Beckett Almanac

of Baseball Cards and Collectibles

Number 9

Edited by Dr. James Beckett,
Rich Klein and Grant Sandground
with the Price Guide staff of
Beckett Baseball

Beckett Publications • Dallas, Texas

BECKETT PUBLICATIONS
DALLAS, TEXAS

Manufactured in the United States of America
First Printing
ISBN 1-930692-34-X

TABLE OF CONTENTS

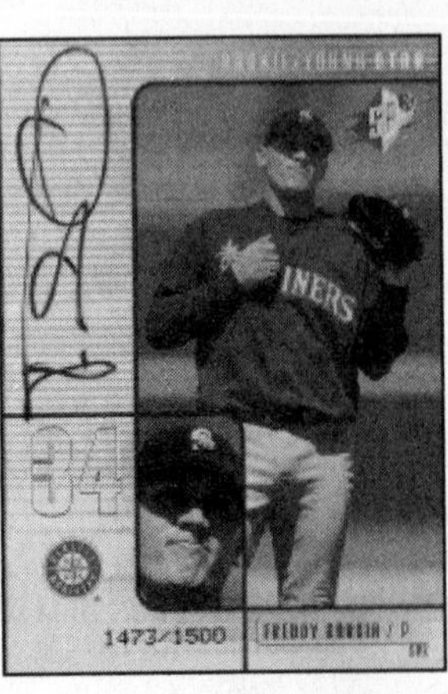

Major League

Minor League Singles

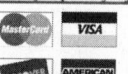

Minor League Team Sets

INTERNATIONAL

MULTI-SPORTS

MEMORABILIA

STATUES

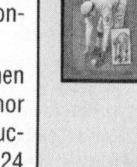

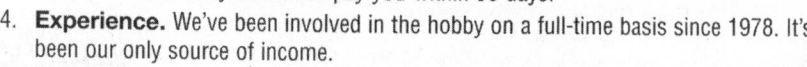

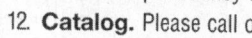

ABOUT THE AUTHOR

Jim Beckett, the leading authority on sport card values in the United States, maintains a wide range of activities in the world of sports. He possesses one of the finest collections of sports cards and autographs in the world, has made numerous appearances on radio and television, and has been frequently cited in many national publications. He was awarded the first "Special Achievement Award" for Contributions to the Hobby by the National Sports Collectors Convention in 1980, the "Jock-Jaspersen Award" for Hobby Dedication in 1983, and the "Buck Barker, Spirit of the Hobby" Award in 1991.

Dr. Beckett is the author of Beckett Baseball Card Price Guide, The Official Price Guide to Baseball Cards, Price Guide to Baseball Collectibles, The Sport Americana Baseball Memorabilia and Autograph Price Guide, Beckett Almanac of Baseball Cards and Collectibles, Beckett Football Card Price Guide, The Official Price Guide to Football Cards, Beckett Hockey Card Price Guide, The Official Price Guide to Hockey Cards, Beckett Basketball Card Price Guide, The Official Price Guide to Basketball Cards, The Beckett Baseball Card Alphabetical Checklist, the Beckett Basketball Card Alphabetical Checklist and the Beckett Football Card Alphabetical Checklist . In addition, he is the founder, publisher, and editor of Beckett Baseball, Beckett Basketball, Beckett Football, Beckett Hockey Beckett and Beckett Racing.

Jim Beckett received his Ph.D. in Statistics from Southern Methodist University . Prior to starting Beckett Publications in 1984, Dr. Beckett served as an Associate Professor of Statistics at Bowling Green State University and as a vice president of a consulting firm in Dallas, Texas.

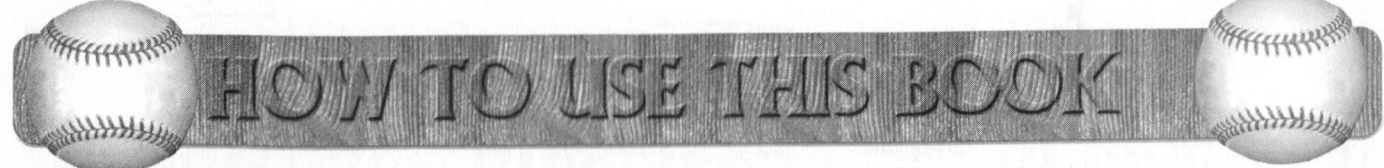

HOW TO USE THIS BOOK

Isn't it great? Every year this book gets better with all the new sets coming out. But even more exciting is that every year there are more options in collecting the cards we love so much. This edition has been enhanced and expanded from the previous edition. The cards you collect who appears on them, what they look like, where they are from, and (most important to most of you) what their current values are are enumerated within. Many of the features contained in the other Beckett Price Guides have been incorporated into this volume since condition grading, terminology, and many other aspects of collecting are common to the card hobby in general. We hope you find the book both interesting and useful in your collecting pursuits.

The Beckett Almanac has been successful where other attempts have failed because it is complete, current, and valid. This Almanac contains not just one, but two prices by condition for all the baseball cards listed. The prices were added to the card lists just prior to printing and reflect not the author's opinions or desires but the going retail prices for each card, based on the marketplace (sports memorabilia conventions and shows, sports card shops, hobby papers, current mail-order catalogs, auction results, and other firsthand reportings of actually realized prices).

What is the best price guide available on the market today? Of course, card sellers prefer the price guide with the highest prices, while card buyers naturally prefer the one with the lowest prices. Accuracy, however, is the true test. Use the price guide trusted by more collectors and dealers than all the others combined. Look for the Beckett® name. I won't put my name on anything I won't stake my reputation on. Not the lowest and not the highest but the most accurate, with integrity.

To facilitate your use of this book, read the complete introductory section on the following pages before going to the pricing pages. Every collectible field has its own terminology; we've tried to capture most of these terms and definitions in our glossary. Please read carefully the section on grading and the condition of your cards, as you cannot determine which price column is appropriate for a given card without first knowing its condition.

Jim Beckett

INTRODUCTION

...e To The World Of Baseball Cards.

...xciting world of baseball card collecting, America's fastest-growing avocation. ...ce in buying this book, since it will open up to you the entire panorama of ...oncise way.

...seball, *Beckett Basketball* , *Beckett Football*, *Beckett Hockey*, ...an indication of the unprecedented popularity of sports cards. ...author of this Almanac, *Beckett Baseball Collector* contains ...rice guide, collectible glossy superstar covers, colorful ...dar, tips for beginners, "Readers Write" letters to and ...varieties, autograph collecting tips and profiles of the sport's Hottest stars. Published every month, BB is the hobby's largest paid circulation periodical. The other five magazines were built on the success of BB.

So collecting baseball cards while still pursued as a hobby with youthful exuberance by kids in the neighborhood has also taken on the trappings of an industry, with thousands of full- and part-time card dealers, as well as vendors of supplies, clubs and conventions. In fact, each year since 1980 thousands of hobbyists have assembled for a National Sports Collectors Convention, at which hundreds of dealers have displayed their wares, seminars have been conducted, autographs penned by sports notables, and millions of cards changed hands. The Beckett Guide is the best annual guide available to the exciting world of baseball cards. Read it and use it. May your enjoyment and your card collection increase in the coming months and years.

...W TO COLLECT

...re no set rules on ...ct, how much ...funds you ...ollect. ...this you some ideas of the various approaches to collecting, we will list some of the more popular areas of specialization.

Many collectors select complete sets from particular years. For example, they may concentrate on assembling complete sets from all the years since their birth or since they became avid sports fans. They may try to collect a card for every player during that specified period of time.

Many others wish to acquire only certain players. Usually such players are the superstars of the sport, but occasionally collectors will specialize in all the cards of players who attended a particular ...llege or came from a certain town. Some collectors are only interested in the first cards or Rookie ...s of certain players. A handy guide for collectors interested in pursuing the hobby this way is the

WANTED! Consignments for Future Auctions

Lot #1
1952 Topps set
$28,535

Lot #31
Old Judge Nichols
$2,593

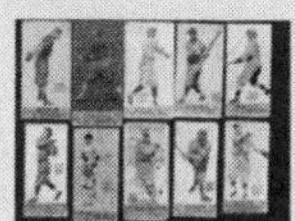

Lot #41
24 Zeenuts w/coupons
$6,268

Lot #54
Gehrig signed envelope
$1,948

Lot #82
Tarzan Bread Card
$1,287

Lot #2
N690 Kal. Bat Cabinet
$25,286

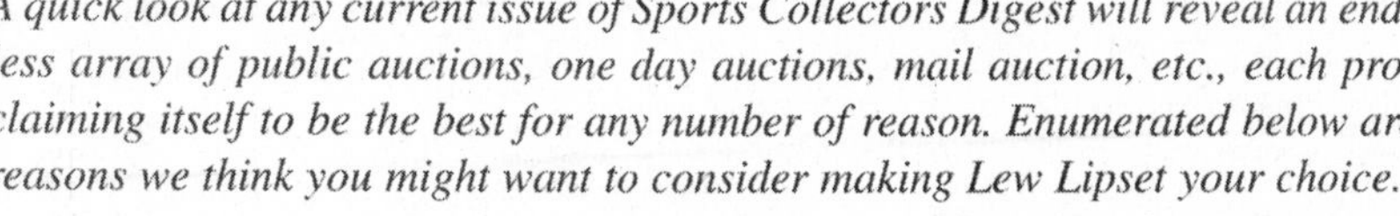

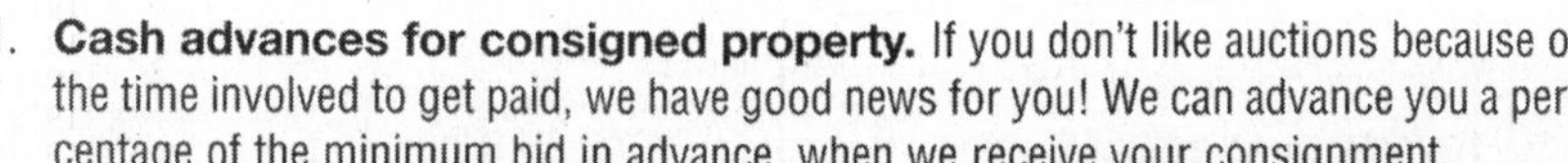

A quick look at any current issue of Sports Collectors Digest will reveal an endless array of public auctions, one day auctions, mail auction, etc., each proclaiming itself to be the best for any number of reason. Enumerated below are reasons we think you might want to consider making Lew Lipset your choice.

1. **Cash advances for consigned property.** If you don't like auctions because of the time involved to get paid, we have good news for you! We can advance you a percentage of the minimum bid in advance, when we receive your consignment.
2. **Ten percent commission and 10% Buyer's Premium.** No other charges. All inclusive includes lotting, photography, advertising and mailing. If unsold, items returned at our expense. Most other major auctions charge 25-30% disguised in consignors charges and buyers fees.
3. **Personalized Service.** We call you when we receive your lots and again when we've reviewed them. When reserves are agreed to, we send you a simple consignor oriented contract outlining the terms and detailing your consignment. Before the auction we send you a listing of the lot numbers of your items in the auction. Within 24 hours of the auction we call you telling you what each item realized, follow that by sending you the realizations on paper for your items as well as the entire auction and we'll almost certainly be able to pay you within 30 days.
4. **Experience.** We've been involved in the hobby on a full-time basis since 1978. It's been our only source of income.
5. **Knowledge.** We've written three books on cards in the form of the Encyclopedia of Baseball Cards and contributed over a hundred articles to the hobby press. In addition to our specialty of pre World War II cards, we've handled large amount of press pins, other pins, advertising, sheet music, postcards, display items and can get authentication on autographed material.
6. **Reasonable reserves.** The norm is to have low reserves to attract bidding, but $100 for a $1,000 item? We'll agree on a reasonable reserve which will attract bidding and protect your interest.
7. **Reasonable lotting.** One auction had 60 Nr Mt T205's 400 T206's, 35 T3s and a group of T210's - all as one lot. We would make these four lots which would mean a greater realization for you.
8. **Reasonably sized auctions.** Our auctions are designed to be a reasonable size, will approximate 300-500 lots and will contain a variety of material in all price rang
9. **Distribution.** Our auctions are produced as full-color catalog supplem Sports Collectors Digest and are sent to 40,000 collectors. In addition own mailing list and the auction is listed in its entirety on ou judge.com.
10. **Selectivity.** We're not interested only in Wagners they're certainly nice to have). We prefer to act a collectors alike and accept a variety of merch
11. **Results.** Last and certainly not least. are illustrated along the perimeter the record prices they brou
12. **Catalog.** Please call or

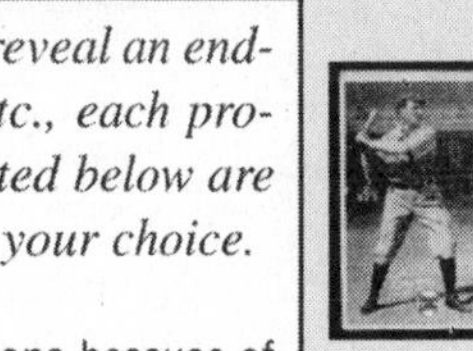

Lot #88
Boston Garter Lajoie
$2,928

Lot #89
H801-7 Old Mill Cabinet
$2,299

Lot #3
Just So McKean
$13,813

Lot #4
Donut Co. Thrilling Moments
$5,856

Lot #91
M110 Sporting Life Lajoie
$2,140

Lot #11
Zeenut DiMaggio w/coupon
$7,594

Lot #95
S81 Silk Rucker
$1,769

Lot #12
Glendale Meat Set
$6,909

Lot #13
Kid Nichols Cabinet
$4,139

Lot #30
Old Judge Kelly Port.
$3,137

"We're not t

Le

P.O. Bo

480-488-9889 • E-MAIL:

26 Topps Set $6,897

Lot #255 8 1950's WS Stubs $2,451

Lot #296 1930 US Amateur program $3,242

w.oldjudge.com

ABOUT THE AUTHOR

Jim Beckett, the leading authority on sport card values in the United States, maintains a wide range of activities in the world of sports. He possesses one of the finest collections of sports cards and autographs in the world, has made numerous appearances on radio and television, and has been frequently cited in many national publications. He was awarded the first "Special Achievement Award" for Contributions to the Hobby by the National Sports Collectors Convention in 1980, the "Jock-Jaspersen Award" for Hobby Dedication in 1983, and the "Buck Barker, Spirit of the Hobby" Award in 1991.

Dr. Beckett is the author of Beckett Baseball Card Price Guide, The Official Price Guide to Baseball Cards, Price Guide to Baseball Collectibles, The Sport Americana Baseball Memorabilia and Autograph Price Guide, Beckett Almanac of Baseball Cards and Collectibles, Beckett Football Card Price Guide, The Official Price Guide to Football Cards, Beckett Hockey Card Price Guide, The Official Price Guide to Hockey Cards, Beckett Basketball Card Price Guide, The Official Price Guide to Basketball Cards, The Beckett Baseball Card Alphabetical Checklist, the Beckett Basketball Card Alphabetical Checklist and the Beckett Football Card Alphabetical Checklist . In addition, he is the founder, publisher, and editor of Beckett Baseball, Beckett Basketball, Beckett Football, Beckett Hockey Beckett and Beckett Racing.

Jim Beckett received his Ph.D. in Statistics from Southern Methodist University . Prior to starting Beckett Publications in 1984, Dr. Beckett served as an Associate Professor of Statistics at Bowling Green State University and as a vice president of a consulting firm in Dallas, Texas.

HOW TO USE THIS BOOK

Isn't it great? Every year this book gets better with all the new sets coming out. But even more exciting is that every year there are more options in collecting the cards we love so much. This edition has been enhanced and expanded from the previous edition. The cards you collect who appears on them, what they look like, where they are from, and (most important to most of you) what their current values are are enumerated within. Many of the features contained in the other Beckett Price Guides have been incorporated into this volume since condition grading, terminology, and many other aspects of collecting are common to the card hobby in general. We hope you find the book both interesting and useful in your collecting pursuits.

The Beckett Almanac has been successful where other attempts have failed because it is complete, current, and valid. This Almanac contains not just one, but two prices by condition for all the baseball cards listed. The prices were added to the card lists just prior to printing and reflect not the author's opinions or desires but the going retail prices for each card, based on the marketplace (sports memorabilia conventions and shows, sports card shops, hobby papers, current mail-order catalogs, auction results, and other firsthand reportings of actually realized prices).

What is the best price guide available on the market today? Of course, card sellers prefer the price guide with the highest prices, while card buyers naturally prefer the one with the lowest prices. Accuracy, however, is the true test. Use the price guide trusted by more collectors and dealers than all the others combined. Look for the Beckett® name. I won't put my name on anything I won't stake my reputation on. Not the lowest and not the highest but the most accurate, with integrity.

To facilitate your use of this book, read the complete introductory section on the following pages before going to the pricing pages. Every collectible field has its own terminology; we've tried to capture most of these terms and definitions in our glossary. Please read carefully the section on grading and the condition of your cards, as you cannot determine which price column is appropriate for a given card without first knowing its condition.

Jim Beckett

INTRODUCTION

...e To The World Of Baseball Cards.

...xciting world of baseball card collecting, America's fastest-growing avocation. ...e in buying this book, since it will open up to you the entire panorama of ...oncise way.

...seball, Beckett Basketball , Beckett Football, Beckett Hockey, ...an indication of the unprecedented popularity of sports cards. ...author of this Almanac, *Beckett Baseball Collector* contains ...rice guide, collectible glossy superstar covers, colorful ...dar, tips for beginners, "Readers Write" letters to and ...l varieties, autograph collecting tips and profiles of the sport's Hottest stars. Published every month, BB is the hobby's largest paid circulation periodical. The other five magazines were built on the success of BB.

So collecting baseball cards while still pursued as a hobby with youthful exuberance by kids in the neighborhood has also taken on the trappings of an industry, with thousands of full- and part-time card dealers, as well as vendors of supplies, clubs and conventions. In fact, each year since 1980 thousands of hobbyists have assembled for a National Sports Collectors Convention, at which hundreds of dealers have displayed their wares, seminars have been conducted, autographs penned by sports notables, and millions of cards changed hands. The Beckett Guide is the best annual guide available to the exciting world of baseball cards. Read it and use it. May your enjoyment and your card collection increase in the coming months and years.

...W TO COLLECT

...re no set rules on ...ct, how much ...funds you ...ollect. ...this you some ideas of the various approaches to collecting, we will list some of the more popular areas of specialization.

Many collectors select complete sets from particular years. For example, they may concentrate on assembling complete sets from all the years since their birth or since they became avid sports fans. They may try to collect a card for every player during that specified period of time.

Many others wish to acquire only certain players. Usually such players are the superstars of the sport, but occasionally collectors will specialize in all the cards of players who attended a particular ...llege or came from a certain town. Some collectors are only interested in the first cards or Rookie ...s of certain players. A handy guide for collectors interested in pursuing the hobby this way is the

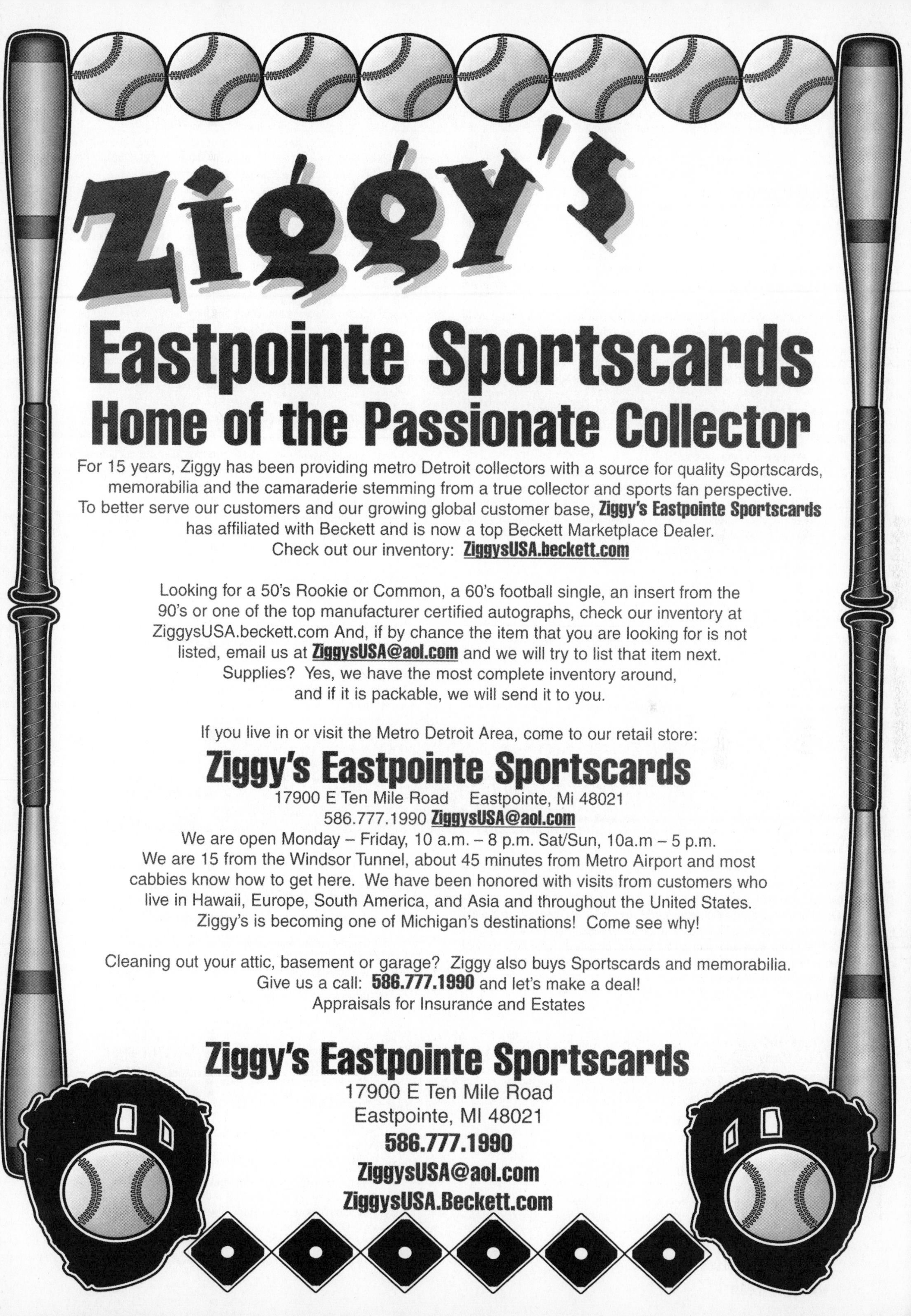

Beckett Baseball Card Alphabetical Checklist.

Another fun way to collect cards is by team. Most fans have a favorite team, and it is natural for that loyalty to be translated into a desire for cards of the players on that favorite team. For most of the recent years, team sets (all the cards from a given team for that year) are readily available at a reasonable price. The Sport Americana Team Baseball Card Checklist will open up this field to the collector.

Obtaining Cards

Several avenues are open to card collectors. Cards still can be purchased in the traditional way: by the pack at the local candy, grocery, drug or major discount stores.

But there are also thousands of card shops across the country that specialize in selling cards individually or by the pack, box, or set. Another alternative is the thousands of card shows held each month around the country, which feature anywhere from eight to 800 tables of sports cards and memorabilia for sale.

For many years, it has been possible to purchase complete sets of baseball cards through mail-order advertisers found in traditional sports media publications, such as The Sporting News, Baseball Digest, Street & Smith yearbooks, and others. These sets also are advertised in the card collecting periodicals. Many collectors will begin by subscribing to at least one of the hobby periodicals, all with good up-to-date information. In fact, subscription offers can be found in the advertising section of this book.

Most serious card collectors obtain old (and new) cards from one or more of several main sources: (1) trading or buying from other collectors or dealers; (2) responding to sale or auction ads in the hobby publications; (3) buying at a local hobby store; (4) attending sports collectibles shows or conventions; and/or (5) purchasing cards over the internet .

We advise that you try all four methods since each has its own distinct advantages: (1) trading is a great way to make new friends; (2) hobby periodicals help you keep up with what's going on in the hobby (including when and where the conventions are happening); (3) stores provide the opportunity to enjoy personalized service and consider a great diversity of material in a relaxed sports-oriented atmosphere; (4) shows allow you to choose from multiple dealers and thousands of cards under one roof in a competitive situation; and (5) the internet allows one to purchase cards in a convenient manner from almost anywhere in the world.

Preserving Your Cards

Cards are fragile. They must be handled properly in order to retain their value. Careless handling can easily result in creased or bent cards. It is, however, not recommended that tweezers or tongs be used to pick up your cards since such utensils might mar or indent card surfaces and thus reduce those cards' conditions and values.

In general, your cards should be handled directly as little as possible. This is sometimes easier to say than to do.

Although there are still many who use custom boxes, storage trays, or even shoe boxes, plastic sheets are the preferred method of many collectors for storing cards.

A collection stored in plastic pages in a three-ring album allows you to view your collection at any time without the need to touch the card itself. Cards can also be kept in single holders (of various types and thickness) designed for the enjoyment of each card individually.

For a large collection, some collectors may use a combination of the above methods. When purchasing plastic sheets for your cards, be sure that you find the pocket size that fits the cards snugly. Don't put your 1951 Bowman in a sheet designed to fit 1981 Topps.

Most hobby and collectibles shops and virtually all collectors' conventions will have these plastic pages available in quantity for the various sizes offered, or you can purchase them directly from the advertisers in this book.

Also, remember that pocket size isn't the only factor to consider when looking for plastic sheets. Other factors such as safety, economy, appearance, availability, or personal preference also may indicate which types of sheets a collector may want to buy.

Damp, sunny and/or hot conditions no, this is not a weather forecast are three elements to avoid in extremes if you are interested in preserving your collection. Too much (or too little) humidity can cause the gradual deterioration of a card. Direct, bright sun (or fluorescent light) over time will bleach out the color of a card. Extreme heat accelerates the decomposition of the card. On the other hand, many cards have lasted more than 75 years without much scientific intervention. So be cautious, even if the above factors typically present a problem only when present in the extreme. It never hurts to be prudent.

Collecting vs. Investing

Collecting individual players and collecting complete sets are both popular vehicles for investment and speculation.

Most investors and speculators stock up on complete sets or on quantities of players they think have good investment potential.

There is obviously no guarantee in this book, or anywhere else for that matter, that cards will outperform the stock market or other investment alternatives in the future. After all, baseball cards do not pay quarterly dividends and cards cannot be sold at their "current values" as easily as stocks or bonds.

Nevertheless, investors have noticed a favorable long-term trend in the past performance of baseball and other sports collectibles, and certain cards and sets have outperformed just about any other investment in some years.

Many hobbyists maintain that the best investment is and always will be the building of a collection, which traditionally has held up better than outright speculation.

Some of the obvious questions are: Which cards? When to buy? When to sell? The best investment you can make is in your own education.

The more you know about your collection and the hobby, the more informed the decisions you will be able to make. We're not selling investment tips. We're selling information about the current value of baseball cards. It's up to you to use that information to your best advantage.

Each hobby has its own language to describe its area of interest. The nomenclature traditionally used for trading cards is derived from the American Card Catalog, published in 1960 by Nostalgia Press. That catalog, written by Jefferson Burdick (who is called the "Father of Card Collecting" for his pioneering work), uses letter and number designations for each separate set of cards. The letter used in the ACC designation refers to the generic type of card. While both sport and non-sport issues are classified in the ACC, we shall confine ourselves to the sport issues. The following list defines the letters and their meanings as used by the American Card Catalog.

(none) or N - 19th Century U.S. Tobacco
B - Blankets
D - Bakery Inserts Including Bread
E - Early Candy and Gum
F - Food Inserts
H - Advertising
M - Periodicals
PC - Postcards
R - Candy and Gum since 1930 Following the letter prefix and an optional hyphen are one-, two-, or three-digit numbers,
R(-)999. These typically represent the company or entity issuing the cards. In several cases, the ACC number is extended by an additional hyphen and another one- or two-digit numerical suffix. For example, the 1957 Topps regular-series baseball card issue carries an ACC designation of
R414-11. The "R" indicates a Candy or Gum card produced since 1930. The "414" is the ACC designation for Topps Chewing Gum baseball card issues, and the "11" is the ACC designation for the 1957 regular issue **(Topps' eleventh baseball set)**. Like other traditional methods of identification, this system provides order to the process of cataloging cards; however, most serious collectors learn the ACC designation of the popular sets by repetition and familiarity, rather than by attempting to "figure out" what they might or should be. From 1948 forward, collectors and dealers commonly refer to all sets by their year, maker, type of issue, and any other distinguishing characteristic. For example, such a characteristic could be an unusual issue or one of several regular issues put out by a specific maker in a single year. Regional issues are usually referred to by year, maker, and sometimes by title or theme of the set.

AMERICAN CARD CATALOG CROSS INDEX

C461912 Imperial Tobacco C46 (minors)
D3101911 Pacific Coast Biscuit D310
D3111911 Pacific Coast Biscuit D311
D3221910 Pirates Tip-Top D322
D3271917 Holsum Bread D327
D3811916 Fleischmann Bread D381
D3821934 Tarzan Thoro Bread D382
D383 1921 Koester's Bread World Series Issue
E90-11909-11 American Caramel E90-1
E90-21910 Pirates American Caramels E90-2
E90-31910 Chicago E90-3
E911908-10 American Caramel E91
E921910 Nadja Caramel E92
E931910 Standard Caramel E93
E951909 Philadelphia Caramel E95
E961912 Philadelphia Caramel E96
E991910 Bishop Coast League E99 (minors)
E1001911 Bishop Coast League E100 (minors)
E1031910 Williams Caramels E103
E1041910 Nadja E104
E1051910 Mello Mints E105
E1061915 American Caramel E106
E1071903-04 Breisch-Williams E107
E1221922 American Caramel E122
E1251910 American Caramel Die Cuts E125
E1261927 American Caramel E126
E1351916 Collins-McCarthy E135
E136-11912 Home Run Kisses E136-1 (minors)
E145-11914 Cracker Jack E145-1
E145-21915 Cracker Jack E145-2.
E2101927 York Caramel E210
E2201921-23 National Caramel E220
E2241914 Texas Tommy E224
E2541909-11 Colgan's Chips E254
E2711910 Darby Chocolates E271
E2851933 Rittenhouse Candy E285
E2861910 Ju Ju Drums E286
E2971909 Briggs E97
E3001911 Plow's Candy E300
H801-61950 Four Mighty Heroes H801-6
M101-21909-13 Sporting News Supplements
M101-41916 Sporting News M101-4
M101-51915 Sporting News M101-5
M101-71926 Sporting News Supplements
M1161911 Sporting Life M116
M1171888-89 Sporting Times M117
N281887 Allen and Ginter N28
N291888 Allen and Ginter N29
N431888 Allen and Ginter N43
N1351893 Duke Talk of the Diamond N135
N1421894 Duke Cabinets N142
N1621888 Goodwin N162
N1671888 Old Judge N167
N1721887-90 Old Judge N172
N1841888 Kimball's N184
N2841887 Buchner N284
N3001895 Mayo N300
N3211888 S.F. Hess and Co. Creole
N338-11893 S.F. Hess and Co. N338-1
N3701887 Lone Jack N370
N4031888 August Beck N403
N5661895 Newsboy N566
N690-11887 Kalamazoo Bats N690-1
690-21887 Kalamazoo Teams N690-2
1910 Sweet Caporal Pins P2
1909 Buster Brown Bread Pins PB2
1909 Morton's Pennant Winner
Bread Pins PB3

PB41922-23 Kolbs Mothers' Bread Pins
PB5-11920 Mrs. Sherlock's Pins PB5-1 (minors)
PB5-21922 Mrs. Sherlock's Pins PB5-2 (minors)
PB5-31933 Mrs. Sherlock's Pins PB5-3 (minors)
PB61934 Ward Baking Sporties Pins PB6
PC7411956-60 Braves Bill and Bob Postcards
PC742-1= 1912 Red Sox Boston American Series
PC742-2= 1912 Red Sox Boston Daily American
Souvenir PC742-2
PC7431909 H.H. Bregstone PC743
PC7441938-59 George Burke PC744
PC7481953-55 Dormand PC748
PC7491959 Tigers Graphic Arts Service PC749
PC7501959 Hayes Company Bauer PC750
PC7511959 Howard Photo Service PC751
PC7531936-52 Albertype Hall of Fame PC753
PC754-21950-69 J.D. McCarthy PC754-2
PC7571915 Sporting News PC757
PC7591949 Solon Sunbeam/Pureta PC759
PC7601908-09 Rose Company PC760
PC7611947 Indians Van Patrick PC-761
PC7621955-62 Don Wingfield PC762
PC7651907 Cubs A.C. Dietsche Postcards PC7651907-09 Tigers A.C. Dietsche Postcards PC7681962 H.F. Gardner Sports Stars PC768
PC7701908 American League Publishing Co. PC773-11909-10 Tigers Topping and Company PC773-21909-11 Tigers H.M. Taylor PC773-2
PC773-11909 Tigers Topping and Company
PC7751907 Cubs G.F. Grignon Co. PC775
PC7821905 Rotograph Co. PC782
PC7831946 Sears-East St. Louis PC783
PC7851905 Souvenir Postcard Shop of
Cleveland PC785
PC7861939 Orcajo Photo Art PC786
PC7961910 Sepia Anon PC796
PE41898 Cameo Pepsin Pins PE4
PM11910 Ornate Oval Pins PM1
PM81938 Our National Game Pins PM8
PR11938 Baseball Tabs PR1
PR21932-34 Orbit Pins Numbered PR2
PR31932-34 Orbit Pins Unnumbered PR3
PR41933 Cracker Jack Pins PR4
PT21910 Luxello Cigars Pins PT2
PX31933 Doubleheader Discs PX3
PX71910 Domino Discs PX7
PM81939 Our National Game Pins PM8
R3001933 George C. Miller R300
R3011936 Overland Candy R301
R302-11943 MP and Co. R302-1
R302-21949 MP and Co. R302-2
R3051933 Tatoo Orbit R305
R3081933 Tatoo Orbit Self Develop R308
R309-11934 Goudey Premiums R309-1
R309-21935 Goudey Premiums R309-2
R3101934 Butterfinger R310
R3131936 National Chicle Fine Pens R313
R313A1935 Gold Medal Flour R313A
R3141936 Goudey Wide Pens R314
R3151928 Portraits and Action R315
R3161929 Portraits and Action R316
R3181934-36 Batter-Up R318
R3191933 Goudey R319
R3201934 Goudey R320
R3211935 Goudey Puzzle R321
R3221936 Goudey B/W R322
R3231938 Goudey Heads Up R323
R3241941 Goudey R324

R3251937 Goudey Knot Hole R325
R3261937 Goudey Flip Movies R326
R3271934-36 Diamond Stars R327
R3281932 U.S. Caramel R328
R3301941 Double Play R330
R3321930 Schutter-Johnson R332
R3331933 Delong R333
R3341939 Play Ball R334
R3351940 Play Ball R335
R3361941 Play Ball R336
R3381933 Sport Kings R338
R3421937 Goudey Thum Movies R342
R3441936 National Chicle Maranville
Secrets R344
R3461948-49 Blue Tint R346
T31911 Turkey Red T3
T2001913 Fatima T200
T2011911 Mecca Double Folders T201
T2021912 Hassan Triple Folders T202
T2031910 Baseball Comics T203
T2041909 Ramly T204
T2081912 1911 A's Fireside T208
T2091910 Contentnea T209 (minors)
T2101910 Old Mill T210 (minors)
T2111910 Red Sun T211 (minors)
T2121909-11 Obak T212 (minors)
T2141915 Victory T214
T2151910-13 Red Cross T215
T2161910-14 People's T216
T2221914 Fatima Players T222
T330-21914 Piedmont Stamps T330-2
V611921 Neilson's V61
V891922 William Paterson V89
V941933 Butterfinger Canadian V94
V1001923 Willards Chocolates V100
V1171923 Maple Crispette V117
V3001937 O-Pee-Chee Batter Ups V300
V351-A1939 World Wide Gum V351A
V351-B1939 World Wide Gum Trimmed
Premiums
V3531933 Goudey Canadian V353
V3541934 Goudey Canadian V354
V3551936 World Wide Gum V355
V3621950 World Wide Gum V362
W463-41934 Exhibits Four-in-One W463-4
W463-51935 Exhibits Four-in-One W463-5
W463-61936 Exhibits Four-in-One W463-6
W5761950-56 Callahan HOF W576
W6001911 Sporting Life Cabinets W600
W6031946-49 Sports Exchange W603
W6051955 Robert Gould W605
W711-11938-39 Cincinnati Orange/Gray
W711-1
W711-21941 Harry Hartman W711-2
W7531941 Browns W753
W7541941 Cardinals W754
WG21904 Fan Craze AL WG2
WG31906 Fan Craze NL WG3
WG41913 Polo Grounds WG4
WG51913 National Game WG5
WG61913 Tom Barker WG6
WG71920 Walter Mails WG7
WG81936 S and S WG8

GLOSSARY/LEGEND

Our glossary defines terms used in the card collecting hobby and in this book. Many of these terms are also common to other types of sports memorabilia collecting. Some terms may have several meanings depending on use and context.

ACETATE—A transparent plastic.

AS— All-Star card. A card portraying an All-Star Player of the previous year that says "All-Star" on its face.

ATG-All-Time Great card.

ATL-All-Time Leaders card.

AU(TO)—Autographed card.

AW—Award Winner

BB—Building Blocks

BC—Bonus card.

BF—Bright Futures

BL—Blue letters.

BNR—Banner Season

BOX CARD—Card issued on a box (e.g., 1987 Topps Box Bottoms).

BRICK—A group of 50 or more cards having common characteristics that is intended to be bought, sold, or traded as a unit.

CABINETS—Popular and highly valuable photographs on thick card stock produced in the 19th and early 20th century.

CC—Curtain Call

CG—Cornerstones of the Game

CHECKLIST—A list of the cards contained in a particular set. The list is always in numerical order if the cards are numbered. Some unnumbered sets are artificially numbered in alphabetical order, by team and alphabetically within the team, or by uniform number for convenience.

CL—Checklist card. A card that lists in order the cards and players in the set or series. Older checklist cards in Mint condition that have not been marked are very desirable and command premiums.

CP—Changing Places

CO—Coach.

COMM—Commissioner.

COMMON CARD—The typical card of any set; it has no premium value accruing from subject matter, numerical scarcity, popular demand, or anomaly.

CONVENTION—A gathering of dealers and collectors at a single location for the purpose of buying, selling, and trading sports memorabilia items. Conventions are open to the public and sometimes feature autograph guests, door prizes, contests, seminars, etc. They are frequently referred to simply as "shows."

COOP—Cooperstown.

COR—Corrected card.

CT—Cooperstown

CY—Cy Young Award.

DD—Decade of Dominance

DEALER—A person who engages in buying, selling, and trading sports collectibles or supplies. A dealer may also be a collector, but as a dealer, his main goal is to earn a profit.

DIE-CUT—A card with part of its stock partially cut, allowing one or more parts to be folded or removed. After removal or appropriate folding, the remaining part of the card can frequently be made to stand up.

DK—Diamond King.

DL—Division Leaders.

DP—Double Print (a card that was printed in double the quantity compared to the other cards in the same series) or a Draft Pick card.

DT—Dream Team

DUFEX—A method of card manufacturing technology patented by Pinnacle Brands, Inc. It involves a refractive quality to a card with a foil coating.

ERA—Earned Run Average.

ERR—Error card. A card with erroneous information, spelling, or depiction on either side of the card. Most errors are not corrected by the producing card company.

FC—Fan Club

FDP—First or First-Round Draft Pick.

FF—Future Foundation

FOIL—Foil embossed stamp on card.

FOLD—Foldout.

FP—Franchise Player

Fran—Franchise

FS—Father/son card.

FS—Future Star

FUN—Fun cards.

FY—First Year

GL—Green letters.

GLOSS—A card with luster; a shiny finish as in a card with UV coating.

GO—could not find on page 202

HG—Heroes of the Game

HIGH NUMBER—The cards in the last series of numbers in a year in which such higher-numbered cards were printed or distributed in significantly lesser amounts than the lower-numbered cards. The high-number designation refers to a scarcity of the high-numbered cards. Not all years have high numbers in terms of this definition.

HL—Highlight card.

HOF—Hall of Fame, or a card that portrays a Hall of Famer (HOFer).

HOLOGRAM—A three-dimensional photographic image.

HH—Hometown Heroes

HOR—Horizontal pose on card as opposed to the standard vertical orientation found on most cards.

IA—In Action card.

IF—Infielder.

INSERT—A card of a different type or any other sports collectible (typically a poster or sticker) contained and sold in the same package along with a card or cards of a major set. An insert card is either unnumbered or not numbered in the same sequence as the major set. Sometimes the inserts are randomly distributed and are not found in every pack.

INTERACTIVE—A concept that involves collector participation.

IRT—International Road Trip

ISSUE—Synonymous with set, but usually used in conjunction with a manufaturer, e.g., a Topps issue.

JSY—means Jersey

KM—K-Men

LHP—Left-handed pitcher.

LL—League Leaders or large letters on card.

LUM—Lumberjack

MAJOR SET—A set produced by a national manufacturer of cards containing a large number of cards. Usually 100 or more different cards constitute a major set.

MB—Master Blasters

MEM—Memorial card. For example, the 1990 Donruss and Topps Bart Giamatti cards.

METALLIC—A glossy design method that enhances card features.

MG—Manager.

MI—Maximum Impact

MINI—A small card; for example, a 1975 Topps card of identical design but smaller dimensions than the regular Topps issue of 1975.

ML—Major League.

MM—Memorable Moments

MULTI-PLAYER CARD—A single card depicting two or more players (but not a team card).

MVP—Most Valuable Player.

NAU—No autograph on card.

NG—Next Game

NH—No-Hitter.

NNOF—No name on front.

NOF—Name on front.

NOTCHING—The grooving of the card, usually caused by fingernails, rubber bands, or bumping card edges against other objects.

NT—Now and Then

NV—Novato

OF—Outfield or Outfielder.

OLY—Olympics Card.

P—Pitcher or Pitching pose.

P1—First Printing.

P2—Second Printing.

P3—Third Printing.

PACKS—A means by which cards are issued in terms of pack type (wax, cello, foil, rack, etc.) and channel of distribution (hobby, retail, etc.).

PARALLEL— A card that is similar in

design to its counterpart from a basic set but offers a distinguishing quality.
PF—Profiles.
PG—Postseason Glory
PLASTIC SHEET—A clear, plastic page that is punched for insertion into a binder (with standard three-ring spacing) containing pockets for displaying cards. Many different styles of sheets exist with pockets of varying sizes to hold the many differing card formats. Also called a display sheet or storage sheet.
PP—Power Passion
PLATINUM—A metallic element used in the process of creating a glossy card.
PR—Printed name on back.
PREMIUM—A card, sometimes on photographic stock, that is purchased or obtained in conjunction with, or redemption for, another card or product. The premium is not packaged in the same unit as the primary item.
PRES—President.
PRISMATIC/PRISM—A glossy or bright design that refracts or disperses light.
PS—Pace Setters
PT—Power Tools
PUZZLE CARD—A card whose back contains a part of a picture which, when joined correctly with other puzzle cards, forms the completed picture.
PUZZLE PIECE—A die-cut piece designed to interlock with similar pieces (e.g., early 1980s Donruss).
PVC—Polyvinyl chloride, a substance used to make many of the popular card display protective sheets. Non-PVC sheets are considered preferable for long-term storage of cards by many.
RARE—A card or series of cards of very limited availability. Unfortunately, "rare" is a subjective term frequently used indiscriminately to hype value. "Rare" cards are harder to obtain than "scarce" cards.
RB—Record Breaker.
RC—Rookie Card
REDEMPTION—A program established by multiple card manufacturers that allows collectors to mail in a special card (usually a random insert) in return for special cards, sets, or other prizes not available through conventional channels.
REFRACTORS—A card that features a design element that enhances (distorts) its color/appearance through deflecting light.
REV NEG—Reversed or flopped photo side of the card. This is a major type of error card, but only some are corrected.
RHP—Right-handed pitcher.
RHW—Rookie Home Whites
RIF—Rifleman
RPM—Rookie Premiere Materials
RR—Rated Rookie
ROO—Rookie
ROY—Rookie of the Year.
RP—Relief pitcher.
RTC—Rookie True Colors
SA—Super Action card.
SASE—Self-Addressed, Stamped Envelope.
SB—Scrapbook
SB—Stolen Bases.
SCARCE—A card or series of cards of limited availability. This subjective term is sometimes used indiscriminately to hype value. "Scarce" cards are not as difficult to obtain as "rare" cards.
SCR—Script name on back.
SD—San Diego Padres.
SEMI-HIGH—A card from the next-to-last series of a sequentially issued set. It has more value than an average card and generally less value than a high number. A card is not called a semi-high unless the next-to-last series in which it exists has an additional premium attached to it.
SERIES—The entire set of cards issued by a particular producer in a particular year; e.g., the 1971 Topps series. Also, within a particular set, series can refer to a group of (consecutively numbered) cards printed at the same time, e.g., the first series of the 1957 Topps issue (#1 through #88).
SET—One each of the entire run of cards of the same type produced by a particular manufacturer during a single year. In other words, if you have a complete set of 1976 Topps then you have every card from #1 up to and including #660; i.e., all the different cards that were produced.
SF—Starflics.
SH—Season Highlight
SHEEN—Brightness or luster emitted by card.
SKIP-NUMBERED—A set that has many unissued card numbers between the lowest number in the set and the highest number in the set, e.g., the 1948 Leaf baseball set contains 98 cards skip-numbered from #1 to #168. A major set in which a few numbers were not printed is not considered to be skip-numbered.
SP—Single or Short Print (a card that was printed in lesser quantity compared to the other cards in the same series; see also DP and TP).
SPECIAL CARD—A card that portrays something other than a single player or team, for example, a card that portrays the previous year's statistical leaders or the results from the previous year's World Series.
SS—Shortstop.
STANDARD SIZE—Most modern sports cards measure 2—1/2 by 3-1/2 inches. Exceptions are noted in card descriptions throughout this book.
STAR CARD—A card that portrays a player of some repute, usually determined by his ability; but, sometimes referring to sheer popularity.
STOCK—The cardboard or paper on which the card is printed.
SUPERIMPOSED—To be affixed on top of something; i.e., a player photo over a solid background.
SUPERSTAR CARD—A card that portrays a superstar, e.g., a Hall of Famer or player with strong Hall of Fame potential.
TC—Team Checklist.
TEAM CARD—A card that depicts an entire team.
THREE-DIMENSIONAL (3D)—A visual image that provides an illusion of depth and perspective.
TOPICAL—A subset or group of cards that have a common theme (e.g., MVP award winners).
TP—Triple Print (a card that was printed in triple the quantity compared to the other cards in the same series).
TR—Trade reference on card.
TRANSPARENT—Clear, see-through.
UDCA—Upper Deck Classic Alumni.
UER—Uncorrected Error.
UMP—Umpire.
USA—Team USA.
UV—Ultraviolet, a glossy coating used in producing cards.
VAR—Variation card. One of two or more cards from the same series with the same number (or player with identical pose if the series is unnumbered) differing from one another by some aspect, the different feature stemming from the printing or stock of the card. This can be caused when the manufacturer of the cards notices an error in one or more of the cards, makes the changes, and then resumes the print run. In this case there will be two versions or variations of the same card. Sometimes one of the variations is relatively scarce.
VERT—Vertical pose on card.
WAS—Washington National League (1974 Topps).
WC—What's the Call?
WL—White letters on front.
WS—World Series card.
YL—Yellow letters on front
YT—Yellow team name on front.
*—to denote multi-sport sets.

UNDERSTANDING CARD VALUES

Determining Value

Why are some cards more valuable than others? Obviously, the economic laws of supply and demand are applicable to card collecting just as they are to any other field where a commodity is bought, sold or traded in a free, unregulated market.

Supply (the number of cards available on the market) is less than the total number of cards originally produced since attrition diminishes that original quantity. Each year a percentage of cards is typically thrown away, destroyed or otherwise lost to collectors. This percentage is much, much smaller today than it was in the past because more and more people have become increasingly aware of the value of their cards.

For those who collect only Mint condition cards, the supply of older cards can be quite small indeed. Until recently, collectors were not so conscious of the need to preserve the condition of their cards. For this reason, it is difficult to know exactly how many 1953 Topps are currently available, Mint or otherwise. It is generally accepted that there are fewer 1953 Topps available than 1963, 1973 or 1983 Topps cards. If demand were equal for each of these sets, the law of supply and demand would increase the price for the least available sets. Demand, however, is never equal for all sets, so price correlations can be complicated. The demand for a card is influenced by many factors. These include: (1) the age of the card; (2) the number of cards printed; (3) the player(s) portrayed on the card; (4) the attractiveness and popularity of the set; and (5) the physical condition of the card.

In general, (1) the older the card, (2) the fewer the number of the cards printed, (3) the more famous, popular and talented the player, (4) the more attractive and popular the set, and (5) the better the condition of the card, the higher the value of the card will be. There are exceptions to all but one of these factors: the condition of the card. Given two cards similar in all respects except condition, the one in the best condition will always be valued higher.

While those guidelines help to establish the value of a card, the countless exceptions and peculiarities make any simple, direct mathematical formula to determine card values impossible.

Regional Variation

Since the market varies from region to region, card prices of local players may be higher. This is known as a regional premium. How significant the premium is and if there is any premium at all depends on the local popularity of the team and the player.

The largest regional premiums usually do not apply to superstars, who often are so well-known nationwide that the prices of their key cards are too high for local dealers to realize a premium.

Lesser stars often command the strongest premiums. Their popularity is concentrated in their home region, creating local demand that greatly exceeds overall demand.

Regional premiums can apply to popular retired players and sometimes can be found in the areas where the players grew up or starred in college.

A regional discount is the converse of a regional premium. Regional discounts occur when a player has been so popular in his region for so long that local collectors and dealers have accumulated quantities of his key cards. The abundant supply may make the cards available in that area at the lowest prices anywhere.

Set Prices

A somewhat paradoxical situation exists in the price of a complete set vs. the combined cost of the individual cards in the set. In nearly every case, the sum of the prices for the individual cards is higher than the cost for the complete set. This is prevalent especially in the cards of the last few years. The reasons for this apparent anomaly stem from the habits of collectors and from the carrying costs to dealers. Today, each card in a set normally is produced in the same quantity as all other cards in its set.

Many collectors pick up only stars, superstars and particular teams. As a result, the dealer is left with a shortage of certain player cards and an abundance of others. He therefore incurs an expense in simply "carrying" these less desirable cards in stock. On the other hand, if he sells a complete set, he gets rid of large numbers of cards at one time. For this reason, he generally is willing to receive less money for a complete set. By doing this, he recovers all of his costs and also makes a profit.

The disparity between the price of the complete set and the sum of the individual cards also has been influenced by the fact that some of the major manufacturers now are pre-collating card sets. Since "pulling" individual cards from the sets involves a specific type of labor (and cost), the singles or star card market is not affected significantly by pre-collation.

Set prices also do not include rare card varieties, unless specifically stated. Of course, the prices for sets do include one example of each type for the given set, but this is the least expensive variety.

Scarce Series

Scarce series occur because cards issued before 1974 were made available to the public each year in several series of finite numbers of cards, rather than all cards of the set being available for purchase at one time. At some point during the year, usually toward the end of the baseball season, interest in current year baseball cards waned. Consequently, the manufacturers produced smaller numbers of these later-series cards.

Nearly all nationwide issues from post-World War II manufacturers (1948 to 1973) exhibit these series variations. In the past, Topps, for example, may have issued series consisting of many different numbers of cards, including 55, 66, 80, 88 and others. Recently, Topps has settled on what is now its standard sheet size of 132 cards, six of which comprise its 792-card set.

While the number of cards within a given series is usually the same as the number of cards on one printed sheet, this is not always the case. For example, Bowman used 36 cards on its standard printed sheets, but in 1948 substituted 12 cards during later print runs of that year's baseball cards. Twelve of the cards from the initial sheet of 36 cards were removed and replaced by 12 different cards giving, in effect, a first series of 36 cards and a second series of 12 new cards. This replacement produced a scarcity of 24 cards the 12 cards removed from the original sheet and the 12 new cards added to the sheet. A full sheet of 1948 Bowman cards (second printing) shows that card numbers 37 through 48 have replaced 12 of the cards on the first printing sheet.

The Topps Company also has created scarcities and/or excesses of certain cards in many of its sets. Topps, however, has most frequently gone the other direction by double printing some of the cards. Double printing causes an abundance of cards of the players who are on the same sheet more than one time. During the years from 1978 to 1981, Topps double printed 66 cards out of their large 726-card set. The Topps practice of double printing cards in earlier years is the most logical explanation for the known scarcities of particular cards in some of these Topps sets.

From 1988 through 1990, Donruss short printed and double printed certain cards in its major sets. Ostensibly this was because of its addition of bonus team MVP cards in its regular-issue wax packs.

We are always looking for information or photographs of printing sheets of cards for research. Each year, we try to update the hobby's knowledge of distribution anomalies. Please let us know at the address in this book if you have first-hand knowledge that would be helpful in this pursuit.

GRADING YOUR CARDS

Each hobby has its own grading terminology stamps, coins, comic books, record collecting, etc. Collectors of sports cards are no exception. The one invariable criterion for determining the value of a card is its condition: The better the condition of the card, the more valuable it is. Condition grading, however, is subjective. Individual card dealers and collectors differ in the strictness of their grading, but the stated condition of a card should be determined without regard to whether it is being bought or sold.

No allowance is made for age. A 1952 card is judged by the same standards as a 2002 card. But there are specific sets and cards that are condition sensitive (marked with "!" in the Price Guide) because of their border color, consistently poor centering, etc. Such cards and sets sometimes command premiums above the listed percentages in Mint condition.

CENTERING

Slightly Off-centered

Off-centered

Well-centered

Badly Off-centered

Miscut

CONDITION GUIDE

Centering

Current centering terminology uses numbers representing the percentage of border on either side of the main design. Obviously, centering is diminished in importance for borderless cards such as Stadium Club.

Slightly Off-Center (60/40): A slightly off-center card is one that, upon close inspection, is found to have one border bigger than the opposite border. This degree once was offensive to only purists, but now some hobbyists try to avoid cards that are anything other than perfectly centered.

Off-Center (70/30): An off-center card has one border that is noticeably more than twice as wide as the opposite border.

Badly Off-Center (80/20 or worse): A badly off-center card has virtually no border on one side of the card.

Miscut: A miscut card actually shows part of the adjacent card in its larger border and consequently a corresponding amount of its card is cut off.

Corner Wear

Corner wear is the most scrutinized grading criteria in the hobby. These are the major categories of corner wear:

- **Corner with a slight touch of wear**: The corner still is sharp, but there is a slight touch of wear showing. On a dark-bordered card, this shows as a dot of white.
- **Fuzzy corner**: The corner still comes to a point, but the point has just begun to fray. A slightly "dinged" corner is considered the same as a fuzzy corner.
- **Slightly rounded corner**: The fraying of the corner has increased to where there is only a hint of a point. Mild layering may be evident. A "dinged" corner is considered the same as a slightly rounded corner.
- **Rounded corner**: The point is completely gone. Some layering is noticeable.
- **Badly rounded corner**: The corner is completely round and rough. Severe layering is evident.

Creases

A third common defect is the crease. The degree of creasing in a card is difficult to show in a drawing or picture. On giving the specific condition of an expensive card for sale, the seller should note any creases additionally. Creases can be categorized as to severity according to the following scale:

Light Crease: A light crease is a crease that is barely noticeable upon close inspection. In fact, when cards are in plastic sheets or holders, a light crease may not be seen (until the card is taken out of the holder). A light crease on the front is much more serious than a light crease on the card back only.

Medium Crease: A medium crease is noticeable when held and studied at arm's length by the naked eye, but does not overly detract from the appearance of the card. It is an obvious crease, but not one that breaks the picture surface of the card.

Heavy Crease: A heavy crease is one that has torn or broken through the card's picture surface, e.g., puts a tear in the photo surface.

Alterations

Deceptive Trimming: This occurs when someone alters the card in order (1) to shave off edge wear, (2) to improve the sharpness of the corners, or (3) to improve centering obviously their objective is to falsely increase the perceived value of the card to an unsuspecting buyer. The shrinkage usually is evident only if the trimmed card is compared to an adjacent full-sized card or if the trimmed card is itself measured.

Obvious Trimming: Obvious trimming is noticeable and unfortunate. It is usually performed by non-collectors who give no thought to the present or future value of their cards.

Deceptively Retouched Borders: This occurs when the borders (especially on those cards with dark borders) are touched up on the edges and corners with magic marker or crayons of appropriate color in order to make the card appear Mint.

Categorization of Defects - Miscellaneous Flaws

The following are common minor flaws that, depending on severity, lower a card's condition by one to four grades and often render it no better than Excellent-Mint: bubbles (lumps in surface), gum and wax stains, diamond cutting (slanted borders), notching, off-centered backs, paper wrinkles, scratched-off cartoons or puzzles on back, rubber band marks, scratches, surface impressions and warping.

The following are common serious flaws that, depending on severity, lower a card's condition at least four grades and often render it no better than Good: chemical or sun fading, erasure marks, mildew, miscutting (severe off-centering), holes, bleached or re-touched borders, tape marks, tears, trimming, water or coffee stains and writing.

Grades

Mint (Mt) - A card with no flaws or wear. The card has four perfect corners, 60/40 or better centering from top to bottom and from left to right, original gloss, smooth edges and original color borders. A Mint card does not have print spots, color or focus imperfections.

Near Mint-Mint (NrMt-Mt) - A card with one minor flaw. Any one of the following would lower a Mint card to Near Mint-Mint: one corner with a slight touch of wear, barely noticeable print spots, color or focus imperfections. The card must have 60/40 or better centering in both directions, original gloss, smooth edges and original color borders.

Near Mint (NrMt) - A card with one minor flaw. Any one of the following would lower a Mint card to Near Mint: one fuzzy corner or two to four corners with slight touches of wear, 70/30 to 60/40 centering, slightly rough edges, minor print spots, color or focus imperfections. The card must have original gloss and original color borders.

Excellent-Mint (ExMt) - A card with two or three fuzzy, but not rounded, corners and centering no worse than 80/20. The card may have no more than two of the following: slightly rough edges, very slightly discolored borders, minor print spots, color or focus imperfections. The card must have original gloss.

Excellent (Ex) - A card with four fuzzy but definitely not rounded corners and centering no worse than 80/20. The card may have a small amount of original gloss lost, rough edges, slightly discolored borders and minor print spots, color or focus imperfections.

Very Good (Vg) - A card that has been handled but not abused: slightly rounded corners with slight layering, slight notching on edges, a significant amount of gloss lost from the surface but no scuffing and moderate discoloration of borders. The card may have a few light creases.

Good (G), Fair (F), Poor (P) - A well-worn, mishandled or abused card: badly rounded and layered corners, scuffing, most or all original gloss missing, seriously discolored borders, moderate or heavy creases, and one or more serious flaws. The grade of Good, Fair or Poor depends on the severity of wear and flaws. Good, Fair and Poor cards generally are used only as fillers.

The most widely used grades are defined above. Obviously, many cards will not perfectly fit one of the definitions.

Therefore, categories between the major grades known as in-between grades are used, such as Good to Very Good (G-Vg), Very Good to Excellent (VgEx), and Excellent-Mint to Near Mint (ExMt-NrMt). Such grades indicate a card with all qualities of the lower category but with at least a few qualities of the higher category.

Beckett Almanac of Baseball Cards and Collectibles lists each card and set in two grades, with the middle grade valued at about 40-45% of the top grade.

The value of cards that fall between the listed columns can also be calculated using a percentage of the top grade. For example, a card that falls between the top and middle grades (Ex, ExMt or NrMt in most cases) will generally be valued at anywhere from 50% to 90% of the top grade.

Similarly, a card that falls between the middle and bottom grades (G-Vg, Vg or VgEx in most cases) will generally be valued at anywhere from 20% to 40% of the top grade.

There are also cases where cards are in better condition than the top grade or worse than the bottom grade. Cards that grade worse than the lowest grade are generally valued at 5-10% of the top grade.

When a card exceeds the top grade by one such as NrMt-Mt when the top grade is NrMt, or Mint when the top grade is NrMt-Mt a premium of up to 50% is possible, with 10-20% the usual norm.

When a card exceeds the top grade by two such as Mint when the top grade is NrMt, or NrMt-Mt when the top grade is ExMt a premium of 25-50% is the usual norm. But certain condition sensitive cards or sets, particularly those from the pre-war era, can bring premiums of up to 100% or even more.

Unopened packs, boxes and factory-collated sets are considered Mint in their unknown (and presumed perfect) state. Once opened, however, each card can be graded (and valued) in its own right by taking into account any defects that may be present in spite of the fact that the card has never been handled.

CORNER WEAR

The partial cards shown at right have been photographed at 300%. This was done in order to magnify each card's corner wear to such a degree that differences could be shown on a printed page.

The 1962 Topps Mickey Mantle card definitely has a rounded corner. Some may say that this card is badly rounded, but that is a judgment call.

The 1962 Topps Hank Aaron card has a slighly rounded corner. Note that there is definite corner wear evident by the fraying and that the corner no longer sports a sharp point.

The 1962 Topps Gil Hodges card has corner wear; it is slightly better than the Aaron card above. Nevertheless, some collectors might classify this Hodges corner as slightly rounded.

The 1962 Topps Manager's Dream card showing Mantle and Mays has slight corner wear. This is not a fuzzy corner as very slight wear is noticeable on the card's photo surface.

The 1962 Topps Don Mossi card has very slight corner wear such that it might be called a fuzzy corner. A close look at the original card shows the corner is not perfect, but almost. However, note that corner wear is somewhat academic on this card. As you can plainly see, the heavy crease going across his name breaks through the photo surface.

SELLING YOUR CARDS

Just about every collector sells cards or will sell cards eventually. Someday you may be interested in selling your duplicates or maybe even your whole collection. You may sell to other collectors, friends or dealers. You may even sell cards you purchased from a certain dealer back to that same dealer. In any event, it helps to know some of the mechanics of the typical transaction between buyer and seller.

Dealers will buy cards in order to resell them to other collectors who are interested in the cards. Dealers will always pay a higher percentage for items that (in their opinion) can be resold quickly, and a much lower percentage for those items that are perceived as having low demand and hence are slow moving. In either case, dealers must buy at a price that allows for the expense of doing business and a margin for profit.

If you have cards for sale, the best advice we can give is that you get several offers for your cards either from card shops or at a card show and take the best offer, all things considered. Note, the "best" offer may not be the one for the highest amount. And remember, if a dealer really wants your cards, he won't let you get away without making his best competitive offer. Another alternative is to place your cards in an auction as one or several lots.

Many people think nothing of going into a department store and paying $15 for an item c clothing for which the store paid $5. But if you were selling your $15 card to a dealer and he offered yo $5 for it, you might consider his mark-up unreasonable. To complete the analogy: Most departme stores (and card dealers) that consistently pay $10 for $15 items eventually go out of business. A exception is when the dealer has lined up a willing buyer for the item(s) you are attempting to sell, or the cards are so Hot that it's likely he'll likely have to hold the cards for just a short period of time.

In those cases, an offer of up to 75 percent of book value still will allow the dealer to make reasonable profit considering the short time he will need to hold the merchandise. In general, howeve most cards and collections will bring offers in the range of 25 to 50 percent of retail price. Also conside that most material from the last five to 10 years is plentiful. If that's what you're selling, don't b surprised if your best offer is well below that range.

INTERESTING NOTES

The first card numerically of an issue is the single card most likely to obtain excessive wear.

Consequently, you typically will find the price on the #1 card (in NrMt or Mint condition) somewhat higher than might otherwise be the case.

Similarly, but to a lesser extent (because normally the less important, reverse side of the card is the one exposed), the last card numerically in an issue also is prone to abnormal wear. This extra wear and tear occurs because the first and last cards are exposed to the elements (human element included) more than any of the other cards. They are generally end cards in any brick formations, rubber bandings, stackings on wet surfaces and like activities.

Sports cards have no intrinsic value. The value of a card, like the value of other collectibles, can be determined only by you and your enjoyment in viewing and possessing these cardboard treasures.

Remember, the buyer ultimately determines the price of each baseball card. You are the determining price factor because you have the ability to say "No" to the price of any card by not exchanging your hard-earned money for a given issue. When the cost of a trading card exceeds the enjoyment you will receive from it, your answer should be "No." We assess and report the prices. You set them!

We are always interested in receiving the price input of collectors and dealers. We happily credit major contributors. We welcome your opinions, since your contributions assist us in ensuring a better guide each year. If you would like to join our survey list for the next editions of this book and others authored by Dr. Beckett, please send your name and address to Dr. James Beckett, 15850 Dallas Parkway, Dallas, TX 75248.

Today's version of the baseball card, with its colorful and oftentimes high-tech front and back, is a far cry from its earliest predecessors. The issue remains cloudy as to which was the very first baseball card ever produced, but the institution of baseball cards dates from the latter half of the 19th century, more than 100 years ago. Early issues, generally printed on heavy cardboard, were of poor quality, with photographs, drawings, and printing far short of today's standards.

Goodwin & Co., of New York, makers of Gypsy Queen, Old Judge, and other cigarette brands, is considered by many to be the first issuer of baseball and other sports cards. Its issues, predominantly sized 1-1/2 by 2-1/2 inches, generally consisted of photographs of baseball players, boxers, wrestlers, and other subjects mounted on stiff cardboard. More than 2,000 different photos of baseball players alone have been identified. These "Old Judges" a collective name commonly used for the Goodwin & Co. cards, were issued from 1886 to 1890 and are treasured parts of many collections today.

Among the other cigarette companies that issued baseball cards still attracting attention today are Allen & Ginter, D. Buchner & Co. (Gold Coin Chewing Tobacco), and P. H. Mayo & Brother. Cards from the first two companies bear colored line drawings, while the Mayos are sepia photographs on black cardboard. In addition to the small-size cards from this era, several tobacco companies issued cabinet-size baseball cards. These "cabinets" were considerably larger than the small cards, usually about 4-1/4 by 6-1/2 inches, and were printed on heavy stock. Goodwin & Co.'s Old Judge cabinets and the National Tobacco Works' "Newsboy" baseball photos are two that remain popular today.

By 1895, the American Tobacco Company began to dominate its competition. They discontinued baseball card inserts in their cigarette packages (actually slide boxes in those days). The lack of competition in the cigarette market had made these inserts unnecessary. This marked the end of the first era of baseball cards. At the dawn of the 20th century, few baseball cards were being issued. But once again, it was the cigarette companies, particularly, the American Tobacco Company, followed to a lesser extent by the candy and gum makers that revived the practice of including baseball cards with their products. The bulk of these cards, identified in the American Card Catalog (designated hereafter as ACC) as T or E cards for 20th century "Tobacco" or "Early Candy and Gum" issues, respectively, were released from 1909 to 1915.

This romantic and popular era of baseball card collecting produced many desirable items. The most outstanding is the fabled T-206 Honus Wagner card. Other perennial favorites among collectors are the T-206 Eddie Plank card, and the T-206 Magee error card. The former was once the second most valuable card and only recently relinquished that position to a more distinctive and aesthetically pleasing Napoleon Lajoie card from the 1933–34 Goudey Gum series. The latter misspells the player's name as "Magie" the most famous and most valuable blooper card.

The ingenuity and distinctiveness of this era has yet to be surpassed. Highlights include:

- The T-202 Hassan triple-folders, one of the best looking and the most distinctive cards ever issued;
- The durable T-201 Mecca double-folders, one of the first sets with players' records on the reverse;
- The T-3 Turkey Reds, the hobby's most popular cabinet card;
- The E-145 Cracker Jacks, the only major set containing Federal League player cards; and
- The T-204 Ramlys, with their distinctive black-and-white oval photos and ornate gold borders.

These are but a few of the varieties issued during this period.

Increasing Popularity

While the American Tobacco Company dominated the field, several other tobacco companies, as well as clothing manufacturers, newspapers and periodicals, game makers, and companies whose identities remain anonymous, also issued cards during this period. In fact, the Collins-McCarthy Candy Company, makers of Zeenuts Pacific Coast League baseball cards, issued cards yearly from 1911 to 1938. Its record for continuous annual card production has been exceeded only by the Topps Chewing Gum Company. The era of the tobacco card issues closed with the onset of World War I, with the exception of the Red Man chewing tobacco sets produced from 1952 to 1955.

The next flurry of card issues broke out in the roaring and prosperous 1920s, the era of the E card. The caramel companies (National Caramel, American Caramel, York Caramel) were the leading distributors of these E cards. In addition, the strip card, a continuos strip with several cards divided by dotted lines or other sectioning features, flourished during this time. While the E cards and the strip cards generally are considered less imaginative than the T cards or the recent candy and gum issues, they still are pursued by many advanced collectors.

Another significant event of the 1920s was the introduction of the arcade card. Taking its designation from its issuer, the Exhibit Supply Company of Chicago, it is usually known as the "Exhibit" card. Once a trademark of the penny arcades, amusement parks, and county fairs across the country, Exhibit machines dispensed nearly postcard-size photos on thick stock for one penny. These picture cards bore likenesses of a favorite cowboy, actor, actress, or baseball player. Exhibit Supply and its associated companies produced baseball cards during a longer time span, although discontinuous, than any other manufacturer. Its first cards appeared in 1921, while its last issue was in 1966. In 1979, the Exhibit Supply Company was bought and somewhat revived by a collector/dealer who has since reprinted Exhibit photos of the past.

If the T card period, from 1909 to 1915, can be designated the "Golden Age" of baseball card collecting, then perhaps the "Silver Age" commenced with the introduction of the Big League Gum series of 239 cards in 1933 (a 240th card was added in 1934). These are the forerunners of today's baseball gum cards, and the Goudey Gum Company of Boston is responsible for their success. This era spanned the period from the Depression days of 1933 to America's formal involvement in World War II in 1941.

Goudey's attractive designs, with full-color line drawings on thick card stock, greatly influenced other cards being issued at that time. As a result, the most attractive and popular vintage cards in history were produced in this "Silver Age." The 1933 Goudey Big League Gum series also owes its popularity to the more than 40 Hall of Fame players in the set. These include four cards of Babe Ruth and two of Lou Gehrig. Goudey's reign continued in 1934, when it issued a 96-card set in color, together with the single remaining card from the 1933 series, #106, the Napoleon Lajoie card.

In addition to Goudey, several other bubblegum manufacturers issued baseball cards during this era. DeLong Gum Company issued an extremely attractive set in 1933. National Chicle Company's 192-card "Batter-Up" series of 1934–1936 became the largest die-cut set in card history. In addition, that company offered the popular "Diamond Stars" series during the same period. Other popular sets included the "Tattoo Orbit" set of 60 color cards issued in 1933 and Gum Products' 75-card "Double Play" set, featuring sepia depictions of two players per card.

In 1939, Gum Inc., which later became Bowman Gum, replaced Goudey Gum as the leading baseball card producer. In 1939 and the following year, it issued two important sets of black-and-white cards. In 1939, its "Play Ball America" set consisted of 162 cards. The larger, 240-card "Play Ball" set of 1940 still is considered by many to be the most attractive black-and-white cards ever produced. That firm introduced its only color set in 1941, consisting of 72 cards titled "Play Ball Sports Hall of Fame." Many of these were colored repeats of poses from the black-and-white 1940 series.

In addition to regular gum cards, many manufacturers distributed premium issues during the 1930s. These premiums were printed on paper or photographic stock, rather than card stock. They were much larger than the regular cards and were sold for a penny across the counter with gum (which was packaged separately from the premium). They often were redeemed at the store or through the mail in

their inventory of sports cards to the point where they were providing both a wider and a deeper selection of trading cards than any site on the Internet. In addition, a company-wide effort to provide daily news content on their site (coupled with a weekly newsletter sent to over 400,000 collectors) began at year's end, and the hobby has reaped the benefits ever since.

As the 2001 season approached, hobbyists waited with bated breath for seven-time Japanese batting champ Ichiro Suzuki to make his debut in the Seattle Mariner's outfield. And what a stunning debut it was. Ichiro led the league in hitting, led the Mariners to their best record ever, and walked off with the A.L. Rookie of the Year and Most Valuable Player awards. Upper Deck obtained the exclusive rights to produce his autograph cards and they hit a grand slam in midsummer by releasing his SPx Rookie Card, featuring a game jersey swatch and a cut signature autograph. In a year studded with notable cards this one was likely the most memorable.

In the National League, 37-year-old San Francisco Giants superstar Barry Bonds captivated the nation by bashing a jaw-dropping 73 home runs, shattering Mark McGwire's 1998 single-season home run record.

Cardinals' rookie Albert Pujols emerged out of the low minor leagues to become an instant hobby superstar and walk away with N.L. Rookie of the Year honors.

The year 2001 was a tumultuous one for sports cards. Topps started the year off with a bang by celebrating their 50th anniversary producing baseball cards. Pacific forfeited its license to make baseball cards after an eight-year run to focus on football and hockey cards. Playoff, a company based out of Grand Prairie, Texas, that had earned its stripes producing football cards in the late 1990s, purchased the rights to the much-hallowed Donruss corporate name and became a formal MLB licensee in the spring of 2001. Their entrance into the baseball card market heralded the return of benchmark brands like Donruss, Donruss Signature and Leaf.

Competition was fiercer than ever amongst the four primary licensees (Donruss-Playoff, Fleer, Topps, and Upper Deck) as they cranked out almost 80 different products over the course of 2001.

Of all these, likely the most historically important product, Upper Deck Prospect Premieres, was widely overlooked upon release. In a bold move, Upper Deck created a set of 102 prospects, none of which had played a day in the majors. Each player was pictured, however, in the major league uniforms of their parent ballclubs and signed to individual contracts. Because no active major leaguers were featured, Upper Deck did not have to include licensing rights from the MLB Players Association, though they did get licensing from Major League Properties. The industry had never seen a major release featuring active ballplayers marketed to the mainstream audience that lacked licensing from the MLBPA. Because of its lack of historical predecessors and a mixed reception from collectors, the cards were tagged by Beckett Baseball Card Monthly as XRC's (or Extended Rookie Cards), a term that had not been used since 1989.

UD's Prospect Premieres was the first major effort by a manufacturer to level the playing field between Topps and everyone else in that Topps has exclusive rights from the MLBPA to include minor leaguers in their basic brands.

Rookie Cards continued to fascinate collectors, especially in a year with talents like Ichiro, Mark Prior and Albert Pujols. The number of players featured on Rookie Cards in 2001 ballooned to an almost absurd figure of 505.

Exchange cards became more prevalent than ever, as manufacturers expanded their use from autograph cards that didn't get returned in time for pack out to slots within basic sets left open in brands released early in the year to fill in with late-season rookie call-ups.

Certified autograph cards remained a huge player in how brands were structured, but the quality of the players suffered greatly as autograph fees continued to spiral out of control. Signatures from superstars like Barry Bonds and Derek Jeter were now being featured on cards with miniscule print runs of 25 or 50 copies while unknown (and often aging and marginal) prospects signed their serial-numbered Rookies Cards by the hundred count.

More serial-numbered Rookie Cards were produced than ever before, but the quantities produced kept sinking lower and lower as companies tried to create secondary market value by simply limiting supply, a dangerous move to say the least. Donruss-Playoff produced the scarcest Rookie Cards of the year, a handful of Game Base cards (including Ichiro) each serial #'d to a scant 100 copies, within their Leaf Limited set.

After a six-month delay, Topps released their much awaited e-Topps program, a product sold entirely on their Web site whereby trading is conducted in a similar fashion to the buying and selling of stocks, in September. The product was met with a reasonable amount of excitement but has struggled to find its place in the market since that point in time.

Several products incorporated non-card memorabilia such as signed caps, bobbing head dolls, and signed baseballs with mixed results.

Memorabilia cards continued to over-saturate the market as the number of cards featuring various bits and pieces of balls, bases, bats, jerseys, pants, shoes, seats, and whatever else could be dreamt up continued to be offered to consumers. To battle consumer apathy, companies often started to offer combination memorabilia cards featuring notable teammates or several pieces of equipment from a notable star.

Retro-themed cards continued to grow in popularity, and some of the innovations seen in these sets were remarkable. Of particular note was Upper Deck's SP Legendary Cuts Autographs set, featuring 84 deceased players. The set required UD to purchase more than 3,300 autograph cuts, which were then incorporated into a windowpane card design. The result was the first certified autograph cards for legends like Roger Maris, Satchell Paige, and Jackie Robinson. Also, Topps Tribute released at year's end and carrying a hefty $40 per pack suggested retail was widely hailed as one of the most beautiful retro-themed cards ever designed, with their crystal-board fronts encasing full-color, razor-sharp photos.

Pack prices continued to escalate, but surprisingly, the public did not balk as long as they delivered value. The most notable high-end product to hit the market in 2001 was Upper Deck Ultimate Collection with a suggested retail of $100 per pack.

September 11th, 2001, is a day that will go down as one of the most devastating in the history of the United States of America. The game of baseball and the hobby of collecting sports cards were rightfully cast aside as the nation mourned the tragic loss of lives in New York, Pennsylvania, and Washington, D.C. America's economy tumbled as airline traveling ground to a near halt and threats of anthrax crippled the mail system. An economy threatening to slip into recession at the beginning of the year dove headlong into it. The sports card market, along with many other industries, felt the hit for several months. Slowly, Americans looked to move past the grief and the sports card industry, steeped in American nostalgia, provided an ideal retreat for many.

The Arizona Diamondbacks beat the New York Yankees in one of the dramatic World Series ever played . . . a much-needed diversion for a grief-stricken nation and a calling card for the dramatic power and glory of our National Pastime.

2002 was a relatively quiet one for baseball cards. Dodger's rookie pitcher Kazuhisa Ishii got off to a blazing first half start and his cards carried many releases through to the All-Star break. Ishii stumbled badly in the second half and no notable rookies were in place to pick up market interest. Cubs hurler Mark Prior created a stir, and his 2001 Rookie Cards were red hot at mid-season. For the second straight season, Barry Bonds was the most dominant star in our sport. His early cards continued to outpace all others in volume trading and professional grading submissions.

The number of players featured on Rookie Cards (or Extended Rookie Cards) reached an all-time high of 524 in 2002 as the manufacturers continued to push the envelope toward more immediate coverage of the current year draft. Though few collectors took notice at the time of release, Upper Deck's incorporation of collegiate Team USA athletes into several year-end brands may take hold and grow into a more prominent position in our industry for collegiate ballplayers. The results of these trends, however, are cards that feature a lot of talented youngsters whom most collectors, unfortunately, have never heard of and won't see in a major league uniform for several years. Brewers second baseman Rickie Weeks, the #2 overall selection in the 2003 MLB draft, was the first Team USA player to reap immediate dividends for Upper Deck as his key early cards surged in value as the draft approached.

In 2002 Topps was the exclusive manufacturer with the licensing rights to produce Rookie Cards for Twins catching prospect Joe Mauer – the #1 overall selection from the 202 MLB draft. Though his cards traded moderately well upon release, it would be over a year later that his name started to show up on the Beckett Baseball Collector Hot List.

To make up for the void in excitement generated by rookies and prospects upon release, the manufacturers made some interesting innovations in product distribution and brand development. In general, base sets got noticeably bigger (including Upper Deck's 1,182 card 40-Man brand and Topps 990-card Topps Total brand). In addition, brands like Topps 206, Leaf Rookies and Stars, and Fleer Fall Classics started to incorporate variations of the base cards directly into the basic issue set (different images, switched out teams, etc.).

One of the bigger surprise hits of the year was the aforementioned Topps 206 brand, of which borrowed design elements and set composition from the legendary T-206 tobacco set. Other brands continued to successfully mine from cards and eras long since passed.

Rookie Cards maintained their status as primary drivers for box sales, exemplified by the incendiary late season release of Bowman Draft and Bowman Chrome Draft (released together in an intermingled pack).

Donruss continued to push the creative envelope by incorporating 8 ½" by 11" framed signature pieces directly into boxes of their Playoff Absolute brand. After a four-year hiatus, Fleer brought back their eponymous "Fleer" name brand with a 540-card set. Donruss introduced their wildly successful Diamond Kings brand, of which featured a 150-card painted set. Fleer's Box Score brand was also a popular debut utilizing a unique box-inside-a-box distribution concept. Popular brands like SP Legendary Cuts, Leaf Certified, Topps Heritage, and Topps Tribute all received warm welcomes for their follow-ups to their successes achieved the prior year.

By 2003 the nation was still struggling to dig out of recession and the sport of baseball narrowly averted a season-ending strike that could have seriously injured the baseball card industry. For the third straight season, the top prospect to have a significant impact on the industry hailed from Japan, slugger Hideki Matsui. Coming off a 50 home run campaign in the Nippon league, Matsui assumed duties as the New York Yankees left fielder and no other first year player was watched more closely. Though he produced 106 RBI's, Matsui lost the A.L. Rookie of the Year award to Kansas City Royals shortstop Angel Berroa in a controversial vote. The influx of talented players from Japan's Nippon League continued in the 2003 off-season as the New York Mets picked up 7-time All-Star shortstop Kazuo Matsui.

Donruss-Playoff had a big year in 2003 highlighted by Leaf Certified, Leaf Limited and Timeles Treasures. Leaf Certified was arguably the product of the year, sporting some of the most beautifu game used and autograph cards ever created within the run of Mirror parallels. Timeless Treasure established an all-time high for suggested retail price per pack at $150 a pop. The product wa consumed with relish as collectors were rewarded with a wide array of attractive cards sporting miniscule print runs.

The Grand Prairie, TX based manufacturer continued to establish themselves as market leader in high-end, game used cards at year's end by purchasing a 1925 Babe Ruth game worn jersey fo $264,000.

Donruss-Playoff also made waves in the world of certified autographs by inking superstars Hide Nomo and Mike Piazza to autograph contracts. Both players had signed very few cards prior to the D/ contract and their newly signed releases were hot commodities at $300-$1000 per throughout the 200 release season.

Despite garnering high praise from dealers and collectors alike for providing exciting product with strong value throughout 2003, some industry experts fear D/P's aggressive redefining of se structure and content may result in short term gains and potential long-term damage to the industry By year's end the secondary market was saturated with variation upon variation of Donruss-Playo autograph and game used cards with print runs of 25 or fewer copies. In addition, their recentl released 2004 Diamond Kings brand has shaken up the secondary market for "1 of 1" cards. B creating an unheard of 79 parallel versions to the base set, the product development team at D/ managed to mass-produce more than 3,500 true 1 of 1's of which were reported as hitting at a rate three per sealed hobby case. Three years ago, a signed card with a print run of 25 copies and a true 1 1 parallel were regarded as truly rare commodities. By 2004, however, these items are being met wi caution by some and apathy by others. It remains to be seen how Donruss-Playoff will continue generate the excitement established within many of their 2003 brands – but their talented produ development staff will likely have some interesting cards to pick up the slack.

2003 was a quiet year for Fleer that ended in widely circulated rumors that the company was fo sale. By early 2004, however, the company was reported to be moving forward with an aggressive campaign to reestablish themselves as a force to be reckoned with in the baseball card market by rejuvenating autograph and game used content and returning from an almost year-long hiatus from advertising.

With the proven success of brands like Timeless Treasures in 2003, the manufacturers continue to push the envelope for high end packs this year. Upper Deck sent shockwaves through the basketball card market by releasing UD Exquisite at $500 per pack. That figure makes the $200 per pack SP Game Patch baseball product seem modest by comparison but the product nonetheless established a new all-time high for SRP's in the baseball card market.

The potentially rich trend of incorporating notable figures from outside the sporting world into trading card sets continued to quietly gain steam in early 2003 with the inclusion of certified autograph cards featuring actors Jason Alexander and John Goodman within Upper Deck's Yankees Legends brand. In November, within packs 2004 Topps series one baseball, Topps included a certified autograph card for every U.S. President from George Washington to George W. Bush in their ground-breaking American Treasures Autograph Relics insert set. In December, Upper Deck quickly followed suit with their Presidential Signature Cuts within their SP Legendary Cuts brand. These cards had a profound effect upon the super high-end market redefining the limits of what could be marketed within a pack of trading cards.

By early 2004, Donruss-Playoff had announced their Fans of the Game insert featuring James Gandolfini (made famous for his Emmy-winning turn as mob boss Tony Soprano on HBO). In addition to Gandolfini, D/P announced intentions to incorporate up to 75 additional entertainment celebrities of whom have connections to America's Pastime.

The 2003 Postseason was one for the ages with the long-suffering Red Sox and Cubs in the mix alongside the New York Yankees and Barry Bonds' San Francisco Giants. An unfortunate chap by the name of Steve Bartman gained infamy as the unfortunate scapegoat for the Cubs demise. Josh Beckett gained notoriety alongside a gritty Ivan Rodriguez as the Florida Marlins snuck up on everyone to beat the Yankees in the World Series.

Marlins rookie hurler Dontrelle Willis, with a colorful delivery that reminded many of Vida Blue and Luis Tiant, dominated the Beckett Baseball Collector Hot List for much of the Summer. Tampa Bay D-Rays prospect Delmon Young and Rickie Weeks picked up the slack for Willis as the year came to a close. Albert Pujols and Mark Prior assumed superstar status in the hobby by the end of the '03 season. Pujol's 2001 Bowman Chrome Rookie Card (of which only 500 serial #'d signed copies were produced) moved up to the $1,000 mark and Prior's 2001 Ultimate Collection RC (250 serial #'d signed copies produced) was a hot ticket at $600.

Barry Bonds shook up the baseball world in the off-season by opting out of his MLB Player's Association contract in an effort to single-handedly monetize his run towards Hank Aaron's All-Time record of 755 home runs. Rumors of steroid usage dogged Bonds throughout the off-season (and to a lesser degree had fans questioning how clean Mark McGwire and Sammy Sosa were in 1998 when they both broke Roger Maris's single-season home run record). All that news was overshadowed when Alex Rodriguez was signed to become the New York Yankees third baseman (after the Red Sox failed to consummate a deal with the Rangers only one month prior).

By 2003 the baseball card market resumed its place at the forefront of the card-collecting hobby, outpacing football, basketball, hockey, golf, and motor sports in volume dollars. In fact, industry experts had estimates of baseball card sales accounting for as much as 60% of total sports card sales as 2004 approached. As the hobby of collecting basebll cards moves towards the 21st century, we face a market that is blessed with bold creativity and superlative quality and also challenged with the need to reach new consumers both in mass retail and in cyberspace to continue its growth.

Finding Out More

The above has been a thumbnail sketch of card collecting from its inception in the 1880s to the present. It is difficult to tell the whole story in just a few pages - there are several other good sources of information. Serious collectors should subscribe to at least one of the excellent hobby periodicals. We also suggest that collectors visit their local card shop(s) and also attend a sports collectibles show in their area. Card collecting is still a young and informal hobby. You can learn more about it in either place. After all, smart dealers realize that spending a few minutes teaching beginners about the hobby often pays off in the long run.

Each year Beckett Publications produces comprehensive annual price guides for these sports: Beckett Almanac of Baseball Cards and Collectibles, Beckett Basketball Card Price Guide, Beckett Football Card Price Guide, Beckett Hockey Card Price Guide, Beckett Racing Price Guide and a line of Beckett Alphabetical Checklists Books have been released as well. The aim of these annual guides is to provide information and accurate pricing on a wide array of sports cards, ranging from main issues by the major card manufacturers to various regional, promotional, and food issues. Also alphabetical checklist books are published to assist the collector in identifying all the cards of any particular player. The seasoned collector will find these tools valuable sources of information that will enable him to pursue his hobby interests.

In addition, abridged editions of the Beckett Price Guides have been published for each of these major sports as part of the House of Collectibles series: The Official Price Guide to Baseball Cards, The Official Price Guide to Football Cards, The Official Price Guide to Basketball Cards. Published in a convenient mass-market paperback format, these price guides provide information and accurate pricing on all the main issues by the major card manufacturers.

Within this Almanac you will find advertisements for sports memorabilia material, mail order, and retail sports collectibles establishments. All advertisements were accepted in good faith based on the reputation of the advertiser; however, neither the author, the publisher, the distributors, nor the other advertisers in this Price Guide accept any responsibility for any particular advertiser not complying with the terms of his or her ad.

Readers also should be aware that prices in advertisements are subject to change over the annual period before a new edition of this volume is issued each spring. When replying to an advertisement late in the baseball year, the reader should take this into account, and contact the dealer by phone or in writing for up-to-date price information. Should you come into contact with any of the advertisers in this guide as a result of their advertisement herein, please mention this source as your contact.

Prices found in this guide reflect current retail rates just prior to the printing of this book. They do not reflect the FOR SALE prices of the author, the publisher, the distributors, the advertisers, or any card dealers associated with this guide. No one is obligated in any way to buy, sell or trade his or her cards based on these prices. The price listings were compiled by the author from actual buy/sell transactions at sports conventions, sports card shops, buy/sell advertisements in the hobby papers, for sale prices from dealer catalogs and price lists, and discussions with leading hobbyists in the U.S. and Canada. All prices are in U.S. dollars.

A great deal of diligence, hard work, and dedicated effort went into this year's volume. However, the high standards to which we hold ourselves could not have been met without the expert input and generous amount of time contributed by many people. Our sincere thanks are extended to each and every one of you.

A complete list of these invaluable contributors appears after the Price Guide section.

MAJOR LEAGUE

1906 A's Postcards

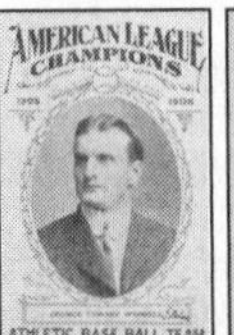

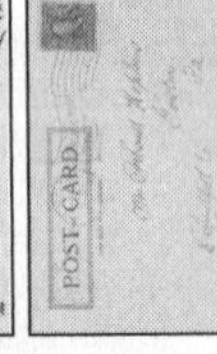

These ornate postcards were issued by the Philadelphia A's to honor the pennant winning team of 1905. The fronts have the words "American League Champions" on the top along with the years 1905 and 1906. Then there is a player photo and then the player is identified along with being a member of the Athetic Baseball team. The backs are blank except for the words post card. These cards were issued by the Lincoln Publishing Co. The cards are unnumbered so we have sequenced them in alphabetical order.

	Ex-Mt	VG
COMPLETE SET	2500.00	1250.00
1 Chief Bender	250.00	125.00
2 Andy Coakley	100.00	50.00
3 Lave Cross	100.00	50.00
4 Monte Cross	100.00	50.00
5 Harry Davis	100.00	50.00
6 Jimmy Dygert	100.00	50.00
7 Topsy Hartsel	100.00	50.00
8 Weldon Henley	100.00	50.00
9 Danny Hoffman	100.00	50.00
10 John Knight	100.00	50.00
11 Bris Lord	100.00	50.00
12 Connie Mack MG	400.00	200.00
13 Danny Murphy	100.00	50.00
14 Joe Myers	100.00	50.00
15 Rube Oldring	100.00	50.00
16 Eddie Plank	300.00	150.00
17 Mike Powers	100.00	50.00
18 Ossie Schreckengost	100.00	50.00
19 Ralph Seybold	100.00	50.00
20 Rube Waddell	300.00	150.00

1911 A's Fireside T208

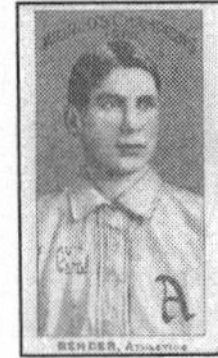

The cards in this 18-card set of color lithographs measure 1 1/2" by 2 5/8"; the cards were marketed in 1911 by Fireside Cigarettes honoring the 1910 World Champion Philadelphia Athletics. This tobacco brand was a product of the Thomas Cullivan Company of Syracuse, New York. The same front designs were also used in the D359 set by Rochester Baking. The players have been alphabetized and numbered for reference in the checklist below since the cards are unnumbered.

	Ex-Mt	VG
COMPLETE SET (18)	20000.00	10000.00
1 Frank Baker	2500.00	1250.00
2 Jack Barry	600.00	300.00
3 Chief Bender	2500.00	1250.00
4 Eddie Collins	3000.00	1500.00
5 Harry Davis	600.00	300.00
6 Jimmy Dygert	600.00	300.00
7 Topsy Hartsel	600.00	300.00
8 Harry Krause	600.00	300.00
9 John Lapp	600.00	300.00
10 Paddy Livingston	600.00	300.00
11 Bris Lord	600.00	300.00
12 Connie Mack MG	2500.00	1250.00
13 Cy Morgan	600.00	300.00
14 Danny Murphy	600.00	300.00
15 Rube Oldring	600.00	300.00
16 Eddie Plank	3000.00	1500.00
17 Amos Strunk	600.00	300.00
18 Ira Thomas	600.00	300.00

1929 A's Villa

Little is known about these postcard size cards issued in the Philadelphia area around 1929. The cards feature a portrait of the player on the front with their name and position on the bottom right. The back mentions a free Saturday matinee on October 12th. The villa logo is on the bottom. This listing may be incomplete so all additions are appreciated.

	Ex-Mt	VG
COMPLETE SET (5)	600.00	300.00
1 Eddie Collins	300.00	150.00
2 Jimmy Dykes	100.00	50.00
3 Mule Haas	100.00	50.00
4 Bing Miller	100.00	50.00
5 Rube Walberg	100.00	50.00

1930 A's Becker

Similar to the 1929 A's Villa cards, these postcard size cards, which feature members of the Philadelphia A's, were used to promote the local Becker Brothers Theatre which were then showing improved talking pictures. The front have a player photo while the back has a movie schedule. Since these cards are unnumbered we have sequenced them in alphabetical order.

	Ex-Mt	VG
COMPLETE SET	1000.00	500.00
1 Max Bishop	100.00	50.00
2 Mickey Cochrane	250.00	125.00
3 Sammy Hale	100.00	50.00
4 Jimmie Foxx	400.00	200.00
5 Al Simmons	250.00	125.00

1942 A's Team Issue

This 38-card set of the 1942 Athletics features black-and-white player posted photos with white borders. The backs are blank. The cards are unnumbered and checklisted below in alphabetical order.

	Ex-Mt	VG
COMPLETE SET (38)	300.00	150.00
1 Johnnie Babich	8.00	4.00
2 Bill Beckman	8.00	4.00
3 Herman Besse	8.00	4.00
4 Lena Blackburne CO	8.00	4.00
5 Buddy Blair	8.00	4.00
6 Al Brancato	8.00	4.00
7 Earle Brucker	8.00	4.00
8 Fred Caligiuri	8.00	4.00
9 Jim Castiglia	8.00	4.00
10 Russell Christopher	8.00	4.00
11 Eddie Collins Jr.	8.00	4.00
12 Lawrence Davis	8.00	4.00
13 Richard Fowler	8.00	4.00
14 Bob Harris	8.00	4.00
15 Lum Harris	10.00	5.00
16 Frank Hayes	8.00	4.00
17 Bob Johnson	12.00	6.00
18 Bill Knickerbocker	8.00	4.00
19 Jack Knott	8.00	4.00
20 Mike Kreevich	8.00	4.00
21 Connie Mack MG	20.00	10.00
22 Earle Mack	8.00	4.00
23 Felix Mackiewicz	8.00	4.00
24 Phil Marchildon	10.00	5.00
25 Benny McCoy	8.00	4.00
26 Dee Miles	8.00	4.00
27 Tex Shirley	8.00	4.00
28 Shibe Park	8.00	4.00
29 Dick Siebert	8.00	4.00
30 Al Simmons CO	20.00	10.00
31 Pete Suder	8.00	4.00
32 Bob Swift	8.00	4.00
33 Elmer Valo	8.00	4.00
34 Porter Vaughn	8.00	4.00
35 Harold Wagner	8.00	4.00
36 Jack Wallaesa	8.00	4.00
37 Roger Wolff	8.00	4.00
38 1942 Athletics Team	10.00	5.00

1943 A's Team Issue

This 28-card set of the Philadelphia Athletics was issued by the club and features 7" by 10" black-and-white player portraits in white borders and with blank backs. The cards are unnumbered and checklisted below in alphabetical order. The team picture (card number 1) measures 7 1/2" by 10 1/2" and the two Connie Mack cards also measure differently than the other cards.

	Ex-Mt	VG
COMPLETE SET (28)	225.00	110.00
1 1943 Athletics Team	25.00	12.50
2 Tal Abernathy	8.00	4.00
3 Orie Arntzen	8.00	4.00
4 Herman Besse	8.00	4.00
5 Don Black	8.00	4.00
6 James Blackburne	8.00	4.00
7 Earle Brucker	8.00	4.00
8 Russ Christopher	8.00	4.00
9 Bobby Estalella	8.00	4.00
10 Everett Fagan	8.00	4.00
11 Jesse Flores	8.00	4.00
12 Irv Hall	8.00	4.00
13 Luman Harris	10.00	5.00
14 Sam Loury	8.00	4.00
15 Connie Mack MG 7 5/8"x9 1/2" with no border and an autograph	25.00	12.50
16 Connie Mack MG 7 3/4"x10 1/2"	25.00	12.50
17 Earle Mack CO	8.00	4.00
18 Eddie Mayo	8.00	4.00
19 Dick Siebert	8.00	4.00
20 Frank Skaff	8.00	4.00
21 Pete Suder	8.00	4.00
22 Bob Swift	8.00	4.00
23 Jim Tyack	8.00	4.00
24 Elmer Valo	10.00	5.00
25 Hal Wagner	8.00	4.00
26 Johnny Welaj	8.00	4.00
27 Jo-Jo White	8.00	4.00
28 Roger Wolff	8.00	4.00

1945 A's Team Issue

This 30-card set of the Philadelphia Athletics was issued by the club and features 7" by 10" black-and-white player portraits in white borders and with blank backs. The cards are unnumbered and checklisted below in alphabetical order.

	Ex-Mt	VG
COMPLETE SET (30)	225.00	110.00
1 1945 Athletics Team Photo	25.00	12.50
2 Charlie Berry CO	8.00	4.00
3 Don Black	8.00	4.00
4 Earle Brucker	8.00	4.00
5 Joe Burns	8.00	4.00
6 Ed Busch	8.00	4.00
7 Russ Christopher	8.00	4.00
8 Joseph Cicero	8.00	4.00
9 Larry Drake	8.00	4.00
10 Hal Epps	8.00	4.00
11 Bobby Estalella	8.00	4.00
12 Jesse Flores	8.00	4.00
13 Mike Garbark	8.00	4.00
14 Charles Gassaway	8.00	4.00
15 Steve Gerkin	8.00	4.00
16 Irv Hall	8.00	4.00
17 Frankie Hayes	8.00	4.00
18 Dave Keefe	8.00	4.00
19 George Kell	20.00	10.00
20 Lou Knerr	8.00	4.00
21 Bill McGhee	8.00	4.00
22 Charles Metro	8.00	4.00
23 Bobo Newsom	10.00	5.00
24 Earle Mack CO	8.00	4.00
25 Hal Peck	8.00	4.00
26 Jim Pruett	8.00	4.00
27 Reidy	8.00	4.00
28 Dick Siebert	8.00	4.00
29 Al Simmons CO	20.00	10.00
30 Bobby Wilkins	8.00	4.00

1946 A's Team Issue

This 15-card set of the Philadelphia Athletics was issued by the club and features 7" by 10" black-and-white player portraits in white borders and with blank backs. The cards are unnumbered and checklisted below in alphabetical order.

	Ex-Mt	VG
COMPLETE SET (15)	150.00	75.00
1 1946 Athletics Team Picture	25.00	12.50
2 Earle Brucker	6.00	3.00
3 Sam Chapman	6.00	3.00
4 Russ Christopher	6.00	3.00
5 Jess Flores	6.00	3.00
6 Richard Fowler	6.00	3.00
7 Luman Harris	8.00	4.00
8 Luther Kaear	6.00	3.00
9 Dave Keefe	6.00	3.00
10 Connie Mack MG	25.00	12.50
11 Phil Marchildon	6.00	3.00
12 Al Simmons CO	20.00	10.00
13 Pete Suder	6.00	3.00
14 Elmer Valo	10.00	5.00
15 Shibe Park	25.00	12.50

1947 A's Team Issue

This 30-card set of the Philadelphia Athletics measures approximately 7" by 10" and features black-and-white player photos with white borders. The backs are blank. The cards are unnumbered and checklisted below in alphabetical order.

	Ex-Mt	VG
COMPLETE SET (30)	175.00	90.00
1 1947 Athletics Team Picture	25.00	12.50
2 Dick Adams	5.00	2.50
3 George Binks	5.00	2.50
4 Earle Brucker	5.00	2.50
5 Sam Chapman	5.00	2.50
6 Russ Christopher	5.00	2.50
7 Joe Coleman	5.00	2.50
8 Bill Dietrich	5.00	2.50
9 Everett Fagan	5.00	2.50
10 Ferris Fain	10.00	5.00
11 Jesse Flores	5.00	2.50
12 Dick Fowler	5.00	2.50
13 Mike Guerra	5.00	2.50
14 Gene Handley	5.00	2.50
15 Eddie Joost	8.00	4.00
16 Dave Keefe	5.00	2.50
17 Bill Knickerbocker	5.00	2.50
18 Connie Mack MG	20.00	10.00
19 Hank Majeski	5.00	2.50
20 Phil Marchildon	5.00	2.50
21 Bill McCahan	5.00	2.50
22 Barney McCosky	5.00	2.50
23 Ray Poole	5.00	2.50
24 Don Richmond	5.00	2.50
25 Buddy Rosar	5.00	2.50
26 Bob Savage	5.00	2.50
27 Carl Scheib	5.00	2.50
28 Al Simmons CO	20.00	10.00
29 Pete Suder	5.00	2.50
30 Elmer Valo	10.00	5.00

1948 A's Team Issue

This 27-card set of the Philadelphia Athletics measures approximately 7" by 10" and features black-and-white player photos with white borders. The backs are blank. The cards are unnumbered and checklisted below in alphabetical order.

	NM	Ex
COMPLETE SET (27)	150.00	75.00
1 1948 Athletics Team Picture	20.00	10.00
2 Leland Brissie	4.00	2.00
3 Earle Brucker	4.00	2.00
4 Sam Chapman	6.00	3.00
5 Joe Coleman	4.00	2.00
6 Billy DeMars	4.00	2.00
7 Ferris Fain	8.00	4.00
8 Dick Fowler	4.00	2.00
9 Herman Franks	5.00	2.50
10 Mike Guerra	4.00	2.00
11 Charles Harris	4.00	2.00
12 Eddie Joost	6.00	3.00
13 David Keefe	4.00	2.00
14 Connie Mack MG	20.00	10.00
15 Hank Majeski	4.00	2.00
16 Phil Marchildon	4.00	2.00
17 Bill McCahan	4.00	2.00
18 Barney McCosky	4.00	2.00
19 Buddy Rosar	4.00	2.00
20 Bob Savage	4.00	2.00
21 Carl Scheib	4.00	2.00
22 Al Simmons CO	20.00	10.00
23 Pete Suder	4.00	2.00
24 Elmer Valo	8.00	4.00
25 Skeeter Webb	4.00	2.00
26 Don White	4.00	2.00
27 Rudy York	5.00	2.50

1949 A's Team Issue

This 33-card set of the Philadelphia Athletics features black-and-white player photos with white borders. Card number 1 measures 8" by 10" and is an actual team photograph. The backs are blank. The cards are unnumbered and checklisted below in alphabetical order. The photos were available direct from the A's for either three cents each or $1 for the set at the time of issue.

	NM	Ex
COMPLETE SET (33)	225.00	110.00
1 1949 Athletics Team. 8x10	25.00	12.50
2 1949 Athletics Team	25.00	12.50
3 Shibe Park	25.00	12.50
4 Joe Astroth	4.00	2.00
5 Henry Biasatti	4.00	2.00
6 Lou Brissie	5.00	2.50
7 Earle Brucker	4.00	2.00
8 Sam Chapman	6.00	3.00
9 Joe Coleman	4.00	2.00
10 Tom Davis	4.00	2.00
11 Jimmie Dykes CO	5.00	2.50
12 Ferris Fain	6.00	3.00
13 Dick Fowler	4.00	2.00
14 Nelson Fox	25.00	12.50
15 Mike Guerra	4.00	2.00
16 Charlie Harris	4.00	2.00
17 Eddie Joost	6.00	3.00
18 David Keefe	4.00	2.00
19 Alex Kellner	4.00	2.00
20 Connie Mack MG	20.00	10.00
21 Earl Mack	4.00	2.00
22 Hank Majeski	4.00	2.00
23 Phil Marchildon	4.00	2.00
24 Barney McCosky	4.00	2.00
25 Lester McCrabb	4.00	2.00
26 Wally Moses	5.00	2.50
27 Buddy Rosar	4.00	2.00
28 Carl Scheib	4.00	2.00
29 Bobby Shantz	8.00	4.00
30 Pete Suder	4.00	2.00
31 Elmer Valo	6.00	3.00
32 Don White	4.00	2.00
33 Taft Wright	4.00	2.00

1950 A's Team Issue

This 28-card set of the Philadelphia Athletics was issued by the club and features black-and-white player portraits that were used previously in the team sets. For a number of years, the A's did not issue new sets, but carried the same cards over several years. The backs are blank. The cards are unnumbered and checklisted below in alphabetical order.

	NM	Ex
COMPLETE SET (27)	125.00	60.00
1 Joseph Astroth	4.00	2.00
3 Lou Brissie	4.00	2.00
4 Samuel Chapman	5.00	2.50
5 Mickey Cochrane CO	20.00	10.00
6 Joseph Coleman	4.00	2.00
7 Bob Dillinger	4.00	2.00
8 Jimmy Dykes CO	5.00	2.50
9 Ferris Fain	5.00	2.50
10 Dick Fowler	4.00	2.00
11 Mike Guerra	4.00	2.00
12 William Hitchcock	4.00	2.00
13 Robert Hooper	4.00	2.00
14 Edwin Joost	5.00	2.50
15 Alex Kellner	4.00	2.00
16 Paul Lehner	4.00	2.00
17 Hank Majeski	4.00	2.00
18 Phil Marchildon	4.00	2.00
19 William McCoskey	4.00	2.00
20 Bing Miller CO	4.00	2.00
21 Wally Moses	5.00	2.50
22 Carl Scheib	4.00	2.00
23 Bobby Shantz	6.00	3.00
24 Pete Suder	4.00	2.00
25 Joe Tipton	4.00	2.00
26 Elmer Valo	5.00	2.50
27 Kermit Wahl	4.00	2.00
28 Henry Wyse	4.00	2.00

1951 A's Team Issue

This 35-card set of the Philadelphia Athletics was issued by the club and features the same photos as in the 1949 or 1950 Athletics team sets. The cards are unnumbered and checklisted below in alphabetical order.

	NM	Ex
COMPLETE SET (35)	140.00	70.00
1 1951 Athletics Team Photo	20.00	10.00
2 Joe Astroth	4.00	2.00
3 Chief Bender CO	10.00	5.00
4 Ed Burtaschy	4.00	2.00
5 Samuel Chapman	5.00	2.50
6 Allie Clark	4.00	2.00
7 Joe Coleman	4.00	2.00
8 Jimmy Dykes MG	5.00	2.50
9 Ferris Fain	5.00	2.50
10 Richard Fowler	4.00	2.00
11 Bill Hitchcock	4.00	2.00
12 Bob Hooper	4.00	2.00
13 Eddie Joost	5.00	2.50
14 Alex Kellner	4.00	2.00
15 Lou Klein	4.00	2.00
16 John Kucab	4.00	2.00
17 Paul Lehner	4.00	2.00
18 Lou Limmer	4.00	2.00
19 Connie Mack OWN	15.00	7.50
20 Earl Mack CO	4.00	2.00
21 Hank Majeski	4.00	2.00
22 Morris Martin	4.00	2.00
23 Bing Miller CO	5.00	2.50
24 Wallace Moses	5.00	2.50
25 Ray Murray	4.00	2.00
26 Tom Oliver CO	4.00	2.00
27 Dave Philley	5.00	2.50
28 Carl Scheib	4.00	2.00
29 Bobby Shantz	6.00	3.00
30 Pete Suder	4.00	2.00
31 Joe Tipton	4.00	2.00
32 Elmer Valo	5.00	2.50
33 Kermit Wahl	4.00	2.00
34 Gus Zernial	6.00	3.00
35 Sam Zoldak	4.00	2.00

1952 A's Team Issue

This 31-card set of the Philadelphia Athletics was issued by the club and features the same photos as in the 1949 and 1951 Athletics team sets. The cards are unnumbered and checklisted below in alphabetical order.

	NM	Ex
COMPLETE SET (31)	125.00	60.00
1 1952 Athletics Team Photo	20.00	10.00
2 Shibe Park	20.00	10.00
3 Joe Astroth	4.00	2.00
4 Hal Bevan	4.00	2.00
5 Harry Byrd	4.00	2.00
6 Allie Clark	4.00	2.00
7 Jimmy Dykes MG	5.00	2.50
8 Ferris Fain	6.00	3.00
9 Dick Fowler	4.00	2.00
10 Bill Hitchcock	4.00	2.00
11 Bob Hooper	4.00	2.00
12 Eddie Joost	5.00	2.50
13 Skeeter Kell	4.00	2.00
14 Alex Kellner	4.00	2.00
15 John Kucab	4.00	2.00
16 Connie Mack OWN	15.00	7.50
17 Morris Martin	4.00	2.00
18 Bing Miller CO	5.00	2.50
19 Wally Moses CO	5.00	2.50
20 Ray Murray	4.00	2.00
21 Bobo Newsom	5.00	2.50
22 Dave Philley	4.00	2.00
23 Sherry Robertson	4.00	2.00
24 Carl Scheib	4.00	2.00
25 Bobby Shantz	6.00	3.00
26 Pete Suder	4.00	2.00
27 Keith Thomas	4.00	2.00
28 Elmer Valo	5.00	2.50
29 Ed Wright	4.00	2.00
30 Gus Zernial	6.00	3.00
31 Sam Zoldak	4.00	2.00

1953 A's Team Issue

This 31-card set of the Philadelphia Athletics was issued by the club and features the same photos as in the 1951 and 1952 Athletics team sets. The cards are unnumbered and checklisted below in alphabetical order.

	NM	Ex
COMPLETE SET (31)	125.00	60.00
1 1953 Athletics Team Photo	20.00	10.00
2 Joe Astroth	4.00	2.00
3 Loren Babe	4.00	2.00
4 Chief Bender CO	10.00	5.00
5 Charlie Bishop	4.00	2.00
6 Harry Byrd	4.00	2.00
7 Joe Coleman	5.00	2.50
8 Joe DeMaestri	4.00	2.00
9 Jimmy Dykes MG	6.00	3.00
10 Frank Fanovich	4.00	2.00
11 Marion Fricano	4.00	2.00
12 Tom Hamilton	4.00	2.00
13 Eddie Joost	6.00	3.00
14 Alex Kellner	4.00	2.00
15 Morris Martin	4.00	2.00
16 Connie Mack OWN	15.00	7.50
17 Ed McGhee	4.00	2.00
18 Cass Michaels	4.00	2.00
19 Bing Miller CO	5.00	2.50
20 Ed Monahan	4.00	2.00
21 Wally Moses CO	5.00	2.50
22 Ray Murray	4.00	2.00
23 Bobo Newsom	5.00	2.50
24 Tom Oliver CO	4.00	2.00
25 Dave Philley	4.00	2.00
26 Ed Robinson	4.00	2.00
27 Carl Scheib	4.00	2.00
28 Bobby Shantz	6.00	3.00
29 Pete Suder	4.00	2.00
30 Elmer Valo	5.00	2.50
31 Gus Zernial	6.00	3.00

1954 A's Team Issue

This 30-card set of the Philadelphia Athletics was issued by the club and features the same photos as in the 1953 Athletics team set. The cards are unnumbered and checklisted below in alphabetical order.

	NM	Ex
COMPLETE SET (30)	125.00	60.00
1 1954 Athletics Team Photo	20.00	10.00
2 Joe Astroth	4.00	2.00
3 Charlie Bishop	4.00	2.00
4 Don Bollweg	4.00	2.00
5 Ed Burtchy	4.00	2.00
6 Joe DeMaestri	4.00	2.00
7 Art Dittmar	4.00	2.00
8 Jim Finigan	4.00	2.00
9 Marion Fricano	4.00	2.00
10 John Gray	4.00	2.00
11 Forest Jacobs	4.00	2.00
12 Eddie Joost	5.00	2.50
13 Alex Kellner	4.00	2.00
14 Lou Limmer	4.00	2.00
15 Wally Moses CO	5.00	2.50
16 Ray Murray	4.00	2.00
17 Dave Philley	4.00	2.00
18 Arnold Portocarrero	4.00	2.00
19 Vic Power	6.00	3.00
20 Bill Renna	4.00	2.00
21 Al Robertson	4.00	2.00
22 Carl Scheib	4.00	2.00
23 Bill Shantz	4.00	2.00
24 Bobby Shantz	6.00	3.00
25 Pete Suder	4.00	2.00
26 Bob Trice	4.00	2.00
27 Elmer Valo	5.00	2.50
28 Ozzie Van Brabant	4.00	2.00
29 Lee Wheat	4.00	2.00
30 Gus Zernial	6.00	3.00

1955 A's Rodeo Meats

The cards in this 47-card set measure 2 1/2" by 3 1/2". The 1955 Rodeo Meats set contains unnumbered, color cards of the first Kansas City A's team. There are many background color variations noted in the checklist, and the card reverses carry a scrapbook offer. The Grimes and Kryhoski cards listed in the scrapbook album were apparently never issued. The catalog number for this set is F152-1. The cards have been arranged in alphabetical order and assigned numbers for reference.

	NM	Ex
COMPLETE SET (47)	5000.00	2500.00
1 Joe Astroth	80.00	40.00
2 Harold Bevan	120.00	60.00
3 Charles Bishop	120.00	60.00
4 Don Bollweg	120.00	60.00
5 Lou Boudreau MG	250.00	125.00
6 Cloyd Boyer (Salmon)	80.00	40.00
7 Cloyd Boyer (Light blue)	150.00	75.00
8 Ed Burtschy	150.00	75.00
9 Art Ceccarelli	120.00	60.00
10 Joe DeMaestri (Yellow)	80.00	40.00
11 Joe DeMaestri (Green)	80.00	40.00
12 Art Ditmar	80.00	40.00
13 John Dixon	120.00	60.00
14 Jim Finigan	80.00	40.00
15 Marion Fricano	120.00	60.00
16 Tom Gorman	80.00	40.00
17 John Gray	120.00	60.00
18 Ray Herbert	80.00	40.00
19 Forrest Jacobs	150.00	75.00
20 Alex Kellner	80.00	40.00
21 Harry Kraft CO (Craft, sic)	80.00	40.00
22 Jack Littrell	80.00	40.00
23 Hector Lopez	100.00	50.00
24 Oscar Melillo CO	80.00	40.00
25 Arnold Portocarrero (Purple)	150.00	75.00
26 Arnold Portocarrero (Gray)	80.00	40.00
27 Vic Power (Yellow)	100.00	50.00
28 Vic Power (Pink)	150.00	75.00
29 Vic Raschi	150.00	75.00
30 Bill Renna (Lavender)	80.00	40.00
31 Bill Renna (Dark pink)	150.00	75.00
32 Al Robertson	120.00	60.00
33 Johnny Sain	200.00	100.00
34 Bobby Schantz ERR (Misspelling)	250.00	125.00
35 Bobby Shantz COR	150.00	75.00
36 Wilmer Shantz (Orange)	80.00	40.00
37 Wilmer Shantz (Lavender)	80.00	40.00
38 Harry Simpson	80.00	40.00
39 Enos Slaughter	250.00	125.00
40 Lou Sleater	80.00	40.00
41 George Susce CO	120.00	60.00
42 Bob Trice	120.00	60.00
43 Elmer Valo (Yellow)	150.00	75.00
44 Elmer Valo (Green sky)	100.00	50.00
45 Bill Wilson (Yellow)	150.00	75.00
46 Bill Wilson (Lavender sky)	80.00	40.00
47 Gus Zernial	120.00	60.00

1955 A's Team Issue

This 29-card set measuring approximately 6 1/4" by 9 1/4" features borderless sepia photos of the Kansas City Athletics. The backs are blank. The cards are unnumbered and checklisted below in alphabetical order.

	NM	Ex
COMPLETE SET (29)	100.00	50.00
1 Joe Asthroth	3.00	1.50
2 Lou Boudreau MG	10.00	5.00
3 Cloyd Boyer	5.00	2.50
4 Art Cecarelli	3.00	1.50
5 Harry Craft CO	3.00	1.50
6 Joe DeMaestri	3.00	1.50
7 Art Dittmar	3.00	1.50
8 Jim Finigan	3.00	1.50
9 Tom Gorman	3.00	1.50
10 Ray Herbert	3.00	1.50
11 Alex Kellner	3.00	1.50
12 Dick Kryhoski	3.00	1.50
13 Jack Littrell	3.00	1.50
14 Hector Lopez	4.00	2.00
15 Oscar Melillo CO	3.00	1.50
16 Arnold Portocarrero	3.00	1.50
17 Vic Power	5.00	2.50
18 Vic Raschi	5.00	2.50
19 Bill Renna	3.00	1.50
20 John Sain	6.00	3.00
21 Bill Shantz	3.00	1.50
22 Bobby Shantz	6.00	3.00
23 Harry Simpson	3.00	1.50
24 Enos Slaughter	8.00	4.00
25 Lou Sleator	3.00	1.50
26 George Susce	3.00	1.50
27 Elmer Valo	4.00	2.00
28 Bill Wilson	3.00	1.50
29 Gus Zernial	5.00	2.50

1956-60 A's Postcards

This multi-year postcard set of the Kansas City Athletics features borderless black-and-white player photos measuring approximately 3 1/4" by 5 1/2". The backs are blank. These set was issued by the club at no charge and issued over a series of years. The cards are unnumbered and checklisted below in alphabetical order.

	NM	Ex
COMPLETE SET	1000.00	500.00
1 Jim Archer	10.00	5.00
2 Hank Bauer	15.00	7.50
3 Mike Baxes Fielding	10.00	5.00
4 Mike Baxes Portrait	10.00	5.00
5 Zeke Bella	10.00	5.00
6 Lou Boudreau MG	20.00	10.00
7 Cletis Boyer	15.00	7.50
8 George Brunet	10.00	5.00
9 Wally Burnette	10.00	5.00
10 Ed Burtschy	10.00	5.00
11 Andy Carey	12.00	6.00
12 Chico Carrasquel	12.00	6.00
13 Robert Cerv Portrait to Letters	10.00	5.00
14 Bob Cerv Portrait to Neck	10.00	5.00
15 Harry Chiti	10.00	5.00
16 Rip Coleman	10.00	5.00
17 Walt Craddock	10.00	5.00
18 Harry Craft CO	10.00	5.00
19 Jack Crimian	10.00	5.00
20 Bud Daley	10.00	5.00
21 Pete Daley	10.00	5.00
22 Bob Davis	10.00	5.00
23 Joe DeMaestri Fielding	10.00	5.00
24 Joe DeMaestri With Bat	10.00	5.00
25 Art Ditmar	10.00	5.00
26 Jim Ewell TR	10.00	5.00
27 Jim Finigan	10.00	5.00
28 Mark Freeman	10.00	5.00
29 Ned Garver	10.00	5.00
30 Bob Giggie	10.00	5.00
31 Joe Ginsberg	10.00	5.00
32 Tom Gorman to hips	10.00	5.00
33 Tom Gorman Pitching	10.00	5.00
34 Tom Gorman Standing with glove	10.00	5.00
35 Bob Grim	10.00	5.00
36 Johnny Groth Portrait	10.00	5.00
37 Johnny Groth Standing with Bat	10.00	5.00
38 Kent Hadley	10.00	5.00
39 Dick Hall	10.00	5.00
40 Ken Hamlin	10.00	5.00
41 Ray Herbert Dark Background	10.00	5.00
42 Ray Herbert White Background	10.00	5.00
43 Troy Herriage	10.00	5.00
44 Whitey Herzog	15.00	7.50
45 Frank House	10.00	5.00
46 Spook Jacobs	10.00	5.00
47 Bob Johnson	10.00	5.00
48 Ken Johnson	10.00	5.00
49 Alex Kellner	10.00	5.00
50 Leo Kiely	10.00	5.00
51 Lou Kretlow	10.00	5.00
52 Johnny Kucks	10.00	5.00
53 Marty Kutnya	10.00	5.00
54 Don Larsen	15.00	7.50
55 Tom Lasorda	25.00	12.50
56 Hec Lopez Batting	10.00	5.00
57 Hector Lopez Portrait	10.00	5.00
58 Jerry Lumpe	10.00	5.00
59 Jack McMahan	10.00	5.00
60 Roger Maris	50.00	25.00
61 Oscar Melillo CO	10.00	5.00
62 Al Pilarick	10.00	5.00
63 Rance Pless	10.00	5.00
64 Vic Power	15.00	7.50
65 Eddie Robinson	10.00	5.00
66 Jose Santiago	10.00	5.00
67 Bobby Shantz	15.00	7.50
68 Norm Siebern	10.00	5.00
69 Harry Simpson Batting	10.00	5.00
70 Harry Simpson Portrait	10.00	5.00
71 Harry Simpson Fielding	10.00	5.00
72 Lou Skizas	10.00	5.00
73 Enos Slaughter Fielding	20.00	10.00
74 Enos Slaughter Batting	20.00	10.00
75 Hal Smith	10.00	5.00
76 Russ Snyder	10.00	5.00
77 George Susce	10.00	5.00
78 Ralph Terry	10.00	5.00
79 Wayne Terwilliger	10.00	5.00
80 Charles Thompson	10.00	5.00
81 Dick Tomanek	10.00	5.00
82 John Tsitouris	10.00	5.00
83 Marv Throneberry	15.00	7.50
84 Bob Trowbridge	10.00	5.00
85 Bill Tuttle	10.00	5.00
86 Jack Urban	10.00	5.00
87 Preston Ward	10.00	5.00
88 Dick Williams	15.00	7.50
89 Gus Zernial (Batting)	15.00	7.50
90 Gus Zernial (Catching)	15.00	7.50

1956 A's Rodeo Meats

The cards in this 12-card set measure 2 1/2" by 3 1/2". The unnumbered, color cards of the 1956 Rodeo baseball series are easily distinguished from their 1955 counterparts by the absence of the scrapbook offer on the reverse. They were available only in packages of Rodeo All-Meat Wieners. The catalog designation for this set is F152-2, and the cards have been assigned numbers in alphabetical order in the checklist below.

	NM	Ex
COMPLETE SET (12)	1200.00	600.00
1 Joe Astroth	60.00	30.00
2 Lou Boudreau MG	250.00	125.00
3 Joe DeMaestri	60.00	30.00
4 Art Ditmar	60.00	30.00
5 Jim Finigan	60.00	30.00
6 Hector Lopez	60.00	30.00
7 Vic Power	60.00	30.00
8 Bobby Shantz	120.00	60.00
9 Harry Simpson	60.00	30.00
10 Enos Slaughter	250.00	125.00
11 Elmer Valo	80.00	40.00
12 Gus Zernial	80.00	40.00

1957 A's Jay Publishing

This 12-card set of the Kansas City Athletics measures approximately 5" by 7" and features black-and-white player photos in a white border. These cards were packaged 12 to a packet. The backs are blank. The cards are unnumbered and checklisted below in alphabetical order. The cards have the player's name and Athletics on the bottom

	NM	Ex
COMPLETE SET	50.00	25.00
1 Lou Boudreau MG	8.00	4.00
2 Bob Cerv	4.00	2.00
3 Tom Gorman	4.00	2.00
4 Milt Graff	4.00	2.00
5 Billy Hunter	4.00	2.00
6 Hector Lopez	4.00	2.00
7 Maury McDermott	4.00	2.00
8 Tom Morgan	4.00	2.00
9 Vic Power	4.00	2.00
10 Harry Simpson	4.00	2.00
11 Lou Skizas	4.00	2.00
12 Hal Smith	4.00	2.00

1958 A's Jay Publishing

This 12-card set of the Kansas City Athletics measures approximately 5" by 7" and features black-and-white player photos in a white border. These cards were packaged 12 to a packet. The backs are blank. The cards are unnumbered and checklisted below in alphabetical order. More than 12 players are listed in this set as it covers players who came to the A's all during the 1958 season.

	NM	Ex
COMPLETE SET	40.00	20.00
1 Harry Craft MG	3.00	1.50
2 Joe DeMaestri	3.00	1.50
3 Ned Garver	3.00	1.50
4 Woody Held	3.00	1.50
5 Frank House	3.00	1.50
6 Hector Lopez	3.00	1.50
7 Vic Power	5.00	2.50
8 Hal Smith	3.00	1.50
9 Ralph Terry	4.00	2.00
10 Virgil Trucks	5.00	2.50
11 Bill Tuttle	3.00	1.50
12 Jack Urban	3.00	1.50

1959 A's Jay Publishing

This 12-card set of the Kansas City Athletics measures approximately 5" by 7" and features black-and-white player photos in a white border. The backs are blank. The cards are unnumbered and checklisted below in alphabetical order.

	NM	Ex
COMPLETE SET (12)	40.00	20.00
1 Bob Cerv	3.00	1.50
2 Harry Craft MG	3.00	1.50
3 Bud Daley	3.00	1.50
4 Ned Garver	3.00	1.50
5 Bob Grim	3.00	1.50
6 Ray Herbert	3.00	1.50
7 Frank House	3.00	1.50
8 Hector Lopez	3.00	1.50
9 Roger Maris	15.00	7.50
10 Hal Smith	3.00	1.50
11 Ralph Terry	4.00	2.00
12 Bill Tuttle	3.00	1.50

1960 A's Jay Publishing

This 12-card set of the Kansas City Athletics measures approximately 5" by 7" and features black-and-white player photos in a white border. The backs are blank. The cards are unnumbered and checklisted below in alphabetical order.

	NM	Ex
COMPLETE SET (11)	30.00	12.00
1 Hank Bauer	5.00	2.00
2 Bud Daley	2.50	1.00
3 Bob Elliott MG	2.50	1.00
4 Ned Garver	2.50	1.00
5 Ray Herbert	2.50	1.00
6 Johnny Kucks	2.50	1.00
7 Don Larsen	4.00	1.60
8 Jerry Lumpe	2.50	1.00
9 Norm Siebern	2.50	1.00
10 Marv Throneberry	5.00	2.00
11 Bill Tuttle	2.50	1.00
12 Dick Williams	5.00	2.00

1960 A's Team Issue

These 3 1/4" by 5 1/2" blank backed cards feature members of the 1960 A's. The fronts have fascimile autographs and we have sequenced the set in alphabetical order

	NM	Ex
COMPLETE SET (18)	35.00	14.00
1 Hank Bauer	5.00	2.00
2 Zeke Bella	2.50	1.00
3 Bob Cerv	2.50	1.00
4 Bud Daley	2.50	1.00
5 Jim Ewell TR	2.50	1.00
6 Ken Hamlin	2.50	1.00
7 Ray Herbert	2.50	1.00
8 Whitey Herzog	5.00	2.00
9 Bob Johnson	2.50	1.00
10 Ken Johnson	2.50	1.00
11 Johnny Kucks	2.50	1.00
12 Marty Kutnya	2.50	1.00
13 Jerry Lumpe	2.50	1.00
14 Norm Siebern	2.50	1.00
15 Russ Snyder	2.50	1.00
16 John Tsitouris	2.50	1.00
17 Bill Tuttle	2.50	1.00
18 Dick Williams	5.00	2.00

1961-62 A's Jay Publishing

This 24-card set of the Kansas City Athletics measures approximately 5" by 7". The fronts feature black-and-white posed player photos with the player's and team name printed below in the white border. These cards were packaged 12 to a packet and originally sold for 25 cents. The backs are blank. The cards are unnumbered and checklisted below in alphabetical order.

	NM	Ex
COMPLETE SET (24)	50.00	20.00
1 Jim Archer	2.00	.80
2 Norm Bass	2.00	.80
3 Hank Bauer 61	4.00	1.60
4 Bob Boyd 61	2.00	.80
5 Wayne Causey	2.00	.80
6 Frank Cipriani	2.00	.80
7 Bud Daley 61	2.00	.80
8 Joe Gordon MG 61	3.00	1.20
9 Ray Herbert 61	2.00	.80
10 Dick Howser	3.00	1.20
11 Manny Jimenez 62	2.00	.80
12 Jerry Lumpe (Head photo)	2.00	.80
13 Jerry Lumpe (At bat)	2.00	.80
14 Joe Nuxhall 61	2.00	.80
15 Joe Pignatano 61	2.00	.80
16 Leo Posada	2.00	.80
17 Ed Rakow	2.00	.80
18 Norm Siebern (At bat)	2.00	.80
19 Norm Siebern (Head photo)	2.00	.80
20 Haywood Sullivan (Waist-up photo)	2.00	.80
21 Haywood Sullivan Head photo)	2.00	.80
22 Marv Throneberry 61	3.00	1.20
23 Bill Tuttle 61	2.00	.80
24 Jerry Walker	2.00	.80

1961 A's Team Issue

These cards measure 3 1/4" by 5 1/2" and are blank backs. The fronts have black and white borderless photos with fascimile autographs. We have sequenced this set in alphabetical order. These cards are usually found with a "red" Kansas City A's envelope. It is believed that these cards were sold as a set at the ballpark and were not used for fan request autographs.

	NM	Ex
COMPLETE SET	60.00	24.00
1 Jim Archer	2.00	.80
2 Norm Bass	2.00	.80
3 Hank Bauer	3.00	1.20
4 Bob Boyd	2.00	.80
5 Andy Carey	2.00	.80
6 Wayne Causey	2.00	.80
7 Clint Courtney	2.00	.80
8 Bud Daley	2.00	.80
9 Joe Gordon MG	3.00	1.20
10 Jay Hankins	2.00	.80
11 Ray Herbert	2.00	.80
12 Dick Howser	3.00	1.20
13 Ken Johnson	2.00	.80
14 Ed Keegan	2.00	.80
15 Lou Klimchock	2.00	.80
16 Bill Kunkel	2.00	.80
17 Frank Lane GM	2.00	.80
18 Don Larsen	4.00	1.60
19 Jerry Lumpe	2.00	.80
20 Joe Nuxhall	2.00	.80
21 Joe Pignatano	2.00	.80
22 Al Pilarcik	2.00	.80
23 Leo Posada	2.00	.80
24 Ed Rakow	2.00	.80

25 Norm Siebern	2.00	.80
26 Haywood Sullivan	2.00	.80
27 Marv Throneberry	3.00	1.20
28 Bill Tuttle	2.00	.80

1962 A's Team Issue

These 4" by 5" black and white cards were used by the Kansas City Athletics to deal with photo requests. These photos have the players name and position on the front surrounded by a white border. Since these cards are unnumbered, we have sequenced them in alphabetical order.

	NM	Ex
COMPLETE SET (32)	60.00	24.00
1 Jim Archer	2.00	.80
2 Joe Azcue	2.00	.80
3 Norm Bass	2.00	.80
4 Hank Bauer MG	2.50	1.00
5 Wayne Causey	2.00	.80
6 Ed Charles	2.50	1.00
7 Gino Cimoli	2.00	.80
8 Bob Del Greco	2.00	.80
9 Art Ditmar	2.00	.80
10 Bob Grim	2.00	.80
11 Dick Howser	2.50	1.00
12 Manny Jimenez	2.00	.80
13 Bill Kunkel	2.00	.80
14 Dario Lodigiani	2.00	.80
15 Ed Lopat CO	3.00	1.20
16 Jerry Lumpe	2.00	.80
17 Danny McDevitt	2.00	.80
18 Gus Niarhos CO	2.00	.80
19 Dan Osinski	2.00	.80
20 Dan Pfister	2.00	.80
21 Leo Posada	2.00	.80
22 Ed Rakow	2.00	.80
23 Diego Segui	2.00	.80
24 Norm Siebern	2.00	.80
25 Gene Stephens	2.00	.80
26 Haywood Sullivan	2.00	.80
27 Jose Tartabull	2.00	.80
28 Jerry Walker	2.00	.80
29 Jo-Jo White CO	2.00	.80
30 Dave Wickersham	2.00	.80
31 Gordon Windhorn	2.00	.80
32 John Wyatt	2.00	.80

1963 A's Jay Publishing

This 12-card set of the Kansas City Athletics measures approximately 5" by 7". The fronts feature black-and-white posed player photos with the player's and team name printed below in the white border. These cards were packaged 12 to a packet. The backs are blank. The cards are unnumbered and checklisted below in alphabetical order.

	NM	Ex
COMPLETE SET (12)	25.00	10.00
1 Jim Archer	2.00	.80
2 Norm Bass	2.00	.80
3 Wayne Causey	2.00	.80
4 Bill Fischer	2.00	.80
5 Dick Howser	3.00	1.20
6 Manny Jiminez	2.00	.80
7 Ed Lopat MG	3.00	1.20
8 Jerry Lumpe	3.00	1.20
9 Norm Siebern	2.00	.80
10 Haywood Sullivan	2.00	.80
11 Jose Tartabull	2.00	.80
12 Jerry Walker	2.00	.80

1964 A's Jay Publishing

This 12-card set of the Kansas City Athletics measures approximately 5" by 7". The fronts feature black-and-white posed player photos with the player's and team name printed below in the white border. These cards were packaged 12 to a packet. The backs are blank. The cards are unnumbered and checklisted below in alphabetical order.

	NM	Ex
COMPLETE SET (12)	25.00	10.00
1 Wayne Causey	2.50	1.00
2 Ed Charles	2.00	.80
3 Moe Drabowsky	2.00	.80
4 Doc Edwards	2.00	.80
5 Jim Gentile	2.50	1.00
6 Ken Harrelson	2.50	1.00
7 Manny Jimenez	2.00	.80
8 Charlie Lau	2.50	1.00
9 Ed Lopat MG	2.50	1.00
10 Orlando Pena	2.00	.80
11 Diego Segui	2.00	.80
12 Jose Tartabull	2.00	.80

1965 A's Jay Publishing

This 12-card set of the Kansas City Athletics measures approximately 5" by 7". The fronts feature black-and-white posed player photos with the player's and team name printed below in the white border. These cards were packaged 12 to a packet. The backs are blank. The cards are unnumbered and checklisted below in alphabetical order.

	NM	Ex
COMPLETE SET (12)	20.00	8.00
1 Bill Bryan	1.50	.60
2 Wayne Causey	1.50	.60
3 Ed Charles	1.50	.60
4 Doc Edwards	1.50	.60
5 Jim Gentile	2.00	.80
6 Dick Green	1.50	.60
7 Ken Harrelson	3.00	1.20
8 Mike Hershberger	1.50	.60
9 Jim Landis	1.50	.60
10 Mel McGaha MG	1.50	.60
11 Wes Stock	1.50	.60
12 Fred Talbot	1.50	.60

1969 A's Black and White

This 15-card set measures approximately 2 1/16" by 3 5/8" and features black-and-white close-up player photos on a white card face. The player's name and position appears below the picture along with the team name. The backs are blank. The cards are unnumbered and checklisted below in alphabetical order. This set features a card of Joe DiMaggio as an A's coach as well as a card from Reggie Jackson's Rookie Card year. The set is dated by the fact that 1969 was the only year Tom Reynolds played for the A's. It is believed that this is a collectors issue set produced by long time collector, Mike Andersen.

	NM	Ex
COMPLETE SET (15)	60.00	24.00
1 Sal Bando	4.00	1.60
2 Hank Bauer MG	3.00	1.20
3 Bert Campaneris	3.00	1.20
4 Danny Cater	2.00	.80
5 Joe DiMaggio CO	30.00	12.00
6 Chuck Dobson	2.00	.80
7 Dick Green	2.00	.80
8 Catfish Hunter	10.00	4.00
9 Reggie Jackson	20.00	8.00
10 Rick Monday	3.00	1.20
11 Jim Nash	2.00	.80
12 Blue Moon Odom	3.00	1.20
13 Tom Reynolds	2.00	.80
14 Phil Roof	2.00	.80
15 Ramon Webster	2.00	.80

1970 A's Black and White

Similar to the set which was issued in 1969 and some collectors call Jack in the Box, this set features members of the 1970 A's. The black and white photos take up most of the card with the players name and Oakland A logo on the bottom. The backs are blank so we have sequenced these cards in alphabetical order.

	NM	Ex
COMPLETE SET	50.00	20.00
1 Felipe Alou	3.00	1.20
2 Sal Bando	2.00	.80
3 Bert Campaneris	2.00	.80
4 Chuck Dobson	1.00	.40
5 Al Downing	1.00	.40
6 Dave Duncan	1.00	.40
7 Frank Fernandez	1.00	.40
8 Tito Francona	1.00	.40
9 Rollie Fingers	6.00	2.40
10 Jim Mudcat Grant	1.00	.40
11 Dick Green	1.00	.40
12 Larry Haney	1.00	.40
13 Catfish Hunter	8.00	3.20
14 Reggie Jackson	15.00	6.00
15 Paul Lindblad	1.00	.40
16 John McNamara MG	1.00	.40
17 Don Mincher	1.00	.40
18 Rick Monday	2.00	.80
19 John Odom	1.00	.40
20 Roberto Pena	1.00	.40
21 Jim Roland	1.00	.40
22 Roberto Rodriguez	1.00	.40
23 Diego Segui	1.00	.40
24 Jose Tartabull	1.00	.40

1973 A's 1874 TCMA Postcards

These nine postcards issued feature members of the National Association Philadelphia Athletics of the 19th century. The fronts feature black and white posed photos while the backs mention these photos are reproduced from the July 25th 1874 Harpers Weekly. Interestingly, these players are from the National Association and this is one of the few sets which features players from that league which existed before the National League was formed.

	NM	Ex
COMPLETE SET(9)	10.00	4.00
1 Cap Anson	3.00	1.20
2 Joseph Battin	1.00	.40
3 John Clapp	1.00	.40
4 Weston Fisler	1.00	.40
5 Count Gedney	1.00	.40
6 Dick McBride	1.00	.40
7 Mike McGeary	1.00	.40
8 John (Lefty) McMullen	1.00	.40
9 Ezra Sutton	1.50	.60

1974 A's 1910-14 TCMA Postcards

This 12-card set features photos of the 1910-1914 Philadelphia A's players printed on postcards. The cards are unnumbered and checklisted below alphabetically.

	NM	Ex
COMPLETE SET (12)	20.00	8.00
1 Frank Baker	6.00	2.40
2 Jack Barry	1.00	.40
3 Chief Bender	6.00	2.40
4 Eddie Collins	8.00	3.20
5 John Coombs	1.00	.40
6 Jack Lapp	1.00	.40
7 Stuffy McInnis	1.00	.40
8 Danny Murphy	1.00	.40
9 Rube Oldring	1.00	.40
10 Eddie Plank	6.00	2.40
11 Amos Strunk	1.00	.40
12 Ira Thomas	1.00	.40

1974 A's 1929-31 TCMA

This 28-card set features photos of the 1929-31 Philadelphia Athletics team and measure approximately 2 1/2" by 4". The cards are unnumbered and checklisted below in alphabetical order.

	NM	Ex
COMPLETE SET (28)	30.00	12.00
1 Max Bishop	1.00	.40
2 Joe Boley	1.00	.40
3 George Burns	1.00	.40
4 Mickey Cochrane	4.00	1.60
5 Eddie Collins Lew Krausse	3.00	1.20
6 Doc Cramer	1.50	.60
7 Jimmy Dykes	2.00	.80
8 George Earnshaw	1.50	.60
9 Howard Ehmke	1.00	.40
10 Lou Finney John Heving	1.00	.40
11 Jimmie Foxx	5.00	2.00
12 Walt French Waite Hoyt	1.50	.60
13 Lefty Grove	4.00	1.60
14 Mule Haas	1.00	.40
15 Sammy Hale	1.00	.40
16 Pinky Higgins Phil Todt	1.00	.40
17 Connie Mack MG Earl Mack	1.50	.60
18 Roy Mahaffey	1.00	.40
19 Eric McNair	1.00	.40
20 Bing Miller	1.00	.40
21 Jack Quinn	2.00	.80
22 Eddie Rommel	1.50	.60
23 Wally Schang	1.50	.60
24 Al Simmons	3.00	1.20
25 Homer Summa	1.00	.40
26 Rube Walberg	1.00	.40
27 Dib Williams	1.00	.40
28 Jim Moore Jim Peterson	1.00	.40
29 A's Team Card Large Photo measures approximately 4 1/2" by 11 3/8"	5.00	2.00

1974 A's 1931 BraMac

This set, which measures 3 1/2" by 5" features members of the 1931 Philadelphia A's and was issued by the Bra-Mac collaboration.

	NM	Ex
COMPLETE SET	15.00	6.00
1 Jimmy Moore	.50	.20
2 Mule Haas	.50	.20
3 Dib Williams	.50	.20
4 Jimmie Foxx	4.00	1.60
5 Al Simmons	2.50	1.00
6 Bing Miller	.50	.20
7 Jimmie Dykes	1.00	.40
8 Eric McNair	.50	.20
9 Joe Boley	.50	.20
10 Mickey Cochrane	2.50	1.00
11 Max Bishop	.50	.20
12 Joe Heving	.50	.20
13 Doc Cramer	1.00	.40
14 Lefty Grove	2.50	1.00
15 Ed Rommel	.50	.20
16 Rube Walberg	.50	.20
17 Roy Mahaffey	.50	.20
18 Lew Krausse	.50	.20
19 Hank McDonald	.50	.20

1975 A's 1913 TCMA

These unnumbered black and white cards, which measure approximately 5 1/8" by 3 1/8" feature members of the 1913 Philadelphia A's. Since these cards are unnumbered, we have sequenced them in alphabetical order.

	NM	Ex
COMPLETE SET	15.00	6.00
1 Frank Baker	2.00	.80
2 Jack Barry	.50	.20
3 Chief Bender	2.00	.80
4 Joe Bush	.75	.30
5 Eddie Collins	3.00	1.20
6 Jack Coombs	.50	.20
7 Connie Mack MG	2.50	1.00
8 Snuffy McInnis	.50	.20
9 Danny Murphy	.50	.20
10 Eddie Murphy	.50	.20
11 Rube Oldring	.50	.20
12 Bill Orr	.50	.20
13 Eddie Plank	2.00	.80
14 Wally Schang	.75	.30
15 Amos Strunk	.50	.20

1976 A's Rodeo Meat Commemorative

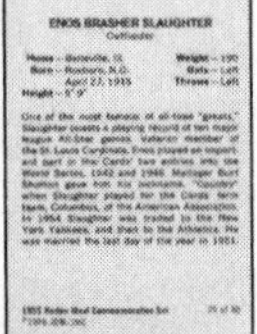

This 30-card standard-sized set commemorates the 1955 Rodeo Meat series. The cards feature posed black-and-white player photos with white borders. The player's name appears in the lower margin. The Rodeo Meat logo is superimposed at the lower left corner of the picture. The backs carry the player's name, biographical information and a player profile. The cards are arranged in alphabetical order and numbered on the back. These cards were also issued in uncut sheet form and the set was available from the producer for $6.50 for the card set or $10 for the uncut sheet.

	NM	Ex
COMPLETE SET (30)	20.00	8.00
1 Title Card	.50	.20
2 Checklist	.50	.20
3 Joe Astroth	.50	.20
4 Lou Boudreau MG	1.50	.60
5 Cloyd Boyer	1.00	.40
6 Art Ceccarelli	.50	.20
7 Harry Craft CO	.50	.20
8 Joe DeMaestri	.50	.20
9 Art Ditmar	1.00	.40
10 Jim Finigan	.50	.20
11 Tom Gorman	1.00	.40
12 Ray Herbert	.75	.30
13 Alex Kellner	.50	.20
14 Jack Littrell	.50	.20
15 Hector Lopez	1.00	.40
16 Oscar Melillo CO	.50	.20
17 Arnold Portocarrero	.50	.20
18 Vic Power	.75	.30
19 Vic Raschi	1.00	.40
20 Bill Renna	.50	.20
21 John Sain	1.00	.40
22 Bobby Shantz	1.00	.40
23 Wilmer Shantz	.50	.20
24 Harry Simpson	.50	.20
25 Enos Slaughter	2.00	.80
26 Lou Sleator	.50	.20
27 George Susce CO	.50	.20
28 Elmer Valo	.75	.30
29 Bill Wilson	.50	.20
30 Gus Zernial	.75	.30

1981 A's Granny Goose

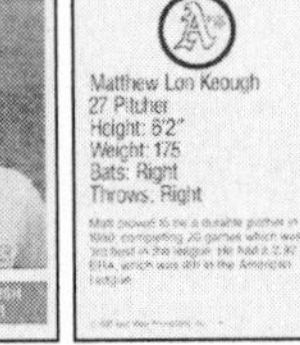

This set is the hardest to obtain of the three years Granny Goose issued cards of the Oakland A's. The Revering card was supposedly destroyed by the printer soon after he was traded away and hence is in shorter supply than the other 14 cards in the set. Wayne Gross is also supposedly available in lesser quantity compared to the other players. The standard-size cards were issued in bags of potato chips. Cards are numbered on the front and back by the player's uniform number.

	Nm-Mt	Ex-Mt
COMPLETE SET (15)	75.00	30.00
1 Billy Martin MG	10.00	4.00
2 Mike Heath	1.50	.60
5 Jeff Newman	1.50	.60
6 Mitchell Page	1.50	.60
8 Rob Picciolo	1.50	.60
10 Wayne Gross SP	5.00	2.00
13 Dave Revering SP	30.00	12.00
17 Mike Norris	1.50	.60
20 Tony Armas	2.00	.80
21 Dwayne Murphy	1.50	.60
22 Rick Langford	1.50	.60
27 Matt Keough	1.50	.60
35 Rickey Henderson	30.00	12.00
39 Dave McKay	1.50	.60
54 Steve McCatty	1.50	.60

1982 A's Granny Goose

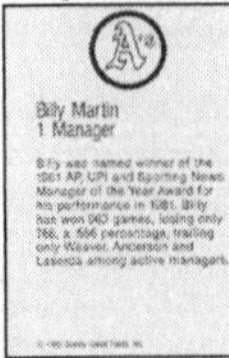

The cards in this 15-card set measure 2 1/2" by 3 1/2". Granny Goose Foods, Inc., a California based company, repeated its successful promotional idea of 1981 by issuing a new set of Oakland A's baseball cards for 1982. Each color player picture is surrounded by white borders and has trim and lettering done in Oakland's green and yellow colors. The cards are, in a sense, numbered according to the uniform number of the player; the card numbering below is according to alphabetical order by name. The card backs carry vital statistics done in black print on a white background. The cards were distributed in packages of potato chips and were also handed out on August 15th at Oakland/Alameda stadium. Although Picciolo was traded, his card was not withdrawn (as was Revering in 1981) and, therefore, its value is no greater than other cards in the set. Blank backs exist for all players; there is no known price differential for these cards.

	Nm-Mt	Ex-Mt
COMPLETE SET (15)	15.00	6.00
1 Tony Armas	.75	.30
2 Wayne Gross	.50	.20
3 Mike Heath	.50	.20
4 Rickey Henderson	8.00	3.20
5 Cliff Johnson	.75	.30
6 Matt Keough	.50	.20
7 Rick Langford	.50	.20
8 Davey Lopes	1.00	.40
9 Billy Martin MG	2.50	1.00
10 Steve McCatty	.50	.20
11 Dwayne Murphy	.50	.20
12 Jeff Newman	.50	.20
13 Mike Norris	.50	.20
14 Rob Picciolo	.50	.20
15 Fred Stanley	.50	.20

1983 A's Granny Goose

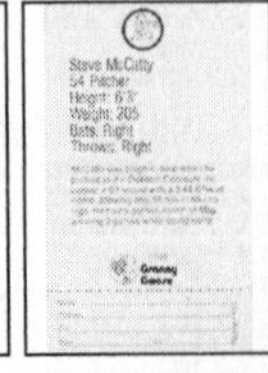

The cards in this 15-card set measure 2 1/2" by 4 1/4". The 1983 Granny Goose Potato Chips set again features Oakland A's players. The cards that were issued in bags of potato chips have a tear off coupon on the bottom with a scratch off section featuring prizes. The grand prize was a World Series trip for two. In addition to their release in bags of potato chips, the Granny Goose cards were also given away (as complete sets with no tabs) to fans attending the Oakland game of July 3, 1983. These give away cards did not contain the coupon on the bottom. Prices listed below are for cards without the detachable tabs that came on the bottom of the cards; cards with tabs intact are valued 50 percent higher than the prices below. The card numbering below is according to uniform number. According to promotional materials, more than one million cards were distributed during the promotion.

	Nm-Mt	Ex-Mt
COMPLETE SET (15)	12.00	4.80
2 Mike Heath	.50	.20
4 Carney Lansford	1.50	.60
10 Wayne Gross	.50	.20
14 Steve Boros MG	.50	.20
15 Davey Lopes	1.00	.40
16 Mike Davis	.50	.20
17 Mike Norris	.50	.20
21 Dwayne Murphy	.50	.20
22 Rick Langford	.50	.20
27 Matt Keough	.50	.20
31 Tom Underwood	.50	.20
33 Dave Beard	.50	.20
35 Rickey Henderson	8.00	3.20
39 Tom Burgmeier	.50	.20
54 Steve McCatty	.50	.20

1983 A's Greats TCMA

This 12-card set features black-and-white photos with red borders of the Athletics

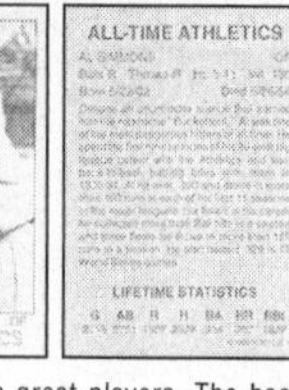

franchise all-time great players. The backs carry player information.

	Nm-Mt	Ex-Mt
COMPLETE SET (12)	8.00	3.20
1 Jimmie Foxx	2.00	.80
2 Eddie Collins	1.50	.60
3 Frank Baker	1.00	.40
4 Jack Barry	.25	.10
5 Al Simmons	1.00	.40
6 Mule Haas	.25	.10
7 Bing Miller	.25	.10
8 Mickey Cochrane	1.25	.50
9 Chief Bender	1.00	.40
10 Lefty Grove	1.50	.60
11 John Wyatt	.25	.10
12 Connie Mack MG	.50	.20

1984 A's Mother's

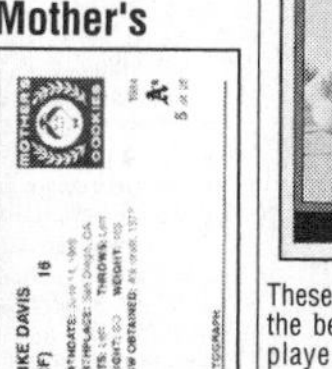

The cards in this 28-card set measure 2 1/2" by 3 1/2". In 1984, the Los Angeles based Mother's Cookies Co. issued five sets of cards featuring players from major league teams. The Oakland A's set features current players depicted by photos. Similar to the Mother's Cookies 1952 and 1953 issues, the cards have rounded corners. The backs of the cards contain the Mother's Cookies logo. The cards were distributed in partial sets to fans at the respective stadiums of the teams involved. Whereas 20 cards were given to each patron, a redemption card, redeemable for eight more cards was included. Unfortunately, the eight cards received by redeeming the coupon were not necessarily the eight needed to complete a set. Hobbyist Barry Colla was involved in the production of these sets.

	Nm-Mt	Ex-Mt
COMPLETE SET (28)	12.50	5.00
1 Steve Boros MG	.25	.10
2 Rickey Henderson	5.00	2.00
3 Joe Morgan	3.00	1.20
4 Dwayne Murphy	.25	.10
5 Mike Davis	.25	.10
6 Bruce Bochte	.25	.10
7 Carney Lansford	.75	.30
8 Steve McCatty	.25	.10
9 Mike Heath	.25	.10
10 Chris Codiroli	.25	.10
11 Bill Almon	.25	.10
12 Bill Caudill	.25	.10
13 Donnie Hill	.25	.10
14 Lary Sorensen	.25	.10
15 Dave Kingman	.75	.30
16 Garry Hancock	.25	.10
17 Jeff Burroughs	.25	.10
18 Tom Burgmeier	.25	.10
19 Jim Essian	.25	.10
20 Mike Warren	.25	.10
21 Davey Lopes	.75	.30
22 Ray Burris	.25	.10
23 Tony Phillips	1.00	.40
24 Tim Conroy	.25	.10
25 Jeff Bettendorf	.25	.10
26 Keith Atherton	.25	.10
27 Ron Schueler CO	.50	.20
Billy Williams CO		
Clete Boyer CO		
Jackie Moore CO		
Bob Didier CO		
28 Oakland Coliseum CL	.25	.10

1985 A's Mother's

The cards in this 28-card set measure 2 1/2" by 3 1/2". In 1985, the Los Angeles based Mother's Cookies Co. again issued five sets of cards featuring players from major league teams. The Oakland A's set features current players depicted by photos on cards with rounded corners. The backs of the cards contain the Mother's Cookies logo. Cards were passed out at the stadium on July 6.

	Nm-Mt	Ex-Mt
COMPLETE SET (28)	10.00	4.00
1 Jackie Moore MG	.25	.10
2 Dave Kingman	.75	.30
3 Don Sutton	1.50	.60
4 Mike Heath	.25	.10
5 Alfredo Griffin	.25	.10
6 Dwayne Murphy	.25	.10
7 Mike Davis	.25	.10
8 Carney Lansford	.75	.30
9 Chris Codiroli	.25	.10
10 Bruce Bochte	.25	.10
11 Mickey Tettleton	1.50	.60
12 Donnie Hill	.25	.10
13 Rob Picciolo	.25	.10
14 Dave Collins	.25	.10
15 Dusty Baker	1.00	.40
16 Tim Conroy	.25	.10
17 Keith Atherton	.25	.10
18 Jay Howell	.25	.10
19 Mike Warren	.25	.10
20 Steve McCatty	.25	.10
21 Bill Krueger	.25	.10
22 Curt Young	.25	.10
23 Dan Meyer	.25	.10
24 Mike Gallego	.25	.10
25 Jeff Kaiser	.25	.10
26 Steve Henderson	.25	.10
27 Clete Boyer CO	.50	.20
Bob Didier CO		
Dave McKay CO		
Wes Stock CO		
Billy Williams CO		
28 Oakland Coliseum CL	.25	.10

1986 A's Greats TCMA

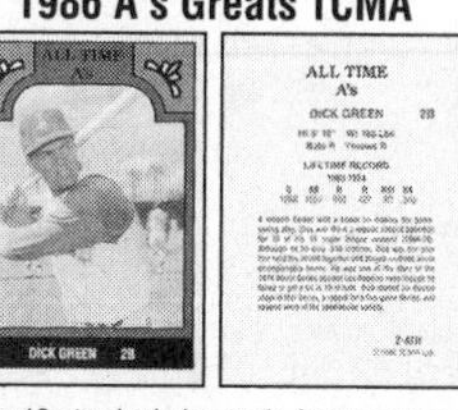

These 12 standard-size cards feature some of the best Oakland A's ever. The fronts feature player photos while the backs have player biographies.

	Nm-Mt	Ex-Mt
COMPLETE SET (12)	5.00	2.00
1 Gene Tenace	.50	.20
2 Dick Green	.25	.10
3 Bert Campaneris	.50	.20
4 Sal Bando	.50	.20
5 Joe Rudi	.25	.10
6 Rick Monday	.25	.10
7 Billy North	.25	.10
8 Dave Duncan	.25	.10
9 Jim "Catfish" Hunter	1.50	.60
10 Ken Holtzman	.50	.20
11 Rollie Fingers	1.00	.40
12 Alvin Dark MG	.25	.10

1986 A's Mother's

This set consists of 28 full-color, rounded-corner cards each measuring the standard size. Starter sets (only 20 cards but also including a certificate for eight more cards) were given out at the ballpark and collectors were encouraged to trade to fill in the rest of their set. The cards were originally given away on July 20th at Oakland Coliseum. Jose Canseco is featured in his rookie season.

	Nm-Mt	Ex-Mt
COMPLETE SET (28)	15.00	6.00
1 Jackie Moore MG	.25	.10
2 Dave Kingman	.75	.30
3 Dusty Baker	1.00	.40
4 Joaquin Andujar	.25	.10
5 Alfredo Griffin	.25	.10
6 Dwayne Murphy	.25	.10
7 Mike Davis	.25	.10
8 Carney Lansford	.75	.30
9 Jose Canseco	8.00	3.20
10 Bruce Bochte	.25	.10
11 Mickey Tettleton	1.00	.40
12 Donnie Hill	.25	.10
13 Jose Rijo	.25	.10
14 Rick Langford	.25	.10
15 Chris Codiroli	.25	.10
16 Moose Haas	.25	.10
17 Keith Atherton	.25	.10
18 Jay Howell	.25	.10
19 Tony Phillips	.75	.30
20 Steve Henderson	.25	.10
21 Bill Krueger	.25	.10
22 Steve Ontiveros	.25	.10
23 Bill Bathe	.25	.10
24 Ricky Peters	.25	.10
25 Tim Birtsas	.25	.10
26 Frank Ciensczyk	.25	.10
Steve Vucinich		
Barry Weinberg TR		
Larry Davis		
27 Bob Didier CO	.50	.20
Dave McKay CO		
Jeff Newman CO		
Ron Plaza CO		
Wes Stock CO		
Bob Watson CO		
28 Oakland Coliseum CL	.25	.10

1987 A's Mother's

This set consists of 28 full-color, rounded-corner cards each measuring the standard size. Starter sets (only 20 cards but also including a certificate for eight more cards) were given out at the ballpark and collectors were encouraged to trade to fill in the rest of their set. The cards were originally given away on July 5th at Oakland Coliseum during a game against the

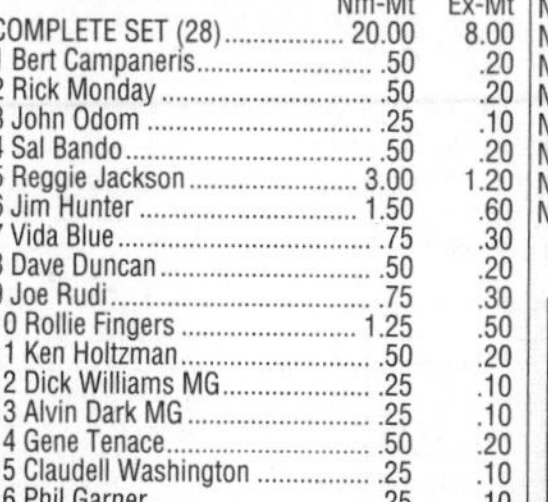

Boston Red Sox. This set is actually an All-Time All-Star set including every A's All-Star player since 1968 (when the franchise moved to Oakland). The vintage photos (each shot during the year of All-Star appearance) were taken from the collection of Doug McWilliams. The set is sequenced by what year the player first made the All-Star team. The sets were reportedly given out free to the first 25,000 paid admissions at the game.

	Nm-Mt	Ex-Mt
COMPLETE SET (28)	20.00	8.00
1 Bert Campaneris	.50	.20
2 Rick Monday	.50	.20
3 John Odom	.25	.10
4 Sal Bando	.50	.20
5 Reggie Jackson	3.00	1.20
6 Jim Hunter	1.50	.60
7 Vida Blue	.75	.30
8 Dave Duncan	.50	.20
9 Joe Rudi	.75	.30
10 Rollie Fingers	1.25	.50
11 Ken Holtzman	.50	.20
12 Dick Williams MG	.25	.10
13 Alvin Dark MG	.25	.10
14 Gene Tenace	.50	.20
15 Claudell Washington	.25	.10
16 Phil Garner	.25	.10
17 Wayne Gross	.25	.10
18 Matt Keough	.25	.10
19 Jeff Newman	.25	.10
20 Rickey Henderson	3.00	1.20
21 Tony Armas	.25	.10
22 Mike Norris	.25	.10
23 Billy Martin MG	1.00	.40
24 Bill Caudill	.25	.10
25 Jay Howell	.25	.10
26 Jose Canseco	4.00	1.60
27 Jose Canseco	3.00	1.20
Reggie Jackson		
28 A's Logo CL	.25	.10

1987 A's Smokey Colorgrams

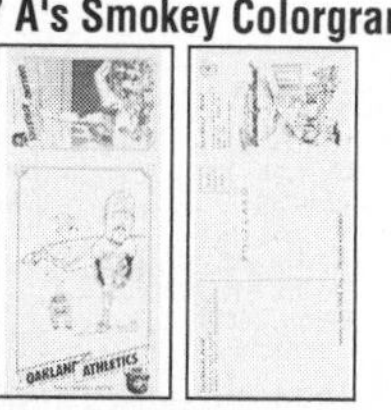

These cards are actually pages of a booklet featuring members of the Oakland A's and Smokey's fire safety tips. The booklet has 12 pages each containing a black and white photo card (approximately 2 1/2" by 3 3/4") and a black and white player caricature (oversized head) postcard (approximately 3 3/4" by 5 5/8"). The cards are unnumbered but they have biographical information and a fire-prevention cartoon on the back of the card.

	Nm-Mt	Ex-Mt
COMPLETE SET (12)	15.00	6.00
1 Joaquin Andujar	.50	.20
2 Jose Canseco	5.00	2.00
3 Mike Davis	.50	.20
4 Alfredo Griffin	.50	.20
5 Moose Haas	.50	.20
6 Jay Howell	.50	.20
7 Reggie Jackson	3.00	1.20
8 Carney Lansford	1.50	.60
9 Dwayne Murphy	.50	.20
10 Tony Phillips	.50	.20
11 Dave Stewart	2.00	.80
12 Curt Young	.50	.20

1988 A's Donruss Team Book

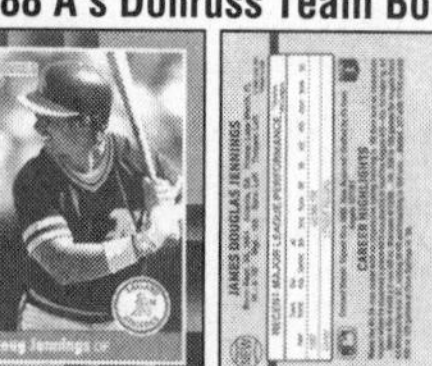

The 1988 Donruss Athletics Team Book set features 27 cards (three pages with nine cards on each page) plus a large full-page puzzle of Stan Musial. Cards are in full color and are standard size. The set was distributed as a four-page book; although the puzzle page was perforated, the card pages were not. The cover of the "Team Collection" book is primarily bright red. Card fronts are very similar in design to the 1988 Donruss regular issue. The card numbers on the backs are the same for those players that are the same as in the regular Donruss set; the new players pictured are numbered on the back as "NEW." In fact 1988 A.L. Rookie of the Year Walt Weiss makes his first Donruss appearance in this set as a "NEW" card. The book is usually sold intact. When cut from the book into individual cards, these cards are distinguishable from the regular 1988 Donruss cards since these have a 1988 copyright on the back whereas the regular issue has a 1987 copyright on the back.

	Nm-Mt	Ex-Mt
COMPLETE SET (27)	6.00	2.40
97 Curt Young	.10	.04
133 Gene Nelson	.10	.04
158 Terry Steinbach	.25	.10
178 Carney Lansford	.25	.10
221 Tony Phillips	.10	.04
256 Mark McGwire	3.00	1.20
302 Jose Canseco	1.50	.60
349 Dennis Eckersley	.75	.30
379 Mike Gallego	.10	.04
425 Luis Polonia	.10	.04
467 Steve Ontiveros	.10	.04
472 Dave Stewart	.25	.10
503 Eric Plunk	.10	.04
528 Greg Cadaret	.10	.04
590 Rick Honeycutt	.10	.04
595 Storm Davis	.10	.04
NEW Don Baylor UER	.25	.10
(Career stats		
are incorrect)		
NEW Ron Hassey	.10	.04
NEW Dave Henderson	.25	.10
NEW Glenn Hubbard	.10	.04
NEW Stan Javier	.10	.04
NEW Doug Jennings	.10	.04
NEW Ed Jurak	.10	.04
NEW Dave Parker	.25	.10
NEW Walt Weiss	.50	.20
NEW Bob Welch	.25	.10
NEW Matt Young	.10	.04

1988 A's Mother's

This set consists of 28 full-color, rounded-corner cards each measuring the standard-size. Starter sets (only 20 cards but also including a certificate for eight more cards) were given out at the ballpark and collectors were encouraged to trade to fill in the rest of their set. The cards were originally given away on July 23rd at Oakland Coliseum during a game. Short sets (20 cards plus certificate) were reportedly given out free to the first 35,000 paid admissions at the game.

	Nm-Mt	Ex-Mt
COMPLETE SET (28)	20.00	8.00
1 Tony LaRussa MG	1.00	.40
2 Mark McGwire	5.00	2.00
3 Dave Stewart	.75	.30
4 Terry Steinbach	.50	.20
5 Dave Parker	1.00	.40
6 Carney Lansford	.75	.30
7 Jose Canseco	2.50	1.00
8 Don Baylor	.75	.30
9 Bob Welch	.50	.20
10 Dennis Eckersley	2.00	.80
11 Walt Weiss	.75	.30
12 Tony Phillips	.50	.20
13 Steve Ontiveros	.25	.10
14 Dave Henderson	.25	.10
15 Stan Javier	.25	.10
16 Ron Hassey	.25	.10
17 Curt Young	.25	.10
18 Glenn Hubbard	.25	.10
19 Storm Davis	.25	.10
20 Eric Plunk	.25	.10
21 Matt Young	.25	.10
22 Mike Gallego	.25	.10
23 Rick Honeycutt	.25	.10
24 Doug Jennings	.25	.10
25 Gene Nelson	.25	.10
26 Greg Cadaret	.25	.10
27 Dave Duncan CO	.50	.20
Rene Lachemann CO		
Jim Lefebvre CO		
Dave McKay CO		
Mike Paul CO		
Bob Watson CO		
28 Jose Canseco	1.50	.60
Mark McGwire CL		

1989 A's Mother's

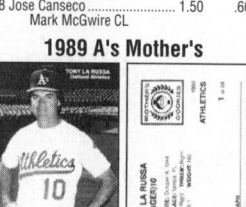

The 1989 Mother's Cookies Oakland A's set contains 28 standard-size cards with rounded corners. The fronts have borderless color photos, and the horizontally oriented backs have biographical information. Starter sets containing 20 of these cards were given away at an A's home game during the 1989 season.

	Nm-Mt	Ex-Mt
COMPLETE SET (28)	15.00	6.00
1 Tony LaRussa MG	1.00	.40
2 Mark McGwire	4.00	1.60
3 Terry Steinbach	.50	.20
4 Dave Parker	1.00	.40
5 Carney Lansford	.75	.30
6 Dave Stewart	.75	.30
7 Jose Canseco	2.00	.80
8 Walt Weiss	.50	.20
9 Bob Welch	.50	.20
10 Dennis Eckersley	1.50	.60
11 Tony Phillips	.50	.20
12 Mike Moore	.50	.20
13 Dave Henderson	.25	.10
14 Curt Young	.25	.10
15 Ron Hassey	.25	.10
16 Eric Plunk	.25	.10
17 Luis Polonia	.25	.10
18 Storm Davis	.25	.10
19 Glenn Hubbard	.25	.10
20 Greg Cadaret	.25	.10
21 Stan Javier	.25	.10
22 Felix Jose	.25	.10
23 Mike Gallego	.25	.10
24 Todd Burns	.25	.10
25 Rick Honeycutt	.25	.10
26 Gene Nelson	.25	.10
27 Dave Duncan CO	.50	.20
Rene Lachemann CO		
Art Kusnyer CO		
Dave McKay CO		
Tommie Reynolds CO		
Merv Rettenmund CO		
28 Walt Weiss	1.50	.60
Mark McGwire		
Jose Canseco CL		

1989 A's Mother's ROY's

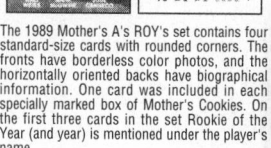

The 1989 Mother's A's ROY's set contains four standard-size cards with rounded corners. The fronts have borderless color photos, and the horizontally oriented backs have biographical information. One card was included in each specially marked box of Mother's Cookies. On the first three cards in the set Rookie of the Year (and year) is mentioned under the player's name.

	Nm-Mt	Ex-Mt
COMPLETE SET (4)	8.00	3.20
1 Jose Canseco	2.00	.80
2 Mark McGwire	4.00	1.60
3 Walt Weiss	1.00	.40
4 Walt Weiss	3.00	1.20
Mark McGwire		
Jose Canseco		

1990 A's Mother's

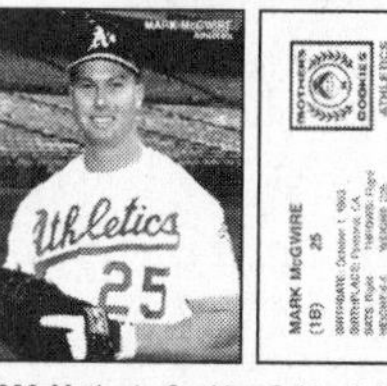

1990 Mother's Cookies Oakland Athletics set contains 28 standard-size cards with rounded corners. The envelope containing the cards honors the 1989 World Championship Oakland Athletics. The A's cards were released at the July 22nd game to the first 35,000 fans to walk through the gates. They were distributed in 20-card random packets at the game and eight more at the redemption booths. However, both groups of cards were random and there was no guarantee of getting a complete set in the cards. The promotional idea was that the only way one could finish the set was to trade for them. The redemption certificates were to be used at the Labor Day San Francisco card show. In addition to this the Mother's Giants cards were also redeemable at that show.

	Nm-Mt	Ex-Mt
COMPLETE SET (28)	15.00	4.50
1 Tony LaRussa MG	1.00	.30
2 Mark McGwire	3.00	.90
3 Terry Steinbach	.50	.15
4 Rickey Henderson	2.50	.75
5 Dave Stewart	.75	.23
6 Jose Canseco	1.50	.45
7 Dennis Eckersley	1.00	.30
8 Carney Lansford	.75	.23
9 Mike Moore	.25	.07
10 Walt Weiss	.25	.07
11 Scott Sanderson	.25	.07
12 Ron Hassey	.25	.07
13 Rick Honeycutt	.25	.07
14 Ken Phelps	.25	.07
15 Jamie Quirk	.25	.07
16 Bob Welch	.50	.15
17 Felix Jose	.25	.07
18 Dave Henderson	.25	.07
19 Mike Norris	.25	.07
20 Todd Burns	.25	.07
21 Lance Blankenship	.25	.07
22 Gene Nelson	.25	.07
23 Stan Javier	.25	.07
24 Curt Young	.25	.07
25 Mike Gallego	.25	.07
26 Joe Klink	.25	.07
27 Rene Lachemann CO	.50	.15
Dave Duncan CO		
Merv Rettenmund CO		
Tommie Reynolds CO		
Art Kusnyer CO		
Dave McKay CO		
28 Larry Davis TR	.25	.07
Steve Vuchinch VC MG		
Frank Cienscyk EQ MG		
Barry Weinberg TR CL		

1991 A's Mother's

The 1991 Mother's Cookies Oakland Athletics set contains 28 standard-size cards with rounded corners. The set includes an additional

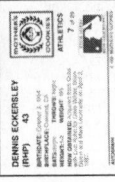

card advertising a trading card collectors album.

	Nm-Mt	Ex-Mt
COMPLETE SET (28)	15.00	4.50
1 Tony LaRussa MG	1.00	.30
2 Mark McGwire	2.50	.75
3 Terry Steinbach	.50	.15
4 Rickey Henderson	2.00	.60
5 Dave Stewart	.75	.23
6 Jose Canseco	1.25	.35
7 Dennis Eckersley	1.00	.30
8 Carney Lansford	.75	.23
9 Bob Welch	.50	.15
10 Walt Weiss	.25	.07
11 Mike Moore	.25	.07
12 Vance Law	.25	.07
13 Rick Honeycutt	.25	.07
14 Harold Baines	.75	.23
15 Jamie Quirk	.25	.07
16 Ernest Riles	.25	.07
17 Willie Wilson	.25	.07
18 Dave Henderson	.25	.07
19 Kirk Dressendorfer	.25	.07
20 Todd Burns	.25	.07
21 Lance Blankenship	.25	.07
22 Gene Nelson	.25	.07
23 Eric Show	.25	.07
24 Curt Young	.25	.07
25 Mike Gallego	.25	.07
26 Joe Klink	.25	.07
27 Steve Chitren	.25	.07
28 Tommie Reynolds CO Art Kusnyer CO Reggie Jackson CO Rick Burleson CO Rene Lachemann CO Dave Duncan CO Dave McKay CO CL	.50	.15

1991 A's S.F. Examiner

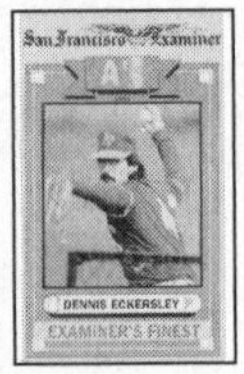

The fifteen 6" by 9" giant-sized cards in this set were issued on yellow cardboard sheets measuring approximately 8 1/2" by 11" and designed for storage in a three-ring binder. The cards are unnumbered and checklisted below in alphabetical order.

	Nm-Mt	Ex-Mt
COMPLETE SET (15)	40.00	12.00
1 Harold Baines	2.00	.60
2 Jose Canseco	6.00	1.80
3 Dennis Eckersley	2.50	.75
4 Mike Gallego	1.00	.30
5 Dave Henderson	1.00	.30
6 Rickey Henderson	8.00	2.40
7 Rick Honeycutt	1.00	.30
8 Mark McGwire	12.00	3.60
9 Mike Moore	1.00	.30
10 Gene Nelson	1.00	.30
11 Eric Show	1.00	.30
12 Terry Steinbach	1.50	.45
13 Dave Stewart	2.50	.75
14 Walt Weiss	1.00	.30
15 Bob Welch	1.50	.45

1992 A's Mother's

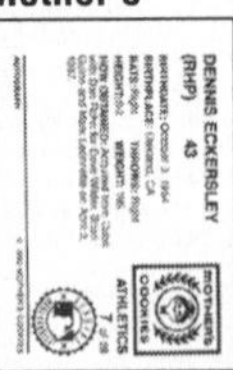

This 28-card standard-size set, sponsored by Mother's Cookies, contains borderless posed color player photos of the Oakland Athletics team. The cards have rounded corners. The red and purple backs include biographical information. The set also includes an order-form card for a Mother's Cookies Oakland Athletics collectors album. The album was available for 3.95.

	Nm-Mt	Ex-Mt
COMPLETE SET (28)	12.00	3.60
1 Tony LaRussa MG	1.00	.30
2 Mark McGwire	2.00	.60
3 Terry Steinbach	.75	.23
4 Rickey Henderson	1.50	.45
5 Dave Stewart	.75	.23
6 Jose Canseco	1.00	.30
7 Dennis Eckersley	1.00	.30
8 Carney Lansford	.75	.23
9 Bob Welch	.50	.15
10 Walt Weiss	.50	.15
11 Mike Moore	.25	.07
12 Goose Gossage	.75	.23
13 Rick Honeycutt	.25	.07
14 Harold Baines	.75	.23
15 Jamie Quirk	.25	.07
16 Jeff Parrett	.25	.07
17 Willie Wilson	.25	.07
18 Dave Henderson	.25	.07
19 Joe Slusarski	.25	.07
20 Mike Bordick	.50	.15
21 Lance Blankenship	.25	.07
22 Gene Nelson	.25	.07
23 Vince Horsman	.25	.07
24 Ron Darling	.25	.07
25 Randy Ready	.25	.07
26 Scott Hemond	.25	.07
27 Scott Brosius	1.50	.45
28 Rene Lachemann CO Art Kusnyer CO Dave McKay CO Tommie Reynolds CO Dave Duncan CO Doug Rader CO CL	.50	.15

1993 A's Mother's

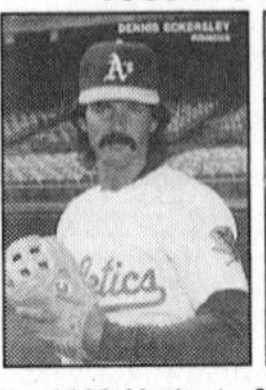

The 1993 Mother's Cookies Athletics set consists of 28 standard-size cards with rounded corners.

	Nm-Mt	Ex-Mt
COMPLETE SET (28)	12.00	3.60
1 Tony LaRussa MG	1.00	.30
2 Mark McGwire	2.50	.75
3 Terry Steinbach	.50	.15
4 Dennis Eckersley	1.00	.30
5 Ruben Sierra	.50	.15
6 Rickey Henderson	2.00	.60
7 Mike Bordick	.25	.07
8 Rick Honeycutt	.25	.07
9 Dave Henderson	.25	.07
10 Bob Welch	.50	.15
11 Dale Sveum	.25	.07
12 Ron Darling	.25	.07
13 Jerry Browne	.25	.07
14 Bobby Witt	.25	.07
15 Troy Neel	.25	.07
16 Goose Gossage	.75	.23
17 Brent Gates	.25	.07
18 Storm Davis	.25	.07
19 Scott Hemond	.25	.07
20 Kelly Downs	.25	.07
21 Kevin Seitzer	.25	.07
22 Lance Blankenship	.25	.07
23 Mike Mohler	.25	.07
24 Edwin Nunez	.25	.07
25 Joe Boever	.25	.07
26 Shawn Hillegas	.25	.07
27 Dave McKay CO Dave Duncan CO Tommie Reynolds CO Art Kusnyer CO Greg Luzinski CO	.50	.15
28 Frank Cienscyzk EQ MG CL	.25	.07

1993 A's Smokey McGwire

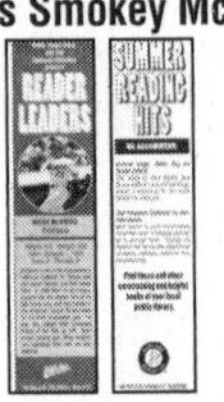

This two-card set measures approximately 2" by 8" and features a small action color photo of Mark McGwire printed above a paragraph about the player. The backs contain recommended reading that could be obtained at the local public library.

	Nm-Mt	Ex-Mt
COMPLETE SET (2)	15.00	4.50
COMMON CARD (1-2)	8.00	2.40

1993 A's Stadium Club

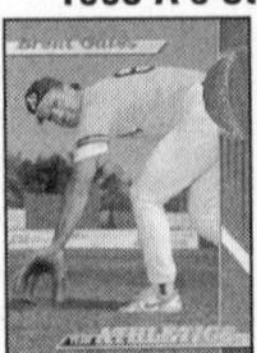

This 30-card standard-size set features the 1993 Oakland Athletics. The set was issued in hobby (plastic box) and retail (blister) form.

	Nm-Mt	Ex-Mt
COMP. FACT SET (30)	6.00	1.80
1 Dennis Eckersley	.25	.07
2 Lance Blankenship	.10	.03
3 Mike Mohler	.10	.03
4 Jerry Browne	.10	.03
5 Kevin Seitzer	.10	.03
6 Storm Davis	.10	.03
7 Mark McGwire	2.50	.75
8 Rickey Henderson	2.00	.60
9 Terry Steinbach	.25	.07
10 Ruben Sierra	.25	.07
11 Dave Henderson	.10	.03
12 Bob Welch	.25	.07
13 Rick Honeycutt	.10	.03
14 Ron Darling	.10	.03
15 Joe Boever	.10	.03
16 Bobby Witt	.10	.03
17 Izzy Molina	.10	.03
18 Mike Bordick	.10	.03
19 Brent Gates	.10	.03
20 Shawn Hillegas	.10	.03
21 Scott Hemond	.10	.03
22 Todd Van Poppel	.10	.03
23 Johnny Guzman	.10	.03
24 Scott Lydy	.10	.03
25 Scott Baker	.10	.03
26 Todd Revenig	.10	.03
27 Scott Brosius	.50	.15
28 Troy Neel	.10	.03
29 Dale Sveum	.10	.03
30 Mike Neill	.10	.03

1994 A's Mother's

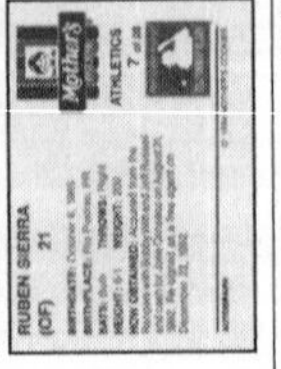

The 1994 Mother's Cookies Athletics set consists of 28 standard-size cards with rounded corners.

	Nm-Mt	Ex-Mt
COMPLETE SET (28)	12.00	3.60
1 Tony LaRussa MG	1.00	.30
2 Mark McGwire	2.50	.75
3 Terry Steinbach	.50	.15
4 Dennis Eckersley	1.00	.30
5 Mike Bordick	.25	.07
6 Rickey Henderson	1.00	.30
7 Ruben Sierra	.50	.15
8 Stan Javier	.25	.07
9 Todd Van Poppel	.25	.07
10 Bob Welch	.50	.15
11 Miguel Jimenez	.25	.07
12 Steve Karsay	.25	.07
13 Geronimo Berroa	.25	.07
14 Bobby Witt	.25	.07
15 Troy Neel	.25	.07
16 Ron Darling	.25	.07
17 Scott Hemond	.25	.07
18 Steve Ontiveros	.25	.07
19 Mike Aldrete	.25	.07
20 Carlos Reyes	.25	.07
21 Brent Gates	.25	.07
22 Mark Acre	.25	.07
23 Eric Helfand	.25	.07
24 Vince Horsman	.25	.07
25 Bill Taylor	.25	.07
26 Scott Brosius	.50	.15
27 John Briscoe	.25	.07
28 Dave Duncan CO Jim Lefebvre CO Carney Lansford CO Tommie Reynolds CO Art Kusnyer CO Dave McKay CO CL	.50	.15

1994 A's Pogs Target

These 30 Pogs were issued in six panels of which five pogs featured members of the A's and the sixth one was the Oakland A's logo. Since the pogs are unnumbered we have sequenced them in alphabetical order. All the player pogs have a fascimile autograph on them.

	Nm-Mt	Ex-Mt
COMPLETE SET (30)	8.00	2.40
1 Mike Aldrete	.10	.03
2 Geronino Berroa	.10	.03
3 Mike Bordick	.10	.03
4 John Briscoe	.10	.03
5 Scott Brosius	.25	.07
6 Ron Darling	.10	.03
7 Dave Duncan CO	.10	.03
8 Dennis Eckersley	.75	.23
9 Brent Gates	.10	.03
10 Scott Hemond	.10	.03
11 Rickey Henderson	2.00	.60
12 Stan Javier	.10	.03
13 Steve Karsay	.10	.03
14 Carney Lansford	.25	.07
15 Jim Lefebvre	.10	.03
16 Tony LaRussa MG	.50	.15
17 Mark McGwire	2.50	.75
18 Dave McKay CO	.10	.03
19 Junior Naboa	.10	.03
20 Troy Neel	.10	.03
21 Edwin Nunez	.10	.03
22 Steve Ontiveros	.10	.03
23 Carlos Reyes	.10	.03
24 Tommy Reynolds CO	.10	.03
25 Ruben Sierra	.25	.07
26 Terry Steinbach	.25	.07
27 Bill Taylor	.10	.03
28 Todd Van Poppel	.10	.03
29 Bob Welch	.25	.07
30 Bobby Witt	.10	.03

1995 A's CHP

Sponsored by the California Highway Patrol, this eight-card set of the Oakland A's features borderless color action player photos. The backs carry player information and a safety message.

	Nm-Mt	Ex-Mt
COMPLETE SET (8)	18.00	5.50
1 Brent Gates	1.00	.30
2 Mark McGwire	6.00	1.80
3 Geronimo Berroa	1.00	.30
4 Jason Giambi	6.00	1.80
5 Terry Steinbach	2.00	.60
6 Mike Bordick	1.00	.30
7 Todd Van Poppel	1.00	.30
8 Ariel Prieto	1.00	.30

1995 A's Mother's

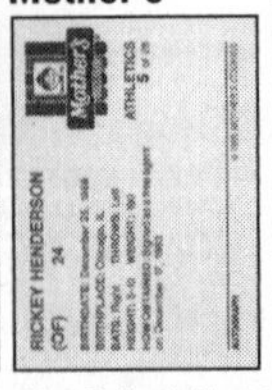

The 1995 Mother's Cookies Oakland A's set consists of 30 standard-size cards with rounded corners. A special card of Ariel Prieto, as well as a special coupon card, was issued in September as part of Hispanic-American night. The complete set includes the Prieto SP card.

	Nm-Mt	Ex-Mt
COMPLETE SET (30)	20.00	6.00
1 Tony LaRussa MG	1.00	.30
2 Mark McGwire	2.50	.75
3 Terry Steinbach	.50	.15
4 Dennis Eckersley	1.00	.30
5 Rickey Henderson	2.00	.60
6 Ron Darling	.25	.07
7 Ruben Sierra	.50	.15
8 Mike Aldrete	.25	.07
9 Stan Javier	.25	.07
10 Mike Bordick	.25	.07
11 Dave Stewart	.75	.23
12 Geronimo Berroa	.25	.07
13 Todd Van Poppel	.25	.07
14 Todd Stottlemyre	.25	.07
15 Eric Helfand	.25	.07
16 Dave Leiper	.25	.07
17 Rick Honeycutt	.25	.07
18 Steve Ontiveros	.25	.07
19 Mike Gallego	.25	.07
20 Carlos Reyes	.25	.07
21 Brent Gates	.25	.07
22 Craig Paquette	.25	.07
23 Mike Harkey	.25	.07
24 Andy Tomberlin	.25	.07
25 Jim Corsi	.25	.07
26 Mark Acre	.25	.07
27 Scott Brosius	.50	.15
28 Jim Lefebvre CO Tommie Reynolds CO Carney Lansford CO Dave Duncan CO Art Kusnyer CO Dave McKay CO CL.	.50	.15
29 Ariel Prieto SP	10.00	3.00
30 Coupon Card	.25	.07

1996 A's Mother's

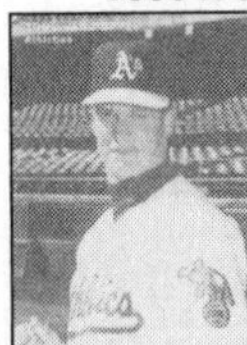

This 28-card set consists of borderless posed color player portraits in stadium settings

	Nm-Mt	Ex-Mt
COMPLETE SET (28)	12.00	3.60
1 Art Howe MG	.50	.15
2 Mark McGwire	3.00	.90
3 Jason Giambi	2.50	.75
4 Terry Steinbach	.50	.15
5 Mike Bordick	.25	.07
6 Brent Gates	.25	.07
7 Scott Brosius	.50	.15
8 Doug Johns	.25	.07
9 Jose Herrera	.25	.07
10 John Wasdin	.25	.07
11 Ernie Young	.25	.07
12 Pedro Munoz	.25	.07
13 Steve Wojciechowski	.25	.07
14 Geronimo Berroa	.25	.07
15 Phil Plantier	.25	.07
16 Bobby Chouinard	.25	.07
17 George Williams	.25	.07
18 Jim Corsi	.25	.07
19 Mike Mohler	.25	.07
20 Torey Lovullo	.25	.07
21 Carlos Reyes	.25	.07
22 Buddy Groom	.25	.07
23 Don Wengert	.25	.07
24 Bill Taylor	.25	.07
25 Todd Van Poppel	.25	.07
26 Rafael Bournigal	.25	.07
27 Damon Mashore	.25	.07
28 Bob Cluck CO Brad Fischer CO Duffy Dyer CO Ron Washington CO Bob Alejo CO Denny Walling CO CL	.25	.07

1996 A's Postcard Team

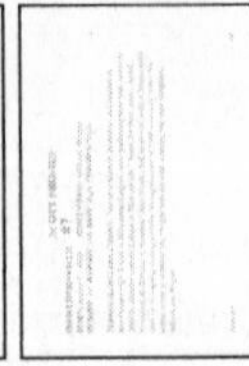

These attractive postcards, which have photographs taken by noted sports photographer Barry Colla, were issued by the Oakland A's in 1996. The full-color, borderless fronts feature color photos while the back has vital stats and biographical information.

	Nm-Mt	Ex-Mt
COMPLETE SET	15.00	4.50
1 Mark McGwire	3.00	.90
2 Mark Acre	.50	.15
3 Mike Bordick	.50	.15
4 John Briscoe	.50	.15
5 Scott Brosius	.75	.23
6 Jim Corsi	.50	.15
7 Brent Gates	.50	.15
8 Jason Giambi	2.50	.75
9 Art Howe MG	.75	.23
10 Doug Johns	.50	.15
11 Steve Karsay	.50	.15
12 Mike Mohler	.50	.15
13 Craig Paquette	.50	.15
14 Ariel Prieto	.50	.15
15 Carlos Reyes	.50	.15
16 Terry Steinbach	.75	.23
17 Dave Stewart	.75	.23
18 Todd Van Poppel	.50	.15
19 John Wasdin	.50	.15
20 George Williams	.50	.15
21 Steve Wojciehowski	.50	.15

1996 A's Postcard Volume

Some of these postcards parallel the regular A's Postcards issued in 1996 while others are new. The difference between these and the regular Postcards are that they are sponsored by Volume Services and there is a note as to a phone number one can call for A's Tickets. Please note that this set is skip numbered.

	Nm-Mt	Ex-Mt
COMPLETE SET	12.00	3.60
3 Mike Bordick	.50	.15
5 Scott Brosius	.75	.23
6 Jim Corsi	.50	.15
7 Brent Gates	.50	.15
8 Jason Giambi	2.50	.75
10 Doug Johns	.50	.15
14 Ariel Prieto	.50	.15
15 Carlos Reyes	.50	.15
16 Terry Steinbach	.75	.23
18 Todd Van Poppel	.50	.15
62 Allen Battle	.50	.15
63 Geronimo Berroa	.50	.15
64 Art Howe MG	.75	.23
65 Mark McGwire	3.00	.90
66 Phil Plantier	.50	.15
67 Ernie Young	.50	.15

1997 A's Mother's

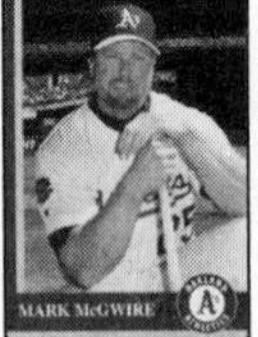

This 28-card set of the Oakland Athletics sponsored by Mother's Cookies consists of posed color player photos with rounded corners. The backs carry biographical information and the sponsor's logo on a white background in red and purple print. A blank slot for the player's autograph rounds out the back.

	Nm-Mt	Ex-Mt
COMPLETE SET (28)	12.00	3.60
1 Art Howe MG	.50	.15
2 Mark McGwire	2.50	.75
3 Jose Canseco	1.00	.30
4 Jason Giambi	2.00	.60
5 Geronimo Berroa	.25	.07
6 Ernie Young	.25	.07
7 Scott Brosius	.50	.15
8 Dave Magadan	.25	.07
9 Mike Mohler	.25	.07
10 George Williams	.25	.07
11 Tony Batista	1.00	.30
12 Steve Karsay	.25	.07
13 Rafael Bournigal	.25	.07
14 Ariel Prieto	.25	.07
15 Buddy Groom	.25	.07
16 Matt Stairs	.25	.07
17 Brent Mayne	.25	.07
18 Bill Taylor	.25	.07
19 Scott Spiezio	.75	.23
20 Richie Lewis	.25	.07
21 Mark Acre	.25	.07
22 Dave Telgheder	.25	.07

23 Willie Adams	.25	.07
24 Izzy Molina	.25	.07
25 Don Wengert	.25	.07
26 Damon Mashore	.25	.07
27 Aaron Small	.25	.07
28 Bob Alejo CO	.25	.07
Bob Cluck CO		
Duffy Dyer CO		
Brad Fischer CO		
Denny Walling CO		
Ron Washington CO CL		

1997 A's Pinnacle Season Ticket McGwire

This two-card set was produced by Pinnacle for the Oakland Athletics and features a 2 1/2" by 3 1/2" color photo of Mark McGwire running with Brent Gates number 13 ready to shake his hand. The picture is printed on a fading green or yellow background on a plastic 3" by 7" card made available to 1997 Season Ticket Holders. The backs are blank. After Brent Gates was traded, the set was pulled off the market and replaced by other passes.

	Nm-Mt	Ex-Mt
COMPLETE SET (2)	30.00	9.00
COMMON CARD (1-2)	15.00	4.50

1998 A's Mother's

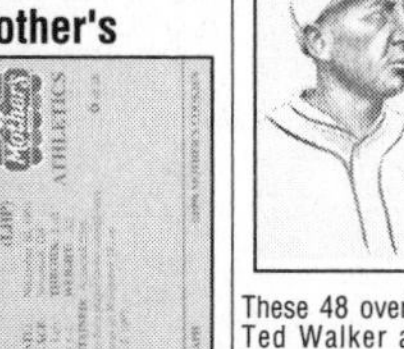

This 28-card set of the Oakland Athletics sponsored by Mother's Cookies consists of posed color player photos with rounded corners.

	Nm-Mt	Ex-Mt
COMPLETE SET (28)	10.00	3.00
1 Art Howe MG	.50	.15
2 Rickey Henderson	2.00	.60
3 Jason Giambi	2.00	.60
4 Tom Candiotti	.25	.07
5 Matt Stairs	.25	.07
6 Kenny Rogers	.50	.15
7 Scott Spiezio	.25	.07
8 Ben Grieve	.50	.15
9 Kevin Mitchell	.25	.07
10 A.J. Hinch	.25	.07
11 Bill Taylor	.25	.07
12 Rafael Bournigal	.25	.07
13 Miguel Tejada	3.00	.90
14 Kurt Abbott	.25	.07
15 Buddy Groom	.25	.07
16 Dave Magadan	.25	.07
17 Mike Oquist	.25	.07
18 Mike Macfarlane	.25	.07
19 Mike Fetters	.25	.07
20 Ryan Christenson	.25	.07
21 T.J. Mathews	.25	.07
22 Mike Mohler	.25	.07
23 Jason McDonald	.25	.07
24 Blake Stein	.25	.07
25 Mike Blowers	.25	.07
26 Jimmy Haynes	.25	.07
27 Aaron Small	.25	.07
28 Duffy Dyer CO	.25	.07
Brad Fischer CO		
Gary Jones CO		
Rick Peterson CO		
Denny Walling CO		
Ron Washington CO CL		

1998-99 A's Historical Society

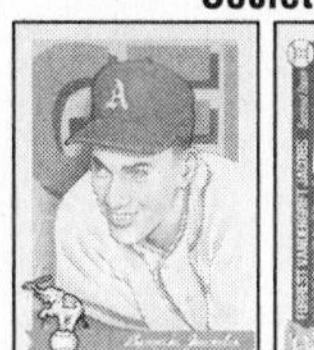

This 41 card set measuring slightly more than the standard size was issued by the Philadelphia A's historical society and honored great and popular players who played for the A's before they moved to Kansas City. The original cost of the set from the A's society was $18.75

	Nm-Mt	Ex-Mt
COMPLETE SET (42)	30.00	9.00
1 Connie Mack MG	2.00	.60
2 Sam Chapman	.50	.15
3 Bobby Shantz	1.00	.30
4 Al Brancato	.50	.15
5 Bob Dillinger	.75	.23
6 Irv Hall	.50	.15
7 Joe Hauser	.50	.15
8 Taffy Wright	.50	.15
9 Gus Zernial	1.00	.30
10 Ray Murray	.50	.15
11 Skeeter Kell	.50	.15
12 Morrie Martin	.50	.15
13 Pete Suder	.50	.15
14 Pinky Higgins	.50	.15
15 Allie Clark	.50	.15
16 Hank Wyse	.50	.15
17 George Kell	1.50	.45
18 Hank Majeski	.50	.15
19 Jimmie Foxx	2.50	.75
20 Crash Davis	.50	.15
21 Elmer Valo	.50	.15
22 Ray Coleman	.50	.15
23 Carl Scheib	.50	.15
24 Billy Hitchcock	.50	.15
25 Earle Brucker Jr.	.50	.15
26 Dave Philley	.50	.15
27 Joe DeMaestri	.50	.15
28 Eddie Collins Jr.	.50	.15
29 Eddie Joost	.75	.23
30 Spook Jacobs	.50	.15
31 Ferris Fain	.75	.23
32 Eddie Robinson	.50	.15
33 Vic Power	.75	.23
34 Lou Brissie	.50	.15
35 Bill Renna	.50	.15
36 Nellie Fox	1.50	.45
37 Lou Limmer	.50	.15
38 Eddie Collins	1.50	.45
39 Roger Cramer	.75	.23
40 Joe Astroth	.50	.15
41 Bill Werber (Issued in 1999)	2.50	.75
42 Rube Oldring	.50	.15
43 Stuffy McInnis	.50	.15
44 Bing Miller	.50	.15
45 Bob Johnson	.75	.23
NNO Joe Jackson	5.00	1.50

1998-99 A's Ted Walker

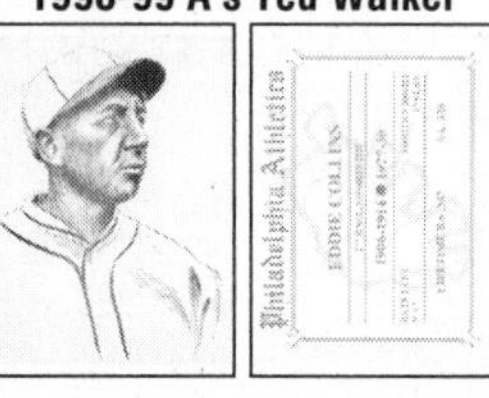

These 48 oversize cards were drawn by artist Ted Walker and featured members of the Philadelphia A's. Ted Walker's grandfather was Tom Walker, a pitcher in the early 20th century with the A's. The cards are unnumbered so we have sequenced them in alphabetical order. The first 44 cards were issued in 1998 and the last four were issued in 1999.

	Nm-Mt	Ex-Mt
COMPLETE SET (48)	40.00	12.00
1 Joe Astroth	.50	.15
2 Frank Baker	1.50	.45
3 Chief Bender	1.50	.45
4 Max Bishop	.50	.15
5 Ty Cobb	5.00	1.50
6 Mickey Cochrane	1.50	.45
7 Eddie Collins	1.50	.45
8 Doc Cramer	.75	.23
9 Joe DeMaestri	.50	.15
10 Bill Dietrich	.50	.15
11 Jimmy Dykes	.75	.23
12 George Earnshaw	.75	.23
13 Elmer Flick	1.00	.30
14 Nellie Fox	1.50	.45
15 Jimmy Foxx	2.50	.75
16 Walter French	.50	.15
17 Lefty Grove	1.50	.45
18 Mule Haas	.50	.15
19 Sammy Hale	.50	.15
20 Joe Jackson	5.00	1.50
21 Bob Johnson	.50	.15
22 Alex Kellner	.50	.15
23 Nap Lajoie	2.50	.75
24 Connie Mack MG	2.00	.60
25 Hank Majeski	.50	.15
26 Stuffy McInnis	.50	.15
27 Bing Miller	.50	.15
28 Wally Moses	.50	.15
29 Dave Philley	.50	.15
30 Eddie Plank	1.50	.45
31 Jack Quinn	.75	.23
32 Eddie Rommell	.75	.23
33 Buddy Rosar	.50	.15
34 Carl Scheib	.50	.15
35 Wally Schang	.50	.15
36 Bobby Shantz	.75	.23
37 Al Simmons	1.50	.45
38 Tris Speaker	2.50	.75
39 Pete Suder	.50	.15
40 Homer Summa	.50	.15
41 Rude Waddell	1.50	.45
42 Rube Walberg	.50	.15
43 Tom Walker	.50	.15
44 Gus Zernial	.75	.23
45 George Burns	.50	.15
46 Ferris Fain	.75	.23
47 Eddie Joost	.75	.23
48 Zack Wheat	1.50	.45

1999 A's Plumbers

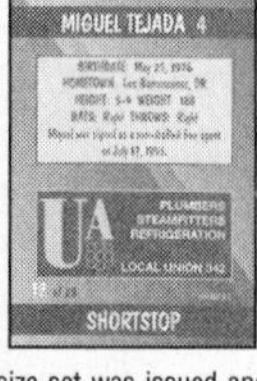

This 28 card standard-size set was issued and featured members of the 1999 Oakland A's. The cards have green amd gold borders and inside the borders are posed shots of the A's. The backs have biographical information and the logo of the Plumbers Steamfitters Refrigeration Local number 342.

	Nm-Mt	Ex-Mt
COMPLETE SET (28)	10.00	3.00
1 Art Howe MG	.50	.15
2 Ben Grieve	.50	.15
3 Jason Giambi	2.00	.60
4 Kenny Rogers	.50	.15
5 Matt Stairs	.25	.07
6 Tom Candiotti	.25	.07
7 Tony Phillips	.25	.07
8 Eric Chavez	1.50	.45
9 Tim Raines	.75	.23
10 A.J. Hinch	.25	.07
11 Bill Taylor	.25	.07
12 Miguel Tejada	1.50	.45
13 Tim Worrell	.25	.07
14 Scott Spiezio	.50	.15
15 Buddy Groom	.25	.07
16 Olmedo Saenz	.25	.07
17 T.J. Mathews	.25	.07
18 Mike Macfarlane	.25	.07
19 Brad Rigby	.25	.07
20 Ryan Christenson	.25	.07
21 Doug Jones	.25	.07
22 Terry Clark	.25	.07
23 Jorge Velandia	.25	.07
24 Gil Heredia	.25	.07
25 John Jaha	.25	.07
26 Jimmy Haynes	.25	.07
27 Jason McDonald	.25	.07
28 Thad Bosley CO	.25	.07
Brad Fischer CO		
Dave Hudgens CO		
Ken Macha CO		
Rick Peterson CO		
Ron Washington CO CL		

2000 A's ATand T Fanfest

These blank-backed cards, which measure 4" by 6 1/2", features a mix of current A's players, coaches and managers and some retired greats. The cards have the player photo, the A's logo and an advertisement for AT and T. Since the cards are unnumbered we have sequenced them in alphabetical order.

	Nm-Mt	Ex-Mt
COMPLETE SET	25.00	7.50
1 Bob Alejo CO	.50	.15
2 Kevin Appier	.50	.15
3 Rich Becker	.50	.15
4 Thad Bosley	.50	.15
5 Eric Chavez	2.00	.60
6 Rollie Fingers	2.00	.60
7 Brad Fischer	.50	.15
8 Jason Giambi	2.50	.75
9 Ben Grieve	.75	.23
10 Chad Harville	.50	.15
11 Gil Heredia	.50	.15
12 A.J. Hinch	.50	.15
13 Ken Holtzman	.75	.23
14 Art Howe MG	.75	.23
15 Tim Hudson	3.00	.90
16 Jason Isringhausen	.75	.23
17 John Jaha	.50	.15
18 Doug Jones	.50	.15
19 Tim Kubinski	.50	.15
20 Brett Laxton	.50	.15
21 Ken Macha CO	.50	.15
22 Mike Magnante	.50	.15
23 Ron Mahay	.50	.15
24 T.J. Mathews	.50	.15
25 Frank Menechino	.50	.15
26 Mark Mulder	2.00	.60
27 Billy North	.50	.15
28 John Odom	.50	.15
29 Adam Piatt	.50	.15
30 Bo Porter	.50	.15
31 Mike Quade CO	.50	.15
32 Matt Stairs	.50	.15
33 Gene Tenace	.75	.23
34 Jorge Velendia	.50	.15
35 Randy Velarde	.50	.15
36 Ron Washington CO	.50	.15

2000 A's Plumbers

This 28 card standard-size set was issued by the Plumbers Steamfitters Refrigeration Local Union 342 and features members of the 2000 Oakland A's. Issued in the style made popular by Mothers Cookies over the previous 15 years, these cards feautre a player photo surrounded by green borders. Unlike most of the other cards though, the corners are not rounded. The photos for this set were taken by noted sports photographer Barry Colla.

	Nm-Mt	Ex-Mt
COMPLETE SET (28)	15.00	4.50
1 Art Howe MG	.50	.15
2 Jason Giambi	2.50	.75
3 Tim Hudson	3.00	.90
4 Matt Stairs	.25	.07
5 Kevin Appier	.50	.15
6 Ben Grieve	.50	.15
7 Randy Velarde	.25	.07
8 Eric Chavez	1.50	.45
9 Mark Mulder	.25	.07
10 Sal Fasano	.25	.07
11 Doug Jones	.25	.07
12 Miguel Tejada	1.50	.45
13 Omar Oliveras	.25	.07
14 Jeremy Giambi	.25	.07
15 Gil Heredia	.25	.07
16 Olmedo Saenz	.25	.07
17 T.J. Mathews	.25	.07
18 Ramon Hernandez	.25	.07
19 Jeff Tam	.25	.07
20 Ryan Christenson	.25	.07
21 John Jaha	.25	.07
22 Rich Saveur	.25	.07
23 Terrence Long	.75	.23
24 Mike Magnante	.25	.07
25 Scott Service	.25	.07
26 Frank Menechino	.25	.07
27 Jason Isringhausen	.50	.15
28 Bob Alejo CO	.25	.07
Rick Peterson CO		
Thad Bosley CO		
Ken Macha CO		
Mike Quade CO		
Brad Fischer CO		
Ron Washington CO CL		

1975 Aaron Magnavox

This promotional photo, which measures approximately 4" by 6 7/8" features Hank Aaron in an Milwaukee Brewer uniform. The photo is surrounded by white borders and the bottom has the facsimile greeting "best wishes, Hank Aaron" on the bottom and the photo is courtesy of the Magnavox Company.

	MINT	NRMT
1 Hank Aaron	10.00	4.50

1984 Aaron Rockstad Poster

This one-card set features a colored painting in a white border of Hank Aaron by artist Stephen D. Rockstad. The poster-size portrait measures approximately 16" by 20". The backs are blank. Only 500 of these portraits were produced and are sequentially numbered as well as signed by the artist.

	Nm-Mt	Ex-Mt
1 Henry"Hank" Aaron	15.00	6.00

1974 Aaron 715 Homer

These 12 black and white postcards, which measure approximately 3" by 5" features highlights from the game where Hank Aaron hit his 715th homer.

	NM	Ex
COMPLETE SET (12)	20.00	8.00
COMMON CARD	2.00	.80

1997 Kyle Abbott

This one-card set was privately printed and published by Kyle Abbott. The front features a color action player photo in a green border. The back displays player information and a religious message from Kyle Abbott.

	Nm-Mt	Ex-Mt
1 Kyle Abbott	1.00	.30

1970-71 Action Cartridge

During the time period of 1970-71 a group of 8 mm cartridges featuring leading players with playing tips were issued. The yellow boxes which measured 2 5/8" by 6" featured the player photo as well as what the tips included. Each player photo includes a fascimile autograph. Since these are unnumbered, we have sequenced them in alphabetical order.

	NM	Ex
COMPLETE SET	400.00	160.00
1 Hank Aaron	80.00	32.00
2 Glenn Beckert	15.00	6.00
Don Kessinger		
3 Lou Brock	40.00	16.00
4 Rod Carew	50.00	20.00
5 Willie Davis	15.00	6.00
6 Bill Freehan	20.00	8.00
7 Reggie Jackson	50.00	20.00
8 Willie McCovey	40.00	16.00
9 Dave McNally	20.00	8.00
10 Brooks Robinson	40.00	16.00
11 Pete Rose	60.00	24.00
12 Tom Seaver	60.00	24.00

1988 Action Packed Test

The 1988 Action Packed Test set contains six standard-size cards with slightly rounded corners. This apparently was the set of cards that Action Packed produced to show their technique to Major League Baseball and the Major League Baseball Players Association in their unsuccessful attempt to seek a baseball card license in 1988. The embossed color

player photos on the fronts are bordered in gold. In black lettering, the player's name appears on a gold plaque above the picture, and the team name on a gold plaque beneath the picture. The card backs have the same design as Score issues, with a color head shot, team logo, biography, and major league batting or pitching statistics, again inside a gold border. The face on the front photo of the Ozzie Smith card was apparently considered too dark and thus reportedly not submitted. The cards are unnumbered and checklisted below in alphabetical order.

	Nm-Mt	Ex-Mt
COMPLETE SET (6)	80.00	32.00
COMMON CARD (1-4)	3.00	1.20
COMMON CARD (5-6)	30.00	12.00
1 Wade Boggs	10.00	4.00
2 Andre Dawson	8.00	3.20
3 Dwight Gooden	5.00	2.00
4 Carney Lansford	3.00	1.20
5 Don Mattingly	30.00	12.00
6 Ozzie Smith SP	50.00	20.00

1992 Action Packed ASG Prototypes

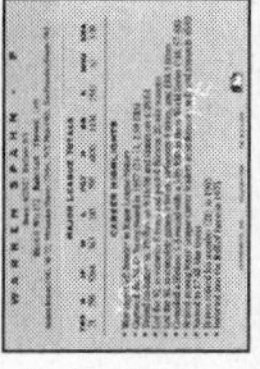

This five-card prototype standard-size set was issued to show the design of the 1992 Action Packed All-Star Gallery regular issue. The prototypes differ from the regular issue in that they are not numbered on the back, and the phrase "1992 Prototype" is printed diagonally in white lettering across the back. The cards are unnumbered and checklisted below in alphabetical order.

	Nm-Mt	Ex-Mt
COMPLETE SET (5)	25.00	7.50
1 Yogi Berra	8.00	2.40
2 Bob Gibson	4.00	1.20
3 Willie Mays	10.00	3.00
4 Warren Spahn	4.00	1.20
5 Willie Stargell	4.00	1.20

1992 Action Packed ASG

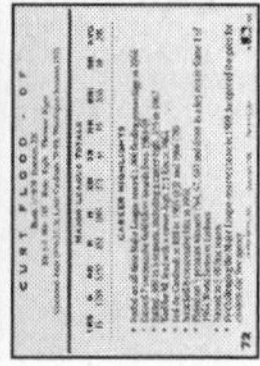

The 1992 Action Packed All-Star Gallery consists of 84 player standard-size cards and pays tribute to former greats of baseball. With the exception of Joe Garagiola, all the players represented appeared in at least one All-Star game. The first 18 cards feature Hall of Famers, and Action Packed guaranteed one Hall of Famer card in each seven-card foil pack. Also 24K gold leaf stamped versions of these Hall of Famer cards were randomly inserted into foil packs. The fronts feature embossed action player photos framed by inner gold border stripes and a black outer border. Most of the photos are color; 13 of them, however, are sepia-toned that have been converted to black and white.

	Nm-Mt	Ex-Mt
COMPLETE SET (84)	15.00	4.50
1 Yogi Berra	1.25	.35
2 Lou Brock	1.00	.30
3 Bob Gibson	1.00	.30
4 Ferguson Jenkins	.75	.23
5 Ralph Kiner	.75	.23
6 Al Kaline	1.00	.30
7 Lou Boudreau	.50	.15
8 Bobby Doerr	.50	.15
9 Billy Herman	.50	.15
10 Monte Irvin	.50	.15
11 George Kell	.50	.15
12 Robin Roberts	.75	.23
13 Johnny Mize	.75	.23
14 Willie Mays	2.50	.75
15 Enos Slaughter	.50	.15
16 Warren Spahn	.75	.23
17 Willie Stargell	.75	.23
18 Billy Williams	.25	.07
19 Vernon Law	.10	.03
20 Virgil Trucks	.10	.03
21 Mel Parnell	.10	.03
22 Wally Moon	.10	.03
23 Gene Woodling	.10	.03
24 Richie Ashburn	1.00	.30
25 Mark Fidrych	.25	.07
26 Roy Face	.10	.03
27 Larry Doby	.25	.07
28 Dick Groat	.10	.03
29 Cesar Cedeno	.10	.03

30 Bob Horner .10 .03
31 Bobby Richardson .25 .07
32 Bobby Murcer .25 .07
33 Gil McDougald .10 .03
34 Roy White .10 .03
35 Bill Skowron .25 .07
36 Mickey Lolich .25 .07
37 Minnie Minoso .25 .07
38 Bill Pierce .25 .07
39 Ron Santo .50 .15
40 Sal Bando .25 .07
41 Ralph Branca .25 .07
42 Bert Campaneris .10 .03
43 Joe Garagiola .50 .15
44 Vida Blue .25 .07
45 Frank Crosetti .50 .15
46 Luis Tiant .10 .03
47 Maury Wills .25 .07
48 Sam McDowell .10 .03
49 Jimmy Piersall .25 .07
50 Jim Lonborg .10 .03
51 Don Newcombe .25 .07
52 Bobby Thomson .25 .07
53 Wilbur Wood .10 .03
54 Carl Erskine .25 .07
55 Chris Chambliss .10 .03
56 Dave Kingman .10 .03
57 Ken Holtzman .10 .03
58 Bud Harrelson .10 .03
59 Clem Labine .25 .07
60 Tony Oliva .25 .07
61 George Foster .10 .03
62 Bobby Bonds .25 .07
63 Harvey Haddix .10 .03
64 Steve Garvey .25 .07
65 Rocky Colavito .50 .15
66 Orlando Cepeda .50 .15
67 Ed Lopat .25 .07
68 Al Oliver .25 .07
69 Bill Mazeroski .75 .23
70 Al Rosen .25 .07
71 Bob Grich .25 .07
72 Curt Flood .25 .07
73 Willie Horton .25 .07
74 Rico Carty .10 .03
75 Davey Johnson .25 .07
76 Don Kessinger .10 .03
77 Frank Thomas .10 .03
78 Bobby Shantz .10 .03
79 Herb Score .25 .07
80 Boog Powell .25 .07
81 Rusty Staub .25 .07
82 Bill Madlock .25 .07
83 Manny Mota .10 .03
84 Bill White .25 .07

1992 Action Packed ASG 24K

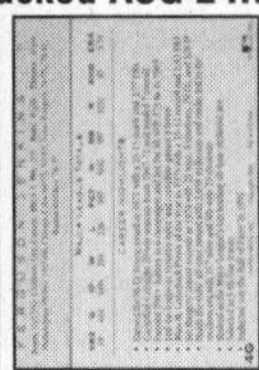

The first 18 cards of the 1992 Action Packed All-Star Gallery feature Hall of Famers and were also produced in a 24K version on a limited basis. These 24K gold-leaf stamped versions of these Hall of Famer cards were randomly inserted into foil packs.

	Nm-Mt	Ex-Mt
COMPLETE SET (18)	300.00	90.00
1G Yogi Berra	40.00	12.00
2G Lou Brock	25.00	7.50
3G Bob Gibson	25.00	7.50
4G Ferguson Jenkins	15.00	4.50
5G Ralph Kiner	20.00	6.00
6G Al Kaline	25.00	7.50
7G Lou Boudreau	15.00	4.50
8G Bobby Doerr	15.00	4.50
9G Billy Herman	15.00	4.50
10G Monte Irvin	15.00	4.50
11G George Kell	15.00	4.50
12G Robin Roberts	20.00	6.00
13G Johnny Mize	20.00	6.00
14G Willie Mays	50.00	15.00
15G Enos Slaughter	15.00	4.50
16G Warren Spahn	20.00	6.00
17G Willie Stargell	20.00	6.00
18G Billy Williams	15.00	4.50

1993 Action Packed ASG

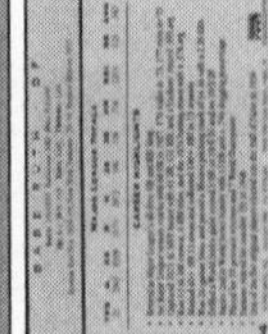

The second series of the Action Packed All-Star Gallery baseball set consists of 84 standard-size cards. Fifty two of the cards are in color, 31 are sepia-tone, and one is a colorized black-and-white. Action Packed included 46 Hall of Famers in the series and guaranteed one of these cards in every pack. Moreover, series II includes randomly inserted 24K cards of these Hall of Famers and contains a card honoring Bud Abbott and Lou Costello, creators of the famous "Who's on First" comedy routine. And as a special bonus for hobby dealers only, each box of cards included two free "Chiptopper" prototype cards of forthcoming Action Packed cards.

	Nm-Mt	Ex-Mt
COMPLETE SET (84)	18.00	5.50
85 Cy Young	.50	.15
86 Honus Wagner	.75	.23
87 Christy Mathewson	.75	.23
88 Ty Cobb	1.50	.45
89 Eddie Collins	.25	.07
90 Walter Johnson	.75	.23
91 Tris Speaker	.50	.15
92 Grover Alexander	.50	.15
93 Edd Roush	.25	.07
94 Babe Ruth	2.00	.60
95 Rogers Hornsby	.75	.23
96 Pie Traynor	.25	.07
97 Lou Gehrig	1.50	.45
98 Mickey Cochrane	.50	.15
99 Lefty Grove	.50	.15
100 Jimmie Foxx	1.00	.30
101 Tony Lazzeri	.25	.07
102 Mel Ott	.50	.15
103 Carl Hubbell	.25	.07
104 Al Lopez	.25	.07
105 Lefty Gomez	.50	.15
106 Dizzy Dean	.75	.23
107 Hank Greenberg	.75	.23
108 Joe Medwick	.25	.07
109 Arky Vaughan	.25	.07
110 Bob Feller	.50	.15
111 Hal Newhouser	.25	.07
112 Early Wynn	.25	.07
113 Bob Lemon	.25	.07
114 Red Schoendienst	.25	.07
115 Satchel Paige	.75	.23
116 Whitey Ford	.50	.15
117 Eddie Mathews	.50	.15
118 Harmon Killebrew	.50	.15
119 Roberto Clemente	2.00	.60
120 Brooks Robinson	.50	.15
121 Don Drysdale	.50	.15
122 Luis Aparicio	.25	.07
123 Willie McCovey	.50	.15
124 Juan Marichal	.25	.07
125 Gaylord Perry	.25	.07
126 Catfish Hunter	.25	.07
127 Jim Palmer	.50	.15
128 Rod Carew	.50	.15
129 Tom Seaver	.50	.15
130 Rollie Fingers	.25	.07
131 Joe Jackson	1.50	.45
132 Pepper Martin	.25	.07
133 Joe Gordon	.40	.12
134 Marty Marion	.25	.07
135 Allie Reynolds	.40	.12
136 Johnny Sain	.40	.12
137 Gil Hodges	.75	.23
138 Ted Kluszewski	.40	.12
139 Nellie Fox	.75	.23
140 Billy Martin	.60	.18
141 Smoky Burgess	.40	.12
142 Lew Burdette	.40	.12
143 Joe Black	.25	.07
144 Don Larsen	.40	.12
145 Ken Boyer	.40	.12
146 Johnny Callison	.25	.07
147 Norm Cash	.40	.12
148 Keith Hernandez	.25	.07
149 Jim Kaat	.40	.12
150 Bill Freehan	.25	.07
151 Joe Torre	.75	.23
152 Bob Uecker	.40	.12
153 Dave McNally	.25	.07
154 Denny McLain	.40	.12
155 Dick Allen	.40	.12
156 Jimmy Wynn	.25	.07
157 Tommy John	.40	.12
158 Paul Blair	.25	.07
159 Reggie Smith	.25	.07
160 Jerry Koosman	.25	.07
161 Thurman Munson	.60	.18
162 Graig Nettles	.40	.12
163 Ron Cey	.25	.07
164 Cecil Cooper	.25	.07
165 Dave Parker	.40	.12
166 Jim Rice	.40	.12
167 Kent Tekulve	.25	.07
168 Who's On First Bud Abbott Lou Costello	.75	.23

1993 Action Packed ASG 24K

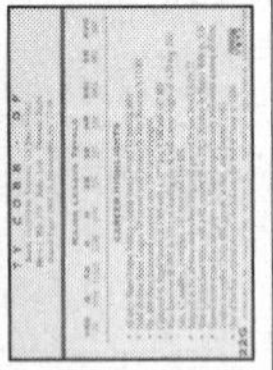

The second series of the 1993 Action Packed All-Star Gallery baseball set included 46 Hall of Famers and a special card honoring Bud Abbott and Lou Costello. Action Packed produced 24K gold leaf versions of all these cards and randomly inserted them throughout the foil packs.

	Nm-Mt	Ex-Mt
COMPLETE SET (47)	800.00	240.00
19G Cy Young	25.00	7.50
20G Honus Wagner	30.00	9.00
21G Christy Mathewson	30.00	9.00
22G Ty Cobb	50.00	15.00
23G Eddie Collins	15.00	4.50
24G Walter Johnson	30.00	9.00
25G Tris Speaker	25.00	7.50
26G Grover Alexander	25.00	7.50
27G Ed Roush	15.00	4.50
28G Babe Ruth	80.00	24.00
29G Rogers Hornsby	30.00	9.00
30G Pie Traynor	15.00	4.50
31G Lou Gehrig	50.00	15.00
32G Mickey Cochrane	25.00	7.50
33G Lefty Grove	25.00	7.50
34G Jimmie Foxx	30.00	9.00
35G Tony Lazzeri	15.00	4.50
36G Mel Ott	25.00	7.50
37G Carl Hubbell	20.00	6.00
38G Al Lopez	15.00	4.50
39G Lefty Gomez	25.00	7.50
40G Dizzy Dean	30.00	9.00
41G Hank Greenberg	30.00	9.00
42G Joe Medwick	15.00	4.50
43G Arky Vaughan	15.00	4.50
44G Bob Feller	30.00	9.00
45G Hal Newhouser	15.00	4.50
46G Early Wynn	15.00	4.50
47G Bob Lemon	15.00	4.50
48G Red Schoendienst	15.00	4.50
49G Satchel Paige	30.00	9.00
50G Whitey Ford	25.00	7.50
51G Eddie Mathews	25.00	7.50
52G Harmon Killebrew	25.00	7.50
53G Roberto Clemente	50.00	15.00
54G Brooks Robinson	30.00	9.00
55G Don Drysdale	25.00	7.50
56G Luis Aparicio	15.00	4.50
57G Willie McCovey	20.00	6.00
58G Juan Marichal	15.00	4.50
59G Gaylord Perry	15.00	4.50
60G Catfish Hunter	15.00	4.50
61G Jim Palmer	20.00	6.00
62G Rod Carew	20.00	6.00
63G Tom Seaver	30.00	9.00
64G Rollie Fingers	15.00	4.50
65G Who's On First	20.00	6.00

1993 Action Packed ASG Coke/Amoco

This 18-card standard-size set pays tribute to former greats of baseball. The cards feature Hall of Fame players and were sponsored by Coca Cola and Amoco. With the purchase of four multi-packs of Coca-Cola products at participating Amoco gas stations, collectors could send in through the mail for a complete set plus a 1.00 off coupon good toward the purchase of Amoco Ultimate gasoline. There was also a pre-promotion set with a red header card, with reportedly only 3000 sets produced, which was not distributed to the public. The red header version was indistinguishable from the gray header set listed below with the exception that Ferguson Jenkins and Billy Herman were replaced in the gray set by Red Schoendienst and Gaylord Perry; Jenkins and Herman were both members of the original 1992 Action Packed ASG set.

	Nm-Mt	Ex-Mt
COMPLETE SET (18)	4.00	1.20
1 Yogi Berra	.50	.15
2 Lou Brock	.25	.07
3 Bob Gibson	.25	.07
4 Red Schoendienst	.10	.03
5 Ralph Kiner	.25	.07
6 Al Kaline	.50	.15
7 Lou Boudreau	.10	.03
8 Bobby Doerr	.10	.03
9 Gaylord Perry	.10	.03
10 Monte Irvin	.10	.03
11 George Kell	.10	.03
12 Robin Roberts	.25	.07
13 Johnny Mize	.10	.03
14 Willie Mays	1.00	.30
15 Enos Slaughter	.10	.03
16 Warren Spahn	.25	.07
17 Willie Stargell	.25	.07
18 Billy Williams	.10	.03

1993 Action Packed Seaver Promos

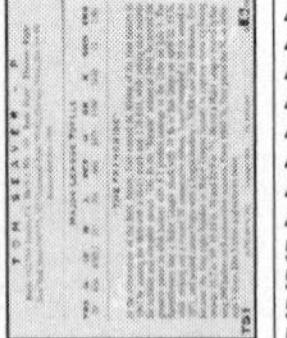

This five-card standard-size promo set features embossed color player photos accented by gold foil and red borders. The player's name appears in the gold foil border at the bottom. The horizontal backs are gray and carry biographical and statistical information, and career highlights. The cards are numbered on the back with a "TS" prefix. Random insertions of these cards were also found in packs of Action Packed racing cards.

	Nm-Mt	Ex-Mt
COMPLETE SET (5)	20.00	6.00
COMMON CARD (TS1-TS5)	5.00	1.50
TS3 Tom Seaver A Tearful Goodbye	2.50	.75

1990 AGFA

This 22-card standard-size set was issued by MSA (Michael Schechter Associates) for AGFA. The promotion reportedly consisted of a three-card pack of these cards given away with any purchase of a three-pack of AGFA film.

	Nm-Mt	Ex-Mt
COMPLETE SET (22)	15.00	4.50
1 Willie Mays	1.50	.45
2 Carl Yastrzemski	1.00	.30
3 Harmon Killebrew	1.00	.30
4 Joe Torre	.75	.23
5 Al Kaline	1.00	.30
6 Hank Aaron	1.50	.45
7 Rod Carew	1.00	.30
8 Roberto Clemente	2.00	.60
9 Luis Aparicio	.50	.15
10 Roger Maris	.75	.23
11 Joe Morgan	.75	.23
12 Maury Wills	.50	.15
13 Brooks Robinson	1.00	.30
14 Tom Seaver	1.00	.30
15 Steve Carlton	.75	.23
16 Whitey Ford	1.00	.30
17 Jim Palmer	1.00	.30
18 Rollie Fingers	.50	.15
19 Bruce Sutter	.25	.07
20 Willie McCovey	1.00	.30
21 Mike Schmidt	1.00	.30
22 Yogi Berra	1.00	.30

1939-52 Albertype Hall of Fame PC754-2

The Albertype Company issued postcards of Hall of Fame inductees from 1936 through 1952. However, since the HOF was not offically opened until 1939, we are dating this set as 1939-52. This black and white postcard set, the cards being called plaques as they feature the Hall of Fame plaque of the player, was addended to each year by new Hall of Fame inductees. Sixty-two Albertype postcards are known and are listed in the checklist below. The set is sequenced in order of induction into the Hall of Fame.

	Ex-Mt	VG
COMPLETE SET (62)	850.00	425.00
1 Ty Cobb	50.00	25.00
2 Walter Johnson	40.00	20.00
3 Christy Mathewson	40.00	20.00
4 Babe Ruth	75.00	38.00
5 Honus Wagner	40.00	20.00
6 Morgan Bulkeley	10.00	5.00
7 Ban Johnson	10.00	5.00
8 Nap Lajoie	20.00	10.00
9 Connie Mack	20.00	10.00
10 John McGraw	20.00	10.00
11 Tris Speaker	20.00	10.00
12 George Wright	10.00	5.00
13 Cy Young	50.00	25.00
14 Grover Cleveland Alexander	20.00	10.00
15 Alexander Cartwright	15.00	7.50
16 Henry Chadwick	10.00	5.00
17 Cap Anson	25.00	12.50
18 Eddie Collins	20.00	10.00
19 Charlie Comiskey	10.00	5.00
20 Candy Cummings	10.00	5.00
21 Buck Ewing	10.00	5.00
22 Lou Gehrig	60.00	30.00
23 Willie Keeler	10.00	5.00
24 Ole Hoss Radbourne	10.00	5.00
25 George Sisler	15.00	7.50
26 Albert Spalding	10.00	5.00
27 Rogers Hornsby	25.00	12.50
28 Kenesaw Mountain Landis	10.00	5.00
29 Roger Bresnahan	10.00	5.00
30 Dan Brouthers	10.00	5.00
31 Fred Clarke	10.00	5.00
32 Jimmy Collins	10.00	5.00
33 Ed Delahanty	10.00	5.00
34 Hugh Duffy	10.00	5.00
35 Hugh Jennings	10.00	5.00
36 King Kelly	10.00	5.00
37 Jimmy O'Rourke	10.00	5.00
38 Wilbert Robinson	10.00	5.00
39 Jesse Burkett	10.00	5.00
40 Frank Chance	20.00	10.00
41 Jack Chesbro	10.00	5.00
42 Johnny Evers	20.00	10.00
43 Clark Griffith	15.00	7.50
44 Tom McCarthy	10.00	5.00
45 Joe McGinnity	10.00	5.00
46 Eddie Plank	20.00	10.00
47 Joe Tinker	20.00	10.00
48 Rube Waddell	10.00	5.00
49 Ed Walsh	15.00	7.50
50 Mickey Cochrane	20.00	10.00
51 Frankie Frisch	20.00	10.00
52 Lefty Grove	25.00	12.50
53 Carl Hubbell	25.00	12.50
54 Herb Pennock	15.00	7.50
55 Pie Traynor	20.00	10.00
56 Mordecai Brown	20.00	10.00
57 Charlie Gehringer	15.00	7.50
58 Kid Nichols	10.00	5.00
59 Jimmy Foxx	25.00	12.50
60 Mel Ott	20.00	10.00
61 Harry Heilmann	10.00	5.00
62 Paul Waner	15.00	7.50
63 Abner Doubleday	10.00	5.00
64 Christy Mathewson BUST	10.00	5.00
65 HOF Exterior	10.00	5.00
66 HOF Interior	10.00	5.00

1971 Aldama Yesterday Heroes

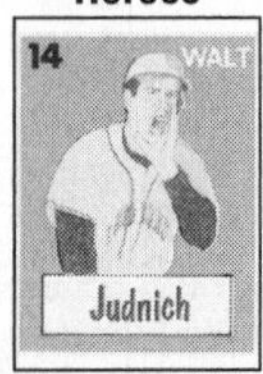

This crude 16 card blank-backed set was issued in the early 1970's and was presumebly issued by Carl Aldama as one of the many collector issue sets he produced around that time period. The fronts have small shots of the player with their first name on top and their last name on the bottom. The purpose of this set was to create cards for players who had never been on a card before.

	NM	Ex
COMPLETE SET (16)	10.00	4.00
1 Wally Hood	.75	.30
2 Jim Westlake	.75	.30
3 Stan McWilliams	.75	.30
4 Les Fleming	.75	.30
5 John Ritchey	.75	.30
6 Steve Nagy	.75	.30
7 Ken Gables	.75	.30
8 Maurice Fisher	.75	.30
9 Don Lang	.75	.30
10 Harry Malmberg	.75	.30
11 Jack Conway	.75	.30
12 Don White	.75	.30
13 Dick Lajeskie	.75	.30
14 Walt Judnich	.75	.30
15 Joe Kirrene	.75	.30
16 Ed Sauer	.75	.30

1990 All-American Baseball Team

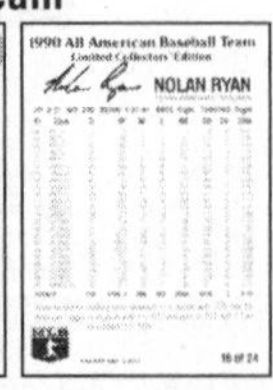

This 24-card, standard-size set was issued by MSA (Michael Schechter Associates) for 7/11, Squirt, and Dr. Pepper, and other carbonated beverages (but there are no markings on the cards whatsoever to indicate who sponsored the set other than MSA). These cards were distributed and issued inside 12-packs of sodas. The 12-packs included a checklist on one panel, and the cards themselves were glued on the inside of the pack so that it was difficult to remove a card without damaging it. The fronts feature a red-white and blue design framing the players photos while the back has major league career statistics and a sentence of career highlights. The back also has a fascimile autograph of the player on the back. Like many of the sets sponsored by MSA there are no team logos on the cards as they have been airbrushed away.

	Nm-Mt	Ex-Mt
COMPLETE SET (24)	20.00	6.00
1 George Brett	2.00	.60
2 Mark McGwire	3.00	.90
3 Wade Boggs	1.50	.45
4 Cal Ripken	4.00	1.20
5 Rickey Henderson	2.00	.60
6 Dwight Gooden	.50	.15
7 Bo Jackson	1.00	.30
8 Roger Clemens	2.00	.60
9 Orel Hershiser	.50	.15
10 Ozzie Smith	2.00	.60
11 Don Mattingly	2.00	.60
12 Kirby Puckett	1.00	.30
13 Robin Yount	1.25	.35
14 Tony Gwynn	2.00	.60
15 Jose Canseco	1.00	.30
16 Nolan Ryan	4.00	1.20
17 Ken Griffey Jr.	3.00	.90
18 Will Clark	1.00	.30
19 Ryne Sandberg	1.50	.45
20 Kent Hrbek	.25	.07
21 Carlton Fisk	1.50	.45
22 Paul Molitor	1.50	.45
23 Dave Winfield	1.00	.30
24 Andre Dawson	1.00	.30

1908 All-American Ladies Baseball Club

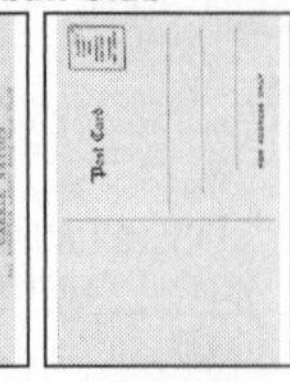

This extremely rare set of printed postcards by an unknown publisher features stars of the All-American Ladies Base Ball Club which toured America early in the 20th century. Although no date is listed on the cards they were produced sometime after 1907 beacuse they have a divided back. Prior to 1907 all postcards backs were undivided and all messages had to be written on the front or picture side of the card. All cards show close up action views of the players on a white background. We have listed the known versions, all additions to this checklist are appreciated.

	Ex-Mt	VG
COMPLETE SET (5)	1000.00	500.00
1 Bessie Barrett	200.00	100.00
2 May Fay	200.00	100.00
3 Harriett Murphy	200.00	100.00
4 Carrie Nation	200.00	100.00
5 Elizabeth Pull	200.00	100.00

1950 All-Star Pinups

These 10 pinups which measure approximately 7" in diameter feature the player photo along with a printed ID on the front and the back features instructions on how to pop out the pin up. These pinups are unnumbered and punched out from a book, which was issued

with a 50 cent cover price, and we have sequenced them in alphabetical order. Ted Williams is the featured player on the book cover.

	NM	Ex
COMPLETE SET (10)	1200.00	600.00
1 Joe DiMaggio	300.00	150.00
2 Jim Hegan	25.00	12.50
3 Gil Hodges	100.00	50.00
4 George Kell	80.00	40.00
5 Ralph Kiner	100.00	50.00
6 Stan Musial	150.00	75.00
7 Mel Parnell	25.00	12.50
8 Phil Rizzuto	100.00	50.00
9 Jackie Robinson	200.00	100.00
10 Ted Williams	300.00	150.00

1971 All-Star Baseball Album

The 1971 All-Star Baseball Album contains two pages of 12 perforated player pictures for a total of 24 cards. Each page has three rows of four cards measuring approximately 7 1/2 by 8 3/4". The individual cards measure 1 7/8" by 2 7/8". The cards are printed on thin paper stock. The fronts feature a posed all star color player photo with the player's autograph facsimile across the bottom of the picture. The backs carry biography, team name, and player profile superimposed over a ghosted team logo. The cards are unnumbered and checklisted below in alphabetical order. On an additional page that follows each of the player picture pages, is a page listing the player's statistics. A 1971 American and National League team schedule appears on the back of the album. The album, titled Today's All-Stars was produced by Dell and originally sold for 39 cents.

	NM	Ex
COMPLETE SET (24)	12.00	4.80
1 Hank Aaron	1.00	.40
2 Luis Aparicio	.40	.16
3 Ernie Banks	.75	.30
4 Johnny Bench	.75	.30
5 Rico Carty	.20	.08
6 Roberto Clemente	1.50	.60
7 Bob Gibson	.40	.16
8 Willie Horton	.20	.08
9 Frank Howard	.30	.12
10 Reggie Jackson	.75	.30
11 Ferguson Jenkins	.40	.16
12 Alex Johnson	.10	.04
13 Al Kaline	.40	.16
14 Harmon Killebrew	.40	.16
15 Willie Mays	1.00	.40
16 Sam McDowell	.20	.08
17 Denny McLain	.30	.12
18 Boog Powell	.30	.12
19 Brooks Robinson	.40	.16
20 Frank Robinson	.40	.16
21 Pete Rose	.75	.30
22 Tom Seaver	.75	.30
23 Rusty Staub	.30	.12
24 Carl Yastrzemski	.40	.16
NNO Album	5.00	2.00

1981 All-Star Game Program Inserts

S. GARVEY 1B

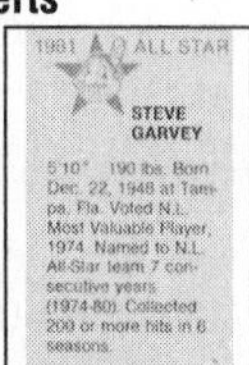

This 180-card set was distributed inside the 1981 All-Star Game Official Program on foldout sheets with each sheet containing 30 cards. Each card measures approximately 1 1/4" by 2" and features color action photos of the American League (numbers 1-90) and the National League All-Star Nominees (numbers 91-181). The cards are unnumbered and checklisted below in alphabetical order by position within each player's respective league.

	Nm-Mt	Ex-Mt
COMPLETE SET (180)	10.00	4.00
1 Willie Aikens	.05	.02
2 Bruce Bochte	.05	.02
3 Rod Carew	.50	.20
4 Cecil Cooper	.10	.04
5 Mike Hargrove	.10	.04
6 Tony Perez	.50	.20
7 John Mayberry	.05	.02
8 Eddie Murray	2.00	.80
9 Bob Watson	.10	.04
10 Julio Cruz	.05	.02
11 Rich Dauer	.05	.02
12 Damaso Garcia	.05	.02
13 Bobby Grich	.10	.04
14 Duane Kuiper	.05	.02
15 Willie Randolph	.10	.04
16 Lou Whitaker	.20	.08
17 Frank White	.05	.02
18 Bump Wills	.05	.02
19 Mark Belanger	.05	.02
20 Rick Burleson	.05	.02
21 Bucky Dent	.05	.02
22 Alfredo Griffin	.05	.02
23 Roy Smalley	.05	.02
24 Alan Trammell	.50	.20
25 Tom Veryzer	.05	.02
26 Robin Yount	1.00	.40
27 U.L. Washington	.05	.02
28 Buddy Bell	.10	.04
29 George Brett	4.00	1.60
30 John Castino	.05	.02
31 Doug DeCinces	.05	.02
32 Wayne Gross	.05	.02
33 Toby Harrah	.05	.02
34 Butch Hobson	.05	.02
35 Carney Lansford	.05	.02
36 Graig Nettles	.15	.06
37 Rick Cerone	.05	.02
38 Rick Dempsey	.05	.02
39 Brian Downing	.10	.04
40 Carlton Fisk	1.00	.40
41 Ron Hassey	.05	.02
42 Lance Parrish	.10	.04
43 Ted Simmons	.10	.04
44 Jim Sundberg	.05	.02
45 Butch Wynegar	.05	.02
46 Tony Armas	.05	.02
47 Don Baylor	.10	.04
48 Al Bumbry	.05	.02
49 Joe Charboneau	.20	.08
50 Miguel Dilone	.05	.02
51 Dan Ford	.05	.02
52 Rickey Henderson	3.00	1.20
53 Reggie Jackson	1.00	.40
54 Steve Kemp	.05	.02
55 Ron LeFlore	.05	.02
56 Chet Lemon	.05	.02
57 Greg Luzinski	.10	.04
58 Fred Lynn	.10	.04
59 Hal McRae	.05	.02
60 Paul Molitor	1.50	.60
61 Dwayne Murphy	.05	.02
62 Ben Oglivie	.05	.02
63 Al Oliver	.15	.06
64 Jorge Orta	.05	.02
65 Amos Otis	.05	.02
66 Jim Rice	.15	.06
67 Mickey Rivers	.05	.02
68 Ken Singleton	.05	.02
69 Gorman Thomas	.05	.02
70 Willie Wilson	.05	.02
71 Dave Winfield	1.00	.40
72 Carl Yastrzemski	1.00	.40
73 Floyd Bannister	.05	.02
74 Len Barker	.05	.02
75 Britt Burns	.05	.02
76 Richard Dotson	.05	.02
77 Dennis Eckersley	.75	.30
78 Rollie Fingers	.50	.20
79 Mike Flanagan	.05	.02
80 Ken Forsch	.05	.02
81 Rich Gossage	.15	.06
82 Ron Guidry	.10	.04
83 Larry Gura	.05	.02
84 Tommy John	.15	.06
85 Matt Keough	.05	.02
86 Dennis Leonard	.05	.02
87 Scott McGregor	.05	.02
88 Mike Norris	.05	.02
89 Dave Stieb	.10	.04
90 Milt Wilcox	.05	.02
91 Bill Buckner	.05	.02
92 Enos Cabell	.05	.02
93 Chris Chambliss	.10	.04
94 Dan Driessen	.05	.02
95 Steve Garvey	.50	.20
96 Keith Hernandez	.10	.04
97 Willie Montanez	.05	.02
98 Pete Rose	2.00	.80
99 Willie Stargell	.75	.30
100 Doug Flynn	.05	.02
101 Phil Garner	.05	.02
102 Glenn Hubbard	.05	.02
103 Rafael Landestoy	.05	.02
104 Davey Lopes	.10	.04
105 Ron Oester	.05	.02
106 Rodney Scott	.05	.02
107 Rennie Stennett	.05	.02
108 Manny Trillo	.05	.02
109 Larry Bowa	.05	.02
110 Dave Concepcion	.10	.04
111 Ivan DeJesus	.05	.02
112 Tim Foli	.05	.02
113 Bill Russell	.05	.02
114 Ozzie Smith	2.50	1.00
115 Chris Speier	.05	.02
116 Frank Taveras	.05	.02
117 Garry Templeton	.05	.02
118 Ron Cey	.10	.04
119 Darrell Evans	.10	.04
120 Bob Horner	.05	.02
121 Ray Knight	.05	.02
122 Bill Madlock	.10	.04
123 Ken Oberkfell	.05	.02
124 Larry Parrish	.05	.02
125 Ken Reitz	.05	.02
126 Mike Schmidt	2.00	.80
127 Alan Ashby	.05	.02
128 Johnny Bench	1.50	.60
129 Bob Boone	.10	.04
130 Gary Carter	1.50	.60
131 Terry Kennedy	.05	.02
132 Milt May	.05	.02
133 Darrell Porter	.05	.02
134 John Stearns	.05	.02
135 Steve Yeager	.05	.02
136 Dusty Baker	.10	.04
137 Cesar Cedeno	.05	.02
138 Jack Clark	.05	.02
139 Dave Collins	.05	.02
140 Warren Cromartie	.05	.02
141 Jose Cruz	.10	.04
142 Andre Dawson	.75	.30
143 Mike Easler	.05	.02
144 George Foster	.05	.02
145 Ken Griffey	.10	.04
146 Steve Henderson	.05	.02
147 George Hendrick	.05	.02
148 Dave Kingman	.15	.06
149 Ken Landreaux	.05	.02
150 Sixto Lezcano	.05	.02
151 Garry Maddox	.05	.02
152 Jerry Martin	.05	.02
153 Gary Matthews	.05	.02
154 Lee Mazzilli	.05	.02
155 Bake McBride	.05	.02
156 Omar Moreno	.05	.02
157 Dale Murphy	.75	.30
158 Dave Parker	.10	.04
159 Terry Puhl	.05	.02
160 Gene Richards	.05	.02
161 Reggie Smith	.05	.02
162 Ellis Valentine	.05	.02
163 Doyle Alexander	.05	.02
164 Neil Allen	.05	.02
165 Jim Bibby	.05	.02
166 Vida Blue	.10	.04
167 Steve Carlton	1.00	.40
168 Juan Eichelberger	.05	.02
169 Burt Hooton	.05	.02
170 Bob Knepper	.05	.02
171 Joe Niekro	.05	.02
172 Rick Rhoden	.05	.02
173 Dick Ruthven	.05	.02
174 Nolan Ryan	4.00	1.60
175 Scott Sanderson	.05	.02
176 Tom Seaver	1.00	.40
177 Lary Sorensen	.05	.02
178 Bruce Sutter	.15	.06
179 Don Sutton	.50	.20
180 Fernando Valenzuela	2.00	.80

1982 All-Star Game Program Inserts

R. CAREW 1B

This 180-card set was distributed inside the 1982 All-Star Game Official Program on foldout sheets with each sheet containing 30 cards. Each card measures approximately 1 1/4" by 2" and features color action photos of the National League All-Star Nominees (numbers 1-90) and the Americanl League All-Star Nominees (numbers 91-181). The cards are unnumbered and checklisted below in alphabetical order by position within each player's respective league.

	Nm-Mt	Ex-Mt
COMPLETE SET	10.00	4.00
1 Bill Buckner	.10	.04
2 Chris Chambliss	.10	.04
3 Dan Driessen	.05	.02
4 Steve Garvey	.50	.20
5 Keith Hernandez	.20	.08
6 Art Howe	.10	.04
7 Dave Kingman	.10	.04
8 Al Oliver	.10	.04
9 Pete Rose	2.00	.80
10 Juan Bonilla	.05	.02
11 Phil Garner	.05	.02
12 Tom Herr	.05	.02
13 Glenn Hubbard	.05	.02
14 Joe Morgan	.50	.20
15 Ron Oester	.05	.02
16 Steve Sax	.50	.20
17 Rodney Scott	.05	.02
18 Manny Trillo	.05	.02
19 Larry Bowa	.10	.04
20 Dave Concepcion	.15	.06
21 Ivan DeJesus	.05	.02
22 Johnnie LeMaster	.05	.02
23 Craig Reynolds	.05	.02
24 Bill Russell	.05	.02
25 Ozzie Smith	2.00	.80
26 Chris Speier	.05	.02
27 Garry Templeton	.05	.02
28 Johnny Bench	1.50	.60
29 Hubie Brooks	.10	.04
30 Ron Cey	.15	.06
31 Darrell Evans	.10	.04
32 Bob Horner	.05	.02
33 Ray Knight	.05	.02
34 Bill Madlock	.10	.04
35 Ken Oberkfell	.05	.02
36 Mike Schmidt	1.50	.60
37 Alan Ashby	.05	.02
38 Bruce Benedict	.05	.02
39 Gary Carter	.75	.30
40 Bo Diaz	.05	.02
41 Terry Kennedy	.05	.02
42 Tony Pena	.15	.06
43 Darrell Porter	.05	.02
44 Mike Scioscia	.15	.06
45 John Stearns	.05	.02
46 Dusty Baker	.10	.04
47 Cesar Cedeno	.10	.04
48 Jack Clark	.10	.04
49 Warren Cromartie	.05	.02
50 Jose Cruz	.05	.02
51 Andre Dawson	.50	.20
52 Leon Durham	.05	.02
53 Mike Easler	.05	.02
54 George Foster	.10	.04
55 Pedro Guerrero	.15	.06
56 Steve Henderson	.05	.02
57 George Hendrick	.05	.02
58 Ken Landreaux	.05	.02
59 Sixto Lezcano	.05	.02
60 Garry Maddox	.05	.02
61 Gary Matthews	.05	.02
62 Omar Moreno	.05	.02
63 Dale Murphy	.50	.20
64 Dave Parker	.20	.08
65 Terry Puhl	.05	.02
66 Tim Raines	.50	.20
67 Gene Richards	.10	.04
68 Tony Scott	.05	.02
69 Lonnie Smith	.05	.02
70 Claudell Washington	.05	.02
71 Mookie Wilson	.10	.04
72 Joel Youngblood	.05	.02
73 Bruce Berenyi	.05	.02
74 Rick Camp	.05	.02
75 Steve Carlton	1.00	.40
76 Bob Forsch	.05	.02
77 Alan Fowlkes	.05	.02
78 Gene Garber	.10	.04
79 Randy Jones	.05	.02
80 Tim Lollar	.05	.02
81 Randy Martz	.05	.02
82 Joe Niekro	.10	.04
83 Jeff Reardon	.15	.06
84 Jerry Reuss	.10	.04
85 Don Robinson	.05	.02
86 Steve Rogers	.05	.02
87 Bruce Sutter	.15	.06
88 Don Sutton	.50	.20
89 Kent Tekulve	.05	.02
90 Fernando Valenzuela	.50	.20
91 Willie Aikens	.05	.02
92 Rod Carew	1.00	.40
93 Dave Collins	.05	.02
94 Cecil Cooper	.10	.04
95 Mike Hargrove	.10	.04
96 John Mayberry	.05	.02
97 Eddie Murray	1.00	.40
98 Tom Paciorek	.05	.02
99 Carl Yastrzemski	2.00	.80
100 Tony Bernazard	.05	.02
101 Julio Cruz	.05	.02
102 Rich Dauer	.05	.02
103 Jim Gantner	.05	.02
104 Bobby Grich	.10	.04
105 Willie Randolph	.15	.06
106 Jerry Remy	.05	.02
107 Lou Whitaker	.15	.06
108 Frank White	.10	.04
109 Bill Almon	.05	.02
110 Rick Burleson	.05	.02
111 Bucky Dent	.10	.04
112 Alfredo Griffin	.05	.02
113 Glenn Hoffman	.05	.02
114 Roy Smalley	.05	.02
115 Alan Trammell	.20	.08
116 U.L. Washington	.05	.02
117 Robin Yount	.50	.20
118 Buddy Bell	.10	.04
119 George Brett	2.50	1.00
120 John Castino	.05	.02
121 Doug DeCinces	.10	.04
122 Toby Harrah	.05	.02
123 Carney Lansford	.10	.04
124 Paul Molitor	.50	.20
125 Graig Nettles	.10	.04
126 Cal Ripken Jr.	5.00	2.00
127 Rick Cerone	.05	.02
128 Rick Dempsey	.05	.02
129 Carlton Fisk	.50	.20
130 Ron Hassey	.05	.02
131 Mike Heath	.05	.02
132 Lance Parrish	.15	.06
133 Ted Simmons	.10	.04
134 Jim Sundberg	.05	.02
135 Butch Wynegar	.05	.02
136 Tony Armas	.05	.02
137 Harold Baines	.15	.06
138 Don Baylor	.10	.04
139 Bruce Bochte	.05	.02
140 Al Bumbry	.05	.02
141 Dwight Evans	.20	.08
142 Dan Ford	.05	.02
143 Kirk Gibson	.50	.20
144 Ken Griffey	.10	.04
145 Rickey Henderson	3.00	1.20
146 Reggie Jackson	2.00	.80
147 Steve Kemp	.05	.02
148 Ron LeFlore	.05	.02
149 Chet Lemon	.05	.02
150 Fred Lynn	.10	.04
151 Bake McBride	.05	.02
152 Jerry Mumphrey	.05	.02
153 Dwayne Murphy	.05	.02
154 Ben Oglivie	.05	.02
155 Amos Otis	.05	.02
156 Jim Rice	.20	.08
157 Mickey Rivers	.10	.04
158 Ken Singleton	.05	.02
159 Gorman Thomas	.05	.02
160 Willie Wilson	.05	.02
161 Dave Winfield	.75	.30
162 Richie Zisk	.05	.02
163 Floyd Bannister	.05	.02
164 Len Barker	.05	.02
165 Britt Burns	.05	.02
166 Bill Caudill	.05	.02
167 Jim Clancy	.05	.02
168 Danny Darwin	.05	.02
169 Ron Davis	.05	.02
170 Rollie Fingers	.50	.20
171 Ron Guidry	.20	.08
172 Larry Gura	.05	.02
173 Lamarr Hoyt	.05	.02
174 Matt Keough	.05	.02
175 Scott McGregor	.05	.02
176 Jack Morris	.15	.06
177 Dave Stieb	.10	.04
178 John Tudor	.05	.02
179 Pete Vuckovich	.05	.02
180 Geoff Zahn	.05	.02

1983 All-Star Game Program Inserts

T. HARRAH 3B

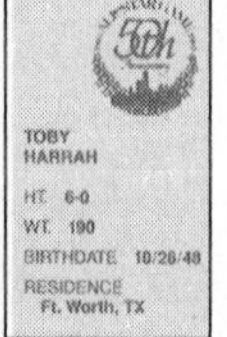

TOBY
HARRAH
HT. 6-0
WT. 190
BIRTHDATE 10/26/48
RESIDENCE
Ft. Worth, TX

This 180-card set was distributed inside the 1983 All-Star Game Official Program on foldout sheets with each sheet containing 30 cards. Each card measures approximately 1 1/4" by 2" and features color action photos of the American League (numbers 1-90) and the National League All-Star Nominees (numbers 91-181). The cards are unnumbered and checklisted below in alphabetical order by position within each player's respective league.

	Nm-Mt	Ex-Mt
COMPLETE SET (180)	10.00	4.00
1 Willie Aikens	.05	.02
2 Rod Carew	.50	.20
3 Cecil Cooper	.10	.04
4 Kent Hrbek	.10	.04
5 Eddie Murray	1.50	.60
6 Tom Paciorek	.05	.02
7 Andre Thornton	.05	.02
8 Willie Upshaw	.05	.02
9 Carl Yastrzemski	.75	.30
10 Rich Dauer	.05	.02
11 Jim Gantner	.05	.02
12 Damaso Garcia	.05	.02
13 Bobby Grich	.10	.04
14 Willie Randolph	.10	.04
15 Jerry Remy	.05	.02
16 Manny Trillo	.05	.02
17 Lou Whitaker	.20	.08
18 Frank White	.05	.02
19 Todd Cruz	.05	.02
20 Tim Foli	.05	.02
21 Alfredo Griffin	.05	.02
22 Glenn Hoffman	.05	.02
23 Cal Ripken	3.00	1.20
24 Roy Smalley	.05	.02
25 Alan Trammell	.50	.20
26 U.L. Washington	.05	.02
27 Robin Yount	.75	.30
28 Buddy Bell	.10	.04
29 Wade Boggs	5.00	2.00
30 George Brett	1.50	.60
31 Doug DeCinces	.05	.02
32 Gary Gaetti	.75	.30
33 Toby Harrah	.05	.02
34 Carney Lansford	.05	.02
35 Paul Molitor	1.25	.50
36 Graig Nettles	.15	.06
37 Bob Boone	.10	.04
38 Rick Cerone	.05	.02
39 Rick Dempsey	.05	.02
40 Carlton Fisk	1.00	.40
41 Mike Heath	.05	.02
42 Lance Parrish	.10	.04
43 Ted Simmons	.10	.04
44 Jim Sundberg	.05	.02
45 John Wathan	.05	.02
46 Tony Armas	.05	.02
47 Harold Baines	.20	.08
48 Barry Bonnell	.05	.02
49 Tom Brunansky	.05	.02
50 Al Cowens	.05	.02
51 Brian Downing	.05	.02
52 Dwight Evans	.10	.04
53 Kirk Gibson	.20	.08
54 Rickey Henderson	2.00	.80
55 Larry Herndon	.05	.02
56 Reggie Jackson	1.00	.40
57 Steve Kemp	.05	.02
58 Chet Lemon	.05	.02
59 Greg Luzinski	.10	.04
60 Fred Lynn	.10	.04
61 Rick Manning	.05	.02
62 Hal McRae	.05	.02
63 Jerry Mumphrey	.05	.02
64 Dwayne Murphy	.05	.02
65 Ben Oglivie	.05	.02
66 Amos Otis	.05	.02
67 Jim Rice	.15	.06
68 Ken Singleton	.05	.02
69 Gorman Thomas	.05	.02
70 Gary Ward	.05	.02
71 Willie Wilson	.05	.02
72 Dave Winfield	1.00	.40
73 Bert Blyleven	.10	.04
74 Bill Caudill	.05	.02
75 Richard Dotson	.05	.02
76 Dennis Eckersley	.75	.30
77 Mike Flanagan	.05	.02
78 Ken Forsch	.05	.02
79 Larry Gura	.05	.02
80 Rick Honeycutt	.05	.02
81 Dennis Lamp	.05	.02
82 Mike Norris	.05	.02
83 Dan Petry	.05	.02
84 Dan Quisenberry	.05	.02
85 Shane Rawley	.05	.02
86 Jim Slaton	.05	.02
87 Bob Stanley	.05	.02
88 Dave Stieb	.05	.02
89 Al Williams	.05	.02
90 Geoff Zahn	.05	.02
91 Bill Buckner	.05	.02
92 Chris Chambliss	.10	.04
93 Dan Driessen	.05	.02
94 Steve Garvey	.20	.08
95 Keith Hernandez	.10	.04
96 Ray Knight	.05	.02
97 Al Oliver	.10	.04
98 Pete Rose	1.00	.40
99 Jason Thompson	.05	.02
100 Juan Bonilla	.05	.02
101 Doug Flynn	.05	.02
102 Tom Herr	.05	.02
103 Glenn Hubbard	.05	.02
104 Joe Morgan	.50	.20
105 Ron Oester	.05	.02
106 Johnny Ray	.05	.02
107 Ryne Sandberg	4.00	1.60
108 Steve Sax	.10	.04
109 Larry Bowa	.05	.02
110 Dave Concepcion	.10	.04
111 Ivan DeJesus	.05	.02
112 Rafael Ramirez	.05	.02
113 Bill Russell	.05	.02
114 Ozzie Smith	2.00	.80
115 Chris Speier	.05	.02
116 Garry Templeton	.05	.02
117 Dickie Thon	.05	.02
118 Hubie Brooks	.05	.02
119 Ron Cey	.10	.04
120 Phil Garner	.05	.02
121 Pedro Guerrero	.10	.04
122 Bob Horner	.05	.02
123 Bill Madlock	.10	.04
124 Ken Oberkfell	.05	.02
125 Mike Schmidt	1.50	.60
126 Tim Wallach	.05	.02
127 Alan Ashby	.05	.02
128 Bruce Benedict	.05	.02
129 Gary Carter	.75	.30
130 Jody Davis	.05	.02
131 Bo Diaz	.05	.02
132 Terry Kennedy	.05	.02
133 Tony Pena	.10	.04
134 Darrell Porter	.05	.02

135 John Stearns .05 .02
136 Dusty Baker .10 .04
137 Cesar Cedeno .05 .02
138 Jack Clark .05 .02
139 Warren Cromartie .05 .02
140 Jose Cruz .10 .04
141 Chili Davis .10 .04
142 Andre Dawson .50 .20
143 Leon Durham .05 .02
144 Mike Easler .05 .02
145 George Foster .05 .02
146 Von Hayes .05 .02
147 George Hendrick .05 .02
148 Ruppert Jones .05 .02
149 Ken Landreaux .05 .02
150 Sixto Lezcano .05 .02
151 Garry Maddox .05 .02
152 Gary Matthews .05 .02
153 Willie McGee 1.00 .40
154 Omar Moreno .05 .02
155 Dale Murphy .50 .20
156 Dave Parker .10 .04
157 Terry Puhl .05 .02
158 Tim Raines .20 .08
159 Gene Richards .05 .02
160 Lonnie Smith .05 .02
161 Claudell Washington .05 .02
162 Mookie Wilson .10 .04
163 Joaquin Andujar .05 .02
164 Rick Camp .05 .02
165 Steve Carlton .75 .30
166 Atlee Hammaker .05 .02
167 Fergie Jenkins .50 .20
168 Bob Knepper .05 .02
169 Charlie Lea .05 .02
170 Larry McWilliams .05 .02
171 Alejandro Pena .05 .02
172 Pascual Perez .05 .02
173 Jerry Reuss .10 .04
174 Steve Rogers .05 .02
175 Nolan Ryan 3.00 1.20
176 Tom Seaver 1.00 .40
177 Rod Scurry .05 .02
178 Eric Show .05 .02
179 Mario Soto .05 .02
180 Bruce Sutter .15 .06

1984 All-Star Game Program Inserts

This 180-card set was distributed inside the 1984 All-Star Game Official Program on foldout sheets with each sheet containing 30 cards. Each card measures approximately 1 3/16" by 1 7/8" and features color photos of the National League (numbers 1-90) and the American League All-Star Nominees (numbers 91-181). The cards are unnumbered and checklisted below in alphabetical order by position within each player's respective league. Inserts listed above number 180 were issued as pitchers and write in candidates.

	Nm-Mt	Ex-Mt
COMPLETE SET (180)	10.00	4.00
1 Bill Buckner	.10	.04
2 Chris Chambliss	.10	.04
3 Dan Driessen	.05	.02
4 Steve Garvey	.15	.06
5 David Green	.05	.02
6 Keith Hernandez	.15	.06
7 Ray Knight	.05	.02
8 Al Oliver	.10	.04
9 Jason Thompson	.05	.02
10 Bill Doran	.05	.02
11 Tommy Herr	.05	.02
12 Glenn Hubbard	.05	.02
13 Ron Oester	.05	.02
14 Johnny Ray	.05	.02
15 Ryne Sandberg	3.00	1.20
16 Steve Sax	.05	.02
17 Manny Trillo	.05	.02
18 Alan Wiggins	.05	.02
19 Dale Berra	.05	.02
20 Dave Concepcion	.10	.04
21 Ivan DeJesus	.05	.02
22 Johnnie LeMaster	.05	.02
23 Rafael Ramirez	.05	.02
24 Bill Russell	.10	.04
25 Ozzie Smith	2.00	.80
26 Garry Templeton	.05	.02
27 Dickie Thon	.05	.02
28 Ron Cey	.10	.04
29 Phil Garner	.05	.02
30 Pedro Guerrero	.05	.02
31 Bob Horner	.05	.02
32 Bill Madlock	.10	.04
33 Graig Nettles	.10	.04
34 Ken Oberkfell	.05	.02
35 Mike Schmidt	1.00	.40
36 Tim Wallach	.05	.02
37 Alan Ashby	.05	.02
38 Bruce Benedict	.05	.02
39 Gary Carter	.20	.08
40 Jody Davis	.05	.02
41 Bo Diaz	.05	.02
42 Terry Kennedy	.05	.02
43 Tony Pena	.10	.04
44 Darrell Porter	.05	.02
45 Steve Yeager	.05	.02
46 Jack Clark	.10	.04
47 Jose Cruz	.10	.04
48 Chili Davis	.10	.04
49 Andre Dawson	.15	.06
50 Leon Durham	.20	.08
51 George Foster	.05	.02
52 Tony Gwynn	3.00	1.20
53 George Hendrick	.05	.02
54 Ken Landreaux	.05	.02
55 Joe Lefebvre	.05	.02
56 Jeff Leonard	.05	.02
57 Willie McGee	.20	.08
58 Mike Marshall	.05	.02
59 Gary Matthews	.05	.02
60 Keith Moreland	.05	.02
61 Jerry Mumphrey	.05	.02
62 Dale Murphy	.20	.08
63 Amos Otis	.05	.02
64 Dave Parker	.15	.06
65 Terry Puhl	.05	.02
66 Tim Raines	.15	.06
67 Gary Redus	.05	.02
68 Pete Rose	1.00	.40
69 Darryl Strawberry	.25	.10
70 Lonnie Smith	.05	.02
71 Claudell Washington	.05	.02
72 Mookie Wilson	.10	.04
73 Joaquin Andujar	.05	.02
74 Steve Bedrosian	.05	.02
75 John Candelaria	.05	.02
76 John Denny	.05	.02
77 Dwight Gooden	1.00	.40
78 Rich Gossage	.15	.06
79 Al Holland	.05	.02
80 Rick Honeycutt	.05	.02
81 Dave LaPoint	.05	.02
82 Gary Lavelle	.05	.02
83 Charlie Lea	.05	.02
84 Jesse Orosco	.10	.04
85 Alejandro Pena	.05	.02
86 Nolan Ryan	3.00	1.20
87 Eric Show	.05	.02
88 Bryn Smith	.05	.02
89 Lee Smith	.15	.06
90 Mario Soto	.05	.02
91 Rod Carew	.50	.20
92 Cecil Cooper	.10	.04
93 Darrell Evans	.10	.04
94 Ken Griffey	.10	.04
95 Kent Hrbek	.05	.02
96 Eddie Murray	1.00	.40
97 Tom Paciorek	.05	.02
98 Andre Thornton	.05	.02
99 Willie Upshaw	.05	.02
100 Julio Cruz	.05	.02
101 Rich Dauer	.05	.02
102 Jim Gantner	.05	.02
103 Damaso Garcia	.05	.02
104 Bobby Grich	.10	.04
105 Willie Randolph	.10	.04
106 Jerry Remy	.05	.02
107 Lou Whitaker	.20	.08
108 Frank White	.10	.04
109 Tim Foli	.05	.02
110 Julio Franco	.15	.06
111 Alfredo Griffin	.05	.02
112 Glenn Hoffman	.05	.02
113 Cal Ripken	3.00	1.20
114 Dick Schofield	.05	.02
115 Alan Trammell	.50	.20
116 Robin Yount	.50	.20
117 U.L. Washington	.05	.02
118 Buddy Bell	.10	.04
119 Wade Boggs	3.00	1.20
120 George Brett	2.00	.80
121 John Castino	.05	.02
122 Doug DeCinces	.05	.02
123 Toby Harrah	.05	.02
124 Carney Lansford	.05	.02
125 Vance Law	.05	.02
126 Paul Molitor	.50	.20
127 Bob Boone	.10	.04
128 Rick Dempsey	.05	.02
129 Carlton Fisk	.50	.20
130 Mike Heath	.05	.02
131 Lance Parrish	.15	.06
132 Jim Sundberg	.05	.02
133 Ted Simmons	.10	.04
134 John Wathan	.05	.02
135 Butch Wynegar	.05	.02
136 Tony Armas	.05	.02
137 Harold Baines	.15	.06
138 Don Baylor	.15	.06
139 Jesse Barfield	.05	.02
140 Tom Brunansky	.05	.02
141 Brian Downing	.05	.02
142 Dwight Evans	.10	.04
143 Rickey Henderson	1.50	.60
144 Larry Herndon	.05	.02
145 Reggie Jackson	.75	.30
146 Steve Kemp	.05	.02
147 Ron Kittle	.05	.02
148 Chet Lemon	.05	.02
149 John Lowenstein	.05	.02
150 Greg Luzinski	.10	.04
151 Fred Lynn	.10	.04
152 Hal McRae	.05	.02
153 Lloyd Moseby	.05	.02
154 Dwayne Murphy	.05	.02
155 Larry Parrish	.05	.02
156 Ben Oglivie	.05	.02
157 Jim Rice	.15	.06
158 Gorman Thomas	.05	.02
159 Ken Singleton	.05	.02
160 Gary Ward	.05	.02
161 Dave Winfield	.75	.30
162 George Wright	.05	.02
163 Dave Beard	.05	.02
164 Bert Blyleven	.15	.06
165 Mike Boddicker	.05	.02
166 Mike Caldwell	.05	.02
167 Bill Caudill	.05	.02
168 Danny Darwin	.05	.02
169 Ron Davis	.05	.02
170 Richard Dotson	.05	.02
171 Larry Gura	.05	.02
172 Bruce Hurst	.05	.02
173 Luis Leal	.05	.02
174 Jack Morris	.15	.06
175 Dan Petry	.05	.02
176 Mike Smithson	.05	.02
177 Sammy Stewart	.05	.02
178 Dave Stieb	.10	.04
179 Milt Wilcox	.05	.02
180 Geoff Zahn	.05	.02
181 Aurelio Lopez	.05	.02
182 Tippy Martinez	.05	.02
183 Don Mattingly	5.00	2.00
184 Pete O'Brien	.05	.02
185 Tom Paciorek	.05	.02
186 Dan Quisenberry	.05	.02
187 Jerry Remy	.05	.02
188 Luis Sanchez	.05	.02
189 Pat Tabler	.05	.02

1985 All-Star Game Program Inserts

D. Mattingly 1B

Don Mattingly NEW YORK YANKEES

This 180-card set was distributed inside the 1985 All-Star Game Official Program on foldout sheets with each sheet containing 30 cards. Each card measures approximately 1 1/4" by 2" and features color photos of the American League (numbers 1-90) and the National League All-Star Nominees (numbers 91-181). The cards are unnumbered and checklisted below in alphabetical order by position within each player's respective league.

	Nm-Mt	Ex-Mt
COMPLETE SET (180)	10.00	4.00
1 Bill Buckner	.05	.02
2 Rod Carew	.50	.20
3 Cecil Cooper	.10	.04
4 Alvin Davis	.10	.04
5 Kent Hrbek	.10	.04
6 Don Mattingly	2.00	.80
7 Eddie Murray	1.00	.40
8 Pete O'Brien	.05	.02
9 Willie Upshaw	.05	.02
10 Marty Barrett	.05	.02
11 Julio Cruz	.05	.02
12 Jim Gantner	.05	.02
13 Damaso Garcia	.05	.02
14 Bobby Grich	.10	.04
15 Willie Randolph	.10	.04
16 Tim Teufel	.05	.02
17 Lou Whitaker	.25	.10
18 Frank White	.05	.02
19 Onix Concepcion	.05	.02
20 Tony Fernandez	.15	.06
21 Julio Franco	.15	.06
22 Alfredo Griffin	.05	.02
23 Jackie Gutierrez	.05	.02
24 Spike Owen	.05	.02
25 Cal Ripken	3.00	1.20
26 Alan Trammell	.50	.20
27 Robin Yount	.75	.30
28 Buddy Bell	.10	.04
29 Wade Boggs	2.00	.80
30 George Brett	1.50	.60
31 Doug DeCinces	.05	.02
32 Darrell Evans	.10	.04
33 Gary Gaetti	.10	.04
34 Carney Lansford	.10	.04
35 Paul Molitor	1.00	.40
36 Rance Mulliniks	.05	.02
37 Bob Boone	.10	.04
38 Rick Dempsey	.05	.02
39 Carlton Fisk	1.00	.40
40 Rich Gedman	.05	.02
41 Mike Heath	.05	.02
42 Lance Parrish	.10	.04
43 Jim Sundberg	.05	.02
44 Ernie Whitt	.05	.02
45 Butch Wynegar	.05	.02
46 Tony Armas	.05	.02
47 Harold Baines	.15	.06
48 Jesse Barfield	.05	.02
49 Don Baylor	.10	.04
50 George Bell	.05	.02
51 Tom Brunansky	.05	.02
52 Brett Butler	.10	.04
53 Dave Collins	.05	.02
54 Brian Downing	.05	.02
55 Mike Easler	.05	.02
56 Dwight Evans	.10	.04
57 Kirk Gibson	.25	.10
58 Rickey Henderson	1.50	.60
59 Reggie Jackson	1.00	.40
60 Ron Kittle	.05	.02
61 Lee Lacy	.05	.02
62 Chet Lemon	.05	.02
63 Fred Lynn	.10	.04
64 Lloyd Moseby	.05	.02
65 Dwayne Murphy	.05	.02
66 Ben Oglivie	.05	.02
67 Larry Parrish	.05	.02
68 Kirby Puckett	3.00	1.20
69 Jim Rice	.15	.06
70 Gary Ward	.05	.02
71 Willie Wilson	.05	.02
72 Dave Winfield	1.00	.40
73 Doyle Alexander	.05	.02
74 Mike Boddicker	.05	.02
75 Oil Can Boyd	.05	.02
76 Danny Darwin	.05	.02
77 Ron Guidry	.10	.04
78 Willie Hernandez	.05	.02
79 Mark Langston	.25	.10
80 Charlie Liebrandt	.05	.02
81 Jack Morris	.10	.04
82 Dickie Noles	.05	.02
83 Dan Petry	.05	.02
84 Dan Quisenberry	.10	.04
85 Dave Righetti	.10	.04
86 Don Schulze	.05	.02
87 Tom Seaver	.75	.30
88 Jim Slaton	.05	.02
89 Frank Viola	.10	.04
90 Geoff Zahn	.05	.02
91 Greg Brock	.05	.02
92 Enos Cabell	.05	.02
93 Dan Driessen	.05	.02
94 Leon Durham	.05	.02
95 Steve Garvey	.25	.10
96 David Green	.05	.02
97 Keith Hernandez	.10	.04
98 Pete Rose	1.00	.40
99 Jason Thompson	.05	.02
100 Bill Doran	.05	.02
101 Tommy Herr	.05	.02
102 Glenn Hubbard	.05	.02
103 Johnny Ray	.05	.02
104 Juan Samuel	.05	.02
105 Ryne Sandberg	2.00	.80
106 Steve Sax	.10	.04
107 Manny Trillo	.05	.02
108 Alan Wiggins	.05	.02
109 Larry Bowa	.10	.04
110 Hubie Brooks	.05	.02
111 Dave Concepcion	.10	.04
112 Ivan DeJesus	.05	.02
113 Rafael Ramirez	.05	.02
114 Craig Reynolds	.05	.02
115 Bill Russell	.05	.02
116 Ozzie Smith	1.50	.60
117 Garry Templeton	.05	.02
118 Ron Cey	.10	.04
119 Phil Garner	.05	.02
120 Bob Horner	.05	.02
121 Ray Knight	.05	.02
122 Bill Madlock	.10	.04
123 Graig Nettles	.15	.06
124 Terry Pendleton	.25	.10
125 Mike Schmidt	.75	.30
126 Tim Wallach	.05	.02
127 Bob Brenly	.10	.04
128 Gary Carter	.50	.20
129 Jody Davis	.05	.02
130 Mike Fitzgerald	.05	.02
131 Terry Kennedy	.05	.02
132 Tony Pena	.10	.04
133 Darrell Porter	.05	.02
134 Mike Scioscia	.15	.06
135 Ozzie Virgil	.05	.02
136 Jack Clark	.05	.02
137 Jose Cruz	.10	.04
138 Chili Davis	.10	.04
139 Andre Dawson	.35	.14
140 Bob Dernier	.05	.02
141 George Foster	.05	.02
142 Pedro Guerrero	.10	.04
143 Tony Gwynn	2.00	.80
144 Von Hayes	.05	.02
145 George Hendrick	.05	.02
146 Steve Kemp	.05	.02
147 Jeff Leonard	.05	.02
148 Mike Marshall	.05	.02
149 Gary Matthews	.05	.02
150 Willie McGee	.25	.10
151 Kevin McReynolds	.05	.02
152 Keith Moreland	.05	.02
153 Jerry Mumphrey	.05	.02
154 Dale Murphy	.25	.10
155 Dave Parker	.10	.04
156 Terry Puhl	.05	.02
157 Tim Raines	.10	.04
158 Lonnie Smith	.05	.02
159 Darryl Strawberry	.10	.04
160 Claudell Washington	.05	.02
161 Mookie Wilson	.10	.04
162 Marvell Wynne	.05	.02
163 Joaquin Andujar	.05	.02
164 Steve Bedrosian	.05	.02
165 John Candelaria	.05	.02
166 Jose DeLeon	.05	.02
167 John Denny	.05	.02
168 Dennis Eckersley	.75	.30
169 Dwight Gooden	1.00	.40
170 Rich Gossage	.15	.06
171 Mike Krukow	.05	.02
172 Rick Mahler	.05	.02
173 Jesse Orosco	.10	.04
174 Shane Rawley	.05	.02
175 Nolan Ryan	3.00	1.20
176 Bryn Smith	.05	.02
177 Lee Smith	.15	.06
178 Mario Soto	.05	.02
179 Steve Trout	.05	.02
180 Fernando Valenzuela	.25	.10

2001 All-Star Game Program Promos

These five blank-backed posters, which measure approximately 8 1/4" by 11" feature drawings of five players as if they were on the cover of the 2001 All-Star Game program. Since these are unnumbered, we have sequenced them in alphabetical order.

	MINT	NRMT
COMPLETE SET	30.00	13.50
1 Ken Griffey Jr.	5.00	2.20
2 Derek Jeter	8.00	3.60
3 Pedro Martinez	4.00	1.80
4 Mike Piazza	5.00	2.20
5 Ichiro Suzuki	10.00	4.50

1991 Alrak Griffey Gazette

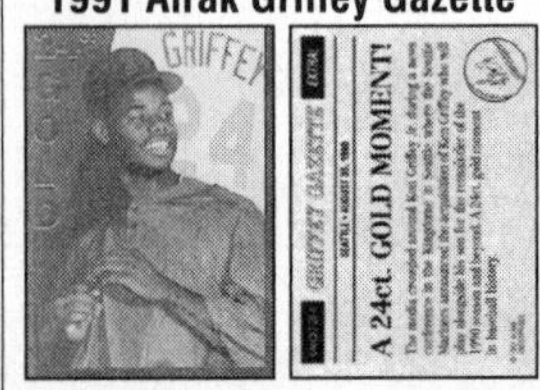

Produced by Alrak Enterprises, these standard-size cards were issued in honor of Ken Griffey Jr. The 3,000 promo sets were distributed at the SuperBowl Sports Collectors Classic III in Bellevue, Washington (January, 1992). These promos carries the following stamp on their backs: "Promo Card, SuperBowl Sports Collectors Classic III, Bellevue, Washington, January 1992 and are valued at double the prices listed below.

	Nm-Mt	Ex-Mt
COMPLETE SET (4)	6.00	1.80
COMMON CARD (1-4)	1.50	.45

1991 Alrak Griffey Postcard

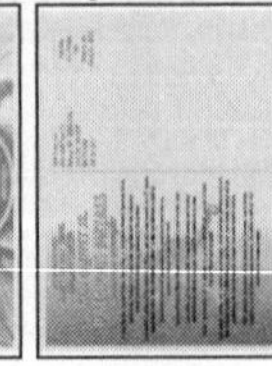

This one card set measures approximately 5 3/8" by 7 1/4" and was distributed by Alrak Enterprises to advertise their Ken Griffey Jr. Solid Brass Monthly Sportcard Series.

	Nm-Mt	Ex-Mt
1 Ken Griffey Jr.	2.00	.60

1992 Alrak Griffey Ace Auto Supply

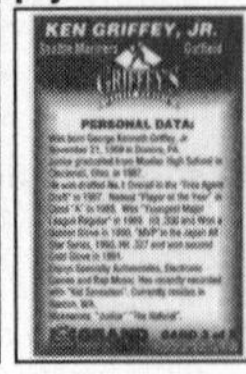

This ten-card set, subtitled "Griffey's Golden Moments," was produced by Alrak Enterprises for Ace Auto Supply and Grand Auto Supply stores. The production run was reportedly 85,000 sets and they were sold at 145 stores in northern California, Nevada Washington and Alaska. The plastic cards measure approximately 3 3/8" by 2 1/8" and resemble plastic credit cards.

	Nm-Mt	Ex-Mt
COMPLETE SET (10)	12.00	3.60
COMMON CARD (1-10)	1.25	.35

1992 Alrak Griffey Golden Moments

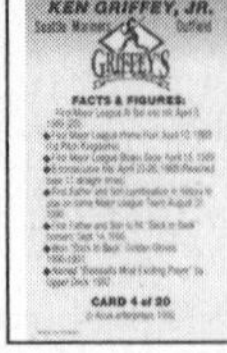

This ten-card set measures approximately 2 1/8" by 3 3/8" and is similar in design and material to credit cards. The cards feature posed and action color photos of Ken Griffey Jr. and Ken Griffey Sr. with white borders. The cards indicate "X of 20" on the back, so a second series of ten more cards was evidently planned.

	Nm-Mt	Ex-Mt
COMPLETE SET (10)	15.00	4.50
COMMON CARD (1-10)	1.50	.45

1992 Alrak Griffey Golden Moments Sheet

This commemorative blank-backed sheet measures approximately 8 1/2" by 10 3/4" and features pictures of the Griffey's Golden Moments limited edition plastic baseball cards from Series I and II. Each sheet is individually numbered with production was limited to 1,000.

	Nm-Mt	Ex-Mt
1 Ken Griffey Jr.	5.00	1.50

1992 Alrak Griffey McDonald's

This set, sponsored by McDonald's, contains three card and pin combinations. The cards are numbered on the front and measure 2 1/2" X 3 1/2". The card back describes the Ronald McDonald Children's Charities program in Western Washington. The set was produced by Alrak Enterprises with a reported production run of 100,000 for each card and pin combination. They were sold in 117 Western McDonald's Washington restaurants.

	Nm-Mt	Ex-Mt
COMPLETE SET (3)	10.00	3.00
COMMON CARD (1-3)	3.50	1.05

1993 Alrak Griffey 24 Taco Time

This six-card standard-size set was issued in the Pacific Northwest at Taco Time restaurants. Three cards have cut-out color player photos against gradated backgrounds of various colors. Color coordinated striped borders edged with gold foil frame the pictures. A gold-foil stamp at the lower right carries the words "Griffey 24" and "One of 24,000." The backs give player profile information and statistics against brightly colored backgrounds with a baseball player icon. The fourth card in the set is a 1992 All-Star MVP commemorative. It features a posed shot of Griffey with the MVP award. The horizontal back carries a color action photo with statistics in a ghosted white box on the left side. The fifth and sixth cards carry the red-foil Taco Time logo in their upper left corners and have red-foil-trimmed borders. The backs carry designs similar to the first three cards described above. The cards are unnumbered.

	Nm-Mt	Ex-Mt
COMPLETE SET (6)	10.00	3.00
COMMON CARD (1-6)	2.00	.60

1993 Alrak Griffey Mt. Vernon Ohio

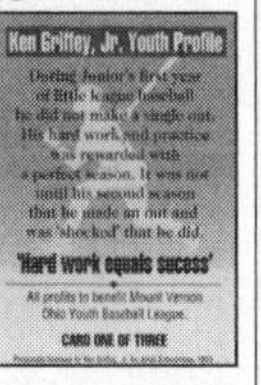

Twenty thousand of these three-card standard-size sets were produced for the city of Mt. Vernon and all profits were to benefit the Mt. Vernon Ohio Youth Baseball League. Two different versions of the cards exist, one with and one without a gold-foil facsimile autograph inscribed across the picture. Either version is valued at the same price.

	Nm-Mt	Ex-Mt
COMPLETE SET (3)	6.00	1.80
COMMON CARD (1-3)	2.00	.60

1993 Alrak Griffey Triple Play

This tri-fold card measures 7 1/2" by 3 1/2" unfolded and features a full-length color action photo of Griffey on one side with the words "Triple Play" appearing above the photo and statistics below. The production run was reportedly 24,000.

	Nm-Mt	Ex-Mt
1 Ken Griffey Jr.	3.00	.90

1993 Alrak Griffey Two-sided

This card measures the standard size and features a cut-out action shot of Griffey batting on one side and three cut-out action photos of Griffey on the other side.

	Nm-Mt	Ex-Mt
1 Ken Griffey Jr.	3.00	.90

1994 Alrak Griffey Jr. Taco Time

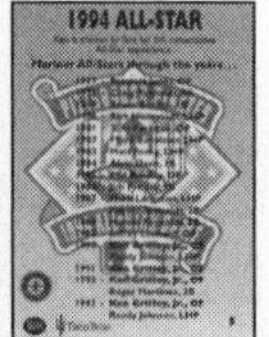

As part of a "Double Play" combination promotion, these 11 cards were specially offered as foil-wrapped singles to purchasers of a a 44 oz. Coke in a special Ken Griffey Jr. Collector's Cup at Taco Time Restaurants of Western Washington. Production of card numbers 1-6 was limited to 35,000 silver foil-accented sets. Additionally, 5,000 special gold foil-accented versions were created and randomly issued. The production run of the silver-foil SP2, SP4, and SP5 was 15,000, while that of the holographic foil SP1-3 was 20,000. Also, 30,000 cards were distributed to kick off the promotion to fans attending the Mariners-White Sox game of June 24. Measuring 3 1/2" by 5", the fronts feature original caricatures of Griffey by sports artist Larry Weber. The backs carry a description of a memorable moment in the career of the Mariners' star, as well as the Mariners, Alrak, and Taco Time logos.

	Nm-Mt	Ex-Mt
COMPLETE SILVER SET (6)	10.00	3.00
COMMON SILVER CARD (1-6)	2.00	.60
*GOLD: 3X VALUE		
COMPLETE SP SET (5)	30.00	9.00
COMMON CARD (SP1-SP5)	6.00	1.80

1908-10 American Caramel E91

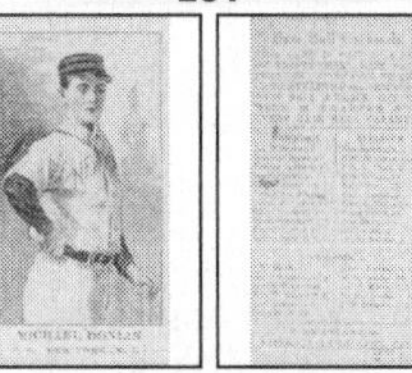

The cards in this 99-card set measure 1 1/2" by 2 3/4". E91 encompasses three separate sets of color cards issued in 1908 and 1910. The 33 ballplayer drawings of the 1908 set were also used in the two 1910 sets. Eleven players were dropped and 11 were added for set 3. There are only 75 different players, so that, for example, there are two cards of Bender with identical fronts, but a different player is "named" in the same pose in set 3. Likewise, there can be three different players assigned to the same pose -- one from each set. The set 1 checklist lists "Athletics" first; set 3 "Pittsburgh" first. Because of these drawings (which are generic and do not specifically resemble the actual player's likeness) the set has never been popular with collectors, hence their relatively low price.

	Ex-Mt	VG
COMPLETE SET (99)	8000.00	4000.00
1 Chief Bender	120.00	60.00
2 Roger Bresnahan	120.00	60.00
3 Al Bridwell	60.00	30.00
4 Mordecai Brown	120.00	60.00
5 Frank Chance	150.00	75.00
6 James Collins	120.00	60.00
7 Harry Davis	60.00	30.00
8 Art Devlin	60.00	30.00
9 Mike Donlin	80.00	40.00
10 Johnny Evers	150.00	75.00
11 Topsy Hartsel	60.00	30.00
12 Johnny Kling	60.00	30.00
13 Christy Mathewson	250.00	125.00
14 Joe McGinnity	120.00	60.00
15 John McGraw MG	150.00	75.00
16 Danny Murphy	60.00	30.00
17 Simon Nichols	60.00	30.00
18 Rube Oldring	60.00	30.00
19 Orval Overall	60.00	30.00
20 Eddie Plank	175.00	90.00
21 Ed Reulbach	60.00	30.00
22 Jimmy Scheckard	60.00	30.00
23 Ossie Schreckengost	60.00	30.00
24 Frank Schulte	80.00	40.00
25 Ralph Seybold	60.00	30.00
26 J.B. Seymore	60.00	30.00
27 Daniel Shay	60.00	30.00
28 James Slagle	60.00	30.00
29 Harry Steinfeldt	80.00	40.00
30 Luther Taylor	60.00	30.00
31 Fred Tenney	60.00	30.00
32 Joe Tinker	150.00	75.00
33 Rube Waddell	120.00	60.00
34 Jimmy Archer	60.00	30.00
35 Frank Baker	120.00	60.00
36 Jack Barry	60.00	30.00
37 Chief Bender	120.00	60.00
38 Al Bridwell	60.00	30.00
39 Mordecai Brown	120.00	60.00
40 Frank Chance	150.00	75.00
41 Eddie Collins	150.00	75.00
42 Harry Davis	60.00	30.00
43 Art Devlin	60.00	30.00
44 Mike Donlin	80.00	40.00
45 Larry Doyle	80.00	40.00
46 Johnny Evers	150.00	75.00
47 Bob Ganley	60.00	30.00
48 Fred Hartzell	60.00	30.00
49 Solly Hoffman	60.00	30.00
50 Harry Krause	60.00	30.00
51 Rube Marquard	120.00	60.00
52 Christy Mathewson	250.00	125.00
53 John McGraw MG	120.00	60.00
54 Chief Meyers	80.00	40.00
55 Danny Murphy	60.00	30.00
56 Red Murray	60.00	30.00
57 Orval Overall	60.00	30.00
58 Eddie Plank	175.00	90.00
59 Ed Reulbach	60.00	30.00
60 Jimmy Scheckard	60.00	30.00
61 Frank Schulte	80.00	40.00
62 J.B. Seymore	60.00	30.00
63 Harry Steinfeldt	80.00	40.00
64 Fred Tenney	60.00	30.00
65 Ira Thomas	60.00	30.00
66 Joe Tinker	150.00	75.00
67 Jap Barbeau	60.00	30.00
68 George Browne	60.00	30.00
69 Ed Carger	60.00	30.00
70 Charlie Chech	60.00	30.00
71 Fred Clarke	120.00	60.00
72 Wid Conroy	60.00	30.00
73 Jim Delehanty	60.00	30.00
74 Jiggs Donahue	60.00	30.00
75 J.A. Donohue	60.00	30.00
76 George Gibson	60.00	30.00
77 Bob Groom	60.00	30.00
78 Harry Hooper	120.00	60.00
79 Tom Hughes	60.00	30.00
80 Walter Johnson	250.00	125.00
81 Tommy Leach	80.00	40.00
82 Sam Leever	60.00	30.00
83 Harry Lord	60.00	30.00
84 George McBride	60.00	30.00
85 Amby McConnell	60.00	30.00
86 Clyde Milan	80.00	40.00
87 J.B. Miller	60.00	30.00
88 Harry Niles	60.00	30.00
89 Deacon Phillippe	80.00	40.00
90 Tris Speaker	150.00	75.00
91 Jack Stahl	80.00	40.00
92 Allen Storke	60.00	30.00
93 Gabby Street	80.00	40.00
94 Bob Unglaub	60.00	30.00
95 Charlie Wagner	60.00	30.00
96 Honus Wagner	300.00	150.00
97 Vic Willis	120.00	60.00
98 Owen Wilson	60.00	30.00
99 Joe Wood	120.00	60.00

1909-11 American Caramel E90-1

The cards in this 120-card set measure 1 1/2" by 2 3/4". The E90-1 set contains in order, the Mitchell of Cincinnati, Sweeney of Boston, and Graham cards which are more difficult to obtain than other cards in the set. In fact, there are many differential levels of scarcity in this set which was issued from 1909 through 1911. Several players exist in more than one pose or color background; these cards are noted in the checklist below.

	Ex-Mt	VG
COMPLETE SET (120)	50000.00	
25000.00		
1 William Bailey	100.00	50.00
2 Frank Baker	250.00	125.00
3 Jack Barry	100.00	50.00
4 George Bell	100.00	50.00
5 Harry Bemis	250.00	125.00
6 Chief Bender	250.00	125.00
7 Bob Bescher	200.00	100.00
8 Cliff Blankenship	100.00	50.00
9 John Bliss	100.00	50.00
10 William J. Bradley	100.00	50.00
11 Kitty Bransfield	100.00	50.00
(blue background)		
12 Kitty Bransfield	150.00	75.00
(pink background)		
13 Roger Bresnahan	250.00	125.00
14 Al Bridwell	100.00	50.00
15 Buster Brown HOR	100.00	50.00
Boston NL		
16 Mordecai Brown	350.00	180.00
Chic NL		
17 Donie Bush	100.00	50.00
18 John A. Butler	100.00	50.00
19 Howie Camnitz	100.00	50.00
20 Frank Chance	350.00	180.00
21 Hal Chase	200.00	100.00
22 Fred Clarke	250.00	125.00
Phila. NL		
23 Fred Clarke	1800.00	900.00
Pitts		
24 Wallace O. Clement	150.00	75.00
25 Ty Cobb	3000.00	1500.00
26 Eddie Collins	350.00	180.00
27 Frank Corridon	100.00	50.00
28 Sam Crawford	250.00	125.00
29 Lou Criger	100.00	50.00
30 Jasper Davis	100.00	50.00
31 George Davis	250.00	125.00
32 Ray Demmitt	200.00	100.00
33 Mike Donlin	150.00	75.00
34 Wild Bill Donovan	150.00	75.00
35 Red Dooin	100.00	50.00
36 Patsy Dougherty	150.00	75.00
37 Hugh Duffy	2000.00	1000.00
38 Jimmy Dygert	100.00	50.00
39 Rube Ellis	100.00	50.00
40 Clyde Engle	100.00	50.00
41 Art Fromme	200.00	100.00
42 George Gibson	300.00	150.00
back view		
43 George Gibson	100.00	50.00
front view		
44 George Graham	2000.00	1000.00
45 Eddie Grant	150.00	75.00
46 Dolly Gray	100.00	50.00
47 Bob Groom	100.00	50.00
48 Charles Hall HOR	100.00	50.00
49 Tippy Hartzell	100.00	50.00
green background		
50 Tippy Hartzell	100.00	50.00
pink background		
51 William Heitmuller	100.00	50.00
52 Harry Howell	100.00	50.00
follow thru		
53 Harry Howell	200.00	100.00
windup		
54 Tex Erwin	100.00	50.00
Sic, Irwin		
55 Frank Isbell	100.00	50.00
56 Joe Jackson	6000.00	3000.00
57 Hugh Jennings	300.00	150.00
58 Tim Jordan	100.00	50.00
59 Addie Joss	400.00	200.00
portrait		
60 Addie Joss HOR	1800.00	900.00
pitching		
61 Ed Karger	750.00	375.00
62 Willie Keeler	400.00	200.00
portrait,		
pink background		
63 Willie Keeler	600.00	300.00
portrait,		
red background		
64 Willie Keeler HOR	2000.00	1000.00
throwing		
65 John Knight	100.00	50.00
66 Harry Krause	100.00	50.00
67 Nap Lajoie	800.00	400.00
68 Tommy Leach	150.00	75.00
batting		
69 Tommy Leach	150.00	75.00
throwing		
70 Sam Leever	100.00	50.00
71 Hans Lobert	200.00	100.00
72 Harry Lumley	100.00	50.00
73 Rube Marquard	250.00	125.00
74 Christy Matthewson	800.00	400.00
(sic, Mathewson)		
75 Stuffy McInnes	150.00	75.00
76 Harry McIntyre	100.00	50.00
(sic, McIntire)		
77 Larry McLean	200.00	100.00
78 George McQuillan	100.00	50.00
79 Dots Miller	100.00	50.00
80 Mike Mitchell	6000.00	3000.00
Cincinnati		
81 Fred Mitchell	100.00	50.00
NY AL		
82 George Mullin	150.00	75.00
83 Rebel Oakes	100.00	50.00
84 Patrick O'Connor	100.00	50.00
85 Charley O'Leary	100.00	50.00
86 Orval Overall	150.00	75.00
87 Jim Pastorius	100.00	50.00
88 Ed Phelps	100.00	50.00
89 Eddie Plank	400.00	200.00
90 Lew Richie	100.00	50.00
91 Germany Schaefer	150.00	75.00
92 Victor Schlitzer	150.00	75.00
93 Johnny Seigle HOR	200.00	100.00
sic, Siegle		
94 Dave Shean	200.00	100.00
95 Jimmy Sheckard	150.00	75.00
96 Tris Speaker	1500.00	750.00
97 Jake Stahl	1250.00	600.00
98 Oscar Stanage	100.00	50.00
99 George Stone	100.00	50.00
green background		
100 George Stone	100.00	50.00
sky background		
101 George Stovall	100.00	50.00
102 Ed Summers	100.00	50.00
103 Bill Sweeney	2000.00	1000.00
Boston		
104 Jeff Sweeney	100.00	50.00
105 Lee Tannehill	100.00	50.00
Chicago AL		
106 Lee Tannehill	100.00	50.00
Chicago NL		
107 Fred Tenney	100.00	50.00
108 Ira Thomas	100.00	50.00
109 Roy Thomas	100.00	50.00
110 Joe Tinker	300.00	150.00
111 Bob Unglaub	100.00	50.00
112 Jerry Upp	100.00	50.00
113 Honus Wagner	1200.00	600.00
batting		
114 Honus Wagner	1200.00	600.00
throwing		
115 Bobby Wallace	250.00	125.00
116 Ed Walsh	2000.00	1000.00
117 Vic Willis	250.00	125.00
118 Hooks Wiltse	200.00	100.00
119 Cy Young	400.00	200.00
Boston AL		
portrait		
120 Cy Young	800.00	400.00
Cleveland		
pitching		

1915 American Caramel E106

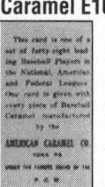

The cards in this 48-card set measure 1 1/2" by 2 3/4". The color cards in this series of "leading Baseball players in the National, American and Federal Leagues" were produced by the American Caramel Company of York, PA. The obverse surfaces appear glazed, a process used in several other sets of this vintage (T213, T216), probably as protection against stain damage. The set was issued in 1915. The cards have been alphabetized and numbered in the checklist below. The complete set price includes all variation cards listed in the checklist below.

	Ex-Mt	VG
COMPLETE SET (48)	12000.00	6000.00
1 Jack Barry	125.00	60.00
2A Chief Bender	250.00	125.00
(blue background)		
2B Chief Bender	250.00	125.00
(green background)		
3 Bob Bescher	125.00	60.00
4 Roger Bresnahan	250.00	125.00
5 Al Bridwell	125.00	60.00
6 Donie Bush	125.00	60.00
7A Hal Chase	150.00	75.00
portrait		
7B Hal Chase	150.00	75.00
catching		
8A Ty Cobb	1500.00	750.00
batting ft		
8B Ty Cobb	1500.00	750.00
batting sd		
9 Eddie Collins	250.00	125.00
10 Sam Crawford	250.00	125.00
11 Ray Demmitt	125.00	60.00
12 Bill Donovan	125.00	60.00
13 Red Dooin	125.00	60.00
14 Mickey Doolan	125.00	60.00
15 Larry Doyle	150.00	75.00
16 Clyde Engle	125.00	60.00
17 Johnny Evers	250.00	125.00
18 Art Fromme	125.00	60.00
19A George Gibson	125.00	60.00
front		
19B George Gibson	125.00	60.00
back		
20 Topsy Hartzell	125.00	60.00
21 Fred Jacklitsch	125.00	60.00
22 Hugh Jennings MG	250.00	125.00
23 Otto Knabe	125.00	60.00
24 Nap Lajoie	400.00	200.00
25 Hans Lobert	125.00	60.00
26 Rube Marquard	250.00	125.00
27 Christy Mathewson	1200.00	600.00
28 John McGraw MG	400.00	200.00
29 George McQuillan	125.00	60.00
30 Dots Miller	125.00	60.00
31 Danny Murphy	125.00	60.00
32 Rebel Oakes	125.00	60.00
33 Eddie Plank	250.00	125.00
34 Germany Schaefer	125.00	60.00
35 Tris Speaker	400.00	200.00
36 Oscar Stanage	125.00	60.00
37 George Stovall	125.00	60.00
38 Jeff Sweeney	125.00	60.00
39A Joe Tinker	250.00	125.00
portrait		
39B Joe Tinker	250.00	125.00
batting		
40A Honus Wagner	800.00	400.00
batting		
40B Honus Wagner	800.00	400.00
throwing		
41 Hooks Wiltse	125.00	60.00
42 Heinie Zimmerman	125.00	60.00

1922 American Caramel E122

The cards in this 79-card set measure 2" by 3 1/2". The principal feature of this re-issue of the "80 series" of set E121 is the cross-hatch pattern or "screen" which covers the obverse of the card. The photos are black and white, and the player's name, position and team appear in a panel under his picture, all enclosed within the rectangular frame line. The set, which is unnumbered, was marketed in 1922 by the American Caramel Company. The cards have been alphabetized and numbered in the checklist below.

	Ex-Mt	VG
COMPLETE SET (79)	8000.00	4000.00
1 Grover C. Alexander	250.00	125.00
2 Jim Bagby	50.00	25.00
3 Frank Baker	150.00	75.00
4 Dave Bancroft	150.00	75.00
5 Ping Bodie	50.00	25.00
6 George Burns	50.00	25.00
7 Geo. J. Burns	50.00	25.00
8 Owen Bush	50.00	25.00
9 Max Carey	150.00	75.00
10 Red Causey	50.00	25.00
11 Ty Cobb	600.00	300.00
12 Eddie Collins	250.00	125.00
13 Jake Daubert	75.00	38.00
14 Hooks Dauss	50.00	25.00
15 Charlie Deal	50.00	25.00
16 Bill Doak	50.00	25.00
17 Bill Donovan MG	50.00	25.00
18 Johnny Evers MG	150.00	75.00
19 Urban Faber	150.00	75.00
20 Eddie Foster	50.00	25.00
21 Larry Gardner	50.00	25.00
22 Kid Gleason MG	75.00	38.00
23 Hank Gowdy	75.00	38.00
24 John Graney	50.00	25.00
25 Tom Griffith	50.00	25.00
26 Harry Heilmann	150.00	75.00
27 Walter Holke	50.00	25.00
28 Charley Hollacher	50.00	25.00
29 Harry Hooper	150.00	75.00
30 Rogers Hornsby	300.00	150.00
31 Baby Doll Jacobson	50.00	25.00
32 Walter Johnson	350.00	180.00
33 James Johnston	50.00	25.00
34 Joe Judge	75.00	38.00
35 George Kelly	150.00	75.00
36 Dick Kerr	75.00	38.00
37 Pete Kilduff	50.00	25.00
38 Bill Killefer	50.00	25.00
39 John Lavan	50.00	25.00
40 Duffy Lewis	50.00	25.00
41 Al Mamaux	50.00	25.00
42 Rabbit Maranville	150.00	75.00
43 Carl Mays	75.00	38.00
44 John McGraw MG	150.00	75.00
45 Snuffy McInnis	75.00	38.00
46 Clyde Milan	75.00	38.00
47 Otto Miller	50.00	25.00
48 Guy Morton	50.00	25.00
49 Eddie Murphy	50.00	25.00
50 Hy Myers	50.00	25.00
51 Steve O'Neill	75.00	38.00
52 Roger Peckinpaugh	75.00	38.00
53 Jeff Pfeffer	50.00	25.00
54 Wally Pipp	75.00	38.00
55 Sam Rice	150.00	75.00

56 Eppa Rixey 150.00 75.00
57 Babe Ruth 1200.00 600.00
58 Slim Sallee 50.00 25.00
59 Ray Schalk 150.00 75.00
60 Walter Schang 50.00 25.00
61 Ferd Schupp 50.00 25.00
62 Fred Schupp 50.00 25.00
63 Everett Scott 75.00 38.00
64 Hank Severeid 50.00 25.00
65 George Sisler 250.00 125.00
(batting)
66 George Sisler 250.00 125.00
(throwing)
67 Tris Speaker 250.00 125.00
68 Milton Stock 50.00 25.00
69 Amos Strunk 50.00 25.00
70 Chester Thomas 50.00 25.00
71 George Tyler 50.00 25.00
72 Jim Vaughn 50.00 25.00
73 Bob Veach 50.00 25.00
74 Bill Wambsganss 75.00 38.00
75 Zach Wheat 150.00 75.00
76 Fred Williams 75.00 38.00
77 Ivy Wingo 50.00 25.00
78 Joe Wood 100.00 50.00
79 Pep Young 50.00 25.00
(2ndB. Detroit)

1910 American Caramel Die Cuts E125

These cards have all been discovered since 1969. Cards from this set have been found from the following teams: Philadelphia A's; Boston Red Sox; New York Giants and Pittsburgh Pirates. The best supposition about this set places it being produced during the 1910 season. The cards are black and white and range as high as 7" and as much as 4" wide. While 41 are supposed to exist according to the checklists only about 1/2 of that amount have been found yet. All cards on the checklist are priced even though not all of them have been found yet.

Ex-Mt VG
COMPLETE SET (41) 50000.00 25000.00
1 Babe Adams 1000.00 500.00
2 Red Ames 800.00 400.00
3 Frank Baker 2000.00 1000.00
4 Jack Barry 800.00 400.00
5 Chief Bender 2000.00 1000.00
6 Al Bridwell 800.00 400.00
7 Bobby Byrne 800.00 400.00
8 Bill Carrigan 800.00 400.00
9 Eddie Cicotte 2000.00 1000.00
10 Fred Clarke 2000.00 1000.00
Sic, Clark
11 Eddie Collins 2500.00 1250.00
12 Harry Davis 800.00 400.00
13 Art Devlin 800.00 400.00
14 Josh Devore 800.00 400.00
15 Larry Doyle 1000.00 500.00
16 John Flynn 800.00 400.00
17 George Gibson 800.00 400.00
18 Topsy Hartsel 800.00 400.00
Sic, Hartsell
19 Harry Hooper 1500.00 750.00
20 Harry Krause 800.00 400.00
21 Tommy Leach 800.00 400.00
22 Harry Lord 800.00 400.00
23 Christy Mathewson 5000.00 2500.00
24 Ambrose McConnell 800.00 400.00
25 Fred Merkle 1000.00 500.00
26 Dots Miller 800.00 400.00
27 Danny Murphy 800.00 400.00
28 Red Murray 800.00 400.00
29 Harry Niles 800.00 400.00
30 Rube Oldring 800.00 400.00
31 Eddie Plank 2500.00 1250.00
32 Cy Seymour 800.00 400.00
33 Tris Speaker 2500.00 1250.00
34 Jake Stahl 800.00 400.00
35 Ira Thomas 800.00 400.00
36 Heinie Wagner 800.00 400.00
37 Honus Wagner 4000.00 2000.00
Batting
38 Honus Wagner 4000.00 2000.00
Throwing
39 Art Wilson 800.00 400.00
40 Owen Wilson 1000.00 500.00
41 Hooks Wiltse 800.00 400.00

1927 American Caramel E126

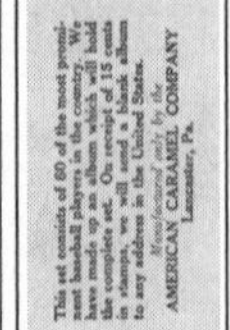

The cards in this 60-card set measure 1 5/8" by 3 1/4". The American Caramel Company released its set of baseball players in 1927. The cards contain black and white pictures, with the individual's name centered underneath, and his team and position to either side below that. This is the only numbered series of baseball cards to be issued by American Caramel; the backs contain advertising for an album designed to hold the set.

Ex-Mt VG
COMPLETE SET (60) 8000.00 4000.00
1 John Gooch 80.00 40.00
2 Clyde Barnhart 80.00 40.00
3 Joe Bush 100.00 50.00
4 Lee Meadows 80.00 40.00
5 Dick Cox 80.00 40.00
6 Red Faber 150.00 75.00
7 Aaron Ward 80.00 40.00
8 Ray Schalk 150.00 75.00
9 Specs Toporcer 80.00 40.00
10 Billy Southworth 100.00 50.00
11 Allen Sothoron 80.00 40.00
12 Will Sherdel 80.00 40.00
13 Grover C. Alexander 200.00 100.00
14 Jack Quinn 100.00 50.00
15 Chick Galloway 80.00 40.00
16 Eddie Collins 200.00 100.00
17 Ty Cobb 1000.00 500.00
18 Percy Jones 80.00 40.00
19 Charlie Grimm 100.00 50.00
20 Bennie Karr 80.00 40.00
21 Charlie Jamieson 80.00 40.00
22 Sherrod Smith 80.00 40.00
23 Vergil Cheeves 80.00 40.00
24 James Ring 80.00 40.00
25 Muddy Ruel 80.00 40.00
26 Joe Judge 100.00 50.00
27 Tris Speaker 250.00 125.00
28 Walter Johnson 400.00 200.00
29 Sam Rice 150.00 75.00
30 Hank DeBerry 80.00 40.00
31 Walter Henline 80.00 40.00
32 Max Carey 150.00 75.00
33 Arnold Statz 80.00 40.00
34 Irish Meusel 100.00 50.00
35 Pat Collins 80.00 40.00
36 Urban Shocker 100.00 50.00
37 Bob Shawkey 100.00 50.00
38 Babe Ruth 1500.00 750.00
39 Bob Meusel 100.00 50.00
40 Alex Ferguson 80.00 40.00
41 Stuffy McInnis 100.00 50.00
42 Cy Williams 100.00 50.00
43 Russell Wrightstone 80.00 40.00
44 John Tobin 100.00 50.00
photo actually Ed Brown
45 Baby Doll Jacobson 80.00 40.00
46 Bryan Harris 80.00 40.00
47 Elam VanGilder 80.00 40.00
48 Ken Williams 100.00 50.00
49 George Sisler 200.00 100.00
50 Ed Brown 100.00 50.00
photo actually John Tobin
51 Jack Smith 80.00 40.00
52 Dave Bancroft 150.00 75.00
53 Larry Woodall 80.00 40.00
54 Lu Blue 80.00 40.00
55 Johnny Bassler 80.00 40.00
56 Jackie May 80.00 40.00
57 Horace Ford 80.00 40.00
58 Curt Walker 80.00 40.00
59 Art Nehf 80.00 40.00
60 George Kelly 150.00 75.00

1908 American League Publishing Co. PC770

This 1908-issued set features a large action shot or pose the player in uniform and also a small portrait of the player in street clothes in an oval at the top of the card. A short biography in a rectangular box is also featured at the base of the front, and the identifying line "American League Pub. Company, Cleveland, O." is located directly below the box.

Ex-Mt VG
COMPLETE SET (15) 3500.00 1800.00
1 Harry Bay 150.00 75.00
2 Charles Berger 150.00 75.00
3 Joe Birmingham 150.00 75.00
4 Bill Bradley 150.00 75.00
5 Walter Clarkson 150.00 75.00
6 Ty Cobb 1000.00 500.00
7 Elmer Flick 250.00 125.00
8 Claude Hickman 150.00 75.00
9 William Hinchman 150.00 75.00
10 Addie Joss 400.00 200.00
11 Nap Lajoie 300.00 150.00
12 Glen Liebhardt 150.00 75.00
13 George Nill 150.00 75.00
14 George Perring 150.00 75.00
15 Honus Wagner 500.00 250.00

1950 American Nut and Chocolate Co. Pennant

This 23-pennant set was distributed by the American Nut and Chocolate Co. and originally sold for 50 cents a set. The pennants measure approximately 1 7/8" by 4" and feature crude line-art drawings of the players with a facsimile autograph. The pennants are unnumbered and checklisted below in alphabetical order.

NM Ex
COMPLETE SET (23) 1200.00 600.00
1 Ewell Blackwell 30.00 15.00
2 Harry Brecheen 30.00 15.00
3 Phil Cavarretta 40.00 20.00
4 Bobby Doerr 50.00 25.00
5 Bob Elliott 30.00 15.00
6 Boo Ferriss 30.00 15.00
7 Joe Gordon 40.00 20.00
8 Tommy Holmes 30.00 15.00
9 Charles Keller 40.00 20.00
10 Ken Keltner 30.00 15.00
11 Whitey Kurowski 30.00 15.00
12 Ralph Kiner 80.00 40.00
13 Johnny Pesky 40.00 20.00
14 Pee Wee Reese 80.00 40.00
15 Phil Pizzuto 80.00 40.00
16 Johnny Sain 40.00 20.00
17 Enos Slaughter 50.00 25.00
18 Warren Spahn 80.00 40.00
19 Vern Stephens 30.00 15.00
20 Earl Torgeson 30.00 15.00
21 Dizzy Trout 30.00 15.00
22 Ted Williams 200.00 100.00
23 Ted Williams CL 100.00 50.00

1962-66 American Tract Society

These cards are quite attractive and feature the "pure card" concept that is always popular with collectors, i.e., no borders or anything else on the card front to detract from the color photo. The cards are numbered on the back and the skip-numbering of the cards below is actually due to the fact that these cards are part of a much larger (sport and non-sport) set with a Christian theme. The set features Christian ballplayers giving first-person testimonies on the card backs telling how their belief in Jesus has changed their lives. These cards are sometimes referred to as "Tracards." The cards measure approximately 2 3/4" X 3 1/2". The set price below refers to only one of each player, not including any variations. These cards were issued throughout the 1960's, as one of the Felipe Alou cards features him in an Atlanta Braves cap (The Braves would not move to Atlanta until 1966)

NM Ex
COMPLETE SET 100.00 40.00
43A Bobby Richardson 12.00 4.80
black print on back
43B Bobby Richardson 12.00 4.80
blue print on back
43C Bobby Richardson 12.00 4.80
black print on back
with Play Ball in red
43D Bobby Richardson 12.00 4.80
black print on back
with exclamation point
after Play Ball
51A Jerry Kindall 6.00 2.40
portrait from chest up
black print on back
51B Jerry Kindall 6.00 2.40
on one knee with bat
blue print on back
52A Felipe Alou 10.00 4.00
on one knee looking up
black print on back
52B Felipe Alou 10.00 4.00
on one knee looking up
blue print on back
52C Felipe Alou 10.00 4.00
Batting pose
red lettering "A Tip for You"
52D Felipe Alou 6.00 2.40
Batting Pose
Name on Front of Card
66 Al Worthington 6.00 2.40
(black print on back)
XX Jim Kaat 12.00 4.80
Black and White

1961 Angels Jay Publishing

This 12-card set of the Los Angeles Angels measures approximately 5" by 7". The fronts feature black-and-white posed player photos with the player's and team name printed below in the white border. These cards were packaged 12 to a packet. The backs are blank. The cards are unnumbered and checklisted below in alphabetical order.

NM Ex
COMPLETE SET (12) 30.00 12.00
1 Ken Aspromonte 2.00 .80
2 Julio Becquer 2.00 .80
3 Steve Bilko 2.00 .80
4 Fritz Brickell 2.00 .80
5 Bob Cerv 2.00 .80
6 Ned Garver 2.00 .80
7 Ted Kluszewski 8.00 3.20
8 Tom Morgan 2.00 .80
9 Albie Pearson 2.00 .80
10 Bill Rigney MG 2.00 .80
11 Faye Throneberry 2.00 .80
12 Ed Yost 2.00 .80

1962 Angels Jay Publishing

This 12-card set of the Los Angeles Angels measures approximately 5" by 7". The fronts feature black-and-white posed player photos with the player's and team name printed below in the white border. These cards were packaged 12 to a packet. The backs are blank. The cards are unnumbered and checklisted below in alphabetical order.

NM Ex
COMPLETE SET (12) 30.00 12.00
1 Earl Averill 2.00 .80
2 Steve Bilko 2.00 .80
3 Ryne Duren 3.00 1.20
4 Eli Grba 2.00 .80
5 Ken Hunt 2.00 .80
6 Ted Kluszewski 8.00 3.20
7 Tom Morgan 2.00 .80
8 Albie Pearson 2.00 .80
9 Bill Rigney MG 2.00 .80
10 Ed Sadowski 2.00 .80
11 Leon Wagner 2.00 .80
12 Eddie Yost 2.00 .80

1963-64 Angels Jay Publishing

This set of the Los Angeles Angels was issued over two years and measures approximately 5" by 7". The fronts feature black-and-white posed player photos with the player's and team name printed below in the white border. These cards were packaged 12 to a packet. The backs are blank. The cards are unnumbered and checklisted below in alphabetical order.

NM Ex
COMPLETE SET (19) 40.00 16.00
1 Bo Belinsky 64 3.00 1.20
2 Dean Chance 4.00 1.60
(Head photo)
3 Dean Chance 4.00 1.60
(Action pose)
4 Charlie Dees 64 2.00 .80
5 Jim Fregosi 4.00 1.60
6 Ken Hunt 63 2.00 .80
7 Don Lee 2.00 .80
8 Ken McBride 64 2.00 .80
9 Billy Moran 2.00 .80
10 Tom Morgan 63 2.00 .80
11 Dan Osinski 64 2.00 .80
12 Albie Pearson 2.00 .80
(Action pose)
13 Albie Pearson 2.00 .80
(Pose with bat)
14 Bill Rigney MG 2.00 .80
15 Bob Rodgers 2.00 .80
16 Ed Sadowski 2.00 .80
17 Lee Thomas 2.00 .80
(Pose with bat)
18 Lee Thomas 2.00 .80
(Closer pose with bat)
19 Leon Wagner 63 2.00 .80

1964 Angels Team Issue

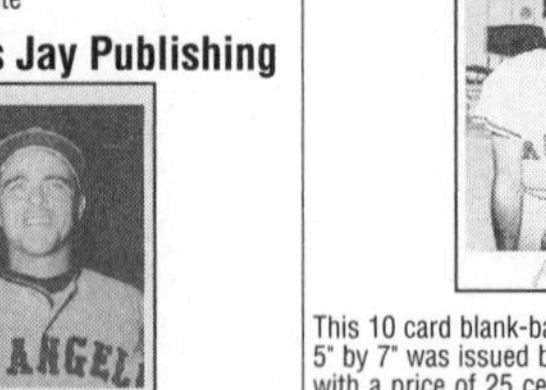

This 10 card blank-backed set, which measures 5" by 7" was issued by the Angels as a package with a price of 25 cents. The fronts have white borders with the player's photo and the fascimile autograph on the bottom. Since the cards are unnumbered, we have sequenced them in alphabetical order.

NM Ex
COMPLETE SET 20.00 8.00
1 Charlie Dees 2.00 .80
2 Jim Fregosi 3.00 1.20
3 Ed Kirkpatrick 2.00 .80
4 Joe Koppe 2.00 .80
5 Barry Latman 2.00 .80
6 Bob Lee 2.00 .80
7 Albie Pearson 2.50 1.00
8 Jimmy Piersall 3.00 1.20
9 Bill Rigney MG 2.00 .80
10 Bob Rodgers 2.00 .80

1965 Angels Matchbooks County National

These matchbooks were issued by County National bank and feature members of the 1965 California Angels. The checklist is incomplete so any additions to finish the set are appreciated.

NM Ex
COMPLETE SET 40.00 16.00
1 Jim Fregosi 8.00 3.20
2 Ed Kirkpatrick 5.00 2.00
3 Bobby Knoop 5.00 2.00
4 Barry Latman 5.00 2.00
5 Fred Newman 5.00 2.00
6 Bob Rodgers 5.00 2.00
7 Tom Satriano 5.00 2.00
8 Willie Smith 5.00 2.00

1965 Angels Matchbook Santa Ana

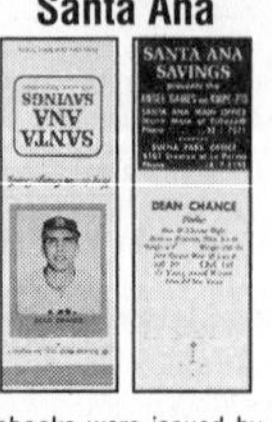

These matchbooks were issued by Santa Ana Savings bank and feature members of the 1965 California Angels. The checklist is incomplete so any additions to finish the set are appreciated.

NM Ex
COMPLETE SET 40.00 16.00
1 Dean Chance 6.00 2.40
2 Jim Fregosi 8.00 3.20
3 Bobby Knoop 5.00 2.00
4 Ken McBride 5.00 2.00
5 Rick Reichardt 5.00 2.00
6 Bill Rigney MG 5.00 2.00
7 Bob Rodgers 5.00 2.00
8 Willie Smith 5.00 2.00

1966 Angels Dexter Press

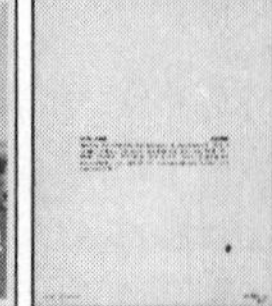

Produced by Dexter Press, Inc. (West Nyack, New York), this sixteen-card set measures approximately 4" by 5 7/8". The fronts feature glossy posed color player photos with white borders. The player's autograph is inscribed in black across the top of the picture. In blue print, the back has the player's name, position, and biographical information. The cards are unnumbered and checklisted below in alphabetical order.

NM Ex
COMPLETE SET (16) 35.00 14.00
1 George Brunet 2.00 .80
2 Jose Cardenal 2.00 .80
3 Dean Chance 3.00 1.20
4 Jim Fregosi 4.00 1.60
5 Ed Kirkpatrick 2.00 .80
6 Bob Knoop 2.00 .80
7 Bob Lee 2.00 .80
8 Marcelino Lopez 2.00 .80
9 Fred Newman 2.00 .80
10 Albie Pearson 2.00 .80
11 Jimmy Piersall 4.00 1.60
12 Rick Reichardt 2.00 .80
13 Bob Rodgers 2.00 .80
14 Paul Schaal 2.00 .80
15 Norm Siebern 2.00 .80
16 Willie Smith 2.00 .80

1966 Angels Matchbook

These matchbooks feature members of the 1966 California Angels and were produced for the County National Bank. This checklist may be incomplete so any additions are appreciated.

NM Ex
COMPLETE SET 30.00 12.00
1 Dean Chance 6.00 2.40
2 Ed Kirkpatrick 5.00 2.00
3 Barry Latman 5.00 2.00
4 Bob Lee 5.00 2.00
5 Fred Newman 5.00 2.00
6 Bill Rigney MG 5.00 2.00
7 Bob Rodgers 5.00 2.00
8 Willie Smith 5.00 2.00

1969 Angels Jack in the Box

This 13-card set measures approximately 2 by 3 1/2" and features black-and-white player photos on a white card face. The cards are unnumbered and checklisted below in alphabetical order.

NM Ex
COMPLETE SET (13) 45.00 18.00
1 Sandy Alomar 3.00 1.20
2 Joe Azcue 2.50 1.00
3 Jim Fregosi 5.00 2.00
4 Lou Johnson 2.50 1.00
5 Jay Johnstone 3.00 1.20
6 Rudy May 2.50 1.00

Card	NM	Ex
7 Jim McGlothlin	2.50	1.00
8 Andy Messersmith	5.00	2.00
9 Tom Murphy	2.50	1.00
10 Rick Reichardt	2.50	1.00
11 Aurelio Rodriguez	2.50	1.00
12 Jim Spencer	2.50	1.00
13 Hoyt Wilhelm	10.00	4.00

1971 Angels Jack in the Box

This 10-card set measures approximately 4 by 2 1/2" and features yellowish tone player photos printed on tan paper stock. The cards are unnumbered and checklisted below in alphabetical order.

	NM	Ex
COMPLETE SET (10)	25.00	10.00
1 Sandy Alomar	2.50	1.00
2 Ken Berry	2.00	.80
3 Tony Conigliaro	6.00	2.40
4 Jim Fregosi	4.00	1.60
5 Alex Johnson	2.00	.80
6 Rudy May	2.00	.80
7 Andy Messersmith	3.00	1.20
8 Lefty Phillips MG	2.00	.80
9 Jim Spencer	2.00	.80
10 Clyde Wright	2.00	.80

1972 Angels Postcards

These 30 black and white 3 1/4" by 4 3/4" blank backed postcards feature members of the 1972 California Angels. A key card in the set is Nolan Ryan, during his first season as a member of the Angels.

	NM	Ex
COMPLETE SET	20.00	8.00
1 Lloyd Allen	.50	.20
2 Sandy Alomar	.75	.30
3 Steve Barber	.50	.20
4 Ken Berry	.50	.20
5 Leo Cardenas	.50	.20
6 Rick Clark	.50	.20
7 Eddie Fisher	.50	.20
8 Art Kusnyer	.50	.20
9 Winston Llenas	.50	.20
10 Rudy May	.50	.20
11 Ken McMullen	.50	.20
12 Andy Messersmith	.50	.20
13 Bob Oliver	.50	.20
14 Vada Pinson	1.00	.40
15 Mel Queen	.50	.20
16 Mickey Rivers	1.50	.60
17 Don Rose	.50	.20
18 Nolan Ryan	10.00	4.00
19 Jim Spencer	.50	.20
20 Lee Stanton	.50	.20
21 John Stephenson	.50	.20
22 Jeff Torborg	.50	.20
23 Clyde Wright	.50	.20
24 Del Rice MG	.50	.20
25 Peanuts Lowrey CO	.50	.20
26 Tom Morgan CO	.50	.20
27 Jimmie Reese CO	.75	.30
28 John Roseboro CO	.50	.20
29 Bobby Winkles CO	.50	.20
30 Gene Autry OWN	.75	.30
Most of tie showing		

1973 Angels Postcards

These 40 3 1/4" by 4 3/4" blank-backed, black and white, postcards feature members of the 1973 California Angels.

	NM	Ex
1 Lloyd Allen	.50	.20
2 Sandy Alomar	.50	.20
3 Steve Barber	.50	.20
4 Ken Berry	.50	.20
5 Jerry DaVanon	.50	.20
6 Mike Epstein	.50	.20
7 Alan Gallagher	.50	.20
8 Bill Grabarkewitz	.50	.20
9 Rich Hand	.50	.20
10 Art Kusnyer	.50	.20
11 Dick Lange	.50	.20
12 Winston Llenas	.50	.20
13 Rudy May	.50	.20
14 Tom McCraw	.50	.20
15 Rudy Meoli	.50	.20
16 Aurelio Monteagudo	.50	.20
17 Tom Morgan CO	.50	.20
18 Bob Oliver	.50	.20
19 Bill Parker	.50	.20
20 Salty Parker CO	.50	.20
21 Ron Perrranoski	.50	.20
22 Vada Pinson	1.00	.40
23 Jimmie Reese CO	.75	.30
24 Frank Robinson	4.00	1.60
25 John Roseboro CO	.50	.20
26 Nolan Ryan	8.00	3.20
27 Richie Scheinblum	.50	.20
28 Dave Sells	.50	.20
29 Bill Singer	.50	.20
30 Jim Spencer	.50	.20
31 Lee Stanton	.50	.20
32 John Stephenson	.50	.20
33 Jeff Torborg	.75	.30
34 Bobby Valentine	.75	.30
35 Bobby Winkles MG	.50	.20
36 Clyde Wright	.50	.20
37 Gene Autry OWN	.75	.30
Close crop		
38 Harry Dalton GM	.50	.20
39 Don Drysdale ANN	1.50	.60
40 Dick Enberg ANN	.75	.30

1974 Angels Postcards

These 39 black and white, blank-backed postcards feature members of the 1974 California Angels. They are unnumbered and we have sequenced them in alphabetical order. Dick Williams replaced Bobby Winkles as manager midway through the season which accounts for the two different manager cards in this set.

	NM	Ex
COMPLETE SET (39)	30.00	12.00
1 Sandy Alomar	.75	.30
2 Dave Chalk	.50	.20
3 John Doherty	.50	.20
4 Denny Doyle	.50	.20
5 Tom Egan	.50	.20
6 Ed Figueroa	.50	.20
7 Andy Hassler	.50	.20
8 Whitey Herzog CO	.75	.30
9 Doug Howard	.50	.20
10 Joe Lahoud	.50	.20
11 Dick Lange	.50	.20
12 Winston Llenas	.50	.20
13 Skip Lockwood	.50	.20
14 Rudy May	.50	.20
15 Tom McCraw	.50	.20
16 Tom Morgan CO	.50	.20
17 Bob Oliver	.50	.20
18 Salty Parker CO	.50	.20
19 Jimmie Reese CO	.75	.30
20 Mickey Rivers	.75	.30
21 Frank Robinson	4.00	1.60
22 Ellie Rodriguez	.50	.20
23 John Roseboro CO	.50	.20
24 Nolan Ryan	8.00	3.20
25 Charlie Sands	.50	.20
26 Paul Schaal	.50	.20
27 Dave Sells	.50	.20
28 Dick Selma	.50	.20
29 Bill Singer	.50	.20
30 Lee Stanton	.50	.20
31 Bill Stoneman	.75	.30
32 Frank Tanana	1.00	.40
33 Bobby Valentine	.75	.30
34 Dick Williams MG	.75	.30
35 Bob Winkles MG	.50	.20
36 Gene Autry OWN	.75	.30
37 Harry Dalton GM	.50	.20
38 Don Drysdale ANN	1.50	.60
39 Dick Enberg ANN	.75	.30

1975 Angels Postcards

This 48-card set of the California Angels features player photos on postcard-size cards. The cards are unnumbered and checklisted in alphabetical order.

	NM	Ex
COMPLETE SET (48)	30.00	12.00
1 Jerry Adair CO	.50	.20
2 Bob Allietta	.50	.20
3 Gene Autry OWN	1.00	.40
4 John Balaz	.50	.20
5 Steve Blateric	.50	.20
6 Bruce Bochte	.75	.30
7 Jim Brewer	.50	.20
8 Dave Chalk	.50	.20
9 Dave Collins	.50	.20
10 Harry Dalton GM	.50	.20
11 Chuck Dobson	.50	.20
12 John Doherty	.50	.20
13 Denny Doyle	.50	.20
14 Don Drysdale ANN	2.00	.80
15 Tom Egan	.50	.20
16 Dick Enberg ANN	.75	.30
17 Ed Figueroa	.50	.20
18 Ike Hampton	.50	.20
19 Tommy Harper	.50	.20
20 Andy Hassler	.50	.20
21 Whitey Herzog MG	1.00	.40
22 Chuck Hockenbery	.50	.20
23 Don Kirkwood	.50	.20
24 Joe Lahoud	.50	.20
25 Dick Lange	.50	.20
26 Winston Llenas	.50	.20
27 Rudy Meoli	.50	.20
28 Mike Miley	.50	.20
29 Billy Muffett CO	.50	.20
30 Morris Nettles	.50	.20
31 Orlando Pena	.50	.20
32 Orlando Ramirez	.50	.20
33 Jimmie Reese CO	.75	.30
34 Jerry Remy	.50	.20
35 Grover Resinger CO	.50	.20
36 Mickey Rivers	.75	.30
37 Ellie Rodriguez	.50	.20
38 Nolan Ryan	7.50	3.00
39 Mickey Scott	.50	.20
40 Dave Sells	.50	.20
41 Bill Singer	.50	.20
42 Billy Smith	.50	.20
43 Lee Stanton	.50	.20
44 Bill Sudakis	.50	.20
45 Frank Tahana	1.00	.40
46 Bob Valentine	.75	.30
47 Dick Williams MG	.75	.30
48 Anaheim Stadium	.50	.20

1976 Angels Postcards

These 39 blank-backed black and white postcards feature membuers of the 1976 California Angels. They measure 3 1/4" by 5 1/2" and we have sequenced them alphabetically.

	NM	Ex
COMPLETE SET (39)	25.00	10.00
1 Orlando Alvarez	.50	.20
2 Bruce Bochte	.50	.20
3 Bobby Bonds	1.00	.40

	NM	Ex
4 Jim Brewer	.50	.20
5 Dan Briggs	.50	.20
6 Dave Chalk	.50	.20
7 Bob Clear CO	.50	.20
8 Dave Collins	.50	.20
9 Paul Dade	.50	.20
10 Dick Drago	.50	.20
11 Andy Etchebarren	.50	.20
12 Adrian Garrett	.50	.20
13 Mario Guerrero	.50	.20
14 Ike Hampton	.50	.20
15 Paul Hartzell	.50	.20
16 Ed Herrmann	.50	.20
17 Vern Hoscheit CO	.50	.20
18 Terry Humphrey	.50	.20
19 Ron Jackson	.50	.20
20 Bob Jones	.50	.20
21 Bill Melton	.50	.20
22 Sid Monge	.50	.20
23 Billy Muffett CO	.50	.20
24 Mike Overy	.50	.20
25 Orlando Ramirez	.50	.20
26 Jimmie Reese CO	.75	.30
27 Jerry Remy	.50	.20
Position listed as 2B		
28 Jerry Remy	.50	.20
Position listed as IF		
29 Grover Resinger CO	.50	.20
30 Gary Ross	.50	.20
31 Nolan Ryan	5.00	2.00
Entire collar on jersey		
32 Nolan Ryan	5.00	2.00
Collar cut off		
33 Mickey Scott	.50	.20
34 Norm Sherry CO	.50	.20
35 Lee Stanton	.50	.20
36 Frank Tanana	.75	.30
37 Rusty Torres	.50	.20
38 John Verhoeven	.50	.20
39 Dick Williams MG	.75	.30

1977 Angels Postcards

These 49 blank backed postcards measure 3 1/4" by 5 1/2" and feature members of the 1977 California Angels. These cards are unnumbered so we have sequenced them alphabetically.

	NM	Ex
COMPLETE SET (49)	30.00	12.00
1 Willie Aikens	.50	.20
2 Mike Barlow	.50	.20
3 Don Baylor	1.50	.60
4 Bruce Bochte	.50	.20
5 Bobby Bonds	1.00	.40
6 Thad Bosley	.50	.20
7 Ken Brett	.50	.20
8 Dan Briggs	.50	.20
9 John Caneira	.50	.20
10 Dave Chalk	.50	.20
11 Bob Clear CO	.50	.20
12 Del Crandall CO	.50	.20
13 Mike Cuellar	.75	.30
14 Dick Drago	.50	.20
15 Andy Etchebarren	.50	.20
16 Gil Flores	.50	.20
17 Dave Garcia MG	.50	.20
18 Dan Goodwin	.50	.20
19 Marv Grissom CO	.50	.20
20 Bobby Grich	.75	.30
21 Mario Guerrero	.50	.20
22 Ike Hampton	.50	.20
23 Paul Hartzell	.50	.20
24 Terry Humphrey	.50	.20
25 Ron Jackson	.50	.20
26 Bob Jones	.50	.20
27 Don Kirkwood	.50	.20
28 Fred Kuhaulua	.50	.20
29 Ken Landreaux	.50	.20
30 Dave LaRoche	.50	.20
31 Carlos May	.50	.20
32 Billy Muffett CO	.50	.20
33 Rance Mulliniks	.50	.20
34 Dyar Miller	.50	.20
35 Gary Nolan	.50	.20
36 Jimmie Reese CO	.75	.30
37 Jerry Remy	.50	.20
38 Frank Robinson CO	2.50	1.00
39 Gary Ross	.50	.20
40 Joe Rudi	.50	.20
41 Nolan Ryan	5.00	2.00
42 Mickey Scott	.50	.20
43 Norm Sherry MG	.50	.20
44 Wayne Simpson	.50	.20
45 Tony Solaita	.50	.20
46 Frank Tanana	.75	.30
47 Rusty Torres	.50	.20
48 John Verhoeven	.50	.20
49 Dick Enberg ANN	.75	.30

1978 Angels Family Fun Centers

This 37-card set features members of the 1978 California Angels. These large cards measure approximately 3 1/2" by 5 1/2" and display sepia tone player photos. The cards are unnumbered and checklisted below in alphabetical order. This set was also available in uncut sheet form.

	NM	Ex
COMPLETE SET (37)	50.00	20.00
1 Don Aase	1.50	.60
2 Mike Barlow	1.50	.60
3 Don Baylor	2.50	1.00
4 Lyman Bostock	5.00	2.00
5 Ken Brett	2.00	.80
6 Dave Chalk	1.50	.60
7 Bob Clear	1.50	.60
8 Brian Downing	2.50	1.00
9 Ron Fairly	2.00	.80
10 Gil Flores	1.50	.60
11 Dave Frost	1.50	.60
12 Dave Garcia	1.50	.60
13 Bobby Grich	2.50	1.00
14 Tom Griffin	1.50	.60
15 Marv Grissom CO	1.50	.60
16 Ike Hampton	1.50	.60
17 Paul Hartzell	1.50	.60
18 Terry Humphrey	1.50	.60
19 Ron Jackson	1.50	.60
20 Chris Knapp	1.50	.60
21 Ken Landreaux	1.50	.60
22 Carney Lansford	3.00	1.20
23 Dave LaRoche	1.50	.60
24 John McNamara MG	2.00	.80
25 Dyar Miller	1.50	.60
26 Rick Miller	1.50	.60
27 Balor Moore	1.50	.60
28 Rance Mulliniks	2.00	.80
29 Floyd Rayford	1.50	.60
30 Jimmie Reese CO	2.50	1.00
31 Merv Rettenmund	1.50	.60
32 Joe Rudi	2.00	.80
33 Nolan Ryan	15.00	6.00
34 Bob Skinner CO	1.50	.60
35 Tony Solaita	1.50	.60
36 Frank Tanana	2.50	1.00
37 Dickie Thon	2.00	.80

1984 Angels Postcards

These 29 postcards, which measure 3 1/2" by 5 1/2", feature members of the 1984 California Angels. The fronts have the player photo, while the backs have the players name, the Angels logo and the year of issue. Since these cards are unnumbered, we have sequenced them in alphabetical order.

	Nm-Mt	Ex-Mt
COMPLETE SET (29)	20.00	8.00
1 Don Aase	.50	.20
2 Mike Barlow	.50	.20
3 Juan Beniquez	.50	.20
4 Bob Boone	.75	.30
5 Rick Burleson	.50	.20
6 Rod Carew	2.00	.80
7 Doug Corbett	.50	.20
8 John Curtis	.50	.20
9 Doug DeCinces	.75	.30
10 Brian Downing	.75	.30
11 Ken Forsch	.50	.20
12 Bobby Grich	.75	.30
13 Reggie Jackson	3.00	1.20
14 Ron Jackson	.50	.20
15 Tommy John	1.50	.60
16 Curt Kaufman	.50	.20
17 Bruce Kison	.50	.20
18 Frank LaCorte	.50	.20
19 Fred Lynn	1.00	.40
20 John McNamara MG	.50	.20
21 Jerry Narron	.75	.30
22 Gary Pettis	.50	.20
23 Rob Picciolo	.50	.20
24 Dick Schofield	.50	.20
25 Jim Slaton	.50	.20
26 Rob Wilfong	.50	.20
27 Ellis Valentine	.50	.20
28 Mike Witt	.50	.20
29 Geoff Zahn	.50	.20

1984 Angels Smokey

The cards in this 32-card set measure approximately 2 1/2" by 3 3/4" and feature the California Angels in full color. Sets were given out to persons 15 and under attending the June 16th game against the Indians. Unlike the Padres set of this year, Smokey the Bear is not featured on these cards. The player's photo, the Angels' logo, and the Smokey the Bear logo appear on the front, in addition to the California Department of Forestry and the U.S. Forest Service logos. The abbreviated backs contain short biographical data, career statistics, and an anti-wildfire hint from the player on the front. Since the cards are unnumbered, they are ordered and numbered below alphabetically by the player's name.

	Nm-Mt	Ex-Mt
COMPLETE SET (32)	10.00	4.00
1 Don Aase	.25	.10
2 Juan Beniquez	.25	.10
3 Bob Boone	1.00	.40
4 Rick Burleson	.25	.10
5 Rod Carew	2.50	1.00
6 John Curtis	.25	.10
7 Doug DeCinces	.75	.30
8 Brian Downing	.75	.30
9 Ken Forsch	.25	.10
10 Bobby Grich	.75	.30
11 Reggie Jackson	3.00	1.20
12 Ron Jackson	.25	.10
13 Tommy John	1.00	.40
14 Curt Kaufman	.25	.10
15 Bruce Kison	.25	.10
16 Frank LaCorte	.25	.10
17 Logo Card	.25	.10
(Forestry Dept.)		
18 Fred Lynn	.50	.20
19 John McNamara MG	.25	.10
20 Jerry Narron	.25	.10
21 Gary Pettis	.25	.10
22 Rob Picciolo	.25	.10
23 Ron Romanick	.25	.10
24 Luis Sanchez	.25	.10
25 Dick Schofield	.25	.10
26 Daryl Sconiers	.25	.10
27 Jim Slaton	.25	.10
28 Smokey the Bear	.25	.10
29 Ellis Valentine	.25	.10
30 Rob Wilfong	.25	.10
31 Mike Witt	.25	.10
32 Geoff Zahn	.25	.10

1985 Angels Smokey

The cards in this 24-card set measure approximately 4 1/4" by 6" and feature the California Angels in full color. The player's photo, the Angels' logo, and the Smokey the Bear logo appear on the front, in addition to the California Department of Forestry and the U.S. Forest Service logos. The abbreviated backs contain short biographical data and an anti-wildfire message.

	Nm-Mt	Ex-Mt
COMPLETE SET (24)	8.00	3.20
1 Mike Witt	.25	.10
2 Reggie Jackson	2.50	1.00
3 Bob Boone	1.00	.40
4 Mike Brown	.25	.10
5 Rod Carew	2.00	.80
6 Doug DeCinces	.75	.30
7 Brian Downing	.75	.30
8 Ken Forsch	.25	.10
9 Gary Pettis	.25	.10
10 Jerry Narron	.25	.10
11 Ron Romanick	.25	.10
12 Bobby Grich	.75	.30
13 Dick Schofield	.25	.10
14 Juan Beniquez	.25	.10
15 Geoff Zahn	.25	.10
16 Luis Sanchez	.25	.10
17 Jim Slaton	.25	.10
18 Doug Corbett	.25	.10
19 Ruppert Jones	.25	.10
20 Rob Wilfong	.25	.10
21 Donnie Moore	.25	.10
22 Pat Clements	.25	.10
23 Tommy John	1.00	.40
24 Gene Mauch MG	.50	.20

1985 Angels Straw Hat

This 13-card set was distributed by Straw Hat Pizza Restaurants and measures approximately 11" by 16". The fronts feature color player drawings with a white border. The bottom part of the card contains a coupon for pizza and a Silver Anniversary Sweepstakes form. The backs are blank. The cards are unnumbered and checklisted below in alphabetical order.

	Nm-Mt	Ex-Mt
COMPLETE SET (13)	40.00	16.00
1 Gene Autry OWN	3.00	1.20
2 Don Baylor	3.00	1.20
3 Bo Belinsky	2.00	.80
4 Rod Carew	5.00	2.00
5 Dean Chance	2.00	.80
6 Jim Fregosi	2.00	.80
7 Bobby Grich	2.00	.80
Bobby Knoop		
8 Reggie Jackson	8.00	3.20
9 Alex Johnson	2.00	.80
10 Ted Kluszewski	3.00	1.20
Albie Pearson		
11 Nolan Ryan	10.00	4.00
12 Frank Tanana	3.00	1.20
13 Mike Witt	2.00	.80

1986 Angels Greats TCMA

This 12-card standard-size set features some of the leading all-time members of the California Angels. The fronts feature a player photo while the backs have a player biography.

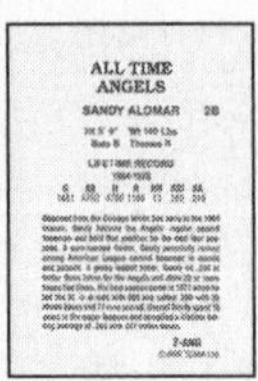

	Nm-Mt	Ex-Mt
COMPLETE SET (12)	5.00	2.00
1 Rod Carew	2.50	1.00
2 Sandy Alomar	.25	.10
3 Jim Fregosi	.75	.30
4 Dave Chalk	.25	.10
5 Leon Wagner	.25	.10
6 Albie Pearson	.25	.10
7 Rick Reichardt	.25	.10
8 Bob Rodgers	.25	.10
9 Dean Chance	.50	.20
10 Clyde Wright	.25	.10
11 Bob Lee	.25	.10
12 Bill Rigney MG	.25	.10

1986 Angels Postcards

These 28 black and white postcards feature members of the division-winning California Angels. These cards measure 3 1/2" by 5 1/2" and are in black and white. The backs have a postcard back, the Angels logo, the player's name and a team logo. Since these cards are unnumbered we have sequenced them in alphabetical order.

	Nm-Mt	Ex-Mt
COMPLETE SET (28)	20.00	8.00
1 Bob Boone	.75	.30
2 Rick Burleson	.50	.20
3 John Candelaria	.50	.20
4 Bob Clear CO	.50	.20
5 Doug Corbett	.50	.20
6 Doug DeCinces	.75	.30
7 Brian Downing	.75	.30
8 Terry Forster	.50	.20
9 Bobby Grich	.75	.30
10 George Hendrick	.75	.30
11 Reggie Jackson	3.00	1.20
12 Ruppert Jones	.50	.20
13 Wally Joyner	2.00	.80
14 Bobby Knoop CO	.50	.20
15 Marcel Lachemann CO	.50	.20
16 Gary Lucas	.50	.20
17 Gene Mauch MG	.50	.20
18 Kirk McCaskill	.50	.20
19 Donnie Moore	.50	.20
20 Jerry Narron	.50	.20
21 Gary Pettis	.50	.20
22 Jimmie Reese CO	.75	.30
23 Ron Romanick	.50	.20
24 Dick Schofield	.50	.20
25 Moose Stubing CO	.50	.20
26 Don Sutton	2.00	.80
27 Rob Wilfong	.50	.20
28 Mike Witt	.50	.20

1986 Angels Smokey

The Forestry Service (in conjunction with the California Angels) produced this large, attractive 24-card set. The cards feature Smokey the Bear pictured in the upper right corner of the card. The card backs give a fire safety tip. The set was given out free at Anaheim Stadium on August 9th. The cards measure approximately 4 1/4" by 6" and are subtitled "Wildfire Prevention" on the front.

	Nm-Mt	Ex-Mt
COMPLETE SET (24)	8.00	3.20
1 Mike Witt	.25	.10
2 Reggie Jackson	2.50	1.00
3 Bob Boone	1.00	.40
4 Don Sutton	1.50	.60
5 Kirk McCaskill	.25	.10
6 Doug DeCinces	.75	.30
7 Brian Downing	.75	.30
8 Doug Corbett	.25	.10
9 Gary Pettis	.25	.10
10 Jerry Narron	.25	.10
11 Ron Romanick	.25	.10
12 Bobby Grich	.75	.30
13 Dick Schofield	.25	.10
14 George Hendrick	.25	.10
15 Rick Burleson	.25	.10
16 John Candelaria	.25	.10
17 Jim Slaton	.25	.10
18 Darrell Miller	.25	.10
19 Ruppert Jones	.25	.10
20 Rob Wilfong	.25	.10
21 Donnie Moore	.25	.10
22 Wally Joyner	1.50	.60
23 Terry Forster	.25	.10
24 Gene Mauch MG	.50	.20

1987 Angels Grich Sheet

Issued to pay tribute to Bobby Grich's last season, this sheet was issued to fans at Bobby Grich Night, May 1, 1987. The perforated sheet measures approximately 10" by 17 1/2" and features 17 different Topps cards of Grich, from his 1971 Rookie Card (number 193) through his 1987 Topps card (number 677). When perforated, each card measured the standard size. This sheet was sponsored by the Sheraton Hotel chain and the top perforated card mentions that.

	Nm-Mt	Ex-Mt
COMPLETE SET	7.50	3.00
COMMON CARD	.50	.20

1987 Angels Promotional Photo Sheet

This 40-card set was distributed on four 8" by 10" sheets with ten photos on each sheet. The photos are black-and-white portraits of the California Angels measuring approximately 1 1/2" by 2 1/4" each. The backs are blank. The cards are unnumbered and checklisted below in alphabetical order.

	Nm-Mt	Ex-Mt
COMPLETE SET (40)	15.00	6.00
1 Gene Autry OWN	.50	.20
2 DeWayne Buice	.25	.10
3 John Candelaria	.25	.10
4 Ray Chadwick	.25	.10
5 Bob Clear CO	.25	.10
6 Stu Cliburn	.25	.10
7 Mike Cook	.25	.10
8 Sherman Corbett	.25	.10
9 Doug DeCinces	.50	.20
10 Rick Down CO	.25	.10
11 Brian Downing	.50	.20
12 Jack Fimple	.25	.10
13 Chuck Finley	1.50	.60
14 Todd Fischer	.25	.10
15 Willie Fraser	.25	.10
16 George Hendrick	.25	.10
17 Jack Howell	.25	.10
18 Ruppert Jones	.25	.10
19 Wally Joyner	1.50	.60
20 Bobby Knoop CO	.25	.10
21 Marcel Lachemann CO	.25	.10
22 Gary Lucas	.25	.10
23 Urbano Lugo	.25	.10
24 Gene Mauch MG	.50	.20
25 Kirk McCaskill	.25	.10
26 Mark McLemore	1.00	.40
27 Darrell Miller	.25	.10
28 Donnie Moore	.25	.10
29 Gary Pettis	.25	.10
30 Gus Polidor	.25	.10
31 Mike Port GM	.25	.10
32 Jimmie Reese CO	.75	.30
33 Vern Ruhle	.25	.10
34 Mark Ryal	.25	.10
35 Dick Schofield	.25	.10
36 Moose Stubing CO	.25	.10
37 Don Sutton	1.50	.60
38 Devon White	1.00	.40
39 Mike Witt	.25	.10
40 Butch Wynegar	.25	.10

1987 Angels Smokey

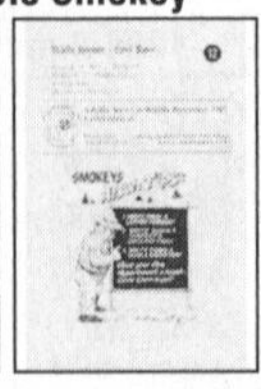

The U.S. Forestry Service (in conjunction with the California Angels) produced this large, attractive 24-card set to commemorate the 43rd birthday of Smokey. The cards feature Smokey the Bear pictured at the bottom of every card. The card backs give a cartoon fire safety tip. The cards measure approximately 4" by 6" and are subtitled "Wildfire Prevention" on the front.

	Nm-Mt	Ex-Mt
COMPLETE SET (24)	8.00	3.20
1 John Candelaria	.25	.10
2 Don Sutton	1.50	.60
3 Mike Witt	.25	.10
4 Gary Lucas	.25	.10
5 Kirk McCaskill	.25	.10
6 Chuck Finley	1.50	.60
7 Willie Fraser	.25	.10
8 Donnie Moore	.25	.10
9 Urbano Lugo	.25	.10
10 Butch Wynegar	.25	.10
11 Darrell Miller	.25	.10
12 Wally Joyner	1.50	.60
13 Mark McLemore	1.00	.40
14 Mark Ryal	.25	.10
15 Dick Schofield	.25	.10
16 Jack Howell	.25	.10
17 Doug DeCinces	.75	.30
18 Gus Polidor	.25	.10
19 Brian Downing	.75	.30
20 Gary Pettis	.25	.10
21 Ruppert Jones	.25	.10
22 George Hendrick	.25	.10
23 Devon White	1.00	.40
24 Checklist Card	.25	.10

1988 Angels Smokey

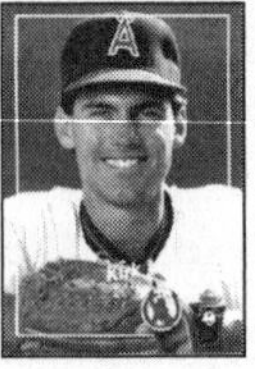

The U.S. Forestry Service (in conjunction with the California Angels) produced this attractive 25-card set. The cards feature Smokey the Bear pictured at the bottom of every card. The card backs give a cartoon fire safety tip. The cards measure approximately 2 1/2" by 3 1/2" and are in full color. The cards are numbered on the back. They were distributed during promotions on August 28, September 4, and September 18.

	Nm-Mt	Ex-Mt
COMPLETE SET (25)	8.00	3.20
1 Cookie Rojas MG	.25	.10
2 Johnny Ray	.25	.10
3 Jack Howell	.25	.10
4 Mike Witt	.25	.10
5 Tony Armas	.25	.10
6 Gus Polidor	.25	.10
7 DeWayne Buice	.25	.10
8 Dan Petry	.25	.10
9 Bob Boone	1.00	.40
10 Chili Davis	1.00	.40
11 Greg Minton	.25	.10
12 Kirk McCaskill	.25	.10
13 Devon White	.50	.20
14 Willie Fraser	.25	.10
15 Chuck Finley	1.00	.40
16 Dick Schofield	.25	.10
17 Wally Joyner	1.00	.40
18 Brian Downing	.75	.30
19 Stu Cliburn	.25	.10
20 Donnie Moore	.25	.10
21 Bryan Harvey	.50	.20
22 Mark McLemore	.50	.20
23 Butch Wynegar	.25	.10
24 George Hendrick	.25	.10
NNO Checklist/Logo Card	.25	.10

1989 Angels Smokey

The 1989 Smokey Angels All-Stars set contains 20 standard-size cards. The fronts have red and white borders. The backs are blue and red and feature career highlights. This set, which depicts current and former Angels who appeared in the All-Star game, was given away at the June 25, 1989 Angels home game. The set numbering is ordered chronologically according to when each subject participated in the respective All-Star Game as an Angel representative.

	Nm-Mt	Ex-Mt
COMPLETE SET (20)	12.00	4.80
1 Bill Rigney MG	.25	.10
2 Dean Chance	.50	.20
3 Jim Fregosi	.50	.20
4 Bobby Knoop	.25	.10
5 Don Mincher	.25	.10
6 Clyde Wright	.25	.10
7 Nolan Ryan	6.00	2.40
8 Frank Robinson	2.00	.80
9 Frank Tanana	.50	.20
10 Rod Carew	2.00	.80
11 Bobby Grich	.75	.30
12 Brian Downing	.50	.20
13 Don Baylor	1.00	.40
14 Fred Lynn	.50	.20
15 Reggie Jackson	2.00	.80
16 Doug DeCinces	.75	.30
17 Bob Boone	1.00	.40
18 Wally Joyner	1.00	.40
19 Mike Witt	.25	.10
20 Johnny Ray	.25	.10

1990 Angels Smokey

The 1990 Smokey Angels set contains standard-size cards which were produced by the U.S. Forest Service and Bureau of Land Management in conjunction with the California Department of Forestry. The first 18 cards in the set are alphabetically arranged. Bailes and McClure were apparently added to the checklist later than these 18, after they were acquired by the Angels.

	Nm-Mt	Ex-Mt
COMPLETE SET (20)	6.00	1.80
1 Jim Abbott	.50	.15
2 Bert Blyleven	.75	.23
3 Chili Davis	1.00	.30
4 Brian Downing	.50	.15
5 Chuck Finley	.75	.23
6 Willie Fraser	.25	.07
7 Bryan Harvey	.25	.07
8 Jack Howell	.25	.07
9 Wally Joyner	.75	.23
10 Mark Langston	.50	.15
11 Kirk McCaskill	.25	.07
12 Mark McLemore	.50	.15
13 Lance Parrish	.50	.15
14 Johnny Ray	.25	.07
15 Dick Schofield	.25	.07
16 Mike Witt	.25	.07
17 Claudell Washington	.25	.07
18 Devon White	.50	.15
19 Scott Bailes	.25	.07
20 Bob McClure	.25	.07

1991 Angels Smokey

This 20-card standard-size set was sponsored by the USDA Forest Service and USDI Bureau of Land Management in cooperation with the California Department of Forestry.

	Nm-Mt	Ex-Mt
COMPLETE SET (20)	6.00	1.80
1 Luis Polonia	.25	.07
2 Junior Felix	.25	.07
3 Dave Winfield	1.25	.35
4 Dave Parker	.75	.23
5 Lance Parrish	.50	.15
6 Wally Joyner	.75	.23
7 Jim Abbott	.50	.15
8 Mark Langston	.50	.15
9 Chuck Finley	.75	.23
10 Kirk McCaskill	.25	.07
11 Jack Howell	.25	.07
12 Donnie Hill	.25	.07
13 Gary Gaetti	.50	.15
14 Dick Schofield	.25	.07
15 Luis Sojo	.25	.07
16 Mark Eichhorn	.25	.07
17 Bryan Harvey	.25	.07
18 Jeff D. Robinson	.25	.07
19 Scott Lewis	.25	.07
20 John Orton	.25	.07

1992 Angels Police

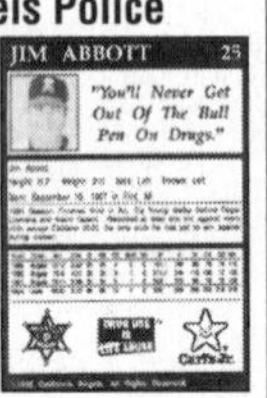

This 18-card standard-size set was cosponsored by the Orange County Sheriff's Department and Carl's Jr. Restaurants in Orange County, California. Deputies and police officers distributed the cards to children in grades K through 6, and 15,000 sets were given out at the September 19 Angel home game. The total number of cards produced was 870,000 individual cards.

	Nm-Mt	Ex-Mt
COMPLETE SET (18)	6.00	1.80
1 Jim Abbott	.50	.15
2 Gene Autry OWN	1.50	.45
3 Bert Blyleven	.75	.23
4 Hubie Brooks	.25	.07
5 Chad Curtis	.50	.15
6 Alvin Davis	.25	.07
7 Gary DiSarcina	.25	.07
8 Junior Felix	.25	.07
9 Chuck Finley	.75	.23
10 Gary Gaetti	.50	.15
11 Rene Gonzales	.25	.07
12 Von Hayes	.25	.07
13 Carl Karcher Founder of Carl's Jr. Restaurants	.25	.07
14 Mark Langston	.50	.15
15 Luis Polonia	.25	.07
16 Bobby Rose	.25	.07
17 Lee Stevens	.25	.07
18 Happy Star (Title Card)	.25	.07

1993 Angels Adohr Farms

Adohr Dairy of Santa Ana, Calif., has produced a four-milk carton set featuring California Angels players. Each carton includes a headshot of Tim Salmon, Chad Curtis, J.T. Snow and Damion Easley, along with the player's name, the Angel's logo and a safety tip on the front of the carton. The cartons were issued during the later half of the 1993 season at schools and hospitals in Los Angeles and Orange Counties. It was not available to the general public. According to one collector two million cartons were filled with milk, while 1,500 were left flat and undistributed. This is the first year that Adohr has highlighted Angels players. Previously the company produced cartons with Raiders, Rams and Clippers players.

	Nm-Mt	Ex-Mt
COMPLETE SET (4)	15.00	4.50
1 Chad Curtis	3.00	.90
2 Damion Easley	3.00	.90
3 Tim Salmon	5.00	1.50
4 J.T. Snow	6.00	1.80

1993 Angels Mother's

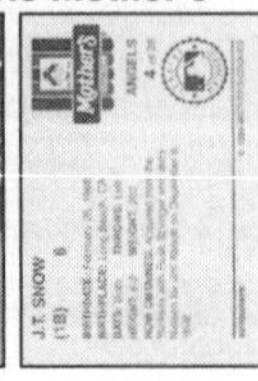

The 1993 Mother's Cookies Angels set consists of 28 standard-size cards with rounded corners.

	Nm-Mt	Ex-Mt
COMPLETE SET (28)	12.00	3.60
1 Buck Rodgers MG	.25	.07
2 Gary DiSarcina	.25	.07
3 Chuck Finley	.75	.23
4 J.T. Snow	1.50	.45
5 Gary Gaetti	.50	.15
6 Chili Davis	.50	.15
7 Tim Salmon	3.00	.90
8 Mark Langston	.50	.15
9 Scott Sanderson	.25	.07
10 John Orton	.25	.07
11 Julio Valera	.25	.07
12 Chad Curtis	.25	.07
13 Kelly Gruber	.25	.07
14 Rene Gonzales	.25	.07
15 Luis Polonia	.25	.07
16 Greg Myers	.25	.07
17 Gene Nelson	.25	.07
18 Torey Lovullo	.25	.07
19 Scott Lewis	.25	.07
20 Chuck Crim	.25	.07
21 John Farrell	.25	.07
22 Steve Frey	.25	.07
23 Stan Javier	.25	.07
24 Ken Patterson	.25	.07
25 Ron Tingley	.25	.07
26 Damion Easley	.50	.15
27 Joe Grahe	.25	.07
28 Chuck Hernandez CO	.75	.23

Jimmie Reese CO
Ken Macha CO
Rod Carew CO
John Wathan CO
Bobby Knoop CO
Rick Turner CO CL

1993 Angels Police

This 21-card standard-size set was sponsored by Carl's Jr. restaurants. The first 11 cards included a paper insert urging the collector to visit any participating Orange Country Carl's Jr. restaurant to receive the rest of the set. Reportedly only 20,000 sets were produced. Card number 21 comes in two different colors, there is no differenation for pricing for either version.

	Nm-Mt	Ex-Mt
COMPLETE SET (21)	25.00	7.50
1 Gene Autry OWN	5.00	1.50
2 Carl Karcher Chairman and Founder, Carl's Jr. Restaurants	1.00	.30
3 Buck Rodgers MG	1.00	.30
4 Rod Carew CO	5.00	1.50
5 Kelly Gruber	1.00	.30
6 Chili Davis	1.25	.35
7 Chad Curtis	1.00	.30
8 Mark Langston	1.25	.35
9 Scott Sanderson	1.00	.30
10 J.T. Snow	5.00	1.50
11 Rene Gonzales	1.00	.30
12 Jimmie Reese CO	1.50	.45
13 Damion Easley	1.25	.35
14 Julio Valera	1.00	.30
15 Luis Polonia	1.00	.30
16 John Orton	1.00	.30
17 Gary DiSarcina	1.00	.30
18 Greg Myers	1.00	.30
19 Chuck Finley	1.50	.45
20 Tim Salmon	5.00	1.50
21 Happy Star (Carl's Jr. mascot)	1.00	.30

1993 Angels Stadium Club

This 30-card standard-size set features the 1993 California Angels. The set was issued in hobby (plastic box) and retail (blister) form.

	Nm-Mt	Ex-Mt
COMP.FACT SET (30)	5.00	1.50
1 J.T. Snow	1.50	.45
2 Chuck Crim	.10	.03
3 Chili Davis	.25	.07
4 Mark Langston	.25	.07
5 Ron Tingley	.10	.03

6 Eduardo Perez .10 .03
7 Scott Sanderson .10 .03
8 Jorge Fabregas .10 .03
9 Troy Percival .50 .15
10 Rod Correia .10 .03
11 Greg Myers .10 .03
12 Steve Frey .10 .03
13 Tim Salmon 2.00 .60
14 Scott Lewis .10 .03
15 Rene Gonzales .10 .03
16 Chuck Finley .25 .07
17 John Orton .10 .03
18 Joe Grahe .10 .03
19 Luis Polonia .10 .03
20 John Farrell .10 .03
21 Damion Easley .10 .03
22 Gene Nelson .10 .03
23 Chad Curtis .10 .03
24 Russ Springer .10 .03
25 DeShawn Warren .10 .03
26 Darryl Scott .10 .03
27 Gary DiSarcina .10 .03
28 Jerry Nielsen .10 .03
29 Torey Lovullo .10 .03
30 Julio Valera .10 .03

1994 Angels Adohr Farms

For the second year, Adohr farms produced a set of milk cartons featuring members of the California Angels. These items were not on milk cartons which were distributed in schools and hospitals.

	Nm-Mt	Ex-Mt
COMPLETE SET (4)	10.00	3.00
1 Gary DiSarcina	2.50	.75
2 Phil Leftwich	2.50	.75
3 Joe Magrane	2.50	.75
4 Greg Myers	2.50	.75

1994 Angels L.A. Times

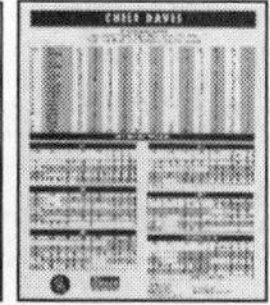

These 26 collector sheets were issued by the Orange County edition of the Los Angeles Times, were printed on semigloss paper, and measure 7 1/2" by 8 3/4". The sheets are numbered on the front as "X of 26." A rack display of 2 feet by 3 feet features four Angels. This item sells for approximately $10.

	Nm-Mt	Ex-Mt
COMPLETE SET (26)	15.00	4.50
1 Chili Davis	1.00	.30
2 Chad Curtis	.50	.15
3 John Dopson	.50	.15
4 Gary DiSarcina	.50	.15
5 Jim Edmonds	2.00	.60
6 Joe Grahe	.50	.15
7 Bo Jackson	1.50	.45
8 Joe Magrane	.50	.15
9 Phil Leftwich	.50	.15
10 Bill Sampen	.50	.15
11 Chuck Finley	1.00	.30
12 Dwight Smith	.50	.15
13 Mark Leiter	.50	.15
14 Mark Langston	.75	.23
15 Mike Butcher	.50	.15
16 Rex Hudler	.75	.23
17 Craig Lefferts	.50	.15
18 Damion Easley	.50	.15
19 Greg Myers	.50	.15
20 Chris Turner	.50	.15
21 Tim Salmon	2.00	.60
22 Harold Reynolds	1.00	.30
23 Bob Patterson	.50	.15
24 Spike Owen	.50	.15
25 Eduardo Perez	.50	.15
26 Marcel Lachemann MG	.50	.15

1994 Angels Mother's

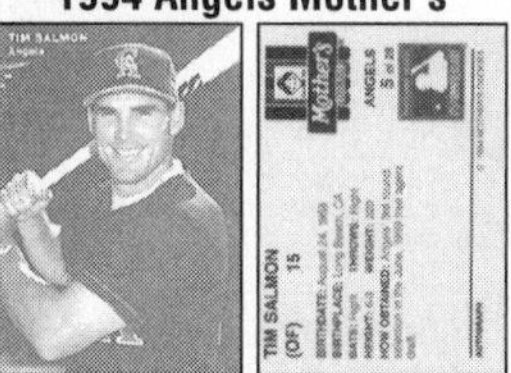

The 1994 Mother's Cookies Angels set consists of 28 standard-size cards with rounded corners.

	Nm-Mt	Ex-Mt
COMPLETE SET (28)	12.00	3.60
1 Marcel Lachemann MG	.25	.07
2 Mark Langston	.50	.15
3 J.T. Snow	1.00	.30
4 Chad Curtis	.25	.07
5 Tim Salmon	3.00	.90
6 Gary DiSarcina	.25	.07
7 Bo Jackson	1.00	.30
8 Dwight Smith	.25	.07
9 Chuck Finley	.75	.23
10- Rod Correia	.25	.07
11 Spike Owen	.25	.07
12 Harold Reynolds	.75	.23
13 Chris Turner	.25	.07
14 Chili Davis	.75	.23
15 Bob Patterson	.25	.07
16 Jim Edmonds	3.00	.90
17 Joe Magrane	.25	.07
18 Craig Lefferts	.25	.07
19 Scott Lewis	.25	.07
20 Rex Hudler	.50	.15
21 Mike Butcher	.25	.07
22 Brian Anderson	.75	.23
23 Greg Myers	.25	.07
24 Mark Leiter	.25	.07
25 Joe Grahe	.25	.07
26 Jorge Fabregas	.25	.07
27 John Dopson	.25	.07
28 Chuck Hernandez CO Ken Macha CO Bobby Knoop CO Joe Maddon CO Rod Carew CO Max Oliveras CO CL	.50	.15

1995 Angels CHP

Sponsored by the California Highway Patrol and commemorating the 35th anniversary of the California Angels, this 16-card set features color action player photos in a silver frame. The backs carry player information and a safety message.

	Nm-Mt	Ex-Mt
COMPLETE SET (16)	20.00	6.00
1 Tim Salmon	4.00	1.20
2 Chuck Finley	2.00	.60
3 Mark Langston	1.50	.45
4 Gary DiSarcina	1.00	.30
5 Damion Easley	1.00	.30
6 Spike Owen	1.00	.30
7 Troy Percival	2.00	.60
8 Chili Davis	2.00	.60
9 Jim Edmonds	4.00	1.20
10 Rex Hudler	1.50	.45
11 Greg Myers	1.00	.30
12 Brian Anderson	1.50	.45
13 J.T. Snow	2.00	.60
14 Tony Phillips	1.00	.30
15 Lee Smith	1.50	.45
16 Marcel Lachemann MG Chief Don Watkins	1.00	.30

1995 Angels Mother's

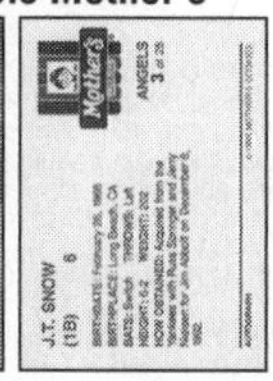

This 1995 Mother's Cookies California Angels set consists of 28 standard-size cards with rounded corners.

	Nm-Mt	Ex-Mt
COMPLETE SET (28)	12.00	3.60
1 Marcel Lachemann MG	.25	.07
2 Mark Langston	.50	.15
3 J.T. Snow	1.00	.30
4 Tim Salmon	2.00	.60
5 Chili Davis	.50	.15
6 Gary DiSarcina	.25	.07
7 Tony Phillips	.25	.07
8 Jim Edmonds	2.00	.60
9 Chuck Finley	.75	.23
10 Mark Dalesandro	.25	.07
11 Greg Myers	.25	.07
12 Spike Owen	.25	.07
13 Lee Smith	.50	.15
14 Eduardo Perez	.25	.07
15 Bob Patterson	.25	.07
16 Mitch Williams	.50	.15
17 Garret Anderson	1.00	.30
18 Mike Bielecki	.25	.07
19 Shawn Boskie	.25	.07
20 Damion Easley	.25	.07
21 Mike Butcher	.25	.07
22 Brian Anderson	.50	.15
23 Andy Allanson	.25	.07
24 Scott Sanderson	.25	.07
25 Troy Percival	.75	.23
26 Rex Hudler	.50	.15
27 Mike James	.25	.07
28 Rod Carew CO Chuck Hernandez CO Rick Burleson CO Bobby Knoop CO Bill Lachemann CO Mick Billmeyer CO Joe Maddon CO CL	.75	.23

1995 Angels Team Issue

This three-card set features a color player photo on the front with a black-and-white elongated photo, player information, statistics and a facsimile autograph on the back. The cards are unnumbered and checklisted below in alphabetical order.

	Nm-Mt	Ex-Mt
COMPLETE SET (3)	5.00	1.50
1 Jim Abbott	2.00	.60
2 Chili Davis	2.00	.60
3 J.T. Snow	2.00	.60

1996 Angels Mother's

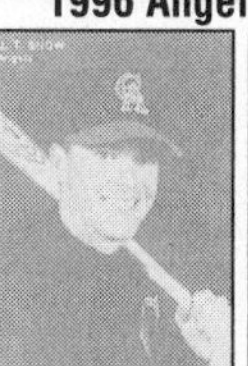
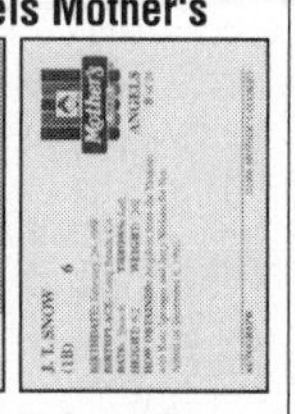

This 28-card set consists of borderless posed color player portraits in stadium settings.

	Nm-Mt	Ex-Mt
COMPLETE SET (28)	10.00	3.00
1 Marcel Lachemann MG	.25	.07
2 Chili Davis	.50	.15
3 Mark Langston	.50	.15
4 Tim Salmon	1.50	.45
5 Jim Abbott	.50	.15
6 Jim Edmonds	1.50	.45
7 Gary DiSarcina	.25	.07
8 J.T. Snow	.75	.23
9 Chuck Finley	.75	.23
10 Tim Wallach	.25	.07
11 Lee Smith	.50	.15
12 George Arias	.25	.07
13 Troy Percival	.75	.23
14 Randy Velarde	.25	.07
15 Garret Anderson	1.50	.45
16 Jorge Fabregas	.25	.07
17 Shawn Boskie	.25	.07
18 Mark Eichhorn	.25	.07
19 Jack Howell	.25	.07
20 Jason Grimsley	.25	.07
21 Rex Hudler	.50	.15
22 Mike Aldrete	.25	.07
23 Mike James	.25	.07
24 Scott Sanderson	.25	.07
25 Don Slaught	.25	.07
26 Mark Holzemer	.25	.07
27 Dick Schofield	.25	.07
28 Mick Billmeyer CO Rick Burleson CO Rod Carew CO Chuck Hernandez CO Bobby Knoop CO Bill Lachemann CO Joe Maddon CO CL	.75	.23

1997 Angels Mother's

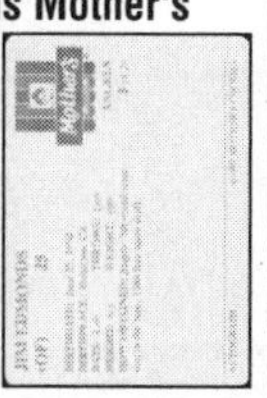

This 28-card set of the Anaheim Angels sponsored by Mother's Cookies consists of posed color player photos with rounded corners.

	Nm-Mt	Ex-Mt
COMPLETE SET (28)	12.00	3.60
1 Terry Collins MG	.25	.07
2 Tim Salmon	1.50	.45
3 Eddie Murray	1.00	.30
4 Mark Langston	.50	.15
5 Jim Edmonds	1.50	.45
6 Tony Phillips	.25	.07
7 Gary DiSarcina	.25	.07
8 Garret Anderson	1.25	.35
9 Chuck Finley	.75	.23
10 Darin Erstad	3.00	.90
11 Jim Leyritz	.25	.07
12 Shigetoshi Hasegawa	1.00	.30
13 Luis Alicea	.25	.07
14 Troy Percival	.75	.23
15 Allen Watson	.25	.07
16 Craig Grebeck	.25	.07
17 Mike Holtz	.25	.07
18 Chad Kreuter	.25	.07
19 Dennis Springer	.25	.07
20 Jason Dickson	.25	.07
21 Mike James	.25	.07
22 Orlando Palmeiro	.25	.07
23 Dave Hollins	.25	.07
24 Mark Gubicza	.25	.07
25 Pep Harris	.25	.07
26 Jack Howell	.25	.07
27 Rich DeLucia	.25	.07
28 Larry Bowa CO Rod Carew CO Joe Coleman CO Marcel Lachemann CO Joe Maddon CO Dave Parker CO CL	.75	.23

1998 Angels Postcards

These 30 blank backed postcards measure 5" by 7" and feature members of the 1998 Anaheim Angels. They are black and white and since they are unnumbered except for a uniform notation on the bottom we have sequenced them in alphabetical order

	Nm-Mt	Ex-Mt
COMPLETE SET	20.00	6.00
1 Garret Anderson	2.00	.60
2 Mike Billmeyer	.50	.15
3 Larry Bowa CO	.75	.23
4 Greg Cadaret	.50	.15
5 Rod Carew CO	1.50	.45
6 Joe Coleman CO	.50	.15
7 Terry Collins MG	.50	.15
8 Jason Dickson	.50	.15
9 Gary DiSarcina	.50	.15
10 Jim Edmonds	2.00	.60
11 Cecil Fielder	.75	.23
12 Chuck Finley	1.00	.30
13 Troy Glaus	5.00	1.50
14 Todd Greene	.50	.15
15 Pep Harris	.50	.15
16 George Hendrick CO	.50	.15
17 Dave Hollins	.50	.15
18 Ken Hill	.50	.15
19 Marcel Lachemann CO	.50	.15
20 Joe Maddon	.50	.15
21 Jack McDowell	.50	.15
22 Orlando Palmeiro	.50	.15
23 Troy Percival	1.00	.30
24 Tim Salmon	1.50	.45
25 Craig Shipley	.50	.15
26 Steve Sparks	.50	.15
27 Randy Velarde	.50	.15
28 Matt Walbeck	.50	.15
29 Jarrod Washburn	1.50	.45
30 Allen Watson	.50	.15

1998 Angels Score

This 15-card set was issued in special retail packs and features color photos of the Anaheim Angels team. The backs carry player information. A special platinum parallel set was also issued and randomly inserted in packs.

	Nm-Mt	Ex-Mt
COMPLETE SET (15)	6.00	1.80
*PLATINUM: 5X BASIC CARDS		
1 Rickey Henderson	2.00	.60
2 Todd Greene	.25	.07
3 Shigetoshi Hasegawa	.50	.15
4 Darin Erstad	2.00	.60
5 Jason Dickson	.25	.07
6 Tim Salmon	1.00	.30
7 Ken Hill	.25	.07
8 Dave Hollins	.25	.07
9 Gary DiSarcina	.25	.07
10 Mike James	.25	.07
11 Jim Edmonds	1.50	.45
12 Troy Percival	1.00	.30
13 Chuck Finley	.50	.15
14 Tony Phillips	.25	.07
15 Garret Anderson	1.50	.45

1999 Angels CHP

This 10 card standard-size set was issued by the California Highway Patrol and featured members of the Angels. Some of the players are posed with officers and some of the players have action shots.

	Nm-Mt	Ex-Mt
COMPLETE SET (10)	40.00	12.00
1 Chuck Finley	2.50	.75
2 Shigetosi Hasegawa	2.50	.75
3 Gary DiSarcina	1.50	.45
4 Darin Erstad	12.00	3.60
5 Mo Vaughn	2.50	.75
6 Tim Salmon Posed with Angel Johnson JoAnn O'Hair	6.00	1.80
7 Troy Percival Posed with Ana Burson Mike Lundquist	2.50	.75
8 Jim Edmonds Posed with Tony Lassos Galen Burson	6.00	1.80
9 Troy Glaus Posed with Keith Bauer Ed Exley	10.00	3.00
10 Santa Ana CHP Mike Lundquist Ana Burson Galen Burson Keith Bauer Ed Exley	1.50	.45

1999 Angels Magnets

These four magnets were sold directly at Edison Field and featured members of the Anaheim Angels. The fronts have the player's last name printed down the side along with a photo and the Angels logo. The backs, are obviously, blank. Since these are unnumbered we have sequenced them in alphabetical order. Please note that Jim Edmonds and Chuck Finley were only available in 1999 so they are slightly tougher than Darin Erstad and Tim Salmon. The magnets are sequenced in alphabetical order.

	Nm-Mt	Ex-Mt
COMPLETE SET (4)	25.00	7.50
1 Jim Edmonds	8.00	2.40
2 Darin Erstad	8.00	2.40
3 Chuck Finley	6.00	1.80
4 Tim Salmon	5.00	1.50

2002 Angels Topps 1982 Commemorative

This nine-card set was given away at the April 14th Anaheim Angels game and honored the 1982 division champion Angels Team. Topps reprinted 1983 Topps cards from nine of the key players from the team and similar to the 2002 Archives set the card number was placed on the side.

	Nm-Mt	Ex-Mt
COMPLETE SET	8.00	2.40
1 Don Baylor	1.00	.30
2 Rod Carew	2.00	.60
3 Doug DeCinces	.50	.15
4 Brian Downing	1.00	.30
5 Reggie Jackson	2.00	.60
6 Fred Lynn	.50	.15
7 Geoff Zahn	.25	.07
8 Bob Boone	.50	.15
9 Bobby Grich	.75	.23
NNO Header Card Fox Sports Net	.25	.07

2000 APBA Superstars

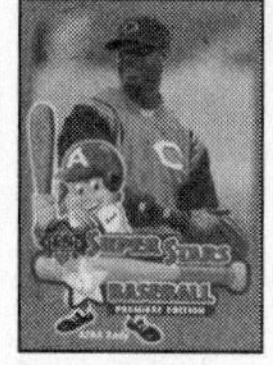

These 30 cards were inserted into the 2000 APBA Superstars board game. These cards were included in the "kids" or beginning game of the long-term popular board game. The fronts have full color photos while the backs are geared to the game.

	Nm-Mt	Ex-Mt
COMPLETE SET (30)	30.00	9.00
1 Roberto Alomar	1.00	.30
2 Jeff Bagwell	1.25	.35
3 Barry Bonds	2.50	.75
4 Jeromy Burnitz	.50	.15
5 Carlos Delgado	1.25	.35
6 Jermaine Dye	.25	.07
7 Cliff Floyd	.50	.15
8 Jason Giambi	1.50	.45
9 Juan Gonzalez	1.00	.30
10 Shawn Green	1.00	.30
11 Ken Griffey Jr.	2.50	.75
12 Vladimir Guerrero	1.50	.45
13 Tony Gwynn	2.50	.75
14 Todd Helton	1.25	.35
15 Derek Jeter	5.00	1.50
16 Randy Johnson	2.00	.60
17 Chipper Jones	1.50	.45
18 Jason Kendall	.50	.15
19 Matt Lawton	.25	.07
20 Pedro Martinez	1.25	.35
21 Mark McGwire	4.00	1.20
22 Mike Piazza	3.00	.90
23 Cal Ripken	5.00	1.50
24 Alex Rodriguez	3.00	.90
25 Ivan Rodriguez	1.25	.35
26 Scott Rolen	1.00	.30
27 Sammy Sosa	2.50	.75
28 Frank Thomas	1.00	.30
29 Greg Vaughn	.25	.07
30 Mo Vaughn	.50	.15

2000 APBA Superstars Cut-outs

These six cardboard cut-outs were inserted into the 2000 APBA Superstars board game. Each cut-out features a major league player, and is used to navigate around the game board. Please note that these cut-outs are not numbered and are listed below in alphabetical order.

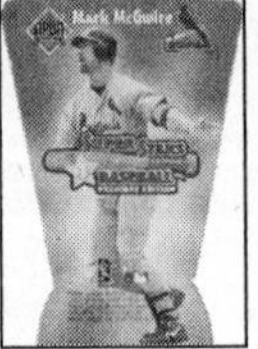

	Nm-Mt	Ex-Mt
COMPLETE SET (6)	6.00	1.80
1 Barry Bonds	2.00	.60
2 Nomar Garciaparra	1.00	.30
3 Ken Griffey Jr.	1.25	.35
4 Mark McGwire	2.00	.60
5 Mike Piazza	1.25	.35
6 Alex Rodriguez	1.25	.35

1996 Arizona Lottery

This three-card set features black-and-white action player photos with black borders. The backs carry player information and career highlights as well as information on what the collector can win playing the lottery scratch-off game, "Diamond Bucks." The cards are unnumbered and checklisted below in alphabetical order.

	Nm-Mt	Ex-Mt
COMPLETE SET (3)	8.00	2.40
1 Ernie Banks	3.00	.90
2 Gaylord Perry	2.00	.60
3 Brooks Robinson	3.00	.90

1953-63 Artvue Hall of Fame Postcards

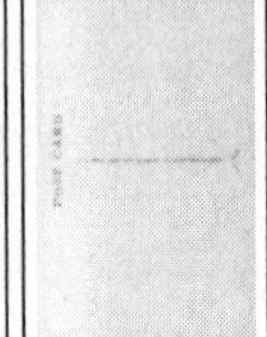

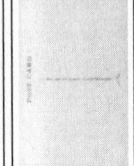

This 91-card set features photos of the members of the Baseball Hall of Fame printed on postcard-size cards. The cards are unnumbered and checklisted below in alphabetical order.

	NM	Ex
COMPLETE SET (91)	600.00	300.00
1 Grover Alexander	12.00	6.00
2 Cap Anson	12.00	6.00
3 Frank Baker	10.00	5.00
4 Ed Barrow	5.00	2.50
5 Chief Bender	6.00	3.00
6 Roger Bresnahan	5.00	2.50
7 Modecai Brown	10.00	5.00
8 Morgan Bulkeley	5.00	2.50
9 Jesse Burkett	5.00	2.50
10 Max Carey	5.00	2.50
11 Alexander Cartwright	5.00	2.50
12 Henry Chadwick	5.00	2.50
13 Frank Chance	6.00	3.00
14 Jack Chesbro	5.00	2.50
15 Fred Clarke	5.00	2.50
16 John Clarkson	5.00	2.50
17 Ty Cobb	25.00	12.50
18 Mickey Cochrane	6.00	3.00
19 Eddie Collins	10.00	5.00
20 Jimmy Collins	5.00	2.50
21 Charlie Comiskey	5.00	2.50
22 Tom Connolly	5.00	2.50
23 Sam Crawford	8.00	4.00
24 Joe Cronin	6.00	3.00
25 Candy Cummings	5.00	2.50
26 Dizzy Dean	6.00	3.00
27 Ed Delehanty	5.00	2.50
28 Bill Dickey	6.00	3.00
29 Joe DiMaggio	40.00	20.00
30 Hugh Duffy	5.00	2.50
31 Johnny Evers	5.00	2.50
32 Buck Ewing	5.00	2.50
33 Bob Feller	10.00	5.00
34 Elmer Flick	5.00	2.50
35 Jimmy Foxx	8.00	4.00
36 Frankie Frisch	6.00	3.00
37 Lou Gehrig	3.00	1.50
38 Charlie Gehringer	10.00	5.00
39 Hank Greenberg	10.00	5.00
40 Clark Griffith	6.00	3.00
41 Lefty Grove	15.00	7.50
42 Billy Hamilton	6.00	3.00
43 Gabby Hartnett	5.00	2.50
44 Harry Heilmann	5.00	2.50
45 Rogers Hornsby	12.00	6.00
46 Carl Hubbell	12.50	6.25
47 Hugh Jennings	5.00	2.50
48 Ban Johnson	5.00	2.50
49 Walter Johnson	20.00	10.00
50 Willie Keeler	6.00	3.00
51 King Kelly	6.00	3.00
52 Bill Klem	5.00	2.50
53 Nap Lajoie	20.00	10.00
54 Kenesaw Mountain Landis	5.00	2.50
55 Ted Lyons	5.00	2.50
56 Connie Mack	10.00	5.00
57 Rabbit Maranville	5.00	2.50
58 Christy Mathewson	15.00	7.50
59 Joe McCarthy	5.00	2.50
60 Tom McCarthy	5.00	2.50
61 Joe McGinnity	5.00	2.50
62 John McGraw	10.00	5.00
63 Bill McKechnie	5.00	2.50
64 Kid Nichols	5.00	2.50
65 Jimmy O'Rourke	5.00	2.50
66 Mel Ott	8.00	4.00
67 Herb Pennock	5.00	2.50
68 Eddie Plank	5.00	2.50
69 Sam Rice	5.00	2.50
70 Eppa Rixey	5.00	2.50
71 Jackie Robinson	25.00	12.50
72 Wilbert Robinson	5.00	2.50
73 Edd Roush	5.00	2.50
74 Babe Ruth	50.00	25.00
75 Ray Schalk	5.00	2.50
76 Al Simmons	6.00	3.00
77 George Sisler	10.00	5.00
78 Albert Spalding	6.00	3.00
79 Tris Speaker	10.00	5.00
80 Bill Terry	6.00	3.00
81 Joe Tinker	6.00	3.00
82 Dazzy Vance	5.00	2.50
83 Rube Waddell	8.00	4.00
84 Honus Wagner	20.00	10.00
85 Bobby Wallace	5.00	2.50
86 Ed Walsh	5.00	2.50
87 Paul Waner	6.00	3.00
88 Zach Wheat	5.00	2.50
89 George Wright	5.00	2.50
90 Harry Wright	5.00	2.50
91 Cy Young	20.00	10.00

1982 ASA Mickey Mantle

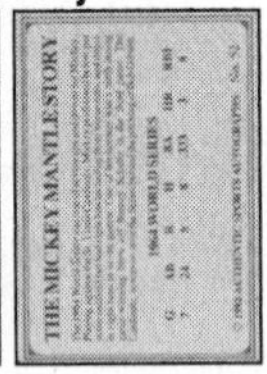

This seventy-two card standard-size set was the first issued by ASA to honor past greats of the game. The first card in this set comes either signed or unsigned. We have priced the set both ways. There were 5,000 numbered sets issued with Mantle autographed cards which were originally issued at $24.99 each and 15,000 unnumbered sets issued with no signed cards at $12.99 each.

	Nm-Mt	Ex-Mt
COMPLETE SET W AU (72)	200.00	80.00
COMPLETE SET W/O AU (72)	100.00	40.00
COMMON CARD (1-72)	1.00	.40
1 Mickey Mantle	2.50	1.00
1AU Mickey Mantle Autographed	100.00	40.00
2 Mickey Mantle Merlyn Mantle, 1951	1.00	.40
5 Mickey Mantle Mrs. Mantle Merlyn Mantle	1.00	.40
7 Mickey Mantle Joe DiMaggio Ted Williams	3.00	1.20
9 Mickey Mantle Billy Mantle Mickey Jr. Born 4/12/52	1.00	.40
10 Mickey Mantle Roy Mantle Ray Mantle	1.00	.40
12 Mickey Mantle Hank Bauer Johnny Hopp	1.00	.40
14 Mickey Mantle Billy Martin on to 1952 Series	1.50	.60
15 Mickey Mantle Billy Martin, 1953	1.50	.60
23 Mickey Mantle Billy Skowron Phil Rizzuto, 1955	2.00	.80
24 Mickey Mantle Jackie Robinson, 1954	2.50	1.00
25 Mickey Mantle Ted Williams, 1956	2.50	1.00
26 Mickey Mantle Bill Skowron Yogi Berra, 1955	2.00	.80
27 Mickey Mantle Bob Lemon Safe at first, 1956	1.50	.60
28 Mickey Mantle Yogi Berra Elston Howard Hank Bauer 1956 World Series	2.00	.80
29 Mickey Mantle Yogi Berra Whitey Ford, 1957	2.00	.80
30 Mickey Mantle Roy Sievers, 1957	1.00	.40
33 Mickey Mantle Cardinal Spellman, 1957	1.00	.40
34 Mickey Mantle Teresa Brewer, 1957	1.00	.40
35 Mickey Mantle Brooks Robinson, 1957	1.50	.60
36 Mickey Mantle 1958 World Series	1.50	.60
37 Mickey Mantle Ernie Banks 1958 All-Star Game	2.00	.80
38 Mickey Mantle Casey Stengel, 1959	2.00	.80
39 Mickey Mantle Roger Maris, 1960	2.00	.80
42 Mickey Mantle Roger Maris Yogi Berra Elston Howard Bill Skowron John Blanchard, 1961	2.00	.80
43 Mickey Mantle Roger Maris Mrs. Babe Ruth, 1961	2.00	.80
44 Mickey Mantle Roger Maris, 1961	2.00	.80
45 Mickey Mantle 54 HRs Roger Maris 61 HRs, 1961	2.00	.80
51 Mickey Mantle Joe Pepitone Whitey Ford 1964 Banner Year	1.50	.60
53 Mickey Mantle Sen. Robert F. Kennedy 1965 Day	2.50	1.00
55 Mickey Mantle Joe DiMaggio, 1966	2.50	1.00
56 Billy Mantle Merlyn Mantle Mickey Mantle Jr. Danny Mantle David Mantle	1.00	.40
58 Mickey Mantle Hits Homerun No. 529, 1968	1.50	.60
66 Mickey Mantle Whitey Ford Casey Stengel 1974 Hall of Fame Inductees	2.50	1.00
67 Mickey Mantle Billy Martin Joe DiMaggio Whitey Ford 1979 Old Timers Game	2.50	1.00
68 Mickey Mantle Don Larsen 1981 Old Timers Game	1.50	.60
69 Mickey Mantle Butch Mantle Roy Mantle Barbara Mantle Mrs. Mantle Ray Mantle Family Day	1.00	.40

1983 ASA Bob Feller

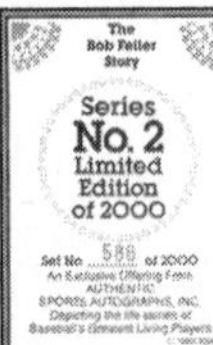

This 12-card standard-size set honors the career of Bob Feller and features fronts of white-bordered and red-trimmed black-and-white photos of him during his career. The backs are red-bordered, trimmed by a black line and carry a story that is continuous from card to card. Card number 1 carries an authentic autograph and is numbered sequentially out of 2,000.

	Nm-Mt	Ex-Mt
COMPLETE SET (12)	25.00	10.00
1 Bob Feller The Bob Feller Story Autograph card	20.00	8.00
2 Bob Feller Steve O'Neill MG 1937	1.00	.40
3 Bob Feller Gene Tunney 1942 Navy Induction	1.50	.60
4 Bob Feller Rollie Hemsley Tommy Bridges Bucky Walters 1946 Bob Owens Baseball School	1.00	.40
5 Bob Feller Satchel Paige 1946	2.50	1.00
6 Bob Feller Bill Veeck OWN 1947	1.00	.40
7 Bob Feller Hal Newhouser 1947	1.50	.60
8 Bob Feller Joe Gordon Kenny Keltner 1947	1.00	.40
9 Bob Feller Bob Lemon 1950	1.50	.60
10 Bob Feller Jim Hegan Al Rosen Luke Easter 200th Victory, 1951	1.00	.40
11 Bob Feller 1954 Indians Pitching Staff	1.50	.60
12 Bob Feller The Feller Style	1.50	.60

1983 ASA Brooks Robinson

This 12-card standard-size set honors the career of Brooks Robinson and features fronts of white-bordered and red-trimmed black-and-white photos of him during his career. The backs are red-bordered, trimmed by a black line and carry a story that is continuous from card to card. Card number 1 carries an authentic autograph and is numbered sequentially out of 2,000.

	Nm-Mt	Ex-Mt
COMPLETE SET (12)	30.00	12.00
COMMON CARD (1-12)	1.00	.40
1AU Brooks Robinson Autograph card	20.00	8.00
2 Brooks Robinson Tito Francona Bob Hale 1956 Spring Training	1.00	.40
6 Brooks Robinson Thurman Munson Luis Aparicio Mickey Lolich Harmon Killebrew 1971 All-Star Game	2.00	.80

1983 ASA Duke Snider

This 12-card standard-size set honors the career of Duke Snider and features fronts of white-bordered and red-trimmed black-and-white photos of him during his career. The backs are red-bordered, trimmed by a black line and carry a story that is continuous from card to card. Card number 1 carries an authentic autograph and is numbered sequentially out of 2,000.

	Nm-Mt	Ex-Mt
COMPLETE SET (12)	30.00	12.00
COMMON CARD (1-12)	1.00	.40
1 Duke Snider Autograph card	20.00	8.00
4 Duke Snider Billy Cox Pee Wee Reese Jackie Robinson Roy Campanella Andy Pafko Gil Hodges Carl Furillo Joe Black	1.00	.40
5 Duke Snider Gil Hodges Carl Furillo Roy Campanella Jackie Robinson Pee Wee Reese Chuck Dressen MG Dick Williams Wes Westrum Hoyt Wilhelm	2.00	.80
6 Duke Snider Gil Hodges Don Hoak Pee Wee Reese	2.00	.80
7 Duke Snider Joe Black Chuck Dressen MG	1.00	.40
9 Duke Snider Gil Hodges Johnny Podres Clem Labine	2.00	.80

1983 ASA Frank Robinson

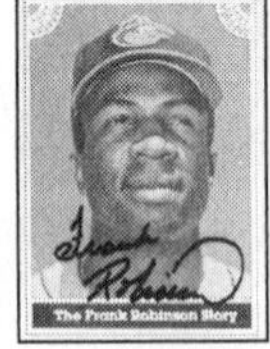

This 12-card standard-size set honors the career of Frank Robinson and features fronts of white-bordered and red-trimmed black-and-white photos of him during his career. The backs are red-bordered, trimmed by a black line and carry a story that is continuous from card to card. Card number 1 carries an authentic autograph and is numbered sequentially out of 2,000.

	Nm-Mt	Ex-Mt
COMPLETE SET (12)	30.00	12.00
COMMON CARD (1-12)	1.00	.40
1AU Frank Robinson The Frank Robinson Story {Autograph card	20.00	8.00
10 Frank Robinson Mike Strahler 1972 Santurce	1.00	.40

1983 ASA Hank Aaron

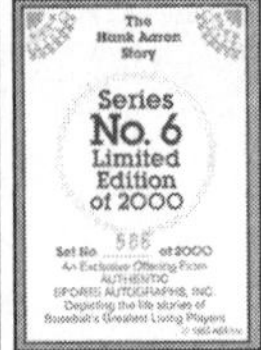

This 12-card standard-size set honors the career of Hank Aaron and features fronts of white-bordered and red-trimmed black-and-white photos of him during his career. The backs are red-bordered, trimmed by a black line and carry a story that is continuous from card to card. Card number 1 carries an authentic autograph and is numbered sequentially out of 2,000.

	Nm-Mt	Ex-Mt
COMPLETE SET (12)	100.00	40.00
COMMON CARD (1-12)	1.00	.40
1 Hank Aaron The Hank Aaron Story Autograph card	100.00	40.00
2 Hank Aaron Ben Geraghty MG 1953 Jacksonville	1.00	.40
4 Hank Aaron Wes Covington Bob Hazle 1957 Braves	1.00	.40
5 Hank Aaron Red Schoendienst Fred Haney MG 1958 Braves	1.00	.40
6 Hank Aaron Mickey Mantle 1958 World Series	2.50	1.00
7 Hank Aaron Eddie Mathews 1965 Braves	1.50	.60
9 Hank Aaron Rico Carty 1970 Braves	1.00	.40
12 Hank Aaron Darrell Evans Dave Johnson 1973 Braves	1.00	.40

1983 ASA Joe DiMaggio

This 12-card standard-size set honors the career of Joe DiMaggio and features fronts of white-bordered and red-trimmed black-and-white photos of him during his career. The backs are red-bordered, trimmed by a black line and carry a story that is continuous from card to card. Card number 1 carries an authentic autograph and is numbered sequentially out of 2,000.

	Nm-Mt	Ex-Mt
COMPLETE SET (12)	200.00	80.00
1 Joe DiMaggio The Joe Dimaggio Story Autograph card	200.00	80.00
2 Joe DiMaggio Dom DiMaggio San Francisco, 1935	2.00	.80
3 Joe DiMaggio Joe McCarthy MG Jacob Ruppert OWN Tony Lazzeri 1936 World Series	2.00	.80
4 Joe DiMaggio Lou Gehrig George Selkirk Bill Dickey 1936	4.00	1.60
5 Joe DiMaggio That Classic Stance 1947	2.00	.80
6 Joe DiMaggio Ted Williams 1942	4.00	1.60
7 Joe DiMaggio Charlie Keller Tommy Henrich 1946	2.00	.80
8 Joe DiMaggio 1950 Spring Training	2.00	.80
9 Joe DiMaggio Mickey Mantle 1951	4.00	1.60
10 Joe DiMaggio Mel Allen ANN 1951	2.00	.80
11 Joe DiMaggio A's 1968	2.00	.80
12 Joe DiMaggio Billy Martin Mickey Mantle Whitey Ford 1978	2.00	.80

1983 ASA Johnny Mize

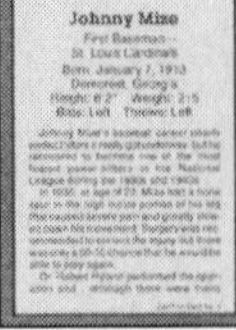

This 12-card standard-size set honors the career of Johnny Mize and features fronts of white-bordered and red-trimmed black-and-white photos of him during his career. The backs are red-bordered, trimmed by a black line and carry a story that is continuous from card No. 2 to card No. 9. The backs of cards 10, 11, and 12 carry his lifetime career and World Series records, respectively. Card number 1 carries an authentic autograph and is numbered sequentially out of 2,000.

	Nm-Mt	Ex-Mt
COMPLETE SET (12)	25.00	10.00
COMMON CARD (1-12)	.50	.20
1 Johnny Mize Autograph card	20.00	8.00
10 Johnny Mize Duke of Windsor Duchess of Windsor	.50	.20
11 Johnny Mize Yogi Berra Ed Lopat Playing Cards	1.00	.40

1983 ASA Juan Marichal

This 12-card standard-size set honors the career of Juan Marichal and features fronts of

white-bordered and red-trimmed black-and-white photos of him during his career. The backs are red-bordered, trimmed by a black line and carry a story that is continuous from card to card. Card number 1 carries an authentic autograph and is numbered sequentially out of 2,000.

	Nm-Mt	Ex-Mt
COMPLETE SET (12)	20.00	8.00
COMMON CARD (1-12)	1.00	.40
1 Juan Marichal	15.00	6.00
The Juan Marichal Story		
Autograph card		
5 Juan Marichal	2.00	.80
Willie Mays		
1971		
7 Juan Marichal	1.50	.60
Willie McCovey		
1973		
9 Juan Marichal	1.00	.40
Walt Alston MG		
1975		
10 Juan Marichal	1.00	.40
Walt Alston MG		
April 17, 1975		

1983 ASA Warren Spahn

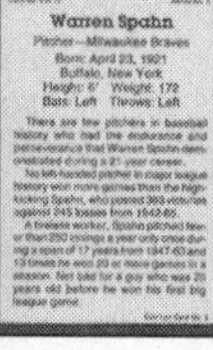

This 12-card standard-size set honors the career of Warren Spahn and features fronts of white-bordered and green-trimmed black-and-white photos of him during his career. The backs are green-bordered, trimmed by a black line and carry a story that is continuous from card No. 2 to card No. 9. The backs of cards 10, 11, and 12 carry his lifetime career and World Series records, respectively.

	Nm-Mt	Ex-Mt
COMPLETE SET (12)	5.00	2.00
COMMON CARD (1-12)	.50	.20
1A Warren Spahn	20.00	8.00
Autographed		
Warren Spahn UER	.75	.30
Vern Bickford		
Johnny Sain		
Misspelled "uupon" on card back		
Warren Spahn	.75	.30
Fred Haney MG		
Bobby Thomson		
Lew Burdette		

1983 ASA Willie Mays 12

This 12-card standard-size set honors the career of Willie Mays and features fronts of white-bordered and red-trimmed black-and-white photos of him during his career. The backs are red-bordered, trimmed by a black line and carry a story that is continuous from card to card. Card number 1 carries an authentic autograph and is numbered sequentially out of 2,000.

	Nm-Mt	Ex-Mt
COMPLETE SET (12)	100.00	40.00
COMMON CARD (1-12)	2.00	.80
Willie Mays	75.00	30.00
The Willie Mays Story		
Autographed Card		
Willie Mays	4.00	1.60
Mickey Mantle		
1951		
Willie Mays	3.00	1.20
Stan Musial		
1956		
Willie Mays	3.00	1.20
Roberto Clemente		
Hank Aaron		
1969		
11 Willie Mays	3.00	1.20
Roberto Clemente		
Sept. 30, 1972		
12 Willie Mays	2.00	.80
Ralph Kiner		
1982		

1983 ASA Yogi Berra

This 12-card standard-size set honors the career of Yogi Berra and features fronts of white-bordered and red-trimmed black-and-white photos of him during his career. The backs are red-bordered, trimmed by a black line and carry a story that is continuous from card to card. Card number 1 carries an

authentic autograph and is numbered sequentially out of 2,000.

	Nm-Mt	Ex-Mt
COMPLETE SET (12)	40.00	16.00
1 Yogi Berra	30.00	12.00
The Yogi Berra Story		
Autograph card		
2 Yogi Berra	1.00	.40
Youthful Yogi		
3 Yogi Berra	2.50	1.00
Mickey Mantle		
Joe Collins		
Hank Bauer		
Gene Woodling		
1953 Yankees		
4 Yogi Berra	1.00	.40
Sal Maglie		
Don Larsen		
1958		
5 Yogi Berra	2.50	1.00
Roger Maris		
Mickey Mantle		
Bobby Richardson		
Bill Skowron		
Tony Kubek		
Art Ditmar		
Hector Lopez		
Clete Boyer		
Casey Stengel MG		
1960		
6 Yogi Berra	2.50	1.00
Roger Maris		
Mickey Mantle		
Elston Howard		
Bill Skowron		
John Blanchard		
1961		
7 Yogi Berra MG	2.50	1.00
Casey Stengel MG		
1964		
8 Yogi Berra	2.50	1.00
Joe DiMaggio		
Red Ruffing		
Whitey Ford		
Charlie Keller		
Don Larsen		
Bobby Richardson		
Tommy Henrich		
Old Timers Day, 1967		
9 Yogi Berra	2.00	.80
Bill Dickey		
Elston Howard		
Thurman Munson		
Yankee Catching Tradition		
10 Yogi Berra CO	1.00	.40
Gil Hodges MG		
Eddie Yost		
Rube Walker		
Joe Pignatano		
11 Yogi Berra MG	1.00	.40
Walter Alston MG		
1973		
12 Yogi Berra CO	1.00	.40
1978 Yankees		

1984 ASA Willie Mays 90

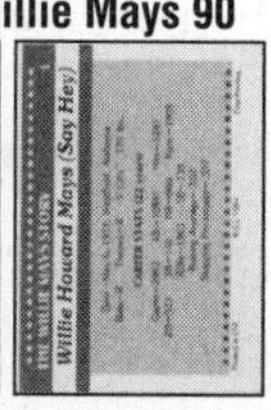

This ninety-card standard-size set was issued by ASA and printed by Renata Gallaso Inc. to honor the life and career of Willie Mays. These cards were issued in set form only. Sets were issued with and without the number one card being signed by Mays. The complete set does not include the autograph card which is valued seperately. Cards 1-45 contain biographical information about Mays while cards 46-90 have a puzzle back. The puzzle when put together features a collage of all Willie Mays baseball cards.

	Nm-Mt	Ex-Mt
COMPLETE SET (90)	15.00	6.00
COMMON CARD (1-90)	.10	.04
1A Willie Mays	75.00	30.00
Say Hey, autographed		
1B Willie Mays	.10	.04
Say Hey		
unautographed		
4 Willie Mays	.40	.16
Leo Durocher		
Hank Thompson		
Monte Irvin		
1951 Rookie Season		
7 Willie Mays	.60	.24
THE Catch		
12 Willie Mays	.25	.10
Horace Stoneham OWN		
A Sportsman and A Gentleman		
13 Willie Mays	.40	.16
Duke Snider		
The Toast of New York		
19 Willie Mays	.40	.16
Roberto Clemente		
3,000 Hitters		
20 Willie Mays	.10	.04
4 Homers in One Game		
24 Willie Mays	.40	.16
Whitey Ford		
Tom Tresh		
Friendly Foes UER		
Tresh is spelled Thresh		
26 Willie Mays	.25	.10
Dick Stuart		
Earl Wilson		
Spring Training		
27 Willie Mays	.25	.10
Warren Giles PRES		
Another MVP Season		
29 Willie Mays	.60	.24
Mickey Mantle		
30 Willie Mays	.60	.24
Stan Musial		
Pride of the N.L.		
31 Willie Mays	.25	.10
Roy Hofheinz OWN		
The Birthday Boy		
32 Willie Mays	.25	.10
Ernie Banks		
500 Home Run Hitters		
35 Willie Mays	.40	.16
Don Drysdale		
All-Stars		
38 Willie Mays	.25	.10
John Lindsay MAYOR		
Willie Mays Day		
39 Willie Mays	.60	.24
Queen Elizabeth		
Ronald Reagan		
Holding Court		
40 Willie Mays	.60	.24
Hank Aaron		
Home Run Kings		
42 Willie Mays	.10	.04
Santa		
43 Willie Mays	.25	.10
Mae Mays		
The Exhibit		
44 Willie Mays	.60	.24
Joe DiMaggio		
Baseball Immortals		
45 Willie Mays	.10	.04
Greatest of Them All		
46 Willie Mays	.60	.24
Mrs. Willie Mays		
Bill Cosby		
52 Willie Mays	.60	.24
Hank Aaron		

1967 Ashland Oil

This 12 card set measures 2" by 7 1/2" and the cards are unnumbered. Therefore, we have sequenced the cards in alphabetical order. Jim Maloney is considered tougher and is notated as a SP in the listings below.

	NM	Ex
COMPLETE SET	200.00	80.00
1 Jim Bunning	25.00	10.00
2 Elston Howard	15.00	6.00
3 Al Kaline	25.00	10.00
4 Harmon Killebrew	25.00	10.00
5 Ed Kranepool	10.00	4.00
6 Jim Maloney SP	50.00	20.00
7 Bill Mazeroski	20.00	8.00
8 Frank Robinson	25.00	10.00
9 Ron Santo	15.00	6.00
10 Joe Torre	20.00	8.00
11 Leon Wagner	10.00	4.00
12 Pete Ward	10.00	4.00

1965 Astros Jay Publishing

This 12-card set of the Houston Astros measures approximately 5" by 7". The fronts feature black-and-white posed player photos with the player's and team name printed below in the white border. These cards were packaged 12 to a packet. The backs are blank. The cards are unnumbered and checklisted below in alphabetical order. This was the debut season for Houston to be named the Astros.

	NM	Ex
COMPLETE SET (12)	20.00	8.00
1 Dave Adlesh	2.00	.80
2 Bob Aspromonte	2.00	.80
3 John Bateman	2.00	.80
4 Walt Bond	2.00	.80
5 Ron Brand	2.00	.80
6 Nellie Fox	6.00	2.40
7 Jerry Grote	2.00	.80
8 Sonny Jackson	2.00	.80
9 Eddie Kasko	2.00	.80
10 Bob Lillis	2.00	.80
11 Mike White	2.00	.80
12 Lum Harris MG	2.00	.80

1965 Astros Team Issue

These blank-back black and white photos measure 3 1/4" by 5 1/2". The photos are facsimile autographs on the bottom and we have sequenced them in alphabetical order. As this set was update during the season, we have many more than 25 players in our checklist.

	NM	Ex
COMPLETE SET	75.00	30.00
1 Jimmie Adair CO	3.00	1.20
2 Bob Aspromonte	4.00	1.60
3 John Bateman	3.00	1.20
4 Walt Bond	3.00	1.20
5 Bob Bruce	3.00	1.20
6 Jim Busby CO	3.00	1.20
7 Danny Coombs	3.00	1.20
8 Larry Dierker	5.00	2.00
9 Dick Farrell	3.00	1.20
10 Nellie Fox CO	15.00	6.00
11 Joe Gaines	3.00	1.20
12 Dave Giusti	4.00	1.60
13 Luman Harris MG	3.00	1.20
14 Eddie Kasko	3.00	1.20
15 Bob Lillis	3.00	1.20
16 Ken Mackenzie	3.00	1.20
17 Joe Morgan	10.00	4.00
18 Don Nottebart	3.00	1.20
19 Jim Owens	3.00	1.20
20 Howie Pollet CO	3.00	1.20
21 Gene Ratliff	3.00	1.20
22 Claude Raymond	3.00	1.20
23 Rusty Staub	8.00	3.20
24 Jim Wynn	6.00	2.40
25 Hal Woodeshick	3.00	1.20

1967 Astros

These 30 blank-backed cards are irregularly cut, but most measure approximately 1 1/4" by 2". They feature white bordered black-and-white posed player photos and carry the player's name and position in black lettering within the lower white margin. The backs are blank. The cards are unnumbered and checklisted below in alphabetical order.

	NM	Ex
COMPLETE SET (30)	60.00	24.00
1 Dave Adlesh	2.00	.80
2 Bob Aspromonte	2.50	1.00
3 John Bateman	2.00	.80
4 Wade Blasingame	2.00	.80
5 John Buzhardt	2.00	.80
6 Danny Coombs	2.00	.80
7 Mike Cuellar	3.00	1.20
8 Ron Davis	2.00	.80
9 Larry Dierker	4.00	1.60
10 Dave Giusti	2.50	1.00
11 Fred Gladding	2.00	.80
12 Julio Gotay	2.00	.80
13 Buddy Hancken CO	2.00	.80
14 Grady Hatton MG	2.00	.80
15 Hal King	2.00	.80
16 Denny Lemaster	2.00	.80
17 Mel McGaha CO	2.00	.80
18 Denis Menke	2.00	.80
19 Norm Miller	2.00	.80
20 Joe Morgan	10.00	4.00
21 Ivan Murrell	2.00	.80
22 Jim Owens CO	2.00	.80
23 Salty Parker CO	2.00	.80
24 Doug Rader	3.00	1.20
25 Jim Ray	2.00	.80
26 Rusty Staub	6.00	2.40
27 Lee Thomas	2.00	.80
28 Hector Torres	2.00	.80
29 Don Wilson	3.00	1.20
30 Jimmy Wynn	4.00	1.60

1967 Astros Team Issue

These cards, which measure just slightly shorter than standard postcards, feature members of the 1967 Houston Astros. These cards have the player's name, position and Houston Astros (in all caps) at the bottom of the white borders. Since these cards are unnumbered, we have sequenced them in alphabetical order.

	NM	Ex
COMPLETE SET	40.00	16.00
1 Bob Aspromonte	1.50	.60
2 Lee Bales	1.00	.40
3 John Bateman	1.00	.40
4 Ron Brand	1.00	.40
5 Bo Belinsky	1.50	.60
6 Mike Cuellar	2.00	.80
7 Ron Davis	1.00	.40
8 Larry Dierker	2.50	1.00
9 Dick Farrell	1.00	.40
10 Dave Giusti	1.00	.40
11 Chuck Harrison	1.00	.40
12 Grady Hatton MG	1.00	.40
13 Bill Heath	1.00	.40
14 Sonny Jackson	1.00	.40
15 Jim Landis	1.00	.40
16 Bob Lillis	1.00	.40
17 Barry Latman	1.00	.40
18 Ed Mathews	5.00	2.00
19 Joe Morgan	8.00	3.20
20 Aaron Pointer	1.00	.40
21 Claude Raymond	1.00	.40
22 Carroll Sembera	1.00	.40
23 Dan Schneider	1.00	.40
24 Rusty Staub	3.00	1.20
25 Don Wilson	2.00	.80
26 Jim Wynn	1.50	.60
27 Chris Zachary	1.00	.40

1967 Astros Team Issue 12

This 12-card team-issued set features the 1967 Houston Astros. The cards measure approximately 2 1/2" by 3" and show signs of perforation on their sides. The reason for the perforations were that the they were issued as a perforated sheet and sold at Astrodome souvenir stands. The posed color player photos have white borders and a facsimile autograph inscribed across them. The horizontally oriented backs have biography and career summary information on a yellow background, and complete statistics. The cards are unnumbered and checklisted below in alphabetical order. This set was available for $1 direct from the Astros.

	NM	Ex
COMPLETE SET (12)	75.00	30.00
1 Bob Aspromonte	5.00	2.00
2 John Bateman	3.00	1.20
3 Mike Cuellar	6.00	2.40
4 Larry Dierker	6.00	2.40
5 Dave Giusti	5.00	2.00
6 Grady Hatton MG	3.00	1.20
7 Bill Heath	3.00	1.20
8 Sonny Jackson	3.00	1.20
9 Eddie Mathews	25.00	10.00
10 Joe Morgan	25.00	10.00
11 Rusty Staub	8.00	3.20
12 Jim Wynn	8.00	3.20

1970 Astros Photos

These photos feature members of the 1970 Houston Astros. The photos are unnumbered and we have sequenced them in alphabetical order. A photo of Cesar Cedeno in his rookie season is included in this set.

	NM	Ex
COMPLETE SET	20.00	8.00
1 Jack Billingham	.50	.20
2 Cesar Cedeno	1.50	.60
3 Ron Cook	.50	.20
4 George Culver	.50	.20
5 Larry Dierker	1.00	.40
6 Jack DiLauro	.50	.20
7 John Edwards	.50	.20
8 Ken Forsch	.75	.30
9 Fred Gladding	.50	.20
10 Tommy Helms	.50	.20
11 Larry Howard	.50	.20
12 Keith Lampard	.50	.20
13 Denny LeMaster	.50	.20
14 Marty Martinez	.50	.20
15 John Mayberry	.75	.30
16 Denis Menke	.50	.20
17 Roger Metzger	.50	.20
18 Jesus Alou	.75	.30
19 Norm Miller	.50	.20
20 Joe Morgan	4.00	1.60
21 Doug Rader	1.00	.40
22 Jim Ray	.50	.20
23 Hector Torres	.50	.20
24 Harry Walker MG	.50	.20
25 Bob Watson	1.00	.40
26 Bob Watson	1.00	.40
27 Don Wilson	.50	.20
28 Jim Wynn	1.00	.40
29 Jim York	.50	.20

1970 Astros Team Issue

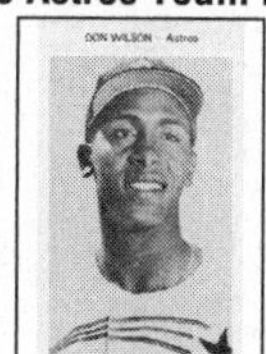

This 12-card set of the Houston Astros measures approximately 4 1/4" by 7". The fronts display black-and-white player portraits bordered in white. The player's name and team are printed in the top margin. The backs are blank. The cards are unnumbered and checklisted below in alphabetical order.

	NM	Ex
COMPLETE SET (10)	20.00	8.00
1 Tommy Davis	2.00	.80
2 Larry Dierker	2.00	.80
3 John Edwards	1.00	.40
4 Fred Gladding	1.00	.40
5 Tom Griffin	1.00	.40
6 Denny Lemaster	1.00	.40
7 Denis Menke	1.00	.40
8 Joe Morgan	5.00	2.00
9 Joe Pepitone	1.50	.60
10 Doug Rader	1.50	.60
11 Don Wilson	1.50	.60
12 Jim Wynn	2.00	.80

1971 Astros Coke

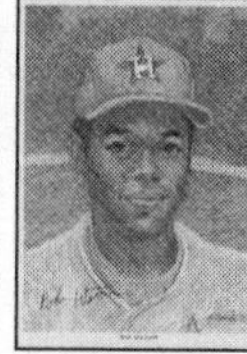

Sponsored by the Houston Coca-Cola Bottling Company, these twelve photos measure approximately 8" by 11" and feature artwork depicting Houston Astro players against stadium backgrounds. The pictures have white borders. A facsimile autograph is printed in black on the picture. The horizontal backs show a pale blue tinted photo of the Astrodome, with player biographical information, statistics and career highlights printed in darker blue over the photo. At the top are the Coca-Cola emblem and slogan. The photos are unnumbered and checklisted below in alphabetical order. Wade Blasingame and Jimmy Wynn are considered to be in shorter supply than the other cards and have been marked with SP in the checklist.

	NM	Ex
COMPLETE SET(12)	50.00	20.00
COMMON CARD (1-12)	2.00	.80
COMMON SP	10.00	4.00
1 Jesus Alou	2.50	1.00
2 Wade Blasingame SP	10.00	4.00
3 Cesar Cedeno	4.00	1.60
4 Larry Dierker	3.00	1.20
5 John Edwards	2.00	.80
6 Denis Menke	2.00	.80
7 Roger Metzger	2.00	.80
8 Joe Morgan	10.00	4.00
9 Doug Rader	2.50	1.00
10 Bob Watson	3.00	1.20
11 Don Wilson	2.00	.80
12 Jim Wynn SP	15.00	6.00

1971 Astros Team Issue

This 24-card set measures approximately 3 1/2" by 5 3/8" and features black-and-white player portraits in a white border. A facsimile autograph is printed across the bottom of the picture. The backs are blank. The cards are unnumbered and checklisted below in alphabetical order.

	NM	Ex
COMPLETE SET (24)	15.00	6.00
1 Wade Blasingame	.50	.20
2 Cesar Cedeno	1.50	.60
3 Rich Chiles	.50	.20
4 George Culver	.50	.20
5 Larry Dierker	1.00	.40
6 John Edwards	.50	.20
7 Ken Forsch	.75	.30
8 Fred Gladding	.50	.20
9 Tom Griffin	.50	.20
10 Buddy Harris	.50	.20
11 Buddy Hancken CO	.50	.20
12 Jack Hiatt	.50	.20
13 Larry Howard	.50	.20
14 Hub Kittle CO	.50	.20
15 Roger Metzger	.75	.30
16 Joe Morgan	3.00	1.20
17 Jim Owens CO	.50	.20
18 Salty Parker CO	.50	.20
19 Doug Rader	.75	.30
20 Jim Ray	.50	.20
21 Harry Walker MG	.75	.30
22 Bob Watson	1.00	.40
23 Don Wilson	.75	.30
24 Jim Wynn	1.00	.40

1972 Astros Team Issue

This 30-card set of the 1972 Houston Astros measures approximately 3 1/2" by 5" and features black-and-white player portraits with white borders. A facsimile autographed is printed across the bottom of the photo. The backs are blank. The cards are unnumbered and checklisted below in alphabetical order.

	NM	Ex
COMPLETE SET (30)	15.00	6.00
1 Jesus Alou	.75	.30
2 Wade Blasingame	.50	.20
3 Cesar Cedeno	1.50	.60
4 George Culver	.50	.20
5 Larry Dierker	1.00	.40
6 John Edwards	.50	.20
7 Robert Fenwick	.50	.20
8 Ken Forsch	.50	.20
9 Fred Gladding	.50	.20
10 Tom Griffin	.50	.20
11 Buddy Hancken CO	.50	.20
12 Tommy Helms	.50	.20
13 Jack Hiatt	.50	.20
14 Hub Kittle CO	.50	.20
15 Lee May	.75	.30
16 Roger Metzger	.50	.20
17 Norm Miller	.50	.20
18 Jim Owens CO	.50	.20
19 Salty Parker CO	.50	.20
20 Doug Rader	.75	.30
21 Jim Ray	.50	.20
22 Jerry Reuss	1.00	.40
23 Dave Roberts	.50	.20
24 Jim Stewart	.50	.20
25 Bob Stinson	.50	.20
26 Harry Walker MG	.50	.20
27 Bob Watson	1.00	.40
28 Don Wilson	.75	.30
29 Jim Wynn	1.00	.40
30 Jim York	.50	.20

1975 Astros Postcards

These photos were issued and featured members of the 1975 Houston Astros. They are unnumbered and we have sequenced them in alphabetical order.

	NM	Ex
COMPLETE SET	15.00	6.00
1 Rob Andrews	.50	.20
2 Rafael Batista	.50	.20
3 Ken Boswell	.50	.20
4 Enos Cabell	.50	.20
5 Cesar Cedeno	1.50	.60
6 Jose Cruz	.75	.30
7 Larry Dierker	1.00	.40
8 Mike Easler	.75	.30
9 Ken Forsch	.50	.20
10 Preston Gomez MG	.50	.20
11 Wayne Granger	.50	.20
12 Tom Griffin	.50	.20
13 Greg Gross	.50	.20
14 Tommy Helms	.50	.20
15 Wilbur Howard	.50	.20
16 Cliff Johnson	.50	.20
17 Skip Jutze	.50	.20
18 Hub Kittle CO	.50	.20
19 Doug Konieczny	.50	.20
20 Bob Lillis CO	.50	.20
21 Milt May	.50	.20
22 Roger Metzger	.50	.20
23 Larry Milbourne	.50	.20
24 Doug Rader	.50	.20
25 J.R. Richard	1.00	.40
26 Dave Roberts	.50	.20
27 Fred Scherman	.50	.20
28 Bob Watson	1.00	.40
29 Jim Williams	.50	.20
30 Jim York	.50	.20

1976 Astros Post Dierker

This one-card set was distributed by the Houston Post and honors Larry Dierker's no hitter.

	NM	Ex
1 Larry Dierker	5.00	2.00

1976 Astros Postcards

This 32-card set of the Houston Astros features player photos on postcard-size cards. The cards are unnumbered and checklisted below in alphabetical order.

	NM	Ex
COMPLETE SET (32)	15.00	6.00
1 Joaquin Andujar	.75	.30
2 Mike Barlow	.50	.20
3 Ken Boswell	.50	.20
4 Enos Cabell	.50	.20
5 Cesar Cedeno	.75	.30
6 Mike Cosgrove	.50	.20
7 Jose Cruz	1.00	.40
8 Larry Dierker	1.00	.40
9 Jerry DaVanon	.50	.20
10 Ken Forsch	.50	.20
11 Tom Griffin	.50	.20
12 Greg Gross	.50	.20
13 Larry Hardy	.50	.20
14 Wilbur Howard	.50	.20
15 Art Howe	1.50	.60
16 Cliff Johnson	.75	.30
17 Deacon Jones CO	.50	.20
18 Skip Jutze	.50	.20
19 Bob Lillis CO	.50	.20
20 Joe McIntosh	.50	.20
21 Roger Metzger	.50	.20
22 Larry Milbourne	.50	.20
23 Joe Niekro	1.00	.40
24 Tony Pacheco	.50	.20
25 Gene Pentz	.50	.20
26 J.R. Richard	1.00	.40
27 Leon Roberts	.50	.20
28 Gil Rondon	.50	.20
29 Jose Sosa	.50	.20
30 Bill Virdon MG	.50	.20
31 Bob Watson	1.00	.40
32 Mel Wright CO	.50	.20

1978 Astros Burger King

The cards in this 23-card set measure 2 1/2" by 3 1/2". Released in local Houston Burger King outlets during the 1978 season, this Houston Astros series contains the standard 22 numbered player cards and one unnumbered checklist. The player poses found to differ from the regular Topps issue are marked with asterisks.

	NM	Ex
COMPLETE SET (23)	16.00	6.50
1 Bill Virdon MG	1.00	.40
2 Joe Ferguson	.50	.20
3 Ed Herrmann	.50	.20
4 J.R. Richard	1.50	.60
5 Joe Niekro	1.00	.40
6 Floyd Bannister	.75	.30
7 Joaquin Andujar	1.50	.60
8 Ken Forsch	.50	.20
9 Mark Lemongello	.50	.20
10 Joe Sambito	.50	.20
11 Gene Pentz	.50	.20
12 Bob Watson	1.50	.60
13 Julio Gonzalez	.50	.20
14 Enos Cabell	.75	.30
15 Roger Metzger	.50	.20
16 Art Howe	1.00	.40
17 Jose Cruz	1.50	.60
18 Cesar Cedeno	1.50	.60
19 Terry Puhl	.75	.30
20 Wilbur Howard	.50	.20
21 Dave Bergman *	.75	.30
22 Jesus Alou *	.75	.30
NNO Checklist Card TP	.25	.10

1978 Astros Postcards

These postcards feature members of the 1978 Houston Astros. They are unnumbered and we have ordered them alphabetically.

	NM	Ex
COMPLETE SET	15.00	6.00
1 Jesus Alou	.50	.20
2 Joaquin Andujar	.50	.20
3 Floyd Bannister	.50	.20
4 Dave Bergman	.50	.20
5 Enos Cabell	.50	.20
6 Cesar Cedeno	1.00	.40
7 Jose Cruz	.75	.30
8 Tom Dixon	.50	.20
9 Ken Forsch	.50	.20
10 Julio Gonzalez	.50	.20
11 Wilbur Howard	.50	.20
12 Art Howe	1.00	.40
13 Deacon Jones CO	.50	.20
14 Rafael Landestoy	.50	.20
15 Mark Lemongello	.50	.20
16 Bob Lillis CO	.50	.20
17 Tony Pacheco CO	.50	.20
18 Terry Puhl	.50	.20
19 Luis Pujols	.50	.20
20 Joe Niekro	.75	.30
21 J. R. Richard	1.00	.40
22 Joe Sambito	.75	.30
23 Jimmy Sexton	.75	.30
24 Bill Virdon MG	.50	.20
25 Dennis Walling	.50	.20
26 Bob Watson	1.00	.40
27 Rick Williams	.50	.20
28 Mel Wright CO	.50	.20

1979 Astros Postcards

These 4" by 5" postcards feature members of the 1979 Houston Astros. They are unnumbered and sequenced them in alphabetical order.

	NM	Ex
COMPLETE SET	15.00	6.00
1 Jesus Alou	.50	.20
2 Joaquin Andujar	.50	.20
3 Alan Ashby	.50	.20
4 Bruce Bochy	.50	.20
5 Enos Cabell	.50	.20
6 Cedar Cedeno	.75	.30
7 Jose Cruz	.75	.30
8 Tom Dixon	.50	.20
9 Ken Forsch	.50	.20
10 Julio Gonzalez	.50	.20
11 Art Howe	.75	.30
12 Rafael Landestoy	.50	.20
13 Jeff Leonard	.50	.20
14 Bo McLaughlin	.50	.20
15 Joe Niekro	.75	.30
16 Randy Niemann	.50	.20
17 Terry Puhl	.50	.20
18 Craig Reynolds	.50	.20
19 Frank Riccelli	.50	.20
20 J.R. Richard	1.00	.40
21 Bert Roberge	.50	.20
22 Vern Ruhle	.50	.20
23 Joe Sambito	.50	.20
24 Jimmy Sexton	.75	.30
25 Bill Virdon MG	.50	.20
26 Denny Walling	.50	.20
27 Bob Watson	1.00	.40
28 Gary Wilson	.50	.20

1980 Astros Team Issue

Measuring 4" by 5", these dull finish cards had a limited distribution. Since they are unnumbered we have sequenced them in alphabetical order.

	NM	Ex
COMPLETE SET	20.00	8.00
1 Joaquin Andujar	.50	.20
2 Alan Ashby	.50	.20
3 Dave Bergman	.50	.20
4 Bruce Bochy	.50	.20
5 Enos Cabell	.50	.20
6 Cesar Cedeno	1.00	.40
7 Jose Cruz	.75	.30
8 Ken Forsch	.50	.20
9 Julio Gonzales	.50	.20
10 Danny Heep	.50	.20
11 Art Howe	.75	.30
12 Deacon Jones CO	.50	.20
13 Frank LaCorte	.50	.20
14 Rafael Landestoy	.50	.20
15 Bob Lillis CO	.50	.20
16 Don Leppert CO	.50	.20
17 Joe Morgan	2.00	.80
18 Joe Niekro	.75	.30
19 Gordon Pladson	.50	.20
20 Terry Puhl	.50	.20
21 Craig Reynolds	.50	.20
22 J.R. Richard	1.00	.40
23 Bert Roberge	.50	.20
24 Nolan Ryan	4.00	1.60
25 Joe Sambito	.50	.20
26 Dave Smith	1.00	.40
27 Bill Virdon MG	.50	.20
28 Denny Walling	.50	.20
29 Mel Wright CO	.50	.20

1981 Astros Postcards

These 30 postcards were issued and featured members of the playoff bound 1981 Houston Astros. They are unnumbered and we have sequenced them in alphabetical order.

	Nm-Mt	Ex-Mt
COMPLETE SET	20.00	8.00
1 Alan Ashby	.50	.20
2 Cesar Cedeno	.75	.30
3 Jose Cruz	.75	.30
4 Kiko Garcia	.50	.20
5 Danny Heep	.50	.20
6 Art Howe	.75	.30
7 Mike Ivie	.50	.20
8 Deacon Jones CO	.50	.20
9 Bob Knepper	.50	.20
10 Frank LaCorte	.50	.20
11 Don Leppert CO	.50	.20
12 Bob Lillis CO	.50	.20
13 Joe Niekro	.75	.30
14 Joe Pittman	.50	.20
15 Terry Puhl	.50	.20
16 Luis Pujols	.50	.01
17 Craig Reynolds	.50	.20
18 J.R. Richard	1.00	.40
19 Dave Roberts	.50	.20
20 Vern Ruhle	.50	.20
21 Nolan Ryan	5.00	2.00
22 Joe Sambito	.50	.20
23 Dave Smith	.75	.30
24 Bobby Sprowl	.50	.20
25 Don Sutton	1.50	.60
26 Dickie Thon	.50	.20
27 Bill Virdon MG	.50	.20
28 Denny Walling	.50	.20
29 Gary Woods	.50	.20
30 Mel Wright CO	.50	.20

1982 Astros Postcards

These postcards feature members of the 1982 Houston Astros. They are unnumbered and we have sequenced them in alphabetical order.

	Nm-Mt	Ex-Mt
COMPLETE SET	15.00	6.00
1 Alan Ashby	.50	.20
2 Jose Cruz	.75	.30
3 Kiko Garcia	.50	.20
4 Phil Garner	.50	.20
5 Danny Heep	.50	.20
6 Art Howe	.75	.30
7 Deacon Jones CO	.50	.20
8 Bob Knepper	.50	.20
9 Alan Knicely	.50	.20
10 Ray Knight	.50	.20
11 Mike LaCoss	.50	.20
12 Frank LaCorte	.50	.20
13 Don Leppert CO	.50	.20
14 Bob Lillis MG	.50	.20
15 Randy Moffitt	.50	.20
16 Joe Niekro	.75	.30
17 Terry Puhl	.50	.20
18 Luis Pujols	.50	.20
19 Craig Reynolds	.50	.20
20 J.R. Richard	.75	.30
21 Vern Ruhle	.50	.20
22 Nolan Ryan	5.00	2.00
23 Joe Sambito	.50	.20
24 Tony Scott	.50	.20
25 Harry Spilman	.50	.20
26 Dave Smith	.50	.20
27 Dickie Thon	.50	.20
28 Denny Walling	.50	.20
29 Mel Wright CO	.50	.20

1983 Astros Postcards

These postcards feature members of the 1983 Houston Astros. They are unnumbered and we have sequenced them in alphabetical order.

	Nm-Mt	Ex-Mt
COMPLETE SET	20.00	8.00
1 Alan Ashby	.50	.20
2 Kevin Bass	.50	.20
3 Jose Cruz	.75	.30
4 Bill Dawley	.50	.20
5 Cot Deal CO	.50	.20
6 Frank DiPino	.50	.20
7 Bill Doran	.75	.30
8 Phil Garner	.50	.20
9 Art Howe	.75	.30
10 Bob Knepper	.50	.20
11 Ray Knight	.50	.20
12 Frank LaCorte	.50	.20
13 Mike LaCoss	.50	.20
14 Don Leppert CO	.50	.20
15 Bob Lillis MG	.50	.20
16 Mike Madden	.50	.20
17 Denis Menke CO	.50	.20
18 Omar Moreno	.50	.20
19 Les Moss CO	.50	.20
20 Joe Niekro	.75	.30
21 Terry Puhl	.50	.20
22 Luis Pujols	.50	.20
23 Craig Reynolds	.50	.20
24 Vern Ruhle	.50	.20
25 Nolan Ryan	5.00	2.00
26 Joe Sambito	.50	.20
27 Mike Scott	1.00	.40
28 Tony Scott	.50	.20
29 Dave Smith	.50	.20
30 Julio Solano	.50	.20
31 Harry Spilman	.50	.20
32 Dickie Thon	.50	.20
33 Tim Tolman	.50	.20
34 Jerry Walker CO	.50	.20
35 Denny Walling	.50	.20

1984 Astros Mother's

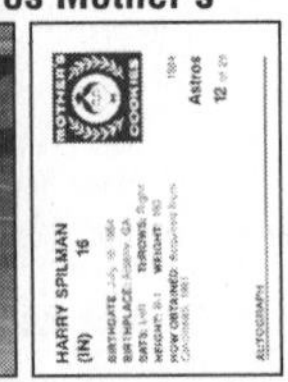

The cards in this 28-card set measure 2 1/2" by 3 1/2". In 1984, the Los Angeles based Mother's Cookies Co. issued five sets of cards featuring players from major league teams. The Houston Astros set features current players depicted by photos. Similar to their 1952 and 1953 issues, the cards have rounded corners. The backs of the cards contain the Mother's Cookies logo. The cards were distributed in partial sets to fans at the respective stadiums of the teams involved. Whereas 20 cards were given to each patron, a redemption card, redeemable for eight more cards was included. Unfortunately, the eight cards received by redeeming the coupon were not necessarily the eight needed to complete a set. Hobbyist Barry Colla was involved in the production of these sets.

	Nm-Mt	Ex-Mt
COMPLETE SET (28)	18.00	7.25
1 Nolan Ryan	10.00	4.00
2 Joe Niekro	.75	.30
3 Alan Ashby	.25	.10
4 Bill Doran	.75	.30
5 Phil Garner	.25	.10
6 Ray Knight	.25	.10
7 Dickie Thon	.25	.10
8 Jose Cruz	1.00	.40
9 Jerry Mumphrey	.25	.10
10 Terry Puhl	.50	.20
11 Enos Cabell	.25	.10
12 Harry Spilman	.50	.20
13 Dave Smith	.50	.20
14 Mike Scott	1.00	.40
15 Bob Lillis MG	.25	.10
16 Bob Knepper	.25	.10
17 Frank DiPino	.25	.10
18 Tom Wieghaus	.25	.10
19 Denny Walling	.25	.10
20 Tony Scott	.25	.10
21 Alan Bannister	.25	.10
22 Bill Dawley	.25	.10
23 Vern Ruhle	.25	.10
24 Mike LaCoss	.25	.10
25 Mike Madden	.25	.10
26 Craig Reynolds	.25	.10
27 Cot Deal CO Don Leppert CO Denis Menke CO Les Moss CO Jerry Walker CO	.50	.20
28 Astros Logo CL	.25	.10

1984 Astros Postcards

These postcards feature members of the 1984 Astros. They are unnumbered so we have sequenced them in alphabetical order.

	Nm-Mt	Ex-Mt
COMPLETE SET	20.00	8.00
1 Alan Ashby	.50	.20
2 Mark Bailey	.50	.20
3 Kevin Bass	.50	.20
4 Enos Cabell	.50	.20
5 Jose Cruz	.75	.30
6 Bill Dawley	.50	.20
7 Cot Deal CO	.50	.20
8 Frank DiPino	.50	.20
9 Bill Doran	.75	.30
10 Phil Garner	.50	.20
11 Bob Knepper	.50	.20
12 Ray Knight	.50	.20
13 Mike LaCoss	.50	.20
14 Don Leppert CO	.50	.20
15 Bob Lillis MG	.50	.20
16 Mike Madden	.50	.20
17 Denis Menke CO	.50	.20
18 Les Moss CO	.50	.20
19 Jerry Mumphrey	.50	.20
20 Joe Niekro	.75	.30
21 Terry Puhl	.50	.20
22 Craig Reynolds	.50	.20
23 Vern Ruhle	.50	.20
24 Nolan Ryan	5.00	2.00
25 Joe Sambito	.50	.20
26 Mike Scott	1.00	.40
27 Dave Smith	.50	.20
28 Julio Solano	.50	.20
29 Harry Spilman	.50	.20
30 Dickie Thon	.50	.20
31 Jerry Walker CO	.50	.20
32 Denny Walling	.50	.20

1985 Astros Mother's

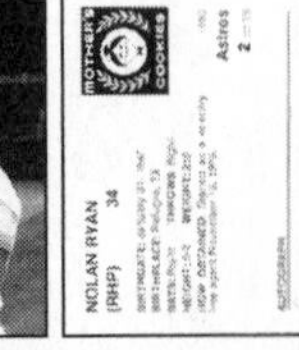

The cards in this 28-card set measure 2 1/2" by 3 1/2". In 1985, the Los Angeles-based Mother's Cookies Co. again issued five sets of cards featuring players from major league teams. The Houston Astros set features current players depicted by photos on cards with rounded corners. The backs of the cards contain the Mother's Cookies logo. Cards were passed out at the stadium on July 13. The checklist card features the Astros logo on the obverse.

	Nm-Mt	Ex-Mt
COMPLETE SET (28)	12.00	4.80
1 Bob Lillis MG	.25	.10
2 Nolan Ryan	8.00	3.20
3 Phil Garner	.25	.10
4 Jose Cruz	1.00	.40
5 Denny Walling	.25	.10
6 Joe Niekro	.75	.30
7 Terry Puhl	.50	.20
8 Bill Doran	.25	.10
9 Dickie Thon	.25	.10
10 Enos Cabell	.25	.10
11 Frank DiPino	.25	.10
12 Julio Solano	.25	.10
13 Alan Ashby	.25	.10
14 Craig Reynolds	.25	.10
15 Jerry Mumphrey	.25	.10
16 Bill Dawley	.25	.10
17 Mark Bailey	.25	.10
18 Mike Scott	1.00	.40
19 Harry Spilman	.25	.10
20 Bob Knepper	.25	.10
21 Dave Smith	.50	.20
22 Kevin Bass	.25	.10
23 Tim Tolman	.25	.10
24 Jeff Calhoun	.25	.10
25 Jim Pankovits	.25	.10
26 Ron Mathis	.25	.10
27 Cot Deal CO Matt Galante CO Don Leppert CO Denis Menke CO Jerry Walker CO	.50	.20
28 Astros Logo CL	.25	.10

1985 Astros Postcards

These black and white blank-backed postcards were issued by the Houston Astros and feature members of the 1985 Astros. Since these photos are unnumbered, we have sequenced them in alphabetical order.

	Nm-Mt	Ex-Mt
COMPLETE SET	20.00	8.00
1 Alan Ashby	.50	.20
2 Mark Bailey	.50	.20
3 Kevin Bass	.50	.20
4 Jeff Calhoun	.50	.20
5 Jose Cruz	.75	.30
6 Bill Dawley	.50	.20
7 Cot Deal CO	.50	.20
8 Frank DiPino	.50	.20
9 Bill Doran	.50	.20
10 Matt Galante CO	.50	.20
11 Phil Garner	.50	.20
12 Chris Jones	.50	.20
13 Bob Knepper	.50	.20
14 Bob Lillis MG	.50	.20
15 Mike Madden	.50	.20
16 Ron Mathis	.50	.20
17 Denis Menke CO	.50	.20
18 Les Moss CO	.50	.20
19 Jerry Mumphrey	.50	.20

Card	Nm-Mt	Ex-Mt
20 Joe Niekro	.75	.30
21 Jim Pankovits	.50	.20
22 Bert Pena	.50	.20
23 Terry Puhl	.50	.20
24 Craig Reynolds	.50	.20
25 Mike Richardt	.50	.20
26 Nolan Ryan	5.00	2.00
27 Mike Scott	1.00	.40
28 Dave Smith	.75	.30
29 Harry Spilman	.50	.20
30 Dickie Thon	.50	.20
31 Jerry Walker CO	.50	.20
32 Denny Walling	.50	.20

1986 Astros Greats TCMA

This 12-card standard-size set features some of the best Astros players since their inception in 1962. The cards feature a player photo on the front. Player information as well as statistics are on the back.

	Nm-Mt	Ex-Mt
COMPLETE SET (12)	5.00	2.00
1 Bob Watson	.75	.30
2 Joe Morgan	2.00	.80
3 Roger Metzger	.25	.10
4 Doug Rader	.25	.10
5 Jimmy Wynn	.75	.30
6 Cesar Cedeno	.75	.30
7 Rusty Staub	1.00	.40
8 Johnny Edwards	.25	.10
9 J.R. Richard	.50	.20
10 Dave Roberts	.25	.10
11 Fred Gladding	.25	.10
12 Bill Virdon MG	.25	.10

1986 Astros Miller Lite

This 22 card set measures 4 1/2" by 6 3/4" and was issued at Astros games. The Nolan Ryan card was not issued at games and is considered a short print as supplies of the card are very limited. The complete set price does include the Ryan card.

	Nm-Mt	Ex-Mt
COMPLETE SET (21)	25.00	10.00
1 Alan Ashby	1.00	.40
2 Mark Bailey	1.00	.40
3 Kevin Bass	1.00	.40
4 Jose Cruz	2.50	1.00
5 Glenn Davis	1.50	.60
6 Jim Deshaies	1.00	.40
7 Frank DiPino	1.00	.40
8 Bill Doran	1.00	.40
9 Phil Garner	1.00	.40
10 Billy Hatcher	1.00	.40
11 Charlie Kerfeld	1.00	.40
12 Bob Knepper	1.00	.40
13 Hal Lanier MG	1.00	.40
14 Mike Madden	1.00	.40
15 Jim Pankovits	1.00	.40
16 Terry Puhl	1.50	.60
17 Craig Reynolds	1.00	.40
18 Nolan Ryan SP	200.00	80.00
19 Mike Scott	2.50	1.00
20 Dave Smith	1.50	.60
21 Dickie Thon	1.00	.40
22 Denny Walling	1.00	.40

1986 Astros Mother's

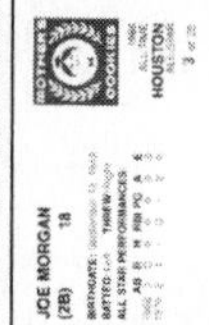

This set consists of 28 full-color, rounded-corner standard-size cards. Starter sets (only 20 cards but also including a certificate for eight more cards) were given out at the ballpark and collectors were encouraged to trade to fill in the rest of their set. Cards were originally given out at the Astrodome on July 10th. Since the 1986 All-Star Game was held in Houston, the set features Astro All-Stars since 1962 as painted by artist Richard Wallich. The set numbering is essentially chronological according to when each player was selected for the All-Star Game as an Astro.

	Nm-Mt	Ex-Mt
COMPLETE SET (28)	12.00	4.80
1 Dick Farrell	.25	.10
2 Hal Woodeshick	.25	.10
3 Joe Morgan	2.00	.80
4 Claude Raymond	.25	.10
5 Mike Cuellar	.50	.20
6 Rusty Staub	1.00	.40
7 Jimmy Wynn	.75	.30
8 Larry Dierker	.75	.30
9 Denis Menke	.25	.10
10 Don Wilson	.25	.10
11 Cesar Cedeno	.50	.20
12 Lee May	.50	.20
13 Bob Watson	1.00	.40
14 Ken Forsch	.25	.10
15 Joaquin Andujar	.25	.10
16 Terry Puhl	.50	.20
17 Joe Niekro	.75	.30
18 Craig Reynolds	.25	.10
19 Joe Sambito	.25	.10
20 Jose Cruz	1.00	.40
21 J.R. Richard	.75	.30
22 Bob Knepper	.25	.10
23 Nolan Ryan	8.00	3.20
24 Ray Knight	.25	.10
25 Bill Dawley	.25	.10
26 Dickie Thon	.25	.10
27 Jerry Mumphrey	.25	.10
28 Astros Logo CL	.25	.10

1986 Astros Police

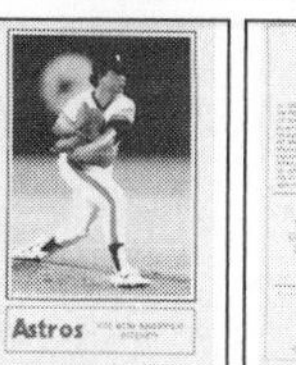

This 26-card safety set was also sponsored by Kool-Aid. The backs contain a biographical paragraph above a "Tip from the Dugout". The front features a full-color photo of the player, his name, and uniform number. The cards are numbered on the back and measure approximately 2 5/8" by 4 1/8". The backs are printed in orange and blue on white card stock. Sets were distributed at the Astrodome on June 14th as well as given away throughout the summer by the Houston Police.

	Nm-Mt	Ex-Mt
COMPLETE SET (26)	8.00	3.20
1 Jim Pankovits	.25	.10
2 Nolan Ryan	4.00	1.60
3 Mike Scott	1.00	.40
4 Kevin Bass	.25	.10
5 Bill Doran	.25	.10
6 Hal Lanier MG	.25	.10
7 Denny Walling	.25	.10
8 Alan Ashby	.25	.10
9 Phil Garner	.25	.10
10 Charlie Kerfeld	.25	.10
11 Dave Smith	.50	.20
12 Jose Cruz	1.00	.40
13 Craig Reynolds	.25	.10
14 Mark Bailey	.25	.10
15 Bob Knepper	.25	.10
16 Julio Solano	.25	.10
17 Dickie Thon	.25	.10
18 Mike Madden	.25	.10
19 Jeff Calhoun	.25	.10
20 Tony Walker	.25	.10
21 Terry Puhl	.50	.20
22 Glenn Davis	.75	.30
23 Billy Hatcher	.25	.10
24 Jim Deshaies	.25	.10
25 Frank DiPino	.25	.10
26 Gene Tenace CO	.75	.30
Matt Galante CO		
Denis Menke CO		
Yogi Berra CO		
Les Moss CO		

1986 Astros Postcards

These blank-backed black and white postcards feature members of the division champion 1986 Houston Astros. The fronts have a posed portrait with the players name at the bottom. Since these are unnumbered, we have sequenced them in alphabetical order.

	Nm-Mt	Ex-Mt
COMPLETE SET	20.00	8.00
1 Larry Andersen	.50	.20
2 Alan Ashby	.50	.20
3 Kevin Bass	.50	.20
4 Yogi Berra CO	2.00	.80
5 Jeff Calhoun	.50	.20
6 Jose Cruz	.75	.30
7 Danny Darwin	.50	.20
8 Jim Deshaies	.50	.20
9 Glenn Davis	.75	.30
10 Bill Doran	.50	.20
11 Dan Driessen	.50	.20
12 Ty Gainey	.50	.20
13 Matt Galante CO	.50	.20
14 Phil Garner	.50	.20
15 Billy Hatcher	.50	.20
16 Charlie Kerfeld	.50	.20
17 Bob Knepper	.50	.20
18 Hal Lanier MG	.50	.20
19 Davey Lopes	.75	.30
20 Aurelio Lopez	.50	.20
21 Denis Menke CO	.50	.20
22 Les Moss CO	.50	.20
23 Jim Pankovits	.50	.20
24 Terry Puhl	.50	.20
25 Craig Reynolds	.50	.20
26 Nolan Ryan	5.00	2.00
27 Mike Scott	1.00	.40
28 Dave Smith	.75	.30
29 Dickie Thon	.50	.20
30 Gene Tenace	.75	.30
31 Tony Walker	.50	.20
32 Denny Walling	.50	.20

1986 Astros Team Issue

These 16 blank-backed photos feature members of the Division Winner '86 Astros. These photos measure 6" by 9" and have full-color photos and a facsimile signature. The photos are unnumbered and we have checklisted them in alphabetical order.

	Nm-Mt	Ex-Mt
COMPLETE SET (16)	10.00	4.00
1 Alan Ashby	.25	.10
2 Kevin Bass	.25	.10
3 Jose Cruz	1.00	.40
4 Glenn Davis	.75	.30
5 Bill Doran	.25	.10
6 Phil Garner	.25	.10
7 Billy Hatcher	.25	.10
8 Charlie Kerfeld	.25	.10
9 Bob Knepper	.25	.10
10 Aurelio Lopez	.25	.10
11 Terry Puhl	.50	.20
12 Craig Reynolds	.25	.10
13 Nolan Ryan	6.00	2.40
14 Mike Scott	.75	.30
15 Dickie Thon	.25	.10
16 Denny Walling	.25	.10

1987 Astros Mother's

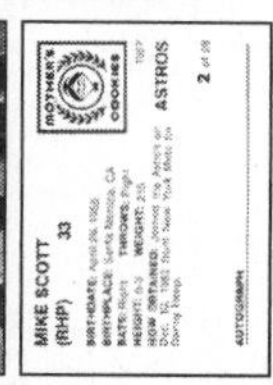

This set consists of 28 full-color, rounded-corner standard-size cards. Starter sets (only 20 cards but also including a certificate for eight more cards) were given out at the ballpark and collectors were encouraged to trade to fill in the rest of their set. Cards were originally given out at the Astrodome on July 17th during a game against the Phillies. Photos were taken by Barry Colla. The sets were reportedly given out free to the first 25,000 paid admissions at the game.

	Nm-Mt	Ex-Mt
COMPLETE SET (28)	12.00	4.80
1 Hal Lanier MG	.25	.10
2 Mike Scott	.75	.30
3 Jose Cruz	1.00	.40
4 Bill Doran	.25	.10
5 Bob Knepper	.25	.10
6 Phil Garner	.25	.10
7 Terry Puhl	.50	.20
8 Nolan Ryan	6.00	2.40
9 Kevin Bass	.25	.10
10 Glenn Davis	.50	.20
11 Alan Ashby	.25	.10
12 Charlie Kerfeld	.25	.10
13 Denny Walling	.25	.10
14 Danny Darwin	.25	.10
15 Mark Bailey	.25	.10
16 Davey Lopes	.75	.30
17 Dave Meads	.25	.10
18 Aurelio Lopez	.25	.10
19 Craig Reynolds	.25	.10
20 Dave Smith	.50	.20
21 Larry Andersen	.25	.10
22 Jim Pankovits	.25	.10
23 Jim Deshaies	.25	.10
24 Bert Pena	.25	.10
25 Dickie Thon	.25	.10
26 Billy Hatcher	.25	.10
27 Yogi Berra CO	1.00	.40
Denis Menke CO		
Gene Tenace CO		
Matt Galante CO		
Les Moss Co		
28 Astrodome CL	.25	.10

1987 Astros 1983-85 Postcard Rerelease`

Issued in 1987, these black and white blank-backed postcards feature members of the 1983-85 Houston Astros. For some reason, these cards were rereleased in 1987. Since the cards are unnumbered, we have sequenced them in alphabetical order.

	Nm-Mt	Ex-Mt
COMPLETE SET	25.00	10.00
1 Alan Ashby	.50	.20
2 Mark Bailey	.50	.20
3 George Bjorkman	.50	.20
4 Enos Cabell	.50	.20
5 Jose Cruz	.75	.30
6 Glenn Davis	.75	.30
7 Bill Dawley	.50	.20
8 Frank DiPino	.50	.20
9 Bill Doran	.50	.20
10 Ty Gainey	.50	.20
11 Phil Garner	.50	.20
12 Art Howe	.75	.30
13 Chris Jones	.50	.20
14 Bob Knepper	.50	.20
15 Ray Knight	.50	.20
16 Frank Lacorte	.50	.20
17 Mike LaCoss	.50	.20
18 Don Leppert CO	.50	.20
19 Bob Lillis MG	.50	.20
20 Mike Madden	.50	.20
21 Omar Moreno	.50	.20
22 Jerry Mumphrey	.50	.20
23 Jim Pankovits	.50	.20
24 Terry Puhl	.50	.20
25 Joe Niekro	.75	.30
26 Bert Pena	.50	.20
27 Luis Pujols	.50	.20
28 Craig Reynolds	.50	.20
29 J.R. Richard	1.00	.40
30 Mike Richardt	.50	.20
31 Mark Ross	.50	.20
32 Vern Ruhle	.50	.20
33 Nolan Ryan	5.00	2.00
34 Joe Sambito	.50	.20
35 Mike Scott	1.00	.40
36 Tony Scott	.50	.20
37 Dave Smith	.75	.30
39 Julio Solano	.50	.20
39 Harry Spilman	.50	.20
40 Stretch Suba	.50	.20
41 Dickie Thon	.50	.20
42 Denny Walling	.50	.20

1987 Astros Police

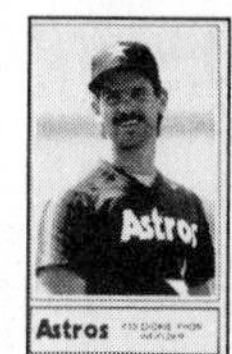

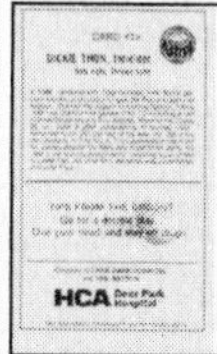

This 26-card safety set was sponsored by the Astros, Deer Park Hospital, and Sportsmedia Presentations. The backs contain a biographical paragraph above a "Tip from the Dugout". The front features a full-color photo of the player, his name, position, and uniform number. The cards are numbered on the back and measure 2 5/8" by 4 1/8". The first twelve cards were distributed at the Astrodome on July 14th and the rest were given away later in the summer by the Deer Park Hospital.

	Nm-Mt	Ex-Mt
COMPLETE SET (26)	8.00	3.20
1 Larry Andersen	.25	.10
2 Mark Bailey	.25	.10
3 Jose Cruz	1.00	.40
4 Danny Darwin	.25	.10
5 Bill Doran	.25	.10
6 Billy Hatcher	.25	.10
7 Hal Lanier MG	.25	.10
8 Davey Lopes	.50	.20
9 Dave Meads	.25	.10
10 Craig Reynolds	.25	.10
11 Mike Scott	.75	.30
12 Denny Walling	.25	.10
13 Aurelio Lopez	.25	.10
14 Dickie Thon	.25	.10
15 Terry Puhl	.50	.20
16 Nolan Ryan	4.00	1.60
17 Dave Smith	.50	.20
18 Julio Solano	.25	.10
19 Jim Deshaies	.25	.10
20 Bob Knepper	.25	.10
21 Alan Ashby	.25	.10
22 Kevin Bass	.25	.10
23 Glenn Davis	.50	.20
24 Phil Garner	.25	.10
25 Jim Pankovits	.25	.10
26 Gene Tenace CO	.50	.20
Matt Galante CO		
Denis Menke CO		
Yogi Berra CO		
Les Moss CO		

1987 Astros Postcards

These blank-backed black and white postcards feature members of the 1987 Houston Astros. The fronts have a posed portrait with the players name at the bottom. Since these are unnumbered, we have sequenced them in alphabetical order.

	Nm-Mt	Ex-Mt
COMPLETE SET	20.00	8.00
1 Larry Andersen	.50	.20
2 Alan Ashby	.50	.20
3 Mark Bailey	.50	.20
4 Kevin Bass	.50	.20
5 Yogi Berra CO	2.00	.80
6 Jose Cruz	.75	.30
7 Danny Darwin	.50	.20
8 Glenn Davis	.75	.30
9 Jim Deshaies	.50	.20
10 Bill Doran	.50	.20
11 Ty Gainey	.50	.20
12 Matt Galante CO	.50	.20
13 Phil Garner	.50	.20
14 Billy Hatcher	.50	.20
15 Charlie Kerfeld	.50	.20
16 Bob Knepper	.50	.20
17 Hal Lanier MG	.50	.20
18 Dave Lopes	.75	.30
19 Aurelio Lopez	.50	.20
20 Dave Meads	.50	.20
21 Denis Menke CO	.50	.20
22 Les Moss CO	.50	.20
23 Jim Pankovits	.50	.20
24 Bert Pena	.50	.20
25 Terry Puhl	.50	.20
26 Craig Reynolds	.50	.20
27 Nolan Ryan	5.00	2.00
28 Mike Scott	1.00	.40
29 Dave Smith	.50	.20
30 Julio Solano	.50	.20
31 Gene Tenace CO	.50	.20
32 Dickie Thon	.50	.20
33 Denny Walling	.50	.20

1987 Astros-Series One

This set features members of the 1965 Houston Astros. The cards are unnumbered, therefore we have sequenced them in alphabetical order.

	Nm-Mt	Ex-Mt
COMPLETE SET (32)	12.00	4.80
1 Bob Aspromonte	.25	.10
2 John Bateman	.25	.10
3 Jim Beauchamp	.25	.10
4 Walt Bond	.25	.10
5 Ron Brand	.25	.10
6 Hal Brown	.25	.10
7 Bob Bruce	.25	.10
8 Larry Dierker	.75	.30
9 Dick (Turk) Farrell	.25	.10
10 Nellie Fox	2.00	.80
11 Dave Giusti	.25	.10
12 Sonny Jackson	.25	.10
13 Ken Johnson	.25	.10
14 Eddie Kasko	.25	.10
15 Don Larsen	.50	.20
16 Bob Lillis	.25	.10
17 Joe Morgan	3.00	1.20
18 Don Nottebart	.25	.10
19 Claude Raymond	.25	.10
20 Al Spangler	.25	.10
21 Rusty Staub	1.00	.40
22 Hal Woodeshick	.25	.10
23 Jim Wynn	.50	.20
24 Don Larsen	.50	.20
Bob Turley		
25 Joe Morgan	2.00	.80
Nellie Fox		
26 Doug Rader	.25	.10
Norm Miller		
27 Jim Owens	.75	.30
Nellie Fox		
Turk Farrell		
28 Al Spangler	.50	.20
Rusty Staub		
Jim Wynn		
29 Bob Aspromonte	1.00	.40
Eddie Kasko		
Joe Morgan		
Walt Bond		
30 Lum Harris MG	.25	.10
Clint Courtney CO		
Jim Busby CO		
Jimmy Adair CO		
Howie Pollet CO		
31 1965 Team Photo	.25	.10
32 Hats Photo	.25	.10

1987 Astros Shooting Stars-Series One

This set features some of the leading all-time Houston Astros. The cards are unnumbered so we have sequenced them in alphabetical order. The shooting stars refers to the uniform worn by the Astros in the late 60's and early 70's.

	Nm-Mt	Ex-Mt
COMPLETE SET (32)	10.00	4.00
1 Cesar Cedeno	.50	.20
2 Danny Coombs	.25	.10
3 Mike Cuellar	.50	.20
4 Larry Dierker	.75	.30
5 John Edwards	.25	.10
6 Dick Farrell	.25	.10
7 Ken Forsch	.25	.10
8 Dave Giusti	.25	.10
9 Fred Gladding	.25	.10
10 Tom Griffin	.25	.10
11 Chuck Harrison	.25	.10
12 Tommy Helms	.25	.10
13 Sonny Jackson	.25	.10
14 Denny Lemaster	.25	.10
15 Lee May	.50	.20
16 Denis Menke	.25	.10
17 Norm Miller	.25	.10
18 Joe Morgan	2.50	1.00
19 Doug Rader	.25	.10
20 J.R. Richard	.50	.20
21 Al Spangler	.25	.10
22 Rusty Staub	1.00	.40
23 Bob Watson	.75	.30
24 Don Wilson	.25	.10
25 Jim Wynn	.50	.20
26 Mickey Mantle	3.00	1.20
Don Drysdale		
Rusty Staub		
27 1969 Pitching Staff	.25	.10
28 Don Wilson	.25	.10
Harry Walker MG		
29 Astro Bullpen Car	.25	.10
30 1966 Team Photo	.25	.10
31 1967 Team Photo	.25	.10
32 1968 Team Photo	.25	.10

1987 Astros Shooting Stars-Series Two

This set in another in the continuation of the Astros Shooting Stars. These cards feature more Houston Astros and are unnumbered. Therefore, we have sequenced them in alphabetical order.

Nm-Mt Ex-Mt
COMPLETE SET (32) 12.00 4.80
1 Jesus Alou .25 .10
2 Jack Billingham .25 .10
3 Jim Bouton 1.00 .40
4 George Culver .25 .10
5 Ron Davis .25 .10
6 Nellie Fox 1.50 .60
7 Cesar Geronimo .25 .10
8 Julio Gotay .25 .10
9 Greg Gross .25 .10
10 Cliff Johnson .50 .20
11 Dave Nicholson .25 .10
12 Claude Osteen .25 .10
13 Claude Raymond .25 .10
14 Dave Roberts .25 .10
15 Fred Scherman .25 .10
16 Hector Torres .25 .10
17 Bob Stinson .25 .01
18 Sandy Valdespino .25 .10
19 Jim York .25 .10
20 Chris Zachary .25 .10
21 Willie Mays 3.00 1.20
Leo Durocher MG
Cesar Cedeno
22 John Mayberry 1.00 .40
Joe Morgan
23 Eddie Mathews .75 .30
Chuck Harrison
24 Doug Rader .25 .10
Harry Walker MG
Curt Blefary
Joe Morgan
Denis Menke
25 Rusty Staub 3.00 1.20
Willie Mays
26 Norm Miller .25 .10
Jesus Alou
Jimmy Stewart
Jim Wynn
Bob Watson
Tommie Agee
Cesar Cedeno
27 Cesar Cedeno 1.00 .40
Joe Morgan
Jim Wynn
Bob Watson
Denis Menke
Doug Rader
Johnny Edwards
Roger Metzger
28 Don Wilson .50 .20
Don Larsen
Bo Belinsky
29 Danny Coombs .50 .20
Dan Schneider
Bo Belinsky
Mike Cuellar
30 1969 Team Photo .25 .10
31 1970 Team Photo .25 .10
32 1971 Team Photo .25 .10

1987 Astros Shooting Stars-Series Three

More Houston Astros of the past are portrayed in this set. These cards are unnumbered so we have sequenced them in alphabetical order.

Nm-Mt Ex-Mt
COMPLETE SET (32) 8.00 3.20
1 Dave Adlesh .25 .10
2 John Bateman .25 .10
3 Bo Belinsky .75 .30
4 Nate Colbert .25 .10
5 Tommy Davis .50 .20
6 Jack DiLauro .25 .10
7 Mike Easler .25 .10
8 Jim Gentile .25 .10
9 Preston Gomez MG .25 .10
10 Jim Landis .25 .10
11 Barry Latman .25 .10
12 Mike Marshall .50 .20
13 Marty Martinez .25 .10
14 Milt May .25 .10
15 John Mayberry .25 .10
16 Larry Milbourne .25 .10
17 Jim Owens .25 .10
18 Joe Pepitone .50 .20
19 Jim Ray .25 .10
20 Jerry Reuss .50 .20
21 Larry Sherry .25 .10
22 Dick Simpson .25 .10
23 Jimmy Stewart .25 .10
24 Robin Roberts .75 .30
Larry Dierker
25 Doug Rader .25 .10
Roger Metzger
Tommy Helms
Lee May
26 Jerry Reuss .25 .10
J.R. Richard
Tom Griffin
Jim Owens CO
Don Wilson
Dave Roberts
Ken Forsch
Larry Dierker
27 John Bateman .25 .10
Dave Adlesh
Ron Brand
Bill Heath
28 Don Wilson .25 .10
Tom Griffin
Larry Dierker
Denny LeMaster
29 Bob Watson .25 .10
Larry Howard
John Edwards
Bob Stinson
Skip Jutze
30 1972 Team Photo .25 .10
31 1973 Team Photo .25 .10
32 1974 Team Photo .25 .10

1987 Astros Rainbow-Series One

This 32-card set was issued in 1987 along with the three Astros Shooting Stars series and features photos of Houston Astros printed on commemorative postcards. The backs are blank. The cards are unnumbered and checklisted below in alphabetical order.

Nm-Mt Ex-Mt
COMPLETE SET (32) 18.00 7.25
1 Jesus Alou .50 .20
2 Joaquin Andujar .50 .20
3 Dave Bergman .50 .20
4 Enos Cabell .50 .20
5 Cesar Cedeno .75 .30
6 Ken Forsch .50 .20
7 Tom Griffin .50 .20
8 Greg Gross .50 .20
9 Wilbur Howard .50 .20
10 Art Howe .75 .30
11 Alan Knicely .50 .20
12 Ray Knight .50 .20
13 Frank Lacorte .50 .20
14 Mike Lacoss .50 .20
15 Rafael Landestoy .50 .20
16 Jeff Leonard .50 .20
17 Bob Lillis .50 .20
18 Milt May .50 .20
19 Larry Milbourne .50 .20
20 Roger Metzger .50 .20
21 Joe Morgan 2.50 1.00
22 Joe Niekro 1.00 .40
23 Phil Niekro 1.50 .60
Donald Davidson FO
Joe Niekro
24 Luis Pujols .50 .20
25 Doug Rader .50 .20
26 J.R. Richard .75 .30
27 Vern Ruhle .50 .20
28 Joe Sambito .50 .20
29 Don Sutton 2.50 1.00
30 Bob Watson 1.00 .40
31 Bob Lillis CO .50 .20
Jesus Alou CO
Bill Virdon MG
Deacon Jones CO
Mel Wright CO
32 1980 Championship Award .50 .20

1987 Astros Rainbow Postcards-Series Two

This 32-card set is a continuation of the Astros Shooting Stars Postcards-Series One set which was issued in 1987 along with the three Astros Shooting Stars series. The fronts feature photos of Houston Astros printed on commemorative postcards. The backs are blank. The cards are unnumbered and checklisted below in alphabetical order.

Nm-Mt Ex-Mt
COMPLETE SET (32) 20.00 8.00
1 Floyd Bannister .50 .20
2 Bruce Bochy .50 .20
3 Ken Boswell .50 .20
4 Tom Dixon .50 .20
5 Joe Ferguson .50 .20
6 Joe Ferguson .50 .20
Deacon Jones
Cesar Cedeno
Bob Watson
Jose Cruz
Leon Roberts
7 Jim Fuller .50 .20
8 Kiko Garcia .50 .20
9 Julio Gonzalez .50 .20
10 Larry Hardy .50 .20
11 Danny Heep .50 .20
12 Ed Hermann .50 .20
13 Wilbur Howard .50 .20
14 Mike Ivie .50 .20
15 Cliff Johnson .75 .30
16 Skip Jutze .50 .20
17 Doug Konieczny .50 .20
18 Pete Ladd .50 .20
19 Mark Lemongello .50 .20
20 Joe Niekro 1.00 .40
21 Randy Niemann .50 .20
22 Johnny Ray .50 .20
23 Nolan Ryan 10.00 4.00
24 Dave Roberts (C) .50 .20
25 Dave Roberts (P) .50 .20
26 Tony Scott .50 .20
27 Harry Spilman .50 .20
28 Bill Virdon .75 .30
29 Bob Watson .75 .30
Millionth Run
30 Gary Woods .50 .20
31 Jim York .50 .20
32 Cot Deal CO .50 .20
Don Leppert CO
Matt Galante CO
Jerry Walker CO
Denis Menke CO
Bob Lillis MG

1987 Astros Rainbow Postcards-Series Three

This 32-card set is a continuation of the Astros Shooting Stars Postcards-Series One and Series Two sets which were issued in 1987 along with the three Astros Shooting Stars series. The fronts feature photos of Houston Astros printed on commemorative postcards. The backs are blank. The cards are unnumbered and checklisted below in alphabetical order.

Nm-Mt Ex-Mt
COMPLETE SET (32) 25.00 10.00
1 Alan Ashby .50 .20
2 Reggie Baldwin .50 .20
3 Mike Cosgrove .50 .20
4 Jose Cruz 1.50 .60
5 Phil Garner .50 .20
6 Bob Knepper .50 .20
7 Dan Larson .50 .20
8 Scott Loucks .50 .20
9 Bo McLaughlin .50 .20
10 Joe Niekro .75 .30
Joe Sambito
11 Joe Pittman .50 .20
12 Terry Puhl .50 .20
13 Craig Reynolds .50 .20
14 J.R. Richard 1.00 .40
15 Nolan Ryan 10.00 4.00
16 Nolan Ryan 6.00 2.40
4000th K
17 Jimmy Sexton .75 .30
18 Paul Siebert .50 .20
19 Dave Smith .50 .20
20 Rob Sperring .50 .20
21 Dickie Thon .50 .20
22 Denny Walling .50 .20
23 Danny Walton .50 .20
24 Rick Williams .50 .20
25 1975 Astros Team Picture .50 .20
26 1976 Astros Team Picture .50 .20
27 1977 Astros Team Picture .50 .20
28 1978 Astros Team Picture .50 .20
29 1979 Astros Team Picture .50 .20
30 1980 Astros Team Picture .50 .20
31 1981 Astros Team Picture .50 .20
32 1982 Astros Team Picture .50 .20

1988 Astros Mother's

This set consists of 28 full-color, rounded-corner standard-size cards. Starter sets (only 20 cards but also including a certificate for eight more cards) were given out at the ballpark and collectors were encouraged to trade to fill in the rest of their set. Cards were originally given out at the Astrodome on August 26th during a game. The sets were reportedly given out free to the first 25,000 paid admissions at the game.

Nm-Mt Ex-Mt
COMPLETE SET (28) 12.00 4.80
1 Hal Lanier MG .25 .10
2 Mike Scott .75 .30
3 Gerald Young .25 .10
4 Bill Doran .25 .10
5 Bob Knepper .25 .10
6 Billy Hatcher .25 .10
7 Terry Puhl .50 .20
8 Nolan Ryan 6.00 2.40
9 Kevin Bass .25 .10
10 Glenn Davis .50 .20
11 Alan Ashby .25 .10
12 Steve Henderson .25 .10
13 Denny Walling .25 .10
14 Danny Darwin .25 .10
15 Mark Bailey .25 .10
16 Ernie Camacho .25 .10
17 Rafael Ramirez .25 .10
18 Jeff Heathcock .25 .10
19 Craig Reynolds .25 .10
20 Dave Smith .50 .20
21 Larry Andersen .25 .10
22 Jim Pankovits .25 .10
23 Jim Deshaies .25 .10
24 Juan Agosto .25 .10
25 Chuck Jackson .25 .10
26 Joaquin Andujar .25 .10
27 Yogi Berra CO 1.00 .40
Gene Clines CO
Matt Galante CO
Marc Hill CO
Denis Menke CO
Les Moss CO
28 Dave Labossiere TR .25 .10
Dennis Liborio EQMG
Doc Ewell TR CL

1988 Astros Police

This 26-card safety set was sponsored by the Astros, Deer Park Hospital, and Sportsmedia Presentations. The backs contain a biographical paragraph above "Tips from the Dugout". The front features a full-color photo of the player,

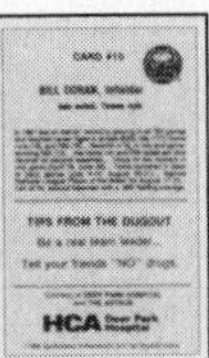

his name, position, and uniform number. The cards are numbered on the back and measure 2 5/8" by 4 1/8". The sets were supposedly distributed to the first 15,000 youngsters attending the New York Mets game against the Astros at the Astrodome on July 9th.

Nm-Mt Ex-Mt
COMPLETE SET (26) 10.00 4.00
1 Juan Agosto .25 .10
2 Larry Andersen .25 .10
3 Joaquin Andujar .25 .10
4 Alan Ashby .25 .10
5 Mark Bailey .25 .10
6 Kevin Bass .25 .10
7 Danny Darwin .25 .10
8 Glenn Davis .50 .20
9 Jim Deshaies .25 .10
10 Bill Doran .25 .10
11 Billy Hatcher .25 .10
12 Jeff Heathcock .25 .10
13 Steve Henderson .25 .10
14 Chuck Jackson .25 .10
15 Bob Knepper .25 .10
16 Jim Pankovits .25 .10
17 Terry Puhl .50 .20
18 Rafael Ramirez .25 .10
19 Craig Reynolds .25 .10
20 Nolan Ryan 6.00 2.40
21 Mike Scott .50 .20
22 Dave Smith .50 .20
23 Denny Walling .25 .10
24 Gerald Young .25 .10
25 Hal Lanier MG .25 .10
26 Coaching Staff .50 .20

1989 Astros Colt .45s Smokey

The 1989 Smokey Houston Colt .45s set contains 29 standard-size cards. The Houston Astros were originally called the Houston Colt .45s. The card fronts have black and white photos with white and light blue borders. This set depicts Houston Colt .45s' players from their inaugural 1962 season.

Nm-Mt Ex-Mt
COMPLETE SET (29) 6.00 2.40
1 Bob Bruce .25 .10
2 Al Cicotte .25 .10
3 Dave Giusti .50 .20
4 Jim Golden .25 .10
5 Ken Johnson .25 .10
6 Tom Borland .25 .10
7 Bobby Shantz .50 .20
8 Dick Farrell .50 .20
9 Jim Umbricht .25 .10
10 Hal Woodeshick .25 .10
11 Merritt Ranew .25 .10
12 Hal Smith .25 .10
13 Jim Campbell .25 .10
14 Norm Larker .25 .10
15 Joe Amalfitano .25 .10
16 Bob Aspromonte .50 .20
17 Bob Lillis .25 .10
18 Dick Gernert .25 .10
19 Don Buddin .25 .10
20 Pidge Browne .25 .10
21 Von McDaniel .25 .10
22 Don Taussig .25 .10
23 Al Spangler .25 .10
24 Al Heist .25 .10
25 Jim Pendleton .25 .10
26 Johnny Weekly .25 .10
27 Harry Craft MG .25 .10
28 Colt Coaches .25 .10
29 1962 Houston Colt 45s .75 .30

1989 Astros Lennox HSE

The 1989 Lennox HSE Astros set contains 26 cards measuring approximately 2 5/8" by 4 1/8". The fronts have color photos with burnt orange and white borders; the backs feature biographical information and career highlights. The set looks very much like the Police Astros sets of the previous years but is not since it was not sponsored by any Police Department and does not have a safety tip anywhere on the card.

Nm-Mt Ex-Mt
COMPLETE SET (26) 8.00 3.20
1 Billy Hatcher .25 .10
2 Greg Gross .25 .10
3 Rick Rhoden .25 .10
4 Mike Scott .50 .20
5 Kevin Bass .25 .10
6 Alex Trevino .25 .10
7 Jim Clancy .25 .10
8 Bill Doran .25 .10
9 Dan Schatzeder .25 .10
10 Bob Knepper .25 .10
11 Jim Deshaies .25 .10
12 Eric Yelding .25 .10
13 Danny Darwin .25 .10
14 Matt Galante CO .50 .20
Yogi Berra CO
Ed Napoleon CO
Ed Ott CO
Phil Garner CO
Les Moss CO
15 Craig Reynolds .25 .10
16 Rafael Ramirez .25 .10
17 Juan Agosto .25 .10
18 Larry Andersen .25 .10
19 Dave Smith .50 .20
20 Gerald Young .25 .10
21 Ken Caminiti 1.00 .40
22 Terry Puhl .50 .20
23 Bob Forsch .25 .10
24 Craig Biggio 2.50 1.00
25 Art Howe MG .50 .20
26 Glenn Davis .50 .20

1989 Astros Mother's

The 1989 Mother's Cookies Houston Astros set contains 28 standard-size cards with rounded corners. The fronts have borderless color photos, and the horizontally oriented backs have biographical information. Starter sets containing 20 of these cards were given away at an Astros home game during the 1989 season.

Nm-Mt Ex-Mt
COMPLETE SET (28) 10.00 4.00
1 Art Howe MG .25 .10
2 Mike Scott .75 .30
3 Gerald Young .25 .10
4 Bill Doran .25 .10
5 Billy Hatcher .25 .10
6 Terry Puhl .50 .20
7 Bob Knepper .25 .10
8 Kevin Bass .25 .10
9 Glenn Davis .50 .20
10 Alan Ashby .25 .10
11 Bob Forsch .25 .10
12 Greg Gross .25 .10
13 Danny Darwin .25 .10
14 Craig Biggio 4.00 1.60
15 Jim Clancy .25 .10
16 Rafael Ramirez .25 .10
17 Alex Trevino .25 .10
18 Craig Reynolds .25 .10
19 Dave Smith .50 .20
20 Larry Andersen .25 .10
21 Eric Yelding .25 .10
22 Jim Deshaies .25 .10
23 Juan Agosto .25 .10
24 Rick Rhoden .25 .10
25 Ken Caminiti 1.00 .40
26 Dave Meads .25 .10
27 Yogi Berra CO 1.00 .40
Ed Napoleon CO
Matt Galante CO
Ed Ott CO
Phil Garner CO
Les Moss CO
28 Dave Labossiere TR .25 .10
Doc Ewell TR
Dennis Liborio EQMG CL

1989 Astros Smokey

These 4" by 6" cards feature members of the Houston Astros. These cards feature player photos on the front and various safety tips on the back. We have sequenced this set in alphabetical order.

Nm-Mt Ex-Mt
COMPLETE SET (40) 10.00 4.00
1 Juan Agosto .25 .10
2 Larry Andersen .25 .10
3 Alan Ashby .25 .10
4 Kevin Bass .25 .10
5 Yogi Berra CO 1.00 .40
6 Craig Biggio 2.50 1.00
7 Ken Caminiti 1.00 .40
8 Casey Candaele .25 .10
9 Jim Clancy .25 .10
10 Danny Darwin .25 .10
11 Glenn Davis .50 .20
12 Jim Deshaies .25 .10
13 Bill Doran .25 .10
14 Bob Forsch .25 .10
15 Matt Galante CO .25 .10
16 Phil Garner CO .25 .10
17 Greg Gross .25 .10
18 Billy Hatcher .25 .10
19 Art Howe MG .25 .10

20 Chuck Jackson .25 .10
21 Charley Kerfeld .25 .10
22 Bob Knepper .25 .10
23 Steve Lombardozzi .25 .10
24 Roger Mason .25 .10
25 Louie Meadows .25 .10
26 Dave Meads .25 .10
27 Brian Meyer .25 .10
28 Les Moss CO .25 .10
29 Ed Napoleon CO .25 .10
30 Ed Ott CO .25 .10
31 Terry Puhl .50 .20
32 Rafael Ramirez .25 .10
33 Craig Reynolds .25 .10
34 Rick Rhoden .25 .10
35 Dan Schatzeder .25 .10
36 Mike Scott .50 .20
37 Dave Smith .50 .20
38 Alex Trevino .25 .10
39 Eric Yelding .25 .10
40 Gerald Young .25 .10

1990 Astros Lennox HSE

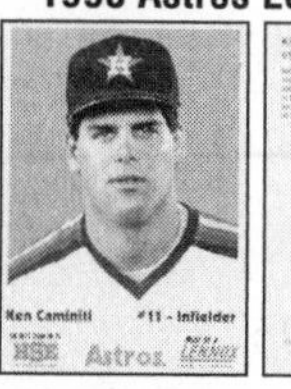

This 28-card, approximately 3 1/2" by 5", set (of 1990 Houston Astros) was issued in conjunction with HSE Cable Network and Lennox Heating and Air Conditioning as indicated on both the front and back of the cards. The front of the cards have full color portraits of the player while the back gives brief information about the player. The set has been checklisted below in alphabetical order.

Nm-Mt Ex-Mt
COMPLETE SET (28) 12.00 3.60
1 Juan Agosto .50 .15
2 Larry Andersen .50 .15
3 Eric Anthony .50 .15
4 Craig Biggio 2.50 .75
5 Ken Caminiti 1.00 .30
6 Casey Candaele .50 .15
7 Jose Cano .50 .15
8 Jim Clancy .50 .15
9 Danny Darwin .50 .15
10 Mark Davidson .50 .15
11 Glenn Davis .75 .23
12 Jim Deshaies .50 .15
13 Bill Doran .50 .15
14 Bill Gullickson .50 .15
15 Xavier Hernandez .50 .15
16 Art Howe MG .50 .15
17 Mark Portugal .50 .15
18 Terry Puhl .75 .23
19 Rafael Ramirez .50 .15
20 David Rohde .50 .15
21 Dan Schatzeder .50 .15
22 Mike Scott .75 .23
23 Dave Smith .75 .23
24 Franklin Stubbs .50 .15
25 Alex Trevino .50 .15
26 Glenn Wilson .50 .15
27 Eric Yelding .50 .15
28 Gerald Young .50 .15

1990 Astros Mother's

This 28-card standard-size set features members of the 1990 Houston Astros. This set features the traditional rounded corners and has biographical information about each player on the back. These Astros cards were given away on July 15th to the first 25,000 fans at the Astrodome. They were distributed in 20 card random packets at the game and eight more at the redemption booths. However, both groups of cards were random and there was no guarantee of getting a complete set in the cards. The promotional idea was that the only way one could finish the set was to trade for them. The certificates of redemption for eight were redeemable at the major card show at the AstroArena on August 24-26, 1990.

Nm-Mt Ex-Mt
COMPLETE SET (28) 8.00 2.40
1 Art Howe MG .25 .07
2 Glenn Davis .50 .15
3 Eric Anthony .25 .07
4 Mike Scott .75 .23
5 Craig Biggio 2.00 .60
6 Ken Caminiti .75 .23
7 Bill Doran .25 .07
8 Gerald Young .25 .07
9 Terry Puhl .50 .15
10 Mark Portugal .25 .07
11 Mark Davidson .25 .07
12 Jim Deshaies .25 .07
13 Bill Gullickson .25 .07
14 Franklin Stubbs .25 .07
15 Danny Darwin .25 .07
16 Ken Oberkfell .25 .07
17 Dave Smith .50 .15
18 Dan Schatzeder .25 .07
19 Rafael Ramirez .25 .07
20 Larry Andersen .25 .07
21 Alex Trevino .25 .07
22 Glenn Wilson .25 .07
23 Jim Clancy .25 .07
24 Eric Yelding .25 .07
25 Casey Candaele .25 .07
26 Juan Agosto .25 .07
27 Billy Bowman CO .50 .15
Bob Cluck CO
Phil Garner CO
Matt Galante CO
Ed Napoleon CO
Rudy Jaramillo CO
28 Dave Labossiere TR .25 .07
Dennis Liborio EQ.MG
Doc Ewell TR

1991 Astros Mother's

The 1991 Mother's Cookies Houston Astros set contains 28 standard-size cards with rounded corners.

Nm-Mt Ex-Mt
COMPLETE SET (28) 10.00 3.00
1 Art Howe MG .25 .07
2 Steve Finley 1.00 .30
3 Pete Harnisch .25 .07
4 Mike Scott .75 .23
5 Craig Biggio 1.50 .45
6 Ken Caminiti .50 .15
7 Eric Yelding .25 .07
8 Jeff Bagwell 5.00 1.50
9 Jim Deshaies .25 .07
10 Mark Portugal .25 .07
11 Mark Davidson .25 .07
12 Jimmy Jones .25 .07
13 Luis Gonzalez 2.00 .60
14 Karl Rhodes .25 .07
15 Curt Schilling 2.00 .60
16 Ken Oberkfell .25 .07
17 Mark McLemore .50 .15
18 Dave Rohde .25 .07
19 Rafael Ramirez .25 .07
20 Al Osuna .25 .07
21 Jim Corsi .25 .07
22 Carl Nichols .25 .07
23 Jim Clancy .25 .07
24 Dwayne Henry .25 .07
25 Casey Candaele .25 .07
26 Xavier Hernandez .25 .07
27 Darryl Kile 1.50 .45
28 Phil Garner CO .50 .15
Bob Cluck CO
Ed Ott CO
Matt Galante CO
Rudy Jaramillo CO

1992 Astros Mother's

The 1992 Mother's Cookies Astros set contains 28 standard-size cards with rounded corners.

Nm-Mt Ex-Mt
COMPLETE SET (28) 10.00 3.00
1 Art Howe MG .25 .07
2 Steve Finley .75 .23
3 Pete Harnisch .25 .07
4 Pete Incaviglia .25 .07
5 Craig Biggio 1.50 .45
6 Ken Caminiti .50 .15
7 Eric Anthony .25 .07
8 Jeff Bagwell 4.00 1.20
9 Andujar Cedeno .25 .07
10 Mark Portugal .25 .07
11 Eddie Taubensee .25 .07
12 Jimmy Jones .25 .07
13 Joe Boever .25 .07
14 Benny Distefano .25 .07
15 Juan Guerrero .25 .07
16 Doug Jones .25 .07
17 Scott Servais .25 .07
18 Butch Henry .25 .07
19 Rafael Ramirez .25 .07
20 Al Osuna .25 .07
21 Rob Murphy .25 .07
22 Chris Jones .25 .07
23 Rob Mallicoat .25 .07
24 Darryl Kile 1.00 .30
25 Casey Candaele .25 .07
26 Xavier Hernandez .25 .07
27 Rudy Jaramillo CO .50 .15
Ed Ott CO
Matt Galante CO
Bob Cluck CO
Tom Spencer CO
28 Dennis Liborio EQMG .25 .07
Dave Labossiere TR
Doc Ewell TR CL

1993 Astros Mother's

The 1993 Mother's Cookies Astros set consists of 28 standard-size cards with rounded corners.

Nm-Mt Ex-Mt
COMPLETE SET (28) 10.00 3.00
1 Art Howe MG .25 .07
2 Steve Finley .75 .23
3 Pete Harnisch .25 .07
4 Craig Biggio 2.00 .60

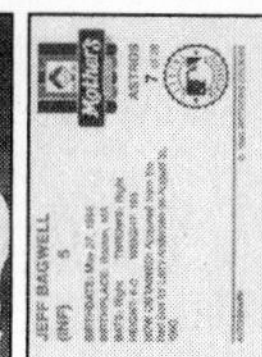

5 Doug Drabek .25 .07
6 Scott Servais .25 .07
7 Jeff Bagwell 3.00 .90
8 Eric Anthony .25 .07
9 Ken Caminiti .50 .15
10 Andujar Cedeno .25 .07
11 Mark Portugal .25 .07
12 Jose Uribe .25 .07
13 Rick Parker .25 .07
14 Doug Jones .25 .07
15 Luis Gonzalez 1.50 .45
16 Kevin Bass .25 .07
17 Greg Swindell .25 .07
18 Eddie Taubensee .25 .07
19 Darryl Kile 1.00 .30
20 Brian Williams .25 .07
21 Chris James .25 .07
22 Chris Donnels .25 .07
23 Xavier Hernandez .25 .07
24 Casey Candaele .25 .07
25 Eric Bell .25 .07
26 Mark Grant .25 .07
27 Tom Edens .25 .07
28 Ed Ott CO .50 .15
Bob Cluck CO
Matt Galante CO
Billy Joe Bowman CO
Rudy Jaramillo CO
Tom Spencer CO CL

1993 Astros Stadium Club

This 30-card standard-size set features the 1993 Houston Astros. The set was issued in hobby (plastic box) and retail (blister) form.

Nm-Mt Ex-Mt
COMP. FACT SET (30) 5.00 1.50
1 Doug Drabek .10 .03
2 Eddie Taubensee .10 .03
3 James Mouton .10 .03
4 Ken Caminiti .25 .07
5 Chris James .10 .03
6 Jeff Juden .10 .03
7 Eric Anthony .10 .03
8 Jeff Bagwell 1.50 .45
9 Greg Swindell .10 .03
10 Steve Finley .50 .15
11 Al Osuna .10 .03
12 Gary Mota .10 .03
13 Scott Servais .10 .03
14 Craig Biggio 1.25 .35
15 Doug Jones .10 .03
16 Rob Mallicoat .10 .03
17 Darryl Kile .75 .23
18 Kevin Bass .10 .03
19 Pete Harnisch .10 .03
20 Andujar Cedeno .10 .03
21 Brian L.Hunter .10 .03
22 Brian Williams .10 .03
23 Chris Donnels .10 .03
24 Xavier Hernandez .10 .03
25 Todd Jones .25 .07
26 Luis Gonzalez 1.00 .30
27 Rick Parker .10 .03
28 Casey Candaele .10 .03
29 Tony Eusebio .10 .03
30 Mark Portugal .10 .03

1994 Astros Mother's

The 1994 Mother's Cookies Astros set consists of 28 standard-size cards with rounded corners.

Nm-Mt Ex-Mt
COMPLETE SET (28) 10.00 3.00
1 Terry Collins MG .25 .07
2 Mitch Williams .50 .15
3 Jeff Bagwell 2.50 .75
4 Luis Gonzalez 1.25 .35
5 Craig Biggio 1.50 .45
6 Darryl Kile 1.00 .30
7 Ken Caminiti .50 .15
8 Steve Finley .75 .23
9 Pete Harnisch .25 .07
10 Sid Bream .25 .07
11 Mike Felder .25 .07
12 Tom Edens .25 .07
13 James Mouton .25 .07
14 Doug Drabek .25 .07
15 Greg Swindell .25 .07
16 Chris Donnels .25 .07
17 John Hudek .25 .07
18 Andujar Cedeno .25 .07
19 Scott Servais .25 .07
20 Todd Jones .50 .15
21 Kevin Bass .25 .07
22 Shane Reynolds .25 .07
23 Brian Williams .25 .07
24 Tony Eusebio .25 .07
25 Mike Hampton .75 .23
26 Andy Stankiewicz .25 .07
27 Matt Galante CO .50 .15
Steve Henderson CO
Ben Hines CO
Julio Linares CO
Mel Stottlemyre CO
28 Dennis Liborio EQMG .25 .07
Dave Labossiere TR
Rex Jones TR

1995 Astros Mother's

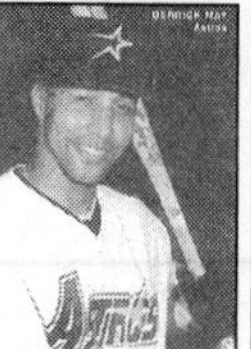
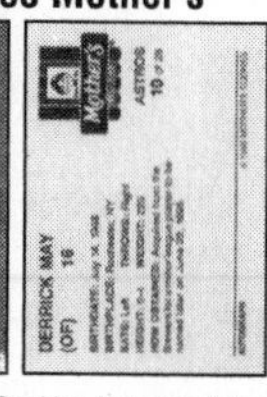

This 1995 Mother's Cookies Houston Astros set consists of 28 standard-size cards with rounded corners.

Nm-Mt Ex-Mt
COMPLETE SET (28) 10.00 3.00
1 Terry Collins MG .25 .07
2 Jeff Bagwell 2.50 .75
3 Luis Gonzalez 1.25 .35
4 Darryl Kile .50 .15
5 Derek Bell .25 .07
6 Scott Servais .25 .07
7 Craig Biggio 1.50 .45
8 Dave Magadan .25 .07
9 Milt Thompson .25 .07
10 Derrick May .25 .07
11 Doug Drabek .25 .07
12 Tony Eusebio .25 .07
13 Phil Nevin .75 .23
14 James Mouton .25 .07
15 Phil Plantier .25 .07
16 Pedro Martinez .25 .07
17 Orlando Miller .25 .07
18 John Hudek .25 .07
19 Doug Brocail .25 .07
20 Craig Shipley .25 .07
21 Shane Reynolds .25 .07
22 Mike Hampton .50 .15
23 Todd Jones .50 .15
24 Greg Swindell .25 .07
25 Jim Dougherty .25 .07
26 Brian L. Hunter .25 .07
27 Dave Veres .25 .07
28 Julio Linares CO .50 .15
Matt Galante CO
Jesse Barfield CO
Mel Stottlemyre CO
Steve Henderson CO CL

1996 Astros Mother's

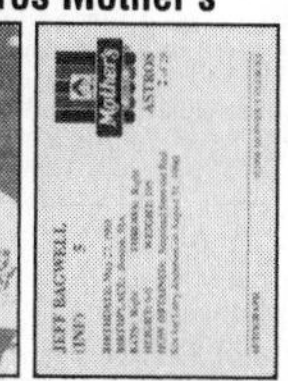

This 28-card set consists of borderless posed color player portraits in stadium settings.

Nm-Mt Ex-Mt
COMPLETE SET (28) 8.00 2.40
1 Terry Collins MG .25 .07
2 Jeff Bagwell 2.50 .75
3 Craig Biggio 1.50 .45
4 Derek Bell .25 .07
5 Darryl Kile .50 .15
6 Sean Berry .25 .07
7 Doug Drabek .25 .07
8 Derrick May .25 .07
9 Orlando Miller .25 .07
10 Mike Hampton .50 .15
11 Rick Wilkins .25 .07
12 Brian Hunter .25 .07
13 Shane Reynolds .25 .07
14 James Mouton .25 .07
15 Greg Swindell .25 .07
16 Bill Spiers .25 .07
17 Alvin Morman .25 .07
18 Tony Eusebio .25 .07
19 John Hudek .25 .07
20 Doug Brocail .25 .07
21 Anthony Young .25 .07
22 John Cangelosi .25 .07
23 Jeff Tabaka .25 .07
24 Mike Simms .25 .07
25 Todd Jones .50 .15
26 Ricky Gutierrez .25 .07
27 Mark Small .25 .07
28 Matt Galante CO .25 .07
Julio Linares CO
Rick Sweet CO
Brent Strom CO
Steve Henderson CO CL

1997 Astros Mother's

This 28-card set of the Houston Astros sponsored by Mother's Cookies consists of posed color player photos with rounded corners.

Nm-Mt Ex-Mt
COMPLETE SET (28) 12.00 3.60
1 Larry Dierker MG .50 .15
2 Jeff Bagwell 3.00 .90

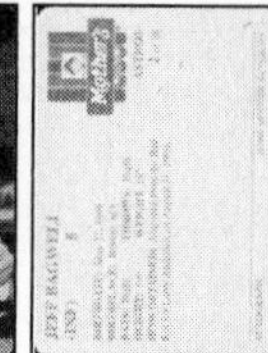

3 Craig Biggio 2.00 .60
4 Darryl Kile 1.00 .30
5 Luis Gonzalez 1.25 .35
6 Shane Reynolds .25 .07
7 James Mouton .25 .07
8 Sean Berry .25 .07
9 Billy Wagner 1.50 .45
10 Ricky Gutierrez .25 .07
11 Mike Hampton .50 .15
12 Tony Eusebio .25 .07
13 Derek Bell .25 .07
14 Ray Montgomery .25 .07
15 Bill Spiers .25 .07
16 Sid Fernandez .50 .15
17 Brad Ausmus .25 .07
18 John Hudek .25 .07
19 Bob Abreu 2.00 .60
20 Russ Springer .25 .07
21 Chris Holt .25 .07
22 Tom Martin .25 .07
23 Donne Wall .25 .07
24 Thomas Howard .25 .07
25 Jose Lima .25 .07
26 Pat Listach .25 .07
27 Ramon Garcia .25 .07
28 Alan Ashby CO .50 .15
Jose Cruz CO
Mike Cubbage CO
Tom McCraw CO
Vern Ruhle CO
Bill Virdon CO CL

1998 Astros Mother's

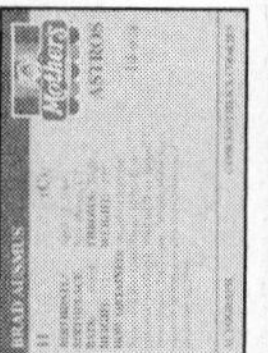

This 28-card set of the Houston Astros sponsored by Mother's Cookies consists of posed color player photos with rounded corners.

Nm-Mt Ex-Mt
COMPLETE SET (28) 10.00 3.00
1 Larry Dierker MG .50 .15
2 Jeff Bagwell 2.00 .60
3 Craig Biggio 1.50 .45
4 Derek Bell .25 .07
5 Shane Reynolds .25 .07
6 Sean Berry .25 .07
7 Moises Alou 1.00 .30
8 Carl Everett .25 .07
9 Billy Wagner .25 .07
10 Tony Eusebio .25 .07
11 Mike Hampton .50 .15
12 Ricky Gutierrez .25 .07
13 Jose Lima .25 .07
14 Brad Ausmus .25 .07
15 Bill Spiers .25 .07
16 C.J. Nitkowski .25 .07
17 Randy Johnson 2.50 .75
18 Mike Magnante .25 .07
19 Dave Clark .25 .07
20 Sean Bergman .25 .07
21 Richard Hidalgo .75 .23
22 Pete Schourek .25 .07
23 Jay Powell .25 .07
24 Trever Miller .25 .07
25 Tim Bogar .25 .07
26 Doug Henry .25 .07
27 Scott Elarton .25 .07
28 Jose Cruz CO .25 .07
Mike Cubbage CO
Dave Engle CO
Matt Galante CO
Tom McCraw CO
Vern Ruhle CO CL

1999 Astros Albertsons

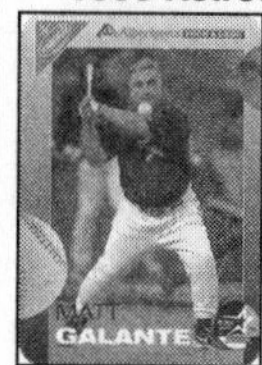

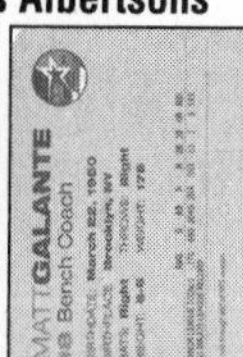

This 34 card standard-size set features members of the 1999 Houson Astros, the last team to play in the Astrodome. The cards have rounded corners and the upper left corner features a Nabisco logo while the lower right corner has the 1999 Astros logo. The cards are unnumbered except for the uniform numbers so we have sequenced them in alphabetical order.

Nm-Mt Ex-Mt
COMPLETE SET (34) 12.00 3.60
1 Moises Alou 1.00 .30
2 Jeff Bagwell 2.00 .60
3 Paul Bako .25 .07
4 Glen Barker .25 .07
5 Derek Bell .25 .07
6 Sean Bergman .25 .07

Card	Nm-Mt	Ex-Mt
7 Craig Biggio	1.25	.35
8 Tim Bogar	.25	.07
9 Ken Caminiti	.50	.15
10 Mike Cubbage CO	.25	.07
11 Jose Cruz CO	.50	.15
12 Larry Dierker MG	.50	.15
13 Scott Elarton	.25	.07
14 Tony Eusebio	.25	.07
15 Carl Everett	.25	.07
16 Matt Galante CO	.25	.07
17 Ricky Gutierrez	.25	.07
18 Mike Hampton	.50	.15
19 Doug Henry	.25	.07
20 Richard Hidalgo	.75	.23
21 Chris Holt	.25	.07
22 Jack Howell	.25	.07
23 Russ Johnson	.25	.07
24 Jose Lima	.25	.07
25 Tom McCraw CO	.25	.07
26 Mitch Meluskey	.25	.07
27 Trever Miller	.25	.07
28 Jay Powell	.25	.07
29 Shane Reynolds	.50	.15
30 Vern Ruhle CO	.25	.07
31 Bill Spiers	.25	.07
32 John Tamargo CO	.25	.07
33 Billy Wagner	1.00	.30
34 Brian Wiliams	.25	.07

1999 Astros Buddies

This five card standard-size set features people involved with the 1999 Houston Astros, either as a player or as a coach/manager. The fronts feature a player photo with the words "Exclusive Edition" on top, the "Astros Buddies Logo" on the upper left and the players name on the bottom.

	Nm-Mt	Ex-Mt
COMPLETE SET	8.00	2.40
1 Larry Dierker	1.00	.30
2 Jose Cruz	1.00	.30
3 Craig Biggio	3.00	.90
4 Jeff Bagwell	4.00	1.20
5 Houston Astrodome	.50	.15

2001 Astros Team Issue

The 30-card postcard sized colored set was issued by Barry Colla. Each card comes two ways: a blank white back; or a "Dear Astro Fan" message on the back with a team logo and a facsimile autograph. The cards with messages are numbered on the back.

	Nm-Mt	Ex-Mt
COMPLETE SET (30)	10.00	3.00
1 Larry Dierker MG	.25	.07
2 Moises Alou	.50	.15
3 Brad Ausmus	.25	.07
4 Jeff Bagwell	1.50	.45
5 Lance Berkman	1.50	.45
6 Craig Biggio	1.25	.35
7 Scott Elarton	.25	.07
8 Tony Eusebio	.25	.07
9 Richard Hidalgo	.50	.15
10 Jose Lima	.25	.07
11 Julio Lugo	.25	.07
12 Shane Reynolds	.25	.07
13 Billy Spiers	.25	.07
14 Chris Truby	.25	.07
15 Jose Vizcaino	.25	.07
16 Billy Wagner	1.00	.30
17 Glen Barker	.25	.07
18 Kent Bottenfield	.25	.07
19 Nelson Cruz	.25	.07
20 Octavio Dotel	.50	.15
21 Morgan Ensberg	.50	.15
22 Adam Everett	.50	.15
23 Keith Ginter	.25	.07
24 Mike Jackson	.25	.07
25 Brad Lidge	.25	.07
26 Tony McKnight	.25	.07
27 Wade Miller	1.00	.30
28 Roy Oswalt	2.00	.60
29 Jay Powell	.25	.07
30 Daryle Ward	.25	.07

2002 Astros Postcards

These postcard-size cards were issued by the Astros and featured the photography of noted hobby figure Barry Colla. The cards have either a fan message on the back or a blank-back. Please note that these each card number ends in an 02 and we are just using the numbers before the 02 (for 2002) designation.

	Nm-Mt	Ex-Mt
COMPLETE SET	20.00	6.00
1 Brad Ausmus	.50	.15
2 Jeff Bagwell	2.50	.75
3 Lance Berkman	1.50	.45
4 Craig Biggio	2.00	.60
5 Doug Brocail	.50	.15
6 Nelson Cruz	.50	.15
7 Richard Hidalgo	1.00	.30
8 Julio Lugo	.50	.15
9 Orlando Merced	.50	.15
10 Wade Miller	1.50	.45
11 Roy Oswalt	1.50	.45
12 Shane Reynolds	.50	.15
13 Jose Vizcaino	.50	.15
14 Billy Wagner	1.50	.45
15 Daryle Ward	.50	.15
16 Jimy Williams MG	.50	.15
70 Octavio Dotel	.75	.23
71 Morgan Ensberg	1.00	.30
72 Adam Everett	.75	.23
73 Carlos Hernandez	.50	.15
74 Brian L. Hunter	.50	.15
75 T.J. Mathews	.50	.15
76 Dave Mlicki	.50	.15
77 Ricky Stone	.50	.15
78 Greg Zaun	.50	.15
79 Jose Cruz CO	.75	.23
80 Burt Hooton CO	.50	.15
81 Gene Lamont CO	.50	.15
82 Tony Pena CO	.75	.23
83 Harry Spilman CO	.50	.15
84 John Tamargo CO	.50	.15

2003 Astros Team Issue

These cards were issued with either "Dear Astros Fans" or blank backs. All of these cards are numbered before the 03 (year of issue).

	MINT	NRMT
COMPLETE SET	20.00	9.00
1 Brad Ausmus	.50	.23
2 Jeff Bagwell	2.50	1.10
3 Lance Berkman	1.50	.70
4 Craig Biggio	2.00	.90
5 Octavio Dotel	.75	.35
6 Richard Hidalgo	1.00	.45
7 Brian L. Hunter	.50	.23
8 Jeff Kent	1.50	.70
9 Julio Lugo	.50	.23
10 Orlando Merced	.50	.23
11 Wade Miller	1.00	.45
12 Roy Oswalt	1.00	.45
13 Shane Reynolds	.50	.23
14 Jose Vizcaino	.50	.23
15 Billy Wagner	1.50	.70
16 Jimy Williams MG	.50	.23
17 Geoff Blum	.50	.23
18 Raul Chavez	.50	.23
19 Bruce Chen	.50	.23
20 Morgan Ensberg	1.00	.45
21 Brad Lidge	.50	.23
22 Brian Moehler	.50	.23
23 Pete Munro	.50	.23
24 Tim Redding	.50	.23
25 Jeriome Robertson	.75	.35
26 Ricky Stone	.50	.23
27 Gregg Zaun	.50	.23
28 Mark Bailey	.50	.23
29 Jose Cruz CO	.75	.35
30 Burt Hooton CO	.50	.23
31 Gene Lamont CO	.50	.23
32 Harry Spilman CO	.50	.23
33 John Tamargo CO	.50	.23

1997 AT and T Ambassadors of Baseball

These four standard-size cards were issued by AT and T featured retired ballplayers whose trips were arranged by the Major League Baseball Players Alumni. The cards have the AT and T logo in the upper right corner and the Ambassadors of Baseball Logo on the lower left corner. The cards are not numbered so we have sequenced them in alphabetical order.

	Nm-Mt	Ex-Mt
COMPLETE SET (4)	20.00	6.00
1 Jesse Barfield	5.00	1.50
2 Darrell Evans	5.00	1.50
3 Al Hrabosky	5.00	1.50
4 Jerry Koosman	5.00	1.50

1968 Atlantic Oil Play Ball Contest Cards

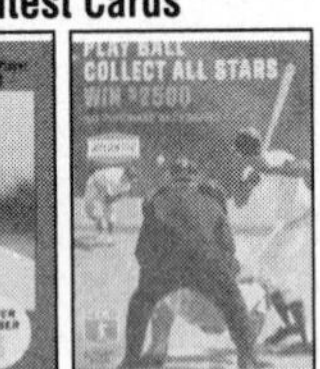

These fifty cards were issued in two-card panels which when split becomes standard-size cards. For easier reference we have sequenced the set in alphabetical order and listed the player number and prize (when applicable) next to the player's name. Winning cards of more than $1 are not priced and not included in the complete set price.

	NM	Ex
COMPLETE SET	225.00	90.00
1 Hank Aaron-4	25.00	10.00
2 Tommy Agee-2 ($2500)		
3 Felipe Alou-3	3.00	1.20
4 Max Alvis-2	1.50	.60
5 Bob Aspromonte-1	1.50	.60
6 Ernie Banks-5 ($100)		
7 Lou Brock-1	15.00	6.00
8 Jim Bunning-9	4.00	1.60
9 Johnny Callison-1	2.00	.80
10 Bert Campaneris-2	2.00	.80
11 Norm Cash-5	3.00	1.20
12 Orlando Cepeda-4	4.00	1.60
13 Dean Chance-9	1.50	.60
14 Roberto Clemente-7	35.00	14.00
15 Tommy Davis-4 ($100)		
16 Andy Etchebarren-8 ($5)		
17 Ron Fairly-6 ($10)		
18 Bill Freehan-3 ($2500)		
19 Jim Fregosi-2	2.00	.80
20 Bob Gibson-9	15.00	6.00
21 Jim Hart-3	1.50	.60
22 Joe Horlen-9	1.50	.60
23 Al Kaline-2	20.00	8.00
24 Jim Lonborg-9	2.00	.80
25 Jim Maloney-9	2.00	.80
26 Roger Maris-7	15.00	6.00
27 Mike McCormick-9	1.50	.60
28 Willie McCovey-4	15.00	6.00
29 Sam McDowell-9	2.00	.80
30 Tug McGraw-7 ($10)		
31 Tony Oliva-1	3.00	1.20
32 Claude Osteen-11 ($1)	4.00	1.60
33 Milt Pappas-10	2.00	.80
34 Joe Pepitone-6	2.00	.80
35 Vada Pinson-3	2.00	.80
36 Boog Powell-6	2.00	.80
37 Brooks Robinson-1	15.00	6.00
38 Frank Robinson-5	15.00	6.00
39 Pete Rose-1	20.00	8.00
40 Jose Santiago-11	1.50	.60
41 Ron Santo-4	3.00	1.20
42 George Scott-6	1.50	.60
43 Ron Swoboda-7	1.50	.60
44 Tom Tresh-2	1.50	.60
45 Fred Valentine-6	1.50	.60
46 Pete Ward-1	1.50	.60
47 Billy Williams-8 ($5)		
48 Maury Wills-1	2.00	.80
49 Earl Wilson-10 ($1)	4.00	1.60
50 Carl Yastrzemski-5	15.00	6.00

1888 August Beck N403

The tobacco brand with the unusual name of Yum Yum was marketed by the August Beck Company of Chicago. The cards are blank-backed with sepia fronts and are not numbered. There are ballplayers known, and the series was released to the public in 1887 or 1888. We have sequenced this set in alphabetical order. There are new additions added to this checklist and more may be out there so any information would be greatly appreciated. The Cap Anson card actually features a photo of Ned Wiliamson which depresses its value slightly.

	Ex-Mt	VG
COMPLETE SET	80000.00	40000.00
1 Cap Anson Ned Williamson pictured on card	4000.00	2000.00
2 Lady Baldwin	1500.00	750.00
3 Dan Brouthers	2500.00	1250.00
4 Bill Brown	1500.00	750.00
5 Charlie Buffington	1500.00	750.00
6A Tommy Burns: Chicago civ. Portrait	1500.00	750.00
6B Tommy Burns: Chicago standing with bat	1500.00	750.00
7A John Clarkson civ. Portrait	2500.00	1250.00
7B John Clarkson throwing	2500.00	1250.00
8 John Coleman	1500.00	750.00
9 Roger Connor	2500.00	1250.00
10 Larry Corcoran	1500.00	750.00
11 Tom Daly: Chicago Picture is Billy Sunday	1500.00	750.00
12 Tom Deasley	1500.00	750.00
13 Mike Dorgan	1500.00	750.00
14 Buck Ewing	2500.00	1250.00
15 Silver Flint	1500.00	750.00
16 Pud Galvin	2500.00	1250.00
17 Pete Gillespie	1500.00	750.00
18 Jack Glasscock	1500.00	750.00
19 George Gore	1500.00	750.00
20 Ed Greer	1500.00	750.00
21 Tim Keefe	2500.00	1250.00
22 Mike (King) Kelly	4000.00	2000.00
23 Gus Krock	1500.00	750.00
24 Connie Mack	4000.00	2000.00
25 Kid Madden	1500.00	750.00
26 George Miller	1500.00	750.00
27 James Mutrie	3000.00	1500.00
28 Bill Nash: Boston	1500.00	750.00
29A Jim O'Rourke New York portrait	2500.00	1250.00
29B Jim O'Rourke no team New York uniform with bat)	2500.00	1250.00
30 Danny Richardson	1500.00	750.00
31 James (Chief) Roseman	1500.00	750.00
32 Jimmy Ryan	2000.00	1000.00
33 Bill Sowders	1500.00	750.00
34 Marty Sullivan	1500.00	750.00
35 Billy Sunday	3000.00	1500.00
36 Ezra Sutton	1500.00	750.00
37 Mike Tiernan (2)	1500.00	750.00
38 George Van Haltren	1500.00	750.00
39A Mickey Welch New York portrait	2500.00	1250.00
39B Mickey Welch New York Pitching, hands at waist	2500.00	1250.00
39C Mickey Welch New York Portrait; right arm extended	2500.00	1250.00
40 Jim Whitney	1500.00	750.00
41 George Wood	1500.00	750.00

1998 Aurora

The 1998 Aurora set (produced by Pacific) was issued in one series totalling 200 cards. The cards were issued in six card packs with a SRP of $2.99. In addition, a Tony Gwynn sample card was issued prior to the product's release. The card was distributed to dealers and hobby media to preview the product. It's identical in design to a standard Aurora card except for the word "SAMPLE" printed on the card back in the area typically designated for a card number. A Magglio Ordonez Rookie Card is the key card in this set.

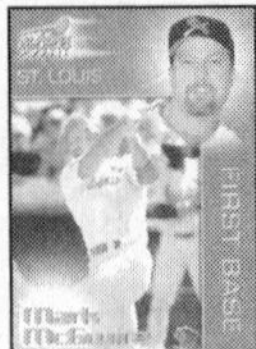

	Nm-Mt	Ex-Mt
COMPLETE SET (200)	40.00	12.00
1 Garret Anderson	.40	.12
2 Jim Edmonds	.40	.12
3 Darin Erstad	.40	.12
4 Cecil Fielder	.40	.12
5 Chuck Finley	.40	.12
6 Todd Greene	.40	.12
7 Ken Hill	.40	.12
8 Tim Salmon	.60	.18
9 Roberto Alomar	1.00	.30
10 Brady Anderson	.40	.12
11 Joe Carter	.40	.12
12 Mike Mussina	1.00	.30
13 Rafael Palmeiro	.60	.18
14 Cal Ripken	3.00	.90
15 B.J. Surhoff	.40	.12
16 Steve Avery	.40	.12
17 Nomar Garciaparra	1.50	.45
18 Pedro Martinez	1.00	.30
19 John Valentin	.40	.12
20 Jason Varitek	.40	.12
21 Mo Vaughn	.40	.12
22 Albert Belle	.40	.12
23 Ray Durham	.40	.12
24 Magglio Ordonez RC	2.00	.60
25 Frank Thomas	1.00	.30
26 Robin Ventura	.40	.12
27 Sandy Alomar Jr.	.40	.12
28 Travis Fryman	.40	.12
29 Dwight Gooden	.40	.12
30 David Justice	.40	.12
31 Kenny Lofton	.40	.12
32 Manny Ramirez	.40	.12
33 Jim Thome	1.00	.30
34 Omar Vizquel	.40	.12
35 Enrique Wilson	.40	.12
36 Jaret Wright	.40	.12
37 Tony Clark	.40	.12
38 Bobby Higginson	.40	.12
39 Brian Hunter	.40	.12
40 Bip Roberts	.40	.12
41 Justin Thompson	.40	.12
42 Jeff Conine	.40	.12
43 Johnny Damon	.40	.12
44 Jermaine Dye	.40	.12
45 Jeff King	.40	.12
46 Jeff Montgomery	.40	.12
47 Hal Morris	.40	.12
48 Dean Palmer	.40	.12
49 Terry Pendleton	.40	.12
50 Rick Aguilera	.40	.12
51 Marty Cordova	.40	.12
52 Paul Molitor	.60	.18
53 Otis Nixon	.40	.12
54 Brad Radke	.40	.12
55 Terry Steinbach	.40	.12
56 Todd Walker	.40	.12
57 Chili Davis	.40	.12
58 Derek Jeter	2.50	.75
59 Chuck Knoblauch	.40	.12
60 Tino Martinez	.60	.18
61 Paul O'Neill	.60	.18
62 Andy Pettitte	.60	.18
63 Mariano Rivera	.60	.18
64 Bernie Williams	.60	.18
65 Jason Giambi	1.00	.30
66 Ben Grieve	.40	.12
67 Rickey Henderson	1.00	.30
68 A.J. Hinch	.40	.12
69 Kenny Rogers	.40	.12
70 Jay Buhner	.40	.12
71 Joey Cora	.40	.12
72 Ken Griffey Jr.	1.50	.45
73 Randy Johnson	1.00	.30
74 Edgar Martinez	.60	.18
75 Jamie Moyer	.40	.12
76 Alex Rodriguez	1.50	.45
77 David Segui	.40	.12
78 Rolando Arrojo RC	.40	.12
79 Wade Boggs	.60	.18
80 Roberto Hernandez	.40	.12
81 Dave Martinez	.40	.12
82 Fred McGriff	.60	.18
83 Paul Sorrento	.40	.12
84 Kevin Stocker	.40	.12
85 Will Clark	1.00	.30
86 Juan Gonzalez	1.00	.30
87 Tom Goodwin	.40	.12
88 Rusty Greer	.40	.12
89 Ivan Rodriguez	1.00	.30
90 John Wetteland	.40	.12
91 Jose Canseco	1.00	.30
92 Roger Clemens	2.00	.60
93 Jose Cruz Jr.	.40	.12
94 Carlos Delgado	.40	.12
95 Pat Hentgen	.40	.12
96 Jay Bell	.40	.12
97 Andy Benes	.40	.12
98 Karim Garcia	.40	.12
99 Travis Lee	.40	.12
100 Devon White	.40	.12
101 Matt Williams	.40	.12
102 Andres Galarraga	.40	.12
103 Tom Glavine	.60	.18
104 Andruw Jones	.40	.12
105 Chipper Jones	1.00	.30
106 Ryan Klesko	.40	.12
107 Javy Lopez	.40	.12
108 Greg Maddux	1.50	.45
109 Walt Weiss	.40	.12
110 Rod Beck	.40	.12
111 Jeff Blauser	.40	.12
112 Mark Grace	.60	.18
113 Lance Johnson	.40	.12
114 Mickey Morandini	.40	.12
115 Henry Rodriguez	.40	.12
116 Sammy Sosa	1.50	.45
117 Kerry Wood	1.00	.30
118 Lenny Harris	.40	.12
119 Damian Jackson	.40	.12
120 Barry Larkin	1.00	.30
121 Reggie Sanders	.40	.12
122 Brett Tomko	.40	.12
123 Dante Bichette	.40	.12
124 Ellis Burks	.40	.12
125 Vinny Castilla	.40	.12
126 Todd Helton	.60	.18
127 Darryl Kile	.40	.12
128 Larry Walker	.60	.18
129 Bobby Bonilla	.40	.12
130 Livan Hernandez	.40	.12
131 Charles Johnson	.40	.12
132 Derrek Lee	.40	.12
133 Edgar Renteria	.40	.12
134 Gary Sheffield	.40	.12
135 Moises Alou	.40	.12
136 Jeff Bagwell	.60	.18
137 Derek Bell	.40	.12
138 Craig Biggio	.60	.18
139 John Halama RC	.40	.12
140 Mike Hampton	.40	.12
141 Richard Hidalgo	.40	.12
142 Wilton Guerrero	.40	.12
143 Todd Hollandsworth	.40	.12
144 Eric Karros	.40	.12
145 Paul Konerko	.40	.12
146 Raul Mondesi	.40	.12
147 Hideo Nomo	1.00	.30
148 Chan Ho Park	.40	.12
149 Mike Piazza	1.50	.45
150 Jeromy Burnitz	.40	.12
151 Todd Dunn	.40	.12
152 Marquis Grissom	.40	.12
153 John Jaha	.40	.12
154 Dave Nilsson	.40	.12
155 Fernando Vina	.40	.12
156 Mark Grudzielanek	.40	.12
157 Vladimir Guerrero	1.00	.30
158 F.P. Santangelo	.40	.12
159 Jose Vidro	.40	.12
160 Rondell White	.40	.12
161 Edgardo Alfonzo	.40	.12
162 Carlos Baerga	.40	.12
163 John Franco	.40	.12
164 Todd Hundley	.40	.12
165 Brian McRae	.40	.12
166 John Olerud	.40	.12
167 Rey Ordonez	.40	.12
168 Masato Yoshii RC	.60	.18
169 Ricky Bottalico	.40	.12
170 Doug Glanville	.40	.12
171 Gregg Jefferies	.40	.12
172 Desi Relaford	.40	.12
173 Scott Rolen	.60	.18
174 Curt Schilling	.60	.18
175 Jose Guillen	.40	.12
176 Jason Kendall	.40	.12
177 Al Martin	.40	.12
178 Doug Strange	.40	.12
179 Kevin Young	.40	.12
180 Royce Clayton	.40	.12
181 Delino DeShields	.40	.12
182 Gary Gaetti	.40	.12
183 Ron Gant	.40	.12
184 Brian Jordan	.40	.12
185 Ray Lankford	.40	.12
186 Willie McGee	.40	.12
187 Mark McGwire	2.50	.75
188 Kevin Brown	.60	.18
189 Ken Caminiti	.40	.12
190 Steve Finley	.40	.12
191 Tony Gwynn	1.25	.35
192 Wally Joyner	.40	.12
193 Ruben Rivera	.40	.12
194 Quilvio Veras	.40	.12
195 Barry Bonds	2.50	.75
196 Shawn Estes	.40	.12
197 Orel Hershiser	.40	.12
198 Jeff Kent	.40	.12
199 Robb Nen	.40	.12
200 J.T. Snow	.40	.12
NNO Tony Gwynn Sample	3.00	.90

1998 Aurora Cubes

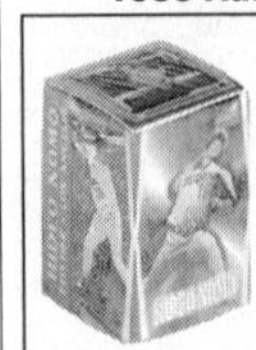

These cubes, inserted one per hobby box, feature 20 of the leading players in baseball in an innovative cube design.

	Nm-Mt	Ex-Mt
COMPLETE SET (20)	120.00	36.00
1 Travis Lee	2.00	.60
2 Chipper Jones	5.00	1.50
3 Greg Maddux	8.00	2.40
4 Cal Ripken	15.00	4.50
5 Nomar Garciaparra	8.00	2.40
6 Frank Thomas	5.00	1.50
7 Manny Ramirez	2.00	.60
8 Larry Walker	3.00	.90
9 Hideo Nomo	5.00	1.50
10 Mike Piazza	8.00	2.40
11 Derek Jeter	12.00	3.60
12 Ben Grieve	2.00	.60
13 Mark McGwire	12.00	3.60
14 Tony Gwynn	6.00	1.80
15 Barry Bonds	12.00	3.60
16 Ken Griffey Jr.	8.00	2.40
17 Alex Rodriguez	8.00	2.40
18 Wade Boggs	3.00	.90
19 Juan Gonzalez	5.00	1.50
20 Jose Cruz Jr.	2.00	.60

1998 Aurora Hardball Cel-Fusions

Randomly inserted in packs at a rate of one in 73, this 20-card set is an insert to the Aurora brand. The cards unique design resembling a baseball features a game action photo of the game's hottest stars.

	Nm-Mt	Ex-Mt
COMPLETE SET (20)	250.00	75.00
1 Travis Lee	5.00	1.50
2 Chipper Jones	12.00	3.60
3 Greg Maddux	20.00	6.00
4 Cal Ripken	40.00	12.00
5 Nomar Garciaparra	20.00	6.00
6 Frank Thomas	12.00	3.60
7 David Justice	5.00	1.50
8 Jeff Bagwell	8.00	2.40
9 Hideo Nomo	12.00	3.60
10 Mike Piazza	20.00	6.00
11 Derek Jeter	30.00	9.00
12 Ben Grieve	5.00	1.50
13 Scott Rolen	8.00	2.40
14 Mark McGwire	30.00	9.00
15 Tony Gwynn	15.00	4.50
16 Ken Griffey Jr.	20.00	6.00
17 Alex Rodriguez	20.00	6.00
18 Ivan Rodriguez	12.00	3.60
19 Roger Clemens	25.00	7.50
20 Jose Cruz Jr.	5.00	1.50

1998 Aurora Kings of the Major Leagues

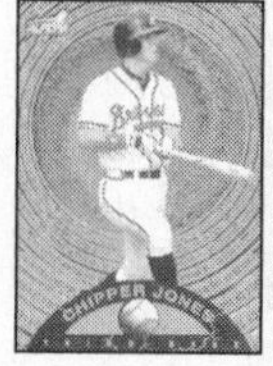

Randomly inserted in packs at a rate of one in 361, this 10-card set is an insert to the Aurora brands. The fronts feature a color action photo on a circular background in full foil design.

	Nm-Mt	Ex-Mt
COMPLETE SET (10)	400.00	120.00
1 Chipper Jones	25.00	7.50
2 Greg Maddux	40.00	12.00
3 Cal Ripken	80.00	24.00
4 Nomar Garciaparra	40.00	12.00
5 Frank Thomas	25.00	7.50
6 Mike Piazza	40.00	12.00
7 Mark McGwire	60.00	18.00
8 Tony Gwynn	30.00	9.00
9 Ken Griffey Jr.	40.00	12.00
10 Alex Rodriguez	40.00	12.00

1998 Aurora On Deck Laser Cuts

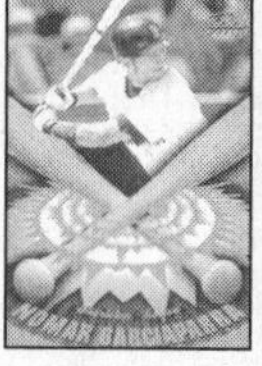

In another example of Pacific using their die-cut technology, these cards featuring 20 of the leading players in baseball were issued four every 37 packs.

	Nm-Mt	Ex-Mt
COMPLETE SET (20)	80.00	24.00
1 Travis Lee	1.25	.35
2 Chipper Jones	3.00	.90
3 Greg Maddux	5.00	1.50
4 Cal Ripken	10.00	3.00
5 Nomar Garciaparra	5.00	1.50
6 Frank Thomas	3.00	.90
7 Manny Ramirez	1.25	.35
8 Larry Walker	2.00	.60
9 Hideo Nomo	3.00	.90
10 Mike Piazza	5.00	1.50
11 Derek Jeter	8.00	2.40
12 Ben Grieve	1.25	.35
13 Mark McGwire	8.00	2.40
14 Tony Gwynn	4.00	1.20
15 Barry Bonds	8.00	2.40
16 Ken Griffey Jr.	5.00	1.50
17 Alex Rodriguez	5.00	1.50
18 Wade Boggs	2.00	.60
19 Juan Gonzalez	3.00	.90
20 Jose Cruz Jr.	1.25	.35

1998 Aurora Pennant Fever

Inserted in packs at a rate of one per pack, this 50-card set features a selection of the league's top stars. The card fronts feature a background of "pennant" design that reads the featured player's team name. A color photo of the player rests in front of the pennant along with the player's name and team position in the lower right corner. In addition, Tony Gwynn signed three extremely rare Pennant Fever inserts (one Copper, one Platinum Blue and one Silver version). All three of these cards are too rare to provide price listings.

	Nm-Mt	Ex-Mt
COMPLETE SET (50)	25.00	7.50
*RED: 1.5X TO 4X BASIC PENNANT ...		
RED STATED ODDS 1:4 RETAIL.........		
*SILVER: 8X TO 20X BASIC PENNANT		
SILVER: RANDOM INSERTS IN RETAIL PACKS		
SILVER PRINT RUN 250 SERIAL #'d SETS		
*PLAT.BLUE: 15X TO 40X BASIC PENNANT		
PLAT.BLUE: RANDOM INSERTS IN ALL PACKS		
PLAT.BLUE PRINT RUN 100 SERIAL #'d SETS		
*COPPER: 40X TO 100X BASIC PENNANT		
COPPER: RANDOM INSERTS IN HOBBY PACKS		
COPPER PRINT RUN 20 SERIAL #'d SETS		
1 Tony Gwynn	1.25	.35
2 Derek Jeter	2.50	.75
3 Alex Rodriguez	1.50	.45
4 Paul Molitor	.60	.18
5 Nomar Garciaparra	1.50	.45
6 Jeff Bagwell	.60	.18
7 Ivan Rodriguez	1.00	.30
8 Cal Ripken	3.00	.90
9 Matt Williams	.40	.12
10 Chipper Jones	1.00	.30
11 Edgar Martinez	.60	.18
12 Wade Boggs	.60	.18
13 Paul Konerko	.40	.12
14 Ben Grieve	.40	.12
15 Sandy Alomar Jr.	.40	.12
16 Travis Lee	.40	.12
17 Scott Rolen	.60	.18
18 Ryan Klesko	.40	.12
19 Juan Gonzalez	1.00	.30
20 Albert Belle	.40	.12
21 Roger Clemens	2.00	.60
22 Javy Lopez	.40	.12
23 Jose Cruz Jr.	.40	.12
24 Ken Griffey Jr.	1.50	.45
25 Mark McGwire	2.50	.75
26 Brady Anderson	.40	.12
27 Jaret Wright	.40	.12
28 Roberto Alomar	1.00	.30
29 Joe Carter	.40	.12
30 Hideo Nomo	1.00	.30
31 Mike Piazza	1.50	.45
32 Andres Galarraga	.40	.12
33 Larry Walker	.60	.18
34 Tim Salmon	.60	.18
35 Frank Thomas	1.00	.30
36 Moises Alou	.40	.12
37 David Justice	.40	.12
38 Manny Ramirez	.40	.12
39 Jim Edmonds	.40	.12
40 Barry Bonds	2.50	.75
41 Jim Thome	1.00	.30
42 Mo Vaughn	.40	.12
43 Rafael Palmeiro	.60	.18
44 Darin Erstad	.40	.12
45 Pedro Martinez	1.00	.30
46 Greg Maddux	1.50	.45
47 Jose Canseco	1.00	.30
48 Vladimir Guerrero	1.00	.30
49 Bernie Williams	.60	.18
50 Randy Johnson	1.00	.30

1999 Aurora

The 1999 Aurora set (produced by Pacific) was issued in April, 1999 in one series totalling 200 cards and was distributed in six-card packs with a SRP of $2.99. Each card features a total of three color photos (two on the front and one on the back) of some of baseball's most popular players.

	Nm-Mt	Ex-Mt
COMPLETE SET (200)	40.00	12.00
1 Garret Anderson	.40	.12
2 Jim Edmonds	.40	.12
3 Darin Erstad	.40	.12
4 Matt Luke	.40	.12
5 Tim Salmon	.60	.18
6 Mo Vaughn	.40	.12
7 Jay Bell	.40	.12
8 David Dellucci	.40	.12
9 Steve Finley	.40	.12
10 Bernard Gilkey	.40	.12
11 Randy Johnson	1.00	.30
12 Travis Lee	.40	.12
13 Matt Williams	.40	.12
14 Andres Galarraga	.40	.12
15 Tom Glavine	.60	.18
16 Andruw Jones	.40	.12
17 Chipper Jones	1.25	.35
18 Brian Jordan	.40	.12
19 Javy Lopez	.40	.12
20 Greg Maddux	1.50	.45
21 Albert Belle	.40	.12
22 Will Clark	1.00	.30
23 Scott Erickson	.40	.12
24 Mike Mussina	1.00	.30
25 Cal Ripken	3.00	.90
26 B.J. Surhoff	.40	.12
27 Nomar Garciaparra	1.50	.45
28 Reggie Jefferson	.40	.12
29 Darren Lewis	.40	.12
30 Pedro Martinez	1.00	.30
31 John Valentin	.40	.12
32 Rod Beck	.40	.12
33 Mark Grace	.60	.18
34 Lance Johnson	.40	.12
35 Mickey Morandini	.40	.12
36 Sammy Sosa	1.50	.45
37 Kerry Wood	1.00	.30
38 James Baldwin	.40	.12
39 Mike Caruso	.40	.12
40 Ray Durham	.40	.12
41 Magglio Ordonez	.40	.12
42 Frank Thomas	1.00	.30
43 Aaron Boone	.40	.12
44 Sean Casey	.40	.12
45 Barry Larkin	1.00	.30
46 Hal Morris	.40	.12
47 Denny Neagle	.40	.12
48 Greg Vaughn	.40	.12
49 Pat Watkins	.40	.12
50 Roberto Alomar	1.00	.30
51 Sandy Alomar Jr.	.40	.12
52 David Justice	.40	.12
53 Kenny Lofton	.40	.12
54 Manny Ramirez	.40	.12
55 Richie Sexson	.40	.12
56 Jim Thome	1.00	.30
57 Omar Vizquel	.40	.12
58 Dante Bichette	.40	.12
59 Vinny Castilla	.40	.12
60 Edgard Clemente	.40	.12
61 Derrick Gibson	.40	.12
62 Todd Helton	.60	.18
63 Darryl Kile	.40	.12
64 Larry Walker	.60	.18
65 Tony Clark	.40	.12
66 Damion Easley	.40	.12
67 Bob Higginson	.40	.12
68 Brian Hunter	.40	.12
69 Dean Palmer	.40	.12
70 Justin Thompson	.40	.12
71 Craig Counsell	.40	.12
72 Todd Dunwoody	.40	.12
73 Cliff Floyd	.40	.12
74 Alex Gonzalez	.40	.12
75 Livan Hernandez	.40	.12
76 Mark Kotsay	.40	.12
77 Derrek Lee	.40	.12
78 Moises Alou	.40	.12
79 Jeff Bagwell	.60	.18
80 Derek Bell	.40	.12
81 Craig Biggio	.60	.18
82 Ken Caminiti	.40	.12
83 Richard Hidalgo	.40	.12
84 Shane Reynolds	.40	.12
85 Jeff Conine	.40	.12
86 Johnny Damon	.40	.12
87 Jermaine Dye	.40	.12
88 Jeff King	.40	.12
89 Jeff Montgomery	.40	.12
90 Mike Sweeney	.40	.12
91 Kevin Brown	.60	.18
92 Mark Grudzielanek	.40	.12
93 Eric Karros	.40	.12
94 Raul Mondesi	.40	.12
95 Chan Ho Park	.40	.12
96 Gary Sheffield	.40	.12
97 Jeromy Burnitz	.40	.12
98 Jeff Cirillo	.40	.12
99 Marquis Grissom	.40	.12
100 Geoff Jenkins	.40	.12
101 Dave Nilsson	.40	.12
102 Jose Valetin	.40	.12
103 Fernando Vina	.40	.12
104 Marty Cordova	.40	.12
105 Matt Lawton	.40	.12
106 David Ortiz	.40	.12
107 Brad Radke	.40	.12
108 Todd Walker	.40	.12
109 Shane Andrews	.40	.12
110 Orlando Cabrera	.40	.12
111 Brad Fullmer	.40	.12
112 Vladimir Guerrero	1.00	.30
113 Wilton Guerrero	.40	.12
114 Carl Pavano	.40	.12
115 Fernando Seguignol	.40	.12
116 Ugueth Urbina	.40	.12
117 Edgardo Alfonzo	.40	.12
118 Bobby Bonilla	.40	.12
119 Rickey Henderson	1.00	.30
120 Hideo Nomo	1.00	.30
121 John Olerud	.40	.12
122 Rey Ordonez	.40	.12
123 Mike Piazza	1.50	.45
124 Masato Yoshii	.40	.12
125 Scott Brosius	.40	.12
126 Orlando Hernandez	.40	.12
127 Hideki Irabu	.40	.12
128 Derek Jeter	2.50	.75
129 Chuck Knoblauch	.40	.12
130 Tino Martinez	.60	.18
131 Jorge Posada	.60	.18
132 Bernie Williams	.60	.18
133 Eric Chavez	.40	.12
134 Ryan Christenson	.40	.12
135 Jason Giambi	1.00	.30
136 Ben Grieve	.40	.12
137 A.J. Hinch	.40	.12
138 Matt Stairs	.40	.12
139 Miguel Tejada	.40	.12
140 Bob Abreu	.40	.12
141 Gary Bennett RC	.40	.12
142 Desi Relaford	.40	.12
143 Scott Rolen	.60	.18
144 Curt Schilling	.60	.18
145 Kevin Sefcik	.40	.12
146 Brian Giles	.40	.12
147 Jose Guillen	.40	.12
148 Jason Kendall	.40	.12
149 Aramis Ramirez	.40	.12
150 Tony Womack	.40	.12
151 Kevin Young	.40	.12
152 Eric Davis	.40	.12
153 J.D. Drew	.40	.12
154 Ray Lankford	.40	.12
155 Eli Marrero	.40	.12
156 Mark McGwire	2.50	.75
157 Luis Ordaz	.40	.12
158 Edgar Renteria	.40	.12
159 Andy Ashby	.40	.12
160 Tony Gwynn	1.25	.35
161 Trevor Hoffman	.40	.12
162 Wally Joyner	.40	.12
163 Jim Leyritz	.40	.12
164 Ruben Rivera	.40	.12
165 Reggie Sanders	.40	.12
166 Quilvio Veras	.40	.12
167 Rich Aurilia	.40	.12
168 Marvin Benard	.40	.12
169 Barry Bonds	2.50	.75
170 Ellis Burks	.40	.12
171 Jeff Kent	.40	.12
172 Bill Mueller	.40	.12
173 J.T. Snow	.40	.12
174 Jay Buhner	.40	.12
175 Jeff Fassero	.40	.12
176 Ken Griffey Jr.	1.50	.45
177 Carlos Guillen	.40	.12
178 Edgar Martinez	.60	.18
179 Alex Rodriguez	1.50	.45
180 David Segui	.40	.12
181 Dan Wilson	.40	.12
182 Rolando Arrojo	.40	.12
183 Wade Boggs	.60	.18
184 Jose Canseco	1.00	.30
185 Aaron Ledesma	.40	.12
186 Dave Martinez	.40	.12
187 Quinton McCracken	.40	.12
188 Fred McGriff	.60	.18
189 Juan Gonzalez	1.00	.30
190 Tom Goodwin	.40	.12
191 Rusty Greer	.40	.12
192 Roberto Kelly	.40	.12
193 Rafael Palmeiro	.60	.18
194 Ivan Rodriguez	1.00	.30
195 Roger Clemens	2.00	.60
196 Jose Cruz Jr.	.40	.12
197 Carlos Delgado	.40	.12
198 Alex Gonzalez	.40	.12
199 Roy Halladay	.40	.12
200 Pat Hentgen	.40	.12

1999 Aurora Opening Day

This parallel set was issued one card per 24-pack hobby box. Because of the number of cases produced, the cards are serial numbered to 31. A gold foil "Opening Day" starburst logo is featured on the front of each card. Within the starburst, the card is serial numbered "X/31". Pacific issued an Opening Day card for each of the rest of their 1999 sets - but it should be noted that the concept debuted in the Aurora brand.

	Nm-Mt	Ex-Mt
*STARS: 20X TO 50X BASIC CARDS..		

1999 Aurora Red

Radomly inserted in Treat Retail packs only at the rate of 4:25, this 200-card set is parallel to the Pacific Aurora base set with red foil highlights.

	Nm-Mt	Ex-Mt
*STARS: 3X TO 8X BASIC CARDS......		

1999 Aurora Complete Players

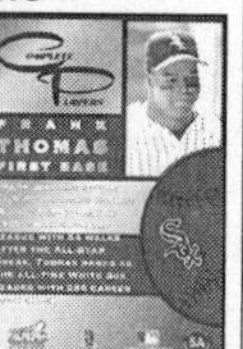

Randomly inserted in packs, this 20 card set features two cards each of ten top stars who have proven they can do it all. Each card features a color player photo printed on fully foiled and etched card stock and designed to fit with its matching same player card. Only 299 serially numbered sets were produced.

	Nm-Mt	Ex-Mt
COMPLETE SET (20)	300.00	90.00
A AND B CARDS ARE EQUALLY VALUED!		
1A Cal Ripken	40.00	12.00
2A Nomar Garciaparra	20.00	6.00
3A Sammy Sosa	20.00	6.00
4A Kerry Wood	6.00	1.80
5A Frank Thomas	6.00	1.80
6A Mike Piazza	20.00	6.00
7A Mark McGwire	30.00	9.00
8A Tony Gwynn	15.00	4.50
9A Ken Griffey Jr.	20.00	6.00
10A Alex Rodriguez	20.00	6.00

1999 Aurora Kings of the Major Leagues

Randomly inserted in packs at the rate of one in 361, this 10-card set features color player images printed on full foil cards with a crown image in the background.

	Nm-Mt	Ex-Mt
1 Cal Ripken	80.00	24.00
2 Nomar Garciaparra	40.00	12.00
3 Sammy Sosa	40.00	12.00
4 Kerry Wood	25.00	7.50
5 Frank Thomas	25.00	7.50
6 Mike Piazza	40.00	12.00
7 Mark McGwire	60.00	18.00
8 Tony Gwynn	30.00	9.00
9 Ken Griffey Jr.	40.00	12.00
10 Alex Rodriguez	40.00	12.00

1999 Aurora On Deck Laser-Cuts

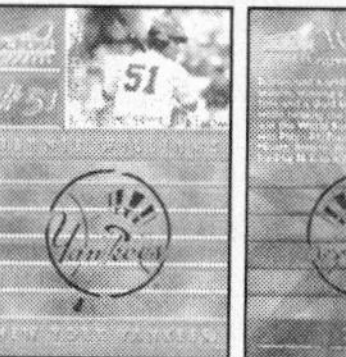

Randomly inserted in hobby packs only at the rate of four in 37, this 20-card set features color photos of some of baseball's favorite players printed on laser cut cards.

	Nm-Mt	Ex-Mt
COMPLETE SET (20)	80.00	24.00
1 Chipper Jones	3.00	.90
2 Cal Ripken	8.00	2.40
3 Nomar Garciaparra	4.00	1.20
4 Sammy Sosa	4.00	1.20
5 Frank Thomas	2.50	.75
6 Manny Ramirez	1.00	.30
7 Todd Helton	1.50	.45
8 Larry Walker	1.50	.45
9 Jeff Bagwell	1.50	.45
10 Vladimir Guerrero	2.50	.75
11 Mike Piazza	4.00	1.20
12 Derek Jeter	6.00	1.80
13 Bernie Williams	1.50	.45
14 J.D. Drew	1.00	.30
15 Mark McGwire	6.00	1.80
16 Tony Gwynn	3.00	.90
17 Ken Griffey Jr.	4.00	1.20
18 Alex Rodriguez	4.00	1.20
19 Juan Gonzalez	2.50	.75
20 Ivan Rodriguez	2.50	.75

1999 Aurora Pennant Fever

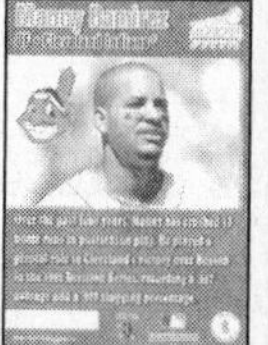

Randomly inserted in packs at the rate of four in 37, this 20-card set features color player images printed on fully foiled and etched cards with shadow photos of the same player as the background. Spokesperson Tony Gwynn signed 97 serial numbered copies of his own card, all of which were randomly seeded into packs.

	Nm-Mt	Ex-Mt
COMPLETE SET (20)	40.00	12.00
*SILVER: 1.5X TO 4X BASIC PEN.FEVER		
SILVER: RANDOM INSERTS IN RETAIL PACKS		
SILVER PRINT RUN 250 SERIAL #d SETS		
*PLAT.BLUE: 3X TO 8X BASIC PEN.FEVER		
PLAT.BLUE: RANDOM INS.IN HOB/RET.PACKS		
PLAT.BLUE PRINT RUN 100 SERIAL #d SETS		
*COPPER: 10X TO 25X BASIC PEN.FEVER		
COPPER: RANDOM INSERTS IN HOBBY PACKS		
COPPER PRINT RUN 20 SERIAL #d SETS		
GWYNN SIGNED 97 P.FEVER BASIC CARDS		
GWYNN SIGNED 1 P.FEVER COPPER CARD		
GWYNN SIGNED 1 P.FEVER P.BLUE CARD		
GWYNN SIGNED 1 P.FEVER SILVER CARD		
1 Chipper Jones	1.50	.45
2 Greg Maddux	2.00	.60
3 Cal Ripken	4.00	1.20
4 Nomar Garciaparra	2.00	.60
5 Sammy Sosa	2.00	.60
6 Kerry Wood	1.25	.35
7 Frank Thomas	1.25	.35
8 Manny Ramirez	.50	.15
9 Todd Helton	.75	.23
10 Jeff Bagwell	.75	.23
11 Mike Piazza	2.00	.60
12 Derek Jeter	3.00	.90
13 Bernie Williams	.75	.23
14 J.D. Drew	.50	.15
15 Mark McGwire	3.00	.90
16 Tony Gwynn	1.50	.45
17 Ken Griffey Jr.	2.00	.60
18 Alex Rodriguez	2.00	.60
19 Juan Gonzalez	1.25	.35
20 Ivan Rodriguez	1.25	.35
S16 Tony Gwynn AU/97	50.00	15.00

1999 Aurora Styrotechs

Randomly inserted in packs at the rate of one in 37, this 20-card set features color photos of some of baseball's top players printed on all-new styrene card stock.

	Nm-Mt	Ex-Mt
COMPLETE SET (20)	200.00	60.00
1 Chipper Jones	8.00	2.40

2 Greg Maddux 10.00 3.00
3 Cal Ripken 20.00 6.00
4 Nomar Garciaparra 10.00 3.00
5 Sammy Sosa 10.00 3.00
6 Kerry Wood 6.00 1.80
7 Frank Thomas 6.00 1.80
8 Manny Ramirez 2.50 .75
9 Larry Walker 4.00 1.20
10 Jeff Bagwell 4.00 1.20
11 Mike Piazza 10.00 3.00
12 Derek Jeter 15.00 4.50
13 Bernie Williams 4.00 1.20
14 J.D. Drew 2.50 .75
15 Mark McGwire 15.00 4.50
16 Tony Gwynn 8.00 2.40
17 Ken Griffey Jr. 10.00 3.00
18 Alex Rodriguez 10.00 3.00
19 Juan Gonzalez 6.00 1.80
20 Ivan Rodriguez 6.00 1.80

1999 Aurora Players Choice

These cards which parallel the regular Aurora cards were given out at the Players Choice award ceremony. The cards have a special "Players Choice" stamp on them but otherwise parallel the regular Aurora cards. We have skip-numbered this set to match the regular card numbers. Varying amounts of each card were issued so we have put the print run next to the players name.

Nm-Mt Ex-Mt
13 Matt Williams/109 10.00 3.00
20 Greg Maddux/79 40.00 12.00
36 Sammy Sosa/82 30.00 9.00
54 Manny Ramirez/100 20.00 6.00
79 Jeff Bagwell/109 20.00 6.00
119 R.Henderson/108 25.00 7.50

2000 Aurora

The 2000 Aurora set was released in March, 2000 as a 151-card set. Each pack contained six cards and carried a suggested retail price of 2.99. Two versions of card number 133 were created to showcase Ken Griffey Jr. on the Mariners and his new team, the Reds. It's worth noting that this was the first MLB licensed card to feature Griffey as a Red and for a short while it traded in the $15-30 range. A promotional sample card featuring Tony Gwynn was distributed to dealers and hobby media several weeks before the product went live. In addition, a last minute card was added to the set featuring Ken Griffey Jr. in a Reds uniform.

Nm-Mt Ex-Mt
COMPLETE SET (151) 40.00 12.00
1 Darin Erstad .40 .12
2 Troy Glaus .60 .18
3 Tim Salmon .60 .18
4 Mo Vaughn .40 .12
5 Jay Bell .40 .12
6 Erubiel Durazo .40 .12
7 Luis Gonzalez .40 .12
8 Randy Johnson 1.00 .30
9 Matt Williams .40 .12
10 Tom Glavine .60 .18
11 Andruw Jones .40 .12
12 Chipper Jones 1.00 .30
13 Brian Jordan .40 .12
14 Greg Maddux 1.50 .45
15 Kevin Millwood .40 .12
16 Albert Belle .40 .12
17 Will Clark 1.00 .30
18 Mike Mussina 1.00 .30
19 Cal Ripken 3.00 .90
20 B.J. Surhoff .40 .12
21 Nomar Garciaparra 1.50 .45
22 Pedro Martinez 1.00 .30
23 Troy O'Leary .40 .12
24 Wilton Veras .40 .12
25 Mark Grace .60 .18
26 Henry Rodriguez .40 .12
27 Sammy Sosa 1.50 .45
28 Kerry Wood 1.00 .30
29 Ray Durham .40 .12
30 Paul Konerko .40 .12
31 Carlos Lee .40 .12
32 Magglio Ordonez .40 .12
33 Chris Singleton .40 .12
34 Frank Thomas 1.00 .30
35 Mike Cameron .40 .12
36 Sean Casey .40 .12
37 Barry Larkin 1.00 .30
38 Pokey Reese .40 .12
39 Eddie Taubensee .40 .12
40 Roberto Alomar 1.00 .30
41 David Justice .40 .12
42 Kenny Lofton .40 .12
43 Manny Ramirez .40 .12
44 Richie Sexson .40 .12
45 Jim Thome 1.00 .30
46 Omar Vizquel .40 .12
47 Todd Helton .60 .18
48 Mike Lansing .40 .12
49 Neifi Perez .40 .12
50 Ben Petrick .40 .12
51 Larry Walker .60 .18
52 Tony Clark .40 .12
53 Damion Easley .40 .12
54 Juan Encarnacion .40 .12
55 Juan Gonzalez 1.00 .30
56 Dean Palmer .40 .12
57 Luis Castillo .40 .12
58 Cliff Floyd .40 .12
59 Alex Gonzalez .40 .12
60 Mike Lowell .40 .12
61 Preston Wilson .40 .12
62 Jeff Bagwell .60 .18
63 Craig Biggio .60 .18
64 Ken Caminiti .40 .12
65 Jose Lima .40 .12
66 Billy Wagner .40 .12
67 Carlos Beltran .40 .12
68 Johnny Damon .40 .12
69 Jermaine Dye .40 .12
70 Mark Quinn .40 .12
71 Mike Sweeney .40 .12
72 Kevin Brown .60 .18
73 Shawn Green .40 .12
74 Eric Karros .40 .12
75 Chan Ho Park .40 .12
76 Gary Sheffield .40 .12
77 Ron Belliard .40 .12
78 Jeromy Burnitz .40 .12
79 Marquis Grissom .40 .12
80 Geoff Jenkins .40 .12
81 David Nilsson .40 .12
82 Ron Coomer .40 .12
83 Jacque Jones .40 .12
84 Brad Radke .40 .12
85 Todd Walker .40 .12
86 Michael Barrett .40 .12
87 Peter Bergeron .40 .12
88 Vladimir Guerrero 1.00 .30
89 Jose Vidro .40 .12
90 Rondell White .40 .12
91 Edgardo Alfonzo .40 .12
92 Darryl Hamilton .40 .12
93 Rey Ordonez .40 .12
94 Mike Piazza 1.50 .45
95 Robin Ventura .60 .18
96 Roger Clemens 2.00 .60
97 Orlando Hernandez .40 .12
98 Derek Jeter 2.50 .75
99 Tino Martinez .60 .18
100 Mariano Rivera .60 .18
101 Bernie Williams .60 .18
102 Eric Chavez .40 .12
103 Jason Giambi 1.00 .30
104 Ben Grieve .40 .12
105 Tim Hudson .60 .18
106 John Jaha .40 .12
107 Matt Stairs .40 .12
108 Bob Abreu .40 .12
109 Doug Glanville .40 .12
110 Mike Lieberthal .40 .12
111 Scott Rolen .60 .18
112 Curt Schilling .60 .18
113 Brian Giles .40 .12
114 Chad Hermansen .40 .12
115 Jason Kendall .40 .12
116 Warren Morris .40 .12
117 Kevin Young .40 .12
118 Rick Ankiel .40 .12
119 J.D. Drew .40 .12
120 Ray Lankford .40 .12
121 Mark McGwire 2.50 .75
122 Edgar Renteria .40 .12
123 Fernando Tatis .40 .12
124 Ben Davis .40 .12
125 Tony Gwynn 1.25 .35
126 Trevor Hoffman .40 .12
127 Phil Nevin .40 .12
128 Barry Bonds 2.50 .75
129 Ellis Burks .40 .12
130 Jeff Kent .40 .12
131 J.T. Snow .40 .12
132 Freddy Garcia .40 .12
133 Ken Griffey Jr. 1.50 .45
133R Ken Griffey Jr. Reds 1.50 .45
134 Edgar Martinez .60 .18
135 Alex Rodriguez 1.50 .45
136 Dan Wilson .40 .12
137 Jose Canseco 1.00 .30
138 Roberto Hernandez .40 .12
139 Dave Martinez .40 .12
140 Fred McGriff .60 .18
141 Rusty Greer .40 .12
142 Ruben Mateo .40 .12
143 Rafael Palmeiro .60 .18
144 Ivan Rodriguez 1.00 .30
145 Jeff Zimmerman .40 .12
146 Homer Bush .40 .12
147 Carlos Delgado .40 .12
148 Raul Mondesi .40 .12
149 Shannon Stewart .40 .12
150 Vernon Wells .40 .12
SAMP Tony Gwynn Samp. 2.00 .60

2000 Aurora Pinstripes

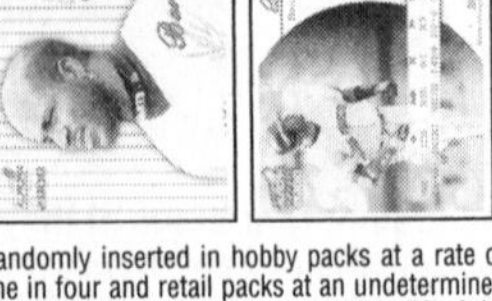

Randomly inserted in hobby packs at a rate of one in four and retail packs at an undetermined rate, this skip-numbered set parallels 50 of the original base cards with pinstriped backgrounds.

Nm-Mt Ex-Mt
COMPLETE SET (50) 100.00 30.00
4 Mo Vaughn 1.25 .35
8 Randy Johnson 3.00 .90
9 Matt Williams 1.25 .35
11 Andruw Jones 1.25 .35
12 Chipper Jones 3.00 .90
14 Greg Maddux 5.00 1.50
19 Cal Ripken 10.00 3.00
21 Nomar Garciaparra 5.00 1.50
22 Pedro Martinez 3.00 .90
27 Sammy Sosa 5.00 1.50
32 Magglio Ordonez 1.25 .35
34 Frank Thomas 3.00 .90
36 Sean Casey 1.25 .35
37 Barry Larkin 3.00 .90
42 Kenny Lofton 1.25 .35
43 Manny Ramirez 1.25 .35
45 Jim Thome 3.00 .90
47 Todd Helton 2.00 .60
51 Larry Walker 2.00 .60
55 Juan Gonzalez 3.00 .90
62 Jeff Bagwell 2.00 .60
63 Craig Biggio 2.00 .60
67 Carlos Beltran 1.25 .35
73 Shawn Green 1.25 .35
76 Gary Sheffield 1.25 .35
78 Jeromy Burnitz 1.25 .35
88 Vladimir Guerrero 3.00 .90
91 Edgardo Alfonzo 1.25 .35
94 Mike Piazza 5.00 1.50
96 Roger Clemens 6.00 1.80
97 Orlando Hernandez 1.25 .35
98 Derek Jeter 8.00 2.40
101 Bernie Williams 2.00 .60
102 Eric Chavez 1.25 .35
105 Tim Hudson 2.00 .60
111 Scott Rolen 2.00 .60
112 Curt Schilling 2.00 .60
113 Brian Giles 1.25 .35
118 Rick Ankiel 1.25 .35
121 Mark McGwire 8.00 2.40
125 Tony Gwynn 4.00 1.20
128 Barry Bonds 8.00 2.40
130 Jeff Kent 1.25 .35
133 Ken Griffey Jr. 5.00 1.50
135 Alex Rodriguez 5.00 1.50
137 Jose Canseco 3.00 .90
140 Fred McGriff 2.00 .60
143 Rafael Palmeiro 2.00 .60
144 Ivan Rodriguez 3.00 .90
147 Carlos Delgado 1.25 .35

2000 Aurora Pinstripes Premiere Date

Randomly inserted at one per hobby box, this insert set parallels 50 of the original base cards with pinstriped backgrounds. Each card is serial numbered to 52.

Nm-Mt Ex-Mt
*PIN.P.DATE: 3X TO 8X BASIC P'STRIPE

2000 Aurora Premiere Date

Randomly inserted in hobby packs at one in 37, this insert set parallels the entire 151-card Aurora base set. Each card is serial numbered to 52.

Nm-Mt Ex-Mt
*STARS: 10X TO 25X BASIC CARDS ..

2000 Aurora Dugout View Net Fusions

Randomly inserted in packs at one in 37, this 20-card insert features some of the best in baseball on cards that contain strips of actual netting.

Nm-Mt Ex-Mt
COMPLETE SET (20) 120.00 36.00
1 Mo Vaughn 2.50 .75
2 Chipper Jones 6.00 1.80
3 Cal Ripken 20.00 6.00
4 Nomar Garciaparra 10.00 3.00
5 Sammy Sosa 10.00 3.00
6 Manny Ramirez 2.50 .75
7 Larry Walker 4.00 1.20
8 Juan Gonzalez 6.00 1.80
9 Jeff Bagwell 4.00 1.20
10 Craig Biggio 4.00 1.20
11 Shawn Green 2.50 .75
12 Vladimir Guerrero 6.00 1.80
13 Mike Piazza 10.00 3.00
14 Derek Jeter 15.00 4.50
15 Scott Rolen 4.00 1.20
16 Mark McGwire 15.00 4.50
17 Tony Gwynn 8.00 2.40
18 Ken Griffey Jr. 10.00 3.00
19 Alex Rodriguez 10.00 3.00
20 Rafael Palmeiro 4.00 1.20

2000 Aurora Pennant Fever

Randomly inserted in packs at four in 37, this insert set features 20 major league player's that are chasing the pennant. Tony Gwynn signed 150 cards for this insert set, 147 of which are the basic Pennant Fever cards and one each of the copper, platinum, blue and silver inserts.

Nm-Mt Ex-Mt
COMPLETE SET (20) 40.00 12.00
*COPPER: 1.5X TO 4X BASIC PEN.FEVER
COPPER RANDOM INSERTS IN HOBBY
COPPER PRINT RUN 399 SERIAL #'d SETS
*PLAT.BLUE: 4X TO 10X BASIC PEN.FEVER
PLAT.BLUE: RANDOM INSERTS IN ALL PACKS
PLAT.BLUE PRINT RUN 67 SERIAL #'d SETS
*SILVER: 2.5X TO 6X BASIC PEN.FEVER
SILVER: RANDOM INSERTS IN RETAIL PACKS
SILVER PRINT RUN 199 SERIAL #'d SETS
GWYNN SIGNED 147 PEN.FEVER BASIC
GWYNN SIGNED 1 PEN.FEVER COPPER
GWYNN SIGNED 1 PEN.FEVER PLAT.BLUE
GWYNN SIGNED 1 PEN.FEVER SILVER
GWYNN AU'S: RANDOM INS.IN ALL PACKS
1 Andruw Jones 1.00 .30
2 Chipper Jones 2.50 .75
3 Greg Maddux 4.00 1.20
4 Cal Ripken 8.00 2.40
5 Nomar Garciaparra 4.00 1.20
6 Pedro Martinez 2.50 .75
7 Sammy Sosa 4.00 1.20
8 Manny Ramirez 1.00 .30
9 Jim Thome 2.50 .75
10 Jeff Bagwell 1.50 .45
11 Mike Piazza 4.00 1.20
12 Roger Clemens 5.00 1.50
13 Derek Jeter 6.00 1.80
14 Bernie Williams 1.50 .45
15 Mark McGwire 6.00 1.80
16 Tony Gwynn 3.00 .90
17 Ken Griffey Jr. 4.00 1.20
18 Alex Rodriguez 4.00 1.20
19 Rafael Palmeiro 1.50 .45
20 Ivan Rodriguez 2.50 .75
AU16 Tony Gwynn AU/147 40.00 12.00

2000 Aurora Scouting Report

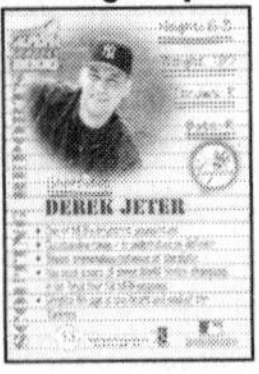

Randomly inserted in hobby packs at four in 37, this insert set features an individual analysis of 20 of the leagues most feared hitters.

Nm-Mt Ex-Mt
COMPLETE SET (20) 50.00 15.00
1 Randy Johnson 2.50 .75
2 Andruw Jones 1.00 .30
3 Chipper Jones 2.50 .75
4 Cal Ripken 8.00 2.40
5 Nomar Garciaparra 4.00 1.20
6 Pedro Martinez 2.50 .75
7 Sammy Sosa 4.00 1.20
8 Sean Casey 1.00 .30
9 Carlos Beltran 1.00 .30
10 Shawn Green 1.00 .30
11 Vladimir Guerrero 2.50 .75
12 Roger Clemens 5.00 1.50
13 Derek Jeter 6.00 1.80
14 Scott Rolen 1.50 .45
15 Rick Ankiel 1.00 .30
16 Mark McGwire 6.00 1.80
17 Ken Griffey Jr. 4.00 1.20
18 Alex Rodriguez 4.00 1.20
19 Ruben Mateo 1.00 .30
20 Ivan Rodriguez 2.50 .75

2000 Aurora Star Factor

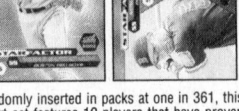

Randomly inserted in packs at one in 361, this insert set features 10 players that have proven to be among the best in baseball.

Nm-Mt Ex-Mt
COMPLETE SET (10) 250.00 75.00
1 Chipper Jones 15.00 4.50
2 Cal Ripken 50.00 15.00
3 Nomar Garciaparra 25.00 7.50
4 Sammy Sosa 25.00 7.50
5 Mike Piazza 25.00 7.50
6 Derek Jeter 40.00 12.00
7 Mark McGwire 40.00 12.00
8 Tony Gwynn 20.00 6.00
9 Ken Griffey Jr. 25.00 7.50
10 Alex Rodriguez 25.00 7.50

2000 Aurora Styrotechs

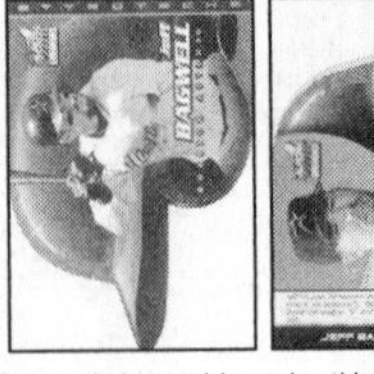

Randomly inserted in packs, this die-cut insert set features 20 helmet-shaped cards that feature some of the best in baseball. Each card is serial numbered to 299.

Nm-Mt Ex-Mt
COMPLETE SET (20) 250.00 75.00
1 Chipper Jones 12.00 3.60
2 Cal Ripken 40.00 12.00
3 Nomar Garciaparra 20.00 6.00
4 Sammy Sosa 20.00 6.00
5 Frank Thomas 12.00 3.60
6 Manny Ramirez 5.00 1.50
7 Larry Walker 8.00 2.40
8 Jeff Bagwell 8.00 2.40
9 Carlos Beltran 5.00 1.50
10 Vladimir Guerrero 12.00 3.60
11 Mike Piazza 20.00 6.00
12 Derek Jeter 30.00 9.00
13 Bernie Williams 8.00 2.40
14 Mark McGwire 30.00 9.00
15 Tony Gwynn 15.00 4.50
16 Barry Bonds 30.00 9.00
17 Ken Griffey Jr. 20.00 6.00
18 Alex Rodriguez 20.00 6.00
19 Jose Canseco 12.00 3.60
20 Ivan Rodriguez 12.00 3.60

1998 Authetic Images

Issued by Authentic Images, these standard-sized metallic cards honors some of the leading players in baseball history. The fronts have ghosted photos of the featured players with the player's name on top, the team logo and a fascimile signature. The back has biographical information, a picture, a write-up and career statistics. The card is serial numbered to 536 copies. Some other cards featuring all time home run heroes were published by Authentic Images in 1998. We have put the print run next to the players name in our checklist

Nm-Mt Ex-Mt
1 Roger Maris/10,000 30.00 9.00
2 Mickey Mantle/536 50.00 15.00
3 Mark McGwire/62,000 30.00 9.00
4 Sammy Sosa 30.00 9.00
25,000

1992 Avery Police

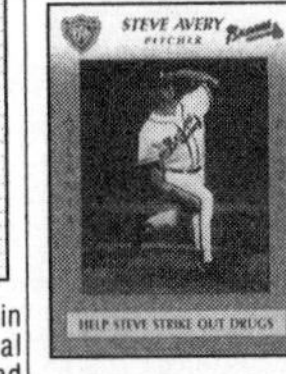

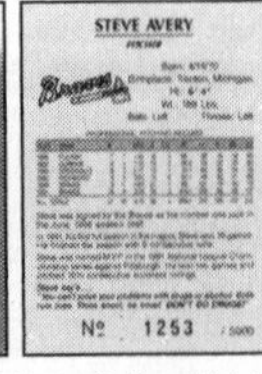

Sponsored by the Atlanta Police Athletic League, this card measures the standard-size. One card was given out with each paid admission to a charity auction and autograph session on June 20, 1992. A total of 5,000 cards were produced and each card bears a serial number on the back. The front features a color action photo; the top border is white, while the borders on the other three sides are turquoise. A neon yellow bar at the bottom contains the words "Help Steve Strike Out Drugs." The back has biography, professional pitching record, career highlights and an anti-drug and alcohol quote by Avery. The card is unnumbered.

Nm-Mt Ex-Mt
1 Steve Avery 3.00 .90

1914 B18 Blankets

This set of felt-type cloth squares was issued in 1914 with several brands of cigarettes. Each blanket is a 5 1/4" square. Each player exists with two different color combinations based on his team; however, only those variations reflecting price differentials are listed in the checklist below. Cleveland players have either yellow or purple bases; New York Yankees players have either blue or green infields; St. Louis Browns players have either red or purple paths; Washington players have either brown or green bases; Brooklyn players have either blue or green infields; New York Giants players have either brown or green paths; Pittsburgh players have either red or purple bases; and St. Louis Cardinals players have either purple or yellow paths. Some blankets are known to exist in a (third) different color scheme -- those with red infields. These blankets are quite scarce and are listed in the checklist below. The complete set price below reflects a set including all variations listed below. The blankets are unnumbered and are ordered below alphabetically within team, i.e., Cleveland Indians (1-9), Detroit Tigers (10-19), New York Yankees (20-28), St. Louis Browns (29-37), Washington Senators (38-46), Boston Bees NL (47-55), Brooklyn Dodgers (56-64), New York Giants (65-73), Pittsburgh Pirates (74-82) and St. Louis Cardinals (83-91).

Ex-Mt VG
COMPLETE SET 12000.00 6000.00
1A Johnny Bassler 50.00 25.00
yellow bases
1B Johnny Bassler 40.00 20.00
purple bases
2A Ray Chapman 50.00 25.00
yellow bases
2B Ray Chapman 40.00 20.00
purple bases
3A Jack Graney 50.00 25.00
yellow bases
3B Jack Graney 40.00 20.00
purple bases
4A Joe Jackson 800.00 400.00
yellow bases
4B Joe Jackson 800.00 400.00
purple bases
5A Nemo Leibold 50.00 25.00
yellow bases
5B Nemo Leibold 40.00 20.00
purple bases
6A Willie Mitchell 50.00 25.00
yellow bases
6B Willie Mitchell 50.00 25.00
purple bases
7A Ivy Olson 50.00 25.00
yellow bases
7B Ivy Olson 40.00 20.00
purple bases
8A Steve O'Neil 50.00 25.00
yellow bases
8B Steve O'Neil 40.00 20.00

purple bases
9A Terry Turner 50.00 25.00
yellow bases
9B Terry Turner 40.00 20.00
purple bases
10A Del Baker 20.00 10.00
white infield
10B Del Baker 60.00 30.00
brown infield
10C Del Baker 300.00 150.00
red infield
11A Paddy Bauman 20.00 10.00
(sic, Baumann)
white infield
11B Paddy Bauman 60.00 30.00
(sic, Baumann)
brown infield
11C Paddy Bauman 300.00 150.00
(sic& Baumann)
red infield
12A George Burns 20.00 10.00
white infield
12B George Burns 60.00 30.00
brown infield
12C George Burns 300.00 150.00
red infield
13A Marty Cavanaugh 20.00 10.00
(sic& Kavanagh)
white infield
13B Marty Cavanaugh 60.00 30.00
(sic& Kavanagh)
brown infield
13C Marty Cavanaugh 300.00 150.00
(sic& Kavanagh)
red infield
14A Ty Cobb 250.00 125.00
white infield
14B Ty Cobb 600.00 300.00
brown infield
14C Ty Cobb 1000.00 500.00
red infield
15A Harry Coveleski 20.00 10.00
white infield
15B Harry Coveleski 60.00 30.00
brown infield
15C Harry Coveleski 300.00 150.00
red infield
16A Ray Demmitt 20.00 10.00
white infield
16B Ray Demmitt 60.00 30.00
brown infield
16C Ray Demmitt 300.00 150.00
red infield
17A Del Gainor 20.00 10.00
white infield
17B Del Gainor 60.00 30.00
brown infield
18 Marty Kavanaugh 20.00 10.00
(sic& Kavanagh)
white infield
19A George Moriarty 20.00 10.00
white infield
19B George Moriarty 60.00 30.00
brown infield
19C George Moriarty 300.00 150.00
red infield
20 Luke Boone 20.00 10.00
21 Frank Chance (3) 50.00 25.00
22 King Cole 20.00 10.00
23 Topsy Hartzell 20.00 10.00
24 Ray Keating 20.00 10.00
25 Fritz Maisel 20.00 10.00
26 Roger Peckinpaugh 30.00 15.00
27 Jeff Sweeney 20.00 10.00
28 Dee Walsh 20.00 10.00
29A Sam Agnew 50.00 25.00
red paths
29B Sam Agnew 50.00 25.00
purple paths
30A Jimmy Austin 50.00 25.00
red paths
30B Jimmy Austin 50.00 25.00
purple paths
31A Earl Hamilton 50.00 25.00
red paths
31B Earl Hamilton 50.00 25.00
purple paths
32A Bill McAllister 50.00 25.00
(McAllester)
red paths
32B Bill McAllister 50.00 25.00
(McAllester)
purple paths
33A Del Pratt 50.00 25.00
red paths
33B Del Pratt 50.00 25.00
purple paths
34A Burt Shotton 50.00 25.00
red paths
34B Burt Shotton 50.00 25.00
purple paths
35A Bobby Wallace 60.00 30.00
red paths
35B Bobby Wallace 60.00 30.00
purple paths
36A Jimmy Walsh 50.00 25.00
red paths
36B Jimmy Walsh 50.00 25.00
purple paths
37A Gus Williams 50.00 25.00
red paths
37B Gus Williams 50.00 25.00
purple paths
38 Eddie Ainsmith 20.00 10.00
39 Eddie Foster 20.00 10.00
40 Chick Gandil 50.00 25.00
41 Walter Johnson 100.00 50.00
42 George McBride 20.00 10.00
43 Clyde Milan 30.00 15.00
44 Danny Moeller 20.00 10.00
45 Ray Morgan 20.00 10.00
46 Howard Shanks 20.00 10.00
47A Joe Connolly 20.00 10.00
white infield
47B Joe Connolly 60.00 30.00
brown infield
48A Hank Gowdy 20.00 10.00
white infield
48B Hank Gowdy 60.00 30.00
brown infield
48C Hank Gowdy 300.00 150.00
red infield
49A Tommy Griffith 20.00 10.00
white infield
49B Tommy Griffith 60.00 30.00
brown infield
49C Tommy Griffith 300.00 150.00
red infield
50A Bill James 20.00 10.00
white infield
50B Bill James 60.00 30.00
brown infield
51A Les Mann 20.00 10.00
white infield
51B Les Mann 60.00 30.00
brown infield
51C Les Mann 300.00 150.00
red infield
52A Rabbit Maranville 40.00 20.00
white infield
52B Rabbit Maranville 100.00 50.00
brown infield
52C Rabbit Maranville 400.00 200.00
red infield
53A Hub Perdue 20.00 10.00
white infield
53B Hub Perdue 60.00 30.00
brown infield
54A Lefty Tyler 20.00 10.00
white infield
54B Lefty Tyler 60.00 30.00
brown infield
54C Lefty Tyler 300.00 150.00
red infield
55A Bart Whaling 20.00 10.00
white infield
55B Bart Whaling 60.00 30.00
brown infield
55C Bart Whaling 300.00 150.00
red infield
56 George Cutshaw 20.00 10.00
57 Jake Daubert 30.00 15.00
58 John Hummel 20.00 10.00
59 Otto Miller 20.00 10.00
60 Nap Rucker 30.00 15.00
61 Red Smith 20.00 10.00
62 Casey Stengel 100.00 50.00
63 Bull Wagner 20.00 10.00
64 Zach Wheat 40.00 20.00
65 George Burns 20.00 10.00
66 Larry Doyle 30.00 15.00
67 Art Fletcher 20.00 10.00
68 Eddie Grant 30.00 15.00
69 Chief Meyers 20.00 10.00
70 Red Murray 20.00 10.00
71 Fred Snodgrass 20.00 10.00
72 Jeff Tesreau 20.00 10.00
73 Hooks Wiltse 20.00 10.00
74A Babe Adams 50.00 25.00
red bases
74B Babe Adams 50.00 25.00
purple bases
75A Max Carey 60.00 30.00
red bases
75B Max Carey 60.00 30.00
purple bases
76A George Gibson 50.00 25.00
red bases
76B George Gibson 50.00 25.00
purple bases
77A Ham Hyatt 50.00 25.00
red bases
77B Ham Hyatt 50.00 25.00
purple bases
78A Joe Kelley (Kelly) 50.00 25.00
red bases
78B Joe Kelley (Kelly) 50.00 25.00
purple bases
79A Ed Konetchy 50.00 25.00
red bases
79B Ed Konetchy 50.00 25.00
purple bases
80A Mike Mowrey 50.00 25.00
red bases
80B Mike Mowrey 50.00 25.00
purple bases
81A Marty O'Toole 50.00 25.00
red bases
81B Marty O'Toole 50.00 25.00
purple bases
82A Jim Viox 50.00 25.00
red bases
82B Jim Viox 50.00 25.00
purple bases
83A Bill Doak 40.00 20.00
red paths
83B Bill Doak 50.00 25.00
yellow paths
84A Cozy Dolan 30.00 15.00
purple paths
84B Cozy Dolan 50.00 25.00
yellow paths
85A Miller Huggins 50.00 25.00
purple paths
85B Miller Huggins 80.00 40.00
yellow paths
86A Dot's Miller 40.00 20.00
purple paths
86B Dot's Miller 50.00 25.00
yellow paths
87A Hank Robinson 40.00 20.00
purple paths
87B Hank Robinson 50.00 25.00
yellow paths
88A Slim Sallee 40.00 20.00
purple paths
88B Slim Sallee 50.00 25.00
yellow paths
89A Bill Steele 40.00 20.00
purple paths
89B Bill Steele 50.00 25.00
yellow paths
90A Possum Whitted 40.00 20.00
purple paths
90B Possum Whitted 50.00 25.00
yellow paths
91A Owen Wilson 40.00 20.00
purple paths
91B Owen Wilson 50.00 25.00
yellow paths

1928 Babe Ruth Candy Company E-Unc.

This six-card set is one of the more obscure candy sets and features cards picturing Babe Ruth which measure approximately 1 7/8" by 4". The cards are sepia in color and depict scenes from either a movie, "Babe Comes Home" (numbers 1, 2 and 4), or scenes from the Yankee Post Season West Coast Exhibition Tour in 1924 (numbers 3 and 6). Each card has "Babe Ruth" below the photo followed by a caption. The backs contain instructions on how to exchange all six cards for a baseball with Babe Ruth's genuine signature on it. Card number six is considerably tougher to find and seems to be a premium card and very difficult to find.

Ex-Mt VG
COMPLETE SET (6) 2000.00 1000.00
1 Babe Ruth 250.00 125.00
In uniform of Los Angeles
2 Babe Ruth 250.00 125.00
Swinging, follow thru
3 Babe Ruth 250.00 125.00
In uniform with a young boy
4 Babe Ruth 250.00 125.00
Anna Q. Nilsson
In civilian dress
5 Babe Ruth 250.00 125.00
In uniform kissing a small girl
6 Babe Ruth 1000.00 500.00
Autographing a ball

1948 Babe Ruth Story

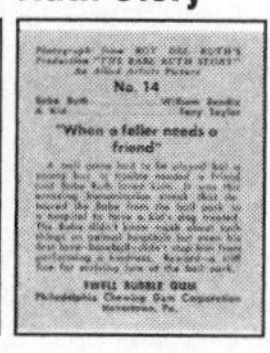

The 1948 Babe Ruth Story set of 28 black and white numbered cards (measuring approximately 2" by 2 1/2") was issued by the Philadelphia Chewing Gum Company to commemorate the 1949 movie of the same name starring William Bendix, Claire Trevor, and Charles Bickford. Babe Ruth himself appears on several cards. The last 12 cards (17 to 28) are more difficult to obtain than other cards in the set and are also more desirable in that most picture actual players as well as actors from the movie. Supposedly these last 12 cards were issued much later after the first 16 cards had already been released and distributed. The last seven cards (22-28) in the set are subtitled "The Babe Ruth Story in the Making" at the top of each reverse. The bottom of every card says "Swell Bubble Gum, Philadelphia Chewing Gum Corporation." The catalog designation for this set is R421.

NM Ex
COMPLETE SET (28) 1500.00 750.00
COMMON CARD (1-16) 20.00 10.00
COMMON CARD (17-24) 50.00 25.00
COMMON CARD (25-28) 200.00 100.00
1 The Babe Ruth Story 150.00 75.00
In the Making
(Babe Ruth shown
with William Bendix)
2 Bat Boy Becomes 25.00 12.50
the Babe
(Facsimile autographed
by William Bendix)
3 Claire Hodgson played 20.00 10.00
by Claire Trevor
4 Babe Ruth played by 20.00 10.00
William Bendix;
Claire Hodgson played
by Claire Trevor
5 Brother Matthias 20.00 10.00
played by
Charles Bickford
6 Phil Conrad played 20.00 10.00
by Sam Levene
7 Night Club Singer 20.00 10.00
played by
Gertrude Niesen
8 Baseball's Famous Deal 20.00 10.00
9 Babe Ruth played by 20.00 10.00
William Bendix;
Mrs.Babe Ruth played
by Claire Trevor
10 Actors for Babe Ruth 20.00 10.00
Mrs. Babe Ruth
Brother Matthias
11 Babe Ruth played by 20.00 10.00
William Bendix;
Miller Huggins played
by Fred Lightner
12 Babe Ruth played by 20.00 10.00
William Bendix;
Johnny Sylvester
played by
George Marshall
13 Actors for Mr. and Mrs. 20.00 10.00
and Johnny Sylvester
14 When A Feller Needs 20.00 10.00
A Friend
15 Dramatic Home Run 20.00 10.00
16 The Homer That Set 20.00 10.00

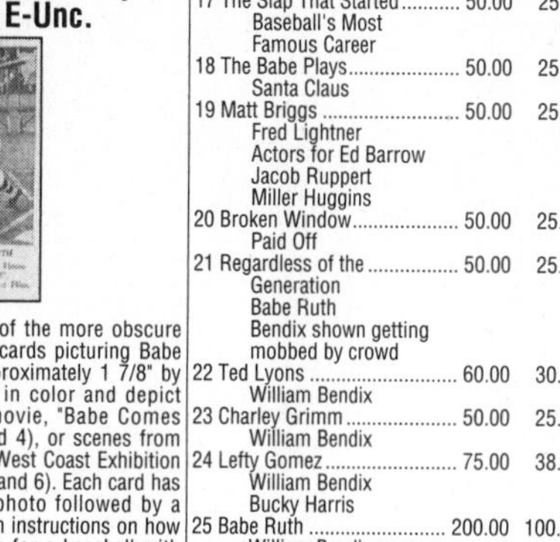

the Record
17 The Slap That Started 50.00 25.00
Baseball's Most
Famous Career
18 The Babe Plays 50.00 25.00
Santa Claus
19 Matt Briggs 50.00 25.00
Fred Lightner
Actors for Ed Barrow
Jacob Ruppert
Miller Huggins
20 Broken Window 50.00 25.00
Paid Off
21 Regardless of the 50.00 25.00
Generation
Babe Ruth
Bendix shown getting
mobbed by crowd
22 Ted Lyons 60.00 30.00
William Bendix
23 Charley Grimm 50.00 25.00
William Bendix
24 Lefty Gomez 75.00 38.00
William Bendix
Bucky Harris
25 Babe Ruth 200.00 100.00
William Bendix
Babe Ruth
pictured with ball
26 Babe Ruth 200.00 100.00
William Bendix
Babe Ruth
pictured with bat
27 Babe Ruth 200.00 100.00
Claire Trevor
28 William Bendix 200.00 100.00
Babe Ruth
Claire Trevor
Babe Ruth pictured
autographing ball

1948 Babe Ruth Story Premium

This 8" by 9 1/2" sepia photo was given away at movie theatre premiers of the "Babe Ruth Story" movie. The front shows long time teammates Lou Gehrig and the Babe in a posed shot. The back has Babe Ruth's career information.

NM Ex
1 Babe Ruth 5000.00 2500.00
Lou Gehrig

1994 Ball Park Franks Will Clark

Measuring the standard-size, this card was sponsored by Ball Park Franks. The front features a full-bleed color action player photo. The player's name and the sponsor name appear at the upper left corner. On a black panel outlined in red, the back carries career highlights. The card is unnumbered.

Nm-Mt Ex-Mt
1 Will Clark 1.00 .30

1995 Ball Park Franks

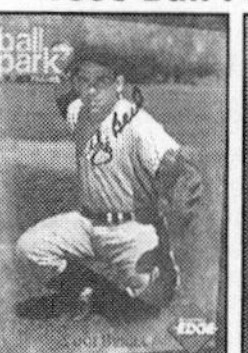

Measuring the standard size, these two autograph cards were produced for Ball Park Franks by Collector's Edge. Collectors could receive the two cards through a mail-in offer for 8 UPC codes from any Ball Park product; for 4 UPC codes and $2.50; or for 2 UPC codes and $5.00. The offer expired on May 31, 1995 or while supplies lasted. The fronts display color action photos that fade to marbleized borders. The player's signature is inscribed across the picture. The cards are unnumbered and checklisted below in alphabetical order. Each card was accompanied by a second card, featuring a ghosted photo and certifying that the signature is authentic.

Nm-Mt Ex-Mt
COMPLETE SET (2) 20.00 6.00
1 Yogi Berra AU 10.00 3.00
2 Frank Robinson AU 10.00 3.00

1997 Bally's Mays Chips

These four $5 chips feature Hall of Famer and one time Bally's spokesperson, Willie Mays. Since they are unnumbered, we have sequenced them in order of playing career

Nm-Mt Ex-Mt
COMPLETE SET 40.00 12.00
COMMON CARD 10.00 3.00

1995 Baltimore Sun Ripken Vending Card

This card appears to be one of a set of eight commemorative cards produced for the Baltimore Sun and measuring approximately 11" by 17". The white-bordered front features a black-and-white player picture on the left half with a commemorative statement on the right. The Baltimore Sun's logo is printed at the bottom. The back is blank.

Nm-Mt Ex-Mt
1 Cal Ripken 5.00 1.50

1911 Baseball Bats E-Unc.

This 44-card set was distributed on candy boxes with the player panel on one side and the name "Baseball Bats" printed on crossed bats and a ball on the opposite side. The two side panels indicate "All Leading Players" and an end flap displays "One Cent." The cards measure approximately 1 3/8" by 2 3/8" and feature a player picture surrounded by either a white or orange border and a thin black line.

Ex-Mt VG
COMPLETE SET (44) 5000.00 2500.00
1 Frank Baker 200.00 100.00
2 Jack Baker 50.00 25.00
3 Chief Bender 100.00 50.00
4 Al Bridwell 50.00 25.00
5 Mordecai Brown 100.00 50.00
6 Bill Corrigan UER 50.00 25.00
misspelled Carrigan
7 Frank Chance 150.00 75.00
8 Hal Chase 150.00 75.00
9 Eddie Cicotte 150.00 75.00
10 Fred Clarke UER 100.00 50.00
misspelled Clark
11 Ty Cobb 1000.00 500.00
12 King Cole 50.00 25.00
13 Shano Collins 50.00 25.00
14 Sam Crawford 150.00 75.00
15 Lou Criger 50.00 25.00
16 Harry Davis 50.00 25.00
17 Jim Delehanty 50.00 25.00
18 Art Devlin 50.00 25.00
19 Josh Devore 50.00 25.00
20 Patsy Donovan 50.00 25.00
21 Larry Doyle 75.00 38.00
22 Johnny Evers 150.00 75.00
23 John Flynn 50.00 25.00
24 Solly Hofman 50.00 25.00
25 Walter Johnson 500.00 250.00
26 Johnny Kling 50.00 25.00
27 Nap Lajoie 250.00 125.00
28 Matthew McIntyre 50.00 25.00
29 Fred Merkle 75.00 38.00
30 Tom Needham 50.00 25.00
31 Rube Oldring 50.00 25.00
32 Frank Schulte 50.00 25.00
33 Cy Seymour 50.00 25.00
34 James Sheckard 50.00 25.00
35 Tris Speaker 150.00 75.00
36 Oscar Stanage 50.00 25.00
(Batting, side)
37 Oscar Stanage 50.00 25.00
(Batting, front)
38 Ira Thomas 50.00 25.00
39 Joe Tinker 150.00 75.00
40 Heinie Wagner 50.00 25.00
41 Honus Wagner 300.00 150.00
42 Ed Walsh 100.00 50.00
43 Chief Wilson 75.00 38.00
44 Art Wilson 50.00 25.00

1910 Baseball Comics T203

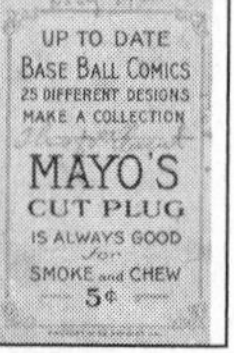

This 25-card set was issued by Winner Cut Plug and Mayo Cut Plug. Measuring 2 1/16" by 3 1/8", each card features a color comic picture relating to a baseball phrase or slogan. The back carries an advertisement inside a picture frame. The cards are unnumbered.

Ex-Mt VG
COMPLETE SET (25) 450.00 220.00
COMMON CARD (1-25) 20.00 10.00

1979 Baseball Greats

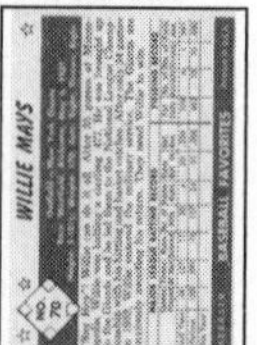

These 2 1/2" by 3 3/4" cards were issued in 1979 by Carl Berg. They have the same design as 53 Bowman Black and White and use photos from that era as well. The cards are numbered 65 through 80 as if they were a continuation of the 53 Bowman Black and White set.

NM Ex
COMPLETE SET (16) 25.00 10.00
65 Monte Irvin .50 .20
66 Early Wynn .50 .20
67 Robin Roberts .50 .20
68 Stan Musial 3.00 1.20

69 Ernie Banks	2.00	.80
70 Willie Mays	5.00	2.00
71 Yogi Berra	2.00	.80
72 Mickey Mantle	8.00	3.20
73 Whitey Ford	2.00	.80
74 Bob Feller	2.00	.80
75 Ted Williams	5.00	2.00
76 Satchel Paige	3.00	1.20
77 Jackie Robinson	5.00	2.00
78 Ed Mathews	.50	.20
79 Warren Spahn	.50	.20
80 Ralph Kiner	.50	.20

1982 Baseball Card News

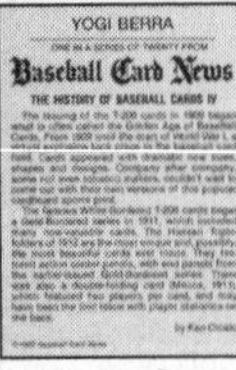
YOGI BERRA
ONE IN A SERIES OF TWENTY FROM
Baseball Card News
THE HISTORY OF BASEBALL CARDS IV

This 20-card standard-size set features glossy, black-and-white posed player photos with rounded corners. Backs display the player's name at the top and below the heading "Baseball Card News," each card carries a portion of a 20-part history of baseball cards by Ken Cicalo. The cards are numbered on the back with Roman numerals. These cards were also issued with subscription offer backs.

	Nm-Mt	Ex-Mt
COMPLETE SET	20.00	8.00
1 Mickey Mantle	4.00	1.60
2 Ted Williams	3.00	1.20
3 Stan Musial	2.00	.80
4 Yogi Berra	1.00	.40
5 Roger Maris	1.00	.40
6 Hank Aaron	2.50	1.00
7 Willie Mays	2.50	1.00
8 Joe DiMaggio Bob Feller	1.50	.60
9 Lou Brock (Portrait)	.50	.20
10 Roberto Clemente	3.00	1.20
11 Ernie Banks	1.00	.40
12 Lou Brock (Holding bat)	.50	.20
13 Jackie Robinson Roy Campanella	1.50	.60
14 Maury Wills	.25	.10
15 Bob Feller	.50	.20
16 Roy Campanella	1.00	.40
17 Sandy Koufax	1.00	.40
18 Joe DiMaggio	3.00	1.20
19 Satchel Paige	2.00	.80
20 Babe Ruth	4.00	1.60

1910 Baseball Fans

These four fans which measure 7 1/2" in diameter and 5 1/4" in length of handles features some of the leading players of the time. On the top of the fan is the expression "A fan for a fan:". The players photo and a fascimile signature is underneath that expression. Since these fans are unnumbered, we have sequenced them in alphabetical order.

	Ex-Mt	VG
COMPLETE SET (4)	6000.00	3000.00
1 Hal Chase	1000.00	500.00
2 Ty Cobb	3000.00	1500.00
3 Larry Doyle	500.00	250.00
4 Christy Mathewson	2000.00	1000.00

1910 Baseball Magazine Premium Posters

Measuring approximately 11 1/2" by 19 1/2" this poster was probably an redemption issued by Baseball Magazine. Little is known about these posters and all future information would be appreciated.

	MINT	NRMT
1 Frank Chance	1000.00	450.00
2 Ty Cobb	2500.00	1100.00

1963 Baseball Magazine M118

These 8 1/2" by 11" photos feature a player portrait surrounded by white borders. The backs are blank

	NM	Ex
COMPLETE SET (88)	800.00	325.00
1 Hank Aaron	20.00	8.00
2 Joe Adcock	6.00	2.40
3 Grover Alexander	10.00	4.00
4 Bob Allison	5.00	2.00
5 George Altman	5.00	2.00
6 Luis Aparicio	10.00	4.00
7 Richie Ashburn	10.00	4.00
8 Ernie Banks	12.00	4.80
9 Steve Barber	5.00	2.00
10 Earl Battey	5.00	2.00
11 Yogi Berra	15.00	6.00
12 Jim Bunning	10.00	4.00
13 Roy Campanella	15.00	6.00
14 Norm Cash	8.00	3.20
15 Orlando Cepeda	10.00	4.00
16 Ty Cobb	20.00	8.00
17 Rocky Colavito	8.00	3.20
18 Bennie Daniels	5.00	2.00
19 Dizzy Dean	10.00	4.00
20 Joe DiMaggio	30.00	12.00
21 Don Drysdale	10.00	4.00
22 Ryne Duren	5.00	2.00
23 Roy Face	6.00	2.40
24 Bob Feller	10.00	4.00
25 Whitey Ford	12.00	4.80
26 Nelson Fox	10.00	4.00
27 Tito Francona	5.00	2.00
28 Bob Friend	5.00	2.00
29 Lou Gehrig	25.00	10.00
30 Jim Gentile	5.00	2.00
31 Hank Greenberg	12.00	4.80
32 Dick Groat	6.00	2.40
33 Lefty Grove	10.00	4.00
34 Ron Hansen	5.00	2.00
35 Woody Held	5.00	2.00
36 Gil Hodges	10.00	4.00
37 Rogers Hornsby	10.00	4.00
38 Elston Howard	8.00	3.20
39 Dick Howser	5.00	2.00
40 Joe Jay	5.00	2.00
41 Jack Jensen	6.00	2.40
42 Walter Johnson	15.00	6.00
43 Al Kaline	10.00	4.00
44 Harmon Killebrew	10.00	4.00
45 Willie Kirkland	5.00	2.00
46 Sandy Koufax	20.00	8.00
47 Ted Kluszewski	8.00	3.20
48 Jim Landis	5.00	2.00
49 Dale Long	5.00	2.00
50 Jerry Lumpe	5.00	2.00
51 Connie Mack	10.00	4.00
52 Art Mahaffey	5.00	2.00
53 Frank Malzone	5.00	2.00
54 Mickey Mantle	30.00	12.00
55 Roger Maris	15.00	6.00
56 Eddie Mathews	10.00	4.00
57 Christy Mathewson	10.00	4.00
58 Willie Mays	20.00	8.00
59 Minnie Minoso	6.00	2.40
60 Wally Moon	5.00	2.00
61 Stan Musial	12.00	4.80
62 Charley Neal	5.00	2.00
63 Mel Ott	10.00	4.00
64 Camilo Pascual	5.00	2.00
65 Albie Pearson	5.00	2.00
66 Jim Piersall	6.00	2.40
67 Vada Pinson	6.00	2.40
68 Paul Richards	5.00	2.00
69 Brooks Robinson	10.00	4.00
70 Frank Robinson	10.00	4.00
71 Jackie Robinson	20.00	8.00
72 Pete Runnels	5.00	2.00
73 Babe Ruth	30.00	12.00
74 Ron Santo	8.00	3.20
75 Norm Siebern	5.00	2.00
76 Roy Sievers	5.00	2.00
77 Duke Snider	12.00	4.80
78 Warren Spahn	10.00	4.00
79 Tris Speaker	10.00	4.00
80 Casey Stengel	10.00	4.00
81 Dick Stuart	5.00	2.00
82 Lee Thomas	5.00	2.00
83 Honus Wagner	10.00	4.00
84 Bill White	6.00	2.40
85 Ted Williams	25.00	10.00
86 Gene Woodling	5.00	2.00
87 Early Wynn	10.00	4.00
88 Cy Young	10.00	4.00

1975 Baseball Royalty

These eight cards were created for and given away to the 1st 500 attendees at the 1975 Mid-Atlantic Sports Collectors Association show. The fronts have the words "Baseball Royalty" on top with the players photo underneath and then the information about the show. These players were selected since each player had a "royal" nickname. Since these cards are unnumbered we have sequenced them in alphabetical order.

	NM	Ex
COMPLETE SET	20.00	8.00
1 Paul Derringer	1.00	.40
2 Roy Face	1.00	.40
3 Rogers Hornsby	4.00	1.60
4 Carl Hubbell	2.50	1.00
5 Charlie Keller	1.50	.60
6 Babe Ruth	8.00	3.20
7 Hal Schumacher	1.00	.40
8 Duke Snider	3.00	1.20

1990 Baseball Wit

The 1990 Baseball Wit set was issued in complete set form only. This set was dedicated to and featured several ex-members of the Little Leagues. This 108-card, standard-size set was available primarily in retail and chain outlets. Most of the older (retired) players in the set are shown in black and white. The card backs typically give three trivia questions with answers following. The object of the game is to collect points by correctly answering any one of the questions on the back of each card or identifying the picture on the front. The first printing of 10,000 sets had several errors, and the cards were not numbered. The second printing corrected these errors and numbered the cards. The number on the front of the card is used when playing the game and is not to be confused with the card number, which is found on the back of all cards. The unnumbered cards have a value of up to 5X the numbered varieties.

	Nm-Mt	Ex-Mt
COMP. FACT SET (108)	8.00	2.40
1 Orel Hershiser	.10	.03
2 Tony Gwynn	1.00	.30
3 Mickey Mantle	2.00	.60
4 Willie Stargell	.15	.04
5 Don Baylor	.10	.03
6 Hank Aaron	1.00	.30
7 Don Larsen	.10	.03
8 Lee Mazzilli	.05	.02
9 Boog Powell	.10	.03
10 Little League World Series	.05	.02
11 Jose Canseco	.50	.15
12 Mike Scott	.05	.02
13 Bob Feller	.15	.04
14 Ron Santo	.25	.07
15A Mel Stottlemyer ERR sic, Stottlemyre	.10	.03
15B Mel Stottlemyre COR	.10	.03
16 Shea Stadium	.05	.02
17 Brooks Robinson	.25	.07
18 Willie Mays	1.00	.30
19 Ernie Banks	.25	.07
20 Keith Hernandez	.10	.03
21 Bret Saberhagen	.10	.03
22 Baseball Hall of Fame	.05	.02
23 Luis Aparicio	.15	.04
24 Yogi Berra	.25	.07
25 Manny Mota	.10	.03
26 Steve Garvey	.10	.03
27 Bill Shea	.05	.02
28 Fred Lynn	.05	.02
29 Todd Worrell	.05	.02
30 Roy Campanella	.25	.07
31 Bob Gibson	.15	.04
32 Gary Carter	.25	.07
33 Jim Palmer	.15	.04
34 Carl Yastrzemski	.15	.04
35 Dwight Gooden	.10	.03
36 Stan Musial	.50	.15
37 Rickey Henderson	.50	.15
38 Dale Murphy	.15	.04
39 Mike Schmidt	.25	.07
40 Gaylord Perry	.15	.04
41 Ozzie Smith	1.00	.30
42 Reggie Jackson	.25	.07
43 Steve Carlton	.15	.04
44 Jim Perry	.05	.02
45 Vince Coleman	.05	.02
46 Tom Seaver	.25	.07
47 Marty Marion	.05	.02
48 Frank Robinson	.15	.04
49 Joe DiMaggio	1.50	.45
50 Ted Williams	1.50	.45
51 Rollie Fingers	.10	.03
52 Jackie Robinson	1.00	.30
53 Vic Raschi	.05	.02
54 Johnny Bench	.25	.07
55 Nolan Ryan	2.00	.60
56 Ty Cobb	1.00	.30
57 Harry Steinfeldt	.05	.02
58 James O'Rourke	.05	.02
59 John McGraw	.15	.04
60 Candy Cummings	.10	.03
61 Jimmie Foxx	.15	.04
62 Walter Johnson	.15	.04
63 1903 World Series	.05	.02
64 Satchel Paige	.25	.07
65 Bobby Wallace	.10	.03
66 Cap Anson	.15	.04
67 Hugh Duffy	.10	.03
68 William(Buck) Ewing	.10	.03
69 Bobo Holloman	.05	.02
70 Ed Delahanty	.10	.03
71 Dizzy Dean	.15	.04
72 Tris Speaker	.15	.04
73 Lou Gehrig	1.25	.35
74 Wee Willie Keeler	.10	.03
75 Cal Hubbard	.10	.03
76 Eddie Collins	.15	.04
77 Chris Von Der Ahe	.05	.02
78 Sam Crawford	.15	.04
79 Cy Young	.15	.04
80 Johnny Vander Meer	.10	.03
81 Joey Jay	.05	.02
82 Zack Wheat	.10	.03
83 Jim Bottomley	.10	.03
84 Honus Wagner	.25	.07
85 Casey Stengel	.25	.07
86 Babe Ruth	2.00	.60
87 John Lindemuth Carl Stotz	.05	.02
88 Max Carey	.10	.03
89 Mordecai Brown	.10	.03
90 Cinc. Red Stockings 1869	.05	.02
91 Rube Marquard	.10	.03
92 Charles Radbourne Horse	.10	.03
93 Hack Wilson	.10	.03
94 Lefty Grove	.15	.04
95 Carl Hubbell	.15	.04
96 A.J. Cartwright	.15	.04
97 Rogers Hornsby	.15	.04
98 Ernest Thayer	.05	.02
99 Connie Mack	.10	.03
100 Cent. Celebration 1939	.50	.15
101 Branch Rickey	.10	.03
102 Dan Brouthers	.10	.03
103 1st Baseball Uniform	.05	.02
104 Christy Mathewson	.15	.04
105 Joe Nuxhall	.05	.02
106 Cent. Celebration 1939	.05	.02
107 William H. Taft PRES.	.15	.04
108 Abner Doubleday	.05	.02

1991 Baseball's Best Aces of the Mound

This 8" by 8" sticker album is 24 pages in length and features 18 of MLB's outstanding pitchers. One page is devoted to each player and includes player profile, a black and white photo, and a slot for the sticker. The stickers measure 2 1/2" square and feature glossy color action player photos with white borders. They appear on two insert sheets in the middle of the album and are arranged alphabetically, with the number appearing on the front.

	Nm-Mt	Ex-Mt
COMPLETE SET	8.00	2.40
1 Rick Aguilera	.25	.07
2 Jack Armstrong	.25	.07
3 Tim Belcher	.25	.07
4 Roger Clemens	3.00	.90
5 Doug Drabek	.25	.07
6 Dennis Eckersley	2.00	.60
7 Chuck Finley	.75	.23
8 Dwight Gooden	.50	.15
9 Neal Heaton	.25	.07
10 Teddy Higuera	.25	.07
11 Dennis Martinez	.75	.23
12 Randy Myers	.25	.07
13 Gregg Olson	.25	.07
14 Bret Saberhagen	.50	.15
15 Mike Scott	.25	.07
16 Dave Stewart	.50	.15
17 Dave Stieb	.25	.07
18 Frank Viola	.25	.07

1991 Baseball's Best Hit Men

This 8" by 8" sticker album is 24 pages in length and features 18 of MLB's outstanding hitters. One page is devoted to each player and includes player profile, a black and white photo, and a slot for the sticker. The stickers measure 2 1/2" square and feature glossy color action player photos with white borders. They appear on two insert sheets in the middle of the album and are arranged alphabetically, with the number appearing on the front.

	Nm-Mt	Ex-Mt
COMPLETE SET (18)	15.00	4.50
1 George Bell	.25	.07
2 Wade Boggs	1.25	.35
3 George Brett	2.50	.75
4 Hubie Brooks	.25	.07
5 Will Clark	1.00	.30
6 Len Dykstra	.50	.15
7 Ken Griffey Jr.	3.00	.90
8 Pedro Guerrero	.50	.15
9 Ozzie Guillen	.25	.07
10 Tony Gwynn	2.50	.75
11 Gregg Jefferies	.25	.07
12 Carney Lansford	.25	.07
13 Barry Larkin	1.25	.35
14 Don Mattingly	2.50	.75
15 Kirby Puckett	1.50	.45
16 Tim Raines	.50	.15
17 Ryne Sandberg	2.50	.75
18 Robin Yount	1.25	.35

1991 Baseball's Best Home Run Kings

This 8" by 8" sticker album is 24 pages in length and features 18 of MLB's home run kings. One page is devoted to each player and includes player profile, a black and white photo, and a slot for the sticker. The stickers measure 2 1/2" square and feature glossy color action player photos with white borders. The stickers are unnumbered and checklisted below in alphabetical order.

	Nm-Mt	Ex-Mt
COMPLETE SET (18)	10.00	3.00
1 Jesse Barfield	.25	.07
2 Jose Canseco	1.50	.45
3 Eric Davis	.50	.15
4 Glenn Davis	.25	.07
5 Andre Dawson	1.00	.30
6 Dwight Evans	.50	.15
7 Cecil Fielder	.50	.15
8 Kelly Gruber	.25	.07
9 Von Hayes	.25	.07
10 Kent Hrbek	.25	.07
11 Bo Jackson	1.00	.30
12 Howard Johnson	.25	.07
13 Mark McGwire	4.00	1.20
14 Kevin Mitchell	.25	.07
15 Eddie Murray	1.50	.45
16 Ruben Sierra	.50	.15
17 Darryl Strawberry	.50	.15
18 Tim Wallach	.25	.07

1991 Baseball's Best Record Breakers

This 8" by 8" sticker album is 24 pages in length and features 18 of MLB's outstanding players. One page is devoted to each player and includes player profile, a black and white photo, and a slot for the sticker. The stickers measure 2 1/2" square and feature glossy color action player photos with white borders. They appear on two insert sheets in the middle of the album and are arranged alphabetically, with the number appearing on the front.

	Nm-Mt	Ex-Mt
COMPLETE SET (18)	15.00	4.50
1 Bert Blyleven	.50	.15
2 Jose Canseco	.75	.23
3 Gary Carter	.75	.23
4 Vince Coleman	.25	.07
5 Mark Davis	.25	.07
6 Carlton Fisk	1.25	.35
7 Rickey Henderson	1.50	.45
8 Reggie Jackson	1.25	.35
9 Howard Johnson	.25	.07
10 Ramon Martinez	.50	.15
11 Don Mattingly	2.50	.75
12 Dave Righetti	.25	.07
13 Cal Ripken Jr.	5.00	1.50
14 Nolan Ryan	5.00	1.50
15 Ryne Sandberg	2.00	.60
16 Mike Schmidt	1.25	.35
17 Ozzie Smith	2.50	.75
18 Fernando Valenzuela	.50	.15

1934-36 Batter-Up R318

The 1934-36 Batter-Up set, issued by National Chicle, contains 192 blank-backed die-cut cards. Numbers 1 to 80 are approximately 2 3/8" by 3 1/4" in size while 81 to 192 are 2 3/8" by 3". The latter are more difficult to find than the former. The pictures come in basic black and white or in tints of blue, brown, green, purple, red, or sepia. There are three combination cards (each featuring two players per card) in the high series (98, 111, and 115). Cards with the die-cut backing removed are graded fair at best.

	Ex-Mt	VG
COMPLETE SET (192)	18000.00	9000.00
COMMON CARD (1-80)	40.00	20.00
COMMON CARD (81-192)	80.00	40.00
WRAP.(1-CENT, CATCHER)	200.00	100.00
WRAP.(1-CENT, BAT)	600.00	300.00
1 Wally Berger	100.00	25.00
2 Ed Brandt	40.00	20.00
3 Al Lopez	90.00	45.00
4 Dick Bartell	50.00	25.00
5 Carl Hubbell	125.00	60.00
6 Bill Terry	150.00	75.00
7 Pepper Martin	60.00	30.00
8 Jim Bottomley	90.00	45.00
9 Tommy Bridges	50.00	25.00
10 Rick Ferrell	90.00	45.00
11 Ray Benge	40.00	20.00
12 Wes Ferrell	50.00	25.00
13 Chalmer Cissell	40.00	20.00
14 Pie Traynor	125.00	60.00
15 Leroy Mahaffey	40.00	20.00
16 Chick Hafey	90.00	45.00
17 Lloyd Waner	90.00	45.00
18 Jack Burns	40.00	20.00
19 Buddy Myer	50.00	25.00
20 Bob Johnson	50.00	25.00
21 Arky Vaughan	90.00	45.00
22 Red Rolfe	50.00	25.00
23 Lefty Gomez	150.00	75.00
24 Earl Averill	125.00	60.00
25 Mickey Cochrane	150.00	75.00
26 Van Lingle Mungo	60.00	30.00
27 Mel Ott	200.00	100.00
28 Jimmie Foxx	275.00	140.00
29 Jimmy Dykes	50.00	25.00
30 Bill Dickey	200.00	100.00
31 Lefty Grove	200.00	100.00
32 Joe Cronin	150.00	75.00
33 Frankie Frisch	125.00	60.00
34 Al Simmons	125.00	60.00
35 Rogers Hornsby	275.00	140.00
36 Ted Lyons	90.00	45.00
37 Rabbit Maranville	90.00	45.00
38 Jimmy Wilson	50.00	25.00
39 Willie Kamm	40.00	20.00
40 Bill Hallahan	40.00	20.00
41 Gus Suhr	40.00	20.00
42 Charley Gehringer	125.00	60.00
43 Joe Heving	40.00	20.00
44 Adam Comorosky	40.00	20.00
45 Tony Lazzeri	175.00	90.00
46 Sam Leslie	40.00	20.00
47 Bob Smith	40.00	20.00
48 Willis Hudlin	40.00	20.00
49 Carl Reynolds	40.00	20.00
50 Fred Schulte	40.00	20.00
51 Cookie Lavagetto	60.00	30.00
52 Hal Schumacher	50.00	25.00
53 Roger Cramer	50.00	25.00
54 Sylvester Johnson	40.00	20.00
55 Ollie Bejma	40.00	20.00
56 Sam Byrd	40.00	20.00
57 Hank Greenberg	275.00	140.00
58 Bill Knickerbocker	40.00	20.00
59 Bill Urbanski	40.00	20.00
60 Eddie Morgan	40.00	20.00
61 Rabbit McNair	40.00	20.00
62 Ben Chapman	50.00	25.00
63 Roy Johnson	40.00	20.00
64 Dizzy Dean	400.00	200.00
65 Zeke Bonura	40.00	20.00

66 Fred Marberry 40.00 20.00
67 Gus Mancuso 40.00 20.00
68 Joe Vosmik 40.00 20.00
69 Earl Grace 40.00 20.00
70 Tony Piet 40.00 20.00
71 Rollie Hemsley 40.00 20.00
72 Fred Fitzsimmons 50.00 25.00
73 Hack Wilson 150.00 75.00
74 Chick Fullis 40.00 20.00
75 Fred Frankhouse 40.00 20.00
76 Ethan Allen 40.00 20.00
77 Heinie Manush 90.00 45.00
78 Rip Collins 40.00 20.00
79 Tony Cuccinello 40.00 20.00
80 Joe Kuhel 40.00 20.00
81 Tommy Bridges 100.00 50.00
82 Clint Brown 80.00 40.00
83 Albert Blanche 80.00 40.00
84 Boze Berger 80.00 40.00
85 Goose Goslin 175.00 90.00
86 Lefty Gomez 225.00 110.00
87 Joe Glenn 80.00 40.00
88 Cy Blanton 80.00 40.00
89 Tom Carey 80.00 40.00
90 Ralph Birkofer 80.00 40.00
91 Fred Gabler 80.00 40.00
92 Dick Coffman 80.00 40.00
93 Ollie Bejma 80.00 40.00
94 Leroy Parmelee 80.00 40.00
95 Carl Reynolds 80.00 40.00
96 Ben Cantwell 80.00 40.00
97 Curtis Davis 80.00 40.00
98 Earl Webb and Wally Moses 125.00 60.00
99 Ray Benge 80.00 40.00
100 Pie Traynor 200.00 100.00
101 Phil Cavarretta 100.00 50.00
102 Pep Young 80.00 40.00
103 Willis Hudlin 80.00 40.00
104 Mickey Haslin 80.00 40.00
105 Ossie Bluege 90.00 45.00
106 Paul Andrews 80.00 40.00
107 Ed Brandt 80.00 40.00
108 Don Taylor 80.00 40.00
109 Thornton Lee 90.00 45.00
110 Hal Schumacher 90.00 45.00
111 Hayes and Ted Lyons 125.00 60.00
112 Odell Hale 80.00 40.00
113 Earl Averill 175.00 90.00
114 Italo Chelini 80.00 40.00
115 Ivy Andrews and Jim Bottomley 125.00 60.00
116 Bill Walker 80.00 40.00
117 Bill Dickey 300.00 150.00
118 Gerald Walker 80.00 40.00
119 Ted Lyons 175.00 90.00
120 Eldon Auker 80.00 40.00
121 Bill Hallahan 90.00 45.00
122 Fred Lindstrom 175.00 90.00
123 Oral Hildebrand 80.00 40.00
124 Luke Appling 225.00 110.00
125 Pepper Martin 100.00 50.00
126 Rick Ferrell 175.00 90.00
127 Ival Goodman 80.00 40.00
128 Joe Kuhel 80.00 40.00
129 Ernie Lombardi 175.00 90.00
130 Charley Gehringer 225.00 110.00
131 Van Lingle Mungo 90.00 45.00
132 Larry French 80.00 40.00
133 Buddy Myer 90.00 45.00
134 Mel Harder 100.00 50.00
135 Augie Galan 80.00 40.00
136 Gabby Hartnett 175.00 90.00
137 Stan Hack 90.00 45.00
138 Billy Herman 175.00 90.00
139 Bill Jurges 80.00 40.00
140 Bill Lee 90.00 45.00
141 Zeke Bonura 80.00 40.00
142 Tony Piet 80.00 40.00
143 Paul Dean 100.00 50.00
144 Jimmie Foxx 400.00 200.00
145 Joe Medwick 225.00 110.00
146 Rip Collins 80.00 40.00
147 Mel Almada 80.00 40.00
148 Allan Cooke 80.00 40.00
149 Moe Berg 425.00 210.00
150 Dolph Camilli 90.00 45.00
151 Oscar Melillo 80.00 40.00
152 Bruce Campbell 80.00 40.00
153 Lefty Grove 300.00 150.00
154 Johnny Murphy 100.00 50.00
155 Luke Sewell 90.00 45.00
156 Leo Durocher 250.00 125.00
157 Lloyd Waner 175.00 90.00
158 Guy Bush 80.00 40.00
159 Jimmy Dykes 90.00 45.00
160 Steve O'Neill 90.00 45.00
161 General Crowder 90.00 45.00
162 Joe Cascarella 90.00 45.00
163 Daniel(Bud) Hafey 90.00 45.00
164 Gilly Campbell 80.00 40.00
165 Ray Hayworth 80.00 40.00
166 Frank Demaree 80.00 40.00
167 John Babich 80.00 40.00
168 Marvin Owen 80.00 40.00
169 Ralph Kress 80.00 40.00
170 Mule Haas 80.00 40.00
171 Frank Higgins 90.00 45.00
172 Wally Berger 100.00 50.00
173 Frankie Frisch 250.00 125.00
174 Wes Ferrell 90.00 45.00
175 Pete Fox 80.00 40.00
176 John Vergez 80.00 40.00
177 Billy Rogell 80.00 40.00
178 Don Brennan 80.00 40.00
179 Jim Bottomley 175.00 90.00
180 Travis Jackson 175.00 90.00
181 Red Rolfe 100.00 50.00
182 Frank Crosetti 125.00 60.00
183 Joe Cronin 175.00 90.00
184 Schoolboy Rowe 100.00 50.00
185 Chuck Klein 225.00 110.00
186 Lon Warneke 90.00 45.00
187 Gus Suhr 80.00 40.00
188 Ben Chapman 90.00 45.00
189 Clint Brown 80.00 40.00
190 Paul Derringer 100.00 50.00
191 John Burns 80.00 40.00
192 John Broaca 125.00 60.00

1959 Bauer Hayes Company PC750

The 1959 Hayes Company postacrd consists of but one card. The Dexter Press printed Hank Bauer card is in full color and features a facsimile autograph of Bauer at the bottom of the card.

	NM	Ex
1 Hank Bauer	15.00	7.50

1959 Bazooka

The 23 full-color, unnumbered cards comprising the 1959 Bazooka set were cut from the bottom of the boxes of gum marketed nationally that year by Topps. Bazooka was the brand name which Topps had been using to sell its one cent bubblegum; this year Topps decided to distribute 25 pieces of Bazooka gum in a box. The cards themselves measure 2 13/16" by 4 15/16". Only nine cards were originally issued; 14 more were added to the set at a later date (these are marked with SP in the checklist). The latter are less plentiful and hence more valuable than the original nine. All the cards are blank backed and the catalog designation is R414-15. The prices below are for the cards cut from the box; complete boxes intact would be worth about 50 percent more.

	NM	Ex
COMPLETE SET (23)	7000.00	3500.00
COMMON CARD (1-23)	50.00	25.00
COMMON CARD SP	200.00	100.00
1 Hank Aaron	500.00	250.00
2 Richie Ashburn SP	400.00	200.00
3 Ernie Banks SP	600.00	300.00
4 Ken Boyer SP	300.00	150.00
5 Orlando Cepeda	200.00	100.00
6 Bob Cerv SP	200.00	100.00
7 Rocky Colavito SP	400.00	200.00
8 Del Crandall	50.00	25.00
9 Jim Davenport	50.00	25.00
10 Don Drysdale SP	500.00	250.00
11 Nellie Fox SP	400.00	200.00
12 Jackie Jensen SP	300.00	150.00
13 Harvey Kuenn SP	250.00	125.00
14 Mickey Mantle	1500.00	750.00
15 Willie Mays	600.00	300.00
16 Bill Mazeroski	200.00	100.00
17 Roy McMillan	50.00	25.00
18 Billy Pierce SP	250.00	125.00
19 Roy Sievers SP	200.00	100.00
20 Duke Snider SP	800.00	400.00
21 Gus Triandos SP	200.00	100.00
22 Bob Turley	100.00	50.00
23 Vic Wertz SP	200.00	100.00

1960 Bazooka

In 1960, Topps introduced a 36-card baseball player set in three card panels on the bottom of Bazooka gum boxes. The cards measure 1 13/16" by 2 3/4" and the panels measure 2 3/4" by 5 1/2". The cards carried full color pictures and were numbered at the bottom underneath the team position. The checklist below contains prices for individual cards. Complete panels of three would have a 50 percent more than the sum of the indiviudal cards (prices) on the panel and complete boxes would command a premium of another 50 percent above those prices.

	NM	Ex
COMPLETE INDIV.SET	1000.00	400.00
1 Ernie Banks	50.00	20.00
2 Bud Daley	12.00	4.80
3 Wally Moon	12.00	4.80
4 Hank Aaron	100.00	40.00
5 Milt Pappas	12.00	4.80
6 Dick Stuart	12.00	4.80
7 Roberto Clemente	200.00	80.00
8 Yogi Berra	70.00	28.00
9 Ken Boyer	15.00	6.00
10 Orlando Cepeda	30.00	12.00
11 Gus Triandos	12.00	4.80
12 Frank Malzone	12.00	4.80
13 Willie Mays	120.00	47.50
14 Camilo Pascual	12.00	4.80
15 Bob Cerv	12.00	4.80
16 Vic Power	12.00	4.80
17 Larry Sherry	12.00	4.80
18 Al Kaline	50.00	20.00
19 Warren Spahn	50.00	20.00
20 Harmon Killebrew	50.00	20.00
21 Jackie Jensen	15.00	6.00
22 Luis Aparicio	30.00	12.00
23 Gil Hodges	30.00	12.00
24 Richie Ashburn	40.00	16.00
25 Nellie Fox	40.00	16.00
26 Robin Roberts	40.00	16.00
27 Joe Cunningham	12.00	4.80
28 Early Wynn	30.00	12.00
29 Frank Robinson	50.00	20.00
30 Rocky Colavito	30.00	12.00
31 Mickey Mantle	300.00	120.00
32 Glen Hobbie	12.00	4.80
33 Roy McMillan	12.00	4.80
34 Harvey Kuenn	12.00	4.80
35 Johnny Antonelli	12.00	4.80
36 Del Crandall	12.00	4.80

1961 Bazooka

The 36 card set issued by Bazooka in 1961 follows the format established in 1960; three full color, numbered cards to each panel found on a Bazooka gum box. The individual cards measure 1 13/16" by 2 3/4" whereas the panels measure 2 3/4" by 5 1/2". The cards of 1960 and 1961 are similar in design but are easily distinguished from one another by their numbers. Complete panels of three would have a value of 40 percent more than the sum of the individual cards (prices) on the panel and complete boxes would command a premium of another 40 percent above those prices.

	NM	Ex
COMPLETE INDIV. SET	800.00	325.00
1 Art Mahaffey	12.00	4.80
2 Mickey Mantle	300.00	120.00
3 Ron Santo	15.00	6.00
4 Bud Daley	12.00	4.80
5 Roger Maris	70.00	28.00
6 Eddie Yost	12.00	4.80
7 Minnie Minoso	15.00	6.00
8 Dick Groat	12.00	4.80
9 Frank Malzone	12.00	4.80
10 Dick Donovan	12.00	4.80
11 Eddie Mathews	50.00	20.00
12 Jim Lemon	12.00	4.80
13 Chuck Estrada	12.00	4.80
14 Ken Boyer	15.00	6.00
15 Harvey Kuenn	12.00	4.80
16 Ernie Broglio	12.00	4.80
17 Rocky Colavito	30.00	12.00
18 Ted Kluszewski	30.00	12.00
19 Ernie Banks	50.00	20.00
20 Al Kaline	50.00	20.00
21 Ed Bailey	12.00	4.80
22 Jim Perry	12.00	4.80
23 Willie Mays	100.00	40.00
24 Bill Mazeroski	30.00	12.00
25 Gus Triandos	12.00	4.80
26 Don Drysdale	40.00	16.00
27 Frank Herrera	12.00	4.80
28 Earl Battey	12.00	4.80
29 Warren Spahn	50.00	20.00
30 Gene Woodling	12.00	4.80
31 Frank Robinson	50.00	20.00
32 Pete Runnels	12.00	4.80
33 Woodie Held	12.00	4.80
34 Norm Larker	12.00	4.80
35 Luis Aparicio	30.00	12.00
36 Bill Tuttle	12.00	4.80

1962 Bazooka

The 1962 Bazooka set of 45 full color, blank backed, unnumbered cards was issued in panels of three on Bazooka bubble gum. The individual cards measure 1 13/16" by 2 3/4" whereas the panels measure 2 3/4" by 5 1/2". The cards below are numbered by panel alphabetically based on the last name of the player pictured on the far left card of the panel. The cards with SP in the checklist below are more difficult to obtain. Complete panels would have a value of 40 percent more than the sum of the individual cards (prices) on the panel and complete boxes would command a premium of another 40 percent above those prices.

	NM	Ex
COMPLETE INDIV. SET	3000.00	1200.00
COMMON CARD (1-45)	12.00	4.80
COMMON SP	70.00	28.00
1 Bob Allison SP	70.00	28.00
2 Eddie Mathews SP	500.00	200.00
3 Vada Pinson SP	100.00	40.00
4 Earl Battey	12.00	4.80
5 Warren Spahn	50.00	20.00
6 Lee Thomas	12.00	4.80
7 Orlando Cepeda	30.00	12.00
8 Woodie Held	12.00	4.80
9 Bob Aspromonte	12.00	4.80
10 Dick Howser	12.00	4.80
11 Roberto Clemente	200.00	80.00
12 Al Kaline	50.00	20.00
13 Joe Jay	12.00	4.80
14 Roger Maris	70.00	28.00
15 Frank Howard	15.00	6.00
16 Sandy Koufax	70.00	28.00
17 Jim Gentile	12.00	4.80
18 Johnny Callison	12.00	4.80
19 Jim Landis	12.00	4.80
20 Ken Boyer	15.00	6.00
21 Chuck Schilling	12.00	4.80
22 Art Mahaffey	12.00	4.80
23 Mickey Mantle	275.00	110.00
24 Dick Stuart	12.00	4.80
25 Ken McBride	12.00	4.80
26 Frank Robinson	50.00	20.00
27 Gil Hodges	40.00	16.00
28 Milt Pappas	12.00	4.80
29 Hank Aaron	100.00	40.00
30 Luis Aparicio	30.00	12.00
31 Johnny Romano SP	70.00	28.00
32 Ernie Banks SP	500.00	200.00
33 Norm Siebern SP	70.00	28.00
34 Ron Santo	20.00	8.00
35 Norm Cash	15.00	6.00
36 Jim Piersall	15.00	6.00
37 Don Schwall	12.00	4.80
38 Willie Mays	110.00	45.00
39 Norm Larker	12.00	4.80
40 Bill White	15.00	6.00
41 Whitey Ford	50.00	20.00
42 Rocky Colavito	30.00	12.00
43 Don Zimmer SP	100.00	40.00
44 Harmon Killebrew SP	500.00	200.00
45 Gene Woodling SP	70.00	28.00

1963 Bazooka

The 1963 Bazooka set of 36 full color, blank backed numbered cards was issued on Bazooka bubble gum boxes. This year marked a change in format from previous Bazooka issues with a smaller sized card being issued. The individual cards measure 1 9/16" by 2 1/2" whereas the panels measure 2 1/2" by 4 11/16". The card features a white strip with the player's name printed in black on the card. The number appears in the white border on the bottom of the card. Three cards were issued per panel. Complete panels of three would have a value of 15 percent more than the sum of the individual cards (prices) on the panel and complete boxes would command a premium of another 30 percent above those prices.

	NM	Ex
COMPLETE INDIV.SET	800.00	325.00
1 Mickey Mantle	200.00	80.00
2 Bob Rodgers	8.00	3.20
3 Ernie Banks	50.00	20.00
4 Norm Siebern	8.00	3.20
5 Warren Spahn	40.00	16.00
6 Bill Mazeroski	20.00	8.00
7 Harmon Killebrew	40.00	16.00
8 Dick Farrell	8.00	3.20
9 Hank Aaron	80.00	32.00
10 Dick Donovan	8.00	3.20
11 Jim Gentile	8.00	3.20
12 Willie Mays	80.00	32.00
13 Camilo Pascual	8.00	3.20
14 Roberto Clemente	100.00	40.00
15 Johnny Callison	8.00	3.20
16 Carl Yastrzemski	40.00	16.00
17 Don Drysdale	30.00	12.00
18 Johnny Romano	8.00	3.20
19 Al Jackson	8.00	3.20
20 Ralph Terry	8.00	3.20
21 Bill Monbouquette	8.00	3.20
22 Orlando Cepeda	20.00	8.00
23 Stan Musial	50.00	20.00
24 Floyd Robinson	8.00	3.20
25 Chuck Hinton	8.00	3.20
26 Bob Purkey	8.00	3.20
27 Ken Hubbs	10.00	4.00
28 Bill White	10.00	4.00
29 Ray Herbert	8.00	3.20
30 Brooks Robinson	50.00	20.00
31 Frank Robinson	50.00	20.00
32 Lee Thomas	8.00	3.20
33 Rocky Colavito	20.00	8.00
34 Al Kaline	50.00	20.00
35 Art Mahaffey	8.00	3.20
36 Tommy Davis	8.00	3.20

1963 Bazooka ATG

The 1963 Bazooka All Time Greats set contains 41 black and white numbered cards issued as inserts in boxes of Bazooka Bubble gum. The cards feature bust shots with gold trim and measure 1 9/16" by 2 1/2". The backs are yellow with black print containing vital information and a biography of the player. Many of the players are pictured not as they looked during their playing careers but as they looked many years after their playing days were through. The cards also exist in a scarcer variety with silver trim instead of gold; the silver trim variety cards are worth approximately double the prices listed below. Cards are numbered on the back.

	NM	Ex
COMPLETE SET (41)	350.00	140.00
1 Joe Tinker	6.00	2.40
2 Harry Heilmann	6.00	2.40
3 Jack Chesbro	4.00	1.60
4 Christy Mathewson	15.00	6.00
5 Herb Pennock	6.00	2.40
6 Cy Young	10.00	4.00
7 Ed Walsh	6.00	2.40
8 Nap Lajoie	10.00	4.00
9 Eddie Plank	6.00	2.40
10 Honus Wagner	20.00	8.00
11 Chief Bender	6.00	2.40
12 Walter Johnson	15.00	6.00
13 Mordecai Brown	6.00	2.40
14 Rabbit Maranville	6.00	2.40
15 Lou Gehrig	50.00	20.00
16 Ban Johnson	4.00	1.60
17 Babe Ruth	80.00	32.00
18 Connie Mack	6.00	2.40
19 Hank Greenberg	6.00	2.40
20 John McGraw	6.00	2.40
21 Johnny Evers	6.00	2.40
22 Al Simmons	6.00	2.40
23 Jimmy Collins	6.00	2.40
24 Tris Speaker	8.00	3.20
25 Frank Chance	6.00	2.40
26 Fred Clarke	6.00	2.40
27 Wilbert Robinson	6.00	2.40
28 Dazzy Vance	6.00	2.40
29 Pete Alexander	8.00	3.20
30 Judge Landis	6.00	2.40
31 Willie Keeler	6.00	2.40
32 Rogers Hornsby	10.00	4.00
33 Hugh Duffy	6.00	2.40
34 Mickey Cochrane	6.00	2.40
35 Ty Cobb	50.00	20.00
36 Mel Ott	10.00	4.00
37 Clark Griffith	6.00	2.40
38 Ted Lyons	6.00	2.40
39 Cap Anson	6.00	2.40
40 Bill Dickey	6.00	2.40
41 Eddie Collins	6.00	2.40

1964 Bazooka

The 1964 Bazooka set of 36 full color, blank backed, numbered cards were issued in panels of three on the backs of Bazooka bubble gum boxes. The individual cards measure 1 9/16" by 2 1/2" whereas the panels measure 2 1/2" by 4 11/16". Many players who were in the 1963 set have the same number in this set; however, the pictures are different. Complete panels of three would have a value of 15 percent more than the sum of the individual cards (prices) on the panel and complete boxes would command a premium of another 40 percent above those prices.

	NM	Ex
COMPLETE INDIV. SET	800.00	325.00
1 Mickey Mantle	200.00	80.00
2 Dick Groat	8.00	3.20
3 Steve Barber	8.00	3.20
4 Ken McBride	8.00	3.20
5 Warren Spahn	40.00	16.00
6 Bob Friend	8.00	3.20
7 Harmon Killebrew	40.00	16.00
8 Dick Farrell	8.00	3.20
9 Hank Aaron	80.00	32.00
10 Rich Rollins	8.00	3.20
11 Jim Gentile	8.00	3.20
12 Willie Mays	80.00	32.00
13 Camilo Pascual	8.00	3.20
14 Roberto Clemente	100.00	40.00
15 Johnny Callison	8.00	3.20
16 Carl Yastrzemski	50.00	20.00
17 Billy Williams	20.00	8.00
18 Johnny Romano	8.00	3.20
19 Jim Maloney	8.00	3.20
20 Norm Cash	10.00	4.00
21 Willie McCovey	20.00	8.00
22 Jim Fregosi	8.00	3.20
23 George Altman	8.00	3.20
24 Floyd Robinson	8.00	3.20
25 Chuck Hinton	8.00	3.20
26 Ron Hunt	8.00	3.20
27 Gary Peters	8.00	3.20
28 Dick Ellsworth	8.00	3.20
29 Elston Howard	10.00	4.00
30 Brooks Robinson	50.00	20.00
31 Frank Robinson	50.00	20.00
32 Sandy Koufax	70.00	28.00
33 Rocky Colavito	20.00	8.00
34 Al Kaline	50.00	20.00
35 Ken Boyer	10.00	4.00
36 Tommy Davis	8.00	3.20

1964 Bazooka Stamps

Many of the 100 color portraits of baseball players featured in this 1964 Topps stamp series show players without caps. Each small stamp is 1" by 1 1/2". The subject's name, team and position are found in a colored rectangle beneath the picture area. Each sheet is numbered in the upper left hand corner outside the picture area. The sheet number is given after the player's name in the checklist below with the prefix S. The stamps were issued in sheets of 10 but an album to hold this particular set has not yet been seen.

	NM	Ex
COMPLETE SET (100)	450.00	180.00
1 Ed Charles	1.00	.40
2 Vada Pinson	2.00	.80
3 Jimmy Hall	1.00	.40
4 Milt Pappas	1.50	.60

5 Dick Ellsworth 1.00 .40
6 Frank Malzone 1.50 .60
7 Max Alvis 1.00 .40
8 Pete Ward 1.00 .40
9 Tony Taylor 1.50 .60
10 Bill White 2.50 1.00
11 Don Zimmer 2.00 .80
12 Bobby Richardson 5.00 2.00
13 Larry Jackson 1.00 .40
14 Norm Siebern 1.00 .40
15 Frank Robinson 15.00 6.00
16 Bob Aspromonte 1.00 .40
17 Al McBean 1.00 .40
18 Floyd Robinson 1.00 .40
19 Bill Monbouquette 1.00 .40
20 Willie Mays 40.00 16.00
21 Brooks Robinson S3 20.00 8.00
22 Joe Pepitone S3 2.50 1.00
23 Carl Yastrzemski S3 20.00 8.00
24 Don Lock S3 1.00 .40
25 Ernie Banks S3 20.00 8.00
26 Dave Nicholson S3 1.00 .40
27 Roberto Clemente S3 50.00 20.00
28 Curt Flood S3 2.50 1.00
29 Woody Held S3 1.00 .40
30 Jesse Gonder S3 1.00 .40
31 Juan Pizarro 1.00 .40
32 Jim Maloney S4 1.50 .60
33 Ron Santo 2.50 1.00
34 Harmon Killebrew 10.00 4.00
35 Ed Roebuck S4 1.00 .40
36 Boog Powell 2.50 1.00
37 Jim Grant S4 1.00 .40
38 Hank Aguirre S4 1.00 .40
39 Juan Marichal 10.00 4.00
40 Bill Mazeroski 3.00 1.20
41 Dick Radatz S5 1.00 .40
42 Albie Pearson S5 1.00 .40
43 Tommy Harper S5 1.50 .60
44 Carl Willey S5 1.00 .40
45 Jim Bouton 2.50 1.00
46 Ron Perranoski S5 1.00 .40
47 Chuck Hinton S5 1.00 .40
48 John Romano S5 1.00 .40
49 Norm Cash 2.50 1.00
50 Orlando Cepeda 5.00 2.00
51 Dick Stuart S6 1.00 .40
52 Rich Rollins S6 1.00 .40
53 Mickey Mantle S6 80.00 32.00
54 Steve Barber S6 1.00 .40
55 Jim O'Toole S6 1.00 .40
56 Gary Peters S6 1.00 .40
57 Warren Spahn S6 12.00 4.80
58 Tony Gonzalez S6 1.00 .40
59 Joe Torre S6 2.50 1.00
60 Jim Fregosi S6 2.00 .80
61 Ken Boyer 2.50 1.00
62 Felipe Alou 1.50 .60
63 Jim Davenport S7 1.00 .40
64 Tommy Davis 2.00 .80
65 Rocky Colavito 4.00 1.60
66 Bob Friend S7 1.50 .60
67 Billy Moran S7 1.00 .40
68 Bill Freehan 2.00 .80
69 George Altman S7 1.00 .40
70 Ken Johnson S7 1.00 .40
71 Earl Battey S8 1.00 .40
72 Elston Howard 2.50 1.00
73 Billy Williams 10.00 4.00
74 Claude Osteen 1.50 .60
75 Jim Gentile 1.50 .60
76 Donn Clendenon 1.50 .60
77 Ernie Broglio 1.00 .40
78 Hal Woodeshick 1.00 .40
79 Don Drysdale 10.00 4.00
80 John Callison 1.50 .60
81 Dick Groat 1.50 .60
82 Moe Drabowsky 1.00 .40
83 Frank Howard 1.50 .60
84 Hank Aaron 40.00 16.00
85 Al Jackson 1.00 .40
86 Jerry Lumpe 1.00 .40
87 Wayne Causey 1.00 .40
88 Rusty Staub 2.50 1.00
89 Ken McBride 1.00 .40
90 Jack Baldschun 1.00 .40
91 Sandy Koufax S10 25.00 10.00
92 Camilo Pascual S10 1.00 .40
93 Ron Hunt S10 1.00 .40
94 Willie McCovey S10 12.00 4.80
95 Al Kaline S10 15.00 6.00
96 Ray Culp S10 1.00 .40
97 Ed Mathews S10 12.00 4.80
98 Dick Farrell S10 1.00 .40
99 Lee Thomas S10 1.50 .60
100 Vic Davalillo S10 1.00 .40

1965 Bazooka

The 1965 Bazooka set of 36 full color, blank backed, numbered cards was issued in panels of three on the backs of Bazooka bubble gum boxes. The individual cards measure 1 9/16" by 2 1/2" whereas the panels measure 2 1/2" by 4 11/16". As in the previous two years some of the players have the same numbers on their cards; however all pictures are different from the previous two years. Complete panels of three would have a value of 15 percent more than the sum of the individual cards (prices) on the panel and complete boxes would command a premium of another 40 percent above those prices.

	NM	Ex
COMPLETE INDIV. SET	800.00	325.00
1 Mickey Mantle	200.00	80.00
2 Larry Jackson	8.00	3.20
3 Chuck Hinton	8.00	3.20
4 Tony Oliva	15.00	6.00
5 Dean Chance	8.00	3.20
6 Jim O'Toole	8.00	3.20
7 Harmon Killebrew	30.00	12.00
8 Pete Ward	8.00	3.20
9 Hank Aaron	80.00	32.00
10 Dick Radatz	8.00	3.20
11 Boog Powell	10.00	4.00
12 Willie Mays	80.00	32.00
13 Bob Veale	8.00	3.20
14 Roberto Clemente	100.00	40.00
15 Johnny Callison	8.00	3.20
16 Joe Torre	15.00	6.00
17 Billy Williams	25.00	10.00
18 Bob Chance	8.00	3.20
19 Bob Aspromonte	8.00	3.20
20 Joe Christopher	8.00	3.20
21 Jim Bunning	20.00	8.00
22 Jim Fregosi	8.00	3.20
23 Bob Gibson	30.00	12.00
24 Juan Marichal	30.00	12.00
25 Dave Wickersham	8.00	3.20
26 Ron Hunt	8.00	3.20
27 Gary Peters	8.00	3.20
28 Ron Santo	15.00	6.00
29 Elston Howard	10.00	4.00
30 Brooks Robinson	40.00	16.00
31 Frank Robinson	40.00	16.00
32 Sandy Koufax	50.00	20.00
33 Rocky Colavito	20.00	8.00
34 Al Kaline	40.00	16.00
35 Ken Boyer	10.00	4.00
36 Tommy Davis	8.00	3.20

1966 Bazooka

The 1966 Bazooka set of 48 full color, blank backed, numbered cards was issued in panels of three on the backs of Bazooka bubble gum boxes. The individual cardsd measure 1 9/16" by 2 1/2" whereas the complete panels measure 2 1/2" by 4 11/16". The set is distinguishable from the previous years by mention of "48 card set" at the bottom of the card. Complete panels of three would have a value of 15 percent more than the sum of the individual cards (prices) on the panel and complete boxes would command a premium of another 40 percent above those prices.

	NM	Ex
COMPLETE INDIV. SET	800.00	325.00
1 Sandy Koufax	50.00	20.00
2 Willie Horton	8.00	3.20
3 Frank Howard	10.00	4.00
4 Richie Allen	10.00	4.00
5 Mel Stottlemyre	10.00	4.00
6 Tony Conigliaro	12.00	4.80
7 Mickey Mantle	200.00	80.00
8 Leon Wagner	8.00	3.20
9 Ed Kranepool	8.00	3.20
10 Juan Marichal	25.00	10.00
11 Harmon Killebrew	25.00	10.00
12 Johnny Callison	8.00	3.20
13 Roy McMillan	8.00	3.20
14 Willie McCovey	25.00	10.00
15 Rocky Colavito	15.00	6.00
16 Willie Mays	80.00	32.00
17 Sam McDowell	8.00	3.20
18 Vern Law	8.00	3.20
19 Jim Fregosi	8.00	3.20
20 Ron Fairly	8.00	3.20
21 Bob Gibson	25.00	10.00
22 Carl Yastrzemski	30.00	12.00
23 Bill White	10.00	4.00
24 Bob Aspromonte	8.00	3.20
25 Dean Chance	8.00	3.20
26 Roberto Clemente	100.00	40.00
27 Tony Cloninger	8.00	3.20
28 Curt Blefary	8.00	3.20
29 Milt Pappas	8.00	3.20
30 Hank Aaron	80.00	32.00
31 Jim Bunning	15.00	6.00
32 Frank Robinson	30.00	12.00
33 Bill Skowron	10.00	4.00
34 Brooks Robinson	30.00	12.00
35 Jim Wynn	8.00	3.20
36 Joe Torre	12.00	4.80
37 Jim Grant	8.00	3.20
38 Pete Rose	60.00	24.00
39 Ron Santo	12.00	4.80
40 Tom Tresh	10.00	4.00
41 Tony Oliva	12.00	4.80
42 Don Drysdale	25.00	10.00
43 Pete Richert	8.00	3.20
44 Bert Campaneris	8.00	3.20
45 Jim Maloney	8.00	3.20
46 Al Kaline	30.00	12.00
47 Eddie Fisher	8.00	3.20
48 Billy Williams	20.00	8.00

1967 Bazooka

The 1967 Bazooka set of 48 full color, blank backed, numbered cards was issued in panels of three on the backs of Bazooka bubble gum boxes. The individual cards measure 1 9/16" by 2 1/2" whereas the complete panels measure 2 1/2" by 4 11/16". This set is virtually identical to the 1966 set with the exception of ten new cards as replacements for ten 1966 cards. The remaining 38 cards are identical in pose and number. The replacement cards are listed in the checklist below with an asterisk. Complete panels of three would have a value of 15 percent more than the sum of the individual cards (prices) on the panel and complete boxes would command a premium of another 40 percent above those prices.

	NM	Ex
COMPLETE INDIV. SET	800.00	325.00
1 Rick Reichardt	8.00	3.20
2 Tommie Agee	8.00	3.20
3 Frank Howard	10.00	4.00
4 Richie Allen	10.00	4.00
5 Mel Stottlemyre	10.00	4.00
6 Tony Conigliaro	12.00	4.80
7 Mickey Mantle	200.00	80.00
8 Leon Wagner	8.00	3.20
9 Gary Peters	8.00	3.20
10 Juan Marichal	25.00	10.00
11 Harmon Killebrew	25.00	10.00
12 Johnny Callison	8.00	3.20
13 Denny McLain	12.00	4.80
14 Willie McCovey	25.00	10.00
15 Rocky Colavito	15.00	6.00
16 Willie Mays	80.00	32.00
17 Sam McDowell	8.00	3.20
18 Jim Kaat	12.00	4.80
19 Jim Fregosi	8.00	3.20
20 Ron Fairly	8.00	3.20
21 Bob Gibson	25.00	10.00
22 Carl Yastrzemski	30.00	12.00
23 Bill White	10.00	4.00
24 Bob Aspromonte	8.00	3.20
25 Dean Chance	8.00	3.20
26 Roberto Clemente	100.00	40.00
27 Tony Cloninger	8.00	3.20
28 Curt Blefary	8.00	3.20
29 Phil Regan	8.00	3.20
30 Hank Aaron	80.00	32.00
31 Jim Bunning	15.00	6.00
32 Frank Robinson	30.00	12.00
33 Ken Boyer	10.00	4.00
34 Brooks Robinson	30.00	12.00
35 Jim Wynn	8.00	3.20
36 Joe Torre	12.00	4.80
37 Tommy Davis	8.00	3.20
38 Pete Rose	60.00	24.00
39 Ron Santo	12.00	4.80
40 Tom Tresh	10.00	4.00
41 Tony Oliva	12.00	4.80
42 Don Drysdale	25.00	10.00
43 Pete Richert	8.00	3.20
44 Bert Campaneris	8.00	3.20
45 Jim Maloney	8.00	3.20
46 Al Kaline	30.00	12.00
47 Matty Alou	8.00	3.20
48 Billy Williams	20.00	8.00

1968 Bazooka

The 1968 Bazooka Tipps from the Topps is a set of 15 numbered boxes (measuring 5 1/2" by 6 1/4" when detached). each containing on the back panel (measuring 3" by 6 1/4") a baseball playing tip from a star, and on the side panels four mini cards, two per side, in full color, measuring 1 1/4" by 3 1/8". Although the set contains a total of 60 of these small cards, 4 are repeated; therefore there are only 56 different small cards. Some collectors cut the panels into individual card; however most collectors retain entire panels or boxes. The prices in the checklist therfore reflect only the values of the complete boxes.

	NM	Ex
COMPLETE BOX SET	1000.00	400.00
COMMON BOX	50.00	20.00
COMMON INDIV. PLAYER	3.00	1.20
1 Maury Wills: Bunting Al Kaline Paul Casanova Clete Boyer Tom Seaver	120.00	47.50
2 C.Yastrzemski: Batting Jim Hunter Bill Freehan Matty Alou Jim Lefebvre	80.00	32.00
3 B.Campaneris: Stealing Tim McCarver Bob Veale Frank Robinson Bobby Knoop	50.00	20.00
4 Maury Wills: Sliding Ken Holtzman Jose Azcue Tony Conigliaro Bill White	50.00	20.00
5 J.Javier: Double Play Juan Marichal Rico Petrocelli Joe Pepitone Hank Aaron	120.00	47.50
6 O.Cepeda: 1st Base Ron Santo Don Drysdale Pete Rose Tommie Agee	80.00	32.00
7 B.Mazeroski: 2nd Base John Roseboro Jim Bunning Frank Howard George Scott	50.00	20.00
8 B.Robinson: 3rd Base Tony Gonzalez Jim McGlothlin Wille Horton Harmon Killebrew	60.00	24.00
9 Jim Fregosi: Shortstop Max Alvis Bob Gibson Tony Oliva Vada Pinson	50.00	20.00
10 Joe Torre: Catching Dean Chance Fergie Jenkins Tommy Davis Rick Monday	50.00	20.00
11 Jim Lonborg: Pitching Joel Horlen Jim Wynn Curt Flood Mickey Mantle	200.00	80.00
12 Mike McCormick: Fielding Pitcher Don Mincher Tony Perez Roberto Clemente Al Downing	50.00	20.00
13 F.Crosetti: Coaching Rod Carew Don Wilson Ron Swoboda Willie McCovey	50.00	20.00
14 Willie Mays: Outfield Richie Allen Gary Peters Billy Williams Rusty Staub	120.00	47.50
15 L.Brock: Base Running Tommie Agee Pete Rose Ron Santo Don Drysdale	120.00	47.50

1969-70 Bazooka

The 1969-70 Bazooka Baseball Extra News set contains 12 complete panels, each comprising a large action shot of a significant event in baseball history and four small cards, comparable to those in the Tipps from the Topps set of 1968, of Hall of Famers. Although some collectors cut the panels into individual cards (measuring 3" by 6 1/4" or 1 1/4" by 3 1/8"), most collectors retain the entire panel, or box (measuring 5 1/2" by 6 1/4"). The prices in the checklist below reflect the value for the entire box, as these cards are more widely seen and collected as complete panels or boxes.

	NM	Ex
COMPLETE PANEL SET	400.00	160.00
COMMON PANEL (1-12)	30.00	12.00
COMMON INDIV. PLAYER	.50	.20
1 No-Hit Duel by Fred Toney Hippo Vaughn: Ty Cobb Willie Keeler Mordecai Brown Eddie Plank	40.00	16.00
2 Alexander Conquers Yankees: Al Simmons Ban Johnson Walter Johnson Rogers Hornsby	30.00	12.00
3 Yanks' Lazzeri Sets AL Record: Christy Mathewson Chief Bender Grover Alexander Cy Young	30.00	12.00
4 Homerun Almost Hit Out of Stadium: Lou Gehrig Hugh Duffy Tris Speaker Joe Tinker	40.00	16.00
5 Four Consecutive Homers by Lou: John McGraw Frank Chance Babe Ruth Mickey Cochrane	100.00	40.00
6 No-Hit Game by Walter Johnson: Cy Young Walter Johnson Johnny Evers John McGraw	30.00	12.00
7 Twelve RBIs by Jim Bottomley: Johnny Evers Eddie Collins Lou Gehrig Ty Cobb	50.00	20.00
8 Ty Cobb Ties Record: Honus Wagner Mickey Cochrane Eddie Collins Mel Ott	40.00	16.00
9 Babe Ruth Hits Three Homers in Game: Cap Anson Tris Speaker Jack Chesbro Al Simmons	50.00	20.00
10 Babe Ruth Calls Shot in Series Game: Rabbit Maranville Ed Walsh Nap Lajoie Connie Mack	50.00	20.00
11 Babe Ruth's 60th Homer Sets New Record: Joe Tinker Nap Lajoie Mel Ott Frank Chance	50.00	20.00
12 Double Shutout by Ed Reulbach: Rogers Hornsby Rabbit Maranville Christy Mathewson Honus Wagner	30.00	12.00

1971 Bazooka Numbered Test

This was supposedly a test issue which was different from the more common unnumbered set and much more difficult to find. There are 48 cards (16 panels) in this numbered set whereas the unnumbered set had only 12 panels or 36 individual cards. Individual cards measure approximately 2" by 2 5/8" whereas the panels measure 2 5/8" by 5 15/16". Complete panels of three would have a value of 10 percent more than the sum of the individual cards (prices) on the panel and complete boxes would command a premium of another 30 percent above those prices.

	NM	Ex
COMPLETE SET (48)	650.00	250.00
1 Tim McCarver	6.00	2.40
2 Frank Robinson	30.00	12.00
3 Bill Mazeroski	20.00	8.00
4 Willie McCovey	20.00	8.00
5 Carl Yastrzemski	30.00	12.00
6 Clyde Wright	4.00	1.60
7 Jim Merritt	4.00	1.60
8 Luis Aparicio	20.00	8.00
9 Bobby Murcer	6.00	2.40
10 Rico Petrocelli	4.00	1.60
11 Sam McDowell	4.00	1.60
12 Clarence Gaston	4.00	1.60
13 Fergie Jenkins	20.00	8.00
14 Al Kaline	30.00	12.00
15 Ken Harrelson	4.00	1.60
16 Tommie Agee	4.00	1.60
17 Harmon Killebrew	20.00	8.00
18 Reggie Jackson	50.00	20.00
19 Juan Marichal	20.00	8.00
20 Frank Howard	6.00	2.40
21 Bill Melton	4.00	1.60
22 Brooks Robinson	30.00	12.00
23 Hank Aaron	50.00	20.00
24 Larry Dierker	4.00	1.60
25 Jim Fregosi	4.00	1.60
26 Billy Williams	20.00	8.00
27 Dave McNally	4.00	1.60
28 Rico Carty	4.00	1.60
29 Johnny Bench	40.00	16.00
30 Tommy Harper	4.00	1.60
31 Bert Campaneris	4.00	1.60
32 Pete Rose	50.00	20.00
33 Orlando Cepeda	20.00	8.00
34 Maury Wills	6.00	2.40
35 Tom Seaver	40.00	16.00
36 Tony Oliva	15.00	6.00
37 Bill Freehan	4.00	1.60
38 Roberto Clemente	90.00	36.00
39 Claude Osteen	4.00	1.60
40 Rusty Staub	6.00	2.40
41 Bob Gibson	20.00	8.00
42 Amos Otis	4.00	1.60
43 Jim Wynn	6.00	2.40
44 Rich Allen	15.00	6.00
45 Tony Conigliaro	15.00	6.00
46 Randy Hundley	4.00	1.60
47 Willie Mays	50.00	20.00
48 Jim Hunter	20.00	8.00

1971 Bazooka Unnumbered

The 1971 Bazooka set of 36 full-color, unnumbered cards was issued in 12 panels of three cards each on the backs of boxes containing one cent Bazooka bubble gum. Individual cards measure approximately 2" by 2 5/8" whereas the panels measure 2 5/8" by 5 15/16". The panels are numbered in the checklist alphabetically by the player's last name on the left most card of the panel. Complete panels of three would have a value of 10 percent more than the sum of the individual cards (prices) on the panel and complete boxes would command a premium of another 30 percent above those prices.

	NM	Ex
COMPLETE INDIV.SET	300.00	120.00
1 Tommie Agee	3.00	1.20
2 Harmon Killebrew	15.00	6.00
3 Reggie Jackson	30.00	12.00
4 Bert Campaneris	3.00	1.20
5 Pete Rose	30.00	12.00
6 Orlando Cepeda	15.00	6.00

7 Rico Carty	3.00	1.20
8 Johnny Bench	25.00	10.00
9 Tommy Harper	3.00	1.20
10 Bill Freehan	3.00	1.20
11 Roberto Clemente	60.00	24.00
12 Claude Osteen	3.00	1.20
13 Jim Fregosi	3.00	1.20
14 Billy Williams	15.00	6.00
15 Dave McNally	3.00	1.20
16 Randy Hundley	3.00	1.20
17 Willie Mays	35.00	14.00
18 Jim Hunter	15.00	6.00
19 Juan Marichal	15.00	6.00
20 Frank Howard	5.00	2.00
21 Bill Melton	3.00	1.20
22 Willie McCovey	15.00	6.00
23 Carl Yastrzemski	20.00	8.00
24 Clyde Wright	3.00	1.20
25 Jim Merritt	3.00	1.20
26 Luis Aparicio	15.00	6.00
27 Bobby Murcer	5.00	2.00
28 Rico Petrocelli	3.00	1.20
29 Sam McDowell	3.00	1.20
30 Clarence Gaston	3.00	1.20
31 Brooks Robinson	20.00	8.00
32 Hank Aaron	30.00	12.00
33 Larry Dierker	3.00	1.20
34 Rusty Staub	5.00	2.00
35 Bob Gibson	15.00	6.00
36 Amos Otis	3.00	1.20

1988 Bazooka

There are 22 standard-size cards in the set. The cards have extra thick white borders. Card backs are printed in blue and red on white card stock. Some sets can also be found with gray backs; these gray backs carry no additional value premium. Cards are numbered on the back; they were numbered by Topps alphabetically. The word "Bazooka" only appears faintly as background for the statistics on the back of the card. Cards were available inside specially marked boxes of Bazooka gum retailing between 59 cents and 99 cents. The emphasis in the player selection for this set is on young stars of baseball.

	Nm-Mt	Ex-Mt
COMPLETE SET (22)	8.00	3.20
1 George Bell	.10	.04
2 Wade Boggs	.75	.30
3 Jose Canseco	.75	.30
4 Roger Clemens	1.25	.50
5 Vince Coleman	.10	.04
6 Eric Davis	.25	.10
7 Tony Fernandez	.10	.04
8 Dwight Gooden	.25	.10
9 Tony Gwynn	1.25	.50
11 Don Mattingly	1.25	.50
13 Mark McGwire	2.00	.80
14 Kirby Puckett	.75	.30
15 Tim Raines	.25	.10
16 Dave Righetti	.10	.04
17 Cal Ripken	2.50	1.00
18 Juan Samuel	.10	.04
19 Ryne Sandberg	.75	.30
20 Benito Santiago	.25	.10
21 Darryl Strawberry	.25	.10
22 Todd Worrell	.10	.04

1989 Bazooka

The 1989 Bazooka Shining Stars set contains 22 standard-size cards. The fronts have white borders and a large yellow stripe; the vertically oriented backs are pink, red and white and have career stats. The cards were inserted one per box of Bazooka Gum. The set is sequenced in alphabetical order.

	Nm-Mt	Ex-Mt
COMPLETE SET (22)	5.00	2.00
1 Tim Belcher	.10	.04
2 Damon Berryhill	.10	.04
3 Wade Boggs	1.00	.40
4 Jay Buhner	.25	.10
5 Jose Canseco	1.00	.40
6 Vince Coleman	.10	.04
7 Cecil Espy	.10	.04
8 Dave Gallagher	.10	.04
9 Ron Gant	.25	.10
10 Kirk Gibson	.25	.10
11 Paul Gibson	.10	.04
12 Mark Grace	1.00	.40
13 Tony Gwynn	1.25	.50
14 Rickey Henderson	1.25	.50
15 Orel Hershiser	.25	.10
16 Gregg Jefferies	.10	.04
17 Ricky Jordan	.10	.04
18 Chris Sabo	.10	.04
19 Gary Sheffield	1.25	.50
20 Darryl Strawberry	.25	.10
21 Frank Viola	.10	.04
22 Walt Weiss	.10	.04

1990 Bazooka

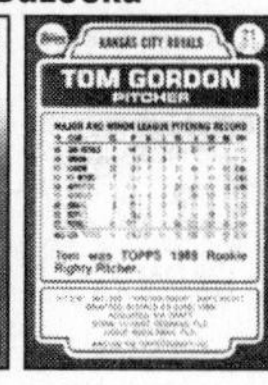

The 1990 Bazooka Shining Stars set contains 22 standard-size cards with a mix of award winners, league leaders, and young stars. This set was issued by Topps using the Bazooka name. Card backs were printed in blue and red on white card stock. The word "Bazooka" appears faintly as background for the statistics on the back of the card as well as appearing prominently on the front of each card.

	Nm-Mt	Ex-Mt
COMPLETE SET (22)	6.00	1.80
1 Kevin Mitchell	.10	.03
2 Robin Yount	.75	.23
3 Mark Davis	.10	.03
4 Bret Saberhagen	.25	.07
5 Fred McGriff	.50	.15
6 Tony Gwynn	1.50	.45
7 Kirby Puckett	.75	.23
8 Vince Coleman	.10	.03
9 Rickey Henderson	1.25	.35
10 Ben McDonald	.10	.03
11 Gregg Olson	.10	.03
12 Todd Zeile	.25	.07
13 Carlos Martinez	.10	.03
14 Gregg Jefferies	.10	.03
15 Craig Worthington	.10	.03
16 Gary Sheffield	1.00	.30
17 Greg Briley	.10	.03
18 Ken Griffey Jr.	2.50	.75
19 Jerome Walton	.10	.03
20 Bob Geren	.10	.03
21 Tom Gordon	.10	.03
22 Jim Abbott	.25	.07

1991 Bazooka

The 1991 Bazooka Shining Stars set contains 22 standard-size cards featuring league leaders and rookie sensations. The set was produced by Topps for Bazooka. One card was inserted in each box of Bazooka Bubble Gum. The fronts are similar to the Topps regular issue, only that the "Shining Star" emblem appears at the card top and the Bazooka logo overlays the lower right corner of the picture. In a blue and red design on white card stock, the backs have statistics and biography.

	Nm-Mt	Ex-Mt
COMPLETE SET (22)	6.00	1.80
1 Barry Bonds	2.00	.60
2 Rickey Henderson	1.25	.35
3 Bob Welch	.10	.03
4 Doug Drabek	.10	.03
5 Alex Fernandez	.10	.03
6 Jose Offerman	.10	.03
7 Frank Thomas	1.00	.30
8 Cecil Fielder	.25	.07
9 Ryne Sandberg	1.00	.30
10 George Brett	1.00	.30
11 Willie McGee	.25	.07
12 Vince Coleman	.10	.03
13 Hal Morris	.10	.03
14 Delino DeShields	.10	.03
15 Robin Ventura	.50	.15
16 Jeff Huson	.10	.03
17 Felix Jose	.10	.03
18 Dave Justice	.50	.15
19 Larry Walker	.75	.23
20 Sandy Alomar Jr.	.25	.07
21 Kevin Appier	.10	.03
22 Scott Radinsky	.10	.03

1992 Bazooka Quadracard '53 Archives

This 22-card set was produced by Topps for Bazooka, and the set is subtitled "Topps Archives Quadracard" on the top of the backs. Each standard-size card features four micro-reproductions of 1953 Topps baseball cards. These front and back borders of the cards are blue.

	Nm-Mt	Ex-Mt
COMPLETE SET (22)	12.00	3.60
1 Joe Adcock	1.00	.30
Bob Lemon		
Willie Mays		
Vic Wertz		
2 Carl Furillo	.50	.15
Don Newcombe		
Phil Rizzuto		
Hank Sauer		
3 Ferris Fain	.50	.15
John Logan		
Ed Mathews		
Bobby Shantz		
4 Yogi Berra	.75	.23
Del Crandall		
Howie Pollet		
Gene Woodling		
5 Richie Ashburn	1.00	.30
Leo Durocher MG		
Allie Reynolds		
Early Wynn		
6 Hank Aaron	1.50	.45
Ray Boone		
Luke Easter		
Dick Williams		
7 Ralph Branca	.75	.23
Bob Feller		
Rogers Hornsby		
Bobby Thomson		
8 Jim Gilliam	.50	.15
Billy Martin		
Minnie Minoso		
Hal Newhouser		
9 Smoky Burgess	.50	.15
John Mize		
Preacher Roe		
Warren Spahn		
10 Monte Irvin	.75	.23
Bobo Newsom		
Duke Snider		
Wes Westrum		
11 Carl Erskine	.50	.15
Jackie Jensen		
George Kell		
Red Schoendienst		
12 Bill Bruton	.50	.15
Whitey Ford		
Ed Lopat		
Mickey Vernon		
13 Joe Black	.25	.07
Lew Burdette		
Johnny Pesky		
Enos Slaughter		
14 Gus Bell	.75	.23
Mike Garcia		
Mel Parnell		
Jackie Robinson		
15 Alvin Dark	.50	.15
Dick Groat		
Pee Wee Reese		
John Sain		
16 Gil Hodges	.50	.15
Sal Maglie		
Wilmer Mizell		
Billy Pierce		
17 Nellie Fox	.50	.15
Ralph Kiner		
Ted Kluszewski		
Eddie Stanky		
18 Ewell Blackwell	.50	.15
Vern Law		
Satchel Paige		
Jim Wilson		
19 Lou Boudreau MG	.25	.07
Roy Face		
Harvey Haddix		
Bill Rigney		
20 Roy Campanella	.50	.15
Walt Dropo		
Harvey Kuenn		
Al Rosen		
21 Joe Garagiola	1.00	.30
Robin Roberts		
Casey Stengel MG		
Hoyt Wilhelm		
22 John Antonelli	1.00	.30
Bob Friend		
Dixie Walker CO		
Ted Williams		

1993 Bazooka Team USA

Originally available only in a special Bazooka collector's box, these 22 standard-size cards were produced by Topps and feature the 1993 Team USA players. The card design is similar to that of the '93 Topps series. The white-bordered fronts feature posed color player photos. The player's name appears in a blue stripe near the bottom; the Bazooka logo appears at the upper right. The colorful white-bordered backs carry a color head shot, biography, statistics, and career highlights. The cards are numbered on the back as "X of 22." Todd Helton has a very early card in this set. The full box this set came in also contained 50 pieces of Bazooka gum.

	Nm-Mt	Ex-Mt
COMP.FACT. SET (22)	100.00	30.00
1 Terry Harvey	.10	.03
2 Dante Powell	.10	.03
3 Andy Barkett	.10	.03
4 Steve Reich	.10	.03
5 Charlie Nelson	.10	.03
6 Todd Walker	6.00	1.80
7 Dustin Hermanson	1.50	.45
8 Pat Clougherty	.10	.03
9 Danny Graves	5.00	1.50
10 Paul Wilson	1.00	.30
11 Todd Helton	80.00	24.00
12 Russ Johnson	.25	.07
13 Darren Grass	.10	.03
14 A.J. Hinch	.25	.07
15 Mark Merila	.10	.03
16 John Powell	.10	.03
17 Bob Scafa	.10	.03
18 Matt Beaumont	.10	.03
19 Todd Dunn	.10	.03
20 Mike Martin	.10	.03
21 Carlton Loewer	.50	.15
22 Bret Wagner	.10	.03

1995 Bazooka

This 132-card standard-size set was issued by Topps. For the previous 35 years, Topps had used the Bazooka label to issue various cards, but this was the first time a mainstream set was issued in pack form. The five-card packs, with a suggested retail price of 50 cents, included an info card as well as a piece of bubble gum. The fronts have an action photo surrounded by white borders. The "Bazooka" label is in the upper left corner, while the player's name and team are on the bottom of the card. The player's position is identified on the right. The backs have a game as well as his previous season and career stats. There are no Rookie Cards in this set. Factory sets included five Red Hot inserts.

	Nm-Mt	Ex-Mt
COMPLETE SET (132)	10.00	3.00
COMP.FACT.SET (137)	10.00	3.00
1 Greg Maddux	.75	.23
2 Cal Ripken Jr.	1.50	.45
3 Lee Smith	.20	.06
4 Sammy Sosa	.75	.23
5 Jason Bere	.10	.03
6 David Justice	.20	.06
7 Kevin Mitchell	.10	.03
8 Ozzie Guillen	.10	.03
9 Roger Clemens	1.00	.30
10 Mike Mussina	.50	.15
11 Sandy Alomar Jr.	.10	.03
12 Cecil Fielder	.20	.06
13 Dennis Martinez	.20	.06
14 Randy Myers	.20	.06
15 Jay Buhner	.20	.06
16 Ivan Rodriguez	.50	.15
17 Mo Vaughn	.20	.06
18 Ryan Klesko	.20	.06
19 Chuck Finley	.20	.06
20 Barry Bonds	1.25	.35
21 Dennis Eckersley	.20	.06
22 Kenny Lofton	.20	.06
23 Rafael Palmeiro	.30	.09
24 Mike Stanley	.10	.03
25 Gregg Jefferies	.10	.03
26 Robin Ventura	.20	.06
27 Mark McGwire	1.25	.35
28 Ozzie Smith	.75	.23
29 Troy Neel	.10	.03
30 Tony Gwynn	.60	.18
31 Ken Griffey Jr.	.75	.23
32 Will Clark	.50	.15
33 Craig Biggio	.30	.09
34 Shawon Dunston	.10	.03
35 Wilson Alvarez	.10	.03
36 Bobby Bonilla	.20	.06
37 Marquis Grissom	.10	.03
38 Ben McDonald	.10	.03
39 Delino DeShields	.10	.03
40 Barry Larkin	.50	.15
41 John Olerud	.20	.06
42 Jose Canseco	.50	.15
43 Greg Vaughn	.20	.06
44 Gary Sheffield	.20	.06
45 Paul O'Neill	.30	.09
46 Bob Hamelin	.10	.03
47 Don Mattingly	1.25	.35
48 John Franco	.20	.06
49 Bret Boone	.20	.06
50 Rick Aguilera	.20	.06
51 Tim Wallach	.10	.03
52 Roberto Kelly	.10	.03
53 Danny Tartabull	.10	.03
54 Randy Johnson	.50	.15
55 Greg McMichael	.10	.03
56 Bip Roberts	.10	.03
57 David Cone	.20	.06
58 Raul Mondesi	.20	.06
59 Travis Fryman	.20	.06
60 Jeff Conine	.20	.06
61 Jeff Bagwell	.30	.09
62 Rickey Henderson	.50	.15
63 Fred McGriff	.30	.09
64 Matt Williams	.20	.06
65 Rick Wilkins	.10	.03
66 Eric Karros	.20	.06
67 Mel Rojas	.10	.03
68 Juan Gonzalez	.50	.15
69 Chuck Carr	.10	.03
70 Moises Alou	.20	.06
71 Mark Grace	.30	.09
72 Alex Fernandez	.10	.03
73 Rod Beck	.10	.03
74 Ray Lankford	.10	.03
75 Dean Palmer	.20	.06
76 Joe Carter	.20	.06
77 Mike Piazza	.75	.23
78 Eddie Murray	.50	.15
79 Dave Nilsson	.10	.03
80 Brett Butler	.20	.06
81 Roberto Alomar	.50	.15
82 Jeff Kent	.20	.06
83 Andres Galarraga	.20	.06
84 Brady Anderson	.20	.06
85 Jimmy Key	.20	.06
86 Bret Saberhagen	.20	.06
87 Chili Davis	.20	.06
88 Jose Rijo	.10	.03
89 Wade Boggs	.30	.09
90 Len Dykstra	.20	.06
91 Steve Howe	.10	.03
92 Hal Morris	.10	.03
93 Larry Walker	.30	.09
94 Jeff Montgomery	.10	.03
95 Wil Cordero	.10	.03
96 Jay Bell	.20	.06
97 Tom Glavine	.30	.09
98 Chris Hoiles	.10	.03
99 Steve Avery	.10	.03
100 Ruben Sierra	.10	.03
101 Mickey Tettleton	.10	.03
102 Paul Molitor	.30	.09
103 Carlos Baerga	.10	.03
104 Walt Weiss	.10	.03
105 Darren Daulton	.20	.06
106 Jack McDowell	.10	.03
107 Doug Drabek	.10	.03
108 Mark Langston	.10	.03
109 Manny Ramirez	.20	.06
110 Kevin Appier	.20	.06
111 Andy Benes	.10	.03
112 Chuck Knoblauch	.20	.06
113 Kirby Puckett	.50	.15
114 Dante Bichette	.20	.06
115 Deion Sanders	.30	.09
116 Albert Belle	.20	.06
117 Todd Zeile	.20	.06
118 Devon White	.10	.03
119 Tim Salmon	.30	.09
120 Frank Thomas	.50	.15
121 John Wetteland	.20	.06
122 James Mouton	.10	.03
123 Javier Lopez	.20	.06
124 Carlos Delgado	.20	.06
125 Cliff Floyd	.20	.06
126 Alex Gonzalez	.10	.03
127 Billy Ashley	.10	.03
128 Rondell White	.20	.06
129 Rico Brogna	.10	.03
130 Melvin Nieves	.10	.03
131 Jose Oliva	.10	.03
132 J.R. Phillips	.10	.03

1995 Bazooka Red Hot

This 22-card standard-size set, featuring some of the most popular players, is similar to the regular issue. Differences between these cards and the regular issue include the photo being shaded in a red background, the position is also in red and the player's name is stamped in gold foil. The backs are numbered with an "RH" prefix.

	Nm-Mt	Ex-Mt
COMPLETE SET (22)	20.00	6.00
RH1 Greg Maddux	1.50	.45
RH2 Cal Ripken Jr.	3.00	.90
RH3 Barry Bonds	2.50	.75
RH4 Kenny Lofton	.40	.12
RH5 Mike Stanley	.40	.12
RH6 Tony Gwynn	1.25	.35
RH7 Ken Griffey Jr.	1.50	.45
RH8 Barry Larkin	.75	.23
RH9 Jose Canseco	.75	.23
RH10 Paul O'Neill	.50	.15
RH11 Randy Johnson	.75	.23
RH12 David Cone	.40	.12
RH13 Jeff Bagwell	.50	.15
RH14 Matt Williams	.40	.12
RH15 Mike Piazza	1.50	.45
RH16 Roberto Alomar	.75	.23
RH17 Jimmy Key	.40	.12
RH18 Wade Boggs	.50	.15
RH19 Paul Molitor	.50	.15
RH20 Carlos Baerga	.40	.12
RH21 Albert Belle	.40	.12
RH22 Frank Thomas	.75	.23

1996 Bazooka

The 1996 Bazooka standard-size set was issued in one series totalling 132 cards. The five-card packs retailed for $.50 each. The set contains baseball's best rookies, rising stars and veterans. The card fronts feature an exciting full-color photo of the player. The back of each card contains one of five different Bazooka Joe characters, along with the Bazooka Ball flipping game, the player's biographical data and 1995 career statistics. Additionally, every card contains a Funny Fortune, which predicts the fate of each player on a particular date. Packs contain five cards plus one chunk of Bazooka gum. Finally, each factory set also included a reprint of Mickey Mantle's 1959 Bazooka card.

	Nm-Mt	Ex-Mt
COMP.FACT.SET (133)	12.00	3.60
COMPLETE SET (132)	10.00	3.00
1 Ken Griffey, Jr.	.75	.23
2 J.T. Snow	.20	.06
3 Rondell White	.20	.06
4 Reggie Sanders	.20	.06
5 Jeff Montgomery	.20	.06
6 Mike Stanley	.20	.06
7 Bernie Williams	.30	.09
8 Mike Piazza	.75	.23
9 Brian L.Hunter	.20	.06
10 Len Dykstra	.20	.06
11 Ray Lankford	.20	.06
12 Kenny Lofton	.20	.06
13 Robin Ventura	.20	.06
14 Devon White	.20	.06
15 Cal Ripken	1.50	.45
16 Heathcliff Slocumb	.20	.06
17 Ryan Klesko	.20	.06
18 Terry Steinbach	.20	.06
19 Travis Fryman	.20	.06
20 Sammy Sosa	.75	.23
21 Jim Thome	.50	.15
22 Kenny Rogers	.20	.06

1996 Bazooka

23 Don Mattingly 1.25 .35
24 Kirby Puckett .50 .15
25 Matt Williams .20 .06
26 Larry Walker .30 .09
27 Tim Wakefield .20 .06
28 Greg Vaughn .20 .06
29 Denny Neagle .20 .06
30 Ken Caminiti .20 .06
31 Garret Anderson .20 .06
32 Brady Anderson .20 .06
33 Carlos Baerga .20 .06
34 Wade Boggs .30 .09
35 Roberto Alomar .50 .15
36 Eric Karros .20 .06
37 Jay Buhner .20 .06
38 Dante Bichette .20 .06
39 Darren Daulton .20 .06
40 Jeff Bagwell .30 .09
41 Jay Bell .20 .06
42 Dennis Eckersley .20 .06
43 Will Clark .50 .15
44 Tom Glavine .30 .09
45 Rick Aguilera .20 .06
46 Kevin Seitzer .20 .06
47 Bret Boone .20 .06
48 Mark Grace .30 .09
49 Ray Durham .20 .06
50 Rico Brogna .20 .06
51 Kevin Appier .20 .06
52 Moises Alou .20 .06
53 Jeff Conine .20 .06
54 Marty Cordova .20 .06
55 Jose Mesa .20 .06
56 Rod Beck .20 .06
57 Marquis Grissom .20 .06
58 David Cone .20 .06
59 Albert Belle .20 .06
60 Lee Smith .20 .06
61 Frank Thomas .50 .15
62 Roger Clemens 1.00 .30
63 Bobby Bonilla .20 .06
64 Paul Molitor .30 .09
65 Chuck Knoblauch .20 .06
66 Steve Finley .20 .06
67 Craig Biggio .30 .09
68 Ramon Martinez .20 .06
69 Jason Isringhausen .20 .06
70 Mark Wohlers .20 .06
71 Vinny Castilla .20 .06
72 Ron Gant .20 .06
73 Juan Gonzalez .50 .15
74 Mark McGwire 1.25 .35
75 Jeff King .20 .06
76 Pedro Martinez .50 .15
77 Chad Curtis .20 .06
78 John Olerud .20 .06
79 Greg Maddux .75 .23
80 Derek Jeter 1.25 .35
81 Mike Mussina .50 .15
82 Gregg Jefferies .20 .06
83 Jim Edmonds .20 .06
84 Carlos Perez .20 .06
85 Mo Vaughn .20 .06
86 Todd Hundley .20 .06
87 Roberto Hernandez .20 .06
88 Derek Bell .20 .06
89 Andres Galarraga .20 .06
90 Brian McRae .20 .06
91 Joe Carter .20 .06
92 Orlando Merced .20 .06
93 Cecil Fielder .20 .06
94 Dean Palmer .20 .06
95 Randy Johnson .50 .15
96 Chipper Jones .50 .15
97 Barry Larkin .50 .15
98 Hideo Nomo .50 .15
99 Gary Gaetti .20 .06
100 Edgar Martinez .30 .09
101 John Wetteland .20 .06
102 Rafael Palmeiro .30 .09
103 Chuck Finley .20 .06
104 Ivan Rodriguez .50 .15
105 Shawn Green .20 .06
106 Manny Ramirez .20 .06
107 Lance Johnson .20 .06
108 Jose Canseco .50 .15
109 Fred McGriff .30 .09
110 David Segui .20 .06
111 Tim Salmon .30 .09
112 Hal Morris .20 .06
113 Tino Martinez .30 .09
114 Bret Saberhagen .20 .06
115 Brian Jordan .20 .06
116 David Justice .20 .06
117 Jack McDowell .20 .06
118 Barry Bonds 1.25 .35
119 Mark Langston .20 .06
120 John Valentin .20 .06
121 Raul Mondesi .20 .06
122 Quilvio Veras .20 .06
123 Randy Myers .20 .06
124 Tony Gwynn .60 .18
125 Johnny Damon .20 .06
126 Doug Drabek .20 .06
127 Bill Pulsipher .20 .06
128 Paul O'Neill .30 .09
129 Rickey Henderson .50 .15
130 Deion Sanders .30 .09
131 Orel Hershiser .20 .06
132 Gary Sheffield .20 .06
NNO Mickey Mantle 10.00 3.00
1959 Bazooka

2003 Bazooka

This 280 card set was released in March, 2003. The set was isssued in eight card packs that had an $2 SRP. These packs came 24 packs to a box and 10 boxes to a case. The Bazooka Joe card (number 7) was issued in a basic version as well as feauturing a logo of all the major league teams. In addition, 20 cards from the set featured a fascimile signature of the featured player as well as a colorized Bazooka logo. These regular and special logo cards of those player were printed to the same quantity.

Nm-Mt Ex-Mt
COMP.SET w/LOGO's (330) 80.00 24.00
COMPLETE SET (310) 60.00 18.00
COMP.SET w/o JOE's (280) 50.00 15.00
COMMON CARD (1-280) .40 .12
COMMON ROOKIE .40 .12
COMMON LOGO .40 .12
1 Luis Castillo .40 .12
2 Randy Winn .40 .12
3 Orlando Hudson .40 .12
3A Orlando Hudson Logo .40 .12
4 Fernando Vina .40 .12
5 Pat Burrell .40 .12
6 Brad Wilkerson .40 .12
7 Bazooka Joe .40 .12
7AN Bazooka Joe Angels .40 .12
7AS Bazooka Joe A's .40 .12
7AT Bazooka Joe Astros .40 .12
7BL Bazooka Joe Blue Jays .40 .12
7BR Bazooka Joe Braves .40 .12
7BW Bazooka Joe Brewers .40 .12
7CA Bazooka Joe Cardinals .40 .12
7CU Bazooka Joe Cubs .40 .12
7DE Bazooka Joe Devil Rays .40 .12
7DI Bazooka Joe Diamondbacks .40 .12
7DO Bazooka Joe Dodgers .40 .12
7EX Bazooka Joe Expos .40 .12
7GI Bazooka Joe Giants .40 .12
7IN Bazooka Joe Indians .40 .12
7MA Bazooka Joe Mariners .40 .12
7ME Bazooka Joe Mets .40 .12
7MR Bazooka Joe Marlins .40 .12
7OR Bazooka Joe Orioles .40 .12
7PA Bazooka Joe Padres .40 .12
7PH Bazooka Joe Phillies .40 .12
7PI Bazooka Joe Pirates .40 .12
7RA Bazooka Joe Rangers .40 .12
7RC Bazooka Joe Rockies .40 .12
7RD Bazooka Joe Reds .40 .12
7RS Bazooka Joe Red Sox .40 .12
7RY Bazooka Joe Royals .40 .12
7TI Bazooka Joe Tigers .40 .12
7TW Bazooka Joe Twins .40 .12
7WS Bazooka Joe White Sox .40 .12
7YA Bazooka Joe Yankees .40 .12
8 Javy Lopez .40 .12
9 Juan Pierre .40 .12
10 Hideo Nomo 1.00 .30
11 Barry Larkin 1.00 .30
12 Alfonso Soriano .60 .18
12A Alfonso Soriano Logo .60 .18
13 Rodrigo Lopez .40 .12
14 Mark Ellis .40 .12
15 Tim Salmon .60 .18
16 Garret Anderson .40 .12
16A Garret Anderson Logo .40 .12
17 Aaron Boone .40 .12
18 Jason Kendall .40 .12
19 Hee Seop Choi .40 .12
20 Jorge Posada .60 .18
21 Sammy Sosa 1.50 .45
22 Mark Prior 2.00 .60
22A Mark Prior Logo 2.00 .60
23 Mark Teixeira .60 .18
24 Manny Ramirez .40 .12
25 Jim Thome 1.00 .30
26 A.J. Pierzynski .40 .12
27 Scott Rolen .60 .18
28 Austin Kearns .40 .12
29 Bret Boone .40 .12
30 Ken Griffey Jr. 1.50 .45
31 Greg Maddux 1.50 .45
32 Derek Lowe .40 .12
33 David Wells .40 .12
34 A.J. Burnett .40 .12
35 Randall Simon .40 .12
36 Nick Johnson .40 .12
37 Junior Spivey .40 .12
38 Eric Gagne .60 .18
39 Darin Erstad .40 .12
40 Marty Cordova .40 .12
41 Brett Myers .40 .12
42 Mo Vaughn .40 .12
43 Randy Wolf .40 .12
44 Vicente Padilla .40 .12
45 Elmer Dessens .40 .12
46 Jason Simontacchi .40 .12
47 John Mabry .40 .12
48 Torii Hunter .40 .12
48A Torii Hunter Logo .40 .12
49 Lyle Overbay .40 .12
50 Kirk Saarloos .40 .12
51 Bernie Williams .60 .18
52 Wade Miller .40 .12
53 Bobby Abreu .40 .12
54 Wilson Betemit .40 .12
55 Edwin Almonte .40 .12
56 Jarrod Washburn .40 .12
57 Drew Henson .40 .12
58 Tony Batista .40 .12
59 Juan Rivera .40 .12
60 Larry Walker .60 .18
61 Brandon Phillips .40 .12
62 Franklyn German .40 .12
63 Victor Martinez .40 .12
63A Victor Martinez Logo .40 .12
64 Moises Alou .40 .12
65 Nomar Garciaparra 1.50 .45
66 Willie Harris .40 .12
67 Sean Casey .40 .12
68 Omar Vizquel .60 .18
69 Robert Fick .40 .12
70 Curt Schilling .60 .18
70A Curt Schilling Logo .60 .18
71 Adam Kennedy .40 .12
72 Scott Hairston .40 .12
73 Jimmy Journell .40 .12
74 Rafael Furcal .40 .12
75 Barry Zito .60 .18
76 Ed Rogers .40 .12
77 Cliff Floyd .40 .12
78 Matt Clement .40 .12
79 Mike Lowell .40 .12
80 Randy Johnson 1.00 .30
81 Craig Biggio .60 .18
82 Carlos Beltran .40 .12
83 Paul Lo Duca .40 .12
84 Jose Vidro .40 .12
85 Gary Sheffield .40 .12
86 Jacque Jones .40 .12
87 Corey Hart .40 .12
88 Roberto Alomar 1.00 .30
89 Robin Ventura .40 .12
90 Pedro Martinez 1.00 .30
91 Scott Hatteberg .40 .12
92 Marlon Byrd .40 .12
93 Pokey Reese .40 .12
94 Sean Burroughs .40 .12
95 Magglio Ordonez .40 .12
96 Mariano Rivera .60 .18
97 John Olerud .40 .12
98 Edgar Renteria .40 .12
99 Ben Grieve .40 .12
100 Barry Bonds 2.50 .75
100A Barry Bonds Logo 2.50 .75
101 Ivan Rodriguez 1.00 .30
102 Josh Phelps .40 .12
103 Nobuaki Yoshida RC .50 .15
103A Nobuaki Yoshida Logo .50 .15
104 Roy Halladay .40 .12
105 Mark Buehrle .40 .12
106 Chan Ho Park .40 .12
107 Joe Kennedy .40 .12
108 Shin-Soo Choo .40 .12
108A Shin-Soo Choo Logo .40 .12
109 Ryan Jensen .40 .12
110 Todd Helton .60 .18
111 Chris Duncan RC .50 .15
112 Taggert Bozied .60 .18
113 Sean Burnett .40 .12
114 Mike Lieberthal .40 .12
115 Josh Beckett .60 .18
116 Andy Pettitte .60 .18
117 Jose Reyes .60 .18
117A Jose Reyes Logo .60 .18
118 Bartolo Colon .40 .12
119 Justin Morneau .40 .12
120 Lance Berkman .40 .12
121 Mike Wodnicki RC .50 .15
122 Craig Brazell RC .75 .23
122A Craig Brazell Logo .75 .23
123 Troy Glaus .60 .18
124 John Smoltz .60 .18
125 Mike Sweeney .40 .12
126 Jay Gibbons .40 .12
127 Kerry Wood 1.00 .30
128 Ellis Burks .40 .12
129 Carlos Pena .40 .12
130 Shawn Green .40 .12
131 Jason Stokes 1.00 .30
131A Jason Stokes Logo 1.00 .30
132 Raul Ibanez .40 .12
133 Francisco Rodriguez .40 .12
133A Francisco Rodriguez Logo .40 .12
134 Adrian Beltre .40 .12
135 Richie Sexson .40 .12
136 Paul Byrd .40 .12
137 Bobby Kielty .40 .12
138 Dewon Brazelton .40 .12
139 Jeremy Griffiths RC .75 .23
140 Vladimir Guerrero 1.00 .30
140A Vladimir Guerrero Logo 1.00 .30
141 Jake Peavy .40 .12
142 Bryan Bullington RC 1.50 .45
143 Orlando Cabrera .40 .12
144 Scott Erickson .40 .12
145 Doug Mientkiewicz .40 .12
146 Derrek Lee .40 .12
147 Daryl Clark RC .75 .23
148 Trevor Hoffman .40 .12
149 Gabe Gross .40 .12
150 Roger Clemens 2.00 .60
151 Khalil Greene .60 .18
151A Khalil Greene Logo .60 .18
152 Cory Doyne RC .50 .15
153 Brandon Roberson RC .50 .15
154 Josh Fogg .40 .12
155 Eric Chavez .40 .12
156 Kris Benson .40 .12
157 Billy Koch .40 .12
158 Jermaine Dye .40 .12
159 Kip Bouknight RC .75 .23
160 Brian Giles .40 .12
161 Justin Huber .40 .12
162 Mike Restovich .40 .12
163 Brandon Webb RC 2.00 .60
164 Odalis Perez .40 .12
165 Phil Nevin .40 .12
166 Dontrelle Willis 1.00 .30
167 Aaron Heilman .40 .12
168 Dustin Moseley RC .75 .23
169 Rylan Reed RC .50 .15
170 Miguel Tejada .40 .12
171 Nic Jackson .40 .12
172 Anthony Webster RC .75 .23
173 Jorge Julio .40 .12
174 Kevin Millwood .40 .12
175 Brian Jordan .40 .12
176 Terry Tiffee RC .75 .23
177 Dallas McPherson .60 .18
178 Freddy Garcia .40 .12
179 Jaime Moyer .40 .12
180 Rafael Palmeiro .60 .18
181 Mike O'Keefe RC .50 .15
182 Kevin Youkilis RC 1.50 .45
183 Kip Wells .40 .12
184 Joe Mauer 1.00 .30
185 Edgar Martinez .60 .18
186 Jamie Bubela RC .50 .15
187 Jose Hernandez .40 .12
188 Josh Hamilton .40 .12
189 Matt Diaz RC .75 .23
190 Chipper Jones 1.00 .30
191 Kevin Mench .40 .12
192 Joey Gomes RC .50 .15
193 Shannon Stewart .40 .12
194 David Eckstein .40 .12
195 Mike Piazza 1.50 .45
196 Damian Moss .40 .12
197 Mike Fontenot .40 .12
198 Shea Hillenbrand .40 .12
199 Evel Bastida-Martinez RC .50 .15
200 Jason Giambi 1.00 .30
201 Aron Weston RC .50 .15
202 Frank Thomas 1.00 .30
203 Carlos Lee .40 .12
204 C.C. Sabathia .40 .12
205 Jim Edmonds .40 .12
206 Jemel Spearman RC .50 .15
207 Jason Jennings .40 .12
208 Jeremy Bonderman RC 1.00 .30
209 Preston Wilson .40 .12
210 Eric Hinske .40 .12
210A Eric Hinske Logo .40 .12
211 Will Smith .40 .12
212 Matthew Hagen RC .75 .23
213 Joe Randa .40 .12
214 James Loney .60 .18
215 Carlos Delgado .40 .12
216 Chris Kroski RC .50 .15
217 Cristian Guzman .40 .12
218 Tomo Ohka .40 .12
219 Al Leiter .40 .12
220 Adam Dunn .40 .12
221 Raul Mondesi .40 .12
222 Donald Hood RC .75 .23
223 Mark Mulder .40 .12
224 Mike Williams .40 .12
225 Ryan Klesko .40 .12
226 Rich Aurilia .40 .12
227 Chris Snelling .40 .12
228 Gary Schneidmiller RC .50 .15
229 Ichiro Suzuki 1.50 .45
229A Ichiro Suzuki Logo 1.50 .45
230 Luis Gonzalez .40 .12
231 Rocco Baldelli 1.50 .45
232 Callix Crabbe RC .75 .23
233 Adrian Gonzalez .40 .12
234 Corey Koskie .40 .12
235 Tom Glavine .60 .18
236 Kevin Beavers RC .50 .15
237 Frank Catalanotto .40 .12
238 Kevin Cash .40 .12
239 Nick Trzesniak RC .50 .15
240 Paul Konerko .40 .12
241 Jose Cruz Jr. .40 .12
242 Hank Blalock .60 .18
243 J.D. Drew .40 .12
244 Kazuhiro Sasaki .40 .12
245 Jeff Bagwell .60 .18
246 Jason Schmidt .40 .12
247 Xavier Nady .40 .12
248 Aramis Ramirez .40 .12
249 Jimmy Rollins .40 .12
250 Alex Rodriguez 1.50 .45
250A Alex Rodriguez Logo 1.50 .45
251 Terrence Long .40 .12
252 Derek Jeter 2.50 .75
253 Edgardo Alfonzo .40 .12
254 Toby Hall .40 .12
255 Kazuhisa Ishii .40 .12
256 Brad Nelson .40 .12
257 Kevin Brown .40 .12
258 Roy Oswalt .40 .12
259 Mike Cameron .40 .12
260 Juan Gonzalez 1.00 .30
261 Dmitri Young .40 .12
262 Jose Jimenez .40 .12
263 Wily Mo Pena .40 .12
264 Joe Borchard .40 .12
265 Mike Mussina 1.00 .30
266 Fred McGriff .60 .18
267 Johnny Damon .40 .12
268 Joel Pineiro .40 .12
269 Andruw Jones .40 .12
270 Tim Hudson .40 .12
271 Chad Tracy .40 .12
272 Brad Fullmer .40 .12
273 Boof Bonser .40 .12
274 Clint Nageotte .40 .12
275 Jeff Kent .40 .12
276 Tino Martinez .60 .18
277 Matt Morris .40 .12
278 Jonny Gomes .40 .12
279 Benito Santiago .40 .12
280 Albert Pujols 2.00 .60
280A Albert Pujols Logo 2.00 .60

2003 Bazooka Minis

Issued at a stated rate of one per pack, this is a complete parallel of the Bazooka set. All the cards were issued in this parallel set including all 31 Bazooka Joe cards as well as the 20 logo variation cards. These cards measure approximately 2 1/4" by 3 1/8"/

Nm-Mt Ex-Mt
*MINIS: .75X TO 2X BASIC
*MINIS JOE'S: .75X TO 2X BASIC JOE'S
*MINIS LOGO'S: .75X TO 2X BASIC LOGO'S
*MINI'S RC'S: .75X TO 2X BASIC RC'S

2003 Bazooka Silver

Issued at a stated rate of almost one per pack, this is a complete parallel to the Bazooka set. These cards can be identified by their silver borders. Again, all the Bazooka Joe varieties as well as the logo cards were issued in a silver version.

Nm-Mt Ex-Mt
*SILVER: .75X TO 2X BASIC
*SILVER JOE'S: .75X TO 2X BASIC JOE'S
*SILVER LOGO'S: .75X TO 2X BASIC LOGO'S
*SILVER RC'S: .75X TO 2X BASIC

2003 Bazooka 4 on 1 Sticker

Inserted at a stated rate of one in four hobby and one in 6 retail packs, these 55 sticker cards feature four players on the front

Nm-Mt Ex-Mt
1 Mark Prior 4.00 1.20
Roy Oswalt
Jarrod Washburn
Barry Zito
2 Troy Glaus 1.25 .35
Shea Hillenbrand
Eric Chavez
Eric Hinske
3 Orlando Hudson 2.00 .60
Alfonso Soriano
Roberto Alomar
Jose Vidro
4 Nomar Garciaparra 5.00 1.50
Derek Jeter
Miguel Tejada
Alex Rodriguez
5 Jason Giambi 2.00 .60
Jim Thome
Todd Helton
Rafael Palmeiro
6 Mike Williams 1.25 .35
Trevor Hoffman
Billy Koch
John Smoltz
7 Jorge Posada 3.00 .90
Mike Piazza
A.J. Pierzynski
Ivan Rodriguez
8 Vladimir Guerrero 2.00 .60
Jim Edmonds
Manny Ramirez
Brad Wilkerson
9 Shawn Green 3.00 .90
Sammy Sosa
Torri Hunter
Larry Walker
10 Bernie Williams 3.00 .90
Ken Griffey Jr.
Ichiro Suzuki
Adam Dunn
11 John Olerud 1.00 .30
Mike Lieberthal
Terrence Long
Drew Henson
12 Edgar Martinez 1.25 .35
Bret Boone
Mo Vaughn
Robert Fick
13 Randy Johnson 4.00 1.20
Roger Clemens
Pedro Martinez
Greg Maddux
14 Curt Schilling 2.00 .60
Tim Hudson
Tom Glavine
Kerry Wood
15 Paul Konerko 1.25 .35
Mike Sweeney
Cristian Guzman
Scott Rolen
16 Josh Phelps 1.25 .35
Brandon Phillips
Hee Seop Choi
Hank Blalock
17 Benito Santiago 2.00 .60
Barry Larkin
Gary Sheffield
Carlos Delgado
18 Juan Rivera 1.25 .35
Jose Reyes
Sean Burroughs
Carlos Pena
19 Tony Batista 1.25 .35
Tim Salmon
Jeff Bagwell
Raul Ibanez
20 Edgardo Alfonzo 1.00 .30
Nic Jackson
Luis Castillo
David Eckstein
21 David Wells 1.00 .30
Ryan Klesko
Phil Nevin
Jeff Kent
22 Derek Lowe 1.00 .30
Vicente Padilla
Kevin Millwood
Joel Pineiro
23 Fernando Vina 1.00 .30
Darin Erstad
Jimmy Rollins
Doug Mientkiewicz
24 Joe Mauer 2.00 .60
Justin Huber
Jason Stokes
Chad Tracy
25 Austin Kearns 1.00 .30
Junior Spivey
Brett Myers
Victor Martinez
26 Khalil Greene 1.25 .35
Gabe Gross
Kevin Cash
James Loney
27 Albert Pujols 4.00 1.20
Mark Buehrle
Chipper Jones
Lance Berkman
28 Adam Kennedy 1.25 .35
Craig Biggio
Johnny Damon
Randy Winn
29 Brian Giles 1.00 .30
J.D. Drew
Marlon Byrd
Joe Borchard
30 Al Leiter 2.00 .60
Mike Mussina
Bartolo Colon
Freddy Garcia
31 Jason Kendall 1.00 .30
Richie Sexson
Mike Lowell
Paul LoDuca
32 Pat Burrell 1.00 .30
Garret Anderson
Cliff Floyd
Andruw Jones
33 Xavier Nady 1.25 .35
Bobby Abreu
Taggert Bozied
Adrian Beltre

34 Rocco Baldelli 4.00 1.20
Dontrelle Willis
Chris Snelling
Mark Teixeira
35 Willie Harris 1.00 .30
Nick Johnson
Jason Jennings
Kazuhisa Ishii
36 Mark Mulder 1.25 .35
Sean Burnett
Paul Byrd
Josh Beckett
37 Corey Koskie 1.25 .35
Aramis Ramirez
Tino Martinez
Moises Alou
38 Jose Cruz Jr. 1.00 .30
Roy Halladay
Dewon Brazelton
Jonny Gomes
39 Odalis Perez 1.00 .30
Kevin Brown
Matt Clement
Randy Wolf
40 Eric Gagne 1.25 .35
Jose Jimenez
Franklyn German
Edwin Almonte
41 Luis Gonzalez 2.00 .60
Shannon Stewart
Brian Jordan
Juan Gonzalez
42 Toby Hall 1.00 .30
Joe Kennedy
Javier Lopez
Damian Moss
43 Magglio Ordonez 1.00 .30
Carlos Lee
Randall Simon
Dmitri Young
44 Sean Casey 1.00 .30
Aaron Boone
Jacque Jones
Michael Restovich
45 Adrian Gonzalez 2.00 .60
Corey Hart
Fred McGriff
Frank Thomas
46 C.C. Sabathia 1.25 .35
Omar Vizquel
Andy Pettitte
Robin Ventura
47 Jason Schmidt 1.00 .30
Ellis Burks
Joe Randa
Kris Benson
48 Mike Cameron 1.00 .30
Pokey Reese
Jermaine Dye
Preston Wilson
49 Chan Ho Park 2.00 .60
Kazuhiro Sasaki
Tomo Ohka
Hideo Nomo
50 Jason Simontacchi 1.00 .30
Kip Wells
Matt Morris
Rodrigo Lopez
51 Dallas McPherson 2.00 .60
Josh Hamilton
Jeremy Bonderman
Aaron Heilman
52 Nobuaki Yoshida 3.00 .90
Chris Duncan
Craig Brazell
Bryan Bullington
53 Daryl Clark 4.00 1.20
Brandon Webb
Dustin Moseley
Mike O'Keefe
54 Kevin Youkilis 3.00 .90
Jaime Bubela
Matt Diaz
Joey Gomes
55 Chris Kroski 1.00 .30
Donald Hood
Gary Schneidmiller
Callix Crabbe

2003 Bazooka Blasts Relics

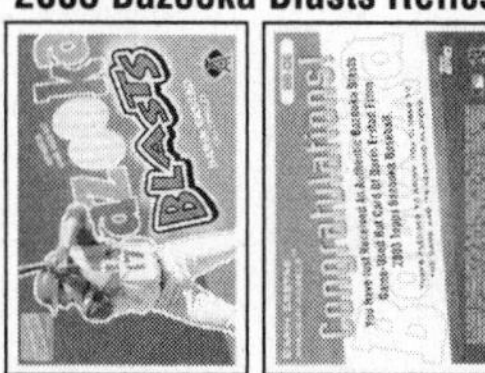

Issued at different odds depending on what group the player belonged to, these 35 cards feature a game-used bat chip of the featured player.

Nm-Mt Ex-Mt
GROUP A STATED ODDS 1:1666
GROUP B STATED ODDS 1:306
GROUP C STATED ODDS 1:197
GROUP D STATED ODDS 1:95
GROUP E STATED ODDS 1:52
GROUP F STATED ODDS 1:76
GROUP G STATED ODDS 1:326
GROUP H STATED ODDS 1:48
PARALLEL 25 ODDS 1:524
PARALLEL 25 PRINT RUN 25 #'d SETS
NO PARALLEL 25 PRICING DUE TO SCARCITY
AG Andres Galarraga C 8.00 2.40
ANR Aramis Ramirez E 8.00 2.40
AR Alex Rodriguez F 15.00 4.50
AS Alfonso Soriano D 10.00 3.00
BB Barry Bonds F 20.00 6.00
BW Bernie Williams D 10.00 3.00
CD Carlos Delgado D 8.00 2.40
CI Cesar Izturis B 10.00 3.00
CJ Chipper Jones E 10.00 3.00
DE Darin Erstad F 8.00 2.40
DH Drew Henson H 8.00 2.40
EM Edgar Martinez D 10.00 3.00
GS Gary Sheffield H 8.00 2.40
IR Ivan Rodriguez G 10.00 3.00
JD Johnny Damon H 8.00 2.40
JDD J.D. Drew B 10.00 3.00
JP Jorge Posada D 10.00 3.00
LB Lance Berkman E 8.00 2.40
LG Luis Gonzalez B 10.00 3.00
MP Mike Piazza H 15.00 4.50
MR Manny Ramirez F 8.00 2.40
MS Mike Sweeney C 8.00 2.40
NJ Nick Johnson B 10.00 3.00
PL Paul Lo Duca A 10.00 3.00
RA Roberto Alomar E 10.00 3.00
RH Rickey Henderson H 10.00 3.00
RK Ryan Klesko E 8.00 2.40
RM Raul Mondesi C 8.00 2.40
RP Rafael Palmeiro E 10.00 3.00
RV Robin Ventura F 8.00 2.40
SG Shawn Green D 8.00 2.40
TG Tony Gwynn H 15.00 4.50
TM Tino Martinez E 10.00 3.00
TS Tsuyoshi Shinjo E 8.00 2.40
WB Wilson Betemit E 8.00 2.40

2003 Bazooka Comics

Issued at a stated rate of one in four, these 24 comics, drawn in the style of the old Bazooka Joe comics, feature some of the leading players in the game.

Nm-Mt Ex-Mt
COMPLETE SET (24) 25.00 7.50
1 Albert Pujols 2.50 .75
2 Alex Rodriguez 2.00 .60
3 Alfonso Soriano 1.00 .30
4 Barry Zito 1.00 .30
5 Chipper Jones 1.25 .35
6 Derek Jeter 3.00 .90
7 Greg Maddux 2.00 .60
8 Ichiro Suzuki 2.00 .60
9 Jason Giambi 1.25 .35
10 Jim Thome 1.25 .35
11 John Smoltz 1.00 .30
12 Mike Piazza 2.00 .60
13 Randy Johnson 1.25 .35
14 Roger Clemens 2.50 .75
15 Sammy Sosa 2.00 .60
16 Shawn Green 1.00 .30
17 Pedro Martinez 1.25 .35
18 Manny Ramirez 1.00 .30
19 Torii Hunter 1.00 .30
20 Ivan Rodriguez 1.25 .35
21 Miguel Tejada 1.00 .30
22 Troy Glaus 1.00 .30
23 Ken Griffey Jr. 2.00 .60
24 Nomar Garciaparra 2.00 .60

2003 Bazooka Piece of Americana Relics

These 30 cards, which feature game-work uniform swatches were issued at different odds depending on which group the card belonged to.

Nm-Mt Ex-Mt
GROUP A STATED ODDS 1:1666
GROUP B STATED ODDS 1:611
GROUP C STATED ODDS 1:226
GROUP D STATED ODDS 1:118
GROUP E STATED ODDS 1:36
GROUP F STATED ODDS 1:73
GROUP G STATED ODDS 1:190
PARALLEL 25 ODDS 1:611
PARALLEL 25 PRINT RUN 25 #'d SETS
NO PARALLEL 25 PRICING DUE TO SCARCITY
AD Adam Dunn G 8.00 2.40
AH Aubrey Huff F 8.00 2.40
AJ Andruw Jones E 8.00 2.40
AL Al Leiter D 8.00 2.40
BB Bret Boone E 8.00 2.40
CB Craig Biggio E 10.00 3.00
CD Carlos Delgado E 8.00 2.40
CG Cristian Guzman E 8.00 2.40
CJ Chipper Jones E 10.00 3.00
CS Curt Schilling D 10.00 3.00
DB Dewon Brazelton F 8.00 2.40
FT Frank Thomas F 10.00 3.00
IR Ivan Rodriguez D 10.00 3.00
JB Jeff Bagwell A 15.00 4.50
JE Jim Edmonds E 8.00 2.40
JK Jeff Kent D 8.00 2.40
LW Larry Walker D 10.00 3.00
MM Mike Mussina C 10.00 3.00
MO Magglio Ordonez E 8.00 2.40
MP Mike Piazza E 15.00 4.50
NG Nomar Garciaparra B 20.00 6.00
PA Albert Pujols E 15.00 4.50
PL Paul Lo Duca B 10.00 3.00
PW Preston Wilson C 8.00 2.40
RF Rafael Furcal C 8.00 2.40
RP Rafael Palmeiro E 10.00 3.00
SG Shawn Green E 8.00 2.40
TG Tony Gwynn G 15.00 4.50
TH Todd Helton E 10.00 3.00
THA Toby Hall F 8.00 2.40

2003 Bazooka Stand-Ups

Issued at a stated rate of one in eight hobby and one in 24 retail, this 25 card set features a design similar to the 1964 Topps Stand-Up set.

Nm-Mt Ex-Mt
1 Albert Pujols 6.00 1.80
2 Alfonso Soriano 2.00 .60
3 Ichiro Suzuki 5.00 1.50
4 Sammy Sosa 5.00 1.50
5 Randy Johnson 3.00 .90
6 Barry Bonds 8.00 2.40
7 Vladimir Guerrero 3.00 .90
8 Nomar Garciaparra 5.00 1.50
9 Alex Rodriguez 5.00 1.50
10 Troy Glaus 2.00 .60
11 Barry Zito 2.00 .60
12 Derek Jeter 8.00 2.40
13 Lance Berkman 2.00 .60
14 Larry Walker 2.00 .60
15 Adam Dunn 2.00 .60
16 Shawn Green 2.00 .60
17 Curt Schilling 2.00 .60
18 Todd Helton 2.00 .60
19 Pedro Martinez 3.00 .90
20 Pat Burrell 2.00 .60
21 Miguel Tejada 2.00 .60
22 Manny Ramirez 2.00 .60
23 Mike Piazza 5.00 1.50
24 Jim Thome 3.00 .90
25 Jason Giambi 3.00 .90

2003 Bazooka Stand-Ups Red

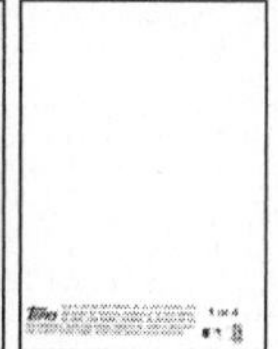

Issued as an unperforated card on top of each Bazooka box, these four cards feature some of the leading players. These cards can be differentiated from the regular stand-ups as they have a red border.

Nm-Mt Ex-Mt
COMPLETE SET (4) 8.00 2.40
1 Barry Bonds 4.00 1.20
2 Albert Pujols 3.00 .90
3 Jim Thome 1.50 .45
4 Barry Zito 1.50 .45

2004 Bazooka

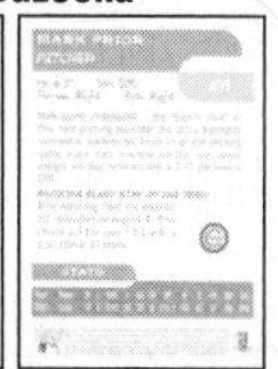

This 300 card set was released in March, 2004. This was issued in eight-card hobby and retail packs with an $2 SRP which came 24 packs to a box and 10 boxes to a case. Cards numbered 1-270 feature veterans while cards 271-300 are all Rookie Cards. It is also important to note that there were 30 variation cards issued as part of this set; each of these variations were produced in the same quantity as their counterpart and thus there is no scarcity and a set is considered complete at 330 cards.

Nm-Mt Ex-Mt
COMPLETE SET (330) 60.00 18.00
COMMON CARD (1-270) .40 .12
COMMON CARD (271-300) .50 .15
1 Bobby Abreu .40 .12
2 Jesse Foppert .40 .12
3 Shea Hillenbrand .40 .12
4 Jose Lima .40 .12
5 Manny Ramirez .40 .12
6 Denny Neagle .40 .12
7 Frank Thomas 1.00 .30
8 A.J. Burnett .40 .12
9 Carl Everett .40 .12
10A Scott Podsednik Blue Jsy 1.00 .30
10B Scott Podsednik White Jsy 1.00 .30
11 Travis Lee .40 .12
12 Mike Mussina 1.00 .30
13 Runelvys Hernandez .40 .12
14 Shannon Stewart .40 .12
15 Miguel Cabrera 1.00 .30
16 Edgardo Alfonzo .40 .12
17 Victor Zambrano .40 .12
18 Rafael Furcal .40 .12
19 Eric Hinske .40 .12
20 Paul Lo Duca .40 .12
21 Phil Nevin .40 .12
22 Aramis Ramirez .40 .12
23 Jim Thome 1.00 .30
24 Jeromy Burnitz .40 .12
25A Mark Prior Glove Chest 2.00 .60
25B Mark Prior Glove Face 2.00 .60
26 Ramon Hernandez .40 .12
27 Cliff Lee .40 .12
28 Greg Myers .40 .12
29 Robert Fick .40 .12
30 Mike Sweeney .40 .12
31 Carlos Zambrano .40 .12
32 Roberto Alomar 1.00 .30
33 Orlando Cabrera .40 .12
34 Orlando Hudson .40 .12
35A Nomar Garciaparra Batting 1.50 .45
35B Nomar Garciaparra Fielding 1.50 .45
36 Esteban Loaiza .40 .12
37 Laynce Nix .40 .12
38 Joe Randa .40 .12
39 Juan Uribe .40 .12
40 Pat Burrell .40 .12
41 Steve Finley .40 .12
42 Livan Hernandez .40 .12
43 Al Leiter .40 .12
44 Brett Myers .40 .12
45 Jody Gerut .40 .12
46 Mark Teixeira .40 .12
47 Barry Zito .60 .18
48 Moises Alou .40 .12
49 Mike Cameron .40 .12
50A Albert Pujols One Hand 2.00 .60
50B Albert Pujols Two Hands 2.00 .60
51 Tim Hudson .40 .12
52 Kenny Lofton .40 .12
53 Trot Nixon .60 .18
54 Tim Redding .40 .12
55 Marlon Byrd .40 .12
56 Javier Vazquez .40 .12
57 Sean Burroughs .40 .12
58 Cliff Floyd .40 .12
59 Juan Rivera .40 .12
60 Mike Lieberthal .40 .12
61 Xavier Nady .40 .12
62 Brad Radke .40 .12
63 Miguel Tejada .40 .12
64A Ichiro Suzuki Running 1.50 .45
64B Ichiro Suzuki Throwing 1.50 .45
65 Garret Anderson .40 .12
66 Sean Casey .40 .12
67A Jason Giambi Fielding 1.00 .30
67B Jason Giambi Hitting 1.00 .30
68 Aubrey Huff .40 .12
69 Javy Lopez .40 .12
70 Hideo Nomo 1.00 .30
71 Mark Redman .40 .12
72 Jose Vidro .40 .12
73 Rich Aurilia .40 .12
74 Luis Castillo .40 .12
75 Jay Gibbons .40 .12
76 Torii Hunter .40 .12
77 Derek Lowe .40 .12
78 Wes Obermueller .40 .12
79 Edgar Renteria .40 .12
80 Jeff Bagwell .60 .18
81 Fernando Vina .40 .12
82 Frank Catalanotto .40 .12
83 Marcus Giles .40 .12
84 Raul Ibanez .40 .12
85 Mike Lowell .40 .12
86 Tomo Ohka .40 .12
87A Jose Reyes w/Bat .60 .18
87B Jose Reyes w/o Bat .60 .18
88 Omar Vizquel .40 .12
89 Shawn Chacon .40 .12
90 Rocco Baldelli 1.00 .30
91A Brian Giles w/Bat .40 .12
91B Brian Giles w/o Bat .40 .12
92 Kazuhisa Ishii .40 .12
93 Greg Maddux 1.50 .45
94 John Olerud .40 .12
95 Eric Chavez .40 .12
96 Doug Waechter .40 .12
97 Tony Batista .40 .12
98 Jeriome Robertson .40 .12
99 Troy Glaus .60 .18
100A Eric Gagne Hand Out .60 .18
100B Eric Gagne Hand Up .60 .18
101A Pedro Martinez Leg Down 1.00 .30
101B Pedro Martinez Leg Up 1.00 .30
102 Magglio Ordonez .40 .12
103A Alex Rodriguez w/Bat 1.50 .45
103B Alex Rodriguez w/o Bat 1.50 .45
104 Jason Bay .60 .18
105 Larry Walker .60 .18
106 Matt Clement .40 .12
107 Tom Glavine .60 .18
108 Geoff Jenkins .40 .12
109 Victor Martinez .40 .12
110 David Ortiz .40 .12
111 Ivan Rodriguez 1.00 .30
112 Jarrod Washburn .40 .12
113 Josh Beckett .60 .18
114 Bartolo Colon .40 .12
115 Juan Gonzalez 1.00 .30
116A Derek Jeter Fielding 2.50 .75
116B Derek Jeter Hitting 2.50 .75
117 Edgar Martinez .60 .18
118 Ramon Ortiz .40 .12
119 Scott Rolen .60 .18
120A Brandon Webb w/Ball .40 .12
120B Brandon Webb w/o Ball .40 .12
121 Carlos Beltran .40 .12
122 Jose Contreras .40 .12
123 Luis Gonzalez .40 .12
124 Jason Johnson .40 .12
125 Luis Matos .40 .12
126 Russ Ortiz .40 .12
127 Damian Rolls .40 .12
128 David Wells .40 .12
129 Adrian Beltre .40 .12
130 Shawn Green .40 .12
131 Nate Cornejo .40 .12
132 Nick Johnson .40 .12
133 Joe Mays .40 .12
134 Roy Oswalt .40 .12
135 C.C. Sabathia .40 .12
136A Vernon Wells Fielding .40 .12
136B Vernon Wells Hitting .40 .12
137 Kris Benson .40 .12
138 Carl Crawford .40 .12
139A Ken Griffey Jr. Fielding 1.50 .45
139B Ken Griffey Jr. Hitting 1.50 .45
140A Randy Johnson Black Jsy 1.00 .30
140B Randy Johnson White Jsy 1.00 .30
141 Fred McGriff .60 .18
142 Vicente Padilla .40 .12
143 Tim Salmon .60 .18
144 Kip Wells .40 .12
145 Lance Berkman .40 .12
146 Jose Cruz Jr. .40 .12
147 Marquis Grissom .40 .12
148 Jacque Jones .40 .12
149 Gil Meche .40 .12
150A Vladimir Guerrero Fielding 1.00 .30
150B Vladimir Guerrero Hitting 1.00 .30
151 Reggie Sanders .40 .12
152 Ty Wigginton .40 .12
153 Angel Berroa .40 .12
154 Johnny Damon .40 .12
155 Rafael Palmeiro .60 .18
156A Chipper Jones w/Bat 1.00 .30
156B Chipper Jones w/o Bat 1.00 .30
157 Kevin Millar .40 .12
158 Corey Patterson .40 .12
159A Johan Santana Both Feet .40 .12
159B Johan Santana One Foot .40 .12
160 Bernie Williams .60 .18
161 Craig Biggio .60 .18
162A Carlos Delgado Blue Jsy .40 .12
162B Carlos Delgado White Jsy .40 .12
163 Aaron Guiel .40 .12
164 Wade Miller .40 .12
165 Andruw Jones .40 .12
166 Jay Payton .40 .12
167 Benito Santiago .40 .12
168 Woody Williams .40 .12
169 Casey Blake .40 .12
170 Adam Dunn .40 .12
171 Jose Guillen .40 .12
172 Brian Jordan .40 .12
173 Kevin Millwood .40 .12
174 Carlos Pena .40 .12
175 Curt Schilling .60 .18
176 Jerome Williams .40 .12
177A Hank Blalock Grey Jsy .40 .12
177B Hank Blalock White Jsy .40 .12
178 Erubiel Durazo .40 .12
179 Cristian Guzman .40 .12
180 Austin Kearns .40 .12
181 Raul Mondesi .40 .12
182 Andy Pettitte .60 .18
183 Jason Schmidt .40 .12
184 Jeremy Bonderman .40 .12
185A Dontrelle Willis w/Ball .40 .12
185B Dontrelle Willis w/o Ball .40 .12
186 Ray Durham .40 .12
187 Jerry Hairston Jr. .40 .12
188 Jason Kendall .40 .12
189 Melvin Mora .40 .12
190 Jeff Kent .40 .12
191 Jae Weong Seo .40 .12
192 Jack Wilson .40 .12
193 Cesar Izturis .40 .12
194 Jermaine Dye .40 .12
195A Roy Halladay w/Ball .40 .12
195B Roy Halladay w/o Ball .40 .12
196 Jason Phillips .40 .12
197 Matt Morris .40 .12
198A Mike Piazza Fielding 1.50 .45
198B Mike Piazza Running 1.50 .45
199 Richie Sexson .40 .12
200 Alfonso Soriano .60 .18
201 Mark Mulder .40 .12
202 David Eckstein .40 .12
203 Mike Hampton .40 .12
204 Ryan Klesko .40 .12
205 Damian Moss .40 .12
206 Juan Pierre .40 .12
207 Ben Sheets .40 .12
208 Randy Winn .40 .12
209 Bret Boone .40 .12
210 Jim Edmonds .40 .12
211 Rich Harden .40 .12
212 Paul Konerko .40 .12
213 Jamie Moyer .40 .12
214 A.J. Pierzynski .40 .12
215 Gary Sheffield .40 .12
216 Randy Wolf .40 .12
217 Kevin Brown .40 .12
218 Morgan Ensberg .40 .12
219 Bo Hart .40 .12
220 Bill Mueller .40 .12
221 Corey Koskie .40 .12
222 Joel Pineiro .40 .12
223 Preston Wilson .40 .12
224 Aaron Boone .40 .12
225 Kerry Wood 1.00 .30
226 Darin Erstad .40 .12
227 Wes Helms .40 .12
228 Brian Lawrence .40 .12
229 Mark Buehrle .40 .12
230A Sammy Sosa w/Ball 1.50 .45
230B Sammy Sosa w/Bat 1.50 .45
231 Sidney Ponson .40 .12
232 Dmitri Young .40 .12
233 Ellis Burks .40 .12
234 Kelvim Escobar .40 .12
235 Todd Helton .60 .18
236 Matt Lawton .40 .12
237 Eric Munson .40 .12
238 Jorge Posada .60 .18
239 Mariano Rivera .60 .18
240 Michael Young .40 .12
241 Ramon Nivar .40 .12
242 Edwin Jackson .60 .18
243 Felix Pie .60 .18
244 Joe Mauer 1.00 .30
245 Grady Sizemore .60 .18
246 Bobby Jenks .40 .12
247 Chad Billingsley .40 .12
248 Casey Kotchman .40 .12
249 Bobby Crosby .40 .12
250 Khalil Greene .40 .12
251 Danny Garcia .40 .12
252 Nick Markakis .40 .12
253 Bernie Castro .40 .12
254 Aaron Hill .40 .12
255 Josh Barfield .40 .12
256 Ryan Wagner .40 .12
257 Ryan Harvey .60 .18
258 Jimmy Gobble .40 .12
259 Ryan Madson .40 .12
260 Zack Greinke .60 .18
261 Rene Reyes .40 .12
262 Eric Duncan .40 .12
263 Chris Lubanski .40 .12
264 Jeff Mathis .40 .12
265 Rickie Weeks 1.00 .30
266 Justin Morneau .40 .12
267 Brian Snyder .40 .12
268 Neal Cotts .40 .12

269 Joe Borchard .40 .12
270 Larry Bigbie .40 .12
271 Marcus McBeth FY RC .50 .15
272 Tydus Meadows FY RC .50 .15
273 Zach Miner FY RC .75 .23
274A A.Lerew w/Ball FY RC .75 .23
274B A.Lerew w/o Ball FY RC .75 .23
275A Y.Molina w/Bat FY RC .75 .23
275B Y.Molina w/o Bat FY RC .75 .23
276A Jon Knott w/Bat FY RC .75 .23
276B Jon Knott w/o Bat FY RC .75 .23
277 Matthew Moses FY RC 2.00 .60
278 Sung Jung FY RC 1.25 .35
279 Mike Gosling FY RC .50 .15
280 David Murphy FY RC 1.50 .45
281 Tim Frend FY RC 2.00 .60
282 Casey Myers FY RC .50 .15
283 Brayan Pena FY RC .50 .15
284 Omar Falcon FY RC .50 .15
285 Blake Hawksworth FY RC .75 .23
286 Jesse Roman FY RC .50 .15
287 Kyle Davies FY RC .75 .23
288 Matt Creighton FY RC .75 .23
289 Rodney Choy Foo FY RC .75 .23
290 Kyle Sleeth FY RC 2.00 .60
291 Carlos Quentin FY RC 1.25 .35
292 Khalid Ballouli FY RC .50 .15
293A Tim Stauffer w/Ball FY RC 1.00 .30
293B Tim Stauffer w/o Ball FY RC 1.00 .30
294 Craig Ansman FY RC .75 .23
295 Dioner Navarro FY RC 1.50 .45
296A Josh Labandeira w/Ball FY RC .50 .15
296B Josh Labandeira w/o Ball FY RC .50 .15
297 Jeffrey Allison FY RC 2.00 .60
298 Anthony Acevedo FY RC 1.25 .35
299 Brad Sullivan FY RC .75 .23
300 Conor Jackson FY RC 1.50 .45

2004 Bazooka Red Border Chunks

Nm-Mt Ex-Mt
*CHUNKS 1-270: .75X TO 2X BASIC
*CHUNKS 271-300: .75X TO 2X BASIC
ONE PER PACK

2004 Bazooka Minis

Nm-Mt Ex-Mt
*MINIS 1-270: .75X TO 2X BASIC
*MINIS 271-300: .75X TO 2X BASIC
ONE PER PACK

2004 Bazooka 4 on 1 Sticker

Nm-Mt Ex-Mt
STATED ODDS 1:4 H, 1:6 R
1 Rich Harden 1.00 .30
Dontrelle Willis
Jerome Williams
Brandon Webb
2 Eric Duncan 5.00 1.50
Derek Jeter
Alfonso Soriano
Jason Giambi
3 Grady Sizemore 3.00 .90
Rocco Baldelli
Ichiro Suzuki
Vladimir Guerrero
4 Roy Halladay 2.00 .60
Pedro Martinez
Curt Schilling
Brett Myers
5 Alex Rodriguez 3.00 .90
Angel Berroa
Jose Reyes
Khalil Greene
6 Kerry Wood 2.00 .60
Adam Dunn
Jeff Kent
Scott Rolen
7 Miguel Cabrera 2.00 .60
Scott Podsednik
Bo Hart
Mark Teixeira
8 Rickie Weeks 4.00 1.20
Josh Barfield
Albert Pujols
Vernon Wells
9 Torii Hunter 3.00 .90
Garret Anderson
Bobby Abreu
Ken Griffey Jr.
10 Jay Gibbons 3.00 .90
Chipper Jones
Mike Piazza
Mike Sweeney
11 David Ortiz 2.00 .60
Nick Johnson
Carlos Delgado
Frank Thomas
12 Todd Helton 1.25 .35
Jose Vidro
Mike Lowell
Miguel Tejada
13 Randy Wolf 2.00 .60
Mark Mulder
Johan Santana
Randy Johnson
14 Bret Boone 1.00 .30
Aubrey Huff
Eric Chavez
Javy Lopez
15 Jason Schmidt 4.00 1.20
Roy Oswalt
Joel Pineiro
Mark Prior
16 Kevin Millwood 1.25 .35
Andy Pettitte
Matt Morris
Tim Hudson
17 Javier Vazquez 2.00 .60
Esteban Loaiza
Orlando Cabrera
Roberto Alomar
18 Al Leiter 1.00 .30
David Wells
Mike Hampton
Jarrod Washburn
19 Paul Lo Duca 1.00 .30
Mike Lieberthal
Brian Giles
Andruw Jones
20 Magglio Ordonez 1.25 .35
Corey Patterson
Aaron Boone
Jeff Bagwell
21 Troy Glaus 1.25 .35
Edgar Martinez
Manny Ramirez
Raul Ibanez
22 Sammy Sosa 3.00 .90
Barry Zito
Bartolo Colon
Austin Kearns
23 Jim Edmonds 1.00 .30
Gary Sheffield
Preston Wilson
Shawn Green
24 Bernie Williams 2.00 .60
Juan Pierre
Josh Beckett
Mike Mussina
25 Ramon Hernandez 1.00 .30
Jason Kendall
Jason Phillips
A.J. Pierzynski
26 Pat Burrell 1.00 .30
Laynce Nix
Mike Cameron
Cliff Floyd
27 Eric Gagne 1.25 .35
Carl Crawford
Jose Guillen
Steve Finley
28 Ellis Burks 1.00 .30
Livan Hernandez
Derek Lowe
Kazuhisa Ishii
29 Jorge Posada 2.00 .60
Jeff Mathis
Victor Martinez
Ivan Rodriguez
30 Jim Thome 3.00 .90
Marcus Giles
Nomar Garciaparra
Hank Blalock
31 Edgar Renteria 1.00 .30
Bobby Crosby
Neal Cotts
Russ Ortiz
32 Zack Greinke 1.25 .35
Cristian Guzman
Cesar Izturis
Kevin Brown
33 Bobby Jenks 1.00 .30
Ramon Nivar
Richie Sexson
Ryan Klesko
34 Omar Vizquel 1.00 .30
Carlos Pena
Rafael Furcal
Gil Meche
35 Kenny Lofton 1.25 .35
Tim Salmon
Marquis Grissom
Craig Biggio
36 Kyle Davies 2.50 .75
Anthony Lerew
Brayan Pena
Sung Jung
37 Rodney Choy Foo 4.00 1.20
Craig Ansman
David Murphy
Matthew Moses
38 Carlos Quentin 3.00 .90
Dioner Navarro
Marcus McBeth
Josh Labandeira
39 Kyle Sleeth 4.00 1.20
Conor Jackson
Brad Sullivan
Jeffrey Allison
40 Yadier Molina 2.00 .60
Jon Knott
Blake Hawksworth
Tim Stauffer

2004 Bazooka Adventures Relics

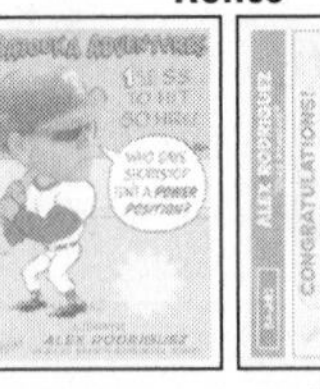

Nm-Mt Ex-Mt
GROUP A ODDS 1:134 H, 1:187 R
GROUP B ODDS 1:207 H, 1:289 R
GROUP C ODDS 1:74 H, 1:104 R
GROUP D ODDS 1:57 H, 1:80 R
GROUP E ODDS 1:86 H, 1:119 R
OVERALL PARALLEL 25 ODDS 1:94
PARALLEL 25 PRINT RUN 25 #'d SETS
NO PARALLEL 25 PRICING DUE TO SCARCITY
AD1 Adam Dunn Stripe Jsy A 8.00 2.40
AD2 Adam Dunn Grey Jsy A 8.00 2.40
AJ Andruw Jones Jsy D 8.00 2.40
AP Albert Pujols Uni D 20.00 6.00
AR1 Alex Rodriguez Blue Jsy E 10.00 3.00
AR2 Alex Rodriguez White Jsy D 10.00 3.00
AS Alfonso Soriano Uni C 10.00 3.00
BG Ben Grieve Jsy A 8.00 2.40
BP Brad Penny Jsy A 8.00 2.40
BW Bernie Williams Jsy B 10.00 3.00
BZ Barry Zito Jsy B 10.00 3.00
CB Craig Biggio Uni A 10.00 3.00
CE Carl Everett Uni D 8.00 2.40
CF Cliff Floyd Jsy B 8.00 2.40
CG Cristian Guzman Jsy C 8.00 2.40
CJ Chipper Jones Jsy D 10.00 3.00
CS Curt Schilling Jsy A 10.00 3.00
DW Dontrelle Willis Uni D 8.00 2.40
EA Edgardo Alfonzo Uni D 8.00 2.40
EC Eric Chavez Uni A 8.00 2.40
GJ Geoff Jenkins Jsy E 8.00 2.40
GM Greg Maddux Jsy D 15.00 4.50
HN Hideo Nomo Jsy C 10.00 3.00
JB Jeff Bagwell Uni A 10.00 3.00
JDG Jeremy Giambi Jsy E 8.00 2.40
JG Jason Giambi Jsy D 10.00 3.00
JK Jason Kendall Jsy B 8.00 2.40
JO John Olerud Jsy E 8.00 2.40
JT Jim Thome Jsy C 10.00 3.00
JW Jarrod Washburn Uni C 8.00 2.40
KB Kevin Brown Jsy A 8.00 2.40
KM Kevin Millwood Jsy E 8.00 2.40
KW Kerry Wood Jsy A 10.00 3.00
LB Lance Berkman Jsy D 8.00 2.40
LC Luis Castillo Jsy D 8.00 2.40
LG Luis Gonzalez Uni A 8.00 2.40
LW Larry Walker Jsy A 10.00 3.00
MB Marlon Byrd Jsy C 8.00 2.40
MCM Mike Mussina Uni C 10.00 3.00
ML Mike Lowell Jsy D 8.00 2.40
MM Mark Mulder Uni A 8.00 2.40
MP1 M.Piazza 2nd Most Jsy C 15.00 4.50
MP2 M.Piazza 10 Straight Jsy D 15.00 4.50
MR Manny Ramirez Uni C 8.00 2.40
MT Miguel Tejada Uni E 8.00 2.40
MV Mo Vaughn Jsy A 8.00 2.40
NG Nomar Garciaparra Uni C 15.00 4.50
PB Pat Burrell Jsy E 8.00 2.40
PK Paul Konerko Jsy B 8.00 2.40
PL Paul Lo Duca Jsy C 8.00 2.40
PW Preston Wilson Jsy E 8.00 2.40
RJ Randy Johnson Jsy C 10.00 3.00
RP1 R.Palmeiro 500th HR Jsy D 10.00 3.00
RP2 R.Palmeiro 9 Straight Jsy D 10.00 3.00
SC Sean Casey Jsy D 8.00 2.40
SG Shawn Green Jsy C 8.00 2.40
TAH1 T.Hudson Most Wins Jsy B 8.00 2.40
TAH2 T.Hudson 3rd Best Uni D 8.00 2.40
TEG Troy Glaus Uni A 10.00 3.00
TG Tom Glavine Jsy A 10.00 3.00
TH Toby Hall Jsy A 8.00 2.40
TJS Tim Salmon Uni B 10.00 3.00
VG Vladimir Guerrero Jsy C 10.00 3.00

2004 Bazooka Blasts Bat Relics

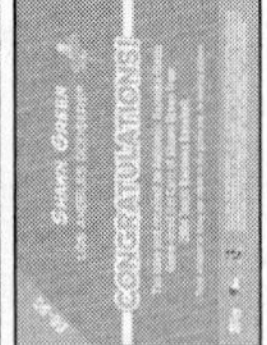

Nm-Mt Ex-Mt
GROUP A ODDS 1:62 H, 1:86 R
GROUP B ODDS 1:29 H, 1:40 R
OVERALL PARALLEL 25 ODDS 1:94
PARALLEL 25 PRINT RUN 25 #'d SETS
NO PARALLEL 25 PRICING DUE TO SCARCITY
AD Adam Dunn A 8.00 2.40
AG Adrian Gonzalez B 8.00 2.40
AH Aubrey Huff A 8.00 2.40
AJG Andres Galarraga A 8.00 2.40
ANR Aramis Ramirez B 8.00 2.40
AP Albert Pujols B 20.00 6.00
AR Alex Rodriguez B 10.00 3.00
AS Alfonso Soriano A 10.00 3.00
BB Bret Boone B 8.00 2.40
BF Brad Fullmer A 8.00 2.40
BW Bernie Williams A 10.00 3.00
CB Craig Biggio A 10.00 3.00
CC Carl Crawford A 8.00 2.40
CE Carl Everett B 8.00 2.40
CG Cristian Guzman A 8.00 2.40
CIB Carlos Beltran A 8.00 2.40
CJ Chipper Jones B 10.00 3.00
CL Carlos Lee A 8.00 2.40
CP Corey Patterson A 8.00 2.40
DM Doug Mientkiewicz A 8.00 2.40
EM Edgar Martinez B 10.00 3.00
FM Fred McGriff A 10.00 3.00
FT Frank Thomas B 10.00 3.00
GS Gary Sheffield B 8.00 2.40
HB Hank Blalock A 8.00 2.40
IR Ivan Rodriguez B 10.00 3.00
JAG Juan Gonzalez B 10.00 3.00
JB Jeff Bagwell A 10.00 3.00
JG Jason Giambi A 10.00 3.00
JNB Jeromy Burnitz A 8.00 2.40
JO John Olerud A 8.00 2.40
JP Jorge Posada A 10.00 3.00
JR Juan Rivera B 8.00 2.40
LB Lance Berkman B 8.00 2.40
LG Luis Gonzalez A 8.00 2.40
LW Larry Walker B 10.00 3.00
MA Moises Alou A 8.00 2.40
MAT Michael Tucker A 8.00 2.40
MCT Mark Teixeira A 8.00 2.40
MG Marquis Grissom B 8.00 2.40
ML Matt Lawton B 8.00 2.40
MO Magglio Ordonez B 8.00 2.40
MP Mike Piazza A 15.00 4.50
MR Manny Ramirez B 8.00 2.40
MT Miguel Tejada A 8.00 2.40
MV Mo Vaughn B 8.00 2.40
NG Nomar Garciaparra A 15.00 4.50
NH Nathan Haynes B 8.00 2.40
OV Omar Vizquel B 8.00 2.40
PK Paul Konerko A 8.00 2.40
PL Paul Lo Duca A 8.00 2.40
RA Roberto Alomar B 10.00 3.00
RB Rocco Baldelli A 10.00 3.00
RF Rafael Furcal B 8.00 2.40
RP Rafael Palmeiro B 10.00 3.00
RS Ruben Sierra B 8.00 2.40
RSA Rich Aurilia B 8.00 2.40
RW Rondell White B 8.00 2.40
SB Sean Burroughs B 8.00 2.40
SG Shawn Green B 8.00 2.40
SR Scott Rolen A 10.00 3.00
SS Shannon Stewart A 8.00 2.40
ST So Taguchi B 8.00 2.40
TB Tony Batista B 8.00 2.40
TG Troy Glaus A 10.00 3.00
TH Torii Hunter A 8.00 2.40
TJS Tim Salmon A 10.00 3.00
TKH Todd Helton B 10.00 3.00
TM Tino Martinez A 10.00 3.00
VG Vladimir Guerrero B 10.00 3.00
VW Vernon Wells A 8.00 2.40

2004 Bazooka Comics

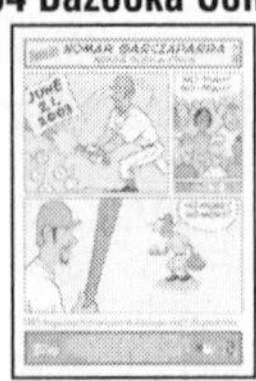

Nm-Mt Ex-Mt
COMPLETE SET (24) 25.00 7.50
STATED ODDS 1:4
BC1 Garret Anderson 1.00 .30
BC2 Jeff Bagwell 1.00 .30
BC3 Hank Blalock 1.00 .30
BC4 Roy Halladay 1.00 .30
BC5 Dontrelle Willis 1.00 .30
BC6 Roger Clemens 2.50 .75
BC7 Carlos Delgado 1.00 .30
BC8 Rafael Furcal 1.00 .30
BC9 Eric Gagne 1.00 .30
BC10 Nomar Garciaparra 2.00 .60
BC11 Derek Jeter 3.00 .90
BC12 Esteban Loaiza 1.00 .30
BC13 Kevin Millwood 1.00 .30
BC14 Bill Mueller 1.00 .30
BC15 Rafael Palmeiro 1.00 .30
BC16 Albert Pujols 2.50 .75
BC17 Jose Reyes 1.00 .30
BC18 Alex Rodriguez 2.00 .60
BC19 Alfonso Soriano 1.00 .30
BC20 Sammy Sosa 2.00 .60
BC21 Ichiro Suzuki 2.00 .60
BC22 Frank Thomas 1.25 .35
BC23 Brad Wilkerson 1.00 .30
BC24 Roy Oswalt 1.00 .30
Pete Munro
Kirk Saarloos
Brad Lidge
Octavio Dotel
Billy Wagner

2004 Bazooka One-Liners Relics

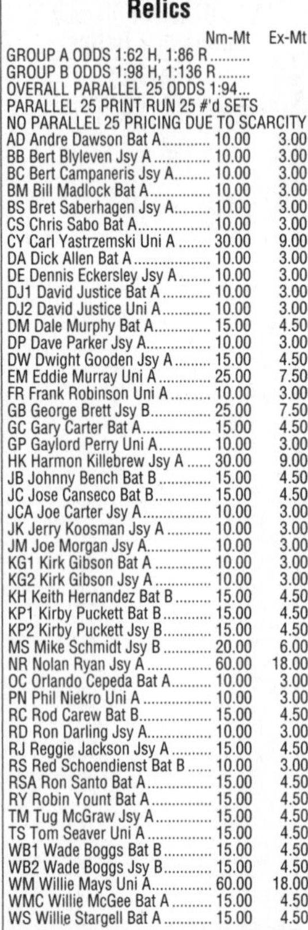

Nm-Mt Ex-Mt
GROUP A ODDS 1:62 H, 1:86 R
GROUP B ODDS 1:98 H, 1:136 R
OVERALL PARALLEL 25 ODDS 1:94
PARALLEL 25 PRINT RUN 25 #'d SETS
NO PARALLEL 25 PRICING DUE TO SCARCITY
AD Andre Dawson Bat A 10.00 3.00
BB Bert Blyleven Jsy A 10.00 3.00
BC Bert Campaneris Jsy A 10.00 3.00
BM Bill Madlock Bat A 10.00 3.00
BS Bret Saberhagen Jsy A 10.00 3.00
CS Chris Sabo Bat A 10.00 3.00
CY Carl Yastrzemski Uni A 30.00 9.00
DA Dick Allen Bat A 10.00 3.00
DE Dennis Eckersley Jsy A 10.00 3.00
DJ1 David Justice Bat A 10.00 3.00
DJ2 David Justice Uni A 10.00 3.00
DM Dale Murphy Bat A 15.00 4.50
DP Dave Parker Jsy A 10.00 3.00
DW Dwight Gooden Jsy A 15.00 4.50
EM Eddie Murray Uni A 25.00 7.50
FR Frank Robinson Uni A 10.00 3.00
GB George Brett Jsy B 25.00 7.50
GC Gary Carter Bat A 15.00 4.50
GP Gaylord Perry Uni A 10.00 3.00
HK Harmon Killebrew Jsy A 30.00 9.00
JB Johnny Bench Bat B 15.00 4.50
JC Jose Canseco Bat B 15.00 4.50
JCA Joe Carter Jsy A 10.00 3.00
JK Jerry Koosman Jsy A 10.00 3.00
JM Joe Morgan Jsy A 10.00 3.00
KG1 Kirk Gibson Bat A 10.00 3.00
KG2 Kirk Gibson Jsy A 10.00 3.00
KH Keith Hernandez Bat B 15.00 4.50
KP1 Kirby Puckett Bat B 15.00 4.50
KP2 Kirby Puckett Jsy B 15.00 4.50
MS Mike Schmidt Jsy B 20.00 6.00
NR Nolan Ryan Jsy A 60.00 18.00
OC Orlando Cepeda Bat A 10.00 3.00
PN Phil Niekro Uni A 10.00 3.00
RC Rod Carew Bat B 15.00 4.50
RD Ron Darling Jsy A 10.00 3.00
RJ Reggie Jackson Jsy A 15.00 4.50
RS Red Schoendienst Bat B 10.00 3.00
RSA Ron Santo Bat A 15.00 4.50
RY Robin Yount Bat A 15.00 4.50
TM Tug McGraw Jsy A 15.00 4.50
TS Tom Seaver Uni A 15.00 4.50
WB1 Wade Boggs Bat B 15.00 4.50
WB2 Wade Boggs Jsy B 15.00 4.50
WM Willie Mays Uni A 60.00 18.00
WMC Willie McGee Bat A 15.00 4.50
WS Willie Stargell Bat A 15.00 4.50

2004 Bazooka Stand-Ups

Nm-Mt Ex-Mt
STATED ODDS 1:8 H, 1:24 R
1 Jose Reyes 2.00 .60

2 Jim Thome 3.00 .90
3 Roy Halladay 2.00 .60
4 Jason Giambi 3.00 .90
5 Dontrelle Willis 2.00 .60
6 Mike Piazza 5.00 1.50
7 Chipper Jones 3.00 .90
8 Mark Prior 6.00 1.80
9 Todd Helton 2.00 .60
10 Miguel Cabrera 3.00 .90
11 Derek Jeter 8.00 2.40
12 Nomar Garciaparra 5.00 1.50
13 Alex Rodriguez 5.00 1.50
14 Miguel Tejada 2.00 .60
15 Carlos Delgado 2.00 .60
16 Pedro Martinez 3.00 .90
17 Sammy Sosa 5.00 1.50
18 Ichiro Suzuki 5.00 1.50
19 Vladimir Guerrero 3.00 .90
20 Alfonso Soriano 2.00 .60
21 Eric Chavez 2.00 .60
22 Albert Pujols 6.00 1.80
23 Ivan Rodriguez 3.00 .90
24 Vernon Wells 2.00 .60
25 Eric Gagne 2.00 .60

2004 Bazooka Tattoos

Nm-Mt Ex-Mt
STATED ODDS 1:4 H, 1:6 R
AD Adam Dunn 1.00 .30
AJ Andruw Jones 1.00 .30
AP Albert Pujols 5.00 1.50
AR Alex Rodriguez 4.00 1.20
AS Alfonso Soriano 1.50 .45
BAZ Bazooka Logo 1.00 .30
BP Brad Penny 1.00 .30
BW Bernie Williams 1.50 .45
BZ Barry Zito 1.50 .45
CB Craig Biggio 1.50 .45
CF Cliff Floyd 1.00 .30
CG Cristian Guzman 1.00 .30
CJ Chipper Jones 2.50 .75
CS Curt Schilling 1.50 .45
DW Dontrelle Willis 1.00 .30
EC Eric Chavez 1.00 .30
GJ Geoff Jenkins 1.00 .30
GM Greg Maddux 4.00 1.20
HN Hideo Nomo 2.50 .75
JB Jeff Bagwell 1.50 .45
JG Jason Giambi 2.50 .75
JK Jason Kendall 1.00 .30
JO John Olerud 1.00 .30
JT Jim Thome 2.50 .75
JW Jarrod Washburn 1.00 .30
KB Kevin Brown 1.00 .30
KM Kevin Millwood 1.00 .30
KW Kerry Wood 2.50 .75
LB Lance Berkman 1.00 .30
LC Luis Castillo 1.00 .30
LG Luis Gonzalez 1.00 .30
LW Larry Walker 1.50 .45
MB Marlon Byrd 1.00 .30
MCM Mike Mussina 2.50 .75
ML Mike Lowell 1.00 .30
MM Mark Mulder 1.00 .30
MP Mike Piazza 4.00 1.20
MR Manny Ramirez 1.00 .30
MT Miguel Tejada 1.00 .30
NG Nomar Garciaparra 4.00 1.20
PB Pat Burrell 1.00 .30
PK Paul Konerko 1.00 .30
PL Paul Lo Duca 1.00 .30
PW Preston Wilson 1.00 .30
RJ Randy Johnson 2.50 .75
RP Rafael Palmeiro 1.50 .45
SC Sean Casey 1.00 .30
SG Shawn Green 1.00 .30
TAH Tim Hudson 1.00 .30
TEG Troy Glaus 1.50 .45
TG Tom Glavine 1.50 .45
TH Toby Hall 1.00 .30
TJS Tim Salmon 1.50 .45
TOP Topps Logo 1.00 .30
VG Vladimir Guerrero 2.50 .75

1976 Cool Papa Bell

This 13 card set features highlights in the career of Negro League great Cool Papa Bell. The set was issued soon after his induction into the Hall of Fame. This set was available from the producer for $2.50 at the time of issue.

	NM	Ex
COMPLETE SET (13)	12.00	4.80
COMMON CARD	1.00	.40
2 Cool Papa Bell	1.00	.40
Lou Brock Sets S.B. Record		
13 Cool Papa Bell	2.00	.80
Josh Gibson		
XX Header Card	.50	.20

1951 Berk Ross *

The 1951 Berk Ross set consists of 72 cards (each measuring approximately 2 1/16" by 2 1/2") with tinted photographs, divided evenly into four series (designated in the checklist as A, B, C and D). The cards were marketed in boxes containing two card panels, without gum, and the set includes stars of other sports as well as baseball players. The set is sometimes still found in the original packaging. Intact panels are worth 25 percent more than the sum of the individual cards. The catalog designation for this set is W532-1. In every series the first ten cards are baseball players; the set has a heavy emphasis on Yankees and Phillies players as they were in the World Series the year before. The set includes the first card of NBA Legend Bob Cousy as well as a card of Yankees Hall of Famer Whitey Ford in his Rookie Card year.

	NM	Ex
COMP.BASEBALL SET (72)	1000.00	500.00
COMMON BASEBALL	10.00	5.00
COMMON FOOTBALL	10.00	5.00
COMMON OTHERS	5.00	2.50
A1 Al Rosen	12.00	6.00
A2 Bob Lemon	25.00	12.50
A3 Phil Rizzuto	25.00	12.50
A4 Hank Bauer	20.00	10.00
A5 Billy Johnson	10.00	5.00
A6 Jerry Coleman	10.00	5.00
A7 Johnny Mize	25.00	12.50
A8 Dom DiMaggio	20.00	10.00
A9 Richie Ashburn	40.00	20.00
A10 Del Ennis	10.00	5.00
B1 Stan Musial	120.00	60.00
B2 Warren Spahn	30.00	15.00
B3 Tom Henrich	12.00	6.00
B4 Yogi Berra	80.00	40.00
B5 Joe DiMaggio	200.00	100.00
B6 Bobby Brown	12.00	6.00
B7 Granny Hamner	10.00	5.00
B8 Willie Jones	10.00	5.00
B9 Stan Lopata	10.00	5.00
B10 Mike Goliat	10.00	5.00
C1 Ralph Kiner	25.00	12.50
C2 Bill Goodman	10.00	5.00
C3 Allie Reynolds	20.00	10.00
C4 Vic Raschi	15.00	7.50
C5 Joe Page	15.00	7.50
C6 Eddie Lopat	20.00	10.00
C7 Andy Seminick	10.00	5.00
C8 Dick Sisler	10.00	5.00
C9 Eddie Waitkus	10.00	5.00
C10 Ken Heintzelman	10.00	5.00
D1 Gene Woodling	15.00	7.50
D2 Cliff Mapes	10.00	5.00
D3 Fred Sanford	10.00	5.00
D4 Tommy Byrne	10.00	5.00
D5 Whitey Ford	100.00	50.00
D6 Jim Konstanty	10.00	5.00
D7 Russ Meyer	12.00	6.00
D8 Robin Roberts	30.00	15.00
D9 Curt Simmons	12.00	6.00
D10 Sam Jethroe	12.00	6.00

1952 Berk Ross

The 1952 Berk Ross set of 72 unnumbered, tinted photocards, each measuring approximately 2" by 3", seems to have been patterned after the highly successful 1951 Bowman set. The reverses of Ewell Blackwell and Nellie Fox are transposed while Phil Rizzuto comes with two different poses. The complete set below includes both poses of Rizzuto. There is a card of Joe DiMaggio even though he retired after the 1951 season. The catalog designation for this set is W532-2, and the cards have been assigned numbers in the alphabetical checklist below.

	NM	Ex
COMPLETE SET (72)	4000.00	2000.00
WRAPPER	60.00	30.00
1 Richie Ashburn	50.00	25.00
2 Hank Bauer	15.00	7.50
3 Yogi Berra	120.00	60.00
4 Ewell Blackwell UER (photo actually Nellie Fox)	20.00	10.00
5 Bobby Brown	15.00	7.50
6 Jim Busby	10.00	5.00
7 Roy Campanella	120.00	60.00
8 Chico Carrasquel	15.00	7.50
9 Jerry Coleman	15.00	7.50
10 Joe Collins	10.00	5.00
11 Alvin Dark	15.00	7.50
12 Dom DiMaggio	20.00	10.00
13 Joe DiMaggio	1000.00	500.00
14 Larry Doby	25.00	12.50
15 Bobby Doerr	25.00	12.50
16 Bob Elliott	10.00	5.00
17 Del Ennis	10.00	5.00
18 Ferris Fain	10.00	5.00
19 Bob Feller	60.00	30.00
20 Nellie Fox UER (photo actually Ewell Blackwell)	40.00	20.00
21 Ned Garver	10.00	5.00
22 Clint Hartung	10.00	5.00
23 Jim Hearn	10.00	5.00
24 Gil Hodges	50.00	25.00
25 Monte Irvin	25.00	12.50
26 Larry Jansen	10.00	5.00
27 Sheldon Jones	10.00	5.00
28 George Kell	25.00	12.50
29 Monte Kennedy	10.00	5.00
30 Ralph Kiner	50.00	25.00
31 Dave Koslo	10.00	5.00
32 Bob Kuzava	10.00	5.00
33 Bob Lemon	25.00	12.50
34 Whitey Lockman	10.00	5.00
35 Ed Lopat	15.00	7.50
36 Sal Maglie	15.00	7.50
37 Mickey Mantle	1200.00	600.00
38 Billy Martin	50.00	25.00
39 Willie Mays	400.00	200.00
40 Gil McDougald	15.00	7.50
41 Minnie Minoso	20.00	10.00
42 Johnny Mize	50.00	25.00
43 Tom Morgan	10.00	5.00
44 Don Mueller	10.00	5.00
45 Stan Musial	200.00	100.00
46 Don Newcombe	20.00	10.00
47 Ray Noble	10.00	5.00
48 Joe Ostrowski	10.00	5.00
49 Mel Parnell	15.00	7.50
50 Vic Raschi	15.00	7.50
51 Pee Wee Reese	50.00	25.00
52 Allie Reynolds	15.00	7.50
53 Bill Rigney	10.00	5.00
54A Phil Rizzuto (bunting)	50.00	25.00
54B Phil Rizzuto (swinging)	50.00	25.00
55 Robin Roberts	40.00	20.00
56 Eddie Robinson UER White Cox on Back	10.00	5.00
57 Jackie Robinson	300.00	150.00
58 Preacher Roe	15.00	7.50
59 Johnny Sain	15.00	7.50
60 Red Schoendienst	25.00	12.50
61 Duke Snider	120.00	60.00
62 George Spencer	10.00	5.00
63 Eddie Stanky	15.00	7.50
64 Hank Thompson	15.00	7.50
65 Bobby Thomson	20.00	10.00
66 Vic Wertz	10.00	5.00
67 Wally Westlake	10.00	5.00
68 Wes Westrum	10.00	5.00
69 Ted Williams	300.00	150.00
70 Gene Woodling	20.00	10.00
71 Gus Zernial	15.00	7.50

1916 BF2 Felt Pennants

These small triangular felt pennants were issued around 1916. The pennants themselves are 8 1/4" in length, whereas the unnumbered paper photos (glued on to the felt pennant) are 1 3/4" by 1 1/4". The photos are black and white and appear to have been taken from Sporting News issues of the same era. These unnumbered pennants are ordered below in alphabetical order within team. The teams themselves are ordered alphabetically within league beginning with the American League.

	Ex-Mt	VG
COMPLETE SET	9000.00	4500.00
1 Jack Barry	50.00	25.00
2 Hick Cady	50.00	25.00
3 Del Gainer	50.00	25.00
4 Harry Hooper	100.00	50.00
5 Dutch Leonard	50.00	25.00
6 Duffy Lewis	50.00	25.00
7 Joe Wood	80.00	40.00
8 Joe Benz	50.00	25.00
9 Eddie Collins	100.00	50.00
10 Shano Collins	50.00	25.00
11 Charles Comiskey OWN	100.00	50.00
12 Red Faber	100.00	50.00
13 Joe Jackson	1500.00	750.00
14 Jack Lapp	50.00	25.00
15 Eddie Murphy	50.00	25.00
16 Pants Rowland MG	50.00	25.00
17 Reb Russell	50.00	25.00
18 Ray Schalk	100.00	50.00
19 Jim Scott	50.00	25.00
20 Ed Walsh	100.00	50.00
21 Buck Weaver	150.00	75.00
22 Ray Chapman	60.00	30.00
23 Chick Gandil	150.00	75.00
24 Guy Morton	50.00	25.00
25 Donie Bush	50.00	25.00
26 Ty Cobb	1200.00	600.00
27 Harry Coveleski	50.00	25.00
28 Sam Crawford	100.00	50.00
29 Jean Dubuc	50.00	25.00
30 Hugh Jennings MG	100.00	50.00
31 Oscar Stanage	50.00	25.00
32 Bobby Veach	50.00	25.00
33 Ralph Young	50.00	25.00
34 Frank Baker	100.00	50.00
35 Joe Gideon	50.00	25.00
36 Wally Pipp	60.00	30.00
37 Napoleon Lajoie	200.00	100.00
38 Connie Mack MG	200.00	100.00
39 Stuffy McInnis	60.00	30.00
40 Rube Oldring	50.00	25.00
41 Wally Schang	60.00	30.00
42 Earl Hamilton	50.00	25.00
43 Fielder Jones	50.00	25.00
44 Doc Lavan	50.00	25.00
45 George Sisler	100.00	50.00
46 Eddie Foster	50.00	25.00
47 Walter Johnson	400.00	200.00
48 Joe Judge	50.00	25.00
49 George McBride	50.00	25.00
50 Clyde Milan	60.00	30.00
51 Ray Morgan	50.00	25.00
52 Johnny Evers	100.00	50.00
53 Hank Gowdy	50.00	25.00
54 Bill James	50.00	25.00
55 Sherry Magee	60.00	30.00
56 Rabbit Maranville	100.00	50.00
57 Dick Rudolph	50.00	25.00
58 George Stallings MG	50.00	25.00
59 Lefty Tyler	50.00	25.00
60 Jake Daubert	50.00	25.00
61 Rube Marquard	100.00	50.00
62 Chief Meyers	60.00	30.00
63 Otto Miller	50.00	25.00
64 Nap Rucker	50.00	25.00
65 Jimmy Archer	50.00	25.00
66 Mordecai Brown	100.00	50.00
67 Claude Hendrix	50.00	25.00
68 Jimmy Lavender	50.00	25.00
69 Vic Saier	50.00	25.00
70 Wildfire Schulte	50.00	25.00
71 Joe Tinker	100.00	50.00
72 Hippo Vaughn	50.00	25.00
73 Heine Zimmerman	50.00	25.00
74 Buck Herzog	50.00	25.00
75 Ivy Wingo	50.00	25.00
76 George Burns	50.00	25.00
77 Red Dooin	50.00	25.00
78 Larry Doyle	60.00	30.00
79 Bennie Kauff	50.00	25.00
80 Hans Lobert	50.00	25.00
81 John McGraw MG	150.00	75.00
82 Fred Merkle	50.00	25.00
83 Jeff Tesreau	50.00	25.00
84 Grover C. Alexander	150.00	75.00
85 Dave Bancroft	100.00	50.00
86 Chief Bender	100.00	50.00
87 Gavvy Cravath	60.00	30.00
88 Josh Devore	50.00	25.00
89 Bill Killefer	50.00	25.00
90 Fred Luderus	50.00	25.00
91 Pat Moran	50.00	25.00
92 Dode Paskert	50.00	25.00
93 Max Carey	100.00	50.00
94 Al Mamaux	50.00	25.00
95 Honus Wagner	400.00	200.00
96 Miller Huggins	100.00	50.00
97 Slim Sallee	50.00	25.00

1937 BF104 Blanket

These blankets, which measure approximately 3 1/2" feature some of the leading players of the late 1930's. The fronts have the player's name on top with his team and league in separate "flags". The player's photo takes up the rest of the blanket. Since these are unnumbered, we have sequenced them in alphabetical order. It is possible this list is incomplete, so all additions are appreciated.

	Ex-Mt	VG
COMPLETE SET	2000.00	1000.00
1 Luke Appling	120.00	60.00
2 Moe Berg	150.00	75.00
3 Cy Blanton	50.00	25.00
4 Mickey Cochrane	120.00	60.00
5 Joe Cronin	120.00	60.00
6 Tony Cuccinello	50.00	25.00
7 Dizzy Dean	200.00	100.00
8 Jimmie Dykes	60.00	30.00
9 Jimmie Foxx	200.00	100.00
10 Frankie Frisch	120.00	60.00
11 Woody Jensen	50.00	25.00
12 Harry Kelly	50.00	25.00
13 Thornton Lee	50.00	25.00
14 Connie Mack MG	150.00	75.00
15 Stu Martin	50.00	25.00
16 Joe Medwick	120.00	60.00
17 Ray Mueller	50.00	25.00
18 Bobo Newsome	60.00	30.00
19 Monty Stratton	80.00	40.00
20 Pie Traynor	120.00	60.00
21 Jim Turner	60.00	30.00
22 Bill Werber	60.00	30.00
23 Rudy York	60.00	30.00

1986 Big League Chew

This 12-card standard-size set was produced by Big League Chew and was inserted in with their packages of Big League Chew gum, which were shaped and styled after a pouch of chewing tobacco. The cards were found one per pouch of shredded gum or were available through a mail-in offer of two coupons and $2.00 for a complete set. The cards in the packs often were damaged in the packaging process. The players featured are members of the 500 career home run club. The backs are printed in blue ink on white card stock. The set is subtitled "Home Run Legends". The front of each card shows a year inside a small flag; the year is the year that player passed 500 homers.

	Nm-Mt	Ex-Mt
COMPLETE SET (12)	6.00	2.40
1 Hank Aaron	1.50	.60
2 Babe Ruth	2.00	.80
3 Willie Mays	1.50	.60
4 Frank Robinson	.50	.20
5 Harmon Killebrew	.50	.20
6 Mickey Mantle	2.00	.80
7 Jimmie Foxx	.50	.20
8 Ted Williams	1.50	.60
9 Ernie Banks	.50	.20
10 Eddie Mathews	.50	.20
11 Mel Ott	.50	.20
12 500 HR Members	.25	.10

1983 Big League Collectibles Original All-Stars

This 40-card set measures approximately 2 1/2" by 3 3/4" and features colorized individual player pictures of the original 1933 All-Star teams of both the American and National leagues. The backs carry player information and either their 1933 batting or pitching record. The set was issued in honor of the 50th Anniversary of the first All-Star Game (popularly known as The Game of the Century) that was played at Comiskey Park in Chicago, Illinois, on July 6, 1933. Only 10,000 of each set were produced and were sequentially numbered on the back of card number 1 which carried the AL All-Star Team photo. The set was originally available from the producer for $8 each.

	Nm-Mt	Ex-Mt
COMP. FACT. SET (40)	25.00	10.00
1 AL All-Star Team	.25	.10
2 Connie Mack MG	.50	.20
3 Alvin Crowder	.25	.10
4 Lefty Gomez	1.00	.40
5 Jimmy Dykes	.25	.10
6 Earl Averill	1.00	.40
7 Charlie Gehringer	1.00	.40
8 Lefty Grove	1.00	.40
9 Lou Gehrig	3.00	1.20
10 Al Simmons	1.00	.40
11 Ben Chapman	.25	.10
12 Jimmie Foxx	1.50	.60
13 Oral Hildebrand	.25	.10
14 Joe Cronin	1.00	.40
15 Bill Dickey	1.00	.40
16 Sam West	.25	.10
17 Rick Ferrell	.50	.20
18 Tony Lazzeri	1.00	.40
19 Wes Ferrell	.25	.10
20 Babe Ruth	5.00	2.00
21 NL All-Star Team CL	.25	.10
22 John McGraw MG	.50	.20
23 Pepper Martin	.25	.10
24 Woody English	.25	.10
25 Paul Waner	1.00	.40
26 Lefty O'Doul	.50	.20
27 Chuck Klein	1.00	.40
28 Tony Cuccinello	.25	.10
29 Frankie Frisch	1.00	.40
30 Gabby Hartnett	1.00	.40
31 Carl Hubbell	1.00	.40
32 Chick Hafey	.50	.20
33 Dick Bartell	.25	.10
34 Bill Hallahan	.25	.10
35 Hal Schumkacher	.25	.10
36 Lon Warneke	.25	.10
37 Wally Berger	.25	.10
38 Bill Terry	1.00	.40
39 Jimmy Wilson	.25	.10
40 Pie Traynor	1.00	.40

1985 Big League Collectibles 30s

This 90-card limited edition set features white-bordered color portraits of players who played in America's National Pastime during the 1930's. The cards measure approximately 2 1/8" by 3 1/8". The backs carry a paragraph about the player and either his pitching or batting record. Only 5,000 sets were produced and are sequentially numbered on the title card.

	Nm-Mt	Ex-Mt
COMP. FACT. SET (90)	40.00	16.00
1 Title Card	.25	.10
2 Bucky Walters	.50	.20
3 Monte Pearson	.25	.10
4 Stan Hack	.50	.20
5 Joe Cronin	1.00	.40
6 Leo Durocher	.75	.30
7 Max Bishop	.25	.10
8 Don Hurst	.25	.10
9 Barney McCosky	.25	.10
10 Remy"Ray" Kremer	.25	.10
11 Julius"Moose" Solters	.25	.10
12 Danny MacFayden	.25	.10
13 Mickey Cochrane	1.00	.40
14 Ethan Allen	.25	.10
15 Lu Blue	.25	.10
16 Johnny Mize	1.00	.40
17 Joe DiMaggio	3.00	1.20
18 George Grantham	.25	.10
19 Willie Kamm	.25	.10
20 Charlie Root	.25	.10
21 Moe Berg	2.00	.80
22 Floyd"Babe" Herman	.50	.20
23 Heinie Manush	1.00	.40
24 Dolf Camilli	.50	.20
25 Rudy York	.50	.20
26 Truett"Rip" Sewell	.25	.10
27 Rick Ferrell	.50	.20
28 Arthur"Pinky" Whitney	.25	.10
29 Edmund"Bing" Miller	.25	.10
30 Gus Mancuso	.25	.10
31 John"Jocko" Conlan	.50	.20
32 Joe Medwick	1.00	.40
33 Johnny Allen	.25	.10
34 Johnny Vander Meer	.50	.20
35 Earl Averill	1.00	.40
36 Taylor Douthit	.25	.10
37 Charles"Buddy" Myer	.25	.10
38 Van Lingle Mungo	.50	.20
39 Smead Jolley	.25	.10
40 Flint Rhem	.25	.10
41 Leon"Goose" Goslin	1.00	.40
42 Adam Comorsky	.25	.10
43 Jack Burns	.25	.10
44 Ed Brandt	.25	.10
45 Bob Johnson	.25	.10
46 Mel Ott	1.00	.40
47 Monty Stratton	.50	.20
48 Paul"Daffy" Dean	.50	.20
49 Lou Gehrig	3.00	1.20
50 Frank"Buck" McCormick	.25	.10
51 Jeff Heath	.25	.10
52 Charles"Gabby" Hartnett	.25	.10
53 Ossie Bluege	.25	.10
54 Babe Ruth	5.00	2.00
55 Bobby Doerr	1.00	.40
56 Virgil"Spud" Davis	.25	.10
57 Dale Alexander	.25	.10
58 Jim Tobin	.25	.10
59 Joseph Vosmik	.25	.10
60 Al Lopez	1.00	.40
61 Jimmie Foxx	2.00	.80
62 Fred Fitzsimmons	.50	.20
63 Bob Fothergill	.25	.10
64 Mort Cooper	.25	.10
65 George"Twinkletoes" Selkirk	.25	.10
66 Burton Shotton	.25	.10
67 Bob Feller	1.50	.60
68 Larry French	.25	.10
69 Joseph Judge	.25	.10
70 Clyde Sukeforth	.25	.10
71 Jim Tabor	.25	.10
72 Silas Johnson	.25	.10
73 Earl Webb	.25	.10
74 Charles"Red" Lucas	.25	.10
75 Ralph Kress	.25	.10
76 Casey Stengel	1.25	.50
77 George"Mule" Haas	.25	.10
78 Joe"Jo-Jo" Moore	.25	.10
79 Carl Reynolds	.25	.10
80 James"Tex" Carleton	.25	.10
81 Johnny Murphy	.25	.10
82 Paul Derringer	.25	.10
83 Harold Trosky	.50	.20
84 Fred Lindstrom	1.00	.40
85 Jack Russell	.25	.10
86 Stan"Frenchy" Bordagaray	.25	.10
87 Roy Johnson	.25	.10
88 Sylvester Johnson	.25	.10
89 Mike"Pinky" Higgins	.25	.10
90 Arky Vaughan	1.00	.40

1989 Bimbo Bread Discs

The 1989 Bimbo Bread set is a 12-disc set issued in Puerto Rico which measured 2 3/4" in diameter. This set features only Puerto Rican players. The top center of the the front of the disk has the Bimbo Bear logo. The previous years stats are on the back.

	Nm-Mt	Ex-Mt
COMPLETE SET (12)	15.00	6.00
1 Carmelo Martinez	.50	.20
2 Candy Maldonado	.50	.20
3 Benito Santiago	.75	.30
4 Rey Quinones	.50	.20
5 Jose Oquendo	.50	.20
6 Ruben Sierra	.75	.30
7 Jose Lind	.50	.20
8 Juan Beniquez	.50	.20
9 Willie Hernandez	.75	.30
10 Juan Nieves	.50	.20
11 Jose Guzman	.50	.20
12 Roberto Alomar	10.00	4.00

1999 Black Diamond

This 120-card set, produced by Upper Deck, was released in December, 1998 in six-card packs with a SRP of $3.99. This set features color player photos of 90 of Baseball's top collectible stars and photos of 30 star rookies and most promising prospects called Diamond Debut. The Diamond Debut cards were seeded into packs at a rate on one in four.

	Nm-Mt	Ex-Mt
COMPLETE SET (120)	80.00	24.00

COMP.SET w/o DD's (90) 25.00 7.50
COMMON CARD (1-90) .40 .12
COMMON DD (91-120) 2.00 .60
1 Darin Erstad .40 .12
2 Tim Salmon .60 .18
3 Jim Edmonds .40 .12
4 Matt Williams .40 .12
5 David Dellucci .40 .12
6 Jay Bell .40 .12
7 Andres Galarraga .40 .12
8 Chipper Jones 1.00 .30
9 Greg Maddux 1.50 .45
10 Andruw Jones .40 .12
11 Cal Ripken 3.00 .90
12 Rafael Palmeiro .60 .18
13 Brady Anderson .40 .12
14 Mike Mussina 1.00 .30
15 Nomar Garciaparra 1.50 .45
16 Mo Vaughn .40 .12
17 Pedro Martinez 1.00 .30
18 Sammy Sosa 1.50 .45
19 Henry Rodriguez .40 .12
20 Frank Thomas 1.00 .30
21 Maggio Ordonez .40 .12
22 Albert Belle .40 .12
23 Paul Konerko .40 .12
24 Sean Casey .40 .12
25 Jim Thome 1.00 .30
26 Kenny Lofton .40 .12
27 Sandy Alomar Jr. .40 .12
28 Jaret Wright .40 .12
29 Larry Walker .60 .18
30 Todd Helton .60 .18
31 Vinny Castilla .40 .12
32 Tony Clark .40 .12
33 Damion Easley .40 .12
34 Mark Kotsay .40 .12
35 Derrek Lee .40 .12
36 Moises Alou .40 .12
37 Jeff Bagwell .60 .18
38 Craig Biggio .60 .18
39 Randy Johnson 1.00 .30
40 Dean Palmer .40 .12
41 Johnny Damon .40 .12
42 Chan Ho Park .40 .12
43 Raul Mondesi .40 .12
44 Gary Sheffield .40 .12
45 Jeromy Burnitz .40 .12
46 Marquis Grissom .40 .12
47 Jeff Cirillo .40 .12
48 Paul Molitor .60 .18
49 Todd Walker .40 .12
50 Vladimir Guerrero 1.00 .30
51 Brad Fullmer .40 .12
52 Mike Piazza 1.50 .45
53 Hideo Nomo 1.00 .30
54 Carlos Baerga .40 .12
55 John Olerud .40 .12
56 Derek Jeter 2.50 .75
57 Hideki Irabu .40 .12
58 Tino Martinez .60 .18
59 Bernie Williams .60 .18
60 Miguel Tejada .40 .12
61 Ben Grieve .40 .12
62 Jason Giambi 1.00 .30
63 Scott Rolen .60 .18
64 Doug Glanville .40 .12
65 Desi Relaford .40 .12
66 Tony Womack .40 .12
67 Jason Kendall .40 .12
68 Jose Guillen .40 .12
69 Tony Gwynn 1.25 .35
70 Ken Caminiti .40 .12
71 Greg Vaughn .40 .12
72 Kevin Brown .60 .18
73 Barry Bonds 2.50 .75
74 J.T. Snow .40 .12
75 Jeff Kent .40 .12
76 Ken Griffey Jr. 1.50 .45
77 Alex Rodriguez 1.50 .45
78 Edgar Martinez .60 .18
79 Jay Buhner .40 .12
80 Mark McGwire 2.50 .75
81 Delino DeShields .40 .12
82 Brian Jordan .40 .12
83 Quinton McCracken .40 .12
84 Fred McGriff .60 .18
85 Juan Gonzalez 1.00 .30
86 Ivan Rodriguez 1.00 .30
87 Will Clark 1.00 .30
88 Roger Clemens 2.00 .60
89 Jose Cruz Jr. .40 .12
90 Babe Ruth 3.00 .90
91 Troy Glaus DD 3.00 .90
92 Jarrod Washburn DD 2.00 .60
93 Travis Lee DD 2.00 .60
94 Bruce Chen DD 2.00 .60
95 Mike Caruso DD 2.00 .60
96 Jim Parque DD 2.00 .60
97 Kerry Wood DD 5.00 1.50
98 Jeremy Giambi DD 2.00 .60
99 Matt Anderson DD 2.00 .60
100 Seth Greisinger DD 2.00 .60
101 Gabe Alvarez DD 2.00 .60
102 Rafael Medina DD 2.00 .60
103 Daryle Ward DD 2.00 .60
104 Alex Cora DD 2.00 .60
105 Adrian Beltre DD 2.00 .60
106 Geoff Jenkins DD 2.00 .60
107 Eric Milton DD 2.00 .60
108 Carl Pavano DD 2.00 .60
109 Eric Chavez DD 2.00 .60
110 Orl. Hernandez DD 2.00 .60
111 A.J. Hinch DD 2.00 .60
112 Carlton Loewer DD 2.00 .60
113 Aramis Ramirez DD 2.00 .60
114 Cliff Politte DD 2.00 .60
115 Matt Clement DD 2.00 .60
116 Alex Gonzalez DD 2.00 .60
117 J.D. Drew DD 2.00 .60
118 Shane Monahan DD 2.00 .60
119 Rolando Arrojo DD 2.00 .60
120 George Lombard DD 2.00 .60

1999 Black Diamond Double

Randomly inserted in packs, this 120-card set is a parallel version of the base set. Cards 1-90 are sequentially numbered to 3,000 and the Diamond Debut cards (91-120) are numbered to 2,500. Mark McGwire, Sammy Sosa and Ken Griffey Jr. the three leading home run hitters of 1998) all had 1,998 cards printed each and therefore are shortprinted compared to the rest of the set.

Nm-Mt Ex-Mt
*STARS: 2.5X TO 6X BASIC CARDS ...
*DIAM.DEB: .6X TO 1.2X BASIC DIAM.DEB.
18 Sammy Sosa/1998 15.00 4.50
76 Ken Griffey Jr./1998 15.00 4.50
80 Mark McGwire/1998 25.00 7.50

1999 Black Diamond Triple

Randomly inserted in packs, this 120-card set is a parallel version of the base set. Cards 1-90 are sequentially numbered to 1,500 and the cards 91-120 are numbered to 1,000. Mark McGwire, Ken Griffey Jr and Sammy Sosa were all printed in quantities equalling their career home run totals at that time. Therefore, those cards are short printed compared to the rest of the set.

Nm-Mt Ex-Mt
*STARS: 4X TO 10X BASIC CARDS ...
*DIAM.DEB: 1X TO 2.5X BASIC DIAM.DEB.
18 Sammy Sosa/273 25.00 7.50
76 Ken Griffey Jr./350 25.00 7.50
80 Mark McGwire/457 40.00 12.00

1999 Black Diamond Quadruple

Randomly inserted in packs, this 120-card set is a parallel version of the base set. Cards 1-90 are sequentially numbered to 150, and cards 91-120 are numbered to 100. Mark McGwire, Sammy Sosa and Ken Griffey Jr. all were printed to the amount of homers they hit in 1998. Therefore these cards are shortprinted compared to the other players in the set.

Nm-Mt Ex-Mt
*STARS: 12.5X TO 25X BASIC CARDS
*DIAM.DEB: 2X TO 4X BASIC DIAM.DEB.
18 Sammy Sosa/66 40.00 12.00
76 Ken Griffey Jr./56 40.00 12.00
80 Mark McGwire/70 60.00 18.00

1999 Black Diamond A Piece of History

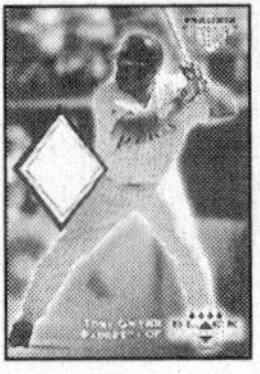

Randomly inserted in packs, this six-card set features color photos of six current top sluggers with one game-used bat piece in the shape of a diamond embedded in each card. Only 350 cards of each player were produced. The Mark McGwire card in this set is one of the most important insert cards issued in the 1990's. This is due to the fact that McGwire did not approve of his game-used bats being cut up after these cards were produced.

Nm-Mt Ex-Mt
BW Bernie Williams 15.00 4.50
JG Juan Gonzalez 15.00 4.50
MM Mark McGwire 200.00 60.00
MV Mo Vaughn 10.00 3.00
SS Sammy Sosa 50.00 15.00
TG Tony Gwynn 20.00 6.00

1999 Black Diamond Dominance

Randomly inserted in packs, this 30-card set features color photos of top stars and is sequentially numbered to 1,500.

Nm-Mt Ex-Mt
COMPLETE SET (30) 400.00 120.00
PARALLEL EMERALD ONE OF ONE'S EXIST
D1 Kerry Wood 6.00 1.80
D2 Derek Jeter 25.00 7.50
D3 Alex Rodriguez 15.00 4.50
D4 Frank Thomas 10.00 3.00
D5 Jeff Bagwell 6.00 1.80
D6 Mo Vaughn 4.00 1.20
D7 Ivan Rodriguez 10.00 3.00
D8 Cal Ripken 30.00 9.00
D9 Rolando Arrojo 2.50 .75
D10 Chipper Jones 10.00 3.00
D11 Kenny Lofton 4.00 1.20
D12 Paul Konerko 4.00 1.20
D13 Mike Piazza 15.00 4.50
D14 Ben Grieve 4.00 1.20
D15 Nomar Garciaparra 15.00 4.50
D16 Travis Lee 2.50 .75
D17 Scott Rolen 6.00 1.80
D18 Juan Gonzalez 10.00 3.00
D19 Tony Gwynn 12.00 3.60
D20 Tony Clark 4.00 1.20
D21 Roger Clemens 20.00 6.00
D22 Sammy Sosa 15.00 4.50
D23 Larry Walker 6.00 1.80
D24 Ken Griffey Jr. 15.00 4.50
D25 Mark McGwire 25.00 7.50
D26 Barry Bonds 25.00 7.50
D27 Vladimir Guerrero 10.00 3.00
D28 Tino Martinez 6.00 1.80
D29 Greg Maddux 15.00 4.50
D30 Babe Ruth 30.00 9.00

1999 Black Diamond Mystery Numbers

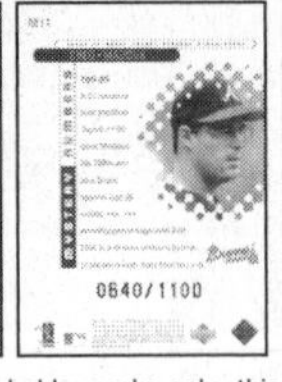

Randomly inserted in hobby packs only, this 30-card set features color photos of top Baseball stars. The numbers after the player's name indicate how many of that card was printed. A total of 46,500 cards were produced.

Nm-Mt Ex-Mt
COMPLETE SET (30) 400.00 120.00
COMMON CARD (M1-M20) 4.00 1.20
COMMON CARD (M20-M30) 2.50 .75
M1 Babe Ruth/100 100.00 30.00
M2 Ken Griffey Jr./200 50.00 15.00
M3 Kerry Wood/300 10.00 3.00
M4 Mark McGwire/400 40.00 12.00
M5 Alex Rodriguez/500 25.00 7.50
M6 Chipper Jones/600 10.00 3.00
M7 N.Garciaparra/700 20.00 6.00
M8 Derek Jeter/800 30.00 9.00
M9 Mike Piazza/900 20.00 6.00
M10 Roger Clemens/1000 20.00 6.00
M11 Greg Maddux/1100 15.00 4.50
M12 Scott Rolen/1200 6.00 1.80
M13 Cal Ripken/1300 30.00 9.00
M14 Ben Grieve/1400 4.00 1.20
M15 Troy Glaus/1500 6.00 1.80
M16 Sammy Sosa/1600 15.00 4.50
M17 Darin Erstad/1700 4.00 1.20
M18 Juan Gonzalez/1800 10.00 3.00
M19 P.Martinez/1900 10.00 3.00
M20 Larry Walker/2000 4.00 1.20
M21 V.Guerrero/2100 6.00 1.80
M22 Jeff Bagwell/2200 4.00 1.20
M23 Jaret Wright/2300 2.50 .75
M24 Travis Lee/2400 2.50 .75
M25 Barry Bonds/2500 15.00 4.50
M26 O.Hernandez/2600 2.50 .75
M27 Frank Thomas/2700 6.00 1.80
M28 Tony Gwynn/2800 8.00 2.40
M29 A.Galarraga/2900 2.50 .75
M30 Craig Biggio/3000 4.00 1.20

1999 Black Diamond Mystery Numbers Emerald

Randomly inserted in hobby packs only, this 30-card set is a very limited parallel version of the base insert set. Only 465 total cards were produced. Each player was produced in a different number of cards equal to the checklist number within the set. Pricing is not available due to scarcity.

Nm-Mt Ex-Mt
M1 Babe Ruth/1
M2 Ken Griffey Jr./2
M3 Kerry Wood/3
M4 Mark McGwire/4
M5 Alex Rodriguez/5
M6 Chipper Jones/6
M7 Nomar Garciaparra/7
M8 Derek Jeter/8
M9 Mike Piazza/9
M10 Roger Clemens/10
M11 Greg Maddux/11
M12 Scott Rolen/12
M13 Cal Ripken/13
M14 Ben Grieve/14
M15 Troy Glaus/15
M16 Sammy Sosa/16
M17 Darin Erstad/17
M18 Juan Gonzalez/18
M19 Pedro Martinez/19
M20 Larry Walker/20
M21 Vladimir Guerrero/21
M22 Jeff Bagwell/22
M23 Jaret Wright/23
M24 Travis Lee/24
M25 Barry Bonds/25
M26 Orlando Hernandez/26
M27 Frank Thomas/27
M28 Tony Gwynn/28
M29 Andres Galarraga/29
M30 Craig Biggio/30

2000 Black Diamond

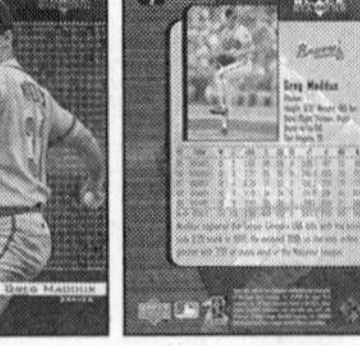

This 120 standard-size set (produced by Upper Deck) was issued in December, 1999 in six card packs which had an SRP of $3.99. The cards were issued 30 packs per box and 12 boxes in a case. Cards numbered one through 90 featured veterans while cards numbered 91 through 120 are a Diamond Debut subset featuring prospects and rookies and were issued one every four packs. 350 Reggie Jackson A Piece of History 500 Club bat cards were randomly seeded into packs. In addition, Jackson signed and numbered 44 copies. Pricing for these bat cards can be referenced under 1999 Upper Deck A Piece of History 500 Club.

Nm-Mt Ex-Mt
COMPLETE SET (120) 120.00 36.00
COMP.SET w/o SP's (90) 25.00 7.50
COMMON CARD (1-90) .40 .12
COMMON DD (91-120) 2.00 .60
1 Darin Erstad .40 .12
2 Tim Salmon .60 .18
3 Mo Vaughn .40 .12
4 Matt Williams .40 .12
5 Travis Lee .40 .12
6 Randy Johnson 1.00 .30
7 Tom Glavine .60 .18
8 Chipper Jones 1.00 .30
9 Greg Maddux 1.50 .45
10 Andruw Jones .40 .12
11 Brian Jordan .40 .12
12 Cal Ripken 3.00 .90
13 Albert Belle .40 .12
14 Mike Mussina 1.00 .30
15 Nomar Garciaparra 1.50 .45
16 Troy O'Leary .40 .12
17 Pedro Martinez 1.00 .30
18 Sammy Sosa 1.50 .45
19 Henry Rodriguez .40 .12
20 Frank Thomas 1.00 .30
21 Magglio Ordonez .40 .12
22 Greg Vaughn .40 .12
23 Barry Larkin 1.00 .30
24 Sean Casey .40 .12
25 Jim Thome 1.00 .30
26 Kenny Lofton .40 .12
27 Roberto Alomar 1.00 .30
28 Manny Ramirez .40 .12
29 Larry Walker .60 .18
30 Todd Helton .60 .18
31 Gabe Kapler .40 .12
32 Tony Clark .40 .12
33 Dean Palmer .40 .12
34 Cliff Floyd .40 .12
35 Alex Gonzalez .40 .12
36 Moises Alou .40 .12
37 Jeff Bagwell .60 .18
38 Craig Biggio .60 .18
39 Richard Hidalgo .40 .12
40 Carlos Beltran .40 .12
41 Johnny Damon .40 .12
42 Adrian Beltre .40 .12
43 Gary Sheffield .40 .12
44 Kevin Brown UER .60 .18
Career strikeout totals are wrong
45 Jeromy Burnitz .40 .12
46 Jeff Cirillo .40 .12
47 Joe Mays .40 .12
48 Todd Walker .40 .12
49 Vladimir Guerrero 1.00 .30
50 Michael Barrett .40 .12
51 Rickey Henderson 1.00 .30
52 Mike Piazza 1.50 .45
53 Robin Ventura .60 .18
54 John Olerud .40 .12
55 Edgardo Alfonzo .40 .12
56 Derek Jeter 2.50 .75
57 Orlando Hernandez .40 .12
58 Tino Martinez .60 .18
59 Bernie Williams .60 .18
60 Roger Clemens 2.00 .60
61 Eric Chavez .40 .12
62 Ben Grieve .40 .12
63 Jason Giambi .60 .18
64 Scott Rolen .60 .18
65 Bob Abreu .40 .12
66 Curt Schilling .60 .18
67 Mike Lieberthal .40 .12
68 Warren Morris .40 .12
69 Brian Giles .40 .12
70 Eric Owens .40 .12
71 Tony Gwynn 1.25 .35
72 Reggie Sanders .40 .12
73 Barry Bonds 2.50 .75
74 J.T. Snow .40 .12
75 Jeff Kent .40 .12
76 Ken Griffey Jr. 1.50 .45
77 Alex Rodriguez 1.50 .45
78 Edgar Martinez .60 .18
79 Jay Buhner .40 .12
80 Mark McGwire 2.50 .75
81 J.D. Drew .40 .12
82 Eric Davis .40 .12
83 Fernando Tatis .40 .12
84 Wade Boggs .60 .18
85 Fred McGriff .60 .18
86 Juan Gonzalez 1.00 .30
87 Ivan Rodriguez 1.00 .30
88 Rafael Palmeiro .60 .18
89 Shawn Green .40 .12
90 Carlos Delgado .40 .12
91 Pat Burrell DD 2.50 .75
92 Eric Munson DD 2.00 .60
93 Jorge Toca DD 2.00 .60
94 Rick Ankiel DD 2.00 .60
95 Tony Armas Jr. DD 2.00 .60
96 Byung-Hyun Kim DD 2.00 .60
97 Alfonso Soriano DD 4.00 1.20
98 Mark Quinn DD 2.00 .60
99 Ryan Rupe DD 2.00 .60
100 Adam Kennedy DD 2.00 .60
101 Jeff Weaver DD 2.00 .60
102 Ramon Ortiz DD 2.00 .60
103 Eugene Kingsale DD 2.00 .60
104 Josh Beckett DD 5.00 1.50
105 Eric Gagne DD 4.00 1.20
106 Peter Bergeron DD 2.00 .60
107 Erubiel Durazo DD 2.00 .60
108 Chad Meyers DD 2.00 .60
109 Kip Wells DD 2.00 .60
110 Chad Harville DD 2.00 .60
111 Matt Riley DD 2.00 .60
112 Ben Petrick DD 2.00 .60
113 Ed Yarnall DD 2.00 .60
114 Calvin Murray DD 2.00 .60
115 Vernon Wells DD 2.00 .60
116 A.J. Burnett DD 2.00 .60
117 Jacque Jones DD 2.00 .60
118 F.Cordero DD 2.00 .60
119 Tomo Ohka DD RC 2.00 .60
120 Julio Ramirez DD 2.00 .60

2000 Black Diamond Final Cut

Randomly inserted into packs, these cards parallel the regular Upper Deck Black Diamond set. Each card features gold foil fronts, a die cut edge and is numbered to 100 on the front.

Nm-Mt Ex-Mt
*STARS 1-90: 10X TO 25X BASIC CARDS
*DIAM.DEB 91-120: 2.5X TO 6X BASIC DD

2000 Black Diamond Reciprocal Cut

These cards parallel the regular Black Diamond set. The cards have an interesting twist in which the front and back picture images have been flip-flopped from the basic cards. They are printed in a super-premium die cut and rainbow foil coverage and were insered at two different ratios. The regular cards (1-90) were inserted one every seven packs while the Diamond Debut cards (91-120) were inserted one every 12 packs.

Nm-Mt Ex-Mt
*STARS 1-90: 2X TO 5X BASIC CARDS
*DIAM.DEB 91-120: .6X TO 1.5X BASIC DD

2000 Black Diamond A Piece of History

Inserted into packs at a rate of one every 179 hobby and one every 359 retail packs, these 19 cards feature diamond-shaped pieces of game-used bats used by a selection of major league stars.

Nm-Mt Ex-Mt
*DOUBLE: .6X TO 1.5X BASIC APH ....
DOUBLE STATED ODDS 1:1079 HOBBY
TRIPLE: RANDOM INSERT IN PACKS
TRIPLE PRINT RUN 1 SERIAL #'d SET
NO TRIPLE PRICING DUE TO SCARCITY
AB Albert Belle 10.00 3.00
AJ Andruw Jones 10.00 3.00
AR Alex Rodriguez 25.00 7.50
BB Barry Bonds 40.00 12.00
CAL Cal Ripken 50.00 15.00
CJ Chipper Jones 15.00 4.50
DE Darin Erstad 10.00 3.00
DJ Derek Jeter 40.00 12.00
IR Ivan Rodriguez 15.00 4.50
JC Jose Canseco 15.00 4.50
JR Ken Griffey Jr. 25.00 7.50
MP Mike Piazza 25.00 7.50
MV Mo Vaughn 10.00 3.00
RM Raul Mondesi 10.00 3.00
SR Scott Rolen 15.00 4.50
TG Tony Gwynn 25.00 7.50
TH Todd Helton 15.00 4.50
TL Travis Lee 10.00 3.00
VG Vladimir Guerrero 15.00 4.50

2000 Black Diamond Barrage

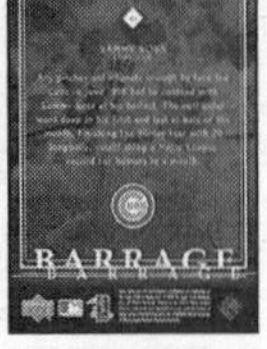

Inserted one every 29 packs, these 10 cards feature some of baseball's leading hitters.

Nm-Mt Ex-Mt
COMPLETE SET (10) 50.00 15.00
B1 Mark McGwire 10.00 3.00
B2 Ken Griffey Jr. 6.00 1.80
B3 Sammy Sosa 6.00 1.80
B4 Jeff Bagwell 2.50 .75
B5 Juan Gonzalez 4.00 1.20
B6 Alex Rodriguez 6.00 1.80
B7 Manny Ramirez 1.50 .45
B8 Ivan Rodriguez 4.00 1.20
B9 Chipper Jones 4.00 1.20
B10 Mike Piazza 6.00 1.80

2000 Black Diamond Constant Threat

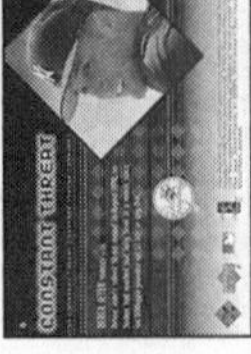

Inserted one every 29 packs, these 10 cards feature some of baseball's superstars.

Nm-Mt Ex-Mt
COMPLETE SET (10) 50.00 15.00
T1 Ken Griffey Jr. 6.00 1.80
T2 Vladimir Guerrero 4.00 1.20
T3 Alex Rodriguez 6.00 1.80
T4 Sammy Sosa 6.00 1.80
T5 Juan Gonzalez 4.00 1.20
T6 Derek Jeter 10.00 3.00

T7 Nomar Garciaparra 6.00 1.80
T8 Barry Bonds 10.00 3.00
T9 Chipper Jones 4.00 1.20
T10 Mike Piazza 6.00 1.80

2000 Black Diamond Diamonation

Inserted one every four packs, these 10 cards feature players who are among the best in the game. The fronts have a posed action shot while the back has a player photo, a brief blurb and the team's logo.

	Nm-Mt	Ex-Mt
COMPLETE SET (10)	10.00	3.00
D1 Ken Griffey Jr.	2.00	.60
D2 Randy Johnson	1.25	.35
D3 Mark McGwire	3.00	.90
D4 Manny Ramirez	.50	.15
D5 Scott Rolen	.75	.23
D6 Bernie Williams	.75	.23
D7 Roger Clemens	2.50	.75
D8 Mo Vaughn	.50	.15
D9 Frank Thomas	1.25	.35
D10 Sean Casey	.50	.15

2000 Black Diamond Diamonds in the Rough

Inserted one every nine packs, these ten cards feature some of baseball's leading prospects. The cards are printed on rainbow foil.

	Nm-Mt	Ex-Mt
COMPLETE SET (10)	15.00	4.50
R1 Pat Burrell	1.50	.45
R2 Eric Munson	1.00	.30
R3 Alfonso Soriano	2.50	.75
R4 Ruben Mateo	1.00	.30
R5 A.J. Burnett	1.00	.30
R6 Ben Davis	1.00	.30
R7 Lance Berkman	1.00	.30
R8 Ed Yarnall	1.00	.30
R9 Rick Ankiel	1.00	.30
R10 Ryan Bradley	1.00	.30

2000 Black Diamond Gallery

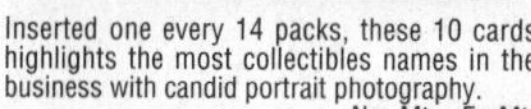

Inserted one every 14 packs, these 10 cards highlights the most collectibles names in the business with candid portrait photography.

	Nm-Mt	Ex-Mt
COMPLETE SET (10)	40.00	12.00
G1 Derek Jeter	8.00	2.40
G2 Alex Rodriguez	5.00	1.50
G3 Nomar Garciaparra	5.00	1.50
G4 Cal Ripken	10.00	3.00
G5 Sammy Sosa	5.00	1.50
G6 Tony Gwynn	4.00	1.20
G7 Mark McGwire	8.00	2.40
G8 Roger Clemens	6.00	1.80
G9 Greg Maddux	5.00	1.50
G10 Pedro Martinez	3.00	.90

2000 Black Diamond Might

Inserted one every fourteen packs, these 10 cards feature some of baseball's leading sluggers.

	Nm-Mt	Ex-Mt
COMPLETE SET (10)	30.00	9.00
M1 Ken Griffey Jr.	4.00	1.20
M2 Mark McGwire	6.00	1.80
M3 Sammy Sosa	4.00	1.20
M4 Manny Ramirez	1.00	.30
M5 Jeff Bagwell	1.50	.45
M6 Frank Thomas	2.50	.75
M7 Mike Piazza	4.00	1.20
M8 Juan Gonzalez	2.50	.75
M9 Barry Bonds	6.00	1.80
M10 Alex Rodriguez	4.00	1.20

2000 Black Diamond Rookie Edition

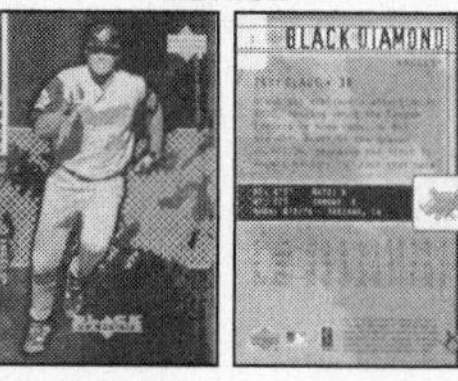

The 2000 Black Diamond Rookie Edition product, produced by Upper Deck, was released in December, 2000 and featured a 154-card base set. The set is broken into tiers as follows: Base Veterans (1-90), Rookie Gems (91-120) that are serial numbered to 1000, Rookie Jerseys (121-136), and USA Jersey cards (137-154). Each pack contained six cards, and carried a suggested retail price of $2.99. Notable Rookie Cards include Brad Cresse, Xavier Nady, Kazuhiro Sasaki, Ben Sheets and Barry Zito.

	Nm-Mt	Ex-Mt
COMP.SET w/o SP's (90)	25.00	7.50
COMMON CARD (1-90)	.40	.12
COMMON GEMS (91-120)	5.00	1.50
COMMON JSY. (121-136)	8.00	2.40
COMMON USA (137-154)	8.00	2.40
1 Troy Glaus	.60	.18
2 Mo Vaughn	.40	.12
3 Darin Erstad	.40	.12
4 Jason Giambi	1.00	.30
5 Tim Hudson	.60	.18
6 Ben Grieve	.40	.12
7 Eric Chavez	.40	.12
8 Tony Batista	.40	.12
9 Carlos Delgado	.40	.12
10 David Wells	.40	.12
11 Greg Vaughn	.40	.12
12 Fred McGriff	.60	.18
13 Manny Ramirez	.40	.12
14 Roberto Alomar	1.00	.30
15 Jim Thome	1.00	.30
16 Alex Rodriguez	1.50	.45
17 Edgar Martinez	.60	.18
18 John Olerud	.40	.12
19 Albert Belle	.40	.12
20 Mike Mussina	1.00	.30
21 Cal Ripken	3.00	.90
22 Ivan Rodriguez	1.00	.30
23 Rafael Palmeiro	.60	.18
24 Pedro Martinez	1.00	.30
25 Nomar Garciaparra	1.50	.45
26 Carl Everett	.40	.12
27 Jermaine Dye	.40	.12
28 Mike Sweeney	.40	.12
29 Juan Gonzalez	1.00	.30
30 Bobby Higginson	.40	.12
31 Dean Palmer	.40	.12
32 Jacque Jones	.40	.12
33 Eric Milton	.40	.12
34 Matt Lawton	.40	.12
35 Magglio Ordonez	.40	.12
36 Paul Konerko	.40	.12
37 Frank Thomas	1.00	.30
38 Ray Durham	.40	.12
39 Roger Clemens	2.00	.60
40 Derek Jeter	2.50	.75
41 Bernie Williams	.60	.18
42 Jose Canseco	1.00	.30
43 Craig Biggio	.60	.18
44 Richard Hidalgo	.40	.12
45 Jeff Bagwell	.60	.18
46 Greg Maddux	1.50	.45
47 Chipper Jones	1.00	.30
48 Rafael Furcal	.40	.12
49 Andruw Jones	.40	.12
50 Geoff Jenkins	.40	.12
51 Jeromy Burnitz	.40	.12
52 Mark McGwire	2.50	.75
53 Rick Ankiel	.40	.12
54 Jim Edmonds	.40	.12
55 Kerry Wood	1.00	.30
56 Sammy Sosa	1.50	.45
57 Matt Williams	.40	.12
58 Randy Johnson	1.00	.30
59 Steve Finley	.40	.12
60 Curt Schilling	.60	.18
61 Kevin Brown	.40	.12
62 Gary Sheffield	.40	.12
63 Shawn Green	.40	.12
64 Jose Vidro	.40	.12
65 Vladimir Guerrero	1.00	.30
66 Jeff Kent	.40	.12
67 Barry Bonds	2.50	.75
68 Ryan Dempster	.40	.12
69 Cliff Floyd	.40	.12
70 Preston Wilson	.40	.12
71 Mike Piazza	1.50	.45
72 Al Leiter	.40	.12
73 Edgardo Alfonzo	.40	.12
74 Derek Bell	.40	.12
75 Ryan Klesko	.40	.12
76 Tony Gwynn	1.25	.35
77 Bob Abreu	.40	.12
78 Pat Burrell	.60	.18
79 Scott Rolen	.60	.18
80 Mike Lieberthal	.40	.12
81 Jason Kendall	.40	.12
82 Brian Giles	.40	.12
83 Ken Griffey Jr.	1.50	.45
84 Pokey Reese	.40	.12
85 Dmitri Young	.40	.12
86 Sean Casey	.40	.12
87 Jeff Cirillo	.40	.12
88 Todd Helton	.60	.18
89 Jeffrey Hammonds	.40	.12
90 Larry Walker	.60	.18
91 Barry Zito RC	20.00	6.00
92 Keith Ginter RC	5.00	1.50
93 Dane Sardinha RC	5.00	1.50
94 Kenny Kelly RC	5.00	1.50
95 Ryan Kohlmeier RC	5.00	1.50
96 Leo Estrella RC	5.00	1.50
97 Danys Baez RC	8.00	2.40
98 Paul Rigdon RC	5.00	1.50
99 Mike Lamb RC	5.00	1.50
100 Aaron McNeal RC	5.00	1.50
101 Juan Pierre RC	10.00	3.00
102 Rico Washington RC	5.00	1.50
103 Luis Matos RC	10.00	3.00
104 Adam Bernero RC	5.00	1.50
105 Wascar Serrano RC	5.00	1.50
106 Chris Richard RC	5.00	1.50
107 Justin Miller RC	5.00	1.50
108 Julio Zuleta RC	5.00	1.50
109 Alex Cabrera RC	5.00	1.50
110 G.Stechschulte RC	5.00	1.50
111 Tony Mota RC	5.00	1.50
112 Tomo Ohka RC	5.00	1.50
113 Geraldo Guzman RC	5.00	1.50
114 Scott Downs RC	5.00	1.50
115 Timo Perez RC	5.00	1.50
116 Chad Durbin RC	5.00	1.50
117 Sun-Woo Kim RC	5.00	1.50
118 Tomas De la Rosa RC	5.00	1.50
119 Javier Cardona RC	5.00	1.50
120 Kazuhiro Sasaki RC	8.00	2.40
121 Brad Cresse JSY RC	8.00	2.40
122 M.Wheatland JSY RC	8.00	2.40
123 Joe Torres JSY RC	8.00	2.40
124 Dave Krynzel JSY RC	8.00	2.40
125 Ben Diggins JSY RC	8.00	2.40
126 Sean Burnett JSY RC	15.00	4.50
127 D.Espinosa JSY RC	8.00	2.40
128 Scott Heard JSY RC	8.00	2.40
129 Daylan Holt JSY RC	8.00	2.40
130 Koyie Hill JSY RC	10.00	3.00
131 Mark Buehrle JSY RC	15.00	4.50
132 Xavier Nady JSY RC	15.00	4.50
133 Mike Tonis JSY RC	10.00	3.00
134 Matt Ginter JSY RC	8.00	2.40
135 L.Barcelo JSY RC	8.00	2.40
136 Cory Vance JSY RC	8.00	2.40
137 Sean Burroughs USA	10.00	3.00
138 Todd Williams USA	8.00	2.40
139 B.Wilkerson USA RC	10.00	3.00
140 Ben Sheets USA RC	15.00	4.50
141 K.Ainsworth USA RC	10.00	3.00
142 Anthony Sanders USA	8.00	2.40
143 R.Franklin USA RC	8.00	2.40
144 S.Heams USA RC	8.00	2.40
145 Roy Oswalt USA RC	20.00	6.00
146 Jon Rauch USA RC	8.00	2.40
147 B.Abernathy USA RC	8.00	2.40
148 Ernie Young USA	8.00	2.40
149 Chris George USA	8.00	2.40
150 Gookie Dawkins USA	8.00	2.40
151 Adam Everett USA	8.00	2.40
152 John Cotton USA RC	8.00	2.40
153 Pat Borders USA	8.00	2.40
154 D.Mientkiewicz USA	8.00	2.40

2000 Black Diamond Rookie Edition Gold

Randomly inserted into packs, this 136-card set is a partial parallel to the Black Diamond Rookie Edition base set. The set was produced with gold foil, and is broken into tiers as follows: Base Veterans (1-90) numbered to 1000, Rookie Gems (91-120) numbered to 500, and Rookie Jerseys (121-136) numbered to 100.

Nm-Mt Ex-Mt
*STARS 1-90: 3X TO 8X BASIC CARDS
*GEMS 91-120: .4X TO 1X BASIC CARDS
*JERSEYS 121-136: 1.25X TO 3X BASIC

2000 Black Diamond Rookie Edition Authentic Pinstripes

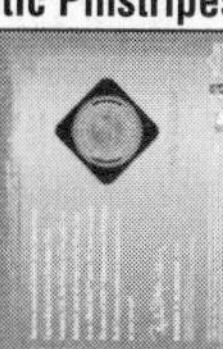

Randomly inserted into packs, this nine-card insert features game-used memorabilia cards of Derek Jeter and various other Yankee greats. Production numbers are listed below.

	Nm-Mt	Ex-Mt
APB Derek Jeter Bat/1000	40.00	12.00
APC Derek Jeter Cap/200	80.00	24.00
APG D.Jeter Glove/200	80.00	24.00
APJ Derek Jeter Jsy/1000	40.00	12.00
DJJD Derek Jeter Joe DiMaggio Bat/25		
DJMM Derek Jeter Mickey Mantle Bat/25		
DJRM Derek Jeter Roger Maris Bat/25		
JDMB Derek Jeter Bat Joe DiMaggio Bat Mickey Mantle Bat/25		
JWOJ Derek Jeter Bernie Williams Paul O'Neill Jsy/100	120.00	36.00

2000 Black Diamond Rookie Edition Diamonation

Randomly inserted into packs at one in 12, this nine-card insert set features some of the most dominating players in the game of baseball. Card backs carry a "D" prefix.

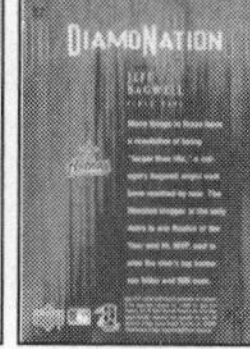

	Nm-Mt	Ex-Mt
COMPLETE SET (9)	30.00	9.00
D1 Pedro Martinez	2.50	.75
D2 Derek Jeter	6.00	1.80
D3 Jason Giambi	2.50	.75
D4 Todd Helton	1.50	.45
D5 Nomar Garciaparra	4.00	1.20
D6 Randy Johnson	2.50	.75
D7 Jeff Bagwell	1.50	.45
D8 Cal Ripken	8.00	2.40
D9 Ivan Rodriguez	2.50	.75

2000 Black Diamond Rookie Edition Gallery

Randomly inserted into packs at one in 20, this six-card insert features a gallery of superstar players. Card backs carry a "G" prefix.

	Nm-Mt	Ex-Mt
COMPLETE SET (6)	30.00	9.00
G1 Sammy Sosa	5.00	1.50
G2 Barry Bonds	8.00	2.40
G3 Vladimir Guerrero	3.00	.90
G4 Cal Ripken	10.00	3.00
G5 Mike Piazza	5.00	1.50
G6 Mark McGwire	8.00	2.40

2000 Black Diamond Rookie Edition Might

Randomly inserted into packs at one in 12, this nine-card insert features some of the most powerful players in the game of baseball. Card backs carry a "M" prefix.

	Nm-Mt	Ex-Mt
COMPLETE SET (9)	40.00	12.00
M1 Mark McGwire	6.00	1.80
M2 Mike Piazza	4.00	1.20
M3 Frank Thomas	2.50	.75
M4 Ken Griffey Jr.	4.00	1.20
M5 Sammy Sosa	4.00	1.20
M6 Alex Rodriguez	4.00	1.20
M7 Carlos Delgado	1.00	.30
M8 Vladimir Guerrero	2.50	.75
M9 Barry Bonds	6.00	1.80

2000 Black Diamond Rookie Edition Skills

Randomly inserted into packs at one in 20, this six-card insert features some of the most skilled players in the game of baseball. Card backs carry a "S" prefix.

	Nm-Mt	Ex-Mt
COMPLETE SET (6)	30.00	9.00
S1 Alex Rodriguez	5.00	1.50
S2 Chipper Jones	3.00	.90
S3 Ken Griffey Jr.	5.00	1.50
S4 Pedro Martinez	3.00	.90
S5 Ivan Rodriguez	3.00	.90
S6 Derek Jeter	8.00	2.40

1975 Blankback Discs

This six-disc baseball-designed set measures approximately 3 3/8" in diameter. The fronts feature a black-and-white player head photo on a white background in the center with the player's name, position, and team name below. The blue and red sides contain biographical information. The backs are blank. The discs are unnumbered and checklisted below in alphabetical order. Bench and Seaver are available in lesser quantities than other players so they are labeled as SP's in the checklist below

	NM	Ex
COMPLETE SET (6)	500.00	200.00
1 Henry Aaron	50.00	20.00
2 Johnny Bench SP	150.00	60.00
3 Catfish Hunter	25.00	10.00
4 Fred Lynn	5.00	2.00
5 Pete Rose	80.00	32.00
6 Tom Seaver SP	250.00	100.00

1976 Blankback Discs

These discs are similar to the Crane Discs except they have blank backs. They are valued evenly with Crane Discs

	NM	Ex
COMPLETE SET (70)	20.00	8.00
1 Hank Aaron	2.50	1.00
2 Johnny Bench	1.50	.60
3 Vida Blue	.25	.10
4 Larry Bowa	.25	.10
5 Lou Brock	1.50	.60
6 Jeff Burroughs	.10	.04
7 John Candelaria	.10	.04
8 Jose Cardenal	.10	.04
9 Rod Carew	1.50	.60
10 Steve Carlton	1.50	.60
11 Dave Cash	.10	.04
12 Cesar Cedeno	.25	.10
13 Ron Cey	.25	.10
14 Carlton Fisk	2.00	.80
15 Tito Fuentes	.10	.04
16 Steve Garvey	1.00	.40
17 Ken Griffey	.25	.10
18 Don Gullett	.10	.04
19 Willie Horton	.10	.04
20 Al Hrabosky	.10	.04
21 Catfish Hunter	1.50	.60
22A Reggie Jackson Oakland Athletics	5.00	2.00
22B Reggie Jackson Baltimore Orioles	1.50	.60
23 Randy Jones	.10	.04
24 Jim Kaat	.50	.20
25 Don Kessinger	.10	.04
26 Dave Kingman	.50	.20
27 Jerry Koosman	.25	.10
28 Mickey Lolich	.25	.10
29 Greg Luzinski	.50	.20
30 Fred Lynn	.50	.20
31 Bill Madlock	.25	.10
32A Carlos May Chicago White Sox	1.00	.40
32B Carlos May New York Yankees	.10	.04
33 John Mayberry	.10	.04
34 Bake McBride	.10	.04
35 Doc Medich	.10	.04
36A Andy Messersmith Los Angeles Dodgers	1.00	.40
36B Andy Messersmith Atlanta Braves	.10	.04
37 Rick Monday	.10	.04
38 John Montefusco	.10	.04
39 Jerry Morales	.10	.04
40 Joe Morgan	1.50	.60
41 Thurman Munson	1.00	.40
42 Bobby Murcer	.50	.20
43 Al Oliver	.50	.20
44 Jim Palmer	1.50	.60
45 Dave Parker	.75	.30
46 Tony Perez	1.00	.40
47 Jerry Reuss	.10	.04
48 Brooks Robinson	1.50	.60
49 Frank Robinson	1.50	.60
50 Steve Rogers	.10	.04
51 Pete Rose	2.00	.80
52 Nolan Ryan	4.00	1.60
53 Manny Sanguillen	.10	.04
54 Mike Schmidt	2.50	1.00
55 Tom Seaver	2.00	.80
56 Ted Simmons	.50	.20
57 Reggie Smith	.25	.10
58 Willie Stargell	1.50	.60
59 Rusty Staub	.50	.20
60 Rennie Stennett	.10	.04
61 Don Sutton	1.50	.60
62A Andre Thornton Chicago Cubs	1.00	.40
62B Andre Thornton Montreal Expos	.10	.04
63 Luis Tiant	.50	.20
64 Joe Torre	.75	.30
65 Mike Tyson	.10	.04
66 Bob Watson	.25	.10
67 Wilbur Wood	.10	.04
68 Jimmy Wynn	.10	.04
69 Carl Yastrzemski	1.50	.60
70 Richie Zisk	.10	.04

1991 Bleachers 23K Griffey Jr.

These three 23-karat gold standard-size cards were issued by Bleachers. The production run was reported to be 10,000 numbered sets and 1,500 uncut numbered strips. On white, green, yellow and blue bars, the backs carry the player's name, biography, statistics, highlights and a serial number ("X of 10,000") inside a black border.

	Nm-Mt	Ex-Mt
COMPLETE SET (3)	30.00	9.00
COMMON CARD (1-3)	10.00	3.00

1991 Bleachers 23K Thomas

These three 23-karat gold standard-size cards were produced by Bleachers. On gray, yellow,

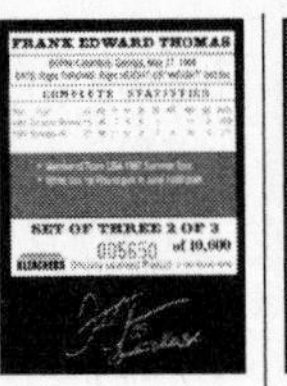

white and red stripes, the back has the player's name, biography, statistics, highlights and the serial number (1 of 10,000), inside a black border. It was reported that the production run was limited to 10,000 sets and 1,500 uncut numbered strips.

	Nm-Mt	Ex-Mt
COMPLETE SET (3)	30.00	9.00
COMMON CARD (1-3)	10.00	3.00

1991-92 Bleachers Promos

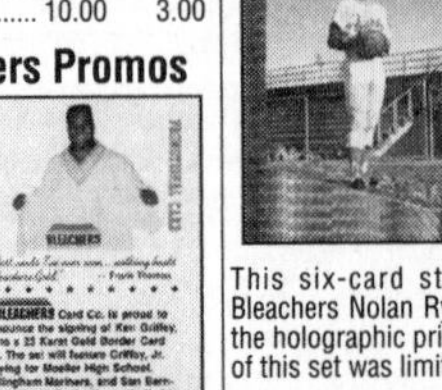

These promo standard-size cards were distributed to dealers to promote the new forthcoming Bleachers 23K card sets. The card backs contain order information as well as information about Bleachers upcoming releases.

	Nm-Mt	Ex-Mt
COMPLETE SET (7)	18.00	5.50
COMMON RYAN (3-7)	3.00	.90
1 Ken Griffey Jr. Spirit jersey 1991 copyright Frank Thomas pictured on back	3.00	.90
2 Dave Justice 1992 copyright wearing Bleachers t-shirt	2.00	.60

1992 Bleachers 23K Justice

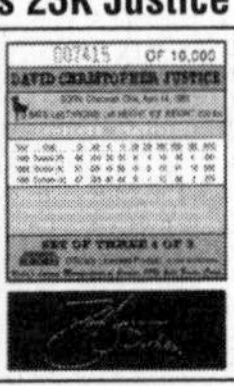

These three 23-karat gold standard-size cards were issued by Bleachers. The production run was reported to be 10,000 numbered sets and 1,500 uncut numbered strips. On white, pink, and orange bars, the backs carry the player's name, biography, statistics, highlights, and a serial number ("X of 10,000") inside a black border. Prism cards (silver prism border instead of gold) were randomly inserted in sets on a limited basis. These prism versions are valued at double the prices listed in our checklist.

	Nm-Mt	Ex-Mt
COMPLETE SET (3)	15.00	4.50
COMMON CARD (1-3)	5.00	1.50

1992 Bleachers 23K Ryan

These three 23-karat gold standard-size standard-size cards were issued by Bleachers. The sets were packaged in a cardboard sleeve and shrink wrapped; promo cards and prism cards were randomly inserted. The production run is reported to be 10,000 numbered sets and 1,500 uncut numbered strips. On white, purple, and orange bars, the backs carry the player's name, biography, statistics, highlights, and a serial number ("X of 10,000") inside a black border. Prism cards (silver prism border instead of gold) were randomly inserted in sets on a limited basis. These prism versions are valued at double the prices listed in our checklist.

	Nm-Mt	Ex-Mt
COMPLETE SET (3)	30.00	9.00
COMMON CARD (1-3)	10.00	3.00

1993 Bleachers Promos

These thirteen promo standard-size cards were distributed to dealers to promote the new upcoming Bleachers 23K card sets. The card backs contain order information as well as information about Bleachers upcoming releases.

	Nm-Mt	Ex-Mt
COMPLETE SET (13)	40.00	12.00
COMMON BONDS (1-3)	3.00	.90
COMMON RYAN (4-6)	6.00	1.80

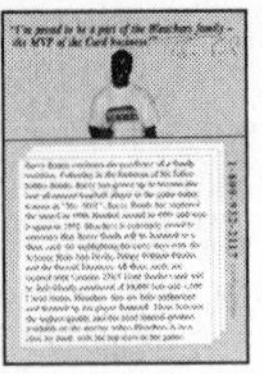

COMMON RYAN (7-9)	6.00	1.80
COMMON SANDBERG (10-13)	3.00	.90

1993 Bleachers Ryan 6

This six-card standard-size set of 1993 Bleachers Nolan Ryan is the premier edition of the holographic prism border cards. Production of this set was limited to 10,000 sets.

	Nm-Mt	Ex-Mt
COMPLETE SET (6)	30.00	9.00
COMMON CARD (1-6)	5.00	1.50

1993-00 Bleachers

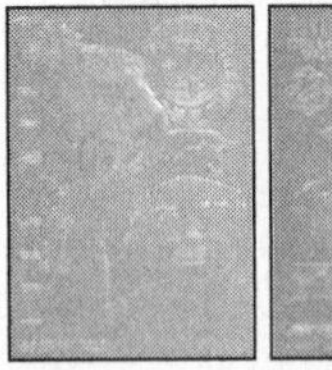

These cards feature embossed player images on 23 Karat all-gold sculptured cards. Each card was sold individually and packaged in a clear acrylic holder along with a Certificate of Authenticity inside a collectible foil-stamped box. The set is unnumbered and checklisted below in alphabetical order. Each card is serially numbered. The continuation line includes: year, brand, and number of cards issued. No complete set price is used since these cards were issued in individual fashion.

	Nm-Mt	Ex-Mt
1 Hank Aaron 1995 Classic 2,297	30.00	9.00
2 Hank Aaron 1995 Classic 10,000	10.00	3.00
3 Hank Aaron(Diamond Star) 1996 10,000	10.00	3.00
4 Hank Aaron 755 Homers Game Used Piece 1,000	40.00	12.00
5 Barry Bonds Arizona State Sun Devil 1993 10,000	6.00	1.80
6 Barry Bonds Prince William Pirates 1993 10,000	6.00	1.80
7 Barry Bonds Hawaii Islanders 1993 10,000	6.00	1.80
8 Barry Bonds(Diamond Star) 1996 Classic 4,995	15.00	4.50
9 Roberto Clemente Diamond Star 1997 10,000	10.00	3.00
10 Whitey Ford 1996 25,000	6.00	1.80
11 Ken Griffey Jr. Mega Star Sculptured Card 1993 10,000	6.00	1.80
12 Ken Griffey Jr. Mega Star Sculptured Card 1993 10,000	6.00	1.80
13 Ken Griffey Jr.(Silver/Gold) 1995 10,000	15.00	4.50
14 Ken Griffey Jr.(Triple Image) 1996 10,000	15.00	4.50
15 Ken Griffey Jr.(Diamond Star) 1996 10,000	15.00	4.50
16 Ken Griffey Jr.(#1) 1997 4,997	30.00	9.00
17 Ken Griffey Jr.(#2) 1997 4,997	30.00	9.00
18 Ken Griffey Jr.(#3) 1997 4,997	30.00	9.00
19 Ken Griffey Jr. Chasing 61, 1998 9861	6.00	1.80
20 Derek Jeter 1997 10,000	10.00	3.00
21 Mickey Mantle(#1) 1996 25,000	10.00	3.00
22 Mickey Mantle(#2) 1996 10,000	15.00	4.50
23 Mickey Mantle(#3) 1996 10,000	15.00	4.50
24 Mickey Mantle(#4) 1996 10,000	15.00	4.50
25 Mickey Mantle(#5) 1996 10,000	15.00	4.50
26 Mickey Mantle(Diamond Star) 1996 10,000	15.00	4.50
27 Roger Maris 61 Homers with Gemstone 1998: 1,000	30.00	9.00
28 Don Mattingly 1997 10,000	6.00	1.80
29 Mark McGwire Chasing 61, 1998 9861	6.00	1.80
30 Mark McGwire Sammy Sosa Breaking History	20.00	6.00
31 Mark McGwire 70 Homers with Gemstone 1998, 9,870	50.00	15.00
32 Mark McGwire 70 homers Game Used Piece 2000 1,000	100.00	30.00
33 Mark McGwire Record Setting 70th Homer	20.00	6.00
34 Eddie Murray(#1) 1996 10,000	10.00	3.00
35 Eddie Murray(#2) 1996 5,000	15.00	4.50
36 Cal Ripken(#1) 1995 75,000	6.00	1.80
37 Cal Ripken(#2) 1996 10,000	15.00	4.50
38 Cal Ripken Ironman 1995	6.00	1.80
39 Cal Ripken(Japanese) 1996 10,000	30.00	9.00
40 Cal Ripken(Diamond Star) 1996 21,310	15.00	4.50
41 Cal Ripken Lou Gehrig 1995 10,000	30.00	9.00
42 Cal Ripken Lou Gehrig (Iron Men) 1995 20,000	15.00	4.50
43 Cal Ripken 2,131 Games Game Used Piece 2000 1,000	50.00	15.00
44 Jackie Robinson 1997 Gold Performance Mint 25,000	10.00	3.00
45 Alex Rodriguez Black Autograph 1996 5,000	15.00	4.50
46 Alex Rodriguez Pearl Autograph 1996 5,000	30.00	9.00
47 Pete Rose 4,256 Hits Game Used Piece 2000 1,000	30.00	9.00
48 Babe Ruth (Diamond Star) 1997 10,000	30.00	9.00
49 Nolan Ryan Little League Highlights 1993 10,000	6.00	1.80
50 Nolan Ryan High School Highlights 1993 10,000	6.00	1.80
51 Nolan Ryan Minor League Highlights 1993 10,000	6.00	1.80
52 Nolan Ryan Minor League Statistics 1993 10,000	6.00	1.80
53 Nolan Ryan International Strikeout King 1993 10,000	6.00	1.80
54 Nolan Ryan Career Highlights 1993 10,000	6.00	1.80
55 Nolan Ryan(#1) 1993 10,000	15.00	4.50
56 Nolan Ryan(#2) 1993 5,714	15.00	4.50
57 Nolan Ryan All-Time Strikeout King 1996 50,000	15.00	4.50
58 Nolan Ryan(Diamond Star) 1996 10,000	15.00	4.50
59 Nolan Ryan Laser Cut Diamond Star 1996 10,000	18.00	5.50
60 Nolan Ryan 5,714 K's Game Used Piece 2000 1,000	50.00	15.00
61 Ryne Sandberg North Central High School 1993 10,000	6.00	1.80
62 Ryne Sandberg Helena Phillies 1993 10,000	6.00	1.80
63 Ryne Sandberg Reading Phillies 1993 10,000	6.00	1.80
64 Sammy Sosa Chasing 61, 1998 9862	6.00	1.80
65 Frank Thomas 1995 10,000	15.00	4.50
66 Frank Thomas(Diamond Star) 1996 10,000	15.00	4.50
67 Ted Williams 1996 25,000	15.00	4.50
68 Ted Williams(Diamond Star) 1996 10,000	30.00	9.00
P1 Ken Griffey Jr. Promo Card Moeller High School	6.00	1.80

1982 Cy Block

This one card standard-size set features insurance agent Cy Block who had a brief major leaguer career in the 1940's. The black and white card has a photo of Block on the front and complete career statistics on the back. The card, although it does not say on it, was produced by Topps for Block who used it as a buisness card during his prosperous post-playing career in insurance.

	Nm-Mt	Ex-Mt
1 Cy Block	1.00	.40

1979 Blue Jays Bubble Yum

These 20 white-bordered posed black-and-white player photographs measure approximately 5 1/2" by 8 1/2". The player's name and position along with the Blue Jays logo and a picture of a pack of Bubble Yum, appear within the wide lower white margin. The white back carries the player's name and position at the top, followed below by his uniform number, biography and statistics. The photos are unnumbered and checklisted below in alphabetical order.

	NM	Ex
COMPLETE SET (20)	30.00	12.00
1 Bob Bailor	2.50	1.00
2 Rick Bosetti	1.50	.60
3 Tom Buskey	1.50	.60
4 Rico Carty	3.00	1.20
5 Rick Cerone	2.00	.80
6 Jim Clancy	1.50	.60
7 Bobby Doerr CO	4.00	1.60
8 Dave Freisleben	1.50	.60
9 Luis Gomez	1.50	.60
10 Alfredo Griffin	3.00	1.20
11 Roy Hartsfield MG	1.50	.60
12 Roy Howell	1.50	.60
13 Phil Huffman	1.50	.60
14 Jesse Jefferson	1.50	.60
15 Dave Lemanczyk	1.50	.60
16 John Mayberry	3.00	1.20
17 Balor Moore	1.50	.60
18 Tom Underwood	1.50	.60
19 Otto Velez	2.00	.80
20 Al Woods	1.50	.60

1979 Blue Jays McCarthy Postcards

In the early days of the Blue Jays, they used postcards of sports photographer J.D. McCarthy as promotional team issues. These were the new photos issued in 1979, since they are unnumbered we have sequenced them in alphabetical order. The Dave Stieb postcard predates his Rookie Card by one year while the Danny Ainge predates his Rookie Card by two years.

	NM	Ex
COMPLETE SET	20.00	8.00
1 Danny Ainge	6.00	2.40
2 Bob Bailor	.50	.20
3 Rick Bosetti	.50	.20
4 Bobby Brown	.50	.20
5 Tom Buskey	.50	.20
6 Joe Cannon	.50	.20
7 Rico Carty	.75	.30
8 Rick Cerone	.75	.30
9 Jim Clancy	.50	.20
10 Bob Davis	.50	.20
11 Dave Freisleben	.50	.20
12 Luis Gomez	.50	.20
13 Alfredo Griffin	.50	.20
14 Roy Lee Howell	.50	.20
15 Phil Huffman	.50	.20
16 Tim Johnson	.50	.20
17 Craig Kusick	.50	.20
18 Dave Lemancyzk	.50	.20
19 Mark Lemongello	.50	.20
20 Dave McKay	.50	.20
21 John Mayberry	.75	.30
22 Balor Moore	.50	.20
23 Tom Murphy	.50	.20
24 Dave Stieb	5.00	2.00
25 Tom Underwood	.50	.20
26 Otto Velez	.50	.20
27 Ted Wilborn	.50	.20
28 Al Woods	.50	.20

1982 Blue Jays Sun

This 18-card set features blue-bordered color player photos of the 1982 Toronto Blue Jays. The set was inserted for several weeks into the newspaper and could be cut out of the Sports section of the Sunday Sun. The cards are unnumbered and checklisted below in alphabetical order.

	Nm-Mt	Ex-Mt
COMPLETE SET (18)	15.00	6.00
1 Jesse Barfield	2.00	.80
2 Barry Bonnell	1.00	.40
3 Jim Clancy	1.00	.40
4 Damaso Garcia	1.00	.40
5 Jerry Garvin	1.00	.40
6 Jim Gott	1.00	.40
7 Alfredo Griffin	1.00	.40
8 Garth Iorg	1.00	.40
9 Roy Lee Jackson	1.00	.40
10 Buck Martinez	1.00	.40
11 John Mayberry	1.00	.40
12 Joey McLaughlin	1.00	.40
13 Lloyd Moseby	1.00	.40
14 Rance Mulliniks	1.00	.40
15 Dale Murray	1.00	.40
16 Dave Stieb	2.00	.80
17 Willie Upshaw	1.00	.40
18 Ernie Whitt	1.50	.60

1984 Blue Jays Fire Safety

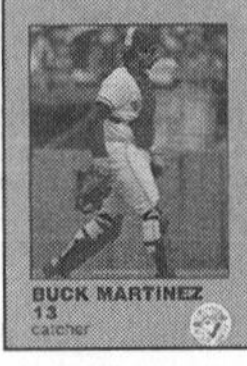

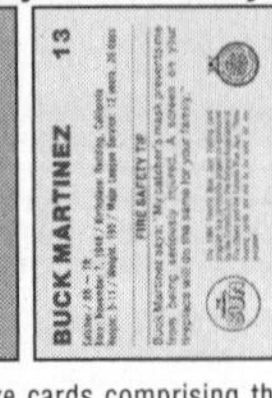

The 35 standard-size cards comprising this 1984 Blue Jays Fire Safety set feature on their fronts blue-bordered, color player action shots. The player's name, position, and uniform number appear in black lettering within the lower blue margin. The circular Blue Jays' logo rests at the bottom right. The horizontal white back carries the player's name and uniform number at the top, followed below by biography and a fire safety tip. The logos at the bottom for the Ontario Association of Fire Chiefs and The Toronto Sun round out the card. The cards are unnumbered and checklisted below in alphabetical order.

	Nm-Mt	Ex-Mt
COMPLETE SET (35)	15.00	6.00
1 Jim Acker	.50	.20
2 Willie Aikens	.50	.20
3 Doyle Alexander	.75	.30
4 Jesse Barfield	1.00	.40
5 George Bell	.75	.30
6 Jim Clancy	.50	.20
7 Bryan Clark	.50	.20
8 Stan Clarke	.50	.20
9 Dave Collins	.75	.30
10 Bobby Cox MG	1.00	.40
11 Tony Fernandez	1.50	.60
12 Damaso Garcia	.75	.30
13 Cito Gaston CO	.75	.30
14 Jim Gott	.50	.20
15 Alfredo Griffin	.75	.30
16 Kelly Gruber	1.00	.40
17 Garth Iorg	.50	.20
18 Roy Lee Jackson	.50	.20
19 Cliff Johnson	.75	.30
20 Jimmy Key	3.00	1.20
21 Dennis Lamp	.50	.20
22 Rick Leach	.50	.20
23 Luis Leal	.50	.20
24 Buck Martinez	.75	.30
25 Lloyd Moseby	1.00	.40
26 Rance Mulliniks	.75	.30
27 Billy Smith CO	.50	.20
28 Dave Stieb	1.00	.40
29 John Sullivan CO	.50	.20
30 Willie Upshaw	.75	.30
31 Mitch Webster	.50	.20
32 Ernie Whitt	.75	.30
33 Al Widmar CO	.50	.20
34 Jimy Williams CO	.50	.20
35 Blue Jays Logo	.50	.20

1985 Blue Jays Fire Safety

The 36 standard-size cards comprising this 1985 Blue Jays Fire Safety set feature on their fronts blue-bordered posed color player photos. The player's name, position, and uniform number appear in black lettering within the lower blue margin. The circular Blue Jays' logo rests at the bottom right. The horizontal white back carries the player's name and uniform number at the top, followed below by biography, statistics, and a fire safety tip. The logos at the bottom for the Ontario Association of Fire Chiefs, the Ontario Ministry of the Solicitor General, The Toronto Star, and Midas round out the card. The cards are unnumbered and checklisted below in alphabetical order.

	Nm-Mt	Ex-Mt
COMPLETE SET (36)	10.00	4.00
1 Jim Acker	.25	.10
2 Willie Aikens	.25	.10
3 Doyle Alexander	.50	.20
4 Jesse Barfield	.75	.30
5 George Bell	.50	.20
6 Jeff Burroughs	.50	.20
7 Bill Caudill	.25	.10
8 Jim Clancy	.25	.10
9 Bobby Cox MG	1.00	.40
10 Tony Fernandez	1.00	.40
11 Damaso Garcia	.50	.20
12 Cito Gaston CO	.50	.20
13 Kelly Gruber	.75	.30
14 Tom Henke	1.00	.40
15 Garth Iorg	.25	.10
16 Jimmy Key	1.50	.60
17 Dennis Lamp	.25	.10
18 Gary Lavelle	.25	.10
19 Luis Leal	.25	.10
20 Manny Lee	.25	.10

21 Buck Martinez .50 .20
22 Len Matuszek .25 .10
23 Lloyd Moseby .50 .20
24 Rance Mulliniks .25 .10
25 Ron Musselman .25 .10
26 Billy Smith CO .25 .10
27 Dave Stieb .75 .30
28 John Sullivan CO .25 .10
29 Lou Thornton .25 .10
30 Willie Upshaw .50 .20
31 Mitch Webster .25 .10
32 Ernie Whitt .50 .20
33 Al Widmar CO .25 .10
34 Jimy Williams CO .25 .10
35 Blue Jays Logo .25 .10
(Unnumbered checklist back)
36 Blue Jays Team Photo .50 .20
(Schedule on back)

1985 Blue Jays Pepsi/Frito Lay Pennants

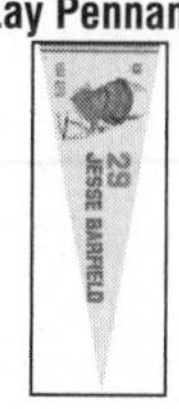

This five-pennant set was produced by Pepsi Cola and Frito Lay and measures approximately 9 1/2" by 26". The fronts display a color drawing of the player's head alongside a full player image with the player's name and jersey number and a facsimile autograph. The cards are unnumbered and checklisted below in alphabetical order.

Nm-Mt Ex-Mt
COMPLETE SET (5) 10.00 4.00
1 Jesse Barfield 3.00 1.20
2 Bill Caudill 2.00 .80
3 Dave Stieb 4.00 1.60
4 Willie Upshaw 2.00 .80
5 Ernie Whitt 2.00 .80

1986 Blue Jays Ault Foods

The 24 stickers in this set, featuring members of the Toronto Blue Jays, measure approximately 2" by 3" and were to be pasted in a 9" by 12", 20-page album. Ault Foods were sold under several brands, e.g., Sealtest, Silverwood, Royal Oak, and Copper Cliff. The stickers are unnumbered and checklisted below in alphabetical order. The set is also noteworthy in that it contains Cecil Fielder appearing in his Rookie Card year.

Nm-Mt Ex-Mt
COMPLETE SET (24) 20.00 8.00
1 Jim Acker .50 .20
2 Doyle Alexander .50 .20
3 Jesse Barfield 1.50 .60
4 George Bell 1.50 .60
5 Bill Caudill .50 .20
6 Jim Clancy .50 .20
7 Steve Davis .50 .20
8 Tony Fernandez 1.50 .60
9 Cecil Fielder 6.00 2.40
10 Damaso Garcia 1.00 .40
11 Don Gordon .50 .20
12 Kelly Gruber 1.50 .60
13 Tom Henke 1.50 .60
14 Garth Iorg .50 .20
15 Cliff Johnson 1.00 .40
16 Jimmy Key 2.00 .80
17 Dennis Lamp .50 .20
18 Gary Lavelle .50 .20
19 Buck Martinez 1.00 .40
20 Lloyd Moseby 1.00 .40
21 Rance Mulliniks 1.00 .40
22 Dave Stieb 1.50 .60
23 Willie Upshaw 1.00 .40
24 Ernie Whitt 1.00 .40
NNO Ault Album 2.50 1.00

1986 Blue Jays Fire Safety

The 36 standard-size cards comprising this 1986 Toronto Blue Jays Fire set feature on their fronts blue-bordered, posed color player photos. The cards are unnumbered and checklisted below in alphabetical order. The set is also noteworthy in that it contains Cecil Fielder appearing in his Rookie Card year.

Nm-Mt Ex-Mt
COMPLETE SET (36) 12.00 4.80
1 Jim Acker .25 .10
2 Doyle Alexander .50 .20
3 Jesse Barfield .75 .30
4 George Bell .75 .30
5 Bill Caudill .25 .10
6 Jim Clancy .25 .10
7 Steve Davis .25 .10
8 Mark Eichhorn .50 .20
9 Tony Fernandez .75 .30
10 Cecil Fielder 5.00 2.00
11 Tom Filer .25 .10
12 Damaso Garcia .50 .20
13 Cito Gaston CO .75 .30
14 Don Gordon .25 .10
15 Kelly Gruber .50 .20
16 Jeff Hearron .25 .10
17 Tom Henke .75 .30
18 Garth Iorg .25 .10
19 Cliff Johnson .50 .20
20 Jimmy Key 1.00 .40
21 Dennis Lamp .25 .10
22 Gary Lavelle .25 .10
23 Rick Leach .25 .10
24 Buck Martinez .50 .20
25 John McLaren CO .25 .10
26 Lloyd Moseby .50 .20
27 Rance Mulliniks .25 .10
28 Billy Smith CO .25 .10
29 Dave Stieb .75 .30
30 John Sullivan CO .25 .10
31 Willie Upshaw .50 .20
32 Ernie Whitt .50 .20
33 Al Widmar CO .25 .10
34 Jimy Williams MG .25 .10
35 Blue Jays LOGO .25 .10
(Won-Lost Record)
36 Blue Jays Team Photo CL .25 .10

1986 Blue Jays Greats TCMA

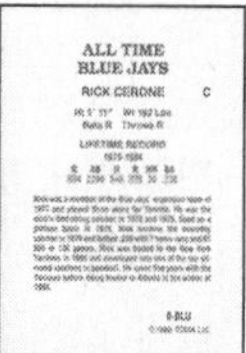

These 12 standard-size cards honor the best players of the Toronto Blue Jays first decade. The players are pictured on the front. The backs have a biography and career statistics.

Nm-Mt Ex-Mt
COMPLETE SET (12) 3.00 1.20
1 John Mayberry .50 .20
2 Bob Bailor .25 .10
3 Luis Gomez .25 .10
4 Roy Howell .25 .10
5 Otto Velez .25 .10
6 Rick Bosetti .25 .10
7 Al Woods .25 .10
8 Rick Cerone .50 .20
9 Dave Lemanczyk .25 .10
10 Tom Underwood .25 .10
11 Joey McLaughlin .25 .10
12 Bobby Cox MG .75 .30

1987 Blue Jays Fire Safety

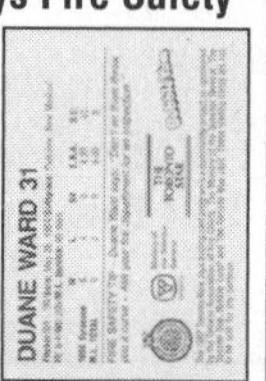

The 36 standard-size cards comprising this 1987 Toronto Blue Jays Fire Safety set feature on their fronts white-bordered, posed color player photos. The cards are unnumbered and checklisted below in alphabetical order.

Nm-Mt Ex-Mt
COMPLETE SET (36) 8.00 3.20
1 Jesse Barfield .75 .30
2 George Bell .75 .30
3 John Cerutti .25 .10
4 Toronto Blue Jays CL .50 .20
5 Jim Clancy .25 .10
6 Rob Ducey .25 .10
7 Mark Eichhorn .50 .20
8 Tony Fernandez .75 .30
9 Cecil Fielder 1.50 .60
10 Cito Gaston CO .75 .30
11 Kelly Gruber .50 .20
12 Tom Henke .75 .30
13 Jeff Hearron .25 .10
14 Garth Iorg .25 .10
15 Joe Johnson .25 .10
16 Jimmy Key 1.00 .40
17 Gary Lavelle .25 .10
18 Rick Leach .25 .10
19 Logo Card .25 .10
(Franchise yearly record on back)
20 Fred McGriff 4.00 1.60
21 John McLaren CO .25 .10
22 Craig McMurtry .25 .10
23 Lloyd Moseby .50 .20
24 Rance Mulliniks .25 .10
25 Jeff Musselman .25 .10
26 Jose Nunez .25 .10
27 Mike Sharperson .25 .10
28 Billy Smith CO .25 .10
29 Matt Stark .25 .10
30 Dave Stieb .75 .30
31 John Sullivan CO .25 .10
32 Willie Upshaw .50 .20
33 Duane Ward .50 .20
34 Ernie Whitt .50 .20
35 Al Widmar CO .25 .10
36 Jimy Williams MG .25 .10

1988 Blue Jays 5x7

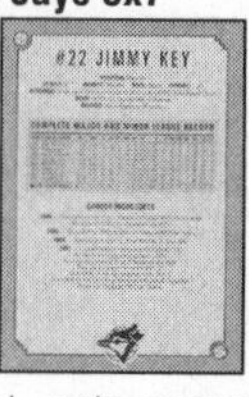

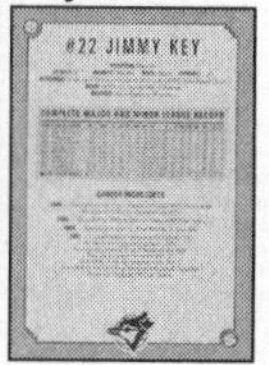

These 14 oversized cards measure approximately 5" by 7" and feature turquoise-bordered retouched posed color player photos. The cards are unnumbered and checklisted below in alphabetical order.

Nm-Mt Ex-Mt
COMPLETE SET (14) 16.00 6.50
1 Jesse Barfield 1.50 .60
2 George Bell 1.50 .60
3 Jim Clancy .50 .20
4 Mark Eichhorn .50 .20
5 Tony Fernandez 1.50 .60
6 Tom Henke 1.50 .60
7 Jimmy Key 2.00 .80
8 Nelson Liriano .50 .20
9 Lloyd Moseby 1.50 .60
10 Dave Stieb 1.50 .60
11 Willie Upshaw 1.00 .40
12 Jimy Williams MG .50 .20
13 1988 Schedule .50 .20
14 1988 Season Ticket .50 .20
Packages/Single Game
Ticket Prices

1988 Blue Jays Fire Safety

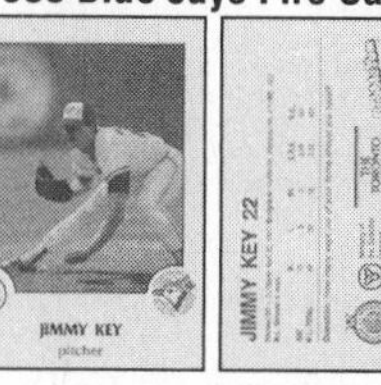

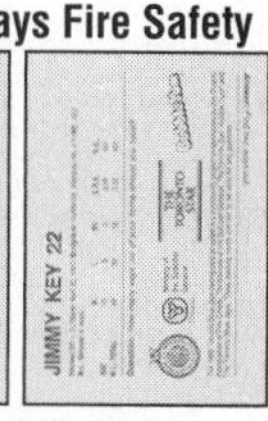

This attractive, white-bordered, 36-card set features Toronto Blue Jays, their coaches and manager. The cards (measuring 3 1/2" by 5") are over-sized. The cards are unnumbered and checklisted below in alphabetical order.

Nm-Mt Ex-Mt
COMPLETE SET (36) 10.00 4.00
*FRENCH: 1.5X BASIC CARDS
1 Jesse Barfield .75 .30
2 George Bell .75 .30
3 Juan Beniquez .25 .10
4 Pat Borders .50 .20
5 Sil Campusano .25 .10
6 John Cerutti .25 .10
7 Jim Clancy .25 .10
8 Rob Ducey .25 .10
9 Mark Eichhorn .25 .10
10 Tony Fernandez .75 .30
11 Cecil Fielder 1.00 .40
12 Mike Flanagan .50 .20
13 Cito Gaston CO .75 .30
14 Kelly Gruber .50 .20
15 Tom Henke .75 .30
16 Jimmy Key 1.00 .40
17 Rick Leach .25 .10
18 Manny Lee .25 .10
19 Nelson Liriano .25 .10
20 Winston Llenas CO .25 .10
21 Fred McGriff 3.00 1.20
22 John McLaren CO .25 .10
23 Lloyd Moseby .50 .20
24 Rance Mulliniks .50 .20
25 Jeff Musselman .25 .10
26 Billy Smith CO .25 .10
27 Dave Stieb .75 .30
28 Todd Stottlemyre 1.25 .50
29 John Sullivan CO .25 .10
30 Duane Ward .25 .10
31 David Wells 1.00 .40
32 Ernie Whitt .50 .20
33 Al Widmar CO .25 .10
34 Jimy Williams MG .25 .10
35 Team Card CL .50 .20
36 Title/Logo Card .50 .20
(Year by year record on back)

1989 Blue Jays Fire Safety

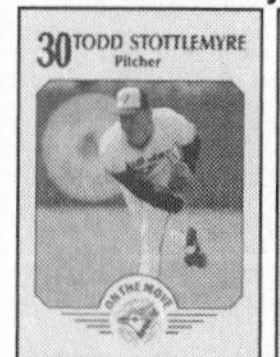

The 36 standard-size cards comprising this 1989 Toronto Blue Jays Fire Safety set feature on their fronts white-bordered, color player action shots. The cards are unnumbered and checklisted below in alphabetical order.

Nm-Mt Ex-Mt
COMPLETE SET (36) 8.00 3.20
1 Jesse Barfield .75 .30
2 George Bell .75 .30
3 Pat Borders .50 .20
4 Bob Brenly .50 .20
5 Sal Butera .25 .10
6 Sil Campusano .25 .10
7 John Cerutti .25 .10
8 Rob Ducey .25 .10
9 Tony Fernandez .75 .30
10 Mike Flanagan .50 .20
11 Cito Gaston CO .75 .30
12 Kelly Gruber .50 .20
13 Tom Henke .75 .30
14 Jimmy Key 1.00 .40
15 Tom Lawless .25 .10
16 Manny Lee .25 .10
17 Nelson Liriano .25 .10
18 Fred McGriff 2.00 .80
19 John McLaren CO .25 .10
20 Lloyd Moseby .50 .20
21 Rance Mulliniks .25 .10
22 Jeff Musselman .25 .10
23 Greg Myers .25 .10
24 Jose Nunez .25 .10
25 Mike Squires CO .25 .10
26 Dave Stieb .75 .30
27 Todd Stottlemyre 1.00 .40
28 John Sullivan CO .25 .10
29 Duane Ward .25 .10
30 David Wells .75 .30
31 Ernie Whitt .50 .20
32 Al Widmar CO .25 .10
33 Jimy Williams MG .25 .10
34 Frank Wills .25 .10
35 Team Logo .25 .10
(W-L record on back)
36 Team Photo CL .50 .20

1990 Blue Jays Fire Safety

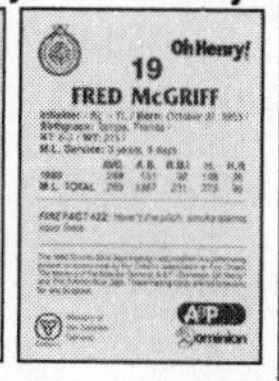

The 36 standard-size cards comprising this 1990 Blue Jays Fan Club set feature on their fronts white-bordered color player action shots. The cards are unnumbered and checklisted below in alphabetical order. The set is also noteworthy in that it contains John Olerud appearing in his Rookie Card year.

Nm-Mt Ex-Mt
COMPLETE SET (36) 8.00 2.40
1 Jim Acker .25 .07
2 George Bell .75 .23
3 Willie Blair .25 .07
4 Pat Borders .25 .07
5 John Cerutti .25 .07
6 Galen Cisco CO .25 .07
7 Junior Felix .25 .07
8 Tony Fernandez .75 .23
9 Cito Gaston MG .75 .23
10 Kelly Gruber .50 .15
11 Tom Henke .75 .23
12 Glenallen Hill .50 .15
13 Jimmy Key 1.00 .30
14 Paul Kilgus .25 .07
15 Tom Lawless .25 .07
16 Manny Lee .25 .07
17 Al Leiter 1.00 .30
18 Nelson Liriano .25 .07
19 Fred McGriff 1.50 .45
20 John McLaren CO .25 .07
21 Rance Mulliniks .25 .07
22 Greg Myers .25 .07
23 John Olerud 2.50 .75
24 Alex Sanchez .25 .07
25 Mike Squires CO .25 .07
26 Dave Stieb .75 .23
27 Todd Stottlemyre .75 .23
28 John Sullivan CO .25 .07
29 Gene Tenace CO .50 .15
30 Ozzie Virgil .25 .07
31 Duane Ward .25 .07
32 David Wells 1.00 .30
33 Frank Wills .25 .07
34 Mookie Wilson .50 .15
35 Schedule Card .25 .07
36 Skydome CL .50 .15

1990 Blue Jays Hostess Stickers

These six strips of three stickers each feature color player action shots depicting great moments for the Blue Jays. Each strip measures approximately 7" by 3 1/4"; each sticker measures approximately 2 1/4" by 3 1/4". A brief description in English of the great moment, along with the Blue Jays logo, appears within the blue stripe across the top. The same description, in French, appears within the blue stripe at the bottom, along with the Hostess logo. The stickers are unnumbered and checklisted below by strip.

Nm-Mt Ex-Mt
COMPLETE SET (6) 20.00 6.00
1 Damaso Garcia 4.00 1.20
George Bell
Kelly Gruber
2 George Bell 4.00 1.20
Lloyd Moseby
Jesse Barfield
Jesse Barfield
3 Fred McGriff 6.00 1.80
Tom Henke
Jimmy Key
4 Jim Clancy 4.00 1.20
Ernie Whitt
Tom Henke
5 Dave Collins 5.00 1.50
Jesse Barfield
Tony Fernandez
Junior Felix
Tony Fernandez
Kelly Gruber
George Bell
Fred McGriff
6 Junior Felix 4.00 1.20
Dave Stieb

1991 Blue Jays Fire Safety

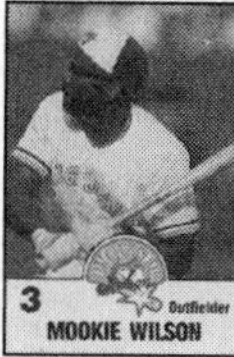

This 36-card standard-size set was jointly sponsored by the Ontario Association of Fire Chiefs, the Ministry of the Solicitor General, A and P/Dominion, Oh Henry, and the Toronto Blue Jays. The cards are unnumbered and checklisted below in alphabetical order.

Nm-Mt Ex-Mt
COMPLETE SET (36) 10.00 3.00
1 Jim Acker .25 .07
2 Roberto Alomar 2.00 .60
3 Pat Borders .25 .07
4 Denis Boucher .25 .07
5 Joe Carter 1.50 .45
6 Galen Cisco CO .25 .07
7 Ken Dayley .25 .07
8 Rob Ducey .25 .07
9 Cito Gaston MG .50 .15
10 Rene Gonzales .25 .07
11 Kelly Gruber .50 .15
12 Rich Hacker CO .25 .07
13 Tom Henke .75 .23
14 Glenallen Hill .50 .15
15 Jimmy Key 1.00 .30
16 Manny Lee .25 .07
17 Al Leiter 1.00 .30
18 Rance Mulliniks .50 .15
19 Greg Myers .25 .07
20 John Olerud 1.00 .30
21 Mike Squires CO .25 .07
22 Dave Stieb .75 .23
23 Todd Stottlemyre .50 .15
24 John Sullivan CO .25 .07
25 Pat Tabler .25 .07
26 Gene Tenace CO .25 .07
27 Hector Torres CO .25 .07
28 Duane Ward .25 .07
29 David Wells 1.00 .30
30 Devon White .50 .15
31 Mark Whiten .25 .07
32 Kenny Williams .50 .15
33 Frank Wills .25 .07
34 Mookie Wilson .50 .15
35 B.J. Burdy (Mascot) .25 .07
36 Checklist Card .50 .15

1991 Blue Jays Score

The 1991 Score Toronto Blue Jays set contains 40 player cards plus five magic motion trivia cards. The standard-size cards feature on the fronts glossy color action photos with white borders.

Nm-Mt Ex-Mt
COMPLETE SET (40) 14.00 4.20
1 Joe Carter 1.50 .45
2 Tom Henke .75 .23
3 Jimmy Key 1.00 .30
4 Al Leiter 1.00 .30
5 Dave Stieb 1.00 .30
6 Todd Stottlemyre .50 .15
7 Mike Timlin .50 .15
8 Duane Ward .25 .07
9 David Wells 1.00 .30
10 Frank Wills .25 .07
11 Pat Borders .25 .07
12 Greg Myers .25 .07
13 Roberto Alomar 2.50 .75
14 Rene Gonzales .25 .07
15 Kelly Gruber .50 .15
16 Manny Lee .25 .07
17 Rance Mulliniks .25 .07
18 John Olerud 1.00 .30
19 Pat Tabler .25 .07
20 Derek Bell .50 .15
21 Jim Acker .25 .07
22 Rob Ducey .25 .07
23 Devon White .50 .15
24 Mookie Wilson .50 .15
25 Juan Guzman .50 .15
26 Ed Sprague .50 .15
27 Ken Dayley .25 .07
28 Tom Candiotti .25 .07
29 Candy Maldonado .25 .07
30 Eddie Zosky .25 .07
31 Steve Karsay .50 .15
32 Bob MacDonald .25 .07
33 Ray Giannelli .25 .07
34 Jerry Schunk .25 .07
35 Dave Weathers .25 .07
36 Cito Gaston MG .50 .15
37 Joe Carter AS .50 .15

38 Jimmy Key AS	.50	.15
39 Roberto Alomar AS	1.25	.35
40 1991 All-Star Game	.25	.07

1992 Blue Jays Fire Safety

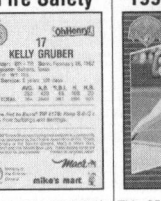

This 36-card standard-size set was jointly sponsored by the Ontario Association of Fire Chiefs, The Ministry of the Solicitor General, Mac's Milk, Mike's Mart, and Oh Henry. The cards are printed on recycled paper and are thinner than most sports cards. The cards are unnumbered and checklisted below in alphabetical order.

	Nm-Mt	Ex-Mt
COMPLETE SET (36)	12.50	3.70
1 Roberto Alomar	2.00	.60
2 Bob Bailor CO	.25	.07
3 Derek Bell	.25	.07
4 Pat Borders	.25	.07
5 Joe Carter	1.25	.35
6 Galen Cisco CO	.25	.07
7 Ken Dayley	.25	.07
8 Rob Ducey	.25	.07
9 Cito Gaston MG	.75	.23
10 Alfredo Griffin	.25	.07
11 Kelly Gruber	.50	.15
12 Juan Guzman	.25	.07
13 Rich Hacker CO	.25	.07
14 Tom Henke	.75	.23
15 Larry Hisle CO	.25	.07
16 Jimmy Key	1.00	.30
17 Manny Lee	.25	.07
18 Bob MacDonald	.25	.07
19 Candy Maldonado	.25	.07
20 Jack Morris	1.00	.30
21 Rance Mulliniks	.50	.15
22 Greg Myers	.25	.07
23 John Olerud	1.00	.30
24 Dave Stieb	.75	.23
25 Todd Stottlemyre	.50	.15
26 John Sullivan CO	.25	.07
27 Pat Tabler	.25	.07
28 Gene Tenace CO	.25	.07
29 Mike Timlin	.25	.07
30 Duane Ward	.25	.07
31 Turner Ward	.25	.07
32 David Wells	1.00	.30
33 Devon White	.50	.15
34 Dave Winfield	1.50	.45
35 Eddie Zosky	.25	.07
36 Checklist Card	.25	.07

1992 Blue Jays Maxwell House

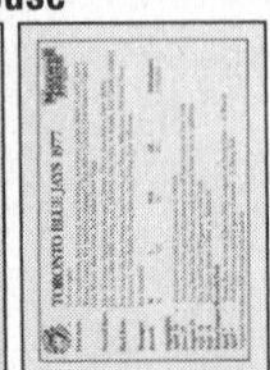

Sponsored by Maxwell House Coffee, this 18-card standard-size set celebrates the first fifteen years of the Toronto Blue Jays. The set includes a mail-in offer for a commemorative team card album. The cards are unnumbered and checklisted below in year order.

	Nm-Mt	Ex-Mt
COMPLETE SET (18)	15.00	4.50
1 1977 Team Photo	1.50	.45
9 1985 Team Photo	1.50	.45
16 1992 Team Photo	1.50	.45
17 Title Card	1.00	.30
18 Album Offer Card	1.00	.30

1993 Blue Jays Colla Postcards 15

This 15-card set is borderless, without the player's name on the front. Eight cards are marked "WC" for "World Champions", in a border across the front corner. Backs contain the player's name, the Bluejays' logo and are all numbered alphabetically as described below.

	Nm-Mt	Ex-Mt
COMPLETE SET (15)	7.50	2.20
1 Roberto Alomar	2.00	.60
2 Pat Borders	.50	.15
3 Joe Carter	1.50	.45
4 Roberto Alomar WC	1.50	.45
5 Pat Borders WC	.50	.15
6 Joe Carter WC	.75	.23
7 Juan Guzman WC	.50	.15
8 Jack Morris WC	1.00	.30
9 John Olerud WC	.75	.23
10 Todd Stottlemyre WC	.75	.23
11 Devon White WC	.50	.15
12 Juan Guzman	.50	.15
13 Paul Molitor	2.00	.60
14 Dave Stewart	.75	.23
15 Devon White	.75	.23

1993 Blue Jays Dempster's

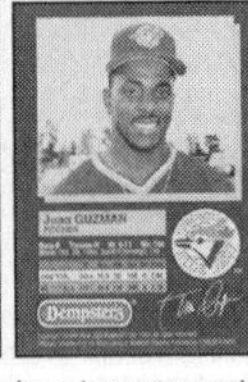

This 25-card standard-size set commemorates the 1992 World Series Champion Toronto Blue Jays and was sponsored by Dempster's. The cards are numbered on the front.

	Nm-Mt	Ex-Mt
COMPLETE SET (25)	15.00	4.50
1 Juan Guzman	.50	.15
2 Roberto Alomar	2.00	.60
3 Danny Cox	.50	.15
4 Paul Molitor	2.00	.60
5 Todd Stottlemyre	.75	.23
6 Joe Carter	1.50	.45
7 Jack Morris	1.00	.30
8 Ed Sprague	.50	.15
9 Turner Ward	.50	.15
10 John Olerud	1.50	.45
11 Duane Ward	.50	.15
12 Alfredo Griffin	.50	.15
13 Cito Gaston MG	.75	.23
14 Dave Stewart	1.00	.30
15 Mark Eichhorn	.50	.15
16 Darnell Coles	.50	.15
17 Randy Knorr	.50	.15
18 Al Leiter	1.50	.45
19 Pat Hentgen	1.50	.45
20 Devon White	.75	.23
21 Pat Borders	.50	.15
22 Darrin Jackson	.50	.15
23 Dick Schofield	.50	.15
24 Luis Sojo	.50	.15
25 Mike Timlin	.75	.23

1993 Blue Jays Donruss 45

This standard-size 45-card gold-boxed set showcases the 1992 Blue Jays with full-bleed action color photos.

	Nm-Mt	Ex-Mt
COMP.FACT SET (45)	15.00	4.50
1 Checklist Card	.25	.07
2 Roberto Alomar	1.50	.45
3 Derek Bell	.25	.07
4 Pat Borders	.25	.07
5 Joe Carter	1.25	.35
6 Alfredo Griffin	.25	.07
7 Kelly Gruber	.25	.07
8 Manny Lee	.25	.07
9 Candy Maldonado	.25	.07
10 John Olerud	1.00	.30
11 Ed Sprague	.25	.07
12 Pat Tabler	.25	.07
13 Devon White	.50	.15
14 Dave Winfield	1.50	.45
15 David Cone	1.00	.30
16 Mark Eichhorn	.25	.07
17 Juan Guzman	.25	.07
18 Tom Henke	.25	.07
19 Jimmy Key	.50	.15
20 Jack Morris	.75	.23
21 Todd Stottlemyre	.50	.15
22 Mike Timlin	.50	.15
23 Duane Ward	.25	.07
24 David Wells	1.00	.30
25 Randy Knorr	.25	.07
26 Rance Mulliniks	.25	.07
27 Tom Quinlan	.25	.07
28 Cito Gaston MG	.50	.15
29 Dave Stieb	.75	.23
30 Ken Dayley	.25	.07
31 Turner Ward	.25	.07
32 Eddie Zosky	.25	.07
33 Pat Hentgen	1.50	.45
34 Al Leiter	1.00	.30
35 Doug Linton	.25	.07
36 Bob MacDonald	.25	.07
37 Rick Trlicek	.25	.07
38 Domingo Martinez	.25	.07
39 Mike Maksudian	.25	.07
40 Rob Ducey	.25	.07
41 Jeff Kent	4.00	1.20
42 Greg Myers	.25	.07
43 Dave Weathers	.25	.07
44 Skydome	.25	.07
45 Trophy Presentation	.25	.07

1993 Blue Jays Donruss McDonald's

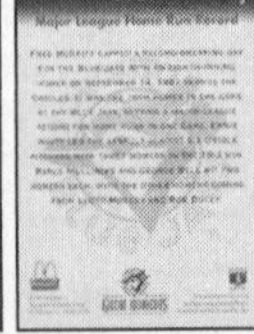

This 36-card standard-size set was produced by Donruss for McDonald's and recognizes "Great Moments" of the Blue Jays. Foil packs sold for 45 cents Canadian with purchase of fries or hash browns. In terms of design, the set subdivides into three sections: 1985-92 Team Highlights (1-13); 1992 World Series (14-26); and regular-issue player cards (27-35). The cards have fronts depicting significant plays and players from 1985 to 1992 in action photos. The McDonald's logo is located in the top left. On cards 1-26, the gold-foil stamped "Great Moments" appears near the bottom with the name of the great moment listed below, while the back describes the event pictured on the front and is superimposed on a ghosted logo of the Blue Jays, with the date in gold lettering across the top.

	Nm-Mt	Ex-Mt
COMPLETE SET (36)	18.00	5.50
1 Willie Upshaw	.50	.15
2 Jesse Barfield	.75	.23
3 Fred McGriff	2.50	.75
4 George Bell	.75	.23
5 Kelly Gruber	.50	.15
6 Ernie Whitt	.25	.07
7 Tom Henke	.25	.07
8 Dave Stieb	.50	.15
9 Jack Morris	.75	.23
10 Team salutes fans 1992-FANtastic	.25	.07
11 Pat Borders Mark McGwire	2.00	.60
12 Roberto Alomar	2.00	.60
13 Candy Maldonado	.25	.07
14 Ed Sprague	.50	.15
15 Bobby Cox MG Cito Gaston MG	.25	.07
16 Devon White	.75	.23
17 Kelly Gruber Deion Sanders	2.00	.60
18A Roberto Alomar ERR Winning Welcome missing from front) Kelly Gruber	2.00	.60
18B Roberto Alomar COR Kelly Gruber 1992-Winning Welcome	2.00	.60
19 Kelly Gruber Damon Berryhill	.25	.07
20 Jimmy Key	.50	.15
21 Devon White Candy Maldonado	.50	.15
22 Joe Carter Otis Nixon	.75	.23
23 Blue Jays COR 1992-World Champions	.75	.23
23A Blue Jays ERR 1992-World Champions (Front is Jimmy Key photo from card 20)	.75	.23
24 Paul Beeston PR Cito Gaston MG 1992-WS Trophy	.25	.07
25 Pat Borders MVP	.25	.07
26 SkyDome victory parade 1992-WS Heroes	.25	.07
27 John Olerud	.75	.23
28 Roberto Alomar	2.00	.60
29 Ed Sprague	.25	.07
30 Dick Schofield	.25	.07
31 Devon White	.50	.15
32 Joe Carter	1.50	.45
33 Darrin Jackson	.25	.07
34 Pat Borders	.25	.07
35 Paul Molitor	2.00	.60
36 Checklist 1-36	.25	.07

1993 Blue Jays Donruss World Series

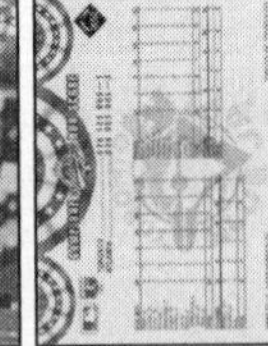

This nine-card horizontally oriented set captures highlights from the 1992 World Series. The cards are numbered on the back with a "WS" prefix.

	Nm-Mt	Ex-Mt
COMPLETE SET (9)	6.00	1.80
1 Series Opener (Blue Jays-Braves)	.50	.15
2 Joe Carter	1.00	.30
3 Ed Sprague Derek Bell	.50	.15
4 Candy Maldonado	.50	.15
5 Jimmy Key	.75	.23
6 John Olerud	1.00	.30
7 Dave Winfield Derek Bell	1.50	.45
8 Pat Borders	.75	.23
9 Blue Jays celebrate	.75	.23

1993 Blue Jays Fire Safety

This 36-card standard-size set commemorates the 1992 World Series Champion Toronto Blue Jays. The set was jointly sponsored by the Ontario Association of Fire Chiefs, The Office of the Fire Marshal, Becker's, Oh Henry, and the Blue Jays. The cards are unnumbered and checklisted below in alphabetical order.

	Nm-Mt	Ex-Mt
COMPLETE SET (36)	10.00	3.00
1 Roberto Alomar	1.50	.45
2 Bob Bailor CO	.25	.07
3 Pat Borders	.25	.07
4 Joe Carter	1.00	.30
5 Galen Cisco CO	.25	.07
6 Darnell Coles	.25	.07
7 Danny Cox	.25	.07
8 Ken Dayley	.25	.07
9 Mark Eichhorn	.25	.07
10 Cito Gaston MG	.75	.23
11 Alfredo Griffin	.25	.07
12 Juan Guzman	.25	.07
13 Rich Hacker CO	.25	.07
14 Pat Hentgen	.50	.15
15 Larry Hisle CO	.25	.07
16 Darrin Jackson	.25	.07
17 Randy Knorr	.25	.07
18 Al Leiter	1.00	.30
19 Domingo Martinez	.25	.07
20 Paul Molitor	1.50	.45
21 Jack Morris	.75	.23
22 John Olerud	1.00	.30
23 Tom Quinlan	.25	.07
24 Dick Schofield	.25	.07
25 Luis Sojo	.25	.07
26 Ed Sprague	.25	.07
27 Dave Stewart	.75	.23
28 Todd Stottlemyre	.50	.15
29 John Sullivan CO	.25	.07
30 Gene Tenace CO	.25	.07
31 Mike Timlin	.50	.15
32 Duane Ward	.25	.07
33 Turner Ward	.25	.07
34 Devon White	.50	.15
35 Eddie Zosky	.25	.07
36 Checklist 1-36	.25	.07

1994 Blue Jays Postcards

This 12-postcard set of Toronto Blue Jays was issued in a cardboard sleeve. Each postcard measures 4" by 6". The postcards are unnumbered and checklisted below in alphabetical order.

	Nm-Mt	Ex-Mt
COMPLETE SET (12)	8.00	2.40
1 Roberto Alomar	2.00	.60
2 Pat Borders	.50	.15
3 Joe Carter	1.50	.45
4 Carlos Delgado	3.00	.90
5 Juan Guzman	.50	.15
6 Paul Molitor	2.50	.75
7 John Olerud	1.50	.45
8 Ed Sprague	.50	.15
9 Devon White	1.00	.30
10 1992, 1993 WS Trophies	.50	.15
11 World Series Rings	.50	.15
12 1993 WS Champions Logo	.50	.15

1994 Blue Jays U.S. Playing Cards

These 56 playing standard-size cards have rounded corners, and feature borderless color posed and action player photos on their fronts. The player's name and position appear near the bottom. The two-tone blue backs carry logos for the Blue Jays, MLB, MLBPA, and Bicycle Sports Collection. The set is checklisted below in playing card order by suits and assigned numbers to aces (1), jacks (11), queens (12), and kings (13).

	Nm-Mt	Ex-Mt
COMP. FACT SET (56)	4.00	1.20
1C John Olerud	.25	.07
1D Roberto Alomar	.40	.12
1H Joe Carter	.30	.09
1S Paul Molitor	.40	.12
2C Al Leiter	.25	.07
2D Eddie Zosky	.05	.02
2H Woody Williams	.10	.03
2S Michael Timlin	.05	.02
3C Dave Stewart	.10	.03
3D Rob Butler	.05	.02
3H Danny Cox	.05	.02
3S Randy Knorr	.05	.02
4C Pat Borders	.05	.02
4D Tony Castillo	.05	.02
4H Todd Stottlemyre	.10	.03
4S Pat Hentgen	.25	.07
5C Devon White	.10	.03
5D Duane Ward	.05	.02
5H Ed Sprague	.05	.02
5S Darnell Coles	.05	.02
6C Joe Carter	.30	.09
6D Paul Molitor	.40	.12
6H John Olerud	.25	.07
6S Juan Guzman	.05	.02
7C Roberto Alomar	.40	.12
7D John Olerud	.25	.07
7H Paul Molitor	.40	.12
7S Roberto Alomar	.40	.12
8C Woody Williams	.10	.03
8D Carlos Delgado	.75	.23
8H Scott Brow	.05	.02
8S Joe Carter	.30	.09
9C Eddie Zosky	.05	.02
9D Michael Timlin	.10	.03
9H Pat Hentgen	.25	.07
9S Scott Brow	.05	.02
10C Willie Canate	.05	.02
10D Randy Knorr	.05	.02
10H Al Leiter	.15	.04
10S Dick Schofield	.05	.02
11C Danny Cox	.05	.02
11D Pat Hentgen	.25	.07
11H Dave Stewart	.10	.03
11S Rob Butler	.05	.02
12C Todd Stottlemyre	.10	.03
12D Darnell Coles	.05	.02
12H Pat Borders	.05	.02
12S Tony Castillo	.05	.02
13C Ed Sprague	.05	.02
13D Juan Guzman	.05	.02
13H Devon White	.10	.03
13S Duane Ward	.05	.02
NNO Featured Players	.05	.02

1995 Blue Jays Becker

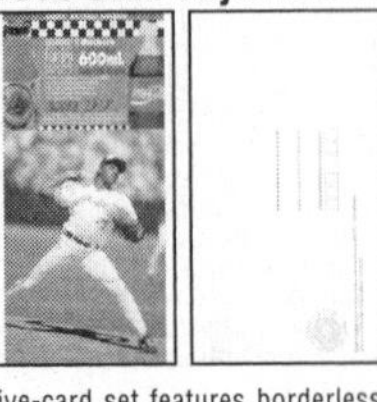

This five-card set features borderless color player photos distributed in a booklet and sponsored by Becker's stores. The backs display a postcard format and player information. The top portion of each page displays a perforated coupon redeemable for a certain food item at participating Becker's stores. The cards are unnumbered and checklisted below according to where they appear in the booklet.

	Nm-Mt	Ex-Mt
COMPLETE SET (5)	10.00	3.00
1 Roberto Alomar	3.00	.90
2 Juan Guzman	1.00	.30
3 Paul Molitor	3.00	.90
4 John Olerud	1.50	.45
5 Joe Carter	2.50	.75

1995 Blue Jays Oh Henry!

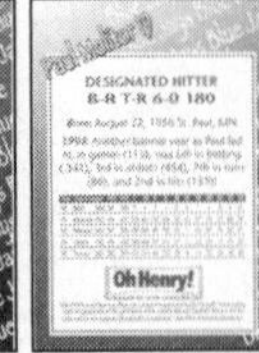

This 36-card set of the Toronto Blue Jays was sponsored by Oh Henry Candy Bars and features color player action photos. The backs carry player information and career statistics. The cards are unnumbered and checklisted below in alphabetical order.

	Nm-Mt	Ex-Mt
COMPLETE SET (36)	12.00	3.60
1 Roberto Alomar	1.50	.45
2 Bob Bailor CO	.25	.07
3 Howard Battle	.25	.07
4 Joe Carter	1.00	.30
5 Tony Castillo	.25	.07
6 Domingo Cedeno	.25	.07
7 Galen Cisco CO	.25	.07
8 David Cone	1.00	.30
9 Brad Cornett	.25	.07
10 Danny Cox	.25	.07
11 Tim Crabtree	.25	.07
12 Carlos Delgado	1.50	.45
13 Cito Gaston MG	.75	.23
14 Alex Gonzalez	.50	.15
15 Shawn Green	2.00	.60
16 Juan Guzman	.25	.07
17 Darren Hall	.25	.07
18 Pat Hentgen	.50	.15
19 Larry Hisle CO	.25	.07
20 Dennis Holmberg CO	.25	.07
21 Michael Huff	.25	.07
22 Randy Knorr	.25	.07
23 Al Leiter	1.00	.30
24 Nick Leyva CO	.25	.07
25 Angel Martinez	.25	.07
26 Paul Molitor	1.50	.45
27 John Olerud	.75	.23
28 Tomas Perez	.25	.07
29 Aaron Small	.25	.07
30 Paul Spoljaric	.25	.07
31 Ed Sprague	.25	.07
32 Gene Tenace CO	.25	.07
33 Mike Timlin	.50	.15
34 Duane Ward	.25	.07
35 Devon White	.50	.15
36 Woody Williams	.50	.15

1995 Blue Jays Postcards

This five-card set of collector postcards comes in a stapled booklet which measures 4" by 8 1/2". The fronts feature borderless color player photos attached by perforation to a sponsor's coupon at the top. After perforation, the postcards measure 4" by 5 1/2".

	Nm-Mt	Ex-Mt
COMPLETE SET (5)	5.00	1.50

1 Roberto Alomar 2.00 .60
2 Joe Carter 1.50 .45
3 Juan Guzman 1.00 .30
4 Paul Molitor 2.00 .60
5 John Olerud 1.50 .45

1995 Blue Jays U.S. Playing Cards

These 56 standard-size playing cards have rounded corners, and feature color player photos on their white-bordered fronts. The player's name and position appear in a red bar near the bottom. The blue and gray backs carry the logos for the Toronto Blue Jays, MLBPA, and Bicycle Sports Collection. The set is checklisted below in playing card order by suits and assigned numbers to aces (1), jacks (11), queens (12), and kings (13).

Nm-Mt Ex-Mt
COMP. FACT SET (56) 5.00 1.50
1C John Olerud .25 .07
1D Joe Carter .30 .09
1H Roberto Alomar .40 .12
1S Paul Molitor .40 .12
2C Pat Hentgen .10 .03
2D Duane Ward .05 .02
2H Candy Maldonado .05 .02
2S Todd Stottlemyre .10 .03
3C Juan Guzman .05 .02
3D Dave Stewart .10 .03
3H Mike Timlin .05 .02
3S Rickey Henderson .75 .23
4C Cecil Fielder .25 .07
4D Tony Fernandez .10 .03
4H Ed Sprague .05 .02
4S Tom Henke .10 .03
5C Roberto Alomar .40 .12
5D Jack Morris .10 .03
5H Pat Borders .05 .02
5S Fred McGriff .40 .12
6C Joe Carter .30 .09
6D Dave Winfield .50 .15
6H Jimmy Key .10 .03
6S Devon White .05 .02
7C Mark Eichhorn .05 .02
7D John Olerud .25 .07
7H Paul Molitor .40 .12
7S Duane Ward .05 .02
8C Carlos Delgado .60 .18
8D Manny Lee .05 .02
8H Candy Maldonado .05 .02
8S David Wells .15 .04
9C Tom Candiotti .05 .02
9D Pat Hentgen .25 .07
9H Danny Cox .05 .02
9S David Cone .25 .07
10C Dave Stewart .10 .03
10D Randy Knorr .05 .02
10H Todd Stottlemyre .10 .03
10S Mike Timlin .10 .03
11C Tony Fernandez .15 .04
11D Juan Guzman .05 .02
11H Rickey Henderson .75 .23
11S Ed Sprague .05 .02
12C Pat Borders .05 .02
12D Fred McGriff .40 .12
12H Tom Henke .10 .03
12S Jack Morris .30 .09
13C Dave Winfield .50 .15
13D Devon White .05 .02
13H Cecil Fielder .25 .07
13S Jimmy Key .25 .07
NNO Title Card .05 .02
NNO Team Logo .05 .02
NNO Team Name .05 .02
NNO Featured players .05 .02

1996 Blue Jays Becker

This five-card set features borderless color action player photos distributed in a booklet and sponsored by Becker's stores. The backs display a postcard format and player information. The last two pages of the booklet carry perforated coupons redeemable for certain food items at participating Becker's stores. The cards are unnumbered and checklisted below according to where they appear in the booklet.

Nm-Mt Ex-Mt
COMPLETE SET (5) 8.00 2.40
1 Alfredo Griffin 1.00 .30
2 Jesse Barfield 2.00 .60
3 George Bell 2.00 .60
4 Kelly Gruber 1.50 .45
5 Dave Stieb 1.50 .45

1996 Blue Jays Bookmarks

This six-card set of the Toronto Blue Jays measures approximately 2 1/2" by 6 1/4". One side features a color player portrait with personal statistics in English and a facsimile autograph. The other side displays color action player photos with personal statistics in French and a facsimile autograph. The cards are unnumbered and checklisted below in alphabetical order.

Nm-Mt Ex-Mt
COMPLETE SET (6) 5.00 1.50
1 Joe Carter 1.50 .45
2 Pat Hentgen 1.00 .30
3 Otis Nixon .25 .07
4 John Olerud .75 .23
5 Ed Sprague .25 .07
6 Woody Williams .50 .15

1996 Blue Jays Oh Henry!

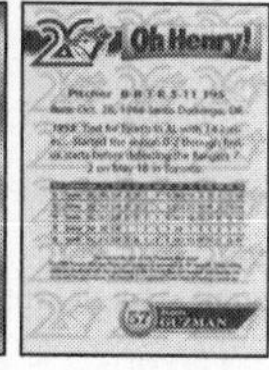

This 36-card set commemorates the 20th anniversary of the Toronto Blue Jays and features color player photos with player information and statistics on the backs.

Nm-Mt Ex-Mt
COMPLETE SET (36) 12.00 3.60
1 George Bell .75 .23
2 Brian Bohanon .25 .07
3 Joe Carter 1.25 .35
4 Tony Castillo .25 .07
5 Domingo Cedeno .25 .07
6 Tim Crabtree .25 .07
7 Felipe Crespo .25 .07
8 Carlos Delgado 1.50 .45
9 Cito Gaston MG .25 .07
10 Alex Gonzalez .50 .15
11 Shawn Green 2.00 .60
12 Alfredo Griffin CO .25 .07
13 Kelly Gruber .50 .15
14 Juan Guzman .25 .07
15 Erik Hanson .25 .07
16 Pat Hentgen .50 .15
17 Marty Janzen .25 .07
18 Nick Leyva CO .25 .07
19 Sandy Martinez .25 .07
20 Lloyd Moseby .50 .15
21 Otis Nixon .25 .07
22 Charlie O'Brien .25 .07
23 John Olerud 1.00 .30
24 Robert Perez .25 .07
25 Mel Queen CO .25 .07
26 Paul Quantrill .75 .23
27 Bill Risley .25 .07
28 Juan Samuel .25 .07
29 Ed Sprague .25 .07
30 Dave Stieb .75 .23
31 Gene Tenace CO .25 .07
32 Mike Timlin .50 .15
33 Willie Upshaw CO .25 .07
34 Jeff Ware .25 .07
35 Ernie Whitt .50 .15
36 Woody Williams .50 .15

1997 Blue Jays Bookmarks

This 12-card set of the Toronto Blue Jays measures approximately 2 7/16" by 6 1/4". One side features a color player portrait with personal statistics in English and a facsimile autograph. The other side displays the same color portrait with personal statistics in French and a facsimile autograph. The cards are unnumbered and checklisted below in alphabetical order.

Nm-Mt Ex-Mt
COMPLETE SET (12) 15.00 4.50
1 Joe Carter 2.00 .60
2 Roger Clemens 5.00 1.50
3 Tim Crabtree 1.00 .30
4 Cito Gaston MG 1.50 .45
5 Alex Gonzalez 1.50 .45
6 Shawn Green 3.00 .90
7 Juan Guzman 1.00 .30
8 Pat Hentgen 1.50 .45
9 Otis Nixon 1.00 .30
10 Charlie O'Brien 1.00 .30
11 Benito Santiago 2.00 .60
12 Mike Timlin 1.50 .45

1997 Blue Jays Cash Converters

This one-card set was distributed by the Toronto Blue Jays and displays color photos of four Blue Jays pitchers on a blue "K" and solid red background. The back displays an advertisement for the "K for Kids" program sponsored by Cash Converters.

Nm-Mt Ex-Mt
1 Juan Guzman 3.00 .90
Erik Hansen
Roger Clemens
Pat Hentgen

1997 Blue Jays Copi Quik Interleague

This one-card set was sponsored by Copi Quik and commemorates the Inaugural interleague play games between the Toronto Blue Jays and the Philadelphia Phillies at Veterans Stadium on June 13-15, 1997. The front features an action image of Roger Clemens on a blue background. The back displays information about the player and the interleague games. Only 7,000 of this card were printed and are sequentially numbered.

Nm-Mt Ex-Mt
1 Roger Clemens 5.00 1.50

1997 Blue Jays Jackie Robinson

This one-card set commemorates the 50th anniversary of Jackie Robinson becoming the first man to cross Major League Baseball's race barrier. The front features a sepia tone player portrait with a thin black inner border and a wider blue outer border. The back displays player information below a statement by Brooklyn Dodgers owner Branch Rickey about Jackie Robinson.

Nm-Mt Ex-Mt
1 Jackie Robinson 5.00 1.50

1997 Blue Jays Oh Henry!

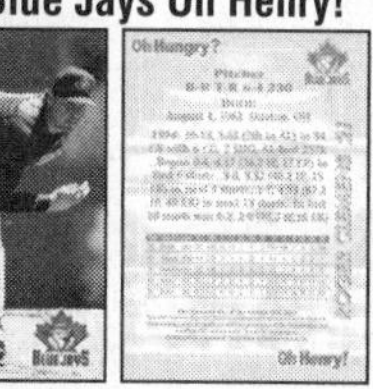

This 36-card set of the Toronto Blue Jays was sponsored by Oh Henry Candy Bars and features color player action photos. The backs carry player information and career statistics.

Nm-Mt Ex-Mt
COMPLETE SET (36) 12.00 3.60
1 Luis Andujar .25 .07
2 Tilson Brito .25 .07
3 Jacob Brumfield .25 .07
4 Joe Carter 1.00 .30
5 Roger Clemens 2.50 .75
6 Tim Crabtree .25 .07
7 Felipe Crespo .25 .07
8 Carlos Delgado 1.25 .35
9 Carlos Garcia .25 .07
10 Cito Gaston MG .50 .15
11 Alex Gonzalez .50 .15
12 Shawn Green 1.50 .45
13 Alfredo Griffin CO .25 .07
14 Juan Guzman .25 .07
15 Erik Hanson .25 .07
16 Pat Hentgen 1.00 .30
17 Jim Lett CO .25 .07
18 Nick Leyva CO .25 .07
19 Orlando Merced .25 .07
20 Otis Nixon .25 .07
21 Charlie O'Brien .25 .07
22 Robert Perez .25 .07
23 Robert Person .25 .07
24 Dan Plesac .25 .07
25 Paul Quantrill .50 .15
26 Mel Queen CO .25 .07
27 Bill Risley .25 .07
28 Juan Samuel .25 .07
29 Benito Santiago .50 .15
30 Paul Spoljaric .25 .07
31 Ed Sprague .25 .07
32 Shannon Stewart 1.00 .30
33 Gene Tenace CO .25 .07
34 Mike Timlin .50 .15
35 Willie Upshaw CO .25 .07
36 Woody Williams .50 .15

1997 Blue Jays Sizzler

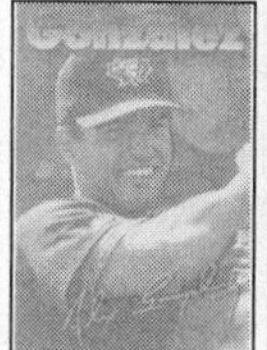
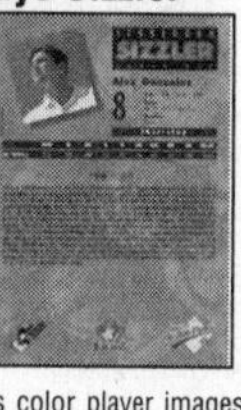

This 60-card set features color player images on various colored borderless backgrounds with faint baseball images. A facsimile gold autograph is printed across the bottom of the front. The backs carry a small player photo with player information and statistics. Cards numbered 32-50 display "Magic Moments" in the team's history. For $19.95, the collector could obtain a black "Pleather" album with archival-approved sleeves to keep the cards in.

Nm-Mt Ex-Mt
COMPLETE SET (60) 25.00 7.50
1 Alex Gonzalez .50 .15
2 Pat Hentgen 1.00 .30
3 Joe Carter 1.00 .30
4 Ed Sprague .25 .07
5 Benito Santiago .75 .23
6 Roger Clemens 5.00 1.50
7 Carlos Garcia .25 .07
8 Juan Guzman .25 .07
9 Dan Plesac .25 .07
10 Carlos Delgado 1.50 .45
11 Orlando Merced .25 .07
12 Woody Williams .50 .15
13 Shawn Green 2.00 .60
14 Erik Hanson .25 .07
15 Charlie O'Brien .25 .07
16 Otis Nixon .25 .07
17 Paul Spoljaric .25 .07
18 Jacob Brumfield .25 .07
19 Mike Timlin .50 .15
20 Tilson Brito .25 .07
21 Paul Quantrill .50 .15
22 Tim Crabtree .25 .07
23 Jim Lett .25 .07
24 Cito Gaston MG .50 .15
25 Alfredo Griffin CO .25 .07
26 Nick Leyva CO .25 .07
27 Mel Queen CO .25 .07
28 Gene Tenace CO .25 .07
29 Willie Upshaw CO .25 .07
30 Pat Hentgen .50 .15
31 Roger Clemens 2.50 .75
32 First Pitch '77 .25 .07
33 Dave Stieb's No Hitter .25 .07
34 George Bell .25 .07
Lloyd Moseby
Jesse Barfield
35 1992 World Series .25 .07
36 1985 Pennant Win .25 .07
37 Paul Molitor 1.50 .45
38 Tom Henke .25 .07
Duane Ward
39 Ernie Whitt .50 .15
40 Joe Carter 1.00 .30
Home Run, 1993
41 Jack Morris .75 .23
42 Pat Borders .25 .07
43 Dave Winfield 1.25 .35
44 Damaso Garcia .25 .07
45 Tony Fernandez .50 .15
46 Roberto Alomar 1.25 .35
47 Dave Stewart .50 .15
48 John Olerud .75 .23
Paul Molitor
Roberto Alomar
49 Fred McGriff 1.25 .35
50 Kelly Gruber .25 .07
51 Alex Gonzalez .50 .15
52 Huck Flener .25 .07
53 Marty Janzen .25 .07
54 Sandy Martinez .25 .07
55 Felipe Crespo .25 .07
56 Tomas Perez .25 .07
57 Shannon Stewart 1.25 .35
58 Billy Koch 1.00 .30
59 Roy Halladay 3.00 .90
60 Chris Carpenter .50 .15

1997 Blue Jays Sun

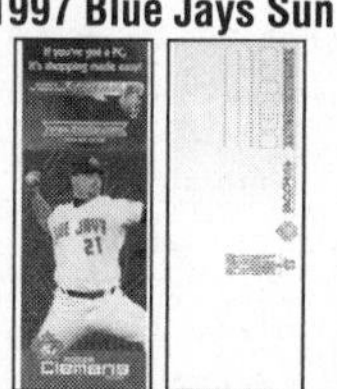

This nine-card set was used to commemorate "Designated Driver Day at SkyDome." The fronts feature color action player photos printed on cards measuring approximately 3" by 8". The top section of the card is perforated and contains sponsor advertisements. A contest entry card was enclosed to be returned with a new slogan for the next "Designated Driver Day" and a chance to win two tickets to the Toronto Blue Jays Skybox for that day. The cards are unnumbered and checklisted below in alphabetical order.

Nm-Mt Ex-Mt
COMPLETE SET (8) 15.00 4.50
1 Title Card 1.00 .30
2 Joe Carter 2.00 .60
3 Roger Clemens 4.00 1.20
4 Carlos Delgado 3.00 .90
5 Alex Gonzalez 1.50 .45
6 Pat Hentgen 2.50 .75
7 Otis Nixon 1.00 .30
8 Charlie O'Brien 1.00 .30
9 Ed Sprague 1.00 .30

1998 Blue Jays Labatt

These five color 4" by 6" cards feature members of the Toronto Blue Jays. The backs feature a post card back along with a safety tip

Nm-Mt Ex-Mt
COMPLETE SET (5) 10.00 3.00
1 Jose Cruz Jr. 2.00 .60
Shawn Green
Shannon Stewart
2 Carlos Delgado 3.00 .90
3 Alex Gonzalez 1.00 .30
4 Roger Clemens 3.00 .90
Pat Hentgen
5 Set Montage 1.50 .45

2002 Blue Jays Team Issue

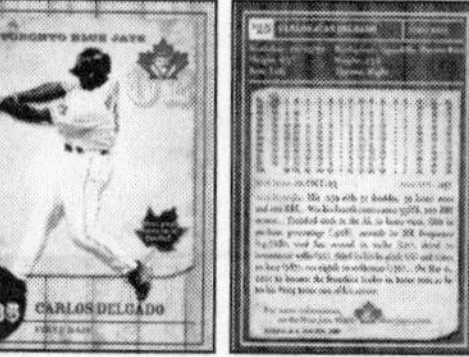

This standard-size set was given away at just one Toronto Blue Jay game this year. The fronts have the player photo set against a wall-like background. The player's name and position in on the bottom of the card with their uniform number in the left corner. The back has biographical information along with seasonal and career stats to go with a brief biography. Since these cards are unnumbered, we have sequenced them in alphabetical order. In addition, four figures from the 1992 World Champs are honored with alumni cards.

Nm-Mt Ex-Mt
COMPLETE SET 10.00 3.00
1 Mike Barnett CO .25 .07
2 Dave Berg .25 .07
3 Brian Butterfield CO .25 .07
4 Chris Carpenter .25 .07
5 Scott Cassidy .25 .07
6 Jose Cruz Jr. .50 .15
7 Carlos Delgado 1.50 .45
8 Kelvim Escobar .75 .23
9 Scott Eyre .25 .07
10 Darrin Fletcher .25 .07
11 Cito Gaston ALUM MG .50 .15
12 John Gibbons .25 .07
13 Roy Halladay 1.25 .35
14 Tom Henke .75 .23
15 Felix Heredia .25 .07
16 Eric Hinske 1.25 .35
17 Ken Huckaby .25 .07
18 Joe Lawrence .75 .23
19 Esteban Loaiza .75 .23
20 Felipe Lopez .75 .23
21 Jack Morris .75 .23
22 Steve Parris .25 .07
23 Gil Patterson .25 .07
24 Cliff Politte .25 .07
25 Luke Prokopec .25 .07
26 Shannon Stewart 1.00 .30
27 Corey Thurman .50 .15
28 Carlos Tosca .25 .07
29 Pete Walker .25 .07
30 Bruce Walton .25 .07
31 Vernon Wells 1.25 .35
32 Devon White .50 .15
33 Tom Wilson .25 .07
34 Chris Woodward .25 .07

1948-49 Blue Tint R346

The cards in this 48-card set measure 2" by 2 5/8". The "Blue Tint" set derives its name from its distinctive coloration. Collector Ralph Triplette has pointed out in his research that the set was issued during 1948 and 1949, not in 1947 as had been previously commonly thought. The cards are blank-backed and unnumbered, and were issued in strips of six or eight. The set was probably produced in Brooklyn and hence has a heavy emphasis on New York teams, especially the Yankees. Known variations are No. 2, Durocher, listed with Brooklyn or New York Giants, and No. 18, Ott, listed with Giants or no team designation. The set was initially listed in the catalog as R346 as well as being listed as W518. Although the W categorization is undoubtedly the more correct, nevertheless, the R listing has become the popularly referenced designation for the set. The complete set price below includes all listed variations. Numbers 41 through 48 exist with or without numbers on the front.

NM Ex
COMPLETE SET 1200.00 600.00
1 Bill Johnson 10.00 5.00
2A Leo Durocher 20.00 10.00
(Brooklyn Dodgers)
2B Leo Durocher 20.00 10.00
(New York Giants)
3 Marty Marion 12.00 6.00
4 Ewell Blackwell 12.00 6.00
5 John Lindell 10.00 5.00
6 Larry Jansen 10.00 5.00
7 Ralph Kiner 20.00 10.00
8 Chuck Dressen CO 12.00 6.00
9 Bobby Brown 12.00 6.00
10 Luke Appling 20.00 10.00
11 Bill Nicholson 12.00 6.00

12 Phil Masi	10.00	5.00
13 Frank Shea	10.00	5.00
14 Bob Dillinger	10.00	5.00
15 Pete Suder	10.00	5.00
16 Joe DiMaggio	200.00	100.00
17 John Corriden CO	10.00	5.00
18A Mel Ott MG (New York Giants)	40.00	20.00
18B Mel Ott (no team designation)	40.00	20.00
19 Warren Rosar	10.00	5.00
20 Warren Spahn	25.00	12.50
21 Allie Reynolds	12.00	6.00
22 Lou Boudreau	20.00	10.00
23 Hank Majeski (photo actually Randy Gumpert)	10.00	5.00
24 Frank Crosetti	15.00	7.50
25 Gus Niarhos	10.00	5.00
26 Bruce Edwards	10.00	5.00
27 Rudy York	10.00	5.00
28 Don Black	10.00	5.00
29 Lou Gehrig	200.00	100.00
30 Johnny Mize	20.00	10.00
31 Ed Stanky	12.00	6.00
32 Vic Raschi	12.00	6.00
33 Cliff Mapes	10.00	5.00
34 Enos Slaughter	20.00	10.00
35 Hank Greenberg	20.00	10.00
36 Jackie Robinson	120.00	60.00
37 Frank Hiller	10.00	5.00
38 Bob Elliott	12.00	6.00
39 Harry Walker	10.00	5.00
40 Ed Lopat	15.00	7.50
41 Bobby Thomson	15.00	7.50
42 Tommy Henrich	12.00	6.00
43 Bobby Feller	50.00	25.00
44 Ted Williams	150.00	75.00
45 Dixie Walker	12.00	6.00
46 Johnny Vander Meer	12.00	6.00
47 Clint Hartung	10.00	5.00
48 Charlie Keller	12.00	6.00

1929 Blum's Baseball Bulletin

These black-backed photos, which measure 9 1/2" by 13 5/8" feature leading players of the past and present. The players photo is on the top with his name and brief biography on the bottom. The Groh card measure 11 1/2" by 13 3/4". Since these are unnumbered, we have sequenced them in alphabetical order.

	Ex-Mt	VG
COMPLETE SET	1200.00	600.00
1 Eddie Collins	300.00	150.00
2 Jake Daubert	100.00	50.00
3 Heinie Groh	100.00	50.00
4 Nap Lajoie	300.00	150.00
5 Rabbit Maranville	250.00	125.00
6 Tris Speaker	300.00	150.00

1987 Boardwalk and Baseball

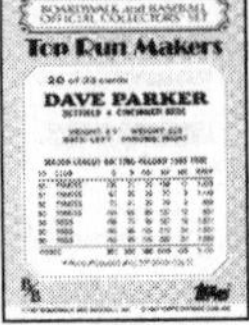

This 33-card standard-size set was produced by Topps for distribution by the "Boardwalk and Baseball" Theme Park which was located in Haines City, Florida. The set comes in a custom blue collector box. The full-color fronts are surrounded by a pink and black frame border. The card backs are printed in pink and black on white card stock. The set is subtitled "Top Run Makers." Hence no pitchers are included in the set. The checklist for the set is given on the back panel of the box.

	Nm-Mt	Ex-Mt
COMP. FACT. SET (33)	5.00	2.00
1 Mike Schmidt	.50	.20
2 Eddie Murray	.50	.20
3 Dale Murphy	.40	.16
4 Dave Winfield	.30	.12
5 Jim Rice	.10	.04
6 Cecil Cooper	.05	.02
7 Dwight Evans	.05	.02
8 Rickey Henderson	1.00	.40
9 Robin Yount	.30	.12
10 Andre Dawson	.30	.12
11 Gary Carter	.20	.08
12 Keith Hernandez	.10	.04
13 George Brett	1.25	.50
14 Bill Buckner	.05	.02
15 Tony Armas	.05	.02
16 Harold Baines	.20	.08
17 Don Baylor	.10	.04
18 Steve Garvey	.20	.08
19 Lance Parrish	.10	.04
20 Dave Parker	.10	.04
21 Buddy Bell	.05	.02
22 Cal Ripken	2.50	1.00
23 Bob Horner	.05	.02
24 Tim Raines	.10	.04
25 Jack Clark	.05	.02
26 Leon Durham	.05	.02
27 Pedro Guerrero	.05	.02
28 Kent Hrbek	.05	.02
29 Kirk Gibson	.10	.04
30 Ryne Sandberg	1.25	.50
31 Wade Boggs	.60	.24
32 Don Mattingly	1.25	.50
33 Darryl Strawberry	.10	.04

1984 Boggs Dental Group

This one card set, which measures 8 1/2" by 5 1/2" features on the front information about two dentists four offices in Connecticut as well as a color photo of Wade Boggs. The back of this

card is a promotion for these dentist fourth office they opened.

	Nm-Mt	Ex-Mt
1 Wade Boggs	5.00	2.00

2003 Bonds SBC

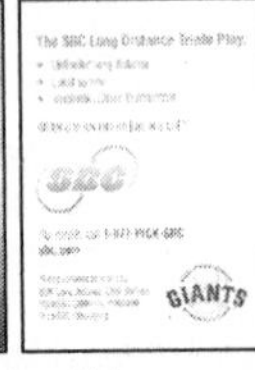

This one card set, which measures approximately 2 1/2" by 3 1/2" was issued to promote SBC Communications and featured all-time great Barry Bonds. The front has an action photo of bonds with the year 2003 on the left and the player's name on the right with his uniform number on the bottom. The back has information about how one can sign up with SBC communications

	MINT	NRMT
1 Barry Bonds	5.00	2.20

1973-02 Book Promotional Cards

This set features various cards used to promote baseball books. We have sequenced them in year order. Cards number two through number 13 all were used to promote "Who was Harry Steinfeldt? and other baseball trivia.". All of these cards measure the standard size. We are not using a complete set price for this set because of the vide variance in years and availability of how these cards were released.

	NM	Ex
1 Bo Belinsky 1973 Pitching and Wooing	5.00	2.00
2 Frank Baumholtz	3.00	1.20
3 Jim Bouton	5.00	2.00
4 Tony Conigliaro	5.00	2.00
5 Don Drysdale	10.00	4.00
6 Hank Greenberg	10.00	4.00
7 Walter Johnson	15.00	6.00
8 Billy Loes	3.00	1.20
9 Johnny Mize	10.00	4.00
10 Lefty O'Doul	5.00	2.00
11 Babe Ruth	25.00	10.00
12 Johnny Sain	5.00	2.00
13 Jim Thorpe	20.00	8.00
14 Jim Bouton 1979 Ball Four Plus Ball Five	3.00	1.20
15 Billy Martin 1980 Number One	5.00	2.00
16 Mickey Mantle 1986 The Mick	10.00	4.00
17 Gary Carter 1987 A Dream Season	4.00	1.60
17 Babe Ruth 1988 Babe Ruth's Book of Baseball Audio Cassette	5.00	2.00
18 Nolan Ryan 1988 Throwing Heat	10.00	4.00
19 Orel Hershiser 1989 Out of the Blue	3.00	1.20
20 Gil Hodges 1992 The Quiet Man	5.00	2.00
21 Joe Morgan 1993 A Life in Baseball	3.00	1.20
22 Jim Bouton 1994 Strike Zone	2.00	.80
23 Eliot Asinof 1994 Strike Zone	2.00	.80
24 Charles Lupica 1997 The Cleveland Indians Flagpole Sitter	1.00	.40
25 Joe Dittmar 1999 Baseball Records Registry Postcard features Randy Johnson	2.00	.80
26 Big Book of Jewish Baseball 2001 Sandy Koufax Pictured	1.00	.40
27 The Big Book of Jewish Baseball Uncut Sheet Sandy Koufax Lipman Pike Moe Berg Jesse Levis Harry Shuman Hank Greenberg Harry Danning Cy Malis Hy Cohen	10.00	4.00
28 Lou Gehrig Breaking the Slump 2002	1.00	.40
29 Babe Ruth Breaking the Slump 2002	1.00	.40
30 Hack Wilson Rogers Hornsby Breaking the Slump 2002	1.00	.40

1912 Boston Garter

These oversize gorgeous full color cards from the early part of the 20th century feature some of the leading players in the game. The front shows a drawing of the player along with a suitcase showing who they are. In the background one can see some ball field activities. The Back lists details about how to use these cards to promote a storefront as well as a checklist on the back.

	Ex-Mt	VG
COMPLETE SET (16)	140000.00	70000.00
1 Bob Bescher	6000.00	3000.00
2 Roger Breshnahan	10000.00	5000.00
3 Frank Chance	12000.00	6000.00
4 Hal Chase	8000.00	4000.00
5 Fred Clarke	12000.00	6000.00
6 Eddie Collins	12000.00	6000.00
7 Red Dooin	6000.00	3000.00
8 Hugh Jennings MG	10000.00	5000.00
9 Walter Johnson	18000.00	9000.00
10 Johnny Kling	6000.00	3000.00
11 Larry Lajoie	12000.00	6000.00
12 Frank LaPorte	6000.00	3000.00
13 Christy Mathewson	18000.00	9000.00
14 Nap Rucker	8000.00	4000.00
15 Tris Speaker	12000.00	6000.00
16 Ed Walsh	12000.00	6000.00

1913 Boston Garter

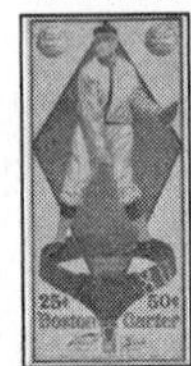

This 12 card oversize set features some of the leading players of the 1910's. These cards were issued free to retailers who sold the "Boston Garter" products. The front of the cards have a player photo in a "diamond" with the words "Boston Garter" written on baseballs located at the top. On the bottom are the words 25 and 50 cents as well as the design of the Boston Garter. The back gives career information about the player as well as has a checklist of the cards.

	Ex-Mt	VG
COMPLETE SET (10)	70000.00	35000.00
1 Tris Speaker	8000.00	4000.00
2 Ty Cobb	12000.00	6000.00
3 Burt Shotton Sic, Shotten	3000.00	1500.00
4 Joe Tinker	6000.00	3000.00
5 Johnny Evers	6000.00	3000.00
6 Joe Jackson	15000.00	7500.00
7 Rabbit Maranville	5000.00	2500.00
8 Larry Doyle	4000.00	2000.00
9 Frank Baker	5000.00	2500.00
10 Ed Konetchy	3000.00	1500.00
11 Walter Johnson	10000.00	5000.00
12 Buck Herzog	3000.00	1500.00

1914 Boston Garter

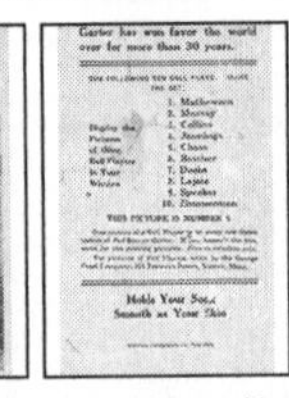

This ten card white bordered set has a black and white portrait on the front with the players name and the Boston Garter logo in a baseball on the bottom. The back has information about the Boston Garter product along with a checklist and information on how to acquire these photos.

	Ex-Mt	VG
COMPLETE SET (10)	35000.00	17500.00
1 Christy Mathewson	6000.00	3000.00
2 Red Murray	2500.00	1250.00
3 Eddie Collins	5000.00	2500.00
4 Hugh Jennings MG	4000.00	2000.00
5 Hal Chase	3000.00	1500.00
6 Bob Bescher	2500.00	1250.00
7 Red Dooin	2500.00	1250.00
8 Nap Lajoie	5000.00	2500.00
9 Tris Speaker	6000.00	3000.00
10 Henie Zimmerman	2500.00	1250.00

1948 Bowman

The 48-card Bowman set of 1948 was the first major set of the post-war period. Each 2 1/16" by 2 1/2" card had a black and white photo of a current player, with his biographical information printed in black ink on a gray back.

Due to the printing process and the 36-card sheet size upon which Bowman was then printing, the 12 cards marked with an SP in the checklist are scarcer numerically, as they were removed from the printing sheet in order to make room for the 12 high numbers (37-48). Cards were issued in one-card penny packs. Many cards are found with over-printed, transposed, or blank backs. The set features the Rookie Cards of Hall of Famers Yogi Berra, Ralph Kiner, Stan Musial, Red Schoendienst, and Warren Spahn. Half of the cards in the set feature New York players (Yankees or Giants).

	NM	Ex
COMPLETE SET (48)	3600.00	1800.00
COMMON CARD (1-36)	20.00	10.00
COMMON CARD (37-48)	30.00	15.00
WRAPPER (5-CENT)	700.00	350.00
WRAPPER (1-CENT)		
1 Bob Elliott RC	125.00	19.00
2 Ewell Blackwell RC	60.00	30.00
3 Ralph Kiner RC	150.00	75.00
4 Johnny Mize RC	125.00	60.00
5 Bob Feller RC	250.00	125.00
6 Yogi Berra RC	500.00	250.00
7 Pete Reiser SP	125.00	60.00
8 Phil Rizzuto SP RC	350.00	180.00
9 Walker Cooper RC	20.00	10.00
10 Buddy Rosar	20.00	10.00
11 Johnny Lindell	25.00	12.50
12 Johnny Sain RC	80.00	40.00
13 Willard Marshall SP	40.00	20.00
14 Allie Reynolds RC	60.00	30.00
15 Eddie Joost	20.00	10.00
16 Jack Lohrke SP	40.00	20.00
17 Enos Slaughter RC	100.00	50.00
18 Warren Spahn RC	300.00	150.00
19 Tommy Henrich	60.00	30.00
20 Buddy Kerr SP	40.00	20.00
21 Ferris Fain RC	40.00	20.00
22 Floyd Bevens SP RC	50.00	25.00
23 Larry Jansen RC	25.00	12.50
24 Dutch Leonard SP	40.00	20.00
25 Barney McCosky	20.00	10.00
26 Frank Shea SP RC	50.00	25.00
27 Sid Gordon RC	25.00	12.50
28 Emil Verban SP	40.00	20.00
29 Joe Page SP RC	80.00	40.00
30 W.Lockman SP RC	50.00	25.00
31 Bill McCahan	20.00	10.00
32 Bill Rigney RC	20.00	10.00
33 Bill Johnson	25.00	12.50
34 Sheldon Jones SP	40.00	20.00
35 Snuffy Stirnweiss RC	40.00	20.00
36 Stan Musial RC	800.00	400.00
37 Clint Hartung RC	30.00	15.00
38 Red Schoendienst RC	200.00	100.00
39 Augie Galan	30.00	15.00
40 Marty Marion RC	80.00	40.00
41 Rex Barney RC	60.00	30.00
42 Ray Poat	30.00	15.00
43 Bruce Edwards	40.00	20.00
44 Johnny Wyrostek	30.00	15.00
45 Hank Sauer RC	60.00	30.00
46 Herman Wehmeier	30.00	15.00
47 Bobby Thomson RC	100.00	50.00
48 Dave Koslo RC	80.00	19.50

1949 Bowman

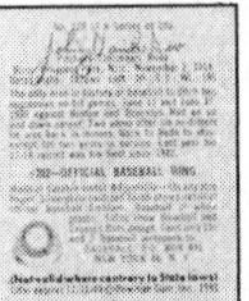

The cards in this 240-card set measure approximately 2 1/16" by 2 1/2". In 1949 Bowman took an intermediate step between black and white and full color with this set of tinted photos on colored backgrounds. Collectors should note the series price variations, which reflect some inconsistencies in the printing process. There are four major varieties in name printing, which are noted in the checklist below: NOF: name on front; NNOF: no name on front; PR: printed name on back; and SCR: script name on back. Cards were issued in five cent nickel packs. These variations resulted when Bowman used twelve of the lower numbers to fill out the last press sheet of 36 cards, adding to numbers 217-240. Cards 1-3 and 5-73 can be found with either gray or white backs. Certain cards have been seen with a "gray" or "slate" background on the front. These cards are a result of a color printing error and are rarely seen on the secondary market so no value is established for them. Not all numbers are known to exist in this fashion. However, within the numbers between 75 and 107, slightly more of these cards have appeared on the market. Within the high numbers series (145-240), these cards have been seen but the appearance of these cards are very rare. Other cards are known to be extant with double printed backs. The set features the Rookie Cards of Hall of Famers Roy Campanella, Bob Lemon, Robin Roberts, Duke Snider, and Early Wynn as well as Rookie Cards of Richie Ashburn and Gil Hodges.

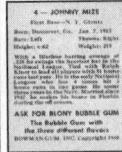

	NM	Ex
COMP. MASTER SET (252)	16000.00	8000.00
COMPLETE SET (240)	15000.00	7500.00
COMMON CARD (1-144)	15.00	7.50
COMMON (145-240)	50.00	25.00
WRAPPER (1-CENT,Rd,Wh,Bl)		
WRAP.(5-CENT,GREEN)	250.00	125.00
WRAP.(5-CENT,BLUE)	200.00	100.00
1 Vern Bickford RC	125.00	25.00
2 Whitey Lockman	40.00	20.00
3 Bob Porterfield	15.00	7.50
4A Jerry Priddy NNOF	15.00	7.50
4B Jerry Priddy NOF	50.00	25.00
5 Hank Sauer	40.00	20.00
6 Phil Cavarretta	40.00	20.00
7 Joe Dobson	15.00	7.50
8 Murry Dickson	15.00	7.50
9 Ferris Fain	40.00	20.00
10 Ted Gray	15.00	7.50
11 Lou Boudreau	80.00	40.00
12 Cass Michaels	15.00	7.50
13 Bob Chesnes	15.00	7.50
14 Curt Simmons RC	40.00	20.00
15 Ned Garver	15.00	7.50
16 Al Kozar	15.00	7.50
17 Earl Torgeson	15.00	7.50
18 Bobby Thomson	40.00	20.00
19 Bobby Brown RC	60.00	30.00
20 Gene Hermanski	15.00	7.50
21 Frank Baumholtz	25.00	12.50
22 Peanuts Lowrey	15.00	7.50
23 Bobby Doerr	80.00	40.00
24 Stan Musial	600.00	300.00
25 Carl Scheib	15.00	7.50
26 George Kell RC	80.00	40.00
27 Bob Feller	300.00	150.00
28 Don Kolloway	15.00	7.50
29 Ralph Kiner	125.00	60.00
30 Andy Seminick	40.00	20.00
31 Dick Kokos	15.00	7.50
32 Eddie Yost RC	60.00	30.00
33 Warren Spahn	200.00	100.00
34 Dave Koslo	15.00	7.50
35 Vic Raschi RC	60.00	30.00
36 Pee Wee Reese	200.00	100.00
37 Johnny Wyrostek	15.00	7.50
38 Emil Verban	15.00	7.50
39 Billy Goodman	25.00	12.50
40 George Munger	15.00	7.50
41 Lou Brissie	15.00	7.50
42 Hoot Evers	15.00	7.50
43 Dale Mitchell RC	40.00	20.00
44 Dave Philley	15.00	7.50
45 Wally Westlake	15.00	7.50
46 Robin Roberts RC	250.00	125.00
47 Johnny Sain	60.00	30.00
48 Willard Marshall	15.00	7.50
49 Frank Shea	25.00	12.50
50 Jackie Robinson RC	1200.00	600.00
51 Herman Wehmeier	15.00	7.50
52 Johnny Schmitz	15.00	7.50
53 Jack Kramer	15.00	7.50
54 Marty Marion	60.00	30.00
55 Eddie Joost	15.00	7.50
56 Pat Mullin	15.00	7.50
57 Gene Bearden	40.00	20.00
58 Bob Elliott	40.00	20.00
59 Jack Lohrke	15.00	7.50
60 Yogi Berra	300.00	150.00
61 Rex Barney	40.00	20.00
62 Grady Hatton	15.00	7.50
63 Andy Pafko	40.00	20.00
64 Dom DiMaggio	60.00	30.00
65 Enos Slaughter	80.00	40.00
66 Elmer Valo	15.00	7.50
67 Alvin Dark RC	40.00	20.00
68 Sheldon Jones	15.00	7.50
69 Tommy Henrich	40.00	20.00
70 Carl Furillo RC	125.00	60.00
71 Vern Stephens	15.00	7.50
72 Tommy Holmes	40.00	20.00
73 Billy Cox RC	40.00	20.00
74 Tom McBride	15.00	7.50
75 Eddie Mayo	15.00	7.50
76 Bill Nicholson RC	25.00	12.50
77 Ernie Bonham	15.00	7.50
78A Sam Zoldak NNOF	15.00	7.50
78B Sam Zoldak NOF	50.00	25.00
79 Ron Northey	15.00	7.50
80 Bill McCahan	15.00	7.50
81 Virgil Stallcup	15.00	7.50
82 Joe Page	60.00	30.00
83A Bob Scheffing NNOF	15.00	7.50
83B Bob Scheffing NOF	50.00	25.00
84 Roy Campanella RC	800.00	400.00
85A Johnny Mize NNOF	100.00	50.00
85B Johnny Mize NOF	150.00	75.00
86 Johnny Pesky	60.00	30.00
87 Randy Gumpert	15.00	7.50
88A Bill Salkeld NNOF	15.00	7.50
88B Bill Salkeld NOF	50.00	25.00
89 Mizell Platt	15.00	7.50
90 Gil Coan	15.00	7.50
91 Dick Wakefield	15.00	7.50
92 Willie Jones	40.00	20.00
93 Ed Stevens	15.00	7.50
94 Mickey Vernon RC	40.00	20.00
95 Howie Pollet RC	15.00	7.50
96 Taft Wright	15.00	7.50
97 Danny Litwhiler	15.00	7.50
98A Phil Rizzuto NNOF	200.00	100.00
98B Phil Rizzuto NOF	250.00	125.00
99 Frank Gustine	15.00	7.50
100 Gil Hodges RC	250.00	125.00
101 Sid Gordon	15.00	7.50
102 Stan Spence	15.00	7.50
103 Joe Tipton	15.00	7.50
104 Eddie Stanky RC	40.00	20.00
105 Bill Kennedy	15.00	7.50
106 Jake Early	15.00	7.50
107 Eddie Lake	15.00	7.50
108 Ken Heintzelman	15.00	7.50
109A Ed Fitzgerald SCR	15.00	7.50
109B Ed Fitzgerald PR	60.00	30.00
110 Early Wynn RC	150.00	75.00
111 Red Schoendienst	100.00	50.00
112 Sam Chapman	40.00	20.00
113 Ray LaManno	15.00	7.50
114 Allie Reynolds	60.00	30.00
115 Dutch Leonard	15.00	7.50
116 Joe Hatton	15.00	7.50
117 Walker Cooper	15.00	7.50
118 Sam Mele	15.00	7.50
119 Floyd Baker	15.00	7.50
120 Cliff Fannin	15.00	7.50

121 Mark Christman 15.00 7.50
122 George Vico 15.00 7.50
123 Johnny Blatnick 15.00 7.50
124A D.Murtaugh SCR RC 50.00 25.00
124B D.Murtaugh PR RC 60.00 30.00
125 Ken Keltner 25.00 12.50
126A Al Brazle SCR 15.00 7.50
126B Al Brazle PR 60.00 30.00
127A Hank Majeski SCR 15.00 7.50
127B Hank Majeski PR 60.00 30.00
128 Johnny VanderMeer 60.00 30.00
129 Bill Johnson 40.00 20.00
130 Harry Walker 15.00 7.50
131 Paul Lehner 15.00 7.50
132A Al Evans SCR 15.00 7.50
132B Al Evans PR 60.00 30.00
133 Aaron Robinson 15.00 7.50
134 Hank Borowy 15.00 7.50
135 Stan Rojek 15.00 7.50
136 Hank Edwards 15.00 7.50
137 Ted Wilks 15.00 7.50
138 Buddy Rosar 15.00 7.50
139 Hank Arft 15.00 7.50
140 Ray Scarborough 15.00 7.50
141 Tony Lupien 15.00 7.50
142 Eddie Waitkus RC 40.00 20.00
143A B.Dillinger RC SCR 25.00 12.50
143B Bob Dillinger RC PR 60.00 30.00
144 Mickey Haefner 15.00 7.50
145 Sylvester Donnelly 50.00 25.00
146 Mike McCormick 50.00 25.00
147 Bert Singleton 50.00 25.00
148 Bob Swift 50.00 25.00
149 Roy Partee 50.00 25.00
150 Allie Clark 50.00 25.00
151 Mickey Harris 50.00 25.00
152 Clarence Maddern 50.00 25.00
153 Phil Masi 50.00 25.00
154 Clint Hartung 60.00 30.00
155 Mickey Guerra 50.00 25.00
156 Al Zarilla 50.00 25.00
157 Walt Masterson 50.00 25.00
158 Harry Brecheen 60.00 30.00
159 Glen Moulder 50.00 25.00
160 Jim Blackburn 50.00 25.00
161 Jocko Thompson 50.00 25.00
162 Preacher Roe RC 125.00 60.00
163 Clyde McCullough 50.00 25.00
164 Vic Wertz RC 80.00 40.00
165 Snuffy Stirnweiss 80.00 40.00
166 Mike Tresh 50.00 25.00
167 Babe Martin 50.00 25.00
168 Doyle Lade 50.00 25.00
169 Jeff Heath 60.00 30.00
170 Bill Rigney 60.00 30.00
171 Dick Fowler 50.00 25.00
172 Eddie Pellagrini 50.00 25.00
173 Eddie Stewart 50.00 25.00
174 Terry Moore RC 80.00 40.00
175 Luke Appling 125.00 60.00
176 Ken Raffensberger 50.00 25.00
177 Stan Lopata 60.00 30.00
178 Tom Brown 60.00 30.00
179 Hugh Casey 80.00 40.00
180 Connie Berry 50.00 25.00
181 Gus Niarhos 50.00 25.00
182 Hal Peck 50.00 25.00
183 Lou Stringer 50.00 25.00
184 Bob Chipman 50.00 25.00
185 Pete Reiser 80.00 40.00
186 Buddy Kerr 50.00 25.00
187 Phil Marchildon 50.00 25.00
188 Karl Drews 50.00 25.00
189 Earl Wooten 50.00 25.00
190 Jim Hearn 50.00 25.00
191 Joe Haynes 50.00 25.00
192 Harry Gumbert 50.00 25.00
193 Ken Trinkle 50.00 25.00
194 Ralph Branca RC 100.00 50.00
195 Eddie Bockman 50.00 25.00
196 Fred Hutchinson 60.00 30.00
197 Johnny Lindell 60.00 30.00
198 Steve Gromek 50.00 25.00
199 Tex Hughson 50.00 25.00
200 Jess Dobernic 50.00 25.00
201 Sibby Sisti 50.00 25.00
202 Larry Jansen 60.00 30.00
203 Barney McCosky 50.00 25.00
204 Bob Savage 50.00 25.00
205 Dick Sisler 60.00 30.00
206 Bruce Edwards 50.00 25.00
207 Johnny Hopp 50.00 25.00
208 Dizzy Trout 60.00 30.00
209 Charlie Keller 80.00 40.00
210 Joe Gordon 80.00 40.00
211 Boo Ferriss 50.00 25.00
212 Ralph Hamner 50.00 25.00
213 Red Barrett 50.00 25.00
214 Richie Ashburn RC 600.00 300.00
215 Kirby Higbe 50.00 25.00
216 Schoolboy Rowe 60.00 30.00
217 Marino Pieretti 50.00 25.00
218 Dick Kryhoski 50.00 25.00
219 Virgil Fire Trucks 60.00 30.00
220 Johnny McCarthy 50.00 25.00
NY Giants Cap but listed as Sioux City MG
221 Bob Muncrief 50.00 25.00
222 Alex Kellner 50.00 25.00
223 Bobby Hofman 50.00 25.00
224 Satchell Paige RC 1500.00 750.00
225 Jerry Coleman RC 80.00 40.00
226 Duke Snider RC 1000.00 500.00
227 Fritz Ostermueller 50.00 25.00
228 Jackie Mayo 50.00 25.00
229 Ed Lopat RC 125.00 60.00
230 Augie Galan 60.00 30.00
231 Earl Johnson 60.00 30.00
232 George McQuinn 60.00 30.00
233 Larry Doby RC 200.00 100.00
234 Rip Sewell 50.00 25.00
235 Jim Russell 50.00 25.00
236 Fred Sanford 50.00 25.00
237 Monte Kennedy 50.00 25.00
238 Bob Lemon RC 200.00 100.00
239 Frank McCormick 50.00 25.00
240 Babe Young UER 100.00 25.00
(Photo actually Bobby Young)

1950 Bowman

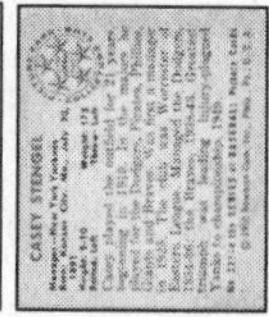

The cards in this 252-card set measure approximately 2 1/16" by 2 1/2". This set, marketed in 1950 by Bowman, represented a major improvement in terms of quality over their previous efforts. Each card was a beautifully colored line drawing developed from a simple photograph. The first 72 cards are the scarcest in the set, while the final 72 cards may be found with or without the copyright line. This was the only Bowman sports set to carry the famous "5-Star" logo. Cards were issued in five-card nickel packs. Key rookies in this set are Hank Bauer, Don Newcombe, and Al Rosen.

NM Ex
COMPLETE SET (252) 8500.00 4200.00
COMMON CARD (1-72) 50.00 25.00
COMMON CARD (73-252) 15.00 7.50
WRAPPER (1-cent) 250.00 125.00
WRAPPER (5-cent) 250.00 125.00
1 Mel Parnell RC 150.00 30.00
2 Vern Stephens 60.00 30.00
3 Dom DiMaggio 80.00 40.00
4 Gus Zernial RC 60.00 30.00
5 Bob Kuzava 50.00 25.00
6 Bob Feller 300.00 150.00
7 Jim Hegan 60.00 30.00
8 George Kell 80.00 40.00
9 Vic Wertz 60.00 30.00
10 Tommy Henrich 80.00 40.00
11 Phil Rizzuto 300.00 150.00
12 Joe Page 80.00 40.00
13 Ferris Fain 60.00 30.00
14 Alex Kellner 50.00 25.00
15 Al Kozar 50.00 25.00
16 Roy Sievers RC 80.00 40.00
17 Sid Hudson 50.00 25.00
18 Eddie Robinson 50.00 25.00
19 Warren Spahn 300.00 150.00
20 Bob Elliott 60.00 30.00
21 Pee Wee Reese 300.00 150.00
22 Jackie Robinson 1200.00 600.00
23 Don Newcombe RC 150.00 75.00
24 Johnny Schmitz 50.00 25.00
25 Hank Sauer 60.00 30.00
26 Grady Hatton 50.00 25.00
27 Herman Wehmeier 50.00 25.00
28 Bobby Thomson 80.00 40.00
29 Eddie Stanky 60.00 30.00
30 Eddie Waitkus 60.00 30.00
31 Del Ennis 80.00 40.00
32 Robin Roberts 150.00 75.00
33 Ralph Kiner 100.00 50.00
34 Murry Dickson 50.00 25.00
35 Enos Slaughter 100.00 50.00
36 Eddie Kazak 60.00 30.00
37 Luke Appling 80.00 40.00
38 Bill Wight 50.00 25.00
39 Larry Doby 100.00 50.00
40 Bob Lemon 80.00 40.00
41 Hoot Evers 50.00 25.00
42 Art Houtteman 50.00 25.00
43 Bobby Doerr 80.00 40.00
44 Joe Dobson 50.00 25.00
45 Al Zarilla 50.00 25.00
46 Yogi Berra 400.00 200.00
47 Jerry Coleman 80.00 40.00
48 Lou Brissie 50.00 25.00
49 Elmer Valo 50.00 25.00
50 Dick Kokos 50.00 25.00
51 Ned Garver 60.00 30.00
52 Sam Mele 60.00 30.00
53 Clyde Vollmer 50.00 25.00
54 Gil Coan 50.00 25.00
55 Buddy Kerr 50.00 25.00
56 Del Crandall RC 60.00 30.00
57 Vern Bickford 50.00 25.00
58 Carl Furillo 80.00 40.00
59 Ralph Branca 80.00 40.00
60 Andy Pafko 60.00 30.00
61 Bob Rush 50.00 25.00
62 Ted Kluszewski 125.00 60.00
63 Ewell Blackwell 60.00 30.00
64 Alvin Dark 60.00 30.00
65 Dave Koslo 50.00 25.00
66 Larry Jansen 60.00 30.00
67 Willie Jones 60.00 30.00
68 Curt Simmons 60.00 30.00
69 Wally Westlake 50.00 25.00
70 Bob Chesnes 50.00 25.00
71 Red Schoendienst 80.00 40.00
72 Howie Pollet 50.00 25.00
73 Willard Marshall 15.00 7.50
74 Johnny Antonelli RC 60.00 30.00
75 Roy Campanella 300.00 150.00
76 Rex Barney 40.00 20.00
77 Duke Snider 300.00 150.00
78 Mickey Owen 25.00 12.50
79 Johnny VanderMeer 40.00 20.00
80 Howard Fox 15.00 7.50
81 Ron Northey 15.00 7.50
82 Whitey Lockman 25.00 12.50
83 Sheldon Jones 15.00 7.50
84 Richie Ashburn 125.00 60.00
85 Ken Heintzelman 15.00 7.50
86 Stan Rojek 15.00 7.50
87 Bill Werle 15.00 7.50
88 Marty Marion 40.00 20.00
89 George Munger 15.00 7.50
90 Harry Brecheen 40.00 20.00
91 Cass Michaels 15.00 7.50
92 Hank Majeski 15.00 7.50
93 Gene Bearden 40.00 20.00
94 Lou Boudreau 60.00 30.00
95 Aaron Robinson 15.00 7.50
96 Virgil Trucks 25.00 12.50
97 Maurice McDermott RC 15.00 7.50
98 Ted Williams 1000.00 500.00
99 Billy Goodman 25.00 12.50
100 Vic Raschi 60.00 30.00
101 Bobby Brown 60.00 30.00
102 Billy Johnson 25.00 12.50
103 Eddie Joost 15.00 7.50
104 Sam Chapman 15.00 7.50
105 Bob Dillinger 15.00 7.50
106 Cliff Fannin 15.00 7.50
107 Sam Dente 15.00 7.50
108 Ray Scarborough 15.00 7.50
109 Sid Gordon 15.00 7.50
110 Tommy Holmes 25.00 12.50
111 Walker Cooper 15.00 7.50
112 Gil Hodges 125.00 60.00
113 Gene Hermanski 15.00 7.50
114 Wayne Terwilliger RC 15.00 7.50
115 Roy Smalley 15.00 7.50
116 Virgil Stallcup 15.00 7.50
117 Bill Rigney 15.00 7.50
118 Clint Hartung 15.00 7.50
119 Dick Sisler 25.00 12.50
120 John Thompson 15.00 7.50
121 Andy Seminick 25.00 12.50
122 Johnny Hopp 25.00 12.50
123 Dino Restelli 15.00 7.50
124 Clyde McCullough 15.00 7.50
125 Del Rice 15.00 7.50
126 Al Brazle 15.00 7.50
127 Dave Philley 15.00 7.50
128 Phil Masi 15.00 7.50
129 Joe Gordon 25.00 12.50
130 Dale Mitchell 25.00 12.50
131 Steve Gromek 15.00 7.50
132 Mickey Vernon 25.00 12.50
133 Don Kolloway 15.00 7.50
134 Paul Trout 15.00 7.50
135 Pat Mullin 15.00 7.50
136 Warren Rosar 15.00 7.50
137 Johnny Pesky 25.00 12.50
138 Allie Reynolds 60.00 30.00
139 Johnny Mize 80.00 40.00
140 Pete Suder 15.00 7.50
141 Joe Coleman 25.00 12.50
142 Sherman Lollar RC 40.00 20.00
143 Eddie Stewart 15.00 7.50
144 Al Evans 15.00 7.50
145 Jack Graham 15.00 7.50
146 Floyd Baker 15.00 7.50
147 Mike Garcia RC 40.00 20.00
148 Early Wynn 80.00 40.00
149 Bob Swift 15.00 7.50
150 George Vico 15.00 7.50
151 Fred Hutchinson 25.00 12.50
152 Ellis Kinder RC 25.00 12.50
153 Walt Masterson 15.00 7.50
154 Gus Niarhos 15.00 7.50
155 Frank Shea 25.00 12.50
156 Fred Sanford 25.00 12.50
157 Mike Guerra 15.00 7.50
158 Paul Lehner 15.00 7.50
159 Joe Tipton 15.00 7.50
160 Mickey Harris 15.00 7.50
161 Sherry Robertson 15.00 7.50
162 Eddie Yost 25.00 12.50
163 Earl Torgeson 15.00 7.50
164 Sibby Sisti 15.00 7.50
165 Bruce Edwards 15.00 7.50
166 Joe Hatton 15.00 7.50
167 Preacher Roe 60.00 30.00
168 Bob Scheffing 15.00 7.50
169 Hank Edwards 15.00 7.50
170 Dutch Leonard 15.00 7.50
171 Harry Gumbert 15.00 7.50
172 Peanuts Lowrey 15.00 7.50
173 Lloyd Merriman 15.00 7.50
174 Hank Thompson RC 40.00 20.00
175 Monte Kennedy 15.00 7.50
176 Sylvester Donnelly 15.00 7.50
177 Hank Borowy 15.00 7.50
178 Ed Fitzgerald 15.00 7.50
179 Chuck Diering 15.00 7.50
180 Harry Walker 25.00 12.50
181 Marino Pieretti 15.00 7.50
182 Sam Zoldak 15.00 7.50
183 Mickey Haefner 15.00 7.50
184 Randy Gumpert 15.00 7.50
185 Howie Judson 15.00 7.50
186 Ken Keltner 25.00 12.50
187 Lou Stringer 15.00 7.50
188 Earl Johnson 15.00 7.50
189 Owen Friend 15.00 7.50
190 Ken Wood 15.00 7.50
191 Dick Starr 15.00 7.50
192 Bob Chipman 15.00 7.50
193 Pete Reiser 40.00 20.00
194 Billy Cox 60.00 30.00
195 Phil Cavarretta 40.00 20.00
196 Doyle Lade 15.00 7.50
197 Johnny Wyrostek 15.00 7.50
198 Danny Litwhiler 15.00 7.50
199 Jack Kramer 15.00 7.50
200 Kirby Higbe 25.00 12.50
201 Pete Castiglione 15.00 7.50
202 Cliff Chambers 15.00 7.50
203 Danny Murtaugh 25.00 12.50
204 Granny Hamner RC 40.00 20.00
205 Mike Goliat 15.00 7.50
206 Stan Lopata 25.00 12.50
207 Max Lanier 15.00 7.50
208 Jim Hearn 15.00 7.50
209 Johnny Lindell 15.00 7.50
210 Ted Gray 15.00 7.50
211 Charlie Keller 40.00 20.00
212 Jerry Priddy 15.00 7.50
213 Carl Scheib 15.00 7.50
214 Dick Fowler 15.00 7.50
215 Ed Lopat 60.00 30.00
216 Bob Porterfield 25.00 12.50
217 Casey Stengel MG 125.00 60.00
218 Cliff Mapes RC 25.00 12.50
219 Hank Bauer RC 100.00 50.00
220 Leo Durocher MG 60.00 30.00
221 Don Mueller RC 40.00 20.00
222 Bobby Morgan 15.00 7.50
223 Jim Russell 15.00 7.50
224 Jack Banta 15.00 7.50
225 Eddie Sawyer MG 25.00 12.50
226 Jim Konstanty RC 60.00 30.00
227 Bob Miller 25.00 12.50
228 Bill Nicholson 25.00 12.50
229 Frank Frisch MG 60.00 30.00
230 Bill Serena 15.00 7.50
231 Preston Ward 15.00 7.50
232 Al Rosen RC 60.00 30.00
233 Allie Clark 15.00 7.50
234 Bobby Shantz RC 60.00 30.00
235 Harold Gilbert 15.00 7.50
236 Bob Cain 15.00 7.50
237 Bill Salkeld 15.00 7.50
238 Nippy Jones 15.00 7.50
239 Bill Howerton 15.00 7.50
240 Eddie Lake 15.00 7.50
241 Neil Berry 15.00 7.50
242 Dick Kryhoski 15.00 7.50
243 Johnny Groth 15.00 7.50
244 Dale Coogan 15.00 7.50
245 Al Papai 15.00 7.50
246 Walt Dropo RC 40.00 20.00
247 Irv Noren RC 25.00 12.50
248 Sam Jethroe RC 60.00 30.00
249 Snuffy Stirnweiss 25.00 12.50
250 Ray Coleman 15.00 7.50
251 Les Moss 15.00 7.50
252 Billy DeMars RC 60.00 16.50

1951 Bowman

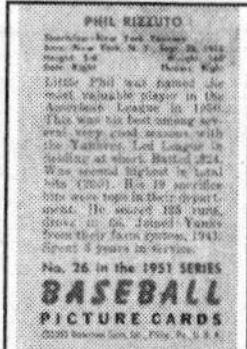

The cards in this 324-card set measure approximately 2 1/16" by 3 1/8". Many of the obverses of the cards appearing in the 1951 Bowman set are enlargements of those appearing in the previous year. The high number series (253-324) is highly valued and contains the true "Rookie" cards of Mickey Mantle and Willie Mays. Card number 195 depicts Paul Richards in caricature. George Kell's card (number 46) incorrectly lists him as being in the "1941" Bowman series. Cards were issued either in one card penny packs which came 120 to a box or in six-card nickel packs which came 24 to a box. Player names are found printed in a panel on the front of the card. These cards were supposedly also sold in sheets in variety stores in the Philadelphia area.

NM Ex
COMPLETE SET (324) 20000.00 10000.00
COMMON CARD (1-252) 20.00 10.00
COMMON (253-324) 50.00 25.00
WRAPPER (1-cent) 200.00 100.00
WRAPPER (5-cent) 250.00 125.00
1 Whitey Ford RC 2000.00 500.00
2 Yogi Berra 400.00 200.00
3 Robin Roberts 80.00 40.00
4 Del Ennis 25.00 12.50
5 Dale Mitchell 25.00 12.50
6 Don Newcombe 60.00 30.00
7 Gil Hodges 125.00 60.00
8 Paul Lehner 20.00 10.00
9 Sam Chapman 20.00 10.00
10 Red Schoendienst 60.00 30.00
11 George Munger 20.00 10.00
12 Hank Majeski 20.00 10.00
13 Eddie Stanky 25.00 12.50
14 Alvin Dark 40.00 20.00
15 Johnny Pesky 25.00 12.50
16 Maurice McDermott 20.00 10.00
17 Pete Castiglione 20.00 10.00
18 Gil Coan 20.00 10.00
19 Sid Gordon 20.00 10.00
20 Del Crandall UER 25.00 12.50
(Misspelled Crandell on card)
21 Snuffy Stirnweiss 25.00 12.50
wearing St.L.Browns hat
22 Hank Sauer 25.00 12.50
23 Hoot Evers 20.00 10.00
24 Ewell Blackwell 40.00 20.00
25 Vic Raschi 60.00 30.00
26 Phil Rizzuto 125.00 60.00
27 Jim Konstanty 25.00 12.50
28 Eddie Waitkus 20.00 10.00
29 Allie Clark 20.00 10.00
30 Bob Feller 125.00 60.00
31 Roy Campanella 300.00 150.00
32 Duke Snider 250.00 125.00
33 Bob Hooper 20.00 10.00
34 Marty Marion 40.00 20.00
35 Al Zarilla 20.00 10.00
36 Joe Dobson 20.00 10.00
37 Whitey Lockman 40.00 20.00
38 Al Evans 20.00 10.00
39 Ray Scarborough 20.00 10.00
40 Gus Bell RC 60.00 30.00
41 Eddie Yost 25.00 12.50
42 Vern Bickford 20.00 10.00
43 Billy DeMars 20.00 10.00
44 Roy Smalley 20.00 10.00
45 Art Houtteman 20.00 10.00
46 George Kell 1941 UER 60.00 30.00
47 Grady Hatton 20.00 10.00
48 Ken Raffensberger 20.00 10.00
49 Jerry Coleman 25.00 12.50
50 Johnny Mize 80.00 40.00
51 Andy Seminick 20.00 10.00
52 Dick Sisler 40.00 20.00
53 Bob Lemon 60.00 30.00
54 Ray Boone RC 40.00 20.00
55 Gene Hermanski 20.00 10.00
56 Ralph Branca 60.00 30.00
57 Alex Kellner 20.00 10.00
58 Enos Slaughter 60.00 30.00
59 Randy Gumpert 20.00 10.00
60 Chico Carrasquel RC 60.00 30.00
61 Jim Hearn 25.00 12.50
62 Lou Boudreau 60.00 30.00
63 Bob Dillinger 20.00 10.00
64 Bill Werle 20.00 10.00
65 Mickey Vernon 40.00 20.00
66 Bob Elliott 25.00 12.50
67 Roy Sievers 25.00 12.50
68 Dick Kokos 20.00 10.00
69 Johnny Schmitz 20.00 10.00
70 Ron Northey 20.00 10.00
71 Jerry Priddy 20.00 10.00
72 Lloyd Merriman 20.00 10.00
73 Tommy Byrne 20.00 10.00
74 Billy Johnson 25.00 12.50
75 Russ Meyer RC 25.00 12.50
76 Stan Lopata 25.00 12.50
77 Mike Goliat 20.00 10.00
78 Early Wynn 60.00 30.00
79 Jim Hegan 25.00 12.50
80 Pee Wee Reese 200.00 100.00
81 Carl Furillo 60.00 30.00
82 Joe Tipton 20.00 10.00
83 Carl Scheib 20.00 10.00
84 Barney McCosky 20.00 10.00
85 Eddie Kazak 20.00 10.00
86 Harry Brecheen 25.00 12.50
87 Floyd Baker 20.00 10.00
88 Eddie Robinson 20.00 10.00
89 Hank Thompson 25.00 12.50
90 Dave Koslo 20.00 10.00
91 Clyde Vollmer 20.00 10.00
92 Vern Stephens 25.00 12.50
93 Danny O'Connell 20.00 10.00
94 Clyde McCullough 20.00 10.00
95 Sherry Robertson 20.00 10.00
96 Sandy Consuegra 20.00 10.00
97 Bob Kuzava 20.00 10.00
98 Willard Marshall 20.00 10.00
99 Earl Torgeson 20.00 10.00
100 Sherm Lollar 25.00 12.50
101 Owen Friend 20.00 10.00
102 Dutch Leonard 20.00 10.00
103 Andy Pafko 40.00 20.00
104 Virgil Trucks 25.00 12.50
105 Don Kolloway 20.00 10.00
106 Pat Mullin 20.00 10.00
107 Johnny Wyrostek 20.00 10.00
108 Virgil Stallcup 20.00 10.00
109 Allie Reynolds 60.00 30.00
110 Bobby Brown 40.00 20.00
111 Curt Simmons 25.00 12.50
112 Willie Jones 20.00 10.00
113 Bill Nicholson 20.00 10.00
114 Sam Zoldak 20.00 10.00
Pictured in Indians uniform
115 Steve Gromek 20.00 10.00
116 Bruce Edwards 20.00 10.00
117 Eddie Miksis 20.00 10.00
118 Preacher Roe 60.00 30.00
119 Eddie Joost 20.00 10.00
120 Joe Coleman 25.00 12.50
121 Gerry Staley 20.00 10.00
122 Joe Garagiola RC 100.00 50.00
123 Howie Judson 20.00 10.00
124 Gus Niarhos 20.00 10.00
125 Bill Rigney 25.00 12.50
126 Bobby Thomson 60.00 30.00
127 Sal Maglie RC 60.00 30.00
128 Ellis Kinder 20.00 10.00
129 Matt Batts 20.00 10.00
130 Tom Saffell 20.00 10.00
131 Cliff Chambers 20.00 10.00
132 Cass Michaels 20.00 10.00
133 Sam Dente 20.00 10.00
134 Warren Spahn 125.00 60.00
135 Walker Cooper 20.00 10.00
136 Ray Coleman 20.00 10.00
137 Dick Starr 20.00 10.00
138 Phil Cavarretta 25.00 12.50
139 Doyle Lade 20.00 10.00
140 Eddie Lake 20.00 10.00
141 Fred Hutchinson 25.00 12.50
142 Aaron Robinson 20.00 10.00
143 Ted Kluszewski 80.00 40.00
144 Herman Wehmeier 20.00 10.00
145 Fred Sanford 25.00 12.50
146 Johnny Hopp 25.00 12.50
147 Ken Heintzelman 20.00 10.00
148 Granny Hamner 20.00 10.00
149 Bubba Church 20.00 10.00
150 Mike Garcia 25.00 12.50
151 Larry Doby 60.00 30.00
152 Cal Abrams 20.00 10.00
153 Rex Barney 25.00 12.50
154 Pete Suder 20.00 10.00
155 Lou Brissie 20.00 10.00
156 Del Rice 20.00 10.00
157 Al Brazle 20.00 10.00
158 Chuck Diering 20.00 10.00
159 Eddie Stewart 20.00 10.00
160 Phil Masi 20.00 10.00
161 Wes Westrum RC 20.00 10.00
162 Larry Jansen 25.00 12.50
163 Monte Kennedy 20.00 10.00
164 Bill Wight 20.00 10.00
165 Ted Williams UER 800.00 400.00
Wrong birthdate
166 Stan Rojek 20.00 10.00
Pictured in Pirates uniform
167 Murry Dickson 20.00 10.00
168 Sam Mele 20.00 10.00
169 Sid Hudson 20.00 10.00
170 Sibby Sisti 20.00 10.00
171 Buddy Kerr 20.00 10.00
172 Ned Garver 20.00 10.00
173 Hank Arft 20.00 10.00
174 Mickey Owen 25.00 12.50
175 Wayne Terwilliger 20.00 10.00
176 Vic Wertz 40.00 20.00
177 Charlie Keller 25.00 12.50
178 Ted Gray 20.00 10.00
179 Danny Litwhiler 20.00 10.00
180 Howie Fox 20.00 10.00
181 Casey Stengel MG 80.00 40.00
182 Tom Ferrick 20.00 10.00
183 Hank Bauer 60.00 30.00
184 Eddie Sawyer MG 40.00 20.00
185 Jimmy Bloodworth 20.00 10.00
186 Richie Ashburn 100.00 50.00
187 Al Rosen 40.00 20.00
188 Bobby Avila RC 25.00 12.50
189 Erv Palica 20.00 10.00
190 Joe Hatten 20.00 10.00
191 Billy Hitchcock 20.00 10.00
192 Hank Wyse 20.00 10.00
193 Ted Wilks 20.00 10.00

194 Peanuts Lowrey	20.00	10.00
195 Paul Richards MG	25.00	12.50
(Caricature)		
196 Billy Pierce RC	60.00	30.00
197 Bob Cain	20.00	10.00
198 Monte Irvin RC	100.00	50.00
199 Sheldon Jones	20.00	10.00
200 Jack Kramer	20.00	10.00
Pictured in NY Giants uniform		
201 Steve O'Neill MG	20.00	10.00
202 Mike Guerra	20.00	10.00
203 Vernon Law RC	60.00	30.00
204 Vic Lombardi	20.00	10.00
205 Mickey Grasso	20.00	10.00
206 Conrado Marrero	20.00	10.00
207 Billy Southworth MG	20.00	10.00
208 Blix Donnelly	20.00	10.00
209 Ken Wood	20.00	10.00
210 Les Moss	20.00	10.00
Pictured in St.L.Browns uniform		
211 Hal Jeffcoat	20.00	10.00
212 Bob Rush	20.00	10.00
213 Neil Berry	20.00	10.00
214 Bob Swift	20.00	10.00
215 Ken Peterson	20.00	10.00
216 Connie Ryan	20.00	10.00
217 Joe Page	25.00	12.50
218 Ed Lopat	60.00	30.00
219 Gene Woodling RC	60.00	30.00
220 Bob Miller	20.00	10.00
221 Dick Whitman	20.00	10.00
222 Thurman Tucker	20.00	10.00
223 Johnny VanderMeer	40.00	20.00
224 Billy Cox	25.00	12.50
225 Dan Bankhead	40.00	20.00
226 Jimmy Dykes MG	20.00	10.00
227 Bobby Shantz UER	25.00	12.50
Sic, Schantz		
228 Cloyd Boyer	25.00	12.50
229 Bill Howerton	20.00	10.00
Pictured in St.L.Cardinals uniform		
230 Max Lanier	20.00	10.00
231 Luis Aloma	20.00	10.00
232 Nelson Fox RC	250.00	125.00
233 Leo Durocher MG	60.00	30.00
234 Clint Hartung	25.00	12.50
235 Jack Lohrke	20.00	10.00
236 Warren Rosar	20.00	10.00
237 Billy Goodman	25.00	12.50
238 Pete Reiser	40.00	20.00
239 Bill MacDonald	20.00	10.00
240 Joe Haynes	20.00	10.00
241 Irv Noren	25.00	12.50
242 Sam Jethroe	25.00	12.50
243 Johnny Antonelli	25.00	12.50
244 Cliff Fannin	20.00	10.00
245 John Berardino RC	60.00	30.00
246 Bill Serena	20.00	10.00
247 Bob Ramazzotti	20.00	10.00
248 Johnny Klippstein	20.00	10.00
249 Johnny Groth	20.00	10.00
250 Hank Borowy	20.00	10.00
251 Willard Ramsdell	20.00	10.00
252 Dixie Howell	20.00	10.00
253 Mickey Mantle RC	8500.00	4200.00
254 Jackie Jensen RC	100.00	50.00
255 Milo Candini	50.00	25.00
256 Ken Sylvestri	50.00	25.00
257 Birdie Tebbetts RC	60.00	30.00
258 Luke Easter RC	60.00	30.00
259 Chuck Dressen MG	60.00	30.00
260 Carl Erskine RC	100.00	50.00
261 Wally Moses	60.00	30.00
262 Gus Zernial	60.00	30.00
263 Howie Pollet	60.00	30.00
Pictured in Cardinals uniform		
264 Don Richmond	50.00	25.00
265 Steve Bilko	50.00	25.00
266 Harry Dorish	50.00	25.00
267 Ken Holcombe	50.00	25.00
268 Don Mueller	60.00	30.00
269 Ray Noble	50.00	25.00
270 Willard Nixon	50.00	25.00
271 Tommy Wright	50.00	25.00
272 Billy Meyer MG	50.00	25.00
273 Danny Murtaugh	60.00	30.00
274 George Metkovich	50.00	25.00
275 Bucky Harris MG	80.00	40.00
276 Frank Quinn	50.00	25.00
277 Roy Hartsfield	50.00	25.00
278 Norman Roy	50.00	25.00
279 Jim Delsing	50.00	25.00
280 Frank Overmire	50.00	25.00
Pictured in Browns uniform		
281 Al Widmar	50.00	25.00
282 Frank Frisch MG	100.00	50.00
283 Walt Dubiel	50.00	25.00
284 Gene Bearden	60.00	30.00
285 Johnny Lipon	50.00	25.00
286 Bob Usher	50.00	25.00
287 Jim Blackburn	50.00	25.00
288 Bobby Adams	50.00	25.00
289 Cliff Mapes	60.00	30.00
290 Bill Dickey CO	100.00	50.00
291 Tommy Henrich CO	80.00	40.00
292 Eddie Pellegrini	50.00	25.00
293 Ken Johnson	50.00	25.00
294 Jocko Thompson	50.00	25.00
295 Al Lopez MG	125.00	60.00
296 Bob Kennedy	60.00	30.00
297 Dave Philley	50.00	25.00
298 Joe Astroth	50.00	25.00
299 Clyde King	50.00	25.00
300 Hal Rice	50.00	25.00
301 Tommy Glaviano	50.00	25.00
302 Jim Busby	50.00	25.00
303 Marv Rotblatt	50.00	25.00
304 Al Gettel	50.00	25.00
305 Willie Mays RC	3000.00	1500.00
306 Jim Piersall RC	125.00	60.00
307 Walt Masterson	50.00	25.00
308 Ted Beard	50.00	25.00
309 Mel Queen	50.00	25.00
310 Erv Dusak	50.00	25.00
311 Mickey Harris	50.00	25.00
312 Gene Mauch RC	60.00	30.00
313 Ray Mueller	50.00	25.00
314 Johnny Sain	80.00	40.00
315 Zack Taylor MG	50.00	25.00
316 Duane Pillette	50.00	25.00
317 Smoky Burgess RC	80.00	40.00
318 Warren Hacker	50.00	25.00
319 Red Rolfe MG	60.00	30.00
320 Hal White	50.00	25.00
321 Earl Johnson	50.00	25.00
322 Luke Sewell MG	60.00	30.00
323 Joe Adcock RC	80.00	40.00
324 Johnny Pramesa RC	125.00	38.00

1952 Bowman

The cards in this 252-card set measure approximately 2 1/16" by 3 1/8". While the Bowman set of 1952 retained the card size introduced in 1951, it employed a modification of color tones from the two preceding years. The cards also appeared with a facsimile autograph on the front and, for the first time since 1949, premium advertising on the back. The 1952 set was apparently sold in sheets as well as in gum packs. Artwork for 15 cards that were never issued was discovered in the early 1980s. Cards were issued in one card penny packs or five card nickel packs. The five cent packs came 24 to a box. Notable Rookie Cards in this set are Lew Burdette, Gil McDougald, and Minnie Minoso.

	NM	Ex
COMPLETE SET (252)	8500.00	4200.00
COMMON CARD (1-216)	15.00	6.75
COMMON (217-252)	60.00	30.00
WRAPPER (1-cent)	200.00	100.00
WRAPPER (5-cent)	100.00	50.00
1 Yogi Berra	700.00	220.00
2 Bobby Thomson	40.00	20.00
3 Fred Hutchinson	25.00	12.50
4 Robin Roberts	80.00	40.00
5 Minnie Minoso RC	125.00	60.00
6 Virgil Stallcup	15.00	7.50
7 Mike Garcia	25.00	12.50
8 Pee Wee Reese	150.00	75.00
9 Vern Stephens	25.00	12.50
10 Bob Hooper	15.00	7.50
11 Ralph Kiner	60.00	30.00
12 Max Surkont	15.00	7.50
13 Cliff Mapes	15.00	7.50
14 Cliff Chambers	15.00	7.50
15 Sam Mele	15.00	7.50
16 Turk Lown	15.00	7.50
17 Ed Lopat	40.00	20.00
18 Don Mueller	25.00	12.50
19 Bob Cain	15.00	7.50
20 Willie Jones	15.00	7.50
21 Nellie Fox	100.00	50.00
22 Willard Ramsdell	15.00	7.50
23 Bob Lemon	60.00	30.00
24 Carl Furillo	40.00	20.00
25 Mickey McDermott	15.00	7.50
26 Eddie Joost	15.00	7.50
27 Joe Garagiola	40.00	20.00
28 Roy Hartsfield	15.00	7.50
29 Ned Garver	15.00	7.50
30 Red Schoendienst	60.00	30.00
31 Eddie Yost	25.00	12.50
32 Eddie Miksis	15.00	7.50
33 Gil McDougald RC	80.00	40.00
34 Alvin Dark	25.00	12.50
35 Granny Hamner	15.00	7.50
36 Cass Michaels	15.00	7.50
37 Vic Raschi	25.00	12.50
38 Whitey Lockman	25.00	12.50
39 Vic Wertz	25.00	12.50
40 Bubba Church	15.00	7.50
41 Chico Carrasquel	25.00	12.50
42 Johnny Wyrostek	15.00	7.50
43 Bob Feller	150.00	75.00
44 Roy Campanella	250.00	125.00
45 Johnny Pesky	25.00	12.50
46 Carl Scheib	15.00	7.50
47 Pete Castiglione	15.00	7.50
48 Vern Bickford	15.00	7.50
49 Jim Hearn	15.00	7.50
50 Gerry Staley	15.00	7.50
51 Gil Coan	15.00	7.50
52 Phil Rizzuto	150.00	75.00
53 Richie Ashburn	125.00	60.00
54 Billy Pierce	25.00	12.50
55 Ken Raffensberger	15.00	7.50
56 Clyde King	25.00	12.50
57 Clyde Vollmer	15.00	7.50
58 Hank Majeski	15.00	7.50
59 Murry Dickson	15.00	7.50
60 Sid Gordon	15.00	7.50
61 Tommy Byrne	15.00	7.50
62 Joe Presko	15.00	7.50
63 Irv Noren	15.00	7.50
64 Roy Smalley	15.00	7.50
65 Hank Bauer	40.00	20.00
66 Sal Maglie	25.00	12.50
67 Johnny Groth	15.00	7.50
68 Jim Busby	15.00	7.50
69 Joe Adcock	25.00	12.50
70 Carl Erskine	40.00	20.00
71 Vernon Law	25.00	12.50
72 Earl Torgeson	15.00	7.50
73 Jerry Coleman	25.00	12.50
74 Wes Westrum	25.00	12.50
75 George Kell	60.00	30.00
76 Del Ennis	25.00	12.50
77 Eddie Robinson	15.00	7.50
78 Lloyd Merriman	15.00	7.50
79 Lou Brissie	15.00	7.50
80 Gil Hodges	100.00	50.00
81 Billy Goodman	25.00	12.50
82 Gus Zernial	25.00	12.50
83 Howie Pollet	15.00	7.50
84 Sam Jethroe	25.00	12.50
85 Marty Marion CO	25.00	12.50
86 Cal Abrams	15.00	7.50
87 Mickey Vernon	25.00	12.50
88 Bruce Edwards	15.00	7.50
89 Billy Hitchcock	15.00	7.50
90 Larry Jansen	25.00	12.50
91 Don Kolloway	15.00	7.50
92 Eddie Waitkus	25.00	12.50
93 Paul Richards MG	25.00	12.50
94 Luke Sewell MG	25.00	12.50
95 Luke Easter	25.00	12.50
96 Ralph Branca	25.00	12.50
97 Willard Marshall	15.00	7.50
98 Jimmy Dykes MG	25.00	12.50
99 Clyde McCullough	15.00	7.50
100 Sibby Sisti	15.00	7.50
101 Mickey Mantle	2500.00	1250.00
102 Peanuts Lowrey	15.00	7.50
103 Joe Haynes	15.00	7.50
104 Hal Jeffcoat	15.00	7.50
105 Bobby Brown	25.00	12.50
106 Randy Gumpert	15.00	7.50
107 Del Rice	15.00	7.50
108 George Metkovich	15.00	7.50
109 Tom Morgan	15.00	7.50
110 Max Lanier	15.00	7.50
111 Hoot Evers	15.00	7.50
112 Smoky Burgess	25.00	12.50
113 Al Zarilla	15.00	7.50
114 Frank Hiller	15.00	7.50
115 Larry Doby	60.00	30.00
116 Duke Snider	200.00	100.00
117 Bill Wight	15.00	7.50
118 Ray Murray	15.00	7.50
119 Bill Howerton	15.00	7.50
120 Chet Nichols	15.00	7.50
121 Al Corwin	15.00	7.50
122 Billy Johnson	15.00	7.50
123 Sid Hudson	15.00	7.50
124 Birdie Tebbetts	15.00	7.50
125 Howie Fox	15.00	7.50
126 Phil Cavarretta	25.00	12.50
127 Dick Sisler	15.00	7.50
128 Don Newcombe	60.00	30.00
129 Gus Niarhos	15.00	7.50
130 Allie Clark	15.00	7.50
131 Bob Swift	15.00	7.50
132 Dave Cole	15.00	7.50
133 Dick Kryhoski	15.00	7.50
134 Al Brazle	15.00	7.50
135 Mickey Harris	15.00	7.50
136 Gene Hermanski	15.00	7.50
137 Stan Rojek	15.00	7.50
138 Ted Wilks	15.00	7.50
139 Jerry Priddy	15.00	7.50
140 Ray Scarborough	15.00	7.50
141 Hank Edwards	15.00	7.50
142 Early Wynn	60.00	30.00
143 Sandy Consuegra	15.00	7.50
144 Joe Hatton	15.00	7.50
145 Johnny Mize	60.00	30.00
146 Leo Durocher MG	60.00	30.00
147 Marlin Stuart	15.00	7.50
148 Ken Heintzelman	15.00	7.50
149 Howie Judson	15.00	7.50
150 Herman Wehmeier	15.00	7.50
151 Al Rosen	25.00	12.50
152 Billy Cox	15.00	7.50
153 Fred Hatfield	15.00	7.50
154 Ferris Fain	25.00	12.50
155 Billy Meyer MG	15.00	7.50
156 Warren Spahn	125.00	60.00
157 Jim Delsing	15.00	7.50
158 Bucky Harris MG	40.00	20.00
159 Dutch Leonard	15.00	7.50
160 Eddie Stanky	25.00	12.50
161 Jackie Jensen	40.00	20.00
162 Monte Irvin	60.00	30.00
163 Johnny Lipon	15.00	7.50
164 Connie Ryan	15.00	7.50
165 Saul Rogovin	15.00	7.50
166 Bobby Adams	15.00	7.50
167 Bobby Avila	25.00	12.50
168 Preacher Roe	25.00	12.50
169 Walt Dropo	25.00	12.50
170 Joe Astroth	15.00	7.50
171 Mel Queen	15.00	7.50
172 Ebba St.Claire	15.00	7.50
173 Gene Bearden	15.00	7.50
174 Mickey Grasso	15.00	7.50
175 Randy Jackson	15.00	7.50
176 Harry Brecheen	25.00	12.50
177 Gene Woodling	25.00	12.50
178 Dave Williams RC	25.00	12.50
179 Pete Suder	15.00	7.50
180 Ed Fitzgerald	15.00	7.50
181 Joe Collins RC	25.00	12.50
182 Dave Koslo	15.00	7.50
183 Pat Mullin	15.00	7.50
184 Curt Simmons	25.00	12.50
185 Eddie Stewart	15.00	7.50
186 Frank Smith	15.00	7.50
187 Jim Hegan	25.00	12.50
188 Chuck Dressen MG	25.00	12.50
189 Jimmy Piersall	25.00	12.50
190 Dick Fowler	15.00	7.50
191 Bob Friend RC	40.00	20.00
192 John Cusick	15.00	7.50
193 Bobby Young	15.00	7.50
194 Bob Porterfield	15.00	7.50
195 Frank Baumholtz	15.00	7.50
196 Stan Musial	600.00	300.00
197 Charlie Silvera RC	15.00	7.50
198 Chuck Diering	15.00	7.50
199 Ted Gray	15.00	7.50
200 Ken Silvestri	15.00	7.50
201 Ray Coleman	15.00	7.50
202 Harry Perkowski	15.00	7.50
203 Steve Gromek	15.00	7.50
204 Andy Pafko	25.00	12.50
205 Walt Masterson	15.00	7.50
206 Elmer Valo	15.00	7.50
207 George Strickland	15.00	7.50
208 Walker Cooper	15.00	7.50
209 Dick Littlefield	15.00	7.50
210 Archie Wilson	15.00	7.50
211 Paul Minner	15.00	7.50
212 Solly Hemus RC	15.00	7.50
213 Monte Kennedy	15.00	7.50
214 Ray Boone	15.00	7.50
215 Sheldon Jones	15.00	7.50
216 Matt Batts	15.00	7.50
217 Casey Stengel MG	150.00	75.00
218 Willie Mays	1500.00	750.00
219 Neil Berry	60.00	30.00
220 Russ Meyer	60.00	30.00
221 Lou Kretlow	60.00	30.00
222 Dixie Howell	60.00	30.00
223 Harry Simpson	60.00	30.00
224 Johnny Schmitz	60.00	30.00
225 Del Wilber	60.00	30.00
226 Alex Kellner	60.00	30.00
227 Clyde Sukeforth CO	60.00	30.00
228 Bob Chipman	60.00	30.00
229 Hank Arft	60.00	30.00
230 Frank Shea	60.00	30.00
231 Dee Fondy	60.00	30.00
232 Enos Slaughter	100.00	50.00
233 Bob Kuzava	60.00	30.00
234 Fred Fitzsimmons CO	60.00	30.00
235 Steve Souchock	60.00	30.00
236 Tommy Brown	60.00	30.00
237 Sherm Lollar	60.00	30.00
238 Roy McMillan RC	60.00	30.00
239 Dale Mitchell	60.00	30.00
240 Billy Loes RC	60.00	30.00
241 Mel Parnell	60.00	30.00
242 Everett Kell	60.00	30.00
243 George Munger	60.00	30.00
244 Lew Burdette RC	80.00	40.00
245 George Schmees	60.00	30.00
246 Jerry Snyder	60.00	30.00
247 Johnny Pramesa	60.00	30.00
248 Bill Werle	60.00	30.00
Full name in signature		
248A Bill Werle	60.00	30.00
Signature on front has no W		
249 Hank Thompson	60.00	30.00
250 Ike Delock	60.00	30.00
251 Jack Lohrke	60.00	30.00
252 Frank Crosetti CO	125.00	31.00

1953 Bowman B/W

The cards in this 64-card set measure approximately 2 1/2" by 3 3/4". Some collectors believe that the high cost of producing the 1953 color series forced Bowman to issue this set in black and white, since the two sets are identical in design except for the element of color. This set was also produced in fewer numbers than its color counterpart, and is popular among collectors for the challenge involved in completing it and the lack of short prints. Cards were issued in five-card nickel packs. There are no key Rookie Cards in this set. Recently, a variation of the Hal Bevan card (number 43) was discovered, that card exists with him being born in either 1930 or 1950. The 1950 version is much more difficult.

	NM	Ex
COMPLETE SET (64)	3000.00	1500.00
WRAPPER (1-CENT)	350.00	180.00
1 Gus Bell	125.00	25.00
2 Willard Nixon	40.00	20.00
3 Bill Rigney	40.00	20.00
4 Pat Mullin	40.00	20.00
5 Dee Fondy	40.00	20.00
6 Ray Murray	40.00	20.00
7 Andy Seminick	40.00	20.00
8 Pete Suder	40.00	20.00
9 Walt Masterson	40.00	20.00
10 Dick Sisler	60.00	30.00
11 Dick Gernert	40.00	20.00
12 Randy Jackson	40.00	20.00
13 Joe Tipton	40.00	20.00
14 Bill Nicholson	60.00	30.00
15 Johnny Mize	125.00	60.00
16 Stu Miller RC	60.00	30.00
17 Virgil Trucks	60.00	30.00
18 Billy Hoeft	40.00	20.00
19 Paul LaPalme	40.00	20.00
20 Eddie Robinson	40.00	20.00
21 Clarence Podbielan	40.00	20.00
22 Matt Batts	40.00	20.00
23 Wilmer Mizell	60.00	30.00
24 Del Wilber	40.00	20.00
25 Johnny Sain	80.00	40.00
26 Preacher Roe	80.00	40.00
27 Bob Lemon	175.00	90.00
28 Hoyt Wilhelm	125.00	60.00
29 Sid Hudson	40.00	20.00
30 Walker Cooper	40.00	20.00
31 Gene Woodling	80.00	40.00
32 Rocky Bridges	40.00	20.00
33 Bob Kuzava	40.00	20.00
34 Ebba St.Claire	40.00	20.00
35 Johnny Wyrostek	40.00	20.00
36 Jimmy Piersall	80.00	40.00
37 Hal Jeffcoat	40.00	20.00
38 Dave Cole	40.00	20.00
39 Casey Stengel MG	350.00	180.00
40 Larry Jansen	60.00	30.00
41 Bob Ramazzotti	40.00	20.00
42 Howie Judson	40.00	20.00
43 Hal Bevan ERR		
Born in 1950		
43A Hal Bevan COR	40.00	20.00
Born in 1930		
44 Jim Delsing	40.00	20.00
45 Irv Noren	60.00	30.00
46 Bucky Harris MG	80.00	40.00
47 Jack Lohrke	40.00	20.00
48 Steve Ridzik	40.00	20.00
49 Floyd Baker	40.00	20.00
50 Dutch Leonard	40.00	20.00
51 Lou Burdette	80.00	40.00
52 Ralph Branca	80.00	40.00
53 Morrie Martin	40.00	20.00
54 Bill Miller	40.00	20.00
55 Don Johnson	40.00	20.00
56 Roy Smalley	40.00	20.00
57 Andy Pafko	60.00	30.00
58 Jim Konstanty	60.00	30.00
59 Duane Pillette	40.00	20.00
60 Billy Cox	80.00	40.00
61 Tom Gorman	40.00	20.00
62 Keith Thomas	40.00	20.00
63 Steve Gromek	40.00	20.00
64 Andy Hansen	80.00	26.00

1953 Bowman Color

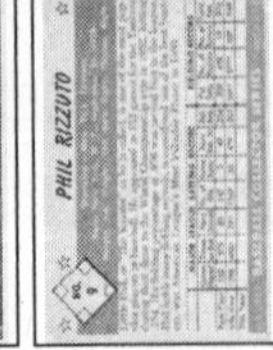

The cards in this 160-card set measure approximately 2 1/2" by 3 3/4". The 1953 Bowman Color set, considered by many to be the best looking set of the modern era, contains Kodachrome photographs with no names or facsimile autographs on the face. Cards were issued in five-card nickel packs in a 24 pack box with each pack having gum in it. The entire low number run were also printed in three card strips; it is believed that these three card strips in numerical order were box toppers to retailers. The box features an endorsement from Joe DiMaggio. Numbers 113 to 160 are somewhat more difficult to obtain, with numbers 113 to 128 being the most difficult. There are two cards of Al Corwin (126 and 149). There are no key Rookie Cards in this set.

	NM	Ex
COMPLETE SET (160)	15000.00	7500.00
COMMON CARD (1-112)	40.00	20.00
COMMON (113-128)	80.00	40.00
COMMON (129-160)	75.00	38.00
WRAPPER (1-cent)	400.00	200.00
WRAPPER (5-CENT)	300.00	150.00
1 Dave Williams	175.00	35.00
2 Vic Wertz	50.00	25.00
3 Sam Jethroe	50.00	25.00
4 Art Houtteman	40.00	20.00
5 Sid Gordon	40.00	20.00
6 Joe Ginsberg	40.00	20.00
7 Harry Chiti	40.00	20.00
8 Al Rosen	50.00	25.00
9 Phil Rizzuto	225.00	110.00
10 Richie Ashburn	150.00	75.00
11 Bobby Shantz	50.00	25.00
12 Carl Erskine	60.00	30.00
13 Gus Zernial	50.00	25.00
14 Billy Loes	50.00	25.00
15 Jim Busby	40.00	20.00
16 Bob Friend	50.00	25.00
17 Gerry Staley	40.00	20.00
18 Nellie Fox	150.00	75.00
19 Alvin Dark	50.00	25.00
20 Don Lenhardt	40.00	20.00
21 Joe Garagiola	60.00	30.00
22 Bob Porterfield	40.00	20.00
23 Herman Wehmeier	40.00	20.00
24 Jackie Jensen	60.00	30.00
25 Hoot Evers	40.00	20.00
26 Roy McMillan	40.00	20.00
27 Vic Raschi	60.00	30.00
28 Smoky Burgess	50.00	25.00
29 Bobby Avila	50.00	25.00
30 Phil Cavarretta	50.00	25.00
31 Jimmy Dykes MG	50.00	25.00
32 Stan Musial	800.00	400.00
33 Pee Wee Reese	1000.00	500.00
34 Gil Coan	40.00	20.00
35 Maurice McDermott	40.00	20.00
36 Minnie Minoso	80.00	40.00
37 Jim Wilson	40.00	20.00
38 Harry Byrd	40.00	20.00
39 Paul Richards MG	50.00	25.00
40 Larry Doby	100.00	50.00
41 Sammy White	40.00	20.00
42 Tommy Brown	40.00	20.00
43 Mike Garcia	50.00	25.00
44 Yogi Berra	800.00	400.00
Hank Bauer		
Mickey Mantle		
45 Walt Dropo	50.00	25.00
46 Roy Campanella	350.00	180.00
47 Ned Garver	40.00	20.00
48 Hank Sauer	50.00	25.00
49 Eddie Stanky MG	50.00	25.00
50 Lou Kretlow	40.00	20.00
51 Monte Irvin	80.00	40.00
52 Marty Marion MG	50.00	25.00
53 Del Rice	40.00	20.00
54 Chico Carrasquel	40.00	20.00
55 Leo Durocher MG	80.00	40.00
56 Bob Cain	40.00	20.00
57 Lou Boudreau MG	80.00	40.00
58 Willard Marshall	40.00	20.00
59 Mickey Mantle	2000.00	1000.00
60 Granny Hamner	40.00	20.00
61 George Kell	80.00	40.00
62 Ted Kluszewski	100.00	50.00
63 Gil McDougald	80.00	40.00
64 Curt Simmons	50.00	25.00
65 Robin Roberts	125.00	60.00
66 Mel Parnell	50.00	25.00
67 Mel Clark	40.00	20.00
68 Allie Reynolds	60.00	30.00
69 Charlie Grimm MG	50.00	25.00
70 Clint Courtney	40.00	20.00
71 Paul Minner	40.00	20.00
72 Ted Gray	40.00	20.00
73 Billy Pierce	50.00	25.00
74 Don Mueller	50.00	25.00
75 Saul Rogovin	40.00	20.00
76 Jim Hearn	40.00	20.00
77 Mickey Grasso	40.00	20.00
78 Carl Furillo	60.00	30.00
79 Ray Boone	50.00	25.00
80 Ralph Kiner	100.00	50.00

81 Enos Slaughter.................. 100.00 50.00
82 Joe Astroth.......................... 40.00 20.00
83 Jack Daniels 40.00 20.00
84 Hank Bauer............................ 60.00 30.00
85 Solly Hemus........................... 40.00 20.00
86 Harry Simpson 40.00 20.00
87 Harry Perkowski.................... 40.00 20.00
88 Joe Dobson............................ 40.00 20.00
89 Sandy Consuegra 40.00 20.00
90 Joe Nuxhall 50.00 25.00
91 Steve Souchock..................... 40.00 20.00
92 Gil Hodges.......................... 300.00 150.00
93 Phil Rizzuto and 300.00 150.00
Billy Martin
94 Bob Addis............................. 40.00 20.00
95 Wally Moses CO 50.00 25.00
96 Sal Maglie 50.00 25.00
97 Eddie Mathews................... 350.00 180.00
98 Hector Rodriguez 40.00 20.00
99 Warren Spahn 350.00 180.00
100 Bill Wight............................ 40.00 20.00
101 Red Schoendienst 80.00 40.00
102 Jim Hegan 50.00 25.00
103 Del Ennis............................. 50.00 25.00
104 Luke Easter 50.00 25.00
105 Eddie Joost 40.00 20.00
106 Ken Raffensberger................ 40.00 20.00
107 Alex Kellner 40.00 20.00
108 Bobby Adams........................ 40.00 20.00
109 Ken Wood 40.00 20.00
110 Bob Rush 40.00 20.00
111 Jim Dyck 40.00 20.00
112 Toby Atwell 40.00 20.00
113 Karl Drews............................ 80.00 40.00
114 Bob Feller........................ 500.00 250.00
115 Cloyd Boyer.......................... 80.00 40.00
116 Eddie Yost 100.00 50.00
117 Duke Snider..................... 600.00 300.00
118 Billy Martin 400.00 200.00
119 Dale Mitchell 100.00 50.00
120 Marlin Stuart 80.00 40.00
121 Yogi Berra 800.00 400.00
122 Bill Serena 80.00 40.00
123 Johnny Lipon 80.00 40.00
124 Charlie Dressen MG 100.00 50.00
125 Fred Hatfield......................... 80.00 40.00
126 Al Corwin 80.00 40.00
127 Dick Kryhoski 80.00 40.00
128 Whitey Lockman 100.00 50.00
129 Russ Meyer........................... 75.00 38.00
130 Cass Michaels 75.00 38.00
131 Connie Ryan.......................... 75.00 38.00
132 Fred Hutchinson................... 90.00 45.00
133 Willie Jones.......................... 75.00 38.00
134 Johnny Pesky........................ 90.00 45.00
135 Bobby Morgan....................... 75.00 38.00
136 Jim Brideweser 75.00 38.00
137 Sam Dente............................. 75.00 38.00
138 Bubba Church 75.00 38.00
139 Pete Runnels......................... 90.00 45.00
140 Al Brazle 75.00 38.00
141 Frank Shea 75.00 38.00
142 Larry Miggins........................ 75.00 38.00
143 Al Lopez MG...................... 110.00 55.00
144 Warren Hacker 75.00 38.00
145 George Shuba 90.00 45.00
146 Early Wynn....................... 200.00 100.00
147 Clem Koshorek...................... 75.00 38.00
148 Billy Goodman....................... 90.00 45.00
149 Al Corwin 75.00 38.00
150 Carl Scheib 75.00 38.00
151 Joe Adcock....................... 110.00 55.00
152 Clyde Vollmer 75.00 38.00
153 Whitey Ford...................... 800.00 400.00
154 Turk Lown 75.00 38.00
155 Allie Clark 75.00 38.00
156 Max Surkont.......................... 75.00 38.00
157 Sherm Lollar 90.00 45.00
158 Howard Fox 75.00 38.00
159 Mickey Vernon UER 90.00 45.00
(Photo actually
Floyd Baker)
160 Cal Abrams..................... 500.00 170.00

1954 Bowman

The cards in this 224-card set measure approximately 2 1/2" by 3 3/4". The set was distributed in two separate series: 1-128 in first series and 129-224 in second series. A contractual problem apparently resulted in the deletion of the number 66 Ted Williams card from this Bowman set, thereby creating a scarcity that is highly valued among collectors. The set price below does NOT include number 66 Williams but does include number 66 Jim Piersall, the apparent replacement for Williams in spite of the fact that Piersall was already number 210 to appear later in the set. Many errors in players' statistics exist (and some were corrected) while a few players' names were printed on the front, instead of appearing as a facsimile autograph. Most of these differences are so minor that there is no price differential for either card. The cards which changes were made on are numbers 12, 22,25,26,35,38,41,43,47,53,61,67,80,81,82,85, 93,94,99,103,105,124,138,139, 140,145,153,156,174,179,185,212,216 and 217. The set was issued in seven-card nickel packs and one-card penny packs. The one cent packs were issued 120 to a box. The notable Rookie Cards in this set are Harvey Kuenn and Don Larsen.

NM Ex
COMPLETE SET (224).......... 4000.00 2000.00
WRAP.(1-CENT, DATED)........ 150.00 75.00
WRAP.(1-CENT, UNDATED).... 200.00 100.00
WRAP.(5-CENT, DATED)......... 150.00 75.00
WRAP.(5-CENT, UNDATED)...... 60.00 30.00
1 Phil Rizzuto 175.00 52.50
2 Jackie Jensen 30.00 15.00
3 Marion Fricano 12.00 6.00
4 Bob Hooper............................ 12.00 6.00
5 Billy Hunter 12.00 6.00
6 Nellie Fox............................... 80.00 40.00
7 Walt Dropo 20.00 10.00
8 Jim Busby 12.00 6.00
9 Dave Williams 12.00 6.00
10 Carl Erskine......................... 20.00 10.00
11 Sid Gordon........................... 12.00 6.00
12 Roy McMillan 20.00 10.00
13 Paul Minner.......................... 12.00 6.00
14 Gerry Staley.......................... 12.00 6.00
15 Richie Ashburn..................... 80.00 40.00
16 Jim Wilson 12.00 6.00
17 Tom Gorman......................... 12.00 6.00
18 Hoot Evers............................ 12.00 6.00
19 Bobby Shantz 20.00 10.00
20 Art Houtteman....................... 12.00 6.00
21 Vic Wertz............................... 20.00 10.00
22 Sam Mele 12.00 6.00
23 Harvey Kuenn RC 30.00 15.00
24 Bob Porterfield 12.00 6.00
25 Wes Westrum 20.00 10.00
26 Billy Cox 20.00 10.00
27 Dick Cole 12.00 6.00
28 Jim Greengrass 12.00 6.00
29 Johnny Klippstein................. 12.00 6.00
30 Del Rice................................. 12.00 6.00
31 Smoky Burgess 20.00 10.00
32 Del Crandall.......................... 20.00 10.00
33A Vic Raschi 20.00 10.00
(No mention of
trade on back)
33B Vic Raschi.......................... 30.00 15.00
(Traded to St.Louis)
34 Sammy White........................ 12.00 6.00
35 Eddie Joost 12.00 6.00
36 George Strickland................. 12.00 6.00
37 Dick Kokos 12.00 6.00
38 Minnie Minoso 30.00 15.00
39 Ned Garver 12.00 6.00
40 Gil Coan................................ 12.00 6.00
41 Alvin Dark............................. 20.00 10.00
42 Billy Loes.............................. 20.00 10.00
43 Bob Friend............................ 20.00 10.00
44 Harry Perkowski................... 12.00 6.00
45 Ralph Kiner 50.00 25.00
46 Rip Repulski 12.00 6.00
47 Granny Hamner 12.00 6.00
48 Jack Dittmer.......................... 12.00 6.00
49 Harry Byrd............................ 12.00 6.00
50 George Kell........................... 50.00 25.00
51 Alex Kellner.......................... 12.00 6.00
52 Joe Ginsberg 12.00 6.00
53 Don Lenhardt 12.00 6.00
54 Chico Carrasquel 12.00 6.00
55 Jim Delsing 12.00 6.00
56 Maurice McDermott 12.00 6.00
57 Hoyt Wilhelm........................ 50.00 25.00
58 Pee Wee Reese.................... 80.00 40.00
59 Bob Schultz 12.00 6.00
60 Fred Baczewski.................... 12.00 6.00
61 Eddie Miksis......................... 12.00 6.00
62 Enos Slaughter..................... 50.00 25.00
63 Earl Torgeson....................... 12.00 6.00
64 Eddie Mathews..................... 80.00 40.00
65 Mickey Mantle................. 1500.00 750.00
66A Ted Williams 3000.00 1500.00
66B Jimmy Piersall 80.00 40.00
67 Carl Scheib........................... 12.00 6.00
68 Bobby Avila 20.00 10.00
69 Clint Courtney 12.00 6.00
70 Willard Marshall 12.00 6.00
71 Ted Gray............................... 12.00 6.00
72 Eddie Yost 20.00 10.00
73 Don Mueller.......................... 20.00 10.00
74 Jim Gilliam 30.00 15.00
75 Max Surkont......................... 12.00 6.00
76 Joe Nuxhall 20.00 10.00
77 Bob Rush 12.00 6.00
78 Sal Yvars 12.00 6.00
79 Curt Simmons....................... 20.00 10.00
80 Johnny Logan 20.00 10.00
81 Jerry Coleman...................... 20.00 10.00
82 Billy Goodman...................... 20.00 10.00
83 Ray Murray 12.00 6.00
84 Larry Doby 50.00 25.00
85 Jim Dyck 12.00 6.00
86 Harry Dorish......................... 12.00 6.00
87 Don Lund 12.00 6.00
88 Tom Umphlett 12.00 6.00
89 Willie Mays..................... 500.00 250.00
90 Roy Campanella 150.00 75.00
91 Cal Abrams........................... 12.00 6.00
92 Ken Raffensberger................ 12.00 6.00
93 Bill Serena 12.00 6.00
94 Solly Hemus 12.00 6.00
95 Robin Roberts 50.00 25.00
96 Joe Adcock........................... 20.00 10.00
97 Gil McDougald...................... 20.00 10.00
98 Ellis Kinder 12.00 6.00
99 Pete Suder............................ 12.00 6.00
100 Mike Garcia 20.00 10.00
101 Don Larsen RC 80.00 40.00
102 Billy Pierce 20.00 10.00
103 Steve Souchock.................. 12.00 6.00
104 Frank Shea 12.00 6.00
105 Sal Maglie 20.00 10.00
106 Clem Labine 20.00 10.00
107 Paul LaPalme 12.00 6.00
108 Bobby Adams...................... 12.00 6.00
109 Roy Smalley 12.00 6.00
110 Red Schoendienst 50.00 25.00
111 Murry Dickson..................... 12.00 6.00
112 Andy Pafko 20.00 10.00
113 Allie Reynolds 20.00 10.00
114 Willard Nixon...................... 12.00 6.00
115 Don Bollweg 12.00 6.00
116 Luke Easter 20.00 10.00
117 Dick Kryhoski 12.00 6.00
118 Bob Boyd 12.00 6.00
119 Fred Hatfield....................... 12.00 6.00
120 Mel Hoderlein...................... 12.00 6.00
121 Ray Katt.............................. 12.00 6.00
122 Carl Furillo.......................... 30.00 15.00
123 Toby Atwell 12.00 6.00
124 Gus Bell.............................. 20.00 10.00
125 Warren Hacker 12.00 6.00
126 Cliff Chambers.................... 12.00 6.00
127 Del Ennis............................ 20.00 10.00
128 Ebba St.Claire.................... 12.00 6.00
129 Hank Bauer......................... 30.00 15.00
130 Milt Bolling......................... 12.00 6.00
131 Joe Astroth......................... 12.00 6.00
132 Bob Feller 80.00 40.00
133 Duane Pillette 12.00 6.00
134 Luis Aloma 12.00 6.00
135 Johnny Pesky 20.00 10.00
136 Clyde Vollmer..................... 12.00 6.00
137 Al Corwin 12.00 6.00
138 Gil Hodges.......................... 80.00 40.00
139 Preston Ward 12.00 6.00
140 Saul Rogovin...................... 12.00 6.00
141 Joe Garagiola 30.00 15.00
142 Al Brazle 12.00 6.00
143 Willie Jones........................ 12.00 6.00
144 Ernie Johnson RC............... 30.00 15.00
145 Billy Martin 80.00 40.00
146 Dick Gernert 12.00 6.00
147 Joe DeMaestri 12.00 6.00
148 Dale Mitchell 20.00 10.00
149 Bob Young 12.00 6.00
150 Cass Michaels 12.00 6.00
151 Pat Mullin 12.00 6.00
152 Mickey Vernon 20.00 10.00
153 Whitey Lockman 20.00 10.00
154 Don Newcombe.................. 30.00 15.00
155 Frank Thomas RC............... 20.00 10.00
156 Rocky Bridges.................... 12.00 6.00
157 Turk Lown 12.00 6.00
158 Stu Miller............................ 20.00 10.00
159 Johnny Lindell.................... 12.00 6.00
160 Danny O'Connell................. 12.00 6.00
161 Yogi Berra 175.00 90.00
162 Ted Lepcio.......................... 12.00 6.00
163A Dave Philley 20.00 10.00
(No mention of
trade on back)
163B Dave Philley 30.00 15.00
(Traded to
Cleveland)
164 Early Wynn......................... 50.00 25.00
165 Johnny Groth 12.00 6.00
166 Sandy Consuegra 12.00 6.00
167 Billy Hoeft.......................... 12.00 6.00
168 Ed Fitzgerald...................... 12.00 6.00
169 Larry Jansen 20.00 10.00
170 Duke Snider.................... 175.00 90.00
171 Carlos Bernier 12.00 6.00
172 Andy Seminick 12.00 6.00
173 Dee Fondy 12.00 6.00
174 Pete Castiglione................. 12.00 6.00
175 Mel Clark............................ 12.00 6.00
176 Vern Bickford 12.00 6.00
177 Whitey Ford.................... 100.00 50.00
178 Del Wilber 12.00 6.00
179 Morrie Martin 12.00 6.00
180 Joe Tipton 12.00 6.00
181 Les Moss............................ 12.00 6.00
182 Sherm Lollar....................... 20.00 10.00
183 Matt Batts........................... 12.00 6.00
184 Mickey Grasso.................... 12.00 6.00
185 Daryl Spencer..................... 12.00 6.00
186 Russ Meyer........................ 12.00 6.00
187 Vern Law............................ 20.00 10.00
188 Frank Smith........................ 12.00 6.00
189 Randy Jackson.................... 12.00 6.00
190 Joe Presko 12.00 6.00
191 Karl Drews.......................... 12.00 6.00
192 Lou Burdette 20.00 10.00
193 Eddie Robinson.................. 12.00 6.00
194 Sid Hudson 12.00 6.00
195 Bob Cain............................. 12.00 6.00
196 Bob Lemon.......................... 50.00 25.00
197 Lou Kretlow........................ 12.00 6.00
198 Virgil Trucks....................... 12.00 6.00
199 Steve Gromek..................... 12.00 6.00
200 Conrado Marrero................ 12.00 6.00
201 Bobby Thomson.................. 30.00 15.00
202 George Shuba 20.00 10.00
203 Vic Janowicz 20.00 10.00
204 Jack Collum........................ 12.00 6.00
205 Hal Jeffcoat 12.00 6.00
206 Steve Bilko 12.00 6.00
207 Stan Lopata........................ 12.00 6.00
208 Johnny Antonelli 20.00 10.00
209 Gene Woodling................... 20.00 10.00
210 Jimmy Piersall.................... 30.00 15.00
211 Al Robertson 12.00 6.00
212 Owen Friend 12.00 6.00
213 Dick Littlefield 12.00 6.00
214 Ferris Fain 20.00 10.00
215 Johnny Bucha 12.00 6.00
216 Jerry Snyder....................... 12.00 6.00
217 Hank Thompson................. 20.00 10.00
218 Preacher Roe...................... 20.00 10.00
219 Hal Rice.............................. 12.00 6.00
220 Hobie Landrith.................... 12.00 6.00
221 Frank Baumholtz 12.00 6.00
222 Memo Luna 12.00 6.00
223 Steve Ridzik....................... 12.00 6.00
224 Bill Bruton 50.00 12.50

1955 Bowman

The cards in this 320-card set measure approximately 2 1/2" by 3 3/4". The Bowman set of 1955 is known as the "TV set" because each player photograph is cleverly shown within a television set design. The set contains umpire cards, some transposed pictures (e.g., Johnsons and Bollings), an incorrect spelling for Harvey Kuenn, and a traded line for Palica (all of which are noted in the checklist below). Some three-card advertising strips exist, the backs of these panels contain advertising for Bowman products. Print advertisments for these cards featured Willie Mays along with publicizing the great value in nine cards for a nickel. Advertising panels seen include Nellie Fox/Carl Furillo/Carl Erskine; Hank Aaron/Johnny Logan/Eddie Miksis; Bob Rush/Ray Katt/Willie Mays; Steve Gromek/Milt Bolling/Vern Stephens, Russ Kemmemer/ Hal Jeffcoat/Dee Fondy and a Bob Darnell/Early Wynn/Pee Wee Reese. Cards were issued either in nine-card nickel packs or one card penny packs. Cello packs containing approximately 20 cards have also been seen, albeit on a very limited basis. The notable Rookie Cards in this set are Elston Howard and Don Zimmer. Hall of Fame umpires pictured in the set are Al Barlick, Jocko Conlon and Cal Hubbard. Undated five cent wrappers are also known to exist for this set.

NM Ex
COMPLETE SET (320)........... 5000.00 2500.00
COMMON CARD (1-96)......... 12.00 6.00
COMMON CARD (97-224)....... 10.00 5.00
COMMON (225-320)............. 15.00 7.50
COMMON UMP. 225-320......... 30.00 15.00
WRAPPER (1-CENT)............... 60.00 30.00
WRAPPER (5-CENT)............... 60.00 30.00
1 Hoyt Wilhelm..................... 100.00 22.00
2 Alvin Dark............................ 15.00 7.50
3 Joe Coleman 15.00 7.50
4 Eddie Waitkus 15.00 7.50
5 Jim Robertson...................... 12.00 6.00
6 Pete Suder........................... 12.00 6.00
7 Gene Baker.......................... 12.00 6.00
8 Warren Hacker 12.00 6.00
9 Gil McDougald..................... 20.00 10.00
10 Phil Rizzuto 125.00 60.00
11 Bill Bruton 15.00 7.50
12 Andy Pafko......................... 15.00 7.50
13 Clyde Vollmer..................... 12.00 6.00
14 Gus Keriazakos.................. 12.00 6.00
15 Frank Sullivan.................... 12.00 6.00
16 Jimmy Piersall.................... 20.00 10.00
17 Del Ennis............................ 15.00 7.50
18 Stan Lopata 12.00 6.00
19 Bobby Avila 15.00 7.50
20 Al Smith 15.00 7.50
21 Don Hoak 12.00 6.00
22 Roy Campanella 125.00 60.00
23 Al Kaline 150.00 75.00
24 Al Aber 12.00 6.00
25 Minnie Minoso 30.00 15.00
26 Virgil Trucks 15.00 7.50
27 Preston Ward 12.00 6.00
28 Dick Cole 12.00 6.00
29 Red Schoendienst 30.00 15.00
30 Bill Sarni............................. 12.00 6.00
31 Johnny Temple RC 15.00 7.50
32 Wally Post 15.00 7.50
33 Nellie Fox........................... 50.00 25.00
34 Clint Courtney 12.00 6.00
35 Bill Tuttle............................ 12.00 6.00
36 Wayne Belardi 12.00 6.00
37 Pee Wee Reese............. 1000.00 50.00
38 Early Wynn 30.00 15.00
39 Bob Darnell 15.00 7.50
40 Vic Wertz 15.00 7.50
41 Mel Clark 12.00 6.00
42 Bob Greenwood 12.00 6.00
43 Bob Buhl 15.00 7.50
44 Danny O'Connell................ 12.00 6.00
45 Tom Umphlett 12.00 6.00
46 Mickey Vernon 15.00 7.50
47 Sammy White..................... 12.00 6.00
48A Milt Bolling ERR 20.00 10.00
(Name on back is
Frank Bolling)
48B Milt Bolling COR 20.00 10.00
49 Jim Greengrass.................. 12.00 6.00
50 Hobie Landrith.................... 12.00 6.00
51 Elvin Tappe........................ 12.00 6.00
52 Hal Rice.............................. 12.00 6.00
53 Alex Kellner 12.00 6.00
54 Don Bollweg 12.00 6.00
55 Cal Abrams......................... 12.00 6.00
56 Billy Cox............................. 15.00 7.50
57 Bob Friend.......................... 15.00 7.50
58 Frank Thomas 15.00 7.50
59 Whitey Ford.................... 100.00 50.00
60 Enos Slaughter.................. 30.00 15.00
61 Paul LaPalme 12.00 6.00
62 Royce Lint 12.00 6.00
63 Irv Noren 15.00 7.50
64 Curt Simmons..................... 15.00 7.50
65 Don Zimmer RC 20.00 10.00
66 George Shuba 20.00 10.00
67 Don Larsen......................... 20.00 10.00
68 Elston Howard RC 80.00 40.00
69 Billy Hunter 12.00 6.00
70 Lou Burdette 20.00 10.00
71 Dave Jolly........................... 12.00 6.00
72 Chet Nichols 12.00 6.00
73 Eddie Yost 15.00 7.50
74 Jerry Snyder....................... 12.00 6.00
75 Brooks Lawrence RC.......... 12.00 6.00
76 Tom Poholsky 12.00 6.00
77 Jim McDonald 12.00 6.00
78 Gil Coan.............................. 12.00 6.00
79 Willie Miranda 12.00 6.00
80 Lou Limmer......................... 12.00 6.00
81 Bobby Morgan.................... 12.00 6.00
82 Lee Walls............................ 12.00 6.00
83 Max Surkont....................... 12.00 6.00
84 George Freese 12.00 6.00
85 Cass Michaels 12.00 6.00
86 Ted Gray............................. 12.00 6.00
87 Randy Jackson 12.00 6.00
88 Steve Bilko 12.00 6.00
89 Lou Boudreau MG 30.00 15.00
90 Art Ditmar 12.00 6.00
91 Dick Marlowe 12.00 6.00
92 George Zuverink................. 12.00 6.00
93 Andy Seminick 12.00 6.00
94 Hank Thompson.................. 15.00 7.50
95 Sal Maglie 15.00 7.50
96 Ray Narleski RC 12.00 6.00
97 Johnny Podres.................... 30.00 15.00
98 Jim Gilliam 20.00 10.00
99 Jerry Coleman 15.00 7.50
100 Tom Morgan 10.00 5.00
101A Don Johnson ERR........... 20.00 10.00
(Photo actually
Ernie Johnson)
101B Don Johnson COR 20.00 10.00
102 Bobby Thomson................ 15.00 7.50
103 Eddie Mathews.................. 80.00 40.00
104 Bob Porterfield 10.00 5.00
105 Johnny Schmitz.................. 10.00 5.00
106 Del Rice............................. 10.00 5.00
107 Solly Hemus...................... 10.00 5.00
108 Lou Kretlow....................... 10.00 5.00
109 Vern Stephens................... 15.00 7.50
110 Bob Miller.......................... 10.00 5.00
111 Steve Ridzik....................... 10.00 5.00
112 Granny Hamner 10.00 5.00
113 Bob Hall............................. 10.00 5.00
114 Vic Janowicz 15.00 7.50
115 Roger Bowman 10.00 5.00
116 Sandy Consuegra 10.00 5.00
117 Johnny Groth 10.00 5.00
118 Bobby Adams.................... 10.00 5.00
119 Joe Astroth........................ 10.00 5.00
120 Ed Burtschy........................ 10.00 5.00
121 Rufus Crawford.................. 10.00 5.00
122 Al Corwin 10.00 5.00
123 Marv Grissom 10.00 5.00
124 Johnny Antonelli 15.00 7.50
125 Paul Giel............................ 15.00 7.50
126 Billy Goodman.................... 15.00 7.50
127 Hank Majeski 10.00 5.00
128 Mike Garcia 15.00 7.50
129 Hal Naragon 10.00 5.00
130 Richie Ashburn.................. 50.00 25.00
131 Willard Marshall 10.00 5.00
132A Harvey Kueen ERR.......... 50.00 25.00
(Sic& Kuenn)
132B Harvey Kuenn COR.......... 30.00 15.00
133 Charles King...................... 10.00 5.00
134 Bob Feller.......................... 80.00 40.00
135 Lloyd Merriman.................. 10.00 5.00
136 Rocky Bridges.................... 10.00 5.00
137 Bob Talbot......................... 10.00 5.00
138 Davey Williams.................. 15.00 7.50
139 Shantz Brothers................. 15.00 7.50
Wilmer Shantz
Bobby Shantz
140 Bobby Shantz 15.00 7.50
141 Wes Westrum 15.00 7.50
142 Rudy Regalado................... 10.00 5.00
143 Don Newcombe.................. 30.00 15.00
144 Art Houtteman.................... 10.00 5.00
145 Bob Nieman........................ 10.00 5.00
146 Don Liddle.......................... 10.00 5.00
147 Sam Mele 10.00 5.00
148 Bob Chakales...................... 10.00 5.00
149 Cloyd Boyer........................ 10.00 5.00
150 Billy Klaus 10.00 5.00
151 Jim Brideweser 10.00 5.00
152 Johnny Klippstein.............. 10.00 5.00
153 Eddie Robinson.................. 10.00 5.00
154 Frank Lary RC..................... 15.00 7.50
155 Gerry Staley....................... 10.00 5.00
156 Jim Hughes 15.00 7.50
157A Ernie Johnson ERR 20.00 10.00
(Photo actually
Don Johnson)
157B Ernie Johnson COR.......... 20.00 10.00
158 Gil Hodges......................... 50.00 25.00
159 Harry Byrd......................... 10.00 5.00
160 Bill Skowron....................... 20.00 10.00
161 Matt Batts........................... 10.00 5.00
162 Charlie Maxwell................. 10.00 5.00
163 Sid Gordon 15.00 7.50
164 Toby Atwell 10.00 5.00
165 Maurice McDermott 10.00 5.00
166 Jim Busby 10.00 5.00
167 Bob Grim RC 20.00 10.00
168 Yogi Berra 125.00 60.00
169 Carl Furillo........................ 30.00 15.00
170 Carl Erskine....................... 20.00 10.00
171 Robin Roberts 50.00 25.00
172 Willie Jones....................... 10.00 5.00
173 Chico Carrasquel............... 10.00 5.00
174 Sherm Lollar 15.00 7.50
175 Wilmer Shantz................... 10.00 5.00
176 Joe DeMaestri 10.00 5.00
177 Willard Nixon..................... 10.00 5.00
178 Tom Brewer....................... 10.00 5.00
179 Hank Aaron 250.00 125.00
180 Johnny Logan 15.00 7.50
181 Eddie Miksis...................... 10.00 5.00
182 Bob Rush 10.00 5.00
183 Ray Katt............................. 10.00 5.00
184 Willie Mays.................... 250.00 125.00
185 Vic Raschi 10.00 5.00
186 Alex Grammas.................... 10.00 5.00
187 Fred Hatfield...................... 10.00 5.00
188 Ned Garver 10.00 5.00
189 Jack Collum....................... 10.00 5.00
190 Fred Baczewski.................. 10.00 5.00
191 Bob Lemon......................... 30.00 15.00
192 George Strickland.............. 10.00 5.00
193 Howie Judson 10.00 5.00
194 Joe Nuxhall 15.00 7.50
195A Erv Palica 15.00 7.50
(Without trade)
195B Erv Palica 40.00 20.00
(With trade)
196 Russ Meyer........................ 15.00 7.50
197 Ralph Kiner 30.00 15.00
198 Dave Pope.......................... 10.00 5.00
199 Vern Law............................ 15.00 7.50
200 Dick Littlefield 10.00 5.00
201 Allie Reynolds 20.00 10.00
202 Mickey Mantle UER 800.00 400.00
Birthdate listed as 10/30/31
Should be 10/20/31
203 Steve Gromek.................... 10.00 5.00
204A Frank Bolling ERR 20.00 10.00
(Name on back is
Milt Bolling)
204B Frank Bolling COR........... 20.00 10.00
205 Rip Repulski....................... 10.00 5.00
206 Ralph Beard........................ 10.00 5.00
207 Frank Shea 10.00 5.00
208 Ed Fitzgerald...................... 10.00 5.00
209 Smoky Burgess 15.00 7.50
210 Earl Torgeson.................... 10.00 5.00
211 Sonny Dixon....................... 10.00 5.00
212 Jack Dittmer....................... 10.00 5.00
213 George Kell........................ 30.00 15.00

Card	NM	Ex
214 Billy Pierce	15.00	7.50
215 Bob Kuzava	10.00	5.00
216 Preacher Roe	20.00	10.00
217 Del Crandall	15.00	7.50
218 Joe Adcock	15.00	7.50
219 Whitey Lockman	15.00	7.50
220 Jim Hearn	10.00	5.00
221 Hector Brown	10.00	5.00
222 Russ Kemmerer	10.00	5.00
223 Hal Jeffcoat	10.00	5.00
224 Dee Fondy	10.00	5.00
225 Paul Richards MG	15.00	7.50
226 Bill McKinley UMP RC	30.00	15.00
227 Frank Baumholtz	15.00	7.50
228 John Phillips	15.00	7.50
229 Jim Brosnan RC	20.00	10.00
230 Al Brazle	15.00	7.50
231 Jim Konstanty	20.00	10.00
232 Birdie Tebbetts MG	20.00	10.00
233 Bill Serena	15.00	7.50
234 Dick Bartell CO	20.00	10.00
235 Joe Paparella UMP RC	30.00	15.00
236 Murry Dickson	15.00	7.50
237 Johnny Wyrostek	15.00	7.50
238 Eddie Stanky MG	20.00	10.00
239 Edwin Rommel UMP	40.00	20.00
240 Billy Loes	20.00	10.00
241 Johnny Pesky CO	20.00	10.00
242 Ernie Banks	350.00	180.00
243 Gus Bell	20.00	10.00
244 Duane Pillette	15.00	7.50
245 Bill Miller	15.00	7.50
246 Hank Bauer	30.00	15.00
247 Dutch Leonard CO	15.00	7.50
248 Harry Dorish	15.00	7.50
249 Billy Gardner RC	20.00	10.00
250 Larry Napp UMP RC	30.00	15.00
251 Stan Jok	15.00	7.50
252 Roy Smalley	15.00	7.50
253 Jim Wilson	15.00	7.50
254 Bennett Flowers	15.00	7.50
255 Pete Runnels	20.00	10.00
256 Owen Friend	15.00	7.50
257 Tom Alston	15.00	7.50
258 John Stevens UMP RC	30.00	15.00
259 Don Mossi RC	30.00	15.00
260 Edwin Hurley UMP RC	30.00	15.00
261 Walt Moryn	20.00	10.00
262 Jim Lemon	15.00	7.50
263 Eddie Joost	15.00	7.50
264 Bill Henry	15.00	7.50
265 Albert Barlick UMP RC	80.00	40.00
266 Mike Fornieles	15.00	7.50
267 Jim Honochick UMP RC	80.00	40.00
268 Roy Lee Hawes	15.00	7.50
269 Joe Amalfitano RC	20.00	10.00
270 Chico Fernandez	20.00	10.00
271 Bob Hooper	15.00	7.50
272 John Flaherty UMP RC	30.00	15.00
273 Bubba Church	15.00	7.50
274 Jim Delsing	15.00	7.50
275 William Grieve UMP RC	30.00	15.00
276 Ike Delock	15.00	7.50
277 Ed Runge UMP RC	30.00	15.00
278 Charlie Neal RC	40.00	20.00
279 Hank Soar UMP RC	40.00	20.00
280 Clyde McCullough	15.00	7.50
281 Charles Berry UMP	40.00	20.00
282 Phil Cavarretta	20.00	10.00
283 Nestor Chylak UMP RC	80.00	40.00
284 Bill Jackowski UMP RC	30.00	15.00
285 Walt Dropo	20.00	10.00
286 Frank Secory UMP RC	30.00	15.00
287 Ron Mrozinski	15.00	7.50
288 Dick Smith	15.00	7.50
289 Arthur Gore UMP RC	30.00	15.00
290 Hershell Freeman	15.00	7.50
291 Frank Dascoli UMP RC	30.00	15.00
292 Marv Blaylock	15.00	7.50
293 Thomas Gorman UMP RC	40.00	20.00
294 Wally Moses CO	15.00	7.50
295 Lee Ballanfant UMP RC	30.00	15.00
296 Bill Virdon RC	30.00	15.00
297 Dusty Boggess UMP RC	30.00	15.00
298 Charlie Grimm MG	20.00	10.00
299 Lon Warneke UMP	40.00	20.00
300 Tommy Byrne	20.00	10.00
301 William Engeln UMP RC	30.00	15.00
302 Frank Malzone RC	30.00	15.00
303 Jocko Conlan UMP	80.00	40.00
304 Harry Chiti	15.00	7.50
305 Frank Umont UMP RC	30.00	15.00
306 Bob Cerv	20.00	10.00
307 Babe Pinelli UMP	40.00	20.00
308 Al Lopez MG	50.00	25.00
309 Hal Dixon UMP RC	30.00	15.00
310 Ken Lehman	15.00	7.50
311 Lawrence Goetz UMP RC	30.00	15.00
312 Bill Wight	15.00	7.50
313 Augie Donatelli UMP RC	50.00	25.00
314 Dale Mitchell	20.00	10.00
315 Cal Hubbard UMP RC	80.00	40.00
316 Marion Fricano	15.00	7.50
317 W. Summers UMP	20.00	10.00
318 Sid Hudson	15.00	7.50
319 Al Schroll	15.00	7.50
320 George Susce RC	50.00	10.00

1955 Bowman Advertising Strips

For Bowman's final set; these advertising panels have been seen. The fronts are standard 1955 Bowman cards while the backs have advertising information.

	NM	Ex
COMPLETE SET	500.00	250.00
1 Nellie Fox	100.00	50.00
Carl Furillo		
Carl Erskine		
2 Hank Aaron	150.00	75.00
Johnny Logan		
Eddie Miksis		
3 Bob Rush	150.00	75.00
Ray Katt		
Willie Mays		
4 Steve Gromek	50.00	25.00
Milt Bolling		
Vern Stephens		
5 Bob Darnell	120.00	60.00
Early Wynn		
Pee Wee Reese		
6 Russ Kemmerer	50.00	25.00
Hal Jeffcoat		
Dee Fondy		
7 Don Bollweg	50.00	25.00
Cal Abrams		
Billy Cox		

1982 Bowman 1952 Extension

In 1980, 15 unissued pieces of artwork initially intended to be used by Bowman Gum in their 1952 baseball card set were discovered. This set consists of 15 cards made from this original artwork. The backs have been created to resemble the original 1952 series, and the set has been numbered 253-267 (the next 15 cards in the 1952 Bowman sequence). The facsimile autograph on the original 1952 Bowmans has been omitted from the cards in this set. This set was originally available from the producer for $3 per set.

	Nm-Mt	Ex-Mt
COMPLETE SET (15)	5.00	2.00
253 Bob Kennedy	.25	.10
254 Barney McCosky	.25	.10
255 Chris Van Cuyk	.25	.10
256 Morrie Martin	.25	.10
257 Jim Wilson	.25	.10
258 Bob Thorpe	.25	.10
259 Bill Henry	.25	.10
260 Bob Addis	.25	.10
261 Terry Moore CO	.75	.30
262 Joe Dobson	.25	.10
263 John Merson	.25	.10
264 Virgil Trucks	.50	.20
265 Johnny Hopp	.25	.10
267 George Shuba	.50	.20

1989 Bowman

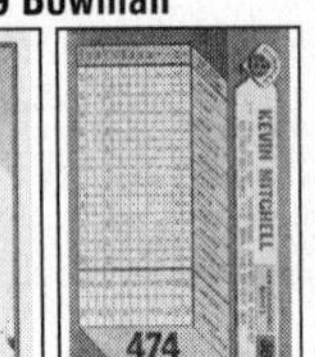

The 1989 Bowman set, produced by Topps, contains 484 slightly oversized cards (measuring 2 1/2" by 3 3/4"). The cards were released in midseason 1989 in wax, rack, cello and factory set formats. The fronts have white-bordered color photos with facsimile autographs and small Bowman logos. The backs feature charts detailing 1988 player performances vs. each team. The cards are ordered alphabetically according to teams in the AL and NL. Cards 258-261 form a father/son subset. Rookie Cards in this set include Sandy Alomar Jr., Steve Finley, Ken Griffey Jr., Tino Martinez, Gary Sheffield, John Smoltz and Robin Ventura.

	Nm-Mt	Ex-Mt
COMPLETE SET (484)	25.00	10.00
COMP.FACT.SET (484)	25.00	10.00
1 Oswald Peraza	.05	.02
2 Brian Holton	.05	.02
3 Jose Bautista RC	.10	.04
4 Pete Harnisch RC	.25	.10
5 Dave Schmidt	.05	.02
6 Gregg Olson RC	.25	.10
7 Jeff Ballard	.05	.02
8 Bob Melvin	.05	.02
9 Cal Ripken	.75	.30
10 Randy Milligan	.05	.02
11 Juan Bell RC	.10	.04
12 Billy Ripken	.05	.02
13 Jim Traber	.05	.02
14 Pete Stanicek	.05	.02
15 Steve Finley RC	.50	.20
16 Larry Sheets	.05	.02
17 Phil Bradley	.05	.02
18 Brady Anderson RC	.50	.20
19 Lee Smith	.10	.04
20 Tom Fischer	.05	.02
21 Mike Boddicker	.05	.02
22 Rob Murphy	.05	.02
23 Wes Gardner	.05	.02
24 John Dopson	.05	.02
25 Bob Stanley	.05	.02
26 Roger Clemens	.50	.20
27 Rich Gedman	.05	.02
28 Marty Barrett	.05	.02
29 Luis Rivera	.05	.02
30 Jody Reed	.05	.02
31 Nick Esasky	.05	.02
32 Wade Boggs	.15	.06
33 Jim Rice	.10	.04
34 Mike Greenwell	.05	.02
35 Dwight Evans	.10	.04
36 Ellis Burks	.15	.06
37 Chuck Finley	.10	.04
38 Kirk McCaskill	.05	.02
39 Jim Abbott RC*	.50	.20
40 Bryan Harvey RC *	.25	.10
41 Bert Blyleven	.10	.04
42 Mike Witt	.05	.02
43 Bob McClure	.05	.02
44 Bill Schroeder	.05	.02
45 Lance Parrish	.05	.02
46 Dick Schofield	.05	.02
47 Wally Joyner	.10	.04
48 Jack Howell	.05	.02
49 Johnny Ray	.05	.02
50 Chili Davis	.10	.04
51 Tony Armas	.05	.02
52 Claudell Washington	.05	.02
53 Brian Downing	.05	.02
54 Devon White	.10	.04
55 Bobby Thigpen	.05	.02
56 Bill Long	.05	.02
57 Jerry Reuss	.05	.02
58 Shawn Hillegas	.05	.02
59 Melido Perez	.05	.02
60 Jeff Bittiger	.05	.02
61 Jack McDowell	.10	.04
62 Carlton Fisk	.15	.06
63 Steve Lyons	.05	.02
64 Ozzie Guillen	.05	.02
65 Robin Ventura RC	.75	.30
66 Fred Manrique	.05	.02
67 Dan Pasqua	.05	.02
68 Ivan Calderon	.05	.02
69 Ron Kittle	.05	.02
70 Daryl Boston	.05	.02
71 Dave Gallagher	.05	.02
72 Harold Baines	.10	.04
73 Charles Nagy RC	.25	.10
74 John Farrell	.05	.02
75 Kevin Wickander	.05	.02
76 Greg Swindell	.05	.02
77 Mike Walker	.05	.02
78 Doug Jones	.05	.02
79 Rich Yett	.05	.02
80 Tom Candiotti	.05	.02
81 Jesse Orosco	.05	.02
82 Bud Black	.05	.02
83 Andy Allanson	.05	.02
84 Pete O'Brien	.05	.02
85 Jerry Browne	.05	.02
86 Brook Jacoby	.05	.02
87 Mark Lewis RC	.10	.04
88 Luis Aguayo	.05	.02
89 Cory Snyder	.05	.02
90 Oddibe McDowell	.05	.02
91 Joe Carter	.15	.06
92 Frank Tanana	.05	.02
93 Jack Morris	.10	.04
94 Doyle Alexander	.05	.02
95 Steve Searcy	.05	.02
96 Randy Bockus	.05	.02
97 Jeff M. Robinson	.05	.02
98 Mike Henneman	.05	.02
99 Paul Gibson	.05	.02
100 Frank Williams	.05	.02
101 Matt Nokes	.05	.02
102 Rico Brogna RC UER (Misspelled Ricco on card back)	.40	.16
103 Lou Whitaker	.10	.04
104 Al Pedrique	.05	.02
105 Alan Trammell	.15	.06
106 Chris Brown	.05	.02
107 Pat Sheridan	.05	.02
108 Chet Lemon	.05	.02
109 Keith Moreland	.05	.02
110 Mel Stottlemyre Jr.	.05	.02
111 Bret Saberhagen	.10	.04
112 Floyd Bannister	.05	.02
113 Jeff Montgomery	.10	.04
114 Steve Farr	.05	.02
115 Tom Gordon UER RC (Front shows autograph of Don Gordon)	.25	.10
116 Charlie Leibrandt	.05	.02
117 Mark Gubicza	.05	.02
118 Mike Macfarlane RC	.25	.10
119 Bob Boone	.10	.04
120 Kurt Stillwell	.05	.02
121 George Brett	.60	.24
122 Frank White	.10	.04
123 Kevin Seitzer	.05	.02
124 Willie Wilson	.05	.02
125 Pat Tabler	.05	.02
126 Bo Jackson	.25	.10
127 Hugh Walker RC	.10	.04
128 Danny Tartabull	.05	.02
129 Teddy Higuera	.05	.02
130 Don August	.05	.02
131 Juan Nieves	.05	.02
132 Mike Birkbeck	.05	.02
133 Dan Plesac	.05	.02
134 Chris Bosio	.05	.02
135 Bill Wegman	.05	.02
136 Chuck Crim	.05	.02
137 B.J. Surhoff	.10	.04
138 Joey Meyer	.05	.02
139 Dale Sveum	.05	.02
140 Paul Molitor	.15	.06
141 Jim Gantner	.05	.02
142 Gary Sheffield RC	1.50	.60
143 Greg Brock	.05	.02
144 Robin Yount	.40	.16
145 Glenn Braggs	.05	.02
146 Rob Deer	.05	.02
147 Fred Toliver	.05	.02
148 Jeff Reardon	.10	.04
149 Allan Anderson	.05	.02
150 Frank Viola	.05	.02
151 Shane Rawley	.05	.02
152 Juan Berenguer	.05	.02
153 Johnny Ard	.05	.02
154 Tim Laudner	.05	.02
155 Brian Harper	.05	.02
156 Al Newman	.05	.02
157 Kent Hrbek	.10	.04
158 Gary Gaetti	.10	.04
159 Wally Backman	.05	.02
160 Gene Larkin	.05	.02
161 Greg Gagne	.05	.02
162 Kirby Puckett	.25	.10
163 Dan Gladden	.05	.02
164 Randy Bush	.05	.02
165 Dave LaPoint	.05	.02
166 Andy Hawkins	.05	.02
167 Dave Righetti	.05	.02
168 Lance McCullers	.05	.02
169 Jimmy Jones	.05	.02
170 Al Leiter	.25	.10
171 John Candelaria	.05	.02
172 Don Slaught	.05	.02
173 Jamie Quirk	.05	.02
174 Rafael Santana	.05	.02
175 Mike Pagliarulo	.05	.02
176 Don Mattingly	.60	.24
177 Ken Phelps	.05	.02
178 Steve Sax	.05	.02
179 Dave Winfield	.10	.04
180 Stan Jefferson	.05	.02
181 Rickey Henderson	.25	.10
182 Bob Brower	.05	.02
183 Roberto Kelly	.10	.04
184 Curt Young	.05	.02
185 Gene Nelson	.05	.02
186 Bob Welch	.05	.02
187 Rick Honeycutt	.05	.02
188 Dave Stewart	.10	.04
189 Mike Moore	.05	.02
190 Dennis Eckersley	.10	.04
191 Eric Plunk	.05	.02
192 Storm Davis	.05	.02
193 Terry Steinbach	.10	.04
194 Ron Hassey	.05	.02
195 Stan Royer RC	.10	.04
196 Walt Weiss	.05	.02
197 Mark McGwire	1.00	.40
198 Carney Lansford	.10	.04
199 Glenn Hubbard	.05	.02
200 Dave Henderson	.05	.02
201 Jose Canseco	.25	.10
202 Dave Parker	.10	.04
203 Scott Bankhead	.05	.02
204 Tom Niedenfuer	.05	.02
205 Mark Langston	.05	.02
206 Erik Hanson RC	.25	.10
207 Mike Jackson	.05	.02
208 Dave Valle	.05	.02
209 Scott Bradley	.05	.02
210 Harold Reynolds	.10	.04
211 Tino Martinez RC	.75	.30
212 Rich Renteria	.05	.02
213 Rey Quinones	.05	.02
214 Jim Presley	.05	.02
215 Alvin Davis	.05	.02
216 Edgar Martinez	.25	.10
217 Darnell Coles	.05	.02
218 Jeffrey Leonard	.05	.02
219 Jay Buhner	.10	.04
220 Ken Griffey Jr. RC	8.00	3.20
221 Drew Hall	.05	.02
222 Bobby Witt	.05	.02
223 Jamie Moyer	.10	.04
224 Charlie Hough	.10	.04
225 Nolan Ryan	1.00	.40
226 Jeff Russell	.05	.02
227 Jim Sundberg	.05	.02
228 Julio Franco	.05	.02
229 Buddy Bell	.10	.04
230 Scott Fletcher	.05	.02
231 Jeff Kunkel	.05	.02
232 Steve Buechele	.05	.02
233 Monty Fariss	.05	.02
234 Rick Leach	.05	.02
235 Ruben Sierra	.05	.02
236 Cecil Espy	.05	.02
237 Rafael Palmeiro	.25	.10
238 Pete Incaviglia	.05	.02
239 Dave Stieb	.05	.02
240 Jeff Musselman	.05	.02
241 Mike Flanagan	.05	.02
242 Todd Stottlemyre	.15	.06
243 Jimmy Key	.10	.04
244 Tony Castillo RC	.10	.04
245 Alex Sanchez	.05	.02
246 Tom Henke	.05	.02
247 John Cerutti	.05	.02
248 Ernie Whitt	.05	.02
249 Bob Brenly	.05	.02
250 Rance Mulliniks	.05	.02
251 Kelly Gruber	.05	.02
252 Ed Sprague RC	.25	.10
253 Fred McGriff	.25	.10
254 Tony Fernandez	.05	.02
255 Tom Lawless	.05	.02
256 George Bell	.05	.02
257 Jesse Barfield	.05	.02
258 Roberto Alomar	.25	.10
Sandy Alomar		
259 Ken Griffey Jr.	1.00	.40
Ken Griffey Sr.		
260 Cal Ripken Jr.	.25	.10
Cal Ripken Sr.		
261 Mel Stottlemyre Jr.	.05	.02
Mel Stottlemyre Sr.		
262 Zane Smith	.05	.02
263 Charlie Puleo	.05	.02
264 Derek Lilliquist RC	.10	.04
265 Paul Assenmacher	.05	.02
266 John Smoltz RC	1.00	.40
267 Tom Glavine	.25	.10
268 Steve Avery RC	.25	.10
269 Pete Smith	.05	.02
270 Jody Davis	.05	.02
271 Bruce Benedict	.05	.02
272 Andres Thomas	.05	.02
273 Gerald Perry	.05	.02
274 Ron Gant	.10	.04
275 Darrell Evans	.10	.04
276 Dale Murphy	.25	.10
277 Dion James	.05	.02
278 Lonnie Smith	.05	.02
279 Geronimo Berroa	.05	.02
280 Steve Wilson RC	.10	.04
281 Rick Sutcliffe	.10	.04
282 Kevin Coffman	.05	.02
283 Mitch Williams	.05	.02
284 Greg Maddux	.50	.20
285 Paul Kilgus	.05	.02
286 Mike Harkey RC	.10	.04
287 Lloyd McClendon	.05	.02
288 Damon Berryhill	.05	.02
289 Ty Griffin	.05	.02
290 Ryne Sandberg	.40	.16
291 Mark Grace	.25	.10
292 Curt Wilkerson	.05	.02
293 Vance Law	.05	.02
294 Shawon Dunston	.05	.02
295 Jerome Walton	.25	.10
296 Mitch Webster	.05	.02
297 Dwight Smith RC	.10	.04
298 Andre Dawson	.10	.04
299 Jeff Sellers	.05	.02
300 Jose Rijo	.05	.02
301 John Franco	.10	.04
302 Rick Mahler	.05	.02
303 Ron Robinson	.05	.02
304 Danny Jackson	.05	.02
305 Rob Dibble RC *	.50	.20
306 Tom Browning	.05	.02
307 Bo Diaz	.05	.02
308 Manny Trillo	.05	.02
309 Chris Sabo RC *	.40	.16
310 Ron Oester	.05	.02
311 Barry Larkin	.25	.10
312 Todd Benzinger	.05	.02
313 Paul O'Neill	.15	.06
314 Kal Daniels	.05	.02
315 Joel Youngblood	.05	.02
316 Eric Davis	.10	.04
317 Dave Smith	.05	.02
318 Mark Portugal	.05	.02
319 Brian Meyer	.05	.02
320 Jim Deshaies	.05	.02
321 Juan Agosto	.05	.02
322 Mike Scott	.05	.02
323 Rick Rhoden	.05	.02
324 Jim Clancy	.05	.02
325 Larry Andersen	.05	.02
326 Alex Trevino	.05	.02
327 Alan Ashby	.05	.02
328 Craig Reynolds	.05	.02
329 Bill Doran	.05	.02
330 Rafael Ramirez	.05	.02
331 Glenn Davis	.05	.02
332 Willie Ansley RC	.10	.04
333 Gerald Young	.05	.02
334 Cameron Drew	.05	.02
335 Jay Howell	.05	.02
336 Tim Belcher	.05	.02
337 Fernando Valenzuela	.10	.04
338 Ricky Horton	.05	.02
339 Tim Leary	.05	.02
340 Bill Bene	.05	.02
341 Orel Hershiser	.10	.04
342 Mike Scioscia	.05	.02
343 Rick Dempsey	.05	.02
344 Willie Randolph	.10	.04
345 Alfredo Griffin	.05	.02
346 Eddie Murray	.25	.10
347 Mickey Hatcher	.05	.02
348 Mike Sharperson	.05	.02
349 John Shelby	.05	.02
350 Mike Marshall	.05	.02
351 Kirk Gibson	.10	.04
352 Mike Davis	.05	.02
353 Bryn Smith	.05	.02
354 Pascual Perez	.05	.02
355 Kevin Gross	.05	.02
356 Andy McGaffigan	.05	.02
357 Brian Holman RC *	.10	.04
358 Dave Wainhouse RC	.10	.04
359 Dennis Martinez	.10	.04
360 Tim Burke	.05	.02
361 Nelson Santovenia	.05	.02
362 Tim Wallach	.05	.02
363 Spike Owen	.05	.02
364 Rex Hudler	.05	.02
365 Andres Galarraga	.10	.04
366 Otis Nixon	.05	.02
367 Hubie Brooks	.05	.02
368 Mike Aldrete	.05	.02
369 Tim Raines	.10	.04
370 Dave Martinez	.05	.02
371 Bob Ojeda	.05	.02
372 Ron Darling	.05	.02
373 Wally Whitehurst RC	.10	.04
374 Randy Myers	.10	.04
375 David Cone	.10	.04
376 Dwight Gooden	.15	.06
377 Sid Fernandez	.05	.02
378 Dave Proctor	.05	.02
379 Gary Carter	.15	.06
380 Keith Miller	.05	.02
381 Gregg Jefferies	.10	.04
382 Tim Teufel	.05	.02
383 Kevin Elster	.05	.02
384 Dave Magadan	.05	.02
385 Keith Hernandez	.15	.06
386 Mookie Wilson	.10	.04
387 Darryl Strawberry	.15	.06
388 Kevin McReynolds	.05	.02
389 Mark Carreon	.05	.02
390 Jeff Parrett	.05	.02
391 Mike Maddux	.05	.02
392 Don Carman	.05	.02
393 Bruce Ruffin	.05	.02
394 Ken Howell	.05	.02
395 Steve Bedrosian	.05	.02
396 Floyd Youmans	.05	.02
397 Larry McWilliams	.05	.02
398 Pat Combs RC *	.10	.04
399 Steve Lake	.05	.02
400 Dickie Thon	.05	.02
401 Ricky Jordan RC *	.25	.10
402 Mike Schmidt	.50	.20
403 Tom Herr	.05	.02
404 Chris James	.05	.02
405 Juan Samuel	.05	.02
406 Von Hayes	.05	.02
407 Ron Jones	.05	.02
408 Curt Ford	.05	.02
409 Bob Walk	.05	.02
410 Jeff D. Robinson	.05	.02
411 Jim Gott	.05	.02
412 Scott Medvin	.05	.02
413 John Smiley	.05	.02
414 Bob Kipper	.05	.02
415 Brian Fisher	.05	.02
416 Doug Drabek	.05	.02
417 Mike LaValliere	.05	.02
418 Ken Oberkfell	.05	.02

419 Sid Bream .05 .02
420 Austin Manahan .05 .02
421 Jose Lind .05 .02
422 Bobby Bonilla .10 .04
423 Glenn Wilson .05 .02
424 Andy Van Slyke .10 .04
425 Gary Redus .05 .02
426 Barry Bonds 1.25 .50
427 Don Heinkel .05 .02
428 Ken Dayley .05 .02
429 Todd Worrell .05 .02
430 Brad DuVall .05 .02
431 Jose DeLeon .05 .02
432 Joe Magrane .05 .02
433 John Ericks .05 .02
434 Frank DiPino .05 .02
435 Tony Pena .05 .02
436 Ozzie Smith .40 .16
437 Terry Pendleton .10 .04
438 Jose Oquendo .05 .02
439 Tim Jones .05 .02
440 Pedro Guerrero .05 .02
441 Milt Thompson .05 .02
442 Willie McGee .10 .04
443 Vince Coleman .05 .02
444 Tom Brunansky .05 .02
445 Walt Terrell .05 .02
446 Eric Show .05 .02
447 Mark Davis .05 .02
448 Andy Benes RC .40 .16
449 Ed Whitson .05 .02
450 Dennis Rasmussen .05 .02
451 Bruce Hurst .05 .02
452 Pat Clements .05 .02
453 Benito Santiago .10 .04
454 Sandy Alomar Jr. RC .40 .16
455 Garry Templeton .05 .02
456 Jack Clark .05 .02
457 Tim Flannery .05 .02
458 Roberto Alomar .30 .12
459 Carmelo Martinez .05 .02
460 John Kruk .10 .04
461 Tony Gwynn .30 .12
462 Jerald Clark RC .10 .04
463 Don Robinson .05 .02
464 Craig Lefferts .05 .02
465 Kelly Downs .05 .02
466 Rick Reuschel .05 .02
467 Scott Garrelts .05 .02
468 Wil Tejada .05 .02
469 Kirt Manwaring .05 .02
470 Terry Kennedy .05 .02
471 Jose Uribe .05 .02
472 Royce Clayton RC .40 .16
473 Robby Thompson .05 .02
474 Kevin Mitchell .10 .04
475 Ernie Riles .05 .02
476 Will Clark .25 .10
477 Donell Nixon .05 .02
478 Candy Maldonado .05 .02
479 Tracy Jones .05 .02
480 Brett Butler .10 .04
481 Checklist 1-121 .05 .02
482 Checklist 122-242 .05 .02
483 Checklist 243-363 .05 .02
484 Checklist 364-484 .05 .02

1989 Bowman Tiffany

This is a parallel to the regular 1989 Bowman set. This set was issued with a glossy front and white-stock backs, thus joining other sets known in the Topps family as "Tiffany" sets. The set measure 2 1/2" by 3 3/4" and was issued in factory set form only. In addition to the 484 regular cards, the 11 Reprint inserts were also included in the factory set. Reportedly, only 6,000 factory sets were printed.

Nm-Mt Ex-Mt
COMP.FACT.SET (495) 300.00 120.00
*STARS: 8X TO 20X BASIC CARDS
*ROOKIES: 8X TO 20X BASIC CARDS

1989 Bowman Reprint Inserts

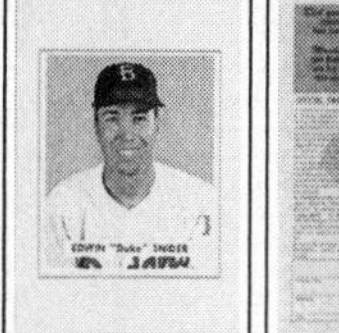
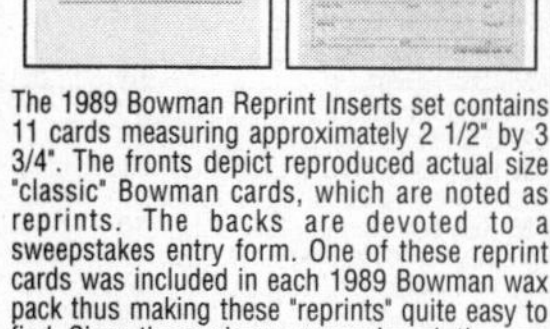

The 1989 Bowman Reprint Inserts set contains 11 cards measuring approximately 2 1/2" by 3 3/4". The fronts depict reproduced actual size "classic" Bowman cards, which are noted as reprints. The backs are devoted to a sweepstakes entry form. One of these reprint cards was included in each 1989 Bowman wax pack thus making these "reprints" quite easy to find. Since the cards are unnumbered, they are ordered below in alphabetical order by player's name and year within player.

Nm-Mt Ex-Mt
*TIFFANY: 10X TO 20X HI COLUMN
ONE TIFF.REP.SET PER TIFF.FACT.SET
1 Richie Ashburn 49 .25 .10
2 Yogi Berra 48 .25 .10
3 Whitey Ford 51 .25 .10
4 Gil Hodges 49 .30 .12
5 Mickey Mantle 51 1.00 .40
6 Mickey Mantle 53 1.00 .40
7 Willie Mays 51 .50 .20
8 Satchel Paige 49 .25 .10
9 Jackie Robinson 50 .50 .20
10 Duke Snider 49 .25 .10
11 Ted Williams 54 .50 .20

1990 Bowman

The 1990 Bowman set (produced by Topps) consists of 528 standard-size cards. The cards were issued in wax packs and factory sets. Each wax pack contained one of 11 different 1950's retro art cards. Unlike most sets, player selection focused primarily on rookies instead

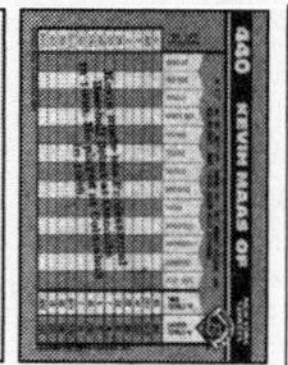

of proven major leaguers. The cards feature a white border with the player's photo inside and the Bowman logo on top. The card numbering is in team order with the teams themselves being ordered alphabetically within each league. Notable Rookie Cards include Moises Alou, Travis Fryman, Juan Gonzalez, Chuck Knoblauch, Ray Lankford, Sammy Sosa, Frank Thomas, Mo Vaughn, Larry Walker, and Bernie Williams.

Nm-Mt Ex-Mt
COMPLETE SET (528) 25.00 7.50
COMP.FACT.SET (528) 25.00 7.50
1 Tommy Greene RC .10 .03
2 Tom Glavine .15 .04
3 Andy Nezelek .05 .02
4 Mike Stanton RC .25 .07
5 Rick Luecken .05 .02
6 Kent Mercker RC .25 .07
7 Derek Lilliquist .05 .02
8 Charlie Leibrandt .05 .02
9 Steve Avery .05 .02
10 John Smoltz .25 .07
11 Mark Lemke .05 .02
12 Lonnie Smith .05 .02
13 Oddibe McDowell .05 .02
14 Tyler Houston RC .25 .07
15 Jeff Blauser .05 .02
16 Ernie Whitt .05 .02
17 Alexis Infante .05 .02
18 Jim Presley .05 .02
19 Dale Murphy .25 .07
20 Nick Esasky .05 .02
21 Rick Sutcliffe .10 .03
22 Mike Bielecki .05 .02
23 Steve Wilson .05 .02
24 Kevin Blankenship .05 .02
25 Mitch Williams .05 .02
26 Dean Wilkins .05 .02
27 Greg Maddux .40 .12
28 Mike Harkey .05 .02
29 Mark Grace .15 .04
30 Ryne Sandberg .40 .12
31 Greg Smith .05 .02
32 Dwight Smith .05 .02
33 Damon Berryhill .05 .02
34 E.Cunningham UER RC .10 .03
(Errant * by the word "in")
35 Jerome Walton .05 .02
36 Lloyd McClendon .05 .02
37 Ty Griffin .05 .02
38 Shawon Dunston .05 .02
39 Andre Dawson .10 .03
40 Luis Salazar .05 .02
41 Tim Layana .05 .02
42 Rob Dibble .10 .03
43 Tom Browning .05 .02
44 Danny Jackson .05 .02
45 Jose Rijo .05 .02
46 Scott Scudder .05 .02
47 Randy Myers UER .10 .03
(Career ERA .274& should be 2.74)
48 Brian Lane RC .10 .03
49 Paul O'Neill .15 .04
50 Barry Larkin .25 .07
51 Reggie Jefferson RC .25 .07
52 Jeff Branson RC** .10 .03
53 Chris Sabo .05 .02
54 Joe Oliver .05 .02
55 Todd Benzinger .05 .02
56 Rolando Roomes .05 .02
57 Hal Morris .05 .02
58 Eric Davis .10 .03
59 Scott Bryant .05 .02
60 Ken Griffey Sr. .10 .03
61 Darryl Kile RC 1.00 .30
62 Dave Smith .05 .02
63 Mark Portugal .05 .02
64 Jeff Juden RC .10 .03
65 Bill Gullickson .05 .02
66 Danny Darwin .05 .02
67 Larry Andersen .05 .02
68 Jose Cano .05 .02
69 Dan Schatzeder .05 .02
70 Jim Deshaies .05 .02
71 Mike Scott .05 .02
72 Gerald Young .05 .02
73 Ken Caminiti .10 .03
74 Ken Oberkfell .05 .02
75 Dave Rohde .05 .02
76 Bill Doran .05 .02
77 Andujar Cedeno RC .10 .03
78 Craig Biggio .15 .04
79 Karl Rhodes RC .25 .07
80 Glenn Davis .05 .02
81 Eric Anthony RC .10 .03
82 John Wetteland .25 .07
83 Jay Howell .05 .02
84 Orel Hershiser .10 .03
85 Tim Belcher .05 .02
86 Kiki Jones .05 .02
87 Mike Hartley .05 .02
88 Ramon Martinez .05 .02
89 Mike Scioscia .05 .02
90 Willie Randolph .10 .03
91 Juan Samuel .05 .02
92 Jose Offerman RC .25 .07
93 Dave Hansen RC .25 .07
94 Jeff Hamilton .05 .02
95 Alfredo Griffin .05 .02
96 Tom Goodwin RC .25 .07
97 Kirk Gibson .10 .03
98 Jose Vizcaino RC .25 .07
99 Kal Daniels .05 .02
100 Hubie Brooks .05 .02
101 Eddie Murray .25 .07
102 Dennis Boyd .05 .02
103 Tim Burke .05 .02
104 Bill Sampen .05 .02
105 Brett Gideon .05 .02
106 Mark Gardner RC .10 .03
107 Howard Farmer .05 .02
108 Mel Rojas RC .10 .03
109 Kevin Gross .05 .02
110 Dave Schmidt .05 .02
111 Dennis Martinez .10 .03
112 Jerry Goff .05 .02
113 Andres Galarraga .10 .03
114 Tim Wallach .05 .02
115 Marquis Grissom RC .25 .07
116 Spike Owen .05 .02
117 Larry Walker RC 1.50 .45
118 Tim Raines .10 .03
119 Delino DeShields RC .25 .07
120 Tom Foley .05 .02
121 Dave Martinez .05 .02
122 Frank Viola UER .05 .02
(Career ERA .384 should be 3.84)
123 Julio Valera RC .05 .02
124 Alejandro Pena .05 .02
125 David Cone .10 .03
126 Dwight Gooden .15 .04
127 Kevin D. Brown .05 .02
128 John Franco .10 .03
129 Terry Bross .05 .02
130 Blaine Beatty .05 .02
131 Sid Fernandez .05 .02
132 Mike Marshall .05 .02
133 Howard Johnson .05 .02
134 Jaime Roseboro .05 .02
135 Alan Zinter RC .10 .03
136 Keith Miller .05 .02
137 Kevin Elster .05 .02
138 Kevin McReynolds .05 .02
139 Barry Lyons .05 .02
140 Gregg Jefferies .10 .03
141 Darryl Strawberry .15 .04
142 Todd Hundley RC .25 .07
143 Scott Service .05 .02
144 Chuck Malone .05 .02
145 Steve Ontiveros .05 .02
146 Roger McDowell .05 .02
147 Ken Howell .05 .02
148 Pat Combs .05 .02
149 Jeff Parrett .05 .02
150 Chuck McElroy RC .10 .03
151 Jason Grimsley RC .10 .03
152 Len Dykstra .10 .03
153 M.Morandini RC .25 .07
154 John Kruk .10 .03
155 Dickie Thon .05 .02
156 Ricky Jordan .05 .02
157 Jeff Jackson RC .10 .03
158 Darren Daulton .10 .03
159 Tom Herr .05 .02
160 Von Hayes .05 .02
161 Dave Hollins RC .25 .07
162 Carmelo Martinez .05 .02
163 Bob Walk .05 .02
164 Doug Drabek .05 .02
165 Walt Terrell .05 .02
166 Bill Landrum .05 .02
167 Scott Ruskin .05 .02
168 Bob Patterson .05 .02
169 Bobby Bonilla .10 .03
170 Jose Lind .05 .02
171 Andy Van Slyke .10 .03
172 Mike LaValliere .05 .02
173 Willie Greene RC .10 .03
174 Jay Bell .10 .03
175 Sid Bream .05 .02
176 Tom Prince .05 .02
177 Wally Backman .05 .02
178 Moises Alou RC .50 .15
179 Steve Carter .05 .02
180 Gary Redus .05 .02
181 Barry Bonds .60 .18
182 Don Slaught UER .05 .02
(Card back shows headings for a pitcher)
183 Joe Magrane .05 .02
184 Bryn Smith .05 .02
185 Todd Worrell .05 .02
186 Jose DeLeon .05 .02
187 Frank DiPino .05 .02
188 John Tudor .05 .02
189 Howard Hilton .05 .02
190 John Ericks .05 .02
191 Ken Dayley .05 .02
192 Ray Lankford RC .25 .07
193 Todd Zeile .10 .03
194 Willie McGee .10 .03
195 Ozzie Smith .40 .12
196 Milt Thompson .05 .02
197 Terry Pendleton .10 .03
198 Vince Coleman .05 .02
199 Paul Coleman RC .10 .03
200 Jose Oquendo .05 .02
201 Pedro Guerrero .05 .02
202 Tom Brunansky .05 .02
203 Roger Smithberg .05 .02
204 Eddie Whitson .05 .02
205 Dennis Rasmussen .05 .02
206 Craig Lefferts .05 .02
207 Andy Benes .10 .03
208 Bruce Hurst .05 .02
209 Eric Show .05 .02
210 Rafael Valdez .05 .02
211 Joey Cora .10 .03
212 Thomas Howard .05 .02
213 Rob Nelson .05 .02
214 Jack Clark .10 .03
215 Garry Templeton .05 .02
216 Fred Lynn .05 .02
217 Tony Gwynn .30 .09
218 Benito Santiago .10 .03
219 Mike Pagliarulo .05 .02
220 Joe Carter .10 .03
221 Roberto Alomar .25 .07
222 Bip Roberts .05 .02
223 Rick Reuschel .05 .02
224 Russ Swan .05 .02
225 Eric Gunderson .05 .02
226 Steve Bedrosian .05 .02
227 Mike Remlinger .05 .02
228 Scott Garrelts .05 .02
229 Ernie Camacho .05 .02
230 Andres Santana RC .10 .03
231 Will Clark .25 .07
232 Kevin Mitchell .05 .02
233 Robby Thompson .05 .02
234 Bill Bathe .05 .02
235 Tony Perezchica .05 .02
236 Gary Carter .15 .04
237 Brett Butler .10 .03
238 Matt Williams .10 .03
239 Earnie Riles .05 .02
240 Kevin Bass .05 .02
241 Terry Kennedy .05 .02
242 Steve Hosey RC .10 .03
243 Ben McDonald RC .25 .07
244 Jeff Ballard .05 .02
245 Joe Price .05 .02
246 Curt Schilling 1.00 .30
247 Pete Harnisch .05 .02
248 Mark Williamson .05 .02
249 Gregg Olson .10 .03
250 Chris Myers .05 .02
251 David Segui RC ERR .25 .07
(Missing vital stats at top of card back under name)
251B David Segui COR RC .25 .07
252 Joe Orsulak .05 .02
253 Craig Worthington .05 .02
254 Mickey Tettleton .05 .02
255 Cal Ripken .75 .23
256 Bill Ripken .05 .02
257 Randy Milligan .05 .02
258 Brady Anderson .10 .03
259 Chris Hoiles RC UER .25 .07
Baltimore is spelled Balitmore
260 Mike Devereaux .05 .02
261 Phil Bradley .05 .02
262 Leo Gomez RC .10 .03
263 Lee Smith .10 .03
264 Mike Rochford .05 .02
265 Jeff Reardon .10 .03
266 Wes Gardner .05 .02
267 Mike Boddicker .05 .02
268 Roger Clemens .50 .15
269 Rob Murphy .05 .02
270 Mickey Pina .05 .02
271 Tony Pena .05 .02
272 Jody Reed .05 .02
273 Kevin Romine .05 .02
274 Mike Greenwell .05 .02
275 Maurice Vaughn RC 1.00 .30
276 Danny Heep .05 .02
277 Scott Cooper RC .10 .03
278 Greg Blosser RC .10 .03
279 Dwight Evans UER .10 .03
(* by "1990 Team Breakdown")
280 Ellis Burks .15 .04
281 Wade Boggs .15 .04
282 Marty Barrett .05 .02
283 Kirk McCaskill .05 .02
284 Mark Langston .05 .02
285 Bert Blyleven .10 .03
286 Mike Fetters RC .25 .07
287 Kyle Abbott .05 .02
288 Jim Abbott .15 .04
289 Chuck Finley .10 .03
290 Gary DiSarcina RC .25 .07
291 Dick Schofield .05 .02
292 Devon White .05 .02
293 Bobby Rose .05 .02
294 Brian Downing .05 .02
295 Lance Parrish .05 .02
296 Jack Howell .05 .02
297 Claudell Washington .05 .02
298 John Orton RC .10 .03
299 Wally Joyner .10 .03
300 Lee Stevens .10 .03
301 Chili Davis .10 .03
302 Johnny Ray .05 .02
303 Greg Hibbard RC .10 .03
304 Eric King .05 .02
305 Jack McDowell .05 .02
306 Bobby Thigpen .05 .02
307 Adam Peterson .05 .02
308 Scott Radinsky RC .25 .07
309 Wayne Edwards .05 .02
310 Melido Perez .05 .02
311 Robin Ventura .25 .07
312 Sammy Sosa RC 10.00 3.00
313 Dan Pasqua .05 .02
314 Carlton Fisk .15 .04
315 Ozzie Guillen .05 .02
316 Ivan Calderon .05 .02
317 Daryl Boston .05 .02
318 Craig Grebeck RC .25 .07
319 Scott Fletcher .05 .02
320 Frank Thomas RC 2.00 .60
321 Steve Lyons .05 .02
322 Carlos Martinez .05 .02
323 Joe Skalski .05 .02
324 Tom Candiotti .05 .02
325 Greg Swindell .05 .02
326 Steve Olin RC .25 .07
327 Kevin Wickander .05 .02
328 Doug Jones .05 .02
329 Jeff Shaw .05 .02
330 Kevin Bearse .05 .02
331 Dion James .05 .02
332 Jerry Browne .05 .02
333 Joey Belle .25 .07
334 Felix Fermin .05 .02
335 Candy Maldonado .05 .02
336 Cory Snyder .05 .02
337 Sandy Alomar Jr. .10 .03
338 Mark Lewis .05 .02
339 Carlos Baerga RC .25 .07
340 Chris James .05 .02
341 Brook Jacoby .05 .02
342 Keith Hernandez .15 .04
343 Frank Tanana .05 .02
344 Scott Aldred .05 .02
345 Mike Henneman .05 .02
346 Steve Wapnick .05 .02
347 Greg Gohr RC .10 .03
348 Eric Stone .05 .02
349 Brian DuBois .05 .02
350 Kevin Ritz .05 .02
351 Rico Brogna .25 .07
352 Mike Heath .05 .02
353 Alan Trammell .15 .04
354 Chet Lemon .05 .02
355 Dave Bergman .05 .02
356 Lou Whitaker .10 .03
357 Cecil Fielder UER .10 .03
* by 1990 Team Breakdown
358 Milt Cuyler RC .10 .03
359 Tony Phillips .05 .02
360 Travis Fryman RC .50 .15
361 Ed Romero .05 .02
362 Lloyd Moseby .05 .02
363 Mark Gubicza .05 .02
364 Bret Saberhagen .10 .03
365 Tom Gordon .10 .03
366 Steve Farr .05 .02
367 Kevin Appier .25 .07
368 Storm Davis .05 .02
369 Mark Davis .05 .02
370 Jeff Montgomery .10 .03
371 Frank White .10 .03
372 Brent Mayne RC .25 .07
373 Bob Boone .10 .03
374 Jim Eisenreich .05 .02
375 Danny Tartabull .05 .02
376 Kurt Stillwell .05 .02
377 Bill Pecota .05 .02
378 Bo Jackson .25 .07
379 Bob Hamelin RC .25 .07
380 Kevin Seitzer .05 .02
381 Rey Palacios .05 .02
382 George Brett .60 .18
383 Gerald Perry .05 .02
384 Teddy Higuera .05 .02
385 Tom Filer .05 .02
386 Dan Plesac .05 .02
387 Cal Eldred RC .25 .07
388 Jaime Navarro .05 .02
389 Chris Bosio .05 .02
390 Randy Veres .05 .02
391 Gary Sheffield .25 .07
392 George Canale .05 .02
393 B.J. Surhoff .10 .03
394 Tim McIntosh .05 .02
395 Greg Brock .05 .02
396 Greg Vaughn .10 .03
397 Darryl Hamilton .05 .02
398 Dave Parker .10 .03
399 Paul Molitor .15 .04
400 Jim Gantner .05 .02
401 Rob Deer .05 .02
402 Billy Spiers .05 .02
403 Glenn Braggs .05 .02
404 Robin Yount .40 .12
405 Rick Aguilera .10 .03
406 Johnny Ard .05 .02
407 Kevin Tapani RC .25 .07
408 Park Pittman .05 .02
409 Allan Anderson .05 .02
410 Juan Berenguer .05 .02
411 Willie Banks RC .10 .03
412 Rich Yett .05 .02
413 Dave West .05 .02
414 Greg Gagne .05 .02
415 Chuck Knoblauch RC .50 .15
416 Randy Bush .05 .02
417 Gary Gaetti .10 .03
418 Kent Hrbek .10 .03
419 Al Newman .05 .02
420 Danny Gladden .05 .02
421 Paul Sorrento RC .25 .07
422 Derek Parks RC .10 .03
423 Scott Leius RC .10 .03
424 Kirby Puckett .25 .07
425 Willie Smith .05 .02
426 Dave Righetti .05 .02
427 Jeff D. Robinson .05 .02
428 Alan Mills RC .10 .03
429 Tim Leary .05 .02
430 Pascual Perez .05 .02
431 Alvaro Espinoza .05 .02
432 Dave Winfield .10 .03
433 Jesse Barfield .05 .02
434 Randy Velarde .05 .02
435 Rick Cerone .05 .02
436 Steve Balboni .05 .02
437 Mel Hall .05 .02
438 Bob Geren .05 .02
439 Bernie Williams RC 1.50 .45
440 Kevin Maas RC .25 .07
441 Mike Blowers RC .10 .03
442 Steve Sax .05 .02
443 Don Mattingly .60 .18
444 Roberto Kelly .05 .02
445 Mike Moore .05 .02
446 Reggie Harris RC .10 .03
447 Scott Sanderson .05 .02
448 Dave Otto .05 .02
449 Dave Stewart .10 .03
450 Rick Honeycutt .05 .02
451 Dennis Eckersley .10 .03
452 Carney Lansford .10 .03
453 Scott Hemond RC .10 .03
454 Mark McGwire .60 .18
455 Felix Jose .05 .02
456 Terry Steinbach .05 .02
457 Rickey Henderson .25 .07
458 Dave Henderson .05 .02
459 Mike Gallego .05 .02
460 Jose Canseco .25 .07
461 Walt Weiss .05 .02
462 Ken Phelps .05 .02
463 Darren Lewis RC .10 .03
464 Ron Hassey .05 .02
465 Roger Salkeld RC .10 .03
466 Scott Bankhead .05 .02
467 Keith Comstock .05 .02
468 Randy Johnson .40 .12
469 Erik Hanson .05 .02
470 Mike Schooler .05 .02
471 Gary Eave .05 .02
472 Jeffrey Leonard .05 .02
473 Dave Valle .05 .02
474 Omar Vizquel .25 .07
475 Pete O'Brien .05 .02
476 Henry Cotto .05 .02
477 Jay Buhner .10 .03
478 Harold Reynolds .10 .03
479 Alvin Davis .05 .02
480 Darnell Coles .05 .02
481 Ken Griffey Jr. .75 .23
482 Greg Briley .05 .02

483 Scott Bradley .05 .02
484 Tino Martinez .25 .07
485 Jeff Russell .05 .02
486 Nolan Ryan 1.00 .30
487 Robb Nen RC 1.00 .30
488 Kevin Brown .10 .03
489 Brian Bohanon RC .10 .03
490 Ruben Sierra .05 .02
491 Pete Incaviglia .05 .02
492 Juan Gonzalez RC 2.00 .60
493 Steve Buechele .05 .02
494 Scott Coolbaugh .05 .02
495 Geno Petralli .05 .02
496 Rafael Palmeiro .15 .04
497 Julio Franco .05 .02
498 Gary Pettis .05 .02
499 Donald Harris .05 .02
500 Monty Fariss .05 .02
501 Harold Baines .10 .03
502 Cecil Espy .05 .02
503 Jack Daugherty .05 .02
504 Willie Blair RC .10 .03
505 Dave Stieb .10 .03
506 Tom Henke .05 .02
507 John Cerutti .05 .02
508 Paul Kilgus .05 .02
509 Jimmy Key .10 .03
510 John Olerud RC 1.00 .30
511 Ed Sprague .10 .03
512 Manuel Lee .05 .02
513 Fred McGriff .25 .07
514 Glenallen Hill .05 .02
515 George Bell .05 .02
516 Mookie Wilson .10 .03
517 Luis Sojo RC .25 .07
518 Nelson Liriano .05 .02
519 Kelly Gruber .05 .02
520 Greg Myers .05 .02
521 Pat Borders .05 .02
522 Junior Felix .05 .02
523 Eddie Zosky RC .10 .03
524 Tony Fernandez .05 .02
525 Checklist 1-132 UER .05 .02
(No copyright mark on the back)
526 Checklist 133-264 .05 .02
527 Checklist 265-396 .05 .02
528 Checklist 397-528 .05 .02

1990 Bowman Tiffany

These 528 standard-size cards were issued as a factory set by Topps. These cards parallel the regular Bowman issue except they have glossy fronts and a very easy to read white stock back. In addition to the 528 basic cards, the 11 insert art cards were also included in the factory set. According to published reports at the time, approximately 3,000 of these sets were produced.

	Nm-Mt	Ex-Mt
COMP.FACT.SET (539)	250.00	75.00

*STARS: 8X TO 20X BASIC CARDS ....
*ROOKIES: 5X TO 12X BASIC CARDS

1990 Bowman Art Inserts

These standard-size cards were included as an insert in every 1990 Bowman pack. This set, which consists of 11 superstars, depicts drawings by Craig Pursley with the backs being descriptions of the 1990 Bowman sweepstakes. We have checklisted the set alphabetically by player. All the cards in this set can be found with either one asterisk or two on the back.

	Nm-Mt	Ex-Mt
COMPLETE SET (11)	2.00	.60

*TIFFANY: 8X TO 20X BASIC ART INSERT
ONE TIFF.REP.SET PER TIFF.FACT.SET
1 Will Clark .25 .07
2 Mark Davis .05 .02
3 Dwight Gooden .15 .04
4 Bo Jackson .25 .07
5 Don Mattingly .60 .18
6 Kevin Mitchell .05 .02
7 Gregg Olson .10 .03
8 Nolan Ryan 1.00 .30
9 Bret Saberhagen .10 .03
10 Jerome Walton .05 .02
11 Robin Yount .40 .12

1990 Bowman Insert Lithographs

These 11" by 14" lithographs were issued through both Topps dealer network and through a pack/wrapper redemption. The fronts of the lithographs are larger versions of the 1990 Bowman insert sets. These lithos were drawn by Craig Pursley and are signed by the artist and are come either with or without serial numbering to 500. The backs are blank but we are sequencing them in the same order as the 1990 Bowman inserts. The lithos which the artist signed are worth approximately 2X to 3X the regular lithographs.

	Nm-Mt	Ex-Mt
COMPLETE SET (11)	600.00	180.00
1 Will Clark	50.00	15.00
2 Mark Davis	25.00	7.50
3 Dwight Gooden	30.00	9.00
4 Bo Jackson	30.00	9.00
5 Don Mattingly	100.00	30.00
6 Kevin Mitchell	25.00	7.50
7 Gregg Olson	25.00	7.50
8 Nolan Ryan	250.00	75.00
9 Bret Saberhagen	30.00	9.00
10 Jerome Walton	25.00	7.50
11 Robin Yount	50.00	15.00

1991 Bowman

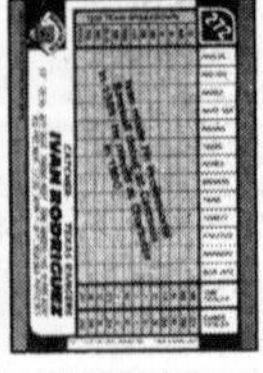

This single-series 704-card standard-size set marked the third straight year that Topps issued a set weighted towards prospects using the Bowman name. Cards were issued in wax packs and factory sets. The cards share a design very similar to the 1990 Bowman set with white borders enframing a color photo. The player name, however, is more prominent than in the previous year set. The cards are arranged in team order by division as follows: AL East, AL West, NL East, and NL West. Subsets include Rod Carew Tribute (1-5), Minor League MVP's (180-185/693-698), AL Silver Sluggers (367-375), NL Silver Sluggers (376-384) and checklists (699-704). Rookie Cards in this set include Jeff Bagwell, Jeromy Burnitz, Carl Everett, Chipper Jones, Eric Karros, Ryan Klesko, Kenny Lofton, Javier Lopez, Raul Mondesi, Mike Mussina, Ivan "Pudge" Rodriguez, Tim Salmon, Jim Thome, and Rondell White. There are two instances of misnumbering in the set; Ken Griffey (should be 255) and Ken Griffey Jr. are both numbered 246 and Donovan Osborne (should be 406) and Thomson/Branca share number 410.

	Nm-Mt	Ex-Mt
COMPLETE SET (704)	40.00	12.00
COMP.FACT.SET (704)	40.00	12.00

1 Rod Carew I .15 .04
2 Rod Carew II .15 .04
3 Rod Carew III .15 .04
4 Rod Carew IV .15 .04
5 Rod Carew V .15 .04
6 Willie Fraser .05 .02
7 John Olerud .10 .03
8 William Suero .05 .02
9 Roberto Alomar .25 .07
10 Todd Stottlemyre .05 .02
11 Joe Carter .10 .03
12 Steve Karsay RC .50 .15
13 Mark Whiten .05 .02
14 Pat Borders .05 .02
15 Mike Timlin RC .50 .15
16 Tom Henke .05 .02
17 Eddie Zosky .05 .02
18 Kelly Gruber .05 .02
19 Jimmy Key .10 .03
20 Jerry Schunk .05 .02
21 Manuel Lee .05 .02
22 Dave Stieb .05 .02
23 Pat Hentgen RC .50 .15
24 Glenallen Hill .05 .02
25 Rene Gonzales .05 .02
26 Ed Sprague .05 .02
27 Ken Dayley .05 .02
28 Pat Tabler .05 .02
29 Denis Boucher RC .15 .04
30 Devon White .05 .02
31 Dante Bichette .10 .03
32 Paul Molitor .15 .04
33 Greg Vaughn .10 .03
34 Dan Plesac .05 .02
35 Chris George RC .15 .04
36 Tim McIntosh .05 .02
37 Franklin Stubbs .05 .02
38 Bo Dodson RC .15 .04
39 Ron Robinson .05 .02
40 Ed Nunez .05 .02
41 Greg Brock .05 .02
42 Jaime Navarro .05 .02
43 Chris Bosio .05 .02
44 B.J. Surhoff .10 .03
45 Chris Johnson .05 .02
46 Willie Randolph .10 .03
47 Narciso Elvira .05 .02
48 Jim Gantner .05 .02
49 Kevin Brown .05 .02
50 Julio Machado .05 .02
51 Chuck Crim .05 .02
52 Gary Sheffield .10 .03
53 Angel Miranda RC .15 .04
54 Ted Higuera .05 .02
55 Robin Yount .40 .12
56 Cal Eldred .05 .02
57 Sandy Alomar Jr .05 .02
58 Greg Swindell .05 .02
59 Brook Jacoby .05 .02
60 Efrain Valdez .05 .02
61 Ever Magallanes .05 .02
62 Tom Candiotti .05 .02
63 Eric King .05 .02
64 Alex Cole .05 .02
65 Charles Nagy .05 .02
66 Mitch Webster .05 .02
67 Chris James .05 .02
68 Jim Thome RC 4.00 1.20
69 Carlos Baerga .05 .02
70 Mark Lewis .05 .02
71 Jerry Browne .05 .02
72 Jesse Orosco .05 .02
73 Mike Huff .05 .02
74 Jose Escobar .05 .02
75 Jeff Manto .05 .02
76 Turner Ward RC .15 .04
77 Doug Jones .05 .02
78 Bruce Egloff .05 .02
79 Tim Costo RC .15 .04
80 Beau Allred .05 .02
81 Albert Belle .10 .03
82 John Farrell .05 .02
83 Glenn Davis .05 .02
84 Joe Orsulak .05 .02
85 Mark Williamson .05 .02
86 Ben McDonald .05 .02
87 Billy Ripken .05 .02
88 Leo Gomez UER .05 .02
Baltimore is spelled Balitmore
89 Bob Melvin .05 .02
90 Jeff M. Robinson .05 .02
91 Jose Mesa .05 .02
92 Gregg Olson .05 .02
93 Mike Devereaux .05 .02
94 Luis Mercedes RC .15 .04
95 Arthur Rhodes RC .50 .15
96 Juan Bell .05 .02
97 Mike Mussina RC 3.00 .90
98 Jeff Ballard .05 .02
99 Chris Hoiles .05 .02
100 Brady Anderson .10 .03
101 Bob Milacki .05 .02
102 David Segui .05 .02
103 Dwight Evans .10 .03
104 Cal Ripken .75 .23
105 Mike Linskey .05 .02
106 Jeff Tackett RC .15 .04
107 Jeff Reardon .10 .03
108 Dana Kiecker .05 .02
109 Ellis Burks .10 .03
110 Dave Owen .05 .02
111 Danny Darwin .05 .02
112 Mo Vaughn .10 .03
113 Jeff McNeely RC .15 .04
114 Tom Bolton .05 .02
115 Greg Blosser .05 .02
116 Mike Greenwell .05 .02
117 Phil Plantier RC .15 .04
118 Roger Clemens .50 .15
119 John Marzano .05 .02
120 Jody Reed .05 .02
121 Scott Taylor RC .15 .04
122 Jack Clark .10 .03
123 Derek Livernois .05 .02
124 Tony Pena .05 .02
125 Tom Brunansky .05 .02
126 Carlos Quintana .05 .02
127 Tim Naehring .05 .02
128 Matt Young .05 .02
129 Wade Boggs .15 .04
130 Kevin Morton .05 .02
131 Pete Incaviglia .05 .02
132 Rob Deer .05 .02
133 Bill Gullickson .05 .02
134 Rico Brogna .05 .02
135 Lloyd Moseby .05 .02
136 Cecil Fielder .10 .03
137 Tony Phillips .05 .02
138 Mark Leiter RC .15 .04
139 John Cerutti .05 .02
140 Mickey Tettleton .05 .02
141 Milt Cuyler .05 .02
142 Greg Gohr .05 .02
143 Tony Bernazard .05 .02
144 Dan Gakeler .05 .02
145 Travis Fryman .10 .03
146 Dan Petry .05 .02
147 Scott Aldred .05 .02
148 John DeSilva .05 .02
149 Rusty Meacham RC .15 .04
150 Lou Whitaker .10 .03
151 Dave Haas .05 .02
152 Luis de los Santos .05 .02
153 Ivan Cruz .05 .02
154 Alan Trammell .15 .04
155 Pat Kelly RC .05 .02
156 Carl Everett RC 1.00 .30
157 Greg Cadaret .05 .02
158 Kevin Maas .05 .02
159 Jeff Johnson .05 .02
160 Willie Smith .05 .02
161 Gerald Williams RC .50 .15
162 Mike Humphreys RC .15 .04
163 Alvaro Espinoza .05 .02
164 Matt Nokes .05 .02
165 Wade Taylor .05 .02
166 Roberto Kelly .05 .02
167 John Habyan .05 .02
168 Steve Farr .05 .02
169 Jesse Barfield .05 .02
170 Steve Sax .05 .02
171 Jim Leyritz .05 .02
172 Robert Eenhoorn RC .15 .04
173 Bernie Williams .25 .07
174 Scott Lusader .05 .02
175 Torey Lovullo .05 .02
176 Chuck Cary .05 .02
177 Scott Sanderson .05 .02
178 Don Mattingly .60 .18
179 Mel Hall .05 .02
180 Juan Gonzalez .25 .07
181 Hensley Meulens .05 .02
182 Jose Offerman .05 .02
183 Jeff Bagwell RC 2.00 .60
184 Jeff Conine RC 1.00 .30
185 Henry Rodriguez RC .50 .15
186 Jimmie Reese CO .10 .03
187 Kyle Abbott .05 .02
188 Lance Parrish .10 .03
189 Rafael Montalvo .05 .02
190 Floyd Bannister .05 .02
191 Dick Schofield .05 .02
192 Scott Lewis .05 .02
193 Jeff D. Robinson .05 .02
194 Kent Anderson .05 .02
195 Wally Joyner .10 .03
196 Chuck Finley .10 .03
197 Luis Sojo .05 .02
198 Jeff Richardson .05 .02
199 Dave Parker .10 .03
200 Jim Abbott .15 .04
201 Junior Felix .05 .02
202 Mark Langston .05 .02
203 Tim Salmon RC 2.00 .60
204 Cliff Young .05 .02
205 Scott Bailes .05 .02
206 Bobby Rose .05 .02
207 Gary Gaetti .10 .03
208 Ruben Amaro RC .15 .04
209 Luis Polonia .05 .02
210 Dave Winfield .10 .03
211 Bryan Harvey .05 .02
212 Mike Moore .05 .02
213 Rickey Henderson .25 .07
214 Steve Chitren .05 .02
215 Bob Welch .05 .02
216 Terry Steinbach .05 .02
217 Earnest Riles .05 .02
218 Todd Van Poppel RC .50 .15
219 Mike Gallego .05 .02
220 Curt Young .05 .02
221 Todd Burns .05 .02
222 Vance Law .05 .02
223 Eric Show .05 .02
224 Don Peters .05 .02
225 Dave Stewart .10 .03
226 Dave Henderson .05 .02
227 Jose Canseco .25 .07
228 Walt Weiss .05 .02
229 Dann Howitt .05 .02
230 Willie Wilson .05 .02
231 Harold Baines .10 .03
232 Scott Hemond .05 .02
233 Joe Slusarski .05 .02
234 Mark McGwire .60 .18
235 K.Dressendorfer RC .15 .04
236 Craig Paquette RC .50 .15
237 Dennis Eckersley .10 .03
238 Dana Allison .05 .02
239 Scott Bradley .05 .02
240 Brian Holman .05 .02
241 Mike Schooler .05 .02
242 Rich DeLucia .05 .02
243 Edgar Martinez .15 .04
244 Henry Cotto .05 .02
245 Omar Vizquel .10 .03
246 Ken Griffey Jr. .50 .15
(See also 255)
247 Jay Buhner .10 .03
248 Bill Krueger .05 .02
249 Dave Fleming RC .15 .04
250 Patrick Lennon .05 .02
251 Dave Valle .05 .02
252 Harold Reynolds .10 .03
253 Randy Johnson .30 .09
254 Scott Bankhead .05 .02
255 Ken Griffey Sr. UER .05 .02
(Card number is 246)
256 Greg Briley .05 .02
257 Tino Martinez .15 .04
258 Alvin Davis .05 .02
259 Pete O'Brien .05 .02
260 Erik Hanson .05 .02
261 Bret Boone RC 3.00 .90
262 Roger Salkeld .05 .02
263 Dave Burba RC .50 .15
264 Kerry Woodson RC .15 .04
265 Julio Franco .10 .03
266 Dan Peltier RC .15 .04
267 Jeff Russell .05 .02
268 Steve Buechele .05 .02
269 Donald Harris .05 .02
270 Robb Nen .15 .04
271 Rich Gossage .10 .03
272 Ivan Rodriguez RC 2.50 .75
273 Jeff Huson .05 .02
274 Kevin Brown .10 .03
275 Dan Smith RC .15 .04
276 Gary Pettis .05 .02
277 Jack Daugherty .05 .02
278 Mike Jeffcoat .05 .02
279 Brad Arnsberg .05 .02
280 Nolan Ryan 1.00 .30
281 Eric McCray .05 .02
282 Scott Chiamparino .05 .02
283 Ruben Sierra .05 .02
284 Geno Petralli .05 .02
285 Monty Fariss .05 .02
286 Rafael Palmeiro .15 .04
287 Bobby Witt .05 .02
288 Dean Palmer UER .10 .03
Photo is Dan Peltier
289 Tony Scruggs .05 .02
290 Kenny Rogers .10 .03
291 Bret Saberhagen .10 .03
292 Brian McRae RC .50 .15
293 Storm Davis .05 .02
294 Danny Tartabull .05 .02
295 David Howard .05 .02
296 Mike Boddicker .05 .02
297 Joel Johnston RC .15 .04
298 Tim Spehr .05 .02
299 Hector Wagner .05 .02
300 George Brett .60 .18
301 Mike Macfarlane .05 .02
302 Kirk Gibson .10 .03
303 Harvey Pulliam RC .15 .04
304 Jim Eisenreich .05 .02
305 Kevin Seitzer .05 .02
306 Mark Davis .05 .02
307 Kurt Stillwell .05 .02
308 Jeff Montgomery .05 .02
309 Kevin Appier .10 .03
310 Bob Hamelin .05 .02
311 Tom Gordon .05 .02
312 Kerwin Moore RC .15 .04
313 Hugh Walker .05 .02
314 Terry Shumpert .05 .02
315 Warren Cromartie .05 .02
316 Gary Thurman .05 .02
317 Steve Bedrosian .05 .02
318 Danny Gladden .05 .02
319 Jack Morris .10 .03
320 Kirby Puckett .25 .07
321 Kent Hrbek .10 .03
322 Kevin Tapani .05 .02
323 Denny Neagle RC .50 .15
324 Rich Garces RC .15 .04
325 Larry Casian .05 .02
326 Shane Mack .05 .02
327 Allan Anderson .05 .02
328 Junior Ortiz .05 .02
329 Paul Abbott RC .50 .15
330 Chuck Knoblauch .10 .03
331 Chili Davis .10 .03
332 Todd Ritchie RC .50 .15
333 Brian Harper .05 .02
334 Rick Aguilera .10 .03
335 Scott Erickson .05 .02
336 Pedro Munoz RC .15 .04
337 Scott Leius .05 .02
338 Greg Gagne .05 .02
339 Mike Pagliarulo .05 .02
340 Terry Leach .05 .02
341 Willie Banks .05 .02
342 Bobby Thigpen .05 .02
343 R.Hernandez RC .50 .15
344 Melido Perez .05 .02
345 Carlton Fisk .15 .04
346 Norberto Martin .05 .02
347 Johnny Ruffin RC .15 .04
348 Jeff Carter .05 .02
349 Lance Johnson .05 .02
350 Sammy Sosa .50 .15
351 Alex Fernandez .05 .02
352 Jack McDowell .05 .02
353 Bob Wickman RC .15 .04
354 Wilson Alvarez .05 .02
355 Charlie Hough .10 .03
356 Ozzie Guillen .05 .02
357 Cory Snyder .05 .02
358 Robin Ventura .10 .03
359 Scott Fletcher .05 .02
360 Cesar Bernhardt .05 .02
361 Dan Pasqua .05 .02
362 Tim Raines .10 .03
363 Brian Drahman .05 .02
364 Wayne Edwards .05 .02
365 Scott Radinsky .05 .02
366 Frank Thomas .25 .07
367 Cecil Fielder SLUG .05 .02
368 Julio Franco SLUG .05 .02
369 Kelly Gruber SLUG .05 .02
370 Alan Trammell SLUG .10 .03
371 R.Henderson SLUG .15 .04
372 Jose Canseco SLUG .10 .03
373 Ellis Burks SLUG .05 .02
374 Lance Parrish SLUG .05 .02
375 Dave Parker SLUG .05 .02
376 Eddie Murray SLUG .15 .04
377 Ryne Sandberg SLUG .25 .07
378 Matt Williams SLUG .05 .02
379 Barry Larkin SLUG .10 .03
380 Barry Bonds SLUG .30 .09
381 Bobby Bonilla SLUG .05 .02
382 D.Strawberry SLUG .10 .03
383 Benny Santiago SLUG .05 .02
384 Don Robinson SLUG .05 .02
385 Paul Coleman .05 .02
386 Milt Thompson .05 .02
387 Lee Smith .10 .03
388 Ray Lankford .05 .02
389 Tom Pagnozzi .05 .02
390 Ken Hill .05 .02
391 Jamie Moyer .10 .03
392 Greg Carmona .05 .02
393 John Ericks .05 .02
394 Bob Tewksbury .05 .02
395 Jose Oquendo .05 .02
396 Rheal Cormier RC .15 .04
397 Mike Milchin .05 .02
398 Ozzie Smith .40 .12
399 Aaron Holbert RC .15 .04
400 Jose DeLeon .05 .02
401 Felix Jose .05 .02
402 Juan Agosto .05 .02
403 Pedro Guerrero .10 .03
404 Todd Zeile .05 .02
405 Gerald Perry .05 .02
406 D.Osborne UER RC .15 .04
Card number is 410
407 Bryn Smith .05 .02
408 Bernard Gilkey .05 .02
409 Rex Hudler .05 .02
410 Bobby Thomson .25 .07
Ralph Branca
Shot Heard Round the World
See also 406
411 Lance Dickson RC .15 .04
412 Danny Jackson .05 .02
413 Jerome Walton .05 .02
414 Sean Cheetham .05 .02
415 Joe Girardi .05 .02
416 Ryne Sandberg .40 .12
417 Mike Harkey .05 .02
418 George Bell .05 .02
419 Rick Wilkins RC .15 .04
420 Earl Cunningham .05 .02
421 H.Slocumb RC .15 .04
422 Mike Bielecki .05 .02
423 Jessie Hollins RC .15 .04
424 Shawon Dunston .05 .02
425 Dave Smith .05 .02
426 Greg Maddux .40 .12
427 Jose Vizcaino .05 .02
428 Luis Salazar .05 .02
429 Andre Dawson .10 .03
430 Rick Sutcliffe .10 .03
431 Paul Assenmacher .05 .02
432 Erik Pappas .05 .02
433 Mark Grace .15 .04
434 Dennis Martinez .10 .03
435 Marquis Grissom .05 .02
436 Wil Cordero RC .50 .15
437 Tim Wallach .05 .02
438 Brian Barnes RC .05 .02
439 Barry Jones .05 .02
440 Ivan Calderon .05 .02
441 Stan Spencer .05 .02
442 Larry Walker .25 .07
443 Chris Haney RC .15 .04
444 Hector Rivera .05 .02
445 Delino DeShields .10 .03
446 Andres Galarraga .10 .03
447 Gilberto Reyes .05 .02
448 Willie Greene .05 .02
449 Greg Colbrunn RC .50 .15
450 Rondell White RC .75 .23
451 Steve Frey .05 .02
452 Shane Andrews RC .15 .04
453 Mike Fitzgerald .05 .02
454 Spike Owen .05 .02
455 Dave Martinez .05 .02
456 Dennis Boyd .05 .02
457 Eric Bullock .05 .02
458 Reid Cornelius RC .15 .04
459 Chris Nabholz .05 .02

460 David Cone .10 .03
461 Hubie Brooks .05 .02
462 Sid Fernandez .05 .02
463 Doug Simons .05 .02
464 Howard Johnson .05 .02
465 Chris Donnels .05 .02
466 Anthony Young RC .15 .04
467 Todd Hundley .05 .02
468 Rick Cerone .05 .02
469 Kevin Elster .05 .02
470 Wally Whitehurst .05 .02
471 Vince Coleman .05 .02
472 Dwight Gooden .15 .04
473 Charlie O'Brien .05 .02
474 Jeromy Burnitz RC .75 .23
475 John Franco .10 .03
476 Daryl Boston .05 .02
477 Frank Viola .10 .03
478 D.J. Dozier .05 .02
479 Kevin McReynolds .05 .02
480 Tom Herr .05 .02
481 Gregg Jefferies .05 .02
482 Pete Schourek RC .15 .04
483 Ron Darling .05 .02
484 Dave Magadan .05 .02
485 Andy Ashby RC .50 .15
486 Dale Murphy .25 .07
487 Von Hayes .05 .02
488 Kim Batiste RC .15 .04
489 Tony Longmire RC .15 .04
490 Wally Backman .05 .02
491 Jeff Jackson .05 .02
492 Mickey Morandini .05 .02
493 Darrel Akerfelds .05 .02
494 Ricky Jordan .05 .02
495 Randy Ready .05 .02
496 Darrin Fletcher .05 .02
497 Chuck Malone .05 .02
498 Pat Combs .05 .02
499 Dickie Thon .05 .02
500 Roger McDowell .05 .02
501 Len Dykstra .10 .03
502 Joe Boever .05 .02
503 John Kruk .10 .03
504 Terry Mulholland .05 .02
505 Wes Chamberlain RC .15 .04
506 Mike Lieberthal RC .75 .23
507 Darren Daulton .10 .03
508 Charlie Hayes .05 .02
509 John Smiley .05 .02
510 Gary Varsho .05 .02
511 Curt Wilkerson .05 .02
512 Orlando Merced RC .15 .04
513 Barry Bonds .60 .18
514 Mike LaValliere .05 .02
515 Doug Drabek .05 .02
516 Gary Redus .05 .02
517 W.Pennyfeather RC .15 .04
518 Randy Tomlin RC .05 .02
519 Mike Zimmerman RC .15 .04
520 Jeff King .05 .02
521 Kurt Miller RC .15 .04
522 Jay Bell .10 .03
523 Bill Landrum .05 .02
524 Zane Smith .05 .02
525 Bobby Bonilla .10 .03
526 Bob Walk .05 .02
527 Austin Manahan .05 .02
528 Joe Ausanio .05 .02
529 Andy Van Slyke .10 .03
530 Jose Lind .05 .02
531 Carlos Garcia RC .15 .04
532 Don Slaught .05 .02
533 Gen.Colin Powell .50 .15
534 Frank Bolick RC .15 .04
535 Gary Scott .05 .02
536 Nikco Riesgo .05 .02
537 Reggie Sanders RC .75 .23
538 Tim Howard RC .15 .04
539 Ryan Bowen RC .15 .04
540 Eric Anthony .05 .02
541 Jim Deshaies .05 .02
542 Tom Nevers RC .15 .04
543 Ken Caminiti .10 .03
544 Karl Rhodes .05 .02
545 Xavier Hernandez .05 .02
546 Mike Scott .05 .02
547 Jeff Juden .05 .02
548 Darryl Kile .10 .03
549 Willie Ansley .05 .02
550 Luis Gonzalez RC 1.50 .45
551 Mike Simms .05 .02
552 Mark Portugal .05 .02
553 Jimmy Jones .05 .02
554 Jim Clancy .05 .02
555 Pete Harnisch .05 .02
556 Craig Biggio .15 .04
557 Eric Yelding .05 .02
558 Dave Rohde .05 .02
559 Casey Candaele .05 .02
560 Curt Schilling .15 .04
561 Steve Finley .10 .03
562 Javier Ortiz .05 .02
563 Andujar Cedeno .05 .02
564 Rafael Ramirez .05 .02
565 Kenny Lofton RC 1.00 .30
566 Steve Avery .05 .02
567 Lonnie Smith .05 .02
568 Kent Mercker .05 .02
569 Chipper Jones RC 4.00 1.20
570 Terry Pendleton .10 .03
571 Otis Nixon .05 .02
572 Juan Berenguer .05 .02
573 Charlie Leibrandt .05 .02
574 David Justice .10 .03
575 Keith Mitchell RC .15 .04
576 Tom Glavine .15 .04
577 Greg Olson .05 .02
578 Rafael Belliard .05 .02
579 Ben Rivera RC .15 .04
580 John Smoltz .15 .04
581 Tyler Houston .05 .02
582 Mark Wohlers RC .50 .15
583 Ron Gant .10 .03
584 Ramon Caraballo RC .15 .04
585 Sid Bream .05 .02
586 Jeff Treadway .05 .02
587 Javy Lopez RC 3.00 .90
588 Deion Sanders .15 .04
589 Mike Heath .05 .02
590 Ryan Klesko RC 1.00 .30
591 Bob Ojeda .05 .02
592 Alfredo Griffin .05 .02
593 Raul Mondesi RC 1.00 .30
594 Greg Smith .05 .02
595 Orel Hershiser .10 .03
596 Juan Samuel .05 .02
597 Brett Butler .10 .03
598 Gary Carter .15 .04
599 Stan Javier .05 .02
600 Kal Daniels .05 .02
601 Jamie McAndrew RC .15 .04
602 Mike Sharperson .05 .02
603 Jay Howell .05 .02
604 Eric Karros RC 1.00 .30
605 Tim Belcher .05 .02
606 Dan Opperman .05 .02
607 Lenny Harris .05 .02
608 Tom Goodwin .05 .02
609 Darryl Strawberry .15 .04
610 Ramon Martinez .05 .02
611 Kevin Gross .05 .02
612 Zakary Shinall .05 .02
613 Mike Scioscia .05 .02
614 Eddie Murray .25 .07
615 Ronnie Walden RC .15 .04
616 Will Clark .25 .07
617 Adam Hyzdu RC .50 .15
618 Matt Williams .10 .03
619 Don Robinson .05 .02
620 Jeff Brantley .05 .02
621 Greg Litton .05 .02
622 Steve Decker .05 .02
623 Robby Thompson .05 .02
624 Mark Leonard .05 .02
625 Kevin Bass .05 .02
626 Scott Garrelts .05 .02
627 Jose Uribe .05 .02
628 Eric Gunderson .05 .02
629 Steve Hosey .05 .02
630 Trevor Wilson .05 .02
631 Terry Kennedy .05 .02
632 Dave Righetti .10 .03
633 Kelly Downs .05 .02
634 Johnny Ard .05 .02
635 E.Christopherson RC .15 .04
636 Kevin Mitchell .05 .02
637 John Burkett .05 .02
638 Kevin Rogers RC .15 .04
639 Bud Black .05 .02
640 Willie McGee .10 .03
641 Royce Clayton .05 .02
642 Tony Fernandez .05 .02
643 Ricky Bones RC .15 .04
644 Thomas Howard .05 .02
645 Dave Staton RC .15 .04
646 Jim Presley .05 .02
647 Tony Gwynn .30 .09
648 Marty Barrett .05 .02
649 Scott Coolbaugh .05 .02
650 Craig Lefferts .05 .02
651 Eddie Whitson .05 .02
652 Oscar Azocar .05 .02
653 Wes Gardner .05 .02
654 Bip Roberts .05 .02
655 Robbie Beckett RC .15 .04
656 Benito Santiago .10 .03
657 Greg W.Harris .05 .02
658 Jerald Clark .05 .02
659 Fred McGriff .15 .04
660 Larry Andersen .05 .02
661 Bruce Hurst .05 .02
662 Steve Martin UER RC .15 .04
Card said he pitched at Waterloo
He's an outfielder
663 Rafael Valdez .05 .02
664 Paul Faries .05 .02
665 Andy Benes .05 .02
666 Randy Myers .05 .02
667 Rob Dibble .10 .03
668 Glenn Sutko .05 .02
669 Glenn Braggs .05 .02
670 Billy Hatcher .05 .02
671 Joe Oliver .05 .02
672 Freddie Benavides RC .15 .04
673 Barry Larkin .25 .07
674 Chris Sabo .05 .02
675 Mariano Duncan .05 .02
676 Chris Jones RC .05 .02
677 Gino Minutelli .05 .02
678 Reggie Jefferson .05 .02
679 Jack Armstrong .05 .02
680 Chris Hammond .05 .02
681 Jose Rijo .05 .02
682 Bill Doran .05 .02
683 Terry Lee .05 .02
684 Tom Browning .05 .02
685 Paul O'Neill .15 .04
686 Eric Davis .10 .03
687 Dan Wilson RC .50 .15
688 Ted Power .05 .02
689 Tim Layana .05 .02
690 Norm Charlton .05 .02
691 Hal Morris .05 .02
692 Rickey Henderson .15 .04
693 Sam Militello RC .15 .04
694 Matt Mieske RC .15 .04
695 Paul Russo RC .15 .04
696 Domingo Mota MVP .05 .02
697 Todd Guggiana RC .15 .04
698 Marc Newfield RC .15 .04
699 Checklist 1-122 .05 .02
700 Checklist 123-244 .05 .02
701 Checklist 245-366 .05 .02
702 Checklist 367-471 .05 .02
703 Checklist 472-593 .05 .02
704 Checklist 594-704 .05 .02

1992 Bowman

This 705-card standard-size set was issued in one comprehensive series. Unlike the previous Bowman issues, the 1992 set was radically upgraded to slick stock with gold foil subset cards in an attempt to reposition the brand as a premium level product. It initially stumbled out of the gate, but its superior selection of prospects enabled it to eventually gain acceptance in the hobby and now stands as one of the more important issues of the 1990's. Cards were distributed in plastic wrap packs, retail jumbo packs and special 80-card retail carton packs. Card fronts feature posed and action color player photos on a UV-coated white card face. . Forty-five foil cards inserted at a stated rate of one per wax pack and two per jumbo (23 regular cards) pack. These foil cards feature past and present Team USA players and minor league POY Award winners. Each foil card has an extremely slight variation in that the photos are cropped differently. There is no additional value to either version. Some of the regular and special cards picture prospects in civilian clothing who were still in the farm system. Rookie Cards in this set include Garret Anderson, Carlos Delgado, Mike Hampton, Brian Jordan, Mike Piazza, Manny Ramirez and Mariano Rivera.

Nm-Mt Ex-Mt
COMPLETE SET (705) 150.00 45.00
1 Ivan Rodriguez 1.25 .35
2 Kirk McCaskill .50 .15
3 Scott Livingstone .50 .15
4 Salomon Torres RC .50 .15
5 Carlos Hernandez .50 .15
6 Dave Hollins .50 .15
7 Scott Fletcher .50 .15
8 Jorge Fabregas RC 1.00 .30
9 Andujar Cedeno .50 .15
10 Howard Johnson .50 .15
11 Trevor Hoffman RC 5.00 1.50
12 Roberto Kelly .50 .15
13 Gregg Jefferies .50 .15
14 Marquis Grissom .50 .15
15 Mike Ignasiak .50 .15
16 Jack Morris .50 .15
17 William Pennyfeather .50 .15
18 Todd Stottlemyre .50 .15
19 Chito Martinez .50 .15
20 Roberto Alomar 1.25 .35
21 Sam Militello .50 .15
22 Hector Fajardo RC .50 .15
23 Paul Quantrill RC .50 .15
24 Chuck Knoblauch .50 .15
25 Reggie Jefferson .50 .15
26 Jeremy McGarity RC .50 .15
27 Jerome Walton .50 .15
28 Chipper Jones 8.00 2.40
29 Brian Barber RC .50 .15
30 Ron Darling .50 .15
31 Roberto Petagine RC 1.00 .30
32 Chuck Finley .50 .15
33 Edgar Martinez .75 .23
34 Napoleon Robinson .50 .15
35 Andy Van Slyke .50 .15
36 Bobby Thigpen .50 .15
37 Travis Fryman .50 .15
38 Eric Christopherson .50 .15
39 Terry Mulholland .50 .15
40 Darryl Strawberry .75 .23
41 Manny Alexander RC .50 .15
42 Tracy Sanders RC .50 .15
43 Pete Incaviglia .50 .15
44 Kim Batiste .50 .15
45 Frank Rodriguez .50 .15
46 Greg Swindell .50 .15
47 Delino DeShields .50 .15
48 John Ericks .50 .15
49 Franklin Stubbs .50 .15
50 Tony Gwynn 1.50 .45
51 Clifton Garrett RC .50 .15
52 Mike Gardella .50 .15
53 Scott Erickson .50 .15
54 Gary Caraballo RC .50 .15
55 Jose Oliva RC .50 .15
56 Brook Fordyce .50 .15
57 Mark Whiten .50 .15
58 Joe Slusarski .50 .15
59 J.R. Phillips RC 1.00 .30
60 Barry Bonds 3.00 .90
61 Bob Milacki .50 .15
62 Keith Mitchell .50 .15
63 Angel Miranda .50 .15
64 Raul Mondesi 5.00 1.50
65 Brian Koelling RC .50 .15
66 Brian McRae .50 .15
67 John Patterson RC .50 .15
68 John Wetteland .50 .15
69 Wilson Alvarez .50 .15
70 Wade Boggs .75 .23
71 Darryl Ratliff RC .50 .15
72 Jeff Jackson .50 .15
73 Jeremy Hernandez RC .50 .15
74 Darryl Hamilton .50 .15
75 Rafael Belliard .50 .15
76 Rick Trlicek RC .50 .15
77 Felipe Crespo RC .50 .15
78 Carney Lansford .50 .15
79 Ryan Long RC .50 .15
80 Kirby Puckett 1.25 .35
81 Earl Cunningham .50 .15
82 Pedro Martinez 15.00 4.50
83 Scott Hatteberg RC 1.00 .30
84 Juan Gonzalez UER 1.25 .35
(65 doubles vs. Tigers)
85 Robert Nutting RC .50 .15
86 Pokey Reese RC 1.00 .30
87 Dave Silvestri .50 .15
88 Scott Ruffcorn RC .50 .15
89 Rick Aguilera .50 .15
90 Cecil Fielder .50 .15
91 Kirk Dressendorfer .50 .15
92 Jerry DiPoto RC .50 .15
93 Mike Felder .50 .15
94 Craig Paquette .50 .15
95 Elvin Paulino RC .50 .15
96 Donovan Osborne .50 .15
97 Hubie Brooks .50 .15
98 Derek Lowe RC 5.00 1.50
99 David Zancanaro .50 .15
100 Ken Griffey Jr. 2.00 .60
101 Todd Hundley .50 .15
102 Mike Trombley RC .50 .15
103 Ricky Gutierrez RC 1.00 .30
104 Braulio Castillo .50 .15
105 Craig Lefferts .50 .15
106 Rick Sutcliffe .50 .15
107 Dean Palmer .50 .15
108 Henry Rodriguez .50 .15
109 Mark Clark RC 1.00 .30
110 Kenny Lofton .75 .23
111 Mark Carreon .50 .15
112 J.T. Bruett .50 .15
113 Gerald Williams .50 .15
114 Frank Thomas 1.25 .35
115 Kevin Reimer .50 .15
116 Sammy Sosa 2.00 .60
117 Mickey Tettleton .50 .15
118 Reggie Sanders .50 .15
119 Trevor Wilson .50 .15
120 Cliff Brantley .50 .15
121 Spike Owen .50 .15
122 Jeff Montgomery .50 .15
123 Alex Sutherland .50 .15
124 Brien Taylor RC 1.00 .30
125 Brian Williams RC .50 .15
126 Kevin Seitzer .50 .15
127 Carlos Delgado RC 20.00 6.00
128 Gary Scott .50 .15
129 Scott Cooper .50 .15
130 Domingo Jean RC .50 .15
131 Pat Mahomes RC 1.00 .30
132 Mike Boddicker .50 .15
133 Roberto Hernandez .50 .15
134 Dave Valle .50 .15
135 Kurt Stillwell .50 .15
136 Brad Pennington RC .50 .15
137 Jermaine Swinton RC .50 .15
138 Ryan Hawblitzel RC .50 .15
139 Tito Navarro RC .50 .15
140 Sandy Alomar Jr. .50 .15
141 Todd Benzinger .50 .15
142 Danny Jackson .50 .15
143 Melvin Nieves RC .50 .15
144 Jim Campanis .50 .15
145 Luis Gonzalez .75 .23
146 D.Doorneweerd RC .50 .15
147 Charlie Hayes .50 .15
148 Greg Maddux 2.00 .60
149 Brian Harper .50 .15
150 Brent Miller RC .50 .15
151 Shawn Estes RC 1.00 .30
152 Mike Williams RC 1.00 .30
153 Charlie Hough .50 .15
154 Randy Myers .50 .15
155 Kevin Young RC 1.00 .30
156 Rick Wilkins .50 .15
157 Terry Shumpert .50 .15
158 Steve Karsay .50 .15
159 Gary DiSarcina .50 .15
160 Deion Sanders .75 .23
161 Tom Browning .50 .15
162 Dickie Thon .50 .15
163 Luis Mercedes .50 .15
164 Riccardo Ingram .50 .15
165 Tavo Alvarez RC .50 .15
166 Rickey Henderson 1.25 .35
167 Jaime Navarro .50 .15
168 Billy Ashley RC .50 .15
169 Phil Dauphin RC .50 .15
170 Ivan Cruz .50 .15
171 Harold Baines .50 .15
172 Bryan Harvey .50 .15
173 Alex Cole .50 .15
174 Curtis Shaw RC .50 .15
175 Matt Williams .50 .15
176 Felix Jose .50 .15
177 Sam Horn .50 .15
178 Randy Johnson 1.25 .35
179 Ivan Calderon .50 .15
180 Steve Avery .50 .15
181 William Suero .50 .15
182 Bill Swift .50 .15
183 Howard Battle RC .50 .15
184 Ruben Amaro .50 .15
185 Jim Abbott .75 .23
186 Mike Fitzgerald .50 .15
187 Bruce Hurst .50 .15
188 Jeff Juden .50 .15
189 Jeromy Burnitz 1.25 .35
190 Dave Burba .50 .15
191 Kevin Brown .50 .15
192 Patrick Lennon .50 .15
193 Jeff McNeely .50 .15
194 Wil Cordero .50 .15
195 Chili Davis .50 .15
196 Milt Cuyler .50 .15
197 Von Hayes .50 .15
198 Todd Revenig RC .50 .15
199 Joel Johnston .50 .15
200 Jeff Bagwell 1.25 .35
201 Alex Fernandez .50 .15
202 Todd Jones RC 1.00 .30
203 Charles Nagy .50 .15
204 Tim Raines .50 .15
205 Kevin Maas .50 .15
206 Julio Franco .50 .15
207 Randy Velarde .50 .15
208 Lance Johnson .50 .15
209 Scott Leius .50 .15
210 Derek Lee .50 .15
211 Joe Sondrini RC .50 .15
212 Royce Clayton .50 .15
213 Chris George .50 .15
214 Gary Sheffield .50 .15
215 Mark Gubicza .50 .15
216 Mike Moore .50 .15
217 Rick Huisman RC .50 .15
218 Jeff Russell .50 .15
219 D.J. Dozier .50 .15
220 Dave Martinez .50 .15
221 Alan Newman RC .50 .15
222 Nolan Ryan 4.00 1.20
223 Teddy Higuera .50 .15
224 Damon Buford RC .50 .15
225 Ruben Sierra .50 .15
226 Tom Nevers .50 .15
227 Tommy Greene .50 .15
228 Nigel Wilson RC 1.00 .30
229 John DeSilva .50 .15
230 Bobby Witt .50 .15
231 Greg Cadaret .50 .15
232 John Vander Wal RC 1.00 .30
233 Jack Clark .50 .15
234 Bill Doran .50 .15
235 Bobby Bonilla .50 .15
236 Steve Olin .50 .15
237 Derek Bell .50 .15
238 David Cone .50 .15
239 Victor Cole .50 .15
240 Rod Bolton RC .50 .15
241 Tom Pagnozzi .50 .15
242 Rob Dibble .50 .15
243 Michael Carter RC .50 .15
244 Don Peters .50 .15
245 Mike LaValliere .50 .15
246 Joe Perona RC .50 .15
247 Mitch Williams .50 .15
248 Jay Buhner .50 .15
249 Andy Benes .50 .15
250 Alex Ochoa RC 1.00 .30
251 Greg Blosser .50 .15
252 Jack Armstrong .50 .15
253 Juan Samuel .50 .15
254 Terry Pendleton .50 .15
255 Ramon Martinez .50 .15
256 Rico Brogna .50 .15
257 John Smiley .50 .15
258 Carl Everett .75 .23
259 Tim Salmon 1.25 .35
260 Will Clark 1.25 .35
261 Ugueth Urbina RC 1.00 .30
262 Jason Wood RC .50 .15
263 Dave Magadan .50 .15
264 Dante Bichette .50 .15
265 Jose DeLeon .50 .15
266 Mike Neill RC 1.00 .30
267 Paul O'Neill .75 .23
268 Anthony Young .50 .15
269 Greg W. Harris .50 .15
270 Todd Van Poppel .50 .15
271 Pedro Castellano RC .50 .15
272 Tony Phillips .50 .15
273 Mike Gallego .50 .15
274 Steve Cooke RC .50 .15
275 Robin Ventura .50 .15
276 Kevin Mitchell .50 .15
277 Doug Linton RC .50 .15
278 Robert Eenhoorn .50 .15
279 Gabe White RC .50 .15
280 Dave Stewart .50 .15
281 Mo Sanford .50 .15
282 Greg Perschke .50 .15
283 Kevin Flora RC .50 .15
284 Jeff Williams RC 1.00 .30
285 Keith Miller .50 .15
286 Andy Ashby .50 .15
287 Doug Dascenzo .50 .15
288 Eric Karros .50 .15
289 Glenn Murray RC .50 .15
290 Troy Percival RC 3.00 .90
291 Orlando Merced .50 .15
292 Peter Hoy .50 .15
293 Tony Fernandez .50 .15
294 Juan Guzman .50 .15
295 Jesse Barfield .50 .15
296 Sid Fernandez .50 .15
297 Scott Cepicky .50 .15
298 Garret Anderson RC 10.00 3.00
299 Cal Eldred .50 .15
300 Ryne Sandberg 2.50 .75
301 Jim Gantner .50 .15
302 Mariano Rivera RC 10.00 3.00
303 Ron Lockett RC .50 .15
304 Jose Offerman .50 .15
305 Dennis Martinez .50 .15
306 Luis Ortiz RC .50 .15
307 David Howard .50 .15
308 Russ Springer RC 1.00 .30
309 Chris Howard .50 .15
310 Kyle Abbott .50 .15
311 Aaron Sele RC 2.00 .60
312 David Justice .50 .15
313 Pete O'Brien .50 .15
314 Greg Hansell RC .50 .15
315 Dave Winfield .50 .15
316 Lance Dickson .50 .15
317 Eric King .50 .15
318 Vaughn Eshelman RC .50 .15
319 Tim Belcher .50 .15
320 Andres Galarraga .50 .15
321 Scott Bullett RC .50 .15
322 Doug Strange .50 .15
323 Jerald Clark .50 .15
324 Dave Righetti .50 .15
325 Greg Hibbard .50 .15
326 Eric Hillman RC .50 .15
327 Shane Reynolds RC 1.00 .30
328 Chris Hammond .50 .15
329 Albert Belle .50 .15
330 Rich Becker RC .50 .15
331 Eddie Williams RC .50 .15
332 Donald Harris .50 .15
333 Dave Smith .50 .15
334 Steve Fireovid .50 .15
335 Steve Buechele .50 .15
336 Mike Schooler .50 .15
337 Kevin McReynolds .50 .15
338 Hensley Meulens .50 .15
339 Benji Gil RC 1.00 .30
340 Don Mattingly 3.00 .90
341 Alvin Davis .50 .15
342 Alan Mills .50 .15
343 Kelly Downs .50 .15
344 Leo Gomez .50 .15
345 Tarrik Brock RC .50 .15
346 Ryan Turner RC .50 .15
347 John Smoltz .75 .23
348 Bill Sampen .50 .15
349 Paul Byrd RC 1.00 .30
350 Mike Bordick .50 .15
351 Jose Lind .50 .15
352 David Wells .50 .15
353 Barry Larkin 1.25 .35
354 Bruce Ruffin .50 .15
355 Luis Rivera .50 .15
356 Sid Bream .50 .15
357 Julian Vasquez RC .50 .15
358 Jason Bere RC 1.00 .30
359 Ben McDonald .50 .15
360 Scott Stahoviak RC .50 .15
361 Kirt Manwaring .50 .15
362 Jeff Johnson .50 .15

363 Rob Deer .50 .15
364 Tony Pena .50 .15
365 Melido Perez .50 .15
366 Clay Parker .50 .15
367 Dale Sveum .50 .15
368 Mike Scioscia .50 .15
369 Roger Salkeld .50 .15
370 Mike Stanley .50 .15
371 Jack McDowell .50 .15
372 Tim Wallach .50 .15
373 Billy Ripken .50 .15
374 Mike Christopher .50 .15
375 Paul Molitor .75 .23
376 Dave Stieb .50 .15
377 Pedro Guerrero .50 .15
378 Russ Swan .50 .15
379 Bob Ojeda .50 .15
380 Donn Pall .50 .15
381 Eddie Zosky .50 .15
382 Darnell Coles .50 .15
383 Tom Smith RC .50 .15
384 Mark McGwire 3.00 .90
385 Gary Carter .75 .23
386 Rich Amaral RC .50 .15
387 Alan Embree RC .50 .15
388 Jonathan Hurst RC .50 .15
389 Bobby Jones RC 1.00 .30
390 Rico Rossy .50 .15
391 Dan Smith .50 .15
392 Terry Steinbach .50 .15
393 Jon Farrell RC .50 .15
394 Dave Anderson .50 .15
395 Benny Santiago .50 .15
396 Mark Wohlers .50 .15
397 Mo Vaughn .50 .15
398 Randy Kramer .50 .15
399 John Jaha RC 1.00 .30
400 Cal Ripken 4.00 1.20
401 Ryan Bowen .50 .15
402 Tim McIntosh .50 .15
403 Bernard Gilkey .50 .15
404 Junior Felix .50 .15
405 Cris Colon RC .50 .15
406 Marc Newfield .50 .15
407 Bernie Williams .75 .23
408 Jay Howell .50 .15
409 Zane Smith .50 .15
410 Jeff Shaw .50 .15
411 Kerry Woodson .50 .15
412 Wes Chamberlain .50 .15
413 Dave Mlicki RC 1.00 .30
414 Benny Distefano .50 .15
415 Kevin Rogers .50 .15
416 Tim Naehring .50 .15
417 Clemente Nunez RC .50 .15
418 Luis Sojo .50 .15
419 Kevin Ritz .50 .15
420 Omar Olivares .50 .15
421 Manuel Lee .50 .15
422 Julio Valera .50 .15
423 Omar Vizquel .50 .15
424 Darren Burton RC .50 .15
425 Mel Hall .50 .15
426 Dennis Powell .50 .15
427 Lee Stevens .50 .15
428 Glenn Davis .50 .15
429 Willie Greene .50 .15
430 Kevin Wickander .50 .15
431 Dennis Eckersley .50 .15
432 Joe Orsulak .50 .15
433 Eddie Murray 1.25 .35
434 Matt Stairs RC 1.00 .30
435 Wally Joyner .50 .15
436 Rondell White 1.25 .35
437 Rob Maurer .50 .15
438 Joe Redfield .50 .15
439 Mark Lewis .50 .15
440 Darren Daulton .50 .15
441 Mike Henneman .50 .15
442 John Cangelosi .50 .15
443 Vince Moore RC .50 .15
444 John Wehner .50 .15
445 Kent Hrbek .50 .15
446 Mark McLemore .50 .15
447 Bill Wegman .50 .15
448 Robby Thompson .50 .15
449 Mark Anthony RC .50 .15
450 Archi Cianfrocco RC .50 .15
451 Johnny Ruffin .50 .15
452 Javy Lopez 2.50 .75
453 Greg Gohr .50 .15
454 Tim Scott .50 .15
455 Stan Belinda .50 .15
456 Darrin Jackson .50 .15
457 Chris Gardner .50 .15
458 Esteban Beltre .50 .15
459 Phil Plantier .50 .15
460 Jim Thome 8.00 2.40
461 Mike Piazza RC 40.00 12.00
462 Matt Sinatro .50 .15
463 Scott Servais .50 .15
464 Brian Jordan RC 3.00 .90
465 Doug Drabek .50 .15
466 Carl Willis .50 .15
467 Bret Barberie .50 .15
468 Hal Morris .50 .15
469 Steve Sax .50 .15
470 Jerry Willard .50 .15
471 Dan Wilson .50 .15
472 Chris Hoiles .50 .15
473 Rheal Cormier .50 .15
474 John Morris .50 .15
475 Jeff Reardon .50 .15
476 Mark Leiter .50 .15
477 Tom Gordon .50 .15
478 Kent Bottenfield RC 1.00 .30
479 Gene Larkin .50 .15
480 Dwight Gooden .75 .23
481 B.J. Surhoff .50 .15
482 Andy Stankiewicz .50 .15
483 Tino Martinez .75 .23
484 Craig Biggio .75 .23
485 Denny Neagle .50 .15
486 Rusty Meacham .50 .15
487 Kal Daniels .50 .15
488 Dave Henderson .50 .15
489 Tim Costo .50 .15
490 Doug Davis .50 .15
491 Frank Viola .50 .15
492 Cory Snyder .50 .15
493 Chris Martin .50 .15
494 Dion James .50 .15
495 Randy Tomlin .50 .15
496 Greg Vaughn .50 .15
497 Dennis Cook .50 .15
498 Rosario Rodriguez .50 .15
499 Dave Staton .50 .15
500 George Brett 3.00 .90
501 Brian Barnes .50 .15
502 Butch Henry RC .50 .15
503 Harold Reynolds .50 .15
504 David Nied RC 1.00 .30
505 Lee Smith .50 .15
506 Steve Chitren .50 .15
507 Ken Hill .50 .15
508 Robbie Beckett .50 .15
509 Troy Afenir .50 .15
510 Kelly Gruber .50 .15
511 Bret Boone 1.25 .35
512 Jeff Branson .50 .15
513 Mike Jackson .50 .15
514 Pete Harnisch .50 .15
515 Chad Kreuter .50 .15
516 Joe Vitko RC .50 .15
517 Orel Hershiser .50 .15
518 John Doherty RC .50 .15
519 Jay Bell .50 .15
520 Mark Langston .50 .15
521 Dann Howitt .50 .15
522 Bobby Reed RC .50 .15
523 Bobby Munoz RC .50 .15
524 Todd Ritchie .50 .15
525 Bip Roberts .50 .15
526 Pat Listach RC 1.00 .30
527 Scott Brosius RC 3.00 .90
528 John Roper RC .50 .15
529 Phil Hiatt RC .50 .15
530 Denny Walling .50 .15
531 Carlos Baerga .50 .15
532 Manny Ramirez RC 20.00 6.00
533 Pat Clements UER .50 .15
(Mistakenly numbered 553)
534 Ron Gant .50 .15
535 Pat Kelly .50 .15
536 Bill Spiers .50 .15
537 Darren Reed .50 .15
538 Ken Caminiti .50 .15
539 Butch Huskey RC .50 .15
540 Matt Nokes .50 .15
541 John Kruk .50 .15
542 John Jaha FOIL .50 .15
543 Justin Thompson RC .50 .15
544 Steve Hosey .50 .15
545 Joe Kmak .50 .15
546 John Franco .50 .15
547 Devon White .50 .15
548 E.Hansen FOIL RC .50 .15
549 Ryan Klesko 1.25 .35
550 Danny Tartabull .50 .15
551 Frank Thomas FOIL 1.25 .35
552 Kevin Tapani .50 .15
553 Willie Banks .50 .15
(See also 533)
554 B.J. Wallace RC FOIL .50 .15
555 Orlando Miller RC .50 .15
556 Mark Smith RC .50 .15
557 Tim Wallach FOIL .50 .15
558 Bill Gullickson .50 .15
559 Derek Bell FOIL .50 .15
560 Joe Randa FOIL RC 1.00 .30
561 Frank Seminara RC .50 .15
562 Mark Gardner .50 .15
563 Rick Greene RC FOIL .50 .15
564 Gary Gaetti .50 .15
565 Ozzie Guillen .50 .15
566 Charles Nagy FOIL .50 .15
567 Mike Milchin .50 .15
568 Ben Shelton RC .50 .15
569 Chris Roberts FOIL .50 .15
570 Ellis Burks .50 .15
571 Scott Scudder .50 .15
572 Jim Abbott FOIL .75 .23
573 Joe Carter .50 .15
574 Steve Finley .50 .15
575 Jim Olander FOIL .50 .15
576 Carlos Garcia .50 .15
577 Gregg Olson .50 .15
578 Greg Swindell FOIL .50 .15
579 Matt Williams FOIL .50 .15
580 Mark Grace .75 .23
581 Howard House FOIL RC .50 .15
582 Luis Polonia .50 .15
583 Erik Hanson .50 .15
584 Salomon Torres FOIL .50 .15
585 Carlton Fisk .75 .23
586 Bret Saberhagen .50 .15
587 C.McConnell FOIL RC .50 .15
588 Jimmy Key .50 .15
589 Mike Macfarlane .50 .15
590 Barry Bonds FOIL 3.00 .90
591 Jamie McAndrew .50 .15
592 Shane Mack .50 .15
593 Kerwin Moore .50 .15
594 Joe Oliver .50 .15
595 Chris Sabo .50 .15
596 Alex Gonzalez RC 2.00 .60
597 Brett Butler .50 .15
598 Mark Hutton RC .50 .15
599 Andy Benes FOIL .50 .15
600 Jose Canseco 1.25 .35
601 Darryl Kile .50 .15
602 Matt Stairs FOIL .50 .15
603 R.Butler RC FOIL .50 .15
604 Willie McGee .50 .15
605 Jack McDowell FOIL .50 .15
606 Tom Candiotti .50 .15
607 Ed Martel RC .50 .15
608 Matt Mieske FOIL .50 .15
609 Darrin Fletcher .50 .15
610 Rafael Palmeiro .75 .23
611 Bill Swift FOIL .50 .15
612 Mike Mussina 1.25 .35
613 Vince Coleman .50 .15
614 Scott Cepicky COR .50 .15
614A S.Cepicky FOIL UER .50 .15
Bats: LEFLT
615 Mike Greenwell .50 .15
616 Kevin McGehee RC .50 .15
617 J.Hammonds FOIL .50 .15
618 Scott Taylor .50 .15
619 Dave Otto .50 .15
620 Mark McGwire FOIL 3.00 .90
621 Kevin Tatar RC .50 .15
622 Steve Farr .50 .15
623 Ryan Klesko FOIL .50 .15
624 Dave Fleming .50 .15
625 Andre Dawson .50 .15
626 Tino Martinez FOIL .75 .23
627 Chad Curtis RC 1.00 .30
628 Mickey Morandini .50 .15
629 Gregg Olson FOIL .50 .15
630 Lou Whitaker .50 .15
631 Arthur Rhodes .50 .15
632 Brandon Wilson RC .50 .15
633 Lance Jennings RC .50 .15
634 Allen Watson RC .50 .15
635 Len Dykstra .50 .15
636 Joe Girardi .50 .15
637 K.Hernandez RC FOIL .50 .15
638 Mike Hampton RC 3.00 .90
639 Al Osuna .50 .15
640 Kevin Appier .50 .15
641 Rick Helling FOIL .50 .15
642 Jody Reed .50 .15
643 Ray Lankford .50 .15
644 John Olerud .50 .15
645 Paul Molitor FOIL .75 .23
646 Pat Borders .50 .15
647 Mike Morgan .50 .15
648 Larry Walker .75 .23
649 P.Castellano FOIL .50 .15
650 Fred McGriff .75 .23
651 Walt Weiss .50 .15
652 C.Murray RC FOIL 1.00 .30
653 Dave Nilsson .50 .15
654 Greg Pirkl RC .50 .15
655 Robin Ventura FOIL .50 .15
656 Mark Portugal .50 .15
657 Roger McDowell .50 .15
658 Rick Hirtensteiner FOIL RC .50 .15
659 Glenallen Hill .50 .15
660 Greg Gagne .50 .15
661 Charles Johnson FOIL .75 .23
662 Brian Hunter .50 .15
663 Mark Lemke .50 .15
664 Tim Belcher FOIL .50 .15
665 Rich DeLucia .50 .15
666 Bob Walk .50 .15
667 Joe Carter FOIL .50 .15
668 Jose Guzman .50 .15
669 Otis Nixon .50 .15
670 Phil Nevin FOIL .75 .23
671 Eric Davis .50 .15
672 Damion Easley RC 1.00 .30
673 Will Clark FOIL 1.25 .35
674 Mark Kiefer RC .50 .15
675 Ozzie Smith 2.00 .60
676 Manny Ramirez FOIL 5.00 1.50
677 Gregg Olson .50 .15
678 Cliff Floyd RC 5.00 1.50
679 Duane Singleton RC .50 .15
680 Jose Rijo .50 .15
681 Willie Randolph .50 .15
682 M.Tucker FOIL RC 1.00 .30
683 Darren Lewis .50 .15
684 Dale Murphy 1.25 .35
685 Mike Pagliarulo .50 .15
686 Paul Miller RC .50 .15
687 Mike Robertson RC .50 .15
688 Mike Devereaux .50 .15
689 Pedro Astacio RC 1.00 .30
690 Alan Trammell .75 .23
691 Roger Clemens 2.50 .75
692 Bud Black .50 .15
693 Turk Wendell RC 1.00 .30
694 Barry Larkin FOIL 1.25 .35
695 Todd Zeile .50 .15
696 Pat Hentgen .50 .15
697 Eddie Taubensee RC 1.00 .30
698 G.Velasquez RC .50 .15
699 Tom Glavine .75 .23
700 Robin Yount 2.00 .60
701 Checklist 1-141 .50 .15
702 Checklist 142-282 .50 .15
703 Checklist 283-423 .50 .15
704 Checklist 424-564 .50 .15
705 Checklist 565-705 .50 .15

1993 Bowman

This 708-card standard-size set (produced by Topps) was issued in one series and features one of the more comprehensive selection of prospects and rookies available that year. Cards were distributed in 14-card plastic wrapped packs and jumbo packs. Each 14-card pack contained one silver foil bordered subset card. The basic issue card fronts feature white-bordered color action player photos. The 48 foil subset cards (339-374 and 693-704) feature sixteen 1992 MVPs of the Minor Leagues, top prospects and a few father/son combinations. Rookie Cards in this set include James Baldwin, Roger Cedeno, Derek Jeter, Jason Kendall, Andy Pettitte, Jose Vidro and Preston Wilson.

Nm-Mt Ex-Mt
COMPLETE SET (708) 50.00 15.00
1 Glenn Davis .15 .04
2 Hector Roa RC .25 .07
3 Ken Ryan RC .25 .07
4 Derek Wallace RC .25 .07
5 Jorge Fabregas .15 .04
6 Joe Oliver .15 .04
7 Brandon Wilson .15 .04
8 Mark Thompson RC .25 .07
9 Tracy Sanders .15 .04
10 Rich Renteria .15 .04
11 Lou Whitaker .30 .09
12 Brian L. Hunter RC .50 .15
13 Joe Vitiello .15 .04
14 Eric Karros .30 .09
15 Joe Kmak .15 .04
16 Tavo Alvarez .15 .04
17 Steve Dunn RC .25 .07
18 Tony Fernandez .15 .04
19 Melido Perez .15 .04
20 Mike Lieberthal .30 .09
21 Terry Steinbach .15 .04
22 Stan Belinda .15 .04
23 Jay Buhner .30 .09
24 Allen Watson .15 .04
25 Daryl Henderson RC .25 .07
26 Ray McDavid RC .25 .07
27 Shawn Green 1.00 .30
28 Bud Black .15 .04
29 Sherman Obando RC .25 .07
30 Mike Hostetler RC .25 .07
31 Nate Minchey RC .25 .07
32 Randy Myers .15 .04
33 Brian Grebeck .15 .04
34 John Roper .15 .04
35 Larry Thomas .15 .04
36 Alex Cole .15 .04
37 Tom Kramer RC .25 .07
38 Matt Whisenant RC .25 .07
39 Chris Gomez RC .50 .15
40 Luis Gonzalez .30 .09
41 Kevin Appier .30 .09
42 Omar Daal RC .50 .15
43 Duane Singleton .15 .04
44 Bill Risley .15 .04
45 Pat Meares RC .50 .15
46 Butch Huskey .15 .04
47 Bobby Munoz .15 .04
48 Juan Bell .15 .04
49 Scott Lydy RC .25 .07
50 Dennis Moeller .15 .04
51 Marc Newfield .15 .04
52 Tripp Cromer RC .25 .07
53 Kurt Miller .15 .04
54 Jim Pena .15 .04
55 Juan Guzman .15 .04
56 Matt Williams .30 .09
57 Harold Reynolds .30 .09
58 Donnie Elliott RC .25 .07
59 Jon Shave RC .25 .07
60 Kevin Roberson RC .25 .07
61 Hilly Hathaway RC .25 .07
62 Jose Rijo .15 .04
63 Kerry Taylor RC .15 .04
64 Ryan Hawblitzel .15 .04
65 Glenallen Hill .15 .04
66 Ramon Martinez RC .25 .07
67 Travis Fryman .30 .09
68 Tom Nevers .15 .04
69 Phil Hiatt .15 .04
70 Tim Wallach .15 .04
71 B.J. Surhoff .30 .09
72 Rondell White .30 .09
73 Denny Hocking RC .50 .15
74 Mike Oquist RC .25 .07
75 Paul O'Neill .50 .15
76 Willie Banks .15 .04
77 Bob Welch .15 .04
78 Jose Sandoval RC .25 .07
79 Bill Haselman .15 .04
80 Rheal Cormier .15 .04
81 Dean Palmer .30 .09
82 Pat Gomez RC .25 .07
83 Steve Karsay .15 .04
84 Carl Hanselman RC .25 .07
85 T.R. Lewis RC .25 .07
86 Chipper Jones .75 .23
87 Scott Hatteberg .15 .04
88 Greg Hibbard .15 .04
89 Lance Painter RC .25 .07
90 Chad Mottola RC .50 .15
91 Jason Bere .15 .04
92 Dante Bichette .30 .09
93 Sandy Alomar Jr. .15 .04
94 Carl Everett .30 .09
95 Danny Bautista RC 1.00 .30
96 Steve Finley .30 .09
97 David Cone .30 .09
98 Todd Hollandsworth .15 .04
99 Matt Mieske .15 .04
100 Larry Walker .50 .15
101 Shane Mack .15 .04
102 Aaron Ledesma RC .25 .07
103 Andy Pettitte RC 8.00 2.40
104 Kevin Stocker .15 .04
105 Mike Mohler RC .25 .07
106 Tony Menendez .15 .04
107 Derek Lowe .30 .09
108 Basil Shabazz .15 .04
109 Dan Smith .15 .04
110 Scott Sanders RC .50 .15
111 Todd Stottlemyre .15 .04
112 Benji Simonton RC .25 .07
113 Rick Sutcliffe .30 .09
114 Lee Heath RC .25 .07
115 Jeff Russell .15 .04
116 Dave Stevens RC .25 .07
117 Mark Holzemer RC .25 .07
118 Tim Belcher .15 .04
119 Bobby Thigpen .15 .04
120 Roger Bailey RC .25 .07
121 Tony Mitchell RC .25 .07
122 Junior Felix .15 .04
123 Rich Robertson RC .25 .07
124 Andy Cook RC .25 .07
125 Brian Bevil RC .25 .07
126 Darryl Strawberry .50 .15
127 Cal Eldred .15 .04
128 Cliff Floyd .50 .15
129 Alan Newman .15 .04
130 Howard Johnson .15 .04
131 Jim Abbott .50 .15
132 Chad McConnell .15 .04
133 Miguel Jimenez RC .25 .07
134 Brett Backlund RC .25 .07
135 John Cummings RC .25 .07
136 Brian Barber .15 .04
137 Rafael Palmeiro .50 .15
138 Tim Worrell RC .25 .07
139 Jose Pett RC .25 .07
140 Barry Bonds 2.00 .60
141 Damon Buford .15 .04
142 Jeff Blauser .15 .04
143 Frankie Rodriguez .15 .04
144 Mike Morgan .15 .04
145 Gary DiSarcina .15 .04
146 Pokey Reese .15 .04
147 Johnny Ruffin .15 .04
148 David Nied .15 .04
149 Charles Nagy .15 .04
150 Mike Myers RC .25 .07
151 Kenny Carlyle RC .25 .07
152 Eric Anthony .15 .04
153 Jose Lind .15 .04
154 Pedro Martinez 1.50 .45
155 Mark Kiefer .15 .04
156 Tim Laker RC .25 .07
157 Pat Mahomes .15 .04
158 Bobby Bonilla .30 .09
159 Domingo Jean .15 .04
160 Darren Daulton .30 .09
161 Mark McGwire 2.00 .60
162 Jason Kendall RC 1.50 .45
163 Desi Relaford .15 .04
164 Ozzie Canseco .15 .04
165 Rick Helling .15 .04
166 Steve Pegues RC .25 .07
167 Paul Molitor .50 .15
168 Larry Carter RC .15 .04
169 Arthur Rhodes .15 .04
170 Damon Hollins RC .50 .15
171 Frank Viola .30 .09
172 Steve Trachsel RC .50 .15
173 J.T. Snow RC 1.50 .45
174 Keith Gordon RC .25 .07
175 Carlton Fisk .50 .15
176 Jason Bates RC .25 .07
177 Mike Crosby RC .25 .07
178 Benny Santiago .30 .09
179 Mike Moore .15 .04
180 Jeff Juden .15 .04
181 Darren Burton .15 .04
182 Todd Williams RC .50 .15
183 John Jaha .15 .04
184 Mike Lansing RC .50 .15
185 Pedro Grifol RC .25 .07
186 Vince Coleman .15 .04
187 Pat Kelly .15 .04
188 Clemente Alvarez RC .25 .07
189 Ron Darling .15 .04
190 Orlando Merced .15 .04
191 Chris Bosio .15 .04
192 Steve Dixon RC .25 .07
193 Doug Dascenzo .15 .04
194 Ray Holbert RC .25 .07
195 Howard Battle .15 .04
196 Willie McGee .30 .09
197 John O'Donoghue RC .25 .07
198 Steve Avery .15 .04
199 Greg Blosser .15 .04
200 Ryne Sandberg 1.25 .35
201 Joe Grahe .15 .04
202 Dan Wilson .30 .09
203 Domingo Martinez RC .25 .07
204 Andres Galarraga .30 .09
205 Jamie Taylor RC .25 .07
206 Darrell Whitmore RC .25 .07
207 Ben Blomdahl RC .25 .07
208 Doug Drabek .15 .04
209 Keith Miller .15 .04
210 Billy Ashley .15 .04
211 Mike Farrell RC .25 .07
212 John Wetteland .30 .09
213 Randy Tomlin .15 .04
214 Sid Fernandez .15 .04
215 Quilvio Veras RC .50 .15
216 Dave Hollins .15 .04
217 Mike Neill .15 .04
218 Andy Van Slyke .30 .09
219 Bret Boone .50 .15
220 Tom Pagnozzi .15 .04
221 Mike Welch RC .25 .07
222 Frank Seminara .15 .04
223 Ron Villone .15 .04
224 D.J. Thielen RC .25 .07
225 Cal Ripken 2.50 .75
226 Pedro Borbon Jr. RC .25 .07
227 Carlos Quintana .15 .04
228 Tommy Shields .15 .04
229 Tim Salmon .50 .15
230 John Smiley .15 .04
231 Ellis Burks .30 .09
232 Pedro Castellano .15 .04
233 Paul Byrd .15 .04
234 Bryan Harvey .15 .04
235 Scott Livingstone .15 .04
236 James Mouton RC .25 .07
237 Joe Randa .30 .09
238 Pedro Astacio .15 .04
239 Darryl Hamilton .15 .04
240 Joey Eischen RC .25 .07
241 Edgar Herrera RC .25 .07
242 Dwight Gooden .50 .15
243 Sam Militello .15 .04
244 Ron Blazier RC .25 .07
245 Ruben Sierra .15 .04
246 Al Martin .15 .04
247 Mike Felder .15 .04
248 Bob Tewksbury .15 .04
249 Craig Lefferts .15 .04
250 Luis Lopez RC .25 .07
251 Devon White .15 .04
252 Will Clark .75 .23
253 Mark Smith .15 .04
254 Terry Pendleton .30 .09
255 Aaron Sele .15 .04
256 Jose Viera RC .25 .07
257 Damion Easley .15 .04
258 Rod Lofton RC .25 .07
259 Chris Snopek RC .25 .07
260 Q.McCracken RC .50 .15
261 Mike Matthews RC .25 .07
262 Hector Carrasco RC .25 .07
263 Rick Greene .15 .04
264 Chris Holt RC .50 .15
265 George Brett 2.00 .60
266 Rick Gorecki RC .25 .07
267 Francisco Gamez RC .25 .07
268 Marquis Grissom .15 .04
269 Kevin Tapani UER .15 .04
(Misspelled Tapan on card front)
270 Ryan Thompson .15 .04
271 Gerald Williams .15 .04
272 Paul Fletcher RC .25 .07

273 Lance Blankenship .15 .04
274 Marty Neff RC .25 .07
275 Shawn Estes .15 .04
276 Rene Arocha RC .50 .15
277 Scott Eyre RC .25 .07
278 Phil Plantier .15 .04
279 Paul Spoljaric RC .25 .07
280 Chris Gambs .15 .04
281 Harold Baines .30 .09
282 Jose Oliva .15 .04
283 Matt Whiteside RC .25 .07
284 Brant Brown RC .50 .15
285 Russ Springer .15 .04
286 Chris Sabo .15 .04
287 Ozzie Guillen .15 .04
288 Marcus Moore RC .25 .07
289 Chad Ogea .15 .04
290 Walt Weiss .15 .04
291 Brian Edmondson .15 .04
292 Jimmy Gonzalez .15 .04
293 Danny Miceli RC .50 .15
294 Jose Offerman .15 .04
295 Greg Vaughn .30 .09
296 Frank Bolick .15 .04
297 Mike Maksudian RC .25 .07
298 John Franco .30 .09
299 Danny Tartabull .15 .04
300 Len Dykstra .30 .09
301 Bobby Witt .15 .04
302 Trey Beamon RC .25 .07
303 Tino Martinez .50 .15
304 Aaron Holbert .15 .04
305 Juan Gonzalez .75 .23
306 Billy Hall RC .25 .07
307 Duane Ward .15 .04
308 Rod Beck .15 .04
309 Jose Mercedes RC .25 .07
310 Otis Nixon .15 .04
311 Gettys Glaze RC .25 .07
312 Candy Maldonado .15 .04
313 Chad Curtis .15 .04
314 Tim Costo .15 .04
315 Mike Robertson .15 .04
316 Nigel Wilson .15 .04
317 Greg McMichael RC .50 .15
318 Scott Pose RC .25 .07
319 Ivan Cruz .15 .04
320 Greg Swindell .15 .04
321 Kevin McReynolds .15 .04
322 Tom Candiotti .15 .04
323 Rob Wishnevski RC .25 .07
324 Ken Hill .15 .04
325 Kirby Puckett .75 .23
326 Tim Bogar RC .25 .07
327 Mariano Rivera 1.00 .30
328 Mitch Williams .15 .04
329 Craig Paquette .15 .04
330 Jay Bell .30 .09
331 Jose Martinez RC .25 .07
332 Rob Deer .15 .04
333 Brook Fordyce .15 .04
334 Matt Nokes .15 .04
335 Derek Lee .15 .04
336 Paul Ellis RC .25 .07
337 Desi Wilson RC .25 .07
338 Roberto Alomar .75 .23
339 Jim Tatum FOIL RC .25 .07
340 J.T. Snow FOIL .75 .23
341 Tim Salmon FOIL .50 .15
342 Russ Davis FOIL RC .50 .15
343 Javy Lopez FOIL .50 .15
344 Troy O'Leary FOIL RC .50 .15
345 M.Cordova FOIL RC 1.00 .30
346 Bubba Smith RC FOIL .25 .07
347 Chipper Jones FOIL .75 .23
348 Jessie Hollins FOIL .15 .04
349 Willie Greene FOIL .15 .04
350 Mark Thompson FOIL .15 .04
351 Nigel Wilson FOIL .15 .04
352 Todd Jones FOIL .15 .04
353 Raul Mondesi FOIL .30 .09
354 Cliff Floyd FOIL .50 .15
355 Bobby Jones FOIL .30 .09
356 Kevin Stocker FOIL .15 .04
357 M.Cummings FOIL .15 .04
358 Allen Watson FOIL .15 .04
359 Ray McDavid FOIL .15 .04
360 Steve Hosey FOIL .15 .04
361 B.Pennington FOIL .15 .04
362 F.Rodriguez FOIL .15 .04
363 Troy Percival FOIL .50 .15
364 Jason Bere FOIL .15 .04
365 Manny Ramirez FOIL .75 .23
366 J.Thompson FOIL .15 .04
367 Joe Vitiello FOIL .15 .04
368 Tyrone Hill FOIL .15 .04
369 David McCarty FOIL .15 .04
370 Brien Taylor FOIL .15 .04
371 T.Van Poppel FOIL .15 .04
372 Marc Newfield FOIL .15 .04
373 T.Lowery RC FOIL .50 .15
374 Alex Gonzalez FOIL .15 .04
375 Ken Griffey Jr. 1.25 .35
376 Donovan Osborne .15 .04
377 Ritchie Moody RC .25 .07
378 Shane Andrews .15 .04
379 Carlos Delgado .75 .23
380 Bill Swift .15 .04
381 Leo Gomez .15 .04
382 Ron Gant .30 .09
383 Scott Fletcher .15 .04
384 Matt Walbeck RC .50 .15
385 Chuck Finley .30 .09
386 Kevin Mitchell .15 .04
387 Wilson Alvarez UER .15 .04
(Misspelled Alverez on card front)
388 John Burke RC .25 .07
389 Alan Embree .15 .04
390 Trevor Hoffman .30 .09
391 Alan Trammell .50 .15
392 Todd Jones .15 .04
393 Felix Jose .15 .04
394 Orel Hershiser .30 .09
395 Pat Listach .15 .04
396 Gabe White .15 .04
397 Dan Serafini RC .25 .07
398 Todd Hundley .15 .04
399 Wade Boggs .50 .15
400 Tyler Green .15 .04
401 Mike Bordick .15 .04
402 Scott Bullett .15 .04
403 LaGrande Russell RC .25 .07
404 Ray Lankford .15 .04
405 Nolan Ryan 3.00 .90
406 Robbie Beckett .15 .04
407 Brent Bowers RC .25 .07
408 Adell Davenport RC .25 .07
409 Brady Anderson .30 .09
410 Tom Glavine .50 .15
411 Doug Hecker RC .25 .07
412 Jose Guzman .15 .04
413 Luis Polonia .15 .04
414 Brian Williams .15 .04
415 Bo Jackson .75 .23
416 Eric Young .15 .04
417 Kenny Lofton .30 .09
418 Orestes Destrade .15 .04
419 Tony Phillips .15 .04
420 Jeff Bagwell .50 .15
421 Mark Gardner .15 .04
422 Brett Butler .30 .09
423 Graeme Lloyd RC .50 .15
424 Delino DeShields .15 .04
425 Scott Erickson .15 .04
426 Jeff Kent .75 .23
427 Jimmy Key .30 .09
428 Mickey Morandini .15 .04
429 Marcos Armas RC .25 .07
430 Don Slaught .15 .04
431 Randy Johnson .75 .23
432 Omar Olivares .15 .04
433 Charlie Leibrandt .15 .04
434 Kurt Stillwell .15 .04
435 Scott Brow RC .25 .07
436 Robby Thompson .15 .04
437 Ben McDonald .15 .04
438 Deion Sanders .50 .15
439 Tony Pena .15 .04
440 Mark Grace .50 .15
441 Eduardo Perez .15 .04
442 Tim Pugh RC .25 .07
443 Scott Ruffcorn .15 .04
444 Jay Gainer RC .25 .07
445 Albert Belle .30 .09
446 Bret Barberie .15 .04
447 Justin Mashore .15 .04
448 Pete Harnisch .15 .04
449 Greg Gagne .15 .04
450 Eric Davis .30 .09
451 Dave Mlicki .15 .04
452 Moises Alou .30 .09
453 Rick Aguilera .15 .04
454 Eddie Murray .75 .23
455 Bob Wickman .15 .04
456 Wes Chamberlain .15 .04
457 Brent Gates .15 .04
458 Paul Wagner .15 .04
459 Mike Hampton .30 .09
460 Ozzie Smith 1.25 .35
461 Tom Henke .15 .04
462 Ricky Gutierrez .15 .04
463 Jack Morris .30 .09
464 Joel Chimelis .15 .04
465 Gregg Olson .15 .04
466 Javy Lopez .50 .15
467 Scott Cooper .15 .04
468 Willie Wilson .15 .04
469 Mark Langston .15 .04
470 Barry Larkin .75 .23
471 Rod Bolton .15 .04
472 Freddie Benavides .15 .04
473 Ken Ramos RC .25 .07
474 Chuck Carr .15 .04
475 Cecil Fielder .30 .09
476 Eddie Taubensee .15 .04
477 Chris Eddy RC .25 .07
478 Greg Hansell .15 .04
479 Kevin Reimer .15 .04
480 Dennis Martinez .30 .09
481 Chuck Knoblauch .30 .09
482 Mike Draper .15 .04
483 Spike Owen .15 .04
484 Terry Mulholland .15 .04
485 Dennis Eckersley .30 .09
486 Blas Minor .15 .04
487 Dave Fleming .15 .04
488 Dan Cholowsky .15 .04
489 Ivan Rodriguez .75 .23
490 Gary Sheffield .30 .09
491 Ed Sprague .15 .04
492 Steve Hosey .15 .04
493 Jimmy Haynes RC .50 .15
494 John Smoltz .50 .15
495 Andre Dawson .30 .09
496 Rey Sanchez .15 .04
497 Ty Van Burkleo .15 .04
498 Bobby Ayala RC .25 .07
499 Tim Raines .30 .09
500 Charlie Hayes .15 .04
501 Paul Sorrento .15 .04
502 Richie Lewis RC .25 .07
503 Jason Pfaff RC .25 .07
504 Ken Caminiti .30 .09
505 Mike Macfarlane .15 .04
506 Jody Reed .15 .04
507 Bobby Hughes RC .25 .07
508 Wil Cordero .15 .04
509 George Tsamis RC .25 .07
510 Bret Saberhagen .30 .09
511 Derek Jeter RC 25.00 7.50
512 Gene Schall .15 .04
513 Curtis Shaw .15 .04
514 Steve Cooke .15 .04
515 Edgar Martinez .50 .15
516 Mike Milchin .15 .04
517 Billy Ripken .15 .04
518 Andy Benes .15 .04
519 Juan de la Rosa RC .25 .07
520 John Burkett .15 .04
521 Alex Ochoa .15 .04
522 Tony Tarasco RC .50 .15
523 Luis Ortiz .15 .04
524 Rick Wilkins .15 .04
525 Chris Turner RC .25 .07
526 Rob Dibble .30 .09
527 Jack McDowell .15 .04
528 Daryl Boston .15 .04
529 Bill Wertz RC .25 .07
530 Charlie Hough .30 .09
531 Sean Bergman .15 .04
532 Doug Jones .15 .04
533 Jeff Montgomery .15 .04
534 Roger Cedeno RC .50 .15
535 Robin Yount 1.25 .35
536 Mo Vaughn .30 .09
537 Brian Harper .15 .04
538 Juan Castillo RC .15 .04
539 Steve Farr .15 .04
540 John Kruk .30 .09
541 Troy Neel .15 .04
542 Danny Clyburn RC .25 .07
543 Jim Converse RC .25 .07
544 Gregg Jefferies .15 .04
545 Jose Canseco .75 .23
546 Julio Bruno RC .25 .07
547 Rob Butler .15 .04
548 Royce Clayton .15 .04
549 Chris Hoiles .15 .04
550 Greg Maddux 1.25 .35
551 Joe Ciccarella RC .25 .07
552 Ozzie Timmons .15 .04
553 Chili Davis .30 .09
554 Brian Koelling .15 .04
555 Frank Thomas .75 .23
556 Vinny Castilla .30 .09
557 Reggie Jefferson .15 .04
558 Rob Natal .15 .04
559 Mike Henneman .15 .04
560 Craig Biggio .50 .15
561 Billy Brewer .15 .04
562 Dan Melendez .15 .04
563 Kenny Felder RC .25 .07
564 Miguel Batista RC 1.00 .30
565 Dave Winfield .30 .09
566 Al Shirley .15 .04
567 Robert Eenhoorn .15 .04
568 Mike Williams .15 .04
569 Tanyon Sturtze RC .50 .15
570 Tim Wakefield .30 .09
571 Greg Pirkl .15 .04
572 Sean Lowe RC .25 .07
573 Terry Burrows RC .25 .07
574 Kevin Higgins .15 .04
575 Joe Carter .30 .09
576 Kevin Rogers .15 .04
577 Manny Alexander .15 .04
578 David Justice .30 .09
579 Brian Conroy RC .25 .07
580 Jessie Hollins .15 .04
581 Ron Watson RC .25 .07
582 Bip Roberts .15 .04
583 Tom Urbani RC .25 .07
584 Jason Hutchins RC .25 .07
585 Carlos Baerga .15 .04
586 Jeff Mutis .15 .04
587 Justin Thompson .15 .04
588 Orlando Miller .15 .04
589 Brian McRae .15 .04
590 Ramon Martinez .15 .04
591 Dave Nilsson .15 .04
592 Jose Vidro RC 4.00 1.20
593 Rich Becker .15 .04
594 Preston Wilson RC 3.00 .90
595 Don Mattingly 2.00 .60
596 Tony Longmire .15 .04
597 Kevin Seitzer .15 .04
598 Midre Cummings RC .25 .07
599 Omar Vizquel .30 .09
600 Lee Smith .30 .09
601 David Hulse RC .25 .07
602 Darrell Sherman RC .25 .07
603 Alex Gonzalez .15 .04
604 Geronimo Pena .15 .04
605 Mike Devereaux .15 .04
606 S.Hitchcock RC .50 .15
607 Mike Greenwell .15 .04
608 Steve Buechele .15 .04
609 Troy Percival .50 .15
610 Roberto Kelly .15 .04
611 James Baldwin RC .50 .15
612 Jerald Clark .15 .04
613 Albie Lopez RC .50 .15
614 Dave Magadan .15 .04
615 Mickey Tettleton .15 .04
616 Sean Runyan RC .25 .07
617 Bob Hamelin .15 .04
618 Raul Mondesi .30 .09
619 Tyrone Hill .15 .04
620 Darrin Fletcher .15 .04
621 Mike Trombley .15 .04
622 Jeromy Burnitz .30 .09
623 Bernie Williams .50 .15
624 Mike Farmer RC .25 .07
625 Rickey Henderson .75 .23
626 Carlos Garcia .15 .04
627 Jeff Darwin RC .25 .07
628 Todd Zeile .15 .04
629 Benji Gil .15 .04
630 Tony Gwynn 1.00 .30
631 Aaron Small RC .25 .07
632 Joe Rosselli RC .25 .07
633 Mike Mussina .75 .23
634 Ryan Klesko .30 .09
635 Roger Clemens 1.50 .45
636 Sammy Sosa 1.25 .35
637 Orlando Palmeiro RC .25 .07
638 Willie Greene .15 .04
639 George Bell .15 .04
640 Garvin Alston RC .25 .07
641 Pete Janicki RC .25 .07
642 Chris Sheff RC .25 .07
643 Felipe Lira RC .25 .07
644 Roberto Petagine .15 .04
645 Wally Joyner .30 .09
646 Mike Piazza 2.00 .60
647 Jaime Navarro .15 .04
648 Jeff Hartsock .15 .04
649 David McCarty .15 .04
650 Bobby Jones .30 .09
651 Mark Hutton .15 .04
652 Kyle Abbott .15 .04
653 Steve Cox RC .50 .15
654 Jeff King .15 .04
655 Norm Charlton .15 .04
656 Mike Gulan RC .25 .07
657 Julio Franco .30 .09
658 C.Cairncross RC .25 .07
659 John Olerud .30 .09
660 Salomon Torres .15 .04
661 Brad Pennington .15 .04
662 Melvin Nieves .15 .04
663 Ivan Calderon .15 .04
664 Turk Wendell .15 .04
665 Chris Pritchett .15 .04
666 Reggie Sanders .30 .09
667 Robin Ventura .30 .09
668 Joe Girardi .15 .04
669 Manny Ramirez .75 .23
670 Jeff Conine .30 .09
671 Greg Gohr .15 .04
672 Andujar Cedeno .15 .04
673 Les Norman RC .25 .07
674 Mike James RC .25 .07
675 Marshall Boze RC .25 .07
676 B.J. Wallace .15 .04
677 Kent Hrbek .30 .09
678 Jack Voigt RC .25 .07
679 Brien Taylor .15 .04
680 Curt Schilling .50 .15
681 Todd Van Poppel .15 .04
682 Kevin Young .30 .09
683 Tommy Adams .15 .04
684 Bernard Gilkey .15 .04
685 Kevin Brown .30 .09
686 Fred McGriff .50 .15
687 Pat Borders .15 .04
688 Kirt Manwaring .15 .04
689 Sid Bream .15 .04
690 John Valentin .15 .04
691 Steve Olsen RC .25 .07
692 Roberto Mejia RC .25 .07
693 Carlos Delgado FOIL .75 .23
694 S.Gibralter FOIL RC .25 .07
695 Gary Mota FOIL RC .25 .07
696 Jose Malave FOIL RC .25 .07
697 Larry Sutton FOIL RC .25 .07
698 Dan Frye FOIL RC .25 .07
699 Tim Clark FOIL RC .25 .07
700 Brian Rupp FOIL RC .25 .07
701 Felipe Alou FOIL .30 .09
Moises Alou
702 Barry Bonds FOIL .75 .23
Bobby Bonds
703 Ken Griffey Sr. FOIL .75 .23
Ken Griffey Jr.
704 Brian McRae FOIL .15 .04
Hal McRae
705 Checklist 1 .15 .04
706 Checklist 2 .15 .04
707 Checklist 3 .15 .04
708 Checklist 4 .15 .04

1994 Bowman Previews

This 10-card standard-size set served as a preview to the 1994 Bowman set. The cards were randomly inserted one in every 24 1994 Stadium Club second series pack. The backs are identical to the basic issue with a horizontal layout containing a player photo, text and statistics.

	Nm-Mt	Ex-Mt
COMPLETE SET (10)	25.00	7.50
1 Frank Thomas	5.00	1.50
2 Mike Piazza	10.00	3.00
3 Albert Belle	2.00	.60
4 Javier Lopez	2.00	.60
5 Cliff Floyd	2.00	.60
6 Alex Gonzalez	1.25	.35
7 Ricky Bottalico	2.00	.60
8 Tony Clark	2.00	.60
9 Mac Suzuki	2.00	.60
10 James Mouton Foil	1.25	.35

1994 Bowman

The 1994 Bowman set consists of 682 standard-size, full-bleed cards primarily distributed in plastic wrap packs and jumbo packs. There are 52 Foil cards (337-388) that include a number of top young stars and prospects. These foil cards were issued one per foil pack and two per jumbo. Rookie Cards of note include Edgardo Alfonzo, Tony Clark, Jermaine Dye, Brad Fullmer, Richard Hidalgo, Derrek Lee, Chan Ho Park, Jorge Posada and Edgar Renteria.

	Nm-Mt	Ex-Mt
COMPLETE SET (682)	60.00	18.00

1 Joe Carter .40 .12
2 Marcus Moore .25 .07
3 Doug Creek RC .50 .15
4 Pedro Martinez 1.00 .30
5 Ken Griffey Jr. 1.50 .45
6 Greg Swindell .25 .07
7 J.J. Johnson .25 .07
8 Homer Bush RC 1.00 .30
9 Arquimedez Pozo RC .50 .15
10 Bryan Harvey .25 .07
11 J.T. Snow .40 .12
12 Alan Benes RC 1.00 .30
13 Chad Kreuter .25 .07
14 Eric Karros .40 .12
15 Frank Thomas 1.00 .30
16 Bret Saberhagen .40 .12
17 Terrell Lowery .25 .07
18 Rod Bolton .25 .07
19 Harold Baines .40 .12
20 Matt Walbeck .25 .07
21 Tom Glavine .60 .18
22 Todd Jones .25 .07
23 Alberto Castillo RC .50 .15
24 Ruben Sierra .25 .07
25 Don Mattingly 2.50 .75
26 Mike Morgan .25 .07
27 Jim Musselwhite RC .50 .15
28 Matt Brunson RC .50 .15
29 A.Meinershagen RC .50 .15
30 Joe Girardi .25 .07
31 Shane Halter .25 .07
32 Jose Paniagua RC 1.00 .30
33 Paul Perkins RC .50 .15
34 John Hudek RC .50 .15
35 Frank Viola .40 .12
36 David Lamb RC .50 .15
37 Marshall Boze .25 .07
38 Jorge Posada RC 8.00 2.40
39 Brian Anderson RC 1.00 .30
40 Mark Whiten .25 .07
41 Sean Bergman .25 .07
42 Jose Parra RC .50 .15
43 Mike Robertson .25 .07
44 Pete Walker RC .50 .15
45 Juan Gonzalez 1.00 .30
46 Cleveland Ladell RC .50 .15
47 Mark Smith .25 .07
48 Kevin Jarvis UER .50 .15
(team listed as Yankees on back)
49 Amaury Telemaco RC .50 .15
50 Andy Van Slyke .40 .12
51 Rikkert Faneyte RC .50 .15
52 Curtis Shaw .25 .07
53 Matt Drews RC .50 .15
54 Wilson Alvarez .25 .07
55 Manny Ramirez .60 .18
56 Bobby Munoz .25 .07
57 Ed Sprague .25 .07
58 Jamey Wright RC 1.00 .30
59 Jeff Montgomery .25 .07
60 Kirk Rueter .40 .12
61 Edgar Martinez .60 .18
62 Luis Gonzalez .40 .12
63 Tim Vanegmond RC .50 .15
64 Bip Roberts .25 .07
65 John Jaha .25 .07
66 Chuck Carr .25 .07
67 Chuck Finley .40 .12
68 Aaron Holbert .25 .07
69 Cecil Fielder .40 .12
70 Tom Engle RC .50 .15
71 Ron Karkovice .25 .07
72 Joe Orsulak .25 .07
73 Duff Brumley RC .50 .15
74 Craig Clayton RC .50 .15
75 Cal Ripken 3.00 .90
76 Brad Fullmer RC 2.50 .75
77 Tony Tarasco .25 .07
78 Terry Farrar RC .50 .15
79 Matt Williams .40 .12
80 Rickey Henderson 1.00 .30
81 Terry Mulholland .25 .07
82 Sammy Sosa 1.50 .45
83 Paul Sorrento .25 .07
84 Pete Incaviglia .25 .07
85 Darren Hall RC .50 .15
86 Scott Klingenbeck .25 .07
87 Dario Perez RC .50 .15
88 Ugueth Urbina .25 .07
89 Dave Vanhof RC .50 .15
90 Domingo Jean .25 .07
91 Otis Nixon .25 .07
92 Andres Berumen .25 .07
93 Jose Valentin .25 .07
94 Edgar Renteria RC 8.00 2.40
95 Chris Turner .25 .07
96 Ray Lankford .25 .07
97 Danny Bautista .25 .07
98 Chan Ho Park RC 2.50 .75
99 Glenn DiSarcina RC .50 .15
100 Butch Huskey .25 .07
101 Ivan Rodriguez 1.00 .30
102 Johnny Ruffin .25 .07
103 Alex Ochoa .25 .07
104 Torii Hunter RC 10.00 3.00
105 Ryan Klesko .40 .12
106 Jay Bell .40 .12
107 Kurt Peltzer RC .50 .15
108 Miguel Jimenez .25 .07
109 Russ Davis .25 .07
110 Derek Wallace .25 .07
111 Keith Lockhart RC 1.00 .30
112 Mike Lieberthal .40 .12
113 Dave Stewart .40 .12
114 Tom Schmidt .25 .07
115 Brian McRae .25 .07
116 Moises Alou .40 .12
117 Dave Fleming .25 .07
118 Jeff Bagwell .60 .18
119 Luis Ortiz .25 .07
120 Tony Gwynn 1.25 .35
121 Jaime Navarro .25 .07
122 Benito Santiago .40 .12
123 Darrell Whitmore .25 .07
124 John Mabry RC 1.00 .30
125 Mickey Tettleton .25 .07
126 Tom Candiotti .25 .07
127 Tim Raines .40 .12
128 Bobby Bonilla .40 .12
129 John Dettmer .25 .07
130 Hector Carrasco .25 .07
131 Chris Hoiles .25 .07
132 Rick Aguilera .25 .07
133 David Justice .40 .12
134 Esteban Loaiza RC 8.00 2.40
135 Barry Bonds 2.50 .75
136 Bob Welch .25 .07
137 Mike Stanley .25 .07
138 Roberto Hernandez .25 .07
139 Sandy Alomar Jr. .25 .07
140 Darren Daulton .40 .12
141 Angel Martinez RC .50 .15
142 Howard Johnson .25 .07
143 Bob Hamelin UER .25 .07
(name and card number colors don't match)
144 J.J. Thobe RC .50 .15
145 Roger Salkeld .25 .07
146 Orlando Miller .25 .07
147 Dmitri Young .40 .12
148 Tim Hyers RC .50 .15
149 Mark Loretta RC 1.50 .45
150 Chris Hammond .25 .07
151 Joel Moore RC .50 .15
152 Todd Zeile .25 .07
153 Wil Cordero .25 .07
154 Chris Smith .25 .07
155 James Baldwin .25 .07
156 Edgardo Alfonzo RC 2.50 .75
157 Kym Ashworth RC .50 .15
158 Paul Bako RC .50 .15
159 Rick Krivda RC .50 .15
160 Pat Mahomes .25 .07

161 Damon Hollins .40 .12
162 Felix Martinez RC .50 .15
163 Jason Myers RC .50 .15
164 Izzy Molina RC .50 .15
165 Brien Taylor .25 .07
166 Kevin Orie RC .50 .15
167 Casey Whitten RC .50 .15
168 Tony Longmire .25 .07
169 John Olerud .40 .12
170 Mark Thompson .25 .07
171 Jorge Fabregas .25 .07
172 John Wetteland .40 .12
173 Dan Wilson .25 .07
174 Doug Drabek .25 .07
175 Jeff McNeely .25 .07
176 Melvin Nieves .25 .07
177 Doug Glanville RC 1.00 .30
178 Javier De La Hoya RC .50 .15
179 Chad Curtis .25 .07
180 Brian Barber .25 .07
181 Mike Henneman .25 .07
182 Jose Offerman .25 .07
183 Robert Ellis RC .50 .15
184 John Franco .40 .12
185 Benji Gil .25 .07
186 Hal Morris .25 .07
187 Chris Sabo .25 .07
188 Blaise Ilsley RC .50 .15
189 Steve Avery .25 .07
190 Rick White RC .50 .15
191 Rod Beck .25 .07
192 Mark McGwire UER 2.50 .75
(No card number on back)
193 Jim Abbott .60 .18
194 Randy Myers .25 .07
195 Kenny Lofton .40 .12
196 Mariano Duncan .25 .07
197 Lee Daniels RC .50 .15
198 Armando Reynoso .25 .07
199 Joe Randa .40 .12
200 Cliff Floyd .40 .12
201 Tim Harkrider RC .50 .15
202 Kevin Gallaher RC .50 .15
203 Scott Cooper .25 .07
204 Phil Stidham RC .50 .15
205 Jeff D'Amico RC 1.00 .30
206 Matt Whisenant .25 .07
207 De Shawn Warren .25 .07
208 Rene Arocha .25 .07
209 Tony Clark RC 1.00 .30
210 Jason Jacome RC .50 .15
211 Scott Christman RC .50 .15
212 Bill Pulsipher .40 .12
213 Dean Palmer .40 .12
214 Chad Mottola .25 .07
215 Manny Alexander .25 .07
216 Rich Becker .25 .07
217 Andre King RC .50 .15
218 Carlos Garcia .25 .07
219 Ron Pezzoni RC .50 .15
220 Steve Karsay .25 .07
221 Jose Musset RC .50 .15
222 Karl Rhodes .25 .07
223 Frank Cimorelli RC .50 .15
224 Kevin Jordan RC .50 .15
225 Duane Ward .25 .07
226 John Burke .25 .07
227 Mike Macfarlane .25 .07
228 Mike Lansing .25 .07
229 Chuck Knoblauch .40 .12
230 Ken Caminiti .40 .12
231 Gar Finnvold RC .50 .15
232 Derrek Lee RC 3.00 .90
233 Brady Anderson .40 .12
234 Vic Darensbourg RC .50 .15
235 Mark Langston .25 .07
236 T.J. Mathews RC .50 .15
237 Lou Whitaker .40 .12
238 Roger Cedeno .25 .07
239 Alex Fernandez .25 .07
240 Ryan Thompson .25 .07
241 Kerry Lacy RC .50 .15
242 Reggie Sanders .40 .12
243 Brad Pennington .25 .07
244 Bryan Eversgerd RC .50 .15
245 Greg Maddux 1.50 .45
246 Jason Kendall .40 .12
247 J.R. Phillips .25 .07
248 Bobby Witt .25 .07
249 Paul O'Neill .60 .18
250 Ryne Sandberg 1.50 .45
251 Charles Nagy .25 .07
252 Kevin Stocker .25 .07
253 Shawn Green 1.00 .30
254 Charlie Hayes .25 .07
255 Donnie Elliott .25 .07
256 Rob Fitzpatrick RC .50 .15
257 Tim Davis .25 .07
258 James Mouton .25 .07
259 Mike Greenwell .25 .07
260 Ray McDavid .25 .07
261 Mike Kelly .25 .07
262 Andy Larkin RC .50 .15
263 Marquis Riley UER .25 .07
(No card number on back)
264 Bob Tewksbury .25 .07
265 Brian Edmondson .25 .07
266 Eduardo Lantigua RC .50 .15
267 Brandon Wilson .25 .07
268 Mike Welch .25 .07
269 Tom Henke .25 .07
270 Pokey Reese .25 .07
271 Greg Zaun RC 1.00 .30
272 Todd Ritchie .25 .07
273 Javier Lopez .40 .12
274 Kevin Young .25 .07
275 Kirt Manwaring .25 .07
276 Bill Taylor RC .50 .15
277 Robert Eenhoorn .25 .07
278 Jessie Hollins .25 .07
279 Julian Tavarez RC 1.00 .30
280 Gene Schall .25 .07
281 Paul Molitor .60 .18
282 Neifi Perez RC 1.00 .30
283 Greg Gagne .25 .07
284 Marquis Grissom .25 .07
285 Randy Johnson 1.00 .30
286 Pete Harnisch .25 .07
287 Joel Bennett RC .50 .15
288 Derek Bell .25 .07
289 Darryl Hamilton .25 .07
290 Gary Sheffield .40 .12
291 Eduardo Perez .25 .07
292 Basil Shabazz .25 .07
293 Eric Davis .40 .12
294 Pedro Astacio .25 .07
295 Robin Ventura .40 .12
296 Jeff Kent .40 .12
297 Rick Helling .40 .12
298 Joe Oliver .25 .07
299 Lee Smith .40 .12
300 Dave Winfield .40 .12
301 Deion Sanders .60 .18
302 R.Manzanillo RC .50 .15
303 Mark Portugal .25 .07
304 Brent Gates .25 .07
305 Wade Boggs .60 .18
306 Rick Wilkins .25 .07
307 Carlos Baerga .25 .07
308 Curt Schilling .60 .18
309 Shannon Stewart 1.00 .30
310 Darren Holmes .25 .07
311 Robert Toth RC .50 .15
312 Gabe White .25 .07
313 Mac Suzuki RC 1.00 .30
314 Alvin Morman RC .50 .15
315 Mo Vaughn .40 .12
316 Bryce Florie RC .50 .15
317 Gabby Martinez RC .50 .15
318 Carl Everett .40 .12
319 Kerwin Moore .25 .07
320 Tom Pagnozzi .25 .07
321 Chris Gomez .25 .07
322 Todd Williams .25 .07
323 Pat Hentgen .25 .07
324 Kirk Presley RC .50 .15
325 Kevin Brown .40 .12
326 J.Isringhausen RC 1.50 .45
327 Rick Forney RC .50 .15
328 Carlos Pulido RC .50 .15
329 Terrell Wade RC .50 .15
330 Al Martin .25 .07
331 Dan Carlson RC .50 .15
332 Mark Acre RC .50 .15
333 Sterling Hitchcock .25 .07
334 Jon Ratliff RC .50 .15
335 Alex Ramirez RC .50 .15
336 Phil Geisler RC .50 .15
337 E.Zambrano FOIL RC .50 .15
338 Jim Thome FOIL 1.00 .30
339 James Mouton FOIL .25 .07
340 Cliff Floyd FOIL .40 .12
341 Carlos Delgado FOIL .60 .18
342 R.Petagine FOIL .25 .07
343 Tim Clark FOIL .25 .07
344 Bubba Smith FOIL .25 .07
345 Randy Curtis FOIL RC .50 .15
346 Joe Biasucci FOIL RC .50 .15
347 D.J. Boston FOIL RC .50 .15
348 R.Rivera FOIL RC .50 .15
349 Bryan Link FOIL RC .50 .15
350 Mike Bell FOIL RC .50 .15
351 M.Watson FOIL RC .50 .15
352 Jason Myers FOIL .25 .07
353 Chipper Jones FOIL 1.00 .30
354 B.Kieschnick FOIL .25 .07
355 Pokey Reese FOIL .25 .07
356 John Burke FOIL .25 .07
357 Kurt Miller FOIL .25 .07
358 Orlando Miller FOIL .25 .07
359 T.Hollandsworth FOIL .25 .07
360 Rondell White FOIL .40 .12
361 Bill Pulsipher FOIL .40 .12
362 Tyler Green FOIL .25 .07
363 M.Cummings FOIL .25 .07
364 Brian Barber FOIL .25 .07
365 Melvin Nieves FOIL .25 .07
366 Salomon Torres FOIL .25 .07
367 Alex Ochoa FOIL .25 .07
368 F.Rodriguez FOIL .25 .07
369 Brian Anderson FOIL .40 .12
370 James Baldwin FOIL .25 .07
371 Manny Ramirez FOIL .60 .18
372 J.Thompson FOIL .25 .07
373 Johnny Damon FOIL 1.00 .30
374 Jeff D'Amico FOIL 1.00 .30
375 Rich Becker FOIL .25 .07
376 Derek Jeter FOIL 3.00 .90
377 Steve Karsay FOIL .25 .07
378 Mac Suzuki FOIL .40 .12
379 Benji Gil FOIL .25 .07
380 Alex Gonzalez FOIL .25 .07
381 Jason Bere FOIL .25 .07
382 Brett Butler FOIL .40 .12
383 Jeff Conine FOIL .40 .12
384 Darren Daulton FOIL .40 .12
385 Jeff Kent FOIL .40 .12
386 Don Mattingly FOIL 2.50 .75
387 Mike Piazza FOIL 2.00 .60
388 Ryne Sandberg FOIL 1.50 .45
389 Rich Amaral .25 .07
390 Craig Biggio .60 .18
391 Jeff Suppan RC 1.00 .30
392 Andy Benes .25 .07
393 Cal Eldred .25 .07
394 Jeff Conine .40 .12
395 Tim Salmon .60 .18
396 Ray Suplee RC .50 .15
397 Tony Phillips .25 .07
398 Ramon Martinez .25 .07
399 Julio Franco .40 .12
400 Dwight Gooden .60 .18
401 Kevin Lomon RC .50 .15
402 Jose Rijo .25 .07
403 Mike Devereaux .25 .07
404 Mike Zolecki RC .50 .15
405 Fred McGriff .60 .18
406 Danny Clyburn .25 .07
407 Robby Thompson .25 .07
408 Terry Steinbach .25 .07
409 Luis Polonia .25 .07
410 Mark Grace .60 .18
411 Albert Belle .40 .12
412 John Kruk .40 .12
413 Scott Spiezio RC 2.50 .75
414 Ellis Burks UER .40 .12
(Name spelled Elkis on front)
415 Joe Vitiello .25 .07
416 Tim Costo .25 .07
417 Marc Newfield .25 .07
418 Oscar Henriquez RC .50 .15
419 Matt Perisho RC .50 .15
420 Julio Bruno .25 .07
421 Kenny Felder .25 .07
422 Tyler Green .25 .07
423 Jim Edmonds .60 .18
424 Ozzie Smith 1.50 .45
425 Rick Greene .25 .07
426 Todd Hollandsworth .25 .07
427 Eddie Pearson RC .50 .15
428 Quilvio Veras .25 .07
429 Kenny Rogers .40 .12
430 Willie Greene .25 .07
431 Vaughn Eshelman .25 .07
432 Pat Meares .25 .07
433 Jermaine Dye RC 8.00 2.40
434 Steve Cooke .25 .07
435 Bill Swift .25 .07
436 Fausto Cruz RC .50 .15
437 Mark Hutton .25 .07
438 B.Kieschnick RC 1.00 .30
439 Yorkis Perez .25 .07
440 Len Dykstra .40 .12
441 Pat Borders .25 .07
442 Doug Walls RC .50 .15
443 Wally Joyner .40 .12
444 Ken Hill .25 .07
445 Eric Anthony .25 .07
446 Mitch Williams .25 .07
447 Cory Bailey RC .50 .15
448 Dave Staton .25 .07
449 Greg Vaughn .40 .12
450 Dave Magadan .25 .07
451 Chili Davis .40 .12
452 Gerald Santos RC .50 .15
453 Joe Perona .25 .07
454 Delino DeShields .25 .07
455 Jack McDowell .25 .07
456 Todd Hundley .25 .07
457 Ritchie Moody .25 .07
458 Bret Boone .40 .12
459 Ben McDonald .25 .07
460 Kirby Puckett 1.00 .30
461 Gregg Olson .25 .07
462 Rich Aude RC .50 .15
463 John Burkett .25 .07
464 Troy Neel .25 .07
465 Jimmy Key .40 .12
466 Ozzie Timmons .25 .07
467 Eddie Murray 1.00 .30
468 Mark Tranberg RC .50 .15
469 Alex Gonzalez .25 .07
470 David Nied .25 .07
471 Barry Larkin 1.00 .30
472 Brian Looney RC .50 .15
473 Shawn Estes .25 .07
474 A.J. Sager RC .50 .15
475 Roger Clemens 2.00 .60
476 Vince Moore .25 .07
477 Scott Karl RC .50 .15
478 Kurt Miller .25 .07
479 Garret Anderson 1.00 .30
480 Allen Watson .25 .07
481 Jose Lima RC 1.50 .45
482 Rick Gorecki .25 .07
483 Jimmy Hurst RC .50 .15
484 Preston Wilson .60 .18
485 Will Clark 1.00 .30
486 Mike Ferry RC .50 .15
487 Curtis Goodwin RC .50 .15
488 Mike Myers .25 .07
489 Chipper Jones 1.00 .30
490 Jeff King .25 .07
491 W.VanLandingham RC .50 .15
492 Carlos Reyes RC .50 .15
493 Andy Pettitte 1.00 .30
494 Brant Brown .25 .07
495 Daron Kirkreit .25 .07
496 Ricky Bottalico RC 1.00 .30
497 Devon White .25 .07
498 Jason Johnson RC .50 .15
499 Vince Coleman .25 .07
500 Larry Walker .60 .18
501 Bobby Ayala .25 .07
502 Steve Finley .40 .12
503 Scott Fletcher .25 .07
504 Brad Ausmus .25 .07
505 Scott Talanoa RC .50 .15
506 Orestes Destrade .25 .07
507 Gary DiSarcina .25 .07
508 Willie Smith RC .50 .15
509 Alan Trammell .60 .18
510 Mike Piazza 2.00 .60
511 Ozzie Guillen .25 .07
512 Jeromy Burnitz .40 .12
513 Darren Oliver RC 1.00 .30
514 Kevin Mitchell .25 .07
515 Rafael Palmeiro .60 .18
516 David McCarty .25 .07
517 Jeff Blauser .25 .07
518 Trey Beamon .25 .07
519 Royce Clayton .25 .07
520 Dennis Eckersley .40 .12
521 Bernie Williams .60 .18
522 Steve Buechele .25 .07
523 Dennis Martinez .40 .12
524 Dave Hollins .25 .07
525 Joey Hamilton .25 .07
526 Andres Galarraga .40 .12
527 Jeff Granger .25 .07
528 Joey Eischen .25 .07
529 Desi Relaford .25 .07
530 Roberto Petagine .25 .07
531 Andre Dawson .40 .12
532 Ray Holbert .25 .07
533 Duane Singleton .25 .07
534 Kurt Abbott RC 1.00 .30
535 Bo Jackson 1.00 .30
536 Gregg Jefferies .25 .07
537 David Mysel .25 .07
538 Raul Mondesi .40 .12
539 Chris Snopek .25 .07
540 Brook Fordyce .25 .07
541 Ron Frazier RC .50 .15
542 Brian Koelling .25 .07
543 Jimmy Haynes .25 .07
544 Marty Cordova .25 .07
545 Jason Green RC .50 .15
546 Orlando Merced .25 .07
547 Lou Pote RC .50 .15
548 Todd Van Poppel .25 .07
549 Pat Kelly .25 .07
550 Turk Wendell .25 .07
551 Herbert Perry RC 1.00 .30
552 Ryan Karp RC .50 .15
553 Juan Guzman .25 .07
554 Bryan Rekar RC .50 .15
555 Kevin Appier .40 .12
556 Chris Schwab RC .50 .15
557 Jay Buhner .40 .12
558 Andujar Cedeno .25 .07
559 Ryan McGuire RC .50 .15
560 Ricky Gutierrez .25 .07
561 Keith Kimsey RC .50 .15
562 Tim Clark .25 .07
563 Damion Easley .25 .07
564 Clint Davis RC .50 .15
565 Mike Moore .25 .07
566 Orel Hershiser .40 .12
567 Jason Bere .25 .07
568 Kevin McReynolds .25 .07
569 Leland Macon RC .50 .15
570 John Courtright RC .50 .15
571 Sid Fernandez .25 .07
572 Chad Roper .25 .07
573 Terry Pendleton .40 .12
574 Danny Miceli .25 .07
575 Joe Rosselli .25 .07
576 Mike Bordick .25 .07
577 Danny Tartabull .25 .07
578 Jose Guzman .25 .07
579 Omar Vizquel .40 .12
580 Tommy Greene .25 .07
581 Paul Spoljaric .25 .07
582 Walt Weiss .25 .07
583 Oscar Jimenez RC .50 .15
584 Rod Henderson .25 .07
585 Derek Lowe .40 .12
586 Richard Hidalgo RC 4.00 1.20
587 Shayne Bennett RC .50 .15
588 Tim Belk RC .50 .15
589 Matt Mieske .25 .07
590 Nigel Wilson .25 .07
591 Jeff Knox RC .50 .15
592 Bernard Gilkey .25 .07
593 David Cone .40 .12
594 Paul LoDuca RC 8.00 2.40
595 Scott Ruffcorn .25 .07
596 Chris Roberts .25 .07
597 Oscar Munoz RC .50 .15
598 Scott Sullivan RC .50 .15
599 Matt Jarvis RC .50 .15
600 Jose Canseco 1.00 .30
601 Tony Graffanino RC 1.00 .30
602 Don Slaught .25 .07
603 Brett King RC .50 .15
604 Jose Herrera RC .50 .15
605 Melido Perez .25 .07
606 Mike Hubbard RC .50 .15
607 Chad Ogea .25 .07
608 Wayne Gomes RC 1.00 .30
609 Roberto Alomar 1.00 .30
610 Angel Echevarria RC .50 .15
611 Jose Lind .25 .07
612 Darrin Fletcher .25 .07
613 Chris Bosio .25 .07
614 Darryl Kile .40 .12
615 Frankie Rodriguez .25 .07
616 Phil Plantier .25 .07
617 Pat Listach .25 .07
618 Charlie Hough .40 .12
619 Ryan Hancock RC .50 .15
620 Darrel Deak RC .50 .15
621 Travis Fryman .40 .12
622 Brett Butler .40 .12
623 Lance Johnson .25 .07
624 Pete Smith .25 .07
625 James Hurst RC .50 .15
626 Roberto Kelly .25 .07
627 Mike Mussina 1.00 .30
628 Kevin Tapani .25 .07
629 John Smoltz .60 .18
630 Midre Cummings .25 .07
631 Salomon Torres .25 .07
632 Willie Adams .25 .07
633 Derek Jeter 3.00 .90
634 Steve Trachsel .25 .07
635 Albie Lopez .25 .07
636 Jason Moler .25 .07
637 Carlos Delgado .60 .18
638 Roberto Mejia .25 .07
639 Darren Burton .25 .07
640 B.J. Wallace .25 .07
641 Brad Clontz RC .50 .15
642 Billy Wagner RC 2.50 .75
643 Aaron Sele .25 .07
644 Cameron Cairncross .25 .07
645 Brian Harper .25 .07
646 Marc Valdes UER .25 .07
(No card number on back)
647 Mark Ratekin .25 .07
648 Terry Bradshaw RC .50 .15
649 Justin Thompson .25 .07
650 Mike Busch RC .50 .15
651 Joe Hall RC .50 .15
652 Bobby Jones .25 .07
653 Kelly Stinnett RC 1.00 .30
654 Rod Steph RC .50 .15
655 Jay Powell RC 1.00 .30
656 K.Garagozzo RC UER .50 .15
No card number on back
657 Todd Dunn .25 .07
658 Charles Peterson RC .50 .15
659 Darren Lewis .25 .07
660 John Wasdin RC .50 .15
661 Tate Seefried RC .50 .15
662 Hector Trinidad RC .50 .15
663 John Carter RC .25 .07
664 Larry Mitchell .25 .07
665 David Catlett RC .50 .15
666 Dante Bichette .40 .12
667 Felix Jose .25 .07
668 Rondell White .40 .12
669 Tino Martinez .60 .18
670 Brian L. Hunter .25 .07
671 Jose Malave .25 .07
672 Archi Cianfrocco .25 .07
673 Mike Matheny RC 1.00 .30
674 Bret Barberie .25 .07
675 Andrew Lorraine RC .50 .15
676 Brian Jordan .40 .12
677 Tim Belcher .25 .07
678 Antonio Osuna RC .50 .15
679 Checklist .25 .07
680 Checklist .25 .07
681 Checklist .25 .07
682 Checklist .25 .07

1995 Bowman

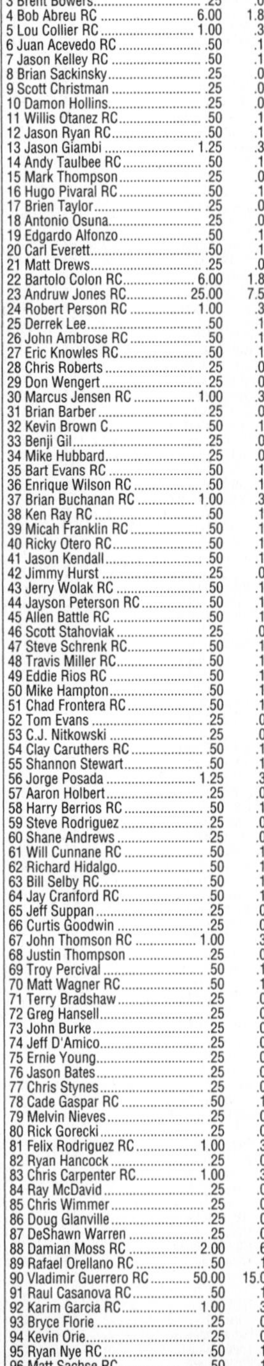

Cards from this 439-card standard-size prospect-oriented set were primarily issued in plastic wrapped packs and jumbo packs. Card fronts feature white borders enframing full color photos. The left border is a reversed negative of the photo. The set includes 54 silver foil subset cards (221-274). The foil subset, largely comprising of minor league stars, have embossed borders and are found one per pack and two per jumbo pack. Rookie Cards of note include Bob Abreu, Bartolo Colon, Vladmir Guerrero, Andruw Jones, Hideo Nomo and Scott Rolen.

	Nm-Mt	Ex-Mt
COMPLETE SET (439)	200.00	60.00
1 Billy Wagner	.50	.15
2 Chris Widger	.25	.07
3 Brent Bowers	.25	.07
4 Bob Abreu RC	6.00	1.80
5 Lou Collier RC	1.00	.30
6 Juan Acevedo RC	.50	.15
7 Jason Kelley RC	.50	.15
8 Brian Sackinsky	.25	.07
9 Scott Christman	.25	.07
10 Damon Hollins	.25	.07
11 Willis Otanez RC	.50	.15
12 Jason Ryan RC	.50	.15
13 Jason Giambi	1.25	.35
14 Andy Taulbee RC	.50	.15
15 Mark Thompson	.25	.07
16 Hugo Pivaral RC	.50	.15
17 Brien Taylor	.25	.07
18 Antonio Osuna	.25	.07
19 Edgardo Alfonzo	.50	.15
20 Carl Everett	.50	.15
21 Matt Drews	.25	.07
22 Bartolo Colon RC	6.00	1.80
23 Andruw Jones RC	25.00	7.50
24 Robert Person RC	1.00	.30
25 Derrek Lee	.50	.15
26 John Ambrose RC	.50	.15
27 Eric Knowles RC	.50	.15
28 Chris Roberts	.25	.07
29 Don Wengert	.25	.07
30 Marcus Jensen RC	1.00	.30
31 Brian Barber	.25	.07
32 Kevin Brown C	.50	.15
33 Benji Gil	.25	.07
34 Mike Hubbard	.25	.07
35 Bart Evans RC	.50	.15
36 Enrique Wilson RC	.50	.15
37 Brian Buchanan RC	1.00	.30
38 Ken Ray RC	.50	.15
39 Micah Franklin RC	.50	.15
40 Ricky Otero RC	.50	.15
41 Jason Kendall	.50	.15
42 Jimmy Hurst	.25	.07
43 Jerry Wolak RC	.50	.15
44 Jayson Peterson RC	.50	.15
45 Allen Battle RC	.50	.15
46 Scott Stahoviak	.25	.07
47 Steve Schrenk RC	.50	.15
48 Travis Miller RC	.50	.15
49 Eddie Rios RC	.50	.15
50 Mike Hampton	.50	.15
51 Chad Frontera RC	.50	.15
52 Tom Evans	.25	.07
53 C.J. Nitkowski	.25	.07
54 Clay Caruthers RC	.50	.15
55 Shannon Stewart	.50	.15
56 Jorge Posada	1.25	.35
57 Aaron Holbert	.25	.07
58 Harry Berrios RC	.50	.15
59 Steve Rodriguez	.25	.07
60 Shane Andrews	.25	.07
61 Will Cunnane RC	.50	.15
62 Richard Hidalgo	.50	.15
63 Bill Selby RC	.50	.15
64 Jay Cranford RC	.50	.15
65 Jeff Suppan	.25	.07
66 Curtis Goodwin	.25	.07
67 John Thomson RC	1.00	.30
68 Justin Thompson	.25	.07
69 Troy Percival	.50	.15
70 Matt Wagner RC	.50	.15
71 Terry Bradshaw	.25	.07
72 Greg Hansell	.25	.07
73 John Burke	.25	.07
74 Jeff D'Amico	.25	.07
75 Ernie Young	.25	.07
76 Jason Bates	.25	.07
77 Chris Stynes	.25	.07
78 Cade Gaspar RC	.50	.15
79 Melvin Nieves	.25	.07
80 Rick Gorecki	.25	.07
81 Felix Rodriguez RC	1.00	.30
82 Ryan Hancock	.25	.07
83 Chris Carpenter RC	1.00	.30
84 Ray McDavid	.25	.07
85 Chris Wimmer	.25	.07
86 Doug Glanville	.25	.07
87 DeShawn Warren	.25	.07
88 Damian Moss RC	2.00	.60
89 Rafael Orellano RC	.50	.15
90 Vladimir Guerrero RC	50.00	15.00
91 Raul Casanova RC	.50	.15
92 Karim Garcia RC	1.00	.30
93 Bryce Florie	.25	.07
94 Kevin Orie	.25	.07
95 Ryan Nye RC	.50	.15
96 Matt Sachse RC	.50	.15
97 Ivan Arteaga RC	.50	.15

98 Glenn Murray	.25	.07
99 Stacy Hollins RC	.50	.15
100 Jim Pittsley	.25	.07
101 Craig Mattson RC	.50	.15
102 Neifi Perez	.25	.07
103 Keith Williams	.25	.07
104 Roger Cedeno	.25	.07
105 Tony Terry RC	.50	.15
106 Jose Malave	.25	.07
107 Joe Rosselli	.25	.07
108 Kevin Jordan	.25	.07
109 Sid Roberson RC	.50	.15
110 Alan Embree	.25	.07
111 Terrell Wade	.25	.07
112 Bob Wolcott	.25	.07
113 Carlos Perez RC	1.00	.30
114 Mike Bovee RC	.50	.15
115 Tommy Davis RC	.50	.15
116 Jeremey Kendall RC	.50	.15
117 Rich Aude	.25	.07
118 Rick Huisman	.25	.07
119 Tim Belk	.25	.07
120 Edgar Renteria	.75	.23
121 Calvin Maduro RC	.50	.15
122 Jerry Martin RC	.50	.15
123 Ramon Fermin RC	.50	.15
124 Kimera Bartee RC	.50	.15
125 Mark Farris	.25	.07
126 Frank Rodriguez	.25	.07
127 Bobby Higginson RC	3.00	.90
128 Bret Wagner	.25	.07
129 Edwin Diaz RC	.50	.15
130 Jimmy Haynes	.25	.07
131 Chris Weinke RC	2.00	.60
132 Damian Jackson RC	1.00	.30
133 Felix Martinez	.25	.07
134 Edwin Hurtado RC	.50	.15
135 Matt Raleigh RC	.50	.15
136 Paul Wilson	.25	.07
137 Ron Villone	.25	.07
138 E.Stuckenschneider RC	.50	.15
139 Tate Seefried	.25	.07
140 Rey Ordonez RC	2.00	.60
141 Eddie Pearson	.25	.07
142 Kevin Gallaher	.25	.07
143 Torii Hunter	.75	.23
144 Daron Kirkreit	.25	.07
145 Craig Wilson	.25	.07
146 Ugueth Urbina	.25	.07
147 Chris Snopek	.25	.07
148 Kym Ashworth	.25	.07
149 Wayne Gomes	.25	.07
150 Mark Loretta	.25	.07
151 Ramon Morel RC	.50	.15
152 Trot Nixon	.75	.23
153 Desi Relaford	.25	.07
154 Scott Sullivan	.25	.07
155 Marc Barcelo	.25	.07
156 Willie Adams	.25	.07
157 Derrick Gibson RC	.50	.15
158 Brian Meadows RC	.50	.15
159 Julian Tavarez	.25	.07
160 Bryan Rekar	.25	.07
161 Steve Gibralter	.25	.07
162 Esteban Loaiza	.50	.15
163 John Wasdin	.25	.07
164 Kirk Presley	.25	.07
165 Mariano Rivera	.75	.23
166 Andy Larkin	.25	.07
167 Sean Whiteside RC	.50	.15
168 Matt Apana RC	.50	.15
169 Shawn Senior RC	.50	.15
170 Scott Gentile	.25	.07
171 Quilvio Veras	.25	.07
172 Eli Marrero RC	1.50	.45
173 Mendy Lopez RC	.50	.15
174 Homer Bush	.25	.07
175 Brian Stephenson RC	.50	.15
176 Jon Nunnally	.25	.07
177 Jose Herrera	.25	.07
178 Corey Avrard RC	.50	.15
179 David Bell	.25	.07
180 Jason Isringhausen	.50	.15
181 Jamey Wright	.25	.07
182 Lonell Roberts RC	.25	.07
183 Marty Cordova	.25	.07
184 Amaury Telemaco	.25	.07
185 John Mabry	.25	.07
186 Andrew Vessel RC	.50	.15
187 Jim Cole RC	.50	.15
188 Marquis Riley	.25	.07
189 Todd Dunn	.25	.07
190 John Carter	.25	.07
191 Donnie Sadler RC	1.00	.30
192 Mike Bell	.25	.07
193 Chris Cumberland RC	.50	.15
194 Jason Schmidt	1.50	.45
195 Matt Brunson	.25	.07
196 James Baldwin	.25	.07
197 Bill Simas RC	.50	.15
198 Gus Gandarillas	.25	.07
199 Mac Suzuki	.25	.07
200 Rick Holifield RC	.50	.15
201 Fernando Lunar RC	.50	.15
202 Kevin Jarvis	.25	.07
203 Everett Stull	.25	.07
204 Steve Wojciechowski	.25	.07
205 Shawn Estes	.25	.07
206 Jermaine Dye	.50	.15
207 Marc Kroon	.25	.07
208 Peter Munro RC	1.00	.30
209 Pat Watkins	.25	.07
210 Matt Smith	.25	.07
211 Joe Vitiello	.25	.07
212 Gerald Witasick Jr.	.25	.07
213 Freddy A. Garcia RC	.50	.15
214 Glenn Dishman RC	.50	.15
215 Jay Canizaro RC	.50	.15
216 Angel Martinez	.25	.07
217 Yamil Benitez RC	.50	.15
218 Fausto Macey RC	.50	.15
219 Eric Owens	.25	.07
220 Checklist	.25	.07
221 D.Hosey FOIL RC	.50	.15
222 B.Woodall FOIL RC	.50	.15
223 Billy Ashley FOIL	.25	.07
224 M.Grudzielanek FOIL RC	2.00	.60
225 M.Johnson FOIL RC	1.00	.30
226 Tim Unroe FOIL RC	.50	.15
227 Todd Greene FOIL	.25	.07
228 Larry Sutton FOIL	.25	.07
229 Derek Jeter FOIL	4.00	1.20
230 Sal Fasano FOIL RC	.50	.15
231 Ruben Rivera FOIL	.25	.07
232 Chris Truby FOIL RC	1.00	.30
233 John Donati FOIL	.25	.07
234 D.Conner FOIL RC	.50	.15
235 Sergio Nunez FOIL RC	.50	.15
236 Ray Brown FOIL RC	.50	.15
237 Juan Melo FOIL RC	.50	.15
238 Hideo Nomo FOIL RC	5.00	1.50
239 Jamie Bluma RC FOIL	.50	.15
240 Jay Payton FOIL RC	2.00	.60
241 Paul Konerko FOIL	1.00	.30
242 Scott Elarton FOIL RC	1.00	.30
243 Jeff Abbott FOIL RC	1.00	.30
244 Jim Brower FOIL RC	.50	.15
245 Geoff Blum FOIL RC	1.00	.30
246 Aaron Boone FOIL RC	10.00	3.00
247 J.R. Phillips FOIL	.25	.07
248 Alex Ochoa FOIL	.25	.07
249 N.Garciaparra FOIL	8.00	2.40
250 Garret Anderson FOIL	.50	.15
251 Ray Durham FOIL	.50	.15
252 Paul Shuey FOIL	.25	.07
253 Tony Clark FOIL	.25	.07
254 Johnny Damon FOIL	.75	.23
255 Duane Singleton FOIL	.25	.07
256 LaTroy Hawkins FOIL	.25	.07
257 Andy Pettitte FOIL	.75	.23
258 Ben Grieve FOIL	.50	.15
259 Marc Newfield FOIL	.25	.07
260 Terrell Lowery FOIL	.25	.07
261 Shawn Green FOIL	.50	.15
262 Chipper Jones FOIL	1.25	.35
263 B.Kieschnick FOIL	.25	.07
264 Pokey Reese FOIL	.25	.07
265 Doug Million FOIL	.25	.07
266 Marc Valdes FOIL	.25	.07
267 Brian L.Hunter FOIL	.25	.07
268 T.Hollandsworth FOIL	.25	.07
269 Rod Henderson FOIL	.25	.07
270 Bill Pulsipher FOIL	.25	.07
271 Scott Rolen FOIL RC	15.00	4.50
272 Trey Beamon FOIL	.25	.07
273 Alan Benes FOIL	.25	.07
274 D.Hermanson FOIL	.25	.07
275 Ricky Bottalico	.25	.07
276 Albert Belle	.50	.15
277 Deion Sanders	.75	.23
278 Matt Williams	.50	.15
279 Jeff Bagwell	.75	.23
280 Kirby Puckett	1.25	.35
281 Dave Hollins	.25	.07
282 Don Mattingly	3.00	.90
283 Joey Hamilton	.25	.07
284 Bobby Bonilla	.50	.15
285 Moises Alou	.50	.15
286 Tom Glavine	.75	.23
287 Brett Butler	.50	.15
288 Chris Hoiles	.25	.07
289 Kenny Rogers	.50	.15
290 Larry Walker	.75	.23
291 Tim Raines	.50	.15
292 Kevin Appier	.50	.15
293 Roger Clemens	2.50	.75
294 Chuck Carr	.25	.07
295 Randy Myers	.25	.07
296 Dave Nilsson	.25	.07
297 Joe Carter	.50	.15
298 Chuck Finley	.50	.15
299 Ray Lankford	.50	.15
300 Roberto Kelly	.25	.07
301 Jon Lieber	.25	.07
302 Travis Fryman	.50	.15
303 Mark McGwire	3.00	.90
304 Tony Gwynn	1.50	.45
305 Kenny Lofton	.50	.15
306 Mark Whiten	.25	.07
307 Doug Drabek	.25	.07
308 Terry Steinbach	.25	.07
309 Ryan Klesko	.50	.15
310 Mike Piazza	2.00	.60
311 Ben McDonald	.25	.07
312 Reggie Sanders	.50	.15
313 Alex Fernandez	.25	.07
314 Aaron Sele	.25	.07
315 Gregg Jefferies	.25	.07
316 Rickey Henderson	1.25	.35
317 Brian Anderson	.50	.15
318 Jose Valentin	.25	.07
319 Rod Beck	.25	.07
320 Marquis Grissom	.50	.15
321 Ken Griffey Jr.	2.00	.60
322 Bret Saberhagen	.50	.15
323 Juan Gonzalez	1.25	.35
324 Paul Molitor	.75	.23
325 Gary Sheffield	.50	.15
326 Darren Daulton	.50	.15
327 Bill Swift	.25	.07
328 Brian McRae	.25	.07
329 Robin Ventura	.50	.15
330 Lee Smith	.50	.15
331 Fred McGriff	.75	.23
332 Delino DeShields	.25	.07
333 Edgar Martinez	.75	.23
334 Mike Mussina	1.25	.35
335 Orlando Merced	.25	.07
336 Carlos Baerga	.25	.07
337 Wil Cordero	.25	.07
338 Tom Pagnozzi	.25	.07
339 Pat Hentgen	.25	.07
340 Chad Curtis	.25	.07
341 Darren Lewis	.25	.07
342 Jeff Kent	.50	.15
343 Bip Roberts	.50	.15
344 Ivan Rodriguez	1.25	.35
345 Jeff Montgomery	.25	.07
346 Hal Morris	.25	.07
347 Danny Tartabull	.25	.07
348 Raul Mondesi	.50	.15
349 Ken Hill	.25	.07
350 Pedro Martinez	1.25	.35
351 Frank Thomas	1.25	.35
352 Manny Ramirez	.50	.15
353 Tim Salmon	.75	.23
354 W. VanLandingham	.25	.07
355 Andres Galarraga	.50	.15
356 Paul O'Neill	.75	.23
357 Brady Anderson	.50	.15
358 Ramon Martinez	.25	.07
359 John Olerud	.50	.15
360 Ruben Sierra	.25	.07
361 Cal Eldred	.25	.07
362 Jay Buhner	.50	.15
363 Jay Bell	.50	.15
364 Wally Joyner	.50	.15
365 Chuck Knoblauch	.50	.15
366 Len Dykstra	.50	.15
367 John Wetteland	.50	.15
368 Roberto Alomar	1.25	.35
369 Craig Biggio	.75	.23
370 Ozzie Smith	2.00	.60
371 Terry Pendleton	.50	.15
372 Sammy Sosa	2.00	.60
373 Carlos Garcia	.25	.07
374 Jose Rijo	.25	.07
375 Chris Gomez	.25	.07
376 Barry Bonds	3.00	.90
377 Steve Avery	.25	.07
378 Rick Wilkins	.25	.07
379 Pete Harnisch	.25	.07
380 Dean Palmer	.50	.15
381 Bob Hamelin	.25	.07
382 Jason Bere	.25	.07
383 Jimmy Key	.50	.15
384 Dante Bichette	.50	.15
385 Rafael Palmeiro	.75	.23
386 David Justice	.50	.15
387 Chili Davis	.50	.15
388 Mike Greenwell	.25	.07
389 Todd Zeile	.25	.07
390 Jeff Conine	.50	.15
391 Rick Aguilera	.25	.07
392 Eddie Murray	1.25	.35
393 Mike Stanley	.25	.07
394 Cliff Floyd UER (numbered 294)	.50	.15
395 Randy Johnson	1.25	.35
396 David Nied	.25	.07
397 Devon White	.50	.15
398 Royce Clayton	.25	.07
399 Andy Benes	.25	.07
400 John Hudek	.25	.07
401 Bobby Jones	.25	.07
402 Eric Karros	.50	.15
403 Will Clark	1.25	.35
404 Mark Langston	.25	.07
405 Kevin Brown	.50	.15
406 Greg Maddux	2.00	.60
407 David Cone	.50	.15
408 Wade Boggs	.75	.23
409 Steve Trachsel	.25	.07
410 Greg Vaughn	.50	.15
411 Mo Vaughn	.50	.15
412 Wilson Alvarez	.25	.07
413 Cal Ripken	4.00	1.20
414 Rico Brogna	.25	.07
415 Barry Larkin	1.25	.35
416 Cecil Fielder	.50	.15
417 Jose Canseco	1.25	.35
418 Jack McDowell	.25	.07
419 Mike Lieberthal	.50	.15
420 Andrew Lorraine	.25	.07
421 Rich Becker	.25	.07
422 Tony Phillips	.25	.07
423 Scott Ruffcorn	.25	.07
424 Jeff Granger	.25	.07
425 Greg Pirkl	.25	.07
426 Dennis Eckersley	.50	.15
427 Jose Lima	.25	.07
428 Russ Davis	.25	.07
429 Armando Benitez	.25	.07
430 Alex Gonzalez	.25	.07
431 Carlos Delgado	.50	.15
432 Chan Ho Park	.50	.15
433 Mickey Tettleton	.25	.07
434 Dave Winfield	.50	.15
435 John Burkett	.25	.07
436 Orlando Miller	.25	.07
437 Rondell White	.50	.15
438 Jose Oliva	.25	.07
439 Checklist	.25	.07

1995 Bowman Gold Foil

Numbered 221-274, this 54-card standard-size set is the gold insert parallel version of the silver foil subset found in the basic issue. The odds of finding a gold foil version are one in six packs.

	Nm-Mt	Ex-Mt
COMPLETE SET (54)	150.00	45.00
*STARS: .6X TO 1.5X BASIC CARDS		
*ROOKIES: .5X TO 1.2X BASIC		

1996 Bowman

The 1996 Bowman set was issued in one series totalling 385 cards. The 11-card packs retailed for $2.50 each. The fronts feature color action player photos in a tan-checkered frame with the player's name printed in silver foil at the bottom. The backs carry another color player photo with player information, 1995 and career player statistics. Each pack contained 10 regular issue cards plus either one foil parallel or an insert card. In a special promotional program, Topps offered collector's a $100 guarantee on complete sets. To get the guarantee, collectors had to mail in a Guaranteed Value Certificate request form, found in packs, along with a $5 processing and registration fee before the December 31st, 1996 deadline. Collectors would then receive a $100 Guaranteed Value Certificate, of which they could mail back to Topps between August 31st, 1999 and December 31st, 1999, along with their complete set, to receive $100. A reprint version of the 1952 Bowman Mickey Mantle card was randomly inserted into packs. Rookie Cards in this set include Russell Branyan, Mike Cameron, Luis Castillo, Ryan Dempster, Livan Hernandez, Geoff Jenkins, Ben Petrick and Mike Sweeney

	Nm-Mt	Ex-Mt
COMPLETE SET (385)	60.00	18.00
1 Cal Ripken	2.50	.75
2 Ray Durham	.30	.09
3 Ivan Rodriguez	.75	.23
4 Fred McGriff	.50	.15
5 Hideo Nomo	.75	.23
6 Troy Percival	.30	.09
7 Moises Alou	.30	.09
8 Mike Stanley	.30	.09
9 Jay Buhner	.30	.09
10 Shawn Green	.30	.09
11 Ryan Klesko	.30	.09
12 Andres Galarraga	.30	.09
13 Dean Palmer	.30	.09
14 Jeff Conine	.30	.09
15 Brian L.Hunter	.30	.09
16 J.T. Snow	.30	.09
17 Larry Walker	.50	.15
18 Barry Larkin	.75	.23
19 Alex Gonzalez	.30	.09
20 Edgar Martinez	.50	.15
21 Mo Vaughn	.30	.09
22 Mark McGwire	2.00	.60
23 Jose Canseco	.75	.23
24 Jack McDowell	.30	.09
25 Dante Bichette	.30	.09
26 Wade Boggs	.50	.15
27 Mike Piazza	1.25	.35
28 Ray Lankford	.30	.09
29 Craig Biggio	.50	.15
30 Rafael Palmeiro	.50	.15
31 Ron Gant	.30	.09
32 Javy Lopez	.30	.09
33 Brian Jordan	.30	.09
34 Paul O'Neill	.50	.15
35 Mark Grace	.50	.15
36 Matt Williams	.30	.09
37 Pedro Martinez	.75	.23
38 Rickey Henderson	.75	.23
39 Bobby Bonilla	.30	.09
40 Todd Hollandsworth	.30	.09
41 Jim Thome	.75	.23
42 Gary Sheffield	.75	.23
43 Tim Salmon	.50	.15
44 Gregg Jefferies	.30	.09
45 Roberto Alomar	.75	.23
46 Carlos Baerga	.30	.09
47 Mark Grudzielanek	.30	.09
48 Randy Johnson	.75	.23
49 Tino Martinez	.50	.15
50 Robin Ventura	.30	.09
51 Ryne Sandberg	1.25	.35
52 Jay Bell	.30	.09
53 Jason Schmidt	.30	.09
54 Frank Thomas	.75	.23
55 Kenny Lofton	.30	.09
56 Ariel Prieto	.30	.09
57 David Cone	.30	.09
58 Reggie Sanders	.30	.09
59 Michael Tucker	.30	.09
60 Vinny Castilla	.30	.09
61 Len Dykstra	.30	.09
62 Todd Hundley	.30	.09
63 Brian McRae	.30	.09
64 Dennis Eckersley	.30	.09
65 Rondell White	.30	.09
66 Eric Karros	.30	.09
67 Greg Maddux	1.25	.35
68 Kevin Appier	.30	.09
69 Eddie Murray	.75	.23
70 John Olerud	.30	.09
71 Tony Gwynn	1.00	.30
72 David Justice	.30	.09
73 Ken Caminiti	.30	.09
74 Terry Steinbach	.30	.09
75 Alan Benes	.30	.09
76 Chipper Jones	.75	.23
77 Jeff Bagwell	.50	.15
78 Barry Bonds	2.00	.60
79 Ken Griffey Jr.	1.50	.45
80 Roger Cedeno	.30	.09
81 Joe Carter	.30	.09
82 Henry Rodriguez	.30	.09
83 Jason Isringhausen	.30	.09
84 Chuck Knoblauch	.30	.09
85 Manny Ramirez	.30	.09
86 Tom Glavine	.50	.15
87 Jeffrey Hammonds	.30	.09
88 Paul Molitor	.50	.15
89 Roger Clemens	1.50	.45
90 Greg Vaughn	.30	.09
91 Marty Cordova	.30	.09
92 Albert Belle	.30	.09
93 Mike Mussina	.75	.23
94 Garret Anderson	.30	.09
95 Juan Gonzalez	.75	.23
96 John Valentin	.30	.09
97 Jason Giambi	.75	.23
98 Kirby Puckett	.75	.23
99 Jim Edmonds	.30	.09
100 Cecil Fielder	.30	.09
101 Mike Aldrete	.30	.09
102 Marquis Grissom	.30	.09
103 Derek Bell	.30	.09
104 Raul Mondesi	.30	.09
105 Sammy Sosa	1.25	.35
106 Travis Fryman	.30	.09
107 Rico Brogna	.30	.09
108 Will Clark	.75	.23
109 Bernie Williams	.50	.15
110 Brady Anderson	.30	.09
111 Torii Hunter	.30	.09
112 Derek Jeter	2.00	.60
113 Mike Kusiewicz RC	.50	.15
114 Scott Rolen	.75	.23
115 Ramon Castro	.30	.09
116 Jose Guillen RC	3.00	.90
117 Wade Walker RC	.50	.15
118 Shawn Senior	.30	.09
119 Onan Masaoka RC	.75	.23
120 Marlon Anderson RC	1.50	.45
121 Katsuhiro Maeda RC	.75	.23
122 G.Stephenson RC	.75	.23
123 Butch Huskey	.30	.09
124 D'Angelo Jimenez RC	1.50	.45
125 Tony Mounce RC	.50	.15
126 Jay Canizaro	.30	.09
127 Juan Melo	.30	.09
128 Steve Gibralter	.30	.09
129 Freddy Garcia	.30	.09
130 Julio Santana UER	.30	.09
Card has him born in 1993		
131 Richard Hidalgo	.30	.09
132 Jermaine Dye	.30	.09
133 Willie Adams	.30	.09
134 Everett Stull	.30	.09
135 Ramon Morel	.30	.09
136 Chan Ho Park	.30	.09
137 Jamey Wright	.30	.09
138 Luis R.Garcia RC	.50	.15
139 Dan Serafini	.30	.09
140 Ryan Dempster RC	1.00	.30
141 Tate Seefried	.30	.09
142 Jimmy Hurst	.30	.09
143 Travis Miller	.30	.09
144 Curtis Goodwin	.30	.09
145 Rocky Coppinger RC	.50	.15
146 Enrique Wilson	.30	.09
147 Jaime Bluma	.30	.09
148 Andrew Vessel	.30	.09
149 Damian Moss	.30	.09
150 Shawn Gallagher RC	.50	.15
151 Pat Watkins	.30	.09
152 Jose Paniagua	.30	.09
153 Danny Graves	.30	.09
154 Bryon Gainey RC	.50	.15
155 Steve Soderstrom	.30	.09
156 Cliff Brumbaugh RC	.50	.15
157 Eugene Kingsale RC	.75	.23
158 Lou Collier	.30	.09
159 Todd Walker	.50	.15
160 Kris Detmers RC	.50	.15
161 Josh Booty RC	.75	.23
162 Greg Whiteman RC	.50	.15
163 Damian Jackson	.30	.09
164 Tony Clark	.30	.09
165 Jeff D'Amico	.30	.09
166 Johnny Damon	.30	.09
167 Rafael Orellano	.30	.09
168 Ruben Rivera	.30	.09
169 Alex Ochoa	.30	.09
170 Jay Powell	.30	.09
171 Tom Evans	.30	.09
172 Ron Villone	.30	.09
173 Shawn Estes	.30	.09
174 John Wasdin	.30	.09
175 Bill Simas	.30	.09
176 Kevin Brown	.30	.09
177 Shannon Stewart	.30	.09
178 Todd Greene	.30	.09
179 Bob Wolcott	.30	.09
180 Chris Snopek	.30	.09
181 Nomar Garciaparra	1.50	.45
182 Cameron Smith RC	.50	.15
183 Matt Drews	.30	.09
184 Jimmy Haynes	.30	.09
185 Chris Carpenter	.30	.09
186 Desi Relaford	.30	.09
187 Ben Grieve	.30	.09
188 Mike Bell	.30	.09
189 Luis Castillo RC	3.00	.90
190 Ugueth Urbina	.30	.09
191 Paul Wilson	.30	.09
192 Andruw Jones	1.25	.35
193 Wayne Gomes	.30	.09
194 Craig Counsell RC	2.00	.60
195 Jim Cole	.30	.09
196 Brooks Kieschnick	.30	.09
197 Trey Beamon	.30	.09
198 Marino Santana RC	.50	.15
199 Bob Abreu	.30	.09
200 Pokey Reese	.30	.09
201 Dante Powell	.30	.09
202 George Arias	.30	.09
203 Jorge Velandia RC	.50	.15
204 George Lombard RC	.75	.23
205 Byron Browne RC	.50	.15
206 John Frascatore	.30	.09
207 Terry Adams	.30	.09
208 Wilson Delgado RC	.50	.15
209 Billy McMillon	.30	.09
210 Jeff Abbott	.30	.09
211 Trot Nixon	.50	.15
212 Amaury Telemaco	.30	.09
213 Scott Sullivan	.30	.09
214 Justin Thompson	.30	.09
215 Decomba Conner	.30	.09
216 Ryan McGuire	.30	.09
217 Matt Luke	.30	.09
218 Doug Million	.30	.09
219 Jason Dickson RC	.50	.15
220 Ramon Hernandez RC	1.50	.45
221 Mark Bellhorn RC	2.00	.60
222 Eric Ludwick RC	.50	.15
223 Luke Wilcox RC	.50	.15
224 Marty Malloy RC	.50	.15
225 Gary Coffee RC	.50	.15
226 Wendell Magee RC	.50	.15
227 Brett Tomko RC	.75	.23
228 Derek Lowe	.30	.09
229 Jose Rosado RC	.50	.15
230 Steve Bourgeois RC	.50	.15
231 Neil Weber RC	.50	.15
232 Jeff Ware	.30	.09
233 Edwin Diaz	.30	.09
234 Greg Norton	.30	.09
235 Aaron Boone	.30	.09
236 Jeff Suppan	.30	.09
237 Bret Wagner	.30	.09
238 Elieser Marrero	.30	.09
239 Will Cunnane	.30	.09
240 Brian Barkley RC	.50	.15
241 Jay Payton	.30	.09
242 Marcus Jensen	.30	.09
243 Ryan Nye	.30	.09
244 Chad Mottola	.30	.09
245 Scott McClain RC	.50	.15
246 Jessie Ibarra RC	.50	.15
247 Mike Darr RC	.75	.23
248 Bobby Estalella RC	.75	.23
249 Michael Barrett	.30	.09
250 Jamie Lopiccolo RC	.50	.15
251 Shane Spencer RC	2.00	.60
252 Ben Petrick RC	.75	.23
253 Jason Bell RC	.50	.15
254 Arnold Gooch RC	.50	.15
255 T.J. Mathews	.30	.09

256 Jason Ryan .30 .09
257 Pat Cline RC .50 .15
258 Rafael Carmona RC .50 .15
259 Carl Pavano RC 1.00 .30
260 Ben Davis .30 .09
261 Matt Lawton RC .75 .23
262 Kevin Sefcik RC .50 .15
263 Chris Fussell RC .50 .15
264 Mike Cameron RC 3.00 .90
265 Marty Janzen RC .50 .15
266 Livan Hernandez RC 1.00 .30
267 Raul Ibanez RC 2.00 .60
268 Juan Encarnacion .30 .09
269 David Yocum RC .50 .15
270 Jonathan Johnson RC .50 .15
271 Reggie Taylor .30 .09
272 Danny Buxbaum RC .50 .15
273 Jacob Cruz .30 .09
274 Bobby Morris RC .50 .15
275 Andy Fox RC .50 .15
276 Greg Keagle .30 .09
277 Charles Peterson .30 .09
278 Derrek Lee .30 .09
279 Bryant Nelson RC .50 .15
280 Antone Williamson .30 .09
281 Scott Elarton .30 .09
282 Shad Williams RC .50 .15
283 Rich Hunter RC .50 .15
284 Chris Sheff .30 .09
285 Derrick Gibson .30 .09
286 Felix Rodriguez .30 .09
287 Brian Banks RC .50 .15
288 Jason McDonald .30 .09
289 Glendon Rusch RC .75 .23
290 Gary Rath .30 .09
291 Peter Munro .30 .09
292 Tom Fordham .30 .09
293 Jason Kendall .30 .09
294 Russ Johnson .30 .09
295 Joe Long .30 .09
296 Robert Smith RC .75 .23
297 Jarrod Washburn RC 2.00 .60
298 Dave Coggin RC .50 .15
299 Jeff Yoder RC .50 .15
300 Jed Hansen RC .50 .15
301 Matt Morris RC 4.00 1.20
302 Josh Bishop RC .50 .15
303 Dustin Hermanson .30 .09
304 Mike Gulan .30 .09
305 Felipe Crespo .30 .09
306 Quinton McCracken .30 .09
307 Jim Bonnici RC .50 .15
308 Sal Fasano .30 .09
309 Gabe Alvarez RC .50 .15
310 Heath Murray RC .50 .15
311 Javier Valentin RC .50 .15
312 Bartolo Colon .30 .09
313 Olmedo Saenz .30 .09
314 Norm Hutchins RC .50 .15
315 Chris Holt .30 .09
316 David Doster RC .50 .15
317 Robert Person .30 .09
318 Donne Wall RC .50 .15
319 Adam Riggs RC .50 .15
320 Homer Bush .30 .09
321 Brad Rigby RC .50 .15
322 Lou Merloni RC .75 .23
323 Neifi Perez .30 .09
324 Chris Cumberland .30 .09
325 Alvie Shepherd RC .50 .15
326 Jarrod Patterson RC .50 .15
327 Ray Ricken RC .50 .15
328 Danny Klassen RC .50 .15
329 David Miller RC .50 .15
330 Chad Alexander RC .50 .15
331 Matt Beaumont .30 .09
332 Damon Hollins .30 .09
333 Todd Dunn .30 .09
334 Mike Sweeney RC 5.00 1.50
335 Richie Sexson .50 .15
336 Billy Wagner .30 .09
337 Ron Wright RC .50 .15
338 Paul Konerko .30 .09
339 Tommy Phelps RC .50 .15
340 Karim Garcia .30 .09
341 Mike Grace RC .50 .15
342 Russell Branyan RC .75 .23
343 Randy Winn RC 1.50 .45
344 A.J. Pierzynski RC 4.00 1.20
345 Mike Busby RC .50 .15
346 Matt Beech RC .50 .15
347 Jose Cepeda RC .50 .15
348 Brian Stephenson .30 .09
349 Rey Ordonez .30 .09
350 Rich Aurilla RC 2.50 .75
351 Edgard Velazquez RC .50 .15
352 Raul Casanova .30 .09
353 Carlos Guillen RC 1.50 .45
354 Bruce Aven RC .50 .15
355 Ryan Jones RC .50 .15
356 Derek Aucoin RC .50 .15
357 Brian Rose RC .50 .15
358 Richard Almanzar RC .50 .15
359 Fletcher Bates RC .50 .15
360 Russ Ortiz RC 3.00 .90
361 Wilton Guerrero RC .75 .23
362 Geoff Jenkins RC 2.50 .75
363 Pete Janicki .30 .09
364 Yamil Benitez .30 .09
365 Aaron Holbert .30 .09
366 Tim Belk .30 .09
367 Terrell Wade .30 .09
368 Terrence Long .30 .09
369 Brad Fullmer .30 .09
370 Matt Wagner .30 .09
371 Craig Wilson RC .50 .15
372 Mark Loretta .30 .09
373 Eric Owens .30 .09
374 Vladimir Guerrero 1.50 .45
375 Tommy Davis .30 .09
376 Donnie Sadler .30 .09
377 Edgar Renteria .30 .09
378 Todd Helton 1.50 .45
379 Ralph Milliard RC .50 .15
380 Darin Blood RC .50 .15
381 Shayne Bennett .30 .09
382 Mark Redman .30 .09
383 Felix Martinez .30 .09
384 Sean Watkins RC .50 .15
385 Oscar Henriquez .30 .09
M20 Mickey Mantle 5.00 1.50

1952 Bowman Reprint
NNO Checklists .30 .09

1996 Bowman Foil

These parallel foil cards were seeded at an approximate rate of one per pack. Packs that did not contain a Foil card had a Bowman's Best Preview or Minor League Player of the Year insert card instead. The striking silver foil card fronts differ them from the base 1996 Bowman cards.

	Nm-Mt	Ex-Mt
COMPLETE SET (385)	300.00	90.00

*STARS: 1X TO 2.5X BASIC CARDS ...
*ROOKIES: 1.25X TO 2.5X BASIC CARDS

1996 Bowman Minor League POY

Randomly inserted in packs at a rate of one in 12, this 15-card set features top minor league prospects for Player of the Year Candidates. The fronts carry a color player photo with red-and-silver foil printing. The backs display player information including his career bests.

	Nm-Mt	Ex-Mt
COMPLETE SET (15)	25.00	7.50
1 Andruw Jones	3.00	.90
2 Derrick Gibson	.75	.23
3 Bob Abreu	.75	.23
4 Todd Walker	1.25	.35
5 Jamey Wright	.75	.23
6 Wes Helms	1.00	.30
7 Karim Garcia	.75	.23
8 Bartolo Colon	.75	.23
9 Alex Ochoa	.75	.23
10 Mike Sweeney	5.00	1.50
11 Ruben Rivera	.75	.23
12 Gabe Alvarez	.50	.15
13 Billy Wagner	.75	.23
14 Vladimir Guerrero	4.00	1.20
15 Edgard Velazquez	.50	.15

1997 Bowman

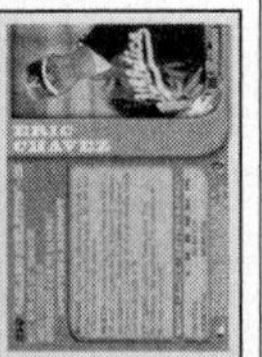

The 1997 Bowman set was issued in two series (series one numbers 1-221, series two numbers 222-441) and was distributed in 10 card packs with a suggested retail price of $2.50. The 441-card set features color photos of 300 top prospects with silver and blue foil stamping and 140 veteran stars designated by silver and red foil stamping. An unannounced Hideki Irabu red bordered card (number 441) was also included in series two packs. Players that were featured for the first time on a Bowman card also carried a blue foil "1st Bowman Card" logo on the card front. Topps offered collectors a $125 guarantee on complete sets. To get the guarantee, collectors had to mail in the Guaranteed Certificate Request Form which was found in every three packs of either series along with a $5 registration and processing fee. To redeem the guarantee, collectors had to send a complete set of Bowman regular cards (441 cards in both series) along with the certificate to Topps between August 31 and December 31 in the year 2000. Rookie Cards in this set include Adrian Beltre, Kris Benson, Eric Chavez, Jose Cruz Jr, Travis Lee, Aramis Ramirez, Miguel Tejada and Kerry Wood. Please note that cards 155 and 158 don't exist. Calvin "Pokey" Reese and George Arias are both numbered 156 (Reese is an uncorrected error - should be numbered 155). Chris Carpenter and Eric Milton are both numbered 159 (Carpenter is an uncorrected error - should be numbered 158).

	Nm-Mt	Ex-Mt
COMPLETE SET (441)	50.00	15.00
COMP. SERIES 1 (221)	25.00	7.50
COMP. SERIES 2 (220)	25.00	7.50

1 Derek Jeter 2.00 .60
2 Edgar Renteria .30 .09
3 Chipper Jones .75 .23
4 Hideo Nomo .75 .23
5 Tim Salmon .50 .15
6 Jason Giambi .75 .23
7 Robin Ventura .30 .09
8 Tony Clark .30 .09
9 Barry Larkin .75 .23
10 Paul Molitor .50 .15
11 Bernard Gilkey .30 .09
12 Jack McDowell .30 .09
13 Andy Benes .30 .09
14 Ryan Klesko .30 .09
15 Mark McGwire 2.00 .60
16 Ken Griffey Jr. 1.25 .35
17 Robb Nen .30 .09
18 Cal Ripken 2.50 .75
19 John Valentin .30 .09
20 Ricky Bottalico .30 .09
21 Mike Lansing .30 .09
22 Ryne Sandberg 1.25 .35
23 Carlos Delgado .30 .09
24 Craig Biggio .50 .15
25 Eric Karros .30 .09
26 Kevin Appier .30 .09
27 Mariano Rivera .50 .15
28 Vinny Castilla .30 .09
29 Juan Gonzalez .75 .23
30 Al Martin .30 .09
31 Jeff Cirillo .30 .09
32 Eddie Murray .75 .23
33 Ray Lankford .30 .09
34 Manny Ramirez .30 .09
35 Roberto Alomar .75 .23
36 Will Clark .75 .23
37 Chuck Knoblauch .30 .09
38 Harold Baines .30 .09
39 Trevor Hoffman .30 .09
40 Edgar Martinez .50 .15
41 Geronimo Berroa .30 .09
42 Rey Ordonez .30 .09
43 Mike Stanley .30 .09
44 Mike Mussina .75 .23
45 Kevin Brown .30 .09
46 Dennis Eckersley .30 .09
47 Henry Rodriguez .30 .09
48 Tino Martinez .50 .15
49 Eric Young .30 .09
50 Bret Boone .30 .09
51 Raul Mondesi .30 .09
52 Sammy Sosa 1.25 .35
53 John Smoltz .50 .15
54 Billy Wagner .30 .09
55 Jeff D'Amico .30 .09
56 Ken Caminiti .30 .09
57 Jason Kendall .30 .09
58 Wade Boggs .50 .15
59 Andres Galarraga .30 .09
60 Jeff Brantley .30 .09
61 Mel Rojas .30 .09
62 Brian L. Hunter .30 .09
63 Bobby Bonilla .30 .09
64 Roger Clemens 1.50 .45
65 Jeff Kent .30 .09
66 Matt Williams .30 .09
67 Albert Belle .30 .09
68 Jeff King .30 .09
69 John Wetteland .30 .09
70 Deion Sanders .50 .15
71 Bubba Trammell RC .50 .15
72 Felix Heredia RC .50 .15
73 Billy Koch RC .75 .23
74 Sidney Ponson RC 1.25 .35
75 Ricky Ledee RC .50 .15
76 Brett Tomko .30 .09
77 Braden Looper RC .50 .15
78 Damian Jackson .30 .09
79 Jason Dickson .30 .09
80 Chad Green RC .50 .15
81 R.A. Dickey RC .50 .15
82 Jeff Liefer .30 .09
83 Matt Wagner .30 .09
84 Richard Hidalgo .30 .09
85 Adam Riggs .30 .09
86 Robert Smith .30 .09
87 Chad Hermansen RC .50 .15
88 Felix Martinez .30 .09
89 J.J. Johnson .30 .09
90 Todd Dunwoody .30 .09
91 Katsuhiro Maeda .30 .09
92 Darin Erstad .30 .09
93 Elieser Marrero .30 .09
94 Bartolo Colon .30 .09
95 Chris Fussell .30 .09
96 Ugueth Urbina .30 .09
97 Josh Paul RC .50 .15
98 Jaime Bluma .30 .09
99 Seth Greisinger RC .50 .15
100 Jose Cruz Jr. RC 2.00 .60
101 Todd Dunn .30 .09
102 Joe Young RC .50 .15
103 Jonathan Johnson .30 .09
104 Justin Towle RC .50 .15
105 Brian Rose .30 .09
106 Jose Guillen .30 .09
107 Andruw Jones .30 .09
108 Mark Kotsay RC .50 .15
109 Wilton Guerrero .30 .09
110 Jacob Cruz .30 .09
111 Mike Sweeney .30 .09
112 Julio Mosquera .30 .09
113 Matt Morris .30 .09
114 Wendell Magee .30 .09
115 John Thomson .30 .09
116 Javier Valentin .30 .09
117 Tom Fordham .30 .09
118 Ruben Rivera .30 .09
119 Mike Drumright RC .50 .15
120 Chris Holt .30 .09
121 Sean Maloney .30 .09
122 Michael Barrett .30 .09
123 Tony Saunders RC .50 .15
124 Kevin Brown C .30 .09
125 Richard Almanzar .30 .09
126 Mark Redman .30 .09
127 Anthony Sanders RC .50 .15
128 Jeff Abbott .30 .09
129 Eugene Kingsale .30 .09
130 Paul Konerko .30 .09
131 Randall Simon RC .75 .23
132 Andy Larkin .30 .09
133 Rafael Medina .30 .09
134 Mendy Lopez .30 .09
135 Freddy Adrian Garcia .30 .09
136 Karim Garcia .30 .09
137 Larry Rodriguez RC .50 .15
138 Carlos Guillen .30 .09
139 Aaron Boone .30 .09
140 Donnie Sadler .30 .09
141 Brooks Kieschnick .30 .09
142 Scott Spiezio .30 .09
143 Everett Stull .30 .09
144 Enrique Wilson .30 .09
145 Milton Bradley RC 4.00 1.20
146 Kevin Orie .30 .09
147 Derek Wallace .30 .09
148 Russ Johnson .30 .09
149 Joe Lagarde RC .50 .15
150 Luis Castillo .30 .09
151 Jay Payton .30 .09
152 Joe Long .30 .09
153 Livan Hernandez .30 .09
154 Vladimir Nunez RC .50 .15
155 Pokey Reese UER .30 .09
Card actually numbered 156
156 George Arias .30 .09
157 Homer Bush .30 .09
158 Chris Carpenter UER .30 .09
Card numbered 159
159 Eric Milton RC 1.25 .35
160 Richie Sexson .30 .09
161 Carl Pavano .30 .09
162 Chris Gissell RC .50 .15
163 Mac Suzuki .30 .09
164 Pat Cline .30 .09
165 Ron Wright .30 .09
166 Dante Powell .30 .09
167 Mark Bellhorn .30 .09
168 George Lombard .30 .09
169 Pee Wee Lopez RC .50 .15
170 Paul Wilder RC .50 .15
171 Brad Fullmer .30 .09
172 Willie Martinez RC .50 .15
173 Dario Veras RC .50 .15
174 Dave Coggin .30 .09
175 Kris Benson RC .75 .23
176 Torii Hunter .30 .09
177 D.T. Cromer .30 .09
178 Nelson Figueroa RC .50 .15
179 Hiram Bocachica RC .50 .15
180 Shane Monahan .30 .09
181 Jimmy Anderson RC .50 .15
182 Juan Melo .30 .09
183 Pablo Ortega RC .50 .15
184 Calvin Pickering RC .50 .15
185 Reggie Taylor .30 .09
186 Jeff Farnsworth RC .50 .15
187 Terrence Long .30 .09
188 Geoff Jenkins .30 .09
189 Steve Rain RC .50 .15
190 Nerio Rodriguez RC .50 .15
191 Derrick Gibson .30 .09
192 Darin Blood .30 .09
193 Ben Davis .30 .09
194 Adrian Beltre RC 2.00 .60
195 Damian Sapp RC UER .50 .15
196 Kerry Wood RC 10.00 3.00
197 Nate Rolison RC .50 .15
198 Fernando Tatis RC .50 .15
199 Brad Penny RC 2.00 .60
200 Jake Westbrook RC .50 .15
201 Edwin Diaz .30 .09
202 Joe Fontenot RC .50 .15
203 Matt Halloran RC .50 .15
204 Blake Stein RC .50 .15
205 Onan Masaoka .30 .09
206 Ben Petrick .30 .09
207 Matt Clement RC 1.50 .45
208 Todd Greene .30 .09
209 Ray Ricken .30 .09
210 Eric Chavez RC 5.00 1.50
211 Edgard Velazquez .30 .09
212 Bruce Chen RC .50 .15
213 Danny Patterson .30 .09
214 Jeff Yoder .30 .09
215 Luis Ordaz RC .50 .15
216 Chris Widger .30 .09
217 Jason Brester .30 .09
218 Carlton Loewer .30 .09
219 Chris Reitsma RC .50 .15
220 Neifi Perez .30 .09
221 Hideki Irabu RC .50 .15
222 Ellis Burks .30 .09
223 Pedro Martinez .75 .23
224 Kenny Lofton .30 .09
225 Randy Johnson .75 .23
226 Terry Steinbach .30 .09
227 Bernie Williams .50 .15
228 Dean Palmer .30 .09
229 Alan Benes .30 .09
230 Marquis Grissom .30 .09
231 Gary Sheffield .50 .15
232 Curt Schilling .50 .15
233 Reggie Sanders .30 .09
234 Bobby Higginson .30 .09
235 Moises Alou .30 .09
236 Tom Glavine .50 .15
237 Mark Grace .50 .15
238 Ramon Martinez .30 .09
239 Rafael Palmeiro .50 .15
240 John Olerud .30 .09
241 Dante Bichette .30 .09
242 Greg Vaughn .30 .09
243 Jeff Bagwell .50 .15
244 Barry Bonds 2.00 .60
245 Pat Hentgen .30 .09
246 Jim Thome .75 .23
247 J.Allensworth .30 .09
248 Andy Pettitte .50 .15
249 Jay Bell .30 .09
250 John Jaha .30 .09
251 Jim Edmonds .30 .09
252 Ron Gant .30 .09
253 David Cone .30 .09
254 Jose Canseco .75 .23
255 Jay Buhner .30 .09
256 Greg Maddux 1.25 .35
257 Brian McRae .30 .09
258 Lance Johnson .30 .09
259 Travis Fryman .30 .09
260 Paul O'Neill .50 .15
261 Ivan Rodriguez .75 .23
262 Gregg Jefferies .30 .09
263 Fred McGriff .50 .15
264 Derek Bell .30 .09
265 Jeff Conine .30 .09
266 Mike Piazza 1.25 .35
267 Mark Grudzielanek .30 .09
268 Brady Anderson .30 .09
269 Marty Cordova .30 .09
270 Ray Durham .30 .09
271 Joe Carter .30 .09
272 Brian Jordan .30 .09
273 David Justice .30 .09
274 Tony Gwynn 1.00 .30
275 Larry Walker .50 .15
276 Cecil Fielder .30 .09
277 Mo Vaughn .30 .09
278 Alex Fernandez .30 .09
279 Michael Tucker .30 .09
280 Jose Valentin .30 .09
281 Sandy Alomar Jr. .30 .09
282 Todd Hollandsworth .30 .09
283 Rico Brogna .30 .09
284 Rusty Greer .30 .09
285 Roberto Hernandez .30 .09
286 Hal Morris .30 .09
287 Johnny Damon .30 .09
288 Todd Hundley .30 .09
289 Rondell White .30 .09
290 Frank Thomas .75 .23
291 Don Denbow RC .50 .15
292 Derrek Lee .30 .09
293 Todd Walker .30 .09
294 Scott Rolen .50 .15
295 Wes Helms .30 .09
296 Bob Abreu .30 .09
297 John Patterson RC .75 .23
298 Alex Gonzalez RC 1.25 .35
299 Grant Roberts RC .50 .15
300 Jeff Suppan .30 .09
301 Luke Wilcox .30 .09
302 Marlon Anderson .30 .09
303 Ray Brown .30 .09
304 Mike Caruso RC .50 .15
305 Sam Marsonek RC .50 .15
306 Brady Raggio RC .50 .15
307 Kevin McGlinchy RC .50 .15
308 Roy Halladay RC 4.00 1.20
309 Jeremi Gonzalez RC .50 .15
310 Aramis Ramirez RC 2.50 .75
311 Dee Brown RC .50 .15
312 Justin Thompson .30 .09
313 Jay Tessmer RC .50 .15
314 Mike Johnson RC .50 .15
315 Danny Clyburn .30 .09
316 Bruce Aven .30 .09
317 Keith Foulke RC 1.25 .35
318 Jimmy Osting RC .50 .15
319 Val.De Los Santos RC .50 .15
320 Shannon Stewart .30 .09
321 Willie Adams .30 .09
322 Larry Barnes RC .50 .15
323 Mark Johnson RC .50 .15
324 Chris Stowers RC .50 .15
325 Brandon Reed .30 .09
326 Randy Winn .30 .09
327 Steve Chavez RC .50 .15
328 Nomar Garciaparra 1.25 .35
329 Jacque Jones RC 1.50 .45
330 Chris Clemons .30 .09
331 Todd Helton .75 .23
332 Ryan Brannan RC .50 .15
333 Alex Sanchez RC .50 .15
334 Arnold Gooch .30 .09
335 Russell Branyan .30 .09
336 Daryle Ward .50 .15
337 John LeRoy RC .50 .15
338 Steve Cox .30 .09
339 Kevin Witt .30 .09
340 Norm Hutchins .30 .09
341 Gabby Martinez .30 .09
342 Kris Detmers .30 .09
343 Mike Villano RC .50 .15
344 Preston Wilson .30 .09
345 James Manias RC .50 .15
346 Deivi Cruz RC .50 .15
347 Donzell McDonald RC .50 .15
348 Rod Myers RC .50 .15
349 Shawn Chacon RC 2.50 .75
350 Elvin Hernandez RC .50 .15
351 Orlando Cabrera RC .75 .23
352 Brian Banks .30 .09
353 Robbie Bell .50 .15
354 Brad Rigby .30 .09
355 Scott Elarton .30 .09
356 Kevin Sweeney RC .50 .15
357 Steve Soderstrom .30 .09
358 Ryan Nye .30 .09
359 Marlon Allen RC .50 .15
360 Donny Leon RC .75 .23
361 Garrett Neubart RC .50 .15
362 Abraham Nunez RC .50 .15
363 Adam Eaton RC .50 .15
364 Octavio Dotel RC .50 .15
365 Dean Crow RC .50 .15
366 Jason Baker RC .50 .15
367 Sean Casey .50 .15
368 Joe Lawrence RC .50 .15
369 Adam Johnson RC .50 .15
370 S.Schoeneweis RC .50 .15
371 Gerald Witasick Jr. .30 .09
372 Ronnie Belliard RC .50 .15
373 Russ Ortiz .30 .09
374 Robert Stratton RC .50 .15
375 Bobby Estalella .30 .09
376 Corey Lee RC .50 .15
377 Carlos Beltran .75 .23
378 Mike Cameron .30 .09
379 Scott Randall RC .50 .15
380 Corey Erickson RC .50 .15
381 Jay Canizaro .30 .09
382 Kerry Robinson RC .50 .15
383 Todd Noel RC .50 .15
384 A.J. Zapp RC .50 .15
385 Jarrod Washburn .30 .09
386 Ben Grieve .30 .09
387 Javier Vazquez RC 4.00 1.20
388 Tony Graffanino .30 .09
389 Travis Lee RC .50 .15
390 DaRond Stovall .30 .09
391 Dennis Reyes RC .50 .15
392 Danny Buxbaum .30 .09
393 Marc Lewis RC .50 .15
394 Kelvim Escobar RC .50 .15
395 Danny Klassen .30 .09
396 Ken Cloude RC .50 .15
397 Gabe Alvarez .30 .09
398 Jaret Wright RC .50 .15
399 Raul Casanova .30 .09
400 Clayton Bruner RC .50 .15
401 Jason Marquis RC .50 .15
402 Marc Kroon .30 .09
403 Jamey Wright .30 .09
404 Matt Snyder RC .50 .15
405 Josh Garrett RC .50 .15
406 Juan Encarnacion .30 .09
407 Heath Murray .30 .09
408 Brett Herbison RC .50 .15
409 Brent Butler RC .50 .15
410 Danny Peoples RC .50 .15
411 Miguel Tejada RC 5.00 1.50
412 Damian Moss .30 .09
413 Jim Pittsley .30 .09
414 Dmitri Young .30 .09

415 Glendon Rusch .30 .09
416 Vladimir Guerrero .75 .23
417 Cole Liniak RC .50 .15
418 R.Hernandez UER .30 .09
Card back says 1st Bowman card is 1997, he had a 1996 Bowman
419 Cliff Politte RC .50 .15
420 Mel Rosario RC .50 .15
421 Jorge Carrion RC .50 .15
422 John Barnes RC .50 .15
423 Chris Stowe RC .50 .15
424 Vernon Wells RC 5.00 1.50
425 Brett Caradonna RC .50 .15
426 Scott Hodges RC .50 .15
427 Jon Garland RC .75 .23
428 Nathan Haynes RC .50 .15
429 Geoff Goetz RC .50 .15
430 Adam Kennedy RC 1.25 .35
431 T.J. Tucker RC .50 .15
432 Aaron Akin RC .50 .15
433 Jayson Werth RC .50 .15
434 Glenn Davis RC .50 .15
435 Mark Mangum RC .50 .15
436 Troy Cameron RC .50 .15
437 J.J. Davis RC .50 .15
438 Lance Berkman RC 5.00 1.50
439 Jason Standridge RC .50 .15
440 Jason Dellaero RC .50 .15
441 Hideki Irabu .50 .15

1997 Bowman International

Inserted one in every pack, this 441-card set is parallel to the regular Bowman set. The difference is found in the flag in the background of each card that tells in what country the pictured player was born.

Nm-Mt Ex-Mt
COMPLETE SET (441) 160.00 47.50
COMP.SERIES 1 (221) 80.00 24.00
COMP.SERIES 2 (220) 80.00 24.00
*STARS: 1X TO 2.5X BASIC CARDS...
*ROOKIES: .5X TO 1.2X BASIC CARDS

1997 Bowman 1998 ROY Favorites

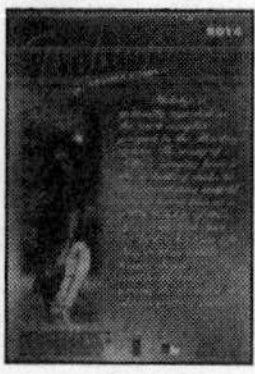

Randomly inserted in 1997 Bowman Series two packs at the rate of one in 12, this 15-card set features color photos of prospective 1998 Rookie of the Year candidates.

Nm-Mt Ex-Mt
COMPLETE SET (15) 15.00 4.50
ROY1 Jeff Abbott 1.00 .30
ROY2 Karim Garcia 1.00 .30
ROY3 Todd Helton 2.50 .75
ROY4 Richard Hidalgo 1.00 .30
ROY5 Geoff Jenkins 1.00 .30
ROY6 Russ Johnson 1.00 .30
ROY7 Paul Konerko 1.00 .30
ROY8 Mark Kotsay .60 .18
ROY9 Ricky Ledee .60 .18
ROY10 Travis Lee .60 .18
ROY11 Derrek Lee 1.00 .30
ROY12 Elieser Marrero 1.00 .30
ROY13 Juan Melo 1.00 .30
ROY14 Brian Rose 1.00 .30
ROY15 Fernando Tatis .60 .18

1997 Bowman Certified Blue Ink Autographs

Randomly inserted in first and second series packs at a rate of one in 96 and ANCO packs at one in 115, this 90-card set features color player photos of top prospects with blue ink autographs and printed on sturdy 16 pt. card stock with the Topps Certified Autograph Issue Stamp. The Derek Jeter blue ink and green ink versions are seeded in every 1,928 packs.

Nm-Mt Ex-Mt
*BLACK INK: .5X TO 1.2X BLUE INK...
BLACK STATED ODDS 1:503, ANCO 1:600
*GOLD INK: 1X TO 2.5X BLUE INK.....
GOLD: STATED ODDS 1:1509, ANCO 1:1795
*GREEN JETER: SAME VALUE AS BLUE INK
D.JETER BLUE SER.1 ODDS 1:1928...
D.JETER GREEN SER.2 ODDS 1:1928.
CA1 Jeff Abbott 10.00 3.00
CA2 Bob Abreu 20.00 6.00
CA3 Willie Adams 10.00 3.00
CA4 Brian Banks 10.00 3.00
CA5 Kris Benson 20.00 6.00
CA6 Darin Blood 10.00 3.00
CA7 Jaime Bluma 10.00 3.00
CA8 Kevin L. Brown 10.00 3.00
CA9 Ray Brown 10.00 3.00
CA10 Homer Bush 10.00 3.00
CA11 Mike Cameron 20.00 6.00
CA12 Jay Canizaro 10.00 3.00
CA13 Luis Castillo 20.00 6.00
CA14 Dave Coggin 10.00 3.00
CA15 Bartolo Colon 20.00 6.00
CA16 Rocky Coppinger 10.00 3.00
CA17 Jacob Cruz 10.00 3.00
CA18 Jose Cruz Jr. 25.00 7.50
CA19 Jeff D'Amico 10.00 3.00
CA20 Ben Davis 10.00 3.00
CA21 Mike Drumright 10.00 3.00
CA22 Scott Elarton 10.00 3.00
CA23 Darin Erstad 20.00 6.00
CA24 Bobby Estalella 10.00 3.00
CA25 Joe Fontenot 10.00 3.00
CA26 Tom Fordham 10.00 3.00
CA27 Brad Fullmer 10.00 3.00
CA28 Chris Fussell 10.00 3.00
CA29 Karim Garcia 10.00 3.00
CA30 Kris Detmers 10.00 3.00
CA31 Todd Greene 10.00 3.00
CA32 Ben Grieve 10.00 3.00
CA33 Vladimir Guerrero 50.00 15.00
CA34 Jose Guillen 20.00 6.00
CA35 Roy Halladay 60.00 18.00
CA36 Wes Helms 10.00 3.00
CA37 Chad Hermansen 15.00 4.50
CA38 Richard Hidalgo 20.00 6.00
CA39 Todd Hollandsworth 10.00 3.00
CA40 Damian Jackson 10.00 3.00
CA41 Derek Jeter 120.00 36.00
CA42 Andruw Jones 30.00 9.00
CA43 Brooks Kieschnick 10.00 3.00
CA44 Eugene Kingsale 10.00 3.00
CA45 Paul Konerko 20.00 6.00
CA46 Marc Kroon 10.00 3.00
CA47 Derrek Lee 20.00 6.00
CA48 Travis Lee 15.00 4.50
CA49 Terrence Long 20.00 6.00
CA50 Curt Lyons 10.00 3.00
CA51 Eli Marrero 10.00 3.00
CA52 Rafael Medina 10.00 3.00
CA53 Juan Melo 10.00 3.00
CA54 Shane Monahan 10.00 3.00
CA55 Julio Mosquera 10.00 3.00
CA56 Heath Murray 10.00 3.00
CA57 Ryan Nye 10.00 3.00
CA58 Kevin Orie 10.00 3.00
CA59 Russ Ortiz 20.00 6.00
CA60 Carl Pavano 20.00 6.00
CA61 Jay Payton 10.00 3.00
CA62 Neifi Perez 10.00 3.00
CA63 Sidney Ponson 25.00 7.50
CA64 Pokey Reese 10.00 3.00
CA65 Ray Ricken 10.00 3.00
CA66 Brad Rigby 10.00 3.00
CA67 Adam Riggs 10.00 3.00
CA68 Ruben Rivera 10.00 3.00
CA69 J.J. Johnson 10.00 3.00
CA70 Scott Rolen 30.00 9.00
CA71 Tony Saunders 10.00 3.00
CA72 Donnie Sadler 10.00 3.00
CA73 Richie Sexson 20.00 6.00
CA74 Scott Spiezio 10.00 3.00
CA75 Everett Stull 10.00 3.00
CA76 Mike Sweeney 20.00 6.00
CA77 Fernando Tatis 15.00 4.50
CA78 Miguel Tejada 60.00 18.00
CA79 Justin Thompson 10.00 3.00
CA80 Justin Towle 10.00 3.00
CA81 Billy Wagner 30.00 9.00
CA82 Todd Walker 20.00 6.00
CA83 Luke Wilcox 10.00 3.00
CA84 Paul Wilder 10.00 3.00
CA85 Enrique Wilson 10.00 3.00
CA86 Kerry Wood 150.00 45.00
CA87 Jamey Wright 10.00 3.00
CA88 Ron Wright 10.00 3.00
CA89 Dmitri Young 20.00 6.00
CA90 Nelson Figueroa 10.00 3.00

1997 Bowman International Best

Randomly inserted in series two packs at the rate of one in 12, this 20-card set features color photos of both prospects and veterans from far and wide who have made an impact on the game.

Nm-Mt Ex-Mt
COMPLETE SET (20) 50.00 15.00
*ATOMIC: 1.5X TO 4X BASIC INT.BEST
ATOMIC SER.2 STATED ODDS 1:96 ...
*REFRACTORS: .75X TO 2X BASIC INT.BEST
REFRACTOR SER.2 STATED ODDS 1:48
BBI1 Frank Thomas 3.00 .90
BBI2 Ken Griffey Jr. 5.00 1.50
BBI3 Juan Gonzalez 3.00 .90
BBI4 Bernie Williams 2.00 .60
BBI5 Hideo Nomo 3.00 .90
BBI6 Sammy Sosa 5.00 1.50
BBI7 Larry Walker 2.00 .60
BBI8 Vinny Castilla 1.25 .35
BBI9 Mariano Rivera 2.00 .60
BBI10 Rafael Palmeiro 2.00 .60
BBI11 Nomar Garciaparra 5.00 1.50
BBI12 Todd Walker 1.25 .35
BBI13 Andruw Jones 1.25 .35
BBI14 Vladimir Guerrero 3.00 .90
BBI15 Ruben Rivera 1.25 .35
BBI16 Bob Abreu 1.25 .35
BBI17 Karim Garcia 1.25 .35
BBI18 Katsuhiro Maeda 1.25 .35
BBI19 Jose Cruz Jr. 3.00 .90
BBI20 Damian Moss 1.25 .35

1997 Bowman Scout's Honor Roll

Randomly inserted in first series packs at a rate of one in 12, this 15-card set features color photos of top prospects and rookies printed on double-etched foil cards.

Nm-Mt Ex-Mt
COMPLETE SET (15) 25.00 7.50

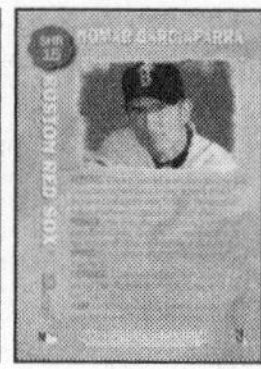

1 Dmitri Young .75 .23
2 Bob Abreu .75 .23
3 Vladimir Guerrero 2.00 .60
4 Paul Konerko .75 .23
5 Kevin Orie .75 .23
6 Todd Walker .75 .23
7 Ben Grieve .75 .23
8 Darin Erstad .75 .23
9 Derrek Lee .75 .23
10 Jose Cruz Jr. 2.50 .75
11 Scott Rolen 1.25 .35
12 Travis Lee 1.00 .30
13 Andruw Jones .75 .23
14 Wilton Guerrero .75 .23
15 Nomar Garciaparra 3.00 .90

1998 Bowman Previews

Randomly inserted in Stadium Club first series hobby and retail packs at the rate of one in 12 and first series Home Team Advantage packs at a rate of one in four, this 10-card set is a sneak preview of the Bowman series and features color photos of top players. The cards are numbered with a BP prefix on the backs.

Nm-Mt Ex-Mt
COMPLETE SET (10) 25.00 7.50
BP1 Nomar Garciaparra 4.00 1.20
BP2 Scott Rolen 1.50 .45
BP3 Ken Griffey Jr. 4.00 1.20
BP4 Frank Thomas 2.50 .75
BP5 Larry Walker 1.50 .45
BP6 Mike Piazza 4.00 1.20
BP7 Chipper Jones 2.50 .75
BP8 Tino Martinez 1.50 .45
BP9 Mark McGwire 6.00 1.80
BP10 Barry Bonds 6.00 1.80

1998 Bowman Prospect Previews

Randomly seeded in Stadium Club second series hobby and retail packs at a rate of one in twelve and second series Home Team Advantage packs at a rate of one in four, this ten card set previewed the upcoming 1998 Bowman brand, featuring a selection of top youngsters expected to make an impact in 1998.

Nm-Mt Ex-Mt
COMPLETE SET (10) 10.00 3.00
BP1 Ben Grieve 1.00 .30
BP2 Brad Fullmer 1.00 .30
BP3 Ryan Anderson 1.25 .35
BP4 Mark Kotsay 1.00 .30
BP5 Bobby Estalella 1.00 .30
BP6 Juan Encarnacion 1.00 .30
BP7 Todd Helton 1.50 .45
BP8 Mike Lowell 4.00 1.20
BP9 A.J. Hinch 1.00 .30
BP10 Richard Hidalgo 1.25 .35

1998 Bowman

The complete 1998 Bowman set was distributed amongst two series with a total of 441 cards. The 10-card packs retailed for $2.50 each. Series one contains 221 cards while series two contains 220 cards. Each player's facsimile signature taken from the contract they signed with Topps is also on the left border. Players new to Bowman are marked with the new Bowman Rookie Card stamp. Notable Rookie Cards include Ryan Anderson. Jack Cust, Troy Glaus, Orlando Hernandez, Gabe Kapler, Ruben Mateo, Kevin Millwood and Magglio Ordonez. The 1991 BBM (Major Japanese Card set) cards of Shigetoshi Hasegawa, Hideki Irabu and Hideo Nomo (All of which are considered Japanese Rookie Cards) were randomly inserted into these packs.

Nm-Mt Ex-Mt
COMPLETE SET (441) 50.00 15.00
COMP. SERIES 1 (221) 25.00 7.50
COMP. SERIES 2 (220) 25.00 7.50
1 Nomar Garciaparra 1.25 .35
2 Scott Rolen .50 .15
3 Andy Pettitte .50 .15
4 Ivan Rodriguez .75 .23
5 Mark McGwire 2.00 .60
6 Jason Dickson .30 .09
7 Jose Cruz Jr. .30 .09
8 Jeff Kent .30 .09
9 Mike Mussina .75 .23
10 Jason Kendall .30 .09
11 Brett Tomko .30 .09
12 Jeff King .30 .09
13 Brad Radke .30 .09
14 Robin Ventura .30 .09
15 Jeff Bagwell .50 .15
16 Greg Maddux 1.25 .35
17 John Jaha .30 .09
18 Mike Piazza 1.25 .35
19 Edgar Martinez .50 .15
20 David Justice .30 .09
21 Todd Hundley .30 .09
22 Tony Gwynn 1.00 .30
23 Larry Walker .50 .15
24 Bernie Williams .50 .15
25 Edgar Renteria .30 .09
26 Rafael Palmeiro .50 .15
27 Tim Salmon .50 .15
28 Matt Morris .30 .09
29 Shawn Estes .30 .09
30 Vladimir Guerrero .75 .23
31 Fernando Tatis .30 .09
32 Justin Thompson .30 .09
33 Ken Griffey Jr. 1.25 .35
34 Edgardo Alfonzo .30 .09
35 Mo Vaughn .30 .09
36 Marty Cordova .30 .09
37 Craig Biggio .50 .15
38 Roger Clemens 1.50 .45
39 Mark Grace .50 .15
40 Ken Caminiti .30 .09
41 Tony Womack .30 .09
42 Albert Belle .30 .09
43 Tino Martinez .50 .15
44 Sandy Alomar Jr. .30 .09
45 Jeff Cirillo .30 .09
46 Jason Giambi .75 .23
47 Darin Erstad .30 .09
48 Livan Hernandez .30 .09
49 Mark Grudzielanek .30 .09
50 Sammy Sosa 1.25 .35
51 Curt Schilling .50 .15
52 Brian Hunter .30 .09
53 Neifi Perez .30 .09
54 Todd Walker .30 .09
55 Jose Guillen .30 .09
56 Jim Thome .75 .23
57 Tom Glavine .50 .15
58 Todd Greene .30 .09
59 Rondell White .30 .09
60 Roberto Alomar .75 .23
61 Tony Clark .30 .09
62 Vinny Castilla .30 .09
63 Barry Larkin .75 .23
64 Hideki Irabu .30 .09
65 Johnny Damon .30 .09
66 Juan Gonzalez .75 .23
67 John Olerud .30 .09
68 Gary Sheffield .30 .09
69 Raul Mondesi .30 .09
70 Chipper Jones .75 .23
71 David Ortiz .30 .09
72 Warren Morris RC .30 .09
73 Alex Gonzalez .30 .09
74 Nick Bierbrodt .30 .09
75 Roy Halladay .30 .09
76 Danny Buxbaum .30 .09
77 Adam Kennedy .30 .09
78 Jared Sandberg .30 .09
79 Michael Barrett .30 .09
80 Gil Meche 1.50 .45
81 Jayson Werth .30 .09
82 Abraham Nunez .30 .09
83 Ben Petrick .30 .09
84 Brett Caradonna .30 .09
85 Mike Lowell RC 2.00 .60
86 Clayton Bruner .30 .09
87 John Curtice RC .40 .12
88 Bobby Estalella .30 .09
89 Juan Melo .30 .09
90 Arnold Gooch .30 .09
91 Kevin Millwood RC 1.50 .45
92 Richie Sexson .30 .09
93 Orlando Cabrera .30 .09
94 Pat Cline .30 .09
95 Anthony Sanders .30 .09
96 Russ Johnson .30 .09
97 Ben Grieve .30 .09
98 Kevin McGlinchy .30 .09
99 Paul Wilder .30 .09
100 Russ Ortiz .30 .09
101 Ryan Jackson RC .30 .09
102 Heath Murray .30 .09
103 Brian Rose .30 .09
104 R.Radmanovich RC .30 .09
105 Ricky Ledee .30 .09
106 Jeff Wallace RC .30 .09
107 Ryan Minor RC .30 .09
108 Dennis Reyes .30 .09
109 James Manias .30 .09
110 Chris Carpenter .30 .09
111 Daryle Ward .30 .09
112 Vernon Wells .50 .15
113 Chad Green .30 .09
114 Mike Stoner RC .30 .09
115 Brad Fullmer .30 .09
116 Adam Eaton .30 .09
117 Jeff Liefer .30 .09
118 Corey Koskie RC 1.25 .35
119 Todd Helton .50 .15
120 Jaime Jones RC .30 .09
121 Mel Rosario .30 .09
122 Geoff Goetz .30 .09
123 Adrian Beltre .30 .09
124 Jason Dellaero .30 .09
125 Gabe Kapler RC .60 .18
126 Scott Schoeneweis .30 .09
127 Ryan Brannan .30 .09
128 Aaron Akin .30 .09
129 Ryan Anderson RC .40 .12
130 Brad Penny .30 .09
131 Bruce Chen .30 .09
132 Eli Marrero .30 .09
133 Eric Chavez .50 .15
134 Troy Glaus RC 4.00 1.20
135 Troy Cameron .30 .09
136 Brian Sikorski RC .30 .09
137 Mike Kinkade RC .30 .09
138 Braden Looper .30 .09
139 Mark Mangum .30 .09
140 Danny Peoples .30 .09
141 J.J. Davis .30 .09
142 Ben Davis .30 .09
143 Jacque Jones .30 .09
144 Derrick Gibson .30 .09
145 Bronson Arroyo .30 .09
146 L.De Los Santos RC UER .30 .09
has hitting stat line instead of pitching
147 Jeff Abbott .30 .09
148 Mike Cuddyer RC 1.00 .30
149 Jason Romano .30 .09
150 Shane Monahan .30 .09
151 Ntema Ndungidi RC .30 .09
152 Alex Sanchez .30 .09
153 Jack Cust RC .40 .12
154 Brent Butler .30 .09
155 Ramon Hernandez .30 .09
156 Norm Hutchins .30 .09
157 Jason Marquis .30 .09
158 Jacob Cruz .30 .09
159 Rob Burger RC .30 .09
160 Dave Coggin .30 .09
161 Preston Wilson .30 .09
162 Jason Fitzgerald RC .30 .09
163 Dan Serafini .30 .09
164 Peter Munro .30 .09
165 Trot Nixon .50 .15
166 Homer Bush .30 .09
167 Dermal Brown .30 .09
168 Chad Hermansen .30 .09
169 Julio Moreno RC .30 .09
170 John Roskos RC .30 .09
171 Grant Roberts .30 .09
172 Ken Cloude .30 .09
173 Jason Brester .30 .09
174 Jason Conti .30 .09
175 Jon Garland .30 .09
176 Robbie Bell .30 .09
177 Nathan Haynes .30 .09
178 Ramon Ortiz RC 1.00 .30
179 Shannon Stewart .30 .09
180 Pablo Ortega .30 .09
181 Jimmy Rollins RC 1.25 .35
182 Sean Casey .30 .09
183 Ted Lilly RC .60 .18
184 Chris Enochs RC .30 .09
185 M.Ordonez RC UER 3.00 .90
Front photo is Mario Valdez
186 Mike Drumright .30 .09
187 Aaron Boone .30 .09
188 Matt Clement .30 .09
189 Todd Dunwoody .30 .09
190 Larry Rodriguez .30 .09
191 Todd Noel .30 .09
192 Geoff Jenkins .30 .09
193 George Lombard .30 .09
194 Lance Berkman .50 .15
195 Marcus McCain .30 .09
196 Ryan McGuire .30 .09
197 Jhensy Sandoval .30 .09
198 Corey Lee .30 .09
199 Mario Valdez .30 .09
200 Robert Fick RC 1.25 .35
201 Donnie Sadler .30 .09
202 Marc Kroon .30 .09
203 David Miller .30 .09
204 Jarrod Washburn .30 .09
205 Miguel Tejada .50 .15
206 Raul Ibanez .30 .09
207 John Patterson .30 .09
208 Calvin Pickering .30 .09
209 Felix Martinez .30 .09
210 Mark Redman .30 .09
211 Scott Elarton .30 .09
212 Jose Amado RC .30 .09
213 Kerry Wood .75 .23
214 Dante Powell .30 .09
215 Aramis Ramirez .30 .09
216 A.J. Hinch .30 .09
217 Dustin Carr RC .30 .09
218 Mark Kotsay .30 .09
219 Jason Standridge .30 .09
220 Luis Ordaz .30 .09
221 O.Hernandez RC 1.25 .35
222 Cal Ripken 2.50 .75
223 Paul Molitor .50 .15
224 Derek Jeter 2.00 .60
225 Barry Bonds 2.00 .60
226 Jim Edmonds .30 .09
227 John Smoltz .50 .15
228 Eric Karros .30 .09
229 Ray Lankford .30 .09
230 Rey Ordonez .30 .09
231 Kenny Lofton .30 .09
232 Alex Rodriguez 1.25 .35
233 Dante Bichette .30 .09
234 Pedro Martinez .75 .23
235 Carlos Delgado .30 .09
236 Rod Beck .30 .09
237 Matt Williams .30 .09
238 Charles Johnson .30 .09
239 Rico Brogna .30 .09
240 Frank Thomas .75 .23
241 Paul O'Neill .50 .15
242 Jaret Wright .30 .09
243 Brant Brown .30 .09
244 Ryan Klesko .30 .09
245 Chuck Finley .30 .09
246 Derek Bell .30 .09
247 Delino DeShields .30 .09
248 Chan Ho Park .30 .09
249 Wade Boggs .50 .15
250 Jay Buhner .30 .09
251 Butch Huskey .30 .09
252 Steve Finley .30 .09
253 Will Clark .75 .23
254 John Valentin .30 .09
255 Bobby Higginson .30 .09
256 Darryl Strawberry .50 .15
257 Randy Johnson .75 .23
258 Al Martin .30 .09
259 Travis Fryman .30 .09
260 Fred McGriff .50 .15
261 Jose Valentin .30 .09
262 Andruw Jones .50 .15
263 Kenny Rogers .30 .09
264 Moises Alou .30 .09
265 Denny Neagle .30 .09
266 Ugueth Urbina .30 .09
267 Derrek Lee .30 .09
268 Ellis Burks .30 .09
269 Mariano Rivera .50 .15
270 Dean Palmer .30 .09
271 Eddie Taubensee .30 .09
272 Brady Anderson .30 .09
273 Brian Giles .30 .09
274 Quinton McCracken .30 .09
275 Henry Rodriguez .30 .09
276 Andres Galarraga .30 .09
277 Jose Canseco .75 .23
278 David Segui .30 .09
279 Bret Saberhagen .30 .09
280 Kevin Brown .50 .15
281 Chuck Knoblauch .30 .09

282 Jeromy Burnitz .30 .09
283 Jay Bell .30 .09
284 Manny Ramirez .30 .09
285 Rick Helling .30 .09
286 Francisco Cordova .30 .09
287 Bob Abreu .30 .09
288 J.T. Snow .30 .09
289 Hideo Nomo .75 .23
290 Brian Jordan .30 .09
291 Javy Lopez .30 .09
292 Travis Lee .30 .09
293 Russell Branyan .30 .09
294 Paul Konerko .30 .09
295 Masato Yoshii RC .60 .18
296 Kris Benson .30 .09
297 Juan Encarnacion .30 .09
298 Eric Milton .30 .09
299 Mike Caruso .30 .09
300 R.Aramboles RC .40 .12
301 Bobby Smith .30 .09
302 Billy Koch .30 .09
303 Richard Hidalgo .30 .09
304 Justin Baughman RC .30 .09
305 Chris Gissell .30 .09
306 Donnie Bridges RC .40 .12
307 Nelson Lara RC .30 .09
308 Randy Wolf RC 1.00 .30
309 Jason LaRue RC .40 .12
310 Jason Gooding RC .30 .09
311 Edgard Clemente .30 .09
312 Andrew Vessel .30 .09
313 Chris Reitsma .30 .09
314 Jesus Sanchez RC .30 .09
315 Buddy Carlyle RC .30 .09
316 Randy Winn .30 .09
317 Luis Rivera RC .30 .09
318 Marcus Thames RC .40 .12
319 A.J. Pierzynski .30 .09
320 Scott Randall .30 .09
321 Damian Sapp .30 .09
322 Ed Yarnall RC .30 .09
323 Luke Allen RC .40 .12
324 J.D. Smart .30 .09
325 Willie Martinez .30 .09
326 Alex Ramirez .30 .09
327 Eric DuBose RC .40 .12
328 Kevin Witt .30 .09
329 Dan McKinley RC .30 .09
330 Cliff Politte .30 .09
331 Vladimir Nunez .30 .09
332 John Halama RC .40 .12
333 Nerio Rodriguez .30 .09
334 Desi Relaford .30 .09
335 Robinson Checo .30 .09
336 John Nicholson .50 .15
337 Tom LaRosa RC .30 .09
338 Kevin Nicholson RC .30 .09
339 Javier Vazquez .30 .09
340 A.J. Zapp .30 .09
341 Tom Evans .30 .09
342 Kerry Robinson .30 .09
343 Gabe Gonzalez RC .30 .09
344 Ralph Milliard .30 .09
345 Enrique Wilson .30 .09
346 Elvin Hernandez .30 .09
347 Mike Lincoln RC .30 .09
348 Cesar King RC .30 .09
349 Cristian Guzman RC 1.25 .35
350 Donzell McDonald .30 .09
351 Jim Parque RC .40 .12
352 Mike Saipe RC .30 .09
353 Carlos Febles RC .40 .12
354 Dernell Stenson RC .40 .12
355 Mark Osborne RC .30 .09
356 Odalis Perez RC .60 .18
357 Jason Dewey RC .30 .09
358 Joe Fontenot .30 .09
359 Jason Grilli RC .30 .09
360 Kevin Haverbusch RC .30 .09
361 Jay Yennaco RC .30 .09
362 Brian Buchanan .30 .09
363 John Barnes .30 .09
364 Chris Fussell .30 .09
365 Kevin Gibbs RC .30 .09
366 Joe Lawrence .30 .09
367 DaRond Stovall .30 .09
368 Brian Fuentes RC .30 .09
369 Jimmy Anderson .30 .09
370 Lariel Gonzalez RC .30 .09
371 Scott Williamson RC .40 .12
372 Milton Bradley .30 .09
373 Jason Halper RC .30 .09
374 Brent Billingsley RC .30 .09
375 Joe DePastino RC .30 .09
376 Jake Westbrook .30 .09
377 Octavio Dotel .30 .09
378 Jason Williams RC .30 .09
379 Julio Ramirez RC .30 .09
380 Seth Greisinger .30 .09
381 Mike Judd RC .30 .09
382 Ben Ford RC .30 .09
383 Tom Bennett RC .30 .09
384 Adam Butler RC .30 .09
385 Wade Miller RC 1.25 .35
386 Kyle Peterson RC .30 .09
387 Tommy Peterman RC .30 .09
388 Onan Masaoka .30 .09
389 Jason Rakers RC .30 .09
390 Rafael Medina .30 .09
391 Luis Lopez RC .30 .09
392 Jeff Yoder .30 .09
393 Vance Wilson RC .30 .09
394 F.Seguignol RC .30 .09
395 Ron Wright .30 .09
396 Ruben Mateo RC .40 .12
397 Steve Lomasney RC .40 .12
398 Damian Jackson .30 .09
399 Mike Jerzembeck RC .30 .09
400 Luis Rivas RC 1.00 .30
401 Kevin Burford RC .30 .09
402 Glenn Davis .30 .09
403 Robert Luce RC .30 .09
404 Cole Liniak .30 .09
405 Matt LeCroy RC .40 .12
406 Jeremy Giambi RC .40 .12
407 Shawn Chacon .30 .09
408 Dewayne Wise RC .30 .09
409 Steve Woodard .30 .09
410 F.Cordero RC .40 .12
411 Damon Minor RC .40 .12
412 Lou Collier .30 .09
413 Justin Towle .30 .09
414 Juan LeBron .30 .09
415 Michael Coleman .30 .09
416 Felix Rodriguez .30 .09
417 Paul Ah Yat RC .30 .09
418 Kevin Barker RC .30 .09
419 Brian Meadows .30 .09
420 Darnell McDonald RC .40 .12
421 Matt Kinney RC .40 .12
422 Mike Vavrek RC .30 .09
423 Courtney Duncan RC .30 .09
424 Kevin Millar RC 1.25 .35
425 Ruben Rivera .30 .09
426 Steve Shoemaker RC .30 .09
427 Dan Reichert RC .40 .12
428 Carlos Lee RC 1.25 .35
429 Rod Barajas .30 .09
430 Pablo Ozuna RC .40 .12
431 Todd Belitz RC .30 .09
432 Sidney Ponson .30 .09
433 Steve Carver RC .30 .09
434 Esteban Yan RC .40 .12
435 Cedrick Bowers .30 .09
436 Marlon Anderson .30 .09
437 Carl Pavano .30 .09
438 Jae Weong Seo RC .60 .18
439 Jose Taveras RC .30 .09
440 Matt Anderson RC .40 .12
441 Darron Ingram RC .30 .09
NNO S.Hasegawa '91 BBM 10.00 3.00
NNO H.Irabu '91 BBM 10.00 3.00
NNO H.Nomo '91 BBM 25.00 7.50

1998 Bowman Golden Anniversary

Randomly inserted in first series packs at a rate of one in 237 and second series packs at a rate of one in 194, this 441-card set is a parallel to the Bowman base set. The set celebrates Bowman's 50th birthday. Each card is highlighted by gold-stamped facsimile autographs (instead of silver foil on the basic cards) and are sequentially numbered to 50.

Nm-Mt Ex-Mt
*STARS: 15X TO 40X BASIC CARDS ..
*ROOKIES: 7.5X TO 15X BASIC CARDS

1998 Bowman International

Inserted one per pack, this 441-card set is a parallel to the Bowman base set. The set allows collectors to see where their favorite players were born and learn the vitals on each of them as translated in the player's home language.

Nm-Mt Ex-Mt
COMPLETE SET (441) 200.00 60.00
COMP. SERIES 1 (221) 120.00 36.00
COMP. SERIES 2 (220) 80.00 24.00
*STARS: 1.25X TO 3X BASIC CARDS .
*ROOKIES: .6X TO 1.5X BASIC CARDS

1998 Bowman 1999 ROY Favorites

Randomly inserted in second series packs at a rate of one in 12, this 10-card insert features color action photography on borderless, double-etched foil cards. The players featured on these cards were among the leading early candidates for the 1999 ROY award.

Nm-Mt Ex-Mt
COMPLETE SET (10) 20.00 6.00
ROY1 Adrian Beltre 1.25 .35
ROY2 Troy Glaus 6.00 1.80
ROY3 Chad Hermansen 1.25 .35
ROY4 Matt Clement 1.25 .35
ROY5 Eric Chavez 2.00 .60
ROY6 Kris Benson 1.25 .35
ROY7 Richie Sexson 1.25 .35
ROY8 Randy Wolf 4.00 1.20
ROY9 Ryan Minor 1.25 .35
ROY10 Alex Gonzalez 1.25 .35

1998 Bowman Certified Blue Autographs

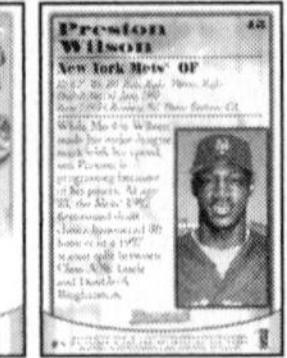

Randomly inserted in first series packs at a rate of one in 149 and second series packs at a rate of one in 122.

Nm-Mt Ex-Mt
*GOLD FOIL: 1.5X TO 4X BLUE AU'S..
SER.1 GOLD FOIL STATED ODDS 1:2976
SER.2 GOLD FOIL STATED ODDS 1:2445
*SILVER FOIL: .75X TO 2X BLUE AU'S
SER.1 SILVER FOIL STATED ODDS 1:992
SER.2 SILVER FOIL STATED ODDS 1:815
1 Adrian Beltre 15.00 4.50
2 Brad Fullmer 10.00 3.00
3 Ricky Ledee 10.00 3.00
4 David Ortiz 25.00 7.50
5 Fernando Tatis 10.00 3.00
6 Kerry Wood 60.00 18.00
7 Mel Rosario 10.00 3.00
8 Cole Liniak 10.00 3.00
9 A.J. Hinch 10.00 3.00
10 Jhensy Sandoval 10.00 3.00
11 Jose Cruz Jr. 15.00 4.50
12 Richard Hidalgo 15.00 4.50
13 Geoff Jenkins 15.00 4.50
14 Carl Pavano 15.00 4.50
15 Richie Sexson 15.00 4.50
16 Tony Womack 10.00 3.00
17 Scott Rolen 25.00 7.50
18 Ryan Minor 10.00 3.00
19 Eli Marrero 10.00 3.00
20 Jason Marquis 10.00 3.00
21 Mike Lowell 20.00 6.00
22 Todd Helton 25.00 7.50
23 Chad Green 10.00 3.00
24 Scott Elarton 10.00 3.00
25 Russell Branyan 10.00 3.00
26 Mike Drumright 10.00 3.00
27 Ben Grieve 10.00 3.00
28 Jacque Jones 15.00 4.50
29 Jared Sandberg 10.00 3.00
30 Grant Roberts 10.00 3.00
31 Mike Stoner 10.00 3.00
32 Brian Rose 10.00 3.00
33 Randy Winn 10.00 3.00
34 Justin Towle 10.00 3.00
35 Anthony Sanders 10.00 3.00
36 Rafael Medina 10.00 3.00
37 Corey Lee 10.00 3.00
38 Mike Kinkade 15.00 4.50
39 Norm Hutchins 10.00 3.00
40 Jason Brester 10.00 3.00
41 Ben Davis 10.00 3.00
42 Nomar Garciaparra 120.00 36.00
43 Jeff Liefer 10.00 3.00
44 Eric Milton 10.00 3.00
45 Preston Wilson 15.00 4.50
46 Miguel Tejada 25.00 7.50
47 Luis Ordaz 10.00 3.00
48 Travis Lee 10.00 3.00
49 Kris Benson 10.00 3.00
50 Jacob Cruz 10.00 3.00
51 Dermal Brown 10.00 3.00
52 Marc Kroon 10.00 3.00
53 Chad Hermansen 10.00 3.00
54 Roy Halladay 25.00 7.50
55 Eric Chavez 25.00 7.50
56 Jason Conti 10.00 3.00
57 Juan Encarnacion 10.00 3.00
58 Paul Wilder 10.00 3.00
59 Aramis Ramirez 15.00 4.50
60 Cliff Politte 10.00 3.00
61 Todd Dunwoody 10.00 3.00
62 Paul Konerko 15.00 4.50
63 Shane Monahan 10.00 3.00
64 Alex Sanchez 10.00 3.00
65 Jeff Abbott 10.00 3.00
66 John Patterson 10.00 3.00
67 Peter Munro 10.00 3.00
68 Jarrod Washburn 15.00 4.50
69 Derrek Lee 15.00 4.50
70 Ramon Hernandez 10.00 3.00

1998 Bowman Minor League MVP's

Randomly inserted in second series packs at a rate of one in 12, this 11-card insert features former Minor League MVP award winners in color action photography.

Nm-Mt Ex-Mt
COMPLETE SET (11) 25.00 7.50
MVP1 Jeff Bagwell 1.50 .45
MVP2 Andres Galarraga 1.00 .30
MVP3 Juan Gonzalez 2.50 .75
MVP4 Tony Gwynn 3.00 .90
MVP5 Vladimir Guerrero 2.50 .75
MVP6 Derek Jeter 6.00 1.80
MVP7 Andruw Jones 1.00 .30
MVP8 Tino Martinez 1.50 .45
MVP9 Manny Ramirez 1.00 .30
MVP10 Gary Sheffield 1.00 .30
MVP11 Jim Thome 2.50 .75

1998 Bowman Scout's Choice

Randomly inserted in first series packs at a rate of one in 12, this borderless 21-card set is an insert featuring leading minor league prospects.

Nm-Mt Ex-Mt
COMPLETE SET (21) 25.00 7.50
SC1 Paul Konerko 2.00 .60
SC2 Richard Hidalgo 2.00 .60
SC3 Mark Kotsay 2.00 .60
SC4 Ben Grieve 2.00 .60
SC5 Chad Hermansen 2.00 .60
SC6 Matt Clement 2.00 .60
SC7 Brad Fullmer 2.00 .60
SC8 Eli Marrero 2.00 .60
SC9 Kerry Wood 5.00 1.50
SC10 Adrian Beltre 2.00 .60
SC11 Ricky Ledee 2.00 .60
SC12 Travis Lee 2.00 .60
SC13 Abraham Nunez 2.00 .60
SC14 Brian Rose 2.00 .60
SC15 Dermal Brown 2.00 .60
SC16 Juan Encarnacion 2.00 .60
SC17 Aramis Ramirez 2.00 .60
SC18 Todd Helton 3.00 .90
SC19 Kris Benson 2.00 .60
SC20 Russell Branyan 2.00 .60
SC21 Mike Stoner 2.00 .60

1999 Bowman Pre-Production

This six-card set was issued to preview the 1999 Bowman set. The cards are numbered with a "PP" prefix and feature a mixture of veterans and young players. The set was distributed to dealers and hobby media in complete set form within a clear cello wrap several months prior to the shipping of 1999 Bowman series one.

Nm-Mt Ex-Mt
COMPLETE SET (6) 5.00 1.50
PP1 Andres Galarraga 1.50 .45
PP2 Raul Mondesi 1.00 .30
PP3 Vinny Castilla 1.00 .30
PP4 Corey Koskie UER 1.00 .30
Birthyear listed as 1967
PP5 Octavio Dotel 1.00 .30
PP6 Dernell Stenson .50 .15

1999 Bowman

The 1999 Bowman set was issued in two series and was distributed in 10 card packs with a suggested retail price of $3.00. The 440-card set featured the newest faces and potential talent that would carry Major League Baseball into the next millennium. This set features 300 top prospects and and 140 veterans. Prospect cards are designated with a silver and blue design while the veteran cards are shown with a silver and red design. Prospects making their debut on a Bowman card each featured a "Bowman Rookie Card" stamp on front. Notable Rookie Cards include Pat Burrell, Sean Burroughs, Adam Dunn, Rafael Furcal, Tim Hudson, Nick Johnson, Austin Kearns, Corey Patterson, Wily Mo Pena, Adam Piatt and Alfonso Soriano.

Nm-Mt Ex-Mt
COMPLETE SET (440) 100.00 30.00
COMP. SERIES 1 (220) 40.00 12.00
COMP. SERIES 2 (220) 60.00 18.00
1 Ben Grieve .30 .09
2 Kerry Wood .75 .23
3 Ruben Rivera .30 .09
4 Sandy Alomar Jr. .30 .09
5 Cal Ripken 2.50 .75
6 Mark McGwire 2.00 .60
7 Vladimir Guerrero .75 .23
8 Moises Alou .30 .09
9 Jim Edmonds .30 .09
10 Greg Maddux 1.25 .35
11 Gary Sheffield .30 .09
12 John Valentin .30 .09
13 Chuck Knoblauch .30 .09
14 Tony Clark .30 .09
15 Rusty Greer .30 .09
16 Al Leiter .30 .09
17 Travis Lee .30 .09
18 Jose Cruz Jr. .30 .09
19 Pedro Martinez .75 .23
20 Paul O'Neill .50 .15
21 Todd Walker .30 .09
22 Vinny Castilla .30 .09
23 Barry Larkin .75 .23
24 Curt Schilling .50 .15
25 Jason Kendall .30 .09
26 Scott Erickson .30 .09
27 Andres Galarraga .30 .09
28 Jeff Shaw .30 .09
29 John Olerud .30 .09
30 Orlando Hernandez .30 .09
31 Larry Walker .50 .15
32 Andruw Jones .30 .09
33 Jeff Cirillo .30 .09
34 Barry Bonds 2.00 .60
35 Manny Ramirez .30 .09
36 Mark Kotsay .30 .09
37 Ivan Rodriguez .75 .23
38 Jeff King .30 .09
39 Brian Hunter .30 .09
40 Ray Durham .30 .09
41 Bernie Williams .50 .15
42 Darin Erstad .30 .09
43 Chipper Jones .75 .23
44 Pat Hentgen .30 .09
45 Eric Young .30 .09
46 Jaret Wright .30 .09
47 Juan Guzman .30 .09
48 Jorge Posada .50 .15
49 Bobby Higginson .30 .09
50 Jose Guillen .30 .09
51 Trevor Hoffman .30 .09
52 Ken Griffey Jr. 1.25 .35
53 David Justice .30 .09
54 Matt Williams .30 .09
55 Eric Karros .30 .09
56 Derek Bell .30 .09
57 Ray Lankford .30 .09
58 Mariano Rivera .50 .15
59 Brett Tomko .30 .09
60 Mike Mussina .75 .23
61 Kenny Lofton .30 .09
62 Chuck Finley .30 .09
63 Alex Gonzalez .30 .09
64 Mark Grace .50 .15
65 Raul Mondesi .30 .09
66 David Cone .30 .09
67 Brad Fullmer .30 .09
68 Andy Benes .30 .09
69 John Smoltz .50 .15
70 Shane Reynolds .30 .09
71 Bruce Chen .30 .09
72 Adam Kennedy .30 .09
73 Jack Cust .30 .09
74 Matt Clement .30 .09
75 Derrick Gibson .30 .09
76 Darnell McDonald .30 .09
77 Adam Everett RC .40 .12
78 Ricardo Aramboles .30 .09
79 Mark Quinn RC .40 .12
80 Jason Rakers .30 .09
81 Seth Etherton RC .40 .12
82 Jeff Urban RC .40 .12
83 Manny Aybar .30 .09
84 Mike Nannini RC .40 .12
85 Onan Masaoka .30 .09
86 Rod Barajas .30 .09
87 Mike Frank .30 .09
88 Scott Randall .30 .09
89 Justin Bowles RC .30 .09
90 Chris Haas .30 .09
91 Arturo McDowell RC .40 .12
92 Matt Belisle RC .40 .45
93 Scott Elarton .30 .09
94 Vernon Wells .30 .09
95 Pat Cline .30 .09
96 Ryan Anderson .30 .09
97 Kevin Barker .30 .09
98 Ruben Mateo .30 .09
99 Robert Fick .30 .09
100 Corey Koskie .30 .09
101 Ricky Ledee .30 .09
102 Rick Elder RC .40 .12
103 Jack Cressend RC .30 .09
104 Joe Lawrence .30 .09
105 Mike Lincoln .30 .09
106 Kit Pellow RC .30 .09
107 Matt Burch RC .40 .12
108 Cole Liniak .30 .09
109 Jason Dewey .30 .09
110 Cesar King .30 .09
111 Julio Ramirez .30 .09
112 Jake Westbrook .30 .09
113 Eric Valent RC .40 .12
114 Roosevelt Brown RC .40 .12
115 Choo Freeman RC .40 .12
116 Juan Melo .30 .09
117 Jason Grilli .30 .09
118 Jared Sandberg .30 .09
119 Glenn Davis .30 .09
120 David Riske RC .30 .09
121 Jacque Jones .30 .09
122 Corey Lee .30 .09
123 Michael Barrett .30 .09
124 Lariel Gonzalez .30 .09
125 Mitch Meluskey .30 .09
126 Freddy Adrian Garcia .30 .09
127 Tony Torcato RC .40 .12
128 Jeff Liefer .30 .09
129 Ntema Ndungidi .30 .09
130 Andy Brown RC .40 .12
131 Ryan Mills RC .40 .12
132 Andy Abad RC .30 .09
133 Carlos Febles .30 .09
134 Jason Tyner RC .40 .12
135 Mark Osborne .30 .09
136 Phil Norton RC .30 .09
137 Nathan Haynes .30 .09
138 Roy Halladay .30 .09
139 Juan Encarnacion .30 .09
140 Brad Penny .30 .09
141 Grant Roberts .30 .09
142 Aramis Ramirez .30 .09
143 Cristian Guzman .30 .09
144 Mamon Tucker RC .40 .12
145 Ryan Bradley .30 .09
146 Brian Simmons .30 .09
147 Dan Reichert .30 .09
148 Russ Branyan .30 .09
149 Victor Valencia RC .30 .09
150 Scott Schoeneweis .30 .09
151 Sean Spencer RC .30 .09
152 Odalis Perez .30 .09
153 Joe Fontenot .30 .09
154 Milton Bradley .30 1.30
155 Josh McKinley RC .40 .12
156 Terrence Long .30 .09
157 Danny Klassen .30 .09
158 Paul Hoover RC .40 .12
159 Ron Belliard .30 .09
160 Armando Rios .30 .09
161 Ramon Hernandez .30 .09
162 Jason Conti .30 .09
163 Chad Hermansen .30 .09
164 Jason Standridge .30 .09
165 Jason Dellaero .30 .09
166 John Curtice .30 .09
167 Clayton Andrews RC .40 .12
168 Jeremy Giambi .30 .09
169 Alex Ramirez .30 .09
170 Gabe Molina RC .30 .09
171 M.Encarnacion RC .30 .09
172 Mike Zywica RC .30 .09
173 Chip Ambres RC .40 .12
174 Trot Nixon .50 .15
175 Pat Burrell RC 4.00 1.20
176 Jeff Yoder .30 .09
177 Chris Jones RC .40 .12
178 Kevin Witt .30 .09
179 Keith Luuloa RC .30 .09
180 Billy Koch .30 .09
181 Damaso Marte RC .30 .09
182 Ryan Glynn RC .30 .09
183 Calvin Pickering .30 .09
184 Michael Cuddyer .30 .09
185 Nick Johnson RC 2.00 .60
186 D.Mientkiewicz RC 1.25 .35
187 Nate Cornejo RC .60 .18
188 Octavio Dotel .30 .09
189 Wes Helms .30 .09
190 Nelson Lara .30 .09
191 Chuck Abbott RC .30 .09
192 Tony Armas Jr. .30 .09
193 Gil Meche .30 .09
194 Ben Petrick .30 .09
195 Chris George RC .40 .12
196 Scott Hunter RC .30 .09
197 Ryan Brannan .30 .09
198 Amaury Garcia RC .40 .12
199 Chris Gissell .30 .09

200 Austin Kearns RC 5.00 1.50
201 Alex Gonzalez .30 .09
202 Wade Miller .30 .09
203 Scott Williamson .30 .09
204 Chris Enochs .30 .09
205 Fernando Seguignol .30 .09
206 Marlon Anderson .30 .09
207 Todd Sears RC .40 .12
208 Nate Bump RC .30 .09
209 J.M. Gold RC .40 .12
210 Matt LeCroy .30 .09
211 Alex Hernandez .30 .09
212 Luis Rivera .30 .09
213 Troy Cameron .30 .09
214 Alex Escobar RC .40 .12
215 Jason LaRue .30 .09
216 Kyle Peterson .30 .09
217 Brent Butler .30 .09
218 Dernell Stenson .30 .09
219 Adrian Beltre .30 .09
220 Daryle Ward .30 .09
221 Jim Thome .75 .23
222 Cliff Floyd .30 .09
223 Rickey Henderson .75 .23
224 Garret Anderson .30 .09
225 Ken Caminiti .30 .09
226 Bret Boone .30 .09
227 Jeromy Burnitz .30 .09
228 Steve Finley .30 .09
229 Miguel Tejada .30 .09
230 Greg Vaughn .30 .09
231 Jose Offerman .30 .09
232 Andy Ashby .30 .09
233 Albert Belle .30 .09
234 Fernando Tatis .30 .09
235 Todd Helton .50 .15
236 Sean Casey .30 .09
237 Brian Giles .30 .09
238 Andy Pettitte .50 .15
239 Fred McGriff .50 .15
240 Roberto Alomar .75 .23
241 Edgar Martinez .50 .15
242 Lee Stevens .30 .09
243 Shawn Green .30 .09
244 Ryan Klesko .30 .09
245 Sammy Sosa 1.25 .35
246 Todd Hundley .30 .09
247 Shannon Stewart .30 .09
248 Randy Johnson .75 .23
249 Rondell White .30 .09
250 Mike Piazza 1.25 .35
251 Craig Biggio .50 .15
252 David Wells .30 .09
253 Brian Jordan .30 .09
254 Edgar Renteria .30 .09
255 Bartolo Colon .30 .09
256 Frank Thomas .75 .23
257 Will Clark .75 .23
258 Dean Palmer .30 .09
259 Dmitri Young .30 .09
260 Scott Rolen .50 .15
261 Jeff Kent .30 .09
262 Dante Bichette .30 .09
263 Nomar Garciaparra 1.25 .35
264 Tony Gwynn 1.00 .30
265 Alex Rodriguez 1.25 .35
266 Jose Canseco .75 .23
267 Jason Giambi .75 .23
268 Jeff Bagwell .50 .15
269 Carlos Delgado .30 .09
270 Tom Glavine .50 .15
271 Eric Davis .30 .09
272 Edgardo Alfonzo .30 .09
273 Tim Salmon .50 .15
274 Johnny Damon .30 .09
275 Rafael Palmeiro .50 .15
276 Denny Neagle .30 .09
277 Neifi Perez .30 .09
278 Roger Clemens 1.50 .45
279 Brant Brown .30 .09
280 Kevin Brown .50 .15
281 Jay Bell .30 .09
282 Jay Buhner .30 .09
283 Matt Lawton .30 .09
284 Robin Ventura .30 .09
285 Juan Gonzalez .75 .23
286 Mo Vaughn .30 .09
287 Kevin Millwood .30 .09
288 Tino Martinez .50 .15
289 Justin Thompson .30 .09
290 Derek Jeter 2.00 .60
291 Ben Davis .30 .09
292 Mike Lowell .30 .09
293 Calvin Murray .30 .09
294 Micah Bowie RC .30 .09
295 Lance Berkman .30 .09
296 Jason Marquis .30 .09
297 Chad Green .30 .09
298 Dee Brown .30 .09
299 Jerry Hairston Jr. .30 .09
300 Gabe Kapler .30 .09
301 Brent Stentz RC .40 .12
302 Scott Mullen RC .30 .09
303 Brandon Reed .30 .09
304 Shea Hillenbrand RC 2.00 .60
305 J.D. Closser RC .40 .12
306 Gary Matthews Jr. .30 .09
307 Toby Hall RC .60 .18
308 Jason Phillips RC .30 .09
309 Jose Macias RC .30 .09
310 Jung Bong RC .40 .12
311 Ramon Soler RC .40 .12
312 Kelly Dransfeldt RC .30 .09
313 Carl. E. Hernandez RC .40 .12
314 Kevin Haverbusch .30 .09
315 Aaron Myette RC .40 .12
316 Chad Harville RC .30 .09
317 Kyle Farnsworth RC 1.00 .30
318 Gookie Dawkins RC .40 .12
319 Willie Martinez .30 .09
320 Carlos Lee .30 .09
321 Carlos Pena RC 1.00 .30
322 Peter Bergeron RC .40 .12
323 A.J. Burnett RC 1.00 .30
324 Bucky Jacobsen RC .40 .12
325 Mo Bruce RC .30 .09
326 Reggie Taylor .30 .09
327 Jackie Rexrode .30 .09
328 Alvin Morrow RC .30 .09
329 Carlos Beltran .30 .09
330 Eric Chavez .30 .09
331 John Patterson .30 .09
332 Jayson Werth .30 .09
333 Richie Sexson .30 .09
334 Randy Wolf .30 .09
335 Eli Marrero .30 .09
336 Paul LoDuca .30 .09
337 J.D Smart .30 .09
338 Ryan Minor .30 .09
339 Kris Benson .30 .09
340 George Lombard .30 .09
341 Troy Glaus .50 .15
342 Eddie Yarnall .30 .09
343 Kip Wells RC .60 .18
344 C.C. Sabathia RC 1.00 .30
345 Sean Burroughs RC 3.00 .90
346 Felipe Lopez RC .40 .12
347 Ryan Rupe RC .40 .12
348 Orber Moreno RC .30 .09
349 Rafael Roque RC .30 .09
350 Alfonso Soriano RC 8.00 2.40
351 Pablo Ozuna .30 .09
352 Corey Patterson RC 4.00 1.20
353 Braden Looper .30 .09
354 Robbie Bell .30 .09
355 Mark Mulder RC 4.00 1.20
356 Angel Pena .30 .09
357 Kevin McGlinchy .30 .09
358 M.Restovich RC 1.25 .35
359 Eric DuBose .30 .09
360 Geoff Jenkins .30 .09
361 Mark Harriger RC .30 .09
362 Junior Herndon RC .40 .12
363 Tim Raines Jr. RC .40 .12
364 Rafael Furcal RC 2.00 .60
365 Marcus Giles RC 2.50 .75
366 Ted Lilly .30 .09
367 Jorge Toca RC .40 .12
368 David Kelton RC .60 .18
369 Adam Dunn RC 6.00 1.80
370 Guillermo Mota RC .30 .09
371 Brett Laxton RC .30 .09
372 Travis Harper RC .40 .12
373 Tom Davey RC .30 .09
374 Darren Blakely RC .30 .09
375 Tim Hudson RC 4.00 1.20
376 Jason Romano .30 .09
377 Dan Reichert .30 .09
378 Julio Lugo RC .40 .12
379 Jose Garcia RC .30 .09
380 Erubiel Durazo RC 1.25 .35
381 Jose Jimenez .30 .09
382 Chris Fussell .30 .09
383 Steve Lomasney .30 .09
384 Juan Pena RC .40 .12
385 Allen Levrault RC .40 .12
386 Juan Rivera RC .60 .18
387 Steve Colyer RC .40 .12
388 Joe Nathan RC .40 .12
389 Ron Walker RC .30 .09
390 Nick Bierbrodt .30 .09
391 Luke Prokopec RC .40 .12
392 Dave Roberts RC .60 .18
393 Mike Darr .30 .09
394 Abraham Nunez RC 1.00 .30
395 G.Chiaramonte RC .30 .09
396 J.Van Buren RC .40 .12
397 Mike Kusiewicz .30 .09
398 Matt Wise RC .30 .09
399 Joe McEwing RC .40 .12
400 Matt Holliday RC .40 .12
401 Willi Mo Pena RC 1.25 .35
402 Ruben Quevedo RC .40 .12
403 Rob Ryan RC .30 .09
404 Freddy Garcia RC 1.00 .30
405 Kevin Eberwein RC .40 .12
406 Jesus Colome RC .30 .09
407 Chris Singleton .30 .09
408 Bubba Crosby RC 1.00 .30
409 Jesus Cordero RC .40 .12
410 Donny Leon .30 .09
411 G.Tomlinson RC .40 .12
412 Jeff Winchester RC .40 .12
413 Adam Piatt RC .40 .12
414 Robert Stratton .30 .09
415 T.J. Tucker .30 .09
416 Ryan Langerhans RC .40 .12
417 A.Shumaker RC .30 .09
418 Matt Miller RC .30 .09
419 Doug Clark RC .30 .09
420 Kory DeHaan RC .30 .09
421 David Eckstein RC 1.00 .30
422 Brian Cooper RC .30 .09
423 Brady Clark RC .30 .09
424 Chris Magruder RC .40 .12
425 Bobby Seay RC .40 .12
426 Aubrey Huff RC 2.50 .75
427 Mike Jerzembeck .30 .09
428 Matt Blank RC .40 .12
429 Benny Agbayani RC .40 .12
430 Kevin Beirne RC .40 .12
431 Josh Hamilton RC 1.00 .30
432 Josh Girdley RC .40 .12
433 Kyle Snyder RC .40 .12
434 Mike Paradis RC .40 .12
435 Jason Jennings RC .60 .18
436 David Walling RC .40 .12
437 Omar Ortiz RC .40 .12
438 Jay Gehrke RC .40 .12
439 Casey Burns RC .40 .12
440 Carl Crawford RC 2.00 .60

1999 Bowman Gold

Randomly inserted in first series packs at a rate of one in 111 and second series packs at a rate of one in 59, this 440-card set is a parallel to the Bowman base set. The set features facsimile autographs printed in gold foil with gold border designs. Each card is serial numbered to 99 on the back.

Nm-Mt Ex-Mt
*STARS: 10X TO 25X BASIC CARDS ..
*ROOKIES: 4X TO 10X BASIC CARDS

1999 Bowman International

Inserted one per pack, this 440-card set is a parallel to the Bowman base set. Card fronts contain each player's nationality with a background photograph of a landmark native to his homeland. Card backs contain vital information which are translated into the player's home language giving the collector insight into the player's background. Card fronts are printed on a distinctive foil board.

Nm-Mt Ex-Mt
COMPLETE SET (440) 200.00 60.00
COMP.SERIES 1 (220) 80.00 24.00
COMP.SERIES 2 (220) 120.00 36.00
*STARS: 1X TO 2.5X BASIC CARDS ...
*ROOKIES: .6X TO 1.5X BASIC CARDS

1999 Bowman Autographs

This set contains a selection of top young prospects, all of whom participated by signing their cards in blue ink. Card rarity is differentiated by either a blue, silver or gold foil Topps Certified Autograph Issue Stamp. The insert rates for Blue are at a rate of one in 162; Silver one in 485 and Gold one in 1,194.

Nm-Mt Ex-Mt
BA1 Ruben Mateo B 10.00 3.00
BA2 Troy Glaus G 40.00 12.00
BA3 Ben Davis G 15.00 4.50
BA4 Jayson Werth B 10.00 3.00
BA5 Jerry Hairston Jr. S 10.00 1.50
BA6 Darnell McDonald B 10.00 3.00
BA7 Calvin Pickering S 15.00 4.50
BA8 Ryan Minor S 15.00 4.50
BA9 Alex Escobar B 15.00 4.50
BA10 Grant Roberts B 10.00 3.00
BA11 Carlos Guillen B 10.00 3.00
BA12 Ryan Anderson S 15.00 4.50
BA13 Gil Meche S 40.00 12.00
BA14 Russell Branyan S 15.00 4.50
BA15 Alex Ramirez S 15.00 4.50
BA16 Jason Rakers S 15.00 4.50
BA17 Eddie Yarnall B 15.00 4.50
BA18 Freddy Garcia B 20.00 6.00
BA19 Jason Conti B 10.00 3.00
BA20 Corey Koskie B 15.00 4.50
BA21 Roosevelt Brown B 15.00 4.50
BA22 Willie Martinez B 10.00 3.00
BA23 Mike Jerzembeck B 10.00 3.00
BA24 Lariel Gonzalez B 10.00 3.00
BA25 F.Seguignol B 10.00 3.00
BA26 Robert Fick S 25.00 7.50
BA27 J.D. Smart B 10.00 3.00
BA28 Ryan Mills B 15.00 4.50
BA29 Chad Hermansen G 15.00 4.50
BA30 Jason Grilli B 10.00 3.00
BA31 Michael Cuddyer B 10.00 3.00
BA32 Jacque Jones S 25.00 7.50
BA33 Reggie Taylor B 10.00 3.00
BA34 Richie Sexson G 25.00 7.50
BA35 Michael Barrett B 10.00 3.00
BA36 Paul LoDuca B 15.00 4.50
BA37 Adrian Beltre G 25.00 7.50
BA38 Peter Bergeron B 15.00 4.50
BA39 Joe Fontenot B 10.00 3.00
BA40 Randy Wolf B 15.00 4.50
BA41 Nick Johnson B 40.00 12.00
BA42 Ryan Bradley B 10.00 3.00
BA43 Mike Lowell S 25.00 7.50
BA44 Ricky Ledee G 10.00 2.00
BA45 Mike Lincoln S 15.00 4.50
BA46 Jeremy Giambi B 10.00 3.00
BA47 Dermal Brown S 15.00 4.50
BA48 Derrick Gibson B 10.00 3.00
BA49 Scott Randall B 10.00 3.00
BA50 Ben Petrick S 15.00 4.50
BA51 Jason LaRue B 10.00 3.00
BA52 Cole Liniak B 10.00 3.00
BA53 John Curtice B 10.00 3.00
BA54 Jackie Rexrode B 10.00 3.00
BA55 John Patterson B 10.00 3.00
BA56 Brad Penny S 25.00 7.50
BA57 Jared Sandberg B 10.00 3.00
BA58 Kerry Wood G 40.00 12.00
BA59 Eli Marrero S 15.00 4.50
BA60 Jason Marquis B 10.00 3.00
BA61 George Lombard S 15.00 4.50
BA62 Bruce Chen S 15.00 4.50
BA63 Kevin Witt S 15.00 4.50
BA64 Vernon Wells B 20.00 6.00
BA65 Billy Koch B 15.00 4.50
BA66 Roy Halladay G 40.00 12.00
BA67 Nathan Haynes B 15.00 4.50
BA68 Ben Grieve G 15.00 4.50
BA69 Eric Chavez G 25.00 7.50
BA70 Lance Berkman S 25.00 7.50

1999 Bowman 2000 ROY Favorites

Randomly inserted in second series packs at a rate of one in twelve, this 10-card insert set features borderless, double-etched foil cards and feature players that had serious potential to win the 2000 Rookie of the Year award.

Nm-Mt Ex-Mt
COMPLETE SET (10) 10.00 3.00
ROY1 Ryan Anderson .50 .15
ROY2 Pat Burrell 2.00 .60
ROY3 A.J. Burnett .75 .23
ROY4 Ruben Mateo .50 .15
ROY5 Alex Escobar .50 .15
ROY6 Pablo Ozuna .50 .15
ROY7 Mark Mulder 2.50 .75
ROY8 Corey Patterson 2.50 .75
ROY9 George Lombard .50 .15
ROY10 Nick Johnson 1.25 .35

1999 Bowman Early Risers

Randomly inserted in second series packs at a rate of one in twelve, this 11-card insert set features current superstars who have already won a ROY award and who continue to prove their worth on the diamond.

Nm-Mt Ex-Mt
COMPLETE SET (11) 25.00 7.50
ER1 Mike Piazza 2.50 .75
ER2 Cal Ripken 5.00 1.50
ER3 Jeff Bagwell 1.00 .30
ER4 Ben Grieve .60 .18
ER5 Kerry Wood 1.50 .45
ER6 Mark McGwire 4.00 1.20
ER7 Nomar Garciaparra 2.50 .75
ER8 Derek Jeter 4.00 1.20
ER9 Scott Rolen 1.00 .30
ER10 Jose Canseco 1.50 .45
ER11 Raul Mondesi .60 .18

1999 Bowman Late Bloomers

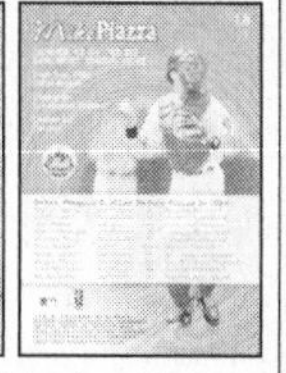

Randomly inserted in first series packs at a rate of one in twelve, this 10-card insert set features late round picks from previous drafts. Players featured include Mike Piazza and Jim Thome.

Nm-Mt Ex-Mt
COMPLETE SET (10) 8.00 2.40
LB1 Mike Piazza 2.50 .75
LB2 Jim Thome 1.50 .45
LB3 Larry Walker 1.00 .30
LB4 Vinny Castilla .60 .18
LB5 Andy Pettitte 1.00 .30
LB6 Jim Edmonds .60 .18
LB7 Kenny Lofton .60 .18
LB8 John Smoltz 1.00 .30
LB9 Mark Grace 1.00 .30
LB10 Trevor Hoffman .60 .18

1999 Bowman Scout's Choice

Randomly inserted in first series packs at a rate of one in twelve, this 21-card insert set features a selection of gifted prospects.

Nm-Mt Ex-Mt
COMPLETE SET (21) 20.00 6.00
SC1 Ruben Mateo 1.00 .30
SC2 Ryan Anderson 1.00 .30
SC3 Pat Burrell 3.00 .90
SC4 Troy Glaus 1.50 .45
SC5 Eric Chavez 1.00 .30
SC6 Adrian Beltre 1.00 .30
SC7 Bruce Chen 1.00 .30
SC8 Carlos Beltran 1.00 .30
SC9 Alex Gonzalez 1.00 .30
SC10 Carlos Lee 1.00 .30
SC11 George Lombard 1.00 .30
SC12 Matt Clement 1.00 .30
SC13 Calvin Pickering 1.00 .30
SC14 Marlon Anderson 1.00 .30
SC15 Chad Hermansen 1.00 .30
SC16 Russell Branyan 1.00 .30
SC17 Jeremy Giambi 1.00 .30
SC18 Ricky Ledee 1.00 .30
SC19 John Patterson 1.00 .30
SC20 Roy Halladay 1.00 .30
SC21 Michael Barrett 1.00 .30

2000 Bowman Pre-Production

This three card set of sample cards was distributed within a sealed, clear, cello poly-wrap to dealers and hobby media several weeks prior to the national release of 2000 Bowman.

Nm-Mt Ex-Mt
COMPLETE SET (3) 4.00 1.20
PP1 Chipper Jones 2.00 .60
PP2 Adam Piatt 1.00 .30
PP3 Josh Hamilton 1.00 .30

2000 Bowman

The 2000 Bowman product was released in May, 2000 as a 440-card set. The set features 140 veteran players and 300 rookies and prospects. Each pack contained 10 cards and carried a suggested retail price of $3.00. Rookie Cards include Rick Asadoorian, Bobby Bradley, Kevin Mench, Nick Neugebauer, Ben Sheets and Barry Zito.

Nm-Mt Ex-Mt
COMPLETE SET (440) 80.00 24.00
1 Vladimir Guerrero .75 .23
2 Chipper Jones .75 .23
3 Todd Walker .30 .09
4 Barry Larkin .75 .23
5 Bernie Williams .50 .15
6 Todd Helton .50 .15
7 Jermaine Dye .30 .09
8 Brian Giles .30 .09
9 Freddy Garcia .30 .09
10 Greg Vaughn .30 .09
11 Alex Gonzalez .30 .09
12 Luis Gonzalez .30 .09
13 Ron Belliard .30 .09
14 Ben Grieve .30 .09
15 Carlos Delgado .30 .09
16 Brian Jordan .30 .09
17 Fernando Tatis .30 .09
18 Ryan Rupe .30 .09
19 Miguel Tejada .30 .09
20 Mark Grace .50 .15
21 Kenny Lofton .30 .09
22 Eric Karros .30 .09
23 Cliff Floyd .30 .09
24 John Halama .30 .09
25 Cristian Guzman .30 .09
26 Scott Williamson .30 .09
27 Mike Lieberthal .30 .09
28 Tim Hudson .50 .15
29 Warren Morris .30 .09
30 Pedro Martinez .75 .23
31 John Smoltz .50 .15
32 Ray Durham .30 .09
33 Chad Allen .30 .09
34 Tony Clark .30 .09
35 Tino Martinez .50 .15
36 J.T. Snow .30 .09
37 Kevin Brown .30 .09
38 Bartolo Colon .30 .09
39 Rey Ordonez .30 .09
40 Jeff Bagwell .50 .15
41 Ivan Rodriguez .75 .23
42 Eric Chavez .30 .09
43 Eric Milton .30 .09
44 Jose Canseco .75 .23
45 Shawn Green .30 .09
46 Rich Aurilia .30 .09
47 Roberto Alomar .75 .23
48 Brian Daubach .30 .09
49 Magglio Ordonez .30 .09
50 Derek Jeter 2.00 .60
51 Kris Benson .30 .09
52 Albert Belle .30 .09
53 Rondell White .30 .09
54 Justin Thompson .30 .09
55 Nomar Garciaparra 1.25 .35
56 Chuck Finley .30 .09
57 Omar Vizquel .30 .09
58 Luis Castillo .30 .09
59 Richard Hidalgo .30 .09
60 Barry Bonds 2.00 .60
61 Craig Biggio .50 .15
62 Doug Glanville .30 .09
63 Gabe Kapler .30 .09
64 Johnny Damon .30 .09
65 Pokey Reese .30 .09
66 Andy Pettitte .50 .15
67 B.J. Surhoff .30 .09
68 Richie Sexson .30 .09
69 Javy Lopez .30 .09
70 Raul Mondesi .30 .09
71 Darin Erstad .30 .09
72 Kevin Millwood .30 .09
73 Ricky Ledee .30 .09
74 John Olerud .30 .09
75 Sean Casey .30 .09
76 Carlos Febles .30 .09
77 Paul O'Neill .50 .15
78 Bob Abreu .30 .09
79 Neifi Perez .30 .09
80 Tony Gwynn 1.00 .30
81 Russ Ortiz .30 .09
82 Matt Williams .30 .09
83 Chris Carpenter .30 .09
84 Roger Cedeno .30 .09
85 Tim Salmon .50 .15
86 Billy Koch .30 .09
87 Jeromy Burnitz .30 .09
88 Edgardo Alfonzo .30 .09
89 Jay Bell .30 .09
90 Manny Ramirez .30 .09
91 Frank Thomas .75 .23
92 Mike Mussina .75 .23
93 J.D. Drew .30 .09
94 Adrian Beltre .30 .09
95 Alex Rodriguez 1.25 .35
96 Larry Walker .50 .15
97 Juan Encarnacion .30 .09
98 Mike Sweeney .30 .09
99 Rusty Greer .30 .09
100 Randy Johnson .75 .23
101 Jose Vidro .30 .09
102 Preston Wilson .30 .09
103 Greg Maddux 1.25 .35
104 Jason Giambi .75 .23
105 Cal Ripken 2.50 .75
106 Carlos Beltran .30 .09
107 Vinny Castilla .30 .09
108 Mariano Rivera .50 .15
109 Mo Vaughn .30 .09
110 Rafael Palmeiro .50 .15
111 Shannon Stewart .30 .09
112 Mike Hampton .30 .09
113 Joe Nathan .30 .09
114 Ben Davis .30 .09
115 Andruw Jones .30 .09
116 Robin Ventura .30 .09
117 Damion Easley .30 .09
118 Jeff Cirillo .30 .09
119 Kerry Wood .75 .23
120 Scott Rolen .50 .15
121 Sammy Sosa 1.25 .35
122 Ken Griffey Jr. 1.25 .35
123 Shane Reynolds .30 .09
124 Troy Glaus .50 .15
125 Tom Glavine .50 .15
126 Michael Barrett .30 .09

Card	Nm-Mt	Ex-Mt
127 Al Leiter	.30	.09
128 Jason Kendall	.30	.09
129 Roger Clemens	1.50	.45
130 Juan Gonzalez	.75	.23
131 Corey Koskie	.30	.09
132 Curt Schilling	.50	.15
133 Mike Piazza	1.25	.35
134 Gary Sheffield	.30	.09
135 Jim Thome	.75	.23
136 Orlando Hernandez	.30	.09
137 Ray Lankford	.30	.09
138 Geoff Jenkins	.30	.09
139 Jose Lima	.30	.09
140 Mark McGwire	2.00	.60
141 Adam Piatt	.30	.09
142 Pat Manning RC	.40	.12
143 Marcos Castillo RC	.40	.12
144 Lesli Brea RC	.40	.12
145 Humberto Cota RC	.40	.12
146 Ben Petrick	.30	.09
147 Kip Wells	.30	.09
148 Wily Pena	.30	.09
149 Chris Wakeland RC	.30	.09
150 Brad Baker RC	.40	.12
151 Robbie Morrison RC	.40	.12
152 Reggie Taylor	.30	.09
153 Matt Ginter RC	.40	.12
154 Peter Bergeron	.30	.09
155 Roosevelt Brown	.30	.09
156 Matt Cepicky RC	.40	.12
157 Ramon Castro	.30	.09
158 Brad Baisley RC	.40	.12
159 Jeff Goldbach RC	.40	.12
160 Mitch Meluskey	.30	.09
161 Chad Harville	.30	.09
162 Brian Cooper	.30	.09
163 Marcus Giles	.30	.09
164 Jim Morris	2.00	.60
165 Geoff Goetz	.30	.09
166 Bobby Bradley RC	.40	.12
167 Rob Bell	.30	.09
168 Joe Crede	.30	.09
169 Michael Restovich	.30	.09
170 Quincy Foster RC	.30	.09
171 Enrique Cruz RC	.40	.12
172 Mark Quinn	.30	.09
173 Nick Johnson	.30	.09
174 Jeff Liefer	.30	.09
175 Kevin Mench RC	.60	.18
176 Steve Lomasney	.30	.09
177 Jayson Werth	.30	.09
178 Tim Drew	.30	.09
179 Chip Ambres	.30	.09
180 Ryan Anderson	.30	.09
181 Matt Blank	.30	.09
182 G.Chiaramonte	.30	.09
183 Corey Myers RC	.40	.12
184 Jeff Yoder	.30	.09
185 Craig Dingman RC	.30	.09
186 Jon Hamilton RC	.30	.09
187 Toby Hall	.30	.09
188 Russell Branyan	.30	.09
189 Brian Falkenborg RC	.40	.12
190 Aaron Harang RC	.40	.12
191 Juan Pena	.30	.09
192 Travis Thompson RC	.30	.09
193 Alfonso Soriano	.75	.23
194 Alejandro Diaz RC	.40	.12
195 Carlos Pena	.30	.09
196 Kevin Nicholson	.30	.09
197 Mo Bruce	.30	.09
198 C.C. Sabathia	.30	.09
199 Carl Crawford	.30	.09
200 Rafael Furcal	.30	.09
201 Andrew Beinbrink RC	.30	.09
202 Jimmy Osting	.30	.09
203 Aaron McNeal RC	.40	.12
204 Brett Laxton	.30	.09
205 Chris George	.30	.09
206 Felipe Lopez	.30	.09
207 Ben Sheets RC	1.25	.35
208 Mike Meyers RC	.40	.12
209 Jason Conti	.30	.09
210 Milton Bradley	.30	.09
211 Chris Mears RC	.40	.12
212 Carlos Hernandez RC	.60	.18
213 Jason Romano	.30	.09
214 Geoffrey Tomlinson	.30	.09
215 Jimmy Rollins	.30	.09
216 Pablo Ozuna	.30	.09
217 Steve Cox	.30	.09
218 Terrence Long	.30	.09
219 Jeff DaVanon RC	.40	.12
220 Rick Ankiel	.30	.09
221 Jason Standridge	.30	.09
222 Tony Armas Jr.	.30	.09
223 Jason Tyner	.30	.09
224 Ramon Ortiz	.30	.09
225 Daryle Ward	.30	.09
226 Enger Veras RC	.40	.12
227 Chris Jones	.30	.09
228 Eric Cammack RC	.30	.09
229 Ruben Mateo	.30	.09
230 Ken Harvey RC	1.25	.35
231 Jake Westbrook	.30	.09
232 Rob Purvis RC	.30	.09
233 Choo Freeman	.30	.09
234 Aramis Ramirez	.30	.09
235 A.J. Burnett	.30	.09
236 Kevin Barker	.30	.09
237 Chance Caple RC	.40	.12
238 Jarrod Washburn	.30	.09
239 Lance Berkman	.30	.09
240 Michael Wenner RC	.30	.09
241 Alex Sanchez	.30	.09
242 Pat Daneker	.30	.09
243 Grant Roberts	.30	.09
244 Mark Ellis RC	.60	.18
245 Donny Leon	.30	.09
246 David Eckstein	.30	.09
247 Dicky Gonzalez RC	.40	.12
248 John Patterson	.30	.09
249 Chad Green	.30	.09
250 Scot Shields RC	.30	.09
251 Troy Cameron	.30	.09
252 Jose Molina	.30	.09
253 Rob Pugmire RC	.40	.12
254 Rick Elder	.30	.09
255 Sean Burroughs	.50	.15
256 Josh Kalinowski RC	.30	.09
257 Matt LeCroy	.30	.09
258 Alex Graman RC	.30	.09
259 Tomo Ohka RC	.40	.12
260 Brady Clark	.30	.09
261 Rico Washington RC	.40	.12
262 Gary Matthews Jr.	.30	.09
263 Matt Wise	.30	.09
264 Keith Reed RC	.40	.12
265 Santiago Ramirez RC	.30	.09
266 Ben Broussard RC	.40	.12
267 Ryan Langerhans	.30	.09
268 Juan Rivera	.30	.09
269 Shawn Gallagher	.30	.09
270 Jorge Toca	.30	.09
271 Brad Lidge	.30	.09
272 Leoncio Estrella RC	.30	.09
273 Ruben Quevedo	.30	.09
274 Jack Cust	.30	.09
275 T.J. Tucker	.30	.09
276 Mike Colangelo	.30	.09
277 Brian Schneider	.30	.09
278 Calvin Murray	.30	.09
279 Josh Girdley	.30	.09
280 Mike Paradis	.30	.09
281 Chad Hermansen	.30	.09
282 Ty Howington RC	.40	.12
283 Aaron Myette	.30	.09
284 D'Angelo Jimenez	.30	.09
285 Dernell Stenson	.30	.09
286 Jerry Hairston Jr.	.30	.09
287 Gary Majewski RC	.40	.12
288 Derrin Ebert	.30	.09
289 Steve Fish RC	.30	.09
290 Carlos E. Hernandez	.30	.09
291 Allen Levrault	.30	.09
292 Sean McNally RC	.30	.09
293 Randey Dorame RC	.40	.12
294 Wes Anderson RC	.40	.12
295 B.J. Ryan	.30	.09
296 Alan Webb RC	.40	.12
297 Brandon Inge RC	.40	.12
298 David Walling	.30	.09
299 Sun Woo Kim RC	.40	.12
300 Pat Burrell	.50	.15
301 Rick Guttormson RC	.30	.09
302 Gil Meche	.30	.09
303 Carlos Zambrano RC	2.50	.75
304 Eric Byrnes UER RC	1.25	.35
Bo Porter pictured		
305 Robb Quinlan RC	.40	.12
306 Jackie Rexrode	.30	.09
307 Nate Bump	.30	.09
308 Sean DePaula RC	.30	.09
309 Matt Riley	.30	.09
310 Ryan Minor	.30	.09
311 J.J. Davis	.30	.09
312 Randy Wolf	.30	.09
313 Jason Jennings	.30	.09
314 Scott Seabol RC	.30	.09
315 Doug Davis	.30	.09
316 Todd Moser RC	.30	.09
317 Rob Ryan	.30	.09
318 Bubba Crosby	.30	.09
319 Ryan Knox RC	.60	.18
320 Mario Encarnacion	.30	.09
321 F.Rodriguez RC	2.00	.60
322 Michael Cuddyer	.30	.09
323 Ed Yarnall	.30	.09
324 Cesar Saba RC	.40	.12
325 Gookie Dawkins	.30	.09
326 Alex Escobar	.30	.09
327 Julio Zuleta RC	.40	.12
328 Josh Hamilton	.30	.09
329 Nick Neugebauer RC	.40	.12
330 Matt Belisle	.30	.09
331 Kurt Ainsworth RC	1.00	.30
332 Tim Raines Jr.	.30	.09
333 Eric Munson	.30	.09
334 Donzell McDonald	.30	.09
335 Larry Bigbie RC	.60	.18
336 Matt Watson RC	.40	.12
337 Aubrey Huff	.30	.09
338 Julio Ramirez	.30	.09
339 Jason Grabowski RC	.40	.12
340 Jon Garland	.30	.09
341 Austin Kearns	.50	.15
342 Josh Pressley RC	.40	.12
343 Miguel Olivo RC	.40	.12
344 Julio Lugo	.30	.09
345 Roberto Vaz	.30	.09
346 Ramon Soler	.30	.09
347 Brandon Phillips RC	1.25	.35
348 Vince Faison RC	.40	.12
349 Mike Venafro	.30	.09
350 Rick Asadoorian RC	.40	.12
351 B.J. Garbe RC	.40	.12
352 Dan Reichert	.30	.09
353 Jason Stumm RC	.40	.12
354 Ruben Salazar RC	.40	.12
355 Francisco Cordero	.30	.09
356 Juan Guzman RC	.40	.12
357 Mike Bacsik RC	.30	.09
358 Jared Sandberg	.30	.09
359 Rod Barajas	.30	.09
360 Junior Brignac RC	.40	.12
361 J.M. Gold	.30	.09
362 Octavio Dotel	.30	.09
363 David Kelton	.30	.09
364 Scott Morgan	.30	.09
365 Wascar Serrano RC	.40	.12
366 Wilton Veras	.30	.09
367 Eugene Kingsale	.30	.09
368 Ted Lilly	.30	.09
369 George Lombard	.30	.09
370 Chris Haas	.30	.09
371 Wilton Pena RC	.30	.09
372 Vernon Wells	.30	.09
373 Jason Royer RC	.40	.12
374 Jeff Heaverlo RC	.40	.12
375 Calvin Pickering	.30	.09
376 Mike Lamb RC	.40	.12
377 Kyle Snyder	.30	.09
378 Javier Cardona RC	.30	.09
379 Aaron Rowand RC	.40	.12
380 Dee Brown	.30	.09
381 Brett Myers RC	2.50	.75
382 Abraham Nunez	.30	.09
383 Eric Valent	.30	.09
384 Jody Gerut RC	2.50	.75
385 Adam Dunn	.75	.23
386 Jay Gehrke	.30	.09
387 Omar Ortiz	.30	.09
388 Darnell McDonald	.30	.09
389 Tony Schrager RC	.30	.09
390 J.D. Closser	.30	.09
391 Ben Christensen RC	.40	.12
392 Adam Kennedy	.30	.09
393 Nick Green RC	.30	.09
394 Ramon Hernandez	.30	.09
395 Roy Oswalt RC	4.00	1.20
396 Andy Tracy RC	.30	.09
397 Eric Gagne	.75	.23
398 Michael Tejera RC	.30	.09
399 Adam Everett	.30	.09
400 Corey Patterson	.50	.15
401 Gary Knotts RC	.30	.09
402 Ryan Christianson RC	.40	.12
403 Eric Ireland RC	.30	.09
404 Andrew Good RC	.40	.12
405 Brad Penny	.30	.09
406 Jason LaRue	.30	.09
407 Kit Pellow	.30	.09
408 Kevin Beirne	.30	.09
409 Kelly Dransfeldt	.30	.09
410 Jason Grilli	.30	.09
411 Scott Downs RC	.30	.09
412 Jesus Colome	.30	.09
413 John Sneed RC	.30	.09
414 Tony McKnight	.30	.09
415 Luis Rivera	.30	.09
416 Adam Eaton	.30	.09
417 Mike MacDougal RC	.60	.18
418 Mike Nannini	.30	.09
419 Barry Zito RC	5.00	1.50
420 DeWayne Wise	.30	.09
421 Jason Dellaero	.30	.09
422 Chad Moeller	.30	.09
423 Jason Marquis	.30	.09
424 Tim Redding RC	1.00	.30
425 Mark Mulder	.50	.15
426 Josh Paul	.30	.09
427 Chris Enochs	.30	.09
428 W.Rodriguez RC	.40	.12
429 Kevin Witt	.30	.09
430 Scott Sobkowiak RC	.30	.09
431 McKay Christensen	.30	.09
432 Jung Bong	.30	.09
433 Keith Evans RC	.30	.09
434 Garry Maddox Jr. RC	.30	.09
435 Ramon Santiago RC	.40	.12
436 Alex Cora	.30	.09
437 Carlos Lee	.30	.09
438 Jason Repko RC	.40	.12
439 Matt Burch	.30	.09
440 Shawn Sonnier RC	.30	.09

2000 Bowman Gold

Randomly inserted into hobby/retail packs at one in 64, this 440-card insert is a complete parallel of the Bowman base set. Each card features a gold facsimile autograph that runs down the right side of the card. Each card in the set is also individually serial numbered to 99.

	Nm-Mt	Ex-Mt
*STARS: 10X TO 25X BASIC CARDS		
*ROOKIES: 5X TO 12X BASIC CARDS		

2000 Bowman Retro/Future

Randomly inserted into hobby/retail packs at one per pack, this 440-card insert is a complete parallel of the Bowman base set. Each card features a television border similar to that of the classic 1955 Bowman set.

	Nm-Mt	Ex-Mt
COMPLETE SET (440)	300.00	90.00
*STARS: 1X TO 2.5X BASIC CARDS		
*ROOKIES: .6X TO 1.5X BASIC CARDS		

2000 Bowman Autographs

Randomly inserted into packs, this 40-card insert features autographed cards from young players like Corey Patterson, Ruben Mateo, and Alfonso Soriano. Please note that this is a three tiered autographed set. Cards that are marked with a "B" are part of the Blue Tier (1:144 HOB/RET, 1:69 HTC). Cards marked with an "S" are part of the Silver Tier (1:312 HOB/RET, 1:148 HTC), and cards marked with a "G" are part of the Gold Tier (1:1604 HOB/RET, 1:762 HTC).

Card	Nm-Mt	Ex-Mt
AD Adam Dunn B	20.00	6.00
AH Aubrey Huff B	10.00	3.00
AK Austin Kearns B	15.00	4.50
AP Adam Piatt S	15.00	4.50
AS Alfonso Soriano S	40.00	12.00
BP Ben Petrick G	25.00	7.50
BS Ben Sheets B	15.00	4.50
BWP Brad Penny B	10.00	3.00
CA Chip Ambres B	10.00	3.00
CB Carlos Beltran G	30.00	9.00
CF Choo Freeman B	10.00	3.00
CP Corey Patterson S	25.00	7.50
DB Dee Brown S	15.00	4.50
DK David Kelton B	10.00	3.00
EV Eric Valent B	10.00	3.00
EY Ed Yarnall S	15.00	4.50
JC Jack Cust S	15.00	4.50
JDC J.D. Closser B	10.00	3.00
JDD J.D. Drew G	30.00	9.00
JJ Jason Jennings B	10.00	3.00
JR Jason Romano B	10.00	3.00
JV Jose Vidro S	20.00	6.00
JZ Julio Zuleta B	10.00	3.00
KJW Kevin Witt S	15.00	4.50
KLW Kerry Wood S	30.00	9.00
LB Lance Berkman S	20.00	6.00
MC Michael Cuddyer S	15.00	4.50
MJR Mike Restovich B	10.00	3.00
MM Mike Meyers B	10.00	3.00
MQ Mark Quinn S	15.00	4.50
MR Matt Riley S	20.00	6.00
NJ Nick Johnson S	20.00	6.00
RA Rick Ankiel G	25.00	7.50
RF Rafael Furcal S	20.00	6.00
RM Ruben Mateo G	25.00	7.50
SB Sean Burroughs S	25.00	7.50
SC Steve Cox B	10.00	3.00
SD Scott Downs S	15.00	4.50
SW Scott Williamson G	25.00	7.50
VW Vernon Wells G	30.00	9.00

2000 Bowman Early Indications

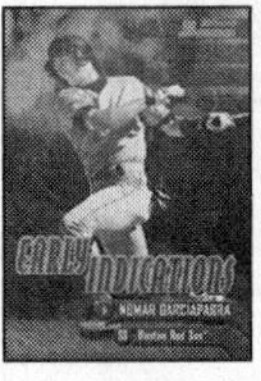

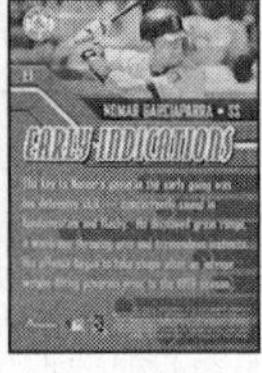

Randomly inserted into hobby/retail packs at one in 24, this 10-card insert features players that put up big numbers early on in their careers. Card backs carry an "E" prefix.

Card	Nm-Mt	Ex-Mt
COMPLETE SET (10)	50.00	15.00
E1 Nomar Garciaparra	5.00	1.50
E2 Cal Ripken	10.00	3.00
E3 Derek Jeter	8.00	2.40
E4 Mark McGwire	8.00	2.40
E5 Alex Rodriguez	5.00	1.50
E6 Chipper Jones	3.00	.90
E7 Todd Helton	2.00	.60
E8 Vladimir Guerrero	3.00	.90
E9 Mike Piazza	5.00	1.50
E10 Jose Canseco	3.00	.90

2000 Bowman Major Power

Randomly inserted into hobby/retail packs at one in 24, this 10-card insert features the major league's top sluggers. Card backs carry a "MP" prefix.

Card	Nm-Mt	Ex-Mt
COMPLETE SET (10)	50.00	15.00
MP1 Mark McGwire	8.00	2.40
MP2 Chipper Jones	3.00	.90
MP3 Alex Rodriguez	5.00	1.50
MP4 Sammy Sosa	5.00	1.50
MP5 Rafael Palmeiro	2.00	.60
MP6 Ken Griffey Jr.	5.00	1.50
MP7 Nomar Garciaparra	5.00	1.50
MP8 Barry Bonds	8.00	2.40
MP9 Derek Jeter	8.00	2.40
MP10 Jeff Bagwell	2.00	.60

2000 Bowman Tool Time

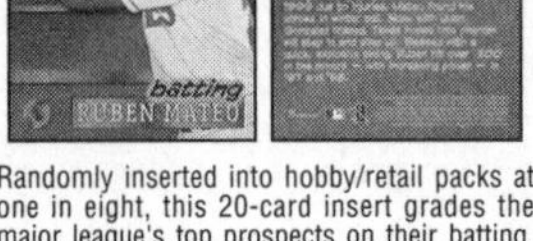

Randomly inserted into hobby/retail packs at one in eight, this 20-card insert grades the major league's top prospects on their batting, power, speed, arm strength, and defensive skills. Card backs carry a "TT" prefix.

Card	Nm-Mt	Ex-Mt
COMPLETE SET (20)	20.00	6.00
TT1 Pat Burrell	1.00	.30
TT2 Aaron Rowand	1.00	.30
TT3 Chris Wakeland	1.00	.30
TT4 Ruben Mateo	1.00	.30
TT5 Pat Burrell	1.00	.30
TT6 Adam Piatt	1.00	.30
TT7 Nick Johnson	1.00	.30
TT8 Jack Cust	1.00	.30
TT9 Rafael Furcal	1.00	.30
TT10 Julio Ramirez	1.00	.30
TT11 Gookie Dawkins	1.00	.30
TT12 Corey Patterson	1.00	.30
TT13 Ruben Mateo	1.00	.30
TT14 Jason Dellaero	1.00	.30
TT15 Sean Burroughs	1.00	.30
TT16 Ryan Langerhans	1.00	.30
TT17 D'Angelo Jimenez	1.00	.30
TT18 Corey Patterson	1.00	.30
TT19 Troy Cameron	1.00	.30
TT20 Michael Cuddyer	1.00	.30

2000 Bowman Draft Picks

The 2000 Bowman Draft Picks set was released in November, 2000 as a 110-card set. Each factory set was initially distributed in a tight, clear cello wrap and contained the 110-card set plus one of 60 different autographs. Topps announced that due to the unavailability of certain players previously scheduled to sign autographs, a small quantity (less than ten

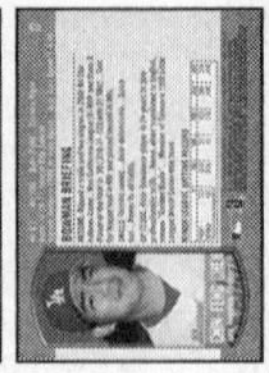

percent) of autographed cards from the 2000 Topps Baseball Rookies/Traded set were be included into its 2000 Bowman Baseball Draft Picks set. Rookie Cards include Chin-Feng Chen, Adrian Gonzalez, Kazuhiro Sasaki, Grady Sizemore and Chin-Hui Tsao.

Card	Nm-Mt	Ex-Mt
COMP.FACT.SET (111)	40.00	12.00
COMPLETE SET (110)	30.00	9.00
1 Pat Burrell	.50	.15
2 Rafael Furcal	.30	.09
3 Grant Roberts	.30	.09
4 Barry Zito	2.00	.60
5 Julio Zuleta	.30	.09
6 Mark Mulder	.50	.15
7 Rob Bell	.30	.09
8 Adam Piatt	.30	.09
9 Mike Lamb	.30	.09
10 Pablo Ozuna	.30	.09
11 Jason Tyner	.30	.09
12 Jason Marquis	.30	.09
13 Eric Munson	.30	.09
14 Seth Etherton	.30	.09
15 Milton Bradley	.30	.09
16 Nick Green	.30	.09
17 Chin-Feng Chen RC	1.00	.30
18 Matt Boone RC	.40	.12
19 Kevin Gregg RC	.40	.12
20 Eddy Garabito RC	.40	.12
21 Aaron Capista RC	.40	.12
22 Esteban German RC	.40	.12
23 Derek Thompson RC	.40	.12
24 Phil Merrell RC	.30	.09
25 Brian O'Connor RC	.30	.09
26 Yamid Haad	.30	.09
27 Hector Mercado RC	.30	.09
28 Jason Woolf RC	.30	.09
29 Eddy Furniss RC	.30	.09
30 Cha Sueng Baek RC	.40	.12
31 Colby Lewis RC	.50	.15
32 Pasqual Coco RC	.30	.09
33 Jorge Cantu RC	.40	.12
34 Erasmo Ramirez RC	.30	.09
35 Bobby Kielty RC	.50	.15
36 Joaquin Benoit RC	.40	.12
37 Brian Esposito RC	.40	.12
38 Michael Wenner	.30	.09
39 Juan Rincon RC	.40	.12
40 Yorvit Torrealba RC	.40	.12
41 Chad Durham RC	.40	.12
42 Jim Mann RC	.30	.09
43 Shane Loux RC	.40	.12
44 Luis Rivas	.30	.09
45 Ken Chenard RC	.40	.12
46 Mike Lockwood RC	.40	.12
47 Yovanny Lara RC	.30	.09
48 Bubba Carpenter RC	.30	.09
49 Ryan Dittfurth RC	.40	.12
50 John Stephens RC	.40	.12
51 Pedro Feliz RC	.40	.12
52 Kenny Kelly RC	.40	.12
53 Neil Jenkins RC	.40	.12
54 Mike Glendenning RC	.30	.09
55 Bo Porter	.30	.09
56 Eric Byrnes	1.00	.30
57 Tony Alvarez RC	.40	.12
58 Kazuhiro Sasaki RC	1.00	.30
59 Chad Durbin RC	.30	.09
60 Mike Bynum RC	.40	.12
61 Travis Wilson RC	.40	.12
62 Jose Leon RC	.30	.09
63 Ryan Vogelsong RC	.40	.12
64 Geraldo Guzman RC	.30	.09
65 Craig Anderson RC	.40	.12
66 Carlos Silva RC	.40	.12
67 Brad Thomas RC	.30	.09
68 Chin-Hui Tsao RC	1.50	.45
69 Mark Buehrle RC	1.25	.35
70 Juan Salas RC	.40	.12
71 Denny Abreu RC	.40	.12
72 Keith McDonald RC	.30	.09
73 Chris Richard RC	.40	.12
74 Tomas De la Rosa RC	.30	.09
75 Vicente Padilla RC	.75	.23
76 Justin Brunette RC	.30	.09
77 Scott Linebrink RC	.30	.09
78 Jeff Sparks RC	.30	.09
79 Tike Redman RC	.40	.12
80 John Lackey RC	.50	.15
81 Joe Strong RC	.30	.09
82 Brian Tollberg RC	.30	.09
83 Steve Sisco RC	.30	.09
84 Chris Clapinski RC	.30	.09
85 Augie Ojeda RC	.30	.09
86 Adrian Gonzalez RC	1.50	.45
87 Mike Stodolka RC	.40	.12
88 Adam Johnson RC	.40	.12
89 Matt Wheatland RC	.30	.09
90 Corey Smith RC	.50	.15
91 Rocco Baldelli RC	10.00	3.00
92 Keith Bucktrot RC	.40	.12
93 Adam Wainwright RC	1.50	.45
94 Blaine Boyer RC	.40	.12
95 Aaron Herr RC	.40	.12
96 Scott Thorman RC	.50	.15
97 Bryan Digby RC	.40	.12
98 Josh Shortslef RC	.40	.12
99 Sean Smith RC	.40	.12
100 Alex Cruz RC	.40	.12
101 Marc Love RC	.40	.12
102 Kevin Lee RC	.40	.12
103 Victor Ramos RC	.40	.12
104 Jason Kaanoi RC	.30	.09
105 Luis Escobar RC	.40	.12
106 Tripper Johnson RC	.50	.15
107 Phil Dumatrait RC	.40	.12
108 Bryan Edwards RC	.40	.12

109 Grady Sizemore RC 12.00 3.60
110 Thomas Mitchell RC .40 .12

2000 Bowman Draft Picks Autographs

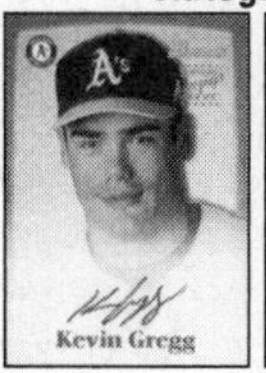

Inserted into 2000 Bowman Draft Pick sets at one per set, this 55-card insert features autographed cards of some of the hottest prospects in baseball. Card backs carry a "BDPA" prefix. Please note that cards BDPA16, BDPA32, BDPA34, BDPA45, BDPA56 do not exist.

	Nm-Mt	Ex-Mt
BDPA1 Pat Burrell	20.00	6.00
BDPA2 Rafael Furcal	15.00	4.50
BDPA3 Grant Roberts	10.00	3.00
BDPA4 Barry Zito	50.00	15.00
BDPA5 Julio Zuleta	10.00	3.00
BDPA6 Mark Mulder	25.00	7.50
BDPA7 Rob Bell	10.00	3.00
BDPA8 Adam Piatt	10.00	3.00
BDPA9 Mike Lamb	10.00	3.00
BDPA10 Pablo Ozuna	10.00	3.00
BDPA11 Jason Tyner	10.00	3.00
BDPA12 Jason Marquis	10.00	3.00
BDPA13 Eric Munson	15.00	4.50
BDPA14 Seth Etherton	10.00	3.00
BDPA15 Milton Bradley	15.00	4.50
BDPA16 Does Not Exist		
BDPA17 Michael Wenner	10.00	3.00
BDPA18 M.Glendenning	10.00	3.00
BDPA19 Tony Alvarez	10.00	3.00
BDPA20 Adrian Gonzalez	30.00	9.00
BDPA21 Corey Smith	15.00	4.50
BDPA22 Matt Wheatland	10.00	3.00
BDPA23 Adam Johnson	10.00	3.00
BDPA24 Mike Stodolka	10.00	3.00
BDPA25 Rocco Baldelli	120.00	36.00
BDPA26 Juan Rincon	10.00	3.00
BDPA27 Chad Durbin	10.00	3.00
BDPA28 Yorvit Torrealba	10.00	3.00
BDPA29 Nick Green	10.00	3.00
BDPA30 Derek Thompson	10.00	3.00
BDPA31 John Lackey	15.00	4.50
BDPA32 Does Not Exist		
BDPA33 Kevin Gregg	10.00	3.00
BDPA34 Does Not Exist		
BDPA35 Denny Abreu	10.00	3.00
BDPA36 Brian Tollberg	10.00	3.00
BDPA37 Yamid Haad	10.00	3.00
BDPA38 Grady Sizemore	100.00	30.00
BDPA39 Carlos Silva	10.00	3.00
BDPA40 Jorge Cantu	10.00	3.00
BDPA41 Bobby Kielty	15.00	4.50
BDPA42 Scott Thorman	15.00	4.50
BDPA43 Juan Salas	10.00	3.00
BDPA44 Phil Dumatrait	10.00	3.00
BDPA45 Does Not Exist		
BDPA46 Mike Lockwood	10.00	3.00
BDPA47 Yovanny Lara	10.00	3.00
BDPA48 Tripper Johnson	15.00	4.50
BDPA49 Colby Lewis	15.00	4.50
BDPA50 Neil Jenkins	10.00	3.00
BDPA51 Keith Bucktrot	10.00	3.00
BDPA52 Eric Byrnes	25.00	7.50
BDPA53 Aaron Herr	10.00	3.00
BDPA54 Erasmo Ramirez	10.00	3.00
BDPA55 Chris Richard	10.00	3.00
BDPA56 Does Not Exist		
BDPA57 Mike Bynum	10.00	3.00
BDPA58 Brian Esposito	10.00	3.00
BDPA59 Chris Clapinski	10.00	3.00
BDPA60 Augie Ojeda	10.00	3.00

2001 Bowman Promos

This three-card set was distributed in a sealed plastic cello wrap to dealers and hobby media a few months prior to the release of 2001 Bowman to allow a sneak preview of the upcoming brand. The promos can be readily identified from base issue cards by their PP prefixed numbering on back.

	Nm-Mt	Ex-Mt
COMPLETE SET (3)	6.00	1.80
PP1 Barry Bonds	2.00	.60
PP2 Roger Clemens	3.00	.90
PP3 Adrian Gonzalez	1.50	.45

2001 Bowman

Issued in one series, this 440 card set features a mix of 140 veteran cards along with 300 cards of young players. The cards were issued in either 10-card retail or hobby packs or 21-card hobby collector packs. The 10 card packs had an SRP of $3 while the jumbo packs had an SRP of $6. The 10 card packs were inserted 24 packs to a box and 12 boxes to a case. The 21 card packs were inserted 12 packs per box and eight boxes per case. An exchange card with a redemption deadline of May 31st, 2002, good for a signed Sean Burroughs baseball, was randomly seeded into packs at a miniscule rate of 1:30,432. Only eighty exchange cards were produced. In addition, a special card featuring game-used jersey swatches of A.L. and N.L. Rookie of the Year winners Kazuhiro Sasaki and Rafael Furcal was randomly seeded into packs at the following rates; hobby 1:2,202 and Home Team Advantage 1:1,045.

	Nm-Mt	Ex-Mt
COMPLETE SET (440)	100.00	30.00
COMMON CARD (1-440)	.30	.09
COMMON RC	.30	.09
1 Jason Giambi	.75	.23
2 Rafael Furcal	.30	.09
3 Rick Ankiel	.30	.09
4 Freddy Garcia	.30	.09
5 Magglio Ordonez	.30	.09
6 Bernie Williams	.50	.15
7 Kenny Lofton	.30	.09
8 Al Leiter	.30	.09
9 Albert Belle	.30	.09
10 Craig Biggio	.50	.15
11 Mark Mulder	.30	.09
12 Carlos Delgado	.30	.09
13 Darin Erstad	.30	.09
14 Richie Sexson	.30	.09
15 Randy Johnson	.75	.23
16 Greg Maddux	1.25	.35
17 Cliff Floyd	.30	.09
18 Mark Buehrle	.30	.09
19 Chris Singleton	.30	.09
20 Orlando Hernandez	.30	.09
21 Javier Vazquez	.30	.09
22 Jeff Kent	.30	.09
23 Jim Thome	.75	.23
24 John Olerud	.30	.09
25 Jason Kendall	.30	.09
26 Scott Rolen	.50	.15
27 Tony Gwynn	1.00	.30
28 Edgardo Alfonzo	.30	.09
29 Pokey Reese	.30	.09
30 Todd Helton	.50	.15
31 Mark Quinn	.30	.09
32 Dan Tosca RC	.40	.12
33 Dean Palmer	.30	.09
34 Jacque Jones	.30	.09
35 Ray Durham	.30	.09
36 Rafael Palmeiro	.50	.15
37 Carl Everett	.30	.09
38 Ryan Dempster	.30	.09
39 Randy Wolf	.30	.09
40 Vladimir Guerrero	.75	.23
41 Livan Hernandez	.30	.09
42 Mo Vaughn	.30	.09
43 Shannon Stewart	.30	.09
44 Preston Wilson	.30	.09
45 Jose Vidro	.30	.09
46 Fred McGriff	.50	.15
47 Kevin Brown	.30	.09
48 Peter Bergeron	.30	.09
49 Miguel Tejada	.30	.09
50 Chipper Jones	.75	.23
51 Edgar Martinez	.50	.15
52 Tony Batista	.30	.09
53 Jorge Posada	.50	.15
54 Ricky Ledee	.30	.09
55 Sammy Sosa	1.25	.35
56 Steve Cox	.30	.09
57 Tony Armas Jr.	.30	.09
58 Gary Sheffield	.30	.09
59 Bartolo Colon	.30	.09
60 Pat Burrell	.30	.09
61 Jay Payton	.30	.09
62 Sean Casey	.30	.09
63 Larry Walker	.50	.15
64 Mike Mussina	.75	.23
65 Nomar Garciaparra	1.25	.35
66 Darren Dreifort	.30	.09
67 Richard Hidalgo	.30	.09
68 Troy Glaus	.50	.15
69 Ben Grieve	.30	.09
70 Jim Edmonds	.30	.09
71 Raul Mondesi	.30	.09
72 Andruw Jones	.30	.09
73 Luis Castillo	.30	.09
74 Mike Sweeney	.30	.09
75 Derek Jeter	2.00	.60
76 Ruben Mateo	.30	.09
77 Carlos Lee	.30	.09
78 Cristian Guzman	.30	.09
79 Mike Hampton	.30	.09
80 J.D. Drew	.30	.09
81 Matt Lawton	.30	.09
82 Moises Alou	.30	.09
83 Terrence Long	.30	.09
84 Geoff Jenkins	.30	.09
85 Manny Ramirez	.30	.09
86 Johnny Damon	.30	.09
87 Barry Larkin	.75	.23
88 Pedro Martinez	.75	.23
89 Juan Gonzalez	.75	.23
90 Roger Clemens	1.50	.45
91 Carlos Beltran	.30	.09
92 Brad Radke	.30	.09
93 Orlando Cabrera	.30	.09
94 Roberto Alomar	.75	.23
95 Barry Bonds	2.00	.60
96 Tim Hudson	.30	.09
97 Tom Glavine	.50	.15
98 Jeromy Burnitz	.30	.09
99 Adrian Beltre	.30	.09
100 Mike Piazza	1.25	.35
101 Kerry Wood	.75	.23
102 Steve Finley	.30	.09
103 Alex Cora	.30	.09
104 Bob Abreu	.30	.09
105 Neifi Perez	.30	.09
106 Mark Redman	.30	.09
107 Paul Konerko	.30	.09
108 Jermaine Dye	.30	.09
109 Brian Giles	.30	.09
110 Ivan Rodriguez	.75	.23
111 Vinny Castilla	.30	.09
112 Adam Kennedy	.30	.09
113 Eric Chavez	.30	.09
114 Billy Koch	.30	.09
115 Shawn Green	.30	.09
116 Matt Williams	.30	.09
117 Greg Vaughn	.30	.09
118 Gabe Kapler	.30	.09
119 Jeff Cirillo	.30	.09
120 Frank Thomas	.75	.23
121 David Justice	.30	.09
122 Cal Ripken	2.50	.75
123 Rich Aurilia	.30	.09
124 Curt Schilling	.50	.15
125 Barry Zito	.75	.23
126 Brian Jordan	.30	.09
127 Chan Ho Park	.30	.09
128 J.T. Snow	.30	.09
129 Kazuhiro Sasaki	.30	.09
130 Alex Rodriguez	1.25	.35
131 Mariano Rivera	.50	.15
132 Eric Milton	.30	.09
133 Andy Pettitte	.50	.15
134 Scott Elarton	.30	.09
135 Ken Griffey Jr.	1.25	.35
136 Bengie Molina	.30	.09
137 Jeff Bagwell	.50	.15
138 Kevin Millwood	.30	.09
139 Tino Martinez	.50	.15
140 Mark McGwire	2.00	.60
141 Larry Barnes	.30	.09
142 John Buck RC	.60	.18
143 Freddie Bynum RC	.40	.12
144 Abraham Nunez	.30	.09
145 Felix Diaz RC	.40	.12
146 Horacio Estrada	.30	.09
147 Ben Diggins	.30	.09
148 Tsuyoshi Shinjo RC	1.25	.35
149 Rocco Baldelli	2.00	.60
150 Rod Barajas	.30	.09
151 Luis Terrero	.30	.09
152 Milton Bradley	.30	.09
153 Kurt Ainsworth	.30	.09
154 Russell Branyan	.30	.09
155 Ryan Anderson	.30	.09
156 Mitch Jones RC	.40	.12
157 Chip Ambres	.30	.09
158 Steve Bennett RC	.30	.09
159 Ivanon Coffie	.30	.09
160 Sean Burroughs	.30	.09
161 Keith Bucktrot	.30	.09
162 Tony Alvarez	.30	.09
163 Joaquin Benoit	.30	.09
164 Rick Asadoorian	.30	.09
165 Ben Broussard	.30	.09
166 Ryan Madson RC	.40	.12
167 Dee Brown	.30	.09
168 Sergio Contreras RC	.40	.12
169 John Barnes	.30	.09
170 Ben Washburn RC	.40	.12
171 Erick Almonte RC	.40	.12
172 Shawn Fagan RC	.30	.09
173 Gary Johnson RC	.40	.12
174 Brady Clark	.30	.09
175 Grant Roberts	.30	.09
176 Tony Torcato	.30	.09
177 Ramon Castro	.30	.09
178 Esteban German	.30	.09
179 Joe Hamer RC	.40	.12
180 Nick Neugebauer	.30	.09
181 Dernell Stenson	.30	.09
182 Yhency Brazoban RC	.40	.12
183 Aaron Myette	.30	.09
184 Juan Sosa	.30	.09
185 Brandon Inge	.30	.09
186 Domingo Guante RC	.40	.12
187 Adrian Brown	.30	.09
188 Deivi Mendez RC	.40	.12
189 Luis Matos	.30	.09
190 Pedro Liriano RC	.40	.12
191 Donnie Bridges	.30	.09
192 Alex Cintron	.30	.09
193 Jace Brewer	.30	.09
194 Ron Davenport RC	.40	.12
195 Jason Belcher RC	.40	.12
196 Adrian Hernandez RC	.30	.09
197 Bobby Kielty	.30	.09
198 Reggie Griggs RC	.40	.12
199 R. Abercrombie RC	.40	.12
200 Troy Farnsworth RC	.40	.12
201 Matt Belisle	.30	.09
202 Miguel Villilo RC	.40	.12
203 Adam Everett	.30	.09
204 John Lackey	.30	.09
205 Pasqual Coco	.30	.09
206 Adam Wainwright	.30	.09
207 Matt White RC	.40	.12
208 Chin-Feng Chen	.30	.09
209 Jeff Andra RC	.40	.12
210 Willie Bloomquist	.30	.09
211 Wes Anderson	.30	.09
212 Enrique Cruz	.30	.09
213 Jerry Hairston Jr.	.30	.09
214 Mike Bynum	.30	.09
215 Brian Hitchcox RC	.40	.12
216 Ryan Christianson	.30	.09
217 J.J. Davis	.30	.09
218 Jovanny Cedeno	.30	.09
219 Elvin Nina	.30	.09
220 Alex Graman	.30	.09
221 Arturo McDowell	.30	.09
222 Deivis Santos RC	.40	.12
223 Jody Gerut	.30	.09
224 Sun Woo Kim	.30	.09
225 Jimmy Rollins	.30	.09
226 Ntema Ndungidi	.30	.09
227 Ruben Salazar	.30	.09
228 Josh Girdley	.30	.09
229 Carl Crawford	.30	.09
230 Luis Montanez RC	.40	.12
231 Ramon Carvajal RC	.40	.12
232 Matt Riley	.30	.09
233 Ben Davis	.30	.09
234 Jason Grabowski	.30	.09
235 Chris George	.30	.09
236 Hank Blalock RC	6.00	1.80
237 Roy Oswalt	.50	.15
238 Eric Reynolds RC	.40	.12
239 Brian Cole	.30	.09
240 Denny Bautista RC	1.25	.35
241 Hector Garcia RC	.40	.12
242 Joe Thurston RC	1.00	.30
243 Brad Cresse	.30	.09
244 Corey Patterson	.30	.09
245 Brett Evert RC	.40	.12
246 Elpidio Guzman RC	.40	.12
247 Vernon Wells	.30	.09
248 Roberto Miniel RC	.40	.12
249 Brian Bass RC	.40	.12
250 Mark Burnett RC	.40	.12
251 Juan Silvestre	.30	.09
252 Pablo Ozuna	.30	.09
253 Jayson Werth	.30	.09
254 Russ Jacobson	.30	.09
255 Chad Hermansen	.30	.09
256 Travis Hafner RC	1.50	.45
257 Brad Baker	.30	.09
258 Gookie Dawkins	.30	.09
259 Michael Cuddyer	.30	.09
260 Mark Buehrle	.30	.09
261 Ricardo Aramboles	.30	.09
262 Esix Snead RC	.40	.12
263 Wilson Betemit RC	.40	.12
264 Albert Pujols RC	40.00	12.00
265 Joe Lawrence	.30	.09
266 Ramon Ortiz	.30	.09
267 Ben Sheets	.30	.09
268 Luke Lockwood RC	.40	.12
269 Toby Hall	.30	.09
270 Jack Cust	.30	.09
271 Pedro Feliz UER	.30	.09
No facsimile signature on card		
272 Noel Devarez RC	.40	.12
273 Josh Beckett	.50	.15
274 Alex Escobar	.30	.09
275 Doug Gredvig RC	.40	.12
276 Marcus Giles	.30	.09
277 Jon Rauch	.30	.09
278 Brian Schmitt RC	.40	.12
279 Seung Song RC	1.00	.30
280 Kevin Mench	.30	.09
281 Adam Eaton	.30	.09
282 Shawn Sonnier	.30	.09
283 Andy Van Hekken RC	.40	.12
284 Aaron Rowand	.30	.09
285 Tony Blanco RC	.60	.18
286 Ryan Kohlmeier	.30	.09
287 C.C. Sabathia	.30	.09
288 Bubba Crosby	.30	.09
289 Josh Hamilton	.30	.09
290 Dee Haynes RC	.60	.18
291 Jason Marquis	.30	.09
292 Julio Zuleta	.30	.09
293 Carlos Hernandez	.30	.09
294 Matt Lecroy	.30	.09
295 Andy Beal RC	.40	.12
296 Carlos Pena	.30	.09
297 Reggie Taylor	.30	.09
298 Bob Keppel RC	.60	.18
299 Miguel Cabrera UER	2.50	.75
Photo is Manuel Esquivia		
300 Ryan Franklin	.30	.09
301 Brandon Phillips	.30	.09
302 Victor Hall RC	.40	.12
303 Tony Pena Jr.	.30	.09
304 Jim Journell RC	.40	.12
305 Cristian Guerrero	.30	.09
306 Miguel Olivo	.30	.09
307 Jin Ho Cho	.30	.09
308 Choo Freeman	.30	.09
309 Danny Borrell RC	.40	.12
310 Doug Mientkiewicz	.30	.09
311 Aaron Herr	.30	.09
312 Keith Ginter	.30	.09
313 Felipe Lopez	.30	.09
314 Jeff Goldbach	.30	.09
315 Travis Harper	.30	.09
316 Paul LoDuca	.30	.09
317 Joe Torres	.30	.09
318 Eric Byrnes	.30	.09
319 George Lombard	.30	.09
320 Dave Krynzel	.30	.09
321 Ben Christensen	.30	.09
322 Aubrey Huff	.30	.09
323 Lyle Overbay	.30	.09
324 Sean McGowan	.30	.09
325 Jeff Heaverlo	.30	.09
326 Timo Perez	.30	.09
327 Octavio Martinez RC	.40	.12
328 Vince Faison	.30	.09
329 David Parrish RC	.40	.12
330 Bobby Bradley	.30	.09
331 Jason Miller RC	.40	.12
332 Corey Spencer RC	.40	.12
333 Craig House	.30	.09
334 Maxim St. Pierre RC	.40	.12
335 Adam Johnson	.30	.09
336 Joe Crede	.30	.09
337 Greg Nash RC	.40	.12
338 Chad Durbin	.30	.09
339 Pat Magness RC	.40	.12
340 Matt Wheatland	.30	.09
341 Julio Lugo	.30	.09
342 Grady Sizemore	1.00	.30
343 Adrian Gonzalez	.30	.09
344 Tim Raines Jr.	.30	.09
345 Ranier Olmedo RC	.40	.12
346 Phil Dumatrait	.30	.09
347 Brandon Mims RC	.40	.12
348 Jason Jennings	.30	.09
349 Phil Wilson RC	.40	.12
350 Jason Hart	.30	.09
351 Cesar Izturis	.30	.09
352 Matt Butler RC	.40	.12
353 David Kelton	.30	.09
354 Luke Prokopec	.30	.09
355 Corey Smith	.30	.09
356 Joel Pineiro	1.00	.30
357 Ken Chenard	.30	.09
358 Keith Reed	.30	.09
359 David Walling	.30	.09
360 Alexis Gomez RC	.40	.12
361 Justin Morneau RC	3.00	.90
362 Josh Fogg RC	.40	.12
363 J.R. House	.30	.09
364 Andy Tracy	.30	.09
365 Kenny Kelly	.30	.09
366 Aaron McNeal	.30	.09
367 Nick Johnson	.30	.09
368 Brian Esposito	.30	.09
369 Charles Frazier RC	.40	.12
370 Scott Heard	.30	.09
371 Pat Strange	.30	.09
372 Mike Meyers	.30	.09
373 Ryan Ludwick RC	.40	.12
374 Brad Wilkerson	.30	.09
375 Allen Levrault	.30	.09
376 Seth McClung RC	.40	.12
377 Joe Nathan	.30	.09
378 Rafael Soriano RC	1.50	.45
379 Chris Richard	.30	.09
380 Jared Sandberg	.30	.09
381 Tike Redman	.30	.09
382 Adam Dunn UER	.30	.09
Card lists him as a pitcher		
383 Jared Abruzzo RC	.40	.12
384 Jason Richardson RC	.40	.12
385 Matt Holliday	.30	.09
386 Darwin Cubillan RC	.40	.12
387 Mike Nannini	.30	.09
388 Blake Williams RC	.40	.12
389 V. Pascucci RC	.40	.12
390 Jon Garland	.30	.09
391 Josh Pressley	.30	.09
392 Jose Ortiz	.30	.09
393 Ryan Hannaman RC	.40	.12
394 Steve Smyth RC	.40	.12
395 John Patterson	.30	.09
396 Chad Petty RC	.40	.12
397 Jake Peavy RC	1.50	.45
UER last name misspelled Peavey		
398 Onix Mercado RC	.40	.12
399 Jason Romano	.30	.09
400 Luis Torres RC	.40	.12
401 Casey Fossum RC	.40	.12
402 Eduardo Figueroa RC	.40	.12
403 Bryan Barnowski RC	.40	.12
404 Tim Redding	.30	.09
405 Jason Standridge	.30	.09
406 Marvin Seale RC	.40	.12
407 Todd Moser	.30	.09
408 Alex Gordon	.30	.09
409 Steve Smitherman RC	1.50	.45
410 Ben Petrick	.30	.09
411 Eric Munson	.30	.09
412 Luis Rivas	.30	.09
413 Matt Ginter	.30	.09
414 Alfonso Soriano	.50	.15
415 Rafael Boitel RC	.40	.12
416 Dany Morban RC	.40	.12
417 Justin Woodrow RC	.40	.12
418 Wilfredo Rodriguez	.30	.09
419 Derrick Van Dusen RC	.40	.12
420 Josh Spoerl RC	.40	.12
421 Juan Pierre	.30	.09
422 J.C. Romero	.30	.09
423 Ed Rogers RC	.40	.12
424 Tomo Ohka	.30	.09
425 Ben Hendrickson RC	.40	.12
426 Carlos Zambrano	.30	.09
427 Brett Myers	.30	.09
428 Scott Seabol	.30	.09
429 Thomas Mitchell	.30	.09
430 Jose Reyes RC	5.00	1.50
431 Kip Wells	.30	.09
432 Donzell McDonald	.30	.09
433 Adam Pettyjohn RC	.40	.12
434 Austin Kearns	.30	.09
435 Rico Washington	.30	.09
436 Doug Nickle RC	.30	.09
437 Steve Lomasney	.30	.09
438 Jason Jones RC	.40	.12
439 Bobby Seay	.30	.09
440 Justin Wayne RC	.60	.18
ROYR Kazuhiro Sasaki	25.00	7.50
Rafael Furcal ROY Jsy		
NNO Sean Burroughs Ball/80	40.00	12.00

2001 Bowman Gold

Inserted one per pack, these 440 cards are a parallel to the basic Bowman set.

Nm-Mt Ex-Mt

*STARS: 1.25X TO 3X BASIC CARDS.
*ROOKIES: 1X TO 2.5X BASIC CARDS

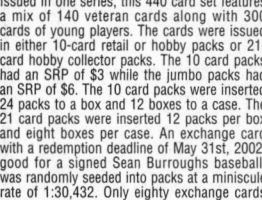

2001 Bowman Autographs

Inserted at a rate of one in 74 hobby packs and one in 35 HTA packs, these 40 cards feature autographs from some of the leading prospects in the Bowman set. Dustin McGowan did not return his cards in time for inclusion in the product and exchange cards with a redemption deadline of April 30th, 2003 were seeded into packs in their place.

	Nm-Mt	Ex-Mt
BA-AE Alex Escobar	10.00	3.00
BA-AG Adrian Gonzalez	10.00	3.00
BA-AJ Adam Johnson	10.00	3.00
BA-AP Albert Pujols	250.00	75.00
BA-ADP Adam Piatt	10.00	3.00
BA-AJG Alex Graman	10.00	3.00
BA-AKG Alex Gordon	10.00	3.00
BA-BB Brian Barnowski	10.00	3.00
BA-BD Ben Diggins	10.00	3.00
BA-BS Ben Sheets	10.00	3.00
BA-BW Brad Wilkerson	10.00	3.00
BA-BZ Barry Zito	25.00	7.50
BA-CG Cristian Guerrero	10.00	3.00
BA-DK Dave Krynzel	10.00	3.00
BA-DM D. McGowan EXCH	30.00	9.00
BA-DWK David Kelton	10.00	3.00
BA-FB Freddie Bynum	10.00	3.00
BA-JB Jason Botts	10.00	3.00
BA-JD Jose Diaz	10.00	3.00
BA-JH Josh Hamilton	10.00	3.00
BA-JM Justin Morneau	25.00	7.50
BA-JP Josh Pressley	10.00	3.00
BA-JRH J.R. House	10.00	3.00
BA-JWH Jason Hart	10.00	3.00
BA-KM Kevin Mench	10.00	3.00
BA-LM Luis Montanez	10.00	3.00
BA-LO Lyle Overbay	10.00	3.00
BA-MV Miguel Villilo	10.00	3.00
BA-ND Noel Devarez	10.00	3.00
BA-PL Pedro Liriano	10.00	3.00
BA-RF Rafael Furcal	10.00	3.00
BA-RJ Russ Jacobson	10.00	3.00
BA-SB Sean Burroughs	10.00	3.00
BA-SM S. McGowan EXCH	10.00	3.00
BA-SS Shawn Sonnier	10.00	3.00

BA-SU Sixto Urena 10.00 3.00
BA-SDS Steve Smyth 10.00 3.00
BA-TH Travis Hafner 25.00 7.50
BA-TJ Tripper Johnson 10.00 3.00
BA-WB Wilson Betemit 10.00 3.00

2001 Bowman AutoProofs

Inserted at a rate of 1 in 18,239 hobby packs and 1 in 8,306 HTA packs; these 10 cards feature players signing their actual Bowman Rookie Cards. Each player signed 25 cards for this promotion. Hank Bauer, Pat Burrell, Carlos Delgado, Chipper Jones, Ralph Kiner, Gil McDougald, and Ivan Rodriguez did not return their cards in time for inclusion in this product and exchange cards with a redemption deadline of April 30th, 2003 were seeded in to packs in their place.

Nm-Mt Ex-Mt
1 Hank Bauer 50
2 Pat Burrell 99
3 Carlos Delgado 92
4 Carl Erskine 51
5 Rafael Furcal 99
6 Chipper Jones 91
7 Ralph Kiner 48
8 Don Larsen 54
9 Gil McDougald 52
10 Ivan Rodriguez EXCH

2001 Bowman Futures Game Relics

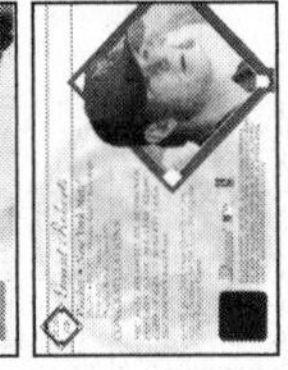

Inserted at overall odds of one in 82 hobby packs and one in 39 HTA packs, these 34 cards feature relics used by the featured players in the futures game. These cards were inserted at different ratios and our checklist provides that information as to what group each insert belongs to.

Nm-Mt Ex-Mt
FGRAE Alex Escobar A 10.00 3.00
FGRAM Aaron Myette B 10.00 3.00
FGRBB Bobby Bradley B 10.00 3.00
FGRBP Ben Petrick C 10.00 3.00
FGRBS Ben Sheets B 10.00 3.00
FGRBW Brad Wilkerson C 10.00 3.00
FGRBZ Barry Zito B 15.00 4.50
FGRCA Craig Anderson B 10.00 3.00
FGRCC Chin-Feng Chen A 30.00 9.00
FGRCG Chris George D 10.00 3.00
FGRCH C. Hernandez D 10.00 3.00
FGRCP Corey Patterson A 10.00 3.00
FGRCP Carlos Pena A 10.00 3.00
FGRCT Chin-Hui Tsao D 25.00 7.50
FGREM Eric Munson A 10.00 3.00
FGRFL Felipe Lopez A 10.00 3.00
FGRGR Grant Roberts D 10.00 3.00
FGRJC Jack Cust A 10.00 3.00
FGRJH Josh Hamilton A 10.00 3.00
FGRJR Jason Romano C 10.00 3.00
FGRJZ Julio Zuleta A 10.00 3.00
FGRKA Kurt Ainsworth B 10.00 3.00
FGRMB Mike Bynum D 10.00 3.00
FGRMG Marcus Giles A 10.00 3.00
FGRNN N. Ndungidi A 10.00 3.00
FGRRA Ryan Anderson B 10.00 3.00
FGRRC Ramon Castro C 10.00 3.00
FGRRD R. Dorame D 10.00 3.00
FGRRO Ramon Ortiz D 10.00 3.00
FGRSK Sun Woo Kim D 10.00 3.00
FGRTD Travis Dawkins C 10.00 3.00
FGRTO Tomokazu Ohka B 10.00 3.00
FGRTW Travis Wilson A 10.00 3.00
FGRVW Vernon Wells C 10.00 3.00

2001 Bowman Multiple Game Relics

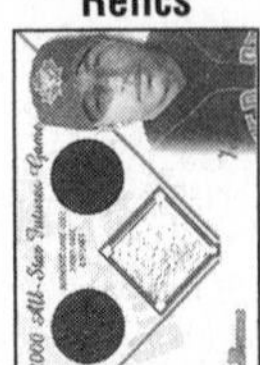

Issued at overall odds of one in 1,476 hobby packs and one in 701 HTA packs, these cards have three different pieces of memorabilia on them. These cards feature a piece of a jersey, helmet and a base fragment.

Nm-Mt Ex-Mt
MGR-AE Alex Escobar B 25.00 7.50
MGR-BP Ben Petrick A 25.00 7.50
MGR-BW B. Wilkerson B 25.00 7.50
MGR-CC C. Chen A 150.00 45.00
MGR-CP Carlos Pena A 25.00 7.50
MGR-EM Eric Munson B 25.00 7.50
MGR-FL Felipe Lopez A 25.00 7.50
MGR-JC Jack Cust A 25.00 7.50
MGR-JH Josh Hamilton B 25.00 7.50
MGR-JR Jason Romano A 25.00 7.50
MGR-JZ Julio Zuleta A 25.00 7.50
MGR-MG Marcus Giles A 25.00 7.50
MGR-NN N. Ndungidi A 25.00 7.50
MGR-RC Ramon Castro A 25.00 7.50
MGR-TD Travis Dawkins A 25.00 7.50
MGR-TW Travis Wilson A 25.00 7.50
MGR-VW Vernon Wells A 25.00 7.50
MGR-DCP C. Patterson B 25.00 7.50

2001 Bowman Multiple Game Relics Autograph

Inserted in packs at a rate of one in 18,259 Hobby and one in 8,306 HTA packs, these five cards feature not only three pieces of memorabilia from the featured players but also included an authentic signature.

Nm-Mt Ex-Mt
AMGR-AE Alex Escobar
AMGR-BW Brad Wilkerson
AMGR-CP Corey Patterson
AMGR-EM Eric Munson
AMGR-JH Josh Hamilton

2001 Bowman Rookie Reprints

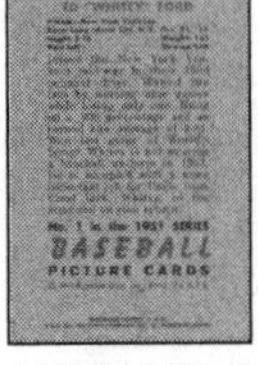

Inserted at a rate of one in 12, these 25 cards feature reprint cards of various stars who made their debut between 1948 and 1955.

Nm-Mt Ex-Mt
COMPLETE SET (25) 60.00 18.00
1 Yogi Berra 5.00 1.50
2 Ralph Kiner 3.00 .90
3 Stan Musial 10.00 3.00
4 Warren Spahn 3.00 .90
5 Roy Campanella 5.00 1.50
6 Bob Lemon 3.00 .90
7 Robin Roberts 3.00 .90
8 Duke Snider 3.00 .90
9 Early Wynn 3.00 .90
10 Richie Ashburn 3.00 .90
11 Gil Hodges 5.00 1.50
12 Hank Bauer 3.00 .90
13 Don Newcombe 3.00 .90
14 Al Rosen 3.00 .90
15 Willie Mays 12.00 3.60
16 Joe Garagiola 3.00 .90
17 Whitey Ford 3.00 .90
18 Lew Burdette 3.00 .90
19 Gil McDougald 3.00 .90
20 Minnie Minoso 3.00 .90
21 Eddie Mathews 5.00 1.50
22 Harvey Kuenn 3.00 .90
23 Don Larsen 5.00 1.50
24 Elston Howard 3.00 .90
25 Don Zimmer 3.00 .90

2001 Bowman Rookie Reprints Autographs

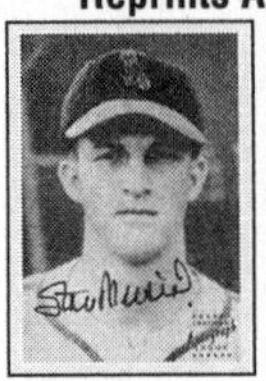
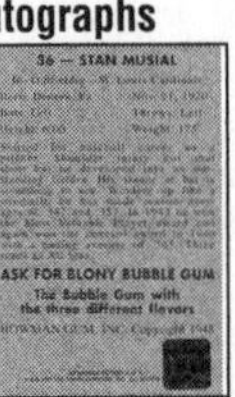

Inserted at a rate of one in 2,467 hobby packs and one in 1,162 HTA packs, these 10 cards feature the players signing their rookie reprint cards. Duke Snider did not return his card in time for inclusion in packs. His card was redeemable until April 30, 2003. Please note that card number 7 does not exist.

Nm-Mt Ex-Mt
1 Yogi Berra 80.00 24.00
2 Willie Mays 200.00 60.00
3 Stan Musial 120.00 36.00
4 Duke Snider EXCH 40.00 12.00
5 Warren Spahn 60.00 18.00
6 Ralph Kiner 25.00 7.50
7 Does Not Exist
8 Don Larsen 25.00 7.50
9 Don Zimmer 25.00 7.50
10 Minnie Minoso 25.00 7.50

2001 Bowman Rookie Reprints Relic Bat

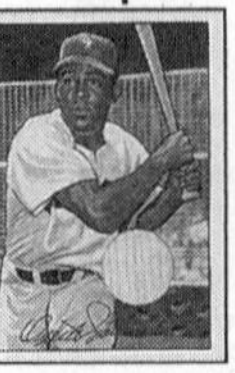
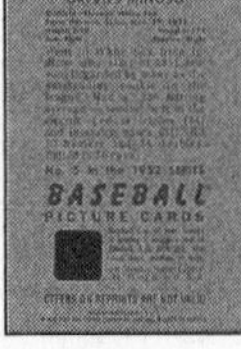

Issued at a rate of one in 1,954 hobby packs and one in 928 HTA packs, these five cards feature not only the rookie reprint of these players but also a piece of a bat they used during their career.

Nm-Mt Ex-Mt
1 Willie Mays 80.00 24.00
2 Duke Snider 25.00 7.50
3 Minnie Minoso 15.00 4.50
4 Hank Bauer 15.00 4.50
5 Gil McDougald 15.00 4.50

2001 Bowman Rookie Reprints Relic Bat Autographs

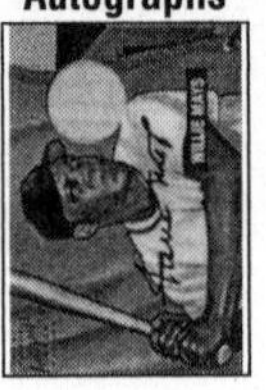

Issued at a rate of one in 18,259 hobby packs and one in 8,306 HTA packs, these five cards feature not only the rookie reprint of these players but also a piece of a bat they used during their career as well as an authentic autograph.

Nm-Mt Ex-Mt
1 Willie Mays
2 Duke Snider
3 Minnie Minoso
4 Hank Bauer
5 Gil McDougald

2001 Bowman Draft Picks

Issued as a 112-card factory set with a SRP of $45.99, these sets feature 100 cards of young players along with an autograph and relic card in each box. Twelve sets were included in each case. Cards BDP51 and BDP71 featuring Alex Herrera and Brad Thomas are uncorrected errors in that the card backs were switched for each player.

Nm-Mt Ex-Mt
COMP.FACT.SET (112) 30.00 9.00
COMPLETE SET (110) 20.00 6.00
BDP1 Alfredo Amezaga RC .50 .15
BDP2 Andrew Good .30 .09
BDP3 Kelly Johnson RC .40 .12
BDP4 Larry Bigbie .30 .09
BDP5 Matt Thompson RC .40 .12
BDP6 Wilton Chavez RC .40 .12
BDP7 Joe Borchard RC 1.25 .35
BDP8 David Espinosa .30 .09
BDP9 Zach Day RC .50 .15
BDP10 Brad Hawpe RC 2.00 .60
BDP11 Nate Cornejo .30 .09
BDP12 Matt Cooper RC .40 .12
BDP13 Brad Lidge .30 .09
BDP14 Angel Berroa RC 1.50 .45
BDP15 L. Matthews RC .40 .12
BDP16 Jose Garcia .30 .09
BDP17 Grant Balfour RC .30 .09
BDP18 Ron Chiavacci RC .30 .09
BDP19 Jae Seo .30 .09
BDP20 Juan Rivera .30 .09
BDP21 D'Angelo Jimenez .30 .09
BDP22 Juan A.Pena RC .40 .12
BDP23 Marlon Byrd RC 2.00 .60
BDP24 Sean Burnett .30 .09
BDP25 Josh Pearce RC .40 .12
BDP26 B. Duckworth RC .40 .12
BDP27 Jack Taschner RC .40 .12
BDP28 Marcus Thames .30 .09
BDP29 Brent Abernathy .30 .09
BDP30 David Elder RC .40 .12
BDP31 Scott Cassidy RC .40 .12
BDP32 D. Tankersley RC .40 .12
BDP33 Denny Stark .30 .09
BDP34 Dave Williams RC .40 .12
BDP35 Boof Bonser RC .50 .15
BDP36 Kris Foster RC .30 .09
BDP37 Luis Garcia RC .40 .12
BDP38 Shawn Chacon .30 .09
BDP39 Mike Rivera RC .40 .12
BDP40 Will Smith RC .40 .12
BDP41 M. Ensberg RC 1.00 .30
BDP42 Ken Harvey .30 .09
BDP43 R. Rodriguez RC .40 .12
BDP44 Jose Mieses RC .40 .12
BDP45 Luis Maza RC .40 .12
BDP46 Julio Perez RC .40 .12
BDP47 Dustan Mohr RC .40 .12
BDP48 Randy Flores RC .30 .09
BDP49 Covelli Crisp RC .75 .23
BDP50 Kevin Reese RC .40 .12
BDP51 Brad Thomas UER .30 .09
Card back is BDP71 Alex Herrera
BDP52 Xavier Nady .30 .09
BDP53 Ryan Vogelsong .30 .09
BDP54 Carlos Silva .30 .09
BDP55 Dan Wright .30 .09
BDP56 Brent Butler .30 .09
BDP57 Brandon Knight RC .30 .09
BDP58 Brian Reith RC .40 .12
BDP59 M. Valenzuela RC .40 .12
BDP60 Bobby Hill RC .75 .23
BDP61 Rich Rundles RC .40 .12
BDP62 Rick Elder .30 .09
BDP63 J.D. Closser .30 .09
BDP64 Scot Shields .30 .09
BDP65 Miguel Olivo .30 .09
BDP66 Stubby Clapp RC .30 .09
BDP67 J. Williams RC 2.50 .75
BDP68 Jason Lane RC .50 .15
BDP69 Chase Utley RC 2.00 .60
BDP70 Erik Bedard RC .75 .23
BDP71 A. Herrera UER RC .30 .09
Card back is BDP51 Brad Thomas
BDP72 Juan Cruz RC .40 .12
BDP73 Billy Martin RC .40 .12
BDP74 Ronnie Merrill RC .40 .12
BDP75 Jason Kinchen RC .40 .12
BDP76 Wilkin Ruan RC .40 .12
BDP77 Cody Ransom RC .30 .09
BDP78 Bud Smith RC .40 .12
BDP79 Wily Mo Pena .30 .09
BDP80 Jeff Nettles RC .40 .12
BDP81 Jamal Strong RC .40 .12
BDP82 Bill Ortega RC .40 .12
BDP83 Mike Bell .30 .09
BDP84 Ichiro Suzuki RC 5.00 1.50
BDP85 F. Rodney RC .40 .12
BDP86 Chris Smith RC .40 .12
BDP87 J.VanBenschoten RC 1.25 .35
BDP88 Bobby Crosby RC 10.00 3.00
BDP89 Kenny Baugh RC .40 .12
BDP90 Jake Gautreau RC .40 .12
BDP91 Gabe Gross RC .50 .15
BDP92 Kris Honel RC 1.50 .45
BDP93 Dan Denham RC .40 .12
BDP94 Aaron Heilman RC .75 .23
BDP95 Irvin Guzman RC 2.00 .60
BDP96 Mike Jones RC .50 .15
BDP97 J. Griffin RC .50 .15
BDP98 Macay McBride RC .40 .12
BDP99 J. Rheinecker RC .40 .12
BDP100 B. Sardinha RC .50 .15
BDP101 J. Weintraub RC .40 .12
BDP102 J.D. Martin RC .40 .12
BDP103 Jayson Nix RC .75 .23
BDP104 Noah Lowry RC .40 .12
BDP105 Richard Lewis RC .40 .12
BDP106 B. Hennessey RC .40 .12
BDP107 Jeff Mathis RC 2.00 .60
BDP108 Jon Skaggs RC .40 .12
BDP109 Justin Pope RC .40 .12
BDP110 Josh Burrus RC .40 .12

2001 Bowman Draft Picks Autographs

Inserted one per Bowman draft pick factory set, these 37 cards feature autographs of some of the leading players from the Bowman Draft Pick set.

Nm-Mt Ex-Mt
BDPAAA A. Amezaga 15.00 4.50
BDPAAC Alex Cintron 15.00 4.50
BDPAAE Adam Everett 10.00 3.00
BDPAAF Alex Fernandez 10.00 3.00
BDPAAG Alexis Gomez 10.00 3.00
BDPAAH Aaron Herr 10.00 3.00
BDPAAK Austin Kearns 15.00 4.50
BDPABB Bobby Bradley 10.00 3.00
BDPABH Beau Hale 10.00 3.00
BDPABP Brandon Phillips 10.00 3.00
BDPABS Bud Smith 10.00 3.00
BDPACG C. Guerrero 10.00 3.00
BDPACI Cesar Izturis 10.00 3.00
BDPACP Christian Parra 10.00 3.00
BDPAER Ed Rogers 10.00 3.00
BDPAFL Felipe Lopez 10.00 3.00
BDPAGA Garrett Atkins 15.00 4.50
BDPAGJ Gary Johnson 10.00 3.00
BDPAJA Jared Abruzzo 10.00 3.00
BDPAJK Joe Kennedy 10.00 3.00
BDPAJL John Lackey 10.00 3.00
BDPAJP Joel Pineiro 25.00 7.50
BDPAJT Joe Torres 10.00 3.00
BDPANJ Nick Johnson 15.00 4.50
BDPANR Nick Regilio 10.00 3.00
BDPARC Ryan Church 15.00 4.50
BDPARD Ryan Dittfurth 10.00 3.00
BDPARL Ryan Ludwick 10.00 3.00
BDPARO Roy Oswalt 20.00 6.00
BDPASH Scott Heard 10.00 3.00
BDPASS Scott Seabol 10.00 3.00
BDPATO Tomo Ohka 15.00 4.50
BDPAANC A. Cameron 10.00 3.00
BDPABJS Brian Specht 10.00 3.00
BDPAJMW Justin Wayne 15.00 4.50
BDPARMM Ryan Madson 10.00 3.00
BDPAROC R. Carvajal 10.00 3.00

2001 Bowman Draft Picks Futures Game Relics

Inserted one per factory set, these 26 cards feature relics from the futures game.

Nm-Mt Ex-Mt
FGRAA Alfredo Amezaga 10.00 3.00
FGRAD Adam Dunn 8.00 2.40
FGRAG Adrian Gonzalez 8.00 2.40
FGRAH Alex Herrera 8.00 2.40
FGRBM Brett Myers 8.00 2.40
FGRCD Cody Ransom 8.00 2.40
FGRCG Chris George 8.00 2.40
FGRCH Carlos Hernandez 8.00 2.40
FGRCU Chase Utley 20.00 6.00
FGREB Erik Bedard 10.00 3.00
FGRGB Grant Balfour 8.00 2.40
FGRHB Hank Blalock 25.00 7.50
FGRJB Joe Borchard 10.00 3.00
FGRJC Juan Cruz 8.00 2.40
FGRJP Josh Pearce 8.00 2.40
FGRJR Juan Rivera 8.00 2.40
FGRJAP Juan A.Pena 8.00 2.40
FGRLG Luis Garcia 8.00 2.40
FGRMC Miguel Cabrera 25.00 7.50
FGRMR Mike Rivera 8.00 2.40
FGRRR R. Rodriguez 8.00 2.40
FGRSC Scott Chiasson 8.00 2.40
FGRSS Seung Song 10.00 3.00
FGRTB Toby Hall 8.00 2.40
FGRWB Wilson Betemit 8.00 2.40
FGRWP Wily Mo Pena 8.00 2.40

2001 Bowman Draft Picks Relics

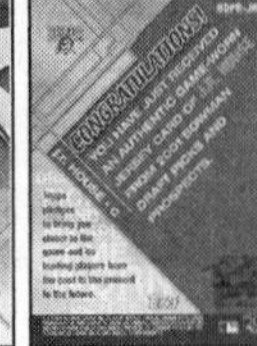

Inserted one per factory set, these six cards feature relics from some of the most popular prospects in the Bowman Draft Pick set.

Nm-Mt Ex-Mt
BDPRCI Cesar Izturis 10.00 3.00
BDPRGJ Gary Johnson 10.00 3.00
BDPRNR Nick Regilio 10.00 3.00
BDPRRC Ryan Church 15.00 4.50
BDPRBJS Brian Specht 10.00 3.00
BDPRJRH J.R. House 10.00 3.00

2002 Bowman

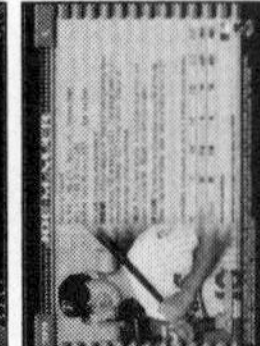

This 440 card set was issued in May, 2002. It was issued in 10 card packs which were packed 24 packs to a box and 12 boxes per case. These packs had an SRP of $3 per pack. The first 110 cards of this set featured veterans while the rest of the set featured rookies and prospects.

Nm-Mt Ex-Mt
COMPLETE SET (440) 80.00 24.00
COMMON CARD (1-110) .30 .09
COMMON CARD (111-440) .30 .09
1 Adam Dunn .30 .09
2 Derek Jeter 2.00 .60
3 Alex Rodriguez 1.25 .35
4 Miguel Tejada .30 .09
5 Nomar Garciaparra 1.25 .35
6 Toby Hall .30 .09
7 Brandon Duckworth .30 .09
8 Paul LoDuca .30 .09
9 Brian Giles .30 .09
10 C.C. Sabathia .30 .09
11 Curt Schilling .50 .15
12 Tsuyoshi Shinjo .30 .09
13 Ramon Hernandez .30 .09
14 Jose Cruz Jr. .30 .09
15 Albert Pujols 1.50 .45
16 Joe Mays .30 .09
17 Javy Lopez .30 .09
18 J.T. Snow .30 .09
19 David Segui .30 .09
20 Jorge Posada .50 .15
21 Doug Mientkiewicz .30 .09
22 Jerry Hairston Jr. .30 .09
23 Bernie Williams .50 .15
24 Mike Sweeney .30 .09
25 Jason Giambi .75 .23
26 Ryan Dempster .30 .09
27 Ryan Klesko .30 .09
28 Mark Quinn .30 .09
29 Jeff Kent .30 .09
30 Eric Chavez .30 .09
31 Adrian Beltre .30 .09
32 Andruw Jones .30 .09
33 Alfonso Soriano .50 .15
34 Aramis Ramirez .30 .09
35 Greg Maddux 1.25 .35
36 Andy Pettitte .50 .15
37 Bartolo Colon .30 .09
38 Ben Sheets .30 .09
39 Bobby Higginson .30 .09
40 Ivan Rodriguez .75 .23
41 Brad Penny .30 .09
42 Carlos Lee .30 .09
43 Damion Easley .30 .09
44 Preston Wilson .30 .09
45 Jeff Bagwell .50 .15
46 Eric Milton .30 .09
47 Rafael Palmeiro .50 .15
48 Gary Sheffield .30 .09
49 J.D. Drew .30 .09
50 Jim Thome .75 .23
51 Ichiro Suzuki 1.25 .35
52 Bud Smith .30 .09
53 Chan Ho Park .30 .09
54 D'Angelo Jimenez .30 .09
55 Ken Griffey Jr. 1.25 .35
56 Wade Miller .30 .09
57 Vladimir Guerrero .75 .23
58 Troy Glaus .50 .15
59 Shawn Green .30 .09
60 Kerry Wood .75 .23

61 Jack Wilson .30 .09
62 Kevin Brown .30 .09
63 Marcus Giles .30 .09
64 Pat Burrell .30 .09
65 Larry Walker .50 .15
66 Sammy Sosa 1.25 .35
67 Raul Mondesi .30 .09
68 Tim Hudson .30 .09
69 Lance Berkman .30 .09
70 Mike Mussina .75 .23
71 Barry Zito .50 .15
72 Jimmy Rollins .30 .09
73 Barry Bonds 2.00 .60
74 Craig Biggio .50 .15
75 Todd Helton .50 .15
76 Roger Clemens 1.50 .45
77 Frank Catalanotto .30 .09
78 Josh Towers .30 .09
79 Roy Oswalt .30 .09
80 Chipper Jones .75 .23
81 Cristian Guzman .30 .09
82 Darin Erstad .30 .09
83 Freddy Garcia .30 .09
84 Jason Tyner .30 .09
85 Carlos Delgado .30 .09
86 Jon Lieber .30 .09
87 Juan Pierre .30 .09
88 Matt Morris .30 .09
89 Phil Nevin .30 .09
90 Jim Edmonds .30 .09
91 Magglio Ordonez .30 .09
92 Mike Hampton .30 .09
93 Rafael Furcal .30 .09
94 Richie Sexson .30 .09
95 Luis Gonzalez .30 .09
96 Scott Rolen .50 .15
97 Tim Redding .30 .09
98 Moises Alou .30 .09
99 Jose Vidro .30 .09
100 Mike Piazza 1.25 .35
101 Pedro Martinez UER .75 .23
Career strikeout total incorrect
102 Geoff Jenkins .30 .09
103 Johnny Damon .30 .09
104 Mike Cameron .30 .09
105 Randy Johnson .75 .23
106 David Eckstein .30 .09
107 Javier Vazquez .30 .09
108 Mark Mulder .30 .09
109 Robert Fick .30 .09
110 Roberto Alomar .75 .23
111 Wilson Betemit .30 .09
112 Chris Tritle RC .50 .15
113 Ed Rogers .30 .09
114 Juan Pena .30 .09
115 Josh Beckett .60 .18
116 Juan Cruz .30 .09
117 Noochie Varner RC .50 .15
118 Taylor Buchholz RC .75 .23
119 Mike Rivera .30 .09
120 Hank Blalock 1.00 .30
121 Hansel Izquierdo RC .50 .15
122 Orlando Hudson .30 .09
123 Bill Hall .30 .09
124 Jose Reyes 1.00 .30
125 Juan Rivera .30 .09
126 Eric Valent .30 .09
127 Scotty Layfield RC .50 .15
128 Austin Kearns .40 .12
129 Nic Jackson RC .50 .15
130 Chris Baker RC .50 .15
131 Chad Qualls RC .50 .15
132 Marcus Thames .30 .09
133 Nathan Haynes .30 .09
134 Brett Evert .30 .09
135 Joe Borchard .40 .12
136 Ryan Christianson .30 .09
137 Josh Hamilton .30 .09
138 Corey Patterson .40 .12
139 Travis Wilson .30 .09
140 Alex Escobar .30 .09
141 Alexis Gomez .30 .09
142 Nick Johnson .40 .12
143 Kenny Kelly .30 .09
144 Marlon Byrd .40 .12
145 Kory DeHaan .30 .09
146 Matt Belisle .30 .09
147 Carlos Hernandez .30 .09
148 Sean Burroughs .40 .12
149 Angel Berroa .40 .12
150 Aubrey Huff .40 .12
151 Travis Hafner .40 .12
152 Brandon Berger .30 .09
153 David Krynzel .30 .09
154 Ruben Salazar .30 .09
155 J.R. House .30 .09
156 Juan Silvestre .30 .09
157 Dewon Brazelton .30 .09
158 Jayson Werth .30 .09
159 Larry Barnes .30 .09
160 Elvis Pena .30 .09
161 Ruben Gotay RC .50 .15
162 Tommy Marx RC .50 .15
163 John Suomi RC .50 .15
164 Javier Colina .30 .09
165 Greg Sain RC .50 .15
166 Robert Cosby RC .50 .15
167 Angel Pagan RC .50 .15
168 Ralph Santana RC .50 .15
169 Joe Orloski RC .50 .15
170 Shayne Wright RC .50 .15
171 Jay Caligiuri RC .50 .15
172 Greg Montalbano RC .75 .23
173 Rich Harden RC 5.00 1.50
174 Rich Thompson RC .50 .15
175 Fred Bastardo RC .50 .15
176 Alejandro Giron RC .50 .15
177 Jesus Medrano RC .50 .15
178 Kevin Deaton RC .50 .15
179 Mike Rosamond RC .50 .15
180 Jon Guzman RC .50 .15
181 Gerard Oakes RC .50 .15
182 Francisco Liriano RC .75 .23
183 Matt Allegra RC .50 .15
184 Mike Snyder RC .50 .15
185 James Shanks RC .50 .15
186 Anderson Hernandez RC .50 .15
187 Dan Trumble RC .50 .15
188 Luis DePaula RC .50 .15
189 Randall Shelley RC .50 .15
190 Richard Lane RC .50 .15
191 Antwon Rollins RC .50 .15
192 Ryan Bukvich RC .50 .15
193 Derrick Lewis .30 .09
194 Eric Miller RC .50 .15
195 Justin Schuda RC .50 .15
196 Brian West RC .50 .15
197 Adam Roller RC .50 .15
198 Neal Frendling RC .50 .15
199 Jeremy Hill RC .50 .15
200 James Barrett RC .50 .15
201 Brett Kay RC .50 .15
202 Ryan Mottl RC .50 .15
203 Brad Nelson RC 1.50 .45
204 Juan M. Gonzalez RC .50 .15
205 Curtis Legendre RC .50 .15
206 Ronald Acuna RC .50 .15
207 Chris Flinn RC .50 .15
208 Nick Alvarez RC .50 .15
209 Jason Ellison RC .50 .15
210 Blake McGinley RC .50 .15
211 Dan Phillips RC .50 .15
212 Demetrius Heath RC .50 .15
213 Eric Bruntlett RC .50 .15
214 Joe Jiannetti RC .50 .15
215 Mike Hill RC .50 .15
216 Ricardo Cordova RC .50 .15
217 Mark Hamilton RC .50 .15
218 David Mattox RC .50 .15
219 Jose Morban RC .50 .15
220 Scott Wiggins RC .50 .15
221 Steve Green .30 .09
222 Brian Rogers .30 .09
223 Chin-Hui Tsao .40 .12
224 Kenny Baugh .30 .09
225 Nate Teut .30 .09
226 Josh Wilson RC .50 .15
227 Christian Parker .30 .09
228 Tim Raines Jr. .30 .09
229 Anastacio Martinez RC .50 .15
230 Richard Lewis .30 .09
231 Tim Kalita RC .50 .15
232 Edwin Almonte RC .50 .15
233 Hee-Seop Choi .60 .18
234 Ty Howington .30 .09
235 Victor Alvarez RC .50 .15
236 Morgan Ensberg .40 .12
237 Jeff Austin RC .50 .15
238 Luis Terrero .30 .09
239 Adam Wainwright .40 .12
240 Clint Weibl RC .50 .15
241 Eric Cyr .30 .09
242 Marlyn Tisdale RC .50 .15
243 John VanBenschoten .60 .18
244 Ryan Raburn RC .50 .15
245 Miguel Cabrera 2.00 .60
246 Jung Bong .30 .09
247 Raul Chavez RC .50 .15
248 Erik Bedard .30 .09
249 Chris Snelling RC 1.25 .35
250 Joe Rogers RC .50 .15
251 Nate Field RC .50 .15
252 Matt Herges RC .50 .15
253 Matt Childers RC .50 .15
254 Erick Almonte .30 .09
255 Nick Neugebauer .30 .09
256 Ron Calloway RC .50 .15
257 Seung Song .30 .09
258 Brandon Phillips .30 .09
259 Cole Barthel RC .50 .15
260 Jason Lane .30 .09
261 Jae Seo .30 .09
262 Randy Flores .30 .09
263 Scott Chiasson .30 .09
264 Chase Utley .60 .18
265 Tony Alvarez .30 .09
266 Ben Howard RC .50 .15
267 Nelson Castro RC .50 .15
268 Mark Lukasiewicz RC .50 .15
269 Eric Glaser RC .50 .15
270 Rob Henkel RC .50 .15
271 Jose Valverde RC .75 .23
272 Ricardo Rodriguez .30 .09
273 Chris Smith .30 .09
274 Mark Prior 2.50 .75
275 Miguel Olivo .30 .09
276 Ben Broussard .30 .09
277 Zach Sorensen .30 .09
278 Brian Mallette RC .50 .15
279 Brad Wilkerson .30 .09
280 Carl Crawford .40 .12
281 Chone Figgins RC .50 .15
282 Jimmy Alvarez RC .50 .15
283 Gavin Floyd RC 2.50 .75
284 Josh Bonifay RC .50 .15
285 Garrett Guzman RC .50 .15
286 Blake Williams .30 .09
287 Matt Holliday .30 .09
288 Ryan Madson .30 .09
289 Luis Torres .30 .09
290 Jeff Verplancke RC .50 .15
291 Nate Espy RC .50 .15
292 Jeff Lincoln RC .50 .15
293 Ryan Snare RC .50 .15
294 Jose Ortiz .30 .09
295 Eric Munson .30 .09
296 Denny Bautista .40 .12
297 Willy Aybar .30 .09
298 Kelly Johnson .30 .09
299 Justin Morneau .60 .18
300 Derrick Van Dusen .30 .09
301 Chad Petty .40 .12
302 Mike Restovich .30 .09
303 Shawn Fagan .30 .09
304 Yurendell DeCaster RC .50 .15
305 Justin Wayne .30 .09
306 Mike Peeples RC .50 .15
307 Joel Guzman .40 .12
308 Ryan Vogelsong .30 .09
309 Jorge Padilla RC .50 .15
310 Grady Sizemore .60 .18
311 Joe Jester RC .50 .15
312 Jim Journell .30 .09
313 Bobby Seay .30 .09
314 Ryan Church RC .60 .18
315 Grant Balfour .30 .09
316 Mitch Jones .30 .09
317 Travis Foley RC .50 .15
318 Bobby Crosby 1.00 .30
319 Adrian Gonzalez .40 .12
320 Ronnie Merrill .30 .09
321 Joel Pineiro .40 .12
322 John-Ford Griffin .30 .09
323 Brian Forystek RC .50 .15
324 Sean Douglass .30 .09
325 Manny Delcarmen RC .50 .15
326 Donnie Bridges .30 .09
327 Jim Kavourias RC .50 .15
328 Gabe Gross .30 .09
329 Jon Rauch .30 .09
330 Bill Ortega .30 .09
331 Joey Hammond RC .50 .15
332 Ramon Moreta RC .50 .15
333 Ron Davenport .30 .09
334 Brett Myers .40 .12
335 Carlos Pena .30 .09
336 Ezequiel Astacio RC .50 .15
337 Edwin Yan RC .50 .15
338 Josh Girdley .30 .09
339 Shaun Boyd .30 .09
340 Juan Rincon .30 .09
341 Chris Duffy RC .50 .15
342 Jason Kinchen .30 .09
343 Brad Thomas .30 .09
344 David Kelton .30 .09
345 Rafael Soriano .40 .12
346 Colin Young RC .50 .15
347 Eric Byrnes .30 .09
348 Chris Narveson RC .75 .23
349 John Rheinecker .30 .09
350 Mike Wilson RC .50 .15
351 Justin Sherrod RC .50 .15
352 Deivi Mendez .30 .09
353 Wily Mo Pena .30 .09
354 Brett Roneberg RC .50 .15
355 Trey Lunsford RC .50 .15
356 Jimmy Gobble RC 1.50 .45
357 Brent Butler .30 .09
358 Aaron Heilman .30 .09
359 Wilkin Ruan .30 .09
360 Brian Wolfe RC .50 .15
361 Cody Ransom .30 .09
362 Koyie Hill .30 .09
363 Scott Cassidy .50 .15
364 Tony Fontana RC .50 .15
365 Mark Teixeira 1.00 .30
366 Doug Sessions RC .50 .15
367 Victor Hall .30 .09
368 Josh Cisneros RC .50 .15
369 Kevin Mench .30 .09
370 Tike Redman .30 .09
371 Jeff Heaverlo .30 .09
372 Carlos Brackley RC .50 .15
373 Brad Hawpe .30 .09
374 Jesus Colome .30 .09
375 David Espinosa .30 .09
376 Jesse Foppert RC 2.00 .60
377 Ross Peeples RC .50 .15
378 Alex Requena RC .50 .15
379 Joe Mauer RC 8.00 2.40
380 Carlos Silva .30 .09
381 David Wright RC 2.50 .75
382 Craig Kuzmic RC .50 .15
383 Pete Zamora RC .50 .15
384 Matt Parker RC .50 .15
385 Keith Ginter .30 .09
386 Gary Cates Jr. .50 .15
387 Justin Reid RC .50 .15
388 Jake Mauer RC .50 .15
389 Dennis Tankersley .30 .09
390 Josh Barfield RC 3.00 .90
391 Luis Maza .30 .09
392 Henry Pichardo RC .50 .15
393 Michael Floyd RC .50 .15
394 Clint Nageotte RC 1.25 .35
395 Raymond Cabrera RC .50 .15
396 Mauricio Lara RC .50 .15
397 Alejandro Cadena RC .50 .15
398 Jonny Gomes RC 1.25 .35
399 Jason Bulger RC .50 .15
400 Bobby Jenks RC 1.50 .45
401 David Gil RC .50 .15
402 Joel Crump RC .50 .15
403 Kazuhisa Ishii RC 1.50 .45
404 So Taguchi RC 1.50 .45
405 Ryan Doumit RC .75 .23
406 Macay McBride .30 .09
407 Brandon Claussen 1.00 .30
408 Chin-Feng Chen .40 .12
409 Josh Phelps .30 .09
410 Freddie Money RC .75 .23
411 Cliff Bartosh RC .50 .15
412 Josh Pearce .30 .09
413 Lyle Overbay .30 .09
414 Ryan Anderson .30 .09
415 Terrance Hill RC .50 .15
416 John Rodriguez RC .50 .15
417 Richard Stahl .30 .09
418 Brian Specht .30 .09
419 Chris Latham RC .50 .15
420 Carlos Cabrera RC .50 .15
421 Jose Bautista RC 1.25 .35
422 Kevin Frederick RC .50 .15
423 Jerome Williams 1.00 .30
424 Napoleon Calzado RC .50 .15
425 Benito Baez .30 .09
426 Xavier Nady .30 .09
427 Jason Botts RC .50 .15
428 Steve Bechler RC .50 .15
429 Reed Johnson RC .75 .23
430 Mark Outlaw RC .50 .15
431 Billy Sylvester .30 .09
432 Luke Lockwood .30 .09
433 Jake Peavy .40 .12
434 Alfredo Amezaga .30 .09
435 Aaron Cook RC .50 .15
436 Josh Shaffer RC .50 .15
437 Dan Wright .30 .09
438 Ryan Gripp RC .50 .15
439 Alex Herrera .30 .09
440 Jason Bay RC 1.50 .45

2002 Bowman Gold

Inserted one per pack, this is a parallel to the 2002 Bowman set. These cards can be differentiated by the Bowman logo and the facsimile signature in gold foil stamping.

Nm-Mt Ex-Mt
*RED 1-110: 1.25X TO 3X BASIC
*BLUE 111-440: .75X TO 2X BASIC
*BLUE ROOKIES 111-440: .75X TO 2X BASIC

2002 Bowman Uncirculated

Inserted at a stated rate of one per box, these cards were issued as redemptions through the Pit.Com. These cards were printed to a stated print run of 672 sets and could be redeemed and were kept in special holders. The cards could be exchanged until December 31, 2002 with delivery beginning July 7, 2002.

Nm-Mt Ex-Mt
112 Chris Tritle
117 Noochie Varner
118 Taylor Buchholz
121 Hansel Izquierdo
123 Bill Hall
127 Scotty Layfield
129 Nic Jackson
130 Chris Baker
131 Chad Qualls
161 Ruben Gotay
162 Tommy Marx
163 John Suomi
164 Javier Colina
165 Greg Sain
222 Brian Rogers
229 Anastacio Martinez
230 Richard Lewis
231 Tim Kalita
232 Edwin Almonte
235 Victor Alvarez
237 Jeff Austin
240 Clint Weibl
244 Ryan Raburn
249 Chris Snelling
250 Joe Rogers
251 Nate Field
253 Matt Childers
256 Ron Calloway
259 Cole Barthel
266 Ben Howard
267 Nelson Castro
269 Eric Glaser
270 Rob Henkel
271 Jose Valverde
278 Brian Mallette
281 Chone Figgins
282 Jimmy Alvarez
283 Gavin Floyd
284 Josh Bonifay
285 Garrett Guzman
290 Jeff Verplancke
291 Nate Espy
293 Ryan Snare
304 Yurendell De Caster
306 Mike Peeples
309 Jorge Padilla
311 Joe Jester
314 Ryan Church
317 Travis Foley
323 Brian Forystek
325 Manny Delcarmen
327 Jim Kavourias
331 Joey Hammond
336 Ezequiel Astacio
337 Edwin Yan
341 Chris Duffy
348 Chris Narveson
351 Justin Sherrod
354 Brett Roneberg
355 Trey Lunsford
356 Jimmy Gobble
360 Brian Wolfe
362 Koyie Hill
364 Tony Fontana
366 Doug Sessions
372 Carlos Brackley
376 Jesse Foppert
377 Ross Peeples
378 Alex Requena
379 Joe Mauer
381 David Wright
382 Craig Kuzmic
383 Pete Zamora
384 Matt Parker
386 Gary Cates Jr.
387 Justin Reid
388 Jake Mauer
390 Josh Barfield
392 Henry Pichardo
393 Michael Floyd
394 Clint Nageotte
395 Raymond Cabrera
396 Mauricio Lara
397 Alejandro Cadena
398 Jonny Gomes
399 Jason Bulger
400 Bobby Jenks
401 David Gil
402 Joel Crump
403 Kazuhisa Ishii
404 So Taguchi
405 Ryan Doumit
410 Freddie Money
411 Cliff Bartosh
415 Terrance Hill
416 John Rodriguez
419 Chris Latham
420 Carlos Cabrera
421 Jose Bautista
422 Kevin Frederick
424 Napoleon Calzado
425 Benito Baez
427 Jason Botts
428 Steve Bechler
429 Reed Johnson
430 Mark Outlaw
436 Josh Shaffer
437 Dan Wright
438 Ryan Gripp
440 Jason Bay
NNO Exchange Card

2002 Bowman Autographs

Inserted in packs at overall odds of one in 40 hobby packs, one in 24 HTA packs and one in 53 retail packs, this 45 card set featued autographs of leading rookies and prospects.

Nm-Mt Ex-Mt
GROUP A 1:67 H, 1:39 HTA, 1:89 R
GROUP B 1:129 H, 1:74 HTA, 1:170 R

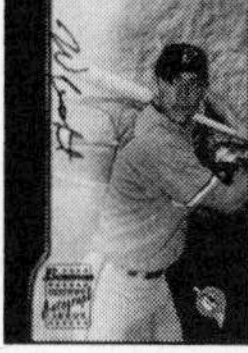

GROUP C 1:881 H, 1:507 HTA, 1:1165 R
GROUP D 1:1558 H, 1:896 HTA, 1:2060 R
GROUP E 1:1685 H, 1:968 HTA, 1:2238 R
OVERALL ODDS 1:40 H, 1:24 HTA, 1:53 R
ONE ADD'L AUTO PER SEALED HTA BOX
BA-AA Alfredo Amezaga A 10.00 3.00
BA-AH Aubrey Huff A 15.00 4.50
BA-BA Brandon Claussen A 15.00 4.50
BA-BC Ben Christensen A 10.00 3.00
BA-BD Brian Cardwell A 10.00 3.00
BA-BBC Boof Bonser A 10.00 3.00
BA-BJC Brian Specht C 10.00 3.00
BA-BSS Bud Smith B 10.00 3.00
BA-CK Charles Kegley A 10.00 3.00
BA-CR Cody Ransom B 10.00 3.00
BA-CS Chris Smith B 10.00 3.00
BA-CT Chris Tritle B 10.00 3.00
BA-CU Chase Utley A 25.00 7.50
BA-DV Domingo Valdez A 10.00 3.00
BA-DW Dan Wright B 10.00 3.00
BA-GA Garrett Atkins A 15.00 4.50
BA-GJ Gary Johnson C 10.00 3.00
BA-HB Hank Blalock B 25.00 7.50
BA-JB Josh Beckett B 40.00 12.00
BA-JD Jeff Davanon A 10.00 3.00
BA-JL Jason Lane A 10.00 3.00
BA-JP Juan Pena A 10.00 3.00
BA-JS Juan Silvestre A 10.00 3.00
BA-JAB Jason Botts B 10.00 3.00
BA-JLW Jerome Williams A 15.00 4.50
BA-KG Keith Ginter B 10.00 3.00
BA-LB Larry Bigbie A 10.00 3.00
BA-MB Marlon Byrd B 15.00 4.50
BA-MC Matt Cooper A 10.00 3.00
BA-MD Manny Delcarmen A 10.00 3.00
BA-ME Morgan Ensberg A 15.00 4.50
BA-MP Mark Prior B 80.00 24.00
BA-NJ Nick Johnson B 15.00 4.50
BA-NN Nick Neugebauer E 10.00 3.00
BA-NV Noochie Varner B 10.00 3.00
BA-RF Randy Flores D 10.00 3.00
BA-RF Ryan Franklin B 10.00 3.00
BA-RH Ryan Hannaman A 10.00 3.00
BA-RO Roy Oswalt B 15.00 4.50
BA-RV Ryan Vogelsong B 10.00 3.00
BA-TB Tony Blanco A 10.00 3.00
BA-TH Toby Hall B 10.00 3.00
BA-TS Terrmel Sledge B 15.00 4.50
BA-WB Wilson Betemit B 10.00 3.00
BA-WS Will Smith A 10.00 3.00

2002 Bowman Futures Game Autograph Relics

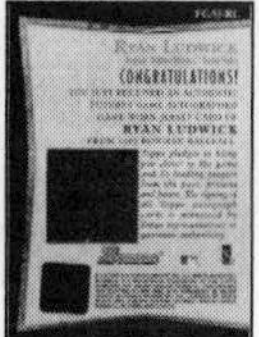

Inserted at overall odds of one in 196 hobby packs, one in 113 HTA packs and one in 259 retail packs for jersey cards and one in 126 HTA packs for base cards, these cards feature pieces of memorabilia and the player's autograph from the 2001 Futures Game.

Nm-Mt Ex-Mt
GROUP A JSY 1:2193 H, 1:1262 HTA, 1:2898 R
GROUP B JSY 1:1599 H, 1:923 HTA, 1:2125 R
GROUP C JSY 1:522 H, 1:301 HTA, 1:688 R
GROUP D JSY 1:1533 H, 1:882 HTA, 1:2028 R
GROUP E JSY 1:1425 H, 1:822 HTA, 1:1882 R
GROUP F JSY 1:1316 H, 1:759 HTA, 1:1738 R
CH Carlos Hernandez Jsy B 25.00 7.50
CP Carlos Pena Jsy D 25.00 7.50
DT Dennis Tankersley Jsy E 25.00 7.50
JRH J.R. House Jsy C 25.00 7.50
JW Jerome Williams Jsy F 30.00 9.00
NJ Nick Johnson Jsy C 25.00 7.50
RL Ryan Ludwick Jsy C 25.00 7.50
TH Toby Hall Base 25.00 7.50
WB Wilson Betemit Jsy A 25.00 7.50

2002 Bowman Game Used Relics

Inserted at an overall stated odd of one in 74 hobby packs, one in 43 HTA packs and one in 99 retail packs, these 26 cards features some of the leading prospects from the set along a piece of game-used memorabilia.

Nm-Mt Ex-Mt
GROUP A BAT 1:3236 H, 1:1866 HTA, 1:4331 R
GROUP B BAT 1:1472 H, 1:849 HTA, 1:1949 R
GROUP C BAT 1:1647 H, 1:948 HTA, 1:2180 R
GROUP D BAT 1:894 H, 1:515 HTA, 1:1180 R
GROUP E BAT 1:375 H, 1:216 HTA, 1:496 R
GROUP F BAT 1:1042 H, 1:601 HTA, 1:1381 R

GROUP G BAT 1:939 H, 1:541 HTA, 1:1237 R
OVERALL BAT 1:135 H, 1:78 HTA, 1:179 R
GROUP A JSY 1:2085 H,1:1202 HTA,1:2762 R
GROUP B JSY 1:1916 H, 1:528 HTA, 1:1213 R
GROUP C JSY 1:223 H, 1:129 HTA, 1:295 R
OVERALL JSY 1:165 H, 1:95 HTA, 1:219 R
BR-AB Angel Berroa Bat B 15.00 4.50
BR-AC Antoine Cameron Bat C 10.00 3.00
BR-AE Adam Everett Bat E 8.00 2.40
BR-AF Alex Fernandez Bat B 10.00 3.00
BR-AF Alex Fernandez Jsy C 8.00 2.40
BR-AG Alexis Gomez Bat A 10.00 3.00
BR-AK Austin Kearns Bat E 8.00 2.40
BR-ALC Alex Cintron Bat E 8.00 2.40
BR-CG Cristian Guerrero Bat E 8.00 2.40
BR-CI Cesar Izturis Bat D 8.00 2.40
BR-CP Corey Patterson Bat B 15.00 4.50
BR-CY Colin Young Jsy C 8.00 2.40
BR-DJ D'Angelo Jimenez Bat C 10.00 3.00
BR-FJ Forrest Johnson Bat G 8.00 2.40
BR-GA Garrett Atkins Bat F 10.00 3.00
BR-JA Jared Abruzzo Bat D 8.00 2.40
BR-JA Jared Abruzzo Jsy C 8.00 2.40
BR-JL Jason Lane Jsy B 8.00 2.40
BR-JS Jamal Strong Jsy A 8.00 2.40
BR-NC Nate Cornejo Jsy C 8.00 2.40
BR-NN Nick Neugebauer Jsy C 8.00 2.40
BR-RC Ryan Church Bat D 10.00 3.00
BR-RD Ryan Dittfurth Jsy C 8.00 2.40
BR-RM Ryan Madson Bat E 8.00 2.40
BR-RS Ruben Salazar Bat A 10.00 3.00
BR-RST Richard Stahl Jsy B 8.00 2.40

2002 Bowman Draft

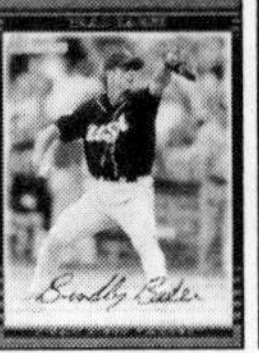
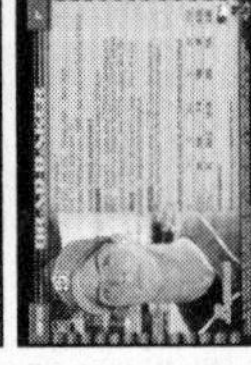

This 165 card set was issued in December, 2002. These cards were issued in seven card packs which came 24 packs to a box and 10 boxes to a case. Each pack contained four regular Bowman Draft Pick Cards, two Bowman Chrome Draft cards and one Bowman gold card.

Nm-Mt Ex-Mt
COMPLETE SET (165) 40.00 12.00
BDP1 Clint Everts RC 1.25 .35
BDP2 Fred Lewis RC .40 .12
BDP3 Jon Broxton RC .40 .12
BDP4 Jason Anderson RC .40 .12
BDP5 Mike Eusebio RC .40 .12
BDP6 Zack Greinke RC 5.00 1.50
BDP7 Joe Blanton RC 3.00 .90
BDP8 Sergio Santos RC 2.00 .60
BDP9 Jason Cooper RC .40 .12
BDP10 Delwyn Young RC 1.50 .45
BDP11 Jeremy Hermida RC 2.50 .75
BDP12 Dan Ortmeier RC .75 .23
BDP13 Kevin Jepsen RC .40 .12
BDP14 Russ Adams RC .75 .23
BDP15 Mike Nixon RC .40 .12
BDP16 Nick Swisher RC 1.50 .45
BDP17 Cole Hamels RC 5.00 1.50
BDP18 Brian Dopirak RC 1.50 .45
BDP19 James Loney RC 3.00 .90
BDP20 Denard Span RC .40 .12
BDP21 Billy Petrick RC .40 .12
BDP22 Jared Doyle RC .40 .12
BDP23 Jeff Francoeur RC 4.00 1.20
BDP24 Nick Bourgeois RC .40 .12
BDP25 Matt Cain RC 1.50 .45
BDP26 John McCurdy RC .40 .12
BDP27 Mark Kiger RC .40 .12
BDP28 Bill Murphy RC .40 .12
BDP29 Matt Craig RC .40 .12
BDP30 Mike Megrew RC .40 .12
BDP31 Ben Crockett RC .40 .12
BDP32 Luke Hagerty RC .40 .12
BDP33 Matt Whitney RC 1.25 .35
BDP34 Dan Meyer RC .75 .23
BDP35 Jeremy Brown RC 1.00 .30
BDP36 Doug Johnson RC .40 .12
BDP37 Steve Obenchain RC .40 .12
BDP38 Matt Clanton RC .40 .12
BDP39 Mark Teahen RC .40 .12
BDP40 Tom Carrow RC .40 .12
BDP41 Micah Schilling RC .40 .12
BDP42 Blair Johnson RC .40 .12
BDP43 Jason Pridie RC 1.25 .35
BDP44 Joey Votto RC .50 .15
BDP45 Taber Lee RC .40 .12
BDP46 Adam Peterson RC .40 .12
BDP47 Adam Donachie RC .40 .12
BDP48 Josh Murray RC .40 .12
BDP49 Brent Clevlen RC 1.25 .35
BDP50 Chad Pleiness RC .40 .12
BDP51 Zach Hammes RC .50 .15
BDP52 Chris Snyder RC .40 .12
BDP53 Chris Smith RC .40 .12
BDP54 Justin Maureau RC .40 .12
BDP55 David Bush RC 1.50 .45
BDP56 Tim Gilhooly RC .40 .12
BDP57 Blair Barbier RC .40 .12
BDP58 Zach Segovia RC .75 .23
BDP59 Jeremy Reed RC 4.00 1.20
BDP60 Matt Pender RC .40 .12
BDP61 Eric Thomas RC .40 .12
BDP62 Justin Jones RC 1.50 .45
BDP63 Brian Slocum RC .40 .12
BDP64 Larry Broadway RC 1.50 .45
BDP65 Bo Flowers RC .40 .12
BDP66 Scott White RC .40 .12
BDP67 Steve Stanley RC .40 .12
BDP68 Alex Merricks RC .40 .12
BDP69 Josh Womack RC .40 .12
BDP70 Dave Jensen RC .40 .12
BDP71 Curtis Granderson RC 1.00 .30
BDP72 Pat Osborn RC .40 .12
BDP73 Nic Carter RC .40 .12
BDP74 Mitch Talbot RC .40 .12
BDP75 Don Murphy RC .40 .12
BDP76 Val Majewski RC .75 .23
BDP77 Javy Rodriguez RC .40 .12
BDP78 Fernando Pacheco RC .40 .12
BDP79 Steve Russell RC .40 .12
BDP80 Jon Slack RC .40 .12
BDP81 John Baker RC .40 .12
BDP82 Aaron Coonrod RC .40 .12
BDP83 Josh Johnson RC .40 .12
BDP84 Jake Blalock RC 2.00 .60
BDP85 Alex Hart RC 1.00 .30
BDP86 Wes Bankston RC 1.50 .45
BDP87 Josh Rupe RC .40 .12
BDP88 Dan Cevette RC .40 .12
BDP89 Kiel Fisher RC .50 .15
BDP90 Alan Rick RC .40 .12
BDP91 Charlie Morton RC .40 .12
BDP92 Chad Spann RC 1.00 .30
BDP93 Kyle Boyer RC .40 .12
BDP94 Bob Malek RC .40 .12
BDP95 Ryan Rodriguez RC .40 .12
BDP96 Jordan Renz RC .40 .12
BDP97 Randy Frye RC .40 .12
BDP98 Rich Hill RC .40 .12
BDP99 B.J. Upton RC 6.00 1.80
BDP100 Dan Christensen RC .40 .12
BDP101 Casey Kotchman RC 3.00 .90
BDP102 Eric Good RC .30 .09
BDP103 Mike Fontenot RC .40 .12
BDP104 John Webb RC .40 .12
BDP105 Jason Dubois RC 1.50 .45
BDP106 Ryan Kibler RC .40 .12
BDP107 John Peralta RC .40 .12
BDP108 Kirk Saarloos RC .40 .12
BDP109 Rhett Parrott RC .40 .12
BDP110 Jason Grove RC .40 .12
BDP111 Colt Griffin RC 1.00 .30
BDP112 Dallas McPherson RC 2.50 .75
BDP113 Oliver Perez RC .50 .15
BDP114 Mar. McDougall RC .40 .12
BDP115 Mike Wood RC .40 .12
BDP116 Scott Hairston RC 1.50 .45
BDP117 Jason Simontacchi RC .40 .12
BDP118 Taggert Bozied RC 1.50 .45
BDP119 Shelley Duncan RC .40 .12
BDP120 Dontrelle Willis RC 8.00 2.40
BDP121 Sean Burnett .30 .09
BDP122 Aaron Cook .30 .09
BDP123 Brett Evert .30 .09
BDP124 Jimmy Journell .30 .09
BDP125 Brett Myers .30 .09
BDP126 Brad Baker .30 .09
BDP127 Billy Traber RC 1.00 .30
BDP128 Adam Wainwright .30 .09
BDP129 Jason Young RC .40 .12
BDP130 John Buck .30 .09
BDP131 Kevin Cash RC .40 .12
BDP132 Jason Stokes RC 4.00 1.20
BDP133 Drew Henson .30 .09
BDP134 Chad Tracy RC 1.50 .45
BDP135 Orlando Hudson .30 .09
BDP136 Brandon Phillips .30 .09
BDP137 Joe Borchard .30 .09
BDP138 Marlon Byrd .30 .09
BDP139 Carl Crawford .30 .09
BDP140 Michael Restovich .30 .09
BDP141 Corey Hart RC 1.50 .45
BDP142 Edwin Almonte .30 .09
BDP143 Francis Beltran RC .40 .12
BDP144 Jorge De La Rosa RC .40 .12
BDP145 Gerardo Garcia RC .40 .12
BDP146 Franklyn German RC .40 .12
BDP147 Francisco Liriano .50 .15
BDP148 Francisco Rodriguez .30 .09
BDP149 Ricardo Rodriguez .30 .09
BDP150 Seung Song .30 .09
BDP151 John Stephens .30 .09
BDP152 Justin Huber RC 1.00 .30
BDP153 Victor Martinez .30 .09
BDP154 Hee Seop Choi .50 .15
BDP155 Justin Morneau .50 .15
BDP156 Miguel Cabrera 1.50 .45
BDP157 Victor Diaz RC 1.50 .45
BDP158 Jose Reyes .75 .23
BDP159 Omar Infante .30 .09
BDP160 Angel Berroa .30 .09
BDP161 Tony Alvarez .30 .09
BDP162 Shin Soo Choo RC 1.50 .45
BDP163 Wily Mo Pena .30 .09
BDP164 Andres Torres .30 .09
BDP165 Jose Lopez RC 2.50 .75

2002 Bowman Draft Gold

Issued one per pack, this is a parallel to the Bowman Draft Set. These cards have the player's fascimile autograph set off in gold foil.

Nm-Mt Ex-Mt
*GOLD: 1.25X TO 3X BASIC
*GOLD RC'S: .6X TO 1.5X BASIC

2002 Bowman Draft Fabric of the Future Relics

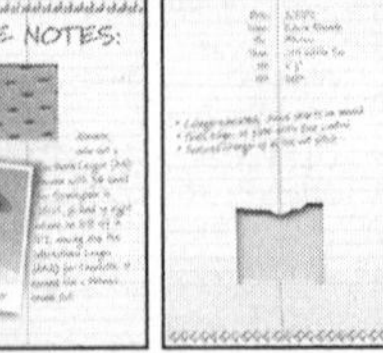

Inserted at a stated rate of one in 55, these 28 cards feature prospects from the 2002 All-Star Futures Game who are very close to be major leaguers. All of these cards have a game-worn jersey relic piece on them.

Nm-Mt Ex-Mt
AB Angel Berroa 10.00 3.00
AT Andres Torres 8.00 2.40
AW Adam Wainwright 10.00 3.00
BM Brett Myers 10.00 3.00
BT Billy Traber 10.00 3.00
CC Carl Crawford 10.00 3.00
CH Corey Hart 10.00 3.00
CT Chad Tracy 10.00 3.00
DH Drew Henson 10.00 3.00
EA Edwin Almonte 8.00 2.40
FB Francis Beltran 8.00 2.40
FG Franklyn German 8.00 2.40
FL Francisco Liriano 8.00 2.40
GG Gerardo Garcia 8.00 2.40
HC Hee Seop Choi 15.00 4.50
JH Justin Huber 8.00 2.40
JK Josh Karp 8.00 2.40
JL Jose Lopez 12.00 3.60
JR Jorge De La Rosa 8.00 2.40
JS1 Jason Stokes 15.00 4.50
JS2 John Stephens 8.00 2.40
KC Kevin Cash 8.00 2.40
MR Michael Restovich 8.00 2.40
SB Sean Burnett 8.00 2.40
SC Shin Soo Choo 10.00 3.00
TA Tony Alvarez 8.00 2.40
VD Victor Diaz 10.00 3.00
WP Wily Mo Pena 8.00 2.40

2002 Bowman Draft Freshman Fiber

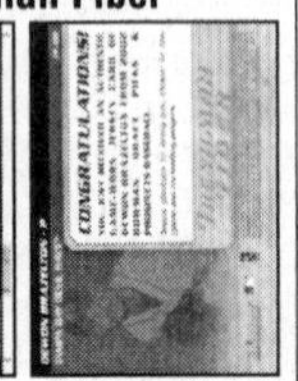

Issued at a stated rate of one in 605 for the bat cards and one in 45 for the jersey cards, these 13 cards feature some of the leading young players in the game along with a game-worn piece.

Nm-Mt Ex-Mt
AH Aubrey Huff Jsy 5.00 1.50
AK Austin Kearns Bat 8.00 2.40
BA Brent Abernathy Jsy 5.00 1.50
DB Dewon Brazelton Jsy 5.00 1.50
JH Josh Hamilton Jsy 5.00 1.50
JK Joe Kennedy Jsy 5.00 1.50
JS Jared Sandberg Jsy 5.00 1.50
JV John VanBenschoten Jsy 8.00 2.40
JWS Jason Standridge Jsy 5.00 1.50
MB Marlon Byrd Bat 8.00 2.40
MT Mark Teixeira Bat 15.00 4.50
NB Nick Bierbrodt Jsy 5.00 1.50
TH Toby Hall Jsy 5.00 1.50

2002 Bowman Draft Signs of the Future

Inserted at different odds depending on what group the player belonged to, these 21 cards feature authentic autographs of the featured player.

Nm-Mt Ex-Mt
GROUP A ODDS 1:100
GROUP B ODDS 1:110
GROUP C ODDS 1:1028
GROUP D ODDS 1:1103
GROUP E ODDS 1:386
GROUP F ODDS 1:2807
BI Brandon Inge E 10.00 3.00
BK Bob Keppel C 10.00 3.00
BP Brandon Phillips B 10.00 3.00
BS Bud Smith E 10.00 3.00
CP Christian Parra D 10.00 3.00
CT Chad Tracy A 15.00 4.50
DD Dan Denham A 10.00 3.00
EB Erik Bedard A 10.00 3.00
JEM Justin Morneau B 15.00 4.50
JM Jake Mauer B 10.00 3.00
JR Juan Rivera B 10.00 3.00
JW Jerome Williams F 15.00 4.50
KH Kris Honel A 10.00 3.00
LB Larry Bigbie E 10.00 3.00
LN Lance Niekro A 10.00 3.00
ME Morgan Ensberg E 10.00 3.00
MF Mike Fontenot A 15.00 4.50
MJ Mitch Jones A 10.00 3.00
NJ Nic Jackson B 10.00 3.00
TB Taylor Buchholz B 15.00 4.50
TL Todd Linden B 25.00 7.50

2002 Bowman Draft Team Topps Legends Autographs

Nm-Mt Ex-Mt
SEE 2001 TOPPS TEAM TOPPS FOR PRICING

2003 Bowman

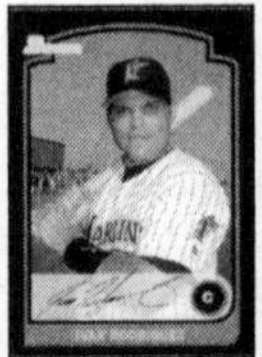

This 330 card set was released in May, 2003. These cards were mixed between veteran cards with red borders on the bottom (1-155) and rookie/prospect cards with blue on the bottom (156-330). This set was issued in 10 card packs which came 24 packs to a box and 12 boxes to a case with an $3 SRP per pack. A special card was inserted featured game-used relics of the two 2002 Major League Rookie of the Years.

Nm-Mt Ex-Mt
COMPLETE SET (330) 80.00 24.00
COMMON CARD (1-155) .30 .09
COMMON CARD (156-330) .30 .09
1 Garret Anderson .30 .09
2 Derek Jeter 2.00 .60
3 Gary Sheffield .30 .09
4 Matt Morris .30 .09
5 Derek Lowe .30 .09
6 Andy Van Hekken .30 .09
7 Sammy Sosa 1.25 .35
8 Ken Griffey Jr. 1.25 .35
9 Omar Vizquel .30 .09
10 Jorge Posada .50 .15
11 Lance Berkman .30 .09
12 Mike Sweeney .30 .09
13 Adrian Beltre .30 .09
14 Richie Sexson .30 .09
15 A.J. Pierzynski .30 .09
16 Bartolo Colon .30 .09
17 Mike Mussina .75 .23
18 Paul Byrd .30 .09
19 Bobby Abreu .30 .09
20 Miguel Tejada .30 .09
21 Aramis Ramirez .30 .09
22 Edgardo Alfonzo .30 .09
23 Edgar Martinez .50 .15
24 Albert Pujols 1.50 .45
25 Carl Crawford .30 .09
26 Eric Hinske .30 .09
27 Tim Salmon .50 .15
28 Luis Gonzalez .30 .09
29 Jay Gibbons .30 .09
30 John Smoltz .50 .15
31 Tim Wakefield .30 .09
32 Mark Prior 1.50 .45
33 Magglio Ordonez .30 .09
34 Adam Dunn .30 .09
35 Larry Walker .50 .15
36 Luis Castillo .30 .09
37 Wade Miller .30 .09
38 Carlos Beltran .30 .09
39 Odalis Perez .30 .09
40 Alex Sanchez .30 .09
41 Torii Hunter .30 .09
42 Cliff Floyd .30 .09
43 Andy Pettitte .50 .15
44 Francisco Rodriguez .30 .09
45 Eric Chavez .30 .09
46 Kevin Millwood .30 .09
47 Dennis Tankersley .30 .09
48 Hideo Nomo .75 .23
49 Freddy Garcia .30 .09
50 Randy Johnson .75 .23
51 Aubrey Huff .30 .09
52 Carlos Delgado .30 .09
53 Troy Glaus .50 .15
54 Junior Spivey .30 .09
55 Mike Hampton .30 .09
56 Sidney Ponson .30 .09
57 Aaron Boone .30 .09
58 Kerry Wood .75 .23
59 Runelvys Hernandez .30 .09
60 Nomar Garciaparra 1.25 .35
61 Todd Helton .50 .15
62 Mike Lowell .30 .09
63 Roy Oswalt .30 .09
64 Raul Ibanez .30 .09
65 Brian Jordan .30 .09
66 Geoff Jenkins .30 .09
67 Jermaine Dye .30 .09
68 Tom Glavine .50 .15
69 Bernie Williams .50 .15
70 Vladimir Guerrero .75 .23
71 Mark Mulder .30 .09
72 Jimmy Rollins .30 .09
73 Oliver Perez .30 .09
74 Rich Aurilia .30 .09
75 Joel Pineiro .30 .09
76 J.D. Drew .30 .09
77 Ivan Rodriguez .75 .23
78 Josh Phelps .30 .09
79 Darin Erstad .30 .09
80 Curt Schilling .50 .15
81 Paul Lo Duca .30 .09
82 Marty Cordova .30 .09
83 Manny Ramirez .30 .09
84 Bobby Hill .30 .09
85 Paul Konerko .30 .09
86 Austin Kearns .30 .09
87 Jason Jennings .30 .09
88 Brad Penny .30 .09
89 Jeff Bagwell .50 .15
90 Shawn Green .30 .09
91 Jason Schmidt .30 .09
92 Doug Mientkiewicz .30 .09
93 Jose Vidro .30 .09
94 Bret Boone .30 .09
95 Jason Giambi .75 .23
96 Barry Zito .50 .15
97 Roy Halladay .30 .09
98 Pat Burrell .30 .09
99 Sean Burroughs .30 .09
100 Barry Bonds 2.00 .60
101 Kazuhiro Sasaki .30 .09
102 Fernando Vina .30 .09
103 Chan Ho Park .30 .09
104 Andruw Jones .30 .09
105 Adam Kennedy .30 .09
106 Shea Hillenbrand .30 .09
107 Greg Maddux 1.25 .35
108 Jim Edmonds .30 .09
109 Pedro Martinez .75 .23
110 Moises Alou .30 .09
111 Jeff Weaver .30 .09
112 C.C. Sabathia .30 .09
113 Robert Fick .30 .09
114 A.J. Burnett .30 .09
115 Jeff Kent .30 .09
116 Kevin Brown .30 .09
117 Rafael Furcal .30 .09
118 Cristian Guzman .30 .09
119 Brad Wilkerson .30 .09
120 Mike Piazza 1.25 .35
121 Alfonso Soriano .50 .15
122 Mark Ellis .30 .09
123 Vicente Padilla .30 .09
124 Eric Gagne .50 .15
125 Ryan Klesko .30 .09
126 Ichiro Suzuki 1.25 .35
127 Tony Batista .30 .09
128 Roberto Alomar .75 .23
129 Alex Rodriguez 1.25 .35
130 Jim Thome .75 .23
131 Jarrod Washburn .30 .09
132 Orlando Hudson .30 .09
133 Chipper Jones .75 .23
134 Rodrigo Lopez .30 .09
135 Johnny Damon .30 .09
136 Matt Clement .30 .09
137 Frank Thomas .75 .23
138 Ellis Burks .30 .09
139 Carlos Pena .30 .09
140 Josh Beckett .50 .15
141 Joe Randa .30 .09
142 Brian Giles .30 .09
143 Kazuhisa Ishii .30 .09
144 Corey Koskie .30 .09
145 Orlando Cabrera .30 .09
146 Mark Buehrle .30 .09
147 Roger Clemens 1.50 .45
148 Tim Hudson .30 .09
149 Randy Wolf UER .30 .09
resume says AL leaders; he pitches in NL
150 Josh Fogg .30 .09
151 Phil Nevin .30 .09
152 John Olerud .30 .09
153 Scott Rolen .50 .15
154 Joe Kennedy .30 .09
155 Rafael Palmeiro .50 .15
156 Chad Hutchinson .30 .09
157 Quincy Carter XRC .60 .18
158 Hee Seop Choi .30 .09
159 Joe Borchard .30 .09
160 Brandon Phillips .30 .09
161 Wily Mo Pena .30 .09
162 Victor Martinez .30 .09
163 Jason Stokes .75 .23
164 Ken Harvey .30 .09
165 Juan Rivera .30 .09
166 Jose Contreras RC 2.00 .60
167 Dan Haren RC 1.25 .35
168 Michel Hernandez RC .40 .12
169 Eider Torres RC .40 .12
170 Chris De La Cruz RC .40 .12
171 Ramon Nivar-Martinez RC 1.00 .30
172 Mike Adams RC .40 .12
173 Justin Arneson RC .40 .12
174 Jamie Athas RC .40 .12
175 Dwaine Bacon RC .40 .12
176 Clint Barmes RC .60 .18
177 B.J. Barns RC .40 .12
178 Tyler Johnson RC .40 .12
179 Bobby Basham RC 1.00 .30
180 T.J. Bohn RC .40 .12
181 J.D. Durbin RC 1.00 .30
182 Brandon Bowe RC .40 .12
183 Craig Brazell RC .60 .18
184 Dusty Brown RC .40 .12
185 Brian Bruney RC .60 .18
186 Greg Bruso RC .40 .12
187 Jaime Bubela RC .40 .12
188 Bryan Bullington RC 2.00 .60
189 Brian Burgamy RC .40 .12
190 Eny Cabreja RC .40 .12
191 Daniel Cabrera RC .40 .12
192 Ryan Cameron RC .40 .12
193 Lance Caraccioli RC .40 .12
194 David Cash RC .40 .12
195 Bernie Castro RC .40 .12
196 Ismael Castro RC .60 .18
197 Daryl Clark RC .60 .18
198 Jeff Clark RC .40 .12
199 Chris Colton RC .40 .12
200 Dexter Cooper RC .40 .12
201 Callix Crabbe RC .60 .18
202 Chien-Ming Wang RC 2.00 .60
203 Eric Crozier RC .60 .18
204 Nook Logan RC .40 .12
205 David DeJesus RC 1.00 .30
206 Matt DeMarco RC .40 .12
207 Chris Duncan RC .40 .12
208 Eric Eckenstahler .30 .09
209 Willie Eyre RC .40 .12
210 Evel Bastida-Martinez RC .40 .12
211 Chris Fallon RC .40 .12
212 Mike Flannery RC .40 .12
213 Mike O'Keefe RC .40 .12
214 Ben Francisco RC .60 .18
215 Kason Gabbard RC .40 .12
216 Mike Gallo RC .40 .12
217 Jairo Garcia RC .40 .12
218 Angel Garcia RC .60 .18
219 Michael Garciaparra RC 1.25 .35
220 Joey Gomes RC .40 .12
221 Dusty Gomon RC 1.00 .30
222 Bryan Grace RC .40 .12
223 Tyson Graham RC .40 .12
224 Henry Guerrero RC .40 .12
225 Franklin Gutierrez RC 2.50 .75
226 Carlos Guzman RC .60 .18
227 Matthew Hagen RC 1.00 .30
228 Josh Hall RC .60 .18
229 Rob Hammock RC .60 .18
230 Brendan Harris RC .60 .18
231 Gary Harris RC .40 .12
232 Clay Hensley RC .40 .12
233 Michael Hinckley RC 1.00 .30
234 Luis Hodge RC .40 .12
235 Donnie Hood RC .60 .18
236 Travis Ishikawa RC .60 .18
237 Edwin Jackson RC 3.00 .90
238 Ardley Jansen RC .60 .18
239 Ferenc Jongejan RC .40 .12
240 Matt Kata RC 1.00 .30
241 Kazuhiro Takeoka RC .40 .12
242 Beau Kemp RC .40 .12
243 Il Kim RC .40 .12
244 Brennan King RC .40 .12
245 Chris Kroski RC .40 .12
246 Jason Kubel RC 1.00 .30
247 Pete LaForest RC .60 .18
248 Wil Ledezma RC .40 .12
249 Jeremy Bonderman RC 1.25 .35

250 Gonzalo Lopez RC .40 .12
251 Brian Luderer RC .40 .12
252 Ruddy Lugo RC .40 .12
253 Wayne Lydon RC .40 .12
254 Mark Malaska RC .40 .12
255 Andy Marte RC 3.00 .90
256 Tyler Martin RC .40 .12
257 Branden Florence RC .40 .12
258 Aneudis Mateo RC .40 .12
259 Derell McCall RC .40 .12
260 Brian McCann RC 1.00 .30
261 Mike McNutt RC .40 .12
262 Jacabo Meque RC .40 .12
263 Derek Michaelis RC .60 .18
264 Aaron Miles RC 1.25 .35
265 Jose Morales RC .40 .12
266 Dustin Moseley RC .60 .18
267 Adrian Myers RC .40 .12
268 Dan Neil RC .40 .12
269 Jon Nelson RC .60 .18
270 Mike Neu RC .40 .12
271 Leigh Neuage RC .40 .12
272 Wes O'Brien RC .40 .12
273 Trent Oeltjen RC .60 .18
274 Tim Olson RC .60 .18
275 David Pahucki RC .40 .12
276 Nathan Panther RC 1.00 .30
277 Arnie Munoz RC .40 .12
278 Dave Pember RC .40 .12
279 Jason Perry RC 1.25 .35
280 Matthew Peterson RC .40 .12
281 Ryan Shealy RC 1.00 .30
282 Jorge Piedra RC .60 .18
283 Simon Pond RC 1.00 .30
284 Aaron Rakers RC .40 .12
285 Hanley Ramirez RC 2.00 .60
286 Manuel Ramirez RC .60 .18
287 Kevin Randel RC .40 .12
288 Darrell Rasner RC .40 .12
289 Prentice Redman RC .40 .12
290 Eric Reed RC 1.00 .30
291 Wilton Reynolds RC .60 .18
292 Eric Riggs RC .60 .18
293 Carlos Rijo RC .40 .12
294 Rajai Davis RC .60 .18
295 Aron Weston RC .40 .12
296 Arturo Rivas RC .40 .12
297 Kyle Roat RC .40 .12
298 Bubba Nelson RC .75 .23
299 Levi Robinson RC .40 .12
300 Ray Sadler RC .40 .12
301 Gary Schneidmiller RC .40 .12
302 Jon Schuerholz RC .40 .12
303 Corey Shafer RC .60 .18
304 Brian Shackelford RC .40 .12
305 Bill Simon RC .40 .12
306 Haj Turay RC .60 .18
307 Sean Smith RC .60 .18
308 Ryan Spataro RC .40 .12
309 Jemel Spearman RC .40 .12
310 Keith Stamler RC .40 .12
311 Luke Steidlmayer RC .40 .12
312 Adam Stern RC .40 .12
313 Jay Sitzman RC .40 .12
314 Thomari Story-Harden RC .60 .18
315 Terry Tiffee RC .60 .18
316 Nick Trzesniak RC .40 .12
317 Denny Tussen RC .40 .12
318 Scott Tyler RC .60 .18
319 Shane Victorino RC .40 .12
320 Doug Waechter RC .60 .18
321 Brandon Watson RC .40 .12
322 Todd Wellemeyer RC .60 .18
323 Eli Whiteside RC .40 .12
324 Josh Willingham RC 1.50 .45
325 Travis Wong RC .60 .18
326 Brian Wright RC .40 .12
327 Kevin Youkilis RC 2.00 .60
328 Andy Sisco RC 1.50 .45
329 Dustin Yount RC 1.00 .30
330 Andrew Dominique RC .40 .12
NNO Eric Hinske Bat 15.00 4.50
Jason Jennings Jsy
ROY Relic

2003 Bowman Gold

Nm-Mt Ex-Mt
COMPLETE SET (330) 250.00 75.00
*RED 1-155: 1.25X TO 3X BASIC
*BLUE 156-330: 1.25X TO 3X BASIC
*BLUE ROOKIES: .75X TO 2X BASIC
ONE PER PACK

2003 Bowman Uncirculated Metallic Gold

These cards were originally issued as exchange cards in the silver packs which were inserted one per hobby box. In addition, these exchange cards were seeded into retail packs at a stated rate of one in 49. These cards could be mailed into the Pit.Com for redemption for a hermetically sealed card. Please note that the original stated print run for these cards are 230 sets. These cards could be redeemed until April 30th, 2004.

Nm-Mt Ex-Mt
NNO Exchange Card 10.00 3.00

2003 Bowman Uncirculated Silver

These cards were issued at a stated rate of one per silver pack, which were inserted one per sealed hobby box. This is a parallel set to the basic Bowman set and each card was issued in already sealed holder. Please note that each card was issued to a stated print run of 250 serial numbered sets. In addition, a few cards were issued as redemption cards for the entire Uncirculated Silver set. These cards could be redeemed until April 30th, 2004.

Nm-Mt Ex-Mt
*UNC.SILVER 1-155: 6X TO 15X BASIC
*UNC.SILVER 156-330: 6X TO 15X BASIC
*UNC.SILVER ROOKIES: 4X TO 10X BASIC
NNO Set Exchange Card

2003 Bowman Future Fiber Bats

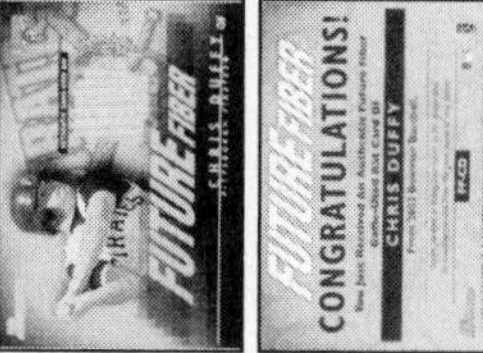

Nm-Mt Ex-Mt
GROUP A ODDS 1:96 H, 1:34 HTA, 1:196 R
GROUP B ODDS 1:393 H, 1:140 HTA, 1:803 R
AG Adrian Gonzalez A 8.00 2.40
AH Aubrey Huff A 8.00 2.40
AK Austin Kearns A 8.00 2.40
BS Bud Smith B 8.00 2.40
CD Chris Duffy B 8.00 2.40
CK Casey Kotchman A 10.00 3.00
DH Drew Henson A 8.00 2.40
DW David Wright A 8.00 2.40
ES Esix Snead A 8.00 2.40
EY Edwin Yan B 8.00 2.40
FS Freddy Sanchez A 8.00 2.40
HB Hank Blalock A 10.00 3.00
JB Jason Botts A 8.00 2.40
JDM Jake Mauer A 8.00 2.40
JG Jason Grove A 8.00 2.40
JH Josh Hamilton A 8.00 2.40
JM Joe Mauer A 20.00 6.00
JW Justin Wayne B 8.00 2.40
KC Kevin Cash B 8.00 2.40
KD Kory DeHaan A 8.00 2.40
MR Michael Restovich A 8.00 2.40
NH Nathan Haynes A 8.00 2.40
PF Pedro Feliz A 8.00 2.40
RB Rocco Baldelli B 20.00 6.00
RJ Reed Johnson A 8.00 2.40
RK Ryan Langerhans A 8.00 2.40
RS Randall Shelley A 8.00 2.40
SB Sean Burroughs A 8.00 2.40
ST So Taguchi A 8.00 2.40
TW Travis Wilson A 8.00 2.40
WB Wilson Betemit A 8.00 2.40
WR Wilkin Ruan B 8.00 2.40
XN Xavier Nady A 8.00 2.40

2003 Bowman Futures Game Base Autograph

Nm-Mt Ex-Mt
STATED ODDS 1:141 HTA
JR Jose Reyes 30.00 9.00

2003 Bowman Futures Game Gear Jersey Relics

Nm-Mt Ex-Mt
STATED ODDS 1:26 H, 1:9 HTA, 1:52 R
AC Aaron Cook 8.00 2.40
AW Adam Wainwright 8.00 2.40
BB Brad Baker 8.00 2.40
BE Brett Evert 8.00 2.40
BH Bill Hall 8.00 2.40
BM Brett Myers 8.00 2.40
BP Brandon Phillips 8.00 2.40
BT Billy Traber 8.00 2.40
CC Carl Crawford 8.00 2.40
CH Corey Hart 8.00 2.40
CT Chad Tracy 8.00 2.40
DH Drew Henson 8.00 2.40
EA Edwin Almonte 8.00 2.40
FB Francis Beltran 8.00 2.40
FL Francisco Liriano 8.00 2.40
FR Francisco Rodriguez 8.00 2.40
GG Gerardo Garcia 8.00 2.40
HC Hee Seop Choi 8.00 2.40
JB John Buck 8.00 2.40
JDR Jorge De La Rosa 8.00 2.40
JEB Joe Borchard 8.00 2.40
JH Justin Huber 8.00 2.40
JJ Jimmy Journell 8.00 2.40
JK Josh Karp 8.00 2.40
JL Jose Lopez 10.00 3.00
JM Justin Morneau 15.00 4.50
JMS John Stephens 8.00 2.40
JR Jose Reyes 10.00 3.00
JS Jason Stokes 10.00 3.00
JY Jason Young 8.00 2.40
KC Kevin Cash 8.00 2.40
LO Lyle Overbay 8.00 2.40
MB Marlon Byrd 8.00 2.40
MC Miguel Cabrera 20.00 6.00
MR Michael Restovich 8.00 2.40
OH Orlando Hudson 8.00 2.40
OI Omar Infante 8.00 2.40
RD Ryan Dittfurth 8.00 2.40
RR Ricardo Rodriguez 8.00 2.40
SB Sean Burnett 8.00 2.40
SC Shin Soo Choo 8.00 2.40
SS Seung Song 8.00 2.40
TA Tony Alvarez 8.00 2.40
VD Victor Diaz 8.00 2.40
VM Victor Martinez 8.00 2.40
WP Wily Mo Pena 8.00 2.40

2003 Bowman Signs of the Future

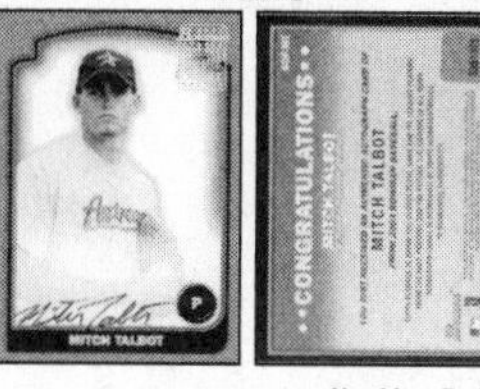

Nm-Mt Ex-Mt
GROUP A ODDS 1:39 H, 1:13 HTA, 1:79 R
GROUP B ODDS 1:183 H, 1:65 HTA, 1:374 R
GROUP C ODDS 1:2288 H, 1:816 HTA, 1:4720 R
*RED INK: 1.25X TO 3X GROUP A
*RED INK: 1.25X TO 3X GROUP B
*RED INK: .75X TO 2X GROUP C
RED INK ODDS 1:687 H, 1:245 HTA, 1:1402 R
AV Andy Van Hekken A 8.00 2.40
BB Bryan Bullington A 20.00 6.00
BJ Bobby Jenks B 10.00 3.00
BK Ben Kozlowski A 8.00 2.40
BL Brandon League B 8.00 2.40
BS Brian Slocum A 8.00 2.40
CH Cole Hamels A 30.00 9.00
CJH Corey Hart A 10.00 3.00
CMH Chad Hutchinson C 15.00 4.50
CP Chris Piersoll B 8.00 2.40
DG Doug Gredvig A 8.00 2.40
DHM Dustin McGowan A 10.00 3.00
DL Donald Levinski A 8.00 2.40
DS Doug Sessions B 8.00 2.40
FL Fred Lewis A 8.00 2.40
FS Freddy Sanchez B 8.00 2.40
HR Hanley Ramirez A 20.00 6.00
JA Jason Arnold B 10.00 3.00
JB John Buck A 8.00 2.40
JC Jesus Cota B 8.00 2.40
JG Jason Grove B 8.00 2.40
JGU Jeremy Guthrie A 8.00 2.40
JL James Loney A 15.00 4.50
JOG Jonny Gomes B 10.00 3.00
JR Jose Reyes A 25.00 7.50
JRH Joel Hanrahan A 10.00 3.00
JSC Jason St. Clair B 8.00 2.40
KG Khalil Greene A 15.00 4.50
KH Koyie Hill B 8.00 2.40
MT Mitch Talbot A 8.00 2.40
NC Nelson Castro B 8.00 2.40
OV Oscar Villareal A 8.00 2.40
PR Prentice Redman A 8.00 2.40
QC Quincy Carter C 20.00 6.00
RC Ryan Church B 8.00 2.40
RS Ryan Snare B 8.00 2.40
TL Todd Linden B 10.00 3.00
VM Val Majewski A 10.00 3.00
ZG Zack Greinke A 25.00 7.50
ZS Zach Segovia A 8.00 2.40

2003 Bowman Signs of the Future Dual

Nm-Mt Ex-Mt
STATED ODDS 1:9220 H,1:3264 HTA,1:20,390 R
CH Quincy Carter 100.00 30.00
Chad Hutchinson

2003 Bowman Draft

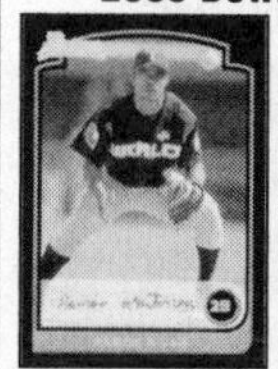

This 165-card standard-size set was released in December, 2003. The set was issued in 10 card packs with a $2.99 SRP which came 24 packs to a box and 10 boxes to a case. Please note that each Draft pack included 2 Chrome cards.

MINT NRMT
COMPLETE SET (165) 40.00 18.00
1 Dontrelle Willis .75 .35
2 Freddy Sanchez .30 .14
3 Miguel Cabrera .75 .35
4 Ryan Ludwick .30 .14
5 Ty Wigginton .30 .14
6 Mark Teixeira .50 .23
7 Trey Hodges .30 .14
8 Laynce Nix .75 .35
9 Antonio Perez .30 .14
10 Jody Gerut .30 .14
11 Jae Weong Seo .30 .14
12 Erick Almonte .30 .14
13 Lyle Overbay .30 .14
14 Billy Traber .30 .14
15 Andres Torres .30 .14
16 Jose Valverde .30 .14
17 Aaron Heilman .30 .14
18 Brandon Larson .30 .14
19 Jung Bong .30 .14
20 Jesse Foppert .30 .14
21 Angel Berroa .30 .14
22 Jeff DaVanon .30 .14
23 Kurt Ainsworth .30 .14
24 Brandon Claussen .30 .14
25 Xavier Nady .30 .14
26 Travis Hafner .30 .14
27 Jerome Williams .30 .14
28 Jose Reyes .50 .23
29 Sergio Mitre RC .75 .35
30 Bo Hart RC 1.50 .70
31 Adam Miller RC .75 .35
32 Brian Finch RC .40 .18
33 Taylor Mattingly RC 2.50 1.10
34 Daric Barton RC 1.50 .70
35 Chris Ray RC .50 .23
36 Jarrod Saltalamacchia RC .75 .35
37 Dennis Dove RC .50 .23
38 James Houser RC .75 .35
39 Clint King RC 1.25 .55
40 Lou Palmisano RC 2.00 .90
41 Dan Moore RC .40 .18
42 Craig Stansberry RC .75 .35
43 Jo Jo Reyes RC .75 .35
44 Jake Stevens RC .50 .23
45 Tom Gorzelanny RC .50 .23
46 Brian Marshall RC .40 .18
47 Scott Beerer RC .40 .18
48 Javi Herrera RC .50 .23
49 Steve LeRud RC .75 .35
50 Josh Banks RC 1.00 .45
51 Jon Papelbon RC .40 .18
52 Juan Valdes RC .50 .23
53 Beau Vaughan RC .50 .23
54 Matt Chico RC .75 .35
55 Todd Jennings RC .50 .23
56 Anthony Gwynn RC 1.50 .70
57 Matt Harrison RC .50 .23
58 Aaron Marsden RC .50 .23
59 Casey Abrams RC .40 .18
60 Cory Stuart RC .40 .18
61 Mike Wagner RC .40 .18
62 Jordan Pratt RC .50 .23
63 Andre Randolph RC .50 .23
64 Blake Balkcom RC .75 .35
65 Josh Muecke RC .40 .18
66 Jamie D'Antona RC 2.00 .90
67 Cole Seifrig RC 2.00 .90
68 Josh Anderson RC .50 .23
69 Matt Lorenzo RC .50 .23
70 Nate Spears RC .75 .35
71 Chris Goodman RC .40 .18
72 Brian McFall RC .75 .35
73 Billy Hogan RC 1.00 .45
74 Jamie Romak RC .75 .35
75 Jeff Cook RC .50 .23
76 Brooks McNiven RC .40 .18
77 Xavier Paul RC 2.50 1.10
78 Bob Zimmermann RC .40 .18
79 Mickey Hall RC 1.00 .45
80 Shaun Marcum RC .40 .18
81 Matt Nachreiner RC .75 .35
82 Chris Kinsey RC .40 .18
83 Jonathan Fulton RC .50 .23
84 Edgardo Baez RC .75 .35
85 Robert Valido RC 2.50 1.10
86 Kenny Lewis RC .75 .35
87 Trent Peterson RC .40 .18
88 Johnny Woodard RC .50 .23
89 Wes Littleton RC .75 .35
90 Sean Rodriguez RC 1.00 .45
91 Kyle Pearson RC .40 .18
92 Josh Rainwater RC .75 .35
93 Travis Schlichting RC .75 .35
94 Tim Battle RC .50 .23
95 Aaron Hill RC 1.50 .70
96 Bob McCrory RC .40 .18
97 Rick Guarno RC .50 .23
98 Brandon Yarbrough RC .40 .18
99 Peter Stonard RC .40 .18
100 Darin Downs RC .75 .35
101 Matt Bruback RC .30 .14
102 Danny Garcia RC .40 .18
103 Cory Stewart RC .40 .18
104 Ferdin Tejeda RC .40 .18
105 Kade Johnson RC .40 .18
106 Andrew Brown RC .40 .18
107 Aquilino Lopez RC .40 .18
108 Stephen Randolph RC .40 .18
109 Dave Matranga RC .40 .18
110 Dustin McGowan RC 1.00 .45
111 Juan Camacho RC .40 .18
112 Cliff Lee .30 .14
113 Jeff Duncan RC .50 .23
114 C.J. Wilson .30 .14
115 Brandon Roberson RC .40 .18
116 David Corrente RC .40 .18
117 Kevin Beavers RC .40 .18
118 Anthony Webster RC .75 .35
119 Oscar Villarreal RC .40 .18
120 Hong-Chih Kuo RC .75 .35
121 Josh Barfield .50 .23
122 Denny Bautista .30 .14
123 Chris Burke RC .50 .23
124 Robinson Cano RC .50 .23
125 Jose Castillo .30 .14
126 Neal Cotts .30 .14
127 Jorge De La Rosa .30 .14
128 J.D. Durbin 1.00 .45
129 Edwin Encarnacion .30 .14
130 Gavin Floyd .30 .14
131 Alexis Gomez .30 .14
132 Edgar Gonzalez RC .40 .18
133 Khalil Greene .50 .23
134 Zack Greinke .75 .35
135 Franklin Gutierrez .75 .35
136 Rich Harden .50 .23
137 J.J. Hardy RC 2.00 .90
138 Ryan Howard RC 1.00 .45
139 Justin Huber .30 .14
140 David Kelton .30 .14
141 Dave Krynzel .30 .14
142 Pete LaForest .60 .25
143 Adam LaRoche .50 .23
144 Preston Larrison RC .50 .23
145 John Maine RC 2.00 .90
146 Andy Marte 1.25 .55
147 Jeff Mathis .30 .14
148 Joe Mauer UER .75 .35
Card has playing for New Haven
149 Clint Nageotte .30 .14
150 Chris Narveson .30 .14
151 Ramon Nivar 1.00 .45
152 Felix Pie RC 2.50 1.10
153 Guillermo Quiroz RC 1.25 .55
154 Rene Reyes .30 .14
155 Royce Ring .30 .14
156 Alexis Rios 1.00 .45
157 Grady Sizemore .50 .23
158 Stephen Smitherman .30 .14
159 Seung Song .30 .14
160 Scott Thorman .30 .14
161 Chad Tracy .30 .14
162 Chin-Hui Tsao .30 .14
163 John VanBenschoten .30 .14
164 Kevin Youkilis .75 .35
165 Chien-Ming Wang .75 .35

2003 Bowman Draft Gold

MINT NRMT
COMPLETE SET (165) 100.00 45.00
*GOLD: 1.25X TO 3X BASIC
*GOLD RC'S: 6X TO 1.5X BASIC
*GOLD RC YR: .6X TO 1.5X BASIC
ONE PER PACK

2003 Bowman Draft Fabric of the Future Jersey Relics

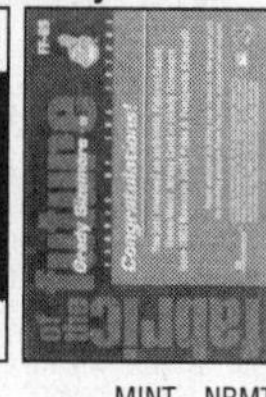

MINT NRMT
GROUP A ODDS 1:721 H, 1:720 R
GROUP B ODDS 1:315 H/R
GROUP C ODDS 1:98 H/R
GROUP D ODDS 1:81 H, 1:82 R
GROUP E ODDS 1:263 H/R
GROUP F ODDS 1:241 H, 1:240 R
AL Adam LaRoche D 10.00 4.50
AM Andy Marte D 15.00 6.75
CN Chris Narveson C 5.00 2.20
EG Edgar Gonzalez D 5.00 2.20
FG Franklin Gutierrez C 8.00 3.60
FP Felix Pie A 15.00 6.75
GF Gavin Floyd E 8.00 3.60
GS Grady Sizemore D 10.00 4.50
JB Josh Barfield B 10.00 4.50
JD J.D. Durbin D 8.00 3.60
JH Justin Huber D 8.00 3.60
JM Joe Mauer C 15.00 6.75
JSM Jeff Mathis B 8.00 3.60
KG Khalil Greene D 10.00 4.50
RC Robinson Cano C 8.00 3.60
RH Rich Harden C 10.00 4.50
RJH Ryan Howard F 8.00 3.60
RR Rene Reyes E 5.00 2.20
RRR Royce Ring F 5.00 2.20
ZG Zack Greinke C 10.00 4.50

2003 Bowman Draft Prospect Premiums Relics

MINT NRMT
GROUP A ODDS 1:216 H/R
GROUP B ODDS 1:470 H, 1:469 R
AK Austin Kearns Jsy B 5.00 2.20
BH Brendan Harris Bat A 8.00 3.60
BM Brett Myers Jsy B 5.00 2.20
CC Carl Crawford Bat A 8.00 3.60
CS Chris Snelling Bat A 8.00 3.60
CU Chase Utley Bat A 8.00 3.60
HB Hank Blalock Bat A 10.00 4.50
JM Justin Morneau Bat A 8.00 3.60
JT Joe Thurston Bat A 8.00 3.60
NH Nathan Haynes Bat A 8.00 3.60
RB Rocco Baldelli Bat A 15.00 6.75
TH Travis Hafner Bat A 8.00 3.60

2003 Bowman Draft Signs of the Future

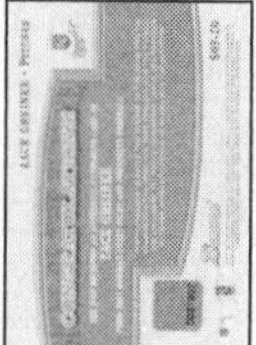

MINT NRMT
GROUP A ODDS 1:385 H, 1:720 R
GROUP B ODDS 1:491 H, 1:491 R
GROUP C ODDS 1:2160 H, 1:12,185 R
AT Andres Torres A 10.00 4.50
CS Cory Stewart B 10.00 4.50
DT Dennis Tankersley A 10.00 4.50
JA Jason Arnold B 10.00 4.50
ZG Zack Greinke C 25.00 11.00

2003 Bowman Draft Team Topps Blue Chips Autographs

MINT NRMT
STATED ODDS 1:216 H/R
SEE 03 TEAM TOPPS BLUE CHIP FOR PRICES

1997 Bowman Chrome

The 1997 Bowman Chrome set was issued in one series totalling 300 cards and was distributed in four-card packs with a suggested retail price of $3.00. The cards parallel the 1997 Bowman brand and the 300 card set represents a selection of top cards taken from the 441-card 1997 Bowman set. The product was released in the Winter, after the end of the 1997 season. The fronts feature color action player photos printed on dazzling chromium stock. The backs carry player information. Rookie Cards in this set include Adrian Beltre, Kris Benson, Lance Berkman, Kris Benson, Eric Chavez, Jose Cruz Jr., Travis Lee, Aramis Ramirez, Miguel Tejada, Vernon Wells and Kerry Wood.

Nm-Mt Ex-Mt
COMPLETE SET (300) 180.00 55.00
1 Derek Jeter 3.00 .90
2 Chipper Jones 1.25 .35
3 Hideo Nomo 1.25 .35
4 Tim Salmon .75 .23
5 Robin Ventura .50 .15
6 Tony Clark .50 .15
7 Barry Larkin 1.25 .35
8 Paul Molitor .75 .23
9 Andy Benes .50 .15
10 Ryan Klesko .50 .15
11 Mark McGwire 3.00 .90
12 Ken Griffey Jr. 2.00 .60
13 Robb Nen .50 .15
14 Cal Ripken 4.00 1.20
15 John Valentin .50 .15
16 Ricky Bottalico .50 .15
17 Mike Lansing .50 .15
18 Ryne Sandberg 2.00 .60
19 Carlos Delgado .50 .15
20 Craig Biggio .75 .23
21 Eric Karros .50 .15
22 Kevin Appier .50 .15
23 Mariano Rivera .75 .23
24 Vinny Castilla .50 .15
25 Juan Gonzalez 1.25 .35
26 Al Martin .50 .15
27 Jeff Cirillo .50 .15
28 Ray Lankford .50 .15
29 Manny Ramirez .50 .15
30 Roberto Alomar 1.25 .35
31 Will Clark 1.25 .35
32 Chuck Knoblauch .50 .15
33 Harold Baines .50 .15
34 Edgar Martinez .75 .23
35 Mike Mussina 1.25 .35
36 Kevin Brown .50 .15
37 Dennis Eckersley .50 .15
38 Tino Martinez .75 .23
39 Raul Mondesi .50 .15
40 Sammy Sosa 2.00 .60
41 John Smoltz .75 .23
42 Billy Wagner .50 .15
43 Ken Caminiti .50 .15
44 Wade Boggs .75 .23
45 Andres Galarraga .50 .15
46 Roger Clemens 2.50 .75
47 Matt Williams .50 .15
48 Albert Belle .50 .15
49 Jeff King .50 .15
50 John Wetteland .50 .15
51 Deion Sanders .75 .23
52 Ellis Burks .50 .15
53 Pedro Martinez 1.25 .35
54 Kenny Lofton .50 .15
55 Randy Johnson 1.25 .35
56 Bernie Williams .75 .23
57 Marquis Grissom .50 .15
58 Gary Sheffield .50 .15
59 Curt Schilling .75 .23
60 Reggie Sanders .50 .15
61 Bobby Higginson .50 .15
62 Moises Alou .50 .15
63 Tom Glavine .75 .23
64 Mark Grace .75 .23
65 Rafael Palmeiro .75 .23
66 John Olerud .50 .15
67 Dante Bichette .50 .15
68 Jeff Bagwell .75 .23
69 Barry Bonds 3.00 .90
70 Pat Hentgen .50 .15
71 Jim Thome 1.25 .35
72 Andy Pettitte .75 .23
73 Jay Bell .50 .15
74 Jim Edmonds .50 .15
75 Ron Gant .50 .15
76 David Cone .50 .15
77 Jose Canseco 1.25 .35
78 Jay Buhner .50 .15
79 Greg Maddux 2.00 .60
80 Lance Johnson .50 .15
81 Travis Fryman .50 .15
82 Paul O'Neill .75 .23
83 Ivan Rodriguez 1.25 .35
84 Fred McGriff .75 .23
85 Mike Piazza 2.00 .60
86 Brady Anderson .50 .15
87 Marty Cordova .50 .15
88 Joe Carter .50 .15
89 Brian Jordan .50 .15
90 David Justice .50 .15
91 Tony Gwynn 1.50 .45
92 Larry Walker .75 .23
93 Mo Vaughn .50 .15
94 Sandy Alomar Jr. .50 .15
95 Rusty Greer .50 .15
96 Roberto Hernandez .50 .15
97 Hal Morris .50 .15
98 Todd Hundley .50 .15
99 Rondell White .50 .15
100 Frank Thomas 1.25 .35
101 Bubba Trammell RC 1.50 .45
102 Sidney Ponson RC 4.00 1.20
103 Ricky Ledee RC 1.50 .45
104 Brett Tomko .50 .15
105 Braden Looper RC 1.00 .30
106 Jason Dickson .50 .15
107 Chad Green RC 1.00 .30
108 R.A. Dickey RC 1.00 .30
109 Jeff Liefer .50 .15
110 Richard Hidalgo .50 .15
111 Chad Hermansen RC 1.50 .45
112 Felix Martinez .50 .15
113 J.J. Johnson .50 .15
114 Todd Dunwoody .50 .15
115 Katsuhiro Maeda .50 .15
116 Darin Erstad .50 .15
117 Elieser Marrero .50 .15
118 Bartolo Colon .50 .15
119 Ugueth Urbina .50 .15
120 Jaime Bluma .50 .15
121 Seth Greisinger RC 1.50 .45
122 Jose Cruz Jr. RC 8.00 2.40
123 Todd Dunn .50 .15
124 Justin Towle RC 1.00 .30
125 Brian Rose .50 .15
126 Jose Guillen .50 .15
127 Andruw Jones .50 .15
128 Mark Kotsay RC 1.50 .45
129 Wilton Guerrero .50 .15
130 Jacob Cruz .50 .15
131 Mike Sweeney .50 .15
132 Matt Morris .50 .15
133 John Thomson .50 .15
134 Javier Valentin .50 .15
135 Mike Drumright RC 1.00 .30
136 Michael Barrett .50 .15
137 Tony Saunders RC 1.00 .30
138 Kevin Brown .50 .15
139 Anthony Sanders RC 1.00 .30
140 Jeff Abbott .50 .15
141 Eugene Kingsale .50 .15
142 Paul Konerko .50 .15
143 Randall Simon RC 2.50 .75
144 Freddy Adrian Garcia .50 .15
145 Karim Garcia .50 .15
146 Carlos Guillen .50 .15
147 Aaron Boone .50 .15
148 Donnie Sadler .50 .15
149 Brooks Kieschnick .50 .15
150 Scott Spiezio .50 .15
151 Kevin Orie .50 .15
152 Russ Johnson .50 .15
153 Livan Hernandez .50 .15
154 Vladimir Nunez RC 1.00 .30
155 Pokey Reese .50 .15
156 Chris Carpenter .50 .15
157 Eric Milton RC 4.00 1.20
158 Richie Sexson .50 .15
159 Carl Pavano .50 .15
160 Pat Cline .50 .15
161 Ron Wright .50 .15
162 Dante Powell .50 .15
163 Mark Bellhorn .50 .15
164 George Lombard .50 .15
165 Paul Wilder RC 1.00 .30
166 Brad Fullmer .50 .15
167 Kris Benson RC 2.50 .75
168 Torii Hunter .50 .15
169 D.T. Cromer RC 1.00 .30
170 Nelson Figueroa RC 1.50 .45
171 Hiram Bocachica RC 1.50 .45
172 Shane Monahan .50 .15
173 Juan Melo .50 .15
174 Calvin Pickering RC 1.50 .45
175 Reggie Taylor .50 .15
176 Geoff Jenkins .50 .15
177 Steve Rain RC 1.00 .30
178 Nerio Rodriguez RC 1.00 .30
179 Derrick Gibson .50 .15
180 Darin Blood .50 .15
181 Ben Davis .50 .15
182 Adrian Beltre RC 8.00 2.40
183 Kerry Wood RC 40.00 12.00
184 Nate Rolison RC 1.00 .30
185 Fernando Tatis RC 1.50 .45
186 Jake Westbrook RC 1.50 .45
187 Edwin Diaz .50 .15
188 Joe Fontenot RC 1.00 .30
189 Matt Halloran RC 1.00 .30
190 Matt Clement RC 5.00 1.50
191 Todd Greene .50 .15
192 Eric Chavez RC 20.00 6.00
193 Edgard Velazquez .50 .15
194 Bruce Chen RC 1.50 .45
195 Jason Brester .50 .15
196 Chris Reitsma RC 1.50 .45
197 Neifi Perez .50 .15
198 Hideki Irabu RC 1.50 .45
199 Don Denbow RC 1.00 .30
200 Derrek Lee .50 .15
201 Todd Walker .50 .15
202 Scott Rolen .75 .23
203 Wes Helms .50 .15
204 Bob Abreu .50 .15
205 John Patterson RC 2.50 .75
206 Alex Gonzalez RC 4.00 1.20
207 Grant Roberts RC 1.50 .45
208 Jeff Suppan .50 .15
209 Luke Wilcox .50 .15
210 Marlon Anderson .50 .15
211 Mike Caruso RC 1.00 .30
212 Roy Halladay RC 15.00 4.50
213 Jeremi Gonzalez RC 1.00 .30
214 Aramis Ramirez RC 10.00 3.00
215 Dee Brown RC 1.50 .45
216 Justin Thompson .50 .15
217 Danny Clyburn .50 .15
218 Bruce Aven .50 .15
219 Keith Foulke RC 4.00 1.20
220 Shannon Stewart .50 .15
221 Larry Barnes RC 1.00 .30
222 Mark Johnson RC 1.00 .30
223 Randy Winn .50 .15
224 Nomar Garciaparra 2.00 .60
225 Jacque Jones RC 6.00 1.80
226 Chris Clemons .50 .15
227 Todd Helton 1.25 .35
228 Ryan Brannan RC 1.00 .30
229 Alex Sanchez RC 1.50 .45
230 Russell Branyan .50 .15
231 Daryle Ward 1.00 .30
232 Kevin Witt .50 .15
233 Gabby Martinez .50 .15
234 Preston Wilson .50 .15
235 Donzell McDonald RC 1.00 .30
236 Orlando Cabrera RC 2.50 .75
237 Brian Banks .50 .15
238 Robbie Bell 1.00 .30
239 Brad Rigby .50 .15
240 Scott Elarton .50 .15
241 Donny Leon RC 1.50 .45
242 Abraham Nunez RC 1.00 .30
243 Adam Eaton RC 1.50 .45
244 Octavio Dotel RC 1.50 .45
245 Sean Casey 1.50 .45
246 Joe Lawrence RC 1.50 .45
247 Adam Johnson RC 1.00 .30
248 Ronnie Belliard RC 1.50 .45
249 Bobby Estalella .50 .15
250 Corey Lee RC 1.00 .30
251 Mike Cameron .50 .15
252 Kerry Robinson RC 1.00 .30
253 A.J. Zapp RC 1.50 .45
254 Jarrod Washburn .50 .15
255 Ben Grieve .50 .15
256 Javier Vazquez RC 15.00 4.50
257 Travis Lee RC 1.50 .45
258 Dennis Reyes RC 1.00 .30
259 Danny Buxbaum .50 .15
260 Kelvim Escobar RC 1.50 .45
261 Danny Klassen .50 .15
262 Ken Cloude RC 1.50 .45
263 Gabe Alvarez .50 .15
264 Clayton Bruner RC 1.00 .30
265 Jason Marquis RC 1.50 .45
266 Jamey Wright .50 .15
267 Matt Snyder RC 1.00 .30
268 Josh Garrett RC 1.00 .30
269 Juan Encarnacion .50 .15
270 Heath Murray .50 .15
271 Brent Butler RC 1.50 .45
272 Danny Peoples RC 1.00 .30
273 Miguel Tejada RC 20.00 6.00
274 Jim Pittsley .50 .15
275 Dmitri Young .50 .15
276 Vladimir Guerrero 1.25 .35
277 Cole Liniak RC 1.00 .30
278 Ramon Hernandez .50 .15
279 Cliff Politte RC 1.00 .30
280 Mel Rosario RC 1.00 .30
281 Jorge Carrion RC 1.00 .30
282 John Barnes RC 1.00 .30
283 Chris Stowe RC 1.00 .30
284 Vernon Wells RC 20.00 6.00
285 Brett Caradonna RC 1.00 .30
286 Scott Hodges RC 1.50 .45
287 Jon Garland RC 2.50 .75
288 Nathan Haynes RC 1.50 .45
289 Geoff Goetz RC 1.00 .30
290 Adam Kennedy RC 4.00 1.20
291 T.J. Tucker RC 1.00 .30
292 Aaron Akin RC 1.00 .30
293 Jayson Werth RC 1.50 .45
294 Glenn Davis RC 1.00 .30
295 Mark Mangum RC 1.00 .30
296 Troy Cameron RC 1.50 .45
297 J.J. Davis RC 1.50 .45
298 Lance Berkman RC 20.00 6.00
299 Jason Standridge RC 1.50 .45
300 Jason Dellaero RC 1.00 .30

1997 Bowman Chrome International

Randomly inserted in packs at the rate of one in four, this 300-card set is parallel to the base set and is distinguished by the flag on the background of each card front identifying the country where that player was born.

Nm-Mt Ex-Mt
*STARS: 1.25X TO 3X BASIC CARDS .
*ROOKIES: .4X TO 1X BASIC CARDS .

1997 Bowman Chrome International Refractors

Randomly inserted in packs at the rate of one in 24, this 300-card set is a parallel version of the Bowman Chrome International set and is similar in design. The difference is found in the refractive quality of the card front.

Nm-Mt Ex-Mt
*STARS: 6X TO 15X BASIC CARDS ....
*ROOKIES: 1.5X TO 4X BASIC CARDS

1997 Bowman Chrome Refractors

Randomly inserted in packs at the rate of one in 12, this 300-card set is parallel to the base set and is similar in design. The difference can be found in the refractive quality of the cards fronts.

Nm-Mt Ex-Mt
*STARS: 3X TO 8X BASIC CARDS .....
*ROOKIES: 1.25X TO 3X BASIC CARDS

1997 Bowman Chrome 1998 ROY Favorites

Randomly inserted in packs at the rate of one in 24, cards from this 15-card set features color action photos of 1998 Rookie of the Year prospective candidtates printed on chromium cards.

Nm-Mt Ex-Mt
COMPLETE SET (15) 25.00 7.50
*REFRACTORS: .75X TO 2X BASIC ROY
REFRACTOR STATED ODDS 1:72
ROY1 Jeff Abbott 1.50 .45
ROY2 Karim Garcia 1.50 .45
ROY3 Todd Helton 4.00 1.20
ROY4 Richard Hidalgo 1.50 .45
ROY5 Geoff Jenkins 1.50 .45
ROY6 Russ Johnson 1.50 .45
ROY7 Paul Konerko 1.50 .45
ROY8 Mark Kotsay 1.00 .30
ROY9 Ricky Ledee 1.00 .30
ROY10 Travis Lee 1.00 .30
ROY11 Derrek Lee 1.50 .45
ROY12 Elieser Marrero 1.50 .45
ROY13 Juan Melo 1.50 .45
ROY14 Brian Rose 1.50 .45
ROY15 Fernando Tatis 1.00 .30

1997 Bowman Chrome Scout's Honor Roll

Randomly inserted in packs at a rate of one in 12, this 15-card set features color photos of top prospects and rookies printed on chromium cards. The backs carry player information.

Nm-Mt Ex-Mt
COMPLETE SET (15) 30.00 9.00
*REF: .75X TO 2X BASIC CHR.HONOR
REFRACTOR STATED ODDS 1:36
SHR1 Dmitri Young 1.25 .35
SHR2 Bob Abreu 1.25 .35
SHR3 Vladimir Guerrero 3.00 .90
SHR4 Paul Konerko 1.25 .35
SHR5 Kevin Orie 1.25 .35
SHR6 Todd Walker 1.25 .35
SHR7 Ben Grieve 1.25 .35
SHR8 Darin Erstad 1.25 .35
SHR9 Derrek Lee 1.25 .35
SHR10 Jose Cruz Jr. 3.00 .90
SHR11 Scott Rolen 2.00 .60
SHR12 Travis Lee 1.50 .45
SHR13 Andruw Jones 1.25 .35
SHR14 Wilton Guerrero 1.25 .35
SHR15 Nomar Garciaparra 5.00 1.50

1998 Bowman Chrome

The 1998 Bowman Chrome set was issued in two separate series with a total of 441 cards. The four-card packs retailed for $3.00 each. These cards are parallel to the regular Bowman set but with a premium Chrome finish. Unlike the 1997 brand, the 1998 issue parallels the entire Bowman brand. Rookie Cards include Ryan Anderson, Jack Cust, Troy Glaus, Orlando Hernandez, Gabe Kapler, Carlos Lee, Ruben Mateo, Kevin Millwood, Magglio Ordonez and Jimmy Rollins.

Nm-Mt Ex-Mt
COMPLETE SET (441) 160.00 47.50
COMP. SERIES 1 (221) 80.00 24.00
COMP. SERIES 2 (220) 80.00 24.00
1 Nomar Garciaparra 2.00 .60
2 Scott Rolen .75 .23
3 Andy Pettitte .75 .23
4 Ivan Rodriguez 1.25 .35
5 Mark McGwire 3.00 .90
6 Jason Dickson .50 .15
7 Jose Cruz Jr. .50 .15
8 Jeff Kent .50 .15
9 Mike Mussina 1.25 .35
10 Jason Kendall .50 .15
11 Brett Tomko .50 .15
12 Jeff King .50 .15
13 Brad Radke .50 .15
14 Robin Ventura .50 .15
15 Jeff Bagwell .75 .23
16 Greg Maddux 2.00 .60
17 John Jaha .50 .15
18 Mike Piazza 2.00 .60
19 Edgar Martinez .75 .23
20 David Justice .50 .15
21 Todd Hundley .50 .15
22 Tony Gwynn 1.50 .45
23 Larry Walker .75 .23
24 Bernie Williams .75 .23
25 Edgar Renteria .50 .15
26 Rafael Palmeiro .75 .23
27 Tim Salmon .75 .23
28 Matt Morris .50 .15
29 Shawn Estes .50 .15
30 Vladimir Guerrero 1.25 .35
31 Fernando Tatis .50 .15
32 Justin Thompson .50 .15
33 Ken Griffey Jr. 2.00 .60
34 Edgardo Alfonzo .50 .15
35 Mo Vaughn .50 .15
36 Marty Cordova .50 .15
37 Craig Biggio .75 .23
38 Roger Clemens 2.50 .75
39 Mark Grace .75 .23
40 Ken Caminiti .50 .15
41 Tony Womack .50 .15
42 Albert Belle .50 .15
43 Tino Martinez .75 .23
44 Sandy Alomar Jr. .50 .15
45 Jeff Cirillo .50 .15
46 Jason Giambi 1.25 .35
47 Darin Erstad .50 .15
48 Livan Hernandez .50 .15
49 Mark Grudzielanek .50 .15
50 Sammy Sosa 2.00 .60
51 Curt Schilling .75 .23
52 Brian Hunter .50 .15
53 Neifi Perez .50 .15
54 Todd Walker .50 .15
55 Jose Guillen .50 .15
56 Jim Thome 1.25 .35
57 Tom Glavine .75 .23
58 Todd Greene .50 .15
59 Rondell White .50 .15
60 Roberto Alomar 1.25 .35
61 Tony Clark .50 .15
62 Vinny Castilla .50 .15
63 Barry Larkin 1.25 .35
64 Hideki Irabu .50 .15
65 Johnny Damon .50 .15
66 Juan Gonzalez 1.25 .35
67 John Olerud .50 .15
68 Gary Sheffield .50 .15
69 Raul Mondesi .50 .15
70 Chipper Jones 1.25 .35
71 David Ortiz 2.50 .75
72 Warren Morris RC 1.00 .30
73 Alex Gonzalez .50 .15
74 Nick Bierbrodt .50 .15
75 Roy Halladay .50 .15
76 Danny Buxbaum .50 .15
77 Adam Kennedy .50 .15
78 Jared Sandberg .50 .15
79 Michael Barrett .50 .15
80 Gil Meche 5.00 1.50
81 Jayson Werth .50 .15
82 Abraham Nunez .50 .15
83 Ben Petrick .50 .15
84 Brett Caradonna .50 .15
85 Mike Lowell RC 8.00 2.40
86 Clay Bruner .50 .15
87 John Curtice RC 1.50 .45
88 Bobby Estalella .50 .15
89 Juan Melo .50 .15
90 Arnold Gooch .50 .15
91 Kevin Millwood RC 6.00 1.80
92 Richie Sexson .50 .15
93 Orlando Cabrera .50 .15
94 Pat Cline .50 .15
95 Anthony Sanders .50 .15
96 Russ Johnson .50 .15
97 Ben Grieve .50 .15
98 Kevin McGlinchy .50 .15
99 Paul Wilder .50 .15
100 Russ Ortiz .50 .15
101 Ryan Jackson RC 1.00 .30
102 Heath Murray .50 .15
103 Brian Rose .50 .15
104 R.Radmanovich RC 1.00 .30
105 Ricky Ledee .50 .15
106 Jeff Wallace RC 1.00 .30
107 Ryan Minor RC 1.00 .30
108 Dennis Reyes .50 .15
109 James Manias .50 .15
110 Chris Carpenter .50 .15
111 Daryle Ward .50 .15
112 Vernon Wells .75 .23
113 Chad Green .50 .15
114 Mike Stoner RC 1.00 .30
115 Brad Fullmer .50 .15
116 Adam Eaton .50 .15
117 Jeff Liefer .50 .15
118 Corey Koskie RC 5.00 1.50
119 Todd Helton .75 .23
120 Jaime Jones RC 1.00 .30
121 Mel Rosario .50 .15
122 Geoff Goetz .50 .15
123 Adrian Beltre .50 .15
124 Jason Dellaero .50 .15
125 Gabe Kapler RC 2.50 .75
126 Scott Schoeneweis .50 .15
127 Ryan Brannan .50 .15
128 Aaron Akin .50 .15
129 Ryan Anderson RC 1.50 .45
130 Brad Penny .50 .15
131 Bruce Chen .50 .15
132 Eli Marrero .50 .15
133 Eric Chavez .75 .23
134 Troy Glaus RC 15.00 4.50
135 Troy Cameron .50 .15
136 Brian Sikorski RC 1.00 .30
137 Mike Kinkade RC 1.00 .30
138 Braden Looper .50 .15
139 Mark Mangum .50 .15
140 Danny Peoples .50 .15
141 J.J. Davis .50 .15
142 Ben Davis .50 .15
143 Jacque Jones .50 .15
144 Derrick Gibson .50 .15
145 Bronson Arroyo 1.00 .30
146 L.De Los Santos RC 1.00 .30
147 Jeff Abbott .50 .15
148 Mike Cuddyer RC 4.00 1.20
149 Jason Romano .50 .15
150 Shane Monahan .50 .15
151 Ntema Ndungidi RC 1.00 .30

152 Alex Sanchez .50 .15
153 Jack Cust RC 1.50 .45
154 Brent Butler .50 .15
155 Ramon Hernandez .50 .15
156 Norm Hutchins .50 .15
157 Jason Marquis .50 .15
158 Jacob Cruz .50 .15
159 Rob Burger RC 1.00 .30
160 Dave Coggin .50 .15
161 Preston Wilson .50 .15
162 Jason Fitzgerald RC 1.00 .30
163 Dan Serafini .50 .15
164 Pete Munro .50 .15
165 Trot Nixon .75 .23
166 Homer Bush .50 .15
167 Dermal Brown .50 .15
168 Chad Hermansen .50 .15
169 Julio Moreno RC 1.00 .30
170 John Roskos RC 1.00 .30
171 Grant Roberts .50 .15
172 Ken Cloude .50 .15
173 Jason Brester .50 .15
174 Jason Conti .50 .15
175 Jon Garland .50 .15
176 Robbie Bell .50 .15
177 Nathan Haynes .50 .15
178 Ramon Ortiz RC 4.00 1.20
179 Shannon Stewart .50 .15
180 Pablo Ortega .50 .15
181 Jimmy Rollins RC 5.00 1.50
182 Sean Casey .50 .15
183 Ted Lilly RC 2.50 .75
184 Chris Enochs RC 1.00 .30
185 M.Ordonez RC UER 10.00 3.00
Front photo is Mario Valdez
186 Mike Drumright .50 .15
187 Aaron Boone .50 .15
188 Matt Clement .50 .15
189 Todd Dunwoody .50 .15
190 Larry Rodriguez .50 .15
191 Todd Noel .50 .15
192 Geoff Jenkins .50 .15
193 George Lombard .50 .15
194 Lance Berkman .75 .23
195 Marcus McCain .50 .15
196 Ryan McGuire .50 .15
197 Jhensy Sandoval .50 .15
198 Corey Lee .50 .15
199 Mario Valdez .50 .15
200 Robert Fick RC 5.00 1.50
201 Donnie Sadler .50 .15
202 Marc Kroon .50 .15
203 David Miller .50 .15
204 Jarrod Washburn .50 .15
205 Miguel Tejada .75 .23
206 Raul Ibanez .50 .15
207 John Patterson .50 .15
208 Calvin Pickering .50 .15
209 Felix Martinez .50 .15
210 Mark Redman .50 .15
211 Scott Elarton .50 .15
212 Jose Amado RC 1.00 .30
213 Kerry Wood 1.25 .35
214 Dante Powell .50 .15
215 Aramis Ramirez .50 .15
216 A.J. Hinch .50 .15
217 Dustin Carr RC 1.00 .30
218 Mark Kotsay .50 .15
219 Jason Standridge .50 .15
220 Luis Ordaz .50 .15
221 O.Hernandez RC 5.00 1.50
222 Cal Ripken 4.00 1.20
223 Paul Molitor .75 .23
224 Derek Jeter 3.00 .90
225 Barry Bonds 3.00 .90
226 Jim Edmonds .50 .15
227 John Smoltz .75 .23
228 Eric Karros .50 .15
229 Ray Lankford .50 .15
230 Rey Ordonez .50 .15
231 Kenny Lofton .50 .15
232 Alex Rodriguez 2.00 .60
233 Dante Bichette .50 .15
234 Pedro Martinez 1.25 .35
235 Carlos Delgado .50 .15
236 Rod Beck .50 .15
237 Matt Williams .50 .15
238 Charles Johnson .50 .15
239 Rico Brogna .50 .15
240 Frank Thomas 1.25 .35
241 Paul O'Neill .75 .23
242 Jaret Wright .50 .15
243 Brant Brown .50 .15
244 Ryan Klesko .50 .15
245 Chuck Finley .50 .15
246 Derek Bell .50 .15
247 Delino DeShields .50 .15
248 Chan Ho Park .50 .15
249 Wade Boggs .75 .23
250 Jay Buhner .50 .15
251 Butch Huskey .50 .15
252 Steve Finley .50 .15
253 Will Clark 1.25 .35
254 John Valentin .50 .15
255 Bobby Higginson .50 .15
256 Darryl Strawberry .75 .23
257 Randy Johnson 1.25 .35
258 Al Martin .50 .15
259 Travis Fryman .50 .15
260 Fred McGriff .75 .23
261 Jose Valentin .50 .15
262 Andruw Jones .50 .15
263 Kenny Rogers .50 .15
264 Moises Alou .50 .15
265 Denny Neagle .50 .15
266 Ugueth Urbina .50 .15
267 Derrek Lee .50 .15
268 Ellis Burks .50 .15
269 Mariano Rivera .75 .23
270 Dean Palmer .50 .15
271 Eddie Taubensee .50 .15
272 Brady Anderson .50 .15
273 Brian Giles .50 .15
274 Quinton McCracken .50 .15
275 Henry Rodriguez .50 .15
276 Andres Galarraga .50 .15
277 Jose Canseco 1.25 .35
278 David Segui .50 .15
279 Bret Saberhagen .50 .15
280 Kevin Brown .75 .23
281 Chuck Knoblauch .50 .15
282 Jeromy Burnitz .50 .15
283 Jay Bell .50 .15
284 Manny Ramirez .50 .15
285 Rick Helling .50 .15
286 Francisco Cordova .50 .15
287 Bob Abreu .50 .15
288 J.T. Snow .50 .15
289 Hideo Nomo 1.25 .35
290 Brian Jordan .50 .15
291 Javy Lopez .50 .15
292 Travis Lee .50 .15
293 Russell Branyan .50 .15
294 Paul Konerko .50 .15
295 Masato Yoshii RC 2.50 .75
296 Kris Benson .50 .15
297 Juan Encarnacion .50 .15
298 Eric Milton .50 .15
299 Mike Caruso .50 .15
300 R. Aramboles RC 1.50 .45
301 Bobby Smith .50 .15
302 Billy Koch .50 .15
303 Richard Hidalgo .50 .15
304 Justin Baughman RC 1.00 .30
305 Chris Gissell .50 .15
306 Donnie Bridges RC 1.50 .45
307 Nelson Lara RC 1.00 .30
308 Randy Wolf RC 4.00 1.20
309 Jason LaRue RC 1.50 .45
310 Jason Gooding RC 1.00 .30
311 Edgard Clemente .50 .15
312 Andrew Vessel .50 .15
313 Chris Reitsma .50 .15
314 Jesus Sanchez RC 1.00 .30
315 Buddy Carlyle RC 1.00 .30
316 Randy Winn .50 .15
317 Luis Rivera RC 1.00 .30
318 Marcus Thames RC 1.50 .45
319 A.J. Pierzynski .50 .15
320 Scott Randall .50 .15
321 Damian Sapp .50 .15
322 Ed Yarnall RC 1.00 .30
323 Luke Allen RC 1.50 .45
324 J.D. Smart .50 .15
325 Willie Martinez .50 .15
326 Alex Ramirez .50 .15
327 Eric DuBose RC 1.50 .45
328 Kevin Witt .50 .15
329 Dan McKinley RC 1.00 .30
330 Cliff Politte .50 .15
331 Vladimir Nunez .50 .15
332 John Halama RC 1.50 .45
333 Nerio Rodriguez .50 .15
334 Desi Relaford .50 .15
335 Robinson Checo .50 .15
336 John Nicholson .75 .23
337 Tom LaRosa RC 1.00 .30
338 Kevin Nicholson RC 1.00 .30
339 Javier Vazquez .50 .15
340 A.J. Zapp .50 .15
341 Tom Evans .50 .15
342 Kerry Robinson .50 .15
343 Gabe Gonzalez RC 1.00 .30
344 Ralph Milliard .50 .15
345 Enrique Wilson .50 .15
346 Elvin Hernandez .50 .15
347 Mike Lincoln RC 1.00 .30
348 Cesar King RC 1.00 .30
349 Cristian Guzman RC 5.00 1.50
350 Donzell McDonald .50 .15
351 Jim Parque RC 1.50 .45
352 Mike Saipe RC 1.00 .30
353 Carlos Febles RC 1.50 .45
354 Dernell Stenson RC 1.50 .45
355 Mark Osborne RC 1.00 .30
356 Odalis Perez RC 2.50 .75
357 Jason Dewey RC 1.00 .30
358 Joe Fontenot .50 .15
359 Jason Grilli RC 1.00 .30
360 Kevin Haverbusch RC 1.00 .30
361 Jay Yennaco RC 1.00 .30
362 Brian Buchanan .50 .15
363 John Barnes .50 .15
364 Chris Fussell .50 .15
365 Kevin Gibbs RC 1.00 .30
366 Joe Lawrence .50 .15
367 DaRond Stovall .50 .15
368 Brian Fuentes RC 1.00 .30
369 Jimmy Anderson .50 .15
370 Lariel Gonzalez RC 1.00 .30
371 Scott Williamson RC 1.50 .45
372 Milton Bradley .50 .15
373 Jason Halper RC 1.00 .30
374 Brent Billingsley RC 1.00 .30
375 Joe DePastino RC 1.00 .30
376 Jake Westbrook .50 .15
377 Octavio Dotel .50 .15
378 Jason Williams RC 1.00 .30
379 Julio Ramirez RC 1.00 .30
380 Seth Greisinger .50 .15
381 Mike Judd RC 1.00 .30
382 Ben Ford RC 1.00 .30
383 Tom Bennett RC 1.00 .30
384 Adam Butler RC 1.00 .30
385 Wade Miller RC 5.00 1.50
386 Kyle Peterson RC 1.00 .30
387 Tommy Peterman RC 1.00 .30
388 Onan Masaoka .50 .15
389 Jason Rakers RC 1.00 .30
390 Rafael Medina .50 .15
391 Luis Lopez RC 1.00 .30
392 Jeff Yoder .50 .15
393 Vance Wilson RC 1.00 .30
394 F. Seguignol RC 1.00 .30
395 Ron Wright .50 .15
396 Ruben Mateo RC 1.50 .45
397 Steve Lomasney RC 1.50 .45
398 Damian Jackson .50 .15
399 Mike Jerzembeck RC 1.00 .30
400 Luis Rivas RC 4.00 1.20
401 Kevin Burford RC 1.00 .30
402 Glenn Davis 1.00 .30
403 Robert Luce RC 1.00 .30
404 Cole Liniak .50 .15
405 Matt LeCroy RC 1.50 .45
406 Jeremy Giambi RC 1.50 .45
407 Shawn Chacon .50 .15
408 Dewayne Wise RC 1.00 .30
409 Steve Woodard .50 .15
410 F.Cordero RC 1.50 .45
411 Damon Minor RC 1.50 .45
412 Lou Collier .50 .15
413 Justin Towle .50 .15
414 Juan LeBron .50 .15
415 Michael Coleman .50 .15
416 Felix Rodriguez .50 .15
417 Paul Ah Yat RC 1.00 .30
418 Kevin Barker RC 1.00 .30
419 Brian Meadows .50 .15
420 Darnell McDonald RC 1.50 .45
421 Matt Kinney RC 1.50 .45
422 Mike Vavrek RC 1.00 .30
423 Courtney Duncan RC 1.00 .30
424 Kevin Millar RC 5.00 1.50
425 Ruben Rivera .50 .15
426 Steve Shoemaker RC 1.00 .30
427 Dan Reichert RC 1.50 .45
428 Carlos Lee RC 5.00 1.50
429 Rod Barajas 1.00 .30
430 Pablo Ozuna RC 1.50 .45
431 Todd Belitz RC 1.00 .30
432 Sidney Ponson .50 .15
433 Steve Carver RC 1.00 .30
434 Esteban Yan RC 1.50 .45
435 Cedrick Bowers .50 .15
436 Marlon Anderson .50 .15
437 Carl Pavano .50 .15
438 Jae Weong Seo RC 2.50 .75
439 Jose Taveras RC 1.00 .30
440 Matt Anderson RC 1.50 .45
441 Darron Ingram RC 1.00 .30

1998 Bowman Chrome Golden Anniversary

Randomly inserted in first series packs at a rate of one in 164 and second series packs at a rate of one in 133, this 441-card set is a parallel to the Bowman Chrome base set. The set is sequentially numbered to 50 and is highlighted by gold facsimile signatures.

Nm-Mt Ex-Mt
*STARS: 6X TO 15X BASIC CARDS
*ROOKIES: 3X TO 8X BASIC CARDS
GOLD.ANN.REF.SER.1 ODDS 1:1279
GOLD.ANN.REF.SER.2 ODDS 1:1022
GOLD.ANN.REF.PRINT RUN 5 SERIAL #'d SETS
GOLD.ANN.REF.NOT PRICED DUE TO SCARCITY

1998 Bowman Chrome International

Randomly inserted in packs at a rate of one in four, this 441-card set is a parallel to the Bowman Chrome base set. These cards are differentiated by maps of the player's hometown area in the background of each card front.

	Nm-Mt	Ex-Mt
COMPLETE SET (441)	700.00	210.00
COMP. SERIES 1 (221)	400.00	120.00
COMP. SERIES 2 (220)	300.00	90.00

*STARS: 1.5X TO 4X BASIC CARDS
*ROOKIES: .4X TO 1X BASIC CARDS

1998 Bowman Chrome International Refractors

Randomly inserted in packs at a rate of one in 24, this 441-card set is a parallel to the Bowman Chrome base set. These cards are differentiated by maps of the player's hometown area in the background of each card front.

Nm-Mt Ex-Mt
*STARS: 5X TO 12X BASIC CARDS
*ROOKIES: 1.5X TO 4X BASIC CARDS

1998 Bowman Chrome Refractors

Randomly inserted in packs at a rate of one in 12, this 441-card set is a parallel of the Bowman Chrome base set. The refractive quality of the card fronts differentiate themselves from basic issue cards.

Nm-Mt Ex-Mt
*STARS: 3X TO 8X BASIC CARDS
*ROOKIES: 1.25X TO 3X BASIC CARDS

1998 Bowman Chrome Reprints

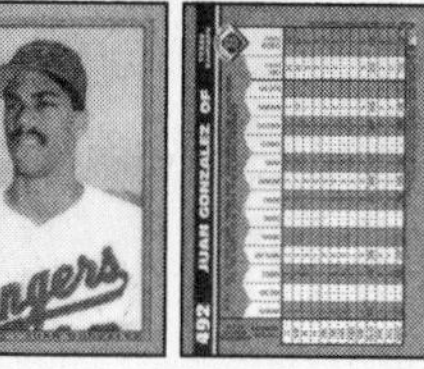

Randomly inserted in first and second packs at a rate of one in 12, these cards are replicas of classic Bowman Rookie Cards from 1948-1955 and 1989-present. Odd numbered cards (1, 3, 5 etc) were distributed in first series packs and even numbered cards in second series packs. The upgraded Chrome silver-colored stock gives them a striking appearance and makes them easy to differentiate from the originals.

	Nm-Mt	Ex-Mt
COMPLETE SET (50)	160.00	47.50
COMPLETE SERIES 1 (25)	80.00	24.00
COMPLETE SERIES 2 (25)	80.00	24.00

*REFRACTORS: 1X TO 2.5X BASIC REPRINTS
REFRACTOR STATED ODDS 1:36

1 Yogi Berra 4.00 1.20
2 Jackie Robinson 5.00 1.50
3 Don Newcombe 1.50 .45
4 Satchell Paige 4.00 1.20
5 Willie Mays 10.00 3.00
6 Gil McDougald 1.50 .45
7 Don Larsen 1.50 .45
8 Elston Howard 2.50 .75
9 Robin Ventura 1.50 .45
10 Brady Anderson 1.50 .45
11 Gary Sheffield 1.50 .45
12 Tino Martinez 2.50 .75
13 Ken Griffey Jr. 6.00 1.80
14 John Smoltz 2.50 .75
15 Sandy Alomar Jr. 1.00 .30
16 Larry Walker 2.50 .75
17 Todd Hundley 1.00 .30
18 Mo Vaughn 1.50 .45
19 Sammy Sosa 6.00 1.80
20 Frank Thomas 4.00 1.20
21 Chuck Knoblauch 1.50 .45
22 Bernie Williams 2.50 .75
23 Juan Gonzalez 4.00 1.20
24 Mike Mussina 4.00 1.20
25 Jeff Bagwell 2.50 .75
26 Tim Salmon 2.50 .75
27 Ivan Rodriguez 4.00 1.20
28 Kenny Lofton 1.50 .45
29 Chipper Jones 4.00 1.20
30 Javy Lopez 1.50 .45
31 Ryan Klesko 1.50 .45
32 Raul Mondesi 1.50 .45
33 Jim Thome 4.00 1.20
34 Carlos Delgado 1.50 .45
35 Mike Piazza 6.00 1.80
36 Manny Ramirez 1.50 .45
37 Andy Pettitte 2.50 .75
38 Derek Jeter 10.00 3.00
39 Brad Fullmer 1.00 .30
40 Richard Hidalgo 1.50 .45
41 Tony Clark 1.00 .30
42 Andruw Jones 1.50 .45
43 Vladimir Guerrero 4.00 1.20
44 Nomar Garciaparra 6.00 1.80
45 Paul Konerko 1.50 .45
46 Ben Grieve 1.00 .30
47 Hideo Nomo 4.00 1.20
48 Scott Rolen 2.50 .75
49 Jose Guillen 1.00 .30
50 Livan Hernandez 1.00 .30

1998 Bowman Chrome Reprints Refractors

Randomly inserted in packs at a rate of one in 36, this 50-card set is a parallel insert to the Bowman Chrome Reprints set.

Nm-Mt Ex-Mt
*REFRACTORS: 1X TO 2.5X BASIC REPRINTS

1999 Bowman Chrome

The 1999 Bowman Chrome set was issued in two distinct series and were distributed in four card packs with a suggested retail price of $3.00. The set contains 440 regular cards printed on brilliant chromium 18-pt. Stock. Within the set are 300 top prospects that are designated with silver and blue foil. Each player's facsimile rookie signature are featured on these cards. There are also 140 vereran stars designated with a red and silver foil stamp. The backs contain information on each player's rookie and most recent season, career statistics and a scouting report from early league days Rookie Cards include Pat Burrell, Adam Dunn, Rafael Furcal, Freddy Garcia, Tim Hudson, Nick Johnson, Austin Kearns, Willy Mo Pena, Adam Piatt, Corey Patterson and Alfonso Soriano.

	Nm-Mt	Ex-Mt
COMPLETE SET (440)	300.00	90.00
COMP. SERIES 1 (220)	100.00	30.00
COMP. SERIES 2 (220)	200.00	60.00

1 Ben Grieve .50 .15
2 Kerry Wood 1.25 .35
3 Ruben Rivera .50 .15
4 Sandy Alomar Jr. .50 .15
5 Cal Ripken 4.00 1.20
6 Mark McGwire 3.00 .90
7 Vladimir Guerrero 1.25 .35
8 Moises Alou .50 .15
9 Jim Edmonds .50 .15
10 Greg Maddux 2.00 .60
11 Gary Sheffield .50 .15
12 John Valentin .50 .15
13 Chuck Knoblauch .50 .15
14 Tony Clark .50 .15
15 Rusty Greer .50 .15
16 Al Leiter .50 .15
17 Travis Lee .50 .15
18 Jose Cruz Jr. .50 .15
19 Pedro Martinez 1.25 .35
20 Paul O'Neill .75 .23
21 Todd Walker .50 .15
22 Vinny Castilla .50 .15
23 Barry Larkin 1.25 .35
24 Curt Schilling .75 .23
25 Jason Kendall .50 .15
26 Scott Erickson .50 .15
27 Andres Galarraga .50 .15
28 Jeff Shaw .50 .15
29 John Olerud .50 .15
30 Orlando Hernandez .50 .15
31 Larry Walker .75 .23
32 Andruw Jones .50 .15
33 Jeff Cirillo .50 .15
34 Barry Bonds 3.00 .90
35 Manny Ramirez .50 .15
36 Mark Kotsay .50 .15
37 Ivan Rodriguez 1.25 .35
38 Jeff King .50 .15
39 Brian Hunter .50 .15
40 Ray Durham .50 .15
41 Bernie Williams .75 .23
42 Darin Erstad .50 .15
43 Chipper Jones 1.25 .35
44 Pat Hentgen .50 .15
45 Eric Young .50 .15
46 Jaret Wright .50 .15
47 Juan Guzman .50 .15
48 Jorge Posada .75 .23
49 Bobby Higginson .50 .15
50 Jose Guillen .50 .15
51 Trevor Hoffman .50 .15
52 Ken Griffey Jr. 2.00 .60
53 David Justice .50 .15
54 Matt Williams .50 .15
55 Eric Karros .50 .15
56 Derek Bell .50 .15
57 Ray Lankford .50 .15
58 Mariano Rivera .75 .23
59 Brett Tomko .50 .15
60 Mike Mussina 1.25 .35
61 Kenny Lofton .50 .15
62 Chuck Finley .50 .15
63 Alex Gonzalez .50 .15
64 Mark Grace .75 .23
65 Raul Mondesi .50 .15
66 David Cone .50 .15
67 Brad Fullmer .50 .15
68 Andy Benes .50 .15
69 John Smoltz .75 .23
70 Shane Reynolds .50 .15
71 Bruce Chen .50 .15
72 Adam Kennedy .50 .15
73 Jack Cust .50 .15
74 Matt Clement .50 .15
75 Derrick Gibson .50 .15
76 Darnell McDonald .50 .15
77 Adam Everett RC 1.50 .45
78 Ricardo Aramboles .50 .15
79 Mark Quinn RC 1.50 .45
80 Jason Rakers .50 .15
81 Seth Etherton RC 1.50 .45
82 Jeff Urban RC 1.00 .30
83 Manny Aybar .50 .15
84 Mike Nannini RC 1.50 .45
85 Onan Masaoka .50 .15
86 Rod Barajas .50 .15
87 Mike Frank .50 .15
88 Scott Randall .50 .15
89 Justin Bowles RC 1.00 .30
90 Chris Haas .50 .15
91 Arturo McDowell RC 1.50 .45
92 Matt Belisle RC 1.50 .45
93 Scott Elarton .50 .15
94 Vernon Wells .50 .15
95 Pat Cline .50 .15
96 Ryan Anderson .50 .15
97 Kevin Barker .50 .15
98 Ruben Mateo .50 .15
99 Robert Fick .50 .15
100 Corey Koskie .50 .15
101 Ricky Ledee .50 .15
102 Rick Elder RC 1.50 .45
103 Jack Cressend RC 1.00 .30
104 Joe Lawrence .50 .15
105 Mike Lincoln .50 .15
106 Kit Pellow RC 1.00 .30
107 Matt Burch RC 1.00 .30
108 Cole Liniak .50 .15
109 Jason Dewey .50 .15
110 Cesar King .50 .15
111 Julio Ramirez .50 .15
112 Jake Westbrook .50 .15
113 Eric Valent RC 1.50 .45
114 Roosevelt Brown RC 1.50 .45
115 Choo Freeman RC 1.50 .45
116 Juan Melo .50 .15
117 Jason Grilli .50 .15
118 Jared Sandberg .50 .15
119 Glenn Davis .50 .15
120 David Riske RC 1.00 .30
121 Jacque Jones .50 .15
122 Corey Lee .50 .15
123 Michael Barrett .50 .15
124 Lariel Gonzalez .50 .15
125 Mitch Meluskey .50 .15
126 Freddy Adrian Garcia .50 .15
127 Tony Torcato RC 1.50 .45
128 Jeff Liefer .50 .15
129 Ntema Ndungidi .50 .15
130 Andy Brown RC 1.50 .45
131 Ryan Mills RC 1.50 .45
132 Andy Abad RC 1.00 .30
133 Carlos Febles .50 .15
134 Jason Tyner RC 1.50 .45
135 Mark Osborne .50 .15
136 Phil Norton RC 1.00 .30
137 Nathan Haynes .50 .15
138 Roy Halladay .50 .15
139 Juan Encarnacion .50 .15
140 Brad Penny .50 .15
141 Grant Roberts .50 .15
142 Aramis Ramirez .50 .15
143 Cristian Guzman .50 .15
144 Mamon Tucker RC 1.50 .45
145 Ryan Bradley .50 .15
146 Brian Simmons .50 .15
147 Dan Reichert .50 .15
148 Russell Branyan .50 .15
149 Victor Valencia RC 1.00 .30
150 Scott Schoeneweis .50 .15
151 Sean Spencer RC 1.00 .30
152 Odalis Perez .50 .15
153 Joe Fontenot .50 .15
154 Milton Bradley .50 .15
155 Josh McKinley RC 1.50 .45
156 Terrence Long .50 .15
157 Danny Klassen .50 .15
158 Paul Hoover RC 1.00 .30
159 Ron Belliard .50 .15
160 Armando Rios .50 .15
161 Ramon Hernandez .50 .15
162 Jason Conti .50 .15
163 Chad Hermansen .50 .15
164 Jason Standridge .50 .15
165 Jason Dellaero .50 .15
166 John Curtice .50 .15
167 Clayton Andrews RC 1.50 .45
168 Jeremy Giambi .50 .15
169 Alex Ramirez .50 .15
170 Gabe Molina RC 1.00 .30
171 M.Encarnacion RC 1.00 .30
172 Mike Zywica RC 1.00 .30
173 Chip Ambres RC 1.50 .45
174 Trot Nixon .75 .23

175 Pat Burrell RC 15.00 4.50
176 Jeff Yoder .50 .15
177 Chris Jones RC 1.50 .45
178 Kevin Witt .50 .15
179 Keith Luuloa RC 1.00 .30
180 Billy Koch .50 .15
181 Damaso Marte RC 1.00 .30
182 Ryan Glynn RC 1.00 .30
183 Calvin Pickering .50 .15
184 Michael Cuddyer .50 .15
185 Nick Johnson RC 8.00 2.40
186 D.Mientkiewicz RC 5.00 1.50
187 Nate Cornejo RC 2.50 .75
188 Octavio Dotel .50 .15
189 Wes Helms .50 .15
190 Nelson Lara .50 .15
191 Chuck Abbott RC 1.00 .30
192 Tony Armas Jr. .50 .15
193 Gil Meche .50 .15
194 Ben Petrick .50 .15
195 Chris George RC 1.50 .45
196 Scott Hunter RC 1.00 .30
197 Ryan Brannan .50 .15
198 Amaury Garcia RC 1.00 .30
199 Chris Gissell .50 .15
200 Austin Kearns RC 20.00 6.00
201 Alex Gonzalez .50 .15
202 Wade Miller .50 .15
203 Scott Williamson .50 .15
204 Chris Enochs .50 .15
205 Fernando Seguignol .50 .15
206 Marlon Anderson .50 .15
207 Todd Sears RC 1.50 .45
208 Nate Bump RC 1.00 .30
209 J.M. Gold RC 1.50 .45
210 Matt LeCroy .50 .15
211 Alex Hernandez .50 .15
212 Luis Rivera .50 .15
213 Troy Cameron .50 .15
214 Alex Escobar RC 1.50 .45
215 Jason LaRue .50 .15
216 Kyle Peterson .50 .15
217 Brent Butler .50 .15
218 Dernell Stenson .50 .15
219 Adrian Beltre .50 .15
220 Daryle Ward .50 .15
221 Jim Thome 1.25 .35
222 Cliff Floyd .50 .15
223 Rickey Henderson 1.25 .35
224 Garret Anderson .50 .15
225 Ken Caminiti .50 .15
226 Bret Boone .50 .15
227 Jeromy Burnitz .50 .15
228 Steve Finley .50 .15
229 Miguel Tejada .50 .15
230 Greg Vaughn .50 .15
231 Jose Offerman .50 .15
232 Andy Ashby .50 .15
233 Albert Belle .50 .15
234 Fernando Tatis .50 .15
235 Todd Helton .75 .23
236 Sean Casey .50 .15
237 Brian Giles .50 .15
238 Andy Pettitte .75 .23
239 Fred McGriff .75 .23
240 Roberto Alomar 1.25 .35
241 Edgar Martinez .75 .23
242 Lee Stevens .50 .15
243 Shawn Green .50 .15
244 Ryan Klesko .50 .15
245 Sammy Sosa 2.00 .60
246 Todd Hundley .50 .15
247 Shannon Stewart .50 .15
248 Randy Johnson 1.25 .35
249 Rondell White .50 .15
250 Mike Piazza 2.00 .60
251 Craig Biggio .75 .23
252 David Wells .50 .15
253 Brian Jordan .50 .15
254 Edgar Renteria .50 .15
255 Bartolo Colon .50 .15
256 Frank Thomas 1.25 .35
257 Will Clark 1.25 .35
258 Dean Palmer .50 .15
259 Dmitri Young .50 .15
260 Scott Rolen .75 .23
261 Jeff Kent .50 .15
262 Dante Bichette .50 .15
263 Nomar Garciaparra 2.00 .60
264 Tony Gwynn 1.50 .45
265 Alex Rodriguez 2.00 .60
266 Jose Canseco 1.25 .35
267 Jason Giambi 1.25 .35
268 Jeff Bagwell .75 .23
269 Carlos Delgado .50 .15
270 Tom Glavine .75 .23
271 Eric Davis .50 .15
272 Edgardo Alfonzo .50 .15
273 Tim Salmon .75 .23
274 Johnny Damon .50 .15
275 Rafael Palmeiro .75 .23
276 Denny Neagle .50 .15
277 Neifi Perez .50 .15
278 Roger Clemens 2.50 .75
279 Brant Brown .50 .15
280 Kevin Brown .75 .23
281 Jay Bell .50 .15
282 Jay Buhner .50 .15
283 Matt Lawton .50 .15
284 Robin Ventura .50 .15
285 Juan Gonzalez 1.25 .35
286 Mo Vaughn .50 .15
287 Kevin Millwood .50 .15
288 Tino Martinez .75 .23
289 Justin Thompson .50 .15
290 Derek Jeter 3.00 .90
291 Ben Davis .50 .15
292 Mike Lowell .50 .15
293 Calvin Murray .50 .15
294 Micah Bowie RC 1.00 .30
295 Lance Berkman .50 .15
296 Jason Marquis .50 .15
297 Chad Green .50 .15
298 Dee Brown .50 .15
299 Jerry Hairston Jr. .50 .15
300 Gabe Kapler .50 .15
301 Brent Stentz RC 1.00 .30
302 Scott Mullen RC 1.00 .30
303 Brandon Reed .50 .15
304 Shea Hillenbrand RC 8.00 2.40
305 J.D. Closser RC 1.50 .45
306 Gary Matthews Jr. .50 .15
307 Toby Hall RC 2.50 .75
308 Jason Phillips RC 1.00 .30
309 Jose Macias RC 1.00 .30
310 Jung Bong RC 1.50 .45
311 Ramon Soler RC 1.50 .45
312 Kelly Dransfeldt RC 1.00 .30
313 Carlos E. Hernandez RC 1.50 .45
314 Kevin Haverbusch .50 .15
315 Aaron Myette RC 1.50 .45
316 Chad Harville RC 1.00 .30
317 Kyle Farnsworth RC 4.00 1.20
318 Gookie Dawkins RC 1.50 .45
319 Willie Martinez .50 .15
320 Carlos Lee .50 .15
321 Carlos Pena RC 4.00 1.20
322 Peter Bergeron RC 1.50 .45
323 A.J. Burnett RC 4.00 1.20
324 Bucky Jacobsen RC 1.50 .45
325 Mo Bruce RC 1.00 .30
326 Reggie Taylor .50 .15
327 Jackie Rexrode .50 .15
328 Alvin Morrow RC 1.00 .30
329 Carlos Beltran .50 .15
330 Eric Chavez .50 .15
331 John Patterson .50 .15
332 Jayson Werth .50 .15
333 Richie Sexson .50 .15
334 Randy Wolf .50 .15
335 Eli Marrero .50 .15
336 Paul LoDuca .50 .15
337 J.D Smart .50 .15
338 Ryan Minor .50 .15
339 Kris Benson .50 .15
340 George Lombard .50 .15
341 Troy Glaus .75 .23
342 Eddie Yarnall .50 .15
343 Kip Wells RC 2.50 .75
344 C.C. Sabathia RC 4.00 1.20
345 Sean Burroughs RC 12.00 3.60
346 Felipe Lopez RC 1.50 .45
347 Ryan Rupe RC 1.50 .45
348 Orber Moreno RC 1.00 .30
349 Rafael Roque RC 1.00 .30
350 Alfonso Soriano RC 40.00 12.00
351 Pablo Ozuna .50 .15
352 Corey Patterson RC 15.00 4.50
353 Braden Looper .50 .15
354 Robbie Bell .50 .15
355 Mark Mulder RC 15.00 4.50
356 Angel Pena .50 .15
357 Kevin McGlinchy .50 .15
358 M.Restovich RC 5.00 1.50
359 Eric DuBose .50 .15
360 Geoff Jenkins .50 .15
361 Mark Harriger RC 1.00 .30
362 Junior Herndon RC 1.50 .45
363 Tim Raines Jr. RC 1.50 .45
364 Rafael Furcal RC 8.00 2.40
365 Marcus Giles RC 8.00 2.40
366 Ted Lilly .50 .15
367 Jorge Toca RC 1.50 .45
368 David Kelton RC 2.50 .75
369 Adam Dunn RC 25.00 7.50
370 Guillermo Mota RC 1.00 .30
371 Brett Laxton RC 1.00 .30
372 Travis Harper RC 1.00 .30
373 Tom Davey RC 1.00 .30
374 Darren Blakely RC 1.00 .30
375 Tim Hudson RC 15.00 4.50
376 Jason Romano .50 .15
377 Dan Reichert .50 .15
378 Julio Lugo RC 1.50 .45
379 Jose Garcia RC 1.00 .30
380 Erubiel Durazo RC 5.00 1.50
381 Jose Jimenez .50 .15
382 Chris Fussell .50 .15
383 Steve Lomasney .50 .15
384 Juan Pena RC 1.00 .30
385 Allen Levrault RC 1.50 .45
386 Juan Rivera RC 2.50 .75
387 Steve Colyer RC 1.50 .45
388 Joe Nathan RC 1.00 .30
389 Ron Walker RC 1.00 .30
390 Nick Bierbrodt .50 .15
391 Luke Prokopec RC 1.50 .45
392 Dave Roberts RC 2.50 .75
393 Mike Darr .50 .15
394 Abraham Nunez RC 4.00 1.20
395 G.Chiaramonte RC 1.00 .30
396 J.Van Buren RC 1.50 .45
397 Mike Kusiewicz .50 .15
398 Matt Wise RC 1.00 .30
399 Joe McEwing RC 1.50 .45
400 Matt Holliday RC 1.50 .45
401 Willi Mo Pena RC 5.00 1.50
402 Ruben Quevedo RC 1.50 .45
403 Rob Ryan RC 1.00 .30
404 Freddy Garcia RC 4.00 1.20
405 Kevin Eberwein RC 1.50 .45
406 Jesus Colome RC 1.00 .30
407 Chris Singleton .50 .15
408 Bubba Crosby RC 4.00 1.20
409 Jesus Cordero RC 1.50 .45
410 Donny Leon .50 .15
411 G.Tomlinson RC 1.00 .30
412 Jeff Winchester RC 1.50 .45
413 Adam Piatt RC 1.50 .45
414 Robert Stratton .50 .15
415 T.J. Tucker .50 .15
416 Ryan Langerhans RC 1.50 .45
417 A.Shumaker RC 1.00 .30
418 Matt Miller RC 1.00 .30
419 Doug Clark RC 1.00 .30
420 Kory DeHaan RC 1.00 .30
421 David Eckstein RC 4.00 1.20
422 Brian Cooper RC 1.00 .30
423 Brady Clark RC 1.00 .30
424 Chris Magruder RC 1.00 .30
425 Bobby Seay RC 1.50 .45
426 Aubrey Huff RC 10.00 3.00
427 Mike Jerzembeck .50 .15
428 Matt Blank RC 1.00 .30
429 Benny Agbayani RC 1.50 .45
430 Kevin Beirne RC 1.50 .45
431 Josh Hamilton RC 4.00 1.20
432 Josh Girdley RC 1.50 .45
433 Kyle Snyder RC 1.50 .45
434 Mike Paradis RC 1.50 .45
435 Jason Jennings RC 2.50 .75
436 David Walling RC 1.50 .45
437 Omar Ortiz RC 1.00 .30
438 Jay Gehrke RC 1.50 .45
439 Casey Burns RC 1.00 .30
440 Carl Crawford RC 8.00 2.40

1999 Bowman Chrome Gold

Randomly inserted in first series packs a rate of one in twelve , and second series packs at one in 24, this 440-card set is highlighted by gold facsimile signatures and borders and is a parallel to the 1999 Bowman Chrome base set.

Nm-Mt Ex-Mt
*SER.1 STARS: 2.5X TO 6X BASIC CARDS
*SER.1 ROOKIES: .75X TO 2X BASIC .
*SER.2 STARS: 3X TO 8X BASIC CARDS
*SER.2 ROOKIES: 1X TO 2.5X BASIC .

1999 Bowman Chrome Gold Refractors

Randomly inserted in first series packs at a rate of one in 305 and second series packs at a rate of one in 200, this 440-card set is a parallel insert to the Bowman Chrome base set. Gold foil fascimile signatures and refractive chrome fronts highlight the design. In addition, only 25 serial numbered sets were printed.

Nm-Mt Ex-Mt
*STARS: 20X TO 50X BASIC CARDS ..

1999 Bowman Chrome International

Randomly inserted in first series packs at a rate of one in four, and second series packs at a rate of one in 12, this 440-card set is a parallel insert to the Bowman Chrome Base set. Metallic foil fronts and backgrounds taken from notable scenes of the featured players hometown highlight the design.

Nm-Mt Ex-Mt
COMPLETE SET (440) 900.00 275.00
COMP. SERIES 1 (220) 300.00 90.00
COMP. SERIES 2 (220) 600.00 180.00
*SER.1 STARS: 1.25X TO 3X BASIC CARDS
*SER.1 ROOKIES: .4X TO 1X BASIC ...
*SER.2 STARS: 2X TO 5X BASIC CARDS
*SER.2 ROOKIES: .5X TO 1.2X BASIC

1999 Bowman Chrome International Refractors

Randomly inserted in first series packs at a rate of one in 76 and second series packs at a rate of one in 50, this 440-card set is a refractive parallel insert to the Bowman Chrome International set. Only 100 serial numbered sets were printed.

Nm-Mt Ex-Mt
*STARS: 8X TO 20X BASIC CARDS ....
*ROOKIES: 2.5X TO 5X BASIC ....

1999 Bowman Chrome Refractors

Randomly inserted at a rate of one in twelve, this 440-card set is a refractive parallel insert to the Bowman Chrome base set. The refractive sheen of each card highlights the design.

Nm-Mt Ex-Mt
*STARS: 4X TO 10X BASIC CARDS ....
*ROOKIES: 1.25X TO 3X BASIC ....

1999 Bowman Chrome 2000 ROY Favorites

Randomly inserted in second series packs at a rate of one in 20, this 10-card insert set features borderless, double-etched foil cards and feature players that had potential to win Rookie of the Year honors for the 2000 seasons.

Nm-Mt Ex-Mt
COMPLETE SET (10) 20.00 6.00
*REF: .75X TO 2X BASIC CHR.2000 ROY
REFRACTOR SER.2 STATED ODDS 1:100
ROY1 Ryan Anderson 1.00 .30
ROY2 Pat Burrell 4.00 1.20
ROY3 A.J. Burnett 1.50 .45
ROY4 Ruben Mateo 1.00 .30
ROY5 Alex Escobar 1.00 .30
ROY6 Pablo Ozuna 1.00 .30
ROY7 Mark Mulder 4.00 1.20
ROY8 Corey Patterson 4.00 1.20
ROY9 George Lombard 1.00 .30
ROY10 Nick Johnson 2.00 .60

1999 Bowman Chrome Diamond Aces

Randomly inserted in first series packs at the rate of one in 21, this 18-card set features nine emerging stars such as Pat Burrell and Troy Glaus as well as nine proven veterans including Derek Jeter and Ken Griffey Jr.

Nm-Mt Ex-Mt
COMPLETE SET (18) 80.00 24.00
*REF: .75X TO 2X BASIC CHR.ACES ...
REFRACTOR SER.1 ODDS 1:84.........
DA1 Troy Glaus 2.50 .75
DA2 Eric Chavez 1.50 .45
DA3 Fernando Seguignol 1.50 .45
DA4 Ryan Anderson 1.50 .45
DA5 Ruben Mateo 1.50 .45
DA6 Carlos Beltran 1.50 .45
DA7 Adrian Beltre 1.50 .45
DA8 Bruce Chen 1.50 .45
DA9 Pat Burrell 8.00 2.40
DA10 Mike Piazza 6.00 1.80
DA11 Ken Griffey Jr. 6.00 1.80
DA12 Chipper Jones 4.00 1.20
DA13 Derek Jeter 10.00 3.00
DA14 Mark McGwire 10.00 3.00
DA15 Nomar Garciaparra 6.00 1.80
DA16 Sammy Sosa 6.00 1.80
DA17 Juan Gonzalez 4.00 1.20
DA18 Alex Rodriguez 6.00 1.80

1999 Bowman Chrome Impact

Randomly inserted in second series packs at the rate of one in 15, this 15-card insert set features 20 players separated into three distinct categories; Early Impact, Initial Impact and Lasting Impact.

Nm-Mt Ex-Mt
COMPLETE SET (20) 80.00 24.00
*REF 1-10: .75X TO 2X BASIC IMPACT
*REF 11-20: .75X TO 2X BASIC IMPACT
REFRACTOR SER.2 STATED ODDS 1:75
I1 Alfonso Soriano 10.00 3.00
I2 Pat Burrell 5.00 1.50
I3 Ruben Mateo 1.25 .35
I4 A.J. Burnett 1.25 .35
I5 Corey Patterson 5.00 1.50
I6 Daryle Ward 1.25 .35
I7 Eric Chavez 1.25 .35
I8 Troy Glaus 2.00 .60
I9 Sean Casey 1.25 .35
I10 Joe McEwing .50 .15
I11 Gabe Kapler 1.25 .35
I12 Michael Barrett 1.25 .35
I13 Sammy Sosa 5.00 1.50
I14 Alex Rodriguez 5.00 1.50
I15 Mark McGwire 8.00 2.40
I16 Derek Jeter 8.00 2.40
I17 Nomar Garciaparra 5.00 1.50
I18 Mike Piazza 5.00 1.50
I19 Chipper Jones 3.00 .90
I20 Ken Griffey Jr. 5.00 1.50

1999 Bowman Chrome Scout's Choice

Randomly inserted in first series packs at the rate of one in twelve, this 21-card insert set features borderless, double-etched foil cards showcase a selection of the game's top young prospects.

Nm-Mt Ex-Mt
COMPLETE SET (21) 25.00 7.50
*REFRACTORS: .75X TO 2X BASIC SCOUT'S
REFRACTOR SER.1 ODDS 1:48..........
SC1 Ruben Mateo 1.50 .45
SC2 Ryan Anderson 1.50 .45
SC3 Pat Burrell 5.00 1.50
SC4 Troy Glaus 2.50 .75
SC5 Eric Chavez 1.50 .45
SC6 Adrian Beltre 1.50 .45
SC7 Bruce Chen 1.50 .45
SC8 Carlos Beltran 1.50 .45
SC9 Alex Gonzalez 1.50 .45
SC10 Carlos Lee 1.50 .45
SC11 George Lombard 1.50 .45
SC12 Matt Clement 1.50 .45
SC13 Calvin Pickering 1.50 .45
SC14 Marlon Anderson 1.50 .45
SC15 Chad Hermansen 1.50 .45
SC16 Russell Branyan 1.50 .45
SC17 Jeremy Giambi 1.50 .45
SC18 Ricky Ledee 1.50 .45
SC19 John Patterson 1.50 .45
SC20 Roy Halladay 1.50 .45
SC21 Michael Barrett 1.50 .45

2000 Bowman Chrome

The 2000 Bowman Chrome product was released in late July, 2000 as a 440-card set that featured 140 veteran players (1-140), and 300 rookies and prospects (141-440). Each pack contained four cards, and carried a suggested retail price of $3.00. Rookie Cards include Rick Asadoorian, Bobby Bradley, Kevin Mench, Ben Sheets and Barry Zito. In addition, Topps designated five prospects as Bowman Chrome "exclusives" whereby their only appearance in a Topps brand for the year 2000 would be in this set. Jason Hart and Chin-Hui Tsao highlight this selection of Bowman Chrome exclusive Rookie Cards.

Nm-Mt Ex-Mt
COMPLETE SET (440) 120.00 36.00
1 Vladimir Guerrero 1.25 .35
2 Chipper Jones 1.25 .35
3 Todd Walker .50 .15
4 Barry Larkin 1.25 .35
5 Bernie Williams .75 .23
6 Todd Helton .75 .23
7 Jermaine Dye .50 .15
8 Brian Giles .50 .15
9 Freddy Garcia .50 .15
10 Greg Vaughn .50 .15
11 Alex Gonzalez .50 .15
12 Luis Gonzalez .50 .15
13 Ron Belliard .50 .15
14 Ben Grieve .50 .15
15 Carlos Delgado .50 .15
16 Brian Jordan .50 .15
17 Fernando Tatis .50 .15
18 Ryan Rupe .50 .15
19 Miguel Tejada .50 .15
20 Mark Grace .75 .23
21 Kenny Lofton .50 .15
22 Eric Karros .50 .15
23 Cliff Floyd .50 .15
24 John Halama .50 .15
25 Cristian Guzman .50 .15
26 Scott Williamson .50 .15
27 Mike Lieberthal .50 .15
28 Tim Hudson .75 .23
29 Warren Morris .50 .15
30 Pedro Martinez 1.25 .35
31 John Smoltz .75 .23
32 Ray Durham .50 .15
33 Chad Allen .50 .15
34 Tony Clark .50 .15
35 Tino Martinez .75 .23
36 J.T. Snow .50 .15
37 Kevin Brown .75 .23
38 Bartolo Colon .50 .15
39 Rey Ordonez .50 .15
40 Jeff Bagwell .75 .23
41 Ivan Rodriguez 1.25 .35
42 Eric Chavez .50 .15
43 Eric Milton .50 .15
44 Jose Canseco 1.25 .35
45 Shawn Green .50 .15
46 Rich Aurilia .50 .15
47 Roberto Alomar 1.25 .35
48 Brian Daubach .50 .15
49 Magglio Ordonez .50 .15
50 Derek Jeter 3.00 .90
51 Kris Benson .50 .15
52 Albert Belle .50 .15
53 Rondell White .50 .15
54 Justin Thompson .50 .15
55 Nomar Garciaparra 2.00 .60
56 Chuck Finley .50 .15
57 Omar Vizquel .50 .15
58 Luis Castillo .50 .15
59 Richard Hidalgo .50 .15
60 Barry Bonds 3.00 .90
61 Craig Biggio .75 .23
62 Doug Glanville .50 .15
63 Gabe Kapler .50 .15
64 Johnny Damon .50 .15
65 Pokey Reese .50 .15
66 Andy Pettitte .75 .23
67 B.J. Surhoff .50 .15
68 Richie Sexson .50 .15
69 Javy Lopez .50 .15
70 Raul Mondesi .50 .15
71 Darin Erstad .50 .15
72 Kevin Millwood .50 .15
73 Ricky Ledee .50 .15
74 John Olerud .50 .15
75 Sean Casey .50 .15
76 Carlos Febles .50 .15
77 Paul O'Neill .75 .23
78 Bob Abreu .50 .15
79 Neifi Perez .50 .15
80 Tony Gwynn 1.50 .45
81 Russ Ortiz .50 .15
82 Matt Williams .50 .15
83 Chris Carpenter .50 .15
84 Roger Cedeno .50 .15
85 Tim Salmon .75 .23
86 Billy Koch .50 .15
87 Jeromy Burnitz .50 .15
88 Edgardo Alfonzo .50 .15
89 Jay Bell .50 .15
90 Manny Ramirez .50 .15
91 Frank Thomas 1.25 .35
92 Mike Mussina 1.25 .35
93 J.D. Drew .50 .15
94 Adrian Beltre .50 .15
95 Alex Rodriguez 2.00 .60
96 Larry Walker .75 .23
97 Juan Encarnacion .50 .15
98 Mike Sweeney .50 .15
99 Rusty Greer .50 .15
100 Randy Johnson 1.25 .35
101 Jose Vidro .50 .15
102 Preston Wilson .50 .15
103 Greg Maddux 2.00 .60
104 Jason Giambi 1.25 .35
105 Cal Ripken 4.00 1.20
106 Carlos Beltran .50 .15
107 Vinny Castilla .50 .15
108 Mariano Rivera .75 .23
109 Mo Vaughn .50 .15
110 Rafael Palmeiro .75 .23
111 Shannon Stewart .50 .15
112 Mike Hampton .50 .15
113 Joe Nathan .50 .15

114 Ben Davis .50 .15
115 Andruw Jones .50 .15
116 Robin Ventura .50 .15
117 Damion Easley .50 .15
118 Jeff Cirillo .50 .15
119 Kerry Wood 1.25 .35
120 Scott Rolen .75 .23
121 Sammy Sosa 2.00 .60
122 Ken Griffey Jr. 2.00 .60
123 Shane Reynolds .50 .15
124 Troy Glaus .75 .23
125 Tom Glavine .75 .23
126 Michael Barrett .50 .15
127 Al Leiter .50 .15
128 Jason Kendall .50 .15
129 Roger Clemens 2.50 .75
130 Juan Gonzalez 1.25 .35
131 Corey Koskie .50 .15
132 Curt Schilling .75 .23
133 Mike Piazza 2.00 .60
134 Gary Sheffield .50 .15
135 Jim Thome 1.25 .35
136 Orlando Hernandez .50 .15
137 Ray Lankford .50 .15
138 Geoff Jenkins .50 .15
139 Jose Lima .50 .15
140 Mark McGwire 3.00 .90
141 Adam Piatt .50 .15
142 Pat Manning RC 1.50 .45
143 Marcos Castillo RC 1.50 .45
144 Lesli Brea RC 1.50 .45
145 Humberto Cota RC 1.50 .45
146 Ben Petrick .50 .15
147 Kip Wells .50 .15
148 Wily Pena .50 .15
149 Chris Wakeland RC 1.00 .30
150 Brad Baker RC 1.50 .45
151 Robbie Morrison RC 1.00 .30
152 Reggie Taylor .50 .15
153 Matt Ginter RC 1.50 .45
154 Peter Bergeron .50 .15
155 Roosevelt Brown .50 .15
156 Matt Cepicky RC 1.50 .45
157 Ramon Castro .50 .15
158 Brad Baisley RC 1.50 .45
159 Jason Hart RC 1.50 .45
160 Mitch Meluskey .50 .15
161 Chad Harville .50 .15
162 Brian Cooper .50 .15
163 Marcus Giles .50 .15
164 Jim Morris 6.00 1.80
165 Geoff Goetz .50 .15
166 Bobby Bradley RC 1.50 .45
167 Rob Bell .50 .15
168 Joe Crede .50 .15
169 Michael Restovich .50 .15
170 Quincy Foster RC 1.00 .30
171 Enrique Cruz RC 1.50 .45
172 Mark Quinn .50 .15
173 Nick Johnson .50 .15
174 Jeff Liefer .50 .15
175 Kevin Mench RC 2.50 .75
176 Steve Lomasney .50 .15
177 Jayson Werth .50 .15
178 Tim Drew .50 .15
179 Chip Ambres .50 .15
180 Ryan Anderson .50 .15
181 Matt Blank .50 .15
182 G. Chiaramonte .50 .15
183 Corey Myers RC 1.50 .45
184 Jeff Yoder .50 .15
185 Craig Dingman RC 1.00 .30
186 Jon Hamilton RC 1.00 .30
187 Toby Hall .50 .15
188 Russell Branyan .50 .15
189 Brian Falkenborg RC 1.50 .45
190 Aaron Harang RC 1.50 .45
191 Juan Pena .50 .15
192 Chin-Hui Tsao RC 8.00 2.40
193 Alfonso Soriano 1.25 .35
194 Alejandro Diaz RC 1.50 .45
195 Carlos Pena .50 .15
196 Kevin Nicholson .50 .15
197 Mo Bruce .50 .15
198 C.C. Sabathia .50 .15
199 Carl Crawford .50 .15
200 Rafael Furcal .50 .15
201 Andrew Beinbrink RC 1.00 .30
202 Jimmy Osting .50 .15
203 Aaron McNeal RC 1.50 .45
204 Brett Laxton .50 .15
205 Chris George .50 .15
206 Felipe Lopez .50 .15
207 Ben Sheets RC 5.00 1.50
208 Mike Meyers RC 1.50 .45
209 Jason Conti .50 .15
210 Milton Bradley .50 .15
211 Chris Mears RC 1.50 .45
212 Carlos Hernandez RC 1.50 .45
213 Jason Romano .50 .15
214 Geofrey Tomlinson .50 .15
215 Jimmy Rollins .50 .15
216 Pablo Ozuna .50 .15
217 Steve Cox .50 .15
218 Terrence Long .50 .15
219 Jeff DaVanon RC 1.50 .45
220 Rick Ankiel .50 .15
221 Jason Standridge .50 .15
222 Tony Armas Jr. .50 .15
223 Jason Tyner .50 .15
224 Ramon Ortiz .50 .15
225 Daryle Ward .50 .15
226 Enger Veras RC 1.50 .45
227 Chris Jones .50 .15
228 Eric Cammack RC 1.00 .30
229 Ruben Mateo .50 .15
230 Ken Harvey RC 5.00 1.50
231 Jake Westbrook .50 .15
232 Rob Purvis RC 1.00 .30
233 Choo Freeman .50 .15
234 Aramis Ramirez .50 .15
235 A.J. Burnett .50 .15
236 Kevin Barker .50 .15
237 Chance Caple RC 1.50 .45
238 Jarrod Washburn .50 .15
239 Lance Berkman .50 .15
240 Michael Wenner RC 1.00 .30
241 Alex Sanchez .50 .15
242 Pat Daneker .50 .15
243 Grant Roberts .50 .15
244 Mark Ellis RC 2.50 .75
245 Donny Leon .50 .15
246 David Eckstein .50 .15
247 Dicky Gonzalez RC 1.50 .45
248 John Patterson .50 .15
249 Chad Green .50 .15
250 Scot Shields RC 1.00 .30
251 Troy Cameron .50 .15
252 Jose Molina .50 .15
253 Rob Pugmire RC 1.50 .45
254 Rick Elder .50 .15
255 Sean Burroughs .75 .23
256 Josh Kalinowski RC 1.00 .30
257 Matt LeCroy .50 .15
258 Alex Graman RC 1.00 .30
259 Juan Silvestre RC 1.50 .45
260 Brady Clark .50 .15
261 Rico Washington RC 1.50 .45
262 Gary Matthews Jr. .50 .15
263 Matt Wise .50 .15
264 Keith Reed RC 1.50 .45
265 Santiago Ramirez RC 1.00 .30
266 Ben Broussard RC 1.50 .45
267 Ryan Langerhans .50 .15
268 Juan Rivera .50 .15
269 Shawn Gallagher .50 .15
270 Jorge Toca .50 .15
271 Brad Lidge .50 .15
272 Leoncio Estrella RC 1.00 .30
273 Ruben Quevedo .50 .15
274 Jack Cust .50 .15
275 T.J. Tucker .50 .15
276 Mike Colangelo .50 .15
277 Brian Schneider .50 .15
278 Calvin Murray .50 .15
279 Josh Girdley .50 .15
280 Mike Paradis .50 .15
281 Chad Hermansen .50 .15
282 Ty Howington RC 1.50 .45
283 Aaron Myette .50 .15
284 D'Angelo Jimenez .50 .15
285 Dernell Stenson .50 .15
286 Jerry Hairston Jr. .50 .15
287 Gary Majewski RC 1.50 .45
288 Derrin Ebert .50 .15
289 Steve Fish RC 1.00 .30
290 Carlos E. Hernandez .50 .15
291 Allen Levrault .50 .15
292 Sean McNally RC 1.00 .30
293 Randey Dorame RC 1.50 .45
294 Wes Anderson RC 1.50 .45
295 B.J. Ryan .50 .15
296 Alan Webb RC 1.50 .45
297 Brandon Inge RC 1.50 .45
298 David Walling .50 .15
299 Sun Woo Kim RC 1.50 .45
300 Pat Burrell .75 .23
301 Rick Guttormson RC 1.00 .30
302 Gil Meche .50 .15
303 Carlos Zambrano RC 10.00 3.00
304 Eric Byrnes UER RC 5.00 1.50
Bo Porter pictured
305 Robb Quinlan RC 1.50 .45
306 Jackie Rexrode .50 .15
307 Nate Bump .50 .15
308 Sean DePaula RC 1.00 .30
309 Matt Riley .50 .15
310 Ryan Minor .50 .15
311 J.J. Davis .50 .15
312 Randy Wolf .50 .15
313 Jason Jennings .50 .15
314 Scott Seabol RC 1.00 .30
315 Doug Davis .50 .15
316 Todd Moser RC 1.00 .30
317 Rob Ryan .50 .15
318 Bubba Crosby .50 .15
319 Lyle Overbay RC 2.50 .75
320 Mario Encarnacion .50 .15
321 F.Rodriguez RC 8.00 2.40
322 Michael Cuddyer .50 .15
323 Ed Yarnall .50 .15
324 Cesar Saba RC 1.50 .45
325 Gookie Dawkins .50 .15
326 Alex Escobar .50 .15
327 Julio Zuleta RC 1.50 .45
328 Josh Hamilton .50 .15
329 Carlos Urquiola RC 1.50 .45
330 Matt Belisle .50 .15
331 Kurt Ainsworth RC 4.00 1.20
332 Tim Raines Jr. .50 .15
333 Eric Munson .50 .15
334 Donzell McDonald .50 .15
335 Larry Bigbie RC 2.50 .75
336 Matt Watson RC 1.50 .45
337 Aubrey Huff .50 .15
338 Julio Ramirez .50 .15
339 Jason Grabowski RC 1.50 .45
340 Jon Garland .50 .15
341 Austin Kearns .75 .23
342 Josh Pressley RC 1.50 .45
343 Miguel Olivo RC 1.50 .45
344 Julio Lugo .50 .15
345 Roberto Vaz .50 .15
346 Ramon Soler .50 .15
347 Brandon Phillips RC 5.00 1.50
348 Vince Faison RC 1.50 .45
349 Mike Venafro .50 .15
350 Rick Asadoorian RC 1.50 .45
351 B.J. Garbe RC 1.50 .45
352 Dan Reichert .50 .15
353 Jason Stumm RC 1.50 .45
354 Ruben Salazar RC 1.50 .45
355 Francisco Cordero .50 .15
356 Juan Guzman RC 1.50 .45
357 Mike Bacsik RC 1.00 .30
358 Jared Sandberg .50 .15
359 Rod Barajas .50 .15
360 Junior Brignac RC 1.50 .45
361 J.M. Gold .50 .15
362 Octavio Dotel .50 .15
363 David Kelton .50 .15
364 Scott Morgan .50 .15
365 Wascar Serrano RC 1.50 .45
366 Wilton Veras .50 .15
367 Eugene Kingsale .50 .15
368 Ted Lilly .50 .15
369 George Lombard .50 .15
370 Chris Haas .50 .15
371 Wilton Pena RC 1.00 .30
372 Vernon Wells .50 .15
373 Keith Ginter RC 1.00 .30
374 Jeff Heaverlo RC 1.50 .45
375 Calvin Pickering .50 .15
376 Mike Lamb RC 1.50 .45
377 Kyle Snyder .50 .15
378 Javier Cardona RC 1.00 .30
379 Aaron Rowand RC 1.50 .45
380 Dee Brown .50 .15
381 Brett Myers RC 10.00 3.00
382 Abraham Nunez .50 .15
383 Eric Valent .50 .15
384 Jody Gerut RC 10.00 3.00
385 Adam Dunn 1.25 .35
386 Jay Gehrke .50 .15
387 Omar Ortiz .50 .15
388 Darnell McDonald .50 .15
389 Tony Schrager RC 1.00 .30
390 J.D. Closser .50 .15
391 Ben Christensen RC 1.50 .45
392 Adam Kennedy .50 .15
393 Nick Green RC 1.00 .30
394 Ramon Hernandez .50 .15
395 Roy Oswalt RC 15.00 4.50
396 Andy Tracy RC 1.00 .30
397 Eric Gagne 1.25 .35
398 Michael Tejera RC 1.00 .30
399 Adam Everett .50 .15
400 Corey Patterson .75 .23
401 Gary Knotts RC 1.00 .30
402 Ryan Christianson RC 1.50 .45
403 Eric Ireland RC 1.00 .30
404 Andrew Good RC 1.50 .45
405 Brad Penny .50 .15
406 Jason LaRue .50 .15
407 Kit Pellow .50 .15
408 Kevin Beirne .50 .15
409 Kelly Dransfeldt .50 .15
410 Jason Grilli .50 .15
411 Scott Downs RC 1.00 .30
412 Jesus Colome .50 .15
413 John Sneed RC 1.00 .30
414 Tony McKnight .50 .15
415 Luis Rivera .50 .15
416 Adam Eaton .50 .15
417 Mike MacDougal RC 2.50 .75
418 Mike Nannini .50 .15
419 Barry Zito RC 20.00 6.00
420 DeWayne Wise .50 .15
421 Jason Dellaero .50 .15
422 Chad Moeller .50 .15
423 Jason Marquis .50 .15
424 Tim Redding RC 4.00 1.20
425 Mark Mulder .75 .23
426 Josh Paul .50 .15
427 Chris Enochs .50 .15
428 W.Rodriguez RC 1.50 .45
429 Kevin Witt .50 .15
430 Scott Sobkowiak RC 1.00 .30
431 McKay Christensen .50 .15
432 Jung Bong .50 .15
433 Keith Evans RC 1.00 .30
434 Garry Maddox Jr. RC 1.00 .30
435 Ramon Santiago RC 1.50 .45
436 Alex Cora .50 .15
437 Carlos Lee .50 .15
438 Jason Repko RC 1.50 .45
439 Matt Burch .50 .15
440 Shawn Sonnier RC 1.00 .30

2000 Bowman Chrome Oversize

Inserted into hobby boxes as a chip-topper at one per box, this eight-card oversized set features some of the Major Leagues most promising young players.

Nm-Mt Ex-Mt
COMPLETE SET (8) 15.00 4.50
1 Pat Burrell 1.25 .35
2 Josh Hamilton 1.25 .35
3 Rafael Furcal .50 .15
4 Corey Patterson 1.25 .35
5 A.J. Burnett .75 .23
6 Eric Munson .75 .23
7 Nick Johnson .50 .15
8 Alfonso Soriano .50 .15

2000 Bowman Chrome Refractors

Randomly inserted into packs at one in 12, this 440-card insert is a complete parallel of the Bowman Chrome base set. This parallel was produced using Topps' refractor technology.

Nm-Mt Ex-Mt
*STARS: 4X TO 10X BASIC CARDS
*ROOKIES: 2X TO 5X BASIC CARDS

2000 Bowman Chrome Retro/Future

Randomly inserted into hobby/retail packs at one in six, this 440-card insert is a complete parallel of the Bowman Chrome base set. Each card features a television border similar to that of the 1955 Bowman set.

Nm-Mt Ex-Mt
*STARS: 1.5X TO 4X BASIC CARDS
*ROOKIES: .5X TO 1.2X BASIC CARDS

2000 Bowman Chrome Retro/Future Refractors

Randomly inserted into hobby/retail packs at one in 60, this 440-card insert is a complete parallel of the Bowman Chrome base set. Each card features a television border similar to that of the 1955 Bowman set. These cards were produced using Topps' refractor technology.

Nm-Mt Ex-Mt
*STARS: 8X TO 20X BASIC CARDS
*ROOKIES: 2.5X TO 6X BASIC CARDS

2000 Bowman Chrome Bidding for the Call

Randomly inserted into packs at one in 16, this 15-card insert features players that are looking to break into the Major Leagues during the 2000 season. Card backs carry a "BC" prefix. It's worth noting that top prospect Chin-Feng

Chen's very first MLB-licensed card was included in this set.

Nm-Mt Ex-Mt
COMPLETE SET (15) 30.00 9.00
*REFFRACTORS: 1.25X TO 3X BASIC BID
REFRACTOR STATED ODDS 1:160
BC1 Adam Piatt 1.00 .30
BC2 Pat Burrell 1.25 .35
BC3 Mark Mulder 1.25 .35
BC4 Nick Johnson 1.00 .30
BC5 Alfonso Soriano 2.00 .60
BC6 Chin-Feng Chen 2.50 .75
BC7 Scott Sobkowiak 1.00 .30
BC8 Corey Patterson 1.25 .35
BC9 Jack Cust 1.00 .30
BC10 Sean Burroughs 1.25 .35
BC11 Josh Hamilton 1.00 .30
BC12 Corey Myers 1.00 .30
BC13 Eric Munson 1.00 .30
BC14 Wes Anderson 1.50 .45
BC15 Lyle Overbay 1.25 .35

2000 Bowman Chrome Meteoric Rise

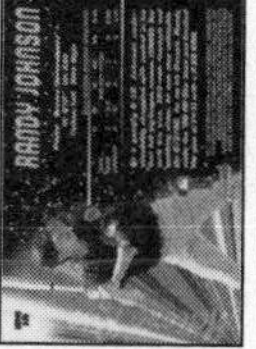

Randomly inserted into packs at one in 24, this 10-card insert features players that have risen to the occasion during their careers. Card backs carry a "MR" prefix.

Nm-Mt Ex-Mt
COMPLETE SET (10) 50.00 15.00
*REF: 1.25X TO 3X BASIC METEORIC
REFRACTOR STATED ODDS 1:240
MR1 Nomar Garciaparra 5.00 1.50
MR2 Mark McGwire 8.00 2.40
MR3 Ken Griffey Jr. 5.00 1.50
MR4 Chipper Jones 3.00 .90
MR5 Manny Ramirez 1.25 .35
MR6 Mike Piazza 5.00 1.50
MR7 Cal Ripken 10.00 3.00
MR8 Ivan Rodriguez 3.00 .90
MR9 Greg Maddux 5.00 1.50
MR10 Randy Johnson 3.00 .90

2000 Bowman Chrome Rookie Class 2000

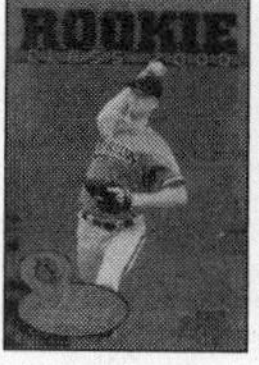

Randomly inserted into packs at one in 24, this 10-card insert features players that made their Major League debuts in 2000. Card backs carry a "RC" prefix.

Nm-Mt Ex-Mt
COMPLETE SET (10) 20.00 6.00
*REF: 1.25X TO 3X BASIC ROOKIE CLASS
REFRACTOR STATED ODDS 1:240
RC1 Pat Burrell 2.50 .75
RC2 Rick Ankiel 1.50 .45
RC3 Ruben Mateo 1.50 .45
RC4 Vernon Wells 1.50 .45
RC5 Mark Mulder 2.50 .75
RC6 A.J. Burnett 1.50 .45
RC7 Chad Hermansen 1.50 .45
RC8 Corey Patterson 2.50 .75
RC9 Rafael Furcal 1.50 .45
RC10 Mike Lamb 1.00 .30

2000 Bowman Chrome Teen Idols

Randomly inserted into packs at one in 16, this 15-card insert set features Major League players that either made it to the majors as teenagers or are top current prospects who are still in their teens in 2000. Card backs carry a "TI" prefix.

Nm-Mt Ex-Mt
COMPLETE SET (15) 50.00 15.00
*SINGLES: 1X TO 2.5X BASIC CARDS
*REFRACTORS: 1.25X TO 3X BASIC TEEN
REFRACTOR STATED ODDS 1:160
TI1 Alex Rodriguez 6.00 1.80
TI2 Andruw Jones 1.50 .45
TI3 Juan Gonzalez 4.00 1.20
TI4 Ivan Rodriguez 4.00 1.20
TI5 Ken Griffey Jr. 6.00 1.80
TI6 Bobby Bradley 1.50 .45
TI7 Brett Myers 4.00 1.20
TI8 C.C. Sabathia 1.50 .45
TI9 Ty Howington 1.50 .45
TI10 Brandon Phillips 2.00 .60
TI11 Rick Asadoorian 1.50 .45
TI12 Wily Mo Pena 1.50 .45
TI13 Sean Burroughs 2.50 .75
TI14 Josh Hamilton 1.50 .45
TI15 Rafael Furcal 1.50 .45

2000 Bowman Chrome Draft Picks

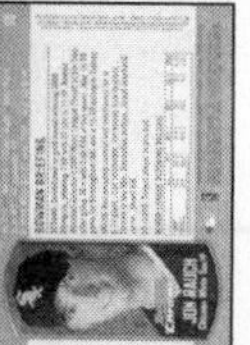

The 2000 Bowman Chrome Draft Picks and Prospects set was released in December, 2000 as a 110-card parallel of the 2000 Bowman Draft Picks set. This product was distributed only in factory set form. Each set features Topps' Chrome technology. A limited selection of prospects were switched out from the Bowman checklist and are featured exclusively in this Bowman Chrome set. The most notable of these players include Timo Perez and Jon Rauch. Other notable Rookie Cards include Chin-Feng Chen and Adrian Gonzalez.

Nm-Mt Ex-Mt
COMP.FACT.SET (110) 60.00 18.00
1 Pat Burrell .75 .23
2 Rafael Furcal .50 .15
3 Grant Roberts .50 .15
4 Barry Zito 8.00 2.40
5 Julio Zuleta 1.00 .30
6 Mark Mulder .75 .23
7 Rob Bell .50 .15
8 Adam Piatt .50 .15
9 Mike Lamb .50 .15
10 Pablo Ozuna .50 .15
11 Jason Tyner .50 .15
12 Jason Marquis .50 .15
13 Eric Munson .50 .15
14 Seth Etherton .50 .15
15 Milton Bradley .50 .15
16 Nick Green .50 .15
17 Chin-Feng Chen RC 3.00 .90
18 Matt Boone RC 1.00 .30
19 Kevin Gregg RC 1.00 .30
20 Eddy Garabito RC 1.00 .30
21 Aaron Capista RC 1.00 .30
22 Esteban German RC 1.00 .30
23 Derek Thompson RC 1.00 .30
24 Phil Merrell RC .50 .15
25 Brian O'Connor RC .50 .15
26 Yamid Haad .50 .15
27 Hector Mercado RC .50 .15
28 Jason Woolf RC .50 .15
29 Eddy Furniss RC .50 .15
30 Cha Sueng Baek RC 1.00 .30
31 Colby Lewis RC 1.50 .45
32 Pasqual Coco RC .50 .15
33 Jorge Cantu RC 1.00 .30
34 Erasmo Ramirez RC .50 .15
35 Bobby Kielty RC 1.50 .45
36 Joaquin Benoit RC 1.00 .30
37 Brian Esposito RC 1.00 .30
38 Michael Wenner .50 .15
39 Juan Rincon RC 1.00 .30
40 Yorvit Torrealba RC 1.00 .30
41 Chad Durham RC 1.00 .30
42 Jim Mann RC .50 .15
43 Shane Loux RC 1.00 .30
44 Luis Rivas .50 .15
45 Ken Chenard RC 1.00 .30
46 Mike Lockwood RC .50 .15
47 Yovanny Lara RC .50 .15
48 Bubba Carpenter RC .50 .15
49 Ryan Dittfurth RC 1.00 .30
50 John Stephens RC 1.00 .30
51 Pedro Feliz RC 1.00 .30
52 Kenny Kelly RC 1.00 .30
53 Neil Jenkins RC 1.00 .30
54 Mike Glendenning RC .50 .15
55 Bo Porter .50 .15
56 Eric Byrnes 2.00 .60
57 Tony Alvarez RC 1.00 .30
58 Kazuhiro Sasaki RC 3.00 .90
59 Chad Durbin RC .50 .15
60 Mike Bynum RC 1.00 .30
61 Travis Wilson RC .50 .15
62 Jose Leon RC .50 .15
63 Ryan Vogelsong RC 1.00 .30
64 Geraldo Guzman RC .50 .15
65 Craig Anderson RC 1.00 .30
66 Carlos Silva RC 1.00 .30
67 Brad Thomas RC .50 .15
68 Chin-Hui Tsao 3.00 .90
69 Mark Buehrle RC 4.00 1.20
70 Juan Salas RC 1.00 .30
71 Denny Abreu RC 1.00 .30
72 Keith McDonald RC .50 .15
73 Chris Richard RC 1.00 .30
74 Tomas De la Rosa RC .50 .15
75 Vicente Padilla RC 2.50 .75
76 Justin Brunette RC .50 .15
77 Scott Linebrink RC .50 .15
78 Jeff Sparks RC .50 .15
79 Tike Redman RC 1.00 .30
80 John Lackey RC 1.50 .45
81 Joe Strong RC .50 .15
82 Brian Tollberg RC .50 .15
83 Steve Sisco RC .50 .15
84 Chris Clapinski RC .50 .15
85 Augie Ojeda RC .50 .15

86 Adrian Gonzalez RC 5.00 1.50
87 Mike Stodolka RC 1.00 .30
88 Adam Johnson RC 1.00 .30
89 Matt Wheatland RC .50 .15
90 Corey Smith RC 1.50 .45
91 Rocco Baldelli RC 25.00 7.50
92 Keith Bucktrot RC 1.00 .30
93 Adam Wainwright RC 5.00 1.50
94 Blaine Boyer RC 1.00 .30
95 Aaron Herr RC 1.00 .30
96 Scott Thorman RC 1.50 .45
97 Bryan Digby RC 1.00 .30
98 Josh Shortslef RC 1.00 .30
99 Sean Smith RC 1.00 .30
100 Alex Cruz RC 1.00 .30
101 Marc Love RC 1.00 .30
102 Kevin Lee RC 1.00 .30
103 Timo Perez RC 1.00 .30
104 Alex Cabrera RC 1.00 .30
105 Shane Heams RC .50 .15
106 Tripper Johnson RC 1.50 .45
107 Brent Abernathy RC 1.00 .30
108 John Cotton RC .50 .15
109 Brad Wilkerson RC 1.50 .45
110 Jon Rauch RC 1.00 .30

2001 Bowman Chrome

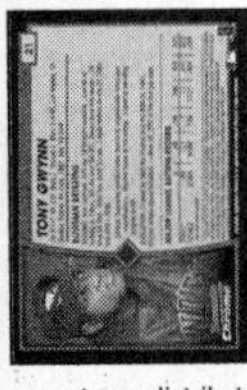

The 2001 Bowman Chrome set was distributed in four-card packs with a suggested retail price of $3.99. This 352-card set consists of 110 leading hitters and pitchers (1-110), 110 rising young stars (201-310), 110 top rookies including 20 not found in the regular Bowman set (111-200, 311-330), 20 autographed rookie refractor cards (331-350) each serial numbered to 500 copies and two Ichiro Suzuki Rookie Cards (351) in available in English and Japanese text variations. Both Ichiro cards were only available via mail redemption whereby exchange cards were seeded into packs. In addition, an exchange card was seeded into packs for the Albert Pujols signed Rookie Card. The deadline to send these cards in was June 30th, 2003.

Nm-Mt Ex-Mt
COMP.SET w/o SP's (220) 50.00 15.00
COMMON (1-110/201-310) .50 .15
COMMON (111-200/311-330) 5.00 1.50
COMMON (331-350) 25.00 7.50
1 Jason Giambi 1.25 .35
2 Rafael Furcal .50 .15
3 Bernie Williams .75 .23
4 Kenny Lofton .50 .15
5 Al Leiter .50 .15
6 Albert Belle .50 .15
7 Craig Biggio .75 .23
8 Mark Mulder .50 .15
9 Carlos Delgado .50 .15
10 Darin Erstad .50 .15
11 Richie Sexson .50 .15
12 Randy Johnson 1.25 .35
13 Greg Maddux 2.00 .60
14 Orlando Hernandez .50 .15
15 Javier Vazquez .50 .15
16 Jeff Kent .50 .15
17 Jim Thome 1.25 .35
18 John Olerud .50 .15
19 Jason Kendall .50 .15
20 Scott Rolen .75 .23
21 Tony Gwynn 1.50 .45
22 Edgardo Alfonzo .50 .15
23 Pokey Reese .50 .15
24 Todd Helton .75 .23
25 Mark Quinn .50 .15
26 Dean Palmer .50 .15
27 Ray Durham .50 .15
28 Rafael Palmeiro .75 .23
29 Carl Everett .50 .15
30 Vladimir Guerrero 1.25 .35
31 Livan Hernandez .50 .15
32 Preston Wilson .50 .15
33 Jose Vidro .50 .15
34 Fred McGriff .75 .23
35 Kevin Brown .50 .15
36 Miguel Tejada .50 .15
37 Chipper Jones 1.25 .35
38 Edgar Martinez .75 .23
39 Tony Batista .50 .15
40 Jorge Posada .75 .23
41 Sammy Sosa 2.00 .60
42 Gary Sheffield .50 .15
43 Bartolo Colon .50 .15
44 Pat Burrell .50 .15
45 Jay Payton .50 .15
46 Mike Mussina 1.25 .35
47 Nomar Garciaparra 2.00 .60
48 Darren Dreifort .50 .15
49 Richard Hidalgo .50 .15
50 Troy Glaus .75 .23
51 Ben Grieve .50 .15
52 Jim Edmonds .50 .15
53 Raul Mondesi .50 .15
54 Andruw Jones .50 .15
55 Mike Sweeney .50 .15
56 Derek Jeter 3.00 .90
57 Ruben Mateo .50 .15
58 Cristian Guzman .50 .15
59 Mike Hampton .50 .15
60 J.D. Drew .50 .15
61 Matt Lawton .50 .15
62 Moises Alou .50 .15
63 Terrence Long .50 .15
64 Geoff Jenkins .50 .15
65 Manny Ramirez .50 .15
66 Johnny Damon .50 .15
67 Pedro Martinez 1.25 .35
68 Juan Gonzalez 1.25 .35
69 Roger Clemens 2.50 .75
70 Carlos Beltran .50 .15
71 Roberto Alomar 1.25 .35
72 Barry Bonds 3.00 .90
73 Tim Hudson .50 .15
74 Tom Glavine .75 .23
75 Jeromy Burnitz .50 .15
76 Adrian Beltre .50 .15
77 Mike Piazza 2.00 .60
78 Kerry Wood 1.25 .35
79 Steve Finley .50 .15
80 Bob Abreu .50 .15
81 Neifi Perez .50 .15
82 Mark Redman .50 .15
83 Paul Konerko .50 .15
84 Jermaine Dye .50 .15
85 Brian Giles .50 .15
86 Ivan Rodriguez 1.25 .35
87 Adam Kennedy .50 .15
88 Eric Chavez .50 .15
89 Billy Koch .50 .15
90 Shawn Green .50 .15
91 Matt Williams .50 .15
92 Greg Vaughn .50 .15
93 Jeff Cirillo .50 .15
94 Frank Thomas 1.25 .35
95 David Justice .50 .15
96 Cal Ripken 4.00 1.20
97 Curt Schilling .75 .23
98 Barry Zito 1.25 .35
99 Brian Jordan .50 .15
100 Chan Ho Park .50 .15
101 J.T. Snow .50 .15
102 Kazuhiro Sasaki .50 .15
103 Alex Rodriguez 2.00 .60
104 Mariano Rivera .75 .23
105 Eric Milton .50 .15
106 Andy Pettitte .75 .23
107 Ken Griffey Jr. 2.00 .60
108 Bengie Molina .50 .15
109 Jeff Bagwell .75 .23
110 Mark McGwire 3.00 .90
111 Dan Tosca RC 8.00 2.40
112 Sergio Contreras RC 8.00 2.40
113 Mitch Jones RC 8.00 2.40
114 Ramon Carvajal RC 8.00 2.40
115 Ryan Madson RC 8.00 2.40
116 Hank Blalock RC 100.00 30.00
117 Ben Washburn RC 8.00 2.40
118 Erick Almonte RC 8.00 2.40
119 Shawn Fagan RC 8.00 2.40
120 Gary Johnson RC 8.00 2.40
121 Brett Evert RC 8.00 2.40
122 Joe Hamer RC 8.00 2.40
123 Yhency Brazoban RC 8.00 2.40
124 Domingo Guante RC 8.00 2.40
125 Deivi Mendez RC 8.00 2.40
126 Adrian Hernandez RC 8.00 2.40
127 R. Abercrombie RC 8.00 2.40
128 Steve Bennett RC 5.00 1.50
129 Matt White RC 8.00 2.40
130 Brian Hitchcox RC 5.00 1.50
131 Deivis Santos RC 8.00 2.40
132 Luis Montanez RC 8.00 2.40
133 Eric Reynolds RC 5.00 1.50
134 Denny Bautista RC 15.00 4.50
135 Hector Garcia RC 8.00 2.40
136 Joe Thurston RC 12.00 3.60
137 Tsuyoshi Shinjo RC 15.00 4.50
138 Elpidio Guzman RC 8.00 2.40
139 Brian Bass RC 8.00 2.40
140 Mark Burnett RC 8.00 2.40
141 Russ Jacobson UER 5.00 1.50
Last name misspelled Jacobsen on front
142 Travis Hafner RC 25.00 7.50
143 Wilson Betemit RC 8.00 2.40
144 Luke Lockwood RC 8.00 2.40
145 Noel Devarez RC 8.00 2.40
146 Doug Gredvig RC 8.00 2.40
147 Seung Song RC 12.00 3.60
148 Andy Van Hekken RC 8.00 2.40
149 Ryan Kohlmeier 5.00 1.50
150 Dee Haynes RC 8.00 2.40
151 Jim Journell RC 8.00 2.40
152 Chad Petty RC 8.00 2.40
153 Danny Borrell RC 8.00 2.40
154 Dave Krynzel 5.00 1.50
155 Octavio Martinez RC 8.00 2.40
156 David Parrish RC 8.00 2.40
157 Jason Miller RC 8.00 2.40
158 Corey Spencer RC 5.00 1.50
159 Maxim St. Pierre RC 8.00 2.40
160 Pat Magness RC 8.00 2.40
161 Ranier Olmedo RC 8.00 2.40
162 Brandon Mims RC 8.00 2.40
163 Phil Wilson RC 8.00 2.40
164 Jose Reyes RC 70.00 21.00
165 Matt Butler RC 8.00 2.40
166 Joel Pineiro 15.00 4.50
167 Ken Chenard 5.00 1.50
168 Alexis Gomez RC 8.00 2.40
169 Justin Morneau RC 40.00 12.00
170 Josh Fogg RC 8.00 2.40
171 Charles Frazier RC 8.00 2.40
172 Ryan Ludwick RC 8.00 2.40
173 Seth McClung RC 8.00 2.40
174 Justin Wayne RC 8.00 2.40
175 Rafael Soriano RC 20.00 6.00
176 Jared Abruzzo RC 8.00 2.40
177 Jason Richardson RC 8.00 2.40
178 Darwin Cubillan RC 5.00 1.50
179 Blake Williams RC 8.00 2.40
180 V. Pascucci RC 8.00 2.40
181 Ryan Hannaman RC 8.00 2.40
182 Steve Smyth RC 8.00 2.40
183 Jake Peavy RC 20.00 6.00
184 Onix Mercado RC 8.00 2.40
185 Luis Torres RC 8.00 2.40
186 Casey Fossum RC 8.00 2.40
187 Eduardo Figueroa RC 8.00 2.40
188 Bryan Barnowski RC 8.00 2.40
189 Jason Standridge 5.00 1.50
190 Marvin Seale RC 8.00 2.40
191 Steve Smitherman RC 20.00 6.00
192 Rafael Boitel RC 8.00 2.40
193 Dany Morban RC 8.00 2.40
194 Justin Woodrow RC 8.00 2.40
195 Ed Rogers RC 8.00 2.40
196 Ben Hendrickson RC 8.00 2.40
197 Thomas Mitchell 5.00 1.50
198 Adam Pettyjohn RC 8.00 2.40
199 Doug Nickle RC 5.00 1.50
200 Jason Jones RC 8.00 2.40
201 Larry Barnes .50 .15
202 Ben Diggins .50 .15
203 Dee Brown .50 .15
204 Rocco Baldelli 4.00 1.20
205 Luis Terrero .50 .15
206 Milton Bradley .50 .15
207 Kurt Ainsworth .50 .15
208 Sean Burroughs .50 .15
209 Rick Asadoorian .50 .15
210 Ramon Castro .50 .15
211 Nick Neugebauer .50 .15
212 Aaron Myette .50 .15
213 Luis Matos .50 .15
214 Donnie Bridges .50 .15
215 Alex Cintron .50 .15
216 Bobby Kielty .50 .15
217 Matt Belisle .50 .15
218 Adam Everett .50 .15
219 John Lackey .50 .15
220 Adam Wainwright .50 .15
221 Jerry Hairston Jr. .50 .15
222 Mike Bynum .50 .15
223 Ryan Christianson .50 .15
224 J.J. Davis .50 .15
225 Alex Graman .50 .15
226 Abraham Nunez .50 .15
227 Sun Woo Kim .50 .15
228 Jimmy Rollins .50 .15
229 Ruben Salazar .50 .15
230 Josh Girdley .50 .15
231 Carl Crawford .50 .15
232 Ben Davis .50 .15
233 Jason Grabowski .50 .15
234 Chris George .50 .15
235 Roy Oswalt .75 .23
236 Brian Cole .50 .15
237 Corey Patterson .50 .15
238 Vernon Wells .50 .15
239 Brad Baker .50 .15
240 Gookie Dawkins .50 .15
241 Michael Cuddyer .50 .15
242 Ricardo Aramboles .50 .15
243 Ben Sheets .50 .15
244 Toby Hall .50 .15
245 Jack Cust .50 .15
246 Pedro Feliz .50 .15
247 Josh Beckett .75 .23
248 Alex Escobar .50 .15
249 Marcus Giles .50 .15
250 Jon Rauch .50 .15
251 Kevin Mench .50 .15
252 Shawn Sonnier .50 .15
253 Aaron Rowand .50 .15
254 C.C. Sabathia .50 .15
255 Bubba Crosby .50 .15
256 Josh Hamilton .50 .15
257 Carlos Hernandez .50 .15
258 Carlos Pena .50 .15
259 Miguel Cabrera 5.00 1.50
260 Brandon Phillips .50 .15
261 Tony Pena Jr. .50 .15
262 Cristian Guerrero .50 .15
263 Jin Ho Cho .50 .15
264 Aaron Herr .50 .15
265 Keith Ginter .50 .15
266 Felipe Lopez .50 .15
267 Travis Harper .50 .15
268 Joe Torres .50 .15
269 Eric Byrnes .50 .15
270 Ben Christensen .50 .15
271 Aubrey Huff .50 .15
272 Lyle Overbay .50 .15
273 Vince Faison .50 .15
274 Bobby Bradley .50 .15
275 Joe Crede .50 .15
276 Matt Wheatland .50 .15
277 Grady Sizemore 1.50 .45
278 Adrian Gonzalez .50 .15
279 Tim Raines Jr. .50 .15
280 Phil Dumatrait .50 .15
281 Jason Hart .50 .15
282 David Kelton .50 .15
283 David Walling .50 .15
284 J.R. House .50 .15
285 Kenny Kelly .50 .15
286 Aaron McNeal .50 .15
287 Nick Johnson .50 .15
288 Scott Heard .50 .15
289 Brad Wilkerson .50 .15
290 Allen Levrault .50 .15
291 Chris Richard .50 .15
292 Jared Sandberg .50 .15
293 Tike Redman .50 .15
294 Adam Dunn .50 .15
295 Josh Pressley .50 .15
296 Jose Ortiz .50 .15
297 Jason Romano .50 .15
298 Tim Redding .50 .15
299 Alex Gordon .50 .15
300 Ben Petrick .50 .15
301 Eric Munson .50 .15
302 Luis Rivas .50 .15
303 Matt Ginter .50 .15
304 Alfonso Soriano .75 .23
305 Wilfredo Rodriguez .50 .15
306 Brett Myers .50 .15
307 Scott Seabol .50 .15
308 Tony Alvarez .50 .15
309 Donzell McDonald .50 .15
310 Austin Kearns .50 .15
311 Will Ohman RC 8.00 2.40
312 Ryan Soules RC 5.00 1.50
313 Cody Ross RC 8.00 2.40
314 Bill Whitecotton RC 8.00 2.40
315 Mike Burns RC 8.00 2.40
316 Manuel Acosta RC 8.00 2.40
317 Lance Niekro RC 8.00 2.40
318 Travis Thompson RC 8.00 2.40
319 Zach Sorensen RC 8.00 2.40
320 Austin Evans RC 5.00 1.50
321 Brad Stiles RC 8.00 2.40
322 Joe Kennedy RC 8.00 2.40
323 Luke Martin RC 8.00 2.40
324 Juan Diaz RC 8.00 2.40
325 Pat Hallmark RC 5.00 1.50
326 Christian Parker RC 5.00 1.50
327 Ronny Corona RC 8.00 2.40
328 Jermaine Clark RC 5.00 1.50
329 Scott Dunn RC 8.00 2.40
330 Scott Chiasson RC 8.00 2.40
331 Greg Nash AU RC 25.00 7.50
332 Brad Cresse AU 25.00 7.50
333 John Buck AU RC 40.00 12.00
334 Freddie Bynum AU RC 25.00 7.50
335 Felix Diaz AU RC 25.00 7.50
336 Jason Belcher AU RC 25.00 7.50
337 T.Farnsworth AU RC 25.00 7.50
338 Roberto Miniel AU RC 25.00 7.50
339 Esix Snead AU RC 25.00 7.50
340 Albert Pujols AU RC 1200.00 350.00
341 Jeff Andra AU RC 25.00 7.50
342 Victor Hall AU RC 25.00 7.50
343 Pedro Liriano AU RC 25.00 7.50
344 Andy Beal AU RC 25.00 7.50
345 Bob Keppel AU RC 40.00 12.00
346 Brian Schmitt AU RC 25.00 7.50
347 Ron Davenport AU RC 150.00 45.00
348 Tony Blanco AU RC 40.00 12.00
349 Reggie Griggs AU RC 25.00 7.50
350 D. Van Dusen AU RC 25.00 7.50
351A I. Suzuki English RC 60.00 18.00
351B I. Suzuki Japan RC 60.00 18.00

2001 Bowman Chrome Gold Refractors

Randomly inserted in packs at the rate of one in 47, this 330-card set is a parallel version of the base set with a distinctive gold refractive quality. Only 99 serially numbered sets were produced. Exchange cards with a redemption deadline of June 30th, 2003 for two separate Ichiro Suzuki issues (English text was numbered to 50 and Japanese text was numbered to 49) were randomly seeded into packs.

Nm-Mt Ex-Mt
*STARS: 8X TO 20X BASIC CARDS
*ROOKIES: 1.5X TO 4X BASIC CARDS
NNO-A Ichiro Suzuki 300.00 90.00
English/50 EXCH
NNO-B Ichiro Suzuki 300.00 90.00
Japan/49 EXCH

2001 Bowman Chrome X-Fractors

Randomly inserted in packs at the rate of one in 23, this 330-card set is a parallel version of the base set highlighted by a distinct background pattern. Exchange cards with a redemption deadline of June 30th, 2003 for two separate Ichiro Suzuki issues (English text and Japanese text) were randomly seeded into packs.

Nm-Mt Ex-Mt
*STARS: 4X TO 10X BASIC CARDS
*ROOKIES: .75X TO 2X BASIC CARDS

2001 Bowman Chrome Futures Game Relics

Randomly inserted in packs at the rate of one in 460, this 30-card set features color photos of players who participated in the 2000 Futures Game in Atlanta with pieces of game-worn uniform numbers and letters embedded in the cards.

Nm-Mt Ex-Mt
FGR-AE Alex Escobar 10.00 3.00
FGR-AM Aaron Myette 10.00 3.00
FGR-BB Bobby Bradley 10.00 3.00
FGR-BP Ben Petrick 10.00 3.00
FGR-BS Ben Sheets 15.00 4.50
FGR-BW Brad Wilkerson 10.00 3.00
FGR-BZ Barry Zito 25.00 7.50
FGR-CA Craig Anderson 10.00 3.00
FGR-CC Chin-Feng Chen 40.00 12.00
FGR-CG Chris George 10.00 3.00
FGR-CH Carlos Hernandez 15.00 4.50
FGR-CP Carlos Pena 10.00 3.00
FGR-CT Chin-Hui Tsao 40.00 12.00
FGR-EM Eric Munson 10.00 3.00
FGR-FL Felipe Lopez 10.00 3.00
FGR-JC Jack Cust 10.00 3.00
FGR-JH Josh Hamilton 10.00 3.00
FGR-JR Jason Romano 10.00 3.00
FGR-JZ Julio Zuleta 10.00 3.00
FGR-KA Kurt Ainsworth 10.00 3.00
FGR-MB Mike Bynum 10.00 3.00
FGR-MG Marcus Giles 15.00 4.50
FGR-NN Ntema Ndungidi 10.00 3.00
FGR-RA Ryan Anderson 10.00 3.00
FGR-RC Ramon Castro 10.00 3.00
FGR-RD Randey Dorame 10.00 3.00
FGR-SK Sun Woo Kim 10.00 3.00
FGR-TO Tomo Ohka 10.00 3.00
FGR-TW Travis Wilson 10.00 3.00
FGR-DCP Corey Patterson 15.00 4.50

2001 Bowman Chrome Rookie Reprints

Randomly inserted in packs at the rate of one in 12, this 25-card set features reprints of classic 1948-1955 Bowman rookies printed on polished Chrome finishes.

Nm-Mt Ex-Mt
COMPLETE SET (25) 60.00 18.00
*REFRACTORS: .75X TO 2X BASIC REPRINT
REFRACTOR STATED ODDS 1:203
REF.PRINT RUN 299 SERIAL #'d SETS
1 Yogi Berra 8.00 2.40
2 Ralph Kiner 4.00 1.20
3 Stan Musial 12.00 3.60
4 Warren Spahn 4.00 1.20
5 Roy Campanella 8.00 2.40
6 Bob Lemon 4.00 1.20
7 Robin Roberts 4.00 1.20
8 Duke Snider 4.00 1.20
9 Early Wynn 4.00 1.20
10 Richie Ashburn 4.00 1.20
11 Gil Hodges 6.00 1.80
12 Hank Bauer 4.00 1.20
13 Don Newcombe 4.00 1.20
14 Al Rosen 4.00 1.20
15 Willie Mays 15.00 4.50
16 Joe Garagiola 4.00 1.20
17 Whitey Ford 4.00 1.20
18 Lew Burdette 4.00 1.20
19 Gil McDougald 4.00 1.20
20 Minnie Minoso 4.00 1.20
21 Eddie Mathews 6.00 1.80
22 Harvey Kuenn 4.00 1.20
23 Don Larsen 6.00 1.80
24 Elston Howard 4.00 1.20
25 Don Zimmer 4.00 1.20

2001 Bowman Chrome Rookie Reprints Relics

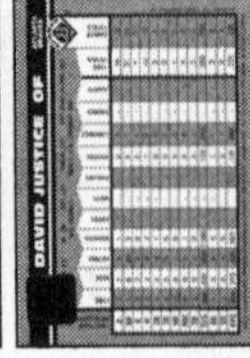

This six-card insert set features color player photos with pieces of their Rookie Season game-worn jerseys or game-used bats embedded in the cards. The insertion rate for the Mike Piazza Bat card is one in 3674 and one in 244 for the jersey cards. Three cards are Bowman Rookie card reprints and three cards are re-created "cards that never were."

Nm-Mt Ex-Mt
1 David Justice Jsy 10.00 3.00
2 Richie Sexson Jsy 10.00 3.00
3 Sean Casey Jsy 10.00 3.00
4 Mike Piazza Bat 40.00 12.00
5 Carlos Delgado Jsy 10.00 3.00
6 Chipper Jones Jsy 15.00 4.50

2002 Bowman Chrome

This 405 card set was issued in July, 2002. It was issued in four card packs with an SRP of $4 which were packed 18 packs to a box and 12 boxes to a case. The first 110 card of the set featured veteran players. The next grouping of cards (111-383) featured a mix of rookies and prospect cards. The then final grouping (384-405) featured signed rookie cards. Both So Taguchi and Kazuhisa Ishii were also printed without autographs on their cards. An exchange was inserted into packs for Jake Mauer's autographed RC. The exchange card was intended to be card number 388 in the checklist but the actual Mauer autograph mailed out to collectors was card number 324. Thus, this set actually has two cards numbered 324 (the Jake Mauer autograph and a basic-issue Ben Broussard card) and no number 388.

Nm-Mt Ex-Mt
COMP.RED SET (110) 40.00 12.00
COMP.BLUE w/o SP's (110) 40.00 12.00
COMMON RED (1-110) .50 .15
COMMON BLUE (111-383) .75 .23
COMMON AU (324B/384-405) 10.00 3.00
324B/384-405 GROUP A AUTO ODDS 1:28
403-404 GROUP B AUTO ODDS 1:1290
324B/384-405 OVERALL AUTO ODDS 1:27
1 Adam Dunn .50 .15
2 Derek Jeter 3.00 .90
3 Alex Rodriguez 2.00 .60
4 Miguel Tejada .50 .15
5 Nomar Garciaparra 2.00 .60
6 Toby Hall .50 .15
7 Brandon Duckworth .50 .15
8 Paul LoDuca .50 .15
9 Brian Giles .50 .15
10 C.C. Sabathia .50 .15
11 Curt Schilling .75 .23
12 Tsuyoshi Shinjo .50 .15
13 Ramon Hernandez .50 .15
14 Jose Cruz Jr. .50 .15
15 Albert Pujols 2.50 .75
16 Joe Mays .50 .15
17 Javy Lopez .50 .15
18 J.T. Snow .50 .15
19 David Segui .50 .15
20 Jorge Posada .75 .23
21 Doug Mientkiewicz .50 .15
22 Jerry Hairston Jr. .50 .15
23 Bernie Williams .75 .23
24 Mike Sweeney .50 .15
25 Jason Giambi 1.25 .35

26 Ryan Dempster .50 .15
27 Ryan Klesko .50 .15
28 Mark Quinn .50 .15
29 Jeff Kent .50 .15
30 Eric Chavez .50 .15
31 Adrian Beltre .50 .15
32 Andruw Jones .50 .15
33 Alfonso Soriano .75 .23
34 Aramis Ramirez .50 .15
35 Greg Maddux 2.00 .60
36 Andy Pettitte .75 .23
37 Bartolo Colon .50 .15
38 Ben Sheets .50 .15
39 Bobby Higginson .50 .15
40 Ivan Rodriguez 1.25 .35
41 Brad Penny .50 .15
42 Carlos Lee .50 .15
43 Damion Easley .50 .15
44 Preston Wilson .50 .15
45 Jeff Bagwell .75 .23
46 Eric Milton .50 .15
47 Rafael Palmeiro .75 .23
48 Gary Sheffield .50 .15
49 J.D. Drew .50 .15
50 Jim Thome 1.25 .35
51 Ichiro Suzuki 2.00 .60
52 Bud Smith .50 .15
53 Chan Ho Park .50 .15
54 D'Angelo Jimenez .50 .15
55 Ken Griffey Jr. 2.00 .60
56 Wade Miller .50 .15
57 Vladimir Guerrero 1.25 .35
58 Troy Glaus .75 .23
59 Shawn Green .50 .15
60 Kerry Wood 1.25 .35
61 Jack Wilson .50 .15
62 Kevin Brown .50 .15
63 Marcus Giles .50 .15
64 Pat Burrell .50 .15
65 Larry Walker .75 .23
66 Sammy Sosa 2.00 .60
67 Raul Mondesi .50 .15
68 Tim Hudson .50 .15
69 Lance Berkman .50 .15
70 Mike Mussina 1.25 .35
71 Barry Zito .75 .23
72 Jimmy Rollins .50 .15
73 Barry Bonds 3.00 .90
74 Craig Biggio .75 .23
75 Todd Helton .75 .23
76 Roger Clemens 2.50 .75
77 Frank Catalanotto .50 .15
78 Josh Towers .50 .15
79 Roy Oswalt .50 .15
80 Chipper Jones 1.25 .35
81 Cristian Guzman .50 .15
82 Darin Erstad .50 .15
83 Freddy Garcia .50 .15
84 Jason Tyner .50 .15
85 Carlos Delgado .50 .15
86 Jon Lieber .50 .15
87 Juan Pierre .50 .15
88 Matt Morris .50 .15
89 Phil Nevin .50 .15
90 Jim Edmonds .50 .15
91 Maggio Ordonez .50 .15
92 Mike Hampton .50 .15
93 Rafael Furcal .50 .15
94 Richie Sexson .50 .15
95 Luis Gonzalez .50 .15
96 Scott Rolen .75 .23
97 Tim Redding .50 .15
98 Moises Alou .50 .15
99 Jose Vidro .50 .15
100 Mike Piazza 2.00 .60
101 Pedro Martinez 1.25 .35
102 Geoff Jenkins .50 .15
103 Johnny Damon .50 .15
104 Mike Cameron .50 .15
105 Randy Johnson 1.25 .35
106 David Eckstein .50 .15
107 Javier Vazquez .50 .15
108 Mark Mulder .50 .15
109 Robert Fick .50 .15
110 Roberto Alomar 1.25 .35
111 Wilson Betemit .75 .23
112 Chris Tritle SP RC 5.00 1.50
113 Ed Rogers .75 .23
114 Juan Pena .75 .23
115 Josh Beckett 2.00 .60
116 Juan Cruz .75 .23
117 Noochie Varner SP RC 5.00 1.50
118 Blake Williams .75 .23
119 Mike Rivera .75 .23
120 Hank Blalock 3.00 .90
121 Hansel Izquierdo SP RC 5.00 1.50
122 Orlando Hudson .75 .23
123 Bill Hall SP 5.00 1.50
124 Jose Reyes 3.00 .90
125 Juan Rivera .75 .23
126 Eric Valent .75 .23
127 Scotty Layfield SP RC 5.00 1.50
128 Austin Kearns 1.25 .35
129 Nic Jackson SP RC 5.00 1.50
130 Scott Chiasson .75 .23
131 Chad Qualls SP RC 5.00 1.50
132 Marcus Thames .75 .23
133 Nathan Haynes .75 .23
134 Joe Borchard 1.25 .35
135 Josh Hamilton .75 .23
136 Corey Patterson 1.25 .35
137 Travis Wilson .75 .23
138 Alex Escobar .75 .23
139 Alexis Gomez .75 .23
140 Nick Johnson 1.25 .35
141 Marlon Byrd 1.25 .35
142 Kory DeHaan .75 .23
143 Carlos Hernandez .75 .23
144 Sean Burroughs 1.25 .35
145 Angel Berroa 1.25 .35
146 Aubrey Huff 1.25 .35
147 Travis Hafner 1.25 .35
148 Brandon Berger .75 .23
149 J.R. House .75 .23
150 Dewon Brazelton .75 .23
151 Jayson Werth .75 .23
152 Larry Barnes .75 .23
153 Ruben Gotay SP RC 5.00 1.50
154 Tommy Marx SP RC 5.00 1.50
155 John Suomi SP RC 5.00 1.50
156 Javier Colina SP 5.00 1.50
157 Greg Sain SP RC 5.00 1.50
158 Robert Cosby SP RC 5.00 1.50
159 Angel Pagan SP RC 5.00 1.50
160 Ralph Santana RC 1.25 .35
161 Joe Orloski RC 1.25 .35
162 Shayne Wright SP RC 5.00 1.50
163 Jay Caligiuri SP RC 5.00 1.50
164 Greg Montalbano SP RC 8.00 2.40
165 Rich Harden SP RC 30.00 9.00
166 Rich Thompson SP RC 5.00 1.50
167 Fred Bastardo SP RC 5.00 1.50
168 Alejandro Giron SP RC 5.00 1.50
169 Jesus Medrano SP RC 5.00 1.50
170 Kevin Deaton SP RC 5.00 1.50
171 Mike Rosamond RC 1.25 .35
172 Jon Guzman SP RC 5.00 1.50
173 Gerard Oakes SP RC 5.00 1.50
174 Francisco Liriano SP RC 8.00 2.40
175 Matt Allegra SP RC 5.00 1.50
176 Mike Snyder SP RC 5.00 1.50
177 James Shanks SP RC 5.00 1.50
178 And. Hernandez SP RC 5.00 1.50
179 Dan Trumble SP RC 5.00 1.50
180 Luis DePaula SP RC 5.00 1.50
181 Randall Shelley SP RC 5.00 1.50
182 Richard Lane SP RC 5.00 1.50
183 Antwon Rollins SP RC 5.00 1.50
184 Ryan Bukvich SP RC 5.00 1.50
185 Derrick Lewis SP 5.00 1.50
186 Eric Miller SP RC 5.00 1.50
187 Justin Schuda SP RC 5.00 1.50
188 Brian West SP RC 5.00 1.50
189 Brad Wilkerson .75 .23
190 Neal Frendling SP RC 5.00 1.50
191 Jeremy Hill SP RC 5.00 1.50
192 James Barrett SP RC 5.00 1.50
193 Brett Kay SP RC 5.00 1.50
194 Ryan Mottl SP RC 5.00 1.50
195 Brad Nelson SP RC 15.00 4.50
196 Juan M. Gonzalez SP RC 5.00 1.50
197 Curtis Legendre SP RC 5.00 1.50
198 Ronald Acuna SP RC 5.00 1.50
199 Chris Flinn SP RC 5.00 1.50
200 Nick Alvarez SP RC 5.00 1.50
201 Jason Ellison SP RC 5.00 1.50
202 Blake McGinley SP RC 5.00 1.50
203 Dan Phillips SP RC 5.00 1.50
204 Demetrius Heath SP RC 5.00 1.50
205 Eric Bruntlett SP RC 5.00 1.50
206 Joe Jiannetti SP RC 5.00 1.50
207 Mike Hill SP RC 5.00 1.50
208 Ricardo Cordova SP RC 5.00 1.50
209 Mark Hamilton SP RC 5.00 1.50
210 David Mattox SP RC 5.00 1.50
211 Jose Morban SP RC 5.00 1.50
212 Scott Wiggins SP RC 5.00 1.50
213 Steve Green .75 .23
214 Brian Rogers SP 5.00 1.50
215 Kenny Baugh .75 .23
216 Anastacio Martinez SP RC 5.00 1.50
217 Richard Lewis .75 .23
218 Tim Kalita SP RC 5.00 1.50
219 Edwin Almonte SP RC 5.00 1.50
220 Hee Seop Choi 2.00 .60
221 Ty Howington .75 .23
222 Victor Alvarez SP RC 5.00 1.50
223 Morgan Ensberg 1.25 .35
224 Jeff Austin SP RC 5.00 1.50
225 Clint Weibl SP RC 5.00 1.50
226 Eric Cyr .75 .23
227 Marlyn Tisdale SP RC 5.00 1.50
228 John VanBenschoten 2.00 .60
229 David Krynzel .75 .23
230 Raul Chavez SP RC 5.00 1.50
231 Brett Evert .75 .23
232 Joe Rogers SP RC 5.00 1.50
233 Adam Wainwright 1.25 .35
234 Matt Herges RC .75 .23
235 Matt Childers SP RC 5.00 1.50
236 Nick Neugebauer .75 .23
237 Carl Crawford 1.25 .35
238 Seung Song .75 .23
239 Randy Flores .75 .23
240 Jason Lane .75 .23
241 Chase Utley 2.00 .60
242 Ben Howard SP RC 5.00 1.50
243 Eric Glaser SP RC 5.00 1.50
244 Josh Wilson RC 1.25 .35
245 Jose Valverde SP RC 8.00 2.40
246 Chris Smith .75 .23
247 Mark Prior 10.00 3.00
248 Brian Mallette SP RC 5.00 1.50
249 Chone Figgins SP RC 5.00 1.50
250 Jimmy Alvarez SP RC 5.00 1.50
251 Luis Terrero .75 .23
252 Josh Bonifay SP RC 5.00 1.50
253 Garrett Guzman SP RC 5.00 1.50
254 Jeff Verplancke SP RC 5.00 1.50
255 Nate Espy SP RC 5.00 1.50
256 Jeff Lincoln SP RC 5.00 1.50
257 Ryan Snare SP RC 5.00 1.50
258 Jose Ortiz .75 .23
259 Denny Bautista 1.25 .35
260 Willy Aybar .75 .23
261 Kelly Johnson .75 .23
262 Shawn Fagan 5.00 1.50
263 Yurendell DeCaster SP RC 5.00 1.50
264 Mike Peeples SP RC 5.00 1.50
265 Joel Guzman 1.25 .35
266 Ryan Vogelsong .75 .23
267 Jorge Padilla SP RC 5.00 1.50
268 Joe Jester SP RC 5.00 1.50
269 Ryan Church SP RC 8.00 2.40
270 Mitch Jones .75 .23
271 Travis Foley SP RC 5.00 1.50
272 Bobby Crosby 5.00 1.50
273 Adrian Gonzalez 1.25 .35
274 Ronnie Merrill .75 .23
275 Joel Pineiro 1.25 .35
276 John-Ford Griffin .75 .23
277 Brian Forystek SP RC 5.00 1.50
278 Sean Douglass .75 .23
279 Manny Delcarmen SP RC 5.00 1.50
280 Jim Kavourias SP RC 5.00 1.50
281 Gabe Gross .75 .23
282 Bill Ortega .75 .23
283 Joey Hammond SP RC 5.00 1.50
284 Brett Myers 1.25 .35
285 Carlos Pena .75 .23
286 Ezequiel Astacio SP RC 5.00 1.50
287 Edwin Yan SP RC 5.00 1.50
288 Chris Duffy SP RC 5.00 1.50
289 Jason Kinchen .75 .23
290 Rafael Soriano 1.25 .35
291 Colin Young RC 5.00 1.50
292 Eric Byrnes .75 .23
293 Chris Narveson SP RC 8.00 2.40
294 John Rheinecker .75 .23
295 Mike Wilson SP RC 5.00 1.50
296 Justin Sherrod SP RC 5.00 1.50
297 Deivi Mendez .75 .23
298 Wily Mo Pena .75 .23
299 Brett Roneberg SP RC 5.00 1.50
300 Trey Lunsford SP RC 5.00 1.50
301 Christian Parker .75 .23
302 Brent Butler .75 .23
303 Aaron Heilman .75 .23
304 Wilkin Ruan .75 .23
305 Kenny Kelly .75 .23
306 Cody Ransom .75 .23
307 Koyie Hill SP 5.00 1.50
308 Tony Fontana SP RC 5.00 1.50
309 Mark Teixeira 3.00 .90
310 Doug Sessions SP RC 5.00 1.50
311 Josh Cisneros SP RC 5.00 1.50
312 Carlos Brackley SP RC 5.00 1.50
313 Tim Raines Jr. .75 .23
314 Ross Peeples SP RC 5.00 1.50
315 Alex Requena SP RC 5.00 1.50
316 Chin-Hui Tsao 1.25 .35
317 Tony Alvarez .75 .23
318 Craig Kuzmic SP RC 5.00 1.50
319 Pete Zamora SP RC 5.00 1.50
320 Matt Parker SP RC 5.00 1.50
321 Keith Ginter .75 .23
322 Gary Cates Jr. SP RC 5.00 1.50
323 Matt Belisle .75 .23
324A Ben Broussard .75 .23
324B Ja.Mauer AU A RC EXCH UER 10.00 3.00
Card was mistakenly numbered as 324
325 Dennis Tankersley .75 .23
326 Juan Silvestre .75 .23
327 Henry Pichardo SP RC 5.00 1.50
328 Michael Floyd SP RC 5.00 1.50
329 Clint Nageotte SP RC 12.00 3.60
330 Raymond Cabrera SP RC 5.00 1.50
331 Mauricio Lara SP RC 5.00 1.50
332 Alejandro Cadena SP RC 5.00 1.50
333 Jonny Gomes SP RC 12.00 3.60
334 Jason Bulger SP RC 5.00 1.50
335 Nate Teut .75 .23
336 David Gil SP RC 5.00 1.50
337 Joel Crump SP RC 5.00 1.50
338 Brandon Phillips .75 .23
339 Macay McBride .75 .23
340 Brandon Claussen 5.00 1.50
341 Josh Phelps .75 .23
342 Freddie Money SP RC 5.00 1.50
343 Cliff Bartosh SP RC 5.00 1.50
344 Terrance Hill SP RC 5.00 1.50
345 John Rodriguez SP RC 5.00 1.50
346 Chris Latham SP RC 5.00 1.50
347 Carlos Cabrera SP RC 5.00 1.50
348 Jose Bautista SP RC 10.00 3.00
349 Kevin Frederick SP RC 5.00 1.50
350 Jerome Williams 3.00 .90
351 Napoleon Calzado SP RC 5.00 1.50
352 Benito Baez SP 5.00 1.50
353 Xavier Nady .75 .23
354 Jason Botts SP RC 5.00 1.50
355 Steve Bechler SP RC 5.00 1.50
356 Reed Johnson SP RC 8.00 2.40
357 Mark Outlaw SP RC 5.00 1.50
358 Jake Peavy 1.25 .35
359 Josh Shaffer SP RC 5.00 1.50
360 Dan Wright SP 5.00 1.50
361 Ryan Gripp SP RC 5.00 1.50
362 Nelson Castro SP RC 5.00 1.50
363 Jason Bay SP RC 15.00 4.50
364 Franklyn German SP RC 5.00 1.50
365 Corwin Malone SP RC 5.00 1.50
366 Kelly Ramos SP RC 5.00 1.50
367 John Ennis SP RC 5.00 1.50
368 George Perez SP 5.00 1.50
369 Rene Reyes SP RC 5.00 1.50
370 Rolando Viera SP RC 5.00 1.50
371 Earl Snyder SP RC 5.00 1.50
372 Kyle Kane SP RC 5.00 1.50
373 Mario Ramos SP RC 8.00 2.40
374 Tyler Yates SP RC 10.00 3.00
375 Jason Young SP RC 5.00 1.50
376 Chris Bootcheck SP RC 5.00 1.50
377 Jesus Cota SP RC 5.00 1.50
378 Corky Miller SP 5.00 1.50
379 Matt Erickson SP RC 5.00 1.50
380 Justin Huber SP RC 15.00 4.50
381 Felix Escalona SP RC 5.00 1.50
382 Kevin Cash SP RC 5.00 1.50
383 J.J. Putz SP RC 5.00 1.50
384 Chris Snelling AU A RC 20.00 6.00
385 David Wright AU A RC 40.00 12.00
386 Brian Wolfe AU A RC 10.00 3.00
387 Justin Reid AU A RC 10.00 3.00
389 Ryan Raburn AU A RC 10.00 3.00
390 Josh Barfield AU A RC 50.00 15.00
391 Joe Mauer AU A RC 100.00 30.00
392 Bobby Jenks AU A RC 25.00 7.50
393 Rob Henkel AU A RC 10.00 3.00
394 Jimmy Gobble AU A RC 25.00 7.50
395 Jesse Foppert AU A RC 30.00 9.00
396 Gavin Floyd AU A RC 40.00 12.00
397 Nate Field AU A RC 10.00 3.00
398 Ryan Doumit AU A RC 15.00 4.50
399 Ron Calloway AU A RC 10.00 3.00
400 Taylor Buchholz AU A RC 15.00 4.50
401 Adam Roller AU A RC 10.00 3.00
402 Cole Barthel AU A RC 10.00 3.00
403 Kazuhisa Ishii SP RC 10.00 3.00
403 Kazuhisa Ishii AU B 60.00 18.00
404 So Taguchi SP RC 8.00 2.40
404 So Taguchi AU B 40.00 12.00
405 Chris Baker AU A RC 10.00 3.00

2002 Bowman Chrome Facsimile Autograph Variations

This 20 card partial parallel to the Bowman Chrome set were issued in this special version with a facsimile autograph as part of the card. These cards were not originally expected to be

issued and caused some confusion in the secondary market upon the product's release.

Nm-Mt Ex-Mt

118 Taylor Buchholz
130 Chris Baker
189 Adam Roller
229 Ryan Raburn
231 Chris Snelling
233 Nate Field
237 Ron Calloway
239 Cole Barthel
244 Rob Henkel
251 Gavin Floyd
301 Jimmy Gobble
305 Brian Wolfe
313 Jesse Foppert
316 Joe Mauer
317 David Wright
323 Justin Reid
324 Jake Mauer
326 Josh Barfield
335 Bobby Jenks
338 Ryan Doumit

2002 Bowman Chrome Gold Refractors

This is a complete parallel set to the Bowman Chrome set. These cards were issued in several different tiers but it is important to note that most of these cards have a stated print run of 50 sets. The Ishii and Taguchi autograph cards have a stated print run of 10 sets.

Nm-Mt Ex-Mt

*GOLD REF RED: 8X TO 20X BASIC ...
*GOLD REF BLUE: 4X TO 10X BASIC..
*GOLD REF BLUE SP: 2X TO 5X BASIC
*GOLD REF AU: 2X TO 5X BASIC.
384-405 GROUP A AUTO ODDS 1:879
403-404 GROUP B AUTO ODDS 1:59,616
324B/384-405 OVERALL AUTO ODDS 1:866
1-383/403-404 PRINT 50 SERIAL #'d SETS
324B/384-405 GROUP A AU PRINT 50 SETS
403-404 GROUP B AU PRINT RUN 10 SETS
403 Kazuhisa Ishii 50.00 15.00
403 Kazuhisa Ishii AU B
404 So Taguchi 40.00 12.00
404 So Taguchi AU B

2002 Bowman Chrome Refractors

This is a complete parallel set to the Bowman Chrome set. These cards were issued in several different tiers but it is important to note that most of these cards have a stated print run of 500 sets. The Ishii and Taguchi autograph cards have a stated print run of 100 sets.

Nm-Mt Ex-Mt

*REF RED: 1.5X TO 4X BASIC
*REF BLUE: 1X TO 2.5X BASIC
*REF BLUE SP: .6X TO 1.5X BASIC ....
*REF AU: .5X TO 1.2X BASIC AU'S
324B/384-405 GROUP A AUTO ODDS 1:88
403-404 GROUP B AUTO ODDS 1:4392
324B/384-405 OVERALL AUTO ODDS 1:86
1-383/403-404 PRINT 500 SERIAL #'d SETS
324B/384-405 GROUP A PRINT RUN 500 SETS
403-404 GROUP B PRINT RUN 100 SETS
403 Kazuhisa Ishii 15.00 4.50
403 Kazuhisa Ishii AU B 100.00 30.00
404 So Taguchi 12.00 3.60
404 So Taguchi AU B 60.00 18.00

2002 Bowman Chrome Uncirculated

Issued as one per box chip topper exchange cards, these cards parallel the Bowman Chrome Rookie Cards. Each card, which needed to be redeemed from ThePit.Com comes in a special "case" which guarantees the card has never been handled. Most of these cards are traded there so we will only price copies which are actually "in-hand" or actually physically owned by the user. 350 of each basic card was produced and a mere 10 of each autograph card was made in Uncirculated format. The deadline to redeem the scratch off exchange cards was December 31st, 2002.

Nm-Mt Ex-Mt

112 Chris Tritle
117 Noochie Varner
121 Hansel Izquierdo
123 Bill Hall
127 Scotty Layfield
129 Nic Jackson
131 Chad Qualls
153 Ruben Gotay
154 Tommy Marx
155 John Suomi
156 Javier Colina
157 Greg Sain
158 Robert Crosby
159 Angel Pagan
162 Shayne Wright
163 Jay Caligiuri
164 Greg Montalbano
165 Rich Harden
166 Rich Thompson
167 Fred Bastardo
168 Alejandro Giron
169 Jesus Medrano
170 Kevin Deaton
172 Jon Guzman
173 Gerard Oakes
174 Francisco Liriano
175 Matt Allegra
176 Mike Snyder
178 Anderson Hernandez
179 Dan Trumble
180 Luis DePaula
181 Randall Shelley
182 Richard Lane
183 Antwon Rollins
184 Ryan Bukvich
185 Derrick Lewis
186 Eric Miller
187 Justin Schuda
188 Brian West
190 Neal Frendling
191 Jeremy Hill
192 James Barrett
193 Brett Kay
194 Ryan Mottl
195 Brad Nelson
196 Juan M. Gonzalez
197 Curtis Legendre
198 Ronald Acuna
199 Chris Flinn
200 Nick Alvarez
201 Jason Ellison
202 Blake McGinley
203 Dan Phillips
204 Demetrius Heath
205 Eric Bruntlett
206 Joe Jiannetti
207 Mike Hill
208 Ricardo Cordova
209 Mark Hamilton
210 David Mattox
211 Jose Morban
212 Scott Wiggins
214 Brian Rogers
216 Anastacio Martinez
218 Tim Kalita
219 Edwin Almonte
222 Victor Alvarez
224 Jeff Austin
225 Clint Weibl
227 Marlyn Tisdale
230 Raul Chavez
232 Joe Rogers
235 Matt Childers
242 Ben Howard
243 Eric Glaser
245 Jose Valverde
248 Brian Mallette
249 Chone Figgins
250 Jimmy Alvarez
252 Josh Bonifay
253 Garrett Guzman
254 Jeff Verplancke
255 Nate Espy
256 Jeff Lincoln
257 Ryan Snare
263 Yurendell DeCaster
264 Mike Peeples
267 Jorge Padilla
268 Joe Jester
269 Ryan Church
271 Travis Foley
277 Brian Forystek
279 Manny Delcarmen
280 Jim Kavourias
283 Joey Hammond
286 Ezequiel Astacio
287 Edwin Yan
288 Chris Duffy
293 Chris Narveson
295 Mike Wilson
296 Justin Sherrod
299 Brett Roneberg
300 Trey Lunsford
307 Koyie Hill
308 Tony Fontana
310 Doug Sessions
311 Josh Cisneros
312 Carlos Brackley
314 Ross Peeples
315 Alex Requena
318 Craig Kuzmic
319 Pete Zamora
320 Matt Parker
322 Gary Cates Jr.
324 Jake Mauer AU
327 Henry Pichardo
328 Michael Floyd
329 Clint Nageotte
330 Raymond Cabrera
331 Mauricio Lara
332 Alejandro Cadena
333 Jonny Gomes
334 Jason Bulger
336 David Gil
337 Joel Crump
342 Freddie Money
343 Cliff Bartosh
344 Terrance Hill
345 John Rodriguez
346 Chris Latham
347 Carlos Cabrera
348 Jose Bautista
349 Kevin Frederick
351 Napolean Calzado
352 Benito Baez
354 Jason Botts
355 Steve Bechler
356 Reed Johnson
357 Mark Outlaw
359 Josh Shaffer
360 Dan Wright
361 Ryan Gripp
362 Nelson Castro
363 Jason Bay
364 Franklyn German
365 Corwin Malone
366 Kelly Ramos
367 John Ennis
368 George Perez
369 Rene Reyes
370 Rolando Viera
371 Earl Snyder
372 Kyle Kane
373 Mario Ramos
374 Tyler Yates
375 Jason Young
376 Chris Bootcheck

377 Jesus Cota
378 Corky Miller
379 Matt Erickson
380 Justin Huber
381 Felix Escalona
382 Kevin Cash
383 J.J. Putz
384 Chris Snelling AU
385 David Wright AU
386 Brian Wolfe AU
387 Justin Reid AU
389 Ryan Raburn AU
390 Josh Barfield AU
391 Joe Mauer AU
392 Bobby Jenks AU
393 Rob Henkel AU
394 Jimmy Gobble AU
395 Jesse Foppert AU
396 Gavin Floyd AU
397 Nate Field AU
398 Ryan Doumit AU
399 Ron Calloway AU
400 Taylor Buchholz AU
401 Adam Roller AU
402 Cole Barthel AU
403 Kazuhisa Ishii
403A Kazuhisa Ishii AU
404 So Taguchi
404A So Taguchi AU
405 Chris Baker AU
NNO Exchange Card

2002 Bowman Chrome X-Fractors

This is a complete parallel set to the Bowman Chrome set. These cards were issued in several different tiers but it is important to note that most of these cards have a stated print run of 250 sets. The Ishii and Taguchi autograph cards have a stated print run of 50 sets.

Nm-Mt Ex-Mt
*XFRACT RED: 3X TO 8X BASIC
*XFRACT BLUE: 1.5X TO 4X BASIC
*XFRACT BLUE SP: .75X TO 2X BASIC
*XFRACT AU: .75X TO 2X BASIC
324B/384-405 GROUP A AUTO ODDS 1:176
403-404 GROUP B AUTO ODDS 1:9072
324B/384-405 OVERALL AUTO ODDS 1:173
1-383/403-404 PRINT 250 SERIAL #'d SETS
324B/384-405 GROUP A PRINT RUN 250 SETS
403-404 GROUP B PRINT RUN 50 SETS
403 Kazuhisa Ishii 20.00 6.00
403 Kazuhisa Ishii AU B 120.00 36.00
404 So Taguchi 15.00 4.50
404 So Taguchi AU B 80.00 24.00

2002 Bowman Chrome Reprints

Isssued at stated odds of one in six, these 20 cards feature reprint cards of players who have made their debut since Bowman was reintroduced as a major brand in 1989.

Nm-Mt Ex-Mt
COMPLETE SET (20) 25.00 7.50
*BLACK REF: .6X TO 1.5X BASIC REPRINTS
BLACK REFRACTOR ODDS 1:18
BCR-AJ Andruw Jones 95 2.00 .60
BCR-BC Bartolo Colon 95 2.00 .60
BCR-BW Bernie Williams 90 2.00 .60
BCR-CD Carlos Delgado 92 2.00 .60
BCR-CJ Chipper Jones 91 2.50 .75
BCR-DJ Derek Jeter 93 8.00 2.40
BCR-FT Frank Thomas 90 2.50 .75
BCR-GS Gary Sheffield 89 2.00 .60
BCR-IR Ivan Rodriguez 91 2.50 .75
BCR-JB Jeff Bagwell 91 2.00 .60
BCR-JG Juan Gonzalez 90 2.50 .75
BCR-JK Jason Kendall 93 2.00 .60
BCR-JP Jorge Posada 94 2.00 .60
BCR-KG Ken Griffey Jr. 89 5.00 1.50
BCR-LG Luis Gonzalez 91 2.00 .60
BCR-LW Larry Walker 90 2.00 .60
BCR-MP Mike Piazza 92 5.00 1.50
BCR-MS Mike Sweeney 96 2.00 .60
BCR-SR Scott Rolen 95 2.00 .60
BCR-VG Vladimir Guerrero 95 2.50 .75

2002 Bowman Chrome Draft

Inserted one per pack, this is a parallel to the Bowman Draft Pick set. Each of these cards uses the Topps "Chrome" technology and these cards were inserted two per bowman draft pack. Cards numbered 166 through 175 are not parallels to the regular Bowman cards and they feature autographs of the players. Those ten cards were issued at a stated rate of one in 45 Bowman Draft packs.

Nm-Mt Ex-Mt
COMPLETE SET (175) 300.00 90.00
COMP.SET w/o AU's (165) 160.00 47.50
COMMON CARD (1-165) .40 .12
COMMON CARD (166-175) 15.00 4.50
1 Clint Everts RC 4.00 1.20
2 Fred Lewis RC 1.00 .30
3 Jon Broxton RC 1.00 .30
4 Jason Anderson RC 1.00 .30
5 Mike Eusebio RC 1.00 .30
6 Zack Greinke RC 15.00 4.50
7 Joe Blanton RC 8.00 2.40
8 Sergio Santos RC 6.00 1.80
9 Jason Cooper RC 1.00 .30
10 Delwyn Young RC 5.00 1.50
11 Jeremy Hermida RC 8.00 2.40
12 Dan Ortmeier RC 2.50 .75
13 Kevin Jepsen RC 1.00 .30
14 Russ Adams RC 2.50 .75
15 Mike Nixon RC 1.00 .30
16 Nick Swisher RC 5.00 1.50
17 Cole Hamels RC 15.00 4.50
18 Brian Dopirak RC 5.00 1.50
19 James Loney RC 10.00 3.00
20 Denard Span RC 1.00 .30
21 Billy Petrick RC 1.00 .30
22 Jared Doyle RC 1.00 .30
23 Jeff Francoeur RC 15.00 4.50
24 Nick Bourgeois RC 1.00 .30
25 Matt Cain RC 5.00 1.50
26 John McCurdy RC 1.00 .30
27 Mark Kiger RC 1.00 .30
28 Bill Murphy RC 1.00 .30
29 Matt Craig RC 1.00 .30
30 Mike Megrew RC 1.00 .30
31 Ben Crockett RC 1.00 .30
32 Luke Hagerty RC 1.00 .30
33 Matt Whitney RC 4.00 1.20
34 Dan Meyer RC 2.50 .75
35 Jeremy Brown RC 3.00 .90
36 Doug Johnson RC 1.00 .30
37 Steve Obenchain RC 1.00 .30
38 Matt Clanton RC 1.00 .30
39 Mark Teahen RC 1.00 .30
40 Tom Carrow RC 1.00 .30
41 Micah Schilling RC 1.00 .30
42 Blair Johnson RC 1.00 .30
43 Jason Pridie RC 4.00 1.20
44 Joey Votto RC 1.50 .45
45 Taber Lee RC 1.00 .30
46 Adam Peterson RC 1.00 .30
47 Adam Donachie RC 1.00 .30
48 Josh Murray RC 1.00 .30
49 Brent Clevlen RC 4.00 1.20
50 Chad Pleiness RC 1.00 .30
51 Zach Hammes RC 1.50 .45
52 Chris Snyder RC 1.00 .30
53 Chris Smith RC 1.00 .30
54 Justin Maureau RC 1.00 .30
55 David Bush RC 5.00 1.50
56 Tim Gilhooly RC 1.00 .30
57 Blair Barbier RC 1.00 .30
58 Zach Segovia RC 2.50 .75
59 Jeremy Reed RC 15.00 4.50
60 Matt Pender RC 1.00 .30
61 Eric Thomas RC 1.00 .30
62 Justin Jones RC 5.00 1.50
63 Brian Slocum RC 1.00 .30
64 Larry Broadway RC 5.00 1.50
65 Bo Flowers RC 1.00 .30
66 Scott White RC 1.00 .30
67 Steve Stanley RC 1.00 .30
68 Alex Merricks RC 1.00 .30
69 Josh Womack RC 1.00 .30
70 Dave Jensen RC 1.00 .30
71 Curtis Granderson RC 3.00 .90
72 Pat Osborn RC 1.00 .30
73 Nic Carter RC 1.00 .30
74 Mitch Talbot RC 1.00 .30
75 Don Murphy RC 1.00 .30
76 Val Majewski RC 2.50 .75
77 Javy Rodriguez RC 1.00 .30
78 Fernando Pacheco RC 1.00 .30
79 Steve Russell RC 1.00 .30
80 Jon Slack RC 1.00 .30
81 John Baker RC 1.00 .30
82 Aaron Coonrod RC 1.00 .30
83 Josh Johnson RC 1.00 .30
84 Jake Blalock RC 6.00 1.80
85 Alex Hart RC 3.00 .90
86 Wes Bankston RC 5.00 1.50
87 Josh Rupe RC 1.00 .30
88 Dan Cevette RC 1.00 .30
89 Kiel Fisher RC 1.50 .45
90 Alan Rick RC 1.00 .30
91 Charlie Morton RC 1.00 .30
92 Chad Spann RC 3.00 .90
93 Kyle Boyer RC 1.00 .30
94 Bob Malek RC 1.00 .30
95 Ryan Rodriguez RC 1.00 .30
96 Jordan Renz RC 1.00 .30
97 Randy Frye RC 1.00 .30
98 Rich Hill RC 1.00 .30
99 B.J. Upton RC 20.00 6.00
100 Dan Christensen RC 1.00 .30
101 Casey Kotchman RC 10.00 3.00
102 Eric Good RC 1.00 .30
103 Mike Fontenot RC 1.00 .30
104 John Webb RC 1.00 .30
105 Jason Dubois RC 5.00 1.50
106 Ryan Kibler RC 1.00 .30
107 John Peralta RC 1.00 .30
108 Kirk Saarloos RC 1.00 .30
109 Rhett Parrott RC 1.00 .30
110 Jason Grove RC 1.00 .30
111 Colt Griffin RC 3.00 .90
112 Dallas McPherson RC 8.00 2.40
113 Oliver Perez RC 1.50 .45
114 Marshall McDougall RC 1.00 .30
115 Mike Wood RC 1.00 .30
116 Scott Hairston RC 5.00 1.50
117 Jason Simontacchi RC 1.00 .30
118 Taggert Bozied RC 5.00 1.50
119 Shelley Duncan RC 1.00 .30
120 Dontrelle Willis RC 25.00 7.50
121 Sean Burnett .40 .12
122 Aaron Cook .60 .18
123 Brett Evert .40 .12
124 Jimmy Journell .40 .12
125 Brett Myers .60 .18
126 Brad Baker .40 .12
127 Billy Traber RC 3.00 .90
128 Adam Wainwright .60 .18
129 Jason Young 1.00 .30
130 John Buck .40 .12
131 Kevin Cash 1.00 .30
132 Jason Stokes RC 15.00 4.50
133 Drew Henson .60 .18
134 Chad Tracy RC 5.00 1.50
135 Orlando Hudson .40 .12
136 Brandon Phillips .40 .12
137 Joe Borchard .60 .18
138 Marlon Byrd .60 .18
139 Carl Crawford .60 .18
140 Michael Restovich .40 .12
141 Corey Hart RC 5.00 1.50
142 Edwin Almonte .60 .18
143 Francis Beltran RC 1.00 .30
144 Jorge De La Rosa RC 1.00 .30
145 Gerardo Garcia RC 1.00 .30
146 Franklyn German RC 1.00 .30
147 Francisco Liriano .60 .18
148 Francisco Rodriguez .60 .18
149 Ricardo Rodriguez .40 .12
150 Seung Song .40 .12
151 John Stephens .40 .12
152 Justin Huber RC 3.00 .90
153 Victor Martinez .60 .18
154 Hee Seop Choi 1.00 .30
155 Justin Morneau 1.00 .30
156 Miguel Cabrera 3.00 .90
157 Victor Diaz RC 5.00 1.50
158 Jose Reyes 1.50 .45
159 Omar Infante .40 .12
160 Angel Berroa .60 .18
161 Tony Alvarez .40 .12
162 Shin Soo Choo RC 5.00 1.50
163 Wily Mo Pena .40 .12
164 Andres Torres .40 .12
165 Jose Lopez RC 8.00 2.40
166 Scott Moore AU RC 20.00 6.00
167 Chris Gruler AU RC 15.00 4.50
168 Joe Saunders AU RC 15.00 4.50
169 Jeff Francis AU RC 15.00 4.50
170 Royce Ring AU RC 15.00 4.50
171 Greg Miller AU RC 40.00 12.00
172 Brandon Weeden AU RC 15.00 4.50
173 Drew Meyer AU RC 15.00 4.50
174 Khalil Greene AU RC 50.00 15.00
175 Mark Schramek AU RC 15.00 4.50

2002 Bowman Chrome Draft Gold Refractors

Issued at a stated rate of one in 67 Bowman Draft packs, these cards are gold refractors of the Bowman Chrome Draft set. Those cards have a stated print run of 50 serial numbered sets. Cards numbered 166 through 175, which are autographed were issued at a stated rate of one in 1546 Bowman Draft cards and there is no pricing provided on these cards due to market scarcity.

Nm-Mt Ex-Mt
*GOLD REF 1-165: 8X TO 20X BASIC
*GOLD REF RC 1-165: 7.5X TO 15X BASIC
1-165 ODDS 1:67 BOWMAN DRAFT
166-175 AU ODDS 1:1546 BOWMAN DRAFT
1-165 PRINT RUN 50 SERIAL #'d SETS
166-175 ARE NOT SERIAL-NUMBERED
166-175 NO PRICING DUE TO SCARCITY

2002 Bowman Chrome Draft Refractors

Issued at a stated rate of one in 11 Bowman Draft packs, these cards are refractor parallels of the Bowman Chrome Draft set. Those cards have a stated print run of 300 serial numbered sets. Cards numbered 166 through 175, which are autographed were issued at a stated rate of one in 154 Bowman Draft packs.

Nm-Mt Ex-Mt
*REFRACTOR 1-165: 2.5X TO 6X BASIC
*REFRACTOR RC 1-165: 2X TO 5X BASIC
*REFRACTOR 166-175: .6X TO 1.2X BASIC

2002 Bowman Chrome Draft X-Fractors

Issued at a stated rate of one in 22 Bowman Draft packs, these cards are x-fractor parallels of the Bowman Chrome Draft set. Those cards have a stated print run of 150 serial numbered sets. Cards numbered 166 through 175, which are autographed were issued at a stated rate of one in 309 Bowman Draft packs.

Nm-Mt Ex-Mt
*X-FRACTOR 1-165: 3X TO 8X BASIC
*X-FRACTOR RC 1-165: 3X TO 6X BASIC
*X-FRACTOR 166-175: .75X TO 1.5X BASIC

2003 Bowman Chrome

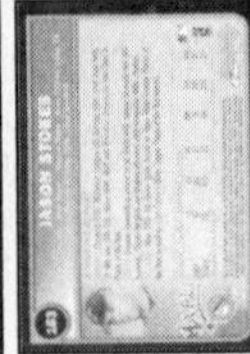

This 351 card set was released in July, 2003. The set was issued in four-card packs with an $4 SRP which came 18 to a box and 12 boxes to a case. Cards numbered 1 through 165 feature veteran players while cards 166 through 330 feature rookie players. Cards numbered 331 through 350 feature autograph cards of Rookie Cards. Each of those cards, with the exception of Jose Contreras (number 332) was issued to a stated print run of 1700 sets and were seeded at a stated rate of one in 26. The Contreras card was issued to a stated print run of 340 cards and was issued at a stated rate of one in 3,3351 packs. The final card of the set features baseball legend Willie Mays. That card was issued as a box-loader and an authentic autograph on that card was also randomly inserted into packs. The autograph card was inserted at a stated rate of one in 384 box loader packs and was issued to a stated print run of 150 sets. Bryan Bullington did not return his cards in time for pack out and those cards could be redeemed until July 31, 2005.

MINT NRMT
COMPLETE SET (351) 600.00 275.00
COMP.SET w/o AU's (331) 200.00 90.00
COMMON CARD (1-165) .50 .23
COMMON CARD (166-330) .50 .23
COMMON RC (156-330) 1.00 .45
COMP.SET w/o AU'S INCLUDES 351 MAYS
MAYS AU IS NOT PART OF 351-CARD SET
1 Garret Anderson .50 .23
2 Derek Jeter 3.00 1.35
3 Gary Sheffield .50 .23
4 Matt Morris .50 .23
5 Derek Lowe .50 .23
6 Andy Van Hekken .50 .23
7 Sammy Sosa 2.00 .90
8 Ken Griffey Jr. 2.00 .90
9 Omar Vizquel .50 .23
10 Jorge Posada .75 .35
11 Lance Berkman .50 .23
12 Mike Sweeney .50 .23
13 Adrian Beltre .50 .23
14 Richie Sexson .50 .23
15 A.J. Pierzynski .50 .23
16 Bartolo Colon .50 .23
17 Mike Mussina 1.25 .55
18 Paul Byrd .50 .23
19 Bobby Abreu .50 .23
20 Miguel Tejada .50 .23
21 Aramis Ramirez .50 .23
22 Edgardo Alfonzo .50 .23
23 Edgar Martinez .75 .35
24 Albert Pujols 2.50 1.10
25 Carl Crawford .50 .23
26 Eric Hinske .50 .23
27 Tim Salmon .75 .35
28 Luis Gonzalez .50 .23
29 Jay Gibbons .50 .23
30 John Smoltz .50 .23
31 Tim Wakefield .50 .23
32 Mark Prior 2.50 1.10
33 Magglio Ordonez .50 .23
34 Adam Dunn .50 .23
35 Larry Walker .75 .35
36 Luis Castillo .50 .23
37 Wade Miller .50 .23
38 Carlos Beltran .50 .23
39 Odalis Perez .50 .23
40 Alex Sanchez .50 .23
41 Torii Hunter .50 .23
42 Cliff Floyd .50 .23
43 Andy Pettitte .75 .35
44 Francisco Rodriguez .50 .23
45 Eric Chavez .50 .23
46 Kevin Millwood .50 .23
47 Dennis Tankersley .50 .23
48 Hideo Nomo 1.25 .55
49 Freddy Garcia .50 .23
50 Randy Johnson 1.25 .55
51 Aubrey Huff .50 .23
52 Carlos Delgado .50 .23
53 Troy Glaus .75 .35
54 Junior Spivey .50 .23
55 Mike Hampton .50 .23
56 Sidney Ponson .50 .23
57 Aaron Boone .50 .23
58 Kerry Wood 1.25 .55
59 Willie Harris .50 .23
60 Nomar Garciaparra 2.00 .90
61 Todd Helton .75 .35
62 Mike Lowell .50 .23
63 Roy Oswalt .50 .23
64 Raul Ibanez .50 .23
65 Brian Jordan .50 .23
66 Geoff Jenkins .50 .23
67 Jermaine Dye .50 .23
68 Tom Glavine .75 .35
69 Bernie Williams .75 .35
70 Vladimir Guerrero 1.25 .55
71 Mark Mulder .50 .23
72 Jimmy Rollins .50 .23
73 Oliver Perez .50 .23
74 Rich Aurilia .50 .23
75 Joel Pineiro .50 .23
76 J.D. Drew .50 .23
77 Ivan Rodriguez 1.25 .55
78 Josh Phelps .50 .23
79 Darin Erstad .50 .23
80 Curt Schilling .75 .35
81 Paul Lo Duca .50 .23
82 Marty Cordova .50 .23
83 Manny Ramirez .50 .23
84 Bobby Hill .50 .23
85 Paul Konerko .50 .23
86 Austin Kearns .50 .23
87 Jason Jennings .50 .23
88 Brad Penny .50 .23
89 Jeff Bagwell .75 .35
90 Shawn Green .50 .23
91 Jason Schmidt .50 .23
92 Doug Mientkiewicz .50 .23
93 Jose Vidro .50 .23
94 Bret Boone .50 .23
95 Jason Giambi 1.25 .55
96 Barry Zito .50 .23
97 Roy Halladay .50 .23
98 Pat Burrell .50 .23
99 Sean Burroughs .50 .23
100 Barry Bonds 3.00 1.35
101 Kazuhiro Sasaki .50 .23
102 Fernando Vina .50 .23
103 Chan Ho Park .50 .23
104 Andruw Jones .50 .23
105 Adam Kennedy .50 .23
106 Shea Hillenbrand .50 .23
107 Greg Maddux 2.00 .90
108 Jim Edmonds .50 .23
109 Pedro Martinez 1.25 .55
110 Moises Alou .50 .23
111 Jeff Weaver .50 .23
112 C.C. Sabathia .50 .23
113 Robert Fick .50 .23
114 A.J. Burnett .50 .23
115 Jeff Kent .50 .23
116 Kevin Brown .50 .23
117 Rafael Furcal .50 .23
118 Cristian Guzman .50 .23
119 Brad Wilkerson .50 .23
120 Mike Piazza 2.00 .90
121 Alfonso Soriano .75 .35
122 Mark Ellis .50 .23
123 Vicente Padilla .50 .23
124 Eric Gagne .75 .35
125 Ryan Klesko .50 .23
126 Ichiro Suzuki 2.00 .90
127 Tony Batista .50 .23
128 Roberto Alomar 1.25 .55
129 Alex Rodriguez 2.00 .90
130 Jim Thome 1.25 .55
131 Jarrod Washburn .50 .23
132 Orlando Hudson .50 .23
133 Chipper Jones 1.25 .55
134 Rodrigo Lopez .50 .23
135 Johnny Damon .50 .23
136 Matt Clement .50 .23
137 Frank Thomas 1.25 .55
138 Ellis Burks .50 .23
139 Carlos Pena .50 .23
140 Josh Beckett .75 .35
141 Joe Randa .50 .23
142 Brian Giles .50 .23
143 Kazuhisa Ishii .50 .23
144 Corey Koskie .50 .23
145 Orlando Cabrera .50 .23
146 Mark Buehrle .50 .23
147 Roger Clemens 2.50 1.10
148 Tim Hudson .50 .23
149 Randy Wolf .50 .23
150 Josh Fogg .50 .23
151 Phil Nevin .50 .23
152 John Olerud .50 .23
153 Scott Rolen .75 .35
154 Joe Kennedy .50 .23
155 Rafael Palmeiro .75 .35
156 Chad Hutchinson .50 .23
157 Quincy Carter XRC 2.00 .90
158 Hee Seop Choi .50 .23
159 Joe Borchard .50 .23
160 Brandon Phillips .50 .23
161 Wily Mo Pena .50 .23
162 Victor Martinez .50 .23
163 Jason Stokes 1.25 .55
164 Ken Harvey .50 .23
165 Juan Rivera .50 .23
166 Joe Valentine RC 1.50 .70
167 Dan Haren RC 4.00 1.80
168 Michel Hernandez RC 1.50 .70
169 Eider Torres RC 1.50 .70
170 Chris De La Cruz RC 1.50 .70
171 Ramon Nivar-Martinez RC 3.00 1.35
172 Mike Adams RC 1.50 .70
173 Justin Arneson RC 1.50 .70
174 Jamie Athas RC 1.50 .70
175 Dwaine Bacon RC 1.50 .70
176 Clint Barmes RC 2.00 .90
177 B.J. Barns RC 1.50 .70
178 Tyler Johnson RC 1.50 .70
179 Brandon Webb RC 10.00 4.50
180 T.J. Bohn RC 1.50 .70
181 Ozzie Chavez RC 1.50 .70
182 Brandon Bowe RC 1.50 .70
183 Craig Brazell RC 2.00 .90
184 Dusty Brown RC 1.50 .70
185 Brian Bruney RC 2.00 .90
186 Greg Bruso RC 1.50 .70
187 Jaime Bubela RC 1.50 .70
188 Matt Diaz RC 3.00 1.35
189 Brian Burgamy RC 1.50 .70
190 Eny Cabreja RC 1.50 .70
191 Daniel Cabrera RC 1.50 .70
192 Ryan Cameron RC 1.50 .70
193 Lance Caracciolі RC 1.50 .70
194 David Cash RC 1.50 .70
195 Bernie Castro RC 1.50 .70
196 Ismael Castro RC 2.00 .90
197 Cory Doyne RC 1.50 .70
198 Jeff Clark RC 1.50 .70
199 Chris Colton RC 1.50 .70
200 Dexter Cooper RC 1.50 .70
201 Callix Crabbe RC 2.00 .90
202 Chien-Ming Wang RC 6.00 2.70
203 Eric Crozier RC 2.00 .90
204 Nook Logan RC 1.50 .70
205 David DeJesus RC 3.00 1.35
206 Matt DeMarco RC 1.50 .70
207 Chris Duncan RC 1.50 .70
208 Eric Eckenstahler .50 .23
209 Willie Eyre RC 1.50 .70
210 Evel Bastida-Martinez RC 1.50 .70
211 Chris Fallon RC 1.50 .70
212 Mike Flannery RC 1.50 .70
213 Mike O'Keefe RC 1.50 .70
214 Levi Ford RC 2.00 .90
215 Kason Gabbard RC 1.50 .70
216 Mike Gallo RC 1.50 .70
217 Jairo Garcia RC 1.50 .70
218 Angel Garcia RC 2.00 .90
219 Michael Garciaparra RC 3.00 1.35
220 Jeremy Griffiths RC 2.00 .90
221 Dusty Gomon RC 3.00 1.35
222 Bryan Grace RC 1.50 .70
223 Tyson Graham RC 1.50 .70
224 Henry Guerrero RC 1.50 .70
225 Franklin Gutierrez RC 10.00 4.50
226 Carlos Guzman RC 2.00 .90
227 Matthew Hagen RC 3.00 1.35
228 Josh Hall RC 2.00 .90
229 Rob Hammock RC 2.00 .90
230 Brendan Harris RC 2.00 .90
231 Gary Harris RC 1.50 .70
232 Clay Hensley RC 1.50 .70
233 Michael Hinckley RC 3.00 1.35
234 Luis Hodge RC 1.50 .70
235 Donnie Hood RC 2.00 .90
236 Matt Hensley RC 1.50 .70
237 Edwin Jackson RC 10.00 4.50
238 Ardley Jansen RC 2.00 .90
239 Ferenc Jongejan RC 1.50 .70
240 Matt Kata RC 3.00 1.35
241 Kazuhiro Takeoka RC 1.50 .70
242 Charlie Manning RC 1.50 .70
243 Il Kim RC 1.50 .70
244 Brennan King RC 1.50 .70
245 Chris Kroski RC 1.50 .70
246 David Martinez RC 1.50 .70
247 Pete LaForest RC 2.00 .90
248 Wil Ledezma RC 1.50 .70
249 Jeremy Bonderman RC 4.00 1.80
250 Gonzalo Lopez RC 1.50 .70
251 Brian Luderer RC 1.50 .70

252 Ruddy Lugo RC 1.50 .70
253 Wayne Lydon RC 1.50 .70
254 Mark Malaska RC 1.50 .70
255 Andy Marte RC 15.00 6.75
256 Tyler Martin RC 1.50 .70
257 Branden Florence RC 1.50 .70
258 Aneudis Mateo RC 1.50 .70
259 Derell McCall RC 1.50 .70
260 Elizardo Ramirez RC 4.00 1.80
261 Mike McNutt RC 1.50 .70
262 Jacobo Meque RC 1.50 .70
263 Derek Michaelis RC 2.00 .90
264 Aaron Miles RC 4.00 1.80
265 Jose Morales RC 1.50 .70
266 Dustin Moseley RC 2.00 .90
267 Adrian Myers RC 1.50 .70
268 Dan Neil RC 1.50 .70
269 Jon Nelson RC 2.00 .90
270 Mike Neu RC 1.50 .70
271 Leigh Neuage RC 1.50 .70
272 Wes O'Brien RC 1.50 .70
273 Trent Oeltjen RC 2.00 .90
274 Tim Olson RC 2.00 .90
275 David Pahucki RC 1.50 .70
276 Nathan Panther RC 3.00 1.35
277 Arnie Munoz RC 1.50 .70
278 Dave Pember RC 1.50 .70
279 Jason Perry RC 3.00 1.35
280 Matthew Peterson RC 1.50 .70
281 Greg Aquino RC 1.50 .70
282 Jorge Piedra RC 2.00 .90
283 Simon Pond RC 3.00 1.35
284 Aaron Rakers RC 1.50 .70
285 Felix Sanchez RC 1.50 .70
286 Manuel Ramirez RC 2.00 .90
287 Kevin Randel RC 1.50 .70
288 Kelly Shoppach RC 5.00 2.20
289 Prentice Redman RC 1.50 .70
290 Eric Reed RC 3.00 1.35
291 Wilton Reynolds RC 2.00 .90
292 Eric Riggs RC 2.00 .90
293 Carlos Rijo RC 1.50 .70
294 Tyler Adamczyk RC 1.50 .70
295 Jon-Mark Sprowl RC 3.00 1.35
296 Arturo Rivas RC 1.50 .70
297 Kyle Roat RC 1.50 .70
298 Bubba Nelson RC 1.25 .55
299 Levi Robinson RC 1.50 .70
300 Ray Sadler RC 1.50 .70
301 Rylan Reed RC 1.50 .70
302 Jon Schuerholz RC 1.50 .70
303 Nobuaki Yoshida RC 1.50 .70
304 Brian Shackelford RC 1.50 .70
305 Bill Simon RC 1.50 .70
306 Haj Turay RC 2.00 .90
307 Sean Smith RC 2.00 .90
308 Ryan Spataro RC 1.50 .70
309 Jemel Spearman RC 1.50 .70
310 Keith Stamler RC 1.50 .70
311 Luke Steidlmayer RC 1.50 .70
312 Adam Stern RC 1.50 .70
313 Jay Sitzman RC 1.50 .70
314 Mike Wodnicki RC 1.50 .70
315 Terry Tiffee RC 2.00 .90
316 Nick Trzesniak RC 1.50 .70
317 Denny Tussen RC 1.50 .70
318 Scott Tyler RC 2.00 .90
319 Shane Victorino RC 1.50 .70
320 Doug Waechter RC 2.00 .90
321 Brandon Watson RC 1.50 .70
322 Todd Wellemeyer RC 2.00 .90
323 Eli Whiteside RC 1.50 .70
324 Josh Willingham RC 5.00 2.20
325 Travis Wong RC 2.00 .90
326 Brian Wright RC 1.50 .70
327 Felix Pie RC 12.00 5.50
328 Andy Sisco RC 5.00 2.20
329 Dustin Yount RC 3.00 1.35
330 Andrew Dominique RC 1.50 .70
331 Brian McCann AU A RC 20.00 9.00
332 Jose Contreras AU B RC 200.00 90.00
333 Corey Shafer AU A RC 20.00 9.00
334 Hanley Ramirez AU A RC 40.00 18.00
335 Ryan Shealy AU A RC 20.00 9.00
336 Kevin Youkilis AU A RC 40.00 18.00
337 Jason Kubel AU A RC 20.00 9.00
338 Aron Weston AU A RC 15.00 6.75
338B Rajai Davis AU A ERR
339 J.D. Durbin AU A RC 20.00 9.00
340 G. Schneidmiller AU A RC 15.00 6.75
341 Travis Ishikawa AU A RC 20.00 9.00
342 Ben Francisco AU A RC 20.00 9.00
343 Bobby Basham AU A RC 20.00 9.00
344 Joey Gomes AU A RC 15.00 6.75
345 Beau Kemp AU A RC 15.00 6.75
346 T.Story-Harden AU A RC 15.00 6.75
347 Daryl Clark AU A RC 20.00 9.00
348 B.Bullington AU A RC EXCH 30.00 13.50
349 Rajai Davis AU A RC 20.00 9.00
350 Darrell Rasner AU A RC 15.00 6.75
351 Willie Mays 2.00 .90
351AU Willie Mays AU 300.00 135.00

2003 Bowman Chrome Blue Refractors

These cards were issued at a stated rate of one per box loader pack. Each of those packs contained an exchange card for an uncirculated card of which had to be redeemed from ThePit.Com by November, 30, 2005.

MINT NRMT
SEE WWW.THEPIT.COM FOR PRICING
NNO Exchange Card 15.00 6.75

2003 Bowman Chrome Gold Refractors

This is a full parallel to the 2003 Bowman Chrome set. Cards 1-330 were issued at a stated rate of one per box loader pack. The cards 331-350 were inserted at much tougher odds. Cards 331-350 (except for number 332) were issued at a stated rate of one in 1202 hobby packs and were issued to a stated print run of 50 sets. Card number 332 was issued at a stated rate of one in 177,606 hobby packs and was issued to a stated rate of 10 sets. The Willie Mays card (number 351) was issued at a stated rate of one in 116 box loader packs. There were also cards inserted for a complete set of these randomly inserted in packs at a stated rate of one in 78,936 packs. That exchange card was issued to a stated print run on 10 sets and those cards could be redeemed until November 30, 2005.

MINT NRMT
*GOLD REF 1-155: 4X TO 10X BASIC
*GOLD REF 156-330: 4X TO 10X BASIC
*GOLD REF RC'S 156-330: 3X TO 8X BASIC
1-330 ODDS ONE PER BOX LOADER PACK
1-330 PRINT RUN 170 SERIAL #'d SETS
*GOLD REF AU A 331/333-350: 2X TO 4X BASIC
NNO Set Exchange Card

2003 Bowman Chrome Refractors

This is a complete parallel to the regular Bowman Chrome set. Cards numbered 1-330 were issued at a stated rate of one in four hobby packs. Cards numbers 331-350 (with the exception of number 332) were issued at a stated rate of one in 92 packs. Those cards were issued to a stated print run of 500 sets. Card number 332 was issued at a stated rate of one in 11,479 packs and was issued to a stated print run of 100 sets. Card number 351 featuring Willie Mays was issued at a stated rate of one in 12 box loader packs.

MINT NRMT
*REF 1-155: 2X TO 5X BASIC
*REF 156-330: 2X TO 5X BASIC
*REF 156-330 RC'S: 1X TO 2.5X BASIC
*REF AU A 331/333-350: .5X TO 1.2X BASIC
*REF.MAYS: 2X TO 5X BASIC

2003 Bowman Chrome X-Fractors

This is a complete parallel to the basic Bowman Chrome set. Cards numbered 1-330 were issued at a stated rate of one in nine hobby packs. Cards numbered 331-350 (with the exception of number 332) were issued at a stated rate of one in 199 hobby packs and were issued to a stated print run of 250 sets. The Jose Contreras Card (number 332) was issued at a stated rate of one in 22,959 sets and was issued to a stated print run of 50 sets. The Willie Mays card (number 351) was issued at a stated rate of one in 58 box loader packs.

MINT NRMT
*X-FR 1-155: 2.5X TO 6X BASIC
*X-FR 156-330: 2.5X TO 6X BASIC
*X-FR RC'S 156-330: 1.25X TO 3X BASIC
*X-FR AU A 331/333-350: .6X TO 1.5X BASIC
*X-FR MAYS: 4X TO 10X BASIC

2003 Bowman Chrome Draft

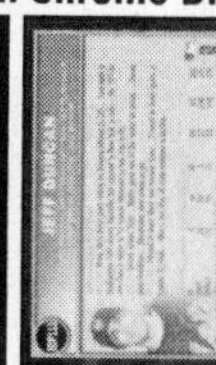

This 176-card set was inserted as part of the 2003 Bowman Draft Packs. Each pack contained 2 Bowman Chrome Cards numbered between 1-165. In addition, cards numbered 166 through 176 were inserted at a stated rate of one in 41 packs. Each of those cards can be easily idenitifed as they were autographed. Please note that these cards were issued as a mix of live and exchange cards with a deadline for redeeming the exchange cards of November 30, 2005.

MINT NRMT
COMPLETE SET (176) 350.00 160.00
COMP.SET w/o AU's (165) 120.00 55.00
COMMON CARD (1-165) .40 .18
1-165 TWO PER BOWMAN DRAFT PACK
COMMON CARD (166-176) 20.00 9.00
166-176 STATED ODDS 1:41 H/R
168-176 ARE ALL PARTIAL LIVE/EXCH DIST.
168-176 EXCH.DEADLINE 11/30/05
1 Dontrelle Willis 1.50 .70
2 Freddy Sanchez .40 .18
3 Miguel Cabrera 1.50 .70
4 Ryan Ludwick .40 .18
5 Ty Wigginton .60 .25
6 Mark Teixeira 1.00 .45
7 Trey Hodges .40 .18
8 Laynce Nix 1.50 .70
9 Antonio Perez .40 .18
10 Jody Gerut .60 .25
11 Jae Weong Seo .40 .18
12 Erick Almonte .40 .18
13 Lyle Overbay .40 .18
14 Billy Traber .40 .18
15 Andres Torres .40 .18
16 Jose Valverde .40 .18
17 Aaron Heilman .40 .18
18 Brandon Larson .40 .18
19 Jung Bong .40 .18
20 Jesse Foppert .60 .25
21 Angel Berroa .60 .25
22 Jeff DaVanon .40 .18
23 Kurt Ainsworth .40 .18
24 Brandon Claussen .60 .25
25 Xavier Nady .40 .18
26 Travis Hafner .60 .25
27 Jerome Williams .60 .25
28 Jose Reyes 1.00 .45
29 Sergio Mitre RC 2.50 1.10
30 Bo Hart RC 5.00 2.20
31 Adam Miller RC 2.50 1.10
32 Brian Finch RC 1.00 .45
33 Taylor Mattingly RC 8.00 3.60
34 Daric Barton RC 5.00 2.20
35 Chris Ray RC 1.50 .70
36 Jarrod Saltalamacchia RC 2.50 1.10
37 Dennis Dove RC 1.50 .70
38 James Houser RC 2.50 1.10
39 Clint King RC 4.00 1.80
40 Lou Palmisano RC 6.00 2.70
41 Dan Moore RC 1.00 .45
42 Craig Stansberry RC 2.50 1.10
43 Jo Jo Reyes RC 2.50 1.10
44 Jake Stevens RC 1.50 .70
45 Tom Gorzelanny RC 1.50 .70
46 Brian Marshall RC 1.00 .45
47 Scott Beerer RC 1.00 .45
48 Javi Herrera RC 1.50 .70
49 Steve LeRud RC 2.50 1.10
50 Josh Banks RC 3.00 1.35
51 Jon Papelbon RC 1.00 .45
52 Juan Valdes RC 1.50 .70
53 Beau Vaughan RC 1.50 .70
54 Matt Chico RC 2.50 1.10
55 Todd Jennings RC 1.50 .70
56 Anthony Gwynn RC 5.00 2.20
57 Matt Harrison RC 1.50 .70
58 Aaron Marsden RC 1.50 .70
59 Casey Abrams RC 1.00 .45
60 Cory Stuart RC 1.00 .45
61 Mike Wagner RC 1.00 .45
62 Jordan Pratt RC 1.50 .70
63 Andre Randolph RC 1.50 .70
64 Blake Balkcom RC 2.50 1.10
65 Josh Muecke RC 1.00 .45
66 Jamie D'Antona RC 6.00 2.70
67 Cole Seifrig RC 6.00 2.70
68 Josh Anderson RC 1.50 .70
69 Matt Lorenzo RC 1.50 .70
70 Nate Spears RC 2.50 1.10
71 Chris Goodman RC 1.00 .45
72 Brian McFall RC 2.50 1.10
73 Billy Hogan RC 3.00 1.35
74 Jamie Romak RC 2.50 1.10
75 Jeff Cook RC 1.50 .70
76 Brooks McNiven RC 1.00 .45
77 Xavier Paul RC 8.00 3.60
78 Bob Zimmerman RC 1.00 .45
79 Mickey Hall RC 3.00 1.35
80 Shaun Marcum RC 1.00 .45
81 Matt Nachreiner RC 2.50 1.10
82 Chris Kinsey RC 1.00 .45
83 Jonathan Fulton RC 1.50 .70
84 Edgardo Baez RC 2.50 1.10
85 Robert Valido RC 8.00 3.60
86 Kenny Lewis RC 2.50 1.10
87 Trent Peterson RC 1.00 .45
88 Johnny Woodard RC 1.50 .70
89 Wes Littleton RC 2.50 1.10
90 Sean Rodriguez RC 3.00 1.35
91 Kyle Pearson RC 1.00 .45
92 Josh Rainwater RC 2.50 1.10
93 Travis Schlichting RC 2.50 1.10
94 Tim Battle RC 1.50 .70
95 Aaron Hill RC 5.00 2.20
96 Bob McCrory RC 1.00 .45
97 Rick Guarno RC 1.00 .45
98 Brandon Yarbrough RC 1.00 .45
99 Peter Stonard RC 1.00 .45
100 Darin Downs RC 2.50 1.10
101 Matt Bruback RC 1.00 .45
102 Danny Garcia RC 1.00 .45
103 Cory Stewart RC 1.00 .45
104 Ferdin Tejeda RC 1.00 .45
105 Kade Johnson RC 1.00 .45
106 Andrew Brown RC 1.00 .45
107 Aquilino Lopez RC 1.00 .45
108 Stephen Randolph RC 1.00 .45
109 Dave Matranga RC 1.00 .45
110 Dustin McGowan RC 3.00 1.35
111 Juan Camacho RC 1.00 .45
112 Cliff Lee .40 .18
113 Jeff Duncan RC 1.50 .70
114 C.J. Wilson .40 .18
115 Brandon Roberson RC 1.00 .45
116 David Corrente RC 1.00 .45
117 Kevin Beavers RC 1.00 .45
118 Anthony Webster RC 2.50 1.10
119 Oscar Villarreal RC 1.00 .45
120 Hong-Chih Kuo RC 2.50 1.10
121 Josh Barfield 1.00 .45
122 Denny Bautista .40 .18
123 Chris Burke RC 1.50 .70
124 Robinson Cano RC 1.50 .70
125 Jose Castillo .60 .25
126 Neal Cotts .40 .18
127 Jorge De La Rosa .40 .18
128 J.D. Durbin .40 .18
129 Edwin Encarnacion .40 .18
130 Gavin Floyd .60 .25
131 Alexis Gomez .40 .18
132 Edgar Gonzalez RC 1.00 .45
133 Khalil Greene 1.00 .45
134 Zack Greinke 1.50 .70
135 Franklin Gutierrez 2.50 1.10
136 Rich Harden 1.00 .45
137 J.J. Hardy RC 6.00 2.70
138 Ryan Howard RC 3.00 1.35
139 Justin Huber .60 .25
140 David Kelton .40 .18
141 Dave Krynzel .40 .18
142 Pete LaForest 1.00 .45
143 Adam LaRoche 1.00 .45
144 Preston Larrison RC 1.50 .70
145 John Maine RC 6.00 2.70
146 Andy Marte 5.00 2.20
147 Jeff Mathis .60 .25
148 Joe Mauer 1.50 .70
149 Clint Nageotte .60 .25
150 Chris Narveson .40 .18
151 Ramon Nivar 1.50 .70
152 Felix Pie 4.00 1.80
153 Guillermo Quiroz RC 4.00 1.80
154 Rene Reyes .40 .18
155 Royce Ring .40 .18
156 Alexis Rios 8.00 3.60
157 Grady Sizemore 1.00 .45
158 Stephen Smitherman .40 .18
159 Seung Song .40 .18
160 Scott Thorman .40 .18
161 Chad Tracy .60 .25
162 Chin-Hui Tsao .60 .25
163 John VanBenschoten .60 .25
164 Kevin Youkilis 2.50 1.10
165 Chien-Ming Wang 2.50 1.10
166 Chris Lubanski AU RC 25.00 11.00
167 Ryan Harvey AU RC 50.00 22.00
168 Matt Murton AU RC 20.00 9.00
169 Jay Sborz AU RC 20.00 9.00
170 Brandon Wood AU RC 25.00 11.00
171 Nick Markakis AU RC 25.00 11.00
172 Rickie Weeks AU RC 60.00 27.00
173 Eric Duncan AU RC 30.00 13.50
174 Chad Billingsley AU RC 20.00 9.00
175 Ryan Wagner AU RC 25.00 11.00
176 Delmon Young AU RC 70.00 32.00

2003 Bowman Chrome Draft Gold Refractors

MINT NRMT
*GOLD REF 1-165: 8X TO 20X BASIC
*GOLD REF RC 1-165: 10X TO 20X BASIC
*GOLD REF RC YR 1-165: 7.5X TO 15X BASIC
1-165 ODDS 1:98 BOWMAN DRAFT HOBBY
166-176 AU ODDS 1:1479 BOW.DRAFT HOBBY
1-165 PRINT RUN 50 SERIAL #'d SETS
166-176 AU PRINT RUN 50 SETS
166-176 AU PRINT RUN PROVIDED BY TOPPS
166-176 AU'S ARE NOT SERIAL-NUMBERED
GOLD.REF ARE HOBBY-ONLY DISTRIBUTION

2003 Bowman Chrome Draft Refractors

MINT NRMT
*REFRACTOR 1-165: 1.5X TO 4X BASIC
*REFRACTOR RC 1-165: 1.25X TO 3X BASIC
*REFRACTOR RC YR 1-165: 1.5X TO 4X BASIC
*REFRACTOR AU 166-176: .5X TO 1.2X BASIC
1-165 ODDS 1:11 BOWMAN DRAFT H/R
166-176 AU ODDS 1:196 BOW.DRAFT HOBBY
166-176 AU ODDS 1:197 BOW.DRAFT RETAIL
166-176 AU PRINT RUN 500 SETS
166-176 AU PRINT RUN PROVIDED BY TOPPS
166-176 AU'S ARE NOT SERIAL-NUMBERED

2003 Bowman Chrome Draft X-Fractors

MINT NRMT
*X-FRACTOR 1-165: 3X TO 8X BASIC
*X-FRACTOR RC 1-165: 2.5X TO 6X BASIC
*X-FRACTOR RC YR 1-165: 2.5X TO 6X BASIC
*X-FRACTOR AU 166-176: .75X TO 2X BASIC
1-165 ODDS 1:50 BOWMAN DRAFT HOBBY
1-165 ODDS 1:52 BOWMAN DRAFT RETAIL
166-176 AU ODDS 1:393 BOW.DRAFT HOBBY
166-176 AU ODDS 1:394 BOW.DRAFT RETAIL
1-165 PRINT RUN 130 SERIAL #'d SETS
166-176 AU PRINT RUN 250 SETS
166-176 AU PRINT RUN PROVIDED BY TOPPS
166-176 AU'S ARE NOT SERIAL-NUMBERED

2001 Bowman Heritage Promos

This five-card set was distributed in a sealed plastic cello wrap to dealers and people that attended the 2001 National Convention in Cleveland, a few months prior to the release of 2001 Bowman Heritage to allow a sneak preview of the upcoming brand. Please note that a sealed piece of gum was issued in the cello packs.

Nm-Mt Ex-Mt
COMPLETE SET (5) 100.00 30.00
1 Roberto Alomar 10.00 3.00
2 Albert Pujols 50.00 15.00
3 C.C. Sabathia 10.00 3.00
4 Mark McGwire 25.00 7.50
5 Juan Gonzalez 8.00 2.40

2001 Bowman Heritage

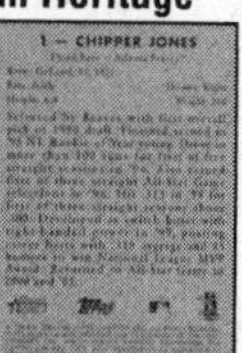

This 440-card product was issued in 10 card packs, along with a slab of gum, with an SRP of $3 per pack. The packs were issued 16 to a box with 24 boxes to a case. Cards numbered 331-440 were inserted at a rate of one every two packs.

Nm-Mt Ex-Mt
COMPLETE SET (440) 250.00 75.00
COMP.SET w/o SP's (330) 50.00 15.00
COMMON CARD (1-330) .40 .12
COMMON RC (1-330) .50 .15
COMMON (331-440) 2.00 .60
1 Chipper Jones 1.00 .30
2 Pete Harnisch .40 .12
3 Brian Giles .75 .23
4 J.T. Snow .75 .23
5 Bartolo Colon .75 .23
6 Jorge Posada .60 .18
7 Shawn Green .75 .23
8 Derek Jeter 2.50 .75
9 Benito Santiago .75 .23
10 Ramon Hernandez .40 .12
11 Bernie Williams .60 .18
12 Greg Maddux 1.50 .45
13 Barry Bonds 2.50 .75
14 Roger Clemens 2.00 .60
15 Miguel Tejada .75 .23
16 Pedro Feliz .40 .12
17 Jim Edmonds .75 .23
18 Tom Glavine .60 .18
19 David Justice .75 .23
20 Rich Aurilia .75 .23
21 Jason Giambi 1.00 .30
22 Orlando Hernandez .75 .23
23 Shawn Estes .40 .12
24 Nelson Figueroa .40 .12
25 Terrence Long .75 .23
26 Mike Mussina 1.00 .30
27 Eric Davis .75 .23
28 Jimmy Rollins .75 .23
29 Andy Pettitte .60 .18
30 Shawon Dunston .40 .12
31 Tim Hudson .75 .23
32 Jeff Kent .75 .23
33 Scott Brosius .75 .23
34 Livan Hernandez .40 .12
35 Alfonso Soriano .60 .18
36 Mark McGwire 2.50 .75
37 Russ Ortiz .75 .23
38 Fernando Vina .75 .23
39 Ken Griffey Jr. 1.50 .45
40 Edgar Renteria .75 .23
41 Kevin Brown .75 .23
42 Robb Nen .75 .23
43 Paul LoDuca .75 .23
44 Bobby Abreu .75 .23
45 Adam Dunn .75 .23
46 Osvaldo Fernandez .40 .12
47 Marvin Benard .40 .12
48 Mark Gardner .40 .12
49 Alex Rodriguez 1.50 .45
50 Preston Wilson .75 .23
51 Roberto Alomar 1.00 .30
52 Ben Davis .40 .12
53 Derek Bell .40 .12
54 Ken Caminiti .75 .23
55 Barry Zito 1.00 .30
56 Scott Rolen .60 .18
57 Geoff Jenkins .75 .23
58 Mike Cameron .75 .23
59 Ben Grieve .40 .12
60 Chuck Knoblauch .75 .23
61 Matt Lawton .40 .12
62 Chan Ho Park .75 .23
63 Lance Berkman .75 .23
64 Carlos Beltran .75 .23
65 Dean Palmer .75 .23
66 Alex Gonzalez .40 .12
67 Larry Walker .60 .18
68 Magglio Ordonez .75 .23
69 Ellis Burks .75 .23
70 Mark Mulder .75 .23
71 Randy Johnson 1.00 .30
72 John Smoltz .60 .18
73 Jerry Hairston Jr. .40 .12
74 Pedro Martinez 1.00 .30
75 Fred McGriff .60 .18
76 Sean Casey .75 .23
77 C.C. Sabathia .75 .23
78 Todd Helton .60 .18
79 Brad Penny .40 .12
80 Mike Sweeney .75 .23
81 Billy Wagner .75 .23
82 Mark Buehrle .75 .23
83 Cristian Guzman .75 .23
84 Jose Vidro .75 .23
85 Pat Burrell .75 .23
86 Jermaine Dye .75 .23
87 Brandon Inge .40 .12
88 David Wells .75 .23
89 Mike Piazza 1.50 .45
90 Jose Cabrera .40 .12
91 Cliff Floyd .75 .23
92 Matt Morris .75 .23
93 Raul Mondesi .75 .23
94 Joe Kennedy RC .50 .15
95 Jack Wilson RC .50 .15
96 Andruw Jones .75 .23
97 Mariano Rivera .60 .18
98 Mike Hampton .75 .23
99 Roger Cedeno .40 .12
100 Jose Cruz .75 .23
101 Mike Lowell .75 .23
102 Pedro Astacio .40 .12
103 Joe Mays .40 .12
104 John Franco .75 .23
105 Tim Redding .40 .12
106 Sandy Alomar Jr. .40 .12
107 Bret Boone .75 .23
108 Josh Towers RC .50 .15
109 Matt Stairs .40 .12
110 Chris Truby .40 .12
111 Jeff Suppan .40 .12
112 J.C. Romero .40 .12
113 Felipe Lopez .40 .12
114 Ben Sheets .75 .23
115 Frank Thomas 1.00 .30
116 A.J. Burnett .40 .12
117 Tony Clark .40 .12
118 Mac Suzuki .40 .12
119 Brad Radke .75 .23
120 Jeff Shaw .40 .12
121 Nick Neugebauer .40 .12
122 Kenny Lofton .75 .23
123 Jacque Jones .75 .23
124 Brent Mayne .40 .12
125 Carlos Hernandez .40 .12
126 Shane Spencer .40 .12
127 John Lackey .40 .12
128 Sterling Hitchcock .40 .12
129 Darren Dreifort .40 .12
130 Rusty Greer .75 .23
131 Michael Cuddyer .40 .12
132 Tyler Houston .40 .12
133 Chin-Feng Chen .75 .23
134 Ken Harvey .40 .12
135 Marquis Grissom .40 .12
136 Russell Branyan .40 .12
137 Eric Karros .75 .23
138 Josh Beckett .60 .18
139 Todd Zeile .75 .23
140 Corey Koskie .75 .23
141 Steve Sparks .40 .12
142 Bobby Seay .40 .12
143 Tim Raines Jr. .40 .12
144 Julio Zuleta .40 .12
145 Jose Lima .40 .12
146 Dante Bichette .75 .23
147 Randy Keisler .40 .12
148 Brent Butler .40 .12
149 Antonio Alfonseca .40 .12
150 Bryan Rekar .40 .12
151 Jeffrey Hammonds .40 .12
152 Larry Bigbie .40 .12
153 Blake Stein .40 .12
154 Robin Ventura .75 .23
155 Rondell White .75 .23
156 Juan Silvestre .40 .12
157 Marcus Thames .40 .12
158 Sidney Ponson .75 .23
159 Juan A. Pena RC .50 .15

160 C.J. Nitkowski .40 .12
161 Adam Everett .40 .12
162 Eric Munson .40 .12
163 Jason Isringhausen .75 .23
164 Brad Fullmer .40 .12
165 Miguel Olivo .40 .12
166 Fernando Tatis .40 .12
167 Freddy Garcia .75 .23
168 Tom Goodwin .40 .12
169 Armando Benitez .75 .23
170 Paul Konerko .75 .23
171 Jeff Cirillo .40 .12
172 Shane Reynolds .40 .12
173 Kevin Tapani .40 .12
174 Joe Crede .40 .12
175 Omar Infante RC 1.50 .45
176 Jake Peavy RC 2.00 .60
177 Corey Patterson .75 .23
178 Mike Penney RC .50 .15
179 Jeromy Burnitz .75 .23
180 David Segui .40 .12
181 Marcus Giles .75 .23
182 Paul O'Neill .60 .18
183 John Olerud .75 .23
184 Andy Benes .40 .12
185 Brad Cresse .40 .12
186 Ricky Ledee .40 .12
187 Allen Levrault UER .40 .12
Last name misspelled Leveralt
188 Royce Clayton .40 .12
189 Kelly Johnson RC .50 .15
190 Quilvio Veras .40 .12
191 Mike Williams .40 .12
192 Jason Lane RC .75 .23
193 Rick Helling .40 .12
194 Tim Wakefield .75 .23
195 James Baldwin .40 .12
196 Cody Ransom RC .50 .15
197 Bobby Kielty .40 .12
198 Bobby Jones .40 .12
199 Steve Cox .40 .12
200 Jamal Strong RC .50 .15
201 Steve Lomasney .40 .12
202 Brian Cardwell RC .50 .15
203 Mike Matheny .40 .12
204 Jeff Randazzo RC .50 .15
205 Aubrey Huff .75 .23
206 Chuck Finley .75 .23
207 Denny Bautista RC 1.50 .45
208 Terry Mulholland .40 .12
209 Rey Ordonez .40 .12
210 Keith Surkont RC .50 .15
211 Orlando Cabrera .40 .12
212 Juan Encarnacion .40 .12
213 Dustin Hermanson .40 .12
214 Luis Rivas .40 .12
215 Mark Quinn .40 .12
216 Randy Velarde .40 .12
217 Billy Koch .40 .12
218 Ryan Rupe .40 .12
219 Keith Ginter .40 .12
220 Woody Williams .40 .12
221 Ryan Franklin .40 .12
222 Aaron Myette .40 .12
223 Joe Borchard RC 2.00 .60
224 Nate Cornejo .40 .12
225 Julian Tavarez .40 .12
226 Kevin Millwood .75 .23
227 Travis Hafner RC 2.00 .60
228 Charles Nagy .40 .12
229 Mike Lieberthal .75 .23
230 Jeff Nelson .40 .12
231 Ryan Dempster .40 .12
232 Andres Galarraga .75 .23
233 Chad Durbin .40 .12
234 Timo Perez .40 .12
235 Troy O'Leary .40 .12
236 Kevin Young .40 .12
237 Gabe Kapler .40 .12
238 Juan Cruz RC .50 .15
239 Masato Yoshii .40 .12
240 Aramis Ramirez .75 .23
241 Matt Cooper RC .50 .15
242 Randy Flores RC .50 .15
243 Rafael Furcal .75 .23
244 David Eckstein .40 .12
245 Matt Clement .75 .23
246 Craig Biggio .60 .18
247 Rick Reed .40 .12
248 Jose Macias .40 .12
249 Alex Escobar .40 .12
250 Roberto Hernandez .40 .12
251 Andy Ashby .40 .12
252 Tony Armas Jr. .40 .12
253 Jamie Moyer .75 .23
254 Jason Tyner .40 .12
255 Charles Kegley RC .50 .15
256 Jeff Conine .75 .23
257 Francisco Cordova .40 .12
258 Ted Lilly .40 .12
259 Joe Randa .40 .12
260 Jeff D'Amico .40 .12
261 Albie Lopez .40 .12
262 Kevin Appier .75 .23
263 Richard Hidalgo .75 .23
264 Omar Daal .40 .12
265 Ricky Gutierrez .40 .12
266 John Rocker .40 .12
267 Ray Lankford .40 .12
268 Beau Hale RC .50 .15
269 Tony Blanco RC .75 .23
270 Derrek Lee UER .75 .23
First name misspelled Derrick
271 Jamey Wright .40 .12
272 Alex Gordon .40 .12
273 Jeff Weaver .40 .12
274 Jaret Wright .40 .12
275 Jose Hernandez .40 .12
276 Bruce Chen .40 .12
277 Todd Hollandsworth .40 .12
278 Wade Miller .75 .23
279 Luke Prokopec .40 .12
280 Rafael Soriano RC 2.00 .60
281 Damion Easley .40 .12
282 Darren Oliver .40 .12
283 B. Duckworth RC .50 .15
284 Aaron Herr .40 .12
285 Ray Durham .75 .23
286 Wilmy Caceras RC .50 .15
287 Ugueth Urbina .40 .12
288 Scott Seabol .40 .12
289 Lance Niekro RC .50 .15
290 Trot Nixon .60 .18
291 Adam Kennedy .40 .12
292 Brian Schmitt RC .50 .15
293 Grant Roberts .40 .12
294 Benny Agbayani .40 .12
295 Travis Lee .40 .12
296 Erick Almonte RC .50 .15
297 Jim Thome 1.00 .30
298 Eric Young .40 .12
299 Dan Denham RC .50 .15
300 Boof Bonser RC .75 .23
301 Denny Neagle .40 .12
302 Kenny Rogers .75 .23
303 J.D. Closser .40 .12
304 Chase Utley RC 2.50 .75
305 Rey Sanchez .40 .12
306 Sean McGowan .40 .12
307 Justin Pope RC .50 .15
308 Torii Hunter .75 .23
309 B.J. Surhoff .75 .23
310 Aaron Heilman RC 1.25 .35
311 Gabe Gross RC .75 .23
312 Lee Stevens .40 .12
313 Todd Hundley .40 .12
314 Macay McBride RC .50 .15
315 Edgar Martinez .60 .18
316 Omar Vizquel .75 .23
317 Reggie Sanders .75 .23
318 John-Ford Griffin RC .75 .23
319 Tim Salmon UER .60 .18
Photo is Troy Glaus
320 Pokey Reese .40 .12
321 Jay Payton .40 .12
322 Doug Glanville .40 .12
323 Greg Vaughn .75 .23
324 Ruben Sierra .40 .12
325 Kip Wells .40 .12
326 Carl Everett .75 .23
327 Garret Anderson .75 .23
328 Jay Bell .75 .23
329 Barry Larkin 1.00 .30
330 Jeff Mathis RC 2.50 .75
331 Adrian Gonzalez SP 2.00 .60
332 Juan Rivera SP 2.00 .60
333 Tony Alvarez SP 2.00 .60
334 Xavier Nady SP 2.00 .60
335 Josh Hamilton SP 2.00 .60
336 Will Smith SP RC 2.00 .60
337 Israel Alcantara SP 2.00 .60
338 Chris George SP 2.00 .60
339 Sean Burroughs SP 2.00 .60
340 Jack Cust SP 2.00 .60
341 Henry Mateo SP RC 2.00 .60
342 Carlos Pena SP 2.00 .60
343 J.R. House SP 2.00 .60
344 Carlos Silva SP 2.00 .60
345 Mike Rivera SP RC 2.00 .60
346 Adam Johnson SP 2.00 .60
347 Scott Heard SP 2.00 .60
348 Alex Cintron SP 2.00 .60
349 Miguel Cabrera SP 10.00 3.00
350 Nick Johnson SP 2.00 .60
351 Albert Pujols SP RC 40.00 12.00
352 Ichiro Suzuki SP RC 25.00 7.50
353 Carlos Delgado SP 2.00 .60
354 Troy Glaus SP 3.00 .90
355 Sammy Sosa SP 5.00 1.50
356 Ivan Rodriguez SP 3.00 .90
357 Vladimir Guerrero SP 3.00 .90
358 Manny Ramirez SP 2.00 .60
359 Luis Gonzalez SP 2.00 .60
360 Roy Oswalt SP 3.00 .90
361 Moises Alou SP 2.00 .60
362 Juan Gonzalez SP 3.00 .90
363 Tony Gwynn SP 4.00 1.20
364 Hideo Nomo SP 3.00 .90
365 T. Shinjo SP RC 4.00 1.20
366 Kazuhiro Sasaki SP 2.00 .60
367 Cal Ripken SP 10.00 3.00
368 Rafael Palmeiro SP 3.00 .90
369 J.D. Drew SP 2.00 .60
370 Doug Mientkiewicz SP 2.00 .60
371 Jeff Bagwell SP 3.00 .90
372 Darin Erstad SP 2.00 .60
373 Tom Gordon SP 2.00 .60
374 Ben Petrick SP 2.00 .60
375 Eric Milton SP 2.00 .60
376 N. Garciaparra SP 5.00 1.50
377 Julio Lugo SP 2.00 .60
378 Tino Martinez SP 3.00 .90
379 Javier Vazquez SP 2.00 .60
380 Jeremy Giambi SP 2.00 .60
381 Marty Cordova SP 2.00 .60
382 Adrian Beltre SP 2.00 .60
383 John Burkett SP 2.00 .60
384 Aaron Boone SP 2.00 .60
385 Eric Chavez SP 2.00 .60
386 Curt Schilling SP 3.00 .90
387 Cory Lidle UER 2.00 .60
First name misspelled Corey
388 Jason Schmidt SP 2.00 .60
389 Johnny Damon SP 2.00 .60
390 Steve Finley SP 2.00 .60
391 Edgardo Alfonzo SP 2.00 .60
392 Jose Valentin SP 2.00 .60
393 Jose Canseco SP 3.00 .90
394 Ryan Klesko SP 2.00 .60
395 David Cone SP 2.00 .60
396 Jason Kendall UER 2.00 .60
Last name misspelled Kendell
397 Placido Polanco SP 2.00 .60
398 Glendon Rusch SP 2.00 .60
399 Aaron Sele SP 2.00 .60
400 D'Angelo Jimenez SP 2.00 .60
401 Mark Grace SP 3.00 .90
402 Al Leiter SP 2.00 .60
403 Brian Jordan SP 2.00 .60
404 Phil Nevin SP 2.00 .60
405 Brent Abernathy SP 2.00 .60
406 Kerry Wood SP 3.00 .90
407 Alex Gonzalez SP 2.00 .60
408 Robert Fick SP 2.00 .60
409 Dmitri Young UER 2.00 .60
First name misspelled Dimitri
410 Wes Helms SP 2.00 .60
411 Trevor Hoffman SP 2.00 .60
412 Rickey Henderson SP 3.00 .90
413 Bobby Higginson SP 2.00 .60
414 Gary Sheffield SP 2.00 .60
415 Darryl Kile SP 2.00 .60
416 Richie Sexson SP 2.00 .60
417 F. Menechino SP RC 2.00 .60
418 Javy Lopez SP 2.00 .60
419 Carlos Lee SP 2.00 .60
420 Jon Lieber SP 2.00 .60
421 Hank Blalock SP RC 15.00 4.50
422 Marlon Byrd SP RC 8.00 2.40
423 Jason Kinchen SP RC 2.00 .60
424 M. Ensberg SP RC 4.00 1.20
425 Greg Nash SP RC 2.00 .60
426 D. Tankersley SP RC 2.00 .60
427 Nate Murphy SP RC 2.00 .60
428 Chris Smith SP RC 2.00 .60
429 Jake Gautreau SP RC 2.00 .60
430 J. VanBenschoten SP RC 5.00 1.50
431 T.Thompson SP RC 2.00 .60
432 O.Hudson SP RC 2.00 .60
433 J.Williams SP RC 10.00 3.00
434 Kevin Reese SP RC 2.00 .60
435 Ed Rogers SP RC 2.00 .60
436 Ryan Jamison SP RC 2.00 .60
437 A. Pettyjohn SP RC 2.00 .60
438 Hee Seop Choi SP RC 10.00 3.00
439 J. Morneau SP RC 10.00 3.00
440 Mitch Jones SP RC 2.00 .60

2001 Bowman Heritage Chrome

Inserted at a rate of one in 12 packs, the first 110 cards of this set are featured in this partial parallel set. Please see the multipliers to assess the values for the individual cards.

Nm-Mt Ex-Mt
*CHROME STARS: 4X TO 10X BASIC CARDS
*CHROME RC'S: 2.5X TO 6X BASIC CARDS

2001 Bowman Heritage 1948 Reprints

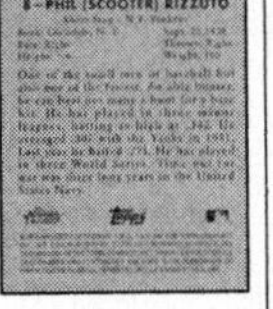

Issued one per two packs, these 13 cards feature reprints of the featured players 1948 Bowman card.

Nm-Mt Ex-Mt
COMPLETE SET (13) 10.00 3.00
1 Ralph Kiner 1.00 .30
2 Johnny Mize 1.00 .30
3 Bobby Thomson 1.00 .30
4 Yogi Berra 1.50 .45
5 Phil Rizzuto 1.25 .35
6 Bob Feller 1.00 .30
7 Enos Slaughter 1.00 .30
8 Stan Musial 2.00 .60
9 Hank Sauer 1.00 .30
10 Ferris Fain 1.00 .30
11 Red Schoendienst 1.00 .30
12 Allie Reynolds UER 1.00 .30
Original Card number is incorrect
13 Johnny Sain 1.00 .30

2001 Bowman Heritage 1948 Reprints Autographs

Inserted at an overall rate of one in 1,523 these two cards have autographs from the feature players on their 1948 reprint cards.

Nm-Mt Ex-Mt
1 Warren Spahn 1 60.00 18.00
2 Bob Feller 2 50.00 15.00

2001 Bowman Heritage 1948 Reprints Relics

Issued at an overall odds of one in 53, these 12 cards feature relic cards from the featured players. The cards featuring pieces of actual seats were inserted at a rate of one in 291 while the odds for bats were one in 2,113 and the odds for jerseys were one in 2,905.

Nm-Mt Ex-Mt
BHM-BF Bob Feller Seat A 20.00 6.00
BHM-BT Bobby Thomson 15.00 4.50
Seat C
BHM-ES Enos Slaughter 15.00 4.50
Seat C
BHM-FF Ferris Fain Seat A 15.00 4.50
BHM-HS Hank Sauer 15.00 4.50
Seat A
BHM-JM Johnny Mize 20.00 6.00
Seat C
BHM-PR Phil Rizzuto 20.00 6.00
Seat B
BHM-RK Ralph Kiner 15.00 4.50
Seat B
BHM-RS R.Schoendienst 15.00 4.50
Bat
BHM-SM1 Stan Musial 30.00 9.00
Seat C
BHM-YB1 Yogi Berra 25.00 7.50
Seat B
BHM-YB2 Yogi Berra Jsy 40.00 12.00

2001 Bowman Heritage Autographs

Inserted at overall odds of one in 358, these three cards feature active players who signed cards for the Bowman Heritage set.

Nm-Mt Ex-Mt
HAAR Alex Rodriguez B 100.00 30.00
HABB Barry Bonds A 175.00 52.50
HARC Roger Clemens A 100.00 30.00

2002 Bowman Heritage

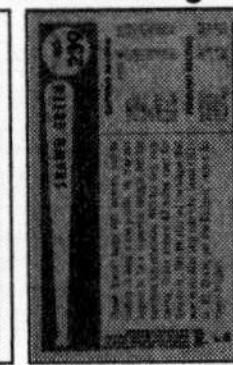

This 440 card standard-size, designed in the style of the 1954 Bowman set, was released in August, 2002. The 10-card packs had an SRP of $3 per pack and were issued 24 packs to a box and 16 boxes to a case. 110 cards were issued in shorter supply than the rest of the set and we have notated that information next to the player's name in our checklist. There were two versions of card number 66 which paid tribute to the Ted Williams/Jim Piersall numbering issue in the original 1954 Bowman set.

Nm-Mt Ex-Mt
COMP.SET w/o SP's (324) 50.00 15.00
COMMON CARD (1-439) .40 .12
COMMON SP 2.00 .60
1 Brent Abernathy .40 .12
2 Jermaine Dye .40 .12
3 James Shanks RC .50 .15
4 Chris Flinn RC .50 .15
5 Mike Peeples SP RC 2.00 .60
6 Gary Sheffield .40 .12
7 Livan Hernandez SP 2.00 .60
8 Jeff Austin RC .50 .15
9 Jeremy Giambi .40 .12
10 Adam Roller RC .50 .15
11 Sandy Alomar Jr. SP 2.00 .60
12 Matt Williams SP 2.00 .60
13 Hee Seop Choi .60 .18
14 Jose Offerman .40 .12
15 Robin Ventura .40 .12
16 Craig Biggio .60 .18
17 David Wells .40 .12
18 Rob Henkel RC .50 .15
19 Edgar Martinez .60 .18
20 Matt Morris SP 2.00 .60
21 Jose Valentin .40 .12
22 Barry Bonds 2.50 .75
23 Justin Schuda RC .50 .15
24 Josh Phelps .40 .12
25 John Rodriguez RC .50 .15
26 Angel Pagan RC .50 .15
27 Aramis Ramirez .40 .12
28 Jack Wilson .40 .12
29 Roger Clemens 2.00 .60
30 Kazuhisa Ishii RC 2.00 .60
31 Carlos Beltran .40 .12
32 Drew Henson SP 2.00 .60
33 Kevin Young SP 2.00 .60
34 Juan Cruz SP 2.00 .60
35 Curtis Legendre RC .50 .15
36 Jose Morban RC .50 .15
37 Ricardo Cordova SP RC 2.00 .60
38 Adam Everett .40 .12
39 Mark Prior 4.00 1.20
40 Jose Bautista RC 1.25 .35
41 Travis Foley RC .50 .15
42 Kerry Wood 1.00 .30
43 B.J. Surhoff .40 .12
44 Moises Alou .40 .12
45 Joey Hammond .40 .12
46 Eric Bruntlett RC .50 .15
47 Carlos Guillen .40 .12
48 Joe Crede .40 .12
49 Dan Phillips RC .50 .15
50 Jason LaRue .40 .12
51 Javy Lopez .40 .12
52 Larry Bigbie SP 2.00 .60
53 Chris Baker RC .50 .15
54 Marty Cordova .40 .12
55 C.C. Sabathia .40 .12
56 Mike Piazza 1.50 .45
57 Brian Giles .40 .12
58 Mike Bordick SP 2.00 .60
59 Tyler Houston SP 2.00 .60
60 Gabe Kapler .40 .12
61 Ben Broussard .40 .12
62 Steve Finley SP 2.00 .60
63 Koyie Hill .40 .12
64 Jeff D'Amico .40 .12
65 Edwin Almonte RC .50 .15
66 Pedro Martinez 1.00 .30
66B Nomar Garciaparra 66 1.50 .45
67 Travis Fryman SP 2.00 .60
68 Brady Clark SP 2.00 .60
69 Reed Johnson SP RC 3.00 .90
70 Mark Grace SP 3.00 .90
71 Tony Batista SP 2.00 .60
72 Roy Oswalt .40 .12
73 Pat Burrell SP 2.00 .60
74 Dennis Tankersley .40 .12
75 Ramon Ortiz .40 .12
76 Neal Frendling SP RC 2.00 .60
77 Omar Vizquel SP 2.00 .60
78 Hideo Nomo 1.00 .30
79 Orlando Hernandez SP 2.00 .60
80 Andy Pettitte .60 .18
81 Cole Barthel RC .50 .15
82 Bret Boone .40 .12
83 Alfonso Soriano .60 .18
84 Brandon Duckworth .40 .12
85 Ben Grieve .40 .12
86 Mike Rosamond SP RC 2.00 .60
87 Luke Prokopec .40 .12
88 Chone Figgins RC .50 .15
89 Rick Ankiel SP 2.00 .60
90 David Eckstein .40 .12
91 Corey Koskie .40 .12
92 David Justice .40 .12
93 Jimmy Alvarez RC .50 .15
94 Jason Schmidt .40 .12
95 Reggie Sanders .40 .12
96 Victor Alvarez RC .50 .15
97 Brett Roneberg RC .50 .15
98 D'Angelo Jimenez .40 .12
99 Hank Blalock 1.00 .30
100 Juan Rivera .40 .12
101 Mark Buehrle SP 2.00 .60
102 Juan Uribe .40 .12
103 Royce Clayton SP 2.00 .60
104 Brett Kay RC .50 .15
105 John Olerud .40 .12
106 Richie Sexson .40 .12
107 Chipper Jones 1.00 .30
108 Adam Dunn .40 .12
109 Tim Salmon SP 3.00 .90
110 Eric Karros .40 .12
111 Jose Vidro .40 .12
112 Jerry Hairston Jr. .40 .12
113 Anastacio Martinez RC .50 .15
114 Robert Fick SP 2.00 .60
115 Randy Johnson 1.00 .30
116 Trot Nixon SP 3.00 .90
117 Nick Bierbrodt SP 2.00 .60
118 Jim Edmonds .40 .12
119 Rafael Palmeiro .60 .18
120 Jose Macias .40 .12
121 Josh Beckett .60 .18
122 Sean Douglass .40 .12
123 Jeff Kent .40 .12
124 Tim Redding .40 .12
125 Xavier Nady .40 .12
126 Carl Everett .40 .12
127 Joe Randa .40 .12
128 Luke Hudson SP 2.00 .60
129 Eric Miller RC .50 .15
130 Melvin Mora .40 .12
131 Adrian Gonzalez .40 .12
132 Larry Walker SP 3.00 .90
133 Nic Jackson SP RC 2.00 .60
134 Mike Lowell SP 2.00 .60
135 Jim Thome 1.00 .30
136 Eric Milton .40 .12
137 Rich Thompson SP RC 2.00 .60
138 Placido Polanco SP 2.00 .60
139 Juan Pierre .40 .12
140 David Segui .40 .12
141 Chuck Finley .40 .12
142 Felipe Lopez .40 .12
143 Toby Hall .40 .12
144 Fred Bastardo RC .50 .15
145 Troy Glaus .60 .18
146 Todd Helton .60 .18
147 Ruben Gotay SP RC 2.00 .60
148 Darin Erstad .40 .12
149 Ryan Gripp SP RC 2.00 .60
150 Orlando Cabrera .40 .12
151 Jason Young RC .50 .15
152 Sterling Hitchcock SP 2.00 .60
153 Miguel Tejada .40 .12
154 Al Leiter .40 .12
155 Taylor Buchholz RC .75 .23
156 Juan M. Gonzalez RC .50 .15
157 Damion Easley .40 .12
158 Jimmy Gobble RC 2.00 .60
159 Dennis Ulacia SP RC 2.00 .60
160 Shane Reynolds SP 2.00 .60
161 Javier Colina .40 .12
162 Frank Thomas 1.00 .30
163 Chuck Knoblauch .40 .12
164 Sean Burroughs .40 .12
165 Greg Maddux 1.50 .45
166 Jason Ellison RC .50 .15
167 Tony Womack .40 .12
168 Randall Shelley SP RC 2.00 .60
169 Jason Marquis .40 .12
170 Brian Jordan .40 .12
171 Vicente Padilla .40 .12
172 Barry Zito .60 .18
173 Matt Allegra SP RC 2.00 .60
174 Ralph Santana SP RC 2.00 .60
175 Carlos Lee .40 .12
176 Richard Hidalgo SP 2.00 .60
177 Kevin Deaton RC .50 .15
178 Juan Encarnacion .40 .12
179 Mark Quinn .40 .12
180 Rafael Furcal .40 .12
181 Garret Anderson UER .40 .12
Photo is Chone Figgins
182 David Wright RC 3.00 .90
183 Jose Reyes 1.00 .30
184 Mario Ramos SP RC 3.00 .90
185 J.D. Drew .40 .12
186 Juan Gonzalez 1.00 .30
187 Nick Neugebauer .40 .12
188 Alejandro Giron RC .50 .15
189 John Burkett .40 .12
190 Ben Sheets .40 .12
191 Vinny Castilla SP 2.00 .60
192 Cory Lidle .40 .12
193 Fernando Vina .40 .12
194 Russell Branyan SP 2.00 .60
195 Ben Davis .40 .12
196 Angel Berroa .40 .12
197 Alex Gonzalez .40 .12

198 Jared Sandberg .40 .12
199 Travis Lee SP 2.00 .60
200 Luis DePaula SP 2.00 .60
201 Ramon Hernandez SP 2.00 .60
202 Brandon Inge .40 .12
203 Aubrey Huff .40 .12
204 Mike Rivera .40 .12
205 Brad Nelson RC 2.00 .60
206 Colt Griffin SP RC 6.00 1.80
207 Joel Pineiro .40 .12
208 Adam Pettyjohn .40 .12
209 Mark Redman .40 .12
210 Roberto Alomar SP 5.00 1.50
211 Denny Neagle .40 .12
212 Adam Kennedy .40 .12
213 Jason Arnold SP RC 6.00 1.80
214 Jamie Moyer .40 .12
215 Aaron Boone .40 .12
216 Doug Glanville .40 .12
217 Nick Johnson SP 2.00 .60
218 Mike Cameron SP 2.00 .60
219 Tim Wakefield SP 2.00 .60
220 Todd Stottlemyre SP 2.00 .60
221 Mo Vaughn SP 2.00 .60
222 Vladimir Guerrero 1.00 .30
223 Bill Ortega .40 .12
224 Kevin Brown .40 .12
225 Peter Bergeron SP 2.00 .60
226 Shannon Stewart SP 2.00 .60
227 Eric Chavez .40 .12
228 Clint Weibl RC .50 .15
229 Todd Hollandsworth SP 2.00 .60
230 Jeff Bagwell .60 .18
231 Chad Qualls RC .50 .15
232 Ben Howard RC .50 .15
233 Rondell White SP 2.00 .60
234 Fred McGriff .60 .18
235 Steve Cox SP 2.00 .60
236 Chris Tritle RC .50 .15
237 Eric Valent .40 .12
238 Joe Mauer RC 8.00 2.40
239 Shawn Green .40 .12
240 Jimmy Rollins .40 .12
241 Edgar Renteria .40 .12
242 Edwin Yan RC .50 .15
243 Noochie Varner RC .50 .15
244 Kris Benson SP 2.00 .60
245 Mike Hampton .40 .12
246 So Taguchi RC .75 .23
247 Sammy Sosa 1.50 .45
248 Terrence Long .40 .12
249 Jason Bay RC 2.00 .60
250 Kevin Millar SP 2.00 .60
251 Albert Pujols 2.00 .60
252 Chris Latham RC .50 .15
253 Eric Byrnes .40 .12
254 Napoleon Calzado SP RC 2.00 .60
255 Bobby Higginson .40 .12
256 Ben Molina .40 .12
257 Torii Hunter SP 2.00 .60
258 Jason Giambi 1.00 .30
259 Bartolo Colon .40 .12
260 Benito Baez .40 .12
261 Ichiro Suzuki 1.50 .45
262 Mike Sweeney .40 .12
263 Brian West RC .50 .15
264 Brad Penny .40 .12
265 Kevin Millwood SP 2.00 .60
266 Orlando Hudson .40 .12
267 Doug Mientkiewicz .40 .12
268 Luis Gonzalez SP 2.00 .60
269 Jay Caligiuri RC .50 .15
270 Nate Cornejo SP 2.00 .60
271 Lee Stevens .40 .12
272 Eric Hinske .40 .12
273 Antwon Rollins RC .50 .15
274 Bobby Jenks RC 2.00 .60
275 Joe Mays .40 .12
276 Josh Shaffer RC .50 .15
277 Jonny Gomes RC 1.50 .45
278 Bernie Williams .60 .18
279 Ed Rogers .40 .12
280 Carlos Delgado .40 .12
281 Raul Mondesi SP 2.00 .60
282 Jose Ortiz .40 .12
283 Cesar Izturis .40 .12
284 Ryan Dempster SP 2.00 .60
285 Brian Daubach .40 .12
286 Hansel Izquierdo RC .50 .15
287 Mike Lieberthal SP 2.00 .60
288 Marcus Thames .40 .12
289 Nomar Garciaparra 1.50 .45
290 Brad Fullmer .40 .12
291 Tino Martinez .60 .18
292 James Barrett RC .50 .15
293 Jacque Jones .40 .12
294 Nick Alvarez SP RC 2.00 .60
295 Jason Grove SP RC 2.00 .60
296 Mike Wilson SP RC 2.00 .60
297 J.T. Snow .40 .12
298 Cliff Floyd .40 .12
299 Todd Hundley SP 2.00 .60
300 Tony Clark SP 2.00 .60
301 Demetrius Heath RC .50 .15
302 Morgan Ensberg .40 .12
303 Cristian Guzman .40 .12
304 Frank Catalanotto .40 .12
305 Jeff Weaver .40 .12
306 Tim Hudson .40 .12
307 Scott Wiggins SP RC 2.00 .60
308 Shea Hillenbrand SP 2.00 .60
309 Todd Walker SP 2.00 .60
310 Tsuyoshi Shinjo .40 .12
311 Adrian Beltre .40 .12
312 Craig Kuzmic RC .50 .15
313 Paul Konerko .40 .12
314 Scott Hairston RC 2.50 .75
315 Chan Ho Park .40 .12
316 Jorge Posada .60 .18
317 Chris Snelling RC 1.50 .45
318 Keith Foulke .40 .12
319 John Smoltz .60 .18
320 Ryan Church SP RC 3.00 .90
321 Mike Mussina 1.00 .30
322 Tony Armas Jr. SP 2.00 .60
323 Craig Counsell .40 .12
324 Marcus Giles .40 .12
325 Greg Vaughn .40 .12
326 Curt Schilling .60 .18
327 Jeromy Burnitz .40 .12
328 Eric Byrnes .40 .12
329 Johnny Damon .40 .12
330 Michael Floyd SP RC 2.00 .60
331 Edgardo Alfonzo .40 .12
332 Jeremy Hill RC .50 .15
333 Josh Bonifay RC .50 .15
334 Byung-Hyun Kim .40 .12
335 Keith Ginter .40 .12
336 Ronald Acuna SP RC 2.00 .60
337 Mike Hill SP RC 2.00 .60
338 Sean Casey .40 .12
339 Matt Anderson SP 2.00 .60
340 Dan Wright .40 .12
341 Ben Petrick .40 .12
342 Mike Sirotka SP 2.00 .60
343 Alex Rodriguez 1.50 .45
344 Einar Diaz .40 .12
345 Derek Jeter 2.50 .75
346 Jeff Conine .40 .12
347 Ray Durham SP 2.00 .60
348 Wilson Betemit SP 2.00 .60
349 Jeffrey Hammonds .40 .12
350 Dan Trumble RC .50 .15
351 Phil Nevin SP 2.00 .60
352 A.J. Burnett .40 .12
353 Bill Mueller .40 .12
354 Charles Nagy .40 .12
355 Rusty Greer SP 2.00 .60
356 Jason Botts RC .50 .15
357 Magglio Ordonez .40 .12
358 Kevin Appier .40 .12
359 Brad Radke .40 .12
360 Chris George .40 .12
361 Chris Piersoll RC .50 .15
362 Ivan Rodriguez 1.00 .30
363 Jim Kavourias RC .50 .15
364 Rick Helling SP 2.00 .60
365 Dean Palmer .40 .12
366 Rich Aurilia SP 2.00 .60
367 Ryan Vogelsong .40 .12
368 Matt Lawton .40 .12
369 Wade Miller .40 .12
370 Dustin Hermanson .40 .12
371 Craig Wilson .40 .12
372 Todd Zeile SP 2.00 .60
373 Jon Guzman RC .50 .15
374 Ellis Burks .40 .12
375 Robert Cosby SP RC 2.00 .60
376 Jason Kendall .40 .12
377 Scott Rolen SP 3.00 .90
378 Andruw Jones .40 .12
379 Greg Sain RC .50 .15
380 Paul LoDuca .40 .12
381 Scotty Layfield RC .50 .15
382 Tomo Ohka .40 .12
383 Garrett Guzman RC .50 .15
384 Jack Cust SP 2.00 .60
385 Shayne Wright RC .50 .15
386 Derrek Lee .40 .12
387 Jesus Medrano RC .50 .15
388 Javier Vazquez .40 .12
389 Preston Wilson SP 2.00 .60
390 Gavin Floyd RC 3.00 .90
391 Sidney Ponson SP 2.00 .60
392 Jose Hernandez .40 .12
393 Scott Erickson SP 2.00 .60
394 Jose Valverde RC .75 .23
395 Mark Hamilton SP RC 2.00 .60
396 Brad Cresse .40 .12
397 Danny Bautista .40 .12
398 Ray Lankford SP 2.00 .60
399 Miguel Batista SP 2.00 .60
400 Brent Butler .40 .12
401 Manny Delcarmen SP RC 2.00 .60
402 Kyle Farnsworth SP 2.00 .60
403 Freddy Garcia .40 .12
404 Joe Jiannetti RC .50 .15
405 Josh Barfield RC 4.00 1.20
406 Corey Patterson .40 .12
407 Josh Towers .40 .12
408 Carlos Pena .40 .12
409 Jeff Cirillo .40 .12
410 Jon Lieber .40 .12
411 Woody Williams SP 2.00 .60
412 Richard Lane SP RC 2.00 .60
413 Alex Gonzalez .40 .12
414 Wilkin Ruan .40 .12
415 Geoff Jenkins .40 .12
416 Carlos Hernandez .40 .12
417 Matt Clement SP 2.00 .60
418 Jose Cruz Jr. .40 .12
419 Jake Mauer RC .50 .15
420 Matt Childers RC .50 .15
421 Tom Glavine SP 3.00 .90
422 Ken Griffey Jr. 1.50 .45
423 Anderson Hernandez RC .50 .15
424 John Suomi RC .50 .15
425 Doug Sessions RC .50 .15
426 Jaret Wright .40 .12
427 Rolando Viera SP RC 2.00 .60
428 Aaron Sele .40 .12
429 Dmitri Young .40 .12
430 Ryan Klesko .40 .12
431 Kevin Tapani SP 2.00 .60
432 Joe Kennedy .40 .12
433 Austin Kearns .40 .12
434 Roger Cedeno SP 2.00 .60
435 Lance Berkman .40 .12
436 Frank Menechino .40 .12
437 Brett Myers .40 .12
438 Bob Abreu .40 .12
439 Shawn Estes SP 2.00 .60

2002 Bowman Heritage Black Box

Issued at stated odds of one in two packs, these 55 cards form a partial parallel of the Bowman Heritage set. These cards can be notated by the players "signature" being placed in a black box.

Nm-Mt Ex-Mt
13 Hee Seop Choi 1.25 .35
22 Barry Bonds 5.00 1.50
23 Justin Schuda .75 .23
27 Aramis Ramirez .75 .23
30 Kazuhisa Ishii 3.00 .90
39 Mark Prior 8.00 2.40
41 Travis Foley .75 .23
56 Mike Piazza 3.00 .90
66 Nomar Garciaparra 2.00 .60
72 Roy Oswalt .75 .23
96 Victor Alvarez .75 .23
99 Hank Blalock 2.00 .60
107 Chipper Jones 2.00 .60
108 Adam Dunn .75 .23
120 Jose Macias .75 .23
121 Josh Beckett 1.25 .35
139 Juan Pierre .75 .23
143 Toby Hall .75 .23
145 Troy Glaus 1.25 .35
146 Todd Helton 1.25 .35
153 Miguel Tejada .75 .23
167 Tony Womack .75 .23
180 Rafael Furcal .75 .23
182 David Wright 5.00 1.50
185 J.D. Drew .75 .23
222 Vladimir Guerrero 2.00 .60
227 Eric Chavez .75 .23
238 Joe Mauer 12.00 3.60
240 Jimmy Rollins .75 .23
246 So Taguchi 1.25 .35
247 Sammy Sosa 3.00 .90
251 Albert Pujols 4.00 1.20
258 Jason Giambi 2.00 .60
261 Ichiro Suzuki 3.00 .90
266 Orlando Hudson .75 .23
269 Jay Caligiuri .75 .23
274 Bobby Jenks 3.00 .90
275 Joe Mays .75 .23
277 Jonny Gomes 2.50 .75
310 Tsuyoshi Shinjo .75 .23
314 Scott Hairston 4.00 1.20
316 Jorge Posada 1.25 .35
317 Chris Snelling 2.50 .75
335 Keith Ginter .75 .23
343 Alex Rodriguez 3.00 .90
345 Derek Jeter 5.00 1.50
362 Ivan Rodriguez 2.00 .60
390 Gavin Floyd 5.00 1.50
396 Brad Cresse .75 .23
405 Josh Barfield 6.00 1.80
414 Wilkin Ruan .75 .23
416 Carlos Hernandez .75 .23
418 Jose Cruz Jr. .75 .23
422 Ken Griffey Jr. 3.00 .90
433 Austin Kearns .75 .23

2002 Bowman Heritage Chrome Refractors

Issued at stated odds of one in 16, these 110 cards partially parallel the regular Bowman Heritage set. Please note that although the numbering is different, the cards are the same as the regular cards except for the Chrome technology used. These cards were issued to a stated print run of 350 serial numbered sets.

Nm-Mt Ex-Mt
*CHROME: 4X TO 10X BASIC CARDS.
*CHROME SP'S: .75X TO 2X BASIC SP'S
*CHROME RC'S: 3X TO 8X BASIC RC'S

2002 Bowman Heritage Gold Chrome Refractors

Issued at stated odds of one in 32, these 110 cards partially parallel the regular Bowman Heritage set. Please note that although the numbering is different, the cards are the same as the regular cards except for the Chrome technology used. Each card was issued to a stated print run of 175 serial numbered sets.

Nm-Mt Ex-Mt
*GOLD: 6X TO 15X BASIC CARDS
*GOLD SP'S: 1.25X TO 3X BASIC SP'S
*GOLD RC'S: 5X TO 12X BASIC RC'S

2002 Bowman Heritage 1954 Reprints

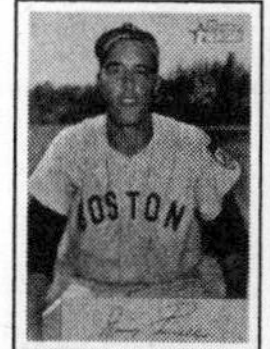

Issued at stated odds of one in 12, these 20 cards feature reprinted versions of the featured player 1954 Bowman card.

Nm-Mt Ex-Mt
COMPLETE SET (20) 50.00 15.00
BHR-AR Allie Reynolds 2.00 .60
BHR-BF Bob Feller 3.00 .90
BHR-CL Clem Labine 3.00 .90
BHR-DC Del Crandall 2.00 .60
BHR-DL Don Larsen 3.00 .90
BHR-DM Don Mueller 2.00 .60
BHR-DS Duke Snider 5.00 1.50
BHR-DW Dave Williams 2.00 .60
BHR-ES Enos Slaughter 2.00 .60
BHR-GM Gil McDougald 2.00 .60
BHR-HW Hoyt Wilhelm 2.00 .60
BHR-JL Johnny Logan 2.00 .60
BHR-JP Jim Piersall 2.00 .60
BHR-NF Nellie Fox 3.00 .90
BHR-PR Phil Rizzuto 3.00 .90
BHR-RA Richie Ashburn 3.00 .90
BHR-WF Whitey Ford 3.00 .90
BHR-WM Willie Mays 10.00 3.00
BHR-WW Wes Westrum 2.00 .60
BHR-YB Yogi Berra 5.00 1.50

2002 Bowman Heritage 1954 Reprints Autographs

Inserted at stated odds of one in 126, these six cards have autographs of the featured player on their 1954 Reprint card.

Nm-Mt Ex-Mt
*SPEC.ED: 1.25X TO 3X BASIC AUTOS
SPEC.ED STATED ODDS 1:1910
SPEC.ED. PRINT RUN 54 SERIAL #'d SETS
BHRA-CL Clem Labine 25.00 7.50

BHRA-DC Del Crandall 25.00 7.50
BHRA-DM Don Mueller 15.00 4.50
BHRA-DW Dave Williams 15.00 4.50
BHRA-JL Johnny Logan 25.00 7.50
BHRA-YB Yogi Berra 60.00 18.00

2002 Bowman Heritage Autographs

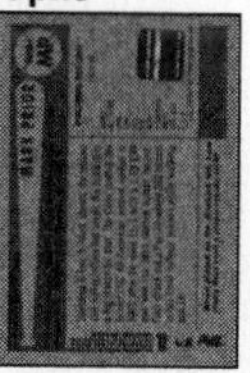

Issued at overall stated odds of one in 45, these 13 cards feature players signing copies of their Bowman Heritage card. Please note that these cards were issued in three different groups with differing odds and we have noted which players belong to which group in our checklist.

Nm-Mt Ex-Mt
GROUP A STATED ODDS 1:620
GROUP B STATED ODDS 1:89
GROUP C STATED ODDS 1:103
OVERALL STATED ODDS 1:45
BHA-AP Albert Pujols A 150.00 45.00
BHA-CI Cesar Izturis B 10.00 3.00
BHA-DH Drew Henson B 20.00 6.00
BHA-HB Hank Blalock C 20.00 6.00
BHA-JM Joe Mauer C 60.00 18.00
BHA-JR Juan Rivera C 15.00 4.50
BHA-KG Keith Ginter B 10.00 3.00
BHA-KI Kazuhisa Ishii A 40.00 12.00
BHA-LB Lance Berkman B 15.00 4.50
BHA-MP Mark Prior B 100.00 30.00
BHA-PL Paul LoDuca C 15.00 4.50
BHA-RO Roy Oswalt B 15.00 4.50
BHA-TH Toby Hall B 10.00 3.00

2002 Bowman Heritage Relics

Inserted in packs at overall stated odds of one in 47 for Jersey cards and one in 75 for Uniform cards, these 26 cards feature game-worn swatches on them. Many cards belong to different groups and we have noted that information next to their name in our checklist.

Nm-Mt Ex-Mt
GROUP A JSY ODDS 1:1910
GROUP B JSY ODDS 1:1551
GROUP C JSY ODDS 1:138
GROUP D JSY ODDS 1:207
GROUP E JSY ODDS 1:165
GROUP F JSY ODDS 1:2072
GROUP G JSY ODDS 1:653
GROUP A UNI ODDS 1:1551
GROUP B UNI ODDS 1:855
GROUP C UNI ODDS 1:124
GROUP D UNI ODDS 1:284
BH-AP Albert Pujols Uni C 20.00 6.00
BH-BB Barry Bonds Uni D 25.00 7.50
BH-CD Carlos Delgado Jsy G 10.00 3.00
BH-CJ Chipper Jones Jsy C 15.00 4.50
BH-DE Darin Erstad Uni C 10.00 3.00
BH-EA Edgardo Alfonzo Jsy C 10.00 3.00
BH-EC Eric Chavez Jsy C 10.00 3.00
BH-EM Edgar Martinez Jsy C 15.00 4.50
BH-FT Frank Thomas Jsy F 15.00 4.50
BH-GM Greg Maddux Jsy C 15.00 4.50
BH-IR Ivan Rodriguez Uni B 15.00 4.50
BH-JB Josh Beckett Jsy E 15.00 4.50
BH-JE Jim Edmonds Jsy D 10.00 3.00
BH-JS John Smoltz Jsy C 15.00 4.50
BH-JT Jim Thome Jsy E 15.00 4.50
BH-KS Kazuhiro Sasaki Jsy C 10.00 3.00
BH-LW Larry Walker Jsy C 15.00 4.50
BH-MP Mike Piazza Uni A 15.00 4.50
BH-MR Mariano Rivera Uni C 15.00 4.50
BH-NG Nomar Garciaparra Jsy A 20.00 6.00
BH-PK Paul Konerko Jsy E 10.00 3.00
BH-PW Preston Wilson Jsy B 10.00 3.00
BH-SR Scott Rolen Jsy C 15.00 4.50
BH-TG Tony Gwynn Jsy D 15.00 4.50
BH-TH Todd Helton Jsy D 15.00 4.50
BH-TS Tim Salmon Uni C 15.00 4.50

2003 Bowman Heritage

This 300-card standard-size set was released in December, 2003. The set was issued in four-card packs with an $3 SRP which came 24 packs to a box and 10 boxes to a case. This set was designed in the style of what the 1956 Bowman set would have been if that set had been issued. Cards numbered 161 through 170

feature players who debuted in the 2003 season and each of those players have a double image. Cards numbered 171-180 featured retired greats and those cards were issued in three styles: Regular design, Double Image and Knothole Design, Cards number 180 through 300 are all Rookie Cards and all those cards are issued in the knothole design.

MINT NRMT
COMPLETE SET (300) 100.00 45.00
1 Jorge Posada .60 .25
2 Todd Helton .60 .25
3 Marcus Giles .40 .18
4 Eric Chavez .40 .18
5 Edgar Martinez .60 .25
6 Luis Gonzalez .40 .18
7 Corey Patterson .40 .18
8 Preston Wilson .40 .18
9 Ryan Klesko .40 .18
10 Randy Johnson 1.00 .45
11 Jose Guillen .40 .18
12 Carlos Lee .40 .18
13 Steve Finley .40 .18
14 A.J. Pierzynski .40 .18
15 Troy Glaus .60 .25
16 Darin Erstad .40 .18
17 Moises Alou .40 .18
18 Torii Hunter .40 .18
19 Marlon Byrd .40 .18
20 Mark Prior 2.00 .90
21 Shannon Stewart .40 .18
22 Craig Biggio .60 .25
23 Johnny Damon .40 .18
24 Robert Fick .40 .18
25 Jason Giambi 1.00 .45
26 Fernando Vina .40 .18
27 Aubrey Huff .40 .18
28 Benito Santiago .40 .18
29 Jay Gibbons .40 .18
30 Ken Griffey Jr. 1.50 .70
31 Rocco Baldelli 1.50 .70
32 Pat Burrell .40 .18
33 A.J. Burnett .40 .18
34 Omar Vizquel .40 .18
35 Greg Maddux 1.50 .70
36 Cliff Floyd .40 .18
37 C.C. Sabathia .40 .18
38 Geoff Jenkins .40 .18
39 Ty Wigginton .40 .18
40 Jeff Kent .40 .18
41 Orlando Hudson .40 .18
42 Edgardo Alfonzo .40 .18
43 Greg Myers .40 .18
44 Melvin Mora .40 .18
45 Sammy Sosa 1.50 .70
46 Russ Ortiz .40 .18
47 Josh Beckett .60 .25
48 David Wells .40 .18
49 Woody Williams .40 .18
50 Alex Rodriguez 1.50 .70
51 Randy Wolf .40 .18
52 Carlos Beltran .40 .18
53 Austin Kearns .40 .18
54 Trot Nixon .60 .25
55 Ivan Rodriguez 1.00 .45
56 Shea Hillenbrand .40 .18
57 Roberto Alomar 1.00 .45
58 John Olerud .40 .18
59 Michael Young .40 .18
60 Garret Anderson .40 .18
61 Mike Lieberthal .40 .18
62 Adam Dunn .40 .18
63 Raul Ibanez .40 .18
64 Kenny Lofton .40 .18
65 Ichiro Suzuki 1.50 .70
66 Jarrod Washburn .40 .18
67 Shawn Chacon .40 .18
68 Alex Gonzalez .40 .18
69 Roy Halladay .40 .18
70 Vladimir Guerrero 1.00 .45
71 Hee Seop Choi .40 .18
72 Jody Gerut .40 .18
73 Ray Durham .40 .18
74 Mark Teixeira .60 .25
75 Hank Blalock .60 .25
76 Jerry Hairston Jr. .40 .18
77 Erubiel Durazo .40 .18
78 Frank Catalanotto .40 .18
79 Jacque Jones .40 .18
80 Bobby Abreu .40 .18
81 Mike Hampton .40 .18
82 Zach Day .40 .18
83 Jimmy Rollins .40 .18
84 Joel Pineiro .40 .18
85 Brett Myers .40 .18
86 Frank Thomas 1.00 .45
87 Aramis Ramirez .40 .18
88 Paul Lo Duca .40 .18
89 Dmitri Young .40 .18
90 Brian Giles .40 .18
91 Jose Cruz Jr. .40 .18
92 Derek Lowe .40 .18
93 Mark Buehrle .40 .18
94 Wade Miller .40 .18
95 Derek Jeter 2.50 1.10
96 Bret Boone .40 .18
97 Tony Batista .40 .18
98 Sean Casey .40 .18
99 Eric Hinske .40 .18
100 Albert Pujols 2.00 .90
101 Runelvys Hernandez .40 .18
102 Vernon Wells .40 .18
103 Kerry Wood 1.00 .45
104 Lance Berkman .40 .18
105 Alfonso Soriano .60 .25
106 Bill Mueller .40 .18
107 Bartolo Colon .40 .18
108 Andy Pettitte .60 .25

109 Rafael Furcal .40 .18
110 Dontrelle Willis 1.00 .45
111 Carl Crawford .40 .18
112 Scott Rolen .60 .25
113 Chipper Jones 1.00 .45
114 Magglio Ordonez .40 .18
115 Bernie Williams .60 .25
116 Roy Oswalt .40 .18
117 Kevin Brown .40 .18
118 Cristian Guzman .40 .18
119 Kazuhisa Ishii .40 .18
120 Larry Walker .60 .25
121 Miguel Tejada .40 .18
122 Manny Ramirez .40 .18
123 Mike Mussina 1.00 .45
124 Mike Lowell .40 .18
125 Scott Podsednik 1.00 .45
126 Aaron Boone .40 .18
127 Carlos Delgado .40 .18
128 Jose Vidro .40 .18
129 Brad Radke .40 .18
130 Rafael Palmeiro .60 .25
131 Mark Mulder .40 .18
132 Jason Schmidt .40 .18
133 Gary Sheffield .40 .18
134 Richie Sexson .40 .18
135 Barry Zito .60 .25
136 Tom Glavine .60 .25
137 Jim Edmonds .40 .18
138 Andruw Jones .40 .18
139 Pedro Martinez 1.00 .45
140 Curt Schilling .60 .25
141 Phil Nevin .40 .18
142 Nomar Garciaparra 1.50 .70
143 Vicente Padilla .40 .18
144 Kevin Millwood .40 .18
145 Shawn Green .40 .18
146 Jeff Bagwell .60 .25
147 Hideo Nomo 1.00 .45
148 Fred McGriff .60 .25
149 Matt Morris .40 .18
150 Roger Clemens 2.00 .90
151 Jerome Williams .40 .18
152 Orlando Cabrera .40 .18
153 Tim Hudson .40 .18
154 Mike Sweeney .40 .18
155 Jim Thome 1.00 .45
156 Rich Aurilia .40 .18
157 Mike Piazza 1.50 .70
158 Edgar Renteria .40 .18
159 Javy Lopez .40 .18
160 Jamie Moyer .40 .18
161 Miguel Cabrera DI 1.50 .70
162 Adam Loewen DI RC 2.50 1.10
163 Jose Reyes DI .60 .25
164 Zack Greinke DI 1.00 .45
165 Gavin Floyd DI .40 .18
166 Jeremy Guthrie DI .40 .18
167 Victor Martinez DI .40 .18
168 Rich Harden DI .60 .25
169 Joe Mauer DI 1.00 .45
170 Khalil Greene DI .60 .25
171A Willie Mays 2.00 .90
171B Willie Mays DI 2.00 .90
171C Willie Mays KN 2.00 .90
172A Phil Rizzuto .60 .25
172B Phil Rizzuto DI .60 .25
172C Phil Rizzuto KN .60 .25
173A Al Kaline 1.00 .45
173B Al Kaline DI 1.00 .45
173C Al Kaline KN 1.00 .45
174A Warren Spahn .60 .25
174B Warren Spahn DI .60 .25
174C Warren Spahn KN .60 .25
175A Jimmy Piersall .40 .18
175B Jimmy Piersall DI .40 .18
175C Jimmy Piersall KN .40 .18
176A Luis Aparicio .40 .18
176B Luis Aparicio DI .40 .18
176C Luis Aparicio KN .60 .25
177A Whitey Ford .60 .25
177B Whitey Ford DI .60 .25
177C Whitey Ford KN .60 .25
178A Harmon Killebrew 1.00 .45
178B Harmon Killebrew DI 1.00 .45
178C Harmon Killebrew KN 1.00 .45
179A Duke Snider .60 .25
179B Duke Snider DI .60 .25
179C Duke Snider KN .60 .25
180A Roberto Clemente 2.50 1.10
180B Roberto Clemente DI 2.50 1.10
180C Roberto Clemente KN 2.50 1.10
181 David Martinez KN RC .40 .18
182 Felix Pie KN RC 3.00 1.35
183 Kevin Correia KN RC .40 .18
184 Brandon Webb KN RC 2.50 1.10
185 Matt Diaz KN RC 1.00 .45
186 Lew Ford KN RC .60 .25
187 Jeremy Griffiths KN RC .60 .25
188 Matt Hensley KN RC .40 .18
189 Danny Garcia KN RC .40 .18
190 Elizardo Ramirez KN RC 1.25 .55
191 Greg Aquino KN RC .40 .18
192 Felix Sanchez KN RC .40 .18
193 Kelly Shoppach KN RC 1.50 .70
194 Bubba Nelson KN RC 1.00 .45
195 Mike O'Keefe KN RC .40 .18
196 Hanley Ramirez KN RC 2.00 .90
197 Todd Wellemeyer KN RC .60 .25
198 Dustin Moseley KN RC .60 .25
199 Eric Crozier KN RC .60 .25
200 Ryan Shealy KN RC 1.00 .45
201 Jeremy Bonderman KN RC 1.25 .55
202 Bo Hart KN RC 2.00 .90
203 Dusty Brown KN RC .40 .18
204 Rob Hammock KN RC .60 .25
205 Jorge Piedra KN RC .60 .25
206 Jason Kubel KN RC .60 .25
207 Stephen Randolph KN RC .40 .18
208 Andy Sisco KN RC 1.50 .70
209 Matt Kata KN RC 1.00 .45
210 Robinson Cano KN RC .60 .25
211 Ben Francisco KN RC .60 .25
212 Arnie Munoz KN RC .40 .18
213 Ozzie Chavez KN RC .40 .18
214 Beau Kemp KN RC .40 .18
215 Travis Wong KN RC .60 .25
216 Brian McCann KN RC 1.00 .45
217 Aquilino Lopez KN RC .40 .18
218 Bobby Basham KN RC 1.00 .45
219 Tim Olson KN RC .60 .25
220 Nathan Panther KN RC 1.00 .45
221 Wil Ledezma KN RC .40 .18
222 Josh Willingham KN RC 1.50 .70
223 David Cash KN RC .40 .18
224 Oscar Villarreal KN RC .40 .18
225 Jeff Duncan KN RC .60 .25
226 Dan Haren KN RC 1.25 .55
227 Michel Hernandez KN RC .40 .18
228 Matt Murton KN RC 1.00 .45
229 Clay Hensley KN RC .40 .18
230 Tyler Johnson KN RC .40 .18
231 Tyler Martin KN RC .40 .18
232 J.D. Durbin KN RC 1.00 .45
233 Shane Victorino KN RC .40 .18
234 Rajai Davis KN RC .60 .25
235 Chien-Ming Wang KN RC 2.00 .90
236 Travis Ishikawa KN RC .60 .25
237 Eric Eckenstahler KN RC .40 .18
238 Dustin McGowan KN RC 1.25 .55
239 Prentice Redman KN RC .40 .18
240 Haj Turay KN RC .60 .25
241 Matt DeMarco KN RC .40 .18
242 Lou Palmisano KN RC 2.50 1.10
243 Eric Reed KN RC 1.00 .45
244 Willie Eyre KN RC .40 .18
245 Ferdin Tejeda KN RC .40 .18
246 Michael Garciaparra KN RC 1.25 .55
247 Michael Hinckley KN RC 1.00 .45
248 Branden Florence KN RC .40 .18
249 Trent Oeltjen KN RC .60 .25
250 Mike Neu KN RC .40 .18
251 Chris Lubanski KN RC 2.00 .90
252 Brandon Wood KN RC 1.50 .70
253 Delmon Young KN RC 8.00 3.60
254 Matt Harrison KN RC .60 .25
255 Chad Billingsley KN RC 1.25 .55
256 Josh Anderson KN RC .60 .25
257 Brian McFall KN RC 1.00 .45
258 Ryan Wagner KN RC 1.50 .70
259 Billy Hogan KN RC 1.25 .55
260 Nate Spears KN RC 1.00 .45
261 Ryan Harvey KN RC 3.00 1.35
262 Wes Littleton KN RC 1.00 .45
263 Xavier Paul KN RC 3.00 1.35
264 Sean Rodriguez KN RC 1.25 .55
265 Brian Finch KN RC .40 .18
266 Josh Rainwater KN RC 1.00 .45
267 Brian Snyder KN RC .60 .25
268 Eric Duncan KN RC 2.00 .90
269 Rickie Weeks KN RC 5.00 2.20
270 Tim Battle KN RC .60 .25
271 Scott Beerer KN RC .40 .18
272 Aaron Hill KN RC 2.00 .90
273 Casey Abrams KN RC .40 .18
274 Jonathan Fulton KN RC .60 .25
275 Todd Jennings KN RC .60 .25
276 Jordan Pratt KN RC .60 .25
277 Tom Gorzelanny KN RC .60 .25
278 Matt Lorenzo KN RC .60 .25
279 Jarrod Saltalamacchia KN RC 1.00 .45
280 Mike Wagner KN RC .40 .18

2003 Bowman Heritage Autographs

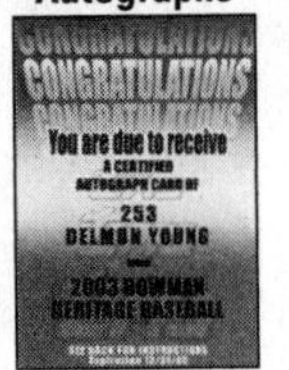

MINT NRMT
STATED ODDS 1:1014
EXCHANGE DEADLINE 12/31/05
253 Delmon Young KN EXCH 60.00 27.00

2003 Bowman Heritage Box Toppers

MINT NRMT
COMPLETE SET (8) 25.00 11.00
*BOX TOPPER: .4X TO 1X BASIC
ONE PER SEALED BOX

2003 Bowman Heritage Facsimile Signature

MINT NRMT
*FACSIMILE 161-170: 1X TO 2.5X BASIC
*FACSIMILE 171A-180C: 1X TO 2.5X BASIC
*FACSIMILE 181-280: .6X TO 1.5X BASIC
ONE PER PACK

2003 Bowman Heritage Gold Rainbow

MINT NRMT
STATED ODDS 1:4178
STATED PRINT RUN 1 SERIAL #'d SET
NO PRICING DUE TO SCARCITY

2003 Bowman Heritage Rainbow

MINT NRMT
COMPLETE SET (100) 80.00 36.00
*RAINBOW: .4X TO 1X BASIC
ONE PER PACK

2003 Bowman Heritage Diamond Cuts Relics

MINT NRMT
BAT ODDS 1:133
JSY GROUP A ODDS 1:28
JSY GROUP B ODDS 1:936
JSY GROUP C ODDS 1:626
UNI ODDS 1:35
GOLD STATED ODDS 1:8193
GOLD PRINT RUN 1 SERIAL #'d SET
NO GOLD PRICING DUE TO SCARCITY
*RED BAT: .6X TO 1.5X BASIC BAT
*RED JSY: 1X TO 2.5X BASIC JSY

*RED UNI: 1X TO 2.5X BASIC UNI
RED STATED ODDS 1:143
RED PRINT RUN 56 SERIAL #'d SETS
AJ Andruw Jones Jsy A 8.00 3.60
AK Austin Kearns Jsy A 8.00 3.60
AP Albert Pujols Bat 25.00 11.00
AR1 Alex Rodriguez Bat 15.00 6.75
AR2 Alex Rodriguez Jsy A 10.00 4.50
AS Alfonso Soriano Bat 15.00 6.75
BB Bret Boone Jsy A 8.00 3.60
BM Brett Myers Jsy A 8.00 3.60
BW Bernie Williams Uni 10.00 4.50
BZ Barry Zito Uni 10.00 4.50
CB Craig Biggio Uni 10.00 4.50
CF Cliff Floyd Uni 8.00 3.60
CG Cristian Guzman Jsy A 8.00 3.60
CJ1 Chipper Jones Bat 15.00 6.75
CJ2 Chipper Jones Jsy A 10.00 4.50
EC Eric Chavez Uni 8.00 3.60
GS Gary Sheffield Uni 8.00 3.60
HB Hank Blalock Bat 15.00 6.75
HN Hideo Nomo Jsy A 10.00 4.50
JA Jeremy Affeldt Uni 8.00 3.60
JB Jeff Bagwell Jsy A 10.00 4.50
JE Jim Edmonds Uni 8.00 3.60
JG Jason Giambi Uni 10.00 4.50
JJ Jason Jennings Jsy A 8.00 3.60
JL Javy Lopez Jsy A 8.00 3.60
JLP Josh Phelps Jsy C 8.00 3.60
JR Jose Reyes Jsy A 10.00 4.50
JV Javier Vazquez Jsy A 8.00 3.60
JW Jarrod Washburn Uni 8.00 3.60
KI Kazuhiro Sasaki Jsy A 8.00 3.60
KM Kevin Millwood Jsy A 8.00 3.60
KW Kerry Wood Uni 10.00 4.50
MA Moises Alou Jsy C 8.00 3.60
MG Mark Grace Jsy B 10.00 4.50
ML Mike Lowell Jsy A 8.00 3.60
MM Mark Mulder Uni 8.00 3.60
MS Mike Sweeney Jsy A 8.00 3.60
MT Miguel Tejada Uni 8.00 3.60
PL Paul Lo Duca Jsy A 8.00 3.60
PM Pedro Martinez Jsy A 10.00 4.50
RC Roberto Clemente Bat 80.00 36.00
RH Rickey Henderson Bat 15.00 6.75
RP1 Rafael Palmeiro Bat 15.00 6.75
RP2 Rafael Palmeiro Uni 10.00 4.50
SR1 Scott Rolen Bat 15.00 6.75
SR2 Scott Rolen Uni 10.00 4.50
SS1 Sammy Sosa Bat 15.00 6.75
SS2 Sammy Sosa Jsy A 10.00 4.50
TA Tony Armas Jr. Jsy A 8.00 3.60
TG Troy Glaus Uni 10.00 4.50
TH Todd Helton Jsy A 10.00 4.50
THA Tim Hudson Uni 8.00 3.60
TW Ty Wigginton Uni 8.00 3.60
VG Vladimir Guerrero Bat 15.00 6.75
VW Vernon Wells Jsy A 8.00 3.60

2003 Bowman Heritage Olbermann Autograph

MINT NRMT
STATED ODDS 1:1421
KOA Keith Olbermann 80.00 36.00

2003 Bowman Heritage Signs of Greatness

MINT NRMT
STATED ODDS 1:30
RED INK STATED ODDS 1:32,141
RED INK PRINT RUN 1 SERIAL #'d SET
NO RED INK PRICING DUE TO SCARCITY
BF Brian Finch 10.00 4.50
BS Brian Snyder 10.00 4.50
CB Chad Billingsley 15.00 6.75
DW Dontrelle Willis 30.00 13.50
FP Felix Pie 25.00 11.00
JD Jeff Duncan 10.00 4.50
KY Kevin Youkilis 25.00 11.00
MM Matt Murton 10.00 4.50
RC Robinson Cano 10.00 4.50
RH Rich Harden 20.00 9.00
RW Rickie Weeks 30.00 13.50
TG Tom Gorzelanny 10.00 4.50

2003 Bowman Heritage Team Topps Blue Chips Autographs

MINT NRMT
GROUP A ODDS 1:709

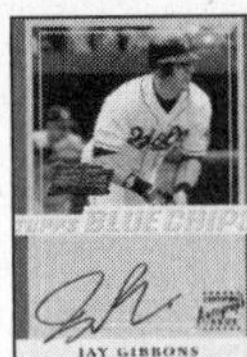

GROUP B ODDS 1:142
SEE 03 TEAM TOPPS BLUE CHIP FOR PRICES

1994 Bowman's Best

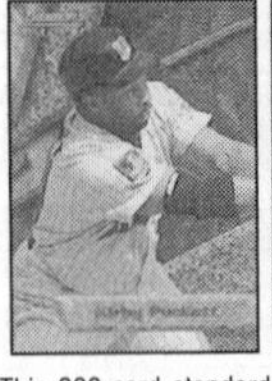

This 200-card standard-size set (produced by Topps) consists of 90 veteran stars, 90 rookies and prospects and 20 Mirror Image cards. The veteran cards have red fronts and are designated 1R-90R. The rookies and prospects cards have blue fronts and are designated 1B-90B. The Mirror Image cards feature a veteran star and a prospect matched by position in a horizontal design. These cards are numbered 91-110. Subsets featured are Super Vet (1R-6R), Super Rookie (82R-90R), and Blue Chip (1B-11B). Rookie Cards include Edgardo Alfonzo, Tony Clark, Brad Fullmer, Chan Ho Park, Jorge Posada and Edgar Renteria.

Nm-Mt Ex-Mt
COMPLETE SET (200) 40.00 12.00
B1 Chipper Jones 1.25 .35
B2 Derek Jeter 4.00 1.20
B3 Bill Pulsipher .50 .15
B4 James Baldwin .25 .07
B5 Brooks Kieschnick RC 1.00 .30
B6 Justin Thompson .25 .07
B7 Midre Cummings .25 .07
B8 Joey Hamilton .25 .07
B9 Pokey Reese .25 .07
B10 Brian Barber .25 .07
B11 John Burke .25 .07
B12 DeShawn Warren .25 .07
B13 Edgardo Alfonzo RC 2.50 .75
B14 Eddie Pearson RC .50 .15
B15 Jimmy Haynes .25 .07
B16 Danny Bautista .25 .07
B17 Roger Cedeno .25 .07
B18 Jon Lieber .25 .07
B19 Billy Wagner RC 2.50 .75
B20 Tate Seefried RC .50 .15
B21 Chad Mottola .25 .07
B22 Jose Malave .25 .07
B23 Terrell Wade RC .50 .15
B24 Shane Andrews .25 .07
B25 Chan Ho Park RC 2.50 .75
B26 Kirk Presley RC .50 .15
B27 Robbie Beckett .25 .07
B28 Orlando Miller .25 .07
B29 Jorge Posada RC 8.00 2.40
B30 Frankie Rodriguez .25 .07
B31 Brian L. Hunter .25 .07
B32 Billy Ashley .25 .07
B33 Rondell White .50 .15
B34 John Roper .25 .07
B35 Marc Valdes .25 .07
B36 Scott Ruffcorn .25 .07
B37 Rod Henderson .25 .07
B38 Curtis Goodwin RC .50 .15
B39 Russ Davis .25 .07
B40 Rick Gorecki .25 .07
B41 Johnny Damon 1.25 .35
B42 Roberto Petagine .25 .07
B43 Chris Snopek .25 .07
B44 Mark Acre RC .50 .15
B45 Todd Hollandsworth .25 .07
B46 Shawn Green 1.25 .35
B47 John Carter RC .50 .15
B48 Jim Pittsley RC .50 .15
B49 John Wasdin RC .50 .15
B50 D.J. Boston RC .50 .15
B51 Tim Clark .25 .07
B52 Alex Ochoa .25 .07
B53 Chad Roper .25 .07
B54 Mike Kelly .25 .07
B55 Brad Fullmer RC 2.50 .75
B56 Carl Everett .50 .15
B57 Tim Belk RC .50 .15
B58 Jimmy Hurst RC .50 .15
B59 Mac Suzuki RC 1.00 .30
B60 Mike Moore .25 .07
B61 Alan Benes RC .50 .15
B62 Tony Clark RC 1.00 .30
B63 Edgar Renteria RC 8.00 2.40
B64 Trey Beamon .25 .07
B65 LaTroy Hawkins RC 1.00 .30
B66 Wayne Gomes RC 1.00 .30
B67 Ray McDavid .25 .07
B68 John Dettmer .25 .07
B69 Willie Greene .25 .07
B70 Dave Stevens .25 .07
B71 Kevin Orie RC .25 .07
B72 Chad Ogea .25 .07
B73 Ben Van Ryn RC .50 .15
B74 Kym Ashworth RC .50 .15
B75 Dmitri Young .50 .15
B76 Herbert Perry RC 1.00 .30
B77 Joey Eischen .25 .07
B78 Arquimedez Pozo RC .50 .15
B79 Ugueth Urbina .25 .07
B80 Keith Williams RC .50 .15
B81 John Frascatore RC .50 .15
B82 Garey Ingram RC .50 .15
B83 Aaron Small .25 .07
B84 Olmedo Saenz RC .50 .15
B85 Jesus Tavarez RC .50 .15
B86 Jose Silva RC 1.00 .30
B87 Jay Witasick RC .50 .15
B88 Jay Maldonado RC .50 .15
B89 Keith Heberling RC .50 .15
B90 Rusty Greer RC 1.50 .45
R1 Paul Molitor .75 .23
R2 Eddie Murray 1.25 .35
R3 Ozzie Smith 2.00 .60
R4 Rickey Henderson 1.25 .35
R5 Lee Smith .50 .15
R6 Dave Winfield .50 .15
R7 Roberto Alomar 1.25 .35
R8 Matt Williams .50 .15
R9 Mark Grace .75 .23
R10 Lance Johnson .25 .07
R11 Darren Daulton .50 .15
R12 Tom Glavine .75 .23
R13 Gary Sheffield .50 .15
R14 Rod Beck .25 .07
R15 Fred McGriff .75 .23
R16 Joe Carter .50 .15
R17 Dante Bichette .50 .15
R18 Danny Tartabull .25 .07
R19 Juan Gonzalez 1.25 .35
R20 Steve Avery .25 .07
R21 John Wetteland .50 .15
R22 Ben McDonald .25 .07
R23 Jack McDowell .25 .07
R24 Jose Canseco 1.25 .35
R25 Tim Salmon .75 .23
R26 Wilson Alvarez .25 .07
R27 Gregg Jefferies .25 .07
R28 John Burkett .25 .07
R29 Greg Vaughn .50 .15
R30 Robin Ventura .50 .15
R31 Paul O'Neill .75 .23
R32 Cecil Fielder .50 .15
R33 Kevin Mitchell .25 .07
R34 Jeff Conine .50 .15
R35 Carlos Baerga .25 .07
R36 Greg Maddux 2.00 .60
R37 Roger Clemens 2.50 .75
R38 Deion Sanders .75 .23
R39 Delino DeShields .25 .07
R40 Ken Griffey Jr. 2.00 .60
R41 Albert Belle .50 .15
R42 Wade Boggs .75 .23
R43 Andres Galarraga .50 .15
R44 Aaron Sele .25 .07
R45 Don Mattingly 3.00 .90
R46 David Cone .50 .15
R47 Len Dykstra .50 .15
R48 Brett Butler .50 .15
R49 Bill Swift .25 .07
R50 Bobby Bonilla .50 .15
R51 Rafael Palmeiro .75 .23
R52 Moises Alou .50 .15
R53 Jeff Bagwell .75 .23
R54 Mike Mussina 1.25 .35
R55 Frank Thomas 1.25 .35
R56 Jose Rijo .25 .07
R57 Ruben Sierra .25 .07
R58 Randy Myers .25 .07
R59 Barry Bonds 3.00 .90
R60 Jimmy Key .50 .15
R61 Travis Fryman .50 .15
R62 John Olerud .50 .15
R63 David Justice .50 .15
R64 Ray Lankford .25 .07
R65 Bob Tewksbury .25 .07
R66 Chuck Carr .25 .07
R67 Jay Buhner .50 .15
R68 Kenny Lofton .50 .15
R69 Marquis Grissom .25 .07
R70 Sammy Sosa 2.00 .60
R71 Cal Ripken 4.00 1.20
R72 Ellis Burks .50 .15
R73 Jeff Montgomery .25 .07
R74 Julio Franco .50 .15
R75 Kirby Puckett 1.25 .35
R76 Larry Walker .75 .23
R77 Andy Van Slyke .50 .15
R78 Tony Gwynn 1.50 .45
R79 Will Clark 1.25 .35
R80 Mo Vaughn .50 .15
R81 Mike Piazza 2.50 .75
R82 James Mouton .25 .07
R83 Carlos Delgado .75 .23
R84 Ryan Klesko .50 .15
R85 Javier Lopez .50 .15
R86 Raul Mondesi .50 .15
R87 Cliff Floyd .50 .15
R88 Manny Ramirez .75 .23
R89 Hector Carrasco .25 .07
R90 Jeff Granger .25 .07
X91 Frank Thomas .75 .23
Dmitri Young
X92 Fred McGriff .50 .15
Brooks Kieschnick
X93 Matt Williams .25 .07
Shane Andrews
X94 Cal Ripken 2.00 .60
Kevin Orie
X95 Barry Larkin 2.00 .60
Derek Jeter
X96 Ken Griffey Jr. 1.00 .30
Johnny Damon
X97 Barry Bonds 1.50 .45
Rondell White
X98 Albert Belle .50 .15
Jimmy Hurst
X99 Raul Mondesi .50 .15
Ruben Rivera RC
X100 Roger Clemens 1.25 .35
Scott Ruffcorn
X101 Greg Maddux 1.25 .35
John Wasdin
X102 Tim Salmon .75 .23
Chad Mottola
X103 Carlos Baerga .25 .07
Arquimedez Pozo
X104 Mike Piazza 1.25 .35
Bobby Hughes
X105 Carlos Delgado .75 .23
Melvin Nieves
X106 Javier Lopez 2.50 .75
Jorge Posada
X107 Manny Ramirez .75 .23
Jose Malave
X108 Travis Fryman .75 .23

Chipper Jones
X109 Steve Avery .25 .07
Bill Pulsipher
X110 John Olerud 1.25 .35
Shawn Green

1994 Bowman's Best Refractors

This 200-card standard-size set is a parallel to the basic Bowman's Best issue. The cards were randomly inserted in packs at a rate of one in nine packs. The only difference is the refractive coating on front that allows for a brighter, shinier appearance.

Nm-Mt Ex-Mt
*RED STARS: 4X TO 10X BASIC CARDS
*BLUE STARS: 4X TO 10X BASIC CARDS
*BLUE ROOKIES: 1.5X TO 4X BASIC ..
*MIRROR IMAGE STARS: 2X TO 5X BASIC

1995 Bowman's Best

This 195 card standard-size set (produced by Topps) consists of 90 veteran stars, 90 rookies and prospects and 15 dual player Mirror Image cards. The packs contain seven cards and the suggested retail price was $5. The veteran cards have red fronts and are designated R1-R90. Cards of rookies and prospects have blue fronts and are designated B1-B90. The Mirror Image cards feature a veteran star and a prospect matched by position in a horizontal design. These cards are numbered X1-X15. Rookie Cards include Bob Abreu, Bartolo Colon, Scott Elarton, Juan Encarnacion, Vladimir Guerrero, Andruw Jones, Hideo Nomo, Rey Ordonez, Scott Rolen and Richie Sexson.

Nm-Mt Ex-Mt
COMPLETE SET (195) 250.00 75.00
COMMON CARD (B1-R90) .50 .15
COMMON CARD (X1-X15) .50 .15
B1 Derek Jeter 3.00 .90
B2 Vladimir Guerrero RC 80.00 24.00
B3 Bob Abreu RC 10.00 3.00
B4 Chan Ho Park .50 .15
B5 Paul Wilson .50 .15
B6 Chad Ogea .50 .15
B7 Andruw Jones RC 50.00 15.00
B8 Brian Barber .50 .15
B9 Andy Larkin .50 .15
B10 Richie Sexson RC 15.00 4.50
B11 Everett Stull .50 .15
B12 Brooks Kieschnick .50 .15
B13 Matt Murray .50 .15
B14 John Wasdin .50 .15
B15 Shannon Stewart .50 .15
B16 Luis Ortiz .50 .15
B17 Marc Kroon .50 .15
B18 Todd Greene .50 .15
B19 Juan Acevedo RC 1.00 .30
B20 Tony Clark .50 .15
B21 Jermaine Dye .50 .15
B22 Derrek Lee .50 .15
B23 Pat Watkins .50 .15
B24 Pokey Reese .50 .15
B25 Ben Grieve .50 .15
B26 Julio Santana RC .50 .15
B27 Felix Rodriguez RC 2.00 .60
B28 Paul Konerko 2.00 .60
B29 Nomar Garciaparra 8.00 2.40
B30 Pat Ahearne .50 .15
B31 Jason Schmidt 1.50 .45
B32 Billy Wagner .50 .15
B33 Rey Ordonez RC 3.00 .90
B34 Curtis Goodwin .50 .15
B35 Sergio Nunez RC 1.00 .30
B36 Tim Belk .50 .15
B37 Scott Elarton RC 2.00 .60
B38 Jason Isringhausen .50 .15
B39 Trot Nixon .75 .23
B40 Sid Roberson RC 1.00 .30
B41 Ron Villone .50 .15
B42 Ruben Rivera .50 .15
B43 Rick Huisman .50 .15
B44 Todd Hollandsworth .50 .15
B45 Johnny Damon .75 .23
B46 Garret Anderson .50 .15
B47 Jeff D'Amico .50 .15
B48 Dustin Hermanson .50 .15
B49 Juan Encarnacion RC 5.00 1.50
B50 Andy Pettitte .75 .23
B51 Chris Stynes .50 .15
B52 Troy Percival .50 .15
B53 LaTroy Hawkins .50 .15
B54 Roger Cedeno .50 .15
B55 Alan Benes .50 .15
B56 Karim Garcia RC 2.00 .60
B57 Andrew Lorraine .50 .15
B58 Gary Rath RC 1.00 .30
B59 Bret Wagner .50 .15
B60 Jeff Suppan .50 .15
B61 Bill Pulsipher .50 .15
B62 Jay Payton RC 3.00 .90
B63 Alex Ochoa .50 .15
B64 Ugueth Urbina .50 .15
B65 Armando Benitez .50 .15
B66 George Arias .50 .15
B67 Raul Casanova RC 1.00 .30
B68 Matt Drews .50 .15
B69 Jimmy Haynes .50 .15
B70 Jimmy Hurst .50 .15
B71 C.J. Nitkowski .50 .15
B72 Tommy Davis RC 1.00 .30
B73 Bartolo Colon RC 10.00 3.00
B74 Chris Carpenter RC 2.00 .60
B75 Trey Beamon .50 .15
B76 Bryan Rekar .50 .15
B77 James Baldwin .50 .15
B78 Marc Valdes .50 .15
B79 Tom Fordham RC 1.00 .30
B80 Marc Newfield .50 .15
B81 Angel Martinez .50 .15
B82 Brian L. Hunter .50 .15
B83 Jose Herrera .50 .15
B84 Glenn Dishman RC 1.00 .30
B85 Jacob Cruz RC 2.00 .60
B86 Paul Shuey .50 .15
B87 Scott Rolen RC 30.00 9.00
B88 Doug Million .50 .15
B89 Desi Relaford .50 .15
B90 Michael Tucker .50 .15
R1 Randy Johnson 1.25 .35
R2 Joe Carter .50 .15
R3 Chili Davis .50 .15
R4 Moises Alou .50 .15
R5 Gary Sheffield .50 .15
R6 Kevin Appier .50 .15
R7 Denny Neagle .50 .15
R8 Ruben Sierra .50 .15
R9 Darren Daulton .50 .15
R10 Cal Ripken 4.00 1.20
R11 Bobby Bonilla .50 .15
R12 Manny Ramirez .50 .15
R13 Barry Bonds 3.00 .90
R14 Eric Karros .50 .15
R15 Greg Maddux 2.00 .60
R16 Jeff Bagwell .75 .23
R17 Paul Molitor .75 .23
R18 Ray Lankford .50 .15
R19 Mark Grace .75 .23
R20 Kenny Lofton .50 .15
R21 Tony Gwynn 1.50 .45
R22 Will Clark 1.25 .35
R23 Roger Clemens 2.50 .75
R24 Dante Bichette .50 .15
R25 Barry Larkin 1.25 .35
R26 Wade Boggs .75 .23
R27 Kirby Puckett 1.25 .35
R28 Cecil Fielder .50 .15
R29 Jose Canseco 1.25 .35
R30 Juan Gonzalez 1.25 .35
R31 David Cone .50 .15
R32 Craig Biggio .75 .23
R33 Tim Salmon .75 .23
R34 David Justice .50 .15
R35 Sammy Sosa 2.00 .60
R36 Mike Piazza 2.00 .60
R37 Carlos Baerga .50 .15
R38 Jeff Conine .50 .15
R39 Rafael Palmeiro .75 .23
R40 Bret Saberhagen .50 .15
R41 Len Dykstra .50 .15
R42 Mo Vaughn .50 .15
R43 Wally Joyner .50 .15
R44 Chuck Knoblauch .50 .15
R45 Robin Ventura .50 .15
R46 Don Mattingly 3.00 .90
R47 Dave Hollins .50 .15
R48 Andy Benes .50 .15
R49 Ken Griffey Jr. 2.00 .60
R50 Albert Belle .50 .15
R51 Matt Williams .50 .15
R52 Rondell White .50 .15
R53 Raul Mondesi .50 .15
R54 Brian Jordan .50 .15
R55 Greg Vaughn .50 .15
R56 Fred McGriff .75 .23
R57 Roberto Alomar 1.25 .35
R58 Dennis Eckersley .50 .15
R59 Lee Smith .50 .15
R60 Eddie Murray 1.25 .35
R61 Kenny Rogers .50 .15
R62 Ron Gant .50 .15
R63 Larry Walker .75 .23
R64 Chad Curtis .50 .15
R65 Frank Thomas 1.25 .35
R66 Paul O'Neill .75 .23
R67 Kevin Seitzer .50 .15
R68 Marquis Grissom .50 .15
R69 Mark McGwire 4.00 1.20
R70 Travis Fryman .50 .15
R71 Andres Galarraga .50 .15
R72 Carlos Perez RC 2.00 .60
R73 Tyler Green .50 .15
R74 Marty Cordova .50 .15
R75 Shawn Green .50 .15
R76 Vaughn Eshelman .50 .15
R77 John Mabry .50 .15
R78 Jason Bates .50 .15
R79 Jon Nunnally .50 .15
R80 Ray Durham .50 .15
R81 Edgardo Alfonzo .50 .15
R82 Esteban Loaiza .50 .15
R83 Hideo Nomo RC 12.00 3.60
R84 Orlando Miller .50 .15
R85 Alex Gonzalez .50 .15
R86 M.Grudzielanek RC 3.00 .90
R87 Julian Tavarez .50 .15
R88 Benji Gil .50 .15
R89 Quilvio Veras .50 .15
R90 Ricky Bottalico .50 .15
X1 Ben Davis RC 1.50 .45
Ivan Rodriguez
X2 Mark Redman RC 2.50 .75
Manny Ramirez
X3 Reggie Taylor RC 1.50 .45
Deion Sanders
X4 Ryan Jaroncyk RC .50 .15
Shawn Green
X5 Juan LeBron RC 2.00 .60
Juan Gonzalez UER
Card pictures Carlos Beltran instead of Juan LeBron.
X6 Tony McKnight RC .50 .15
Craig Biggio
X7 Michael Barrett RC 2.50 .75
Travis Fryman
X8 Corey Jenkins RC .50 .15
Mo Vaughn
X9 Ruben Rivera 1.25 .35
Frank Thomas
X10 Curtis Goodwin .50 .15
Kenny Lofton
X11 Brian L. Hunter .75 .23
Tony Gwynn
X12 Todd Greene 1.25 .35
Ken Griffey Jr.
X13 Karim Garcia .50 .15
Matt Williams
X14 Billy Wagner .75 .23
Randy Johnson
X15 Pat Watkins .75 .23
Jeff Bagwell

1995 Bowman's Best Refractors

Randomly inserted at a rate of one in six packs, this set is a parallel to the basic Bowman's Best issue. As far as the refractive qualities, the final 15 Mirror Image cards (X1-X15) are considered diffractors which reflects light in a different manner than the typical refractor. Unlike the 180 red and blue Refractors, the Mirror Image Diffractors are seeded into packs at a rate of 1:12. The veteran red refractor cards have been seen with or without the word refractor on the back. These cards without the refractor markings are valued at the same price as the regular refractors.

Nm-Mt Ex-Mt
*STARS: 4X TO 10X BASIC CARDS ....
*RCs: 1.5X TO 4X BASIC CARDS........
*MIRROR IMAGE: 1.25X TO 3X BASIC CARDS

1995 Bowman's Best Jumbo Refractors

This ten-card set was produced for various retail outlets. One card was inserted into each specially marked retail Topps box. According to Treat, Inc. there are no more than 9,000 of each card issued. Each over-sized card measures approximately 4" by 6". The most available of these cards are Albert Belle and Greg Maddux since they were distributed nationally. The other eight players were issued on a more regional basis. The cards are an exact parallel of the standard-size Refractor inserts except for their larger size.

Nm-Mt Ex-Mt
COMPLETE SET (10) 125.00 38.00
1 Albert Belle DP 4.00 1.20
2 Ken Griffey Jr 20.00 6.00
3 Tony Gwynn 15.00 4.50
4 Greg Maddux DP 8.00 2.40
5 Hideo Nomo 15.00 4.50
6 Mike Piazza 20.00 6.00
7 Cal Ripken 30.00 9.00
8 Sammy Sosa 15.00 4.50
9 Frank Thomas 8.00 2.40
10 Mo Vaughn 5.00 1.50

1996 Bowman's Best Previews

Printed with Finest technology, this 30-card set features the hottest 15 top prospects and 15 veterans and was randomly inserted in 1996 Bowman packs at the rate of one in 12. The fronts display a color action player photo. The backs carry player information.

Nm-Mt Ex-Mt
COMPLETE SET (30) 60.00 18.00
*REFRACTORS: .5X TO 1.2X BASIC PREVIEWS
REFRACTOR STATED ODDS 1:24 ......
*ATOMIC: 1X TO 2.5X BASIC PREVIEWS
ATOMIC STATED ODDS 1:48 ....
BBP1 Chipper Jones 2.50 .75
BBP2 Alan Benes 1.00 .30
BBP3 Brooks Kieschnick 1.00 .30
BBP4 Barry Bonds 6.00 1.80
BBP5 Rey Ordonez 1.00 .30
BBP6 Tim Salmon 1.50 .45
BBP7 Mike Piazza 4.00 1.20
BBP8 Billy Wagner 1.00 .30
BBP9 Andruw Jones 4.00 1.20
BBP10 Tony Gwynn 3.00 .90
BBP11 Paul Wilson 1.00 .30
BBP12 Pokey Reese 1.00 .30
BBP13 Frank Thomas 2.50 .75
BBP14 Greg Maddux 4.00 1.20
BBP15 Derek Jeter 6.00 1.80
BBP16 Jeff Bagwell 1.50 .45
BBP17 Barry Larkin 2.50 .75
BBP18 Todd Greene 1.00 .30
BBP19 Ruben Rivera 1.00 .30
BBP20 Richard Hidalgo 1.00 .30
BBP21 Larry Walker 1.50 .45
BBP22 Carlos Baerga 1.00 .30
BBP23 Derrick Gibson 1.00 .30
BBP24 Richie Sexson 1.50 .45
BBP25 Mo Vaughn 1.00 .30
BBP26 Hideo Nomo 2.50 .75
BBP27 N.Garciaparra 5.00 1.50
BBP28 Cal Ripken 8.00 2.40
BBP29 Karim Garcia 1.00 .30
BBP30 Ken Griffey Jr 4.00 1.20

1996 Bowman's Best

This 180-card set was (produced by Topps) issued in packs of six cards at the cost of $4.99 per pack. The fronts feature a color action player cutout of 90 outstanding veteran players on a chromium gold background design and 90 up and coming prospects and rookies on a silver design. The backs carry a color player portrait, player information and statistics. Card number 33 was never actually issued. Instead, both Roger Clemens and Rafael Palmeiro are erroneously numbered 32. A chrome reprint of the 1952 Bowman Mickey Mantle was inserted at the rate of one in 24 packs. A Refractor version of the Mantle was seeded at 1:96 packs and an Atomic Refractor version was seeded at 1:192. Notable Rookie Cards include Geoff Jenkins and Mike Sweeney.

Nm-Mt Ex-Mt
COMPLETE SET (180) 40.00 12.00
1 Hideo Nomo 1.00 .30
2 Edgar Martinez .60 .18
3 Cal Ripken 3.00 .90
4 Wade Boggs .60 .18
5 Cecil Fielder .40 .12
6 Albert Belle .40 .12
7 Chipper Jones 1.00 .30
8 Ryne Sandberg 1.50 .45
9 Tim Salmon .60 .18
10 Barry Bonds 2.50 .75
11 Ken Caminiti .40 .12
12 Ron Gant .40 .12
13 Frank Thomas 1.00 .30
14 Dante Bichette .40 .12
15 Jason Kendall .40 .12
16 Mo Vaughn .40 .12
17 Rey Ordonez .40 .12
18 Henry Rodriguez .40 .12
19 Ryan Klesko .40 .12
20 Jeff Bagwell .60 .18
21 Randy Johnson 1.00 .30
22 Jim Edmonds .40 .12
23 Kenny Lofton .40 .12
24 Andy Pettitte .60 .18
25 Brady Anderson .40 .12
26 Mike Piazza 1.50 .45
27 Greg Vaughn .40 .12
28 Joe Carter .40 .12
29 Jason Giambi 1.00 .30
30 Ivan Rodriguez 1.00 .30
31 Jeff Conine .40 .12
32 Rafael Palmeiro .60 .18
33 Roger Clemens 2.00 .60
34 Chuck Knoblauch .40 .12
35 Reggie Sanders .40 .12
36 Andres Galarraga .40 .12
37 Paul O'Neill .60 .18
38 Tony Gwynn 1.25 .35
39 Paul Wilson .40 .12
40 Garret Anderson .40 .12
41 David Justice .40 .12
42 Eddie Murray 1.00 .30
43 Mike Grace RC .50 .15
44 Marty Cordova .40 .12
45 Kevin Appier .40 .12
46 Raul Mondesi .40 .12
47 Jim Thome 1.00 .30
48 Sammy Sosa 1.50 .45
49 Craig Biggio .60 .18
50 Marquis Grissom .40 .12
51 Alan Benes .40 .12
52 Manny Ramirez .40 .12
53 Gary Sheffield .40 .12
54 Mike Mussina 1.00 .30
55 Robin Ventura .40 .12
56 Johnny Damon .40 .12
57 Jose Canseco 1.00 .30
58 Juan Gonzalez 1.00 .30
59 Tino Martinez .60 .18
60 Brian Hunter .40 .12
61 Fred McGriff .60 .18
62 Jay Buhner .40 .12
63 Carlos Delgado .40 .12
64 Moises Alou .40 .12
65 Roberto Alomar 1.00 .30
66 Barry Larkin 1.00 .30
67 Vinny Castilla .40 .12
68 Ray Durham .40 .12
69 Travis Fryman .40 .12
70 Jason Isringhausen .40 .12
71 Ken Griffey Jr. 1.50 .45
72 John Smoltz .60 .18
73 Matt Williams .40 .12
74 Chan Ho Park .40 .12
75 Mark McGwire 3.00 .90
76 Jeffrey Hammonds .40 .12
77 Will Clark 1.00 .30
78 Kirby Puckett 1.00 .30
79 Derek Jeter 2.50 .75
80 Derek Bell .40 .12
81 Eric Karros .40 .12
82 Len Dykstra .40 .12
83 Larry Walker .60 .18
84 Mark Grudzielanek .40 .12
85 Greg Maddux 1.50 .45
86 Carlos Baerga .40 .12
87 Paul Molitor .60 .18
88 John Valentin .40 .12
89 Mark Grace .60 .18
90 Ray Lankford .40 .12
91 Andruw Jones 1.50 .45
92 Nomar Garciaparra 2.00 .60
93 Alex Ochoa .40 .12
94 Derrick Gibson .40 .12
95 Jeff D'Amico .40 .12
96 Ruben Rivera .40 .12
97 Vladimir Guerrero 2.00 .60
98 Pokey Reese .40 .12
99 Richard Hidalgo .40 .12
100 Bartolo Colon .40 .12
101 Karim Garcia .40 .12
102 Ben Davis .40 .12
103 Jay Powell .40 .12
104 Chris Snopek .40 .12
105 Glendon Rusch RC .75 .23
106 Enrique Wilson .40 .12
107 A.Alfonseca RC .75 .23
108 Wilton Guerrero RC .75 .23
109 Jose Guillen RC 4.00 1.20
110 Miguel Mejia RC .50 .15
111 Jay Payton .40 .12
112 Scott Elarton .40 .12
113 Brooks Kieschnick .40 .12
114 Dustin Hermanson .40 .12
115 Roger Cedeno .40 .12
116 Matt Wagner .40 .12
117 Lee Daniels .40 .12
118 Ben Grieve .40 .12
119 Ugueth Urbina .40 .12
120 Danny Graves .40 .12
121 Dan Donato RC .50 .15
122 Matt Ruebel RC .50 .15
123 Mark Sievert RC .50 .15
124 Chris Stynes .40 .12
125 Jeff Abbott .40 .12
126 Rocky Coppinger RC .50 .15
127 Jermaine Dye .40 .12
128 Todd Greene .40 .12
129 Chris Carpenter .40 .12
130 Edgar Renteria .40 .12
131 Matt Drews .40 .12
132 Edgard Velazquez RC .50 .15
133 Casey Whitten .40 .12
134 Ryan Jones RC .50 .15
135 Todd Walker .60 .18
136 Geoff Jenkins RC 4.00 1.20
137 Matt Morris RC 5.00 1.50
138 Richie Sexson .60 .18
139 Todd Dunwoody RC .50 .15
140 Gabe Alvarez RC .50 .15
141 J.J. Johnson .40 .12
142 Shannon Stewart .40 .12
143 Brad Fullmer .40 .12
144 Julio Santana .40 .12
145 Scott Rolen 1.25 .35
146 Amaury Telemaco .40 .12
147 Trey Beamon .40 .12
148 Billy Wagner .40 .12
149 Todd Hollandsworth .40 .12
150 Doug Million .40 .12
151 Javier Valentin RC .50 .15
152 Wes Helms RC 1.25 .35
153 Jeff Suppan .40 .12
154 Luis Castillo RC 4.00 1.20
155 Bob Abreu .40 .12
156 Paul Konerko .40 .12
157 Jamey Wright .40 .12
158 Eddie Pearson .40 .12
159 Jimmy Haynes .40 .12
160 Derrek Lee .40 .12
161 Damian Moss .40 .12
162 Carlos Guillen RC 2.00 .60
163 Chris Fussell RC .50 .15
164 Mike Sweeney RC 6.00 1.80
165 Donnie Sadler .40 .12
166 Desi Relaford .40 .12
167 Steve Gibralter .40 .12
168 Neifi Perez .40 .12
169 Antone Williamson .40 .12
170 Marty Janzen RC .50 .15
171 Todd Helton 2.00 .60
172 Raul Ibanez RC 2.50 .75
173 Bill Selby .40 .12
174 Shane Monahan RC .50 .15
175 Robin Jennings .40 .12
176 Bobby Chouinard .40 .12
177 Einar Diaz .40 .12
178 Jason Thompson .40 .12
179 Rafael Medina RC .50 .15
180 Kevin Orie .40 .12
NNO Mickey Mantle 10.00 3.00
1952 Bowman Atomic Ref.
NNO Mickey Mantle 5.00 1.50
1952 Bowman Refractor
NNO Mickey Mantle 2.50 .75
1952 Bowman Chrome

1996 Bowman's Best Atomic Refractors

Inserted one in every 48 hobby packs and one in every 80 retail packs, this 180-card set is parallel to the 1996 Bowman's Best set. It is similar in design to the regular set but was printed with sparkling refractor technology.

Nm-Mt Ex-Mt
*GOLD STARS: 6X TO 15X BASIC CARDS
*SILVER STARS: 6X TO 15X BASIC CARDS
*ROOKIES: 3X TO 8X BASIC CARDS ..

1996 Bowman's Best Refractors

This 180-card set is parallel to the regular 1996 Bowman Best set and is similar in design. The difference is in the refractive quality of the cards. The cards were inserted at the rate of one in every 12 hobby packs and one in every 20 retail packs.

Nm-Mt Ex-Mt
*GOLD STARS: 3X TO 8X BASIC CARDS
*SILVER STARS: 3X TO 8X BASIC CARDS
*ROOKIES: 1.5X TO 4X BASIC CARDS

1996 Bowman's Best Cuts

Randomly inserted in hobby packs at a rate of one in 24 and retail packs at a rate on one in 40, this chromium card die-cut set features 15 top hobby stars.

Nm-Mt Ex-Mt
COMPLETE SET (15) 80.00 24.00
*REFRACTORS: .6X TO 1.5X BASIC CUTS
REF.STATED ODDS 1:48 HOB, 1:80 RET
*ATOMIC: 1X TO 2.5X BASIC CUTS....
ATOMIC STATED ODDS 1:96 HOB, 1:160 RET
1 Ken Griffey Jr. 6.00 1.80
2 Jason Isringhausen 1.50 .45
3 Derek Jeter 10.00 3.00
4 Andruw Jones 6.00 1.80
5 Chipper Jones 4.00 1.20
6 Ryan Klesko 1.50 .45
7 Raul Mondesi 1.50 .45
8 Hideo Nomo 4.00 1.20
9 Mike Piazza 6.00 1.80
10 Manny Ramirez 1.50 .45
11 Cal Ripken 12.00 3.60
12 Ruben Rivera 1.50 .45
13 Tim Salmon 2.50 .75
14 Frank Thomas 4.00 1.20
15 Jim Thome 4.00 1.20

1996 Bowman's Best Mirror Image

Randomly inserted in hobby packs at a rate of one in 48 and retail packs at a rate of one in 80, this 10-card set features four top players on a single card at one of ten different positions. The fronts display a color photo of an AL veteran with a semicircle containing a color portrait of a prospect who plays the same position. The backs carry a color photo of an NL veteran with a semicircle color portrait of a prospect.

Nm-Mt Ex-Mt
COMPLETE SET (10) 80.00 24.00
*REFRACTORS: .6X TO 1.5X BASIC CARDS
REFRACTOR ODDS 1:96 HOB, 1:160 RET
*ATOMIC REFRACTORS: 1.25X TO 3X BASIC CARDS
ATOMIC ODDS 1:192 HOB, 1:320 RET
1 Jeff Bagwell 5.00 1.50
Todd Helton
Frank Thomas
Richie Sexson
2 Craig Biggio 2.50 .75
Luis Castillo
Roberto Alomar
Desi Relaford
3 Chipper Jones 5.00 1.50
Scott Rolen
Wade Boggs
George Arias
4 Barry Larkin 20.00 6.00
Neifi Perez
Cal Ripken
Mark Bellhorn
5 Larry Walker 4.00 1.20
Karim Garcia
Albert Belle
Ruben Rivera
6 Barry Bonds 20.00 6.00
Andruw Jones
Kenny Lofton
Donnie Sadler
7 Tony Gwynn 10.00 3.00
Vladimir Guerrero
Ken Griffey
Ben Grieve
8 Mike Piazza 10.00 3.00
Ben Davis
Ivan Rodriguez
Javier Valentin
9 Greg Maddux 12.00 3.60
Jamey Wright
Mike Mussina
Bartolo Colon
10 Tom Glavine 5.00 1.50
Billy Wagner
Randy Johnson
Jarrod Washburn

1997 Bowman's Best Preview

Randomly inserted in 1997 Bowman Series 1 packs at a rate of one in 12, this 20-card set features color photos of 10 rookies and 10 veterans that would be appearing in the 1997 Bowman's Best set. The background of each card features a flag of the featured player's homeland.

Nm-Mt Ex-Mt
COMPLETE SET (20) 80.00 24.00
*REF: .75X TO 2X BASIC PREVIEWS
REFRACTOR STATED ODDS 1:48
*ATOMIC REF: 1.5X TO 4X BASIC PREVIEWS
ATOMIC STATED ODDS 1:96
1 Frank Thomas 4.00 1.20
2 Ken Griffey Jr. 6.00 1.80
3 Barry Bonds 10.00 3.00
4 Derek Jeter 10.00 3.00
5 Chipper Jones 4.00 1.20
6 Mark McGwire 12.00 3.60
7 Cal Ripken 12.00 3.60
8 Kenny Lofton 1.50 .45
9 Gary Sheffield 1.50 .45
10 Jeff Bagwell 2.50 .75
11 Wilton Guerrero 1.50 .45
12 Scott Rolen 2.50 .75
13 Todd Walker 1.50 .45
14 Ruben Rivera 1.50 .45
15 Andruw Jones 1.50 .45
16 Nomar Garciaparra 6.00 1.80
17 Vladimir Guerrero 4.00 1.20
18 Miguel Tejada 6.00 1.80
19 Bartolo Colon 1.50 .45
20 Katsuhiro Maeda 1.50 .45

1997 Bowman's Best

The 1997 Bowman's Best set (produced by Topps) was issued in one series totalling 200 cards and was distributed in six-card packs (SRP $4.99). The fronts feature borderless color player photos printed on chromium card stock. The cards of the 100 current veteran stars display a classic gold design while the cards of the 100 top prospects carry a sleek silver design. Rookie Cards include Adrian Beltre, Kris Benson, Jose Cruz Jr., Travis Lee, Fernando Tatis, Miguel Tejada and Kerry Wood.

Nm-Mt Ex-Mt
COMPLETE SET (200) 40.00 12.00
1 Ken Griffey Jr. 1.50 .45
2 Cecil Fielder .40 .12
3 Albert Belle .40 .12
4 Todd Hundley .40 .12
5 Mike Piazza 1.50 .45
6 Matt Williams .40 .12
7 Mo Vaughn .40 .12
8 Ryne Sandberg 1.50 .45
9 Chipper Jones 1.00 .30
10 Edgar Martinez .60 .18
11 Kenny Lofton .40 .12
12 Ron Gant .40 .12
13 Moises Alou .40 .12
14 Pat Hentgen .40 .12
15 Steve Finley .40 .12
16 Mark Grace .60 .18
17 Jay Buhner .40 .12
18 Jeff Conine .40 .12
19 Jim Edmonds .40 .12
20 Todd Hollandsworth .40 .12
21 Andy Pettitte .60 .18
22 Jim Thome 1.00 .30
23 Eric Young .40 .12
24 Ray Lankford .40 .12
25 Marquis Grissom .40 .12
26 Tony Clark .40 .12
27 Jermaine Allensworth .40 .12
28 Ellis Burks .40 .12
29 Tony Gwynn 1.25 .35
30 Barry Larkin 1.00 .30
31 John Olerud .40 .12
32 Mariano Rivera .60 .18
33 Paul Molitor .60 .18
34 Ken Caminiti .40 .12
35 Gary Sheffield .40 .12
36 Al Martin .40 .12
37 John Valentin .40 .12
38 Frank Thomas 1.00 .30
39 John Jaha .40 .12
40 Greg Maddux 1.50 .45
41 Alex Fernandez .40 .12
42 Dean Palmer .40 .12
43 Bernie Williams .60 .18
44 Deion Sanders .60 .18
45 Mark McGwire 3.00 .90
46 Brian Jordan .40 .12
47 Bernard Gilkey .40 .12
48 Will Clark 1.00 .30
49 Kevin Appier .40 .12
50 Tom Glavine .60 .18
51 Chuck Knoblauch .40 .12
52 Rondell White .40 .12
53 Greg Vaughn .40 .12
54 Mike Mussina 1.00 .30
55 Brian McRae .40 .12
56 Chili Davis .40 .12
57 Wade Boggs .60 .18
58 Jeff Bagwell .60 .18
59 Roberto Alomar 1.00 .30
60 Dennis Eckersley .40 .12
61 Ryan Klesko .40 .12
62 Manny Ramirez .40 .12
63 John Wetteland .40 .12
64 Cal Ripken 3.00 .90
65 Edgar Renteria .40 .12
66 Tino Martinez .60 .18
67 Larry Walker .60 .18
68 Gregg Jefferies .40 .12
69 Lance Johnson .40 .12
70 Carlos Delgado .40 .12
71 Craig Biggio .60 .18
72 Jose Canseco 1.00 .30
73 Barry Bonds 2.50 .75
74 Juan Gonzalez 1.00 .30
75 Eric Karros .40 .12
76 Reggie Sanders .40 .12
77 Robin Ventura .40 .12
78 Hideo Nomo 1.00 .30
79 David Justice .40 .12
80 Vinny Castilla .40 .12
81 Travis Fryman .40 .12
82 Derek Jeter 2.50 .75
83 Sammy Sosa 1.50 .45
84 Ivan Rodriguez 1.00 .30
85 Rafael Palmeiro .60 .18
86 Roger Clemens 2.00 .60
87 Jason Giambi 1.00 .30
88 Andres Galarraga .40 .12
89 Jermaine Dye .40 .12
90 Joe Carter .40 .12
91 Brady Anderson .40 .12
92 Derek Bell .40 .12
93 Randy Johnson 1.00 .30
94 Fred McGriff .60 .18
95 John Smoltz .60 .18
96 Harold Baines .40 .12
97 Raul Mondesi .40 .12
98 Tim Salmon .60 .18
99 Carlos Baerga .40 .12
100 Dante Bichette .40 .12
101 Vladimir Guerrero 1.00 .30
102 Richard Hidalgo .40 .12
103 Paul Konerko .40 .12
104 Alex Gonzalez RC 1.00 .30
105 Jason Dickson .40 .12
106 Jose Rosado .40 .12
107 Todd Walker .40 .12
108 Seth Greisinger RC .50 .15
109 Todd Helton 1.00 .30
110 Ben Davis .40 .12
111 Bartolo Colon .40 .12
112 Elieser Marrero .40 .12
113 Jeff D'Amico .40 .12
114 Miguel Tejada RC 5.00 1.50
115 Darin Erstad .40 .12
116 Kris Benson RC .75 .23
117 Adrian Beltre RC 2.00 .60
118 Neifi Perez .40 .12
119 Pokey Reese .40 .12
120 Carl Pavano .40 .12
121 Juan Melo .40 .12
122 Kevin McGlinchy RC .40 .12
123 Pat Cline .40 .12
124 Felix Heredia RC .40 .12
125 Aaron Boone .40 .12
126 Glendon Rusch .40 .12
127 Mike Cameron .40 .12
128 Justin Thompson .40 .12
129 Chad Hermansen RC .50 .15
130 Sidney Ponson RC 1.00 .30
131 Willie Martinez RC .40 .12
132 Paul Wilder RC .40 .12
133 Geoff Jenkins .40 .12
134 Roy Halladay RC 4.00 1.20
135 Carlos Guillen .40 .12
136 Tony Batista .40 .12
137 Todd Greene .40 .12
138 Luis Castillo .40 .12
139 Jimmy Anderson RC .40 .12
140 Edgard Velazquez .40 .12
141 Chris Snopek .40 .12
142 Ruben Rivera .40 .12
143 Javier Valentin .40 .12
144 Brian Rose .40 .12
145 Fernando Tatis RC .50 .15
146 Dean Crow RC .40 .12
147 Karim Garcia .40 .12
148 Dante Powell .40 .12
149 Hideki Irabu RC .50 .15
150 Matt Morris .40 .12
151 Wes Helms .40 .12
152 Russ Johnson .40 .12
153 Jarrod Washburn .40 .12
154 Kerry Wood RC 10.00 3.00
155 Joe Fontenot RC .40 .12
156 Eugene Kingsale .40 .12
157 Terrence Long .40 .12
158 Calvin Maduro .40 .12
159 Jeff Suppan .40 .12
160 DaRond Stovall .40 .12
161 Mark Redman .40 .12
162 Ken Cloude RC .50 .15
163 Bobby Estalella .40 .12
164 Abraham Nunez RC .40 .12
165 Derrick Gibson .40 .12
166 Mike Drumright RC .40 .12
167 Katsuhiro Maeda .40 .12
168 Jeff Liefer .40 .12
169 Ben Grieve .40 .12
170 Bob Abreu .40 .12
171 Shannon Stewart .40 .12
172 Braden Looper RC .40 .12
173 Brant Brown .40 .12
174 Marlon Anderson .40 .12
175 Brad Fullmer .40 .12
176 Carlos Beltran 1.00 .30
177 Nomar Garciaparra 1.50 .45
178 Derrek Lee .40 .12
179 Val.De Los Santos RC .40 .12
180 Dmitri Young .40 .12
181 Jamey Wright .40 .12
182 Hiram Bocachica RC .50 .15
183 Wilton Guerrero .40 .12
184 Chris Carpenter .40 .12
185 Scott Spiezio .40 .12
186 Andruw Jones .40 .12
187 Travis Lee RC .50 .15
188 Jose Cruz Jr. RC 2.00 .60
189 Jose Guillen .40 .12
190 Jeff Abbott .40 .12
191 Ricky Ledee RC .50 .15
192 Mike Sweeney .40 .12
193 Donnie Sadler .40 .12
194 Scott Rolen .60 .18
195 Kevin Orie .40 .12
196 Jason Conti RC .40 .12
197 Mark Kotsay RC .50 .15
198 Eric Milton RC 1.00 .30
199 Russell Branyan .40 .12
200 Alex Sanchez RC .50 .15

1997 Bowman's Best Atomic Refractors

Randomly inserted in packs at a rate of one in 24, cards from this 200 card set parallel the regular Bowman's Best set and were printed with sparkling cross-weave refractor technology.

Nm-Mt Ex-Mt
*STARS: 6X TO 15X BASIC CARDS
*ROOKIES: 4X TO 10X BASIC CARDS

1997 Bowman's Best Refractors

Randomly inserted in packs at a rate of one in 12, this 200 card set is parallel to the regular set and is similar in design. The difference is found in the refractive quality of the cards.

Nm-Mt Ex-Mt
*STARS: 3X TO 8X BASIC CARDS
*ROOKIES: 2X TO 5X BASIC CARDS

1997 Bowman's Best Autographs

Randomly inserted in packs at a rate of 1:170, this 10-card set features five silver rookie cards and five gold veteran cards with authentic autographs and a "Certified Autograph Issue" stamp.

Nm-Mt Ex-Mt
*REF.STARS: .75X TO 2X BASIC CARDS
REFRACTOR STATED ODDS 1:2036
*ATOMIC STARS: 1.5X TO 4X BASIC CARDS
ATOMIC STATED ODDS 1:6107
SKIP-NUMBERED 10-CARD SET
29 Tony Gwynn 40.00 12.00
33 Paul Molitor 25.00 7.50
82 Derek Jeter 100.00 30.00
91 Brady Anderson 15.00 4.50
98 Tim Salmon 25.00 7.50
107 Todd Walker 15.00 4.50
183 Wilton Guerrero 5.00 1.50
185 Scott Spiezio 5.00 1.50
188 Jose Cruz Jr. 25.00 7.50
194 Scott Rolen 40.00 12.00

1997 Bowman's Best Best Cuts

Randomly inserted in packs at a rate of one in 24, this 20-card set features color player photos printed on intricate, Laser Cut Chromium card stock.

Nm-Mt Ex-Mt
COMPLETE SET (20) 150.00 45.00
*REFRACTOR: .6X TO 1.5X BASIC CUTS
REFRACTOR STATED ODDS 1:48
*ATOMIC: 1X TO 2.5X BASIC CUTS
ATOMIC STATED ODDS 1:96
BC1 Derek Jeter 15.00 4.50
BC2 Chipper Jones 6.00 1.80
BC3 Frank Thomas 6.00 1.80
BC4 Cal Ripken 20.00 6.00
BC5 Mark McGwire 20.00 6.00
BC6 Ken Griffey Jr. 10.00 3.00
BC7 Jeff Bagwell 4.00 1.20
BC8 Mike Piazza 10.00 3.00
BC9 Ken Caminiti 2.50 .75
BC10 Albert Belle 2.50 .75
BC11 Jose Cruz Jr. 4.00 1.20
BC12 Wilton Guerrero 2.50 .75
BC13 Darin Erstad 2.50 .75
BC14 Andruw Jones 2.50 .75
BC15 Scott Rolen 4.00 1.20
BC16 Jose Guillen 2.50 .75
BC17 Bob Abreu 2.50 .75
BC18 Vladimir Guerrero 6.00 1.80
BC19 Todd Walker 2.50 .75
BC20 Nomar Garciaparra 10.00 3.00

1997 Bowman's Best Mirror Image

Randomly inserted in packs at a rate of one in 48, this 10-card set features color photos of four of the best players in the same position printed on double-sided chromium card stock. Two veterans and two rookies appear on each card. The veteran players are displayed in the larger photos with the rookies appearing in smaller corner photos.

Nm-Mt Ex-Mt
COMPLETE SET (10) 80.00 24.00
*REFRACTORS: .6X TO 1.5X BASIC CARDS
REFRACTOR STATED ODDS 1:96
*ATOMIC REF: 1.25X TO 3X BASIC MI
ATOMIC STATED ODDS 1:192
*INVERTED: 2X VALUE OF NON-INVERTED
INVERTED: RANDOM INSERTS IN PACKS
INVERTED HAVE LARGER ROOKIE PHOTOS
MI1 Nomar Garciaparra 12.00 3.60
Derek Jeter
Hiram Bocachica
Barry Larkin
MI2 Travis Lee 5.00 1.50
Frank Thomas
Derrick Lee
Jeff Bagwell
MI3 Kerry Wood 8.00 2.40
Greg Maddux
Kris Benson
John Smoltz
MI4 Kevin Brown 8.00 2.40
Ivan Rodriguez
Eli Marrero
Mike Piazza
MI5 Jose Cruz Jr. 12.00 3.60
Ken Griffey Jr.
Andruw Jones
Barry Bonds
MI6 Jose Guillen 5.00 1.50
Juan Gonzalez
Richard Hidalgo
Gary Sheffield
MI7 Paul Konerko 12.00 3.60
Mark McGwire
Todd Helton
Rafael Palmeiro
MI8 Wilton Guerrero 3.00 .90
Craig Biggio
Donnie Sadler
Chuck Knoblauch
MI9 Russell Branyan 5.00 1.50
Matt Williams
Adrian Beltre
Chipper Jones
MI10 Bob Abreu 5.00 1.50
Kenny Lofton
Vladimir Guerrero
Albert Belle

1997 Bowman's Best Jumbo

This 16-card set features selected cards from the 1997 regular Bowman's Best set in a 4" by 6" jumbo version available to Stadium Club members only by mail. Only 675 of each of the 16 cards were produced for this jumbo version. The cards are checklisted according to their number in the regular size set.

Nm-Mt Ex-Mt
*REFRACTORS: 4X BASIC JUMBOS
*ATOMIC REFRACTORS: 8X BASIC JUMBOS
1 Ken Griffey Jr. 10.00 3.00
5 Mike Piazza 10.00 3.00
9 Chipper Jones 8.00 2.40
11 Kenny Lofton 2.00 .60
29 Tony Gwynn 8.00 2.40
33 Paul Molitor 4.00 1.20
38 Frank Thomas 4.00 1.20
45 Mark McGwire 12.00 3.60
64 Cal Ripken Jr. 15.00 4.50
73 Barry Bonds 8.00 2.40
74 Juan Gonzalez 3.00 .90
82 Derek Jeter 15.00 4.50
101 Vladimir Guerrero 4.00 1.20
177 Nomar Garciaparra 8.00 2.40
186 Andruw Jones 4.00 1.20
188 Jose Cruz Jr. 2.00 .60

1998 Bowman's Best

The 1998 Bowman's Best set (produced by Topps) consists of 200 standard size cards and was released in August, 1998. The six-card packs retailed for a suggested price of $5 each. The card fronts feature 100 action photos with a gold background showcasing today's veteran players and 100 photos (combining posed shots with action shots) with a silver background showcasing rookies. The Bowman's Best logo sits in the upper right corner and the featured player's name sits in the lower left corner. Rookie Cards include Ryan Anderson, Troy Glaus, Orlando Hernandez, Carlos Lee, Ruben Mateo and Magglio Ordonez.

Nm-Mt Ex-Mt
COMPLETE SET (200) 40.00 12.00
1 Mark McGwire 2.50 .75
2 Jeromy Burnitz .40 .12
3 Barry Bonds 2.50 .75
4 Dante Bichette .40 .12
5 Chipper Jones 1.00 .30
6 Frank Thomas 1.00 .30
7 Kevin Brown .60 .18
8 Juan Gonzalez 1.00 .30
9 Jay Buhner .40 .12
10 Chuck Knoblauch .40 .12
11 Cal Ripken 3.00 .90
12 Matt Williams .40 .12
13 Jim Edmonds .40 .12
14 Manny Ramirez .40 .12
15 Tony Clark .40 .12
16 Mo Vaughn .40 .12
17 Bernie Williams .60 .18
18 Scott Rolen .60 .18
19 Gary Sheffield .40 .12
20 Albert Belle .40 .12
21 Mike Piazza 1.50 .45
22 John Olerud .40 .12
23 Tony Gwynn 1.25 .35
24 Jay Bell .40 .12
25 Jose Cruz Jr. .40 .12
26 Justin Thompson .40 .12
27 Ken Griffey Jr. 1.50 .45
28 Sandy Alomar Jr. .40 .12
29 Mark Grudzielanek .40 .12
30 Mark Grace .60 .18
31 Ron Gant .40 .12
32 Javy Lopez .40 .12
33 Jeff Bagwell .60 .18
34 Fred McGriff .60 .18
35 Rafael Palmeiro .60 .18
36 Vinny Castilla .40 .12
37 Andy Benes .40 .12
38 Pedro Martinez 1.00 .30
39 Andy Pettitte .60 .18
40 Marty Cordova .40 .12
41 Rusty Greer .40 .12
42 Kevin Orie .40 .12
43 Chan Ho Park .40 .12
44 Ryan Klesko .40 .12
45 Alex Rodriguez 1.50 .45
46 Travis Fryman .40 .12
47 Jeff King .40 .12
48 Roger Clemens 2.00 .60
49 Darin Erstad .40 .12
50 Brady Anderson .40 .12
51 Jason Kendall .40 .12
52 John Valentin .40 .12
53 Ellis Burks .40 .12
54 Brian Hunter .40 .12
55 Paul O'Neill .60 .18
56 Ken Caminiti .40 .12
57 David Justice .40 .12
58 Eric Karros .40 .12
59 Pat Hentgen .40 .12
60 Greg Maddux 1.50 .45
61 Craig Biggio .60 .18
62 Edgar Martinez .60 .18
63 Mike Mussina 1.00 .30
64 Larry Walker .60 .18
65 Tino Martinez .60 .18
66 Jim Thome 1.00 .30
67 Tom Glavine .60 .18
68 Raul Mondesi .40 .12
69 Marquis Grissom .40 .12
70 Randy Johnson 1.00 .30
71 Steve Finley .40 .12
72 Jose Guillen .40 .12
73 Nomar Garciaparra 1.50 .45

74 Wade Boggs .60 .18
75 Bobby Higginson .40 .12
76 Robin Ventura .40 .12
77 Derek Jeter 2.50 .75
78 Andruw Jones .40 .12
79 Ray Lankford .40 .12
80 Vladimir Guerrero 1.00 .30
81 Kenny Lofton .40 .12
82 Ivan Rodriguez 1.00 .30
83 Neifi Perez .40 .12
84 John Smoltz .60 .18
85 Tim Salmon .60 .18
86 Carlos Delgado .40 .12
87 Sammy Sosa 1.50 .45
88 Jaret Wright .40 .12
89 Roberto Alomar 1.00 .30
90 Paul Molitor .60 .18
91 Dean Palmer .40 .12
92 Barry Larkin 1.00 .30
93 Jason Giambi 1.00 .30
94 Curt Schilling .60 .18
95 Eric Young .40 .12
96 Denny Neagle .40 .12
97 Moises Alou .40 .12
98 Livan Hernandez .40 .12
99 Todd Hundley .40 .12
100 Andres Galarraga .40 .12
101 Travis Lee .40 .12
102 Lance Berkman .60 .18
103 Orlando Cabrera .40 .12
104 Mike Lowell RC 3.00 .90
105 Ben Grieve .40 .12
106 Jae Weong Seo RC 1.00 .30
107 Richie Sexson .40 .12
108 Eli Marrero .40 .12
109 Aramis Ramirez .40 .12
110 Paul Konerko .40 .12
111 Carl Pavano .40 .12
112 Brad Fullmer .40 .12
113 Matt Clement .40 .12
114 Donzell McDonald .40 .12
115 Todd Helton .60 .18
116 Mike Caruso .40 .12
117 Donnie Sadler .40 .12
118 Bruce Chen .40 .12
119 Jarrod Washburn .40 .12
120 Adrian Beltre .40 .12
121 Ryan Jackson RC .40 .12
122 Kevin Millar RC 2.00 .60
123 Corey Koskie RC 2.00 .60
124 Dermal Brown .40 .12
125 Kerry Wood 1.00 .30
126 Juan Melo .40 .12
127 Ramon Hernandez .40 .12
128 Roy Halladay .40 .12
129 Ron Wright .40 .12
130 Darnell McDonald RC .60 .18
131 Odalis Perez RC 1.00 .30
132 Alex Cora RC .60 .18
133 Justin Towle .40 .12
134 Juan Encarnacion .40 .12
135 Brian Rose .40 .12
136 Russell Branyan .40 .12
137 Cesar King RC .40 .12
138 Ruben Rivera .40 .12
139 Ricky Ledee .40 .12
140 Vernon Wells .60 .18
141 Luis Rivas RC 1.50 .45
142 Brent Butler .40 .12
143 Karim Garcia .40 .12
144 George Lombard .40 .12
145 Masato Yoshii RC 1.00 .30
146 Braden Looper .40 .12
147 Alex Sanchez .40 .12
148 Kris Benson .40 .12
149 Mark Kotsay .40 .12
150 Richard Hidalgo .40 .12
151 Scott Elarton .40 .12
152 Ryan Minor RC .40 .12
153 Troy Glaus RC 5.00 1.50
154 Carlos Lee RC 2.00 .60
155 Michael Coleman .40 .12
156 Jason Grilli RC .40 .12
157 Julio Ramirez RC .40 .12
158 Randy Wolf RC 1.50 .45
159 Ryan Brannan .40 .12
160 Edgard Clemente .40 .12
161 Miguel Tejada .60 .18
162 Chad Hermansen .40 .12
163 Ryan Anderson RC .60 .18
164 Ben Petrick .40 .12
165 Alex Gonzalez .40 .12
166 Ben Davis .40 .12
167 John Patterson .40 .12
168 Cliff Politte .40 .12
169 Randall Simon .40 .12
170 Javier Vazquez .40 .12
171 Kevin Witt .40 .12
172 Geoff Jenkins .40 .12
173 David Ortiz .40 .12
174 Derrick Gibson .40 .12
175 Abraham Nunez .40 .12
176 A.J. Hinch .40 .12
177 Ruben Mateo RC .60 .18
178 Magglio Ordonez RC 3.00 .90
179 Todd Dunwoody .40 .12
180 Daryle Ward .40 .12
181 Mike Kinkade RC .40 .12
182 Willie Martinez .40 .12
183 O.Hernandez RC 2.00 .60
184 Eric Milton .40 .12
185 Eric Chavez .60 .18
186 Damian Jackson .40 .12
187 Jim Parque RC .60 .18
188 Dan Reichert RC .60 .18
189 Mike Drumright .40 .12
190 Todd Walker .40 .12
191 Shane Monahan .40 .12
192 Derrek Lee .40 .12
193 Jeremy Giambi RC .60 .18
194 Dan McKinley RC .40 .12
195 Tony Armas Jr. RC .60 .18
196 Matt Anderson RC .60 .18
197 Jim Chamblee RC .40 .12
198 F.Cordero RC .60 .18
199 Calvin Pickering .40 .12
200 Reggie Taylor .40 .12

1998 Bowman's Best Atomic Refractors

The 1998 Bowman's Best Atomic Refractor set consists of 200 cards and is a parallel to the 1998 Bowman's Best base set. The cards are randomly inserted in packs at a rate of one in 82. The entire set is sequentially numbered to 100. Each card front featured a kaleidescopic refractive background.

Nm-Mt Ex-Mt
*STARS: 8X TO 20X BASIC CARDS
*ROOKIES: 5X TO 12X BASIC CARDS

1998 Bowman's Best Refractors

The 1998 Bowman's Best Refractor set consists of 200 cards and is a parallel to the 1998 Bowman's Best base set. The cards are randomly inserted in packs at a rate of one in 20. The entire set is sequentially numbered to 400.

Nm-Mt Ex-Mt
*STARS: 5X TO 12X BASIC CARDS
*ROOKIES: 2.5X TO 6X BASIC CARDS

1998 Bowman's Best Autographs

Randomly inserted in packs at a rate of one in 180, this 10-card set is an insert to the 1998 Bowman's Best brand. The fronts feature five gold veteran and five silver prospect cards sporting a Topps "Certified Autograph Issue" logo for authentication. The cards are designed in an identical manner to the basic issue 1998 Bowman's Best set except, of course, for the autograph and the certification logo.

Nm-Mt Ex-Mt
*REFRACTORS: 1X TO 2.5X BASIC AU'S
REFRACTOR STATED ODDS 1:2158
*ATOMICS: 2X TO 5X BASIC AU'S
ATOMIC STATED ODDS 1:6437
SKIP-NUMBERED 10-CARD SET
5 Chipper Jones 40.00 12.00
10 Chuck Knoblauch 15.00 4.50
15 Tony Clark 10.00 3.00
20 Albert Belle 15.00 4.50
25 Jose Cruz Jr. 15.00 4.50
105 Ben Grieve 10.00 3.00
110 Paul Konerko 15.00 4.50
115 Todd Helton 25.00 7.50
120 Adrian Beltre 15.00 4.50
125 Kerry Wood 40.00 12.00

1998 Bowman's Best Mirror Image Fusion

Randomly inserted in packs at a rate of one in 12, this 20-card set is an insert to the 1998 Bowman's Best brand. The fronts feature a Major League veteran player with his positional protégé on the flip side. The player's name runs along the bottom of the card.

Nm-Mt Ex-Mt
COMPLETE SET (20) 150.00 45.00
*REFRACTORS: 1.25X TO 3X BASIC MIRROR
REFRACTOR STATED ODDS 1:809
REF.PRINT RUN 100 SERIAL #'d SETS
ATOMIC STATED ODDS 1:3237
ATOMIC PRINT RUN 25 SERIAL #'d SETS
NO ATOMIC PRICING DUE TO SCARCITY
MI1 Frank Thomas 5.00 1.50
David Ortiz
MI2 Chuck Knoblauch 2.50 .75
Enrique Wilson
MI3 Nomar Garciaparra 10.00 3.00
Miguel Tejada
MI4 Alex Rodriguez 10.00 3.00
Mike Caruso
MI5 Cal Ripken 20.00 6.00
Ryan Minor
MI6 Ken Griffey Jr. 10.00 3.00
Ben Grieve
MI7 Juan Gonzalez 5.00 1.50
Juan Encarnacion
MI8 Jose Cruz Jr. 2.50 .75
Ruben Mateo
MI9 Randy Johnson 5.00 1.50
Ryan Anderson
MI10 Ivan Rodriguez 5.00 1.50
A.J. Hinch
MI11 Jeff Bagwell 4.00 1.20
Paul Konerko
MI12 Mark McGwire 15.00 4.50
Travis Lee
MI13 Craig Biggio 4.00 1.20
Chad Hermansen
MI14 Mark Grudzielanek 2.50 .75
Alex Gonzalez
MI15 Chipper Jones 5.00 1.50
Adrian Beltre
MI16 Larry Walker 4.00 1.20
Mark Kotsay
MI17 Tony Gwynn 8.00 2.40
George Lombard
MI18 Barry Bonds 15.00 4.50
Richard Hidalgo
MI19 Greg Maddux 10.00 3.00
Kerry Wood
MI20 Mike Piazza 10.00 3.00
Ben Petrick

1998 Bowman's Best Performers

Randomly inserted in packs at a rate of one in six, this 10-card set is an insert to the 1998 Bowman's Best brand. The card fronts feature full color game-action photos of ten players with the best Minor League stats of 1997. The featured player's name is found below the photo with both Bowman's Best logo and the team logo above the photo.

Nm-Mt Ex-Mt
COMPLETE SET (10) 15.00 4.50
*REFRACTORS: 5X TO 12X BASIC PERF.
REFRACTOR STATED ODDS 1:809
REF.PRINT RUN 200 SERIAL #'d SETS
*ATOMIC: 12.5X TO 30X BASIC PERF.
ATOMIC STATED ODDS 1:3237
ATOMIC PRINT RUN 50 SERIAL #'d SETS
BP1 Ben Grieve 1.50 .45
BP2 Travis Lee 1.50 .45
BP3 Ryan Minor 1.50 .45
BP4 Todd Helton 2.50 .75
BP5 Brad Fullmer 1.50 .45
BP6 Paul Konerko 1.50 .45
BP7 Adrian Beltre 1.50 .45
BP8 Richie Sexson 1.50 .45
BP9 Aramis Ramirez 1.50 .45
BP10 Russell Branyan 1.50 .45

1999 Bowman's Best Pre-Production

These three cards were distributed as a complete set in a sealed poly-bag and sent to dealers and hobby media several weeks prior to the national release of 1999 Bowman's Best. The cards were created to preview the upcoming product and are almost identical in design to their basic issue counterparts. The key difference is the card numbering. These pre-production cards are numbered PP1-PP3, whereas the basic issue cards of Anderson, Lopez and Gold are all numbered within the context of the 180-card standard set.

Nm-Mt Ex-Mt
COMPLETE SET (3) 2.50 .75
PP1 Javy Lopez 1.50 .45
PP2 Marlon Anderson 1.00 .30
PP3 J.M. Gold .50 .15

1999 Bowman's Best

The 1999 Bowman's Best set (produced by Topps) consists of 200 standard size cards. The six-card packs, released in August, 1999, retailed for a suggested price of $5 each. The cards are printed on 27-pt. Serillusion stock and feature 85 veteran stars in a striking gold series, 15 Best Performers bonus subset captured in a bronze series, 50 rookies highlighted in a brilliant blue series and 50 prospects shown in a captivating silver series. The fifty rookies and prospects (cards 151-200) were seeded at a rate of one per pack. Notable Rookie Cards included Pat Burrell, Sean Burroughs, Nick Johnson, Austin Kearns, Corey Patterson and Alfonso Soriano.

Nm-Mt Ex-Mt
COMPLETE SET (200) 50.00 15.00
COMP.SET w/o SP's (150) 25.00 7.50
COMMON CARD (1-150) .40 .12
COMMON (151-200) .50 .15
1 Chipper Jones 1.00 .30
2 Brian Jordan .40 .12
3 David Justice .40 .12
4 Jason Kendall .40 .12
5 Mo Vaughn .40 .12
6 Jim Edmonds .40 .12
7 Wade Boggs .60 .18
8 Jeromy Burnitz .40 .12
9 Todd Hundley .40 .12
10 Rondell White .40 .12
11 Cliff Floyd .40 .12
12 Sean Casey .40 .12
13 Bernie Williams .60 .18
14 Dante Bichette .40 .12
15 Greg Vaughn .40 .12
16 Andres Galarraga .40 .12
17 Ray Durham .40 .12
18 Jim Thome 1.00 .30
19 Gary Sheffield .40 .12
20 Frank Thomas 1.00 .30
21 Orlando Hernandez .40 .12
22 Ivan Rodriguez 1.00 .30
23 Jose Cruz Jr. .40 .12
24 Jason Giambi 1.00 .30
25 Craig Biggio .60 .18
26 Kerry Wood 1.00 .30
27 Manny Ramirez .40 .12
28 Curt Schilling .60 .18
29 Mike Mussina 1.00 .30
30 Tim Salmon .60 .18
31 Mike Piazza 1.50 .45
32 Roberto Alomar 1.00 .30
33 Larry Walker .60 .18
34 Barry Larkin 1.00 .30
35 Nomar Garciaparra 1.50 .45
36 Paul O'Neill .60 .18
37 Todd Walker .40 .12
38 Eric Karros .40 .12
39 Brad Fullmer .40 .12
40 John Olerud .40 .12
41 Todd Helton .60 .18
42 Raul Mondesi .40 .12
43 Jose Canseco 1.00 .30
44 Matt Williams .40 .12
45 Ray Lankford .40 .12
46 Carlos Delgado .40 .12
47 Darin Erstad .40 .12
48 Vladimir Guerrero 1.00 .30
49 Robin Ventura .40 .12
50 Alex Rodriguez 1.50 .45
51 Vinny Castilla .40 .12
52 Tony Clark .40 .12
53 Pedro Martinez 1.00 .30
54 Rafael Palmeiro .60 .18
55 Scott Rolen .60 .18
56 Tino Martinez .60 .18
57 Tony Gwynn 1.25 .35
58 Barry Bonds 2.50 .75
59 Kenny Lofton .40 .12
60 Javy Lopez .40 .12
61 Mark Grace .60 .18
62 Travis Lee .40 .12
63 Kevin Brown .60 .18
64 Al Leiter .40 .12
65 Albert Belle .40 .12
66 Sammy Sosa 1.50 .45
67 Greg Maddux 1.50 .45
68 Mark Kotsay .40 .12
69 Dmitri Young .40 .12
70 Mark McGwire 2.50 .75
71 Juan Gonzalez 1.00 .30
72 Andruw Jones .40 .12
73 Derek Jeter 2.50 .75
74 Randy Johnson 1.00 .30
75 Cal Ripken 3.00 .90
76 Shawn Green .40 .12
77 Moises Alou .40 .12
78 Tom Glavine .60 .18
79 Sandy Alomar Jr. .40 .12
80 Ken Griffey Jr. 1.50 .45
81 Ryan Klesko .40 .12
82 Jeff Bagwell .60 .18
83 Ben Grieve .40 .12
84 John Smoltz .60 .18
85 Roger Clemens 2.00 .60
86 Ken Griffey Jr. BP 1.00 .30
87 Roger Clemens BP 1.00 .30
88 Derek Jeter BP 1.25 .35
89 Nomar Garciaparra BP .75 .23
90 Mark McGwire BP 1.25 .35
91 Sammy Sosa BP 1.00 .30
92 Alex Rodriguez BP .75 .23
93 Greg Maddux BP .75 .23
94 Vladimir Guerrero BP .60 .18
95 Chipper Jones BP .60 .18
96 Kerry Wood BP .60 .18
97 Ben Grieve BP .40 .12
98 Tony Gwynn BP .60 .18
99 Juan Gonzalez BP .60 .18
100 Mike Piazza BP .75 .23
101 Eric Chavez .40 .12
102 Billy Koch .40 .12
103 Dernell Stenson .40 .12
104 Marlon Anderson .40 .12
105 Ron Belliard .40 .12
106 Bruce Chen .40 .12
107 Carlos Beltran .40 .12
108 Chad Hermansen .40 .12
109 Ryan Anderson .40 .12
110 Michael Barrett .40 .12
111 Matt Clement .40 .12
112 Ben Davis .40 .12
113 Calvin Pickering .40 .12
114 Brad Penny .40 .12
115 Paul Konerko .40 .12
116 Alex Gonzalez .40 .12
117 George Lombard .40 .12
118 John Patterson .40 .12
119 Rob Bell .40 .12
120 Ruben Mateo .40 .12
121 Troy Glaus .60 .18
122 Ryan Bradley .40 .12
123 Carlos Lee .40 .12
124 Gabe Kapler .40 .12
125 Ramon Hernandez .40 .12
126 Carlos Febles .40 .12
127 Mitch Meluskey .40 .12
128 Michael Cuddyer .40 .12
129 Pablo Ozuna .40 .12
130 Jayson Werth .40 .12
131 Ricky Ledee .40 .12
132 Jeremy Giambi .40 .12
133 Danny Klassen .40 .12
134 Mark DeRosa .40 .12
135 Randy Wolf .40 .12
136 Roy Halladay .40 .12
137 Derrick Gibson .40 .12
138 Ben Petrick .40 .12
139 Warren Morris .40 .12
140 Lance Berkman .40 .12
141 Russell Branyan .40 .12
142 Adrian Beltre .40 .12
143 Juan Encarnacion .40 .12
144 Fernando Seguignol .40 .12
145 Corey Koskie .40 .12
146 Preston Wilson .40 .12
147 Homer Bush .40 .12
148 Daryle Ward .40 .12
149 Joe McEwing RC .50 .15
150 Peter Bergeron RC .50 .15
151 Pat Burrell RC 5.00 1.50
152 Choo Freeman RC .50 .15
153 Matt Belisle RC .50 .15
154 Carlos Pena RC 1.25 .35
155 A.J. Burnett RC 1.25 .35
156 D.Mientkiewicz RC 1.50 .45
157 Sean Burroughs RC 4.00 1.20
158 Mike Zywica RC .50 .15
159 Corey Patterson RC 5.00 1.50
160 Austin Kearns RC 6.00 1.80
161 Chip Ambres RC .50 .15
162 Kelly Dransfeldt RC .50 .15
163 Mike Nannini RC .50 .15
164 Mark Mulder RC 5.00 1.50
165 Jason Tyner RC .50 .15
166 Bobby Seay RC .50 .15
167 Alex Escobar RC .50 .15
168 Nick Johnson RC 2.50 .75
169 Alfonso Soriano RC 10.00 3.00
170 Clayton Andrews RC .50 .15
171 C.C. Sabathia RC 1.25 .35
172 Matt Holliday RC .50 .15
173 Brad Lidge RC .50 .15
174 Kit Pellow RC .50 .15
175 J.M. Gold RC .50 .15
176 Roosevelt Brown RC .50 .15
177 Eric Valent RC .50 .15
178 Adam Everett RC .50 .15
179 Jorge Toca RC .50 .15
180 Matt Roney RC .50 .15
181 Andy Brown RC .50 .15
182 Phil Norton RC .50 .15
183 Mickey Lopez RC .50 .15
184 Chris George RC .50 .15
185 Arturo McDowell RC .50 .15
186 Jose Fernandez RC .50 .15
187 Seth Etherton RC .50 .15
188 Josh McKinley RC .50 .15
189 Nate Cornejo RC .75 .23
190 G.Chiaramonte RC .50 .15
191 Mamon Tucker RC .50 .15
192 Ryan Mills RC .50 .15
193 Chad Moeller RC .50 .15
194 Tony Torcato RC .50 .15
195 Jeff Winchester RC .50 .15
196 Rick Elder RC .50 .15
197 Matt Burch RC .50 .15
198 Jeff Urban RC .50 .15
199 Chris Jones RC .50 .15
200 Masao Kida RC .50 .15

1999 Bowman's Best Atomic Refractors

Randomly inserted at a rate of one in 62, this 200-card set is a parallel of the Bowman's Best Base set. Each card in this set is sequentially numbered to 100 and feature a refractive kaleidescope treatment on front.

Nm-Mt Ex-Mt
*STARS: 10X TO 25X BASIC CARDS
*ROOKIES: 7.5X TO 15X BASIC CARDS

1999 Bowman's Best Refractors

Randomly inserted at a rate of one in 15, this 200-card set is a parallel of the Bowman's Best Base set and features iridescent select metallization technology. Each card in this set is sequentially numbered to 400.

Nm-Mt Ex-Mt
*STARS: 5X TO 12X BASIC CARDS
*ROOKIES: 4X TO 8X BASIC CARDS

1999 Bowman's Best Franchise Best Mach I

Randomly inserted in packs at the rate of one in 41, this 10-card set features color photos of some of the Major's top stars printed on die-cut Serillusion stock and sequentially nubered to 3,000.

Nm-Mt Ex-Mt
COMPLETE SET (10) 60.00 18.00
*MACH II: .75X TO 2X MACH I
MACH II STATED ODDS 1:124
MACH II PRINT RUN 1000 SERIAL #'d SETS
*MACH III: 1.25X TO 3X MACH I
MACH III STATED ODDS 1:248
MACH III PRINT RUN 500 SERIAL #'d SETS
FB1 Mark McGwire 10.00 3.00
FB2 Ken Griffey Jr. 6.00 1.80
FB3 Sammy Sosa 6.00 1.80
FB4 Nomar Garciaparra 6.00 1.80
FB5 Alex Rodriguez 6.00 1.80
FB6 Derek Jeter 10.00 3.00
FB7 Mike Piazza 6.00 1.80
FB8 Frank Thomas 4.00 1.20
FB9 Chipper Jones 4.00 1.20
FB10 Juan Gonzalez 4.00 1.20

1999 Bowman's Best Franchise Favorites

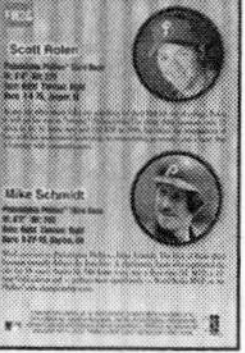

Randomly inserted in packs at the rate of one in 40, this six-card set features color photos of retired legends and current stars in three versions. Version A pictures the current star; Version B, a retired great; and Version C pairs the current star with the retired legend.

	Nm-Mt	Ex-Mt
COMPLETE SET (6)	80.00	24.00
FR1A Derek Jeter	20.00	6.00
FR1B Don Mattingly	20.00	6.00
FR1C Derek Jeter Don Mattingly	25.00	7.50
FR2A Scott Rolen	8.00	2.40
FR2B Mike Schmidt	12.00	3.60
FR2C Scott Rolen Mike Schmidt	20.00	6.00

1999 Bowman's Best Franchise Favorites Autographs

This six-card set is an autographed parallel version of the regular insert set with the "Topps Certified Autograph Issue" stamp. The insertion rate for these cards are: Versions A and B, 1:1550 packs; and Version C, 1:6174. Version C cards feature autographs from both players.

	Nm-Mt	Ex-Mt
FR1A Derek Jeter	120.00	36.00
FR1B Don Mattingly	60.00	18.00
FR1C Derek Jeter Don Mattingly	300.00	90.00
FR2A Scott Rolen	25.00	7.50
FR2B Mike Schmidt	50.00	15.00
FR2C Scott Rolen Mike Schmidt	120.00	36.00

1999 Bowman's Best Future Foundations Mach I

Randomly inserted into packs at the rate of one in 41, this 10-card set features color photos of some of the top young stars printed on die-cut Serillusion stock and sequentially numbered to 3,000.

	Nm-Mt	Ex-Mt
COMPLETE SET (10)	30.00	9.00
*MACH II: .75X TO 2X MACH I		
MACH II STATED ODDS 1:124		
MACH II PRINT RUN 1000 SERIAL #'d SETS		
*MACH III: 1.25X TO 3X MACH I		
MACH III STATED ODDS 1:248		
MACH III PRINT RUN 500 SERIAL #'d SETS		
FF1 Ruben Mateo	1.00	.30
FF2 Troy Glaus	2.50	.75
FF3 Eric Chavez	1.50	.45
FF4 Pat Burrell	6.00	1.80
FF5 Adrian Beltre	1.50	.45
FF6 Ryan Anderson	1.00	.30
FF7 Alfonso Soriano	8.00	2.40
FF8 Brad Penny	1.00	.30
FF9 Derrick Gibson	1.00	.30
FF10 Bruce Chen	1.00	.30

1999 Bowman's Best Mirror Image

Randomly inserted into packs at the rate of one in 24, this 10-card double-sided set features color photos of a veteran ballplayer on one side and a hot prospect on the other.

	Nm-Mt	Ex-Mt
COMPLETE SET (10)	60.00	18.00
*REFRACTORS: .75X TO 2X BASIC MIR.IMAGE		
REFRACTOR STATED ODDS 1:96		
*ATOMIC: 1.25X TO 3X BASIC MIR.IMAGE		
ATOMIC STATED ODDS 1:192		
M1 Alex Rodriguez Alex Gonzalez	5.00	1.50
M2 Ken Griffey Jr. Ruben Mateo	5.00	1.50
M3 Derek Jeter Alfonso Soriano	10.00	3.00
M4 Sammy Sosa Corey Patterson	5.00	1.50
M5 Greg Maddux Bruce Chen	5.00	1.50
M6 Chipper Jones Eric Chavez	2.50	.75
M7 Vladimir Guerrero Carlos Beltran	2.50	.75
M8 Frank Thomas Nick Johnson	2.50	.75
M9 Nomar Garciaparra Pablo Ozuna	5.00	1.50
M10 Mark McGwire Pat Burrell	6.00	1.80

1999 Bowman's Best Rookie Locker Room Autographs

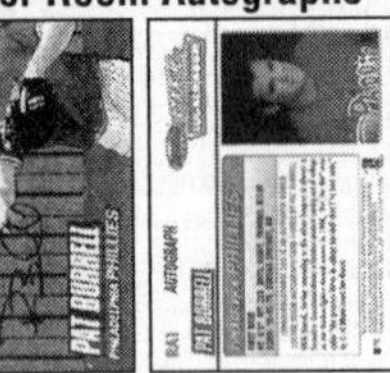

Randomly inserted into packs at the rate of one in 248, this five-card set features autographed color photos of top prospects with the "Topps Certified Autograph Issue" logo stamp.

	Nm-Mt	Ex-Mt
RA1 Pat Burrell	25.00	7.50
RA2 Michael Barrett	10.00	3.00
RA3 Troy Glaus	25.00	7.50
RA4 Gabe Kapler	10.00	3.00
RA5 Eric Chavez	15.00	4.50

1999 Bowman's Best Rookie Locker Room Game Used Bats

Randomly inserted into packs at the rate of one in 517, this six-card set features color photos of top players with pieces of game-used bats embedded into the cards.

	Nm-Mt	Ex-Mt
RB1 Pat Burrell	20.00	6.00
RB2 Michael Barrett	8.00	2.40
RB3 Troy Glaus	15.00	4.50
RB4 Gabe Kapler	8.00	2.40
RB5 Eric Chavez	10.00	3.00
RB6 Richie Sexson	10.00	3.00

1999 Bowman's Best Rookie Locker Room Game Worn Jerseys

Randomly inserted into packs at the rate of one in 538, this four-card set features color photos of some of the hottest young stars with pieces of their game-used jerseys embedded in the cards.

	Nm-Mt	Ex-Mt
RJ1 Richie Sexson	10.00	3.00
RJ2 Michael Barrett	10.00	3.00
RJ3 Troy Glaus	15.00	4.50
RJ4 Eric Chavez	10.00	3.00

1999 Bowman's Best Rookie of the Year

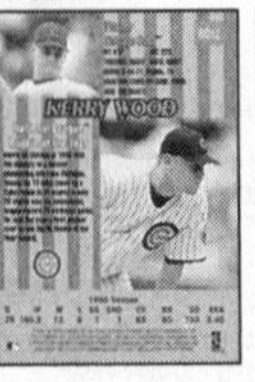

Randomly inserted into packs at the rate of one in 95, this two-card set features color photos of the 1998 American and National League Rookies of the Year printed on Serillusion card stock. An autographed version of Ben Grieve's card with the "Topps Certified Autograph Issue" stamp was inserted at the rate of 1:1239 packs.

	Nm-Mt	Ex-Mt
COMPLETE SET (2)	5.00	1.50
ROY1 Ben Grieve	2.50	.75
ROY2 Kerry Wood	2.50	.75
ROY1A Ben Grieve AU	15.00	4.50

2000 Bowman's Best Pre-Production

This three card set of sample cards was distributed within a sealed, clear, cello poly-wrap to dealers and hobby media several weeks prior to the national release of 2000 Bowman's Best.

	Nm-Mt	Ex-Mt
COMPLETE SET (3)	6.00	1.80
PP1 Larry Walker	1.00	.30
PP2 Adam Dunn	4.00	1.20
PP3 Brett Myers	2.00	.60

2000 Bowman's Best Previews

Randomly inserted into Bowman hobby/retail packs at one in 18, this 10-card insert set features preview cards from the 2000 Bowman's Best product. Card backs carry a "BB" prefix.

	Nm-Mt	Ex-Mt
COMPLETE SET (10)	40.00	12.00
BB1 Derek Jeter	6.00	1.80
BB2 Ken Griffey Jr.	4.00	1.20
BB3 Nomar Garciaparra	4.00	1.20
BB4 Mike Piazza	4.00	1.20
BB5 Alex Rodriguez	4.00	1.20
BB6 Sammy Sosa	4.00	1.20
BB7 Mark McGwire	6.00	1.80
BB8 Pat Burrell	1.50	.45
BB9 Josh Hamilton	1.00	.30
BB10 Adam Piatt	1.00	.30

2000 Bowman's Best

The 2000 Bowman's Best set (produced by Topps) was released in early August, 2000 and features a 200-card base set broken into tiers as follows: Base Veterans/Prospects (1-150) and Rookies (151-200) which were serial numbered to 2999. Each pack contained four cards, and carried a suggested retail of $5.00. Rookie Cards include Rick Asadoorian, Willie Bloomquist, Bobby Bradley, Ben Broussard, Chin-Feng Chen and Barry Zito. The added element of serial-numbered Rookie Cards was extremely popular with collectors and a much-need jolt of life for the Bowman's Best brand (which has been badly overshadowed for two years by the Bowman Chrome Brand).

	Nm-Mt	Ex-Mt
COMP.SET w/o RC's (150)	50.00	15.00
COMMON CARD (1-150)	.40	.12
COMMON (151-200)	5.00	1.50
1 Nomar Garciaparra	1.50	.45
2 Chipper Jones	1.00	.30
3 Tony Clark	.40	.12
4 Bernie Williams	.60	.18
5 Barry Bonds	2.50	.75
6 Jermaine Dye	.40	.12
7 John Olerud	.40	.12
8 Mike Hampton	.40	.12
9 Cal Ripken	3.00	.90
10 Jeff Bagwell	.60	.18
11 Troy Glaus	.60	.18
12 J.D. Drew	.40	.12
13 Jeromy Burnitz	.40	.12
14 Carlos Delgado	.40	.12
15 Shawn Green	.40	.12
16 Kevin Millwood	.40	.12
17 Rondell White	.40	.12
18 Scott Rolen	.60	.18
19 Jeff Cirillo	.40	.12
20 Barry Larkin	1.00	.30
21 Brian Giles	.40	.12
22 Roger Clemens	2.00	.60
23 Manny Ramirez	.40	.12
24 Alex Gonzalez	.40	.12
25 Mark Grace	.60	.18
26 Fernando Tatis	.40	.12
27 Randy Johnson	1.00	.30
28 Roger Cedeno	.40	.12
29 Brian Jordan	.40	.12
30 Kevin Brown	.40	.12
31 Greg Vaughn	.40	.12
32 Roberto Alomar	1.00	.30
33 Larry Walker	.60	.18
34 Rafael Palmeiro	.60	.18
35 Curt Schilling	.60	.18
36 Orlando Hernandez	.40	.12
37 Todd Walker	.40	.12
38 Juan Gonzalez	1.00	.30
39 Sean Casey	.40	.12
40 Tony Gwynn	1.25	.35
41 Albert Belle	.40	.12
42 Gary Sheffield	.40	.12
43 Michael Barrett	.40	.12
44 Preston Wilson	.40	.12
45 Jim Thome	1.00	.30
46 Shannon Stewart	.40	.12
47 Mo Vaughn	.40	.12
48 Ben Grieve	.40	.12
49 Adrian Beltre	.40	.12
50 Sammy Sosa	1.50	.45
51 Bob Abreu	.40	.12
52 Edgardo Alfonzo	.40	.12
53 Carlos Febles	.40	.12
54 Frank Thomas	1.00	.30
55 Alex Rodriguez	1.50	.45
56 Cliff Floyd	.40	.12
57 Jose Canseco	1.00	.30
58 Erubiel Durazo	.40	.12
59 Tim Hudson	.60	.18
60 Craig Biggio	.60	.18
61 Eric Karros	.40	.12
62 Mike Mussina	1.00	.30
63 Robin Ventura	.40	.12
64 Carlos Beltran	.40	.12
65 Pedro Martinez	1.00	.30
66 Gabe Kapler	.40	.12
67 Jason Kendall	.40	.12
68 Derek Jeter	2.50	.75
69 Magglio Ordonez	.40	.12
70 Mike Piazza	1.50	.45
71 Mike Lieberthal	.40	.12
72 Andres Galarraga	.40	.12
73 Raul Mondesi	.40	.12
74 Eric Chavez	.40	.12
75 Greg Maddux	1.50	.45
76 Matt Williams	.40	.12
77 Kris Benson	.40	.12
78 Ivan Rodriguez	1.00	.30
79 Pokey Reese	.40	.12
80 Vladimir Guerrero	1.00	.30
81 Mark McGwire	2.50	.75
82 Vinny Castilla	.40	.12
83 Todd Helton	.60	.18
84 Andruw Jones	.40	.12
85 Ken Griffey Jr.	1.50	.45
86 Mark McGwire BP	1.25	.35
87 Derek Jeter BP	1.25	.35
88 Chipper Jones BP	.60	.18
89 Nomar Garciaparra BP	1.00	.30
90 Sammy Sosa BP	1.00	.30
91 Cal Ripken BP	1.50	.45
92 Juan Gonzalez BP	.60	.18
93 Alex Rodriguez BP	1.00	.30
94 Barry Bonds BP	1.25	.35
95 Sean Casey BP	.40	.12
96 Vladimir Guerrero BP	.60	.18
97 Mike Piazza BP	1.00	.30
98 Shawn Green BP	.40	.12
99 Jeff Bagwell BP	.40	.12
100 Ken Griffey Jr. BP	1.00	.30
101 Rick Ankiel	.40	.12
102 John Patterson	.40	.12
103 David Walling	.40	.12
104 Michael Restovich	.40	.12
105 A.J. Burnett	.40	.12
106 Pablo Ozuna	.40	.12
107 Chad Hermansen	.40	.12
108 Choo Freeman	.40	.12
109 Mark Quinn	.40	.12
110 Corey Patterson	.60	.18
111 Ramon Ortiz	.40	.12
112 Vernon Wells	.40	.12
113 Milton Bradley	.40	.12
114 Gookie Dawkins	.40	.12
115 Sean Burroughs	.60	.18
116 Wily Mo Pena	.40	.12
117 Dee Brown	.40	.12
118 C.C. Sabathia	.40	.12
119 Adam Kennedy	.40	.12
120 Octavio Dotel	.40	.12
121 Kip Wells	.40	.12
122 Ben Petrick	.40	.12
123 Mark Mulder	.60	.18
124 Jason Standridge	.40	.12
125 Adam Piatt	.40	.12
126 Steve Lomasney	.40	.12
127 Jayson Werth	.40	.12
128 Alex Escobar	.40	.12
129 Ryan Anderson	.40	.12
130 Adam Dunn	1.00	.30
131 Ted Lilly	.40	.12
132 Brad Penny	.40	.12
133 Daryle Ward	.40	.12
134 Eric Munson	.40	.12
135 Nick Johnson	.40	.12
136 Jason Jennings	.40	.12
137 Tim Raines Jr.	.40	.12
138 Ruben Mateo	.40	.12
139 Jack Cust	.40	.12
140 Rafael Furcal	.40	.12
141 Eric Gagne	1.00	.30
142 Tony Armas Jr.	.40	.12
143 Mike Paradis	.40	.12
144 Peter Bergeron	.40	.12
145 Alfonso Soriano	1.00	.30
146 Josh Hamilton	.40	.12
147 Michael Cuddyer	.40	.12
148 Jay Gehrke	.40	.12
149 Josh Girdley	.40	.12
150 Pat Burrell	.60	.18
151 Brett Myers RC	25.00	7.50
152 Scott Seabol RC	5.00	1.50
153 Keith Reed RC	5.00	1.50
154 F.Rodriguez RC	20.00	6.00
155 Barry Zito RC	40.00	12.00
156 Pat Manning RC	5.00	1.50
157 Ben Christensen RC	5.00	1.50
158 Corey Myers RC	5.00	1.50
159 Wascar Serrano RC	5.00	1.50
160 Wes Anderson RC	5.00	1.50
161 Andy Tracy RC	5.00	1.50
162 Cesar Saba RC	5.00	1.50
163 Mike Lamb RC	5.00	1.50
164 Bobby Bradley RC	5.00	1.50
165 Vince Faison RC	5.00	1.50
166 Ty Howington RC	5.00	1.50
167 Ken Harvey RC UER Card has pitching stats on the back	12.00	3.60
168 Josh Kalinowski RC	5.00	1.50
169 Ruben Salazar RC	5.00	1.50
170 Aaron Rowand RC	5.00	1.50
171 Ramon Santiago RC	5.00	1.50
172 Scott Sobkowiak RC	5.00	1.50
173 Lyle Overbay RC	8.00	2.40
174 Rico Washington RC	5.00	1.50
175 Rick Asadoorian RC	5.00	1.50
176 Matt Ginter RC	5.00	1.50
177 Jason Stumm RC	5.00	1.50
178 B.J. Garbe RC	5.00	1.50
179 Mike MacDougal RC	8.00	2.40
180 Ryan Christianson RC	5.00	1.50
181 Kurt Ainsworth RC	10.00	3.00
182 Brad Baisley RC	5.00	1.50
183 Ben Broussard RC	5.00	1.50
184 Aaron McNeal RC	5.00	1.50
185 John Sneed RC	5.00	1.50
186 Junior Brignac RC	5.00	1.50
187 Chance Caple RC	5.00	1.50
188 Scott Downs RC	5.00	1.50
189 Matt Cepicky RC	5.00	1.50
190 Chin-Feng Chen RC	30.00	9.00
191 Johan Santana RC	30.00	9.00
192 Brad Baker RC	5.00	1.50
193 Jason Repko RC	5.00	1.50
194 Craig Dingman RC	5.00	1.50
195 Chris Wakeland RC	5.00	1.50
196 Rogelio Arias RC	5.00	1.50
197 Luis Matos RC	15.00	4.50
198 Rob Ramsay	5.00	1.50
199 Willie Bloomquist RC	30.00	9.00
200 Tony Pena Jr. RC	5.00	1.50

2000 Bowman's Best Autographed Baseball Redemptions

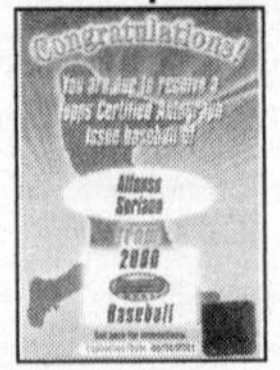

Randomly inserted into packs at one in 688, this five-card insert features exchange cards for actual autographed baseballs from some of the Major League's hottest prospects. Please note the deadline to return these cards to Topps was June 30th, 2001.

	Nm-Mt	Ex-Mt
1 Josh Hamilton	40.00	12.00
2 Rick Ankiel	40.00	12.00
3 Alfonso Soriano	60.00	18.00
4 Nick Johnson	40.00	12.00
5 Corey Patterson	40.00	12.00

2000 Bowman's Best Bets

Randomly inserted into packs at one in 15, this 10-card insert features prospects that are sure bets to excel at the Major League level. Card backs carry a "BBB" prefix.

	Nm-Mt	Ex-Mt
COMPLETE SET (10)	25.00	7.50
BBB1 Pat Burrell	2.50	.75
BBB2 Alfonso Soriano	4.00	1.20
BBB3 Corey Patterson	2.50	.75
BBB4 Eric Munson	1.50	.45
BBB5 Sean Burroughs	2.50	.75
BBB6 Rafael Furcal	1.50	.45
BBB7 Rick Ankiel	1.50	.45
BBB8 Nick Johnson	1.50	.45
BBB9 Ruben Mateo	1.50	.45
BBB10 Josh Hamilton	1.50	.45

2000 Bowman's Best Franchise 2000

Randomly inserted into packs at one in 18, this 25-card set features players that teams build around. Card backs carry an "F" prefix.

	Nm-Mt	Ex-Mt
COMPLETE SET (25)	150.00	45.00
F1 Cal Ripken	20.00	6.00
F2 Nomar Garciaparra	10.00	3.00
F3 Frank Thomas	6.00	1.80
F4 Manny Ramirez	2.50	.75
F5 Juan Gonzalez	6.00	1.80
F6 Carlos Beltran	2.50	.75
F7 Derek Jeter	15.00	4.50
F8 Alex Rodriguez	10.00	3.00
F9 Ben Grieve	2.50	.75
F10 Jose Canseco	6.00	1.80
F11 Ivan Rodriguez	6.00	1.80
F12 Mo Vaughn	2.50	.75
F13 Randy Johnson	6.00	1.80
F14 Chipper Jones	6.00	1.80
F15 Sammy Sosa	10.00	3.00
F16 Ken Griffey Jr.	10.00	3.00
F17 Larry Walker	4.00	1.20
F18 Preston Wilson	2.50	.75
F19 Jeff Bagwell	4.00	1.20
F20 Shawn Green	2.50	.75
F21 Vladimir Guerrero	6.00	1.80
F22 Mike Piazza	10.00	3.00
F23 Scott Rolen	4.00	1.20
F24 Tony Gwynn	8.00	2.40
F25 Barry Bonds	15.00	4.50

2000 Bowman's Best Franchise Favorites

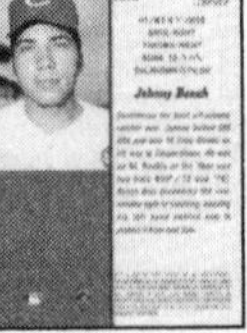

Randomly inserted into packs at one in 17, this six-card insert features players (past and present) that are franchise favorites. Card backs carry a "FR" prefix.

	Nm-Mt	Ex-Mt
COMPLETE SET (6)	30.00	9.00

FR1A Sean Casey .... 2.50 .75
FR1B Johnny Bench 4.00 1.20
FR1C Sean Casey 4.00 1.20
Johnny Bench
FR2A Cal Ripken 10.00 3.00
FR2B Brooks Robinson 4.00 1.20
FR2C Cal Ripken 10.00 3.00
Brooks Robinson

2000 Bowman's Best Franchise Favorites Autographs

Randomly inserted into packs, this six-card insert is a complete parallel of the Franchise Favorites insert. Each of these cards were autographed by the players, and the set was broken into tiers as folllows: Group A (Sean Casey and Cal Ripken) were inserted at one in 1291, Group B (Johnny Bench and Brooks Robinson) were inserted at one in 1291, and Group C (Casey/Bench, and Ripken/Robinson) were inserted into packs at one in 1,513. The overall odds of getting an autograph cards were one in 574. Card backs carry a "FR" prefix.

	Nm-Mt	Ex-Mt
FR1A Sean Casey A	30.00	9.00
FR1B Johnny Bench B	60.00	18.00
FR1C Sean Casey Johnny Bench	120.00	36.00
FR2A Cal Ripken A	120.00	36.00
FR2B Brooks Robinson B	60.00	18.00
FR2C Cal Ripken Brooks Robinson	300.00	90.00

2000 Bowman's Best Locker Room Collection Autographs

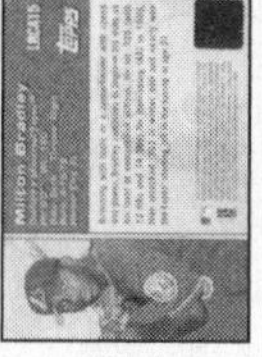

Randomly inserted into packs, this 19-card insert features autographed cards of top Major League prospects. Card backs carry an "LRCA" prefix. Please note that these cards were broken into two groups. Group A cards were inserted at one in 1033 packs, and Group B cards were inserted at one in 61.

	Nm-Mt	Ex-Mt
LRCA1 Carlos Beltran B	15.00	4.50
LRCA2 Rick Ankiel A	10.00	3.00
LRCA3 Vernon Wells A	15.00	4.50
LRCA4 Ruben Mateo A	10.00	3.00
LRCA5 Ben Petrick A	10.00	3.00
LRCA6 Adam Piatt A	10.00	3.00
LRCA7 Eric Munson A	15.00	4.50
LRCA8 Alfonso Soriano A	40.00	12.00
LRCA9 Kerry Wood B	30.00	9.00
LRCA10 Jack Cust A	10.00	3.00
LRCA11 Rafael Furcal A	15.00	4.50
LRCA12 Josh Hamilton A	10.00	3.00
LRCA13 Brad Penny A	15.00	4.50
LRCA14 Dee Brown A	10.00	3.00
LRCA15 Milton Bradley A	15.00	4.50
LRCA16 Ryan Anderson A	10.00	3.00
LRCA17 John Patterson A	10.00	3.00
LRCA18 Nick Johnson A	15.00	4.50
LRCA19 Peter Bergeron A	10.00	3.00

2000 Bowman's Best Locker Room Collection Bats

Randomly inserted into packs at one in 376, this 11-card insert features game-used bat cards of some of the hottest prospects in baseball. Card backs carry a "LRCL" prefix.

	Nm-Mt	Ex-Mt
LRCL-AP Adam Piatt	8.00	2.40
LRCL-BP Ben Petrick	8.00	2.40
LRCL-BP Brad Penny	10.00	3.00
LRCL-CB Carlos Beltran	10.00	3.00
LRCL-DB Dee Brown	8.00	2.40
LRCL-EM Eric Munson	8.00	2.40
LRCL-JD J.D. Drew	10.00	3.00
LRCL-PB Pat Burrell	15.00	4.50
LRCL-RA Rick Ankiel	8.00	2.40
LRCL-RF Rafael Furcal	10.00	3.00
LRCL-VW Vernon Wells	10.00	3.00

2000 Bowman's Best Locker Room Collection Jerseys

Randomly inserted into packs at one in 206, this five-card insert features swatches from

actual game-used jerseys. Card backs carry a "LRCJ" prefix.

	Nm-Mt	Ex-Mt
LRCJ1 Carlos Beltran	10.00	3.00
LRCJ2 Rick Ankiel	8.00	2.40
LRCJ3 Mark Quinn	8.00	2.40
LRCJ4 Ben Petrick	8.00	2.40
LRCJ5 Adam Piatt	8.00	2.40

2000 Bowman's Best Selections

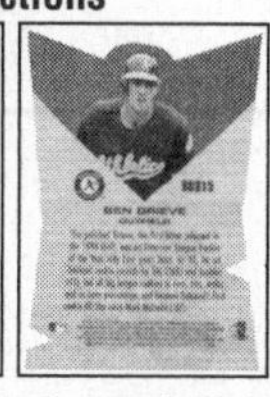

Randomly inserted into packs at one in 30, this 15-card insert features players that turned out to be outstanding draft selections. Card backs carry a "BBS" prefix.

	Nm-Mt	Ex-Mt
COMPLETE SET (15)	120.00	36.00
BBS1 Alex Rodriguez	10.00	3.00
BBS2 Ken Griffey Jr.	10.00	3.00
BBS3 Pat Burrell	4.00	1.20
BBS4 Mark McGwire	15.00	4.50
BBS5 Derek Jeter	15.00	4.50
BBS6 Nomar Garciaparra	10.00	3.00
BBS7 Mike Piazza	10.00	3.00
BBS8 Josh Hamilton	2.50	.75
BBS9 Cal Ripken	20.00	6.00
BBS10 Jeff Bagwell	4.00	1.20
BBS11 Chipper Jones	6.00	1.80
BBS12 Jose Canseco	6.00	1.80
BBS13 Carlos Beltran	2.50	.75
BBS14 Kerry Wood	2.50	.75
BBS15 Ben Grieve	2.50	.75

2000 Bowman's Best Year by Year

Randomly inserted into packs at one in 23, this 10-card insert features duos that made their Major League debuts in the same year. Card backs carry a "YY" prefix.

	Nm-Mt	Ex-Mt
COMPLETE SET (10)	80.00	24.00
YY1 Sammy Sosa Ken Griffey Jr.	8.00	2.40
YY2 Nomar Garciaparra Vladimir Guerrero	8.00	2.40
YY3 Alex Rodriguez Jeff Cirillo	8.00	2.40
YY4 Mike Piazza Pedro Martinez	8.00	2.40
YY5 Derek Jeter Edgardo Alfonzo	12.00	3.60
YY6 Alfonso Soriano Rick Ankiel	2.00	.60
YY7 Mark McGwire Barry Bonds	12.00	3.60
YY8 Juan Gonzalez Larry Walker	5.00	1.50
YY9 Ivan Rodriguez Jeff Bagwell	5.00	1.50
YY10 Shawn Green Manny Ramirez	2.00	.60

2001 Bowman's Best Promos

This three-card set was distributed in a sealed plastic cello wrap to dealers and hobby media a few months prior to the release of 2001 Bowman's Best to allow a sneak preview of the upcoming brand. The promos can be readily identified from base issue cards by their PP prefixed numbering on back.

	Nm-Mt	Ex-Mt
COMPLETE SET (3)	5.00	1.50
PP1 Todd Helton	2.00	.60
PP2 Tim Hudson	2.00	.60
PP3 Vernon Wells	1.00	.30

2001 Bowman's Best

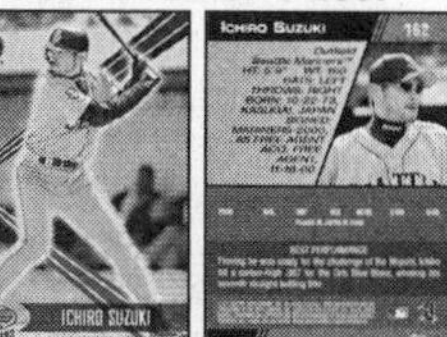

This 200-card set features color action player photos printed in an all new design and leading technology. The set was distributed in five-card packs with a suggested retial price of $5 and includes 35 Rookie and 15 Exclusive Rookie cards sequentially numbered to 2,999.

	Nm-Mt	Ex-Mt
COMP.SET w/o SP's (150)	50.00	15.00
COMMON CARD (1-150)	.40	.12
COMMON (151-200)	8.00	2.40
1 Vladimir Guerrero	1.00	.30
2 Miguel Tejada	.40	.12
3 Geoff Jenkins	.40	.12
4 Jeff Bagwell	.60	.18
5 Todd Helton	.60	.18
6 Ken Griffey Jr.	1.50	.45
7 Nomar Garciaparra	1.50	.45
8 Chipper Jones	1.00	.30
9 Darin Erstad	.40	.12
10 Frank Thomas	1.00	.30
11 Jim Thome	1.00	.30
12 Preston Wilson	.40	.12
13 Kevin Brown	.40	.12
14 Derek Jeter	2.50	.75
15 Scott Rolen	.60	.18
16 Ryan Klesko	.40	.12
17 Jeff Kent	.40	.12
18 Raul Mondesi	.40	.12
19 Greg Vaughn	.40	.12
20 Bernie Williams	.60	.18
21 Mike Piazza	1.50	.45
22 Richard Hidalgo	.40	.12
23 Dean Palmer	.40	.12
24 Roberto Alomar	1.00	.30
25 Sammy Sosa	1.50	.45
26 Randy Johnson	1.00	.30
27 Manny Ramirez	.40	.12
28 Roger Clemens	2.00	.60
29 Terrence Long	.40	.12
30 Jason Kendall	.40	.12
31 Richie Sexson	.40	.12
32 David Wells	.40	.12
33 Andruw Jones	.40	.12
34 Pokey Reese	.40	.12
35 Juan Gonzalez	1.00	.30
36 Carlos Beltran	.40	.12
37 Shawn Green	.40	.12
38 Mariano Rivera	.60	.18
39 John Olerud	.40	.12
40 Jim Edmonds	.40	.12
41 Andres Galarraga	.40	.12
42 Carlos Delgado	.40	.12
43 Kris Benson	.40	.12
44 Andy Pettitte	.60	.18
45 Jeff Cirillo	.40	.12
46 Magglio Ordonez	.40	.12
47 Tom Glavine	.60	.18
48 Garret Anderson	.40	.12
49 Cal Ripken	3.00	.90
50 Pedro Martinez	1.00	.30
51 Barry Bonds	2.50	.75
52 Alex Rodriguez	1.50	.45
53 Ben Grieve	.40	.12
54 Edgar Martinez	.60	.18
55 Jason Giambi	1.00	.30
56 Jeromy Burnitz	.40	.12
57 Mike Mussina	1.00	.30
58 Moises Alou	.40	.12
59 Sean Casey	.40	.12
60 Greg Maddux	1.50	.45
61 Tim Hudson	.40	.12
62 Mark McGwire	2.50	.75
63 Rafael Palmeiro	.60	.18
64 Tony Batista	.40	.12
65 Kazuhiro Sasaki	.40	.12
66 Jorge Posada	.60	.18
67 Johnny Damon	.40	.12
68 Brian Giles	.40	.12
69 Jose Vidro	.40	.12
70 Jermaine Dye	.40	.12
71 Craig Biggio	.60	.18
72 Larry Walker	.60	.18
73 Eric Chavez	.40	.12
74 David Segui	.40	.12
75 Tim Salmon	.60	.18
76 Javy Lopez	.40	.12
77 Paul Konerko	.40	.12
78 Barry Larkin	1.00	.30
79 Mike Hampton	.40	.12
80 Bobby Higginson	.40	.12
81 Mark Mulder	.40	.12
82 Pat Burrell	.40	.12
83 Kerry Wood	1.00	.30
84 J.T. Snow	.40	.12
85 Ivan Rodriguez	1.00	.30
86 Edgardo Alfonzo	.40	.12
87 Orlando Hernandez	.40	.12
88 Gary Sheffield	.40	.12
89 Mike Sweeney	.40	.12
90 Carlos Lee	.40	.12
91 Rafael Furcal	.40	.12
92 Troy Glaus	.60	.18
93 Bartolo Colon	.40	.12
94 Cliff Floyd	.40	.12
95 Barry Zito	1.00	.30
96 J.D. Drew	.40	.12
97 Eric Karros	.40	.12
98 Jose Valentin	.40	.12
99 Ellis Burks	.40	.12
100 David Justice	.40	.12
101 Larry Barnes	.40	.12
102 Rod Barajas	.40	.12
103 Tony Pena Jr.	.40	.12
104 Jerry Hairston Jr.	.40	.12
105 Keith Ginter	.40	.12
106 Corey Patterson	.40	.12
107 Aaron Rowand	.40	.12
108 Miguel Olivo	.40	.12
109 Gookie Dawkins	.40	.12
110 C.C. Sabathia	.40	.12
111 Ben Patrick	.40	.12
112 Eric Munson	.40	.12
113 Ramon Castro	.40	.12
114 Alex Escobar	.40	.12
115 Josh Hamilton	.40	.12
116 Jason Marquis	.40	.12
117 Ben Davis	.40	.12
118 Alex Cintron	.40	.12
119 Julio Zuleta	.40	.12
120 Ben Broussard	.40	.12
121 Adam Everett	.40	.12
122 Ramon Carvajal RC	.40	.12
123 Felipe Lopez	.40	.12
124 Alfonso Soriano	.60	.18
125 Jayson Werth	.40	.12
126 Donzell McDonald	.40	.12
127 Jason Hart	.40	.12
128 Joe Crede	.40	.12
129 Sean Burroughs	.40	.12
130 Jack Cust	.40	.12
131 Corey Smith	.40	.12
132 Adrian Gonzalez	.40	.12
133 J.R. House	.40	.12
134 Steve Lomasney	.40	.12
135 Tim Raines Jr.	.40	.12
136 Tony Alvarez	.40	.12
137 Doug Mientkiewicz	.40	.12
138 Rocco Baldelli	3.00	.90
139 Jason Romano	.40	.12
140 Vernon Wells	.40	.12
141 Mike Bynum	.40	.12
142 Xavier Nady	.40	.12
143 Brad Wilkerson	.40	.12
144 Ben Diggins	.40	.12
145 Aubrey Huff	.40	.12
146 Eric Byrnes	.40	.12
147 Alex Gordon	.40	.12
148 Roy Oswalt	.60	.18
149 Brian Esposito	.40	.12
150 Scott Seabol	.40	.12
151 Erick Almonte RC	8.00	2.40
152 Gary Johnson RC	8.00	2.40
153 Pedro Liriano RC	8.00	2.40
154 Matt White RC	8.00	2.40
155 Luis Montanez RC	8.00	2.40
156 Brad Cresse	8.00	2.40
157 Wilson Betemit RC	8.00	2.40
158 Octavio Martinez RC	8.00	2.40
159 Adam Pettyjohn RC	8.00	2.40
160 Corey Spencer RC	8.00	2.40
161 Mark Burnett RC	8.00	2.40
162 Ichiro Suzuki RC	40.00	12.00
163 Alexis Gomez RC	8.00	2.40
164 Greg Nash RC	8.00	2.40
165 Roberto Miniel RC	8.00	2.40
166 Justin Morneau RC	25.00	7.50
167 Ben Washburn RC	8.00	2.40
168 Bob Keppel RC	8.00	2.40
169 Deivi Mendez RC	8.00	2.40
170 Tsuyoshi Shinjo RC	12.00	3.60
171 Jared Abruzzo RC	8.00	2.40
172 Derrick Van Dusen RC	8.00	2.40
173 Hee Seop Choi RC	25.00	7.50
174 Albert Pujols RC	100.00	30.00
175 Travis Hafner RC	15.00	4.50
176 Ron Davenport RC	8.00	2.40
177 Luis Torres RC	8.00	2.40
178 Jake Peavy RC	15.00	4.50
179 Elvis Corporan RC	8.00	2.40
180 Dave Krynzel	8.00	2.40
181 Tony Blanco RC	8.00	2.40
182 Elpidio Guzman RC	8.00	2.40
183 Matt Butler RC	8.00	2.40
184 Joe Thurston RC	10.00	3.00
185 Andy Beal RC	8.00	2.40
186 Kevin Nulton RC	8.00	2.40
187 Sneideer Santos RC	8.00	2.40
188 Joe Dillon RC	8.00	2.40
189 Jeremy Blevins RC	8.00	2.40
190 Chris Amador RC	8.00	2.40
191 Mark Hendrickson RC	8.00	2.40
192 Willy Aybar RC	15.00	4.50
193 Antoine Cameron RC	8.00	2.40
194 J.J. Johnson RC	8.00	2.40
195 Ryan Ketchner RC	25.00	7.50
196 Bjorn Ivy RC	8.00	2.40
197 Josh Kroeger RC	15.00	4.50
198 Ty Wigginton RC	20.00	6.00
199 Stubby Clapp RC	8.00	2.40
200 Jerrod Riggan RC	8.00	2.40

2001 Bowman's Best Autographs

Randomly inserted in packs at the rate of one in 95, this seven-card set features autographed photos of top players.

	Nm-Mt	Ex-Mt
BBAAG Adrian Gonzalez	10.00	3.00
BBABC Brad Cresse	10.00	3.00
BBAJH Josh Hamilton	10.00	3.00
BBAJR Jon Rauch	10.00	3.00
BBAJRH J.R. House	10.00	3.00
BBASB Sean Burroughs	10.00	3.00
BBATL Terrence Long	10.00	3.00

2001 Bowman's Best Exclusive Autographs

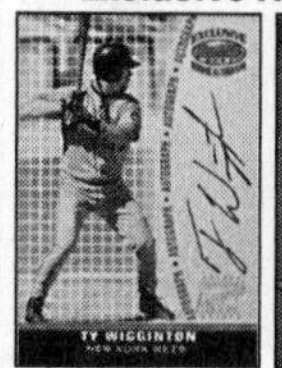

Randomly inserted in packs at the rate of one in 50, this nine-card set features autographed player photos.

	Nm-Mt	Ex-Mt
BBEABI Bjorn Ivy	10.00	3.00
BBEAJB Jeremy Blevins	10.00	3.00
BBEAJJ J.J. Johnson	10.00	3.00
BBEAJR Jerrod Riggan	10.00	3.00
BBEAMH M. Hendrickson	10.00	3.00
BBEASC S. Clapp EXCH	10.00	3.00
BBEASS Sneideer Santos	10.00	3.00
BBEATW Ty Wigginton	20.00	6.00
BBEAWA Willy Aybar	15.00	4.50

2001 Bowman's Best Franchise Favorites

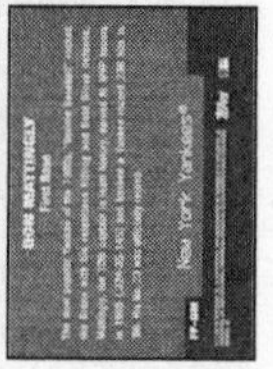

Randomly inserted in packs at the rate of one in 16, this nine-card set features color photos of past and present players that are franchise favorites.

	Nm-Mt	Ex-Mt
COMPLETE SET (9)	50.00	15.00
FF-AR Alex Rodriguez	8.00	2.40
FF-DE Darin Erstad	4.00	1.20
FF-DM Don Mattingly	12.00	3.60
FF-DW Dave Winfield	4.00	1.20
FF-EJ Darin Erstad Reggie Jackson	4.00	1.20
FF-MW Don Mattingly Dave Winfield	12.00	3.60
FF-NR Nolan Ryan	12.00	3.60
FF-RJ Reggie Jackson	4.00	1.20
FF-RR Nolan Ryan Alex Rodriguez	12.00	3.60

2001 Bowman's Best Franchise Favorites Autographs

Randomly inserted in packs, this nine-card set is an autographed parallel version of the regular insert set.

	Nm-Mt	Ex-Mt
FFAAR Alex Rodriguez	100.00	30.00
FFADE Darin Erstad	25.00	7.50
FFADM Don Mattingly	100.00	30.00
FFADW Dave Winfield	40.00	12.00
FFAEJ Darin Erstad Reggie Jackson	100.00	30.00
FFAMW Don Mattingly Dave Winfield	200.00	60.00
FFANR Nolan Ryan	120.00	36.00
FFARJ Reggie Jackson	60.00	18.00
FFARR Nolan Ryan Alex Rodriguez	400.00	120.00

2001 Bowman's Best Franchise Favorites Relics

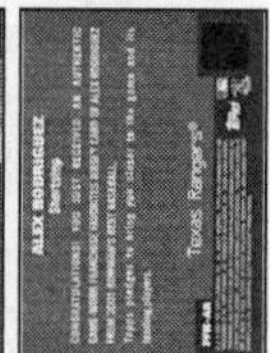

Randomly inserted in packs at the rate of one in 58, this 12-card set features color player photos of franchise favorites along with memorabilia pieces.

	Nm-Mt	Ex-Mt
FFRAR Alex Rodriguez Jsy	25.00	7.50
FFRBB Craig Biggio Jeff Bagwell	40.00	12.00
FFRCB Craig Biggio Uniform	15.00	4.50
FFRDE Darin Erstad Jsy	10.00	3.00
FFRDM Don Mattingly Jsy	40.00	12.00
FFRDW Dave Winfield Jsy	10.00	3.00
FFREJ Darin Erstad Reggie Jackson	40.00	12.00
FFRJB Jeff Bagwell Uniform	15.00	4.50
FFRMW Don Mattingly Dave Winfield	100.00	30.00
FFRNR Nolan Ryan Jsy	50.00	15.00
FFRRJ Reggie Jackson Jsy	15.00	4.50
FFRRR Nolan Ryan Alex Rodriguez	80.00	24.00

2001 Bowman's Best Franchise Futures

Randomly inserted into packs at the rate of one in 24, this 12-card set displays color photos of top young players.

	Nm-Mt	Ex-Mt
COMPLETE SET (12)	30.00	9.00
FF1 Josh Hamilton	2.00	.60
FF2 Wes Helms	2.00	.60
FF3 Alfonso Soriano	3.00	.90

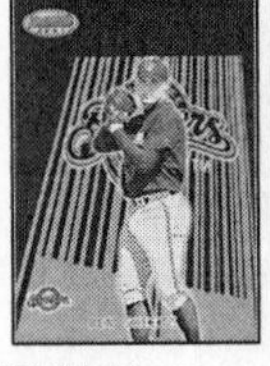

FF4 Nick Johnson 2.00 .60
FF5 Jose Ortiz 2.00 .60
FF6 Ben Sheets 2.00 .60
FF7 Sean Burroughs 2.00 .60
FF8 Ben Petrick 2.00 .60
FF9 Corey Patterson 2.00 .60
FF10 J.R. House 2.00 .60
FF11 Alex Escobar 2.00 .60
FF12 Travis Hafner 6.00 1.80

2001 Bowman's Best Impact Players

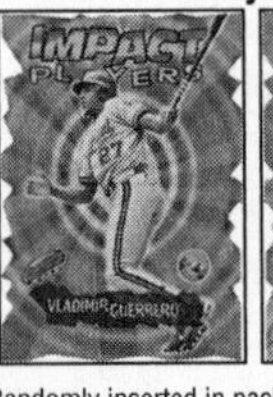
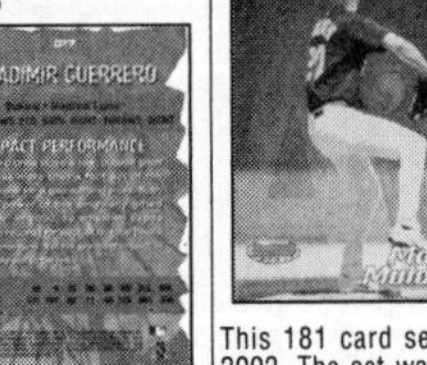

Randomly inserted in packs at the rate of one in seven, this 20-card set features color action photos of top players who have made their mark on the game.

	Nm-Mt	Ex-Mt
COMPLETE SET (20)	30.00	9.00
IP1 Mark McGwire	5.00	1.50
IP2 Sammy Sosa	3.00	.90
IP3 Manny Ramirez	1.00	.30
IP4 Troy Glaus	1.25	.35
IP5 Ken Griffey Jr.	3.00	.90
IP6 Gary Sheffield	1.00	.30
IP7 Vladimir Guerrero	2.00	.60
IP8 Carlos Delgado	1.00	.30
IP9 Jason Giambi	2.00	.60
IP10 Frank Thomas	2.00	.60
IP11 Vernon Wells	1.00	.30
IP12 Carlos Pena	1.00	.30
IP13 Joe Crede	1.00	.30
IP14 Keith Ginter	1.00	.30
IP15 Aubrey Huff	1.00	.30
IP16 Brad Cresse	1.00	.30
IP17 Austin Kearns	1.00	.30
IP18 Nick Johnson	1.00	.30
IP19 Josh Hamilton	1.00	.30
IP20 Corey Patterson	1.00	.30

2001 Bowman's Best Locker Room Collection Jerseys

Randomly inserted in packs at the rate of one in 133, this five-card set features color player photos with swatches of jerseys embedded in the cards and carry the "LRCL" prefix.

	Nm-Mt	Ex-Mt
LRCJEC Eric Chavez	10.00	3.00
LRCJJP Jay Payton	8.00	2.40
LRCJMM Mark Mulder	10.00	3.00
LRCJPR Pokey Reese	8.00	2.40
LRCJPW Preston Wilson	10.00	3.00

2001 Bowman's Best Locker Room Collection Lumber

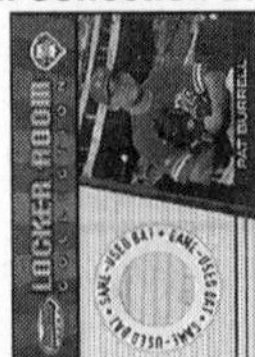

Randomly inserted in packs at the rate of one in 267, this five-card set features color player photos with pieces of actual bats embedded in the cards and carry the "LRCL" prefix.

	Nm-Mt	Ex-Mt
LRCLAG Adrian Gonzalez	10.00	3.00
LRCLCP Corey Patterson	10.00	3.00
LRCLEM Eric Munson	8.00	2.40
LRCLPB Pat Burrell	10.00	3.00
LRCLSB Sean Burroughs	10.00	3.00

2001 Bowman's Best Rookie Fever

Randomly inserted in packs at the rate of one in 10, this 10-card set features color photos of top players during their rookie year. Card backs display the "RF" prefix.

	Nm-Mt	Ex-Mt
COMPLETE SET (10)	15.00	4.50
RF1 Chipper Jones	1.50	.45
RF2 Preston Wilson	1.00	.30

RF3 Todd Helton	1.00	.30
RF4 Jay Payton	1.00	.30
RF5 Ivan Rodriguez	1.50	.45
RF6 Manny Ramirez	1.00	.30
RF7 Derek Jeter	4.00	1.20
RF8 Orlando Hernandez	1.00	.30
RF9 Mark Quinn	1.00	.30
RF10 Terrence Long	1.00	.30

2002 Bowman's Best

This 181 card set was released in August, 2002. The set was issued in five card packs which were issued 10 packs to a box and 10 boxes to a case with an SRP of $15. The first 90 cards of the set featured veteran players while cards 91 through 181 featured prospects or rookies along with either an autograph or a game-used bat piece of the featured player. The higher numbered cards were issued in different seeding ratios and we have noted the group the player belongs to next to their name in our checklist. Card number 181 features Kaz Ishii and was issued as an exchange card which could be redeemed until December 31, 2002.

	Nm-Mt	Ex-Mt
COMP.SET w/o SP's (90)	100.00	30.00
COMMON CARD (1-90)	.75	.23
COMMON AUTO A (91-180)	8.00	2.40
AUTO GROUP A ODDS 1:3		
COMMON AUTO B (91-180)	10.00	3.00
AUTO GROUP B ODDS 1:19		
COMMON BAT (91-180)	5.00	1.50
91-180 BAT STATED ODDS 1:5		
181 ISHII BAT EXCHANGE ODDS 1:131		
1 Josh Beckett	1.25	.35
2 Derek Jeter	5.00	1.50
3 Alex Rodriguez	3.00	.90
4 Miguel Tejada	.75	.23
5 Nomar Garciaparra	3.00	.90
6 Aramis Ramirez	.75	.23
7 Jeremy Giambi	.75	.23
8 Bernie Williams	1.25	.35
9 Juan Pierre	.75	.23
10 Chipper Jones	2.00	.60
11 Jimmy Rollins	.75	.23
12 Alfonso Soriano	1.25	.35
13 Mark Prior	4.00	1.20
14 Paul Konerko	.75	.23
15 Tim Hudson	.75	.23
16 Doug Mientkiewicz	.75	.23
17 Todd Helton	1.25	.35
18 Moises Alou	.75	.23
19 Juan Gonzalez	2.00	.60
20 Jorge Posada	1.25	.35
21 Jeff Kent	.75	.23
22 Roger Clemens	4.00	1.20
23 Phil Nevin	.75	.23
24 Brian Giles	.75	.23
25 Carlos Delgado	.75	.23
26 Jason Giambi	2.00	.60
27 Vladimir Guerrero	2.00	.60
28 Cliff Floyd	.75	.23
29 Shea Hillenbrand	.75	.23
30 Ken Griffey Jr.	3.00	.90
31 Mike Piazza	3.00	.90
32 Carlos Pena	.75	.23
33 Larry Walker	1.25	.35
34 Magglio Ordonez	.75	.23
35 Mike Mussina	2.00	.60
36 Andruw Jones	.75	.23
37 Nick Johnson	.75	.23
38 Curt Schilling	1.25	.35
39 Eric Chavez	.75	.23
40 Bartolo Colon	.75	.23
41 Eric Hinske	.75	.23
42 Sean Burroughs	.75	.23
43 Randy Johnson	2.00	.60
44 Adam Dunn	.75	.23
45 Pedro Martinez	2.00	.60
46 Garret Anderson	.75	.23
47 Jim Thome	2.00	.60
48 Gary Sheffield	.75	.23
49 Tsuyoshi Shinjo	.75	.23
50 Albert Pujols	4.00	1.20
51 Ichiro Suzuki	3.00	.90
52 C.C. Sabathia	.75	.23
53 Bobby Abreu	.75	.23
54 Ivan Rodriguez	2.00	.60
55 J.D. Drew	.75	.23
56 Jacque Jones	.75	.23
57 Jason Kendall	.75	.23
58 Javier Vazquez	.75	.23
59 Jeff Bagwell	1.25	.35
60 Greg Maddux	3.00	.90
61 Jim Edmonds	.75	.23
62 Hank Blalock	2.00	.60
63 Jose Vidro	.75	.23
64 Kevin Brown	.75	.23
65 Mark Teixeira	2.00	.60
66 Sammy Sosa	3.00	.90
67 Lance Berkman	.75	.23
68 Mark Mulder	.75	.23
69 Marty Cordova	.75	.23
70 Frank Thomas	2.00	.60
71 Mike Cameron	.75	.23
72 Mike Sweeney	.75	.23
73 Barry Bonds	5.00	1.50
74 Troy Glaus	1.25	.35
75 Barry Zito	1.25	.35
76 Pat Burrell	.75	.23
77 Paul LoDuca	.75	.23
78 Rafael Palmeiro	1.25	.35
79 Austin Kearns	.75	.23
80 Darin Erstad	.75	.23
81 Richie Sexson	.75	.23
82 Roberto Alomar	2.00	.60
83 Roy Oswalt	.75	.23
84 Ryan Klesko	.75	.23
85 Luis Gonzalez	.75	.23
86 Scott Rolen	1.25	.35
87 Shannon Stewart	.75	.23
88 Shawn Green	.75	.23
89 Toby Hall	.75	.23
90 Bret Boone	.75	.23
91 Casey Kotchman Bat RC	15.00	4.50
92 Jose Valverde AU A RC	10.00	3.00
93 Cole Barthel Bat RC	5.00	1.50
94 Brad Nelson AU A RC	15.00	4.50
95 Mauricio Lara AU A RC	8.00	2.40
96 Ryan Gripp Bat RC	5.00	1.50
97 Brian West AU A RC	8.00	2.40
98 Chris Piersoll AU B RC	10.00	3.00
99 Ryan Church AU B RC	15.00	4.50
100 Javier Colina AU A	8.00	2.40
101 Juan M. Gonzalez AU A RC	8.00	2.40
102 Benito Baez AU A	8.00	2.40
103 Mike Hill Bat RC	5.00	1.50
104 Jason Grove AU B RC	10.00	3.00
105 Koyie Hill AU B	10.00	3.00
106 Mark Outlaw AU A RC	8.00	2.40
107 Jason Bay Bat RC	10.00	3.00
108 Jorge Padilla AU A RC	8.00	2.40
109 Pete Zamora AU A RC	8.00	2.40
110 Joe Mauer AU A RC	70.00	21.00
111 Franklyn German AU A RC	8.00	2.40
112 Chris Flinn AU A RC	8.00	2.40
113 David Wright Bat RC	15.00	4.50
114 An. Martinez AU A RC	8.00	2.40
115 Nic Jackson Bat RC	5.00	1.50
116 Rene Reyes AU A RC	8.00	2.40
117 Colin Young AU A RC	8.00	2.40
118 Joe Orloski AU A RC	8.00	2.40
119 Mike Wilson AU A RC	8.00	2.40
120 Rich Thompson AU A RC	8.00	2.40
121 Jake Mauer AU B RC	10.00	3.00
122 Mario Ramos AU A RC	8.00	2.40
123 Doug Sessions AU B RC	10.00	3.00
124 Doug Devore Bat RC	5.00	1.50
125 Travis Foley AU A RC	8.00	2.40
126 Chris Baker AU A RC	8.00	2.40
127 Michael Floyd AU A RC	8.00	2.40
128 Josh Barfield Bat RC	15.00	4.50
129 Jose Bautista Bat RC	8.00	2.40
130 Gavin Floyd AU A RC	25.00	7.50
131 Jason Botts Bat RC	5.00	1.50
132 Clint Nageotte AU A RC	12.00	3.60
133 Jesus Cota AU B RC	10.00	3.00
134 Ron Calloway Bat RC	5.00	1.50
135 Kevin Cash Bat RC	5.00	1.50
136 Jonny Gomes AU B RC	20.00	6.00
137 Dennis Ulacia AU A RC	8.00	2.40
138 Ryan Snare AU A RC	8.00	2.40
139 Kevin Deaton AU A RC	8.00	2.40
140 Bobby Jenks AU B RC	25.00	7.50
141 Casey Kotchman AU A RC	30.00	9.00
142 Adam Walker AU A RC	8.00	2.40
143 Mike Gonzalez AU A RC	8.00	2.40
144 Ruben Gotay Bat RC	5.00	1.50
145 Jason Grove Bat RC	5.00	1.50
146 Freddy Sanchez AU B RC	10.00	3.00
147 Jason Arnold AU B RC	20.00	6.00
148 Scott Hairston AU A RC	20.00	6.00
149 Jason St. Clair AU B RC	10.00	3.00
150 Chris Tritle Bat RC	5.00	1.50
151 Edwin Yan Bat RC	5.00	1.50
152 Freddy Sanchez Bat RC	5.00	1.50
153 Greg Sain Bat RC	5.00	1.50
154 Yurendell De Caster Bat RC	5.00	1.50
155 Noochie Varner Bat RC	5.00	1.50
156 Nelson Castro AU B RC	10.00	3.00
157 Randall Shelley Bat RC	5.00	1.50
158 Reed Johnson Bat RC	8.00	2.40
159 Ryan Raburn AU A RC	8.00	2.40
160 Jose Morban Bat RC	5.00	1.50
161 Justin Schuda AU A RC	8.00	2.40
162 Henry Pichardo AU A RC	8.00	2.40
163 Josh Bard AU A RC	8.00	2.40
164 Josh Bonifay AU A RC	8.00	2.40
165 Brandon League AU B RC	10.00	3.00
166 Jorge-Julio DePaula AU A RC	15.00	4.50
167 Todd Linden AU B RC	40.00	12.00
168 Francisco Liriano AU A RC	10.00	3.00
169 Chris Snelling AU A RC	12.00	3.60
170 Blake McGinley AU A RC	8.00	2.40
171 Cody McKay AU A RC	8.00	2.40
172 Jason Stanford AU A RC	8.00	2.40
173 Lenny Dinardo AU A RC	8.00	2.40
174 Greg Montalbano AU A RC	8.00	2.40
175 Earl Snyder AU A RC	8.00	2.40
176 Justin Huber AU A RC	12.00	3.60
177 Chris Narveson AU A RC	8.00	2.40
178 Jon Switzer AU A RC	8.00	2.40
179 Ronald Acuna AU A RC	8.00	2.40
180 Chris Duffy Bat RC	5.00	1.50
181 Kazuhisa Ishii Bat RC	10.00	3.00

2002 Bowman's Best Blue

This 181 card set is a parallel of the regular Bowman's Best set. These cards were seeded into packs at different rates which we have notated. These card can be differentiated by their "blue" coloring. Cards numbered from 1 through 90 were issued to a stated print run of 300 serial numbered sets. Card number 181 features Kaz Ishii and was issued as an exchange card which could be redeemed until December 31, 2002.

	Nm-Mt	Ex-Mt
*BLUE 1-90: 1X TO 2.5X BASIC		
1-90 STATED ODDS 1:6		
1-90 PRINT RUN 300 SERIAL #'d SETS		
*BLUE AUTO: .4X TO 1X BASIC AU A		
*BLUE AUTO: .3X TO .8X BASIC AU B		
AUTO STATED ODDS 1:6		
*BLUE BAT: .4X TO 1X BASIC BAT		
BAT STATED ODDS 1:14		
ISHII BAT EXCHANGE ODDS 1:335		
ISHII BAT EXCHANGE DEADLINE 12/31/02		
BLUE BATS FEATURE TEAM LOGOS!		
181 Kazuhisa Ishii Bat	10.00	3.00

2002 Bowman's Best Gold

This 181 card set is a parallel of the regular Bowman's Best set. These cards were seeded into packs at different rates which we have notated. These card can be differentiated by their "gold" coloring. Cards numbered from 1 through 90 were limited to a stated print run of 50 serial numbered sets. Card number 181 features Kaz Ishii and was issued as an exchange card which could be redeemed until December 31, 2002.

	Nm-Mt	Ex-Mt
*GOLD 1-90: 3X TO 8X BASIC		
1-90 STATED ODDS 1:31		
1-90 PRINT RUN 50 SERIAL #'d SETS		
*GOLD AUTO: 1X TO 2.5X BASIC AU A		
*GOLD AUTO: .75X TO 2X BASIC AU B		
GOLD AUTO STATED ODDS 1:51		
*GOLD BAT: 1X TO 2.5X BASIC BAT		
GOLD BAT STATED ODDS 1:115		
ISHII BAT EXCHANGE ODDS 1:3444		
ISHII BAT EXCHANGE DEADLINE 12/31/02		
GOLD BATS FEATURE FACSIMILE AUTOS!		
181 Kazuhisa Ishii Bat	25.00	7.50

2002 Bowman's Best Red

This 181 card set is a parallel of the regular Bowman's Best set. These cards were seeded into packs at different rates which we have notated. These card can be differentiated by their "red" coloring. Cards numbered from 1 through 90 were limited to a stated print run of 200 serial numbered sets. Card number 181 features Kaz Ishii and was issued as an exchange card which could be redeemed until December 31, 2002.

	Nm-Mt	Ex-Mt
*RED 1-90: 1.25X TO 3X BASIC		
1-90 PRINT RUN 200 SERIAL #'d SETS		
*RED AUTO: .6X TO 1.5X BASIC AU A		
*RED AUTO: .5X TO 1.2X BASIC AU B		
AUTO STATED ODDS 1:17		
*RED BATS: .6X TO 1.5X BASIC BATS		
BAT STATED ODDS 1:39		
ISHII BAT EXCHANGE ODDS 1:1117		
ISHII BAT EXCHANGE DEADLINE 12/31/02		
RED BATS FEATURE STATISTICS!		
181 Kazuhisa Ishii Bat	15.00	4.50

2002 Bowman's Best Uncirculated

Ninety-one different scratch-off redemption cards were inserted into packs at overall odds of one in 92. Once the cards were scratched, a code number was revealed whereby collectors could enter the code at the Topps website to reveal which specific player they had won the rights to. The actual "Uncirculated" cards were straight parallels of the basic Bowman's Best autographed rookie cards - except these were sealed inside a hard plastic case of which was affixed with a tamper-proof Topps holographic logo. These cards were printed to a stated print run of 20 sets and there is no pricing provided due to scarcity. The deadline to redeem the cards was December 31st, 2002.

	Nm-Mt	Ex-Mt
COMMON EXCH		
AU STATED ODDS 1:129		
BAT STATED ODDS 1:322		
OVERALL STATED ODDS 1:92		

2003 Bowman's Best

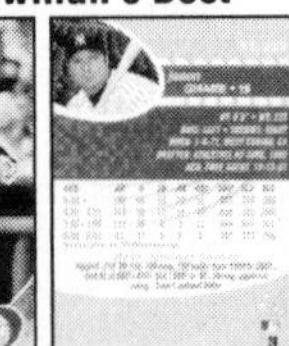

This 130 card set was released in September, 2003. This set was issued in five card packs which contained an autograph card. Each of these packs had an SRP of $15 and these packs were issued 10 to a box and 10 boxes to a case. This set was designed to be checklisted alphabetically as no numbering was used for this set. The first year cards which are autographed have the lettering FY AU RC after their name in the checklist. A few first year players had some cards issued with an bat piece included. Those bat cards were issued one per box-loader pack. In addition, high draft pick Bryan Bullington signed some of the actual boxes and those boxes were issued at a stated rate of one in 106.

	MINT	NRMT
COMP.SET w/o SP's (50)	40.00	18.00
COMMON CARD	.60	.25
COMMON AUTO	8.00	3.60
COMMON BAT	4.00	1.80
AB Andrew Brown FY AU RC	8.00	3.60
AK Austin Kearns	.60	.25
AM Aneudis Mateo FY AU RC	8.00	3.60
AP Albert Pujols	3.00	1.35
AR Alex Rodriguez	2.50	1.10
AS Alfonso Soriano	1.00	.45
AW Aron Weston FY AU RC	8.00	3.60
BB Bryan Bullington FY AU RC	20.00	9.00
BC Bernie Castro FY RC	1.00	.45
BFL Br. Florence FY AU RC	8.00	3.60
BFR Ben Francisco FY AU RC	10.00	4.50
BH Brendan Harris FY AU RC	10.00	4.50
BJH Bo Hart FY RC	3.00	1.35
BK Beau Kemp FY AU RC	8.00	3.60
BLB Barry Bonds	4.00	1.80
BM Brian McCann FY AU RC	10.00	4.50
BSG Brian Giles	.60	.25
BWB Bobby Basham FY AU RC	10.00	4.50
BZ Barry Zito	1.00	.45
CAD Carlos Duran FY AU RC	8.00	3.60
CDC C. De La Cruz FY AU RC	8.00	3.60
CJ Chipper Jones	1.50	.70
CJW C.J. Wilson FY AU	8.00	3.60
CM Charlie Manning FY AU RC	8.00	3.60
CMS Curt Schilling	1.00	.45
CS Cory Stewart FY AU RC	8.00	3.60
CSS Corey Shafer FY AU RC	10.00	4.50
CW Chien-Ming Wang FY RC	4.00	1.80
CWA Chien-Ming Wang FY AU	40.00	18.00
DAM D. Moseley FY AU RC	10.00	4.50
DC David Cash FY AU RC	8.00	3.60
DH Dan Haren FY AU RC	10.00	4.50
DJ Derek Jeter	4.00	1.80
DM David Martinez FY AU RC	8.00	3.60
DMM D. McGowan FY AU RC	10.00	4.50
DR Darrell Rasner FY AU RC	8.00	3.60
DW Doug Waechter FY AU RC	10.00	4.50
DY Dustin Yount FY RC	1.50	.70
ERA El. Ramirez FY AU RC	15.00	6.75
ERI Eric Riggs FY AU RC	10.00	4.50
ET Eider Torres FY AU RC	8.00	3.60
FP Felix Pie FY AU RC	40.00	18.00
FS Felix Sanchez FY AU RC	8.00	3.60
FT Ferdin Tejeda FY AU RC	8.00	3.60
GA Greg Aquino FY AU RC	8.00	3.60
GB Gregor Blanco FY AU RC	8.00	3.60
GJA Garret Anderson	.60	.25
GM Greg Maddux	2.50	1.10
GS G. Schneidmiller FY AU RC	8.00	3.60
HR Hanley Ramirez FY AU RC	20.00	9.00
HRB Hanley Ramirez FY Bat	10.00	4.50
HT Haj Turay FY RC	1.50	.70
IS Ichiro Suzuki	2.50	1.10
JB Jeremy Bonderman FY RC	2.00	.90
JC Jose Contreras FY RC	3.00	1.35
JDD J.D. Durbin FY AU RC	10.00	4.50
JFK Jeff Kent	.60	.25
JG Joey Gomes FY AU RC	8.00	3.60
JGB Joey Gomes FY Bat	4.00	1.80
JGG Jason Giambi	1.50	.70
JK Jason Kubel FY AU RC	10.00	4.50
JKB Jason Kubel FY Bat	5.00	2.20
JLB Jaime Bubela FY AU RC	8.00	3.60
JM Jose Morales FY AU RC	8.00	3.60
JMS Jon-Mark Sprowl FY RC	1.50	.70
JRG Jeremy Griffiths FY AU RC	10.00	4.50
JT Jim Thome	1.50	.70
JV Joe Valentine FY AU RC	8.00	3.60
JW Josh Willingham FY AU RC	15.00	6.75
KG Ken Griffey Jr.	2.50	1.10
KJ Kade Johnson FY AU RC	8.00	3.60
KS Kelly Shoppach FY AU RC	15.00	6.75
KY Kevin Youkilis FY AU RC	20.00	9.00
KYE Kevin Youkilis FY Bat	10.00	4.50
LB Lance Berkman	.60	.25
LF Lew Ford FY AU RC	10.00	4.50
LFJ Lew Ford FY Bat	5.00	2.20
LW Larry Walker	1.00	.45
MB Matt Bruback FY RC	1.00	.45
MD Matt Diaz FY RC	1.50	.70
MDA Matt Diaz FY AU	10.00	4.50
MDH Matt Hensley FY AU RC	8.00	3.60
MDM Mark Malaska FY AU RC	8.00	3.60
MH Mi. Hernandez FY AU RC	8.00	3.60
MHI Mi. Hinckley FY AU RC	10.00	4.50
MJP Mike Piazza	2.50	1.10
MK Matt Kata FY AU RC	10.00	4.50
MNH Matt Hagen FY AU RC	10.00	4.50
MO Mike O'Keefe FY RC	1.00	.45
MOR Magglio Ordonez	.60	.25
MP Mark Prior	3.00	1.35
MR Manny Ramirez	.60	.25
MS Mike Sweeney	.60	.25
MT Miguel Tejada	.60	.25
NG Nomar Garciaparra	2.50	1.10
NL Nook Logan FY AU RC	8.00	3.60
OC Ozzie Chavez FY AU RC	8.00	3.60
PB Pat Burrell	.60	.25
PL Pete LaForest FY AU RC	10.00	4.50
PM Pedro Martinez	1.50	.70
PR Prentice Redman FY AU RC	8.00	3.60
RC Ryan Cameron FY AU RC	8.00	3.60
RD Rajai Davis FY AU RC	10.00	4.50
RH Ryan Howard FY AU RC	12.00	5.50
RHJ Ryan Howard FY Bat	6.00	2.70
RJ Randy Johnson	1.50	.70
RM R. Nivar-Martinez FY RC	1.50	.70
RS Ryan Shealy FY AU RC	10.00	4.50
RSB Ryan Shealy FY Bat	5.00	2.20
RWH Rob. Hammock FY AU RC	10.00	4.50
SG Shawn Green	.60	.25
SS Sammy Sosa	2.50	1.10
ST Scott Tyler FY AU RC	10.00	4.50
SV Shane Victorino FY RC	1.00	.45
TA Tyler Adamczyk FY AU RC	8.00	3.60
TH Todd Helton	1.00	.45
TI Travis Ishikawa FY AU RC	10.00	4.50
TJ Tyler Johnson FY AU RC	8.00	3.60
TJB T.J. Bohn FY RC	1.00	.45
TKH Torii Hunter	.60	.25
TO Tim Olson FY AU RC	10.00	4.50
TS T.Story-Harden FY AU RC	8.00	3.60
TSB T.Story-Harden FY Bat	4.00	1.80
TT Terry Tiffee FY RC	1.50	.70
VG Vladimir Guerrero	1.50	.70
WE Willie Eyre FY AU RC	8.00	3.60
WL Wil Ledezma FY AU RC	8.00	3.60
WRC Roger Clemens	3.00	1.35
KBS Kelly Shoppach FY Bat	8.00	3.60
RLD Rajai Davis FY Bat	5.00	2.20
NNO Bryan Bullington Opened Box AU	25.00	11.00
NNO Bryan Bullington Sealed Box AU		

2003 Bowman's Best Blue

	MINT	NRMT
*BLUE: 1.5X TO 4X BASIC		
*BLUE FY: 2.5X TO 6X BASIC FY		
BLUE STATED ODDS 1:28		
BLUE PRINT RUN 100 SERIAL #'d SETS		
*BLUE AUTO: .75X TO 2X BASIC AUTO		
BLUE AUTO ODDS 1:32		
BLUE AUTO PRINT RUN 50 SETS		

BLUE AUTO'S NOT SERIAL-NUMBERED
BLUE AU PRINT RUNS PROVIDED BY TOPPS
*BLUE BAT: 1X TO 2.5X BASIC FY BAT
BLUE BAT ODDS 1:22 BOXLOADER PACKS
BLUE BAT PRINT RUN 50 SETS.........
BLUE BATS NOT SERIAL-NUMBERED
BLUE BAT PRINTS PROVIDED BY TOPPS

2003 Bowman's Best Red

	MINT	NRMT
*RED: 3X TO 8X BASIC RED		
*RED FY: 4X TO 10X BASIC FY		
RED STATED ODDS 1:55		
RED STATED PRINT RUN 50 SERIAL #'d SETS		
RED AUTO ODDS 1:63		
RED AUTO PRINT RUN 25 SETS		
RED AU PRINT RUNS PROVIDED BY TOPPS		
RED AUTOS NOT SERIAL-NUMBERED		
NO RED AUTO PRICING DUE TO SCARCITY		
RED BAT ODDS 1:44 BOXLOADER PACKS		
RED BAT PRINT RUN 25 SETS		
RED BAT PRINT RUNS PROVIDED BY TOPPS		
RED BATS NOT SERIAL-NUMBERED..		
NO RED BAT PRICING DUE TO SCARCITY		
BWB Bobby Basham FY AU		

2003 Bowman's Best Double Play Autographs

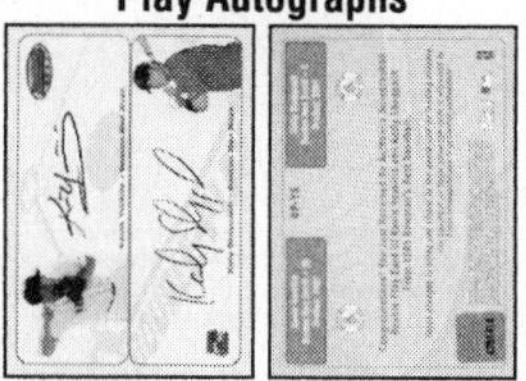

	MINT	NRMT
STATED ODDS 1:55		
EB Elizardo Ramirez Bryan Bullington	40.00	18.00
GK Joey Gomes Jason Kubel	25.00	11.00
HV Dan Haren Joe Valentine	25.00	11.00
LL Nook Logan Wil Ledezma	15.00	6.75
RS Prentice Redman Gary Schneidmiller	15.00	6.75
SB Corey Shafer Gregor Blanco	25.00	11.00
SR Felix Sanchez Darrell Rasner	15.00	6.75
YS Kevin Youkilis Kelly Shoppach	60.00	27.00

2003 Bowman's Best Triple Play Autographs

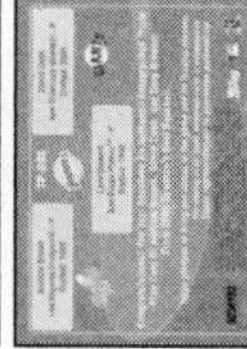

	MINT	NRMT
STATED ODDS 1:219		
BCS Andrew Brown David Cash Cory Stewart	50.00	22.00
DRS Rajai Davis Hanley Ramirez Ryan Shealy	80.00	36.00

1974 Bramac 1933 National League All-Stars

This 18-card set features black-and-white photos of the 1933 All-Stars of the National League. The set measures approximately 2 1/2" by 3 1/4" and was originally available from the producers for $3.

	NM	Ex
COMPLETE SET (18)	30.00	12.00
1 Paul Waner	2.50	1.00
2 Woody English	1.00	.40
3 Dick Bartell	1.00	.40
4 Chuck Klein	2.50	1.00
5 Tony Cuccinello	1.00	.40
6 Lefty O'Doul	1.50	.60
7 Gabby Hartnett	2.50	1.00
8 Lon Warneke	1.00	.40
9 Walter Berger	1.50	.60
10 Chick Hafey	2.00	.80
11 Frank Frisch	2.50	1.00
12 Carl Hubbell	4.00	1.60
13 Bill Hallahan	1.00	.40
14 Hal Schumacher	1.50	.60
15 Pie Traynor	2.50	1.00
16 Bill Terry	2.50	1.00
17 Pepper Martin	2.00	.80
18 Jimmy Wilson	1.50	.60

1889 Braves Cabinets Smith

These three cabinets feature members of the 1889 Boston Beaneaters and were produced by the G. Walden Smith studio in Boston. Each of these cabinets measure approximately 4 1/4" by 6 1/2" and feature the player a posed shot in their uniforms. Since the cards are unnumbered, we have sequenced them in alphabetical order.vThere should be more to this set so any additions are greatly appreciated.

	MINT	NRMT
COMPLETE SET	4000.00	1800.00
1 Tom Brown	1500.00	700.00
2 Charlie Ganzel	1500.00	700.00
3 Charles Smith	1500.00	700.00

1891 Braves Conly Cabinets

These Cabinets feature members of the 1891 Boston NL team. The players are all pictured in suit and tie. The back features an ad for Conly studios. This set is not numbered so we have sequenced them in alphabetical order.

	Ex-Mt	VG
COMPLETE SET	6000.00	3000.00
1 Hugh Duffy	3000.00	1500.00
2 George Haddock	1500.00	750.00
3 John Irwin	1500.00	750.00

1899 Braves Chickering Cabinets

These cabinets, which measure approximately 8" by 9 1/2", feature members of the 1899 Boston team which was known as the Beaneaters at that time. The photographs were taken by the Elmer Chickering studio at that time, which was one of the leading photo studios of the time. Since these cabinets are unnumbered, we have sequenced them in alphabetical order. It is very possible that there are other cabinets so any further information is greatly appreciated.

	Ex-Mt	VG
COMPLETE SET	15000.00	7500.00
1 Harvey Bailey	1000.00	500.00
2 Marty Bergen	1000.00	500.00
3 William Clarke	1000.00	500.00
4 Jimmy Collins	2000.00	1000.00
5 Hugh Duffy	2000.00	1000.00
6 Billy Hamilton	2000.00	1000.00
7 Frank Killen	1000.00	500.00
8 Edward Lewis	1000.00	500.00
9 Herman Long	1200.00	600.00
10 Robert Lowe	1200.00	600.00
11 Jouett Meekin	1000.00	500.00
12 Kid Nichols	2000.00	1000.00
13 Fred Tenney	1200.00	600.00

1932 Braves Team Issue

These blank-backed photos which measure 9" by 12" are a sepia color against cream borders. All photos are copyright 1932 by "Gowell Studios." Since they are unnumbered we have sequenced them in alphabetical order.

	Ex-Mt	VG
COMPLETE SET	150.00	75.00
1 Wally Berger	20.00	10.00
2 Huck Betts	10.00	5.00
3 Ed Brandt	10.00	5.00
4 Bobby Brown	10.00	5.00
5 Ben Cantwell	10.00	5.00
6 Pinky Hargrave	15.00	7.50
7 Fritz Knothe	10.00	5.00
8 Freddie Leach	10.00	5.00
9 Rabbit Maranville	25.00	12.50
10 Bill McKechnie MG	25.00	12.50
11 Randy Moore	10.00	5.00
12 Art Shires	15.00	7.50
13 Al Spohrer	10.00	5.00
14 Bill Urbanski	10.00	5.00
15 Red Worthington	10.00	5.00

1948 Braves Gentles Bread Label

These bread labels were issued one per loaf of Gentles bread. They feature a player photo with a fascimile signature on either the top or bottom with the "Gentles Bread" logo on the other end. These cards are unnumbered so we have sequenced them in alphabetical order. We suspect there might be more additions so any help is appreciated.

	NM	Ex
COMPLETE SET	1200.00	600.00
1 Tommy Holmes	250.00	125.00
2 Phil Masi	200.00	100.00
3 John Sain	400.00	200.00
4 Warren Spahn	500.00	250.00

1953 Braves Johnston Cookies

The cards in this 25-card set measure approximately 2 9/16" by 3 5/8". The 1953 Johnston's Cookies set of numbered cards features Milwaukee Braves players only. This set is the most plentiful of the three Johnston's Cookies sets and no known scarcities exist. The catalog designation for this set is D356-1.

	NM	Ex
COMPLETE SET (25)	450.00	220.00
1 Charlie Grimm MG	15.00	7.50
2 John Antonelli	15.00	7.50
3 Vern Bickford	12.00	6.00
4 Bob Buhl	15.00	7.50
5 Lew Burdette	20.00	10.00
6 Dave Cole	12.00	6.00
7 Ernie Johnson	15.00	7.50
8 Dave Jolly	12.00	6.00
9 Don Liddle	12.00	6.00
10 Warren Spahn	80.00	40.00
11 Max Surkont	12.00	6.00
12 Jim Wilson	12.00	6.00
13 Sibbi Sisti	12.00	6.00
14 Walker Cooper	12.00	6.00
15 Del Crandall	15.00	7.50
16 Ebba St.Claire	12.00	6.00
17 Joe Adcock	20.00	10.00
18 George Crowe	12.00	6.00
19 Jack Dittmer	12.00	6.00
20 Johnny Logan	15.00	7.50
21 Ed Mathews	80.00	40.00
22 Bill Bruton	15.00	7.50
23 Sid Gordon	12.00	6.00
24 Andy Pafko	15.00	7.50
25 Jim Pendleton	12.00	6.00

1953 Braves Merrell

This 17-card set features black-and-white art work of the Milwaukee Braves drawn by Marshall Merrell. The set measures 8" by 10" and was printed on heavy card stock. The prints originally were sold for 25 cents each. The cards are unnumbered and checklisted below in alphabetical order.

	NM	Ex
COMPLETE SET (17)	200.00	100.00
1 Joe Adcock	15.00	7.50
2 Johnny Antonelli	12.00	6.00
3 Billy Bruton	10.00	5.00
4 Bob Buhl	10.00	5.00
5 Lou Burdette	15.00	7.50
6 Del Crandall	12.00	6.00
7 Jack Dittmer	10.00	5.00
8 Sid Gordon	10.00	5.00
9 Charlie Grimm MG	12.00	6.00
10 Don Liddle	10.00	5.00
11 Johnny Logan	10.00	5.00
12 Ed Mathews	25.00	12.50
13 Andy Pafko	12.00	6.00
14 Jim Pendleton	10.00	5.00
15 Warren Spahn	40.00	20.00
16 Max Surkont	10.00	5.00
17 Jim Wilson	10.00	5.00

1953-54 Braves Spic and Span 3x5

This 27-card set features only members of the Milwaukee Braves. The cards are black and white and approximately 3 1/4" by 5 1/2". Some of the photos in the set are posed against blank backgrounds, but most are posed against seats and a chain link fence, hence the set is sometimes referred to as the "chain link fence" set. There is a facsimile autograph at the bottom of the card. The set was probably issued in 1953 and 1954 since Hank Aaron is not included in the set and Don Liddle, Ebba St.Claire, and Johnny Antonelli were traded from the Braves on February 1, 1954 for Bobby Thomson (who is also in the set). Cards can be found either blank back or with player's name, comment, and logo in blue on the back

	NM	Ex
COMPLETE SET (28)	1000.00	500.00
1 Joe Adcock	35.00	17.50
2 Johnny Antonelli	30.00	15.00
3 Vern Bickford	25.00	12.50
4 Bill Bruton	30.00	15.00
5 Bob Buhl	30.00	15.00
6 Lew Burdette	35.00	17.50
7 Dick Cole	25.00	12.50
8 Walker Cooper	25.00	12.50
9 Del Crandall	30.00	15.00
10 George Crowe	25.00	12.50
11 Jack Dittmer	25.00	12.50
12 Sid Gordon	25.00	12.50
13 Ernie Johnson	30.00	15.00
14 Dave Jolly	25.00	12.50
15 Don Liddle	25.00	12.50
16 Johnny Logan	30.00	15.00
17 Ed Mathews	150.00	75.00
18 Danny O'Connell	25.00	12.50
19 Andy Pafko	30.00	15.00
20 Jim Pendleton	25.00	12.50
21 Ebba St.Claire	25.00	12.50
22 Warren Spahn	150.00	75.00
23 Max Surkont	25.00	12.50
24 Bobby Thomson	35.00	17.50
25 Bob Thorpe	25.00	12.50
26 Roberto Vargas	25.00	12.50
27 Jim Wilson	25.00	12.50
28 Hank Aaron	300.00	150.00

1953-56 Braves Spic and Span 7x10

This 13-card set features only members of the Milwaukee Braves. The set was issued beginning in 1953 but may have been issued for several years as they seem to be the most common of all the Spic and Span issues. In addition, Danny O'Connell and Bobby Thomson were not on the '53 Braves team. The front of each card shows the logo, "Spic and Span Dry Cleaners ... the Choice of Your Favorite Braves." There is a thick white border around the cards with facsimile autograph in black in the bottom border. The cards have blank backs and are approximately 7" by 10".

	NM	Ex
COMPLETE SET (13)	200.00	100.00
1 Joe Adcock	12.00	6.00
2 Billy Bruton	10.00	5.00
3 Bob Buhl	10.00	5.00
4 Lew Burdette	12.00	6.00
5 Del Crandall	10.00	5.00
6 Jack Dittmer	8.00	4.00
7 Johnny Logan	10.00	5.00
8 Eddie Mathews	50.00	25.00
9 Chet Nichols	8.00	4.00
10 Danny O'Connell	8.00	4.00
11 Andy Pafko	10.00	5.00
12 Warren Spahn	50.00	25.00
13 Bobby Thomson	12.00	6.00

1954 Braves Douglas Felts

These circular oversize felts feature members of the 1954 Milwaukee Braves. Against a white baseball background, the player's photo and fascimile signature is set. The backs are blank and since these are unnumbered, we have sequenced them in alphabetical order.

	NM	Ex
COMPLETE SET	150.00	75.00
1 Joe Adcock	15.00	7.50
2 Bill Bruton	12.00	6.00
3 Bob Buhl	10.00	5.00
4 Lew Burdette	12.00	6.00
5 Del Crandall	12.00	6.00
6 Johnny Logan	10.00	5.00
7 Eddie Mathews	25.00	12.50
8 Danny O'Connell	10.00	5.00
9 Andy Pafko	12.00	6.00
10 Jim Pendleton	10.00	5.00
11 Warren Spahn	25.00	12.50
12 Bobby Thomson	20.00	10.00

1954 Braves Douglas Portraits

These 8" by 10" portraits feature members of the 1954 Milwaukee Braves. The checklist is identical to the Douglas Felt checklist of the same year. The drawings are oin Sepia-toned paper and the backs are blank

	NM	Ex
COMPLETE SET	175.00	90.00
1 Joe Adcock	15.00	7.50
2 Bill Bruton	12.00	6.00
3 Bob Buhl	12.00	6.00
4 Lew Burdette	20.00	10.00
5 Del Crandall	12.00	6.00
6 Johnny Logan	12.00	6.00
7 Eddie Mathews	25.00	12.50
8 Danny O'Connell	10.00	5.00
9 Andy Pafko	12.00	6.00
10 Jim Pendleton	10.00	5.00
11 Warren Spahn	30.00	15.00
12 Bobby Thomson	15.00	7.50

1954 Braves Johnston Cookies

The cards in this 35-card set measure approximately 2" by 3 7/8". The 1954 Johnston's Cookies set of color cards of Milwaukee Braves are numbered according to the player's uniform number, except for the non-players, Lacks and Taylor, who are found at the end of the set. The Bobby Thomson card was withdrawn early in the year after his injury and is scarce. The catalog number for this set is D356-2. The Hank Aaron card shows him with uniform number 5, rather than the more familiar 44, that he switched to shortly thereafter.

	NM	Ex
COMPLETE SET (35)	1100.00	550.00
COMMON SP	200.00	100.00
1 Del Crandall	20.00	10.00
3 Jim Pendleton	12.00	6.00
4 Danny O'Connell	12.00	6.00
5 Hank Aaron	500.00	250.00
6 Jack Dittmer	12.00	6.00
9 Joe Adcock	20.00	10.00
10 Bob Buhl	15.00	7.50
11 Phil Paine	12.00	6.00
12 Ben Johnson	12.00	6.00
13 Sibbi Sisti	12.00	6.00
15 Charles Gorin	12.00	6.00
16 Chet Nichols	12.00	6.00
17 Dave Jolly	12.00	6.00
19 Jim Wilson	12.00	6.00
20 Ray Crone	12.00	6.00
21 Warren Spahn	80.00	40.00
22 Gene Conley	15.00	7.50
23 Johnny Logan	20.00	10.00
24 Charlie White	12.00	6.00
27 George Metkovich	12.00	6.00
28 Johnny Cooney CO	12.00	6.00
29 Paul Burris	12.00	6.00
31 Bucky Walters CO	15.00	7.50
32 Ernie Johnson	15.00	7.50
33 Lou Burdette	20.00	10.00
34 Bobby Thomson SP	200.00	100.00
35 Bob Keely	12.00	6.00
38 Bill Bruton	15.00	7.50
40 Charlie Grimm MG	20.00	10.00
41 Eddie Mathews	80.00	40.00
42 Sam Calderone	12.00	6.00
47 Joey Jay	15.00	7.50
48 Andy Pafko	15.00	7.50
49 Dr. Charles Lacks (Unnumbered)	12.00	6.00
50 Joseph F. Taylor (Unnumbered)	12.00	6.00

1954 Braves Merrell

This set of the Milwaukee Braves measures approximately 8" by 10" and features black-and-white drawings of players by artist, Marshall Merrell. The cards are unnumbered and checklisted below in alphabetical order. This checklist may be incomplete and additions are welcome.

	NM	Ex
COMPLETE SET	150.00	75.00
1 Hank Aaron	40.00	20.00
2 Joe Adcock	15.00	7.50
3 Bob Buhl	10.00	5.00
4 Charlie Grimm MG	12.00	6.00
5 Johnny Logan	10.00	5.00
6 Ed Mathews	25.00	12.50
7 Danny O'Connell	10.00	5.00
8 Andy Pafko	12.00	6.00
9 Warren Spahn	30.00	15.00
10 Jim Wilson	10.00	5.00

1954 Braves Spic and Span Postcards

This black and white set features only members of the Milwaukee Braves. The cards have postcard backs and measure approximately 3 11/16" by 6". The postcards were issued beginning in 1954. There is a facsimile autograph on the front in black or white ink. The set apparently was also issued with white borders in a 5" by 7" size. The catalog designation for this set is PC756. The front of each card shows the logo, "Spic and Span Dry Cleaners ... the Choice of Your Favorite Braves."

	NM	Ex
COMPLETE SET (18)	500.00	250.00
1 Henry Aaron	250.00	125.00
2 Joe Adcock	25.00	12.50
3 Billy Bruton	20.00	10.00
4 Bob Buhl	20.00	10.00
5 Lew Burdette	25.00	12.50
6 Gene Conley	20.00	10.00
7 Del Crandall	25.00	12.50
8 Ray Crone	15.00	7.50
9 Jack Dittmer	15.00	7.50
10 Ernie Johnson	20.00	10.00
11 Dave Jolly	15.00	7.50
12 Johnny Logan	20.00	10.00
13 Eddie Mathews	80.00	40.00
14 Chet Nichols	15.00	7.50
15 Danny O'Connell	15.00	7.50
16 Andy Pafko	20.00	10.00
17 Warren Spahn	80.00	40.00
18 Bobby Thomson	25.00	12.50

1955 Braves Golden Stamps

This 32-stamp set features color photos of the Milwaukee Braves and measures approximately

1 15/16" by 2 5/8". The stamps are designed to be placed in a 32-page album which measures approximately 8 3/8" by 10 15/16". The album contains black-and-white drawings of players with their batting averages and life stories. The team's history and other information is also printed in the album. The stamps are unnumbered and listed below according to where they fall in the album.

	NM	Ex
COMPLETE SET (32)	100.00	50.00
1 1954 Team Photo	10.00	5.00
2 Charlie Grimm MG	10.00	5.00
3 Warren Spahn	15.00	7.50
4 Lew Burdette	8.00	4.00
5 Chet Nichols	2.00	1.00
6 Gene Conley	2.00	1.00
7 Bob Buhl	2.00	1.00
8 Jim Wilson	2.00	1.00
9 Dave Jolly	2.00	1.00
10 Ernie Johnson	3.00	1.50
11 Joey Jay	3.00	1.50
12 Dave Koslo	2.00	1.00
13 Charlie Gorin	2.00	1.00
14 Ray Crone	2.00	1.00
15 Del Crandall	3.00	1.50
16 Joe Adcock	4.00	2.00
17 Jack Dittmer	2.00	1.00
18 Eddie Mathews	20.00	10.00
19 Johnny Logan	3.00	1.50
20 Andy Pafko	3.00	1.50
21 Bill Bruton	2.00	1.00
22 Bobby Thomson	4.00	2.00
23 Charlie White	2.00	1.00
24 Danny O'Connell	2.00	1.00
25 Henry Aaron	25.00	12.50
26 Jim Pendleton	2.00	1.00
27 George Metkovich	2.00	1.00
28 Mel Roach	2.00	1.00
29 John Cooney CO	2.00	1.00
30 Bucky Walters CO	3.00	1.50
31 Charles Lacks TR	2.00	1.00
32 Milwaukee County Stadium	10.00	5.00
XX Album	5.00	2.50

1955 Braves Johnston Cookies

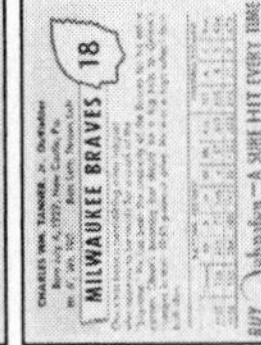

The cards in this 35-card set measure approximately 2 3/4" by 4". This set of Milwaukee Braves issued in 1955 by Johnston Cookies are numbered by the uniform number of the player depicted, except for non-players Lacks, Lewis and Taylor. The cards were issued in strips of six which accounts for the rouletted edges found on single cards. They are larger in size than the two previous sets but are printed on thinner cardboard. Each player in the checklist has been marked to show on which panel or strip he appeared (Pafko appears twice). A complete panel of six cards is worth 25 percent more than the sum of the individual players. The catalog designation for this set is D356-3.

	NM	Ex
COMPLETE SET (35)	1100.00	550.00
1 Del Crandall P1	25.00	12.50
3 Jim Pendleton P3	15.00	7.50
4 Danny O'Connell P1	15.00	7.50
6 Jack Dittmer P6	15.00	7.50
9 Joe Adcock P2	25.00	12.50
10 Bob Buhl P6	20.00	10.00
11 Phil Paine P5	15.00	7.50
12 Ray Crone P5	15.00	7.50
15 Charlie Gorin P1	15.00	7.50
16 Dave Jolly P4	15.00	7.50
17 Chet Nichols P2	15.00	7.50
18 Chuck Tanner P5	30.00	15.00
19 Jim Wilson P6	15.00	7.50
20 Dave Koslo P4	15.00	7.50
21 Warren Spahn P3	75.00	38.00
22 Gene Conley P3	20.00	10.00
23 Johnny Logan P4	25.00	12.50
24 Charlie White P2	15.00	7.50
28 Johnny Cooney CO P4	15.00	7.50
30 Roy Smalley P3	15.00	7.50
31 Bucky Walters CO P6	20.00	10.00
32 Ernie Johnson P5	20.00	10.00
33 Lew Burdette P1	25.00	12.50
34 Bobby Thomson P6	25.00	12.50
35 Bob Keely P1	15.00	7.50
38 Bill Bruton P4	20.00	10.00
39 George Crowe P3	15.00	7.50
40 Charlie Grimm MG P6	20.00	10.00
41 Eddie Mathews P5	75.00	38.00
44 Hank Aaron P1	400.00	200.00
47 Joey Jay P2	20.00	10.00
48 Andy Pafko P2 P4	20.00	10.00
49 Dr. Charles Leaks P2 (Unnumbered)	15.00	7.50
50 Duffy Lewis P5 Trav.Sec. (Unnumbered)	20.00	10.00
51 Joe Taylor P3 (Unnumbered)	15.00	7.50

1955 Braves Spic and Span Die-Cut

This 18-card, die-cut, set features only members of the Milwaukee Braves. Each player measures differently according to the pose but they are, on average, approximately 8" by 8". The cards could be folded together to stand up. Each card contains a logo in the middle at the bottom and a copyright notice, "1955 Spic and Span Cleaners" in the lower right corner.

	NM	Ex
COMPLETE SET (18)	3000.00	1500.00
1 Hank Aaron	800.00	400.00
2 Joe Adcock	150.00	75.00
3 Billy Bruton	100.00	50.00
4 Bob Buhl	100.00	50.00
5 Lew Burdette	150.00	75.00
6 Gene Conley	100.00	50.00
7 Del Crandall	150.00	75.00
8 Jack Dittmer	100.00	50.00
9 Ernie Johnson	120.00	60.00
10 Dave Jolly	100.00	50.00
11 Johnny Logan	120.00	60.00
12 Eddie Mathews	300.00	150.00
13 Chet Nichols	100.00	50.00
14 Danny O'Connell	100.00	50.00
15 Andy Pafko	120.00	60.00
16 Warren Spahn	300.00	150.00
17 Bob Thomson	150.00	75.00
18 Jim Wilson	100.00	50.00

1956-60 Braves Bill and Bob Postcards PPC-741

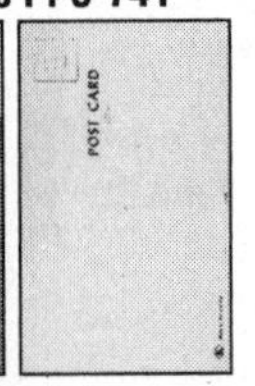

The Bill and Bob postcards issued during the 1956-60 time period features only Milwaukee Braves. The cards are unnumbered, other than the K card number at the middle base on the reverse, and present some of the most attractive color postcards issued in the postwar period. Three poses of Adcock and two poses each of Bruton and Crandall exist. The Torre card has been seen with a Pepsi advertisment on the reverse. The complete set price includes only one of each player.

	NM	Ex
COMPLETE SET (15)	1200.00	600.00
1 Hank Aaron	400.00	200.00
2 Joe Adcock (3)	50.00	25.00
3 Bill Bruton (2)	60.00	30.00
4 Bob Buhl	25.00	12.50
5 Lew Burdette	50.00	25.00
6 Gene Conley	40.00	20.00
7 Wes Covington	40.00	20.00
8 Del Crandall (2)	25.00	12.50
9 Chuck Dressen MG	40.00	20.00
10 Charlie Grimm MG	60.00	30.00
11 Fred Haney MG	50.00	25.00
12 Bobby Keely CO	25.00	12.50
13 Ed Mathews	150.00	75.00
14 Warren Spahn	150.00	75.00
15 Frank Torre	60.00	30.00

1957 Braves 8x10

This 12-card set features reddish sepia portraits of the Milwaukee Braves in a combination of photos and drawings printed on a yellowish card. The backs are blank. The cards are unnumbered and checklisted below in alphabetical order.

	NM	Ex
COMPLETE SET (12)	150.00	75.00
1 Joe Adcock	15.00	7.50
2 Bill Bruton	12.00	6.00
3 Bob Buhl	12.00	6.00
4 Lew Burdette	15.00	7.50
5 Del Crandall	12.00	6.00
6 Johnny Logan	12.00	6.00
7 Ed Mathews	25.00	12.50
8 Danny O'Connell	10.00	5.00
9 Andy Pafko	12.00	6.00
10 Jim Pendleton	10.00	5.00
11 Warren Spahn	30.00	15.00
12 Bob Thomson	15.00	7.50

1957 Braves Spic and Span 4x5

This set contains 20 black and white photos each with a blue-printed message such as "Stay in There and Pitch" and blue facsimile autograph The set features only members of the Milwaukee Braves. Red Schoendienst was traded to the Braves on June 15, 1957 in exchange for Danny O'Connell, Ray Crone, and Bobby Thomson. Wes Covington, Felix Mantilla, and Bob Trowbridge are also listed as shorter-printed (SP) cards as they were apparently mid-season call-ups. The cards are approximately 4 5/16" by 5" with a thick white border and are blank backed. Spic and Span appears in blue in the white border in the lower right corner of the card. Since the cards are unnumbered, they are numbered in alphabetical order in the checklist below.

	NM	Ex
COMPLETE SET (20)	500.00	250.00
COMMON CARD (1-20)	10.00	5.00
COMMON CARD SP	25.00	12.50
1 Henry Aaron	150.00	75.00
2 Joe Adcock	15.00	7.50
3 Billy Bruton	12.00	6.00
4 Bob Buhl	12.00	6.00
5 Lew Burdette	15.00	7.50
6 Gene Conley	12.00	6.00
7 Wes Covington SP	30.00	15.00
8 Del Crandall	15.00	7.50
9 Ray Crone	10.00	5.00
10 Fred Haney MG	10.00	5.00
11 Ernie Johnson	12.00	6.00
12 Johnny Logan	12.00	6.00
13 Felix Mantilla SP	25.00	12.50
14 Ed Mathews	50.00	25.00
15 Danny O'Connell	10.00	5.00
16 Andy Pafko	12.00	6.00
17 Red Schoendienst SP	60.00	30.00
18 Warren Spahn	50.00	25.00
19 Bobby Thomson	15.00	7.50
20 Bob Trowbridge SP	25.00	12.50

1958 Braves Jay Publishing

This 12-card set of the Milwaukee Braves measures approximately 5" by 7" and features black-and-white player photos in a white border. These cards were packaged 12 to a packet. The backs are blank. The cards are unnumbered and checklisted below in alphabetical order.

	NM	Ex
COMPLETE SET (12)	60.00	30.00
1 Hank Aaron	15.00	7.50
2 Joe Adcock	5.00	2.50
3 Lew Burdette	5.00	2.50
4 Wes Covington	4.00	2.00
5 Del Crandall	3.00	1.50
6 Robert Hazle	3.00	1.50
7 John Logan	3.00	1.50
8 Eddie Mathews	10.00	5.00
9 Donald McMahon	3.00	1.50
10 Andy Pafko	3.00	1.50
11 Red Schoendienst	8.00	4.00
12 Warren Spahn	10.00	5.00

1959 Braves Jay Publishing

This 12-card set of the Milwaukee Braves measures approximately 5" by 7" and features black-and-white player photos in a white border. These cards were packaged 12 to a packet. The backs are blank. The cards are unnumbered and checklisted below in alphabetical order.

	NM	Ex
COMPLETE SET	40.00	20.00
1 Joe Adcock	5.00	2.50
2 Billy Bruton	3.00	1.50
3 Wes Covington	3.00	1.50
4 Johnny Logan	4.00	2.00
5 Stan Lopata	3.00	1.50
6 Eddie Mathews	8.00	4.00
7 Don McMahon	3.00	1.50
8 Del Rice	3.00	1.50
9 Mel Roach	3.00	1.50
10 Bob Rush	3.00	1.50
11 Bob Trowbridge	3.00	1.50
12 Casey Wise	3.00	1.50

1960 Braves Davison's

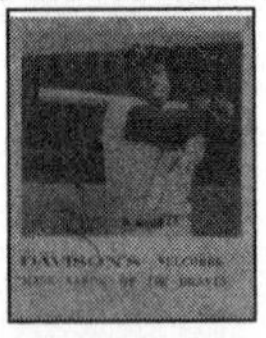

These cards measure approximately 3" by 3 5/8" and features black-and-white player photos. The cards are unnumbered and checklisted below in alphabetical order. The checklist may be incomplete and additions are welcome.

	NM	Ex
COMPLETE SET	50.00	20.00
1 Hank Aaron	30.00	12.00
2 Eddie Mathews	20.00	8.00

1960 Braves Jay Publishing

This 12-card set of the Milwaukee Braves measures approximately 5" by 7" and features black-and-white player photos in a white border. These cards were packaged 12 to a packet. The backs are blank. The cards are unnumbered and checklisted below in alphabetical order.

	NM	Ex
COMPLETE SET (12)	40.00	16.00
1 Hank Aaron	10.00	4.00
2 Billy Bruton	3.00	1.20
3 Wes Covington	3.00	1.20
4 Charlie Dressen MG	3.00	1.20
5 Bob Giggie	2.00	.80
6 Joey Jay	3.00	1.20
7 Stan Lopata	2.00	.80
8 Felix Mantilla	2.00	.80
9 Bob Rush	2.00	.80
10 Red Schoendienst	4.00	1.60
11 Warren Spahn	8.00	3.20
12 Frank Torre	3.00	1.20

1960 Braves Lake to Lake

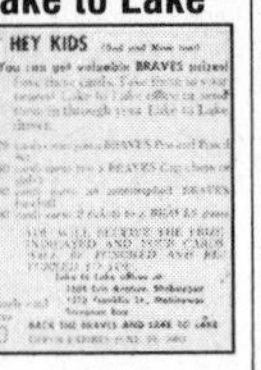

The cards in this 28-card set measure 2 1/2" by 3 1/4". The 1960 Lake to Lake set of unnumbered, blue tinted cards features Milwaukee Braves players only. For some reason, this set of Braves does not include Eddie Mathews. The cards were issued on milk cartons by Lake to Lake Dairy. Most cards have staple holes in the upper right corner. The backs are in red and give details and prizes associated with the card promotion. Cards with staple holes can be considered very good to excellent at best. The catalog designation for this set is F102-1.

	NM	Ex
COMPLETE SET (28)	1200.00	475.00
1 Hank Aaron	400.00	160.00
2 Joe Adcock	25.00	10.00
3 Ray Boone	125.00	50.00
4 Bill Bruton	300.00	120.00
5 Bob Buhl	20.00	8.00
6 Lew Burdette	25.00	10.00
7 Chuck Cottier	15.00	6.00
8 Wes Covington	20.00	8.00
9 Del Crandall	25.00	10.00
10 Chuck Dressen MG	20.00	8.00
11 Bob Giggie	15.00	6.00
12 Joey Jay	20.00	8.00
13 Johnny Logan	20.00	8.00
14 Felix Mantilla	15.00	6.00
15 Lee Maye	15.00	6.00
16 Don McMahon	15.00	6.00
17 George Myatt CO	15.00	6.00
18 Andy Pafko CO	20.00	8.00
19 Juan Pizarro	15.00	6.00
20 Mel Roach	15.00	6.00
21 Bob Rush	15.00	6.00
22 Bob Scheffing CO	15.00	6.00
23 Red Schoendienst	40.00	16.00
24 Warren Spahn	80.00	32.00
25 Al Spangler	15.00	6.00
26 Frank Torre	20.00	8.00
27 Carlton Willey	15.00	6.00
28 Whit Wyatt CO	20.00	8.00

1960 Braves Spic and Span

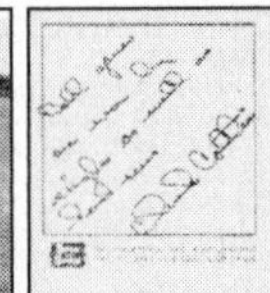

This set features only members of the Milwaukee Braves. These small cards each measure approximately 2 13/16" by 3 1/16". The cards have a thin white border around a black and white photo with no other writing or words on the front. The card backs have the Spic and Span logo at the bottom along with "Photographed and Autographed Exclusively for Spic and Span". A message and facsimile autograph from the player is presented inside a square box all in blue on the card back.

	NM	Ex
COMPLETE SET (27)	500.00	200.00
1 Henry Aaron	150.00	60.00
2 Joe Adcock	15.00	6.00
3 Billy Bruton	12.00	4.80
4 Bob Buhl	12.00	4.80
5 Lew Burdette	15.00	6.00
6 Chuck Cottier	10.00	4.00
7A Del Crandall ERR (Reversed negative)	50.00	20.00
7B Del Crandall COR	15.00	6.00
8 Charlie Dressen MG	12.00	4.80
9 Joey Jay	12.00	4.80
10 Johnny Logan	12.00	4.80
11 Felix Mantilla	10.00	4.00
12 Ed Mathews	50.00	20.00
13 Lee Maye	10.00	4.00
14 Don McMahon	10.00	4.00
15 George Myatt CO	10.00	4.00
16 Andy Pafko CO	12.00	4.80
17 Juan Pizarro	10.00	4.00
18 Mel Roach	10.00	4.00
19 Bob Rush	10.00	4.00
20 Bob Scheffing CO	10.00	4.00
21 Red Schoendienst	20.00	8.00
22 Warren Spahn	50.00	20.00
23 Al Spangler	10.00	4.00
24 Frank Torre	12.00	4.80
25 Carl Willey	10.00	4.00
26 Whit Wyatt CO	12.00	4.80

1962 Braves Jay Publishing

This 12-card set of the Milwaukee Braves measures approximately 5" by 7". The fronts feature black-and-white posed player photos with the player's and team name printed below in the white border. These cards were packaged 12 to a packet. The backs are blank. The cards are unnumbered and checklisted below in alphabetical order.

	NM	Ex
COMPLETE SET (12)	40.00	16.00
1 Hank Aaron	15.00	6.00
2 Joe Adcock	4.00	1.60
3 Frank Bolling	2.00	.80
4 Lou Burdette	4.00	1.60
5 Del Crandall	4.00	1.60
6 Eddie Mathews	8.00	3.20
7 Lee Maye	2.00	.80
8 Roy McMillan	3.00	1.20
9 Warren Spahn	8.00	3.20
10 George (Birdie) Tebbetts MG	2.00	.80
11 Joe Torre	5.00	2.00
12 Carl Willey	2.00	.80

1963 Braves Jay Publishing

This set of the Milwaukee Braves measures approximately 5" by 7". The fronts feature black-and-white posed player photos with the player's and team name printed below in the white border. These cards were packaged 12 to a packet. The backs are blank. The cards are unnumbered and checklisted below in alphabetical order. More than the standard 12 cards are listed as the Braves updated this set throughout the 1963 season.

	NM	Ex
COMPLETE SET	60.00	24.00
1 Hank Aaron	15.00	6.00
2 Tommie Aaron	3.00	1.20
3 Gus Bell	3.00	1.20
4 Frank Bolling	2.00	.80
5 Lew Burdette	4.00	1.60
6 Cecil Butler	2.00	.80
7 Tony Cloninger	3.00	1.20
8 Jim Constable	2.00	.80
9 Del Crandall	3.00	1.20
10 Frank Funk	2.00	.80
11 Bob Hendley	2.00	.80
12 Norm Larker	2.00	.80
13 Eddie Mathews	10.00	4.00
14 Roy McMillan	2.00	.80
15 Denis Menke	2.00	.80
16 Ron Piche	2.00	.80
17 Claude Raymond	2.00	.80
18 Amado Samuel	2.00	.80
19 Bob Shaw	2.00	.80
20 Warren Spahn	10.00	4.00
21 Joe Torre	6.00	2.40
22 Bob Uecker	5.00	2.00

1964 Braves Jay Publishing

This 12-card set of the Milwaukee Braves measures approximately 5" by 7". The fronts feature black-and-white posed player photos with the player's and team name printed below in the white border. These cards were packaged 12 to a packet. The backs are blank. The cards are unnumbered and checklisted below in alphabetical order.

	NM	Ex
COMPLETE SET (12)	50.00	20.00
1 Hank Aaron	15.00	6.00
2 Frank Bolling	2.00	.80
3 Bobby Bragan MG	2.00	.80
4 Tony Cloninger	2.00	.80
5 Denny Lemaster	2.00	.80
6 Eddie Mathews	10.00	4.00
7 Lee Maye	2.00	.80
8 Roy McMillan	3.00	1.20
9 Denis Menke	2.00	.80
10 Bob Sadowski	2.00	.80
11 Warren Spahn	10.00	4.00
12 Joe Torre	5.00	2.00

1965 Braves Jay Publishing

This 12-card set of the Milwaukee Braves measures approximately 5" by 7". The fronts feature black-and-white posed player photos with the player's and team name printed below in the white border. These cards were packaged 12 to a packet. The backs are blank. The cards are unnumbered and checklisted below in alphabetical order. 1965 would prove to be the Braves final season in Milwaukee.

	NM	Ex
COMPLETE SET (12)	50.00	20.00
1 Hank Aaron	15.00	6.00
2 Wade Blasingame	2.00	.80
3 Frank Bolling	2.00	.80
4 Bobby Bragan MG	2.00	.80
5 Hank Fischer	2.00	.80
6 Mack Jones	2.00	.80
7 Denny LeMaster	2.00	.80
8 Eddie Mathews	8.00	3.20
9 Phil Niekro	10.00	4.00
10 Billy O'Dell	2.00	.80
11 Dan Osinski	2.00	.80
12 Joe Torre	6.00	2.40

1965 Braves Team Issue

This 12-card set of the 1965 Milwaukee Braves measures approximately 4 7/8" by 7 1/8" and features black-and-white player photos with white borders. The backs are blank. The cards are unnumbered and checklisted below in alphabetical order.

	NM	Ex
COMPLETE SET (12)	20.00	8.00
1 Sandy Alomar	2.00	.80
2 Frank Bolling	2.00	.80
3 Ty Cline	2.00	.80
4 Mike De La Hoz	2.00	.80
5 Hank Fischer	2.00	.80
6 Mack Jones	2.00	.80
7 Gary Kolb	2.00	.80
8 Billy O'Dell	2.00	.80
9 Chi Chi Olivo	2.00	.80
10 Dan Osinski	2.00	.80
11 Bob Sadowski	2.00	.80
12 Bob Tiefenauer	2.00	.80

1966 Braves Postcards

This 27-card set of the Atlanta Braves features black-and-white player portraits in white borders and measures approximately 4" by 5". The backs are blank. The cards are unnumbered and checklisted below in alphabetical order.

	NM	Ex
COMPLETE SET (27)	200.00	80.00
1 Hank Aaron	30.00	12.00
2 Ted Abernathy	8.00	3.20
3 Felipe Alou	12.00	4.80
4 Wade Blasingame	8.00	3.20
5 Frank Bolling	8.00	3.20
6 Bobby Bragan MG	10.00	4.00
7 Clay Carroll	8.00	3.20
8 Rico Carty	10.00	4.00
9 Tony Cloninger	8.00	3.20
10 Mike de la Hoz	8.00	3.20
11 Gary Geiger	8.00	3.20
12 John Herrnstein	8.00	3.20
13 Billy Hitchcock CO	8.00	3.20
14 Ken Johnson	8.00	3.20
15 Mack Jones	8.00	3.20
16 Denver LeMaster	8.00	3.20
17 Eddie Mathews	25.00	10.00
18 Denis Menke	8.00	3.20
19 Felix Millan	10.00	4.00
20 Gene Oliver	8.00	3.20
21 Grover Resinger CO	8.00	3.20
22 Dan Schneider	8.00	3.20
23 Ken Silvestri CO	8.00	3.20
24 Joe Torre	20.00	8.00
25 Arnold Umbach	8.00	3.20
26 Jo Jo White CO	8.00	3.20
27 Whitlow Wyatt CO	10.00	4.00

1966 Braves Volpe

These 12 cards, which measure 8 1/2" by 11" feature members of the 1966 Atlanta Braves in their first year in Atlanta. These cards are unnumbered, so we have sequenced them in alphabetical order. The fronts feature drawings of the players while the back has biographical information, information blurbs and career statistics.

	NM	Ex
COMPLETE SET	120.00	47.50
1 Hank Aaron	30.00	12.00
2 Felipe Alou	12.00	4.80
3 Frank Bolling	8.00	3.20
4 Bobby Bragan MG	8.00	3.20
5 Rico Carty	10.00	4.00
6 Tony Cloninger	8.00	3.20
7 Mack Jones	8.00	3.20
8 Denny Lemaster	8.00	3.20
9 Eddie Mathews	20.00	8.00
10 Denis Menke	8.00	3.20
11 Lee Thomas	8.00	3.20
12 Joe Torre	12.00	4.80

1967 Braves Irvingdale Dairy

Four Atlanta Braves were featured on the back of one milk carton. If each player photo were cut, it would measure 1 3/4" by 2 5/8". The fronts feature a brown-tinted head-and-shoulders shot, with the player's name below. The backs are blank. The cards are unnumbered and checklisted below in alphabetical order.

	NM	Ex
COMPLETE SET (4)	30.00	12.00
1 Clete Boyer	12.00	4.80
2 Mack Jones	8.00	3.20
3 Denis Menke	8.00	3.20
4 Joe Torre	15.00	6.00

1967 Braves Photos

These photos were issued by the Atlanta Braves and features members of the 1967 Braves. The tops are black and white portrait photos with

the players name on the bottom. The backs are blank so we have sequenced these cards in alphabetical order.

	NM	Ex
COMPLETE SET (29)	175.00	70.00
1 Hank Aaron	20.00	8.00
2 Felipe Alou	10.00	4.00
3 Wade Blasingame	5.00	2.00
4 Clete Boyer	8.00	3.20
5 Bob Bruce	5.00	2.00
6 Clay Carroll	5.00	2.00
7 Rico Carty	8.00	3.20
8 Ty Cline	5.00	2.00
9 Tony Cloninger	5.00	2.00
10 Mike de la Hoz	5.00	2.00
11 Gary Geiger	5.00	2.00
12 Ramon Hernandez	5.00	2.00
13 Billy Hitchcock MG	5.00	2.00
14 Pat Jarvis	5.00	2.00
15 Ken Johnson	5.00	2.00
16 Mack Jones	5.00	2.00
17 Dick Kelley	5.00	2.00
18 Bob Kennedy CO	5.00	2.00
19 Denver Lemaster	5.00	2.00
20 Orlando Martinez	5.00	2.00
21 Denis Menke	5.00	2.00
22 Felix Millan	5.00	2.00
23 Phil Niekro	20.00	8.00
24 Gene Oliver	5.00	2.00
25 Jay Ritchie	5.00	2.00
26 Joe Torre	20.00	8.00
27 Ken Silvestri CO	5.00	2.00
28 Woody Woodward	5.00	2.00
29 Whitlow Wyatt CO	8.00	3.20

1968 Braves Postcards

This 33-card set of the Atlanta Braves features black-and-white player portraits with white borders. The backs are blank. The cards are unnumbered and checklisted below in alphabetical order.

	NM	Ex
COMPLETE SET (33)	175.00	70.00
1 Hank Aaron	20.00	8.00
2 Tommie Aaron	6.00	2.40
3 Felipe Alou	8.00	3.20
4 Clete Boyer	6.00	2.40
5 Jim Britton	5.00	2.00
6 Jim Busby CO	5.00	2.00
7 Clay Carroll	5.00	2.00
8 Rico Carty	6.00	2.40
9 Tony Cloninger	5.00	2.00
10 Harry Dorish CO	5.00	2.00
11 Tito Francona	5.00	2.00
12 Billy Goodman CO	5.00	2.00
13 Luman Harris MG	5.00	2.00
14 Sonny Jackson	5.00	2.00
15 Pat Jarvis	5.00	2.00
16 Bob Johnson	5.00	2.00
17 Deron Johnson	5.00	2.00
18 Ken Johnson	5.00	2.00
19 Dick Kelley	5.00	2.00
20 Mike Lum	5.00	2.00
21 Marty Martinez	5.00	2.00
22 Felix Millan	6.00	2.40
23 Phil Niekro	15.00	6.00
24 Mike Page	5.00	2.00
25 Milt Pappas	6.00	2.40
26 Claude Raymond	5.00	2.00
27 Ron Reed	5.00	2.00
28 Ken Silvestri CO	5.00	2.00
29 George Stone	5.00	2.00
30 Bob Tillman	5.00	2.00
31 Joe Torre	12.00	4.80
32 Bob Uecker	8.00	3.20
33 Cecil Upshaw	5.00	2.00

1969 Braves Birthday Party Photo Stamps

This 25-stamp set was distributed as one sheet of postage-size stamps and features black-and-white portraits of the Atlanta Braves. The stamps are unnumbered and checklisted below in alphabetical order.

	NM	Ex
COMPLETE SET (25)	100.00	40.00
1 Hank Aaron	20.00	8.00
(dark photo)		
2 Hank Aaron	20.00	8.00
(light photo)		
3 Tommie Aaron	4.00	1.60
4 Clete Boyer	4.00	1.60
5 Rico Carty	4.00	1.60
6 Orlando Cepeda	8.00	3.20
7 Bob Didier	3.00	1.20
8 Ralph Garr	5.00	2.00
9 Gil Garrido	3.00	1.20
10 Tony Gonzalez	3.00	1.20
11 Luman Harris MG	3.00	1.20
12 Sonny Jackson	3.00	1.20
13 Pat Jarvis	3.00	1.20
14 Larry Jaster	3.00	1.20
15 Mike Lum	3.00	1.20
16 Felix Millan	4.00	1.60
17 Jim Nash	3.00	1.20
18 Phil Niekro	8.00	3.20
19 Milt Pappas	4.00	1.60
20 Ron Reed	3.00	1.20
21 George Stone	3.00	1.20
22 Bob Tillman	3.00	1.20
23 Cecil Upshaw	3.00	1.20
24 Hoyt Wilhelm	6.00	2.40
25 Title Stamp	3.00	1.20

1970 Braves Stamps

This eight-stamp set of the Atlanta Braves features black-and-white player portraits measuring approximately 1 1/4" by 1 3/4" with rounded corners. The stamps are unnumbered and checklisted below in alphabetical order.

	NM	Ex
COMPLETE SET (8)	25.00	10.00
1 Hank Aaron	10.00	4.00
2 Rico Carty	3.00	1.20
3 Orlando Cepeda	6.00	2.40
4 Luman Harris MG	2.00	.80
5 Pat Jarvis	2.00	.80
6 Felix Millan	3.00	1.20
7 Cecil Upshaw	2.00	.80
8 Hoyt Wilhelm	5.00	2.00

1974 Braves Photo Cards

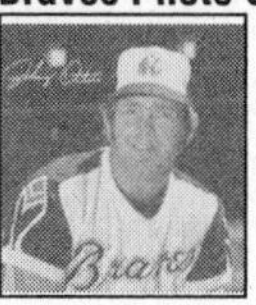

This set of six photo cards was produced by the Atlanta Braves Sales Department. The photos were included in a special brochure promoting the 1974 season. The photo cards measure approximately 7" by 7 1/2" and feature full-bleed color portraits of the Braves' star players. A player autograph facsimile is superimposed on the photo in the upper left corner in white lettering. The backs have a ghosted baseball icon with the words "take 'em out to..." in bold black lettering in the upper left corner. Each card has promotional information regarding season tickets or player highlights from previous seasons. The cards are unnumbered and checklisted below alphabetically.

	NM	Ex
COMPLETE SET (6)	20.00	8.00
1 Hank Aaron	8.00	3.20
2 Dusty Baker	4.00	1.60
3 Darrell Evans	3.00	1.20
4 Eddie Mathews MG	5.00	2.00
5 Phil Niekro	6.00	2.40
6 Johnny Oates	2.00	.80

1974 Braves Team Issue

These 7" by 9" blank-backed full color photos feature members of the Atlanta Braves. The fronts have a full color photo with the players name and team on the bottom. There may be more players in this set so all additions are appreciated. Since these are unnumbered, we have sequenced these photos in alphabetical order.

	NM	Ex
COMPLETE SET	15.00	6.00
1 Dusty Baker	3.00	1.20
2 Darrell Evans	3.00	1.20
3 Ralph Garr	2.00	.80
4 Dave Johnson	3.00	1.20
5 Phil Niekro	5.00	2.00

1975 Braves Postcards

This 38-card set of the Atlanta Bravesw features player photos on postcard-size cards. The cards are unnumbered and checklisted below in alphabetical order.

	NM	Ex
COMPLETE SET (38)	20.00	8.00
1 Dusty Baker	1.00	.40
2 Larvell Blanks	.50	.20
3 Bob Beale	.50	.20
4 Mike Beard	.50	.20
5 Jim Busby CO	.50	.20
6 Buzz Capra	.50	.20
7 Vic Correll	.50	.20
8 Bruce Dal Canton	.50	.20
9 Jamie Easterly	.50	.20
10 Darrell Evans	1.50	.60
11 Ralph Garr	.75	.30
12 Clarence Gaston	.75	.30
13 Gary Gentry	.50	.20
14 Rod Gilbreath	.50	.20
15 Ed Goodson	.50	.20
16 Eddie Haas CO	.50	.20
17 Roric Harrison	.50	.20
18 Tom House	.75	.30
19 Clyde King CO	.50	.20
20 Dave Johnson	1.50	.60
21 Mike Lum	.50	.20
22 Dave May	.50	.20
23 Carl Morton	.50	.20
24 Phil Niekro	4.00	1.60
25 Johnny Oates	.50	.20
26 John Odom	.50	.20
27 Rowland Office	.50	.20
28 Marty Perez	.50	.20
29 Biff Pocoroba	.50	.20
30 Ron Reed	.50	.20
31 Craig Robinson	.50	.20
32 Ray Sadecki	.50	.20
33 Ken Silvestri CO	.50	.20
34 Elias Sosa	.50	.20
35 Herm Starrette CO	.50	.20
36 Frank Tepedino	.75	.30
37 Mike Thompson	.50	.20
38 Earl Williams	.50	.20

1976 Braves Postcards

This 34-card set of the Atlanta Braves features player photos on postcard-size cards. The cards are unnumbered and checklisted below in alphabetical order.

	NM	Ex
COMPLETE SET (34)	20.00	8.00
1 Mike Beard	.50	.20
2 Vern Benson CO	.50	.20
3 Dave Bristol CO	.50	.20
4 Chris Cannizzaro	.50	.20
5 Buzz Capra	.50	.20
6 Darrel Chaney	.50	.20
7 Vic Correll	.50	.20
8 Terry Crowley	.50	.20
9 Bruce Dal Canton	.50	.20
10 Adrian Devine	.50	.20
11 Darrell Evans	1.50	.60
12 Cito Gaston	.50	.20
13 Rod Gilbreath	.50	.20
14 Eddie Haas CO	.50	.20
15 Ken Henderson	.50	.20
16 Lee Lacy	.50	.20
17 Max Leon	.50	.20
18 Dave May	.50	.20
19 Andy Messersmith	.50	.20
20 Roger Moret	.50	.20
21 Carl Morton	.50	.20
22 Phil Niekro	4.00	1.60
23 Rowland Office	.50	.20
24 Marty Perez	.50	.20
25 Biff Pocoroba	.50	.20
26 Luis Quintana	.50	.20
27 Craig Robinson	.50	.20
28 Jerry Royster	.50	.20
29 Dick Ruthven	.50	.20
30 Elias Sosa	.50	.20
31 Herm Starrette CO	.50	.20
32 Pablo Torrealba	.50	.20
33 Earl Williams	.50	.20
34 Jim Wynn	.75	.30

1978 Braves Coke

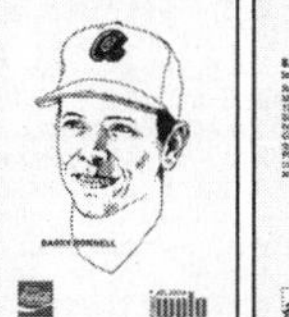

This 14-card set of the Atlanta Braves measures approximately 3" by 4 1/4" and was sponsored by Coca-Cola and Atlanta Radio Station WPLO. The white fronts feature black-and-white drawings of player heads with the player's name and sponsor logos below. The backs carry the player's name, position, biography, and career information with the team and sponsor logos on a white background. The cards are unnumbered and checklisted below in alphabetical order. A poster was also made for this promotion, it has a value of $15.

	NM	Ex
COMPLETE SET (14)	20.00	8.00
1 Barry Bonnell	1.00	.40
2 Jeff Burroughs	1.50	.60
3 Rick Camp	1.00	.40
4 Gene Garber	1.50	.60
5 Rod Gilbreath	1.00	.40
6 Bob Horner	2.00	.80
7 Glenn Hubbard	1.00	.40
8 Gary Matthews	2.00	.80
9 Larry McWilliams	1.00	.40
10 Dale Murphy	5.00	2.00
11 Phil Niekro	4.00	1.60
12 Rowland Office	1.00	.40
13 Biff Pocoroba	1.00	.40
14 Jerry Royster	1.00	.40

1978 Braves TCC

These 16 standard-size cards feature past members of the Milwaukee Braves. Although the checklist mentions that uniform and card number are the same we have sequenced this set in alphabetical order.

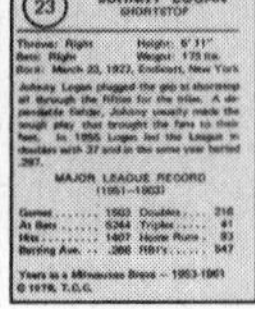

	NM	Ex
COMPLETE SET (16)	7.50	3.00
1 Hank Aaron	2.00	.80
2 Joe Adcock	.75	.30
3 Billy Bruton	.25	.10
4 Bob Buhl	.25	.10
5 Lou Burdette	.50	.20
6 Wes Covington	.25	.10
7 Del Crandall	.50	.20
8 Johnny Logan	.25	.10
9 Eddie Mathews	1.00	.40
10 Andy Pafko	.25	.10
11 Red Schoendienst	.75	.30
12 Warren Spahn	1.00	.40
13 Joe Torre	1.25	.50
14 Bob Uecker	1.00	.40
15 Carl Willey	.25	.10
16 Checklist	.25	.10

1979 Braves Team Issue

These cards, issued on a light stock black and white, actually measure slightly smaller than a postcard. While many of the cards did have the players name printed on them, some did not. These cards are unnumbered so we have sequenced them in alphabetical order.

	NM	Ex
COMPLETE SET	25.00	10.00
1 Tommy Aaron CO	.50	.20
2 Barry Bonnell	.50	.20
3 Jeff Burroughs	.75	.30
4 Bobby Cox MG	.75	.30
Dark Background		
5 Bobby Cox MG	.75	.30
White Background		
6 Bobby Dews CO	.50	.20
7 Pepe Frias	.50	.20
8 Gene Garber	.50	.20
Portrait		
9 Gene Garber	.50	.20
Kneeling		
10 Cito Gaston	.50	.20
11 Alex Grammas CO	.50	.20
12 Bob Horner	1.00	.40
13 Glenn Hubbard	.50	.20
14 Mike Lum	.50	.20
Portrait		
15 Mike Lum	.50	.20
Ready to hit		
16 Gary Matthews	.75	.30
17 Gary Matthews	.75	.30
Close up		
18 Rick Matula	.50	.20
19 Joe McLaughlin	.50	.20
20 Larry McWilliams	.50	.20
21 Ed Miller	.50	.20
22 Dale Murphy	5.00	2.00
Name on Card		
23 Dale Murphy	5.00	2.00
No Name on Card		
24 Phil Niekro	3.00	1.20
Name on Card		
25 Phil Niekro	3.00	1.20
No Name on Card		
26 Rowland Office	.50	.20
27 Biff Pocoroba	.50	.20
28 Jerry Royster	.50	.20
29 Hank Small	.50	.20
30 Charlie Spikes	.50	.20

1980 Braves 1914 TCMA

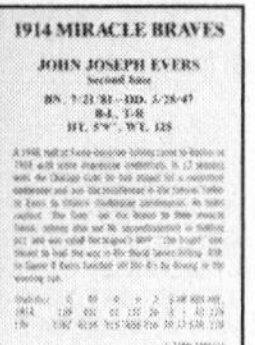

This 33-card set features sepia tinted photos of the 1914 World Champion "Miracle Braves" with black-and-white designed borders. The backs carry player information and career statistics. We are missing cards #9 and #31, we would appreciate any identification.

	NM	Ex
COMPLETE SET (31)	10.00	4.00
1 Joe Connolly	.25	.10
2 Lefty Tyler	.25	.10
3 Tom Hughes	.25	.10
4 Hank Gowdy	.50	.20
5 Gene Cocreham	.25	.10
6 Larry Gilbert	.25	.10
7 George Davis	.25	.10
8 Hub Perdue	.25	.10
10 Clarence Kraft	.25	.10
11 Tommy Griffith	.25	.10
12 Johnny Evers	1.00	.40
Ira Thomas		
Bill Klem		
Unknown Umpires		
13 Oscar Dugen	.25	.10
14 Josh Devore	.25	.10
15 George Stallings MG	.50	.20
16 Rabbit Maranville	1.00	.40
17 Paul Strand	.25	.10
18 Charlie Deal	.25	.10
19 Dick Rudolph	.50	.20
20 Butch Schmidt	.25	.10
21 Johnny Evers	1.50	.60
22 Dick Crutcher	.25	.10
23 Possum Whitted	.25	.10
24 Fred Mitchell CO	.25	.10
25 Herbie Moran	.25	.10
26 Bill James	.25	.10

27 Ted Cather	.25	.10
28 Red Smith	.25	.10
29 Les Mann	.25	.10
30 Herbie Moran	.25	.10
Wally Schang		
32 Johnny Evers MVP	.50	.20
Receives Gift of Car		
33 Jim Gafney OWN	.25	.10

1980 Braves 1957 TCMA

This 42-card set features photos of the 1957 Milwaukee Braves team with blue lettering. The backs carry player information.

	NM	Ex
COMPLETE SET (42)	20.00	8.00
1 Don McMahon	.25	.10
2 Joey Jay	.25	.10
3 Phil Paine	.25	.10
4 Bob Trowbridge	.25	.10
5 Bob Buhl	.25	.10
6 Lew Burdette	.75	.30
7 Ernie Johnson	.25	.10
8 Ray Crone	.25	.10
9 Taylor Phillips	.25	.10
10 Johnny Logan	.50	.20
11 Frank Torre	.50	.20
12 John DeMerit	.25	.10
13 Red Murff	.25	.10
14 Nippy Jones	.25	.10
15 Bobby Thomson	.75	.30
16 Chuck Tanner	.25	.10
17 Charlie Root CO	.50	.20
18 Juan Pizarro	.25	.10
19 Hawk Taylor	.25	.10
20 Mel Roach	.25	.10
21 Bob Hazle	.25	.10
22 Del Rice	.25	.10
23 Felix Mantilla	.25	.10
24 Andy Pafko	.50	.20
25 Del Crandall	.50	.20
26 Wes Covington	.25	.10
27 Eddie Mathews	2.00	.80
28 Joe Adcock	1.00	.40
29 Dick Cole	.25	.10
30 Carl Sawatski	.25	.10
31 Warren Spahn	2.00	.80
32 Hank Aaron	5.00	2.00
33 Bob Keely	.25	.10
34 Johnny Riddle CO	.25	.10
35 Connie Ryan	.25	.10
36 Harry Hanebrink	.25	.10
37 Danny O'Connell	.25	.10
38 Fred Haney MG	.25	.10
39 Dave Jolly	.25	.10
40 Red Schoendienst	1.50	.60
41 Gene Conley	.25	.10
42 Bill Bruton	.50	.20

1981 Braves Police

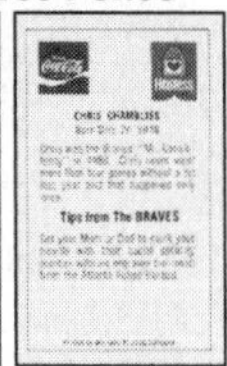

The cards in this 27-card set measure approximately 2 5/8" by 4 1/8". This first Atlanta Police set features full color cards sponsored by the Braves, the Atlanta Police Department, Coca-Cola and Hostess. The cards are numbered by uniform number, which is contained on the front along with an Atlanta Police Athletic League logo, a black and white Braves logo, and a green bow in the upper right corner of the frameline. The backs feature brief player biographies, logos of Coke and Hostess, and Tips from the Braves. It is reported that 33,000 of these sets were printed. The Terry Harper card is supposed to be slightly more difficult to obtain than other cards in the set.

	Nm-Mt	Ex-Mt
COMPLETE SET (27)	15.00	6.00
COMMON SP	1.00	.40
1 Jerry Royster	.25	.10
3 Dale Murphy	4.00	1.60
4 Biff Pocoroba	.25	.10
5 Bob Horner	.50	.20
6 Bobby Cox MG	1.00	.40
9 Luis Gomez	.25	.10
10 Chris Chambliss	.50	.20
15 Bill Nahorodny	.25	.10
16 Rafael Ramirez	.25	.10
17 Glenn Hubbard	.25	.10
18 Claudell Washington	.50	.20
19 Terry Harper SP	1.00	.40
20 Bruce Benedict	.25	.10
24 John Montefusco	.25	.10
25 Rufino Linares	.25	.10
26 Gene Garber	.50	.20
30 Brian Asselstine	.25	.10
34 Larry Bradford	.25	.10
35 Phil Niekro	2.50	1.00
37 Rick Camp	.25	.10
39 Al Hrabosky	.50	.20
40 Tommy Boggs	.25	.10
42 Rick Mahler	.25	.10
44 Hank Aaron CO	4.00	1.60
45 Ed Miller	.25	.10
46 Gaylord Perry	2.50	1.00
49 Preston Hanna	.25	.10

1982 Braves Burger King Lids

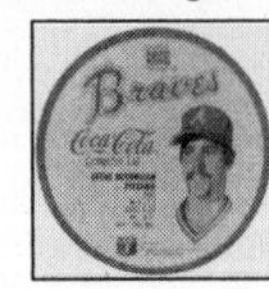

The cards in this 27-card set measure 3 11/16" diameter. During the summer of 1982, the Atlanta-area chain of Burger King restaurants issued a series of 27 "Collector Lids" in honor of the Atlanta Braves baseball team. A special cup listing the scores of the Braves 13-game season-opening win streak and crowned by a baseball player lid was given with the purchase of a large Coca-Cola. The black and white player photos are printed on a sturdy, glazed cardboard disc, the edges of which are attached to a red plastic rim. These lids are blank backed. The individual's name, height, weight and 1981 record are listed, but the lids are not numbered. The MLB and Burger King logos, as well as the Coca-Cola TM line also appear on the disc.

	Nm-Mt	Ex-Mt
COMPLETE SET (27)	40.00	16.00
1 Bruce Benedict	1.00	.40
2 Steve Bedrosian	2.00	.80
3 Tommy Boggs	1.00	.40
4 Brett Butler	4.00	1.60
5 Rick Camp	1.00	.40
6 Chris Chambliss	2.00	.80
7 Ken Dayley	1.00	.40
8 Gene Garber	1.50	.60
9 Preston Hanna	1.00	.40
10 Terry Harper	1.00	.40
11 Bob Horner	1.50	.60
12 Al Hrabosky	1.50	.60
13 Glenn Hubbard	1.00	.40
14 Randy Johnson	1.00	.40
15 Rufino Linares	1.00	.40
16 Rick Mahler	1.00	.40
17 Larry McWilliams	1.00	.40
18 Dale Murphy	15.00	6.00
19 Phil Niekro	8.00	3.20
20 Biff Pocoroba	1.00	.40
21 Rafael Ramirez	1.00	.40
22 Jerry Royster	1.00	.40
23 Ken Smith	1.00	.40
24 Bob Walk	1.00	.40
25 Claudell Washington	1.50	.60
26 Bob Watson	2.00	.80
27 Larry Whisenton	1.00	.40

1982 Braves Police

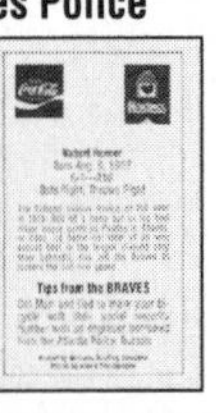

The cards in this 30-card set measure approximately 2 5/8" by 4 1/8". The Atlanta Police Department followed up on their successful 1981 safety set by publishing a new Braves set for 1982. Featured in excellent color photos are manager Joe Torre, 24 players, and 5 coaches. The cards are numbered, by uniform number, on the front only, while the backs contain a short biography of the individual and a Tips from the Braves section. The logos for the Atlanta PAL and the Braves appear on the front; those of Coca-Cola and Hostess are found on the back. A line commemorating Atlanta's record-shattering, season-beginning win streak is located in the upper right corner on every card obverse. The player list on the reverse of the Torre card is a roster list and not a checklist for the set. There were 8,000 sets reportedly printed. The Bob Watson card is supposedly more difficult to obtain than others in this set.

	Nm-Mt	Ex-Mt
COMPLETE SET (30)	20.00	8.00
COMMON CARD	.50	.20
COMMON SP	3.00	1.20
1 Jerry Royster	.50	.20
3 Dale Murphy	5.00	2.00
4 Biff Pocoroba	.50	.20
5 Bob Horner	.75	.30
6 Randy Johnson	.50	.20
8 Bob Watson SP	3.00	1.20
9 Joe Torre MG	1.50	.60
10 Chris Chambliss	1.00	.40
15 Claudell Washington	.75	.30
16 Rafael Ramirez	.50	.20
17 Glenn Hubbard	.50	.20
20 Bruce Benedict	.50	.20
22 Brett Butler	3.00	1.20
23 Tommy Aaron CO	.75	.30
25 Rufino Linares	.50	.20
26 Gene Garber	.75	.30
27 Larry McWilliams	.50	.20
28 Larry Whisenton	.50	.20
32 Steve Bedrosian	1.50	.60
35 Phil Niekro	3.00	1.20
37 Rick Camp	.50	.20
38 Joe Cowley	.50	.20
39 Al Hrabosky	.75	.30
42 Rick Mahler	.50	.20
43 Bob Walk	.50	.20
45 Bob Gibson CO	1.50	.60
49 Preston Hanna	.50	.20
52 Joe Pignatano CO	.50	.20
53 Dal Maxvill CO	.50	.20
54 Rube Walker CO	.50	.20

1982 Braves Team Issue

This set, which measures approximately 3" by 5" features members of the division winning Atlanta Braves team. The fronts have black and white photos on a glossy stock.Since these cards are unnumbered, we have sequenced them in alphabetical order.

	Nm-Mt	Ex-Mt
COMPLETE SET (20)	12.00	4.80
1 Jose Alvarez	.50	.20
2 Steve Bedrosian	1.50	.60
3 Bruce Benedict	.50	.20
4 Brett Butler	2.00	.80
5 Rick Camp	.50	.20
6 Joe Cowley	.50	.20
7 Carlos Diaz	.50	.20
8 Ken Dayley	.50	.20
9 Terry Harper	.50	.20
10 Randy Johnson	.50	.20
11 Rufino Linares	.50	.20
12 Rick Mahler	.50	.20
13 Larry McWilliams	.50	.20
14 Dale Murphy	2.50	1.00
15 Bob Porter	.50	.20
16 Joe Torre MG	1.50	.60
17 Bob Walk	.50	.20
18 Bob Watson	.75	.30
19 Larry Whisenton	.50	.20
20 Chief Noc-a-homa	.50	.20
MASCOT		

1983 Braves 53 Fritsch

This 32 card set measures approximately 2 5/8" by 3 3/4". These cards commemorated the 30th anniversary of the Braves move to Milwaukee. The player photos are surrounded by blue borders all the way around. They are identified in the bottom right corner. The backs have vital statistics and bulletpoint career highlights. The cards are numbered by uniform number.

	Nm-Mt	Ex-Mt
COMPLETE SET (32)	10.00	4.00
1 Del Crandall	.50	.20
2 Billy Klaus	.25	.10
4 Sid Gordon	.50	.20
6 Jack Dittmer	.25	.10
9 Joe Adcock	.75	.30
10 Bob Buhl	.50	.20
11 Murray Wall	.25	.10
13 Sibby Sisti	.25	.10
14 Paul Burris	.25	.10
16 Dave Jolly	.25	.10
18 Bob Thorpe	.25	.10
19 Jim Wilson	.25	.10
20 Dick Donovan	.25	.10
21 Warren Spahn	2.50	1.00
22 Virgil Jester	.25	.10
23 Johnny Logan	.50	.20
28 Johnny Cooney CO	.25	.10
29 Luis Marquez	.25	.10
30 Dave Cole	.25	.10
31 Bucky Walters CO	.50	.20
32 Ernie Johnson	.25	.10
33 Lew Burdette	1.00	.40
34 John Antonelli	.50	.20
36 Max Surkont	.25	.10
37 George Crowe	.25	.10
38 Billy Bruton	.50	.20
39 Walker Cooper	.25	.10
41 Eddie Mathews	2.50	1.00
42 Ebba St. Claire	.25	.10
43 Don Liddle	.25	.10
48 Andy Pafko	.50	.20
53 Jim Pendleton	.25	.10

1983 Braves Police

The cards in this 30-card set measure approximately 2 5/8" by 4 1/8". For the third year in a row, the Atlanta Braves, in cooperation with the Atlanta Police Department, Coca-Cola, and Hostess, issued a full color safety set. The set features Joe Torre, five coaches, and 24 of the Atlanta Braves. Numbered only by uniform number, the statement that the Braves were the 1982 National League Western Division Champions is included on the fronts along with the Braves and Police Athletic biographies, a short narrative on the player, Tips from the Braves, and the Coke and Hostess logos.

	Nm-Mt	Ex-Mt
COMPLETE SET (30)	15.00	6.00
1 Jerry Royster	.25	.10
3 Dale Murphy	4.00	1.60
4 Biff Pocoroba	.25	.10
5 Bob Horner	.50	.20
6 Randy Johnson	.25	.10
8 Bob Watson	.75	.30
9 Joe Torre MG	1.00	.40
10 Chris Chambliss	.75	.30
11 Ken Smith	.25	.10
15 Claudell Washington	.50	.20
16 Rafael Ramirez	.25	.10
17 Glenn Hubbard	.25	.10
19 Terry Harper	.25	.10
20 Bruce Benedict	.25	.10
22 Brett Butler	1.50	.60
24 Larry Owen	.25	.10
26 Gene Garber	.50	.20
27 Pascual Perez	.25	.10
29 Craig McMurtry	.25	.10
32 Steve Bedrosian	.50	.20
33 Pete Falcone	.25	.10
35 Phil Niekro	2.00	.80
36 Sonny Jackson CO	.25	.10
37 Rick Camp	.25	.10
45 Bob Gibson CO	2.00	.80
49 Rick Behenna	.25	.10
51 Terry Forster	.25	.10
52 Joe Pignatano CO	.25	.10
53 Dal Maxvill CO	.25	.10
54 Rube Walker CO	.25	.10

1984 Braves Photos

These 31 photos were issued by the Braves and featur members of the 1984 Atlanta Braves. They are unnumbered so we have sequenced them in alphabetical order.

	Nm-Mt	Ex-Mt
COMPLETE SET	20.00	8.00
1 Luke Appling CO	1.50	.60
2 Len Barker	.50	.20
3 Steve Bedrosian	.75	.30
4 Bruce Benedict	.50	.20
5 Rick Camp	.50	.20
6 Chris Chambliss	.75	.30
7 Jeff Dedmon	.50	.20
8 Pete Falcone	.50	.20
9 Terry Forster	.50	.20
10 Gene Garber	.75	.30
11 Bob Gibson CO	2.00	.80
12 Terry Harper	.50	.20
13 Bob Horner	.50	.20
14 Glenn Hubbard	.75	.30
15 Randy Johnson	.50	.20
16 Brad Komminsk	.50	.20
17 Rufino Linares	.50	.20
18 Rick Mahler	.50	.20
19 Dal Maxvill CO	.50	.20
20 Craig McMurtry	.50	.20
21 Dale Murphy	3.00	1.20
22 Ken Oberkfell	.50	.20
23 Pascual Perez	.50	.20
24 Gerald Perry	.50	.20
25 Joe Pignatano CO	.50	.20
26 Rafael Ramirez	.50	.20
27 Jerry Royster	.50	.20
28 Paul Runge	.50	.20
29 Alex Trevino	.50	.20
30 Claudell Washington	.50	.20
31 Bob Watson	.75	.30

1984 Braves Police

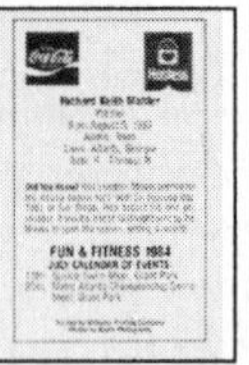

The cards in this 30-card set measure approximately 2 5/8" by 4 1/8". For the fourth straight year, the Atlanta Police Department issued a full color set of Atlanta Braves. The cards were given out two per week by Atlanta police officers. In addition to the police department, the set was sponsored by Coke and Hostess. The backs of the cards of Perez and Ramirez are in Spanish. The Joe Torre card contains the checklist.

	Nm-Mt	Ex-Mt
COMPLETE SET (30)	10.00	4.00
1 Jerry Royster	.25	.10
3 Dale Murphy	3.00	1.20
5 Bob Horner	.50	.20
6 Randy Johnson	.25	.10
8 Bob Watson	.75	.30
9 Joe Torre MG CL	1.00	.40
10 Chris Chambliss	.50	.20
11 Mike Jorgensen	.25	.10
15 Claudell Washington	.50	.20
16 Rafael Ramirez	.25	.10
17 Glenn Hubbard	.25	.10
19 Terry Harper	.25	.10
20 Bruce Benedict	.25	.10
25 Alex Trevino	.25	.10
26 Gene Garber	.50	.20
27 Pascual Perez	.25	.10
28 Gerald Perry	.25	.10
29 Craig McMurtry	.25	.10
31 Donnie Moore	.25	.10
32 Steve Bedrosian	.50	.20
33 Pete Falcone	.25	.10
37 Rick Camp	.25	.10
39 Len Barker	.25	.10
42 Rick Mahler	.25	.10
45 Bob Gibson CO	2.00	.80
51 Terry Forster	.25	.10
52 Joe Pignatano CO	.25	.10
53 Dal Maxvill CO	.25	.10
54 Rube Walker CO	.25	.10
55 Luke Appling CO	1.50	.60

1985 Braves Hostess

The cards in this 22 standard-size set features players of the Atlanta Braves. Cards were produced by Topps for Hostess (Continental Baking Co.) and are quite attractive. The card backs are similar in design to the 1985 Topps regular issue; however all photos are different from those that Topps used as these were apparently taken during Spring Training. Cards were available in boxes of Hostess products in packs of four (three players and a contest card). Other than the manager card, the rest of the set is ordered and numbered alphabetically.

	Nm-Mt	Ex-Mt
COMPLETE SET (22)	8.00	3.20
1 Eddie Haas MG	.25	.10
2 Len Barker	.25	.10
3 Steve Bedrosian	.50	.20
4 Bruce Benedict	.25	.10
5 Rick Camp	.25	.10
6 Rick Cerone	.25	.10
7 Chris Chambliss	.50	.20
8 Terry Forster	.25	.10
9 Gene Garber	.50	.20
10 Albert Hall	.25	.10
11 Bob Horner	.50	.20
12 Glenn Hubbard	.25	.10
13 Brad Komminsk	.25	.10
14 Rick Mahler	.25	.10
15 Craig McMurtry	.25	.10
16 Dale Murphy	1.00	.40
17 Ken Oberkfell	.25	.10
18 Pascual Perez	.25	.10
19 Gerald Perry	.25	.10
20 Rafael Ramirez	.25	.10
21 Bruce Sutter	.75	.30
22 Claudell Washington	.50	.20

1985 Braves Police

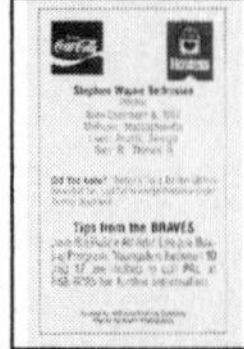

The cards in this 30-card set measure 2 5/8" by 4 1/8". For the fifth straight year, the Atlanta Police Department issued a full color set of Atlanta Braves. The set was also sponsored by Coca Cola and Hostess. In the upper right of the obverse is a logo commemorating the 20th anniversary of the Braves in Atlanta. Cards are numbered by uniform number. Cards feature a safety tip on the back. Each card except for Manager Haas has an interesting "Did You Know" fact about the player.

	Nm-Mt	Ex-Mt
COMPLETE SET (30)	10.00	4.00
2 Albert Hall	.25	.10
3 Dale Murphy	3.00	1.20
5 Rick Cerone	.25	.10
7 Bobby Wine CO	.25	.10
10 Chris Chambliss	.50	.20
11 Bob Horner	.50	.20
12 Paul Runge	.25	.10
15 Claudell Washington	.50	.20
16 Rafael Ramirez	.25	.10
17 Glenn Hubbard	.25	.10
18 Paul Zuvella	.25	.10
19 Terry Harper	.25	.10
20 Bruce Benedict	.25	.10
22 Eddie Haas MG	.25	.10
24 Ken Oberkfell	.25	.10
26 Gene Garber	.50	.20
27 Pascual Perez	.25	.10
28 Gerald Perry	.25	.10
29 Craig McMurtry	.25	.10
32 Steve Bedrosian	.50	.20
33 Johnny Sain CO	.75	.30
34 Zane Smith	.50	.20
36 Brad Komminsk	.25	.10
37 Rick Camp	.25	.10
39 Len Barker	.25	.10
40 Bruce Sutter	1.00	.40
42 Rick Mahler	.25	.10
51 Terry Forster	.25	.10
52 Leo Mazzone CO	.25	.10
53 Bobby Dews CO	.25	.10

1985 Braves TBS America's Team

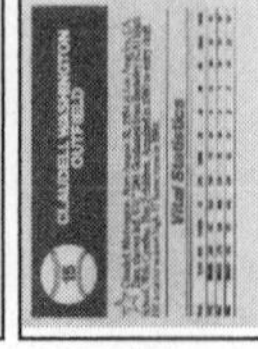

This set features four close-up headshots on painted backgrounds. The photos measure 8 1/4" X 10 3/4". In a star-studded rectangular box, the words "America's Team" are emblazoned across the bottom of each picture. The horizontally oriented backs have biography and statistics for the last three seasons (1982-84). The photos are unnumbered and checklisted below alphabetically.

	Nm-Mt	Ex-Mt
COMPLETE SET (4)	6.00	2.40
1 Brad Komminsk	1.00	.40
2 Dale Murphy	4.00	1.60
3 Bruce Sutter	2.50	1.00
4 Claudell Washington	1.50	.60

1986 Braves Greats TCMA

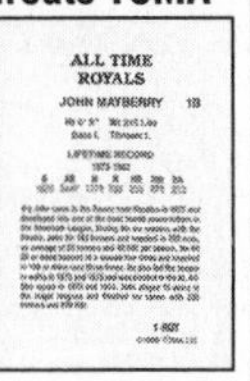

This 12-card standard-size set features leading Braves players from all three cities (Boston, Atlanta and Milwaukee). The fronts have player photos, while the backs have a biography, and career statistics.

	Nm-Mt	Ex-Mt
COMPLETE SET (12)	6.00	2.40
1 Joe Adcock	.50	.20
2 Felix Millan	.25	.10
3 Rabbit Maranville	1.00	.40
4 Eddie Mathews	1.50	.60
5 Hank Aaron	3.00	1.20
6 Wally Berger	.50	.20
7 Tommy Holmes	.50	.20
8 Del Crandall	.50	.20
9 Warren Spahn	1.50	.60
10 Charles "Kid" Nichols	.75	.30
11 Cecil Upshaw	.25	.10
12 Fred Haney MG	.25	.10

1986 Braves Police

This 30-card safety set was also sponsored by Coca-Cola. The backs contain the usual biographical info and safety tip. The front features a full-color photo of the player, his name, and uniform number. The cards measure 2 5/8" by 4 1/8". Cards were freely distributed throughout the summer by the Police Departments in the Atlanta area. Cards are numbered below by uniform number.

	Nm-Mt	Ex-Mt
COMPLETE SET (30)	10.00	4.00
2 Russ Nixon CO	.25	.10
3 Dale Murphy	3.00	1.20
4 Bob Skinner CO	.25	.10
5 Billy Sample	.25	.10
7 Chuck Tanner MG	.50	.20
8 Willie Stargell CO	1.50	.60
9 Ozzie Virgil	.25	.10
10 Chris Chambliss	.50	.20
11 Bob Horner	.50	.20
14 Andres Thomas	.25	.10
15 Claudell Washington	.50	.20
16 Rafael Ramirez	.25	.10
17 Glenn Hubbard	.25	.10
18 Omar Moreno	.25	.10
19 Terry Harper	.25	.10
20 Bruce Benedict	.25	.10
23 Ted Simmons	1.00	.40
24 Ken Oberkfell	.25	.10
26 Gene Garber	.50	.20
29 Craig McMurtry	.25	.10
30 Paul Assenmacher	.50	.20
33 Johnny Sain CO	.75	.30
34 Zane Smith	.25	.10
38 Joe Johnson	.25	.10
40 Bruce Sutter	1.00	.40
42 Rick Mahler	.25	.10
46 David Palmer	.25	.10
48 Duane Ward	.50	.20
49 Jeff Dedmon	.25	.10
52 Al Monchak CO	.25	.10

1987 Braves 1957 TCMA

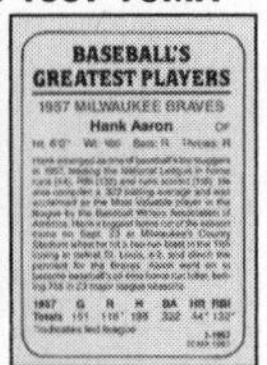

This nine-card standard-size set commemorates the 30th anniversary and members of the 1957 World Champion Milwaukee Braves. The player's name and position are displayed on the front. The backs carry highlights and stats from the 1957 season.

	Nm-Mt	Ex-Mt
COMPLETE SET (9)	6.00	2.40
1 Hank Aaron	3.00	1.20
2 Eddie Mathews	1.50	.60
3 Bob Hazle	.25	.10
4 Johnny Logan	.75	.30
5 Red Schoendienst	1.25	.50
6 Wes Covington	.50	.20
7 Lew Burdette	1.00	.40
8 Warren Spahn	1.50	.60
9 Bob Buhl	.75	.30

1987 Braves Smokey

The U.S. Forestry Service (in conjunction with the Atlanta Braves) produced this large, attractive 27-card set to commemorate the 43rd birthday of Smokey. The cards feature Smokey the Bear pictured in the top right

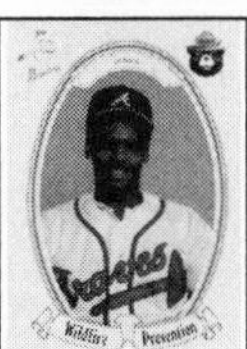

corner of every card. The card backs give a cartoon fire safety tip. The cards measure approximately 4" by 6" and are subtitled "Wildfire Prevention" on the front. Distribution of the cards was gradual at the stadium throughout the summer.

	Nm-Mt	Ex-Mt
COMPLETE SET (27)	30.00	12.00
1 Zane Smith	1.00	.40
2 Charlie Puleo	1.00	.40
3 Randy O'Neal	1.00	.40
4 David Palmer	1.00	.40
5 Rick Mahler	1.00	.40
6 Ed Olwine	1.00	.40
7 Jeff Dedmon	1.00	.40
8 Paul Assenmacher	1.25	.50
9 Gene Garber	1.25	.50
10 Jim Acker	1.00	.40
11 Bruce Benedict	1.00	.40
12 Ozzie Virgil	1.00	.40
13 Ted Simmons	2.00	.80
14 Dale Murphy	10.00	4.00
15 Graig Nettles	1.50	.60
16 Ken Oberkfell	1.00	.40
17 Gerald Perry	1.00	.40
18 Rafael Ramirez	1.00	.40
19 Ken Griffey	1.50	.60
20 Andres Thomas	1.00	.40
21 Glenn Hubbard	1.00	.40
22 Damaso Garcia	1.00	.40
23 Gary Roenicke	1.00	.40
24 Dion James	1.00	.40
25 Albert Hall	1.00	.40
26 Chuck Tanner MG	1.25	.50
NNO Smokey/Checklist	1.00	.40

1989 Braves Dubuque

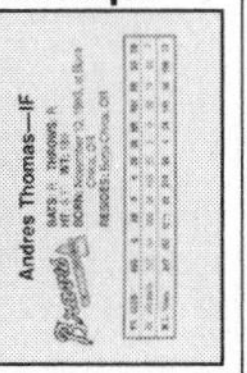

This 30-card set was sponsored by Dubuque, the meat company that makes the hot dogs sold at Atlanta-Fulton County Stadium. The cards were given away at the ballpark on Sundays and at autograph appearances at card stores. Due to the latter, several of these exist in much larger quantities. The cards measure approximately 2 1/4" by 3 1/2". Almost all the photos were taken during spring training, with the exception of Oddibe McDowell, mid-season additions Mark Eichhorn and John Russell, and coach Brian Snitker. The cards are unnumbered and checklisted below in alphabetical order.

	Nm-Mt	Ex-Mt
COMPLETE SET (30)	40.00	16.00
COMMON CARD (1-30)	1.00	.40
COMMON LATE SEASON	2.00	.80
1 Jim Acker	1.00	.40
2 Jose Alvarez	1.00	.40
3 Paul Assenmacher	1.00	.40
4 Bruce Benedict	1.00	.40
5 Jeff Blauser	1.25	.50
6 Joe Boever	1.00	.40
7 Bruce Dal Canton CO	1.00	.40
8 Marty Clary	1.00	.40
9 Jody Davis	1.00	.40
10 Mark Eichhorn SP	2.00	.80
11 Ron Gant	3.00	1.20
12 Tom Glavine	6.00	2.40
13 Tommy Gregg	1.00	.40
14 Clarence Jones CO	1.00	.40
15 Derek Lilliquist	1.00	.40
16 Roy Majtyka TR	1.00	.40
17 Oddibe McDowell SP	2.00	.80
18 Dale Murphy	4.00	1.60
19 Russ Nixon MG	1.00	.40
20 Gerald Perry	1.00	.40
21 John Russell SP	2.00	.80
22 Lonnie Smith	1.25	.50
23 Pete Smith	1.00	.40
24 John Smoltz	8.00	3.20
25 Brian Snitker CO SP	2.00	.80
26 Andres Thomas	1.00	.40
27 Jeff Treadway	1.00	.40
28 Jeff Wetherby	1.00	.40
29 Ed Whited	1.00	.40
30 Bobby Wine CO	1.00	.40

1990 Braves Dubuque Perforated

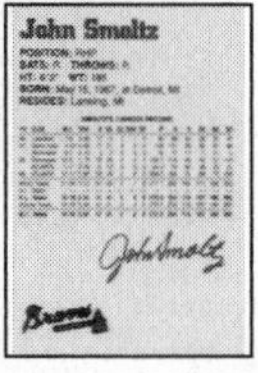

Given out early in the season, this set's 30 cards are slightly smaller than the other Dubuque Singles set, and was part of a perforated sheet that included a team photo. The backs are similar, but the fronts are all different with portrait shots. The cards are unnumbered and checklisted below in alphabetical order.

	Nm-Mt	Ex-Mt
COMPLETE SET (30)	30.00	9.00
1 Jeff Blauser	1.00	.30
2 Joe Boever	.50	.15
3 Francisco Cabrera	.50	.15
4 Tony Castillo	.50	.15
5 Marty Clary	.50	.15
6 Nick Esasky	.50	.15
7 Ron Gant	2.00	.60
8 Tom Glavine	4.00	1.20
9 Tommy Gregg	.50	.15
10 Dwayne Henry	.50	.15
11 Joe Hesketh	.50	.15
12 Alexis Infante	.50	.15
13 David Justice	4.00	1.20
14 Charlie Kerfeld	.50	.15
15 Charlie Leibrandt	.50	.15
16 Mark Lemke	.50	.15
17 Derek Lilliquist	.50	.15
18 Rick Luecken	.50	.15
19 Oddibe McDowell	.50	.15
20 Dale Murphy	4.00	1.20
21 Russ Nixon MG	.50	.15
22 Greg Olson	.50	.15
23 Jim Presley	.50	.15
24 Lonnie Smith	.50	.15
25 Pete Smith	.50	.15
26 John Smoltz	3.00	.90
27 Mike Stanton	1.50	.45
28 Andres Thomas	.50	.15
29 Jeff Treadway	.50	.15
30 Ernie Whitt	.50	.15

1990 Braves Dubuque Singles

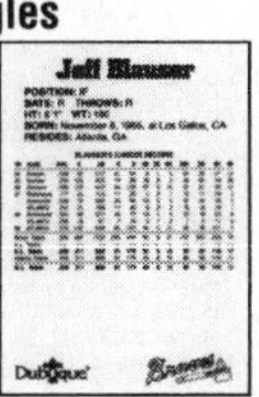

These 35 cards measure approximately 2 1/4" by 3 1/2" and were given out, usually four at a time, on Sundays with subjects available for autographs that day. Several were offered more than once, but Murphy's card was given out once before his trade to the Phillies. The cards issued early in the season featured spring training action shots on their fronts. Those issued later in the season had action photos taken at Atlanta-Fulton County Stadium. The Mark Grant card was given out only on the last Sunday of the season, the only new card to be issued so late. The cards are unnumbered and checklisted below in alphabetical order.

	Nm-Mt	Ex-Mt
COMPLETE SET (35)	50.00	15.00
COMMON CARD (1-35)	1.00	.30
COMMON SP	5.00	1.50
1 Steve Avery	1.25	.35
2 Jeff Blauser	1.25	.35
3 Joe Boever	1.00	.30
4 Francisco Cabrera	1.00	.30
5 Pat Corrales CO	1.00	.30
6 Bobby Cox MG	1.50	.45
7 Nick Esasky	1.00	.30
8 Ron Gant	2.00	.60
9 Tom Glavine	5.00	1.50
10 Mark Grant SP	5.00	1.50
11 Tommy Gregg	1.00	.30
12 Dwayne Henry	1.00	.30
13 Homer the Brave (Mascot)	1.00	.30
14 Alexis Infante	1.00	.30
15 Clarence Jones CO	1.00	.30
16 David Justice	5.00	1.50
17 Jimmy Kremers	1.00	.30
18 Charlie Leibrandt	1.00	.30
19 Mark Lemke	1.00	.30
20 Roy Majtyka TR	1.00	.30
21 Leo Mazzone CO	1.00	.30
22 Oddibe McDowell	1.00	.30
23 Dale Murphy SP	10.00	3.00
24 Phil Niekro	3.00	.90
25 Greg Olson	1.00	.30
26 Jim Presley	1.00	.30
27 Rally (Mascot)	1.00	.30
28 Lonnie Smith	1.25	.35
29 Pete Smith	1.00	.30
30 John Smoltz	4.00	1.20
31 Brian Snitker CO	1.00	.30
32 Andres Thomas	1.00	.30
33 Jeff Treadway	1.00	.30
34 Ernie Whitt	1.00	.30
35 Jimy Williams CO	1.00	.30

1991 Braves Dubuque Perforated

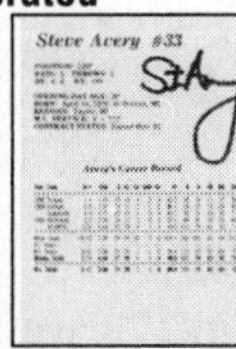

The 1991 Atlanta Braves team set was sponsored by Dubuque. The set was issued in three 10 5/8" by 9 3/8" panels that were attached to form a continuous sheet. The first panel features a team photo. The second and third panels have 15 player cards each; after perforation, the cards measure approximately 2 3/16" by 3 3/16". The front design has a posed head and shoulders color photo, with red borders and diamond designs on the corners of the picture. he cards are unnumbered and checklisted below in alphabetical order.

	Nm-Mt	Ex-Mt
COMPLETE SET (30)	18.00	5.50
1 Steve Avery	.25	.07
2 Rafael Belliard	.25	.07
3 Juan Berenguer	.25	.07
4 Jeff Blauser	.50	.15
5 Sid Bream	.25	.07
6 Francisco Cabrera	.25	.07
7 Bobby Cox MG	.50	.15
8 Nick Esasky	.25	.07
9 Marvin Freeman	.25	.07
10 Ron Gant	1.00	.30
11 Tom Glavine	2.50	.75
12 Mark Grant	.25	.07
13 Tommy Gregg	.25	.07
14 Mike Heath	.25	.07
15 Danny Heep	.25	.07
16 David Justice	2.00	.60
17 Charlie Leibrandt	.25	.07
18 Mark Lemke	.25	.07
19 Kent Mercker	.25	.07
20 Otis Nixon	.50	.15
21 Greg Olson	.25	.07
22 Jeff Parrett	.25	.07
23 Terry Pendleton	1.00	.30
24 Deion Sanders	2.50	.75
25 Doug Sisk	.25	.07
26 Lonnie Smith	.25	.07
27 Pete Smith	.25	.07
28 John Smoltz	2.00	.60
29 Mike Stanton	.50	.15
30 Jeff Treadway	.25	.07

1991 Braves Dubuque Standard

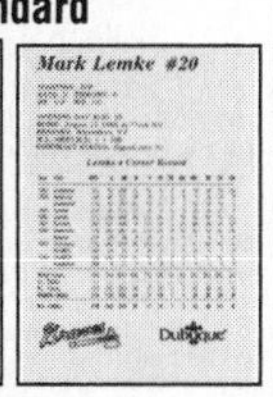

These 39 cards were sponsored by Dubuque Meats and measure approximately 2 1/4" by 3 1/2". They were given out, usually three or six at a time, on Sundays with subjects available for autographs that day. Aside from players' uniform numbers on the back, the cards are unnumbered and checklisted below in alphabetical order. Sunday Aug. 25 had six new cards given out for the first time (Hunter, Mitchell, Clancy, Beauchamp, Esasky, Grant). Sunday Sept. 22 had three new cards issued (Pete Smith, Bell, Reynoso) with three previously released. Two Sundays previous to these had featured three previously issued cards each day. The final day of the season (Oct. 6) featured a Deion Sanders card, along with Glavine, Avery, Cox, Gant, Justice, Pendleton and Treadway. A special "apology" card was issued with the cards this day due to no autographs. Black- and blue-lettered varieties exist on at least 30 cards (different printings).

	Nm-Mt	Ex-Mt
COMPLETE SET (39)	50.00	15.00
1 Steve Avery	1.00	.30
2 Jim Beauchamp CO	1.00	.30
3 Mike Bell	1.00	.30
4 Rafael Belliard	1.00	.30
5 Juan Berenguer	1.00	.30
6 Jeff Blauser	1.25	.35
7 Sid Bream	1.00	.30
8 Francisco Cabrera	1.00	.30
9 Jim Clancy	1.00	.30
10 Pat Corrales CO	1.00	.30
11 Bobby Cox MG	1.25	.35
12 Nick Esasky	1.00	.30
13 Marvin Freeman	1.00	.30
14 Ron Gant	2.00	.60
15 Tom Glavine	5.00	1.50
16 Mark Grant	1.00	.30
17 Tommy Gregg	1.00	.30
18 Mike Heath	1.00	.30
19 Brian Hunter	1.00	.30
20 Clarence Jones CO	1.00	.30
21 David Justice	3.00	.90
22 Charlie Leibrandt	1.00	.30
23 Mark Lemke	1.00	.30
24 Leo Mazzone CO	1.00	.30
25 Kent Mercker	1.00	.30
26 Keith Mitchell	1.00	.30
27 Otis Nixon	1.00	.30
28 Greg Olson	1.00	.30
29 Jeff Parrett	1.00	.30
30 Terry Pendleton	2.00	.60
31 Armando Reynoso	1.00	.30
32 Deion Sanders	5.00	1.50
33 Lonnie Smith	1.00	.30
34 Pete Smith	1.00	.30
35 John Smoltz	4.00	1.20
36 Mike Stanton	1.25	.35
37 Jeff Treadway	1.00	.30
38 Jimy Williams CO	1.00	.30
39 Ned Yost CO	1.00	.30

1992 Braves Krystal Postcard Sanders

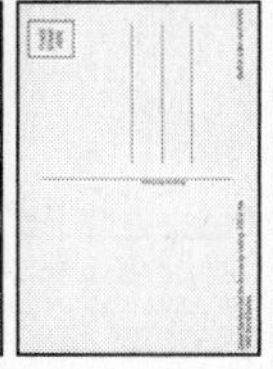

This postcards features two sport athlete Deion Sanders. This postcard was issued by the Krystal food chain.

	Nm-Mt	Ex-Mt
1 Deion Sanders	3.00	.90

1992 Braves Lykes Perforated

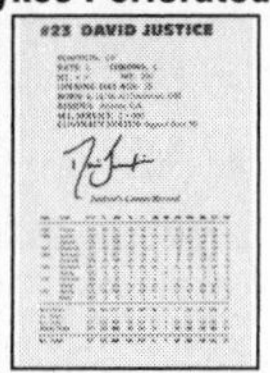

The 1992 Atlanta Braves Team Picture Card set was sponsored by Lykes and distributed as an uncut, perforated sheet before a Braves' home game. It consists of three large sheets (each measuring approximately 10 5/8" by 9 3/8") joined together to form one continuous sheet. The first panel features a team photo, while the second and third panels feature 15 player cards each. After perforation, the cards measure approximately 2 1/8" by 3 1/8". The cards are unnumbered and checklisted below in alphabetical order.

	Nm-Mt	Ex-Mt
COMPLETE SET (30)	14.00	4.20
1 Steve Avery	.25	.07
2 Rafael Belliard	.25	.07
3 Juan Berenguer	.25	.07
4 Damon Berryhill	.25	.07
5 Mike Bielecki	.25	.07
6 Jeff Blauser	.50	.15
7 Sid Bream	.25	.07
8 Francisco Cabrera	.25	.07
9 Bobby Cox MG	.50	.15
10 Nick Esasky	.25	.07
11 Marvin Freeman	.25	.07
12 Ron Gant	1.00	.30
13 Tom Glavine	2.00	.60
14 Tommy Gregg	.25	.07
15 Brian Hunter	.25	.07
16 David Justice	1.25	.35
17 Charlie Leibrandt	.25	.07
18 Mark Lemke	.25	.07
19 Kent Mercker	.25	.07
20 Otis Nixon	.25	.07
21 Greg Olson	.25	.07
22 Alejandro Pena	.25	.07
23 Terry Pendleton	1.00	.30
24 Deion Sanders	2.00	.60
25 Lonnie Smith	.50	.15
26 John Smoltz	1.50	.45
27 Mike Stanton	.50	.15
28 Jeff Treadway	.25	.07
29 Jerry Willard	.25	.07
30 Mark Wohlers	.25	.07

1992 Braves Lykes Standard

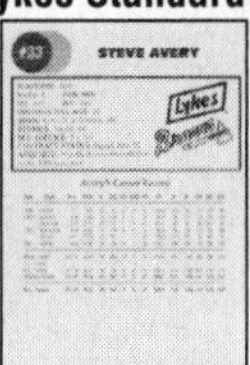

These 37 standard-size cards were given out (some more than once) to fans 12 years old and under on Tuesdays. Two different uncut sheets have surfaced, but no complete sets were sold or given away by the Braves. The mascot cards were available on a daily basis. The cards are unnumbered and checklisted below in alphabetical order.

	Nm-Mt	Ex-Mt
COMPLETE SET (36)	30.00	9.00
COMMON CARD (1-37)	.50	.15
COMMON DP	.25	.07
1 Steve Avery	.50	.15
2 Jim Beauchamp CO	.50	.15
3 Rafael Belliard	.50	.15
4 Juan Berenguer	.50	.15
5 Damon Berryhill	.50	.15
6 Mike Bielecki	.50	.15
7 Jeff Blauser	1.00	.30
8 Sid Bream	.50	.15
9 Francisco Cabrera	.50	.15
10 Pat Corrales CO	.50	.15
11 Bobby Cox MG	1.00	.30
12 Marvin Freeman	.50	.15
13 Ron Gant	2.00	.60
14 Tom Glavine	4.00	1.20
15 Tommy Gregg	.50	.15
16 Homer the Brave DP (Mascot)	.25	.07
17 Brian Hunter	.50	.15
18 Clarence Jones CO	.50	.15
19 David Justice	2.50	.75
20 Charlie Leibrandt	.50	.15
21 Mark Lemke	.50	.15
22 Leo Mazzone CO	.50	.15
23 Kent Mercker	.50	.15
24 Otis Nixon	.50	.15
25 Greg Olson	.50	.15
26 Alejandro Pena	.50	.15
27 Terry Pendleton	2.00	.60
28 Rally (Mascot) DP	.25	.07
29 Deion Sanders	4.00	1.20
30 Lonnie Smith	1.00	.30
31 John Smoltz	3.00	.90
32 Mike Stanton	.50	.15
33 Jeff Treadway	.50	.15
34 Jerry Willard	.50	.15
35 Jimy Williams CO	.50	.15
36 Mark Wohlers	.50	.15
37 Ned Yost CO	.50	.15

1993 Braves Florida Agriculture

These were given out in eight-card perforated sheets at the Sunshine State Games in Tallahassee in July 1993. The sheets measure approximately 7" by 10" and the cards, when cut from the sheets, are the standard size. Within a baseball icon between the two panels is the result of an "at bat" in a game that used an 11" by 8 1/2" game card, which was also distributed at the Games. The cards are numbered on the back with the numbering essentially following alphabetical order.

	Nm-Mt	Ex-Mt
COMPLETE SET (8)	10.00	3.00
1 Title Card	1.00	.30
2 Steve Avery	1.00	.30
3 Jeff Blauser	1.25	.35
4 Sid Bream	1.00	.30
5 Tom Glavine	2.50	.75
6 Mark Lemke	1.00	.30
7 Greg Olson	1.00	.30
8 Terry Pendleton	2.00	.60

1993 Braves Lykes Perforated

These 30 cards measure approximately 2 1/8" by 3 1/8" and feature color player photos that are the same as the Dubuque Meats Tuesday giveaway cards, except that Ryan Klesko was only in this set. The cards were issued late in the season and as a result include an early card of Fred McGriff as a Brave. The cards are unnumbered and checklisted below in alphabetical order.

	Nm-Mt	Ex-Mt
COMPLETE SET (30)	18.00	5.50
1 Steve Avery	.25	.07
2 Steve Bedrosian	.50	.15
3 Rafael Belliard	.25	.07
4 Damon Berryhill	.25	.07
5 Jeff Blauser	.50	.15
6 Sid Bream	.25	.07
7 Francisco Cabrera	.25	.07
8 Bobby Cox MG	.50	.15
9 Marvin Freeman	.25	.07
10 Ron Gant	1.00	.30
11 Tom Glavine	3.00	.90
12 Jay Howell	.25	.07
13 Brian Hunter	.25	.07
14 David Justice	1.50	.45
15 Ryan Klesko	2.00	.60
16 Mark Lemke	.25	.07
17 Greg Maddux	8.00	2.40
18 Fred McGriff	2.00	.60
19 Greg McMichael	.25	.07
20 Kent Mercker	.25	.07
21 Otis Nixon	.25	.07
22 Greg Olson	.25	.07
23 Bill Pecota	.25	.07
24 Terry Pendleton	.75	.23
25 Deion Sanders	3.00	.90
26 Pete Smith	.25	.07
27 John Smoltz	2.00	.60
28 Mike Stanton	.50	.15
29 Tony Tarasco	.25	.07
30 Mark Wohlers	.25	.07

1993 Braves Lykes Standard

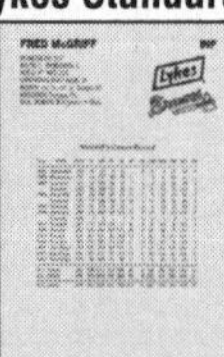

These 38 standard-size cards feature the same portraits as the perforated Dubuque Meats 1993 set, but with a different design. Each Tuesday, the Braves gave out three different cards, and for the first time, did not repeat any player's card during the season. Mascot cards were offered to youngsters on a daily basis. The cards are unnumbered and checklisted below in alphabetical order. Some near-complete sets surfaced following the season, along with some uncut sheets, but neither the near-complete sets nor the sheets included the cards of Javy Lopez, Fred McGriff, and Tony Tarasco, which were the final Tuesday's handout. The uncut sheet had six rows with six slots per row; thirty-five players are featured, and one slot is blank. The printing on the back of these three cards is slightly different from the other 35 cards, indicating a separate printing.

	Nm-Mt	Ex-Mt
COMPLETE SET (38)	40.00	12.00
COMMON CARD (1-38)	.50	.15
COMMON DP	.25	.07
SP COMMONS	4.00	1.20
1 Steve Avery	.50	.15
2 Jim Beauchamp CO	.50	.15
3 Steve Bedrosian	1.00	.30
4 Rafael Belliard	.50	.15
5 Damon Berryhill	.50	.15
6 Jeff Blauser	1.00	.30
7 Sid Bream	.50	.15
8 Francisco Cabrera	.50	.15
9 Pat Corrales CO	.50	.15
10 Bobby Cox MG	1.00	.30
11 Marvin Freeman	.50	.15
12 Ron Gant	2.00	.60
13 Tom Glavine	4.00	1.20
14 Homer the Brave DP (Mascot)	.25	.07
15 Jay Howell	.50	.15
16 Brian Hunter	.50	.15
17 Clarence Jones CO	.50	.15
18 David Justice	2.50	.75
19 Mark Lemke	.50	.15
20 Javy Lopez SP	10.00	3.00
21 Greg Maddux	10.00	3.00
22 Leo Mazzone CO	.50	.15
23 Fred McGriff SP	8.00	2.40
24 Greg McMichael	.50	.15
25 Kent Mercker	.50	.15
26 Otis Nixon	1.00	.30
27 Greg Olson	.50	.15
28 Bill Pecota	.50	.15
29 Terry Pendleton	2.00	.60
30 Rally (Mascot) DP	.25	.07
31 Deion Sanders	4.00	1.20
32 Pete Smith	.50	.15
33 John Smoltz	3.00	.90
34 Mike Stanton	.50	.15
35 Tony Tarasco SP	4.00	1.20
36 Jimy Williams CO	.50	.15
37 Mark Wohlers	.50	.15
38 Ned Yost CO	.50	.15

1993 Braves Postcards

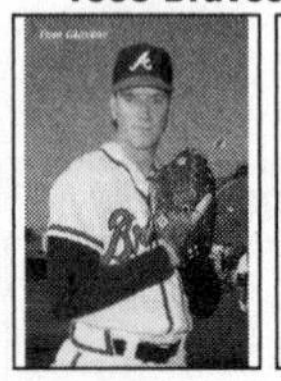

These seven postcards featuring members of the Atlanta Braves, were taken by veteran sports photographer Barry Colla. The full-bleed fronts have the player's photo with their name on the bottom in white letters. The backs are standard postcard backs. Since these cards are unnumbered, we have sequenced them in alphabetical order.

	Nm-Mt	Ex-Mt
COMPLETE SET (7)	8.00	2.40
1 Steve Avery	.50	.15
2 Tom Glavine	2.00	.60
3 David Justice	1.50	.45
4 Otis Nixon	.50	.15
5 Terry Pendleton	.75	.23
6 Deion Sanders	1.50	.45
7 John Smoltz	1.50	.45

1993 Braves Stadium Club

This 30-card standard-size set features the 1993 Atlanta Braves. The set was issued in hobby (plastic box) and retail (blister) form.

	Nm-Mt	Ex-Mt
COMP.FACT SET (30)	10.00	3.00
1 Tom Glavine	1.00	.30
2 Bill Pecota	.10	.03
3 David Justice	.75	.23
4 Mark Lemke	.10	.03
5 Jeff Blauser	.10	.03
6 Ron Gant	.25	.07
7 Greg Olson	.10	.03
8 Francisco Cabrera	.10	.03
9 Chipper Jones	3.00	.90
10 Steve Avery	.10	.03
11 Kent Mercker	.10	.03
12 John Smoltz	.50	.15
13 Pete Smith	.10	.03
14 Damon Berryhill	.10	.03
15 Sid Bream	.10	.03
16 Otis Nixon	.10	.03
17 Mike Stanton	.10	.03
18 Greg Maddux	3.00	.90
19 Jay Howell	.10	.03
20 Rafael Belliard	.10	.03
21 Terry Pendleton	.50	.15
22 Deion Sanders	.75	.23
23 Brian R. Hunter	.10	.03
24 Marvin Freeman	.10	.03
25 Mark Wohlers	.10	.03
26 Ryan Klesko	.75	.23
27 Javier Lopez	1.00	.30
28 Melvin Nieves	.10	.03
29 Tony Tarasco	.10	.03
30 Ramon Caraballo	.10	.03

1994 Braves Lykes Perforated

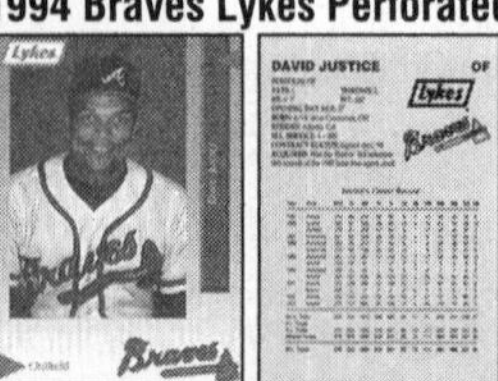

The 1994 Atlanta Braves Team Picture Card set was sponsored by Lykes, the stadium's hot dog maker. It consists of three 10 5/8" by 9 3/8" sheets and one 10 5/8" by 3 1/8" 5-card strip, all joined together to form one continuous sheet. The first panel features a team photo, with each player identified by row. The second and third panels display 15 player cards each, with the 5-card strip for a total of 35 cards. In contrast to the 1994 Braves Standard set, these cards measure 1 1/8" by 3 1/8" and are perforated. The design of these cards is identical to the standard cards, except that the bio and statistics on the card backs are in team color-coded red and blue print rather than black. The difference in player selection between the perforated and standard sets is instructive. The perforated set omits Sanders (traded) but adds Roberto Kelly (acquired), Mike Mordecai (called up), and Jose Oliva (called up). Also Pat Corrales was omitted from the perforated set. The cards are unnumbered but are arranged alphabetically by column beginning in the upper left corner.

	Nm-Mt	Ex-Mt
COMPLETE SET (35)	20.00	6.00
1 Steve Avery	.25	.07
2 Jim Beauchamp CO	.25	.07
3 Steve Bedrosian	.50	.15
4 Rafael Belliard	.25	.07
5 Mike Bielecki	.25	.07
6 Jeff Blauser	.50	.15
7 Bobby Cox MG	.50	.15
8 Dave Gallagher	.25	.07
9 Tom Glavine	2.00	.60
10 Milt Hill	.25	.07
11 Chipper Jones	6.00	1.80
12 Clarence Jones CO	.25	.07
13 David Justice	1.00	.30
14 Mike Kelly	.25	.07
15 Roberto Kelly	.25	.07
16 Ryan Klesko	2.00	.60
17 Mark Lemke	.50	.15
18 Javier Lopez	2.00	.60
19 Greg Maddux	6.00	1.80
20 Leo Mazzone CO	.25	.07
21 Fred McGriff	1.50	.45
22 Greg McMichael	.25	.07
23 Kent Mercker	.25	.07
24 Mike Mordecai	.25	.07
25 Charlie O'Brien	.25	.07
26 Jose Oliva	.25	.07
27 Gregg Olson	.25	.07
28 Bill Pecota	.25	.07
29 Terry Pendleton	1.00	.30
30 John Smoltz	1.50	.45
31 Mike Stanton	.25	.07
32 Tony Tarasco	.25	.07
33 Jimy Williams CO	.25	.07
34 Mark Wohlers	.25	.07
35 Ned Yost CO	.25	.07

1994 Braves Lykes Standard

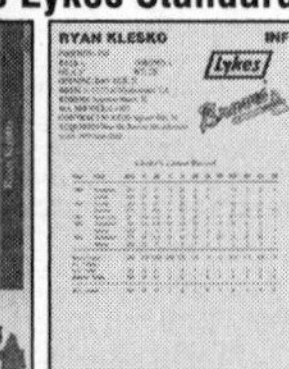

This 34-card standard-size set was sponsored by Lykes, the stadium's hot dog maker. Three cards each were to be given out on nine Tuesdays, but three giveaway dates were lost to the strike. The other seven cards were either of players who were traded (Sanders and Hill) or were not given out at games (Cox, Jones, Kelly, Klesko, and McGriff). These seven cards may be scarcer than the others. The cards are unnumbered and checklisted below in alphabetical order.

	Nm-Mt	Ex-Mt
COMPLETE SET (34)	35.00	10.50
1 Steve Avery	.50	.15
2 Jim Beauchamp CO	.50	.15
3 Steve Bedrosian	1.00	.30
4 Rafael Belliard	.50	.15
5 Mike Bielecki	.50	.15
6 Jeff Blauser	1.00	.30
7 Pat Corrales CO	.50	.15
8 Bobby Cox MG	1.00	.30
9 Dave Gallagher	.50	.15
10 Tom Glavine	3.00	.90
11 Milt Hill	.50	.15
12 Chipper Jones	6.00	1.80
13 Clarence Jones CO	.50	.15
14 David Justice	2.00	.60
15 Mike Kelly	.50	.15
16 Ryan Klesko	2.00	.60
17 Mark Lemke	.50	.15
18 Javy Lopez	2.00	.60
19 Greg Maddux	6.00	1.80
20 Leo Mazzone CO	.50	.15
21 Fred McGriff	2.00	.60
22 Greg McMichael	.50	.15
23 Kent Mercker	.50	.15
24 Charlie O'Brien	.50	.15
25 Gregg Olson	.50	.15
26 Bill Pecota	.50	.15
27 Terry Pendleton	2.00	.60
28 Deion Sanders	2.00	.60
29 John Smoltz	2.00	.60
30 Mike Stanton	.50	.15
31 Tony Tarasco	.50	.15
32 Jimy Williams CO	.50	.15
33 Mark Wohlers	.50	.15
34 Ned Yost CO	.50	.15

1994 Braves U.S. Playing Cards

These 56 playing standard-size cards have rounded corners, and feature color posed and action player photos on their white-bordered fronts.The set is checklisted below in playing card order by suits and assigned numbers to aces (1), jacks (11), queens (12), and kings (13).

	Nm-Mt	Ex-Mt
COMP. FACT SET (56)	6.00	1.80
1C Ron Gant	.25	.07
1D Greg Maddux	1.00	.30
1H Dave Justice	.50	.15
1S Jeff Blauser	.05	.02
2C Chipper Jones	1.00	.30
2D Ron Gant	.25	.07
2H Mark Lemke	.05	.02
2S Mike Stanton	.05	.02
3C Terry Pendleton	.10	.03
3D Kent Mercker	.05	.02
3H Javier Lopez	.40	.12
3S Ryan Klesko	.50	.15
4C Mark Wohlers	.05	.02
4D Greg McMichael	.05	.02
4H Rafael Belliard	.05	.02
4S Michael Potts	.05	.02
5C Pedro Borbon	.05	.02
5D Tony Tarasco	.05	.02
5H Bill Pecota	.05	.02
5S Charlie O'Brien	.05	.02
6C Steve Avery	.25	.07
6D John Smoltz	.25	.07
6H Tom Glavine	.50	.15
6S Steve Bedrosian	.05	.02
7C Deion Sanders	.25	.07
7D Fred McGriff	.25	.07
7H Milt Hill	.05	.02
7S Javier Lopez	.40	.12
8C Dave Justice	.25	.07
8D Ron Gant	.25	.07
8H Jeff Blauser	.10	.03
8S Greg Maddux	1.00	.30
9C Dave Gallagher	.05	.02
9D Mike Kelly	.05	.02
9H Ryan Klesko	.10	.03
9S Deion Sanders	.25	.07
10C Rafael Belliard	.05	.02
10D Steve Bedrosian	.05	.02
10H Terry Pendleton	.10	.03
10S Ramon Caraballo	.05	.02
11C Greg McMichael	.05	.02
11D Bill Pecota	.05	.02
11H Mike Stanton	.05	.02
11S Kent Mercker	.05	.02
12C John Smoltz	.25	.07
12D Mark Lemke	.05	.02
12H Steve Avery	.05	.02
12S Mark Wohlers	.05	.02
13C Fred McGriff	.25	.07
13D Terry Pendleton	.10	.03
13H Deion Sanders	.25	.07
13S Tom Glavine	.50	.15
NNO Featured Players	.05	.02

1995 Braves Atlanta Constitution

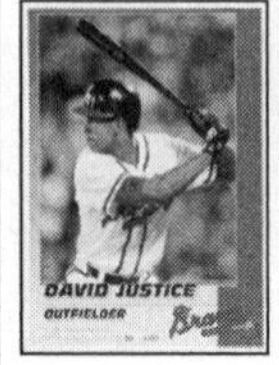

This eight-card set of the Atlanta Braves measuring approximately 8 1/2" by 11" features color action player photos with a red, blue and yellow inner border and a white outer margin. The backs carry player information and career statistics. Only 5,000 of each card were produced and are sequentially numbered. The profits from this set was donated to the Atlanta Braves Foundation. The cards are unnumbered and checklisted below in alphabetical order.

	Nm-Mt	Ex-Mt
COMPLETE SET (8)	12.00	3.60
1 Steve Avery	1.00	.30
2 Tom Glavine	3.00	.90
3 Marquis Grissom	1.00	.30
4 David Justice	2.50	.75
5 Ryan Klesko	2.50	.75
6 Mark Lemke	1.00	.30
7 John Smoltz	2.00	.60
8 Mark Wohlers	1.00	.30

1996 Braves Fleer

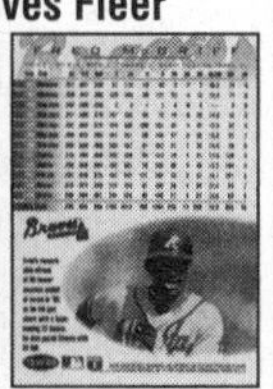

These 20 standard-size cards feature the same design as the regular Fleer issue, except they are UV coated, use silver foil and are numbered "x of 20". The team set packs were available at retail locations and hobby shops in 10-card packs for a suggested retail price of $1.99.

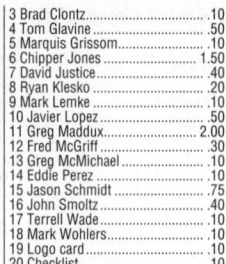

	Nm-Mt	Ex-Mt
COMPLETE SET (20)	6.00	1.80
1 Steve Avery	.10	.03
2 Jeff Blauser	.10	.03
3 Brad Clontz	.10	.03
4 Tom Glavine	.50	.15
5 Marquis Grissom	.10	.03
6 Chipper Jones	1.50	.45
7 David Justice	.40	.12
8 Ryan Klesko	.20	.06
9 Mark Lemke	.10	.03
10 Javier Lopez	.50	.15
11 Greg Maddux	2.00	.60
12 Fred McGriff	.30	.09
13 Greg McMichael	.10	.03
14 Eddie Perez	.10	.03
15 Jason Schmidt	.75	.23
16 John Smoltz	.40	.12
17 Terrell Wade	.10	.03
18 Mark Wohlers	.10	.03
19 Logo card	.10	.03
20 Checklist	.10	.03

1997 Braves Score

This 15-card set of the Atlanta Braves was issued in five-card packs with a suggested retail of $1.30 each. The fronts feature color player photos with special team specific color foil stamping. The backs carry player information. Only 100 cases were made for each team. Platinum parallel cards were inserted at a rate of 1:6, Premier parallel cards at a rate of 1:31.

	Nm-Mt	Ex-Mt
COMPLETE SET (15)	10.00	3.00
*PLATINUM: 4X BASIC CARDS		
*PREMIER: 20X BASIC CARDS		
1 Ryan Klesko	1.00	.30
2 Dave Justice	.75	.23
3 Terry Pendleton	.25	.07
4 Tom Glavine	1.25	.35
5 Javier Lopez	1.00	.30
6 John Smoltz	.75	.23
7 Jermaine Dye	.25	.07
8 Mark Lemke	.25	.07
9 Fred McGriff	.75	.23
10 Chipper Jones	3.00	.90
11 Terrell Wade	.25	.07
12 Greg Maddux	3.00	.90
13 Mark Wohlers	.25	.07
14 Marquis Grissom	.25	.07
15 Andruw Jones	2.00	.60

1998 Braves Score

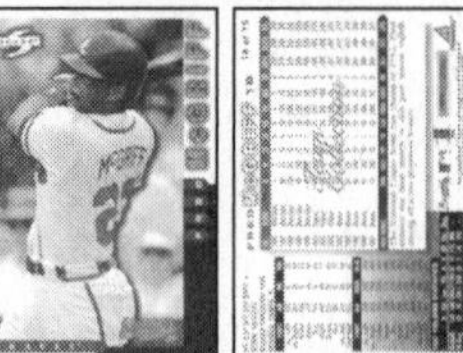

This 15-card set was issued in special retail packs and features color photos of the Atlanta Braves team. The backs carry player information. A special platinum parallel set was also issued and randomly inserted in packs.

	Nm-Mt	Ex-Mt
COMPLETE SET (15)	8.00	2.40
*PLATINUM: 5X BASIC CARDS		
1 Andruw Jones	1.25	.35
2 Greg Maddux	2.50	.75
3 Michael Tucker	.25	.07
4 Denny Neagle	.25	.07
5 Javier Lopez	1.00	.30
6 Ryan Klesko	1.00	.30
7 Chipper Jones	2.50	.75
8 Kenny Lofton	.75	.23
9 John Smoltz	.75	.23
10 Jeff Blauser	.25	.07
11 Tom Glavine	1.25	.35
12 Tony Graffanino	.25	.07
13 Terrell Wade	.25	.07
14 Fred McGriff	.75	.23
15 Mark Wohlers	.25	.07

1999 Braves Atlanta Journal-Constitution Jumbos

This 16-card jumbo set was released in conjunction with the Atlanta Journal-Constitution in 1999, and features 16 jumbo photos of the 1999 Atlanta Braves. The photos measure approximately 8"x10". Please note that only 15,000 of each photo were produced. The photos have been put in alphabetical order below for convenience.

	Nm-Mt	Ex-Mt
COMPLETE SET (16)	50.00	15.00
1 Tom Glavine	6.00	1.80
2 Ozzie Guillen	2.00	.60
3 Brian Hunter	2.00	.60
4 Andruw Jones	6.00	1.80
5 Chipper Jones	8.00	2.40
6 Brian Jordan	2.00	.60
7 Ryan Klesko	5.00	1.50
8 Keith Lockhart	2.00	.60
9 Javy Lopez	3.00	.90
10 Greg Maddux	8.00	2.40
11 Otis Nixon	2.00	.60
12 Eddie Perez	2.00	.60
13 John Rocker	3.00	.90
14 John Smoltz	5.00	1.50
15 Walt Weiss	2.00	.60
16 Gerald Williams	2.00	.60

1909 H.H. Bregstone PC743

The H.H. Bregstone postcards were issued during the 1909-11 time period. They feature St. Louis Browns and St. Louis Cardinals only. The cards are sepia and black in appearance and are of consistent quality in the printing. Each cards features the line "by H.H. Bregstone, St. Louis" at the bottom of the obverse. The player's last name, his position, and his team are enumerated. The reverses features the letters AZO in the stamp area. B. Gregory of the Trolley League is probably Howie Gregory who played for the Browns that year.

	Ex-Mt	VG
COMPLETE SET (53)	12000.00	6000.00
1 Bill Bailey	250.00	125.00
2 Jap Barbeau	250.00	125.00
3 Shad Barry	250.00	125.00
4 Fred Beebe	250.00	125.00
5 Frank Betcher	250.00	125.00
6 Jack Bliss	250.00	125.00
7 Roger Bresnahan	500.00	250.00
8 Bobby Byrne	250.00	125.00
9 Chappy Charles	250.00	125.00
10 Frank Corridon	250.00	125.00
11 Dade Criss	250.00	125.00
12 Lou Criger	250.00	125.00
13 Joe Delahanty	250.00	125.00
14 Bill Dineen	250.00	125.00
15 Rube Ellis	250.00	125.00
16 Steve Evans	250.00	125.00
17 Art Fromme	250.00	125.00
18 Rube Geyer	250.00	125.00
19 Billy Gilbert	250.00	125.00
20 Bert Graham	250.00	125.00
21 B. Gregory Probably Howie Gregory	250.00	125.00
22 Art Griggs	250.00	125.00
23 Bob Harmon	250.00	125.00
24 Roy Hartzell	250.00	125.00
25 Irv Higginbotham	250.00	125.00
26 Thomas Higgins	250.00	125.00
27 Danny Hoffman	250.00	125.00
28 Harry Howell	250.00	125.00
29 Miller Huggins	500.00	250.00
30 Rudy Hulswitt	250.00	125.00
31 Johnson	250.00	125.00
32 Tom Jones	250.00	125.00
33 Ed Konetchy	250.00	125.00
34 Johnny Lush	250.00	125.00
35 Lee Magee	250.00	125.00
36 Jimmy McAleer MG	250.00	125.00
37 Stoney McGlynn	250.00	125.00
38 Rebel Oakes	250.00	125.00
39 Tom O'Hara	250.00	125.00
40 Ham Patterson	250.00	125.00
41 Barney Pelty	250.00	125.00
42 Ed Phelps	250.00	125.00
43 Elmer Rieger	250.00	125.00
44 Charlie Rhodes	250.00	125.00
45 Slim Sallee	250.00	125.00
46 Al Schweitzer	250.00	125.00
47 Wib Smith	250.00	125.00
48 Jim Stephens	250.00	125.00
49 George Stone	250.00	125.00
50 Rube Waddell	500.00	250.00
51 Bobby Wallace	500.00	250.00
52 Jim Williams	250.00	125.00
53 Vic Willis	500.00	250.00

1903-04 Breisch-Williams E107

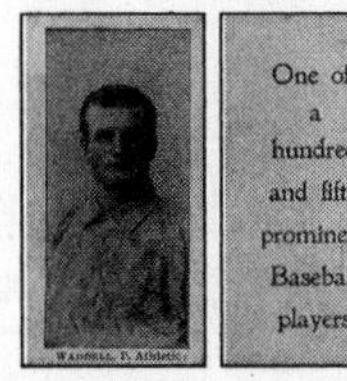
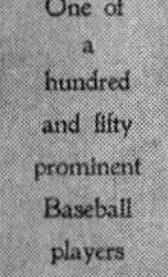

One of
a
hundred
and fifty
prominent
Baseball
players

The cards in this 159-card set measure 1 1/4" by 2 1/2". The black and white cards of this series of "prominent baseball players" were marketed by the Breisch-Williams Company. Judging from the team changes for individual players, the set appears to have been issued in 1903-04. Cards have been found with smaller printing front and back and also with the company name hand stamped on back. There are several names misspelled. The cards have been alphabetized and numbered in the checklist below. A second type of these cards are also known. These cards have a thicker paper stock and narrower borders. However -- there is no definative answer as to how many players are available in this type. Any further information is greatly appreciated.

	Ex-Mt	VG
COMPLETE SET	90000.00	45000.00
1 John Anderson St. Louis AL	400.00	200.00
2 John Anderson NY AL	400.00	200.00
3 Jimmy Barrett: Detroit (sic, Barret)	400.00	200.00
4 Ginger Beaumont	500.00	250.00
5 Erve Beck	400.00	200.00
6 Jake Beckley	1500.00	750.00
7 Harry Bemis: Cleve.	400.00	200.00
8 Chief Bender Phila. AL	1500.00	750.00
9 Bill Bernhard	400.00	200.00
10 Harry Bay sic, Bey)	400.00	200.00
11 Bill Bradley	400.00	200.00
12 Fritz Buelow	400.00	200.00
13 Nixey Callahan	400.00	200.00
14 Scoops Carey	400.00	200.00
15 Charlie Carr	400.00	200.00
16 Bill Carrick	400.00	200.00
17 Doc Casey	400.00	200.00
18 Frank Chance	1500.00	750.00
19 Jack Chesbro	1500.00	750.00
20 Boileryard Clarke sic, Clark	400.00	200.00
21 Fred Clarke	1500.00	750.00
22 Jimmy Collins	1500.00	750.00
23 Duff Cooley	400.00	200.00
24 Tommy Corcoran	400.00	200.00
25 Bill Coughlin sic, Coughlan)	400.00	200.00
26 Lou Criger	400.00	200.00
27 Lave Cross	400.00	200.00
28 Monte Cross	400.00	200.00
29 Bill Dahlen Brooklyn	500.00	250.00
30 Bill Dahlen New York National	1500.00	750.00
31 Tom Daly	400.00	200.00
32 George Davis	1500.00	750.00
33 Harry Davis	400.00	200.00
34 Ed Delahanty	2000.00	1000.00
35 Gene DeMontreville	400.00	200.00
36 Pop Dillon Brooklyn	400.00	200.00
37 Pop Dillon Detroit	400.00	200.00
38 Bill Dinneen (sic, Dineen)	400.00	200.00
39 Jiggs Donahue	400.00	200.00
40 Mike Donlin	500.00	250.00
41 Patsy Donovan	400.00	200.00
42 Patsy Dougherty	400.00	200.00
43 Klondike Douglass sic, Douglas)	400.00	200.00
44 Jack Doyle Brooklyn	400.00	200.00
45 Jack Doyle Phila. NL	400.00	200.00
46 Lew Drill	400.00	200.00
47 Jack Dunn	400.00	200.00
48 Kid Elberfeld sic, Elberfield	400.00	200.00
49 Kid Elberfeld sic, Elberfield	400.00	200.00
50 Duke Farrell	400.00	200.00
51 Hobe Ferris	400.00	200.00
52 Elmer Flick	1500.00	750.00
53 Buck Freeman	400.00	200.00
54 Bill Friel sic, Freil	400.00	200.00
55 Dave Fultz	400.00	200.00
56 Ned Garvin	400.00	200.00
57 Billy Gilbert	400.00	200.00
58 Harry Gleason	400.00	200.00
59 Kid Gleason NY NL	600.00	300.00
60 Kid Gleason Phila. NL	600.00	300.00
61 John Gochnaur Cleve. sic, Gochnauer	400.00	200.00
62 Danny Green	400.00	200.00
63 Noodles Hahn	500.00	250.00
64 Bill Hallman	400.00	200.00
65 Ned Hanlon MG	800.00	400.00
66 Dick Harley	400.00	200.00
67 Jack Harper	400.00	200.00
68 Topsy Hartsel sic, Hartsell	400.00	200.00
69 Emmett Heidrick	400.00	200.00
70 Charlie Hemphill	400.00	200.00
71 Weldon Henley	400.00	200.00
72 Charlie Hickman	400.00	200.00
73 Harry Howell	400.00	200.00
74 Frank Isbell sic, Isabel	400.00	200.00
75 Fred Jacklitsch sic, Jacklitzch	400.00	200.00
76 Charlie Jones	400.00	200.00
77 Fielder Jones	400.00	200.00
78 Addie Joss	1500.00	750.00
79 Mike Kahoe	400.00	200.00
80 Willie Keeler	2500.00	1250.00
81 Joe Kelley	1500.00	750.00
82 Brickyard Kennedy	400.00	200.00
83 Frank Kitson	400.00	200.00
84 Malachi Kittredge Boston NL	400.00	200.00
85 Malachi Kittredge Wash.	400.00	200.00
86 Candy LaChance	400.00	200.00
87 Nap Lajoie	2500.00	1250.00
88 Tommy Leach	400.00	200.00
89 Watty Lee Pittsburgh	400.00	200.00
90 Watty Lee Washington	400.00	200.00
91 Sam Leever	400.00	200.00
92 Herman Long	500.00	250.00
93 Billy Lush Cleveland	400.00	200.00
94 Billy Lush Detroit	400.00	200.00
95 Christy Mathewson	3000.00	1500.00
96 Sport McAllister	400.00	200.00
97 Jack McCarthy	400.00	200.00
98 Barry McCormick	400.00	200.00
99 Ed McFarland	400.00	200.00
100 Herm McFarland	400.00	200.00
101 Joe McGinnity	1500.00	750.00
102 John McGraw	2000.00	1000.00
103 Deacon McGuire Brooklyn	400.00	200.00
104 Deacon McGuire New York		
105 Jock Menefee	400.00	200.00
106 Sam Mertes	400.00	200.00
107 Roscoe Miller	400.00	200.00
108 Fred Mitchell	400.00	200.00
109 Earl Moore	400.00	200.00
110 Danny Murphy	400.00	200.00
111 Jack O'Connor	400.00	200.00
112 Al Orth	400.00	200.00
113 Dick Padden	400.00	200.00
114 Freddy Parent	400.00	200.00
115 Roy Patterson	400.00	200.00
116 Heinie Peitz	400.00	200.00
117 Deacon Phillipe sic, Phillipi	500.00	250.00
118 Wiley Piatt	400.00	200.00
119 Ollie Pickering	400.00	200.00
120 Eddie Plank	2000.00	1000.00
121 Ed Poole Brooklyn	400.00	200.00
122 Ed Poole Cinc.	400.00	200.00
123 Jack Powell New York AL	400.00	200.00
124 Jack Powell StL AL	400.00	200.00
125 Doc Powers	400.00	200.00
126 Claude Ritchey sic, Ritchie	400.00	200.00
127 Jimmy Ryan	500.00	250.00
128 Ossie Schreckengost	400.00	200.00
129 Kip Selbach	400.00	200.00
130 Socks Seybold	400.00	200.00
131 Jimmy Sheckard	400.00	200.00
132 Ed Siever	400.00	200.00
133 Harry Smith	400.00	200.00
134 Tully Sparks	400.00	200.00
135 Jake Stahl	500.00	250.00
136 Harry Steinfeldt	500.00	250.00
137 Sammy Strang	400.00	200.00
138 Willie Sudhoff	400.00	200.00
139 Joe Sugden	400.00	200.00
140 Billy Sullivan	500.00	250.00
141 Jack Taylor	400.00	200.00
142 Fred Tenney	400.00	200.00
143 Roy Thomas	400.00	200.00
144 Jack Thoney Cleve.	400.00	200.00
145 Jack Thoney NY AL	400.00	200.00
146 Happy Townsend	400.00	200.00
147 George Van Haltren	400.00	200.00
148 Rube Waddell	1500.00	750.00
149 Honus Wagner	4000.00	2000.00
150 Bobby Wallace	1500.00	750.00
151 John Warner	400.00	200.00
152 Jimmy Wiggs	400.00	200.00
153 Jimmy Williams	400.00	200.00
154 Vic Willis	1500.00	750.00
155 Hooks Wiltse	400.00	200.00
156 George Winter sic, Winters	400.00	200.00
157 Bob Wood	400.00	200.00
158 Joe Yeager	400.00	200.00
159 Cy Young	2500.00	1250.00
160 Chief Zimmer	400.00	200.00

1981 George Brett Promo

This promo card was distributed at the St. Louis Card Show in 1981. It commemorates his .390 season. It features an artist's rendition with a Sporting News quote on back. Just 5,000 were issued.

	Nm-Mt	Ex-Mt
1 George Brett	10.00	4.00

1982 Brett Spotbilt

This one card standard-size set features Kansas City Royals star George Brett. This card features Brett's picture on the card. The letters GB5 (his uniform number) are on the top with the Spot-Bilt words and logo on the bottom. The horizontal back has vital statistics, career stats as well as some career highlights.

	Nm-Mt	Ex-Mt
5 George Brett	1.00	.40

1993 George Brett 3,000 Hit

This one-card set is actually a 16-page booklet honoring George Brett for his 3,000 hits. The front features a strip depicting Brett at bat with a facsimile autograph below. The back displays a color photo of Brett rejoicing after the hit. The inside carries facts about the player with an autographed picture enclosed.

	Nm-Mt	Ex-Mt
1 George Brett	5.00	1.50

1970 Brewers McDonald's

This 31-card set features cards measuring approximately 2 15/16" by 4 3/8" and was issued during the Brewers' first year in Milwaukee after moving from Seattle. The cards are drawings of the members of the 1970 Milwaukee Brewers and underneath the drawings there is information about the players. These cards are still often found in uncut sheet form and hence have no extra value in that form. The backs are blank. The set is checklisted alphabetically with the number of the sheet being listed next to the players name. There were six different sheets of six cards each although only one sheet contained six players; the other sheets depicted five players and a Brewers' logo.

	NM	Ex
COMPLETE SET (31)	8.00	3.20
1 Max Alvis 6	.25	.10
2 Bob Bolin 1	.25	.10
3 Gene Brabender 3	.25	.10
4 Dave Bristol 5 MG	.50	.20
5 Wayne Comer 2	.25	.10
6 Cal Ermer 3 CO	.25	.10
7 John Gelnar 4	.25	.10
8 Greg Goossen 5	.25	.10
9 Tommy Harper 5	.75	.30
10 Mike Hegan 3	.50	.20
11 Mike Hershberger 3	.25	.10
12 Steve Hovley 2	.25	.10
13 John Kennedy 2	.25	.10
14 Lew Krausse 4	.25	.10
15 Ted Kubiak 1	.25	.10
16 George Lauzerique 6	.25	.10
17 Bob Locker 5	.25	.10
18 Roy McMillan 4 CO	.50	.20
19 Jerry McNertney 4	.25	.10
20 Bob Meyer 2	.25	.10
21 Jackie Moore 6 CO	.50	.20
22 John Morris 1	.25	.10
23 John O'Donoghue 1	.25	.10
24 Marty Pattin 6	.25	.10
25 Rich Rollins 4	.50	.20
26 Phil Roof 5	.25	.10
27 Ted Savage 1	.25	.10
28 Russ Snyder 6	.25	.10
29 Wes Stock 2 CO	.50	.20
30 Sandy Valdespino 2	.25	.10
31 Danny Walton 3	.25	.10

1970 Brewers Milk

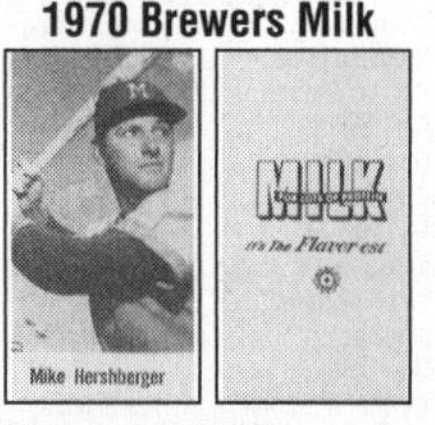

This 24-card set of the Milwaukee Brewers measures approximately 2 5/8" by 4 1/4" and features blue-and-white player photos. The players name is printed in blue in the white wide bottom border. The cards are unnumbered and checklisted below in alphabetical order.

	NM	Ex
COMPLETE SET (24)	10.00	4.00
1 Gene Brabender	.50	.20
2 Dave Bristol MG	.75	.30
3 Wayne Comer	.50	.20
4 Cal Ermer CO	.50	.20
5 Greg Goossen	.50	.20
6 Tom Harper	1.00	.40
7 Mike Hegan	.75	.30
8 Mike Hershberger	.50	.20
9 Steve Hovley	.50	.20
10 John Kennedy	.50	.20
11 Lew Krausse	.50	.20
12 Ted Kubiak	.50	.20
13 Bob Locker	.50	.20
14 Roy McMillan CO	.75	.30
15 Jerry McNertney	.50	.20
16 Bob Meyer	.50	.20
17 John Morris	.50	.20
18 John O'Donoghue	.50	.20
19 Marty Pattin	.50	.20
20 Rich Rollins	.75	.30
21 Phil Roof	.50	.20
22 Ted Savage	.50	.20
23 Russ Snyder	.50	.20
24 Dan Walton	.50	.20

1970 Brewers Team Issue

This 12-card set of the Milwaukee Brewers measures approximately 4 1/4" by 7". The fronts display black-and-white player portraits bordered in white. The player's name and team are printed in the top margin. The backs are blank. The cards are unnumbered and checklisted below in alphabetical order.

	NM	Ex
COMPLETE SET (12)	18.00	7.25
1 Max Alvis	2.00	.80
2 Dave Bristol MG	2.00	.80
3 Tommy Harper	2.50	1.00
4 Mike Hegan	2.00	.80
5 Mike Hershberger	1.50	.60
6 Lew Krausse	1.50	.60
7 Ted Kubiak	1.50	.60
8 Dave May	1.50	.60
9 Jerry McNertney	1.50	.60
10 Phil Roof	1.50	.60
11 Ted Savage	1.50	.60
12 Danny Walton	1.50	.60

1971 Brewers Team Issue

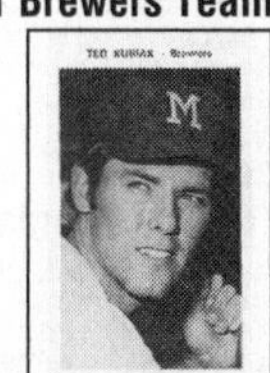

This 18-photo set features members of the Milwaukee Brewers. The photos are not dated, but can be identified as a 1971 issue since Bill Voss' card is included in the set and this was his first year with the team. Additionally, Tommy Harper's card is included and 1971 was his final year with the Brewers. The photos are printed on thin paper stock that has a pebbled texture. They measure approximately 4 1/4" by 7" and display black-and-white portraits edged in white. The player's name and team are printed in the top margin. The cards have blank backs and are numbered and checklisted alphabetically below.

	NM	Ex
COMPLETE SET (18)	20.00	8.00
1 Max Alvis	1.50	.60
2 Dave Bristol MG	1.50	.60
3 Tommy Harper	2.00	.80
4 Mike Hegan	2.00	.80
5 Mike Hershberger	1.50	.60
6 Lew Krausse	1.50	.60
7 Ted Kubiak	1.50	.60
8 Dave May	1.50	.60
9 Jerry McNertney	1.50	.60
10 Bill Parsons	1.50	.60
11 Marty Pattin	1.50	.60
12 Roberto Pena	1.50	.60
13 Ellie Rodriguez	1.50	.60
14 Phil Roof	1.50	.60
15 Ken Sanders	1.50	.60
16 Ted Savage	1.50	.60
17 Bill Voss	1.50	.60
18 Danny Walton	1.50	.60

1975 Brewers Broadcasters

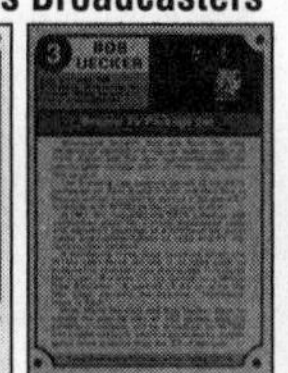

This seven-card standard-size set features four announcer cards and three schedule cards. All the cards have on the fronts black and white photos, with orange picture frame borders on a white card face. The backs are gray and present either comments on the announcers or broadcast schedules. The first four cards are numbered on the back.

	NM	Ex
COMPLETE SET	25.00	10.00
1 Jim Irwin ANN	3.00	1.20
2 Gary Bender ANN	4.00	1.60
3 Bob Uecker ANN	10.00	4.00
4 Merle Harmon ANN	5.00	2.00
x Television Schedule (unnumbered)	3.00	1.20
x Radio Schedule Part 1 (unnumbered)	3.00	1.20
x Radio Schedule Part 2 (unnumbered)	3.00	1.20

1976 Brewers A and P

This 16-card set of the Milwaukee Brewers measures approximately 5 7/8" by 9". The white-bordered fronts feature color player head photos with a facsimile autograph below. The backs are blank. The cards are unnumbered and checklisted below in alphabetical order. They were issued four at a time over a four week period at participating A and P stores. These cards were made available to customers who bought specially marked items.

	NM	Ex
COMPLETE SET (16)	20.00	8.00
1 Hank Aaron	10.00	4.00
2 Pete Broberg	.50	.20
3 Jim Colborn	.50	.20
4 Mike Hegan	.50	.20
5 Von Joshua	.50	.20
6 Tim Johnson	.50	.20
7 Sixto Lezcano	.50	.20
8 Charlie Moore	.50	.20
9 Don Money	.50	.20
10 Darrell Porter	1.50	.60
11 George Scott	1.50	.60
12 Bill Sharp	.50	.20
13 Jim Slaton	.50	.20
14 Bill Travers	.50	.20
15 Robin Yount	8.00	3.20
16 County Stadium	.50	.20

1979 Brewers Team Issue

These cards, which measure 4" by 5 1/2" were issued either on light paper or on card stock. Some of these cards were issued both ways. All values are the same no matter what stock was used. These cards were not numbered so we have sequenced them alphabetically.

	NM	Ex
COMPLETE SET (29)	15.00	6.00
1 Jerry Augustine	.50	.20
2 George Bamberger MG	.50	.20
3 Sal Bando	.75	.30
4 Mike Caldwell	.50	.20
5 Bill Castro	.50	.20
6 Cecil Cooper	1.00	.40
7 Reggie Cleveland	.50	.20
8 Dick Davis	.50	.20
9 Ray Fosse	.50	.20
10 Bob Galasso	.50	.20
11 Jim Gantner	.50	.20

12 Moose Haas .50 .20
13 Larry Haney CO .50 .20
14 Larry Hisle .50 .20
15 Frank Howard CO .75 .30
16 Harvey Kuenn CO .75 .30
17 Sixto Lezcano .50 .20
18 Buck Martinez .50 .20
19 Cal McLish CO .50 .20
20 Bob McClure .50 .20
21 Don Money .50 .20
22 Ben Oglivie .50 .20
23 Buck Rodgers CO .50 .20
24 Jim Slaton .50 .20
25 Lary Sorensen .50 .20
26 Gorman Thomas .75 .30
27 Bill Travers .50 .20
28 Jim Wohlford .50 .20
29 Robin Yount 5.00 2.00

1980 Brewers Team Issue

These 24 photos were issued by the team and feature members of the 1980 Milwaukee Brewers. The photos are unnumbered and sequenced in alphabetical order.

NM Ex
COMPLETE SET 15.00 6.00
1 Jerry Augustine .50 .20
2 George Bamberger MG .50 .20
3 Sal Bando .75 .30
4 Mark Brouhard .50 .20
5 Mike Caldwell .50 .20
6 Bill Castro .50 .20
7 Reggie Cleveland .50 .20
8 Dick Davis .50 .20
9 Jim Gantner .75 .30
10 Moose Haas .50 .20
11 Larry Haney CO .50 .20
12 Ron Hansen CO .50 .20
13 Larry Hisle .50 .20
14 Frank Howard CO .75 .30
15 Harvey Kuenn CO .75 .30
16 Sixto Lezcano .50 .20
17 Buck Martinez .50 .20
18 Cal McLish CO .50 .20
19 Don Money .75 .30
20 Ben Oglivie .75 .30
21 Buck Rodgers CO .50 .20
22 Lary Sorenson .50 .20
23 Gorman Thomas .75 .30
24 Robin Yount 5.00 2.00

1982 Brewers Police

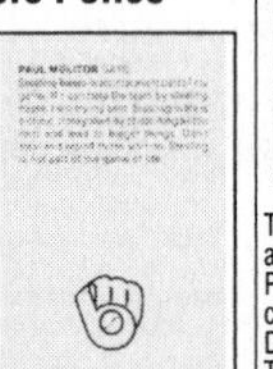

The cards in this 30-card set measure approximately 2 13/16" by 4 1/8". This set of Milwaukee Brewers baseball cards is noted for its excellent color photographs set upon a simple white background. The set was initially distributed at the stadium on May 5th, but was also handed out by several local police departments, and credit lines for the Wisconsin State Fair Park Police (no shield design on reverse), Milwaukee, Brookfield, and Wauwatosa PD's have already been found. The reverses feature advice concerning safety measures, social situations, and crime prevention (Romero card in both Spanish and English). The team card carries a checklist which lists the Brewer's coaches separately although they all appear on a single card; VP/GM Harry Dalton is not mentioned on this list but is included in the set.The prices below are for the basic set without regard to the Police Department listed on the backs. Cards from the more obscure corners and small towns of Wisconsin (where fewer cards were produced) will be valued higher.

Nm-Mt Ex-Mt
COMPLETE SET (30) 20.00 8.00
4 Paul Molitor 8.00 3.20
5 Ned Yost .75 .30
7 Don Money .75 .30
9 Larry Hisle .50 .20
10 Bob McClure .50 .20
11 Ed Romero .50 .20
13 Roy Howell .50 .20
15 Cecil Cooper 1.50 .60
17 Jim Gantner 1.00 .40
19 Robin Yount 6.00 2.40
20 Gorman Thomas 1.00 .40
22 Charlie Moore .75 .30
23 Ted Simmons 1.50 .60
24 Ben Oglivie 1.00 .40
26 Kevin Bass .50 .20
28 Jamie Easterly .50 .20
29 Mark Brouhard .50 .20
30 Moose Haas .50 .20
34 Rollie Fingers 2.50 1.00
35 Randy Lerch .50 .20
41 Jim Slaton .50 .20
45 Doug Jones 1.50 .60
46 Jerry Augustine .50 .20
47 Dwight Bernard .50 .20
48 Mike Caldwell .75 .30
50 Pete Vuckovich 1.00 .40
NNO Team Card 1.00 .40
NNO Harry Dalton GM .50 .20
NNO Buck Rodgers MG .50 .20
NNO Ron Hansen CO .50 .20
Bob Rodgers MG
Harry Warner CO
Larry Haney CO
Cal McLish CO

1983 Brewers Gardner's

The cards in this 22-card set measure 2 1/2" by 3 1/2". The 1983 Gardner's Brewers set features Milwaukee Brewer players and manager Harvey Kuenn. Topps printed the set for the Madison (Wisconsin) bakery, hence, the backs are identical to the 1983 Topps backs except for the card number. The fronts of the cards, however, feature all new photos and include the Gardner's logo and the Brewers' logo. Many of the cards are grease laden, as they were issued with packages of bread and hamburger and hot-dog buns. The card numbering for this set is essentially in alphabetical order by player's name (after the manager is listed first).

Nm-Mt Ex-Mt
COMPLETE SET (22) 25.00 10.00
1 Harvey Kuenn MG 1.50 .60
2 Dwight Bernard .75 .30
3 Mark Brouhard .75 .30
4 Mike Caldwell 1.00 .40
5 Cecil Cooper 1.50 .60
6 Marshall Edwards .75 .30
7 Rollie Fingers 3.00 1.20
8 Jim Gantner 1.25 .50
9 Moose Haas .75 .30
10 Bob McClure .75 .30
11 Paul Molitor 10.00 4.00
12 Don Money 1.00 .40
13 Charlie Moore 1.00 .40
14 Ben Oglivie 1.25 .50
15 Ed Romero .75 .30
16 Ted Simmons 1.50 .60
17 Jim Slaton .75 .30
18 Don Sutton 3.00 1.20
19 Gorman Thomas 1.50 .60
20 Pete Vuckovich 1.25 .50
21 Ned Yost 1.00 .40
22 Robin Yount 8.00 3.20

1983 Brewers Police

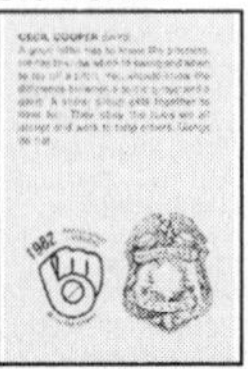

The cards in this 30-card set measure approximately 2 13/16" by 4 1/8". The 1983 Police Milwaukee Brewers set contains full color cards issued by the Milwaukee Police Department in conjunction with the Brewers. The cards are numbered on the fronts by the player uniform number and contain the line, "The Milwaukee Police Department Presents the 1983 Milwaukee Braves." The backs contain a brief narrative attributable to the player on the front, the Milwaukee Police logo, and a Milwaukee Brewers logo stating that they were the 1982 American League Champions. In all, 28 variations of these Police sets have been found to date. Prices below are for the basic set without regard to the Police Department listed on the backs of the cards; cards from the more obscure corners and small towns of Wisconsin (whose cards were produced in lesser quantities) will be valued higher.

Nm-Mt Ex-Mt
COMPLETE SET (30) 12.00 4.80
4 Paul Molitor 4.00 1.60
5 Ned Yost .50 .20
7 Don Money .50 .20
8 Rob Picciolo .25 .10
10 Bob McClure .25 .10
11 Ed Romero .25 .10
13 Roy Howell .25 .10
15 Cecil Cooper .75 .30
16 Marshall Edwards .25 .10
17 Jim Gantner .75 .30
19 Robin Yount 3.00 1.20
20 Gorman Thomas 1.00 .40
21 Don Sutton 1.50 .60
22 Charlie Moore .25 .10
23 Ted Simmons 1.00 .40
24 Ben Oglivie .50 .20
26 Bob Skube .25 .10
27 Pete Ladd .25 .10
28 Jamie Easterly .25 .10
30 Moose Haas .25 .10
32 Harvey Kuenn MG .50 .20
34 Rollie Fingers 1.50 .60
40 Bob L. Gibson .25 .10
41 Jim Slaton .25 .10
42 Tom Tellmann .25 .10
46 Jerry Augustine .25 .10
48 Mike Caldwell .50 .20
50 Pete Vuckovich .50 .20
NNO Pat Dobson CO .50 .20
Ron Hansen CO
Larry Haney CO
Dave Garcia CO
NNO Team Photo CL .50 .20

1984 Brewers Gardner's

The cards in this 22-card set measure 2 1/2" by 3 1/2". For the second year in a row, the Gardner Bakery Company issued a set of cards available in packages of Gardner Bakery products. The set was manufactured by Topps, and the backs of the cards are identical to the Topps cards of this year except for the numbers. The Gardner logo appears on the

fronts of the cards with the player's name, position abbreviation, the name Brewers, and the words 1984 Series II. The card numbering for this set is essentially in alphabetical order by player's name (after the manager is listed first).

Nm-Mt Ex-Mt
COMPLETE SET (22) 12.00 4.80
1 Rene Lachemann MG .25 .10
2 Mark Brouhard .25 .10
3 Mike Caldwell .50 .20
4 Bobby Clark .25 .10
5 Cecil Cooper 1.00 .40
6 Rollie Fingers 2.00 .80
7 Jim Gantner .75 .30
8 Moose Haas .25 .10
9 Roy Howell .25 .10
10 Pete Ladd .25 .10
11 Rick Manning .25 .10
12 Bob McClure .25 .10
13 Paul Molitor 4.00 1.60
14 Charlie Moore .50 .20
15 Ben Oglivie .75 .30
16 Ed Romero .25 .10
17 Ted Simmons 1.00 .40
18 Jim Sundberg .50 .20
19 Don Sutton 2.00 .80
20 Tom Tellmann .25 .10
21 Pete Vuckovich .75 .30
22 Robin Yount 3.00 1.20

1984 Brewers Mr Z's Pizza

These cards were issued as part of a set of Milwaukee Brewers issued as pizza inserts during the 1984 season. These cards feature full color photos of the featured Brewers. There may be additions to this checklist so any help is appreciated. Since these cards are unnumbered, we have sequenced them in alphabetical order.

MINT NRMT
COMPLETE SET 8.00 3.60
1 Cecil Cooper 2.00 .90
2 Jim Gantner 1.25 .55
3 Paul Molitor 4.00 1.80
4 Robin Yount 3.00 1.35

1984 Brewers Police

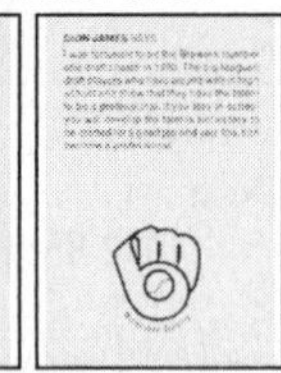

The cards in this 30-card set measure approximately 2 13/16" by 4 1/8". Again this year, the police departments in and around Milwaukee issued sets of the Milwaukee Brewers. Although each set contained the same players and numbers, the individual police departments placed their own name on the fronts of cards to show that they were the particular jurisdiction issuing the set. The backs contain the Brewers logo, a safety tip, and in some cases, a badge of the jurisdiction. To date, 59 variations of this set have been found. Prices below are for the basic set without regard to the Police Department issuing the cards; cards from the more obscure corners and small towns of Wisconsin will be valued higher. Cards are numbered by uniform number.

Nm-Mt Ex-Mt
COMPLETE SET (30) 10.00 4.00
2 Randy Ready .25 .10
4 Paul Molitor 3.00 1.20
8 Jim Sundberg .50 .20
9 Rene Lachemann MG .25 .10
10 Bob McClure .25 .10
11 Ed Romero .25 .10
13 Roy Howell .25 .10
14 Dion James .25 .10
15 Cecil Cooper .75 .30
17 Jim Gantner .75 .30
19 Robin Yount 2.50 1.00
20 Don Sutton 1.50 .60
21 Bill Schroeder .25 .10
22 Charlie Moore .25 .10
23 Ted Simmons 1.00 .40
24 Ben Oglivie .75 .30
25 Bob Clark .25 .10
27 Pete Ladd .25 .10
28 Rick Manning .25 .10
29 Mark Brouhard .25 .10
30 Moose Haas .25 .10
34 Rollie Fingers 1.50 .60
42 Tom Tellmann .25 .10
43 Chuck Porter .25 .10
46 Jerry Augustine .25 .10
47 Jaime Cocanower .25 .10
48 Mike Caldwell .50 .20
50 Pete Vuckovich .50 .20
NNO Dave Garcia CO .25 .10
Pat Dobson CO
Andy Etchebarren CO
Tom Trebelhorn CO
NNO Team Photo CL .50 .20

1985 Brewers Gardner's

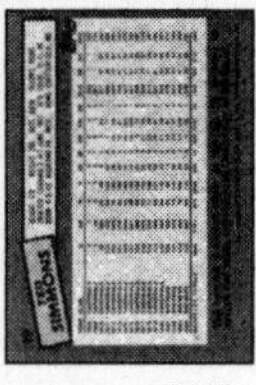

The cards in this 22-card set measure 2 1/2" by 3 1/2". For the third year in a row, the Gardner Bakery Company issued a set of cards available in packages of Gardner Bakery products. The set was manufactured by Topps, and the backs of the cards are identical to the Topps cards of this year except for the card numbers and copyright information. The Gardner logo appears on the fronts of the cards with the player's name, position abbreviation, and the name Brewers. The card numbering for this set is essentially in alphabetical order.

Nm-Mt Ex-Mt
COMPLETE SET (22) 10.00 4.00
1 George Bamberger MG .50 .20
2 Mark Brouhard .25 .10
3 Bobby Clark .25 .10
4 Jaime Cocanower .25 .10
5 Cecil Cooper 1.00 .40
6 Rollie Fingers 1.50 .60
7 Jim Gantner .75 .30
8 Moose Haas .25 .10
9 Dion James .25 .10
10 Pete Ladd .25 .10
11 Rick Manning .25 .10
12 Bob McClure .25 .10
13 Paul Molitor 4.00 1.60
14 Charlie Moore .50 .20
15 Ben Oglivie .75 .30
16 Chuck Porter .25 .10
17 Ed Romero .25 .10
18 Bill Schroeder .25 .10
19 Ted Simmons 1.00 .40
20 Tom Tellmann .25 .10
21 Pete Vuckovich .75 .30
22 Robin Yount 3.00 1.20

1985 Brewers Police

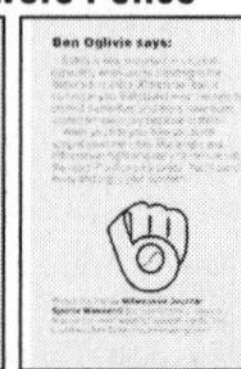

The cards in this 30-card set measure 2 3/4" by 4 1/8". Again this year, the police departments in and around Milwaukee issued sets of the Milwaukee Brewers. The backs contain the Brewers logo, a safety tip, and in some cases, a badge of the jurisdiction. Prices below are for the basic set without regard to the Police Department issuing the cards; cards from the more obscure corners and small towns of Wisconsin (smaller production) will be valued higher. Cards are numbered by uniform number.

Nm-Mt Ex-Mt
COMPLETE SET (30) 8.00 3.20
2 Randy Ready .25 .10
4 Paul Molitor 3.00 1.20
5 Doug Loman .25 .10
7 Paul Householder .25 .10
10 Bob McClure .25 .10
11 Ed Romero .25 .10
14 Dion James .25 .10
15 Cecil Cooper 1.00 .40
17 Jim Gantner .75 .30
18 Danny Darwin .25 .10
19 Robin Yount 2.00 .80
21 Bill Schroeder .25 .10
22 Charlie Moore .25 .10
23 Ted Simmons 1.00 .40
24 Ben Oglivie .50 .20
26 Brian Giles .25 .10
27 Pete Ladd .25 .10
28 Rick Manning .25 .10
29 Mark Brouhard .25 .10
30 Moose Haas .25 .10
31 George Bamberger MG .50 .20
34 Rollie Fingers 1.50 .60
40 Bob L. Gibson .25 .10
41 Ray Searage .25 .10
47 Jaime Cocanower .25 .10
48 Ray Burris .25 .10
49 Ted Higuera .50 .20
50 Pete Vuckovich .50 .20
NNO Team Roster .25 .10
NNO Herm Sterrette CO .25 .10
Tony Muser CO
Frank Howard CO
Larry Haney CO
Andy Etchebarren CO
NNO Newspaper Carrier .25 .10

1986 Brewers Greats TCMA

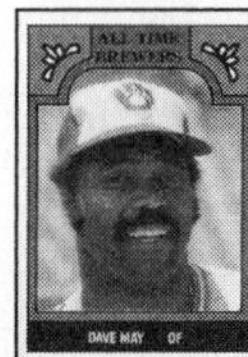

This 12-card standard-size set honors the best retired Brewers of the first two decades. The fronts have a player photo and position while the backs have vital statistics, career information and lifetime statistics.

Nm-Mt Ex-Mt
COMPLETE SET (12) 3.00 1.20
1 George Scott .50 .20
2 Pedro Garcia .25 .10
3 Tim Johnson .25 .10
4 Don Money .25 .10
5 Sixto Lezcano .25 .10
6 John Briggs .25 .10
7 Dave May .25 .10
8 Darrell Porter .50 .20
9 Jim Colborn .25 .10
10 Mike Caldwell .50 .20
11 Rollie Fingers 1.00 .40
12 Harvey Kuenn MG .50 .20

1986 Brewers Police

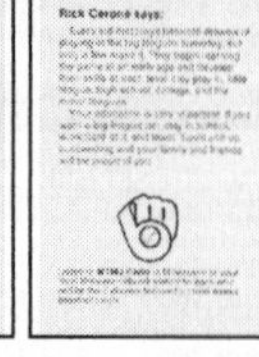

This 32-card safety set was also sponsored by WTMJ Radio and Kinney Shoes. The backs contain the usual biographical info and safety tip. The front features a full-color photo of the player, his name, position, and uniform number. The cards measure approximately 2 5/8" by 4 1/8". Cards were freely distributed throughout the summer by the Police Departments in the Milwaukee area. Cards are numbered in alphabetical order.

Nm-Mt Ex-Mt
COMPLETE SET (32) 8.00 3.20
1 George Bamberger MG .25 .10
2 Juan Castillo .25 .10
3 Rick Cerone .25 .10
4 Mark Clear .25 .10
5 Jaime Cocanower .25 .10
6 Cecil Cooper .75 .30
7 Danny Darwin .25 .10
8 Rob Deer .25 .10
9 Mike Felder .25 .10
10 Jim Gantner .25 .10
11 Ted Higuera .50 .20
12 Paul Householder .25 .10
13 Tim Leary .25 .10
14 Rick Manning .25 .10
15 Bob McClure .25 .10
16 Paul Molitor 3.00 1.20
17 Charlie Moore .25 .10
18 Juan Nieves .25 .10
19 Ben Oglivie .50 .20
20 Dan Plesac .50 .20
21 Chuck Porter .25 .10
22 Randy Ready .25 .10
23 Ernest Riles .25 .10
24 Billy Jo Robidoux .25 .10
25 Bill Schroeder .25 .10
26 Ray Searage .25 .10
27 Bill Wegman .25 .10
28 Robin Yount 2.00 .80
29 Andy Etchebarren CO .25 .10
Larry Haney CO
Frank Howard CO
Tony Muser CO
Herm Starrette CO
30 Milwaukee Brewers .25 .10

1987 Brewers Police

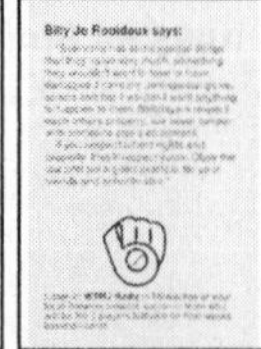

This 30-card safety set was also sponsored by WTMJ Radio and Kinney Shoes. The backs contain the usual biographical info and safety tip. The front features a full-color photo of the player, his name, position, and uniform number. The cards measure approximately 2 5/8" by 4 1/8". Cards were freely distributed throughout the summer by the Police Departments in the Milwaukee area and throughout other parts of Wisconsin. Cards are numbered below by uniform number. Bosio comes as card number #26 or card#29, there is no difference in the values of the Bosio cards.

Nm-Mt Ex-Mt
COMPLETE SET (30) 8.00 3.20
1 Ernest Riles .25 .10
2 Edgar Diaz .25 .10
3 Juan Castillo .25 .10
4 Paul Molitor 2.50 1.00
5 B.J. Surhoff 2.00 .80
7 Dale Sveum .25 .10
9 Greg Brock .25 .10
13 Billy Joe Robidoux .25 .10
14 Jim Paciorek .25 .10
15 Cecil Cooper .75 .30
16 Mike Felder .25 .10
17 Jim Gantner .75 .30
19 Robin Yount 2.00 .80
20 Juan Nieves .25 .10
21 Bill Schroeder .25 .10
25 Mark Clear .25 .10
26 Glenn Braggs .25 .10
28 Chris Bosio .25 .10
28 Rick Manning .25 .10
29 Chris Bosio .50 .20

Card	Nm-Mt	Ex-Mt
32 Chuck Crim	.25	.10
34 Mark Ciardi	.25	.10
37 Dan Plesac	.50	.20
38 John Henry Johnson	.25	.10
40 Mike Birkbeck	.25	.10
42 Tom Trebelhorn MG	.25	.10
45 Rob Deer	.50	.20
46 Bill Wegman	.25	.10
49 Teddy Higuera	.25	.10
NNO Andy Etchebarren CO	.25	.10
Larry Haney CO		
Chuck Hartenstein CO		
Dave Hilton CO		
Tony Muser CO		
NNO Brewers Team CL	.50	.20

1987 Brewers Team Issue

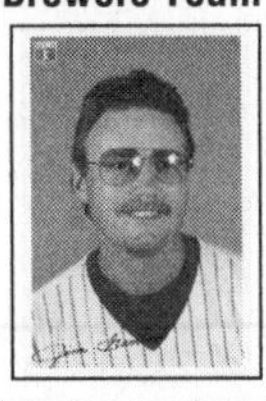

These cards feature members of the 1987 Milwaukee Brewers. These cards are unnumbered and we have checklisted them below in alphabetical order.

	Nm-Mt	Ex-Mt
COMPLETE SET (16)	6.00	2.40
1 Glenn Braggs	.25	.10
2 Greg Brock	.25	.10
3 Mark Clear	.25	.10
4 Cecil Cooper	.75	.30
5 Rob Deer	.25	.10
6 Jim Gantner	.75	.30
7 Teddy Higuera	.25	.10
8 Paul Molitor	2.50	1.00
9 Juan Nieves	.25	.10
10 Dan Plesac	.50	.20
11 Billy Jo Robidoux	.25	.10
12 Bill Schroeder	.25	.10
13 B.J. Surhoff	1.50	.60
14 Dale Sveum	.25	.10
15 Bill Wegman	.25	.10
16 Robin Yount	1.50	.60

1988 Brewers Police

This 30-card safety set was also sponsored by WTMJ Radio and Stadia Athletic Shoes. The backs contain the usual biographical info and safety tip. The front features a full-color photo of the player, his name, position, and uniform number. The cards measure approximately 2 7/8" by 4 1/8". Cards were freely distributed throughout the summer by the Police Departments in the Milwaukee area and throughout other parts of Wisconsin. Cards are numbered below by uniform number.

	Nm-Mt	Ex-Mt
COMPLETE SET (30)	6.00	2.40
1 Ernest Riles	.25	.10
3 Juan Castillo	.25	.10
4 Paul Molitor	2.50	1.00
5 B.J. Surhoff	1.50	.60
7 Dale Sveum	.25	.10
9 Greg Brock	.25	.10
11 Charlie O'Brien	.25	.10
14 Jim Adduci	.25	.10
16 Mike Felder	.25	.10
17 Jim Gantner	.75	.30
19 Robin Yount	1.50	.60
20 Juan Nieves	.25	.10
21 Bill Schroeder	.25	.10
23 Joey Meyer	.25	.10
25 Mark Clear	.25	.10
26 Glenn Braggs	.25	.10
28 Odell Jones	.25	.10
29 Chris Bosio	.25	.10
30 Steve Kiefer	.25	.10
32 Chuck Crim	.25	.10
33 Jay Aldrich	.25	.10
37 Dan Plesac	.50	.20
40 Mike Birkbeck	.25	.10
42 Tom Trebelhorn MG	.25	.10
43 Dave Stapleton	.25	.10
45 Rob Deer	.50	.20
46 Bill Wegman	.25	.10
49 Ted Higuera	.25	.10
NNO Team Photo HOR	.50	.20
NNO Andy Etchebarren CO	.25	.10
Larry Haney CO		
Chuck Hartenstein CO		
Dave Hilton CO		
Tony Muser CO		

1988 Brewers Team Issue

This 37-card set of the 1988 Milwaukee Brewers features black-and-white player portraits with white borders and measures approximately 4" by 5 1/2". The backs are blank. The cards are unnumbered and checklisted below in alphabetical order.

	Nm-Mt	Ex-Mt
COMPLETE SET (37)	10.00	4.00
1 Jim Adduci	.25	.10
2 Don August	.25	.10
3 Mike Birkbeck	.25	.10
4 Chris Bosio	.25	.10
5 Glenn Braggs	.25	.10
6 Greg Brock	.25	.10
7 Juan Castillo	.25	.10
8 Mark Clear	.25	.10
9 Chuck Crim	.25	.10
10 Rob Deer	.25	.10
11 Andy Etchebarren CO	.25	.10
12 Mike Felder	.25	.10
13 Tom Filer	.25	.10
14 Jim Gantner	.75	.30
15 Darryl Hamilton	.25	.10
16 Larry Haney CO	.25	.10
17 Chuck Hartenstein CO	.25	.10
18 Ted Higuera	.25	.10
19 Dave Hilton CO	.25	.10
20 Odell Jones	.25	.10
21 Steve Kiefer	.25	.10
22 Jeffrey Leonard	.25	.10
23 Joey Meyer	.25	.10
24 Paul Mirabella	.25	.10
25 Paul Molitor	1.50	.60
26 Tony Muser CO	.25	.10
27 Juan Nieves	.25	.10
28 Charlie O'Brien	.25	.10
29 Dan Plesac	.25	.10
30 Billy Jo Robidoux	.25	.10
31 Bill Schroeder	.25	.10
32 Dave Stapleton	.25	.10
33 B.J. Surhoff	1.00	.40
34 Dale Sveum	.25	.10
35 Tom Trebelhorn MG	.25	.10
36 Bill Wegman	.25	.10
37 Robin Yount	1.25	.50

1989 Brewers Gardner's

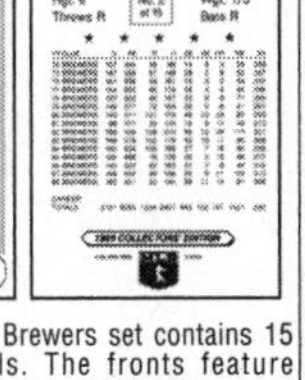

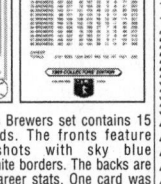

The 1989 Gardner's Brewers set contains 15 standard-size cards. The fronts feature airbrushed mugshots with sky blue backgrounds and white borders. The backs are white and feature career stats. One card was distributed in each specially marked Gardner's bakery product. Cards were issued during the middle of the season. For some reason Riles is included in the set even though he had been traded by the Brewers during the 1988 season.

	Nm-Mt	Ex-Mt
COMPLETE SET (15)	12.50	5.00
1 Paul Molitor	6.00	2.40
2 Robin Yount	4.00	1.60
3 Jim Gantner	1.00	.40
4 Rob Deer	.50	.20
5 B.J. Surhoff	1.50	.60
6 Dale Sveum	.50	.20
7 Ted Higuera	.50	.20
8 Dan Plesac	.75	.30
9 Bill Wegman	.50	.20
10 Juan Nieves	.50	.20
11 Greg Brock	.50	.20
12 Glenn Braggs	.50	.20
13 Joey Meyer	.50	.20
14 Earnest Riles	.50	.20
15 Don August	.50	.20

1989 Brewers Police

The 1989 Police Milwaukee Brewers set contains 30 cards measuring approximately 2 3/4" by 4 1/4". The fronts have color photos with white borders; the backs feature safety tips. The unnumbered cards were given away by various local Wisconsin police departments. The cards are numbered below by uniform number.

	Nm-Mt	Ex-Mt
COMPLETE SET (30)	8.00	3.20
1 Gary Sheffield	4.00	1.60
4 Paul Molitor	2.50	1.00
5 B.J. Surhoff	1.00	.40
6 Bill Spiers	.25	.10
7 Dale Sveum	.25	.10
9 Greg Brock	.25	.10
14 Gus Polidor	.25	.10
16 Mike Felder	.25	.10
17 Jim Gantner	.75	.30
19 Robin Yount	2.00	.80
20 Juan Nieves	.25	.10
22 Charlie O'Brien	.25	.10
23 Joey Meyer	.25	.10
25 Dave Engle	.25	.10
26 Glenn Braggs	.25	.10
27 Paul Mirabella	.25	.10
29 Chris Bosio	.25	.10
30 Terry Francona	.50	.20
32 Chuck Crim	.25	.10
37 Dan Plesac	.25	.10
38 Don August	.25	.10
40 Mike Birkbeck	.25	.10
41 Mark Knudson	.25	.10
42 Tom Trebelhorn MG	.25	.10
45 Rob Deer	.25	.10
46 Bill Wegman	.25	.10
48 Bryan Clutterbuck	.25	.10
49 Teddy Higuera	.25	.10
NNO Team Card CL	.50	.20
NNO Duffy Dyer CO	.25	.10
Andy Etchebarren CO		
Larry Haney CO		
Chuck Hartenstein CO		
Tony Muser CO		

1989 Brewers Yearbook

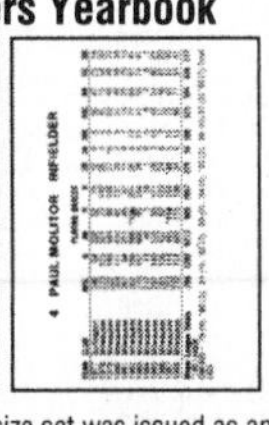

This 18-card standard size set was issued as an insert in the 1989 Milwaukee Brewer Yearbooks. The yearbook itself had a suggested retail price of 4.95. The card set features 17 of the Brewers and their manager. The cards are dominated by a full-color photo of the player on the top two-thirds of the cards along with the uniform number name and position underneath the player. There is also a large logo on the bottom right of the card commemorating the twentieth anniversary of the Brewers in Milwaukee. The backs only contain the player's name and their career statistics. The set is checklisted below by uniform numbers.

	Nm-Mt	Ex-Mt
COMPLETE SET (18)	10.00	4.00
1 Gary Sheffield	4.00	1.60
4 Paul Molitor	3.00	1.20
5 B.J. Surhoff	1.00	.40
7 Dale Sveum	.25	.10
9 Greg Brock	.25	.10
17 Jim Gantner	.75	.30
19 Robin Yount	2.00	.80
20 Juan Nieves	.25	.10
26 Glenn Braggs	.25	.10
29 Chris Bosio	.25	.10
32 Chuck Crim	.25	.10
37 Dan Plesac	.50	.20
38 Don August	.25	.10
40 Mike Birkbeck	.25	.10
42 Tom Trebelhorn MG	.25	.10
45 Rob Deer	.25	.10
46 Bill Wegman	.25	.10
49 Ted Higuera	.25	.10

1990 Brewers Miller Brewing

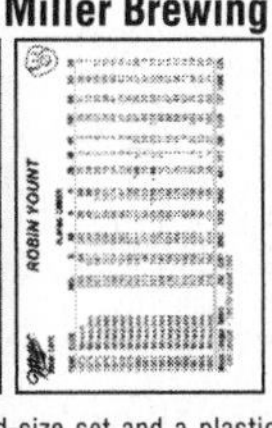

This 32-card standard-size set and a plastic binder were sponsored by Miller Brewing Co. and given away to the first 25,000 adults (21 years and older) attending the Brewers' home game against the White Sox on August 4th. The fronts have either action or posed color player photos, with the player's name and position given in white lettering on a black stripe at the bottom of the card face. The backs have biographical information and player statistics. The cards are unnumbered and checklisted below in alphabetical order. The complete set price below does not include the binder.

	Nm-Mt	Ex-Mt
COMPLETE SET (32)	20.00	6.00
1 Chris Bosio	.25	.07
2 Greg Brock	.25	.07
3 Chuck Crim	.25	.07
4 Rob Deer	.25	.07
5 Edgar Diaz	.25	.07
6 Tom Edens	.25	.07
7 Mike Felder	.25	.07
8 Tom Filer	.25	.07
9 Jim Gantner	.75	.23
10 Darryl Hamilton	.50	.15
11 Teddy Higuera	.25	.07
12 Mark Knudson	.25	.07
13 Bill Krueger	.25	.07
14 Paul Mirabella	.25	.07
15 Paul Molitor	8.00	2.40
16 Jaime Navarro	.25	.07
17 Charlie O'Brien	.25	.07
18 Dave Parker	1.00	.30
19 Dan Plesac	.25	.07
20 Dennis Powell	.25	.07
21 Ron Robinson	.25	.07
22 Bob Sebra	.25	.07
23 Gary Sheffield	3.00	.90
24 Bill Spiers	.25	.07
25 B.J. Surhoff	1.00	.30
26 Dale Sveum	.25	.07
27 Tom Trebelhorn MG	.25	.07
28 Greg Vaughn	1.50	.45
29 Randy Veres	.25	.07
30 Bill Wegman	.25	.07
31 Robin Yount	6.00	1.80
32 Don Baylor CO	.50	.15
Ray Burris CO		
Duffy Dyer CO		
Andy Etchebarren CO		
Larry Haney CO		
XX Album	1.00	.30

1990 Brewers Police

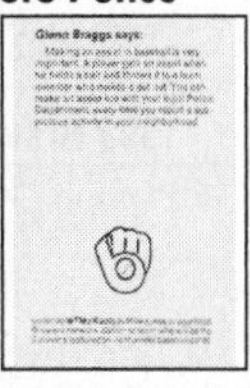

This 30-card police set was issued in conjunction with the Fan Appreciation store of Waukesha, Wisconsin and the Waukesha Police department. This set measures approximately 2 13/16" by 4 1/8" and is checklisted in alphabetical order. The front of the card is a full-color photo surrounded by a blue border while the back has anti-crime tips.

	Nm-Mt	Ex-Mt
COMPLETE SET (30)	8.00	2.40
1 Don August	.25	.07
2 Billy Bates	.25	.07
3 Chris Bosio	.25	.07
4 Glenn Braggs	.25	.07
5 Greg Brock	.25	.07
6 Chuck Crim	.25	.07
7 Rob Deer	.25	.07
8 Eddie Diaz	.25	.07
9 Mike Felder	.25	.07
10 Tom Filer	.25	.07
11 Tony Fossas	.25	.07
12 Jim Gantner	.50	.15
13 Ted Higuera	.25	.07
14 Mark Knudson	.25	.07
15 Paul Mirabella	.25	.07
16 Paul Molitor	2.00	.60
17 Jaime Navarro	.25	.07
18 Charlie O'Brien	.25	.07
19 Dave Parker	1.00	.30
20 Dan Plesac	.25	.07
21 Gus Polidor	.25	.07
22 Gary Sheffield	1.50	.45
23 B.J. Surhoff	.50	.15
24 Dale Sveum	.25	.07
25 Tom Trebelhorn MG	.25	.07
26 Greg Vaughn	1.00	.30
27 Robin Yount	1.50	.45
28 Don Baylor CO	.50	.15
Ray Burris CO		
Duffy Dyer CO		
Andy Etchebarren CO		
Larry Haney CO		
29 Milwaukee Brewers	.50	.15

1991 Brewers Miller Brewing

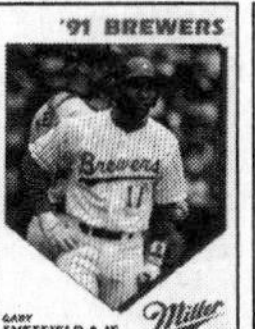

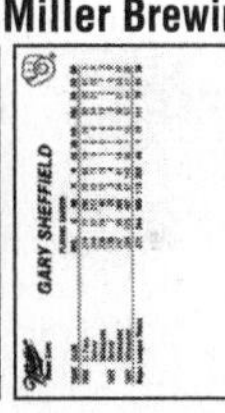

This 32-card set was sponsored by the Miller Brewing Company, and the company logo appears in red lettering at the lower right corner of the front. The sets were given away at the Brewers' home game against the Baltimore Orioles on August 17. The standard-size cards feature on the fronts color action player photos inside a pentagonal-shaped design that resembles home plate. A black border on the right side of the pentagon creates the impression of a shadow. The words "91 Brewers" appears in bluish-purple lettering above the photo, with player information given in black lettering in the lower left corner of the card face. The backs are printed in black and present complete Major League statistics. The cards are unnumbered and checklisted below in alphabetical order, with the coaches' card listed at the end.

	Nm-Mt	Ex-Mt
COMPLETE SET (32)	12.00	3.60
1 Don August	.25	.07
2 Jim Austin	.25	.07
3 Dante Bichette	1.00	.30
4 Chris Bosio	.25	.07
5 Kevin D. Brown	.25	.07
6 Chuck Crim	.25	.07
7 Rick Dempsey	.50	.15
8 Jim Gantner	.75	.23
9 Darryl Hamilton	.25	.07
10 Teddy Higuera	.25	.07
11 Darren Holmes	.25	.07
12 Jim Hunter	.25	.07
13 Mark Knudson	.25	.07
14 Mark Lee	.25	.07
15 Julio Machado	.25	.07
16 Candy Maldonado	.25	.07
17 Paul Molitor	5.00	1.50
18 Jaime Navarro	.25	.07
19 Edwin Nunez	.25	.07
20 Dan Plesac	.50	.15
21 Willie Randolph	.75	.23
22 Ron Robinson	.25	.07
23 Gary Sheffield	3.00	.90
24 Bill Spiers	.25	.07
25 Franklin Stubbs	.25	.07
26 B.J. Surhoff	1.00	.30
27 Dale Sveum	.25	.07
28 Tom Trebelhorn MG	.25	.07
29 Greg Vaughn	.50	.15
30 Bill Wegman	.25	.07
31 Robin Yount	4.00	1.20
32 Don Baylor CO	.50	.15
Fred Stanley CO		
Duffy Dyer CO		
Larry Haney CO		
Andy Etchebarren CO		
Ray Burris CO		
XX Album	1.00	.30

1991 Brewers Police

This 30-card standard-size set was sponsored by the Waukesha Police Department, Waukesha Sportscards, and Delicious Brand Cookies and Crackers. These sponsors are mentioned at the bottom of both sides of the card.

	Nm-Mt	Ex-Mt
COMPLETE SET (30)	8.00	2.40
1 Don August	.25	.07
2 Dante Bichette	1.00	.30
3 Chris Bosio	.25	.07
4 Greg Brock	.25	.07
5 Kevin D. Brown	.25	.07
6 Chuck Crim	.25	.07
7 Rick Dempsey	.50	.15
8 Jim Gantner	.75	.23
9 Darryl Hamilton	.50	.15
10 Teddy Higuera	.25	.07
11 Mark Lee	.25	.07
12 Mark Knudson	.25	.07
13 Julio Machado	.25	.07
14 Candy Maldonado	.25	.07
15 Paul Molitor	2.50	.75
16 Jaime Navarro	.25	.07
17 Edwin Nunez	.25	.07
18 Dan Plesac	.25	.07
19 Willie Randolph	.75	.23
20 Ron Robinson	.25	.07
20 Gary Sheffield	2.00	.60
21 Bill Spiers	.25	.07
22 Franklin Stubbs	.25	.07
23 B.J. Surhoff	1.00	.30
24 Dale Sveum	.25	.07
25 Tom Trebelhorn MG	.25	.07
26 Greg Vaughn	1.00	.30
27 Bill Wegman	.25	.07
28 Robin Yount	2.00	.60
NNO0 Don Baylor CO	.50	.15
Ray Burris CO		
Duffy Dyer CO		
Andy Etchebarren CO		
Larry Haney CO		
Fred Stanley CO		

1992 Brewers Carlson Travel

This 31-card standard-size set was sponsored by Carlson Travel in conjunction with United Airlines and TV Channel 6 (WITI in Milwaukee). It was issued to commemorate the 1982 Milwaukee Brewers team who played in the World Series. The set included a travel coupon entitling the holder to 50.00 off per couple on the next cruise vacation. The cards are unnumbered and checklisted below in alphabetical order.

	Nm-Mt	Ex-Mt
COMPLETE SET (31)	12.50	3.70
1 Jerry Augustine	.25	.07
2 Dwight Bernard	.25	.07
3 Mark Brouhard	.25	.07
4 Mike Caldwell	.50	.15
5 Cecil Cooper	.75	.23
6 Marshall Edwards	.25	.07
7 Rollie Fingers	2.00	.60
8 Jim Gantner	.75	.23
9 Moose Haas	.25	.07
10 Roy Howell	.25	.07
11 Harvey Kuenn MG	.50	.15
12 Pete Ladd	.25	.07
13 Bob McClure	.25	.07
14 Doc Medich	.25	.07
15 Paul Molitor	4.00	1.20
16 Don Money	.50	.15
17 Charlie Moore	.25	.07
18 Ben Oglivie	.75	.23
19 Ed Romero	.25	.07
20 Ted Simmons	1.00	.30
21 Jim Slaton	.25	.07
22 Don Sutton	2.00	.60
23 Gorman Thomas	.75	.23
24 Pete Vuckovich	.50	.15
25 Ned Yost	.25	.07
26 Robin Yount	3.00	.90
xx Bernie Brewer	.25	.07
(Team Mascot)		
XX Larry Haney CO	.25	.07
Ron Hansen CO		
Harry Warner CO		
Cal McLish CO		
Pat Dobson CO		
XX Cecil Cooper PS	.50	.15
xx Team Photo	.50	.15
xx Carlson Travel Coupon	.25	.07

1992 Brewers Police

For the second consecutive year, this 30-card standard-size set was sponsored by the

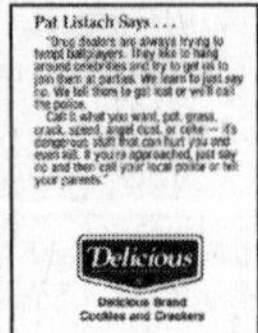

Waukesha Police Department, Waukesha Sports Cards, and Delicious Brand Cookies and Crackers. The cards are unnumbered and checklisted below in alphabetical order.

	Nm-Mt	Ex-Mt
COMPLETE SET (30)	8.00	2.40
1 Andy Allanson	.25	.07
2 Jim Austin	.25	.07
3 Dante Bichette	1.00	.30
4 Ricky Bones	.25	.07
5 Chris Bosio	.25	.07
6 Mike Fetters	.25	.07
7 Scott Fletcher	.25	.07
8 Jim Gantner	.75	.23
9 Phil Garner MG	.25	.07
10 Darryl Hamilton	.25	.07
11 Doug Henry	.25	.07
12 Teddy Higuera	.25	.07
13 Pat Listach	.25	.07
14 Tim McIntosh	.25	.07
15 Paul Molitor	2.50	.75
16 Jaime Navarro	.25	.07
17 Edwin Nunez	.25	.07
18 Jesse Orosco	.50	.15
19 Dan Plesac	.25	.07
20 Ron Robinson	.25	.07
21 Bruce Ruffin	.25	.07
22 Kevin Seitzer	.50	.15
23 Bill Spiers	.25	.07
24 Franklin Stubbs	.25	.07
25 William Suero	.25	.07
26 B.J. Surhoff	1.00	.30
27 Greg Vaughn	.50	.15
28 Bill Wegman	.25	.07
29 Robin Yount	2.00	.60
30 Mike Easler CO Bill Castro CO Don Rowe CO Duffy Dyer CO Tim Foli CO	.25	.07

1992 Brewers Sentry Yount

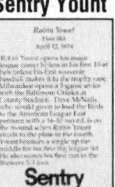

Sponsored by Sentry Foods, this four-card standard-size card captures four moments in the career of Robin Yount, who reached 3,000 career hits during the 1992 season. The cards are unnumbered and checklisted below in chronological order.

	Nm-Mt	Ex-Mt
COMPLETE SET (4)	15.00	4.50
COMMON CARD (1-4)	4.00	1.20

1993 Brewers Police

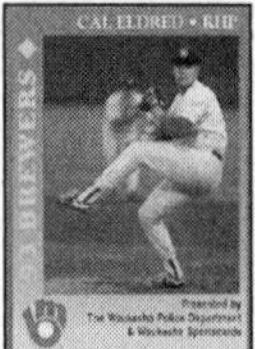

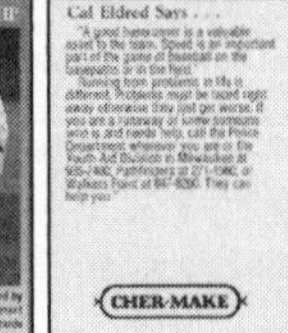

This 30-card standard-size set was sponsored by the Waukesha Police Department, Waukesha Sportscards, and Cher-Make. The fronts display a color action photo on a blue background and are edged in blue. The player's name and position appear in white lettering at the top with "'93 Brewers" and the team logo printed in yellow along the left edge. The sponsors are listed at the bottom of the card. The backs have black print on a white background and feature public service tips from the players. The Cher-Make logo is carried on the bottom. The cards are unnumbered and checklisted below in alphabetical order.

	Nm-Mt	Ex-Mt
COMPLETE SET (30)	8.00	2.40
1 Jim Austin	.25	.07
2 Ricky Bones	.25	.07
3 Tom Brunansky	.50	.15
4 Alex Diaz	.25	.07
5 Bill Doran	.25	.07
6 Cal Eldred	.25	.07
7 Mike Fetters	.25	.07
8 Phil Garner MG	.25	.07
9 Darryl Hamilton	.25	.07
10 Doug Henry	.25	.07
11 Ted Higuera	.25	.07
12 John Jaha	.25	.07
13 Mark Kiefer	.25	.07
14 Joe Kmak	.25	.07
15 Pat Listach	.25	.07
16 Graeme Lloyd	.50	.15
17 Tim McIntosh	.25	.07
18 Jaime Navarro	.25	.07
19 Dave Nilsson	.50	.15
20 Jesse Orosco	.50	.15
21 Kevin Reimer	.25	.07
22 Bill Spiers	.25	.07
23 William Suero	.25	.07
24 B.J. Surhoff	1.00	.30
25 Dickie Thon	.25	.07
26 Greg Vaughn	1.00	.30
27 Bill Wegman	.25	.07
28 Robin Yount	2.00	.60
29 Robin Yount MM	1.00	.30
NNO Title Card	.25	.07

1993 Brewers Sentry

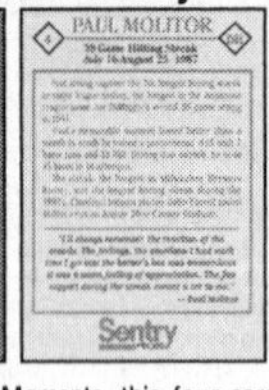

Subtitled "Memorable Moments, this four-card standard-size set was sponsored by Sentry Foods and features color player photos on its fronts. The pictures are edged with dark blue lines and so are the cards. In the light blue area at the top between these darker lines appear the set subtitle and the Brewers logo. Near the bottom of the photo the player's exploit and its date are printed in gold foil. The year of issue appears at the bottom in a gold-foil diamond set off by a gold-foil stripe on either side. The white back carries the player's name, position, uniform number, exploit, and date at the top. The player's career highlights and a quote appear beneath within a red-lined rectangle. The Sentry logo at the bottom rounds out the back. The cards are unnumbered and checklisted below in alphabetical order.

	Nm-Mt	Ex-Mt
COMPLETE SET (4)	8.00	2.40
1 Paul Molitor	4.00	1.20
2 Juan Nieves	1.00	.30
3 Dale Sveum	1.00	.30
4 Robin Yount	3.00	.90

1994 Brewers Miller Brewing

Produced in perforated booklets, these Brewers cards were supposed to be issued in four sets to fans attending four different Brewers games at Milwaukee County Stadium. Set 1 (1-94) was issued at the April 24 game vs. Kansas City; set 2 (95-188) was issued at the June 26 game vs. Boston. Sets 3 (189-282) and 4 (283-376) were to be issued at later games (August 21 vs. Oakland; September 18 vs. Detroit), but the intervention of the baseball strike postponed their release. All four sets combined would include every player in the Brewers' 25-year history. The perforated booklets measure approximately 13" by 7" and each contains 94 cards; the individual cards measure the standard size. The gold-bordered cards feature on their fronts black-and-white player head shots. The player's name appears in black lettering within a white bar at the bottom. The white back carries the player's name, biography, years with the Brewers, and statistics therefrom. The cards are unnumbered and checklisted below in alphabetical order within each set. The final two series were released early in 1995.

	Nm-Mt	Ex-Mt
COMPLETE SET (376)	40.00	12.00
1 Hank Aaron	5.00	1.50
2 Jim Adduci	.10	.03
3 Jay Aldrich	.10	.03
4 Andy Allanson	.10	.03
5 Dave Baldwin	.10	.03
6 Sal Bando	.40	.12
7 Len Barker	.10	.03
8 Kevin Bass	.10	.03
9 Ken Berry	.10	.03
10 George Canale	.10	.03
11 Tom Candiotti	.30	.09
12 Mike Capel	.10	.03
13 Bobby Darwin	.10	.03
14 Danny Darwin	.10	.03
15 Brock Davis	.10	.03
16 Dick Davis	.10	.03
17 Jamie Easterly	.10	.03
18 Tom Edens	.10	.03
19 Marshall Edwards	.10	.03
20 Cal Eldred	.20	.06
21 Rob Ellis	.10	.03
22 Ed Farmer	.10	.03
23 Mike Felder	.10	.03
24 John Felske	.10	.03
25 Mike Ferraro	.10	.03
26 Mike Fetters	.10	.03
27 Danny Frisella	.10	.03
28 Bob Galasso	.10	.03
29 Jim Gantner	.40	.12
30 Pedro Garcia	.10	.03
31 Rob Gardner	.10	.03
32 John Gelnar	.10	.03
33 Moose Haas	.10	.03
34 Darryl Hamilton	.20	.06
35 Larry Haney	.10	.03
36 Jim Hannan	.10	.03
37 Bob Hansen	.10	.03
38 Michael Ignasiak	.10	.03
39 John Jaha	.30	.09
40 Dion James	.10	.03
41 Deron Johnson	.20	.06
42 John Henry Johnson	.10	.03
43 Tim Johnson	.10	.03
44 Rickey Keeton	.10	.03
45 John Kennedy	.10	.03
46 Jim Kern	.10	.03
47 Pete Ladd	.10	.03
48 Joe Lahoud	.10	.03
49 Tom Lampkin	.10	.03
50 Dave LaPoint	.10	.03
51 George Lauzerique	.10	.03
52 Julio Machado	.10	.03
53 Alex Madrid	.10	.03
54 Candy Maldonado	.10	.03
55 Carlos Maldonado	.10	.03
56 Rick Manning	.10	.03
57 Jaime Navarro	.10	.03
58 Ray Newman	.10	.03
59 Juan Nieves	.10	.03
60 Dave Nilsson	.20	.06
61 Charlie O'Brien	.10	.03
62 Syd O'Brien	.10	.03
63 John O'Donoghue	.10	.03
64 Jim Paciorek	.10	.03
65 Dave Parker	.75	.23
66 Bill Parsons	.10	.03
67 Marty Pattin	.10	.03
68 Jamie Quirk	.10	.03
69 Willie Randolph	.40	.12
70 Paul Ratliff	.10	.03
71 Lance Rautzhan	.10	.03
72 Randy Ready	.10	.03
73 Ray Sadecki	.10	.03
74 Lenn Sakata	.10	.03
75 Ken Sanders	.10	.03
76 Ted Savage	.10	.03
77 Dick Schofield	.10	.03
78 Jim Tatum	.10	.03
79 Chuck Taylor	.10	.03
80 Tom Tellmann	.10	.03
81 Frank Tepedino	.20	.06
82 Sandy Valdespino	.10	.03
83 Jose Valentin	.40	.12
84 Greg Vaughn	.75	.23
85 Carlos Velazquez	.10	.03
86 Rick Waits	.10	.03
87 Danny Walton	.10	.03
88 Floyd Weaver	.10	.03
89 Bill Wegman	.10	.03
90 Floyd Wicker	.10	.03
91 Al Yates	.10	.03
92 Ned Yost	.20	.06
93 Mike Young	.10	.03
94 Robin Yount	3.00	.90
95 Hank Allen	.10	.03
96 Felipe Alou	.75	.23
97 Max Alvis	.10	.03
98 Larry Anderson	.10	.03
99 Rick Auerbach	.10	.03
100 Don August	.10	.03
101 Billy Bates	.10	.03
102 Gary Beare	.10	.03
103 Larry Bearnarth	.10	.03
104 Andy Beene	.10	.03
105 Jerry Bell	.10	.03
106 Juan Bell	.10	.03
107 Dwight Bernard	.10	.03
108 Bernie Carbo	.10	.03
109 Jose Cardenal	.20	.06
110 Matias Carrillo	.10	.03
111 Juan Castillo	.10	.03
112 Bill Castro	.10	.03
113 Rick Cerone	.10	.03
114 Rob Deer	.20	.06
115 Rick Dempsey	.20	.06
116 Alex Diaz	.10	.03
117 Dick Ellsworth	.10	.03
118 Narciso Elvira	.10	.03
119 Tom Filer	.10	.03
120 Rollie Fingers	1.50	.45
121 Scott Fletcher	.10	.03
122 John Flinn	.10	.03
123 Rich Folkers	.10	.03
124 Tony Fossas	.10	.03
125 Chris George	.10	.03
126 Bob L. Gibson	.10	.03
127 Gus Gil	.10	.03
128 Tommy Harper	.20	.06
129 Vic Harris	.10	.03
130 Paul Hartzell	.10	.03
131 Tom Hausman	.10	.03
132 Neal Heaton	.10	.03
133 Mike Hegan	.10	.03
134 Jack Heidemann	.10	.03
135 Doug Jones	.40	.12
136 Mark Kiefer	.10	.03
137 Steve Kiefer	.10	.03
138 Ed Kirkpatrick	.10	.03
139 Joe Kmak	.10	.03
140 Mark Knudson	.10	.03
141 Kevin Kobel	.10	.03
142 Pete Koegel	.10	.03
143 Jack Lazorko	.10	.03
144 Tim Leary	.10	.03
145 Mark Lee	.10	.03
146 Jeffrey Leonard	.10	.03
147 Randy Lerch	.10	.03
148 Brad Lesley	.10	.03
149 Sixto Lezcano	.10	.03
150 Josias Manzanillo	.10	.03
151 Buck Martinez	.20	.06
152 Tom Matchick	.10	.03
153 Dave May	.10	.03
154 Matt Maysey	.10	.03
155 Bob McClure	.10	.03
156 Tim McIntosh	.10	.03
157 Tim Nordbrook	.10	.03
158 Ben Oglivie	.30	.09
159 Troy O'Leary	.40	.12
160 Jim Olander	.10	.03
161 Roberto Pena	.10	.03
162 Jeff Peterek	.10	.03
163 Ray Peters	.10	.03
164 Rob Picciolo	.10	.03
165 Dan Plesac	.20	.06
166 John Poff	.10	.03
167 Gus Polidor	.10	.03
168 Kevin Reimer	.10	.03
169 Andy Replogle	.10	.03
170 Jerry Reuss	.20	.06
171 Archie Reynolds	.10	.03
172 Bob Reynolds	.10	.03
173 Ken Reynolds	.10	.03
174 Tommie Reynolds	.10	.03
175 Ernest Riles	.10	.03
176 Bill Schroeder	.10	.03
177 George Scott	.20	.06
178 Ray Searage	.10	.03
179 Bob Sebra	.10	.03
180 Kevin Seitzer	.30	.09
181 Dick Selma	.10	.03
182 Bill Sharp	.10	.03
183 Ron Theobald	.10	.03
184 Dan Thomas	.10	.03
185 Gorman Thomas	.40	.12
186 Randy Veres	.10	.03
187 Bill Voss	.10	.03
188 Jim Wohlford	.10	.03
189 Jerry Augustine	.10	.03
190 Jim Austin	.10	.03
191 Rick Austin	.10	.03
192 Kurt Bevacqua	.20	.06
193 Tommy Bianco	.10	.03
194 Dante Bichette	1.50	.45
195 Mike Birkbeck	.10	.03
196 Dan Boitano	.10	.03
197 Bobby Bolin	.10	.03
198 Mark Bomback	.10	.03
199 Ricky Bones	.10	.03
200 Chris Bosio	.10	.03
201 Thad Bosley	.10	.03
202 Steve Bowling	.10	.03
203 Gene Brabender	.10	.03
204 Glenn Braggs	.10	.03
205 Mike Caldwell	.20	.06
206 Bill Champion	.10	.03
207 Mark Ciardi	.10	.03
208 Bobby Clark	.10	.03
209 Ron Clark	.10	.03
210 Mark Clear	.10	.03
211 Reggie Cleveland	.10	.03
212 Bryan Clutterbuck	.10	.03
213 Jaime Cocanower	.10	.03
214 Jim Colborn	.10	.03
215 Cecil Cooper	.40	.12
216 Edgar Diaz	.10	.03
217 Frank DiPino	.10	.03
218 Dave Engle	.10	.03
219 Ray Fosse	.10	.03
220 Terry Francona	.20	.06
221 Tito Francona	.10	.03
222 La Vel Freeman	.10	.03
223 Brian Giles	.10	.03
224 Bob Heise	.10	.03
225 Doug Henry	.10	.03
226 Mike Hershberger	.10	.03
227 Teddy Higuera	.10	.03
228 Sam Hinds	.10	.03
229 Fred Holdsworth	.10	.03
230 Darren Holmes	.10	.03
231 Paul Householder	.10	.03
232 Odell Jones	.10	.03
233 Brad Komminsk	.10	.03
234 Andy Kosco	.10	.03
235 Lew Krausse	.10	.03
236 Ray Krawczyk	.10	.03
237 Bill Krueger	.10	.03
238 Ted Kubiak	.10	.03
239 Jack Lind	.10	.03
240 Frank Linzy	.10	.03
241 Pat Listach	.10	.03
242 Graeme Lloyd	.10	.03
243 Bob Locker	.10	.03
244 Skip Lockwood	.10	.03
245 Ken McMullen	.10	.03
246 Jerry McNertney	.10	.03
247 Doc Medich	.10	.03
248 Bob Meyer	.10	.03
249 Joey Meyer	.10	.03
250 Matt Mieske	.10	.03
251 Roger Miller	.10	.03
252 Paul Mirabella	.10	.03
253 Angel Miranda	.10	.03
254 Bobby Mitchell	.10	.03
255 Paul Mitchell	.10	.03
256 Paul Molitor	4.00	1.20
257 Rafael Novoa	.10	.03
258 Jesse Orosco	.20	.06
259 Carlos Ponce	.10	.03
260 Chuck Porter	.10	.03
261 Darrell Porter	.20	.06
262 Billy Jo Robidoux	.10	.03
263 Ron Robinson	.10	.03
264 Eduardo Rodriguez	.10	.03
265 Ellie Rodriguez	.10	.03
266 Rich Rollins	.10	.03
267 Ed Romero	.10	.03
268 Gary Sheffield	2.00	.60
269 Bob Sheldon	.10	.03
270 Chris Short	.10	.03
271 Bob Skube	.10	.03
272 Jim Slaton	.10	.03
273 Bernie Smith	.10	.03
274 Russ Snyder	.10	.03
275 Lary Sorensen	.10	.03
276 Bill Spiers	.10	.03
277 Ed Sprague	.20	.06
278 Dickie Thon	.10	.03
279 Bill Travers	.10	.03
280 Pete Vuckovich	.30	.09
281 Clyde Wright	.10	.03
282 Jeff Yurak	.10	.03
283 Joe Azcue	.10	.03
284 Mike Boddicker	.20	.06
285 Ken Brett	.10	.03
286 John Briggs	.10	.03
287 Pete Broberg	.10	.03
288 Greg Brock	.10	.03
289 Jeff Bronkey	.10	.03
290 Mark Brouhard	.10	.03
291 Kevin Brown	.10	.03
292 Ollie Brown	.10	.03
293 Bruce Brubaker	.10	.03
294 Tom Brunansky	.20	.06
295 Steve Brye	.10	.03
296 Bob Burda	.10	.03
297 Ray Burris	.10	.03
298 Jeff Cirillo	1.00	.30
299 Bobby Clark	.10	.03
300 Bob Coluccio	.10	.03
301 Wayne Comer	.10	.03
302 Billy Conigliaro	.10	.03
303 Cecil Cooper	.50	.15
304 Barry Cort	.10	.03
305 Chuck Crim	.10	.03
306 LaFayette Currence	.10	.03
307 Kiki Diaz	.10	.03
308 Bill Doran	.10	.03
309 Al Downing	.10	.03
310 Tom Edens	.10	.03
311 Andy Etchebarren	.10	.03
312 Rollie Fingers	1.50	.45
313 Jim Gantner	.40	.12
314 Greg Goosen	.20	.06
315 Brian Harper	.10	.03
316 Larry Hisle	.10	.03
317 Steve Hovley	.10	.03
318 Wilbur Howard	.10	.03
319 Roy Howell	.10	.03
320 Bob Humphreys	.10	.03
321 Jim Hunter	.10	.03
322 Dave Huppert	.10	.03
323 Von Joshua	.10	.03
324 Art Kusnyer	.10	.03
325 Doug Loman	.10	.03
326 Jim Lonborg	.20	.06
327 Marcelino Lopez	.10	.03
328 Willie Lozado	.10	.03
329 Mike Matheny	.10	.03
330 Ken McMullen	.10	.03
331 Jose Mercedes	.10	.03
332 Paul Molitor	4.00	1.20
333 Don Money (Head Shot)	.20	.06
334 Don Money (Action Shot)	.20	.06
335 Charlie Moore	.20	.06
336 Donnie Moore	.10	.03
337 John Morris	.10	.03
338 Curt Motton	.10	.03
339 Willie Mueller	.10	.03
340 Tom Murphy	.10	.03
341 Tony Muser	.10	.03
342 Edwin Nunez	.10	.03
343 Ben Oglivie	.30	.09
344 Pat Osborn	.10	.03
345 Dennis Powell	.10	.03
346 Jody Reed	.10	.03
347 Phil Roof	.10	.03
348 Jimmy Rosario	.10	.03
349 Bruce Ruffin	.10	.03
350 Gary Ryerson	.10	.03
351 Bob Scanlan	.10	.03
352 Ted Simmons (Head Shot)	.75	.23
353 Ted Simmons (Action Shot)	.75	.23
354 Duane Singleton	.10	.03
355 Steve Stanicek	.10	.03
356 Fred Stanley	.10	.03
357 Dave Stapleton	.10	.03
358 Randy Stein	.10	.03
359 Earl Stephenson	.10	.03
360 Franklin Stubbs	.10	.03
361 William Suero	.10	.03
362 Jim Sundberg	.20	.06
363 B.J. Surhoff	.75	.23
364 Gary Sutherland	.10	.03
365 Don Sutton	1.50	.45
366 Dale Sveum	.10	.03
367 Gorman Thomas	.40	.12
368 Wayne Twitchell	.10	.03
369 Dave Valle	.10	.03
370 Greg Vaughn	.40	.12
371 John Vukovich	.10	.03
372 Danny Walton	.10	.03
373 Turner Ward	.10	.03
374 Rick Wrona	.10	.03
375 Jim Wynn	.20	.06
376 Robin Yount	3.00	.90

1994 Brewers Police

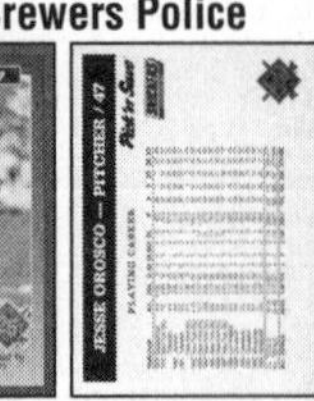

Sponsored by Pick 'n Save and Snickers Ice Cream Bars to celebrate the 25th Anniversary of the Brewers, this 30-card set features, on its fronts, posed color player photos with two-toned green borders. Other than the players' uniform numbers, the cards are unnumbered and checklisted below in alphabetical order.

	Nm-Mt	Ex-Mt
COMPLETE SET (30)	8.00	2.40
1 Bernie Brewer Mascot	.25	.07
2 Ricky Bones	.25	.07
3 Jeff Bronkey	.25	.07
4 Tom Brunansky	.25	.07
5 Jeff D'Amico DP Kelly Wunsch DP	1.50	.45
6 Cal Eldred	.25	.07
7 Mike Fetters	.25	.07
8 Phil Garner MG	.25	.07
9 Darryl Hamilton	.25	.07
10 Brian Harper	.25	.07
11 Doug Henry	.25	.07
12 Teddy Higuera	.25	.07
13 Mike Ignasiak	.25	.07
14 John Jaha	.25	.07
15 Mark Kiefer	.25	.07
16 Pat Listach	.25	.07
17 Graeme Lloyd	.50	.15
18 Matt Mieske	.25	.07
19 Jaime Navarro	.25	.07
20 Dave Nilsson	.50	.15
21 Jesse Orosco	.50	.15
22 Jody Reed	.25	.07
23 Bob Scanlan	.25	.07
24 Kevin Seitzer	.50	.15
25 Bill Spiers	.25	.07
26 B.J. Surhoff	1.00	.30
27 Jose Valentin	.75	.23
28 Greg Vaughn	.50	.15

29 Turner Ward	.25	.07
30 Bill Wegman	.25	.07

1994 Brewers Sentry

This eight-card set was issued to honor outstanding achievements by Milwaukee Brewer players. Though the set is sponsored by Sentry Foods, its logo does not appear on the cards. One card was given out each Tuesday night home game through August 30. The fronts feature color player photos inside a blue border with gold and green. A special Brewers' 25th Anniversary logo appears in the top left, while the player's name is printed on a navy bar beneath the picture. On a white background, the back presents the player's outstanding achievement. The cards are unnumbered and checklisted below in alphabetical order.

	Nm-Mt	Ex-Mt
COMPLETE SET (8)	12.00	3.60
1 Hank Aaron	5.00	1.50
2 Rollie Fingers	2.00	.60
3 Pat Listach	1.00	.30
4 Paul Molitor	4.00	1.20
5 Paul Molitor	4.00	1.20
Robin Yount		
Jim Gantner		
6 Juan Nieves	1.00	.30
7 Don Sutton	2.00	.60
8 Robin Yount	3.00	.90

1994 Brewers Team Issue

This 29-card set of the 1994 Milwaukee Brewers features black-and-white player portraits with white borders and measures approximately 4" by 5 7/16". The backs are blank. The cards are unnumbered and checklisted below in alphabetical order.

	Nm-Mt	Ex-Mt
COMPLETE SET (29)	10.00	3.00
1 Ricky Bones	.25	.07
2 Jeff Bronkey	.25	.07
3 Tom Brunansky	.50	.15
4 Alex Diaz	.25	.07
5 Cal Eldred	.25	.07
6 Mike Fetters	.25	.07
7 Phil Garner MG	.25	.07
8 Darryl Hamilton	.25	.07
9 Brian Harper	.25	.07
10 Doug Henry	.25	.07
11 Ted Higuera	.25	.07
12 John Jaha	.50	.15
13 Mark Kiefer	.25	.07
14 Pat Listach	.25	.07
15 Graeme Lloyd	.25	.07
16 Matt Mieske	.25	.07
17 Angel Miranda	.25	.07
18 Jaime Navarro	.25	.07
19 Dave Nilsson	.50	.15
20 Jesse Orosco	.50	.15
21 Jody Reed	.25	.07
22 Bob Scanlan	.25	.07
23 Kevin Seitzer	.50	.15
24 Bill Spiers	.25	.07
25 B.J. Surhoff	1.00	.30
26 Jose Valentin	.75	.23
27 Greg Vaughn	.50	.15
28 Turner Ward	.25	.07
29 Bill Wegman	.25	.07

1995 Brewers Police

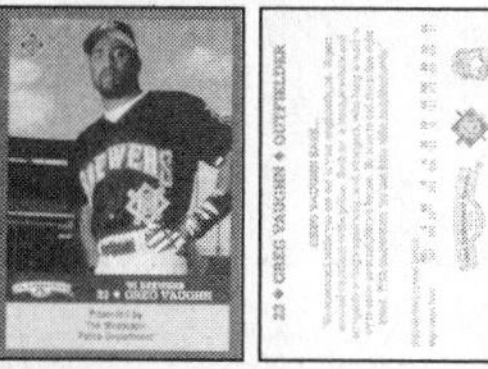

This green bordered standard-size set was issued by Milwaukee area police forces to promote safety among their residents. Since these cards are unnumbered except by uniform number, we have sequenced them in alphabetical order.

	Nm-Mt	Ex-Mt
COMPLETE SET	10.00	3.00
1 Ricky Bones	.25	.07
2 Jeff Bronkey	.25	.07
3 Jeff Cirillo	1.00	.30
Mike Matheny		
4 Cal Eldred	.25	.07
5 Mike Fetters	.25	.07
6 Phil Garner MG	.25	.07
7 Darryl Hamilton	.25	.07
8 David Hulse	.25	.07
9 Mike Ignasiak	.25	.07
10 John Jaha	.50	.15
11 Scott Karl	.50	.15
Steve Sparks		
Alberto Reyes		
12 Mark Kiefer	.25	.07
Jose Mercedes		
13 Pat Listach	.25	.07
14 Graeme Lloyd	.25	.07
15 Derrick May	.25	.07
16 Matt Mieske	.25	.07
17 Angel Miranda	.25	.07
18 Dave Nilsson	.50	.15
19 Joe Oliver	.25	.07
20 Bob Scanlan	.25	.07
21 Kevin Seitzer	.50	.15
21 B.J Surhoff	.75	.23
22 Bob Uecker ANN	1.00	.30
23 Jose Valentin	.50	.15
24 Greg Vaughn	1.00	.30
25 Fernando Vina	.50	.15
26 Turner Ward	.25	.07
27 Bill Wegman	.25	.07
28 Bill Castro CO	.25	.07
Duffy Dyer CO		
Tim Foli CO		
Lamar Johnson CO		
Don Rowe CO		
29 Advertising Card	.25	.07
30 Cheese Sample Card	.25	.07

1996 Brewers Police

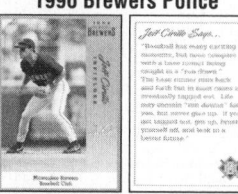

This 30-card set features color action photos of the 1996 Milwaukee Brewers. The backs carry a safety message from the player pictured on the front. The cards are unnumbered and checklisted below in alphabetical order.

	Nm-Mt	Ex-Mt
COMPLETE SET (30)	10.00	3.00
1 Ricky Bones	.25	.07
2 Marshall Boze	.25	.07
3 Chuck Carr	.25	.07
4 Jeff Cirillo	.75	.23
5 Cal Eldred	.25	.07
6 Mike Fetters	.25	.07
7 Ramon Garcia	.25	.07
8 Phil Garner MG	.25	.07
9 David Hulse	.25	.07
10 John Jaha	.50	.15
11 Scott Karl	.25	.07
12 Jesse Levis	.25	.07
13 Pat Listach	.25	.07
14 Graeme Lloyd	.25	.07
15 Mark Loretta	.75	.23
16 Mike Matheny	.25	.07
17 Ben McDonald	.25	.07
18 Matt Mieske	.25	.07
19 Angel Miranda	.25	.07
20 David Nilsson	.50	.15
21 Mike Potts	.25	.07
22 Kevin Seitzer	.50	.15
23 Steve Sparks	.25	.07
24 Jose Valentin	.75	.23
25 Greg Vaughn	.50	.15
26 Fernando Vina	.75	.23
27 Turner Ward	.25	.07
28 Kevin Wickander	.25	.07
29 Coaches Card	.25	.07
30 Miller Park	.25	.07

1997 Brewers Police

This 29-card set of the Milwaukee Brewers was presented by the Waukesha Police Department, Waukesha Sports Cards, and Delzer Lithograph Company. The cards are unnumbered and checklisted below in alphabetical order.

	Nm-Mt	Ex-Mt
COMPLETE SET (29)	12.00	3.60
1 Chris Bando CO	.25	.07
Bill Castro CO		
Jim Gantner CO		
Lamar Johnson CO		
Don Rowe CO		
2 Jeromy Burnitz	.75	.23
3 Chuck Carr	.25	.07
4 Jeff Cirillo	.75	.23
5 Jeff D'Amico	.50	.15
6 Eddy Diaz	.25	.07
7 Mike Fetters	.25	.07
8 Bryce Florie	.25	.07
9 Phil Garner MG	.25	.07
10 Jeff Huson	.25	.07
11 John Jaha	.50	.15
12 Doug Jones	.50	.15
13 Scott Karl	.25	.07
14 Jesse Levis	.25	.07
15 Mark Loretta	.75	.23
16 Mike Matheny	.25	.07
17 Ben McDonald	.25	.07
18 Jose Mercedes	.25	.07
19 Matt Mieske	.25	.07
20 Angel Miranda	.25	.07
21 Marc Newfield	.25	.07
22 David Nilsson	.50	.15
23 Jackie Robinson	3.00	.90
24 Tim Unroe	.25	.07
25 Jose Valentin	.75	.23
26 Ron Villone	.25	.07
27 Fernando Vina	.75	.23
28 Bob Wickman	.50	.15
29 Gerald Williams	.25	.07

1998 Brewers Police

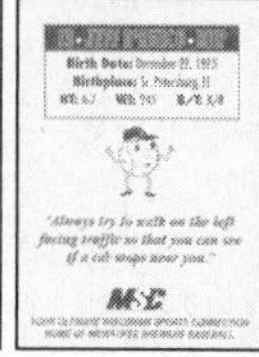

This 30 card standard-size set features members of the 1998 Milwaukee Brewers. The cards care sponsored by the Milwaukee Sports Connection as well as the Waukesha Police Department; Waukesha Sports Cards and Delzer Lithograph Co. Since the cards are unnumbered, we have sequenced them in alphabetical order.

	Nm-Mt	Ex-Mt
COMPLETE SET (30)	8.00	2.40
1 Jeromy Burnitz	.75	.23
2 Jeff Cirillo	.75	.23
3 Jeff D'Amico	.50	.15
4 Cal Eldred	.25	.07
5 Chad Fox	.25	.07
6 Phil Garner MG	.25	.07
7 Marquis Grissom	.50	.15
8 Bob Hamelin	.25	.07
9 Darrin Jackson	.25	.07
10 John Jaha	.50	.15
11 Geoff Jenkins	1.00	.30
12 Doug Jones	.50	.15
13 Jeff Juden	.25	.07
14 Scott Karl	.25	.07
15 Jesse Levis	.25	.07
16 Mark Loretta	.75	.23
17 Mike Matheny	.25	.07
18 Jose Mercedes	.25	.07
19 Mike Myers	.25	.07
20 Marc Newfield	.25	.07
21 David Nilsson	.50	.15
22 Al Reyes	.25	.07
23 Jose Valentin	.75	.23
24 Fernando Vina	.75	.23
25 Paul Wagner	.25	.07
26 Bob Wickman	.50	.15
27 Steve Woodard	.25	.07
28 Bobby Hughes	.50	.15
Eric Owens		
29 Bronswell Patrick	.25	.07
Brad Woodall		
30 Chris Bando CO	.25	.07
Bill Castro CO		
Lamar Johnson CO		
Doug Mansolino CO		
Don Rowe CO		
Joel Youngblood CO		

1999 Brewers Postcards

These 5" by 7" blank backed postcards featured members of the 1999 Milwaukee Brewers. The postcards have a large photo of the player with the Ohio Casualty Group log and Milwaukee County Stadium logo on the bottom. As these cards are unnumbered we have sequenced them in alphabetical order.

	Nm-Mt	Ex-Mt
COMPLETE SET	7.00	2.10
1 Ron Belliard	.50	.15
2 Bill Campbell CO	.25	.07
2 Sean Berry	.25	.07
4 Lou Collier	.25	.07
5 Cal Eldred	.25	.07
6 Phil Garner MG	.25	.07
7 Marquis Grissom	.50	.15
8 Bobby Hughes	.25	.07
9 Ron Jackson CO	.25	.07
10 Geoff Jenkins	1.00	.30
11 Scott Karl	.25	.07
12 Jim Lefebvre CO	.25	.07
13 Mark Loretta	.75	.23
14 Bob Melvin CO	.25	.07
15 Mike Myers	.25	.07
16 Alex Ochoa	.25	.07
17 Eric Plunk	.25	.07
18 Bill Pulsipher	.25	.07
19 Rafael Roque	.25	.07
20 Jose Valentin	.50	.15
21 Fernando Vina	.50	.15
22 David Weathers	.25	.07
23 Bob Wickman	.50	.15
24 Bernie Brewer	.25	.07
Mascot		

1999 Brewers Safety

This 30-card standard-size set was issued to commemorate the 1999 Milwaukee Brewers. The fronts have a player portrait against a ghosted background of the new stadium. The players name and uniform number is printed next to the photo and the cards say on the bottom "Presented by Midwest Sports Channel and the Milwaukee Brewers". The backs have some biographical information as well as a safety tip. The cards are unnumbered so we have sequenced them in alphabetical order.

	Nm-Mt	Ex-Mt
COMPLETE SET (30)	10.00	3.00
1 Jim Abbott	.50	.15
2 Brian Banks	.25	.07
3 Sean Berry	.25	.07
4 Jeromy Burnitz	1.00	.30
5 Jeff Cirillo	1.00	.30
6 Lou Collier	.25	.07
7 Cal Eldred	.25	.07
8 Valerio De Los Santos	.25	.07
9 Chad Fox	.25	.07
10 Phil Garner MG	.25	.07
11 Marquis Grissom	.50	.15
12 Bobby Hughes	.25	.07
13 Geoff Jenkins	1.00	.30
14 Scott Karl	.25	.07
15 Mark Loretta	.75	.23
16 Mike Myers	.25	.07
17 David Nilsson	.50	.15
18 Alex Ochoa	.25	.07
19 Eric Plunk	.25	.07
20 Bill Pulsipher	.25	.07
21 Al Reyes	.25	.07
22 Rafael Roque	.25	.07
23 Jose Valentin	.50	.15
24 Fernando Vina	.50	.15
25 David Weathers	.25	.07
26 Bob Wickman	.50	.15
27 Steve Woodard	.25	.07
28 Steve Faltisek	.25	.07
Rich Becker		
29 Bob Melvin CO	.25	.07
Jim Lefevre CO		
Ron Jackson CO		
Bill Castro CO		
Doug Mansolino CO		
Bill Campbell CO		
30 Milwaukee County Stadium	.25	.07

2000 Brewers All-Decade 70's

This 13 card standard-size set features some of the best Milwaukee Brewer players from the 1970's. The white bordered cards have the all-decades team logo on the top and a gold foild diamond with their name and position. The backs have a blurb as to why the players are remembered for their days with the Brewers. Since the cards are unnumbered, we have sequenced them in alphabetical order.

	Nm-Mt	Ex-Mt
COMPLETE SET (13)	8.00	2.40
1 Hank Aaron	5.00	1.50
2 George Bamberger MG	.25	.07
3 Mike Caldwell	.25	.07
4 Cecil Cooper	1.00	.30
5 Tommy Harper	.25	.07
6 Larry Hisle	.25	.07
7 Charlie Moore	.25	.07
8 Sixto Lezcano	.25	.07
9 Don Money	.50	.15
10 Ken Sanders	.25	.07
11 Jim Slaton	.25	.07
12 Gorman Thomas	.75	.23
13 Robin Yount	4.00	1.20

2000 Brewers All-Decade 80's

This 13 card standard-size set features some of the best Milwaukee Brewer players from the 1980's. The white bordered cards have the all-decades team logo on the bottom and a gold foild diamond with their name and position. The backs have a blurb as to why the players are remembered for their days with the Brewers. Since the cards are unnumbered, we have sequenced them in alphabetical order.

	Nm-Mt	Ex-Mt
COMPLETE SET (13)	8.00	2.40
1 Mike Caldwell	.25	.07
2 Cecil Cooper	.75	.23
3 Rollie Fingers	1.25	.35
4 Jim Gantner	.25	.07
5 Harvey Kuenn MG	.25	.07
6 Paul Molitor	2.50	.75
Batting		
7 Paul Molitor	2.50	.75
Fielding		
8 Ben Oglivie	.50	.15
9 Ted Simmons	.75	.23
10 Gorman Thomas	.50	.15
11 Pete Vuckovich	.25	.07
12 Robin Yount	2.00	.60
Close-Up		
13 Robin Yount	2.00	.60
Batting		

2000 Brewers All-Decade 90's

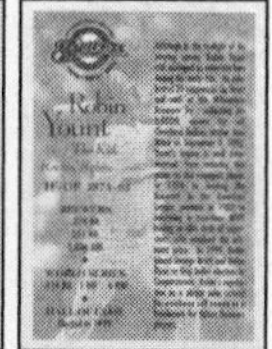

This 13 card standard-size set features some of the best Milwaukee Brewer players from the 1990's. The white bordered cards have the all-decades team logo on the top and a gold foild diamond with their name and position. The backs have a blurb as to why the players are remembered for their days with the Brewers. Since the cards are unnumbered, we have sequenced them in alphabetical order.

	Nm-Mt	Ex-Mt
COMPLETE SET	8.00	2.40
1 Chris Bosio	.25	.07
2 Jeromy Burnitz	.75	.23
3 Jeff Cirillo	.50	.15
4 Phil Garner MG	.25	.07
5 John Jaha	.50	.15
6 Geoff Jenkins	1.00	.30
7 David Nilsson	.50	.15
8 B.J. Surhoff	.75	.23
9 Fernando Vina	.50	.15
10 Jose Valentin	.50	.15
11 Bill Wegman	.25	.07
12 Bob Wickman	.25	.07
13 Robin Yount	2.00	.60

2000 Brewers Police

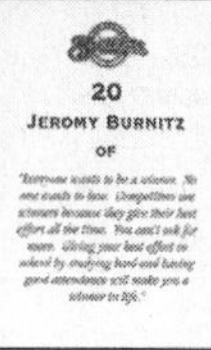

This 30-card standard-sized set was issued by Milwaukee area police departments. The fronts feature pose players portraits against a black background. The backs feature a safety tip. Since the cards are unnumbered except by uniform number; we have sequenced them alphabetically.

	Nm-Mt	Ex-Mt
COMPLETE SET (30)	8.00	2.40
1 Juan Acevedo	.25	.07
2 Kevin Barker	.25	.07
3 Ron Belliard	.50	.15
4 Jason Bere	.25	.07
5 Sean Berry	.25	.07
6 Henry Blanco	.25	.07
7 Jim Bruske	.25	.07
8 Jeromy Burnitz	.75	.23
9 Valerio De Los Santos	.25	.07
10 Marquis Grissom	.50	.15
11 Charlie Hayes	.25	.07
12 Jimmy Haynes	.25	.07
13 Jose Hernandez	.25	.07
14 Tyler Houston	.25	.07
15 Geoff Jenkins	1.00	.30
16 Curtis Leskanic	.25	.07
17 Davey Lopes MG	.50	.15
18 Luis Lopez	.25	.07
19 Mark Loretta	.75	.23
20 James Mouton	.25	.07
21 Lyle Mouton	.25	.07
22 Jaime Navarro	.25	.07
23 John Snyder	.25	.07
24 Everett Stull	.25	.07
25 David Weathers	.25	.07
26 Bob Wickman	.50	.15
27 Matt Williams	.25	.07
28 Steve Woodard	.25	.07
29 Bill Schroeder ANN	.25	.07
Matt Vasgersian ANN		
30 Jerry Royster CO	.75	.23
Rod Carew CO		
Bill Castro CO		
Bob Apodaca CO		
Chris Speier CO		
Gary Allenson CO		

2000 Brewers Postcards

These 26 blank-backed black and white cards featured members of the 2000 Milwaukee Brewers. The player photos take up most of the cards and the players name and position is directly under their photo. Since the cards are unnumbered, we have sequenced them in alphabetical order.

	Nm-Mt	Ex-Mt
COMPLETE SET	15.00	4.50
1 Gary Allenson CO	.50	.15
2 Bob Apodaca CO	.50	.15
3 Juan Acevedo	.50	.15
4 Kevin Barker	.50	.15
5 Ron Belliard	.75	.23
6 Sean Berry	.50	.15
7 Henry Blanco	.50	.15
8 Jeromy Burnitz	1.00	.30
9 Rod Carew CO	2.00	.60
10 Bill Castro CO	.50	.15
11 Valerio de los Santos	.50	.15
12 Marquis Grissom	.75	.23

13 Charlie Hayes .50 .15
14 Jose Hernandez .50 .15
15 Tyler Houston .50 .15
16 Geoff Jenkins 1.50 .45
17 Curtis Leskanic .50 .15
18 Luis Lopez .50 .15
19 Mark Loretta 1.00 .30
20 James Mouton .50 .15
21 Lyle Mouton .50 .15
22 Jerry Royster CO .50 .15
23 Chris Speier CO .50 .15
24 David Weathers .50 .15
25 Bob Wickman .75 .23
26 Steve Woodard .50 .15

2001 Brewers Police

This 30 card standard-size set features members of the 2001 Milwaukee Brewers. The white-bordered fronts feature player photos along with sponsorship of "Fox Sports Net" and the local police department who distibuted the set. The back has safety information. Since these cards are unnumbered, we have sequenced them in alphabetical order.

Nm-Mt Ex-Mt
COMPLETE SET (30) 10.00 3.00
1 Ronnie Belliard .50 .15
2 Henry Blanco .25 .07
3 Raul Casanova .25 .07
4 Will Cunnane .25 .07
5 Jeromy Burnitz .75 .23
6 Jeff D'Amico .25 .07
7 Mike DeJean .25 .07
8 Angel Echevarria .25 .07
9 Tony Fernandez .50 .15
10 Chad Fox .25 .07
11 Jeffrey Hammonds .25 .07
12 Jimmy Haynes .25 .07
13 Jose Hernandez .50 .15
14 Tyler Houston .25 .07
15 Geoff Jenkins 1.00 .30
16 Ray King .25 .07
17 Mark Leiter .25 .07
18 Curtis Leskanic .25 .07
19 Dave Lopes MG .50 .15
20 Luis Lopez .25 .07
21 Mark Loretta .75 .23
22 James Mouton .25 .07
23 Paul Rigdon .25 .07
24 Richie Sexson 1.00 .30
25 Ben Sheets 1.25 .35
26 David Weathers .25 .07
27 Devon White .25 .07
28 Jamey Wright .25 .07
29 Jerry Royster CO .75 .23
Rod Carew CO
Bill Castro CO
Bob Apodaca CO
Luis Salazar CO
Gary Allenson CO
30 Bill Schroeder ANN .25 .07
Matt Vasgersian ANN

2001 Brewers Walk of Fame

This four card standard-size set was given away at the Milwaukee Brewers Stadium on July 12, 2001 when the Walk of Fame was dedicated outside the then newly constructed Miller Park. The fronts have the the player's uniform number as well as the words Walk of Fame on the left and the player's photo on the right. The back has a black and white photo of the player along with the July 12,2001 date. Since these cards are unnumbered, we have sequenced them in alphabetical order.

MINT NRMT
COMPLETE SET 10.00 4.50
1 Hank Aaron 5.00 2.20
2 Rollie Fingers 1.00 .45
3 Paul Molitor 4.00 1.80
4 Robin Yount 2.50 1.10

2002 Brewers Police

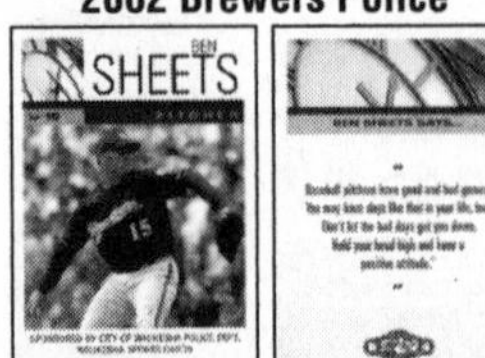

This 30-card standard-size set features members of the 2002 Milwaukee Brewers. The fronts have the player's photo and information about the police area which sponsored the set. The back has a safety tip as well as "Miller Park" logo. Since these cards are unnmbered, we have sequenced them in alphabetical order.

Nm-Mt Ex-Mt
COMPLETE SET 8.00 2.40
1 Paul Bako .25 .07
2 Ron Belliard .50 .15
3 Mike Buddie .25 .07
4 Jose Cabrera .25 .07
5 Raul Casanova .25 .07
6 Mike DeJean .25 .07
7 Nelson Figueroa .25 .07
8 Chad Fox .25 .07
9 Jeffrey Hammonds .25 .07
10 Lenny Harris .25 .07
11 Jose Hernandez .50 .15
12 Tyler Houston .25 .07
13 Geoff Jenkins 1.00 .30
14 Ray King .25 .07
15 Curtis Leskanic .25 .07
16 Luis Lopez .25 .07
17 Mark Loretta .25 .07
18 Nick Neugebauer 1.00 .30
19 Takahito Nomura .50 .15
20 Alex Ochoa .25 .07
21 Ruben Quevedo .25 .07
22 Paul Rigdon .25 .07
23 Glendon Rusch .25 .07
24 Alex Sanchez .50 .15
25 Richie Sexson 1.00 .30
26 Ben Sheets 1.00 .30
27 Matt Stairs .25 .07
28 Luis Vizcaino .25 .07
29 Jamey Wright .25 .07
30 Eric Young .50 .15

2002 Brewers Topps

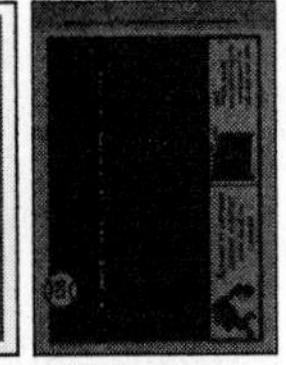

This six card standard-size set was given away at selected Milwaukee Brewer games during the 2002 season. This set honored key members of the 1982 Milwaukee Brewers and featured reprints of a different Topps card for each of them. We have placed the information of what year the reprint card was as well as the day the card was given out next to the player's name in our checklist.

Nm-Mt Ex-Mt
COMPLETE SET 40.00 12.00
1 Don Money 4/19 5.00 1.50
1978 Topps
2 Paul Molitor 5/24 15.00 4.50
1992 Topps
3 Cecil Cooper 6/21 8.00 2.40
4 Robin Yount 7/12 12.00 3.60
1982 Topps
5 Gorman Thomas 8/9 6.00 1.80
1981 Topps
6 Ben Oglivie 9/6 5.00 1.50
1980 Topps

2003 Brewers Police

This 30-card standard-size set features members of the 2003 Milwaukee Brewers. The fronts are very simple with the white borders surrounding a full-color portrait of the player who is identified by his uniform number, name and position at the bottom left corner of the photo. The backs have a safety tip.

Nm-Mt Ex-Mt
COMPLETE SET 8.00 2.40
1 Brady Clark .25 .07
2 Royce Clayton .25 .07
3 Jason Conti .25 .07
4 Enrique Cruz .25 .07
5 Mike DeJean .25 .07
6 Jayson Durocher .25 .07
7 Valerio de los Santos .25 .07
8 Matt Ford .25 .07
9 John Foster .25 .07
10 Wayne Franklin .25 .07
11 Keith Ginter .25 .07
12 Jeffrey Hammonds .25 .07
13 Wes Helms .50 .15
14 Geoff Jenkins 1.00 .30
15 Matt Kinney .25 .07
16 Curtis Leskanic .25 .07
17 Shane Nance .25 .07
18 Keith Osik .25 .07
19 Eddie Perez .25 .07
20 Scott Podsednik .25 .07
21 Todd Ritchie .25 .07
22 Glendon Rusch .25 .07
23 Alex Sanchez .50 .15
24 Richie Sexson 1.00 .30
25 Ben Sheets .75 .23
26 John Vander Wal .25 .07
27 Luis Vizcaino .25 .07
28 Ned Yost MG .25 .07
29 Eric Young .50 .15
30 The Coaches .25 .07

2003 Brewers Team Issue

These blank-backed cards, which measure approximately 5" by 7" feature members of the 2003 Milwaukee Brewers. These cards have a black and white player photo surrounded by white borders. The player's name and position

are on the bottom along with the Brewers logo and a "US Bank" logo. Since these cards are unnumbered, we have sequenced them in alphabetical order.

MINT NRMT
COMPLETE SET 15.00 6.75
1 Dave Burba .50 .23
2 Bill Castro CO .50 .23
3 Brady Clark .50 .23
4 Royce Clayton .50 .23
5 Enrique Cruz .50 .23
6 Rich Donnelly CO .50 .23
7 Leo Estrella .50 .23
8 Wayne Franklin .50 .23
9 Keith Ginter .50 .23
10 Bill Hall .50 .23
11 Brooks Kieschnick .50 .23
11 Geoff Jenkins 1.50 .70
13 Matt Kinney .50 .23
14 Mike Maddux .50 .23
15 Shane Nance .50 .23
16 Dave Nelson CO .50 .23
17 Wes Obermueller .50 .23
18 Keith Osik .50 .23
19 Ulice Payne PRES .50 .23
20 Eddie Perez .50 .23
21 Scott Podsednik 2.50 1.10
22 Richie Sexson 1.50 .70
23 Ben Sheets 1.00 .45
24 John Vander Wal .50 .23
25 Luis Vizcaino .50 .23
26 Butch Wynegar CO .50 .23
27 Ned Yost MG .50 .23

1909 Briggs E97

The cards in this 32-card set measure 1 1/2" by 2 3/4". The C.A. Briggs Company distributed this set in 1909, and it is one of the most highly prized of caramel issues. The cards come in two distinct varieties: one group in color with a brown print checklist on back; the other with identical player poses in black and white with blank backs. A comparison of team and name variations suggests that the black and white set pre-dates the color issue. The list below has been correctly alphabetized and hence does not exactly follow the checklist back order.

Ex-Mt VG
COMPLETE SET (32) 7000.00 3500.00
1 Jimmy Austin 150.00 75.00
2 Joe Birmingham 150.00 75.00
3 William J. Bradley 150.00 75.00
4 Kitty Bransfield 150.00 75.00
5 Howie Camnitz 150.00 75.00
6 Bill Carrigan 150.00 75.00
7 Harry Davis 150.00 75.00
8 Josh Devore 150.00 75.00
9 Mickey Doolan 150.00 75.00
10 Bull Durham 150.00 75.00
11 Jimmy Dygert 150.00 75.00
12 Topsy Hartsel 150.00 75.00
13 Charlie Hemphill 150.00 75.00
14 Bill Hinchman 150.00 75.00
15 Willie Keeler 600.00 300.00
16 Joseph J. Kelley 400.00 200.00
17 Red Kleinow 150.00 75.00
18 Rube Kroh 150.00 75.00
19 Amby McConnell 150.00 75.00
20 Matty McIntyre 150.00 75.00
21 Chief Meyers 200.00 100.00
22 Earl Moore 150.00 75.00
23 George Mullin 150.00 75.00
24 Red Murray 150.00 75.00
25 Simon Nichols (sic) 150.00 75.00
26 Claude Rossman 150.00 75.00
27 Admiral Schlei 150.00 75.00
28A Harry Steinfeldt 200.00 100.00
28B Harry Steinfeldt 500.00 250.00
No T in Steinfeldt
29A Dennis Sullivan: 200.00 100.00
Chicago
29B Dennis Sullivan: 1500.00 750.00
Boston
30A Irv "Cy" Young 600.00 300.00
Boston Nat'l
30B Cy Young: Cleveland 1000.00 500.00

1953-54 Briggs

The cards in this 37-card set measure 2 1/4" by 3 1/2". The 1953-54 Briggs Hot Dog set of color cards contains 25 Senators and 12 known players from the Dodgers, Yankees and Giants. They were issued in two card panels in the Washington, D.C. area as part of the hot dog package itself. The cards are unnumbered and are printed on waxed cardboard, and the style of the Senator cards differs from that of the New York players. The latter appear in poses which also exist in the Dan Dee and Stahl Meyer card sets. The catalog designation is F154. In the checklist below the Washington players are numbered 1-25 alphabetically by name and the New York players are numbered 26-40 similarly.

NM Ex
COMPLETE SET (40) 10000.00 5000.00
COMMON CARD (1-28) 150.00 75.00
COMMON CARD (29-40) 175.00 90.00
1 Jim Busby 150.00 75.00
2 Tommy Byrne 150.00 75.00
3 Gilbert Coan 150.00 75.00
4 Sonny Dixon 150.00 75.00
5 Ed Fitzgerald 150.00 75.00
6 Mickey Grasso 150.00 75.00
7 Mel Hoderlein 150.00 75.00
8 Jackie Jensen 200.00 100.00
9 Connie Marrero 150.00 75.00
10 Carmen Mauro 150.00 75.00
11 Walt Masterson 150.00 75.00
12 Mickey McDermott 150.00 75.00
13 Julio Moreno 150.00 75.00
14 Bob Oldis 150.00 75.00
15 Erwin Porterfield 150.00 75.00
16 Pete Runnels 175.00 90.00
17 Johnny Schmitz 150.00 75.00
18 Angel Scull 150.00 75.00
19 Spec Shea 150.00 75.00
20 Albert Sima 150.00 75.00
21 Chuck Stobbs 150.00 75.00
22 Wayne Terwilliger 150.00 75.00
23 Joe Tipton 150.00 75.00
24 Tom Umphlett 150.00 75.00
25 Mickey Vernon 175.00 90.00
26 Clyde Vollmer 150.00 75.00
27 Gene Verble 150.00 75.00
28 Eddie Yost 150.00 75.00
29 Hank Bauer 200.00 100.00
30 Carl Erskine 200.00 100.00
31 Gil Hodges 300.00 150.00
32 Monte Irvin 300.00 150.00
33 Whitey Lockman 175.00 90.00
34 Mickey Mantle 2500.00 1250.00
35 Willie Mays 1250.00 600.00
36 Gil McDougald 200.00 100.00
37 Don Mueller 175.00 90.00
38 Don Newcombe 200.00 100.00
39 Phil Rizzuto 300.00 150.00
40 Duke Snider 500.00 250.00

1941 Browns W753

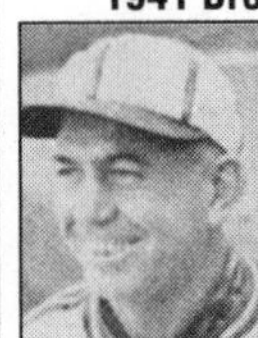
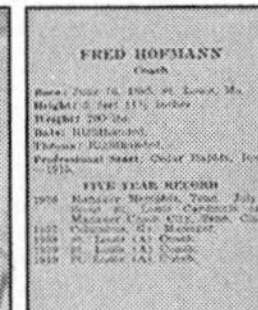

The cards in this 29-card set measure approximately 2 1/8" by 2 5/8". The 1941 W753 set features unnumbered cards of the St. Louis Browns. The cards are numbered below alphabetically by player's name. Similar to the W711-2 set, it was issued in a box with a reverse side resembling a mailing label. These sets were also available via mail-order. This set is valued at an extra $100 when still in its original mailing box.

Ex-Mt VG
COMPLETE SET (30) 500.00 250.00
1 Johnny Allen 20.00 10.00
2 Elden Auker 20.00 10.00
3 Donald L. Barnes OWN 15.00 7.50
4 Johnny Berardino 30.00 15.00
5 George Caster 15.00 7.50
6 Harland Clift 20.00 10.00
7 Roy J. Cullenbine 15.00 7.50
8 William O. DeWitt GM 15.00 7.50
9 Robert Estalella 15.00 7.50
10 Rick Ferrell 60.00 30.00
11 Dennis W. Galehouse 20.00 10.00
12 Joseph L. Grace 15.00 7.50
13 Frank Grube 15.00 7.50
14 Robert A. Harris 15.00 7.50
15 Donald Heffner 15.00 7.50
16 Fred Hofmann 15.00 7.50
17 Walter F. Judnich 15.00 7.50
18 Jack Kramer 15.00 7.50
19 Chester(Chet) Laabs 15.00 7.50
20 John Lucadello 15.00 7.50
21 George H. McQuinn 15.00 7.50
22 Robert Muncrief Jr. 15.00 7.50
23 John Niggeling 15.00 7.50
24 Fritz Ostermueller 15.00 7.50
25 James(Luke) Sewell MG 20.00 10.00
26 Alan C. Strange 15.00 7.50
27 Bob Swift 15.00 7.50
28 James(Zack) Taylor CO 15.00 7.50
29 Bill Trotter 15.00 7.50
30 Title Card 15.00 7.50
(Order Coupon on back)

1952 Browns Postcards

The 12-card set has glossy black and white with PC backs. It appears that backs determine the year. The 1952 cards have "Post Card" in script block lettering over the top if you lay the card down horizontally. There is a line dividing the back on one side"Correspondence" and the other "Address". There is no postage box. The cards are unnumbered and listed alphabetically.

NM Ex
COMPLETE SET (12) 120.00 60.00
1 Tommy Byrne 12.00 6.00
2 Bob Cain 10.00 5.00
3 Clint Courtney 10.00 5.00
4 Jim Delsing 10.00 5.00
5 Jim Dyck 10.00 5.00
6 Marty Marion 20.00 10.00
7 Cass Michaels 10.00 5.00
8 Bob Nieman 10.00 5.00
9 Satchel Paige 30.00 15.00
10 Duane Pillette 10.00 5.00
11 Jim Rivera 10.00 5.00
12 Bobby Young 10.00 5.00

1953 Browns Postcards

All the 1953 cards have divided backs, but "Photo Post Card" in double block lettering and then "Address" under that in smaller lettering. The only variation known is one of Ned Garver where the "Photo Post Card" is in a different type of lettering. Everything else is the same. The set is unnumbered and listed below in alphabetical order. The Don Larsen card predates his Bowman Rookie Card.

NM Ex
COMPLETE SET (31) 400.00 200.00
1 Neil Berry 10.00 5.00
portrait
2 Mike Blyzka 10.00 5.00
pitching
3 Harry Brecheen 15.00 7.50
portrait
4 Bob Cain 10.00 5.00
kneeling
5 Clint Courtney 10.00 5.00
portrait
6 Jim Dyck 10.00 5.00
hitting
7 Hank Edwards 10.00 5.00
portrait
8 Ned Garver 15.00 7.50
portrait
9 Johnny Groth 10.00 5.00
kneeling
10 Bobo Holloman 15.00 7.50
portrait
11 Bill Hunter 10.00 5.00
portrait
12 Dick Kokos 10.00 5.00
portrait
13 Dick Kryhoski 10.00 5.00
leaning
14 Max Lanier 10.00 5.00
portrait
15 Don Larsen 20.00 10.00
pitching
16 Don Lenhardt 10.00 5.00
portrait
17 Dick Littlefield 10.00 5.00
portrait
18 Marty Marion 15.00 7.50
portrait
19 Babe Martin 10.00 5.00
squatting
20 Willie Miranda 10.00 5.00
portrait
21 Les Moss 10.00 5.00
portrait
22 Bill Norman CO 10.00 5.00
23 Satchel Paige 40.00 20.00
pitching
24 Satchel Paige 40.00 20.00
kneeling
25 Duane Pillette 10.00 5.00
portrait
26 Bob Scheffing 10.00 5.00
hands on knees
27 Roy Sievers 15.00 7.50
portrait
28 Marlin Stuart 10.00 5.00
portrait
29 Virgil Trucks 10.00 5.00
portrait
30 Bill Veeck OWN 25.00 12.50
sitting at desk
31 Vic Wertz 15.00 7.50
hitting

1996 Browns '44 Fritsch

This 36-card set of the 1944 American League Champion St. Louis Browns Baseball team with a suggested retail price of $10 features an artist's rendition of the player on the front. The backs carry player information, career statistics, and a small cartoon depicting one aspect of the player's career.

Nm-Mt Ex-Mt
COMPLETE SET (36) 10.00 3.00
1 Team Card .25 .07
2 Don Gutteridge .25 .07
3 Milt Byrnes .25 .07
4 Al Hollingsworth .25 .07
5 Willis Hudlin .25 .07
6 Sid Jakucki .25 .07
7 Nelson Potter .50 .15
8 Len Schulte .25 .07
9 Vern Stephens .75 .23
10 Frank Demaree .25 .07
11 Al Zarilla .25 .07
12 Bob Muncrief .25 .07
13 Steve Sundra .25 .07
14 Jack Kramer .25 .07
15 Lefty West .25 .07
16 Denny Galehouse .25 .07
17 Luke Sewell MG .50 .15
18 Joe Schultz .50 .15
19 George McQuinn .75 .23
20 Ellis Clary .25 .07
21 Babe Martin .25 .07
22 Red Hayworth .25 .07
23 Frank Mancuso .25 .07
24 Tex Shirley .25 .07
25 Mike Chartak .25 .07
26 Mark Christman .25 .07
27 Tom Hafey .25 .07

Card		
28 Tom Turner	.25	.07
29 Floyd Baker	.25	.07
30 Mike Kreevich	.25	.07
31 George Caster	.25	.07
32 Gene Moore	.25	.07
33 Chet Laabs	.25	.07
34 Sam Zoldak	.25	.07
35 Hal Epps	.25	.07
36 Checklist	.25	.07

1998 Browns Heads Up

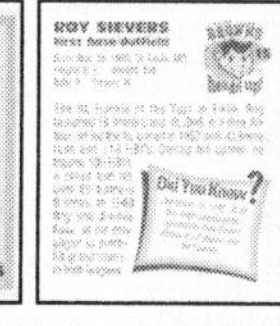

These 20 cards, issued in the style of the 1938 Goudey Heads Up set, was issued by the St. Louis Browns historical society and featured living alumni of the Browns. These cards measure 2 1/2" by 2" and are unnumbered so we have sequenced them in alphabetical order.

	Nm-Mt	Ex-Mt
COMPLETE SET (20)	8.00	2.40
1 Hank Arft	.25	.07
2 Ellis Clary	.25	.07
3 Jim Delsing	.25	.07
4 Ned Garver	.25	.07
5 Don Gutteridge	.25	.07
6 Red Hayworth	.25	.07
7 Bill Jennings	.25	.07
8 Dick Kryhoski	.25	.07
9 Don Lenhardt	.25	.07
10 Bob Mahoney	.25	.07
11 Frank Mancuso	.25	.07
12 Babe Martin	.25	.07
13 Ed Mickelson	.25	.07
14 Stan Musial	5.00	1.50
15 J.W. Porter	.25	.07
16 Arthur Richman	.25	.07
17 Roy Sievers	.50	.15
18 Virgil Trucks	.25	.07
19 Jerry Witte	.25	.07
20 Al Widmar	.25	.07

2003 Browns 1953 50th Anniversary

This 40 card standard-size set features many people associated with the 1953 St Louis Browns who were playing their final season before moving to Baltimore. The fronts feature player drawings along with the player name and a smaller print their position and team. The horizontal backs feature biographical information as well as their 1953 and career stats.

	MINT	NRMT
COMPLETE SET	10.00	4.50
1 Satchel Paige	1.50	.70
2 Les Moss	.25	.11
3 Roy Sievers	.50	.23
4 Bobby Young	.25	.11
5 Marlin Stuart	.25	.11
6 Billy Hunter	.25	.11
7 Don Lenhardt	.25	.11
8 Johnny Groth	.25	.11
9 Vic Wertz	.25	.11
10 Don Larsen	.75	.35
11 Clint Courtney	.25	.11
12 Dick Kryhoski	.25	.11
13 Neil Berry	.25	.11
14 Bob Cain	.25	.11
15 Willie Miranda	.25	.11
16 Hank Edwards	.25	.11
17 Dick Kokos	.25	.11
18 Jim Pisoni	.25	.11
19 Harry Brecheen	.50	.23
20 St Louis Browns	.50	.23
21 St Louis Browns CL	.50	.23
22 Lou Kretlow	.25	.11
23 Babe Martin	.25	.11
24 Ed Mickelson	.25	.11
25 Frank Kellert	.25	.11
26 Virgil Trucks	.25	.11
27 Dick Littlefield	.25	.11
28 Jim Dyck	.25	.11
29 Mike Blyzka	.25	.11
30 Bob Habenicht	.25	.11
31 Max Lanier	.25	.11
32 Bob Elliott	.25	.11
33 Duane Pillette	.25	.11
34 Johnny Lipon	.25	.11
35 Bob Turley	1.00	.45
36 Vern Stephens	.50	.23
37 Hal White	.25	.11
38 Dixie Upright	.25	.11
39 Bobo Holloman	.25	.11
40 Marty Marion MG	.50	.23

1976 Buchman Discs

These discs are a parallel version of the Crane Discs. These are differentiated by saying Buchman on the back and are valued at a multiple of the Crane Discs

	NM	Ex
COMPLETE SET (70)	25.00	10.00
1 Hank Aaron	3.00	1.20
2 Johnny Bench	2.00	.80
3 Vida Blue	.50	.20
4 Larry Bowa	.50	.20
5 Lou Brock	2.00	.80
6 Jeff Burroughs	.25	.10
7 John Candelaria	.25	.10
8 Jose Cardenal	.25	.10
9 Rod Carew	2.00	.80
10 Steve Carlton	2.00	.80
11 Dave Cash	.25	.10
12 Cesar Cedeno	.50	.20
13 Ron Cey	.50	.20
14 Carlton Fisk	2.50	1.00
15 Tito Fuentes	.25	.10
16 Steve Garvey	1.25	.50
17 Ken Griffey	.50	.20
18 Don Gullett	.25	.10
19 Willie Horton	.25	.10
20 Al Hrabosky	.25	.10
21 Catfish Hunter	2.00	.80
22A Reggie Jackson	6.00	2.40
Oakland Athletics		
22B Reggie Jackson	2.00	.80
Baltimore Orioles		
23 Randy Jones	.25	.10
24 Jim Kaat	.75	.30
25 Don Kessinger	.25	.10
26 Dave Kingman	.75	.30
27 Jerry Koosman	.50	.20
28 Mickey Lolich	.50	.20
29 Greg Luzinski	.75	.30
30 Fred Lynn	.75	.30
31 Bill Madlock	.50	.20
32A Carlos May	1.25	.50
Chicago White Sox		
32B Carlos May	.25	.10
New York Yankees		
33 John Mayberry	.25	.10
34 Bake McBride	.25	.10
35 Doc Medich	.25	.10
36A Andy Messersmith	1.25	.50
Los Angeles Dodgers		
36B Andy Messersmith	.25	.10
Atlanta Braves		
37 Rick Monday	.25	.10
38 John Montefusco	.25	.10
39 Jerry Morales	.25	.10
40 Joe Morgan	2.00	.80
41 Thurman Munson	1.25	.50
42 Bobby Murcer	.75	.30
43 Al Oliver	.75	.30
44 Jim Palmer	2.00	.80
45 Dave Parker	1.00	.40
46 Tony Perez	1.25	.50
47 Jerry Reuss	.25	.10
48 Brooks Robinson	2.00	.80
49 Frank Robinson	2.00	.80
50 Steve Rogers	.25	.10
51 Pete Rose	2.50	1.00
52 Nolan Ryan	5.00	2.00
53 Manny Sanguillen	.25	.10
54 Mike Schmidt	3.00	1.20
55 Tom Seaver	2.50	1.00
56 Ted Simmons	.75	.30
57 Reggie Smith	.50	.20
58 Willie Stargell	2.00	.80
59 Rusty Staub	.75	.30
60 Rennie Stennett	.25	.10
61 Don Sutton	2.00	.80
62A Andre Thornton	1.25	.50
Chicago Cubs		
62B Andre Thornton	.25	.10
Montreal Expos		
63 Luis Tiant	.75	.30
64 Joe Torre	1.00	.40
65 Mike Tyson	.25	.10
66 Bob Watson	.50	.20
67 Wilbur Wood	.25	.10
68 Jimmy Wynn	.25	.10
69 Carl Yastrzemski	2.00	.80
70 Richie Zisk	.25	.10

1887 Buchner N284

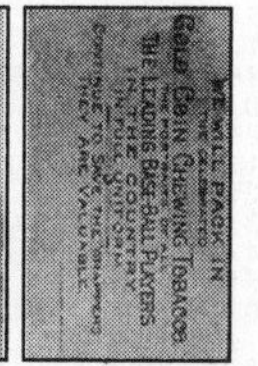

The baseball players found in this Buchner set are a part of a larger group of cards portraying policemen, jockeys and actors, all of which were issued with the tobacco brand "Gold Coin." The set is comprised of three major groupings or types. In the first type, nine players from eight teams, plus three Brooklyn players, are all portrayed in identical poses according to position. In the second type, St. Louis has 14 players depicted in poses which are not repeated. The last group contains 53 additional cards which vary according to pose, team change, spelling, etc. These third type cards are indicated in the checklist below by an asterisk. In all, there are 116 individuals portrayed on 142 cards. The existence of an additional player in the set, McClellan of Brooklyn, has never been verified and the card probably doesn't exist. The set was issued circa 1887. The cards are numbered below in alphabetical order within team with teams themselves listed in alphabetical order: Baltimore (1-4), Boston (5-13), Brooklyn (14-17), Chicago (18-26), Detroit (27-35), Indianapolis (36-47), LaCrosse (48-51), Milwaukee (52-55), New York Mets (56-63), New York (64-73), Philadelphia (74-83), Pittsburg (84-92), St. Louis (93-106), and Washington (107-117).

	Ex-Mt	VG
COMPLETE SET (152)	30000.00	15000.00
COMMON ST. LOUIS	250.00	125.00
COMMON CARD *	150.00	75.00
1 Tommy(Oyster) Burns *	150.00	75.00
2 Chris Fulmer *	150.00	75.00
3 Matt Kilroy	150.00	75.00
4 Blondie Purcell *	150.00	75.00
5 John Burdock	150.00	75.00
6 Bill Daley	150.00	75.00
7 Joe Hornung	150.00	75.00
8 Dick Johnston	150.00	75.00
9A King Kelly: Boston	400.00	200.00
Right field		
9B King Kelly: Boston	600.00	300.00
Catcher *		
10A John Morrell	150.00	75.00
Boston		
Both hands		
out-stretched face high		
10B John Morrell	150.00	75.00
Boston *		
Hands clasped		
near chin		
11A Hoss Radbourn:	400.00	200.00
Boston		
Sic, Radbourne		
11B Hoss Radbourn:	500.00	250.00
Boston *		
Sic, Radbourne;		
hands together		
above waist		
12 Ezra Sutton	150.00	75.00
13 Sam Wise	150.00	75.00
14 Bill McClellan:		
Brooklyn		
Never confirmed		
15 Jimmy Peoples	150.00	75.00
16 Bill Phillips	150.00	75.00
17 Henry Porter	150.00	75.00
18A Cap Anson	800.00	400.00
Chicago		
Both hands out-stretched		
face high		
18B Cap Anson:	1200.00	600.00
Chicago *		
Left hand on hip		
right hand down		
19 Tom Burns	150.00	75.00
20A John Clarkson	400.00	200.00
Chicago		
20B John Clarkson:	500.00	250.00
Chicago *		
Right arm extended		
left arm near side		
21 Silver Flint	150.00	75.00
22 Fred Pfeffer	150.00	75.00
23 Jimmy Ryan	200.00	100.00
24 Billy Sullivan	200.00	100.00
25 Billy Sunday	400.00	200.00
26A Ned Williamson:	150.00	75.00
Chicago		
Shortstop		
26B Ned Williamson:	150.00	75.00
Chicago		
Second base *		
27 Charlie Bennett	200.00	100.00
28A Dan Brouthers:	400.00	200.00
Detroit		
Fielding		
28B Dan Brouthers:	500.00	250.00
Detroit *		
Batting		
29 Fred Dunlap	150.00	75.00
30 Charlie Getzien	150.00	75.00
31 Ned Hanlon	300.00	150.00
32 Jim Manning	150.00	75.00
33A Hardy Richardson:	150.00	75.00
Detroit		
Hands together in		
front of chest		
33B Hardy Richardson:	150.00	75.00
Detroit *		
Right hand holding		
ball above head		
34A Sam Thompson:	400.00	200.00
Detroit		
Looking up with		
hands at waist		
34B Sam Thompson:	500.00	250.00
Detroit *		
Hands chest high		
35 Deacon White	250.00	125.00
36 Tug Arundels	150.00	75.00
37 Charley Bassett	150.00	75.00
38 Henry Boyle *	150.00	75.00
39 John Cahill *	150.00	75.00
40A Jerry Denny:	150.00	75.00
Indianapolis		
Hands on knees		
legs bent		
40B Jerry Denny:	150.00	75.00
Indianapolis *		
Hands on knees		
legs not bent		
41A Jack Glasscock:	200.00	100.00
Indianapolis		
Crouching		
catching a grounder		
41B Jack Glasscock:	200.00	100.00
Indianapolis *		
Hands on knees		
42 John Healy	150.00	75.00
43 George Meyers *	150.00	75.00
44 Jack McGeachy	150.00	75.00
45 Mark Polhemus	150.00	75.00
46A Emmett Seery:	150.00	75.00
Indianapolis		
Hands together in		
front of chest		
46B Emmett Seery:	200.00	100.00
Indianapolis *		
Hands outstretched		
head high		
47 Shomberg	150.00	75.00
48 Corbett *	150.00	75.00
49 Crowley *	150.00	75.00
50 Kennedy *	150.00	75.00
51 Rooks *	150.00	75.00
52 Forster *	150.00	75.00
53 Hart *	150.00	75.00
54 Morrissy *	150.00	75.00
55 Strauss *	150.00	75.00
56 Ed Cushmann *	150.00	75.00
57 Jim Donohue *	150.00	75.00
58 Dude Esterbrooke *	150.00	75.00
59 Joe Gerhardt *	150.00	75.00
60 Frank Hankinson *	150.00	75.00
61 Jack Nelson *	150.00	75.00
62 Dave Orr *	150.00	75.00
63 James Rosemann *	150.00	75.00
64A Roger Connor:	400.00	200.00
New York		
Both hands		
out-stretched face high		
64B Roger Connor:	500.00	250.00
New York *		
Hands outstretched		
palms up		
65 Pat Deasley *	150.00	75.00
66A Mike Dorgan	150.00	75.00
Fielding		
66B Mike Dorgan	150.00	75.00
Batting *		
67A Buck Ewing	400.00	200.00
New York (Ball in left hand		
right arm out shoulder high		
67B Buck Ewing	500.00	250.00
New York *		
Appears ready to clap		
68A Pete Gillespie:	150.00	75.00
New York		
Fielding		
68B Pete Gillespie:	150.00	75.00
New York		
Batting *		
69 George Gore	150.00	75.00
70A Tim Keefe:	400.00	200.00
New York		
70B Tim Keefe:	500.00	250.00
New York *		
Ball just released		
from right hand		
71A Jim O'Rourke:	400.00	200.00
New York		
Hands cupped in		
front, thigh high		
71B Jim O'Rourke:	500.00	250.00
New York *		
Hands on knees		
looking right		
72A Danny Richardson:	150.00	75.00
New York		
Third base		
72B Danny Richardson:	150.00	75.00
New York		
Second base*		
73A John M. Ward:	400.00	200.00
New York		
Crouching, catching a grounder		
73B John M. Ward:	500.00	250.00
New York *		
Hands by left knee		
73C John M. Ward:	400.00	200.00
New York *		
Hands on knees		
74A Ed Andrews:	150.00	75.00
Philadelphia		
Hands together in		
front of neck		
74B Ed Andrews:	150.00	75.00
Philadelphia *		
Catching, hands waist high		
75 Charlie Bastian	150.00	75.00
76 Dan Casey *	150.00	75.00
77 Jack Clements	150.00	75.00
78 Sid Farrar	200.00	100.00
79 Charlie Ferguson	150.00	75.00
80 Jim Fogarty	150.00	75.00
81 Arthur Irwin	150.00	75.00
82A Joel Mulvey:	150.00	75.00
Philadelphia		
Hands on knees		
82B Joel Mulvey:	150.00	75.00
Philadelphia *		
Hands together		
above head		
83A Pete Wood	150.00	75.00
Philadelphia		
Fielding		
83B Pete Wood	200.00	100.00
Philadelphia HOR		
Stealing a Base *		
84 Sam Barkley	150.00	75.00
85 Ed Beecher:	150.00	75.00
86 Tom Brown	150.00	75.00
87 Fred Carroll	150.00	75.00
88 John Coleman	150.00	75.00
89 Jim McCormick	150.00	75.00
90 Doggie Miller	150.00	75.00
91 Pop Smith	150.00	75.00
92 Art Whitney	150.00	75.00
93 Sam Barkley	250.00	125.00
94 Doc Bushong	250.00	125.00
95 Bob Carruthers	300.00	150.00
96 Charles Comiskey	600.00	300.00
97 Dave Foutz	250.00	125.00
98 William Gleason	300.00	150.00
99 Arlie Latham	400.00	200.00
100 Jumbo McGinnis	250.00	125.00
101 Hugh Nicol	250.00	125.00
102 James O'Neil	250.00	125.00
103 Yank Robinson	250.00	125.00
104 Sullivan	250.00	125.00
105 C.Von Der Ahe OWN.	800.00	400.00
Actually a photo		
rather than drawing		
106 Curt Welch	300.00	150.00
107 Cliff Carroll	150.00	75.00
108 Craig *	150.00	75.00
109 Sam Crane *	150.00	75.00
110 Ed Dailey	150.00	75.00
111 Jim Donnelly	150.00	75.00
112A Jack Farrell:	150.00	75.00
Washington		
Ball in left hand		
right arm out shoulder high		
112B Jack Farrell:	150.00	75.00
Washington *		
Ball in hands		
near right knee		
113 Barney Gilligan	150.00	75.00
114A Paul Hines:	150.00	75.00
Washington		
Fielding		
114B Paul Hines:	150.00	75.00
Washington *		
Batting		
115 Al Myers	150.00	75.00
116 Billy O'Brien	150.00	75.00
117 Jim Whitney	150.00	75.00

1977 Burger Chef Discs

The individual discs measure approximately 2 1/2" in diameter and contain a burger-related caricature on the reverse. There were nine discs on each tray; five on the front and four on the back. Each tray contained one team and there were 24 different trays, obviously one for each team. On the tray the copyright notice indicates 1977. The player photos are shown without team logos on their caps. We have sequenced this set in the following order: Houston (1-9), St. Louis (10-18), Texas (19-27), Boston (28-36), Baltimore (37-45), Minnesota (46-54), Cleveland (55-63), Kansas City (64-72), Chicago White Sox (73-81), Milwaukee (82-90), Detroit (91-99), San Francisco (100-108), Oakland (109-117), California (118-126), San Diego (127-135), New York Mets (136-144), Los Angeles (145-153), Montreal (154-162), Philadelphia (163-171), New York Yankees (172-180), Pirates (181-189), Chicago Cubs (190-198), Cincinnati (199-207), Atlanta (208-216). No 1977 expansion teams were featured in this set. Complete Panels are worth twice the amount of the values for each team.

	NM	Ex
COMPLETE SET (216)	150.00	60.00
1 J.R. Richard	.50	.20
2 Enos Cabell	.25	.10
3 Leon Roberts	.25	.10
4 Ken Forsch	.25	.10
5 Roger Metzger	.25	.10
6 Bob Watson	.50	.20
7 Cesar Cedeno	.50	.20
8 Joe Ferguson	.25	.10
9 Jose Cruz	.50	.20
10 Al Hrabosky	.25	.10
11 Keith Hernandez	1.50	.60
12 Pete Falcone	.25	.10
13 Ken Reitz	.25	.10
14 John Denny	.25	.10
15 Lou Brock	4.00	1.60
16 Ted Simmons	1.00	.40
17 Bake McBride	.25	.10
18 Mike Tyson	.25	.10
19 Campy Campaneris	.50	.20
20 Gaylord Perry	3.00	1.20
21 Lenny Randle	.25	.10
22 Bert Blyleven	1.00	.40
23 Jim Sundberg	.50	.20
24 Mike Hargrove	.50	.20
25 Tom Grieve	.50	.20
26 Toby Harrah	.25	.10
27 Juan Beniquez	.25	.10
28 Rick Burleson	.25	.10
29 Jim Rice	1.50	.60
30 Dwight Evans	1.00	.40
31 Fergie Jenkins	3.00	1.20
32 Bill Lee	.25	.10
33 Carlton Fisk	6.00	2.40
34 Luis Tiant	1.00	.40
35 Fred Lynn	.50	.20
36 Carl Yastrzemski	4.00	1.60
37 Al Bumbry	.25	.10
38 Mark Belanger	.50	.20
39 Paul Blair	.25	.10
40 Ross Grimsley	.25	.10
41 Ken Singleton	.50	.20
42 Jim Palmer	4.00	1.60
43 Brooks Robinson	4.00	1.60
44 Doug DeCinces	.50	.20
45 Lee May	.50	.20
46 Tom Johnson	.25	.10
47 Dave Goltz	.25	.10
48 Dan Ford	.25	.10
49 Larry Hisle	.25	.10
50 Mike Cubbage	.25	.10
51 Rod Carew	4.00	1.60
52 Bobby Randall	.25	.10
53 Butch Wynegar	.25	.10
54 Lyman Bostock	.50	.20
55 Duane Kuiper	.25	.10
56 Rick Manning	.25	.10
57 Buddy Bell	1.00	.40
58 Dennis Eckersley	5.00	2.00
59 Wayne Garland	.25	.10
60 Dave LaRoche	.25	.10
61 Rick Waits	.25	.10
62 Ray Fosse	.25	.10
63 Frank Duffy	.25	.10
64 Paul Splittorff	.25	.10
65 Amos Otis	.50	.20
66 Tom Poquette	.25	.10
67 Fred Patek	.25	.10
68 Doug Bird	.25	.10
69 John Mayberry	.25	.10
70 Dennis Leonard	.25	.10
71 George Brett	25.00	10.00
72 Hal McRae	1.00	.40
73 Chet Lemon	.50	.20
74 Jorge Orta	.25	.10
75 Richie Zisk	.25	.10
76 Lamar Johnson	.25	.10
77 Bart Johnson	.25	.01
78 Jack Brohamer	.25	.10
79 Jim Spencer	.25	.10
80 Ralph Garr	.25	.10
81 Bucky Dent	.50	.20
82 Jerry Augustine	.25	.10
83 Jim Slaton	.25	.10
84 Charlie Moore	.25	.10
85 Von Joshua	.25	.10
86 Eduardo Rodriquez	.25	.10
87 Sal Bando	.50	.20
88 Robin Yount	6.00	2.40
89 Sixto Lezcano	.25	.10

90 Bill Travers	.25	.10
91 Ben Oglivie	.25	.10
92 Mark Fidrych	5.00	2.00
93 Aurelio Rodriquez	.25	.10
94 Bill Freehan	1.00	.40
95 John Hiller	.25	.10
96 Rusty Staub	1.00	.40
97 Willie Horton	.50	.20
98 Ron LeFlore	.50	.20
99 Jason Thompson	.50	.20
100 Marty Perez	.25	.10
101 Randy Moffitt	.25	.10
102 Gary Thomasson	.25	.10
103 Jim Barr	.25	.10
104 Larry Herndon	.25	.10
105 Bobby Murcer	1.00	.40
106 John Montefusco	.25	.10
107 Willie Crawford	.25	.10
108 Chris Speier	.25	.10
109 Phil Garner	1.00	.40
110 Mike Torrez	.25	.10
111 Manny Sanguillen	.25	.10
112 Stan Bahnsen	.25	.10
113 Mike Norris	.25	.10
114 Vida Blue	1.00	.40
115 Claudell Washington	.50	.20
116 Bill North	.25	.10
117 Paul Lindblad	.25	.10
118 Paul Hartzell	.25	.10
119 Dave Chalk	.25	.10
120 Ron Jackson	.25	.10
121 Jerry Remy	.25	.10
122 Frank Tanana	1.00	.40
123 Nolan Ryan	25.00	10.00
124 Bobby Bonds	.50	.20
125 Joe Rudi	.50	.20
126 Bobby Grich	1.00	.40
127 Butch Metzger	.25	.10
128 Doug Rader	.25	.10
129 George Hendrick	.50	.20
130 David Winfield	8.00	3.20
131 Gene Tenace	1.00	.40
132 Randy Jones	.25	.10
133 Rollie Fingers	3.00	1.20
134 Mike Ivie	.25	.10
135 Enzo Hernandez	.25	.10
136 Ed Kranepool	.25	.10
137 John Matlack	.25	.10
138 Felix Millan	.25	.10
139 Skip Lockwood	.25	.10
140 John Stearns	.25	.10
141 Dave Kingman	1.50	.60
142 Tom Seaver	6.00	2.40
143 Jerry Koosman	1.00	.40
144 Bud Harrelson	.25	.10
145 Davey Lopes	.50	.20
146 Rick Monday	.25	.10
147 Don Sutton	3.00	1.20
148 Rick Rhoden	.25	.10
149 Doug Rau	.25	.10
150 Steve Garvey	2.00	.80
151 Steve Yeager	.25	.10
152 Reggie Smith	.50	.20
153 Ron Cey	1.00	.40
154 Gary Carter	5.00	2.00
155 Del Unser	.25	.10
156 Tim Foli	.25	.10
157 Barry Foote	.25	.10
158 Ellis Valentine	.25	.10
159 Steve Rogers	.25	.10
160 Tony Perez	2.50	1.00
161 Larry Parrish	.50	.20
162 Dave Cash	.25	.10
163 Greg Luzinski	1.00	.40
164 Bob Boone	1.00	.40
165 Tug McGraw	1.00	.40
166 Jay Johnstone	.50	.20
167 Garry Maddox	.25	.10
168 Mike Schmidt	15.00	6.00
169 Jim Kaat	1.50	.60
170 Larry Bowa	1.00	.40
171 Steve Carlton	6.00	2.40
172 Don Gullett	.25	.10
173 Chris Chambliss	.25	.10
174 Graig Nettles	1.00	.40
175 Willie Randolph	1.50	.60
176 Reggie Jackson	6.00	2.40
177 Thurman Munson	2.50	1.00
178 Catfish Hunter	4.00	1.60
179 Roy White	.50	.20
180 Mickey Rivers	.25	.10
181 Jerry Reuss	.50	.20
182 Rennie Stennett	.25	.10
183 Bill Robinson	.25	.10
184 Frank Taveras	.25	.10
185 Duffy Dyer	.25	.10
186 Willie Stargell	4.00	1.60
187 Dave Parker	2.50	1.00
188 John Candelaria	.50	.20
189 Al Oliver	1.00	.40
190 Joe Wallis	.25	.10
191 Manny Trillo	.25	.10
192 Bill Bonham	.25	.10
193 Rick Reuschel	.50	.20
194 Ray Burris	.25	.10
195 Bill Buckner	.50	.20
196 Jerry Morales	.25	.10
197 Jose Cardenal	.25	.10
198 Bill Madlock	1.00	.40
199 Dan Driessen	.25	.10
200 Dave Concepcion	1.00	.40
201 George Foster	1.00	.40
202 Cesar Geronimo	.25	.10
203 Gary Nolan	.25	.10
204 Pete Rose	10.00	4.00
205 Johnny Bench	6.00	2.40
206 Ken Griffey	1.00	.40
207 Joe Morgan	4.00	1.60
208 Dick Ruthven	.25	.10
209 Phil Niekro	3.00	1.20
210 Gary Matthews	.50	.20
211 Willie Montanez	.25	.10
212 Jerry Royster	.25	.10
213 Andy Messersmith	.25	.10
214 Jeff Burroughs	.50	.20
215 Tom Paciorek	.50	.20
216 Darrel Chaney	.25	.10

1980 Burger King Pitch/Hit/Run

The cards in this 34-card set measure 2 1/2" by 3 1/2". The "Pitch, Hit, and Run" set was a promotion introduced by Burger King in 1980. The cards carry a Burger King logo on the front and those marked by an asterisk in the checklist contain a different photo from that found in the regularly issued Topps series. For example, Nolan Ryan was shown as a California Angel and Joe Morgan was a Cincinnati Red in the 1980 Topps regular set. Cards 1-11 are pitchers, 12-22 are hitters, and 23-33 are speedsters. Within each subgroup, the players are numbered corresponding to the alphabetical order of their names.

	NM	Ex
COMPLETE SET (34)	20.00	8.00
1 Vida Blue *	.50	.20
2 Steve Carlton	1.50	.60
3 Rollie Fingers	1.00	.40
4 Ron Guidry *	.50	.20
5 Jerry Koosman *	.25	.10
6 Phil Niekro	1.00	.40
7 Jim Palmer *	1.50	.60
8 J.R. Richard	.25	.10
9 Nolan Ryan * Houston Astros	10.00	4.00
10 Tom Seaver *	2.00	.80
11 Bruce Sutter	.25	.10
12 Don Baylor	.50	.20
13 George Brett	5.00	2.00
14 Rod Carew	1.25	.50
15 George Foster	.25	.10
16 Keith Hernandez *	.50	.20
17 Reggie Jackson *	3.00	1.20
18 Fred Lynn *	.50	.20
19 Dave Parker	.25	.10
20 Jim Rice	.25	.10
21 Pete Rose	3.00	1.20
22 Dave Winfield *	2.00	.80
23 Bobby Bonds *	.50	.20
24 Enos Cabell	.10	.04
25 Cesar Cedeno	.25	.10
26 Julio Cruz	.10	.04
27 Ron LeFlore *	.25	.10
28 Dave Lopes *	.25	.10
29 Omar Moreno *	.25	.10
30 Joe Morgan * Houston Astros	2.00	.80
31 Bill North	.10	.04
32 Frank Taveras	.10	.04
33 Willie Wilson	.25	.10
NNO Checklist Card TP	.05	.02

1986 Burger King All-Pro

This 20-card standard-size set was distributed in Burger King restaurants across the country. They were produced as panels of three where the middle card was actually a special discount coupon card. The folded panel was given with the purchase of a Whopper. Each individual card measures 2 1/2" by 3 1/2". The team logos have been airbrushed from the pictures. The cards are numbered on the front at the top.

	Nm-Mt	Ex-Mt
COMPLETE SET (20)	10.00	4.00
1 Tony Pena	.10	.04
2 Dave Winfield	.75	.30
3 Fernando Valenzuela	.25	.10
4 Pete Rose	1.25	.50
5 Mike Schmidt	1.25	.50
6 Steve Carlton	.50	.20
7 Glenn Wilson	.10	.04
8 Jim Rice	.25	.10
9 Wade Boggs	1.25	.50
10 Juan Samuel	.10	.04
11 Dale Murphy	.50	.20
12 Reggie Jackson	.75	.30
13 Kirk Gibson	.25	.10
14 Eddie Murray	1.25	.50
15 Cal Ripken	5.00	2.00
16 Willie McGee	.25	.10
17 Dwight Gooden	.25	.10
18 Steve Garvey	.50	.20
19 Don Mattingly	2.50	1.00
20 George Brett	2.50	1.00

1987 Burger King All-Pro

This 20-card set consists of ten panels of two cards each joined together along with a promotional coupon. Individual cards measure 2 1/2" by 3 1/2" whereas the panels measure approximately 3 1/2" by 7 5/8". MSA (Mike Schechter Associates produced the cards for Burger King; there are no Major League logos on the cards. The cards are numbered on the front. The set card numbering is almost (but not quite) in alphabetical order by player's name.

	Nm-Mt	Ex-Mt
COMPLETE SET (20)	6.00	2.40
1 Wade Boggs	.75	.30
2 Gary Carter	.30	.12
3 Will Clark	.75	.30
4 Roger Clemens	1.50	.60
5 Steve Garvey	.30	.12
6 Ron Darling	.10	.04
7 Pedro Guerrero	.10	.04
8 Von Hayes	.10	.04
9 Rickey Henderson	1.00	.40
10 Keith Hernandez	.20	.08
11 Wally Joyner	.50	.20
12 Mike Krukow	.10	.04
13 Don Mattingly	1.50	.60
14 Ozzie Smith	.75	.30
15 Tony Pena	.10	.04
16 Jim Rice	.20	.08
17 Mike Schmidt	.50	.20
18 Ryne Sandberg	1.50	.60
19 Darryl Strawberry	.10	.04
20 Fernando Valenzuela	.20	.08

1994 Burger King Ripken

Co-sponsored by Coca-Cola and Burger King, this nine-card standard-size set was produced by Pinnacle to honor Baltimore Orioles star shortstop, Cal Ripken Jr. Three-card packs were available for 25 cents with the purchase of a large soft drink at Baltimore and Washington, D.C. Burger Kings, beginning May 22. The cards were available until June 19, or while supplies lasted. Each card was issued in two versions: standard and gold-foil, with the three-card packs containing two standard and one gold foil card. Ripken autographed several hundred cards, which were awarded in a drawing held after the promotion to collectors who had mailed in entry forms. The cards are numbered on the back as "X of 9."

	Nm-Mt	Ex-Mt
COMPLETE SET (9)	5.00	1.50
COMMON CARD (1-9)	.75	.23
*GOLD CARDS: 2X BASIC CARDS		

1997 Burger King Ripken

This eight-card set features borderless color action photos of Cal Ripken Jr. and was sponsored by Burger King. The backs carry another photo and a paragraph about an event in the life of Cal Ripken Jr. The set was available in three-card packs beginning August 4, and running through September 13, 1997 at participating Burger Kings for 99 cents a pack with the purchase of a Value Meal. The cards were also available in limited quantities to be purchased separately for $1.15 per pack. Each pack contained a game piece which gave the collector a chance to win a Ripken watch or autographed Ripken balls or jerseys. All proceeds from this promotion benefited the Ripken Charities.

	Nm-Mt	Ex-Mt
COMPLETE SET (8)	6.00	1.80
COMMON CARD (1-8)	1.00	.30
*GOLD: 2X BASIC CARDS		
AU Cal Ripken Jr. AU Certified Autograph	100.00	30.00

1938-59 George Burke PC744

The Burke postcards were issued by Chicago photographer George Burke during the period from 1938 through the 1950's. Because there are hundreds known and new ones are discovered frequently, a checklist has not been provided. The reverses feature the stamped name of "Geo. Burke, his address and the city "Chicago"

	Ex-Mt	VG
COMMON CARD (1938-48)	10.00	5.00
COMMON CARD (1948-on)	5.00	2.50

1978 Burlington Free Press

These newspaper inserts feature members of the Boston Red Sox and the Montreal Expos. Since each team was reasonably near Burlington, Vermont -- that is why the set consists of players from those teams. These cards are unnumbered, so we have sequenced them in alphabetical order. There are probably many additions to this set so any additional information is greatly appreciated.

	NM	Ex
COMPLETE SET	15.00	6.00
1 Bernie Carbo	1.00	.40
2 Dave Cash	1.00	.40
3 Dick Drago	1.00	.40
4 Pepe Frias	1.00	.40
5 Wayne Garrett	1.00	.40
6 Ross Grimsley	1.00	.40
7 Butch Hobson	1.00	.40
8 Bill Lee	1.25	.50
9 Rudy May	1.00	.40
10 Bob Montgomery	1.00	.40
11 Larry Parrish	1.00	.40
12 Jerry Remy	1.00	.40
13 Rodney Scott	1.00	.40
14 Chris Speier	1.00	.40
15 Wayne Twitchell	1.00	.40
16 Del Unser	1.00	.40
17 Ellis Valentine	1.00	.40
18 Dick Williams MG	1.00	.40

1933 Butter Cream R306

The small, elongated (measuring 1 1/4" by 3 1/2") cards of this 30 card set are unnumbered and contain many cut-down, blurry black and white photos. The producer's name is sometimes printed on the reverse. Despite their limitations, Butter Cream cards are highly prized by collectors. The cards have been alphabetized and numbered for reference in the checklist below. The Babe Ruth card is significantly scarcer than the other cards in the set; although almost never seen, we have priced it in this set. The Ruth card is not included in the set price. There are two varieties of the back: One says "Your estimate of this year to Sept 1st; and "Your estimate of this year to Oct. 1st.

	Ex-Mt	VG
COMPLETE SET (29)	8000.00	4000.00
1 Earl Averill	300.00	150.00
2 Ed Brandt	200.00	100.00
3 Guy T. Bush	200.00	100.00
4 Mickey Cochrane	400.00	200.00
5 Joe Cronin	400.00	200.00
6 George Earnshaw	200.00	100.00
7 Wesley Ferrell	250.00	125.00
8 Jimmy Foxx	400.00	200.00
9 Frank Frisch	400.00	200.00
10 Charles M. Gelbert	200.00	100.00
11 Lefty Grove	400.00	200.00
12 Gabby Hartnett	300.00	150.00
13 Babe Herman	300.00	150.00
14 Chuck Klein	300.00	150.00
15 Ray Kremer	200.00	100.00
16 Fred Lindstrom	300.00	150.00
17 Ted Lyons	300.00	150.00
18 Pepper Martin	250.00	125.00
19 Robert O'Farrell	200.00	100.00
20 Ed A. Rommell	200.00	100.00
21 Charles Root	200.00	100.00
22 Harold Ruel	200.00	100.00
23 Babe Ruth SP	15000.00	7500.00
24 Al Simmons	400.00	200.00
25 Bill Terry	400.00	200.00
26 George Uhle	200.00	100.00
27 Lloyd Waner	300.00	150.00
28 Paul Waner	400.00	200.00
29 Hack Wilson	300.00	150.00
30 Glenn Wright	200.00	100.00

1933 Butterfinger Canadian V94

These large photos measure approximately 6 1/2" by 8 1/2" and are printed on thin paper stock. The fronts feature black-and-white posed action shots within white borders. A facsimile autograph is inscribed across the picture. The backs are blank.

	Ex-Mt	VG
COMPLETE SET	4000.00	2000.00
1 Earl Averill	80.00	40.00
2 Larry Benton	40.00	20.00
3 Jim Bottomley	80.00	40.00
4 Tom Bridges	50.00	25.00
5 Bob Brown	40.00	20.00
6 Owen T. Carroll	40.00	20.00
7 Mickey Cochrane	125.00	60.00
8 Roger Cramer	50.00	25.00
9 Joe Cronin	125.00	60.00
10 Alvin Crowder	50.00	25.00
11 Dizzy Dean	150.00	75.00
12 Edward Delker	40.00	20.00
13 Bill Dickey	125.00	60.00
14 Rick Ferrell	80.00	40.00
15 Lew Fonseca	50.00	25.00
16A Jimmy Foxx Name spelled Fox	150.00	75.00
16B Jimmie Foxx Name spelled correctly	40.00	20.00
17 Chuck Fullis	40.00	20.00
18 Lou Gehrig	300.00	150.00
19 Charles Gehringer	125.00	60.00
20 Lefty Gomez	125.00	60.00
21 Lefty Grove	150.00	75.00
22 Mule Haas	40.00	20.00
23 Chick Hafey	80.00	40.00
24 Stanley Harris	80.00	40.00
25 Frank Higgins	40.00	20.00
26 Shorty Hogan	40.00	20.00
27 Ed Holley	40.00	20.00
28 Waite Hoyt	80.00	40.00
29 Jim Jordan	40.00	20.00
30 Hal Lee	40.00	20.00
31 Gus Mancuso	50.00	25.00
32 Oscar Melillo	40.00	20.00
33 Austin Moore	40.00	20.00
34 Randy Moore	40.00	20.00
35 Joe Morrissey	40.00	20.00
36 Joe Mowry	40.00	20.00
37 Bobo Newsom	50.00	25.00
38 Ernest Orsatti	40.00	20.00
39 Carl Reynolds	40.00	20.00
40 Walter Roettger	40.00	20.00
41 Babe Ruth	400.00	200.00
42 Blondy Ryan	40.00	20.00
43 John Salveson	40.00	20.00
44 Al Simmons	125.00	60.00
45 Al Smith	40.00	20.00
46 Harold Smith	40.00	20.00
47 Allyn Stout	40.00	20.00
48 Fresco Thompson	50.00	25.00
49 Art Veltman	40.00	20.00
50 Johnny Vergez	40.00	20.00
51 Gerald Walker	40.00	20.00
52 Paul Waner	80.00	40.00
53 Burgess Whitehead	40.00	20.00
54 Earl Whitehill	40.00	20.00
55 Robert Weiland	40.00	20.00
56 Jimmy Wilson	50.00	25.00
57 Bob Worthington	40.00	20.00
58 Tom Zachary	50.00	25.00

1934 Butterfinger Premiums R310

This large-size premium set comes either i paper or on heavy cardboard stock wit advertising for Butterfinger or other candy a the top. The heavy cardboard Butterfinge display advertising cards are valued at triple th prices in the list below. The cards ar unnumbered and Foxx exists as Fox or Foxx The cards measure approximately 7 3/4" by 3/4" and have a thick off-white border aroun the player photo.

	Ex-Mt	VG
COMPLETE SET (65)	3000.00	1500.00
1 Earl Averill	40.00	20.00
2 Dick Bartell	25.00	12.50
3 Lawrence Benton	25.00	12.50
4 Wally Berger	30.00	15.00
5 Jim Bottomley	40.00	20.00
6 Ralph Boyle	25.00	12.50
7 Tex Carleton	25.00	12.50
8 Owen T. Carroll	25.00	12.5
9 Ben Chapman	25.00	12.5
10 Mickey Cochrane	60.00	30.0
11 Jimmy Collins	25.00	12.5
12 Joe Cronin	60.00	30.0
13 Al Crowder	25.00	12.5
14 Dizzy Dean	125.00	60.0
15 Paul Derringer	30.00	15.0
16 Bill Dickey	60.00	30.0
17 Leo Durocher	60.00	30.0
18 George Earnshaw	25.00	12.5
19 Dick Ferrell	40.00	20.0
20 Lew Fonseca	30.00	15.0
21A Jimmie Fox sic, Foxx	120.00	60.0
21B Jimmie Foxx	120.00	60.00
22 Benny Frey	25.00	12.50
23 Frankie Frisch	60.00	30.00
24 Lou Gehrig	300.00	150.00
25 Charley Gehringer	60.00	30.00
26 Lefty Gomez	60.00	30.00
27 Ray Grabowski	25.00	12.50
28 Lefty Grove	75.00	38.00
29 Mule Haas	25.00	12.5
30 Chick Hafey	40.00	20.0
31 Stanley Harris	40.00	20.0
32 Francis J. Hogan	25.00	12.5
33 Ed Holley	25.00	12.5
34 Rogers Hornsby	100.00	50.0
35 Waite Hoyt	40.00	20.0
36 Walter Johnson	200.00	100.0
37 Jim Jordan	25.00	12.5
38 Joe Kuhel	25.00	12.5
39 Hal Lee	25.00	12.5
40 Gus Mancuso	25.00	12.5
41 Heinie Manush	40.00	20.0
42 Fred Marberry	25.00	12.5
43 Pepper Martin	30.00	15.0
44 Oscar Melillo	25.00	12.5
45 Johnny Moore	25.00	12.5
46 Joe Morrisey	25.00	12.5
47 Joe Mowrey	25.00	12.5
48 Bob O'Farrell	25.00	12.5
49 Mel Ott	80.00	40.0

50 Monte Pearson 30.00 15.00
51 Carl Reynolds 25.00 12.50
52 Red Ruffing 40.00 20.00
53 Babe Ruth 400.00 200.00
54 John Ryan 25.00 12.50
55 Al Simmons 40.00 20.00
56 Al Spohrer 25.00 12.50
57 Gus Suhr 25.00 12.50
58 Steve Swetonic 30.00 15.00
59 Dazzy Vance 40.00 20.00
60 Joe Vosmik 25.00 12.50
61 Lloyd Waner 40.00 20.00
62 Paul Waner 40.00 20.00
63 Sam West 25.00 12.50
64 Earl Whitehill 25.00 12.50
65 Jimmy Wilson 25.00 12.50

1989 Cadaco Ellis Discs

The 1989 Cadaco Ellis discs were designed to be used in a game. These are large-sized discs, measuring approximately 3 1/2" in diameter, the standard size which has been used for many decades by the Cadaco Company for the game which was called at one point the Ethan Allen Cadaco game. This set marks the first time that full color photos were used on the front, but with no team logo. The backs contain complete major league statistics on the back. The set is checklisted in alphabetical order.

Nm-Mt Ex-Mt
COMPLETE SET (63) 60.00 24.00
1 Harold Baines 1.00 .40
2 Wade Boggs 2.00 .80
3 Bobby Bonilla .50 .20
4 George Brett 5.00 2.00
5 Jose Canseco 2.00 .80
6 Gary Carter 2.00 .80
7 Joe Carter .50 .20
8 Will Clark 1.50 .60
9 Roger Clemens 5.00 2.00
10 Vince Coleman .25 .10
11 David Cone .50 .20
12 Eric Davis .50 .20
13 Glenn Davis .25 .10
14 Andre Dawson 1.50 .60
15 Shawon Dunston .25 .10
16 Dennis Eckersley 2.00 .80
17 Carlton Fisk 2.00 .80
18 Scott Fletcher .25 .10
19 John Franco .50 .20
20 Julio Franco .50 .20
21 Gary Gaetti .50 .20
22 Andres Galarraga 1.50 .60
23 Kirk Gibson .50 .20
24 Mike Greenwell .25 .10
25 Mark Gubicza .25 .10
26 Pedro Guerrero .25 .10
27 Tony Gwynn 5.00 2.00
28 Rickey Henderson 3.00 1.20
29 Orel Hershiser .50 .20
30 Kent Hrbek .25 .10
31 Danny Jackson .25 .10
32 Barry Larkin UER 1.50 .60
Terry McGriff pictured on card
33 Greg Maddux 5.00 2.00
34 Don Mattingly 5.00 2.00
35 Fred McGriff 1.50 .60
36 Mark McGwire 8.00 3.20
37 Paul Molitor 2.00 .80
38 Tony Pena .50 .20
39 Gerald Perry .25 .10
40 Dan Plesac .25 .10
41 Kirby Puckett 3.00 1.20
42 Johnny Ray .25 .10
43 Jeff Reardon .25 .10
44 Cal Ripken 10.00 4.00
45 Babe Ruth 10.00 4.00
46 Nolan Ryan 10.00 4.00
47 Juan Samuel .25 .10
48 Ryne Sandberg 3.00 1.20
49 Benito Santiago .25 .10
50 Steve Sax .25 .10
51 Mike Schmidt 3.00 1.20
52 Kevin Seitzer .25 .10
53 Ozzie Smith 5.00 2.00
54 Terry Steinbach .25 .10
55 Dave Stewart .25 .10
56 Darryl Strawberry .50 .20
57 Andres Thomas .25 .10
58 Alan Trammell 1.50 .60
59 Andy Van Slyke .50 .20
60 Frank Viola .25 .10
61 Dave Winfield 2.00 .80
62 Todd Worrell .50 .20
63 Strategy Disc .25 .10

1991 Cadaco Ellis Discs

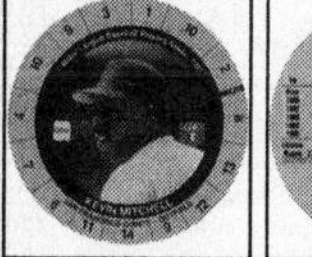

These discs were designed to be used in conjuction with the Cadaco BB game. These discs feature player photos and feature leading stars in the game. Retired superstars Roberto Clemente, Ty Cobb, Lou Gehrig, Babe Ruth and Honus Wagner are also included in this set.

Nm-Mt Ex-Mt
COMPLETE SET (62) 75.00 22.00
1 Roberto Alomar 1.50 .45
2 Harold Baines .50 .15
3 Craig Biggio 1.00 .30
4 Wade Boggs 2.50 .75
5 Barry Bonds 5.00 1.50
6 Bobby Bonilla .25 .07
7 Jose Canseco 2.00 .60
8 Will Clark 1.50 .45
9 Roger Clemens 5.00 1.50
10 Roberto Clemente 8.00 2.40
11 Ty Cobb 6.00 1.80
12 Vince Coleman .25 .07
13 Eric Davis .50 .15
14 Glenn Davis .25 .07
15 Andre Dawson 1.50 .45
16 Delino DeShields .25 .07
17 Shawon Dunston .25 .07
18 Cecil Fielder .50 .15
19 Tony Fernandez .50 .15
20 Carlton Fisk 2.00 .60
21 Julio Franco .50 .15
22 Gary Gaetti .50 .15
23 Lou Gehrig 8.00 2.40
24 Kirk Gibson .50 .15
25 Mark Grace 2.50 .75
26 Ken Griffey Jr. 8.00 2.40
27 Kelly Gruber .25 .07
28 Tony Gwynn 5.00 1.50
29 Rickey Henderson 3.00 .90
30 Orel Hershiser .50 .15
31 David Justice 1.50 .45
32 Bo Jackson 1.50 .45
33 Howard Johnson .25 .07
34 Barry Larkin 1.50 .45
35 Ramon Martinez .25 .07
36 Don Mattingly 5.00 1.50
37 Fred McGriff 1.00 .30
38 Mark McGwire 8.00 2.40
39 Kevin Mitchell .25 .07
40 Lance Parrish .50 .15
41 Tony Pena .50 .15
42 Kirby Puckett 3.00 .90
43 Cal Ripken Jr. 10.00 3.00
44 Babe Ruth 10.00 3.00
45 Nolan Ryan 10.00 3.00
46 Bret Saberhagen .25 .07
47 Chris Sabo .25 .07
48 Ryne Sandberg 4.00 1.20
49 Benito Santiago .50 .15
50 Steve Sax .25 .07
51 Gary Sheffield 2.00 .60
52 Ruben Sierra .50 .15
53 Ozzie Smith 5.00 1.50
54 Terry Steinbach .25 .07
55 Dave Stewart .25 .07
56 Mickey Tettleton .25 .07
57 Alan Trammell 1.00 .30
58 Jose Uribe .25 .07
59 Honus Wagner 3.00 .90
60 Lou Whitaker .50 .15
61 Matt Williams 1.00 .30
62 Robin Yount 2.00 .60

1993 Cadaco Discs

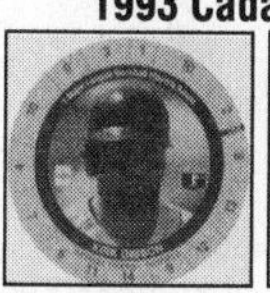
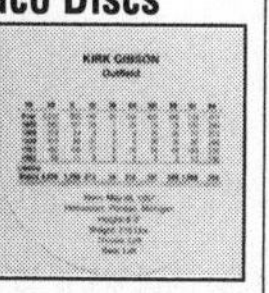

These cards were issued as part of the Cadaco games. These discs feature a mix of active players and a few retired players.

Nm-Mt Ex-Mt
COMPLETE SET (62) 75.00 22.00
1 Kevin Appier .25 .07
2 Carlos Baerga .25 .07
3 Harold Baines .50 .15
4 Derek Bell .25 .07
5 George Bell .25 .07
6 Jay Bell .25 .07
7 Mike Boddicker .25 .07
8 Wade Boggs 2.00 .60
9 Hubie Brooks .25 .07
10 Jose Canseco 1.50 .45
11 Roger Clemens 4.00 1.20
12 Roberto Clemente 6.00 1.80
13 Ty Cobb 5.00 1.50
14 Alex Cole .25 .07
15 Jeff Conine .25 .07
16 Andre Dawson 1.50 .45
17 Shawon Dunston .25 .07
18 Len Dykstra .50 .15
19 Carlton Fisk 2.00 .60
20 Darrin Fletcher .25 .07
21 Gary Gaetti .50 .15
22 Greg Gagne .25 .07
23 Mike Gallego .25 .07
24 Lou Gehrig 6.00 1.80
25 Kirk Gibson .50 .15
26 Tom Glavine 1.50 .45
27 Mark Grace 1.50 .45
28 Ken Griffey Jr. 6.00 1.80
29 Tony Gwynn 4.00 1.20
30 Charles Hayes .25 .07
31 Rickey Henderson 2.50 .75
32 Orel Hershiser .50 .15
33 Bo Jackson 1.50 .45
34 Howard Johnson .25 .07
35 Randy Johnson 2.50 .75
36 Ricky Jordan .25 .07
37 David Justice 1.50 .45
38 Ray Lankford .25 .07
39 Ramon Martinez .25 .07
40 Don Mattingly 4.00 1.20
41 Mark McGwire 6.00 1.80
42 Brian McRae .25 .07
43 Joe Oliver .25 .07
44 Tony Pena .25 .07
45 Kirby Puckett 2.00 .60
46 Cal Ripken 8.00 2.40
47 Babe Ruth 8.00 2.40
48 Nolan Ryan 8.00 2.40
49 Bret Saberhagen .25 .07
50 Chris Sabo .25 .07
51 Ryne Sandberg 4.00 1.20
52 Benito Santiago .50 .15
53 Steve Sax .25 .07
54 Gary Sheffield 1.50 .45
55 Ozzie Smith 4.00 1.20
56 Dave Stewart .25 .07
57 Darryl Strawberry .50 .15
58 Frank Thomas 2.00 .60
59 Robin Ventura .50 .15
60 Hector Villanueva .25 .07
61 Honus Wagner 4.00 1.20
62 Lou Whitaker .50 .15

1997 California Lottery

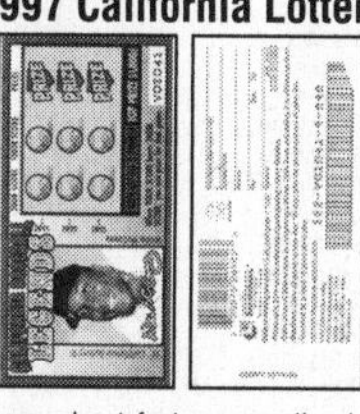

This five-card set features small color head photos of California Baseball Legends. The set measures approximately 4" by 2" and was actually real California scratch-off lottery ticket stubs that could be obtained for $1 a piece. The backs carry the lottery rules and prize information. The cards are unnumbered and checklisted below in alphabetical order.

Nm-Mt Ex-Mt
COMPLETE SET (5) 6.00 1.80
1 Rod Carew 2.00 .60
2 Don Drysdale 2.00 .60
3 Rollie Fingers 1.00 .30
4 Willie McCovey 1.50 .45
5 Gaylord Perry 1.00 .30

1950-56 Callahan HOF W576

The cards in this 82-card set measure approximately 1 3/4" by 2 1/2". The 1950-56 Callahan Hall of Fame set was issued over a number of years at the Baseball Hall of Fame museum in Cooperstown, New York. New cards were added to the set each year when new members were inducted into the Hall of Fame. The cards with (2) in the checklist exist with two different biographies. The year of each card's first inclusion in the set is also given in parentheses; those not listed parenthetically below were issued in 1950 as well as in all the succeeding years and are hence the most common. Naturally the supply of cards is directly related to how many years a player was included in the set; cards that were not issued until 1955 are much scarcer than those printed all the years between 1950 and 1956. The catalog designation is W576. One frequently finds "complete~ sets in the original box; take care to investigate the year of issue, the set may be complete in the sense of all the cards issued up to a certain year, but not all 82 cards below. The box is priced below. For example, a "complete" 1950 set would obviously not include any of the cards marked below with ('52), ('54), or ('55) as none of those cards existed in 1950 since those respective players had not yet been inducted. The complete set price below refers to a set including all 83 cards below. Since the cards are unnumbered, they are numbered below for reference alphabetically by player's name.

NM Ex
COMPLETE SET (83) 800.00 400.00
COMMON CARD '50 2.50 1.25
COMMON CARD '52 3.00 1.50
COMMON CARD '54 4.00 2.00
COMMON CARD '55 6.00 3.00
1 Grover Alexander 4.00 2.00
2 Cap Anson 3.00 1.50
3 Frank Baker '55 6.00 3.00
4 Edward Barrow '54 4.00 2.00
5 Chief Bender (2) '54 4.00 2.00
6 Roger Bresnahan 2.50 1.25
7 Dan Brouthers 2.50 1.25
8 Mordecai Brown 2.50 1.25
9 Morgan Bulkeley 2.50 1.25
10 Jesse Burkett 2.50 1.25
11 Alexander Cartwright 2.50 1.25
12 Henry Chadwick 2.50 1.25
13 Frank Chance 2.50 1.25
14 Happy Chandler '52 75.00 38.00
15 Jack Chesbro 2.50 1.25
16 Fred Clarke 2.50 1.25
17 Ty Cobb 75.00 38.00
18A Mickey Cochrane ERR 5.00 2.50
Name spelled Cochran
18B M.Cochrane COR 30.00 15.00
19 Eddie Collins (2) 2.50 1.25
20 Jimmie Collins 2.50 1.25
21 Charles Comiskey 2.50 1.25
22 Tom Connolly '54 4.00 2.00
23 Candy Cummings 2.50 1.25
24 Dizzy Dean '54 20.00 10.00
25 Ed Delahanty 2.50 1.25
26 Bill Dickey '54 (2) 8.00 4.00
27 Joe DiMaggio '55 200.00 100.00
28 Hugh Duffy 2.50 1.25
29 Johnny Evers 2.50 1.25
30 Buck Ewing 2.50 1.25
31 Jimmie Foxx 5.00 2.50
32 Frank Frisch 2.50 1.25
33 Lou Gehrig 80.00 40.00
34 Charles Gehringer 4.00 2.00
35 Clark Griffith 2.50 1.25
36 Lefty Grove 5.00 2.50
37 Gabby Hartnett '55 6.00 3.00
38 Harry Heilmann '52 3.00 1.50
39 Rogers Hornsby 5.00 2.50
40 Carl Hubbell 3.00 1.50
41 Hughie Jennings 2.50 1.25
42 Ban Johnson 2.50 1.25
43 Walter Johnson 10.00 5.00
44 Willie Keeler 2.50 1.25
45 Mike Kelly 2.50 1.25
46 Bill Klem '54 4.00 2.00
47 Napoleon Lajoie 4.00 2.00
48 Kenesaw Landis 2.50 1.25
49 Ted Lyons '55 6.00 3.00
50 Connie Mack 2.50 1.25
51 Rabbit Maranville '54 4.00 2.00
52 Christy Mathewson 10.00 5.00
53 Tommy McCarthy 2.50 1.25
54 Joe McGinnity 2.50 1.25
55 John McGraw 3.00 1.50
56 Kid Nichols 2.50 1.25
57 Jim O'Rourke 2.50 1.25
58 Mel Ott 4.00 2.00
59 Herb Pennock 2.50 1.25
60 Eddie Plank 2.50 1.25
61 Charles Radbourne 2.50 1.25
62 Wilbert Robinson 2.50 1.25
63 Babe Ruth 120.00 60.00
64 Ray Schalk '55 6.00 3.00
65 Al Simmons '54 4.00 2.00
66 George Sisler (2) 2.50 1.25
67 Albert G. Spalding 2.50 1.25
68 Tris Speaker 4.00 2.00
69 Bill Terry '54 5.00 2.50
70 Joe Tinker 2.50 1.25
71 Pie Traynor 2.50 1.25
72 Dazzy Vance '55 6.00 3.00
73 Rube Waddell 2.50 1.25
74 Hans Wagner 10.00 5.00
75 Bobby Wallace '54 4.00 2.00
76 Ed Walsh 2.50 1.25
77 Paul Waner '52 5.00 2.50
78 George Wright 2.50 1.25
79 Harry Wright '54 4.00 2.00
80 Cy Young 6.00 3.00
81 Museum Interior 4.00 2.00
'54 (2)
82 Museum Exterior 4.00 2.00
'54 (2)
XX Presentation Box 2.50 1.25

1996 Canadian Club

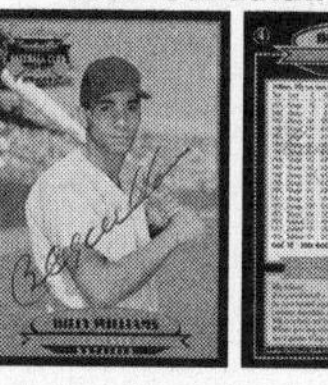

These six cards were issued as premiums by Canadian Club Whiskey. They were available and all the cards were signed by the Hall of Fame players. The cards are also accompanied by a certificate of authenticity.

Nm-Mt Ex-Mt
COMPLETE SET (6) 60.00 18.00
1 Ernie Banks 15.00 4.50
2 Rollie Fingers 6.00 1.80
3 Willie Stargell 15.00 4.50
4 Billy Williams 10.00 3.00
5 Brooks Robinson 15.00 4.50
6 Frank Robinson 15.00 4.50

2000 Capcure

These eight cards, which measure the standard size when removed from a perforated sheet, feature leading hitters of the game. The fronts have a player photo with his name on the bottom. The back feature information about helping the prostate cancer cause. Since these cards are unnumbered, we have sequenced them in alphabetical order.

Nm-Mt Ex-Mt
COMPLETE SET 60.00 18.00
1 Jason Giambi 3.00 .90
2 Ken Griffey Jr 8.00 2.40
3 Tony Gwynn 8.00 2.40
4 Derek Jeter 15.00 4.50
5 Mark McGwire 10.00 3.00
6 Alex Rodriguez 10.00 3.00
7 Sammy Sosa 8.00 2.40
8 Robin Ventura 1.50 .45

2001 Capcure

These eight perforated cards, which measure the standard size when cut from a sheet, feature a star hitter on both sides of the card. Since the cards are unnumbered we have sequenced them based on alphabetical order.

Nm-Mt Ex-Mt
COMPLETE SET (8) 50.00 15.00
1 Jeff Bagwell 3.00 .90
Carlos Delgado
2 Jay Bell 6.00 1.80
Alex Rodriguez
3 Nomar Garciaparra 8.00 2.40
Sammy Sosa
4 Jason Giambi 8.00 2.40
Mark McGwire
5 Tony Gwynn 6.00 1.80
Ivan Rodriguez
6 Ken Griffey Jr. 8.00 2.40
Robin Ventura
7 Derek Jeter 10.00 3.00
Mike Sweeney
8 Chipper Jones 3.00 .90
Jim Thome

1974 Capital Publishing

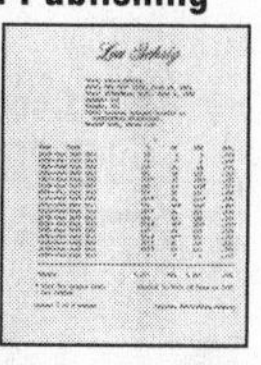

This 110-card set was issued by Capital Publishing Company and features 4 1/8" by 5 1/4" black-and-white photos of great players. The fronts consist of nothing more than the picture of the player while the back has biographical information and statistics. It is believed that cards 106 through 110 are significantly tougher than the rest of the set.

NM Ex
COMPLETE SET (110) 100.00 40.00
1 Babe Ruth 5.00 2.00
2 Lou Gehrig 4.00 1.60
3 Ty Cobb 4.00 1.60
4 Jackie Robinson 4.00 1.60
5 Roger Connor 1.00 .40
6 Harry Heilmann 1.00 .40
7 Clark Griffith 1.00 .40
8 Ed Walsh 1.00 .40
9 Hugh Duffy 1.00 .40
10 Russ Christopher .50 .20
11 Snuffy Stirnweiss .50 .20
12 Willie Keller 1.50 .60
13 Buck Ewing 1.00 .40
14 Tony Lazzeri 1.00 .40
15 King Kelly 1.50 .60
16 Jimmy McAleer .50 .20
17 Frank Chance 2.00 .80
18 Sam Zoldak .50 .20
19 Christy Mathewson 2.00 .80
20 Eddie Collins 2.00 .80
21 Cap Anson 2.00 .80
22 Steve Evans .50 .20
23 Mordecai Brown 1.50 .60
24 Don Black .50 .20
25 Home Run Baker 1.00 .40
26 Jack Chesbro .50 .20
27 Gil Hodges 1.00 .40
28 Dan Brouthers 1.00 .40
29 Don Hoak .50 .20
30 Herb Pennock 1.00 .40
31 Vern Stephens .50 .20
32 Cy Young 2.00 .80
33 Eddie Cicotte 2.00 .80
34 Sam Jones .50 .20
35 Ed Waitkus .50 .20
36 Roger Bresnahan 1.00 .40
37 Fred Merkle .50 .20
38 Ed Delehanty .50 .20
39 Tris Speaker 1.50 .60
40 Fred Clarke 1.00 .40
41 Johnny Evers 2.00 .80
42 Mickey Cochrane 1.50 .60
43 Nap Lajoie 2.00 .80
44 Charles Comiskey 1.00 .40
45 Sam Crawford 1.00 .40
46 Ban Johnson 1.00 .40
47 Ray Schalk 1.00 .40
48 Pat Moran .50 .20
49 Walt Judnich .50 .20
50 Bill Killefer .50 .20
51 Jimmie Foxx 2.00 .80
52 Red Rolfe .50 .20
53 Howie Pollett .50 .20
54 Wally Pipp .50 .20
55 Chief Bender 1.00 .40
56 Connie Mack 2.00 .80
57 Bump Hadley .50 .20
58 Al Simmons 1.50 .60
59 Hughie Jennings 1.00 .40
60 Johnny Allen .50 .20
61 Fred Snodgrass .50 .20
62 Heinie Manush 1.00 .40
63 Dazzy Vance 1.00 .40
64 George Sisler 1.50 .60
65 Jim Bottomley 1.00 .40
66 Roy Chapman .50 .20
67 Hal Chase .50 .20
68 Jack Barry .50 .20
69 George Burns .50 .20
70 Jim Barrett .50 .20
71 Grover Alexander 2.00 .80
72 Elmer Flick .50 .20
73 Jake Flowers .50 .20
74 Al Orth .50 .20
75 Cliff Aberson .50 .20
76 Moe Berg 2.00 .80
77 Bill Bradley .50 .20
78 Max Bishop .50 .20
79 Jimmy Austin .50 .20
80 Beals Becker .50 .20
81 Jack Clements .50 .20
82 Cy Blanton .50 .20
83 Garland Braxton .50 .20
84 Red Ames .50 .20
85 Hippo Vaughn .50 .20
86 Ray Caldwell .50 .20
87 Clint Brown .50 .20
88 Joe Jackson 3.00 1.20
89 Pete Appleton .50 .20
90 Ed Brandt .50 .20
91 Walter Johnson 2.00 .80
92 Dizzy Dean 2.00 .80
93 Nick Altrock .50 .20
94 Buck Weaver 2.00 .80
95 George Blaeholder .50 .20
96 Jim Bagby Sr. .50 .20
97 Ted Blankenship .50 .20
98 Babe Adams .50 .20
99 Lefty Williams 1.50 .60
100 Tommy Bridges .50 .20
101 Rube Benton .50 .20

102 Jim Poole	.50	.20
103 Max Butcher	.50	.20
104 Larry Benton	.50	.20
105 Chick Gandil	1.50	.60
106 Lefty Grove	5.00	2.00
107 Roberto Clemente	10.00	4.00
108 Albert Spalding	5.00	2.00
109 Bill Barrett	1.00	.40
110 Bob O'Farrell	1.00	.40

1986 Card Collectors Company Canseco

These 10 full-bleed standard-size cards features then rookie Jose Canseco. The fronts show the different photos which are available while the backs have information on how to obtain these photos autographed.

	Nm-Mt	Ex-Mt
COMPLETE SET (10)	10.00	4.00
COMMON CARD	1.00	.40

1986 Card Collectors Mantle

This 10-card standard-size set features various photos of Mickey Mantle. The fronts have a mix of photos used by the card companies and more modern photos on front while the back says that these photos are available in an 8" by 10" signed form from Card Collectors for just $15 each or for $139.95 for the group of 10.

	Nm-Mt	Ex-Mt
COMPLETE SET (10)	20.00	8.00
COMMON CARD (1-10)	2.00	.80

1987 Card Collectors McGwire

This 10-card standard-size set features various photos of Mickey Mantle. The fronts have a mix of photos used by the card companies and more modern photos on front while the back says that these photos are available in an 8" by 10" signed form from Card Collectors for just $10 each or for $89.95 for the group of 10. Other than the art-work, all the photos used for this promotion were taken by Barry Colla.

	Nm-Mt	Ex-Mt
COMPLETE SET (10)	20.00	8.00
COMMON CARD (1-10)	2.00	.80

1989 Card Collectors Company Jefferies

This 16-card set features borderless color photos of Gregg Jefferies from childhood to adulthood. The backs carry information about the photos.

	Nm-Mt	Ex-Mt
COMPLETE SET (16)	4.00	1.60
COMMON CARD (1-16)	.25	.10

1990 Card Collectors Company Justice Boyhood

This 16-card set depicts different stages of the boyhood of David Justice. The fronts feature various pictures from his life on a red background. The backs carry information about the picture.

	Nm-Mt	Ex-Mt
COMPLETE SET (16)	4.00	1.20
COMMON CARD (1-16)	.25	.07

1908 Cardinals Republic

Issued as a supplement in the St Louis Republic, these photos feature members of the 1908 St Louis Cardinals. There might be more of these so any additions to this checklist is appreciated. Since these are unnumbered, we have sequenced them in alphabetical order.

	Ex-Mt	VG
COMPLETE SET	400.00	200.00
1 Fred Beebe	100.00	50.00
2 Robert Byrne	100.00	50.00
3 Ed Konetchy	100.00	50.00
4 John Lush	100.00	50.00

1931 Cardinals Metropolitan

This 30-card set features white-bordered, sepia colored blank-backed photos of the 1931 St. Louis Cardinals and measures approximately 6 1/8" by 9 1/2". The cards are unnumbered and checklisted below in alphabetical order. The words "Metropolitan Studios St. Louis" are in the bottom right hand corner. These photos were sent to fans in an manila envelope. One could order another set from the team for 41 cents.

	Ex-Mt	VG
COMPLETE CARD (30)	400.00	200.00
1 Earl"Sparky" Adams	10.00	5.00
2 Ray Blades	10.00	5.00
3 James Bottomley	20.00	10.00
4 Sam Breadon PRES	10.00	5.00
5 James"Rip" Collins	15.00	7.50
6 Dizzy Dean	50.00	25.00
7 Paul Derringer	10.00	5.00
8 Jake Flowers	10.00	5.00
9 Frank Frisch	40.00	20.00
10 Charles Gelbert	10.00	5.00
11 Miguel Gonzales	10.00	5.00
12 Burleigh Grimes	20.00	10.00
13 Charles"Chick" Hafey	20.00	10.00
14 Jesse Haines	20.00	10.00
15 William Hallahan	10.00	5.00
16 Andrew High	10.00	5.00
17 Sylvester Johnson	10.00	5.00
18 Tony Kaufmann	10.00	5.00
19 James Lindsey	10.00	5.00
20 Gus Mancuso	10.00	5.00
21 Pepper Martin	20.00	10.00
22 Ernest Orsatti	10.00	5.00
23 Charles Rhem	10.00	5.00
24 Branch Rickey VP	20.00	10.00
25 Walter Roettger	10.00	5.00
26 Allyn Stout	10.00	5.00
27 Gabby Street MG	10.00	5.00
28 Clyde Wares CO	10.00	5.00
29 George Watkins	10.00	5.00
30 James Wilson	10.00	5.00

1935 Cardinals Rice Stix

This two card set features the Dean brothers who won 49 games for the Cardinals in 1934. These cards measure approximately 2 1/4" by 3" and were issued as premiums when shirts were purchased from that St Louis firm.

	Ex-Mt	VG
COMPLETE SET	1000.00	500.00
1 Paul "Daffy" Dean	400.00	200.00
2 Jay "Dizzy" Dean	600.00	300.00

1941 Cardinals W754

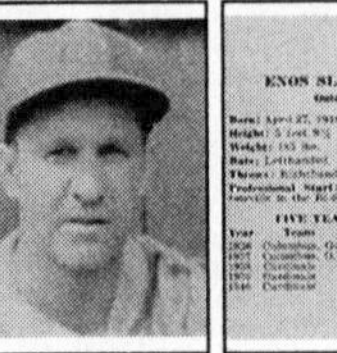

The cards in this 30-card set measure approximately 2 1/8" by 2 5/8". The 1941 W754 set of unnumbered cards features St. Louis Cardinals. The cards are numbered below alphabetically by player's name. This is another set issued in its own box with the other side being a mailing label. This set is worth about $100 more when still in the original box.

	Ex-Mt	VG
COMPLETE SET (30)	600.00	300.00
1 Sam Breadon OWN	15.00	7.50
2 Jimmy Brown	15.00	7.50
3 Mort Cooper	25.00	12.50
4 Walker Cooper	20.00	10.00
5 Estel Crabtree	15.00	7.50
6 Frank Crespi	15.00	7.50
7 Bill Crouch	15.00	7.50
8 Mike Gonzalez CO	20.00	10.00
9 Harry Gumpert	15.00	7.50
10 John Hopp	20.00	10.00
11 Ira Hutchinson	15.00	7.50
12 Howie Krist	15.00	7.50
13 Eddie Lake	15.00	7.50
14 Max Lanier	25.00	12.50
15 Gus Mancuso	15.00	7.50
16 Marty Marion	40.00	20.00
17 Steve Mesner	15.00	7.50
18 John Mize	80.00	40.00
19 Terry Moore	30.00	15.00
20 Sam Nahem	15.00	7.50
21 Don Padgett	15.00	7.50
22 Branch Rickey GM	60.00	30.00
23 Clyde Shoun	15.00	7.50
24 Enos Slaughter	80.00	40.00
25 Billy Southworth MG	20.00	10.00
26 Coaker Triplett	15.00	7.50
27 Buzzy Wares	15.00	7.50
28 Lon Warneke	20.00	10.00
29 Ernie White	15.00	7.50
30 Title Card	15.00	7.50

(Order Coupon on back)

1953 Cardinals Hunter's Wieners

The cards in this 26 card set measure 2 1/4" by 3 1/2". The 1953 Hunter's Wieners set of full color, blank backed unnumbered cards feature St. Louis Cardinal players only. The cards have red borders and were issued in panels of two on hot dog packages. The catalog designation is F 153-1. We have sequenced this set in alphabetical order.

	NM	Ex
COMPLETE SET (26)	3500.00	1800.00
1 Steve Bilko	100.00	50.00
2 Alpha Brazle	100.00	50.00
3 Cloyd Boyer	125.00	60.00
4 Cliff Chambers	100.00	50.00
5 Mike Clark	100.00	50.00
6 Jack Crimian	100.00	50.00
7 Les Fusselman	100.00	50.00
8 Harvey Haddix	150.00	75.00
9 Solly Hemus	100.00	50.00
10 Ray Jablonski	100.00	50.00
11 Will Johnson	100.00	50.00
12 Harry Lowrey	100.00	50.00
13 Larry Miggins	100.00	50.00
14 Stuart Miller	100.00	50.00
15 Wilmer Mizell	100.00	50.00
16 Stan Musial	1000.00	500.00
17 Joe Presko	100.00	50.00
18 Del Rice	100.00	50.00
19 Hal Rice	100.00	50.00
20 Willard Schmidt	100.00	50.00
21 Red Schoendienst	250.00	125.00
22 Dick Sisler	100.00	50.00
23 Enos Slaughter	250.00	125.00
24 Gerry Staley	100.00	50.00
25 Ed Stanky	150.00	75.00
26 John Yuhas	100.00	50.00

1954 Cardinals Hunter's Wieners

The cards in this 30 card set measure 2 1/4" by 3 1/2". The 1954 Hunter's Weiners set of full color, blank backed unnumbered cards features St. Louis Cardinals. They were issued in pairs on the backs of hot dog packages as in 1953; however one of the cards is a statistical record of the player's career. The poses are very similar to those used in the 1953 set; however, there are captions which read "What's My Name" and "What's My Record". The catalog designation is F153-2.

	NM	Ex
COMPLETE SET (30)	3000.00	1500.00
1 Tom Alston	80.00	40.00
2 Steve Bilko	80.00	40.00
3 Alpha Brazle	80.00	40.00
4 Tom Burgess	80.00	40.00
5 Cot Deal	80.00	40.00
6 Alex Grammas	80.00	40.00
7 Harvey Haddix	100.00	50.00
8 Solly Hemus	80.00	40.00
9 Ray Jablonski	80.00	40.00
10 Royce Lint	80.00	40.00
11 Harry Lowrey	80.00	40.00
12 Memo Luna	80.00	40.00
13 Stu Miller	100.00	50.00
14 Stan Musial	800.00	400.00
15 Tom Poholsky	80.00	40.00
16 Bill Posedel CO	80.00	40.00
17 Joe Presko	80.00	40.00
18 Vic Raschi	120.00	60.00
19 Dick Rand	80.00	40.00
20 Rip Repulski	80.00	40.00
21 Del Rice	80.00	40.00
22 John Riddle CO	80.00	40.00
23 Mike Ryba CO	80.00	40.00
24 Red Schoendienst	150.00	75.00
25 Dick Schofield	100.00	50.00
26 Enos Slaughter	150.00	75.00
27 Gerry Staley	80.00	40.00
28 Ed Stanky MG	100.00	50.00
29 Ed Yuhas	80.00	40.00
30 Sal Yvars	80.00	40.00

1954-55 Cardinals Postcards

These postcards were issued over a two year period. The top of the card has a picture of the player on top and a message beginning "Dear Cardinal Fan". The backs are blank. Since these cards are unnumbered, we have sequenced them in alphabetical order.

	NM	Ex
COMPLETE SET	400.00	200.00
1 Luis Arroyo	15.00	7.50
2 Bill Baker	10.00	5.00
3 Ralph Beard	10.00	5.00
4 Ken Boyer	25.00	12.50
5 Al Brazle	10.00	5.00
6 Nelson Burbrink	10.00	5.00
7 Joe Cunningham	12.00	6.00
8 Cot Deal	10.00	5.00
9 Eddie Dyer	10.00	5.00
10 Joe Frazier	10.00	5.00
11 Ben Flowers	10.00	5.00
12 Al Gettel	10.00	5.00
13 Alex Grammas	10.00	5.00
14 Harvey Haddix	12.00	6.00
15 Solly Hemus	10.00	5.00
16 Ray Jablonski	10.00	5.00
17 Larry Jackson	12.00	6.00
18 Gordon Jones	10.00	5.00
19 Paul LaPalme	10.00	5.00
20 Brooks Lawrence	10.00	5.00
21 Royce Lint	10.00	5.00
22 Harry Lowrey	10.00	5.00
23 Wally Moon	12.00	6.00
24 Stan Musial	40.00	20.00
25 Bill Posedel	10.00	5.00
26 Tom Poholsky	10.00	5.00
27 Joe Presko	10.00	5.00
28 Vic Raschi	12.00	6.00
29 Del Rice	10.00	5.00
30 John Riddle	10.00	5.00
31 Rip Repulski	10.00	5.00
32 Mike Ryba	10.00	5.00
33 Bill Sarni	10.00	5.00
34 Will Schmidt	10.00	5.00
35 Red Schoendienst	25.00	12.50
36 Dick Schofield	10.00	5.00
37 Gerry Staley	10.00	5.00
38 Eddie Stanky MG	12.00	6.00
39 Bill Virdon	15.00	7.50
40 Ben Wade	10.00	5.00
41 Pete Whisenant	10.00	5.00
42 Sal Yvars	10.00	5.00

1955 Cardinals Hunter's Wieners

The cards in this 30 card set measure 2" by 4 3/4". The 1955 Hunter's Wieners set of full color, blank backed, unnumbered cards feature St. Louis Cardinals only. This year presented a different format from the previous two years in that there are two pictures on the front of each card, one full figure shot and a close up bust shot. The card was actually the side panel of the hot dog package rather than the back as in the previous two years. The catalog designation of this scarce regional issue is F153-3. Ken Boyer appears in his rookie season.

	NM	Ex
COMPLETE SET (30)	4000.00	2000.00
1 Tom Alston	100.00	50.00
2 Ken Boyer	200.00	100.00
3 Harry Elliott	100.00	50.00
4 Jack Faszholz	100.00	50.00
5 Joe Frazier	100.00	50.00
6 Alex Grammas	100.00	50.00
7 Harvey Haddix	120.00	60.00
8 Solly Hemus	100.00	50.00
9 Larry Jackson	120.00	60.00
10 Tony Jacobs	100.00	50.00
11 Gordon Jones	100.00	50.00
12 Paul LaPalme	100.00	50.00
13 Brooks Lawrence	100.00	50.00
14 Wally Moon	120.00	60.00
15 Stan Musial	1000.00	500.00
16 Tom Poholsky	100.00	50.00
17 Bill Posedel CO	100.00	50.00
18 Vic Raschi	150.00	75.00
19 Rip Repulski	100.00	50.00
20 Del Rice	100.00	50.00
21 John Riddle CO	100.00	50.00
22 Bill Sarni	100.00	50.00
23 Red Schoendienst	200.00	100.00
24 Dick Schofield	120.00	60.00
25 Frank Smith	100.00	50.00
26 Ed Stanky MG	120.00	60.00
27 Bob Tiefenauer	100.00	50.00
28 Bill Virdon	150.00	75.00
29 Fred Walker CO	100.00	50.00
30 Floyd Woolridge	100.00	50.00

1956 Cardinals Postcards

These cards were the first issued in the style the Cardinals would use for many years. The fronts have photos of players in the "Old" Cardinals uniform with Cardinals on it with a thick heavy line right under that word. The backs have postcard backs with a Busch Stadium address. Each card has a 1" border on the bottom which usually contained an fascimile autograph. Since these cards are unnumbered, we have sequenced them in alphabetical order.

	NM	Ex
COMPLETE SET	250.00	125.00
1 Tom Alston	10.00	5.00
2 Don Blasingame	8.00	4.00
3 Ken Boyer	15.00	7.50
4 Jack Brandt	8.00	4.00
5 Jackie Collum	8.00	4.00
6 Walker Cooper	8.00	4.00
7 Al Dark	10.00	5.00
8 Bob Del Greco	8.00	4.00
9 Murry Dickson	8.00	4.00
10 Chuck Harmon	8.00	4.00
11 Grady Hatton	8.00	4.00
12 Johnny Hopp CO	8.00	4.00
13 Fred Hutchinson MG	8.00	4.00
14 Ray Katt	8.00	4.00
15 Ellis Kinder	8.00	4.00
16 Jim Konstanty	10.00	5.00
17 Larry Jackson	8.00	4.00
18 Dick Littlefield	8.00	4.00
19 Lindy McDaniel	10.00	5.00
20 Vinegar Bend Mizell	8.00	4.00
21 Wally Moon	8.00	4.00
22 Terry Moore CO	10.00	5.00
23 Bobby Morgan	8.00	4.00
24 Stan Musial	25.00	12.50
25 Tom Poholsky	8.00	4.00
26 Bill Posedel CO	8.00	4.00
27 Rip Repulski	8.00	4.00
28 Hank Sauer	10.00	5.00
29 Hal Smith	8.00	4.00
30 Herm Wehmeier	8.00	4.00

1957-58 Cardinals Postcards

These postcards were issued by the St Louis Cardinals over a two year period and the players in the set are wearing the uniform that the Cards wore from 1957 through 1971. The only way a collector can tell the difference between the postcards is that the 1957 cards have a notation for a 2 cent stamp while the 1958 cards have a notation for a 3 cent stamp. Since these cards are unnumbered, we have sequenced them in alphabetical order.

	NM	Ex
COMPLETE SET	400.00	200.00
1 Ruben Amaro	8.00	4.00
2 Frank Barnes	8.00	4.00
3 Don Blasingame	8.00	4.00
4 Ken Boyer	15.00	7.50
5 Jim Brosnan	10.00	5.00
6 Tom Cheney	8.00	4.00
7 Nelson Chittum	8.00	4.00
8 Walker Cooper	8.00	4.00
9 Joe Cunningham	10.00	5.00
10 Al Dark	10.00	5.00
11 Jim Davis	8.00	4.00
12 Bing Devine GM	8.00	4.00
13 Murry Dickson	8.00	4.00
14 Del Ennis	10.00	5.00
15 Curt Flood	20.00	10.00
16 Gene Freese	8.00	4.00
17 Gene Green	8.00	4.00
18 Stan Hack CO	8.00	4.00
19 Al Hollingsworth	8.00	4.00
20 Fred Hutchinson MG	8.00	4.00
21 Larry Jackson	8.00	4.00
22 Sam Jones	8.00	4.00
23 Eddie Kasko	8.00	4.00
24 Ray Katt	8.00	4.00
25 Hobie Landrith	8.00	4.00
26 Bob Mabe	8.00	4.00
27 Sal Maglie	12.00	6.00
28 Morrie Martin	8.00	4.00
29 Lindy McDaniel	10.00	5.00
30 Von McDaniel	8.00	4.00
31 Lloyd Merritt	8.00	4.00
32 Eddie Miksis	8.00	4.00
33 Bob Miller	8.00	4.00
34 Vinegar Bend Mizell	8.00	4.00
35 Wally Moon	8.00	4.00
36 Terry Moore CO	8.00	4.00
37 Billy Muffett	8.00	4.00
38 Stan Musial	25.00	12.50
39 Irv Noren	8.00	4.00
40 Phil Paine	8.00	4.00
41 Will Schmidt	8.00	4.00
42 Dick Schofield	8.00	4.00
43 Bobby Gene Smith	8.00	4.00
44 Hal Smith	8.00	4.00
45 Chuck Stobbs	8.00	4.00
46 Joe Taylor	8.00	4.00
47 Herman Wehmeier	8.00	4.00
48 Bill Wight	8.00	4.00
49 Hoyt Wilhelm	20.00	10.00

1958 Cardinals Jay Publishing

This 14-card set of the St. Louis Cardinals measures approximately 5" by 7" and features black-and-white player photos in a white border. These cards were packaged 12 to a packet. The backs are blank. The cards are unnumbered and checklisted below in alphabetical order. Changes to the Cardinals roster during the season accounts for more than 12 cards in this set.

	NM	Ex
COMPLETE SET (14)	50.00	25.00
1 Don Blasingame	3.00	1.50
2 Ken Boyer	8.00	4.00
3 Joe Cunningham	4.00	2.00
4 Alvin Dark	6.00	3.00
5 Del Ennis	3.00	1.50
6 Larry Jackson	3.00	1.50
7 Sam Jones	3.00	1.50
8 Eddie Kasko	3.00	1.50
9 Lindy McDaniel	3.00	1.50
10 Von McDaniel	3.00	1.50
11 Wilmer Mizell	3.00	1.50

	NM	Ex
12 Wally Moon	3.00	1.50
13 Stan Musial	15.00	7.50
14 Hal Smith	3.00	1.50

1959 Cardinals Jay Publishing

This 12-card set of the St. Louis Cardinals measures approximately 5" by 7" and features black-and-white player photos in a white border. These cards were packaged 12 to a packet. The backs are blank. The cards are unnumbered and checklisted below in alphabetical order.

	NM	Ex
COMPLETE SET	50.00	25.00
1 Don Blasingame	3.00	1.50
2 Ken Boyer	6.00	3.00
3 Jim Brosnan	3.00	1.50
4 Gino Cimoli	3.00	1.50
5 Joe Cunningham	4.00	2.00
6 Curt Flood	6.00	3.00
7 Alex Grammas	3.00	1.50
8 Gene Green	3.00	1.50
9 Larry Jackson	3.00	1.50
10 Wilmer Mizell	3.00	1.50
11 Stan Musial	15.00	7.50
12 Hal R. Smith	3.00	1.50

1960 Cardinals Jay Publishing

This 12-card set of the St. Louis Cardinals measures approximately 5" by 7". The fronts feature black-and-white posed player photos with the player's and team name printed below in the white border. These cards were packaged 12 in a packet. The backs are blank. The cards are unnumbered and checklisted below in alphabetical order.

	NM	Ex
COMPLETE SET (12)	35.00	14.00
1 Ken Boyer	5.00	2.00
2 Joe Cunningham	3.00	1.20
3 Curt Flood	4.00	1.60
4 Larry Jackson	2.00	.80
5 Ronnie Kline	2.00	.80
6 Lindy McDaniel	2.00	.80
7 Wilmer Mizell	2.00	.80
8 Stan Musial	15.00	6.00
9 Bob Nieman	2.00	.80
10 Hal Smith	2.00	.80
11 Daryl Spencer	2.00	.80
12 Bill White	4.00	1.60

1961 Cardinals Jay Publishing

This 13-card set of the St. Louis Cardinals measures approximately 5" by 7". The fronts feature black-and-white posed player photos with the player's and team name printed below in the white border. These cards were packaged 12 in a packet. The backs are blank. The cards are unnumbered and checklisted below in alphabetical order. Thirteen cards are listed for this set as Walt Moryn is included this year. Since these sets were issued throughout the years, sometimes more than the 12 players listed are included. Additions to this or any other team issue set in the book is appreciated.

	NM	Ex
COMPLETE SET (13)	35.00	14.00
1 Ken Boyer	5.00	2.00
2 Ernie Broglio	2.00	.80
3 Joe Cunningham	3.00	1.20
4 Curt Flood	4.00	1.60
5 Solly Hemus MG	2.00	.80
6 Larry Jackson	2.00	.80
7 Julian Javier	3.00	1.20
8 Lindy McDaniel	2.00	.80
9 Walt Moryn	2.00	.80
10 Stan Musial	15.00	6.00
11 Hal Smith	2.00	.80
12 Daryl Spencer	2.00	.80
13 Bill White	4.00	1.60

1962 Cardinals Jay Publishing

The 1962 Jay Cardinals set consists of 14 cards produced by Jay Publishing. The Minoso card establishes the year of the set, since 1962 was Minoso's only year with the Cardinals. The cards measure approximately 4 3/4" by 7" and are printed on thin photographic paper stock. The white fronts feature a black-and-white player portrait with the player's name and the team name below. The backs are blank. The cards are packaged 12 to a packet and originally sold for 25 cents. The cards are unnumbered and checklisted below in alphabetical order. Updates during the season account for the additional cards.

	NM	Ex
COMPLETE SET (14)	45.00	18.00
1 Ken Boyer	5.00	2.00
2 Ernie Broglio	2.00	.80
3 Curt Flood	4.00	1.60
4 Bob Gibson	15.00	6.00
4 Julio Gotay	2.00	.80
5 Larry Jackson	2.00	.80
6 Julian Javier	3.00	1.20
7 Johnny Keane MG	2.00	.80
8 Lindy McDaniel	2.00	.80
9 Minnie Minoso	5.00	2.00
10 Stan Musial	15.00	6.00
11 Curt Simmons	3.00	1.20
11 Gene Oliver	2.00	.80
12 Bill White	4.00	1.60

1963-64 Cardinals Jay Publishing

This set of the St. Louis Cardinals measures approximately 5" by 7". The fronts feature black-and-white posed player photos with the player's and team name printed below in the white border. These cards were packaged 12 in a packet. The backs are blank. The cards are unnumbered and checklisted below in alphabetical order. These cards were issued over a two year period and where possible we have identified which year each card was issued.

	NM	Ex
COMPLETE SET (20)	60.00	24.00
1 Ken Boyer (With glove)	5.00	2.00
2 Ken Boyer (With bat)	5.00	2.00
3 Ernie Broglio (Above waist pose)	2.00	.80
4 Ernie Broglio (Action photo with glove)	2.00	.80
5 Curt Flood (Smiling)	4.00	1.60
6 Curt Flood	4.00	1.60
7 Bob Gibson (Head pose)	12.00	4.80
8 Bob Gibson (Action pose)	12.00	4.80
9 Dick Groat 64	4.00	1.60
10 Julian Javier	3.00	1.20
11 John Keane MG (Above waist pose)	2.00	.80
12 John Keane MG (Full shot)	2.00	.80
13 Dal Maxvill 64	2.00	.80
14 Tim McCarver 64	5.00	2.00
15 Stan Musial 63	15.00	6.00
16 Ray Sadecki (Without glasses)	2.00	.80
17 Ray Sadecki (With glasses)	2.00	.80
18 Curt Simmons (Close up head shot)	3.00	1.20
19 Curt Simmons (With glove)	3.00	1.20
20 Bill White	4.00	1.60

1964 Cardinals Team Issue

This eight-card set measures approximately 4" by 5" and features black-and-white player portraits in a white border with the player's name and position in the bottom margin. The backs are blank. The cards are unnumbered and checklisted below in alphabetical order.

	NM	Ex
COMPLETE SET (8)	20.00	8.00
1 Ken Boyer	5.00	2.00
2 Curt Flood	4.00	1.60
3 Dick Groat	3.00	1.20
4 Charley James	2.00	.80
5 Julian Javier	3.00	1.20
6 Tim McCarver	5.00	2.00
7 Ray Sadecki	2.00	.80
8 Bill White	4.00	1.60

1965 Cardinals Jay Publishing

This 12-card set of the St. Louis Cardinals measures approximately 5" by 7". The fronts feature black-and-white posed player photos with the player's and team name printed below in the white border. These cards were packaged

12 in a packet. The backs are blank. The cards are unnumbered and checklisted below in alphabetical order.

	NM	Ex
COMPLETE SET (12)	30.00	12.00
1 Ken Boyer	5.00	2.00
2 Curt Flood	4.00	1.60
3 Bob Gibson	8.00	3.20
4 Dick Groat	3.00	1.20
5 Julian Javier	2.00	.80
6 Tim McCarver	5.00	2.00
7 Bob Purkey	2.00	.80
8 Red Schoendienst MG	5.00	2.00
9 Mike Shannon	4.00	1.60
10 Tracy Stallard	2.00	.80
11 Carl Warwick	2.00	.80
12 Bill White	4.00	1.60

1965 Cardinals Team Issue

The 28-card set of the St. Louis Cardinals measures approximately 3 1/4" by 5 1/2" and features black-and-white player photos in a white border with a facsimile autograph in the wide bottom margin. The backs are blank. The cards are unnumbered and checklisted below in alphabetical order. Steve Carlton has a card in his Rookie Card year.

	NM	Ex
COMPLETE SET (28)	80.00	32.00
1 Dennis Aust	2.00	.80
2 Joe Becker CO	2.00	.80
3 Nellie Briles	2.00	.80
4 Lou Brock	8.00	3.20
5 Jerry Buchek	2.00	.80
6 Steve Carlton	15.00	6.00
7 Don Dennis	2.00	.80
8 Curt Flood	4.00	1.60
9 Bob Gibson	8.00	3.20
10 Tito Francona	2.00	.80
11 Phil Gagliano	2.00	.80
12 Larry Jaster	2.00	.80
13 Julian Javier	3.00	1.20
14 George Kernek	2.00	.80
15 Dal Maxvill	3.00	1.20
16 Tim McCarver	5.00	2.00
17 Bob Milliken	2.00	.80
18 Bob Purkey	2.00	.80
19 Ray Sadecki	2.00	.80
20 Red Schoendienst MG	5.00	2.00
21 Joe Schultz CO	2.00	.80
22 Mike Shannon	4.00	1.60
23 Curt Simmons	3.00	1.20
24 Bob Skinner	2.00	.80
25 Tracy Stallard	2.00	.80
26 Bob Tolan	2.00	.80
27 Ray Washburn	2.00	.80
28 Hal Woodeschick	2.00	.80

1966 Cardinals Team Issue

These 12 black and white photos were available directly from Busch Stadium for twenty-five cents. The cards measure approximately 4 3/4" by 7 and have blank backs. We have dated this set as 1966 was Charlie Smith's last season and Alex Johnson's first season with the Cardinals.

	NM	Ex
COMPLETE SET (12)	30.00	12.00
1 Lou Brock	8.00	3.20
2 Jerry Buchek	2.00	.80
3 Curt Flood	4.00	1.60
4 Phil Gagliano	2.00	.80
5 Bob Gibson	8.00	3.20
6 Julian Javier	3.00	1.20
7 Alex Johnson	2.00	.80
8 Tim McCarver	5.00	2.00
9 Red Schoendienst MG	5.00	2.00
10 Curt Simmons	3.00	1.20
11 Charlie Smith	2.00	.80
12 Tracy Stallard	2.00	.80

1970 Cardinals Team Issue

This 33-card set of the St. Louis Cardinals measures approximately 4 1/4" by 7" and features black-and-white player photos in a white border. These cards were packaged 12 to a packet and some display facsimile autographs. The backs are blank. The cards are unnumbered and checklisted below in alphabetical order. Updates and changes during

the year account for the odd number of cards. This set can be dated to 1970 as that Richie (Dick) Allen's only season with the Cards.

	NM	Ex
COMPLETE SET (33)	80.00	32.00
1 Richie Allen Glasses	5.00	2.00
2 Richie Allen Uniform # showing	5.00	2.00
3 Jim Beauchamp	2.00	.80
4 Lou Brock	8.00	3.20
5 Vern Benson CO	2.00	.80
6 Sal Campisi	2.00	.80
7 Jose Cardenal	3.00	1.20
8 Bob Chlupsa	2.00	.80
9 Ed Crosby	2.00	.80
10 George Culver	2.00	.80
11 Vic Davilillo	3.00	1.20
12 Bob Gibson	8.00	3.20
13 Santiago Guzman	2.00	.80
14 Joe Hague	2.00	.80
15 Julian Javier	3.00	1.20
16 Al Hrabosky	3.00	1.20
17 Leron Lee Head and Shoulders	2.00	.80
18 Leron Lee Uniform # Showing	2.00	.80
19 Frank Linzy	2.00	.80
20 Dal Maxvill	2.00	.80
21 Milt Ramirez	2.00	.80
22 Jerry Reuss	4.00	1.60
23 Cookie Rojas	2.00	.80
24 Red Schoendienst MG	5.00	2.00
25 Mike Shannon	4.00	1.60
26 Ted Simmons	6.00	2.40
27 Dick Sisler CO	2.00	.80
28 Carl Taylor Portrait	2.00	.80
29 Carl Taylor Kneeling	2.00	.80
30 Chuck Taylor	2.00	.80
31 Joe Torre	5.00	2.00
32 Bart Zeller Portrait	2.00	.80
33 Bart Zeller Batting	2.00	.80

1971 Cardinals Team Issue

This 30-card set measures 3 1/4" by 5 1/2" and features black-and-white player portraits with white borders. A facsimile autograph appears in the wider white border area at the bottom. The backs are blank. The cards are unnumbered and checklisted below in alphabetical order.

	NM	Ex
COMPLETE SET (30)	70.00	28.00
1 Matty Alou	3.00	1.20
2 Jim Beauchamp	1.50	.60
3 Vern Benson CO	1.50	.60
4 Ken Boyer CO	4.00	1.60
5 Lou Brock	10.00	4.00
6 Bob Burda	1.50	.60
7 Jose Cardenal	2.00	.80
8 Steve Carlton	10.00	4.00
9 Reggie Cleveland	1.50	.60
10 Moe Drabowsky	1.50	.60
11 Bob Gibson	10.00	4.00
12 Joe Hague	1.50	.60
13 Julian Javier	2.00	.80
14 George Kissell CO	1.50	.60
15 Frank Linzy	1.50	.60
16 Dal Maxvill	2.00	.80
17 Jerry McNertney	1.50	.60
18 Luis Melendez	1.50	.60
19 Jerry Reuss	3.00	1.20
20 Al Santorini	1.50	.60
21 Red Schoendienst MG	4.00	1.60
22 Barney Schultz CO	1.50	.60
23 Don Shaw	1.50	.60
24 Ted Simmons	4.00	1.60
25 Ted Sizemore	1.50	.60
26 Chuck Taylor	1.50	.60
27 Lee Thomas CO	1.50	.60
28 Joe Torre (Profile)	4.00	1.60
29 Joe Torre (Front View)	4.00	1.60
30 Chris Zachary	1.50	.60

1972 Cardinals Team Issue

This 18-card set of the St. Louis Cardinals measures approximately 3 1/4" by 5 1/2" and features black-and-white player portraits with white borders. A facsimile autograph appears in the wide bottom margin. The backs are blank. The cards are unnumbered and checklisted below in alphabetical order.

	NM	Ex
COMPLETE SET (18)	60.00	24.00
1 Nelson Briles	3.00	1.20
2 Lou Brock	8.00	3.20
3 Steve Carlton	8.00	3.20
4 Donn Clendenon	3.00	1.20
5 Tony Cloninger	3.00	1.20
6 Ed Crosby	3.00	1.20
7 Jose Cruz	4.00	1.60
8 Moe Drabowsky	3.00	1.20
9 Bob Gibson	10.00	4.00
10 Joe Grzenda	3.00	1.20
11 George Kissell CO	3.00	1.20
12 Dal Maxvill	3.00	1.20
13 Billy Muffett CO	3.00	1.20
14 Ted Simmons	5.00	2.00
15 Ted Sizemore	3.00	1.20
16 Scipio Spinks	3.00	1.20
17 Mike Torrez	4.00	1.60
18 Rick Wise	4.00	1.60

1974 Cardinals 1931 Bra-Mac

This 20 card set, which measures 3 1/2" by 5" features members of the 1931 World Champion St Louis Cardinals.

	NM	Ex
COMPLETE SET	15.00	6.00
1 Burleigh Grimes	1.50	.60
2 Sparky Adams	.50	.20
3 Jesse Haines	1.50	.60
4 Jimmie Wilson	.75	.30
5 Ernie Orsatti	.50	.20
6 Gus Mancuso	.50	.20
7 Ray Blades	.50	.20
8 Frank Frisch	2.00	.80
9 Bill Hallahan	.50	.20
10 George Watkins	.50	.20
11 Pepper Martin	1.00	.40
12 Charlie Gelbert	.50	.20
13 Jake Flowers	.50	.20
14 Jim Lindsey	.50	.20
15 Rip Collins	.50	.20
16 Flint Rhem	.50	.20
17 Paul Derringer	.50	.20
18 Syl Johnson	.50	.20
19 Chick Hafey	1.00	.40
20 Jim Bottomley	1.50	.60

1974 Cardinals 1934 TCMA

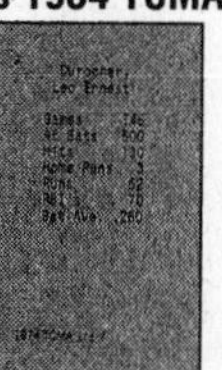

This 31-card set of the 1934 World Champion St. Louis Cardinals measures approximately 2 1/4" by 3 5/8" and features black-and-white player photos. Each set includes four jumbo cards measuring approximately 3 5/8" by 4 1/2" and displaying action photos from the 1934 World Series Games with various information on the backs. The cards are unnumbered and checklisted below with the jumbo cards being the last four cards, numbers 28-31.

	NM	Ex
COMPLETE SET (31)	25.00	10.00
1 Tex Carleton	.50	.20
2 Rip Collins	1.00	.40
3 Cliff Crawford	.50	.20
4 Spud Davis	.50	.20
5 Daffy Dean Dizzy Dean	2.00	.80
6 Paul Dean	1.00	.40
7 Dizzy Dean	3.00	1.20
8 Bill DeLancey	.50	.20
9 Leo Durocher	3.00	1.20
10 Frank Frisch P/MG	2.50	1.00
11 Chick Fullis	.50	.20
12 Mike Gonzalez CO	.50	.20
13 Jesse Haines	2.00	.80
14 Bill Hallahan	1.00	.40
15 Francis Healy	.50	.20
16 Jim Lindsey	.50	.20
17 Pepper Martin	1.50	.60
18 Joe Medwick	2.50	1.00
19 Jim Mooney	.50	.20
20 Ernie Orsatti	.50	.20
21 Flint Rhem	.50	.20
22 John Rothrock	.50	.20
23 Dazzy Vance	2.00	.80
24 Bill Walker	.50	.20
25 Buzzy Wares CO	.50	.20
26 Whitey Whitehead	.50	.20
27 Jim Winford	.50	.20
28 Dizzy Dean Leo Durocher Celebrate	2.00	.80
29 Leo Durocher Scores	2.50	1.00
30 Joe Medwick Mickey Cochrane	2.00	.80
31 1934 St. Louis Cardinals World Champions	1.50	.60

1974 Cardinals Postcards

These postcards, which were available directly from the Cardinals, feature members of the 1974 St Louis Cardinals. Some of the photos used in 1974 were used in previous years. Since these photos are not numbered, we have sequenced them alphabetically.

	NM	Ex
COMPLETE SET	20.00	8.00
1 Vern Benson CO	.50	.20
2 Lou Brock	2.50	1.00
3 Jose Cruz	1.00	.40
4 Joe Cunningham FO	.50	.20
5 John Curtis	.50	.20
6 Rich Folkers	.50	.20
7 Bob Forsch	.50	.20
8 Alan Foster	.50	.20
9 Mike Garman	.50	.20
10 Bob Gibson	3.00	1.20
11 Jim Hickman	.50	.20
12 Marc Hill	.50	.20
13 Al Hrabosky	.50	.20
14 George Kissell CO	.50	.20

15 Johnny Lewis CO	.50	.20
16 Bake McBride	.75	.30
17 Tim McCarver	1.50	.60
18 Lynn McGlothen	.50	.20
19 Luis Melendez	.50	.20
20 Orlando Pena	.50	.20
21 Ken Reitz	.50	.20
22 Pete Richert	.50	.20
23 Dave Ricketts	.50	.20
24 Red Schoendienst MG	1.00	.40
25 Barney Schultz	.50	.20
26 Sonny Siebert	.50	.20
27 Ted Simmons	1.00	.40
28 Ted Sizemore	.50	.20
29 Reggie Smith	.75	.30
30 Joe Torre	1.00	.40
31 Mike Tyson	.50	.20

1975 Cardinals Postcards

This 30-card set of the St Louis Cardinals features player photos on postcard-size cards. The cards are unnumbered and checklisted below in alphabetical order.

	NM	Ex
COMPLETE SET (30)	20.00	8.00
1 Ed Brinkman	.50	.20
2 Lou Brock	3.00	1.20
3 Ron Bryant	.50	.20
4 Danny Cater	.50	.20
5 John Curtis	.50	.20
6 Willie Davis	.75	.30
7 John Denny	.50	.20
8 Jim Dwyer	.50	.20
9 Ron Fairly	.75	.30
10 Bob Forsch	.50	.20
11 Mike Garman	.50	.20
12 Bob Gibson	4.00	1.60
13 Mario Guerrero	.50	.20
14 Keith Hernandez	5.00	2.00
15 Al Hrabosky	.50	.20
16 Teddy Martinez	.50	.20
17 Bake McBride	.50	.20
18 Lynn McGlothen	.50	.20
19 Luis Melendez	.50	.20
20 Tommy Moore	.50	.20
21 Ron Reed	.50	.20
22 Ken Reitz	.50	.20
23 Ken Rudolph	.50	.20
24 Ray Sadecki	.50	.20
25 Ted L. Simmons	1.50	.60
26 Ted Sizemore	.50	.20
27 Reggie Smith	.75	.30
28 Elias Sosa	.50	.20
29 Greg Terlecky	.50	.20
30 Mike Tyson	.50	.20

1976 Cardinals Postcards

This 35-card set of the St. Louis Cardinals features player photos on postcard-size cards. The cards are unnumbered and checklisted below in alphabetical order.

	NM	Ex
COMPLETE SET (35)	20.00	8.00
1 Mike Anderson	.50	.20
2 Lou Brock	4.00	1.60
3 Willie Crawford	.50	.20
4 John Curtis	.50	.20
5 Hector Cruz	.50	.20
6 John Denny	.75	.30
7 Ron Fairly	.75	.30
8 Pete Falcone	.50	.20
9 Joe Ferguson	.50	.20
10 Bob Forsch	.50	.20
11 Danny Frisella	.50	.20
12 Preston Gomez CO	.50	.20
13 Bill Greif	.50	.20
14 Vic Harris	.50	.20
15 Keith Hernandez	3.00	1.20
16 Al Hrabosky	.75	.30
17 Don Kessinger	.50	.20
18 Fred Koenig CO	.50	.20
19 Johnny Lewis	.50	.20
20 Bake McBride	.50	.20
21 Lynn McGlothen	.50	.20
22 Luis Melendez	.50	.20
23 Bob Milliken CO	.50	.20
24 Jerry Mumphrey	.50	.20
25 Mike Proly	.50	.20
26 Harry Rasmussen	.50	.20
27 Lee Richard	.50	.20
28 Ken Rudolph	.50	.20
29 Red Schoendienst MG	1.50	.60
30 Ted Simmons	1.00	.40
31 Reggie Smith	1.00	.40
32 Eddie Solomon	.50	.20
33 Mike Tyson	.50	.20
34 Mike Wallace	.50	.20
35 Tom Zimmer	.50	.20

1977 Cardinals 5x7

This 30-card set features black-and-white player portraits in a white border with the player's name and position printed in the bottom margin. The backs are blank. The cards are unnumbered and checklisted below in alphabetical order.

	NM	Ex
COMPLETE SET (30)	15.00	6.00
1 Mike Anderson	.50	.20
2 Lou Brock	2.00	.80
3 Clay Carroll	.50	.20
4 Heity Cruz	.50	.20
5 John Denny	.50	.20
6 Larry Dierker	1.00	.40
7 Rawly Eastwick	.50	.20
8 Pete Falcone	.50	.20
9 Bob Forsch	.50	.20
10 Roger Freed	.50	.20
11 Keith Hernandez	1.50	.60
12 Al Hrabosky	.75	.30
13 Jack Krol CO	.50	.20
14 Butch Metzger	.50	.20
15 Mo Mozzali CO	.50	.20
16 Jerry Mumphrey	.50	.20
17 Claude Osteen CO	.50	.20
18 Mike Phillips	.50	.20
19 Dave Rader	.50	.20
20 Vern Rapp MG	.50	.20
21 Eric Rasmussen	.50	.20
22 Ken Reitz	.50	.20
23 Sonny Ruberto CO	.50	.20
24 Bobby Schultz	.50	.20
25 Tony Scott	.50	.20
26 Ted Simmons	1.50	.60
27 Garry Templeton	1.00	.40
28 Mike Tyson	.50	.20
29 Tom Underwood	.50	.20
30 John Urrea	.50	.20

1977 Cardinals Team Issue

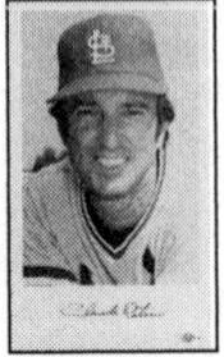

This 28-card set measures approximately 3 1/4" by 5 1/2" and features black-and-white player portraits in a white border. A facsimile autograph is printed in the wide bottom margin. The backs are blank. The cards are unnumbered and checklisted below in alphabetical order.

	NM	Ex
COMPLETE SET (28)	10.00	4.00
1 Mike Anderson	.25	.10
2 Lou Brock	2.50	1.00
3 Clay Carroll	.25	.10
4 Heity Cruz	.25	.10
5 John Denny	.50	.20
6 Larry Dierker	.50	.20
7 Pete Falcone	.25	.10
8 Bob Forsch	.25	.10
9 Roger Freed	.25	.10
10 Keith Hernandez	1.00	.40
11 Al Hrabosky	.50	.20
12 Don Kessinger	.25	.10
13 Jack Krol CO	.25	.10
14 Butch Metzger	.25	.10
15 Maurice"Mo" Mozzali CO	.25	.10
16 Jerry Mumphrey	.25	.10
17 Claude Osteen CO	.25	.10
18 Dave Rader	.25	.10
19 Vern Rapp MG	.25	.10
20 Eric Rasmussen	.25	.10
21 Ken Reitz	.25	.10
22 Sonny Ruberto CO	.25	.10
23 Buddy Schutz	.25	.10
24 Tony Scott	.25	.10
25 Ted Simmons	1.00	.40
26 Garry Templeton	.75	.30
27 Mike Tyson	.25	.10
28 John Urrea	.25	.10

1978 Cardinals Team Issue

This 37-card set measures approximately 3 1/4" by 5 1/2" and features black-and-white player portraits in a white border. A facsimile autograph is printed in the wide bottom margin. The backs are blank. The cards are unnumbered and checklisted below in alphabetical order.

	NM	Ex
COMPLETE SET (37)	12.00	4.80
1 Ken Boyer MG	1.00	.40
2 Lou Brock	2.50	1.00
3 Tom Bruno	.25	.10
4 John Denny	.25	.10
5 Jim Dwyer	.25	.10
6 Pete Falcone	.25	.10
7 Bob Forsch	.25	.10
8 Roger Freed	.25	.10
9 Dave Hamilton	.25	.10
10 George Hendrick	.25	.10
11 Keith Hernandez	1.00	.40
12 Dane Iorg	.25	.10
13 Jack Krol CO	.25	.10
14 Mark Littell	.25	.10
15 Aurelio Lopez	.25	.10
16 Silvio Martinez	.25	.10
17 Dal Maxvill CO	.25	.10
18 Jerry Morales	.25	.10
19 Maurice"Mo" Mozzali CO	.25	.10
20 Jerry Mumphrey	.25	.10
21 Ken Oberkfell	.25	.10
22 Claude Osteen CO	.25	.10
23 Mike Phillips	.25	.10
24 Eric Rasmussen	.25	.10
25 Ken Reitz	.25	.10
26 Dave Ricketts CO	.25	.10
27 Sonny Ruberto CO	.25	.10
28 Red Schoendienst MG	1.00	.40
29 Buddy Schultz	.25	.10
30 Tony Scott	.25	.10
31 Ted Simmons	1.00	.40
32 Gary Sutherland	.25	.10
33 Steve Swisher	.25	.10
34 Garry Templeton	.50	.20
35 Mike Tyson	.25	.10
36 Pete Vuckovich	.50	.20
37 John Urrea	.25	.10

1979 Cardinals 5x7

This 32-card set features black-and-white player portraits in a white border with the player's name and position printed in the bottom margin. The backs are blank. The cards are unnumbered and checklisted below in alphabetical order.

	NM	Ex
COMPLETE SET (36)	20.00	8.00
1 Ken Boyer MG	1.00	.40
2 Lou Brock	2.50	1.00
3 Tom Bruno	.50	.20
4 Bernie Carbo	.50	.20
5 John Denny	.50	.20
6 Bob Forsch	.50	.20
7 George Frazier	.50	.20
8 Roger Freed	.50	.20
9 John Fulgham	.50	.20
10 Tom Grieve	.75	.30
11 George Hendrick	.50	.20
12 Keith Hernandez	1.50	.60
13 Dane Iorg	.50	.20
14 Terry Kennedy	.75	.30
15 Darold Knowles	.50	.20
16 Jack Krol CO	.50	.20
17 Mark Littell	.50	.20
18 Silvio Martinez	.50	.20
19 Dal Maxvill CO	.50	.20
20 Will McEnaney	.50	.20
21 Jerry Mumphrey	.50	.20
22 Ken Oberkfell	.50	.20
23 Claude Osteen CO	.50	.20
24 Mike Phillips	.50	.20
25 Dave Ricketts CO	.50	.20
26 Tony Scott	.50	.20
27 Red Schoendienst CO	1.50	.60
28 Buddy Schultz	.50	.20
29 Ted Simmons	1.00	.40
30 Steve Swisher	.50	.20
number 9 on uniform		
31 Steve Swisher	.50	.20
No number on uniform		
32 Bob Sykes	.50	.20
33 Garry Templeton	.75	.30
34 Roy Thomas	.50	.20
35 Mike Tyson	.50	.20
36 Pete Vuckovich	.75	.30

1981 Cardinals 5x7

This 26-card set features black-and-white player portraits in a white border with the player's name and position printed in the bottom margin. The backs are blank. The cards are unnumbered and checklisted below in alphabetical order.

	Nm-Mt	Ex-Mt
COMPLETE SET (26)	15.00	6.00
1 Steve Braun	.50	.20
2 Glenn Brummer	.50	.20
3 Larry Dierker	1.00	.40
4 Bob Forsch	.50	.20
5 Julio Gonzalez	.50	.20
6 George Hendrick	1.00	.40
7 Keith Hernandez	2.00	.80
8 Tom Herr	1.00	.40
Uniform number visible		
9 Tom Herr	1.00	.40
No number visible		
10 Whitey Herzog MG	1.50	.60
11 Chuck Hiller CO	.50	.20
12 Dane Iorg	.50	.20
13 Jim Kaat	1.50	.60
14 Hub Kittle CO	.50	.20
15 Hal Lanier CO	.50	.20
16 Dave LaPoint	.50	.20
17 John Martin	.50	.20
18 Ken Oberkfell	.50	.20
Uniform number 10		
19 Ken Oberkfell	.50	.20
Uniform number 20		
20 Jim Otten	.50	.20
21 Darrell Porter	1.00	.40
22 Dave Ricketts CO	.50	.20
23 Orlando Sanchez	.50	.20
24 Red Schoendienst CO	2.00	.80
25 Bob Shirley	.50	.20
26 Gene Tenace	1.00	.40

1982 Cardinals Post-Dispatch

Issued after the 1982 World Series as a supplement in the St Louis Post-Dispatch, these inserts feature the members of the 1982 World Champions St Louis Cardinals. These "cards" have a player photo, information about the player's season and 1982 Regular Season and World Series statistics. Since these are unnumbered, we have sequenced them in alphabetical order.

	Nm-Mt	Ex-Mt
COMPLETE SET	30.00	12.00
1 Joaquin Andujar	1.00	.40
2 Doug Bair	1.00	.40
3 Steve Braun	1.00	.40
4 Glenn Brummer	1.00	.40
5 Bob Forsch	1.00	.40
6 Julio Gonzalez	1.00	.40
8 George Hendrick	1.25	.50
9 Keith Hernandez	1.50	.60
10 Tom Herr	1.00	.40
11 Dane Iorg	1.00	.40
12 Jim Kaat	1.50	.60
13 Dave LaPoint	1.00	.40
14 Jeff Lahti	1.00	.40
15 John Martin	1.00	.40
16 Willie McGee	3.00	1.20
17 Steve Mura	1.00	.40
18 Ken Oberkfell	1.00	.40
19 Darrell Porter	1.00	.40
20 Mike Ramsey	1.00	.40
21 Lonnie Smith	1.25	.50
22 Ozzie Smith	4.00	1.60
23 John Stuper	1.00	.40
24 Bruce Sutter	2.00	.80
25 Gene Tenace	1.25	.50

1983 Cardinals

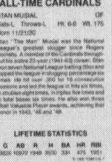

These cards feature members of the 1983 St. Louis Cardinals. These cards are unnumbered and we have sequenced them in alphabetical order.

	Nm-Mt	Ex-Mt
COMPLETE SET (31)	10.00	4.00
1 Joaquin Andujar	.50	.20
2 Doug Bair	.25	.10
3 Steve Braun	.25	.10
4 Glenn Brummer	.25	.10
5 Bob Forsch	.25	.10
6 David Green	.25	.10
7 George Hendrick	.50	.20
8 Keith Hernandez	1.00	.40
9 Tom Herr	.25	.10
10 Whitey Herzog MG	.75	.30
11 Chuck Hiller CO	.25	.10
12 Jim Kaat	.75	.30
13 Hub Kittle CO	.25	.10
14 Jeff Lahti	.25	.10
15 Hal Lanier CO	.25	.10
16 David LaPoint	.25	.10
17 Dane Iorg	.25	.10
18 John Martin	.25	.10
19 Willie McGee	2.50	1.00
20 Ken Oberkfell	.25	.10
21 Darrell Porter	.50	.20
22 Jamie Quirk	.25	.10
23 Mike Ramsey	.25	.10
24 Eric Rasmussen	.25	.10
25 Dave Ricketts CO	.25	.10
26 Rafael Santana	.25	.10
27 Red Schoendienst CO	1.00	.40
28 Lonnie Smith	.50	.20
29 Ozzie Smith	4.00	1.60
30 John Stuper	.25	.10
31 Bruce Sutter	1.00	.40

1983 Cardinals Colonial Bread Porter

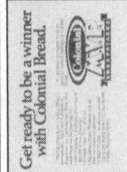

This one-card set features a blue-and-white photo of the 1982 World Series MVP, Darrell Porter of the World Champion St. Louis Cardinals, holding a loaf of Colonial Bread. The back displays sweepstakes rules for a contest sponsored by Colonial Bread.

	Nm-Mt	Ex-Mt
1 Darrell Porter	3.00	1.20

1983 Cardinals Greats TCMA

This 12-card standard-size set honors some leading all-time St. Louis Cardinals. These players are noted with their name and position on the front. The backs have vital statistics, a biography as well as career totals.

	Nm-Mt	Ex-Mt
COMPLETE SET (12)	6.00	2.40
1 Jim Bottomley	.50	.20
2 Rogers Hornsby	1.25	.50
3 Ken Boyer	.75	.30
4 Marty Marion	.75	.30
5 Ducky Medwick	.50	.20
6 Chick Hafey	.50	.20
7 Stan Musial	2.50	1.00
8 Bob Gibson	1.25	.50
9 Harry Brecheen	.25	.10
10 Tim McCarver	.75	.30
11 Alpha Brazle	.25	.10
12 Red Schoendienst MG	.75	.30

1983 Cardinals 1942-1946 TCMA

This 68-card set was printed in 1983 by TCMA and features photos of the 1942-46 St. Louis Cardinals teams. The backs carry player information. Cards numbered 66 and 67 are double-sized cards.

	Nm-Mt	Ex-Mt
COMPLETE SET (68)	12.00	4.80
1 Jimmy Brown	.10	.04
2 Jeff Cross	.10	.04
3 Lou Klein	.10	.04
4 Danny Litwhiler	.10	.04
5 Sam Narron	.10	.04
6 Estel Crabtree	.10	.04
7 Buzzy Wares	.10	.04
8 Ken O'Dea	.10	.04
9 Buddy Blattner	.10	.04
10 Erv Dusak	.10	.04
11 Ray Sanders	.10	.04
12 Harry Walker	.25	.10
13 Coaker Triplett	.10	.04
14 Stan Musial	5.00	2.00
15 Walker Cooper	.10	.04
16 Whitey Kurowski	.25	.10
17 Enos Slaughter	.75	.30
18 Terry Moore	.50	.20
19 Johnny Hopp	.10	.04
20 Creepy Crespi	.10	.04
21 Marty Marion	.75	.30
22 Debs Garms	.10	.04
23 Frank Demaree	.10	.04
24 George Fallon	.10	.04
25 Buster Adams	.10	.04
26 Emil Verban	.10	.04
27 Augie Bergamo	.10	.04
28 Pepper Martin	.75	.30
29 Mike Gonzalez CO	.10	.04
30 Leo Durocher MG	.50	.20
Eddie Dyer MG		
31 Red Schoendienst	1.50	.60
32 Del Rice	.10	.04
33 Joe Garagiola	.75	.30
34 Dick Sisler	.10	.04
35 Clyde Kluttz	.10	.04
36 Bill Endicott	.10	.04
37 Nippy Jones	.10	.04
38 Walter Sessi	.10	.04
39 Del Wilber	.10	.04
40 Mort Cooper	.10	.04
41 John Beazley	.10	.04
42 Howie Krist	.10	.04
43 Max Lanier	.10	.04
44 Harry Gumbert	.10	.04
45 Howie Pollet	.10	.04
46 Ernie White	.10	.04
47 Murry Dickson	.10	.04
48 Lon Warneke	.25	.10
49 Bill Lohrmann	.10	.04
50 Clyde Shoun	.10	.04
51 George Munger	.10	.04
52 Harry Brecheen	.25	.10
53 Alpha Brazle	.10	.04
54 Bud Byerly	.10	.04
55 Ted Wilks	.10	.04
56 Fred Schmidt	.10	.04
57 Al Jurisch	.10	.04
58 Red Barrett	.10	.04
59 Ken Burkhardt	.10	.04
60 Blix Donnelly	.10	.04
61 Johnny Grodzicki	.10	.04
62 Billy Southworth MG	.10	.04
63 Eddie Dyer MG	.10	.04
64 Red Ruffing	.50	.20
Bud Beasley		
65 Stan Musial	.75	.30
Bill Southworth MG		
Johnny Hopp		
66 Sportsman Park	1.00	.40
67 1942 Cardinals Team Picture .	1.00	.40
68 Stan Musial	.75	.30
Bill Southworth MG		
Ray Sanders		

1984 Cardinals

This 32-card set of the St. Louis Cardinals measures approximately 3 1/4" by 5 1/2" and features white-bordered, black-and-white player portraits. A facsimile autograph appears in the wide bottom margin. The backs are blank. Some personnel changes during the season account for more than 30 cards although they were issued in 30 card sets. The cards are unnumbered and checklisted below in alphabetical order.

	Nm-Mt	Ex-Mt
COMPLETE SET (32)	8.00	3.20
1 Neil Allen	.25	.10
2 Joaquin Andujar	.50	.20
3 Steve Braun	.25	.10
4 Glenn Brummer	.25	.10
5 Ralph Citarella	.25	.10
6 Danny Cox	.25	.10
7 Bob Forsch	.25	.10
8 David Green	.25	.10
9 George Hendrick	.50	.20
10 Tom Herr	.25	.10
11 Whitey Herzog MG	.75	.30
12 Rick Horton	.25	.10
13 Art Howe	.50	.20
14 Mike Jorgensen	.25	.10
15 Jeff Lahti	.25	.10
16 Tito Landrum	.25	.10
17 Hal Lanier CO	.25	.10
18 Dave LaPoint	.25	.10
19 Nick Leyva CO	.25	.10
20 Bill Lyons	.25	.10
21 Willie McGee	1.50	.60
22 Darrell Porter	.50	.20
23 Dave Ricketts CO	.25	.10
24 Mike Roarke CO	.25	.10
25 Dave Rucker	.25	.10
26 Mark Salas	.25	.10
27 Red Schoendienst CO	1.00	.40
28 Lonnie Smith	.25	.10
29 Ozzie Smith	3.00	1.20
30 Bruce Sutter	.75	.30
31 Andy Van Slyke	1.50	.60
32 Dave Von Ohlen	.25	.10

1984 Cardinals 5x7

This 30-card set features black-and-white player portraits either borderless or in a white border with the player's name and position printed in the bottom margin. The backs are blank. The cards are unnumbered and checklisted below in alphabetical order.

	Nm-Mt	Ex-Mt
COMPLETE SET (30)	20.00	8.00
1 Neil Allen	.50	.20
2 Joaquin Andujar	.50	.20
3 Steve Braun	.50	.20
4 Glenn Brummer	.50	.20
5 Danny Cox	.50	.20
6 Bob Forsch	.50	.20
7 Jose Gonzalez	.50	.20
8 David Green	.50	.20
9 George Hendrick	.75	.30
10 Tom Herr	.50	.20
11 Whitey Herzog MG	1.00	.40
12 Ricky Horton	.50	.20
13 Art Howe	.75	.30
14 Hal Lanier CO	.50	.20
15 Dave LaPoint	.50	.20
16 Nick Leyva CO	.50	.20
17 Bill Lyons	.50	.20
18 Willie McGee	2.00	.80
19 Tom Nieto	.50	.20
20 Terry Pendleton	2.00	.80
21 Darrell Porter	.75	.30
22 Dave Ricketts CO	.50	.20
23 Mike Roarke CO	.50	.20
24 Dave Rucker	.50	.20
25 Red Schoendienst CO	1.50	.60
26 Lonnie Smith	.75	.30
27 Ozzie Smith	2.50	1.00
28 John Stuper	.50	.20
29 Bruce Sutter	1.00	.40
30 Andy Van Slyke	2.00	.80

1985 Cardinals Team Issue

These 32 cards represent members of the 1985 St. Louis Cardinals. The fronts have black and white photographs and facsimile autographs. The backs are blank. We have checklisted this set in alphabetical order.

	Nm-Mt	Ex-Mt
COMPLETE SET (33)	10.00	4.00
1 Neil Allen	.25	.10
2 Joaquin Andujar	.50	.20
3 Steve Braun	.25	.10
4 Bill Campbell	.25	.10
5 Jack Clark	.75	.30
6 Vince Coleman	1.00	.40
7 Danny Cox	.25	.10
8 Ken Dayley	.25	.10
9 Ivan DeJesus	.25	.10
10 Bob Forsch	.25	.10
11 Brian Harper	.25	.10
12 Andy Hassler	.25	.10
13 Tom Herr	.25	.10
14 Whitey Herzog MG	.75	.30
15 Ricky Horton	.25	.10
16 Mike Jorgensen	.25	.10
17 Kurt Kepshire	.25	.10
18 Hal Lanier CO	.25	.10
19 Jeff Lahti	.25	.10
20 Tito Landrum	.25	.10
21 Tom Lawless	.25	.10
22 Johnny Lewis CO	.25	.10
23 Nick Leyva CO	.25	.10
24 Willie McGee	1.00	.40
25 Tom Nieto	.25	.10
26 Terry Pendleton	1.00	.40
27 Darrell Porter	.50	.20
28 Dave Ricketts CO	.25	.10
29 Mike Roarke CO	.25	.10
30 Red Schoendienst CO	1.00	.40
31 Ozzie Smith	2.50	1.00
32 John Tudor	.50	.20
33 Andy Van Slyke	1.00	.40

1986 Cardinals Team Issue

This 45-card set of the St. Louis Cardinals measures approximately 3 1/4" by 5 1/2" and features white-bordered, black-and-white player portraits. A facsimile autograph appears in the wide bottom margin. The backs are blank. The cards are unnumbered and checklisted below in alphabetical order. This set was updated during the season and that explains the large size of this set.

	Nm-Mt	Ex-Mt
COMPLETE SET (45)	10.00	4.00
1 Nick Allen	.25	.10
2 Joaquin Andujar	.50	.20
3 Greg Bargar	.25	.10
4 Steve Braun	.25	.10
5 Ray Burris	.25	.10
6 Bill Campbell	.25	.10
7 Jack Clark	.75	.30
8 Vince Coleman	1.00	.40
9 Tim Conroy	.25	.10
10 Dan Cox	.25	.10
11 Ken Dayley	.25	.10
12 Ivan DeJesus	.25	.10
13 Bob Forsch	.25	.10
14 Rich Hacker CO	.25	.10
15 Brian Harper	.25	.10
16 Mike Heath	.25	.10
17 Tom Herr	.25	.10
18 Whitey Herzog MG	.75	.30
19 Rick Horton	.25	.10
20 Clint Hurdle	.50	.20
21 Mike Jorgensen	.25	.10
22 Kurt Kepshire	.25	.10
23 Jeff Lahti	.25	.10
24 Tito Landrum	.25	.10
25 Hal Lanier CO	.25	.10
26 Tom Lawless	.25	.10
27 Johnny Lewis CO	.25	.10
28 Nick Leyva CO	.25	.10
29 Greg Mathews	.25	.10
30 Willie McGee	1.00	.40
31 Tom Nieto	.25	.10
32 Jose Oquendo	.25	.10
33 Rick Ownbey	.25	.10
34 Terry Pendleton	.75	.30
35 Pat Perry	.25	.10
36 Darrell Porter	.25	.10
37 Dave Ricketts CO	.25	.10
38 Mike Roarke CO	.25	.10
39 Red Schoendienst CO	1.00	.40
40 Ozzie Smith	2.50	1.00
41 John Tudor	.25	.10
42 Andy Van Slyke	.75	.30
43 Andy Van Slyke	.75	.30
44 Jerry White	.25	.10
45 Todd Worrell	1.00	.40

1986 Cardinals IGA Stores

This 14-card set of the St. Louis Cardinals measures approximately 6" by 9". The fronts feature white-framed color player portraits with a facsimile autographed in the lower left. The backs are blank. The cards are unnumbered and checklisted below in alphabetical order.

	Nm-Mt	Ex-Mt
COMPLETE SET (14)	16.00	6.50
1 Jack Clark	2.00	.80
2 Vince Coleman	2.50	1.00
3 Dan Cox	1.00	.40
4 Bob Forsch	1.00	.40
5 Mike Heath	1.00	.40
6 Tom Herr	1.00	.40
7 Tito Landrum	1.00	.40
8 Jeff Lahti	1.00	.40
9 Willie McGee	2.50	1.00
10 Terry Pendleton	2.00	.80
11 Ozzie Smith	5.00	2.00
12 John Tudor	1.00	.40
13 Andy Van Slyke	2.00	.80
14 Todd Worrell	2.50	1.00

1986 Cardinals KAS Discs

This set of discs was distributed by KAS in 1986 to commemorate the Cardinal's "almost" World Championship in 1985. Each disc measures 2 3/4" in diameter. Each disc has a white border on the front. Inside this white border is a full-color photo of the player with his hat airbrushed to erase the team logo on

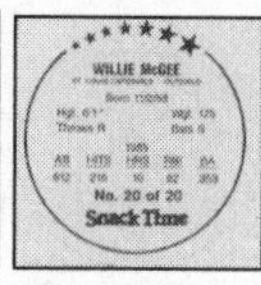

ther hat. The statistics on back of the disc give the player's 1985 pitching or hitting record as well as his vital statistics. The discs are numbered on the back.

	Nm-Mt	Ex-Mt
COMPLETE SET (20)	12.00	4.80
1 Vince Coleman	.50	.20
2 Ken Dayley	.25	.10
3 Tito Landrum	.25	.10
4 Steve Braun	.25	.10
5 Danny Cox	.25	.10
6 Bob Forsch	.25	.10
7 Ozzie Smith	6.00	2.40
8 Brian Harper	.25	.10
9 Jack Clark	.75	.30
10 Todd Worrell	.75	.30
11 Joaquin Andujar	.50	.20
12 Tom Nieto	.25	.10
13 Kurt Kepshire	.25	.10
14 Terry Pendleton	1.00	.40
15 Tom Herr	.25	.10
16 Darrell Porter	.50	.20
17 John Tudor	.50	.20
18 Jeff Lahti	.25	.10
19 Andy Van Slyke	1.00	.40
20 Willie McGee	2.00	.80

1986 Cardinals Schnucks Milk

The cards in this set were printed on the sides of Schnucks milk cartons. The set features only members of the St. Louis Cardinals. The cards measure approximately 3 3/4" by 7 1/2" and have black and white photos. The cards are unnumbered and blank backed. The cards are ordered below according to alphabetical order except for the mascot and schedule cards which are listed last.

	Nm-Mt	Ex-Mt
COMPLETE SET	50.00	20.00
1 Jack Clark	3.00	1.20
2 Vince Coleman	4.00	1.60
3 Tim Conroy	1.50	.60
4 Danny Cox	1.50	.60
5 Ken Dayley	1.50	.60
6 Bob Forsch	1.50	.60
7 Mike Heath	1.50	.60
8 Tom Herr	1.50	.60
9 Rick Horton	1.50	.60
10 Clint Hurdle	2.00	.80
11 Kurt Kepshire	1.50	.60
12 Jeff Lahti	1.50	.60
13 Tito Landrum	1.50	.60
14 Mike Lavalliere	1.50	.60
15 Tom Lawless	1.50	.60
16 Willie McGee	4.00	1.60
17 Jose Oquendo	1.50	.60
18 Rick Ownbey	1.50	.60
19 Terry Pendleton	4.00	1.60
20 Pat Perry	1.50	.60
21 Ozzie Smith	10.00	4.00
22 John Tudor	2.00	.80
23 Andy Van Slyke	3.00	1.20
24 Todd Worrell	4.00	1.60
25 Fred Bird (Mascot)	1.50	.60
26 Cardinals Schedule	1.50	.60

1987 Cardinals 1934 TCMA

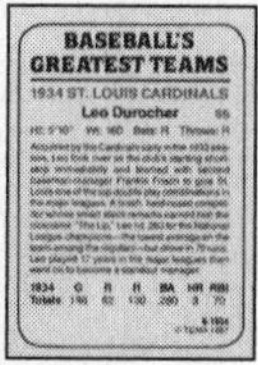

This nine-card standard-size set honors members of the "Gashouse Gang". This team won the world series and was led by the Dean Brothers who combined for 49 wins, 30 by Dizzy. The fronts have a player portrait as well as name and position. The back describes their 1934 season and has stats for that season as well.

	Nm-Mt	Ex-Mt
COMPLETE SET (9)	5.00	2.00
1 Dizzy Dean	2.00	.80
2 Daffy Dean	.50	.20
3 Pepper Martin	.75	.30
4 Ripper Collins	.25	.10
5 Frankie Frisch P/MG	1.00	.40
6 Leo Durocher	1.00	.40
7 Ducky Medwick	1.00	.40
8 Tex Carleton	.25	.10
9 Spud Davis	.25	.10

1987 Cardinals Smokey

The U.S. Forestry Service (in conjunction with the St. Louis Cardinals) produced this large, attractive 25-card set to commemorate the

43rd birthday of Smokey. The cards feature Smokey the Bear pictured in the top right corner of every card. The card backs give a cartoon fire safety tip. The cards measure approximately 4" by 6" and are subtitled "Wildfire Prevention" on the front. Sets were supposedly available from the Cardinals team for 3.50 postpaid. Also a limited number of 8 1/2" by 12" full-color team photos were available from the team to those who sent in a large SASE. The large team photo is not considered part of the complete set.

	Nm-Mt	Ex-Mt
COMPLETE SET (25)	12.00	4.80
1 Ray Soff	.50	.20
2 Todd Worrell	1.00	.40
3 John Tudor	.75	.30
4 Pat Perry	.50	.20
5 Rick Horton	.50	.20
6 Danny Cox	.50	.20
7 Bob Forsch	.75	.30
8 Greg Mathews	.50	.20
9 Bill Dawley	.50	.20
10 Steve Lake	.50	.20
11 Tony Pena	.50	.20
12 Tom Pagnozzi	.75	.30
13 Jack Clark	1.00	.40
14 Jim Lindeman	.50	.20
15 Mike Laga	.50	.20
16 Terry Pendleton	1.00	.40
17 Ozzie Smith	4.00	1.60
18 Jose Oquendo	.50	.20
19 Tom Lawless	.50	.20
20 Tom Herr	.75	.30
21 Curt Ford	.50	.20
22 Willie McGee	1.50	.60
23 Tito Landrum	.50	.20
24 Vince Coleman	.75	.30
25 Whitey Herzog MG	1.00	.40
NNO Team Photo (large)	3.00	1.20

1987 Cardinals Team Issue

This 33-card set of the St. Louis Cardinals features black-and-white player photos measuring approximately 3 1/4" by 5 1/2". The cards are unnumbered and checklisted below in alphabetical order.

	Nm-Mt	Ex-Mt
COMPLETE SET (33)	12.00	4.80
1 Rod Booker	.25	.10
2 Jack Clark	.75	.30
3 Vince Coleman	.25	.10
4 Tim Conroy	.25	.10
5 Dan Cox	.25	.10
6 Bill Dawley	.25	.10
7 Ken Dayley	.25	.10
8 Curt Ford	.25	.10
9 Bob Forsch	.25	.10
10 Richard Hacker CO	.25	.10
11 Tom Herr	.50	.20
12 Whitey Herzog MG	.75	.30
13 Rich Horton	.25	.10
14 Steve Lake	.25	.10
15 Tito Landrum	.25	.10
16 Tom Lawless	.25	.10
17 Johnny Lewis CO	.25	.10
18 Nick Leyva CO	.25	.10
19 Jim Lindeman	.25	.10
20 Joe Magrane	.25	.10
21 Willie McGee	1.50	.60
22 John Morris	.25	.10
23 Jose Oquendo	.25	.10
24 Tony Pena	.50	.20
25 Terry Pendleton	.75	.30
26 Pat Perry	.25	.10
27 Dave Ricketts CO	.25	.10
28 Mike Roarke CO	.25	.10
29 Red Schoendienst CO	1.00	.40
30 Ozzie Smith	3.00	1.20
31 John Tudor	.50	.20
32 Lee Tunnell	.25	.10
33 Todd Worrell	.75	.30

1988 Cardinals Smokey

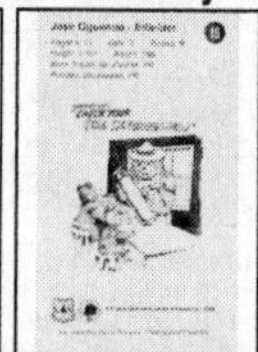

The U.S. Forestry Service (in conjunction with the St. Louis Cardinals) produced this attractive 25-card set. The cards feature Smokey the Bear pictured in the lower right corner of every card. The card backs give a cartoon fire safety tip. The cards measure approximately 3" by 5" and are in full color. The cards are numbered on the backs. The sets were distributed on July 19th during the Cardinals' game against the Los Angeles Dodgers to fans 15 years of age and under.

	Nm-Mt	Ex-Mt
COMPLETE SET (25)	10.00	4.00
1 Whitey Herzog MG	.75	.30
2 Danny Cox	.25	.10
3 Ken Dayley	.25	.10
4 Jose DeLeon	.25	.10
5 Bob Forsch	.50	.20
6 Joe Magrane	.25	.10
7 Greg Mathews	.25	.10
8 Scott Terry	.25	.10
9 John Tudor	.50	.20
10 Todd Worrell	.75	.30
11 Steve Lake	.25	.10
12 Tom Pagnozzi	.50	.20
13 Tony Pena	.50	.20
14 Bob Horner	.25	.10
15 Tom Lawless	.25	.10
16 Jose Oquendo (Ryne Sandberg also shown on card)	1.00	.40
17 Terry Pendleton	.75	.30
18 Ozzie Smith	4.00	1.60
19 Vince Coleman	.50	.20
20 Curt Ford	.25	.10
21 Willie McGee	1.25	.50
22 Larry McWilliams	.25	.10
23 Steve Peters	.25	.10
24 Luis Alicea	.25	.10
25 Tom Brunansky	.25	.10

1988 Cardinals Team Issue

This 36-card set of the St. Louis Cardinals features black-and-white player photos measuring approximately 3 1/4" by 5 1/2". The cards are unnumbered and checklisted below in alphabetical order.

	Nm-Mt	Ex-Mt
COMPLETE SET (36)	12.00	4.80
1 Luis Alicea	.25	.10
2 Tom Brunansky	.50	.20
3 Vince Coleman	.50	.20
4 Dan Cox	.25	.10
5 Ken Dayley	.25	.10
6 Jose DeLeon	.25	.10
7 Curt Ford	.25	.10
8 Bob Forsch	.25	.10
9 Richard Hacker CO	.25	.10
10 Whitey Herzog MG	.75	.30
11 Bob Horner	.25	.10
12 Michael Joyce	.25	.10
13 Steve Lake	.25	.10
14 Tom Lawless	.25	.10
15 Johnny Lewis CO	.25	.10
16 Nick Leyva CO	.25	.10
17 Jim Lindeman	.25	.10
18 Joe Magrane	.25	.10
19 Greg Mathews	.25	.10
20 Willie McGee	1.00	.40
21 Larry McWilliams	.25	.10
22 John Morris	.25	.10
23 Randy O'Neal	.25	.10
24 Jose Oquendo	.25	.10
25 Tom Pagnozzi	.25	.10
26 Tony Pena	.50	.20
27 Terry Pendleton	.75	.30
28 Steve Peters	.25	.10
29 Dave Ricketts CO	.25	.10
30 Mike Roarke CO	.25	.10
31 Red Schoendienst CO	1.00	.40
32 Ozzie Smith	2.50	1.00
33 Scott Terry	.25	.10
34 John Tudor	.25	.10
35 Duane Walker	.25	.10
36 Todd Worrell	.75	.30

1989 Cardinals Smokey

The 1989 Smokey Cardinals set contains 24 cards measuring approximately 4" by 6". The fronts have color photos with white and red borders. The backs feature biographical information. The cards are unnumbered so they are listed below in alphabetical order for reference.

	Nm-Mt	Ex-Mt
COMPLETE SET (24)	10.00	4.00
1 Tom Brunansky	.25	.10
2 Vince Coleman	.75	.30
3 John Costello	.25	.10
4 Ken Dayley	.25	.10
5 Jose DeLeon	.25	.10
6 Frank DiPino	.25	.10
7 Pedro Guerrero	.75	.30
8 Whitey Herzog MG	.75	.30
9 Ken Hill	.50	.20
10 Tim Jones	.25	.10
11 Jim Lindeman	.25	.10
12 Joe Magrane	.25	.10
13 Willie McGee	1.00	.40
14 John Morris	.25	.10
15 Jose Oquendo	.25	.10
16 Tom Pagnozzi	.25	.10
17 Tony Pena	.50	.20
18 Terry Pendleton	.75	.30
19 Dan Quisenberry	.75	.30
20 Ozzie Smith	3.00	1.20
21 Scott Terry	.25	.10
22 Milt Thompson	.25	.10
23 Denny Walling	.25	.10
24 Todd Worrell	.75	.30

1989 Cardinals Team Issue

This 34-card set of the St. Louis Cardinals features black-and-white player photos measuring approximately 3 1/4" by 5 1/2". The cards are unnumbered and checklisted below in alphabetical order.

	Nm-Mt	Ex-Mt
COMPLETE SET (34)	12.00	4.80
1 Tom Brunansky	.50	.20
2 Cris Carpenter	.25	.10
3 Vince Coleman	.50	.20
4 John Costello	.25	.10
5 Dan Cox	.25	.10
6 Ken Dayley	.25	.10

7 Jose DeLeon .25 .10
8 Frank DiPino .25 .10
9 Pedro Guerrero .75 .30
10 Rick Hacker CO .25 .10
11 Whitey Herzog MG .75 .30
12 Ken Hill .50 .20
13 Tim Jones .25 .10
14 Johnny Lewis CO .25 .10
15 Jim Lindeman .25 .10
16 Joe Magrane .25 .10
17 Greg Mathews .25 .10
18 Willie McGee 1.00 .40
19 John Morris .25 .10
20 Jose Oquendo .25 .10
21 Tom Pagnozzi .25 .10
22 Tony Pena .50 .20
23 Terry Pendleton .75 .30
24 Ted Power .25 .10
25 Dan Quisenberry .75 .30
26 Dave Ricketts CO .25 .10
27 Jim Riggelman CO .25 .10
28 Mike Roarke CO .25 .10
29 Red Schoendienst CO 1.00 .40
30 Ozzie Smith 3.00 1.20
31 Scott Terry .25 .10
32 Milt Thompson .25 .10
33 Denny Walling .25 .10
34 Todd Worrell .75 .30

1990 Cardinals Smokey

This 27-card, approximately 3" by 5", set was issued about the 1990 St. Louis Cardinals in conjuction with the US Forest Service which was using the popular character Smokey the Bear. The set has full color action photos of the Cardinals on the front of the card while the back of the card has fire safety tips on the bottom of the card. The set has been checklisted alphabetically for reference. The cards are unnumbered; not even uniform numbers are displayed prominently.

	Nm-Mt	Ex-Mt
COMPLETE SET (27)	15.00	4.50
1 Vince Coleman	1.00	.30
2 Dave Collins	.50	.15
3 Danny Cox	.50	.15
4 Ken Dayley	.50	.15
5 Frank DiPino	.50	.15
6 Jose DeLeon	.50	.15
7 Pedro Guerrero	1.00	.30
8 Whitey Herzog MG	1.00	.30
9 Rick Horton	.50	.15
10 Rex Hudler	.50	.15
11 Tim Jones	.50	.15
12 Joe Magrane	.50	.15
13 Greg Mathews	.50	.15
14 Willie McGee	2.00	.60
15 John Morris	.50	.15
16 Tom Niedenfuer	.50	.15
17 Jose Oquendo	.50	.15
18 Tom Pagnozzi	.50	.15
19 Terry Pendleton	1.00	.30
20 Bryn Smith	.50	.15
21 Lee Smith	1.00	.30
22 Ozzie Smith	3.00	.90
23 Scott Terry	.50	.15
24 Milt Thompson	.50	.15
25 John Tudor	.50	.15
26 Denny Walling	.50	.15
27 Todd Zeile	1.50	.45

1990 Cardinals Topps TV

This Cardinals team set contains 66 cards measuring the standard size. Cards numbered 1-36 were with the parent club, while cards 37-66 were in the farm system.

	Nm-Mt	Ex-Mt
COMPLETE FACT. SET (66)	50.00	15.00
1 Whitey Herzog MG	.50	.15
2 Steve Braun CO	.25	.07
3 Rich Hacker CO	.25	.07
4 Dave Ricketts CO	.25	.07
5 Jim Riggleman CO	.25	.07
6 Mike Roarke CO	.25	.07
7 Cris Carpenter	.25	.07
8 John Costello	.25	.07
9 Danny Cox	.25	.07
10 Ken Dayley	.25	.07
11 Jose DeLeon	.25	.07
12 Frank DiPino	.25	.07
13 Ken Hill	.25	.07
14 Howard Hilton	.25	.07
15 Ricky Horton	.25	.07
16 Joe Magrane	.25	.07
17 Greg Mathews	.25	.07
18 Bryn Smith	.25	.07
19 Scott Terry	.25	.07
20 Bob Tewksbury	.25	.07
21 John Tudor	.25	.07
22 Todd Worrell	.50	.15
23 Tom Pagnozzi	.25	.07
24 Todd Zeile	1.50	.45
25 Pedro Guerrero	.50	.15
26 Tim Jones	.25	.07
27 Jose Oquendo	.25	.07
28 Terry Pendleton	1.50	.45
29 Ozzie Smith	40.00	12.00
30 Denny Walling	.25	.07
31 Tom Brunansky	.50	.15
32 Vince Coleman	.50	.15
33 Dave Collins	.25	.07
34 Willie McGee	1.50	.45
35 John Morris	.25	.07
36 Milt Thompson	.25	.07
37 Gibson Alba	.25	.07
38 Scott Arnold	.25	.07
39 Rod Brewer	.25	.07
40 Greg Carmona	.25	.07
41 Mark Clark	.50	.15
42 Stan Clarke	.25	.07
43 Paul Coleman	.25	.07
44 Todd Crosby	.25	.07
45 Brad DuVall	.25	.07
46 John Ericks	.25	.07
47 Bien Figueroa	.25	.07
48 Terry Francona	.50	.15
49 Ed Fulton	.25	.07
50 Bernard Gilkey	1.50	.45
51 Ernie Camacho	.25	.07
52 Mike Hinkle	.25	.07
53 Ray Lankford	8.00	2.40
54 Julian Martinez	.25	.07
55 Jesus Mendez	.25	.07
56 Mike Milchin	.25	.07
57 Mauricio Nunez	.25	.07
58 Omar Olivares	1.50	.45
59 Geronimo Pena	.25	.07
60 Mike Perez	.25	.07
61 Gaylen Pitts MG	.25	.07
62 Mark Riggins CO	.25	.07
63 Tim Sherrill	.25	.07
64 Roy Silver	.25	.07
65 Ray Stephens	.25	.07
66 Craig Wilson	.25	.07

1991 Cardinals Police

This 24-card police set was sponsored by the Kansas City Life Insurance Company and distributed by Greater St. Louis Law Enforcement Agencies. The cards measure approximately 2 5/8" by 4 1/8" and feature on the fronts a mix of posed and action color player photos with white borders. The cards are checklisted below by uniform number.

	Nm-Mt	Ex-Mt
COMPLETE SET (24)	12.00	3.60
1 Ozzie Smith	3.00	.90
7 Geronimo Pena	.50	.15
9 Joe Torre MG	1.50	.45
10 Rex Hudler	.75	.23
11 Jose Oquendo	.50	.15
12 Craig Wilson	.50	.15
16 Ray Lankford	2.00	.60
19 Tom Pagnozzi	.50	.15
21 Gerald Perry	.50	.15
23 Bernard Gilkey	.75	.23
25 Milt Thompson	.50	.15
27 Todd Zeile	1.50	.45
28 Pedro Guerrero	1.00	.30
29 Rich Gedman	.50	.15
34 Felix Jose	.50	.15
35 Frank DiPino	.50	.15
36 Bryn Smith	.50	.15
37 Scott Terry	.50	.15
38 Todd Worrell	1.00	.30
39 Bob Tewksbury	.50	.15
43 Ken Hill	.50	.15
47 Lee Smith	1.00	.30
48 Jose DeLeon	.50	.15
49 Juan Agosto	.50	.15

1992 Cardinals McDonald's/Pacific

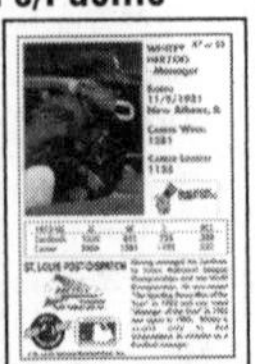

Produced by Pacific, this 55-card standard-size set commemorates the 100th anniversary of the St. Louis Cardinals. The collection was available at McDonald's restaurants in the greater St. Louis area for 1.49 with a purchase, and was distributed to raise money for Ronald McDonald Children's Charities. The set features black-and-white and color action player photos of players throughout Cardinals' history. The pictures are bordered in gold and include the player's name, the Cardinals 100th anniversary logo, and the McDonald's logo. The back design consists of a posed player photo, biographical and statistical information, and a career summary. There was also an album issued to go with this set. The album is not widely available at this time.

	Nm-Mt	Ex-Mt
COMPLETE SET (55)	40.00	12.00
1 Jim Bottomley	1.00	.30
2 Rip Collins	.25	.07
3 Johnny Mize	1.00	.30
4 Rogers Hornsby	1.50	.45
5 Miller Huggins	1.00	.30
6 Marty Marion	.75	.23
7 Frank Frisch	1.00	.30
8 Whitey Kurowski	.25	.07
9 Joe Medwick	1.00	.30
10 Terry Moore	.75	.23
11 Chick Hafey	1.00	.30
12 Pepper Martin	.75	.23
13 Bob O'Farrell	.25	.07
14 Walker Cooper	.25	.07
15 Dizzy Dean	2.00	.60
16 Grover C. Alexander	1.50	.45
17 Jesse Haines	1.00	.30
18 Bill Hallahan	.25	.07
19 Mort Cooper	.50	.15
20 Burleigh Grimes	1.00	.30
21 Red Schoendienst	1.50	.45
22 Stan Musial	8.00	2.40
23 Enos Slaughter	1.50	.45
24 Keith Hernandez	.75	.23
25 Bill White	.75	.23
26 Orlando Cepeda	1.00	.30
27 Julian Javier	.50	.15
28 Dick Groat	.50	.15
29 Ken Boyer	1.00	.30
30 Lou Brock	1.50	.45
31 Mike Shannon	.50	.15
32 Curt Flood	.75	.23
33 Joe Cunningham	.50	.15
34 Reggie Smith	.50	.15
35 Ted Simmons	.75	.23
36 Tim McCarver	.75	.23
37 Tom Herr	.25	.07
38 Ozzie Smith	8.00	2.40
39 Joe Torre	1.00	.30
40 Terry Pendleton	.75	.23
41 Ken Reitz	.25	.07
42 Vince Coleman	.25	.07
43 Willie McGee	1.00	.30
44 Bake McBride	.25	.07
45 George Hendrick	.25	.07
46 Bob Gibson	1.50	.45
47 Whitey Herzog MG	.75	.23
48 Harry Brecheen	.50	.15
49 Howard Pollet	.25	.07
50 John Tudor	.25	.07
51 Bob Forsch	.25	.07
52 Bruce Sutter	.75	.23
53 Lee Smith	.75	.23
54 Todd Worrell	.50	.15
55 Al Hrabosky	.25	.07
XX Album	5.00	1.50

1992 Cardinals Police

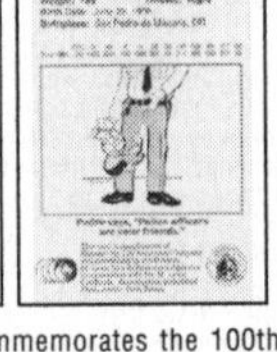

This 26-card set commemorates the 100th anniversary of the Cardinals. The set was sponsored by the Kansas City Life Insurance Company and distributed by the Greater St. Louis Law Enforcement Agencies. The cards measure 2 5/8" by 4 1/8" and feature color action player photos with white borders. The cards are unnumbered and checklisted below in alphabetical order.

	Nm-Mt	Ex-Mt
COMPLETE SET (27)	10.00	3.00
1 Juan Agosto	.25	.07
2 Cris Carpenter	.25	.07
3 Jose DeLeon	.25	.07
4 Andres Galarraga	1.50	.45
5 Rich Gedman	.25	.07
6 Bernard Gilkey	.25	.07
7 Pedro Guerrero	.50	.15
8 Rex Hudler	.50	.15
9 Felix Jose	.25	.07
10 Ray Lankford	1.00	.30
11 Joe Magrane	.25	.07
12 Omar Olivares	.25	.07
13 Jose Oquendo	.25	.07
14 Tom Pagnozzi	.25	.07
15 Geronimo Pena	.25	.07
16 Gerald Perry	.25	.07
17 Bryn Smith	.25	.07
18 Lee Smith	.75	.23
19 Ozzie Smith	3.00	.90
20 Scott Terry	.25	.07
21 Bob Tewksbury	.25	.07
22 Milt Thompson	.25	.07
23 Joe Torre MG	1.00	.30
24 Craig Wilson	.25	.07
25 Todd Worrell	.50	.15
26 Todd Zeile	1.00	.30
27 Checklist	.25	.07

1993 Cardinals Police

Sponsored by the Kansas City Life Insurance Company, the 26 cards comprising this set measure 2 5/8" by 4" and feature on their fronts blue-bordered color player action photos. The cards are unnumbered and checklisted below in alphabetical order.

	Nm-Mt	Ex-Mt
COMPLETE SET (26)	8.00	2.40
1 Luis Alicea	.25	.07
2 Rene Arocha	.25	.07
3 Rod Brewer	.25	.07
4 Ozzie Canseco	.25	.07
5 Rheal Cormier	.25	.07
6 Bernard Gilkey	.25	.07
7 Gregg Jefferies	.25	.07
8 Brian Jordan	1.00	.30
9 Ray Lankford	1.00	.30
10 Rob Murphy	.25	.07
11 Omar Olivares	.25	.07
12 Jose Oquendo	.25	.07
13 Donovan Osborne	.25	.07
14 Tom Pagnozzi	.25	.07
15 Geronimo Pena	.25	.07
16 Mike Perez	.25	.07
17 Gerald Perry	.25	.07
18 Stan Royer	.25	.07
19 Lee Smith	.75	.23
20 Ozzie Smith	3.00	.90
21 Bob Tewksbury	.25	.07
22 Joe Torre MG	1.00	.30
23 Hector Villanueva	.25	.07
24 Tracy Woodson	.25	.07
25 Todd Zeile	1.00	.30
26 Checklist	.25	.07

1993 Cardinals Stadium Club

This 30-card standard-size set features the 1993 St. Louis Cardinals. The set was issued in hobby (plastic box) and retail (blister) form.

	Nm-Mt	Ex-Mt
COMP. FACT SET (30)	4.00	1.20
1 Ozzie Smith	2.00	.60
2 Rene Arocha	.10	.03
3 Bernard Gilkey	.10	.03
4 Jose Oquendo	.10	.03
5 Mike Perez	.10	.03
6 Tom Pagnozzi	.10	.03
7 Rod Brewer	.10	.03
8 Joe Magrane	.10	.03
9 Todd Zeile	.25	.07
10 Bob Tewksbury	.10	.03
11 Darrel Deak	.10	.03
12 Gregg Jefferies	.10	.03
13 Lee Smith	.25	.07
14 Ozzie Canseco	.10	.03
15 Tom Urbani	.10	.03
16 Donovan Osborne	.10	.03
17 Ray Lankford	.50	.15
18 Rheal Cormier	.10	.03
19 Allen Watson	.10	.03
20 Geronimo Pena	.10	.03
21 Rob Murphy	.10	.03
22 Tracy Woodson	.10	.03
23 Basil Shabazz	.10	.03
24 Omar Olivares	.10	.03
25 Brian Jordan	.75	.23
26 Les Lancaster	.10	.03
27 Sean Lowe	.10	.03
28 Hector Villanueva	.10	.03
29 Brian Barber	.10	.03
30 Aaron Holbert	.10	.03

1994 Cardinals Magnets GM

This six-card set featues color action player photos in white borders. The cards are actually magnets that measure approximately 2" by 3". The last two cards of the set were released sparingly because of the Baseball strike of 1994.

	Nm-Mt	Ex-Mt
COMPLETE SET (6)	20.00	6.00
COMMON CARD (1-4)	2.00	.60
COMMON CARD (5-6)	5.00	1.50
1 Ozzie Smith	8.00	2.40
2 Gregg Jefferies	2.00	.60
3 Bob Tewksbury	2.00	.60
4 Ray Lankford	4.00	1.20
5 Rene Arocha	5.00	1.50
6 Tom Pagnozzi	5.00	1.50

1994 Cardinals Police

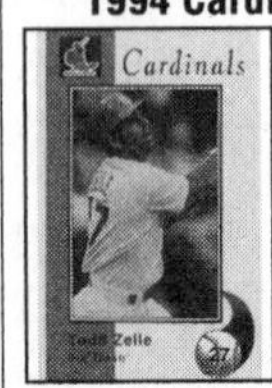

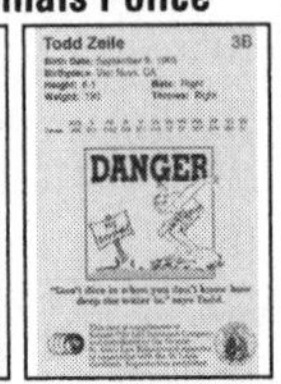

Measuring approximately 2 5/8" by 4", this 26-card set was sponsored by Kansas City Life Insurance Company and distributed by Greater St. Louis Law Enforcement Agencies. The cards are unnumbered and checklisted below in alphabetical order.

	Nm-Mt	Ex-Mt
COMPLETE SET (26)	6.00	1.80
1 Luis Alicea	.25	.07
2 Rene Arocha	.25	.07
3 Rich Batchelor	.25	.07
4 Rheal Cormier	.25	.07
5 Bernard Gilkey	.25	.07
6 Gregg Jefferies	.25	.07
7 Brian Jordan	1.00	.30
8 Paul Kilgus	.25	.07
9 Ray Lankford	.75	.23
10 Rob Murphy	.25	.07
11 Omar Olivares	.25	.07
12 Jose Oquendo	.25	.07
13 Tom Pagnozzi	.25	.07
14 Erik Pappas	.25	.07
15 Geronimo Pena	.25	.07
16 Mike Perez	.25	.07
17 Gerald Perry	.25	.07
18 Stan Royer	.25	.07
19 Ozzie Smith	2.50	.75
20 Rick Sutcliffe	.50	.15
21 Bob Tewksbury	.25	.07
22 Joe Torre MG	1.00	.30
23 Tom Urbani	.25	.07
24 Allen Watson	.25	.07
25 Mark Whiten	.25	.07
26 Todd Zeile	.75	.23

1996 Cardinals Police

This 26-card set measures approximately 2 1/2" by 4". The player's photo, name and uniform number are notated on the front. The back has vital statistics, career stats and a safety tip. The cards are unnumberd so we have sequenced them in alphabetical order.

	Nm-Mt	Ex-Mt
COMPLETE SET (26)	8.00	2.40
1 Alan Benes	.25	.07
2 Andy Benes	.25	.07
3 Pat Borders	.25	.07
4 Royce Clayton	.25	.07
5 Dennis Eckersley	1.00	.30
6 Tony Fossas	.25	.07
7 Fredbird CL Mascot	.25	.07
8 Ron Gant	.50	.15
9 Gary Gaetti	.50	.15
10 Mike Gallego	.25	.07
11 Rick Honeycutt	.25	.07
12 Danny Jackson	.25	.07
13 Brian Jordan	.50	.15
14 Ray Lankford	.75	.23
15 Tony LaRussa MG	.75	.23
16 John Mabry	.25	.07
17 T.J. Mathews	.25	.07
18 Willie McGee	1.00	.30
19 Mike Morgan	.25	.07
20 Donovan Osborne	.25	.07
21 Tom Pagnozzi	.25	.07
22 Mark Petvosek	.25	.07
23 Ozzie Smith	2.50	.75
24 Todd Stottlemyre	.25	.07
25 Mark Sweeney	.25	.07
26 Tom Urbani	.25	.07

1997 Cardinals Police

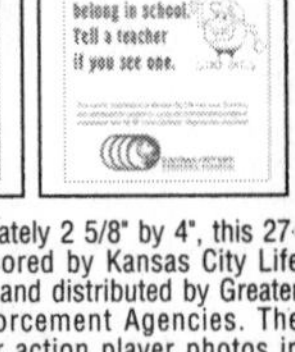

Measuring approximately 2 5/8" by 4", this 27-card set was sponsored by Kansas City Life Insurance Company and distributed by Greate St. Louis Law Enforcement Agencies. The fronts feature color action player photos ir white borders. The backs carry biographica information, statistics, and a picture illustrating a public service announcement. The cards are unnumbered and checklisted below ir alphabetical order.

	Nm-Mt	Ex-Mt
COMPLETE SET (27)	10.00	3.00
1 Alan Benes	.25	.07
2 Andy Benes	.25	.07
3 Royce Clayton	.25	.07
4 Delino DeShields	.50	.15
5 Dennis Eckersley	1.00	.30
6 Tony Fossas	.25	.07
7 Fredbird(Mascot) CL	.25	.07
8 Gary Gaetti	.50	.15
9 Ron Gant	.50	.15
10 Rick Honeycutt	.25	.07
11 Danny Jackson	.25	.07
12 Brian Jordan	.75	.23
13 Tom Lampkin	.25	.07
14 Ray Lankford	.50	.15
15 Tony La Russa MG	.75	.23
16 Eric Ludwick	.25	.07
17 John Mabry	.25	.07
18 T.J. Mathews	.25	.07
19 Willie McGee	1.00	.30
20 Donovan Osborne	.25	.07
21 Tom Pagnozzi	.25	.07
22 Mark Petkovsek	.25	.07
23 Steve Scarsone	.25	.07
24 Danny Sheaffer	.25	.07
25 Todd Stottlemyre	.25	.07
26 Mark Sweeney	.25	.07
27 Dmitri Young	.75	.23

1998-03 Cardinals Fox Sports

Issued over a series of years, these standar size cards were designed to do promotions for

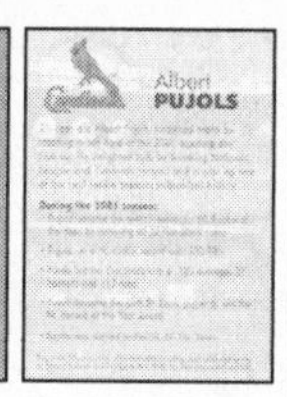

the Fox Sports Network regional coverage of the St. Louis Cardinals. Apparently issued at a rate of one card per year, the front features a Cardinal star while the back features information about that player. This checklist is incomplete and any additional information is appreciated.

MINT NRMT
2 Mark McGwire 2.00 .90
5 Albert Pujols 2.00 .90

1998 Cardinals Hunter

This three item card and pin set features three of the most famous personages in St Louis Cardinal history. The blank-backed card featured a photo, and a brief biography of the person featured. There is also an ad for ""Hunter Meats". Since these items are unnumbered, we have sequenced them in alphabetical order.

Nm-Mt Ex-Mt
COMPLETE SET (3) 10.00 3.00
1 Jack Buck ANN 2.00 .60
2 Bob Gibson 4.00 1.20
3 Stan Musial 5.00 1.50

1998 Cardinals Score

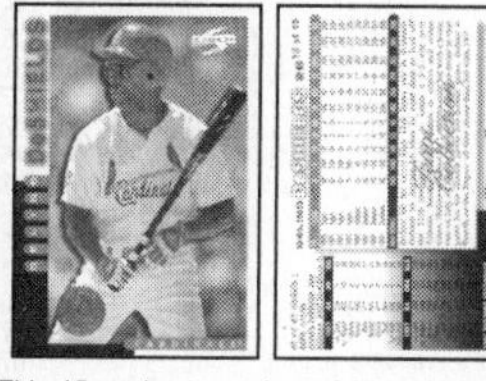

This 15-card set was issued in special retail packs and features color photos of the St. Louis Cardinals team. The backs carry player information. A special platinum parallel set was also issued and randomly inserted in packs.

Nm-Mt Ex-Mt
COMPLETE SET (15) 8.00 2.40
*PLATINUM: 5X BASIC CARDS
1 Andy Benes .25 .07
2 Todd Stottlemyre .25 .07
3 Dennis Eckersley 1.00 .30
4 Mark McGwire 3.00 .90
5 Dmitri Young .75 .23
6 Ron Gant .50 .15
7 Mike Difelice .25 .07
8 Ray Lankford .50 .15
9 John Mabry .25 .07
10 Royce Clayton .25 .07
11 Alan Benes .25 .07
12 Delino DeShields .25 .07
13 Brian Jordan .50 .15
14 Gary Gaetti .50 .15
15 Matt Morris 1.00 .30

1999 Cardinals Safety

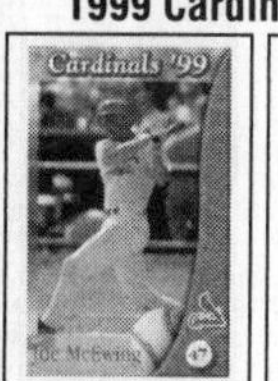

This 26 card set features members of the St Louis Cardinals and was sponsored by the Kansas City Life Insurance Company. The fronts of most of these cards feature blurry photos with the words "Cardinals 99" on top and the player name and uniform number on the bottom. The backs give some biographical information and a life aphorism. Since these cards are unnumbered we have sequenced them in alphabetical order.

Nm-Mt Ex-Mt
COMPLETE SET (26) 10.00 3.00
1 Juan Acevedo .25 .07
2 Manny Aybar .25 .07
3 Alan Benes .25 .07
4 Ricky Bottalico .25 .07
5 Kent Bottenfield .25 .07
6 Darren Bragg .25 .07
7 Alberto Castillo .25 .07
8 Eric Davis .50 .15
9 J.D.Drew 1.00 .30
10 Shawon Dunston .25 .07
11 John Frascatore .25 .07
12 David Howard .25 .07
13 Ray Lankford .50 .15
14 Tony LaRussa MG .75 .23
15 Eli Marrero .50 .15
16 Joe McEwing .25 .07
17 Willie McGee 1.00 .30
18 Mark McGwire 2.50 .75
19 Kent Mercker .25 .07
20 Matt Morris .25 .07
21 Darren Oliver .25 .07
22 Donovan Osborne .25 .07
23 Lance Painter .25 .07
24 Scott Radinsky .25 .07
25 Edgar Renteria .75 .23
26 Fernando Tatis .50 .15

1999 Cardinals Upper Deck McDonalds

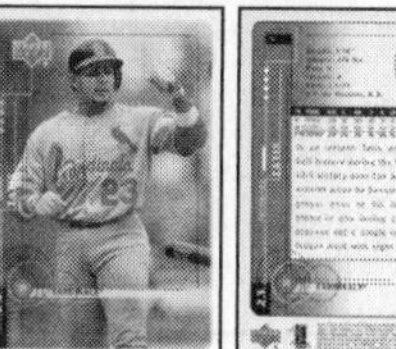

These 15 standard-size cards were available through St. Louis are McDonald restaurants. The cards are similar in design to the 1999 Upper Deck MVP sets.

Nm-Mt Ex-Mt
COMPLETE SET (15) 8.00 2.40
1 J.D. Drew 1.00 .30
2 Jose Jiminez .50 .15
3 Mark McGwire 2.50 .75
4 Fernando Tatis .50 .15
5 Edgar Renteria .75 .23
6 Ray Lankford .50 .15
7 Willie McGee 1.00 .30
8 Ricky Bottalico .25 .07
9 Eli Marrero .50 .15
10 Kent Bottenfield .25 .07
11 Eric Davis .50 .15
12 Darren Bragg .25 .07
13 Joe McEwing .25 .07
14 Shawon Dunston .25 .07
15 Darren Oliver .25 .07

1999 Cardinals Upper Deck McDonalds McGwire Milestones

This nine-card set honoring Mark McGwire was an insert into the 1999 Cardinal Upper Deck packs available in the St. Louis area. The horizontal cards feature a photo of McGwire against a silvery background. The words "McGwire Milestones" are printed in red and the word milestone is printed in a continous line along the bottom of the card. The back has a black box describing a key homer of 1998 and at the bottom there is a description of three various homer highlights of his career.

Nm-Mt Ex-Mt
COMPLETE SET (M1-M9) 25.00 7.50
COMMON CARD (M1-M9) 3.00 .90

2000 Cardinals McDonalds

This four-item card and coin set was issued at four different Cardinal games during the 2000 season. The top part is a card with a player photo and a blurb on the back .Each card also has a McDonald's coupon. The bottom part is dedicated to a coin. Since the items are unnumbered, we have sequenced them in alphabetical order.

Nm-Mt Ex-Mt
COMPLETE SET (4) 40.00 12.00
1 Jim Edmonds 10.00 3.00
2 Willie McGee 10.00 3.00
3 Mark McGwire 15.00 4.50
4 Fernando Vina 6.00 1.80

2002 Cardinals Christian Family Day

This 5" by 7" card features a photo of Albert Pujols on the front and the back features a photo of the Pujols family along with some religious testimony.

MINT NRMT
1 Albert Pujols 3.00 1.35

2002 Cardinals Safety

This set, which measures approximately 2 5/8" by 4" features members of the 2002 St Louis Cardinals. These cards feature a player photo with a mirror-like effect in the background. The player's name and Cardinals 2002 are on the left of the card. The back features biographical information along with career totals and some safety tips. This set was sponsored by the Kansas City Life Insurance Company. Since this set is unnumbered, we have sequenced it in alphabetical order.

Nm-Mt Ex-Mt
COMPLETE SET 8.00 2.40
1 Rick Ankiel .50 .15
2 Andy Benes .25 .07
3 Mike Difelice .25 .07
4 J.D. Drew .75 .23
5 Jim Edmonds 1.00 .30
6 Luther Hackman .25 .07
7 Jason Isringhausen .25 .07
8 Darryl Kile .50 .15
9 Steve Kline .25 .07
10 Tony LaRussa MG .75 .23
11 Eli Marrero .50 .15
12 Mike Matheny .25 .07
13 Mike Matthews .25 .07
14 Matt Morris 1.00 .30
15 Placido Polanco .25 .07
16 Albert Pujols 2.50 .75
17 Edgar Renteria .75 .23
18 Kerry Robinson .25 .07
19 Bud Smith .25 .07
20 Gene Stechschulte .25 .07
21 Garrett Stephenson .25 .07
22 Mike Timlin .25 .07
23 Dave Veres .25 .07
24 Fernando Vina .25 .07
25 Woody Williams .25 .07
26 Fredbird (Mascot) .25 .07

1993 Cardtoons

This 156-card unlicensed standard-size set was distributed in eight-card packs with a suggested retail of $1.29. The set uses fanciful cartoon caricatures on its fronts to parody major league baseball players. The borderless cartoons are framed by a thin gold-colored line that terminates in gold-colored baseball icons, which set off the "player's" name at the bottom. The backs carry comical "career highlights" within silver-colored panels on the left sides and team logo caricatures on the right sides. Cards #1-95 were drawn by sports artist Dayne Dudley. The checklist below contains five subsets and a Promo Set of three cards.The three Promo cards are numbered on the back with a "P" prefix. Cards F1-F10 belong to the Grand Slam Foil Etched Subset which features U-V coated colors and special effects on each card. Cards R1-R8 belong to a subset titled Cardtoons Awards which could be obtained by a special offer found on one of three replacement cards inserted in packs. Cards S1-S11 features cartoons by cartoonist Dave Simpson and carries his views of baseball in 1993. Cards BB1-BB20 display head caricatures of baseball's highest paid players on dollar bill backgrounds. Cards FOG1-FOG9 belong to the subset Field of Greed which fitted together to form a nine-piece puzzle. Even though this set does not have a liscence, it is listed since the company won a suit that allows it to be released as a parody under first admendment rules. The complete set price includes all the insert cards.

Nm-Mt Ex-Mt
COMPLETE SET (156) 75.00 22.00
COMMON CARD (1-95) .10 .03
COMMON CARD (P1-P3) 1.00 .30
COMMON CARD (S1-S7) 1.00 .30
COMMON CARD (FOG1-FOG9) .25 .07
COMMON CARD (BB1-BB20) 1.00 .30
COMMON CARD (F1-F10) 1.00 .30
COMMON CARD (R1-R8) .50 .15
1 Hey Abbott .25 .07
2 Robin Adventura .25 .07
3 Roberto Alamode .75 .23
4 Don Battingly .75 .23
5 Cow Belle .75 .23
6 Jay Bellhop .10 .03
7 Fowl Boggs .75 .23
8 Treasury Bonds .75 .23
9 True Brett .75 .23
10 Wild Pitch Mitch .10 .03
11 Balou's Brothers .10 .03
12 Charlie Bustle .25 .07
13 Brett Butter .10 .03
14 Rambo Canseco .50 .15
15 Roberto Cementie 1.50 .45
16 Roger Clemency .75 .23
17 Will Clock .10 .03
18 David Clone .25 .07
19 Tom Clowning .10 .03
20 Mr. Club .50 .15
21 Joe Crater .25 .07
22 Doolin' Daulton .25 .07
23 Chili Dog Davis .25 .07
24 Doug Drawback .10 .03
25 Dennis Excellency .25 .07
26 Silly Fanatic .10 .03
27 Wand Gonzales .75 .23
28 Amazing Grace .50 .15
29 Tom Grapevine .25 .07
30 Marquis Gruesome .25 .07
31 Homerin' Hank .75 .23
32 Kevin Happier .10 .03
33 Pete Harness .10 .03
34 Charlie Haze .10 .03
35 Egotisticky Henderson .50 .15
36 Sayanora Infielder .10 .03
37 Snoozin' Ted & Tarzan Jane .10 .03
38 Cloud Johnson .10 .03
39 Sandy K-Fax .75 .23
40 The Say What Kid .75 .23
41 Tommy Lasagna .25 .07
42 Greg Maddogs 1.25 .35
43 Stamp the Man .50 .15
44 Mark McBash 1.50 .45
45 Fred McGruff .25 .07
46 Mount Mick 2.00 .60
47 Pat Moustache .10 .03
48 Ozzie Myth .75 .23
49 Bob Nukesbury .10 .03
50 Reggie October .75 .23
51 Doctor OK .25 .07
52 Rafael Palmist .50 .15
53 Lose Pinella .10 .03
54 Vince Poleman .10 .03
55 Charlie Puff .10 .03
56 Rob Quibble .10 .03
57 Darryl Razzberry .10 .03
58 Cal Ripkenwinkle 1.50 .45
59 Budge Rodriguez .75 .23
60 Ryne Sandbox .75 .23
61 Steve Saxophone .10 .03
62 Harry Scaray .10 .03
63 Scary Shefield .50 .15
64 Ruben Siesta .10 .03
65 Dennis Smartinez .10 .03
66 Lee Smite .25 .07
67 Ken Spiffy Jr. 2.00 .60
68 Nails Spikestra .10 .03
69 The Splendid Spinner 1.50 .45
70 Toad Stottlemyre .10 .03
71 Raging Tartabull .10 .03
72 Robbery Thompson .10 .03
73 Alan Trampoline .25 .07
74 Monster Truk .10 .03
75 Shawon Tungsten .10 .03
76 Tony Twynn .75 .23
77 Andy Van Tyke .10 .03
78 Derrick Ventriloquist .10 .03
79 Frankie Violin .10 .03
80 Rap Winfielder .75 .23
81 Robinhood Yount .75 .23
82 Swift Justice .10 .03
83 Brat Saberhagen .10 .03
84 Mike Pizzazz 1.25 .35
85 Andres Colorado .25 .07
86 Money Bagswell 1.25 .35
87 Video Nomo 1.50 .45
88 Out of the Park .10 .03
89 Tim Wallet .10 .03
90 Checklist .10 .03
91 Greenback Jack .10 .03
92 Mighty Matt Power Hitter .10 .03
93 Frankenthomas 2.00 .60
94 Neon Peon Slanders .75 .23
95 Just Air Jordan 2.50 .75
F1 Bo Action 1.00 .30
F2 Andre Awesome 1.50 .45
F3 Bobby Bonus 2.50 .75
F4 Steve Bravery 1.00 .30
F5 Carlton Fist 2.00 .60
F6 E.T. McGee 1.00 .30
F7 Kirbvy Plunkit 3.00 .90
F8 Jose Rheostat 1.00 .30
F9 Sir Noble Ryan 4.00 1.20
F10 Day-Glo Sabo 1.00 .30
P1 Day-Glo Sabo 1.00 .30
P2 Dennis Excellency 1.50 .45
P3 Pledge of Allegiance 1.00 .30
R1 No Ball Peace Prize .50 .15
R2 Forrest Grump .50 .15
R3 Most Virtuous Player .50 .15
R4 Golden Glove Award .50 .15
R5 Comedown Player of the Year .50 .15
R6 Corkville Slugger .50 .15
R7 Can't Get No Relief .50 .15
R8 1994 World Series Champ .50 .15
S1 Pledge of Allegiance 1.00 .30
S2 Th Wave 1.00 .30
S3 Slick Willie 1.00 .30
S4 Umpires Convention 1.00 .30
S5 The Slide 1.00 .30
S6 SH-H-H-H-H-H 1.00 .30
S7 Throwing Out the First Contract 1.00 .30
S8 Babe Rush 3.00 .90
S9 Hot Prospect 1.00 .30
S10 Let's Play Ball 1.00 .30
S11 Role Model 1.00 .30
BB1 Treasury Bonds 2.00 .60
BB2 Sayanora Infielder 1.00 .30
BB3 Cal Ripkenwinkle 4.00 1.20
BB4 Bobby Bonus 1.50 .45
BB5 Joe Crater 1.00 .30
BB6 Kirby Plunkit 2.00 .60
BB7 David Clone 1.00 .30
BB8 Ken Spiffy Jr. 4.00 1.20
BB9 Ruben Siesta 1.00 .30
BB10 Greg Maddogs 2.50 .75
BB11 Mark McBash 1.50 .45
BB12 Rafael Palmist 1.00 .30
BB13 Roberto Alamode 1.50 .45
BB14 Greenback Jack 1.00 .30
BB15 Raging Tartabull 1.00 .30
BB16 Jimmy Kiwi 1.00 .30
BB17 Roger Clemency 2.50 .75
BB18 Rambo Canseco 1.50 .45
BB19 Tom Grapevine 1.25 .35
BB20 John Smileyface 1.00 .30
FOG1 Strike 1 .25 .07
(Top left of puzzle)
FOG2 Strike 2 .25 .07
(Top middle of puzzle)
FOG3 Strike 3 .25 .07
(Top right of puzzle)
FOG4 Strike 4 .25 .07
(Middle left of puzzle)
FOG5 Strike 5 .25 .07
(Middle of puzzle)
FOG6 Strike 6 .25 .07
(Middle right of puzzle)
FOG7 Strike 7 .25 .07
(Bottom left of puzzle)
FOG8 Strike 8 .25 .07
(Bottom middle of puzzle)
FOG9 Strike 9 .25 .07
(Bottom right of puzzle)

1976 Carousel Discs

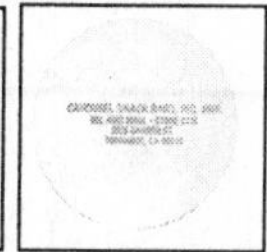

These discs are similar to the 1976 Crane Disc issue. They are differentiated by having a Carousel back and are valued at a multiple of the Crane Discs.

NM Ex
COMPLETE SET (70) 60.00 24.00
1 Hank Aaron 8.00 3.20
2 Johnny Bench 5.00 2.00
3 Vida Blue .75 .30
4 Larry Bowa .75 .30
5 Lou Brock 5.00 2.00
6 Jeff Burroughs .25 .10
7 John Candelaria .25 .10
8 Jose Cardenal .25 .10
9 Rod Carew 5.00 2.00
10 Steve Carlton 5.00 2.00
11 Dave Cash .25 .10
12 Cesar Cedeno .75 .30
13 Ron Cey .75 .30
14 Carlton Fisk 6.00 2.40
15 Tito Fuentes .25 .10
16 Steve Garvey 3.00 1.20
17 Ken Griffey .75 .30
18 Don Gullett .25 .10
19 Willie Horton .25 .10
20 Al Hrabosky .25 .10
21 Catfish Hunter 5.00 2.00
22A Reggie Jackson 15.00 6.00
Oakland Athletics
22B Reggie Jackson 5.00 2.00
Baltimore Orioles
23 Randy Jones .25 .10
24 Jim Kaat 1.50 .60
25 Don Kessinger .25 .10
26 Dave Kingman 1.50 .60
27 Jerry Koosman .75 .30
28 Mickey Lolich .75 .30
29 Greg Luzinski 1.50 .60
30 Fred Lynn 1.50 .60
31 Bill Madlock .75 .30
32A Carlos May 3.00 1.20
Chicago White Sox
32B Carlos May .25 .10
New York Yankees
33 John Mayberry .25 .10
34 Bake McBride .25 .10
35 Doc Medich .25 .10
36A Andy Messersmith 3.00 1.20
Los Angeles Dodgers
36B Andy Messersmith .25 .10
Atlanta Braves
37 Rick Monday .25 .10
38 John Montefusco .25 .10
39 Jerry Morales .25 .10
40 Joe Morgan 5.00 2.00
41 Thurman Munson 3.00 1.20
42 Bobby Murcer 1.50 .60
43 Al Oliver 1.50 .60
44 Jim Palmer 5.00 2.00
45 Dave Parker 2.00 .80
46 Tony Perez 3.00 1.20
47 Jerry Reuss .25 .10
48 Brooks Robinson 5.00 2.00
49 Frank Robinson 5.00 2.00
50 Steve Rogers .25 .10
51 Pete Rose 10.00 4.00
52 Nolan Ryan 12.00 4.80
53 Manny Sanguillen .25 .10
54 Mike Schmidt 8.00 3.20
55 Tom Seaver 6.00 2.40
56 Ted Simmons 1.50 .60
57 Reggie Smith .75 .30
58 Willie Stargell 5.00 2.00
59 Rusty Staub 1.50 .60
60 Rennie Stennett .25 .10
61 Don Sutton 5.00 2.00
62A Andre Thornton 3.00 1.20
Chicago Cubs
62B Andre Thornton .25 .10
Montreal Expos
63 Luis Tiant 1.50 .60
64 Joe Torre 2.00 .80
65 Mike Tyson .25 .10
66 Bob Watson .75 .30
67 Wilbur Wood .25 .10
68 Jimmy Wynn .25 .10
69 Carl Yastrzemski 5.00 2.00
70 Richie Zisk .25 .10

1990 CBS/Fox Video

This one card set which measures 3" by 5" features information about three movies which CBS/Fox had released in video form. There is some basic information about each movie along with a photo of the featured star. The

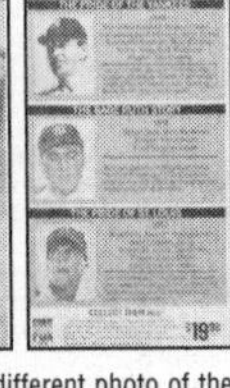

other side features a different photo of the star in an old style baseball card format

Nm-Mt Ex-Mt
1 Pride of the Yankees .... 3.00 .90
Gary Cooper
Babe Ruth Story
William Bendix
Pride of St Louis
Dan Dailey

1989 Cereal Superstars

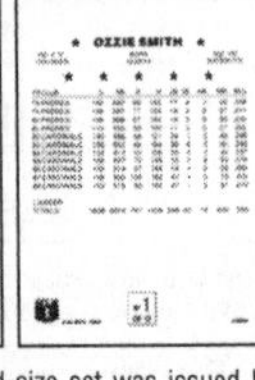

This 12-card, standard-size set was issued by MSA (Michael Schechter Associates) and celebrates some of the baseball's best players as of 1989. The sets have an attractive design of stars in each of the front corners with the word Superstars on the top of the card and players name, team, and position underneath the full color photo of the player. Like most of the MSA sets there are no team logos used. The vertically oriented backs show career statistics. Reportedly two cards were included in each specially marked Ralston Purina cereal box.

Nm-Mt Ex-Mt
COMPLETE SET (12) 12.00 4.80
1 Ozzie Smith 3.00 1.20
2 Andre Dawson .... 1.50 .60
3 Darryl Strawberry .... .50 .20
4 Mike Schmidt .... 1.50 .60
5 Orel Hershiser .... .25 .10
6 Tim Raines .... .50 .20
7 Roger Clemens 4.00 1.60
8 Kirby Puckett .... 2.00 .80
9 George Brett 3.00 1.20
10 Alan Trammell .... 1.50 .60
11 Don Mattingly 4.00 1.60
12 Jose Canseco .... 1.50 .60

1964 Challenge The Yankees

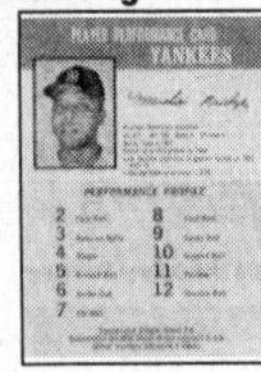

These cards were distributed as part of a baseball game produced in 1964. The cards each measure 4" by 5 3/8" and have square corners. The card fronts show a small black and white inset photo of the player, his name, position, vital statistics and the game outcomes associated with that particular player's card. The colors used on the front of the card are a blue border at the top and a yellow background for the game outcomes at the bottom. The game was played by rolling two dice. The outcomes (two through twelve) on the player's card related to the sum of the two dice. The game was noted for slightly inflated offensive production compared to real life. The cards are blank backed. Since the cards are unnumbered, they are listed below in alphabetical order within group. The first 25 cards are Yankees and the next 25 are All-Stars. Sets were put out in two different years, WG9 1964 and WG10 1965, which are difficult to distinguish. An empty box of either set, with the game pieces intact, is valued at approximately $75.

NM Ex
COMPLETE SET (50) 600.00 240.00
1 Yogi Berra 30.00 12.00
2 Johnny Blanchard 5.00 2.00
3 Jim Bouton 8.00 3.20
4 Clete Boyer 6.00 2.40
5 Marshall Bridges 5.00 2.00
6 Harry Bright 5.00 2.00
7 Al Downing 5.00 2.00
8 Whitey Ford 25.00 10.00
9 Jake Gibbs 5.00 2.00
10 Pedro Gonzalez 5.00 2.00
11 Steve Hamilton 5.00 2.00
12 Elston Howard 10.00 4.00
13 Tony Kubek 10.00 4.00
14 Phil Linz 5.00 2.00
15 Hector Lopez 5.00 2.00
16 Mickey Mantle 150.00 60.00
17 Roger Maris 50.00 20.00
18 Tom Metcalf 5.00 2.00
19 Joe Pepitone 6.00 2.40
20 Hal Reniff 5.00 2.00
21 Bobby Richardson 10.00 4.00
22 Bill Stafford 5.00 2.00
23 Ralph Terry 6.00 2.40
24 Tom Tresh 6.00 2.40
25 Stan Williams 5.00 2.00
26 Hank Aaron 60.00 24.00
27 Tom Cheney 5.00 2.00
28 Del Crandall 5.00 2.00
29 Tito Francona 5.00 2.00
30 Dick Groat 6.00 2.40
31 Al Kaline 25.00 10.00
32 Art Mahaffey 5.00 2.00
33 Frank Malzone 5.00 2.00
34 Juan Marichal 15.00 6.00
35 Eddie Mathews 15.00 6.00
36 Bill Mazeroski 10.00 4.00
37 Ken McBride 5.00 2.00
38 Willie McCovey 15.00 6.00
39 Jim O'Toole 5.00 2.00
40 Milt Pappas 6.00 2.40
41 Ron Perranoski 5.00 2.00
42 Johnny Podres 6.00 2.40
43 Dick Radatz 5.00 2.00
44 Rich Rollins 5.00 2.00
45 Ron Santo 10.00 4.00
46 Moose Skowron 6.00 2.40
47 Duke Snider 25.00 10.00
48 Pete Ward 5.00 2.00
49 Carl Warwick 5.00 2.00
50 Carl Yastrzemski 25.00 10.00

1965 Challenge The Yankees

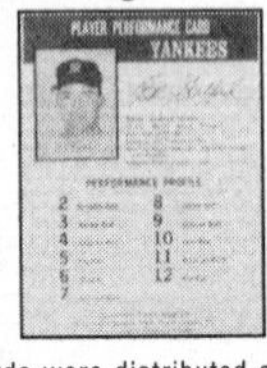

These cards were distributed as part of a baseball game produced in 1965. The cards each measure 4" by 5 3/8" and have square corners. The card fronts show a small black and white inset photo of the player, his name, position, vital statistics, and the game outcomes associated with that particular player's card. The colors used on the front of the card are a blue border at the top and a yellow background for the game outcomes at the bottom. The game was played by rolling two dice. The outcomes (two through twelve) on the player's card related to the sum of the two dice. The game was noted for slightly inflated offensive production compared to real life. The cards are blank backed. Since the cards are unnumbered, they are listed below in alphabetical order within group. The first 23 cards are Yankees and the next 25 are All-Stars. There were also 18 blank cards included in the set for extra players of your choice. These "Challenge The Yankees" sets were put out in two different years, WG9 1964 and WG10 1965, which are difficult to distinguish.

NM Ex
COMPLETE SET (48) 500.00 200.00
1 Johnny Blanchard 5.00 2.00
2 Jim Bouton 8.00 3.20
3 Clete Boyer 6.00 2.40
4 Leon Carmel 5.00 2.00
5 Al Downing 5.00 2.00
6 Whitey Ford 25.00 10.00
7 Jake Gibbs 5.00 2.00
8 Pedro Gonzalez 5.00 2.00
9 Steve Hamilton 5.00 2.00
10 Elston Howard 10.00 4.00
11 Tony Kubek 10.00 4.00
12 Phil Linz 5.00 2.00
13 Mickey Mantle 150.00 60.00
14 Roger Maris 50.00 20.00
15 Tom Metcalf 5.00 2.00
16 Pete Mikkelsen 5.00 2.00
17 Joe Pepitone 6.00 2.40
18 Pedro Ramos 5.00 2.00
19 Hal Reniff 5.00 2.00
20 Bobby Richardson 10.00 4.00
21 Bill Stafford 5.00 2.00
22 Mel Stottlemyre 6.00 2.40
23 Tom Tresh 6.00 2.40
24 Henry Aaron 60.00 24.00
25 Joe Christopher 5.00 2.00
26 Vic Davalillo 5.00 2.00
27 Bill Freehan 6.00 2.40
28 Jim Gentile 5.00 2.00
29 Dick Groat 6.00 2.40
30 Al Kaline 25.00 10.00
31 Don Lock 5.00 2.00
32 Art Mahaffey 5.00 2.00
33 Frank Malzone 5.00 2.00
34 Juan Marichal 15.00 6.00
35 Eddie Mathews 15.00 6.00
36 Bill Mazeroski 10.00 4.00
37 Ken McBride 5.00 2.00
38 Tim McCarver 10.00 4.00
39 Willie McCovey 15.00 6.00
40 Jim O'Toole 5.00 2.00
41 Milt Pappas 6.00 2.40
42 Ron Perranoski 5.00 2.00
43 Johnny Podres 6.00 2.40
44 Dick Radatz 5.00 2.00
45 Rich Rollins 5.00 2.00
46 Ron Santo 10.00 4.00
47 Pete Ward 5.00 2.00
48 Carl Yastrzemski 25.00 10.00

1982 Charboneau Super Joe's

This two-card set features a black-and-white portrait of Cleveland Indians player, Joe Charboneau, on two different size cards. The smaller card is standard size, and the larger one measures approximately 3 1/2" by 5 1/2". The cards are checklisted below with the smaller one listed first.

Nm-Mt Ex-Mt
COMPLETE SET (2) 5.00 2.00
1 Joe Charboneau .... 2.00 .80
(Standard size card)
2 Joe Charboneau 3.00 1.20
(3 1/2" by 5 1/2" size card)

1988 Chef Boyardee

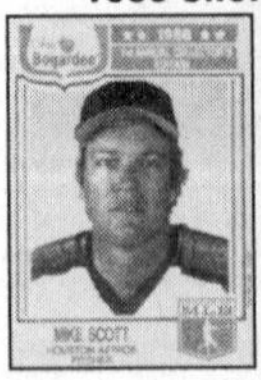

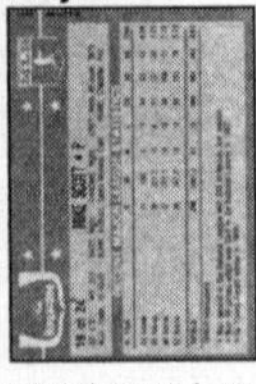

This 24-card set was distributed as a perforated sheet of four rows and six columns of cards in return for ten proofs of purchase of Chef Boyardeee products and 1.50 for postage and handling. The card photos on the fronts are in full color with a light blue border but are not shown with team logos. The card backs are numbered and printed in red and blue on gray card stock. Individual cards measure approximately 2 1/2" by 3 1/2" and show the Chef Boyardee logo in the upper right corner of the obverse. Card backs feature year-by-year season statistics since 1984. There is no additional premium for having the sheet intact as opposed to having individual cards neatly cut.

Nm-Mt Ex-Mt
COMPLETE SET (24) 10.00 4.00
1 Mark McGwire 2.50 1.00
2 Eric Davis .... .50 .20
3 Jack Morris .... .50 .20
4 George Bell .... .25 .10
5 Ozzie Smith .... 1.50 .60
6 Tony Gwynn .... 1.50 .60
7 Cal Ripken 3.00 1.20
8 Todd Worrell .... .50 .20
9 Larry Parrish .... .25 .10
10 Gary Carter .... .75 .30
11 Ryne Sandberg .... 1.00 .40
12 Keith Hernandez .... .50 .20
13 Kirby Puckett .... 1.00 .40
14 Mike Schmidt .... 1.00 .40
15 Frank Viola .... .25 .10
16 Don Mattingly .... 1.50 .60
17 Dale Murphy .... 1.00 .40
18A Andre Dawson ERR .... 1.00 .40
Back lists his 1987 team as the Expos
18B Andre Dawson COR 10.00 4.00
Back lists his 1987 team as the Cubs
19 Mike Scott .... .25 .10
20 Rickey Henderson .... 1.25 .50
21 Jim Rice .... .50 .20
22 Wade Boggs .... 1.25 .50
23 Roger Clemens .... 1.50 .60
24 Fernando Valenzuela .... .50 .20

1976 Chevy Prints

These four prints were drawn by Robert Thon, a noted historical illustrator and were commissioned by Chevrolet in honor of the 100th anniversary of the National League (and what is considered organized ball). The fronts feature four highligts from various times in baseball history and the backs have a description of these events.

NM Ex
COMPLETE SET (4) 10.00 4.00
1 The First Game .... 1.00 .40
2 Pepper Martin .... 2.00 .80
Bill Werber
The Gashouse Gang
3 Babe Ruth 5.00 2.00
The Mighty Babe
4 Hank Aaron 5.00 2.00
The Record Breaker

1910 Chicago E90-3

The E90-3 American Caramels "All the Star Players" set contains 20 unnumbered cards (each measuring 1 1/2" by 2 3/4") featuring the Chicago White Sox and Chicago Cubs. The eleven Cubs are listed first in the checklist below in alphabetical order (1-11), followed by the White Sox (12-20). The backs are slightly different from E90-1 cards and the fronts differ in the use of the team nicknames.

Ex-Mt VG
COMPLETE SET (20) 8000.00 4000.00
1 Jimmy Archer 250.00 125.00
2 Mordecai Brown 800.00 400.00
3 Frank Chance 1000.00 500.00
4 King Cole 250.00 125.00
5 Johnny Evers 800.00 400.00
6 Solly Hoffman 250.00 125.00
7 Orval Overall 250.00 125.00
8 Frank Schulte 300.00 150.00
9 Jimmy Scheckard 250.00 125.00
10 Harry Steinfeldt 300.00 150.00
11 Joe Tinker 800.00 400.00
12 Lena Blackburne 250.00 125.00
13 Patsy Dougherty 250.00 125.00
14 Chick Gandil 800.00 400.00
15 Ed Hahn 250.00 125.00
16 Fred Payne 250.00 125.00
17 Billy Purtell 250.00 125.00
18 Frank (Nig) Smith 250.00 125.00
19 Ed Walsh 800.00 400.00
20 Rollie Zeider 250.00 125.00

1976 Chicago Greats

This standard-size set features black-and-white action player photos with a red baseball and bat border design. A small, square close-up photo is superimposed on one of the upper corners of the picture. "Chicago's Greats" is printed in red at the bottom. The horizontal backs are white and carry the player's name, biographical information, statistics and career highlights. The cards are unnumbered and checklisted below in alphabetical order. The set was originally available for $2.50 from the producers.

NM Ex
COMPLETE SET (24) 12.00 4.80
1 Luke Appling .... .75 .30
2 Ernie Banks .... 1.50 .60
3 Zeke Bonura .... .25 .10
4 Phil Cavarretta .... .50 .20
5 Jimmie Dykes .... .50 .20
6 Nellie Fox .... 1.00 .40
7 Larry French .... .25 .10
8 Charlie Grimm .... .50 .20
9 Gabby Hartnett .... 1.00 .40
10 Billy Herman .... .75 .30
11 Mike Kreevich .... .25 .10
12 Sherm Lollar .... .25 .10
13 Al Lopez .... .75 .30
14 Ted Lyons .... .50 .20
Red Faber
15 Minnie Minoso .... .75 .30
16 Wally Moses .... .25 .10
17 Bill Nicholson .... .25 .10
18 Claude Passeau .... .25 .10
19 Billy Pierce .... .50 .20
20 Ron Santo .... .75 .30
21 Hank Sauer .... .25 .10
22 Riggs Stephenson .... .50 .20
23 Bill Veeck OWN .... .75 .30
24 Philip K. Wrigley OWN .... .50 .20

1977 Chilly Willie Discs

These are the most common of the 1977 MSA Discs. They are valued at the base amount for any 1977 Discs. They were distributed at Chilly Willie outlets.

NM Ex
COMPLETE SET (70) 30.00 12.00
1 Sal Bando .... .25 .10
2 Buddy Bell .... .50 .20
3 Johnny Bench 4.00 1.60
4 Lou Brock 3.00 1.20
5 Larry Bowa .... .50 .20
6 Steve Braun .... .25 .10
7 George Brett 6.00 2.40
8 Jeff Burroughs .... .25 .10
9 Campy Campaneris .... .50 .20
10 John Candelaria .... .25 .10
11 Jose Cardenal .... .25 .10
12 Rod Carew 3.00 1.20
13 Steve Carlton 3.00 1.20
14 Dave Cash .... .25 .10
15 Cesar Cedeno .... .25 .10
16 Ron Cey .... .50 .20
17 Dave Concepcion .... .75 .30
18 Dennis Eckersley 3.00 1.20
19 Mark Fidrych 3.00 1.20
20 Rollie Fingers .... 2.00 .80
21 Carlton Fisk 3.00 1.20
22 George Foster .... .75 .30
23 Wayne Garland .... .25 .10
24 Ralph Garr .... .50 .20
25 Steve Garvey .... 1.50 .60
26 Cesar Geronimo .... .25 .10
27 Bobby Grich .... .50 .20
28 Ken Griffey .... .75 .30
29 Don Gullett .... .25 .10
30 Mike Hargrove .... .50 .20
31 Al Hrabosky .... .25 .10
32 Catfish Hunter .... 2.00 .80
33 Reggie Jackson 4.00 1.60
34 Randy Jones .... .25 .10
35 Dave Kingman .... 1.00 .40
36 Jerry Koosman .... .50 .20
37 Dave LaRoche .... .25 .10
38 Greg Luzinski .... .75 .30
39 Fred Lynn .... .50 .20
40 Bill Madlock .... .50 .20
41 Rick Manning .... .25 .10
42 Jon Matlack .... .25 .10
43 John Mayberry .... .25 .10
44 Hal McRae .... .50 .20
45 Andy Messersmith .... .25 .10
46 Rick Monday .... .25 .10
47 John Montefusco .... .25 .10
48 Joe Morgan .... 2.00 .80
49 Thurman Munson .... 1.50 .60
50 Bobby Murcer .... .75 .30
51 Bill North .... .25 .10
52 Jim Palmer .... 2.00 .80
53 Tony Perez .... 2.00 .80
54 Jerry Reuss .... .25 .10
55 Brooks Robinson 3.00 1.20
56 Pete Rose 4.00 1.60
57 Joe Rudi .... .25 .10
58 Nolan Ryan 8.00 3.20
59 Manny Sanguillen .... .25 .10
60 Mike Schmidt 4.00 1.60
61 Tom Seaver 4.00 1.60
62 Bill Singer .... .25 .10
63 Willie Stargell .... 2.00 .80
64 Rusty Staub .... .75 .30
65 Luis Tiant .... .50 .20
66 Bob Watson .... .50 .20
67 Butch Wynegar .... .25 .10
68 Carl Yastrzemski 3.00 1.20
69 Robin Yount 3.00 1.20
70 Richie Zisk .... .25 .10

1994 Church's Hometown Stars

A pack containing four standard-size cards from the 28-card Hometown Stars set produced by Pinnacle was offered to consumers who bought a nine-piece family meal at Church's Chicken during April and May. Packs were also sold separately for 69 cents each. Each pack contained three regular cards and one gold foil-stamped card from the set. The gold foil cards are valued at two times the regular cards. A portion of the proceeds from card sales went to Habitat for Humanity, a national volunteer organization that helps families build their own homes. The cards are numbered on the back as "X of 28."

Nm-Mt Ex-Mt
COMPLETE SET (28) 12.00 3.60
*GOLD CARDS: 2X BASIC CARDS ....
1 Brian McRae .... .25 .07
2 Dwight Gooden .... .50 .15
3 Ruben Sierra .... .50 .15
4 Greg Maddux .... 2.50 .75
5 Kirby Puckett .... 1.25 .35
6 Jeff Bagwell .... 1.50 .45
7 Cal Ripken 4.00 1.20
8 Lenny Dykstra .... .25 .07
9 Tim Salmon .... .75 .23
10 Matt Williams .... .50 .15
11 Roberto Alomar .... 1.00 .30
12 Barry Larkin .... 1.00 .30
13 Roger Clemens .... 2.50 .75
14 Mike Piazza .... 3.00 .90
15 Travis Fryman .... .50 .15
16 Ryne Sandberg .... 2.00 .60
17 Robin Ventura .... .75 .23
18 Gary Sheffield .... 1.00 .30
19 Carlos Baerga .... .25 .07
20 Jay Bell .... .25 .07
21 Edgar Martinez .... .75 .23
22 Phil Plantier .... .25 .07
23 Danny Tartabull .... .25 .07
24 Marquis Grissom .... .25 .07
25 Robin Yount .... 1.25 .35
26 Ozzie Smith .... 2.00 .60
27 Ivan Rodriguez .... 1.50 .45
28 Dante Bichette .... .50 .15

1994 Church's Show Stoppers

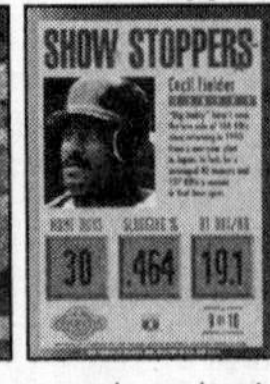

One of ten Show Stoppers cards was inserted in every fourth pack of 1994 Church's Chicken Stars of the Diamond four-card packs. The standard-size inserts were produced by Pinnacle using the "Dufex" printing process and highlight the major leagues' top home run hitters. The colorful metallic fronts feature color player action shots that appear to project from within home plate icons. Team logos are airbrushed away. The player's name appears at the lower right. The light blue back carries a color player head shot on the right, with the player's name, team, and career highlights shown alongside. Statistics for home runs, slugging percentage, and at bat/home run ratio appear near the bottom. The cards are numbered on the back as "X of 10."

Nm-Mt Ex-Mt
COMPLETE SET (10) 20.00 6.00
1 Juan Gonzalez .... 2.50 .75
2 Barry Bonds 5.00 1.50
3 Ken Griffey Jr. 6.00 1.80
4 David Justice .... 2.50 .75
5 Frank Thomas .... 3.00 .90
6 Fred McGriff .... 1.50 .45
7 Albert Belle .... 1.00 .30
8 Joe Carter .... 1.00 .30
9 Cecil Fielder .... 1.00 .30
10 Mickey Tettleton .... .50 .15

1996 Circa

The 1996 Circa set (produced by Fleer/SkyBox) was issued in one series totalling 200 cards. The eight-card packs retailed for $1.99 each. The cards feature color action player photos on one of 28 different background designs and colors indicating the player's major league team. The checklist is grouped alphabetically by team with American League teams preceeding National League teams. The backs carry player information and statistics. Notable Rookie Cards include Darin Erstad and Chris Singleton.

	Nm-Mt	Ex-Mt
COMPLETE SET (200)	25.00	7.50
1 Roberto Alomar	.50	.15
2 Brady Anderson	.20	.06
3 Rocky Coppinger RC	.20	.06
4 Eddie Murray	.50	.15
5 Mike Mussina	.50	.15
6 Randy Myers	.20	.06
7 Rafael Palmeiro	.30	.09
8 Cal Ripken	1.50	.45
9 Jose Canseco	.50	.15
10 Roger Clemens	1.00	.30
11 Mike Greenwell	.20	.06
12 Tim Naehring	.20	.06
13 John Valentin	.20	.06
14 Mo Vaughn	.20	.06
15 Tim Wakefield	.20	.06
16 Jim Abbott	.30	.09
17 Garret Anderson	.20	.06
18 Jim Edmonds	.20	.06
19 Darin Erstad RC	2.00	.60
20 Chuck Finley	.20	.06
21 Troy Percival	.20	.06
22 Tim Salmon	.30	.09
23 J.T. Snow	.20	.06
24 Wilson Alvarez	.20	.06
25 Harold Baines	.20	.06
26 Ray Durham	.20	.06
27 Alex Fernandez	.20	.06
28 Tony Phillips	.20	.06
29 Frank Thomas	.50	.15
30 Robin Ventura	.20	.06
31 Sandy Alomar Jr.	.20	.06
32 Albert Belle	.20	.06
33 Kenny Lofton	.20	.06
34 Dennis Martinez	.20	.06
35 Jose Mesa	.20	.06
36 Charles Nagy	.20	.06
37 Manny Ramirez	.20	.06
38 Jim Thome	.50	.15
39 Travis Fryman	.20	.06
40 Bob Higginson	.20	.06
41 Melvin Nieves	.20	.06
42 Alan Trammell	.30	.09
43 Kevin Appier	.20	.06
44 Johnny Damon	.20	.06
45 Keith Lockhart	.20	.06
46 Jeff Montgomery	.20	.06
47 Joe Randa	.20	.06
48 Bip Roberts	.20	.06
49 Ricky Bones	.20	.06
50 Jeff Cirillo	.20	.06
51 Marc Newfield	.20	.06
52 Dave Nilsson	.20	.06
53 Kevin Seitzer	.20	.06
54 Ron Coomer	.20	.06
55 Marty Cordova	.20	.06
56 Roberto Kelly	.20	.06
57 Chuck Knoblauch	.20	.06
58 Paul Molitor	.30	.09
59 Kirby Puckett	.50	.15
60 Scott Stahoviak	.20	.06
61 Wade Boggs	.30	.09
62 David Cone	.20	.06
63 Cecil Fielder	.20	.06
64 Dwight Gooden	.30	.09
65 Derek Jeter	1.25	.35
66 Tino Martinez	.30	.09
67 Paul O'Neill	.30	.09
68 Andy Pettitte	.30	.09
69 Ruben Rivera	.20	.06
70 Bernie Williams	.30	.09
71 Geronimo Berroa	.20	.06
72 Jason Giambi	.50	.15
73 Mark McGwire	1.25	.35
74 Terry Steinbach	.20	.06
75 Todd Van Poppel	.20	.06
76 Jay Buhner	.20	.06
77 Norm Charlton	.20	.06
78 Ken Griffey Jr.	.75	.23
79 Randy Johnson	.50	.15
80 Edgar Martinez	.30	.09
81 Alex Rodriguez	1.00	.30
82 Paul Sorrento	.20	.06
83 Dan Wilson	.20	.06
84 Will Clark	.50	.15
85 Kevin Elster	.20	.06
86 Juan Gonzalez	.50	.15
87 Rusty Greer	.20	.06
88 Ken Hill	.20	.06
89 Mark McLemore	.20	.06
90 Dean Palmer	.20	.06
91 Roger Pavlik	.20	.06
92 Ivan Rodriguez	.50	.15
93 Joe Carter	.20	.06
94 Carlos Delgado	.20	.06
95 Juan Guzman	.20	.06
96 John Olerud	.20	.06
97 Ed Sprague	.20	.06
98 Jermaine Dye	.20	.06
99 Tom Glavine	.30	.09
100 Marquis Grissom	.20	.06
101 Andruw Jones	.75	.23
102 Chipper Jones	.50	.15
103 David Justice	.20	.06
104 Ryan Klesko	.20	.06
105 Greg Maddux	.75	.23
106 Fred McGriff	.30	.09
107 John Smoltz	.30	.09
108 Brant Brown	.20	.06
109 Mark Grace	.30	.09
110 Brian McRae	.20	.06
111 Ryne Sandberg	.75	.23
112 Sammy Sosa	.75	.23
113 Steve Trachsel	.20	.06
114 Bret Boone	.20	.06
115 Eric Davis	.20	.06
116 Steve Gibralter	.20	.06
117 Barry Larkin	.50	.15
118 Reggie Sanders	.20	.06
119 John Smiley	.20	.06
120 Dante Bichette	.20	.06
121 Ellis Burks	.20	.06
122 Vinny Castilla	.20	.06
123 Andres Galarraga	.20	.06
124 Larry Walker	.30	.09
125 Eric Young	.20	.06
126 Kevin Brown	.20	.06
127 Greg Colbrunn	.20	.06
128 Jeff Conine	.20	.06
129 Charles Johnson	.20	.06
130 Al Leiter	.20	.06
131 Gary Sheffield	.20	.06
132 Devon White	.20	.06
133 Jeff Bagwell	.30	.09
134 Derek Bell	.20	.06
135 Craig Biggio	.30	.09
136 Doug Drabek	.20	.06
137 Brian L.Hunter	.20	.06
138 Darryl Kile	.20	.06
139 Shane Reynolds	.20	.06
140 Brett Butler	.20	.06
141 Eric Karros	.20	.06
142 Ramon Martinez	.20	.06
143 Raul Mondesi	.20	.06
144 Hideo Nomo	.50	.15
145 Chan Ho Park	.20	.06
146 Mike Piazza	.75	.23
147 Moises Alou	.20	.06
148 Yamil Benitez	.20	.06
149 Mark Grudzielanek	.20	.06
150 Pedro Martinez	.50	.15
151 Henry Rodriguez	.20	.06
152 David Segui	.20	.06
153 Rondell White	.20	.06
154 Carlos Baerga	.20	.06
155 John Franco	.20	.06
156 Bernard Gilkey	.20	.06
157 Todd Hundley	.20	.06
158 Jason Isringhausen	.20	.06
159 Lance Johnson	.20	.06
160 Alex Ochoa	.20	.06
161 Rey Ordonez	.20	.06
162 Paul Wilson	.20	.06
163 Ron Blazier	.20	.06
164 Ricky Bottalico	.20	.06
165 Jim Eisenreich	.20	.06
166 Pete Incaviglia	.20	.06
167 Mickey Morandini	.20	.06
168 Ricky Otero	.20	.06
169 Curt Schilling	.30	.09
170 Jay Bell	.20	.06
171 Charlie Hayes	.20	.06
172 Jason Kendall	.20	.06
173 Jeff King	.20	.06
174 Al Martin	.20	.06
175 Alan Benes	.20	.06
176 Royce Clayton	.20	.06
177 Brian Jordan	.20	.06
178 Ray Lankford	.20	.06
179 John Mabry	.20	.06
180 Willie McGee	.20	.06
181 Ozzie Smith	.75	.23
182 Todd Stottlemyre	.20	.06
183 Andy Ashby	.20	.06
184 Ken Caminiti	.20	.06
185 Steve Finley	.20	.06
186 Tony Gwynn	.60	.18
187 Rickey Henderson	.50	.15
188 Wally Joyner	.20	.06
189 Fernando Valenzuela	.20	.06
190 Greg Vaughn	.20	.06
191 Rod Beck	.20	.06
192 Barry Bonds	1.25	.35
193 Shawon Dunston	.20	.06
194 Chris Singleton RC	.30	.09
195 Robby Thompson	.20	.06
196 Matt Williams	.20	.06
197 Barry Bonds CL	.60	.18
198 Ken Griffey Jr. CL	.50	.15
199 Cal Ripken CL	.75	.23
200 Frank Thomas CL	.30	.09

1996 Circa Rave

Randomly inserted in packs at a rate of one in 60, this 200-card set is parallel and similar in design to the regular set except for sparkling foil lettering on front. Each card is individually numbered on back to 150. This set is notable for the fact that it was the one of the earliest parallel sets to feature serial-numbering for each card.

Nm-Mt Ex-Mt

*STARS: 25X TO 60X BASIC CARDS ..
*ROOKIES: 10X TO 25X BASIC CARDS

1996 Circa Access

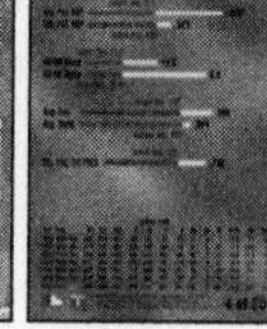

Randomly inserted in packs at a rate of one in 12, this 30-card limited edition set features a fold-out, three-panel card showcasing some of the hottest superstars of the game. The panels display color player photos, player statistics and personal information on team-colored backgrounds. A promotional card featuring Matt Williams was issued to dealers. The card is similar to the basic Access Williams except for the words "Promotional Sample" written across the card front.

	Nm-Mt	Ex-Mt
COMPLETE SET (30)	120.00	36.00
1 Cal Ripken	15.00	4.50
2 Mo Vaughn	2.00	.60
3 Tim Salmon	3.00	.90
4 Frank Thomas	5.00	1.50
5 Albert Belle	2.00	.60
6 Kenny Lofton	2.00	.60
7 Manny Ramirez	2.00	.60
8 Paul Molitor	3.00	.90
9 Kirby Puckett	5.00	1.50
10 Paul O'Neill	3.00	.90
11 Mark McGwire	12.00	3.60
12 Ken Griffey Jr.	8.00	2.40
13 Randy Johnson	5.00	1.50
14 Greg Maddux	8.00	2.40
15 John Smoltz	3.00	.90
16 Sammy Sosa	8.00	2.40
17 Barry Larkin	5.00	1.50
18 Gary Sheffield	2.00	.60
19 Jeff Bagwell	3.00	.90
20 Hideo Nomo	5.00	1.50
21 Mike Piazza	8.00	2.40
22 Moises Alou	2.00	.60
23 Henry Rodriguez	2.00	.60
24 Rey Ordonez	2.00	.60
25 Jay Bell	2.00	.60
26 Ozzie Smith	8.00	2.40
27 Tony Gwynn	6.00	1.80
28 Rickey Henderson	5.00	1.50
29 Barry Bonds	12.00	3.60
30 Matt Williams	2.00	.60
P30 Matt Williams Promo	1.00	.30

1996 Circa Boss

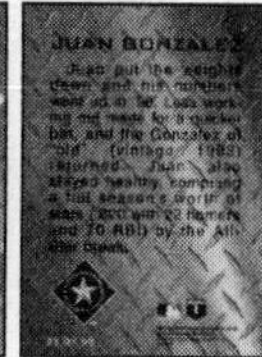

Randomly inserted in packs at a rate of one in six, this 50-card set features a sculpted embossed player image on a team-colored background containing the team logo. The backs carry a information about the player's career. A promotional card featuring Cal Ripken was issued to dealers. The card is similar to the basic Boss Ripken except for the words "Promotional Sample" written across the card front.

	Nm-Mt	Ex-Mt
COMPLETE SET (50)	100.00	30.00
1 Roberto Alomar	2.50	.75
2 Cal Ripken	8.00	2.40
3 Jose Canseco	2.50	.75
4 Mo Vaughn	1.00	.30
5 Tim Salmon	1.50	.45
6 Frank Thomas	2.50	.75
7 Robin Ventura	1.00	.30
8 Albert Belle	1.00	.30
9 Kenny Lofton	1.00	.30
10 Manny Ramirez	1.00	.30
11 Dave Nilsson	1.00	.30
12 Chuck Knoblauch	1.00	.30
13 Paul Molitor	1.50	.45
14 Kirby Puckett	2.50	.75
15 Wade Boggs	1.50	.45
16 Dwight Gooden	1.50	.45
17 Paul O'Neill	1.50	.45
18 Mark McGwire	6.00	1.80
19 Jay Buhner	1.00	.30
20 Ken Griffey Jr.	4.00	1.20
21 Randy Johnson	2.50	.75
22 Will Clark	2.50	.75
23 Juan Gonzalez	2.50	.75
24 Joe Carter	1.00	.30
25 Tom Glavine	1.50	.45
26 Ryan Klesko	1.00	.30
27 Greg Maddux	4.00	1.20
28 John Smoltz	1.50	.45
29 Ryne Sandberg	4.00	1.20
30 Sammy Sosa	4.00	1.20
31 Barry Larkin	2.50	.75
32 Reggie Sanders	1.00	.30
33 Dante Bichette	1.00	.30
34 Andres Galarraga	1.00	.30
35 Charles Johnson	1.00	.30
36 Gary Sheffield	1.00	.30
37 Jeff Bagwell	1.50	.45
38 Hideo Nomo	2.50	.75
39 Mike Piazza	4.00	1.20
40 Moises Alou	1.00	.30
41 Henry Rodriguez	1.00	.30
42 Rey Ordonez	1.00	.30
43 Ricky Otero	1.00	.30
44 Jay Bell	1.00	.30
45 Royce Clayton	1.00	.30
46 Ozzie Smith	4.00	1.20
47 Tony Gwynn	3.00	.90
48 Rickey Henderson	2.50	.75
49 Barry Bonds	6.00	1.80
50 Matt Williams	1.00	.30
P2 Cal Ripken Promo	3.00	.90

1997 Circa

The 1997 Circa set (produced by Fleer/SkyBox) was issued in one series totalling 400 cards and was distributed in eight-card foil packs with a suggested retail price of $1.49. The set contains 393 player cards and seven checklist cards. The fronts feature color player photos with new in-your-face graphics that lift the player off the card. The backs carry in-depth player statistics and "Did you know" information. An Alex Rodriguez promo card (P100) was distributed to dealers. Rookie Cards include Brian Giles.

	Nm-Mt	Ex-Mt
COMPLETE SET (400)	25.00	7.50
1 Kenny Lofton	.20	.06
2 Ray Durham	.20	.06
3 Mariano Rivera	.30	.09
4 Jon Lieber	.20	.06
5 Tim Salmon	.30	.09
6 Mark Grudzielanek	.20	.06
7 Neifi Perez	.20	.06
8 Cal Ripken	1.50	.45
9 John Olerud	.20	.06
10 Edgar Renteria	.20	.06
11 Jose Rosado	.20	.06
12 Mickey Morandini	.20	.06
13 Orlando Miller	.20	.06
14 Ben McDonald	.20	.06
15 Hideo Nomo	.50	.15
16 Fred McGriff	.30	.09
17 Sean Berry	.20	.06
18 Roger Pavlik	.20	.06
19 Aaron Sele	.20	.06
20 Joey Hamilton	.20	.06
21 Roger Clemens	1.00	.30
22 Jose Herrera	.20	.06
23 Ryne Sandberg	.75	.23
24 Ken Griffey Jr.	.75	.23
25 Barry Bonds	1.25	.35
26 Dan Naulty	.20	.06
27 Wade Boggs	.30	.09
28 Ray Lankford	.20	.06
29 Rico Brogna	.20	.06
30 Wally Joyner	.20	.06
31 F.P. Santangelo	.20	.06
32 Vinny Castilla	.20	.06
33 Eddie Murray	.50	.15
34 Kevin Elster	.20	.06
35 Mike Macfarlane	.20	.06
36 Jeff Kent	.20	.06
37 Orlando Merced	.20	.06
38 Jason Isringhausen	.20	.06
39 Chad Ogea	.20	.06
40 Greg Gagne	.20	.06
41 Curt Lyons	.20	.06
42 Mo Vaughn	.20	.06
43 Rusty Greer	.20	.06
44 Shane Reynolds	.20	.06
45 Frank Thomas	.50	.15
46 Chris Hoiles	.20	.06
47 Scott Sanders	.20	.06
48 Mark Lemke	.20	.06
49 Fernando Vina	.20	.06
50 Mark McGwire	1.25	.35
51 Bernie Williams	.30	.09
52 Bobby Higginson	.20	.06
53 Kevin Tapani	.20	.06
54 Rich Becker	.20	.06
55 Felix Heredia RC	.20	.06
56 Delino DeShields	.20	.06
57 Rick Wilkins	.20	.06
58 Edgardo Alfonzo	.20	.06
59 Brett Butler	.20	.06
60 Ed Sprague	.20	.06
61 Joe Randa	.20	.06
62 Ugueth Urbina	.20	.06
63 Todd Greene	.20	.06
64 Devon White	.20	.06
65 Bruce Ruffin	.20	.06
66 Mark Gardner	.20	.06
67 Omar Vizquel	.20	.06
68 Luis Gonzalez	.20	.06
69 Tom Glavine	.30	.09
70 Cal Eldred	.20	.06
71 Wm. VanLandingham	.20	.06
72 Jay Buhner	.20	.06
73 James Baldwin	.20	.06
74 Robin Jennings	.20	.06
75 Terry Steinbach	.20	.06
76 Billy Taylor	.20	.06
77 Armando Benitez	.20	.06
78 Joe Girardi	.20	.06
79 Jay Bell	.20	.06
80 Damon Buford	.20	.06
81 Deion Sanders	.30	.09
82 Bill Haselman	.20	.06
83 John Flaherty	.20	.06
84 Todd Stottlemyre	.20	.06
85 J.T. Snow	.20	.06
86 Felipe Lira	.20	.06
87 Steve Avery	.20	.06
88 Trey Beamon	.20	.06
89 Alex Gonzalez	.20	.06
90 Mark Clark	.20	.06
91 Shane Andrews	.20	.06
92 Randy Myers	.20	.06
93 Gary Gaetti	.20	.06
94 Jeff Blauser	.20	.06
95 Tony Batista	.20	.06
96 Todd Worrell	.20	.06
97 Jim Edmonds	.20	.06
98 Eric Young	.20	.06
99 Roberto Kelly	.20	.06
100 Alex Rodriguez	.75	.23
101 Julio Franco	.20	.06
102 Jeff Bagwell	.30	.09
103 Bobby Witt	.20	.06
104 Tino Martinez	.30	.09
105 Shannon Stewart	.20	.06
106 Brian Banks	.20	.06
107 Eddie Taubensee	.20	.06
108 Terry Mulholland	.20	.06
109 Lyle Mouton	.20	.06
110 Jeff Conine	.20	.06
111 Johnny Damon	.20	.06
112 Quilvio Veras	.20	.06
113 Wilton Guerrero	.20	.06
114 Dmitri Young	.20	.06
115 Garret Anderson	.20	.06
116 Bill Pulsipher	.20	.06
117 Jacob Brumfield	.20	.06
118 Mike Lansing	.20	.06
119 Jose Canseco	.50	.15
120 Mike Bordick	.20	.06
121 Kevin Stocker	.20	.06
122 Frankie Rodriguez	.20	.06
123 Mike Cameron	.20	.06
124 Tony Womack RC	.20	.06
125 Bret Boone	.20	.06
126 Moises Alou	.20	.06
127 Tim Naehring	.20	.06
128 Brant Brown	.20	.06
129 Todd Zeile	.20	.06
130 Dave Nilsson	.20	.06
131 Donne Wall	.20	.06
132 Jose Mesa	.20	.06
133 Mark McLemore	.20	.06
134 Mike Stanton	.20	.06
135 Dan Wilson	.20	.06
136 Jose Offerman	.20	.06
137 David Justice	.20	.06
138 Kirt Manwaring	.20	.06
139 Raul Casanova	.20	.06
140 Ron Coomer	.20	.06
141 Dave Hollins	.20	.06
142 Shawn Estes	.20	.06
143 Darren Daulton	.20	.06
144 Turk Wendell	.20	.06
145 Darrin Fletcher	.20	.06
146 Marquis Grissom	.20	.06
147 Andy Benes	.20	.06
148 Nomar Garciaparra	.75	.23
149 Andy Pettitte	.30	.09
150 Tony Gwynn	.60	.18
151 Robb Nen	.20	.06
152 Kevin Seitzer	.20	.06
153 Ariel Prieto	.20	.06
154 Scott Karl	.20	.06
155 Carlos Baerga	.20	.06
156 Wilson Alvarez	.20	.06
157 Thomas Howard	.20	.06
158 Kevin Appier	.20	.06
159 Russ Davis	.20	.06
160 Justin Thompson	.20	.06
161 Pete Schourek	.20	.06
162 John Burkett	.20	.06
163 Roberto Alomar	.50	.15
164 Darren Holmes	.20	.06
165 Travis Miller	.20	.06
166 Mark Langston	.20	.06
167 Juan Guzman	.20	.06
168 Pedro Astacio	.20	.06
169 Mark Johnson	.20	.06
170 Mark Leiter	.20	.06
171 Heathcliff Slocumb	.20	.06
172 Dante Bichette	.20	.06
173 Brian Giles RC	1.00	.30
174 Paul Wilson	.20	.06
175 Eric Davis	.20	.06
176 Charles Johnson	.20	.06
177 Willie Greene	.20	.06
178 Geronimo Berroa	.20	.06
179 Mariano Duncan	.20	.06
180 Robert Person	.20	.06
181 David Segui	.20	.06
182 Ozzie Guillen	.20	.06
183 Osvaldo Fernandez	.20	.06
184 Dean Palmer	.20	.06
185 Bob Wickman	.20	.06
186 Eric Karros	.20	.06
187 Travis Fryman	.20	.06
188 Andy Ashby	.20	.06
189 Scott Stahoviak	.20	.06
190 Norm Charlton	.20	.06
191 Craig Paquette	.20	.06
192 John Smoltz UER (Name spelled "Smotlz" on back)	.30	.09
193 Orel Hershiser	.20	.06
194 Glenallen Hill	.20	.06
195 George Arias	.20	.06
196 Brian Jordan	.20	.06
197 Greg Vaughn	.20	.06
198 Rafael Palmeiro	.30	.09
199 Darryl Kile	.20	.06
200 Derek Jeter	1.25	.35
201 Jose Vizcaino	.20	.06
202 Rick Aguilera	.20	.06
203 Jason Schmidt	.20	.06
204 Trot Nixon	.30	.09
205 Tom Pagnozzi	.20	.06
206 Mark Wohlers	.20	.06
207 Lance Johnson	.20	.06
208 Carlos Delgado	.20	.06
209 Cliff Floyd	.20	.06
210 Kent Mercker	.20	.06
211 Matt Mieske	.20	.06
212 Ismael Valdes	.20	.06
213 Shawon Dunston	.20	.06
214 Melvin Nieves	.20	.06
215 Tony Phillips	.20	.06
216 Scott Spiezio	.20	.06
217 Michael Tucker	.20	.06
218 Matt Williams	.20	.06
219 Ricky Otero	.20	.06
220 Kevin Ritz	.20	.06
221 Darryl Strawberry	.30	.09
222 Troy Percival	.20	.06
223 Eugene Kingsale	.20	.06
224 Julian Tavarez	.20	.06
225 Jermaine Dye	.20	.06
226 Jason Kendall	.20	.06
227 Sterling Hitchcock	.20	.06
228 Jeff Cirillo	.20	.06
229 Roberto Hernandez	.20	.06
230 Ricky Bottalico	.20	.06
231 Bobby Bonilla	.20	.06
232 Edgar Martinez	.30	.09
233 John Valentin	.20	.06
234 Ellis Burks	.20	.06
235 Benito Santiago	.20	.06
236 Terrell Wade	.20	.06
237 Armando Reynoso	.20	.06
238 Danny Graves	.20	.06
239 Ken Hill	.20	.06

240 Dennis Eckersley .20 .06
241 Darin Erstad .20 .06
242 Lee Smith UER .20 .06
Position 2b
243 Cecil Fielder .20 .06
244 Tony Clark .20 .06
245 Scott Erickson .20 .06
246 Bob Abreu .20 .06
247 Ruben Sierra .20 .06
248 Chili Davis .20 .06
249 Darryl Hamilton .20 .06
250 Albert Belle .20 .06
251 Todd Hollandsworth .20 .06
252 Terry Adams .20 .06
253 Rey Ordonez .20 .06
254 Steve Finley .20 .06
255 Jose Valentin .20 .06
256 Royce Clayton .20 .06
257 Sandy Alomar Jr. .20 .06
258 Mike Lieberthal .20 .06
259 Ivan Rodriguez .50 .15
260 Rod Beck .20 .06
261 Ron Karkovice .20 .06
262 Mark Gubicza .20 .06
263 Chris Holt .20 .06
264 Jaime Bluma UER .20 .06
Name spelled 'Jamie' on front and back
265 Francisco Cordova .20 .06
266 Javy Lopez .20 .06
267 Reggie Jefferson .20 .06
268 Kevin Brown .20 .06
269 Scott Brosius .20 .06
270 Dwight Gooden .30 .09
271 Marty Cordova .20 .06
272 Jeff Brantley .20 .06
273 Joe Carter .20 .06
274 Todd Jones .20 .06
275 Sammy Sosa .75 .23
276 Randy Johnson .50 .15
277 B.J. Surhoff .20 .06
278 Chan Ho Park .20 .06
279 Jamey Wright .20 .06
280 Manny Ramirez .20 .06
281 John Franco .20 .06
282 Tim Worrell .20 .06
283 Scott Rolen .30 .09
284 Reggie Sanders .20 .06
285 Mike Fetters .20 .06
286 Tim Wakefield .20 .06
287 Trevor Hoffman .20 .06
288 Donovan Osborne .20 .06
289 Phil Nevin .20 .06
290 J.Allensworth .20 .06
291 Rocky Coppinger .20 .06
292 Tim Raines .20 .06
293 Henry Rodriguez .20 .06
294 Paul Sorrento .20 .06
295 Tom Goodwin .20 .06
296 Raul Mondesi .20 .06
297 Allen Watson .20 .06
298 Derek Bell .20 .06
299 Gary Sheffield .20 .06
300 Paul Molitor .30 .09
301 Shawn Green .20 .06
302 Darren Oliver .20 .06
303 Jack McDowell .20 .06
304 Denny Neagle .20 .06
305 Doug Drabek .20 .06
306 Mel Rojas .20 .06
307 Andres Galarraga .20 .06
308 Alex Ochoa .20 .06
309 Gary DiSarcina .20 .06
310 Ron Gant .20 .06
311 Gregg Jefferies .20 .06
312 Ruben Rivera .20 .06
313 Vladimir Guerrero .50 .15
314 Willie Adams .20 .06
315 Bip Roberts .20 .06
316 Mark Grace .30 .09
317 Bernard Gilkey .20 .06
318 Marc Newfield .20 .06
319 Al Leiter .20 .06
320 Otis Nixon .20 .06
321 Tom Candiotti .20 .06
322 Mike Stanley .20 .06
323 Jeff Fassero .20 .06
324 Billy Wagner .20 .06
325 Todd Walker .20 .06
326 Chad Curtis .20 .06
327 Quinton McCracken .20 .06
328 Will Clark .50 .15
329 Andruw Jones .20 .06
330 Robin Ventura .20 .06
331 Curtis Pride .20 .06
332 Barry Larkin .50 .15
333 Jimmy Key .20 .06
334 David Wells .20 .06
335 Mike Holtz .20 .06
336 Paul Wagner .20 .06
337 Greg Maddux .75 .23
338 Curt Schilling .30 .09
339 Steve Trachsel .20 .06
340 John Wetteland .20 .06
341 Rickey Henderson .50 .15
342 Ernie Young .20 .06
343 Harold Baines .20 .06
344 Bobby Jones .20 .06
345 Jeff D'Amico .20 .06
346 John Mabry .20 .06
347 Pedro Martinez .50 .15
348 Mark Lewis .20 .06
349 Dan Miceli .20 .06
350 Chuck Knoblauch .20 .06
351 John Smiley .20 .06
352 Brady Anderson .20 .06
353 Jim Leyritz .20 .06
354 Al Martin .20 .06
355 Pat Hentgen .20 .06
356 Mike Piazza .75 .23
357 Charles Nagy .20 .06
358 Luis Castillo .20 .06
359 Paul O'Neill .30 .09
360 Steve Reed .20 .06
361 Tom Gordon .20 .06
362 Craig Biggio .30 .09
363 Jeff Montgomery .20 .06
364 Jamie Moyer .20 .06
365 Ryan Klesko .20 .06
366 Todd Hundley .20 .06
367 Bobby Estalella .20 .06
368 Jason Giambi .50 .15
369 Brian Hunter .20 .06
370 Ramon Martinez .20 .06
371 Carlos Garcia .20 .06
372 Hal Morris .20 .06
373 Juan Gonzalez .50 .15
374 Brian McRae .20 .06
375 Mike Mussina .50 .15
376 John Ericks .20 .06
377 Larry Walker .30 .09
378 Chris Gomez .20 .06
379 John Jaha .20 .06
380 Rondell White .20 .06
381 Chipper Jones .50 .15
382 David Cone .20 .06
383 Alan Benes .20 .06
384 Troy O'Leary .20 .06
385 Ken Caminiti .20 .06
386 Jeff King .20 .06
387 Mike Hampton .20 .06
388 Jaime Navarro .20 .06
389 Brad Radke .20 .06
390 Joey Cora .20 .06
391 Jim Thome .50 .15
392 Alex Fernandez .20 .06
393 Chuck Finley .20 .06
394 Andruw Jones CL .20 .06
395 Ken Griffey Jr. CL .50 .15
396 Frank Thomas CL .30 .09
397 Alex Rodriguez CL .50 .15
398 Cal Ripken CL .75 .23
399 Mike Piazza CL .50 .15
400 Greg Maddux CL .50 .15
P100 A.Rodriguez Promo 2.00 .60

1997 Circa Rave

Randomly inserted in packs at a rate of one in 30, this hobby exclusive set is a parallel version of the regular set and is similar in design. One hundred fifty of this limited edition set were produced and are sequentially numbered.

Nm-Mt Ex-Mt
*STARS: 25X TO 60X BASIC CARDS ..
*ROOKIES: 10X TO 25X BASIC CARDS

1997 Circa Boss

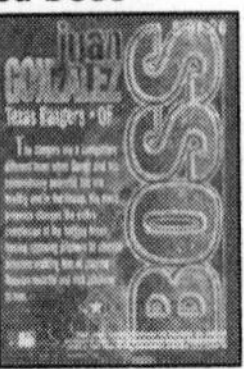

Randomly inserted in packs at a rate of one in six, this 20-card set features color player photos of Baseball's leading men on the field and at bat and are printed on sculpted, embossed cards. The backs carry player information.

Nm-Mt Ex-Mt
COMPLETE SET (20) 40.00 12.00
*SUPER BOSS: 1.5X TO 4X BASIC BOSS
SUPER BOSS STATED ODDS 1:36
1 Jeff Bagwell 1.00 .30
2 Albert Belle .60 .18
3 Barry Bonds 4.00 1.20
4 Ken Caminiti .60 .18
5 Juan Gonzalez 1.50 .45
6 Ken Griffey Jr. 2.50 .75
7 Tony Gwynn 2.00 .60
8 Derek Jeter 4.00 1.20
9 Andruw Jones .60 .18
10 Chipper Jones 1.50 .45
11 Greg Maddux 2.50 .75
12 Mark McGwire 4.00 1.20
13 Mike Piazza 2.50 .75
14 Manny Ramirez .60 .18
15 Cal Ripken 5.00 1.50
16 Alex Rodriguez 2.50 .75
17 John Smoltz 1.00 .30
18 Frank Thomas 1.50 .45
19 Mo Vaughn .60 .18
20 Bernie Williams 1.00 .30

1997 Circa Emerald Autographs

These autographed cards were made available only to those collectors lucky enough to pull one of the scarce Circa Emerald Autograph Redemption cards (randomly seeded into 1:1000 1997 Circa packs). These cards are identical to the regular issue Circa cards except, of course, for the player's autograph on the card front and an embossed Fleer seal for authenticity. The deadline to redeem the cards was May 1st, 1998. In addition, an Emerald Autograph Redemption program entitled "Collect and Win" was featured in 1997 Fleer series two packs. One in every 4 packs contained one of ten different redemption cards. The object was for collectors to piece together all ten cards and then mail them in to receive a complete set of the Circa Emerald Autographs. The catch was that card number seven was extremely shortprinted (official numbers were not released but speculation is that only a handful of number seven cards made their way into packs). The exchange deadline on this "collect and win" promotion was August 1st, 1998.

Nm-Mt Ex-Mt
*EXCH CARDS: .1X TO .25X BASIC AUTO
100 Alex Rodriguez 120.00 36.00
241 Darin Erstad 15.00 4.50
251 T.Hollandsworth AU 10.00 3.00
283 Scott Rolen 25.00 7.50
308 Alex Ochoa 10.00 3.00
325 Todd Walker 15.00 4.50

1997 Circa Fast Track

Randomly inserted in packs at a rate of one in 24, this 10-card set features color player photos of young stars and rookies who will carry baseball into the 21st century. The fronts display the player's image on a flocked background design which shows grass as raised fabric.

Nm-Mt Ex-Mt
COMPLETE SET (10) 40.00 12.00
1 Vladimir Guerrero 4.00 1.20
2 Todd Hollandsworth 1.50 .45
3 Derek Jeter 10.00 3.00
4 Andruw Jones 1.50 .45
5 Chipper Jones 4.00 1.20
6 Andy Pettitte 2.50 .75
7 Mariano Rivera 2.50 .75
8 Alex Rodriguez 6.00 1.80
9 Scott Rolen 2.50 .75
10 Todd Walker 1.50 .45

1997 Circa Icons

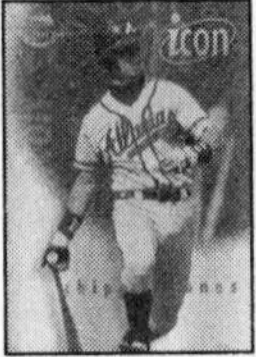

Randomly inserted in packs at a rate of one in 36, this 12-card set features color player images of twelve legendary players printed on 100% holofoil with the word "icon" running across the background. The backs carry player information.

Nm-Mt Ex-Mt
COMPLETE SET (12) 100.00 30.00
1 Juan Gonzalez 5.00 1.50
2 Ken Griffey Jr. 8.00 2.40
3 Tony Gwynn 6.00 1.80
4 Derek Jeter 12.00 3.60
5 Chipper Jones 5.00 1.50
6 Greg Maddux 8.00 2.40
7 Mark McGwire 12.00 3.60
8 Mike Piazza 8.00 2.40
9 Cal Ripken 15.00 4.50
10 Alex Rodriguez 8.00 2.40
11 Frank Thomas 5.00 1.50
12 Matt Williams 2.00 .60

1997 Circa Limited Access

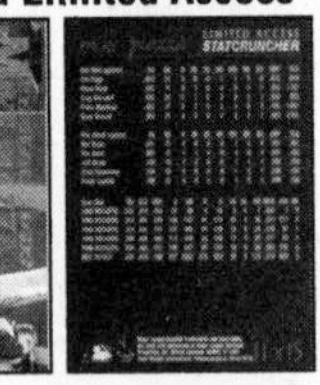

Randomly inserted in retail packs only at a rate of one in 18, this 15-card set features color player photos on die-cut, bi-fold cards which track the players from their youth to the present with in-depth statistical analysis.

Nm-Mt Ex-Mt
COMPLETE SET (15) 150.00 45.00
1 Jeff Bagwell 4.00 1.20
2 Albert Belle 2.50 .75
3 Barry Bonds 15.00 4.50
4 Juan Gonzalez 6.00 1.80
5 Ken Griffey Jr. 10.00 3.00
6 Tony Gwynn 8.00 2.40
7 Derek Jeter 15.00 4.50
8 Chipper Jones 6.00 1.80
9 Greg Maddux 10.00 3.00
10 Mark McGwire 15.00 4.50
11 Mike Piazza 10.00 3.00
12 Cal Ripken 20.00 6.00
13 Alex Rodriguez 10.00 3.00
14 Frank Thomas 6.00 1.80
15 Mo Vaughn 2.50 .75

1997 Circa Rave Reviews

Randomly inserted in packs at a rate of one in 288, this 12-card set features color photos of twelve players who generate incredible numbers off the bat and are printed on 100 percent holofoil. The backs carry player information.

Nm-Mt Ex-Mt
COMPLETE SET (12) 300.00 90.00
1 Albert Belle 6.00 1.80
2 Barry Bonds 40.00 12.00
3 Juan Gonzalez 15.00 4.50
4 Ken Griffey Jr. 25.00 7.50
5 Tony Gwynn 20.00 6.00
6 Greg Maddux 25.00 7.50
7 Mark McGwire 40.00 12.00
8 Eddie Murray 15.00 4.50
9 Mike Piazza 25.00 7.50
10 Cal Ripken 50.00 15.00
11 Alex Rodriguez 25.00 7.50
12 Frank Thomas 15.00 4.50

1998 Circa Thunder

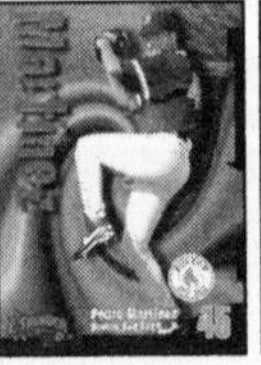

The 1998 Circa Thunder set, produced by Fleer/SkyBox, was issued in one series totalling 300 cards. The eight-card packs retailed for $1.59 each. Collector's should take note that Marquis Grissom's card was erroneously numbered as 8 instead 280. Both Cal Ripken Jr. and Grissom are numbered as 8. In addition, a Cal Ripken promo card was issued prior to the product's public release. The card was distributed in dealer order forms and hobby media releases. It's identical in design to the standard Circa Thunder Ripken except for the text "PROMOTIONAL SAMPLE" written diagonally across the front and back of the card.

Nm-Mt Ex-Mt
COMPLETE SET (300) 25.00 7.50
1 Ben Grieve .20 .06
2 Derek Jeter 1.25 .35
3 Alex Rodriguez .75 .23
4 Paul Molitor .30 .09
5 Nomar Garciaparra .75 .23
6 Fred McGriff .30 .09
7 Kenny Lofton .20 .06
8 Cal Ripken 1.50 .45
9 Matt Williams .20 .06
10 Chipper Jones .50 .15
11 Barry Larkin .50 .15
12 Steve Finley .20 .06
13 Billy Wagner .20 .06
14 Rico Brogna .20 .06
15 Tim Salmon .30 .09
16 Hideo Nomo .50 .15
17 Tony Clark .20 .06
18 Jason Kendall .20 .06
19 Juan Gonzalez .50 .15
20 Jeromy Burnitz .20 .06
21 Roger Clemens 1.00 .30
22 Mark Grace .30 .09
23 Robin Ventura .20 .06
24 Manny Ramirez .20 .06
25 Mark McGwire 1.25 .35
26 Gary Sheffield .20 .06
27 Vladimir Guerrero .50 .15
28 Butch Huskey .20 .06
29 Cecil Fielder .20 .06
30 Rod Myers .20 .06
31 Greg Maddux .75 .23
32 Bill Mueller .20 .06
33 Larry Walker .30 .09
34 Henry Rodriguez .20 .06
35 Mike Mussina .50 .15
36 Ricky Ledee .20 .06
37 Bobby Bonilla .20 .06
38 Curt Schilling .30 .09
39 Luis Gonzalez .20 .06
40 Troy Percival .20 .06
41 Eric Milton .20 .06
42 Mo Vaughn .20 .06
43 Raul Mondesi .20 .06
44 Kenny Rogers .20 .06
45 Frank Thomas .50 .15
46 Jose Canseco .50 .15
47 Tom Glavine .30 .09
48 Rich Butler RC .20 .06
49 Jay Buhner .20 .06
50 Jose Cruz Jr. .20 .06
51 Bernie Williams .30 .09
52 Doug Glanville .20 .06
53 Travis Fryman .20 .06
54 Rey Ordonez .20 .06
55 Jeff Conine .20 .06
56 Trevor Hoffman .20 .06
57 Kirk Rueter .20 .06
UER back Reuter
58 Ron Gant .20 .06
59 Carl Everett .20 .06
60 Joe Carter .20 .06
61 Livan Hernandez .20 .06
62 John Jaha .20 .06
63 Ivan Rodriguez .50 .15
64 Willie Blair .20 .06
65 Todd Helton .30 .09
66 Kevin Young .20 .06
67 Mike Caruso .20 .06
68 Steve Trachsel .20 .06
69 Marty Cordova .20 .06
70 Alex Fernandez .20 .06
71 Eric Karros .20 .06
72 Reggie Sanders .20 .06
73 Russ Davis .20 .06
74 Roberto Hernandez .20 .06
75 Barry Bonds 1.25 .35
76 Alex Gonzalez .20 .06
77 Roberto Alomar .50 .15
78 Troy O'Leary .20 .06
79 Bernard Gilkey .20 .06
80 Ismael Valdes .20 .06
81 Travis Lee .20 .06
82 Brant Brown .20 .06
83 Gary DiSarcina .20 .06
84 Joe Randa .20 .06
85 Jaret Wright .20 .06
86 Quilvio Veras .20 .06
87 Rickey Henderson .50 .15
88 Randall Simon .20 .06
89 Mariano Rivera .30 .09
90 Ugueth Urbina .20 .06
91 Fernando Vina .20 .06
92 Alan Benes .20 .06
93 Dante Bichette .20 .06
94 Karim Garcia .20 .06
95 A.J. Hinch .20 .06
96 Shane Reynolds .20 .06
97 Kevin Stocker .20 .06
98 John Wetteland .20 .06
99 Terry Steinbach .20 .06
100 Ken Griffey Jr. .75 .23
101 Mike Cameron .20 .06
102 Damion Easley .20 .06
103 Randy Myers .20 .06
104 Jason Schmidt .20 .06
105 Jeff King .20 .06
106 Gregg Jefferies .20 .06
107 Sean Casey .20 .06
108 Mark Kotsay .20 .06
109 Brad Fullmer .20 .06
110 Wilson Alvarez .20 .06
111 Sandy Alomar Jr. .20 .06
112 Walt Weiss .20 .06
113 Doug Jones .20 .06
114 Andy Benes .20 .06
115 Paul O'Neill .30 .09
116 Dennis Eckersley .20 .06
117 Todd Greene .20 .06
118 Bobby Jones .20 .06
119 Darrin Fletcher .20 .06
120 Eric Young .20 .06
121 Jeffrey Hammonds .20 .06
122 Mickey Morandini .20 .06
123 Chuck Knoblauch .20 .06
124 Moises Alou .20 .06
125 Miguel Tejada .30 .09
126 Brian Anderson .20 .06
127 Edgar Renteria .20 .06
128 Mike Lansing .20 .06
129 Quinton McCracken .20 .06
130 Ray Lankford .20 .06
131 Andy Ashby .20 .06
132 Kelvim Escobar .20 .06
133 Mike Lowell RC 1.00 .30
134 Randy Johnson .50 .15
135 Andres Galarraga .20 .06
136 Armando Benitez .20 .06
137 Rusty Greer .20 .06
138 Jose Guillen .20 .06
139 Paul Konerko .20 .06
140 Edgardo Alfonzo .20 .06
141 Jim Leyritz .20 .06
142 Mark Clark .20 .06
143 Brian Johnson .20 .06
144 Scott Rolen .30 .09
145 David Cone .20 .06
146 Jeff Shaw .20 .06
147 Shannon Stewart .20 .06
148 Brian Hunter .20 .06
149 Garret Anderson .20 .06
150 Jeff Bagwell .30 .09
151 James Baldwin .20 .06
152 Devon White .20 .06
153 Jim Thome .50 .15
154 Wally Joyner .20 .06
155 Mark Wohlers .20 .06
156 Jeff Cirillo .20 .06
157 Jason Giambi .50 .15
158 Royce Clayton .20 .06
159 Dennis Reyes .20 .06
160 Raul Casanova .20 .06
161 Pedro Astacio .20 .06
162 Todd Dunwoody .20 .06
163 Sammy Sosa .75 .23
164 Todd Hundley .20 .06
165 Wade Boggs .30 .09
166 Robb Nen .20 .06
167 Dan Wilson .20 .06
168 Hideki Irabu .20 .06
169 B.J. Surhoff .20 .06
170 Carlos Delgado .20 .06
171 Fernando Tatis .20 .06
172 Bob Abreu .20 .06
173 David Ortiz .20 .06
174 Tony Womack .20 .06
175 Magglio Ordonez RC 1.25 .35
176 Aaron Boone .20 .06
177 Brian Giles .20 .06
178 Kevin Appier .20 .06
179 Chuck Finley .20 .06
180 Brian Rose .20 .06
181 Ryan Klesko .20 .06
182 Mike Stanley .20 .06
183 Dave Nilsson .20 .06
184 Carlos Perez .20 .06
185 Jeff Blauser .20 .06
186 Richard Hidalgo .20 .06
187 Charles Johnson .20 .06
188 Vinny Castilla .20 .06
189 Joey Hamilton .20 .06
190 Bubba Trammell .20 .06
191 Eli Marrero .20 .06
192 Scott Erickson .20 .06
193 Pat Hentgen .20 .06
194 Jorge Fabregas .20 .06
195 Tino Martinez .30 .09
196 Bobby Higginson .20 .06
197 Dave Hollins .20 .06
198 Rolando Arrojo RC .20 .06
199 Joey Cora .20 .06
200 Mike Piazza .75 .23
201 Reggie Jefferson .20 .06
202 John Smoltz .30 .09
203 Bobby Smith .20 .06
204 Tom Goodwin .20 .06
205 Omar Vizquel .20 .06
206 John Olerud .20 .06
207 Matt Stairs .20 .06
208 Bobby Estalella .20 .06

1997 Circa Rave

209 Miguel Cairo .20 .06
210 Shawn Green .20 .06
211 Jon Nunnally .20 .06
212 Al Leiter .20 .06
213 Matt Lawton .20 .06
214 Brady Anderson .20 .06
215 Jeff Kent .20 .06
216 Ray Durham .20 .06
217 Al Martin .20 .06
218 Jeff D'Amico .20 .06
219 Kevin Tapani .20 .06
220 Jim Edmonds .20 .06
221 Jose Vizcaino .20 .06
222 Jay Bell .20 .06
223 Ken Caminiti .20 .06
224 Craig Biggio .30 .09
225 Bartolo Colon .20 .06
226 Neifi Perez .20 .06
227 Delino DeShields .20 .06
228 Javier Lopez .20 .06
229 David Wells .20 .06
230 Brad Rigby .20 .06
231 John Franco .20 .06
232 Michael Coleman .20 .06
233 Edgar Martinez .30 .09
234 Francisco Cordova .20 .06
235 Johnny Damon .20 .06
236 Deivi Cruz .20 .06
237 J.T. Snow .20 .06
238 Enrique Wilson .20 .06
239 Rondell White .20 .06
240 Aaron Sele .20 .06
241 Tony Saunders .20 .06
242 Ricky Bottalico .20 .06
243 Cliff Floyd .20 .06
244 Chili Davis .20 .06
245 Brian McRae .20 .06
246 Brad Radke .20 .06
247 Chan Ho Park .20 .06
248 Lance Johnson .20 .06
249 Rafael Palmeiro .30 .09
250 Tony Gwynn .60 .18
251 Denny Neagle .20 .06
252 Dean Palmer .20 .06
253 Jose Valentin .20 .06
254 Matt Morris .20 .06
255 Ellis Burks .20 .06
256 Jeff Suppan .20 .06
257 Jimmy Key .20 .06
258 Justin Thompson .20 .06
259 Brett Tomko .20 .06
260 Mark Grudzielanek .20 .06
261 Mike Hampton .20 .06
262 Jeff Fassero .20 .06
263 Charles Nagy .20 .06
264 Pedro Martinez .50 .15
265 Todd Zeile .20 .06
266 Will Clark .50 .15
267 Abraham Nunez .20 .06
268 Dave Martinez .20 .06
269 Jason Dickson .20 .06
270 Eric Davis .20 .06
271 Kevin Orie .20 .06
272 Derrek Lee .20 .06
273 Andruw Jones .20 .06
274 Juan Encarnacion .20 .06
275 Carlos Baerga .20 .06
276 Andy Pettitte .30 .09
277 Brent Brede .20 .06
278 Paul Sorrento .20 .06
279 Mike Lieberthal .20 .06
280 Marquis Grissom .20 .06
UER #'d 8 instead of 280
281 Darin Erstad .20 .06
282 Willie Greene .20 .06
283 Derek Bell .20 .06
284 Scott Spiezio .20 .06
285 David Segui .20 .06
286 Albert Belle .20 .06
287 Ramon Martinez .20 .06
288 Jeremi Gonzalez .20 .06
289 Shawn Estes .20 .06
290 Ron Coomer .20 .06
291 John Valentin .20 .06
292 Kevin Brown .30 .09
293 Michael Tucker .20 .06
294 Brian Jordan .20 .06
295 Darryl Kile .20 .06
296 David Justice .20 .06
297 Frank Thomas CL .30 .09
298 Alex Rodriguez CL .50 .15
299 Ken Griffey Jr. CL .50 .15
300 Jose Cruz Jr. CL .20 .06
P8 Cal Ripken Promo 2.00 .60

1998 Circa Thunder Rave

Randomly inserted into packs at an approximate rate of one in every 36 pack box, cards from this 296-card set parallel the basic set. Please note, the four checklist cards included in the regular set were not created in Rave parallel versions. Only 150 Rave sets were printed and each card is serial numbered "of 150" on back. In addition, special silver sparkling foil is used on the player's name and the Thunder logo on the card front.

Nm-Mt Ex-Mt
*STARS: 20X TO 50X BASIC CARDS
*ROOKIES: 12.5X TO 30X BASIC CARDS

1998 Circa Thunder Boss

Randomly seeded at a rate one in every six packs, cards from this 20-card set feature a collection of the league's top stars.

Nm-Mt Ex-Mt
COMPLETE SET (20) 40.00 12.00
1 Jeff Bagwell 1.00 .30
2 Barry Bonds 4.00 1.20
3 Roger Clemens 3.00 .90
4 Jose Cruz Jr. .60 .18
5 Nomar Garciaparra 2.50 .75
6 Juan Gonzalez 1.50 .45
7 Ken Griffey Jr. 2.50 .75
8 Tony Gwynn 2.00 .60
9 Derek Jeter 4.00 1.20
10 Chipper Jones 1.50 .45
11 Travis Lee .60 .18
12 Greg Maddux 2.50 .75
13 Pedro Martinez 1.50 .45
14 Mark McGwire 4.00 1.20
15 Mike Piazza 2.50 .75
16 Cal Ripken 5.00 1.50
17 Alex Rodriguez 2.50 .75
18 Scott Rolen 1.00 .30
19 Frank Thomas 1.50 .45
20 Larry Walker 1.00 .30

1998 Circa Thunder Fast Track

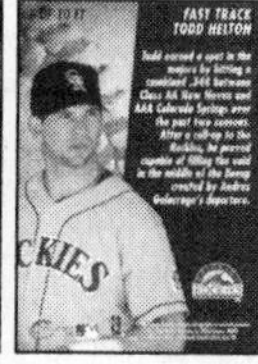

Randomly seeded into packs at a rate of one in 24, cards from this 10-card set feature a selection of talented youngsters on the "fast track" to success. The attractive card fronts feature a color action photo of the player imposed over a glowing gold baseball. In addition, small head shots of all ten players featured in the set are pictured on the right hand side of the card front. The specific player featured on each card has his head shot printed in matching gold holographic imagery.

Nm-Mt Ex-Mt
COMPLETE SET (10) 15.00 4.50
1 Jose Cruz Jr. 1.25 .35
2 Juan Encarnacion 1.25 .35
3 Brad Fullmer 1.25 .35
4 Nomar Garciaparra 5.00 1.50
5 Todd Helton 2.00 .60
6 Livan Hernandez 1.25 .35
7 Travis Lee 1.25 .35
8 Neifi Perez 1.25 .35
9 Scott Rolen 2.00 .60
10 Jaret Wright 1.25 .35

1998 Circa Thunder Limited Access

Randomly seeded into retail packs only at a rate of one in 18, cards from this 15-card set feature a selection of the league's top stars doing there thing. These attractive cards actually open up from top to bottom to feature a full length shot of the featured player with an extensive breakdown of 1997 statistics.

Nm-Mt Ex-Mt
COMPLETE SET (15) 150.00 45.00
1 Jeff Bagwell 4.00 1.20
2 Roger Clemens 12.00 3.60
3 Jose Cruz Jr. 2.50 .75
4 Nomar Garciaparra 10.00 3.00
5 Juan Gonzalez 6.00 1.80
6 Ken Griffey Jr. 10.00 3.00
7 Tony Gwynn 8.00 2.40
8 Derek Jeter 15.00 4.50
9 Greg Maddux 10.00 3.00
10 Pedro Martinez 6.00 1.80
11 Mark McGwire 15.00 4.50
12 Mike Piazza 10.00 3.00
13 Alex Rodriguez 10.00 3.00
14 Frank Thomas 6.00 1.80
15 Larry Walker 4.00 1.20

1998 Circa Thunder Quick Strike

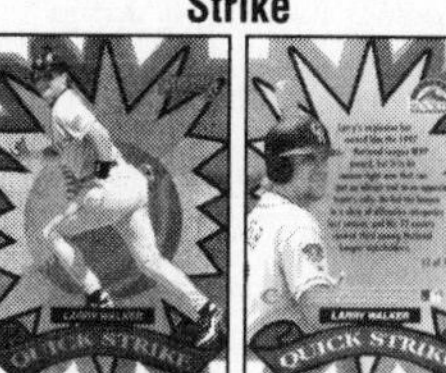

Randomly seeded into packs at a rate of one in 36, cards from this 12-card set feature a selection of the league's top stars printed on colorful foil-board fronts.

Nm-Mt Ex-Mt
COMPLETE SET (12) 80.00 24.00
1 Jeff Bagwell 3.00 .90
2 Roger Clemens 10.00 3.00
3 Jose Cruz Jr. 2.00 .60
4 Nomar Garciaparra 8.00 2.40
5 Ken Griffey Jr. 8.00 2.40
6 Greg Maddux 8.00 2.40
7 Pedro Martinez 5.00 1.50
8 Mark McGwire 12.00 3.60
9 Mike Piazza 8.00 2.40
10 Alex Rodriguez 8.00 2.40
11 Frank Thomas 5.00 1.50
12 Larry Walker 3.00 .90

1998 Circa Thunder Rave Review

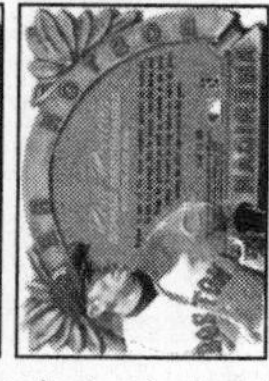

Randomly seeded into packs at a rate of one in 288, cards from this tough 15-card set feature a selection of talented major leaguers. The attractive horizontal images feature a color action shot imposed across a bronze foil plaque with the image of a ball field in the background. The card backs feature the reversed plaque imagery with another player photo.

Nm-Mt Ex-Mt
COMPLETE SET (15) 250.00 75.00
1 Jeff Bagwell 10.00 3.00
2 Barry Bonds 40.00 12.00
3 Roger Clemens 30.00 9.00
4 Jose Cruz Jr. 6.00 1.80
5 Nomar Garciaparra 25.00 7.50
6 Juan Gonzalez 15.00 4.50
7 Ken Griffey Jr. 25.00 7.50
8 Tony Gwynn 20.00 6.00
9 Derek Jeter 40.00 12.00
10 Greg Maddux 25.00 7.50
11 Mark McGwire 40.00 12.00
12 Mike Piazza 25.00 7.50
13 Alex Rodriguez 25.00 7.50
14 Frank Thomas 15.00 4.50
15 Larry Walker 10.00 3.00

1998 Circa Thunder Thunder Boomers

Randomly seeded into packs at a rate of one in 96, cards from this 12-card set feature a selection of top sluggers. Each card features a color action shot imposed over a see-through cloud-like plastic center, encircled by a imagery of a wooden fence with a massive hole smashed through the middle of it.

Nm-Mt Ex-Mt
COMPLETE SET (12) 120.00 36.00
1 Jeff Bagwell 6.00 1.80
2 Barry Bonds 25.00 7.50
3 Jay Buhner 4.00 1.20
4 Andres Galarraga 4.00 1.20
5 Juan Gonzalez 10.00 3.00
6 Ken Griffey Jr. 15.00 4.50
7 Tino Martinez 6.00 1.80
8 Mark McGwire 25.00 7.50
9 Mike Piazza 15.00 4.50
10 Frank Thomas 10.00 3.00
11 Jim Thome 10.00 3.00
12 Larry Walker 6.00 1.80

1998 Circa Thunder Rolen Sportsfest

This one card standard-size set was issued by Fleer/SkyBox and distributed at the inaugural SportsFest show in May 1998. The card features the SportsFest 98 logo on the front and is numbered SF1 on the back. While not serial numbered, the back does state that the production on this card is limited to 5,000 cards.

Nm-Mt Ex-Mt
1 Scott Rolen 5.00 1.50

1985 Circle K

The cards in this 33-card set measure 2 1/2" by 3 1/2" and were issued with an accompanying custom box. In 1985, Topps produced this set for Circle K; cards were printed in Ireland. Cards are numbered on the back according to each player's rank on the all-time career Home Run list. The backs are printed in blue and red on white card stock. The card fronts are glossy and each player is named in the lower left corner. Most of the obverses are in color, although the older vintage players are pictured in black and white. Joe DiMaggio was not included in the set; card number 31 does not exist. It was intended to be DiMaggio but he apparently would not consent to be included in the set.

Nm-Mt Ex-Mt
COMP. FACT. SET (33) 5.00 2.00
1 Hank Aaron .75 .30
2 Babe Ruth 1.50 .60
3 Willie Mays .75 .30
4 Frank Robinson .25 .10
5 Harmon Killebrew .25 .10
6 Mickey Mantle 1.50 .60
7 Jimmie Foxx .25 .10
8 Willie McCovey .25 .10
9 Ted Williams .75 .30
10 Ernie Banks .25 .10
11 Eddie Mathews .25 .10
12 Mel Ott .25 .10
13 Reggie Jackson .50 .20
14 Lou Gehrig .75 .30
15 Stan Musial .50 .20
16 Willie Stargell .25 .10
17 Carl Yastrzemski .25 .10
18 Billy Williams .25 .10
19 Mike Schmidt .50 .20
20 Duke Snider .25 .10
21 Al Kaline .25 .10
22 Johnny Bench .25 .10
23 Frank Howard .10 .04
24 Orlando Cepeda .20 .08
25 Norm Cash .10 .04
26 Dave Kingman .10 .04
27 Rocky Colavito .20 .08
28 Tony Perez .20 .08
29 Gil Hodges .20 .08
30 Ralph Kiner .25 .10
31 Joe DiMaggio
(card does not exist)
32 Johnny Mize .25 .10
33 Yogi Berra .25 .10
34 Lee May .10 .04

1994 Will Clark Kelly Russell Studios

This is a double matted artist's rendering which measures 14" by 11". It is accompanied by a '93 season highlights panel and baseball card panel. This issued is subtitled "The Texas Thrill." This is part of a big set: need complete set information before we price this.

Nm-Mt Ex-Mt
1 Will Clark 5.00 1.50

1972 Classic Cards

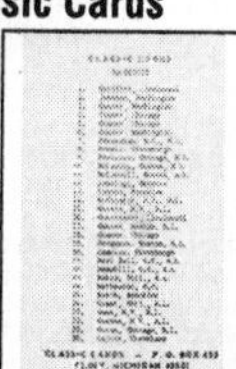

This 120-card set was issued in four series and features sepia player photos printed on beige card stock. The backs carry a checklist of the series in which the player photo displayed on the front is found. The cards are checklisted below according to those checklists. Series 1 consists of cards numbered from 1-30; Series 2, cards numbered from 31-60; Series 3, cards numbered from 61-90; and Series 4, cards numbered from 91-120.

NM Ex
COMPLETE SET (120) 75.00 30.00
1 Clark Griffith 2.00 .80
2 Walter Johnson 3.00 1.20
3 Bob Ganley .50 .20
4 Joe Tinker 2.00 .80
5 Frank Chance 2.00 .80
6 Wid Conroy .50 .20
7 Roger Bresnahan 1.00 .40
8 Jack Powell .50 .20
9 Jack Pfeister .50 .20
10 Tom McCarthy 1.00 .40
11 Amby McConnell .50 .20
12 Hugh Jennings 1.00 .40
13 Ed Lennox .50 .20
14 Moose McCormick .50 .20
15 Fred Merkle .50 .20
16 Dick Hoblitzell .50 .20
17 Bill Dahlen .50 .20
18 Frank Chance 2.00 .80
19 George Ferguson .50 .20
20 Howie Camnitz .50 .20
21 Neal Ball .50 .20
22 Charlie Hemphill .50 .20
23 Frank Baker 1.50 .60
24 Christy Mathewson 2.00 .80
25 Al Burch .50 .20
26 Eddie Grant 1.00 .40
27 Red Ames .50 .20
28 Doc Newton .50 .20
29 Pat Moran .50 .20
30 Nap Lajoie 2.00 .80
31 Mordecai Brown 1.50 .60
32 Bill Abstein .50 .20
33 Ty Cobb 5.00 2.00
34 Billy Campbell .50 .20
35 Claude Rossman .50 .20
36 Topsy Hartsel .50 .20
37 Sam Crawford 1.50 .60
38 Red Dooin .50 .20
39 Jack Dunn .50 .20
40 Tom Downey .50 .20
41 Bill Hinchman .50 .20
42 John Titus .50 .20
43 Patsy Dougherty .50 .20
44 Art Devlin .50 .20
45 Nap Lajoie 2.00 .80
46 Larry Doyle .50 .20
47 Honus Wagner 3.00 1.20
48 Bull Durham 1.00 .40
49 Irv Higginbotham .50 .20
50 George Gibson .50 .20
51 Mike Mowrey .50 .20
52 George Stone .50 .20
53 George Perring .50 .20
54 Orvie Overall .50 .20
55 Hooks Wiltse .50 .20
56 Jack Warhop .50 .20
57 Harry Steinfeldt 1.00 .40
58 Bill O'Hara .50 .20
59 Boss Schmidt .50 .20
60 George Mullin .50 .20
61 Buck Herzog .50 .20
62 John Hummell .50 .20
63 Art Fromme .50 .20
64 Kid Elberfeld .50 .20
65 Frank Bowerman .50 .20
66 Roger Bresnahan 1.00 .40
67 Andy Coakley .50 .20
68 Jim Pastorius .50 .20
69 Tubby Spencer .50 .20
70 Frank Schulte .50 .20
71 Willie Keeler 1.00 .40
72 Joe McGinnity 1.00 .40
73 Harry McIntyre .50 .20
74 Harry Lumley .50 .20
75 Nick Maddox .50 .20
76 Cy Barger .50 .20
77 Bill Donovan .50 .20
78 Tim Jordan .50 .20
79 Johnnie Evers 2.00 .80
80 Zack Wheat 1.00 .40
81 Hippo Vaughn .50 .20
82 Jimmy Sebring .50 .20
83 Tom Tuckey .50 .20
84 Tris Speaker 3.00 1.20
85 John McGraw 2.00 .80
86 Billy Purtell .50 .20
87 George Moriarty .50 .20
88 Charlie Smith .50 .20
89 Bill Bergen .50 .20
90 Kitty Bransfield .50 .20
91 Joe Doyle .50 .20
92 Amos Strunk .50 .20
93 Bob Ewing .50 .20
94 Tom Daley .50 .20
95 Joe Delahanty .50 .20
96 Ed Summers .50 .20
97 Joe Lake .50 .20
98 Dave Altizer .50 .20
99 Roger Bresnahan 1.00 .40
100 Chief Bender 1.50 .60
101 Buck Herzog .50 .20
102 Ira Thomas .50 .20
103 Hal Chase 2.00 .80
104 Tom Needham .50 .20
105 Ducky Pearce .50 .20
106 Rube Ellis .50 .20
107 Ed Konetchy .50 .20
108 Harry Lord .50 .20
109 Ossie Schreck .50 .20
110 Heinie Wagner .50 .20
111 Luther Taylor .50 .20
112 Alan Storke .50 .20
113 Bill Powell .50 .20
114 Ham Hyatt .50 .20
115 George Davis 1.00 .40
116 Bill Grahame .50 .20
117 Larry McLean .50 .20
118 Jiggs Donohue .50 .20
119 Bill Chappelle .50 .20
120 Billy Purtell .50 .20

1987 Classic Game

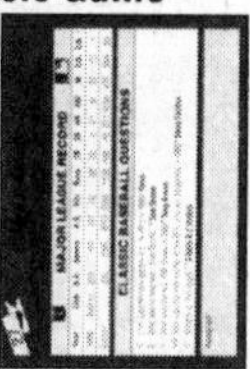

This 100-card standard-size set was actually distributed as part of a trivia board game. The card backs contain several trivia questions (and answers) which are used to play the game. A dark green border frames the full-color photo. The games were produced by Game Time, Ltd. and were available in toy stores as well as from card dealers. According to the producers of this game, only 75,000 sets were distributed. The set features Bo Jackson, Wally Joyner, and Barry Larkin in their Rookie Card year.

Nm-Mt Ex-Mt
COMP.FACT SET (100) 60.00 24.00
1 Pete Rose 2.50 1.00
2 Len Dykstra .25 .10
3 Darryl Strawberry .25 .10
4 Keith Hernandez .25 .10
5 Gary Carter .75 .30
6 Wally Joyner .50 .20
7 Andres Thomas .10 .04
8 Pat Dodson .10 .04
9 Kirk Gibson .25 .10
10 Don Mattingly 5.00 2.00
11 Dave Winfield .75 .30
12 Rickey Henderson 4.00 1.60
13 Dan Pasqua .10 .04
14 Don Baylor .25 .10
15 Bo Jackson 10.00 4.00
(Swinging bat in
Auburn FB uniform)
16 Pete Incaviglia .25 .10
17 Kevin Bass .10 .04
18 Barry Larkin 5.00 2.00
19 Dave Magadan .25 .10
20 Steve Sax .10 .04
21 Eric Davis .25 .10
22 Mike Pagliarulo .10 .04

23 Fred Lynn .25 .10
24 Reggie Jackson 2.00 .80
25 Larry Parrish .10 .04
26 Tony Gwynn 5.00 2.00
27 Steve Garvey .25 .10
28 Glenn Davis .10 .04
29 Tim Raines .25 .10
30 Vince Coleman .10 .04
31 Willie McGee .25 .10
32 Ozzie Smith 4.00 1.60
33 Dave Parker .25 .10
34 Tony Pena .10 .04
35 Ryne Sandberg 4.00 1.60
36 Brett Butler .25 .10
37 Dale Murphy .75 .30
38 Bob Horner .10 .04
39 Pedro Guerrero .10 .04
40 Brook Jacoby .10 .04
41 Carlton Fisk 1.00 .40
42 Harold Baines .50 .20
43 Rob Deer .10 .04
44 Robin Yount 2.50 1.00
45 Paul Molitor 2.50 1.00
46 Jose Canseco 5.00 2.00
47 George Brett 5.00 2.00
48 Jim Presley .10 .04
49 Rich Gedman .10 .04
50 Lance Parrish .25 .10
51 Eddie Murray 2.50 1.00
52 Cal Ripken 10.00 4.00
53 Kent Hrbek .10 .04
54 Gary Gaetti .25 .10
55 Kirby Puckett 5.00 2.00
56 George Bell .10 .04
57 Tony Fernandez .10 .04
58 Jesse Barfield .10 .04
59 Jim Rice .25 .10
60 Wade Boggs 2.50 1.00
61 Marty Barrett .10 .04
62 Mike Schmidt 2.50 1.00
63 Von Hayes .10 .04
64 Jeff Leonard .10 .04
65 Chris Brown .10 .04
66 Dave Smith .10 .04
67 Mike Krukow .10 .04
68 Ron Guidry .25 .10
69 Rob Woodward .10 .04
70 Rob Murphy .10 .04
71 Andres Galarraga 4.00 1.60
72 Dwight Gooden .25 .10
73 Bob Ojeda .10 .04
74 Sid Fernandez .10 .04
75 Jesse Orosco .10 .04
76 Roger McDowell .10 .04
77 John Tudor UER .10 .04
(Misspelled Tutor)
78 Tom Browning .10 .04
79 Rick Aguilera .10 .04
80 Lance McCullers .10 .04
81 Mike Scott .10 .04
82 Nolan Ryan 10.00 4.00
83 Bruce Hurst .10 .04
84 Roger Clemens 6.00 2.40
85 Dennis Boyd .10 .04
86 Dave Righetti .10 .04
87 Dennis Rasmussen .10 .04
88 Bret Saberhagen .25 .10
89 Mark Langston .10 .04
90 Jack Morris .25 .10
91 Fernando Valenzuela .25 .10
92 Orel Hershiser .25 .10
93 Rick Honeycutt .10 .04
94 Jeff Reardon .10 .04
95 John Habyan .10 .04
96 Goose Gossage .25 .10
97 Todd Worrell .25 .10
98 Floyd Youmans .10 .04
99 Don Aase .10 .04
100 John Franco .25 .10

1987 Classic Update Yellow

This 50-card standard-size set was actually distributed as part of an update to a trivia board game, but (unlike the original Classic game) was sold without the game. The set is sometimes referred to as the "Travel Edition" of the game. The card backs contain several trivia questions (and answers) which are used to play the game. A yellow border frames the full-color photo. The games were produced by Game Time, Ltd. and were available in toy stores as well as from card dealers. Cards are numbered beginning with 101, as they are an extension of the original set. According to the set's producers, reportedly about 1/3 of the 150,000 sets printed were error sets in that they had green backs instead of yellow backs. This "green back" variation/error set is valued at approximately double the prices listed below. Early cards of Barry Bonds and Mark McGwire highlight this set. Most cards issued of Barry Bonds tend to be off center. It is believed that the average centering on this card is approximately 80/20.

Nm-Mt Ex-Mt
COMP.FACT.SET (50) 25.00 10.00
101 Mike Schmidt 1.00 .40
102 Eric Davis .25 .10
103 Pete Rose 1.25 .50
104 Don Mattingly 1.25 .50
105 Wade Boggs .25 .10
106 Dale Murphy .40 .16
107 Glenn Davis .10 .04
108 Wally Joyner .40 .16
109 Bo Jackson 1.00 .40
110 Cory Snyder .10 .04
111 Jim Lindeman .15 .06
112 Kirby Puckett .40 .16
113 Barry Bonds 20.00 8.00
114 Roger Clemens 1.00 .40
115 Oddibe McDowell .10 .04
116 Bret Saberhagen .15 .06
117 Joe Magrane .10 .04
118 Scott Fletcher .10 .04
119 Mark McLemore .15 .06
120 Joe Niekro .15 .06
Who Me
121 Mark McGwire 10.00 4.00
122 Darryl Strawberry .25 .10
123 Mike Scott .10 .04
124 Andre Dawson .15 .06
125 Jose Canseco .60 .24
126 Kevin McReynolds .10 .04
127 Joe Carter 2.00 .80
128 Casey Candaele .10 .04
129 Matt Nokes .40 .16
130 Kal Daniels .10 .04
131 Pete Incaviglia .40 .16
132 Benito Santiago .60 .24
133 Barry Larkin 2.00 .80
134 Gary Pettis .10 .04
135 B.J. Surhoff .60 .24
136 Juan Nieves .10 .04
137 Jim Deshaies .10 .04
138 Pete O'Brien .10 .04
139 Kevin Seitzer .40 .16
140 Devon White .60 .24
141 Rob Deer .10 .04
142 Kurt Stillwell .10 .04
143 Edwin Correa .10 .04
144 Dion James .10 .04
145 Danny Tartabull .10 .04
146 Jerry Browne .15 .06
147 Ted Higuera .10 .04
148 Jack Clark .10 .04
149 Ruben Sierra .60 .24
150 Mark McGwire and 1.00 .40
Eric Davis

1987 Classic Update Yellow/Green Backs

These cards parallel the 1987 Classic Yellow set except the backs are in the style of the regular 1987 Classic game set.

Nm-Mt Ex-Mt
COMP.FACT.SET (50) 40.00 16.00
*GREENBACK ERR: .75X TO 2X BASIC CARDS

1988 Classic Blue

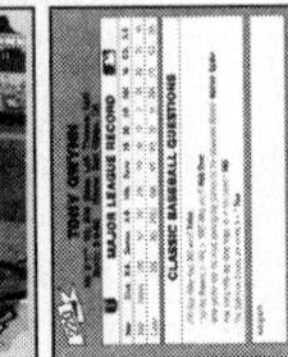

This 50-card blue-bordered standard-size set was actually distributed as part of an update to a trivia board game, but (unlike the original Classic game) was sold without the game. The card backs contain several trivia questions (and answers) which are used to play the game. A blue border frames the full color photo. The games were produced by Game Time, Ltd. and were available in toy stores as well as from card dealers. Cards are numbered beginning with 201 as they are an extension of the original sets.

Nm-Mt Ex-Mt
COMP.FACT. SET (50) 10.00 4.00
201 Eric Davis and .15 .06
Dale Murphy
202 B.J. Surhoff .20 .08
203 John Kruk .15 .06
204 Sam Horn .10 .04
205 Jack Clark .15 .06
206 Wally Joyner .15 .06
207 Matt Nokes .10 .04
208 Bo Jackson .25 .10
209 Darryl Strawberry .10 .04
210 Ozzie Smith 1.50 .60
211 Don Mattingly 2.00 .80
212 Mark McGwire 4.00 1.60
213 Eric Davis .15 .06
214 Wade Boggs .75 .30
215 Dale Murphy .25 .10
216 Andre Dawson .25 .10
217 Roger Clemens 2.50 1.00
218 Kevin Seitzer .10 .04
219 Benito Santiago .15 .06
220 Tony Gwynn 2.00 .80
221 Mike Scott .10 .04
222 Steve Bedrosian .10 .04
223 Vince Coleman .10 .04
224 Rick Sutcliffe .10 .04
225 Will Clark 1.00 .40
226 Pete Rose 1.00 .40
227 Mike Greenwell .10 .04
228 Ken Caminiti .25 .10
229 Ellis Burks 1.00 .40
230 Dave Magadan .10 .04
231 Alan Trammell .25 .10
232 Paul Molitor .50 .20
233 Gary Gaetti .15 .06
234 Rickey Henderson 1.00 .40
235 Danny Tartabull UER .10 .04
(Photo actually
Hal McRae)
236 Bobby Bonilla .15 .06
237 Mike Dunne .10 .04
238 Al Leiter .25 .10
239 John Farrell .10 .04
240 Joe Magrane .10 .04
241 Mike Henneman .15 .06
242 George Bell .10 .04
243 Gregg Jefferies .15 .06
244 Jay Buhner .75 .30
245 Todd Benzinger .10 .04
246 Matt Williams .75 .30
247 Mark McGwire and 2.00 .80
Don Mattingly
(Unnumbered; game
instructions on back)
248 George Brett 1.25 .50
249 Jimmy Key .15 .06
250 Mark Langston .10 .04

1988 Classic Red

This 50-card red-bordered standard-size set was actually distributed as part of an update to a trivia board game, but (unlike the original Classic game) was sold without the game. The card backs contain several trivia questions (and answers) which are used to play the game. A red border frames the full color photo. The games were produced by Game Time, Ltd. and were available in toy stores as well as from card dealers. Cards are numbered beginning with 151 as they are an extension of the original sets.

Nm-Mt Ex-Mt
COMP. FACT. SET (50) 12.00 4.80
151 Mark McGwire and 2.00 .80
Don Mattingly
152 Don Mattingly 1.50 .60
153 Mark McGwire 2.50 1.00
154 Eric Davis .15 .06
155 Wade Boggs .75 .30
156 Dale Murphy .25 .10
157 Andre Dawson .25 .10
158 Roger Clemens 1.50 .60
159 Kevin Seitzer .15 .06
160 Benito Santiago .15 .06
161 Kal Daniels .10 .04
162 John Kruk .15 .06
163 Bill Ripken .10 .04
164 Kirby Puckett 1.00 .40
165 Jose Canseco .50 .20
166 Matt Nokes .10 .04
167 Mike Schmidt .75 .30
168 Tim Raines .15 .06
169 Ryne Sandberg 1.25 .50
170 Dave Winfield .25 .10
171 Dwight Gooden .15 .06
172 Bret Saberhagen .15 .06
173 Willie McGee .15 .06
174 Jack Morris .15 .06
175 Jeff Leonard .10 .04
176 Cal Ripken 3.00 1.20
177 Pete Incaviglia .10 .04
178 Devon White .10 .04
179 Nolan Ryan 3.00 1.20
180 Ruben Sierra .15 .06
181 Todd Worrell .15 .06
182 Glenn Davis .10 .04
183 Frank Viola .10 .04
184 Cory Snyder .10 .04
185 Tracy Jones .10 .04
186 Terry Steinbach .10 .04
187 Julio Franco .15 .06
188 Larry Sheets .10 .04
189 John Marzano .10 .04
190 Kevin Elster .10 .04
191 Vicente Palacios .10 .04
192 Kent Hrbek .10 .04
193 Eric Bell .10 .04
194 Kelly Downs .10 .04
195 Jose Lind .10 .04
196 Dave Stewart .15 .06
197 Mark McGwire and 2.00 .80
Jose Canseco
198 Phil Niekro .50 .20
Cleveland Indians
199 Phil Niekro .50 .20
Toronto Blue Jays
200 Phil Niekro .50 .20
Atlanta Braves

1989 Classic Light Blue

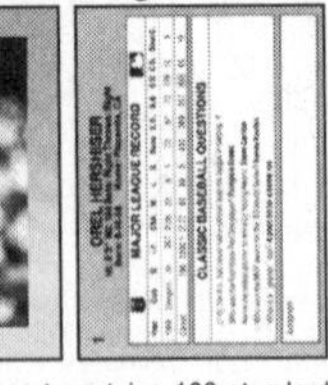

The 1989 Classic set contains 100 standard-size cards. The fronts of these cards have light blue borders. The backs feature 1988 and lifetime stats. The cards were distributed with a baseball boardgame. Reportedly there were 150,000 sets produced.

Nm-Mt Ex-Mt
COMP.FACT.SET (100) 20.00 8.00
1 Orel Hershiser .15 .06
2 Wade Boggs .75 .30
3 Jose Canseco 1.00 .40
4 Mark McGwire 3.00 1.20
5 Don Mattingly 2.00 .80
6 Gregg Jefferies .15 .06
7 Dwight Gooden .15 .06
8 Darryl Strawberry .15 .06
9 Eric Davis .20 .08
10 Joey Meyer .10 .04
11 Joe Carter .20 .08
12 Paul Molitor .75 .30
13 Mark Grace 1.00 .40
14 Kurt Stillwell .10 .04
15 Kirby Puckett 1.00 .40
16 Keith Miller .10 .04
17 Glenn Davis .10 .04
18 Will Clark .50 .20
19 Cory Snyder .10 .04
20 Jose Lind .10 .04
21 Andres Thomas .10 .04
22 Dave Smith .10 .04
23 Mike Scott .10 .04
24 Kevin McReynolds .10 .04
25 B.J. Surhoff .15 .06
26 Mackey Sasser .10 .04
27 Chad Kreuter .10 .04
28 Hal Morris .10 .04
29 Wally Joyner .10 .04
30 Tony Gwynn 2.00 .80
31 Kevin Mitchell .15 .06
32 Dave Winfield .50 .20
33 Billy Bean .20 .08
34 Steve Bedrosian .10 .04
35 Ron Gant .15 .06
36 Len Dykstra .15 .06
37 Andre Dawson .50 .20
38 Brett Butler .15 .06
39 Rob Deer .10 .04
40 Tommy John .15 .06
41 Gary Gaetti .15 .06
42 Tim Raines .15 .06
43 George Bell .10 .04
44 Dwight Evans .15 .06
45 Dennis Martinez .15 .06
46 Andres Galarraga .50 .20
47 George Brett 2.00 .80
48 Mike Schmidt 1.00 .40
49 Dave Stieb .10 .04
50 Rickey Henderson 1.25 .50
51 Craig Biggio 2.00 .80
52 Mark Lemke .10 .04
53 Chris Sabo .10 .04
54 Jeff Treadway .10 .04
55 Kent Hrbek .15 .06
56 Cal Ripken 4.00 1.60
57 Tim Belcher .10 .04
58 Ozzie Smith 1.50 .60
59 Keith Hernandez .15 .06
60 Pedro Guerrero .10 .04
61 Greg Swindell .10 .04
62 Bret Saberhagen .15 .06
63 John Tudor .10 .04
64 Gary Carter .50 .20
65 Kevin Seitzer .10 .04
66 Jesse Barfield .10 .04
67 Luis Medina .10 .04
68 Walt Weiss .10 .04
69 Terry Steinbach .10 .04
70 Barry Larkin .50 .20
71 Pete Rose 1.00 .40
72 Luis Salazar .10 .04
73 Benito Santiago .15 .06
74 Kal Daniels .10 .04
75 Kevin Elster .10 .04
76 Rob Dibble .15 .06
77 Bobby Witt .10 .04
78 Steve Searcy .10 .04
79 Sandy Alomar Jr. .25 .10
80 Chili Davis .15 .06
81 Alvin Davis .10 .04
82 Charlie Leibrandt .10 .04
83 Robin Yount .50 .20
84 Mark Carreon .10 .04
85 Pascual Perez .10 .04
86 Dennis Rasmussen .10 .04
87 Ernie Riles .10 .04
88 Melido Perez .10 .04
89 Doug Jones .10 .04
90 Dennis Eckersley .50 .20
91 Bob Welch .10 .04
92 Bob Milacki .10 .04
93 Jeff Robinson .10 .04
94 Mike Henneman .10 .04
95 Randy Johnson 5.00 2.00
96 Ron Jones .10 .04
97 Jack Armstrong .10 .04
98 Willie McGee .15 .06
99 Ryne Sandberg 1.00 .40
100 David Cone .10 .04
Danny Jackson

1989 Classic Travel Orange

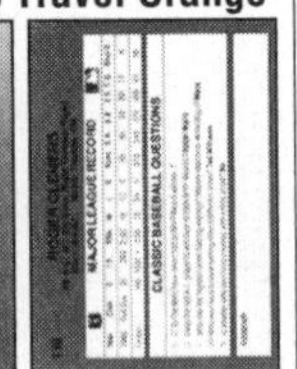

The 1989 Classic Travel Orange set contains 50 standard-size cards. The fronts of the cards have orange borders. The backs feature 1988 and lifetime stats. This subset of cards were distributed as a set in blister packs as "Travel Update I" subsets. Reportedly there were 150,000 sets produced. A first year card of Ken Griffey Jr. highlights this set.

Nm-Mt Ex-Mt
COMP.FACT.SET (50) 15.00 6.00
101 Gary Sheffield 1.50 .60
102 Wade Boggs .15 .06
103 Jose Canseco .25 .10
104 Mark McGwire 1.00 .40
105 Orel Hershiser .10 .04
106 Don Mattingly .60 .24
107 Dwight Gooden .15 .06
108 Darryl Strawberry .15 .06
109 Eric Davis .10 .04
110 H.Meulens UER .05 .02
Listed on card as
Bam Bam Muelens
111 Andy Van Slyke .10 .04
112 Al Leiter .10 .04
113 Matt Nokes .05 .02
114 Mike Krukow .05 .02
115 Tony Fernandez .05 .02
116 Fred McGriff .25 .10
117 Barry Bonds 1.25 .50
118 Gerald Perry .05 .02
119 Roger Clemens .50 .20
120 Kirk Gibson .10 .04
121 Greg Maddux .50 .20
122 Bo Jackson .25 .10
123 Danny Jackson .05 .02
124 Dale Murphy .25 .10
125 David Cone .10 .04
126 Tom Browning .05 .02
127 Roberto Alomar .25 .10
128 Alan Trammell .15 .06
129 Ricky Jordan UER .05 .02
(Misspelled Jordon
on card back)
130 Ramon Martinez .25 .10
131 Ken Griffey Jr. 8.00 3.20
132 Gregg Olson .25 .10
133 Carlos Quintana .05 .02
134 Dave West .05 .02
135 Cameron Drew .05 .02
136 Teddy Higuera .05 .02
137 Sil Campusano .05 .02
138 Mark Gubicza .05 .02
139 Mike Boddicker .05 .02
140 Paul Gibson .05 .02
141 Jose Rijo .05 .02
142 John Costello .05 .02
143 Cecil Espy .05 .02
144 Frank Viola .05 .02
145 Erik Hanson .05 .02
146 Juan Samuel .05 .02
147 Harold Reynolds .10 .04
148 Joe Magrane .05 .02
149 Mike Greenwell .05 .02
150 Darryl Strawberry .10 .04
and Will Clark

1989 Classic Travel Purple

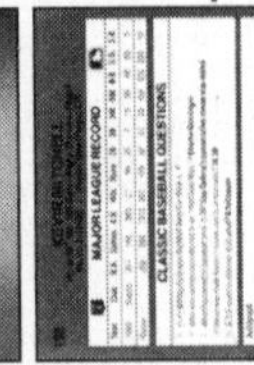

The 1989 Classic "Travel Update II" set contains 50 standard-size cards. The fronts have purple (and gray) borders. The set features "two sport" cards of Bo Jackson and Deion Sanders. In addition, a first year card of Ken Griffey Jr highlights this set. The cards were distributed as a set in blister packs.

Nm-Mt Ex-Mt
COMP.FACT.SET (50) 12.00 4.80
151 Jim Abbott .40 .16
152 Ellis Burks .15 .06
153 Mike Schmidt .50 .20
154 Gregg Jefferies .10 .04
155 Mark Grace .25 .10
156 Jerome Walton .15 .06
157 Bo Jackson .25 .10
158 Jack Clark .05 .02
159 Tom Glavine .25 .10
160 Eddie Murray .25 .10
161 John Dopson .05 .02
162 Ruben Sierra .05 .02
163 Rafael Palmeiro .25 .10
164 Nolan Ryan 1.00 .40
165 Barry Larkin .25 .10
166 Tommy Herr .05 .02
167 Roberto Kelly .10 .04
168 Glenn Davis .05 .02
169 Glenn Braggs .05 .02
170 Juan Bell .05 .02
171 Todd Burns .05 .02
172 Derek Lilliquist .05 .02
173 Orel Hershiser .10 .04
174 John Smoltz .75 .30
175 Ozzie Guillen and .05 .02
Ellis Burks
176 Kirby Puckett .25 .10
177 Robin Ventura .75 .30
178 Allan Anderson .05 .02
179 Steve Sax .05 .02
180 Will Clark .25 .10
181 Mike Devereaux .05 .02
182 Tom Gordon .25 .10
183 Rob Murphy .05 .02
184 Pete O'Brien .05 .02
185 Cris Carpenter .05 .02
186 Tom Brunansky .05 .02
187 Bob Boone .10 .04
188 Lou Whitaker .10 .04
189 Dwight Gooden .15 .06
190 Mark McGwire 1.00 .40
191 John Smiley .05 .02
192 Tommy Gregg .05 .02
193 Ken Griffey Jr. 8.00 3.20
194 Bruce Hurst .05 .02
195 Greg Swindell .05 .02
196 Nelson Liriano .05 .02
197 Randy Myers .10 .04
198 Kevin Mitchell .10 .04
199 Dante Bichette .25 .10
200 Deion Sanders .75 .30

1990 Classic Blue

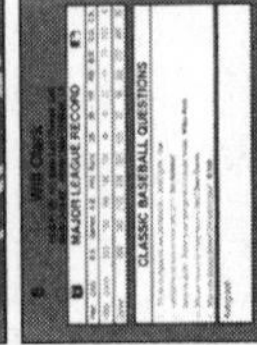

The 1990 Classic Blue (Game) set contains 150 standard-size cards, the largest Classic set to date in terms of player selection. The front borders are blue with magenta splotches. The backs feature 1989 and career total stats. The cards were distributed as a set in blister packs

According to distributors of the set, reportedly there were 200,000 sets produced. Reportedly the Sanders "correction" was made at Sanders own request; less than 10 percent of the sets contain the first version and hence it has the higher value in the checklist below. The complete set price below does not include any of the more difficult variation cards. Early cards of Sammy Sosa and Bernie Williams highlight the set.

	Nm-Mt	Ex-Mt
COMP. FACT SET (150)	10.00	3.00
1 Nolan Ryan	1.00	.30
2 Bo Jackson	.25	.07
3 Gregg Olson	.05	.02
4 Tom Gordon	.05	.02
5 Robin Ventura	.25	.07
6 Will Clark	.25	.07
7 Ruben Sierra	.05	.02
8 Mark Grace	.15	.04
9 Luis DeLosSantos	.05	.02
10 Bernie Williams	1.00	.30
11 Eric Davis	.10	.03
12 Carney Lansford	.10	.03
13 John Smoltz	.25	.07
14 Gary Sheffield	.25	.07
15 Kent Mercker	.10	.03
16 Don Mattingly	.60	.18
17 Tony Gwynn	.30	.09
18 Ozzie Smith	.40	.12
19 Fred McGriff	.15	.04
20 Ken Griffey Jr.	.75	.23
21A Deion Sanders	3.00	.90
Identified only as Prime Time on front		
21B Deion Sanders	.25	.07
Identified as Deion Prime Time Sanders on front of card		
22 Jose Canseco	.25	.07
23 Mitch Williams	.05	.02
24 Cal Ripken UER	.75	.23
Misspelled Ripkin on back		
25 Bob Geren	.05	.02
26 Wade Boggs	.15	.04
27 Ryne Sandberg	.50	.15
28 Kirby Puckett	.25	.07
29 Mike Scott	.10	.03
30 Dwight Smith	.05	.02
31 Craig Worthington	.05	.02
32A Ricky Jordan ERR	.05	.02
Misspelled Jordon on back		
32B Ricky Jordan COR	.05	.02
33 Darryl Strawberry	.15	.04
34 Jerome Walton	.05	.02
35 John Olerud	.50	.15
36 Tom Glavine	.15	.04
37 Rickey Henderson	.25	.07
38 Rolando Roomes	.05	.02
39 Mickey Tettleton	.10	.03
40 Jim Abbott	.15	.04
41 Dave Righetti	.10	.03
42 Mike LaValliere	.05	.02
43 Rob Dibble	.10	.03
44 Pete Harnisch	.05	.02
45 Jose Offerman	.10	.03
46 Walt Weiss	.05	.02
47 Mike Greenwell	.05	.02
48 Barry Larkin	.25	.07
49 Dave Gallagher	.05	.02
50 Junior Felix	.05	.02
51 Roger Clemens	.50	.15
52 Lonnie Smith	.10	.03
53 Jerry Browne	.05	.02
54 Greg Briley	.05	.02
55 Delino DeShields	.10	.03
56 Carmelo Martinez	.05	.02
57 Craig Biggio	.15	.04
58 Dwight Gooden	.15	.04
59 A.L. Fence Busters	1.00	.30
Bo Jackson Ruben Sierra Mark McGwire		
59B Bo/Rubin/Mark	5.00	1.50
Bo Jackson Ruben Sierra Mark McGwire		
60 Greg Vaughn	.10	.03
61 Roberto Alomar	.25	.07
62 Steve Bedrosian	.05	.02
63 Devon White	.05	.02
64 Kevin Mitchell	.05	.02
65 Marquis Grissom	.25	.07
66 Brian Holman	.05	.02
67 Julio Franco	.05	.02
68 Dave West	.05	.02
69 Harold Baines	.10	.03
70 Eric Anthony	.05	.02
71 Glenn Davis	.05	.02
72 Mark Langston	.05	.02
73 Matt Williams	.10	.03
74 Rafael Palmeiro	.25	.07
75 Pete Rose Jr.	.10	.03
76 Ramon Martinez	.05	.02
77 Dwight Evans	.10	.03
78 Mackey Sasser	.05	.02
79 Mike Schooler	.05	.02
80 Dennis Cook	.05	.02
81 Orel Hershiser	.10	.03
82 Barry Bonds	.60	.18
83 Geronimo Berroa	.05	.02
84 George Bell	.10	.03
85 Andre Dawson	.10	.03
86 John Franco	.10	.03
87A Clark/Gwynn	3.00	.90
Will Clark Tony Gwynn		
87B N.L. Hit Kings	.15	.04
Will Clark Tony Gwynn		
88 Glenallen Hill	.05	.02
89 Jeff Ballard	.05	.02
90 Todd Zeile	.10	.03
91 Frank Viola	.10	.03
92 Ozzie Guillen	.05	.02
93 Jeffrey Leonard	.05	.02
94 Dave Smith	.05	.02
95 Dave Parker	.10	.03
96 Jose Gonzalez	.05	.02
97 Dave Stieb	.10	.03
98 Charlie Hayes	.05	.02
99 Jesse Barfield	.10	.03
100 Joey Belle	.10	.03
101 Jeff Reardon	.10	.03
102 Bruce Hurst	.10	.03
103 Luis Medina	.05	.02
104 Mike Moore	.05	.02
105 Vince Coleman	.05	.02
106 Alan Trammell	.15	.04
107 Randy Myers	.05	.02
108 Frank Tanana	.10	.03
109 Craig Lefferts	.05	.02
110 John Wetteland	.10	.03
111 Chris Gwynn	.05	.02
112 Mark Carreon	.05	.02
113 Von Hayes	.10	.03
114 Doug Jones	.05	.02
115 Andres Galarraga	.10	.03
116 Carlton Fisk UER	.15	.04
Bellows Falls misspelled as Bellow Falls on back		
117 Paul O'Neill	.15	.04
118 Tim Raines	.10	.03
119 Tom Brunansky	.05	.02
120 Andy Benes	.10	.03
121 Mark Portugal	.05	.02
122 Willie Randolph	.10	.03
123 Jeff Blauser	.05	.02
124 Don August	.05	.02
125 Chuck Cary	.05	.02
126 John Smiley	.05	.02
127 Terry Mulholland	.05	.02
128 Harold Reynolds	.10	.03
129 Hubie Brooks	.10	.03
130 Ben McDonald	.10	.03
131 Kevin Ritz	.05	.02
132 Luis Quinones	.05	.02
133A H. Meulens ERR	.05	.02
Misspelled Muelens on front		
133B H. Meulens COR	.05	.02
134 Bill Spiers UER	.05	.02
Orangeburg misspelled as Orangburg on back		
135 Andy Hawkins	.05	.02
136 Alvin Davis	.10	.03
137 Lee Smith	.10	.03
138 Joe Carter	.10	.03
139 Bret Saberhagen	.10	.03
140 Sammy Sosa	8.00	2.40
141 Matt Nokes	.05	.02
142 Bert Blyleven	.10	.03
143 Bobby Bonilla	.10	.03
144 Howard Johnson	.10	.03
145 Joe Magrane	.05	.02
146 Pedro Guerrero	.10	.03
147 Robin Yount	.40	.12
148 Dan Gladden	.05	.02
149 Steve Sax	.10	.03
150A Clark/Mitchell	2.00	.60
Will Clark Kevin Mitchell		
150B Bay Bombers	.25	.07
Will Clark Kevin Mitchell		

1990 Classic Update

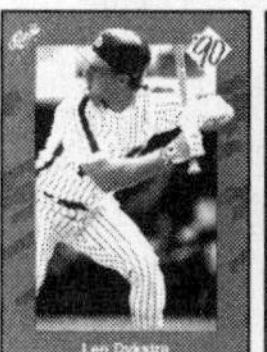
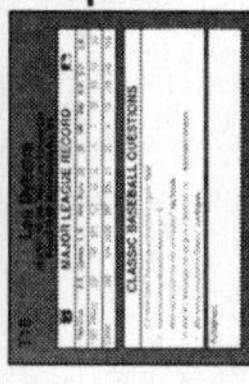

The 1990 Classic Update set was the second set issued by the Classic Game company in 1990. Sometimes referenced as Classic Pink or Red, this set includes a Juan Gonzalez card. This 50-card, standard-size set was issued in late June of 1990. With a few exceptions, the set numbering is in alphabetical order by player's name. Early cards of Juan Gonzalez and Larry Walker highlight this set.

	Nm-Mt	Ex-Mt
COMP. FACT. SET (50)	6.00	1.80
T1 Gregg Jefferies	.05	.02
T2 Steve Adkins	.05	.02
T3 Sandy Alomar Jr.	.10	.03
T4 Steve Avery	.05	.02
T5 Mike Blowers	.05	.02
T6 George Brett	.75	.23
T7 Tom Browning	.05	.02
T8 Ellis Burks	.10	.03
T9 Joe Carter	.10	.03
T10 Jerald Clark	.05	.02
T11 Matt Williams	.75	.23
Will Clark		
T12 Pat Combs	.05	.02
T13 Scott Cooper	.05	.02
T14 Mark Davis	.05	.02
T15 Storm Davis	.05	.02
T16 Larry Walker	1.25	.35
T17 Brian DuBois	.05	.02
T18 Len Dykstra	.10	.03
T19 John Franco	.10	.03
T20 Kirk Gibson	.10	.03
T21 Juan Gonzalez	1.50	.45
T22 Tommy Greene	.05	.02
T23 Kent Hrbek	.10	.03
T24 Mike Huff	.05	.02
T25 Bo Jackson	.20	.06
T26 Nolan Ryan	2.00	.60
Nolan Knows Bo		
T27 Roberto Kelly	.05	.02
T28 Mark Langston	.05	.02
T29 Ray Lankford	.50	.15
T30 Kevin Maas	.05	.02
T31 Julio Machado	.05	.02
T32 Greg Maddux	1.25	.35
T33 Mark McGwire	1.50	.45
T34 Paul Molitor	.20	.06
T35 Hal Morris	.05	.02
T36 Dale Murphy	.20	.06
T37 Eddie Murray	.20	.06
T38 Jaime Navarro	.05	.02
T39 Dean Palmer	.50	.15
T40 Derek Parks	.05	.02
T41 Bobby Rose	.05	.02
T42 Wally Joyner	.05	.02
T43 Chris Sabo	.05	.02
T44 Benito Santiago	.10	.03
T45 Mike Stanton	.05	.02
T46 Terry Steinbach UER	.05	.02
Career BA .725		
T47 Dave Stewart	.10	.03
T48 Greg Swindell	.05	.02
T49 Jose Vizcaino	.10	.03
NNO Mark Davis	.05	.02
Bret Saberhagen (Instructions on back)		

1990 Classic Yellow

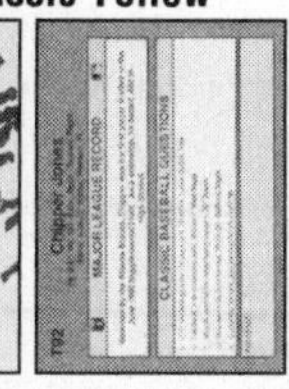

The 1990 Classic III set is also referenced as Classic Yellow. This set also featured number one draft picks of the current year mixed with the other Classic cards. This 100-card standard-size set also contained a special Nolan Ryan commemorative card, Texas Heat. A very early card of Chipper Jones is included in this set. Card T51 was never issued.

	Nm-Mt	Ex-Mt
COMP.FACT.SET (100)	10.00	3.00
T1 Ken Griffey Jr.	.75	.23
T2 John Tudor	.05	.02
T3 John Kruk	.10	.03
T4 Mark Gardner	.05	.02
T5 Scott Radinsky	.05	.02
T6 John Burkett	.05	.02
T7 Will Clark	.25	.07
T8 Gary Carter	.60	.18
T9 Ted Higuera	.05	.02
T10 Dave Parker	.10	.03
T11 Dante Bichette	.25	.07
T12 Don Mattingly	.60	.18
T13 Greg Harris	.05	.02
T14 Dave Hollins	.10	.03
T15 Matt Nokes	.05	.02
T16 Kevin Tapani	.25	.07
T17 Shane Mack	.05	.02
T18 Randy Myers	.10	.03
T19 Greg Olson	.05	.02
T20 Shawn Abner	.05	.02
T21 Jim Presley	.05	.02
T22 Randy Johnson	.40	.12
T23 Edgar Martinez	.15	.04
T24 Scott Coolbaugh	.05	.02
T25 Jeff Treadway	.05	.02
T26 Joe Klink	.05	.02
T27 Rickey Henderson	.25	.07
T28 Sam Horn	.05	.02
T29 Kurt Stillwell	.05	.02
T30 Andy Van Slyke	.10	.03
T31 Willie Banks	.05	.02
T32 Jose Canseco	.25	.07
T33 Felix Jose	.05	.02
T34 Candy Maldonado	.05	.02
T35 Carlos Baerga	.10	.03
T36 Keith Hernandez	.15	.04
T37 Frank Viola	.05	.02
T38 Pete O'Brien	.05	.02
T39 Pat Borders	.05	.02
T40 Mike Heath	.05	.02
T41 Kevin Brown	.10	.03
T42 Chris Bosio	.05	.02
T43 Shawn Boskie	.05	.02
T44 Carlos Quintana	.05	.02
T45 Juan Samuel	.05	.02
T46 Tim Layana	.05	.02
T47 Mike Harkey	.05	.02
T48 Gerald Perry	.05	.02
T49 Mike Witt	.05	.02
T50 Joe Orsulak	.05	.02
T51 Not Issued		
T52 Willie Blair	.05	.02
T53 Gene Larkin	.05	.02
T54 Jody Reed	.05	.02
T55 Jeff Reardon	.10	.03
T56 Kevin McReynolds	.05	.02
T57 Mike Marshall	.05	.02
Unnumbered game instructions on back		
T58 Eric Yelding	.05	.02
T59 Fred Lynn	.05	.02
T60 Jim Leyritz	.25	.07
T61 John Orton	.05	.02
T62 Mike Lieberthal	.40	.12
T63 Mike Hartley	.05	.02
T64 Kal Daniels	.05	.02
T65 Terry Shumpert	.05	.02
T66 Sil Campusano	.05	.02
T67 Tony Pena	.05	.02
T68 Barry Bonds	.60	.18
T69 Roger McDowell	.05	.02
T70 Kelly Gruber	.05	.02
T71 Willie Randolph	.10	.03
T72 Rick Parker	.05	.02
T73 Bobby Bonilla	.10	.03
T74 Jack Armstrong	.05	.02
T75 Hubie Brooks	.05	.02
T76 Sandy Alomar Jr.	.10	.03
T77 Ruben Sierra	.05	.02
T78 Erik Hanson	.05	.02
T79 Tony Phillips	.05	.02
T80 Rondell White	.40	.12
T81 Bobby Thigpen	.05	.02
T82 Ron Walden	.10	.03
T83 Don Peters	.10	.03
T84 Nolan Ryan 6TH	1.00	.30
T85 Lance Dickson	.10	.03
T86 Ryne Sandberg	.40	.12
T87 Eric Christopherson	.10	.03
T88 Shane Andrews	.10	.03
T89 Marc Newfield	.10	.03
T90 Adam Hyzdu	.10	.03
T91 Nolan Ryan	.50	.15
Reid Ryan		
T92 Chipper Jones	3.00	.90
T93 Frank Thomas	1.25	.35
T94 Cecil Fielder	.10	.03
T95 Delino DeShields	.25	.07
T96 John Olerud	.50	.15
T97 David Justice	.50	.15
T98 Joe Oliver	.05	.02
T99 Alex Fernandez	.25	.07
T100 Todd Hundley	.25	.07
NNO Micro Players	1.00	.30
Frank Viola Texas Heat Don Mattingly Chipper Jones (Blue blank back)		

1991 Classic Game

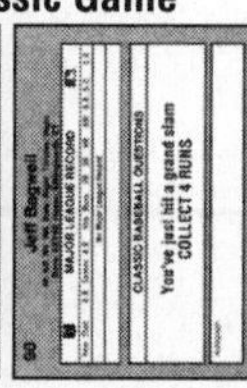

The 1991 Classic Baseball Collector's Edition board game is Classic's first Big Game issue since the 1989 Big Game. 100,000 games were produced, and each one included a board game, action spinner, eight stand-up baseball player pieces, action scoreboard, eight-page picture book with tips from five great baseball players (Carew, Spahn, Schmidt, Brock, and Aaron), 200 player cards, and a certificate of limited edition. The standard-size cards have on the fronts glossy color action photos bordered in purple. The backs are purple and white and have biography, statistics, five trivia questions, and an autograph slot.

	Nm-Mt	Ex-Mt
COMP. FACT SET (200)	20.00	6.00
1 Frank Viola	.05	.02
2 Tim Wallach	.05	.02
3 Lou Whitaker	.10	.03
4 Brett Butler	.10	.03
5 Jim Abbott	.10	.03
6 Jack Armstrong	.05	.02
7 Craig Biggio	.25	.07
8 Brian Barnes	.05	.02
9 Dennis(Oil Can) Boyd	.05	.02
10 Tom Browning	.05	.02
11 Tom Brunansky	.05	.02
12 Ellis Burks	.10	.03
13 Harold Baines	.15	.04
14 Kal Daniels	.05	.02
15 Mark Davis	.05	.02
16 Storm Davis	.05	.02
17 Tom Glavine	.50	.15
18 Mike Greenwell	.05	.02
19 Kelly Gruber	.05	.02
20 Mark Gubicza	.05	.02
21 Pedro Guerrero	.05	.02
22 Mike Harkey	.05	.02
23 Orel Hershiser	.10	.03
24 Ted Higuera	.05	.02
25 Von Hayes	.05	.02
26 Andre Dawson	.25	.07
27 Shawon Dunston	.05	.02
28 Roberto Kelly	.05	.02
29 Joe Magrane	.05	.02
30 Dennis Martinez	.10	.03
31 Kevin McReynolds	.05	.02
32 Matt Nokes	.05	.02
33 Dan Plesac	.05	.02
34 Dave Parker	.10	.03
35 Randy Johnson	.75	.23
36 Bret Saberhagen	.10	.03
37 Mackey Sasser	.05	.02
38 Mike Scott	.05	.02
39 Ozzie Smith	1.00	.30
40 Kevin Seitzer	.05	.02
41 Ruben Sierra	.10	.03
42 Kevin Tapani	.05	.02
43 Danny Tartabull	.05	.02
44 Robby Thompson	.05	.02
45 Andy Van Slyke	.05	.02
46 Greg Vaughn	.10	.03
47 Harold Reynolds	.15	.04
48 Will Clark	.25	.07
49 Gary Gaetti	.10	.03
50 Joe Grahe	.05	.02
51 Carlton Fisk	.50	.15
52 Robin Ventura	.25	.07
53 Ozzie Guillen	.10	.03
54 Tom Candiotti	.05	.02
55 Doug Jones	.05	.02
56 Eric King	.05	.02
57 Kirk Gibson	.10	.03
58 Tim Costo	.05	.02
59 Robin Yount	.50	.15
60 Sammy Sosa	2.00	.60
61 Jesse Barfield	.05	.02
62 Marc Newfield	.05	.02
63 Jimmy Key	.10	.03
64 Felix Jose	.05	.02
65 Mark Whiten	.05	.02
66 Tommy Greene	.05	.02
67 Kent Mercker	.05	.02
68 Greg Maddux	1.50	.45
69 Danny Jackson	.05	.02
70 Reggie Sanders	.10	.03
71 Eric Yelding	.05	.02
72 Karl Rhodes	.05	.02
73 Fernando Valenzuela	.10	.03
74 Chris Nabholz	.05	.02
75 Andres Galarraga	.25	.07
76 Howard Johnson	.05	.02
77 Hubie Brooks	.05	.02
78 Terry Mulholland	.05	.02
79 Paul Molitor	.50	.15
80 Roger McDowell	.05	.02
81 Darren Daulton	.10	.03
82 Zane Smith	.05	.02
83 Ray Lankford	.10	.03
84 Bruce Hurst	.05	.02
85 Andy Benes	.05	.02
86 John Burkett	.05	.02
87 Dave Righetti	.05	.02
88 Steve Karsay	.25	.07
89 D.J. Dozier	.05	.02
90 Jeff Bagwell	2.00	.60
91 Joe Carter	.10	.03
92 Wes Chamberlain	.05	.02
93 Vince Coleman	.05	.02
94 Pat Combs	.05	.02
95 Jerome Walton	.05	.02
96 Jeff Conine	.05	.02
97 Alan Trammell	.15	.04
98 Don Mattingly	1.00	.30
99 Ramon Martinez	.05	.02
100 Dave Magadan	.05	.02
101 Greg Swindell UER	.05	.02
Misnumbered as T10		
102 Dave Stewart	.10	.03
103 Gary Sheffield	.25	.07
104 George Bell	.05	.02
105 Mark Grace	.50	.15
106 Steve Sax	.05	.02
107 Ryne Sandberg	.75	.23
108 Chris Sabo	.05	.02
109 Jose Rijo	.05	.02
110 Cal Ripken	2.50	.75
111 Kirby Puckett	.50	.15
112 Eddie Murray	.50	.15
113 Roberto Alomar	.25	.07
114 Randy Myers	.05	.02
115 Rafael Palmeiro	.25	.07
116 John Olerud	.15	.04
117 Gregg Jefferies	.05	.02
118 Kent Hrbek	.10	.03
119 Marquis Grissom	.10	.03
120 Ken Griffey Jr.	2.00	.60
121 Dwight Gooden	.10	.03
122 Juan Gonzalez	.75	.23
123 Ron Gant	.10	.03
124 Travis Fryman	.25	.07
125 John Franco	.10	.03
126 Dennis Eckersley	.10	.03
127 Cecil Fielder	.10	.03
128 Phil Plantier	.05	.02
129 Kevin Mitchell	.05	.02
130 Kevin Maas	.05	.02
131 Mark McGwire	1.50	.45
132 Ben McDonald	.05	.02
133 Len Dykstra	.10	.03
134 Delino DeShields	.10	.03
135 Jose Canseco	.50	.15
136 Eric Davis	.10	.03
137 George Brett	1.25	.35
138 Steve Avery	.05	.02
139 Eric Anthony	.05	.02
140 Bobby Thigpen	.05	.02
141 Ken Griffey Sr.	.10	.03
142 Barry Larkin	.25	.07
143 Jeff Brantley	.05	.02
144 Bobby Bonilla	.05	.02
145 Jose Offerman	.05	.02
146 Mike Mussina	1.50	.45
147 Erik Hanson	.05	.02
148 Dale Murphy	.40	.12
149 Roger Clemens	1.00	.30
150 Tino Martinez	.25	.07
151 Todd Van Poppel	.25	.07
152 Mo Vaughn	.50	.15
153 Derrick May	.05	.02
154 Jack Clark	.10	.03
155 Dave Hansen	.05	.02
156 Tony Gwynn	1.25	.35
157 Brian McRae	.10	.03
158 Matt Williams	.15	.04
159 Kirk Dressendorfer	.05	.02
160 Scott Erickson	.10	.03
161 Tony Fernandez	.05	.02
162 Willie McGee	.10	.03
163 Fred McGriff	.25	.07
164 Leo Gomez	.05	.02
165 Bernard Gilkey	.05	.02
166 Bobby Witt	.05	.02
167 Doug Drabek	.05	.02
168 Rob Dibble	.05	.02
169 Glenn Davis	.05	.02
170 Danny Darwin	.05	.02
171 Eric Karros	.50	.15
172 Eddie Zosky	.05	.02
173 Todd Zeile	.10	.03
174 Tim Raines	.10	.03
175 Benito Santiago	.10	.03
176 Dan Peltier	.05	.02
177 Darryl Strawberry	.10	.03
178 Hal Morris	.05	.02
179 Hensley Meulens	.05	.02
180 John Smoltz	.25	.07
181 Frank Thomas	1.00	.30
182 Dave Staton	.05	.02
183 Scott Chiamparino	.05	.02
184 Alex Fernandez	.05	.02
185 Mark Lewis	.05	.02
186 Bo Jackson	.25	.07
187 Mickey Morandini UER	.05	.02
Photo is Darren Daulton		
188 Cory Snyder	.05	.02
189 Rickey Henderson	.50	.15
190 Junior Felix	.05	.02
191 Milt Cuyler	.05	.02
192 Wade Boggs	.40	.12
193 Dave Justice	.50	.15
Justice Prevails		
194 Sandy Alomar Jr.	.10	.03
195 Barry Bonds	1.50	.45
196 Nolan Ryan	2.50	.75
197 Rico Brogna	.05	.02
198 Steve Decker	.05	.02
199 Bob Welch	.05	.02
200 Andujar Cedeno	.05	.02

1991 Classic I

This 100-card standard-size set features many of the most popular players in the game of baseball as well as some of the more exciting prospects. The set includes trivia questions on

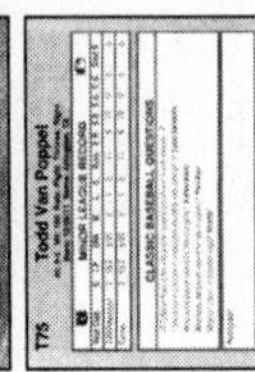

the backs of the cards. For the most part the set is arranged alphabetically by team and then alphabetically by players within that team.

Nm-Mt Ex-Mt
COMP.FACT SET (100) 8.00 2.40
T1 John Olerud .15 .04
T2 Tino Martinez .25 .07
T3 Ken Griffey Jr. 2.00 .60
T4 Jeromy Burnitz .50 .15
T5 Ron Gant .10 .03
T6 Mike Benjamin .05 .02
T7 Steve Decker .05 .02
T8 Matt Williams .15 .04
T9 Rafael Novoa .05 .02
T10 Kevin Mitchell .05 .02
T11 Dave Justice .25 .07
T12 Leo Gomez .05 .02
T13 Chris Hoiles .05 .02
T14 Ben McDonald .05 .02
T15 David Segui .10 .03
T16 Anthony Telford .05 .02
T17 Mike Mussina 1.50 .45
T18 Roger Clemens 1.25 .35
T19 Wade Boggs .50 .15
T20 Tim Naehring .05 .02
T21 Joe Carter .10 .03
T22 Phil Plantier .05 .02
T23 Rob Dibble .05 .02
T24 Mo Vaughn .40 .12
T25 Lee Stevens .05 .02
T26 Chris Sabo .05 .02
T27 Mark Grace .25 .07
T28 Derrick May .05 .02
T29 Ryne Sandberg .50 .15
T30 Matt Stark .05 .02
T31 Bobby Thigpen .05 .02
T32 Frank Thomas .75 .23
T33 Don Mattingly 1.25 .35
T34 Eric Davis .10 .03
T35 Reggie Jefferson .05 .02
T36 Alex Cole .05 .02
T37 Mark Lewis .05 .02
T38 Tim Costo .05 .02
T39 Sandy Alomar Jr. .10 .03
T40 Travis Fryman .25 .07
T41 Cecil Fielder .10 .03
T42 Milt Cuyler .05 .02
T43 Andujar Cedeno .05 .02
T44 Danny Darwin .05 .02
T45 Randy Hennis .05 .02
T46 George Brett 1.00 .30
T47 Jeff Conine .15 .04
T48 Bo Jackson .25 .07
T49 Brian McRae .10 .03
T50 Brent Mayne .05 .02
T51 Eddie Murray .40 .12
T52 Ramon Martinez .05 .02
T53 Jim Neidlinger .05 .02
T54 Jim Poole .05 .02
T55 Tim McIntosh .05 .02
T56 Randy Veres .05 .02
T57 Kirby Puckett .40 .12
T58 Todd Ritchie .15 .04
T59 Rich Garces .05 .02
T60 Moises Alou .25 .07
T61 Delino DeShields .10 .03
T62 Oscar Azocar .05 .02
T63 Kevin Maas .05 .02
T64 Alan Mills .05 .02
T65 John Franco .10 .03
T66 Chris Jelic .05 .02
T67 Dave Magadan .05 .02
T68 Darryl Strawberry .10 .03
T69 Hensley Meulens .05 .02
T70 Juan Gonzalez .75 .23
T71 Reggie Harris .05 .02
T72 Rickey Henderson .50 .15
T73 Mark McGwire 2.00 .60
T74 Willie McGee .10 .03
T75 Todd Van Poppel .05 .02
T76 Bob Welch .05 .02
T77 Todd Van Poppel .05 .02
Don Peters
David Zancanaro
Kirk Dressendorfer
T78 Len Dykstra .10 .03
T79 Mickey Morandini .05 .02
T80 Wes Chamberlain .05 .02
T81 Barry Bonds 1.25 .35
T82 Doug Drabek .05 .02
T83 Randy Tomlin .05 .02
T84 Scott Chiamparino .05 .02
T85 Rafael Palmeiro .25 .07
T86 Nolan Ryan 2.50 .75
T87 Bobby Witt .05 .02
T88 Fred McGriff .25 .07
T89 Dave Stieb .10 .03
T90 Ed Sprague .10 .03
T91 Vince Coleman .05 .02
T92 Rod Brewer .05 .02
T93 Bernard Gilkey .05 .02
T94 Roberto Alomar .25 .07
T95 Chuck Finley .10 .03
T96 Dale Murphy .25 .07
T97 Jose Rijo .05 .02
T98 Hal Morris .05 .02
T99 Friendly Foes .10 .03
Darryl Strawberry
Dwight Gooden
Instructions on back
NNO Todd Van Poppel .10 .03
Dave Justice
Ryne Sandberg
Kevin Maas

1991 Classic II

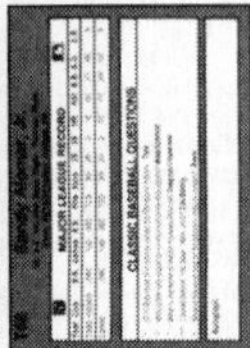
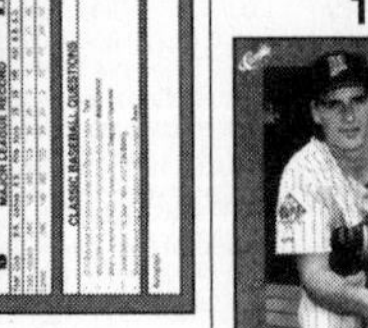

This second issue of the 1991 Classic baseball trivia game contains a small gameboard, accessories, 99 standard-size player cards with trivia questions on the backs, and one "4-in-1" micro player card. The fronts have glossy color action photos with cranberry red borders. The backs have biography, statistics, five trivia questions, and an autograph slot. A first year card of Ivan Rodriguez is featured within this set.

Nm-Mt Ex-Mt
COMP. FACT. SET (100) 8.00 2.40
T1 Ken Griffey Jr. 2.50 .75
T2 Wil Cordero .05 .02
T3 Cal Ripken 3.00 .90
T4 D.J. Dozier .05 .02
T5 Darrin Fletcher .05 .02
T6 Glenn Davis .05 .02
T7 Alex Fernandez .05 .02
T8 Cory Snyder .05 .02
T9 Tim Raines .10 .03
T10 Greg Swindell .05 .02
T11 Mark Lewis .05 .02
T12 Rico Brogna .05 .02
T13 Gary Sheffield .40 .12
T14 Paul Molitor .50 .15
T15 Kent Hrbek .10 .03
T16 Scott Erickson .10 .03
T17 Steve Sax .05 .02
T18 Dennis Eckersley .50 .15
T19 Jose Canseco .40 .12
T20 Kirk Dressendorfer .05 .02
T21 Ken Griffey Sr. .10 .03
T22 Erik Hanson .05 .02
T23 Dan Peltier .05 .02
T24 John Olerud .15 .04
T25 Eddie Zosky .05 .02
T26 Steve Avery .05 .02
T27 John Smoltz .25 .07
T28 Frank Thomas .60 .18
T29 Jerome Walton .05 .02
T30 George Bell .05 .02
T31 Jose Rijo .05 .02
T32 Randy Myers .10 .03
T33 Barry Larkin .25 .07
T34 Eric Anthony .05 .02
T35 Dave Hansen .05 .02
T36 Eric Karros .40 .12
T37 Jose Offerman .05 .02
T38 Marquis Grissom .10 .03
T39 Dwight Gooden .10 .03
T40 Gregg Jefferies .05 .02
T41 Pat Combs .05 .02
T42 Todd Zeile .10 .03
T43 Benito Santiago .10 .03
T44 Dave Staton .05 .02
T45 Tony Fernandez .10 .03
T46 Fred McGriff .15 .04
T47 Jeff Brantley .05 .02
T48 Junior Felix .05 .02
T49 Jack Morris .10 .03
T50 Chris George .05 .02
T51 Henry Rodriguez .10 .03
T52 Paul Marak .05 .02
T53 Ryan Klesko .75 .23
T54 Darren Lewis .05 .02
T55 Lance Dickson .05 .02
T56 Anthony Young .05 .02
T57 Willie Banks .05 .02
T58 Mike Bordick .15 .04
T59 Roger Salkeld .05 .02
T60 Steve Karsay .15 .04
T61 Bernie Williams .25 .07
T62 Mickey Tettleton .10 .03
T63 Dave Justice .25 .07
T64 Steve Decker .05 .02
T65 Roger Clemens 1.25 .35
T66 Phil Plantier .05 .02
T67 Ryne Sandberg .50 .15
T68 Sandy Alomar Jr. .10 .03
T69 Cecil Fielder .10 .03
T70 George Brett 1.25 .35
T71 Delino DeShields .10 .03
T72 Dave Magadan .05 .02
T73 Darryl Strawberry .10 .03
T74 Juan Gonzalez .75 .23
T75 Rickey Henderson .60 .18
T76 Willie McGee .10 .03
T77 Todd Van Poppel .05 .02
T78 Barry Bonds 1.50 .45
T79 Doug Drabek .05 .02
T80 Nolan Ryan 1.25 .35
300 Game Winner
T81 Roberto Alomar .25 .07
T82 Ivan Rodriguez 2.50 .75
T83 Dan Opperman .05 .02
T84 Jeff Bagwell 2.00 .60
T85 Braulio Castillo .05 .02
T86 Doug Simons .05 .02
T87 Wade Taylor .05 .02
T88 Gary Scott .05 .02
T89 Dave Stewart .10 .03
T90 Mike Simms .05 .02
T91 Luis Gonzalez 1.00 .30
T92 Bobby Bonilla .10 .03
T93 Tony Gwynn 1.00 .30
T94 Will Clark .40 .12
T95 Rich Rowland .05 .02
T96 Alan Trammell .15 .04
T97 Nolan Ryan .75 .23
Roger Clemens
T98 Joe Carter .10 .03
T99 Jack Clark .10 .03
T100 Steve Decker .05 .02
NNO John Olerud .50 .15
Dwight Gooden
Jose Canseco
Darryl Strawberry

1991 Classic III

The third issue of the 1991 Classic baseball trivia game contains a small gameboard, accessories, 99 standard-size player cards with trivia questions on the backs, and one "4-in-1" micro player card. The card fronts are glossy color action photos with grayish-green borders. The horizontal backs feature biography, statistics, and five trivia questions. With few exceptions, the cards are arranged in alphabetical order. First year cards of Pedro Martinez and Ivan Rodriguez are featured within this set.

Nm-Mt Ex-Mt
COMP.FACT.SET (100) 5.00 1.50
T1 Jim Abbott .15 .04
T2 Craig Biggio .15 .04
T3 Wade Boggs .15 .04
T4 Bobby Bonilla .10 .03
T5 Ivan Calderon .05 .02
T6 Jose Canseco .25 .07
T7 Andy Benes .05 .02
T8 Wes Chamberlain .05 .02
T9 Will Clark .25 .07
T10 Royce Clayton .05 .02
T11 Gerald Alexander .05 .02
T12 Chili Davis .10 .03
T13 Eric Davis .10 .03
T14 Andre Dawson .10 .03
T15 Rob Dibble .10 .03
T16 Chris Donnels .05 .02
T17 Scott Erickson .05 .02
T18 Monty Fariss .05 .02
T19 Ruben Amaro Jr. .05 .02
T20 Chuck Finley .10 .03
T21 Carlton Fisk .15 .04
T22 Carlos Baerga .05 .02
T23 Ron Gant .10 .03
T24 Dave Justice .10 .03
and Ron Gant
T25 Mike Gardiner .05 .02
T26 Tom Glavine .15 .04
T27 Joe Grahe .05 .02
T28 Derek Bell .10 .03
T29 Mike Greenwell .05 .02
T30 Ken Griffey Jr. .50 .15
T31 Leo Gomez .05 .02
T32 Tom Goodwin .05 .02
T33 Tony Gwynn .30 .09
T34 Mel Hall .05 .02
T35 Brian Harper .05 .02
T36 Dave Henderson .05 .02
T37 Albert Belle .10 .03
T38 Orel Hershiser .10 .03
T39 Brian Hunter .10 .03
T40 Howard Johnson .05 .02
T41 Felix Jose .05 .02
T42 Wally Joyner .10 .03
T43 Jeff Juden .05 .02
T44 Pat Kelly .05 .02
T45 Jimmy Key .10 .03
T46 Chuck Knoblauch .10 .03
T47 John Kruk .10 .03
T48 Ray Lankford .05 .02
T49 Ced Landrum .05 .02
T50 Scott Livingstone .05 .02
T51 Kevin Maas .05 .02
T52 Greg Maddux .40 .12
T53 Dennis Martinez .10 .03
T54 Edgar Martinez .15 .04
T55 Pedro Martinez 3.00 .90
T56 Don Mattingly .60 .18
T57 Orlando Merced .05 .02
T58 Keith Mitchell .05 .02
T59 Kevin Mitchell .05 .02
T60 Paul Molitor .15 .04
T61 Jack Morris .10 .03
T62 Hal Morris .05 .02
T63 Kevin Morton .05 .02
T64 Pedro Munoz .05 .02
T65 Eddie Murray .25 .07
T66 Jack McDowell .05 .02
T67 Jeff McNeely .05 .02
T68 Brian McRae .10 .03
T69 Kevin McReynolds .05 .02
T70 Gregg Olson .05 .02
T71 Rafael Palmeiro .15 .04
T72 Dean Palmer .10 .03
T73 Tony Phillips .05 .02
T74 Kirby Puckett .25 .07
T75 Carlos Quintana .05 .02
T76 Pat Rice .05 .02
T77 Cal Ripken .75 .23
T78 Ivan Rodriguez 2.00 .60
T79 Nolan Ryan 1.00 .30
T80 Bret Saberhagen .10 .03
T81 Tim Salmon 1.00 .30
T82 Juan Samuel .05 .02
T83 Ruben Sierra .05 .02
T84 Heathcliff Slocumb .10 .03
T85 Joe Slusarski .05 .02
T86 John Smiley .05 .02
T87 Dave Smith .05 .02
T88 Ed Sprague .05 .02
T89 Todd Stottlemyre .05 .02
T90 Mike Timlin .10 .03
T91 Greg Vaughn .10 .03
T92 Frank Viola .10 .03
T93 Chico Walker .05 .02
T94 Devon White .05 .02
T95 Matt Williams .10 .03
T96 Rick Wilkins .05 .02
T97 Bernie Williams .25 .07
T98 Nolan Ryan .50 .15
Goose Gossage
T99 Gerald Williams .10 .03
NNO Bobby Bonilla .25 .07
Will Clark
Cal Ripken
Scott Erickson

1991 Classic Nolan Ryan 10

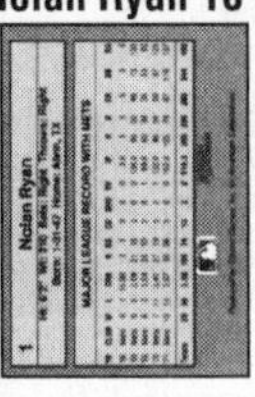

Produced by Classic Games, Inc. and made exclusively for American Collectibles for Shop at Home TV campaign., this ten card limited edition career celebration standard size set highlights Nolan Ryan's achievements. The fronts display posed and action shots with a split design border. The left half of the card has a mottled green and yellow border and the right half displays a teal green one. A black bar overlaid on the photo lists the team he is portrayed playing for, and the years Nolan was a member of that team. The light green horizontal backs carry biography, statistics, and career summary.

Nm-Mt Ex-Mt
COMP. FACT. SET (10) 20.00 6.00
COMMON CARD (1-10) 2.00 .60

1992 Classic Game

The 1992 Classic Baseball Collector's Edition game contains 200 standard-size cards. The cards were issued in two boxes labeled "Trivia Cards A" and "Trivia Cards B." The game also included an official Major League Action Spinner, eight stand-up baseball hero player pieces, an action scoreboard, a hand-illustrated game board, and a collectible book featuring tips from a new group of baseball legends. According to Classic, production has been limited to 125,000 games. The fronts display glossy color action photos bordered in dark purple. The Classic logo and the year "1992" appear in the top border, while the player's name is given in white lettering in the bottom border. The horizontally oriented backs present biography, statistics (1991 and career), and five baseball trivia questions.

Nm-Mt Ex-Mt
COMP. FACT. SET (200) 25.00 7.50
1 Chuck Finley .20 .06
2 Craig Biggio .40 .12
3 Luis Gonzalez .50 .15
4 Pete Harnisch .10 .03
5 Jeff Juden .10 .03
6 Harold Baines .20 .06
7 Kirk Dressendorfer .10 .03
8 Dennis Eckersley .40 .12
9 Dave Henderson .10 .03
10 Dave Stewart .20 .06
11 Joe Carter .20 .06
12 Juan Guzman .10 .03
13 Dave Stieb .10 .03
14 Todd Stottlemyre .10 .03
15 Ron Gant .20 .06
16 Brian Hunter .10 .03
17 Dave Justice .40 .12
18 John Smoltz .20 .06
19 Mike Stanton .20 .06
20 Chris George .10 .03
21 Paul Molitor .50 .15
22 Omar Olivares .10 .03
23 Lee Smith .20 .06
24 Ozzie Smith 1.25 .35
25 Todd Zeile .20 .06
26 George Bell .10 .03
27 Andre Dawson .40 .12
28 Shawon Dunston .10 .03
29 Mark Grace .40 .12
30 Greg Maddux 2.00 .60
31 Dave Smith .10 .03
32 Brett Butler .20 .06
33 Orel Hershiser .20 .06
34 Eric Karros .30 .09
35 Ramon Martinez .10 .03
36 Jose Offerman .10 .03
37 Juan Samuel .10 .03
38 Delino DeShields .20 .06
39 Marquis Grissom .20 .06
40 Tim Wallach .10 .03
41 Eric Gunderson .10 .03
42 Willie McGee .20 .06
43 Dave Righetti .10 .03
44 Robby Thompson .10 .03
45 Matt Williams .30 .09
46 Sandy Alomar Jr. .20 .06
47 Reggie Jefferson .10 .03
48 Mark Lewis .10 .03
49 Robin Ventura .40 .12
50 Tino Martinez .40 .12
51 Roberto Kelly .10 .03
52 Vince Coleman .10 .03
53 Dwight Gooden .20 .06
54 Todd Hundley .20 .06
55 Kevin Maas .10 .03
56 Wade Taylor .10 .03
57 Bryan Harvey .10 .03
58 Leo Gomez .10 .03
59 Ben McDonald .10 .03
60 Ricky Bones .10 .03
61 Tony Gwynn 1.50 .45
62 Benito Santiago .20 .06
63 Wes Chamberlain .10 .03
64 Tommy Greene .10 .03
65 Dale Murphy .40 .12
66 Steve Buechele .10 .03
67 Doug Drabek .10 .03
68 Joe Grahe .10 .03
69 Rafael Palmeiro .40 .12
70 Wade Boggs .75 .23
71 Ellis Burks .20 .06
72 Mike Greenwell .10 .03
73 Mo Vaughn .30 .09
74 Derek Bell .10 .03
75 Rob Dibble .10 .03
76 Barry Larkin .40 .12
77 Jose Rijo .10 .03
78 Doug Henry .10 .03
79 Chris Sabo .10 .03
80 Pedro Guerrero .10 .03
81 George Brett 1.50 .45
82 Tom Gordon .10 .03
83 Mark Gubicza .10 .03
84 Mark Whiten .10 .03
85 Brian McRae .10 .03
86 Danny Jackson .10 .03
87 Milt Cuyler .10 .03
88 Travis Fryman .20 .06
89 Mickey Tettleton .10 .03
90 Alan Trammell .40 .12
91 Lou Whitaker .20 .06
92 Chili Davis .20 .06
93 Scott Erickson .20 .06
94 Kent Hrbek .20 .06
95 Alex Fernandez .10 .03
96 Carlton Fisk .75 .23
97 Ramon Garcia .10 .03
98 Ozzie Guillen .10 .03
99 Tim Raines .20 .06
100 Bobby Thigpen .10 .03
101 Kirby Puckett .75 .23
102 Bernie Williams .75 .23
103 Dave Hansen .10 .03
104 Kevin Tapani .10 .03
105 Don Mattingly 1.50 .45
106 Frank Thomas .75 .23
107 Monty Fariss .10 .03
108 Bo Jackson .20 .06
109 Jim Abbott .20 .06
110 Jose Canseco .40 .12
111 Phil Plantier .10 .03
112 Brian Williams .10 .03
113 Mark Langston .10 .03
114 Wilson Alvarez .10 .03
115 Roberto Hernandez .40 .12
116 Darryl Kile .20 .06
117 Ryan Bowen .10 .03
118 Rickey Henderson 1.00 .30
119 Mark McGwire 2.50 .75
120 Devon White .10 .03
121 Roberto Alomar .40 .12
122 Kelly Gruber .10 .03
123 Eddie Zosky .10 .03
124 Tom Glavine .30 .09
125 Kal Daniels .10 .03
126 Cal Eldred .10 .03
127 Deion Sanders .50 .15
128 Robin Yount .50 .15
129 Cecil Fielder .20 .06
130 Ray Lankford .20 .06
131 Ryne Sandberg .75 .23
132 Darryl Strawberry .20 .06
133 Chris Haney .10 .03
134 Dennis Martinez .20 .06
135 Bryan Hickerson .10 .03
136 Will Clark .75 .23
137 Hal Morris .10 .03
138 Charles Nagy .10 .03
139 Jim Thome 1.00 .30
140 Albert Belle .30 .09
141 Reggie Sanders .10 .03
142 Scott Cooper .10 .03
143 David Cone .40 .12
144 Anthony Young .10 .03
145 Howard Johnson .10 .03
146 Arthur Rhodes .10 .03
147 Scott Aldred .10 .03
148 Mike Mussina 1.25 .35
149 Fred McGriff .30 .09
150 Andy Benes .10 .03
151 Ruben Sierra .20 .06
152 Len Dykstra .20 .06
153 Andy Van Slyke .20 .06
154 Orlando Merced .10 .03
155 Barry Bonds 1.50 .45
156 John Smiley .10 .03
157 Julio Franco .20 .06
158 Juan Gonzalez .40 .12
159 Ivan Rodriguez 1.50 .45
160 Willie Banks .10 .03
161 Eric Davis .30 .09
162 Eddie Murray .40 .12
163 Dave Fleming .10 .03
164 Wally Joyner .10 .03
165 Kevin Mitchell .20 .06
166 Eddie Taubensee .10 .03
167 Danny Tartabull .10 .03
168 Ken Hill .10 .03
169 Willie Randolph .20 .06
170 Kevin McReynolds .10 .03
171 Gregg Jefferies .10 .03
172 Patrick Lennon .10 .03
173 Luis Mercedes .10 .03
174 Glenn Davis .10 .03
175 Bret Saberhagen .20 .06
176 Bobby Bonilla .10 .03
177 Kenny Lofton .40 .12
178 Jose Lind .10 .03
179 Royce Clayton .10 .03
180 Scott Scudder .10 .03
181 Chuck Knoblauch .40 .12
182 Terry Pendleton .10 .03
183 Nolan Ryan 3.00 .90
184 Rob Maurer .10 .03
185 Brian Bohanon .10 .03
186 Ken Griffey Jr. 2.50 .75
187 Jeff Bagwell 1.50 .45
188 Steve Avery .10 .03

189 Roger Clemens 1.50 .45
190 Cal Ripken 3.00 .90
191 Kim Batiste .10 .03
192 Bip Roberts .10 .03
193 Greg Swindell .10 .03
194 Dave Winfield .40 .12
195 Steve Sax .10 .03
196 Frank Viola .10 .03
197 Mo Sanford .10 .03
198 Kyle Abbott .10 .03
199 Jack Morris .20 .06
200 Andy Ashby .10 .03

1992 Classic I

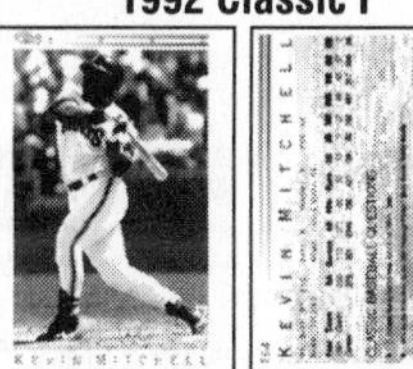

The first issue of the 1992 Classic baseball trivia game contains a small gameboard, accessories, 99 standard-size player cards with trivia questions on the backs, one "4-in-1" micro player card, and four micro player pieces. The cards have on the fronts glossy color action photos bordered in white. A red, gray, and purple stripe with the year "1992" traverses the top of the card. In a horizontal format, the backs feature biography, statistics, and five trivia questions, printed on a ghosted image of the 26 major league city skylines. The cards are numbered on the back and basically arranged in alphabetical order.

Nm-Mt Ex-Mt
COMP. FACT. SET (100) 8.00 2.40
T1 Jim Abbott .10 .03
T2 Kyle Abbott .05 .02
T3 Scott Aldred .05 .02
T4 Roberto Alomar .30 .09
T5 Wilson Alvarez .05 .02
T6 Andy Ashby .05 .02
T7 Steve Avery .05 .02
T8 Jeff Bagwell 1.00 .30
T9 Bret Barberie .05 .02
T10 Kim Batiste .05 .02
T11 Derek Bell .05 .02
T12 Jay Bell .05 .02
T13 Albert Belle .10 .03
T14 Andy Benes .05 .02
T15 Sean Berry .05 .02
T16 Barry Bonds 1.00 .30
T17 Ryan Bowen .05 .02
T18 Alejandro Pena .05 .02
Mark Wohlers
Kent Mercker
T19 Scott Brosius .30 .09
T20 Jay Buhner .10 .03
T21 David Burba .05 .02
T22 Jose Canseco .40 .12
T23 Andujar Cedeno .05 .02
T24 Will Clark .50 .15
T25 Royce Clayton .05 .02
T26 Roger Clemens 1.00 .30
T27 David Cone .30 .09
T28 Scott Cooper .05 .02
T29 Chris Cron .05 .02
T30 Len Dykstra .10 .03
T31 Cal Eldred .05 .02
T32 Hector Fajardo .05 .02
T33 Cecil Fielder .10 .03
T34 Dave Fleming .05 .02
T35 Steve Foster .05 .02
T36 Julio Franco .10 .03
T37 Carlos Garcia .05 .02
T38 Tom Glavine .20 .06
T39 Tom Goodwin .05 .02
T40 Ken Griffey Jr. 1.50 .45
T41 Chris Haney .05 .02
T42 Bryan Harvey .05 .02
T43 Rickey Henderson 939 .75 .23
T44 Carlos Hernandez .05 .02
T45 Roberto Hernandez .30 .09
T46 Brook Jacoby .05 .02
T47 Howard Johnson .05 .02
T48 Pat Kelly .05 .02
T49 Darryl Kile .10 .03
T50 Chuck Knoblauch .30 .09
T51 Ray Lankford .30 .09
With Ozzie Smith
T52 Mark Leiter .05 .02
T53 Darren Lewis .05 .02
T54 Scott Livingstone .05 .02
T55 Shane Mack .05 .02
T56 Chito Martinez .05 .02
T57 Dennis Martinez .10 .03
The Perfect Game
T58 Don Mattingly 1.00 .30
T59 Paul McClellan .05 .02
T60 Chuck McElroy .05 .02
T61 Fred McGriff .20 .06
T62 Orlando Merced .05 .02
T63 Luis Mercedes .05 .02
T64 Kevin Mitchell .10 .03
T65 Hal Morris .05 .02
T66 Jack Morris .10 .03
T67 Mike Mussina .75 .23
T68 Denny Neagle .10 .03
T69 Tom Pagnozzi .05 .02
T70 Terry Pendleton .05 .02
T71 Phil Plantier .05 .02
T72 Kirby Puckett .50 .15
T73 Carlos Quintana .05 .02
T74 Willie Randolph .10 .03
T75 Arthur Rhodes .05 .02
T76 Cal Ripken 2.00 .60
T77 Ivan Rodriguez 1.00 .30
T78 Nolan Ryan 2.00 .60
T79 Ryne Sandberg .60 .18
T80 Deion Sanders .50 .15
Deion Drops In
T81 Reggie Sanders .10 .03
T82 Mo Sanford .05 .02
T83 Terry Shumpert .05 .02
T84 Tim Spehr .05 .02
T85 Lee Stevens .05 .02
T86 Darryl Strawberry .10 .03
T87 Kevin Tapani .05 .02
T88 Danny Tartabull .05 .02
T89 Frank Thomas .60 .18
T90 Jim Thome .75 .23
T91 Todd Van Poppel .05 .02
T92 Andy Van Slyke .05 .02
T93 John Wehner .05 .02
T94 John Wetteland .10 .03
T95 Devon White .05 .02
T96 Brian Williams .05 .02
T97 Mark Wohlers .05 .02
T98 Robin Yount .50 .15
T99 Eddie Zosky .05 .02
NNO0 Barry Bonds 1.00 .30
Roger Clemens
Steve Avery
Nolan Ryan

1992 Classic II

The 1992 Series II baseball trivia board game features 99 standard-size new player trivia standard-size cards, one "4-in-1" micro player card, a gameboard, and a spinner. The cards display color action player photos on the fronts. The horizontal backs have a biography, statistics (1991 and career), five trivia questions, and a color drawing of the team's uniform. According to Classic, the production run was 175,000 games.

Nm-Mt Ex-Mt
COMP. FACT. SET (100) 10.00 3.00
T1 Jim Abbott .10 .03
T2 Jeff Bagwell 1.00 .30
T3 Jose Canseco .40 .12
T4 Julio Valera .05 .02
T5 Scott Brosius .30 .09
T6 Mark Langston .05 .02
T7 Andy Stankiewicz .05 .02
T8 Gary DiSarcina .05 .02
T9 Pete Harnisch .05 .02
T10 Mark McGwire 1.50 .45
T11 Ricky Bones .05 .02
T12 Steve Avery .05 .02
T13 Deion Sanders .40 .12
T14 Mike Mussina .50 .15
T15 Dave Justice .20 .06
T16 Pat Hentgen .30 .09
T17 Tom Glavine .30 .09
T18 Juan Guzman .05 .02
T19 Ron Gant .10 .03
T20 Kelly Gruber .05 .02
T21 Eric Karros .30 .09
T22 Derrick May .05 .02
T23 Dave Hansen .05 .02
T24 Andre Dawson .20 .06
T25 Eric Davis .10 .03
T26 Ozzie Smith .75 .23
T27 Sammy Sosa 1.25 .35
T28 Lee Smith .10 .03
T29 Ryne Sandberg .50 .15
T30 Robin Yount .40 .12
T31 Matt Williams .20 .06
T32 John Vander Wal .05 .02
T33 Bill Swift .05 .02
T34 Delino DeShields .05 .02
T35 Royce Clayton .05 .02
T36 Moises Alou .10 .03
T37 Will Clark .50 .15
T38 Darryl Strawberry .10 .03
T39 Larry Walker .20 .06
T40 Ramon Martinez .05 .02
T41 Howard Johnson .05 .02
T42 Tino Martinez .30 .09
T43 Dwight Gooden .10 .03
T44 Ken Griffey Jr. 1.50 .45
T45 David Cone .30 .09
T46 Kenny Lofton .30 .09
T47 Bobby Bonilla .10 .03
T48 Carlos Baerga .05 .02
T49 Don Mattingly 1.00 .30
T50 Sandy Alomar Jr. .10 .03
T51 Lenny Dykstra .10 .03
T52 Tony Gwynn 1.00 .30
T53 Felix Jose .05 .02
T54 Rick Sutcliffe .05 .02
T55 Wes Chamberlain .05 .02
T56 Cal Ripken 2.00 .60
T57 Kyle Abbott .05 .02
T58 Leo Gomez .05 .02
T59 Gary Sheffield .30 .09
T60 Anthony Young .05 .02
T61 Roger Clemens 1.00 .30
T62 Rafael Palmeiro .30 .09
T63 Wade Boggs .50 .15
T64 Andy Van Slyke .10 .03
T65 Ruben Sierra .05 .02
T66 Denny Neagle .10 .03
T67 Nolan Ryan 2.00 .60
T68 Doug Drabek .05 .02
T69 Ivan Rodriguez 1.25 .35
T70 Barry Bonds 1.00 .30
T71 Chuck Knoblauch .30 .09
T72 Reggie Sanders .10 .03
T73 Cecil Fielder .10 .03
T74 Barry Larkin .30 .09
T75 Scott Aldred .05 .02
T76 Rob Dibble .05 .02
T77 Brian McRae .05 .02
T78 Tim Belcher .05 .02
T79 George Brett 1.00 .30
T80 Frank Viola .05 .02
T81 Roberto Kelly .05 .02
T82 Jack McDowell .05 .02
T83 Mel Hall .05 .02
T84 Esteban Beltre .05 .02
T85 Robin Ventura .30 .09
T86 George Bell .05 .02
T87 Frank Thomas .60 .18
T88 John Smiley .05 .02
T89 Bobby Thigpen .05 .02
T90 Kirby Puckett .50 .15
T91 Kevin Mitchell .10 .03
T92 Peter Hoy .05 .02
T93 Russ Springer .05 .02
T94 Donovan Osborne .05 .02
T95 Dave Silvestri .05 .02
T96 Chad Curtis .10 .03
T97 Pat Mahomes .05 .02
T98 Danny Tartabull .05 .02
T99 John Doherty .05 .02
NNO0 Ryne Sandberg .50 .15
Mike Mussina
Reggie Sanders
Jose Canseco

1993 Classic Game

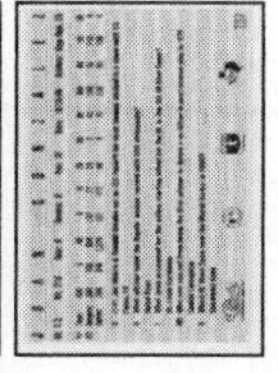

The 1993 Classic Game contains 99 trivia standard-size cards, a micro player card, four micro piece stands, a color game board, and a reusable plastic carrying case. As a special bonus, Classic included highlight trivia cards of George Brett and Robin Yount commemorating their 3,000 hits in the 1992 season. The cards feature color action player photos with navy blue borders.

Nm-Mt Ex-Mt
COMP. FACT. SET (100) 12.00 3.60
1 Jim Abbott .10 .03
2 Roberto Alomar .50 .15
3 Moises Alou .10 .03
4 Brady Anderson .10 .03
5 Eric Anthony .05 .02
6 Alex Arias .05 .02
7 Pedro Astacio .05 .02
8 Steve Avery .05 .02
9 Carlos Baerga .05 .02
10 Jeff Bagwell .75 .23
11 George Bell .05 .02
12 Albert Belle .10 .03
13 Craig Biggio .30 .09
14 Barry Bonds 1.25 .35
15 Bobby Bonilla .10 .03
16 Mike Bordick .05 .02
17 George Brett 1.25 .35
3,000th Hit
18 Jose Canseco .50 .15
19 Joe Carter .10 .03
20 Royce Clayton .05 .02
21 Roger Clemens 1.25 .35
22 Greg Colbrunn .05 .02
23 David Cone .30 .09
24 Darren Daulton .10 .03
25 Delino DeShields .05 .02
26 Rob Dibble .05 .02
27 Dennis Eckersley .20 .06
28 Cal Eldred .05 .02
29 Scott Erickson .10 .03
30 Junior Felix .05 .02
31 Tony Fernandez .05 .02
32 Cecil Fielder .10 .03
33 Steve Finley .10 .03
34 Dave Fleming .05 .02
35 Travis Fryman .05 .02
36 Tom Glavine .30 .09
37 Juan Gonzalez .60 .18
38 Ken Griffey Jr. 1.25 .35
39 Marquis Grissom .10 .03
40 Juan Guzman .05 .02
41 Tony Gwynn 1.25 .35
42 Rickey Henderson 1.00 .30
43 Felix Jose .05 .02
44 Wally Joyner .10 .03
45 David Justice .30 .09
46 Eric Karros .20 .06
47 Roberto Kelly .05 .02
48 Ryan Klesko .10 .03
49 Chuck Knoblauch .10 .03
50 John Kruk .10 .03
51 Ray Lankford .10 .03
52 Barry Larkin .30 .09
53 Pat Listach .05 .02
54 Kenny Lofton .30 .09
55 Shane Mack .05 .02
56 Greg Maddux 1.50 .45
57 Dave Magadan .05 .02
58 Edgar Martinez .20 .06
59 Don Mattingly 1.25 .35
60 Ben McDonald .05 .02
61 Jack McDowell .05 .02
62 Fred McGriff .20 .06
63 Mark McGwire 2.00 .60
64 Kevin McReynolds .05 .02
65 Sam Militello .05 .02
66 Paul Molitor .50 .15
67 Jeff Montgomery .10 .03
68 Jack Morris .10 .03
69 Eddie Murray .50 .15
70 Mike Mussina .75 .23
71 Otis Nixon .05 .02
72 Donovan Osborne .05 .02
73 Terry Pendleton .05 .02
74 Mike Piazza 2.50 .75
75 Kirby Puckett .50 .15
76 Cal Ripken Jr. 2.50 .75
77 Bip Roberts .05 .02
78 Ivan Rodriguez .75 .23
79 Nolan Ryan 2.50 .75
80 Ryne Sandberg 1.00 .30
81 Deion Sanders .30 .09
82 Reggie Sanders .10 .03
83 Frank Seminara .05 .02
84 Gary Sheffield .40 .12
85 Ruben Sierra .10 .03
86 John Smiley .05 .02
87 Lee Smith .10 .03
88 Ozzie Smith .75 .23
89 John Smoltz .20 .06
90 Danny Tartabull .05 .02
91 Bob Tewksbury .05 .02
92 Frank Thomas .75 .23
93 Andy Van Slyke .05 .02
94 Mo Vaughn .10 .03
95 Robin Ventura .10 .03
96 Tim Wakefield .10 .03
97 Larry Walker .10 .03
98 Dave Winfield .50 .15
99 Robin Yount 3,000 .50 .15
NNO Mark McGwire 2.00 .60
Sam Militello
Ryan Klesko
Greg Maddux

1995 Classic $10 Phone Cards Promos

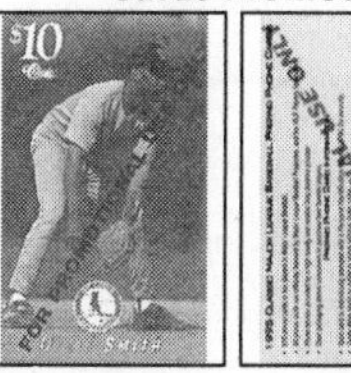
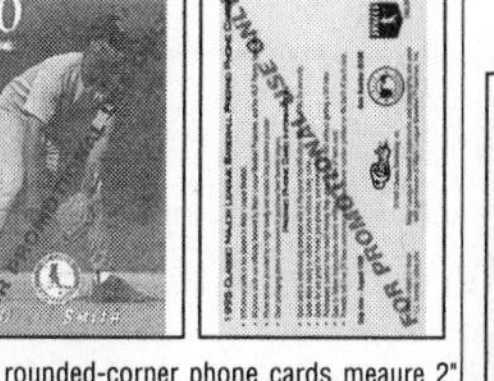

These rounded-corner phone cards meaure 2" by 3 1/4". They were handed out at 1995 FanFest as a redemption when a ticket stub was brought to the Classic booth. Packs handed out to dealers also included an usable $10 phone card. The cards are unnumbered and checklisted below in alphabetical order.

Nm-Mt Ex-Mt
COMPLETE SET (8) 30.00 9.00
1 Barry Bonds 5.00 1.50
2 Will Clark 1.50 .45
3 Juan Gonzalez 2.00 .60
4 Ken Griffey Jr. 6.00 1.80
5 Mike Piazza 6.00 1.80
6 Cal Ripken 10.00 3.00
7 Ozzie Smith 4.00 1.20
8 Frank Thomas 2.50 .75

1995 Classic $10 Phone Cards

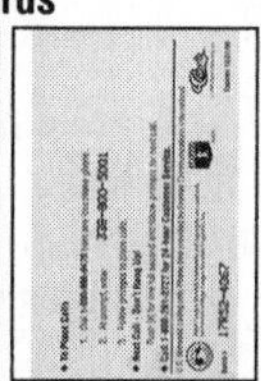

This 57-phone card set measures approximately 2 1/8" by 3 3/8" and features color action player photos with a $10 calling value. The backs carry the instructions on how to use the cards which expired on 12/31/96. The cards are unnumbered and checklisted below alphabetically according to the team's city or state. We have priced the cards as being unused. Cards which has had its PIN used are priced half the value of the unused cards. A Cal Ripken Jr. autographed phone card along with a certificate of authenticity were randomly distributed. As this card is rarely traded on the secondary market, we have no pricing information on this card.

Nm-Mt Ex-Mt
COMPLETE SET (57) 400.00 120.00
1 Chipper Jones 10.00 3.00
2 David Justice 6.00 1.80
3 Greg Maddux 12.00 3.60
4 Fred McGriff 5.00 1.50
5A Cal Ripken 20.00 6.00
Fielding
5B Cal Ripken 20.00 6.00
Follow-through
5C Cal Ripken 20.00 6.00
Catching a pop-up
5D Cal Ripken 20.00 6.00
Swinging
6 Mike Mussina 6.00 1.80
7 Jose Canseco 6.00 1.80
8 Mo Vaughn 4.00 1.20
9 Roger Clemens 10.00 3.00
10 Tim Salmon 4.00 1.20
11 Mark Grace 6.00 1.80
12 Sammy Sosa 10.00 3.00
13 Frank Thomas 8.00 2.40
14 Robin Ventura 4.00 1.20
15 Barry Larkin 6.00 1.80
16 Reggie Sanders 3.00 .90
17 Ron Gant 3.00 .90
18 Manny Ramirez 8.00 2.40
19 Albert Belle 4.00 1.20
20 Carlos Baerga 3.00 .90
21 Eddie Murray 6.00 1.80
22 Kenny Lofton 4.00 1.20
23 Andres Galarraga 6.00 1.80
24 Dante Bichette 4.00 1.20
25 Larry Walker 4.00 1.20
26 Cecil Fielder 4.00 1.20
27 Travis Fryman 4.00 1.20
28 Jeff Conine 3.00 .90
29 Craig Biggio 5.00 1.50
30 Jeff Bagwell 8.00 2.40
31 Kevin Appier 4.00 1.20
32 Hideo Nomo 15.00 4.50
33 Mike Piazza 15.00 4.50
34 Raul Mondesi 5.00 1.50
35 Kirby Puckett 8.00 2.40
36 Carlos Perez 3.00 .90
37 Jeff Kent 5.00 1.50
38 Don Mattingly 10.00 3.00
39 Paul O'Neill 4.00 1.20
40 Wade Boggs 6.00 1.80
41 Mark McGwire 12.00 3.60
42 Rickey Henderson 10.00 3.00
43 Darren Daulton 4.00 1.20
44 Lenny Dykstra 4.00 1.20
45 Denny Neagle 3.00 .90
46 Tony Gwynn 10.00 3.00
47 Barry Bonds 10.00 3.00
48 Matt Williams 4.00 1.20
49 Deion Sanders 4.00 1.20
50 Ken Griffey Jr. 12.00 3.60
51 Randy Johnson 10.00 3.00
52 Ozzie Smith 12.00 3.60
53 Juan Gonzalez 6.00 1.80
54 Will Clark 6.00 1.80
55 Ivan Rodriguez 8.00 2.40
56 Joe Carter 4.00 1.20
57 Roberto Alomar 6.00 1.80
AU5 Cal Ripken Jr AU
Certified Autograph

1996 Classic 7/11 Phone Cards

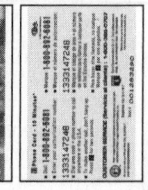

These phone cards feature leading major league players. They were available at all participating 7/11 stores for a cost of $5.99 and are good for 15 minutes of phone time. The cards expired on December 31, 1997. Cards which have been used have half the value of unused cards.

Nm-Mt Ex-Mt
COMPLETE SET 100.00 30.00
1 Cal Ripken 20.00 6.00
2 Frank Thomas 6.00 1.80
3 Hideo Nomo 10.00 3.00
4 Jeff Conine 4.00 1.20
5 Ken Griffey Jr. 12.00 3.60
6 Greg Maddux 12.00 3.60
7 Wade Boggs 8.00 2.40
8 Ivan Rodriguez 8.00 2.40
9 Barry Bonds 10.00 3.00
10 Kirby Puckett 6.00 1.80
11 Mo Vaughn 3.00 .90
12 Tony Gwynn 10.00 3.00

1998 Classic Collectible Ryan Tickets

These oversize commemorative tickets, which measure approximately 4" by 8" feature Nolan Ryan record setting seven no-hitters. The fronts have photos of Ryan along with a photo of an ticket stub from that game. The back has another photo as well as information about that no-hitter. Since these cards are unnumbered, we have sequenced them in order of no-hitter

Nm-Mt Ex-Mt
COMPLETE SET (7) 35.00 10.50
COMMON CARD (1-7) 5.00 1.50

1997 Classic Sports Brooks Robinson

This one card set was issued by Comcast to introduce the new Clasic Sports Network (as well as other all-sports Cable Channels). The horizontal front has an action photo of Brooks Robinson while the back has descriptions of the new cable networks available.

Nm-Mt Ex-Mt
1 Brooks Robinson 5.00 1.50

1997 Clemens A and P

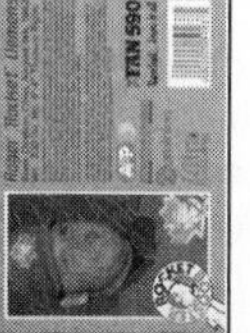

This one-card set measuring approximately 3 1/2" by 5" features a color action photo of Roger Clemens with a blue Toronoto Blue Jays logo as the background in thin inner white and blue borders and a wider red outer border. The back displays a small player portrait and player information along with sponsor logos.

	Nm-Mt	Ex-Mt
1 Roger Clemens	5.00	1.50

1997 Clemens The Fan

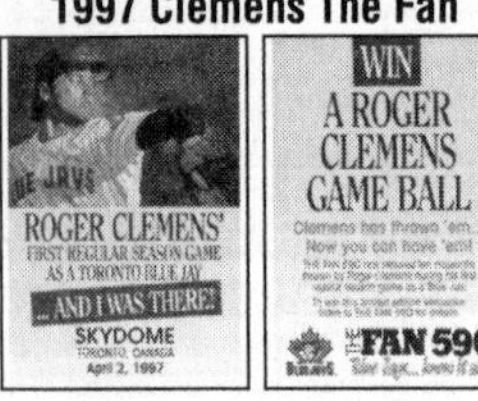

This one-card set was sponsored by THE FAN 590 Radio Station and distributed to fans who attended the first regular season game played by Roger Clemens as a Toronto Blue Jay on April 2, 1997. The front features a small color action painting of the player. The back displays information on how fans could win one of ten baseballs thrown by Roger Clemens during his first regular season game as a Blue Jay.

	Nm-Mt	Ex-Mt
1 Roger Clemens	5.00	1.50

2003 Clemens 300 Upper Deck

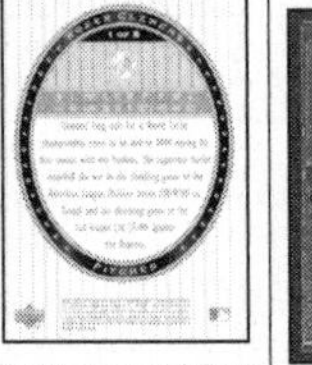

This five card set was given away at an August, 2003 Yankee game to commemorate the 300th career victory of Roger Clemens. Each fan at the game received these five cards along with a drawing of clemens which had a 15% off coupon for Modell's on the back.

	MINT	NRMT
COMPLETE SET	10.00	4.50
COMMON CARD	2.00	.90

1991 Clemente Big League Collectibles

This 19-card set features color photos of Roberto Clemente as he appeared on Topps cards through the years and are printed as stickers. The set was distributed in strips with each strip containing three stickers. The backs are blank. The cards are listed below according to the year of the Topps set in which they originally appeared.

	Nm-Mt	Ex-Mt
COMPLETE SET (19)	20.00	6.00
COMMON CARD (1-19)	1.50	.45

1993 Clemente City Pride

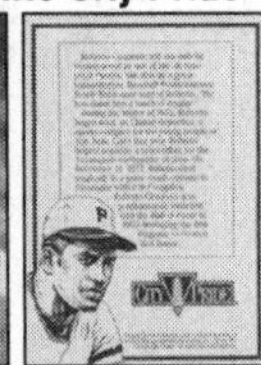

One of these standard-size cards was inserted in a protective sleeve attached to City Pride Bakery plastic bread bags. The bread bag itself contained a "Help Build The Statue" feature, which stated that proceeds from the sale of this bread would go toward constructing a memorial statue to be unveiled before the 1994 All-Star Game at Three Rivers Stadium. Inside team color-coded border stripes (black and mustard), the fronts display full-bleed color or sepia-toned photos. The backs summarize Clemente's life and career with biography, statistics, and career highlights. The cards are unnumbered.

	Nm-Mt	Ex-Mt
COMPLETE SET (6)	15.00	4.50
COMMON CARD (1-6)	2.50	.75

1972 Clemente Daily Juice

This slightly oversized card featured Pirate great Roberto Clemente. The borderless front has a full color photo of Clemente along with a fascimile signature. The horizontal back has information on how to join the Clemente fan club. These cards are still commonly found as part of uncut sheets.

	NM	Ex
1 Roberto Clemente	5.00	2.00

1973 Clemente Pictureform

The Roberto Clemente Pictureform set consists of 12 photos and originally sold for $2.00. The black-and-white action photos are in a circle format and measure approximately 8 3/16" in diameter. The photos are bordered by an orange or light blue 1 3/8" border and printed on medium weight paper stock. There are five scored lines surrounding the photo that indicate where to fold the picture to form the pictureform. Once assembled, the pictures form a twelve-sided sphere. No lettering is printed on the front and the backs are blank. The photos were packaged with a large folder which displayed a color posed photo of Clemente on the front. On the inside left side were Clemente's career highlights and quotes from his peers. The inside right contained instructions for assembling the pictureform with line drawn illustrations above and below.

	NM	Ex
COMPLETE SET (12)	100.00	40.00
COMMON CARD (1-12)	10.00	4.00
XX Album	10.00	4.00

1994 Clemente Wendy's

Sponsored by Wendy's restaurants, this standard-size hologram card commemorates Hall of Famer Roberto Clemente. Reportedly only 90,000 of these hologram cards were produced. Framed by black borders, the horizontal front pictures Clemente in batting posture awaiting the pitch. When the holograph is rotated slightly, he is pictured hitting the ball. His name, the team name, and "3000" are printed in the holograph. The horizontal backs presents two color photos of Clemente and career summary. The card is unnumbered.

	Nm-Mt	Ex-Mt
1 Roberto Clemente	5.00	1.50

1993 Clemente Z-Silk

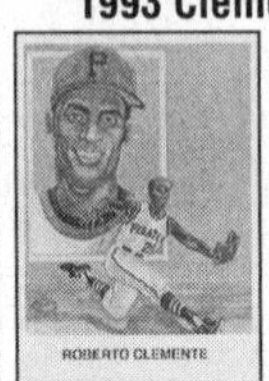

This ten-card set of silk cachets features artist's paintings of Roberto Clemente. The cards measure the standard-size and have white borders. Roberto Clemente's name is printed along the bottom edge. The cards may be most easily distinguished by the differing overlaid action pictures described below.

	Nm-Mt	Ex-Mt
COMPLETE SET (10)	6.00	1.80
COMMON CARD (1-10)	.75	.23

1938 Clopay Foto-Fun R329

This 93-card set features sun-developed blue-tinted photos which are self-developed by the sun. They measure approximately 2 3/16" by 2 3/4". The backs are blank. The cards are unnumbered and checklisted below in alphabetical order. Holders in excellent condition are fairly rare and add a value of at least $25 to any individual clopay.

	Ex-Mt	VG
COMPLETE SET	2500.00	1250.00
1 Luke Appling	50.00	25.00
2 Morris Arnovich	25.00	12.50
3 Eldon Auker	25.00	12.50
4 Jim Bagby	25.00	12.50
5 Red Barrett	25.00	12.50
6 Roy Bell	25.00	12.50
7 Wally Berger	30.00	15.00
8 Oswald Bluege	25.00	12.50
9 Frenchy Bordagaray	25.00	12.50
10 Tom Bridges	30.00	15.00
11 Dolf Camilli	40.00	20.00
12 Ben Chapman	25.00	12.50
13 Harland Clift	30.00	15.00
14 Harry Craft	25.00	12.50
15 Roger Cramer	30.00	15.00
16 Joe Cronin MG	50.00	25.00
17 Kiki Cuyler	50.00	25.00
18 Babe Dahlgren	25.00	12.50
19 Harry Danning	25.00	12.50
20 Frank Demaree	25.00	12.50
21 Gene Desautels	25.00	12.50
22 Jim Deshong	25.00	12.50
23 Bill Dickey	50.00	25.00
24 Jimmy Dykes MG	30.00	15.00
25 Lou Fette	25.00	12.50
26 Louis Finney	25.00	12.50
27 Larry French	25.00	12.50
28 Linus Frey	25.00	12.50
29 Deb Garms	25.00	12.50
30 Charles Gehringer	50.00	25.00
31 Lefty Gomez	50.00	25.00
32 Ival Goodman	25.00	12.50
33 Lee Grissom	25.00	12.50
34 Stanley Hack	30.00	15.00
35 Irving Hadley	25.00	12.50
36 Mel Harder	30.00	15.00
37 Rollie Hemsley	25.00	12.50
38 Tommy Henrich	40.00	20.00
39 Billy Herman	30.00	15.00
40 Willard Hershberger	30.00	15.00
41 Michael Higgins	25.00	12.50
42 Oral Hildebrand	25.00	12.50
43 Carl Hubbell	50.00	25.00
44 Willis Hudlin	25.00	12.50
45 Mike Kreevich	25.00	12.50
46 Ralph Kress	25.00	12.50
47 John Lanning	25.00	12.50
48 Lyn Lary	25.00	12.50
49 Cookie Lavagetto	25.00	12.50
50 Thornton Lee	25.00	12.50
51 Ernie Lombardi	50.00	25.00
52 Al Lopez	50.00	25.00
53 Ted Lyons	50.00	25.00
54 Danny MacFayden	25.00	12.50
55 Max Macon	25.00	12.50
56 Pepper Martin	40.00	20.00
57 Joe Marty	25.00	12.50
58 Frank McCormick	25.00	12.50
59 Bill McKechnie MG	40.00	20.00
60 Joe Medwick	50.00	25.00
61 Cliff Melton	25.00	12.50
62 Charles Meyer	25.00	12.50
63 John Mize	50.00	25.00
64 Terry Moore	25.00	12.50
65 Whitey Moore	25.00	12.50
66 Emmett Mueller	25.00	12.50
67 Hugh Mulcahy	25.00	12.50
68 Van Mungo	30.00	15.00
69 John Murphy	30.00	15.00
70 Lynn Nelson	25.00	12.50
71 Mel Ott	50.00	25.00
72 Monte Pearson	25.00	12.50
73 Bill Rogell	25.00	12.50
74 George Selkirk	25.00	12.50
75 Milt Shoffner	25.00	12.50
76 Clyde Shoun	25.00	12.50
77 Al Simmons	50.00	25.00
78 Gus Suhr	25.00	12.50
79 Bill Sullivan	25.00	12.50
80 Cecil Travis	25.00	12.50
81 Pie Traynor MG	50.00	25.00
82 Harold Trosky	25.00	12.50
83 Jim Turner	25.00	12.50
84 Johnny VanderMeer	40.00	20.00
85 Oscar Vitt MG	25.00	12.50
86 Gerald Walker	25.00	12.50
87 Paul Waner	50.00	25.00
88 Lon Warneke	25.00	12.50
89 Rabbit Warstler	25.00	12.50
90 Bob Weiland	25.00	12.50
91 Burgess Whitehead	25.00	12.50
92 Earl Whitehill	25.00	12.50
93 Rudy York	30.00	15.00
94 Del Young	25.00	12.50

1988 CMC Mattingly

This 20-card set featuring Don Mattingly was distributed as part of a Collecting Kit produced by Collector's Marketing Corp. The cards themselves measure approximately 2 1/2" by 3 1/2" and have a light blue border. The card backs describe some aspect of Mattingly's career. Also in the kit were plastic sheets, a small album, a record, a booklet and information on how to join Don's Fan Club. The set price below is for the whole kit as well as the cards. The set was re-issued with a Line Drive logo in 1993 with a different border.

	Nm-Mt	Ex-Mt
COMPLETE SET (20)	6.00	2.40
COMMON CARD (1-20)	.50	.20
P1 Don Mattingly Promo	.50	.20

1989 CMC Baseball's Greatest

Issued in a cello packs, this four-card, standard-size set was issued by CMC. On a white card face, the fronts feature either color (number 1) or sepia-tone (numbers 2-4) player photos inside a red and white border whose shape resembles the home plate. The set's title appears in the red border above the picture while the player's name appears in a turquoise diamond at the bottom. The backs have the same design, only with a career summary presented on a gray panel instead of the front photo. The cards are unnumbered and checklisted below alphabetically.

	Nm-Mt	Ex-Mt
COMPLETE SET	3.00	1.20
1 Roberto Clemente	.75	.30
2 Ty Cobb	.75	.30
3 Lou Gehrig	.75	.30
4 Babe Ruth	1.00	.40

1989 CMC Canseco

The 1989 CMC Jose Canseco Collector's Kit set contains 20 numbered standard-size cards. The front borders are Oakland A's green and yellow. The backs are green and white, and feature narratives and facsimile signatures. The cards were distributed as a set in a box along with an album and a booklet as well as other elements by CMC, Collectors Marketing Corporation. Since all the cards in the set feature the same player, cards in the checklist below are differentiated by some other characteristic of the particular card.

	Nm-Mt	Ex-Mt
COMPLETE SET (20)	6.00	2.40
COMMON CARD (1-20)	.50	.20
12 Jose Canseco Mark McGwire Bashing after homer	1.00	.40
P1 Jose Canseco Promo	1.00	.40

1989 CMC Mantle

The 1989 CMC Mickey Mantle Collector's Kit set contains 20 numbered standard-size cards. The fronts and backs are white, red and navy. The backs feature narratives and facsimile signatures. The cards were distributed as a set in a box along with an album and a booklet as well as other elements by CMC, Collectors Marketing Corporation. Since all the cards in the set feature the same player, cards in the checklist below are differentiated by some other characteristic of the particular card. Some of the cards in this set are sepia-tone photos as the action predates the widespread use of color film. The set was re-issued with a Line Drive logo in 1993 with a different border.

	Nm-Mt	Ex-Mt
COMPLETE SET (20)	10.00	4.00
COMMON CARD (1-20)	.50	.20
6 Mickey Mantle Roger Maris Posing with bats	1.00	.40
8 Mickey Mantle Joe Cronin Receiving 1962 MVP	.75	.30
10 Mickey Mantle Roger Maris Yogi Berra	.75	.30
15 Mickey Mantle Joe DiMaggio Shaking Hands at Yankee Stadium	1.50	.60
16 Mickey Mantle Giving speech at Yankee Stadium	.50	.20

1989 CMC Ruth

The 1989 CMC Babe Ruth Collector's Kit set contains 20 numbered standard-size cards. The front borders are white, red and navy. The backs are blue and white, and feature narratives and facsimile signatures. The cards were distributed as a set in a box along with an album and a booklet as well as other elements by CMC, Collectors Marketing Corporation. Since all the cards in the set feature the same player, cards in the checklist below are differentiated by some other characteristic of the particular card. All of the cards in this set are sepia-tone photos as the action predates the widespread use of color film.

	Nm-Mt	Ex-Mt
COMPLETE SET (20)	10.00	4.00
COMMON CARD (1-20)	.50	.20
15 Babe Ruth Jacob Ruppert OWN	.75	.30
17 Babe Ruth Miller Huggins MG	.75	.30
P1 Babe Ruth Promo for Set	1.00	.40

1975 Cobb McCallum

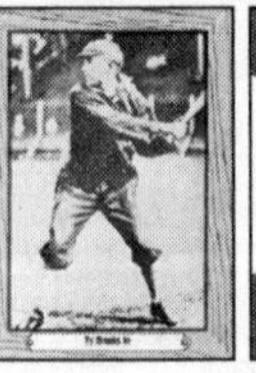

This 20-card set was produced to promote John McCallum's biography on Ty Cobb. The cards measure approximately 2 1/2" X 3 1/2" and feature on the fronts vintage black and white photos, with a hand-drawn artificial wood grain picture frame border. The title to each picture appears in a plaque below the picture. The back has a facsimile autograph and extended caption. The cards are numbered on the back in a baseball icon in the upper right corner. This set was issued at a price of $2.95 upon its release.

	NM	Ex
COMPLETE SET (20)	20.00	8.00
COMMON CARD (1-20)	.75	.30
6 Ty Cobb Walter Johnson	2.00	.80
11 Ty Cobb Paul Cobb	.75	.30
12 Ty Cobb Thomas Edison	1.50	.60
13 Ty Cobb Tangles with John McGraw	1.50	.60
14 John D. McCallum Cy Young	1.00	.40
15 Tris Speaker Joe DiMaggio and Ty Cobb	4.00	1.60
16 Ty Cobb Ted Williams	2.00	.80

1952 Coke Tips

This 10-card set features artwork of various Yankees, Giants and Dodgers and was inserted into regional Coca-Cola bottle cartons. The fronts display the artwork depicting the players and team schedules. The backs carry tips on how to play the pictured player's position and other Big-League tips. The cards are unnumbered and checklisted below in alphabetical order. A Willie Mays card, considered a test for this series, is appended at the end of the checklist. It is possible that the Mays card was actually pulled from this series when he entered military service early during the 1952 season.

	NM	Ex
COMPLETE SET (10)	2500.00	1250.00
1 Hank Bauer	300.00	150.00
2 Carl Furillo	400.00	200.00
3 Gil Hodges	400.00	200.00
4 Ed Lopat	250.00	125.00
5 Gil McDougald	250.00	125.00
6 Don Mueller	200.00	100.00
7 Pee Wee Reese	400.00	200.00
8 Bobby Thomson (Playing 3rd base)	300.00	150.00
9 Bobby Thomson (Hitting)	300.00	150.00
10 Wes Westrum	200.00	100.00
T1 Willie Mays Test	1500.00	750.00

1980 Coke/7-11 NL MVPs

This one-card blank-backed set, sponosred by Coca-Cola and 7-11, features a color posed photo of the co-most valuable players of the 1979 National League.

	NM	Ex
1 Willie Stargell Keith Hernandez	5.00	2.00

1981 Coke Team Sets

The cards in this 132-card set measure 2 1/2" by 3 1/2". In 1981, Topps produced 11 sets of 12 cards each for the Coca-Cola Company. Each set features 11 star players for a particular team plus an advertising card with the team name on the front. Although the cards are numbered in the upper right corner of the back from 1 to 11, they are re-numbered below

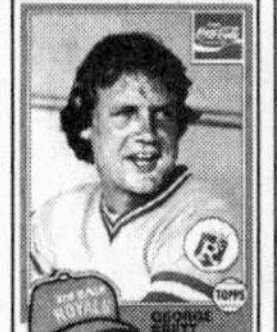

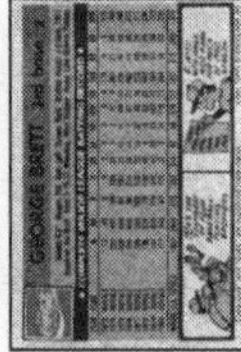

within team, i.e., Boston Red Sox (1-12), Chicago Cubs (13-24), Chicago White Sox (25-36), Cincinnati Reds (37-48), Detroit Tigers (49-60), Houston Astros (61-72), Kansas City Royals (73-84), New York Mets (85-96), Philadelphia Phillies (97-108), Pittsburgh Pirates (109-120), and St. Louis Cardinals (121-132). Within each team the player actually numbered number 1 (on the card back) is the first player below and the player numbered number 11 is the last in that team's list. These player cards are quite similar to the 1981 Topps issue but feature a Coca-Cola logo on both the front and the back. The advertising card for each team features, on its back, an offer for obtaining an uncut sheet of 1981 Topps cards. These promotional cards were actually issued by Coke in only a few of the cities, and most of these cards have reached collectors hands through dealers who have purchased the cards through suppliers. Cards of the following New York Yankees have been discovered: Rick Cerone, Rich Gossage and Reggie Jackson. Since these cards are so infrequently found, we have not yet placed a value on them.

	Nm-Mt	Ex-Mt
COMPLETE SET (132)	40.00	16.00
COMMON CARD (1-132)	.10	.04
COMMON AD CARDS	.05	.02
1 Tom Burgmeier	.10	.04
2 Dennis Eckersley	2.00	.80
3 Dwight Evans	.75	.30
4 Bob Stanley	.10	.04
5 Glenn Hoffman	.10	.04
6 Carney Lansford	.30	.12
7 Frank Tanana	.20	.08
8 Tony Perez	1.50	.60
9 Jim Rice	.40	.16
10 Dave Stapleton	.10	.04
11 Carl Yastrzemski	3.00	1.20
12 Red Sox Ad Card (Unnumbered)	.05	.02
13 Tim Blackwell	.10	.04
14 Bill Buckner	.20	.08
15 Ivan DeJesus	.10	.04
16 Leon Durham	.10	.04
17 Steve Henderson	.10	.04
18 Mike Krukow	.10	.04
19 Ken Reitz	.10	.04
20 Rick Reuschel	.20	.08
21 Scot Thompson	.10	.04
22 Dick Tidrow	.10	.04
23 Mike Tyson	.10	.04
24 Cubs Ad Card (Unnumbered)	.05	.02
25 Britt Burns	.10	.04
26 Todd Cruz	.10	.04
27 Rich Dotson	.10	.04
28 Jim Essian	.10	.04
29 Ed Farmer	.10	.04
30 Lamar Johnson	.10	.04
31 Ron LeFlore	.10	.04
32 Chet Lemon	.10	.04
33 Bob Molinaro	.10	.04
34 Jim Morrison	.10	.04
35 Wayne Nordhagen	.10	.04
36 White Sox Ad Card (Unnumbered)	.05	.02
37 Johnny Bench	4.00	1.60
38 Dave Collins	.10	.04
39 Dave Concepcion	.30	.12
40 Dan Driessen	.10	.04
41 George Foster	.40	.16
42 Ken Griffey	.30	.12
43 Tom Hume	.10	.04
44 Ray Knight	.10	.04
45 Ron Oester	.10	.04
46 Tom Seaver	4.00	1.60
47 Mario Soto	.10	.04
48 Reds Ad Card (Unnumbered)	.05	.02
49 Champ Summers	.10	.04
50 Al Cowens	.10	.04
51 Rich Hebner	.10	.04
52 Steve Kemp	.10	.04
53 Aurelio Lopez	.10	.04
54 Jack Morris	1.50	.60
55 Lance Parrish	.75	.30
56 Johnny Wockenfuss	.10	.04
57 Alan Trammell	4.00	1.60
58 Lou Whitaker	2.00	.80
59 Kirk Gibson	3.00	1.20
60 Tigers Ad Card (Unnumbered)	.05	.02
61 Alan Ashby	.10	.04
62 Cesar Cedeno	.20	.08
63 Jose Cruz	.30	.12
64 Art Howe	.20	.08
65 Rafael Landestoy	.10	.04
66 Joe Niekro	.20	.08
67 Terry Puhl	.10	.04
68 J.R. Richard	.20	.08
69 Nolan Ryan	8.00	3.20
70 Joe Sambito	.10	.04
71 Don Sutton	2.00	.80
72 Astros Ad Card (Unnumbered)	.05	.02
73 Willie Aikens	.10	.04
74 George Brett	8.00	3.20
75 Larry Gura	.10	.04
76 Dennis Leonard	.10	.04
77 Hal McRae	.20	.08
78 Amos Otis	.20	.08
79 Dan Quisenberry	.20	.08
80 U.L. Washington	.10	.04
81 John Wathan	.10	.04
82 Frank White	.20	.08
83 Willie Wilson	.20	.08
84 Royals Ad Card (Unnumbered)	.05	.02
85 Neil Allen	.10	.04
86 Doug Flynn	.10	.04
87 Dave Kingman	.40	.16
88 Randy Jones	.10	.04
89 Pat Zachry	.10	.04
90 Lee Mazzilli	.20	.08
91 Rusty Staub	.30	.12
92 Craig Swan	.10	.04
93 Frank Taveras	.10	.04
94 Alex Trevino	.10	.04
95 Joel Youngblood	.10	.04
96 Mets Ad Card (Unnumbered)	.05	.02
97 Bob Boone	.40	.16
98 Larry Bowa	.20	.08
99 Steve Carlton	2.00	.80
100 Greg Luzinski	.40	.16
101 Garry Maddox	.10	.04
102 Bake McBride	.10	.04
103 Tug McGraw	.20	.08
104 Pete Rose	3.00	1.20
105 Mike Schmidt	3.00	1.20
106 Lonnie Smith	.10	.04
107 Manny Trillo	.10	.04
108 Phillies Ad Card (Unnumbered)	.05	.02
109 Jim Bibby	.10	.04
110 John Candelaria	.10	.04
111 Mike Easler	.10	.04
112 Tim Foli	.10	.04
113 Phil Garner	.10	.04
114 Bill Madlock	.30	.12
115 Omar Moreno	.10	.04
116 Ed Ott	.10	.04
117 Dave Parker	.75	.30
118 Willie Stargell	1.50	.60
119 Kent Tekulve	.20	.08
120 Pirates Ad Card (Unnumbered)	.05	.02
121 Bob Forsch	.10	.04
122 George Hendrick	.20	.08
123 Keith Hernandez	.40	.16
124 Tom Herr	.10	.04
125 Sixto Lezcano	.10	.04
126 Ken Oberkfell	.10	.04
127 Darrell Porter	.20	.08
128 Tony Scott	.10	.04
129 Lary Sorensen	.10	.04
130 Bruce Sutter	.40	.16
131 Garry Templeton	.10	.04
132 Cardinals Ad Card (Unnumbered)	.05	.02
NYY1 Rick Cerone		
NYY2 Rich Gossage		
NYY3 Reggie Jackson		

1991 Coke Mattingly

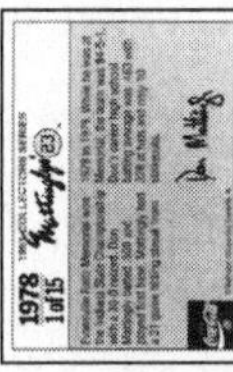

This 15-card standard-size set was sponsored by Coca-Cola. The front design features mostly color action player photos on a white and blue pinstripe card face. Each card has a year number on the top edge of the picture, and the Coke logo is superimposed at the lower left corner. In a horizontal format the backs are printed in blue and red, and present career highlights and statistics.

	Nm-Mt	Ex-Mt
COMPLETE SET (15)	6.00	1.80
COMMON CARD (1-15)	.50	.15

1993 Coke Case Inserts

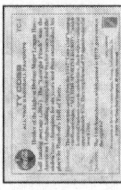

These standard-size cards are one per case inserts in the 1993 Coca-Cola set marketed by Collect-A-Card. The Ty Cobb image on the card is from the 1947 Coca-Cola hanging cardboard signs, "All Time Sports Favorite," which featured various sports celebrities. The variegated gray front has a pair of thin red foil lines surrounding an artist's illustration of the player. Below the picture are the player's name in red foil lettering and the words "All-Time Baseball Favorite." A Coke bottle appears in the lower left corner next to the Coca-Cola logo. The horizontal backs also have a variegated gray background and a thin red line surrounding player profile and a historical trivia question. The card is numbered on the back with a "TC" prefix. The second card features Christy Mathewson in a reprinted ad from 1916. The back describes the ad and gives some more information about Mathewson. The Mathewson card has a "CM" prefix.

	Nm-Mt	Ex-Mt
COMPLETE SET (2)	75.00	22.00
CM1 Christy Mathewson	25.00	7.50
TC1 Ty Cobb	50.00	15.00

1989 Colla Postcards Dawson

These postcards measure 3 1/2" by 5 1/2" and showcase Andre Dawson. The fronts feature color action or posed player shots in a postcard format. The typical postcard backs carry the player's name, position and the team name, along with the team logo.

	Nm-Mt	Ex-Mt
COMPLETE SET (8)	5.00	2.00
COMMON CARD (1-8)	.75	.30

1989 Colla Postcards Greenwell

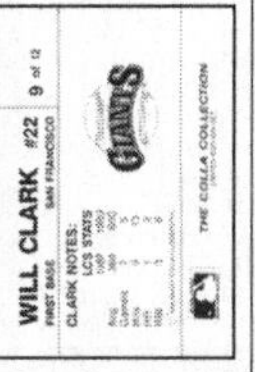

These postcards measure 3 1/2" by 5 1/2" and showcase Mike Greenwell. The fronts feature color action or posed player shots in a postcard format. The typical postcard backs carry the player's name, position and the team name, along with the team logo.

	Nm-Mt	Ex-Mt
COMPLETE SET (8)	4.00	1.60
COMMON CARD (1-8)	.50	.20

1989 Colla Postcards McGwire

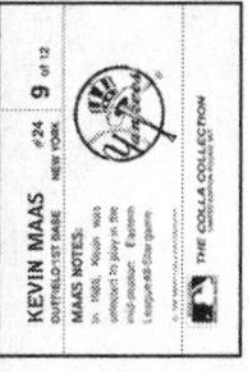

These postcards measure 3 1/2" by 5 1/2" and showcase Mark McGwire. The fronts feature color action or posed player shots in a postcard format. The typical postcard backs carry the player's name, position and the team name, along with the team logo.

	Nm-Mt	Ex-Mt
COMPLETE SET (8)	15.00	6.00
COMMON CARD (1-8)	2.00	.80

1989 Colla Postcards Mitchell

These postcards measure 3 1/2" by 5 1/2" and showcase Kevin Mitchell. The fronts feature color action or posed player shots in a postcard format. The typical postcard backs carry the player's name, position and the team name, along with the team logo.

	Nm-Mt	Ex-Mt
COMPLETE SET (8)	4.00	1.60
COMMON CARD (1-8)	.50	.20

1989 Colla Postcards Ozzie Smith

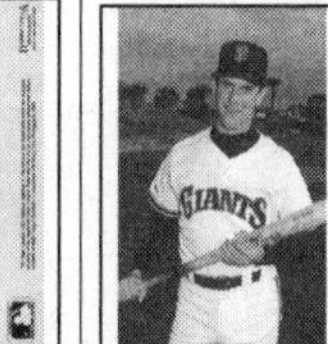

These postcards measure 3 1/2" by 5 1/2" and showcase Ozzie Smith. The fronts feature color action or posed player shots in a postcard format. The typical postcard backs carry the player's name, position and the team name, along with the team logo.

	Nm-Mt	Ex-Mt
COMPLETE SET (8)	10.00	4.00
COMMON CARD (1-8)	1.25	.50

1990 Colla Canseco

This 12-card standard-size set, issued by noted photographer Barry Colla, features Jose Canseco in various poses. The fronts are beautiful full-color photos while the backs contain notes about Canseco. According to the back of the first card in the set, 20,000 numbered sets were issued.

	Nm-Mt	Ex-Mt
COMP.FACT SET (12)	10.00	3.00
COMMON CARD (1-12)	1.00	.30

1990 Colla Will Clark

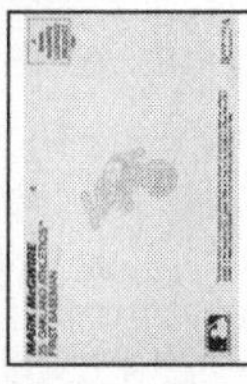

This 12-card standard-size set again features the beautiful photography of Barry Colla; this time Will Clark is the featured player. Again the fronts are borderless photos while the back contains notes about Will Clark. According to card number one, 15,000 numbered sets were produced.

	Nm-Mt	Ex-Mt
COMP. FACT SET (12)	12.00	3.60
COMMON CARD (1-12)	1.25	.35

1990 Colla Maas

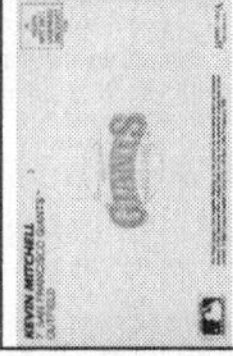

This attractive 12-card standard-size card set was produced by photographer Barry Colla. The set was limited to 7,500 made and each card has some facts relevant to Maas' career on the back of the card. The set was produced to be sold in its own special box and the boxes were issued 24 sets to each bigger box. All of the boxes were produced in the team's colors.

	Nm-Mt	Ex-Mt
COMP. FACT SET (12)	6.00	1.80
COMMON CARD (1-12)	.50	.15

1990 Colla Mattingly

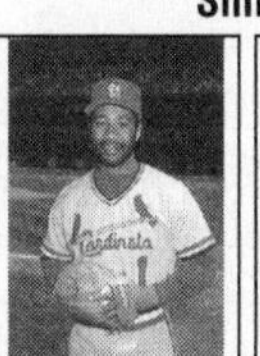

This 12-card standard-size set honoring Yankee great Don Mattingly features the photography of Barry Colla. The set was limited to 15,000 numbered sets and feature full-color photographs on the borderless fronts along with notes about Mattingly on the back.

	Nm-Mt	Ex-Mt
COMP. FACT SET (12)	10.00	3.00
COMMON CARD (1-12)	1.00	.30

1990 Colla Postcards Will Clark

These postcards measure 3 1/2" by 5 1/2" and showcase Will Clark. The fronts feature color action or posed player shots in a postcard format. The typical postcard backs carry the player's name, position and the team name, along with the team logo.

	Nm-Mt	Ex-Mt
COMPLETE SET (8)	10.00	3.00
COMMON CARD (1-8)	1.25	.35

1990 Colla Postcards Grace

These postcards measure 3 1/2" by 5 1/2" and showcase Mark Grace. The fronts feature color action or posed player shots in a postcard format. The typical postcard backs carry the player's name, position and the team name, along with the team logo.

	Nm-Mt	Ex-Mt
COMPLETE SET (8)	7.50	2.20
COMMON CARD (1-8)	1.00	.30

1991 Colla Roberto Alomar

This 13-card standard size set features colorful photos of Roberto Alomar by noted photographer Barry Colla. The high gloss borderless color photos were packed in a full color collector's box. Only 7,500 sets were produced, with 24 sets per display carton. The first card of each set bears the registration number.

	Nm-Mt	Ex-Mt
COMP. FACT SET (13)	10.00	3.00
COMMON CARD (1-12)	1.00	.30

1991 Colla Bonds

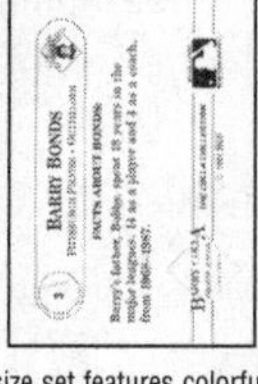

This 13-card standard size set features colorful photos of Barry Bonds by noted photographer Barry Colla. The high gloss borderless color photos were packed in a full color collector's box. Only 7,500 sets were produced, with 24 sets per display carton. The first card of each set bears the registration number. This set was issued so late in 1991 that it was actually January 1992 before the set was in general distribution.

	Nm-Mt	Ex-Mt
COMP. FACT SET (13)	12.00	3.60
COMMON CARD (1-12)	1.00	.30

1991 Colla Joe Carter

This 13-card standard size set features colorful photos of Joe Carter by noted photographer Barry Colla. The high gloss borderless color photos were packed in a full color collector's box. Only 7,500 sets were produced, with 24 sets per display carton. The first card of each set bears the registration number.

	Nm-Mt	Ex-Mt
COMP. FACT SET (13)	10.00	3.00
COMMON CARD (1-12)	1.00	.30

1991 Colla Gooden

This 13-card standard size set features colorful photos of Dwight Gooden by noted photographer Barry Colla. The high gloss borderless color photos were packed in a full color collector's box. Only 15,000 sets were produced, with 24 sets per display carton. The first card of each set bears the registration number.

	Nm-Mt	Ex-Mt
COMP. FACT SET (13)	10.00	3.00
COMMON CARD (1-13)	1.00	.30

1991 Colla Griffey Jr.

This 12-card standard size set features colorful photos of Ken Griffey Jr. by noted photographer Barry Colla. The high gloss borderless color photos were packed in a full color collector's box. Only 15,000 sets were produced, with 24 sets per display carton. The first card of each set bears the registration number.

	Nm-Mt	Ex-Mt
COMP. FACT SET (12)	15.00	4.50
COMMON CARD (1-12)	1.50	.45

1991 Colla Justice

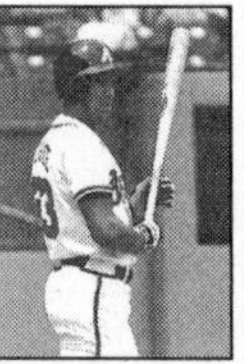

This 13-card standard size set features colorful photos of Dave Justice by noted photographer Barry Colla. The high gloss borderless color photos were packed in a full color collector's box. Only 15,000 sets were produced, with 24 sets per display carton. The first card of each set bears the registration number.

	Nm-Mt	Ex-Mt
COMP. FACT SET (13)	10.00	3.00
COMMON CARD (1-12)	1.00	.30

1991 Colla Sandberg

This 13-card standard size set features colorful photos of Ryne Sandberg by noted photographer Barry Colla. The high gloss borderless color photos were packed in a full color collector's box. Only 15,000 sets were produced, with 24 sets per display carton. The first card of each set bears the registration number.

	Nm-Mt	Ex-Mt
COMP. FACT SET (13)	10.00	3.00
COMMON CARD (1-12)	1.00	.30

1991 Colla Strawberry

This 13-card standard size set features colorful photos of Darryl Strawberry by noted photographer Barry Colla. The high gloss borderless color photos were packed in a full color collector's box. Only 15,000 sets were produced, with 24 sets per display carton. The first card of each set bears the registration number.

	Nm-Mt	Ex-Mt
COMP. FACT SET (13)	8.00	2.40
COMMON CARD (1-12)	.75	.23

1991 Colla Postcards Sandberg

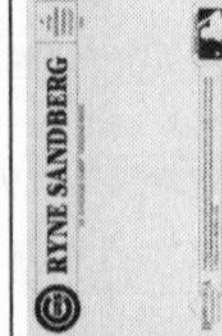

These postcards measure 3 1/2" by 5 1/2" and showcase Ryne Sandberg. The fronts feature color action or posed player shots in a postcard format. The typical postcard backs carry the player's name, position and the team name, along with the team logo.

	Nm-Mt	Ex-Mt
COMPLETE SET (8)	6.00	1.80
COMMON CARD (1-8)	1.00	.30

1992 Colla All-Stars Promos

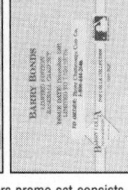

The 1992 Colla All-Stars promo set consists of 25 standard-size cards. The fronts feature full-bleed glossy color photos. The backs carry an advertisement for the cards and logos. Though the cards are unnumbered, they are listed below according to the numbering assigned to them on the checklist card. According to the checklist card, the set was issued July 14, 1992 and limited to 25,000 sets.

	Nm-Mt	Ex-Mt
COMPLETE SET (24)	15.00	4.50
1 Mark McGwire	3.00	.90
2 Will Clark	.75	.23
3 Roberto Alomar	.75	.23
4 Ryne Sandberg	1.00	.30
5 Cal Ripken	4.00	1.20
6 Ozzie Smith	1.50	.45
7 Wade Boggs	.75	.23
8 Terry Pendleton	.20	.06
9 Kirby Puckett	1.00	.30
10 Chuck Knoblauch	.40	.12
11 Ken Griffey Jr.	3.00	.90
12 Joe Carter	.40	.12
13 Sandy Alomar Jr	.20	.06
14 Benito Santiago	.40	.12
15 Mike Mussina	.75	.23
16 Fred McGriff	.60	.18
17 Dennis Eckersley	.40	.12
18 Tony Gwynn	2.00	.60
19 Roger Clemens	2.00	.60
20 Gary Sheffield	1.00	.30
21 Jose Canseco	.75	.23
22 Barry Bonds	2.00	.60
23 Ivan Rodriguez	1.00	.30
24 Tony Fernandez	.20	.06
NNO Juan Guzman CL	.20	.06

1992 Colla All-Star Game

This 24-card standard-size set was made available at the 1992 All-Star game in San Diego. The cards feature All-Stars from the National and American League. Randomly inserted throughout the sets were 200 numbered and autographed Roberto Alomar cards. The production run was limited to 25,000 sets, and the first card (McGwire) of each set bears the set serial number ("X of 25,000"). The fronts display full-bleed glossy color player photos. The All-Star Game logo and the player's name are superimposed across the bottom of the picture. The backs carry a close-up color photo and All-Star statistics. The cards are numbered in a diamond in the upper left corner.

	Nm-Mt	Ex-Mt
COMP. FACT SET (24)	12.50	3.70
1 Mark McGwire	2.50	.75
2 Will Clark	1.00	.30
3 Roberto Alomar	.75	.23
4 Ryne Sandberg	1.00	.30
5 Cal Ripken	3.00	.90
6 Ozzie Smith	1.00	.30
7 Wade Boggs	1.00	.30
8 Terry Pendleton	.25	.07
9 Kirby Puckett	1.00	.30
10 Chuck Knoblauch	.75	.23
11 Ken Griffey Jr.	2.50	.75
12 Joe Carter	.40	.12
13 Sandy Alomar Jr	.25	.07
14 Benito Santiago	.40	.12
15 Mike Mussina	1.00	.30
16 Fred McGriff	.60	.18
17 Dennis Eckersley	1.00	.30
18 Tony Gwynn	1.50	.45
19 Roger Clemens	1.50	.45
20 Gary Sheffield	1.00	.30
21 Jose Canseco	.75	.23
22 Barry Bonds	1.50	.45
23 Ivan Rodriguez	1.25	.35
24 Tony Fernandez	.25	.07

1992 Colla Promos

This 17-card standard-size set consists of promo cards to the various Barry Colla limited edition player sets. The cards feature full-bleed glossy color photos on their fronts. Except for the Thomas card, the backs are horizontally oriented. Some of the backs are gray while others are white. Each back gives the player's name, issue date, production quantity and a toll free phone number for ordering the set. The cards are unnumbered and checklisted below in alphabetical order.

	Nm-Mt	Ex-Mt
COMPLETE SET (17)	40.00	12.00
1A Roberto Alomar	3.00	.90
(English back)		
1B Roberto Alomar	5.00	1.50
(French back)		
2 Jeff Bagwell	2.50	.75
(Bat on right shoulder,& dark blue jersey)		
3 Barry Bonds	3.00	.90
4 Jose Canseco	2.00	.60
5A Joe Carter	1.50	.45
(English back)		
5B Joe Carter	3.00	.90
(French back)		
6 Will Clark	2.00	.60
7 Dwight Gooden	1.50	.45
8 Ken Griffey Jr.	4.00	1.20
9 Dave Justice	2.50	.75
10 Kevin Maas	1.00	.30
11 Don Mattingly	3.00	.90
12 Nolan Ryan	5.00	1.50
(Pitching with arm extended behind body)		
13 Ryne Sandberg	2.50	.75
14 Darryl Strawberry	1.50	.45
15 Frank Thomas	2.00	.60
(Leaning forward, right shoulder nearest camera)		

1992 Colla Bagwell

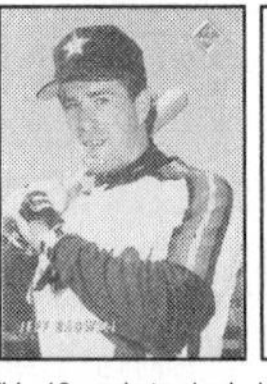

This 12-card standard-size set features colorful photos of Jeff Bagwell by noted sports photographer Barry Colla. Only 25,000 sets were produced, with 24 sets per display carton. Also the set included an Allocation Rights card, which entitled the holder to purchase the Colla Rookie set. The high gloss borderless color photos were packed in a full color collector's box.

	Nm-Mt	Ex-Mt
COMP. FACT SET (12)	10.00	3.00
COMMON CARD (1-12)	1.00	.30
AU Jeff Bagwell AU/200	50.00	15.00

1992 Colla Gwynn

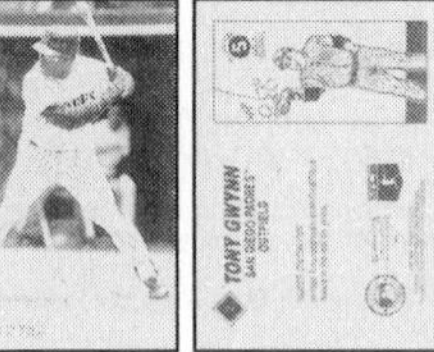

This 12-card standard size set features colorful photos of Tony Gwynn by noted photographer Barry Colla. The high gloss borderless color photos were packed in a full color collector's box. Only 7,500 sets were produced, with the first card of each set carrying the set number. The "92 The Colla Collection" icon appears in an upper corner and the player's name is printed toward the bottom of the picture. In light black lettering on white, the horizontal backs present biography (1), notes on Gwynn (2-11), or major league statistics (12) on the left portion and baseball cartoons on the right portion.

	Nm-Mt	Ex-Mt
COMP. FACT SET (12)	10.00	3.00
COMMON CARD (1-12)	1.00	.30

1992 Colla McGwire

This 12-card standard-size set features colorful photos of Mark McGwire by noted sports photographer Barry Colla. Only 15,000 sets were produced, with 24 sets per display carton. The high gloss borderless color photos were packed in a full color collector's box. The first card of each set bears the set serial number.

	Nm-Mt	Ex-Mt
COMP. FACT SET (12)	10.00	3.00
COMMON CARD (1-12)	1.00	.30
AU Mark McGwire AU/200	750.00	220.00

1992 Colla Ryan

This 12-card standard-size set features colorful photos of Nolan Ryan by noted sports photographer Barry Colla. Only 25,000 sets were produced, with 24 sets per display carton. The high-gloss borderless color photos were packed in a full color collector's box. The first card of each set bears the set serial number.

	Nm-Mt	Ex-Mt
COMP. FACT SET (12)	10.00	3.00
COMMON CARD (1-12)	1.00	.30
AU Nolan Ryan AU/200	200.00	60.00

1992 Colla Thomas

This 12-card standard-size set features colorful photos of Frank Thomas by noted sports photographer Barry Colla. Only 25,000 sets were produced, with 24 sets per display carton. Also the set included an Allocation Rights card, which entitled the holder to purchase the Colla Rookie set. The high gloss borderless color photos were packed in a full color collector's box. The first card of each set bears the set serial number.

	Nm-Mt	Ex-Mt
COMP. FACT SET (12)	10.00	3.00
COMMON CARD (1-12)	1.00	.30
AU Frank Thomas AU/200	60.00	18.00

1993 Colla All-Star Game

Issued by noted photographer Barry Colla, this 24-card boxed set was made available at the 1993 All-Star game in Baltimore. The standard-size cards feature 24 All-Stars from the National and American Leagues.

	Nm-Mt	Ex-Mt
COMP. FACT SET (25)	20.00	6.00
1 Roberto Alomar	1.00	.30
2 Barry Bonds	2.50	.75
3 Ken Griffey Jr.	4.00	1.20
4 John Kruk	.50	.15
5 Kirby Puckett	2.00	.60
6 Darren Daulton	.50	.15
7 Wade Boggs	1.25	.35
8 Matt Williams	.75	.23
9 Cal Ripken	5.00	1.50
10 Ryne Sandberg	2.00	.60
11 Ivan Rodriguez	1.50	.45
12 Andy Van Slyke	.25	.07
13 John Olerud	.50	.15
14 Tom Glavine	1.00	.30
15 Juan Gonzalez	1.00	.30
16 David Justice	1.00	.30
17 Mike Mussina	1.25	.35
18 Tony Gwynn	2.50	.75
19 Joe Carter	.50	.15
20 Barry Larkin	1.00	.30
21 Brian Harper	.25	.07
22 Ozzie Smith	2.00	.60
23 Mark McGwire	4.00	1.20
24 Mike Piazza	5.00	1.50
NNO Checklist Card	.25	.07

1993 Colla Postcards Piazza

These postcards measure 3 1/2" by 5 1/2" and showcase Mike Piazza. The fronts feature color action or posed player shots in a postcard format. The typical postcard backs carry the player's name, position and the team name, along with the team logo.

	Nm-Mt	Ex-Mt
COMPLETE SET (8)	6.00	1.80
COMMON CARD (1-8)	1.00	.30

1993 Colla Postcards Ripken Jr.

These postcards measure 3 1/2" by 5 1/2" and showcase Cal Ripken Jr. The fronts feature color action or posed player shots in a postcard format. The typical postcard backs carry the player's name, position and the team name, along with the team logo.

	Nm-Mt	Ex-Mt
COMPLETE SET (7)	8.00	2.40
COMMON CARD (1-7)	1.25	.35

1990 Collect-A-Books

The 1990 Collect-A-Books set was issued by CMC (Collectors Marketing Corp.) in three different sets (boxes) of 12 players apiece. The sets (boxes) were distinguishable by color, red, yellow, or green. The Collect-A-Books were in the style of the 1970 Topps Comic Book inserts but were much more profesionally made. The cards all fit into a nine-pocket sheet (since they are standard size) even though they can be expanded. The set contains an interesting mixture of retired and current players. The concept for this set was created by former major leaguer Jim Bouton.

	Nm-Mt	Ex-Mt
COMPLETE SET (36)	8.00	2.40
1 Bo Jackson	.20	.06
2 Dwight Gooden	.20	.06
3 Ken Griffey Jr.	1.50	.45
4 Will Clark	.50	.15
5 Ozzie Smith	.75	.23
6 Orel Hershiser	.20	.06
7 Ruben Sierra	.20	.06
8 Rickey Henderson	.50	.15
9 Robin Yount	.40	.12
10 Babe Ruth	1.50	.45
11 Ernie Banks	.40	.12
12 Carl Yastrzemski	.40	.12
13 Don Mattingly	1.00	.30
14 Nolan Ryan	1.50	.45
15 Jerome Walton	.10	.03
16 Kevin Mitchell	.10	.03
17 Tony Gwynn	1.00	.30
18 Dave Stewart	.20	.06
19 Roger Clemens	1.00	.30
20 Darryl Strawberry	.20	.06
21 George Brett	.75	.23
22 Hank Aaron	1.00	.30
23 Ted Williams	1.00	.30
24 Warren Spahn	.40	.12
25 Jose Canseco	.50	.15
26 Wade Boggs	.50	.15
27 Jim Abbott	.20	.06
28 Eric Davis	.20	.06
29 Ryne Sandberg	.75	.23
30 Bret Saberhagen	.20	.06
31 Mark Grace	.40	.12
32 Gregg Olson	.10	.03
33 Kirby Puckett	.60	.18
34 Lou Gehrig	1.25	.35
35 Roberto Clemente	1.25	.35
36 Bob Feller	.40	.12

1991 Collect-A-Books

This 36-card set, which measures the standard size, was issued by Impel for the second consecutive year. Collectors Marketing Corp., the 1990 Collect-a-Book producer, was a division within the Impel Corporâtion. This 1991 set was issued under Impel's Line Drive brand. Each book consists of eight pages and fits into a standard size plastic sheet. The set features 27 active stars and nine famous retired stars. An action shot of the player is pictured on the first two pages. The next four pages has textual information broken down into biographical information& two pages of more detailed personal information and a page of statistics. The inside back cover has a quote from the player pictured while the back cover has an attractive drawing of the player. Unlike the 1990 issue, the Collect-A-Books were issued in random packs.

	Nm-Mt	Ex-Mt
COMPLETE SET (36)	10.00	3.00
1 Roger Clemens	1.00	.30
2 Cal Ripken	2.00	.60
3 Nolan Ryan	2.00	.60
4 Ken Griffey Jr.	1.25	.35
5 Bob Welch	.10	.03
6 Kevin Mitchell	.10	.03
7 Kirby Puckett	.75	.23
8 Len Dykstra	.20	.06
9 Ben McDonald	.10	.03
10 Don Drysdale	.40	.12
11 Lou Brock	.40	.12
12 Ralph Kiner	.40	.12

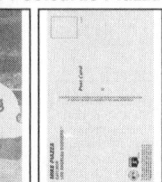

13 Jose Canseco .50 .15
14 Cecil Fielder .20 .06
15 Ryne Sandberg .75 .23
16 Wade Boggs .50 .15
17 Dwight Gooden .20 .06
18 Ramon Martinez .10 .03
19 Tony Gwynn .75 .23
20 Mark Grace .40 .12
21 Kevin Maas .10 .03
22 Thurman Munson .40 .12
23 Bob Gibson .40 .12
24 Bill Mazeroski .30 .09
25 Rickey Henderson .60 .18
26 Barry Bonds 1.00 .30
27 Jose Rijo .10 .03
28 George Brett .75 .23
29 Doug Drabek .10 .03
30 Matt Williams .30 .09
31 Barry Larkin .40 .12
32 Dave Stewart .20 .06
33 Dave Justice .40 .12
34 Harmon Killebrew .40 .12
35 Yogi Berra .40 .12
36 Billy Williams .40 .12

1994 Collector's Choice

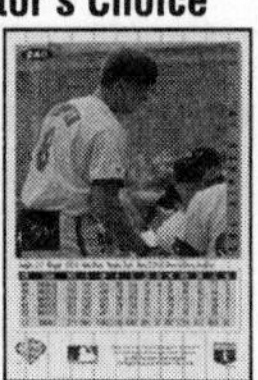

Produced by Upper Deck, this 670 standard-size card set was distributed in two series of 320 and 350. Cards were issued in foil-wrapped 12-card packs and factory sets (of which contained five Gold Signature cards for a total of 675 cards). Basic card fronts feature color player action photos with white borders that are highlighted by vertical gray pinstripes. Subsets include Rookie Class (1-20), First Draft Picks (21-30), Top Performers (306-315), Up Close (631-640) and Future Foundation (641-650). Rookie Cards include Michael Jordan and Alex Rodriguez.

Nm-Mt Ex-Mt
COMPLETE SET (670) 25.00 7.50
COMP.FACT.SET (675) 30.00 9.00
COMP. SERIES 1 (320) 10.00 3.00
COMP. SERIES 2 (350) 15.00 4.50
1 Rich Becker .10 .03
2 Greg Blosser .10 .03
3 Midre Cummings .10 .03
4 Carlos Delgado .30 .09
5 Steve Dreyer RC .10 .03
6 Carl Everett .20 .06
7 Cliff Floyd .20 .06
8 Alex Gonzalez .10 .03
9 Shawn Green .50 .15
10 Butch Huskey .10 .03
11 Mark Hutton .10 .03
12 Miguel Jimenez .10 .03
13 Steve Karsay .10 .03
14 Marc Newfield .10 .03
15 Luis Ortiz .10 .03
16 Manny Ramirez .30 .09
17 Johnny Ruffin .10 .03
18 Scott Stahoviak .10 .03
19 Salomon Torres .10 .03
20 Gabe White .10 .03
21 Brian Anderson RC .25 .07
22 Wayne Gomes RC .10 .03
23 Jeff Granger .10 .03
24 Steve Soderstrom RC .10 .03
25 Trot Nixon RC .50 .15
26 Kirk Presley RC .10 .03
27 Matt Brunson RC .10 .03
28 Brooks Kieschnick RC .25 .07
29 Billy Wagner RC .50 .15
30 Matt Drews RC .10 .03
31 Kurt Abbott RC .25 .07
32 Luis Alicea .10 .03
33 Roberto Alomar .50 .15
34 Sandy Alomar Jr. .10 .03
35 Moises Alou .20 .06
36 Wilson Alvarez .10 .03
37 Rich Amaral .10 .03
38 Eric Anthony .10 .03
39 Luis Aquino .10 .03
40 Jack Armstrong .10 .03
41 Rene Arocha .10 .03
42 Rich Aude RC .10 .03
43 Brad Ausmus .10 .03
44 Steve Avery .10 .03
45 Bob Ayrault .10 .03
46 Willie Banks .10 .03
47 Bret Barberie .10 .03
48 Kim Batiste .10 .03
49 Rod Beck .10 .03
50 Jason Bere .10 .03
51 Sean Berry .10 .03
52 Dante Bichette .20 .06
53 Jeff Blauser .10 .03
54 Mike Blowers .10 .03
55 Tim Bogar .10 .03
56 Tom Bolton .10 .03
57 Ricky Bones .10 .03
58 Bobby Bonilla .20 .06
59 Bret Boone .20 .06
60 Pat Borders .10 .03
61 Mike Bordick .10 .03
62 Daryl Boston .10 .03
63 Ryan Bowen .10 .03
64 Jeff Branson .10 .03
65 George Brett 1.25 .35
66 Steve Buechele .10 .03
67 Dave Burba .10 .03
68 John Burkett .10 .03
69 Jeromy Burnitz .20 .06
70 Brett Butler .20 .06
71 Rob Butler .10 .03
72 Ken Caminiti .20 .06
73 Cris Carpenter .10 .03
74 Vinny Castilla .20 .06
75 Andujar Cedeno .10 .03
76 Wes Chamberlain .10 .03
77 Archi Cianfrocco .10 .03
78 Dave Clark .10 .03
79 Jerald Clark .10 .03
80 Royce Clayton .10 .03
81 David Cone .20 .06
82 Jeff Conine .20 .06
83 Steve Cooke .10 .03
84 Scott Cooper .10 .03
85 Joey Cora .10 .03
86 Tim Costo .10 .03
87 Chad Curtis .10 .03
88 Ron Darling .10 .03
89 Danny Darwin .10 .03
90 Rob Deer .10 .03
91 Jim Deshaies .10 .03
92 Delino DeShields .10 .03
93 Rob Dibble .20 .06
94 Gary DiSarcina .10 .03
95 Doug Drabek .10 .03
96 Scott Erickson .10 .03
97 Rikkert Faneyte RC .10 .03
98 Jeff Fassero .10 .03
99 Alex Fernandez .10 .03
100 Cecil Fielder .20 .06
101 Dave Fleming .10 .03
102 Darrin Fletcher .10 .03
103 Scott Fletcher .10 .03
104 Mike Gallego .10 .03
105 Carlos Garcia .10 .03
106 Jeff Gardner .10 .03
107 Brent Gates .10 .03
108 Benji Gil .10 .03
109 Bernard Gilkey .10 .03
110 Chris Gomez .10 .03
111 Luis Gonzalez .20 .06
112 Tom Gordon .10 .03
113 Jim Gott .10 .03
114 Mark Grace .30 .09
115 Tommy Greene .10 .03
116 Willie Greene .10 .03
117 Ken Griffey Jr. .75 .23
118 Bill Gullickson .10 .03
119 Ricky Gutierrez .10 .03
120 Juan Guzman .10 .03
121 Chris Gwynn .10 .03
122 Tony Gwynn .60 .18
123 Jeffrey Hammonds .10 .03
124 Erik Hanson .10 .03
125 Gene Harris .10 .03
126 Greg W. Harris .10 .03
127 Bryan Harvey .10 .03
128 Billy Hatcher .10 .03
129 Hilly Hathaway .10 .03
130 Charlie Hayes .10 .03
131 Rickey Henderson .50 .15
132 Mike Henneman .10 .03
133 Pat Hentgen .10 .03
134 Roberto Hernandez .10 .03
135 Orel Hershiser .20 .06
136 Phil Hiatt .10 .03
137 Glenallen Hill .10 .03
138 Ken Hill .10 .03
139 Eric Hillman .10 .03
140 Chris Hoiles .10 .03
141 Dave Hollins .10 .03
142 David Hulse .10 .03
143 Todd Hundley .10 .03
144 Pete Incaviglia .10 .03
145 Danny Jackson .10 .03
146 John Jaha .10 .03
147 Domingo Jean .10 .03
148 Gregg Jefferies .10 .03
149 Reggie Jefferson .10 .03
150 Lance Johnson .10 .03
151 Bobby Jones .10 .03
152 Chipper Jones .50 .15
153 Todd Jones .10 .03
154 Brian Jordan .20 .06
155 Wally Joyner .20 .06
156 David Justice .20 .06
157 Ron Karkovice .10 .03
158 Eric Karros .20 .06
159 Jeff Kent .20 .06
160 Jimmy Key .20 .06
161 Mark Kiefer .10 .03
162 Darryl Kile .20 .06
163 Jeff King .10 .03
164 Wayne Kirby .10 .03
165 Ryan Klesko .20 .06
166 Chuck Knoblauch .20 .06
167 Chad Kreuter .10 .03
168 John Kruk .20 .06
169 Mark Langston .10 .03
170 Mike Lansing .10 .03
171 Barry Larkin .50 .15
172 Manuel Lee .10 .03
173 Phil Leftwich RC .10 .03
174 Darren Lewis .10 .03
175 Derek Lilliquist .10 .03
176 Jose Lind .10 .03
177 Albie Lopez .10 .03
178 Javier Lopez .20 .06
179 Torey Lovullo .10 .03
180 Scott Lydy .10 .03
181 Mike Macfarlane .10 .03
182 Shane Mack .10 .03
183 Greg Maddux .75 .23
184 Dave Magadan .10 .03
185 Joe Magrane .10 .03
186 Kirk Manwaring .10 .03
187 Al Martin .10 .03
188 Pedro A. Martinez RC .10 .03
189 Pedro Martinez .50 .15
190 Ramon Martinez .10 .03
191 Tino Martinez .30 .09
192 Don Mattingly 1.25 .35
193 Derrick May .10 .03
194 David McCarty .10 .03
195 Ben McDonald .10 .03
196 Roger McDowell .10 .03
197 Fred McGriff UER .30 .09
(Stats on back have 73 stolen bases for 1989; should be 7)
198 Mark McLemore .10 .03
199 Greg McMichael .10 .03
200 Jeff McNeely .10 .03
201 Brian McRae .10 .03
202 Pat Meares .10 .03
203 Roberto Mejia .10 .03
204 Orlando Merced .10 .03
205 Jose Mesa .10 .03
206 Blas Minor .10 .03
207 Angel Miranda .10 .03
208 Paul Molitor .30 .09
209 Raul Mondesi .20 .06
210 Jeff Montgomery .10 .03
211 Mickey Morandini .10 .03
212 Mike Morgan .10 .03
213 Jamie Moyer .20 .06
214 Bobby Munoz .10 .03
215 Troy Neel .10 .03
216 Dave Nilsson .10 .03
217 John O'Donoghue .10 .03
218 Paul O'Neill .30 .09
219 Jose Offerman .10 .03
220 Joe Oliver .10 .03
221 Greg Olson .10 .03
222 Donovan Osborne .10 .03
223 Jayhawk Owens .10 .03
224 Mike Pagliarulo .10 .03
225 Craig Paquette .10 .03
226 Roger Pavlik .10 .03
227 Brad Pennington .10 .03
228 Eduardo Perez .10 .03
229 Mike Perez .10 .03
230 Tony Phillips .10 .03
231 Hipolito Pichardo .10 .03
232 Phil Plantier .10 .03
233 Curtis Pride RC .25 .07
234 Tim Pugh .10 .03
235 Scott Radinsky .10 .03
236 Pat Rapp .10 .03
237 Kevin Reimer .10 .03
238 Armando Reynoso .10 .03
239 Jose Rijo .10 .03
240 Cal Ripken 1.50 .45
241 Kevin Roberson .10 .03
242 Kenny Rogers .20 .06
243 Kevin Rogers .10 .03
244 Mel Rojas .10 .03
245 John Roper .10 .03
246 Kirk Rueter .20 .06
247 Scott Ruffcorn .10 .03
248 Ken Ryan .10 .03
249 Nolan Ryan 2.00 .60
250 Bret Saberhagen .20 .06
251 Tim Salmon .30 .09
252 Reggie Sanders .20 .06
253 Curt Schilling .30 .09
254 David Segui .10 .03
255 Aaron Sele .10 .03
256 Scott Servais .10 .03
257 Gary Sheffield .20 .06
258 Ruben Sierra .10 .03
259 Don Slaught .10 .03
260 Lee Smith .20 .06
261 Cory Snyder .10 .03
262 Paul Sorrento .10 .03
263 Sammy Sosa .75 .23
264 Bill Spiers .10 .03
265 Mike Stanley .10 .03
266 Dave Staton .10 .03
267 Terry Steinbach .10 .03
268 Kevin Stocker .10 .03
269 Todd Stottlemyre .10 .03
270 Doug Strange .10 .03
271 Bill Swift .10 .03
272 Kevin Tapani .10 .03
273 Tony Tarasco .10 .03
274 Julian Tavarez RC .10 .03
275 Mickey Tettleton .10 .03
276 Ryan Thompson .10 .03
277 Chris Turner .10 .03
278 John Valentin .10 .03
279 Todd Van Poppel .10 .03
280 Andy Van Slyke .20 .06
281 Mo Vaughn .20 .06
282 Robin Ventura .20 .06
283 Frank Viola .20 .06
284 Jose Vizcaino .10 .03
285 Omar Vizquel .20 .06
286 Larry Walker .30 .09
287 Duane Ward .10 .03
288 Allen Watson .10 .03
289 Bill Wegman .10 .03
290 Turk Wendell .10 .03
291 Lou Whitaker .20 .06
292 Devon White .10 .03
293 Rondell White .20 .06
294 Mark Whiten .10 .03
295 Darrel Whitmore .10 .03
296 Bob Wickman .10 .03
297 Rick Wilkins .10 .03
298 Bernie Williams .30 .09
299 Matt Williams .20 .06
300 Woody Williams .20 .06
301 Nigel Wilson .10 .03
302 Dave Winfield .20 .06
303 Anthony Young .10 .03
304 Eric Young .10 .03
305 Todd Zeile .10 .03
306 Jack McDowell TP .20 .06
John Burkett
Tom Glavine
307 Randy Johnson TP .30 .09
308 Randy Myers TP .10 .03
309 Jack McDowell TP .10 .03
310 Mike Piazza TP .50 .15
311 Barry Bonds TP .60 .18
312 Andres Galarraga TP .10 .03
313 Juan Gonzalez TP .60 .18
Barry Bonds
314 Albert Belle TP .20 .06
315 Kenny Lofton TP .10 .03
316 Barry Bonds CL .60 .18
317 Ken Griffey Jr. CL .50 .15
318 Mike Piazza CL .50 .15
319 Kirby Puckett CL .30 .09
320 Nolan Ryan CL .50 .15
321 Roberto Alomar CL .20 .06
322 Roger Clemens CL .50 .15
323 Juan Gonzalez CL .30 .09
324 Ken Griffey Jr. CL .50 .15
325 David Justice CL .10 .03
326 John Kruk CL .10 .03
327 Frank Thomas CL .20 .06
328 Tim Salmon TC .20 .06
329 Jeff Bagwell TC .20 .06
330 Mark McGwire TC .60 .18
331 Roberto Alomar TC .20 .06
332 David Justice TC .10 .03
333 Pat Listach TC .10 .03
334 Ozzie Smith TC .50 .15
335 Ryne Sandberg TC .50 .15
336 Mike Piazza TC .50 .15
337 Cliff Floyd TC .10 .03
338 Barry Bonds TC .60 .18
339 Albert Belle TC .20 .06
340 Ken Griffey Jr. TC .50 .15
341 Gary Sheffield TC .10 .03
342 Dwight Gooden TC .20 .06
343 Cal Ripken TC .75 .23
344 Tony Gwynn TC .30 .09
345 Lenny Dykstra TC .10 .03
346 Andy Van Slyke TC .10 .03
347 Juan Gonzalez TC .30 .09
348 Roger Clemens TC .50 .15
349 Barry Larkin TC .20 .06
350 Andres Galarraga TC .10 .03
351 Kevin Appier TC .10 .03
352 Cecil Fielder TC .10 .03
353 Kirby Puckett TC .30 .09
354 Frank Thomas TC .30 .09
355 Don Mattingly TC .60 .18
356 Bo Jackson .50 .15
357 Randy Johnson .50 .15
358 Darren Daulton .20 .06
359 Charlie Hough .20 .06
360 Andres Galarraga .20 .06
361 Mike Felder .10 .03
362 Chris Hammond .10 .03
363 Shawon Dunston .10 .03
364 Junior Felix .10 .03
365 Ray Lankford .10 .03
366 Darryl Strawberry .30 .09
367 Dave Magadan .10 .03
368 Gregg Olson .10 .03
369 Lenny Dykstra .20 .06
370 Darrin Jackson .10 .03
371 Dave Stewart .20 .06
372 Terry Pendleton .20 .06
373 Arthur Rhodes .10 .03
374 Benito Santiago .20 .06
375 Travis Fryman .20 .06
376 Scott Brosius .20 .06
377 Stan Belinda .10 .03
378 Derek Parks .10 .03
379 Kevin Seitzer .10 .03
380 Wade Boggs .30 .09
381 Wally Whitehurst .10 .03
382 Scott Leius .10 .03
383 Danny Tartabull .10 .03
384 Harold Reynolds .20 .06
385 Tim Raines .20 .06
386 Darryl Hamilton .10 .03
387 Felix Fermin .10 .03
388 Jim Eisenreich .10 .03
389 Kurt Abbott .20 .06
390 Kevin Appier .20 .06
391 Chris Bosio .10 .03
392 Randy Tomlin .10 .03
393 Bob Hamelin .10 .03
394 Kevin Gross .10 .03
395 Wil Cordero .10 .03
396 Joe Girardi .10 .03
397 Orestes Destrade .10 .03
398 Chris Haney .10 .03
399 Xavier Hernandez .10 .03
400 Mike Piazza 1.00 .30
401 Alex Arias .10 .03
402 Tom Candiotti .10 .03
403 Kirk Gibson .20 .06
404 Chuck Carr .10 .03
405 Brady Anderson .20 .06
406 Greg Gagne .10 .03
407 Bruce Ruffin .10 .03
408 Scott Hemond .10 .03
409 Keith Miller .10 .03
410 John Wetteland .20 .06
411 Eric Anthony .10 .03
412 Andre Dawson .20 .06
413 Doug Henry .10 .03
414 John Franco .20 .06
415 Julio Franco .20 .06
416 Dave Hansen .10 .03
417 Mike Harkey .10 .03
418 Jack Armstrong .10 .03
419 Joe Orsulak .10 .03
420 John Smoltz .30 .09
421 Scott Livingstone .10 .03
422 Darren Holmes .10 .03
423 Ed Sprague .10 .03
424 Jay Buhner .20 .06
425 Kirby Puckett .50 .15
426 Phil Clark .10 .03
427 Anthony Young .10 .03
428 Reggie Jefferson .10 .03
429 Mariano Duncan .10 .03
430 Tom Glavine .30 .09
431 Dave Henderson .10 .03
432 Melido Perez .10 .03
433 Paul Wagner .10 .03
434 Tim Worrell .10 .03
435 Ozzie Guillen .10 .03
436 Mike Butcher .10 .03
437 Jim Deshaies .10 .03
438 Kevin Young .10 .03
439 Tom Browning .10 .03
440 Mike Greenwell .10 .03
441 Mike Stanton .10 .03
442 John Doherty .10 .03
443 John Dopson .10 .03
444 Carlos Baerga .10 .03
445 Jack McDowell .10 .03
446 Kent Mercker .10 .03
447 Ricky Jordan .10 .03
448 Jerry Browne .10 .03
449 Fernando Vina .30 .09
450 Jim Abbott .30 .09
451 Teddy Higuera .10 .03
452 Tim Naehring .10 .03
453 Jim Leyritz .10 .03
454 Frank Castillo .10 .03
455 Joe Carter .20 .06
456 Craig Biggio .30 .09
457 Geronimo Pena .10 .03
458 Alejandro Pena .10 .03
459 Mike Moore .10 .03
460 Randy Myers .10 .03
461 Greg Myers .10 .03
462 Greg Hibbard .10 .03
463 Jose Guzman .10 .03
464 Tom Pagnozzi .10 .03
465 Marquis Grissom .10 .03
466 Tim Wallach .10 .03
467 Joe Grahe .10 .03
468 Bob Tewksbury .10 .03
469 B.J. Surhoff .20 .06
470 Kevin Mitchell .10 .03
471 Bobby Witt .10 .03
472 Milt Thompson .10 .03
473 John Smiley .10 .03
474 Alan Trammell .30 .09
475 Mike Mussina .50 .15
476 Rick Aguilera .10 .03
477 Jose Valentin .10 .03
478 Harold Baines .20 .06
479 Bip Roberts .10 .03
480 Edgar Martinez .30 .09
481 Rheal Cormier .10 .03
482 Hal Morris .10 .03
483 Pat Kelly .10 .03
484 Roberto Kelly .10 .03
485 Chris Sabo .10 .03
486 Kent Hrbek .20 .06
487 Scott Kamieniecki .10 .03
488 Walt Weiss .10 .03
489 Karl Rhodes .10 .03
490 Derek Bell .10 .03
491 Chili Davis .20 .06
492 Brian Harper .10 .03
493 Felix Jose .10 .03
494 Trevor Hoffman .20 .06
495 Dennis Eckersley .20 .06
496 Pedro Astacio .10 .03
497 Jay Bell .20 .06
498 Randy Velarde .10 .03
499 David Wells .20 .06
500 Frank Thomas .50 .15
501 Mark Lemke .10 .03
502 Mike Devereaux .10 .03
503 Chuck McElroy .10 .03
504 Luis Polonia .10 .03
505 Damion Easley .10 .03
506 Greg A. Harris .10 .03
507 Chris James .10 .03
508 Terry Mulholland .10 .03
509 Pete Smith .10 .03
510 Rickey Henderson .50 .15
511 Sid Fernandez .10 .03
512 Al Leiter .20 .06
513 Doug Jones .10 .03
514 Steve Farr .10 .03
515 Chuck Finley .20 .06
516 Bobby Thigpen .10 .03
517 Jim Edmonds .30 .09
518 Graeme Lloyd .10 .03
519 Dwight Gooden .30 .09
520 Pat Listach .10 .03
521 Kevin Bass .10 .03
522 Willie Banks .10 .03
523 Steve Finley .20 .06
524 Delino DeShields .10 .03
525 Mark McGwire 1.25 .35
526 Greg Swindell .10 .03
527 Chris Nabholz .10 .03
528 Scott Sanders .10 .03
529 David Segui .10 .03
530 Howard Johnson .10 .03
531 Jaime Navarro .10 .03
532 Jose Vizcaino .10 .03
533 Mark Lewis .10 .03
534 Pete Harnisch .10 .03
535 Robby Thompson .10 .03
536 Marcus Moore .10 .03
537 Kevin Brown .20 .06
538 Mark Clark .10 .03
539 Sterling Hitchcock .10 .03
540 Will Clark .50 .15
541 Denis Boucher .10 .03
542 Jack Morris .20 .06
543 Pedro Munoz .10 .03
544 Bret Boone .20 .06
545 Ozzie Smith .75 .23
546 Dennis Martinez .20 .06
547 Dan Wilson .10 .03
548 Rick Sutcliffe .20 .06
549 Kevin McReynolds .10 .03
550 Roger Clemens 1.00 .30
551 Todd Benzinger .10 .03
552 Bill Haselman .10 .03
553 Bobby Munoz .10 .03
554 Ellis Burks .20 .06
555 Ryne Sandberg .75 .23
556 Lee Smith .20 .06
557 Danny Bautista .10 .03
558 Rey Sanchez .10 .03
559 Norm Charlton .10 .03
560 Jose Canseco .50 .15
561 Tim Belcher .10 .03
562 Denny Neagle .20 .06
563 Eric Davis .20 .06
564 Jody Reed .10 .03
565 Kenny Lofton .20 .06
566 Gary Gaetti .20 .06
567 Todd Worrell .10 .03
568 Mark Portugal .10 .03
569 Dick Schofield .10 .03
570 Andy Benes .10 .03
571 Zane Smith .10 .03
572 Bobby Ayala .10 .03
573 Chip Hale .10 .03
574 Bob Welch .10 .03
575 Deion Sanders .30 .09
576 David Nied .10 .03
577 Pat Mahomes .10 .03
578 Charles Nagy .10 .03
579 Otis Nixon .10 .03
580 Dean Palmer .20 .06
581 Roberto Petagine .10 .03
582 Dwight Smith .10 .03
583 Jeff Russell .10 .03
584 Mark Dewey .10 .03
585 Greg Vaughn .20 .06
586 Brian Hunter .10 .03
587 Willie McGee .20 .06

588 Pedro Martinez .50 .15
589 Roger Salkeld .10 .03
590 Jeff Bagwell .30 .09
591 Spike Owen .10 .03
592 Jeff Reardon .20 .06
593 Erik Pappas .10 .03
594 Brian Williams .10 .03
595 Eddie Murray .50 .15
596 Henry Rodriguez .10 .03
597 Erik Hanson .10 .03
598 Stan Javier .10 .03
599 Mitch Williams .10 .03
600 John Olerud .20 .06
601 Vince Coleman .10 .03
602 Damon Berryhill .10 .03
603 Tom Brunansky .10 .03
604 Robb Nen .20 .06
605 Rafael Palmeiro .30 .09
606 Cal Eldred .10 .03
607 Jeff Brantley .10 .03
608 Alan Mills .10 .03
609 Jeff Nelson .10 .03
610 Barry Bonds 1.25 .35
611 Carlos Pulido RC .10 .03
612 Tim Hyers RC .10 .03
613 Steve Howe .10 .03
614 Brian Turang RC .10 .03
615 Leo Gomez .10 .03
616 Jesse Orosco .10 .03
617 Dan Pasqua .10 .03
618 Marvin Freeman .10 .03
619 Tony Fernandez .10 .03
620 Albert Belle .20 .06
621 Eddie Taubensee .10 .03
622 Mike Jackson .10 .03
623 Jose Bautista .10 .03
624 Jim Thome .50 .15
625 Ivan Rodriguez .50 .15
626 Ben Rivera .10 .03
627 Dave Valle .10 .03
628 Tom Henke .10 .03
629 Omar Vizquel .20 .06
630 Juan Gonzalez .50 .15
631 Roberto Alomar UP .20 .06
632 Barry Bonds UP .60 .18
633 Juan Gonzalez UP .30 .09
634 Ken Griffey Jr. UP .50 .15
635 Michael Jordan UP 1.50 .45
636 David Justice UP .10 .03
637 Mike Piazza UP .50 .15
638 Kirby Puckett UP .30 .09
639 Tim Salmon UP .20 .06
640 Frank Thomas UP .30 .09
641 Alan Benes FF RC .10 .03
642 Johnny Damon FF .50 .15
643 Brad Fullmer FF RC .50 .15
644 Derek Jeter FF 1.50 .45
645 Derrek Lee FF RC .60 .18
646 Alex Ochoa .10 .03
647 Alex Rodriguez FF RC 10.00 3.00
648 Jose Silva FF RC .10 .03
649 Terrell Wade FF RC .10 .03
650 Preston Wilson FF .30 .09
651 Shane Andrews .10 .03
652 James Baldwin .10 .03
653 Ricky Bottalico RC .25 .07
654 Tavo Alvarez .10 .03
655 Donnie Elliott .10 .03
656 Joey Eischen .10 .03
657 Jason Giambi .50 .15
658 Todd Hollandsworth .10 .03
659 Brian L. Hunter .10 .03
660 Charles Johnson .20 .06
661 Michael Jordan RC 3.00 .90
662 Jeff Juden .10 .03
663 Mike Kelly .10 .03
664 James Mouton .10 .03
665 Ray Holbert .10 .03
666 Pokey Reese .10 .03
667 Ruben Santana RC .10 .03
668 Paul Spoljaric .10 .03
669 Luis Lopez .10 .03
670 Matt Walbeck .10 .03
P50 Ken Griffey Jr. Promo 1.00 .30

1994 Collector's Choice Gold Signature

This 670-card Gold Signature set is a parallel to the basic Collector's Choice issue. These cards were randomly inserted into first and second series hobby and retail packs at a rate of one in 36 and jumbo packs at a rate of one in 20. Gold cards were also issued five per factory set. These cards are identical to the basic issue except for gold foil fronts and a facsimile gold foil player's signature. Some subset cards feature borderless designs (unlike the basic player cards), thus their corresponding borderless Gold Foil Signature cards differ only by the gold foil replica autograph. The Jeffrey Hammonds card has the signature of Orioles General Manager Roland Hemond.

Nm-Mt Ex-Mt
*STARS: 12.5X TO 30X BASIC CARDS
*ROOKIES: 10X TO 25X BASIC CARDS

1994 Collector's Choice Silver Signature

This 670-card set is a parallel to the basic Collector's Choice set. One card was inserted into every first and second series pack. Silver cards were also inserted at different rates in other pack forms. Each Silver Foil Signature card is identical in design to its corresponding regular issue card except for the silver borders and silver replica autograph. As with the gold set, the Jeffrey Hammonds card has the signature of Orioles General Manager Roland Hemond.

	Nm-Mt	Ex-Mt
COMPLETE SET (670)	200.00	60.00
COMP. SERIES 1 (320)	80.00	24.00
COMP. SERIES 2 (350)	120.00	36.00

*STARS: 1.5X TO 4X BASIC CARDS
*ROOKIES: 1X TO 2.5X BASIC CARDS

1994 Collector's Choice Home Run All-Stars

This eight-card standard-size set served as the eighth place prize in the Crash the Game contest, which was a promotion in both series of Collector's Choice. The series one expiration was May 18, 1994; series two was Oct. 31, 1994. The cards are numbered with an "HA" prefix.

	Nm-Mt	Ex-Mt
COMPLETE SET (8)	4.00	1.20
HA1 Juan Gonzalez	.75	.23
HA2 Ken Griffey Jr.	1.25	.35
HA3 Barry Bonds	2.00	.60
HA4 Bobby Bonilla	.30	.09
HA5 Cecil Fielder UER (Card number is HA4)	.30	.09
HA6 Albert Belle	.30	.09
HA7 David Justice	.30	.09
HA8 Mike Piazza	1.50	.45

1994 Collector's Choice Team vs. Team

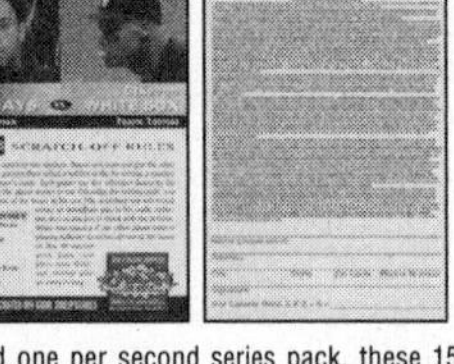

Issued one per second series pack, these 15 foldout, scratch-off game cards feature one team's lineup against the other. Various prizes were available through these game cards. The most plentiful was the eighth place Home Run All-Stars hologram set. Prizes were redeemable through October 31, 1994. Scratch-off rules and two small player photos are on the front with complete rules and provisions on the back. The cards fold out to expose the game portion. Cards that are scratched are half the values below.

	Nm-Mt	Ex-Mt
COMPLETE SET (15)	5.00	1.50
1 Roberto Alomar / Frank Thomas	.25	.07
2 Barry Bonds / Ken Griffey Jr.	.40	.12
3 Roger Clemens / Don Mattingly	.60	.18
4 Lenny Dykstra / David Justice	.10	.03
5 Andres Galarraga / Tony Gwynn	.30	.09
6 Dwight Gooden / Gary Sheffield	.10	.03
7 Ken Griffey Jr. / Juan Gonzalez	.40	.12
8 Barry Larkin / Jeff Bagwell	.15	.04
9 Pat Listach / Albert Belle	.10	.03
10 Mark McGwire / Tim Salmon	.60	.18
11 Mike Piazza / Barry Bonds	.50	.15
12 Kirby Puckett / Brian McRae	.25	.07
13 Cal Ripken / Cecil Fielder	.75	.23
14 Ryne Sandberg / Ozzie Smith	.40	.12
15 Andy Van Slyke / Cliff Floyd	.10	.03

1995 Collector's Choice

Produced by Upper Deck, this set contains 530 standard-size cards issued in 12-card foil hobby and retail packs of which carried a suggested price of 99 cents. The fronts have a color photo with a white border and the player's last name at the bottom in his team's color. The backs have an action photo at the top with statistics and information at the bottom with a silver Upper Deck hologram below that. Subsets featured are Rookie Class (1-27), Future Foundation (28-45), Best of the '90s (51-65) and What's the Call? (86-90). The key Rookie Card in this set is Hideo Nomo. The 55-card Trade set represents the cards a collector received when the five randomly inserted trade cards were redeemed. They are numbered in continuation of the regular Collector's Choice cards but have a "T" suffix. The cards numbered 542-552 were also issued as a bonus to dealers who ordered collector's choice factory sets. The trade cards offer expired on February 1, 1996.

	Nm-Mt	Ex-Mt
COMPLETE SET (530)	20.00	6.00
COMP.FACT.SET (545)	30.00	9.00
COMMON CARD (1-530)	.10	.03
COMP.TRADE SET (55)	10.00	3.00
COMMON TR. (531-585)	.25	.07

1 Charles Johnson .20 .06
2 Scott Ruffcorn .10 .03
3 Ray Durham .20 .06
4 Armando Benitez .20 .06
5 Alex Rodriguez 1.25 .35
6 Julian Tavarez .10 .03
7 Chad Ogea .10 .03
8 Quilvio Veras .10 .03
9 Phil Nevin .20 .06
10 Michael Tucker .10 .03
11 Mark Thompson .10 .03
12 Rod Henderson .10 .03
13 Andrew Lorraine .10 .03
14 Joe Randa .10 .03
15 Derek Jeter 1.25 .35
16 Tony Clark .10 .03
17 Juan Castillo .10 .03
18 Mark Acre .10 .03
19 Orlando Miller .10 .03
20 Paul Wilson .10 .03
21 John Mabry .30 .09
22 Garey Ingram .10 .03
23 Garret Anderson .20 .06
24 Dave Stevens .10 .03
25 Dustin Hermanson .10 .03
26 Paul Shuey .10 .03
27 J.R. Phillips .10 .03
28 Ruben Rivera FF .10 .03
29 Nomar Garciaparra FF 1.50 .45
30 John Wasdin FF .10 .03
31 Jim Pittsley FF .10 .03
32 Scott Elarton FF RC .25 .07
33 Raul Casanova FF RC .10 .03
34 Todd Greene FF .10 .03
35 Bill Pulsipher FF .10 .03
36 Trey Beamon FF .10 .03
37 Curtis Goodwin FF .10 .03
38 Doug Million FF .10 .03
39 Karim Garcia FF RC .25 .07
40 Ben Grieve FF .20 .06
41 Mark Farris FF .10 .03
42 Juan Acevedo FF RC .10 .03
43 C.J. Nitkowski FF .10 .03
44 Travis Miller FF RC .10 .03
45 Reid Ryan FF .20 .06
46 Nolan Ryan 2.00 .60
47 Robin Yount .75 .23
48 Ryne Sandberg .75 .23
49 George Brett 1.25 .35
50 Mike Schmidt .75 .23
51 Cecil Fielder B90 .10 .03
52 Nolan Ryan B90 1.00 .30
53 Rickey Henderson B90 .30 .09
54 George Brett B90 .50 .15
Robin Yount
Dave Winfield
55 Sid Bream B90 .10 .03
56 Carlos Baerga B90 .10 .03
57 Lee Smith B90 .10 .03
58 Mark Whiten B90 .10 .03
59 Joe Carter B90 .10 .03
60 Barry Bonds B90 .60 .18
61 Tony Gwynn B90 .30 .09
62 Ken Griffey Jr. B90 .50 .15
63 Greg Maddux B90 .50 .15
64 Frank Thomas B90 .50 .15
65 Dennis Martinez B90 .10 .03
Kenny Rogers
66 David Cone .20 .06
67 Greg Maddux .75 .23
68 Jimmy Key .20 .06
69 Fred McGriff .30 .09
70 Ken Griffey Jr. .75 .23
71 Matt Williams .20 .06
72 Paul O'Neill .30 .09
73 Tony Gwynn .60 .18
74 Randy Johnson .50 .15
75 Frank Thomas .50 .15
76 Jeff Bagwell .30 .09
77 Kirby Puckett .50 .15
78 Bob Hamelin .10 .03
79 Raul Mondesi .20 .06
80 Mike Piazza .75 .23
81 Kenny Lofton .20 .06
82 Barry Bonds 1.25 .35
83 Albert Belle .20 .06
84 Juan Gonzalez .50 .15
85 Cal Ripken Jr. 1.50 .45
86 Barry Bonds WC .60 .18
87 Mike Piazza WC .50 .15
88 Ken Griffey Jr. WC .50 .15
89 Frank Thomas WC .30 .09
90 Juan Gonzalez WC .30 .09
91 Jorge Fabregas .10 .03
92 J.T. Snow .20 .06
93 Spike Owen .10 .03
94 Eduardo Perez .10 .03
95 Bo Jackson .50 .15
96 Damion Easley .10 .03
97 Gary DiSarcina .10 .03
98 Jim Edmonds .20 .06
99 Chad Curtis .10 .03
100 Tim Salmon .30 .09
101 Chili Davis .20 .06
102 Chuck Finley .20 .06
103 Mark Langston .10 .03
104 Brian Anderson .10 .03
105 Lee Smith .20 .06
106 Phil Leftwich .10 .03
107 Chris Donnels .10 .03
108 John Hudek .10 .03
109 Craig Biggio .30 .09
110 Luis Gonzalez .20 .06
111 Brian L. Hunter .10 .03
112 James Mouton .10 .03
113 Scott Servais .10 .03
114 Tony Eusebio .10 .03
115 Derek Bell .10 .03
116 Doug Drabek .10 .03
117 Shane Reynolds .10 .03
118 Darryl Kile .20 .06
119 Greg Swindell .10 .03
120 Phil Plantier .10 .03
121 Todd Jones .10 .03
122 Steve Ontiveros .10 .03
123 Bobby Witt .10 .03
124 Brent Gates .10 .03
125 Rickey Henderson .50 .15
126 Scott Brosius .20 .06
127 Mike Bordick .10 .03
128 Fausto Cruz .10 .03
129 Stan Javier .10 .03
130 Mark McGwire 1.25 .35
131 Geronimo Berroa .10 .03
132 Terry Steinbach .10 .03
133 Steve Karsay .10 .03
134 Dennis Eckersley .20 .06
135 Ruben Sierra .10 .03
136 Ron Darling .10 .03
137 Todd Van Poppel .10 .03
138 Alex Gonzalez .10 .03
139 John Olerud .20 .06
140 Roberto Alomar .50 .15
141 Darren Hall .10 .03
142 Ed Sprague .10 .03
143 Devon White .20 .06
144 Shawn Green .20 .06
145 Paul Molitor .30 .09
146 Pat Borders .10 .03
147 Carlos Delgado .20 .06
148 Juan Guzman .10 .03
149 Pat Hentgen .10 .03
150 Joe Carter .20 .06
151 Dave Stewart .20 .06
152 Todd Stottlemyre .10 .03
153 Dick Schofield .10 .03
154 Chipper Jones .50 .15
155 Ryan Klesko .20 .06
156 David Justice .20 .06
157 Mike Kelly .10 .03
158 Roberto Kelly .10 .03
159 Tony Tarasco .10 .03
160 Javier Lopez .20 .06
161 Steve Avery .10 .03
162 Greg McMichael .10 .03
163 Kent Mercker .10 .03
164 Mark Lemke .10 .03
165 Tom Glavine .30 .09
166 Jose Oliva .10 .03
167 John Smoltz .30 .09
168 Jeff Blauser .10 .03
169 Troy O'Leary .10 .03
170 Greg Vaughn .20 .06
171 Jody Reed .10 .03
172 Kevin Seitzer .10 .03
173 Jeff Cirillo .10 .03
174 B.J. Surhoff .20 .06
175 Cal Eldred .10 .03
176 Jose Valentin .10 .03
177 Turner Ward .10 .03
178 Darryl Hamilton .10 .03
179 Pat Listach .10 .03
180 Matt Mieske .10 .03
181 Brian Harper .10 .03
182 Dave Nilsson .10 .03
183 Mike Fetters .10 .03
184 John Jaha .10 .03
185 Ricky Bones .10 .03
186 Geronimo Pena .10 .03
187 Bob Tewksbury .10 .03
188 Todd Zeile .10 .03
189 Danny Jackson .10 .03
190 Ray Lankford .10 .03
191 Bernard Gilkey .10 .03
192 Brian Jordan .20 .06
193 Tom Pagnozzi .10 .03
194 Rick Sutcliffe .20 .06
195 Mark Whiten .10 .03
196 Tom Henke .10 .03
197 Rene Arocha .10 .03
198 Allen Watson .10 .03
199 Mike Perez .10 .03
200 Ozzie Smith .75 .23
201 Anthony Young .10 .03
202 Rey Sanchez .10 .03
203 Steve Buechele .10 .03
204 Shawon Dunston .10 .03
205 Mark Grace .30 .09
206 Glenallen Hill .10 .03
207 Eddie Zambrano .10 .03
208 Rick Wilkins .10 .03
209 Derrick May .10 .03
210 Sammy Sosa .75 .23
211 Kevin Roberson .10 .03
212 Steve Trachsel .10 .03
213 Willie Banks .10 .03
214 Kevin Foster .10 .03
215 Randy Myers .10 .03
216 Mike Morgan .10 .03
217 Rafael Bournigal .10 .03
218 Delino DeShields .10 .03
219 Tim Wallach .10 .03
220 Eric Karros .20 .06
221 Jose Offerman .10 .03
222 Tom Candiotti .10 .03
223 Ismael Valdes .10 .03
224 Henry Rodriguez .10 .03
225 Billy Ashley .10 .03
226 Darren Dreifort .10 .03
227 Ramon Martinez .10 .03
228 Pedro Astacio .10 .03
229 Orel Hershiser .20 .06
230 Brett Butler .20 .06
231 Todd Hollandsworth .10 .03
232 Chan Ho Park .20 .06
233 Mike Lansing .10 .03
234 Sean Berry .10 .03
235 Rondell White .20 .06
236 Ken Hill .10 .03
237 Marquis Grissom .10 .03
238 Larry Walker .30 .09
239 John Wetteland .10 .03
240 Cliff Floyd .20 .06
241 Joey Eischen .10 .03
242 Lou Frazier .10 .03
243 Darrin Fletcher .10 .03
244 Pedro Martinez .50 .15
245 Wil Cordero .10 .03
246 Jeff Fassero .10 .03
247 Butch Henry .10 .03
248 Mel Rojas .10 .03
249 Kirk Rueter .10 .03
250 Moises Alou .20 .06
251 Rod Beck .10 .03
252 John Patterson .10 .03
253 Robby Thompson .10 .03
254 Royce Clayton .10 .03
255 Wm. VanLandingham .10 .03
256 Darren Lewis .10 .03
257 Kirt Manwaring .10 .03
258 Mark Portugal .10 .03
259 Bill Swift .10 .03
260 Rikkert Faneyte .10 .03
261 Mike Jackson .10 .03
262 Todd Benzinger .10 .03
263 Bud Black .10 .03
264 Salomon Torres .10 .03
265 Eddie Murray .50 .15
266 Mark Clark .10 .03
267 Paul Sorrento .10 .03
268 Jim Thome .50 .15
269 Omar Vizquel .20 .06
270 Carlos Baerga .10 .03
271 Jeff Russell .10 .03
272 Herbert Perry .10 .03
273 Sandy Alomar Jr. .10 .03
274 Dennis Martinez .20 .06
275 Manny Ramirez .20 .06
276 Wayne Kirby .10 .03
277 Charles Nagy .10 .03
278 Albie Lopez .10 .03
279 Jeromy Burnitz .20 .06
280 Dave Winfield .20 .06
281 Tim Davis .10 .03
282 Marc Newfield .10 .03
283 Tino Martinez .30 .09
284 Mike Blowers .10 .03
285 Goose Gossage .20 .06
286 Luis Sojo .10 .03
287 Edgar Martinez .30 .09
288 Rich Amaral .10 .03
289 Felix Fermin .10 .03
290 Jay Buhner .20 .06
291 Dan Wilson .10 .03
292 Bobby Ayala .10 .03
293 Dave Fleming .10 .03
294 Greg Pirkl .10 .03
295 Reggie Jefferson .10 .03
296 Greg Hibbard .10 .03
297 Yorkis Perez .10 .03
298 Kurt Miller .10 .03
299 Chuck Carr .10 .03
300 Gary Sheffield .20 .06
301 Jerry Browne .10 .03
302 Dave Magadan .10 .03
303 Kurt Abbott .10 .03
304 Pat Rapp .10 .03
305 Jeff Conine .20 .06
306 Benito Santiago .20 .06
307 Dave Weathers .10 .03
308 Robb Nen .20 .06
309 Chris Hammond .10 .03
310 Bryan Harvey .10 .03
311 Charlie Hough .20 .06
312 Greg Colbrunn .10 .03
313 David Segui .10 .03
314 Rico Brogna .10 .03
315 Jeff Kent .20 .06
316 Jose Vizcaino .10 .03
317 Jim Lindeman .10 .03
318 Carl Everett .20 .06
319 Ryan Thompson .10 .03
320 Bobby Bonilla .20 .06
321 Joe Orsulak .10 .03
322 Pete Harnisch .10 .03
323 Doug Linton .10 .03
324 Todd Hundley .10 .03
325 Bret Saberhagen .20 .06
326 Kelly Stinnett .10 .03
327 Jason Jacome .10 .03
328 Bobby Jones .10 .03
329 John Franco .20 .06
330 Rafael Palmeiro .30 .09
331 Chris Hoiles .10 .03
332 Leo Gomez .10 .03
333 Chris Sabo .10 .03
334 Brady Anderson .20 .06
335 Jeffrey Hammonds .10 .03
336 Dwight Smith .10 .03
337 Jack Voigt .10 .03
338 Harold Baines .20 .06
339 Ben McDonald .10 .03
340 Mike Mussina .50 .15
341 Bret Barberie .10 .03
342 Jamie Moyer .20 .06
343 Mike Oquist .10 .03
344 Sid Fernandez .10 .03
345 Eddie Williams .10 .03
346 Joey Hamilton .10 .03
347 Brian Williams .10 .03
348 Luis Lopez .10 .03
349 Steve Finley .20 .06
350 Andy Benes .10 .03
351 Andujar Cedeno .10 .03
352 Bip Roberts .10 .03
353 Ray McDavid .10 .03
354 Ken Caminiti .20 .06
355 Trevor Hoffman .20 .06
356 Mel Nieves .10 .03
357 Brad Ausmus .10 .03
358 Andy Ashby .10 .03
359 Scott Sanders .10 .03
360 Gregg Jefferies .10 .03
361 Mariano Duncan .10 .03
362 Dave Hollins .10 .03
363 Kevin Stocker .10 .03
364 Fernando Valenzuela .20 .06
365 Lenny Dykstra .20 .06
366 Jim Eisenreich .10 .03
367 Ricky Bottalico .10 .03
368 Doug Jones .10 .03
369 Ricky Jordan .10 .03
370 Darren Daulton .20 .06
371 Mike Lieberthal .20 .06
372 Bobby Munoz .10 .03
373 John Kruk .20 .06
374 Curt Schilling .30 .09
375 Orlando Merced .10 .03
376 Carlos Garcia .10 .03
377 Lance Parrish .20 .06
378 Steve Cooke .10 .03
379 Jeff King .10 .03
380 Jay Bell .20 .06
381 Al Martin .10 .03
382 Paul Wagner .10 .03

383 Rick White .10 .03
384 Midre Cummings .10 .03
385 Jon Lieber .10 .03
386 Dave Clark .10 .03
387 Don Slaught .10 .03
388 Denny Neagle .20 .06
389 Zane Smith .10 .03
390 Andy Van Slyke .20 .06
391 Ivan Rodriguez .50 .15
392 David Hulse .10 .03
393 John Burkett .10 .03
394 Kevin Brown .20 .06
395 Dean Palmer .20 .06
396 Otis Nixon .10 .03
397 Rick Helling .10 .03
398 Kenny Rogers .20 .06
399 Darren Oliver .10 .03
400 Will Clark .50 .15
401 Jeff Frye .10 .03
402 Kevin Gross .10 .03
403 John Dettmer .10 .03
404 Manny Lee .10 .03
405 Rusty Greer .20 .06
406 Aaron Sele .10 .03
407 Carlos Rodriguez .10 .03
408 Scott Cooper .10 .03
409 John Valentin .10 .03
410 Roger Clemens 1.00 .30
411 Mike Greenwell .10 .03
412 Tim Vanegmond .10 .03
413 Tom Brunansky .10 .03
414 Steve Farr .10 .03
415 Jose Canseco .50 .15
416 Joe Hesketh .10 .03
417 Ken Ryan .10 .03
418 Tim Naehring .10 .03
419 Frank Viola .20 .06
420 Andre Dawson .20 .06
421 Mo Vaughn .20 .06
422 Jeff Brantley .10 .03
423 Pete Schourek .10 .03
424 Hal Morris .10 .03
425 Deion Sanders .30 .09
426 Brian R. Hunter .10 .03
427 Bret Boone .20 .06
428 Willie Greene .10 .03
429 Ron Gant .20 .06
430 Barry Larkin .50 .15
431 Reggie Sanders .20 .06
432 Eddie Taubensee .10 .03
433 Jack Morris .20 .06
434 Jose Rijo .10 .03
435 Johnny Ruffin .10 .03
436 John Smiley .10 .03
437 John Roper .10 .03
438 Dave Nied .10 .03
439 Roberto Mejia .10 .03
440 Andres Galarraga .20 .06
441 Mike Kingery .10 .03
442 Curt Leskanic .10 .03
443 Walt Weiss .10 .03
444 Marvin Freeman .10 .03
445 Charlie Hayes .10 .03
446 Eric Young .10 .03
447 Ellis Burks .20 .06
448 Joe Girardi .10 .03
449 Lance Painter .10 .03
450 Dante Bichette .20 .06
451 Bruce Ruffin .10 .03
452 Jeff Granger .10 .03
453 Wally Joyner .20 .06
454 Jose Lind .10 .03
455 Jeff Montgomery .10 .03
456 Gary Gaetti .20 .06
457 Greg Gagne .10 .03
458 Vince Coleman .10 .03
459 Mike Macfarlane .10 .03
460 Brian McRae .10 .03
461 Tom Gordon .10 .03
462 Kevin Appier .20 .06
463 Billy Brewer .10 .03
464 Mark Gubicza .10 .03
465 Travis Fryman .20 .06
466 Danny Bautista .10 .03
467 Sean Bergman .10 .03
468 Mike Henneman .10 .03
469 Mike Moore .10 .03
470 Cecil Fielder .20 .06
471 Alan Trammell .30 .09
472 Kirk Gibson .20 .06
473 Tony Phillips .10 .03
474 Mickey Tettleton .10 .03
475 Lou Whitaker .20 .06
476 Chris Gomez .10 .03
477 John Doherty .10 .03
478 Greg Gohr .10 .03
479 Bill Gullickson .10 .03
480 Rick Aguilera .10 .03
481 Matt Walbeck .10 .03
482 Kevin Tapani .10 .03
483 Scott Erickson .10 .03
484 Steve Dunn .10 .03
485 David McCarty .10 .03
486 Scott Leius .10 .03
487 Pat Meares .10 .03
488 Jeff Reboulet .10 .03
489 Pedro Munoz .10 .03
490 Chuck Knoblauch .20 .06
491 Rich Becker .10 .03
492 Alex Cole .10 .03
493 Pat Mahomes .10 .03
494 Ozzie Guillen .10 .03
495 Tim Raines .20 .06
496 Kirk McCaskill .10 .03
497 Olmedo Saenz .10 .03
498 Scott Sanderson .10 .03
499 Lance Johnson .10 .03
500 Michael Jordan 1.50 .45
501 Warren Newson .10 .03
502 Ron Karkovice .10 .03
503 Wilson Alvarez .10 .03
504 Jason Bere .10 .03
505 Robin Ventura .20 .06
506 Alex Fernandez .10 .03
507 Roberto Hernandez .10 .03
508 Norberto Martin .10 .03
509 Bob Wickman .10 .03
510 Don Mattingly 1.25 .35
511 Melido Perez .10 .03
512 Pat Kelly .10 .03
513 Randy Velarde .10 .03
514 Tony Fernandez .10 .03
515 Jack McDowell .10 .03
516 Luis Polonia .10 .03
517 Bernie Williams .30 .09
518 Danny Tartabull .10 .03
519 Mike Stanley .10 .03
520 Wade Boggs .30 .09
521 Jim Leyritz .10 .03
522 Steve Howe .10 .03
523 Scott Kamieniecki .10 .03
524 Russ Davis .10 .03
525 Jim Abbott .30 .09
526 Eddie Murray CL .30 .09
527 Alex Rodriguez CL .50 .15
528 Jeff Bagwell CL .20 .06
529 Joe Carter CL .10 .03
530 Fred McGriff CL .20 .06
531T Tony Phillips TRADE .25 .07
532T D.Magadan TRADE .25 .07
533T Mike Gallego TRADE .25 .07
534T Dave Stewart TRADE .50 .15
535T T.Stottlemyre TRADE .25 .07
536T David Cone TRADE .50 .15
537T M. Grissom TRADE .25 .07
538T Derrick May TRADE .25 .07
539T Joe Oliver TRADE .25 .07
540T Scott Cooper TRADE .25 .07
541T Ken Hill TRADE .25 .07
542T H.Johnson TRADE DP .25 .07
543T B. McRae TRADE DP .25 .07
544T J.Navarro TRADE DP .25 .07
545T O.Timmons TRADE DP .50 .15
546T R. Kelly TRADE DP .25 .07
547T H.Nomo TRADE DP 3.00 .90
548T S.Andrews TRADE DP .25 .07
549T M.Grudzi TRADE DP .75 .23
550T C. Perez TRADE DP .50 .15
551T Henry Rodriguez .25 .07
TRADE DP
552T T.Tarasco TRADE DP .25 .07
553T Glenallen Hill TRADE .25 .07
554T T.Mulholland TRADE .25 .07
555T O.Hershiser TRADE .50 .15
556T Darren Bragg TRADE .25 .07
557T John Burkett TRADE .25 .07
558T Bobby Witt TRADE .25 .07
559T T.Pendleton TRADE .50 .15
560T A.Dawson TRADE .50 .15
561T Brett Butler TRADE .50 .15
562T Kevin Brown TRADE .50 .15
563T Doug Jones TRADE .25 .07
564T A.Van Slyke TRADE .50 .15
565T Jody Reed TRADE .25 .07
566T F. Valenzuela TRADE .50 .15
567T C.Hayes TRADE .25 .07
568T Benji Gil TRADE .25 .07
569T M.McLemore TRADE .25 .07
570T M.Tettleton TRADE .25 .07
571T B.Tewksbury TRADE .25 .07
572T R.Cormier TRADE .25 .07
573T V. Eshelman TRADE .25 .07
574T Mike Macfarlane .25 .07
TRADE
575T Bill Swift TRADE .25 .07
576T Mark Whiten TRADE .25 .07
577T B.Santiago TRADE .50 .15
578T Jason Bates TRADE .25 .07
579T Larry Walker TRADE .75 .23
580T Chad Curtis TRADE .25 .07
581T B.Higginson TRADE 1.25 .35
582T M.Cordova TRADE .25 .07
583T M.Devereaux TRADE .25 .07
584T John Kruk TRADE .50 .15
585T J.Wetteland TRADE .50 .15
P172 K.Griffey Jr. Promo 1.00 .30

1995 Collector's Choice Gold Signature

This set is a parallel of the 530 regular cards from the Collector's Choice set. Gold cards were inserted into one in every 35 packs, 12 per gold super pack and 15 per factory set. Unlike regular issue cards, each Gold Signature card features a gold border (except for a selection of borderless subset cards) and gold facsimile signature on front.

Nm-Mt Ex-Mt
*STARS: 6X TO 15X BASIC CARDS
*ROOKIES: 5X TO 12X BASIC

1995 Collector's Choice Silver Signature

This set is a parallel of the 530 regular cards from the Collector's Choice set. Silver Signature cards were inserted at a rate of one per pack, two per mini jumbo and 12 per silver super pack. Unlike regular issue cards, Silver Signature cards feature silver borders and a silver facsimile signature on front.

Nm-Mt Ex-Mt
COMPLETE SET (530) 60.00 18.00
*STARS: 1.5X TO 4X BASIC CARDS
*ROOKIES: 1.25X TO 3X BASIC

1995 Collector's Choice Crash the All-Star Game

This eight card standard-size set measures the standard size. The cards carry the names of players who participated in the 1995 All-Star game on July 11. The fronts feature color action player photos with a tri-colored border. The player's name and team name are printed in the bottom border. The backs contain the player's name, date of game, and the directions of how to claim a prize if the player hit a home run during the All-Star game. Winner cards could be mailed in, along with 2.00, and redeemed for a gold foil enhanced set. These enhanced cards are valued at the same value as the regular cards. The two winning cards were Mike Piazza and Frank Thomas. The cards are unnumbered and checklisted below in alphabetical order.

Nm-Mt Ex-Mt
COMPLETE SET (8) 20.00 6.00
*REDEMPTION WINNERS: 3X VALUE
1 Albert Belle 1.00 .30
2 Barry Bonds 4.00 1.20
3 Fred McGriff 1.00 .30
4 Mark McGwire 6.00 1.80
5 Raul Mondesi 1.00 .30
6 Mike Piazza 4.00 1.20
7 Manny Ramirez 1.50 .45
8 Frank Thomas 2.00 .60

1995 Collector's Choice Crash the Game

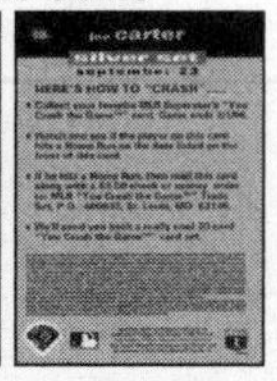

Cards from this 60-card standard-size set were randomly inserted in packs at a rate of one in five. The set was an interactive set in which all 20 players have three cards with a date on it. If the player hit a home run on that date, the collector could redeem the card for a complete enhanced set of all 20 players. The fronts have a color-action photo with the game background in yellow and a large date stamped in silver foil. The expiration date for redeeming these cards was February 1, 1996. Winning cards eligible for redemption at that time have been highlighted with a "W" in our listings below.

Nm-Mt Ex-Mt
COMPLETE SET (60) 30.00 9.00
*GOLD: 2X TO 5X SILVER CRASH
GOLD: RANDOM INSERTS IN PACKS
THREE DATES PER PLAYER
*EXCHANGE: .2X TO .5X SILVER CRASH
*GOLD EXCH: 1.5X TO 4X SILVER CRASH
ONE EXCH.SET VIA MAIL PER WINNER
CG1 Jeff Bagwell 7/30 .30 .09
CG1B Jeff Bagwell 8/13 .30 .09
CG1C Jeff Bagwell 9/28 .30 .09
CG2 Albert Belle 6/18 .20 .06
CG2B Albert Belle 8/26 .20 .06
CG2C Albert Belle 9/20 .20 .06
CG3 Barry Bonds 6/28 1.25 .35
CG3B Barry Bonds 7/9 1.25 .35
CG3C Barry Bonds 9/6 1.25 .35
CG4 Jose Canseco 6/30 W .50 .15
CG4B J.Canseco 7/30 W .50 .15
CG4C Jose Canseco 9/3 .50 .15
CG5 Joe Carter 7/14 .20 .06
CG5B Joe Carter 8/9 .20 .06
CG5C Joe Carter 9/23 .20 .06
CG6 Cecil Fielder 7/4 .20 .06
CG6B Cecil Fielder 8/2 .20 .06
CG6C Cecil Fielder 10/1 .20 .06
CG7 Juan Gonzalez 6/29 .50 .15
CG7B Juan Gonzalez 8/13 .50 .15
CG7C J.Gonzalez 9/3 W .50 .15
CG8 Ken Griffey Jr. 7/2 .75 .23
CG8B K.Griffey Jr. 8/24 W .75 .23
CG8C Ken Griffey Jr. 9/15 .75 .23
CG9 Bob Hamelin 7/23 .10 .03
CG9B Bob Hamelin 8/1 .10 .03
CG9C Bob Hamelin 9/29 .10 .03
CG10 David Justice 6/24 .20 .06
CG10B David Justice 7/25 .20 .06
CG10C David Justice 9/17 .20 .06
CG11 Ryan Klesko 7/13 .20 .06
CG11B Ryan Klesko 8/20 .20 .06
CG11C Ryan Klesko 9/10 .20 .06
CG12 Fred McGriff 8/25 .30 .09
CG12B Fred McGriff 9/8 .30 .09
CG12C Fred McGriff 9/24 .30 .09
CG13 Mark McGwire 7/23 1.25 .35
CG13B M.McGwire 8/3 W 1.25 .35
CG13C M.McGwire 9/27 1.25 .35
CG14 R.Mondesi 7/27 W .20 .06
CG14B Raul Mondesi 8/13 .20 .06
CG14C R.Mondesi 9/15 W .20 .06
CG15 Mike Piazza 7/23 W .75 .23
CG15B Mike Piazza 8/27 .75 .23
CG15C Mike Piazza 9/19 .75 .23
CG16 M.Ramirez 6/21 .20 .06
CG16B M.Ramirez 8/13 .20 .06
CG16C M.Ramirez 9/26 .20 .06
CG17 Alex Rodriguez 9/10 1.25 .35
CG17B A.Rodriguez 9/18 1.25 .35
CG17C A.Rodriguez 9/24 1.25 .35
CG18 Gary Sheffield .20 .06
CG18B Gary Sheffield 8/13 .20 .06
CG18C G.Sheffield 9/4 W .20 .06
CG19 Frank Thomas 7/26 .50 .15
CG19B F.Thomas 8/17 .50 .15
CG19C F.Thomas 9/23 .50 .15
CG20 Matt Williams 7/29 .20 .06
CG20B Matt Williams 8/12 .20 .06
CG20C Matt Williams 9/19 .20 .06

1995 Collector's Choice Trade Cards

To obtain the 55 "Traded and Update" cards for the base 1995 Collector's Choice set (cards 531-585) collectors had to find five different exchange Trade Cards randomly seeded into packs. The Trade exchange cards offer expired on February 1, 1996. Each different Trade exchange card was redeemable for an 11-card run (aka Trade exchange card TC1 could be redeemed for "Trade and Update" cards 531-542).

Nm-Mt Ex-Mt
COMPLETE SET (5) 4.00 1.20
TC1 Larry Walker 2.00 .60
TC2 David Cone 1.25 .35
TC3 Marquis Grissom .60 .18
TC4 Terry Pendleton 1.25 .35
TC5 F.Valenzuela 1.25 .35

1996 Collector's Choice

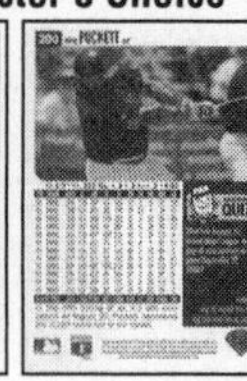

This 790-card standard-size set (produced by Upper Deck) was issued in 12-card packs with 36 packs per box and 20 boxes per case. Suggested retail price on these packs was 99 cents. The fronts of the regular set feature a player photo, his name and team logo. The backs feature another photo, vital stats and a baseball quiz. The set includes the following subsets: 1995 Stat Leaders (2-9), Rookie Class (10-39), Traditional Threads (100-108), Fantasy Team (268-279), International Flavor (325-342), Series 1 Checklists (358-365), Team Checklists (396-423), First HOF Class (500-504), Arizona Fall League (650-666), Award Winners (704-711) and Series 2 Checklists (753-760). Postseason Trade cards were inserted one every 11 packs. These cards had an ordering deadline of May 13 and were each redeemable for 10 cards depicting highlights from the playoffs and World Series, resulting in a 30-card redemption set. Finally, a 30-card Update set was included in each factory set and was also available through a Series 2 wrapper offer. The Cal Ripken Collection cards inserted into these packs, are priced in the Upper Deck area as Upper Deck Ripken Collection. Please check that section for pricing on this set. Notable Rookie Cards include Mike Sweeney.

Nm-Mt Ex-Mt
COMPLETE SET (730) 24.00 7.25
COMP.FACT.SET (790) 30.00 9.00
COMP. SERIES 1 (365) 12.00 3.60
COMP. SERIES 2 (365) 12.00 3.60
COMMON (1-365/396-760) .20 .06
COMP.TRADE SET (30) 15.00 4.50
COMMON (366T-395T) .40 .12
COMP. UPDATE SET (30) 4.00 1.20
COMMON UPD. (761-790) .40 .12
1 Cal Ripken 1.50 .45
2 Edgar Martinez SL .20 .06
Tony Gwynn
3 Albert Belle SL .20 .06
Dante Bichette
4 Albert Belle SL .20 .06
Mo Vaughn
Dante Bichette
5 Kenny Lofton SL .20 .06
Quilvio Veras
6 Mike Mussina SL .50 .15
Greg Maddux
7 Randy Johnson SL .50 .15
Hideo Nomo
8 Randy Johnson SL .50 .15
Greg Maddux
9 Jose Mesa SL .20 .06
Randy Myers
10 Johnny Damon .20 .06
11 Rick Krivda .20 .06
12 Roger Cedeno .20 .06
13 Angel Martinez .20 .06
14 Ariel Prieto .20 .06
15 John Wasdin .20 .06
16 Edwin Hurtado .20 .06
17 Lyle Mouton .20 .06
18 Chris Snopek .20 .06
19 Mariano Rivera .30 .09
20 Ruben Rivera .20 .06
21 Juan Castro RC .20 .06
22 Jimmy Haynes .20 .06
23 Bob Wolcott .20 .06
24 Brian Barber .20 .06
25 Frank Rodriguez .20 .06
26 Jesus Tavarez .20 .06
27 Glenn Dishman .20 .06
28 Jose Herrera .20 .06
29 Chan Ho Park .20 .06
30 Jason Isringhausen .20 .06
31 Doug Johns .20 .06
32 Gene Schall .20 .06
33 Kevin Jordan .20 .06
34 Matt Lawton RC .25 .07
35 Karim Garcia .20 .06
36 George Williams .20 .06
37 Orlando Palmeiro .20 .06
38 Jamie Brewington RC .20 .06
39 Robert Person .20 .06
40 Greg Maddux .75 .23
41 Marquis Grissom .20 .06
42 Chipper Jones .50 .15
43 David Justice .20 .06
44 Mark Lemke .20 .06
45 Fred McGriff .30 .09
46 Javier Lopez .20 .06
47 Mark Wohlers .20 .06
48 Jason Schmidt .20 .06
49 John Smoltz .30 .09
50 Curtis Goodwin .20 .06
51 Greg Zaun .20 .06
52 Armando Benitez .20 .06
53 Manny Alexander .20 .06
54 Chris Hoiles .20 .06
55 Harold Baines .20 .06
56 Ben McDonald .20 .06
57 Scott Erickson .20 .06
58 Jeff Manto .20 .06
59 Luis Alicea .20 .06
60 Roger Clemens 1.00 .30
61 Rheal Cormier .20 .06
62 Vaughn Eshelman .20 .06
63 Zane Smith .20 .06
64 Mike Macfarlane .20 .06
65 Erik Hanson .20 .06
66 Tim Naehring .20 .06
67 Lee Tinsley .20 .06
68 Troy O'Leary .20 .06
69 Garret Anderson .20 .06
70 Chili Davis .20 .06
71 Jim Edmonds .20 .06
72 Troy Percival .20 .06
73 Mark Langston .20 .06
74 Spike Owen .20 .06
75 Tim Salmon .30 .09
76 Brian Anderson .20 .06
77 Lee Smith .20 .06
78 Jim Abbott .30 .09
79 Jim Bullinger .20 .06
80 Mark Grace .30 .09
81 Todd Zeile .20 .06
82 Kevin Foster .20 .06
83 Howard Johnson .20 .06
84 Brian McRae .20 .06
85 Randy Myers .20 .06
86 Jaime Navarro .20 .06
87 Luis Gonzalez .20 .06
88 Ozzie Timmons .20 .06
89 Wilson Alvarez .20 .06
90 Frank Thomas .50 .15
91 James Baldwin .20 .06
92 Ray Durham .20 .06
93 Alex Fernandez .20 .06
94 Ozzie Guillen .20 .06
95 Tim Raines .20 .06
96 Roberto Hernandez .20 .06
97 Lance Johnson .20 .06
98 John Kruk .20 .06
99 Mark Portugal .20 .06
100 Don Mattingly TT .60 .18
101 Roger Clemens TT .50 .15
102 Raul Mondesi TT .20 .06
103 Cecil Fielder TT .20 .06
104 Ozzie Smith TT .50 .15
105 Frank Thomas TT .30 .09
106 Sammy Sosa TT .50 .15
107 Fred McGriff TT .20 .06
108 Barry Bonds TT .60 .18
109 Thomas Howard .20 .06
110 Ron Gant .20 .06
111 Eddie Taubensee .20 .06
112 Hal Morris .20 .06
113 Jose Rijo .20 .06
114 Pete Schourek .20 .06
115 Reggie Sanders .20 .06
116 Benito Santiago .20 .06
117 Jeff Brantley .20 .06
118 Julian Tavarez .20 .06
119 Carlos Baerga .20 .06
120 Jim Thome .50 .15
121 Jose Mesa .20 .06
122 Dennis Martinez .20 .06
123 Dave Winfield .20 .06
124 Eddie Murray .50 .15
125 Manny Ramirez .20 .06
126 Paul Sorrento .20 .06
127 Kenny Lofton .20 .06
128 Eric Young .20 .06
129 Jason Bates .20 .06
130 Bret Saberhagen .20 .06
131 Andres Galarraga .20 .06
132 Joe Girardi .20 .06
133 John Vander Wal .20 .06
134 David Nied .20 .06
135 Dante Bichette .20 .06
136 Vinny Castilla .20 .06
137 Kevin Ritz .20 .06
138 Felipe Lira .20 .06
139 Joe Boever .20 .06
140 Cecil Fielder .20 .06
141 John Flaherty .20 .06
142 Kirk Gibson .20 .06
143 Brian Maxcy .20 .06
144 Lou Whitaker .20 .06
145 Alan Trammell .30 .09
146 Bobby Higginson .20 .06
147 Chad Curtis .20 .06
148 Quilvio Veras .20 .06
149 Jerry Browne .20 .06
150 Andre Dawson .20 .06
151 Robb Nen .20 .06
152 Greg Colbrunn .20 .06
153 Chris Hammond .20 .06
154 Kurt Abbott .20 .06
155 Charles Johnson .20 .06
156 Terry Pendleton .20 .06
157 Dave Weathers .20 .06
158 Mike Hampton .20 .06
159 Craig Biggio .30 .09
160 Jeff Bagwell .30 .09
161 Brian L.Hunter .20 .06
162 Mike Henneman .20 .06
163 Dave Magadan .20 .06
164 Shane Reynolds .20 .06
165 Derek Bell .20 .06
166 Orlando Miller .20 .06
167 James Mouton .20 .06
168 Melvin Bunch .20 .06
169 Tom Gordon .20 .06
170 Kevin Appier .20 .06
171 Tom Goodwin .20 .06
172 Greg Gagne .20 .06
173 Gary Gaetti .20 .06
174 Jeff Montgomery .20 .06
175 Jon Nunnally .20 .06
176 Michael Tucker .20 .06
177 Joe Vitiello .20 .06
178 Billy Ashley .20 .06
179 Tom Candiotti .20 .06
180 Hideo Nomo .50 .15
181 Chad Fonville .20 .06
182 Todd Hollandsworth .20 .06
183 Eric Karros .20 .06
184 Roberto Kelly .20 .06
185 Mike Piazza .75 .23
186 Ramon Martinez .20 .06
187 Tim Wallach .20 .06

188 Jeff Cirillo .20 .06
189 Sid Roberson .20 .06
190 Kevin Seitzer .20 .06
191 Mike Fetters .20 .06
192 Steve Sparks .20 .06
193 Matt Mieske .20 .06
194 Joe Oliver .20 .06
195 B.J. Surhoff .20 .06
196 Alberto Reyes .20 .06
197 Fernando Vina .20 .06
198 LaTroy Hawkins .20 .06
199 Marty Cordova .20 .06
200 Kirby Puckett .50 .15
201 Brad Radke .20 .06
202 Pedro Munoz .20 .06
203 Scott Klingenbeck .20 .06
204 Pat Meares .20 .06
205 Chuck Knoblauch .20 .06
206 Scott Stahoviak .20 .06
207 Dave Stevens .20 .06
208 Shane Andrews .20 .06
209 Moises Alou .20 .06
210 David Segui .20 .06
211 Cliff Floyd .20 .06
212 Carlos Perez .20 .06
213 Mark Grudzielanek .20 .06
214 Butch Henry .20 .06
215 Rondell White .20 .06
216 Mel Rojas .20 .06
217 Ugueth Urbina .20 .06
218 Edgardo Alfonzo .20 .06
219 Carl Everett .20 .06
220 John Franco .20 .06
221 Todd Hundley .20 .06
222 Bobby Jones .20 .06
223 Bill Pulsipher .20 .06
224 Rico Brogna .20 .06
225 Jeff Kent .20 .06
226 Chris Jones .20 .06
227 Butch Huskey .20 .06
228 Robert Eenhoorn .20 .06
229 Sterling Hitchcock .20 .06
230 Wade Boggs .30 .09
231 Derek Jeter 1.25 .35
232 Tony Fernandez .20 .06
233 Jack McDowell .20 .06
234 Andy Pettitte .30 .09
235 David Cone .20 .06
236 Mike Stanley .20 .06
237 Don Mattingly 1.25 .35
238 Geronimo Berroa .20 .06
239 Scott Brosius .20 .06
240 Rickey Henderson .50 .15
241 Terry Steinbach .20 .06
242 Mike Gallego .20 .06
243 Jason Giambi .50 .15
244 Steve Ontiveros .20 .06
245 Dennis Eckersley .20 .06
246 Dave Stewart .20 .06
247 Don Wengert .20 .06
248 Paul Quantrill .20 .06
249 Ricky Bottalico .20 .06
250 Kevin Stocker .20 .06
251 Lenny Dykstra .20 .06
252 Tony Longmire .20 .06
253 Tyler Green .20 .06
254 Mike Mimbs .20 .06
255 Charlie Hayes .20 .06
256 Mickey Morandini .20 .06
257 Heathcliff Slocumb .20 .06
258 Jeff King .20 .06
259 Midre Cummings .20 .06
260 Mark Johnson .20 .06
261 Freddy Adrian Garcia .20 .06
262 Jon Lieber .20 .06
263 Esteban Loaiza .20 .06
264 Dan Miceli .20 .06
265 Orlando Merced .20 .06
266 Denny Neagle .20 .06
267 Steve Parris .20 .06
268 Greg Maddux FT .50 .15
269 Randy Johnson FT .30 .09
270 Hideo Nomo FT .30 .09
271 Jose Mesa FT .20 .06
272 Mike Piazza FT .50 .15
273 Mo Vaughn FT .20 .06
274 Craig Biggio FT .20 .06
275 Edgar Martinez FT .20 .06
276 Barry Larkin FT .20 .06
277 Sammy Sosa FT .50 .15
278 Dante Bichette FT .20 .06
279 Albert Belle FT .20 .06
280 Ozzie Smith .75 .23
281 Mark Sweeney .20 .06
282 Terry Bradshaw .20 .06
283 Allen Battle .20 .06
284 Danny Jackson .20 .06
285 Tom Henke .20 .06
286 Scott Cooper .20 .06
287 Tripp Cromer .20 .06
288 Bernard Gilkey .20 .06
289 Brian Jordan .20 .06
290 Tony Gwynn .60 .18
291 Brad Ausmus .20 .06
292 Bryce Florie .20 .06
293 Andres Berumen .20 .06
294 Ken Caminiti .20 .06
295 Bip Roberts .20 .06
296 Trevor Hoffman .20 .06
297 Roberto Petagine .20 .06
298 Jody Reed .20 .06
299 Fernando Valenzuela .20 .06
300 Barry Bonds 1.25 .35
301 Mark Leiter .20 .06
302 Mark Carreon .20 .06
303 Royce Clayton .20 .06
304 Kirt Manwaring .20 .06
305 Glenallen Hill .20 .06
306 Deion Sanders .30 .09
307 Joe Rosselli .20 .06
308 Robby Thompson .20 .06
309 W. VanLandingham .20 .06
310 Ken Griffey Jr. .75 .23
311 Bobby Ayala .20 .06
312 Joey Cora .20 .06
313 Mike Blowers .20 .06
314 Darren Bragg .20 .06
315 Randy Johnson .50 .15
316 Alex Rodriguez 1.00 .30
317 Andy Benes .40 .12
318 Tino Martinez .30 .09
319 Dan Wilson .20 .06
320 Will Clark .50 .15
321 Jeff Frye .20 .06
322 Benji Gil .20 .06
323 Rick Helling .20 .06
324 Mark McLemore .20 .06
325 Dave Nilsson IF .20 .06
326 Larry Walker IF .20 .06
327 Jose Canseco IF .20 .06
328 Raul Mondesi IF .20 .06
329 Manny Ramirez IF .20 .06
330 Robert Eenhoorn IF .20 .06
331 Chili Davis IF .20 .06
332 Hideo Nomo IF .30 .09
333 Benji Gil IF .20 .06
334 F.Valenzuela IF .20 .06
335 Dennis Martinez IF .20 .06
336 Roberto Kelly IF .20 .06
337 Carlos Baerga IF .20 .06
338 Juan Gonzalez IF .30 .09
339 Roberto Alomar IF .20 .06
340 Chan Ho Park IF .20 .06
341 Andres Galarraga IF .20 .06
342 Midre Cummings IF .20 .06
343 Otis Nixon .20 .06
344 Jeff Russell .20 .06
345 Ivan Rodriguez .50 .15
346 Mickey Tettleton .20 .06
347 Bob Tewksbury .20 .06
348 Domingo Cedeno .20 .06
349 Lance Parrish .20 .06
350 Joe Carter .20 .06
351 Devon White .20 .06
352 Carlos Delgado .20 .06
353 Alex Gonzalez .20 .06
354 Darren Hall .20 .06
355 Paul Molitor .30 .09
356 Al Leiter .20 .06
357 Randy Knorr .20 .06
358 Ken Caminiti CL .20 .06
Steve Finley
Brian Williams
Roberto Petagine
Andujar Cedeno
Phil Plantier
Derek Bell
Pedro A. Martinez
Doug Brocail
Craig Shipley
Ricky Gutierrez
359 Hideo Nomo CL .30 .09
360 Ramon J. Martinez CL .20 .06
Pedro Martinez
361 Robin Ventura CL .20 .06
362 Cal Ripken CL .75 .23
363 Ken Caminiti CL .20 .06
364 Albert Belle CL .30 .09
Eddie Murray
365 Randy Johnson CL .30 .09
366T Tony Pena TRADE .40 .12
367T Jim Thome TRADE 1.00 .30
368T D.Mattingly TRADE 2.50 .75
369T Jim Leyritz TRADE .40 .12
370T K.Griffey Jr. TRADE 1.50 .45
371T E.Martinez TRADE .60 .18
372T P.Schourek TRADE .40 .12
373T Mark Lewis TRADE .40 .12
374T C.Jones TRADE 1.00 .30
375T Fred McGriff TRADE .60 .18
376T Javy Lopez TRADE .40 .12
377T Fred McGriff TRADE .60 .18
378T C.O'Brien TRADE .40 .12
379T M.Devereaux TRADE .40 .12
380T M.Wohlers TRADE .40 .12
381T Bob Wolcott TRADE .40 .12
382T M.Ramirez TRADE .40 .12
383T Jay Buhner TRADE .40 .12
384T O.Hershiser TRADE .40 .12
385T Kenny Lofton TRADE .40 .12
386T G.Maddux TRADE 1.50 .45
387T Javier Lopez TRADE .40 .40
388T Kenny Lofton TRADE .40 .12
389T Eddie Murray TRADE 1.00 .30
390T Luis Polonia TRADE .40 .12
391T P.Borbon TRADE .40 .12
392T Jim Thome TRADE 1.00 .30
393T O.Hershiser TRADE .40 .12
394T David Justice TRADE .40 .12
395T Tom Glavine TRADE .60 .18
396 Greg Maddux TC .50 .15
397 Rico Brogna TC .20 .06
398 Darren Daulton TC .20 .06
399 Gary Sheffield TC .20 .06
400 Moises Alou TC .20 .06
401 Barry Larkin TC .20 .06
402 Jeff Bagwell TC .20 .06
403 Sammy Sosa TC .50 .15
404 Ozzie Smith TC .50 .15
405 Jay Bell TC .20 .06
406 Mike Piazza TC .50 .15
407 Dante Bichette TC .20 .06
408 Tony Gwynn TC .30 .09
409 Barry Bonds TC .60 .18
410 Kenny Lofton TC .20 .06
411 Johnny Damon TC .20 .06
412 Frank Thomas TC .30 .09
413 Greg Vaughn TC .20 .06
414 Paul Molitor TC .20 .06
415 Ken Griffey Jr. TC .50 .15
416 Tim Salmon TC .20 .06
417 Juan Gonzalez TC .30 .09
418 Mark McGwire TC .50 .15
419 Roger Clemens TC .50 .15
420 Wade Boggs TC .20 .06
421 Cal Ripken TC .75 .23
422 Cecil Fielder TC .20 .06
423 Joe Carter TC .20 .06
424 O.Fernandez RC .20 .06
425 Billy Wagner .30 .09
426 George Arias .20 .06
427 Mendy Lopez .20 .06
428 Jeff Suppan .20 .06
429 Rey Ordonez .20 .06
430 Brooks Kieschnick .20 .06
431 Raul Ibanez RC .60 .18
432 Livan Hernandez RC .40 .12
433 Shannon Stewart .20 .06
434 Steve Cox .20 .06
435 Trey Beamon .20 .06
436 Sergio Nunez .20 .06
437 Jermaine Dye .20 .06
438 Mike Sweeney RC 1.25 .35
439 Richard Hidalgo .20 .06
440 Todd Greene .20 .06
441 Robert Smith RC .20 .06
442 Rafael Orellano .20 .06
443 Wilton Guerrero RC .25 .07
444 David Doster .20 .06
445 Jason Kendall .20 .06
446 Edgar Renteria .20 .06
447 Scott Spiezio .20 .06
448 Jay Canizaro .20 .06
449 Enrique Wilson .20 .06
450 Bob Abreu .20 .06
451 Dwight Smith .20 .06
452 Jeff Blauser .20 .06
453 Steve Avery .20 .06
454 Brad Clontz .20 .06
455 Tom Glavine .30 .09
456 Mike Mordecai .20 .06
457 Rafael Belliard .20 .06
458 Greg McMichael .20 .06
459 Pedro Borbon .20 .06
460 Ryan Klesko .20 .06
461 Terrell Wade .20 .06
462 Brady Anderson .20 .06
463 Roberto Alomar .50 .15
464 Bobby Bonilla .20 .06
465 Mike Mussina .50 .15
466 Cesar Devarez .20 .06
467 Jeffrey Hammonds .20 .06
468 Mike Devereaux .20 .06
469 B.J. Surhoff .20 .06
470 Rafael Palmeiro .30 .09
471 John Valentin .20 .06
472 Mike Greenwell .20 .06
473 Dwayne Hosey .20 .06
474 Tim Wakefield .20 .06
475 Jose Canseco .50 .15
476 Aaron Sele .20 .06
477 Stan Belinda .20 .06
478 Mike Stanley .20 .06
479 Jamie Moyer .20 .06
480 Mo Vaughn .20 .06
481 Randy Velarde .20 .06
482 Gary DiSarcina .20 .06
483 Jorge Fabregas .20 .06
484 Rex Hudler .20 .06
485 Chuck Finley .20 .06
486 Tim Wallach .20 .06
487 Eduardo Perez .20 .06
488 Scott Sanderson .20 .06
489 J.T. Snow .20 .06
490 Sammy Sosa .75 .23
491 Terry Adams .20 .06
492 Matt Franco .20 .06
493 Scott Servais .20 .06
494 Frank Castillo .20 .06
495 Ryne Sandberg .75 .23
496 Rey Sanchez .20 .06
497 Steve Trachsel .20 .06
498 Jose Hernandez .20 .06
499 Dave Martinez .20 .06
500 Babe Ruth FC 1.00 .30
501 Ty Cobb FC .50 .15
502 Walter Johnson FC .50 .15
503 C.Mathewson FC .50 .15
504 Honus Wagner FC .50 .15
505 Robin Ventura .30 .09
506 Jason Bere .20 .06
507 Mike Cameron RC 1.00 .30
508 Ron Karkovice .20 .06
509 Matt Karchner .20 .06
510 Harold Baines .20 .06
511 Kirk McCaskill .20 .06
512 Larry Thomas .20 .06
513 Danny Tartabull .20 .06
514 Steve Gibralter .20 .06
515 Bret Boone .20 .06
516 Jeff Branson .20 .06
517 Kevin Jarvis .20 .06
518 Xavier Hernandez .20 .06
519 Eric Owens .20 .06
520 Barry Larkin .50 .15
521 Dave Burba .20 .06
522 John Smiley .20 .06
523 Paul Assenmacher .20 .06
524 Chad Ogea .20 .06
525 Orel Hershiser .20 .06
526 Alan Embree .20 .06
527 Tony Pena .20 .06
528 Omar Vizquel .20 .06
529 Mark Clark .20 .06
530 Albert Belle .20 .06
531 Charles Nagy .20 .06
532 Herbert Perry .20 .06
533 Darren Holmes .20 .06
534 Ellis Burks .20 .06
535 Billy Swift .20 .06
536 Armando Reynoso .20 .06
537 Curtis Leskanic .20 .06
538 Quinton McCracken .20 .06
539 Steve Reed .20 .06
540 Larry Walker .30 .09
541 Walt Weiss .20 .06
542 Bryan Rekar .20 .06
543 Tony Clark .20 .06
544 Steve Rodriguez .20 .06
545 C.J. Nitkowski .20 .06
546 Todd Steverson .20 .06
547 Jose Lima .20 .06
548 Phil Nevin .20 .06
549 Chris Gomez .20 .06
550 Travis Fryman .20 .06
551 Mark Lewis .20 .06
552 Alex Arias .20 .06
553 Marc Valdes .20 .06
554 Kevin Brown .20 .06
555 Jeff Conine .20 .06
556 John Burkett .20 .06
557 Devon White .20 .06
558 Pat Rapp .20 .06
559 Jay Powell .20 .06
560 Gary Sheffield .20 .06
561 Jim Dougherty .20 .06
562 Todd Jones .20 .06
563 Tony Eusebio .20 .06
564 Darryl Kile .20 .06
565 Doug Drabek .20 .06
566 Mike Simms .20 .06
567 Derrick May .20 .06
568 Donne Wall .20 .06
569 Greg Swindell .20 .06
570 Jim Pittsley .20 .06
571 Bob Hamelin .20 .06
572 Mark Gubicza .20 .06
573 Chris Haney .20 .06
574 Keith Lockhart .20 .06
575 Mike Macfarlane .20 .06
576 Les Norman .20 .06
577 Joe Randa .20 .06
578 Chris Stynes .20 .06
579 Greg Gagne .20 .06
580 Raul Mondesi .20 .06
581 Delino DeShields .20 .06
582 Pedro Astacio .20 .06
583 Antonio Osuna .20 .06
584 Brett Butler .20 .06
585 Todd Worrell .20 .06
586 Mike Blowers .20 .06
587 Felix Rodriguez .20 .06
588 Ismael Valdes .20 .06
589 Ricky Bones .20 .06
590 Greg Vaughn .20 .06
591 Mark Loretta .20 .06
592 Cal Eldred .20 .06
593 Chuck Carr .20 .06
594 Dave Nilsson .20 .06
595 John Jaha .20 .06
596 Scott Karl .20 .06
597 Pat Listach .20 .06
598 Jose Valentin .20 .06
599 Mike Trombley .20 .06
600 Paul Molitor .30 .09
601 Dave Hollins .20 .06
602 Ron Coomer .20 .06
603 Matt Walbeck .20 .06
604 Roberto Kelly .20 .06
605 Rick Aguilera .20 .06
606 Pat Mahomes .20 .06
607 Jeff Reboulet .20 .06
608 Rich Becker .20 .06
609 Tim Scott .20 .06
610 Pedro Martinez .50 .15
611 Kirk Rueter .20 .06
612 Tavo Alvarez .20 .06
613 Yamil Benitez .20 .06
614 Darrin Fletcher .20 .06
615 Mike Lansing .20 .06
616 Henry Rodriguez .20 .06
617 Tony Tarasco .20 .06
618 Alex Ochoa .20 .06
619 Tim Bogar .20 .06
620 Bernard Gilkey .20 .06
621 Dave Mlicki .20 .06
622 Brent Mayne .20 .06
623 Ryan Thompson .20 .06
624 Pete Harnisch .20 .06
625 Lance Johnson .20 .06
626 Jose Vizcaino .20 .06
627 Doug Henry .20 .06
628 Scott Kamieniecki .20 .06
629 Jim Leyritz .20 .06
630 Ruben Sierra .20 .06
631 Pat Kelly .20 .06
632 Joe Girardi .20 .06
633 John Wetteland .20 .06
634 Melido Perez .20 .06
635 Paul O'Neill .30 .09
636 Jorge Posada .30 .09
637 Bernie Williams .30 .09
638 Mark Acre .20 .06
639 Mike Bordick .20 .06
640 Mark McGwire 1.25 .35
641 Fausto Cruz .20 .06
642 Ernie Young .20 .06
643 Todd Van Poppel .20 .06
644 Craig Paquette .20 .06
645 Brent Gates .20 .06
646 Pedro Munoz .20 .06
647 Andrew Lorraine .20 .06
648 Sid Fernandez .20 .06
649 Jim Eisenreich .20 .06
650 Johnny Damon AFL .20 .06
651 D.Hermanson AFL .20 .06
652 Joe Randa AFL .20 .06
653 Michael Tucker AFL .20 .06
654 Alan Benes AFL .20 .06
655 Chad Fonville AFL .20 .06
656 David Bell AFL .20 .06
657 Jon Nunnally AFL .20 .06
658 Chan Ho Park AFL .20 .06
659 LaTroy Hawkins AFL .20 .06
660 J.Brewington AFL .20 .06
661 Q.McCracken AFL .20 .06
662 Tim Unroe AFL .20 .06
663 Jeff Ware AFL .20 .06
664 Todd Greene AFL .20 .06
665 Andrew Lorraine AFL .20 .06
666 Ernie Young AFL .20 .06
667 Toby Borland .20 .06
668 Lenny Webster .20 .06
669 Benito Santiago .20 .06
670 Gregg Jefferies .20 .06
671 Darren Daulton .20 .06
672 Curt Schilling .30 .09
673 Mark Whiten .20 .06
674 Todd Zeile .20 .06
675 Jay Bell .20 .06
676 Paul Wagner .20 .06
677 Dave Clark .20 .06
678 Nelson Liriano .20 .06
679 Ramon Morel .20 .06
680 Charlie Hayes .20 .06
681 Angelo Encarnacion .20 .06
682 Al Martin .20 .06
683 Jacob Brumfield .20 .06
684 Mike Kingery .20 .06
685 Carlos Garcia .20 .06
686 Tom Pagnozzi .20 .06
687 David Bell .20 .06
688 Todd Stottlemyre .20 .06
689 Jose Oliva .20 .06
690 Ray Lankford .20 .06
691 Mike Morgan .20 .06
692 John Frascatore .20 .06
693 John Mabry .20 .06
694 Mark Petkovsek .20 .06
695 Alan Benes .20 .06
696 Steve Finley .20 .06
697 Marc Newfield .20 .06
698 Andy Ashby .20 .06
699 Marc Kroon .20 .06
700 Wally Joyner .20 .06
701 Joey Hamilton .20 .06
702 Dustin Hermanson .20 .06
703 Scott Sanders .20 .06
704 Marty Cordova ROY .20 .06
705 Hideo Nomo ROY .30 .09
706 Mo Vaughn MVP .20 .06
707 Barry Larkin MVP .20 .06
708 Randy Johnson CY .30 .09
709 Greg Maddux CY .50 .15
710 Mark McGwire CB .60 .18
711 Ron Gant CB .20 .06
712 Andujar Cedeno .20 .06
713 Brian Johnson .20 .06
714 J.R. Phillips .20 .06
715 Rod Beck .20 .06
716 Sergio Valdez .20 .06
717 Marvin Benard RC .25 .07
718 Steve Scarsone .20 .06
719 Rich Aurilia RC .75 .23
720 Matt Williams .20 .06
721 John Patterson .20 .06
722 Shawn Estes .20 .06
723 Russ Davis .20 .06
724 Rich Amaral .20 .06
725 Edgar Martinez .30 .09
726 Norm Charlton .20 .06
727 Paul Sorrento .20 .06
728 Luis Sojo .20 .06
729 Arquimedez Pozo .20 .06
730 Jay Buhner .20 .06
731 Chris Bosio .20 .06
732 Chris Widger .20 .06
733 Kevin Gross .20 .06
734 Darren Oliver .20 .06
735 Dean Palmer .20 .06
736 Matt Whiteside .20 .06
737 Luis Ortiz .20 .06
738 Roger Pavlik .20 .06
739 Damon Buford .20 .06
740 Juan Gonzalez .50 .15
741 Rusty Greer .20 .06
742 Lou Frazier .20 .06
743 Pat Hentgen .20 .06
744 Tomas Perez .20 .06
745 Juan Guzman .20 .06
746 Otis Nixon .20 .06
747 Robert Perez .20 .06
748 Ed Sprague .20 .06
749 Tony Castillo .20 .06
750 John Olerud .20 .06
751 Shawn Green .20 .06
752 Jeff Ware .20 .06
753 Dante Bichette CL .20 .06
Vinny Castilla
Andres Galarraga
Larry Walker
754 Greg Maddux CL .50 .15
755 Marty Cordova CL .20 .06
756 Ozzie Smith CL .50 .15
757 John Vander Wal CL .20 .06
758 Andres Galarraga CL .20 .06
759 Frank Thomas CL .30 .09
760 Tony Gwynn CL .30 .09
761 Randy Myers UPD .40 .12
762 Kent Mercker UPD .40 .12
763 David Wells UPD .40 .12
764 Tom Gordon UPD .40 .12
765 Wil Cordero UPD .40 .12
766 Dave Magadan UPD .40 .12
767 Doug Jones UPD .40 .12
768 Kevin Tapani UPD .40 .12
769 Curtis Goodwin UPD .40 .12
770 Julio Franco UPD .40 .12
771 Jack McDowell UPD .40 .12
772 Al Leiter UPD .40 .12
773 Sean Berry UPD .40 .12
774 Bip Roberts UPD .40 .12
775 Jose Offerman UPD .40 .12
776 Ben McDonald UPD .40 .12
777 Dan Serafini UPD .40 .12
778 Ryan McGuire UPD .40 .12
779 Tim Raines UPD .40 .12
780 Tino Martinez UPD .60 .18
781 Kenny Rogers UPD .40 .12
782 Bob Tewksbury UPD .40 .12
783 R.Henderson UPD 1.00 .30
784 Ron Gant UPD .40 .12
785 Gary Gaetti UPD .40 .12
786 Andy Benes UPD .40 .12
787 Royce Clayton UPD .40 .12
788 Darryl Hamilton UPD .40 .12
789 Ken Hill UPD .40 .12
790 Erik Hanson UPD .40 .12
P100 K.Griffey Jr. Promo 1.00 .30

1996 Collector's Choice Gold Signature

This 730-card set parallels the basic Collector's Choice issue. These cards were inserted approximately one every 35 packs. Cards 1-365 were issued in first series and 396-730 in second series. The cards are similar to the regular issue except they have gold borders and a gold facsimile player's signature on front. Cards 366-395 do not exist.

Nm-Mt Ex-Mt
*STARS: 10X TO 25X BASIC CARDS ..
*ROOKIES: 6X TO 15X BASIC CARDS

1996 Collector's Choice Silver Signature

This 730-card set parallels the regular Collector's Choice set. These cards were inserted one per pack in both first and second series packs. The cards are similar to the regular issue except for silver borders and a silver foil facsimile player's signature on the card front. Cards 366-395 do not exist.

	Nm-Mt	Ex-Mt
COMPLETE SET (730)	110.00	33.00
COMP. SERIES 1 (365)	60.00	18.00
COMP. SERIES 2 (365)	50.00	15.00

*STARS: 1X TO 2.5X BASIC CARDS ...
*ROOKIES: .75X TO 2X BASIC CARDS

1996 Collector's Choice Crash the Game

Randomly inserted into one in every five series two packs, silver Crash the Game interactive cards feature a selection of thirty of baseball's top stars. If the featured player hit a home run during the series specified on the card, it was then eligible to be redeemed for a super premium Cell Card of the same player. Winning cards have been highlighted with a "W" in the listings below. The postmark expiration date for exchanging winning cards was November 18th, 1996.

	Nm-Mt	Ex-Mt
COMPLETE SET (90)	50.00	15.00
*GOLD: 2X TO 5X BASIC CRASH		
GOLD SER.2 STATED ODDS 1:48		
*EXCH: 2X TO 5X BASIC CRASH		
ONE EXCH.CARD VIA MAIL PER WINNER		
*GOLD EXCH: 6X TO 15X BASIC CRASH		
ONE EXCH.VIA MAIL PER GOLD WINNER		
CG1 C.Jones 7/11 W	.75	.23
CG1B C.Jones 8/27 W	.75	.23
CG1C Chipper Jones 9/19	.75	.23
CG2 Fred McGriff 7/1	.50	.15
CG2B Fred McGriff 8/30	.50	.15
CG2C Fred McGriff 9/10 W	.50	.15
CG3 R.Palmeiro 7/4 W	.50	.15
CG3B R.Palmeiro 8/29	.50	.15
CG3C R.Palmeiro 9/26	.50	.15
CG4 Cal Ripken 6/27	2.50	.75
CG4B Cal Ripken 7/25 W	2.50	.75
CG4C Cal Ripken 9/2	2.50	.75
CG5 Jose Canseco 6/27	.75	.23
CG5B J.Canseco 7/11 W	.75	.23
CG5C Jose Canseco 8/23	.75	.23
CG6 Mo Vaughn 6/21 W	.30	.09
CG6B Mo Vaughn 7/18 W	.30	.09
CG6C Mo Vaughn 9/20	.30	.09
CG7 Jim Edmonds 7/18 W	.30	.09
CG7B J.Edmonds 8/16 W	.30	.09
CG7C Jim Edmonds 9/20	.30	.09
CG8 Tim Salmon 6/20	.50	.15
CG8B Tim Salmon 7/30	.50	.15
CG8C Tim Salmon 9/9	.50	.15
CG9 Sammy Sosa 7/4 W	1.25	.35
CG9B Sammy Sosa 8/1 W	1.25	.35
CG9C Sammy Sosa 9/2	1.25	.35
CG10 Frank Thomas 6/27	.75	.23
CG10B Frank Thomas 7/4	.75	.23
CG10C F.Thomas 9/2 W	.75	.23
CG11 Albert Belle 6/25	.30	.09
CG11B Albert Belle 8/2 W	.30	.09
CG11C Albert Belle 9/6	.30	.09
CG12 M.Ramirez 7/18 W	.30	.09
CG12B M.Ramirez 8/26	.30	.09
CG12C M.Ramirez 9/9 W	.30	.09
CG13 Jim Thome 6/27	.75	.23
CG13B Jim Thome 7/4 W	.75	.23
CG13C Jim Thome 9/23	.75	.23
CG14 D.Bichette 7/11 W	.30	.09
CG14B Dante Bichette 8/9	.30	.09
CG14C Dante Bichette 9/9	.30	.09
CG15 Vinny Castilla 7/1	.30	.09
CG15B V.Castilla 8/23 W	.30	.09
CG15C V.Castilla 9/13 W	.30	.09
CG16 Larry Walker 6/24	.50	.15
CG16B Larry Walker 7/18	.50	.15
CG16C Larry Walker 9/27	.50	.15
CG17 Cecil Fielder 6/27	.30	.09
CG17B C.Fielder 7/30 W	.30	.09
CG17C C.Fielder 9/17 W	.30	.09
CG18 Gary Sheffield 7/4	.30	.09
CG18B Gary Sheffield 8/2	.30	.09
CG18C G.Sheffield 9/5 W	.30	.09
CG19 Jeff Bagwell 7/4 W	.50	.15
CG19B Jeff Bagwell 8/16	.50	.15
CG19C Jeff Bagwell 9/13	.50	.15
CG20 Eric Karros 7/4 W	.30	.09
CG20B Eric Karros 8/13 W	.30	.09
CG20C Eric Karros 9/16	.30	.09
CG21 Mike Piazza 6/27 W	1.25	.35
CG21B Mike Piazza 7/26	1.25	.35
CG21C M.Piazza 9/12 W	1.25	.35
CG22 Ken Caminiti 7/11 W	.30	.09
CG22B K.Caminiti 8/16 W	.30	.09
CG22C K.Caminiti 9/19 W	.30	.09
CG23 Barry Bonds 6/27 W	2.00	.60
CG23B Barry Bonds 7/22	2.00	.60
CG23C Barry Bonds 9/24	2.00	.60
CG24 M.Williams 7/11 W	.30	.09
CG24B Matt Williams 8/19	.30	.09
CG24C Matt Williams 9/27	.30	.09
CG25 Jay Buhner 6/20	.30	.09
CG25B Jay Buhner 7/25	.30	.09
CG25C Jay Buhner 8/29 W	.30	.09
CG26 K.Griffey Jr. 7/18 W	1.25	.35
CG26B Ken Griffey Jr. 8/16 W	1.25	.35
CG26C Ken Griffey Jr. 9/20 W	1.25	.35
CG27 Ron Gant 6/24 W	.30	.09
CG27B Ron Gant 7/11 W	.30	.09
CG27C Ron Gant 9/27 W	.30	.09
CG28 J.Gonzalez 6/28 W	.75	.23
CG28B J. Gonzalez 7/15 W	.75	.23
CG28C Juan Gonzalez 8/6	.75	.23
CG29 M.Tettleton 7/4 W	.30	.09
CG29B M.Tettleton 8/6	.30	.09
CG29C M. Tettleton 9/6 W	.30	.09
CG30 Joe Carter 6/25	.30	.09
CG30B Joe Carter 8/5	.30	.09
CG30C Joe Carter 9/23	.30	.09

1996 Collector's Choice Griffey A Cut Above

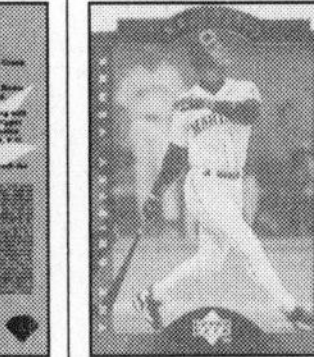

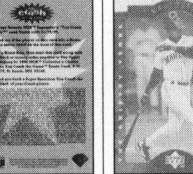

These ten cards focus on Seattle Mariners superstar Ken Griffey Jr. The cards were inserted at a rate of one per pack in special six-card retail packs (five basic CC cards plus one Griffey ACA insert). The packs were sold at Wal-Mart's nationwide and carried a suggested retail price of $0.97.

	Nm-Mt	Ex-Mt
COMPLETE SET (10)	6.00	1.80
COMMON CARD (CA1-CA10)	.75	.23

1996 Collector's Choice Nomo Scrapbook

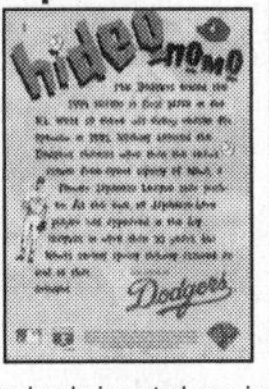

This five-card set was randomly inserted one in every 12 second series packs and features season highlights from Rookie of the Year, Hideo Nomo's first year in the Majors. The fronts display color action player cut-outs with yellow and red shadows on a metallic background. The backs carry a career fact about Nomo.

	Nm-Mt	Ex-Mt
COMPLETE SET (5)	3.00	.90
COMMON (1-5)	1.00	.30

1996 Collector's Choice You Make the Play

Cards from this 90-card set were inserted one per first series pack. Forty-five players are featured and each player is given two outcomes. The cards measure just about the standard-size but have rounded corners. In addition to being inserted into packs, dealers also were offered extra You Make the Play cards depending on how many cases ordered. A dealer who ordered one case received two 12-card packs of these cards for a total of 24 cards. Meanwhile, a dealer who ordered two cases received six 12-card packs for a total of 72 packs. Customers could also receive 12 of these cards by sending 10 wrappers and $2 to an a mail-in order. This offer expired on May 15, 1996.

	Nm-Mt	Ex-Mt
COMPLETE SET (90)	12.00	3.60
*GOLD: 6X TO 15X BASIC PLAY		
GOLD SER.1 STATED ODDS 1:35		
1 Kevin Appier	.20	.06
2 Carlos Baerga	.20	.06
3 Jeff Bagwell	.30	.09
4 Jay Bell	.20	.06
5 Albert Belle	.20	.06
6 Craig Biggio	.30	.09
7 Wade Boggs	.30	.09
8 Barry Bonds	1.25	.35
9 Bobby Bonilla	.20	.06
10 Jose Canseco	.50	.15
11 Joe Carter	.20	.06
12 Darren Daulton	.20	.06
13 Cecil Fielder	.20	.06
14 Ron Gant	.20	.06
15 Juan Gonzalez	.50	.15
16 Ken Griffey Jr.	.75	.23
17 Tony Gwynn	.60	.18
18 Randy Johnson	.50	.15
19 Chipper Jones	.50	.15
20 Barry Larkin	.50	.15
21 Kenny Lofton	.20	.06
22 Greg Maddux	.75	.23
23 Don Mattingly	1.25	.35
24 Fred McGriff	.30	.09
25 Mark McGwire	1.25	.35
26 Paul Molitor	.30	.09
27 Raul Mondesi	.20	.06
28 Eddie Murray	.50	.15
29 Hideo Nomo	.50	.15
30 Jon Nunnally	.20	.06
31 Mike Piazza	.75	.23
32 Kirby Puckett	.50	.15
33 Cal Ripken	1.50	.45
34 Alex Rodriguez	1.00	.30
35 Tim Salmon	.30	.09
36 Gary Sheffield	.20	.06
37 Lee Smith	.20	.06
38 Ozzie Smith	.75	.23
39 Sammy Sosa	.75	.23
40 Frank Thomas	.50	.15
41 Greg Vaughn	.20	.06
42 Mo Vaughn	.20	.06
43 Larry Walker	.30	.09
44 Rondell White	.20	.06
45 Matt Williams	.20	.06

1997 Collector's Choice

This 506-card set (produced by Upper Deck) was distributed in 12-card first series packs with a suggested retail price of $.99 and 14-card second series with a suggested retail price of $1.29. The fronts feature color action player photos while the backs carry player statistics. The first series set contains the following subsets: Rookie Class (1-27), League Leaders (56-63), Postseason (218-224) which recaps action from the 1996 playoffs and World Series Games and Ken Griffey Jr. Checklist (244-249) which also carry collecting tips. The second-series set contains the following: 199 regular player cards, 10 Ken Griffey Jr.'s Hot List (325-334), 18 Rookie Class, 3 Collecting 101 Set checklists, and 30 full-bleed All-Star cards. Notable Rookie Cards include Brian Giles.

	Nm-Mt	Ex-Mt
COMPLETE SET (506)	25.00	7.50
COMP.FACT.SET (516)	25.00	7.50
COMP. SERIES 1 (246)	15.00	4.50
COMP. SERIES 2 (260)	15.00	4.50
1 Andruw Jones	.20	.06
2 Rocky Coppinger	.20	.06
3 Jeff D'Amico	.20	.06
4 Dmitri Young	.20	.06
5 Darin Erstad	.20	.06
6 Jermaine Allensworth	.20	.06
7 Damian Jackson	.20	.06
8 Bill Mueller RC	1.50	.45
9 Jacob Cruz	.20	.06
10 Vladimir Guerrero	.50	.15
11 Marty Janzen	.20	.06
12 Kevin L. Brown	.20	.06
13 Willie Adams	.20	.06
14 Wendell Magee	.20	.06
15 Scott Rolen	.30	.09
16 Matt Beech	.20	.06
17 Neifi Perez	.20	.06
18 Jamey Wright	.20	.06
19 Jose Paniagua	.20	.06
20 Todd Walker	.20	.06
21 Justin Thompson	.20	.06
22 Robin Jennings	.20	.06
23 Dario Veras RC	.20	.06
24 Brian Lesher RC	.20	.06
25 Nomar Garciaparra	.75	.23
26 Luis Castillo	.20	.06
27 Brian Giles RC	1.00	.30
28 Jermaine Dye	.20	.06
29 Terrell Wade	.20	.06
30 Fred McGriff	.30	.09
31 Marquis Grissom	.20	.06
32 Ryan Klesko	.20	.06
33 Javier Lopez	.20	.06
34 Mark Wohlers	.20	.06
35 Tom Glavine	.30	.09
36 Denny Neagle	.20	.06
37 Scott Erickson	.20	.06
38 Chris Hoiles	.20	.06
39 Roberto Alomar	.50	.15
40 Eddie Murray	.50	.15
41 Cal Ripken	1.50	.45
42 Randy Myers	.20	.06
43 B.J. Surhoff	.20	.06
44 Rick Krivda	.20	.06
45 Jose Canseco	.50	.15
46 Heathcliff Slocumb	.20	.06
47 Jeff Suppan	.20	.06
48 Tom Gordon	.20	.06
49 Aaron Sele	.20	.06
50 Mo Vaughn	.20	.06
51 Darren Bragg	.20	.06
52 Wil Cordero	.20	.06
53 Scott Bullett	.20	.06
54 Terry Adams	.20	.06
55 Jackie Robinson	1.00	.30
56 Tony Gwynn LL Alex Rodriguez	.50	.15
57 Andres Galarraga LL Mark McGwire	.60	.18
58 Andres Galarraga LL Albert Belle	.20	.06
59 Eric Young LL Kenny Lofton	.20	.06
60 John Smoltz LL Andy Pettitte	.20	.06
61 John Smoltz LL Roger Clemens	.50	.15
62 Kevin Brown LL Juan Guzman	.20	.06
63 John Wetteland LL Todd Worrell Jeff Brantley	.20	.06
64 Scott Servais	.20	.06
65 Sammy Sosa	.75	.23
66 Ryne Sandberg	.75	.23
67 Frank Castillo	.20	.06
68 Rey Sanchez	.20	.06
69 Steve Trachsel	.20	.06
70 Robin Ventura	.20	.06
71 Wilson Alvarez	.20	.06
72 Tony Phillips	.20	.06
73 Lyle Mouton	.20	.06
74 Mike Cameron	.20	.06
75 Harold Baines	.20	.06
76 Albert Belle	.20	.06
77 Chris Snopek	.20	.06
78 Reggie Sanders	.20	.06
79 Jeff Brantley	.20	.06
80 Barry Larkin	.50	.15
81 Kevin Jarvis	.20	.06
82 John Smiley	.20	.06
83 Pete Schourek	.20	.06
84 Thomas Howard	.20	.06
85 Lee Smith	.20	.06
86 Omar Vizquel	.20	.06
87 Julio Franco	.20	.06
88 Orel Hershiser	.20	.06
89 Charles Nagy	.20	.06
90 Matt Williams	.20	.06
91 Dennis Martinez	.20	.06
92 Jose Mesa	.20	.06
93 Sandy Alomar Jr.	.20	.06
94 Jim Thome	.50	.15
95 Vinny Castilla	.20	.06
96 Armando Reynoso	.20	.06
97 Kevin Ritz	.20	.06
98 Larry Walker	.30	.09
99 Eric Young	.20	.06
100 Dante Bichette	.20	.06
101 Quinton McCracken	.20	.06
102 John Vander Wal	.20	.06
103 Phil Nevin	.20	.06
104 Tony Clark	.20	.06
105 Alan Trammell	.30	.09
106 Felipe Lira	.20	.06
107 Curtis Pride	.20	.06
108 Bobby Higginson	.20	.06
109 Mark Lewis	.20	.06
110 Travis Fryman	.20	.06
111 Al Leiter	.20	.06
112 Devon White	.20	.06
113 Jeff Conine	.20	.06
114 Charles Johnson	.20	.06
115 Andre Dawson	.20	.06
116 Edgar Renteria	.20	.06
117 Robb Nen	.20	.06
118 Kevin Brown	.20	.06
119 Derek Bell	.20	.06
120 Bob Abreu	.20	.06
121 Mike Hampton	.20	.06
122 Todd Jones	.20	.06
123 Billy Wagner	.20	.06
124 Shane Reynolds	.20	.06
125 Jeff Bagwell	.30	.09
126 Brian L. Hunter	.20	.06
127 Jeff Montgomery	.20	.06
128 Rod Myers RC	.20	.06
129 Tim Belcher	.20	.06
130 Kevin Appier	.20	.06
131 Mike Sweeney	.20	.06
132 Craig Paquette	.20	.06
133 Joe Randa	.20	.06
134 Michael Tucker	.20	.06
135 Raul Mondesi	.20	.06
136 Tim Wallach	.20	.06
137 Brett Butler	.20	.06
138 Karim Garcia	.20	.06
139 Todd Hollandsworth	.20	.06
140 Eric Karros	.20	.06
141 Hideo Nomo	.50	.15
142 Ismael Valdes	.20	.06
143 Cal Eldred	.20	.06
144 Scott Karl	.20	.06
145 Matt Mieske	.20	.06
146 Mike Fetters	.20	.06
147 Mark Loretta	.20	.06
148 Fernando Vina	.20	.06
149 Jeff Cirillo	.20	.06
150 Dave Nilsson	.20	.06
151 Kirby Puckett	.50	.15
152 Rich Becker	.20	.06
153 Chuck Knoblauch	.20	.06
154 Marty Cordova	.20	.06
155 Paul Molitor	.30	.09
156 Rick Aguilera	.20	.06
157 Pat Meares	.20	.06
158 Frank Rodriguez	.20	.06
159 David Segui	.20	.06
160 Henry Rodriguez	.20	.06
161 Shane Andrews	.20	.06
162 Pedro Martinez	.50	.15
163 Mark Grudzielanek	.20	.06
164 Mike Lansing	.20	.06
165 Rondell White	.20	.06
166 Ugueth Urbina	.20	.06
167 Rey Ordonez	.20	.06
168 Robert Person	.20	.06
169 Carlos Baerga	.20	.06
170 Bernard Gilkey	.20	.06
171 John Franco	.20	.06
172 Pete Harnisch	.20	.06
173 Butch Huskey	.20	.06
174 Paul Wilson	.20	.06
175 Bernie Williams	.30	.09
175 Dwight Gooden ERR incorrectly numbered 175	.30	.09
177 Wade Boggs	.30	.09
178 Ruben Rivera	.20	.06
179 Jim Leyritz	.20	.06
180 Derek Jeter	1.25	.35
181 Tino Martinez	.30	.09
182 Tim Raines	.20	.06
183 Scott Brosius	.20	.06
184 Jason Giambi	.50	.15
185 Geronimo Berroa	.20	.06
186 Ariel Prieto	.20	.06
187 Scott Spiezio	.20	.06
188 John Wasdin	.20	.06
189 Ernie Young	.20	.06
190 Mark McGwire	1.25	.35
191 Jim Eisenreich	.20	.06
192 Ricky Bottalico	.20	.06
193 Darren Daulton	.20	.06
194 David Doster	.20	.06
195 Gregg Jefferies	.20	.06
196 Lenny Dykstra	.20	.06
197 Curt Schilling	.30	.09
198 Todd Stottlemyre	.20	.06
199 Willie McGee	.20	.06
200 Ozzie Smith	.75	.23
201 Dennis Eckersley	.20	.06
202 Ray Lankford	.20	.06
203 John Mabry	.20	.06
204 Alan Benes	.20	.06
205 Ron Gant	.20	.06
206 Archi Cianfrocco	.20	.06
207 Fernando Valenzuela	.20	.06
208 Greg Vaughn	.20	.06
209 Steve Finley	.20	.06
210 Tony Gwynn	.60	.18
211 Rickey Henderson	.50	.15
212 Trevor Hoffman	.20	.06
213 Jason Thompson	.20	.06
214 Osvaldo Fernandez	.20	.06
215 Glenallen Hill	.20	.06
216 W. VanLandingham	.20	.06
217 Marvin Benard	.20	.06
218 Juan Gonzalez POST	.30	.09
219 Roberto Alomar POST	.30	.09
220 Brian Jordan POST	.20	.06
221 John Smoltz POST	.20	.06
222 Javy Lopez POST	.20	.06
223 Bernie Williams POST	.30	.09
224 Jim Leyritz POST John Wetteland	.20	.06
225 Barry Bonds	1.25	.35
226 Rich Aurilia	.20	.06
227 Jay Canizaro	.20	.06
228 Dan Wilson	.20	.06
229 Bob Wolcott	.20	.06
230 Ken Griffey Jr.	.75	.23
231 Sterling Hitchcock	.20	.06
232 Edgar Martinez	.30	.09
233 Joey Cora	.20	.06
234 Norm Charlton	.20	.06
235 Alex Rodriguez	.75	.23
236 Bobby Witt	.20	.06
237 Darren Oliver	.20	.06
238 Kevin Elster	.20	.06
239 Rusty Greer	.20	.06
240 Juan Gonzalez	.50	.15
241 Will Clark	.50	.15
242 Dean Palmer	.20	.06
243 Ivan Rodriguez	.50	.15
244 Ken Griffey Jr. CL	.25	.07
245 Ken Griffey Jr. CL	.25	.07
246 Ken Griffey Jr. CL	.25	.07
247 Ken Griffey Jr. CL	.25	.07
248 Ken Griffey Jr. CL	.25	.07
249 Ken Griffey Jr. CL	.25	.07
250 Eddie Murray	.50	.15
251 Troy Percival	.20	.06
252 Garret Anderson	.20	.06
253 Allen Watson	.20	.06
254 Jason Dickson	.20	.06
255 Jim Edmonds	.20	.06
256 Chuck Finley	.20	.06
257 Randy Velarde	.20	.06
258 S. Hasegawa RC	.50	.15
259 Todd Greene	.20	.06
260 Tim Salmon	.30	.09
261 Mark Langston	.20	.06
262 Dave Hollins	.20	.06
263 Gary DiSarcina	.20	.06
264 Kenny Lofton	.20	.06
265 John Smoltz	.30	.09
266 Greg Maddux	.75	.23
267 Jeff Blauser	.20	.06
268 Alan Embree	.20	.06
269 Mark Lemke	.20	.06
270 Chipper Jones	.50	.15
271 Mike Mussina	.50	.15
272 Rafael Palmeiro	.30	.09
273 Jimmy Key	.20	.06
274 Mike Bordick	.20	.06
275 Brady Anderson	.20	.06
276 Eric Davis	.20	.06
277 Jeffrey Hammonds	.20	.06
278 Reggie Jefferson	.20	.06
279 Tim Naehring	.20	.06
280 John Valentin	.20	.06
281 Troy O'Leary	.20	.06
282 Shane Mack	.20	.06
283 Mike Stanley	.20	.06
284 Tim Wakefield	.20	.06
285 Brian McRae	.20	.06
286 Brooks Kieschnick	.20	.06
287 Shawon Dunston	.20	.06
288 Kevin Foster	.20	.06
289 Mel Rojas	.20	.06
290 Mark Grace	.30	.09
291 Brant Brown	.20	.06
292 Amaury Telemaco	.20	.06
293 Dave Martinez	.20	.06
294 Jaime Navarro	.20	.06
295 Ray Durham	.20	.06
296 Ozzie Guillen	.20	.06
297 Roberto Hernandez	.20	.06
298 Ron Karkovice	.20	.06
299 James Baldwin	.20	.06
300 Frank Thomas	.50	.15
301 Eddie Taubensee	.20	.06
302 Bret Boone	.20	.06
303 Willie Greene	.20	.06
304 Dave Burba	.20	.06
305 Deion Sanders	.30	.09
306 Reggie Sanders	.20	.06
307 Hal Morris	.20	.06
308 Pokey Reese	.20	.06
309 Tony Fernandez	.20	.06
310 Manny Ramirez	.20	.06
311 Chad Ogea	.20	.06
312 Jack McDowell	.20	.06
313 Kevin Mitchell	.20	.06
314 Chad Curtis	.20	.06
315 Steve Kline	.20	.06
316 Kevin Seitzer	.20	.06
317 Kirt Manwaring	.20	.06
318 Billy Swift	.20	.06
319 Ellis Burks	.20	.06
320 Andres Galarraga	.20	.06
321 Bruce Ruffin	.20	.06
322 Mark Thompson	.20	.06
323 Walt Weiss	.20	.06
324 Todd Jones	.20	.06
325 Andruw Jones GHL	.20	.06
326 Chipper Jones GHL	.30	.09
327 Mo Vaughn GHL	.20	.06
328 Frank Thomas GHL	.30	.09
329 Albert Belle GHL	.20	.06
330 Mark McGwire GHL	.60	.18
331 Derek Jeter GHL	.60	.18
332 Alex Rodriguez GHL	.50	.15
333 Jay Buhner GHL with Ken Griffey Jr.	.20	.06
334 Ken Griffey Jr. GHL	.50	.15
335 Brian L. Hunter	.20	.06
336 Brian Johnson	.20	.06

337 Omar Olivares .20 .06
338 Deivi Cruz RC .30 .09
339 Damion Easley .20 .06
340 Melvin Nieves .20 .06
341 Moises Alou .20 .06
342 Jim Eisenreich .20 .06
343 Mark Hutton .20 .06
344 Alex Fernandez .20 .06
345 Gary Sheffield .20 .06
346 Pat Rapp .20 .06
347 Brad Ausmus .20 .06
348 Sean Berry .20 .06
349 Darryl Kile .20 .06
350 Craig Biggio .30 .09
351 Chris Holt .20 .06
352 Luis Gonzalez .20 .06
353 Pat Listach .20 .06
354 Jose Rosado .20 .06
355 Mike Macfarlane .20 .06
356 Tom Goodwin .20 .06
357 Chris Haney .20 .06
358 Chili Davis .20 .06
359 Jose Offerman .20 .06
360 Johnny Damon .20 .06
361 Bip Roberts .20 .06
362 Ramon Martinez .20 .06
363 Pedro Astacio .20 .06
364 Todd Zeile .20 .06
365 Mike Piazza .75 .23
366 Greg Gagne .20 .06
367 Chan Ho Park .20 .06
368 Wilton Guerrero .20 .06
369 Todd Worrell .20 .06
370 John Jaha .20 .06
371 Steve Sparks .20 .06
372 Mike Matheny .20 .06
373 Marc Newfield .20 .06
374 Jeromy Burnitz .20 .06
375 Jose Valentin .20 .06
376 Ben McDonald .20 .06
377 Roberto Kelly .20 .06
378 Bob Tewksbury .20 .06
379 Ron Coomer .20 .06
380 Brad Radke .20 .06
381 Matt Lawton .20 .06
382 Dan Naulty .20 .06
383 Scott Stahoviak .20 .06
384 Matt Wagner .20 .06
385 Jim Bullinger .20 .06
386 Carlos Perez .20 .06
387 Darrin Fletcher .20 .06
388 Chris Widger .20 .06
389 F.P. Santangelo .20 .06
390 Lee Smith .20 .06
391 Bobby Jones .20 .06
392 John Olerud .20 .06
393 Mark Clark .20 .06
394 Jason Isringhausen .20 .06
395 Todd Hundley .20 .06
396 Lance Johnson .20 .06
397 Edgardo Alfonzo .20 .06
398 Alex Ochoa .20 .06
399 Darryl Strawberry .30 .09
400 David Cone .20 .06
401 Paul O'Neill .30 .09
402 Joe Girardi .20 .06
403 Charlie Hayes .20 .06
404 Andy Pettitte .30 .09
405 Mariano Rivera .30 .09
406 Mariano Duncan .20 .06
407 Kenny Rogers .20 .06
408 Cecil Fielder .20 .06
409 George Williams .20 .06
410 Jose Canseco .50 .15
411 Tony Batista .20 .06
412 Steve Karsay .20 .06
413 Dave Telgheder .20 .06
414 Billy Taylor .20 .06
415 Mickey Morandini .20 .06
416 Calvin Maduro .20 .06
417 Mark Leiter .20 .06
418 Kevin Stocker .20 .06
419 Mike Lieberthal .20 .06
420 Rico Brogna .20 .06
421 Mark Portugal .20 .06
422 Rex Hudler .20 .06
423 Mark Johnson .20 .06
424 Esteban Loaiza .20 .06
425 Lou Collier .20 .06
426 Kevin Elster .20 .06
427 Francisco Cordova .20 .06
428 Marc Wilkins .20 .06
429 Joe Randa .20 .06
430 Jason Kendall .20 .06
431 Jon Lieber .20 .06
432 Steve Cooke .20 .06
433 Emil Brown RC .20 .06
434 Tony Womack RC .30 .09
435 Al Martin .20 .06
436 Jason Schmidt .20 .06
437 Andy Benes .20 .06
438 Delino DeShields .20 .06
439 Royce Clayton .20 .06
440 Brian Jordan .20 .06
441 Donovan Osborne .20 .06
442 Gary Gaetti .20 .06
443 Tom Pagnozzi .20 .06
444 Joey Hamilton .20 .06
445 Wally Joyner .20 .06
446 John Flaherty .20 .06
447 Chris Gomez .20 .06
448 Sterling Hitchcock .20 .06
449 Andy Ashby .20 .06
450 Ken Caminiti .20 .06
451 Tim Worrell .20 .06
452 Jose Vizcaino .20 .06
453 Rod Beck .20 .06
454 Wilson Delgado .20 .06
455 Darryl Hamilton .20 .06
456 Mark Lewis .20 .06
457 Mark Gardner .20 .06
458 Rick Wilkins .20 .06
459 Scott Sanders .20 .06
460 Kevin Orie .20 .06
461 Glendon Rusch .20 .06
462 Juan Melo .20 .06
463 Richie Sexson .20 .06
464 Bartolo Colon .20 .06
465 Jose Guillen .20 .06
466 Heath Murray .20 .06
467 Aaron Boone .20 .06
468 Bubba Trammell RC .30 .09
469 Jeff Abbott .20 .06
470 Derrick Gibson .20 .06
471 Matt Morris .20 .06
472 Ryan Jones .20 .06
473 Pat Cline .20 .06
474 Adam Riggs .20 .06
475 Jay Payton .20 .06
476 Derrek Lee .20 .06
477 Eli Marrero .20 .06
478 Lee Tinsley .20 .06
479 Jamie Moyer .20 .06
480 Jay Buhner .20 .06
481 Bob Wells .20 .06
482 Jeff Fassero .20 .06
483 Paul Sorrento .20 .06
484 Russ Davis .20 .06
485 Randy Johnson .50 .15
486 Roger Pavlik .20 .06
487 Damon Buford .20 .06
488 Julio Santana .20 .06
489 Mark McLemore .20 .06
490 Mickey Tettleton .20 .06
491 Ken Hill .20 .06
492 Benji Gil .20 .06
493 Ed Sprague .20 .06
494 Mike Timlin .20 .06
495 Pat Hentgen .20 .06
496 Orlando Merced .20 .06
497 Carlos Garcia .20 .06
498 Carlos Delgado .20 .06
499 Juan Guzman .20 .06
500 Roger Clemens 1.00 .30
501 Erik Hanson .20 .06
502 Otis Nixon .20 .06
503 Shawn Green .20 .06
504 Charlie O'Brien .20 .06
505 Joe Carter .20 .06
506 Alex Gonzalez .20 .06

1997 Collector's Choice All-Star Connection

Inserted one in every series two packs, this 45-card set celebrates the unique history of Baseball's All Star Game and highlights the League's top All-Star caliber players. The fronts feature color player cut-outs on a big star background.

Nm-Mt Ex-Mt
COMPLETE SET (45) 12.00 3.60
1 Mark McGwire 1.25 .35
2 Chuck Knoblauch .20 .06
3 Jim Thome .50 .15
4 Alex Rodriguez .75 .23
5 Ken Griffey Jr. .75 .23
6 Brady Anderson .20 .06
7 Albert Belle .20 .06
8 Ivan Rodriguez .50 .15
9 Pat Hentgen .20 .06
10 Frank Thomas .50 .15
11 Roberto Alomar .50 .15
12 Robin Ventura .20 .06
13 Cal Ripken 1.50 .45
14 Juan Gonzalez .50 .15
15 Manny Ramirez .20 .06
16 Bernie Williams .30 .09
17 Terry Steinbach .20 .06
18 Andy Pettitte .30 .09
19 Jeff Bagwell .30 .09
20 Craig Biggio .30 .09
21 Ken Caminiti .20 .06
22 Barry Larkin .50 .15
23 Tony Gwynn .60 .18
24 Barry Bonds 1.25 .35
25 Kenny Lofton .20 .06
26 Mike Piazza .75 .23
27 John Smoltz .30 .09
28 Andres Galarraga .20 .06
29 Ryne Sandberg .75 .23
30 Chipper Jones .50 .15
31 Mark Grudzielanek .20 .06
32 Sammy Sosa .75 .23
33 Steve Finley .20 .06
34 Gary Sheffield .20 .06
35 Todd Hundley .20 .06
36 Greg Maddux .75 .23
37 Mo Vaughn .20 .06
38 Eric Young .20 .06
39 Vinny Castilla .20 .06
40 Derek Jeter 1.25 .35
41 Lance Johnson .20 .06
42 Ellis Burks .20 .06
43 Dante Bichette .20 .06
44 Javy Lopez .20 .06
45 Hideo Nomo .50 .15

1997 Collector's Choice Big Shots

Randomly inserted in series two packs at the rate of one in 12, this 19-card set features unique and exciting photos depicting some of the game's most recognized players.

Nm-Mt Ex-Mt
COMPLETE SET (19) 60.00 18.00
*GOLD: 1.5X TO 4X BASIC BIG SHOT.
SER.2 STATED ODDS 1:144
1 Ken Griffey Jr. 4.00 1.20
2 Nomar Garciaparra 4.00 1.20
3 Brian Jordan 1.00 .30
4 Scott Rolen 1.50 .45
5 Alex Rodriguez 4.00 1.20
6 Larry Walker 1.50 .45
7 Mariano Rivera 1.50 .45
8 Cal Ripken 8.00 2.40
9 Deion Sanders 1.50 .45
10 Frank Thomas 2.50 .75
11 Dean Palmer 1.00 .30
12 Ken Caminiti 1.00 .30
13 Derek Jeter 6.00 1.80
14 Barry Bonds 6.00 1.80
15 Chipper Jones 2.50 .75
16 Mo Vaughn 1.00 .30
17 Jay Buhner 1.00 .30
18 Mike Piazza 4.00 1.20
19 Tony Gwynn 3.00 .90

1997 Collector's Choice The Big Show

Inserted one in every first series pack, cards from this 45-card set feature color photos of some of the hottest players in baseball. The backs carry comments about the pictured player by ESPN SportsCenter television sportscasters, Keith Olbermann and Dan Patrick.

Nm-Mt Ex-Mt
COMPLETE SET (45) 10.00 3.00
*WORLD HQ: 15X TO 40X BASIC BIG SHOW
WHQ SER.1 STATED ODDS 1:35
1 Greg Maddux .75 .23
2 Chipper Jones .50 .15
3 Andruw Jones .20 .06
4 John Smoltz .30 .09
5 Cal Ripken 1.50 .45
6 Roberto Alomar .50 .15
7 Rafael Palmeiro .30 .09
8 Eddie Murray .50 .15
9 Jose Canseco .50 .15
10 Roger Clemens 1.00 .30
11 Mo Vaughn .20 .06
12 Jim Edmonds .20 .06
13 Tim Salmon .30 .09
14 Sammy Sosa .75 .23
15 Albert Belle .20 .06
16 Frank Thomas .50 .15
17 Barry Larkin .50 .15
18 Kenny Lofton .20 .06
19 Manny Ramirez .20 .06
20 Matt Williams .20 .06
21 Dante Bichette .20 .06
22 Gary Sheffield .20 .06
23 Craig Biggio .30 .09
24 Jeff Bagwell .30 .09
25 Todd Hollandsworth .20 .06
26 Raul Mondesi .20 .06
27 Hideo Nomo .50 .15
28 Mike Piazza .75 .23
29 Paul Molitor .30 .09
30 Kirby Puckett .50 .15
31 Rondell White .20 .06
32 Rey Ordonez .20 .06
33 Paul Wilson .20 .06
34 Derek Jeter 1.25 .35
35 Andy Pettitte .30 .09
36 Mark McGwire 1.25 .35
37 Jason Kendall .20 .06
38 Ozzie Smith .75 .23
39 Tony Gwynn .60 .18
40 Barry Bonds 1.25 .35
41 Alex Rodriguez .75 .23
42 Jay Buhner .20 .06
43 Ken Griffey Jr. .75 .23
44 Randy Johnson .50 .15
45 Juan Gonzalez .50 .15

1997 Collector's Choice Crash the Game

Inserted in series two packs at the rate of one in five, cards from this interactive game set features three separate cards each of 30 top home run hitters. If the featured player hit a home run during the series specified on the card, the card could than have been redeemed for a special card of the same player. The postmark expiration date for exchanging winning cards was December 1, 1997.

Nm-Mt Ex-Mt
COMPLETE SET (90) 60.00 18.00
*INSTANT WIN: 10X TO 20X BASIC CRASH
INSTANT WIN SER.2 STATED ODDS 1:721
1A Ryan Klesko .40 .12
July 28-30 L
1B Ryan Klesko .40 .12
Aug 8-11 L
1C Ryan Klesko .40 .12
Sept 19-21 L
2A Chipper Jones 1.00 .30
Aug 15-17 L
2B Chipper Jones 1.00 .30
Aug 29-31 L
2C Chipper Jones 1.00 .30
Sept 12-14 L
3A Andruw Jones .40 .12
Aug 22-24 W
3B Andruw Jones .40 .12
Sept 1-3 L
3C Andruw Jones .40 .12
Sept 19-22 L
4A Brady Anderson .40 .12
July 31-Aug 3 W
4B Brady Anderson .40 .12
Sept 4-7 L
4C Brady Anderson .40 .12
Sept 19-22 L
5A Rafael Palmeiro .60 .18
July 29-30 L
5B Rafael Palmeiro .60 .18
Aug 29-31 L
5C Rafael Palmeiro .60 .18
Sept 26-28 L
6A Cal Ripken 3.00 .90
Aug 8-10
6B Cal Ripken 3.00 .90
Sept 1-3 W
6C Cal Ripken 3.00 .90
Sept 11-14 L
7A Mo Vaughn .40 .12
Aug 14-17 L
7B Mo Vaughn .40 .12
Aug 29-31 W
7C Mo Vaughn .40 .12
Sept 23-25 W
8A Sammy Sosa 1.50 .45
Aug 1-3 W
8B Sammy Sosa 1.50 .45
Aug 29-31 L
8C Sammy Sosa 1.50 .45
Sept 19-21 W
9A Albert Belle .40 .12
Aug 7-10 L
9B Albert Belle .40 .12
Sept 11-14 L
9C Albert Belle .40 .12
Sept 19-21 W
10A Frank Thomas 1.00 .30
Aug 29-31 L
10B Frank Thomas 1.00 .30
Sept 1-3 L
10C Frank Thomas 1.00 .30
Sept 23-25 W
11A Manny Ramirez .40 .12
Aug 12-14 W
11B Manny Ramirez .40 .12
Aug 29-31 L
11C Manny Ramirez .40 .12
Sept 11-14 W
12A Jim Thome 1.00 .30
July 28-30 L
12B Jim Thome 1.00 .30
Aug 15-18 W
12C Jim Thome 1.00 .30
Sept 19-22 L
13A Matt Williams .40 .12
Aug 4-5 L
13B Matt Williams .40 .12
Sept 1-3 W
13C Matt Williams .40 .12
Sept 23-25 L
14A Dante Bichette .40 .12
July 24-27 W
14B Dante Bichette .40 .12
Aug 28-29 L
14C Dante Bichette .40 .12
Sept 26-28 W
15A Vinny Castilla .40 .12
Aug 12-13 L
15B Vinny Castilla .40 .12
Sept 4-7 W
15C Vinny Castilla .40 .12
Sept 19-21 L
16A Andres Galarraga .40 .12
Aug 8-10 W
16B Andres Galarraga .40 .12
Aug 30-31 L
16C Andres Galarraga .40 .12
Sept 12-14 L
17A Gary Sheffield .40 .12
Aug 1-3 W
17B Gary Sheffield .40 .12
Sept 1-3 W
17C Gary Sheffield .40 .12
Sept 12-14 W
18A Jeff Bagwell .60 .18
Sept 9-10 L
18B Jeff Bagwell .60 .18
Sept 19-22 W
18C Jeff Bagwell .60 .18
Sept 23-25 W
19A Eric Karros .40 .12
Aug 1-3 L
19B Eric Karros .40 .12
Aug 15-17 L
19C Eric Karros .40 .12
Sept 25-28 W
20A Mike Piazza 1.50 .45
Aug 11-12 L
20B Mike Piazza 1.50 .45
Sept 5-8 W
20C Mike Piazza 1.50 .45
Sept 19-21 W
21A Vladimir Guerrero 1.00 .30
Aug 22-24 L
21B Vladimir Guerrero 1.00 .30
Aug 29-31 L
21C Vladimir Guerrero 1.00 .30
Sept 19-22 L
22A Cecil Fielder .40 .12
Aug 29-31 L
22B Cecil Fielder .40 .12
Sept 4-7 L
22C Cecil Fielder .40 .12
Sept 26-28 L
23A Jose Canseco 1.00 .30
Sept 12-14 L
23B Jose Canseco 1.00 .30
Sept 22-24 L
23C Jose Canseco 1.00 .30
Sept 26-28 L
24A Mark McGwire 2.50 .75
July 31-Aug 3 L
24B Mark McGwire 2.50 .75
Aug 30-31 L
24C Mark McGwire 2.50 .75
Sept 19-22 W
25A Ken Caminiti .40 .12
Aug 8-10 L
25B Ken Caminiti .40 .12
Sept 4-7 W
25C Ken Caminiti .40 .12
Sept 17-18 W
26A Barry Bonds 2.50 .75
Aug 5-7 L
26B Barry Bonds 2.50 .75
Sept 4-7 L
26C Barry Bonds 2.50 .75
Sept 23-24 W
27A Jay Buhner .40 .12
Aug 7-10 L
27B Jay Buhner .40 .12
Aug 28-29 L
27C Jay Buhner .40 .12
Sept 1-3 L
28A Ken Griffey Jr. 1.50 .45
Aug 22-24 W
28B Ken Griffey Jr. 1.50 .45
Aug 28-29 L
28C Ken Griffey Jr. 1.50 .45
Sept 19-22 W
29A Alex Rodriguez 1.50 .45
July 29-31 L
29B Alex Rodriguez 1.50 .45
Aug 30-31 L
29C Alex Rodriguez 1.50 .45
Sept 12-15 L
30A Juan Gonzalez 1.00 .30
Aug 11-13 W
30B Juan Gonzalez 1.00 .30
Aug 30-31 L
30C Juan Gonzalez 1.00 .30
Sept 19-21 W

1997 Collector's Choice Griffey Clearly Dominant

Randomly inserted in first series packs at a rate of one in 144, this five-card set highlights superstar Ken Griffey Jr. with different color photos and information on each card.

Nm-Mt Ex-Mt
COMPLETE SET (5) 40.00 12.00
COMMON (CD1-CD5) 10.00 3.00

1997 Collector's Choice New Frontier

Randomly inserted one in every 69 series two packs, this 40-card set showcases the most anticipated InterLeague match-ups. Each card features a color player cut-out of a great player from either the American or National League on half of a baseball diamond background and is designed to fit with another card displaying a great player match-up from the opposite league to complete the diamond.

Nm-Mt Ex-Mt
COMPLETE SET (40) 500.00 150.00
NF1 Alex Rodriguez 20.00 6.00
NF2 Tony Gwynn 15.00 4.50
NF3 Jose Canseco 12.00 3.60
NF4 Hideo Nomo 12.00 3.60
NF5 Mark McGwire 30.00 9.00
NF6 Barry Bonds 30.00 9.00
NF7 Juan Gonzalez 12.00 3.60
NF8 Ken Caminiti 5.00 1.50
NF9 Tim Salmon 8.00 2.40
NF10 Mike Piazza 20.00 6.00
NF11 Ken Griffey Jr. 20.00 6.00
NF12 Andres Galarraga 5.00 1.50
NF13 Jay Buhner 5.00 1.50
NF14 Dante Bichette 5.00 1.50
NF15 Frank Thomas 12.00 3.60
NF16 Ryne Sandberg 20.00 6.00
NF17 Roger Clemens 25.00 7.50
NF18 Andruw Jones 5.00 1.50
NF19 Jim Thome 12.00 3.60
NF20 Sammy Sosa 20.00 6.00
NF21 Dave Justice 5.00 1.50
NF22 Deion Sanders 8.00 2.40
NF23 Todd Walker 5.00 1.50
NF24 Kevin Orie 5.00 1.50
NF25 Albert Belle 5.00 1.50
NF26 Jeff Bagwell 8.00 2.40
NF27 Manny Ramirez 5.00 1.50
NF28 Brian Jordan 5.00 1.50
NF29 Derek Jeter 30.00 9.00
NF30 Chipper Jones 12.00 3.60
NF31 Mo Vaughn 5.00 1.50
NF32 Gary Sheffield 5.00 1.50
NF33 Carlos Delgado 5.00 1.50
NF34 Vladimir Guerrero 12.00 3.60
NF35 Cal Ripken 40.00 12.00

NF36 Greg Maddux 20.00 6.00
NF37 Cecil Fielder 5.00 1.50
NF38 Todd Hundley 5.00 1.50
NF39 Mike Mussina 12.00 3.60
NF40 Scott Rolen 8.00 2.40

1997 Collector's Choice Premier Power

Randomly inserted in first series packs at a rate of one in 15, this silver version 20-card set features borderless color action player photos and information about the 20 top Major League Home Run hitters.

Nm-Mt Ex-Mt
COMPLETE SET (20) 40.00 12.00
*GOLD: 1.25X TO 3X BASIC PREM.POWER
GOLD SER.1 STATED ODDS 1:69
*JUMBOS: .25X BASIC PREMIER POWER
PP1 Mark McGwire 6.00 1.80
PP2 Brady Anderson 1.00 .30
PP3 Ken Griffey Jr. 4.00 1.20
PP4 Albert Belle 1.00 .30
PP5 Juan Gonzalez 2.50 .75
PP6 Andres Galarraga 1.00 .30
PP7 Jay Buhner 1.00 .30
PP8 Mo Vaughn 1.00 .30
PP9 Barry Bonds 6.00 1.80
PP10 Gary Sheffield 1.00 .30
PP11 Todd Hundley 1.00 .30
PP12 Frank Thomas 2.50 .75
PP13 Sammy Sosa 4.00 1.20
PP14 Ken Caminiti 1.00 .30
PP15 Vinny Castilla 1.00 .30
PP16 Ellis Burks 1.00 .30
PP17 Rafael Palmeiro 1.50 .45
PP18 Alex Rodriguez 4.00 1.20
PP19 Mike Piazza 4.00 1.20
PP20 Eddie Murray 2.50 .75

1997 Collector's Choice Stick'Ums

Randomly inserted in first series packs at a rate of one in three, cards from this 30-card set features color sticker images of star players. These interactive reusable stickers could be used to create mini baseball scenes.

Nm-Mt Ex-Mt
COMPLETE SET (30) 15.00 4.50
1 Ozzie Smith 1.25 .35
2 Andruw Jones .30 .09
3 Alex Rodriguez 1.25 .35
4 Paul Molitor .50 .15
5 Jeff Bagwell .50 .15
6 Manny Ramirez .30 .09
7 Kenny Lofton .30 .09
8 Albert Belle .30 .09
9 Jay Buhner .30 .09
10 Chipper Jones .75 .23
11 Barry Larkin .75 .23
12 Dante Bichette .30 .09
13 Mike Piazza 1.25 .35
14 Andres Galarraga .30 .09
15 Barry Bonds 2.00 .60
16 Brady Anderson .30 .09
17 Gary Sheffield .30 .09
18 Jim Thome .75 .23
19 Tony Gwynn 1.00 .30
20 Cal Ripken 2.50 .75
21 Sammy Sosa 1.25 .35
22 Juan Gonzalez .75 .23
23 Greg Maddux 1.25 .35
24 Ken Griffey Jr. 1.25 .35
25 Mark McGwire 2.00 .60
26 Kirby Puckett .75 .23
27 Mo Vaughn .30 .09
28 Vladimir Guerrero .75 .23
29 Ken Caminiti .30 .09
30 Frank Thomas .75 .23

1997 Collector's Choice Stick'Ums Retail

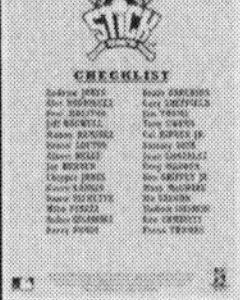

This 28-card set features color sticker images of star players. These interactive reusable stickers could be used to create mini baseball scenes. The back of each sticker displays the checklist for the set. The set was distributed in packs of 15 stickers plus three regular Collector's Choice cards. The stickers are unnumbered and checklisted below in alphabetical order.

Nm-Mt Ex-Mt
COMPLETE SET (28) 10.00 3.00
1 Brady Anderson .25 .07
2 Jeff Bagwell .75 .23
3 Albert Belle .40 .12
4 Dante Bichette .25 .07
5 Barry Bonds 1.50 .45
6 Jay Buhner .25 .07
7 Ken Caminiti .40 .12
8 Andres Galarraga .60 .18
9 Juan Gonzalez .75 .23
10 Ken Griffey Jr. 2.00 .60
11 Vladimir Guerrero 1.00 .30
12 Tony Gwynn 1.50 .45
13 Andruw Jones 1.00 .30
14 Chipper Jones 1.50 .45
15 Barry Larkin .60 .18
16 Kenny Lofton .25 .07
17 Greg Maddux 2.00 .60
18 Mark McGwire 2.50 .75
19 Paul Molitor .60 .18
20 Mike Piazza 2.00 .60
21 Manny Ramirez .60 .18
22 Cal Ripken Jr. 3.00 .90
23 Alex Rodriguez 2.00 .60
24 Gary Sheffield .75 .23
25 Sammy Sosa 1.50 .45
26 Frank Thomas .75 .23
27 Jim Thome .60 .18
28 Mo Vaughn .25 .07

1997 Collector's Choice Toast of the Town

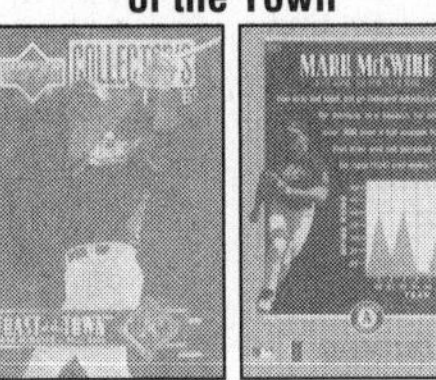

Randomly inserted in series two packs at the rate of one in 35, this 30-card set features color photos of some of the best Major League players printed on premium, foil enhanced card stock.

Nm-Mt Ex-Mt
COMPLETE SET (30) 200.00 60.00
T1 Andruw Jones 2.50 .75
T2 Chipper Jones 6.00 1.80
T3 Greg Maddux 10.00 3.00
T4 John Smoltz 4.00 1.20
T5 Kenny Lofton 2.50 .75
T6 Brady Anderson 2.50 .75
T7 Cal Ripken 20.00 6.00
T8 Mo Vaughn 2.50 .75
T9 Sammy Sosa 10.00 3.00
T10 Albert Belle 2.50 .75
T11 Frank Thomas 6.00 1.80
T12 Barry Larkin 6.00 1.80
T13 Manny Ramirez 2.50 .75
T14 Jeff Bagwell 4.00 1.20
T15 Mike Piazza 10.00 3.00
T16 Paul Molitor 4.00 1.20
T17 Vladimir Guerrero 6.00 1.80
T18 Todd Hundley 2.50 .75
T19 Derek Jeter 15.00 4.50
T20 Andy Pettitte 4.00 1.20
T21 Bernie Williams 4.00 1.20
T22 Mark McGwire 15.00 4.50
T23 Scott Rolen 4.00 1.20
T24 Ken Caminiti 2.50 .75
T25 Tony Gwynn 8.00 2.40
T26 Barry Bonds 15.00 4.50
T27 Ken Griffey Jr. 10.00 3.00
T28 Alex Rodriguez 10.00 3.00
T29 Juan Gonzalez 6.00 1.80
T30 Roger Clemens 12.00 3.60

1997 Collector's Choice Update

This 30-card Update set was made available to collectors who mailed in 10 series two wrappers (plus a check or money order for $3 to cover postage and handling) prior to the December 1st, 1997 deadline. The cards share the same design as the basic issue 1997 Collector's Choice set and content focuses on traded veterans pictured in their new uniforms and a handful of prospects called up during the season (including Jose Cruz Jr. and Hideki Irabu).

Nm-Mt Ex-Mt
COMPLETE SET (30) 5.00 1.50
U1 Jim Leyritz .20 .06
U2 Matt Perisho .20 .06
U3 Michael Tucker .20 .06
U4 Mike Johnson .20 .06
U5 Jaime Navarro .20 .06
U6 Doug Drabek .20 .06
U7 Terry Mulholland .20 .06
U8 Brett Tomko .20 .06
U9 Marquis Grissom .20 .06
U10 David Justice .20 .06
U11 Brian Moehler .20 .06
U12 Bobby Bonilla .20 .06
U13 Todd Dunwoody .20 .06
U14 Tony Saunders .20 .06
U15 Jay Bell .20 .06
U16 Jeff King .20 .06
U17 Terry Steinbach .20 .06
U18 Steve Bieser .20 .06
U19 Takashi Kashiwada .20 .06
U20 Hideki Irabu .20 .06
U21 Damon Mashore .20 .06
U22 Quilvio Veras .20 .06
U23 Will Cunnane .20 .06
U24 Jeff Kent .20 .06
U25 J.T. Snow .20 .06
U26 Dante Powell .20 .06
U27 Jose Cruz Jr. 1.25 .35
U28 John Burkett .20 .06
U29 John Wetteland .20 .06
U30 Benito Santiago .20 .06

1997 Collector's Choice Teams

This set features color action and posed player photos either borderless or in white borders of 13 players each of selected major league baseball teams. The backs carry player information and career statistics. Each set was distributed in a special package along with a foil enhanced die cut 3 1/2" by 5" Home Team Heroes card displaying two star players of that team. The cards are checklisted below by teams with the Home Team Heroes cards, which was also issued seperately, priced as a Upper Deck set.

Nm-Mt Ex-Mt
COMPLETE SET 80.00 24.00
AB Atl. Braves Logo CL .25 .07
AB1 Andruw Jones 1.50 .45
AB2 Kenny Lofton .75 .23
AB3 Fred McGriff .75 .23
AB4 Michael Tucker .50 .15
AB5 Ryan Klesko .50 .15
AB6 Javier Lopez .75 .23
AB7 Mark Wohlers .25 .07
AB8 Tom Glavine 1.00 .30
AB9 Denny Neagle .25 .07
AB10 Chipper Jones 3.00 .90
AB11 Jeff Blauser .25 .07
AB12 Greg Maddux 3.00 .90
AB13 John Smoltz .50 .15
BO Balt. Orioles Logo CL .25 .07
BO1 Rocky Coppinger .25 .07
BO2 Scott Erickson .50 .15
BO3 Chris Hoiles .25 .07
BO4 Roberto Alomar 1.00 .30
BO5 Cal Ripken Jr. 5.00 1.50
BO6 Randy Myers .50 .15
BO7 B.J. Surhoff .50 .15
BO8 Mike Mussina 1.00 .30
BO9 Rafael Palmeiro 1.00 .30
BO10 Jimmy Key .50 .15
BO11 Mike Bordick .25 .07
BO12 Brady Anderson .50 .15
BO13 Eric Davis .50 .15
CI Cleve. Indians Logo CL .25 .07
CI1 Brian Giles 4.00 1.20
CI2 Omar Vizquel .75 .23
CI3 Julio Franco .50 .15
CI4 Orel Hershiser .50 .15
CI5 Charles Nagy .25 .07
CI6 Matt Williams .75 .23
CI7 Jose Mesa .50 .15
CI8 Sandy Alomar Jr. .50 .15
CI9 Jim Thome 1.00 .30
CI10 David Justice 1.00 .30
CI11 Marquis Grissom .50 .15
CI12 Chad Ogea .25 .07
CI13 Manny Ramirez 1.25 .35
CR Colo. Rockies Logo CL .25 .07
CR1 Dante Bichette .50 .15
CR2 Vinny Castilla .50 .15
CR3 Kevin Ritz .25 .07
CR4 Larry Walker .75 .23
CR5 Eric Young .50 .15
CR6 Quinton McCracken .25 .07
CR7 John Vander Wal .25 .07
CR8 Jamey Wright .25 .07
CR9 Mark Thompson .25 .07
CR10 Andres Galarraga 1.00 .30
CR11 Ellis Burks .50 .15
CR12 Kirt Manwaring .25 .07
CR13 Walt Weiss .25 .07
CW Chi. White Sox Logo CL .25 .07
CW1 Robin Ventura 1.00 .30
CW2 Wilson Alvarez .25 .07
CW3 Tony Phillips .25 .07
CW4 Lyle Mouton .25 .07
CW5 James Baldwin .25 .07
CW6 Harold Baines .75 .23
CW7 Albert Belle .50 .15
CW8 Chris Snopek .25 .07
CW9 Ray Durham .50 .15
CW10 Frank Thomas 1.25 .35
CW11 Ozzie Guillen .50 .15
CW12 Roberto Hernandez .50 .15
CW13 Jaime Navarro .25 .07
FM Fla. Marlins Logo CL .25 .07
FM1 Luis Castillo .75 .23
FM2 Al Leiter .50 .15
FM3 Devon White .25 .07
FM4 Jeff Conine .50 .15
FM5 Charles Johnson .25 .07
FM6 Edgar Renteria .75 .23
FM7 Robb Nen .25 .07
FM8 Kevin Brown .75 .23
FM9 Gary Sheffield 1.25 .35
FM10 Alex Fernandez .25 .07
FM11 Pat Rapp .25 .07
FM12 Moises Alou .50 .15
FM13 Bobby Bonilla .50 .15
LA L. A. Dodgers Logo CL .25 .07
LA1 Raul Mondesi .50 .15
LA2 Brett Butler .50 .15
LA3 Todd Hollandsworth .25 .07
LA4 Eric Karros .50 .15
LA5 Hideo Nomo 1.50 .45
LA6 Ismael Valdes .25 .07
LA7 Wilton Guerrero .25 .07
LA8 Ramon Martinez .25 .07
LA9 Greg Gagne .25 .07
LA10 Mike Piazza 3.00 .90
LA11 Chan Ho Park .50 .15
LA12 Todd Worrell .25 .07
LA13 Todd Zeile .50 .15
NY N.Y. Yankees Logo CL .25 .07
NY1 Bernie Williams 1.00 .30
NY2 Dwight Gooden .50 .15
NY3 Wade Boggs 1.25 .35
NY4 Ruben Rivera .25 .07
NY5 Derek Jeter 5.00 1.50
NY6 Tino Martinez .75 .23
NY7 Tim Raines .50 .15
NY8 Joe Girardi .25 .07
NY9 Charlie Hayes .25 .07
NY10 Andy Pettitte .75 .23
NY11 Cecil Fielder .25 .07
NY12 Paul O'Neill .50 .15
NY13 David Cone .75 .23
SM Sea. Mariners Logo CL .25 .07
SM1 Dan Wilson .25 .07
SM2 Ken Griffey Jr. 3.00 .90
SM3 Edgar Martinez .75 .23
SM4 Joey Cora .25 .07
SM5 Norm Charlton .25 .07
SM6 Alex Rodriguez 4.00 1.20
SM7 Randy Johnson 1.50 .45
SM8 Paul Sorrento .25 .07
SM9 Jamie Moyer .50 .15
SM10 Jay Buhner .50 .15
SM11 Russ Davis .25 .07
SM12 Jeff Fassero .25 .07
SM13 Bob Wells .25 .07
TR Tex. Rangers Logo CL .25 .07
TR1 Bobby Witt .25 .07
TR2 Darren Oliver .25 .07
TR3 Rusty Greer .50 .15
TR4 Juan Gonzalez 1.00 .30
TR5 Will Clark 1.00 .30
TR6 Dean Palmer .50 .15
TR7 Ivan Rodriguez 1.25 .35
TR8 John Wetteland .50 .15
TR9 Mark McLemore .25 .07
TR10 John Burkett .25 .07
TR11 Benji Gil .25 .07
TR12 Ken Hill .25 .07
TR13 Mickey Tettleton .50 .15

1998 Collector's Choice

The 1998 Collector's Choice set (produced by Upper Deck) was issued in two separate series, each containing 265 cards. Packs for both first and second series contained 14 cards and carried a suggested retail price of $1.29. First series packs went live around March, 1998 and second series packs followed suit in June, 1998. Card fronts feature color glossy action player photos framed by a clean white border. The backs carry statistical information and another color image. The set contains the topical subsets: Checklists (266-270), Cover Glory (1-18), Golden Jubilee (271-279), Rookie Class (100-126/415-432), Masked Marauders (181-189), and Top of the Charts (253-261). Key Rookie Cards in this set include Kevin Millwood and Magglio Ordonez. Card number 202A featuring Kerry Wood was issued in factory sets to replace Tony Barron

Nm-Mt Ex-Mt
COMPLETE SET (530) 40.00 12.00
COMP. SERIES 1 (265) 20.00 6.00
COMP. SERIES 2 (265) 20.00 6.00
COMP.FACT.SET (530) 50.00 15.00
1 Nomar Garciaparra CG .50 .15
2 Roger Clemens CG .50 .15
3 Larry Walker CG .20 .06
4 Mike Piazza CG .50 .15
5 Mark McGwire CG .60 .18
6 Tony Gwynn CG .30 .09
7 Jose Cruz Jr. CG .20 .06
8 Frank Thomas CG .30 .09
9 Tino Martinez CG .20 .06
10 Ken Griffey Jr. CG .50 .15
11 Barry Bonds CG .50 .15
12 Scott Rolen CG .20 .06
13 Randy Johnson CG .30 .09
14 Ryne Sandberg CG .50 .15
15 Eddie Murray CG .30 .09
16 Kevin Brown CG .20 .06
17 Mike Mussina CG .30 .09
18 Sandy Alomar Jr. CG .20 .06
19 Ken Griffey Jr. CL .30 .09
Adam Riggs
20 Nomar Garciaparra CL .30 .09
Charlie O'Brien
21 Ben Grieve CL .20 .06
Frank Thomas
Tony Gwynn
22 Mark McGwire CL .30 .09
Cal Ripken
23 Tino Martinez CL .20 .06
24 Jason Dickson .20 .06
25 Darin Erstad .20 .06
26 Todd Greene .20 .06
27 Chuck Finley .20 .06
28 Garret Anderson .20 .06
29 Dave Hollins .20 .06
30 Rickey Henderson .50 .15
31 John Smoltz .30 .09
32 Michael Tucker .20 .06
33 Jeff Blauser .20 .06
34 Javier Lopez .20 .06
35 Andruw Jones .20 .06
36 Denny Neagle .20 .06
37 Randall Simon .20 .06
38 Mark Wohlers .20 .06
39 Harold Baines .20 .06
40 Cal Ripken 1.50 .45
41 Mike Bordick .20 .06
42 Jimmy Key .20 .06
43 Armando Benitez .20 .06
44 Scott Erickson .20 .06
45 Eric Davis .20 .06
46 Bret Saberhagen .20 .06
47 Darren Bragg .20 .06
48 Steve Avery .20 .06
49 Jeff Frye .20 .06
50 Aaron Sele .20 .06
51 Scott Hatteberg .20 .06
52 Tom Gordon .20 .06
53 Kevin Orie .20 .06
54 Kevin Foster .20 .06
55 Ryne Sandberg .75 .23
56 Doug Glanville .20 .06
57 Tyler Houston .20 .06
58 Steve Trachsel .20 .06
59 Mark Grace .30 .09
60 Frank Thomas .50 .15
61 Scott Eyre .20 .06
62 Jeff Abbott .20 .06
63 Chris Clemons .20 .06
64 Jorge Fabregas .20 .06
65 Robin Ventura .20 .06
66 Matt Karchner .20 .06
67 Jon Nunnally .20 .06
68 Aaron Boone .20 .06
69 Pokey Reese .20 .06
70 Deion Sanders .30 .09
71 Jeff Shaw .20 .06
72 Eduardo Perez .20 .06
73 Brett Tomko .20 .06
74 Bartolo Colon .20 .06
75 Manny Ramirez .20 .06
76 Jose Mesa .20 .06
77 Brian Giles .20 .06
78 Richie Sexson .20 .06
79 Orel Hershiser .20 .06
80 Matt Williams .20 .06
81 Walt Weiss .20 .06
82 Jerry DiPoto .20 .06
83 Quinton McCracken .20 .06
84 Neifi Perez .20 .06
85 Vinny Castilla .20 .06
86 Ellis Burks .20 .06
87 John Thomson .20 .06
88 Willie Blair .20 .06
89 Bob Hamelin .20 .06
90 Tony Clark .20 .06
91 Todd Jones .20 .06
92 Deivi Cruz .20 .06
93 Frank Catalanotto RC .40 .12
94 Justin Thompson .20 .06
95 Gary Sheffield .20 .06
96 Kevin Brown .30 .09
97 Charles Johnson .20 .06
98 Bobby Bonilla .20 .06
99 Livan Hernandez .20 .06
100 Paul Konerko .20 .06
101 Craig Counsell .20 .06
102 Magglio Ordonez RC 1.00 .30
103 Garrett Stephenson .20 .06
104 Ken Cloude .20 .06
105 Miguel Tejada .30 .09
106 Juan Encarnacion .20 .06
107 Dennis Reyes .20 .06
108 Orlando Cabrera .20 .06
109 Kelvim Escobar .20 .06
110 Ben Grieve .20 .06
111 Brian Rose .20 .06
112 Fernando Tatis .20 .06
113 Tom Evans .20 .06
114 Tom Fordham .20 .06
115 Mark Kotsay .20 .06
116 Mario Valdez .20 .06
117 Jeremi Gonzalez .20 .06
118 Todd Dunwoody .20 .06
119 Javier Valentin .20 .06
120 Todd Helton .30 .09
121 Jason Varitek .20 .06
122 Chris Carpenter .20 .06
123 Kevin Millwood RC 1.00 .30
124 Brad Fullmer .20 .06
125 Jaret Wright .20 .06
126 Brad Rigby .20 .06
127 Edgar Renteria .20 .06
128 Robb Nen .20 .06
129 Tony Pena .20 .06
130 Craig Biggio .30 .09
131 Brad Ausmus .20 .06
132 Shane Reynolds .20 .06
133 Mike Hampton .20 .06
134 Billy Wagner .20 .06
135 Richard Hidalgo .20 .06
136 Jose Rosado .20 .06
137 Yamil Benitez .20 .06
138 Felix Martinez .20 .06
139 Jeff King .20 .06
140 Jose Offerman .20 .06
141 Joe Vitiello .20 .06
142 Tim Belcher .20 .06
143 Brett Butler .20 .06
144 Greg Gagne .20 .06
145 Mike Piazza .75 .23
146 Ramon Martinez .20 .06
147 Raul Mondesi .20 .06
148 Adam Riggs .20 .06
149 Eddie Murray .50 .15
150 Jeff Cirillo .20 .06
151 Scott Karl .20 .06
152 Mike Fetters .20 .06
153 Dave Nilsson .20 .06
154 Antone Williamson .20 .06
155 Jeff D'Amico .20 .06
156 Jose Valentin .20 .06
157 Brad Radke .20 .06
158 Torii Hunter .20 .06
159 Chuck Knoblauch .20 .06
160 Paul Molitor .30 .09
161 Travis Miller .20 .06

162 Rich Robertson .20 .06
163 Ron Coomer .20 .06
164 Mark Grudzielanek .20 .06
165 Lee Smith .20 .06
166 Vladimir Guerrero .50 .15
167 Dustin Hermanson .20 .06
168 Ugueth Urbina .20 .06
169 F.P. Santangelo .20 .06
170 Rondell White .20 .06
171 Bobby Jones .20 .06
172 Edgardo Alfonzo .20 .06
173 John Franco .20 .06
174 Carlos Baerga .20 .06
175 Butch Huskey .20 .06
176 Rey Ordonez .20 .06
177 Matt Franco .20 .06
178 Dwight Gooden .20 .06
179 Chad Curtis .20 .06
180 Tino Martinez .30 .09
181 Charlie O'Brien MM .20 .06
182 Sandy Alomar Jr. MM .20 .06
183 Raul Casanova MM .20 .06
184 Javier Lopez MM .20 .06
185 Mike Piazza MM .50 .15
186 Ivan Rodriguez MM .30 .09
187 Charles Johnson MM .20 .06
188 Brad Ausmus MM .20 .06
189 Brian Johnson MM .20 .06
190 Wade Boggs .30 .09
191 David Wells .20 .06
192 Tim Raines .20 .06
193 Ramiro Mendoza .20 .06
194 Willie Adams .20 .06
195 Matt Stairs .20 .06
196 Jason McDonald .20 .06
197 Dave Magadan .20 .06
198 Mark Bellhorn .20 .06
199 Ariel Prieto .20 .06
200 Jose Canseco .50 .15
201 Bobby Estalella .20 .06
202 Tony Barron RC .20 .06
202A Kerry Wood
203 Midre Cummings .20 .06
204 Ricky Bottalico .20 .06
205 Mike Grace .20 .06
206 Rico Brogna .20 .06
207 Mickey Morandini .20 .06
208 Lou Collier .20 .06
209 Kevin Polcovich .20 .06
210 Kevin Young .20 .06
211 Jose Guillen .20 .06
212 Esteban Loaiza .20 .06
213 Marc Wilkins .20 .06
214 Jason Schmidt .20 .06
215 Gary Gaetti .20 .06
216 Fernando Valenzuela .20 .06
217 Willie McGee .20 .06
218 Alan Benes .20 .06
219 Eli Marrero .20 .06
220 Mark McGwire 1.25 .35
221 Matt Morris .20 .06
222 Trevor Hoffman .20 .06
223 Will Cunnane .20 .06
224 Joey Hamilton .20 .06
225 Ken Caminiti .20 .06
226 Derrek Lee .20 .06
227 Mark Sweeney .20 .06
228 Carlos Hernandez .20 .06
229 Brian Johnson .20 .06
230 Jeff Kent .20 .06
231 Kirk Rueter .20 .06
232 Bill Mueller .20 .06
233 Dante Powell .20 .06
234 J.T. Snow .20 .06
235 Shawn Estes .20 .06
236 Dennis Martinez .20 .06
237 Jamie Moyer .20 .06
238 Dan Wilson .20 .06
239 Joey Cora .20 .06
240 Ken Griffey Jr. .75 .23
241 Paul Sorrento .20 .06
242 Jay Buhner .20 .06
243 Hanley Frias RC .20 .06
244 John Burkett .20 .06
245 Juan Gonzalez .50 .15
246 Rick Helling .20 .06
247 Darren Oliver .20 .06
248 Mickey Tettleton .20 .06
249 Ivan Rodriguez .50 .15
250 Joe Carter .20 .06
251 Pat Hentgen .20 .06
252 Marty Janzen .20 .06
253 Frank Thomas TOP .20 .06
Tony Gwynn
254 Mark McGwire TOP .50 .15
Ken Griffey Jr.
Larry Walker
255 Ken Griffey Jr. TOP .30 .09
Andres Galarraga
256 Brian L.Hunter TOP .20 .06
Tony Womack
257 Roger Clemens TOP .30 .09
Denny Neagle
258 Roger Clemens TOP .50 .15
Curt Schilling
259 Roger Clemens TOP .50 .15
Pedro Martinez
260 Randy Myers TOP .20 .06
Jeff Shaw
261 N. Garciaparra TOP .30 .09
Scott Rolen
262 Charlie O'Brien .20 .06
263 Shannon Stewart .20 .06
264 Robert Person .20 .06
265 Carlos Delgado .20 .06
266 Matt Williams CL .20 .06
Travis Lee
267 Nomar Garciaparra CL .30 .09
Cal Ripken
268 Mark McGwire CL .50 .15
Mike Piazza
269 Tony Gwynn CL .30 .09
Ken Griffey Jr.
270 Fred McGriff CL .20 .06
Jose Cruz Jr.
271 Andruw Jones GJ .20 .06
272 Alex Rodriguez GJ .50 .15
273 Juan Gonzalez GJ .30 .09
274 Nomar Garciaparra GJ .50 .15
275 Ken Griffey Jr. GJ .50 .15
276 Tino Martinez GJ .20 .06
277 Roger Clemens GJ .50 .15
278 Barry Bonds GJ .50 .15
279 Mike Piazza GJ .50 .15
280 Tim Salmon .30 .09
281 Gary DiSarcina .20 .06
282 Cecil Fielder .20 .06
283 Ken Hill .20 .06
284 Troy Percival .20 .06
285 Jim Edmonds .20 .06
286 Allen Watson .20 .06
287 Brian Anderson .20 .06
288 Jay Bell .20 .06
289 Jorge Fabregas .20 .06
290 Devon White .20 .06
291 Yamil Benitez .20 .06
292 Jeff Suppan .20 .06
293 Tony Batista .20 .06
294 Brent Brede .20 .06
295 Andy Benes .20 .06
296 Felix Rodriguez .20 .06
297 Karim Garcia .20 .06
298 Omar Daal .20 .06
299 Andy Stankiewicz .20 .06
300 Matt Williams .20 .06
301 Willie Blair .20 .06
302 Ryan Klesko .20 .06
303 Tom Glavine .30 .09
304 Walt Weiss .20 .06
305 Greg Maddux .75 .23
306 Chipper Jones .50 .15
307 Keith Lockhart .20 .06
308 Andres Galarraga .20 .06
309 Chris Hoiles .20 .06
310 Roberto Alomar .50 .15
311 Joe Carter .20 .06
312 Doug Drabek .20 .06
313 Jeffrey Hammonds .20 .06
314 Rafael Palmeiro .30 .09
315 Mike Mussina .50 .15
316 Brady Anderson .20 .06
317 B.J. Surhoff .20 .06
318 Dennis Eckersley .20 .06
319 Jim Leyritz .20 .06
320 Mo Vaughn .20 .06
321 Nomar Garciaparra .75 .23
322 Reggie Jefferson .20 .06
323 Tim Naehring .20 .06
324 Troy O'Leary .20 .06
325 Pedro Martinez .50 .15
326 John Valentin .20 .06
327 Mark Clark .20 .06
328 Rod Beck .20 .06
329 Mickey Morandini .20 .06
330 Sammy Sosa .75 .23
331 Jeff Blauser .20 .06
332 Lance Johnson .20 .06
333 Scott Servais .20 .06
334 Kevin Tapani .20 .06
335 Henry Rodriguez .20 .06
336 Jaime Navarro .20 .06
337 Benji Gil .20 .06
338 James Baldwin .20 .06
339 Mike Cameron .20 .06
340 Ray Durham .20 .06
341 Chris Snopek .20 .06
342 Eddie Taubensee .20 .06
343 Bret Boone .20 .06
344 Willie Greene .20 .06
345 Barry Larkin .50 .15
346 Chris Stynes .20 .06
347 Pete Harnisch .20 .06
348 Dave Burba .20 .06
349 Sandy Alomar Jr. .20 .06
350 Kenny Lofton .20 .06
351 Geronimo Berroa .20 .06
352 Omar Vizquel .20 .06
353 Travis Fryman .20 .06
354 Dwight Gooden .20 .06
355 Jim Thome .50 .15
356 David Justice .20 .06
357 Charles Nagy .20 .06
358 Chad Ogea .20 .06
359 Pedro Astacio .20 .06
360 Larry Walker .30 .09
361 Mike Lansing .20 .06
362 Kirt Manwaring .20 .06
363 Dante Bichette .20 .06
364 Jamey Wright .20 .06
365 Darryl Kile .20 .06
366 Luis Gonzalez .20 .06
367 Joe Randa .20 .06
368 Raul Casanova .20 .06
369 Damion Easley .20 .06
370 Brian Hunter .20 .06
371 Bobby Higginson .20 .06
372 Brian Moehler .20 .06
373 Scott Sanders .20 .06
374 Jim Eisenreich .20 .06
375 Derrek Lee .20 .06
376 Jay Powell .20 .06
377 Cliff Floyd .20 .06
378 Alex Fernandez .20 .06
379 Felix Heredia .20 .06
380 Jeff Bagwell .30 .09
381 Bill Spiers .20 .06
382 Chris Holt .20 .06
383 Carl Everett .20 .06
384 Derek Bell .20 .06
385 Moises Alou .20 .06
386 Ramon Garcia .20 .06
387 Mike Sweeney .20 .06
388 Glendon Rusch .20 .06
389 Kevin Appier .20 .06
390 Dean Palmer .20 .06
391 Jeff Conine .20 .06
392 Johnny Damon .20 .06
393 Jose Vizcaino .20 .06
394 Todd Hollandsworth .20 .06
395 Eric Karros .20 .06
396 Todd Zeile .20 .06
397 Chan Ho Park .20 .06
398 Ismael Valdes .20 .06
399 Eric Young .20 .06
400 Hideo Nomo .50 .15
401 Mark Loretta .20 .06
402 Doug Jones .20 .06
403 Jeromy Burnitz .20 .06
404 John Jaha .20 .06
405 Marquis Grissom .20 .06
406 Mike Matheny .20 .06
407 Todd Walker .20 .06
408 Marty Cordova .20 .06
409 Matt Lawton .20 .06
410 Terry Steinbach .20 .06
411 Pat Meares .20 .06
412 Rick Aguilera .20 .06
413 Otis Nixon .20 .06
414 Derrick May .20 .06
415 Carl Pavano .20 .06
416 A.J. Hinch .20 .06
417 Dave Dellucci RC .25 .07
418 Bruce Chen .20 .06
419 Darron Ingram RC .20 .06
420 Sean Casey .20 .06
421 Mark L. Johnson .20 .06
422 Gabe Alvarez .20 .06
423 Alex Gonzalez .20 .06
424 Daryle Ward .20 .06
425 Russell Branyan .20 .06
426 Mike Caruso .20 .06
427 Mike Kinkade RC .20 .06
428 Ramon Hernandez .20 .06
429 Matt Clement .20 .06
430 Travis Lee .20 .06
431 Shane Monahan .20 .06
432 Rich Butler RC .20 .06
433 Chris Widger .20 .06
434 Jose Vidro .20 .06
435 Carlos Perez .20 .06
436 Ryan McGuire .20 .06
437 Brian McRae .20 .06
438 Al Leiter .20 .06
439 Rich Becker .20 .06
440 Todd Hundley .20 .06
441 Dave Mlicki .20 .06
442 Bernard Gilkey .20 .06
443 John Olerud .20 .06
444 Paul O'Neill .30 .09
445 Andy Pettitte .30 .09
446 David Cone .20 .06
447 Chili Davis .20 .06
448 Bernie Williams .30 .09
449 Joe Girardi .20 .06
450 Derek Jeter 1.25 .35
451 Mariano Rivera .30 .09
452 George Williams .20 .06
453 Kenny Rogers .20 .06
454 Tom Candiotti .20 .06
455 Rickey Henderson .50 .15
456 Jason Giambi .50 .15
457 Scott Spiezio .20 .06
458 Doug Glanville .20 .06
459 Desi Relaford .20 .06
460 Curt Schilling .30 .09
461 Bob Abreu .20 .06
462 Gregg Jefferies .20 .06
463 Scott Rolen .30 .09
464 Mike Lieberthal .20 .06
465 Tony Womack .20 .06
466 Jermaine Allensworth .20 .06
467 Francisco Cordova .20 .06
468 Jon Lieber .20 .06
469 Al Martin .20 .06
470 Jason Kendall .20 .06
471 Todd Stottlemyre .20 .06
472 Royce Clayton .20 .06
473 Brian Jordan .20 .06
474 John Mabry .20 .06
475 Ray Lankford .20 .06
476 Delino DeShields .20 .06
477 Ron Gant .20 .06
478 Mark Langston .20 .06
479 Steve Finley .20 .06
480 Tony Gwynn .60 .18
481 Andy Ashby .20 .06
482 Wally Joyner .20 .06
483 Greg Vaughn .20 .06
484 Sterling Hitchcock .20 .06
485 Kevin Brown .30 .09
486 Orel Hershiser .20 .06
487 Charlie Hayes .20 .06
488 Darryl Hamilton .20 .06
489 Mark Gardner .20 .06
490 Barry Bonds 1.25 .35
491 Robb Nen .20 .06
492 Kirk Rueter .20 .06
493 Randy Johnson .50 .15
494 Jeff Fassero .20 .06
495 Alex Rodriguez .75 .23
496 David Segui .20 .06
497 Rich Amaral .20 .06
498 Russ Davis .20 .06
499 Bubba Trammell .20 .06
500 Wade Boggs .30 .09
501 Roberto Hernandez .20 .06
502 Dave Martinez .20 .06
503 Dennis Springer .20 .06
504 Paul Sorrento .20 .06
505 Wilson Alvarez .20 .06
506 Mike Kelly .20 .06
507 Albie Lopez .20 .06
508 Tony Saunders .20 .06
509 John Flaherty .20 .06
510 Fred McGriff .30 .09
511 Quinton McCracken .20 .06
512 Terrell Wade .20 .06
513 Kevin Stocker .20 .06
514 Kevin Elster .20 .06
515 Will Clark .50 .15
516 Bobby Witt .20 .06
517 Tom Goodwin .20 .06
518 Aaron Sele .20 .06
519 Lee Stevens .20 .06
520 Rusty Greer .20 .06
521 John Wetteland .20 .06
522 Darrin Fletcher .20 .06
523 Jose Canseco .50 .15
524 Randy Myers .20 .06
525 Jose Cruz Jr. .20 .06
526 Shawn Green .20 .06
527 Tony Fernandez .20 .06
528 Alex Gonzalez .20 .06
529 Ed Sprague .20 .06
530 Roger Clemens 1.00 .30

1998 Collector's Choice Prime Choice Reserve

This special parallel version of the 18-card Rookie Class subset (numbers 415-432) was added to the product at the last minute. Each card is serial numbered to 500 on back.

Nm-Mt Ex-Mt
COMPLETE SET (18) 80.00 24.00
*STARS: 15X TO 40X BASIC CARDS ..
*ROOKIES: 8X TO 20X BASIC CARDS

1998 Collector's Choice Crash the Game

These 90 different game cards were randomly seed at a rate of 1:5 exclusively into second series packs. Thirty different sluggers were each featured on three different parallel cards. The only difference in each card was one of three different game dates printed on front. If the featured player hit a home run during the series specified on the card front, the collector could mail the card in prior to the December 1st, 1998 deadline for a special upgraded Crash the Game Exchange card. Winners and losers are specified below with a "W" or "L" after each card description.

Nm-Mt Ex-Mt
COMPLETE SET (90) 80.00 24.00
*INSTANT WIN: .75X TO 2X BASIC CRASH
INSTANT WIN SER.2 STATED ODDS 1:721
CG1A Ken Griffey Jr. 1.50 .45
June 26-28 W
CG1B Ken Griffey Jr. 1.50 .45
July 7 L
CG1C Ken Griffey Jr. 1.50 .45
Sept 21-24 W
CG2A Travis Lee .40 .12
July 27-30 L
CG2B Travis Lee .40 .12
Aug 27-30 L
CG2C Travis Lee .40 .12
Sept 17-20 L
CG3A Larry Walker .60 .18
July 17-19 L
CG3B Larry Walker .60 .18
Aug 27-30 W
CG3C Larry Walker .60 .18
Sept 25-27 W
CG4A Tony Clark .40 .12
July 9-12 W
CG4B Tony Clark .40 .12
June 30-July 2 L
CG4C Tony Clark .40 .12
Sept 4-6 L
CG5A Cal Ripken 3.00 .90
June 22-25 W
CG5B Cal Ripken 3.00 .90
July 7 L
CG5C Cal Ripken 3.00 .90
Sept 4-6 W
CG6A Tim Salmon .60 .18
June 22-25 L
CG6B Tim Salmon .60 .18
Aug 28-30 L
CG6C Tim Salmon .60 .18
Sept 14-15 L
CG7A Vinny Castilla .40 .12
June30-July2 W
CG7B Vinny Castilla .40 .12
Aug 27-30 W
CG7C Vinny Castilla .40 .12
Sept 7-10 W
CG8A Fred McGriff .60 .18
June 22-25 L
CG8B Fred McGriff .60 .18
July 3-5 L
CG8C Fred McGriff .60 .18
Sept 18-20 W
CG9A Matt Williams .40 .12
July 17-19 L
CG9B Matt Williams .40 .12
Sept 14-16 W
CG9C Matt Williams .40 .12
Sept 18-20 L
CG10A Mark McGwire 2.50 .75
July 7 L
CG10B Mark McGwire 2.50 .75
July 24-26 W
CG10C Mark McGwire 2.50 .75
Aug 18-19 W
CG11A Albert Belle .60 .18
July 3-5 L
CG11B Albert Belle .60 .18
Aug 21-23 W
CG11C Albert Belle .60 .18
Sept 11-13 L
CG12A Jay Buhner .40 .12
July 9-12 W
CG12B Jay Buhner .40 .12
Aug 6-9 L
CG12C Jay Buhner .40 .12
Sept 24-27 L
CG13A Vladimir Guerrero 1.00 .30
June 22-25 L
CG13B Vladimir Guerrero 1.00 .30
Aug 10-12 W
CG13C Vladimir Guerrero 1.00 .30
Sept 14-16 W
CG14A Andruw Jones .40 .12
July 16-19 W
CG14B Andruw Jones .40 .12
Aug 27-30 W
CG14C Andruw Jones .40 .12
Sept 17-20 L
CG15A Nomar Garciaparra 1.50 .45
July 9-12 L
CG15B Nomar Garciaparra 1.50 .45
Aug 13-16 W
CG15C Nomar Garciaparra 1.50 .45
Sept 24-27 W
CG16A Ken Caminiti .40 .12
June 26-28 W
CG16B Ken Caminiti .40 .12
July 13-15 W
CG16C Ken Caminiti .40 .12
Sept 10-13 L
CG17A Sammy Sosa 1.50 .45
July 9-12 W
CG17B Sammy Sosa 1.50 .45
Aug 27-30 W
CG17C Sammy Sosa 1.50 .45
Sept 18-20 L
CG18A Ben Grieve .40 .12
June 30-July 2 W
CG18B Ben Grieve .40 .12
Aug 14-16 L
CG18C Ben Grieve .40 .12
Sept 24-27 L
CG19A Mo Vaughn .40 .12
July 7 L
CG19B Mo Vaughn .40 .12
Sept 7-9 L
CG19C Mo Vaughn .40 .12
Sept 24-27 W
CG20A Frank Thomas 1.00 .30
July 7 L
CG20B Frank Thomas 1.00 .30
July 17-19 W
CG20C Frank Thomas 1.00 .30
Sept 4-6 L
CG21A Manny Ramirez .40 .12
July 9-12 L
CG21B Manny Ramirez .40 .12
Aug 13-16 W
CG21C Manny Ramirez .40 .12
Sept 18-20 W
CG22A Jeff Bagwell .60 .18
July 7 L
CG22B Jeff Bagwell .60 .18
Aug 28-30 W
CG22C Jeff Bagwell .60 .18
Sept 4-6 W
CG23A Jose Cruz Jr. .40 .12
July 9-12 L
CG23B Jose Cruz Jr. .40 .12
Aug 13-16 L
CG23C Jose Cruz Jr. .40 .12
Sept 18-20 L
CG24A Alex Rodriguez 1.50 .45
July 7 W
CG24B Alex Rodriguez 1.50 .45
Aug 6-9 W
CG24C Alex Rodriguez 1.50 .45
Sept 21-23 W
CG25A Mike Piazza 1.50 .45
June 22-25 W
CG25B Mike Piazza 1.50 .45
July 7 L
CG25C Mike Piazza 1.50 .45
Sept 10-13 W
CG26A Tino Martinez .60 .18
June 26-28 W
CG26B Tino Martinez .60 .18
July 9-12 L
CG26C Tino Martinez .60 .18
Aug 13-16 L
CG27A Chipper Jones 1.00 .30
July 3-5 L
CG27B Chipper Jones 1.00 .30
Aug 23-30 L
CG27C Chipper Jones 1.00 .30
Sept 17-20 L
CG28A Juan Gonzalez 1.00 .30
July 7 L
CG28B Juan Gonzalez 1.00 .30
Aug 6-9 W
CG28C Juan Gonzalez 1.00 .30
Sept 11-13 W
CG29A Jim Thome 1.00 .30
June 22-23 L
CG29B Jim Thome 1.00 .30
July 23-26 W
CG29C Jim Thome 1.00 .30
Sept 24-27 L
CG30A Barry Bonds 2.50 .75
July 7 W
CG30B Barry Bonds 2.50 .75
Sept 4-6 L
CG30C Barry Bonds 2.50 .75
Sept 18-20 W

1998 Collector's Choice Evolution Revolution

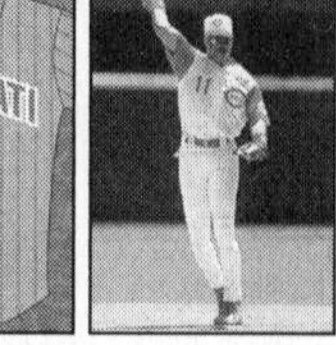

Randomly inserted in series one packs at the rate of one in 13, this 28-card set features a color photo of one player from each of the Major League's 28 teams of 1997 printed on a baseball jersey shaped card which folded out to display the players accomplishments.

Nm-Mt Ex-Mt
COMPLETE SET (28) 60.00 18.00
ER1 Tim Salmon 1.50 .45
ER2 Greg Maddux 4.00 1.20
ER3 Cal Ripken 8.00 2.40
ER4 Mo Vaughn 1.00 .30
ER5 Sammy Sosa 4.00 1.20
ER6 Frank Thomas 2.50 .75
ER7 Barry Larkin 2.50 .75
ER8 Jim Thome 2.50 .75
ER9 Larry Walker 1.50 .45
ER10 Travis Fryman 1.00 .30
ER11 Gary Sheffield 1.50 .45
ER12 Jeff Bagwell 1.50 .45
ER13 Johnny Damon 1.00 .30
ER14 Mike Piazza 4.00 1.20
ER15 Jeff Cirillo 1.00 .30
ER16 Paul Molitor 1.50 .45
ER17 Vladimir Guerrero 2.50 .75
ER18 Todd Hundley 1.00 .30
ER19 Tino Martinez 1.50 .45

ER20 Jose Canseco 2.50 .75
ER21 Scott Rolen 1.50 .45
ER22 Al Martin 1.00 .30
ER23 Mark McGwire 6.00 1.80
ER24 Tony Gwynn 3.00 .90
ER25 Barry Bonds 6.00 1.80
ER26 Ken Griffey Jr. 4.00 1.20
ER27 Juan Gonzalez 2.50 .75
ER28 Roger Clemens 5.00 1.50

1998 Collector's Choice Mini Bobbing Heads

 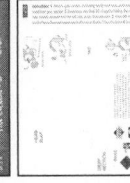

Randomly inserted in packs at a rate of one in three, this 30-card insert set features specially enhanced miniatures that fold into a stand-up figure with a removable bobbing head.

Nm-Mt Ex-Mt
COMPLETE SET (30) 20.00 6.00
1 Tim Salmon .50 .15
2 Travis Lee .30 .09
3 Matt Williams .30 .09
4 Chipper Jones .75 .23
5 Greg Maddux UER 1.25 .35
Card is numbered as 6
6 Cal Ripken 2.50 .75
7 Nomar Garciaparra 1.25 .35
8 Mo Vaughn .30 .09
9 Sammy Sosa 1.25 .35
10 Frank Thomas .75 .23
11 Kenny Lofton .30 .09
12 Jaret Wright .30 .09
13 Larry Walker .50 .15
14 Tony Clark .30 .09
15 Edgar Renteria .30 .09
16 Jeff Bagwell .50 .15
17 Mike Piazza 1.25 .35
18 Vladimir Guerrero .75 .23
19 Derek Jeter 2.00 .60
20 Ben Grieve .30 .09
21 Scott Rolen .50 .15
22 Mark McGwire 2.00 .60
23 Tony Gwynn 1.00 .30
24 Barry Bonds 2.00 .60
25 Ken Griffey Jr. 1.25 .35
26 Alex Rodriguez 1.25 .35
27 Fred McGriff .50 .15
28 Juan Gonzalez .75 .23
29 Roger Clemens 1.50 .45
30 Jose Cruz Jr. .30 .09

1998 Collector's Choice StarQuest

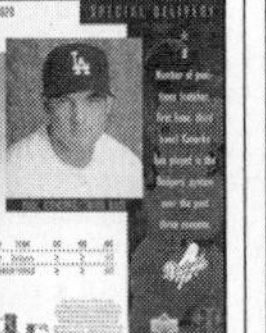

The 1998 Series one Collector's Choice 90-card tiered insert set, StarQuest, features color action player photos with a different number of stars printed below the player's name. The more stars on the card, the more collectible the card. The set contains the following subsets: Special Delivery (SQ1-SQ45), inserted one per pack; Students of the Game (SQ46-SQ65), randomly seeded at a rate of 1:21 packs; Super Powers (SQ66-SQ80), randomly seeded at a rate of 1:71 packs; and Superstar Domain (SQ81-SQ90), randomly seeded at a rate of 1:145 packs.

Nm-Mt Ex-Mt
COMP.DELIV.SET (45) 20.00 6.00
COMMON DELIV (1-45) .15 .04
COMP.STUDENT SET (20) 60.00 18.00
COMMON (46-65) 1.50 .45
COMP.POWERS SET (15) 100.00 30.00
COMM.POWERS (66-80) 3.00 .90
COMP.SUPERSTAR (10) 300.00 90.00
COM.SUPERSTAR (81-90) 5.00 1.50
SQ1 N.Garciaparra SD 1.00 .30
SQ2 Scott Rolen SD .40 .12
SQ3 Jason Dickson SD .25 .07
SQ4 Jaret Wright SD .25 .07
SQ5 Kevin Orie SD .25 .07
SQ6 Jose Guillen SD .25 .07
SQ7 Matt Morris SD .25 .07
SQ8 Mike Cameron SD .25 .07
SQ9 Kevin Polcovich SD .25 .07
SQ10 Jose Cruz Jr. SD .25 .07
SQ11 Miguel Tejada SD .40 .12
SQ12 Fernando Tatis SD .25 .07
SQ13 Todd Helton SD .40 .12
SQ14 Ken Cloude SD .25 .07
SQ15 Ben Grieve SD .25 .07
SQ16 Dante Powell SD .25 .07
SQ17 Bubba Trammell SD .25 .07
SQ18 J.Encarnacion SD .25 .07
SQ19 Derrek Lee SD .25 .07
SQ20 Paul Konerko SD .25 .07
SQ21 Richard Hidalgo SD .25 .07
SQ22 Denny Neagle SD .25 .07
SQ23 David Justice SD .25 .07
SQ24 Pedro Martinez SD .60 .18
SQ25 Greg Maddux SD 1.00 .30
SQ26 Edgar Martinez SD .25 .07
SQ27 Cal Ripken SD 2.00 .60
SQ28 Tim Salmon SD .40 .12
SQ29 Shawn Estes SD .25 .07
SQ30 Ken Griffey Jr. SD 1.00 .30
SQ31 Brad Radke SD .25 .07
SQ32 Andy Pettitte SD .40 .12
SQ33 Curt Schilling SD .40 .12
SQ34 Raul Mondesi SD .25 .07
SQ35 Alex Rodriguez SD 1.00 .30
SQ36 Jeff Kent SD .25 .07
SQ37 Jeff Bagwell SD .40 .12
SQ38 Juan Gonzalez SD .60 .18
SQ39 Barry Bonds SD 1.50 .45
SQ40 Mark McGwire SD 1.50 .45
SQ41 Frank Thomas SD .60 .18
SQ42 Ray Lankford SD .25 .07
SQ43 Tony Gwynn SD .75 .23
SQ44 Mike Piazza SD 1.00 .30
SQ45 Tino Martinez SD .40 .12
SQ46 N.Garciaparra SG 6.00 1.80
SQ47 Paul Molitor SG 2.50 .75
SQ48 C.Knoblauch SG 1.50 .45
SQ49 Rusty Greer SG 1.50 .45
SQ50 Cal Ripken SG 12.00 3.60
SQ51 Roberto Alomar SG 4.00 1.20
SQ52 Scott Rolen SG 2.50 .75
SQ53 Derek Jeter SG 10.00 3.00
SQ54 Mark Grace SG 2.50 .75
SQ55 Randy Johnson SG 4.00 1.20
SQ56 Craig Biggio SG 2.50 .75
SQ57 Kenny Lofton SG 1.50 .45
SQ58 Eddie Murray SG 4.00 1.20
SQ59 Ryne Sandberg SG 6.00 1.80
SQ60 R.Henderson SG 4.00 1.20
SQ61 Darin Erstad SG 1.50 .45
SQ62 Jim Edmonds SG 1.50 .45
SQ63 Ken Caminiti SG 1.50 .45
SQ64 Ivan Rodriguez SG 4.00 1.20
SQ65 Tony Gwynn SG 5.00 1.50
SQ66 Tony Clark SP 4.00 1.20
SQ67 A.Galarraga SP 4.00 1.20
SQ68 Rafael Palmeiro SP 6.00 1.80
SQ69 Manny Ramirez SP 4.00 1.20
SQ70 Albert Belle SP 6.00 1.80
SQ71 Jay Buhner SP 4.00 1.20
SQ72 Mo Vaughn SP 4.00 1.20
SQ73 Barry Bonds SP 25.00 7.50
SQ74 Chipper Jones SP 10.00 3.00
SQ75 Jeff Bagwell SP 6.00 1.80
SQ76 Jim Thome SP 10.00 3.00
SQ77 Sammy Sosa SP 15.00 4.50
SQ78 Todd Hundley SP 4.00 1.20
SQ79 Matt Williams SP 4.00 1.20
SQ80 Vinny Castilla SP 4.00 1.20
SQ81 Jose Cruz Jr. SS 6.00 1.80
SQ82 Frank Thomas SS 15.00 4.50
SQ83 Juan Gonzalez SS 15.00 4.50
SQ84 Mike Piazza SS 25.00 7.50
SQ85 Alex Rodriguez SS 25.00 7.50
SQ86 Larry Walker SS 10.00 3.00
SQ87 Tino Martinez SS 10.00 3.00
SQ88 Greg Maddux SS 25.00 7.50
SQ89 Mark McGwire SS 40.00 12.00
SQ90 Ken Griffey Jr. SS 25.00 7.50

1998 Collector's Choice StarQuest Single

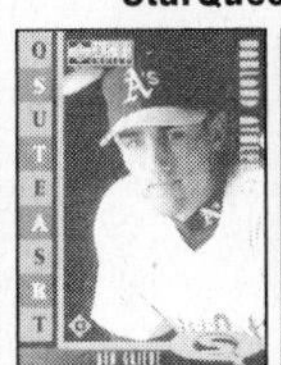

These cards, issued one per second series pack, feature 30 of the leading players in baseball. The fronts of the card have a player photo with the words "Star Quest" spelled down the left side. The player's name and position in on the bottom of the card. In addition, the bottom right corner mentions whether this is a singles, double, triple or home run.

Nm-Mt Ex-Mt
COMPLETE SET (30) 10.00 3.00
*DOUBLE: 4X TO 10X STARQUEST SINGLE
DOUBLES SER.2 STATED ODDS 1:21.
*TRIPLES: 12.5X TO 30X SQ SINGLE.
TRIPLES SER.2 STATED ODDS 1:71...
*HR'S: 30X TO 80X SQ SINGLE.
HOME RUN: RANDOM INS.IN SER.2 PACKS
HOME RUN PRINT RUN 100 SERIAL #'d SETS
1 Ken Griffey Jr. .75 .23
2 Jose Cruz Jr. .20 .06
3 Cal Ripken 1.50 .45
4 Roger Clemens 1.00 .30
5 Frank Thomas .50 .15
6 Derek Jeter 1.25 .35
7 Alex Rodriguez .75 .23
8 Andruw Jones .20 .06
9 Vladimir Guerrero .50 .15
10 Mark McGwire 1.25 .35
11 Kenny Lofton .20 .06
12 Pedro Martinez .50 .15
13 Greg Maddux .75 .23
14 Larry Walker .30 .09
15 Barry Bonds 1.25 .35
16 Chipper Jones .50 .15
17 Jeff Bagwell .30 .09
18 Juan Gonzalez .50 .15
19 Tony Gwynn .60 .18
20 Mike Piazza .75 .23
21 Tino Martinez .30 .09
22 Mo Vaughn .20 .06
23 Ben Grieve .20 .06
24 Scott Rolen .30 .09
25 Nomar Garciaparra .75 .23
26 Paul Konerko .20 .06
27 Jaret Wright .20 .06
28 Gary Sheffield .20 .06
29 Todd Helton .30 .09
30 Travis Lee .20 .06

1998 Collector's Choice Stick 'Ums

Randomly inserted at the rate of one in three first series packs, this 30-card set features color player photos printed on stickers that can be peeled off and restuck anywhere.

Nm-Mt Ex-Mt
COMPLETE SET (30) 20.00 6.00
1 Andruw Jones .30 .09
2 Chipper Jones .75 .23
3 Cal Ripken 2.50 .75
4 Nomar Garciaparra 1.25 .35
5 Mo Vaughn .30 .09
6 Ryne Sandberg 1.25 .35
7 Sammy Sosa 1.25 .35
8 Frank Thomas .75 .23
9 Albert Belle .50 .15
10 Jim Thome .75 .23
11 Manny Ramirez .30 .09
12 Larry Walker .50 .15
13 Gary Sheffield .30 .09
14 Jeff Bagwell .50 .15
15 Mike Piazza 1.25 .35
16 Paul Molitor .50 .15
17 Pedro Martinez .75 .23
18 Todd Hundley .30 .09
19 Derek Jeter 2.00 .60
20 Tino Martinez .50 .15
21 Curt Schilling .50 .15
22 Mark McGwire 2.00 .60
23 Tony Gwynn 1.00 .30
24 Barry Bonds 2.00 .60
25 Ken Griffey Jr. 1.25 .35
26 Alex Rodriguez 1.25 .35
27 Juan Gonzalez .75 .23
28 Ivan Rodriguez .75 .23
29 Roger Clemens 1.50 .45
30 Jose Cruz Jr. .30 .09

1998 Collector's Choice Blowups 5x7

These 10 cards measure approximately 5" by 7". These cards were inserted one per second series retail box and feature oversize parallels of a selection of stars from the basic 1998 Collectors Choice set.

Nm-Mt Ex-Mt
COMPLETE SET (10) 12.00 3.60
306 Chipper Jones 1.50 .45
321 Nomar Garciaparra 1.50 .45
360 Larry Walker .50 .15
450 Derek Jeter 3.00 .90
463 Scott Rolen .75 .23
480 Tony Gwynn 1.50 .45
490 Barry Bonds 1.50 .45
495 Alex Rodriguez 2.00 .60
525 Jose Cruz Jr. .50 .15
530 Roger Clemens 1.50 .45

1998 Collector's Choice Cover Glory 5x7

This 10-card set measures approximately 5" by 7" and features action color player images on a red-and-black background. The backs carry player information with a "headline" and paragraph about the player.

Nm-Mt Ex-Mt
COMPLETE SET (10) 15.00 4.50
1 Nomar Garciaparra 1.50 .45
2 Roger Clemens 1.50 .45
3 Larry Walker .50 .15
4 Mike Piazza 2.00 .60
5 Mark McGwire 3.00 .90
6 Tony Gwynn 1.50 .45
7 Jose Cruz Jr. .50 .15
8 Frank Thomas 1.25 .35
9 Tino Martinez .50 .15
10 Ken Griffey Jr. 3.00 .90

1998 Collector's Choice Golden Jubilee 5x7

These nine oversize cards measure approximately 5" by 7" and feature parallel cards of the golden jubilee subset in second series Collector's Choice.

Nm-Mt Ex-Mt
COMPLETE SET (9) 12.00 3.60
271 Andruw Jones .75 .23
272 Alex Rodriguez 1.50 .45
273 Juan Gonzalez .75 .23
274 Nomar Garciaparra 1.50 .45
275 Ken Griffey Jr. 2.50 .75
276 Tino Martinez .50 .15
277 Roger Clemens 1.50 .45
278 Barry Bonds 1.50 .45
279 Mike Piazza 2.00 .60

1998 Collector's Choice Retail Jumbos

These cards were available as a mail-away from Upper Deck. If a collector mailed in 10 wrappers and an amount for postage and handling they received this skip-numbered set from Upper Deck's redemption center.

Nm-Mt Ex-Mt
COMPLETE SET (33) 30.00 9.00
1 Nomar Garciaparra 1.50 .45
2 Roger Clemens 1.50 .45
3 Larry Walker .25 .07
4 Mike Piazza 2.00 .60
5 Mark McGwire 2.50 .75
6 Tony Gwynn 1.50 .45
7 Jose Cruz Jr. .25 .07
8 Frank Thomas 1.00 .30
35 Andruw Jones .60 .18
40 Cal Ripken 3.00 .90
55 Ryne Sandberg .60 .18
60 Frank Thomas 1.00 .30
95 Gary Sheffield .60 .18
97 Charles Johnson .25 .07
145 Mike Piazza 2.00 .60
160 Paul Molitor .60 .18
180 Tino Martinez .25 .07
220 Mark McGwire 2.50 .75
225 Ken Caminiti .25 .07
240 Ken Griffey Jr. 2.50 .75
242 Jay Buhner .25 .07
245 Juan Gonzalez 1.00 .30
249 Ivan Rodriguez .75 .23
SQ67 Andres Galarraga .40 .12
SQ68 Rafael Palmeiro .60 .18
SQ69 Manny Ramirez .75 .23
SQ70 Albert Belle .25 .07
SQ71 Jay Buhner .25 .07
SQ72 Mo Vaughn .25 .07
SQ73 Barry Bonds 1.50 .45
SQ74 Chipper Jones 1.50 .45
SQ75 Jeff Bagwell .75 .23
SQ76 Jim Thome .60 .18

1995 Collector's Choice SE

The 1995 Collector's Choice SE set (produced by Upper Deck) consists of 265 standard-size cards issued in foil packs. The fronts feature color action player photos with blue borders. The player's name, position and the team name are printed on the bottom of the card. The SE logo in blue-foil appears in a top corner. On a white background, the backs carry another color player photo with a short player biography, career stats and 1994 highlights. Subsets featured include Rookie Class (1-25), Record Pace (26-30), Stat Leaders (137-144), Fantasy Team (249-260). There are no Rookie Cards in this set.

Nm-Mt Ex-Mt
COMPLETE SET (265) 20.00 6.00
1 Alex Rodriguez 2.00 .60
2 Derek Jeter 2.00 .60
3 Dustin Hermanson .15 .04
4 Bill Pulsipher .15 .04
5 Terrell Wade .15 .04
6 Darren Dreifort .15 .04
7 LaTroy Hawkins .15 .04
8 Alex Ochoa .15 .04
9 Paul Wilson .15 .04
10 Ernie Young .15 .04
11 Alan Benes .15 .04
12 Garret Anderson .30 .09
13 Armando Benitez .30 .09
14 Mark Thompson .15 .04
15 Herbert Perry .15 .04
16 Jose Silva .15 .04
17 Orlando Miller .15 .04
18 Russ Davis .15 .04
19 Jason Isringhausen .30 .09
20 Ray McDavid .15 .04
21 Duane Singleton .15 .04
22 Paul Shuey .15 .04
23 Steve Dunn .15 .04
24 Mike Lieberthal .30 .09
25 Chan Ho Park .30 .09
26 Ken Griffey Jr. RP .75 .23
27 Tony Gwynn RP .50 .15
28 Chuck Knoblauch RP .15 .04
29 Frank Thomas RP .50 .15
30 Matt Williams RP .15 .04
31 Chili Davis .30 .09
32 Chad Curtis .15 .04
33 Brian Anderson .15 .04
34 Chuck Finley .30 .09
35 Tim Salmon .50 .15
36 Bo Jackson .75 .23
37 Doug Drabek .15 .04
38 Craig Biggio .50 .15
39 Ken Caminiti .30 .09
40 Jeff Bagwell .50 .15
41 Darryl Kile .30 .09
42 John Hudek .15 .04
43 Brian L. Hunter .15 .04
44 Dennis Eckersley .30 .09
45 Mark McGwire 2.00 .60
46 Brent Gates .15 .04
47 Steve Karsay .15 .04
48 Rickey Henderson .75 .23
49 Terry Steinbach .15 .04
50 Ruben Sierra .15 .04
51 Roberto Alomar .75 .23
52 Carlos Delgado .30 .09
53 Alex Gonzalez .15 .04
54 Joe Carter .30 .09
55 Paul Molitor .50 .15
56 Juan Guzman .15 .04
57 John Olerud .30 .09
58 Shawn Green .30 .09
59 Tom Glavine .50 .15
60 Greg Maddux 1.25 .35
61 Roberto Kelly .15 .04
62 Ryan Klesko .30 .09
63 Javier Lopez .30 .09
64 Jose Oliva .15 .04
65 Fred McGriff .50 .15
66 Steve Avery .15 .04
67 David Justice .30 .09
68 Ricky Bones .15 .04
69 Cal Eldred .15 .04
70 Greg Vaughn .30 .09
71 Dave Nilsson .15 .04
72 Jose Valentin .15 .04
73 Matt Mieske .15 .04
74 Todd Zeile .15 .04
75 Ozzie Smith 1.25 .35
76 Bernard Gilkey .15 .04
77 Ray Lankford .15 .04
78 Bob Tewksbury .15 .04
79 Mark Whiten .15 .04
80 Gregg Jefferies .15 .04
81 Randy Myers .15 .04
82 Shawon Dunston .15 .04
83 Mark Grace .50 .15
84 Derrick May .15 .04
85 Sammy Sosa 1.25 .35
86 Steve Trachsel .15 .04
87 Brett Butler .30 .09
88 Delino DeShields .15 .04
89 Orel Hershiser .30 .09
90 Mike Piazza 1.25 .35
91 Todd Hollandsworth .15 .04
92 Eric Karros .30 .09
93 Ramon Martinez .15 .04
94 Tim Wallach .15 .04
95 Raul Mondesi .30 .09
96 Larry Walker .50 .15
97 Wil Cordero .15 .04
98 Marquis Grissom .15 .04
99 Ken Hill .15 .04
100 Cliff Floyd .30 .09
101 Pedro Martinez .75 .23
102 John Wetteland .30 .09
103 Rondell White .30 .09
104 Moises Alou .30 .09
105 Barry Bonds 2.00 .60
106 Darren Lewis .15 .04
107 Mark Portugal .15 .04
108 Matt Williams .30 .09
109 W.VanLandingham .15 .04
110 Bill Swift .15 .04
111 Robby Thompson .15 .04
112 Rod Beck .15 .04
113 Darryl Strawberry .50 .15
114 Jim Thome .75 .23
115 Dave Winfield .30 .09
116 Eddie Murray .75 .23
117 Manny Ramirez .30 .09
118 Carlos Baerga .15 .04
119 Kenny Lofton .30 .09
120 Albert Belle .30 .09
121 Mark Clark .15 .04
122 Dennis Martinez .30 .09
123 Randy Johnson .75 .23
124 Jay Buhner .30 .09
125 Ken Griffey Jr. 1.25 .35
126 Goose Gossage .30 .09
127 Tino Martinez .50 .15
128 Reggie Jefferson .15 .04
129 Edgar Martinez .50 .15
130 Gary Sheffield .30 .09
131 Pat Rapp .15 .04
132 Bret Barberie .15 .04
133 Chuck Carr .15 .04
134 Jeff Conine .30 .09
135 Charles Johnson .30 .09
136 Benito Santiago .30 .09
137 Matt Williams STL .15 .04
138 Jeff Bagwell STL .30 .09
139 Kenny Lofton STL .15 .04
140 Tony Gwynn STL .50 .15
141 Jimmy Key STL .15 .04
142 Greg Maddux STL .75 .23
143 Randy Johnson STL .50 .15
144 Lee Smith STL .15 .04
145 Bobby Bonilla .30 .09
146 Jason Jacome .15 .04
147 Jeff Kent .30 .09
148 Ryan Thompson .15 .04
149 Bobby Jones .15 .04
150 Bret Saberhagen .30 .09
151 John Franco .30 .09
152 Lee Smith .30 .09
153 Rafael Palmeiro .50 .15
154 Brady Anderson .30 .09
155 Cal Ripken Jr. 2.50 .75
156 Jeffrey Hammonds .15 .04
157 Mike Mussina .75 .23
158 Chris Hoiles .15 .04
159 Ben McDonald .15 .04
160 Tony Gwynn 1.00 .30
161 Joey Hamilton .15 .04
162 Andy Benes .15 .04
163 Trevor Hoffman .30 .09
164 Phil Plantier .15 .04
165 Derek Bell .15 .04
166 Bip Roberts .15 .04
167 Eddie Williams .15 .04
168 Fernando Valenzuela .30 .09
169 Mariano Duncan .15 .04
170 Lenny Dykstra .30 .09
171 Darren Daulton .30 .09
172 Danny Jackson .15 .04
173 Bobby Munoz .15 .04
174 Doug Jones .15 .04
175 Jay Bell .30 .09
176 Zane Smith .15 .04
177 Jon Lieber .15 .04
178 Carlos Garcia .15 .04
179 Orlando Merced .15 .04
180 Andy Van Slyke .30 .09
181 Rick Helling .15 .04
182 Rusty Greer .30 .09
183 Kenny Rogers UER .30 .09
(shows 110 wins in 1990)
184 Will Clark .75 .23
185 Jose Canseco .75 .23
186 Juan Gonzalez .75 .23
187 Dean Palmer .30 .09
188 Ivan Rodriguez .75 .23
189 John Valentin .15 .04
190 Roger Clemens 1.50 .45
191 Aaron Sele .15 .04
192 Scott Cooper .15 .04
193 Mike Greenwell .15 .04
194 Mo Vaughn .30 .09
195 Andre Dawson .30 .09
196 Ron Gant .30 .09
197 Jose Rijo .15 .04
198 Bret Boone .30 .09
199 Deion Sanders .50 .15
200 Barry Larkin .75 .23

201 Hal Morris	.15	.04
202 Reggie Sanders	.30	.09
203 Kevin Mitchell	.15	.04
204 Marvin Freeman	.15	.04
205 Andres Galarraga	.30	.09
206 Walt Weiss	.15	.04
207 Charlie Hayes	.15	.04
208 Dave Nied	.15	.04
209 Dante Bichette	.30	.09
210 David Cone	.30	.09
211 Jeff Montgomery	.15	.04
212 Felix Jose	.15	.04
213 Mike Macfarlane	.15	.04
214 Wally Joyner	.30	.09
215 Bob Hamelin	.15	.04
216 Brian McRae	.15	.04
217 Kirk Gibson	.30	.09
218 Lou Whitaker	.30	.09
219 Chris Gomez	.15	.04
220 Cecil Fielder	.30	.09
221 Mickey Tettleton	.15	.04
222 Travis Fryman	.30	.09
223 Tony Phillips	.15	.04
224 Rick Aguilera	.15	.04
225 Scott Erickson	.15	.04
226 Chuck Knoblauch	.30	.09
227 Kent Hrbek	.30	.09
228 Shane Mack	.15	.04
229 Kevin Tapani	.15	.04
230 Kirby Puckett	.75	.23
231 Julio Franco	.30	.09
232 Jack McDowell	.15	.04
233 Jason Bere	.15	.04
234 Alex Fernandez	.15	.04
235 Frank Thomas	.75	.23
236 Ozzie Guillen	.15	.04
237 Robin Ventura	.30	.09
238 Michael Jordan	2.50	.75
239 Wilson Alvarez	.15	.04
240 Don Mattingly	2.00	.60
241 Jim Abbott	.50	.15
242 Jim Leyritz	.15	.04
243 Paul O'Neill	.50	.15
244 Melido Perez	.15	.04
245 Wade Boggs	.50	.15
246 Mike Stanley	.15	.04
247 Danny Tartabull	.15	.04
248 Jimmy Key	.30	.09
249 Greg Maddux FT	.75	.23
250 Randy Johnson FT	.50	.15
251 Bret Saberhagen FT	.15	.04
252 John Wetteland FT	.15	.04
253 Mike Piazza FT	.75	.23
254 Jeff Bagwell FT	.30	.09
255 Craig Biggio FT	.30	.09
256 Matt Williams FT	.15	.04
257 Wil Cordero FT	.15	.04
258 Kenny Lofton FT	.15	.04
259 Barry Bonds FT	1.00	.30
260 Dante Bichette FT	.15	.04
261 Ken Griffey Jr. CL	.75	.23
262 Goose Gossage CL	.15	.04
263 Cal Ripken CL	1.25	.35
264 Kenny Rogers CL	.15	.04
265 John Valentin CL	.15	.04
P125 K.Griffey Jr. Promo	1.00	.30

1995 Collector's Choice SE Gold Signature

A parallel to the basic 265-card Collector's Choice SE set, each card features a gold-foil replica signature on it. Inserted one in 35 packs, the fronts feature color action player photos with blue borders. Super packs inserted 1:720 contained 12 gold signature cards.

	Nm-Mt	Ex-Mt
*STARS: 10X TO 25X BASIC CARDS		
*ROOKIES: 8X TO 20X BASIC		

1995 Collector's Choice SE Silver Signature

A parallel to the basic 265-card Collector's Choice issue, each card has a silver-foil replica signature on the front. These cards were inserted one in every pack, two per mini jumbo and 12 per super pack (inserted 1:216).

	Nm-Mt	Ex-Mt
COMPLETE SET (265)	60.00	18.00
*STARS: 1.25X TO 3X BASIC CARDS		
*ROOKIES: 1X TO 2.5X BASIC		

1994 Collector's Edge Dial Justice

This card measures the standard size. The fronts feature an action player photo on a clear, blue and green background. The Dial logo and team logo appear at the top. The player's name, position and card name are printed in a blue bar at the bottom. The backs are the reverse of the front with career highlights printed in white.

	Nm-Mt	Ex-Mt
1 David Justice	3.00	.90

1917 Collins-McCarthy E135

The cards in this 200-card set measure 2" by 3 1/4". Collins-McCarthy, the West Coast manufacturer of Zee Nuts (E137), issued the Baseball's Hall of Fame set of players in 1917. These black and white photos of current players were not only numbered but also listed alphabetically. The set is similar to D328, except that E135 is printed on thinner stock. The complete set price includes all variation cards listed in the checklist below. Recent

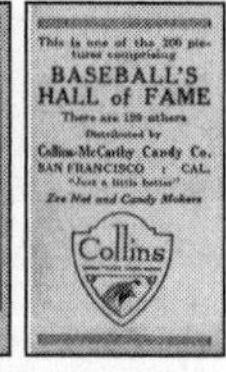

research indicates that this set was issued in 1917, a good example of that is the Ping Bodie card. Bodie played the full 1916 season for San Francisco and his card indicates he is a member of the White Sox. At least four different back varieties are known: A card with a blank back, Collins-McCarthy, Boston Store and Standard Biscuit.

	Ex-Mt	VG
COMPLETE SET (200)	20000.00	10000.00
1 Sam Agnew	80.00	40.00
2 Grover C. Alexander	150.00	75.00
3 W.E. Alexander	80.00	40.00
4 Leon Ames	80.00	40.00
5 Fred Anderson	80.00	40.00
6 Ed Appleton	80.00	40.00
7 Jimmy Archer	80.00	40.00
8 Jimmy Austin	80.00	40.00
9 Jim Bagby	80.00	40.00
10 H.D. Baird	80.00	40.00
11 Frank Baker	150.00	75.00
12 Dave Bancroft	120.00	60.00
13 Jack Barry	80.00	40.00
14 Joe Benz	80.00	40.00
15 Al Betzel	80.00	40.00
16 Ping Bodie	80.00	40.00
17 Joe Boehling	80.00	40.00
18 Eddie Burns	80.00	40.00
19 George Burns (Detroit)	80.00	40.00
20 Geo. J. Burns (NY)	80.00	40.00
21 Joe Bush	100.00	50.00
22 Owen Bush	80.00	40.00
23 Bobbie Byrne	80.00	40.00
24 Forrest Cady	80.00	40.00
25 Max Carey	120.00	60.00
26 Ray Chapman	120.00	60.00
27 Larry Cheney	80.00	40.00
28 Eddie Cicotte	150.00	75.00
29 Tom Clarke	80.00	40.00
30 Ty Cobb	1200.00	600.00
31 Eddie Collins	150.00	75.00
32 Shauno Collins	80.00	40.00
33 Fred Coumbe	80.00	40.00
34 Harry Coveleski	100.00	50.00
35 Gavvy Cravath	100.00	50.00
36 Sam Crawford	150.00	75.00
37 George Cutshaw	100.00	50.00
38 Jack Daubert	100.00	50.00
39 George Dauss	80.00	40.00
40 Charles Deal	80.00	40.00
41 Wheezer Dell	80.00	40.00
42 William Doak	80.00	40.00
43 Bill Donovan	80.00	40.00
44 Larry Doyle	100.00	50.00
45 Johnny Evers	150.00	75.00
46 Urban Faber	120.00	60.00
47 Happy Felsch	150.00	75.00
48 Bill Fischer	80.00	40.00
49 Ray Fisher	80.00	40.00
50 Art Fletcher	80.00	40.00
51 Eddie Foster	80.00	40.00
52 Jacques Fournier	80.00	40.00
53 Del Gainer	80.00	40.00
54 Bert Gallia	80.00	40.00
55 Chick Gandil	150.00	75.00
56 Larry Gardner	80.00	40.00
57 Joe Gedeon	80.00	40.00
58 Gus Getz	80.00	40.00
59 Frank Gilhooley	80.00	40.00
60 Kid Gleason MG	100.00	50.00
61 Mike Gonzales	80.00	40.00
62 Hank Gowdy	100.00	50.00
63 John Graney	80.00	40.00
64 Tom Griffith	80.00	40.00
65 Heinie Groh	100.00	50.00
66 Bob Groom	80.00	40.00
67 Louis Guisto	80.00	40.00
68 Earl Hamilton	80.00	40.00
69 Harry Harper	80.00	40.00
70 Grover Hartley	80.00	40.00
71 Harry Heilmann	120.00	60.00
72 Claude Hendrix	80.00	40.00
73 Olaf Henriksen	80.00	40.00
74 John Henry	80.00	40.00
75 Buck Herzog	80.00	40.00
76A Hugh High ERR (photo actually Claude Williams, white stockings)	150.00	75.00
76B Hugh High COR (black stockings)	100.00	50.00
77 Dick Hoblitzell	80.00	40.00
78 Walter Holke	80.00	40.00
79 Harry Hooper	120.00	60.00
80 Rogers Hornsby	300.00	150.00
81 Ivan Howard	80.00	40.00
82 Joe Jackson	1200.00	600.00
83 Harold Janvrin	80.00	40.00
84 William James	80.00	40.00
85 Charlie Jamieson	80.00	40.00
86 Hugh Jennings MG	120.00	60.00
87 Walter Johnson	400.00	200.00
88 James Johnston	80.00	40.00
89 Fielder Jones	80.00	40.00
90A Joe Judge ERR (photo actually Ray Morgan, bat right shoulder)	150.00	75.00
90B Joe Judge COR (bat left shoulder)	100.00	50.00
91 Hans Lobert	80.00	40.00
92 Benny Kauff	80.00	40.00
93 Wm. Killefer Jr.	80.00	40.00
94 Ed Konetchy	80.00	40.00
95 John Lavan	80.00	40.00
96 Jimmy Lavender	80.00	40.00
97 Nemo Leibold	80.00	40.00
98 Dutch Leonard	100.00	50.00
99 Duffy Lewis	80.00	40.00
100 Tom Long	80.00	40.00
101 Bill Louden	80.00	40.00
102 Fred Luderus	80.00	40.00
103 Lee Magee	80.00	40.00
104 Sherwood Magee	100.00	50.00
105 Al Mamaux	80.00	40.00
106 Leslie Mann	80.00	40.00
107 Rabbit Maranville	120.00	60.00
108 Rube Marquard	150.00	75.00
109 Armando Marsans	80.00	40.00
110 J. Erskine Mayer	80.00	40.00
111 George McBride	80.00	40.00
112 Lew McCarty	80.00	40.00
113 John J. McGraw MG	150.00	75.00
114 Jack McInnis	100.00	50.00
115 Lee Meadows	80.00	40.00
116 Fred Merkle	100.00	50.00
117 Chief Meyers	100.00	50.00
118 Clyde Milan	80.00	40.00
119 Otto Miller	80.00	40.00
120 Clarence Mitchell	80.00	40.00
121A Ray Morgan ERR (photo actually Joe Judge, bat left shoulder)	150.00	75.00
121B Ray Morgan COR (bat right shoulder)	100.00	50.00
122 Guy Morton	80.00	40.00
123 Mike Mowrey	80.00	40.00
124 Elmer Myers	80.00	40.00
125 Hy Myers	80.00	40.00
126 Greasy Neale	100.00	50.00
127 Art Nehf	80.00	40.00
128 J.A. Niehoff	80.00	40.00
129 Steve O'Neill	100.00	50.00
130 Dode Paskert	80.00	40.00
131 Roger Peckinpaugh	100.00	50.00
132 Pol Perritt	80.00	40.00
133 Jeff Pfeffer	80.00	40.00
134 Walter Pipp	120.00	60.00
135 Derril Pratt	80.00	40.00
136 Bill Rariden	80.00	40.00
137 Sam Rice	120.00	60.00
138 Hank Ritter	80.00	40.00
139 Eppa Rixey	120.00	60.00
140 Davey Robertson	80.00	40.00
141 Bob Roth	80.00	40.00
142 Ed Roush	120.00	60.00
143 Clarence Rowland MG	80.00	40.00
144 Dick Rudolph	80.00	40.00
145 William Rumler	80.00	40.00
146A Reb Russell ERR (photo actually Mel Wolfgang& pitching& follow through)	150.00	75.00
146B Reb Russell COR (standing& hands at side)	100.00	50.00
147 Babe Ruth	1500.00	750.00
148 Vic Saier	80.00	40.00
149 Slim Sallee	80.00	40.00
150 Ray Schalk	120.00	60.00
151 Walter Schang	80.00	40.00
152 Frank Schulte	80.00	40.00
153 Ferd Schupp	80.00	40.00
154 Everett Scott	100.00	50.00
155 Hank Severeid	80.00	40.00
156 Howard Shanks	80.00	40.00
157 Bob Shawkey	100.00	50.00
158 Jimmy Sheckard CO	80.00	40.00
159 Ernie Shore	100.00	50.00
160 Chick Shorten	80.00	40.00
161 Burt Shotton	100.00	50.00
162 George Sisler	150.00	75.00
163 Elmer Smith	80.00	40.00
164 J. Carlisle Smith	80.00	40.00
165 Fred Snodgrass	100.00	50.00
166 Tris Speaker	150.00	75.00
167 Oscar Stanage	80.00	40.00
168 Casey Stengel	400.00	200.00
169 Milton Stock	80.00	40.00
170 Amos Strunk	80.00	40.00
171 Zeb Terry	80.00	40.00
172 Jeff Tesreau	80.00	40.00
173 Chester Thomas	80.00	40.00
174 Fred Toney	100.00	50.00
175 Terry Turner	80.00	40.00
176 George Tyler	80.00	40.00
177 Jim Vaughn	80.00	40.00
178 Bob Veach	80.00	40.00
179 Oscar Vitt	100.00	50.00
180 Honus Wagner	600.00	300.00
181 Clarence Walker	80.00	40.00
182 Jim Walsh	80.00	40.00
183 Al Walters	80.00	40.00
184 Bill Wambsganss	80.00	40.00
185 Buck Weaver	150.00	75.00
186 Carl Weilman	80.00	40.00
187 Zack Wheat	150.00	75.00
188 Geo. Whitted	80.00	40.00
189 Joe Wilhoit	80.00	40.00
190A Claude Williams ERR (photo actually Hugh High& black stockings)	150.00	75.00
190B Claude Williams COR (photo correct)	120.00	60.00
191 Fred Williams	100.00	50.00
192 Art Wilson	80.00	40.00
193 Lawton Witt	80.00	40.00
194 Joe Wood	120.00	60.00
195 William Wortman	80.00	40.00
196 Steve Yerkes	80.00	40.00
197 Earl Yingling	80.00	40.00
198 Pep Young (2ndB. Detroit)	80.00	40.00
199 Rollie Zeider	80.00	40.00
200 Heine Zimmerman	80.00	40.00

1962 Colt .45's Booklets

These booklets feature members of the inagural Houston Colt 45's. They were issued and released at various retail outlets. Each booklet is 16 pages and has personal and career information on the players in the set. The following booklets are believed to be in shorter supply: Jim Campbell; J.C. Hartman, Roman Mejias, Jim Pendleton, Paul Richards, Bobby Shantz, Jim Umbricht, Hal Woodeshick, Coaches, Announcers. Umbricht is believed to

be by far the hardest booklet to acquire. Three different versions of each booklet exist: they were sponsored by American Tobacco, Pearl Beer and Phillips 66 respectively. All sponsors are valued the same.

	NM	Ex
COMPLETE SET	250.00	100.00
COMMON CARD	6.00	2.40
COMMON SP'S	15.00	6.00
1 Joe Amalfitano	6.00	2.40
2 Bob Aspromonte	8.00	3.20
3 Bob Bruce	6.00	2.40
4 Jim Campbell SP	15.00	6.00
5 Harry Craft MG	6.00	2.40
6 Dick Farrell	6.00	2.40
7 Dave Giusti	6.00	2.40
8 Jim Golden	6.00	2.40
9 J.C. Hartman SP	15.00	6.00
10 Ken Johnson	6.00	2.40
11 Norm Larker	6.00	2.40
12 Bob Lillis	8.00	3.20
13 Don McMahon	6.00	2.40
14 Roman Mejias SP	15.00	6.00
15 Jim Pendleton SP	15.00	6.00
16 Paul Richards GM SP	20.00	8.00
17 Bobby Shantz SP	20.00	8.00
18 Hal Smith	6.00	2.40
19 Al Spangler	6.00	2.40
20 Jim Umbricht SP	50.00	20.00
21 Carl Warwick	6.00	2.40
22 Hal Woodeshick SP	20.00	8.00
23 The Coaches SP	20.00	8.00
24 The Announcers SP	15.00	6.00

1962 Colt .45's Houston Chronicle

This 20-card set features sketches of the Houston Colt .45's team as drawn by Tony Couch and appeared in the Houston Chronicle newspaper. The cards are unnumbered and checklisted below in alphabetical order.

	NM	Ex
COMPLETE SET (20)	25.00	10.00
1 Joe Amalfitano	1.50	.60
2 Bob Aspromonte	2.00	.80
3 Don Buddin	1.50	.60
4 Al Cicotte	1.50	.60
5 Dick Ferrell(Sic)	1.50	.60
6 Dick Gernert	1.50	.60
7 Jim Golden	1.50	.60
8 Al Heist	1.50	.60
9 Ken Johnson	1.50	.60
10 Norm Larker	1.50	.60
11 Roman Mejias	1.50	.60
12 Ed Olivares	1.50	.60
13 Jim Pendleton	1.50	.60
14 Bobby Shantz	2.00	.80
15 Hal W. Smith	1.50	.60
16 Al Spangler	1.50	.60
17 Don Taussig	1.50	.60
18 Bobby Tiefenauer	1.50	.60
19 Jim Umbricht	1.50	.60
20 Hal Woodeshick	1.50	.60

1962 Colt .45's Jay Publishing

This 12-card set of the Houston Colt .45's measures approximately 5" by 7". The fronts feature black-and-white posed player photos with the player's and team name printed below in the white border. These cards were packaged 12 in a packet. The backs are blank. The cards are unnumbered and checklisted below in alphabetical order. A complete set in the original envelope is valued at fifty percent higher.

	NM	Ex
COMPLETE SET (12)	40.00	16.00
1 Joe Amalfitano	4.00	1.60
2 Bob Aspromonte	5.00	2.00
3 Bob Bruce	3.00	1.20
4 Don Buddin	3.00	1.20
5 Harry Craft MG	3.00	1.20
6 Dick Farrell	3.00	1.20
7 Ken Johnson	3.00	1.20
8 Norm Larker	3.00	1.20
9 Roman Mejias	4.00	1.60
10 Paul Richards GM	5.00	2.00
11 Hal Smith	4.00	1.60
12 Al Spangler	3.00	1.20

1963 Colt .45's Jay Publishing

This 12-card set of the Houston Colt .45's measures approximately 5" by 7". The fronts feature black-and-white posed player photos with the player's and team name printed below in the white border. These cards were packaged 12 in a packet. The backs are blank. The cards are unnumbered and checklisted below in alphabetical order.

	NM	Ex
COMPLETE SET (12)	40.00	16.00
1 Bob Aspromonte	5.00	2.00
2 Bob Bruce	3.00	1.20
3 Harry Craft MG	4.00	1.60
4 Dick Farrell	3.00	1.20
5 Bob Lillis	4.00	1.60
6 Don McMahon	3.00	1.20
7 Jim Pendleton	3.00	1.20
8 Merritt Ranew	3.00	1.20
9 Pete Runnels	3.00	1.20
10 Hal Smith	3.00	1.20
11 Al Spangler	3.00	1.20
12 Carl Warwick	3.00	1.20

1963 Colt .45's Pepsi-Cola

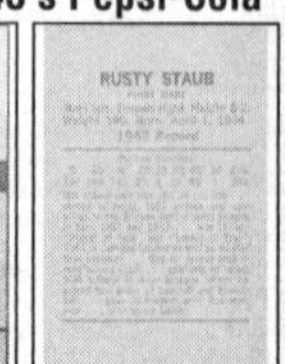

The 1963 Pepsi carton insert set consists of 16 black and white cards portraying Houston Colt 45 players. Cards are often found with the tabs, which contain a schedule and ads. Lillis and Temple are the scarcest commons while Bateman and Warwick were never publicly distributed. The set has a catalog description of F230-3. Rusty Staub appears in his Rookie Card year.

	NM	Ex
COMPLETE SET	1500.00	600.00
COMMON CARD	2.00	.80
COMMON SP'S	25.00	10.00
COMMON 4 BY 6	10.00	4.00
1 Bob Aspromonte	3.00	1.20
2 John Bateman SP	1200.00	475.00
3 Bob Bruce	15.00	6.00
4 Jim Campbell	2.00	.80
5 Dick Farrell	2.00	.80
6 Ernie Fazio	2.00	.80
7 Carroll Hardy	2.00	.80
8 J.C. Hartman	2.00	.80
9 Ken Johnson	2.00	.80
10 Bob Lillis SP	25.00	10.00
11 Don McMahon	2.00	.80
12 Pete Runnels	2.00	.80
13 Al Spangler	2.00	.80
14 Rusty Staub	15.00	6.00
15 Johnny Temple SP	25.00	10.00
16 Carl Warwick SP	300.00	120.00
17 Ernie Fazio(4"x6")	10.00	4.00
18 Pete Runnels(4"x6")	15.00	6.00
19 Al Spangler(4"x6")	10.00	4.00
20 Rusty Staub(4"x6")	25.00	10.00

1964 Colt .45's Jay Publishing

This 12-card set of the Houston Colt .45's measures approximately 5" by 7". The fronts feature black-and-white posed player photos with the player's and team name printed below in the white border. These cards were packaged 12 in a packet. The backs are blank. The cards are unnumbered and checklisted below in alphabetical order.

	NM	Ex
COMPLETE SET (12)	35.00	14.00
1 Bob Aspromonte	4.00	1.60
2 Bob Bruce	3.00	1.20
3 Harry Craft MG	3.00	1.20
4 Dick Farrell	3.00	1.20
5 Ken Johnson	3.00	1.20
6 Pete Runnels	3.00	1.20
7 Al Spangler	3.00	1.20
8 Rusty Staub	8.00	3.20
9 Johnny Temple	4.00	1.60
10 Carl Warwick	3.00	1.20
11 Hal Woodeshick	3.00	1.20
12 Jim Wynn	6.00	2.40

1995 Comic Images Promo

This standard-size promo card was issued to promote the 90-card "Phil Rizzuto's Baseball - The National Pastime" set. Sporting a chromium finish, the front features a full-bleed color shot of Phil Rizzuto. The back presents an advertisement for the card set. The card is unnumbered.

	Nm-Mt	Ex-Mt
1 Phil Rizzuto	3.00	.90

1995 Comic Images

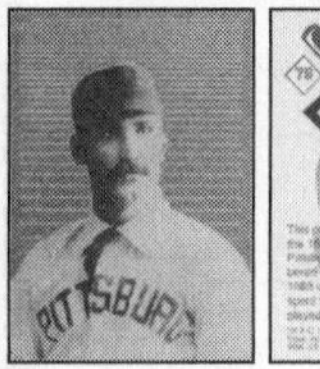

This 90-card standard-size set was produced by Comic Images, who enlisted the help of Hall of Famer Phil Rizzuto. Rizzuto himself autographed 1,000 cards for random insertion. Titled "Phil Rizzuto's Baseball - The National Pastime," set features nostalgic images of players, teams, stadiums, and memorabilia from the turn of the century until the present day.

	Nm-Mt	Ex-Mt
COMPLETE SET (90)	25.00	7.50
1 Sportsman's Park	.25	.07
2 Briggs Stadium	.25	.07
3 Shibe Park	.25	.07
4 Polo Grounds Print	.25	.07
5 Forbes Field	.25	.07
6 Cleveland Stadium	.25	.07
7 League Park	.25	.07
8 Highlander Park	.25	.07
9 South Side Park	.25	.07
10 Catchers' Mitt	.25	.07
11 Baseball Trophy	.25	.07
12 Baseball Plate	.25	.07
13 Bisque Figure	.25	.07
14 Beanbag Toss Game	.25	.07
15 Tobacco Carved Figure	.25	.07
16 Sunday Magazine	.25	.07
17 Street and Smith Sport	.25	.07
18 Collier's	.25	.07
19 Bluebook	.25	.07
20 Chadwick's	.25	.07
21 Harper's Weekly	.25	.07
22 American Magazine	.25	.07
23 Crazy Baseball Stories	.25	.07
24 New York Giants	.25	.07
25 Cincinnati American	.25	.07
26 Chicago White Stockings	.25	.07
27 Baltimore Blues	.25	.07
28 Chicago White Stockings All-American Team	.25	.07
29 Phillipines Baseball	.25	.07
30 Champions	.25	.07
31 John McGraw	1.50	.45
32 Home Run	.25	.07
33 Lorillard Chicago BBC	.25	.07
34 Boston BBC	.25	.07
35 Out at First	.25	.07
36 Coffee Cards	.25	.07
37 Uncut Sheet	.25	.07
38 Tobin Lithographers	.25	.07
39 Uncut Sheet Die Cut	.25	.07
40 Patsy Dougherty	.50	.15
41 A Regular Corker	.25	.07
42 Barker's Advertising Books	.25	.07
43 Toledo BBC Tobacco	.25	.07
44 Shredded Wheat	.25	.07
45 BVS Advertisment	.25	.07
46 Police Gazette Poster	.25	.07
47 Japenese Poster	.25	.07
48 Safe Hit Vegetable Crate	.25	.07
49 Slide, Kelly, Slide Poster	.25	.07
50 Peck and Snyder Hat	.25	.07
51 Reach Gloves Catalog	.25	.07
52 New York Giants Score Card	.25	.07
53 Game Card	.25	.07
54 Wright and Ditson Guide	.25	.07
55 All-Star Game Program	.25	.07
56 Stadium Scene	.25	.07
57 Currier and Ives Print	.25	.07
58 Scorecard Artwork	.25	.07
59 Folk Art	.25	.07
60 Batter	.25	.07
61 Cartoon	.25	.07
62 Teddy Roosevelt Cartoon	.25	.07
63 Uncle Sam Cartoon	.25	.07
64 Casey at the Bat	.25	.07
65 Seymour Church Print	.25	.07
66 Valentine Card	.25	.07
67 Pinup Book	.25	.07
68 Uncle Sam WWI Sheet	.25	.07
69 Baseball Sheet Music	.25	.07
70 Saturday Glove	.25	.07
71 Ft Wayne Woman	.25	.07
72 Spalding Baseball Guide	.25	.07
73 Rally Day Postcard	.25	.07
74 Spalding Advertisment Die Cut	.25	.07
75 Out Baseball Club Cover	.25	.07
76 Jake Beckley	1.00	.30
77 Cap Anson	1.50	.45
78 St Louis Player	.25	.07
79 Sam Thompson	1.00	.30
80 Bobby Wallace	1.00	.30
81 Fogarty and McGuire	.50	.15
82 Yank Robinson	.50	.15
83 Charlie Comiskey	1.00	.30
84 Picked Off	.25	.07
85 Error	.25	.07
86 Third Base	.25	.07
87 Safe at Home	.25	.07
88 Baseball Action	.25	.07
89 Great Fielding	.25	.07
90 Checklist	.25	.07
AU Phil Rizzuto AU	40.00	12.00
NNO Limited Edition Medallion Card		

2000 Cone ALS

This one-card set was issued to bring more publicity to the fight against ALS (Lou Gehrig's Disease). The front has a photo of cone along with a promo for the battle against ALS while the horizontal back has information about ALS.

	Nm-Mt	Ex-Mt
1 David Cone	3.00	.90

1981 Conlon TSN

Issued by The Sporting News, this 100-card set measures approximately 4" by 5" and features the photography of Charles Martin Conlon. The set consists of baseball portraits from 1915-1935. The set was packaged in a brown leatherette case embossed in silver and cost $50 upon issue directly from the Sporting News. The fronts display glossy sepia-tone pictures with white borders on heavy card stock. The words "The Sporting News" are printed at the top and the player's name, position, the year of the photo and the card number are listed at the bottom. The backs are blank. A limited edition set numbered to 1000 and certified was issued in 1993. Those cards are valued the same as the cards issued in 1981

	Nm-Mt	Ex-Mt
COMPLETE SET (100)	100.00	40.00
1 Ty Cobb	8.00	3.20
2 Hugh Jennings	1.50	.60
3 Miller Huggins	1.50	.60
4 Babe Ruth	10.00	4.00
5 Lou Gehrig	8.00	3.20
6 John McGraw	4.00	1.60
7 Bill Terry	2.50	1.00
8 Stan Baumgartner	.50	.20
9 Christy Mathewson	4.00	1.60
10 Grover Alexander	3.00	1.20
11 Tony Lazzeri	1.50	.60
12 Frank Chance Joe Tinker	2.50	1.00
13 Johnny Evers	2.50	1.00
14 Tris Speaker	2.50	1.00
15 Harry Hooper	1.50	.60
16 Duffy Lewis	.50	.20
17 Smokey Joe Wood	1.00	.40
18 Hugh Duffy	1.50	.60
19 Rogers Hornsby	4.00	1.60
20 Earl Averill	1.50	.60
21 Dizzy Dean	4.00	1.60
22 Paul Dean	1.00	.40
23 Frank Frisch	1.50	.60
24 Pepper Martin	1.00	.40
25 Blondy Ryan	.50	.20
26 Hank Gowdy	.50	.20
27 Fred Merkle	1.00	.40
28 Ernie Lombardi	1.50	.60
29 Greasy Neale	1.00	.40
30 Morris Badgro	.50	.20
31 Jim Thorpe	6.00	2.40
32 Roy Johnson	.50	.20
33 Bob Johnson	.50	.20
34 Moose Solters	.50	.20
35 Specs Toporcer	.50	.20
36 Jackie Hayes	.50	.20
37 Walter Johnson	5.00	2.00
38 Lefty Grove	3.00	1.20
39 Eddie Collins	3.00	1.20
40 Buck Weaver	1.50	.60
41 Cozy Dolan	.50	.20
42 Emil Meusel	.50	.20
43 Bob Meusel	1.00	.40
44 Lefty Gomez	1.50	.60
45 Rube Marquard	1.50	.60
46 Jeff Tesreau	.50	.20
47 Joe Heving	.50	.20
48 Johnny Heving	.50	.20
49 Rick Ferrell	1.50	.60
50 Wes Ferrell	1.00	.40
51 Bill Wambsganss	.50	.20
52 Ray Chapman	1.00	.40
53 Joe Sewell	1.50	.60
54 Luke Sewell	.50	.20
55 Odell Hale	.50	.20
56 Sammy Hale	.50	.20
57 Earle Mack	.50	.20
58 Connie Mack	4.00	1.60
59 Rube Walberg	.50	.20
60 Mule Haas	.50	.20
61 Paul Waner	2.50	1.00
62 Lloyd Waner	1.50	.60
63 Pie Traynor	2.50	1.00
64 Honus Wagner	5.00	2.00
65 Joe Cronin	3.00	1.20
66 Moon Harris	.50	.20
67 Sheriff Harris	.50	.20
68 Bucky Harris	1.50	.60
69 Alec Gaston	.50	.20
70 Milt Gaston	.50	.20
71 Casey Stengel	5.00	2.00
72 Amos Rusie	1.50	.60
73 Mickey Welch	1.50	.60
74 Roger Bresnahan	1.50	.60
75 Jesse Burkett	1.50	.60
76 Harry Heilmann	1.50	.60
77 Heinie Manush	1.50	.60
78 Charlie Gehringer	2.50	1.00
79 Hank Greenberg	3.00	1.20
80 Jimmie Foxx	4.00	1.60
81 Al Simmons	2.50	1.00
82 Ed Plank	2.50	1.00
83 George Sisler	2.50	1.00
84 Joe Medwick	1.50	.60
85 Mel Ott	3.00	1.20
86 Hack Wilson	1.50	.60
87 Jimmy Wilson	.50	.20
88 Chuck Klein	1.50	.60
89 Gabby Hartnett	1.50	.60
90 Heinie Groh	.50	.20
91 Ping Bodie	.50	.20
92 Ted Lyons	1.50	.60
93 Jack(Picus) Quinn	.50	.20
94 Oscar Roettger	.50	.20
95 Wally Roettger	.50	.20
96 Bubbles Hargrave	.50	.20
97 Pinky Hargrave	.50	.20
98 Sam Crawford	1.50	.60
99 Gee Walker	.50	.20
100 Homer Summa	.50	.20

1983 Conlon Marketcom

This set of 60 Charles Martin Conlon photo cards was produced by Marketcom in conjunction with The Sporting News. The cards are large size, approximately 4 1/2" X 6 1/8" and are in a sepia tone. The players selected for the set are members of the 1933 American and National League All-Star teams as well as Negro League All-Stars. These cards are numbered at the bottom of each reverse. The set numbering is American League (1-24), National League (25-48) and Negro League (49-60). In the upper right corner of each card's obverse is printed "1933 American (National or Negro League as appropriate) All Stars." Each obverse also features a facsimile autograph of the player pictured.

	Nm-Mt	Ex-Mt
COMPLETE SET (60)	25.00	10.00
1 Jimmy Foxx	.75	.30
2 Heinie Manush	.60	.24
3 Lou Gehrig	2.00	.80
4 Al Simmons	.60	.24
5 Charlie Gehringer	.60	.24
6 Luke Appling	.60	.24
7 Mickey Cochrane	.60	.24
8 Joe Kuhel	.25	.10
9 Bill Dickey	.75	.30
10 Pinky Higgins	.25	.10
11 Roy Johnson	.25	.10
12 Ben Chapman	.25	.10
13 Urban Hodapp	.25	.10
14 Joe Cronin	.60	.24
15 Evar Swanson	.25	.10
16 Earl Averill	.60	.24
17 Babe Ruth	3.00	1.20
18 Tony Lazzeri	.60	.24
19 Alvin Crowder	.25	.10
20 Lefty Grove	.75	.30
21 Earl Whitehill	.25	.10
22 Lefty Gomez	.75	.30
23 Mel Harder	.25	.10
24 Tommy Bridges	.25	.10
25 Chuck Klein	.60	.24
26 Spud Davis	.25	.10
27 Riggs Stephenson	.40	.16
28 Tony Piet	.25	.10
29 Bill Terry	.60	.24
30 Wes Schulmerich	.25	.10
31 Pepper Martin	.40	.16
32 Arky Vaughan	.60	.24
33 Wally Berger	.40	.16
34 Ripper Collins	.25	.10
35 Fred Lindstrom	.60	.24
36 Chick Fullis	.25	.10
37 Paul Waner	.75	.30
38 Johnny Frederick	.25	.10
39 Joe Medwick	.60	.24
40 Pie Traynor	.60	.24
41 Frankie Frisch	.60	.24
42 Chick Hafey	.60	.24
43 Carl Hubbell	.75	.30
44 Guy Bush	.25	.10
45 Dizzy Dean	1.00	.40
46 Hal Schumacher	.25	.10
47 Larry French	.25	.10
48 Lon Warneke	.25	.10
49 Cool Papa Bell	.75	.30
50 Oscar Charleston	.60	.24
51 Josh Gibson	1.25	.50
52 Satchel Paige	1.25	.50
53 Dave Malarcher	.40	.16
54 John Henry Lloyd	.60	.24
55 Rube Foster	.75	.30
56 Buck Leonard	.75	.30
57 Smoky Joe Williams	.75	.30
58 Willie Wells	.60	.24
59 Judy Johnson	.75	.30
60 Martin DiHigo	.60	.24

1986 Conlon Series 1

This 60-card set was produced from the black and white photos in the Charles Martin Conlon collection. Each set comes with a special card which contains the number of that set out of the 12,000 sets which were produced. The cards measure 2 1/2" X 3 1/2" and are printed in sepia tones.

	Nm-Mt	Ex-Mt
COMPLETE SET (60)	20.00	8.00
1 Lou Gehrig	1.50	.60
2 Ty Cobb	1.50	.60
3 Grover C. Alexander	.30	.12
4 Walter Johnson	.75	.30
5 Bill Klem	.30	.12
6 Ty Cobb	1.50	.60
7 Mickey Cochrane	.30	.12
8 Paul Waner	.30	.12
9 Joe Cronin	.30	.12
10 Dizzy Dean	.50	.20
11 Leo Durocher	.30	.12
12 Jimmy Foxx	.50	.20
13 Babe Ruth	2.00	.80
14 Mike Gonzalez Frank Frisch Clyde Ellsworth Wares	.15	.06
15 Carl Hubbell	.30	.12
16 Miller Huggins	.15	.06
17 Lou Gehrig	1.50	.60
18 Connie McGillicuddy (Connie Mack)	.50	.20
19 Heinie Manush	.30	.12
20 Babe Ruth	2.00	.80
22 Pepper Martin	.15	.06
23 Christy Mathewson	.50	.20
24 Ty Cobb	1.50	.60
25 Bucky Harris	.30	.12
26 Waite Hoyt	.30	.12
27 Rube Marquard	.30	.12
28 Joe McCarthy	.30	.12
29 John McGraw	.50	.20
30 Tris Speaker	.50	.20
31 Bill Terry	.30	.12
32 Christy Mathewson	.75	.30
33 Casey Stengel	.75	.30
34 Bob Meusel	.15	.06
35 Rube Waddell	.30	.12
36 Mel Ott	.50	.20
37 Roger Peckinpaugh	.15	.06
38 Pie Traynor	.50	.20
39 Chief Bender	.30	.12
40 Jack Coombs	.15	.06
41 Ty Cobb	1.50	.60
42 Harry Heilmann	.30	.12
43 Charlie Gehringer	.30	.12
44 Rogers Hornsby	.75	.30
45 Lefty Gomez	.30	.12
46 Christy Mathewson	.75	.30
47 Lefty Grove	.50	.20
48 Babe Ruth	2.00	.80
49 Fred Merkle	.15	.06
50 Babe Ruth	2.00	.80
51 Herb Pennock	.30	.12
52 Lou Gehrig	1.50	.60
53 Fred Clarke	.30	.12
54 Babe Ruth	2.00	.80
55 Honus Wagner	.75	.30
56 Hack Wilson	.30	.12
57 Lou Gehrig	1.50	.60
58 Lloyd Waner	.30	.12
59 Charles Martin Conlon	.15	.06
60 Charles Conlon Margie Conlon	.15	.06
NNO Set Number Card	.15	.06

1987 Conlon Series 2

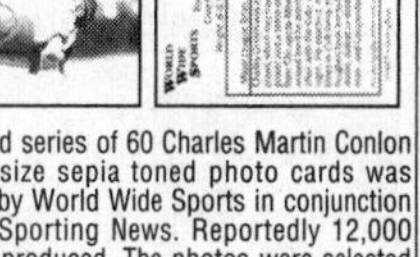

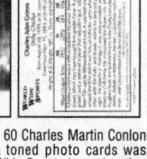

The second series of 60 Charles Martin Conlon standard-size sepia toned photo cards was produced by World Wide Sports in conjunction with The Sporting News. Reportedly 12,000 sets were produced. The photos were selected and background information written by Paul MacFarlane of The Sporting News.

	Nm-Mt	Ex-Mt
COMPLETE SET (60)	12.00	4.80
1 Lou Gehrig	1.50	.60
2 Lefty Gomez	.40	.16
3 Christy Mathewson	.75	.30
4 Grover Alexander	.60	.24
5 Ty Cobb	1.50	.60
6 Walter Johnson	.75	.30
7 Charles(Babe) Adams	.10	.04
8 Nick Altrock	.25	.10
9 Al Schacht	.25	.10
10 Hugh Critz	.10	.04
11 Henry Cullop	.10	.04
12 Jacob Daubert	.10	.04
13 William Donovan	.10	.04
14 Chick Hafey	.25	.10
15 Bill Hallahan	.10	.04
16 Fred Haney	.10	.04
17 Charles Hartnett	.25	.10
18 Walter Henline	.10	.04
19 Edwin Rommel	.10	.04
20 Ralph(Babe) Pinelli	.10	.04
21 Robert Meusel	.25	.10
22 Emil Meusel	.10	.04
23 Smead Jolley	.10	.04
24 Ike Boone	.10	.04
25 Earl Webb	.10	.04
26 Charles Comiskey	.40	.16
27 Eddie Collins	.40	.16
28 George(Buck) Weaver	.40	.16
29 Eddie Cicotte	.40	.16
30 Sam Crawford	.25	.10
31 Charlie Dressen	.10	.04
32 Arthur Fletcher	.10	.04
33 Hugh Duffy	.25	.10
34 Ira Flagstead	.10	.04
35 Harry Hooper	.25	.10
36 George Lewis	.10	.04
37 Jimmie Dykes	.10	.04
38 Goose Goslin	.25	.10
39 Hank Gowdy	.10	.04
40 Charlie Grimm	.10	.04
41 Mark Koenig	.10	.04
42 James Hogan	.10	.04
43 William Jacobson	.10	.04
44 Fielder Jones	.10	.04
45 George Kelly	.25	.10
46 Adolpho Luque	.10	.04
47 Rabbit Maranville	.25	.10
48 Carl Mays	.10	.04
49 Edward Plank	.25	.10
50 Hubert Pruett	.10	.04
51 John(Picus) Quinn	.10	.04
52 Charles(Flint) Rhem	.10	.04
53 Amos Rusie	.25	.10
54 Edd Roush	.25	.10
55 Ray Schalk	.25	.10
56 Ernie Shore	.10	.04
57 Joe Wood	.40	.16
58 George Sisler	.40	.16
59 Jim Thorpe	1.50	.60
60 Earl Whitehill	.10	.04

1988 Conlon American All-Stars

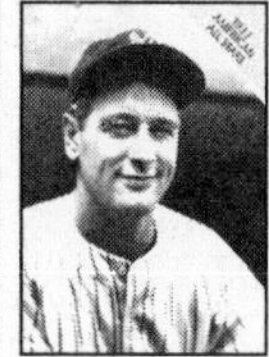

This set of 24 Charles Martin Conlon photo cards was produced by World Wide Sports in conjunction with The Sporting News. The cards are standard size and are in a sepia tone. The photos (members of the 1933 American League All-Star team) were selected and background information written by Paul MacFarlane of The Sporting News. These cards are unnumbered and hence are listed below in alphabetical order. American League is indicated in the lower right corner of each card's reverse. In the upper right corner of each card's obverse is printed "1933 American All Stars."

	Nm-Mt	Ex-Mt
COMPLETE SET (24)	6.00	2.40
1 Luke Appling	.30	.12
2 Earl Averill	.30	.12
3 Tommy Bridges	.15	.06
4 Ben Chapman	.15	.06
5 Mickey Cochrane	.30	.12
6 Joe Cronin	.30	.12
7 Alvin Crowder	.15	.06
8 Bill Dickey	.40	.16
9 James Emory Foxx	.75	.30
10 Lou Gehrig	1.50	.60
11 Charlie Gehringer	.30	.12
12 Lefty Gomez	.30	.12
13 Lefty Grove	.60	.24
14 Mel Harder	.15	.06
15 Pinky Higgins	.15	.06
16 Urban Hodapp	.15	.06
17 Roy Johnson	.15	.06
18 Joe Kuhel	.15	.06
19 Tony Lazzeri	.30	.12
20 Heinie Manush	.30	.12
21 Babe Ruth	2.00	.80
22 Al Simmons	.30	.12
23 Evar Swanson	.15	.06
24 Earl Whitehill	.15	.06

1988 Conlon Hardee's/Coke

This six-card standard-size sepia tone set was issued in 18 central Indiana Hardee's restaurants over a six-week period, a different card per purchase per week. The set features the vintage photography of Charles Martin Conlon, except for the Cool Papa Bell photo which was not shot by Conlon. The card backs contain biographical information, Hardee's logo and a Coca Cola Classic logo. The cards are also copyrighted by The Sporting News.

	Nm-Mt	Ex-Mt
COMPLETE SET (6)	4.50	1.80
1 Cool Papa Bell	.75	.30
2 Ty Cobb	2.00	.80
3 Lou Gehrig	2.00	.80
4 Connie Mack	.75	.30
5 Casey Stengel	.75	.30
6 Rube Waddell	.50	.20

1988 Conlon National All-Stars

This set of 24 Charles Martin Conlon photo cards was produced by World Wide Sports in conjunction with The Sporting News. The cards

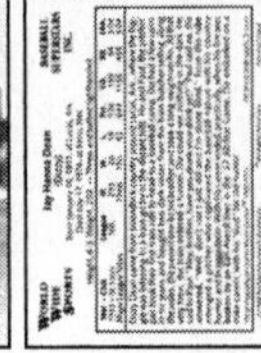

are standard size, and are in a sepia tone. The photos (members of the 1933 National League All-Star team) were selected and background information written by Paul MacFarlane of The Sporting News. These cards are unnumbered and hence are listed below in alphabetical order. National League is indicated in the lower right corner of each card's reverse. In the upper right corner of each card's obverse is printed "1933 National All Stars."

	Nm-Mt	Ex-Mt
COMPLETE SET (24)	5.00	2.00
1 Wally Berger	.15	.06
2 Guy Bush	.15	.06
3 Ripper Collins	.15	.06
4 Spud Davis	.15	.06
5 Dizzy Dean	.50	.20
6 Johnny Frederick	.15	.06
7 Larry French	.15	.06
8 Frankie Frisch	.30	.12
9 Chick Fullis	.15	.06
10 Chick Hafey	.30	.12
11 Carl Hubbell	.50	.20
12 Chuck Klein	.30	.12
13 Fred Lindstrom	.30	.12
14 Pepper Martin	.30	.12
15 Joe Medwick	.30	.12
16 Tony Piet	.15	.06
17 Wes Schulmerich	.15	.06
18 Hal Schumacher	.15	.06
19 Riggs Stephenson	.30	.12
20 Bill Terry	.50	.20
21 Pie Traynor	.50	.20
22 Arky Vaughan	.30	.12
23 Paul Waner	.50	.20
24 Lon Warneke	.15	.06

1988 Conlon Negro All-Stars

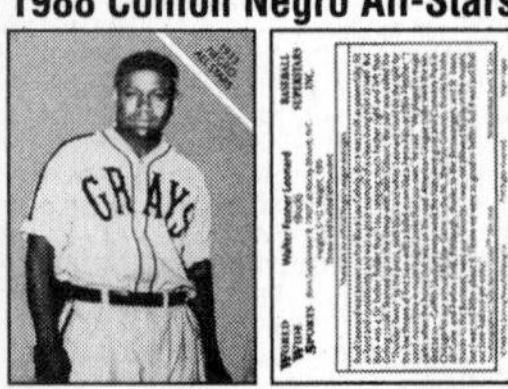

This set of 12 photo cards was produced by World Wide Sports in conjunction with The Sporting News. The cards are standard size, and are in a sepia tone. The photos (Negro League All Stars from 1933) were selected and background information written by Paul MacFarlane of The Sporting News. Despite the stylistic similarity of this set with the other Conlon sets, the photos for this set were not taken by Charles Martin Conlon. These cards are unnumbered and hence are listed below in alphabetical order. Negro League is indicated in the lower right corner of each card's reverse. In the upper right corner of each card's obverse is printed "1933 Negro All Stars." The photo quality on some of the cards is very poor suggesting that the original photo or negative may have been enlarged to an excessive degree.

	Nm-Mt	Ex-Mt
COMPLETE SET (12)	5.00	2.00
1 Cool Papa Bell	.75	.30
2 Oscar Charleston	.50	.20
3 Martin DiHigo	.50	.20
4 Rube Foster	.50	.20
5 Josh Gibson	1.00	.40
6 Judy Johnson	.50	.20
7 Buck Leonard	.50	.20
8 John Henry Lloyd	.50	.20
9 Dave Malarcher	.25	.10
10 Satchel Paige	1.00	.40
11 Willie Wells	.50	.20
12 Smoky Joe Williams	.50	.20

1988 Conlon Series 3

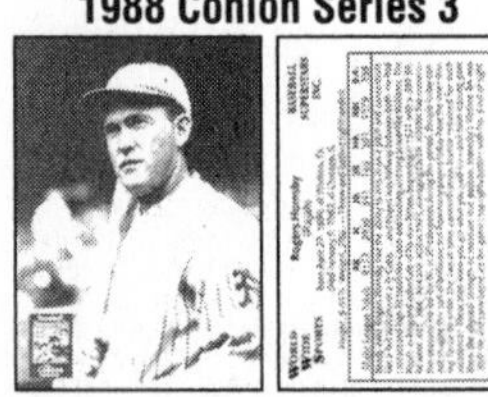

This third series of 30 Charles Martin Conlon photo cards was produced by World Wide Sports in conjunction with The Sporting News. The cards are standard size, and are in a sepia tone. The photos were selected and background information written by Paul MacFarlane of The Sporting News. These cards are unnumbered and hence are listed below in alphabetical order. Series 3 is indicated in the lower right corner of each card's reverse. A black and white logo for the "Baseball Immortals" and The Conlon Collection is overprinted in the lower left corner of each obverse.

	Nm-Mt	Ex-Mt
COMPLETE SET (30)	6.00	2.40
1 Ace Adams	.15	.06
2 Grover C. Alexander	.50	.20
3 Elden Auker	.15	.06
4 Jack Barry	.15	.06
5 Wally Berger	.15	.06
6 Ben Chapman	.15	.06
7 Mickey Cochrane	.30	.12
8 Frankie Crosetti	.15	.06
9 Paul Dean	.15	.06
10 Leo Durocher	.50	.20
11 Wes Ferrell	.30	.12
12 Hank Gowdy	.15	.06
13 Andy High	.15	.06
14 Rogers Hornsby	.75	.30
15 Carl Hubbell	.50	.20
16 Joe Judge	.15	.06
17 Tony Lazzeri	.30	.12
18 Pepper Martin	.30	.12
19 Lee Meadows	.15	.06
20 Johnny Murphy	.15	.06
21 Steve O'Neil	.15	.06
22 Ed Plank	.30	.12
23 Jack(Picus) Quinn	.15	.06
24 Charley Root	.15	.06
25 Babe Ruth	2.00	.80
26 Fred Snodgrass	.15	.06
27 Tris Speaker	.50	.20
28 Bill Terry	.50	.20
29 Jeff Tesreau	.15	.06
30 George Toporcer	.15	.06

1988 Conlon Series 4

This fourth series of 30 Charles Martin Conlon photo cards was produced by World Wide Sports in conjunction with The Sporting News. The cards are standard size, and are in a sepia tone. The photos were selected and background information written by Paul MacFarlane of The Sporting News. These cards are unnumbered and hence are listed below in alphabetical order. Series 4 is indicated in the lower right corner of each card's reverse. A black and white logo for the "Baseball Immortals" and The Conlon Collection is overprinted in the lower left corner of each obverse.

	Nm-Mt	Ex-Mt
COMPLETE SET (30)	6.00	2.40
1 Dale Alexander	.15	.06
2 Morris Badgro	.15	.06
3 Dick Bartell	.15	.06
4 Max Bishop	.15	.06
5 Hal Chase	.30	.12
6 Ty Cobb	1.50	.60
7 Nick Cullop	.15	.06
8 Dizzy Dean	.75	.30
9 Charlie Dressen	.15	.06
10 Jimmy Dykes	.15	.06
11 Art Fletcher	.15	.06
12 Charlie Grimm	.15	.06
13 Lefty Grove	.50	.20
14 Baby Doll Jacobson	.15	.06
15 Bill Klem UMP	.30	.12
16 Mark Koenig	.15	.06
17 Duffy Lewis	.15	.06
18 Carl Mays	.15	.06
19 Fred Merkle	.15	.06
20 Greasy Neale	.30	.12
21 Mel Ott	.50	.20
22 Babe Pinelli	.15	.06
23 Flint Rhem	.15	.06
24 Slim Sallee UER (Misspelled Salee on card back)	.15	.06
25 Al Simmons	.30	.12
26 George Sisler	.30	.12
27 Riggs Stephenson	.15	.06
28 Jim Thorpe	1.50	.60
29 Bill Wambsganss	.15	.06
30 Cy Young	.50	.20

1988 Conlon Series 5

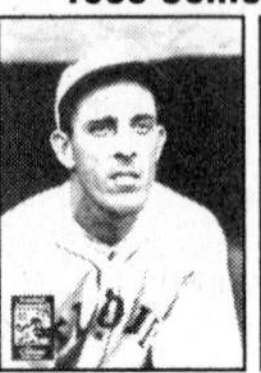

This fifth series of 30 Charles Martin Conlon photo cards was produced by World Wide Sports in conjunction with The Sporting News. The cards are standard size, and are in a sepia tone. The photos were selected and background information written by Paul MacFarlane of The Sporting News. These cards are unnumbered and hence are listed below in alphabetical order. Series 5 is indicated in the lower right corner of each card's reverse. A black and white logo for the "Baseball Immortals" and The Conlon Collection is overprinted in the lower left corner of each obverse.

	Nm-Mt	Ex-Mt
COMPLETE SET (30)	6.00	2.40
1 Nick Altrock	.30	.12
2 Del Baker	.15	.06
3 Moe Berg	1.00	.40
4 Zeke Bonura	.15	.06
5 Eddie Collins	.50	.20
6 Hughie Critz	.15	.06
7 George Dauss	.15	.06
8 Joe Dugan	.15	.06
9 Howard Ehmke	.15	.06
10 James Emory Foxx	.75	.30
11 Frankie Frisch	.30	.12
12 Lou Gehrig	1.50	.60
13 Charlie Gehringer	.50	.20
14 Kid Gleason	.30	.12
15 Lefty Gomez	.50	.20
16 Babe Herman	.30	.12
17 Bill James	.15	.06
18 Joe Kuhel	.15	.06
19 Dolf Luque	.30	.12
20 John McGraw	.50	.20
21 Stuffy McInnis	.15	.06
22 Bob Meusel	.15	.06
23 Lefty O'Doul	.15	.06
24 Hub Pruett	.15	.06
25 Paul Richards	.15	.06
26 Bob Shawkey	.15	.06
27 Gabby Street	.15	.06
28 Johnny Tobin	.15	.06
29 Rube Waddell	.30	.12
30 Billy Werber	.15	.06

1991 Conlon TSN

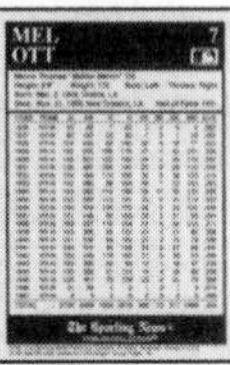

This 330-card standard-size set was issued in black and white and again featured the photography of Charles Conlon. The set was produced by MegaCards in conjunction with The Sporting News. The set was available in both packs as well as factory set form. The card backs contain pertinent information relevant to the front of the cards whether it is career statistics or all-time leaders format or the special cards commemorating the great teams of the first part of the twentieth century.

	Nm-Mt	Ex-Mt
COMPLETE SET (330)	18.00	5.50
1 Rogers Hornsby HOF	.35	.10
2 Jimmie Foxx HOF	.35	.10
3 Dizzy Dean HOF	.40	.12
4 Rabbit Maranville HOF	.20	.06
5 Paul Waner HOF	.20	.06
6 Lloyd Waner HOF	.20	.06
7 Mel Ott HOF	.30	.09
8 Honus Wagner HOF	.40	.12
9 Walter Johnson HOF	.40	.12
10 Carl Hubbell HOF	.25	.07
11 Frank Frisch HOF	.20	.06
12 Kiki Cuyler HOF	.20	.06
13 Red Ruffing HOF	.20	.06
14 Hank Greenberg HOF	.30	.09
15 Johnny Evers HOF	.20	.06
16 Hugh Jennings HOF	.20	.06
17 Dave Bancroft HOF	.20	.06
18 Joe Medwick HOF	.20	.06
19 Ted Lyons HOF	.20	.06
20 Chief Bender HOF	.20	.06
21 Eddie Collins HOF	.20	.06
22 Jim Bottomley HOF	.20	.06
23 Lefty Grove HOF	.30	.09
24 Max Carey HOF	.20	.06
25 Burleigh Grimes HOF	.20	.06
26 Ross Youngs HOF	.20	.06
27 Ernie Lombardi HOF	.20	.06
28 Joe McCarthy HOF	.20	.06
29 Hack Wilson HOF	.25	.07
30 Chuck Klein HOF	.20	.06
31 Earl Averill HOF	.20	.06
32 Grover C. Alexander HOF	.30	.09
33 Chick Hafey HOF	.20	.06
34 Bill McKechnie HOF	.20	.06
35 Bob Feller HOF	.30	.09
36 Pie Traynor HOF	.20	.06
37 Casey Stengel HOF	.30	.09
38 Arky Vaughan HOF	.20	.06
39 Eppa Rixey HOF	.20	.06
40 Joe Sewell HOF	.20	.06
41 Red Faber HOF	.20	.06
42 Travis Jackson HOF	.20	.06
43 Jesse Haines HOF	.20	.06
44 Tris Speaker HOF	.25	.07
45 Connie Mack HOF	.25	.07
46 Connie Mack HOF	.25	.07
47 Connie Mack HOF	.25	.07
48 Ray Schalk HOF	.20	.06
49 Al Simmons HOF	.20	.06
50 Joe Cronin HOF	.20	.06
51 Mickey Cochrane HOF	.25	.07
52 Harry Heilmann HOF	.20	.06
53 Johnny Mize HOF	.25	.07
54 Sam Rice HOF	.20	.06
55 Edd Roush HOF	.20	.06
56 Enos Slaughter HOF	.20	.06
57 Christy Mathewson HOF	.40	.12
58 Fred Lindstrom HOF	.20	.06
59 Gabby Hartnett HOF	.20	.06
60 George Kelly HOF	.20	.06
61 Bucky Harris HOF	.20	.06
62 Goose Goslin HOF	.20	.06
63 Heinie Manush HOF	.20	.06
64 Bill Terry HOF	.25	.07
65 John McGraw HOF	.25	.07
66 George Sisler HOF	.20	.06
67 Lefty Gomez HOF	.25	.07
68 Joe Judge	.10	.03
69 Tommy Thevenow	.05	.02
70 Charlie Gelbert	.05	.02
71 Jackie Hayes	.05	.02
72 Bob Fothergill	.05	.02
73 Adam Comorosky	.05	.02
74 Earl Smith	.05	.02
75 Sam Gray	.05	.02
76 Pete Appleton	.05	.02
77 Gene Moore	.05	.02
78 Art Jorgens	.05	.02
79 Bill Knickerbocker	.05	.02
80 Carl Reynolds	.05	.02
81 Ski Melillo	.05	.02
82 Johnny Burnett	.05	.02
83 Jake Powell	.05	.02
84 Johnny Murphy	.10	.03
85 Roy Parmelee	.05	.02
86 Jimmy Ripple	.05	.02
87 Gee Walker	.05	.02
88 George Earnshaw	.10	.03
89 Billy Southworth	.05	.02
90 Wally Moses	.05	.02
91 Rube Walberg	.05	.02
92 Jimmy Dykes	.10	.03
93 Charlie Root	.05	.02
94 Johnny Cooney	.05	.02
95 Charlie Grimm	.15	.04
96 Bob Johnson	.10	.03
97 Jack Scott	.05	.02
98 Rip Radcliff	.05	.02
99 Fritz Ostermueller	.05	.02
100 Julie Wera '27NY	.05	.02
101 Miller Huggins '27NY	.20	.06
102 Ray Morehart '27NY	.05	.02
103 Benny Bengough '27NY	.10	.03
104 Dutch Ruether '27NY	.05	.02
105 Earle Combs '27NY	.20	.06
106 Myles Thomas '27NY	.05	.02
107 Ben Paschal '27NY	.05	.02
108 Cedric Durst '27NY	.05	.02
109 Wilcy Moore '27NY	.05	.02
110 Babe Ruth '27NY	1.00	.30
111 Lou Gehrig '27NY	.75	.23
112 Joe Dugan '27NY	.10	.03
113 Tony Lazzeri '27NY	.20	.06
114 Urban Shocker '27NY	.10	.03
115 Waite Hoyt '27NY	.20	.06
116 Charley O'Leary '27NY	.05	.02
117 Art Fletcher CO '27NY	.05	.02
118 Pat Collins '27NY	.05	.02
119 Joe Giard '27NY	.05	.02
120 Herb Pennock '27NY	.20	.06
121 Mike Gazella '27NY	.05	.02
122 Bob Meusel '27NY	.15	.04
123 George Pipgras '27NY	.05	.02
124 Johnny Grabowski '27NY	.05	.02
125 Mark Koenig '27NY	.10	.03
126 Stan Hack	.10	.03
127 Earl Whitehill	.05	.02
128 Bill Lee	.05	.02
129 Gus Mancuso	.05	.02
130 Ray Blades	.05	.02
131 Jack Burns	.05	.02
132 Clint Brown	.05	.02
133 Bill Dietrich	.05	.02
134 Cy Blanton	.05	.02
135 Harry Hooper '16 Champs	.20	.06
136 Chick Shorten '16 Champs	.05	.02
137 Tilly Walker '16 Champs	.05	.02
138 Rube Foster '16 Champs	.05	.02
139 Jack Barry '16 Champs	.10	.03
140 Sad Sam Jones '16 Champs	.10	.03
141 Ernie Shore '16 Champs	.10	.03
142 Dutch Leonard '16 Champs	.10	.03
143 Herb Pennock '16 Champs	.20	.06
144 Hal Janvrin '16 Champs	.05	.02
145 Babe Ruth '16 Champs	1.00	.30
146 Duffy Lewis '16 Champs	.10	.03
147 Larry Gardner '16 Champs	.05	.02
148 Doc Hoblitzel '16 Champs	.05	.02
149 Everett Scott '16 Champs	.10	.03
150 Carl Mays '16 Champs	.10	.03
151 Bert Niehoff '16LL	.05	.02
152 Burt Shotton '16LL	.10	.03
153 Red Ames '16LL	.05	.02
154 Cy Williams '16LL	.10	.03
155 Bill Hinchman '16LL	.05	.02
156 Bob Shawkey '16LL	.10	.03
157 Wally Pipp '16LL	.15	.04
158 George J. Burns '16LL	.05	.02
159 Bob Veach '16LL	.05	.02
160 Hal Chase '16LL	.10	.03
161 Tom Hughes '16LL	.05	.02
162 Del Pratt '16LL	.05	.02
163 Heinie Groh '16LL	.10	.03
164 Zack Wheat '16LL	.20	.06
165 Lefty O'Doul Story	.10	.03
166 Willie Kamm Story	.05	.02
167 Paul Waner Story	.20	.06
168 Fred Snodgrass Story	.05	.02
169 Babe Herman Story	.15	.04
170 Al Bridwell Story	.05	.02
171 Chief Meyers Story	.05	.02
172 Hans Lobert Story	.05	.02
173 Rube Bressler Story	.05	.02
174 Sad Sam Jones Story	.10	.03
175 Bob O'Farrell Story	.05	.02
176 Specs Toporcer Story	.05	.02
177 Earl McNeely Story	.05	.02
178 Jack Knott Story	.05	.02
179 Heinie Mueller	.05	.02
180 Tommy Bridges	.10	.03
181 Lloyd Brown	.05	.02
182 Larry Benton	.05	.02
183 Max Bishop	.05	.02
184 Moe Berg	.50	.15
185 Cy Perkins	.05	.02
186 Steve O'Neill	.05	.02
187 Glenn Myatt	.05	.02
188 Joe Kuhel	.05	.02
189 Marty McManus	.05	.02
190 Red Lucas	.05	.02
191 Stuffy McInnis	.05	.02
192 Bing Miller	.05	.02
193 Luke Sewell	.10	.03
194 Bill Sherdel	.05	.02
195 Hal Rhyne	.05	.02
196 Guy Bush	.05	.02
197 Pete Fox	.05	.02
198 Wes Ferrell	.15	.04
199 Roy Johnson	.05	.02
200 Bill Wambsganss Triple Play	.10	.03
201 George H. Burns Triple Play	.05	.02
202 Clarence Mitchell Triple Play	.05	.02
203 Neal Ball Triple Play	.05	.02
204 Johnny Neun Triple Play	.05	.02
205 Homer Summa Triple Play	.05	.02
206 Ernie Padgett Triple Play	.05	.02
207 Walter Holke Triple Play	.05	.02
208 Glenn Wright Triple Play	.05	.02
209 Hank Gowdy	.10	.03
210 Zack Taylor	.05	.02
211 Ben Cantwell	.05	.02
212 Frank Demaree	.05	.02
213 Paul Derringer	.10	.03
214 Bill Hallahan	.05	.02
215 Danny MacFayden	.05	.02
216 Harry Rice	.05	.02
217 Bob Smith	.05	.02
218 Riggs Stephenson	.15	.04
219 Pat Malone	.05	.02
220 Bennie Tate	.05	.02
221 Joe Vosmik	.05	.02
222 George Watkins	.05	.02
223 Jimmie Wilson	.05	.02
224 George Uhle	.05	.02
225 Mel Ott TRIV	.30	.09
226 Nick Altrock TRIV	.05	.02
227 Red Ruffing TRIV	.20	.06
228 Joe Krakauskas TRIV	.05	.02
229 Wally Berger TRIV	.10	.03
230 Bobo Newsom	.15	.04
231 Lon Warneke	.10	.03
232 Frank Snyder	.05	.02
233 Myril Hoag	.05	.02
234 Mel Almada	.05	.02
235 Ivey Wingo	.05	.02
236 Jimmy Austin	.05	.02
237 Zeke Bonura	.05	.02
238 Russ Wrightstone	.05	.02
239 Al Todd	.05	.02
240 Rabbit Warstler	.05	.02
241 Sammy West	.05	.02
242 Art Reinhart	.05	.02
243 Lefty Stewart	.05	.02
244 Johnny Gooch	.05	.02
245 Bubbles Hargrave	.05	.02
246 George Harper	.05	.02
247 Sarge Connally	.05	.02
248 Garland Braxton	.05	.02
249 Wally Schang	.10	.03
250 Ty Cobb ATL	.75	.23
251 Rogers Hornsby ATL	.35	.10
252 Rube Marquard ATL	.20	.06
253 Carl Hubbell ATL	.25	.07
254 Joe Wood ATL	.10	.03
255 Lefty Grove ATL	.30	.09
256 Schoolboy Rowe ATL	.10	.03
257 General Crowder ATL	.05	.02
258 Walter Johnson ATL	.40	.12
259 Chick Hafey ATL	.20	.06
260 Fred Fitzsimmons ATL	.10	.03
261 Earl Webb ATL	.10	.03
262 Earle Combs ATL	.20	.06
263 Ed Konetchy ATL	.05	.02
264 Taylor Douthit ATL	.05	.02
265 Lloyd Waner ATL	.20	.06
266 Mickey Cochrane ATL	.25	.07
267 Hack Wilson ATL	.25	.07
268 Pie Traynor ATL	.20	.06
269 Spud Davis ATL	.05	.02
270 Heinie Manush ATL	.20	.06
271 Pinky Higgins ATL	.05	.02
272 Addie Joss ATL	.20	.06
273 Ed Walsh ATL	.20	.06
274 Pepper Martin ATL	.15	.04
275 Joe Sewell ATL	.20	.06
276 Dutch Leonard ATL	.10	.03
277 Gavvy Cravath ATL	.10	.03
278 Oral Hildebrand	.05	.02
279 Ray Kremer	.05	.02
280 Frankie Pytlak	.05	.02
281 Sammy Byrd	.05	.02
282 Curt Davis	.05	.02
283 Lew Fonseca	.05	.02
284 Muddy Ruel	.05	.02
285 Moose Solters	.05	.02
286 Fred Schulte	.05	.02
287 Jack Quinn	.10	.03
288 Pinky Whitney	.05	.02
289 John Stone	.05	.02
290 Hughie Critz	.05	.02
291 Ira Flagstead	.05	.02
292 George Grantham	.05	.02
293 Sammy Hale	.05	.02
294 Shanty Hogan	.05	.02
295 Ossie Bluege	.05	.02
296 Debs Garms	.05	.02
297 Barney Friberg	.05	.02
298 Ed Brandt	.05	.02
299 Rollie Hemsley	.05	.02
300 Chuck Klein MVP	.20	.06
301 Mort Cooper MVP	.05	.02
302 Jim Bottomley MVP	.20	.06
303 Jimmie Foxx MVP	.35	.10
304 Fred Schulte MVP	.05	.02
305 Frank Frisch MVP	.20	.06
306 Frank McCormick MVP	.10	.03
307 Jake Daubert MVP	.10	.03
308 Roger Peckinpaugh MVP	.05	.02
309 George H. Burns MVP	.05	.02
310 Lou Gehrig MVP	.75	.23
311 Al Simmons MVP	.20	.06
312 Eddie Collins MVP	.20	.06
313 Gabby Hartnett MVP	.20	.06
314 Joe Cronin MVP	.20	.06
315 Paul Waner MVP	.20	.06
316 Bob O'Farrell MVP	.05	.02
317 Larry Doyle MVP	.10	.03
318 Lyn Lary	.05	.02
319 Jakie May	.05	.02
320 Roy Spencer	.05	.02

321 Dick Coffman .05 .02
322 Pete Donohue .05 .02
323 Mule Haas .05 .02
324 Doc Farrell .05 .02
325 Flint Rhem .05 .02
326 Firpo Marberry .05 .02
327 Charles Conlon .05 .02
328 Checklist 1-110 .05 .02
329 Checklist 111-220 .05 .02
330 Checklist 221-330 .05 .02

1991-92 Conlon TSN Prototypes

In conjunction with The Sporting News, Megacards issued various prototype cards to preview their soon to be released regular issue sets. All the cards were standard size. The 1991 Conlon prototypes from the first series were not marked as prototypes, and neither did they have the Major League Baseball logo and the Curtis Management logo on their backs. Their numbering was identical with the regular issue cards, with the exception of Dean (number 3 in the regular issue). The production run was reported to be very limited for these first series cards. The 1991 Conlon Color Babe Ruth prototype has the word "prototype" on its reverse. The 50,000 color Ruth prototype cards produced were distributed to collectors and dealers at the 12th National Sports Collectors Convention in Anaheim in July, 1991. Moreover, five prototypes for the second series (1992 Conlon Collection) were distributed at the same time. The production run was announced to be 20,000 for each card, with the exception of Joe Jackson (67,000). All these cards are marked "prototype" on their backs, and with the exception of the Mathewson card, also bear different card numbers from the regular issues. In general, some subtle differences in photos are found with some of the prototype cards. The second series prototypes show a 1992 copyright on the card back. The Cobb and Jackson cards have a computer color-enhanced photo with white and dark blue borders, while the other cards have black and white photos with white and black borders.

Nm-Mt Ex-Mt
COMPLETE SET (16) 60.00 18.00
13 Ty Cobb 8.00 2.40
Color (Card 250)
14 Joe Jackson 8.00 2.40
Color (Card 444 in regular set, prototype)
34 Dizzy Dean 8.00 2.40
111 Lou Gehrig 10.00 3.00
145 Babe Ruth (Color) DP 15.00 4.50
250 Ty Cobb 10.00 3.00
331 Christy Mathewson 3.00 .90
(Prototype on back)
400 Joe Jackson DP 5.00 1.50
(Prototype on back)
450 Hughie Jennings 1.50 .45
(Prototype on back)
500 Ty Cobb 5.00 1.50
(Prototype on back)
520 Goose Goslin 1.50 .45
(Prototype on back)
661 Bill Terry 2.50 .75
662 Lefty Gomez 2.50 .75
664 Frank Frisch 1.50 .45
710 Red Faber 1.50 .45
905 Lena Blackburne 1.00 .30

1992 Conlon TSN

This 330-card standard-size set is numbered in continuation of the previous year's issue and again features the photography of Charles Conlon. The fronts have either posed or action black and white player photos, enframed by a white line on a black card face. A caption in a diagonal stripe cuts across the upper right corner of the picture. The player's name, team, position, and year the photos were taken appear below the pictures in white lettering. The back has biography, statistics, and career summary. The cards are numbered on the back. Special subsets include No-Hitters (331-372), Two Sports (393-407), Great Stories (421-440), Why Not in Hall of Fame (441-450), Hall of Fame (459-474), 75 Years Ago Highlights (483-492), Triple Crown Winners (525-537), Everyday Heroes (538-550), Nicknames (551-566), Trivia (581-601), and St. Louis Cardinals 1892-1992 (618-657). The set was available in packs as well as in a factory set. Four special gold-border cards previewing the 1993 Conlon Sporting News set were available exclusively in the factory sets. Also randomly inserted in the wax packs were a limited number of personally autographed (but not certified) cards of Bobby Doerr, Bob Feller, Marty Marion, Johnny Mize, Enos Slaughter, and Johnny Vander Meer. These autographed cards range in value from 15.00 to 30.00.

Nm-Mt Ex-Mt
COMPLETE SET (330) 18.00 5.50
COMP.FACT SET (300)
331 Christy Mathewson .40 .12
332 Hooks Wiltse .05 .02
333 Nap Rucker .05 .02
334 Red Ames .05 .02
335 Chief Bender .20 .06
336 Joe Wood .10 .03
337 Ed Walsh .20 .06
338 George Mullin .05 .02
339 Earl Hamilton .05 .02
340 Jeff Tesreau .05 .02
341 Jim Scott .05 .02
342 Rube Marquard .20 .06
343 Claude Hendrix .05 .02
344 Jimmy Lavender .05 .02
345 Joe Bush .10 .03
346 Dutch Leonard .10 .03
347 Fred Toney .05 .02
348 Hippo Vaughn .05 .02
349 Ernie Koob .05 .02
350 Bob Groom .05 .02
351 Ernie Shore .10 .03
352 Hod Eller .05 .02
353 Walter Johnson .40 .12
354 Charles Robertson .05 .02
355 Jesse Barnes .05 .02
356 Sad Sam Jones .10 .03
357 Howard Ehmke .05 .02
358 Jesse Haines .20 .06
359 Ted Lyons .20 .06
360 Carl Hubbell .25 .07
361 Wes Ferrell .15 .04
362 Bobby Burke .05 .02
363 Daffy Dean .10 .03
364 Bobo Newsom .15 .04
365 Vern Kennedy .05 .02
366 Bill Dietrich .05 .02
367 Johnny VanderMeer .15 .04
368 Johnny VanderMeer .15 .04
369 Monte Pearson .05 .02
370 Bob Feller .30 .09
371 Lon Warneke .10 .03
372 Jim Tobin .05 .02
373 Earl Moore .05 .02
374 Bill Dineen .05 .02
375 Mal Eason .05 .02
376 George Mogridge .05 .02
377 Dazzy Vance .20 .06
378 Tex Carleton .05 .02
379 Clyde Shoun .05 .02
380 Frankie Hayes .05 .02
381 Benny Frey .05 .02
382 Hank Johnson .05 .02
383 Red Kress .05 .02
384 Johnny Allen .05 .02
385 Hal Trosky .10 .03
386 Gene Robertson .05 .02
387 Pep Young .05 .02
388 George Selkirk .10 .03
389 Ed Wells .05 .02
390 Jim Weaver .05 .02
391 George McQuinn .05 .02
392 Hans Lobert .05 .02
393 Evar Swanson .05 .02
394 Ernie Nevers .25 .07
395 Jim Levey .05 .02
396 Hugo Bezdek .05 .02
397 Walt French .05 .02
398 Charlie Berry .10 .03
399 Frank Grube .05 .02
400 Chuck Dressen .10 .03
401 Greasy Neale .10 .03
402 Ernie Vick .05 .02
403 Jim Thorpe 1.00 .30
404 Wally Gilbert .05 .02
405 Luke Urban .05 .02
406 Pid Purdy .05 .02
407 Ab Wright .05 .02
408 Billy Urbanski .05 .02
409 Carl Fischer .05 .02
410 Jack Warner .05 .02
411 Bill Cissell .05 .02
412 Merv Shea .05 .02
413 Dolf Luque .10 .03
414 Johnny Bassler .05 .02
415 Odell Hale .05 .02
416 Larry French .05 .02
417 Curt Walker .05 .02
418 Dusty Cooke .05 .02
419 Phil Todt .05 .02
420 Poison Andrews .05 .02
421 Billy Herman .20 .06
422 Tris Speaker .25 .07
423 Al Simmons .20 .06
424 Hack Wilson .25 .07
425 Ty Cobb .75 .23
426 Babe Ruth 1.00 .30
427 Ernie Lombardi .20 .06
428 Dizzy Dean .40 .12
429 Lloyd Waner .20 .06
430 Hank Greenberg .30 .09
431 Lefty Grove .30 .09
432 Mickey Cochrane .25 .07
433 Burleigh Grimes .20 .06
434 Pie Traynor .20 .06
435 Johnny Mize .25 .07
436 Sam Rice .20 .06
437 Goose Goslin .20 .06
438 Chuck Klein .20 .06
439 Connie Mack .25 .07
440 Jim Bottomley .20 .06
441 Riggs Stephenson .15 .04
442 Ken Williams .15 .04
443 Babe Adams .10 .03
444 Joe Jackson 1.00 .30
445 Hal Newhouser .20 .06
446 Wes Ferrell .15 .04
447 Lefty O'Doul .10 .03
448 Wally Schang .10 .03
449 Sherry Magee .05 .02
450 Mike Donlin .10 .03
451 Doc Cramer .10 .03
452 Dick Bartell .05 .02
453 Earle Mack .05 .02
454 Jumbo Brown .05 .02
455 Johnnie Heving .05 .02
456 Percy Jones .05 .02
457 Ted Blankenship .05 .02
458 Al Wingo .05 .02
459 Roger Bresnahan .20 .06
460 Bill Klem .25 .07
461 Charlie Gehringer .25 .07
462 Stan Coveleski .20 .06
463 Eddie Plank .20 .06
464 Clark Griffith .20 .06
465 Herb Pennock .20 .06
466 Earle Combs .20 .06
467 Bobby Doerr .20 .06
468 Waite Hoyt .20 .06
469 Tommy Connolly .20 .06
470 Harry Hooper .20 .06
471 Rick Ferrell .20 .06
472 Billy Evans .15 .04
473 Billy Herman .20 .06
474 Bill Dickey .25 .07
475 Luke Appling .20 .06
476 Babe Pinelli .10 .03
477 Eric McNair .05 .02
478 Sherriff Blake .05 .02
479 Val Picinich .05 .02
480 Fred Heimach .05 .02
481 Jack Graney .05 .02
482 Reb Russell .05 .02
483 Red Faber .20 .06
484 Benny Kauff .10 .03
485 Pants Rowland .05 .02
486 Bobby Veach .05 .02
487 Jim Bagby Sr. .05 .02
488 Pol Perritt .05 .02
489 Buck Herzog .05 .02
490 Art Fletcher .05 .02
491 Walter Holke .05 .02
492 Art Nehf .10 .03
493 Fresco Thompson .05 .02
494 Jimmy Welsh .05 .02
495 Ossie Vitt .05 .02
496 Ownie Carroll .05 .02
497 Ken O'Dea .05 .02
498 Fred Frankhouse .05 .02
499 Jewel Ens .05 .02
500 Morrie Arnovich .05 .02
501 Wally Gerber .05 .02
502 Kiddo Davis .05 .02
503 Buddy Myer .05 .02
504 Sam Leslie .05 .02
505 Cliff Bolton .05 .02
506 Dixie Walker .10 .03
507 Jack Smith .05 .02
508 Bump Hadley .05 .02
509 Buck Crouse .05 .02
510 Joe Glenn .05 .02
511 Chad Kimsey .05 .02
512 Lou Finney .05 .02
513 Roxie Lawson .05 .02
514 Chuck Fullis .05 .02
515 Earl Sheely .05 .02
516 George Gibson .05 .02
517 Johnny Broaca .05 .02
518 Bibb Falk .05 .02
519 Don Hurst .05 .02
520 Grover Hartley .05 .02
521 Don Heffner .05 .02
522 Harvey Hendrick .05 .02
523 Allen Sothoron .05 .02
524 Tony Piet .05 .02
525 Ty Cobb .75 .23
526 Jimmie Foxx .35 .10
527 Rogers Hornsby .35 .10
528 Nap Lajoie .35 .10
529 Lou Gehrig .75 .23
530 Heinie Zimmerman .10 .03
531 Chuck Klein .20 .06
532 Hugh Duffy .20 .06
533 Lefty Grove .30 .09
534 Grover C. Alexander .30 .09
535 Amos Rusie .20 .06
536 Lefty Gomez .25 .07
537 Bucky Walters .15 .04
538 Johnny Hodapp .05 .02
539 Bruce Campbell .05 .02
540 Hod Lisenbee .05 .02
541 Jack Fournier .05 .02
542 Jim Tabor .05 .02
543 Johnny Burnett .05 .02
544 Roy Hartzell .05 .02
545 Doc Gautreau .05 .02
546 Emil Yde .05 .02
547 Bob Johnson .10 .03
548 Joe Hauser .05 .02
549 Ed Reulbach .05 .02
550 Mel Almada .05 .02
551 Mickey Cochrane .25 .07
552 Carl Hubbell .25 .07
553 Charlie Gehringer .25 .07
554 Al Simmons .20 .06
555 Mordecai Brown .20 .06
556 Hugh Jennings .20 .06
557 Kid Elberfeld .05 .02
558 Casey Stengel .30 .09
559 Al Schacht
560 Jimmie Foxx .35 .10
561 George Kelly .20 .06
562 Lloyd Waner .20 .06
563 Paul Waner .20 .06
564 Walter Johnson .40 .12
565 Home Run Baker .20 .06
566 Roy Hughes .05 .02
567 Lew Riggs .05 .02
568 John Whitehead .05 .02
569 Elam Vangilder .05 .02
570 Billy Zitzmann .05 .02
571 Walter Schmidt .05 .02
572 Jackie Tavener .05 .02
573 Joe Genewich .05 .02
574 Johnny Marcum .05 .02
575 Fred Hoffmann .05 .02
576 Red Rolfe .10 .03
577 Vic Sorrell .05 .02
578 Pete Scott .05 .02
579 Tommy Thomas .05 .02
580 Al Smith .05 .02
581 Butch Henline .05 .02
582 Eddie Collins .20 .06
583 Earle Combs .20 .06
584 John McGraw .25 .07
585 Hack Wilson .25 .07
586 Gabby Hartnett .20 .06
587 Kiki Cuyler .20 .06
588 Bill Terry .25 .07
589 Joe McCarthy .20 .06
590 Hank Greenberg .30 .09
591 Tris Speaker .25 .07
592 Bill McKechnie .20 .06
593 Bucky Harris .20 .06
594 Herb Pennock .20 .06
595 George Sisler .20 .06
596 Fred Lindstrom .20 .06
597 Earl Averill .20 .06
598 Dave Bancroft .20 .06
599 Connie Mack .25 .07
600 Joe Cronin .20 .06
601 Ken Ash .05 .02
602 Al Spohrer .05 .02
603 Roy Mahaffey .05 .02
604 Frank O'Rourke .05 .02
605 Lil Stoner .05 .02
606 Frank Gabler .05 .02
607 Tom Padden .05 .02
608 Art Shires .05 .02
609 Sherry Smith .05 .02
610 Phil Weintraub .05 .02
611 Russ Van Atta .05 .02
612 Jo Jo White .05 .02
613 Cliff Melton .05 .02
614 Jimmy Ring .05 .02
615 Heinie Sand .05 .02
616 Dale Alexander .05 .02
617 Kent Greenfield .05 .02
618 Eddie Dyer .05 .02
619 Bill Sherdel .05 .02
620 Max Lanier .05 .02
621 Bob O'Farrell .05 .02
622 Rogers Hornsby .35 .10
623 Bill Beckman .05 .02
624 Mort Cooper .05 .02
625 Bill DeLancey .05 .02
626 Marty Marion .10 .03
627 Billy Southworth .05 .02
628 Johnny Mize .25 .07
629 Joe Medwick .20 .06
630 Grover C. Alexander .30 .09
631 Daffy Dean .10 .03
632 Hi Bell .05 .02
633 Walker Cooper .05 .02
634 Frank Frisch .20 .06
635 Dizzy Dean .40 .12
636 Don Gutteridge .05 .02
637 Pepper Martin .15 .04
638 Ed Konetchy .05 .02
639 Bill Hallahan .05 .02
640 Lon Warneke .10 .03
641 Terry Moore .10 .03
642 Enos Slaughter .20 .06
643 Heinie Mueller .05 .02
644 Specs Toporcer .05 .02
645 Jim Bottomley .20 .06
646 Ray Blades .05 .02
647 Jesse Haines .20 .06
648 Andy High .05 .02
649 Miller Huggins .20 .06
650 Ernie Orsatti .05 .02
651 Les Bell .05 .02
652 Gabby Street .05 .02
653 Wally Roettger .05 .02
654 Syl Johnson .05 .02
655 Mike Gonzalez .05 .02
656 Ripper Collins .05 .02
657 Chick Hafey .20 .06
658 Checklist 331-440 .05 .02
659 Checklist 441-550 .05 .02
660 Checklist 551-660 .05 .02

1992 Conlon TSN 13th National

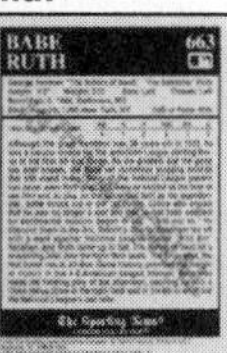

In conjunction with The Sporting News, Megacards issued various prototype cards during 1992 to preview their soon to be released regular issue sets. All the cards were standard size. These cards were given away as promotional items at the 13th National Sports Collectors Convention in Atlanta and therefore have "13th National" stamped on their backs.

Nm-Mt Ex-Mt
COMPLETE SET (4) 10.00 3.00
400 Joe Jackson DP 5.00 1.50
(13th National)
663 Babe Ruth (BW) 8.00 2.40
(13th National)
775 Chief Meyers 1.00 .30
(13th National)
800 Hippo Vaughn 1.00 .30
(13th National)

1992 Conlon TSN All-Star Program

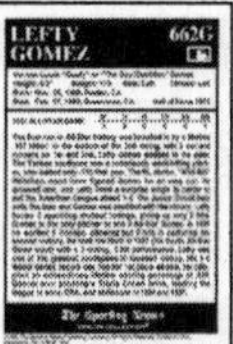

In 1992 several gold-foil edition black and white Conlon Collection cards were released to preview the 1993 Conlon Collection. Cards 661G-664G feature four players who played in the first All-Star Game in 1933. Reportedly 34,000 of each of these cards were produced exclusively for and inserted (one per program) in the 1992 All-Star Game program. These standard-size cards have the same design typical of other Conlon issues, only that the vintage black and white player photos are framed in gold foil.

Nm-Mt Ex-Mt
COMPLETE SET (4) 20.00 6.00
661G Bill Terry 5.00 1.50
662G Lefty Gomez 5.00 1.50
663G Babe Ruth 10.00 3.00
664G Frankie Frisch 3.00 .90

1992-93 Conlon TSN Color Inserts

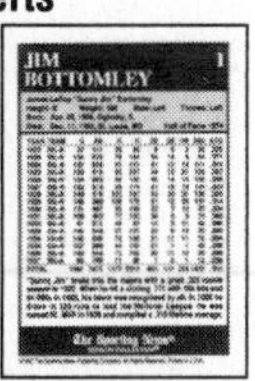

All the cards in this 22-card standard-size set were previously released in black and white in the 1991 or 1992 Conlon regular issue sets. Released on two different occasions, cards 1-6 and 7-12 were issued exclusively as a bonus to collectors who purchased Megacards' hobby accessory products (plastic sheets, card frames, and card sleeves) through retail outlets. The announced production figures for cards 1-6 were 250,000 of each card. For cards 7-12, the announced production run was 252,000 of each card. Cards 13-20 were randomly inserted in 1993 Conlon counter packs and blister packs, with an announced production run of 100,000 of each card. Cards 21-22 were available only through a special send-away offer on the backs of Conlon counter packs and blister packs; 75,000 of each card were produced. There were 60,000 cards of Bob Feller (23) produced exclusively for the Sports Collectors Digest 1993 Price Guide and bound inside copies of that book. The fronts display color player portraits inside a white picture frame on a navy blue card face. A diagonal graphic across the upper right corner of the picture gives the year the player was inducted into the Hall of Fame. The black and white backs are accented in navy blue and provide biography, career statistics, and career summary. The corresponding card number of the black and white regular issue card is given on the line after each player's name.

Nm-Mt Ex-Mt
COMPLETE SET (23) 50.00 15.00
COMMON CARD (1-6) 1.00 .30
COMMON CARD (7-12) 1.00 .30
COMMON CARD (13-20) 2.00 .60
COMMON CARD (21-22) 6.00 1.80
COMMON CARD (23) 5.00 1.50
1 Jim Bottomley 1.00 .30
Card 22
2 Lefty Grove 2.00 .60
Card 23
3 Lou Gehrig 4.00 1.20
Card 111
4 Babe Ruth 6.00 1.80
Card 145
5 Casey Stengel 2.00 .60
Card 37
6 Rube Marquard 1.00 .30
Card 252
7 Walter Johnson 2.00 .60
Card 353
8 Lou Gehrig 4.00 1.20
Card 310
9 Christy Mathewson 2.00 .60
Card 331
10 Ty Cobb 4.00 1.20
Card 250
11 Mel Ott 2.00 .60
Card 225
12 Carl Hubbell 1.00 .30
Card 253
13 Al Simmons 2.00 .60
Card 49
14 Connie Mack 3.00 .90
Card 47
15 Grover C. Alexander 3.00 .90
Card 32
16 Jimmie Foxx 3.00 .90
Card 303
17 Lloyd Waner 2.00 .60
Card 6
18 Tris Speaker 3.00 .90
Card 422
19 Dizzy Dean 4.00 1.20
Card 3
20 Rogers Hornsby 4.00 1.20
Card 1
21 Joe Jackson 6.00 1.80
Card 444
22 Jim Thorpe 6.00 1.80
Card 403
23 Bob Feller 5.00 1.50

1992-93 Conlon TSN Gold Inserts

Several gold-foil edition black and white Conlon Collection standard-size cards were released to preview the 1993 Conlon Collection. Card numbers 665, 770, 820, and 880 were included in 1992 Conlon factory sets; reportedly 90,000 of each card were produced. The factory set cases distributed through hobby dealers also included two additional cards (667 and 730) as a bonus (roughly a dozen of each per case), with a stated production run of 20,000 for each

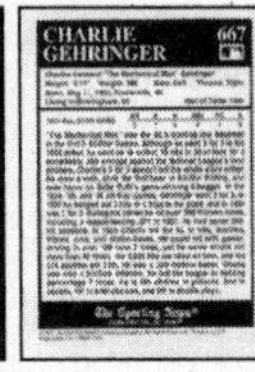

card. Card 1000G, of which 100,000 were produced, was inserted in the 65-card jumbo packs sold only at Toys 'R' Us. Likewise, 100,000 of card 934G were produced and inserted into packs sold only at Eckerd's Drugs. The cards have the same design typical of other Conlon issues, only that the vintage black and white player photos are framed in gold foil.

	Nm-Mt	Ex-Mt
COMPLETE SET (8)	12.00	3.60
665 Carl Hubbell	1.50	.45
667 Charlie Gehringer SP	2.50	.75
730 Luke Appling SP	2.50	.75
(Old Aches and Pains)		
770 Tommy Henrich	1.00	.30
820 John McGraw	2.00	.60
880 Gabby Hartnett	1.50	.45
934G Walter Johnson	5.00	1.50
and Nolan Ryan		
1000G Ty Cobb DP	3.00	.90

1993 Conlon Masters BW

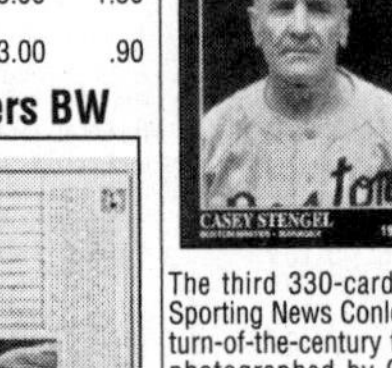

The 1993 Conlon Collection Master Series premier issue consists of nine cards subtitled "The Best There Was". The set production was limited to 25,000, and each set includes a certificate of authenticity with the serial number. The oversize cards measure approximately 8" by 10" and feature the photography of Charles Martin Conlon, the greatest sports photographer of his time. The Sporting News acquired Conlon's work in 1945, and from this archive, Megacards created the Master Series. With the exception of the Johnson and Gehrig card (3), the horizontal backs have a black-and-white close-up player shot on the left. Each set was accompanied by a certificate of authenticity that gave the set number out of a production run of 25,000. By returning the original certificate of authenticity along with 9.95, the collector received a protective portfolio to display the cards and a new deluxe certificate. The portfolio and the cards carried a suggested retail price of 29.95.

	Nm-Mt	Ex-Mt
COMPLETE SET (9)	18.00	5.50
1 The Best There Was	1.50	.45
1905 to 1942		
2 Babe Ruth	6.00	1.80
Outfield		
3 Walter Johnson	3.00	.90
Pitcher		
Lou Gehrig		
First base		
4 Honus Wagner	3.00	.90
Shortstop		
5 Mickey Cochrane	2.00	.60
Catcher		
6 Tris Speaker	2.00	.60
Outfield		
7 Ty Cobb	4.00	1.20
Outfield		
8 Rogers Hornsby	3.00	.90
2nd Base		
9 Pie Traynor	2.00	.60
3rd Base		

1993 Conlon Masters Color

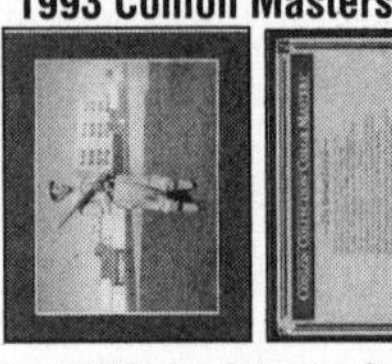

The 1993 Conlon Collection Color Master Series premier issue consists of nine cards. The set production was limited to 25,000, and each set includes a certificate of authenticity with the serial number. The oversize cards measure approximately 8" by 10" and feature the photography of Charles Martin Conlon, the greatest sports photographer of his time. The Sporting News acquired Conlon's work in 1945, and from this archive, Megacards created the Master Series. Using 1993 technology, one special card (3) features Nolan Ryan transported back in time to Yankee Stadium in 1927 in a fantasy conversation with Walter Johnson. Each set was accompanied by a certificate of authenticity that gave the set number out of a production run of 25,000. By returning the original certificate of authenticity along with 9.95, the collector received a protective portfolio to display the cards and a new deluxe certificate. The portfolio and the cards retailed for 29.95.

	Nm-Mt	Ex-Mt
COMPLETE SET (9)	18.00	5.50
1 Title Card	1.00	.30
2 Nap Lajoie	2.00	.60
3 Nolan Ryan	5.00	1.50
Walter Johnson		
4 Hilltop Park	1.00	.30
home of the Highlanders		
5 Babe Ruth	6.00	1.80
6 Frank Baker	2.00	.60
7 John McGraw MG	2.50	.75
8 John McGraw	2.00	.60
Wilbert Robinson		
Christy Mathewson		
9 Hughie Jennings MG	2.00	.60

1993 Conlon TSN Prototypes

These two cards are colorized prototypes, with same design as the regular 888 and 934 from the 1993 Conlon TSN set. The production run for each of these two cards was 52,000.

	Nm-Mt	Ex-Mt
COMPLETE SET	10.00	3.00
888 Babe Ruth	5.00	1.50
934 Walter Johnson	5.00	1.50
with Nolan Ryan		

1993 Conlon TSN

The third 330-card standard-size set of The Sporting News Conlon Collection again features turn-of-the-century to World War II-era players photographed by Charles Conlon, including more than 100 cards of Hall of Famers. Cards from a subset displaying computer color-enhanced photos were randomly inserted in the counter box packs and blister packs. The set contains several subsets continuing from last year's issue and some new subsets unique to this year's set: Game of the Century: 1933 All-Star Game (661-689), Spitballers (702-712), Accused Spitballers (717-725), Nicknames (730-741), Great Stories (751-770), Native Americans: American Indians who played big-league ball (771-777), League Leaders (795-798 and 801-805), Great Managers (817-848), Great Backstops (861-880), Against All Odds (881-894), Trivia (905-918), Nolan Ryan: compares eight Hall of Famers to Ryan (928-935), and First Cards: players for whom cards have never been done before (945-987). The set closes with checklist cards (988-990). The set was also available as a factory set in a special commemorative tin and in the form of three 110-card uncut sheets.

	Nm-Mt	Ex-Mt
COMPLETE SET (330)	18.00	5.50
COMP.FACT (330)	18.00	5.50
661 Bill Terry	.20	.06
662 Lefty Gomez	.20	.06
663 Babe Ruth	1.00	.30
664 Frank Frisch	.20	.06
665 Carl Hubbell	.20	.06
666 Al Simmons	.20	.06
667 Charlie Gehringer	.20	.06
668 Earl Averill	.20	.06
669 Lefty Grove	.30	.09
670 Pie Traynor	.20	.06
671 Chuck Klein	.20	.06
672 Paul Waner	.20	.06
673 Lou Gehrig	.75	.23
674 Rick Ferrell	.20	.06
675 Gabby Hartnett	.20	.06
676 Joe Cronin	.20	.06
677 Chick Hafey	.20	.06
678 Jimmy Dykes	.10	.03
679 Sammy West	.05	.02
680 Pepper Martin	.15	.04
681 Lefty O'Doul	.10	.03
682 General Crowder	.05	.02
683 Jimmie Wilson	.05	.02
684 Dick Bartell	.05	.02
685 Bill Hallahan	.05	.02
686 Wally Berger	.10	.03
687 Lon Warneke	.10	.03
688 Ben Chapman	.05	.02
689 Woody English	.05	.02
690 Jimmy Reese	.10	.03
691 Wattie Holm	.05	.02
692 Charlie Jamieson	.05	.02
693 Tom Zachary	.05	.02
694 Blondy Ryan	.05	.02
695 Sparky Adams	.05	.02
696 Bill Hunnefield	.05	.02
697 Lee Meadows	.05	.02
698 Tom Carey	.05	.02
699 Johnny Rawlings	.05	.02
700 Ken Holloway	.05	.02
701 Lance Richbourg	.05	.02
702 Ray Fisher	.05	.02
703 Ed Walsh	.20	.06
704 Dick Rudolph	.05	.02
705 Ray Caldwell	.05	.02
706 Burleigh Grimes	.20	.06
707 Stan Coveleski	.20	.06
708 George Hildebrand	.05	.02
709 Jack Quinn	.10	.03
710 Red Faber	.20	.06
711 Urban Shocker	.10	.03
712 Dutch Leonard	.10	.03
713 Lou Koupal	.05	.02
714 Jimmy Wasdell	.05	.02
715 Johnny Lindell	.05	.02
716 Don Padgett	.05	.02
717 Nelson Potter	.05	.02
718 Schoolboy Rowe	.10	.03
719 Dave Danforth	.05	.02
720 Claude Passeau	.05	.02
721 Harry Kelley	.05	.02
722 Johnny Allen	.05	.02
723 Tommy Bridges	.10	.03
724 Bill Lee	.05	.02
725 Fred Frankhouse	.05	.02
726 Johnny McCarthy	.05	.02
727 Rip Russell	.05	.02
728 Emory(Topper) Rigney	.05	.02
729 Howie Shanks	.05	.02
730 Luke Appling	.20	.06
731 Bill Byron UMP	.05	.02
732 Earle Combs	.20	.06
733 Hank Greenberg	.30	.09
734 Walter(Boom Boom)	.05	.02
Beck		
735 Sloppy Thurston	.05	.02
736 Hack Wilson	.20	.06
737 Bill McGowan UMP	.20	.06
738 Zeke Bonura	.10	.03
739 Tom Baker	.05	.02
740 Bill(Baby Doll)	.05	.02
Jacobson		
741 Kiki Cuyler	.20	.06
742 George Blaeholder	.05	.02
743 Dee Miles	.05	.02
744 Lee Handley	.05	.02
745 Shano Collins	.05	.02
746 Rosy Ryan	.05	.02
747 Aaron Ward	.05	.02
748 Monte Pearson	.05	.02
749 Jake Early	.05	.02
750 Bill Atwood	.05	.02
751 Mark Koenig	.10	.03
752 Buddy Hassett	.05	.02
753 Davy Jones	.05	.02
754 Honus Wagner	.40	.12
755 Bill Dickey	.20	.06
756 Max Butcher	.05	.02
757 Waite Hoyt	.20	.06
758 Walter Johnson	.40	.12
759 Howard Ehmke	.05	.02
760 Bobo Newsom	.15	.04
761 Tony Lazzeri	.20	.06
762 Tony Lazzeri	.20	.06
763 Spud Chandler	.10	.03
764 Kirby Higbe	.05	.02
765 Paul Richards	.10	.03
766 Rogers Hornsby	.35	.10
767 Joe Vosmik	.05	.02
768 Jesse Haines	.20	.06
769 Bucky Walters	.15	.04
770 Tommy Henrich	.15	.04
771 Jim Thorpe	1.00	.30
772 Euel Moore	.05	.02
773 Rudy York	.10	.03
774 Chief Bender	.20	.06
775 Chief Meyers	.05	.02
776 Bob Johnson	.10	.03
777 Roy Johnson	.05	.02
778 Dick Porter	.05	.02
779 Ethan Allen	.10	.03
780 Slim Sallee	.05	.02
781 Beau Bell	.05	.02
782 Jigger Statz	.05	.02
783 Dutch Henry	.05	.02
784 Larry Woodall	.05	.02
785 Phil Collins	.05	.02
786 Joe Sewell	.20	.06
787 Billy Herman	.20	.06
788 Rube Oldring	.05	.02
789 Bill Walker	.05	.02
790 Joe Schultz	.05	.02
791 Fred Maguire	.05	.02
792 Claude Willoughby	.05	.02
793 Alex Ferguson	.05	.02
794 Johnny Morrison	.05	.02
795 Tris Speaker	.20	.06
796 Ty Cobb	.75	.23
797 Max Carey	.20	.06
798 George Sisler	.20	.06
799 Charlie Hollocher	.05	.02
800 Hippo Vaughn	.05	.02
801 Sad Sam Jones	.10	.03
802 Harry Hooper	.20	.06
803 Gavvy Cravath	.10	.03
804 Walter Johnson	.20	.06
805 Jake Daubert	.10	.03
806 Clyde Milan	.10	.03
807 Hugh McQuillan	.05	.02
808 Fred Brickell	.05	.02
809 Joe Stripp	.05	.02
810 Johnny Hodapp	.05	.02
811 Johnny Vergez	.05	.02
812 Lonny Frey	.05	.02
813 Bill Regan	.05	.02
814 Babe Young	.05	.02
815 Charlie Robertson	.05	.02
816 Walt Judnich	.05	.02
817 Joe Tinker	.20	.06
818 Johnny Evers	.20	.06
819 Frank Chance	.20	.06
820 John McGraw	.20	.06
821 Charlie Grimm	.15	.04
822 Ted Lyons	.20	.06
823 Joe McCarthy MG	.20	.06
824 Connie Mack MG	.20	.06
825 George Gibson	.05	.02
826 Steve O'Neill	.05	.02
827 Tris Speaker	.20	.06
828 Bill Carrigan	.05	.02
829 Casey Stengel	.30	.09
830 Miller Huggins	.20	.06
831 Bill McKechnie MG	.20	.06
832 Chuck Dressen	.10	.03
833 Gabby Street	.05	.02
834 Mel Ott	.30	.09
835 Frank Frisch	.20	.06
836 George Sisler	.20	.06
837 Nap Lajoie	.35	.10
838 Ty Cobb	.75	.23
839 Billy Southworth MG	.05	.02
840 Clark Griffith	.20	.06
841 Bill Terry	.20	.06
842 Rogers Hornsby	.35	.10
843 Joe Cronin	.20	.06
844 Al Lopez	.20	.06
845 Bucky Harris MG	.20	.06
846 Wilbert Robinson MG	.20	.06
847 Hughie Jennings	.20	.06
848 Jimmie Dykes	.10	.03
849 Roy Cullenbine	.05	.02
850 Eddie Moore	.05	.02
851 Jack Rothrock	.05	.02
852 Bill Lamar	.05	.02
853 Monte Weaver	.05	.02
854 Ival Goodman	.05	.02
855 Hank Severeid	.05	.02
856 Fred Haney	.05	.02
857 Joe Shaute	.05	.02
858 Smead Jolley	.05	.02
859 Dib Williams	.05	.02
860 Benny Bengough	.10	.03
861 Rick Ferrell	.20	.06
862 Bob O'Farrell	.05	.02
863 Spud Davis	.05	.02
864 Frankie Hayes	.05	.02
865 Muddy Ruel	.05	.02
866 Mickey Cochrane	.25	.07
867 Johnny Kling	.05	.02
868 Ivey Wingo	.05	.02
869 Bill Dickey	.25	.07
870 Frank Snyder	.05	.02
871 Roger Bresnahan	.20	.06
872 Wally Schang	.10	.03
873 Al Lopez	.20	.06
874 Jimmie Wilson	.05	.02
875 Val Picinich	.05	.02
876 Steve O'Neill	.05	.02
877 Ernie Lombardi	.20	.06
878 Johnny Bassler	.05	.02
879 Ray Schalk	.20	.06
880 Gabby Hartnett	.20	.06
881 Bruce Campbell	.05	.02
882 Red Ruffing	.20	.06
883 Mordecai Brown	.20	.06
884 Jimmy Archer	.05	.02
885 Dave Keefe	.05	.02
886 Nate Andrews	.05	.02
887 Sam Rice	.20	.06
888 Babe Ruth	1.00	.30
889 Chick Hafey	.20	.06
890 Oscar Melillo	.05	.02
891 Joe Wood	.10	.03
892 Johnny Evers	.20	.06
893 Specs Toporcer	.05	.02
894 Myril Hoag	.05	.02
895 Bob Weiland	.05	.02
896 Joe Marty	.05	.02
897 Sherry Magee	.05	.02
898 Danny Taylor	.05	.02
899 Willie Kamm	.05	.02
900 Jimmy Sheckard	.05	.02
901 Syl Johnson	.05	.02
902 Steve Sundra	.05	.02
903 Doc Cramer	.10	.03
904 Hub Pruett	.05	.02
905 Lena Blackburne	.05	.02
906 Eppa Rixey	.20	.06
907 Goose Goslin	.20	.06
908 George Kelly	.20	.06
909 Jim Bottomley	.20	.06
910 Christy Mathewson	.40	.12
911 Tony Lazzeri	.20	.06
912 Johnny Mostil	.05	.02
913 Bobby Doerr	.20	.06
914 Rabbit Maranville	.20	.06
915 Harry Heilmann	.20	.06
916 Bobby Wallace	.20	.06
917 Jimmie Foxx	.35	.10
918 Johnny Mize	.20	.06
919 Jack Bentley	.05	.02
920 Al Schacht	.15	.04
921 Ed Coleman	.05	.02
922 Dode Paskert	.05	.02
923 Hod Ford	.05	.02
924 Randy Moore	.05	.02
925 Milt Shoffner	.05	.02
926 Dick Siebert	.05	.02
927 Tony Kaufmann	.05	.02
928 Dizzy Dean	1.00	.30
with Nolan Ryan		
929 Dazzy Vance	.60	.18
with Nolan Ryan		
930 Lefty Grove	.75	.23
with Nolan Ryan		
931 Rube Waddell	.75	.23
with Nolan Ryan		
932 Grover C. Alexander	.75	.23
with Nolan Ryan		
933 Bob Feller	.75	.23
with Nolan Ryan		
934 Walter Johnson	1.50	.45
with Nolan Ryan		
935 Ted Lyons	.75	.23
with Nolan Ryan		
936 Jim Bagby Jr.	.05	.02
937 Joe Sugden CO	.05	.02
938 Earl Grace	.05	.02
939 Jeff Heath	.05	.02
940 Ken Williams	.15	.04
941 Marv Owen	.05	.02
942 Roy Weatherly	.05	.02
943 Ed Morgan	.05	.02
944 Johnny Rizzo	.05	.02
945 Archie McKain	.05	.02
946 Bob Garbark	.05	.02
947 Bob Osborn	.05	.02
948 Johnny Podgajny	.05	.02
949 Joe Evans	.05	.02
950 Tony Rensa	.05	.02
951 John Humphries	.05	.02
952 Merritt(Sugar) Cain	.05	.02
953 Roy(Snipe) Hansen	.05	.02
954 Johnny Niggeling	.05	.02
955 Hal Wiltse	.05	.02
956 Alex Carrasquel	.10	.03
957 George Grant	.05	.02
958 Lefty Weinert	.05	.02
959 Erv Brame	.05	.02
960 Ray Harrell	.05	.02
961 Ed Linke	.05	.02
962 Sam Gibson	.05	.02
963 Johnny Watwood	.05	.02
964 Doc Prothro	.05	.02
965 Julio Bonetti	.05	.02
966 Lefty Mills	.05	.02
967 Chick Galloway	.05	.02
968 Hal Kelleher	.05	.02
969 Chief Hogsett	.05	.02
970 Ed Heusser	.05	.02
971 Ed Baecht	.05	.02
972 Jack Saltzgaver	.05	.02
973 Leroy Herrmann	.05	.02
974 Belve Bean	.05	.02
975 Harry(Socks) Seibold	.05	.02
976 Vic Keen	.05	.02
977 Bill Barrett	.05	.02
978 Pat McNulty	.05	.02
979 George Turbeville	.05	.02
980 Eddie Phillips	.05	.02
981 Garland Buckeye	.05	.02
982 Vic Frasier	.05	.02
983 Gordon Rhodes	.05	.02
984 Red Barnes	.05	.02
985 Jim Joe Edwards	.05	.02
986 Herschel Bennett	.05	.02
987 Carmen Hill	.05	.02
988 Checklist 661-770	.05	.02
989 Checklist 771-880	.05	.02
990 Checklist 881-990	.05	.02

1994 Conlon TSN Promos

Issued to herald the release of the 330-card 1994 Conlon The Sporting News set, these eight standard-size promos feature black-bordered and white-line-framed black-and-white player photos on their fronts. The player's name, team, position, and year appear in white lettering within the lower black margin. The white and black back carries the player's name, biography, statistics, and career highlights. The faint "For Promotional Use Only" disclaimer appears obliquely. The production run for card numbers 991, 1050, 1105, 1140, 1190, and 1230 was 26,000; for card numbers 1030 and 1170, production was reportedly 52,000.

	Nm-Mt	Ex-Mt
COMPLETE SET (8)	10.00	3.00
991 Pepper Martin	1.00	.30
1030 Joe Jackson DP	3.00	.90
1050 Pie Traynor	2.00	.60
1105 Carl Hubbell	2.00	.60
1140 Lefty Grove	2.00	.60
1170 Dizzy Dean and	2.00	.60
Daffy Dean DP		
1190 Bill Klem	1.50	.45
1230 Mark Koenig	1.00	.30

1994 Conlon TSN

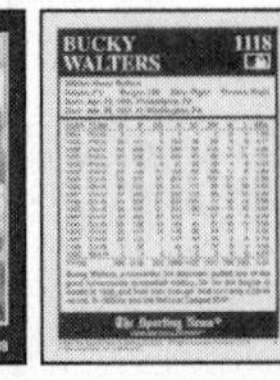

This fourth 330-card standard-size set of The Sporting News Conlon Collection again features the work of noted sports photographer Charles Conlon. The fronts feature black-and-white vintage player photos inside a white frame on a black card face. Subset cards are marked by their title in a black diagonal that cuts across the top right corner. The backs carry biography, statistics, and extended career summary and highlights. Topical subsets featured are Great Stories (991-1007), Hall of Fame (1008-1018), Black Sox Scandal (1019-1042), Nicknames (1050-1066), 1934 All-Star Game (1075-1113), In Memoriam (1121-1128), 1929 Athletics (1135-1159), Double Play Combo (1164-1166), Brothers (1169-1180), Umpires (1185-1212), All-Time Leaders (1217-1223), Switch-Hitters (1229-1237), Trivia (1247-1257), Action (1266-1274), First Card (1282-1317), and Checklists (1318-1320). The cards are numbered on the back in continuation of the previous year's issue. Card 1000 is the famous photo of Ty Cobb sliding. The 1994 Conlon set was issued in 12-card foil packs instead of the 15-card foil packs used in previous years. Reportedly 10,000 gold-bordered burgundy cards were produced for every card in the set. Each foil pack contained one of these cards while two were inserted in each blister pack. According to Megacards, no more than 200,000 of each card were produced. The set was also available in factory set form.

	Nm-Mt	Ex-Mt
COMPLETE SET (330)	18.00	5.50
COMPLETE FACT.SET (330)	18.00	5.50
991 Pepper Martin	.15	.04
992 Joe Sewell	.20	.06
993 Edd Roush	.20	.06
994 Rick Ferrell	.20	.06
995 Johnny Broaca	.05	.02
996 Luke Sewell	.10	.03
997 Burleigh Grimes	.20	.06
998 Hack Wilson	.20	.06
999 Lefty Grove	.30	.09
1000 Ty Cobb	.75	.23
1001 John McGraw	.20	.06
1002 Eddie Plank	.20	.06
1003 Sad Sam Jones	.10	.03
1004 Jim Bottomley	.20	.06
1005 Hank Greenberg	.30	.09
1006 Lloyd Waner	.20	.06
1007 Wilcy Moore	.05	.02
1008 Luke Appling	.20	.06
1009 Hal Newhouser	.20	.06
1010 Al Lopez	.20	.06
1011 Ty Cobb	.75	.23
1012 Kid Nichols	.20	.06
1013 Ed Walsh	.20	.06
1014 Hugh Duffy	.20	.06
1015 Rube Marquard	.20	.06
1016 Addie Joss	.20	.06
1017 Bobby Wallace	.20	.06
1018 Willie Keeler	.20	.06
1019 Jake Daubert	.10	.03
1020 Slim Sallee	.05	.02
1021 Dolf Luque	.10	.03
1022 Ivey Wingo	.05	.02
1023 Edd Roush	.20	.06
1024 Bill Rariden	.05	.02
1025 Sherry Magee	.05	.02
1026 Pat Duncan	.05	.02

1027 Hod Eller .05 .02
1028 Greasy Neale .10 .03
1029 Buck Weaver .20 .06
1030 Joe Jackson 1.00 .30
1031 Chick Gandil .20 .06
1032 Swede Risberg .20 .06
1033 Ray Schalk .20 .06
1034 Eddie Cicotte .15 .04
1035 Bill James .05 .02
1036 Nemo Leibold .05 .02
1037 Dickie Kerr .15 .04
1038 Kid Gleason MG .10 .03
1039 Fred McMullin .05 .02
1040 Eddie Collins .20 .06
1041 Sox Pitchers .15 .04
Lefty Williams
Bill James
Ed Cicotte
Dickie Kerr
1042 Sox Outfielders .20 .06
Nemo Leibold
Happy Felsch
Shano Collins
Joe Jackson
1043 Ken Keltner .10 .03
1044 Charlie Berry .10 .03
1045 Rube Lutzke .05 .02
1046 Johnny Schulte .05 .02
1047 Johnny Welch .05 .02
1048 Jack Russell .05 .02
1049 Red Murray .05 .02
1050 Pie Traynor .20 .06
1051 Mike Donlin .10 .03
1052 Gabby Hartnett .20 .06
1053 Tony Lazzeri .20 .06
1054 Hack Miller .05 .02
1055 Dazzy Vance .20 .06
1056 Bill Carrigan .05 .02
1057 Johnny Murphy .10 .03
1058 Cliff Heathcote .05 .02
1059 Joe Dugan .10 .03
1060 Rabbit Maranville .20 .06
1061 Tommy Henrich .15 .04
1062 Roy Parmelee .05 .02
1063 Lefty Gomez .20 .06
1064 Ernie Lombardi .20 .06
1065 Dave Bancroft .20 .06
1066 Bill McKechnie MG .20 .06
1067 Buddy Hassett .05 .02
1068 Spud Chandler .10 .03
1069 Roy Hughes .05 .02
1070 Hooks Dauss .05 .02
1071 Joe Hauser .05 .02
1072 Spud Davis .05 .02
1073 Max Butcher .05 .02
1074 Lou Chiozza .05 .02
1075 Polo Grounds .05 .02
1934 All-Star Game
1076 Charlie Gehringer .20 .06
1077 Heinie Manush .20 .06
1078 Red Ruffing .20 .06
1079 Mel Harder .10 .03
1080 Babe Ruth 1.00 .30
1081 Ben Chapman .05 .02
1082 Lou Gehrig .75 .23
1083 Jimmie Foxx .35 .10
1084 Al Simmons .20 .06
1085 Joe Cronin .20 .06
1086 Bill Dickey .20 .06
1087 Mickey Cochrane .20 .06
1088 Lefty Gomez .20 .06
1089 Earl Averill Sr. .20 .06
1090 Sammy West .05 .02
1091 Frank Frisch P/MG .20 .06
1092 Billy Herman .20 .06
1093 Pie Traynor .20 .06
1094 Joe Medwick .20 .06
1095 Chuck Klein .20 .06
1096 Kiki Cuyler .20 .06
1097 Mel Ott .30 .09
1098 Wally Berger .10 .03
1099 Paul Waner .20 .06
1100 Bill Terry .20 .06
1101 Travis Jackson .20 .06
1102 Arky Vaughan .20 .06
1103 Gabby Hartnett .20 .06
1104 Al Lopez .20 .06
1105 Carl Hubbell .20 .06
1106 Lon Warneke .10 .03
1107 Van Lingle Mungo .10 .03
1108 Pepper Martin .15 .04
1109 Dizzy Dean .40 .12
1110 Fred Frankhouse .05 .02
1111 Bob Quinn .05 .02
J.G. Taylor Spink
Mrs. J.G. Taylor Spink
1112 Joseph Gilleaudeau .05 .02
Mrs. Joseph Gilleaudeau
Mrs. J.G. Taylor Spink
J.G. Taylor Spink
Mrs. John Heydler
John Heydler
1113 Bill Hinchman .05 .02
Edward Keller
1114 Vic Aldridge .05 .02
1115 Pinky Higgins .05 .02
1116 Hal Carlson .05 .02
1117 Fred Fitzsimmons .10 .03
1118 Bucky Walters .15 .04
1119 Nick Altrock .05 .02
1120 Chuck Dressen .10 .03
1121 Mark Koenig .10 .03
1122 Charlie Gehringer .20 .06
1123 Vern Kennedy .05 .02
1124 Harlond Clift .05 .02
1125 Babe Phelps .05 .02
1126 Johnny Mize .20 .06
1127 Hal Schumacher .10 .03
1128 Ethan Allen .10 .03
1129 Bill Wambsganss .05 .02
1130 Freddy Leach .05 .02
1131 Bud Clancy .05 .02
1132 Stuffy Stewart .05 .02
1133 Bill Brubaker .05 .02
1134 Les Mann .05 .02
1135 Howard Ehmke .05 .02
1136 Al Simmons .20 .06
1137 George Earnshaw .10 .03
1138 Mule Haas .05 .02
1139 Bing Miller .05 .02
1140 Lefty Grove .30 .09
1141 Joe Boley .05 .02
1142 Eddie Collins .20 .06
1143 Walter French .05 .02
1144 Eric McNair .05 .02
1145 Bill Shores .05 .02
1146 Mickey Cochrane .20 .06
1147 Homer Summa .05 .02
1148 Jack Quinn .10 .03
1149 Max Bishop .05 .02
1150 Jimmy Dykes .10 .03
1151 Rube Walberg .05 .02
1152 Jimmie Foxx .35 .10
1153 George H. Burns .05 .02
1154 Doc Cramer .10 .03
1155 Sammy Hale .05 .02
1156 Eddie Rommel .05 .02
1157 Cy Perkins .05 .02
1158 Jim Cronin .05 .02
1159 Connie Mack MG .20 .06
1160 Ray Kolp .05 .02
1161 Clyde Manion .05 .02
1162 Frank Grube .05 .02
1163 Steve Swetonic .05 .02
1164 Joe Tinker .20 .06
1165 Johnny Evers .20 .06
1166 Frank Chance .20 .06
1167 Emerson Dickman .05 .02
1168 Jack Tobin .05 .02
1169 Wes Ferrell .15 .04
Rick Ferrell
1170 Dizzy Dean .20 .06
Daffy Dean
1171 Tony Cuccinello .05 .02
Al Cuccinello
1172 Harry Coveleski .10 .03
Stan Coveleski
1173 Bob Johnson .05 .02
Roy Johnson
1174 Andy High .05 .02
Hugh High
1175 Luke Sewell .15 .04
Joe Sewell
1176 Johnnie Heving .05 .02
Joe Heving
1177 Al Wingo .05 .02
Ivy Wingo
1178 Red Killefer .05 .02
Bill Killefer
1179 Bubbles Hargrave .05 .02
Pinky Hargrave
1180 Paul Waner .15 .04
Lloyd Waner
1181 Johnny VanderMeer .15 .04
1182 Jo Jo Moore .05 .02
1183 Bobby Burke .05 .02
1184 Johnny Moore .05 .02
1185 Jack Egan UMP .05 .02
1186 Tommy Connolly UMP .20 .06
1187 Silk O'Loughlin UMP .20 .06
1188 Beans Reardon UMP .10 .03
1189 Charles Moran UMP .05 .02
1190 Bill Klem UMP .20 .06
1191 Dolly Stark UMP .10 .03
1192 Albert Orth UMP .05 .02
1193 Kitty Bransfield UMP .05 .02
1194 Roy Van Graflan UMP .05 .02
1195 Bob Hart UMP .05 .02
1196 Jocko Conlan UMP .20 .06
1197 Babe Pinelli UMP .10 .03
1198 John Sheridan UMP .05 .02
1199 Dick Nallin UMP .05 .02
1200 Bill Dineen UMP .05 .02
1201 Hank O'Day UMP .10 .03
1202 Cy Rigler UMP .05 .02
1203 Bob Emslie UMP .05 .02
1204 Charles Pfirman UMP .05 .02
1205 Harry Geisel UMP .05 .02
1206 Ernest Quigley UMP .05 .02
1207 Red Ormsby UMP .05 .02
1208 George Hildebrand UMP .05 .02
1209 George Moriarty UMP .10 .03
1210 Billy Evans UMP .15 .04
1211 Brick Owens UMP .05 .02
1212 Bill McGowan UMP .20 .06
1213 Kirby Higbe .05 .02
1214 Taylor Douthit .05 .02
1215 Del Baker .05 .02
1216 Al Demaree .05 .02
1217 Connie Mack MG .20 .06
1218 Nap Lajoie .35 .10
1219 Honus Wagner .40 .12
1220 Christy Mathewson .40 .12
1221 Sam Crawford .20 .06
1222 Tris Speaker .20 .06
1223 Grover C. Alexander .30 .09
1224 Joe Bowman .05 .02
1225 Johnny Rigney .05 .02
1226 Earl Webb .10 .03
1227 Whitey Moore .05 .02
1228 Bruce Campbell .05 .02
1229 Lu Blue .05 .02
1230 Mark Koenig .10 .03
1231 Wally Schang .10 .03
1232 Max Carey .20 .06
1233 Frank Frisch .20 .06
1234 Donie Bush .05 .02
1235 George Davis .05 .02
1236 Billy Rogell .05 .02
1237 Ripper Collins .05 .02
1238 Dick Burrus .05 .02
1239 Evar Swanson .05 .02
1240 Woody English .05 .02
1241 Joe Harris .05 .02
1242 Harry McCurdy .05 .02
1243 Dick Bartell .05 .02
1244 Tommy Thompson .05 .02
1245 Babe Adams .10 .03
1246 Art Nehf .10 .03
1247 Jack Graney .05 .02
1248 Ted Lyons .20 .06
1249 Lou Gehrig .75 .23
1250 Mickey Welch .20 .06
1251 Red Faber .20 .06
1252 Joe McGinnity .20 .06
1253 Rogers Hornsby .35 .10
1254 Mel Ott .30 .09
1255 Walter Johnson .40 .12
1256 Sam Rice .20 .06
1257 Jim Tobin .05 .02
1258 Roger Peckinpaugh .10 .03
1259 George Stovall .05 .02
1260 Fred Merkle .10 .03
1261 Rip Collins .05 .02
1262 Carl Lind .05 .02
1263 Nap Rucker .05 .02
1264 Sloppy Thurston .05 .02
1265 Alex Metzler .05 .02
1266 Charles Conlon .05 .02
1267 Lew McCarty IA .05 .02
Sherry Magee
1268 B.A. Daniels IA .05 .02
1269 Benny Kauff IA .10 .03
1270 Heinie Groh IA .10 .03
1271 Fritz Mollwitz IA .05 .02
1272 George H. Burns IA .05 .02
1273 Lee Magee IA .05 .02
1274 Bill Killefer IA .05 .02
1275 Jack Warhop .05 .02
1276 Dutch Leonard .10 .03
1277 General Crowder .05 .02
1278 Chet Laabs .05 .02
1279 Joe Bush .10 .03
1280 Rube Bressler .05 .02
1281 Bob Brown .05 .02
1282 Bernie DeViveiros .05 .02
1283 Les Tietje .05 .02
1284 Charlie Devens .05 .02
1285 Elliott Bigelow .05 .02
1286 Johnny Dickshot .05 .02
1287 Buster Chatham .05 .02
1288 Walter Beall .05 .02
1289 Dick Attreau .05 .02
1290 Bunny Brief .05 .02
1291 Jim Gleeson .05 .02
1292 Wally Shaner .05 .02
1293 Pat Crawford .05 .02
1294 Manny Salvo .05 .02
1295 Cal Dorsett .05 .02
1296 Rusty Peters .05 .02
1297 Johnny Couch .05 .02
1298 Dutch Ulrich .05 .02
1299 Jim Bivin .05 .02
1300 Paul Strand .05 .02
1301 Johnny Lanning .05 .02
1302 Bill Brenzel .05 .02
1303 Don Songer .05 .02
1304 Dutch Levsen .05 .02
1305 Otto Bluege .05 .02
1306 Fabian Gaffke .05 .02
1307 Flash Archdeacon .05 .02
1308 Tiny Chaplin .05 .02
1309 Larry Rosenthal .05 .02
1310 Bill Bagwell .05 .02
1311 Joe Dawson .05 .02
1312 Johnny Sturm .05 .02
1313 Haskell Billings .05 .02
1314 Whitey Wilshere .05 .02
1315 Asby Asbjornson .05 .02
1316 Hank Steinbacher .05 .02
1317 Stan Baumgartner .05 .02
1318 Checklist 991-1100 .05 .02
1319 Checklist 1101-1210 .05 .02
1320 Checklist 1211-1320 .05 .02

1994 Conlon TSN Burgundy

This set is a parallel to the regular 1994 Conlon issue. Instead of the black and white borders, the borders had a burgundy color. One of these cards were inserted in each 1994 Conlon pack.

Nm-Mt Ex-Mt
*STARS: 2X TO 4X BASIC CARDS

1994 Conlon TSN Color Inserts

All the cards in this 16-card standard-size set were previously released in black and white in the Conlon regular issue sets. The cards are numbered on the back. The corresponding card number of the black and white regular issue card is given on the line after each player's name. Insert cards 24-39 were issued in 1994. Of these, cards 29-30 were available through a send-away offer, while cards 31-33 were inserted exclusively in hobby foil packs. The production figures for cards 24-39 were as follows: 84,000 for card numbers 24-28; 12,000 for card numbers 29-33; 48,000 for card numbers 34-37; and 12,000 for card numbers 38-39. Cards 34-37 were only available with accessory items purchased at Toys'R'Us. Cards 38-39 were available through special offers to be announced. Finally, 24,000 more of card number 28 were printed and have "Conlon Collection Day, Sept. 11, 1994" printed diagonally across their backs. These cards are specially numbered "28CCD" and were to be given out at a Cardinals game against the Dodgers in St. Louis.

Nm-Mt Ex-Mt
COMPLETE SET (16) 40.00 12.00
COMMON CARD (24-28) 1.50 .45
COMMON CARD (29-33) 2.00 .60
COMMON CARD (34-37) 1.50 .45
COMMON CARD (38-39) 3.00 .90
24 Hal Newhouser 2.00 .60
Card 445
25 Hugh Jennings 1.50 .45
Card 556
26 Red Faber 1.50 .45
27 Enos Slaughter 2.00 .60
Card 710
28 Johnny Mize 2.00 .60
Card 56
29 Pie Traynor 3.00 .90
Card 628
30 Walter Johnson 6.00 1.80
Nolan Ryan
Card 268
31 Lou Gehrig 6.00 1.80
Card 529
32 Benny Bengough 2.00 .60
Card 860
33 Babe Ruth 8.00 2.40
Card 888
34 Charlie Gehringer 2.00 .60
Card 667
35 Babe Ruth 8.00 2.40
Card 426
36 Bill Dickey 2.50 .75
Card 869
37 Three Finger Brown 1.50 .45
Card 883
38 Ray Schalk 3.00 .90
Card 48
39 Homerun Baker 4.00 1.20
Card 565

1995 Conlon TSN Prototypes

These 10 standard-size prototype cards were issued by Megacards to preview the design of the 1995 Conlon Collection. The card numbers correspond to the same numbers used in the regular set.

Nm-Mt Ex-Mt
COMPLETE SET (10) 20.00 6.00
3C Babe Ruth 5.00 1.50
100th Anniversary
1337 Bob Feller 3.00 .90
1357 Tris Speaker 2.00 .60
1397 Charles Comisky OWN 2.00 .60
1404 Gabby Hartnett 2.00 .60
1421 Lou Gehrig 4.00 1.20
1425 Lou Boudreau 2.00 .60
1464 Ray Chapman 1.00 .30
1475 Bill Dickey 2.00 .60
1500 Rabbit Maranville 1.50 .45
1535 Babe Ruth 5.00 1.50

1995 Conlon TSN

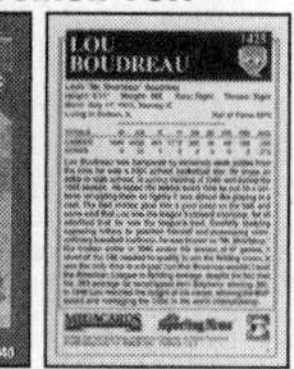

The 1995 Conlon Collection set consists of 110 standard-size cards. This continuation of the Conlon Collection set was supposed to be released in two 110-card series (February and August respectively), but the second series (nor any sets after that) was never released because of the baseball strike. This was the first year that the Conlon Collection did not consist of 330 cards. The set continues to feature the work of noted sports photographer Charles Conlon. No more than 50,000 sets were printed, with a suggested retail price of $19.95 per series. As a special tribute to Conlon and the 100th Anniversary of Babe Ruth's birth, Megacards teamed with Topps to produce a 100th Birthday Card. The card was issued in two forms: a sepia-tone version for 1995 Topps regular series (number 3) and an color-enhanced version (number 3C) inserted in each 1995 Conlon complete set. On the fronts, each black-and-white photo has a gold foil inner border and a forest green outer border. Topical subsets featured are Veterans of World War I and II (1321-1350), '75 Champs (1354-1367), Great Stories (1371-1378), Nicknames (1382-1390), Behind the Scenes (1394-1400), Great Games (1404-1412), and Beating the Odds (1416-1429). Also groups of three "Generic" cards are scattered throughout the set (1351-1352, 1368-1370, 1379-1381, 1391-1393, 1401-1403, 1413-1415).

Nm-Mt Ex-Mt
COMPLETE FACT. SET (110) 50.00 15.00
1321 Grover C. Alexander 1.25 .35
1322 Christy Mathewson 1.25 .35
1323 Eddie Grant .25 .07
1324 Gabby Street .25 .07
1325 Hank Gowdy .25 .07
1326 Jack Bentley .25 .07
1327 Eppa Rixey .75 .23
1328 Bob Shawkey .50 .15
1329 Rabbit Maranville .75 .23
1330 Casey Stengel 1.25 .35
1331 Herb Pennock .75 .23
1332 Eddie Collins Sr. .75 .23
1333 Buddy Hassett .25 .07
1334 Andy Cohen .25 .07
1335 Hank Greenberg 1.25 .35
1336 Andy High .25 .07
1337 Bob Feller 1.25 .35
1338 George Earnshaw .50 .15
1339 Jack Knott .25 .07
1340 Larry French .25 .07
1341 Skippy Roberge .25 .07
1342 Boze Berger .25 .07
1343 Bill Posedel .25 .07
1344 Kirby Higbe .25 .07
1345 Bob Neighbors .25 .07
1346 Hugh Mulcahy .25 .07
1347 Harry Walker .25 .07
1348 Buddy Lewis .25 .07
1349 Cecil Travis .25 .07
1350 Moe Berg 2.50 .75
1351 Nixey Callahan .25 .07
1352 Heinie Peitz .25 .07
1353 Doc White .25 .07
1354 Joe Wood .75 .23
1355 Larry Gardner .25 .07
1356 Steve O'Neill .25 .07
1357 Tris Speaker 1.25 .35
1358 Bill Wambsganss .25 .07
1359 George H. Burns .25 .07
1360 Charlie Jamieson .25 .07
1361 Les Nunamaker .25 .07
1362 Stan Coveleski .75 .23
1363 Joe Sewell .75 .23
1364 Jim Bagby Sr. .25 .07
1365 Duster Mails .25 .07
1366 Jack Graney .25 .07
1367 Elmer Smith .25 .07
1368 Tommy Leach .25 .07
1369 Russ Ford .25 .07
1370 Harry M. Wolter .25 .07
1371 Dazzy Vance .75 .23
1372 Germany Schaefer .50 .15
1373 Elbie Fletcher .25 .07
1374 Clark Griffith .75 .23
1375 Al Simmons .75 .23
1376 Billy Jurges .25 .07
1377 Earl Averill Sr. .75 .23
1378 Bill Klem .75 .23
1379 Armando Marsans .25 .07
1380 Mike Gonzalez .25 .07
1381 Jack Fournier .25 .07
1382 Burleigh Grimes .75 .23
1383 Arlie Latham .25 .07
1384 Ray Schalk .75 .23
1385 Goose Goslin .75 .23
1386 Joe Hauser .25 .07
1387 Dixie Walker .50 .15
1388 Jesse Burkett .25 .07
1389 Cliff Melton .25 .07
1390 Gee Walker .25 .07
1391 Tony Cuccinello .25 .07
1392 Vern Kennedy .25 .07
1393 Tuck Stainback .25 .07
1394 Ed Barrow .50 .15
1395 Ford C. Frick .50 .15
1396 Ban Johnson .50 .15
August Herrmann
1397 Charles Comiskey .50 .15
1398 Jacob Ruppert .50 .15
Joe McCarthy
1399 Branch Rickey .75 .23
1400 Jack Kieran .75 .23
Moe Berg
1401 Mike Ryba .25 .07
1402 Stan Spence .25 .07
1403 Red Barrett .25 .07
1404 Gabby Hartnett .75 .23
1405 Babe Ruth 5.00 1.50
1406 Fred Merkle .50 .15
1407 Claude Passeau .25 .07
1408 Joe Wood .75 .23
1409 Cliff Heathcote .25 .07
1410 Walt Cruise .25 .07
1411 Cookie Lavagetto .25 .07
1412 Tony Lazzeri .75 .23
1413 Atley Donald .25 .07
1414 Ken Raffensberger .25 .07
1415 Dizzy Trout .25 .07
1416 Augie Galan .25 .07
1417 Monty Stratton .25 .07
1418 Claude Passeau .25 .07
1419 Oscar Grimes .25 .07
1420 Rollie Hemsley .25 .07
1421 Lou Gehrig 4.00 1.20
1422 Tom Sunkel .25 .07
1423 Tris Speaker .75 .23
1424 Chick Fewster .25 .07
1425 Lou Boudreau .75 .23
1426 Hank Leiber .25 .07
1427 Eddie Mayo .25 .07
1428 Charley Gelbert .25 .07
1429 Jackie Hayes .25 .07
1430 Checklist .25 .07
NNO Babe Ruth 5.00 1.50
100th Birthday

1995 Conlon TSN Griffey Jr.

Titled "In the Zone," this eight-card standard-size set commemorates legends of the game from different eras by comparing Ken Griffey, Jr. to eight players from the Conlon era. No more than 50,000 sets were printed. Six cards were in each 110-card clamshell package, three were inserted in the 55-card clamshell, and there is one per 22-card clamshell. The other two cards were available through a mail-in offer. The fronts feature a color action cut-out of Ken Griffey superimposed over a color photo of the player mentioned on the card. Both players' names, along with the set logo, also appear on the fronts. On a ghosted color action Ken Griffey photo, the backs carry a small, black-and-white photo of the past player, along with a description of how those two players are alike.

Nm-Mt Ex-Mt
COMPLETE SET (8) 12.50 3.70
1 Ken Griffey Jr. 2.50 .75
Babe Ruth
2 Ken Griffey Jr. 2.50 .75
Lou Gehrig
3 Ken Griffey Jr. 2.00 .60
Ty Cobb
4 Ken Griffey Jr. 1.50 .45
Jimmie Foxx
5 Ken Griffey Jr. 1.50 .45
Mel Ott
6 Ken Griffey Jr. 2.50 .75
Shoeless Joe Jackson
7 Ken Griffey Jr. 1.50 .45
Tris Speaker
8 Ken Griffey Jr. 1.00 .30
Jim(Sunny) Bottomley

1995 Conlon TSN Club Members Promos

Issued to herald the release of the 1995 Conlon series, these two standard-size promos feature black-bordered and white-line-framed black-and-white player photos on their fronts. The player's name, team, position, and year appear in white lettering within the lower black margin. The white and black back carries the player's name, biography, statistics, and career highlights. The faint "Club Members Promo" disclaimer is printed diagonally across the back.

	Nm-Mt	Ex-Mt
COMPLETE SET (2)	5.00	1.50
1387 Rabbit Maranville	2.00	.60
1435 Bob Feller	3.00	.90

1939 Coombs Mobil Booklets

This six-booklet set features tips by Jack Coombs, one of the greatest of all pitchers, on how the stars play the national game. Each pamphlet consists of eight fold-out pages and displays black-and-white photos of players demonstrating the instructions written by Jack Coombs on the various aspects of playing the game. When all six pamphlets were collected, the coupons on the back page of each were to be mailed in with the official contest entry blank printed in booklet No. 6 for a chance to win a trip to two World Series games for that season.

	Ex-Mt	VG
COMPLETE SET (6)	30.00	15.00
COMMON CARD (1-6)	5.00	2.50

1998 Joey Cora Bookmarks

These four small bookmarks feature Joey Cora, who was extremely popular in the Seattle area. The fronts have action photos of Cora while the back makes up a small puzzle. We have sequenced the cards from top to bottom as they appear. These bookmarks were produced by Strategic Pro Marketing.

	Nm-Mt	Ex-Mt
COMPLETE SET (4)	4.00	1.20
COMMON CARD (1-4)	1.00	.30

1979-83 Coral-Lee Postcards

Little is known about this set. Seven of these postcards usually come together as a group and feature players in both game and non-game situations in photos taken by famous photographers such as Annie Leibovitz. Any additional information on these is greatly appreciated. We have sequenced these in alphabetical order. In addition, there have been several recently discovered Coral-Lee Postcards issued after 1981, any further information on those is appreciated as well. The Rose card was apparently issued a couple of years earlier.

	NM	Ex
COMPLETE SET	30.00	12.00
1 Dave Lopes	1.50	.60
2 Billy Martin MG	2.00	.80
3 Willie Mays Ronald Reagan PRES Ed Stack	5.00	2.00
4 Pete Rose Issued in 1979	6.00	2.40
5 George Steinbrenner OWN Billy Martin MG Reggie Jackson Thurman Munson	8.00	3.20
6 Fernando Valenzuela Jose Lopez Portillo PRES Nancy Reagan	3.00	1.20
7 Dave Winfield UER Name spelled Windfield	5.00	2.00
8 Carl Yastrzemski Jimmy Carter PRES	4.00	1.60
9 Bobby Grich Card numbered as number 8 on back	1.50	.60
10 Reggie Jackson Angels	5.00	2.00
11 Joe Morgan Phillies	3.00	1.20
17 Lou Piniella Batting	2.00	.80

1993 Costacos Bros. Promos

These cards measure approximately 4" by 6 1/4" and features a color image of the players. The fronts make it look like these were later issued as posters. Since these cards are unnumbered, we have sequenced thm in alphabetical order.

	Nm-Mt	Ex-Mt
1 Albert Belle	6.00	1.80
2 Kirby Puckett	10.00	3.00

1910-19 Coupon T213

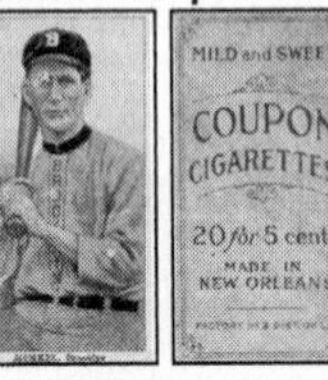

The catalog designation T213, like its predecessor T212, actually contains three separate sets. Set 1 was issued about 1910 and consists of brown-captioned designs taken directly from the T206 set. Set 2 cards are also T206 designs, but with pale blue captions. They were produced in 1914-1915 and contain many team changes and Federal League affiliations. Set 3 cards were produced in 1919 and are physically slightly smaller than the other two sets. Set 1 cards are printed on heavy paper; set 2 cards are printed on cardboard and have a glossy surface, which has resulted in a distinctive type of surface cracking. Each card in Set 1 and 2 measures 1 1/2" by 2 5/8" whereas Set 3 cards are only 1 3/8" by 2 9/16". The "Coupon" brand of cigarettes was manufactured by a branch of the American Tobacco Company located in New Orleans. The different sets can also be distinguished by their back titles, Set 1 (Coupon Mild Cigarettes), Set 2 (Mild and Sweet Coupon Cigarettes 20 for 5 cents), and Set 3 (Coupon Cigarettes 16 for 10 cts.).

	Ex-Mt	VG
COMPLETE SET	45000.00	22500.00
COMMON TYPE 1 (1-68)	100.00	50.00
COMMON TYPE 2 (69-255)	60.00	30.00
COMMON TYPE 3 (256-325)	60.00	30.00
1 Harry Bay Nashville	150.00	75.00
2 Beals Becker	100.00	50.00
3 Chief Bender	200.00	100.00
4 William H. Bernhard Nashville	150.00	75.00
5 Ted Breitenstein New Orleans	150.00	75.00
6 Bobby Byrne	100.00	50.00
7 William J. Campbell	100.00	50.00
8 Max Carey Memphis	200.00	100.00
9 Frank Chance	300.00	150.00
10 Chappy Charles	100.00	50.00
11 Hal Chase (portrait)	150.00	75.00
12 Hal Chase (throwing)	150.00	75.00
13 Ty Cobb	1200.00	600.00
14 Cranston Memphis	100.00	50.00
15 Birdie Cree	100.00	50.00
16 Bill Donovan	100.00	50.00
17 Mickey Doolan	100.00	50.00
18 Jean Dubuc	100.00	50.00
19 Joe Dunn	100.00	50.00
20 Roy Ellam Nashville	150.00	75.00
21 Clyde Engle	100.00	50.00
22 Johnny Evers	300.00	150.00
23 Art Fletcher	100.00	50.00
24 Charles Fritz New Orleans	150.00	75.00
25 Edward Greminger Montgomery	150.00	75.00
26 Hart Little Rock	150.00	75.00
27 Hart Montgomery	150.00	75.00
28 Topsy Hartsel	100.00	50.00
29 Charles Hickman Mobile	150.00	75.00
30 Danny Hoffman	100.00	50.00
31 Harry Howell	100.00	50.00
32 Miller Huggins portrait	200.00	100.00
33 Miller Huggins yelling	200.00	100.00
34 George Hunter	100.00	50.00
35 Dutch Jordan Atlanta	150.00	75.00
36 Ed Killian	100.00	50.00
37 Otto Knabe	100.00	50.00
38 Frank LaPorte	100.00	50.00
39 Ed Lennox	100.00	50.00
40 Harry Lentz Little Rock	150.00	75.00
41 Rube Marquard	200.00	100.00
42 Doc Marshall	100.00	50.00
43 Christy Mathewson	600.00	300.00
44 George McBride	100.00	50.00
45 Pryor McElveen	100.00	50.00
46 Matty McIntyre	100.00	50.00
47 Michael Mitchell	100.00	50.00
48 Carlton Molesworth Birmingham	150.00	75.00
49 Mike Mowrey	100.00	50.00
50 Hy Myers batting	100.00	50.00
51 Hy Myers fielding	100.00	50.00
52 Dode Paskert	100.00	50.00
53 Hub Perdue Nashville	150.00	75.00
54 Archie Persons Montgomery	150.00	75.00
55 Edward Reagan New Orleans	150.00	75.00
56 Robert Rhoades	100.00	50.00
57 Isaac Rockenfeld New Orleans	150.00	75.00
58 Claude Rossman	100.00	50.00
59 Boss Schmidt	100.00	50.00
60 Sid Smith Atlanta	150.00	75.00
61 Charles Starr	100.00	50.00
62 Gabby Street	100.00	50.00
63 Ed Summers	100.00	50.00
64 William Sweeney	100.00	50.00
65 Chester Thomas	100.00	50.00
66 Woodie Thornton Mobile	150.00	75.00
67 Ed Willett	100.00	50.00
68 Owen Wilson	100.00	50.00
69 Red Ames Cincinnati	150.00	75.00
70 Red Ames St. Louis	150.00	75.00
71 Frank Baker New York Amer.	150.00	75.00
72 Frank Baker Philadelphia	150.00	75.00
73 Frank Baker Phila.	150.00	75.00
74 Cy Barger	60.00	30.00
75 Chief Bender trees Baltimore Fed.	150.00	75.00
76 Chief Bender no trees Baltimore Fed.	150.00	75.00
77 Chief Bender trees Philadelphia Amer.	150.00	75.00
78 Chief Bender no trees Philadelphia Amer.	150.00	75.00
79 Chief Bender trees Philadelphia Nat.	150.00	75.00
80 Chief Bender no trees Philadelphia Nat.	150.00	75.00
81 Bill Bradley	60.00	30.00
82 Roger Bresnahan Chicago	150.00	75.00
83 Roger Bresnahan Toledo	150.00	75.00
84 Al Bridwell St. Louis	60.00	30.00
85 Al Bridwell Nashville	60.00	30.00
86 Mordecai Brown Chicago	150.00	75.00
87 Mordecai Brown St. Louis Fed.	150.00	75.00
88 Bobby Byrne	60.00	30.00
89 Howie Camnitz hands over Pittsburgh Fed.	60.00	30.00
90 Howie Camnitz arm at side Pittsburgh Fed.	60.00	30.00
91 Howie Camnitz Savannah	60.00	30.00
92 William J. Campbell	60.00	30.00
93 Frank Chance Los Angeles batting	150.00	75.00
94 Frank Chance Los Angeles portrait	150.00	75.00
95 Frank Chance New York Amer. batting	150.00	75.00
96 Frank Chance New York Amer. portrait	150.00	75.00
97 William Chappelle Brooklyn	60.00	30.00
98 William Chappelle Cleveland	60.00	30.00
99 Hal Chase Buffalo Fed. portrait	100.00	50.00
100 Hal Chase Buffalo Fed. holding cup	100.00	50.00
101 Hal Chase Buffalo Fed. throwing	100.00	50.00
102 Hal Chase Chicago Amer. portrait	100.00	50.00
103 Hal Chase Chicago Amer. holding cup)	100.00	50.00
104 Hal Chase Chicago Amer. throwing	100.00	50.00
105 Ty Cobb batting	3000.00	1500.00
106 Ty Cobb portrait	3000.00	1500.00
107 Eddie Collins Chicago Amer. with A	150.00	75.00
108 Eddie Collins Chicago Amer. without A	150.00	75.00
109 Eddie Collins Philadelphia with A	150.00	75.00
110 Doc Crandall St. Louis Amer.	60.00	30.00
111 Doc Crandall St. Louis Fed.	60.00	30.00
112 Sam Crawford	150.00	75.00
113 Birdie Cree	60.00	30.00
114 Harry Davis Philadelphia	60.00	30.00
115 Harry Davis Phila.	60.00	30.00
116 Ray Demmitt	60.00	30.00
117 Josh Devore Philadelphia	60.00	30.00
118 Josh Devore Chillicothe	60.00	30.00
119 Mike Donlin New York Nat.	80.00	40.00
120 Mike Donlin .300 Batter 7 Years	150.00	75.00
121 Mike Donlin Name spelled Dohlin on card	150.00	75.00
122 Bill Donovan	60.00	30.00
123 Mickey Doolan (batting) Baltimore Fed.	60.00	30.00
124 Mickey Doolan (fielding) Chicago Nat.	60.00	30.00
125 Mickey Doolan (batting) Baltimore Fed.	60.00	30.00
126 Mickey Doolan (fielding) Chicago Nat.	60.00	30.00
127 Tom Downey	60.00	30.00
128 Larry Doyle batting	80.00	40.00
129 Larry Doyle portrait	80.00	40.00
130 Jean Dubuc	60.00	30.00
131 Jack Dunn	60.00	30.00
132 Kid Elberfeld Brooklyn	150.00	75.00
133 Kid Elberfeld Chattanooga	150.00	75.00
134 Steve Evans	60.00	30.00
135 Johnny Evers	150.00	75.00
136 Russ Ford	60.00	30.00
137 Art Fromme	60.00	30.00
138 Chick Gandil Cleveland	150.00	75.00
139 Chick Gandil Washington	150.00	75.00
140 Rube Geyer	60.00	30.00
141 Clark Griffith	150.00	75.00
142 Bob Groom	60.00	30.00
143 Buck Herzog with B	60.00	30.00
144 Buck Herzog without B	60.00	30.00
145 Doc Hoblitzell Boston Amer.	60.00	30.00
146 Doc Hoblitzell Boston Fed.	60.00	30.00
147 Doc Hoblitzell Cincinnati	60.00	30.00
148 Solly Hofman	60.00	30.00
149 Danny Hofmann	60.00	30.00
150 Miller Huggins portrait	150.00	75.00
151 Miller Huggins yelling	150.00	75.00
152 John Hummel Brooklyn	60.00	30.00
153 John Hummel Brooklyn Nat.	60.00	30.00
154 Hugh Jennings yelling	150.00	75.00
155 Hugh Jennings dancing	150.00	75.00
156 Walter Johnson	700.00	350.00
157 Tim Jordan Ft. Worth	60.00	30.00
158 Tim Jordan Toronto	60.00	30.00
159 Joe Kelley New York Amer.	150.00	75.00
160 Joe Kelley Toronto	150.00	75.00
161 Otto Knabe	60.00	30.00
162 Ed Konetchy Boston Nat.	60.00	30.00
163 Ed Konetchy Pittsburgh Fed.	60.00	30.00
164 Ed Konetchy Pittsburgh Nat.	60.00	30.00
165 Harry Krause	60.00	30.00
166 Nap Lajoie Cleveland	350.00	180.00
167 Nap Lajoie Philadelphia	350.00	180.00
168 Nap Lajoie Phila.	350.00	180.00
169 Tommy Leach Chicago	60.00	30.00
170 Tommy Leach Cincinnati	60.00	30.00
171 Tommy Leach Rochester	60.00	30.00
172 Ed Lennox	60.00	30.00
173 Sherry Magee Boston	80.00	40.00
174 Sherry Magee Philadelphia	80.00	40.00
175 Sherry Magee Phila.	80.00	40.00
176 Rube Marquard Brooklyn pitching	150.00	75.00
177 Rube Marquard Brooklyn portrait	150.00	75.00
178 Rube Marquard New York pitching	150.00	75.00
179 Rube Marquard New York portrait	150.00	75.00
180 Christy Mathewson	700.00	350.00
181 John McGraw portrait	150.00	75.00
182 John McGraw glove on hip	150.00	75.00
183 Larry McLean	60.00	30.00
184 George McQuillan Philadelphia	60.00	30.00
185 George McQuillan Phila.	60.00	30.00
186 George McQuillan Pittsburgh	60.00	30.00
187 Fred Merkle	80.00	40.00
188 Chief Meyers Brooklyn T206-249 pose	80.00	40.00
189 Chief Meyers Brooklyn fielding	80.00	40.00
190 Chief Meyers New York T206-249 pose	80.00	40.00
191 Chief Meyers New York fielding	80.00	40.00
192 Dots Miller	60.00	30.00
193 Michael Mitchell	60.00	30.00
194 Mike Mowrey Brooklyn	60.00	30.00
195 Mike Mowrey Pittsburgh Fed.	60.00	30.00
196 Mike Mowrey Pittsburgh Nat.	60.00	30.00
197 George Mullin Indianapolis	60.00	30.00
198 George Mullin Newark	60.00	30.00
199 Danny Murphy	60.00	30.00
200 Red Murray Chicago	60.00	30.00
201 Red Murray Kansas City	60.00	30.00
202 Red Murray New York	60.00	30.00
203 Tom Needham	60.00	30.00
204 Rebel Oakes	60.00	30.00
205 Rube Oldring Philadelphia	80.00	40.00
206 Rube Oldring Phila.	80.00	40.00
207 Dode Paskert Philadelphia	60.00	30.00
208 Dode Paskert Phila.	60.00	30.00
209 William Purtell	60.00	30.00
210 Jack Quinn Baltimore	80.00	40.00
211 Jack Quinn Vernon	80.00	40.00
212 Ed Reulbach Brooklyn Fed.	80.00	40.00
213 Ed Reulbach Pittsburgh	80.00	40.00
214 Ed Reulbach Brooklyn Nat.	80.00	40.00
215 Nap Rucker Brooklyn	80.00	40.00
216 Nap Rucker Brooklyn Nat.	80.00	40.00
217 Dick Rudolph	60.00	30.00
218 Germany Schaefer Kansas City	80.00	40.00
219 Germany Schaefer New York	80.00	40.00
220 Germany Schaefer Washington	80.00	40.00
221 Admiral Schlei portrait	60.00	30.00
222 Admiral Schlei batting	60.00	30.00
223 Boss Schmidt	60.00	30.00
224 Frank Schulte	80.00	40.00
225 Nig Smith	60.00	30.00
226 Tris Speaker	350.00	180.00
227 George Stovall	60.00	30.00
228 Gabby Street catching	60.00	30.00
229 Gabby Street portrait	60.00	30.00
230 Ed Summers	60.00	30.00
231 Ed Sweeney Boston	80.00	40.00
232 Ed Sweeney Chicago	80.00	40.00
233 Ed Sweeney New York	80.00	40.00
234 Ed Sweeney Richmond	80.00	40.00
235 Chester Thomas Philadelphia	60.00	30.00
236 Chester Thomas Phila.	60.00	30.00
237 Joe Tinker Chicago Fed. bat on shoulder	150.00	75.00
238 Joe Tinker Chicago Fed. swinging	150.00	75.00
239 Joe Tinker Chicago Nat. bat on shoulder	150.00	75.00
240 Joe Tinker Chicago Nat. swinging	150.00	75.00
241 Honus Wagner	350.00	180.00
242 Jack Warhop New York	60.00	30.00
243 Jack Warhop St. Louis	60.00	30.00
244 Zack Wheat Brooklyn	150.00	75.00
245 Zack Wheat Brooklyn Nat.	150.00	75.00
246 Kaiser Wilhelm	60.00	30.00
247 Ed Willett Memphis	60.00	30.00
248 Ed Willett St. Louis	60.00	30.00
249 Owen Wilson St. Louis	60.00	30.00
250 Hooks Wiltse Brooklyn Fed. pitching	60.00	30.00
251 Hooks Wiltse Brooklyn Fed. portrait	60.00	30.00
252 Hooks Wiltse Jersey City pitching	60.00	30.00
253 Hooks Wiltse	60.00	30.00

Jersey City
portrait
254 Hooks Wiltse 60.00 30.00
New York
pitching
255 Hooks Wiltse 60.00 30.00
New York
portrait
256 Heinie Zimmerman 60.00 30.00
257 Red Ames 60.00 30.00
258 Frank Baker 150.00 75.00
New York Amer.
259 Chief Bender 150.00 75.00
260 Chief Bender 150.00 75.00
261 Roger Bresnahan 150.00 75.00
Toledo
262 Al Bridwell 60.00 30.00
263 Mordecai Brown 150.00 75.00
264 Bobby Byrne 60.00 30.00
St.Louis Nat.
265 Frank Chance 150.00 75.00
266 Frank Chance 150.00 75.00
267 Hal Chase 100.00 50.00
N.Y. Nat.
268 Hal Chase 100.00 50.00
N.Y. Nat.
269 Hal Chase 100.00 50.00
N.Y. Nat.
270 Ty Cobb 4000.00 2000.00
Detroit
271 Ty Cobb 4000.00 2000.00
Detroit
272 Eddie Collins 150.00 75.00
Chicago Amer.
273 Sam Crawford 150.00 75.00
274 Harry Davis 60.00 30.00
Philadelphia Amer.
275 Mike Donlin 80.00 40.00
276 Bill Donovan 60.00 30.00
Jersey City
277 Mickey Doolan 60.00 30.00
Reading
278 Mickey Doolan 60.00 30.00
Reading
279 Larry Doyle 80.00 40.00
N.Y. Nat.
280 Larry Doyle 80.00 40.00
N.Y. Nat.
281 Jean Dubuc 60.00 30.00
N.Y. Nat.
282 Jack Dunn 80.00 40.00
Baltimore
283 Kid Elberfeld 60.00 30.00
284 Johnny Evers 150.00 75.00
285 Chick Gandil 150.00 75.00
Chicago Amer.
286 Clark Griffith 150.00 75.00
Washington
287 Buck Herzog 60.00 30.00
Boston Nat.
288 Doc Hoblitzell 60.00 30.00
Boston Amer.
289 Miller Huggins 150.00 75.00
N.Y. Amer.
290 Miller Huggins 150.00 75.00
N.Y. Amer.
291 John Hummel 60.00 30.00
292 Hugh Jennings MG 150.00 75.00
Detroit
293 Hugh Jennings MG 150.00 75.00
Detroit
294 Walter Johnson 700.00 350.00
Washington
295 Tim Jordan 60.00 30.00
296 Joe Kelley 150.00 75.00
297 Ed Konetchy 60.00 30.00
Brooklyn
298 Nap Lajoie 350.00 180.00
299 Sherry Magee 80.00 40.00
Cincinnati
300 Rube Marquard 150.00 75.00
Brooklyn
301 Rube Marquard 150.00 75.00
Brooklyn
302 Christy Mathewson 400.00 200.00
New York Nat.
303 John McGraw MG 150.00 75.00
New York Nat.
304 John McGraw MG 150.00 75.00
New York Nat.
305 George McQuillan 60.00 30.00
Boston Nat.
306 Fred Merkle 80.00 40.00
Chicago Nat.
307 Dots Miller 60.00 30.00
St. Louis Nat.
308 Mike Mowrey 60.00 30.00
Brooklyn
309 Hy Myers 60.00 30.00
New Haven
310 Hy Myers 60.00 30.00
Brooklyn
311 Dode Paskert 60.00 30.00
Chicago Nat.
312 Jack Quinn 80.00 40.00
N.Y. Nat.
313 Ed Reulbach 80.00 40.00
314 Nap Rucker 80.00 40.00
315 Dick Rudolph 60.00 30.00
Boston Nat.
316 Germany Schaeffer 60.00 30.00
317 Frank Schulte 80.00 40.00
Binghamton
318 Tris Speaker 350.00 180.00
Cleveland
319 Gabby Street 60.00 30.00
Nashville
320 Gabby Street 60.00 30.00
Nashville
321 Ed Sweeney 80.00 40.00
Pittsburg
322 Ira Thomas 60.00 30.00
323 Joe Tinker 150.00 75.00
324 Zack Wheat 150.00 75.00
Brooklyn
325 Hooks Wiltse 60.00 30.00
326 Heinie Zimmerman 60.00 30.00
N.Y. Nat.

1914 Cracker Jack E145-1

The cards in this 144-card set measure approximately 2 1/4" by 3". This "Series of colored pictures of Famous Ball Players and Managers" was issued in packages of Cracker Jack in 1914. The cards have tinted photos set against red backgrounds and many are found with caramel stains. The set also contains Federal League players. The company claims to have printed 15 million cards. The 1914 series can be distinguished from the 1915 issue by the advertising found on the back of the cards. Team names are included for some players to show differences between the 1914 and 1915 issue.

Ex-Mt VG
COMPLETE SET (144) 45000.00 22500.00
1 Otto Knabe 250.00 125.00
2 Frank Baker 400.00 200.00
3 Joe Tinker 400.00 200.00
4 Larry Doyle 175.00 90.00
5 Ward Miller 150.00 75.00
6 Eddie Plank 600.00 300.00
Phila. AL
7 Eddie Collins 450.00 220.00
Phila. AL
8 Rube Oldring 150.00 75.00
9 Artie Hoffman 150.00 75.00
10 John McInnis 150.00 75.00
11 George Stovall 150.00 75.00
12 Connie Mack MG 500.00 250.00
13 Art Wilson 150.00 75.00
14 Sam Crawford 300.00 150.00
15 Reb Russell 150.00 75.00
16 Howie Camnitz 150.00 75.00
17 Roger Bresnahan 350.00 180.00
Catcher
18 Johnny Evers 350.00 180.00
19 Chief Bender 450.00 220.00
Phila. AL
20 Cy Falkenberg 150.00 75.00
21 Heinie Zimmerman 150.00 75.00
22 Joe Wood 300.00 150.00
23 Chas.Comiskey OWN 350.00 180.00
24 George Mullen 150.00 75.00
25 Michael Simon 150.00 75.00
26 James Scott 150.00 75.00
27 Bill Carrigan 150.00 75.00
28 Jack Barry 150.00 75.00
29 Vean Gregg 200.00 100.00
Cleveland
30 Ty Cobb 6000.00 3000.00
31 Heinie Wagner 150.00 75.00
32 Mordecai Brown 350.00 180.00
33 Amos Strunk 150.00 75.00
34 Ira Thomas 150.00 75.00
35 Harry Hooper 300.00 150.00
36 Ed Walsh 300.00 150.00
37 Grover C. Alexander 800.00 400.00
38 Red Dooin 200.00 100.00
Phila. NL
39 Chick Gandil 350.00 180.00
40 Jimmy Austin 200.00 100.00
St.L. AL
41 Tommy Leach 150.00 75.00
42 Al Bridwell 150.00 75.00
43 Rube Marquard 350.00 180.00
NY NL
44 Charles Tesreau 150.00 75.00
45 Fred Luderus 150.00 75.00
46 Bob Groom 150.00 75.00
47 Josh Devore 200.00 100.00
Phila. NL
48 Harry Lord 250.00 125.00
49 John Miller 150.00 75.00
50 John Hummell 150.00 75.00
51 Nap Rucker 175.00 90.00
52 Zach Wheat 350.00 180.00
53 Otto Miller 150.00 75.00
54 Marty O'Toole 150.00 75.00
55 Dick Hoblitzel 200.00 100.00
Cinc.
56 Clyde Milan 175.00 90.00
57 Walter Johnson 2000.00 1000.00
58 Wally Schang 175.00 90.00
59 Harry Gessler 150.00 75.00
60 Rollie Zeider 250.00 125.00
61 Ray Schalk 300.00 150.00
62 Jay Cashion 300.00 150.00
63 Babe Adams 175.00 90.00
64 Jimmy Archer 150.00 75.00
65 Tris Speaker 700.00 350.00
66 Napoleon Lajoie 800.00 400.00
Cleve.
67 Otis Crandall 150.00 75.00
68 Honus Wagner 2500.00 1250.00
69 John McGraw 450.00 220.00
70 Fred Clarke 300.00 150.00
71 Chief Meyers 175.00 90.00
72 John Boehling 150.00 75.00
73 Max Carey 300.00 150.00
74 Frank Owens 150.00 75.00
75 Miller Huggins 300.00 150.00
76 Claude Hendrix 150.00 75.00
77 Hughie Jennings MG 300.00 150.00
78 Fred Merkle 200.00 100.00
79 Ping Bodie 175.00 90.00
80 Ed Ruelbach 175.00 90.00
81 Jim C. Delehanty 175.00 90.00
82 Gavvy Cravath 200.00 100.00
83 Russ Ford 150.00 75.00
84 Elmer E. Knetzer 150.00 75.00
85 Buck Herzog 150.00 75.00
86 Burt Shotton 150.00 75.00
87 Forrest Cady 150.00 75.00
88 Christy Mathewson 3000.00 1500.00
Pitching
89 Lawrence Cheney 150.00 75.00
90 Frank Smith 150.00 75.00
91 Roger Peckinpaugh 175.00 90.00
92 Al Demaree N.Y. NL 200.00 100.00
93 Del Pratt 250.00 125.00
Throwing
94 Eddie Cicotte 325.00 160.00
95 Ray Keating 150.00 75.00
96 Beals Becker 150.00 75.00
97 John(Rube) Benton 150.00 75.00
98 Frank LaPorte 150.00 75.00
99 Frank Chance 1500.00 750.00
100 Thomas Seaton 150.00 75.00
101 Frank Schulte 150.00 75.00
102 Ray Fisher 150.00 75.00
103 Joe Jackson 8000.00 4000.00
104 Vic Saier 150.00 75.00
105 James Lavender 150.00 75.00
106 Joe Birmingham 150.00 75.00
107 Tom Downey 150.00 75.00
108 Sherry Magee 200.00 100.00
Phila. NL
109 Fred Blanding 150.00 75.00
110 Bob Bescher 150.00 75.00
111 Jim Callahan 300.00 150.00
112 Ed Sweeney 150.00 75.00
113 George Suggs 150.00 75.00
114 Geo.J. Moriarty 175.00 90.00
115 Addison Brennan 150.00 75.00
116 Rollie Zeider 150.00 75.00
117 Ted Easterly 150.00 75.00
118 Ed Konetchy 200.00 100.00
Pittsburgh
119 George Perring 150.00 75.00
120 Mike Doolan 150.00 75.00
121 Hub Perdue 200.00 100.00
Boston NL
122 Owen Bush 150.00 75.00
123 Slim Sallee 150.00 75.00
124 Earl Moore 150.00 75.00
125 Bert Niehoff 200.00 100.00
126 Walter Blair 150.00 75.00
127 Butch Schmidt 150.00 75.00
128 Steve Evans 150.00 75.00
129 Ray Caldwell 150.00 75.00
130 Ivy Wingo 150.00 75.00
131 George Baumgardner 150.00 75.00
132 Les Nunamaker 150.00 75.00
133 Branch Rickey MG 450.00 220.00
134 Armando Marsans 200.00 100.00
Cincinnati
135 Bill Killefer 150.00 75.00
136 Rabbit Maranville 350.00 180.00
137 William Rariden 150.00 75.00
138 Hank Gowdy 150.00 75.00
139 Rebel Oakes 150.00 75.00
140 Danny Murphy 150.00 75.00
141 Cy Barger 150.00 75.00
142 Eugene Packard 150.00 75.00
143 Jake Daubert 175.00 90.00
144 James C. Walsh 200.00 100.00

1915 Cracker Jack E145-2

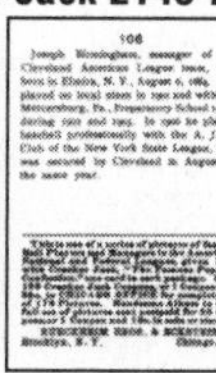

The cards in this 176-card set measure approximately 2 1/4" by 3". When turned over in a lateral motion, a 1915 "series of 176" Cracker Jack card shows the back printing upside-down. Cards were available in boxes of Cracker Jack or from the company for "100 Cracker Jack coupons, or one coupon and 25 cents." An album was available for "50 coupons or one coupon and 10 cents." Because of this send-in offer, the 1915 Cracker Jack cards are noticeably easier to find than the 1914 Cracker Jack cards, although obviously neither set is plentiful. The set essentially duplicates E145-1 (1914 Cracker Jack) except for some additional cards and new poses. Players in the Federal League are indicated by FED in the checklist below.

Ex-Mt VG
COMPLETE SET (176) 35000.00 17500.00
COMMON CARD (1-144) 100.00 50.00
COMM. CARD (145-176) 125.00 60.00
1 Otto Knabe 175.00 90.00
2 Frank Baker 350.00 180.00
3 Joe Tinker 350.00 180.00
4 Larry Doyle 100.00 50.00
5 Ward Miller 100.00 50.00
6 Eddie Plank 500.00 250.00
St.L. FED
7 Eddie Collins 350.00 180.00
Chicago AL
8 Rube Oldring 100.00 50.00
9 Artie Hoffman 100.00 50.00
10 John McInnis 100.00 50.00
11 George Stovall 100.00 50.00
12 Connie Mack MG 400.00 200.00
13 Art Wilson 100.00 50.00
14 Sam Crawford 300.00 150.00
15 Reb Russell 100.00 50.00
16 Howie Camnitz 100.00 50.00
17 Roger Bresnahan 300.00 150.00
18 Johnny Evers 300.00 150.00
19 Chief Bender 350.00 180.00
Baltimore FED
20 Cy Falkenberg 100.00 50.00
21 Heinie Zimmerman 100.00 50.00
22 Joe Wood 250.00 125.00
23 C. Comiskey OWN 300.00 150.00
24 George Mullen 100.00 50.00
25 Michael Simon 100.00 50.00
26 James Scott 100.00 50.00
27 Bill Carrigan 100.00 50.00
28 Jack Barry 100.00 50.00
29 Vean Gregg 125.00 60.00
Boston AL
30 Ty Cobb 4000.00 2000.00
31 Heinie Wagner 100.00 50.00
32 Mordecai Brown 300.00 150.00
33 Amos Strunk 100.00 50.00
34 Ira Thomas 100.00 50.00
35 Harry Hooper 250.00 125.00
36 Ed Walsh 300.00 150.00
37 Grover C. Alexander 600.00 300.00
38 Red Dooin 125.00 60.00
Cincinnati
39 Chick Gandil 300.00 150.00
40 Jimmy Austin 125.00 60.00
Pitts. FED
41 Tommy Leach 100.00 50.00
42 Al Bridwell 100.00 50.00
43 Rube Marquard 350.00 180.00
Brooklyn FED
44 Charles(Jeff) Tesreau 100.00 50.00
45 Fred Luderus 100.00 50.00
46 Bob Groom 100.00 50.00
47 Josh Devore 125.00 60.00
Boston NL
48 Steve O'Neill 125.00 60.00
49 John Miller 100.00 50.00
50 John Hummell 100.00 50.00
51 Nap Rucker 125.00 60.00
52 Zach Wheat 300.00 150.00
53 Otto Miller 100.00 50.00
54 Marty O'Toole 100.00 50.00
55 Dick Hoblitzel 125.00 60.00
Boston AL
56 Clyde Milan 125.00 60.00
57 Walter Johnson 1500.00 750.00
58 Wally Schang 125.00 60.00
59 Harry Gessler 100.00 50.00
60 Oscar Dugey 125.00 60.00
61 Ray Schalk 250.00 125.00
62 Willie Mitchell 125.00 60.00
63 Babe Adams 125.00 60.00
64 Jimmy Archer 100.00 50.00
65 Tris Speaker 600.00 300.00
66 Napoleon Lajoie 600.00 300.00
Phila. AL
67 Otis Crandall 100.00 50.00
68 Honus Wagner 1500.00 750.00
69 John McGraw MG 300.00 150.00
70 Fred Clarke 250.00 125.00
71 Chief Meyers 100.00 50.00
72 John Boehling 100.00 50.00
73 Max Carey 250.00 125.00
74 Frank Owens 100.00 50.00
75 Miller Huggins 300.00 150.00
76 Claude Hendrix 100.00 50.00
77 Hughie Jennings MG 300.00 150.00
78 Fred Merkle 125.00 60.00
79 Ping Bodie 125.00 60.00
80 Ed Ruelbach 125.00 60.00
81 Jim C. Delehanty 125.00 60.00
82 Gavvy Cravath 125.00 60.00
83 Russ Ford 100.00 50.00
84 Elmer E. Knetzer 100.00 50.00
85 Buck Herzog 100.00 50.00
86 Burt Shotton 100.00 50.00
87 Forrest Cady 100.00 50.00
88 Christy Mathewson 1500.00 750.00
Portrait
89 Lawrence Cheney 100.00 50.00
90 Frank Smith 100.00 50.00
91 Roger Peckinpaugh 125.00 60.00
92 Al Demaree 125.00 60.00
Phila. NL
93 Del Pratt 175.00 90.00
Portrait
94 Eddie Cicotte 300.00 150.00
95 Ray Keating 100.00 50.00
96 Beals Becker 100.00 50.00
97 John(Rube) Benton 100.00 50.00
98 Frank LaPorte 100.00 50.00
99 Hal Chase 300.00 150.00
100 Thomas Seaton 100.00 50.00
101 Frank Schulte 100.00 50.00
102 Ray Fisher 100.00 50.00
103 Joe Jackson 8000.00 4000.00
104 Vic Saier 100.00 50.00
105 James Lavender 100.00 50.00
106 Joe Birmingham MG 100.00 50.00
107 Thomas Downey 100.00 50.00
108 Sherry Magee 125.00 60.00
Boston NL
109 Fred Blanding 100.00 50.00
110 Bob Bescher 100.00 50.00
111 Herbie Moran 125.00 60.00
112 Ed Sweeney 100.00 50.00
113 George Suggs 100.00 50.00
114 Geo.J. Moriarty 125.00 60.00
115 Addison Brennan 100.00 50.00
116 Rollie Zeider 100.00 50.00
117 Ted Easterly 100.00 50.00
118 Ed Konetchy 125.00 60.00
Pitts. FED
119 George Perring 100.00 50.00
120 Mike Doolan 100.00 50.00
121 Hub Perdue 125.00 60.00
St. Louis NL
122 Owen Bush 100.00 50.00
123 Slim Sallee 100.00 50.00
124 Earl Moore 100.00 50.00
125 Bert Niehoff 125.00 60.00
Phila. NL
126 Walter Blair 100.00 50.00
127 Butch Schmidt 100.00 50.00
128 Steve Evans 100.00 50.00
129 Ray Caldwell 100.00 50.00
130 Ivy Wingo 100.00 50.00
131 Geo. Baumgardner 100.00 50.00
132 Les Nunamaker 100.00 50.00
133 Branch Rickey MG 300.00 150.00
134 Armando Marsans 125.00 60.00
St.L. FED
135 William Killefer 100.00 50.00
136 Rabbit Maranville 250.00 125.00
137 William Rariden 100.00 50.00
138 Hank Gowdy 100.00 50.00
139 Rebel Oakes 100.00 50.00
140 Danny Murphy 100.00 50.00
141 Cy Barger 100.00 50.00
142 Eugene Packard 100.00 50.00
143 Jake Daubert 100.00 50.00
144 James C. Walsh 100.00 50.00
145 Ted Cather 125.00 60.00
146 George Tyler 125.00 60.00
147 Lee Magee 125.00 60.00
148 Owen Wilson 125.00 60.00
149 Hal Janvrin 125.00 60.00
150 Doc Johnston 125.00 60.00
151 George Whitted 125.00 60.00
152 George McQuillen 125.00 60.00
153 Bill James 125.00 60.00
154 Dick Rudolph 125.00 60.00
155 Joe Connolly 125.00 60.00
156 Jean Dubuc 125.00 60.00
157 George Kaiserling 125.00 60.00
158 Fritz Maisel 125.00 60.00
159 Heinie Groh 125.00 60.00
160 Benny Kauff 125.00 60.00
161 Edd Roush 300.00 150.00
162 George Stallings MG 125.00 60.00
163 Bert Whaling 125.00 60.00
164 Bob Shawkey 125.00 60.00
165 Eddie Murphy 125.00 60.00
166 Joe Bush 125.00 60.00
167 Clark Griffith 300.00 150.00
168 Vin Campbell 125.00 60.00
169 Raymond Collins 125.00 60.00
170 Hans Lobert 125.00 60.00
171 Earl Hamilton 125.00 60.00
172 Erskine Mayer 125.00 60.00
173 Tilly Walker 125.00 60.00
174 Robert Veach 125.00 60.00
175 Joseph Benz 125.00 60.00
176 Hippo Vaughn 175.00 90.00

1982 Cracker Jack

The cards in this 16-card set measure 2 1/2" by 3 1/2"; cards came in two sheets of eight cards, plus an advertising card with a title in the center, which measured approximately 7 1/2" by 10 1/2". Cracker Jack reentered the baseball card market for the first time since 1915 to promote the first "Old Timers Baseball Classic" held July 19, 1982. The color player photos have a Cracker Jack border and have either green (NL) or red (AL) frame lines and name panels. The Cracker Jack logo appears on both sides of each card, with AL players numbered 1-8 and NL players numbered 9-16. Of the 16 ballplayers pictured, five did not appear at the game. At first, the two sheets were available only through the mail but are now commonly found in hobby circles. The set was prepared for Cracker Jack by Topps. The prices below reflect individual card prices; the price for complete panels would be about the same as the sum of the card prices for those players on the panel due to the easy availability of uncut sheets.

Nm-Mt Ex-Mt
COMPLETE SET (16) 10.00 4.00
1 Larry Doby .75 .30
2 Bob Feller 1.00 .40
3 Whitey Ford 1.00 .40
4 Al Kaline 1.00 .40
5 Harmon Killebrew .50 .20
6 Mickey Mantle 5.00 2.00
7 Tony Oliva .25 .10
8 Brooks Robinson 1.00 .40
9 Hank Aaron 3.00 1.20
10 Ernie Banks 1.50 .60
11 Ralph Kiner .50 .20
12 Ed Mathews .50 .20
13 Willie Mays 3.00 1.20
14 Robin Roberts .75 .30
15 Duke Snider 1.50 .60
16 Warren Spahn .75 .30

1993 Cracker Jack 1915 Reprints

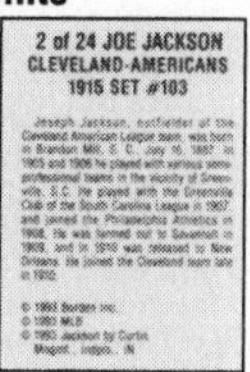

To commemorate its 100th anniversary, Cracker Jack issued a 24-card set of miniature replicas of its 1915 set. One mini-card was inserted into each specially marked single, triple, and value-pack box. A mini-card holder album and a fact booklet that includes each player's lifetime stats were available for 6.95 through a mail-in offer. The album features room for 72 cards implying that Cracker Jack would like to continue this series into future years as well. Each minicard measures approximately 1 1/4" by 1 3/4" and features on its front a white-bordered color portrait of the player on a brick-colored background. The player's name, team, and league appear in the white margin below the picture and "Cracker Jack Ball Players" appears at the top. The white back displays the player's name, team, and league at the top, along with his card number from the 1915 set, followed below by a biography.

Nm-Mt Ex-Mt
COMPLETE SET (24) 15.00 4.50
1 Ty Cobb 3.00 .90
2 Joe Jackson 3.00 .90
3 Honus Wagner 1.50 .45

4 Christy Mathewson 1.25 .35
5 Walter Johnson 1.50 .45
6 Tris Speaker 1.00 .30
7 Grover Alexander 1.00 .30
8 Nap Lajoie 1.00 .30
9 Rube Marquard .50 .15
10 Connie Mack MG .75 .23
11 Johnny Evers .75 .23
12 Branch Rickey .50 .15
13 Fred Clarke MG .50 .15
14 Harry Hooper .50 .15
15 Zack Wheat .50 .15
16 Joe Tinker .50 .15
17 Eddie Collins 1.00 .30
18 Mordecai Brown .50 .15
19 Eddie Plank .50 .15
20 Rabbit Maranville .50 .15
21 John McGraw MG .75 .23
22 Miller Huggins .50 .15
23 Ed Walsh .50 .15
24 Joe Bush .25 .07

1997 Cracker Jack

This 20-card set was distributed in Cracker Jack boxes and measures approximately 1 5/16" by 1 3/4". The fronts feature color action player photos in white borders. The backs carry player information and statistics.

Nm-Mt Ex-Mt
COMPLETE SET (20) 25.00 7.50
1 Jeff Bagwell 1.50 .45
2 Chuck Knoblauch .50 .15
3 Cal Ripken 5.00 1.50
4 Chipper Jones 2.50 .75
5 Derek Jeter 5.00 1.50
6 Barry Larkin 1.00 .30
7 Bernie Williams 1.00 .30
8 Barry Bonds 2.50 .75
9 Kenny Lofton .75 .23
10 Gary Sheffield 1.25 .35
11 Sammy Sosa 2.50 .75
12 Paul Molitor 1.25 .35
13 Andres Galarraga 1.00 .30
14 Ivan Rodriguez 1.25 .35
15 Mike Piazza 3.00 .90
16 Andy Pettitte .50 .15
17 Tom Glavine 1.00 .30
18 Albert Belle .50 .15
19 Mark McGwire 4.00 1.20
20 Mo Vaughn .50 .15

2002 Cracker Jack

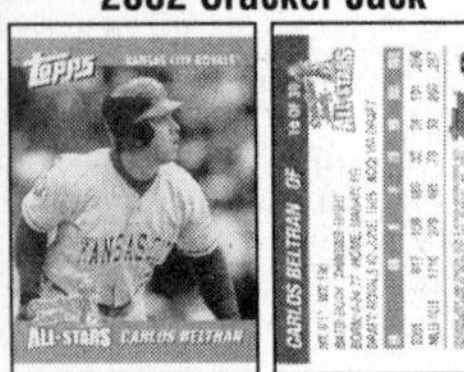

Topps has teamed with Frito Lay, Inc. to create a special 30-card Cracker Jack set. The mini-sized baseball cards were available in specially marked packages of Cracker Jack.

Nm-Mt Ex-Mt
COMPLETE SET (30) 25.00 7.50
1 Roger Clemens 1.50 .45
2 Pedro Martinez 1.25 .35
3 Carlos Delgado 1.00 .30
4 Jeff Conine .25 .07
5 Greg Vaughn .25 .07
6 Jim Thome 1.00 .30
7 Brad Radke .25 .07
8 Frank Thomas 1.00 .30
9 Steve Sparks .25 .07
10 Carlos Beltran .75 .23
11 Ichiro Suzuki 3.00 .90
12 Mark Mulder .75 .23
13 Troy Glaus 1.00 .30
14 Alex Rodriguez 1.50 .45
15 Chipper Jones 1.50 .45
16 Bobby Abreu 1.00 .30
17 Mike Piazza 2.00 .60
18 Cliff Floyd 1.00 .30
19 Vladimir Guerrero 1.50 .45
20 Jeff Bagwell 1.25 .35
21 Albert Pujols 1.50 .45
22 Sammy Sosa 1.50 .45
23 Richie Sexson .75 .23
24 Sean Casey .25 .07
25 Brian Giles 1.00 .30
26 Randy Johnson 1.25 .35
27 Barry Bonds 1.50 .45
28 Kevin Brown .50 .15
29 Phil Nevin .50 .15
30 Todd Helton 1.00 .30

1976 Crane Discs

Produced by MSA, these discs were distributed by a wide variety of advertisers and can be found in various regions of the country. There are many different versions of this set, however, we are only pricing the Crane version. Several players changed teams during the printing of this set, however only the more commonly found version is included in the complete set price. These sets are unnumbered and sequenced in alphabetical order. Some of the other sponsors include Buchmans, Carousel (of which many different locations are known), Dairy Isle, Isaly, Orbakers, Red Barn, Safelon and Towne Club. All multiplier values are notated before.

NM Ex
COMPLETE SET (70) 20.00 8.00
1 Hank Aaron 2.50 1.00
2 Johnny Bench 1.50 .60
3 Vida Blue .25 .10
4 Larry Bowa .25 .10
5 Lou Brock 1.50 .60
6 Jeff Burroughs .10 .04
7 John Candelaria .10 .04
8 Jose Cardenal .10 .04
9 Rod Carew 1.50 .60
10 Steve Carlton 1.50 .60
11 Dave Cash .10 .04
12 Cesar Cedeno .25 .10
13 Ron Cey .25 .10
14 Carlton Fisk 2.00 .80
15 Tito Fuentes .10 .04
16 Steve Garvey .75 .30
17 Ken Griffey .25 .10
18 Don Gullett .10 .04
19 Willie Horton .10 .04
20 Al Hrabosky .10 .04
21 Catfish Hunter 1.50 .60
22A Reggie Jackson 5.00 2.00
Oakland Athletics
22B Reggie Jackson 1.50 .60
Baltimore Orioles
23 Randy Jones .10 .04
24 Jim Kaat .50 .20
25 Don Kessinger .10 .04
26 Dave Kingman .50 .20
27 Jerry Koosman .25 .10
28 Mickey Lolich .25 .10
29 Greg Luzinski .50 .20
30 Fred Lynn .50 .20
31 Bill Madlock .25 .10
32A Carlos May .75 .30
Chicago White Sox
32B Carlos May .10 .04
New York Yankees
33 John Mayberry .10 .04
34 Bake McBride .10 .04
35 Doc Medich .10 .04
36A Andy Messersmith .75 .30
Los Angeles Dodgers
36B Andy Messersmith .10 .04
Atlanta Braves
37 Rick Monday .10 .04
38 John Montefusco .10 .04
39 Jerry Morales .10 .04
40 Joe Morgan 1.50 .60
41 Thurman Munson .75 .30
42 Bobby Murcer .50 .20
43 Al Oliver .50 .20
44 Jim Palmer 1.50 .60
45 Dave Parker .75 .30
46 Tony Perez .75 .30
47 Jerry Reuss .10 .04
48 Brooks Robinson 1.50 .60
49 Frank Robinson 1.50 .60
50 Steve Rogers .10 .04
51 Pete Rose 2.00 .80
52 Nolan Ryan 4.00 1.60
53 Manny Sanguillen .10 .04
54 Mike Schmidt 2.50 1.00
55 Tom Seaver 2.00 .80
56 Ted Simmons .50 .20
57 Reggie Smith .25 .10
58 Willie Stargell 1.50 .60
59 Rusty Staub .50 .20
60 Rennie Stennett .10 .04
61 Don Sutton 1.50 .60
62A Andre Thornton .75 .30
Chicago Cubs
62B Andre Thornton .10 .04
Montreal Expos
63 Luis Tiant .50 .20
64 Joe Torre .75 .30
65 Mike Tyson .10 .04
66 Bob Watson .25 .10
67 Wilbur Wood .10 .04
68 Jimmy Wynn .10 .04
69 Carl Yastrzemski 1.50 .60
70 Richie Zisk .10 .04

1998 Crown Royale

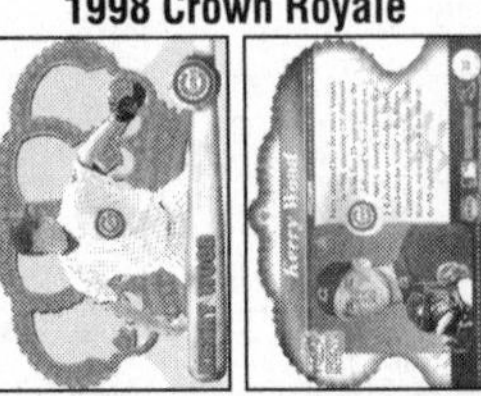

The 1998 Crown Royale set (produced by Pacific) consists of 144 standard size cards. The six-card hobby-only packs retailed for a suggested price of $5.99. The card fronts feature game-action color photos of today's top baseball stars on the distinctively unique horizontal, die cut Crown Royale design. The featured player's name is printed across the bottom of the card along with the team name. The release date was September, 1998. Orlando Hernandez is the most notable Rookie Card in this set.

Nm-Mt Ex-Mt
COMPLETE SET (144) 100.00 30.00
1 Garret Anderson 1.00 .30
2 Jim Edmonds 1.00 .30
3 Darin Erstad 1.00 .30
4 Tim Salmon 1.50 .45
5 Jarrod Washburn 1.00 .30
6 Dave Dellucci RC 1.00 .30
7 Travis Lee 1.00 .30
8 Devon White 1.00 .30
9 Matt Williams 1.00 .30
10 Andres Galarraga 1.00 .30
11 Tom Glavine 1.50 .45
12 Andruw Jones 1.00 .30
13 Chipper Jones 2.50 .75
14 Ryan Klesko 1.00 .30
15 Javy Lopez 1.00 .30
16 Greg Maddux 4.00 1.20
17 Walt Weiss 1.00 .30
18 Roberto Alomar 2.50 .75
19 Harold Baines 1.00 .30
20 Eric Davis 1.00 .30
21 Mike Mussina 2.50 .75
22 Rafael Palmeiro 1.50 .45
23 Cal Ripken 8.00 2.40
24 Nomar Garciaparra 4.00 1.20
25 Pedro Martinez 2.50 .75
26 Troy O'Leary 1.00 .30
27 Mo Vaughn 1.00 .30
28 Tim Wakefield 1.00 .30
29 Mark Grace 1.50 .45
30 Mickey Morandini 1.00 .30
31 Sammy Sosa 4.00 1.20
32 Kerry Wood 2.50 .75
33 Albert Belle 1.00 .30
34 Mike Caruso 1.00 .30
35 Ray Durham 1.00 .30
36 Frank Thomas 2.50 .75
37 Robin Ventura 1.00 .30
38 Bret Boone 1.00 .30
39 Sean Casey 1.00 .30
40 Barry Larkin 2.50 .75
41 Reggie Sanders 1.00 .30
42 Sandy Alomar Jr. 1.00 .30
43 David Justice 1.00 .30
44 Kenny Lofton 1.00 .30
45 Manny Ramirez 1.00 .30
46 Jim Thome 2.50 .75
47 Omar Vizquel 1.00 .30
48 Jaret Wright 1.00 .30
49 Dante Bichette 1.00 .30
50 Ellis Burks 1.00 .30
51 Vinny Castilla 1.00 .30
52 Todd Helton 1.50 .45
53 Larry Walker 1.50 .45
54 Tony Clark 1.00 .30
55 Damion Easley 1.00 .30
56 Bobby Higginson 1.00 .30
57 Cliff Floyd 1.00 .30
58 Livan Hernandez 1.00 .30
59 Derrek Lee 1.00 .30
60 Edgar Renteria 1.00 .30
61 Moises Alou 1.00 .30
62 Jeff Bagwell 1.50 .45
63 Derek Bell 1.00 .30
64 Craig Biggio 1.50 .45
65 Johnny Damon 1.00 .30
66 Jeff King 1.00 .30
67 Hal Morris 1.00 .30
68 Dean Palmer 1.00 .30
69 Bobby Bonilla 1.00 .30
70 Eric Karros 1.00 .30
71 Raul Mondesi 1.00 .30
72 Gary Sheffield 1.00 .30
73 Jeromy Burnitz 1.00 .30
74 Jeff Cirillo 1.00 .30
75 Marquis Grissom 1.00 .30
76 Fernando Vina 1.00 .30
77 Marty Cordova 1.00 .30
78 Pat Meares 1.00 .30
79 Paul Molitor 1.50 .45
80 Terry Steinbach 1.00 .30
81 Todd Walker 1.00 .30
82 Brad Fullmer 1.00 .30
83 Vladimir Guerrero 2.50 .75
84 Carl Pavano 1.00 .30
85 Rondell White 1.00 .30
86 Carlos Baerga 1.00 .30
87 Hideo Nomo 2.50 .75
88 John Olerud 1.00 .30
89 Rey Ordonez 1.00 .30
90 Mike Piazza 4.00 1.20
91 Masato Yoshii RC 1.50 .45
92 Orlando Hernandez RC 2.50 .75
93 Hideki Irabu 1.00 .30
94 Derek Jeter 6.00 1.80
95 Chuck Knoblauch 1.00 .30
96 Ricky Ledee 1.00 .30
97 Tino Martinez 1.50 .45
98 Paul O'Neill 1.50 .45
99 Bernie Williams 1.50 .45
100 Jason Giambi 2.50 .75
101 Ben Grieve 1.00 .30
102 Rickey Henderson 2.50 .75
103 Matt Stairs 1.00 .30
104 Bob Abreu 1.00 .30
105 Doug Glanville 1.00 .30
106 Scott Rolen 1.50 .45
107 Curt Schilling 1.50 .45
108 Jose Guillen 1.00 .30
109 Jason Kendall 1.00 .30
110 Jason Schmidt 1.00 .30
111 Kevin Young 1.00 .30
112 Delino DeShields 1.00 .30
113 Brian Jordan 1.00 .30
114 Ray Lankford 1.00 .30
115 Mark McGwire 6.00 1.80
116 Tony Gwynn 3.00 .90
117 Wally Joyner 1.00 .30
118 Ruben Rivera 1.00 .30
119 Greg Vaughn 1.00 .30
120 Rich Aurilia 1.00 .30
121 Barry Bonds 6.00 1.80
122 Bill Mueller 1.00 .30
123 Robb Nen 1.00 .30
124 Jay Buhner 1.00 .30
125 Ken Griffey Jr. 4.00 1.20
126 Edgar Martinez 1.50 .45
127 Shane Monahan 1.00 .30
128 Alex Rodriguez 4.00 1.20
129 David Segui 1.00 .30
130 Rolando Arrojo RC 1.00 .30
131 Wade Boggs 1.50 .45
132 Quinton McCracken 1.00 .30
133 Fred McGriff 1.50 .45
134 Bobby Smith 1.00 .30
135 Will Clark 2.50 .75
136 Juan Gonzalez 2.50 .75
137 Rusty Greer 1.00 .30
138 Ivan Rodriguez 2.50 .75
139 Aaron Sele 1.00 .30
140 John Wetteland 1.00 .30
141 Jose Canseco 2.50 .75
142 Roger Clemens 5.00 1.50
143 Carlos Delgado 1.00 .30
144 Shawn Green 1.00 .30

1998 Crown Royale All-Stars

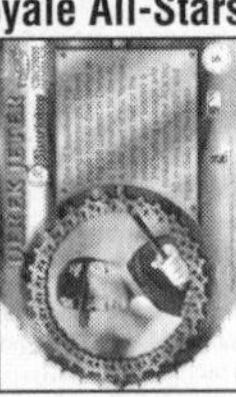

The 1998 Crown Royale All-Stars set consists of 20 cards and is an insert to the 1998 Crown Royale base set. The cards were randomly inserted in hobby packs at a rate of one in 25. The fronts feature a tribute to 20 of 1998's American League and National League All-Stars with color photography and "mountain peak" design in the background commemorating the city of Denver where the All-Star game was held. The player's name is printed across the bottom border along with the player's team logo and team position.

Nm-Mt Ex-Mt
COMPLETE SET (20) 250.00 75.00
1 Roberto Alomar 10.00 3.00
2 Cal Ripken 30.00 9.00
3 Kenny Lofton 4.00 1.20
4 Jim Thome 10.00 3.00
5 Derek Jeter 25.00 7.50
6 David Wells 4.00 1.20
7 Ken Griffey Jr. 15.00 4.50
8 Alex Rodriguez 15.00 4.50
9 Juan Gonzalez 10.00 3.00
10 Ivan Rodriguez 10.00 3.00
11 Gary Sheffield 4.00 1.20
12 Chipper Jones 10.00 3.00
13 Greg Maddux 15.00 4.50
14 Walt Weiss 4.00 1.20
15 Larry Walker 6.00 1.80
16 Craig Biggio 6.00 1.80
17 Mike Piazza 15.00 4.50
18 Mark McGwire 25.00 7.50
19 Tony Gwynn 12.00 3.60
20 Barry Bonds 25.00 7.50

1998 Crown Royale Cramer's Choice Premiums

These premium sized cards were issued one per box. Pacific CEO and founder Mike Cramer personally selected 10 players as being worthy of these specially inserted cards. The card is designed like a trophy with the words "1998 Cramer's Choice Award" on the top along with the players photo. The bottom gives the players name and position. The back explains why the player is worthy of this high honor.

Nm-Mt Ex-Mt
COMPLETE SET (10) 100.00 30.00
CRAMER AU'S RANDOM IN BOXES....
CRAMER AU'S PR.RUN 10 SERIAL #'d SETS
CRAMER AU'S TOO SCARCE TO PRICE
1 Cal Ripken 20.00 6.00
2 Ken Griffey Jr. 10.00 3.00
3 Alex Rodriguez 10.00 3.00
4 Juan Gonzalez 6.00 1.80
5 Travis Lee 2.50 .75
6 Chipper Jones 6.00 1.80
7 Greg Maddux 10.00 3.00
8 Kerry Wood 6.00 1.80
9 Mark McGwire 15.00 4.50
10 Tony Gwynn 8.00 2.40

1998 Crown Royale Diamond Knights

The 1998 Crown Royale Diamond Knights set consists of 25 cards and is an insert to the 1998 Crown Royale base set. The cards are seeded at a rate of one per hobby pack. The card fronts feature game-action color photography of baseball's brightest stars. The featured player's name is written caligraphy style across the bottom border along with the player's team logo.

Nm-Mt Ex-Mt
COMPLETE SET (25) 40.00 12.00
1 Andres Galarraga .50 .15
2 Chipper Jones 1.25 .35
3 Greg Maddux 2.00 .60
4 Cal Ripken 4.00 1.20
5 Nomar Garciaparra 2.00 .60
6 Mo Vaughn .50 .15
7 Kerry Wood 1.25 .35
8 Frank Thomas 1.25 .35
9 Vinny Castilla .50 .15
10 Jeff Bagwell .75 .23
11 Craig Biggio .75 .23
12 Paul Molitor .75 .23
13 Mike Piazza 2.00 .60
14 Orlando Hernandez 1.25 .35
15 Derek Jeter 3.00 .90
16 Ricky Ledee .50 .15
17 Mark McGwire 3.00 .90
18 Tony Gwynn 1.50 .45
19 Barry Bonds 3.00 .90
20 Ken Griffey Jr. 2.00 .60
21 Alex Rodriguez 2.00 .60
22 Wade Boggs .75 .23
23 Juan Gonzalez 1.25 .35
24 Ivan Rodriguez 1.25 .35
25 Jose Canseco 1.25 .35

1998 Crown Royale Firestone on Baseball

The 1998 Crown Royale Firestone on Baseball set consists of 26 cards and is an insert to the 1998 Crown Royale base set. The cards are randomly inserted in hobby packs at a rate of two in 25. The card fronts feature 25 color action photos of baseball's top players selected by respected sports broadcaster and commentator Roy Firestone. The Crown Royale logo sits in the upper left corner and a color photo of Roy Firestone himself sits in the lower right corner. The backs provide commentaries by Roy Firestone on each of the featured players.

Nm-Mt Ex-Mt
COMPLETE SET (26) 200.00 60.00
1 Travis Lee 2.50 .75
2 Chipper Jones 6.00 1.80
3 Greg Maddux 10.00 3.00
4 Cal Ripken 20.00 6.00
5 Nomar Garciaparra 10.00 3.00
6 Mo Vaughn 2.50 .75
7 Kerry Wood 6.00 1.80
8 Frank Thomas 6.00 1.80
9 Manny Ramirez 2.50 .75
10 Larry Walker 4.00 1.20
11 Gary Sheffield 2.50 .75
12 Paul Molitor 4.00 1.20
13 Hideo Nomo 6.00 1.80
14 Mike Piazza 10.00 3.00
15 Ben Grieve 2.50 .75
16 Mark McGwire 15.00 4.50
17 Tony Gwynn 8.00 2.40
18 Barry Bonds 15.00 4.50
19 Ken Griffey Jr. 10.00 3.00
20 Randy Johnson 4.00 1.20
21 Alex Rodriguez 10.00 3.00
22 Wade Boggs 4.00 1.20
23 Juan Gonzalez 6.00 1.80
24 Ivan Rodriguez 6.00 1.80
25 Roger Clemens 12.00 3.60
26 Roy Firestone 5.00 1.50
Tony Gwynn
26A Roy Firestone AU300 40.00 12.00

1998 Crown Royale Home Run Fever

The 1998 Crown Royale Home Run Fever insert set consists of 10 cards and is a serially numbered to 374. The cards are randomly inserted in packs at a rate of one in 73. The fronts feature color game-action photography of 10 superstar sluggers. Play a part in the slugging race by pressing the disappearing ink dots on each card.

Nm-Mt Ex-Mt
COMPLETE SET (10) 150.00 45.00
1 Andres Galarraga 6.00 1.80
2 Sammy Sosa 25.00 7.50
3 Albert Belle 6.00 1.80
4 Jim Thome 15.00 4.50
5 Mark McGwire 40.00 12.00
6 Greg Vaughn 6.00 1.80
7 Ken Griffey Jr. 25.00 7.50
8 Alex Rodriguez 25.00 7.50
9 Juan Gonzalez 15.00 4.50
10 Jose Canseco 15.00 4.50

1998 Crown Royale Pillars of the Game

The 1998 Pacific Crown Royale Pillars of the Game set consists of 25 cards and is an insert to the 1998 Pacific Crown Royale base set. The cards are seeded at a rate of one per hobby pack. The fronts feature color action photography on a background of "marble pillar" design. The featured player's name runs vertical along the right side border with both the player's team logo and the Pacific Crown Royale logo in the left bottom and top corners respectively.

	Nm-Mt	Ex-Mt
COMPLETE SET (25)	25.00	7.50
1 Jim Edmonds	.50	.15
2 Travis Lee	.50	.15
3 Chipper Jones	1.25	.35
4 Tom Glavine	2.00	.60
John Smoltz		
Greg Maddux		
5 Cal Ripken	4.00	1.20
6 Nomar Garciaparra	2.00	.60
7 Roberto Alomar	1.25	.35
8 Sammy Sosa	2.00	.60
9 Kerry Wood	1.25	.35
10 Frank Thomas	1.25	.35
11 Jim Thome	1.25	.35
12 Larry Walker	.75	.23
13 Moises Alou	.50	.15
14 Raul Mondesi	.50	.15
15 Mike Piazza	2.00	.60
16 Hideki Irabu	.50	.15
17 Bernie Williams	.75	.23
18 Ben Grieve	.50	.15
19 Scott Rolen	.75	.23
20 Mark McGwire	3.00	.90
21 Tony Gwynn	1.50	.45
22 Ken Griffey Jr.	2.00	.60
23 Alex Rodriguez	2.00	.60
24 Juan Gonzalez	1.25	.35
25 Roger Clemens	2.50	.75

1999 Crown Royale

The 1999 Crown Royale set (produced by Pacific) was issued in one series totalling 144 cards and distributed exclusively to hobby dealers in six-card packs with a suggested retail price of $5.99. The set features color action player photos printed on die-cut dual-foiled card stock. The set also includes 18 short-printed rookies and prospects with an insertion rate of 1:8 packs. Notable Rookie Cards include Freddy Garcia.

	Nm-Mt	Ex-Mt
COMPLETE SET (144)	200.00	60.00
COMP.SET w/o SP's (126)	120.00	36.00
COMMON CARD (1-144)	.75	.23
COMMON PROSPECT SP	5.00	1.50
1 Jim Edmonds	.75	.23
2 Darin Erstad	.75	.23
3 Troy Glaus	1.25	.35
4 Tim Salmon	1.25	.35
5 Mo Vaughn	.75	.23
6 Jay Bell	.75	.23
7 Steve Finley	.75	.23
8 Randy Johnson	2.00	.60
9 Travis Lee	.75	.23
10 Matt Williams	.75	.23
11 Andruw Jones	.75	.23
12 Chipper Jones	2.00	.60
13 Brian Jordan	.75	.23
14 Ryan Klesko	.75	.23
15 Javy Lopez	.75	.23
16 Greg Maddux	3.00	.90
17 Randall Simon SP	5.00	1.50
18 Albert Belle	.75	.23
19 Will Clark	2.00	.60
20 Delino DeShields	.75	.23
21 Mike Mussina	2.00	.60
22 Cal Ripken	6.00	1.80
23 Nomar Garciaparra	3.00	.90
24 Pedro Martinez	2.00	.60
25 Jose Offerman	.75	.23
26 John Valentin	.75	.23
27 Mark Grace	1.25	.35
28 Lance Johnson	.75	.23
29 Henry Rodriguez	.75	.23
30 Sammy Sosa	3.00	.90
31 Kerry Wood	2.00	.60
32 Mike Caruso	.75	.23
33 Ray Durham	.75	.23
34 Magglio Ordonez	.75	.23
35 Brian Simmons SP	5.00	1.50
36 Frank Thomas	2.00	.60
37 Mike Cameron	.75	.23
38 Barry Larkin	2.00	.60
39 Greg Vaughn	.75	.23
40 Dmitri Young	.75	.23
41 Roberto Alomar	2.00	.60
42 Sandy Alomar Jr.	.75	.23
43 David Justice	.75	.23
44 Kenny Lofton	.75	.23
45 Manny Ramirez	.75	.23
46 Jim Thome	2.00	.60
47 Dante Bichette	.75	.23
48 Vinny Castilla	.75	.23
49 Todd Helton	1.25	.35
50 Larry Walker	1.25	.35
51 Tony Clark	.75	.23
52 Damion Easley	.75	.23
53 Bob Higginson	.75	.23
54 Brian Hunter	.75	.23
55 Gabe Kapler SP	5.00	1.50
56 Jeff Weaver SP RC	8.00	2.40
57 Cliff Floyd	.75	.23
58 Alex Gonzalez SP	5.00	1.50
59 Mark Kotsay	.75	.23
60 Derrek Lee	.75	.23
61 Preston Wilson SP	5.00	1.50
62 Moises Alou	.75	.23
63 Jeff Bagwell	1.25	.35
64 Derek Bell	.75	.23
65 Craig Biggio	1.25	.35
66 Ken Caminiti	.75	.23
67 Carlos Beltran SP	5.00	1.50
68 Johnny Damon	.75	.23
69 Carlos Febles SP	5.00	1.50
70 Jeff King	.75	.23
71 Kevin Brown	1.25	.35
72 Todd Hundley	.75	.23
73 Eric Karros	.75	.23
74 Raul Mondesi	.75	.23
75 Gary Sheffield	.75	.23
76 Jeromy Burnitz	.75	.23
77 Jeff Cirillo	.75	.23
78 Marquis Grissom	.75	.23
79 Fernando Vina	.75	.23
80 Chad Allen SP RC	5.00	1.50
81 Matt Lawton	.75	.23
82 D.Mientkiewicz SP RC	10.00	3.00
83 Brad Radke	.75	.23
84 Todd Walker	.75	.23
85 Michael Barrett SP	5.00	1.50
86 Brad Fullmer	.75	.23
87 Vladimir Guerrero	2.00	.60
88 Wilton Guerrero	.75	.23
89 Ugueth Urbina	.75	.23
90 Bobby Bonilla	.75	.23
91 Rickey Henderson	2.00	.60
92 Rey Ordonez	.75	.23
93 Mike Piazza	3.00	.90
94 Robin Ventura	.75	.23
95 Roger Clemens	4.00	1.20
96 Orlando Hernandez	.75	.23
97 Derek Jeter	5.00	1.50
98 Chuck Knoblauch	.75	.23
99 Tino Martinez	1.25	.35
100 Bernie Williams	1.25	.35
101 Eric Chavez SP	5.00	1.50
102 Jason Giambi	2.00	.60
103 Ben Grieve	.75	.23
104 Tim Raines	.75	.23
105 Marlon Anderson SP	5.00	1.50
106 Doug Glanville	.75	.23
107 Scott Rolen	1.25	.35
108 Curt Schilling	1.25	.35
109 Brian Giles	.75	.23
110 Jose Guillen	.75	.23
111 Jason Kendall	.75	.23
112 Kevin Young	.75	.23
113 J.D. Drew SP	5.00	1.50
114 Jose Jimenez SP	5.00	1.50
115 Ray Lankford	.75	.23
116 Mark McGwire	5.00	1.50
117 Fernando Tatis	.75	.23
118 Matt Clement SP	5.00	1.50
119 Tony Gwynn	2.50	.75
120 Trevor Hoffman	.75	.23
121 Wally Joyner	.75	.23
122 Reggie Sanders	.75	.23
123 Barry Bonds	5.00	1.50
124 Ellis Burks	.75	.23
125 Jeff Kent	.75	.23
126 J.T. Snow	.75	.23
127 Freddy Garcia SP RC	8.00	2.40
128 Ken Griffey Jr.	3.00	.90
129 Edgar Martinez	1.25	.35
130 Alex Rodriguez	3.00	.90
131 David Segui	.75	.23
132 Rolando Arrojo	.75	.23
133 Wade Boggs	1.25	.35
134 Jose Canseco	2.00	.60
135 Quinton McCracken	.75	.23
136 Fred McGriff	1.25	.35
137 Juan Gonzalez	2.00	.60
138 Rusty Greer	.75	.23
139 Rafael Palmeiro	1.25	.35
140 Ivan Rodriguez	2.00	.60
141 Jose Cruz Jr.	.75	.23
142 Carlos Delgado	.75	.23
143 Shawn Green	.75	.23
144 Roy Halladay SP	5.00	1.50

1999 Crown Royale Limited

Randomly inserted into packs at an approximate rate of one in 32, this 144-card set is parallel to the Crown Royale base set and is printed on thick 24-point card stock. Only 99 serial-numbered sets were produced.

Nm-Mt Ex-Mt
*STARS: 4X TO 10X BASIC CARDS....
*SP'S: .6X TO 1.5X BASIC SP'S ....

1999 Crown Royale Opening Day

Randomly inserted into hobby packs at the rate of one in 25, this 144-card set is parallel to the Crown Royale base set. Only 72 serial-numbered sets were produced.

Nm-Mt Ex-Mt
*STARS: 5X TO 12X BASIC CARDS....
*SP'S: 1X TO 2.5X BASIC SP'S ....

1999 Crown Royale Century 21

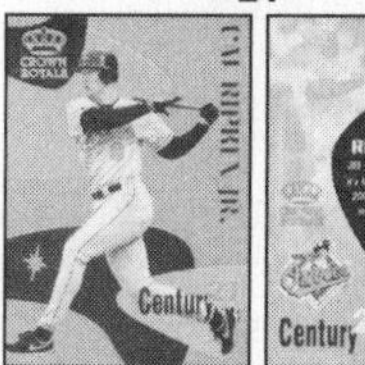

Randomly inserted into packs at the rate of one in 25, this 10-card set features color photos of some of the League's most dominating players printed on full foil cards.

	Nm-Mt	Ex-Mt
COMPLETE SET (10)	100.00	30.00
1 Cal Ripken	20.00	6.00
2 Nomar Garciaparra	10.00	3.00
3 Sammy Sosa	10.00	3.00
4 Frank Thomas	6.00	1.80
5 Mike Piazza	10.00	3.00
6 J.D. Drew	4.00	1.20
7 Mark McGwire	15.00	4.50
8 Tony Gwynn	8.00	2.40
9 Ken Griffey Jr.	10.00	3.00
10 Alex Rodriguez	10.00	3.00

1999 Crown Royale Cramer's Choice Premiums

Inserted one per box, this 10-card premium-size set features action color photos of players chosen by Pacific Trading Cards president/founder/CEO Michael Cramer printed on die-cut pyramid-shaped cards. Six serial-numbered premium-size parallel sets were also produced.

	Nm-Mt	Ex-Mt
COMPLETE SET (10)	120.00	36.00

*DARK BLUE: 2.5X TO 6X PREMIUMS
*GOLD: 6X TO 15X PREMIUMS.........
*GREEN: 3X TO 8X PREMIUMS..........
*LIGHT BLUE: 5X TO 12X PREMIUMS
*RED: 4X TO 10X PREMIUMS...........
DARK BLUE PRINT RUN 35 SERIAL #'d SETS
GOLD PRINT RUN 10 SERIAL #'d SETS
GREEN PRINT RUN 30 SERIAL #'d SETS
LIGHT BLUE PRINT RUN 20 SERIAL #'d SETS
PURPLE AU PRINT RUN 1 SERIAL #'d SET
RED PRINT RUN 25 SERIAL #'d SETS
PARALLELS ARE RANDOM INSERTS IN PACKS...
PURPLE AU'S NOT PRICED DUE TO SCARCITY
BASIC PREMIUMS LISTED BELOW!...

	Nm-Mt	Ex-Mt
1 Cal Ripken	20.00	6.00
2 Nomar Garciaparra	10.00	3.00
3 Sammy Sosa	10.00	3.00
4 Frank Thomas	6.00	1.80
5 Mike Piazza	10.00	3.00
6 Derek Jeter	15.00	4.50
7 J.D. Drew	6.00	1.80
8 Mark McGwire	15.00	4.50
9 Tony Gwynn	8.00	2.40
10 Ken Griffey Jr.	10.00	3.00

1999 Crown Royale Gold Crown Die Cut Premiums

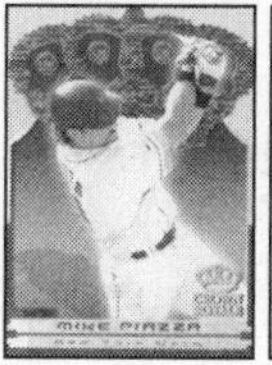

Randomly inserted at the rate of six in 10 boxes, this six-card set features color photos of top players printed on die-cut premium sized cards with gold foil highlights. This was an unannounced insert designed to be a surprise bonus to collectors.

	Nm-Mt	Ex-Mt
COMPLETE SET (6)	80.00	24.00
1 Cal Ripken	25.00	7.50
2 Mike Piazza	12.00	3.60
3 Ken Griffey Jr.	12.00	3.60
4 Tony Gwynn	10.00	3.00
5 Mark McGwire	20.00	6.00
6 J.D. Drew	6.00	1.80

1999 Crown Royale Living Legends

Randomly inserted into packs, this 10-card set features color photos of ten superstars. Only 375 serial-numbered sets were produced.

	Nm-Mt	Ex-Mt
COMPLETE SET (10)	150.00	45.00
1 Greg Maddux	15.00	4.50
2 Cal Ripken	30.00	9.00
3 Nomar Garciaparra	15.00	4.50
4 Sammy Sosa	15.00	4.50
5 Frank Thomas	10.00	3.00
6 Mike Piazza	15.00	4.50
7 Mark McGwire	25.00	7.50
8 Tony Gwynn	12.00	3.60
9 Ken Griffey Jr.	15.00	4.50
10 Alex Rodriguez	15.00	4.50

1999 Crown Royale Master Performers

Randomly inserted into packs at the rate of two in 25, this 20-card set features color photos of

some of the most popular players printed on fully foiled etched cards.

	Nm-Mt	Ex-Mt
COMPLETE SET (20)	150.00	45.00
1 Chipper Jones	5.00	1.50
2 Greg Maddux	8.00	2.40
3 Cal Ripken	15.00	4.50
4 Nomar Garciaparra	8.00	2.40
5 Sammy Sosa	8.00	2.40
6 Frank Thomas	5.00	1.50
7 Raul Mondesi	2.00	.60
8 Vladimir Guerrero	5.00	1.50
9 Mike Piazza	8.00	2.40
10 Roger Clemens	10.00	3.00
11 Derek Jeter	12.00	3.60
12 Scott Rolen	3.00	.90
13 J.D. Drew	1.50	.45
14 Mark McGwire	12.00	3.60
15 Tony Gwynn	6.00	1.80
16 Barry Bonds	12.00	3.60
17 Ken Griffey Jr.	8.00	2.40
18 Alex Rodriguez	8.00	2.40
19 Juan Gonzalez	5.00	1.50
20 Ivan Rodriguez	5.00	1.50

1999 Crown Royale Pillars of the Game

Inserted one per pack, this 25-card set features color photos of top players and rising stars printed on holographic silver foil cards.

	Nm-Mt	Ex-Mt
COMPLETE SET (25)	40.00	12.00
1 Mo Vaughn	.50	.15
2 Chipper Jones	1.25	.35
3 Greg Maddux	2.00	.60
4 Albert Belle	.50	.15
5 Cal Ripken	4.00	1.20
6 Nomar Garciaparra	2.00	.60
7 Sammy Sosa	2.00	.60
8 Frank Thomas	1.25	.35
9 Manny Ramirez	.50	.15
10 Jeff Bagwell	.75	.23
11 Raul Mondesi	.50	.15
12 Vladimir Guerrero	1.25	.35
13 Mike Piazza	2.00	.60
14 Roger Clemens	2.50	.75
15 Derek Jeter	3.00	.90
16 Bernie Williams	.75	.23
17 Ben Grieve	.50	.15
18 J.D. Drew	.50	.15
19 Mark McGwire	3.00	.90
20 Tony Gwynn	1.50	.45
21 Barry Bonds	3.00	.90
22 Ken Griffey Jr.	2.00	.60
23 Alex Rodriguez	2.00	.60
24 Juan Gonzalez	1.25	.35
25 Ivan Rodriguez	1.25	.35

1999 Crown Royale Pivotal Players

Inserted one per pack, this 25-card set features color photos of some of the great superstars of the game printed on holographic silver foil cards.

	Nm-Mt	Ex-Mt
COMPLETE SET (25)	30.00	9.00
1 Mo Vaughn	.50	.15
2 Chipper Jones	1.25	.35
3 Greg Maddux	2.00	.60
4 Albert Belle	.50	.15
5 Cal Ripken	4.00	1.20
6 Nomar Garciaparra	2.00	.60
7 Sammy Sosa	2.00	.60
8 Frank Thomas	1.25	.35
9 Manny Ramirez	.50	.15
10 Craig Biggio	.75	.23
11 Raul Mondesi	.50	.15
12 Vladimir Guerrero	1.25	.35
13 Mike Piazza	2.00	.60
14 Roger Clemens	2.50	.75
15 Derek Jeter	3.00	.90
16 Bernie Williams	.75	.23
17 Ben Grieve	.50	.15
18 Scott Rolen	.75	.23
19 J.D. Drew	.50	.15
20 Mark McGwire	3.00	.90
21 Tony Gwynn	1.50	.45
22 Ken Griffey Jr.	2.00	.60
23 Alex Rodriguez	2.00	.60
24 Juan Gonzalez	1.25	.35
25 Ivan Rodriguez	1.25	.35

1999 Crown Royale Pivotal Players FanFest

This 20 card standard-size set was issued by Pacific at the 1999 All-Star FanFest and was given away to collectors who opened a box of any Pacific product at the 1999 FanFest. This set is a direct parallel of the Pivotal Players insert set.

	Nm-Mt	Ex-Mt
COMPLETE SET (25)	1800.00	550.00
1 Mo Vaughn	20.00	6.00
2 Chipper Jones	100.00	30.00
3 Greg Maddux	120.00	36.00
4 Albert Belle	20.00	6.00
5 Cal Ripken	200.00	60.00
6 Nomar Garciaparra	100.00	30.00
7 Sammy Sosa	100.00	30.00
8 Frank Thomas	50.00	15.00
9 Manny Ramirez	50.00	15.00
10 Craig Biggio	30.00	9.00
11 Raul Mondesi	20.00	6.00
12 Vladimir Guerrero	50.00	15.00
13 Mike Piazza	120.00	36.00
14 Roger Clemens	100.00	30.00
15 Derek Jeter	200.00	60.00
16 Bernie Williams	40.00	12.00
17 Ben Grieve	20.00	6.00
18 Scott Rolen	40.00	12.00
19 J.D. Drew	20.00	6.00
20 Mark McGwire	150.00	45.00
21 Tony Gwynn	100.00	30.00
22 Ken Griffey Jr.	150.00	45.00
23 Alex Rodriguez	100.00	30.00
24 Juan Gonzalez	40.00	12.00
25 Ivan Rodriguez	50.00	15.00

1999 Crown Royale Pivotal Players National

This set was issued through a Pacific wax redemption program at the 1999 Atlanta National. This is a parallel set of the 1999 Crown Royale set but in the front in large letters the words "Pacific Trading Cards, 20th National, Atlanta Ga., July 1999" are printed in the middle. Underneath that description, the cards in the set are all serial numbered out of 20. Due to scarcity, no pricing is provided

	Nm-Mt	Ex-Mt
COMPLETE SET (25)		
1 Mo Vaughn		
2 Chipper Jones		
3 Greg Maddux		
4 Albert Belle		
5 Cal Ripken		
6 Nomar Garciaparra		
7 Sammy Sosa		
8 Frank Thomas		
9 Manny Ramirez		
10 Craig Biggio		
11 Raul Mondesi		
12 Vladimir Guerrero		
13 Mike Piazza		
14 Roger Clemens		
15 Derek Jeter		
16 Bernie Williams		
17 Ben Grieve		
18 Scott Rolen		
19 J.D. Drew		
20 Mark McGwire		
21 Tony Gwynn		
22 Ken Griffey Jr.		
23 Alex Rodriguez		
24 Juan Gonzalez		
25 Ivan Rodriguez		

1999 Crown Royale Player's Choice

These cards, which parallel the regular Crown Royale cards were issued by Pacific to be given away at the Players Choice award ceremony. The cards have a "Players Choice" stamp on them and are skip numbered to match their number from the basic 1999 Crown Royale set. These cards were produced in varying quantites so we have put the print run next to the players name

	Nm-Mt	Ex-Mt
COMPLETE SET	250.00	75.00
8 Randy Johnson/43	25.00	7.50
10 Matt Williams/40	20.00	6.00
16 Greg Maddux/24		
22 Cal Ripken/156	40.00	12.00
30 Sammy Sosa/193	30.00	9.00
41 Roberto Alomar/79	20.00	6.00
61 Preston Wilson/31	20.00	6.00
67 Carlos Beltran/68	20.00	6.00
91 Rickey Henderson/57	50.00	15.00
127 Freddy Garcia/47	20.00	6.00
139 Rafael Palmeiro/52	20.00	6.00

2000 Crown Royale

The 2000 Crown Royale product was released in June, 2000 as a 144-card set. The set features 119 veteran cards and 25 short-printed prospect cards. Each pack contained six cards and carried a suggested retail price of $2.99 per pack. Notable Rookie Cards include Kazuhiro Sasaki.

	Nm-Mt	Ex-Mt
COMPLETE SET (144)	120.00	36.00

COMMON CARD (1-144)	.40	.12
COMMON ROOKIE SP	2.00	.60
1 Darin Erstad	.60	.18
2 Troy Glaus	1.00	.30
3 Adam Kennedy SP	2.00	.60
4 Derrick Turnbow SP RC	2.00	.60
5 Mo Vaughn	.60	.18
6 Erubiel Durazo	.40	.12
7 Steve Finley	.60	.18
8 Randy Johnson	1.50	.45
9 Travis Lee	.40	.12
10 Matt Williams	.60	.18
11 Rafael Furcal SP	2.00	.60
12 Andres Galarraga	.60	.18
13 Andruw Jones	.60	.18
14 Chipper Jones	1.50	.45
15 Javy Lopez	.60	.18
16 Greg Maddux	3.00	.90
17 Albert Belle	.60	.18
18 Will Clark	1.50	.45
19 Mike Mussina	1.50	.45
20 Cal Ripken	6.00	1.80
21 Carl Everett	.60	.18
22 Nomar Garciaparra	3.00	.90
23 Pedro Martinez	1.50	.45
24 Jason Varitek	.60	.18
25 Scott Downs SP RC	2.00	.60
26 Mark Grace	1.00	.30
27 Sammy Sosa	3.00	.90
28 Kerry Wood	1.50	.45
29 Ray Durham	.60	.18
30 Paul Konerko	.60	.18
31 Carlos Lee	.60	.18
32 Magglio Ordonez	.60	.18
33 Frank Thomas	1.50	.45
34 Rob Bell SP	2.00	.60
35 Sean Casey	.60	.18
36 Ken Griffey Jr.	3.00	.90
37 Barry Larkin	1.50	.45
38 Pokey Reese	.40	.12
39 Roberto Alomar	1.50	.45
40 David Justice	.60	.18
41 Kenny Lofton	.60	.18
42 Manny Ramirez	.60	.18
43 Richie Sexson	.60	.18
44 Jim Thome	1.50	.45
45 Rolando Arrojo	.40	.12
46 Jeff Cirillo	.40	.12
47 Tom Goodwin	.40	.12
48 Todd Helton	1.00	.30
49 Larry Walker	1.00	.30
50 Tony Clark	.40	.12
51 Juan Encarnacion	.40	.12
52 Juan Gonzalez	1.50	.45
53 Hideo Nomo	1.50	.45
54 Dean Palmer	.60	.18
55 Cliff Floyd	.60	.18
56 Alex Gonzalez	.40	.12
57 Mike Lowell	.60	.18
58 Brad Penny SP	2.00	.60
59 Preston Wilson	.60	.18
60 Moises Alou	.60	.18
61 Jeff Bagwell	1.00	.30
62 Craig Biggio	1.00	.30
63 Roger Cedeno	.40	.12
64 Julio Lugo SP	2.00	.60
65 Carlos Beltran	.60	.18
66 Johnny Damon	.60	.18
67 Jermaine Dye	.60	.18
68 Carlos Febles	.40	.12
69 Mark Quinn SP	2.00	.60
70 Kevin Brown	1.00	.30
71 Shawn Green	.60	.18
72 Eric Karros	.60	.18
73 Gary Sheffield	.60	.18
74 Kevin Barker SP	2.00	.60
75 Ron Belliard	.40	.12
76 Jeromy Burnitz	.60	.18
77 Geoff Jenkins	.60	.18
78 Jacque Jones	.60	.18
79 Corey Koskie	.60	.18
80 Matt LeCroy SP	2.00	.60
81 Brad Radke	.60	.18
82 Peter Bergeron SP	2.00	.60
83 Matt Blank SP	2.00	.60
84 Vladimir Guerrero	1.50	.45
85 Hideki Irabu	.40	.12
86 Rondell White	.60	.18
87 Edgardo Alfonzo	.60	.18
88 Mike Hampton	.60	.18
89 Rickey Henderson	1.50	.45
90 Rey Ordonez	.40	.12
91 Jay Payton SP	2.00	.60
92 Mike Piazza	3.00	.90
93 Roger Clemens	4.00	1.20
94 Orlando Hernandez	.60	.18
95 Derek Jeter	5.00	1.50
96 Tino Martinez	1.00	.30
97 Alfonso Soriano SP	2.50	.75
98 Bernie Williams	1.00	.30
99 Eric Chavez	.60	.18
100 Jason Giambi	1.50	.45
101 Ben Grieve	.40	.12
102 Tim Hudson	1.00	.30
103 Terrence Long SP	2.00	.60
104 Mark Mulder SP	2.00	.60
105 Adam Piatt SP	2.00	.60
106 Bobby Abreu	.60	.18
107 Doug Glanville	.40	.12
108 Mike Lieberthal	.60	.18
109 Scott Rolen	1.00	.30
110 Brian Giles	.60	.18
111 Chad Hermansen SP	2.00	.60
112 Jason Kendall	.60	.18
113 Warren Morris	.40	.12
114 Rick Ankiel SP	2.00	.60
115 Justin Brunette SP RC	2.00	.60
116 J.D. Drew	.60	.18
117 Mark McGwire	5.00	1.50
118 Fernando Tatis	.40	.12
119 Wiki Gonzalez SP	2.00	.60
120 Tony Gwynn	2.50	.75
121 Trevor Hoffman	.60	.18
122 Ryan Klesko	.60	.18
123 Barry Bonds	5.00	1.50
124 Ellis Burks	.40	.12
125 Jeff Kent	.60	.18
126 Calvin Murray SP	2.00	.60
127 J.T. Snow	.60	.18
128 Freddy Garcia	.60	.18
129 John Olerud	.60	.18
130 Alex Rodriguez	3.00	.90
131 K.Sasaki SP RC	5.00	1.50
132 Jose Canseco	1.50	.45
133 Vinny Castilla	.60	.18
134 Fred McGriff	1.00	.30
135 Greg Vaughn	.60	.18
136 Gabe Kapler	.40	.12
137 M.Lamb SP RC UER Rusty Greer pictured on front	2.00	.60
138 Ruben Mateo SP	2.00	.60
139 Rafael Palmeiro	1.00	.30
140 Ivan Rodriguez	1.50	.45
141 Tony Batista	.60	.18
142 Carlos Delgado	.60	.18
143 Raul Mondesi	.60	.18
144 Shannon Stewart	.60	.18

2000 Crown Royale Limited

Randomly inserted into packs, this 144-card set is a complete parallel of the Crown Royale base set. These cards are individually serial numbered to 144.

	Nm-Mt	Ex-Mt
*STARS: 3X TO 8X BASIC CARDS		
*SP's: 1.5X TO 4X BASIC SP's		

2000 Crown Royale Platinum Blue

Randomly inserted into hobby packs, this 144-card set is a complete parallel of the Crown Royale base set. These cards feature a platinum blue foil, and are individually serial numbered to 75.

	Nm-Mt	Ex-Mt
*STARS: 5X TO 12X BASIC CARDS		
*SP's: 2.5X TO 6X BASIC SP's		
*SP RC's: 4X TO 10X BASIC SP RC's.		

2000 Crown Royale Premiere Date

Randomly inserted into hobby packs at a rate of 1:25, this 144-card set is a complete parallel of the Crown Royale base set. These cards feature a "Premiere Date" stamp on the front of the card, and are individually serial numbered to 121.

	Nm-Mt	Ex-Mt
*STARS: 3X TO 8X BASIC CARDS		
*SP's: 1.5X TO 4X BASIC SP's		
*SP RC's: 2X TO 5X BASIC RC SP's..		

2000 Crown Royale Red

Inserted into retail packs, this 144-card set is a complete parallel of the hobby Crown Royale base set. These cards are the retail version of the base set.

	Nm-Mt	Ex-Mt
COMPLETE SET (144)	300.00	90.00
*STARS: .75X TO 2X BASIC CARDS		
*SP's: .75X TO 2X BASIC SP's		
*SP RC's: .75X TO 2X BASIC SP RC's		

2000 Crown Royale Rookie 499

Randomly inserted into hobby packs, this 25-card set is a complete parallel of all the base rookies. Please note that these cards individually serial numbered to 499.

	Nm-Mt	Ex-Mt
COMPLETE SET (25)	120.00	36.00
*ROOKIE 499's: .75X TO 2X BASIC SP's		
*ROOKIE 499 RC's: .75X TO 2X BASIC SP RC's		

2000 Crown Royale Card-Supials

Randomly inserted into packs at two in 25, this 20-card set features some of the greatest players in the game. These cards also have a mini-version which accompany the regular base version by matching a veteran and a prospect from the same team.

	Nm-Mt	Ex-Mt
COMPLETE SET (20)	120.00	36.00
1 Randy Johnson	4.00	1.20
2 Chipper Jones	4.00	1.20
3 Cal Ripken	15.00	4.50
4 Nomar Garciaparra	8.00	2.40
5 Sammy Sosa	8.00	2.40
6 Frank Thomas	4.00	1.20
7 Ken Griffey Jr.	8.00	2.40
8 Manny Ramirez	1.50	.45
9 Larry Walker	2.50	.75
10 Juan Gonzalez	4.00	1.20
11 Jeff Bagwell	2.50	.75
12 Shawn Green	1.50	.45
13 Vladimir Guerrero	4.00	1.20
14 Mike Piazza	8.00	2.40
15 Derek Jeter	12.00	3.60
16 Scott Rolen	2.50	.75
17 Mark McGwire	12.00	3.60
18 Tony Gwynn	6.00	1.80
19 Alex Rodriguez	8.00	2.40
20 Ivan Rodriguez	4.00	1.20

2000 Crown Royale Card-Supials Minis

Randomly inserted into packs at two in 25, this 20-card set features prospects from the same team as the veteran player in the larger size card.

	Nm-Mt	Ex-Mt
COMPLETE SET (20)	40.00	12.00
1 Erubiel Durazo	2.00	.60
2 Andruw Jones	2.00	.60
3 Matt Riley	2.00	.60
4 Jason Varitek	2.00	.60
5 Kerry Wood	5.00	1.50
6 Magglio Ordonez	2.00	.60
7 Sean Casey	2.00	.60
8 Richie Sexson	2.00	.60
9 Ben Petrick	2.00	.60
10 Juan Encarnacion	2.00	.60
11 Lance Berkman	2.00	.60
12 Eric Gagne	5.00	1.50
13 Peter Bergeron	2.00	.60
14 Edgardo Alfonzo	2.00	.60
15 Alfonso Soriano	5.00	1.50
16 Bob Abreu	2.00	.60
17 Rick Ankiel	2.00	.60
18 Ben Davis	2.00	.60
19 Freddy Garcia	2.00	.60
20 Ruben Mateo	2.00	.60

2000 Crown Royale Cramer's Choice Premiums

Inserted into hobby boxes as chip-toppers, these 10 oversized cards features superstars of the major leagues.

	Nm-Mt	Ex-Mt
COMPLETE SET (10)	100.00	30.00
*AQUA: 5X TO 12X BASIC PREMIUMS		
*BLUE: 2.5X TO 6X BASIC PREMIUMS		
*GOLD: 8X TO 20X BASIC PREMIUMS		
*GREEN: 3X TO 8X BASIC PREMIUMS		
*RED: 4X TO 10X BASIC PREMIUMS .		
AQUA PRINT RUN 20 SERIAL #'d SETS		
BLUE PRINT RUN 35 SERIAL #'d SETS		
GOLD PRINT RUN 10 SERIAL #'d SETS		
GREEN PRINT RUN 30 SERIAL #'d SETS		
PURPLE PRINT RUN 1 SERIAL #'d SETS		
RED PRINT RUN 25 SERIAL #'d SETS		
PARALLELS ARE RANDOM INSERTS IN PACKS		
PURPLE AU'S NOT PRICED DUE TO SCARCITY		
BASIC PREMIUMS LISTED BELOW!...		
1 Cal Ripken	20.00	6.00
2 Nomar Garciaparra	10.00	3.00
3 Ken Griffey Jr.	10.00	3.00
4 Sammy Sosa	10.00	3.00
5 Mike Piazza	10.00	3.00
6 Derek Jeter	15.00	4.50
7 Rick Ankiel	4.00	1.20
8 Mark McGwire	15.00	4.50
9 Tony Gwynn	8.00	2.40
10 Alex Rodriguez	10.00	3.00

2000 Crown Royale Feature Attractions

Randomly inserted into packs at 1:1 hobby and 1:2 retail packs, this 25-card insert features players that attract fans to ballgames.

	Nm-Mt	Ex-Mt
COMPLETE SET (25)	20.00	6.00
*EXCL.SHOW: 30X TO 80X BASIC FEATURE		
EXCL.SHOW RANDOM INSERTS IN PACKS		
EXCL.SHOW PRINT RUN 20 SERIAL #'d SETS		
1 Erubiel Durazo	.25	.07
2 Chipper Jones	1.00	.30
3 Greg Maddux	2.00	.60
4 Cal Ripken	4.00	1.20
5 Nomar Garciaparra	2.00	.60
6 Pedro Martinez	1.00	.30
7 Sammy Sosa	2.00	.60
8 Frank Thomas	1.00	.30
9 Ken Griffey Jr.	2.00	.60
10 Manny Ramirez	.40	.12
11 Larry Walker	.60	.18
12 Juan Gonzalez	1.00	.30
13 Jeff Bagwell	.60	.18
14 Carlos Beltran	.40	.12
15 Shawn Green	.40	.12
16 Vladimir Guerrero	1.00	.30
17 Mike Piazza	2.00	.60
18 Roger Clemens	2.50	.75
19 Derek Jeter	3.00	.90
20 Ben Grieve	.25	.07
21 Rick Ankiel	.50	.15
22 Mark McGwire	3.00	.90
23 Tony Gwynn	1.50	.45
24 Alex Rodriguez	2.00	.60
25 Ivan Rodriguez	1.00	.30

2000 Crown Royale Final Numbers

Randomly inserted into packs at 1:1 hobby 1:2 retail, this 25-card insert features players that have put up great numbers in their career. Please note that there is a parallel version of this card that is serial numbered to 10.

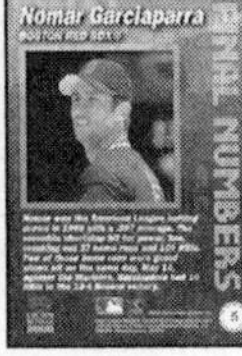

	Nm-Mt	Ex-Mt
COMPLETE SET (25)	20.00	6.00
HOLOGRAPHIC RANDOM INSERTS IN PACKS		
HOLO.PRINT RUN 10 SERIAL #'d SETS		
HOLO.NO PRICING DUE TO SCARCITY		
1 Randy Johnson	1.00	.30
2 Andruw Jones	.40	.12
3 Chipper Jones	1.00	.30
4 Cal Ripken	4.00	1.20
5 Nomar Garciaparra	2.00	.60
6 Pedro Martinez	1.00	.30
7 Sammy Sosa	2.00	.60
8 Ken Griffey Jr.	2.00	.60
9 Sean Casey	.40	.12
10 Manny Ramirez	.40	.12
11 Larry Walker	.60	.18
12 Jeff Bagwell	.60	.18
13 Craig Biggio	.60	.18
14 Shawn Green	.40	.12
15 Vladimir Guerrero	1.00	.30
16 Mike Piazza	2.00	.60
17 Derek Jeter	3.00	.90
18 Bernie Williams	.60	.18
19 Scott Rolen	.60	.18
20 Mark McGwire	3.00	.90
21 Tony Gwynn	1.50	.45
22 Barry Bonds	3.00	.90
23 Alex Rodriguez	2.00	.60
24 Jose Canseco	1.00	.30
25 Ivan Rodriguez	1.00	.30

2000 Crown Royale Final Numbers FanFest

Serial numbered to 20, these cards were distibuted at the 2000 FanFest event. Due to scarcity no pricing is provided.

	Nm-Mt	Ex-Mt
1 Randy Johnson		
2 Andruw Jones		
3 Chipper Jones		
4 Cal Ripken		
5 Nomar Garciaparra		
6 Pedro Martinez		
7 Sammy Sosa		
8 Ken Griffey Jr.		
9 Sean Casey		
10 Manny Ramirez		
11 Larry Walker		
12 Jeff Bagwell		
13 Craig Biggio		
14 Shawn Green		
15 Vladimir Guerrero		
16 Mike Piazza		
17 Derek Jeter		
18 Bernie Williams		
19 Scott Rolen		
20 Mark McGwire		
21 Tony Gwynn		
22 Barry Bonds		
23 Alex Rodriguez		
24 Jose Canseco		
25 Ivan Rodriguez		

2000 Crown Royale Premiums

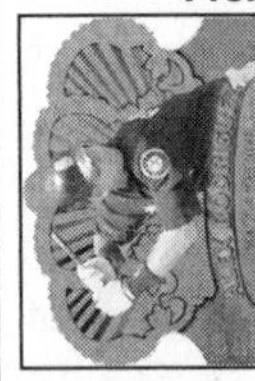

Inserted into hobby boxes as a chip-topper in six out of ten boxes, this six-card insert is an oversized version of the Crown Royale base set.

	Nm-Mt	Ex-Mt
COMPLETE SET (6)	80.00	24.00
1 Cal Ripken	20.00	6.00
2 Nomar Garciaparra	10.00	3.00
3 Ken Griffey Jr.	10.00	3.00
4 Alex Rodriguez	10.00	3.00
5 Mark McGwire	15.00	4.50
6 Derek Jeter	15.00	4.50

2000 Crown Royale Proofs

Randomly inserted into packs at one in 25, this 36-card insert features superstar caliber players.

	Nm-Mt	Ex-Mt
COMPLETE SET (36)	200.00	60.00
*SERIAL 50: 2X TO 5X BASIC PROOFS		
SERIAL 50 RANDOM INSERTS IN PACKS		
SERIAL 50 PRINT RUN 50 SERIAL #'d SETS		
1 Erubiel Durazo	1.50	.45
2 Randy Johnson	6.00	1.80
3 Chipper Jones	6.00	1.80
4 Greg Maddux	12.00	3.60
5 Cal Ripken	25.00	7.50
6 Nomar Garciaparra	12.00	3.60
7 Pedro Martinez	6.00	1.80
8 Sammy Sosa	12.00	3.60
9 Frank Thomas	6.00	1.80
10 Sean Casey	2.50	.75
11 Ken Griffey Jr.	12.00	3.60
12 Manny Ramirez	2.50	.75
13 Jim Thome	6.00	1.80
14 Larry Walker	4.00	1.20
15 Juan Gonzalez	6.00	1.80
16 Jeff Bagwell	4.00	1.20
17 Craig Biggio	4.00	1.20
18 Carlos Beltran	2.50	.75
19 Shawn Green	2.50	.75
20 Vladimir Guerrero	6.00	1.80
21 Edgardo Alfonzo	2.50	.75
22 Mike Piazza	12.00	3.60
23 Roger Clemens	15.00	4.50
24 Derek Jeter	20.00	6.00
25 Alfonso Soriano	10.00	3.00
26 Bernie Williams	4.00	1.20
27 Ben Grieve	1.50	.45
28 Rick Ankiel	8.00	2.40
29 Mark McGwire	20.00	6.00
30 Tony Gwynn	10.00	3.00
31 Barry Bonds	20.00	6.00
32 Alex Rodriguez	12.00	3.60
33 Jose Canseco	6.00	1.80
34 Vinny Castilla	2.50	.75
35 Ivan Rodriguez	6.00	1.80
36 Rafael Palmeiro	4.00	1.20

2000 Crown Royale Sweet Spot Signatures

Randomly inserted into packs, this 30-card insert features autographed cards of some of the hottest names in baseball.

	Nm-Mt	Ex-Mt
1 Adam Kennedy	15.00	4.50
2 Trot Nixon	25.00	7.50
3 Magglio Ordonez	15.00	4.50
4 Sean Casey	15.00	4.50
5 Gookie Dawkins	10.00	3.00
6 Todd Helton	25.00	7.50
7 Ben Petrick	10.00	3.00
8 Jeff Weaver	15.00	4.50
9 Preston Wilson	15.00	4.50
10 Lance Berkman	15.00	4.50
11 Roger Cedeno	10.00	3.00
12 Eric Gagne	40.00	12.00
13 Kevin Barker	10.00	3.00
14 Kyle Peterson	10.00	3.00
15 Tony Armas Jr.	10.00	3.00
16 Peter Bergeron	10.00	3.00
17 Alfonso Soriano	40.00	12.00
18 Ben Grieve	10.00	3.00
19 Ramon Hernandez	10.00	3.00
20 Brian Giles	15.00	4.50
21 Chad Hermansen	10.00	3.00
22 Warren Morris	10.00	3.00
23 Ben Davis	10.00	3.00
24 Chad Hutchinson	10.00	3.00
25 Rick Ankiel	10.00	3.00
26 Freddy Garcia	15.00	4.50
27 Gabe Kapler	10.00	3.00
28 Ruben Mateo	10.00	3.00
29 Billy Koch	15.00	4.50
30 Vernon Wells	15.00	4.50

1907 Cubs A.C. Dietsche Postcards PC765

This set of black and white Dietsche postcards was issued in 1907 and feature Chicago Cubs only. Cards have been seen with and without the player's name on the front. There is no current price differential for either variation.

	Ex-Mt	VG
COMPLETE SET	1400.00	700.00
1 Mordecai Brown	150.00	75.00
2 Frank Chance	200.00	100.00
3 Johnny Evers	200.00	100.00
4 Arthur F. Hoffman	80.00	40.00
5 John Kling	80.00	40.00
6 Carl Lundgren	80.00	40.00
7 Patrick J. Moran	80.00	40.00
8 Orvall Overall	100.00	50.00
9 John A. Pfeister	80.00	40.00
10 Ed Reulbach	100.00	50.00
11 Frank Schulte	100.00	50.00
12 James T. Sheckard	80.00	40.00
13 Harry Steinfeldt	100.00	50.00
14 James Slagle	80.00	40.00
15 Joseph B. Tinker	200.00	100.00

1907 Cubs G.F. Grignon Co. PC775

This rather interesting postcard set measures 1/2" by 5 1/2", was issued in 1907 and features a Chicago Cub player in a circle in the upper right corner of the front of the card. These cards have green backgrounds featuring a teddy bear in different poses. There is also head shot in the upper right corner blending comic and photo art. Cards are known to come with an ad for the Boston Oyster House, a popular Chicago restaurant at the time.

	Ex-Mt	VG
COMPLETE SET (16)	2000.00	1000.00
1 Mordecai Brown	250.00	125.00
2 Frank Chance	300.00	150.00
3 Johnny Evers	300.00	150.00
4 Arthur Hoffman	100.00	50.00
5 John Kling	100.00	50.00
6 Carl Lundgren	100.00	50.00
7 Pat Moran	150.00	75.00
8 Orvall Overall	150.00	75.00
9 Jack Pfiester	100.00	50.00
10 Ed Reulbach	150.00	75.00
11 Frank Schulte	150.00	75.00
12 Jimmy Sheckard	100.00	50.00
13 James Slagle	100.00	50.00
14 Harry Steinfeldt	150.00	75.00
15 Jack Taylor	100.00	50.00
16 Joe Tinker	300.00	150.00

1908 Cubs Postcards

An unknown Chicago Publisher using a logo of a dollar sign inside a shield produced an attractive set of Cubs players on a gray background in 1908. The known cards in this set are listed below any additions to this checklist are appreciated.

	Ex-Mt	VG
COMPLETE SET (4)	750.00	375.00
1 Frank Chance	300.00	150.00
2 Artie Hoffman	150.00	75.00
3 John Kling	150.00	75.00
4 Harry Steinfeldt	175.00	90.00

1930 Cubs Blue Ribbon Malt

These photographs, which measure 6 1/4" by 8 3/4" and feature fascimile autographs are surrounded by plain white borders. Both Chicago Teams are included in this set. The cards have black backs and are therefore sequenced in alphabetical order. It is possible that other cards may be in the set so all additional information is appreciated. These cards were sent out in special envelopes which included an advertising drawing of Charlie Grimm.

	Ex-Mt	VG
COMPLETE SET	400.00	200.00
1 Clyde Beck	10.00	5.00
2 Les Bell	10.00	5.00
3 Clarence Blair	10.00	5.00
4 Fred Blake	10.00	5.00
5 Jimmy Burke CO	10.00	5.00
6 Guy Bush	10.00	5.00
7 Hal Carlson	10.00	5.00
8 Kiki Cuyler	25.00	12.50
9 Woody English	15.00	7.50
10 Charlie Grimm	20.00	10.00
11 Gabby Hartnett	30.00	15.00
12 Cliff Heathcote	10.00	5.00
13 Rogers Hornsby	50.00	25.00
14 Pat Malone	10.00	5.00
15 Joe McCarthy MG	25.00	12.50
16 Malcolm Moss	10.00	5.00
17 Lynn Nelson	10.00	5.00
18 Bob Osborn	10.00	5.00
19 Bobby Smith	10.00	5.00
19 Charlie Root	15.00	7.50
20 Ray Schalk CO	25.00	12.50
21 John Schulte	10.00	5.00
22 Al Shealy	10.00	5.00
23 Riggs Stephenson	20.00	10.00
24 Dan Taylor	10.00	5.00
25 Zach Taylor	10.00	5.00
26 Charles Tolson	10.00	5.00
27 Hal Totten ANN	10.00	5.00
28 Hack Wilson	25.00	12.50

1930 Cubs Team Issue

This 21-card set of the Chicago Cubs features black-and-white player photos with facsimile autographs. The backs are blank. The cards are all 3 1/2" high but have various widths ranging from 1 3/8" to 3". The cards are unnumbered and checklisted below in alphabetical order. A few uncut sheets of this set have survivied.

	Ex-Mt	VG
COMPLETE SET (21)	175.00	90.00
1 Clyde Beck	5.00	2.50
2 Les Bell	5.00	2.50
3 Clarence Blair	5.00	2.50
4 John Blake	5.00	2.50
5 Woody English	8.00	4.00
6 Doc Farrell	5.00	2.50
7 Gabby Hartnett	25.00	12.50
8 Clifton Heathcote	5.00	2.50
9 Rogers Hornsby	50.00	25.00
10 George Kelly	10.00	5.00
11 Pat Malone	5.00	2.50
12 Joe McCarthy MG	10.00	5.00
13 Bob Osborn	5.00	2.50
14 Jesse Petty	5.00	2.50
15 Charlie Root	8.00	4.00
16 Ray Schalk CO	10.00	5.00
17 Fred Schulte	5.00	2.50
18 Al Shealy	5.00	2.50
19 Zack Taylor	5.00	2.50
20 Bud Teachout	5.00	2.50
21 Hack Wilson	20.00	10.00

1931 Cubs Team Issue

These 30 photos feature players and club personnel involved with the 1931 Chicago Cubs. They measure approximately 6" by 9 1/2" and all the photos have a facsimile autograph as well. All of this is surrounded by white borders. The backs are black and we have sequenced the photos in alphabetical order.

	Ex-Mt	VG
COMPLETE SET (30)	150.00	75.00
1 Ed Baecht	3.00	1.50
2 Les Bell	3.00	1.50
3 Clarence Blair	3.00	1.50
4 Sheriff Blake	3.00	1.50
5 Guy Bush	5.00	2.50
6 Margaret Donahue FO	3.00	1.50
7 Woody English	5.00	2.50
8 Charlie Grimm	6.00	3.00
9 Gabby Hartnett	15.00	7.50
10 Rollie Helmsley	3.00	1.50
11 Rogers Hornsby	40.00	20.00
12 Billy Jurges	5.00	2.50
13 Bob Lewis TS	3.00	1.50
14 Andy Lotshaw TR	3.00	1.50
15 Pat Malone	3.00	1.50
16 Frank May	3.00	1.50
17 John Moore	3.00	1.50
18 Charlie Root	5.00	2.50
19 Bob Smith	3.00	1.50
20 Ray Schalk CO	8.00	4.00
21 John Seys FO	3.00	1.50
22 Riggs Stephenson	6.00	3.00
23 Les Sweetland	3.00	1.50
24 Zack Taylor	3.00	1.50
25 Bud Teachout	3.00	1.50
26 William Veeck PRES	5.00	2.50
27 W.M. Warner FO	3.00	1.50
28 Hack Wilson	15.00	7.50
29 Phil Wrigley	5.00	2.50
30 William Wrigley OWN	5.00	2.50

1932 Cubs Team Issue

These 27 photos feature members of the 1932 Chicago Cubs. The photos are shot against a black background and feature a player photo and a facsimile signature. The cards measure approximately 6" by 9" are unnumbered and we have sequenced them in alphabetical order. This set was issued late in the season as Mark Koenig who only spent the last part of the season with the Cubs was included.

	Ex-Mt	VG
COMPLETE SET (27)	150.00	75.00
1 Guy Bush	5.00	2.50
2 Red Corriden CO	3.00	1.50
3 Kiki Cuyler	15.00	7.50
4 Frank Demaree	3.00	1.50
5 Woody English	5.00	2.50
6 Charlie Grimm	8.00	4.00
7 Marv Gudat	3.00	1.50
8 Burleigh Grimes	15.00	7.50
9 Stanley Hack	5.00	2.50
10 Gabby Hartnett	20.00	10.00
11 Rollie Helmsley	3.00	1.50
12 Billy Herman	15.00	7.50
13 Leroy Herrmann	3.00	1.50
14 Billy Jurges	5.00	2.50
15 Mark Koenig	5.00	2.50
16 Pat Malone	3.00	1.50
17 Jake May	3.00	1.50
18 Johnny Moore	3.00	1.50
19 Charley O'Leary CO	3.00	1.50
20 Charlie Root	5.00	2.50
21 Bob Smith	3.00	1.50
22 Riggs Stephenson	6.00	3.00
23 Zack Taylor	3.00	1.50
24 Bud Tinning	3.00	1.50
25 William Veeck GM	5.00	2.50
26 Lon Warneke	5.00	2.50
27 William Wrigley OWN	5.00	2.50

1936 Cubs Team Issue

This 32-card set of the Chicago Cubs measures approximately 6" by 9" and is printed on black paper with a facimile autograph in white. The backs are blank. The cards are unnumbered and checklisted below in alphabetical order.

	Ex-Mt	VG
COMPLETE SET (32)	200.00	100.00
1 Clay Bryant	5.00	2.50
2 Tex Carleton	5.00	2.50
3 Phil Carvaretta	10.00	5.00
4 John Corriden CO	5.00	2.50
5 Frank Demaree	5.00	2.50
6 Margaret Donohue FO	5.00	2.50
7 Woody English	5.00	2.50
8 Larry French	6.00	3.00
9 Augie Galan	6.00	3.00
10 Johnny Gill	5.00	2.50
11 Charlie Grimm MG	8.00	4.00
12 Stanley Hack	10.00	5.00
13 Leo"Gabby" Hartnett	15.00	7.50
14 Roy Henshaw	5.00	2.50
15 Billy Herman	15.00	7.50
16 Roy Johnson	5.00	2.50
17 Bill Jurges	8.00	4.00
18 Chuck Klein	20.00	10.00
19 Fabian Kowalick	5.00	2.50
20 Bill Lee	5.00	2.50
21 Robert Lewis TS	5.00	2.50
22 Gene Lillard	5.00	2.50
23 Andy Lotshaw TR	5.00	2.50
24 Jim O'Dea	5.00	2.50
25 Charlie Root	8.00	4.00
26 John Seys	5.00	2.50
27 Clyde Shoun	5.00	2.50
28 Tuck Stainback	5.00	2.50
29 Riggs Stephenson	10.00	5.00
30 Lon Warneke	8.00	4.00
31 Charles Weber	5.00	2.50
32 Wrigley Field	25.00	12.50

1939 Cubs Team Issue

This set of the Chicago Cubs measures approximately 6 1/2" by 9". The black and white photos display fascimile autographs. The backs are blank. The cards are unnumbered and are checklisted below in alphabetical order.

	Ex-Mt	VG
COMPLETE SET (25)	100.00	50.00
1 Dick Bartell	5.00	2.50
2 Clay Bryant	3.00	1.50
3 Phil Cavarretta	5.00	2.50
4 John Corriden CO	3.00	1.50
5 Dizzy Dean	20.00	10.00
6 Larry French	4.00	2.00
7 Augie Galan	5.00	2.50
8 Bob Garbark	3.00	1.50
9 Jim Gleeson	3.00	1.50
10 Stanley Hack	5.00	2.50
11 Leo Hartnett	15.00	7.50
12 Billy Herman	15.00	7.50
13 Roy Johnson	3.00	1.50
14 Bill Lee	4.00	2.00
15 Hank Lieber	3.00	1.50
16 Gene Lillard	3.00	1.50
17 Gus Mancuso	3.00	1.50
18 Bobby Mattick	3.00	1.50
19 Vance Page	3.00	1.50
20 Claude Passeau	5.00	2.50
21 Carl Reynolds	3.00	1.50
22 Charlie Root	5.00	2.50
23 Glen "Rip" Russell	3.00	1.50
24 Jack Russell	3.00	1.50
25 Earl Whitehill	3.00	1.50

1941 Cubs Team Issue

These photos measure approximately 6 1/2" by 9". They feature members of the 1941 Chicago Cubs. The set is dated by the appearence of Greek George. The backs are blank and we have sequenced them in alphabetical order. This set was issued twice so there are more than the normal amount of players in this set due to roster manipulations during the season.

	Ex-Mt	VG
COMPLETE SET (25)	100.00	50.00
1 Phil Cavarretta	6.00	3.00
2 Dom Dallessandro	3.00	1.50
3 Paul Erickson	3.00	1.50
4 Larry French	5.00	2.50
5 Augie Galan	5.00	2.50
6 Greek George	3.00	1.50
7 Charlie Gilbert	3.00	1.50
8 Stan Hack	5.00	2.50
9 Johnny Hudson	3.00	1.50
10 Bill Lee	5.00	2.50
11 Hank Leiber	3.00	1.50
12 Clyde McCullough	3.00	1.50
13 Jake Mooty	3.00	1.50
14 Bill Myers	3.00	1.50
15 Bill Nicholson	6.00	3.00
16 Lou Novikoff	4.00	2.00
17 Vern Olsen	3.00	1.50
18 Vance Page	3.00	1.50
19 Claude Passeau	5.00	2.50
20 Tot Pressnell	3.00	1.50
21 Charlie Root	5.00	2.50
22 Bob Scheffing	3.00	1.50
23 Lou Stringer	3.00	1.50
24 Bob Sturgeon	3.00	1.50
25 Dick Spalding CO Jimmie Wilson CO Charlie Grimm MG Dizzy Dean CO	15.00	7.50

1942 Cubs Team Issue

These 25 photos were issued by the Chicago Cubs. The black and white blank back photos measure 6 1/2" by 9". Since they are unnumbered we have sequenced them in alphabetical order.

	Ex-Mt	VG
COMPLETE SET (25)	80.00	40.00
1 Hiram Bithorn	3.00	1.50
2 Phil Cavarretta	5.00	2.50
3 Dom Dallessandro	3.00	1.50
4 Paul Erickson	3.00	1.50
5 Bill Fleming	3.00	1.50
6 Charlie Gilbert	3.00	1.50
7 Stanley Hack	5.00	2.50
8 Edward Hanyzewski	3.00	1.50
9 Chico Hernandez	3.00	1.50
10 Bill Lee	4.00	2.00
11 Peanuts Lowrey	3.00	1.50
12 Clyde McCullough	3.00	1.50
13 Jake Mooty	3.00	1.50
14 Lennie Merullo	3.00	1.50
15 Bill Nicholson	6.00	3.00
16 Louie Novikoff	3.00	1.50
17 Vern Olsen	3.00	1.50
18 Claude Passeau	5.00	2.50
19 Tot Pressnell	3.00	1.50
20 Glen Russell	3.00	1.50
21 Bob Scheffing	3.00	1.50
22 John Schmitz	3.00	1.50
23 Lou Stringer	3.00	1.50
24 Bob Sturgeon	3.00	1.50
25 KiKi Cuyler CO Jimmie Wilson CO Dick Spalding CO Cubs Coaches	12.00	6.00

1943 Cubs Team Issue

This set of photographs measure approximately 6 1/2" by 9". They feature members of the 1943 Chicago Cubs. The black and white photos also feature fascimile autographs. The backs are blank and we have sequenced this set in alphabetical order.

	Ex-Mt	VG
COMPLETE SET (24)	100.00	50.00
1 Dick Barrett	3.00	1.50
2 Heinz Becker	3.00	1.50
3 Hi Bithorn	3.00	1.50
4 Phil Cavarretta	6.00	3.00
5 Dom Dallessandro	3.00	1.50
6 Paul Derringer	5.00	2.50
7 Paul Erickson	3.00	1.50
8 Bill Fleming	3.00	1.50
9 Stan Hack	5.00	2.50
10 Ed Hanyzewski	3.00	1.50
11 Chico Hernandez	3.00	1.50
12 Bill Lee	3.00	1.50
13 Peanuts Lowery	4.00	2.00
14 Stu Martin	3.00	1.50
15 Clyde McCullough	3.00	1.50
16 Lennie Merullo	3.00	1.50
17 Bill Nicholson	6.00	3.00
18 Lou Novikoff	3.00	1.50
19 Claude Passeau	5.00	2.50
20 Ray Prim	3.00	1.50
21 Eddie Stanky	6.00	3.00
22 Al Todd	3.00	1.50
23 Lon Warneke	5.00	2.50
24 Hank Wyse	3.00	1.50
25 Kiki Cuyler CO Jimmie Wilson CO Dick Spalding CO	12.00	6.00

1944 Cubs Team Issue

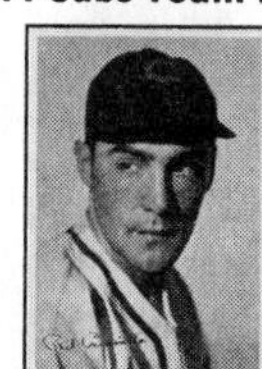

These 1944 Chicago Cub team photos are printed on thin paper stock and measure approximately 6" by 8 1/2". The photos feature a black and white head and shoulders shot, with white borders and the player's autograph inscribed across the picture. The backs are blank. The photos are unnumbered and checklisted below in alphabetical order.

	Ex-Mt	VG
COMPLETE SET (26)	75.00	38.00
1 Heinz Becker	3.00	1.50
2 John Burrows	3.00	1.50
3 Phil Cavarretta	5.00	2.50
4 Dom Dallessandro	3.00	1.50
5 Paul Denuege	3.00	1.50
6 Paul Derringer	5.00	2.50
7 Roy Easterwood	3.00	1.50
8 Paul Erickson	3.00	1.50
9 Bill Fleming	3.00	1.50
10 Jimmie Foxx	15.00	7.50
11 Ival Goodman	3.00	1.50
12 Edward Hanyzewski	3.00	1.50
13 William Holm	3.00	1.50
14 Don Johnson	3.00	1.50
15 Garth Mann	3.00	1.50
16 Lennie Merullo	3.00	1.50
17 John Miklos	3.00	1.50
18 Bill Nicholson	5.00	2.50
19 Lou Novikoff	4.00	2.00
20 Andy Pafko	5.00	2.50
21 Eddie Sauer	3.00	1.50
22 William Schuster	3.00	1.50
23 Eddie Stanky	6.00	3.00
24 Hy Vandenberg	3.00	1.50
25 Hank Wyse	3.00	1.50
26 Tony York	3.00	1.50

1950 Cubs Greats Brace

These 18 photos were issued by noted Chicago photographer George Brace and honored some of the leading players in Cub history. The fronts have a photo of the player along with how long they were in the majors and what years they spent with the Cubs. The backs are blank so we have sequenced this set in alphabetical order.

	NM	Ex
COMPLETE SET (18)	150.00	75.00
1 Grover C. Alexander	12.00	6.00
2 Cap Anson	12.00	6.00
3 Mordecai Brown	12.00	6.00
4 Frank Chance	12.00	6.00
5 John Evers	12.00	6.00
6 Charlie Grimm	10.00	5.00
7 Stan Hack	8.00	4.00
8 Gabby Hartnett	12.00	6.00
9 Billy Herman	12.00	6.00
10 Charlie Hollocher	6.00	3.00
11 Billy Jurges	8.00	4.00
12 Johnny Kling	6.00	3.00
13 Joe McCarthy MG	10.00	5.00
14 Ed Reulbach	8.00	4.00
15 Albert Spalding	12.00	6.00
16 Joe Tinker	12.00	6.00
17 Hippo Vaughn	6.00	3.00
18 Hack Wilson	12.00	6.00

1952 Cubs Ben Bey

These 8" by 11" photos were issued by Ben Bey and featured members of the Chicago Cubs. The front has a player photo as well as a fascimile signature. The back has the notation; "courtesy of Ben Bey, Lucky Fan WBKB Chicago." Since the photos are unnumbered we have sequenced them in alphabetical order. It is possible that there are more photos in this set so please send any additions you might have.

	NM	Ex
COMPLETE SET (26)	120.00	60.00
1 Frank Baumholtz	5.00	2.50
2 Bob Borkowski	5.00	2.50
3 Smoky Burgess	6.00	3.00
4 Phil Cavaretta	8.00	4.00
5 Chuck Connors	10.00	5.00
6 Jack Cusick	5.00	2.50
7 Bruce Edwards	5.00	2.50
8 Dee Fondy	5.00	2.50
9 Joe Hatten	5.00	2.50
10 Gene Hermanski	5.00	2.50
11 Frank Hiller	5.00	2.50
12 Ransom Jackson	5.00	2.50
13 Hal Jeffcoat	5.00	2.50
14 Bob Kelly	5.00	2.50
15 John Klippstein	5.00	2.50
16 Dutch Leonard	5.00	2.50
17 Turk Lown	5.00	2.50
18 Cal McLish	5.00	2.50
19 Eddie Miksis	5.00	2.50
20 Paul Minner	5.00	2.50
21 Bob Ramazzotti	5.00	2.50
22 Bob Rush	5.00	2.50
23 Hank Sauer	10.00	5.00
24 Bob Schultz	5.00	2.50
25 Bill Serena	5.00	2.50
26 Roy Smalley	5.00	2.50

1960 Cubs Jay Publishing

This 12-card set of the Chicago Cubs measures approximately 5" by 7" and features black-and-white player photos in a white border. These cards were packaged 12 to a packet. The backs are blank. The cards are unnumbered and checklisted below in alphabetical order.

	NM	Ex
COMPLETE SET (12)	35.00	14.00
1 George Altman	2.00	.80
2 Bob Anderson	2.00	.80
3 Richie Ashburn	6.00	2.40
4 Ernie Banks	12.00	4.80
5 Moe Drabowsky	2.00	.80
6 Don Elston	2.00	.80
7 Glen Hobbie	2.00	.80
8 Dale Long	2.00	.80
9 Walt Moryn	2.00	.80
10 Sam Taylor	2.00	.80
11 Tony Taylor	2.00	.80
12 Frank Thomas	3.00	1.20

1961 Cubs Jay Publishing

This 12-card set of the Chicago Cubs measures approximately 5" by 7". The fronts feature black-and-white posed player photos with the player's and team name printed below in the white border. These cards were packaged 12 in a packet. The backs are blank. The cards are unnumbered and checklisted below in alphabetical order.

	NM	Ex
COMPLETE SET	35.00	14.00
1 George Altman	2.00	.80
2 Bob Anderson	2.00	.80
3 Richie Ashburn	6.00	2.40
4 Ernie Banks	12.00	4.80
5 Ed Bouchee	2.00	.80
6 Dick Ellsworth	2.00	.80
7 Don Elston	2.00	.80
8 Glen Hobbie	2.00	.80
9 Jerry Kindall	2.00	.80
10 Ron Santo	6.00	2.40
11 Moe Thacker	2.00	.80
12 Don Zimmer	3.00	1.20

1962 Cubs Jay Publishing

This 12-card set of the Chicago Cubs measures approximately 5" by 7". The fronts feature black-and-white posed player photos with the player's and team name printed below in the white border. These cards were packaged 12 in a packet. The backs are blank. The cards are unnumbered and checklisted below in alphabetical order.

	NM	Ex
COMPLETE SET (12)	35.00	14.00
1 George Altman	2.00	.80
2 Bob Anderson	2.00	.80
3 Ernie Banks	12.00	4.80
4 Don Cardwell	2.00	.80
5 Jack Curtis	2.00	.80
6 Don Elston	2.00	.80
7 Glen Hobbie	2.00	.80
8 Ken Hubbs	5.00	2.00
9 Ron Santo	5.00	2.00
10 Barney Schultz	2.00	.80
11 Sam Taylor	2.00	.80
12 Billy Williams	8.00	3.20

1963 Cubs Jay Publishing

This 12-card set of the Chicago Cubs measures approximately 5" by 7". The fronts feature black-and-white posed player photos with the player's and team name printed below in the white border. These cards were packaged 12 in a packet. The backs are blank. The cards are unnumbered and checklisted below in alphabetical order.

	NM	Ex
COMPLETE SET (12)	40.00	16.00
1 Ernie Banks	12.00	4.80
2 Dick Bertell	2.00	.80
3 Lou Brock	12.00	4.80
4 Bob Buhl	2.00	.80
5 Dick Ellsworth	2.00	.80
6 Glen Hobbie	2.00	.80
7 Larry Jackson	2.00	.80
8 Bob Kennedy CO	2.00	.80
9 Lindy McDaniel	2.00	.80
10 Andre Rodgers	2.00	.80
11 Ron Santo	5.00	2.00
12 Billy Williams	8.00	3.20

1964 Cubs Jay Publishing

This 12-card set of the Chicago Cubs measures approximately 5" by 7". The fronts feature black-and-white posed player photos with the player's and team name printed below in the white border. These cards were packaged 12 in a packet. The backs are blank. The cards are unnumbered and checklisted below in alphabetical order.

	NM	Ex
COMPLETE SET (12)	40.00	16.00
1 Ernie Banks	12.00	4.80
2 Dick Bertell	2.00	.80
3 Lou Brock	10.00	4.00
4 Bob Buhl	2.00	.80
5 Don Elston	2.00	.80
6 Ken Hubbs	5.00	2.00
7 Larry Jackson	2.00	.80
8 Don Landrum	2.00	.80
9 Lindy McDaniel	2.00	.80
10 Andre Rodgers	2.00	.80
11 Ron Santo	5.00	2.00
12 Billy Williams	8.00	3.20

1965 Cubs Announcers

Issued to promote the announcers of the 1965 Chicago Cubs. These two postcards feature both announcers.

	NM	Ex
COMPLETE SET	15.00	6.00
1 Lou Boudreau Vince Lloyd Color photo in the dugout	5.00	2.00
2 Lou Bourdreau Vince Lloyd Black and White Photo, on the field	10.00	4.00

1965 Cubs Jay Publishing

This 12-card set of the Chicago Cubs measures approximately 5" by 7". The fronts feature black-and-white posed player photos with the player's and team name printed below in the white border. These cards were packaged 12 in a packet. The backs are blank. The cards are unnumbered and checklisted below in alphabetical order.

	NM	Ex
COMPLETE SET (12)	40.00	16.00
1 George Altman	2.00	.80
2 Ernie Banks	12.00	4.80
3 Dick Bertell	2.00	.80
4 Ernie Broglio	2.00	.80
5 Bob Buhl	2.00	.80
6 Lou Burdette	3.00	1.20
7 Dick Ellsworth	2.00	.80
8 Larry Jackson	2.00	.80
9 Bob Kennedy CO	2.00	.80
10 Ron Santo	5.00	2.00
11 Jim Stewart	2.00	.80
12 Billy Williams	8.00	3.20

1966 Cubs Team Issue

These 12 cards feature members of the 1966 Chicago Cubs, who by finishing last, enabled the New York Mets to finally not finish in the cellar. The cards are unnumbered and we have sequenced them in alphabetical order.

	NM	Ex
COMPLETE SET (12)	35.00	14.00
1 Ted Abernathy	2.00	.80
2 George Altman	3.00	1.20
3 Ernie Banks	10.00	4.00
4 Glenn Beckert	3.00	1.20
5 Ernie Broglio	2.00	.80
6 Leo Durocher MG	5.00	2.00
7 Dick Ellsworth	2.00	.80
8 Larry Jackson	2.00	.80
9 Chris Krug	2.00	.80
10 Harvey Kuenn	3.00	1.20
11 Ron Santo	5.00	2.00
12 Billy Williams	5.00	2.00

1968 Cubs Pro's Pizza

This 12-card set measures 4 3/4: in diameter and featured members of the Chicago Cubs. Only the Cubs players are included in this listing.

	NM	Ex
COMPLETE SET (12)	1500.00	600.00
1 Joe Amalfitano	50.00	20.00
2 Ernie Banks	300.00	120.00
3 Glenn Beckert	75.00	30.00
4 John Boccabella	50.00	20.00
5 Bill Hands	50.00	20.00
6 Ken Holtzman	75.00	30.00
7 Randy Hundley	75.00	30.00
8 Fergie Jenkins	250.00	100.00
9 Don Kessinger	75.00	30.00
10 Adolfo Phillips	50.00	20.00
11 Ron Santo	250.00	100.00
12 Billy Williams	250.00	100.00

1969 Cubs Bumper Stickers

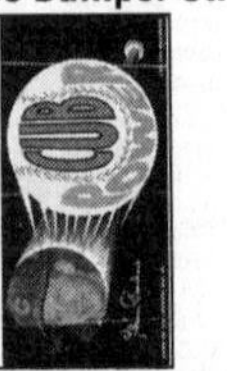

This six-sticker set of the Chicago Cubs measures approximately 7 7/8" by 4" and features color player head photos printed at the end of a baseball bat drawing. Two versions of this set were issued with either "Cub Power" or "Dunkin Donuts" printed inside a ball that looked as if it was being hit by the bat. The stickers are unnumbered and checklisted below in alphabetical order.

	NM	Ex
COMPLETE SET (6)	75.00	30.00
1 Ernie Banks	20.00	8.00
2 Glenn Beckert	10.00	4.00
3 Randy Hundley	10.00	4.00
4 Don Kessinger	10.00	4.00
5 Ron Santo	15.00	6.00
6 Billy Williams	15.00	6.00

1969 Cubs Jewel Tea

This 20-card set of the Chicago Cubs measures approximately 6" by 9" and were given away over a five week period in 1969. The white-bordered fronts feature color player action and posed photos with a facsimile autograph across the picture. The backs are blank. The cards are unnumbered and checklisted below in alphabetical order.

	NM	Ex
COMPLETE SET (20)	45.00	18.00
1 Ted Abernathy	1.50	.60
2 Hank Aguirre	1.50	.60
3 Ernie Banks	10.00	4.00
4 Glenn Beckert	2.00	.80
5 Bill Hands	1.50	.60
6 Jim Hickman	1.50	.60
7 Kenny Holtzman	2.00	.80
8 Randy Hundley	2.00	.80
9 Fergie Jenkins	8.00	3.20
10 Don Kessinger	2.50	1.00
11 Rich Nye	1.50	.60
12 Paul Popovich	1.50	.60
13 Jim Qualls	1.50	.60
14 Phil Regan	1.50	.60
15 Ron Santo	3.00	1.20
16 Dick Selma	1.50	.60
17 Willie Smith	1.50	.60
18 Al Spangler	1.50	.60
19 Billy Williams	6.00	2.40
20 Don Young	1.50	.60

1969 Cubs Photos

These photos feature members of the 1969 Chicago Cubs, best known as the team which lost a huge lead so the Miracle Mets could win the pennant. These photos are unnumbered and we have sequenced them in alphabetical order.

	NM	Ex
COMPLETE SET (12)	25.00	10.00
1 Ted Abernathy	1.50	.60
2 Ernie Banks	8.00	3.20
3 Glenn Beckert	1.50	.60
4 Leo Durocher MG	3.00	1.20
5 Ken Holtzman	2.00	.80
6 Randy Hundley	2.00	.80
7 Ferguson Jenkins	5.00	2.00
8 Don Kessinger	2.50	1.00
9 Phil Regan	1.50	.60
10 Ron Santo	3.00	1.20
11 Al Spangler	1.50	.60
12 Billy Williams	5.00	2.00

1969 Cubs Team Issue Color

This 10-card set of the Chicago Cubs measures approximately 7" by 8 3/4" with the fronts featuring white-bordered color player photos. The player's name and team is printed in black in the white margin below the picture. The backs are blank. The cards are unnumbered and checklisted below in alphabetical order.

	NM	Ex
COMPLETE SET	30.00	12.00
1 Ernie Banks	8.00	3.20
2 Glenn Beckert	1.50	.60
3 Ken Holtzman	2.00	.80
4 Randy Hundley	2.50	1.00
5 Ferguson Jenkins	5.00	2.00
6 Don Kessinger	2.50	1.00
7 Phil Regan	1.50	.60
8 Ron Santo	3.00	1.20
9 Willie Smith	1.50	.60
10 Billy Williams	5.00	2.00

1970 Cubs Dunkin Donuts

This set of six bumper stickers (apparently commemorating the Cubs near-miss in 1969) was produced and distributed by Dunkin Donuts. The stickers are approximately 4 1/16" by 8 1/16" and are in color. Each sticker features a facsimile autograph in the upper left

hand corner. The stickers are unnumbered and are listed below in alphabetical order according to the player's name.

	NM	Ex
COMPLETE SET (6)	25.00	10.00
1 Ernie Banks	15.00	6.00
2 Glenn Beckert	1.50	.60
3 Randy Hundley	1.50	.60
4 Don Kessinger	2.50	1.00
5 Ron Santo	4.00	1.60
6 Billy Williams	8.00	3.20

1972 Cubs Chi-Foursome

These 11" by 14" drawings feature Chicago Cubs players. The attractive color drawings also have a facimilie signature. The backs are blank and we have sequenced this set in alphabetical order.

	NM	Ex
COMPLETE SET (8)	15.00	6.00
1 Ernie Banks	5.00	2.00
2 Glenn Beckert	1.00	.40
3 Fergie Jenkins	2.50	1.00
4 Don Kessinger	1.00	.40
5 Milt Pappas	1.00	.40
6 Joe Pepitone	2.00	.80
7 Ron Santo	2.50	1.00
8 Billy Williams	2.50	1.00

1972 Cubs Team Issue

These 12 photos feature members of the 1972 Chicago Cubs. The photos measure approximately 4 1/4" by 7". The black and white photos are surrounded by white borders and feature a facsimile autograph. The backs are blank and we have sequenced this set in alphabetical order.

	NM	Ex
COMPLETE SET (12)	20.00	8.00
1 Ernie Banks CO	6.00	2.40
2 Glenn Beckert	2.00	.80
3 Bill Hands	1.50	.60
4 Jim Hickman	1.50	.60
5 Randy Hundley	2.00	.80
6 Fergie Jenkins	5.00	2.00
7 Don Kessinger	2.00	.80
8 Rick Monday	2.50	1.00
9 Milt Pappas	1.50	.60
10 Joe Pepitone	2.00	.80
11 Ron Santo	2.50	1.00
12 Billy Williams	5.00	2.00

1973 Cubs Jewel

These blank-backed photos, which measure approximately 6" by 9", feature members of the 1973 Chicago Cubs. These fronts have white borders which surround a full-color player portrait as well as a fascimile autograph. These cards are unnumbered, so we have sequenced them in alphabetical order.

	NM	Ex
COMPLETE SET	15.00	6.00
1 Jack Aker	.50	.20
2 Glenn Beckert	1.00	.40
3 Jose Cardenal	1.00	.40
4 Carmen Fanzone	.50	.20
5 Jim Hickman	.50	.20
6 Burt Hooton	.50	.20
7 Randy Hundley	1.00	.40
8 Fergie Jenkins	3.00	1.20
9 Don Kessinger	1.00	.40
10 Bob Locker	.50	.20
11 Rick Monday	1.00	.40
12 Milt Pappas	1.00	.40
13 Rick Reuschel	2.00	.80
14 Ken Rudolph	.50	.20
15 Ron Santo	2.50	1.00
16 Billy Williams	3.00	1.20

1974 Cubs 1938 Bra-Mac

These 29 photos, which measure 3 1/2" by 5" feature members of the 1938 Chicago Cubs and were issued by Bra-Mac using negatives they had in their massive photo file.

	NM	Ex
COMPLETE SET	25.00	10.00
1 Phil Cavaretta	1.50	.60
2 Bob Garbark	.50	.20
3 Jack Russell	.50	.20
4 Tony Lazzeri	2.00	.80
5 Dizzy Dean	3.00	1.20
6 Coaker Triplett	.50	.20
7 Ken O'Dea	.50	.20
8 Larry French	1.00	.40
9 Stan Hack	1.00	.40
10 Gabby Hartnett	2.00	.80
11 Bill Lee	1.50	.60
12 Kirby Higbe	1.00	.40
13 Bobby Mattick	.50	.20
14 Tex Carleton	.50	.20
15 Charlie Root	1.00	.40
16 Bob Logan	.50	.20
17 Steve Mesner	.50	.20
18 Newt Kimball	.50	.20
19 Clay Bryant	.50	.20
20 Rip Collins	1.00	.40
21 Augie Galan	1.00	.40
22 Frank Demaree	.50	.20
23 Al Epperly	.50	.20
24 Billy Herman	2.00	.80
25 Jim Asbell	.50	.20
26 Carl Reynolds	.50	.20
27 Vance Page	.50	.20
28 Billy Jurges	1.00	.40
29 Joe Marty	.50	.20

1974 Cubs Team Issue

These blank-backed photos, which measure approximately 7" by 9", feature members of the 1974 Chicago Cubs. The fronts have full color photos surrounded by white borders with the players name and team on the bottom. Since these photos are unnumbered, we have sequenced them in alphabetical order.

	NM	Ex
COMPLETE SET	8.00	3.20
1 Ray Burris	.50	.20
2 Jose Cardenal	.75	.30
3 Carmen Fanzone	.50	.20
4 Vic Harris	.50	.20
5 Burt Hooten UER Spelled Houton	.75	.30
6 Don Kessinger	.50	.20
7 Bill Madlock	1.50	.60
8 George Mitterwald	.50	.20
9 Rick Monday	.75	.30
10 Jerry Morales	.50	.20
11 Steve Stone	.75	.30
12 Billy Williams	2.00	.80

1976 Cubs TCMA 1938

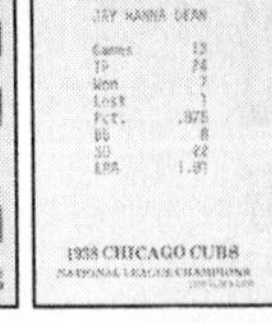

These cards were issued by TCMA and feature members of the pennant winning 1938 Chicago Cubs. These cards are unnumbered and we have sequenced them in alphabetical order.

	NM	Ex
COMPLETE SET (33)	20.00	8.00
1 Jim Ashbell	.50	.20
2 Clay Bryant	.50	.20
3 Tex Carleton	.50	.20
4 Phil Cavaretta	1.00	.40
5 Ripper Collins	.50	.20
6 Red Corriden	.50	.20
7 Dizzy Dean	3.00	1.20
8 Frank Demaree	.50	.20
9 Al Epperly	.50	.20
10 Larry French	.75	.30
11 Augie Galan	.75	.30
12 Bob Garback	.50	.20
13 Charlie Grimm MG	1.50	.60
14 Stan Hack	1.00	.40
15 Gabby Hartnett P/MG	2.00	.80
16 Billy Herman	2.00	.80
17 Kirby Higbe	.75	.30
18 Roy Johnson CO	.50	.20
19 Billy Jurges	.75	.30
20 Newt Kimball	.50	.20
21 Tony Lazzeri	2.00	.80
22 Bill Lee	.50	.20
23 Bob Logan	.50	.20
24 Joe Marty	.50	.20
25 Bobby Mattick	.50	.20
26 Steve Mesner	.50	.20
27 Ken O'Dea	.50	.20
28 Vance Page	.50	.20
29 Carl Reynolds	.50	.20
30 Charlie Root	.75	.30
31 Jack Russell	.50	.20
32 Coaker Triplett	.50	.20
33 Chicago Cub Unidentified Player	.50	.20

1976 Cubs Tribune

These 26 cards were issued by the Chicago Tribune and features the members of the 1976 Cubs. They are unnumbered and we have sequenced them in alphabetical order.

	NM	Ex
COMPLETE SET	25.00	10.00
1 Larry Biittner	1.00	.40
2 Bill Bonham	1.00	.40
3 Pete Broberg	1.00	.40
4 Ray Burris	1.00	.40
5 Jose Cardenal	1.50	.60
6 Gene Clines	1.00	.40
7 Bobby Darwin	1.00	.40
8 Ivan DeJesus	1.00	.40
9 Herman Franks MG	1.00	.40
10 Greg Gross	1.00	.40
11 Willie Hernandez	2.50	1.00
12 Mick Kelleher	1.00	.40
13 Mike Krukow	1.00	.40
14 George Mitterwald	1.00	.40
15 Donnie Moore	1.00	.40
16 Jerry Morales	1.00	.40
17 Bobby Murcer	2.00	.80
18 Steve Ontiveros	1.00	.40
19 Steve Renko	1.00	.40
20 Rick Reuschel	2.00	.80
21 Dave Rosello	1.00	.40
22 Bruce Sutter	5.00	2.00
23 Steve Swisher	1.00	.40
24 Jim Todd	1.00	.40
25 Manny Trillo	1.50	.60
26 Joe Wallis	1.00	.40

1977 Cubs All-Time TCMA

This 13-card set features black-and-white photos with wide white and thin black borders of Chicago Cubs players considered to be the best at their respective positions.The backs carry the checklist for the set. The cards are unnumbered and checklisted below in alphabetical order.

	NM	Ex
COMPLETE SET (13)	8.00	3.20
1 Ernie Banks	1.50	.60
2 Kiki Cuyler	.75	.30
3 Larry French	.50	.20
4 Charlie Grimm	.50	.20
5 Charlie Grimm MG	.50	.20
6 Gabby Hartnett	.75	.30
7 Billy Herman	.75	.30
8 Rogers Hornsby	1.50	.60
9 Emil Kush	.50	.20
10 Charlie Root	.50	.20
11 Ron Santo	1.00	.40
12 Billy Williams	1.00	.40
13 Hack Wilson	.75	.30

1977 Cubs Jewel Tea

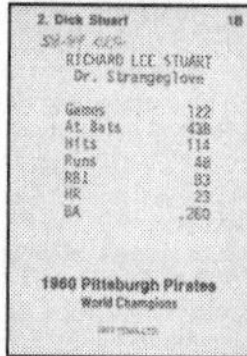

This 15-card set of the Chicago Cubs measures approximately 5 7/8" by 9". The white-bordered fronts feature color player head photos with a facsimile autograph. The backs are blank. The cards are unnumbered and checklisted below in alphabetical order.

	NM	Ex
COMPLETE SET (15)	12.50	5.00
1 Larry Biittner	.75	.30
2 Bill Bonham	.75	.30
3 Bill Buckner	1.50	.60
4 Ray Burris	.75	.30
5 Gene Clines	.75	.30
6 Ivan DeJesus	.75	.30
7 Willie Hernandez	1.50	.60
8 Mike Krukow	.75	.30
9 George Mitterwald	.75	.30
10 Jerry Morales	.75	.30
11 Bobby Murcer	1.00	.40
12 Steve Ontiveros	.75	.30
13 Paul Reuschel	.75	.30
14 Bruce Sutter	2.50	1.00
15 Manny Trillo	1.00	.40

1980 Cubs Greats TCMA

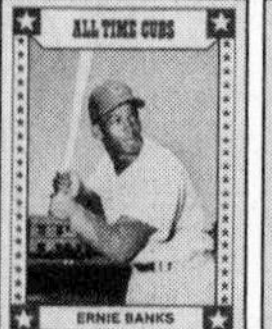

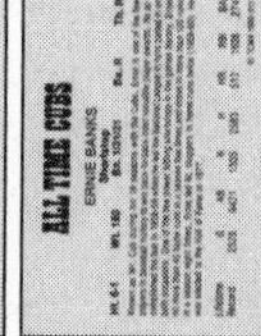

This 12-card standard-size set honors some all-time Chicago Cubs greats. The fronts have a player photo, his name and position. The backs have vital statistics, career totals and a brief biography.

	NM	Ex
COMPLETE SET (12)	5.00	2.00
1 Billy Williams	1.00	.40
2 Charlie Root	.50	.20
3 Ron Santo	.75	.30
4 Larry French	.25	.10
5 Gabby Hartnett	1.00	.40
6 Emil Kush	.25	.10
7 Charlie Grimm	.50	.20
8 Kiki Cuyler	.75	.30
9 Billy Herman	.75	.30
10 Hack Wilson	.75	.30
11 Rogers Hornsby	1.00	.40
12 Ernie Banks	1.50	.60

1981 Cubs Tribune

These photos were inserted daily into the Chicago Tribune and featured members of the 1981 Chicago Cubs. Most of the newspaper cutout is dedicated to the players photo while the bottom of the section featured biographical information about the player and career stats. We have sequenced what we have information on in alphabetical order but this information is incomplete so any additional help is appreciated.

	Nm-Mt	Ex-Mt
COMPLETE SET	3.00	1.20
1 Larry Biittner	.50	.20
2 Bill Caudill	.50	.20
3 Jesus Figeruoa	.50	.20
4 Ken Henderson	.50	.20
5 Willie Hernandez	1.00	.40
6 Mick Kelleher	.50	.20
7 Mike O'Berry	.50	.20

1982 Cubs Red Lobster

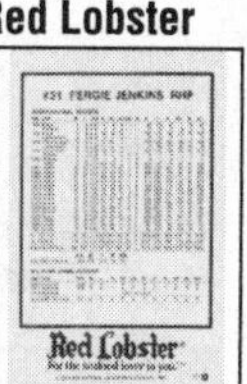

The cards in this 28-card set measure 2 1/4" by 3 1/2". This set of Chicago Cubs players was co-produced by the Cubs and Chicago-area Red Lobster restaurants and was introduced as a promotional giveaway on August 20, 1982, at Wrigley Field. The cards contain borderless color photos of 25 players, manager Lee Elia, the coaching staff, and a team picture. A facsimile autograph appears on the front, and the cards run in sequence by uniform number. While the coaches have a short biographical sketch on back, the player cards simply list the individual's professional record. The key card in the set is obviously Ryne Sandberg's as it predates his Donruss, Fleer, and Topps Rookie Cards by one year. Lee Smith also appears in this set in his Rookie Card year.

	Nm-Mt	Ex-Mt
COMPLETE SET (28)	75.00	30.00
1 Larry Bowa	1.00	.40
4 Lee Elia MG	.50	.20
6 Keith Moreland	.75	.30
7 Jody Davis	1.00	.40
10 Leon Durham	.75	.30
15 Junior Kennedy	.50	.20
17 Bump Wills	.50	.20
18 Scot Thompson	.50	.20
21 Jay Johnstone	1.00	.40
22 Bill Buckner	1.25	.50
23 Ryne Sandberg	60.00	24.00
24 Jerry Morales	.50	.20
25 Gary Woods	.50	.20
28 Steve Henderson	.50	.20
29 Bob Molinaro	.50	.20
31 Fergie Jenkins	4.00	1.60
33 Al Ripley	.50	.20
34 Randy Martz	.50	.20
36 Mike Proly	.50	.20
37 Ken Kravec	.50	.20
38 Willie Hernandez	1.00	.40
39 Bill Campbell	.50	.20
41 Dick Tidrow	.50	.20
46 Lee Smith	8.00	3.20
47 Doug Bird	.50	.20
48 Dickie Noles	.50	.20
NNO Team Picture	4.00	1.60
NNO0 John Vukovich CO	1.00	.40
Gordy MacKenzie CO		
Billy Williams CO		
Billy Connors CO		
Tom Harmon CO		

1983 Cubs Thorn Apple Valley

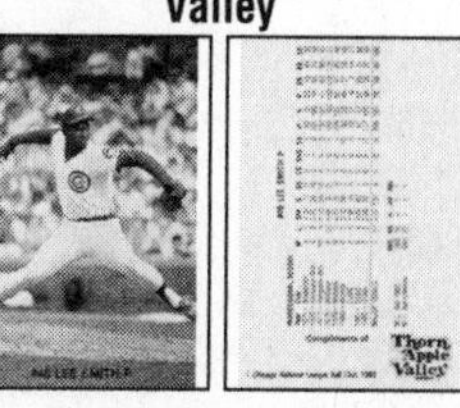

This set of 27 Chicago Cubs features full-color action photos on the front and was sponsored by Thorn Apple Valley. The cards measure approximately 2 1/4" by 3 1/2". The backs provide year-by-year statistics. The cards are unnumbered except for uniform number; they are listed below by uniform with the special cards listed at the end. The card of Joe Carter predates his Donruss Rookie Card by one year.

	Nm-Mt	Ex-Mt
COMPLETE SET (27)	30.00	12.00
1 Larry Bowa	.75	.30
6 Keith Moreland	.25	.10
7 Jody Davis	.50	.20
10 Leon Durham	.50	.20
11 Ron Cey	.75	.30
16 Steve Lake	.25	.10
20 Thad Bosley	.25	.10
21 Jay Johnstone	.50	.20
22 Bill Buckner	.75	.30
23 Ryne Sandberg	12.00	4.80
24 Jerry Morales	.25	.10
25 Gary Woods	.25	.10
27 Mel Hall	.50	.20
29 Tom Veryzer	.25	.10
30 Chuck Rainey	.25	.10
31 Fergie Jenkins	2.00	.80
32 Craig Lefferts	.25	.10
33 Joe Carter	10.00	4.00
34 Steve Trout	.25	.10
36 Mike Proly	.25	.10
39 Bill Campbell	.25	.10
41 Warren Brusstar	.25	.10
44 Dick Ruthven	.25	.10
46 Lee Smith	3.00	1.20
48 Dickie Noles	.25	.10
NNO Lee Elia MG	.25	.10
Ruben Amaro CO		
Billy Connors CO		
Duffy Dyer CO		
Fred Koenig CO		
John Vukovich CO		
NNO Team Photo	1.00	.40

1984 Cubs Brickhouse Playing Cards

This 58-card set features black-and-white photos in white borders with rounded corners of top players who have played with the Chicago Cubs at some time during their careers. The backs display a picture of Jack Brickhouse in a circle with crossed baseball bats behind it on a blue background with red and white printing. The cards are checklisted below in playing card order by suits and assigned numbers to aces (1), jacks (11), queens (12), and kings (13).

	Nm-Mt	Ex-Mt
COMP. FACT SET (58)	12.00	4.80
1C Lon Warneke	.10	.04
1D Burt Hooten	.10	.04
1H Jack Brickhouse ANN	.10	.04
1S Leon Durham	.10	.04
2C Augie Galan	.25	.10
2D Fergie Jenkins	.75	.30
2H 1876 Champions	.10	.04
2S Keith Moreland	.10	.04
3C 1935 Pennant Winning Cubs	.10	.04
3D Ron Santo	.50	.20
3H Cap Anson	1.25	.50
3S Gary Matthews	.10	.04
4C Dizzy Dean	1.50	.60
4D Ken Holtzman	.10	.04
4H Joe Tinker	.50	.20
Johnny Evers		
Frank Chance		
Harry Steinfeldt		
4S Bob Dernier	.10	.04
5C Gabby Hartnett	.75	.30
5D 1969 Cubs	.10	.04
5H Ed Reulbach	.25	.10
5S Eastern Division Champs 1984	.10	.04
6C Billy Herman	.75	.30
6D Billy Williams	1.00	.40
6H Mordecai Brown	.75	.30
6S Ryne Sandberg	3.00	1.20
7C Charlie Root	.10	.04
7D Ken Hubbs	.50	.20
7H Jim "Hippo" Vaughn	.10	.04
7S Jim Frey MG	.10	.04
8C Charlie Grimm	.25	.10
8D Don Cardwell	.10	.04
8H Joe McCarthy MG	.50	.20
8S Rick Sutcliffe	.10	.04
9C Andy Pafko	.10	.04
9D Lou Boudreau	.50	.20
9H Jimmy Cooney	.10	.04
9S Jody Davis	.10	.04
10C Stan Hack	.10	.04
10D Dale Long	.10	.04
10H Rogers Hornsby	1.00	.40
10S Dallas Green GM	.10	.04
11C Phil Cavarretta	.50	.20
11D Sam Jones	.10	.04
11H Hack Wilson	.50	.20
11S Bill Madlock	.25	.10
12C 1945 N.L. Champs	.10	.04
12D Ernie Banks	2.50	1.00
12H Hack Wilson	2.00	.80
Babe Ruth		
Lou Gehrig		
12S Rick Reuschel	.10	.04
13C Bill Nicholson	.10	.04
13D Hank Sauer	.10	.04
13H Babe Ruth	4.00	1.60
13S Milt Pappas	.10	.04
JKO Hey Hey! And Holy Cow!	.10	.04
JKO Ron Cey	.10	.04
NNO Moments in History	.10	.04
1945-1972		
NNO Moments in History	.10	.04
1876-1925		
NNO Moments in History	.10	.04
1972-1984		
NNO Moments in History	.10	.04
1927-1945		

1984 Cubs Chicago Tribune

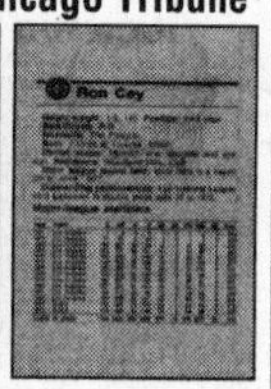

The 1984 Chicago Tribune set was issued in the sports section of the newspaper and features 34 Chicago Cub players. The posed color headshots measure 3 1/4" by 4 5/8" and have blue borders. Next to the photo in a section of equal dimensions appears player information, including position, date of birth, playing experience, baseball career and Major-league playing record. The pictures are unnumbered and checklisted below in alphabetical order.

	Nm-Mt	Ex-Mt
COMPLETE SET (34)	25.00	10.00
1 Ruben Amaro CO	.50	.20
2 Rich Bordi	.50	.20
3 Thad Bosley	.50	.20
4 Larry Bowa	1.00	.40
5 Warren Brusstar	.50	.20
6 Ron Cey	1.00	.40
7 Billy Connors CO	.50	.20
8 Henry Cotto	.50	.20
9 Jody Davis	.75	.30
10 Bob Dernier	.50	.20
11 Dennis Eckersley	2.00	.80
12 George Frazier	.50	.20
13 Jim Frey MG	.50	.20
14 Ron Hassey	.50	.20
15 Richie Hebner	.75	.30
16 Steve Lake	.50	.20
17 Davey Lopes	.75	.30
18 Gary Matthews	1.00	.40
19 Keith Moreland	.50	.20
20 Johnny Oates CO	.50	.20
21 Dave Owen	.50	.20
22 Rick Reuschel	1.00	.40
23 Dan Rohn	.50	.20
24 Dick Ruthven	.50	.20
25 Ryne Sandberg	8.00	3.20
26 Scott Sanderson	.50	.20
27 Lee Smith	1.50	.60
28 Tim Stoddard	.50	.20
29 Rick Sutcliffe	1.00	.40
30 Steve Trout	.50	.20
31 Tom Veryzer	.50	.20
32 John Vukovich CO	.50	.20
33 Gary Woods	.50	.20
34 Don Zimmer CO	.75	.30

1984 Cubs Seven-Up

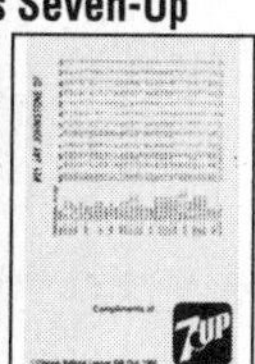

This 28-card set was sponsored by 7-Up. The cards are in full color and measure approximately 2 1/4" by 3 1/2". The card backs are printed in black on white card stock. This set is tougher to find than the other similar Cubs sets since the Cubs were more successful (on the field) in 1984 winning their division, that is, virtually all of the cards printed were distributed during the "Baseball Card Day" promotion (August 12th) which was much better attended that year. There actually were two additional cards produced (in limited quantities) later which some collectors consider part of this set; these late issue cards show four Cubs rookies on each card.

	Nm-Mt	Ex-Mt
COMPLETE SET (28)	30.00	12.00
1 Larry Bowa	1.50	.60
6 Keith Moreland	.50	.20
7 Jody Davis	1.00	.40
10 Leon Durham	1.00	.40
11 Ron Cey	1.50	.60
15 Ron Hassey	.50	.20
18 Richie Hebner	1.00	.40
19 Dave Owen	.50	.20
20 Bob Dernier	.50	.20
21 Jay Johnstone	1.50	.60
23 Ryne Sandberg	15.00	6.00
24 Scott Sanderson	.50	.20
25 Gary Woods	.50	.20
27 Thad Bosley	.50	.20
28 Henry Cotto	.50	.20
34 Steve Trout	.50	.20
36 Gary Matthews	1.50	.60
39 George Frazier	.50	.20
40 Rick Sutcliffe	2.00	.80
41 Warren Brusstar	.50	.20
42 Rich Bordi	.50	.20
43 Dennis Eckersley	4.00	1.60
44 Dick Ruthven	.50	.20
46 Lee Smith	3.00	1.20
47 Rick Reuschel	1.50	.60
49 Tim Stoddard	.50	.20
NNO Ruben Amaro CO	.50	.20
Billy Connors CO		
Johnny Oates CO		
John Vukovich CO		
Don Zimmer CO		
NNO Jim Frey MG	.50	.20

1984 Cubs Unocal

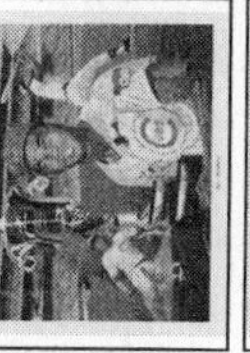

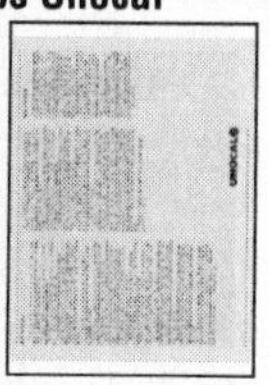

Unocal 76 sponsored this set of 16 color paintings by several different artists. The paintings have white borders and are printed on 11" by 8 1/2" glossy paper. They capture memorable events and players in Chicago Cub history. The backs have an extended caption. The paintings are unnumbered and checklisted below in alphabetical order.

	Nm-Mt	Ex-Mt
COMPLETE SET (16)	15.00	6.00
1 Billy Williams	1.50	.60
2 Bob Dernier	1.50	.60
Ryne Sandberg		
Ernie Banks		
Ken Hubbs		
Larry Jackson		
Ron Santo		
Randy Hundley		
Glenn Beckert		
Don Kessinger		
3 Rogers Hornsby	2.50	1.00
Gabby Hartnett		
Phil Cavarretta		
Hank Sauer		
Ernie Banks		
Ryne Sandberg		
4 Ernie Banks	3.00	1.20
5 Fergie Jenkins	1.50	.60
6 Gabby Hartnett	1.00	.40
Randy Hundley		
Jody Davis		
7 Frank Chance	2.00	.80
Johnny Evers		
Joe Tinker		
Harry Steinfeldt		
Ernie Banks		
Glenn Beckert		
Don Kessinger		
Ron Santo		
Leon Durham		
Ryne Sandberg		
Larry Bowa		
Ron Cey		
8 Frank Chance	1.00	.40
Joe McCarthy		
Charlie Grimm		
Leo Durocher		
Jim Frey		
9 Don Elston	.75	.30
Lindy McDaniel		
Ted Abernathy		
Phil Regan		
Bruce Sutter		
Lee Smith		
10 Jim Frey	.50	.20
11 Memorable High Scoring	.50	.20
Games		
12 Ryne Sandberg	1.50	.60
Rick Sutcliffe		
Dallas Green		
Jim Frey		
13 '84 Clincher	.50	.20
at Pittsburgh		
14 Rick Sutcliffe	.75	.30
15 Ryne Sandberg	1.50	.60
16 Wrigley Field	.50	.20

1985 Cubs Lion Photo

This 27-card set of the Chicago Cubs measures approximately 3 1/2" by 5". The fronts feature color player portraits on a blue background with a white border. The player's name is printed in blue in the wide bottom margin. The white backs carry sponsor information. The cards are unnumbered and checklisted below in alphabetical order.

	Nm-Mt	Ex-Mt
COMPLETE SET (27)	12.00	4.80
1 Larry Bowa	1.00	.40
2 Thad Bosley	.50	.20
3 Warren Brusstar	.50	.20
4 Ron Cey	1.00	.40
5 Jody Davis	.50	.20
6 Brian Dayett	.50	.20
7 Bob Dernier	.50	.20
8 Shawon Dunston	1.50	.60
9 Leon Durham	.50	.20
10 Dennis Eckersley	2.00	.80
11 Ray Fontenot	.50	.20
12 George Frazier	.50	.20
13 Jim Frey MG	.50	.20
14 Steve Lake	.50	.20
15 Davey Lopes	.75	.30
16 Gary Matthews	.75	.30
17 Keith Moreland	.50	.20
18 Dick Ruthven	.50	.20

19 Ryne Sandberg	3.00	1.20
20 Scott Sanderson	.50	.20
21 Lee Smith	1.50	.60
22 Lary Sorensen	.50	.20
23 Chris Speier	.50	.20
24 Rick Sutcliffe	1.00	.40
25 Steve Trout	.50	.20
26 Gary Woods	.50	.20
27 Don Zimmer CO	.75	.30

1985 Cubs Seven-Up

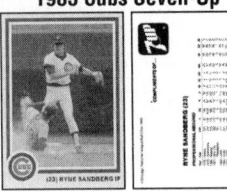

This 28-card set was distributed on August 14th at Wrigley Field for the game against the Expos. The cards measure 2 1/2" by 3 1/2" and were distributed wrapped in cellophane. The cards are unnumbered except for uniform number. The card backs are printed in black on white with a 7-Up logo in the upper right hand corner.

	Nm-Mt	Ex-Mt
COMPLETE SET (28)	15.00	6.00
1 Larry Bowa	.75	.30
6 Keith Moreland	.25	.10
7 Jody Davis	.50	.20
10 Leon Durham	.50	.20
11 Ron Cey	.75	.30
15 Davey Lopes	.50	.20
16 Steve Lake	.25	.10
18 Rich Hebner	.50	.20
20 Bob Dernier	.25	.10
21 Scott Sanderson	.25	.10
22 Billy Hatcher	.25	.10
23 Ryne Sandberg	8.00	3.20
24 Brian Dayett	.25	.10
25 Gary Woods	.25	.10
27 Thad Bosley	.25	.10
28 Chris Speier	.25	.10
31 Ray Fontenot	.25	.10
34 Steve Trout	.25	.10
36 Gary Matthews	.75	.30
39 George Frazier	.25	.10
40 Rick Sutcliffe	.75	.30
41 Warren Brusstar	.25	.10
42 Lary Sorensen	.25	.10
43 Dennis Eckersley	2.50	1.00
44 Dick Ruthven	.25	.10
46 Lee Smith	1.50	.60
NNO Jim Frey MG	.25	.10
NNO Ruben Amaro CO	.50	.20
Billy Connors CO		
Johnny Oates CO		
John Vukovich CO		
Don Zimmer CO		

1986 Cubs Gatorade

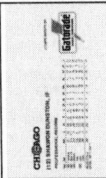

This 28-card set was given out at Wrigley Field on the Cubs' special "baseball card" promotion held July 17th for the game against the Giants. The set was sponsored by Gatorade. The cards are unnumbered except for uniform number. Card backs feature blue print on white card stock. The cards measure approximately 2 7/8" by 4 1/4" and are in full color.

	Nm-Mt	Ex-Mt
COMPLETE SET (28)	12.00	4.80
4 Gene Michael MG	.25	.10
6 Keith Moreland	.25	.10
7 Jody Davis	.50	.20
10 Leon Durham	.50	.20
11 Ron Cey	.75	.30
12 Shawon Dunston	.50	.20
15 Davey Lopes	.75	.30
16 Terry Francona	.25	.10
18 Steve Christmas	.25	.10
19 Manny Trillo	.25	.10
20 Bob Dernier	.25	.10
21 Scott Sanderson	.25	.10
22 Jerry Mumphrey	.25	.10
23 Ryne Sandberg	6.00	2.40
27 Thad Bosley	.25	.10
28 Chris Speier	.25	.10
29 Steve Lake	.25	.10
31 Ray Fontenot	.25	.10
34 Steve Trout	.25	.10
36 Gary Matthews	.50	.20
39 George Frazier	.25	.10
40 Rick Sutcliffe	.75	.30
43 Dennis Eckersley	2.00	.80
46 Lee Smith	1.50	.60
48 Jay Baller	.25	.10
49 Jamie Moyer	2.50	1.00
50 Guy Hoffman	.25	.10
NNO Ruben Amaro CO	.50	.20
Billy Connors CO		
Johnny Oates CO		
John Vukovich CO		
Billy Williams CO		

1986 Cubs Unocal

This set of 20 color action player photos was sponsored by Unocal 76. They are bordered in black and are printed on (approximately) 8 1/2" by 11" glossy paper sheets. A color headshot is

superimposed on each front. The backs contain extensive player information, including biography, performance in the 1985 season, complete Major League statistics, and career summary. The player photos are unnumbered and checklisted below in alphabetical order.

	Nm-Mt	Ex-Mt
COMPLETE SET (20)	10.00	4.00
1 Jay Baller	.25	.10
2 Thad Bosley	.25	.10
3 Ron Cey	.75	.30
4 Jody Davis	.50	.20
5 Bob Dernier	.25	.10
6 Shawon Dunston	.50	.20
7 Leon Durham	.25	.10
8 Dennis Eckersley	2.00	.80
9 Ray Fontenot	.25	.10
10 George Frazier	.25	.10
11 Davey Lopes	.50	.20
12 Gary Matthews	.50	.20
13 Keith Moreland	.25	.10
14 Jerry Mumphrey	.25	.10
15 Ryne Sandberg	5.00	2.00
16 Scott Sanderson	.25	.10
17 Lee Smith	1.50	.60
18 Rick Sutcliffe	.75	.30
19 Manny Trillo	.25	.10
20 Steve Trout	.25	.10

1987 Cubs 1907 TCMA

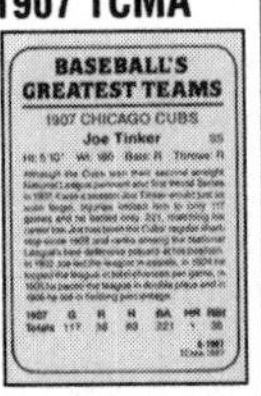

This nine-card standard-size set features some of the 1907 Chicago Cubs stars. The fronts have player photo and identification, while the backs have vital statistics, a biography and 1907 stats.

	Nm-Mt	Ex-Mt
COMPLETE SET (9)	5.00	2.00
1 Harry Steinfeldt	.50	.20
2 Three-Finger Brown	1.00	.40
3 Ed Reulbach	.50	.20
4 Johnny Kling	.50	.20
5 Orvie Overall	.25	.10
6 Joe Tinker	1.00	.40
7 Wildfire Schulte	.75	.30
8 Frank Chance P/MG	1.00	.40
9 Johnny Evers	1.00	.40

1987 Cubs Canon

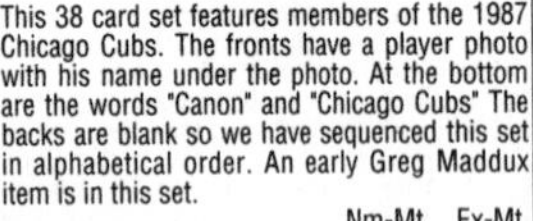

This 38 card set features members of the 1987 Chicago Cubs. The fronts have a player photo with his name under the photo. At the bottom are the words "Canon" and "Chicago Cubs" The backs are blank so we have sequenced this set in alphabetical order. An early Greg Maddux item is in this set.

	Nm-Mt	Ex-Mt
COMPLETE SET (38)	20.00	8.00
2 Glenn Brummer	.50	.20
3 Phil Claussen	.50	.20
3 Jody Davis	.75	.30
4 Ron Davis	.50	.20
5 Andre Dawson	3.00	1.20
6 Brian Dayett	.50	.20
7 Bob Dernier	.50	.20
8 Frank DiPino	.50	.20
9 Shawon Dunston	.50	.20
10 Leon Durham	.75	.30
11 John Fierro TR	.50	.20
12 Dallas Green GM	.75	.30
13 Les Lancaster	.50	.20
14 Frank Lucchesi CO	.50	.20
15 Ed Lynch	.50	.20
16 Greg Maddux	10.00	4.00
17 David Martinez	1.50	.60
18 Gary Matthews	1.00	.40
19 Gene Michael MG	.50	.20
20 Keith Moreland	.50	.20
21 Jamie Moyer	2.50	1.00
22 Jerry Mumphrey	.50	.20
23 Dickie Noles	.50	.20
24 Johnny Oates CO	.50	.20
25 Jimmy Piersall ANN	1.00	.40
26 Ryne Sandberg	5.00	2.00
27 Scott Sanderson	.50	.20
28 Bob Searles	.50	.20
29 Lee Smith	1.50	.60
30 Jim Snyder CO	.50	.20
31 Herm Starrette CO	.50	.20
32 Jim Sundberg	.50	.20
33 Rick Sutcliffe	1.00	.40
34 Manny Trillo	.50	.20
35 Steve Trout	.50	.20
36 John Vukovich CO	.50	.20
37 Chico Walker	.50	.20
38 Billy Williams CO	1.50	.60

1987 Cubs David Berg

This 26-card set was given out at Wrigley Field on the Cubs' special "baseball card" promotion held July 29th. The set was sponsored by David Berg Pure Beef Hot Dogs. The cards are unnumbered except for uniform number. Card backs feature red and blue print on white card stock. The cards measure approximately 2 7/8" by 4 1/4" and are in full color. The set features Greg Maddux in his Rookie Card year.

	Nm-Mt	Ex-Mt
COMPLETE SET (26)	18.00	7.25
1 Dave Martinez	1.00	.40
4 Gene Michael MG	.25	.10
6 Keith Moreland	.25	.10
7 Jody Davis	.50	.20
8 Andre Dawson	2.00	.80
10 Leon Durham	.50	.20
11 Jim Sundberg	.50	.20
12 Shawon Dunston	.75	.30
19 Manny Trillo	.50	.20
20 Bob Dernier	.25	.10
21 Scott Sanderson	.25	.10
22 Jerry Mumphrey	.25	.10
23 Ryne Sandberg	5.00	2.00
24 Brian Dayett	.25	.10
29 Chico Walker	.25	.10
31 Greg Maddux	8.00	3.20
33 Frank DiPino	.25	.10
34 Steve Trout	.25	.10
36 Gary Matthews	.75	.30
37 Ed Lynch	.25	.10
39 Ron Davis	.25	.10
40 Rick Sutcliffe	.75	.30
46 Lee Smith	1.50	.60
47 Dickie Noles	.25	.10
49 Jamie Moyer	1.50	.60
NNO Johnny Oates CO	.50	.20
Jim Snyder CO		
Herm Starrette CO		
John Vukovich CO		
Billy Williams CO		

1988 Cubs David Berg

This 27-card set was given out at Wrigley Field with every paid admission on the Cubs' special "baseball card" promotion held August 24th. The set was sponsored by David Berg Pure Beef Hot Dogs and the Venture store chain. The cards are unnumbered except for uniform number. Card backs feature primarily black print on white card stock. The cards measure approximately 2 7/8" by 4 1/4" and are in full color. Mark Grace makes an early card appearance in this set.

	Nm-Mt	Ex-Mt
COMPLETE SET (27)	15.00	6.00
2 Vance Law	.25	.10
4 Don Zimmer MG	.50	.20
7 Jody Davis	.50	.20
8 Andre Dawson	1.50	.60
9 Damon Berryhill	.25	.10
12 Shawon Dunston	.75	.30
17 Mark Grace	5.00	2.00
18 Angel Salazar	.25	.10
19 Manny Trillo	.25	.10
21 Scott Sanderson	.25	.10
22 Jerry Mumphrey	.25	.10
23 Ryne Sandberg	4.00	1.60
24 Gary Varsho	.25	.10
25 Rafael Palmeiro	5.00	2.00
28 Mitch Webster	.25	.10
30 Darrin Jackson	.25	.10
31 Greg Maddux	6.00	2.40
32 Calvin Schiraldi	.25	.10
33 Frank DiPino	.25	.10
37 Pat Perry	.25	.10
40 Rick Sutcliffe	.75	.30
41 Jeff Pico	.25	.10
45 Al Nipper	.25	.10
49 Jamie Moyer	1.00	.40
50 Les Lancaster	.25	.10
54 Rich Gossage	.75	.30
NNO Joe Altobelli CO	.25	.10
Chuck Cottier CO		
Larry Cox CO		
Jose Martinez CO		
Dick Pole CO		

1988 Cubs Donruss Team Book

The 1988 Donruss Cubs Team Book set features 27 cards (three pages with nine cards on each page) plus a large full-page puzzle of Stan Musial. Cards are in full color and are standard size. The set was distributed as a four-page book; although the puzzle page was perforated, the card pages were not. The cover

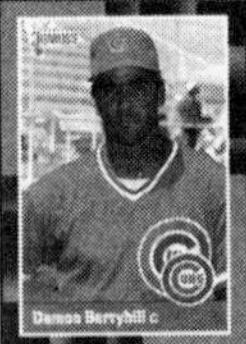

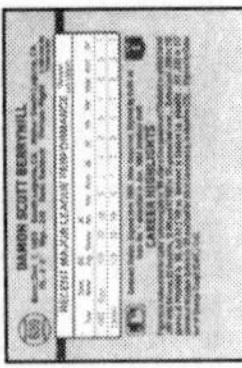

of the "Team Collection" book is primarily bright red. Card fronts are very similar in design to the 1988 Donruss regular issue. The card numbers on the backs are the same for those players that are the same as in the regular Donruss set; the new players pictured are numbered on the back as "NEW." The book is usually sold intact. When cut from the book into individual cards, these cards are distinguishable from the regular 1988 Donruss cards since these have a 1988 copyright on the back whereas the regular issue has a 1987 copyright on the back.

	Nm-Mt	Ex-Mt
COMPLETE SET (27)	6.00	2.40
40 Mark Grace RR	2.50	1.00
68 Rick Sutcliffe	.10	.04
119 Jody Davis	.10	.04
146 Shawon Dunston	.10	.04
169 Jamie Moyer	.75	.30
191 Leon Durham	.10	.04
242 Ryne Sandberg	1.00	.40
269 Andre Dawson	.75	.30
315 Paul Noce	.10	.04
324 Rafael Palmeiro	2.00	.80
438 Dave Martinez	.10	.04
447 Jerry Mumphrey	.10	.04
488 Jim Sundberg	.10	.04
516 Manny Trillo	.10	.04
539 Greg Maddux	4.00	1.60
561 Les Lancaster	.10	.04
570 Frank DiPino	.10	.04
639 Damon Berryhill	.10	.04
646 Scott Sanderson	.10	.04
NEW Mike Bielecki	.10	.04
NEW Rich Gossage	.25	.10
NEW Drew Hall	.10	.04
NEW Darrin Jackson	.25	.10
NEW Vance Law	.10	.04
NEW Al Nipper	.10	.04
NEW Angel Salazar	.10	.04
NEW Calvin Schiraldi	.10	.04

1988 Cubs Vance Law Smokey

These cards which measure 3 3/4" by 5 1/2" feature Cub player Vance Law. He is in several different poses.

	Nm-Mt	Ex-Mt
COMPLETE SET (4)	4.00	1.60
1 Vance Law Smokey Bear	1.50	.60
2 Vance Law Fielding	1.25	.50
3 Vance Law Batting	1.25	.50
4 Smokey Bear	1.00	.40

1989 Cubs Marathon

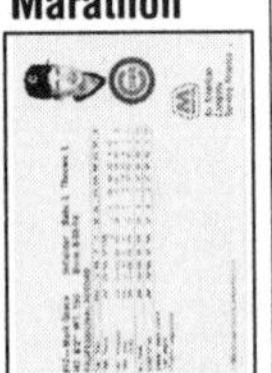

The 1989 Marathon Cubs set features 25 cards measuring approximately 2 3/4" by 4 1/4". The fronts are green and white, and feature facsimile autographs. The backs show black and white mug shots and career stats. The set was given away at the August 10, 1989 Cubs' home game. The cards are numbered by the players' uniform numbers.

	Nm-Mt	Ex-Mt
COMPLETE SET (25)	18.00	7.25
2 Vance Law	.25	.10
4 Don Zimmer MG	.50	.20
7 Joe Girardi	.25	.10
8 Andre Dawson	2.00	.80
9 Damon Berryhill	.25	.10
10 Lloyd McClendon	.50	.20
12 Shawon Dunston	.75	.30
15 Domingo Ramos	.25	.10
17 Mark Grace	5.00	2.00
18 Dwight Smith	.50	.20
19 Curt Wilkerson	.25	.10
20 Jerome Walton	.75	.30
21 Scott Sanderson	.25	.10
23 Ryne Sandberg	5.00	2.00
28 Mitch Williams	.50	.20
31 Greg Maddux	8.00	3.20
32 Calvin Schiraldi	.25	.10
33 Mitch Webster	.25	.10
36 Mike Bielecki	.25	.10
39 Paul Kilgus	.25	.10
40 Rick Sutcliffe	.75	.30
41 Jeff Pico	.25	.10
44 Steve Wilson	.25	.10
50 Les Lancaster	.25	.10
NNO Joe Altobelli CO	.25	.10
Chuck Cottier CO		
Larry Cox CO		
Jose Martinez CO		
Dick Pole CO		

1990 Cubs Marathon

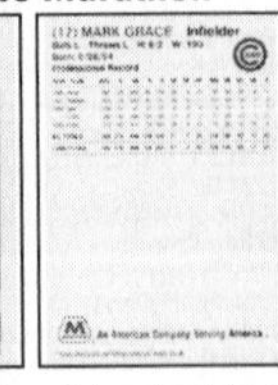

The Marathon Oil Chicago Cubs set contains 28 cards measuring approximately 2 7/8" by 4 1/4" which was given away at the August 17th Cubs' home game. Since the cards are unnumbered, the set is checklisted alphabetically below.

	Nm-Mt	Ex-Mt
COMPLETE SET (28)	12.00	3.60
1 Paul Assenmacher	.25	.07
2 Mike Bielecki	.25	.07
3 Shawn Boskie	.25	.07
4 Dave Clark	.25	.07
5 Doug Dascenzo	.25	.07
6 Andre Dawson	1.50	.45
7 Shawon Dunston	.75	.23
8 Joe Girardi	.50	.15
9 Mark Grace	.75	.23
10 Mike Harkey	.25	.07
11 Les Lancaster	.25	.07
12 Bill Long	.25	.07
13 Greg Maddux	4.00	1.20
14 Lloyd McClendon	.50	.15
15 Jeff Pico	.25	.07
16 Domingo Ramos	.25	.07
17 Luis Salazar	.25	.07
18 Ryne Sandberg	3.00	.90
19 Dwight Smith	.25	.07
20 Rick Sutcliffe	.75	.23
21 Hector Villanueva	.25	.07
22 Jerome Walton	.25	.07
23 Curtis Wilkerson	.25	.07
24 Mitch Williams	.50	.15
25 Steve Wilson	.25	.07
26 Marvell Wynne	.25	.07
27 Don Zimmer MG	.50	.15
28 Joe Altobelli CO	.25	.07
Jose Martinez CO		
Phil Roof CO		
Chuck Cottier CO		
Dick Pole CO		

1990 Cubs Topps TV

This Cubs team set contains 66 standard-size cards. Cards numbered 1-35 were with the parent club, while cards 36-66 were in the farm system. The key card in this set is Greg Maddux

	Nm-Mt	Ex-Mt
COMPLETE FACT. SET (66)	125.00	38.00
1 Don Zimmer MG	.50	.15
2 Joe Altobelli CO	.25	.07
3 Chuck Cottier CO	.25	.07
4 Jose Martinez CO	.25	.07
5 Dick Pole CO	.25	.07
6 Phil Roof CO	.25	.07
7 Paul Assenmacher	.25	.07
8 Mike Bielecki	.25	.07
9 Mike Harkey	.25	.07
10 Joe Kraemer	.25	.07
11 Les Lancaster	.25	.07
12 Greg Maddux	80.00	24.00
13 Jose Nunez	.25	.07
14 Jeff Pico	.25	.07
15 Rick Sutcliffe	.50	.15
16 Dean Wilkins	.25	.07
17 Mitch Williams	.25	.07
18 Steve Wilson	.25	.07
19 Damon Berryhill	.25	.07
20 Joe Girardi	1.50	.45
21 Rick Wrona	.25	.07
22 Shawon Dunston	.50	.15
23 Mark Grace	20.00	6.00
24 Domingo Ramos	.25	.07
25 Luis Salazar	.25	.07
26 Ryne Sandberg	50.00	15.00
27 Greg Smith	.25	.07
28 Curtis Wilkerson	.25	.07
29 Dave Clark	.25	.07
30 Doug Dascenzo	.25	.07
31 Andre Dawson	8.00	2.40
32 Lloyd McClendon	.50	.15
33 Dwight Smith	.25	.07
34 Jerome Walton	.25	.07
35 Marvell Wynne	.25	.07
36 Alex Arias	.25	.07
37 Bob Bafia	.25	.07
38 Brad Bierley	.25	.07
39 Shawn Boskie	.25	.07
40 Danny Clay	.25	.07
41 Rusty Crockett	.25	.07
42 Earl Cunningham	.25	.07
43 Len Damian	.25	.07
44 Darrin Duffy	.25	.07
45 Ty Griffin	.25	.07
46 Brian Guinn	.25	.07
47 Phil Hannon	.25	.07

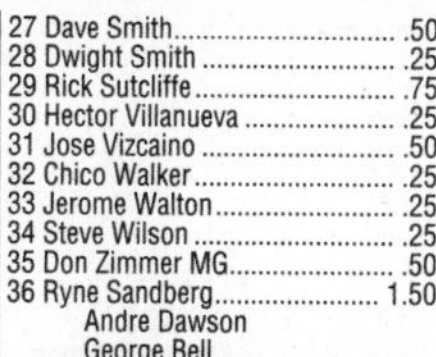

48 Phil Harrison .25 .07
49 Jeff Hearron .25 .07
50 Greg Kallevig .25 .07
51 Ced Landrum .25 .07
52 Bill Long .25 .07
53 Derrick May .25 .07
54 Ray Mullino .25 .07
55 Erik Pappas .25 .07
56 Steve Parker .25 .07
57 Dave Pavlas .25 .07
58 Laddie Renfroe .25 .07
59 Jeff Small .25 .07
60 Doug Strange .25 .07
61 Gary Varsho .25 .07
62 Hector Villanueva .25 .07
63 Rick Wilkins .25 .07
64 Dana Williams .25 .07
65 Bill Wrona .25 .07
66 Fernando Zarranz .25 .07

1991 Cubs Marathon

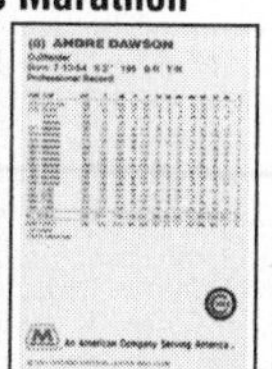

This 28-card set was produced by Marathon Oil, and its company logo appears at the bottom of card back. The cards were given away at the Cubs' home game against Montreal Expos on August 14, 1991. The oversized cards measure approximately 2 7/8" by 4 1/4" and feature on the fronts color action player photos with white borders. The set can also be found with blank backs. The cards are skip-numbered by uniform number and checklisted below accordingly.

Nm-Mt Ex-Mt
COMPLETE SET (28) 12.00 3.60
7 Joe Girardi .50 .15
8 Andre Dawson 1.00 .30
9 Damon Berryhill .25 .07
10 Luis Salazar .25 .07
11 George Bell .25 .07
12 Shawon Dunston .50 .15
16 Jose Vizcaino .50 .15
17 Mark Grace 1.00 .30
18 Dwight Smith .25 .07
19 Hector Villanueva .25 .07
20 Jerome Walton .25 .07
22 Mike Harkey .25 .07
23 Ryne Sandberg 3.00 .90
24 Chico Walker .25 .07
29 Doug Dascenzo .25 .07
30 Bob Scanlan .25 .07
31 Greg Maddux 4.00 1.20
32 Danny Jackson .25 .07
33 Chuck McElroy .25 .07
36 Mike Bielecki .25 .07
40 Rick Sutcliffe .50 .15
41 Jim Essian MG .25 .07
42 Dave Smith .25 .07
45 Paul Assenmacher .25 .07
47 Shawn Boskie .25 .07
50 Les Lancaster .25 .07
51 Heathcliff Slocumb .50 .15
NNO Joe Altobelli CO .25 .07
Chuck Cottier CO
Jose Martinez CO
Billy Connors CO
Phil Roof CO
Richie Zisk CO

1991 Cubs Vine Line

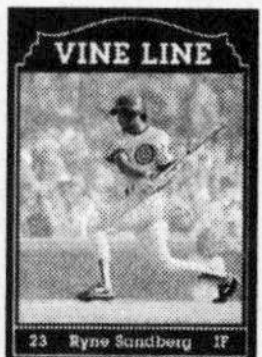

This 36-card set was issued as insert sheets in the Cubs' Vine Line fan news magazine. Each sheet measures approximately 7 1/2" by 10 1/2" and features nine different player cards. After perforation, the cards measure the standard size. The cards are unnumbered and checklisted below in alphabetical order.

Nm-Mt Ex-Mt
COMPLETE SET (36) 20.00 6.00
1 Paul Assenmacher .25 .07
2 Joe Altobelli CO .25 .07
3 George Bell .25 .07
4 Damon Berryhill .25 .07
5 Mike Bielecki .25 .07
6 Shawn Boskie .25 .07
7 Chuck Cottier CO .25 .07
8 Doug Dascenzo .25 .07
9 Andre Dawson 2.00 .60
10 Shawon Dunston .75 .23
11 Joe Girardi .75 .23
12 Mark Grace 2.50 .75
13 Mike Harkey .25 .07
14 Danny Jackson .25 .07
15 Ferguson Jenkins CO 1.50 .45
16 Les Lancaster .25 .07
17 Greg Maddux 8.00 2.40
18 Jose Martinez CO .25 .07
19 Chuck McElroy .25 .07
20 Erik Pappas .25 .07
21 Dick Pole CO .25 .07
22 Phil Roof CO .25 .07
23 Ryne Sandberg 5.00 1.50
24 Luis Salazar .25 .07
25 Gary Scott .25 .07
26 Heathcliff Slocumb .50 .15
27 Dave Smith .50 .15
28 Dwight Smith .25 .07
29 Rick Sutcliffe .75 .23
30 Hector Villanueva .25 .07
31 Jose Vizcaino .50 .15
32 Chico Walker .25 .07
33 Jerome Walton .25 .07
34 Steve Wilson .25 .07
35 Don Zimmer MG .50 .15
36 Ryne Sandberg 1.50 .45
Andre Dawson
George Bell

1992 Cubs Marathon

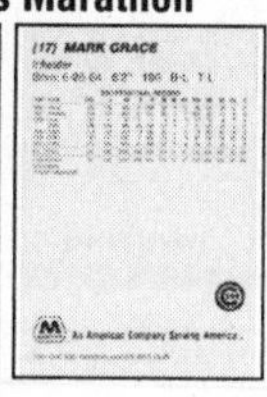

This 28-card set was produced by Marathon Oil, and its company logo appears at the bottom of the card back. The cards measure approximately 2 7/8" by 4 1/4". The cards are skip-numbered on the back by uniform number and checklisted below accordingly.

Nm-Mt Ex-Mt
COMPLETE SET (28) 12.00 3.60
1 Doug Strange .25 .07
5 Jim Lefebvre MG .25 .07
6 Rey Sanchez .25 .07
7 Joe Girardi .25 .07
8 Andre Dawson 1.00 .30
10 Luis Salazar .25 .07
12 Shawon Dunston .50 .15
16 Jose Vizcaino .50 .15
17 Mark Grace 2.00 .60
18 Dwight Smith .25 .07
19 Hector Villanueva .25 .07
20 Jerome Walton .25 .07
21 Sammy Sosa 4.00 1.20
23 Ryne Sandberg 2.50 .75
27 Derrick May .25 .07
29 Doug Dascenzo .25 .07
30 Bob Scanlan .25 .07
31 Greg Maddux 4.00 1.20
32 Danny Jackson .25 .07
34 Ken Patterson .25 .07
35 Chuck McElroy .25 .07
36 Mike Morgan .25 .07
38 Jeff D. Robinson .25 .07
42 Dave Smith .50 .15
45 Paul Assenmacher .25 .07
47 Shawn Boskie .25 .07
49 Frank Castillo .25 .07
NNO Tom Trebelhorn CO .50 .15
Jose Martinez CO
Billy Williams CO
Sammy Ellis CO
Chuck Cottier CO
Billy Connors CO

1992 Cubs Old Style

This 28-card set measures the standard size and features sepia-tone player photos with tan borders. The cards are unnumbered and checklisted below in alphabetical order.

Nm-Mt Ex-Mt
COMPLETE SET (28) 15.00 4.50
1 Grover C. Alexander 1.50 .45
2 Cap Anson 1.00 .30
3 Ernie Banks 3.00 .90
4 Mordecai Brown .75 .23
5 Phil Cavarretta .50 .15
6 Frank Chance 1.00 .30
7 Kiki Cuyler .75 .23
8 Johnny Evers 1.00 .30
9 Charlie Grimm .50 .15
10 Stan Hack .25 .07
11 Gabby Hartnett .75 .23
12 Billy Herman .75 .23
13 Rogers Hornsby 1.50 .45
14 Ken Hubbs .50 .15
15 Randy Hundley .25 .07
16 Ferguson Jenkins 1.00 .30
17 Bill Lee .25 .07
18 Andy Pafko .25 .07
19 Rick Reuschel .25 .07
20 Charlie Root .25 .07
21 Ron Santo .75 .23
22 Hank Sauer .25 .07
23 Riggs Stephenson .50 .15
24 Bruce Sutter .50 .15
25 Joe Tinker 1.00 .30
26 Jim(Hippo) Vaughn .25 .07
27 Billy Williams 1.50 .45
28 Hack Wilson 1.00 .30

1993 Cubs Marathon

This 32-card set was produced by Marathon Oil, and its company logo appears at the bottom of the card back. The cards measure approximately 2 7/8" by 4 1/4". The backs present biographical and statistical information. The cards are checklisted below in alphabetical order.

Nm-Mt Ex-Mt
COMPLETE SET (32) 12.00 3.60
1 Paul Assenmacher .25 .07
2 Jose Bautista .25 .07
3 Steve Buechele .25 .07
4 Frank Castillo .25 .07
5 Billy Connors CO .25 .07
6 Chuck Cottier CO .25 .07
7 Mark Grace 2.50 .75
8 Jose Guzman .25 .07
9 Mike Harkey .25 .07
10 Greg Hibbard .25 .07
11 Doug Jennings .25 .07
12 Steve Lake .25 .07
13 Jim Lefebvre MG .25 .07
14 Candy Maldonado .25 .07
15 Jose Martinez CO .25 .07
16 Derrick May .25 .07
17 Mike Morgan .25 .07
18 Randy Myers .75 .23
19 Tony Muser CO .25 .07
20 Dan Plesac .25 .07
21 Ryne Sandberg 4.00 1.20
22 Rey Sanchez .25 .07
23 Bob Scanlan .25 .07
24 Dan Simonds .25 .07
25 Dwight Smith .25 .07
26 Sammy Sosa 4.00 1.20
27 Tom Trebelhorn CO .25 .07
28 Jose Vizcaino .50 .15
29 Rick Wilkins .25 .07
30 Billy Williams CO 1.00 .30
31 Willie Wilson .25 .07
32 Eric Yelding .25 .07

1993 Cubs Old Style Billy Williams

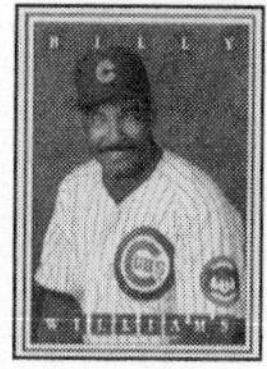
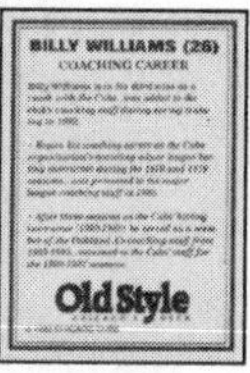

These four standard-size cards feature on their red, white, and blue-bordered fronts black-and-white action shots (except for number 1 below, which carries a posed color photo) of Billy Williams. His first and last name appear in white lettering in blue boxes above and below his image, respectively. The white backs are framed in red and blue lines and carry career highlights. The cards are unnumbered.

Nm-Mt Ex-Mt
COMPLETE SET (4) 10.00 3.00
COMMON CARD (1-4) 3.00 .90

1993 Cubs Rolaids

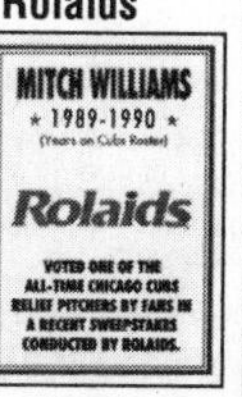

This four-card standard-size set is subtitled "All-Time Cubs Relief Pitchers" and was given away at Wrigley Field on Sept. 4, 1993. The cards are unnumbered and checklisted below in alphabetical order.

Nm-Mt Ex-Mt
COMPLETE SET (4) 4.00 1.20
1 Randy Myers 1.25 .35
2 Lee Smith 1.25 .35
3 Bruce Sutter 1.50 .45
4 Mitch Williams 1.00 .30

1993 Cubs Stadium Club

This 30-card standard-size set features the 1993 Chicago Cubs. The set was issued in hobby (plastic box) and retail (blister) form.

Nm-Mt Ex-Mt
COMP. FACT SET (30) 4.00 1.20
1 Ryne Sandberg 2.00 .60
2 Sammy Sosa 2.00 .60
3 Greg Hibbard .10 .03
4 Candy Maldonado .10 .03
5 Willie Wilson .25 .07
6 Dan Plesac .10 .03
7 Steve Buechele .10 .03
8 Mark Grace 1.00 .30
9 Shawon Dunston .25 .07
10 Steve Lake .10 .03
11 Dwight Smith .10 .03
12 Derrick May .10 .03
13 Paul Assenmacher .10 .03
14 Mike Harkey .10 .03
15 Lance Dickson .10 .03
16 Randy Myers .25 .07
17 Mike Morgan .10 .03
18 Chuck McElroy .10 .03
19 Jose Guzman .10 .03
20 Jose Vizcaino .25 .07
21 Frank Castillo .10 .03
22 Bob Scanlan .10 .03
23 Rick Wilkins .10 .03
24 Rey Sanchez .10 .03
25 Phil Dauphin .10 .03
26 Jim Bullinger .10 .03
27 Jessie Hollins .10 .03
28 Matt Walbeck .10 .03
29 Fernando Ramsey .10 .03
30 Jose Bautista .10 .03

1994 Cubs WGN/Pepsi

These 5" by 7" cards featured members of the 1994 Chicago Cubs. There was supposed to be a series of 30 cards which were sponsored by WGN Television Station, Pepsi Cola, and Taco Bell. However, due to the strike of 1994 it is actually unknown if the entire set as planned was actually released. Any additions to this checklist are very appreciated. The fronts feature a black-and-white player photo with a gray border and sponsor logos. The backs display information about the player as well as some of his favorite things and people.

Nm-Mt Ex-Mt
COMPLETE SET 20.00 6.00
1 Mark Grace 1.50 .45
2 Chicago Cubs 1984 .75 .23
3 Ryne Sandberg 2.50 .75
4 Randy Myers .75 .23
5 Rick Wilkins .50 .15
6 Tom Trebelhorn MG .50 .15
7 Mike Morgan .50 .15
8 Ernie Banks 4.00 1.20
9 Steve Stone ANN .75 .23
10 Steve Trachsel .75 .23
11 Jose Guzman .50 .15
12 Sammy Sosa 5.00 1.50
13 Steve Buechele .50 .15
14 Jose Bautista .50 .15
17 Glenallen Hill .50 .15
19 Ron Santo 1.50 .45
20 Shawon Dunston .75 .23
21 Tuffy Rhodes .50 .15
22 Thom Brennaman ANN .50 .15
24 Ryne Sandberg GAME 1.50 .45
29 Jack Brickhouse ANN .75 .23

1995 Cubs Gatorade

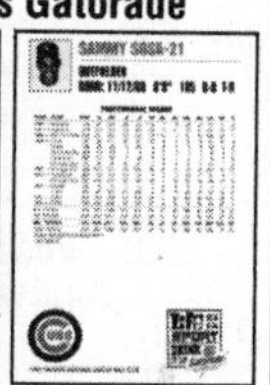

This set, which measures 2 7/8" by 4 1/4" feature members of the 1995 Chicago Cubs. The fronts have full color photos surrounded by white borders with the player's name, uniform number and position on the bottom. The backs have biographical information and year by year statistics. Since these cards are unnumbered, we have sequenced them in alphabetical order.

MINT NRMT
COMPLETE SET 15.00 6.75
1 Scott Bullett .50 .23
2 Jim Bullinger .50 .23
3 Larry Casian .50 .23
4 Frank Castillo .50 .23
5 Shawon Dunston .75 .35
6 Kevin Foster .50 .23
7 Rich Garces .50 .23
8 Luis Gonzalez 1.50 .70
9 Mark Grace 2.00 .90
10 Jose Guzman .50 .23
11 Jose Hernandez .50 .23
12 Howard Johnson .75 .35
13 Brian McRae .75 .35
14 Randy Myers .75 .35
15 Chris Nabholz .50 .23
16 Jaime Navarro .50 .23
17 Mike Perez .50 .23
18 Jim Riggleman MG .50 .23
19 Rey Sanchez .50 .23
20 Scott Servais .50 .23
21 Sammy Sosa 3.00 1.35
22 Ozzie Timmons .50 .23
23 Steve Trachsel .75 .35
24 Turk Wendell .50 .23
25 Anthony Young .50 .23
26 Todd Zeile .50 .23
27 Dave Bialas CO 1.00 .45
Fergie Jenkins CO
Tony Muser CO
Mako Oliveras CO
Dan Radison CO
Billy Williams CO

1995 Cubs Police

These 16 cards were issued by the Illinois State Police and feature members of the 1995 Chicago Cubs. There are black and white photos on the front and the bottom of the card has the Illinois State Police logo as well as the Cub logo. The back has vital statistics as well as having six ways to prevent conflicts. Since the cards are unnumbered we have sequenced them in alphabetical order. There is a possibility there are more cards in this set so any additions to this checklist are appreciated.

Nm-Mt Ex-Mt
COMPLETE SET 10.00 3.00
1 Dave Bialas .25 .07
2 Scott Bullett .25 .07
3 Jim Bullinger .25 .07
4 Larry Casian .25 .07
5 Frank Castillo .25 .07
6 Shawon Dunston .50 .15
7 Kevin Foster .25 .07
8 Mark Grace 1.00 .30
9 Jose Guzman .25 .07
10 Jose Hernandez .25 .07
11 Bryan Hickerson .25 .07
12 Fergie Jenkins CO 1.00 .30
13 Howard Johnson .50 .15
14 Brian McRae .25 .07
15 Tony Muser CO .25 .07
16 Randy Myers .50 .15
17 Jaime Navarro .25 .07
18 Chris Nabholz .25 .07
19 Mako Oliveras .25 .07
20 Mike Perez .25 .07
21 Todd Pratt .25 .07
22 Dan Radison .25 .07
23 Jim Riggleman MG .25 .07
24 Rey Sanchez .25 .07
25 Sammy Sosa 2.50 .75
26 Ozzie Timmons .25 .07
27 Steve Trachsel .25 .07
28 Mike Walker .25 .07
29 Turk Wendell .25 .07
30 Billy Williams CO 1.00 .30
31 Anthony Young .25 .07
32 Todd Zeile .50 .15

1996 Cubs Convention

These black and white photos were given out to fans attending the 1996 Cubs Convention so attendees could have an item for players to sign. The fronts have a player photo along with the Chicago Cubs logo and the player name on top. Inset in the photo is the logo for the Cubs Convention. The horizontal backs feature information about the player as well as his career stats. This checklist is incomplete so any additions are appreciated.

Nm-Mt Ex-Mt
COMPLETE SET 5.00 1.50
1 Mark Grace 2.50 .75
2 Randy Hundley 1.00 .30
3 Steve Stone 1.50 .45

1996 Cubs Fleer

These 20 standard-size cards feature the same design as the regular Fleer issue, except they are UV coated, use silver foil and are numbered "x of 20". The team set packs were available at retail locations and hobby shops in 10-card packs for a suggested retail price of $1.99.

Nm-Mt Ex-Mt
COMPLETE SET (20) 5.00 1.50
1 Terry Adams .10 .03
2 Jim Bullinger .10 .03
3 Frank Castillo .10 .03
4 Kevin Foster .10 .03
5 Leo Gomez .10 .03
6 Luis Gonzalez .50 .15
7 Mark Grace .50 .15
8 Jose Hernandez .10 .03
9 Robin Jennings .10 .03
10 Doug Jones .10 .03
11 Brooks Kieschnick .10 .03
12 Brian McRae .10 .03
13 Jaime Navarro .10 .03
14 Rey Sanchez .10 .03
15 Ryne Sandberg .75 .23
16 Scott Servais .10 .03
17 Sammy Sosa 1.50 .45
18 Steve Trachsel .10 .03
19 Logo card .10 .03
20 Checklist .10 .03

1997 Cubs Gatorade

This 26 card postcard size set features members of the 1997 Chicago Cubs. The cards are unnumbered and we have sequenced them in alphabetical order. The fronts have green borders surrounding an action photo of the player. The backs have the players vital statistics as well as complete season and career statistics.

	Nm-Mt	Ex-Mt
COMPLETE SET (26)	10.00	3.00
1 Terry Adams	.25	.07
2 Kent Bottenfield	.25	.07
3 Brant Brown	.25	.07
4 Dave Clark	.25	.07
5 Shawon Dunston	.50	.15
6 Kevin Foster	.25	.07
7 Doug Glanville	.75	.23
8 Jeremi Gonzalez	.25	.07
9 Mark Grace	1.00	.30
10 Dave Hansen	.25	.07
11 Jose Hernandez	.25	.07
12 Tyler Houston	.25	.07
13 Brian McRae	.25	.07
14 Kevin Orie	.25	.07
15 Bob Patterson	.25	.07
16 Jim Riggleman MG	.25	.07
17 Mel Rojas	.25	.07
18 Rey Sanchez	.25	.07
19 Ryne Sandberg	1.50	.45
20 Scott Servais	.25	.07
21 Sammy Sosa	2.00	.60
22 Kevin Tapani	.25	.07
23 Ramon Tatis	.25	.07
24 Steve Traschel	.50	.15
25 Turk Wendell	.25	.07
26 Dave Bialas CO	.50	.15
Rick Kranitz CO		
Jeff Pentland CO		
Mako Oliveras CO		
Dan Radison CO		
Phil Regan CO		
Billy Williams CO		

1998 Cubs Fan Convention

These 30 cards were issued during the 1998 Cubs Fan Convention and featured players and other members of the Cubs organization past and present. The fronts have the players name on top along with 2 Cubs logos. The 13th Cubs Convention logo is also on the front along with a photo(s) of the people involved. The cards are unnumbered so we have sequenced the individual cards alphabetically and the multi-player card in alphabetical order of the headline on the top. The backs have biographical information and statistics where appropriate.

	Nm-Mt	Ex-Mt
COMPLETE SET (30)	25.00	7.50
1 Terry Adams	.50	.15
2 Ernie Banks	2.50	.75
3 Jack Brickhouse ANN	1.00	.30
4 Harry Caray ANN	1.50	.45
5 Andre Dawson	1.50	.45
6 Mark Grace	1.50	.45
7 Kevin Orie	.50	.15
8 Jim Riggleman MG	.50	.15
9 Ron Santo	1.50	.45
10 Scott Servais	.50	.15
11 Sammy Sosa	4.00	1.20
12 Rick Sutcliffe	.50	.15
13 Steve Trachsel	.50	.15
14 Billy Williams	1.50	.45
15 Carmen Fanzone	.50	.15
Paul Reuschel		
16 Oscar Gamble	.50	.15
Larry Bowa		
17 Randy Hundley	.50	.15
Jody Davis		
18 Pat Hughes ANN	.50	.15
Josh Lewin ANN		
19 Mike Hubbard	.50	.15
Tyler Houston		
20 Mike Bielecki	.50	.15
Vance Law		
21 Kerry Wood	5.00	1.50
Pat Cline		
22 Kevin Foster	.50	.15
Marc Pisciotta		
23 Robin Jennings	.50	.15
Rodney Myers		
24 Mark Clark	.50	.15
Jeremi Gonzalez		
25 Jeff Blauser	.50	.15
Mickey Morandini		
26 Dick Selma	.50	.15
Willie Smith		
27 Glenn Beckert UER	1.00	.30
Don Kessinger		
Glenn is spelled Glen		
28 Milt Pappas	.50	.15
Don Cardwell		
29 Andy Pafko	.75	.23
Gary Matthews		
30 Bob Patterson	.50	.15
Kevin Tapani		

1998 Cubs Sosa ComEd

This one card standard-size set was among items given out by the Cubs to honor Sammy Sosa's 66 homer season. An action shot of Sosa is framed by blue borders with the words 'Slammin' Sammy" on top and the Cubs logo and 1998 on the bottom. The back features biographical information as well as highlights from the 1998 season.

	Nm-Mt	Ex-Mt
1 Sammy Sosa	5.00	1.50

1999 Cubs Old Style All-Century Team

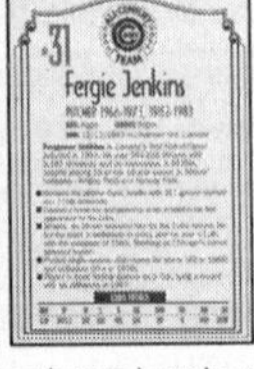

These 21 standard-size cards were issued over three different Cub games. They were issued in seven card packs sequenced in alphabetical order except for the Frank Chance manager card being included in the third pack. Since the cards are unnumbered we have sequenced them in alphabetical order.

	Nm-Mt	Ex-Mt
COMPLETE SET (21)	25.00	7.50
1 Grover Alexander	1.50	.45
2 Ernie Banks	1.50	.45
3 Mordecai Brown	1.50	.45
4 Phil Cavaretta	.75	.23
5 Frank Chance MG/P	1.50	.45
6 Andre Dawson	1.00	.30
7 Mark Grace	1.50	.45
8 Charlie Grimm	.75	.23
9 Stan Hack	.75	.23
10 Gabby Hartnett	1.50	.45
11 Billy Herman	.75	.23
12 Fergie Jenkins	1.50	.45
13 Andy Pafko	.50	.15
14 Ryne Sandberg	1.50	.45
15 Ron Santo	1.00	.30
16 Lee Smith	.75	.23
17 Sammy Sosa	4.00	1.20
18 Bruce Sutter	1.00	.30
19 Joe Tinker	1.50	.45
20 Billy Williams	1.50	.45
21 Hack Wilson	1.50	.45

2001 Cubs Topps 50th Anniversary

This 10 card set features reprints of leading Cub players from the past 50 years. These cards, which are all serial numbered to 30,000 were designed to be given away at various games during the 2001 season. Each player pre-signed 200 of these cards which were also randomly given away at the gate of these games. Since these cards have the original numbers, for our data base purposes we are sequencing them in alphabetical order. Please note that the Andy Pafko card does not picture him as a Cub. However, Pafko was selected to the Cubs All-Century team and combined with the significance in the hobby of his 1952 Topps card, the decision was made to include this card in this series.

	Nm-Mt	Ex-Mt
COMPLETE SET (10)	80.00	24.00
1 Ernie Banks 58	12.00	3.60
2 Andre Dawson 88	8.00	2.40
3 Fergie Jenkins 71	10.00	3.00
4 Andy Pafko 52	5.00	1.50
5 Ryne Sandberg 84	12.00	3.60
6 Ron Santo 61	12.00	3.60
7 Sammy Sosa 98	15.00	4.50
8 Rick Sutcliffe 85	5.00	1.50
9 Bruce Sutter 79	5.00	1.50
10 Billy Williams 72	12.00	3.60

2001 Cubs Topps 50th Anniversary Autographs

Out of the 30,000 of each card produced for the Cubs/Topps 50th Anniversary set, 200 of each card was autographed.

	Nm-Mt	Ex-Mt
COMPLETE SET (10)	800.00	240.00
1 Ernie Banks 58	150.00	45.00
2 Andre Dawson 88	80.00	24.00
3 Fergie Jenkins 71	100.00	30.00
4 Andy Pafko 52	50.00	15.00
5 Ryne Sandberg 84	120.00	36.00
6 Ron Santo 61	120.00	36.00
7 Sammy Sosa 98	150.00	45.00
8 Rick Sutcliffe 85	50.00	15.00
9 Bruce Sutter 79	50.00	15.00
10 Billy Williams 72	100.00	30.00

2002 Cubs Topps Best Moments

These nine standard-size cards were given away at various Chicago Cubs games during the 2002 season. These cards are reprints of Topps cards in seasons in which the featured player completed an important feat in baseball history. These cards were sponsored by various advertisers and came sealed in protective wrappers.

	Nm-Mt	Ex-Mt
COMPLETE SET	80.00	24.00
1 Ernie Banks	15.00	4.50
1954 card, 4/21		
2 Kerry Wood	10.00	3.00
1998 card, 5/6		
3 Don Cardwell	5.00	1.50
1961 card, 5/7		
4 Billy Williams	12.00	3.60
1961 card, 6/19		
5 Bill Buckner	6.00	1.80
1980 card, 6/24		
6 Ken Hubbs	8.00	2.40
1962 card, 6/26		
7 Dave Kingman	6.00	1.80
1979 card, 7/25		
8 Sammy Sosa	15.00	4.50
2002 card, 8/16		
9 Ken Holtzman	5.00	1.50
1969 card, 9/1		
10 Milt Pappas	5.00	1.50
1972 card, 9/2		
11 Lee Smith	6.00	1.80
1984 card, 9/28		

2003 Cubs Santo

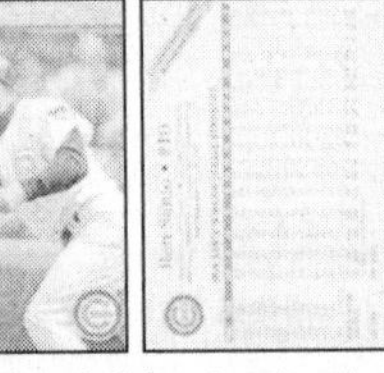

This one card standard-size set was issued as a special giveaway at the September 28, 2003 game in which Ron Santo's uniform number was retired by the Chicago Cubs. The front has an action photo of Santo while the back has personal information as well as seasonal and career stats.

	Nm-Mt	Ex-Mt
1 Ron Santo	10.00	3.00

2000 Cubs Sosa Commemorative

This one-card set was given away at a 2000 Cubs game to celebrate Sammy Sosa hitting more than 60 homers in both the 1998 and 1999 season. The front shows Sosa about to step into his home run "hop" while the horizontal back has information about Sosa as well as his 1999 and career stats.

	MINT	NRMT
1 Sammy Sosa	10.00	4.50

2003 Cubs Sweepstakes

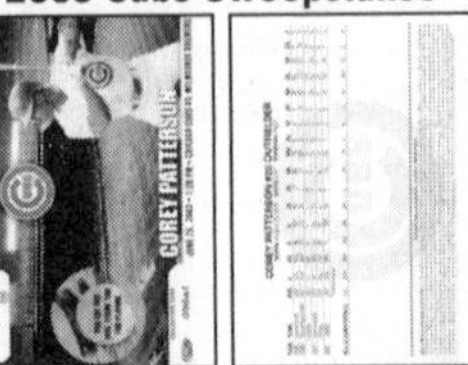

These six cards, which measure 5" by 3" were given away at various Cubs games during the 2003 season and were used as sweepstakes entries to see if lucky fans won an authentic autographed baseball. These cards feature a player photo superimposed on Wrigley Field as well as a space for the fan to rub off the part which indicated whether they won the autographed ball. Please note that each card had a different corporate sponsor. We have sequenced this set in order of what games they were given out at. These prices are based on cards for cards that have been scratched-off.

	MINT	NRMT
COMPLETE SET	30.00	13.50
1 Sammy Sosa	5.00	2.20
2 Billy Williams	2.50	1.10
3 Mark Prior	5.00	2.20
4 Jody Davis	1.00	.45
5 Ron Santo	2.50	1.10
6 Ryne Sandberg	4.00	1.80
7 Corey Patterson	1.50	.70
8 Dusty Baker MG	1.50	.70
9 Ernie Banks	5.00	2.20
10 Kerry Wood	3.00	1.35
11 Fergie Jenkins	2.50	1.10

2003 Cubs Topps

These cards, which were produced by Topps, were given away at selected Cubs home games during the 2003 season. Each card featured a reprint of an older Topps card with a special "2003 Wrigley Field edition" imprint on the front. Each of these cards were sponsored by a different corporate sponsor and were handed out in special holders which were serial numbered to 20,000. We have sequenced these cards in order of what game they were given out at

	MINT	NRMT
COMPLETE SET	30.00	13.50
1 Steve Stone	6.00	2.70
2 Bobby Hill	5.00	2.20
3 Hee Seop Choi	6.00	2.70
4 Glenn Beckert	6.00	2.70
5 Bill Madlock	8.00	3.60
6 Ron Santo	10.00	4.50

1996 CUI Metal Cards Griffey

This metal card set was issued in a tin box with a suggested retail price of $9.95. The fronts feature color player photos of Ken Griffey Jr. on a blue and green background. The backs carry information about different phases of his life. The cards are unnumbered and checklisted below according to what is taking place on the card.

	Nm-Mt	Ex-Mt
COMPLETE SET (5)	10.00	3.00
COMMON CARD (1-4)	2.50	.75
NNO Ken Griffey Tin Box	2.00	.60

1996 CUI Metal Cards Ripken

This metal card set was issued in a tin-holder with a suggested retail price of $9.95 and was primarily sold in retail outlets such as K-Mart. The fronts feature color action photos of Cal Ripken Jr. with the backs displaying something about his life. The cards are unnumbered.

	Nm-Mt	Ex-Mt
COMPLETE SET (5)	10.00	3.00
COMMON CARD (1-4)	2.50	.75
NNO Cal Ripken Tin Box	2.00	.60

1977 Customized Discs

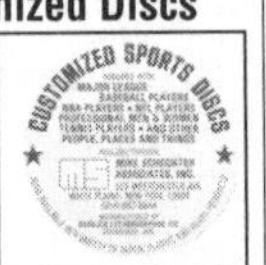

These are among the most difficult of the 1977 MSA Discs. They were issued by MSA to show what products they could produce for potential liscencees.

	NM	Ex
COMPLETE SET (70)	450.00	180.00
1 Sal Bando	4.00	1.60
2 Buddy Bell	8.00	3.20
3 Johnny Bench	60.00	24.00
4 Lou Brock	50.00	20.00
5 Larry Bowa	8.00	3.20
6 Steve Braun	4.00	1.60
7 George Brett	90.00	36.00
8 Jeff Burroughs	4.00	1.60
9 Campy Campaneris	8.00	3.20
10 John Candelaria	4.00	1.60
11 Jose Cardenal	4.00	1.60
12 Rod Carew	50.00	20.00
13 Steve Carlton	50.00	20.00
14 Dave Cash	4.00	1.60
15 Cesar Cedeno	4.00	1.60
16 Ron Cey	8.00	3.20
17 Dave Concepcion	10.00	4.00
18 Dennis Eckersley	50.00	20.00
19 Mark Fidrych	50.00	20.00
20 Rollie Fingers	30.00	12.00
21 Carlton Fisk	50.00	20.00
22 George Foster	10.00	4.00
23 Wayne Garland	4.00	1.60
24 Ralph Garr	8.00	3.20
25 Steve Garvey	20.00	8.00
26 Cesar Geronimo	4.00	1.60
27 Bobby Grich	8.00	3.20
28 Ken Griffey	10.00	4.00
29 Don Gullett	4.00	1.60
30 Mike Hargrove	8.00	3.20
31 Al Hrabosky	4.00	1.60
32 Catfish Hunter	30.00	12.00
33 Reggie Jackson	60.00	24.00
34 Randy Jones	4.00	1.60
35 Dave Kingman	15.00	6.00
36 Jerry Koosman	8.00	3.20
37 Dave LaRoche	4.00	1.60
38 Greg Luzinski	10.00	4.00
39 Fred Lynn	8.00	3.20
40 Bill Madlock	8.00	3.20
41 Rick Manning	4.00	1.60
42 Jon Matlack	4.00	1.60
43 John Mayberry	4.00	1.60
44 Hal McRae	8.00	3.20
45 Andy Messersmith	4.00	1.60
46 Rick Monday	4.00	1.60
47 John Montefusco	4.00	1.60
48 Joe Morgan	30.00	12.00
49 Thurman Munson	20.00	8.00
50 Bobby Murcer	10.00	4.00
51 Bill North	4.00	1.60
52 Jim Palmer	30.00	12.00
53 Tony Perez	30.00	12.00
54 Jerry Reuss	4.00	1.60
55 Brooks Robinson	50.00	20.00
56 Pete Rose	60.00	24.00
57 Joe Rudi	4.00	1.60
58 Nolan Ryan	125.00	50.00
59 Manny Sanguillen	4.00	1.60
60 Mike Schmidt	60.00	24.00
61 Tom Seaver	60.00	24.00
62 Bill Singer	4.00	1.60
63 Willie Stargell	30.00	12.00
64 Rusty Staub	10.00	4.00
65 Luis Tiant	8.00	3.20
66 Bob Watson	8.00	3.20
67 Butch Wynegar	4.00	1.60
68 Carl Yastrzemski	50.00	20.00
69 Robin Yount	50.00	20.00
70 Richie Zisk	4.00	1.60

1976 Dairy Isle Discs

These discs are another variety of the Crane Discs. These have a Dairy Isle back and are worth a multiple of the Crane issue.

	NM	Ex
COMPLETE SET (70)	40.00	16.00
1 Hank Aaron	5.00	2.00
2 Johnny Bench	3.00	1.20
3 Vida Blue	.50	.20
4 Larry Bowa	.50	.20
5 Lou Brock	3.00	1.20
6 Jeff Burroughs	.25	.10
7 John Candelaria	.25	.10
8 Jose Cardenal	.25	.10
9 Rod Carew	3.00	1.20
10 Steve Carlton	3.00	1.20
11 Dave Cash	.25	.10
12 Cesar Cedeno	.50	.20
13 Ron Cey	.50	.20
14 Carlton Fisk	4.00	1.60
15 Tito Fuentes	.25	.10
16 Steve Garvey	1.50	.60
17 Ken Griffey	.50	.20
18 Don Gullett	.25	.10
19 Willie Horton	.25	.10
20 Al Hrabosky	.25	.10
21 Catfish Hunter	3.00	1.20
22A Reggie Jackson	10.00	4.00
Oakland Athletics		
22B Reggie Jackson	3.00	1.20
Baltimore Orioles		
23 Randy Jones	.25	.10
24 Jim Kaat	1.00	.40
25 Don Kessinger	.25	.10
26 Dave Kingman	1.00	.40
27 Jerry Koosman	.50	.20
28 Mickey Lolich	.50	.20
29 Greg Luzinski	1.00	.40
30 Fred Lynn	1.00	.40
31 Bill Madlock	.50	.20
32A Carlos May	1.50	.60
Chicago White Sox		
32B Carlos May	.25	.10
New York Yankees		
33 John Mayberry	.25	.10
34 Bake McBride	.25	.10
35 Doc Medich	.25	.10
36A Andy Messersmith	1.50	.60
Los Angeles Dodgers		
36B Andy Messersmith	.25	.10
Atlanta Braves		
37 Rick Monday	.25	.10
38 John Montefusco	.25	.10
39 Jerry Morales	.25	.10
40 Joe Morgan	3.00	1.20
41 Thurman Munson	1.50	.60
42 Bobby Murcer	1.00	.40
43 Al Oliver	1.00	.40
44 Jim Palmer	3.00	1.20
45 Dave Parker	1.50	.60
46 Tony Perez	1.50	.60
47 Jerry Reuss	.25	.10
48 Brooks Robinson	3.00	1.20
49 Frank Robinson	3.00	1.20
50 Steve Rogers	.25	.10
51 Pete Rose	4.00	1.60

52 Nolan Ryan	8.00	3.20
53 Manny Sanguillen	.25	.10
54 Mike Schmidt	5.00	2.00
55 Tom Seaver	4.00	1.60
56 Ted Simmons	1.00	.40
57 Reggie Smith	.50	.20
58 Willie Stargell	3.00	1.20
59 Rusty Staub	1.00	.40
60 Rennie Stennett	.25	.10
61 Don Sutton	3.00	1.20
62A Andre Thornton	1.50	.60
Chicago Cubs		
62B Andre Thornton	.25	.10
Montreal Expos		
63 Luis Tiant	1.00	.40
64 Joe Torre	1.50	.60
65 Mike Tyson	.25	.10
66 Bob Watson	.50	.20
67 Wilbur Wood	.25	.10
68 Jimmy Wynn	.25	.10
69 Carl Yastrzemski	3.00	1.20
70 Richie Zisk	.25	.10

1977 Dairy Isle Discs

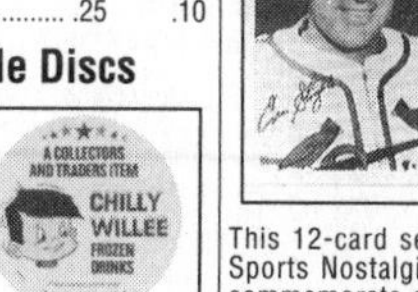

These discs were issued with the Dairy Isle name. Dairy Isle was one of the few issuers of these discs in both 1976 and 1977.

	NM	Ex
COMPLETE SET (70)	150.00	60.00
1 Sal Bando	1.00	.40
2 Buddy Bell	2.50	1.00
3 Johnny Bench	20.00	8.00
4 Lou Brock	15.00	6.00
5 Larry Bowa	2.50	1.00
6 Steve Braun	1.00	.40
7 George Brett	30.00	12.00
8 Jeff Burroughs	1.00	.40
9 Campy Campaneris	2.50	1.00
10 John Candelaria	1.00	.40
11 Jose Cardenal	1.00	.40
12 Rod Carew	15.00	6.00
13 Steve Carlton	15.00	6.00
14 Dave Cash	1.00	.40
15 Cesar Cedeno	1.00	.40
16 Ron Cey	2.50	1.00
17 Dave Concepcion	4.00	1.60
18 Dennis Eckersley	15.00	6.00
19 Mark Fidrych	15.00	6.00
20 Rollie Fingers	10.00	4.00
21 Carlton Fisk	15.00	6.00
22 George Foster	4.00	1.60
23 Wayne Garland	1.00	.40
24 Ralph Garr	2.50	1.00
25 Steve Garvey	8.00	3.20
26 Cesar Geronimo	1.00	.40
27 Bobby Grich	2.50	1.00
28 Ken Griffey	4.00	1.60
29 Don Gullett	1.00	.40
30 Mike Hargrove	2.50	1.00
31 Al Hrabosky	1.00	.40
32 Catfish Hunter	10.00	4.00
33 Reggie Jackson	20.00	8.00
34 Randy Jones	1.00	.40
35 Dave Kingman	5.00	2.00
36 Jerry Koosman	2.50	1.00
37 Dave LaRoche	1.00	.40
38 Greg Luzinski	4.00	1.60
39 Fred Lynn	2.50	1.00
40 Bill Madlock	2.50	1.00
41 Rick Manning	1.00	.40
42 Jon Matlack	1.00	.40
43 John Mayberry	1.00	.40
44 Hal McRae	2.50	1.00
45 Andy Messersmith	1.00	.40
46 Rick Monday	1.00	.40
47 John Montefusco	1.00	.40
48 Joe Morgan	10.00	4.00
49 Thurman Munson	8.00	3.20
50 Bobby Murcer	4.00	1.60
51 Bill North	1.00	.40
52 Jim Palmer	10.00	4.00
53 Tony Perez	10.00	4.00
54 Jerry Reuss	1.00	.40
55 Brooks Robinson	15.00	6.00
56 Pete Rose	20.00	8.00
57 Joe Rudi	1.00	.40
58 Nolan Ryan	40.00	16.00
59 Manny Sanguillen	1.00	.40
60 Mike Schmidt	20.00	8.00
61 Tom Seaver	20.00	8.00
62 Bill Singer	1.00	.40
63 Willie Stargell	10.00	4.00
64 Rusty Staub	4.00	1.60
65 Luis Tiant	2.50	1.00
66 Bob Watson	2.50	1.00
67 Butch Wynegar	1.00	.40
68 Carl Yastrzemski	15.00	6.00
69 Robin Yount	15.00	6.00
70 Richie Zisk	1.00	.40

1976 Dallas Convention

This nine-card slightly oversized set features local Dallas players and was issued in conjunction with the annual Dallas Sports Card Convention hosted by noted hobbyist Gervise Ford. Mr. Ford also produced the set with "Life of the Southwest Insurance Co.".

	NM	Ex
COMPLETE SET (9)	2.00	.80
1 Paul Aube	.25	.10
2 Jodie Beeler	.25	.10
3 Edward Borom	.25	.10
(Red)		
4 Sal Gliatto	.25	.10
5 Richard Herrscher	.25	.10
6 Joe Kotrany	.25	.10
7 Joe Macko	.25	.10
8 Frank Murray	.25	.10
9 Ron Samford	.25	.10

1985 Dallas National Collectors Convention

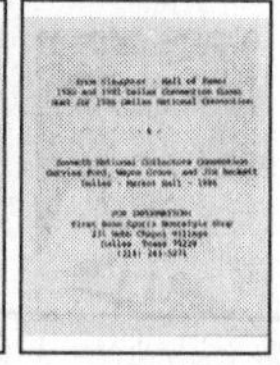

This 12-card set was issued by First Base Sports Nostalgia Shop in Dallas, Texas, to commemorate a bid for the Dallas National Collectors Convention. The black-and-white cards measure approximately 2" by 2 1/2" and include various photos relating to their National Convention bid including a photo of the proposed 1986 Convention hosts (Jim Beckett, Wayne Grove, and Gervise Ford) along with Dallas Maverick star Brad Davis, a shot of the Dallas Marriott, Market Hall and several Baseball legends who were guests of honor of the convention. The backs list the subject of the card front with a brief description and the First Base Sports Nostalgia Shop address.

	Nm-Mt	Ex-Mt
COMPLETE SET (12)	5.00	2.00
1 Stan Musial	1.50	.60
2 Ted Williams	2.00	.80
3 Bob Gibson	.75	.30
4 Brooks Robinson	.75	.30
5 Warren Spahn	.75	.30
6 Enos Slaughter	.75	.30
7 The Famous Chicken	.50	.20
8 Lou Brock	.75	.30
9 Market Hall	.25	.10
1986 Dallas Natl.		
Convention Facility		
10 Texas Ranger	.25	.10
Scoreboard		
11 Dallas Marriott	.25	.10
Market Center		
12 Jim Beckett	.50	.20
Wayne Grove		
Brad Davis (Dallas Maverick)		
Gervise Ford		

1954 Dan Dee

The cards in this 29-card set measure approximately 2 1/2" by 3 5/8". Most of the cards marketed by Dan Dee in bags of potato chips in 1954 depict players from the Cleveland Indians or Pittsburgh Pirates. The Pitttsburgh Pirates players in the set are much tougher to find than the Cleveland Indians players. The pictures used for New York Yankees players were also employed in the Briggs and Stahl-Meyer sets. Dan Dee cards have a waxed surface, but are commonly found with product stains. Paul Smith and Walker Cooper are considered the known scarcities. The catalog designation for this set is F342. These unnumbered cards are listed below in alphabetical order.

	NM	Ex
COMPLETE SET (29)	4500.00	2200.00
COMMON CARD (1-29)	50.00	25.00
COMMON PIRATE CARD	60.00	30.00
1 Bobby Avila	60.00	30.00
2 Hank Bauer	60.00	30.00
3 Walker Cooper SP	300.00	150.00
Pittsburgh Pirates		
4 Larry Doby	100.00	50.00
5 Luke Easter	60.00	30.00
6 Bob Feller	150.00	75.00
7 Bob Friend	100.00	50.00
Pittsburgh Pirates		
8 Mike Garcia	60.00	30.00
9 Sid Gordon	80.00	40.00
Pittsburgh Pirates		
10 Jim Hegan	50.00	25.00
11 Gil Hodges	120.00	60.00
12 Art Houtteman	50.00	25.00
13 Monte Irvin	100.00	50.00
14 Paul LaPalme	60.00	30.00
Pittsburgh Pirates		
15 Bob Lemon	100.00	50.00
16 Al Lopez MG	80.00	40.00
17 Mickey Mantle	2000.00	1000.00
18 Dale Mitchell	50.00	25.00
19 Phil Rizzuto	200.00	100.00
20 Curt Roberts	60.00	30.00
Pittsburgh Pirates		
21 Al Rosen	80.00	40.00
22 Red Schoendienst	100.00	50.00
23 Paul Smith SP	500.00	250.00
Pittsburgh Pirates		
24 Duke Snider	250.00	125.00
25 George Strickland	50.00	25.00
26 Max Surkont	60.00	30.00
Pittsburgh Pirates		
27 Frank Thomas	150.00	75.00
Pittsburgh Pirates		
28 Wally Westlake	50.00	25.00
29 Early Wynn	100.00	50.00

1910 Darby Chocolates E271

These 34 cards listed below are what are known of this very scarce set. A major help in cataloguing this set was a find of 22 cards in 1982. Some new cards are always being discovered. We understand that this checklist may be incomplete therefore verified copies of unlisted cards are appreciated. Uncut complete boxes are more desirable when found and are worth a little more than twice the value of the combined cards.

	Ex-Mt	VG
COMPLETE SET (34)	35000.00	17500.00
1 Jimmy Archer	600.00	300.00
2 Chief Bender	1200.00	600.00
3 Bob Bescher	600.00	300.00
4 Roger Bresnahan	1200.00	600.00
5 Al Bridwell	600.00	300.00
6 Mordecai Brown	1200.00	600.00
7 Eddie Cicotte	1200.00	600.00
8 Fred Clarke	1200.00	600.00
9 Ty Cobb	5000.00	2500.00
10 King Cole	600.00	300.00
11 Eddie Collins	1500.00	750.00
12 Wid Conroy	600.00	300.00
13 Sam Crawford	1200.00	600.00
14 Bill Dahlen	600.00	300.00
15 Bill Donovan	600.00	300.00
16 Patsy Dougherty	600.00	300.00
17 Kid Elberfeld	600.00	300.00
18 Johnny Evers	1200.00	600.00
19 Buck Herzog	600.00	300.00
20 Hugh Jennings MG	1200.00	600.00
21 Walter Johnson	3000.00	1500.00
22 Ed Konetchy	600.00	300.00
23 Tommy Leach	600.00	300.00
24 Fred Luderus	600.00	300.00
Sic, Luderous		
25 John McGraw MG	1500.00	750.00
26 Mike Mowrey	600.00	300.00
27 Jack Powell	600.00	300.00
28 Slim Sallee	600.00	300.00
29 Jimmy Sheckard	600.00	300.00
Sic, Scheckard		
30 Fred Snodgrass	800.00	400.00
31 Tris Speaker	1500.00	750.00
32 Charlie Suggs	600.00	300.00
33 Fred Tenney	600.00	300.00
34 Honus Wagner	3000.00	1500.00

1982 Davco Hall of Fame Boxes

This 25-card set features color drawings of Hall of Fame Baseball Stars measuring approximately 4 1/4" by 7 1/4". The fronts carry both an action drawing of the player and a drawn portrait with blue borders and a red, white, and blue facsimile ribbon around the top and sides of the picture. The player's name and why he is in the Hall of Fame is printed below. The backs are blank. The cards are unnumbered and checklisted below in alphabetical order.

	Nm-Mt	Ex-Mt
COMPLETE SET (25)	50.00	20.00
1 Hank Aaron	3.00	1.20
2 Grover C. Alexander	1.50	.60
3 Roy Campanella	2.50	1.00
4 Ty Cobb	3.00	1.20
5 Joe DiMaggio	4.00	1.60
6 Bob Feller	1.50	.60
7 Jimmy Foxx	2.50	1.00
8 Frank Frisch	1.00	.40
9 Lou Gehrig	3.00	1.20
10 Bob Gibson	1.50	.60
11 Hank Greenberg	2.50	1.00
12 Rogers Hornsby	2.00	.80
13 Walter Johnson	2.50	1.00
14 Sandy Koufax	2.50	1.00
15 Mickey Mantle	5.00	2.00
16 Christy Mathewson	2.00	.80
17 Willie Mays	3.00	1.20
18 Stan Musial	2.50	1.00
19 Jackie Robinson	3.00	1.20
20 Babe Ruth	5.00	2.00
21 Tris Speaker	1.50	.60
22 Pie Traynor	1.50	.60
23 Honus Wagner	2.00	.80
24 Ted Williams	3.00	1.20
25 Cy Young	2.50	1.00

2000 Eric Davis Colon Cancer

This one card standard-size set was issued to promote the need for colon cancer screening. The front of the card has a photo of Davis

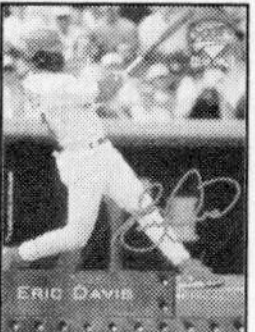

swinging while the back has carrer highlights, biographical information and some information about colon cancer.

	Nm-Mt	Ex-Mt
1 Eric Davis	1.00	.30

1993 Leon Day Commemorative Card

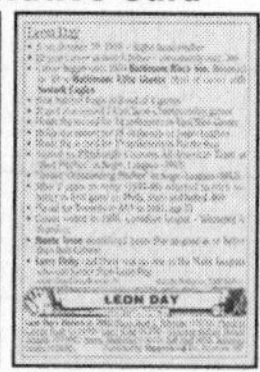

Published by Hieronimus and Co., this card measures 2 1/2" by 3 1/2" and features a portrait of Leon Day on a white background by artist Gary Cieradkowski Jr. The player's name appears in a black-and-white banner that includes drawings of a glove, bat, ball and face mask. The back is printed in black ink and carries biography and career highlights.

	Nm-Mt	Ex-Mt
1 Leon Day	10.00	3.00

1970 Dayton Daily News M137

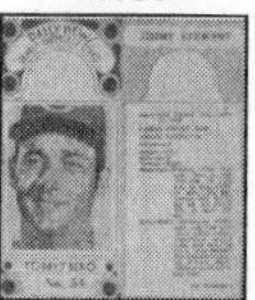

These 3 3/4" by 3 1/2" cards were issued inside issues of the Dayton Daily News. The newsprint-stock cards were issued on successive days and were numbered in that order. Tony Perez, card number 11, has been seen with a light or dark cap. There is no pricing difference for either card. The Dave Concepcion card predates his Topps Rookie Card by one year.

	NM	Ex
COMPLETE SET (160)	450.00	180.00
1 Pete Rose	15.00	6.00
2 Johnny Bench	8.00	3.20
3 Maury Wills	4.00	1.60
4 Harmon Killebrew	5.00	2.00
5 Frank Robinson	8.00	3.20
6 Willie Mays	10.00	4.00
7 Hank Aaron	15.00	6.00
8 Tom Seaver	8.00	3.20
9 Sam McDowell	3.00	1.20
10 Rico Petrocelli	3.00	1.20
11 Tony Perez	5.00	2.00
Dark Cap		
11A Tony Perez	5.00	2.00
White Cap		
12 Hoyt Wilhelm	5.00	2.00
13 Alex Johnson	2.00	.80
14 Gary Nolan	2.00	.80
15 Al Kaline	8.00	3.20
16 Bob Gibson	8.00	3.20
17 Larry Dierker	3.00	1.20
18 Ernie Banks	8.00	3.20
19 Lee May	3.00	1.20
20 Claude Osteen	2.00	.80
21 Tony Horton	2.00	.80
22 Mack Jones	2.00	.80
23 Wally Bunker	2.00	.80
24 Bill Hands	2.00	.80
25 Bobby Tolan	2.00	.80
26 Jim Wynn	3.00	1.20
27 Tom Haller	2.00	.80
28 Carl Yastrzemski	8.00	3.20
29 Jim Merritt	2.00	.80
30 Tony Oliva	4.00	1.60
31 Reggie Jackson	15.00	6.00
32 Bob Clemente	25.00	10.00
33 Tommy Helms	2.00	.80
34 Boog Powell	4.00	1.60
35 Mickey Lolich	3.00	1.20
36 Frank Howard	3.00	1.20
37 Jim McGlothlin	2.00	.80
38 Rusty Staub	3.00	1.20
39 Mel Stottlemyre	3.00	1.20
40 Rico Carty	2.00	.80
41 Nate Colbert	2.00	.80
42 Wayne Granger	2.00	.80
43 Mike Hegan	2.00	.80
44 Jerry Koosman	3.00	1.20
45 Jim Perry	2.00	.80
46 Pat Corrales	2.00	.80
47 Dick Bosman	2.00	.80
48 Bert Campaneris	3.00	1.20
49 Larry Hisle	2.00	.80
50 Bernie Carbo	2.00	.80
51 Wilbur Wood	2.00	.80
52 Dave McNally	3.00	1.20
53 Andy Messersmith	3.00	1.20
54 Jimmy Stewart	2.00	.80
55 Luis Aparicio	5.00	2.00
56 Mike Cuellar	2.00	.80
57 Bill Grabarkewitz	2.00	.80
58 Dick Dietz	2.00	.80
59 Dave Concepcion	5.00	2.00
60 Gary Gentry	2.00	.80
61 Don Money	2.00	.80
62 Rod Carew	8.00	3.20
63 Denis Menke	2.00	.80
64 Hal McRae	3.00	1.20
65 Felipe Alou	3.00	1.20
66 Richie Hebner	2.00	.80
67 Don Sutton	5.00	2.00
68 Wayne Simpson	2.00	.80
69 Art Shamsky	2.00	.80
70 Luis Tiant	4.00	1.60
71 Clay Carroll	2.00	.80
72 Jim Hickman	2.00	.80
73 Clarence Gaston	3.00	1.20
74 Angel Bravo	2.00	.80
75 Jim Hunter	5.00	2.00
76 Lou Piniella	4.00	1.60
77 Jim Bunning	5.00	2.00
78 Don Gullett	2.00	.80
80 Richie Allen	4.00	1.60
81 Jim Bouton	3.00	1.20
82 Jim Palmer	8.00	3.20
83 Woody Woodward	2.00	.80
84 Tom Agee	2.00	.80
85 Carlos May	2.00	.80
86 Ray Washburn	2.00	.80
87 Denny McLain	3.00	1.20
88 Lou Brock	8.00	3.20
89 Ken Henderson	2.00	.80
90 Roy White	3.00	1.20
91 Chris Cannizzaro	2.00	.80
92 Willie Horton	3.00	1.20
93 Jose Cardenal	2.00	.80
94 Jim Fregosi	3.00	1.20
95 Richie Hebner	2.00	.80
96 Tony Conigliaro	4.00	1.60
97 Tony Cloninger	2.00	.80
98 Mike Epstein	2.00	.80
99 Ty Cline	2.00	.80
100 Tommy Harper	2.00	.80
101 Jose Azcue	2.00	.80
102a Ray Fosse	2.00	.80
102b Glenn Beckert	2.00	.80
103 not issued		
104 Gerry Moses	2.00	.80
105 Bud Harrelson	2.00	.80
106 Joe Torre	5.00	2.00
107 Dave Johnson	3.00	1.20
108 Don Kessinger	3.00	1.20
109 Bill Freehan	3.00	1.20
110 Sandy Alomar	2.00	.80
111 Matty Alou	2.00	.80
112 Joe Morgan	5.00	2.00
113 John Odom	2.00	.80
114 Amos Otis	3.00	1.20
115 Jay Johnstone	2.00	.80
116 Ron Perranoski	2.00	.80
117 Manny Mota	2.00	.80
118 Billy Conigliaro	2.00	.80
119 Leo Cardenas	2.00	.80
120 Rich Reese	2.00	.80
121 Ron Santo	4.00	1.60
122 Gene Michael	2.00	.80
123 Milt Pappas	2.00	.80
124 Joe Pepitone	3.00	1.20
125 Jose Cardenal	2.00	.80
126 Jim Northrup	3.00	1.20
127 Wes Parker	2.00	.80
128 Fritz Peterson	2.00	.80
129 Phil Regan	2.00	.80
130 John Callison	2.00	.80
131 Cookie Rojas	2.00	.80
132 Claude Raymond	2.00	.80
133 Darrell Chaney	2.00	.80
134 Gary Peters	2.00	.80
135 Del Unser	2.00	.80
136 Joey Foy	2.00	.80
137 Luke Walker	2.00	.80
138 Bill Mazeroski	5.00	2.00
139 Tony Taylor	2.00	.80
140 Leron Lee	2.00	.80
141 Jesus Alou	3.00	1.20
142 Donn Clendenon	2.00	.80
143 Merv Rettenmund	2.00	.80
144 Bob Moose	2.00	.80
145 Jim Kaat	4.00	1.60
146 Randy Hundley	2.00	.80
147 Jim McAndrew	2.00	.80
148 Manny Sanguillen	2.00	.80
149 Bob Allison	2.00	.80
150 Jim Maloney	2.00	.80
151 Don Buford	2.00	.80
152 Gene Alley	2.00	.80
153 Cesar Tovar	2.00	.80
154 Brooks Robinson	8.00	3.20
155 Milt Wilcox	2.00	.80
156 Willie Stargell	5.00	2.00
157 Paul Blair	2.00	.80
158 Andy Etchebarren	2.00	.80
159 Mark Belanger	2.00	.80
160 Elrod Hendricks	2.00	.80

1933 Delong R333

The cards in this 24-card set measure approximately 2" by 3". The 1933 Delong Gum set of 24 multi-colored cards was, along with the 1933 Goudey Big League series, one of the first baseball card sets issued with chewing gum. It was the only card set issued by this company. The reverse text was written by Austen Lake, who also wrote the sports tips found on the Diamond Stars series which began in 1934, leading to speculation that Delong was bought out by National Chicle.

	Ex-Mt	VG
COMPLETE SET (24)	10000.00	5000.00
1 Marty McManus	200.00	100.00
2 Al Simmons	500.00	250.00
3 Oscar Melillo	150.00	75.00
4 Bill Terry	400.00	200.00
5 Charlie Gehringer	400.00	200.00
6 Mickey Cochrane	500.00	250.00
7 Lou Gehrig	4000.00	2000.00
8 Kiki Cuyler	300.00	150.00
9 Bill Urbanski	150.00	75.00
10 Lefty O'Doul	250.00	125.00
11 Fred Lindstrom	300.00	150.00
12 Pie Traynor	400.00	200.00
13 Rabbit Maranville	300.00	150.00
14 Lefty Gomez	400.00	200.00
15 Riggs Stephenson	200.00	100.00
16 Lon Warneke	150.00	75.00
17 Pepper Martin	200.00	100.00
18 Jimmy Dykes	200.00	100.00
19 Chick Hafey	300.00	150.00
20 Joe Vosmik	150.00	75.00
21 Jimmie Foxx	600.00	300.00
22 Chuck Klein	300.00	150.00
23 Lefty Grove	60.00	30.00
24 Goose Goslin	400.00	200.00

1935 Al Demaree Die Cuts R304

These cards are drawings which were produced approximately in 1935; other cards may exist in this scarce set. The cards measure 1" x 4 1/2". This listing may be incomplete. All additions are welcome and appreciated. A few cards have not yet been discovered with the tab that would enable us to ID the card numbers. They are listed at the end as NNO's

	Ex-Mt	VG
COMPLETE SET	20000.00	10000.00
4 Babe Ruth	2000.00	1000.00
5 Sam Byrd	200.00	100.00
6 Tony Lazzeri	300.00	150.00
7 Frank Crosetti	250.00	125.00
9 Lou Gehrig	1500.00	750.00
11 Mule Haas	200.00	100.00
12 Evar Swanson	200.00	100.00
13 Merv Shea	200.00	100.00
14 Al Simmons throwing	300.00	150.00
15 Minter Hayes	200.00	100.00
16 Al Simmons batting	300.00	150.00
17 Jimmy Dykes	250.00	125.00
18 Luke Appling	300.00	150.00
19 Ted Lyons	300.00	150.00
20 Red Kress	200.00	100.00
21 Gee Walker	200.00	100.00
23 Mickey Cochrane catcher uniform	400.00	200.00
24 Mickey Cochrane batting possibly Gehringer picture	400.00	200.00
25 Pete Fox	200.00	100.00
26 Firpo Marberry	200.00	100.00
28 Mickey Owen	200.00	100.00
35 Joe Vosmik	200.00	100.00
41 Jack Burns	200.00	100.00
45 Ray Pepper	200.00	100.00
46 Bruce Campbell	200.00	100.00
48 Art Scharein	200.00	100.00
49 George Blaeholder	200.00	100.00
50 Rogers Hornsby	1000.00	500.00
54 Jimmie Foxx	600.00	300.00
56 Dib Williams	200.00	100.00
57 Lou Finney	200.00	100.00
61 Ossie Bluege	200.00	100.00
64 Joe Cronin	300.00	150.00
66 Buddy Myer	200.00	100.00
67 Earl Whitehill	200.00	100.00
71 Ed Morgan	200.00	100.00
74 Carl Reynolds	200.00	100.00
76 Bill Cissell	200.00	100.00
77 Johnny Hodapp	200.00	100.00
78 Dusty Cooke	200.00	100.00
79 Lefty Grove	400.00	200.00
82 Gus Mancuso	200.00	100.00
83 Kiddo Davis	200.00	100.00
84 Blondy Ryan	200.00	100.00
86 Travis Jackson	300.00	150.00
89 Bill Terry	400.00	200.00
91 Tony Cuccinello	200.00	100.00
97 Danny Taylor	200.00	100.00
99 Johnny Frederick	200.00	100.00
100 Sam Leslie	200.00	100.00
102 Mark Koenig	200.00	100.00
107 Syl Johnson	200.00	100.00
108 Jim Bottomley	300.00	150.00
112 Harvey Hendrick	200.00	100.00
115 Don Hurst	200.00	100.00
117 Prince Oana	200.00	100.00
121 Spud Davis	200.00	100.00
122 George Watkins	200.00	100.00
123 Frankie Frisch	300.00	150.00
125 Rip Collins	200.00	100.00
126 Dizzy Dean	600.00	300.00
127 Pepper Martin	250.00	125.00
128 Joe Medwick	300.00	150.00
129 Leo Durocher	300.00	150.00
130 Ernie Orsatti	200.00	100.00
132 Shanty Hogan	200.00	100.00
137 Wally Berger	250.00	125.00
141 Gus Suhr	200.00	100.00
142 Earl Grace	200.00	100.00
152 Gabby Hartnett	300.00	150.00
154 Chuck Klein	300.00	150.00
158 Billy Herman	300.00	150.00
160 Charlie Grimm	250.00	125.00
162 Bill Klem UMP	300.00	150.00
167 George Hildebrand UMP	200.00	100.00
NNO Willie Kamm	200.00	100.00
NNO Roy Mahaffey	200.00	100.00
NNO Bob Johnson	200.00	100.00
NNO Pinky Higgins	200.00	100.00
NNO Roy Johnson	200.00	100.00

1991 Denny's Holograms

The 1991 Denny's Grand Slam hologram baseball card set was produced by Upper Deck. The 26-card standard-size set contains one player from each major league team, who was selected on the basis of the number and circumstances of his grand slam home runs. These cards were available at Denny's only with the purchase of a meal from the restaurant's Grand Slam menu; each card came sealed in a plastic bag that prevents prior identification. It is estimated that two million cards were printed. In 1991, if the contest card was a winner, the collector was entitled to a free meal. By the end of the contest, almost half the teams had hit grand slams during the length of the contest. So many teams hit grand slams in that time frame which caused Denny's never to run that aspect of the promotion again.

	Nm-Mt	Ex-Mt
COMPLETE SET (26)	20.00	6.00
1 Ellis Burks	.60	.18
2 Cecil Fielder	.40	.12
3 Will Clark	.75	.23
4 Eric Davis	.40	.12
5 Dave Parker	.40	.12
6 Kelly Gruber	.20	.06
7 Kent Hrbek	.40	.12
8 Don Mattingly	4.00	1.20
9 Brook Jacoby	.20	.06
10 Mark McGwire	5.00	1.50
11 Howard Johnson	.20	.06
12 Tim Wallach	.20	.06
13 Ricky Jordan	.20	.06
14 Andre Dawson	.75	.23
15 Eddie Murray	1.00	.30
16 Danny Tartabull	.20	.06
17 Bobby Bonilla	.20	.06
18 Benito Santiago	.40	.12
19 Alvin Davis	.20	.06
20 Cal Ripken	8.00	2.40
21 Ruben Sierra	.40	.12
22 Pedro Guerrero	.20	.06
23 Wally Joyner	.40	.12
24 Craig Biggio	.60	.18
25 Dave Justice	.40	.12
26 Tim Raines	.40	.12

1992 Denny's Holograms

This 26-card standard-size set of holographic cards was produced by Upper Deck for Denny's. The set features one player from each major league team, who was selected on the basis of the number and circumstances of his grand slam home runs. With each order of a Grand Slam meal, the customer received one hologram card.

	Nm-Mt	Ex-Mt
COMPLETE SET (26)	15.00	4.50
1 Marquis Grissom	.20	.06
2 Ken Caminiti	.40	.12
3 Fred McGriff	.60	.18
4 Felix Jose	.20	.06
5 Jack Clark	.40	.12
6 Albert Belle	.40	.12
7 Sid Bream	.20	.06
8 Robin Ventura	.40	.12
9 Cal Ripken	6.00	1.80
10 Ryne Sandberg	2.50	.75
11 Paul O'Neill	.40	.12
12 Luis Polonia	.20	.06
13 Cecil Fielder	.40	.12
14 Kal Daniels	.20	.06
15 Brian McRae	.20	.06
16 Howard Johnson	.20	.06
17 Greg Vaughn	.40	.12
18 Dale Murphy	.75	.23
19 Kent Hrbek	.40	.12
20 Barry Bonds	3.00	.90
21 Matt Nokes	.20	.06
22 Jose Canseco	1.00	.30
23 Jay Buhner	.40	.12
24 Will Clark	1.50	.45
25 Ruben Sierra	.40	.12
26 Joe Carter	.40	.12

1993 Denny's Holograms

This 28-card standard-size set of holographic cards was produced by Upper Deck for Denny's. The set features one player from each major league team who was selected on the basis of the number and circumstances of his grand slam home runs. With each order of a Grand Slam meal and a Coca-Cola Classic, the

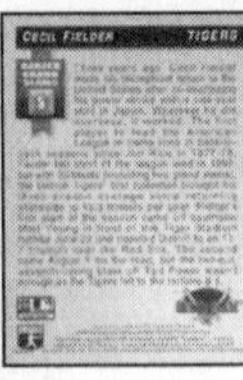

customer received one lithogram card. The set ordering follows alphabetical order of team nicknames.

	Nm-Mt	Ex-Mt
COMPLETE SET (28)	15.00	4.50
1 Chili Davis	.40	.12
2 Eric Anthony	.20	.06
3 Rickey Henderson	1.50	.45
4 Joe Carter	.40	.12
5 Terry Pendleton	.20	.06
6 Robin Yount	1.00	.30
7 Ray Lankford	.40	.12
8 Ryne Sandberg	2.00	.60
9 Darryl Strawberry	.40	.12
10 Marquis Grissom	.20	.06
11 Will Clark	1.50	.45
12 Albert Belle	.40	.12
13 Edgar Martinez	.60	.18
14 Benito Santiago	.40	.12
15 Eddie Murray	1.00	.30
16 Cal Ripken	4.00	1.20
17 Gary Sheffield	1.00	.30
18 Dave Hollins	.20	.06
19 Andy Van Slyke	.20	.06
20 Juan Gonzalez	.75	.23
21 John Valentin	.20	.06
22 Joe Oliver	.20	.06
23 Dante Bichette	.40	.12
24 Wally Joyner	.40	.12
25 Cecil Fielder	.40	.12
26 Kirby Puckett	1.00	.30
27 Robin Ventura	.60	.18
28 Danny Tartabull	.20	.06

1994 Denny's Holograms

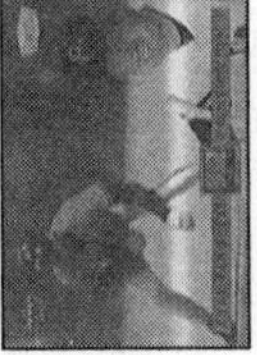

This 28-card standard-size set of holographic cards was produced by Upper Deck for Denny's and features a star player from each of the 28 Major League baseball teams. With each order of any "Classic Hits" entree, the customer received one hologram card in a blue poly pack. There was also a Reggie Jackson Hologram printed. The Jackson card was a contest giveaway for each participating Denny's.

	Nm-Mt	Ex-Mt
COMP FACT. SET (29)	50.00	15.00
COMPLETE SET (28)	15.00	4.50
1 Jim Abbott	.40	.12
2 Roberto Alomar	.75	.23
3 Kevin Appier	.40	.12
4 Jeff Bagwell	1.00	.30
5 Albert Belle	.40	.12
6 Barry Bonds	1.50	.45
7 Bobby Bonilla	.20	.06
8 Lenny Dykstra	.40	.12
9 Cal Eldred	.20	.06
10 Cecil Fielder	.40	.12
11 Andres Galarraga	.75	.23
12 Ken Griffey Jr.	2.00	.60
13 Juan Gonzalez	.75	.23
14 Tony Gwynn	1.50	.45
15 Rickey Henderson	1.25	.35
16 Kent Hrbek	.40	.12
17 David Justice	.75	.23
18 Mike Piazza	2.00	.60
19 Jose Rijo	.20	.06
20 Cal Ripken	3.00	.90
21 Tim Salmon	.75	.23
22 Ryne Sandberg	1.50	.45
23 Gary Sheffield	1.00	.30
24 Ozzie Smith	1.50	.45
25 Frank Thomas	.75	.23
26 Andy Van Slyke	.40	.12
27 Mo Vaughn	.20	.06
28 Larry Walker	.40	.12
XX Reggie Jackson Issued in Giveaway sets	40.00	12.00

1995 Denny's Holograms

This 28-card standard-size set of holographic cards was produced by Upper Deck for Denny's and features a star player from each of the 28 Major League baseball teams. With each order of an "Classic Hits" entree and a non-alcoholic beverage, the customer received one hologram card in a blue poly pack. Also guests at the restaurants could enter a sweepstakes drawing for a complete set of cards, to be given away by each participating restaurant at the end of the promotion after September 30.

	Nm-Mt	Ex-Mt
COMPLETE SET (28)	15.00	4.50
1 Roberto Alomar	.75	.23
2 Moises Alou	.40	.12
3 Jeff Bagwell	1.00	.30
4 Albert Belle	.40	.12
5 Jason Bere	.20	.06
6 Roger Clemens	1.50	.45
7 Darren Daulton	.40	.12
8 Cecil Fielder	.40	.12
9 Andres Galarraga	.40	.12
10 Juan Gonzalez	.75	.23
11 Ken Griffey Jr.	2.00	.60
12 Tony Gwynn	1.50	.45
13 Barry Larkin	.75	.23
14 Greg Maddux	1.50	.45
15 Don Mattingly	1.50	.45
16 Mark McGwire	2.50	.75
17 Orlando Merced	.20	.06
18 Jeff Montgomery	.20	.06
19 Rafael Palmeiro	.75	.23
20 Mike Piazza	2.00	.60
21 Kirby Puckett	1.00	.30
22 Bret Saberhagen	.40	.12
23 Tim Salmon	.75	.23
24 Gary Sheffield	1.00	.30
25 Ozzie Smith	1.50	.45
26 Sammy Sosa	1.50	.45
27 Greg Vaughn	.20	.06
28 Matt Williams	.60	.18

1996 Denny's Holograms

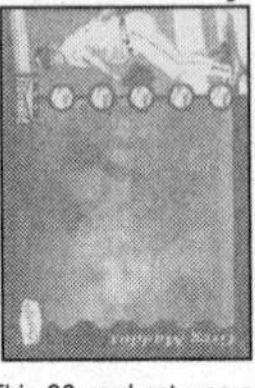

This 28-card set was produced by Pinnacle for Denny's and features a star player from each of the Major League baseball teams. The fronts feature a full motion hologram player image. The backs carry player information. By ordering anything on the menu, a customer could buy two packs. Each Denny's also sponsored a drawing to win all 48 cards (the regular set and both insert sets).

	Nm-Mt	Ex-Mt
COMPLETE SET (28)	12.00	3.60
1 Greg Maddux	1.50	.45
2 Cal Ripken	3.00	.90
3 Frank Thomas	.75	.23
4 Albert Belle	.40	.12
5 Mo Vaughn	.40	.12
6 Jeff Bagwell	1.00	.30
7 Jay Buhner	.40	.12
8 Barry Bonds	1.50	.45
9 Ryne Sandberg	1.50	.45
10 Hideo Nomo	1.50	.45
11 Kirby Puckett	1.00	.30
12 Gary Sheffield	1.00	.30
13 Barry Larkin	.75	.23
14 Wade Boggs	1.00	.30
15 Tony Gwynn	1.50	.45
16 Tim Salmon	.60	.18
17 Jason Isringhausen	.40	.12
18 Cecil Fielder	.40	.12
19 Dante Bichette	.40	.12
20 Ozzie Smith	1.50	.45
21 Ivan Rodriguez	1.00	.30
22 Kevin Appier	.20	.06
23 Joe Carter	.40	.12
24 Moises Alou	.40	.12
25 Mark McGwire	2.50	.75
26 Kevin Seitzer	.20	.06
27 Darren Daulton	.40	.12
28 Jay Bell	.20	.06

1996 Denny's Holograms Grand Slam

Randomly inserted in packs, this 10-card set features star players from several of the Major League baseball teams. The fronts display a holographic player image with bursting fireworks in the background, while the backs carry player information.

	Nm-Mt	Ex-Mt
COMPLETE SET (10)	40.00	12.00
*ARTIST PROOF: 5X BASIC CARDS....		
1 Cal Ripken	10.00	3.00
2 Frank Thomas	3.00	.90
3 Mike Piazza	6.00	1.80
4 Tony Gwynn	5.00	1.50
5 Sammy Sosa	5.00	1.50
6 Barry Bonds	5.00	1.50
7 Jeff Bagwell	4.00	1.20
8 Albert Belle	2.00	.60
9 Mo Vaughn	2.00	.60
10 Kirby Puckett	3.00	.90

1997 Denny's Holograms

This 29-card set was produced by Pinnacle for Denny's Restaurants and features a star player from each of the Major League baseball teams. Card number 29 is a commemorative Jackie Robinson card and card number 30 was only distributed in the Cleveland area. The fronts feature 3-D lenticular color player photos. The backs carry a 3-D hologram and player

statistics. By purchasing any entree and non-alcoholic beverage, a collector could purchase a card for 59 cents. A significant portion of the proceeds went to support Denny's national charity, Save the Children. The complete set price does not include the regional Larry Doby card

	Nm-Mt	Ex-Mt
COMPLETE SET (29)	25.00	7.50
1 Tim Salmon	.50	.15
2 Rafael Palmeiro	1.00	.30
3 Mo Vaughn	.25	.07
4 Frank Thomas	1.25	.35
5 Dave Justice	1.00	.30
6 Travis Fryman	.50	.15
7 Johnny Damon	.75	.23
8 John Jaha	.25	.07
9 Chuck Knoblauch	.50	.15
10 Mark McGwire	4.00	1.20
11 Alex Rodriguez	3.00	.90
12 Juan Gonzalez	1.00	.30
13 Roger Clemens	2.50	.75
14 Derek Jeter	5.00	1.50
15 Andruw Jones	1.50	.45
16 Sammy Sosa	2.50	.75
17 Barry Larkin	1.00	.30
18 Dante Bichette	.50	.15
19 Jeff Bagwell	1.50	.45
20 Mike Piazza	3.00	.90
21 Gary Sheffield	1.25	.35
22 Vladimir Guerrero	1.50	.45
23 Todd Hundley	.50	.15
24 Jason Kendall	.75	.23
25 Ray Lankford	.50	.15
26 Ken Caminiti	.50	.15
27 Barry Bonds	2.50	.75
28 Scott Rolen	1.00	.30
29 Jackie Robinson 50th Anniversary Commemorative	5.00	1.50
30 Larry Doby 50th Anniversary	2.50	.75

1986 DeSa Commemorative

This one-card set measures approximately 4" by 6 " and commemorates Baseball player Joe DeSa. The front features a color player photo with a red border and the words "Joe DeSa Remembered" printed in white at the top. The back displays information about the player and career statistics.

	Nm-Mt	Ex-Mt
1 Joe DeSa	3.00	1.20

1977 Detroit Caesars Discs

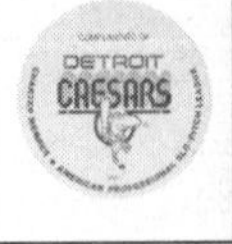

These discs, another of the 1977 MSA Discs were released with Detroit Caesar Backs.

	NM	Ex
COMPLETE SET (70)	150.00	60.00
1 Sal Bando	1.00	.40
2 Buddy Bell	2.50	1.00
3 Johnny Bench	20.00	8.00
4 Lou Brock	15.00	6.00
5 Larry Bowa	2.50	1.00
6 Steve Braun	1.00	.40
7 George Brett	30.00	12.00
8 Jeff Burroughs	1.00	.40
9 Campy Campaneris	2.50	1.00
10 John Candelaria	1.00	.40
11 Jose Cardenal	1.00	.40
12 Rod Carew	15.00	6.00
13 Steve Carlton	15.00	6.00
14 Dave Cash	1.00	.40
15 Cesar Cedeno	1.00	.40
16 Ron Cey	2.50	1.00
17 Dave Concepcion	4.00	1.60
18 Dennis Eckersley	15.00	6.00
19 Mark Fidrych	15.00	6.00
20 Rollie Fingers	10.00	4.00
21 Carlton Fisk	15.00	6.00
22 George Foster	4.00	1.60
23 Wayne Garland	1.00	.40
24 Ralph Garr	2.50	1.00
25 Steve Garvey	7.50	3.00
26 Cesar Geronimo	1.00	.40
27 Bobby Grich	2.50	1.00
28 Ken Griffey	4.00	1.60
29 Don Gullett	1.00	.40
30 Mike Hargrove	2.50	1.00
31 Al Hrabosky	1.00	.40
32 Catfish Hunter	10.00	4.00
33 Reggie Jackson	20.00	8.00
34 Randy Jones	1.00	.40
35 Dave Kingman	5.00	2.00
36 Jerry Koosman	2.50	1.00

37 Dave LaRoche 1.00 .40
38 Greg Luzinski 4.00 1.60
39 Fred Lynn 2.50 1.00
40 Bill Madlock 2.50 1.00
41 Rick Manning 1.00 .40
42 Jon Matlack 1.00 .40
43 John Mayberry 1.00 .40
44 Hal McRae 2.50 1.00
45 Andy Messersmith 1.00 .40
46 Rick Monday 1.00 .40
47 John Montefusco 1.00 .40
48 Joe Morgan 10.00 4.00
49 Thurman Munson 7.50 3.00
50 Bobby Murcer 4.00 1.60
51 Bill North 1.00 .40
52 Jim Palmer 10.00 4.00
53 Tony Perez 10.00 4.00
54 Jerry Reuss 1.00 .40
55 Brooks Robinson 15.00 6.00
56 Pete Rose 20.00 8.00
57 Joe Rudi 1.00 .40
58 Nolan Ryan 40.00 16.00
59 Manny Sanguillen 1.00 .40
60 Mike Schmidt 20.00 8.00
61 Tom Seaver 20.00 8.00
62 Bill Singer 1.00 .40
63 Willie Stargell 10.00 4.00
64 Rusty Staub 4.00 1.60
65 Luis Tiant 2.50 1.00
66 Bob Watson 2.50 1.00
67 Butch Wynegar 1.00 .40
68 Carl Yastrzemski 15.00 6.00
69 Robin Yount 15.00 6.00
70 Richie Zisk 1.00 .40

1979 Detroit Convention

This 20 card 3 1/2" by 5" set was issued to commemorate the 10th annual Detroit show. The cards are reproductions of photos provided by various fans and the Detroit Tigers. An interesting mix of players and media members are commemorated in this set. The cards are unnumbered so we have sequenced them in alphabetical order. The set was originally available for $3.

NM Ex
COMPLETE SET 10.00 4.00
1 Gates Brown .50 .20
2 Norm Cash 1.50 .60
3 Al Cicotte .50 .20
4 Roy Cullenbine .75 .30
5 Gene Desaultes .50 .20
6 Hoot Evers .50 .20
7 Joe Falls .50 .20
Columnist
8 Joe Ginsberg .50 .20
9 Ernie Harwell ANN 1.00 .40
10 Ray Herbert .50 .20
11 John Hiller .50 .20
12 Billy Hoeft .50 .20
13 Ralph Houk MG .75 .30
14 Cliff Kachline .50 .20
Writer
15 George Kell 1.50 .60
16 Ron LeFlore .50 .20
17 Barney McCoskey .50 .20
18 Jim Northrup .50 .20
19 Dick Radatz .50 .20
20 Tom Timmerman .50 .20

1998 Devil Rays Pinnacle

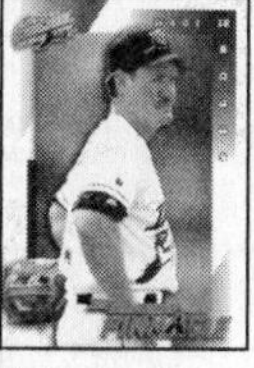
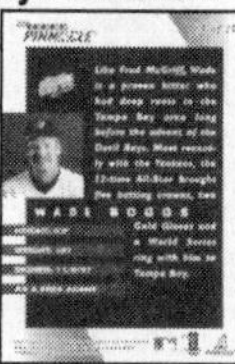

This 26-card set was produced by Pinnacle to commemorate the Devil Rays first team and was distributed in a Collector's Edition box. The fronts feature color action player photos in a blue, purple, and gray-spotted white border. The backs carry a small player head shot and player information. Only 3000 of the set were produced with the boxes serially numbered.

Nm-Mt Ex-Mt
COMPLETE SET (26) 3.00 .90
1 Wilson Alvarez .25 .07
2 Rolando Arrojo .75 .23
3 Dan Carlson .10 .03
4 Rick Gorecki .10 .03
5 Roberto Hernandez .25 .07
6 Albie Lopez .10 .03
7 Jim Mecir .10 .03
8 Tony Saunders .10 .03
9 Dennis Springer .10 .03
10 Ramon Tatis .10 .03
11 Esteban Yan .10 .03
12 Mike Difelice .10 .03
13 John Flaherty .10 .03
14 Wade Boggs 1.00 .30
15 Miguel Cairo .25 .07
16 Aaron Ledesma .10 .03
17 Fred McGriff .50 .15
18 Bobby Smith .10 .03
19 Paul Sorrento .10 .03
20 Kevin Stocker .10 .03
21 Rich Butler .10 .03
22 Mike Kelly .10 .03
23 Dave Martinez .10 .03
24 Quinton McCracken .10 .03
25 Bubba Trammell .10 .03
NNO Team Logo CL .10 .03

1998-99 Devil Rays Postcards

These 4" by 6" blank-backed color postcards have a player photo with the sponsoring information of St Anthony's Health Care on the bottom. The photos were credited to Robert Rogers. It is believed that some of these cards

were issued during the 1999 season, thus we are listing this as a split-year set.

Nm-Mt Ex-Mt
COMPLETE SET 15.00 4.50
1 Scott Aldred .25 .07
2 Wilson Alvarez .25 .07
3 Rolando Arrojo 1.00 .30
4 Wade Boggs 1.50 .45
5 Rich Butler .25 .07
6 Miguel Cairo .50 .15
7 Jose Canseco 2.00 .60
8 Dan Carlson .25 .07
9 Mike DiFelice .25 .07
10 Dave Eiland .25 .07
11 Vaughn Eshelman .25 .07
12 John Flaherty .25 .07
13 Orlando Gomez CO .25 .07
14 Rick Gorecki .25 .07
15 Billy Hatcher CO .25 .07
16 Steve Henderson CO .25 .07
17 Roberto Hernandez .50 .15
18 Frank Howard CO .50 .15
19 Mike Kelly .25 .07
20 Chuck LaMar GM .25 .07
21 Aaron Ledesma .25 .07
22 Albie Lopez .25 .07
23 Joe Magrane CO .25 .07
24 Dave Martinez .25 .07
25 Quinton McCracken .25 .07
26 Fred McGriff .75 .23
27 Jim Mecir .25 .07
28 Jim Morris 2.00 .60
29 Vincent Naimoli OWN .25 .07
30 Bryan Rekar .25 .07
31 Greg Riddoch CO .25 .07
32 Larry Rothschild MG .25 .07
33 Ryan Rupe .25 .07
34 Julio Santana .25 .07
35 Tony Saunders .25 .07
36 Bobby Smith .25 .07
37 Paul Sorrento .25 .07
38 Jeff Sparks .25 .07
39 Dennis Springer .25 .07
40 Dewayne Staats ANN .25 .07
41 Kevin Stocker .25 .07
42 Bubba Trammell .25 .07
43 Terrell Wade .25 .07
44 Dan Wheeler .25 .07
45 Rick White .25 .07
46 Randy Williams .25 .07
47 Rick Williams CO .25 .07
48 Randy Winn .75 .23
49 Esteban Yan .25 .07

2000 Devil Rays Verizon

These 28 standard-size cards feature members of the 2000 Devil Rays and were issued in conjunction with Verizon. The borderless fronts have a color player photo with circles around the players head. The player's name is on the bottom of the card. The back of the card has a small player photo, biographical information as well as career statistics. Since the cards are unnumbered, we have sequenced them in alphabetical order.

Nm-Mt Ex-Mt
COMPLETE SET (28) 10.00 3.00
1 Wilson Alvarez .50 .15
2 Miguel Cairo .25 .07
3 Jose Canseco 1.25 .35
4 Vinny Castilla .50 .15
5 Steve Cox .25 .07
6 Mike DiFelice .25 .07
7 John Flaherty .25 .07
8 Jose Guillen .75 .23
9 Ozzie Guillen .50 .15
10 Juan Guzman .25 .07
11 Roberto Hernandez .50 .15
12 Russ Johnson .25 .07
13 Albie Lopez .25 .07
14 Felix Martinez .25 .07
15 Fred McGriff .75 .23
16 Raymond .25 .07
Mascot
17 Brian Rekar .25 .07
18 Larry Rothschild MG .25 .07
19 Steve Traschel .50 .15
20 Bubba Trammell .25 .07
21 Greg Vaughn .50 .15
22 Rick White .25 .07
23 Gerald Williams .25 .07
24 Randy Winn .50 .15
25 Esteban Yan .25 .07
26 Jose Cardenal CO .25 .07
Bill Fischer CO
Orlando Gomez CO
Billy Hatcher CO
Leon Roberts CO
Bill Russell CO
27 Wade Boggs 1.50 .45
GTE Reading
28 Header Card .25 .07

2001 Devil Rays Team Issue

The 51-card set is 4"x6" and is blank backed. The unnumbered cards are listed below in alphabetical order. The set was sponsored by Bayfront/St. Anthony's.

Nm-Mt Ex-Mt
COMPLETE SET (51) 15.00 4.50
1 Brent Abernathy .25 .07
2 Wilson Alvarez .25 .07
3 Nick Bierbrodt .25 .07
4 Wade Boggs CO 1.00 .30
5 Terry Collins CO .25 .07
6 Jesus Colome .25 .07
7 Steve Cox .25 .07
8 Doug Creek .25 .07
white jersey
9 Doug Creek .25 .07
black jersey
10 Mike DiFelice .25 .07
11 Bill Fischer CO .25 .07
12 John Flaherty .25 .07
13 Chris Gomez .25 .07
14 Ben Grieve .50 .15
15 Jose Guillen .75 .23
16 Juan Guzman .25 .07
17 Toby Hall 1.00 .30
batting
18 Toby Hall 1.00 .30
portrait
19 Josh Hamilton .50 .15
20 Travis Harper .25 .07
21 Billy Hatcher CO .25 .07
22 Frank Howard CO .50 .15
23 Aubrey Huff 1.00 .30
24 Russ Johnson .25 .07
white jersey
25 Russ Johnson .25 .07
black jersey
26 Joe Kennedy .50 .15
27 Albie Lopez .25 .07
28 Felix Martinez .25 .07
29 Fred McGriff .75 .23
30 Hal McRae MGR .25 .07
31 Travis Phelps .25 .07
32 Bryan Rekar .25 .07
33 Damian Rolls .25 .07
34 Ryan Rupe .25 .07
35 Alex Sanchez .25 .07
36 Jared Sandberg .50 .15
37 Bobby Seay .25 .07
38 Jason Standridge .50 .15
39 Tanyon Sturtze .25 .07
vertical
40 Tanyon Sturtze .25 .07
horizontal
41 Jason Tyner .25 .07
taking lead
42 Jason Tyner .25 .07
running
43 Greg Vaughn .50 .15
44 Jeff Wallace .25 .07
45 Dan Wheeler .25 .07
46 Matt White .25 .07
47 Gerald Williams .25 .07
48 Paul Wilson .25 .07
49 Randy Winn .50 .15
50 Esteban Yan .25 .07
51 Victor Zambrano .25 .07

2003 Devil Rays Baldelli DAV

This one card standard-size set was given away at a Devils Ray game during the 2003 season. The front has an action photo of Baldelli while the back has some information about the DAV with information about how to contact them. There is no mention of baseball at the back of this card

MINT NRMT
1 Rocco Baldelli 3.00 1.35

1967 Dexter Press

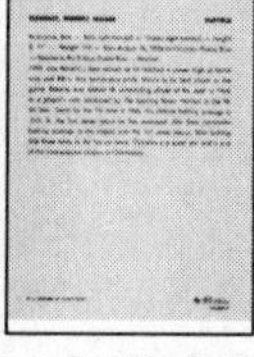

This 228-card set was produced by Dexter Press and issued in team sets as a premium by the Coca-Cola Bottling Co. Eighteen Major League teams participated in the promotion. The set measures approximately 5 1/2" by 7" and features glossy color waist-to-cap player photos in a white border with a black facsimile autograph at the top. The white backs display player biographical details and career highlights printed in blue. An all-star set was also produced with these players' cards differentiated from their regular cards in the team sets by the lengthier biographies on the back. The cards are unnumbered and checklisted below in alphabetical order. Paul Schaal was also issued as a sample print. This card is considered a SP and is not included in the checklist.

NM Ex
COMPLETE SET (228) 800.00 325.00
1 Hank Aaron 20.00 8.00
2 Tommie Agee 4.00 1.60
3 Jack Aker 3.00 1.20
4 Bernie Allen 3.00 1.20
5 Richie Allen 5.00 2.00
6 Gene Alley 3.00 1.20
7 Bob Allison 4.00 1.60
8 Felipe Alou 5.00 2.00
9 Jesus Alou 4.00 1.60
10 Matty Alou 4.00 1.60
11 George Altman 3.00 1.20
12 Max Alvis 3.00 1.20
13 Luis Aparicio 10.00 4.00
14 Bob Aspromonte 3.00 1.20
15 Joe Azcue 3.00 1.20
16 Bob Bailey 3.00 1.20
17 Ernie Banks 15.00 6.00
18 John Bateman 3.00 1.20
19 Earl Battey 3.00 1.20
20 Glenn Beckert 3.00 1.20
21 Gary Bell 3.00 1.20
22 Ken Berry 3.00 1.20
23 Wade Blasingame 3.00 1.20
24 Curt Blefary 3.00 1.20
25 John Boccabella 3.00 1.20
26 Dave Boswell 3.00 1.20
27 Jim Bouton 4.00 1.60
28 Clete Boyer 4.00 1.60
29 Ken Boyer 5.00 2.00
30 Ed Bressoud 3.00 1.20
31 John Briggs 3.00 1.20
32 Ed Brinkman 3.00 1.20
33 Larry Brown 3.00 1.20
34 Ollie Brown 3.00 1.20
35 Bob Bruce 3.00 1.20
36 Don Buford 3.00 1.20
37 Wally Bunker 3.00 1.20
38 Jim Bunning 10.00 4.00
39 Jim Bunning AS 5.00 2.00
40 Johnny Callison 4.00 1.60
41 Bert Campaneris 3.00 1.20
42 Leo Cardenas 3.00 1.20
43 Paul Casanova 3.00 1.20
44 Norm Cash 5.00 2.00
45 Danny Cater 3.00 1.20
46 Dean Chance 3.00 1.20
47 Ed Charles 3.00 1.20
48 Ossie Chavarria 3.00 1.20
49 Horace Clarke 3.00 1.20
50 Roberto Clemente 25.00 10.00
51 Roberto Clemente AS 12.00 4.80
52 Donn Clendenon 3.00 1.20
53 Ty Cline 3.00 1.20
54 Tony Cloninger 3.00 1.20
55 Rocky Colavito 8.00 3.20
56 Gordy Coleman 3.00 1.20
57 Ray Culp 3.00 1.20
58 Clay Dalrymple 3.00 1.20
59 Vic Davalillo 3.00 1.20
60 Jim Davenport 3.00 1.20
61 Ron Davis 3.00 1.20
62 Tommy Davis 4.00 1.60
63 Willie Davis 4.00 1.60
64 Willie Davis AS 4.00 1.60
65 Don Demeter 3.00 1.20
66 Larry Dierker 5.00 2.00
67 Al Downing 3.00 1.20
68 Johnny Edwards 3.00 1.20
69 Andy Etchebarren 3.00 1.20
70 Ron Fairly 4.00 1.60
71 Dick Farrell 3.00 1.20
72 Bill Fischer 3.00 1.20
73 Eddie Fisher 3.00 1.20
74 Jack Fisher 3.00 1.20
75 Joe Foy 3.00 1.20
76 Bill Freehan 4.00 1.60
77 Woodie Fryman 3.00 1.20
78 Tito Fuentes 3.00 1.20
79 Dave Giusti 3.00 1.20
80 Pedro Gonzalez 3.00 1.20
81 Mudcat Grant 3.00 1.20
82 Dick Green 3.00 1.20
83 Dick Groat 4.00 1.60
84 Jerry Grote 3.00 1.20
85 Tom Haller 3.00 1.20
86 Jack Hamilton 3.00 1.20
87 Steve Hamilton 3.00 1.20
88 Ron Hansen 3.00 1.20
89 Tommy Harper 3.00 1.20
90 Ken Harrelson 4.00 1.60
91 Chuck Harrison 3.00 1.20
92 Jim Hart 3.00 1.20
93 Tommy Helms 3.00 1.20
94 Mike Hershberger 3.00 1.20
95 Chuck Hinton 3.00 1.20
96 Ken Holtzman 3.00 1.20
97 Joe Horlen 3.00 1.20
98 Willie Horton 4.00 1.60
99 Elston Howard 5.00 2.00
100 Frank Howard 5.00 2.00
101 Randy Hundley 3.00 1.20
102 Ron Hunt 3.00 1.20
103 Larry Jackson 3.00 1.20
104 Sonny Jackson 3.00 1.20
105 Tommy John 5.00 2.00
106 Davey Johnson 4.00 1.60
107 Deron Johnson 3.00 1.20
108 Ken Johnson 3.00 1.20
109 Lou Johnson 3.00 1.20
110 Cleon Jones 3.00 1.20
111 Dalton Jones 3.00 1.20
112 Al Kaline 15.00 6.00
113 Al Kaline AS 8.00 3.20
114 John Kennedy 3.00 1.20
115 Harmon Killebrew 15.00 6.00
116 Harmon Killebrew AS 8.00 3.20
117 Jim King 3.00 1.20
118 Cal Koonce 3.00 1.20
119 Ed Kranepool 3.00 1.20
120 Lew Krausse 3.00 1.20
121 Jim Landis 3.00 1.20
122 Hal Lanier 3.00 1.20
123 Vern Law 3.00 1.20
124 Jim Lefebvre 3.00 1.20
125 Johnny Lewis 3.00 1.20
126 Don Lock 3.00 1.20
127 Bob Locker 3.00 1.20
128 Mickey Lolich 8.00 3.20
129 Jim Lonborg 4.00 1.60
130 Jerry Lumpe 3.00 1.20
131 Jim Maloney 3.00 1.20
132 Mickey Mantle 50.00 20.00
133 Eddie Mathews 15.00 6.00
134 Willie Mays 30.00 12.00
135 Willie Mays AS 15.00 6.00
136 Bill Mazeroski 8.00 3.20
137 Dick McAuliffe 3.00 1.20
138 Bill McCool 3.00 1.20
139 Mike McCormick 3.00 1.20
140 Willie McCovey 10.00 4.00
141 Tommy McCraw 3.00 1.20
142 Sam McDowell 3.00 1.20
143 Ken McMullen 3.00 1.20
144 Dave McNally 3.00 1.20
145 Jerry McNertney 3.00 1.20
146 Dennis Menke 3.00 1.20
147 Jim Merritt 3.00 1.20
148 Joe Morgan 10.00 4.00
149 Manny Mota 4.00 1.60
150 Jim Nash 3.00 1.20
151 Dick Nen 3.00 1.20
152 Joe Nossek 3.00 1.20
153 Tony Oliva 5.00 2.00
154 Gene Oliver 3.00 1.20
155 Phil Ortega 3.00 1.20
156 Claude Osteen 3.00 1.20
157 Jim O'Toole 3.00 1.20
158 Jim Pagliaroni 3.00 1.20
159 Jim Palmer 15.00 6.00
160 Milt Pappas 3.00 1.20
161 Wes Parker 3.00 1.20
162 Joe Pepitone 4.00 1.60
163 Joe Pepitone AS 3.00 1.20
164 Ron Perranoski 3.00 1.20
165 Gaylord Perry 10.00 4.00
166 Fritz Peterson 3.00 1.20
167 Rico Petrocelli 3.00 1.20
168 Adolfo Phillips 3.00 1.20
169 Vada Pinson 5.00 2.00
170 Johnny Podres 4.00 1.60
171 Boog Powell 5.00 2.00
172 Phil Regan 3.00 1.20
173 Roger Repoz 3.00 1.20
174 Pete Richert 3.00 1.20
175 Brooks Robinson 15.00 6.00
176 Brooks Robinson AS 8.00 3.20
177 Frank Robinson 15.00 6.00
178 Frank Robinson AS 8.00 3.20
179 Cookie Rojas 3.00 1.20
180 Rich Rollins 3.00 1.20
181 Phil Roof 3.00 1.20
182 Pete Rose 20.00 8.00
183 Jose Santiago 3.00 1.20
184 Ron Santo 10.00 4.00
185 Ron Santo AS 5.00 2.00
186 Bob Saverine 3.00 1.20
187 George Scott 3.00 1.20
188 Art Shamsky 3.00 1.20
189 Bob Shaw 3.00 1.20
190 Chris Short 3.00 1.20
191 Norman Siebern 3.00 1.20
192 Moose Skowron 4.00 1.60
193 Charley Smith 3.00 1.20
194 George Smith 3.00 1.20
195 Russ Snyder 3.00 1.20
196 Joe Sparma 3.00 1.20
197 Willie Stargell 10.00 4.00
198 Rusty Staub 5.00 2.00
199 John Stephenson 3.00 1.20
200 Mel Stottlemyre 4.00 1.60
201 Don Sutton 10.00 4.00
202 Ron Swoboda 3.00 1.20
203 Jose Tartabull 3.00 1.20
204 Tony Taylor 3.00 1.20
205 Lee Thomas 3.00 1.20
206 Luis Tiant 5.00 2.00
207 Bob Tillman 3.00 1.20
208 Joe Torre 6.00 2.40
209 Joe Torre AS 5.00 2.00
210 Tom Tresh 4.00 1.60
211 Ted Uhlaender 3.00 1.20
212 Sandy Valdespino 3.00 1.20
213 Fred Valentine 3.00 1.20
214 Bob Veale 3.00 1.20
215 Zoilo Versalles 3.00 1.20
216 Leon Wagner 3.00 1.20
217 Pete Ward 3.00 1.20
218 Don Wert 3.00 1.20
219 Bill White 5.00 2.00
220 Roy White 3.00 1.20
221 Fred Whitfield 3.00 1.20
222 Dave Wickersham 3.00 1.20
223 Billy Williams 10.00 4.00
224 Maury Wills 5.00 2.00
225 Earl Wilson 3.00 1.20
226 Woody Woodward 3.00 1.20
227 Carl Yastrzemski 15.00 6.00
228 Carl Yastrzemski AS 8.00 3.20

1968 Dexter Press

This 77-card set, which measures approximately 3 1/2" by 5 1/2", has beautiful full-color photos on the front of the card with biographical and career information on the back of the card. There are no year by year statistical lines on the back of the card. Dexter

Press is another name for cards which the Coca-Cola Company helped to distribute during the mid sixties. The backs of the cards have a facsimile autograph. Dexter Press was located in West Nyack, New York. These unnumbered cards are listed below in alphabetical order.

	NM	Ex
COMPLETE SET (77)	250.00	100.00
1 Hank Aaron	20.00	8.00
2 Jerry Adair	3.00	1.20
3 Richie Allen	5.00	2.00
4 Bob Allison	4.00	1.60
5 Felipe Alou	5.00	2.00
6 Jesus Alou	3.00	1.20
7 Mike Andrews	3.00	1.20
8 Bob Aspromonte	3.00	1.20
9 Johnny Bateman	3.00	1.20
10 Mark Belanger	3.00	1.20
11 Gary Bell	3.00	1.20
12 Paul Blair	3.00	1.20
13 Curt Blefary	3.00	1.20
14 Bobby Bolin	3.00	1.20
15 Ken Boswell	3.00	1.20
16 Clete Boyer	4.00	1.60
17 Ron Brand	3.00	1.20
18 Darrell Brandon	3.00	1.20
19 Don Buford	3.00	1.20
20 Rod Carew	20.00	8.00
21 Clay Carroll	3.00	1.20
22 Rico Carty	4.00	1.60
23 Dean Chance	3.00	1.20
24 Roberto Clemente	25.00	10.00
25 Tony Cloninger	3.00	1.20
26 Mike Cuellar	3.00	1.20
27 Jim Davenport	3.00	1.20
28 Ron Davis	3.00	1.20
29 Moe Drabowsky	3.00	1.20
30 Dick Ellsworth	3.00	1.20
31 Andy Etchebarren	3.00	1.20
32 Joe Foy	3.00	1.20
33 Bill Freehan	4.00	1.60
34 Jim Fregosi	4.00	1.60
35 Julio Gotay	3.00	1.20
36 Dave Giusti	3.00	1.20
37 Jim Ray Hart	3.00	1.20
38 Jack Hiatt	3.00	1.20
39 Ron Hunt	3.00	1.20
40 Sonny Jackson	3.00	1.20
41 Pat Jarvis	3.00	1.20
42 Davey Johnson	4.00	1.60
43 Ken Johnson	3.00	1.20
44 Dalton Jones	3.00	1.20
45 Jim Kaat	5.00	2.00
46 Harmon Killebrew	12.00	4.80
47 Denny Lemaster	3.00	1.20
48 Frank Linzy	3.00	1.20
49 Jim Lonborg	4.00	1.60
50 Juan Marichal	12.00	4.80
51 Willie Mays	20.00	8.00
52 Bill Mazeroski	6.00	2.40
53 Mike McCormick	3.00	1.20
54 Dave McNally	4.00	1.60
55 Denis Menke	3.00	1.20
56 Joe Morgan	10.00	4.00
57 Dave Morehead	3.00	1.20
58 Phil Niekro	10.00	4.00
59 Russ Nixon	3.00	1.20
60 Tony Oliva	5.00	2.00
61 Gaylord Perry	10.00	4.00
62 Rico Petrocelli	4.00	1.60
63 Tom Phoebus	3.00	1.20
64 Boog Powell	4.00	1.60
65 Brooks Robinson	12.00	4.80
66 Frank Robinson	12.00	4.80
67 Rich Rollins	3.00	1.20
68 John Roseboro	3.00	1.20
69 Ray Sadecki	3.00	1.20
70 George Scott	4.00	1.60
71 Rusty Staub	5.00	2.00
72 Cesar Tovar	3.00	1.20
73 Joe Torre	6.00	2.40
74 Ted Uhlaender	3.00	1.20
75 Woody Woodward	3.00	1.20
76 John Wyatt	3.00	1.20
77 Jimmy Wynn	4.00	1.60

1978 Dexter Hall of Fame Postcards

This 53-card set was produced by Dexter Press and measures approximately 3 1/2" by 5 1/2". The fronts feature a facsimile Cooperstown National Baseball Hall of Fame player's plaque. The backs display a postcard format. The cards are unnumbered and checklisted below in alphabetical order.

	NM	Ex
COMPLETE SET (53)	75.00	30.00
1 Grover Alexander	1.50	.60
2 Lou Boudreau	.50	.20
3 Roy Campanella	1.00	.40
4 Roberto Clemente	5.00	2.00
5 Ty Cobb	8.00	3.20
6 Stan Coveleskie	.50	.20
7 Sam Crawford	.50	.20
8 Martin Dihigo	.50	.20
9 Joe DiMaggio	8.00	3.20
10 Billy Evans	.50	.20
11 Johnny Evers	.50	.20
12 Red Faber	.50	.20
13 Elmer Flick	.50	.20
14 Ford Frick	.50	.20
15 Frankie Frisch	.50	.20
16 Pud Galvin	.50	.20
17 Lou Gehrig	8.00	3.20
18 Warren Giles	.50	.20
19 Will Harridge	.50	.20
20 Harry Heilmann	.50	.20
21 Harry Hooper	.50	.20
22 Waite Hoyt	.50	.20
23 Miller Huggins	.50	.20
24 Judy Johnson	.50	.20
25 Addie Joss	.50	.20
26 Tim Keefe	.50	.20
27 Willie Keeler	.50	.20
28 George Kelly	.50	.20
29 Sandy Koufax	3.00	1.20
30 Nap Lajoie	.50	.20
31 Pop Lloyd	.50	.20
32 Connie Mack	2.00	.80
33 Larry MacPhail	.50	.20
34 Mickey Mantle	8.00	3.20
35 Heinie Manush	.50	.20
36 Eddie Mathews	2.00	.80
37 Willie Mays	5.00	2.00
38 Ducky Medwick	.50	.20
39 Stan Musial	3.00	1.20
40 Herb Pennock	.50	.20
41 Edd Roush	.50	.20
42 Amos Rusie	.50	.20
43 Babe Ruth	10.00	4.00
44 Ray Schalk	.50	.20
45 Al Simmons	.50	.20
46 Albert Spalding	.50	.20
47 Joe Tinker	1.00	.40
48 Harold Traynor	.50	.20
49 Dazzy Vance	.50	.20
50 Lloyd Waner	.50	.20
51 Ted Williams	8.00	3.20
52 Hack Wilson	.50	.20
53 Ross Youngs	.50	.20

2003 Diamond Action

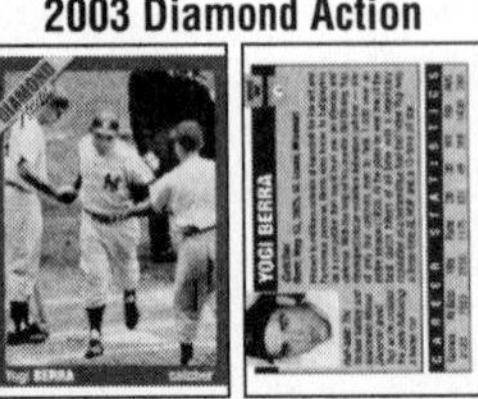

This 28 card set, which measures 2 1/2" by 1 7/8" features black and white photos of old time baseball stars. The photos are surrounded by green borders, while the backs have a player portrait, some biographical information as well as career statistics.

	MINT	NRMT
COMPLETE SET	20.00	9.00
1 Richie Ashburn	1.00	.45
2 Ernie Banks	1.50	.70
3 Yogi Berra	2.00	.90
4 Smoky Burgess	.50	.23
5 Phil Cavarretta	.50	.23
6 Frank Crosetti	.50	.23
7 Don Demeter	.25	.11
8 Sam Dente	.25	.11
9 Joe DiMaggio	3.00	1.35
10 Jim Gilliam	.50	.23
11 Don Hoak	.25	.11
12 Eddie Kasko	.25	.11
13 Dale Long	.25	.11
14 Roger Maris	2.00	.90
15 Eddie Mathews	1.50	.70
16 Lee Maye	.25	.11
17 Willie Mays	2.50	1.10
18 Roy McMillan	.25	.11
19 Wally Moon	.50	.23
20 Bobby Richardson	.75	.35
21 Jackie Robinson	2.50	1.10
22 Bill Serena	.25	.11
23 Birdie Tebbetts	.25	.11
24 Tom Tresh	.50	.23
25 Gee Walker	.25	.11
26 Vic Wertz	.25	.11
27 Maury Wills	.75	.35
28 Ed Yost	.25	.11

1982-83 Diamond Classics

These very attractive cards measure 2 1/2" by 3 3/4" and feature drawings of all-time stars on the front. The drawings cover almost all the front of the cards. The backs give a history of the player as well as some important statistics. Upon release, the 1st series was offered for $8 plus postage. The second series was available for $10 upon release. These cards were produced from original art work and distributed by collector Steve Mitchell.

	Nm-Mt	Ex-Mt
COMPLETE SET (110)	40.00	16.00
1 Joe DiMaggio	2.00	.80
2 Enos Slaughter	.25	.10
3 Smokey Joe Wood	.25	.10
4 Roy Campanella	.50	.20
5 Charlie Gehringer	.25	.10
6 Carl Hubbell	.50	.20
7 Rogers Hornsby	.50	.20
8 Arky Vaughan	.25	.10
9 Al Simmons	.25	.10
10 Wally Berger	.10	.04
11 Sam Rice	.25	.10
12 Dizzy Dean	.50	.20
13 Babe Ruth	3.00	1.20
14 Frankie Frisch	.25	.10
15 George Kell	.25	.10
16 Pee Wee Reese	.50	.20
17 Earl Averill	.25	.10
18 Willie Mays	1.50	.60
19 Frank Baker	.25	.10
20 Hack Wilson	.25	.10
21 Ted Williams	2.00	.80
22 Chuck Klein	.25	.10
23 Bill Dickey	.25	.10
24 Johnny Mize	.25	.10
25 Luke Appling	.25	.10
26 Duke Snider	.50	.20
27 Wahoo Sam Crawford	.50	.20
28 Waite Hoyt	.25	.10
29 Eddie Collins	.50	.20
30 Warren Spahn	.50	.20
31 Satchel Paige	1.00	.40
32 Ernie Lombardi	.25	.10
33 Dom DiMaggio	.25	.10
34 Joe Garagiola	.50	.20
35 Lou Gehrig	2.00	.80
36 Burleigh Grimes	.25	.10
37 Walter Johnson	.50	.20
38 Bill Terry	.25	.10
39 Ty Cobb	2.00	.80
40 Pie Traynor	.25	.10
41 Ted Lyons	.25	.10
42 Richie Ashburn	.50	.20
43 Lefty Grove	.50	.20
44 Edd Roush	.25	.10
45 Phil Rizzuto	.50	.20
46 Stan Musial	1.00	.40
47 Bob Feller	.50	.20
48 Jackie Robinson	2.00	.80
49 Hank Greenberg	.50	.20
50 Mel Ott	.50	.20
51 Joe Cronin	.25	.10
52 Lefty O'Doul	.25	.10
53 Indian Bob Johnson	.10	.04
54 Kiki Cuyler	.25	.10
55 Mickey Mantle	3.00	1.20
56 Ernie Banks	1.00	.40
57 Stan Coveleskie	.25	.10
58 Vince DiMaggio	.25	.10
59 Jim Bottomley	.25	.10
60 Sandy Koufax	1.00	.40
61 Doc Cramer	.10	.04
62 Ted Kluszewski	.50	.20
63 Zeke Bonura	.10	.04
64 Spud Davis	.10	.04
65 Jackie Jensen	.10	.04
66 Honus Wagner	.75	.30
67 Brooks Robinson	.50	.20
68 Dazzy Vance	.25	.10
69 George Uhle	.10	.04
70 Juan Marichal	.50	.20
71 Bobo Newsom	.10	.04
72 Billy Herman	.25	.10
73 Al Rosen	.25	.10
74 Roberto Clemente	2.00	.80
75 George Case	.10	.04
76 Bill Nicholson	.10	.04
77 Tommy Bridges	.10	.04
78 Rabbit Maranville	.25	.10
79 Bob Lemon	.25	.10
80 Heinie Groh	.10	.04
81 Tris Speaker	.50	.20
82 Hank Aaron	1.50	.60
83 Whitey Ford	.50	.20
84 Guy Bush	.10	.04
85 Jimmie Foxx	.50	.20
86 Marty Marion	.25	.10
87 Hal Newhouser	.25	.10
88 George Kelly	.25	.10
89 Harmon Killebrew	.50	.20
90 Willie McCovey	.50	.20
91 Mel Harder	.10	.04
92 Vada Pinson	.25	.10
93 Luis Aparicio	.50	.20
94 Grover Alexander	.50	.20
95 Joe Kuhel	.10	.04
96 Casey Stengel	.50	.20
97 Joe Sewell	.25	.10
98 Red Lucas	.10	.04
99 Luke Sewell	.10	.04
100 Charlie Grimm	.10	.04
101 Cecil Travis	.10	.04
102 Travis Jackson	.25	.10
103 Lou Boudreau	.25	.10
104 Nap Rucker	.10	.04
105 Chief Bender	.25	.10
106 Riggs Stephenson	.10	.04
107 Red Ruffing	.25	.10
108 Robin Roberts	.50	.20
109 Harland Clift	.10	.04
110 Ralph Kiner	.50	.20
XX Certificate Card	.10	.04
NNO Checklist Card	.10	.04

1979 Diamond Greats

This 400-card set features black-and-white player portraits with the player's name, lifetime statistics, team name, and playing position printed in black in the white margins. The backs are blank.

	NM	Ex
COMPLETE SET (400)	75.00	30.00
1 Joe DiMaggio	5.00	2.00
2 Ben Chapman	.10	.04
3 Joe Dugan	.10	.04
4 Bob Shawkey	.25	.10
5 Joe Sewell	.50	.20
6 George Pipgras	.10	.04
7 George Selkirk	.10	.04
8 Babe Dahlgren	.10	.04
9 Spud Chandler	.25	.10
10 Duffy Lewis	.10	.04
11 Lefty Gomez	.75	.30
12 Atley Donald	.10	.04
13 Whitey Witt	.10	.04
14 Marius Russo	.10	.04
15 Buddy Rosar	.10	.04
16 Russ Van Atta	.10	.04
17 Johnny Lindell	.10	.04
18 Bobby Brown	.25	.10
19 Tony Kubek	.25	.10
20 Joe Beggs	.10	.04
21 Don Larsen	.25	.10
22 Andy Carey	.10	.04
23 Johnny Kucks	.10	.04
24 Elston Howard	.25	.10
25 Roger Maris	1.50	.60
26 Rube Marquard	.75	.30
27 Sam Leslie	.10	.04
28 Freddy Leach	.10	.04
29 Fred Fitzsimmons	.25	.10
30 Bill Terry	.75	.30
31 Joe Moore	.10	.04
32 Waite Hoyt	.50	.20
33 Travis Jackson	.50	.20
34 Gus Mancuso	.10	.04
35 Carl Hubbell	1.25	.50
36 Bill Voiselle	.10	.04
37 Hank Leiber	.10	.04
38 Burgess Whitehead	.10	.04
39 Johnny Mize	.75	.30
40 Bill Lohrman	.10	.04
41 Bill Rigney	.10	.04
42 Cliff Melton	.10	.04
43 Willard Marshall	.10	.04
44 Wes Westrum	.10	.04
45 Monte Irvin	.75	.30
46 Marv Grissom	.10	.04
47 Clyde Castleman	.10	.04
48 Harry Gumbert	.10	.04
49 Daryl Spencer	.10	.04
50 Willie Mays	4.00	1.60
51 Sam West	.10	.04
52 Fred Schulte	.10	.04
53 Cecil Travis	.10	.04
54 Tommy Thomas	.10	.04
55 Dutch Leonard	.10	.04
56 Jimmy Wasdell	.10	.04
57 Doc Cramer	.25	.10
58 Harland Clift	.25	.10
59 Ken Chase	.10	.04
60 Buddy Lewis	.10	.04
61 Ossie Bluege	.10	.04
62 Chuck Stobbs	.10	.04
63 Jimmy DeShong	.10	.04
64 Roger Wolff	.10	.04
65 Luke Sewell	.10	.04
66 Sid Hudson	.10	.04
67 Jack Russell	.10	.04
68 Walt Masterson	.10	.04
69 George Myatt	.10	.04
70 Monte Weaver	.10	.04
71 Cliff Bolton	.10	.04
72 Ray Scarborough	.10	.04
73 Albie Pearson	.10	.04
74 Gil Coan	.10	.04
75 Roy Sievers	.25	.10
76 Burleigh Grimes	.50	.20
77 Charlie Hargreaves	.10	.04
78 Babe Herman	.25	.10
79 Fred Frankhouse	.10	.04
80 Al Lopez	.50	.20
81 Lonny Frey	.10	.04
82 Dixie Walker	.10	.04
83 Kirby Higbe	.10	.04
84 Bobby Bragan	.10	.04
85 Leo Durocher	.50	.20
86 Woody English	.10	.04
87 Preacher Roe	.10	.04
88 Vic Lombardi	.10	.04
89 Clyde Sukeforth	.10	.04
90 Pee Wee Reese	2.00	.80
91 Joe Hatten	.10	.04
92 Gene Hermanski	.10	.04
93 Ray Benge	.10	.04
94 Duke Snider	2.00	.80
95 Walter Alston MG	.50	.20
96 Don Drysdale	1.50	.60
97 Andy Pafko	.25	.10
98 Don Zimmer	.25	.10
99 Carl Erskine	.25	.10
100 Dick Williams	.25	.10
101 Charlie Grimm	.25	.10
102 Clarence Blair	.10	.04
103 Johnny Moore	.10	.04
104 Clay Bryant	.10	.04
105 Billy Herman	.50	.20
106 Hy Vandenberg	.10	.04
107 Lennie Merullo	.10	.04
108 Hank Wyse	.10	.04
109 Dom Dallessandro	.10	.04
110 Al Epperly	.10	.04
111 Bill Nicholson	.10	.04
112 Vern Olsen	.10	.04
113 Johnny Schmitz	.10	.04
114 Bob Scheffing	.10	.04
115 Bob Rush	.10	.04
116 Roy Smalley	.10	.04
117 Ransom Jackson	.10	.04
118 Cliff Chambers	.10	.04
119 Harry Chiti	.10	.04
120 Johnny Klippstein	.10	.04
121 Gene Baker	.10	.04
122 Walt Moryn	.10	.04
123 Dick Littlefield	.10	.04
124 Bob Speake	.10	.04
125 Hank Sauer	.10	.04
126 Monty Stratton	.25	.10
127 Johnny Kerr	.10	.04
128 Milt Gaston	.10	.04
129 Eddie Smith	.10	.04
130 Larry Rosenthal	.10	.04
131 Orval Grove	.10	.04
132 Johnny Hodapp	.10	.04
133 Johnny Rigney	.10	.04
134 Willie Kamm	.10	.04
135 Ed Lopat	.25	.10
136 Smead Jolley	.10	.04
137 Ralph Hodgin	.10	.04
138 Ollie Bejma	.10	.04
139 Zeke Bonura	.10	.04
140 Al Hollingsworth	.10	.04
141 Thurman Tucker	.10	.04
142 Cass Michaels	.10	.04
143 Bill Wight	.10	.04
144 Don Lenhardt	.10	.04
145 Sammy Esposito	.10	.04
146 Jack Harshman	.10	.04
147 Turk Lown	.10	.04
148 Jim Landis	.10	.04
149 Bob Shaw	.10	.04
150 Minnie Minoso	.50	.20
151 Les Bell	.10	.04
152 Taylor Douthit	.10	.04
153 Jack Rothrock	.10	.04
154 Terry Moore	.25	.10
155 Max Lanier	.10	.04
156 Don Gutteridge	.10	.04
157 Stu Martin	.10	.04
158 Stan Musial	2.00	.80
159 Frank Crespi	.10	.04
160 Johnny Hopp	.10	.04
161 Ernie Koy	.10	.04
162 Joe Garagiola	.75	.30
163 Joe Orengo	.10	.04
164 Ed Kazak	.10	.04
165 Howie Krist	.10	.04
166 Enos Slaughter	.50	.20
167 Ray Sanders	.10	.04
168 Walker Cooper	.10	.04
169 Nippy Jones	.10	.04
170 Dick Sisler	.10	.04
171 Harvey Haddix	.10	.04
172 Solly Hemus	.10	.04
173 Ray Jablonski	.10	.04
174 Alex Grammas	.10	.04
175 Joe Cunningham	.10	.04
176 Debs Garms	.10	.04
177 Chief Hogsett	.10	.04
178 Alan Strange	.10	.04
179 Rick Ferrell	.50	.20
180 Jack Kramer	.10	.04
181 Jack Knott	.10	.04
182 Bob Harris	.10	.04
183 Billy Hitchcock	.10	.04
184 Jim Walkup	.10	.04
185 Roy Cullenbine	.10	.04
186 Bob Muncrief	.10	.04
187 Chet Laabs	.10	.04
188 Vern Kennedy	.10	.04
189 Bill Trotter	.10	.04
190 Denny Galehouse	.10	.04
191 Al Zarilla	.10	.04
192 Hank Arft	.10	.04
193 Nelson Potter	.10	.04
194 Ray Coleman	.10	.04
195 Bob Dillinger	.25	.10
196 Dick Kokos	.10	.04
197 Bob Cain	.10	.04
198 Virgil Trucks	.10	.04
199 Duane Pillette	.10	.04
200 Bob Turley	.25	.10
201 Wally Berger	.25	.10
202 John Lanning	.10	.04
203 Buck Jordan	.10	.04
204 Jim Turner	.10	.04
205 Johnny Cooney	.10	.04
206 Hank Majeski	.10	.04
207 Phil Masi	.10	.04
208 Tony Cuccinello	.10	.04
209 Whitey Wietelman	.10	.04
210 Lou Fette	.10	.04
211 Vince DiMaggio	.10	.04
212 Huck Betts	.10	.04
213 Red Barrett	.10	.04
214 Pinkey Whitney	.10	.04
215 Tommy Holmes	.25	.10
216 Ray Berres	.10	.04
217 Mike Sandlock	.10	.04
218 Max Macon	.10	.04
219 Sibby Sisti	.10	.04
220 Johnny Beazley	.10	.04
221 Bill Posedel	.10	.04
222 Connie Ryan	.10	.04
223 Del Crandall	.10	.04
224 Bob Addis	.10	.04
225 Warren Spahn	1.25	.50
227 Dom DiMaggio	.25	.10
228 Emerson Dickman	.10	.04
229 Bobby Doerr	.50	.20
230 Tony Lupien	.10	.04
231 Roy Partee	.10	.04
232 Stan Spence	.10	.04
233 Jim Bagby	.10	.04
234 Buster Mills	.10	.04
235 Fabian Gaffke	.10	.04
236 George Metkovich	.10	.04
237 Tom McBride	.10	.04
238 Charlie Wagner	.10	.04
239 Eddie Pellegrini	.10	.04
240 Harry Dorish	.10	.04
241 Ike Delock	.10	.04
242 Mel Parnell	.10	.04
243 Matt Batts	.10	.04
244 Gene Stephens	.10	.04
245 Milt Bolling	.10	.04
246 Charlie Maxwell	.10	.04
247 Willard Nixon	.10	.04
248 Sammy White	.10	.04
249 Dick Gernert	.10	.04
250 Rico Petrocelli	.10	.04
251 Edd Roush	.50	.20
252 Mark Koenig	.25	.10
253 Jimmy Outlaw	.10	.04
254 Ethan Allen	.10	.04
255 Tony Freitas	.10	.04
256 Frank McCormick	.10	.04
257 Bucky Walters	.25	.10
258 Harry Craft	.10	.04
259 Nate Andrews	.10	.04
260 Ed Lukon	.10	.04
261 Elmer Riddle	.10	.04
262 Lee Grissom	.10	.04
263 Johnny Vander Meer	.25	.10
264 Eddie Joost	.10	.04
265 Kermit Wahl	.10	.04
266 Ival Goodman	.10	.04
267 Clyde Vollmer	.10	.04
268 Grady Hatten	.10	.04
269 Ted Kluszewski	.75	.30
270 Johnny Pramesa	.10	.04
271 Joe Black	.25	.10
272 Roy McMillan	.10	.04
273 Wally Post	.10	.04
274 Joe Nuxhall	.10	.04
275 Jerry Lynch	.10	.04
276 Stan Coveleski	.50	.20
277 Bill Wambsganss	.25	.10
278 Bruce Campbell	.10	.04
279 George Uhle	.10	.04
280 Earl Averill	.50	.20
281 Whit Wyatt	.10	.04
282 Oscar Grimes	.10	.04
283 Roy Weatherly	.10	.04
284 Joe Dobson	.10	.04
285 Bob Feller	1.50	.60
286 Jim Hegan	.10	.04
287 Mel Harder	.25	.10
288 Ken Keltner	.10	.04
289 Red Embree	.10	.04

290 Al Milnar .10 .04
291 Lou Boudreau .75 .30
292 Ed Klieman .10 .04
293 Steve Gromek .10 .04
294 George Strickland .10 .04
295 Gene Woodling .10 .04
296 Hank Edwards .10 .04
297 Don Mossi .25 .10
298 Eddie Robinson .10 .04
299 Sam Dente .10 .04
300 Herb Score .25 .10
301 Dolf Camilli .25 .10
302 Jack Warner .10 .04
303 Ike Pearson .10 .04
304 Johnny Peacock .10 .04
305 Gene Corbett .10 .04
306 Walt Millies .10 .04
307 Vance Dinges .10 .04
308 Joe Marty .10 .04
309 Hugh Mulcahy .10 .04
310 Boom Boom Beck .10 .04
311 Charley Schanz .10 .04
312 John Bolling .10 .04
313 Danny Litwhiler .10 .04
314 Emil Verban .10 .04
315 Andy Seminick .10 .04
316 John Antonelli .10 .04
317 Robin Roberts 1.50 .60
318 Richie Ashburn .75 .30
319 Curt Simmons .10 .04
320 Murry Dickson .10 .04
321 Jim Greengrass .10 .04
322 Gene Freese .10 .04
323 Bobby Morgan .10 .04
324 Don Demeter .10 .04
325 Eddie Sawyer .10 .04
326 Bob Johnson .10 .04
327 Ace Parker .50 .20
328 Joe Hauser .10 .04
329 Walt French .10 .04
330 Tom Ferrick .10 .04
331 Bill Werber .10 .04
332 Walt Masters .10 .04
333 Les McCrabb .10 .04
334 Ben McCoy .10 .04
335 Eric Tipton .10 .04
336 Al Rubeling .10 .04
337 Nick Etten .10 .04
338 Carl Scheib .10 .04
339 Dario Lodigiani .10 .04
340 Earle Brucker .10 .04
341 Al Brancato .10 .04
342 Lou Limmer .10 .04
343 Elmer Valo .10 .04
344 Bob Hooper .10 .04
345 Joe Astroth .10 .04
346 Pete Suder .10 .04
347 Dave Philley .10 .04
348 Gus Zernial .10 .04
349 Bobby Shantz .10 .04
350 Joe DeMaestri .10 .04
351 Fred Lindstrom .50 .20
352 Red Lucas .10 .04
353 Clyde Barnhart .10 .04
354 Nick Strincevich .10 .04
355 Lloyd Waner .50 .20
356 Guy Bush .10 .04
357 Joe Bowman .10 .04
358 Al Todd .10 .04
359 Mace Brown .10 .04
360 Larry French .10 .04
361 Elbie Fletcher .10 .04
362 Woody Jensen .10 .04
363 Rip Sewell .10 .04
364 Johnny Dickshot .10 .04
365 Pete Coscarart .10 .04
366 Bud Hafey .10 .04
367 Ken Heintzelman .10 .04
368 Wally Westlake .10 .04
369 Frank Gustine .10 .04
370 Smoky Burgess .25 .10
371 Vernon Law .25 .10
372 Dick Groat .25 .10
373 Bob Skinner .10 .04
374 Don Cardwell .10 .04
375 Bob Friend .10 .04
376 Frank O'Rourke .10 .04
377 Birdie Tebbetts .10 .04
378 Charlie Gehringer .75 .30
379 Eldon Auker .10 .04
380 Tuck Stainback .10 .04
381 Chet Morgan .10 .04
382 Johnny Lipon .10 .04
383 Paul Richards .10 .04
384 Johnny Gorsica .10 .04
385 Ray Hayworth .10 .04
386 Jimmy Bloodworth .10 .04
387 Gene Desautels .10 .04
388 Jo Jo White .10 .04
389 Boots Poffenberger .10 .04
390 Barney McCoskey .10 .04
391 Dick Wakefield .10 .04
392 Johnny Groth .10 .04
393 Steve Souchock .10 .04
394 George Vico .10 .04
395 Hal Newhouser .50 .20
396 Ray Herbert .10 .04
397 Jim Bunning .75 .30
398 Frank Lary .10 .04
399 Harvey Kuenn .25 .10
400 Eddie Mathews 1.50 .60

2002 Diamond Kings Samples

These cards were distributed in Beckett Baseball Card Monthly issue numbers 206 (May, 2002 cover date) and 208 (July, 2002 cover date) in an effort to preview the upcoming Donruss Diamond Kings baseball product. Each magazine was sealed with a clear plastic poly-bag and contained one Diamond Kings sample card (of which was affixed with rubber glue to a subscription offer bound in the middle of the magazine). The cards are straight parallels of the basic issue 2002 Donruss Diamond Kings issued later that year, but can be readily distinguished by the silver foil "SAMPLE" wording stamped on each card back.

Nm-Mt Ex-Mt
*SAMPLES: 1.5X TO 4X BASIC DK'S..
ONE PER BECKETT ISSUE 206 AND 208

2002 Diamond Kings Samples Gold

These cards were distributed in Beckett Baseball Card Monthly issue number 206 (May, 2002 cover date) and issue number 208 (July, 2002 cover date) in an effort to preview the upcoming Donruss Diamond Kings baseball product. Each magazine was sealed with a clear plastic poly-bag and contained one Diamond Kings sample card (of which was affixed with rubber glue to a subscription offer bound in the middle of the magazine). Ninety percent of the magazines contained basic silver-foil stamped samples and only ten percent of the copies contained these scarce gold-foil versions. The cards are straight parallels of the basic issue 2002 Donruss Diamond Kings issued later that year, but can be readily distinguished by the gold foil "SAMPLE" wording stamped on each card back.

Nm-Mt Ex-Mt
*GOLD SAMPLES: 1X TO 2.5X BASIC SAMPLES

2002 Diamond Kings

This 160 card set was issued in two separate series. The first 150 cards were issued within the Diamond Kings brand of which was distributed in May, 2002. These cards were issued in four card packs with an SRP of $3.99 which came 24 packs to a box and 20 boxes to a case. Cards numbered 101 through 150 were printed in shorter supply than the other cards. Cards numbered 101 through 121 feature prospect while cards numbered 122 through 150 featured retired veterans. These cards were all issued at a stated rate of one in three packs. Cards 151-160 were issued within packs of 2002 Donruss the Rookies in mid-December, 2002 at the following ratios: hobby 1:10, retail 1:12. This set was noteworthy as Donruss/Playoff created a full set based on the tradition began in 1982 when the first Diamond King cards were created.

Nm-Mt Ex-Mt
COMP.LOW SET (150) 200.00 60.00
COMP.LOW w/o SP's (100) 50.00 15.00
COMP.UPDATE SET (10) 40.00 12.00
COMMON CARD (1-100) .50 .15
COMMON PROSPECT (101-150) 4.00 1.20
COMMON RETIRED (101-150) 4.00 1.20
COMMON CARD (151-160) 5.00 1.50
1 Vladimir Guerrero 1.25 .35
2 Adam Dunn .50 .15
3 Tsuyoshi Shinjo .50 .15
4 Adrian Beltre .50 .15
5 Troy Glaus .75 .23
6 Albert Pujols 2.50 .75
7 Trot Nixon .75 .23
8 Alex Rodriguez 2.00 .60
9 Tom Glavine .75 .23
10 Alfonso Soriano .75 .23
11 Todd Helton .75 .23
12 Joe Torre 1.25 .35
13 Tim Hudson .50 .15
14 Andruw Jones .50 .15
15 Shawn Green .50 .15
16 Aramis Ramirez .50 .15
17 Shannon Stewart .50 .15
18 Barry Bonds 3.00 .90
19 Sean Casey .50 .15
20 Barry Larkin 1.25 .35
21 Scott Rolen .75 .23
22 Barry Zito .75 .23
23 Sammy Sosa 2.00 .60
24 Bartolo Colon .50 .15
25 Ryan Klesko .50 .15
26 Ben Grieve .50 .15
27 Roy Oswalt .50 .15
28 Kazuhiro Sasaki .50 .15
29 Roger Clemens 2.50 .75
30 Bernie Williams .75 .23
31 Roberto Alomar 1.25 .35
32 Bobby Abreu .50 .15
33 Robert Fick .50 .15
34 Bret Boone .50 .15
35 Rickey Henderson 1.25 .35
36 Brian Giles .50 .15
37 Richie Sexson .50 .15
38 Bud Smith .50 .15
39 Richard Hidalgo .50 .15
40 C. C. Sabathia .50 .15
41 Rich Aurilia .50 .15
42 Carlos Beltran .50 .15
43 Raul Mondesi .50 .15
44 Carlos Delgado .50 .15
45 Randy Johnson 1.25 .35
46 Chan Ho Park .50 .15
47 Rafael Palmeiro .75 .23
48 Chipper Jones 1.25 .35
49 Phil Nevin .50 .15
50 Cliff Floyd .50 .15
51 Pedro Martinez 1.25 .35
52 Craig Biggio .75 .23
53 Paul LoDuca .50 .15
54 Cristian Guzman .50 .15
55 Pat Burrell .50 .15
56 Curt Schilling .75 .23
57 Orlando Cabrera .50 .15
58 Darin Erstad .50 .15
59 Omar Vizquel .50 .15
60 Derek Jeter 3.00 .90
61 Nomar Garciaparra 2.00 .60
62 Edgar Martinez .75 .23
63 Moises Alou .50 .15
64 Eric Chavez .50 .15
65 Mike Sweeney .50 .15
66 Frank Thomas 1.25 .35
67 Mike Piazza 2.00 .60
68 Gary Sheffield .50 .15
69 Mike Mussina 1.25 .35
70 Greg Maddux 2.00 .60
71 Juan Gonzalez 1.25 .35
72 Hideo Nomo 1.25 .35
73 Miguel Tejada .50 .15
74 Ichiro Suzuki 2.00 .60
75 Matt Morris .50 .15
76 Ivan Rodriguez 1.25 .35
77 Mark Mulder .50 .15
78 J.D. Drew .50 .15
79 Mark Grace .75 .23
80 Jason Giambi 1.25 .35
81 Mark Buehrle .50 .15
82 Jose Vidro .50 .15
83 Manny Ramirez .50 .15
84 Jeff Bagwell .75 .23
85 Magglio Ordonez .50 .15
86 Ken Griffey Jr. 2.00 .60
87 Luis Gonzalez .50 .15
88 Jim Edmonds .50 .15
89 Larry Walker .75 .23
90 Jim Thome 1.25 .35
91 Lance Berkman .50 .15
92 Jorge Posada .75 .23
93 Kevin Brown .50 .15
94 Joe Mays .50 .15
95 Kerry Wood 1.25 .35
96 Mark Ellis .50 .15
97 Austin Kearns .50 .15
98 Jorge De La Rosa RC .50 .15
99 Brandon Berger .50 .15
100 Ryan Ludwick .50 .15
101 Marlon Byrd SP 4.00 1.20
102 Brandon Backe SP RC 4.00 1.20
103 Juan Cruz SP 4.00 1.20
104 Anderson Machado SP RC 4.00 1.20
105 So Taguchi SP RC 4.00 1.20
106 Dewon Brazelton SP 4.00 1.20
107 Josh Beckett SP 4.00 1.20
108 John Buck SP 4.00 1.20
109 Jorge Padilla SP RC 4.00 1.20
110 Hee Seop Choi SP 4.00 1.20
111 Angel Berroa SP 4.00 1.20
112 Mark Teixeira SP 5.00 1.50
113 Victor Martinez SP 4.00 1.20
114 Kazuhisa Ishii SP RC 6.00 1.80
115 Dennis Tankersley SP 4.00 1.20
116 Wilson Valdez SP RC 4.00 1.20
117 Antonio Perez SP 4.00 1.20
118 Ed Rogers SP 4.00 1.20
119 Wilson Betemit SP 4.00 1.20
120 Mike Rivera SP 4.00 1.20
121 Mark Prior SP 10.00 3.00
122 Roberto Clemente SP 8.00 2.40
123 Roberto Clemente SP 8.00 2.40
124 Roberto Clemente SP 8.00 2.40
125 Roberto Clemente SP 8.00 2.40
126 Roberto Clemente SP 8.00 2.40
127 Babe Ruth SP 10.00 3.00
128 Ted Williams SP 10.00 3.00
129 Andre Dawson SP 4.00 1.20
130 Eddie Murray SP 5.00 1.50
131 Juan Marichal SP 4.00 1.20
132 Kirby Puckett SP 5.00 1.50
133 Alan Trammell SP 4.00 1.20
134 Bobby Doerr SP 4.00 1.20
135 Carlton Fisk SP 4.00 1.20
136 Eddie Mathews SP 5.00 1.50
137 Mike Schmidt SP 10.00 3.00
138 Catfish Hunter SP 4.00 1.20
139 Nolan Ryan SP 12.00 3.60
140 George Brett SP 12.00 3.60
141 Gary Carter SP 4.00 1.20
142 Paul Molitor SP 4.00 1.20
143 Lou Gehrig SP 6.00 1.80
144 Ryne Sandberg SP 10.00 3.00
145 Tony Gwynn SP 6.00 1.80
146 Ron Santo SP 4.00 1.20
147 Cal Ripken SP 15.00 4.50
148 Al Kaline SP 5.00 1.50
149 Bo Jackson SP 5.00 1.50
150 Don Mattingly SP 12.00 3.60
151 Chris Snelling RC 6.00 1.80
152 Satoru Komiyama RC 5.00 1.50
153 Oliver Perez RC 6.00 1.80
154 Kirk Saarloos RC 5.00 1.50
155 Rene Reyes RC 5.00 1.50
156 Runelvys Hernandez RC 5.00 1.50
157 Rodrigo Rosario RC 5.00 1.50
158 Jason Simontacchi RC 5.00 1.50
159 Miguel Asencio RC 5.00 1.50
160 Aaron Cook RC 5.00 1.50

2002 Diamond Kings Bronze Foil

Inserted at a stated rate of one in six packs, this is a parallel to the Diamond King sets. These cards have white frames with bronze highlights.

Nm-Mt Ex-Mt
*BRONZE 1-100: 1.5X TO 4X BASIC...
*BRONZE 101-121: .4X TO 1X BASIC.
*BRONZE 122-150: .4X TO 1X BASIC.
*BRONZE 151-160: 1X TO 2.5X BASIC

2002 Diamond Kings Gold Foil

Randomly inserted in packs, this is a parallel to the Diamond Kings set. These cards can be differentiated by their having black frames with gold accents. 100 serial-numbered sets were printed.

Nm-Mt Ex-Mt
*GOLD 1-100: 6X TO 15X BASIC
*GOLD 101-121: 1.5X TO 4X BASIC...
*GOLD 122-150: 2.5X TO 6X BASIC...
*GOLD 151-160: 1.5X TO 4X BASIC...
1-150 RANDOM INSERTS IN PACKS
151-160 RANDOM IN DONRUSS ROOK.PACKS

2002 Diamond Kings Silver Foil

Randomly inserted in packs, this is a parallel to the Diamond Kings set. These cards can be differentiated by the grey frames and with silver accents.

Nm-Mt Ex-Mt
*SILVER 1-100: 3X TO 8X BASIC
*SILVER 101-121: .75X TO 2X BASIC
*SILVER 122-150: 1.25X TO 3X BASIC
*SILVER 151-160: 1.25X TO 3X BASIC
151-160 PRINT RUN 250 SERIAL #'d SETS

2002 Diamond Kings Diamond Cut Collection

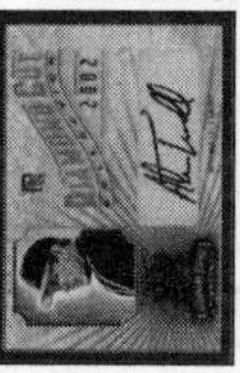

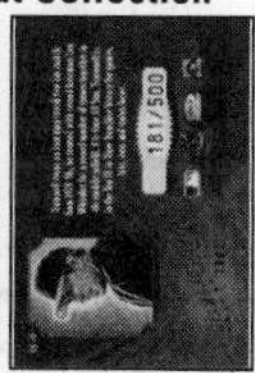

These 100 cards were inserted at an approximate rate of one per hobby box and as random inserts in retail packs. These cards feature a mix of autograph and memorabilia cards. The bat cards of Tony Gwynn and Kazuhisa Ishii were not ready by the time this product packed out. Thus, exchange cards with a deadline of November 1st, 2003 were seeded into packs.

Nm-Mt Ex-Mt
DC1 Vladimir Guerrero AU/400 40.00 12.00
DC2 Mark Prior AU/400 100.00 30.00
DC3 Victor Martinez AU/500 15.00 4.50
DC4 Marlon Byrd AU/500 15.00 4.50
DC5 Bud Smith AU/400 15.00 4.50
DC6 Joe Mays AU/500 15.00 4.50
DC7 Troy Glaus AU/500 25.00 7.50
DC8 Ron Santo AU/500 25.00 7.50
DC9 Roy Oswalt AU/500 25.00 7.50
DC10 Angel Berroa AU/500 15.00 4.50
DC11 Mark Buehrle AU/500 15.00 4.50
DC12 John Buck AU/500 15.00 4.50
DC13 Barry Larkin AU/250 50.00 15.00
DC14 Gary Carter AU/250 40.00 12.00
DC15 Mark Teixeira AU/300 25.00 7.50
DC16 Alan Trammell AU/500 25.00 7.50
DC17 Kazuhisa Ishii AU/100 80.00 24.00
DC18 Rafael Palmeiro AU/125 60.00 18.00
DC19 Austin Kearns AU/500 15.00 4.50
DC20 Joe Torre AU/125 60.00 18.00
DC21 J.D. Drew AU/400 15.00 4.50
DC22 So Taguchi AU/400 30.00 9.00
DC23 Juan Marichal AU/500 15.00 4.50
DC24 Bobby Doerr AU/500 25.00 7.50
DC25 Carlos Beltran AU/500 15.00 4.50
DC26 Robert Fick AU/500 15.00 4.50
DC27 Albert Pujols AU/200 120.00 36.00
DC28 Shannon Stewart AU/500 15.00 4.50
DC29 Antonio Perez AU/500 15.00 4.50
DC30 Wilson Betemit AU/500 15.00 4.50
DC31 Alex Rodriguez Jsy/500 15.00 4.50
DC32 Curt Schilling Jsy/500 15.00 4.50
DC33 George Brett Jsy/300 40.00 12.00
DC34 Hideo Nomo Jsy/100 25.00 7.50
DC35 Ivan Rodriguez Jsy/500 15.00 4.50
DC36 Don Mattingly Jsy/200 50.00 15.00
DC37 Joe Mays Jsy/500 10.00 3.00
DC38 Lance Berkman Jsy/400 10.00 3.00
DC39 Tony Gwynn Jsy/500 15.00 4.50
DC40 Darin Erstad Jsy/400 10.00 3.00
DC41 Adrian Beltre Jsy/400 10.00 3.00
DC42 Frank Thomas Jsy/500 15.00 4.50
DC43 Cal Ripken Jsy/300 50.00 15.00
DC44 Jose Vidro Jsy/500 10.00 3.00
DC45 Randy Johnson Jsy/300 15.00 4.50
DC46 Carlos Delgado Jsy/500 10.00 3.00
DC47 Roger Clemens Jsy/400 25.00 7.50
DC48 Luis Gonzalez Jsy/500 10.00 3.00
DC49 Marlon Byrd Jsy/500 10.00 3.00
DC50 Carlton Fisk Jsy/500 15.00 4.50
DC51 Manny Ramirez Jsy/500 10.00 3.00
DC52 Vladimir Guerrero Jsy/500 15.00 4.50
DC53 Barry Larkin Jsy/500 15.00 4.50
DC54 Aramis Ramirez Jsy/500 10.00 3.00
DC55 Todd Helton Jsy/300 15.00 4.50
DC56 Carlos Beltran Jsy/250 10.00 3.00
DC57 Jeff Bagwell Jsy/250 15.00 4.50
DC58 Larry Walker Jsy/500 15.00 4.50
DC59 Al Kaline Jsy/200 15.00 4.50
DC60 Chipper Jones Jsy/500 15.00 4.50
DC61 Bernie Williams Jsy/500 15.00 4.50
DC62 Bud Smith Jsy/500 10.00 3.00
DC63 Edgar Martinez Jsy/500 15.00 4.50
DC64 Pedro Martinez Jsy/500 15.00 4.50
DC65 Andre Dawson Jsy/200 10.00 3.00
DC66 Mike Piazza Jsy/100 50.00 15.00
DC67 Barry Zito Jsy/500 15.00 4.50
DC68 Bo Jackson Jsy/300 15.00 4.50
DC69 Nolan Ryan Jsy/400 50.00 15.00
DC70 Troy Glaus Jsy/500 15.00 4.50
DC71 Jorge Posada Jsy/500 15.00 4.50
DC72 Ted Williams Jsy/100 150.00 45.00
DC73 N.Garciaparra Jsy/500 15.00 4.50
DC74 Catfish Hunter Jsy/100 25.00 7.50
DC75 Gary Carter Jsy/500 15.00 4.50
DC76 Craig Biggio Jsy/500 15.00 4.50
DC77 Andruw Jones Jsy/500 10.00 3.00
DC78 R.Henderson Jsy/300 15.00 4.50
DC79 Greg Maddux Jsy/400 15.00 4.50
DC80 Kerry Wood Jsy/500 15.00 4.50
DC81 Alex Rodriguez Bat/500 15.00 4.50
DC82 Don Mattingly Bat/425 40.00 12.00
DC83 Craig Biggio Bat/500 25.00 7.50
DC84 Kazuhisa Ishii Bat/375 15.00 4.50
DC85 Eddie Murray Bat/500 25.00 7.50
DC86 Carlton Fisk Bat/500 25.00 7.50
DC87 Tsuyoshi Shinjo Bat/500 15.00 4.50
DC88 Bo Jackson Bat/500 25.00 7.50
DC89 Eddie Mathews Bat/100 25.00 7.50
DC90 Chipper Jones Bat/500 25.00 7.50
DC91 Adam Dunn Bat/375 15.00 4.50
DC92 Tony Gwynn Bat/200 15.00 4.50
DC93 Kirby Puckett Bat/500 25.00 7.50
DC94 Andre Dawson Bat/500 15.00 4.50
DC95 Bernie Williams Bat/500 25.00 7.50
DC96 Rob. Clemente Bat/300 100.00 30.00
DC97 Babe Ruth Bat/100 250.00 75.00
DC98 Roberto Alomar Bat/500 25.00 7.50
DC99 Frank Thomas Bat/500 25.00 7.50
DC100 So Taguchi Bat/500 25.00 7.50

2002 Diamond Kings DK Originals

Randomly inserted in packs, these 15 cards are printed to a stated print run of 1000 serial numbered sets. These cards are printed on canvas board with a vintage Diamond King look to them.

Nm-Mt Ex-Mt
COMPLETE SET (15) 150.00 45.00
DK1 Alex Rodriguez 12.00 3.60
DK2 Kazuhisa Ishii 10.00 3.00
DK3 Pedro Martinez 8.00 2.40
DK4 Nomar Garciaparra 12.00 3.60
DK5 Albert Pujols 15.00 4.50
DK6 Chipper Jones 8.00 2.40
DK7 So Taguchi 8.00 2.40
DK8 Jeff Bagwell 8.00 2.40
DK9 Vladimir Guerrero 8.00 2.40
DK10 Derek Jeter 20.00 6.00
DK11 Sammy Sosa 12.00 3.60
DK12 Ichiro Suzuki 12.00 3.60
DK13 Barry Bonds 20.00 6.00
DK14 Jason Giambi 8.00 2.40
DK15 Mike Piazza 12.00 3.60

2002 Diamond Kings Heritage Collection

Inserted in packs to a stated rate of one in 23 hobby and one in 46 retail packs, these 25 cards featue many of baseball's all-time greats highlighted on canvas board stock.

Nm-Mt Ex-Mt
COMPLETE SET (25) 200.00 60.00
HC1 Lou Gehrig 10.00 3.00
HC2 Nolan Ryan 15.00 4.50
HC3 Ryne Sandberg 10.00 3.00
HC4 Ted Williams 15.00 4.50
HC5 Roberto Clemente 15.00 4.50
HC6 Mike Schmidt 12.00 3.60
HC7 Roger Clemens 12.00 3.60
HC8 Kirby Puckett 5.00 1.50
HC9 Andre Dawson 4.00 1.20
HC10 Carlton Fisk 4.00 1.20
HC11 Don Mattingly 15.00 4.50
HC12 Juan Marichal 4.00 1.20
HC13 George Brett 15.00 4.50
HC14 Bo Jackson 5.00 1.50
HC15 Eddie Mathews 5.00 1.50
HC16 Randy Johnson 5.00 1.50
HC17 Alan Trammell 4.00 1.20
HC18 Tony Gwynn 8.00 2.40
HC19 Paul Molitor 4.00 1.20
HC20 Barry Bonds 15.00 4.50
HC21 Eddie Murray 5.00 1.50
HC22 Catfish Hunter 4.00 1.20
HC23 Rickey Henderson 5.00 1.50
HC24 Cal Ripken 20.00 6.00
HC25 Babe Ruth 15.00 4.50

2002 Diamond Kings Recollection Autographs

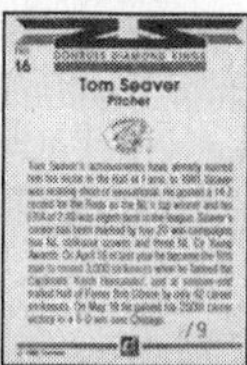

Randomly inserted in packs, these cards are original Diamond Kings which Donruss/Playoff bought back and had the feature player sign. These cards are all numbered to differing amounts and we have notated that information in our checklist. No pricing is provided on quantities of 25 or less.

Nm-Mt Ex-Mt
47 Alan Trammell 88 DK/110 50.00 15.00

2002 Diamond Kings T204

Randomly inserted in packs, these 25 cards are printed to a stated print run of 1000 serial numbered sets. These cards are designed just

like the Ramly T204 set which was issued early in the 20th century.

	Nm-Mt	Ex-Mt
COMPLETE SET (25)	250.00	75.00
RC1 Vladimir Guerrero	8.00	2.40
RC2 Jeff Bagwell	5.00	1.50
RC3 Barry Bonds	20.00	6.00
RC4 Rickey Henderson	8.00	2.40
RC5 Mike Piazza	12.00	3.60
RC6 Derek Jeter	20.00	6.00
RC7 Kazuhisa Ishii	10.00	3.00
RC8 Ichiro Suzuki	12.00	3.60
RC9 Chipper Jones	8.00	2.40
RC10 Sammy Sosa	12.00	3.60
RC11 Don Mattingly	20.00	6.00
RC12 Shawn Green	5.00	1.50
RC13 Nomar Garciaparra	12.00	3.60
RC14 Luis Gonzalez	5.00	1.50
RC15 Albert Pujols	15.00	4.50
RC16 Cal Ripken	25.00	7.50
RC17 Todd Helton	5.00	1.50
RC18 Hideo Nomo	8.00	2.40
RC19 Alex Rodriguez	12.00	3.60
RC20 So Taguchi	5.00	1.50
RC21 Lance Berkman	5.00	1.50
RC22 Tony Gwynn	10.00	3.00
RC23 Roger Clemens	15.00	4.50
RC24 Jason Giambi	8.00	2.40
RC25 Ken Griffey Jr.	12.00	3.60

2002 Diamond Kings Timeline

Issued at a stated rate of one in 60 hobby and one in 120 retail packs, these 10 cards feature two players who have something in common.

	Nm-Mt	Ex-Mt
COMPLETE SET (10)	120.00	36.00
TL1 Lou Gehrig Don Mattingly	15.00	4.50
TL2 Hideo Nomo Ichiro Suzuki	10.00	3.00
TL3 Cal Ripken Alex Rodriguez	20.00	6.00
TL4 Mike Schmidt Scott Rolen	12.00	3.60
TL5 Ichiro Suzuki Albert Pujols	12.00	3.60
TL6 Curt Schilling Randy Johnson	10.00	3.00
TL7 Chipper Jones Eddie Mathews	10.00	3.00
TL8 Lou Gehrig Cal Ripken	20.00	6.00
TL9 Derek Jeter Roger Clemens	15.00	4.50
TL10 Kazuhisa Ishii SoTaguchi	10.00	3.00

2002 Diamond Kings Hawaii

These cards were distributed in six-card cello-wrapped packets at the eBay booth of the Hawaii Trade Conference "Meet the Industry" event in late February, 2002. Each attendee received one packet at the presentation. The cards parallel the basic issue 2002 Donruss Diamond Kings distributed later that year, but can be readily distinguished by the "2002 Hawaii Trade Conference" gold foil logo stamped on the front.

Nm-Mt Ex-Mt

*PARALLEL 20'S RANDOMLY INSERTED INTO PACKS
*PARALLEL: NO PRICING DUE TO SCARCITY
*BLUE PORT: RANDOMLY INSERTED INTO PACKS
*BLUE PORT: SERIAL #'D TO 1 OR 5 .
*BLUE PORT: NO PRICING DUE TO SCARCITY

2002 Diamond Kings Hawaii Parallel 20

These cards area straight parallel of the more common Donruss Diamond Kings Hawaii cards and were randomly seeded into the 6-card packets of Donruss Diamond Kings Hawaii distributed at the eBay booth of the 2002 Hawaii Trade Conference. Each "Parallel 20" version is serial-numbered "of 20" in gold foil on the card back.

Nm-Mt Ex-Mt

*HAWAII DK 20: X TO X BASIC HAWAII DK'S

2003 Diamond Kings Samples

Issued one per Beckett Baseball Card Magazine, these cards were issued to preview the 2003 Donruss Diamond Kings set. These cards parallel the regular set except the word "sample" is stamped in silver on the back.

Nm-Mt Ex-Mt

*SAMPLES: 1.5X TO 4X BASIC CARDS

2003 Diamond Kings Samples Gold

Randomly inserted in Beckett Baseball Card Magazine, these cards feature the word "sample" on the back printed in gold. Usually the gold samples comprise 10 percent of all the samples produced.

Nm-Mt Ex-Mt

*GOLD SAMPLES: 4X TO 10X BASIC CARDS

2003 Diamond Kings

This 200-card set was released in two separate series. The primary Diamond Kings product - containing cards 1-176 from the basic set - was issued in March, 2003. These cards were issued in five card packs with an $4 SRP. These packs came 24 packs to a box and 20 boxes to a case. Cards numbered 151 through 158 feature some of the leading rookie prospects and those cards were issued at a stated rate of one in six. Cards numbered 159 through 175 feature retired greats and those cards were also issued at a stated rate of one in six. Card number 176 feature Cuban refugee Jose Contreras who was signed to a major free agent contract before the 2003 season began. The Contreras card was not on the original checklist. Cards 177-189/191-201 were distributed at a rate of 1:24 packs of DLP Rookies and Traded in December, 2003. Please note, card 190 does not exist.

	Nm-Mt	Ex-Mt
COMP.LO SET (176)	150.00	45.00
COMP.LO SET w/o SP's (150)	50.00	15.00
COMMON CARD (1-150)	.50	.15
COMMON CARD (151-158)	2.00	.60
COMMON CARD (159-175)	4.00	1.20
COMMON CARD (177-201)	4.00	1.20
1 Darin Erstad	.50	.15
2 Garret Anderson	.50	.15
3 Troy Glaus	.75	.23
4 David Eckstein	.50	.15
5 Jarrod Washburn	.50	.15
6 Adam Kennedy	.50	.15
7 Jay Gibbons	.50	.15
8 Tony Batista	.50	.15
9 Melvin Mora	.50	.15
10 Rodrigo Lopez	.50	.15
11 Manny Ramirez	.50	.15
12 Pedro Martinez	1.25	.35
13 Nomar Garciaparra	2.00	.60
14 Rickey Henderson	1.25	.35
15 Johnny Damon	.50	.15
16 Derek Lowe	.50	.15
17 Cliff Floyd	.50	.15
18 Frank Thomas	1.25	.35
19 Magglio Ordonez	.50	.15
20 Paul Konerko	.50	.15
21 Mark Buehrle	.50	.15
22 C.C. Sabathia	.50	.15
23 Omar Vizquel	.50	.15
24 Jim Thome	1.25	.35
25 Ellis Burks	.50	.15
26 Robert Fick	.50	.15
27 Bobby Higginson	.50	.15
28 Randall Simon	.50	.15
29 Carlos Pena	.50	.15
30 Carlos Beltran	.50	.15
31 Paul Byrd	.50	.15
32 Raul Ibanez	.50	.15
33 Mike Sweeney	.50	.15
34 Torii Hunter	.50	.15
35 Corey Koskie	.50	.15
36 A.J. Pierzynski	.50	.15
37 Cristian Guzman	.50	.15
38 Jacque Jones	.50	.15
39 Derek Jeter	3.00	.90
40 Bernie Williams	.75	.23
41 Roger Clemens	2.50	.75
42 Mike Mussina	1.25	.35
43 Jorge Posada	.75	.23
44 Alfonso Soriano	.75	.23
45 Jason Giambi	1.25	.35
46 Robin Ventura	.50	.15
47 David Wells	.50	.15
48 Tim Hudson	.50	.15
49 Barry Zito	.75	.23
50 Mark Mulder	.50	.15
51 Miguel Tejada	.50	.15
52 Eric Chavez	.50	.15
53 Jermaine Dye	.50	.15
54 Ichiro Suzuki	2.00	.60
55 Edgar Martinez	.75	.23
56 John Olerud	.50	.15
57 Dan Wilson	.50	.15
58 Joel Pineiro	.50	.15
59 Kazuhiro Sasaki	.50	.15
60 Freddy Garcia	.50	.15
61 Aubrey Huff	.50	.15
62 Steve Cox	.50	.15
63 Randy Winn	.50	.15
64 Alex Rodriguez	2.00	.60
65 Juan Gonzalez	1.25	.35
66 Rafael Palmeiro	.75	.23
67 Ivan Rodriguez	1.25	.35
68 Kenny Rogers	.50	.15
69 Carlos Delgado	.50	.15
70 Eric Hinske	.50	.15
71 Roy Halladay	.50	.15
72 Vernon Wells	.50	.15
73 Shannon Stewart	.50	.15
74 Curt Schilling	.75	.23
75 Randy Johnson	1.25	.35
76 Luis Gonzalez	.50	.15
77 Mark Grace	.75	.23
78 Junior Spivey	.50	.15
79 Greg Maddux	2.00	.60
80 Tom Glavine	.75	.23
81 John Smoltz	.75	.23
82 Chipper Jones	1.25	.35
83 Gary Sheffield	.50	.15
84 Andruw Jones	.50	.15
85 Kerry Wood	1.25	.35
86 Fred McGriff	.75	.23
87 Sammy Sosa	2.00	.60
88 Mark Prior	2.50	.75
89 Ken Griffey Jr.	2.00	.60
90 Barry Larkin	1.25	.35
91 Adam Dunn	.50	.15
92 Sean Casey	.50	.15
93 Austin Kearns	.50	.15
94 Aaron Boone	.50	.15
95 Larry Walker	.75	.23
96 Todd Helton	.75	.23
97 Jason Jennings	.50	.15
98 Jay Payton	.50	.15
99 Josh Beckett	.75	.23
100 Mike Lowell	.50	.15
101 A.J. Burnett	.50	.15
102 Jeff Bagwell	.75	.23
103 Craig Biggio	.75	.23
104 Lance Berkman	.50	.15
105 Roy Oswalt	.50	.15
106 Wade Miller	.50	.15
107 Shawn Green	.50	.15
108 Adrian Beltre	.50	.15
109 Hideo Nomo	1.25	.35
110 Kazuhisa Ishii	.50	.15
111 Odalis Perez	.50	.15
112 Paul Lo Duca	.50	.15
113 Ben Sheets	.50	.15
114 Richie Sexson	.50	.15
115 Jose Hernandez	.50	.15
116 Vladimir Guerrero	1.25	.35
117 Jose Vidro	.50	.15
118 Tomo Ohka	.50	.15
119 Andres Galarraga	.50	.15
120 Bartolo Colon	.50	.15
121 Mike Piazza	2.00	.60
122 Roberto Alomar	1.25	.35
123 Mo Vaughn	.50	.15
124 Al Leiter	.50	.15
125 Edgardo Alfonzo	.50	.15
126 Pat Burrell	.50	.15
127 Bobby Abreu	.50	.15
128 Mike Lieberthal	.50	.15
129 Vicente Padilla	.50	.15
130 Marlon Byrd	.50	.15
131 Jason Kendall	.50	.15
132 Brian Giles	.50	.15
133 Aramis Ramirez	.50	.15
134 Kip Wells	.50	.15
135 Ryan Klesko	.50	.15
136 Phil Nevin	.50	.15
137 Brian Lawrence	.50	.15
138 Sean Burroughs	.50	.15
139 Mark Kotsay	.50	.15
140 Barry Bonds	3.00	.90
141 Jeff Kent	.50	.15
142 Benito Santiago	.50	.15
143 Kirk Rueter	.50	.15
144 Jason Schmidt	.50	.15
145 Jim Edmonds	.50	.15
146 J.D. Drew	.50	.15
147 Albert Pujols	2.50	.75
148 Tino Martinez	.75	.23
149 Matt Morris	.50	.15
150 Scott Rolen	.75	.23
151 Joe Borchard ROO	2.00	.60
152 Cliff Lee ROO	2.00	.60
153 Brian Tallet ROO	2.00	.60
154 Freddy Sanchez ROO	2.00	.60
155 Chone Figgins ROO	2.00	.60
156 Kevin Cash ROO	2.00	.60
157 Justin Wayne ROO	2.00	.60
158 Ben Kozlowski ROO	2.00	.60
159 Babe Ruth RET	10.00	3.00
160 Jackie Robinson RET	6.00	1.80
161 Ozzie Smith RET	8.00	2.40
162 Lou Gehrig RET	6.00	1.80
163 Stan Musial RET	6.00	1.80
164 Mike Schmidt RET	10.00	3.00
165 Carlton Fisk RET	5.00	1.50
166 George Brett RET	12.00	3.60
167 Dale Murphy RET	8.00	2.40
168 Cal Ripken RET	12.00	3.60
169 Tony Gwynn RET	5.00	1.50
170 Don Mattingly RET	10.00	3.00
171 Jack Morris RET	4.00	1.20
172 Ty Cobb RET	5.00	1.50
173 Nolan Ryan RET	10.00	3.00
174 Ryne Sandberg RET	8.00	2.40
175 Thurman Munson RET	6.00	1.80
176 Jose Contreras ROO RC	10.00	3.00
177 Hideki Matsui ROO RC	15.00	4.50
178 Jeremy Bonderman ROO RC	5.00	1.50
179 Brandon Webb ROO RC	8.00	2.40
180 Adam Loewen ROO RC	8.00	2.40
181 Chien-Ming Wang ROO RC	6.00	1.80
182 Hong-Chih Kuo ROO RC	5.00	1.50
183 Clint Barmes ROO RC	5.00	1.50
184 Guillermo Quiroz ROO RC	5.00	1.50
185 Edgar Gonzalez ROO RC	4.00	1.20
186 Todd Wellemeyer ROO RC	5.00	1.50
187 Dan Haren ROO RC	5.00	1.50
188 Dustin McGowan ROO RC	5.00	1.50
189 Preston Larrison ROO RC	5.00	1.50
190 Does Not Exist		
191 Kevin Youkilis ROO RC	15.00	4.50
192 Bubba Nelson ROO RC	5.00	1.50
193 Chris Burke ROO RC	5.00	1.50
194 J.D. Durbin ROO RC	5.00	1.50
195 Ryan Howard ROO RC	5.00	1.50
196 Jason Kubel ROO RC	5.00	1.50
197 Brendan Harris ROO RC	5.00	1.50
198 Brian Bruney ROO RC	5.00	1.50
199 Ramon Nivar ROO RC	5.00	1.50
200 Rickie Weeks ROO RC	15.00	4.50
201 Delmon Young ROO RC	15.00	4.50

2003 Diamond Kings Bronze Foil

Randomly inserted in packs, this is a parallel to the Diamond Kings set. Cards 177-201 were randomly seeded into packs of DLP Rookies and Traded and unlike the first 176 cards are serial numbered to 200 copies per. The bronze cards can be identified by the white frames and the bronze foil used for the cards.

Nm-Mt Ex-Mt

*BRONZE 1-150: 1.5X TO 4X BASIC...
*BRONZE 151-158: .6X TO 1.5X BASIC
*BRONZE 159-175: .6X TO 1.5X BASIC
*BRONZE 176: .4X TO 1X BASIC ....
*BRONZE 177-189/191-201: .5X TO 1.2X BASIC

2003 Diamond Kings Gold Foil

Randomly inserted into packs, this is a parallel to the Diamond Kings insert set. Cards 177-201 were randomly seeded into packs of DLP Rookies and Traded. These cards feature black frames which surround the gold foil usage. Cards 1-176 were issued to a stated print run of 100 serial numbered sets and 177-201 to a stated print run of 50 serial numbered copies per.

Nm-Mt Ex-Mt

*GOLD 1-150: 6X TO 15X BASIC ....
*GOLD 151-158: 2X TO 5X BASIC ......
*GOLD 176: 1X TO 2.5X BASIC ....
*GOLD 177-201: 1.25X TO 3X BASIC .

	Nm-Mt	Ex-Mt
159 Babe Ruth RET	50.00	15.00
160 Jackie Robinson RET	30.00	9.00
161 Ozzie Smith RET	40.00	12.00
162 Lou Gehrig RET	30.00	9.00
163 Stan Musial RET	40.00	12.00
164 Mike Schmidt RET	50.00	15.00
165 Carlton Fisk RET	25.00	7.50
166 George Brett RET	60.00	18.00
167 Dale Murphy RET	60.00	18.00
168 Cal Ripken RET	80.00	24.00
169 Tony Gwynn RET	30.00	9.00
170 Don Mattingly RET	60.00	18.00
171 Jack Morris RET	20.00	6.00
172 Ty Cobb RET	40.00	12.00
173 Nolan Ryan RET	60.00	18.00
174 Ryne Sandberg RET	60.00	18.00
175 Thurman Munson RET	40.00	12.00

2003 Diamond Kings Silver Foil

Randomly inserted into packs, this is a parallel to the Diamond Kings set. Cards 177-201 were randomly seeded into packs of DLP Rookies and Traded. These cards can be identified by the grey frames surrounding the silver foil. Cards 1-176 were serial numbered to 400 and 177-201 were serial numbered to 100.

Nm-Mt Ex-Mt

*SILVER 1-150: 3X TO 8X BASIC ....
*SILVER 151-158: 1X TO 2.5X BASIC
*SILVER 159-175: 1X TO 2.5X BASIC
*SILVER 176: .5X TO 1.2X BASIC.......
*SILVER 177-201: .6X TO 1.5X BASIC

2003 Diamond Kings Diamond Cut Collection

Randomly inserted into packs, this 110 card set features either an autograph or a game-used memorabilia piece. Since these cards are issued to a varying amount of cards, we have notated that information next to the player's name in our checklist.

	Nm-Mt	Ex-Mt
1 Barry Zito AU/75	80.00	24.00
2 Edgar Martinez AU/125	50.00	15.00
3 Jay Gibbons AU/150	30.00	9.00
4 Joe Borchard AU/150	30.00	9.00
5 Marlon Byrd AU/150	30.00	9.00
6 Adam Dunn AU/150	40.00	12.00
7 Torii Hunter AU/150	40.00	12.00
8 Vladimir Guerrero AU/25		
9 Wade Miller AU/150	30.00	9.00
10 Alfonso Soriano AU/100	60.00	18.00
11 Brian Lawrence AU/150	25.00	7.50
12 Cliff Floyd AU/100	30.00	9.00
13 Dale Murphy AU/75	80.00	24.00
14 Jack Morris AU/150	30.00	9.00
15 Eric Hinske AU/150	25.00	7.50
16 Jason Jennings AU/150	25.00	7.50
17 Mark Buehrle AU/150	30.00	9.00
18 Mark Prior AU/150	100.00	30.00
19 Mark Mulder AU/150	30.00	9.00
20 Mike Sweeney AU/150	30.00	9.00
21 Nolan Ryan AU/50	300.00	90.00
22 Don Mattingly AU/75	150.00	45.00
23 Andruw Jones AU/75	60.00	18.00
24 Aubrey Huff AU/150	30.00	9.00
25 Rickey Henderson AU/25		
26 Nolan Ryan Jsy/250	50.00	15.00
27 Ozzie Smith Jsy/400	15.00	4.50
28 Rickey Henderson Jsy/300	15.00	4.50
29 Jack Morris Jsy/500	10.00	3.00
30 George Brett Jsy/350	25.00	7.50
31 Cal Ripken Jsy/300	40.00	12.00
32 Ryne Sandberg Jsy/450	20.00	6.00
33 Don Mattingly Jsy/400	25.00	7.50
34 Tony Gwynn Jsy/400	15.00	4.50
35 Dale Murphy Jsy/350	15.00	4.50
36 Carlton Fisk Jsy/400	15.00	4.50
37 Stan Musial Jsy/50		
38 Lou Gehrig Jsy/50	300.00	90.00
39 Garret Anderson Jsy/450	10.00	3.00
40 Pedro Martinez Jsy/400	15.00	4.50
41 Nomar Garciaparra Jsy/350	15.00	4.50
42 Magglio Ordonez Jsy/450	10.00	3.00
43 C.C. Sabathia Jsy/500	10.00	3.00
44 Omar Vizquel Jsy/250	15.00	4.50
45 Jim Thome Jsy/500	15.00	4.50
46 Torii Hunter Jsy/500	10.00	3.00
47 Roger Clemens Jsy/500	15.00	4.50
48 Alfonso Soriano Jsy/400	15.00	4.50
49 Tim Hudson Jsy/500	10.00	3.00
50 Barry Zito Jsy/350	15.00	4.50
51 Mark Mulder Jsy/500	10.00	3.00
52 Miguel Tejada Jsy/400	10.00	3.00
53 John Olerud Jsy/350	10.00	3.00
54 Alex Rodriguez Jsy/500	15.00	4.50
55 Rafael Palmeiro Jsy/500	15.00	4.50
56 Curt Schilling Jsy/500	15.00	4.50
57 Randy Johnson Jsy/400	15.00	4.50
58 Greg Maddux Jsy/350	15.00	4.50
59 John Smoltz Jsy/400	15.00	4.50
60 Chipper Jones Jsy/450	15.00	4.50
61 Andruw Jones Jsy/500	10.00	3.00
62 Kerry Wood Jsy/500	15.00	4.50
63 Mark Prior Jsy/500	20.00	6.00
64 Adam Dunn Jsy/350	10.00	3.00
65 Larry Walker Jsy/500	15.00	4.50
66 Todd Helton Jsy/500	15.00	4.50
67 Jeff Bagwell Jsy/500	15.00	4.50
68 Roy Oswalt Jsy/500	10.00	3.00
69 Hideo Nomo Jsy/150	20.00	6.00
70 Kazuhisa Ishii Jsy/250	15.00	4.50
71 Vladimir Guerrero Jsy/500	15.00	4.50
72 Mike Piazza Jsy/500	15.00	4.50
73 Joe Borchard Jsy/500	10.00	3.00
74 Ryan Klesko Jsy/500	10.00	3.00
75 Shawn Green Jsy/500	10.00	3.00
76 George Brett Bat/350	25.00	7.50
77 Ozzie Smith Bat/450	15.00	4.50
78 Cal Ripken Bat/150	50.00	15.00
79 Don Mattingly Bat/400	25.00	7.50
80 Babe Ruth Bat/50	250.00	75.00
81 Dale Murphy Bat/350	15.00	4.50
82 Rickey Henderson Bat/500	15.00	4.50
83 Ivan Rodriguez Bat/500	15.00	4.50
84 Marlon Byrd Bat/500	10.00	3.00
85 Eric Chavez Bat/500	10.00	3.00
86 Nomar Garciaparra Bat/500	15.00	4.50
87 Alex Rodriguez Bat/500	15.00	4.50
88 Vladimir Guerrero Bat/500	15.00	4.50
89 Paul Lo Duca Bat/500	10.00	3.00
90 Richie Sexson Bat/500	10.00	3.00
91 Mike Piazza Bat/350	15.00	4.50
92 J.D. Drew Bat/500	10.00	3.00
93 Juan Gonzalez Bat/500	15.00	4.50
94 Pat Burrell Bat/500	10.00	3.00
95 Adam Dunn Bat/250	15.00	4.50
96 Mike Schmidt Bat/500	20.00	6.00
97 Ryne Sandberg Bat/500	20.00	6.00
98 Edgardo Alfonzo Bat/500	10.00	3.00
99 Andruw Jones Bat/500	10.00	3.00
100 Carlos Beltran Bat/500	10.00	3.00
101 Jeff Bagwell Bat/500	15.00	4.50
102 Lance Berkman Bat/500	10.00	3.00
103 Luis Gonzalez Bat/500	10.00	3.00
104 Carlos Delgado Bat/500	10.00	3.00
105 Jim Edmonds Bat/250	15.00	4.50
106 Alf Soriano Hat-Jsy/75	40.00	12.00
107 Greg Maddux Jsy-AU/50	200.00	60.00
108 Ty Cobb Pants-Bat/25		
109 Adam Dunn Bat-AU/50	80.00	24.00
110 R.Henderson Jsy-Bat/50	40.00	12.00

2003 Diamond Kings DK Evolution

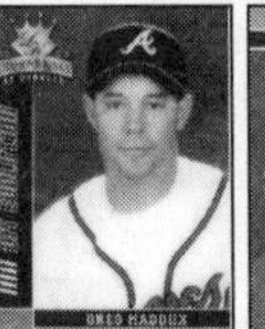

Issued at a stated rate of one in 18 hobby and one in 36 retail, this 25 card set features both the original photo as well as the artwork.

	Nm-Mt	Ex-Mt
1 Cal Ripken	20.00	6.00
2 Ichiro Suzuki	10.00	3.00
3 Randy Johnson	6.00	1.80
4 Pedro Martinez	6.00	1.80
5 Nolan Ryan	15.00	4.50
6 Derek Jeter	15.00	4.50
7 Kerry Wood	6.00	1.80
8 Alex Rodriguez	10.00	3.00
9 Magglio Ordonez	5.00	1.50
10 Greg Maddux	10.00	3.00
11 Todd Helton	5.00	1.50
12 Sammy Sosa	10.00	3.00
13 Lou Gehrig	12.00	3.60
14 Lance Berkman	5.00	1.50
15 Barry Zito	5.00	1.50
16 Barry Bonds	15.00	4.50
17 Tom Glavine	5.00	1.50
18 Shawn Green	5.00	1.50
19 Roger Clemens	12.00	3.60
20 Nomar Garciaparra	10.00	3.00
21 Tony Gwynn	8.00	2.40
22 Vladimir Guerrero	6.00	1.80
23 Albert Pujols	12.00	3.60
24 Chipper Jones	6.00	1.80
25 Alfonso Soriano	5.00	1.50

2003 Diamond Kings Heritage Collection

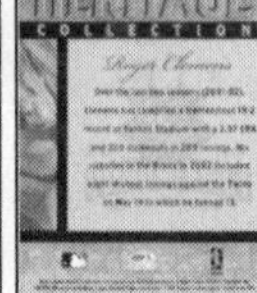

Issued at a stated rate of one in 23, this 25 card set features a mix of past and present superstars spotlighted with silver holo-foil on canvas board.

Nm-Mt Ex-Mt
1 Ozzie Smith 10.00 3.00
2 Lou Gehrig 12.00 3.60
3 Stan Musial 10.00 3.00
4 Mike Schmidt 12.00 3.60
5 Carlton Fisk 5.00 1.50
6 George Brett 15.00 4.50
7 Dale Murphy 6.00 1.80
8 Cal Ripken 20.00 6.00
9 Tony Gwynn 8.00 2.40
10 Don Mattingly 15.00 4.50
11 Jack Morris 5.00 1.50
12 Ty Cobb 10.00 3.00
13 Nolan Ryan 15.00 4.50
14 Ryne Sandberg 12.00 3.60
15 Thurman Munson 8.00 2.40
16 Ichiro Suzuki 10.00 3.00
17 Derek Jeter 15.00 4.50
18 Greg Maddux 10.00 3.00
19 Sammy Sosa 10.00 3.00
20 Pedro Martinez 6.00 1.80
21 Alex Rodriguez 10.00 3.00
22 Roger Clemens 12.00 3.60
23 Barry Bonds 15.00 4.50
24 Lance Berkman 5.00 1.50
25 Vladimir Guerrero 6.00 1.80

2003 Diamond Kings HOF Heroes Reprints

Issued in the style of the 1983 Donruss Hall of Fame Heroes set, this set was issued at a stated rate of one in 43 hobby and one in 67 retail.

Nm-Mt Ex-Mt
1 Bob Feller 8.00 2.40
2 Al Kaline 8.00 2.40
3 Lou Boudreau 8.00 2.40
4 Duke Snider 8.00 2.40
5 Jackie Robinson 10.00 3.00
6 Early Wynn 8.00 2.40
7 Yogi Berra 8.00 2.40
8 Stan Musial 10.00 3.00
9 Ty Cobb 10.00 3.00
10 Ted Williams 15.00 4.50

2003 Diamond Kings HOF Heroes Reprints Materials

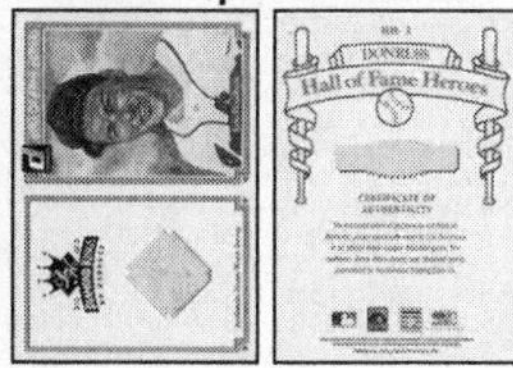

Randomly inserted into packs, these cards parallel the HOF Heroes Reprint set. Each card has a game-used memorabilia piece used by that player during his career. Each of these cards were issued to a stated print run of 50 serial numbered sets.

Nm-Mt Ex-Mt
1 Bob Feller Jsy
2 Al Kaline Bat
3 Lou Boudreau Jsy
4 Duke Snider Bat
5 Jackie Robinson Jsy
6 Early Wynn Jsy
7 Yogi Berra Bat
8 Stan Musial Bat
9 Ty Cobb Bat
10 Ted Williams Jsy

2003 Diamond Kings Recollection

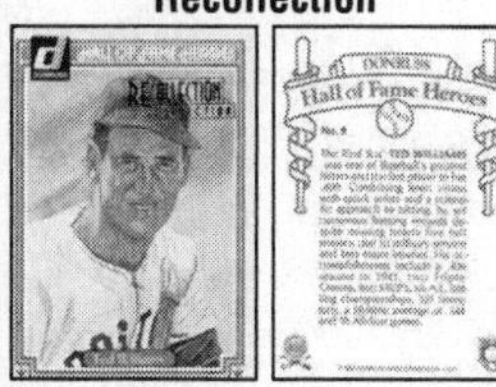

Randomly inserted into packs, these 14 cards feature older repurchased Diamond King subset cards or 1983 Hall of Fame Heroes cards. As each of these cards were issued to a stated print run of 15 or fewer copies, no pricing is available due to market scarcity.

Nm-Mt Ex-Mt
5 Lou Boudreau 83 HOF/3
15 Roberto Clemente 83 HOF/5
16 Roberto Clemente 87 DK/9
17 Ty Cobb 83 DK/10
18 Ty Cobb 83 HOF/5
34 Lou Gehrig 85 DK/10
44 Monte Irvin 83 HOF/5
48 Bob Lemon 83 HOF/5
66 Dan Quisenberry 85 DK/2
69 Jackie Robinson 83 HOF/5
82 Willie Stargell 83 DK/15
83 Willie Stargell 91 DK/6
90 Ted Williams 83 HOF/4
92 Early Wynn 83 HOF/5

2003 Diamond Kings Recollection Autographs

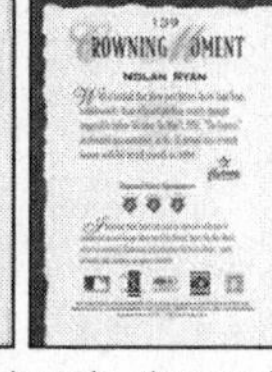

Randomly inserted in packs, these cards feature not only repurchased Donruss Diamond King cards but also an authentic autograph of the featured player. These cards were issued to a varying print run amount and we have notated that information next to the player's name in our checklist. Please note that for cards with a print run of 40 of fewer, no pricing is provided due to market scarcity.

Nm-Mt Ex-Mt
SEE BECKETT.COM FOR PRINT RUNS
NO PRICING ON QTY OF 40 OR LESS.
2 Brandon Berger 02 DK/99 15.00 4.50

2003 Diamond Kings Team Timeline

Randomly inserted into packs, these 10 cards feature both an active and retired player from the same team. Each of these cards are printed on canvas board and were issued to a stated print run of 1000 sets.

Nm-Mt Ex-Mt
1 Nolan Ryan 15.00 4.50
Roy Oswalt
2 Dale Murphy 8.00 2.40
Chipper Jones
3 Stan Musial 10.00 3.00
Jim Edmonds
4 George Brett 15.00 4.50
Mike Sweeney
5 Tony Gwynn 8.00 2.40
Ryan Klesko
6 Carlton Fisk 8.00 2.40
Magglio Ordonez
7 Mike Schmidt 20.00 6.00
Pat Burrell
8 Don Mattingly 20.00 6.00
Bernie Williams
9 Ryne Sandberg 15.00 4.50
Kerry Wood
10 Lou Gehrig 12.00 3.60
Alfonso Soriano

2003 Diamond Kings Team Timeline Jerseys

Randomly inserted into packs, this is a parallel to the Team Timeline insert set. Each of these cards feature two game-worn jersey swatches and were issued to a stated print run of 100 serial numbered sets.

Nm-Mt Ex-Mt
1 Nolan Ryan 120.00 36.00
Roy Oswalt
2 Dale Murphy 40.00 12.00
Chipper Jones
3 Stan Musial 50.00 15.00
Jim Edmonds
4 George Brett 80.00 24.00
Mike Sweeney
5 Tony Gwynn 50.00 15.00
Ryan Klesko
6 Carlton Fisk 40.00 12.00
Magglio Ordonez
7 Mike Schmidt 100.00 30.00
Pat Burrell
8 Don Mattingly 100.00 30.00
Bernie Williams
9 Ryne Sandberg 80.00 24.00
Kerry Wood
10 Lou Gehrig 250.00 75.00
Alfonso Soriano/50

2003 Diamond Kings Atlantic City National

Collectors who opened enough packs of Donruss product at the Donruss corporate booth at the 2003 National held in Atlantic City received copies of these Diamond King cards. The fronts of the card had special Atlantic City embossing while the backs were serial numbered to a stated print of five serial numbered copies. Due to market scarcity, no pricing is provided for these cards.

MINT NRMT
PRINT RUN 5 SERIAL #'d SETS

2003 Diamond Kings Chicago Collection

These cards were issued at the March, 2003 Chicago Sun-Times show. These cards parallel the Donruss Diamond King set and were available to collectors who opened three packs at the Donruss booth. For each three packs collectors opened, they received a specially stamped Diamond Kings cards stamped as "March Chicago Collection" and also with a stamped serial number. Each of these cards were issued to a stated print run of five serial numbered sets and no pricing is available due to market scarcity.

Nm-Mt Ex-Mt
DIST.AT MARCH 03 SUN TIMES SHOW
STATED PRINT RUN 5 SERIAL #'d SETS
NO PRICING DUE TO SCARCITY

2003 Diamond Kings Heritage Collection Hawaii

These cards, which parallel the Diamond Kings Heritage Collection set were distributed at the Hawaii Trade Show conference. These cards were issued to a stated print run of 20 serial numbered sets and no pricing is available due to market scarcity.

Nm-Mt Ex-Mt
DISTRIBUTED AT 2003 HAWAII CONFERENCE
STATED PRINT RUN 20 SERIAL #'d SETS
NO PRICING DUE TO SCARCITY

2003 Diamond Kings Team Timeline Hawaii

This set parallels the Team Timeline insert set. Each of these cards were specially distributed at the Hawaii Conference and were issued to a stated print run of 50 serial numbered sets.

Nm-Mt Ex-Mt
*HAWAII: 2X TO 5X BASIC TIMELINE.
DISTRIBUTED AT 2003 HAWAII CONFERENCE
STATED PRINT RUN 50 SERIAL #'d SETS

2003 Diamond Kings HOF Heroes Reprints Hawaii

These cards, which parallel the HOF Heroes Reprint set was distributed at the 2003 Hawaii Conference. These cards were issued to a stated print run of 50 serial numbered sets.

Nm-Mt Ex-Mt
*HAWAII: 1X TO 2.5X BASIC HOF REPRINTS
DISTRIBUTED AT 2003 HAWAII CONFERENCE
STATED PRINT RUN 50 SERIAL #'d SETS

2004 Diamond Kings

This 175-card set was released in February, 2004. This set was issued in five-card packs with an $6 SRP which came 12 packs to a box and 16 boxes to a case. This product has a dizzying amount of parallels and insert cards which included DK Materials which had two memorabilia pieces on each card and DK Combos which had not only those two memorabilia pieces but also had an authentic autograph from the player. In addition, many other insert sets were issued including a 134-card recollection autograph insert set as well as many other insert sets. This product; despite the seeming never-ending array of parallel and insert sets which made identifying cards difficult actually became one of the hobby hits of the first part of 2004. Cards numbered 1 through 150 feature current major leaguers while cards 151 through 158 are a flashback featuring some of today's players in an then and now format and cards numbered 159 through 175 is a legends subset. Cards numbered 151 through 175 were randomly inserted into packs.

Nm-Mt Ex-Mt
COMPLETE SET w/Sepia (200) 200.00 60.00
COMPLETE SET (175) 100.00 30.00
COMP.SET w/o SP's (150) 40.00 12.00
COMMON CARD (1-150) .50 .15
COMMON CARD (151-175) 3.00 .90
151-175 RANDOM INSERTS IN PACKS
1 Alex Rodriguez 2.00 .60
2 Andruw Jones .50 .15
3 Nomar Garciaparra 2.00 .60
4 Kerry Wood 1.25 .35
5 Magglio Ordonez .50 .15
6 Victor Martinez .50 .15
7 Jeremy Bonderman .50 .15
8 Josh Beckett .75 .23
9 Jeff Kent .50 .15
10 Carlos Beltran .50 .15
11 Hideo Nomo 1.25 .35
12 Richie Sexson .50 .15
13 Jose Vidro .50 .15
14 Jae Weong Seo .50 .15
15 Alfonso Soriano .75 .23
16 Barry Zito .75 .23
17 Brett Myers .50 .15
18 Brian Giles .50 .15
19 Edgar Martinez .75 .23
20 Jim Edmonds .50 .15
21 Rocco Baldelli 1.25 .35
22 Mark Teixeira .50 .15
23 Carlos Delgado .50 .15
24 Julius Matos .50 .15
25 Jose Reyes .75 .23
26 Marlon Byrd .50 .15
27 Albert Pujols 2.50 .75
28 Vernon Wells .50 .15
29 Garret Anderson .50 .15
30 Jerome Williams .50 .15
31 Chipper Jones 1.25 .35
32 Rich Harden .50 .15
33 Manny Ramirez .50 .15
34 Derek Jeter 3.00 .90
35 Brandon Webb .50 .15
36 Mark Prior 2.50 .75
37 Roy Halladay .50 .15
38 Frank Thomas 1.25 .35
39 Rafael Palmeiro .75 .23
40 Adam Dunn .50 .15
41 Aubrey Huff .50 .15
42 Todd Helton .75 .23
43 Matt Morris .50 .15
44 Dontrelle Willis .50 .15
45 Lance Berkman .50 .15
46 Mike Sweeney .50 .15
47 Kazuhisa Ishii .50 .15
48 Torii Hunter .50 .15
49 Vladimir Guerrero 1.25 .35
50 Mike Piazza 2.00 .60
51 Alexis Rios 1.25 .35
52 Shannon Stewart .50 .15
53 Eric Hinske .50 .15
54 Jason Jennings .50 .15
55 Jason Giambi 1.25 .35
56 Brandon Claussen .50 .15
57 Joe Thurston .50 .15
58 Ramon Nivar .50 .15
59 Jay Gibbons .50 .15
60 Eric Chavez .50 .15
61 Jimmy Gobble .50 .15
62 Walter Young .50 .15
63 Mark Grace .75 .23
64 Austin Kearns .50 .15
65 Bob Abreu .50 .15
66 Hee Seop Choi .50 .15
67 Brandon Phillips .50 .15
68 Rickie Weeks 1.25 .35
69 Luis Gonzalez .50 .15
70 Mariano Rivera .75 .23
71 Jason Lane .50 .15
72 Xavier Nady .50 .15
73 Runelvys Hernandez .50 .15
74 Aramis Ramirez .50 .15
75 Ichiro Suzuki 2.00 .60
76 Cliff Lee .50 .15
77 Chris Snelling .50 .15
78 Ryan Wagner .50 .15
79 Miguel Tejada .50 .15
80 Juan Gonzalez 1.25 .35
81 Joe Borchard .50 .15
82 Gary Sheffield .50 .15
83 Wade Miller .50 .15
84 Jeff Bagwell .75 .23
85 Ryan Church .50 .15
86 Adrian Beltre .50 .15
87 Jeff Baker .50 .15
88 Adam Loewen .50 .15
89 Bernie Williams .75 .23
90 Pedro Martinez 1.25 .35
91 Carlos Rivera .50 .15
92 Junior Spivey .50 .15
93 Tim Hudson .50 .15
94 Troy Glaus .75 .23
95 Ken Griffey Jr. 2.00 .60
96 Alexis Gomez .50 .15
97 Antonio Perez .50 .15
98 Dan Haren .50 .15
99 Ivan Rodriguez 1.25 .35
100 Randy Johnson 1.25 .35
101 Lyle Overbay .50 .15
102 Oliver Perez .50 .15
103 Miguel Cabrera 1.25 .35
104 Scott Rolen .75 .23
105 Roger Clemens 2.50 .75
106 Brian Tallet .50 .15
107 Nic Jackson .50 .15
108 Angel Berroa .50 .15
109 Hank Blalock .50 .15
110 Ryan Klesko .50 .15
111 Jose Castillo .50 .15
112 Paul Konerko .50 .15
113 Greg Maddux 2.00 .60
114 Mark Mulder .50 .15
115 Pat Burrell .50 .15
116 Garrett Atkins .50 .15
117 Jeremy Guthrie .50 .15
118 Orlando Cabrera .50 .15
119 Nick Johnson .50 .15
120 Tom Glavine .75 .23
121 Morgan Ensberg .50 .15
122 Sean Casey .50 .15
123 Orlando Hudson .50 .15
124 Hideki Matsui 2.00 .60
125 Craig Biggio .75 .23
126 Adam LaRoche .50 .15
127 Hong-Chih Kuo .50 .15
128 Paul Lo Duca .50 .15
129 Shawn Green .50 .15
130 Luis Castillo .50 .15
131 Joe Crede .50 .15
132 Ken Harvey .50 .15
133 Freddy Sanchez .50 .15
134 Roy Oswalt .50 .15
135 Curt Schilling .75 .23
136 Alfredo Amezaga .50 .15
137 Chien-Ming Wang .50 .15
138 Barry Larkin 1.25 .35
139 Trot Nixon .75 .23
140 Jim Thome 1.25 .35
141 Bret Boone .50 .15
142 Jacque Jones .50 .15
143 Travis Hafner .50 .15
144 Sammy Sosa 2.00 .60
145 Mike Mussina 1.25 .35
146 Vinny Chulk .50 .15
147 Chad Gaudin .50 .15
148 Delmon Young 1.25 .35
149 Mike Lowell .50 .15
150 Rickey Henderson 1.25 .35
151 Roger Clemens FB 6.00 1.80
152 Mark Grace FB 4.00 1.20
153 Rickey Henderson FB 4.00 1.20
154 Alex Rodriguez FB 5.00 1.50
155 Rafael Palmeiro FB 4.00 1.20
156 Greg Maddux FB 5.00 1.50
157 Mike Piazza FB 5.00 1.50
158 Mike Mussina FB 4.00 1.20
159 Dale Murphy LGD 4.00 1.20
160 Cal Ripken LGD 10.00 3.00
161 Carl Yastrzemski LGD 5.00 1.50
162 Marty Marion LGD 3.00 .90
163 Don Mattingly LGD 8.00 2.40
164 Robin Yount LGD 5.00 1.50
165 Andre Dawson LGD 3.00 .90
166 Jim Palmer LGD 3.00 .90
167 George Brett LGD 8.00 2.40
168 Whitey Ford LGD 4.00 1.20
169 Roy Campanella LGD 4.00 1.20
170 Roger Maris LGD 5.00 1.50
171 Duke Snider LGD 4.00 1.20
172 Steve Carlton LGD 3.00 .90
173 Stan Musial LGD 5.00 1.50
174 Nolan Ryan LGD 8.00 2.40
175 Deion Sanders LGD 4.00 1.20

2004 Diamond Kings Sepia

Nm-Mt Ex-Mt
*SEPIA: .75X TO 2X BASIC
RANDOM INSERTS IN PACKS

2004 Diamond Kings Bronze

Nm-Mt Ex-Mt
*BRONZE 1-150: 3X TO 8X BASIC
*BRONZE 151-175: 1.25X TO 3X BASIC
RANDOM INSERTS IN PACKS
STATED PRINT RUN 100 SERIAL #'d SETS

2004 Diamond Kings Bronze Sepia

Nm-Mt Ex-Mt
*BRONZE SEPIA: 1.25X TO 3X BASIC
RANDOM INSERTS IN PACKS
STATED PRINT RUN 100 SERIAL #'d SETS

2004 Diamond Kings Platinum

Nm-Mt Ex-Mt
RANDOM INSERTS IN PACKS
STATED PRINT RUN 1 SERIAL #'d SET
NO PRICING DUE TO SCARCITY

2004 Diamond Kings Platinum Sepia

Nm-Mt Ex-Mt
RANDOM INSERTS IN PACKS
STATED PRINT RUN 1 SERIAL #'d SET
NO PRICING DUE TO SCARCITY

2004 Diamond Kings Silver

Nm-Mt Ex-Mt
*SILVER 1-150: 5X TO 12X BASIC
*SILVER 151-175: 2X TO 5X BASIC
RANDOM INSERTS IN PACKS
STATED PRINT RUN 50 SERIAL #'d SETS

2004 Diamond Kings Silver Sepia

Nm-Mt Ex-Mt
*SILVER SEPIA: 2X TO 5X BASIC
RANDOM INSERTS IN PACKS
STATED PRINT RUN 50 SERIAL #'d SETS

2004 Diamond Kings Framed Platinum Grey

Nm-Mt Ex-Mt
RANDOM INSERTS IN PACKS
STATED PRINT RUN 1 SERIAL #'d SET
NO PRICING DUE TO SCARCITY

2004 Diamond Kings Framed Bronze

Nm-Mt Ex-Mt
*FRAMED BRZ 1-150: 1.5X TO 4X BASIC
*FRAMED BRZ 151-175: .75X TO 2X BASIC
STATED ODDS 1:6

2004 Diamond Kings Framed Bronze Sepia

Nm-Mt Ex-Mt
*FRAMED BRZ.SEPIA: .75X TO 2X BASIC
STATED ODDS 1:6

2004 Diamond Kings Framed Gold

Nm-Mt Ex-Mt
*FRAMED GOLD 1-150: 10X TO 25X BASIC
*FRAMED GOLD 150-175: 4X TO 10X BASIC
RANDOM INSERTS IN PACKS
STATED PRINT RUN 25 SERIAL #'d SETS

2004 Diamond Kings Framed Gold Sepia

Nm-Mt Ex-Mt
*FRAMED GOLD SEPIA: 4X TO 10X BASIC
RANDOM INSERTS IN PACKS
STATED PRINT RUN 25 SERIAL #'d SETS

2004 Diamond Kings Framed Platinum Black

Nm-Mt Ex-Mt
RANDOM INSERTS IN PACKS
STATED PRINT RUN 1 SERIAL #'d SET
NO PRICING DUE TO SCARCITY

2004 Diamond Kings Framed Platinum Black Sepia

Nm-Mt Ex-Mt
RANDOM INSERTS IN PACKS
STATED PRINT RUN 1 SERIAL #'d SET
NO PRICING DUE TO SCARCITY

2004 Diamond Kings Framed Platinum Grey Sepia

Nm-Mt Ex-Mt
RANDOM INSERTS IN PACKS
STATED PRINT RUN 1 SERIAL #'d SET
NO PRICING DUE TO SCARCITY

2004 Diamond Kings Framed Platinum White

Nm-Mt Ex-Mt
RANDOM INSERTS IN PACKS
STATED PRINT RUN 1 SERIAL #'d SET
NO PRICING DUE TO SCARCITY

2004 Diamond Kings Framed Platinum White Sepia

Nm-Mt Ex-Mt
RANDOM INSERTS IN PACKS
STATED PRINT RUN 1 SERIAL #'d SET
NO PRICING DUE TO SCARCITY

2004 Diamond Kings Framed Silver

Nm-Mt Ex-Mt
*FRAMED SLV 1-150: 4X TO 10X BASIC
*FRAMED SLV 151-175: 1.5X TO 4X BASIC
RANDOM INSERTS IN PACKS
STATED PRINT RUN 100 SERIAL #'d SETS

2004 Diamond Kings Framed Silver Sepia

Nm-Mt Ex-Mt
*FRAMED SLV SEPIA: 1.5X TO 4X BASIC
RANDOM INSERTS IN PACKS
STATED PRINT RUN 100 SERIAL #'d SETS

2004 Diamond Kings DK Combos Bronze

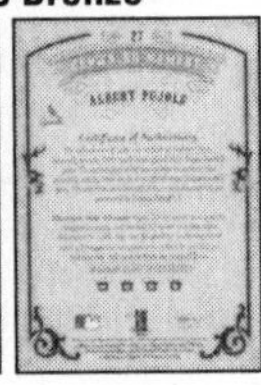

Nm-Mt Ex-Mt
RANDOM INSERTS IN PACKS
PRINT RUNS B/WN 1-30 COPIES PER
NO PRICING ON QTY OF 10 OR LESS.
26 Marlon Byrd Bat-Jsy/30 ... 30.00 9.00
32 Rich Harden Jsy-Jsy/15 ... 80.00 24.00
35 Brandon Webb Bat-Jsy/15 ... 80.00 24.00
41 Aubrey Huff Bat-Jsy/15 ... 50.00 15.00
53 Eric Hinske Bat-Jsy/30 ... 30.00 9.00
57 Joe Thurston Bat-Jsy/25 ... 30.00 9.00
59 Jay Gibbons Jsy-Jsy/15 ... 50.00 15.00
62 Walter Young Bat-Bat/15 ... 40.00 12.00
65 Bob Abreu Bat-Jsy/15 ... 50.00 15.00
71 Jason Lane Bat-Hat/15 ... 40.00 12.00
73 Run Hernandez Jsy-Jsy/15 ... 40.00 12.00
74 Aramis Ramirez Bat-Bat/15 .. 50.00 15.00
77 Chris Snelling Bat-Bat/15 ... 40.00 12.00
81 Joe Borchard Bat-Jsy/15 ... 50.00 15.00
92 Junior Spivey Bat-Jsy/15 ... 40.00 12.00
98 Dan Haren Bat-Jsy/15 ... 50.00 15.00
101 Lyle Overbay Bat-Jsy/30 ... 30.00 9.00
103 Miguel Cabrera Bat-Jsy/30. 80.00 24.00
108 Angel Berroa Bat-Pants/30. 40.00 12.00
109 Hank Blalock Bat-Jsy/30 ... 60.00 18.00
111 Jose Castillo Bat-Bat/15 ... 40.00 12.00
121 Morgan Ensberg Bat-Jsy/30 40.00 12.00
123 Orlando Hudson Bat-Jsy/30 30.00 9.00
126 Adam LaRoche Bat-Bat/30. 40.00 12.00
127 Hong-Chih Kuo Bat-Bat/15. 80.00 24.00
130 Luis Castillo Bat-Jsy/30 ... 40.00 12.00
133 Freddy Sanchez Bat-Bat/15 40.00 12.00
136 Alfredo Amezaga Bat-Jsy/15 40.00 12.00
143 Travis Hafner Bat-Jsy/30 ... 40.00 12.00
147 Chad Gaudin Jsy-Jsy/25 ... 30.00 9.00

2004 Diamond Kings DK Combos Bronze Sepia

Nm-Mt Ex-Mt
RANDOM INSERTS IN PACKS
PRINT RUNS B/WN 1-5 COPIES PER..
NO PRICING DUE TO SCARCITY

2004 Diamond Kings DK Combos Gold

Nm-Mt Ex-Mt
RANDOM INSERTS IN PACKS
PRINT RUNS B/WN 1-5 COPIES PER..
NO PRICING DUE TO SCARCITY

2004 Diamond Kings DK Combos Gold Sepia

Nm-Mt Ex-Mt
RANDOM INSERTS IN PACKS
STATED PRINT RUN 1 SERIAL #'d SET
NO PRICING DUE TO SCARCITY

2004 Diamond Kings DK Combos Platinum

Nm-Mt Ex-Mt
RANDOM INSERTS IN PACKS
STATED PRINT RUN 1 SERIAL #'d SET
NO PRICING DUE TO SCARCITY

2004 Diamond Kings DK Combos Platinum Sepia

Nm-Mt Ex-Mt
RANDOM INSERTS IN PACKS
STATED PRINT RUN RUN 1 SERIAL #'d SET
NO PRICING DUE TO SCARCITY

2004 Diamond Kings DK Combos Silver

Nm-Mt Ex-Mt
RANDOM INSERTS IN PACKS
PRINT RUNS B/WN 1-15 COPIES PER
NO PRICING ON QTY OF 10 OR LESS.
26 Marlon Byrd Bat-Jsy/15 ... 40.00 12.00
101 Lyle Overbay Bat-Jsy/15 ... 40.00 12.00
103 Miguel Cabrera Bat-Jsy/15 100.00 30.00
108 Angel Berroa Bat-Pants/15. 50.00 15.00
109 Hank Blalock Bat-Jsy/15 ... 80.00 24.00
121 Morgan Ensberg Bat-Jsy/15 50.00 15.00
123 Orlando Hudson Bat-Jsy/15 40.00 12.00
126 Adam LaRoche Bat-Bat/15 . 50.00 15.00
130 Luis Castillo Bat-Jsy/15 ... 50.00 15.00
143 Travis Hafner Bat-Jsy/15 ... 50.00 15.00

2004 Diamond Kings DK Combos Silver Sepia

Nm-Mt Ex-Mt
RANDOM INSERTS IN PACKS
PRINT RUNS B/WN 1-3 COPIES PER..
NO PRICING DUE TO SCARCITY

2004 Diamond Kings DK Combos Framed Bronze

Nm-Mt Ex-Mt
RANDOM INSERTS IN PACKS
PRINT RUNS B/WN 1-25 COPIES PER
NO PRICING ON QTY OF 10 OR LESS.
26 Marlon Byrd Bat-Jsy/25 ... 30.00 9.00
35 Brandon Webb Bat-Jsy/25 ... 60.00 18.00
53 Eric Hinske Bat-Jsy/25 ... 30.00 9.00
57 Joe Thurston Bat-Jsy/25 ... 30.00 9.00
59 Jay Gibbons Jsy-Jsy/25 ... 40.00 12.00
62 Walter Young Bat-Bat/25 ... 30.00 9.00
65 Bob Abreu Bat-Jsy/25 ... 40.00 12.00
71 Jason Lane Bat-Hat/25 ... 30.00 9.00
74 Aramis Ramirez Bat-Bat/25 .. 40.00 12.00
77 Chris Snelling Bat-Bat/25 ... 30.00 9.00
81 Joe Borchard Bat-Jsy/25 ... 40.00 12.00
92 Junior Spivey Bat-Jsy/25 ... 30.00 9.00
97 Antonio Perez Bat-Pants/25 . 30.00 9.00
98 Dan Haren Bat-Jsy/25 ... 40.00 12.00
101 Lyle Overbay Bat-Jsy/25 ... 30.00 9.00
103 Miguel Cabrera Bat-Jsy/25. 80.00 24.00
107 Nic Jackson Bat-Bat/25 ... 30.00 9.00
108 Angel Berroa Bat-Pants/25. 40.00 12.00
109 Hank Blalock Bat-Jsy/25 ... 60.00 18.00
110 Ryan Klesko Bat-Jsy/15 ... 50.00 15.00
111 Jose Castillo Bat-Bat/25 ... 30.00 9.00
112 Paul Konerko Bat-Jsy/15 ... 50.00 15.00
121 Morgan Ensberg Bat-Jsy/25 40.00 12.00
123 Orlando Hudson Bat-Jsy/25 30.00 9.00
126 Adam LaRoche Bat-Bat/25 . 40.00 12.00
127 Hong-Chih Kuo Bat-Bat/25. 60.00 18.00
130 Luis Castillo Bat-Jsy/25 ... 40.00 12.00
133 Freddy Sanchez Bat-Bat/15 40.00 12.00
136 Alfredo Amezaga Bat-Jsy/15 40.00 12.00
143 Travis Hafner Bat-Jsy/15 ... 50.00 15.00
147 Chad Gaudin Jsy-Jsy/25 ... 30.00 9.00

2004 Diamond Kings DK Combos Framed Bronze Sepia

Nm-Mt Ex-Mt
RANDOM INSERTS IN PACKS
PRINT RUNS B/WN 1-5 COPIES PER..
NO PRICING DUE TO SCARCITY

2004 Diamond Kings DK Combos Framed Gold

Nm-Mt Ex-Mt
RANDOM INSERTS IN PACKS
PRINT RUNS B/WN 1-5 COPIES PER..
NO PRICING DUE TO SCARCITY

2004 Diamond Kings DK Combos Framed Gold Sepia

Nm-Mt Ex-Mt
RANDOM INSERTS IN PACKS
PRINT RUNS B/WN 1-5 COPIES PER..
NO PRICING DUE TO SCARCITY

2004 Diamond Kings DK Combos Framed Platinum Black

Nm-Mt Ex-Mt
RANDOM INSERTS IN PACKS
STATED PRINT RUN 1 SERIAL #'d SET
NO PRICING DUE TO SCARCITY

2004 Diamond Kings DK Combos Framed Platinum Black Sepia

Nm-Mt Ex-Mt
RANDOM INSERTS IN PACKS
STATED PRINT RUN 1 SERIAL #'d SET
NO PRICING DUE TO SCARCITY

2004 Diamond Kings DK Combos Framed Platinum Grey

Nm-Mt Ex-Mt
RANDOM INSERTS IN PACKS
STATED PRINT RUN 1 SERIAL #'d SET
NO PRICING DUE TO SCARCITY

2004 Diamond Kings DK Combos Framed Platinum Grey Sepia

Nm-Mt Ex-Mt
RANDOM INSERTS IN PACKS
STATED PRINT RUN 1 SERIAL #'d SET
NO PRICING DUE TO SCARCITY

2004 Diamond Kings DK Combos Framed Platinum White

Nm-Mt Ex-Mt
RANDOM INSERTS IN PACKS
STATED PRINT RUN 1 SERIAL #'d SET
NO PRICING DUE TO SCARCITY

2004 Diamond Kings DK Combos Framed Platinum White Sepia

Nm-Mt Ex-Mt
RANDOM INSERTS IN PACKS
STATED PRINT RUN 1 SERIAL #'d SET
NO PRICING DUE TO SCARCITY

2004 Diamond Kings DK Combos Framed Silver

Nm-Mt Ex-Mt
RANDOM INSERTS IN PACKS
PRINT RUNS B/WN 1-15 COPIES PER
NO PRICING ON QTY OF 10 OR LESS.
110 Ryan Klesko Bat-Jsy/15 ... 50.00 15.00

2004 Diamond Kings DK Combos Framed Silver Sepia

Nm-Mt Ex-Mt
RANDOM INSERTS IN PACKS
PRINT RUNS B/WN 1-5 COPIES PER..
NO PRICING DUE TO SCARCITY

2004 Diamond Kings DK Materials Bronze

Nm-Mt Ex-Mt
RANDOM INSERTS IN PACKS
PRINT RUNS B/WN 1-150 COPIES PER
NO PRICING ON QTY OF 5 OR LESS...
1 Alex Rodriguez Bat-Jsy/150 ... 25.00 7.50
2 Andruw Jones Bat-Jsy/150 ... 10.00 3.00
3 Nomar Garciaparra Bat-Jsy/150 25.00 7.50
4 Kerry Wood Bat-Jsy/150 ... 20.00 6.00
5 Magglio Ordonez Bat-Jsy/150 10.00 3.00
6 Victor Martinez Bat-Bat/100 ... 10.00 3.00
7 Jeremy Bonderman Jsy-Jsy/30 15.00 4.50
8 Josh Beckett Bat-Jsy/150 ... 15.00 4.50
9 Jeff Kent Bat-Jsy/150 ... 10.00 3.00
10 Carlos Beltran Bat-Jsy/150 ... 10.00 3.00
11 Hideo Nomo Bat-Jsy/150 ... 20.00 6.00
12 Richie Sexson Bat-Jsy/150 ... 10.00 3.00
13 Jose Vidro Bat-Jsy/50 ... 10.00 3.00
14 Jae Seo Jsy-Jsy/100 ... 10.00 3.00
15 Alfonso Soriano Bat-Jsy/150 15.00 4.50
16 Barry Zito Bat-Jsy/100 ... 15.00 4.50
17 Brett Myers Jsy-Jsy/30 ... 15.00 4.50
18 Brian Giles Bat-Bat/100 ... 10.00 3.00
19 Edgar Martinez Bat-Jsy/150. 15.00 4.50
20 Jim Edmonds Bat-Jsy/150 ... 10.00 3.00
21 Rocco Baldelli Bat-Jsy/100 ... 20.00 6.00
22 Mark Teixeira Bat-Jsy/100 ... 10.00 3.00
23 Carlos Delgado Bat-Jsy/150. 10.00 3.00
25 Jose Reyes Bat-Jsy/100 ... 15.00 4.50
26 Marlon Byrd Bat-Jsy/100 ... 10.00 3.00
27 Albert Pujols Bat-Jsy/150 ... 40.00 12.00
28 Vernon Wells Bat-Jsy/150 ... 10.00 3.00
29 Garret Anderson Bat-Jsy/15. 25.00 7.50
30 Jerome Williams Jsy-Jsy/100 10.00 3.00
31 Chipper Jones Bat-Jsy/150 .. 20.00 6.00
32 Rich Harden Jsy-Jsy/100 ... 10.00 3.00
33 Manny Ramirez Bat-Jsy/150 10.00 3.00
34 Derek Jeter Base-Base/100 .. 30.00 9.00
35 Brandon Webb Bat-Jsy/100 . 10.00 3.00
36 Mark Prior Bat-Jsy/100 ... 40.00 12.00
37 Roy Halladay Jsy-Jsy/100 ... 10.00 3.00
38 Frank Thomas Bat-Jsy/150 ... 20.00 6.00
39 Rafael Palmeiro Bat-Jsy/150 15.00 4.50
40 Adam Dunn Bat-Jsy/150 ... 10.00 3.00
41 Aubrey Huff Bat-Jsy/30 ... 15.00 4.50
42 Todd Helton Bat-Jsy/150 ... 15.00 4.50
43 Matt Morris Jsy-Jsy/100 ... 10.00 3.00
44 Dontrelle Willis Bat-Jsy/100. 10.00 3.00
45 Lance Berkman Bat-Jsy/150. 10.00 3.00
46 Mike Sweeney Bat-Jsy/100 .. 10.00 3.00
47 Kazuhisa Ishii Bat-Jsy/100 ... 10.00 3.00
48 Torii Hunter Bat-Jsy/100 ... 10.00 3.00
49 Vladimir Guerrero Bat-Jsy/100 20.00 6.00
50 Mike Piazza Bat-Jsy/150 ... 25.00 7.50
51 Alexis Rios Bat-Bat/150 ... 20.00 6.00
52 Shannon Stewart Bat-Bat/100 10.00 3.00
53 Eric Hinske Bat-Jsy/100 ... 10.00 3.00
54 Jason Jennings Bat-Jsy/150 10.00 3.00
55 Jason Giambi Bat-Jsy/150 ... 20.00 6.00
56 Brandon Claussen Fld Glv-Shoe/5..
57 Joe Thurston Bat-Jsy/150 ... 10.00 3.00
58 Ramon Nivar Bat-Jsy/150 ... 10.00 3.00
59 Jay Gibbons Jsy-Jsy/100 ... 10.00 3.00
60 Eric Chavez Bat-Jsy/150 ... 10.00 3.00
62 Walter Young Bat-Bat/100 ... 10.00 3.00
63 Mark Grace Bat-Jsy/150 ... 15.00 4.50
64 Austin Kearns Bat-Jsy/150 ... 10.00 3.00
65 Bob Abreu Bat-Jsy/150 ... 10.00 3.00
66 Hee Seop Choi Bat-Jsy/100 .. 10.00 3.00
67 Brandon Phillips Bat-Bat/100 10.00 3.00
68 Rickie Weeks Bat-Bat/100 ... 20.00 6.00
69 Luis Gonzalez Bat-Jsy/150 ... 10.00 3.00
70 Mariano Rivera Jsy-Jsy/100. 15.00 4.50
71 Jason Lane Bat-Hat/15 ... 25.00 7.50
72 Xavier Nady Bat-Hat/5
73 Run Hernandez Jsy-Jsy/30 ... 15.00 4.50
74 Aramis Ramirez Bat-Bat/1
75 Ichiro Suzuki Ball-Base/15 . 100.00 30.00
77 Chris Snelling Bat-Bat/30 ... 15.00 4.50
79 Miguel Tejada Bat-Jsy/150 ... 10.00 3.00
80 Juan Gonzalez Bat-Jsy/150 .. 20.00 6.00
81 Joe Borchard Bat-Jsy/15 ... 25.00 7.50
82 Gary Sheffield Bat-Jsy/150 ... 10.00 3.00
83 Wade Miller Bat-Jsy/50 ... 10.00 3.00
84 Jeff Bagwell Bat-Jsy/150 ... 15.00 4.50
86 Adrian Beltre Bat-Jsy/100 ... 10.00 3.00
87 Jeff Baker Bat-Bat/100 ... 10.00 3.00
89 Bernie Williams Bat-Jsy/150 15.00 4.50
90 Pedro Martinez Bat-Jsy/100. 20.00 6.00
92 Junior Spivey Bat-Jsy/100 ... 10.00 3.00
93 Tim Hudson Bat-Jsy/150 ... 10.00 3.00
94 Troy Glaus Bat-Jsy/100 ... 15.00 4.50
95 Ken Griffey Jr. Base-Base/100 20.00 6.00
96 Alexis Gomez Bat-Bat/30 ... 15.00 4.50
97 Antonio Perez Bat-Pants/100 10.00 3.00
98 Dan Haren Bat-Jsy/100 ... 10.00 3.00
99 Ivan Rodriguez Bat-Jsy/150 . 20.00 6.00
100 Randy Johnson Bat-Jsy/100 20.00 6.00
101 Lyle Overbay Bat-Jsy/100 ... 10.00 3.00
103 Miguel Cabrera Bat-Jsy/100 20.00 6.00
104 Scott Rolen Bat-Jsy/100 ... 15.00 4.50
105 Roger Clemens Bat-Jsy/100 30.00 9.00
107 Nic Jackson Bat-Bat/100 ... 10.00 3.00
108 Angel Berroa Bat-Pants/30. 15.00 4.50
109 Hank Blalock Bat-Jsy/100 ... 10.00 3.00
110 Ryan Klesko Bat-Jsy/100 ... 10.00 3.00
111 Jose Castillo Bat-Bat/100 ... 10.00 3.00
112 Paul Konerko Bat-Jsy/100 .. 10.00 3.00
113 Greg Maddux Bat-Jsy/100 .. 25.00 7.50
114 Mark Mulder Bat-Jsy/100 ... 10.00 3.00
115 Pat Burrell Bat-Jsy/100 ... 10.00 3.00
116 Garrett Atkins Jsy-Jsy/100. 10.00 3.00
118 Orlando Cabrera Bat-Jsy/100 10.00 3.00
119 Nick Johnson Bat-Jsy/100 . 10.00 3.00
120 Tom Glavine Bat-Jsy/100 ... 15.00 4.50
121 Morgan Ensberg Bat-Jsy/100 10.00 3.00
122 Sean Casey Bat-Hat/15 ... 25.00 7.50
123 Orlando Hudson Bat-Jsy/100 10.00 3.00
124 Hideki Matsui Ball-Base/15 120.00 36.00
125 Craig Biggio Bat-Jsy/100 ... 15.00 4.50
126 Adam LaRoche Bat-Bat/100 10.00 3.00
127 Hong-Chih Kuo Bat-Bat/100 10.00 3.00
128 Paul LoDuca Bat-Jsy/100 ... 10.00 3.00
129 Shawn Green Bat-Jsy/100 .. 10.00 3.00
130 Luis Castillo Bat-Jsy/100 ... 10.00 3.00
131 Joe Crede Bat-Btg Glv/5
132 Ken Harvey Bat-Bat/100 ... 10.00 3.00
133 Freddy Sanchez Bat-Bat/100 10.00 3.00
134 Roy Oswalt Bat-Jsy/100 ... 10.00 3.00
135 Curt Schilling Bat-Jsy/100 .. 15.00 4.50
136 Alfredo Amezaga Bat-Jsy/15 25.00 7.50
138 Barry Larkin Bat-Jsy/15 ... 50.00 15.00
139 Trot Nixon Bat-Bat/100 ... 15.00 4.50
140 Jim Thome Bat-Jsy/100 ... 20.00 6.00
141 Bret Boone Bat-Jsy/100 ... 10.00 3.00
142 Jacque Jones Bat-Jsy/100 . 10.00 3.00
143 Travis Hafner Bat-Jsy/100 . 10.00 3.00
144 Sammy Sosa Bat-Jsy/100 .. 25.00 7.50
145 Mike Mussina Bat-Jsy/100. 20.00 6.00
147 Chad Gaudin Jsy-Jsy/100 ... 10.00 3.00
149 Mike Lowell Bat-Jsy/100 ... 10.00 3.00
150 R.Henderson Bat-Jsy/100 .. 20.00 6.00
151 R.Clemens FB Bat-Jsy/100. 30.00 9.00
152 Mark Grace FB Bat-Jsy/15 .. 40.00 12.00
153 R.Henderson FB Bat-Jsy/30 30.00 9.00
154 A.Rodriguez FB Bat-Jsy/100 25.00 7.50
155 R.Palmeiro FB Bat-Jsy/100 15.00 4.50
156 G.Maddux FB Bat-Bat/100 .. 25.00 7.50
157 Mike Piazza FB Bat-Jsy/100 25.00 7.50
158 M.Mussina FB Bat-Jsy/100 20.00 6.00
159 Dale Murphy LGD Bat-Jsy/30 30.00 9.00
160 Cal Ripken LGD Bat-Jsy/100 50.00 15.00
161 C.Yaz LGD Bat-Jsy/100 ... 25.00 7.50
162 M.Marion LGD Jsy-Jsy/30 .. 15.00 4.50
163 D.Mattingly LGD Bat-Jsy/100 40.00 12.00
164 R.Yount LGD Bat-Jsy/100 .. 25.00 7.50
165 A.Dawson LGD Bat-Jsy/30. 15.00 4.50
166 Jim Palmer LGD Jsy-Jsy/5
167 George Brett LGD Bat-Jsy/30 60.00 18.00
168 W.Ford LGD Jsy-Pants/30 .. 25.00 7.50
169 R.Campy LGD Bat-Pants/15 50.00 15.00
170 R.Maris LGD Bat-Jsy/15 ... 120.00 36.00
171 Duke Snider LGD Bat-Jsy/4
172 S.Carlton LGD Bat-Jsy/100 10.00 3.00
173 Stan Musial LGD Bat-Jsy/30 50.00 15.00
174 Nolan Ryan LGD Bat-Jsy/30 60.00 18.00
175 D.Sanders LGD Bat-Jsy/100 15.00 4.50

2004 Diamond Kings DK Materials Bronze Sepia

Nm-Mt Ex-Mt
RANDOM INSERTS IN PACKS
PRINT RUNS B/WN 4-50 COPIES PER
NO PRICING ON QTY OF 5 OR LESS...
151 R.Clemens FB Bat-Jsy/30 ... 50.00 15.00
152 Mark Grace FB Bat-Jsy/15 .. 40.00 12.00
153 R.Henderson FB Bat-Jsy/15 50.00 15.00
154 A.Rodriguez FB Bat-Jsy/30. 50.00 15.00
155 R.Palmeiro FB Bat-Jsy/50 .. 15.00 4.50
156 G.Maddux FB Bat-Bat/50 ... 40.00 12.00
157 Mike Piazza FB Bat-Jsy/50 .. 40.00 12.00
158 M.Mussina FB Bat-Jsy/50 .. 25.00 7.50
159 Dale Murphy LGD Bat-Jsy/50 50.00 15.00
160 Cal Ripken LGD Bat-Jsy/50 80.00 24.00
161 C.Yaz LGD Bat-Jsy/50 ... 40.00 12.00
162 M.Marion LGD Jsy-Jsy/15 .. 25.00 7.50
163 D.Mattingly LGD Bat-Jsy/50 50.00 15.00
164 R.Yount LGD Bat-Jsy/50 ... 40.00 12.00
165 A.Dawson LGD Bat-Jsy/15 . 25.00 7.50
166 Jim Palmer LGD Jsy-Jsy/5
167 G.Brett LGD Bat-Jsy/15 ... 100.00 30.00
168 W.Ford LGD Jsy-Pants/15 .. 40.00 12.00
169 R.Campy LGD Bat-Pants/15 50.00 15.00
170 R.Maris LGD Bat-Jsy/15 ... 120.00 36.00
171 Duke Snider LGD Bat-Jsy/4
172 S.Carlton LGD Bat-Jsy/50 ... 10.00 3.00
173 Stan Musial LGD Bat-Jsy/15 80.00 24.00
174 Nolan Ryan LGD Bat-Jsy/15 100.00 30.00
175 D.Sanders LGD Bat-Jsy/50. 15.00 4.50

2004 Diamond Kings DK Materials Gold

Nm-Mt Ex-Mt
RANDOM INSERTS IN PACKS
PRINT RUNS B/WN 1-50 COPIES PER
NO PRICING ON QTY OF 5 OR LESS...
1 Alex Rodriguez Bat-Jsy/25 ... 50.00 15.00
2 Andruw Jones Bat-Jsy/25 ... 15.00 4.50
3 Nomar Garciaparra Bat-Jsy/25 50.00 15.00
4 Kerry Wood Bat-Jsy/25 ... 30.00 9.00
5 Magglio Ordonez Bat-Jsy/25 .. 15.00 4.50
6 Victor Martinez Bat-Bat/50 ... 10.00 3.00
7 Jeremy Bonderman Jsy-Jsy/5
8 Josh Beckett Bat-Jsy/25 ... 25.00 7.50
9 Jeff Kent Bat-Jsy/25 ... 15.00 4.50
10 Carlos Beltran Bat-Jsy/25 ... 15.00 4.50
11 Hideo Nomo Bat-Jsy/25 ... 30.00 9.00
12 Richie Sexson Bat-Jsy/25 ... 15.00 4.50
13 Jose Vidro Bat-Jsy/25 ... 15.00 4.50
14 Jae Seo Jsy-Jsy/25 ... 15.00 4.50
15 Alfonso Soriano Bat-Jsy/25 .. 25.00 7.50
16 Barry Zito Bat-Jsy/25 ... 25.00 7.50
17 Brett Myers Jsy-Jsy/5
18 Brian Giles Bat-Bat/25 ... 15.00 4.50
19 Edgar Martinez Bat-Jsy/25 ... 25.00 7.50
20 Jim Edmonds Bat-Jsy/25 ... 15.00 4.50
21 Rocco Baldelli Bat-Jsy/25 ... 30.00 9.00
22 Mark Teixeira Bat-Jsy/25 ... 15.00 4.50
23 Carlos Delgado Bat-Jsy/25
25 Jose Reyes Bat-Jsy/25 ... 25.00 7.50
26 Marlon Byrd Bat-Jsy/25 ... 15.00 4.50
27 Albert Pujols Bat-Jsy/25 ... 60.00 18.00
28 Vernon Wells Bat-Jsy/25 ... 15.00 4.50
29 Garret Anderson Bat-Jsy/3
30 Jerome Williams Jsy-Jsy/50 10.00 3.00
31 Chipper Jones Bat-Jsy/25 ... 30.00 9.00
32 Rich Harden Jsy-Jsy/50 ... 10.00 3.00
33 Manny Ramirez Bat-Jsy/25 .. 15.00 4.50
34 Derek Jeter Base-Base/50 ... 40.00 12.00
35 Brandon Webb Bat-Jsy/50 ... 10.00 3.00
36 Mark Prior Bat-Jsy/25 ... 60.00 18.00
37 Roy Halladay Jsy-Jsy/25 ... 15.00 4.50
38 Frank Thomas Bat-Jsy/25 ... 30.00 9.00
39 Rafael Palmeiro Bat-Jsy/50 .. 15.00 4.50
40 Adam Dunn Bat-Jsy/25 ... 15.00 4.50
41 Aubrey Huff Bat-Jsy/5
42 Todd Helton Bat-Jsy/25 ... 25.00 7.50
43 Matt Morris Jsy-Jsy/25 ... 15.00 4.50
44 Dontrelle Willis Bat-Jsy/25 ... 15.00 4.50
45 Lance Berkman Bat-Jsy/25 ... 15.00 4.50
46 Mike Sweeney Bat-Jsy/25 ... 15.00 4.50
47 Kazuhisa Ishii Bat-Jsy/25 ... 15.00 4.50
48 Torii Hunter Bat-Jsy/25 ... 15.00 4.50
49 Vladimir Guerrero Bat-Jsy/25 30.00 9.00
50 Mike Piazza Bat-Jsy/25 ... 50.00 15.00
51 Alexis Rios Bat-Bat/25 ... 30.00 9.00
52 Shannon Stewart Bat-Bat/50 10.00 3.00
53 Eric Hinske Bat-Jsy/50 ... 10.00 3.00
54 Jason Jennings Bat-Jsy/25 .. 15.00 4.50
55 Jason Giambi Bat-Jsy/25 ... 30.00 9.00
56 Brandon Claussen Fld Glv-Shoe/1 ..
57 Joe Thurston Bat-Jsy/50 ... 10.00 3.00
58 Ramon Nivar Bat-Jsy/50 ... 10.00 3.00
59 Jay Gibbons Jsy-Jsy/25 ... 15.00 4.50
60 Eric Chavez Bat-Jsy/25 ... 15.00 4.50
62 Walter Young Bat-Bat/50 ... 10.00 3.00
63 Mark Grace Bat-Jsy/25 ... 25.00 7.50
64 Austin Kearns Bat-Jsy/25 ... 15.00 4.50
65 Bob Abreu Bat-Jsy/25 ... 15.00 4.50
66 Hee Seop Choi Bat-Jsy/25 ... 15.00 4.50
67 Brandon Phillips Bat-Bat/50 . 10.00 3.00
68 Rickie Weeks Bat-Bat/50 ... 25.00 7.50
69 Luis Gonzalez Bat-Jsy/25 ... 15.00 4.50
70 Mariano Rivera Jsy-Jsy/50 ... 15.00 4.50
71 Jason Lane Bat-Hat/3
72 Xavier Nady Bat-Hat/2
73 Run Hernandez Jsy-Jsy/5
74 Aramis Ramirez Bat-Bat/1
75 Ichiro Suzuki Ball-Base/3
77 Chris Snelling Bat-Bat/5
79 Miguel Tejada Bat-Jsy/50 ... 10.00 3.00
80 Juan Gonzalez Bat-Jsy/25 ... 30.00 9.00
81 Joe Borchard Bat-Jsy/3
82 Gary Sheffield Bat-Jsy/25 ... 15.00 4.50
83 Wade Miller Bat-Jsy/3
84 Jeff Bagwell Bat-Jsy/25 ... 25.00 7.50
86 Adrian Beltre Bat-Jsy/25 ... 15.00 4.50
87 Jeff Baker Bat-Bat/50 ... 10.00 3.00
89 Bernie Williams Bat-Jsy/25 .. 25.00 7.50
90 Pedro Martinez Bat-Jsy/25 ... 30.00 9.00
92 Junior Spivey Bat-Jsy/25 ... 15.00 4.50
93 Tim Hudson Bat-Jsy/25 ... 15.00 4.50
94 Troy Glaus Bat-Jsy/25 ... 25.00 7.50
95 Ken Griffey Jr. Base-Base/50 30.00 9.00
96 Alexis Gomez Bat-Bat/5
97 Antonio Perez Bat-Pants/50 . 10.00 3.00
98 Dan Haren Bat-Jsy/25 ... 15.00 4.50
99 Ivan Rodriguez Bat-Jsy/25 ... 30.00 9.00
100 Randy Johnson Bat-Jsy/25 30.00 9.00
101 Lyle Overbay Bat-Jsy/50 ... 10.00 3.00
103 Miguel Cabrera Bat-Jsy/25 . 30.00 9.00
104 Scott Rolen Bat-Jsy/25 ... 25.00 7.50
105 Roger Clemens Bat-Jsy/25. 50.00 15.00
107 Nic Jackson Bat-Bat/30 ... 15.00 4.50
108 Angel Berroa Bat-Pants/3
109 Hank Blalock Bat-Jsy/25 ... 15.00 4.50
110 Ryan Klesko Bat-Jsy/25 ... 15.00 4.50
111 Jose Castillo Bat-Bat/50 ... 10.00 3.00
112 Paul Konerko Bat-Jsy/25 ... 15.00 4.50
113 Greg Maddux Bat-Jsy/25 ... 50.00 15.00
114 Mark Mulder Bat-Jsy/25 ... 15.00 4.50
115 Pat Burrell Bat-Jsy/25 ... 15.00 4.50
116 Garrett Atkins Jsy-Jsy/50 ... 10.00 3.00
118 Orlando Cabrera Bat-Jsy/25 15.00 4.50
119 Nick Johnson Bat-Jsy/25 ... 15.00 4.50
120 Tom Glavine Bat-Jsy/25 ... 25.00 7.50
121 Morgan Ensberg Bat-Jsy/25 15.00 4.50
122 Sean Casey Bat-Hat/3
123 Orlando Hudson Bat-Jsy/25 15.00 4.50
124 Hideki Matsui Ball-Base/3
125 Craig Biggio Bat-Jsy/25 ... 25.00 7.50
126 Adam LaRoche Bat-Bat/50 . 10.00 3.00
127 Hong-Chih Kuo Bat-Bat/50 . 10.00 3.00
128 Paul LoDuca Bat-Jsy/25 ... 15.00 4.50
129 Shawn Green Bat-Jsy/25 ... 15.00 4.50
130 Luis Castillo Bat-Jsy/25 ... 15.00 4.50

131 Joe Crede Bat-Btg Glv/1
132 Ken Harvey Bat-Bat/50 10.00 3.00
133 Freddy Sanchez Bat-Bat/50 10.00 3.00
134 Roy Oswalt Bat-Jsy/50 10.00 3.00
135 Curt Schilling Bat-Jsy/25 25.00 7.50
136 Alfredo Amezaga Bat-Jsy/3
138 Barry Larkin Bat-Jsy/3
139 Trot Nixon Bat-Bat/25 25.00 7.50
140 Jim Thome Bat-Jsy/25 30.00 9.00
141 Bret Boone Bat-Jsy/5
142 Jacque Jones Bat-Jsy/50 10.00 3.00
143 Travis Hafner Bat-Jsy/50 10.00 3.00
144 Sammy Sosa Bat-Jsy/25 50.00 15.00
145 Mike Mussina Bat-Jsy/50 25.00 7.50
147 Chad Gaudin Jsy-Jsy/25 15.00 4.50
149 Mike Lowell Bat-Jsy/25 15.00 4.50
150 R.Henderson Bat-Jsy/25 30.00 9.00
151 R.Clemens FB Bat-Jsy/25 50.00 15.00
152 Mark Grace FB Bat-Jsy/3
153 R.Henderson FB Bat-Jsy/5
154 A.Rodriguez FB Bat-Jsy/25 50.00 15.00
155 R.Palmeiro FB Bat-Jsy/50 25.00 7.50
156 G.Maddux FB Bat-Bat/50 40.00 12.00
157 Mike Piazza FB Bat-Jsy/50 40.00 12.00
158 M.Mussina FB Bat-Jsy/50 30.00 9.00
159 Dale Murphy LGD Bat-Jsy/5
160 Cal Ripken LGD Bat-Jsy/50 80.00 24.00
161 C.Yaz LGD Bat-Jsy/50 40.00 12.00
162 M.Marion LGD Jsy-Jsy/5
163 D.Mattingly LGD Bat-Jsy/50 50.00 15.00
164 R.Yount LGD Bat-Jsy/50 40.00 12.00
165 A.Dawson LGD Bat-Jsy/5
166 Jim Palmer LGD Jsy-Jsy/2
167 George Brett LGD Bat-Jsy/5
168 W.Ford LGD Jsy-Pants/5
169 R.Campy LGD Bat-Pants/3
170 Roger Maris LGD Bat-Jsy/3
171 Duke Snider LGD Bat-Jsy/1
172 S.Carlton LGD Bat-Jsy/50 10.00 3.00
173 Stan Musial LGD Bat-Jsy/5
174 Nolan Ryan LGD Bat-Jsy/5
175 D.Sanders LGD Bat-Jsy/50 15.00 4.50

2004 Diamond Kings DK Materials Gold Sepia

Nm-Mt Ex-Mt
RANDOM INSERTS IN PACKS
PRINT RUNS B/WN 1-15 COPIES PER
NO PRICING ON QTY OF 5 OR LESS
151 R.Clemens FB Bat-Jsy/5
152 Mark Grace FB Bat-Jsy/3
153 R.Henderson FB Bat-Jsy/3
154 A.Rodriguez FB Bat-Jsy/5
155 R.Palmeiro FB Bat-Jsy/15 40.00 12.00
156 G.Maddux FB Bat-Bat/15 60.00 18.00
157 Mike Piazza FB Bat-Jsy/15 60.00 18.00
158 M.Mussina FB Bat-Jsy/15 50.00 15.00
159 Dale Murphy LGD Bat-Jsy/3
160 Cal Ripken LGD Bat-Jsy/15 150.00 45.00
161 C.Yaz LGD Bat-Jsy/15 80.00 24.00
162 M.Marion LGD Jsy-Jsy/3
163 D.Mattingly LGD Bat-Jsy/15 100.00 30.00
164 R.Yount LGD Bat-Jsy/15 80.00 24.00
165 A.Dawson LGD Bat-Jsy/3
166 Jim Palmer LGD Jsy-Jsy/2
167 George Brett LGD Bat-Jsy/3
168 W.Ford LGD Jsy-Pants/3
169 R.Campy LGD Bat-Pants/3
170 Roger Maris LGD Bat-Jsy/3
171 Duke Snider LGD Bat-Jsy/1
172 S.Carlton LGD Bat-Jsy/15 25.00 7.50
173 Stan Musial LGD Bat-Jsy/3
174 Nolan Ryan LGD Bat-Jsy/3
175 D.Sanders LGD Bat-Jsy/15 40.00 12.00

2004 Diamond Kings DK Materials Platinum

Nm-Mt Ex-Mt
RANDOM INSERTS IN PACKS
STATED PRINT RUN 1 SERIAL #'d SET
NO PRICING DUE TO SCARCITY

2004 Diamond Kings DK Materials Platinum Sepia

Nm-Mt Ex-Mt
RANDOM INSERTS IN PACKS
STATED PRINT RUN 1 SERIAL #'d SET
NO PRICING DUE TO SCARCITY

2004 Diamond Kings DK Materials Silver

Nm-Mt Ex-Mt
RANDOM INSERTS IN PACKS
PRINT RUNS B/WN 1-50 COPIES PER
NO PRICING ON QTY OF 6 OR LESS
1 Alex Rodriguez Bat-Jsy/50 40.00 12.00
2 Andruw Jones Bat-Jsy/50 10.00 3.00
3 Nomar Garciaparra Bat-Jsy/50 40.00 12.00
4 Kerry Wood Bat-Jsy/50 25.00 7.50
5 Magglio Ordonez Bat-Jsy/50 10.00 3.00
6 Victor Martinez Bat-Bat/50 10.00 3.00
7 Jeremy Bonderman Jsy-Jsy/15 25.00 7.50
8 Josh Beckett Bat-Jsy/50 15.00 4.50
9 Jeff Kent Bat-Jsy/50 10.00 3.00
10 Carlos Beltran Bat-Jsy/50 10.00 3.00
11 Hideo Nomo Bat-Jsy/50 25.00 7.50
12 Richie Sexson Bat-Jsy/50 10.00 3.00
13 Jose Vidro Bat-Jsy/30 15.00 4.50
14 Jae Seo Jsy-Jsy/50 10.00 3.00
15 Alfonso Soriano Bat-Jsy/50 15.00 4.50
16 Barry Zito Bat-Jsy/50 15.00 4.50
17 Brett Myers Jsy-Jsy/15 25.00 7.50
18 Brian Giles Bat-Bat/50 10.00 3.00
19 Edgar Martinez Bat-Jsy/50 15.00 4.50
20 Jim Edmonds Bat-Jsy/50 10.00 3.00
21 Rocco Baldelli Bat-Jsy/50 25.00 7.50
22 Mark Teixeira Bat-Jsy/50 10.00 3.00
23 Carlos Delgado Bat-Jsy/50 10.00 3.00
25 Jose Reyes Bat-Jsy/50 15.00 4.50
26 Marlon Byrd Bat-Jsy/50 10.00 3.00
27 Albert Pujols Bat-Jsy/50 50.00 15.00
28 Vernon Wells Bat-Jsy/50 10.00 3.00
29 Garret Anderson Bat-Jsy/6
30 Jerome Williams Jsy-Jsy/50 10.00 3.00
31 Chipper Jones Bat-Jsy/50 25.00 7.50
32 Rich Harden Jsy-Jsy/50 10.00 3.00
33 Manny Ramirez Bat-Jsy/50 10.00 3.00
34 Derek Jeter Base-Base/50 40.00 12.00
35 Brandon Webb Bat-Jsy/50 10.00 3.00
36 Mark Prior Bat-Jsy/50 50.00 15.00
37 Roy Halladay Jsy-Jsy/50 10.00 3.00
38 Frank Thomas Bat-Jsy/50 25.00 7.50
39 Rafael Palmeiro Bat-Jsy/50 15.00 4.50
40 Adam Dunn Bat-Jsy/50 10.00 3.00
41 Aubrey Huff Bat-Jsy/15 25.00 7.50
42 Todd Helton Bat-Jsy/50 15.00 4.50
43 Matt Morris Jsy-Jsy/50 10.00 3.00
44 Dontrelle Willis Bat-Jsy/50 10.00 3.00
45 Lance Berkman Bat-Jsy/50 10.00 3.00
46 Mike Sweeney Bat-Jsy/50 10.00 3.00
47 Kazuhisa Ishii Bat-Jsy/50 10.00 3.00
48 Torii Hunter Bat-Jsy/50 10.00 3.00
49 Vladimir Guerrero Bat-Jsy/50 25.00 7.50
50 Mike Piazza Bat-Jsy/50 40.00 12.00
51 Alexis Rios Bat-Bat/50 25.00 7.50
52 Shannon Stewart Bat-Bat/50 10.00 3.00
53 Eric Hinske Bat-Jsy/50 10.00 3.00
54 Jason Jennings Bat-Jsy/50 10.00 3.00
55 Jason Giambi Bat-Jsy/50 25.00 7.50
56 Brandon Claussen Fld Glv-Shoe/1
57 Joe Thurston Bat-Jsy/50 10.00 3.00
58 Ramon Nivar Bat-Jsy/50 10.00 3.00
59 Jay Gibbons Jsy-Jsy/50 10.00 3.00
60 Eric Chavez Bat-Jsy/50 10.00 3.00
62 Walter Young Bat-Bat/50 10.00 3.00
63 Mark Grace Bat-Jsy/50 15.00 4.50
64 Austin Kearns Bat-Jsy/50 10.00 3.00
65 Bob Abreu Bat-Jsy/50 10.00 3.00
66 Hee Seop Choi Bat-Jsy/50 10.00 3.00
67 Brandon Phillips Bat-Bat/50 10.00 3.00
68 Rickie Weeks Bat-Bat/50 25.00 7.50
69 Luis Gonzalez Bat-Jsy/50 10.00 3.00
70 Mariano Rivera Jsy-Jsy/50 15.00 4.50
71 Jason Lane Bat-Hat/5
72 Xavier Nady Bat-Hat/3
73 Run Hernandez Jsy-Jsy/15 25.00 7.50
74 Aramis Ramirez Bat-Bat/1
75 Ichiro Suzuki Ball-Base/6
77 Chris Snelling Bat-Bat/15 25.00 7.50
79 Miguel Tejada Bat-Jsy/50 10.00 3.00
80 Juan Gonzalez Bat-Jsy/50 25.00 7.50
81 Joe Borchard Bat-Jsy/6
82 Gary Sheffield Bat-Jsy/50 10.00 3.00
83 Wade Miller Bat-Jsy/6
84 Jeff Bagwell Bat-Jsy/50 15.00 4.50
86 Adrian Beltre Bat-Jsy/50 10.00 3.00
87 Jeff Baker Bat-Bat/50 10.00 3.00
89 Bernie Williams Bat-Jsy/50 15.00 4.50
90 Pedro Martinez Bat-Jsy/50 25.00 7.50
92 Junior Spivey Bat-Jsy/50 10.00 3.00
93 Tim Hudson Bat-Jsy/50 10.00 3.00
94 Troy Glaus Bat-Jsy/50 15.00 4.50
95 Ken Griffey Jr. Base-Base/50 30.00 9.00
96 Alexis Gomez Bat-Bat/15 25.00 7.50
97 Antonio Perez Bat-Pants/50 10.00 3.00
98 Dan Haren Bat-Jsy/50 10.00 3.00
99 Ivan Rodriguez Bat-Jsy/50 25.00 7.50
100 Randy Johnson Bat-Jsy/50 25.00 7.50
101 Lyle Overbay Bat-Jsy/50 10.00 3.00
103 Miguel Cabrera Bat-Jsy/50 25.00 7.50
104 Scott Rolen Bat-Jsy/50 15.00 4.50
105 Roger Clemens Bat-Jsy/50 40.00 12.00
107 Nic Jackson Bat-Bat/50 10.00 3.00
108 Angel Berroa Bat-Pants/6
109 Hank Blalock Bat-Jsy/50 10.00 3.00
110 Ryan Klesko Bat-Jsy/50 10.00 3.00
111 Jose Castillo Bat-Bat/50 10.00 3.00
112 Paul Konerko Bat-Jsy/50 10.00 3.00
113 Greg Maddux Bat-Jsy/50 40.00 12.00
114 Mark Mulder Bat-Jsy/50 10.00 3.00
115 Pat Burrell Bat-Jsy/50 10.00 3.00
116 Garrett Atkins Jsy-Jsy/50 10.00 3.00
118 Orlando Cabrera Bat-Jsy/50 10.00 3.00
119 Nick Johnson Bat-Jsy/50 10.00 3.00
120 Tom Glavine Bat-Jsy/50 15.00 4.50
121 Morgan Ensberg Bat-Jsy/50 10.00 3.00
122 Sean Casey Bat-Hat/6
123 Orlando Hudson Bat-Jsy/50 10.00 3.00
124 Hideki Matsui Ball-Base/6
125 Craig Biggio Bat-Jsy/50 15.00 4.50
126 Adam LaRoche Bat-Bat/50 10.00 3.00
127 Hong-Chih Kuo Bat-Bat/50 10.00 3.00
128 Paul LoDuca Bat-Jsy/50 10.00 3.00
129 Shawn Green Bat-Jsy/50 10.00 3.00
130 Luis Castillo Bat-Jsy/50 10.00 3.00
131 Joe Crede Bat-Btg Glv/1
132 Ken Harvey Bat-Bat/50 10.00 3.00
133 Freddy Sanchez Bat-Bat/50 10.00 3.00
134 Roy Oswalt Bat-Jsy/50 10.00 3.00
135 Curt Schilling Bat-Jsy/50 15.00 4.50
136 Alfredo Amezaga Bat-Jsy/6
138 Barry Larkin Bat-Jsy/6
139 Trot Nixon Bat-Bat/50 15.00 4.50
140 Jim Thome Bat-Jsy/50 25.00 7.50
141 Bret Boone Bat-Jsy/50 10.00 3.00
142 Jacque Jones Bat-Jsy/50 10.00 3.00
143 Travis Hafner Bat-Jsy/50 10.00 3.00
144 Sammy Sosa Bat-Jsy/50 40.00 12.00
145 Mike Mussina Bat-Jsy/50 25.00 7.50
147 Chad Gaudin Jsy-Jsy/50 10.00 3.00
149 Mike Lowell Bat-Jsy/50 10.00 3.00
150 R.Henderson Bat-Jsy/50 25.00 7.50
151 R.Clemens FB Bat-Jsy/50 40.00 12.00
152 Mark Grace FB Bat-Jsy/6
153 R.Henderson FB Bat-Jsy/15 50.00 15.00
154 A.Rodriguez FB Bat-Jsy/30 50.00 15.00
155 R.Palmeiro FB Bat-Jsy/50 15.00 4.50
156 G.Maddux FB Bat-Bat/50 40.00 12.00
157 Mike Piazza FB Bat-Jsy/50 40.00 12.00
158 M.Mussina FB Bat-Jsy/50 25.00 7.50
159 Dale Murphy LGD Bat-Jsy/15
160 Cal Ripken LGD Bat-Jsy/50 80.00 24.00
161 C.Yaz LGD Bat-Jsy/50 40.00 12.00
162 M.Marion LGD Jsy-Jsy/15 25.00 7.50
163 D.Mattingly LGD Bat-Jsy/50 50.00 15.00
164 R.Yount LGD Bat-Jsy/50 40.00 12.00
165 A.Dawson LGD Bat-Jsy/15 25.00 7.50
166 Jim Palmer LGD Jsy-Jsy/3
167 G.Brett LGD Bat-Jsy/15 100.00 30.00
168 W.Ford LGD Jsy-Pants/15 40.00 12.00
169 R.Campy LGD Bat-Pants/6
170 Roger Maris LGD Bat-Jsy/6
171 Duke Snider LGD Bat-Jsy/1
172 S.Carlton LGD Bat-Jsy/50 10.00 3.00
173 Stan Musial LGD Bat-Jsy/15 80.00 24.00
174 Nolan Ryan LGD Bat-Jsy/15 100.00 30.00
175 D.Sanders LGD Bat-Jsy/50 15.00 4.50

2004 Diamond Kings DK Materials Silver Sepia

Nm-Mt Ex-Mt
RANDOM INSERTS IN PACKS
PRINT RUNS B/WN 1-30 COPIES PER
NO PRICING ON QTY OF 6 OR LESS
151 R.Clemens FB Bat-Jsy/15 60.00 18.00
152 Mark Grace FB Bat-Jsy/6
153 R.Henderson FB Bat-Jsy/6
154 A.Rodriguez FB Bat-Jsy/15 60.00 18.00
155 R.Palmeiro FB Bat-Jsy/30 25.00 7.50
156 G.Maddux FB Bat-Bat/30 50.00 15.00
157 Mike Piazza FB Bat-Jsy/30 50.00 15.00
158 M.Mussina FB Bat-Jsy/30 30.00 9.00
159 Dale Murphy LGD Bat-Jsy/6
160 Cal Ripken LGD Bat-Jsy/30 100.00 30.00
161 C.Yaz LGD Bat-Jsy/30 50.00 15.00
162 M.Marion LGD Jsy-Jsy/6
163 D.Mattingly LGD Bat-Jsy/30 60.00 18.00
164 R.Yount LGD Bat-Jsy/30 50.00 15.00
165 A.Dawson LGD Bat-Jsy/6
166 Jim Palmer LGD Jsy-Jsy/3
167 George Brett LGD Bat-Jsy/6
168 W.Ford LGD Jsy-Pants/6
169 R.Campy LGD Bat-Pants/6
170 Roger Maris LGD Bat-Jsy/6
171 Duke Snider LGD Bat-Jsy/1
172 S.Carlton LGD Bat-Jsy/30 15.00 4.50
173 Stan Musial LGD Bat-Jsy/6
174 Nolan Ryan LGD Bat-Jsy/6
175 D.Sanders LGD Bat-Jsy/30 25.00 7.50

2004 Diamond Kings DK Materials Framed Bronze

Nm-Mt Ex-Mt
RANDOM INSERTS IN PACKS
PRINT RUNS B/WN 1-100 COPIES PER
NO PRICING ON QTY OF 10 OR LESS.
1 Alex Rodriguez Bat-Jsy/100 25.00 7.50
2 Andruw Jones Bat-Jsy/100 10.00 3.00
3 Nomar Garciaparra Bat-Jsy/100 25.00 7.50
4 Kerry Wood Bat-Jsy/100 20.00 6.00
5 Magglio Ordonez Bat-Jsy/100 10.00 3.00
6 Victor Martinez Bat-Bat/100 10.00 3.00
7 Jeremy Bonderman Jsy-Jsy/25 15.00 4.50
8 Josh Beckett Bat-Jsy/100 15.00 4.50
9 Jeff Kent Bat-Jsy/100 10.00 3.00
10 Carlos Beltran Bat-Jsy/100 10.00 3.00
11 Hideo Nomo Bat-Jsy/100 20.00 6.00
12 Richie Sexson Bat-Jsy/100 10.00 3.00
13 Jose Vidro Bat-Jsy/50 10.00 3.00
14 Jae Seo Jsy-Jsy/100 10.00 3.00
15 Alfonso Soriano Bat-Jsy/100 15.00 4.50
16 Barry Zito Bat-Jsy/100 15.00 4.50
17 Brett Myers Jsy-Jsy/25 15.00 4.50
18 Brian Giles Bat-Bat/100 10.00 3.00
19 Edgar Martinez Bat-Jsy/100 15.00 4.50
20 Jim Edmonds Bat-Jsy/100 10.00 3.00
21 Rocco Baldelli Bat-Jsy/100 20.00 6.00
22 Mark Teixeira Bat-Jsy/100 10.00 3.00
23 Carlos Delgado Bat-Jsy/100 10.00 3.00
25 Jose Reyes Bat-Jsy/100 15.00 4.50
26 Marlon Byrd Bat-Jsy/100 10.00 3.00
27 Albert Pujols Bat-Jsy/100 40.00 12.00
28 Vernon Wells Bat-Jsy/100 10.00 3.00
29 Garret Anderson Bat-Jsy/25 15.00 4.50
30 Jerome Williams Jsy-Jsy/100 10.00 3.00
31 Chipper Jones Bat-Jsy/100 20.00 6.00
32 Rich Harden Jsy-Jsy/100 10.00 3.00
33 Manny Ramirez Bat-Jsy/100 10.00 3.00
34 Derek Jeter Base-Base/100 30.00 9.00
35 Brandon Webb Bat-Jsy/100 10.00 3.00
36 Mark Prior Bat-Jsy/100 40.00 12.00
37 Roy Halladay Jsy-Jsy/75 10.00 3.00
38 Frank Thomas Bat-Jsy/100 20.00 6.00
39 Rafael Palmeiro Bat-Jsy/100 15.00 4.50
40 Adam Dunn Bat-Jsy/100 10.00 3.00
41 Aubrey Huff Bat-Jsy/25 15.00 4.50
42 Todd Helton Bat-Jsy/100 15.00 4.50
43 Matt Morris Jsy-Jsy/100 10.00 3.00
44 Dontrelle Willis Bat-Jsy/100 10.00 3.00
45 Lance Berkman Bat-Jsy/100 10.00 3.00
46 Mike Sweeney Bat-Jsy/100 10.00 3.00
47 Kazuhisa Ishii Bat-Jsy/100 10.00 3.00
48 Torii Hunter Bat-Jsy/100 10.00 3.00
49 Vladimir Guerrero Bat-Jsy/100 20.00 6.00
50 Mike Piazza Bat-Jsy/100 25.00 7.50
51 Alexis Rios Bat-Bat/100 20.00 6.00
52 Shannon Stewart Bat-Bat/100 10.00 3.00
53 Eric Hinske Bat-Jsy/100 10.00 3.00
54 Jason Jennings Bat-Jsy/100 10.00 3.00
55 Jason Giambi Bat-Jsy/100 20.00 6.00
56 Brandon Claussen Fld Glv-Shoe/5
57 Joe Thurston Bat-Jsy/100 10.00 3.00
58 Ramon Nivar Bat-Jsy/100 10.00 3.00
59 Jay Gibbons Jsy-Jsy/100 10.00 3.00
60 Eric Chavez Bat-Jsy/100 10.00 3.00
62 Walter Young Bat-Bat/100 10.00 3.00
63 Mark Grace Bat-Jsy/100 15.00 4.50
64 Austin Kearns Bat-Jsy/50 10.00 3.00
65 Bob Abreu Bat-Jsy/100 10.00 3.00
66 Hee Seop Choi Bat-Jsy/100 10.00 3.00
67 Brandon Phillips Bat-Bat/100 10.00 3.00
68 Rickie Weeks Bat-Bat/100 20.00 6.00
69 Luis Gonzalez Bat-Jsy/100 10.00 3.00
70 Mariano Rivera Jsy-Jsy/100 15.00 4.50
71 Jason Lane Bat-Hat/25 15.00 4.50
72 Xavier Nady Bat-Hat/10
73 Run Hernandez Jsy-Jsy/50 10.00 3.00
74 Aramis Ramirez Bat-Bat/1
75 Ichiro Suzuki Ball-Base/25 80.00 24.00
77 Chris Snelling Bat-Bat/25 15.00 4.50
79 Miguel Tejada Bat-Jsy/100 10.00 3.00
80 Juan Gonzalez Bat-Jsy/100 20.00 6.00
81 Joe Borchard Bat-Jsy/25 15.00 4.50
82 Gary Sheffield Bat-Jsy/100 10.00 3.00
83 Wade Miller Bat-Jsy/25 15.00 4.50
84 Jeff Bagwell Bat-Jsy/100 15.00 4.50
86 Adrian Beltre Bat-Jsy/100 10.00 3.00
87 Jeff Baker Bat-Bat/100 10.00 3.00
89 Bernie Williams Bat-Jsy/100 15.00 4.50
90 Pedro Martinez Bat-Jsy/100 20.00 6.00
92 Junior Spivey Bat-Jsy/100 10.00 3.00
93 Tim Hudson Bat-Jsy/100 10.00 3.00
94 Troy Glaus Bat-Jsy/100 15.00 4.50
95 Ken Griffey Jr. Base-Base/100 20.00 6.00
96 Alexis Gomez Bat-Bat/30 15.00 4.50
97 Antonio Perez Bat-Pants/100 10.00 3.00
98 Dan Haren Bat-Jsy/100 10.00 3.00
99 Ivan Rodriguez Bat-Jsy/100 20.00 6.00
100 Randy Johnson Bat-Jsy/100 20.00 6.00
101 Lyle Overbay Bat-Jsy/100 10.00 3.00
103 Miguel Cabrera Bat-Jsy/100 20.00 6.00
104 Scott Rolen Bat-Jsy/100 15.00 4.50
105 Roger Clemens Bat-Jsy/100 30.00 9.00
107 Nic Jackson Bat-Bat/100 10.00 3.00
108 Angel Berroa Bat-Pants/25 15.00 4.50
109 Hank Blalock Bat-Jsy/100 10.00 3.00
110 Ryan Klesko Bat-Jsy/100 10.00 3.00
111 Jose Castillo Bat-Bat/100 10.00 3.00
112 Paul Konerko Bat-Jsy/50 10.00 3.00
113 Greg Maddux Bat-Jsy/100 25.00 7.50
114 Mark Mulder Bat-Jsy/100 10.00 3.00
115 Pat Burrell Bat-Jsy/100 10.00 3.00
116 Garrett Atkins Jsy-Jsy/100 10.00 3.00
118 Orlando Cabrera Bat-Jsy/100 10.00 3.00
119 Nick Johnson Bat-Jsy/100
120 Tom Glavine Bat-Jsy/100 15.00 4.50
121 Morgan Ensberg Bat-Jsy/100 10.00 3.00
122 Sean Casey Bat-Hat/25 15.00 4.50
123 Orlando Hudson Bat-Jsy/100 10.00 3.00
124 Hideki Matsui Ball-Base/25 80.00 24.00
125 Craig Biggio Bat-Jsy/25 25.00 7.50
126 Adam LaRoche Bat-Bat/100 10.00 3.00
127 Hong-Chih Kuo Bat-Bat/100 10.00 3.00
128 Paul LoDuca Bat-Jsy/100 10.00 3.00
129 Shawn Green Bat-Jsy/100 10.00 3.00
130 Luis Castillo Bat-Jsy/100 10.00 3.00
131 Joe Crede Bat-Btg Glv/5
132 Ken Harvey Bat-Bat/100 10.00 3.00
133 Freddy Sanchez Bat-Bat/100 10.00 3.00
134 Roy Oswalt Bat-Jsy/100 10.00 3.00
135 Curt Schilling Bat-Jsy/100 15.00 4.50
136 Alfredo Amezaga Bat-Jsy/25 15.00 4.50
138 Barry Larkin Bat-Jsy/25 30.00 9.00
139 Trot Nixon Bat-Bat/100 15.00 4.50
140 Jim Thome Bat-Jsy/100 20.00 6.00
141 Bret Boone Bat-Jsy/100 10.00 3.00
142 Jacque Jones Bat-Jsy/100 10.00 3.00
143 Travis Hafner Bat-Jsy/100 10.00 3.00
144 Sammy Sosa Bat-Jsy/100 25.00 7.50
145 Mike Mussina Bat-Jsy/100 20.00 6.00
147 Chad Gaudin Jsy-Jsy/50 10.00 3.00
149 Mike Lowell Bat-Jsy/100 10.00 3.00
150 R.Henderson Bat-Jsy/100 20.00 6.00
151 R.Clemens FB Bat-Jsy/25 50.00 15.00
152 Mark Grace FB Bat-Jsy/25 25.00 7.50
153 R.Henderson FB Bat-Jsy/25 30.00 9.00
154 A.Rodriguez FB Bat-Jsy/25 50.00 15.00
155 R.Palmeiro FB Bat-Jsy/100 15.00 4.50
156 G.Maddux FB Bat-Bat/100 25.00 7.50
157 Mike Piazza FB Bat-Jsy/100 25.00 7.50
158 M.Mussina FB Bat-Jsy/100 20.00 6.00
159 Dale Murphy LGD Bat-Jsy/25 30.00 9.00
160 Cal Ripken LGD Bat-Jsy/100 50.00 15.00
161 C.Yaz LGD Bat-Jsy/100 25.00 7.50
162 M.Marion LGD Jsy-Jsy/25 15.00 4.50
163 D.Mattingly LGD Bat-Jsy/100 40.00 12.00
164 R.Yount LGD Bat-Jsy/100 25.00 7.50
165 A.Dawson LGD Bat-Jsy/25 15.00 4.50
166 Jim Palmer LGD Jsy-Jsy/5
167 George Brett LGD Bat-Jsy/25 60.00 18.00
168 W.Ford LGD Jsy-Pants/25 25.00 7.50
169 R.Campy LGD Bat-Pants/25 30.00 9.00
170 R. Maris LGD Bat-Jsy/25 100.00 30.00
171 Duke Snider LGD Bat-Jsy/4
172 S.Carlton LGD Bat-Jsy/100 10.00 3.00
173 Stan Musial LGD Bat-Jsy/25 50.00 15.00
174 Nolan Ryan LGD Bat-Jsy/25 60.00 18.00
175 D.Sanders LGD Bat-Jsy/100 15.00 4.50

2004 Diamond Kings DK Materials Framed Bronze Sepia

Nm-Mt Ex-Mt
RANDOM INSERTS IN PACKS
PRINT RUNS B/WN 4-50 COPIES PER
NO PRICING ON QTY OF 5 OR LESS
151 R.Clemens FB Bat-Jsy/25 50.00 15.00
152 Mark Grace FB Bat-Jsy/25 25.00 7.50
153 R.Henderson FB Bat-Jsy/25 30.00 9.00
154 A.Rodriguez FB Bat-Jsy/25 50.00 15.00
155 R.Palmeiro FB Bat-Jsy/50 15.00 4.50
156 G.Maddux FB Bat-Bat/50 40.00 12.00
157 Mike Piazza FB Bat-Jsy/50 40.00 12.00
158 M.Mussina FB Bat-Jsy/50 25.00 7.50
159 Dale Murphy LGD Bat-Jsy/15 50.00 15.00
160 Cal Ripken LGD Bat-Jsy/50 80.00 24.00
161 C.Yaz LGD Bat-Jsy/50 40.00 12.00
162 M.Marion LGD Jsy-Jsy/15 25.00 7.50
163 D.Mattingly LGD Bat-Jsy/50 50.00 15.00
164 R.Yount LGD Bat-Jsy/50 40.00 12.00
165 A.Dawson LGD Bat-Jsy/15 25.00 7.50
166 Jim Palmer LGD Jsy-Jsy/5
167 G.Brett LGD Bat-Jsy/15 100.00 30.00
168 W.Ford LGD Jsy-Pants/15 40.00 12.00
169 R.Campy LGD Bat-Pants/15 50.00 15.00
170 R.Maris LGD Bat-Jsy/15 120.00 36.00
171 Duke Snider LGD Bat-Jsy/5
172 S.Carlton LGD Bat-Jsy/15 25.00 7.50
173 Stan Musial LGD Bat-Jsy/15 80.00 24.00
174 Nolan Ryan LGD Bat-Jsy/15 100.00 30.00
175 D.Sanders LGD Bat-Jsy/50 15.00 4.50

2004 Diamond Kings DK Materials Framed Gold

Nm-Mt Ex-Mt
RANDOM INSERTS IN PACKS
PRINT RUNS B/WN 1-50 COPIES PER
NO PRICING ON QTY OF 10 OR LESS.
1 Alex Rodriguez Bat-Jsy/10
2 Andruw Jones Bat-Jsy/10
3 Nomar Garciaparra Bat-Jsy/10
4 Kerry Wood Bat-Jsy/10
5 Magglio Ordonez Bat-Jsy/10
6 Victor Martinez Bat-Bat/50 10.00 3.00
7 Jeremy Bonderman Jsy-Jsy/5
8 Josh Beckett Bat-Jsy/10
9 Jeff Kent Bat-Jsy/10
10 Carlos Beltran Bat-Jsy/10
11 Hideo Nomo Bat-Jsy/10
12 Richie Sexson Bat-Jsy/5
13 Jose Vidro Bat-Jsy/5
14 Jae Seo Jsy-Jsy/10
15 Alfonso Soriano Bat-Jsy/10
16 Barry Zito Bat-Jsy/10
17 Brett Myers Jsy-Jsy/5
18 Brian Giles Bat-Bat/10
19 Edgar Martinez Bat-Jsy/5
20 Jim Edmonds Bat-Jsy/5
21 Rocco Baldelli Bat-Jsy/5
22 Mark Teixeira Bat-Jsy/5
23 Carlos Delgado Bat-Jsy/10
25 Jose Reyes Bat-Jsy/10
26 Marlon Byrd Bat-Jsy/25 15.00 4.50
27 Albert Pujols Bat-Jsy/10
28 Vernon Wells Bat-Jsy/10
29 Garret Anderson Bat-Jsy/10
31 Chipper Jones Bat-Jsy/10
32 Rich Harden Jsy-Jsy/50 10.00 3.00
33 Manny Ramirez Bat-Jsy/10
34 Derek Jeter Base-Base/50 40.00 12.00
35 Brandon Webb Bat-Jsy/50 10.00 3.00
36 Mark Prior Bat-Jsy/10
37 Roy Halladay Jsy-Jsy/5
38 Frank Thomas Jsy-Jsy/10
39 Rafael Palmeiro Bat-Jsy/50 15.00 4.50
40 Adam Dunn Bat-Jsy/10
41 Aubrey Huff Bat-Jsy/5
42 Todd Helton Bat-Jsy/10
43 Matt Morris Jsy-Jsy/10
44 Dontrelle Willis Bat-Jsy/10
45 Lance Berkman Bat-Jsy/10
46 Mike Sweeney Bat-Jsy/10
47 Kazuhisa Ishii Bat-Jsy/10
48 Torii Hunter Bat-Jsy/10
49 Vladimir Guerrero Bat-Jsy/10
50 Mike Piazza Bat-Jsy/50 40.00 12.00
51 Alexis Rios Bat-Bat/50 25.00 7.50
52 Shannon Stewart Bat-Bat/50 10.00 3.00
53 Eric Hinske Bat-Jsy/50 10.00 3.00
54 Jason Jennings Bat-Jsy/10
55 Jason Giambi Bat-Jsy/10
56 Brandon Claussen Fld Glv-Shoe/5
57 Joe Thurston Bat-Jsy/50 10.00 3.00
58 Ramon Nivar Bat-Jsy/50 10.00 3.00
59 Jay Gibbons Jsy-Jsy/10
60 Eric Chavez Bat-Jsy/10
62 Walter Young Bat-Bat/50 10.00 3.00
63 Mark Grace Bat-Jsy/5
64 Austin Kearns Bat-Jsy/5
65 Bob Abreu Bat-Jsy/10
66 Hee Seop Choi Bat-Jsy/10
67 Brandon Phillips Bat-Bat/50 10.00 3.00
68 Rickie Weeks Bat-Bat/50 25.00 7.50
69 Luis Gonzalez Bat-Jsy/10
70 Mariano Rivera Jsy-Jsy/50 15.00 4.50
71 Jason Lane Bat-Hat/5
72 Xavier Nady Bat-Hat/5
73 Run Hernandez Jsy-Jsy/5
74 Aramis Ramirez Bat-Bat/1
75 Ichiro Suzuki Ball-Base/5
77 Chris Snelling Bat-Bat/5
79 Miguel Tejada Bat-Jsy/50 10.00 3.00
80 Juan Gonzalez Bat-Jsy/10
81 Joe Borchard Bat-Jsy/5
82 Gary Sheffield Bat-Jsy/10
83 Wade Miller Bat-Jsy/5
84 Jeff Bagwell Bat-Jsy/10
86 Adrian Beltre Bat-Jsy/5
87 Jeff Baker Bat-Bat/50 10.00 3.00
89 Bernie Williams Bat-Jsy/10
90 Pedro Martinez Bat-Jsy/10
92 Junior Spivey Bat-Jsy/5
93 Tim Hudson Bat-Jsy/5
94 Troy Glaus Bat-Jsy/10
95 Ken Griffey Jr. Base-Base/50 30.00 9.00
96 Alexis Gomez Bat-Bat/5
97 Antonio Perez Bat-Pants/50 10.00 3.00
98 Dan Haren Bat-Jsy/50 10.00 3.00
99 Ivan Rodriguez Bat-Jsy/10
100 Randy Johnson Bat-Jsy/10
101 Lyle Overbay Bat-Jsy/50 10.00 3.00
103 Miguel Cabrera Bat-Jsy/10
104 Scott Rolen Bat-Jsy/10
105 Roger Clemens Bat-Jsy/10
107 Nic Jackson Bat-Bat/30 15.00 4.50
108 Angel Berroa Bat-Pants/5
109 Hank Blalock Bat-Jsy/5
110 Ryan Klesko Bat-Jsy/10
111 Jose Castillo Bat-Bat/50 10.00 3.00
112 Paul Konerko Bat-Jsy/10
113 Greg Maddux Bat-Jsy/10
114 Mark Mulder Bat-Jsy/10
115 Pat Burrell Bat-Jsy/10
116 Garrett Atkins Jsy-Jsy/50 10.00 3.00
118 Orlando Cabrera Bat-Jsy/5
119 Nick Johnson Bat-Jsy/10
120 Tom Glavine Bat-Jsy/10
121 Morgan Ensberg Bat-Jsy/10
122 Sean Casey Bat-Hat/5
123 Orlando Hudson Bat-Jsy/10
124 Hideki Matsui Ball-Base/5
125 Craig Biggio Bat-Jsy/10
126 Adam LaRoche Bat-Bat/25
127 Hong-Chih Kuo Bat-Bat/50 10.00 3.00
128 Paul LoDuca Bat-Jsy/10
129 Shawn Green Bat-Jsy/10
130 Luis Castillo Bat-Jsy/10
131 Joe Crede Bat-Btg Glv/5
132 Ken Harvey Bat-Bat/50 10.00 3.00
133 Freddy Sanchez Bat-Bat/50 10.00 3.00
134 Roy Oswalt Bat-Jsy/50 10.00 3.00
135 Curt Schilling Bat-Jsy/10
136 Alfredo Amezaga Bat-Jsy/5
138 Barry Larkin Bat-Jsy/5
139 Trot Nixon Bat-Bat/10
140 Jim Thome Bat-Jsy/10
141 Bret Boone Bat-Jsy/5
142 Jacque Jones Bat-Jsy/50 10.00 3.00
143 Travis Hafner Bat-Jsy/50 10.00 3.00
144 Sammy Sosa Bat-Jsy/10
145 Mike Mussina Bat-Jsy/50 25.00 7.50
147 Chad Gaudin Jsy-Jsy/10
149 Mike Lowell Bat-Jsy/10
150 R.Henderson Bat-Jsy/10
151 R.Clemens FB Bat-Jsy/5
152 Mark Grace FB Bat-Jsy/5
153 R.Henderson FB Bat-Jsy/5
154 A.Rodriguez FB Bat-Jsy/5
155 R.Palmeiro FB Bat-Jsy/50 15.00 4.50
156 G.Maddux FB Bat-Bat/50 40.00 12.00

157 Mike Piazza FB Bat-Jsy/50.. 40.00 12.00
158 M.Mussina FB Bat-Jsy/50 .. 25.00 7.50
159 Dale Murphy LGD Bat-Jsy/5
160 Cal Ripken LGD Bat-Jsy/50 80.00 24.00
161 C.Yaz LGD Bat-Jsy/50 .... 40.00 12.00
162 M.Marion LGD Jsy-Jsy/5
163 D.Mattingly LGD Bat-Jsy/50 50.00 15.00
164 R.Yount LGD Bat-Jsy/50 .... 40.00 12.00
165 A.Dawson LGD Bat-Jsy/5
166 Jim Palmer LGD Jsy-Jsy/5
167 George Brett LGD Bat-Jsy/5
168 W.Ford LGD Jsy-Pants/5
169 R.Campy LGD Bat-Pants/5
170 Roger Maris LGD Bat-Jsy/5
171 Duke Snider LGD Bat-Jsy/1
172 S.Carlton LGD Bat-Jsy/15 .. 25.00 7.50
173 Stan Musial LGD Bat-Jsy/5
174 Nolan Ryan LGD Bat-Jsy/5
175 D.Sanders LGD Bat-Jsy/50. 15.00 4.50

2004 Diamond Kings DK Materials Framed Gold Sepia

Nm-Mt Ex-Mt
RANDOM INSERTS IN PACKS
PRINT RUNS B/WN 1-15 COPIES PER
NO PRICING ON QTY OF 5 OR LESS...
151 R.Clemens FB Bat-Jsy/5
152 Mark Grace FB Bat-Jsy/5
153 R.Henderson FB Bat-Jsy/5
154 A.Rodriguez FB Bat-Jsy/5
155 R.Palmeiro FB Bat-Jsy/15 .. 40.00 12.00
156 G.Maddux FB Bat-Bat/15 .... 60.00 18.00
157 Mike Piazza FB Bat-Jsy/15.. 60.00 18.00
158 M.Mussina FB Bat-Jsy/15 .. 50.00 15.00
159 Dale Murphy LGD Bat-Jsy/5
160 Cal Ripken LGD Bat-Jsy/15 150.00 45.00
161 C.Yaz LGD Bat-Jsy/15 .... 80.00 24.00
162 M.Marion LGD Jsy-Jsy/5
163 D.Mattingly LGD Bat-Jsy/15 100.00 30.00
164 R.Yount LGD Bat-Jsy/15
165 A.Dawson LGD Bat-Jsy/5
166 Jim Palmer LGD Jsy-Jsy/5
167 George Brett LGD Bat-Jsy/5
168 W.Ford LGD Jsy-Pants/5
169 R.Campy LGD Bat-Pants/5
170 Roger Maris LGD Bat-Jsy/5
171 Duke Snider LGD Bat-Jsy/1
172 S.Carlton LGD Bat-Jsy/5
173 Stan Musial LGD Bat-Jsy/5
174 Nolan Ryan LGD Bat-Jsy/5
175 D.Sanders LGD Bat-Jsy/15. 40.00 12.00

2004 Diamond Kings DK Materials Framed Platinum Black

Nm-Mt Ex-Mt
RANDOM INSERTS IN PACKS
STATED PRINT RUN 1 SERIAL #'d SET
NO PRICING DUE TO SCARCITY

2004 Diamond Kings DK Materials Framed Platinum Black Sepia

Nm-Mt Ex-Mt
RANDOM INSERTS IN PACKS
STATED PRINT RUN 1 SERIAL #'d SET
NO PRICING DUE TO SCARCITY

2004 Diamond Kings DK Materials Framed Platinum Grey

Nm-Mt Ex-Mt
RANDOM INSERTS IN PACKS
STATED PRINT RUN 1 SERIAL #'d SET
NO PRICING DUE TO SCARCITY

2004 Diamond Kings DK Materials Framed Platinum Grey Sepia

Nm-Mt Ex-Mt
RANDOM INSERTS IN PACKS
STATED PRINT RUN 1 SERIAL #'d SET
NO PRICING DUE TO SCARCITY

2004 Diamond Kings DK Materials Framed Platinum White

Nm-Mt Ex-Mt
RANDOM INSERTS IN PACKS
STATED PRINT RUN 1 SERIAL #'d SET
NO PRICING DUE TO SCARCITY

2004 Diamond Kings DK Materials Framed Platinum White Sepia

Nm-Mt Ex-Mt
RANDOM INSERTS IN PACKS
STATED PRINT RUN 1 SERIAL #'d SET
NO PRICING DUE TO SCARCITY

2004 Diamond Kings DK Materials Framed Silver

Nm-Mt Ex-Mt
RANDOM INSERTS IN PACKS
PRINT RUNS B/WN 1-75 COPIES PER
NO PRICING ON QTY OF 10 OR LESS.
1 Alex Rodriguez Bat-Jsy/25 ..... 50.00 15.00
2 Andruw Jones Bat-Jsy/25 ...... 15.00 4.50
3 Nomar Garciaparra Bat-Jsy/25 50.00 15.00
4 Kerry Wood Bat-Jsy/25 .... 30.00 9.00
5 Magglio Ordonez Bat-Jsy/25 .. 15.00 4.50
6 Victor Martinez Bat-Bat/50 ..... 10.00 3.00
7 Jeremy Bonderman Jsy-Jsy/10
8 Josh Beckett Bat-Jsy/25 .... 25.00 7.50
9 Jeff Kent Bat-Jsy/25 .... 15.00 4.50
10 Carlos Beltran Bat-Jsy/25 ...... 15.00 4.50
11 Hideo Nomo Bat-Jsy/25 .... 30.00 9.00
12 Richie Sexson Bat-Jsy/25 .... 15.00 4.50
13 Jose Vidro Bat-Jsy/25 .... 15.00 4.50
14 Jae Seo Jsy-Jsy/25 .... 15.00 4.50
15 Alfonso Soriano Bat-Jsy/25.. 25.00 7.50
16 Barry Zito Bat-Jsy/25 .... 25.00 7.50
17 Brett Myers Jsy-Jsy/10
18 Brian Giles Bat-Bat/25 .... 15.00 4.50
19 Edgar Martinez Bat-Jsy/25 .. 25.00 7.50
20 Jim Edmonds Bat-Jsy/25 ...... 15.00 4.50
21 Rocco Baldelli Bat-Jsy/25...... 30.00 9.00
22 Mark Teixeira Bat-Jsy/25 ...... 15.00 4.50
23 Carlos Delgado Bat-Jsy/25 ... 15.00 4.50
25 Jose Reyes Bat-Jsy/25 .... 25.00 7.50
26 Marlon Byrd Bat-Jsy/50 .... 10.00 3.00
27 Albert Pujols Bat-Jsy/25....... 60.00 18.00
28 Vernon Wells Bat-Jsy/25 .... 15.00 4.50
29 Garret Anderson Bat-Jsy/25. 15.00 4.50
31 Chipper Jones Bat-Jsy/25 .... 30.00 9.00
32 Rich Harden Jsy-Jsy/50 .... 10.00 3.00
33 Manny Ramirez Bat-Jsy/25 .. 15.00 4.50
34 Derek Jeter Base-Base/50 .... 40.00 12.00
35 Brandon Webb Bat-Jsy/50 ... 10.00 3.00
36 Mark Prior Bat-Jsy/25 .... 60.00 18.00
37 Roy Halladay Jsy-Jsy/10
38 Frank Thomas Bat-Jsy/25..... 30.00 9.00
39 Rafael Palmeiro Bat-Jsy/50.. 15.00 4.50
40 Adam Dunn Bat-Jsy/25 .... 15.00 4.50
41 Aubrey Huff Bat-Jsy/10
42 Todd Helton Bat-Jsy/25........ 25.00 7.50
43 Matt Morris Jsy-Jsy/25 .... 15.00 4.50
44 Dontrelle Willis Bat-Jsy/25 ... 15.00 4.50
45 Lance Berkman Bat-Jsy/25... 15.00 4.50
46 Mike Sweeney Bat-Jsy/25
47 Kazuhisa Ishii Bat-Jsy/25 ..... 15.00 4.50
48 Torii Hunter Bat-Jsy/25 .... 15.00 4.50
49 Vladimir Guerrero Bat-Jsy/25 30.00 9.00
50 Mike Piazza Bat-Jsy/50......... 40.00 12.00
51 Alexis Rios Bat-Bat/50.......... 25.00 7.50
52 Shannon Stewart Bat-Bat/50 10.00 3.00
53 Eric Hinske Bat-Jsy/50 .... 10.00 3.00
54 Jason Jennings Bat-Jsy/25 .. 15.00 4.50
55 Jason Giambi Bat-Jsy/25 .... 30.00 9.00
56 Brandon Claussen Fld Glv-Shoe/5
57 Joe Thurston Bat-Jsy/50 ...... 10.00 3.00
58 Ramon Nivar Bat-Jsy/50 ...... 10.00 3.00
59 Jay Gibbons Bat-Jsy/25 .... 15.00 4.50
60 Eric Chavez Bat-Jsy/25 .... 15.00 4.50
62 Walter Young Bat-Bat/50...... 10.00 3.00
63 Mark Grace Bat-Jsy/25 .... 25.00 7.50
64 Austin Kearns Bat-Jsy/25..... 15.00 4.50
65 Bob Abreu Bat-Jsy/25 .... 15.00 4.50
66 Hee Seop Choi Bat-Jsy/25.... 15.00 4.50
67 Brandon Phillips Bat-Bat/50. 10.00 3.00
68 Rickie Weeks Bat-Bat/50 ...... 25.00 7.50
69 Luis Gonzalez Bat-Jsy/25 .... 15.00 4.50
70 Mariano Rivera Jsy-Jsy/75... 15.00 4.50
71 Jason Lane Bat-Hat/25 .... 15.00 4.50
72 Xavier Nady Bat-Hat/10
73 Run Hernandez Jsy-Jsy/10
74 Aramis Ramirez Bat-Bat/1
75 Ichiro Suzuki Ball-Base/10
77 Chris Snelling Bat-Bat/10
79 Miguel Tejada Bat-Jsy/50..... 10.00 3.00
80 Juan Gonzalez Bat-Jsy/25 .... 30.00 9.00
81 Joe Borchard Bat-Jsy/25 ...... 15.00 4.50
82 Gary Sheffield Bat-Jsy/25...... 15.00 4.50
83 Wade Miller Bat-Jsy/25 .... 15.00 4.50
84 Jeff Bagwell Bat-Jsy/25 .... 25.00 7.50
86 Adrian Beltre Bat-Jsy/25....... 15.00 4.50
87 Jeff Baker Bat-Bat/50 .... 10.00 3.00
89 Bernie Williams Bat-Jsy/25 .. 25.00 7.50
90 Pedro Martinez Bat-Jsy/25 ... 30.00 9.00
92 Junior Spivey Bat-Jsy/25 ...... 15.00 4.50
93 Tim Hudson Bat-Jsy/25 .... 15.00 4.50
94 Troy Glaus Bat-Jsy/25 .... 25.00 7.50
95 Ken Griffey Jr. Base-Base/50 30.00 9.00
96 Alexis Gomez Bat-Bat/15
97 Antonio Perez Bat-Pants/50 . 10.00 3.00
98 Dan Haren Bat-Jsy/50 .... 10.00 3.00
99 Ivan Rodriguez Bat-Jsy/25 ... 30.00 9.00
100 Randy Johnson Bat-Jsy/25 30.00 9.00
101 Lyle Overbay Bat-Jsy/50..... 10.00 3.00
103 Miguel Cabrera Bat-Jsy/25 . 30.00 9.00
104 Scott Rolen Bat-Jsy/25 .... 25.00 7.50
105 Roger Clemens Bat-Jsy/25. 50.00 15.00
107 Nic Jackson Bat-Bat/50 ...... 10.00 3.00
108 Angel Berroa Bat-Pants/25 . 15.00 4.50
109 Hank Blalock Bat-Jsy/25..... 15.00 4.50
110 Ryan Klesko Bat-Jsy/25 ...... 15.00 4.50
111 Jose Castillo Bat-Bat/50 ..... 10.00 3.00
112 Paul Konerko Bat-Jsy/25 .... 15.00 4.50
113 Greg Maddux Bat-Jsy/25..... 50.00 15.00
114 Mark Mulder Bat-Jsy/25..... 15.00 4.50
115 Pat Burrell Bat-Jsy/25 .... 15.00 4.50
116 Garrett Atkins Jsy-Jsy/50... 10.00 3.00
118 Orlando Cabrera Bat-Jsy/25 15.00 4.50
119 Nick Johnson Bat-Jsy/25 ... 15.00 4.50
120 Tom Glavine Bat-Jsy/25 ..... 25.00 7.50
121 Morgan Ensberg Bat-Jsy/25 15.00 4.50
122 Sean Casey Bat-Hat/25....... 15.00 4.50
123 Orlando Hudson Bat-Jsy/25 15.00 4.50
124 Hideki Matsui Ball-Base/10
125 Craig Biggio Bat-Jsy/25...... 25.00 7.50
126 Adam LaRoche Bat-Bat/50 . 10.00 3.00
127 Hong-Chih Kuo Bat-Bat/50. 10.00 3.00
128 Paul LoDuca Bat-Jsy/25 .... 15.00 4.50
129 Shawn Green Bat-Jsy/25.... 15.00 4.50
130 Luis Castillo Bat-Jsy/25..... 15.00 4.50
131 Joe Crede Bat-Btg Glv/5
132 Ken Harvey Bat-Bat/50 .... 10.00 3.00
133 Freddy Sanchez Bat-Bat/50 10.00 3.00
134 Roy Oswalt Bat-Jsy/50 ...... 10.00 3.00
135 Curt Schilling Bat-Jsy/25.... 25.00 7.50
136 Alfredo Amezaga Bat-Jsy/25 15.00 4.50
138 Barry Larkin Bat-Jsy/25 ..... 30.00 9.00
139 Trot Nixon Bat/25.............. 25.00 7.50
140 Jim Thome Bat-Jsy/25 .... 30.00 9.00
141 Bret Boone Bat-Jsy/50 .... 10.00 3.00
142 Jacque Jones Bat-Jsy/50 ... 10.00 3.00
143 Travis Hafner Bat-Jsy/50.... 10.00 3.00
144 Sammy Sosa Bat-Jsy/25 .... 50.00 15.00
145 Mike Mussina Bat-Jsy/50 ... 25.00 7.50
147 Chad Gaudin Jsy-Jsy/25..... 15.00 4.50
149 Mike Lowell Bat-Jsy/25 ...... 15.00 4.50
150 R.Henderson Bat-Jsy/25 .... 30.00 9.00
151 R.Clemens FB Bat-Jsy/15... 60.00 18.00
152 Mark Grace FB Bat-Jsy/15.. 40.00 12.00
153 R.Henderson FB Bat-Jsy/15 25.00 7.50
154 A.Rodriguez FB Bat-Jsy/15. 60.00 18.00
155 R.Palmeiro FB Bat-Jsy/50 .. 15.00 4.50
156 G.Maddux FB Bat-Bat/50.... 40.00 12.00
157 Mike Piazza FB Bat-Jsy/50.. 40.00 12.00
158 M.Mussina FB Bat-Jsy/50 .. 25.00 7.50
159 Dale Murphy LGD Bat-Jsy/15 50.00 15.00
160 Cal Ripken LGD Bat-Jsy/50 80.00 24.00
161 C.Yaz LGD Bat-Jsy/50 .... 40.00 12.00
162 M.Marion LGD Jsy-Jsy/15.. 25.00 7.50
163 D.Mattingly LGD Bat-Jsy/50 50.00 15.00
164 R.Yount LGD Bat-Jsy/50 .... 40.00 12.00
165 A.Dawson LGD Bat-Jsy/15 . 25.00 7.50
166 Jim Palmer LGD Jsy-Jsy/5
167 G.Brett LGD Bat-Jsy/15 .... 100.00 30.00
168 W.Ford LGD Jsy-Pants/15.. 40.00 12.00
169 R.Campy LGD Bat-Pants/15 50.00 15.00
170 R.Maris LGD Bat-Jsy/15... 120.00 36.00
171 Duke Snider LGD Bat-Jsy/1
172 S.Carlton LGD Bat-Jsy/50 .. 10.00 3.00
173 Stan Musial LGD Bat-Jsy/15 80.00 24.00
174 Nolan Ryan LGD Bat-Jsy/15 100.00 30.00
175 D.Sanders LGD Bat-Jsy/50. 15.00 4.50

2004 Diamond Kings DK Materials Framed Silver Sepia

Nm-Mt Ex-Mt
RANDOM INSERTS IN PACKS
PRINT RUNS B/WN 1-30 COPIES PER
NO PRICING ON QTY OF 10 OR LESS.
151 R.Clemens FB Bat-Jsy/15 ... 60.00 18.00
152 Mark Grace FB Bat-Jsy/15.. 40.00 12.00
153 R.Henderson FB Bat-Jsy/15 50.00 15.00
154 A.Rodriguez FB Bat-Jsy/15. 60.00 18.00
155 R.Palmeiro FB Bat-Jsy/30 .. 25.00 7.50
156 G.Maddux FB Bat-Bat/30 .... 50.00 15.00
157 Mike Piazza FB Bat-Jsy/30.. 50.00 15.00
158 M.Mussina FB Bat-Jsy/30 .. 30.00 9.00
159 Dale Murphy LGD Bat-Jsy/10
160 Cal Ripken LGD Bat-Jsy/30 100.00 30.00
161 C.Yaz LGD Bat-Jsy/30 .... 50.00 15.00
162 M.Marion LGD Jsy-Jsy/10
163 D.Mattingly LGD Bat-Jsy/30 60.00 18.00
164 R.Yount LGD Bat-Jsy/30 .... 50.00 15.00
165 A.Dawson LGD Bat-Jsy/10
166 Jim Palmer LGD Jsy-Jsy/5
167 George Brett LGD Bat-Jsy/10
168 W.Ford LGD Jsy-Pants/10
169 R.Campy LGD Bat-Pants/10
170 Roger Maris LGD Bat-Jsy/10
171 Duke Snider LGD Bat-Jsy/1
172 S.Carlton LGD Bat-Jsy/10
173 Stan Musial LGD Bat-Jsy/10
174 Nolan Ryan LGD Bat-Jsy/10
175 D.Sanders LGD Bat-Jsy/30. 25.00 7.50

2004 Diamond Kings DK Signatures Bronze

Nm-Mt Ex-Mt
RANDOM INSERTS IN PACKS
PRINT RUNS B/WN 1-200 COPIES PER
NO PRICING ON QTY OF 10 OR LESS.
1 Alex Rodriguez/1
2 Andruw Jones/2
4 Kerry Wood/1
5 Magglio Ordonez/2
6 Victor Martinez/200 .... 15.00 4.50
7 Jeremy Bonderman/1
8 Josh Beckett/2
9 Jeff Kent/2
10 Carlos Beltran/8
11 Hideo Nomo/1
12 Richie Sexson/5
13 Jose Vidro/200 .... 15.00 4.50
14 Jae Seo/200 .... 25.00 7.50
17 Brett Myers/200 .... 15.00 4.50
19 Edgar Martinez/25 .... 60.00 18.00
20 Jim Edmonds/1
21 Rocco Baldelli/10
22 Mark Teixeira/5
26 Marlon Byrd/200 .... 10.00 3.00
27 Albert Pujols/1
28 Vernon Wells/10
29 Garret Anderson/5
31 Chipper Jones/1
32 Rich Harden/200 .... 25.00 7.50
35 Brandon Webb/25 .... 40.00 12.00
36 Mark Prior/1
38 Frank Thomas/2
39 Rafael Palmeiro/1
40 Adam Dunn/5
41 Aubrey Huff/100 .... 15.00 4.50
42 Todd Helton/1
44 Dontrelle Willis/15 .... 50.00 15.00
45 Lance Berkman/1
46 Mike Sweeney/8
48 Torii Hunter/100 .... 25.00 7.50
49 Vladimir Guerrero/1
50 Mike Piazza/1
51 Alexis Rios/200 .... 25.00 7.50
52 Shannon Stewart/200 .... 15.00 4.50
53 Eric Hinske/25 .... 20.00 6.00
54 Jason Jennings/15 .... 25.00 7.50
56 Brandon Claussen/200 .... 15.00 4.50
57 Joe Thurston/200 .... 10.00 3.00
58 Ramon Nivar/100 .... 10.00 3.00
59 Jay Gibbons/25 .... 25.00 7.50
60 Eric Chavez/2
61 Jimmy Gobble/100 .... 15.00 4.50
62 Walter Young/200 .... 10.00 3.00
63 Mark Grace/1
64 Austin Kearns/2
65 Bob Abreu/15 .... 30.00 9.00
67 Brandon Phillips/100 .... 10.00 3.00
68 Rickie Weeks/30 .... 60.00 18.00
70 Mariano Rivera/10
71 Jason Lane/200 .... 10.00 3.00
72 Xavier Nady/1
73 Runelvys Hernandez/50........ 15.00 4.50
74 Aramis Ramirez/100............ 15.00 4.50
76 Cliff Lee/200..................... 10.00 3.00
77 Chris Snelling/200.............. 10.00 3.00
78 Ryan Wagner/100 .... 15.00 4.50
80 Juan Gonzalez/5
81 Joe Borchard/200 .... 15.00 4.50
82 Gary Sheffield/10
83 Wade Miller/5
84 Jeff Bagwell/1
85 Ryan Church/200 .... 10.00 3.00
86 Adrian Beltre/5
87 Jeff Baker/100 .... 10.00 3.00
88 Adam Loewen/100 .... 25.00 7.50
90 Pedro Martinez/1
91 Carlos Rivera/100............... 10.00 3.00
92 Junior Spivey/25 .... 20.00 6.00
93 Tim Hudson/2
94 Troy Glaus/5
96 Alexis Gomez/200 .... 10.00 3.00
97 Antonio Perez/46................ 15.00 4.50
98 Dan Haren/100 .... 15.00 4.50
99 Ivan Rodriguez/5
100 Randy Johnson/1
101 Lyle Overbay/200 .... 10.00 3.00
102 Oliver Perez/200............... 10.00 3.00
103 Miguel Cabrera/100........... 40.00 12.00
104 Scott Rolen/2
106 Brian Tallet/200 .... 10.00 3.00
107 Nic Jackson/200............... 10.00 3.00
108 Angel Berroa/25 .... 25.00 7.50
109 Hank Blalock/25 .... 40.00 12.00
110 Ryan Klesko/8
111 Jose Castillo/200.............. 10.00 3.00
112 Paul Konerko/8
113 Greg Maddux/1
114 Mark Mulder/25................ 40.00 12.00
116 Garrett Atkins/100............ 10.00 3.00
117 Jeremy Guthrie/200.......... 10.00 3.00
118 Orlando Cabrera/75 .... 15.00 4.50
120 Tom Glavine/2
121 Morgan Ensberg/200.......... 15.00 4.50
122 Sean Casey/10
123 Orlando Hudson/100.......... 10.00 3.00
125 Craig Biggio/2
126 Adam LaRoche/100........... 15.00 4.50
127 Hong-Chih Kuo/25 .... 40.00 12.00
128 Paul LoDuca/1
130 Luis Castillo/25 .... 25.00 7.50
131 Joe Crede/100 .... 10.00 3.00
132 Ken Harvey/200................ 10.00 3.00
133 Freddy Sanchez/50 .... 15.00 4.50
134 Roy Oswalt/8
135 Curt Schilling/1
136 Alfredo Amezaga/90 .... 10.00 3.00
137 Chien-Ming Wang/25 .... 60.00 18.00
139 Trot Nixon/15 .... 80.00 24.00
142 Jacque Jones/25 .... 25.00 7.50
143 Travis Hafner/200............. 15.00 4.50
144 Sammy Sosa/1
145 Mike Mussina/1
146 Vinny Chulk/200............... 10.00 3.00
147 Chad Gaudin/100.............. 10.00 3.00
148 Delmon Young/25 .... 60.00 18.00
149 Mike Lowell/25 .... 25.00 7.50
151 Roger Clemens FB/1
152 Mark Grace FB/1
154 Alex Rodriguez FB/1
155 Rafael Palmeiro FB/1
156 Greg Maddux FB/1
157 Mike Piazza FB/1
158 Mike Mussina FB/1
159 Dale Murphy LGD/1
160 Cal Ripken LGD/1
161 Carl Yastrzemski LGD/1
162 Marty Marion LGD/15......... 30.00 9.00
163 Don Mattingly LGD/1
164 Robin Yount LGD/1
166 Jim Palmer LGD/1
168 Whitey Ford LGD/1
171 Duke Snider LGD/1
172 Steve Carlton LGD/1
173 Stan Musial LGD/1
174 Nolan Ryan LGD/1
175 Deion Sanders LGD/1

2004 Diamond Kings DK Signatures Bronze Sepia

Nm-Mt Ex-Mt
RANDOM INSERTS IN PACKS
PRINT RUNS B/WN 1-15 COPIES PER
NO PRICING ON QTY OF 1 OR LESS...
162 Marty Marion LGD/15......... 30.00 9.00

2004 Diamond Kings DK Signatures Gold

Nm-Mt Ex-Mt
RANDOM INSERTS IN PACKS
PRINT RUNS B/WN 1-50 COPIES PER
NO PRICING ON QTY OF 12 OR LESS.
26 Marlon Byrd/15 .... 25.00 7.50
32 Rich Harden/50 .... 30.00 9.00
51 Alexis Rios/50 .... 30.00 9.00
56 Brandon Claussen/50 .... 20.00 6.00
57 Joe Thurston/50............... 15.00 4.50
62 Walter Young/50 .... 15.00 4.50
71 Jason Lane/40.................. 15.00 4.50
77 Chris Snelling/50.............. 15.00 4.50
81 Joe Borchard/50 .... 20.00 6.00
85 Ryan Church/50 .... 15.00 4.50
96 Alexis Gomez/50 .... 15.00 4.50
101 Lyle Overbay/50 .... 15.00 4.50
102 Oliver Perez/50 .... 15.00 4.50
106 Brian Tallet/50................ 15.00 4.50
107 Nic Jackson/50............... 15.00 4.50
121 Morgan Ensberg/48.......... 20.00 6.00
146 Vinny Chulk/50 .... 15.00 4.50

2004 Diamond Kings DK Signatures Gold Sepia

Nm-Mt Ex-Mt
RANDOM INSERTS IN PACKS
PRINT RUNS B/WN 1-3 COPIES PER..
NO PRICING DUE TO SCARCITY

2004 Diamond Kings DK Signatures Platinum

Nm-Mt Ex-Mt
RANDOM INSERTS IN PACKS
STATED PRINT RUN 1 SERIAL #'d SET
NO PRICING DUE TO SCARCITY

2004 Diamond Kings DK Signatures Platinum Sepia

Nm-Mt Ex-Mt
RANDOM INSERTS IN PACKS
STATED PRINT RUN 1 SERIAL #'d SET
NO PRICING DUE TO SCARCITY

2004 Diamond Kings DK Signatures Silver

Nm-Mt Ex-Mt
RANDOM INSERTS IN PACKS
PRINT RUNS B/WN 1-100 COPIES PER
NO PRICING ON QTY OF 10 OR LESS.
1 Alex Rodriguez/1
2 Andruw Jones/1
4 Kerry Wood/1
5 Magglio Ordonez/1
6 Victor Martinez/49 .... 20.00 6.00
7 Jeremy Bonderman/1
8 Josh Beckett/1
9 Jeff Kent/1
10 Carlos Beltran/5
11 Hideo Nomo/1
12 Richie Sexson/3
13 Jose Vidro/20 .... 25.00 7.50
14 Jae Seo/80 .... 25.00 7.50
17 Brett Myers/90 .... 15.00 4.50
19 Edgar Martinez/15 .... 80.00 24.00
20 Jim Edmonds/1
21 Rocco Baldelli/5
22 Mark Teixeira/3
26 Marlon Byrd/100 .... 10.00 3.00
27 Albert Pujols/1
28 Vernon Wells/5
29 Garret Anderson/3
31 Chipper Jones/1
32 Rich Harden/100 .... 25.00 7.50
35 Brandon Webb/15 .... 50.00 15.00
36 Mark Prior/1
38 Frank Thomas/1
39 Rafael Palmeiro/1
40 Adam Dunn/3
41 Aubrey Huff/40 .... 25.00 7.50
42 Todd Helton/1
44 Dontrelle Willis/5
45 Lance Berkman/1
46 Mike Sweeney/5
48 Torii Hunter/30 .... 40.00 12.00
49 Vladimir Guerrero/1
50 Mike Piazza/1
51 Alexis Rios/100 .... 25.00 7.50
52 Shannon Stewart/30............ 25.00 7.50
53 Eric Hinske/15 .... 25.00 7.50
54 Jason Jennings/5
56 Brandon Claussen/100 .... 15.00 4.50
57 Joe Thurston/100 .... 10.00 3.00
58 Ramon Nivar/30 .... 20.00 6.00
59 Jay Gibbons/15 .... 30.00 9.00
60 Eric Chavez/1
61 Jimmy Gobble/30 .... 25.00 7.50
62 Walter Young/100 .... 10.00 3.00
63 Mark Grace/1
64 Austin Kearns/1
65 Bob Abreu/6
67 Brandon Phillips/30 .... 20.00 6.00
68 Rickie Weeks/20 .... 60.00 18.00
70 Mariano Rivera/5
71 Jason Lane/100 .... 10.00 3.00
72 Xavier Nady/1
73 Runelvys Hernandez/30........ 20.00 6.00
74 Aramis Ramirez/30.............. 25.00 7.50
76 Cliff Lee/100 .... 10.00 3.00
77 Chris Snelling/100 .... 10.00 3.00
78 Ryan Wagner/30 .... 25.00 7.50
80 Juan Gonzalez/3
81 Joe Borchard/100 .... 15.00 4.50
82 Gary Sheffield/5
83 Wade Miller/3
84 Jeff Bagwell/1
85 Ryan Church/100 .... 10.00 3.00
86 Adrian Beltre/3
87 Jeff Baker/30 .... 20.00 6.00
88 Adam Loewen/30 .... 40.00 12.00
90 Pedro Martinez/1
91 Carlos Rivera/15
92 Junior Spivey/15 .... 25.00 7.50
93 Tim Hudson/1
94 Troy Glaus/3
96 Alexis Gomez/100 .... 10.00 3.00
97 Antonio Perez/15................ 25.00 7.50
98 Dan Haren/30 .... 25.00 7.50
99 Ivan Rodriguez/3
100 Randy Johnson/1
101 Lyle Overbay/100 .... 10.00 3.00
102 Oliver Perez/100 .... 10.00 3.00
103 Miguel Cabrera/30............. 60.00 18.00
104 Scott Rolen/1
105 Roger Clemens/1
106 Brian Tallet/100................ 10.00 3.00
107 Nic Jackson/100............... 10.00 3.00
108 Angel Berroa/5
109 Hank Blalock/30 .... 40.00 12.00
110 Ryan Klesko/5
111 Jose Castillo/100.............. 10.00 3.00
112 Paul Konerko/5
113 Greg Maddux/1
114 Mark Mulder/15................ 50.00 15.00
116 Garrett Atkins/30.............. 20.00 6.00
117 Jeremy Guthrie/30............ 20.00 6.00
118 Orlando Cabrera/15 .... 25.00 7.50
120 Tom Glavine/1
121 Morgan Ensberg/50........... 20.00 6.00
122 Sean Casey/5
123 Orlando Hudson/30 .... 20.00 6.00
125 Craig Biggio/1
126 Adam LaRoche/30............. 25.00 7.50
127 Hong-Chih Kuo/15 .... 50.00 15.00
128 Paul LoDuca/1
130 Luis Castillo/15 .... 30.00 9.00
131 Joe Crede/35 .... 20.00 6.00

132 Ken Harvey/30 20.00 6.00
133 Freddy Sanchez/15 25.00 7.50
134 Roy Oswalt/5
135 Curt Schilling/1
136 Alfredo Amezaga/30 20.00 6.00
137 Chien-Ming Wang/15 80.00 24.00
139 Trot Nixon/6
142 Jacque Jones/10
143 Travis Hafner/30 25.00 7.50
144 Sammy Sosa/1
145 Mike Mussina/1
146 Vinny Chulk/100 10.00 3.00
147 Chad Gaudin/30 20.00 6.00
148 Delmon Young/10
149 Mike Lowell/15 30.00 9.00
151 Roger Clemens FB/1
152 Mark Grace FB/1
154 Alex Rodriguez FB/1
155 Rafael Palmeiro FB/1
156 Greg Maddux FB/1
157 Mike Piazza FB/1
158 Mike Mussina FB/1
159 Dale Murphy LGD/1
160 Cal Ripken LGD/1
161 Carl Yastrzemski LGD/1
162 Marty Marion LGD/10
163 Don Mattingly LGD/1
164 Robin Yount LGD/1
166 Jim Palmer LGD/1
167 George Brett LGD/1
168 Whitey Ford LGD/1
171 Duke Snider LGD/1
172 Steve Carlton LGD/1
173 Stan Musial LGD/1
174 Nolan Ryan LGD/1
175 Deion Sanders LGD/1

2004 Diamond Kings DK Signatures Silver Sepia

Nm-Mt Ex-Mt
RANDOM INSERTS IN PACKS
PRINT RUNS B/WN 1-10 COPIES PER
NO PRICING DUE TO SCARCITY

2004 Diamond Kings DK Signatures Framed Bronze

Nm-Mt Ex-Mt
RANDOM INSERTS IN PACKS
PRINT RUNS B/WN 1-50 COPIES PER
NO PRICING ON QTY OF 10 OR LESS.
1 Alex Rodriguez/1
2 Andruw Jones/5
4 Kerry Wood/1
5 Magglio Ordonez/10
6 Victor Martinez/50 20.00 6.00
7 Jeremy Bonderman/1
8 Josh Beckett/5
9 Jeff Kent/5
10 Carlos Beltran/10
11 Hideo Nomo/1
12 Richie Sexson/10
13 Jose Vidro/25 25.00 7.50
14 Jae Seo/25 30.00 9.00
17 Brett Myers/25 25.00 7.50
19 Edgar Martinez/25 60.00 18.00
20 Jim Edmonds/1
21 Rocco Baldelli/25 60.00 18.00
22 Mark Teixeira/1
26 Marlon Byrd/50 15.00 4.50
27 Albert Pujols/1
28 Vernon Wells/25 40.00 12.00
29 Garret Anderson/10
31 Chipper Jones/1
32 Rich Harden/50 30.00 9.00
35 Brandon Webb/25 40.00 12.00
36 Mark Prior/1
38 Frank Thomas/5
39 Rafael Palmeiro/1
40 Adam Dunn/25 40.00 12.00
41 Aubrey Huff/25 25.00 7.50
42 Todd Helton/1
44 Dontrelle Willis/25 40.00 12.00
45 Lance Berkman/1
46 Mike Sweeney/10
48 Torii Hunter/25 40.00 12.00
49 Vladimir Guerrero/1
50 Mike Piazza/1
51 Alexis Rios/50 30.00 9.00
52 Shannon Stewart/25 25.00 7.50
53 Eric Hinske/25 20.00 6.00
54 Jason Jennings/25 20.00 6.00
56 Brandon Claussen/50 20.00 6.00
57 Joe Thurston/50 15.00 4.50
58 Ramon Nivar/25 20.00 6.00
59 Jay Gibbons/25 25.00 7.50
60 Eric Chavez/10
61 Jimmy Gobble/50 20.00 6.00
62 Walter Young/50 15.00 4.50
63 Mark Grace/1
64 Austin Kearns/5
65 Bob Abreu/25 25.00 7.50
67 Brandon Phillips/50 15.00 4.50
68 Rickie Weeks/25 60.00 18.00
70 Mariano Rivera /10
71 Jason Lane/25 20.00 6.00
72 Xavier Nady/1
73 Runelvys Hernandez/25 20.00 6.00
74 Aramis Ramirez/25 25.00 7.50
76 Cliff Lee/50 15.00 4.50
77 Chris Snelling/50 15.00 4.50
78 Ryan Wagner/25 25.00 7.50
80 Juan Gonzalez/5
81 Joe Borchard/50 20.00 6.00
82 Gary Sheffield/10
83 Wade Miller/5
84 Jeff Bagwell/1
85 Ryan Church/50 15.00 4.50
86 Adrian Beltre/10
87 Jeff Baker/25 20.00 6.00
88 Adam Loewen/25 40.00 12.00
90 Pedro Martinez/1
91 Carlos Rivera/50 15.00 4.50
92 Junior Spivey/25
93 Tim Hudson/10
94 Troy Glaus/25 60.00 18.00
96 Alexis Gomez/50 15.00 4.50
97 Antonio Perez/25 20.00 6.00
98 Dan Haren/25 25.00 7.50
99 Ivan Rodriguez/5
100 Randy Johnson/1
101 Lyle Overbay/50 15.00 4.50
102 Oliver Perez/50 15.00 4.50
103 Miguel Cabrera/50 50.00 15.00
104 Scott Rolen/5
106 Brian Tallet/50 15.00 4.50
107 Nic Jackson/50 15.00 4.50
108 Angel Berroa/25 25.00 7.50
109 Hank Blalock/25 40.00 12.00
110 Ryan Klesko/5
111 Jose Castillo/50 15.00 4.50
112 Paul Konerko/15 30.00 9.00
113 Greg Maddux/1
114 Mark Mulder/25 40.00 12.00
116 Garrett Atkins/50 15.00 4.50
117 Jeremy Guthrie/25 20.00 6.00
118 Orlando Cabrera/25 20.00 6.00
120 Tom Glavine/5
121 Morgan Ensberg/50 20.00 6.00
122 Sean Casey/5
123 Orlando Hudson/50 15.00 4.50
125 Craig Biggio/5
126 Adam LaRoche/50 20.00 6.00
127 Hong-Chih Kuo/25 40.00 12.00
128 Paul LoDuca/1
130 Luis Castillo/25 25.00 7.50
131 Joe Crede/50 15.00 4.50
132 Ken Harvey/25 20.00 6.00
133 Freddy Sanchez/25 20.00 6.00
134 Roy Oswalt/20 40.00 12.00
135 Curt Schilling/1
136 Alfredo Amezaga/25 20.00 6.00
137 Chien-Ming Wang/25 60.00 18.00
139 Trot Nixon/25 60.00 18.00
142 Jacque Jones/25 25.00 7.50
143 Travis Hafner/25 25.00 7.50
144 Sammy Sosa/1
145 Mike Mussina/1
146 Vinny Chulk/50 15.00 4.50
147 Chad Gaudin/25 20.00 6.00
148 Delmon Young/25 60.00 18.00
149 Mike Lowell/25 25.00 7.50
151 Roger Clemens FB/1
152 Mark Grace FB/1
154 Alex Rodriguez FB/1
155 Rafael Palmeiro FB/1
156 Greg Maddux FB/1
157 Mike Piazza FB/1
158 Mike Mussina FB/1
159 Dale Murphy LGD/1
160 Cal Ripken LGD/1
161 Carl Yastrzemski LGD/1
162 Marty Marion LGD/25 25.00 7.50
163 Don Mattingly LGD/1
164 Robin Yount LGD/1
166 Jim Palmer LGD/1
167 George Brett LGD/1
168 Whitey Ford LGD/1
171 Duke Snider LGD/1
172 Steve Carlton LGD/1
173 Stan Musial LGD/1
174 Nolan Ryan LGD/1
175 Deion Sanders LGD/1

2004 Diamond Kings DK Signatures Framed Bronze Sepia

Nm-Mt Ex-Mt
RANDOM INSERTS IN PACKS
PRINT RUNS B/WN 1-25 COPIES PER
NO PRICING ON QTY OF 1 OR LESS
162 Marty Marion LGD/25 25.00 7.50

2004 Diamond Kings DK Signatures Framed Gold

Nm-Mt Ex-Mt
RANDOM INSERTS IN PACKS
PRINT RUNS B/WN 1-5 COPIES PER
NO PRICING DUE TO SCARCITY

2004 Diamond Kings DK Signatures Framed Gold Sepia

Nm-Mt Ex-Mt
RANDOM INSERTS IN PACKS
PRINT RUNS B/WN 1-5 COPIES PER
NO PRICING DUE TO SCARCITY

2004 Diamond Kings DK Signatures Framed Platinum Black

Nm-Mt Ex-Mt
RANDOM INSERTS IN PACKS
STATED PRINT RUN 1 SERIAL #'d SET
NO PRICING DUE TO SCARCITY

2004 Diamond Kings DK Signatures Framed Platinum Black Sepia

Nm-Mt Ex-Mt
RANDOM INSERTS IN PACKS
STATED PRINT RUN 1 SERIAL #'d SET
NO PRICING DUE TO SCARCITY

2004 Diamond Kings DK Signatures Framed Platinum Grey

Nm-Mt Ex-Mt
RANDOM INSERTS IN PACKS
STATED PRINT RUN 1 SERIAL #'d SET
NO PRICING DUE TO SCARCITY

2004 Diamond Kings DK Signatures Framed Platinum Grey Sepia

Nm-Mt Ex-Mt
RANDOM INSERTS IN PACKS
STATED PRINT RUN 1 SERIAL #'d SET
NO PRICING DUE TO SCARCITY

2004 Diamond Kings DK Signatures Framed Platinum White

Nm-Mt Ex-Mt
RANDOM INSERTS IN PACKS
STATED PRINT RUN 1 SERIAL #'d SET
NO PRICING DUE TO SCARCITY

2004 Diamond Kings DK Signatures Framed Platinum White Sepia

Nm-Mt Ex-Mt
RANDOM INSERTS IN PACKS
STATED PRINT RUN 1 SERIAL #'d SET
NO PRICING DUE TO SCARCITY

2004 Diamond Kings DK Signatures Framed Silver

Nm-Mt Ex-Mt
RANDOM INSERTS IN PACKS
PRINT RUNS B/WN 1-25 COPIES PER
NO PRICING ON QTY OF 10 OR LESS.
1 Alex Rodriguez/1
2 Andruw Jones/5
4 Kerry Wood/1
5 Magglio Ordonez/10
6 Victor Martinez/15 30.00 9.00
7 Jeremy Bonderman/1
8 Josh Beckett/5
9 Jeff Kent/5
10 Carlos Beltran/10
11 Hideo Nomo/1
12 Richie Sexson/10
13 Jose Vidro/10
14 Jae Seo/15 50.00 15.00
17 Brett Myers/10
19 Edgar Martinez/10
20 Jim Edmonds/1
21 Rocco Baldelli/15 80.00 24.00
22 Mark Teixeira/1
26 Marlon Byrd/15 25.00 7.50
27 Albert Pujols/1
28 Vernon Wells/10
29 Garret Anderson/10
31 Chipper Jones/1
32 Rich Harden/25 40.00 12.00
35 Brandon Webb/15 50.00 15.00
36 Mark Prior/1
38 Frank Thomas/5
39 Rafael Palmeiro/1
40 Adam Dunn/5
41 Aubrey Huff/10
42 Todd Helton/1
44 Dontrelle Willis/10
45 Lance Berkman/1
46 Mike Sweeney/10
47 Kazuhisa Ishii/1
48 Torii Hunter/10
49 Vladimir Guerrero/1
50 Mike Piazza/1
51 Alexis Rios/25 40.00 12.00
52 Shannon Stewart/5
53 Eric Hinske/15
54 Jason Jennings/10
56 Brandon Claussen/25 25.00 7.50
57 Joe Thurston/25 20.00 6.00
58 Ramon Nivar/25 25.00 7.50
59 Jay Gibbons/15 30.00 9.00
60 Eric Chavez/10
61 Jimmy Gobble/15 30.00 9.00
62 Walter Young/25 20.00 6.00
63 Mark Grace/1
64 Austin Kearns/5
65 Bob Abreu/10
67 Brandon Phillips/15 25.00 7.50
68 Rickie Weeks/10
70 Mariano Rivera/5
71 Jason Lane/10
72 Xavier Nady/1
73 Runelvys Hernandez/15 25.00 7.50
74 Aramis Ramirez/10
76 Cliff Lee/15 25.00 7.50
77 Chris Snelling/25 20.00 6.00
78 Ryan Wagner/10
80 Juan Gonzalez/5
81 Joe Borchard/25 25.00 7.50
82 Gary Sheffield/5
83 Wade Miller/3
84 Jeff Bagwell/1
85 Ryan Church/25 20.00 6.00
86 Adrian Beltre/10
87 Jeff Baker/10
88 Adam Loewen/10
90 Pedro Martinez/1
91 Carlos Rivera/15 25.00 7.50
92 Junior Spivey/10
93 Tim Hudson/10
94 Troy Glaus/5
96 Alexis Gomez/25 20.00 6.00
97 Antonio Perez/10
98 Dan Haren/15
99 Ivan Rodriguez/5
100 Randy Johnson/1
101 Lyle Overbay/25 20.00 6.00
102 Oliver Perez/25 20.00 6.00
103 Miguel Cabrera/10
104 Scott Rolen/5
105 Roger Clemens/1
106 Brian Tallet/25 20.00 6.00
107 Nic Jackson/25 20.00 6.00
108 Angel Berroa/5
109 Hank Blalock/10
110 Ryan Klesko/5
111 Jose Castillo/15 25.00 7.50
112 Paul Konerko/10
113 Greg Maddux/1
114 Mark Mulder/10
116 Garrett Atkins/15
117 Jeremy Guthrie/10
118 Orlando Cabrera/10
120 Tom Glavine/5
121 Morgan Ensberg/15 30.00 9.00
122 Sean Casey/5
123 Orlando Hudson/15 25.00 7.50
125 Craig Biggio/5
126 Adam LaRoche/15 30.00 9.00
127 Hong-Chih Kuo/10
128 Paul LoDuca/1
130 Luis Castillo/15 30.00 9.00
131 Joe Crede/10
132 Ken Harvey/15
133 Freddy Sanchez/15 25.00 7.50
134 Roy Oswalt/10
135 Curt Schilling/1
136 Alfredo Amezaga/15 25.00 7.50
137 Chien-Ming Wang/15 80.00 24.00
139 Trot Nixon/10
142 Jacque Jones/10
143 Travis Hafner/10
144 Sammy Sosa/1
145 Mike Mussina/1
146 Vinny Chulk/25 20.00 6.00
147 Chad Gaudin/15 25.00 7.50
148 Delmon Young/10
149 Mike Lowell/15 30.00 9.00
151 Roger Clemens FB/1
152 Mark Grace FB/1
154 Alex Rodriguez FB/1
155 Rafael Palmeiro FB/1
156 Greg Maddux FB/1
157 Mike Piazza FB/1
158 Mike Mussina FB/1
159 Dale Murphy LGD/1
160 Cal Ripken LGD/1
161 Carl Yastrzemski LGD/1
162 Marty Marion LGD/10
163 Don Mattingly LGD/1
164 Robin Yount LGD/1
166 Jim Palmer LGD/1
167 George Brett LGD/1
168 Whitey Ford LGD/1
171 Duke Snider LGD/1
172 Steve Carlton LGD/1
173 Stan Musial LGD/1
174 Nolan Ryan LGD/1
175 Deion Sanders LGD/1

2004 Diamond Kings DK Signatures Framed Silver Sepia

Nm-Mt Ex-Mt
RANDOM INSERTS IN PACKS
PRINT RUNS B/WN 1-10 COPIES PER
NO PRICING DUE TO SCARCITY

2004 Diamond Kings Diamond Cut Bats

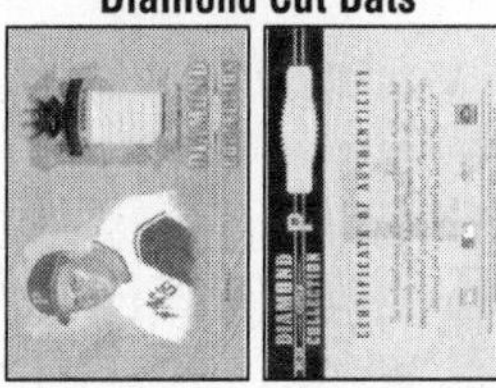

Nm-Mt Ex-Mt
RANDOM INSERTS IN PACKS
PRINT RUNS B/WN 1-100 COPIES PER
NO PRICING ON QTY OF 1 OR LESS
1 Alex Rodriguez/100 25.00 7.50
2 Nomar Garciaparra/100 25.00 7.50
3 Hideo Nomo/100 15.00 4.50
4 Alfonso Soriano/100 15.00 4.50
6 Edgar Martinez/100 15.00 4.50
7 Rocco Baldelli/100 15.00 4.50
8 Mark Teixeira/100 10.00 3.00
9 Albert Pujols/100 30.00 9.00
10 Vernon Wells/100 10.00 3.00
11 Garret Anderson/100 10.00 3.00
14 Brandon Webb/100 10.00 3.00
15 Mark Prior/100 25.00 7.50
16 Rafael Palmeiro/100 15.00 4.50
17 Adam Dunn/100 10.00 3.00
18 Dontrelle Willis/100 10.00 3.00
19 Kazuhisa Ishii/100 10.00 3.00
20 Torii Hunter/100 10.00 3.00
21 Vladimir Guerrero/100 15.00 4.50
22 Mike Piazza/100 25.00 7.50
23 Jason Giambi/100 15.00 4.50
26 Bob Abreu/100 10.00 3.00
27 Hee Seop Choi/100 10.00 3.00
28 Rickie Weeks/100 15.00 4.50
30 Troy Glaus/100 15.00 4.50
31 Ivan Rodriguez/100 15.00 4.50
32 Hank Blalock/100 10.00 3.00
33 Greg Maddux/100 25.00 7.50
34 Nick Johnson/100 10.00 3.00
35 Shawn Green/100 10.00 3.00
36 Sammy Sosa/100 25.00 7.50
37 Dale Murphy/50 25.00 7.50
38 Cal Ripken/50 60.00 18.00
39 Carl Yastrzemski/100 25.00 7.50
41 Don Mattingly/100 30.00 9.00
43 George Brett/50 40.00 12.00
45 Duke Snider/1
46 Steve Carlton/50 15.00 4.50
47 Stan Musial/25 50.00 15.00
48 Nolan Ryan/50 50.00 15.00
49 Deion Sanders/50 25.00 7.50
50 Roberto Clemente/25 150.00 45.00

2004 Diamond Kings Diamond Cut Combos Material

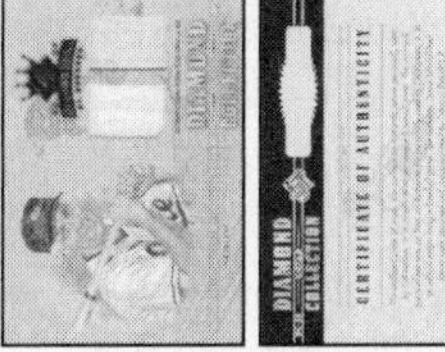

Nm-Mt Ex-Mt
RANDOM INSERTS IN PACKS
PRINT RUNS B/WN 1-50 COPIES PER
NO PRICING ON QTY OF 8 OR LESS
1 Alex Rodriguez Bat-Jsy/50 40.00 12.00
2 Nomar Garciaparra Bat-Jsy/50 40.00 12.00
3 Hideo Nomo Bat-Jsy/25 40.00 12.00
4 Alfonso Soriano Bat-Jsy/50 25.00 7.50
6 Edgar Martinez Bat-Jsy/25 40.00 12.00
7 Rocco Baldelli Bat-Jsy/25 40.00 12.00
8 Mark Teixeira Bat-Jsy/25 25.00 7.50
9 Albert Pujols Bat-Jsy/50 50.00 15.00
10 Vernon Wells Bat-Jsy/25 25.00 7.50
11 Garret Anderson Bat-Jsy/25 25.00 7.50
14 Brandon Webb Bat-Jsy/25 25.00 7.50
15 Mark Prior Bat-Jsy/50 50.00 15.00
16 Rafael Palmeiro Bat-Jsy/25 40.00 12.00
17 Adam Dunn Bat-Jsy/25 25.00 7.50
18 Dontrelle Willis Bat-Jsy/25 25.00 7.50
19 Kazuhisa Ishii Bat-Jsy/25 25.00 7.50
20 Torii Hunter Bat-Jsy/25 25.00 7.50
21 Vladimir Guerrero Bat-Jsy/25 40.00 12.00
22 Mike Piazza Bat-Jsy/50 40.00 12.00
23 Jason Giambi Bat-Jsy/25 40.00 12.00
26 Bob Abreu Bat-Jsy/50 15.00 4.50
27 Hee Seop Choi Bat-Jsy/50 15.00 4.50
30 Troy Glaus Bat-Jsy/25 40.00 12.00
31 Ivan Rodriguez Bat-Jsy/25 40.00 12.00
32 Hank Blalock Bat-Jsy/25 25.00 7.50
33 Greg Maddux Bat-Jsy/50 40.00 12.00
34 Nick Johnson Bat-Jsy/25 25.00 7.50
35 Shawn Green Bat-Jsy/25 25.00 7.50
36 Sammy Sosa Bat-Jsy/50 40.00 12.00
37 Dale Murphy Bat-Jsy/3
38 Cal Ripken Bat-Jsy/8
39 Carl Yastrzemski Bat-Jsy/8
41 Don Mattingly Bat-Jsy/23 80.00 24.00
42 Jim Palmer Jsy-Jsy/22 30.00 9.00
43 George Brett Bat-Jsy/5
44 Whitey Ford Jsy-Pants/16 50.00 15.00
45 Duke Snider Bat-Jsy/1
46 Steve Carlton Bat-Jsy/32 25.00 7.50
47 Stan Musial Bat-Jsy/6
48 Nolan Ryan Bat-Jsy/34 60.00 18.00
49 Deion Sanders Bat-Jsy/24 50.00 15.00
50 Roberto Clemente Bat-Jsy/21

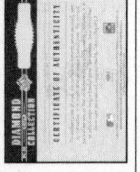

2004 Diamond Kings Diamond Cut Combos Signature

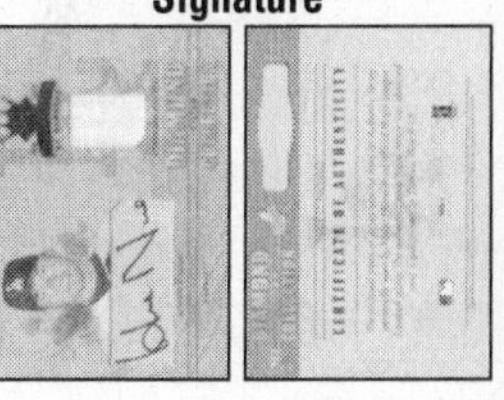

Nm-Mt Ex-Mt
RANDOM INSERTS IN PACKS
PRINT RUNS B/WN 1-32 COPIES PER
NO PRICING ON QTY OF 10 OR LESS.
1 Alex Rodriguez Jsy/3
3 Hideo Nomo Jsy/1
5 Brett Myers Jsy/5
6 Edgar Martinez Jsy/5
7 Rocco Baldelli Jsy/10
8 Mark Teixeira Jsy/10
9 Albert Pujols Jsy/5
10 Vernon Wells Jsy/5
11 Garret Anderson Jsy/5
13 Rich Harden Jsy/1
14 Brandon Webb Jsy/10
15 Mark Prior Jsy/5
16 Rafael Palmeiro Jsy/5
17 Adam Dunn Jsy/5
18 Dontrelle Willis Jsy/10
19 Kazuhisa Ishii Jsy/1
20 Torii Hunter Jsy/5
21 Vladimir Guerrero Jsy/5
22 Mike Piazza Jsy/1
26 Bob Abreu Jsy/10
30 Troy Glaus Jsy/10
31 Ivan Rodriguez Jsy/10
32 Hank Blalock Jsy/10
33 Greg Maddux Jsy/1
37 Dale Murphy Jsy/3
38 Cal Ripken Jsy/8
39 Carl Yastrzemski Jsy/8
40 Marty Marion Jsy/25 40.00 12.00
41 Don Mattingly Jsy/23 150.00 45.00
42 Jim Palmer Jsy/22 50.00 15.00
43 George Brett Jsy/1
44 Whitey Ford Jsy/16 80.00 24.00
45 Duke Snider Jsy/4
46 Steve Carlton Jsy/32 60.00 18.00
47 Stan Musial Jsy/6
48 Nolan Ryan Jsy/1
49 Deion Sanders Jsy/1

2004 Diamond Kings Diamond Cut Jerseys

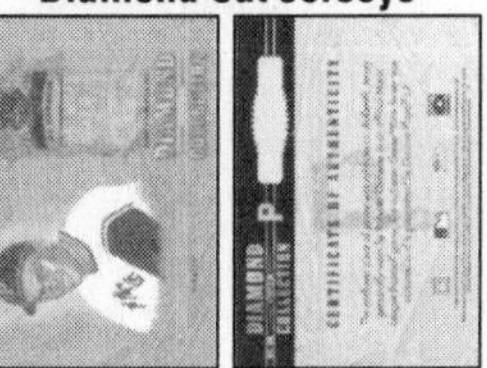

Nm-Mt Ex-Mt
RANDOM INSERTS IN PACKS
PRINT RUNS B/WN 10-100 COPIES PER
NO PRICING ON QTY OF 10 OR LESS.
1 Alex Rodriguez/100 25.00 7.50
2 Nomar Garciaparra/100 25.00 7.50
3 Hideo Nomo/50 25.00 7.50
4 Alfonso Soriano/100 15.00 4.50

5 Brett Myers/50 15.00 4.50
6 Edgar Martinez/100 15.00 4.50
7 Rocco Baldelli/100 15.00 4.50
8 Mark Teixeira/100 10.00 3.00
9 Albert Pujols/100 30.00 9.00
10 Vernon Wells/100 10.00 3.00
11 Garret Anderson/50 15.00 4.50
12 Jerome Williams/100 10.00 3.00
13 Rich Harden/100 10.00 3.00
14 Brandon Webb/100 10.00 3.00
15 Mark Prior/100 25.00 7.50
16 Rafael Palmeiro/100 15.00 4.50
17 Adam Dunn/100 10.00 3.00
18 Dontrelle Willis/100 10.00 3.00
19 Kazuhisa Ishii/100 10.00 3.00
20 Torii Hunter/100 10.00 3.00
21 Vladimir Guerrero/50 25.00 7.50
22 Mike Piazza/100 25.00 7.50
23 Jason Giambi/100 15.00 4.50
25 Ramon Nivar/100 10.00 3.00
26 Bob Abreu/100 10.00 3.00
27 Hee Seop Choi/100 10.00 3.00
30 Troy Glaus/100 15.00 4.50
31 Ivan Rodriguez/100 15.00 4.50
32 Hank Blalock/100 10.00 3.00
33 Greg Maddux/100 25.00 7.50
34 Nick Johnson/100 10.00 3.00
35 Shawn Green/100 10.00 3.00
36 Sammy Sosa/100 25.00 7.50
37 Dale Murphy/50 25.00 7.50
38 Cal Ripken/50 60.00 18.00
39 Carl Yastrzemski/100 25.00 7.50
40 Marty Marion/50 15.00 4.50
41 Don Mattingly/100 30.00 9.00
42 Jim Palmer/25 25.00 7.50
43 George Brett/50 40.00 12.00
44 Whitey Ford/25 40.00 12.00
45 Duke Snider/10
46 Steve Carlton/50 15.00 4.50
47 Stan Musial/10
48 Nolan Ryan/50 50.00 15.00
49 Deion Sanders/50 25.00 7.50
50 Roberto Clemente/10

2004 Diamond Kings Diamond Cut Signatures

Nm-Mt Ex-Mt
RANDOM INSERTS IN PACKS
PRINT RUNS B/WN 1-50 COPIES PER
NO PRICING ON QTY OF 10 OR LESS.
1 Alex Rodriguez/1
3 Hideo Nomo/1
5 Brett Myers/10
6 Edgar Martinez/5
7 Rocco Baldelli/25 60.00 18.00
8 Mark Teixeira/25 40.00 12.00
9 Albert Pujols/1
10 Vernon Wells/5
11 Garret Anderson/5
13 Rich Harden/50 30.00 9.00
14 Brandon Webb/50 30.00 9.00
15 Mark Prior/5
16 Rafael Palmeiro/5
17 Adam Dunn/5
18 Dontrelle Willis/10
19 Kazuhisa Ishii/1
20 Torii Hunter/25 40.00 12.00
21 Vladimir Guerrero/5
22 Mike Piazza/1
24 Ryan Wagner/50 20.00 6.00
25 Ramon Nivar/50 15.00 4.50
26 Bob Abreu/10
28 Rickie Weeks/50 50.00 15.00
29 Adam Loewen/50 30.00 9.00
30 Troy Glaus/10
31 Ivan Rodriguez/10
32 Hank Blalock/25 40.00 12.00
33 Greg Maddux/1
36 Sammy Sosa/1
37 Dale Murphy/3
38 Cal Ripken/8
39 Carl Yastrzemski/8
40 Marty Marion/25 25.00 7.50
41 Don Mattingly/23 120.00 36.00
42 Jim Palmer/22 30.00 9.00
43 George Brett/1
44 Whitey Ford/16 50.00 15.00
45 Duke Snider/4
46 Steve Carlton/32 40.00 12.00
47 Stan Musial/6
48 Nolan Ryan/34 150.00 45.00
49 Deion Sanders/1

2004 Diamond Kings Gallery of Stars

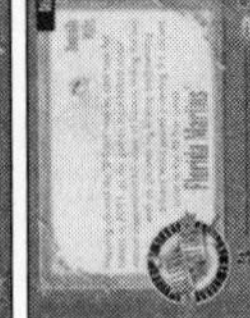

Nm-Mt Ex-Mt
STATED ODDS 1:37
1 Nolan Ryan 10.00 3.00
2 Cal Ripken 12.00 3.60
3 George Brett 10.00 3.00
4 Don Mattingly 10.00 3.00
5 Deion Sanders 4.00 1.20
6 Mike Piazza 6.00 1.80
7 Hideo Nomo 4.00 1.20
8 Rickey Henderson 4.00 1.20
9 Roger Clemens 8.00 2.40
10 Greg Maddux 6.00 1.80
11 Albert Pujols 8.00 2.40
12 Alex Rodriguez 6.00 1.80
13 Dale Murphy 4.00 1.20
14 Mark Prior 8.00 2.40
15 Dontrelle Willis 3.00 .90

2004 Diamond Kings Gallery of Stars Signatures

Nm-Mt Ex-Mt
RANDOM INSERTS IN PACKS
PRINT RUNS B/WN 1-10 COPIES PER
NO PRICING DUE TO SCARCITY

2004 Diamond Kings Heritage Collection

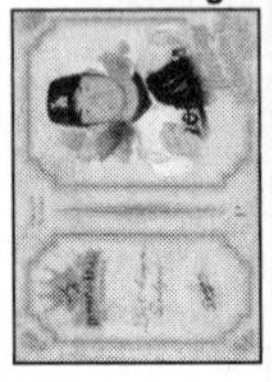

Nm-Mt Ex-Mt
RANDOM INSERTS IN PACKS
1 Dale Murphy 4.00 1.20
2 Cal Ripken 12.00 3.60
3 Carl Yastrzemski 6.00 1.80
4 Don Mattingly 10.00 3.00
5 Jim Palmer 3.00 .90
6 Andre Dawson 3.00 .90
7 Roy Campanella 4.00 1.20
8 George Brett 10.00 3.00
9 Duke Snider 4.00 1.20
10 Marty Marion 3.00 .90
11 Deion Sanders 4.00 1.20
12 Whitey Ford 4.00 1.20
13 Stan Musial 6.00 1.80
14 Nolan Ryan 10.00 3.00
15 Steve Carlton 3.00 .90
16 Robin Yount 6.00 1.80
17 Albert Pujols 8.00 2.40
18 Alex Rodriguez 6.00 1.80
19 Mike Piazza 6.00 1.80
20 Roger Clemens 8.00 2.40
21 Hideo Nomo 4.00 1.20
22 Mark Prior 8.00 2.40
23 Roger Maris 6.00 1.80
24 Greg Maddux 6.00 1.80
25 Mark Grace 4.00 1.20

2004 Diamond Kings Heritage Collection Bats

Nm-Mt Ex-Mt
RANDOM INSERTS IN PACKS
PRINT RUNS B/WN 1-50 COPIES PER
NO PRICING ON QTY OF 1 OR LESS...
1 Dale Murphy/50 25.00 7.50
2 Cal Ripken/50 60.00 18.00
3 Carl Yastrzemski/50 30.00 9.00
4 Don Mattingly/50 40.00 12.00
6 Andre Dawson/25 25.00 7.50
7 Roy Campanella/25 40.00 12.00
8 George Brett/25 60.00 18.00
9 Duke Snider/1
11 Deion Sanders/50 25.00 7.50
13 Stan Musial/25 50.00 15.00
14 Nolan Ryan/25 60.00 18.00
15 Steve Carlton/25 25.00 7.50
16 Robin Yount/50 30.00 9.00
17 Albert Pujols/50 40.00 12.00
18 Alex Rodriguez/50 30.00 9.00
19 Mike Piazza/50 30.00 9.00
20 Roger Clemens/50 30.00 9.00
21 Hideo Nomo/50 25.00 7.50
22 Mark Prior/50 40.00 12.00
23 Roger Maris/25 80.00 24.00
24 Greg Maddux/50 30.00 9.00
25 Mark Grace/50 25.00 7.50

2004 Diamond Kings Heritage Collection Jerseys

Nm-Mt Ex-Mt
RANDOM INSERTS IN PACKS
PRINT RUNS B/WN 10-50 COPIES PER
NO PRICING ON QTY OF 10 OR LESS.
1 Dale Murphy/50 25.00 7.50
2 Cal Ripken/50 60.00 18.00
3 Carl Yastrzemski/50 30.00 9.00
4 Don Mattingly/50 40.00 12.00
5 Jim Palmer/10
6 Andre Dawson/25 25.00 7.50

7 Roy Campanella Pants/25 40.00 12.00
8 George Brett/25 60.00 18.00
9 Duke Snider/10
10 Marty Marion/50 15.00 4.50
11 Deion Sanders/50 25.00 7.50
12 Whitey Ford/25 40.00 12.00
13 Stan Musial/10
14 Nolan Ryan/25 60.00 18.00
15 Steve Carlton/25 25.00 7.50
16 Robin Yount/50 30.00 9.00
17 Albert Pujols/50 40.00 12.00
18 Alex Rodriguez/50 40.00 12.00
19 Mike Piazza/50 30.00 9.00
20 Roger Clemens/50 30.00 9.00
21 Hideo Nomo/50 25.00 7.50
22 Mark Prior/50 40.00 12.00
23 Roger Maris/25 80.00 24.00
24 Greg Maddux/50 30.00 9.00
25 Mark Grace/50 25.00 7.50

2004 Diamond Kings Heritage Collection Signatures

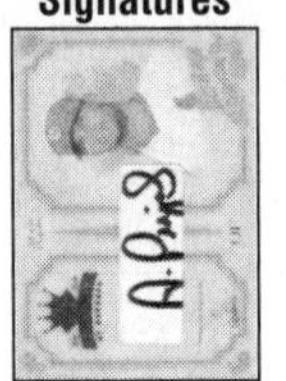

Nm-Mt Ex-Mt
RANDOM INSERTS IN PACKS
PRINT RUNS B/WN 1-16 COPIES PER
NO PRICING ON QTY OF 10 OR LESS.
12 Whitey Ford/16 50.00 15.00

2004 Diamond Kings HOF Heroes

Nm-Mt Ex-Mt
RANDOM INSERTS IN PACKS
PRINT RUNS B/WN 100-1000 COPIES PER
1 George Brett #45/1000 10.00 3.00
2 George Brett #45/500 15.00 4.50
3 George Brett #45/250 25.00 7.50
4 Mike Schmidt #46/1000 8.00 2.40
5 Mike Schmidt #46/250 20.00 6.00
6 Nolan Ryan #47/1000 10.00 3.00
7 Nolan Ryan #47/500 15.00 4.50
8 Nolan Ryan #47/250 25.00 7.50
9 Roberto Clemente #48/1000 10.00 3.00
10 Roberto Clemente #48/500 15.00 4.50
11 Roberto Clemente #48/250 25.00 7.50
12 Roberto Clemente #48/100 30.00 9.00
13 Carl Yastrzemski #49/1000 6.00 1.80
14 Robin Yount #50/1000 6.00 1.80
15 Whitey Ford #51/1000 5.00 1.50
16 Duke Snider #52/1000 5.00 1.50
17 Duke Snider #52/250 15.00 4.50
18 Carlton Fisk #53/1000 5.00 1.50
19 Ozzie Smith #54/1000 6.00 1.80
20 Kirby Puckett #55/1000 5.00 1.50
21 Bobby Doerr #56/1000 4.00 1.20
22 Frank Robinson #57/1000 4.00 1.20
23 Ralph Kiner #58/1000 4.00 1.20
24 Al Kaline #59/1000 5.00 1.50
25 Bob Feller #60/1000 5.00 1.50
26 Yogi Berra #61/1000 5.00 1.50
27 Stan Musial #62/1000 6.00 1.80
28 Stan Musial #62/500 10.00 3.00
29 Stan Musial #62/250 15.00 4.50
30 Jim Palmer #63/1000 4.00 1.20
31 Johnny Bench #64/1000 5.00 1.50
32 Steve Carlton #65/1000 4.00 1.20
33 Gary Carter #66/1000 5.00 1.50
34 Roy Campanella #67/1000 5.00 1.50
35 Roy Campanella #67/250 15.00 4.50

2004 Diamond Kings HOF Heroes Bats

Nm-Mt Ex-Mt
RANDOM INSERTS IN PACKS
PRINT RUNS B/WN 1-25 COPIES PER
NO PRICING ON QTY OF 5 OR LESS...
1 George Brett #45/25 50.00 15.00
2 George Brett #45/25 50.00 15.00
3 George Brett #45/25 50.00 15.00
4 Mike Schmidt #46/25 50.00 15.00
5 Mike Schmidt #46/25 50.00 15.00
6 Nolan Ryan #47/25 60.00 18.00
7 Nolan Ryan #47/25 60.00 18.00
8 Nolan Ryan #47/25 60.00 18.00
9 Roberto Clemente #48/5
10 Roberto Clemente #48/5
11 Roberto Clemente #48/5
12 Roberto Clemente #48/5
13 Carl Yastrzemski #49/25 50.00 15.00
14 Robin Yount #50/25 50.00 15.00
16 Duke Snider #52/1
17 Duke Snider #52/1
18 Carlton Fisk #53/25 40.00 12.00
19 Ozzie Smith #54/25 50.00 15.00
20 Kirby Puckett #55/25 40.00 12.00
21 Bobby Doerr #56/25 25.00 7.50
22 Frank Robinson #57/25 25.00 7.50
23 Ralph Kiner #58/25 25.00 7.50
24 Al Kaline #59/25 40.00 12.00
26 Yogi Berra #61/5
27 Stan Musial #62/5
28 Stan Musial #62/5
29 Stan Musial #62/5
31 Johnny Bench #64/25 40.00 12.00
32 Steve Carlton #65/25 25.00 7.50
33 Gary Carter #66/25 40.00 12.00
34 Roy Campanella #67/25 40.00 12.00
35 Roy Campanella #67/25 40.00 12.00

2004 Diamond Kings HOF Heroes Combos

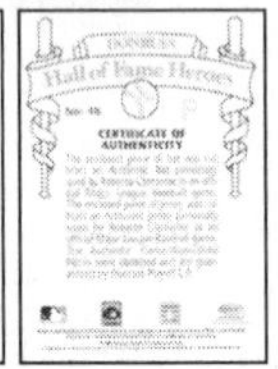

Nm-Mt Ex-Mt
RANDOM INSERTS IN PACKS
PRINT RUNS B/WN 1-25 COPIES PER
NO PRICING ON QTY OF 10 OR LESS.
1 George Brett #45 Bat-Jsy/25 60.00 18.00
2 George Brett #45 Bat-Jsy/25 60.00 18.00
3 George Brett #45 Bat-Jsy/25 60.00 18.00
4 Mike Schmidt #46 Bat-Jsy/25 60.00 18.00
5 Mike Schmidt #46 Bat-Jsy/25 60.00 18.00
6 Nolan Ryan #47 Bat-Jsy/25 80.00 24.00
7 Nolan Ryan #47 Bat-Jsy/25 80.00 24.00
8 Nolan Ryan #47 Bat-Jsy/25 80.00 24.00
9 Roberto Clemente #48 Bat-Jsy/5
10 Roberto Clemente #48 Bat-Jsy/5
11 Roberto Clemente #48 Bat-Jsy/5
12 Roberto Clemente #48 Bat-Jsy/5
13 C.Yastrzemski #49 Bat-Jsy/25 60.00 18.00
14 Robin Yount #50 Bat-Jsy/25 60.00 18.00
15 Whitey Ford #51 Jsy-Pants/25 50.00 15.00
16 Duke Snider #52 Bat-Jsy/1
17 Duke Snider #52 Bat-Jsy/1
18 Carlton Fisk #53 Bat-Jsy/25 50.00 15.00
19 Ozzie Smith #54 Bat-Jsy/25 50.00 15.00
20 Kirby Puckett #55 Bat-Jsy/25 50.00 15.00
21 Bobby Doerr #56 Bat-Jsy/25 30.00 9.00
22 Frank Robinson #57 Bat-Jsy/10
23 Ralph Kiner #58 Bat-Bat/25 30.00 9.00
24 Al Kaline #59 Bat-Jsy/25 50.00 15.00
25 Bob Feller #60 Jsy-Jsy/10
26 Yogi Berra #61 Bat-Jsy/5
27 Stan Musial #62 Bat-Jsy/5
28 Stan Musial #62 Bat-Jsy/5
29 Stan Musial #62 Bat-Jsy/5
30 Jim Palmer #63 Jsy-Jsy/5
31 Johnny Bench #64 Bat-Jsy/1
32 Steve Carlton #65 Bat-Jsy/25 30.00 9.00
33 Gary Carter #66 Bat-Jsy/25 50.00 15.00
34 R.Campy #67 Bat-Pants/25 50.00 15.00
35 R.Campy #67 Bat-Pants/25 50.00 15.00

2004 Diamond Kings HOF Heroes Jerseys

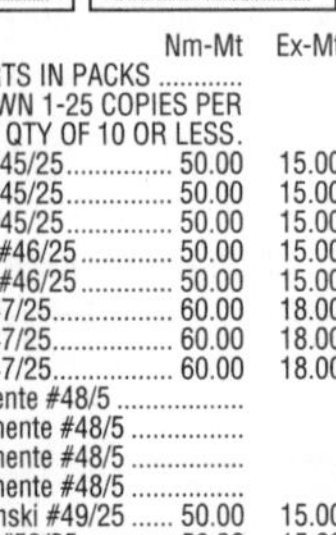

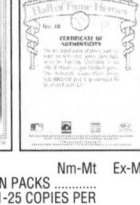

Nm-Mt Ex-Mt
RANDOM INSERTS IN PACKS
PRINT RUNS B/WN 1-25 COPIES PER
NO PRICING ON QTY OF 10 OR LESS.
1 George Brett #45/25 50.00 15.00
2 George Brett #45/25 50.00 15.00
3 George Brett #45/25 50.00 15.00
4 Mike Schmidt #46/25 50.00 15.00
5 Mike Schmidt #46/25 50.00 15.00
6 Nolan Ryan #47/25 60.00 18.00
7 Nolan Ryan #47/25 60.00 18.00
8 Nolan Ryan #47/25 60.00 18.00
9 Roberto Clemente #48/5
10 Roberto Clemente #48/5
11 Roberto Clemente #48/5
12 Roberto Clemente #48/5
13 Carl Yastrzemski #49/25 50.00 15.00
14 Robin Yount #50/25 50.00 15.00
15 Whitey Ford #51/25 40.00 12.00
16 Duke Snider #52/10
17 Duke Snider #52/10
18 Carlton Fisk #53/25 40.00 12.00
19 Ozzie Smith #54/25 50.00 15.00
20 Kirby Puckett #55/25 40.00 12.00
21 Bobby Doerr #56/25 25.00 7.50
22 Frank Robinson #57/10
24 Al Kaline #59/25 40.00 12.00
25 Bob Feller #60/10
26 Yogi Berra #61/5
27 Stan Musial #62/5
28 Stan Musial #62/5
29 Stan Musial #62/5
30 Jim Palmer #63/5
31 Johnny Bench #64/1
32 Steve Carlton #65/25 25.00 7.50
33 Gary Carter #66/25 40.00 12.00
34 Roy Campanella #67/25 40.00 12.00
35 Roy Campanella #67/25 40.00 12.00

2004 Diamond Kings HOF Heroes Signatures

Nm-Mt Ex-Mt
RANDOM INSERTS IN PACKS
PRINT RUNS B/WN 4-32 COPIES PER
NO PRICING ON QTY OF 10 OR LESS.
1 George Brett #45/5
2 George Brett #45/5
3 George Brett #45/5
6 Nolan Ryan #47/5
7 Nolan Ryan #47/5
8 Nolan Ryan #47/5
13 Carl Yastrzemski #49/8
14 Robin Yount #50/19 100.00 30.00
15 Whitey Ford #51/16 50.00 15.00
16 Duke Snider #52/4
17 Duke Snider #52/4
18 Carlton Fisk #53/5
19 Ozzie Smith #54/5
20 Kirby Puckett #55/5
21 Bobby Doerr #56/10
22 Frank Robinson #57/20 50.00 15.00
23 Ralph Kiner #58/4
24 Al Kaline #59/6
25 Bob Feller #60/19 50.00 15.00
26 Yogi Berra #61/8
27 Stan Musial #62/6
28 Stan Musial #62/6
29 Stan Musial #62/6
30 Jim Palmer #63/22 30.00 9.00
31 Johnny Bench #64/5
32 Steve Carlton #65/32 40.00 12.00
33 Gary Carter #66/5

2004 Diamond Kings Recollection Autographs

Nm-Mt Ex-Mt
RANDOM INSERTS IN PACKS
PRINT RUNS B/WN 1-159 COPIES PER
NO PRICING ON QTY OF 14 OR LESS.
1 Sandy Alomar Jr. 91 DK/8
2 Rich Aurilia 02 DK/2
3 Jeff Bagwell 93 TP Gall/1
4 Jeff Bagwell 02 DK/2
5 Jeff Bagwell 03 DK/1
6 Clint Barmes 03 DK Black/82 15.00 4.50
7 Clint Barmes 03 DK Blue/72 15.00 4.50
8 Carlos Beltran 02 DK/23 30.00 9.00
9 Carlos Beltran 03 DK/99 15.00 4.50
10 Adrian Beltre 02 DK/40 25.00 7.50
11 Johnny Bench 83 DK/3
12 Johnny Bench 01 DK Rep/1
13 Yogi Berra 83 HOF/4
14 Craig Biggio 91 DK/10
15 Craig Biggio 03 DK/1
16 Wade Boggs 84 DK/13
17 George Brett 03 DK/1
18 John Buck 02 DK/13
19 Chris Burke 03 DK/150 15.00 4.50
20 Marlon Byrd 02 DK/23 20.00 6.00
21 Marlon Byrd 03 DK/100 15.00 4.50
22 Rod Carew 01 DK Rep/1
23 Steve Carlton 01 DK Rep/6
24 Kevin Cash 03 DK/103 15.00 4.50
25 Jose Cruz 85 DK/59 15.00 4.50
26 J.D. Durbin 03 DK/151 25.00 7.50
27 Jim Edmonds 03 DK/24 30.00 9.00
28 Bob Feller 84 HOF/8
29 Bob Feller 03 DK HOF/18 60.00 18.00
30 Carlton Fisk 02 DK/13
31 Carlton Fisk 02 DK Her/5
32 Julio Franco 87 DK/25 30.00 9.00
33 Freddy Garcia 03 DK/50 25.00 7.50
34 Jay Gibbons 03 DK/100 15.00 4.50
35 Juan Gonzalez 03 DK/10
36 Mark Grace 02 DK/5
37 Mark Grace 03 DK/7
38 Shawn Green 02 DK/2
39 Brendan Harris 03 DK/150 15.00 4.50
40 Rickey Henderson 02 DK/1
41 Rickey Henderson 03 DK/2
42 Ru.Hernandez 02 DK/100 15.00 4.50
43 Eric Hinske 03 DK/20 20.00 6.00
44 Tim Hudson 02 DK/25 50.00 15.00
45 Tim Hudson 03 DK/25 50.00 15.00
46 Aubrey Huff 03 DK/99 15.00 4.50
47 Monte Irvin 84 HOF/7
48 Bo Jackson 02 DK/5
49 Jason Jennings 03 DK/50 15.00 4.50
50 Tommy John 88 DK Black/62 20.00 6.00

51 Tommy John 88 DK Blue/7
52 Howard Johnson 90 DK/52 15.00 4.50
53 Andruw Jones 03 DK/14
54 Austin Kearns 02 DK/25 30.00 9.00
55 Austin Kearns 03 DK/25 30.00 9.00
56 Ralph Kiner 83 HOF/5
57 Carney Lansford 85 DK Black/12
58 Carney Lansford 85 DK Blue/4
59 P.Larrison 03 DK Black/74 20.00 6.00
60 Pr.Larrison 03 DK Blue/77 20.00 6.00
61 Greg Maddux 02 DK/1
62 Greg Maddux 03 DK/2
63 Don Mattingly 85 DK/4
64 Don Mattingly 89 DK/5
65 Don Mattingly 02 DK Time/1
66 Don Mattingly 03 DK/5
67 Dustin McGowan 03 DK/159 15.00 4.50
68 Paul Molitor 02 DK Her/5
69 Melvin Mora 03 DK/101 15.00 4.50
70 Joe Morgan 01 DK Rep/2
71 Jack Morris 03 DK/60 20.00 6.00
72 Jack Morris 03 DK Her/19 40.00 12.00
73 Dale Murphy 03 DK Black/3
74 Dale Murphy 03 DK Blue/47 50.00 15.00
75 Dale Murphy 03 DK Her Black/8
76 Dale Murphy 03 DK Her Blue/10
77 Dale Murphy 03 DK Time/18 80.00 24.00
78 Stan Musial 83 HOF/3
79 Stan Musial 03 DK/2
80 Mike Mussina 03 DK/1
81 Phil Niekro 82 DK/10
82 Magglio Ordonez 03 DK/25 50.00 15.00
83 Magglio Ordonez 03 DK Ins/10
84 Roy Oswalt 03 DK/10
85 Dave Parker 82 DK/20 30.00 9.00
86 Dave Parker 90 DK/18 40.00 12.00
87 Tony Pena 85 DK/7
88 Jorge Posada 02 DK/25 50.00 15.00
89 Mark Prior 03 DK/25 175.00 52.50
90 Cal Ripken 02 DK/2
91 Cal Ripken 03 DK/3
92 Mike Rivera 02 DK/24 20.00 6.00
93 Robin Roberts 84 HOF Black/6
94 Robin Roberts 84 HOF Blue/1
95 Frank Robinson 83 HOF/8
96 Alex Rodriguez 03 DK/1
97 Ivan Rodriguez 03 DK/22 60.00 18.00
98 Scott Rolen 02 DK/5
99 Scott Rolen 03 DK/2
100 Rodrigo Rosario 02 DK/50 15.00 4.50
101 Nolan Ryan 02 DK/3
102 Nolan Ryan 03 DK/5
103 Nolan Ryan 03 DK Bronze/1
104 Nolan Ryan 03 DK Evol/1
105 Ron Santo 02 DK/29 50.00 15.00
106 Richie Sexson 02 DK/25 30.00 9.00
107 Richie Sexson 03 DK/25 30.00 9.00
108 Gary Sheffield 03 DK/11
109 Chris Snelling 02 DK/46 25.00 7.50
110 Duke Snider 83 HOF/4
111 J.T. Snow 93 TP Gall Black/1
112 J.T. Snow 93 TP Gall Blue/1
113 Sammy Sosa 99 Retro DK/2
114 Sammy Sosa 01 DK/2
115 Sammy Sosa 03 DK/3
116 Sammy Sosa 03 DK Ins/1
117 Junior Spivey 03 DK Black/12
118 Junior Spivey 03 DK Blue/13
119 Shannon Stewart 02 DK/50 25.00 7.50
120 S.Stewart 03 DK Black/92 15.00 4.50
121 Shannon Stewart 03 DK Blue/9
122 Frank Thomas 01 DK Black/1
123 Frank Thomas 01 DK Blue/1
124 Frank Thomas 00 Retro DK Black/2
125 Frank Thomas 00 Retro DK Blue/1
126 G.Thomas 82 DK Black/22 20.00 6.00
127 G.Thomas 82 DK Blue/20 20.00 6.00
128 Alan Trammell 02 DK/29 50.00 15.00
129 Alan Trammell 02 DK Her/25 50.00 15.00
130 Robin Ventura 03 DK/25 30.00 9.00
131 Jose Vidro 03 DK/25 30.00 9.00
132 Rickie Weeks 03 DK/52 80.00 24.00
133 Kevin Youkilis 03 DK/153 25.00 7.50
134 Barry Zito 03 DK/5

2004 Diamond Kings Team Timeline

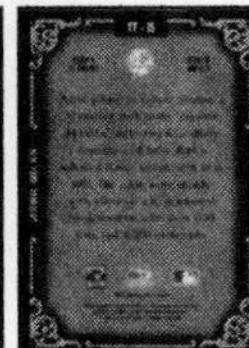

Nm-Mt Ex-Mt
STATED ODDS 1:29
1 Deion Sanders 4.00 1.20
Andruw Jones
2 Rickie Weeks 6.00 1.80
Robin Yount
3 Don Mattingly 10.00 3.00
Whitey Ford
4 Chipper Jones 4.00 1.20
Dale Murphy
5 Nomar Garciaparra 6.00 1.80
Bobby Doerr
6 Mark Prior 8.00 2.40
Sammy Sosa
7 Hideo Nomo 4.00 1.20
Kazuhisa Ishii
8 Andre Dawson 4.00 1.20
Mark Grace
9 Roger Clemens 8.00 2.40
Carl Yastrzemski
10 Mike Mussina 12.00 3.60
Cal Ripken
11 Stan Musial 8.00 2.40
Albert Pujols
12 Jim Palmer 4.00 1.20
Mike Mussina
13 Marty Marion 6.00 1.80
Stan Musial
14 George Brett 10.00 3.00
Mike Sweeney
15 Roger Clemens 8.00 2.40
Roger Maris
16 Duke Snider 4.00 1.20
Shawn Green
17 Jim Thome 8.00 2.40
Mike Schmidt
18 Nolan Ryan 10.00 3.00
Alex Rodriguez
19 Roy Campanella 6.00 1.80
Mike Piazza

2004 Diamond Kings Team Timeline Bats

Nm-Mt Ex-Mt
RANDOM INSERTS IN PACKS
STATED PRINT RUN 25 SERIAL #'d SETS
SNIDER/GREEN TOO SCARCE TO PRICE
SNIDER/GREEN PRINT 1 SERIAL #'d CARD
1 Deion Sanders 30.00 9.00
Andruw Jones
2 Rickie Weeks 80.00 24.00
Robin Yount
3 Don Mattingly 100.00 30.00
Whitey Ford
4 Chipper Jones 60.00 18.00
Dale Murphy
5 Nomar Garciaparra 50.00 15.00
Bobby Doerr
6 Mark Prior 100.00 30.00
Sammy Sosa
7 Hideo Nomo 60.00 18.00
Kazuhisa Ishii
8 Andre Dawson 30.00 9.00
Mark Grace
9 Roger Clemens 60.00 18.00
Carl Yastrzemski
10 Mike Mussina 120.00 36.00
Cal Ripken
11 Stan Musial 100.00 30.00
Albert Pujols
12 Jim Palmer 50.00 15.00
Mike Mussina
13 Marty Marion
Stan Musial
14 George Brett 50.00 15.00
Mike Sweeney
15 Roger Clemens 100.00 30.00
Roger Maris
16 Duke Snider/1
Shawn Green
17 Jim Thome 60.00 18.00
Mike Schmidt
18 Nolan Ryan 80.00 24.00
Alex Rodriguez
19 Roy Campanella 60.00 18.00
Mike Piazza

2004 Diamond Kings Team Timeline Jerseys

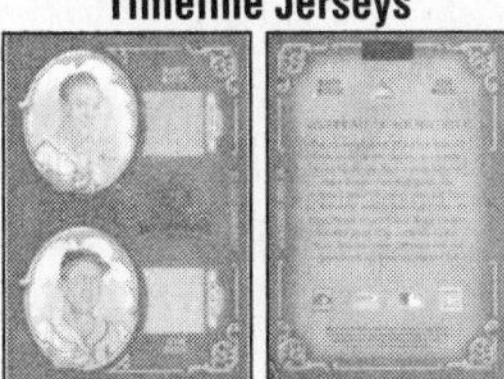

Nm-Mt Ex-Mt
PRINT RUNS B/WN 10-25 COPIES PER
NO PRICING ON QTY OF 10 OR LESS.
PRIME PRINT RUN 1 SERIAL #'d SET
NO PRIME PRICING DUE TO SCARCITY
RANDOM INSERTS IN PACKS
R.WEEKS IS A BAT SWATCH
R.CAMPANELLA IS A PANTS SWATCH
1 Deion Sanders/25 30.00 9.00
Andruw Jones
2 Rickie Weeks/25 80.00 24.00
Robin Yount
3 Don Mattingly/25 100.00 30.00
Whitey Ford
4 Chipper Jones/25 60.00 18.00
Dale Murphy
5 Nomar Garciaparra/25 50.00 15.00
Bobby Doerr
6 Mark Prior/25 100.00 30.00
Sammy Sosa
7 Hideo Nomo/25 60.00 18.00
Kazuhisa Ishii
8 Andre Dawson/25 30.00 9.00
Mark Grace
9 Roger Clemens/25 60.00 18.00
Carl Yastrzemski
10 Mike Mussina/25 120.00 36.00
Cal Ripken
11 Stan Musial/10
Albert Pujols
12 Jim Palmer/10
Mike Mussina
13 Marty Marion/10
Stan Musial
14 George Brett/25 50.00 15.00
Mike Sweeney
15 Roger Clemens/25 100.00 30.00
Roger Maris
16 Duke Snider/10
Shawn Green
17 Jim Thome/25 60.00 18.00
Mike Schmidt
18 Nolan Ryan/25 80.00 24.00
Alex Rodriguez
19 Roy Campanella/25 60.00 18.00
Mike Piazza

2004 Diamond Kings Timeline

Nm-Mt Ex-Mt
STATED ODDS 1:92
1 Roger Clemens 8.00 2.40
2 Mark Grace 4.00 1.20
3 Mike Mussina 4.00 1.20
4 Mike Piazza 6.00 1.80
5 Nolan Ryan 10.00 3.00
6 Rickey Henderson 4.00 1.20

2004 Diamond Kings Timeline Bats

Nm-Mt Ex-Mt
RANDOM INSERTS IN PACKS
STATED PRINT RUN 25 SERIAL #'d SETS
1 Roger Clemens Sox-Yanks 50.00 15.00
2 Mark Grace Cubs-D'backs 40.00 12.00
3 Mike Mussina O's-Yanks 40.00 12.00
4 Mike Piazza Dodgers-Mets 50.00 15.00
5 Nolan Ryan Astros-Rangers 80.00 24.00
6 Rickey Henderson A's-Dodgers 40.00 12.00

2004 Diamond Kings Timeline Jerseys

Nm-Mt Ex-Mt
STATED PRINT RUN 25 SERIAL #'d SETS
PRIME PRINT RUN 1 SERIAL #'d SET
NO PRIME PRICING DUE TO SCARCITY
RANDOM INSERTS IN PACKS
1 Roger Clemens Sox-Yanks 60.00 18.00
2 Mark Grace Cubs-D'backs 50.00 15.00
3 Mike Mussina O's-Yanks 50.00 15.00
4 Mike Piazza Dodgers-Mets 60.00 18.00
5 Nolan Ryan Astros-Rangers 100.00 30.00
6 Rickey Henderson A's-Dodgers 50.00 15.00

1993 Diamond Marks Prototypes

This eight-bookmark prototype set was a collaboration of Barry Colla and Terry Smith. It was produced to gain approval from MLB, and reportedly less than 600 of each card was printed. Dealers who responded to the initial promotional offer from Card Collectors Co., the principal distributor, were given one prototype card with their order. The bookmarks measure approximately 2 1/2" by 5" and feature black-bordered color player shots, some action, others posed, on their fronts. The backs also state "1993 Diamond Marks Prototype." The bookmarks are unnumbered and checklisted below in alphabetical order.

Nm-Mt Ex-Mt
COMPLETE SET (8) 80.00 24.00
1 Roberto Alomar 10.00 3.00
2 Will Clark 10.00 3.00
3 Dennis Eckersley 5.00 1.50
4 Juan Gonzalez 10.00 3.00
5 Ken Griffey Jr. 25.00 7.50
6 Kirby Puckett 10.00 3.00
7 Ryne Sandberg 20.00 6.00
8 Frank Thomas 12.00 3.60

1993 Diamond Marks

This 120-card bookmark set was a collaboration of Barry Colla and Terry Smith. Ten bookmarks and an ad card came in each cello pack. A total production run of only 2,500 cases were produced, and no factory sets were issued. The bookmarks measure approximately

2 1/2" by 5" and feature black-bordered color player shots, some action. others posed, on their fronts. The bookmarks are unnumbered and checklisted below in alphabetical order.

Nm-Mt Ex-Mt
COMPLETE SET (120) 20.00 6.00
1 Roberto Alomar .75 .23
2 Sandy Alomar Jr. .20 .06
3 Moises Alou .20 .06
4 Brady Anderson .20 .06
5 Steve Avery .10 .03
6 Carlos Baerga .10 .03
7 Jeff Bagwell 1.50 .45
8 Derek Bell .10 .03
9 Jay Bell .10 .03
10 Albert Belle .20 .06
11 Dante Bichette .20 .06
12 Craig Biggio .50 .15
13 Wade Boggs 1.25 .35
14 Barry Bonds 2.50 .75
15 Bobby Bonilla .10 .03
16 Pat Borders .10 .03
17 Daryl Boston .10 .03
18 George Brett 2.50 .75
19 John Burkett .10 .03
20 Brett Butler .20 .06
21 Ken Caminiti .20 .06
22 Jose Canseco 1.00 .30
23 Joe Carter .20 .06
24 Will Clark .75 .23
25 Roger Clemens 2.50 .75
26 Chad Curtis .10 .03
27 Darren Daulton .20 .06
28 Eric Davis .20 .06
29 Andre Dawson .30 .09
30 Delino DeShields .10 .03
31 Orestes Destrade .10 .03
32 Gary DiSarcina .10 .03
33 Len Dykstra .20 .06
34 Dennis Eckersley .50 .15
35 Cecil Fielder .20 .06
36 Andres Galarraga .40 .12
37 Ron Gant .20 .06
38 Tom Glavine .50 .15
39 Luis Gonzalez .40 .12
40 Juan Gonzalez 1.00 .30
41 Dwight Gooden .20 .06
42 Mark Grace .30 .09
43 Mike Greenwell .10 .03
44 Ken Griffey Jr. 3.00 .90
45 Marquis Grissom .20 .06
46 Juan Guzman .10 .03
47 Tony Gwynn 2.50 .75
48 Darryl Hamilton .10 .03
49 Charlie Hayes .10 .03
50 Rickey Henderson 1.25 .35
51 Orel Hershiser .20 .06
52 Dave Hollins .10 .03
53 Kent Hrbek .20 .06
54 Bo Jackson .40 .12
55 Gregg Jefferies .10 .03
56 Howard Johnson .10 .03
57 Wally Joyner .20 .06
58 David Justice .30 .09
59 Eric Karros .30 .09
60 Roberto Kelly .10 .03
61 Chuck Knoblauch .20 .06
62 John Kruk .20 .06
63 Barry Larkin .40 .12
64 Pat Listach .10 .03
65 Kenny Lofton .30 .09
66 Mike Macfarlane .10 .03
67 Al Martin .10 .03
68 Dennis Martinez .20 .06
69 Edgar Martinez .20 .06
70 Ramon Martinez .20 .06
71 Don Mattingly 2.50 .75
72 Fred McGriff .30 .09
73 Mark McGwire 4.00 1.20
74 Brian McRae .10 .03
75 Orlando Merced .10 .03
76 Kevin Mitchell .20 .06
77 Paul Molitor .75 .23
78 Eddie Murray .75 .23
79 Mike Mussina .40 .12
80 Randy Myers .10 .03
81 Pete O'Brien .10 .03
82 John Olerud .20 .06
83 Tom Pagnozzi .10 .03
84 Terry Pendleton .10 .03
85 Tony Phillips .10 .03
86 Mike Piazza 3.00 .90
87 Kirby Puckett 1.25 .35
88 Jose Rijo .10 .03
89 Cal Ripken 5.00 1.50
90 Ivan Rodriguez 1.25 .35
91 Nolan Ryan 5.00 1.50
92 Tim Salmon .40 .12
93 Ryne Sandberg 2.00 .60
94 Deion Sanders .30 .09
95 Reggie Sanders .20 .06
96 Benito Santiago .20 .06
97 Gary Sheffield .50 .15
98 Ruben Sierra .20 .06
99 Ozzie Smith 2.00 .60
100 John Smoltz .40 .12
101 J.T. Snow .75 .23
102 Terry Steinbach .10 .03
103 Dave Stewart .20 .06
104 Darryl Strawberry .20 .06
105 B.J. Surhoff .20 .06
106 Danny Tartabull .10 .03
107 Mickey Tettleton .10 .03
108 Frank Thomas 1.50 .45
109 Alan Trammell .40 .12
110 David Valle .10 .03
111 Andy Van Slyke .10 .03
112 Mo Vaughn .20 .06
113 Robin Ventura .30 .09
114 Jose Vizcaino .10 .03
115 Larry Walker .40 .12
116 Walt Weiss .10 .03
117 Matt Williams .30 .09
118 Dave Winfield .75 .23
119 Robin Yount 1.00 .30
120 Todd Zeile .10 .03

1993 Diamond Marks Art

Complimenting the 120-card bookmark set, this eight-bookmark art card set was a collaboration of Barry Colla and Terry Smith. One of the special art cards is included in each 48-pack carton. The bookmark art cards measure approximately 2 1/2" by 5" and feature black-bordered fanciful color player paintings by Terry Smith on their fronts. The bookmarks are unnumbered and checklisted below in alphabetical order. There are reports in the hobby that no more than 3,000 of each card were produced.

Nm-Mt Ex-Mt
COMPLETE SET (8) 175.00 52.50
1 Roberto Alomar 20.00 6.00
2 Barry Bonds 25.00 7.50
3 Ken Griffey Jr. 30.00 9.00
4 David Justice 10.00 3.00
5 John Olerud 10.00 3.00
6 Nolan Ryan 50.00 15.00
7 Frank Thomas 20.00 6.00
8 Robin Yount 25.00 7.50

1934 Diamond Match Co. Silver Border

Issued in 1934, the 200-cover Silver-Bordered set includes many of the day's premier ballplayers. Each cover features four different background colors, red, green, blue and orange. Charlie Grimm is shown in two different poses. Players are listed in alphabetical order. All color variations are equally valued. The complete set price includes both Grimm covers. Complete matchbooks are valued fifty percent higher.

Ex-Mt VG
COMPLETE SET (200) 1000.00 500.00
1 Earl Adams 8.00 4.00
2 Ethan Allen 8.00 4.00
3 Eldon Auker 8.00 4.00
4 Del Baker 8.00 4.00
5 Dick Bartell 8.00 4.00
6 Walter Beck 8.00 4.00
7 Herman Bell 8.00 4.00
8 Ray Benge 8.00 4.00
9 Larry Benton 8.00 4.00
10 Louis Berger 8.00 4.00
11 Wally Berger 10.00 5.00
12 Ray Berres 8.00 4.00
13 Charlie Berry 8.00 4.00
14 Walter Betts 8.00 4.00
15 Ralph Birkofer 8.00 4.00
16 George Blaeholder 8.00 4.00
17 Jim Bottomley 20.00 10.00
18 Ralph Boyle 8.00 4.00
19 Ed Brandt 8.00 4.00
20 Don Brennan 8.00 4.00
21 Jack Burns 8.00 4.00
22 Guy Bush 8.00 4.00
23 Dolph Camilli 10.00 5.00
24 Ben Cantwell 8.00 4.00
25 Tex Carleton 8.00 4.00
26 Owen Carroll 8.00 4.00
27 Louis Chiozza 8.00 4.00
28 Watson Clark 8.00 4.00
29 James A. Collins 10.00 5.00
30 Phil Collins 8.00 4.00
31 Edward Connolly 8.00 4.00
32 Raymond Coombs 8.00 4.00
33 Roger "Doc" Cramer 10.00 5.00
34 Cliff Crawford 8.00 4.00
35 Hugh Critz 8.00 4.00
36 General Crowder 8.00 4.00
37 Tony Cuccinello 8.00 4.00
38 Kiki Cuyler 20.00 10.00
39 Virgil Davis 8.00 4.00
40 Dizzy Dean 30.00 15.00
41 Paul Dean 15.00 7.50
42 Edward Delker 8.00 4.00
43 Paul Derringer 15.00 7.50
44 Gene DeSautel 8.00 4.00
45 Bill Dietrich 8.00 4.00
46 Frank F. Doljack 8.00 4.00
47 Edward Durham 8.00 4.00
48 Leo Durocher 20.00 10.00
49 Jim Elliott 8.00 4.00
50 Woody English 8.00 4.00
51 Woody English 8.00 4.00
52 Rick Ferrell 15.00 7.50
53 Wes Ferrell 12.00 6.00
54 Charles Fischer 8.00 4.00
55 Freddy Fitzsimmons 10.00 5.00

56 Lew Fonseca 10.00 5.00
57 Fred Frankhouse 8.00 4.00
58 John Frederick 8.00 4.00
59 Benny Frey 8.00 4.00
60 Linus Frey 8.00 4.00
61 Frankie Frisch 40.00 20.00
62 Chick Fullis 8.00 4.00
63 Augie Galan 8.00 4.00
64 Milton Galatzer 8.00 4.00
65 Dennis Galehouse 8.00 4.00
66 Milton Gaston 8.00 4.00
67 Charlie Gehringer 20.00 10.00
68 Edward Gharrity 8.00 4.00
69 George Gibson 8.00 4.00
70 Isidore Goldstein 8.00 4.00
71 Hank Gowdy 8.00 4.00
72 Earl Grace 8.00 4.00
73 Charlie Grimm 15.00 7.50
74 Charlie Grimm 15.00 7.50
75 Frank Grube 8.00 4.00
76 Richard Gyselman 8.00 4.00
77 Stan Hack 15.00 7.50
78 Bump Hadley 8.00 4.00
79 Chick Hafey 20.00 10.00
80 Harold Haid 8.00 4.00
81 Jesse Haines 20.00 10.00
82 Odell Hale 8.00 4.00
83 Bill Hallahan 8.00 4.00
84 Luke Hamlin 8.00 4.00
85 Roy Hansen 8.00 4.00
86 Mel Harder 10.00 5.00
87 William Harris 20.00 10.00
88 Gabby Hartnett 15.00 7.50
89 Harvey Hendrick 8.00 4.00
90 Babe Herman 15.00 7.50
91 Billy Herman 20.00 10.00
92 Shanty Hogan 8.00 4.00
93 Chief Hogsett 8.00 4.00
94 Waite Hoyt 20.00 10.00
95 Carl Hubbell 25.00 12.50
96 Si Johnson 8.00 4.00
97 Syl Johnson 8.00 4.00
98 Roy Joiner 8.00 4.00
99 Baxter Jordan 8.00 4.00
100 Arndt Jorgens 8.00 4.00
101 Billy Jurges 10.00 5.00
102 Vern Kennedy 8.00 4.00
103 John Kerr 8.00 4.00
104 Chuck Klein 25.00 12.50
105 Ted Kleinhans 8.00 4.00
106 Bill Klem UMP 15.00 7.50
107 Robert Kline 8.00 4.00
108 William Knickerbocker 8.00 4.00
109 Jack Knott 8.00 4.00
110 Mark Koenig 10.00 5.00
111 William Lawrence 8.00 4.00
112 Thornton Lee 8.00 4.00
113 Bill Lee 8.00 4.00
114 Dutch Leonard 8.00 4.00
115 Ernie Lombardi 25.00 12.50
116 Al Lopez 20.00 10.00
117 Red Lucas 8.00 4.00
118 Ted Lyons 20.00 10.00
119 Daniel MacFayden 8.00 4.00
120 Ed. Majeski 8.00 4.00
121 Leroy Mahaffey 8.00 4.00
122 Pat Malone 8.00 4.00
123 Leo Mangum 8.00 4.00
124 Rabbit Maranville 25.00 12.50
125 Charles Marrow 8.00 4.00
126 Bill McKechnie MG 15.00 7.50
127 Justin McLaughlin 8.00 4.00
128 Marty McManus 8.00 4.00
129 Eric McNair 8.00 4.00
130 Joe Medwick 20.00 10.00
131 Jim Mooney 8.00 4.00
132 Joe Moore 8.00 4.00
133 John Moore 8.00 4.00
134 Randy Moore 8.00 4.00
135 Joe Morrisey 8.00 4.00
136 Joseph Mowrey 8.00 4.00
137 Fred Muller 8.00 4.00
138 Van Lingle Mungo 12.00 6.00
139 Glenn Myatt 8.00 4.00
140 Lynn Nelson 8.00 4.00
141 Prince Oana 8.00 4.00
142 Lefty O'Doul 15.00 7.50
143 Robert O'Farrell 8.00 4.00
144 Ernest Orsatti 8.00 4.00
145 Fritz Ostermueller 8.00 4.00
146 Mel Ott 25.00 12.50
147 Roy Parmelee 8.00 4.00
148 Ralph Perkins 8.00 4.00
149 Frank Pytlak 8.00 4.00
150 Ernest Quigley 8.00 4.00
151 George Rensa 8.00 4.00
152 Harry Rice 8.00 4.00
153 Walter Roettger 10.00 5.00
154 William Rogell 8.00 4.00
155 Edwin Rommel 8.00 4.00
156 Charlie Root 10.00 5.00
157 John Rothrock 8.00 4.00
158 Jack Russell 8.00 4.00
159 Blondy Ryan 8.00 4.00
160 Al Schacht CO 10.00 5.00
161 Wes Schultmerick 8.00 4.00
162 Rip Sewell 8.00 4.00
163 Gordon Slade 8.00 4.00
164 Bob Smith 8.00 4.00
165 Moose Solters 8.00 4.00
166 Glenn Spencer 8.00 4.00
167 Al Spohrer 8.00 4.00
168 George Stainback 10.00 5.00
169 Dolly Stark 15.00 7.50
170 Casey Stengel MG 30.00 15.00
171 Riggs Stephenson 15.00 7.50
172 Walter Stewart 8.00 4.00
173 Lin Storti 8.00 4.00
174 Allyn Stout 8.00 4.00
175 Joe Stripp 8.00 4.00
176 Gus Suhr 10.00 5.00
177 Billy Sullivan Jr. 8.00 4.00
178 Benny Tate 8.00 4.00
179 Danny Taylor 8.00 4.00
180 Tommy Thevenow 8.00 4.00
181 Bud Tinning 8.00 4.00
182 Cecil Travis 8.00 4.00
183 Forest Twogood 8.00 4.00
184 Bill Urbanski 8.00 4.00
185 Dazzy Vance 15.00 7.50
186 Arthur Veltman 8.00 4.00
187 John Vergez 8.00 4.00
188 Gee Walker 8.00 4.00
189 Bill Walker 10.00 5.00
190 Lloyd Waner 20.00 10.00
191 Paul Waner 20.00 10.00
192 Lon Warnecke 10.00 5.00
193 Rabbit Warstler 8.00 4.00
194 Bill Werber 10.00 5.00
195 Jo Jo White 8.00 4.00
196 Pinky Whitney 8.00 4.00
197 Jimmy Wilson 8.00 4.00
198 Hack Wilson 20.00 10.00
199 Ralph Winegarner 8.00 4.00
200 Thomas Zachary 10.00 5.00

1935 Diamond Match Co. Series 2

The Second baseball set was issued circa 1935 by the Diamond Match Company. Each cover in the 24-cover set features a black border on the front and a brief player biography on the reverse. Covers are either green, red or blue in color. A crossed-bat design appears on the front-side of each cover. Players are listed in alphabetical order. Complete matchbooks are valued at fifty percent higher.

Ex-Mt VG
COMPLETE SET (24) 300.00 150.00
1 Ethan Allen (red) 15.00 7.50
2 Wally Berger (red) 15.00 7.50
3 Tommy Carey (blue) 10.00 5.00
4 Louis Chiozza (blue) 10.00 5.00
5 Dizzy Dean (green) 40.00 20.00
6 Frankie Frisch (red) 30.00 15.00
7 Charlie Grimm (blue) 20.00 10.00
8 Chick Hafey (red) 20.00 10.00
9 Francis Hogan (red) 10.00 5.00
10 Carl Hubbell (green) 25.00 12.50
11 Chuck Klein (green) 25.00 12.50
12 Ernie Lombardi (blue) 20.00 10.00
13 Al Lopez (blue) 25.00 12.50
14 Rabbit Maranville (green) 25.00 12.50
15 Joe Moore (red) 10.00 5.00
16 Van Lingle Mungo (green) 15.00 7.50
17 Mel Ott (blue) 30.00 15.00
18 Gordon Slade (green) 10.00 5.00
19 Casey Stengel MG (green) 30.00 15.00
20 Tommy Thevenow (red) 10.00 5.00
21 Lloyd Waner (red) 25.00 12.50
22 Paul Waner (green) 25.00 12.50
23 Lon Warnecke (blue) 12.00 6.00
24 James Wilson (blue) 10.00 5.00

1935-36 Diamond Match Co. Series 3 Type 1

This set was released over two years (1935-36) by the Diamond Match Company. This set varies from the First and Second set in that the saddle has the "ball" with the players name and team only. Covers come in red, green and blue. Players are listed in alphabetical order. Complete matchbooks are valued fifty percent higher.

Ex-Mt VG
COMPLETE SET (151) 1000.00 500.00
1 Ethan Allen 8.00 4.00
2 Melo Almada 8.00 4.00
3 Eldon Auker 8.00 4.00
4 Dick Bartell 8.00 4.00
5 Aloysius Bejma 8.00 4.00
6 Ollie Bejma 8.00 4.00
7 Roy Bell 8.00 4.00
8 Louis Berger 8.00 4.00
9 Wally Berger 10.00 5.00
10 Ralph Birkofer 8.00 4.00
11 Max Bishop 8.00 4.00
12 George Blaeholder 8.00 4.00
13 Zeke Bonura 10.00 5.00
14 Jim Bottomley 20.00 10.00
15 Ed Brandt 8.00 4.00
16 Don Brennan 8.00 4.00
17 Lloyd Brown 8.00 4.00
18 Walter Brown 8.00 4.00
19 Claiborne Bryant 8.00 4.00
20 Jim Bucher 8.00 4.00
21 John Burnett 8.00 4.00
22 Irving Burns 8.00 4.00
23 Merritt Cain 8.00 4.00
24 Ben Cantwell 8.00 4.00
25 Tommy Carey 8.00 4.00
26 Tex Carleton 8.00 4.00
27 Joseph Cascarella 8.00 4.00
28 Thomas Casey 8.00 4.00
29 George Caster 8.00 4.00
30 Phil Cavaretta 15.00 7.50
31 Louis Chiozza 8.00 4.00
32 Edward Cihocki 8.00 4.00
33 Herman E. Clifton 8.00 4.00
34 Richard Coffman 8.00 4.00
35 Edward Coleman 8.00 4.00
36 James A. Collins 10.00 5.00
37 Jocko Conlon 15.00 7.50
38 Roger Cramer 10.00 5.00
39 Hugh Critz 8.00 4.00
40 Alvin Crowder 8.00 4.00
41 Tony Cuccinello 8.00 4.00
42 Kiki Cuyler 20.00 10.00
43 Virgil Davis 8.00 4.00
44 Dizzy Dean 30.00 15.00
45 Paul Derringer 10.00 5.00
46 James DeShong 8.00 4.00
47 Billy Dietrich 8.00 4.00
48 Leo Durocher 25.00 12.50
49 George Earnshaw 12.00 6.00
50 Woody English 8.00 4.00
51 Louis Finney 8.00 4.00
52 Charles Fischer 8.00 4.00
53 Freddy Fitzsimmons 12.00 6.00
54 Linus Frey 8.00 4.00
55 Frankie Frisch 25.00 12.50
56 Augie Galan 10.00 5.00
57 Milton Galatzer 8.00 4.00
58 Dennis Galehouse 8.00 4.00
59 Debs Garms 8.00 4.00
60 Angelo Giuliani 8.00 4.00
61 Earl Grace 8.00 4.00
62 Charlie Grimm 15.00 7.50
63 Frank Grube 8.00 4.00
64 Stan Hack 15.00 7.50
65 Bump Hadley 8.00 4.00
66 Odell Hale 8.00 4.00
67 Bill Hallahan 8.00 4.00
68 Roy Hanson 8.00 4.00
69 Mel Harder 10.00 5.00
70 Gabby Hartnett 20.00 10.00
71 Clyde Hatter 8.00 4.00
72 Raymond Hayworth 8.00 4.00
73 Babe Herman 15.00 7.50
74 Gordon Hinkle 8.00 4.00
75 George Hockette 8.00 4.00
76 James Holbrook 8.00 4.00
77 Alex Hooks 8.00 4.00
78 Waite Hoyt 15.00 7.50
79 Carl Hubbell 20.00 10.00
80 Roy Joiner 8.00 4.00
81 Sam Jones 10.00 5.00
82 Baxter Jordan 8.00 4.00
83 Arndt Jorgens 8.00 4.00
84 Billy Jurges 10.00 5.00
85 Willie Kamm 10.00 5.00
86 Vern Kennedy 8.00 4.00
87 John Kerr 8.00 4.00
88 Chuck Klein 20.00 10.00
89 Ted Kleinhans 8.00 4.00
90 William Knickerbocker 8.00 4.00
91 Jack Knott 8.00 4.00
92 Mark Koenig 10.00 5.00
93 Fabian Kowalik 8.00 4.00
94 Red Kress 8.00 4.00
95 Bill Lee 8.00 4.00
96 Louis Legett 8.00 4.00
97 Dutch Leonard 8.00 4.00
98 Fred Lindstrom 15.00 7.50
99 Edward Linke 8.00 4.00
100 Ernie Lombardi 15.00 7.50
101 Al Lopez 20.00 10.00
102 John Marcum 8.00 4.00
103 Bill McKechnie MG 15.00 7.50
104 Eric McNair 8.00 4.00
105 Joe Medwick 20.00 10.00
106 Oscar Melillo 8.00 4.00
107 John Michaels 8.00 4.00
108 Joe Moore 8.00 4.00
109 John Moore 8.00 4.00
110 Wally Moses 10.00 5.00
111 Joseph Milligan 8.00 4.00
112 Van Lingle Mungo 12.00 6.00
113 Glenn Myatt 8.00 4.00
114 James O'Dea 8.00 4.00
115 Ernest Orsatti 8.00 4.00
116 Fred Ostermueller 8.00 4.00
117 Mel Ott 25.00 12.50
118 LeRoy Parmelee 8.00 4.00
119 Monte Pearson 8.00 4.00
120 Raymond Pepper 8.00 4.00
121 Raymond Phelps 8.00 4.00
122 George Pipgras 8.00 4.00
123 Frank Pytlak 8.00 4.00
124 Gordon Rhodes 8.00 4.00
125 Charlie Root 10.00 5.00
126 John Rothrock 8.00 4.00
127 Muddy Ruel 8.00 4.00
128 Jack Saltzgaver 8.00 4.00
129 Fred Schulte 8.00 4.00
130 George Selkirk 10.00 5.00
131 Mervyn Shea 8.00 4.00
132 Al Spoher 8.00 4.00
133 George Stainback 8.00 4.00
134 Casey Stengel MG 25.00 12.50
135 Walter Stephenson 8.00 4.00
136 Lee Stine 8.00 4.00
137 John Stone 8.00 4.00
138 Gus Suhr 8.00 4.00
139 Tommy Thevenow 8.00 4.00
140 Fay Thomas 8.00 4.00
141 Leslie Tietje 8.00 4.00
142 Bill Urbanski 8.00 4.00
143 William Walker 8.00 4.00
144 Lloyd Waner 20.00 10.00
145 Paul Waner 20.00 10.00
146 Lon Warnecke 10.00 5.00
147 Harold Warstler 8.00 4.00
148 Bill Werber 10.00 5.00
149 Vernon Wiltshere 8.00 4.00
150 James Wilson 8.00 4.00
151 Ralph Winegarner 8.00 4.00

1936 Diamond Match Co. Series 3 Type 2

This 23-player set was issued by the Diamond Match Company around 1936. Each player's cover is featured in three different colors, red, green and blue, All player photos, except "Dizzy" Dean, feature head and shoulders shot. The set was released with two different colors of ink, brown and black. All players are listed in alphabetical order. Complete matchbooks are valued fifty percent higher.

Ex-Mt VG
COMPLETE SET (23) 200.00 100.00
1 Claiborne Bryant 8.00 4.00
2 Tex Carleton 8.00 4.00
3 Phil Cavaretta 12.00 6.00
4 James A. Collins 10.00 5.00
5 Curt Davis 8.00 4.00
6 Dizzy Dean 25.00 12.50
7 Frank Demaree 8.00 4.00
8 Larry French 8.00 4.00
9 Linus Frey 8.00 4.00
10 Augie Galan 10.00 5.00
11 Bob Garbark 8.00 4.00
12 Stan Hack 12.00 6.00
13 Gabby Hartnett 20.00 10.00
14 Billy Herman 20.00 10.00
15 Billy Jurges 10.00 5.00
16 Bill Lee 8.00 4.00
17 Joe Marty 8.00 4.00
18 James O'Dea 8.00 4.00
19 LeRoy Parmelee 8.00 4.00
20 Charlie Root 10.00 5.00
21 Clyde Shoun 8.00 4.00
22 George Stainback 10.00 5.00
23 Paul Waner 20.00 10.00

1936 Diamond Match Co. Series 4

This is by far the smallest matchcover set released by the Diamond Match Company during the 1930's. The set is similar to the Third Baseball set other than the players team name shows under his name on the back. All of the covers minus Charlie Grimm were printed using brown ink. The three different Grimm cover feature black ink. The players are listed in alphabetical order. Complete matchbooks are valued fifty percent higher.

Ex-Mt VG
COMPLETE SET (12) 150.00 75.00
1 Tommy Carey 8.00 4.00
2 Tony Cuccinello 8.00 4.00
3 Freddy Fitzsimmons 10.00 5.00
4 Frankie Frisch 25.00 12.50
5 Charlie Grimm (3) 15.00 7.50
6 Carl Hubbell 20.00 10.00
7 Baxter Jordan 8.00 4.00
8 Chuck Klein 20.00 10.00
9 Al Lopez 15.00 7.50
10 Joe Medwick 15.00 7.50
11 Van Lingle Mungo 12.00 6.00
12 Mel Ott 25.00 12.50

1934-36 Diamond Stars R327

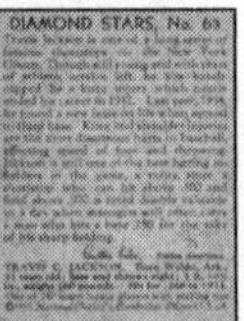

The cards in this 108-card set measure approximately 2 3/8" by 2 7/8". The Diamond Stars set, produced by National Chicle from 1934-36, is also commonly known by its catalog designation, R327. The year of production can be determined by the statistics contained on the back of the card. There are 170 possible front/back combinations counting blue (B) and green (G) backs over all three years. The last twelve cards are repeat players and are quite scarce. The checklist below lists the year(s) and back color(s) for the cards. Cards 32 through 72 were issued only in 1935 with green ink on back. Cards 73 through 84 were issued three ways: 35B, 35G, and 36B. Card numbers 85 through 108 were issued only in 1936 with blue ink on back. The complete set price below refers to the set of all variations listed explicitly below. A blank-backed proof sheet of 12 additional (never-issued) cards was discovered in 1980.

Ex-Mt VG
COMPLETE SET (119) 15000.00 7500.00
COMMON CARD (1-31) 50.00 25.00
COMMON CARD (32-84) 60.00 30.00
COMMON CARD (85-96) 110.00 55.00
COMMON CARD (97-108) 225.00 110.00
WRAP.(1-CENT, BLUE) 250.00 125.00
WRAP.(1-CENT, YELLOW) 200.00 100.00
WRAP.(1-CENT, CLEAR) 200.00 100.00
1 Lefty Grove 750.00 375.00
34G, 35G
2A Al Simmons 150.00 75.00
34G, 35G
Sox on uniform
2B Al Simmons 200.00 100.00
36B
No name on uniform
3 Rabbit Maranville 150.00 75.00
34G, 35G
4 Buddy Myer 60.00 30.00
34G, 35G, 36B
5 Tommy Bridges 60.00 30.00
34G, 35G, 36B
6 Max Bishop 60.00 30.00
34G, 35G
7 Lew Fonseca 60.00 30.00
34G, 35G
8 Joe Vosmik 50.00 25.00
34G, 35G, 36B
9 Mickey Cochrane 175.00 90.00
34G, 35G, 36B
10A Leroy Mahaffey 50.00 25.00
34G, 35G
A's on uniform
10B Leroy Mahaffey 80.00 40.00
36B
No name on uniform
11 Bill Dickey 225.00 110.00
34G, 35G
12A Fred Walker 34G 80.00 40.00
Ruth retires
mentioned on back
12B Fred Walker 35G 80.00 40.00
(Ruth to Boston
mentioned on back
12C Fred Walker 36B 100.00 50.00
13 George Blaeholder 50.00 25.00
34G, 35G
14 Bill Terry 175.00 90.00
34G, 35G
15A Dick Bartell 34G 100.00 50.00
Philadelphia Phillies
on card back
15B Dick Bartell 35G 80.00 40.00
New York Giants
on card back
16 Lloyd Waner 125.00 60.00
34G, 35G, 36B
17 Frankie Frisch 125.00 60.00
34G, 35G
18 Chick Hafey 125.00 60.00
34G, 35G
19 Van Lingle Mungo 80.00 40.00
34G, 35G
20 Frank Hogan 60.00 30.00
34G, 35G
21A Johnny Vergez 34G 80.00 40.00
New York Giants
on card back
21B Johnny Vergez 35G 60.00 30.00
Philadelphia Phillies
on card back
22 Jimmy Wilson 60.00 30.00
34G, 35G, 36B
23 Bill Hallahan 50.00 25.00
34G, 35G
24 Earl Adams 50.00 25.00
34G, 35G
25 Wally Berger 35G 60.00 30.00
26 Pepper Martin 80.00 40.00
35G, 36B
27 Pie Traynor 35G 150.00 75.00
28 Al Lopez 35G 150.00 75.00
29 Red Rolfe 35G 80.00 40.00
30A Heinie Manush 35G 150.00 75.00
W on sleeve
30B Heinie Manush 36B 200.00 100.00
No W on sleeve
31A Kiki Cuyler 35G 125.00 60.00
Chicago Cubs
31B Kiki Cuyler 36B 175.00 90.00
Cincinnati Reds
32 Sam Rice 125.00 60.00
33 Schoolboy Rowe 80.00 40.00
34 Stan Hack 80.00 40.00
35 Earl Averill 125.00 60.00
36A Earnie Lombardi 300.00 150.00
(Sic, Ernie)
36B Ernie Lombardi 200.00 100.00
37 Billy Urbanski 60.00 30.00
38 Ben Chapman 80.00 40.00
39 Carl Hubbell 225.00 110.00
40 Blondy Ryan 60.00 30.00
41 Harvey Hendrick 60.00 30.00
42 Jimmy Dykes 80.00 40.00
43 Ted Lyons 125.00 60.00
44 Rogers Hornsby 400.00 200.00
45 Jo Jo White 60.00 30.00
46 Red Lucas 60.00 30.00
47 Bob Bolton 60.00 30.00
48 Rick Ferrell 125.00 60.00
49 Buck Jordan 60.00 30.00
50 Mel Ott 275.00 140.00
51 Burgess Whitehead 60.00 30.00
52 Tuck Stainback 60.00 30.00
53 Oscar Melillo 60.00 30.00
54A Hank Greenburg 600.00 300.00
(Sic, Greenberg)
54B Hank Greenberg 400.00 200.00
55 Tony Cuccinello 80.00 40.00
56 Gus Suhr 60.00 30.00
57 Cy Blanton 60.00 30.00
58 Glenn Myatt 60.00 30.00
59 Jim Bottomley 125.00 60.00
60 Red Ruffing 150.00 75.00
61 Bill Werber 80.00 40.00
62 Fred Frankhouse 60.00 30.00
63 Travis Jackson 125.00 60.00
64 Jimmie Foxx 450.00 220.00
65 Zeke Bonura 60.00 30.00
66 Ducky Medwick 200.00 100.00
67 Marvin Owen 80.00 40.00
68 Sam Leslie 60.00 30.00
69 Earl Grace 60.00 30.00
70 Hal Trosky 80.00 40.00
71 Ossie Bluege 80.00 40.00
72 Tony Piet 60.00 30.00
73 Fritz Ostermueller 80.00 40.00
35G, 35B, 36B
74 Tony Lazzeri 200.00 100.00
35G, 35B, 36B
75 Jack Burns 80.00 40.00
35G, 35B, 36B
76 Billy Rogell 80.00 40.00
35G, 35B, 36B
77 Charley Gehringer 175.00 90.00
35G, 35B, 36B
78 Joe Kuhel 80.00 40.00
35G, 35B, 36B
79 Willis Hudlin 80.00 40.00
35G, 35B, 36B
80 Lou Chiozza 80.00 40.00
35G, 35B, 36B
81 Bill Delancey 60.00 30.00
35G, 35B, 36B
82A Johnny Babich 80.00 40.00
(Dodgers on uniorm
35G, 35B)
82B Johnny Babich 125.00 60.00
(No name on
uniform; 36B)
83 Paul Waner 150.00 75.00
35G, 35B, 36B
84 Sam Byrd 80.00 40.00
35G, 35B, 36B

85 Moose Solters 110.00 55.00
86 Frank Crosetti 150.00 75.00
87 Steve O'Neill MG 125.00 60.00
88 George Selkirk 125.00 60.00
89 Joe Stripp 125.00 60.00
90 Ray Hayworth 125.00 60.00
91 Bucky Harris MG 225.00 110.00
92 Ethan Allen 110.00 55.00
93 General Crowder 110.00 55.00
94 Wes Ferrell 150.00 75.00
95 Luke Appling 275.00 140.00
96 Lew Riggs 110.00 55.00
97 Al Lopez 450.00 220.00
98 Schoolboy Rowe 225.00 110.00
99 Pie Traynor 500.00 250.00
100 Earl Averill 450.00 220.00
101 Dick Bartell 225.00 110.00
102 Van Lingle Mungo 250.00 125.00
103 Bill Dickey 700.00 350.00
104 Red Rolfe 225.00 110.00
105 Ernie Lombardi 450.00 220.00
106 Red Lucas 225.00 110.00
107 Stan Hack 225.00 110.00
108 Wally Berger 300.00 150.00

1993 Diamond Stars Extension Set

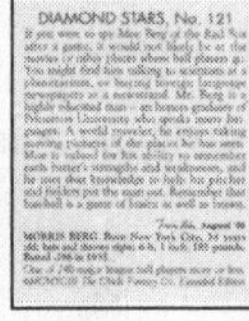

This 36-card set measures 2 3/8" by 2 7/8" and was issued by The Chicle Fantasy Company. These cards did not exist in 1936, but might have, had the National Chicle Co. of Cambridge, Mass. not been on the verge of bankruptcy. Only 108 of a proposed 240 cards were issued from 1934-36. These 36 cards are an idealized version of what might have been. The colorful fronts feature art by D'August Roth Martin and are edged in white. The back carries a descriptive summary of the player's career with biography below. The cards are arranged alphabetically and are numbered on their backs, beginning with number 121. Additionally, three cards (1-3) are included that feature Negro League stars.

Nm-Mt Ex-Mt
COMPLETE SET (36) 10.00 3.00
COMMON CARD (N1-N3) .50 .15
COMMON CARD (121-153) .25 .07
121 Moe Berg 1.50 .45
122 Harlond Clift .25 .07
123 Joe Cronin MG .75 .23
124 Dizzy Dean .75 .23
125 Paul Dean .50 .15
126 Joe DiMaggio 2.00 .60
127 Leo Durocher .75 .23
128 Bob Feller 1.00 .30
129 Carl Fisher .25 .07
130 Lou Gehrig 2.00 .60
131 Bump Hadley .25 .07
132 Jesse Haines .50 .15
133 Bad News Hale .25 .07
134 Gabby Hartnett .75 .23
135 Babe Herman .50 .15
136 Billy Herman .75 .23
137 Waite Hoyt .75 .23
138 Bob Johnson .50 .15
139 Chuck Klein .75 .23
140 Mike Kreevich .25 .07
141 Fred Lindstrom .50 .15
142 Connie Mack MG .75 .23
143 Joe McCarthy MG .75 .23
144 Bill McKechnie MG .50 .15
145 Johnny Mize .75 .23
146 Johnny Moore .25 .07
147 Hugh Mulcahy .25 .07
148 Buck Newsom .50 .15
149 Al Smith .25 .07
150 Casey Stengel MG .75 .23
151 Arky Vaughan .75 .23
152 Gee Walker .25 .07
153 Kenesaw M. Landis COMM .50 .15
N1 Cool Papa Bell .50 .15
N2 Josh Gibson .75 .23
N3 Satchel Paige .75 .23
NNO Title card .50 .15

1981 Diamond Stars Continuation Den's

These 2 1/2" by 3" cards feature reproductions of cards which were prepared by Diamond Stars but never printed. These cards were on a twelve-card sheet and continue the numbering of already existing Diamond Stars cards. This set was created and produced by Denny Eckes. Hobbyist Mike Galella was involved in bringing this sheet to the public. These cards were originally available from the producer for $3.

Nm-Mt Ex-Mt
COMPLETE SET (12) 5.00 2.00
109 Benny Frey .25 .10
110 Pete Fox .25 .10
111 Phil Cavaretta .50 .20
112 Goose Goslin .75 .30
113 Mel Harder .50 .20
114 Doc Cramer .50 .20
115 Gene Moore .25 .10
116 Rip Collins .25 .10
117 Linus Frey .25 .10
118 Lefty Gomez 1.00 .40
119 Jim Bottomley 1.00 .40
Rogers Hornsby
120 Lon Warneke .50 .20

1998 Diamondbacks McDaddy

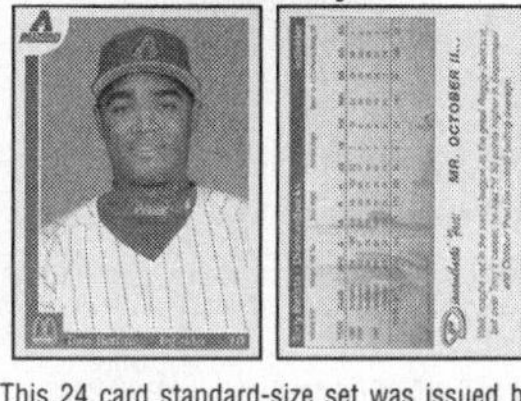

This 24 card standard-size set was issued by the McDonald restaurant chain in the Arizona area and features members of the Arizona Diamondbacks in their inagural season. The cards are unnumbered so we have sequenced them in alphabetical order.

Nm-Mt Ex-Mt
COMPLETE SET (24) 8.00 2.40
1 Joel Adamson .25 .07
2 Brian Anderson .25 .07
3 Tony Batista .50 .15
4 Jay Bell .25 .07
5 Andy Benes .25 .07
6 Yamil Benitez .25 .07
7 Willie Blair .25 .07
8 Brent Brede .25 .07
9 Omar Daal .25 .07
10 David Dellucci .50 .15
11 Jorge Fabregas .25 .07
12 Andy Fox .25 .07
13 Karim Garcia .50 .15
14 Travis Lee 1.00 .30
15 Damian Miller .75 .23
16 Gregg Olson .25 .07
17 Felix Rodriguez .25 .07
18 Buck Showalter MG .25 .07
19 Clint Sodowsky .25 .07
20 Andy Stankiewicz .25 .07
21 Kelly Stinnett .25 .07
22 Jeff Suppan .25 .07
23 Devon White .25 .07
24 Matt Williams .75 .23

1998 Diamondbacks Pinnacle

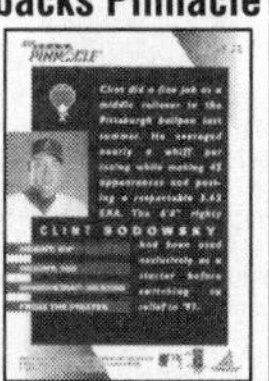

This 26-card set was produced by Pinnacle to commemorate the Diamondbacks first team and was distributed in a Collector's Edition box. The fronts feature color action player photos in a green, purple, and white border. The backs carry a small player head shot and player information. Only 3000 of the set were produced with the boxes serially numbered.

Nm-Mt Ex-Mt
COMPLETE SET (26) 6.00 1.80
1 Chris Clemons .25 .07
2 Brian Anderson .25 .07
3 Andy Benes .25 .07
4 Willie Blair .25 .07
5 Scott Brow .25 .07
6 Omar Daal .25 .07
7 Barry Manuel .25 .07
8 Gregg Olson .25 .07
9 Felix Rodriguez .25 .07
10 Clint Sodowsky .25 .07
11 Russ Springer .25 .07
12 Jeff Suppan .25 .07
13 Jorge Fabregas .25 .07
14 Kelly Stinnett .25 .07
15 Tony Batista .50 .15
16 Jay Bell .25 .07
17 Andy Fox .25 .07
18 Travis Lee 1.00 .30
19 Matt Williams .75 .23
20 Yamil Benitez .25 .07
21 Brent Brede .25 .07
22 David Dellucci .50 .15
23 Karim Garcia .25 .07
24 Chris Jones .25 .07
25 Devon White .25 .07
NNO Team Logo CL .25 .07

1999 Diamondbacks Pepsi Fleer

This set features members of the Arizona Diamond Backs and the players photos is situated against a red, white and blue background with the players name and uniform number in the background. The Pepsi logo in in the bottom left while the Fleer logo is on the upper right. The back has a player photo, some information and complete statistics. The Steve Finley card was pulled early during the run and was only available at the ballpark. The cards were issued in three card packs with one checklist so the checklist should be considered a Double print. Kelly Stinnett and Omar Daal apparently are among the toughest ones to acquire from the packs.

Nm-Mt Ex-Mt
COMPLETE SET (15) 10.00 3.00
1 Jay Bell .25 .07
2 Andy Benes .25 .07
3 Randy Johnson 2.00 .60
4 Matt Williams .75 .23
5 Steve Finley 5.00 1.50
6 Todd Stottlemyre .25 .07
7 Omar Daal .25 .07
8 Travis Lee .50 .15
9 Armando Reynoso .25 .07
10 Gregg Olson .25 .07
11 Tony Batista .50 .15
12 Greg Swindell .25 .07
13 Greg Colbrunn .25 .07
14 Damian Miller .50 .15
15 Kelly Stinnett .25 .07
NNO Checklist .25 .07

2000 Diamondbacks Circle K

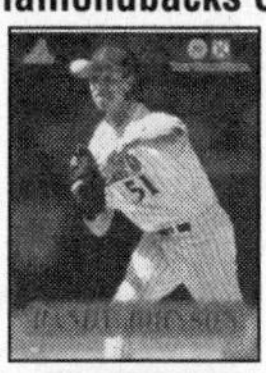

These 8" by 11" photos were distributed at an September 15th, 2000 Arizona Diamondbacks game. Four different people signed cards for this promotion: Greg Colbrunn, Matt Mantei and Damian Miller all signed 4250 cards or less while Randy Johnson is reported to have signed less than 200 cards. Since these cards are unnumbered we have sequenced them in alphabetical order. This was the second year this type of set was distributed at a Diamonback game.

Nm-Mt Ex-Mt
COMPLETE SET (4) 40.00 12.00
1 Greg Colbrunn 5.00 1.50
2 Randy Johnson 25.00 7.50
3 Matt Mantei 6.00 1.80
4 Damian Miller 5.00 1.50

2000 Diamondbacks Keebler

This 28 standard-size set was issued by Keebler in conjunction with the Diammond Backs. The full-bleed cards have round corners with the player's name and position on the bottom. The backs have player information.

Nm-Mt Ex-Mt
COMPLETE SET (28) 30.00 9.00
1 Buck Showalter MG 1.00 .30
2 Randy Johnson 6.00 1.80
3 Luis Gonzalez 3.00 .90
4 Todd Stottlemyre 1.00 .30
5 Matt Williams 2.00 .60
6 Curt Schilling 3.00 .90
7 Jay Bell 1.00 .30
8 Steve Finley 2.00 .60
9 Brian Anderson 1.00 .30
10 Tony Womack 1.00 .30
11 Mike Morgan 1.00 .30
12 Damian Miller 1.50 .45
13 Greg Swindell 1.00 .30
14 Greg Colbrunn 1.00 .30
15 Dan Plesac 1.00 .30
16 Craig Counsell 1.00 .30
17 Russ Springer 1.00 .30
18 Kelly Stinnett 1.00 .30
19 Alex Cabrera 1.00 .30
20 Matt Mantei 1.50 .45
21 Danny Klassen 1.00 .30
22 Hanley Frias 1.00 .30
23 Byung-Hyun Kim 3.00 .90
24 Jason Conti 1.00 .30
25 Danny Bautista 1.00 .30
26 Eurbiel Durazo 1.50 .45
27 Armando Reynoso 1.00 .30
28 Brian Butterfield CO 1.00 .30
Mark Connor CO
Dwayne Murphy CO
Jim Presley CO
Glenn Sherlock CO
Carlos Tosca CO

2000 Diamondbacks Pepsi Upper Deck

This 15 card standard-size set was issued by Upper Deck and featured members of the 2000 Arizona Diamondbacks. The horizontal fronts feature a player portrait as well as an action shot. The Upper Deck logo is in the upper left corner while the Pepsi logo is in on the bottom left. The horizontal backs have a player photo, a brief blurb and career statistics. This set was issued in three separate groups of five cards. Each group was redeemed for five Pepsi labels by the 15th of each month. According to reports, they also were issued in 12-pack cans and Stottlemyre appears to be the toughest of the group.

Nm-Mt Ex-Mt
COMPLETE SET (15) 12.00 3.60
1 Jay Bell .50 .15
2 Matt Mantei 1.00 .30
3 Greg Swindell .50 .15
4 Matt Williams 1.50 .45
5 Erubiel Durazo 1.00 .30
6 Todd Stottlemyre .50 .15
7 Randy Johnson 5.00 1.50
8 Tony Womack .50 .15
9 Greg Colbrunn .50 .15
10 Brian Anderson .50 .15
11 Omar Daal .50 .15
12 Travis Lee 1.00 .30
13 Steve Finley 1.50 .45
14 Luis Gonzalez 2.00 .60
15 Kelly Stinnett .50 .15

2001 Diamondbacks Keebler

These 28 standard-size cards, which all have rounded corners feature members of the 2001 Arizona Diamondbacks. The borderless fronts have the players photo as well as the the name on the bottom while the backs have biographical information as well as the Keebler logo.

Nm-Mt Ex-Mt
COMPLETE SET (28) 12.00 3.60
1 Bob Brenly MG .50 .15
2 Randy Johnson 2.50 .75
3 Luis Gonzalez 1.25 .35
4 Curt Schilling 1.25 .35
5 Matt Williams .75 .23
6 Todd Stottlemyre .25 .07
7 Jay Bell .25 .07
8 Steve Finley .75 .23
9 Mark Grace 1.00 .30
10 Brian Anderson .25 .07
11 Tony Womack .25 .07
12 Damian Miller .25 .07
13 Russ Springer .25 .07
14 Greg Colbrunn .25 .07
15 Craig Counsell .25 .07
16 Greg Swindell .25 .07
17 Reggie Sanders .50 .15
18 Matt Mantei .50 .15
19 Danny Bautista .25 .07
20 Mike Morgan .25 .07
21 Erubiel Durazo .50 .15
22 Troy Brohawn .25 .07
23 Byung-Hyun Kim 1.00 .30
24 David Dellucci .50 .15
25 Robert Ellis .25 .07
26 Rod Barajas .25 .07
27 Armando Reynoso .25 .07
28 Bob Melvin CO .25 .07
Dwayne Murphy CO
Eddie Rodriguez CO
Glenn Sherlock CO
Chris Speier CO
Bob Welch

2001 Diamondbacks Upper Deck Pepsi

Similar to the 2000 set, these cards featured members of the Diamondbacks and were sponsored by Pepsi. The busy horizontal fronts feature the player's name and uniform number on the left. There is a small photo in the middle of the card. The right side of the card has the Pepsi logo, Diamondback logo and the Upper Deck logo. The backs have a small inset photo as well as a brief blurb and stats for the last few seasons

Nm-Mt Ex-Mt
COMPLETE SET 12.00 3.60
1 Randy Johnson 4.00 1.20
2 Matt Williams 1.00 .30
3 Greg Colbrunn .50 .15
4 Mark Grace 1.50 .45
5 Armando Reynoso .50 .15
6 Matt Mantei .75 .23
7 Curt Schilling 2.00 .60
8 Jay Bell .50 .15
9 Reggie Sanders .75 .23
10 Steve Finley 1.00 .30
11 Todd Stottlemyre .50 .15
12 Greg Swindell .50 .15
13 Luis Gonzalez 1.50 .45
14 Brian Anderson .50 .15
15 Tony Womack .50 .15

2002 Diamondbacks ALS

This one card standard-size set features photos of Curt Schilling and Lou Gehrig on the front. The back features information on eight special items up for auction during the game to benefit the ALS foundation and the AZDB Charities.

Nm-Mt Ex-Mt
1 Curt Schilling 5.00 1.50
Lou Gehrig

2002 Diamondbacks Keebler

This 28 card standard-size set features members of the 2002 Arizona Diamondbacks, has rounded corners and was issued in conjuction with Keebler foods. The front of the borderless cards have a player photo with the bottom devoted to the player's name, The Diamondbacks logo and the player's position. The back has vital stats.

Nm-Mt Ex-Mt
COMPLETE SET (28) 10.00 3.00
1 Bob Brenly MG .50 .15
2 Luis Gonzalez 1.25 .35
3 Randy Johnson 2.50 .75
4 Curt Schilling 1.25 .35
5 Matt Williams .75 .23
6 Todd Stottlemyre .25 .07
7 Jay Bell .25 .07
8 Steve Finley .75 .23
9 Mark Grace 1.00 .30
10 Brian Anderson .25 .07
11 Tony Womack .25 .07
12 Damian Miller .25 .07
13 Erubiel Durazo .50 .15
14 Craig Counsell .25 .07
15 David Dellucci .50 .15
16 Greg Swindell .25 .07
17 Greg Colbrunn .25 .07
18 Rick Helling .25 .07
19 Danny Bautista .25 .07
20 Mike Morgan .25 .07
21 Rod Barajas .25 .07
22 Byung-Hyun Kim 1.00 .30
23 Mike Myers .25 .07
24 Jose Guillen .75 .23
25 Miguel Batista .25 .07
26 Junior Spivey .50 .15
27 Quinton McCracken .25 .07
28 Chuck Kniffin CO .25 .07
Bob Melvin CO
Dwayne Murphy CO
Eddie Rodriguez CO
Glenn Sherlock CO
Robin Yount CO

2003 Diamondbacks Keebler

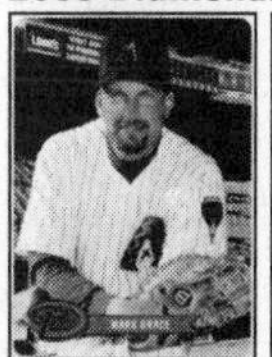
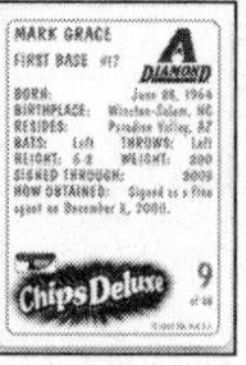

This 28 card standard-size set with rounded corners features members of the 2003 Arizona Diamondback. These cards were given away at a Dodgers game with each fan receiving 20 different cards and eight of the same card they could trade to finish their set.

MINT NRMT
COMPLETE SET 15.00 6.75
1 Bob Brenly MG .50 .23
2 Luis Gonzalez 1.25 .55
3 Randy Johnson 2.00 .90
4 Curt Schilling 2.00 .90
5 Danny Bautista .25 .11
6 Matt Mantei .50 .23
7 Craig Counsell .50 .23
8 Steve Finley .75 .35
9 Mark Grace 1.00 .45
10 Alex Cintron .25 .11
11 Tony Womack .25 .11
12 Chad Moeller .25 .11
13 Shea Hillenbrand .50 .23
14 Miguel Batista .25 .11
15 David Dellucci .50 .23
16 Elmer Dessens .25 .11
17 Lyle Overbay .50 .23
18 Mike Myers .25 .11
19 Quinton McCracken .25 .11
20 Rod Barajas .25 .11
21 Junior Spivey .50 .23
22 Stephen Randolph .25 .11
23 Carlos Baerga .25 .11
24 Mike Koplove .25 .11
25 Brandon Webb 2.50 1.10
26 Oscar Villarreal .25 .11
27 Bret Prinz .25 .11
28 Mark Davis CO .75 .35
Chuck Kniffin CO
Dwayne Murphy CO
Eddie Rodriguez CO
Glenn Sherlock CO
Robin Yount Co

1924 Diaz Cigarettes

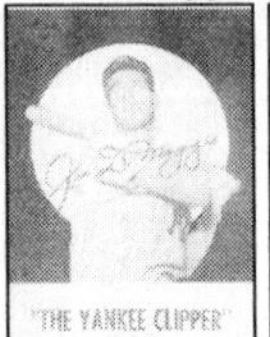

These 136 cards measure 1 3/4" by 2 1/4" with a white band on the top and the bottom. The team name is on the top while the players name is on the bottom. The middle has a player portrait. The back of the card has some information in Spanish Interestingly enough, all the players in this set are pitchers.

	Ex-Mt	VG
COMPLETE SET (136)	30000.00	15000.00
1 Walter Johnson	2000.00	1000.00
2 Waite Hoyt	400.00	200.00
3 Grover Alexander	1000.00	500.00
4 Tom Sheehan	200.00	100.00
5 Pete Donohue	200.00	100.00
6 Herb Pennock	400.00	200.00
7 Adolfo Luque	300.00	150.00
8 Carl Mays	250.00	125.00
9 Fred Marberry	250.00	125.00
10 Red Faber	400.00	200.00
11 William Piercy	200.00	100.00
12 Curt Fullerton	200.00	100.00
13 Sloppy Thurston	200.00	100.00
14 Rube Walberg	200.00	100.00
15 Fred Heimach	200.00	100.00
16 Sherry Smith	200.00	100.00
17 Warren Ogden	200.00	100.00
18 Ernest Osborne	200.00	100.00
19 Dutch Ruether	200.00	100.00
20 Burleigh Grimes	400.00	200.00
21 Joe Genewich	200.00	100.00
22 Vic Aldridge	200.00	100.00
23 Arnold Stone	200.00	100.00
24 Les Howe	200.00	100.00
25 George Murry	200.00	100.00
26 Herman Pillette	200.00	100.00
27 John Couch	200.00	100.00
28 Tony Kaufmann	200.00	100.00
29 Frank May	200.00	100.00
30 Howard Ehmke	250.00	125.00
31 Bob Hasty	200.00	100.00
32 Dazzy Vance	500.00	250.00
33 Gorham Leverette	200.00	100.00
34 Bryan Harris	200.00	100.00
35 Paul Schreiber	200.00	100.00
36 Dewey Hinkle	200.00	100.00
37 Byron Yarrison	200.00	100.00
38 Jesse Haines	400.00	200.00
39 Earl Hamilton	200.00	100.00
40 Wilbur Cooper	250.00	125.00
41 Tom Long	200.00	100.00
42 Alex Ferguson	200.00	100.00
43 Chet Ross	200.00	100.00
44 Jack Quinn	250.00	125.00
45 Ray Kolp	200.00	100.00
46 Art Nehf	250.00	125.00
47 Hugh McQuillan	200.00	100.00
48 George Uhle	250.00	125.00
49 Ed Rommel	250.00	125.00
50 Ted Lyons	400.00	200.00
51 Roy Meeker	200.00	100.00
52 John Stuart	200.00	100.00
53 Joe Oeshger	200.00	100.00
54 Wayland Dean	200.00	100.00
55 Guy Morton	200.00	100.00
56 Bill Doak	200.00	100.00
57 Ed Pfeffer	200.00	100.00
58 Sam Gray	200.00	100.00
59 Lou North	200.00	100.00
60 Godfrey Brogan	200.00	100.00
61 Jimmy Ring	200.00	100.00
62 Rube Marquard	400.00	200.00
63 Bert Lewis	200.00	100.00
64 Frank Henry	200.00	100.00
65 Dennis Burns	200.00	100.00
66 Roline Naylor	200.00	100.00
67 Walt Huntzinger	200.00	100.00
68 Stan Baumgartner	200.00	100.00
69 Virgil Barnes	200.00	100.00
70 Clarence Mitchell	200.00	100.00
71 Lee Meadows	200.00	100.00
72 Charles Clazner	200.00	100.00
73 Jesse Barnes	200.00	100.00
74 Sam Jones	250.00	125.00
75 Dennis Gearin	200.00	100.00
76 Tom Zachary	250.00	125.00
77 Larry Benton	200.00	100.00
78 Jess Winter	200.00	100.00
79 Red Ruffing	500.00	250.00
80 John Cooney	200.00	100.00
81 Joe Bush	250.00	125.00
82 William Harris	200.00	100.00
83 Joe Shaute	200.00	100.00
84 George Pipgras	250.00	125.00
85 Eppa Rixey	400.00	200.00
86 Bill Sherdel	200.00	100.00
87 John Benton	200.00	100.00
88 Art Decatur	200.00	100.00
89 Harry Shriver	200.00	100.00
90 John Morrison	200.00	100.00
91 Walter Betts	200.00	100.00
92 Oscar Roettger	200.00	100.00
93 Bob Shawkey	400.00	200.00
94 Mike Cvengros	200.00	100.00
95 Leo Dickerman	200.00	100.00
96 Phillip Weinert	200.00	100.00
97 Nicholas Dumovich	200.00	100.00
98 Herb McQuaid	200.00	100.00
99 Tim McNamara	200.00	100.00
100 Alan Russell	200.00	100.00
101 Ted Blankenship	200.00	100.00
102 Howard Baldwin	200.00	100.00
103 Frank Davis	200.00	100.00
104 James Edwards	200.00	100.00
105 Hub Pruett	250.00	125.00
106 Dick Rudolph	200.00	100.00
107 Allan Sothoron	200.00	100.00
108 Claude Jonnard	200.00	100.00
109 Joubert Davenport	200.00	100.00
110 Paul Zahnser	200.00	100.00
111 John Bentley	200.00	100.00
112 Wilfred Ryan	200.00	100.00
113 George Metevier	200.00	100.00
114 John Watson	200.00	100.00
115 Syl Johnson	200.00	100.00
116 Oscar Fuhr	200.00	100.00
117 Warren Collins	200.00	100.00
118 Stan Covelskie	400.00	200.00
119 Dave Danforth	200.00	100.00
120 Elam Van Gilder	200.00	100.00
121 Bert Cole	200.00	100.00
122 Ken Holoway	200.00	100.00
123 Charles Robertson	200.00	100.00
124 Ed Wells	200.00	100.00
125 George Davis	200.00	100.00
126 William Bayne	200.00	100.00
127 Urban Shocker	300.00	150.00
128 Slim McGrew	200.00	100.00
129 Philip Bedgood	200.00	100.00
130 Fred Wingfield	200.00	100.00
131 George Modridge	200.00	100.00
132 Joe Martina	200.00	100.00
133 Byron Speece	200.00	100.00
134 Hal Carlson	200.00	100.00
135 Wilbur Hubbell	200.00	100.00
136 Milt Gaston	200.00	100.00

1951 DiMaggio Yankee Clipper Shoes

This one card set, which measures approximately 2 1/2" by 3 1/2" was issued as part of the shoe purchase. These cards were supposed to be tied to the shoe strings. The front has a batting portrait shot of DiMaggio set against a green background while the back a bullet point assortment of career highlights

	Nm-Mt	Ex-Mt
1 Joe DiMaggio	50.00	15.00

1972-87 DiMaggio Bowery Bank

This one-card standard-size set was actually released three times. The first time was is 1972, the second was in 1979 and third was in 1987. We have priced the 1987 version here. The 1979 version is valued at $25 and the 1972 version is at $50. The front features a full-color photo of Dimaggio framed by the words Yankees on top and his name and position on the bottom. The horizontal backs has his career numbers, a brief biography and his vital statistics.

	NM	Ex
1 Joe DiMaggio	12.00	4.80

1988 Disney World Series

These two cards were issued during the 1988 season and featured three star members of various teams. The fronts have the players pictured with Mickey Mouse and the backs have the name of the team, the names of the Disney Palaces and are sponsored by Delta.

	Nm-Mt	Ex-Mt
COMPLETE SET (2)	15.00	6.00
1 Kevin Bass Nolan Ryan Mike Scott	10.00	4.00
2 Jack Clark Don Mattingly Willie Randolph	5.00	2.00

1952 Dixie Lids

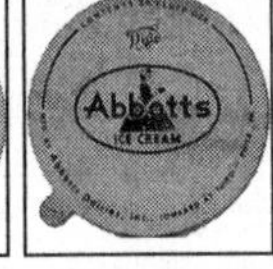

This scarce 24-lid set features all baseball subjects each measuring 2 11/16". The 1952 set was released very late in the year and in only one size; it is undoubtedly the toughest Dixie baseball set. The lids are found with a blue tint. The catalog designation for this set is F7-2A. Lids found with the tab removed would suffer an approximate 25 percent in value. The asterisked lids below are those that were only available in 1952. The 50s Dixie Lids are distinguished from the 30's lids also by the fact that the 50s lids have the circular picture portion abruptly squared off near the bottom end of the lid where the player's name appears.

	NM	Ex
COMPLETE SET (24)	2700.00	1350.00
1 Richie Ashburn	150.00	75.00
2 Tommy Byrne	100.00	50.00
3 Chico Carrasquel	80.00	40.00
4 Pete Castiglione	80.00	40.00
5 Walker Cooper	100.00	50.00
6 Billy Cox	80.00	40.00
7 Ferris Fain	80.00	40.00
8 Bobby Feller	250.00	125.00
9 Nellie Fox	150.00	75.00
10 Monte Irvin	150.00	75.00
11 Ralph Kiner	150.00	75.00
12 Cass Michaels	80.00	40.00
13 Don Mueller	80.00	40.00
14 Mel Parnell	80.00	40.00
15 Allie Reynolds	120.00	60.00
16 Preacher Roe	120.00	60.00
17 Connie Ryan	80.00	40.00
18 Hank Sauer	100.00	50.00
19 Al Schoendienst	150.00	75.00
20 Andy Seminick	100.00	50.00
21 Bobby Shantz	100.00	50.00
22 Enos Slaughter	150.00	75.00
23 Virgil Trucks	80.00	40.00
24 Gene Woodling	100.00	50.00

1952 Dixie Premiums

The catalog designation is F7-2A. The 1952 Dixie Cup Baseball Premiums contain 1951 statistics. There are 24 (sepia-tinted) black and white photos each measuring approximately 8" by 10". Each photo has a facsimile autograph at the bottom. These large premium photos are blank backed and were printed on thick paper stock.

	NM	Ex
COMPLETE SET (24)	700.00	350.00
1 Richie Ashburn	60.00	30.00
2 Tommy Byrne	25.00	12.50
3 Chico Carrasquel	25.00	12.50
4 Pete Castiglione	25.00	12.50
5 Walker Cooper	25.00	12.50
6 Billy Cox	25.00	12.50
7 Ferris Fain	25.00	12.50
8 Bob Feller	100.00	50.00
9 Nellie Fox	60.00	30.00
10 Monte Irvin	60.00	30.00
11 Ralph Kiner	60.00	30.00
12 Cass Michaels	25.00	12.50
13 Don Mueller	25.00	12.50
14 Mel Parnell	25.00	12.50
15 Allie Reynolds	35.00	17.50
16 Preacher Roe	35.00	17.50
17 Connie Ryan	25.00	12.50
18 Hank Sauer	30.00	15.00
19 Al Schoendienst	60.00	30.00
20 Andy Seminick	25.00	12.50
21 Bobby Shantz	30.00	15.00
22 Enos Slaughter	60.00	30.00
23 Virgil Trucks	25.00	12.50
24 Gene Woodling	30.00	15.00

1953 Dixie Lids

This 24-lid set features all baseball subjects each measuring 2 11/16". There are many different back types in existence. The lids are found with a wine tint. The catalog designation for this set is F7-2. Lids found without the tab attached are considered good condition at best. There is also a smaller size variation, 2 5/16" in diameter. These smaller lids are worth an additional 50 percent more than the prices listed below.

	NM	Ex
COMPLETE SET (24)	800.00	400.00
1 Richie Ashburn	50.00	25.00
2 Chico Carrasquel	25.00	12.50
3 Billy Cox	25.00	12.50
4 Ferris Fain	25.00	12.50
5 Nellie Fox	50.00	25.00
6A Sid Gordon Boston Braves	50.00	25.00
6B Sid Gordon Milwaukee Braves	25.00	12.50
7 Warren Hacker	25.00	12.50
8 Monte Irvin	50.00	25.00
9 Jackie Jensen	40.00	20.00
10 Ralph Kiner	50.00	25.00
11 Ted Kluszewski	50.00	25.00
12 Bob Lemon	50.00	25.00
13 Don Mueller	25.00	12.50
14 Mel Parnell	25.00	12.50
15 Jerry Priddy	25.00	12.50
16 Allie Reynolds	40.00	20.00
17 Preacher Roe	40.00	20.00
18 Hank Sauer	25.00	12.50
19 Al Schoendienst	50.00	25.00
20 Bobby Shantz	25.00	12.50
21 Enos Slaughter	50.00	25.00
22A Warren Spahn Boston Braves	100.00	50.00
22B Warren Spahn Milwaukee Braves	100.00	50.00
23A Virgil Trucks Chicago White Sox	25.00	12.50
23B Virgil Trucks St. Louis Browns	25.00	12.50
24 Gene Woodling	25.00	12.50

1953 Dixie Premiums

The catalog designation is F7-2A. The 1953 Dixie Cup Baseball Premiums contain 1952 statistics. There are 24 (sepia-tinted) black and white photos each measuring approximately 8" by 10". Each photo has a facsimile autograph at the bottom. These large premium photos are blank backed and were printed on thick paper stock.

	NM	Ex
COMPLETE SET (24)	400.00	200.00
1 Richie Ashburn	40.00	20.00
2 Chico Carrasquel	15.00	7.50
3 Billy Cox	20.00	10.00
4 Ferris Fain	15.00	7.50
5 Nellie Fox	40.00	20.00
6 Sid Gordon	15.00	7.50
7 Warren Hacker	15.00	7.50
8 Monte Irvin	40.00	20.00
9 Jack Jensen	25.00	12.50
10 Ralph Kiner	40.00	20.00
11 Ted Kluszewski	30.00	15.00
12 Bob Lemon	40.00	20.00
13 Don Mueller	15.00	7.50
14 Mel Parnell	15.00	7.50
15 Jerry Priddy	15.00	7.50
16 Allie Reynolds	25.00	12.50
17 Preacher Roe	25.00	12.50
18 Hank Sauer	20.00	10.00
19 Al Schoendienst	30.00	15.00
20 Bobby Shantz	20.00	10.00
21 Enos Slaughter	30.00	15.00
22 Warren Spahn	50.00	25.00
23 Virgil Trucks	15.00	7.50
24 Gene Woodling	20.00	10.00

1954 Dixie Lids

This 18 lid set features all baseball subjects each measuring 2 11/16". There are many different back types in existence. The lids are typically found with a brown sepia tint. The catalog designation for this set is F7-4. Lids found without the tab attached are considered good condition at best. This year is distinguishable by the fact that the lids say "Get Dixie Lid 3-D Starviewer. Send 25 cents, this lid, name, address, to DIXIE, Box 630, New York 17, N.Y." around the border on the front. The lids have an "L" or "R" on the tab, which distinguished which side of the 3-D viewer was to be used for that particular card. The lids are also seen in a small (2 5/16") and large (3 3/16") size; these variations carry approximately double the prices below.

	NM	Ex
COMPLETE SET (18)	550.00	275.00
1 Richie Ashburn	40.00	20.00
2 Clint Courtney	20.00	10.00
3 Sid Gordon	20.00	10.00
4 Billy Hoeft	20.00	10.00
5 Monte Irvin	40.00	20.00
6 Jackie Jensen	30.00	15.00
7 Ralph Kiner	40.00	20.00
8 Ted Kluszewski	40.00	20.00
9 Gil McDougald	30.00	15.00
10 Minnie Minoso	40.00	20.00
11 Danny O'Connell	20.00	10.00
12 Mel Parnell	20.00	10.00
13 Preacher Roe	30.00	15.00
14 Al Rosen	25.00	12.50
15 Al Schoendienst	40.00	20.00
16 Enos Slaughter	40.00	20.00
17 Gene Woodling	20.00	10.00
18 Gus Zernial	20.00	10.00

1969-72 Dodge Promo Postcards

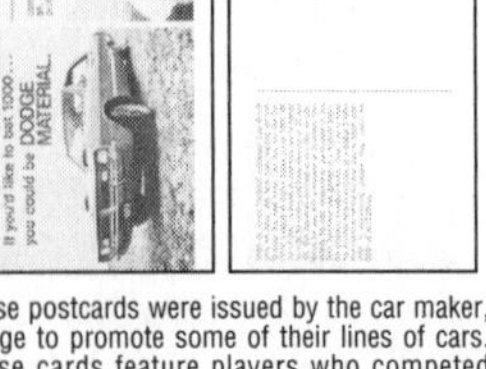

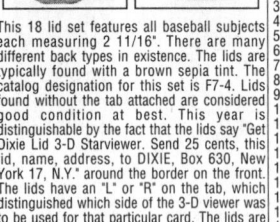

These postcards were issued by the car maker, Dodge to promote some of their lines of cars. These cards feature players who competed against each other in the 1968 World Series (Lou Brock and Bill Freehan) and feature a player photo as well as a photo of the card being promoted. The back is blank except for a brief description of the player as well as how it relates to the "Dodge car" pictured on the front. The cards are unnumbered so we have sequenced them in alphabetical order.

	NM	Ex
COMPLETE SET (4)	35.00	14.00
1 Lou Brock	10.00	4.00
2 Bill Freehan	8.00	3.20
3 Joe Garagiola	10.00	4.00
4 Mickey Lolich	8.00	3.20

1909 Dodgers Daily Eagle Supplement

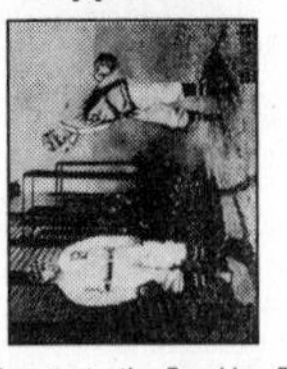

These supplments to the Brooklyn Daily Eagle are sepia toned photos and measure approximately 7" by 9 1/2" and feature members of the Brooklyn Dodgers. Since the photos are unnumbered, we have sequenced them in alphabetical order. Also, it is possible that there are more cards in this set so any additions to this checklist is appreciated.

	Ex-Mt	VG
COMPLETE SET	500.00	250.00
1 George Bell	100.00	50.00
2 George Hunter	100.00	50.00
3 Doc Scanlon	100.00	50.00
4 Kaiser Wilhelm	100.00	50.00
5 Harry McIntire Jimmy Pastorious	100.00	50.00

1940 Dodgers Team Issue

These photos measure approximately 6 1/2" by 9". They feature members of the 1940 Brooklyn Dodgers. The photos take up nearly all of the card except for a small white border. There is also a facsimile signature of each player. The backs are blank and we have sequenced them in alphabetical order. Pee Wee Reese appears in his rookie season in this set.

	Ex-Mt	VG
COMPLETE SET (25)	150.00	75.00
1 Dolph Camilli	10.00	5.00
2 Tex Carleton	5.00	2.50
3 Hugh Casey	8.00	4.00
4 Pete Coscarart	5.00	2.50
5 Curt Davis	5.00	2.50
6 Leo Durocher	15.00	7.50
7 Fred Fitzsimmons	8.00	4.00
8 Herman Franks	5.00	2.50
9 Joe Gallagher	5.00	2.50
10 Charlie Gilbert	5.00	2.50
11 Luke Hamlin	5.00	2.50
12 Johnny Hudson	5.00	2.50
13 Newt Kimball	5.00	2.50
14 Cookie Lavagetto	8.00	4.00
15 Gus Mancuso	5.00	2.50
16 Joe Medwick	15.00	7.50
17 Van Lingle Mungo	8.00	4.00
18 Babe Phelps	5.00	2.50
19 Tot Pressnell	5.00	2.50
20 Pee Wee Reese	25.00	12.50
21 Vito Tamulis	5.00	2.50
22 Joe Vosmik	5.00	2.50
23 Dixie Walker	10.00	5.00
24 Jimmy Wasdell	5.00	2.50
25 Whit Wyatt	8.00	4.00

1941 Dodgers Team Issue

These are blank-backed, white-bordered, 6 1/2 X 9" black-and-white photos. The photos have facsimile autographs, are unnumbered and checklisted below in alphabetical order.

	Ex-Mt	VG
COMPLETE SET (28)	175.00	90.00
1 Mace Brown	5.00	2.50
2 Dolph Camilli	8.00	4.00
3 Tex Carleton	5.00	2.50
4 Hugh Casey	5.00	2.50
5 Pete Coscarart	5.00	2.50
6 Curt Davis	5.00	2.50
7 Leo Durocher MG	15.00	7.50
8 Fred Fitzsimmons	6.00	3.00
9 Herman Franks	5.00	2.50
10 Joe Gallagher	5.00	2.50
10 Jimmy Wasdell	5.00	2.50
11 Charlie Gilbert	5.00	2.50
11 Kemp Wicker	5.00	2.50
12 Luke Hamlin	5.00	2.50
13 Johnny Hudson	5.00	2.50
14 Newill Kimball	5.00	2.50
15 Cookie Lavagetto	6.00	3.00
16 Gus Mancuso	6.00	3.00
17 Joe Medwick	15.00	7.50
18 Van Mungo	8.00	4.00
19 Babe Phelps	5.00	2.50
20 Tot Pressnell	5.00	2.50
21 Pee Wee Reese	20.00	10.00
22 Lew Riggs	5.00	2.50
23 Bill Swift	5.00	2.50
24 Vito Tamulis	5.00	2.50
25 Joe Vosmik	5.00	2.50
26 Dixie Walker	8.00	4.00
27 Jimmy Wasdell	5.00	2.50
28 Whit Wyatt	5.00	2.50

1942 Dodgers Team Issue

This 25-card set of the Brooklyn Dodger measures approximately 6 1/2" by 9" and features black-and-white player portraits with facsimile autograph. The cards are unnumbered and checklisted below in alphabetical order.

	Ex-Mt	VG
COMPLETE SET (25)	175.00	90.00

1 Johnny Allen 5.00 2.50
2 Frenchy Bordagaray 5.00 2.50
3 Dolph Camilli 8.00 4.00
4 Hugh Casey 5.00 2.50
5 Curt Davis 5.00 2.50
6 Leo Durocher 15.00 7.50
7 Larry French 8.00 4.00
8 Augie Galan 5.00 2.50
9 Ed Head 5.00 2.50
10 Billy Herman 15.00 7.50
11 Kirby Higbe 8.00 4.00
12 Alex Kampouris 5.00 2.50
13 Newell Kimball 5.00 2.50
14 Joe Medwick 15.00 7.50
15 Mickey Owen 8.00 4.00
16 Pee Wee Reese 15.00 7.50
17 Pete Reiser 10.00 5.00
18 Lew Riggs 5.00 2.50
19 Johnny Rizzo 5.00 2.50
20 Schoolboy Rowe 8.00 4.00
21 Bill Sullivan 5.00 2.50
22 Arky Vaughn 15.00 7.50
23 Dixie Walker 10.00 5.00
24 Les Webber 5.00 2.50
25 Whitlow Wyatt 8.00 4.00

1943 Dodgers Team Issue

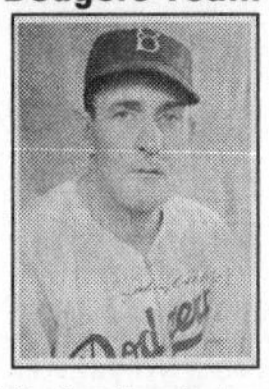

This set of the Brooklyn Dodgers measures approximately 6 1/2" by 9". The black-and-white player photos display fascimile autographs. The backs are blank. The cards are unnumbered and checklisted below in alphabetical order.

Ex-Mt VG
COMPLETE SET (25) 150.00 75.00
1 Johnny Allen 8.00 4.00
2 Frenchy Bordagaray 5.00 2.50
3 Bob Bragan 8.00 4.00
4 Dolph Camilli 10.00 5.00
5 John Cooney 5.00 2.50
6 John Corriden 5.00 2.50
7 Curt Davis 5.00 2.50
8 Leo Durocher MG 15.00 7.50
9 Fred Fitzimmons 8.00 4.00
10 Augie Galan 8.00 4.00
11 Al Glossop 5.00 2.50
12 Ed Head 5.00 2.50
13 Billy Herman 15.00 7.50
14 Kirby Higbe 8.00 4.00
15 Max Macon 5.00 2.50
16 Joe Medwick 15.00 7.50
17 Rube Melton 5.00 2.50
18 Dee Moore 5.00 2.50
19 Bobo Newsom 10.00 5.00
20 Mickey Owen 8.00 4.00
21 Arky Vaughan 15.00 7.50
22 Dixie Walker 10.00 5.00
23 Paul Waner 15.00 7.50
24 Les Webber 5.00 2.50
25 Whitlow Wyatt 5.00 2.50

1943 Dodgers War Bonds

Issued in conjunction with a war bonds drive in 1943, this card, which measure 2 1/2" by 4 3/8" features a team photo of the 1943 Brooklyn Dodgers. Because of the nature of how it was issued, not many of these cards have survived.

Ex-Mt VG
1 Brooklyn Dodgers 500.00 250.00

1946 Dodgers Team Issue

This 25-card set of the Brooklyn Dodgers measures approximately 6 1/2" by 9" and features black-and-white player portraits with white borders. The backs are blank. The cards are unnumbered and checklisted below in alphabetical order.

Ex-Mt VG
COMPLETE SET (25) 150.00 75.00
1 Ferrell(Andy) Anderson 5.00 2.50
2 Henry Behrman 5.00 2.50
3 Ralph Branca 15.00 7.50
4 Hugh Casey 5.00 2.50
5 Leo Durocher MG 15.00 7.50
6 Carl Furillo 15.00 7.50
7 Augie Galan 8.00 4.00
8 Hal Gregg 5.00 2.50
9 Joe Hatten 5.00 2.50
10 Ed Head 5.00 2.50
11 Billy Herman 15.00 7.50
12 Gene Hermanski 5.00 2.50
13 Art Herring 5.00 2.50
14 Kirby Higbe 8.00 4.00
15 Cookie Lavagetto 10.00 5.00
16 Vic Lombardi 5.00 2.50
17 Pee Wee Reese 20.00 10.00
18 Pete Reiser 10.00 5.00
19 Stan Rojek 5.00 2.50
20 Mike Sandlock 5.00 2.50
21 Eddie Stanky 15.00 7.50
22 Ed Stevens 5.00 2.50
23 Dixie Walker 10.00 5.00
24 Les Webber 5.00 2.50
25 Dick Whitman 5.00 2.50

1947 Dodgers Team Issue

This 25-card set of the Brooklyn Dodgers measures approximately 6 1/2" by 9" and features black-and-white player portraits with white borders and facsimile autographs. The backs are blank. The cards are unnumbered and checklisted below in alphabetical order. Carl Furillo, Gil Hodges and Duke Snider are featured in this set, two years before their Rookie Cards. Jackie Robinson is featured in this set as well during his rookie season.

Ex-Mt VG
COMPLETE SET (25) 200.00 100.00
1 Ray Blades CO 5.00 2.50
2 Bob Bragan 8.00 4.00
3 Ralph Branca 10.00 5.00
4 Tommy Brown 5.00 2.50
5 Hugh Casey 5.00 2.50
6 Eddie Chandler 5.00 2.50
7 Carl Furillo 15.00 7.50
8 Hal Gregg 5.00 2.50
9 Joe Hatten 5.00 2.50
10 Gene Hermanski 5.00 2.50
11 Gil Hodges 15.00 7.50
12 John Jorgensen 5.00 2.50
13 Clyde King 5.00 2.50
14 Vic Lombardi 5.00 2.50
15 Rube Melton 5.00 2.50
16 Eddie Miksis 5.00 2.50
17 Pee Wee Reese 15.00 7.50
18 Pete Reiser 10.00 5.00
19 Jackie Robinson 50.00 25.00
20 Stan Rojek 5.00 2.50
21 Burt Shotton MG 5.00 2.50
22 Duke Snider 15.00 7.50
23 Eddie Stanky 10.00 5.00
24 Harry Taylor 5.00 2.50
25 Dixie Walker 8.00 4.00

1948 Dodgers Team Issue

This 26-card set of the Brooklyn Dodgers measures approximately 6 1/2" by 9" and features black-and-white player portraits with white borders. The backs are blank. The cards are unnumbered and checklisted below in alphabetical order. This set can be datec to 1948 with the inclusion of Preston Ward in his only season in Brooklyn.

NM Ex
COMPLETE SET (26) 200.00 100.00
1 Rex Barney 8.00 4.00
2 Ray Blades CO 5.00 2.50
3 Bob Bragan 5.00 2.50
4 Ralph Branca 10.00 5.00
5 Tommy Brown 5.00 2.50
6 Hugh Casey 5.00 2.50
7 Billy Cox 10.00 5.00
8 Leo Durocher MG 15.00 7.50
9 Bruce Edwards 5.00 2.50
10 Carl Furillo 10.00 5.00
11 Joe Hatten 5.00 2.50
12 Gene Hermanski 5.00 2.50
13 Gil Hodges 15.00 7.50
14 John Jorgensen 5.00 2.50
15 Don Lund 5.00 2.50
16 Eddie Miksis 5.00 2.50
17 Jake Pitler CO 5.00 2.50
18 Pee Wee Reese 25.00 12.50
19 Pete Reiser 10.00 5.00
20 Jackie Robinson 40.00 20.00
21 Preacher Roe 10.00 5.00
22 Burt Shotton MG 5.00 2.50
23 Clyde Sukeforth CO 5.00 2.50
24 Harry Taylor 5.00 2.50
25 Arky Vaughan 15.00 7.50
26 Preston Ward 5.00 2.50

1949 Dodgers Team Issue

This 25-card set of the Brooklyn Dodgers measures approximately 6 1/2" by 9" and features black-and-white player portraits with white borders. The backs are blank. The cards are unnumbered and checklisted below in alphabetical order. Roy Campanella is featured in his Rookie Card year. Don Newcombe is featured in this set a year prior to his Rookie Card. The Dodgers, Giants, Red Sox and Yankees Team Issue sets were all available at time of issue from Harry M Stevens for 68 cents per set.

NM Ex
COMPLETE SET (25) 250.00 125.00
1 Jack Banta 5.00 2.50
2 Rex Barney 8.00 4.00
3 Ralph Branca 10.00 5.00
4 Tommy Brown 5.00 2.50
5 Roy Campanella 15.00 7.50
6 Billy Cox 10.00 5.00
7 Bruce Edwards 5.00 2.50
8 Carl Furillo 15.00 7.50
9 Joe Hatten 5.00 2.50
10 Gene Hermanski 5.00 2.50
11 Gil Hodges 15.00 7.50
12 Johnny Hopp 5.00 2.50
13 Spider Jorgensen 5.00 2.50
14 Mike McCormick 5.00 2.50
15 Eddie Miksis 5.00 2.50
16 Don Newcombe 15.00 7.50
17 Erv Palica 5.00 2.50
18 Jake Pitler CO 5.00 2.50
19 Pee Wee Reese 25.00 12.50
20 Jackie Robinson 40.00 20.00
21 Preacher Roe 5.00 2.50
22 Burt Shotton MG 5.00 2.50
23 Duke Snider 25.00 12.50
24 Milt Stock CO 5.00 2.50
25 Clyde Sukeforth CO 5.00 2.50

1955 Dodgers Golden Stamps

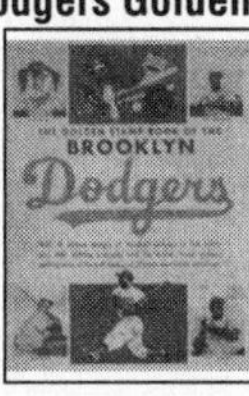

This 32-stamp set features color photos of the Brooklyn Dodgers and measures approximately 2" by 2 5/8". The stamps are designed to be placed in a 32-page album which measures approximately 8 3/8" by 10 15/16". The album contains black-and-white drawings of players with statistics and life stories. The stamps are unnumbered and listed below according to where they fall in the album.

NM Ex
COMPLETE SET (32) 150.00 75.00
1 Walt Alston MG 10.00 5.00
2 Don Newcombe 4.00 2.00
3 Carl Erskine 4.00 2.00
4 Johnny Podres 4.00 2.00
5 Billy Loes 2.00 1.00
6 Russ Meyer 2.00 1.00
7 Jim Hughes 2.00 1.00
8 Sandy Koufax 30.00 15.00
9 Joe Black 3.00 1.50
10 Karl Spooner 2.00 1.00
11 Clem Labine 3.00 1.50
12 Roy Campanella 15.00 7.50
13 Gil Hodges 10.00 5.00
14 Jim Gilliam 5.00 2.50
15 Jackie Robinson 30.00 15.00
16 Pee Wee Reese 15.00 7.50
17 Duke Snider 15.00 7.50
18 Carl Furillo 5.00 2.50
19 Sandy Amoros 4.00 2.00
20 Frank Kellert 2.00 1.00
21 Don Zimmer 4.00 2.00
22 Al Walker 2.00 1.00
23 Tom Lasorda 15.00 7.50
24 Ed Roebuck 2.00 1.00
25 Don Hoak 2.00 1.00
26 George Shuba 3.00 1.50
27 Billy Herman CO 4.00 2.00
28 Jake Pitler CO 2.00 1.00
29 Joe Becker CO 2.00 1.00
30 Doc Wendler TR 3.00 1.50
Carl Furillo
31 Charlie Di Giovanna BB 2.00 1.00
32 Ebbets Field 15.00 7.50
XX Album 5.00 2.50

1956-57 Dodgers

This 28-piece set features blank-backed, white-bordered, 5 X 7 black-and-white photos. The player's name and team appear in black lettering within the lower margin. The photos are unnumbered and checklisted below in alphabetical order.

NM Ex
COMPLETE SET (28) 400.00 200.00
1 Walter Alston MG 15.00 7.50
2 Sandy Amoros 10.00 5.00
3 Joe Becker CO 5.00 2.50
4 Don Bessent 5.00 2.50
5 Roy Campanella 40.00 20.00
6 Roger Craig 8.00 4.00
7 Don Drysdale 25.00 12.50
8 Carl Erskine 10.00 5.00
9 Chico Fernandez 5.00 2.50
10 Carl Furillo 10.00 5.00
11 Jim Gilliam 10.00 5.00
12 Billy Herman CO 10.00 5.00
13 Gil Hodges 25.00 12.50
14 Randy Jackson 5.00 2.50
15 Sandy Koufax 50.00 25.00
16 Clem Labine 8.00 4.00
(Uniform)
17 Clem Labine 8.00 4.00
(T-shirt)
18 Sal Maglie 10.00 5.00
19 Charlie Neal 8.00 4.00
20 Don Newcombe 10.00 5.00
(Uniform)
21 Don Newcombe 10.00 5.00
(T-shirt)
22 Jake Pitler CO 5.00 2.50
23 Johnny Podres 10.00 5.00
24 Pee Wee Reese 25.00 12.50
25 Jackie Robinson 50.00 25.00
26 Ed Roebuck 5.00 2.50
27 Duke Snider 25.00 12.50
28 Al Walker 5.00 2.50

1958 Dodgers Bell Brand

The 1958 Bell Brand Potato Chips set of ten unnumbered cards features members of the Los Angeles Dodgers exclusively. Each card has a 1/4" green border, and the Gino Cimoli, Johnny Podres, Pee Wee Reese and Duke Snider cards are more difficult to find; they are marked with an SP (short printed) in the checklist below. The cards measure approximately 3" by 4". This set marks the first year for the Dodgers in Los Angeles and

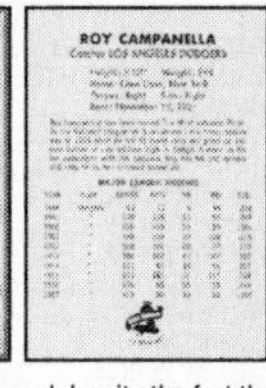

includes a Campanella card despite the fact that he never played for the team in California. The catalog designation for this set is F339-1. Cards found still inside the original cellophane wrapper are valued at double the prices below. According to printed reports, the promotion went badly for Bell Brand and much of the product was destroyed. The cards were found in both 29 cent and 49 cent packages.

NM Ex
COMPLETE SET (10) 1400.00 700.00
COMMON CARD (1-10) 50.00 25.00
COMMON SP 100.00 50.00
1 Roy Campanella 200.00 100.00
2 Gino Cimoli SP 100.00 50.00
3 Don Drysdale 100.00 50.00
4 Jim Gilliam 50.00 25.00
5 Gil Hodges 100.00 50.00
6 Sandy Koufax 250.00 125.00
7 Johnny Podres SP 150.00 75.00
8 Pee Wee Reese SP 200.00 100.00
9 Duke Snider SP 300.00 150.00
10 Don Zimmer 50.00 25.00

1958 Dodgers Jay Publishing

This 12-card set of the Los Angeles Dodgers measures approximately 5" by 7" and features black-and-white player photos in a white border. These cards were packaged 12 to a packet. The backs are blank. The cards are unnumbered and checklisted below in alphabetical order.

NM Ex
COMPLETE SET (12) 75.00 38.00
1 Walt Alston MG 5.00 2.50
2 Roy Campanella 15.00 7.50
3 Gino Cimoli 3.00 1.50
4 Don Drysdale 10.00 5.00
5 Carl Furillo 5.00 2.50
6 Gil Hodges 10.00 5.00
7 Clem Labine 3.00 1.50
8 Charley Neal 3.00 1.50
9 Don Newcombe 5.00 2.50
10 Johnny Podres 5.00 2.50
11 Pee Wee Reese 15.00 7.50
12 Duke Snider 10.00 5.00

1958 Dodgers Team Issue

This 25-card set features black-and-white photos of the Los Angeles Dodgers in white borders. The backs are blank. The set could originally be obtained through the mail for $1. Later on this set was also sold at the park for $1 and due to lack of early sales was later reduced to $.50. The cards are unnumbered and checklisted below in alphabetical order.

NM Ex
COMPLETE SET (25) 125.00 60.00
1 Walt Alston MG 6.00 3.00
2 Joe Becker CO 3.00 1.50
3 Don Bessent 3.00 1.50
4 Roger Craig 5.00 2.50
5 Charlie Dressen CO 5.00 2.50
6 Don Drysdale 10.00 5.00
7 Carl Erskine 5.00 2.50
8 Carl Furillo 5.00 2.50
9 Junior Gilliam 5.00 2.50
10 Gil Hodges 10.00 5.00
11 Randy Jackson 3.00 1.50
12 Sandy Koufax 20.00 10.00
13 Clem Labine 5.00 2.50
14 Danny McDevitt 3.00 1.50
15 Greg Mulleavy CO 3.00 1.50
16 Charlie Neal 3.00 1.50
17 Don Newcombe 5.00 2.50
18 Joe Pignatano 3.00 1.50
19 Johnny Podres 5.00 2.50
20 Pee Wee Reese 10.00 5.00
21 Ed Roebuck 3.00 1.50
22 Duke Snider 10.00 5.00
23 Elmer Valo 4.00 2.00
24 Rube Walker 3.00 1.50
25 Don Zimmer 5.00 2.50

1958 Dodgers Volpe

Printed on heavy paper stock, these blank-backed reproductions of artist Nicholas Volpe's charcoal portraits of the 1958 Los Angeles Dodgers were issued in two sizes, 2 5/8" by 3 3/4" and 8" by 10". The player's name appears near the bottom. The smaller size was sold by mail at a cost of 50 cents a protrait. The larger size was also sold by mail by the club for $1.00 a card. The portraits are unnumbered and checklisted below in alphabetical order.

NM Ex
COMPLETE SET (12) 150.00 75.00
1 Walter Alston MG 15.00 7.50
2 Gino Cimolli 10.00 5.00
3 Don Drysdale 20.00 10.00
4 Carl Erskine 12.00 6.00
5 Carl Furillo 15.00 7.50
6 Jim Gilliam 15.00 7.50
7 Gil Hodges 20.00 10.00
8 Clem Labine 12.00 6.00
9 Don Newcombe 15.00 7.50
10 Johnny Podres 15.00 7.50
11 Pee Wee Reese 20.00 10.00
12 Duke Snider 20.00 10.00

1959 Dodgers Morrell

The cards in this 12-card set measure 2 1/2" by 3 1/2". The 1959 Morrell Meats set of full color, unnumbered cards features Los Angeles Dodger players only. The photos used are the

same as those selected for the Dodger team issue postcards in 1959. The Morrell Meats logo is on the backs of the cards. The Clem Labine card actually features a picture of Stan Williams and the Norm Larker card actually features a picture of Joe Pignatano as indicated in the checklist below. The catalog designation is F172-1.

NM Ex
COMPLETE SET (12) 1250.00 600.00
1 Don Drysdale 125.00 60.00
2 Carl Furillo 100.00 50.00
3 Jim Gilliam 100.00 50.00
4 Gil Hodges 125.00 60.00
5 Sandy Koufax 250.00 125.00
6 Clem Labine UER 60.00 30.00
(Photo actually Stan Williams)
7 Norm Larker UER 60.00 30.00
(Photo actually Joe Pignatano)
8 Charlie Neal 60.00 30.00
9 Johnny Podres 100.00 50.00
10 John Roseboro 80.00 40.00
11 Duke Snider 250.00 125.00
12 Don Zimmer 80.00 40.00

1959 Dodgers Postcards

These 12 postcards were issued by the Dodgers during the 1959 season and feature some of the leading players from the team. The cards have color photos on the front and brown printing on the back and were produced by the H.S. Crocker Co. in LA. A couple of the players are misidentified and we have notated them as such.

NM Ex
COMPLETE SET (12) 200.00 100.00
1 Duke Snider 25.00 12.50
2 Gil Hodges 20.00 10.00
3 Johnny Podres 12.00 6.00
4 Carl Furillo 12.00 6.00
5 Don Drysdale 25.00 12.50
6 Sandy Koufax 50.00 25.00
7 Jim Gilliam 12.00 6.00
8 Don Zimmer 12.00 6.00
9 Charlie Neal 10.00 5.00
10 Norm Larker UER 10.00 5.00
Card pictures Joe Pignatano
11 Clem Labine 12.00 6.00
12 John Roseboro 10.00 5.00

1959 Dodgers Team Issue

This 26-card set of the Los Angeles Dodgers measures approximately 5" by 7" and features black-and-white player photos in a white border. The backs are blank. The cards are unnumbered and checklisted below in alphabetical order.

NM Ex
COMPLETE SET (26) 75.00 38.00
1 Walter Alston MG 6.00 3.00
2 Don Bessent 3.00 1.50
3 Roger Craig 3.00 1.50
4 Charlie Dressen CO 3.00 1.50
5 Don Drysdale 10.00 5.00
6 Carl Erskine 5.00 2.50
7 Ron Fairly 5.00 2.50
8 Carl Furillo 5.00 2.50
9 Junior Gilliam 5.00 2.50
10 Gil Hodges 6.00 3.00
11 Fred Kipp 3.00 1.50
12 Sandy Koufax 15.00 7.50
13 Clem Labine 4.00 2.00
14 Norm Larker 3.00 1.50
15 Bob Lillis 3.00 1.50
16 Danny McDevitt 3.00 1.50
17 Wally Moon 3.00 1.50
18 Greg Mulleavy CO 3.00 1.50
19 Charlie Neal 3.00 1.50
20 Joe Pignatano 3.00 1.50
21 Johnny Podres 5.00 2.50
22 Pee Wee Reese 6.00 3.00
23 Rip Repulski 3.00 1.50
24 John Roseboro 3.00 1.50
25 Duke Snider 6.00 3.00
26 Don Zimmer 4.00 2.00

1959 Dodgers Volpe

Issued on thin paper stock, these blank-backed reproductions of artist Nicholas Volpe's charcoal portraits of the 1959 Dodgers measure approximately 8" by 10". The player's name appears near the bottom. The portraits are unnumbered and checklisted below in alphabetical order. The Campanella portrait has his career stats on the back.

NM Ex
COMPLETE SET (15) 150.00 75.00
1 Walter Alston MG 10.00 5.00
2 Roy Campnella TRIB 15.00 7.50
3 Don Drysdale 15.00 7.50
4 Carl Erskine 10.00 5.00
5 Carl Furillo 10.00 5.00

Card	NM	Ex
6 Jim Gilliam	10.00	5.00
7 Gil Hodges	15.00	7.50
8 Clem Labine	8.00	4.00
9 Wally Moon	6.00	3.00
10 Don Newcombe	10.00	5.00
11 Johnny Podres	8.00	4.00
12 Pee Wee Reese CO	20.00	10.00
13 Rip Repulski	6.00	3.00
14 Vin Scully ANN Jerry Doggett ANN	8.00	4.00
15 Duke Snider	20.00	10.00

1960 Dodgers Bell Brand

The 1960 Bell Brand Potato Chips set of 20 full color, numbered cards features Los Angeles Dodgers only. Because these cards, measuring approximately 2 1/2" by 3 1/2", were issued in packages of potato chips, many cards suffered from stains. Clem Labine, Johnny Klippstein, and Walt Alston are somewhat more difficult to obtain than other cards in the set; they are marked with SP (short printed) in the checklist below. The catalog designation for this set is F339-2.

	NM	Ex
COMPLETE SET (20)	900.00	350.00
COMMON CARD (1-20)	20.00	8.00
COMMON SP	100.00	40.00
1 Norm Larker	20.00	8.00
2 Duke Snider	100.00	40.00
3 Danny McDevitt	20.00	8.00
4 Jim Gilliam	30.00	12.00
5 Rip Repulski	20.00	8.00
6 Clem Labine SP	120.00	47.50
7 John Roseboro	20.00	8.00
8 Carl Furillo	25.00	10.00
9 Sandy Koufax	200.00	80.00
10 Joe Pignatano	20.00	8.00
11 Chuck Essegian	20.00	8.00
12 John Klippstein SP	100.00	40.00
13 Ed Roebuck	20.00	8.00
14 Don Demeter	20.00	8.00
15 Roger Craig	25.00	10.00
16 Stan Williams	20.00	8.00
17 Don Zimmer	25.00	10.00
18 Walt Alston SP MG	150.00	60.00
19 Johnny Podres	30.00	12.00
20 Maury Wills	40.00	16.00

1960 Dodgers Jay Publishing

This set of the Los Angeles Dodgers measures approximately 5" by 7" and features black-and-white player photos in a white border. The backs are blank. These cards were originally packaged 12 to a packet. The set is more than 12 cards as changes during the season necessitated a second printing. The cards are unnumbered and checklisted below in alphabetical order.

	NM	Ex
COMPLETE SET (16)	50.00	20.00
1 Roger Craig	3.00	1.20
2 Don Demeter	3.00	1.20
3 Don Drysdale	6.00	2.40
4 Ron Fairly	4.00	1.60
5 Junior Gilliam	5.00	2.00
6 Gil Hodges	6.00	2.40
7 Frank Howard	5.00	2.00
8 Norm Larker	3.00	1.20
9 Wally Moon	4.00	1.60
10 Charlie Neal	3.00	1.20
11 Johnny Podres	5.00	2.00
12 John Roseboro	4.00	1.60
13 Larry Sherry	3.00	1.20
14 Duke Snider	6.00	2.40
15 Stan Williams	3.00	1.20
16 Maury Wills	5.00	2.00

1960 Dodgers Morrell

The cards in this 12-card set measure 2 1/2" by 3 1/2". The 1960 Morrell Meats set of full color, unnumbered cards is similar in format to the 1959 Morrell set but can be distinguished from the 1959 set by a red heart which appears in the Morrell logo on the back. The photos used are the same as those selected for the Dodger team issue postcards in 1960. The Furillo, Hodges, and Snider cards received limited distribution and are hence more scarce. The catalog designation is F172-2. The cards were printed in Japan.

	NM	Ex
COMPLETE SET (12)	900.00	350.00
COMMON CARD (1-12)	20.00	8.00
COMMON SP	50.00	20.00
1 Walt Alston MG	50.00	20.00
2 Roger Craig	25.00	10.00
3 Don Drysdale	75.00	30.00
4 Carl Furillo SP	100.00	40.00
5 Gil Hodges SP	150.00	60.00
6 Sandy Koufax	200.00	80.00
7 Wally Moon	20.00	8.00
8 Charlie Neal	20.00	8.00
9 Johnny Podres	30.00	12.00
10 John Roseboro	20.00	8.00
11 Larry Sherry	20.00	8.00
12 Duke Snider SP	250.00	100.00

1960 Dodgers Postcards

These 12 postcards feature members of the 1960 Los Angeles Dodgers. These cards are unnumbered and we have sequenced them in alphabetical order. The Furillo card is very scarce as he was released midway through the season and this card is thereford presumed no longer circulated after that point. We are considering the Furillo card a SP

	NM	Ex
COMPLETE SET (12)	40.00	16.00
1 Walt Alston MG	5.00	2.00
2 Roger Craig	3.00	1.20
3 Don Drysdale	8.00	3.20
4 Carl Furillo SP	10.00	4.00
5 Gil Hodges	5.00	2.00
6 Sandy Koufax	10.00	4.00
7 Wally Moon	3.00	1.20
8 Charlie Neal	2.50	1.00
9 Johnny Podres	4.00	1.60
10 Johnny Roseboro	3.00	1.20
11 Larry Sherry	2.50	1.00
12 Duke Snider	8.00	3.20

1960 Dodgers Team Issue

These 20 blank-backed, black-and-white photos of the 1960 Dodgers have white borders around posed player shots and measure approximately 5" by 7". The pictures came in a manila envelope that carried the year of issue. The player's facsimile autograph appears in the margin below each photo. The photos are unnumbered and checklisted below in alphabetical order.

	NM	Ex
COMPLETE SET (20)	75.00	30.00
1 Walter Alston MG	5.00	2.00
2 Bob Bragan CO	2.50	1.00
3 Roger Craig	3.00	1.20
4 Don Demeter	2.50	1.00
5 Don Drysdale	8.00	3.20
6 Chuck Essegian	2.50	1.00
7 Jim Gilliam	4.00	1.60
8 Gil Hodges	8.00	3.20
9 Frank Howard	4.00	1.60
10 Sandy Koufax	15.00	6.00
11 Norm Larker	2.50	1.00
12 Wally Moon	2.50	1.00
13 Charlie Neal	2.50	1.00
14 Johnny Podres	4.00	1.60
15 Pete Reiser CO	2.50	1.00
16 John Roseboro	3.00	1.20
17 Larry Sherry	3.00	1.20
18 Duke Snider	8.00	3.20
19 Stan Williams	2.50	1.00
20 Maury Wills	5.00	2.00

1960 Dodgers Union Oil

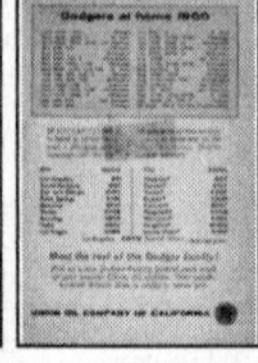

The set contains 23, 16-page unnumbered booklets which describe and give more detailed biographies of the player on the front covers. These booklets were given away at Union Oil gas stations and covered members of the 1960 Los Angeles Dodgers. The back page of the booklets had the Dodger schedule on it along with an ad for Union Oil. They are sometimes referenced as "Meet the Dodger Family" booklets. Each booklet measures approximately 5 3/8" by 7 1/2".

	NM	Ex
COMPLETE SET (23)	75.00	30.00
1 Walt Alston MG	5.00	2.00
2 Roger Craig	3.00	1.20
3 Tom Davis	4.00	1.60
4 Don Demeter	2.00	.80
5 Don Drysdale	10.00	4.00
6 Chuck Essegian	2.00	.80
7 Jim Gilliam	4.00	1.60
8 Gil Hodges	10.00	4.00
9 Frank Howard	4.00	1.60
10 Sandy Koufax	20.00	8.00
11 Norm Larker	2.00	.80
12 Wally Moon	3.00	1.20
13 Charlie Neal	2.00	.80
14 Johnny Podres	4.00	1.60
15 Ed Roebuck	2.00	.80
16 John Roseboro	3.00	1.20
17 Larry Sherry	2.00	.80
18 Norm Sherry	2.00	.80
19 Duke Snider	10.00	4.00
20 Stan Williams	2.00	.80
21 Maury Wills	5.00	2.00
22 Vin Scully ANN Jerry Doggett ANN	3.00	1.20
23 Greg Mulleavy CO Joe Becker CO Bobby Bragan CO Pete Reiser CO	2.00	.80

1961 Dodgers Bell Brand

The 1961 Bell Brand Potato Chips set of 20 full color cards features Los Angeles Dodger players only and is numbered by the uniform numbers of the players. The cards are slightly smaller (approximately 2 7/16" by 3 1/2") than the 1960 Bell Brand cards and are on thinner paper stock. The catalog designation is F339-3.

	NM	Ex
COMPLETE SET (20)	500.00	200.00
3 Willie Davis	25.00	10.00
4 Duke Snider	80.00	32.00
5 Norm Larker	15.00	6.00
8 John Roseboro	20.00	8.00
9 Wally Moon	20.00	8.00
11 Bob Lillis	15.00	6.00
12 Tommy Davis	25.00	10.00
14 Gil Hodges	30.00	12.00
16 Don Demeter	15.00	6.00
19 Jim Gilliam	25.00	10.00
22 John Podres	25.00	10.00
24 Walt Alston MG	30.00	12.00
30 Maury Wills	30.00	12.00
32 Sandy Koufax	120.00	47.50
34 Norm Sherry	15.00	6.00
37 Ed Roebuck	15.00	6.00
38 Roger Craig	20.00	8.00
40 Stan Williams	15.00	6.00
43 Charlie Neal	15.00	6.00
51 Larry Sherry	15.00	6.00

1961 Dodgers Jay Publishing

This 12-card set of the Los Angeles Dodgers measures approximately 5" by 7". The fronts feature black-and-white posed player portraits with the player's and team name printed below in the white border. The backs are blank. The cards are unnumbered and checklisted below in alphabetical order.

	NM	Ex
COMPLETE SET (12)	35.00	14.00
1 Walt Alston MG	5.00	2.00
2 Don Drysdale	8.00	3.20
3 Junior Gilliam	4.00	1.60
4 Frank Howard	4.00	1.60
5 Norm Larker	2.00	.80
6 Wally Moon	2.00	.80
7 Charlie Neal	2.00	.80
8 Johnny Podres	4.00	1.60
9 John Roseboro	2.00	.80
10 Larry Sherry	2.00	.80
11 Stan Williams	2.00	.80
12 Maury Wills	5.00	2.00

1961 Dodgers Morrell

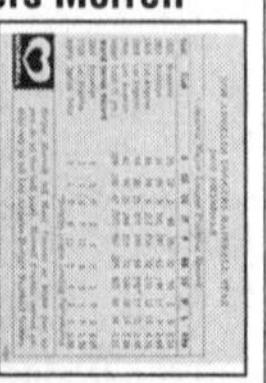

The cards in this six-card set measure 2 1/2" by 3 1/2". The 1961 Morrell Meats set of full color, unnumbered cards features Los Angeles Dodger players only and contains statistical information on the backs of the cards in brown print. The catalog designation is F172-3.

	NM	Ex
COMPLETE SET (6)	275.00	110.00
1 Tommy Davis	25.00	10.00
2 Don Drysdale	80.00	32.00
3 Frank Howard	30.00	12.00
4 Sandy Koufax	150.00	60.00
5 Norm Larker	20.00	8.00
6 Maury Wills	40.00	16.00

1961 Dodgers Union Oil

The set contains 24, 16-page unnumbered booklets which describe and give more detailed biographies of the player on the front covers. These booklets were given away by Union Oil at gas stations and covered members of the 1961 Los Angeles Dodgers. The back page of the booklets had the Dodger schedule on it along with an ad for Union Oil. They are sometimes referenced as "Meet the Dodger Family" booklets. Each booklet measures approximately 5 3/8" by 7 1/2".

	NM	Ex
COMPLETE SET (24)	75.00	30.00
1 Walt Alston MG	5.00	2.00
2 Roger Craig	4.00	1.60
3 Tommy Davis	4.00	1.60
4 Willie Davis	4.00	1.60
5 Don Drysdale	10.00	4.00
6 Dick Farrell	2.00	.80
7 Ron Fairly	3.00	1.20
8 Jim Gilliam	4.00	1.60
9 Gil Hodges	10.00	4.00
10 Frank Howard	5.00	2.00
11 Sandy Koufax	20.00	8.00
12 Norm Larker	2.00	.80
13 Wally Moon	3.00	1.20
14 Charlie Neal	2.00	.80
15 Ron Perranoski	3.00	1.20
16 Johnny Podres	4.00	1.60
17 John Roseboro	3.00	1.20
18 Larry Sherry	2.00	.80
19 Norm Sherry	2.00	.80
20 Duke Snider	10.00	4.00
21 Daryl Spencer	2.00	.80
22 Stan Williams	2.00	.80
23 Maury Wills	5.00	2.00
24 Vin Scully ANN Jerry Doggett ANN	3.00	1.20

1962 Dodgers Bell Brand

The 1962 Bell Brand Potato Chips set of 20 full color cards features Los Angeles Dodger players only and is numbered by the uniform numbers of the players. These cards were printed on a high quality glossy paper, much better than the previous two years, virtually eliminating the grease stains. This set is distinguished by a 1962 Home schedule on the backs of the cards. The cards measure 2 7/16" by 3 1/2", the same size as the year before. The catalog designation is F339-4.

	NM	Ex
COMPLETE SET (20)	500.00	200.00
3 Willie Davis	25.00	10.00
4 Duke Snider	80.00	32.00
6 Ron Fairly	20.00	8.00
8 John Roseboro	20.00	8.00
9 Wally Moon	20.00	8.00
12 Tommy Davis	25.00	10.00
16 Ron Perranoski	20.00	8.00
19 Jim Gilliam	25.00	10.00
20 Daryl Spencer	15.00	6.00
22 John Podres	25.00	10.00
24 Walt Alston MG	30.00	12.00
25 Frank Howard	25.00	10.00
30 Maury Wills	30.00	12.00
32 Sandy Koufax	125.00	50.00
34 Norm Sherry	15.00	6.00
37 Ed Roebuck	15.00	6.00
40 Stan Williams	15.00	6.00
51 Larry Sherry	15.00	6.00
53 Don Drysdale	50.00	20.00
56 Lee Walls	15.00	6.00

1962 Dodgers Jay Publishing

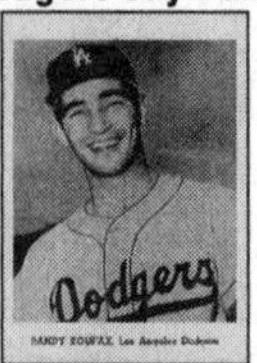

This 12-card set of the Los Angeles Dodgers measures approximately 5" by 7". The fronts feature black-and-white posed player photos with the player's and team name printed below in the white border. These cards were packaged 12 in a packet. The backs are blank. The cards are unnumbered and checklisted below in alphabetical order.

	NM	Ex
COMPLETE SET (12)	45.00	18.00
1 Walt Alston MG	5.00	2.00
2 Don Drysdale	8.00	3.20
3 Ron Fairly	3.00	1.20
4 Jim Gilliam	4.00	1.60
5 Frank Howard	3.00	1.20
6 Sandy Koufax	15.00	6.00
7 Wally Moon	2.50	1.00
8 John Podres	3.00	1.20
9 John Roseboro	3.00	1.20
10 Duke Snider	8.00	3.20
11 Stan Williams	2.50	1.00
12 Maury Wills	5.00	2.00

1962-65 Dodgers Postcards

These ten cards were printed by "Plastic Chrome" and distributed by Mitock and Sons Postcards. All the photos were taken at Dodger Stadium. The backs are red and black with a sketch of Dodgers Stadium on the back in the early cards. These same cards were issued through 1965 so it is really difficult to tell the years apart. We are using the last three numbers printed on the postcard to identify the card number.

	NM	Ex
COMPLETE SET (10)	80.00	32.00
315 Willie Davis	8.00	3.20
316 Larry Sherry	5.00	2.00
317 Ron Perranoski	5.00	2.00
318 Sandy Koufax	20.00	8.00
319 Frank Howard	10.00	4.00
320 Tommy Davis	6.00	2.40
321 Don Drysdale	15.00	6.00
322 John Roseboro	6.00	2.40
323 Ron Fairly	5.00	2.00
324 Maury Wills	10.00	4.00

1962 Dodgers Volpe

These cards measure 8 3/4" by 11". This set, like many others of the period, were drawn by noted sports artist Nicholas Volpe. They were issued by Union Oil Co/Phillips 76. The backs have a brief biography of Volpe. This set was released one per week during the 1962 season.

	NM	Ex
COMPLETE SET (24)	300.00	120.00
1 Sandy Koufax	50.00	20.00
2 Wally Moon	10.00	4.00
3 Don Drysdale	25.00	10.00
4 Jim Gilliam	15.00	6.00
5 Larry Sherry	10.00	4.00
6 John Roseboro	12.00	4.80
7 Willie Davis	12.00	4.80
8 Norm Sherry	10.00	4.00
9 Lee Walls	10.00	4.00
10 Stan Williams	10.00	4.00
11 Tommy Davis	12.00	4.80
12 Ron Fairly	12.00	4.80
13 Larry Burright	10.00	4.00
14 Duke Snider	25.00	10.00
15 Ron Perranoski	10.00	4.00
16 Maury Wills	20.00	8.00
17 Frank Howard	15.00	6.00
18 Joe Moeller	10.00	4.00
19 Ed Roebuck	10.00	4.00
20 Andy Carey	10.00	4.00
21 Johnny Podres	15.00	6.00
22 Daryl Spencer	10.00	4.00
23 Doug Camilli	10.00	4.00
24 Tim Harkness	10.00	4.00

1963 Dodgers Jay Publishing

The 1963 Dodgers Jay set consists of 13 cards produced by Jay Publishing. The Skowron card establishes the year of the set, since 1963 was Skowron's only year with the Dodgers. The cards measure approximately 4 3/4" by 7 1/4" and are printed on thin photographic paper stock. The white fronts feature a black-and-white player portrait with the player's name and the team name below. The backs are blank. The cards are packaged 12 to a packet. The cards are unnumbered and checklisted below in alphabetical order. As far as we can tell, the Bill Skowron card was added and the Wally Moon card not issued in the second printing.

	NM	Ex
COMPLETE SET (13)	40.00	16.00
1 Walt Alston MG	5.00	2.00
2 Tom Davis	3.00	1.20
3 Willie Davis	3.00	1.20
4 Don Drysdale	8.00	3.20
5 Ron Fairly	3.00	1.20
6 Jim Gilliam	3.00	1.20
7 Frank Howard	4.00	1.60
8 Sandy Koufax	15.00	6.00
9 Wally Moon	3.00	1.20
10 Johnny Podres	3.00	1.20
11 John Roseboro	2.50	1.00
12 Bill Skowron	3.00	1.20
13 Maury Wills	5.00	2.00

1964 Dodgers Heads-Up

This ten-card blank-backed set was issued in 1964 as a way to further merchandise some of the Los Angeles stars. This set features a large full-color head shot of a player which came with instructiions on how to push out the players face and the rest of the torso. The whole cardboard sheet measures approximately 7 1/4" by 8 1/2". There was a quantity of these items found in the late 1980's. Since these are unnumbered, they are checklisted below alphabetically.

	NM	Ex
COMPLETE SET (10)	40.00	16.00
1 Tom Davis	3.00	1.20
2 Willie Davis	3.00	1.20
3 Don Drysdale	8.00	3.20
4 Ron Fairly	3.00	1.20
5 Frank Howard	4.00	1.60
6 Sandy Koufax	15.00	6.00
7 Joe Moeller	2.50	1.00
8 Ron Perranoski	2.50	1.00
9 John Roseboro	3.00	1.20
10 Maury Wills	5.00	2.00

1964 Dodgers Jay Publishing

This 12-card set of the Los Angeles Dodgers measures approximately 5" by 7". The fronts feature black-and-white posed player photos with the player's and team name printed below in the white border. These cards were packaged 12 to a packet. The backs are blank. The cards are unnumbered and checklisted below in alphabetical order.

	NM	Ex
COMPLETE SET (12)	50.00	20.00
1 Walt Alston MG	5.00	2.00
2 Tom Davis	3.00	1.20
3 Willie Davis	3.00	1.20
4 Don Drysdale	8.00	3.20
5 Ron Fairly	3.00	1.20
6 Jim Gilliam	4.00	1.60
7 Frank Howard	4.00	1.60
8 Sandy Koufax	15.00	6.00
9 Wally Moon	2.50	1.00
10 John Podres	4.00	1.60
11 John Roseboro	2.50	1.00
12 Maury Wills	5.00	2.00

1964 Dodgers Volpe

This set which measure approximately 8 1/2" by 11" features members of the L.A. Dodgers and were drawn by noted sports artist Nicholas Volpe. These posters were distributed at local Union 76 gas stations. The drawings featured a large full-size facial shot while the background had the player dressed in street clothes.

	NM	Ex
COMPLETE SET	200.00	80.00
1 Willie Davis	10.00	4.00
2 Tommy Davis	15.00	6.00
3 Don Drysdale	20.00	8.00
4 Ron Fairly	10.00	4.00
5 Jim Gilliam	10.00	4.00
6 Frank Howard	15.00	6.00
7 Sandy Koufax	30.00	12.00
8 Bob Miller	8.00	3.20
9 Joe Moeller	8.00	3.20
10 Wally Moon	10.00	4.00
11 Phil Ortega	8.00	3.20
12 Wes Parker	10.00	4.00
13 Ron Perranoski	8.00	3.20
14 Johnny Podres	10.00	4.00
15 John Roseboro	10.00	4.00
16 Dick Tracewski	8.00	3.20
17 Lee Walls	8.00	3.20
18 Maury Wills	15.00	6.00

1965 Dodgers Jay Publishing

These 12 cards feature members of the World Champion Los Angeles Dodgers. They were issued in a pack as a 12 card set and the cards are unnumbered and checklisted below in alphabetical order. This set was issued twice to correct the Tommy and Willie Davis misidentifications.

	NM	Ex
COMPLETE SET (14)	60.00	24.00
1 Walter Alston MG	5.00	2.00
2A Tommy Davis ERR	5.00	2.00
Photo is Willie Davis		
2B Tommy Davis COR	5.00	2.00
3A Willie Davis ERR	5.00	2.00
Photo is Tommy Davis		
3B Willie Davis COR	5.00	2.00
4 Don Drysdale	8.00	3.20
5 Ron Fairly	3.00	1.20
6 Lou Johnson	2.50	1.00
7 Sandy Koufax	15.00	6.00
8 Jim Lefebvre	3.00	1.20
9 Claude Osteen	2.50	1.00
10 Wes Parker	3.00	1.20
11 John Roseboro	3.00	1.20
12 Maury Wills	5.00	2.00

1965 Dodgers Team Issue

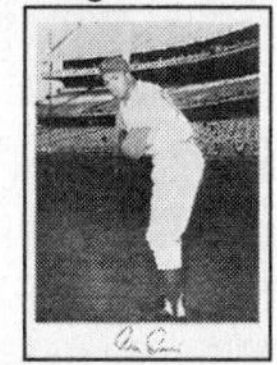

These 21 blank-backed, black-and-white photos of the 1965 Los Angeles Dodgers have white borders around posed player shots and measure approximately 5" by 7". The player's facsimile autograph appears in the bottom margin on each photo. The pictures came in an undated manila envelope. The year of issue was determined to be 1965 because that was Dick Tracewski's last year with the Dodgers and Lou Johnson's first. The photos are unnumbered and checklisted below in alphabetical order.

	NM	Ex
COMPLETE SET (21)	35.00	14.00
1 Walter Alston MG	4.00	1.60
2 Willie Crawford	1.50	.60
3 Tommy Davis	3.00	1.20
4 Willie Davis	3.00	1.20
5 Don Drysdale	6.00	2.40
6 Ron Fairly	2.00	.80
7 Derrell Griffith	1.50	.60
8 Lou Johnson	1.50	.60
9 John Kennedy	1.50	.60
10 Sandy Koufax	15.00	6.00
11 Bob Miller	1.50	.60
12 Nate Oliver	1.50	.60
13 Claude Osteen	2.00	.80
14 Wes Parker	2.00	.80
15 Ron Perranoski	2.00	.80
16 Johnny Podres	3.00	1.20
17 John Purdin	1.50	.60
18 Howie Reed	1.50	.60
19 John Roseboro	2.00	.80
20 Dick Tracewski	1.50	.60
21 Maury Wills	4.00	1.60

1970 Dodgers Team Issue

These blank-backed cards featured members of the 1970 Los Angeles Dodgers. The fronts have a player photo with the fascimile autograph on the bottom. These photos were sold in a special envelope which said 20 individual pictures 50 cents and photo of the stadium and a drawing on the envelope. Since these cards are unnumbered, we have sequenced them in alphabetical order.

	NM	Ex
COMPLETE SET	40.00	16.00
1 Walt Alston MG	3.00	1.20
2 Jim Brewer	2.00	.80
3 Willie Crawford	2.00	.80
4 Willie Davis	2.50	1.00
5 Alan Foster	2.00	.80
6 Len Gabrielson	2.00	.80
7 Bill Grabarkewitz	2.00	.80
8 Tom Haller	2.00	.80
9 Andy Kosco	2.00	.80
10 Ray Lamb	2.00	.80
11 Jim Lefebvre	2.00	.80
12 Joe Moeller	2.00	.80
13 Manny Mota	2.50	1.00
14 Fred Norman	2.00	.80
15 Claude Osteen	2.00	.80
16 Wes Parker	2.00	.80
17 Bill Singer	2.00	.80
18 Ted Sizemore	2.00	.80
19 Bill Sudakis	2.00	.80
20 Maury Wills	4.00	1.60

1971 Dodgers Photos

These photos featured the members of the 1971 Los Angeles Dodgers. They are unnumbered and are therefore sequenced alphabetically. It is possible there are more photos so any additions to this list is appreciated.

	NM	Ex
COMPLETE SET	40.00	16.00
1 Walt Alston MG	5.00	2.00
2 Bill Buckner	4.00	1.60
3 Jim Brewer	2.00	.80
4 Willie Crawford	2.00	.80
5 Bill Grabarkewitz	2.00	.80
6 Jim Lefebvre	3.00	1.20
7 Pete Mikkelsen	2.00	.80
8 Joe Moeller	2.00	.80
9 Manny Mota	3.00	1.20
10 Danny Ozark CO	2.00	.80
11 Jose Pena	2.00	.80
12 Bill Russell	4.00	1.60
13 Duke Sims	2.00	.80
14 Bill Singer	3.00	1.20
15 Mike Strahler	2.00	.80
16 Billy Sudakis	2.00	.80
17 Don Sutton	6.00	2.40
18 Bobby Valentine	4.00	1.60

1971 Dodgers Ticketron

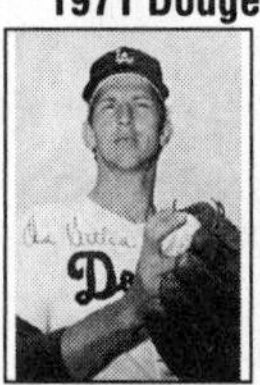

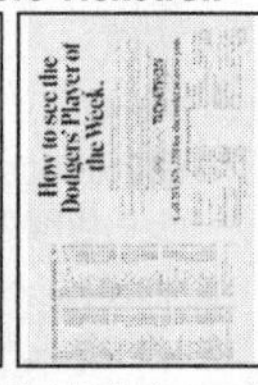

How to see the Dodgers' Player of the Week.

The 1971 Ticketron Los Angeles Dodgers set is a 20-card set with cards measuring approximately 4" by 6". This set has a 1971 Garvey rookie year card as well as 18 other players including Richie Allen in his only year as a Dodger. The fronts are beautiful full-color photos which also have a facsimile autograph on the front and are borderless while the backs contain an advertisement for Ticketron, the 1971 Dodger home schedule and a list of promotional events scheduled for 1971. These unnumbered cards are listed in alphabetical order for convenience.

	NM	Ex
COMPLETE SET (20)	75.00	30.00
1 Richie Allen	5.00	2.00
2 Walt Alston MG	5.00	2.00
3 Jim Brewer	2.00	.80
4 Willie Crawford	2.00	.80
5 Willie Davis	3.00	1.20
6 Steve Garvey	15.00	6.00
7 Bill Grabarkewitz	2.00	.80
8 Jim Lefebvre	3.00	1.20
9 Pete Mikkelsen	2.00	.80
10 Joe Moeller	2.00	.80
11 Manny Mota	3.00	1.20
12 Claude Osteen	3.00	1.20
13 Wes Parker	3.00	1.20
14 Bill Russell	4.00	1.60
15 Duke Sims	2.00	.80
16 Bill Singer	2.00	.80
17 Bill Sudakis	2.00	.80
18 Don Sutton	8.00	3.20
19 Maury Wills	5.00	2.00
20 Vic Scully ANN	4.00	1.60
Jerry Doggett ANN		

1972 Dodgers McDonald's

These borderless discs have color player photos on the front. The backs have the player's name, some biographical information and the 1971 statistics. Since these discs are unnumbered, we have sequenced them in alphabetical order. These items are also known as photoballs.

	NM	Ex
COMPLETE SET	200.00	80.00
1 Walter Alston MG	15.00	6.00
2 Red Adams CO	10.00	4.00
3 Willie Crawford	10.00	4.00
4 Willie Davis	12.00	4.80
5 Al Downing	10.00	4.00
6 Jim Gilliam CO	12.00	4.80
7 Jim LeFebvre	10.00	4.00
8 Pete Mikkelsen	10.00	4.00
9 Manny Mota	12.00	4.80
10 Wes Parker	12.00	4.80
11 Claude Osteen	10.00	4.00
12 Bill Russell	10.00	4.00
13 Duke Sims	10.00	4.00
14 Bill Sudakis	10.00	4.00
15 Don Sutton	20.00	8.00
16 Bobby Valentine	15.00	6.00
17 Maury Wills	20.00	8.00

1973 Dodgers 1941 TCMA

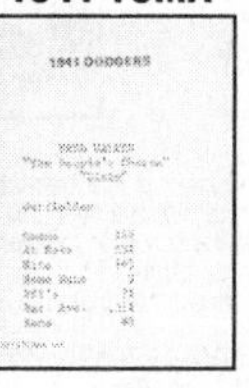

This 32-card set features blue tinted photos of the 1941 National League Champion Brooklyn Dodgers. The backs carry player information. The cards are unnumbered and checklisted below alphabetically.

	NM	Ex
COMPLETE SET (32)	30.00	12.00
1 John Allen	1.00	.40
2 Mace Brown	1.00	.40
3 Dolf Camilli	2.00	.80
4 Hugh Casey	1.50	.60
5 Curtis Davis	1.00	.40
6 Thomas Drake	1.00	.40
7 Leo Durocher P/MG	4.00	1.60
8 Fred Fitzsimmons	2.50	1.00
9 Herman Franks	1.00	.40
10 August Galan	1.50	.60
11 Angelo Giuliani	1.00	.40
12 Luke Hamlin	1.00	.40
13 Billy Herman	2.50	1.00
14 Kirby Higby	1.00	.40
15 Alex Kampouris	1.00	.40
16 Newell Kimball	1.00	.40
17 Cookie Lavagetto	1.50	.60
18 Joseph Medwick	2.50	1.00
19 Van Lingle Mungo	1.50	.60
20 N.L. Champion Card	1.00	.40
21 Mickey Owen	1.00	.40
22 Babe Phelps	1.00	.40
23 Pee Wee Reese	5.00	2.00
24 Pete Reiser	1.50	.60
25 Lewis Riggs	1.00	.40
26 William Swift	1.00	.40
27 Vitautis Tamulis	1.00	.40
28 Joseph Vosmik	1.00	.40
29 Dixie Walker	2.00	.80
30 Paul Waner	3.00	1.20
31 James Wasdell	1.00	.40
32 Whit Wyatt	1.50	.60

1973 Dodgers Postcards

These fifteen cards were created by Kolor View Press and were distributed by Mitock and Sonds. The fronts show clear photographs and the backs are in black print and all these cards are labeled KV5251. Since these cards are unnumbered, we have sequenced them in alphabetical order.

	NM	Ex
COMPLETE SET	30.00	12.00
1 Bill Buckner	2.50	1.00
2 Ron Cey	4.00	1.60
3 Willie Davis	2.50	1.00
4 Joe Ferguson	2.00	.80
5 Tommy John	3.00	1.20
6 Lee Lacy	2.00	.80
7 Tom Lasorda CO	4.00	1.60
8 Dave Lopes	3.00	1.20
9 Andy Messersmith	2.00	.80
10 Manny Mota	2.50	1.00
11 Claude Osteen	2.00	.80
12 Tom Paciorek	2.00	.80
13 Bill Russell	2.00	.80
14 Don Sutton	4.00	1.60
15 Steve Yeager	2.50	1.00

1973 Dodgers Team Issue

These 20 5" by 7" blank-backed black and white photos with fascimile autographs on the

bottom feature members of the 1973 Los Angeles Dodgers. They were sold at the ballpark for 50 cents for the 20 photos. Since the photos are unnumbered, we have sequenced them in alphabetical order.

	NM	Ex
COMPLETE SET (20)	15.00	6.00
1 Walt Alston MG	1.50	.60
2 Red Adams CO	.50	.20
3 Jim Brewer	.50	.20
4 Bill Buckner	1.00	.40
5 Ron Cey	1.50	.60
6 Willie Davis	.75	.30
7 Joe Ferguson	.50	.20
8 Steve Garvey	3.00	1.20
9 Jim Gilliam CO	.75	.30
10 Charlie Hough	.75	.30
11 Tommy John	1.50	.60
12 Lee Lacy	.50	.20
13 Tom Lasorda CO	1.50	.60
14 Davey Lopes	1.00	.40
15 Manny Mota	.50	.20
16 Tom Paciorek	.50	.20
17 Doug Rau	.50	.20
18 Pete Richert	.50	.20
19 Bill Russell	.50	.20
20 Don Sutton	2.00	.80

1974 Dodgers 1952 TCMA

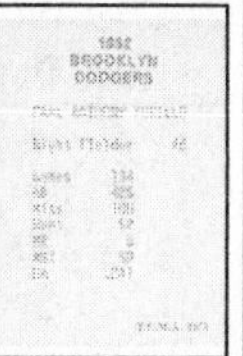

This 40-card set features blue tinted photos of the the 1952 Brooklyn Dodgers team. The backs carry player information.

	NM	Ex
COMPLETE SET (40)	50.00	20.00
1 1952 Cover Card	1.50	.60
2 Cal Abrams	1.00	.40
3 Sandy Amoros	1.50	.60
4 Joe Black	2.50	1.00
5 Rocky Bridges	1.00	.40
6 Ralph Branca	1.50	.60
7 Roy Campanella	5.00	2.00
8 Billy Cox	2.00	.80
9 Chuck Dressen MG	1.50	.60
10 Carl Furillo	2.50	1.00
11 Jim Hughes	1.00	.40
12 Billy Herman CO	1.50	.60
13 Carl Erskine	2.50	1.00
14 Gil Hodges	3.00	1.20
15 Thomas Holmes	1.00	.40
16 Dick Williams	1.50	.60
17 Clyde King	1.00	.40
18 Stephen Lembo	1.00	.40
19 Ken Lehman	1.00	.40
20 Joe Landrum	1.00	.40
21 Clem Labine	2.00	.80
22 Ray Moore	1.00	.40
23 Bob Morgan	1.00	.40
24 Ron Negray	1.00	.40
25 Rocky Nelson	1.00	.40
26 Jake Pitler CO	1.00	.40
27 Billy Loes	1.00	.40
28 Cookie Lavagetto CO	1.50	.60
29 Andy Pafko	1.50	.60
30 Bud Podbielan	1.00	.40
31 Preacher Roe	2.50	1.00
32 John Rutherford	1.00	.40
33 Pee Wee Reese	3.00	1.20
34 Jackie Robinson	5.00	2.00
35 George Shuba	1.00	.40
36 Johnny Schmitz	1.00	.40
37 Duke Snider	3.00	1.20
38 Chris Van Cuyk	1.00	.40
39 Ben Wade	1.00	.40
40 Rube Walker	1.00	.40

1974 Dodgers 1890 Program TCMA

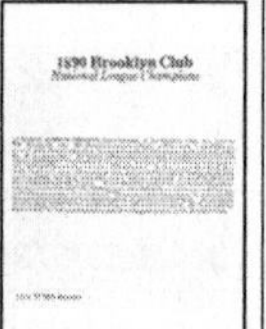

This 16-card set contains copies of information included in the 1890 Brooklyn Dodgers programs. The cards measure approximately 4" by 4 1/4" and feature black-and-white player photos with artistically designed borders. The backs carry a paragraph about the player. The cards are unnumbered and checklisted below in alphabetical order.

	NM	Ex
COMPLETE SET (16)	8.00	3.20
1 Oyster Burns	.75	.30
2 Doc Bushong	.75	.30
3 Robert Lee Caruthers	1.50	.60
4 Robert H. Clark	.50	.20
5 Hubbert Collins	.50	.20
6 John S. Corkhill	.50	.20
7 Thomas P. Daly	.50	.20
8 Dave Foutz	.50	.20
9 Michael F. Hughes	.50	.20
10 Thomas J. Lovett	.50	.20
11 Bill McGunnigle MG	.50	.20
12 Wm. D. O'Brien	.50	.20
13 George Burton Pinkney	.50	.20
14 George J. Smith	.50	.20
15 George T. Stallings	.75	.30
16 Adonis Terry	.50	.20

1975 Dodgers All-Time TCMA

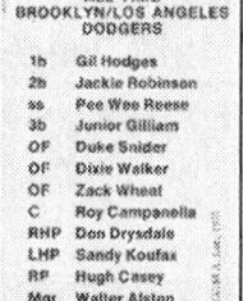

ALL TIME
BROOKLYN/LOS ANGELES
DODGERS
1b Gil Hodges
2b Jackie Robinson
ss Pee Wee Reese
3b Junior Gilliam
OF Duke Snider
OF Dixie Walker
OF Zack Wheat
C Roy Campanella
RHP Don Drysdale
LHP Sandy Koufax
RP Hugh Casey
Mgr Walter Alston

This 12-card set features black-and-white photos with white borders of all-time Dodgers great players. The cards are unnumbered and checklisted below in alphabetical order.

	NM	Ex
COMPLETE SET (12)	20.00	8.00
1 Walter Alston MG	.50	.20
2 Roy Campanella	2.00	.80
3 Hugh Casey	.50	.20
4 Don Drysdale	2.00	.80
5 Junior Gilliam	1.00	.40
6 Gil Hodges	2.00	.80
7 Sandy Koufax	3.00	1.20
8 Pee Wee Reese	2.50	1.00
9 Jackie Robinson	5.00	2.00
10 Duke Snider	3.00	1.20
11 Dixie Walker	1.00	.40
12 Zack Wheat	1.50	.60

1975 Dodgers Postcards

These 15 postcards were issued by Kolor View Press and featured members of the 1975 Dodgers. The fronts feature full-color photos while the backs were issued in black print. The Garvey card has the line "1974 National League MVP" added to the back. These cards are numbered with the prefix "KV7813" and we have used the final number in that sequence as our numbering of this set.

	NM	Ex
COMPLETE SET (15)	20.00	8.00
1 Bill Buckner	1.50	.60
2 Jim Wynn	1.50	.60
3 Henry Cruz	1.00	.40
4 Rick Auerbach	1.00	.40
5 Bill Russell	1.00	.40
6 Tom Paciorek	1.00	.40
7 Steve Yeager	1.50	.60
8 Don Sutton	2.50	1.00
9 Mike Marshall	1.50	.60
10 Ron Cey	2.00	.80
11 Rick Rhoden	1.00	.40
13 Joe Ferguson	1.00	.40
15 Davey Lopes	2.00	.80
31 Doug Rau	1.00	.40
57 Willie Crawford	1.00	.40

1976 Dodgers Postcards

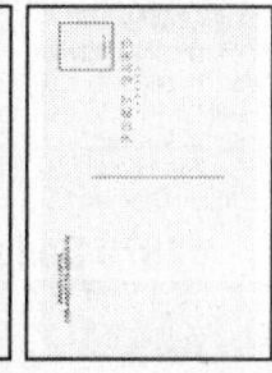

This 10-card set of the Los Angeles Dodgers measures approximately 3 1/2" by 5 1/2" and features borderless color player photos with a facsimile player autograph printed in white. The backs carry a postcard format.

	NM	Ex
COMPLETE SET (10)	12.00	4.80
1 Walt Alston MG	2.00	.80
2 Ron Cey	2.00	.80
3 Tommy John	2.00	.80
4 Davey Lopes	1.50	.60
5 Charlie Hough	1.25	.50
6 Steve Garvey	3.00	1.20
7 Mike Marshall	1.00	.40
8 Joe Ferguson	1.00	.40
9 Dusty Baker	1.50	.60
10 Burt Hooton	1.00	.40

1977-78 Dodgers Photos

This 15-card set of the Los Angeles Dodgers features color player photos in white borders measuring approximately 8" by 10" and with a facsimile autograph. The backs are blank. There is no way to tell if the set was produced in 1977 or 1978. It could be either year. The cards are unnumbered and checklisted below in alphabetical order.

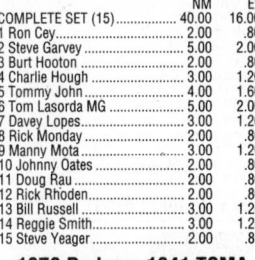

	NM	Ex
COMPLETE SET (15)	40.00	16.00
1 Ron Cey	2.00	.80
2 Steve Garvey	5.00	2.00
3 Burt Hooton	2.00	.80
4 Charlie Hough	3.00	1.20
5 Tommy John	4.00	1.60
6 Tom Lasorda MG	5.00	2.00
7 Davey Lopes	3.00	1.20
8 Rick Monday	2.00	.80
9 Manny Mota	3.00	1.20
10 Johnny Oates	2.00	.80
11 Doug Rau	2.00	.80
12 Rick Rhoden	2.00	.80
13 Bill Russell	3.00	1.20
14 Reggie Smith	3.00	1.20
15 Steve Yeager	2.00	.80

1978 Dodgers 1941 TCMA

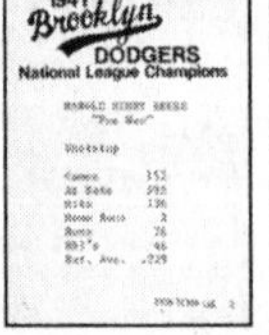

This 43-card set features blue-and-white action photos of the 1941 National League Champion Brooklyn Dodgers in white borders. The backs carry player information. Cards numbers 39 and 40 are currently unknown, any information is greatly appreciated.

	NM	Ex
COMPLETE SET (43)	15.00	6.00
1 Mickey Owen	.25	.10
2 Pee Wee Reese	2.00	.80
3 Hugh Casey	.25	.10
4 Larry French	.25	.10
5 Tom Drake	.25	.10
6 Ed Albasta	.25	.10
7 Tommy Tatum	.25	.10
8 Paul Waner	1.50	.60
9 Van Lingle Mungo	.50	.20
10 Bill Swift	.25	.10
11 Dolph Camilli	.75	.30
12 Pete Coscarart	.25	.10
13 Vito Tamulis	.25	.10
14 Johnny Allen	.25	.10
15 Lee Grissom	.25	.10
16 Billy Herman	1.00	.40
17 Joe Vosmik	.25	.10
18 Babe Phelps	.25	.10
19 Mace Brown	.25	.10
20 Freddie Fitzsimmons	.50	.20
21 Tony Giuliani	.25	.10
22 Lew Riggs	.25	.10
23 Jimmy Wasdell	.25	.10
24 Herman Franks	.25	.10
25 Alex Kampouris	.25	.10
26 Kirby Higby	.25	.10
27 Ducky Medwick	1.00	.40
28 Newt Kimbell	.25	.10
29 Curt Davis	.25	.10
30 Augie Galan	.25	.10
31 Luke Hamlin	.25	.10
32 Cookie Lavagetto	.25	.10
33 Joe Gallagher	.25	.10
34 Whit Wyatt	.50	.20
35 Dixie Walker	.75	.30
36 Pete Reiser	1.00	.40
37 Leo Durocher MG	1.00	.40
38 Pee Wee Reese Ducky Medwick	1.50	.60
39 Unknown		
40 Unknown		
41 Kemp Wicker	.25	.10
42 George Pfister CO	.25	.10
43 Chuck Dressen CO	.25	.10

1979 Dodgers Blue

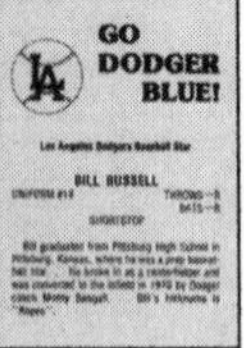

This 15-card standard-size set features full-bleed posed color player photos. The backs are white and carry the slogan "Go Dodger Blue," the player's name, uniform number, batting and throwing preference and a player profile. The cards are unnumbered and checklisted below in alphabetical order.

	NM	Ex
COMPLETE SET (15)	10.00	4.00
1 Dusty Baker	1.00	.40
2 Ron Cey	1.00	.40
3 Terry Forster	.50	.20
4 Steve Garvey	1.50	.60
5 Burt Hooton	.50	.20
6 Charlie Hough	.75	.30
7 Tom Lasorda MG	1.50	.60
8 Davey Lopes	1.00	.40
9 Rick Monday	.75	.30
10 Manny Mota	.75	.30
11 Doug Rau	.50	.20
12 Bill Russell	.75	.30
13 Reggie Smith	1.00	.40
14 Don Sutton	1.50	.60
15 Steve Yeager	.75	.30

1979 Dodgers Postcards

These were the only new postcards issued of Dodger players in 1979. Other than Bob Welch who was playing his first full season, most of the other players were acquired from other teams.

	NM	Ex
COMPLETE SET	3.00	1.20
1 Joe Ferguson	.50	.20
2 Charlie Hough	.75	.30
3 Andy Messersmith	.50	.20
4 Derrek Thomas	.50	.20
5 Gary Thomasson	.50	.20
6 Bob Welch	1.00	.40

1980 Dodgers Greats TCMA

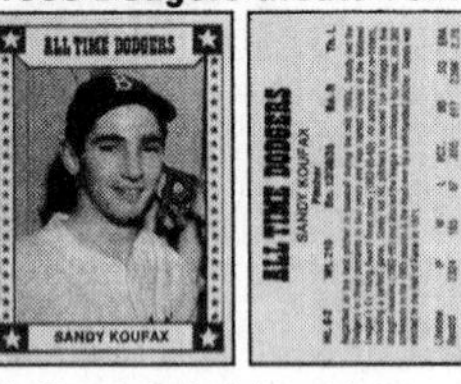

This 12-card standard-size set features some leading all-time Brooklyn Dodgers. The fronts have a player photo in the middle with the words "All-Time Dodgers" on top and his name on the bottom. The backs have vital statistics, a biography as well as career totals.

	NM	Ex
COMPLETE SET (12)	8.00	3.20
1 Gil Hodges	1.00	.40
2 Jim Gilliam	.50	.20
3 Pee Wee Reese	1.50	.60
4 Jackie Robinson	2.50	1.00
5 Sandy Koufax	2.00	.80
6 Zach Wheat	.50	.20
7 Dixie Walker	.50	.20
8 Hugh Casey	.25	.10
9 Dazzy Vance	.50	.20
10 Duke Snider	1.50	.60
11 Roy Campanella	1.50	.60
12 Walter Alston MG	.50	.20

1980 Dodgers Police

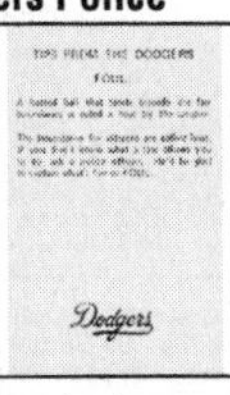

The cards in this 30-card set measure approximately 2 13/16" by 4 1/8". The full color 1980 Police Los Angeles Dodgers set features the player's name, uniform number, position, and biographical data on the fronts in addition to the photo. The backs feature Tips from the Dodgers, the LAPD logo, and the Dodgers' logo. The cards are listed below according to uniform number.

	NM	Ex
COMPLETE SET (30)	12.00	4.80
5 Johnny Oates	.25	.10
6 Steve Garvey	1.00	.40
7 Steve Yeager	.50	.20
8 Reggie Smith	.75	.30
9 Gary Thomasson	.25	.10
10 Ron Cey	.75	.30
12 Dusty Baker	.75	.30
13 Joe Ferguson	.25	.10
15 Davey Lopes	.75	.30
16 Rick Monday	.50	.20
18 Bill Russell	.50	.20
20 Don Sutton	1.50	.60
21 Jay Johnstone	.50	.20
23 Teddy Martinez	.25	.10
27 Joe Beckwith	.25	.10
28 Pedro Guerrero	1.25	.50
29 Don Stanhouse	.25	.10
30 Derrel Thomas	.25	.10
31 Doug Rau	.25	.10
34 Ken Brett	.25	.10
35 Bob Welch	.50	.20
37 Robert Castillo	.25	.10
38 Dave Goltz	.25	.10
41 Jerry Reuss	.50	.20
43 Rick Sutcliffe	1.50	.60
44 Mickey Hatcher	.25	.10
46 Burt Hooton	.50	.20
49 Charlie Hough	.75	.30
51 Terry Forster	.50	.20
NNO Team Card	.50	.20

1980 Dodgers TCMA 1959

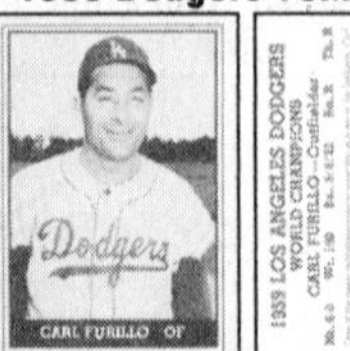

This 40-card standard-size set features members of the 1959 Los Angeles Dodgers, who became the first team to win a World Series while playing on the West Coast. The cards have white blue with Dodger Blue borders inside them. There is a player photo and his name and position are on the bottom. The horizontal backs have vital stats as well as a blurb about the player and his 1959 and career stats

	NM	Ex
COMPLETE SET (40)	20.00	8.00
1 Joe Pignatano	.25	.10
2 Carl Furillo	.75	.30
3 Bob Lillis	.25	.10
4 Chuck Essegian	.25	.10
5 Dick Gray	.25	.10
6 Rip Repulski	.25	.10
7 Jim Baxes	.25	.10
8 Frank Howard	1.00	.40
9 Solly Drake	.25	.10
10 Sandy Amoros	.25	.10
11 Norm Sherry	.25	.10
12 Tommy Davis	.50	.20
13 Jim Gilliam	.50	.20
14 Duke Snider	1.50	.60
15 Maury Wills	1.00	.40
16 Don Demeter	.25	.10
17 Wally Moon	.50	.20
18 John Roseboro	.50	.20
19 Ron Fairly	.50	.20
20 Norm Larker	.25	.10
21 Charlie Neal	.25	.10
22 Don Zimmer	.75	.30
23 Chuck Dressen CO	.50	.20
24 Gil Hodges	1.00	.40
25 Joe Becker CO	.25	.10
26 Walter Alston MG	1.00	.40
27 Greg Mulleavy	.25	.10
28 Don Drysdale	1.50	.60
29 Johnny Podres	.25	.10
30 Sandy Koufax	2.50	1.00
31 Roger Craig	.25	.10
32 Danny McDevitt	.25	.10
33 Bill Harris	.25	.10
34 Larry Sherry	.25	.10
35 Stan Williams	.25	.10
36 Clem Labine	.50	.20
37 Chuck Churn	.25	.10
38 Johnny Klippstein	.25	.10
39 Carl Erskine	.50	.20
40 Fred Kipp	.25	.10

1981 Dodgers

This 12-card set of the Los Angeles Dodgers measures approximately 8" by 10" and features white-bordered color action player photos with a facsimile autograph on the front. The backs are blank. The cards are unnumbered and checklisted below in alphabetical order.

	Nm-Mt	Ex-Mt
COMPLETE SET (12)	10.00	4.00
1 Dusty Baker	1.00	.40
2 Ron Cey	1.00	.40
3 Terry Forster	.50	.20
4 Steve Garvey	2.00	.80
5 Pedro Guerrero	1.50	.60
6 Burt Hooton	.50	.20
7 Davey Lopes	1.00	.40
8 Rick Monday	.75	.30
9 Jerry Reuss	1.00	.40
10 Don Sutton	2.50	1.00
11 Derrel Thomas	.50	.20
12 Fernando Valenzuela	3.00	1.20

1981 Dodgers Photos

These photos feature members of the World Champion 1981 Los Angeles Dodgers. They are unnumbered so we have sequenced them alphabetically.

	Nm-Mt	Ex-Mt
COMPLETE SET	25.00	10.00
1 Dusty Baker	1.00	.40
2 Monty Basgall CO	.50	.20
3 Joe Beckwith	.50	.20
4 Robert Castillo	.50	.20
5 Ron Cey	1.00	.40
6 Mark Cresse CO	.50	.20
7 Joe Ferguson	.50	.20
8 Terry Forster	.50	.20
9 Pepe Frias	.50	.20
10 Steve Garvey	1.50	.60
11 Dave Goltz	.50	.20
12 Pedro Guerrero	1.50	.60
13 Burt Hooten	.50	.20
14 Steve Howe	.50	.20
15 Jay Johnstone	.75	.30
16 Ken Landreaux	.50	.20
17 Tommy Lasorda MG	1.50	.60
18 Rudy Law	.50	.20
19 Davey Lopes	1.00	.40
20 Rick Monday	.75	.30
21 Manny Mota CO	.75	.30
22 Danny Ozark CO	.50	.20
23 Ron Perranoski CO	.50	.20
24 Jerry Reuss	.75	.30
25 Bill Russell	.75	.30
26 Mike Scioscia	2.00	.80
27 Reggie Smith	.75	.30
28 Dave Stewart	1.50	.60
29 Rick Sutcliffe	1.00	.40
30 Derrel Thomas	.50	.20
31 Fernando Valenzuela	2.00	.80
32 Bob Welch	1.00	.40
33 Steve Yeager	.75	.30

1981 Dodgers Police

The cards in this 32-card set measure approximately 2 13/16" by 4 1/8". The full color set of 1981 Los Angeles Dodgers features the player's name, number, position and a line stating that the LAPD salutes the 1981 Dodgers, in addition to the player's photo. The backs feature the LAPD logo and short narratives, attributable to the player on the front of the card, revealing police associated tips. The cards of Ken Landreaux and Dave Stewart are reported to be more difficult to obtain than other cards in this set due to the fact that they are replacements for Stanhouse (released 4/17/81) and Hatcher (traded for Landreaux 3/30/81). The complete set price below refers to all 32 cards, i.e., including the variations. The Dave Stewart card pre-dates his Rookie Card.

	Nm-Mt	Ex-Mt
COMPLETE SET (32)	15.00	6.00
COMMON CARD	.25	.10
COMMON SP	2.50	1.00
2 Tom Lasorda MG	1.00	.40
3 Rudy Law	.25	.10
6 Steve Garvey	1.00	.40
7 Steve Yeager	.50	.20
8 Reggie Smith	.75	.30
10 Ron Cey	.75	.30
12 Dusty Baker	.75	.30
13 Joe Ferguson	.25	.10
14 Mike Scioscia	1.25	.50
15 Davey Lopes	.75	.30
16 Rick Monday	.50	.20
18 Bill Russell	.50	.20
21 Jay Johnstone	.50	.20
26 Don Stanhouse	.25	.10
27 Joe Beckwith	.25	.10
28 Pedro Guerrero	1.00	.40
30 Derrel Thomas	.25	.10
34 Fernando Valenzuela	1.25	.50
35 Bob Welch	.75	.30
36 Pepe Frias	.25	.10
37 Robert Castillo	.25	.10
38 Dave Goltz	.25	.10
41 Jerry Reuss	.50	.20
43 Rick Sutcliffe	1.00	.40
44A Mickey Hatcher	.25	.10
44B Ken Landreaux SP	2.50	1.00
46 Burt Hooton	.50	.20
48 Dave Stewart SP	5.00	2.00
51 Terry Forster	.25	.10
57 Steve Howe	.25	.10
NNO Team Photo CL	.50	.20
NNO Monty Basgall CO Tom Lasorda MG Danny Ozark CO Ron Perranoski CO Manny Mota CO Mark Creese CO	.50	.20

1981 Dodgers Postcards

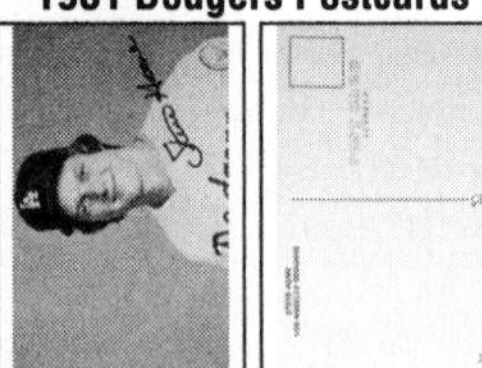

This 11-card set of the Los Angeles Dodgers measures approximately 3 1/2" by 5 1/2" and features borderless color player photos with a facsimile autograph. The backs display a postcard format. The cards are unnumbered and checklisted below in alphabetical order.

	Nm-Mt	Ex-Mt
COMPLETE SET (11)	10.00	4.00
1 Dusty Baker	1.00	.40
2 Steve Garvey	1.50	.60
3 Pedro Guerrero	1.50	.60
4 Steve Howe	.50	.20
5 Ken Landreaux	.50	.20
6 Davey Lopes	1.00	.40
7 Jerry Reuss	1.00	.40
8 Mike Scioscia	2.00	.80
9 Fernando Valenzuela	2.00	.80
10 Bob Welch	1.00	.40
11 Steve Yeager	.75	.30

1982 Dodgers Builders Emporium

This seven-card set of the Los Angeles Dodgers was sponsored by Builders Emporium. The fronts feature black-and-white player action pictures with a small black-and-white head photo of the player on the left. The player's name, team, and sponsor name are printed below this small photo. The backs are blank. The cards are unnumbered and checklisted below in alphabetical order.

	Nm-Mt	Ex-Mt
COMPLETE SET (7)	7.50	3.00
1 Dusty Baker	1.50	.60
2 Ron Cey	1.50	.60
3 Steve Garvey	2.00	.80
4 Pedro Guerrero	1.25	.50
5 Tommy Lasorda MG	2.00	.80
6 Jerry Reuss	1.25	.50
7 Steve Sax	2.00	.80

1982 Dodgers Police

The cards in this 30-card set measure approximately 2 13/16" by 4 1/8". The 1982 Los Angeles Dodgers police set depicts the players and events of the 1981 season. There is a World Series trophy card, three cards

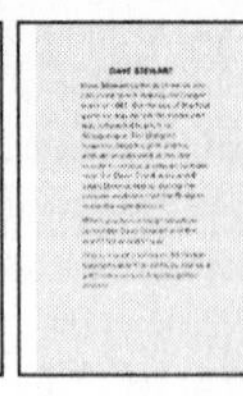

commemorating the Division, League, and World Series wins, one manager card, and 25 player cards. The obverses have brilliant color photos set on white, and the player cards are numbered according to the uniform number of the individual. The reverses contain biographical material, information about stadium events, and a safety feature emphasizing "the team that wouldn't quit." According to published reports, 4.5 million cards were produced for this promotion.

	Nm-Mt	Ex-Mt
COMPLETE SET (30)	10.00	4.00
2 Tom Lasorda MG	1.00	.40
6 Steve Garvey	1.00	.40
7 Steve Yeager	.50	.20
8 Mark Belanger	.25	.10
10 Ron Cey	1.00	.40
12 Dusty Baker	.75	.30
14 Mike Scioscia	.75	.30
16 Rick Monday	.50	.20
18 Bill Russell	.50	.20
21 Jay Johnstone	.50	.20
26 Alejandro Pena	.25	.10
28 Pedro Guerrero	.75	.30
30 Derrel Thomas	.25	.10
31 Jorge Orta	.25	.10
34 Fernando Valenzuela	1.00	.40
35 Bob Welch	.75	.30
38 Dave Goltz	.25	.10
40 Ron Roenicke	.25	.10
41 Jerry Reuss	.50	.20
44 Ken Landreaux	.25	.10
46 Burt Hooton	.50	.20
48 Dave Stewart	1.00	.40
49 Tom Niedenfuer	.25	.10
51 Terry Forster	.25	.10
52 Steve Sax	1.00	.40
57 Steve Howe	.25	.10
NNO World Series Trophy CL	.50	.20
NNO World Series Commemorative	.25	.10
NNO NL Champions	.25	.10
NNO Division Champs	.25	.10

1982 Dodgers Postcards

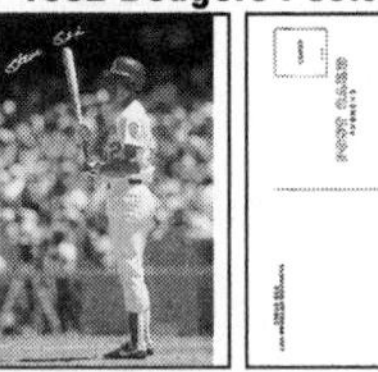

These postcards feature members of the 1982 Los Angeles Dodgers. These cards are unnumbered and we have sequenced them in alphabetical order.

	Nm-Mt	Ex-Mt
COMPLETE SET (10)	6.00	2.40
1 Terry Forster	.50	.20
2 Steve Garvey	1.50	.60
3 Pedro Guerrero	.75	.30
4 Steve Howe	.50	.20
5 Tom Lasorda MG	1.50	.60
6 Tom Neidenfuer	.50	.20
7 Steve Sax	1.50	.60
8 Mike Scioscia	1.00	.40
9 Bob Welch	.75	.30
10 Steve Yeager	.75	.30

1982 Dodgers Union Oil Volpe

Artist Nicholas Volpe drew members of the Dodgers for a Union Oil giveaway. These color portraits are painted in pastel; one portrait a week was given away at the stations. The cards measure 8 1/2" x 11" and the backs contain statistics and other biographical inforamtion. An album which contained 20 plastic sheets to hold these cards was sold by the Dodgers for $6.

	Nm-Mt	Ex-Mt
COMPLETE SET	12.00	4.80
1 Dusty Baker	1.00	.40
2 Mark Belanger	.50	.20
3 Ron Cey	1.00	.40
4 Terry Forster	.50	.20
5 Steve Garvey	1.50	.60
6 Pedro Guerrero	1.00	.40
7 Burt Hooton	.50	.20
8 Steve Howe	.50	.20
9 Ken Landreaux	.50	.20
10 Tom Lasorda MG	1.50	.60
11 Mike Marshall	.75	.30
12 Rick Monday	.75	.30
13 Jose Morales	.50	.20
14 Tom Niedenfuer	.50	.20
15 Jorge Orta	.50	.20
16 Jerry Reuss	.75	.30
17 Ron Roenicke	.50	.20
18 Bill Russell	.75	.30
19 Steve Sax	1.50	.60
20 Mike Scioscia	1.00	.40
21 Vin Scully ANN	1.50	.60
22 Dave Stewart	1.50	.60
23 Derrell Thomas	.50	.20
24 Fernando Valenzuela	1.50	.60
25 Bob Welch	.75	.30
26 Steve Yeager	.75	.30

1983 Dodgers Boys of Summer TCMA

This set of the Los Angeles Dodgers was issued on October 8, 1983. The cards were distributed on sheets measuring approximately 10" by 3 1/2". The fronts feature two color or black-and-white action player photos with a picture of Ebbets Field in the middle. The backs carry the pictured players' names. There maybe more cards in the set and any confirmed additions would be appreciated. The cards are unnumbered and checklisted below in alphabetical order.

Nm-Mt Ex-Mt
COMPLETE SET 15.00 6.00
1 Clem Labine 10.00 4.00
Jackie Robinson
2 Sal Maglie 5.00 2.00
George Shuba

1983 Dodgers Police

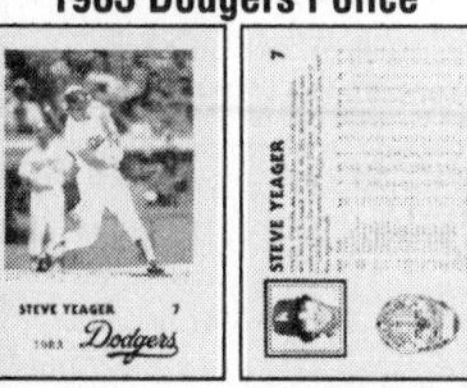

The cards in this 30-card set measure approximately 2 13/16" by 4 1/8". The full color Police Los Angeles Dodgers set of 1983 features the player's name and uniform number on the front along with the Dodger's logo, the year, and the player's photo. The backs feature a small insert portrait picture of the player, player biographies, and career statistics. The logo of the Los Angeles Police Department, the sponsor of the set, is found on the backs of the cards.

Nm-Mt Ex-Mt
COMPLETE SET (30) 8.00 3.20
Tom Lasorda MG 1.00 .40
Steve Sax .50 .20
Mike Marshall .25 .10
Steve Yeager .50 .20
2 Dusty Baker .75 .30
4 Mike Scioscia .75 .30
6 Rick Monday .50 .20
7 Greg Brock .25 .10
8 Bill Russell .50 .20
0 Candy Maldonado .50 .20
1 Ricky Wright .25 .10
2 Mark Bradley .25 .10
3 Dave Sax .25 .10
6 Alejandro Pena .25 .10
7 Joe Beckwith .25 .10
8 Pedro Guerrero .75 .30
0 Derrel Thomas .25 .10
4 Fernando Valenzuela 1.00 .40
5 Bob Welch .75 .30
8 Pat Zachry .25 .10
0 Ron Roenicke .25 .10
1 Jerry Reuss .50 .20
3 Jose Morales .25 .10
4 Ken Landreaux .25 .10
6 Burt Hooton .25 .10
7 Larry White .25 .10
8 Dave Stewart 1.00 .40
9 Tom Niedenfuer .25 .10
7 Steve Howe .25 .10
NNO Ron Perranoski CO .25 .10
Joe Amalfitano CO
Monty Basgall CO
Mark Cresse CO
Manny Mota CO

1983 Dodgers Postcards

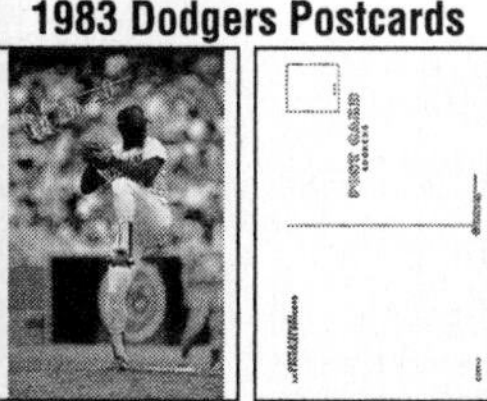

These postcards feature members of the 1983 Los Angeles Dodgers. These cards are unnumbered and checklisted below in alphabetical order.

Nm-Mt Ex-Mt
COMPLETE SET 10.00 4.00
Dusty Baker 1.00 .40
Greg Brock .50 .20
Pedro Guerrero 1.00 .40
Burt Hooton .50 .20
Steve Howe .50 .20
Ken Landreaux .50 .20
Tommy Lasorda MG 1.50 .60
Mike Marshall .50 .20
Rick Monday .75 .30
Manny Mota CO .75 .30
Tom Neidenfuer .50 .20
2 Jerry Reuss .75 .30
3 Bill Russell .75 .30
4 Steve Sax .75 .30
5 Mike Scioscia 1.00 .40
6 Dave Stewart .75 .30
7 Derrel Thomas .50 .20
8 Fernando Valenzuela 1.50 .60
9 Bob Welch .75 .30
0 Steve Yeager .75 .30

1984 Dodgers Coke

These 30 postcards, which measure 3 1/2" by 5 1/4" were issued by the Los Angeled Dodgers. The fronts have the player photo and his name. The backs have a message to Dodger fans, a facsimile autograph and the Coke logo. Some cards were issued with blank backs. Since these cards are unnumbered, we have sequenced them in alphabetical order.

Nm-Mt Ex-Mt
COMPLETE SET 15.00 6.00
1 Joe Amalfitano CO .50 .20
2 Dave Anderson .50 .20
3 Bob Bailor .50 .20
4 Monty Basgall CO .50 .20
5 Greg Brock .50 .20
6 Mark Cresse CO .50 .20
7 Carlos Diaz .50 .20
8 Pedro Guerrero 1.00 .40
9 Orel Hershiser 2.00 .80
10 Rick Honeycutt .50 .20
11 Burt Hooton .50 .20
12 Ken Landreaux .50 .20
13 Rafael Landestoy .50 .20
14 Tom Lasorda MG 1.50 .60
15 Candy Maldonado .50 .20
16 Mike Marshall .50 .20
17 Manny Mota CO .75 .30
18 Jose Morales .50 .20
19 Tom Niedenfuer .50 .20
20 Alejandro Pena .50 .20
21 Ron Perranoski CO .50 .20
22 Jerry Reuss .75 .30
23 German Rivera .50 .20
24 Bill Russell .50 .20
25 Steve Sax .75 .30
26 Mike Scioscia 1.00 .40
27 Bob Welch .75 .30
28 Terry Whitfield .50 .20
29 Steve Yeager .75 .30
30 Pat Zachry .50 .20

1984 Dodgers Police

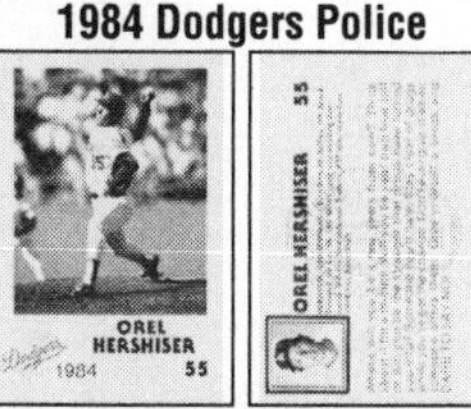

The cards in this 30-card set measure 2 13/16" by 4 1/8". For the fifth straight year, the Los Angeles Police Department sponsored a set of Dodger baseball cards. The set is numbered by player uniform number, which is featured on both the fronts and backs of the cards. The set features an early card of Orel Hershiser predating his Rookie Cards issued the following year.

Nm-Mt Ex-Mt
COMPLETE SET (30) 8.00 3.20
2 Tom Lasorda MG 1.00 .40
3 Steve Sax .75 .30
5 Mike Marshall .25 .10
7 Steve Yeager .50 .20
9 Greg Brock .25 .10
10 Dave Anderson .25 .10
14 Mike Scioscia .75 .30
16 Rick Monday .50 .20
17 Rafael Landestoy .25 .10
18 Bill Russell .50 .20
20 Candy Maldonado .25 .10
21 Bob Bailor .25 .10
25 German Rivera .25 .10
26 Alejandro Pena .25 .10
27 Carlos Diaz .25 .10
28 Pedro Guerrero .75 .30
31 Jack Fimple .25 .10
34 Fernando Valenzuela 1.00 .40
35 Bob Welch .75 .30
38 Pat Zachry .25 .10
40 Rick Honeycutt .25 .10
41 Jerry Reuss .50 .20
43 Jose Morales .25 .10
44 Ken Landreaux .25 .10
45 Terry Whitfield .25 .10
46 Burt Hooton .50 .20
49 Tom Niedenfuer .25 .10
55 Orel Hershiser 4.00 1.60
56 Richard Rodas .25 .10
NNO Monty Basgall CO .25 .10
Joe Amalfitano CO
Mark Cresse CO
Manny Mota CO
Ron Perranoski CO

1984 Dodgers Smokey

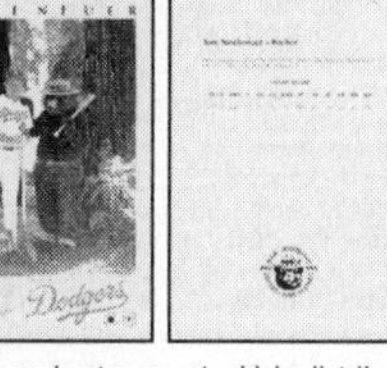

This four-card set was not widely distributed and has not proven to be very popular with collectors. Cards were supposedly distributed by fire agencies in Southern California at fairs, mall displays, and special events. Cards measure approximately 5" by 7" and feature a color picture of Smokey the Bear with a Dodger. The cards were printed on relatively thin card stock; printing on the back is black on white.

Nm-Mt Ex-Mt
COMPLETE SET (4) 18.00 7.25
1 Ken Landreaux 5.00 2.00
with Smokey
2 Tom Niedenfuer 5.00 2.00
with Smokey
3 Steve Sax 6.00 2.40
with Smokey
4 Smokey the Bear 4.00 1.60
(Batting pose)

1984 Dodgers Union Oil

Distributed by Union Oil, this 16-card set measures approximately 8 1/2" by 11" and features color drawings of some of the great moments in Dodgers history. The backs carry text discribing the significance of the drawing. A variety of artists drew these posters. An album was also available to contain these oversized cards.

Nm-Mt Ex-Mt
COMPLETE SET (16) 20.00 8.00
1 Record-Setting Infield 1.00 .40
2 Roy Campanella 5.00 2.00
3 Willie Davis 1.50 .60
4 Don Drysdale 3.00 1.20
5 Manny Mota 1.50 .60
6 Jerry Reuss 1.50 .60
Bill Singer
7 The Tenth Player 1.00 .40
8 Dusty Baker 2.00 .80
Ron Cey
Steve Garvey
Reggie Smith
9 Fernando Valenzuela 2.50 1.00
10 Bob Welch 1.50 .60
Strikes Out Reggie Jackson
11 Maury Wills 2.50 1.00
12 1959 World Championship 1.00 .40
13 1963 World Championship 1.00 .40
14 1965 World Championship 1.00 .40
15 1977 NLCS 1.00 .40
16 1981 World Championship 1.00 .40

1985 Dodgers Coke Postcards

This 34-card set was sponsored by Coke, and the company logo appears on the back of the cards. These oversized cards measure approximately 3 1/2" by 5 1/2". The front design features glossy color player photos, bordered in white and with the player's name below the pictures. Except for the sponsor's logo, the backs are blank. The cards are unnumbered and checklisted below in alphabetical order.

Nm-Mt Ex-Mt
COMPLETE SET (34) 20.00 8.00
1 Joe Amalfitano CO .50 .20
2 Dave Anderson .50 .20
3 Bob Bailor .50 .20
4 Monty Basgall CO .50 .20
5 Tom Brennan .50 .20
6 Greg Brock .50 .20
7 Bobby Castillo .50 .20
8 Mark Cresse CO .50 .20
9 Carlos Diaz .50 .20
10 Mariano Duncan 1.50 .60
11 Pedro Guerrero 1.50 .60
12 Orel Hershiser 2.00 .80
13 Rick Honeycutt .50 .20
14 Steve Howe .50 .20
15 Ken Howell .50 .20
16 Jay Johnstone 1.00 .40
17 Ken Landreaux .50 .20
18 Tom Lasorda MG 2.00 .80
19 Candy Maldonado .50 .20
20 Mike Marshall .50 .20
21 Manny Mota CO 1.00 .40
22 Tom Niedenfuer .50 .20
23 Al Oliver 1.50 .60
24 Alejandro Pena .50 .20
25 Ron Perranoski CO .50 .20
26 Jerry Reuss 1.00 .40
27 R.J. Reynolds .50 .20
28 Bill Russell 1.00 .40
29 Steve Sax 1.00 .40
30 Mike Scioscia 1.50 .60
31 Fernando Valenzuela 1.50 .60
32 Bob Welch 1.00 .40
33 Terry Whitfield .50 .20
34 Steve Yeager 1.00 .40

1986 Dodgers Coke Postcards

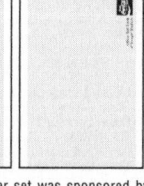

This 33-card Dodger set was sponsored by Coke, and the company logo appears on the back of the cards. The oversized cards measure approximately 3 1/2" by 5 1/2". The front design features glossy color player photos (mostly action), bordered in white and with the player's name below the picture. The backs are blank except for a small Coca-Cola logo. The cards are unnumbered and checklisted below in alphabetical order.

Nm-Mt Ex-Mt
COMPLETE SET (33) 15.00 6.00
1 Joe Amalfitano CO .50 .20
2 Dave Anderson .50 .20
3 Monty Basgall CO .50 .20
4 Greg Brock .50 .20
5 Enos Cabell .50 .20
6 Cesar Cedeno .75 .30
7 Mark Cresse CO .50 .20
8 Mariano Duncan 1.00 .40
9 Carlos Diaz .50 .20
10 Pedro Guerrero 1.00 .40
11 Orel Hershiser 2.50 1.00
12 Ben Hines TR .50 .20
13 Rick Honeycutt .50 .20
14 Ken Howell .50 .20
15 Ken Landreaux .50 .20
16 Tom Lasorda MG 1.50 .60
17 Bill Madlock .75 .30
18 Mike Marshall .50 .20
19 Len Matuszek .50 .20
20 Manny Mota CO .75 .30
21 Tom Niedenfuer .50 .20
22 Alejandro Pena .50 .20
23 Ron Perranoski CO .50 .20
24 Dennis Powell .50 .20
25 Jerry Reuss .75 .30
26 Bill Russell .75 .30
27 Steve Sax .75 .30
28 Mike Scioscia 1.00 .40
29 Alex Trevino .50 .20
30 Fernando Valenzuela 1.00 .40
31 Ed VandeBerg .50 .20
32 Bob Welch .75 .30
33 Terry Whitfield .50 .20

1986 Dodgers Police

This 30-card set features full-color cards each measuring 2 13/16" by 4 1/8". The cards are unnumbered except for uniform numbers. The backs give a safety tip as well as a short capsule biography. The sets were given away at Dodger Stadium on May 18th.

Nm-Mt Ex-Mt
COMPLETE SET (30) 6.00 2.40
2 Tom Lasorda MG 1.00 .40
3 Steve Sax .75 .30
5 Mike Marshall .25 .10
9 Greg Brock .25 .10
10 Dave Anderson .25 .10
12 Bill Madlock .50 .20
14 Mike Scioscia .75 .30
17 Len Matuszek .25 .10
18 Bill Russell .75 .30
22 Franklin Stubbs .25 .10
23 Enos Cabell .25 .10
25 Mariano Duncan .75 .30
26 Alejandro Pena .25 .10
27 Carlos Diaz .25 .10
28 Pedro Guerrero .75 .30
29 Alex Trevino .25 .10
31 Ed VandeBerg .25 .10
34 Fernando Valenzuela .75 .30
35 Bob Welch .75 .30
40 Rick Honeycutt .25 .10
41 Jerry Reuss .50 .20
43 Ken Howell .25 .10
44 Ken Landreaux .25 .10
45 Terry Whitfield .25 .10
48 Dennis Powell .25 .10
49 Tom Niedenfuer .25 .10
51 Reggie Williams .25 .10
55 Orel Hershiser 1.00 .40
NNO Don McMahon CO .25 .10
Mark Cresse CO
Ben Hines CO
Ron Perranoski CO
Monty Basgall CO
Manny Mota CO
Joe Amalfitano CO
NNO Team Photo CL .50 .20

1986 Dodgers Union Oil Photos

This 24-card set features color photos of the 1986 Los Angeles Dodgers and measures approximately 8 1/2" by 11". Player information is printed on the backs. The cards are unnumbered and checklisted below in alphabetical order.

Nm-Mt Ex-Mt
COMPLETE SET (24) 10.00 4.00
1 Dave Anderson .25 .10
2 Greg Brock .25 .10
3 Enos Cabell .25 .10
4 Carlos Diaz .25 .10
5 Mariano Duncan .50 .20
6 Pedro Guerrero .75 .30
7 Orel Hershiser 1.00 .40
8 Rick Honeycutt .25 .10
9 Ken Howell .25 .10
10 Tommy Lasorda MG 1.00 .40
11 Ken Landreaux .25 .10
12 Bill Madlock .50 .20
13 Mike Marshall .25 .10
14 Tom Niedenfuer .25 .10
15 Jerry Reuss .50 .20
16 Bill Russell .50 .20
17 Steve Sax .50 .20
18 Mike Scioscia .75 .30
19 Franklin Stubbs .25 .10
20 Alex Trevino .25 .10
21 Fernando Valenzuela .75 .30
22 Ed Vandeberg .25 .10
23 Bob Welch .50 .20
24 Reggie Williams .25 .10

1987 Dodgers 1955 TCMA

This nine-card standard-size set feature members of the 1955 Brooklyn Dodgers. That team was the only Brooklyn Dodger team to win the World Series. The fronts have player photos, while the backs have information about the players as well as their 1955 statistics.

Nm-Mt Ex-Mt
COMPLETE SET (9) 5.00 2.00
1 Duke Snider .75 .30
Walter Alston MG
2 Roy Campanella 1.00 .40
3 Jackie Robinson 2.00 .80
4 Carl Furillo .75 .30
5 Gil Hodges 1.00 .40
6 Pee Wee Reese .75 .30
Jim Gilliam
7 Don Newcombe .75 .30
8 Ed Roebuck .25 .10
Clem Labine
9 Carl Erskine .50 .20

1987 Dodgers Mother's

This set consists of 28 full-color, rounded-corner cards each measuring 2 1/2" by 3 1/2". Starter sets (only 20 cards but also including a certificate for eight more cards) were given out at the ballpark and collectors were encouraged to trade to fill in the rest of their set. Cards were originally given out at Dodger Stadium on August 9th. Photos were taken by Barry Colla. The sets were reportedly given out free to all game attendees 14 years of age and under.

Nm-Mt Ex-Mt
COMPLETE SET (28) 8.00 3.20
1 Tom Lasorda MG 1.00 .40
2 Pedro Guerrero .75 .30
3 Steve Sax .75 .30
4 Fernando Valenzuela .75 .30
5 Mike Marshall .25 .10
6 Orel Hershiser 1.00 .40
7 Mariano Duncan .25 .10
8 Bill Madlock .50 .20
9 Bob Welch .50 .20
10 Mike Scioscia .75 .30
11 Mike Ramsey .25 .10
12 Matt Young .25 .10
13 Franklin Stubbs .25 .10
14 Tom Niedenfuer .25 .10
15 Reggie Williams .25 .10
16 Rick Honeycutt .25 .10
17 Dave Anderson .25 .10
18 Alejandro Pena .25 .10
19 Ken Howell .25 .10
20 Len Matuszek .25 .10
21 Tim Leary .25 .10
22 Tracy Woodson .25 .10
23 Alex Trevino .25 .10
24 Ken Landreaux .25 .10
25 Mickey Hatcher .25 .10
26 Brian Holton .25 .10
27 Ron Perranoski CO .25 .10
Manny Mota CO
Don McMahon CO
Joe Amalfitano CO
Mark Cresse CO
Bill Russell CO
28 Checklist Card .25 .10

1987 Dodgers Photos

These photos feature members of the 1987 Los Angeles Dodgers. The photos are unnumbered so we have sequenced them in alphabetical order.

Nm-Mt Ex-Mt
COMPLETE SET 10.00 4.00
1 Dave Anderson .50 .20
2 Mariano Duncan .50 .20
3 Pedro Guerrero 1.00 .40
4 Orel Hershiser 1.00 .40
5 Brian Holton .50 .20
6 Rick Honeycutt .50 .20
7 Ken Howell .50 .20
8 Tommy Larsorda MG 1.50 .60
9 Tim Leary .50 .20
10 Len Matuszek .50 .20
11 Alejandro Pena .50 .20
12 Steve Sax .75 .30
13 Mike Scioscia 1.00 .40

Card	Nm-Mt	Ex-Mt
14 Franklin Stubbs	.50	.20
15 Alex Trevino	.50	.20
16 Fernando Valenzuela	1.00	.40
17 Matt Young	.50	.20

1987 Dodgers Police

This 30-card set features full-color cards each measuring approximately 2 13/16" by 4 1/8". The cards are unnumbered except for uniform numbers. The backs give a safety tip as well as a short capsule biography. Cards were given away at Dodger Stadium on April 24th and later during the summer by LAPD officers at a rate of two cards per week.

	Nm-Mt	Ex-Mt
COMPLETE SET (30)	6.00	2.40
1 Tom Lasorda MG	1.00	.40
2 Steve Sax	.50	.20
3 Mike Marshall	.25	.10
4 Dave Anderson	.25	.10
5 Bill Madlock	.50	.20
6 Mike Scioscia	.75	.30
7 Gilberto Reyes	.25	.10
8 Len Matuszek	.25	.10
9 Reggie Williams	.25	.10
10 Franklin Stubbs	.25	.10
11 Tim Leary	.25	.10
12 Mariano Duncan	.25	.10
13 Alejandro Pena	.25	.10
14 Pedro Guerrero	.75	.30
15 Alex Trevino	.25	.10
16 Jeff Hamilton	.25	.10
17 Fernando Valenzuela	.75	.30
18 Bob Welch	.75	.30
19 Matt Young	.25	.10
20 Rick Honeycutt	.25	.10
21 Jerry Reuss	.50	.20
22 Ken Howell	.25	.10
23 Ken Landreaux	.25	.10
24 Ralph Bryant	.25	.10
25 Jose Gonzalez	.25	.10
26 Tom Niedenfuer	.25	.10
27 Brian Holton	.25	.10
28 Orel Hershiser	1.00	.40
29 Ron Perranoski CO	.50	.20
Tom Lasorda MG		
Joe Amalfitano CO		
Don McMahon CO		
Manny Mota CO		
Bill Russell CO		
Mark Cresse CO		
30 Dodgers Stadium	.25	.10
(25th Anniversary)		

1987 Dodgers Smokey All-Stars

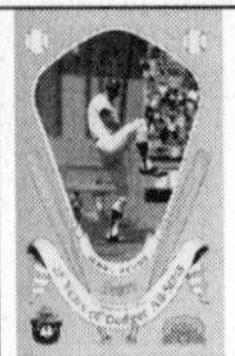

This 40-card set was issued by the U.S. Forestry Service to commemorate the Los Angeles Dodgers selected for the All-Star game over the past 25 years. The cards measure approximately 2 1/2" by 3 3/4" and have full-color fronts. The card fronts are distinguished by their thick silver borders and the bats, balls, and stadium design layout. The 25th anniversary logo for Dodger Stadium is in the lower right corner of each card. The set numbering is alphabetical by subject's name.

	Nm-Mt	Ex-Mt
COMPLETE SET (40)	15.00	6.00
1 Walt Alston MG	1.00	.40
2 Dusty Baker	.75	.30
3 Jim Brewer	.25	.10
4 Ron Cey	.75	.30
5 Tommy Davis	.50	.20
6 Willie Davis	.50	.20
7 Don Drysdale	1.50	.60
8 Steve Garvey	1.00	.40
9 Bill Grabarkewitz	.25	.10
10 Pedro Guerrero	.75	.30
11 Tom Haller	.25	.10
12 Orel Hershiser	.75	.30
13 Burt Hooton	.25	.10
14 Steve Howe	.25	.10
15 Tommy John	.75	.30
16 Sandy Koufax	2.00	.80
17 Tom Lasorda MG	1.00	.40
18 Jim Lefebvre	.25	.10
19 Davey Lopes	.50	.20
20 Mike G. Marshall	.25	.10
21 Mike A. Marshall	.25	.10
22 Andy Messersmith	.25	.10
23 Rick Monday	.25	.10
24 Manny Mota	.50	.20
25 Claude Osteen	.25	.10
26 Johnny Podres	.50	.20
27 Phil Regan	.25	.10
28 Jerry Reuss	.25	.10
29 Rick Rhoden	.25	.10
30 John Roseboro	.50	.20
31 Bill Russell	.50	.20
32 Steve Sax	.50	.20
33 Bill Singer	.25	.10
34 Reggie Smith	.50	.20
35 Don Sutton	1.25	.50
36 Fernando Valenzuela	.75	.30
37 Bob Welch	.50	.20
38 Maury Wills	.75	.30
39 Jim Wynn	.25	.10
40 Checklist Card	.25	.10

1988 Dodgers Mother's

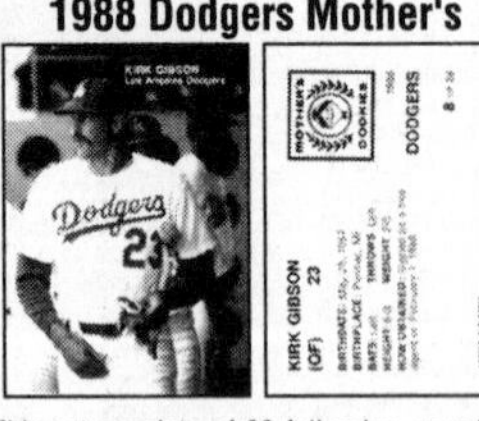

This set consists of 28 full-color, rounded-corner cards each measuring 2 1/2" by 3 1/2". Starter sets (only 20 cards but also including a certificate for eight more cards) were given out at the ballpark and collectors were encouraged to trade to fill in the rest of their set. Cards were originally given out at Dodger Stadium on July 31st. Photos were taken by Barry Colla. The sets were reportedly given out free to the first 25,000 game attendees 14 years of age and under.

	Nm-Mt	Ex-Mt
COMPLETE SET (28)	10.00	4.00
1 Tom Lasorda MG	1.00	.40
2 Pedro Guerrero	.75	.30
3 Steve Sax	.50	.20
4 Fernando Valenzuela	.75	.30
5 Mike Marshall	.25	.10
6 Orel Hershiser	.75	.30
7 Alfredo Griffin	.25	.10
8 Kirk Gibson	1.00	.40
9 Don Sutton	1.00	.40
10 Mike Scioscia	.75	.30
11 Franklin Stubbs	.25	.10
12 Mike Davis	.25	.10
13 Jesse Orosco	.50	.20
14 John Shelby	.25	.10
15 Rick Dempsey	.50	.20
16 Jay Howell	.25	.10
17 Dave Anderson	.25	.10
18 Alejandro Pena	.25	.10
19 Jeff Hamilton	.25	.10
20 Danny Heep	.25	.10
21 Tim Leary	.25	.10
22 Brad Havens	.25	.10
23 Tim Belcher	.50	.20
24 Ken Howell	.25	.10
25 Mickey Hatcher	.25	.10
26 Brian Holton	.25	.10
27 Mike Devereaux	.25	.10
28 Joe Ferguson CO	.25	.10
Mark Cresse CO		
Ron Perranoski CO		
Bill Russell CO		
Joe Amalfitano CO		
Manny Mota CO		
Ben Hines CO CL		

1988 Dodgers Police

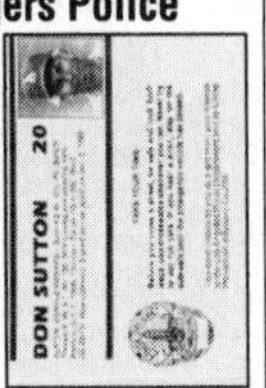

This 30-card set features full-color cards each measuring approximately 2 13/16" by 4 1/8". The cards are unnumbered except for uniform numbers. The backs give a safety tip as well as a short capsule biography. Cards were given during the summer by LAPD officers. The set is very similar to the 1987 set, the 1988 set is distinguished by the fact that it does not have the 25th anniversary (of Dodger Stadium) logo on the card front.

	Nm-Mt	Ex-Mt
COMPLETE SET (30)	6.00	2.40
2 Tom Lasorda MG	1.00	.40
3 Steve Sax	.50	.20
5 Mike Marshall	.25	.10
7 Alfredo Griffin	.25	.10
9 Mickey Hatcher	.25	.10
10 Dave Anderson	.25	.10
12 Danny Heep	.25	.10
14 Mike Scioscia	.75	.30
20 Don Sutton	1.00	.40
21 Tito Landrum and	.25	.10
17 Len Matuszek		
22 Franklin Stubbs	.25	.10
23 Kirk Gibson	1.00	.40
25 Mariano Duncan	.25	.10
26 Alejandro Pena	.25	.10
27 Mike Sharperson and	.25	.10
52 Tim Crews		
28 Pedro Guerrero	.75	.30
29 Alex Trevino	.25	.10
31 John Shelby	.25	.10
33 Jeff Hamilton	.25	.10
34 Fernando Valenzuela	.75	.30
37 Mike Davis	.25	.10
41 Brad Havens	.25	.10
43 Ken Howell	.25	.10
47 Jesse Orosco	.50	.20
49 Tim Belcher and	.25	.10
57 Shawn Hillegas		
50 Jay Howell	.25	.10
51 Brian Holton	.25	.10
54 Tim Leary	.25	.10
55 Orel Hershiser	1.00	.40
NNO Tom Lasorda MG	1.00	.40
and Coaches		

1988 Dodgers Rini Postcards 1

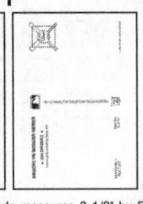

This set of 36 postcards measures 3 1/2" by 5 1/2" and showcases the Brooklyn Dodgers. On a blue background, the horizontal fronts feature color drawings by Susan Rini. There were three subsets in the first series, with 12 cards each. The cards are numbered on the back as "X of 12." Suffixes (A, B, and C) have been arbitrarily assigned to the card numbers below to distinguish between the three subsets.

	Nm-Mt	Ex-Mt
COMPLETE SET (36)	15.00	6.00
1A Dodgers Sym-Phony Band	.50	.20
1B Tom Lasorda	2.00	.80
1C Carl Erskine	1.50	.60
2A Sandy Amoros	.50	.20
2B Carl Furillo	1.50	.60
2C Ebbets Field	.50	.20
3A Don Newcombe	1.50	.60
3B Roger Craig	.75	.30
3C Jackie Robinson	4.00	1.60
4A Duke Snider	3.00	1.20
4B Andy Pafko	.75	.30
4C Red Barber ANN	1.00	.40
Leo Durocher		
5A Harold(Pee Wee) Reese	3.00	1.20
5B George Shuba	.50	.20
5C Red Barber ANN	1.00	.40
6A Johnny Podres	1.50	.60
6B Jackie Robinson	2.00	.80
Branch Rickey		
6C Leo Durocher	2.00	.80
7A Ralph Branca	.75	.30
7B Clem Labine	1.50	.60
7C Gil Hodges	2.00	.80
8A Don Drysdale	2.00	.80
8B Larry MacPhail OWN	.75	.30
8C Mickey Owen	.50	.20
9A Roy Campanella	3.00	1.20
9B Chuck Connors	1.50	.60
9C Preacher Roe	1.50	.60
10A Cookie Lavagetto	.50	.20
10B Walter O'Malley OWN	1.00	.40
10C Cal Abrams	.50	.20
11A Sal Maglie	1.00	.40
11B Carl Erskine	1.50	.60
11C Cookie Lavagetto	.75	.30
12A Clyde King	.50	.20
12B Eddie Miksis	.50	.20
12C Gene Hermanski	.50	.20

1988 Dodgers Smokey

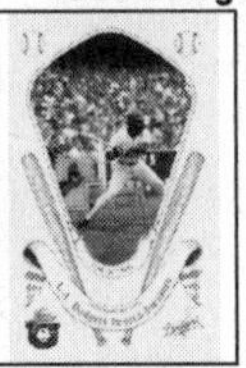
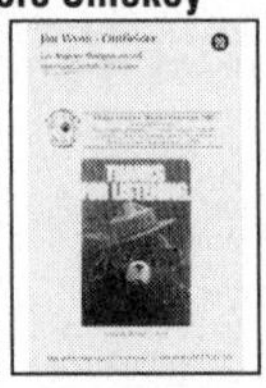

This 32-card set was issued by the U.S. Forestry Service as a perforated sheet that could be separated into individual cards. The set commemorates Los Angeles Dodgers who hold various team and league records, i.e., "L.A. Dodgers Record-Breakers." The cards measure approximately 2 1/2" by 4" and have full-color fronts. The card fronts are distinguished by their thick light blue borders and the bats, balls, and stadium design layout. The sheets of cards were distributed at the Dodgers' Smokey Bear Day game on September 9th.

	Nm-Mt	Ex-Mt
COMPLETE SET (32)	12.00	4.80
1 Walter Alston MG	.75	.30
2 John Roseboro	.25	.10
3 Frank Howard	.50	.20
4 Sandy Koufax	2.00	.80
5 Manny Mota	.50	.20
6 Sandy Koufax	.75	.30
Jerry Reuss		
Bill Singer		
7 Maury Wills	.75	.30
8 Tommy Davis	.50	.20
9 Phil Regan	.25	.10
10 Wes Parker	.25	.10
11 Don Drysdale	1.25	.50
12 Willie Davis	.50	.20
13 Bill Russell	.50	.20
14 Jim Brewer	.25	.10
15 Steve Garvey	.75	.30
Davey Lopes		
Bill Russell		
Ron Cey		
16 Mike Marshall	.25	.10
17 Steve Garvey	1.00	.40
18 Davey Lopes	.50	.20
19 Burt Hooton	.25	.10
20 Jim Wynn	.25	.10
21 Dusty Baker	.50	.20
Ron Cey		
Steve Garvey		
Reggie Smith		
22 Dusty Baker	.75	.30
23 Tommy Lasorda MG	1.00	.40
24 Fernando Valenzuela	.75	.30
25 Steve Sax	.50	.20
26 Dodger Stadium	.25	.10
27 Ron Cey	.50	.20
28 Pedro Guerrero	.50	.20
29 Mike Marshall	.25	.10
30 Don Sutton	1.25	.50
NNO Checklist Card	.50	.20
NNO Smokey Bear	.25	.10

1989 Dodgers Mother's

The 1989 Mother's Los Angeles Dodgers set contains 28 standard-size cards with rounded corners. The fronts have borderless color photos, and the horizontally oriented backs have biographical information. Starter sets containing 20 of these cards were given away at a Dodgers home game during the 1989 season.

	Nm-Mt	Ex-Mt
COMPLETE SET (28)	8.00	3.20
1 Tom Lasorda MG	1.00	.40
2 Eddie Murray	1.00	.40
3 Mike Scioscia	.50	.20
4 Fernando Valenzuela	.75	.30
5 Mike Marshall	.25	.10
6 Orel Hershiser	.75	.30
7 Alfredo Griffin	.25	.10
8 Kirk Gibson	.75	.30
9 John Tudor	.25	.10
10 Willie Randolph	.50	.20
11 Franklin Stubbs	.25	.10
12 Mike Davis	.25	.10
13 Mike Morgan	.25	.10
14 John Shelby	.25	.10
15 Rick Dempsey	.50	.20
16 Jay Howell	.25	.10
17 Dave Anderson	.25	.10
18 Alejandro Pena	.25	.10
19 Jeff Hamilton	.25	.10
20 Ricky Horton	.25	.10
21 Tim Leary	.25	.10
22 Ray Searage	.25	.10
23 Tim Belcher	.25	.10
24 Tim Crews	.25	.10
25 Mickey Hatcher	.25	.10
26 Mariano Duncan	.25	.10
27 Joe Amalfitano CO	.25	.10
Manny Mota CO		
Joe Ferguson CO		
Ron Perranoski CO		
Bill Russell CO		
Mark Cresse CO		
Ben Hines CO		
28 Checklist Card	.25	.10
World Championship Trophy		

1989 Dodgers Police

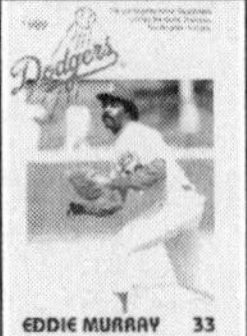

The 1989 Police Los Angeles Dodgers set contains 30 cards measuring approximately 2 5/8" by 4 1/4". The fronts have color photos with white borders; the backs feature safety tips and biographical information. The unnumbered cards were given away by various Los Angeles-area police departments. The cards were also issued as an uncut, perforated sheet to children (age 14 and under) at Dodger Stadium on Baseball Card Night, May 5, 1989.

	Nm-Mt	Ex-Mt
COMPLETE SET (30)	6.00	2.40
1 Ben Hines CO	.50	.20
Ron Perranoski CO		
Tom Lasorda MG		
Joe Amalfitano CO		
Joe Ferguson CO		
Mark Cresse CO		
Bill Russell CO		
Manny Mota CO		
2 Tom Lasorda MG	1.00	.40
3 Jeff Hamilton	.25	.10
4 Mike Marshall	.25	.10
5 Alfredo Griffin	.25	.10
6 Mickey Hatcher	.25	.10
7 Dave Anderson	.25	.10
8 Willie Randolph	.50	.20
9 Mike Scioscia	.75	.30
10 Rick Dempsey	.50	.20
11 Mike Davis	.25	.10
12 Tracy Woodson	.25	.10
13 Franklin Stubbs	.25	.10
14 Kirk Gibson	.75	.30
15 Mariano Duncan	.25	.10
16 Alejandro Pena	.25	.10
17 Mike Sharperson	.25	.10
18 Ricky Horton	.25	.10
19 John Tudor	.25	.10
20 John Shelby	.25	.10
21 Eddie Murray	1.00	.40
22 Fernando Valenzuela	.75	.30
23 Mike Morgan	.25	.10
24 Ramon Martinez	1.00	.40
25 Tim Belcher	.25	.10
26 Jay Howell	.25	.10
27 Tim Crews	.25	.10
28 Tim Leary	.25	.10
29 Orel Hershiser	.75	.30
30 Ray Searage	.25	.10

1989 Dodgers Smokey Greats

The 1989 Smokey Dodger Greats set contain 104 standard-size cards. The fronts and back have white and blue borders. The backs a vertically oriented and feature career totals an fire prevention cartoons. The set depict notable Dodgers of all eras, and was distribute in perforated sheet format. Cards 1-36 a ordered alphabetically and (except for numbe 31) depict Dodger members of the Hall Fame. Cards 37-64 (except for number 57 represent Brooklyn Dodgers whereas cards 65 101 represent Los Angeles Dodgers. The las three cards in the set (102-104) are Hall Famers apparently overlooked in the firs group.

	Nm-Mt	Ex-M
COMPLETE SET (104)	20.00	8.0
COMMON CARD (1-100)	.10	.0
COMMON CARD (101-104)	.30	.1
1 Walter Alston MG	.50	.2
2 David Bancroft	.35	.1
3 Dan Brouthers	.35	.1
4 Roy Campanella	1.00	.4
5 Max Carey	.35	.1
6 Hazen(Kiki) Cuyler	.35	.1
7 Don Drysdale	.75	.3
8 Burleigh Grimes	.35	.1
9 Billy Herman	.35	.1
10 Waite Hoyt	.35	.1
11 Hughie Jennings	.35	.1
12 Willie Keeler	.35	.1
13 Joseph Kelley	.35	.1
14 George Kelly	.35	.1
15 Sandy Koufax	1.50	.6
16 Heinie Manush	.35	.1
17 Juan Marichal	.50	.2
18 Rabbit Maranville	.35	.1
19 Rube Marquard	.35	.1
20 Thomas McCarthy	.35	.1
21 Joseph McGinnity	.35	.1
22 Joe Medwick	.35	.1
23 Pee Wee Reese	.75	.3
24 Frank Robinson	.75	.3
25 Jackie Robinson	2.00	.8
26 Babe Ruth	3.00	1.2
27 Duke Snider	1.00	.4
28 Casey Stengel	.75	.3
29 Dazzy Vance	.35	.1
30 Arky Vaughan	.35	.1
31 Mike Scioscia	.10	.0
32 Lloyd Waner	.35	.1
33 John Montgemery Ward	.35	.1
34 Zack Wheat	.35	.1
35 Hoyt Wilhelm	.35	.1
36 Hack Wilson	.35	.1
37 Tony Cuccinello	.10	.0
38 Al Lopez	.35	.1
39 Leo Durocher	.35	.1
40 Cookie Lavagetto	.10	.0
41 Babe Phelps	.10	.0
42 Dolph Camilli	.20	.0
43 Whitlow Wyatt	.10	.0
44 Mickey Owen	.10	.0
45 Van Mungo	.10	.0
46 Pete Coscarart	.10	.0
47 Pete Reiser	.20	.0
48 Augie Galan	.10	.0
49 Dixie Walker	.20	.0
50 Kirby Higbe	.10	.0
51 Ralph Branca	.20	.0
52 Bruce Edwards	.10	.0
53 Eddie Stanky	.20	.0
54 Gil Hodges	.35	.1
55 Don Newcombe	.20	.0
56 Preacher Roe	.20	.0
57 Willie Randolph	.20	.0
58 Carl Furillo	.20	.0
59 Charlie Dressen	.10	.0
60 Carl Erskine	.20	.0
61 Clem Labine	.10	.0
62 Gino Cimoli	.10	.0
63 Johnny Podres	.20	.0
64 Johnny Roseboro	.10	.0
65 Wally Moon	.20	.0
66 Charlie Neal	.10	.0
67 Norm Larker	.10	.0
68 Stan Williams	.10	.0
69 Maury Wills	.35	.1
70 Tommy Davis	.20	.0
71 Jim Lefebvre	.10	.0
72 Phil Regan	.10	.0
73 Claude Osteen	.10	.0
74 Tom Haller	.10	.0
75 Bill Singer	.10	.0
76 Bill Grabarkewitz	.10	.0
77 Willie Davis	.20	.0
78 Don Sutton	.35	.1
79 Jim Brewer	.10	.0
80 Manny Mota	.20	.0
81 Bill Russell	.20	.0
82 Ron Cey	.20	.0
83 Steve Garvey	.35	.1
84 Mike G. Marshall	.10	.0
85 Andy Messersmith	.10	.0
86 Jimmy Wynn	.10	.0
87 Rick Rhoden	.10	.0
88 Reggie Smith	.20	.0
89 Jay Howell	.10	.0
90 Rick Monday	.20	.0
91 Tommy John	.20	.0
92 Bob Welch	.20	.0
93 Dusty Baker	.20	.0
94 Pedro Guerrero	.20	.0
95 Burt Hooton	.10	.0
96 Davey Lopes	.20	.0
97 Fernando Valenzuela	.35	.1

98 Steve Howe .10 .04
99 Steve Sax .20 .08
100 Orel Hershiser .35 .14
101 Mike A. Marshall .30 .12
102 Ernie Lombardi .75 .30
103 Fred Lindstrom .75 .30
104 Wilbert Robinson .75 .30

1989 Dodgers Stamps St. Vincent

This 18-stamp set was issued by the government of the Caribbean Island of St. Vincent and distributed by Empire of America Federal Savings Bank. The stamps were designed to be placed in a commemorative folder with the 1989 Dodgers team photo printed in the center section. Two players' photos appear on most of the stamps. The stamps are unnumbered and checklisted below in alphabetical order according to the name of the player on the left of the stamp.

Nm-Mt Ex-Mt
COMPLETE SET (18) 10.00 4.00
1 Dave Anderson .50 .20
Alfredo Griffin
2 Tim Belcher .50 .20
Tim Crews
3 Coaches Stamp .50 .20
4 Kal Daniels .50 .20
Mike Marshall
5 Mike Davis 1.00 .40
Kirk Gibson
6 Jeff Hamilton .50 .20
Franklin Stubbs
7 Lenny Harris .50 .20
Chris Gwynn
Billy Bean
8 Orel Hershiser .75 .30
Mike Morgan
9 Jay Howell .50 .20
Alejandro Pena
10 Tom Lasorda MG .75 .30
Jose Gonzalez
11 Eddie Murray 1.50 .60
Willie Randolph
12 Mike Scioscia .50 .20
Rick Dempsey
13 Ray Searage .50 .20
John Tudor
14 Mike Sharperson .50 .20
Mickey Hatcher
15 Fernando Valenzuela .75 .30
John Shelby
16 John Wetteland 1.25 .50
Ramon Martinez
17 Stadium Stamp .50 .20
18 Team Logo .50 .20

1990 Dodgers Mother's

The 1990 Mother's Cookies Los Angeles Dodgers set contains 28 standard-size cards issued with rounded corners and beautiful full color fronts with biographical information on the back. These Dodgers cards were given away at Chavez Ravine to all fans fourteen and under at the August 19th game. They were distributed in 20-card random packets at the game and eight more at the redemption booths. However, both groups of cards were random and there was no guarantee of getting a complete set in the cards. The promotional idea was that the only way one could finish the set was to trade for them. The redemption for eight more cards was done at the 22nd Annual Labor Day card show at the Anaheim Convention Center.

Nm-Mt Ex-Mt
COMPLETE SET (28) 8.00 2.40
1 Tom Lasorda MG 1.00 .30
2 Fernando Valenzuela .75 .23
3 Kal Daniels .25 .07
4 Mike Scioscia .75 .23
5 Eddie Murray 1.00 .30
6 Mickey Hatcher .25 .07
7 Juan Samuel .25 .07
8 Alfredo Griffin .25 .07
9 Tim Belcher .25 .07
10 Hubie Brooks .25 .07
11 Jose Gonzalez .25 .07
12 Orel Hershiser .75 .23
13 Kirk Gibson .75 .23
14 Chris Gwynn .25 .07
15 Jay Howell .25 .07
16 Rick Dempsey .50 .15
17 Ramon Martinez 1.00 .30
18 Lenny Harris .25 .07
19 John Wetteland 1.00 .30
20 Mike Sharperson .25 .07
21 Mike Morgan .25 .07
22 Ray Searage .25 .07
23 Jeff Hamilton .25 .07
24 Jim Gott .25 .07
25 John Shelby .25 .07
26 Tim Crews .25 .07
27 Don Aase .25 .07
28 Joe Ferguson CO .25 .07
Ron Perranoski CO
Mark Cresse CO
Ben Hines CO
Joe Amalfitano CO
Bill Russell CO
Manny Mota CO

1990 Dodgers Police

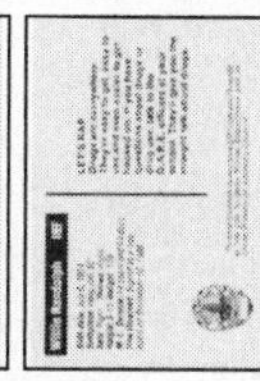

This 30-card set measures approximately 2 3/16" by 4 1/8" and was distributed by both the Los Angeles Police Department and at a pre-season Dodger-Angel exhibition game. This set also commemorated the 100th anniversary of the Dodgers existence. The front has a full-color photo of the player on the front while the back has a brief profile of the player with an anti-crime message. This set is checklisted below by uniform number.

Nm-Mt Ex-Mt
COMPLETE SET (30) 6.00 1.80
1 Tommy Lasorda MG 1.00 .30
3 Jeff Hamilton .25 .07
7 Alfredo Griffin .25 .07
8 Mickey Hatcher .25 .07
10 Juan Samuel .25 .07
12 Willie Randolph .50 .15
14 Mike Scioscia .75 .23
15 Chris Gwynn .25 .07
17 Rick Dempsey .25 .07
21 Hubie Brooks .25 .07
22 Franklin Stubbs .25 .07
23 Kirk Gibson .75 .23
27 Mike Sharperson .25 .07
28 Kal Daniels .25 .07
29 Lenny Harris .25 .07
31 John Shelby .25 .07
33 Eddie Murray 1.00 .30
34 Fernando Valenzuela .75 .23
35 Jim Gott .25 .07
36 Mike Morgan .25 .07
38 Jose Gonzalez .25 .07
39 Jim Neidlinger .25 .07
46 Mike Hartley .25 .07
49 Tim Belcher .25 .07
50 Jay Howell .25 .07
52 Tim Crews .25 .07
55 Orel Hershiser .75 .23
57 John Wetteland 1.00 .30
59 Ray Searage .25 .07
NNO Ben Hines CO .50 .15
Ron Perranowski CO
Mark Cresse CO
Manny Mota CO
Tommy Lasorda MG
Joe Amalfitano CO
Joe Ferguson CO
Bill Russell CO

1990 Dodgers Target

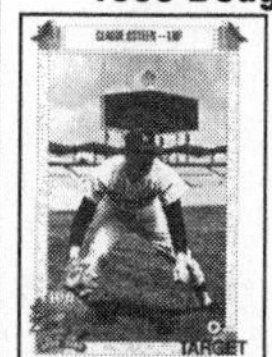
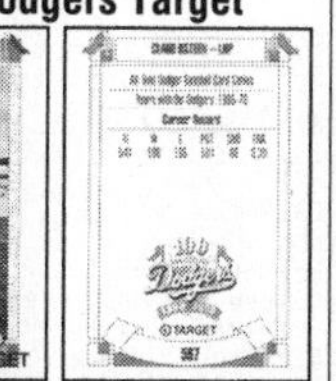

The 1990 Target Dodgers is one of the largest sets ever made. This (more than) 1000-card set features cards each measuring approximately 2" by 3" individually and was issued in large perforated sheets of 15 cards. Players in the set played at one time or another for one of the Dodgers franchises. As such many of the players in the set are older and relatively unknown to today's younger collectors. The set was apparently intended to be arranged in alphabetical order. There were several numbers not used (408, 458, 463, 792, 902, 907, 969, 996, 1031, 1054, 1061, and 1098) as well as a few instances of duplicated numbers.

Nm-Mt Ex-Mt
COMPLETE SET (1106) 125.00 38.00
1 Bert Abbey .10 .03
2 Cal Abrams .10 .03
3 Hank Aguirre .10 .03
4 Eddie Ainsmith .10 .03
5 Ed Albosta .10 .03
6 Luis Alcaraz .10 .03
7 Doyle Alexander .20 .06
8 Dick Allen .50 .15
9 Frank Allen .10 .03
10 Johnny Allen .20 .06
11 Mel Almada .10 .03
12 Walt Alston 1.00 .30
13 Ed Amelung .10 .03
14 Sandy Amoros .20 .06
15 Dave Anderson .10 .03
16 Ferrell Anderson .10 .03
17 John Anderson .10 .03
18 Stan Andrews .10 .03
19 Bill Antonello .10 .03
20 Jimmy Archer .20 .06
21 Bob Aspromonte .10 .03
22 Rick Auerbach .10 .03
23 Charlie Babb .10 .03
24 Johnny Babich .10 .03
25 Bob Bailey .10 .03
26 Bob Bailor .10 .03
27 Dusty Baker .50 .15
28 Tom Baker .10 .03
29 Dave Bancroft .50 .15
30 Dan Bankhead .10 .03
31 Jack Banta .10 .03
32 Jim Barbieri .10 .03
33 Red Barkley .10 .03
34 Jesse Barnes .10 .03
35 Rex Barney .20 .06
36 Billy Barnie .10 .03
37 Bob Barrett .10 .03
38 Jim Baxes .10 .03
39 Billy Bean .50 .15
40 BoomBoom Beck .10 .03
41 Joe Beckwith .10 .03
42 Hank Behrman .10 .03
43 Mark Belanger .20 .06
44 Wayne Belardi .10 .03
45 Tim Belcher .10 .03
46 George Bell .10 .03
47 Ray Benge .10 .03
48 Moe Berg 2.00 .60
49 Bill Bergen .10 .03
50 Ray Berres .10 .03
51 Don Bessent .10 .03
52 Steve Bilko .10 .03
53 Jack Billingham .10 .03
54 Babe Birrer .10 .03
55 Del Bissonette .10 .03
56 Joe Black .20 .06
57 Lu Blue .10 .03
58 George Boehler .10 .03
59 Sammy Bohne .10 .03
60 John Bolling .10 .03
61 Ike Boone .10 .03
62 Frenchy Bordagaray .10 .03
63 Ken Boyer .30 .09
64 Buzz Boyle .10 .03
65 Mark Bradley .10 .03
66 Bobby Bragan .20 .06
67 Ralph Branca .30 .09
68 Ed Brandt .10 .03
69 Sid Bream .10 .03
70 Marv Breeding .10 .03
71 Tom Brennan .10 .03
72 William Brennan .10 .03
73 Rube Bressler .10 .03
74 Ken Brett .10 .03
75 Jim Brewer .10 .03
76 Tony Brewer .10 .03
77 Rocky Bridges .10 .03
78 Greg Brock .10 .03
79 Dan Brouthers .50 .15
80 Eddie Brown .10 .03
81 Elmer Brown .10 .03
82 Lindsay Brown .10 .03
83 Lloyd Brown .10 .03
84 Mace Brown .10 .03
85 Tommy Brown .10 .03
86 Pete Browning .50 .15
87 Ralph Bryant .10 .03
88 Jim Bucher .10 .03
89 Bill Buckner .30 .09
90 Jim Bunning .50 .15
91 Jack Burdock .10 .03
92 Glenn Burke .10 .03
93 Buster Burrell .10 .03
94 Larry Burright .10 .03
95 Doc Bushong .10 .03
96 Max Butcher .10 .03
97 Johnny Butler .10 .03
98 Enos Cabell .10 .03
99 Leon Cadore .10 .03
100 Bruce Caldwell .10 .03
101 Dick Calmus .10 .03
102 Dolf Camilli .20 .06
103 Doug Camilli .10 .03
104 Roy Campanella 5.00 1.50
105 Al Campanis .20 .06
106 Jim Campanis .10 .03
107A Leo Callahan .10 .03
107B Gilly Campbell .10 .03
108 Jimmy Canavan .10 .03
109 Chris Cannizzaro .10 .03
110 Guy Cantrell .10 .03
111 Ben Cantwell .10 .03
112 Andy Carey .10 .03
113 Max Carey .50 .15
114 Tex Carleton .10 .03
115 Ownie Carroll .10 .03
116 Bob Caruthers .20 .06
117 Doc Casey .10 .03
118 Hugh Casey .20 .06
119 Bobby Castillo .10 .03
120 Cesar Cedeno .20 .06
121 Ron Cey .30 .09
122 Ed Chandler .10 .03
123 Ben Chapman .20 .06
124 Larry Cheney .10 .03
125 Bob Chipman .10 .03
126 Chuck Churn .10 .03
127 Gino Cimoli .10 .03
128 Moose Clabaugh .10 .03
129 Bud Clancy .10 .03
130 Bob Clark .10 .03
131 Watty Clark .10 .03
132 Alta Cohen .10 .03
133 Rocky Colavito 1.00 .30
134 Jackie Collum .10 .03
135 Chuck Connors 1.50 .45
136 Jack Coombs .30 .09
137 Johnny Cooney .10 .03
138 Tommy Corcoran .10 .03
139 Pop Corkhill .10 .03
140 John Corriden .10 .03
141 Pete Coscarart .10 .03
142 Wes Covington .10 .03
143 Billy Cox .20 .06
144 Roger Craig .20 .06
146 Willie Crawford .10 .03
147 Tim Crews .10 .03
148 John Cronin .10 .03
149 Lave Cross .10 .03
150 Bill Crouch .10 .03
151 Don Crow .10 .03
152 Henry Cruz .10 .03
153 Tony Cuccinello .10 .03
154 Roy Cullenbine .10 .03
155 George Culver .10 .03
156 Nick Cullop .10 .03
157 George Cutshaw .10 .03
158 Kiki Cuyler .50 .15
159 Bill Dahlen .20 .06
160 Babe Dahlgren .20 .06
161 Jack Dalton .10 .03
162 Tom Daly .10 .03
163 Cliff Dapper .10 .03
164 Bob Darnell .10 .03
165 Bobby Darwin .10 .03
166 Jake Daubert .20 .06
167 Vic Davalillo .20 .06
168 Curt Davis .10 .03
169 Mike Davis .10 .03
170 Ron Davis .10 .03
171 Tommy Davis .30 .09
172 Willie Davis .20 .06
173 Pea Ridge Day .10 .03
174 Tommy Dean .10 .03
175 Hank DeBerry .10 .03
176 Art Decatur .10 .03
177 Raoul(Rod) Dedeaux 1.00 .30
178 Ivan DeJesus .10 .03
179 Don Demeter .10 .03
180 Gene DeMontreville .10 .03
181 Rick Dempsey .20 .06
182 Eddie Dent .10 .03
183 Mike Devereaux .10 .03
184 Carlos Diaz .10 .03
185 Dick Dietz .10 .03
186 Pop Dillon .10 .03
187 Bill Doak .10 .03
188 John Dobbs .10 .03
189 George Dockins .10 .03
190 Cozy Dolan .10 .03
191 Patsy Donovan .10 .03
192 Wild Bill Donovan .20 .06
193 Mickey Doolan .10 .03
194 Jack Doscher .10 .03
195 Phil Douglas .10 .03
196 Snooks Dowd .10 .03
197 Al Downing .20 .06
198 Red Downs .10 .03
199 Jack Doyle .10 .03
200 Solly Drake .10 .03
201 Tom Drake .10 .03
202 Chuck Dressen .20 .06
203 Don Drysdale 2.50 .75
204 Clise Dudley .10 .03
205 Mariano Duncan .20 .06
206 Jack Dunn .10 .03
207 Bull Durham .20 .06
208 Leo Durocher 1.00 .30
209 Billy Earle .10 .03
210 George Earnshaw .20 .06
211 Ox Eckhardt .10 .03
212 Bruce Edwards .10 .03
213 Hank Edwards .10 .03
214 Dick W. Egan .10 .03
215 Harry Eisenstat .10 .03
216 Kid Elberfeld .10 .03
217 Jumbo Elliot .10 .03
218 Don Elston .10 .03
219 Gil English .10 .03
220 Johnny Enzmann .10 .03
221 Al Epperly .10 .03
222 Carl Erskine .30 .09
223 Tex Erwin .10 .03
224 Cecil Espy .10 .03
225 Chuck Essegian .10 .03
226 Dude Esterbrook .10 .03
227 Red Evans .10 .03
228 Bunny Fabrique .10 .03
229 Jim Fairey .10 .03
230 Ron Fairly .20 .06
231 George Fallon .10 .03
232 Turk Farrell .20 .06
233 Duke Farrell .10 .03
234 Jim Faulkner .10 .03
235 Alex Ferguson .10 .03
236 Joe Ferguson .10 .03
237 Chico Fernandez .10 .03
238 Sid Fernandez .20 .06
239 Al Ferrara .10 .03
240 Wes Ferrell .30 .09
241 Lou Fette .10 .03
242 Chick Fewster .10 .03
243 Jack Fimple .10 .03
244 Neal Mickey Finn .10 .03
245 Bob Fisher .10 .03
246 Freddie Fitzsimmons .20 .06
247 Tim Flood .10 .03
248 Jake Flowers .10 .03
249 Hod Ford .10 .03
250 Terry Forster .20 .06
251 Alan Foster .10 .03
252 Jack Fournier .10 .03
253 Dave Foutz .10 .03
254 Art Fowler .10 .03
255 Fred Frankhouse .10 .03
256 Herman Franks .10 .03
257 Johnny Frederick .10 .03
258 Larry French .10 .03
259 Lonny Frey .10 .03
260 Pepe Frias .10 .03
261 Charlie Fuchs .10 .03
262 Carl Furillo .30 .09
263 Len Gabrielson .10 .03
264 Augie Galan .10 .03
265 Joe Gallagher .10 .03
266 Phil Gallivan .10 .03
267 Balvino Galvez .10 .03
268 Mike Garman .10 .03
269 Phil Garner .20 .06
270 Steve Garvey 1.00 .30
271 Ned Garvin .10 .03
272 Hank Gastright .10 .03
273 Sid Gautreaux .10 .03
274 Jim Gentile .20 .06
275 Greek George .10 .03
276 Ben Geraghty .10 .03
277 Gus Getz .10 .03
278 Bob Giallombardo .10 .03
279 Kirk Gibson .30 .09
280 Charlie Gilbert .10 .03
281 Jim Gilliam .20 .06
282 Al Gionfriddo .20 .06
283 Tony Giuliani .10 .03
284 Al Glossop .10 .03
285 John Gochnaur .10 .03
286 Jim Golden .10 .03
287 Dave Goltz .10 .03
288 Jose Gonzalez .10 .03
289 Johnny Gooch .10 .03
290 Ed Goodson .10 .03
291 Billy Grabarkewitz .10 .03
292 Jack Graham .10 .03
293 Mudcat Grant .20 .06
294 Dick Gray .10 .03
295 Kent Greenfield .10 .03
296 Hal Gregg .10 .03
297 Alfredo Griffin .10 .03
298 Mike Griffin .10 .03
299 Derrell Griffith .10 .03
300 Tommy Griffith .10 .03
301 Burleigh Grimes .50 .15
302 Lee Grissom .10 .03
303 Jerry Grote .20 .06
304 Pedro Guerrero .30 .09
305 Brad Gulden .10 .03
306 Ad Gumbert .10 .03
307 Chris Gwynn .10 .03
308 Bert Haas .10 .03
309 John Hale .10 .03
310 Tom Haller .20 .06
311 Bill Hallman .10 .03
312 Jeff Hamilton .10 .03
313 Luke Hamlin .10 .03
314 Ned Hanlon .50 .15
315 Gerald Hannahs .10 .03
316 Charlie Hargreaves .10 .03
317 Tim Harkness .10 .03
318 Harry Harper .10 .03
319 Joe Harris .10 .03
320 Lenny Harris .10 .03
321 Bill F. Hart .10 .03
322 Buddy Hassett .10 .03
323 Mickey Hatcher .10 .03
324 Joe Hatten .10 .03
325 Phil Haugstad .10 .03
326 Brad Havens .10 .03
327 Ray Hayworth .10 .03
328 Ed Head .10 .03
329 Danny Heep .10 .03
330 Fred Heimach .10 .03
331 Harvey Hendrick .10 .03
332 Weldon Henley .10 .03
333 Butch Henline .10 .03
334 Dutch Henry .10 .03
335 Roy Henshaw .10 .03
336 Babe Herman .30 .09
337 Billy Herman .50 .15
338 Gene Hermanski .10 .03
339 Enzo Hernandez .10 .03
340 Art Herring .10 .03
341 Orel Hershiser .75 .23
342 Dave J. Hickman .10 .03
343 Jim Hickman .10 .03
344 Kirby Higbe .20 .06
345 Andy High .10 .03
346 George Hildebrand .10 .03
347 Hunkey Hines .10 .03
348 Don Hoak .20 .06
349 Oris Hockett .10 .03
350 Gil Hodges 2.50 .75
351 Glenn Hoffman .10 .03
352 Al Hollingsworth .10 .03
353 Tommy Holmes .20 .06
354 Brian Holton .10 .03
355 Rick Honeycutt .10 .03
356 Burt Hooton .20 .06
357 Gail Hopkins .10 .03
358 Johnny Hopp .10 .03
359 Charlie Hough .30 .09
360 Frank Howard .30 .09
361 Steve Howe .10 .03
362 Dixie Howell .10 .03
363 Harry Howell .10 .03
364 Jay Howell .20 .06
365 Ken Howell .10 .03
366 Waite Hoyt .50 .15
367 Johnny Hudson .10 .03
368 Jim J. Hughes .10 .03
369 Jim R. Hughes .10 .03
370 Mickey Hughes .10 .03
371 John Hummel .10 .03
372 Ron Hunt .10 .03
373 Willard Hunter .10 .03
374 Ira Hutchinson .10 .03
375 Tom Hutton .10 .03
376 Charlie Irwin .10 .03
377 Fred Jacklitsch .10 .03
378 Randy Jackson .10 .03
379 Merwin Jacobson .10 .03
380 Cleo James .10 .03
381 Hal Janvrin .10 .03
382 Roy Jarvis .10 .03
383 George Jeffcoat .10 .03
384 Jack Jenkins .10 .03
385 Hughie Jennings .50 .15
386 Tommy John .50 .15
387 Lou Johnson .20 .06
388 Fred Ivy Johnston .10 .03
389 Jimmy Johnston .10 .03
390 Jay Johnstone .30 .09
391 Fielder Jones .10 .03
392 Oscar Jones .10 .03
393 Tim Jordan .10 .03
394 Spider Jorgensen .10 .03
395 Von Joshua .10 .03
396 Bill Joyce .10 .03
397 Joe Judge .20 .06
398 Alex Kampouris .10 .03
399 Willie Keeler .50 .15
400 Mike Kekich .10 .03
401 John Kelleher .10 .03
402 Frank Kellert .10 .03
403 Joe Kelley .50 .15
404 George Kelly .50 .15
405 Bob Kennedy .10 .03
406 Brickyard Kennedy .10 .03
407 John Kennedy .10 .03
408 Not issued
409 Newt Kimball .10 .03
410 Clyde King .10 .03
411 Enos Kirkpatrick .10 .03
412 Frank Kitson .10 .03
413 Johnny Klippstein .10 .03
414 Elmer Klumpp .10 .03
415 Len Koenecke .10 .03
416 Ed Konetchy .10 .03
417 Andy Kosco .10 .03
418 Sandy Koufax 8.00 2.40
419 Ernie Koy .20 .06
420 Charlie Kress .10 .03
421 Bill Krueger .10 .03
422 Ernie Krueger .10 .03
423 Clem Labine .20 .06
424 Candy LaChance .10 .03
425 Lee Lacy .10 .03
426 Lerrin LaGrow .10 .03
427 Bill Lamar .10 .03
428 Wayne LaMaster .10 .03
429 Ray Lamb .10 .03

Card		
430 Rafael Landestoy	.10	.03
431 Ken Landreaux	.10	.03
432 Tito Landrum	.10	.03
433 Norm Larker	.10	.03
434 Lyn Lary	.10	.03
435 Tom Lasorda	2.00	.60
436 Cookie Lavagetto	.20	.06
437 Rudy Law	.10	.03
438 Tony Lazzeri	.75	.23
439 Tim Leary	.10	.03
440 Bob Lee	.10	.03
441 Hal Lee	.10	.03
442 Leron Lee	.10	.03
443 Jim Lefebvre	.20	.06
444 Ken Lehman	.10	.03
445 Don LeJohn	.10	.03
446 Steve Lembo	.10	.03
447 Ed Lennox	.10	.03
448 Dutch Leonard	.20	.06
449 Jeffrey Leonard	.20	.06
451 Dennis Lewallyn	.10	.03
452 Bob Lillis	.10	.03
453 Jim Lindsey	.10	.03
454 Fred Lindstrom	.50	.15
455 Billy Loes	.20	.06
456 Bob Logan	.10	.03
457 Bill Lohrman	.10	.03
458 Not issued		
459 Vic Lombardi	.10	.03
460 Davey Lopes	.30	.09
461 Al Lopez	.50	.15
462 Ray Lucas	.10	.03
463 Not issued		
464 Harry Lumley	.10	.03
465 Don Lund	.10	.03
466 Dolf Luque	.30	.09
467 Jim Lyttle	.10	.03
468 Max Macon	.10	.03
469 Bill Madlock	.30	.09
470 Lee Magee	.10	.03
471 Sal Maglie	.30	.09
472 George Magoon	.10	.03
473 Duster Mails	.10	.03
474 Candy Maldonado	.10	.03
475 Tony Malinosky	.10	.03
476 Lew Malone	.10	.03
477 Al Mamaux	.10	.03
478 Gus Mancuso	.10	.03
479 Charlie Manuel	.10	.03
480 Heinie Manush	.50	.15
481 Rabbit Maranville	.50	.15
482 Juan Marichal	1.00	.30
483 Rube Marquard	.50	.15
484 Bill Marriott	.10	.03
485 Buck Marrow	.10	.03
486 Mike A. Marshall	.20	.06
487 Mike G. Marshall	.20	.06
488 Morrie Martin	.10	.03
489 Ramon Martinez	.75	.23
490 Teddy Martinez	.10	.03
491 Earl Mattingly	.10	.03
492 Len Matuszek	.10	.03
493 Gene Mauch	.20	.06
494 Al Maul	.10	.03
495 Carmen Mauro	.10	.03
496 Alvin McBean	.10	.03
497 Bill McCarren	.10	.03
498 Jack McCarthy	.10	.03
499 Tommy McCarthy	.50	.15
500 Lew McCarty	.10	.03
501 Mike J. McCormick	.10	.03
502 Judge McCreedie	.10	.03
503 Tom McCreery	.10	.03
504 Danny McDevitt	.10	.03
505 Chappie McFarland	.10	.03
506 Joe McGinnity	.50	.15
507 Bob McGraw	.10	.03
508 Deacon McGuire	.10	.03
509 Bill McGunnigle	.10	.03
510 Harry McIntire	.10	.03
511 Cal McLish	.10	.03
512 Ken McMullen	.10	.03
513 Doug McWeeny	.10	.03
514 Joe Medwick	.50	.15
515 Rube Melton	.10	.03
516 Fred Merkle	.20	.06
517 Orlando Mercado	.10	.03
518 Andy Messersmith	.20	.06
519 Irish Meusel	.10	.03
520 Benny Meyer	.10	.03
521 Russ Meyer	.10	.03
522 Chief Meyers	.20	.06
523 Gene Michael	.20	.06
524 Pete Mikkelsen	.10	.03
525 Eddie Miksis	.10	.03
526 Johnny Miljus	.10	.03
527 Bob Miller	.10	.03
528 Larry Miller	.10	.03
Wearing a N.Y. Mets uniform		
529 Otto Miller	.10	.03
530 Ralph Miller	.10	.03
531 Walt Miller	.10	.03
532 Wally Millies	.10	.03
533 Bob Milliken	.10	.03
534 Buster Mills	.10	.03
535 Paul Minner	.10	.03
536 Bobby Mitchell	.10	.03
537 Clarence Mitchell	.10	.03
538 Dale Mitchell	.20	.06
539 Fred Mitchell	.10	.03
540 Johnny Mitchell	.10	.03
541 Joe Moeller	.10	.03
542 Rick Monday	.20	.06
543 Wally Moon	.20	.06
544 Cy Moore	.10	.03
545 Dee Moore	.10	.03
546 Eddie Moore	.10	.03
547 Gene Moore	.10	.03
548 Randy Moore	.10	.03
549 Ray Moore	.10	.03
550 Jose Morales	.10	.03
551 Bobby Morgan	.10	.03
552 Eddie Morgan	.10	.03
553 Mike Morgan	.10	.03
554 Johnny Morrison	.10	.03
555 Walt Moryn	.10	.03
556 Ray Moss	.10	.03
557 Manny Mota	.20	.06
558 Joe Mulvey	.10	.03
559 Van Lingle Mungo	.20	.06
560 Les Munns	.10	.03
561 Mike Munoz	.10	.03
562 Simmy Murch	.10	.03
563 Eddie Murray	1.50	.45
564 Hy Myers	.10	.03
565 Sam Nahem	.10	.03
566 Earl Naylor	.10	.03
567 Charlie Neal	.20	.06
568 Ron Negray	.10	.03
569 Bernie Neis	.10	.03
570 Rocky Nelson	.10	.03
571 Dick Nen	.10	.03
572 Don Newcombe	.50	.15
573 Bobo Newsom	.30	.09
574 Doc Newton	.10	.03
575 Tom Niedenfuer	.10	.03
576 Otho Nitcholas	.10	.03
577 Al Nixon	.10	.03
578 Jerry Nops	.10	.03
579 Irv Noren	.10	.03
580 Fred Norman	.10	.03
581 Bill North	.10	.03
582 Johnny Oates	.10	.03
583 Bob O'Brien	.10	.03
584 John O'Brien	.10	.03
585 Lefty O'Doul	.30	.09
586 Joe Oeschger	.10	.03
587 Al Oliver	.30	.09
588 Nate Oliver	.10	.03
589 Luis Olmo	.10	.03
590 Ivy Olson	.10	.03
591 Mickey O'Neil	.10	.03
592 Joe Orengo	.10	.03
593 Jesse Orosco	.20	.06
594 Frank O'Rourke	.10	.03
595 Jorge Orta	.10	.03
596 Phil Ortega	.10	.03
597 Claude Osteen	.20	.06
598 Fritz Ostermueller	.10	.03
599 Mickey Owen	.20	.06
600 Tom Paciorek	.10	.03
601 Don Padgett	.10	.03
602 Andy Pafko	.20	.06
603 Erv Palica	.10	.03
604 Ed Palmquist	.10	.03
605 Wes Parker	.20	.06
606 Jay Partridge	.10	.03
607 Camilo Pascual	.20	.06
608 Kevin Pasley	.10	.03
609 Dave Patterson	.10	.03
610 Harley Payne	.10	.03
611 Johnny Peacock	.10	.03
612 Hal Peck	.10	.03
613 Stu Pederson	.10	.03
614 Alejandro Pena	.10	.03
615 Jose Pena	.10	.03
616 Jack Perconte	.10	.03
617 Charlie Perkins	.10	.03
618 Ron Perranoski	.20	.06
619 Jim Peterson	.10	.03
620 Jesse Petty	.10	.03
621 Jeff Pfeffer	.10	.03
622 Babe Phelps	.10	.03
623 Val Picinich	.10	.03
624 Joe Pignatano	.10	.03
625 George Pinkney	.10	.03
626 Ed Pipgras	.10	.03
627 Bud Podbielan	.10	.03
628 Johnny Podres	.20	.06
629 Boots Poffenberger	.10	.03
630 Nick Polly	.10	.03
631 Paul Popovich	.10	.03
632 Bill Posedel	.10	.03
633 Boog Powell	.30	.09
634 Dennis Powell	.10	.03
635 Paul Ray Powell	.10	.03
636 Ted Power	.10	.03
637 Tot Pressnell	.10	.03
638 John Purdin	.10	.03
639 Jack Quinn	.20	.06
640 Marv Rackley	.10	.03
641 Jack Radtke	.10	.03
642 Pat Ragan	.10	.03
643 Ed Rakow	.10	.03
644 Bob Ramazzotti	.10	.03
645 Willie Ramsdell	.10	.03
646 Mike James Ramsey	.10	.03
647 Mike Jeffery Ramsey	.10	.03
648 Willie Randolph	.20	.06
649 Doug Rau	.10	.03
650 Lance Rautzhan	.10	.03
651 Howie Reed	.10	.03
652 Pee Wee Reese	3.00	.90
653 Phil Regan	.20	.06
654 Bill Reidy	.10	.03
655 Bobby Reis	.10	.03
656 Pete Reiser	.30	.09
657 Rip Repulski	.10	.03
658 Ed Reulbach	.20	.06
659 Jerry Reuss	.20	.06
660 R.J. Reynolds	.10	.03
661 Billy Rhiel	.10	.03
662 Rick Rhoden	.10	.03
663 Paul Richards	.20	.06
664 Danny Richardson	.10	.03
665 Pete Richert	.10	.03
666 Harry Riconda	.10	.03
667 Joe Riggert	.10	.03
668 Lew Riggs	.10	.03
669 Jimmy Ripple	.10	.03
670 Lou Ritter	.10	.03
671 German Rivera	.10	.03
672 Johnny Rizzo	.10	.03
673 Jim Roberts	.10	.03
674 Earl Robinson	.10	.03
675 Frank Robinson	3.00	.90
676 Jackie Robinson	8.00	2.40
677A Wilbert Robinson	1.00	.30
678 Rich Rodas	.10	.03
678B Sergio Robles	.10	.03
679 Ellie Rodriguez	.10	.03
680 Preacher Roe	.30	.09
681 Ed Roebuck	.20	.06
682 Ron Roenicke	.10	.03
683 Oscar Roettger	.10	.03
684 Lee Rogers	.10	.03
685 Packy Rogers	.10	.03
686 Stan Rojek	.10	.03
687 Vicente Romo	.10	.03
688 Johnny Roseboro	.20	.06
689 Goody Rosen	.10	.03
690 Don Ross	.10	.03
691 Ken Rowe	.10	.03
692 Schoolboy Rowe	.20	.06
693 Luther Roy	.10	.03
694 Jerry Royster	.10	.03
695 Nap Rucker	.20	.06
696 Dutch Ruether	.10	.03
697 Bill Russell	.30	.09
698 Jim Russell	.10	.03
699 John Russell UER (Photo actually current catcher John Russell)	.10	.03
700 Johnny Rutherford	.10	.03
701 John Ryan	.10	.03
702 Rosy Ryan	.10	.03
703 Mike Sandlock	.10	.03
704 Ted Savage	.10	.03
705 Dave Sax	.10	.03
706 Steve Sax	.20	.06
707 Bill Sayles	.10	.03
708 Bill Schardt	.10	.03
709 Johnny Schmitz	.10	.03
710 Dick Schofield	.10	.03
711 Howie Schultz	.10	.03
712 Ferdie Schupp	.10	.03
713 Mike Scioscia	.50	.15
714 Dick Scott	.10	.03
715 Tom Seats	.10	.03
716 Jimmy Sebring	.10	.03
717 Larry See	.10	.03
718 Dave Sells	.10	.03
719 Greg Shanahan	.10	.03
720 Mike Sharperson	.10	.03
721 Joe Shaute	.10	.03
722 Merv Shea	.10	.03
723 Jimmy Sheckard	.10	.03
724 Jack Sheehan	.10	.03
725 John Shelby	.10	.03
726 Vince Sherlock	.10	.03
727 Larry Sherry	.20	.06
728 Norm Sherry	.10	.03
729 Bill Shindle	.10	.03
730 Craig Shipley	.10	.03
731 Bart Shirley	.10	.03
732 Steve Shirley	.10	.03
733 Burt Shotton	.20	.06
734 George Shuba	.20	.06
735 Dick Siebert	.10	.03
736 Joe Simpson	.10	.03
737 Duke Sims	.10	.03
738 Bill Singer	.20	.06
739 Fred Sington	.10	.03
740 Ted Sizemore	.10	.03
741 Frank Skaff	.10	.03
742 Bill Skowron	.20	.06
743 Gordon Slade	.10	.03
744 Dwain Lefty Sloat	.10	.03
745 Charley Smith	.10	.03
746 Dick Smith	.10	.03
Wearing a N.Y. Mets uniform		
747 George Smith	.10	.03
748 Germany Smith	.10	.03
749 Jack Smith	.10	.03
750 Reggie Smith	.20	.06
751 Sherry Smith	.10	.03
752 Harry Smythe	.10	.03
753 Duke Snider	4.00	1.20
754 Eddie Solomon	.10	.03
755 Elias Sosa	.10	.03
756 Daryl Spencer	.10	.03
757 Roy Spencer	.10	.03
758 Karl Spooner	.20	.06
759 Eddie Stack	.10	.03
760 Tuck Stainback	.10	.03
761 George Stallings	.20	.06
762 Jerry Standaert	.10	.03
763 Don Stanhouse	.10	.03
764 Eddie Stanky	.20	.06
765 Dolly Stark	.20	.06
766 Jigger Statz	.10	.03
767 Casey Stengel	1.50	.45
768 Jerry Stephenson	.10	.03
769 Ed Stevens	.10	.03
770 Dave Stewart	.30	.09
771 Stuffy Stewart	.10	.03
772 Bob Stinson	.10	.03
773 Milt Stock	.10	.03
774 Harry Stovey	.20	.06
775 Mike Strahler	.10	.03
776 Sammy Strang	.10	.03
777 Elmer Stricklett	.10	.03
778 Joe Stripp	.10	.03
779 Dick Stuart	.20	.06
Wearing a N.Y. Mets uniform		
780 Franklin Stubbs	.10	.03
781 Bill Sudakis	.10	.03
782 Clyde Sukeforth	.10	.03
783 Billy Sullivan	.20	.06
784 Tom Sunkel	.10	.03
785 Rick Sutcliffe	.20	.06
786 Don Sutton	1.00	.30
787 Bill Swift	.10	.03
788 Vito Tamulis	.10	.03
789 Danny Taylor	.10	.03
790 Harry Taylor	.10	.03
791 Zack Taylor	.10	.03
792 Not issued		
793 Chuck Templeton	.10	.03
794 Wayne Terwilliger	.10	.03
795 Derrel Thomas	.10	.03
796 Fay Thomas	.10	.03
797 Gary Thomasson	.10	.03
798 Don Thompson	.10	.03
799 Fresco Thompson	.20	.06
800 Tim Thompson	.10	.03
801 Hank Thormahlen	.10	.03
802 Sloppy Thurston	.10	.03
803 Cotton Tierney	.10	.03
804 Al Todd	.10	.03
805 Bert Tooley	.10	.03
806 Jeff Torborg	.20	.06
807 Dick Tracewski	.10	.03
808 Nick Tremark	.10	.03
809 Alex Trevino	.10	.03
810 Tommy Tucker	.10	.03
811 John Tudor	.10	.03
812 Mike Vail	.10	.03
813 Rene Valdes	.10	.03
814 Bobby Valentine	.20	.06
815 Fernando Valenzuela	.30	.09
816 Elmer Valo	.10	.03
817 Dazzy Vance	.50	.15
818 Sandy Vance	.10	.03
819 Chris Van Cuyk	.10	.03
820 Ed VandeBerg	.10	.03
821 Arky Vaughan	.50	.15
822 Zoilo Versalles	.20	.06
823 Joe Vosmik	.10	.03
824 Ben Wade	.10	.03
825 Dixie Walker	.30	.09
826 Rube Walker	.10	.03
827 Stan Wall	.10	.03
828 Lee Walls	.10	.03
829 Danny Walton	.10	.03
830 Lloyd Waner	.50	.15
831 Paul Waner	.50	.15
832 Chuck Ward	.10	.03
833 John Monte Ward	.50	.15
834 Preston Ward	.10	.03
835 Jack Warner	.10	.03
836 Tommy Warren	.10	.03
837 Carl Warwick	.10	.03
838 Jimmy Wasdell	.10	.03
839 Ron Washington	.10	.03
840 George Watkins	.10	.03
841 Hank Webb	.10	.03
842 Les Webber	.10	.03
843 Gary Weiss	.10	.03
844 Bob Welch	.30	.09
845 Brad Wellman	.10	.03
846 John Werhas	.10	.03
847 Max West	.10	.03
848 Gus Weyhing	.10	.03
849 Mack Wheat	.10	.03
850 Zack Wheat	.50	.15
851 Ed Wheeler	.10	.03
852 Larry White	.10	.03
853 Myron White	.10	.03
854 Terry Whitfield	.10	.03
855 Dick Whitman	.10	.03
856 Possum Whitted	.10	.03
857 Kemp Wicker	.10	.03
858 Hoyt Wilhelm	.50	.15
859 Kaiser Wilhelm	.10	.03
860 Nick Willhite	.10	.03
861 Dick Williams	.20	.06
862 Reggie Williams	.10	.03
863 Stan Williams	.20	.06
864 Woody Williams	.10	.03
865 Maury Wills	1.00	.30
866 Hack Wilson	.75	.23
867 Robert Wilson	.10	.03
868 Gordon Windhorn	.10	.03
869 Jim Winford	.10	.03
870 Lave Winham	.10	.03
871 Tom Winsett	.10	.03
872 Hank Winston	.10	.03
873 Whitey Witt	.20	.06
874 Pete Wojey	.10	.03
875 Tracy Woodson	.10	.03
876 Clarence Wright	.10	.03
877 Glenn Wright	.20	.06
878 Ricky Wright	.10	.03
879 Whit Wyatt	.20	.06
880 Jimmy Wynn	.20	.06
881 Joe Yeager	.10	.03
882 Steve Yeager	.20	.06
883 Matt Young	.10	.03
884 Tom Zachary	.10	.03
885 Pat Zachry	.10	.03
886 Geoff Zahn	.10	.03
887 Don Zimmer		
888 Morrie Aderholt	.10	.03
889 Raleigh Aitchison	.10	.03
890 Whitey Alperman	.10	.03
891 Orlando Alvarez	.10	.03
892 Pat Ankenman	.10	.03
893 Ed Appleton	.10	.03
894 Doug Baird	.10	.03
895 Lady Baldwin	.10	.03
896 Win Ballou	.10	.03
897 Bob Barr	.10	.03
898 Boyd Bartley	.10	.03
899 Eddie Basinski	.10	.03
900 Erve Beck	.10	.03
901 Ralph Birkofer	.10	.03
902 Not issued		
903 Joe Bradshaw	.10	.03
904 Bruce Brubaker	.10	.03
905 Oyster Burns	.10	.03
906 John Butler	.10	.03
907 Not issued		
908 Kid Carsey	.10	.03
909 Pete Cassidy	.10	.03
910 Tom Catterson	.10	.03
911 Glenn Chapman	.10	.03
912 Paul Chervinko	.10	.03
913 George Cisar	.10	.03
914 Wally Clement	.10	.03
915 Bill Collins	.10	.03
916 Chuck Corgan	.10	.03
917 Dick Cox	.10	.03
918 George Crable	.10	.03
919 Sam Crane	.10	.03
920 Cliff Curtis	.10	.03
921 Fats Dantonio	.10	.03
922 Con Daily	.10	.03
923 Jud Daley	.10	.03
924 Jake Daniel	.10	.03
925 Kal Daniels	.10	.03
926 Dan Daub	.10	.03
927 Lindsay Deal	.10	.03
928 Artie Dede	.10	.03
929 Pat Deisel	.10	.03
930 Bert Delmas	.10	.03
931 Rube Dessau	.10	.03
932 Leo Dickerman	.10	.03
933 John Douglas	.10	.03
934 Red Downey	.10	.03
935 Carl Doyle	.10	.03
936 John Duffie	.10	.03
937 Dick Durning	.10	.03
938 Red Durrett	.10	.03
939 Mal Eason	.10	.03
940 Charlie Ebbetts	.30	.09
941 Rube Ehardt	.10	.03
942 Rowdy Elliot	.10	.03
943 Bones Ely	.10	.03
944 Woody English	.20	.06
945 Roy Evans	.10	.03
946 Gus Felix	.10	.03
947 Bill Fischer	.10	.03
948 Jeff Fischer	.10	.03
949 Chauncey Fisher	.10	.03
950 Tom Fitzsimmons	.10	.03
951 Darrin Fletcher	.10	.03
952 Wes Flowers	.10	.03
953 Howard Freigau	.10	.03
954 Nig Fuller	.10	.03
955 John Gaddy	.10	.03
956 Welcome Gaston	.10	.03
957 Frank Gatins	.10	.03
958 Pete Gilbert	.10	.03
959 Wally Gilbert	.10	.03
960 Carden Gillenwater	.10	.03
961 Roy Gleason	.10	.03
962 Harvey Green	.10	.03
963 Nelson Greene	.10	.03
964 John Grim	.10	.03
965 Dan Griner	.10	.03
967 Bill Hall	.10	.03
968 Johnny Hall	.10	.03
969 Not issued		
970 Pat Hanifin	.10	.03
971 Bill Harris	.10	.03
972 Bill W. Hart	.10	.03
973 Chris Hartje	.10	.03
974 Mike Hartley	.10	.03
975 Gil Hatfield	.10	.03
976 Chris Haughey	.10	.03
977 Hugh Hearne	.10	.03
978 Mike Hechinger	.10	.03
979 Jake Hehl	.10	.03
980 Bob Higgins	.10	.03
981 Still Bill Hill	.10	.03
982 Shawn Hillegas	.10	.03
983 Wally Hood	.10	.03
984 Lefty Hopper	.10	.03
985 Ricky Horton	.10	.03
986 Ed Householder	.10	.03
987 Bill Hubbell	.10	.03
988 Al Humphrey	.10	.03
989 Bernie Hungling	.10	.03
990 George Hunter	.10	.03
991 Pat Hurley	.10	.03
992 Joe Hutcheson	.10	.03
993 Roy Hutson	.10	.03
994 Bert Inks	.10	.03
995 Dutch Jordan	.10	.03
996 Not issued		
997 Frank Kane	.10	.03
998 Chet Kehn	.10	.03
999 Maury Kent	.10	.03
1000 Tom Kinslow	.10	.03
1001 Fred Kipp	.10	.03
1002 Joe Klugman	.10	.03
1003 Elmer Knetzer	.10	.03
1004 Barney Koch	.10	.03
1005 Jim Korwan	.10	.03
1006 Joe Koukalik	.10	.03
1007 Lou Koupal	.10	.03
1008 Joe Kustus	.10	.03
1009 Frank Lamanske	.10	.03
1010 Tacks Latimer	.10	.03
1011 Bill Leard	.10	.03
1012 Phil Lewis	.10	.03
1013 Mickey Livingston	.10	.03
1014 Dick Loftus	.10	.03
1015 Charlie Loudenslager	.10	.03
1016 Tom Lovett	.10	.03
1017 Charlie Malay	.10	.03
1018 Mal Mallette	.10	.03
1019 Ralph Mauriello	.10	.03
1020 Bill McCabe	.10	.03
1021 Gene McCann	.10	.03
1022 Mike W. McCormick	.10	.03
1023 Terry McDermott	.10	.03
1024 John McDougal	.10	.03
1025 Pryor McElveen	.10	.03
1026 Dan McGann	.10	.03
1027 Pat McGlothin	.10	.03
1028 Doc McJames	.10	.03
1029 Kit McKenna	.10	.03
1030 Sadie McMahon	.10	.03
1031 Not issued		
1032 Tommy McMillan	.10	.03
1033 Glenn Mickens	.10	.03
1034 Don Miles	.10	.03
1035 Hack Miller	.10	.03
1036 John Miller	.10	.03
1037 Lemmie Miller	.10	.03
1038 George Mohart	.10	.03
1039 Gary Moore	.10	.03
1040 Herbie Moran	.10	.03
1041 Earl Mossor	.10	.03
1042 Glen Moulder	.10	.03
1043 Billy Mullen	.10	.03
1045 Curly Onis	.10	.03
1046 Tiny Osborne	.10	.03
1047 Jim Pastorius	.10	.03
1048 Art Parks	.10	.03
1049 Chink Outen	.10	.03
1050 Jimmy Pattison	.10	.03
1051 Norman Plitt	.10	.03
1052 Doc Reisling	.10	.03
1053 Gilberto Reyes	.10	.03
1054 Not issued		
1055 Lou Rochelli	.10	.03
1056 Jim Romano	.10	.03
1057 Max Rosenfeld	.10	.03
1058 Andy Rush	.10	.03
1059 Jack Ryan	.10	.03
1060 Jack Savage	.10	.03
1061 Not issued		
1062 Ray Schmandt	.10	.03
1063 Henry Schmidt	.10	.03
1064 Charlie Schmutz	.10	.03
1065 Joe Schultz	.10	.03
1066 Ray Searage	.10	.03
1067 Elmer Sexauer	.10	.03
1068 George Sharrott	.10	.03
1069 Tommy Sheehan	.10	.03
1071 George Shoch	.10	.03
1072 Broadway Aleck Smith	.10	.03
1073 Hap Smith	.10	.03
1074 Red Smith	.10	.03
1075 Tony Smith	.10	.03
1076 Gene Snyder	.10	.03
1077 Denny Sothern	.10	.03
1078 Bill Steele	.10	.03
1080 Farmer Steelman	.10	.03
1081 Dutch Stryker	.10	.03
1082 Tommy Tatum	.10	.03

1084 Adonis Terry	.10	.03
1085 Ray Thomas	.10	.03
1086 George Treadway	.10	.03
1087 Overton Tremper	.10	.03
1088 Ty Tyson	.10	.03
1089 Rube Vickers	.10	.03
1090 Jose Vizcaino	.30	.09
1091 Bull Wagner	.10	.03
1092 Butts Wagner	.10	.03
1093 Rube Ward	.10	.03
1094 John Wetteland	.50	.15
1095 Eddie Wilson	.10	.03
1096 Tex Wilson	.10	.03
1097 Zeke Wrigley	.10	.03
1098 Not issued		
1099 Rube Yarrison	.10	.03
1100 Earl Yingling	.10	.03
1101 Chink Zachary	.10	.03
1102 Lefty Davis	.10	.03
1103 Bob Hall	.10	.03
1104 Darby O'Brien	.10	.03
1105 Larry LeJeune	.10	.03
1144 Hub Northen	.10	.03

1991 Dodgers Mother's

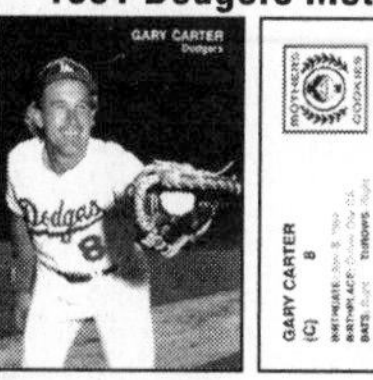

The 1991 Mother's Cookies Los Angeles Dodgers set contains 28 standard-size cards with rounded corners.

	Nm-Mt	Ex-Mt
COMPLETE SET (28)	8.00	2.40
1 Tom Lasorda MG	1.00	.30
2 Darryl Strawberry	.50	.15
3 Kal Daniels	.25	.07
4 Mike Scioscia	.75	.23
5 Eddie Murray	1.00	.30
6 Brett Butler	.75	.23
7 Juan Samuel	.25	.07
8 Alfredo Griffin	.25	.07
9 Tim Belcher	.25	.07
10 Ramon Martinez	.50	.15
11 Jose Gonzalez	.25	.07
12 Orel Hershiser	.75	.23
13 Bob Ojeda	.25	.07
14 Chris Gwynn	.25	.07
15 Jay Howell	.25	.07
16 Gary Carter	1.25	.35
17 Kevin Gross	.25	.07
18 Lenny Harris	.25	.07
19 Mike Hartley	.25	.07
20 Mike Sharperson	.25	.07
21 Mike Morgan	.25	.07
22 John Candelaria	.25	.07
23 Jeff Hamilton	.25	.07
24 Jim Gott	.25	.07
25 Barry Lyons	.25	.07
26 Tim Crews	.25	.07
27 Stan Javier	.25	.07
28 Joe Ferguson CO	.25	.07
Ben Hines CO		
Mark Cresse CO		
Joe Amalfitano CO		
Ron Perranoski CO		
Manny Mota CO		
Bill Russell CO CL		

1991 Dodgers Photos

These photos were issued and feature members of the 1991 Los Angeles Dodgers. They are sequenced in manager and coach order and then alphabetical order by player.

	Nm-Mt	Ex-Mt
COMPLETE SET	20.00	6.00
Tommy Lasorda MG	1.50	.45
Joe Amalfitano CO	.50	.15
Mark Cresse CO	.50	.15
Manny Mota CO	.75	.23
Ron Perranoski CO	.50	.15
Bill Russell CO	.75	.23
Tim Belcher	.50	.15
John Canderlaria	.50	.15
Gary Carter	2.00	.60
0 Kal Daniels	.50	.15
1 Butch Davis	.50	.15
2 Chris Gwynn	.50	.15
3 Carlos Hernandez	.50	.15
4 Orel Hershiser	1.00	.30
5 Jay Howell	.50	.15
6 Stan Javier	.50	.15
7 Eric Karros	2.00	.60
8 Ramon Martinez	.75	.23
9 Mike Morgan	.50	.15
0 Eddie Murray	2.00	.60
1 Jose Offerman	.50	.15
2 Bob Ojeda	.50	.15
3 Juan Samuel	.50	.15
4 Henry Rodriguez	.75	.23
5 Mike Scioscia	1.00	.30
6 Zakary Shinall	.50	.15
7 Greg Smith	.50	.15
8 Darryl Strawberry	.75	.23
9 Dave Walsh	.50	.15
0 Mitch Webster	.50	.15
1 John Wetteland	1.00	.30

1991 Dodgers Police

This 30-card set was sponsored by the Los Angeles Police Department and its Crime Prevention Advisory Council. The cards measure approximately 2 13/16" by 4 1/8". The cards are skip-numbered by uniform number on the fronts.

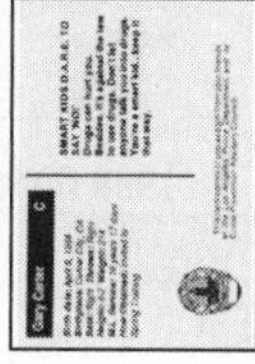

	Nm-Mt	Ex-Mt
COMPLETE SET (30)	6.00	1.80
Jeff Hamilton	.25	.07
Stan Javier	.25	.07
Alfredo Griffin	.25	.07
10 Juan Samuel	.25	.07
12 Gary Carter	1.25	.35
14 Mike Scioscia	.75	.23
15 Chris Gwynn	.25	.07
17 Bob Ojeda	.25	.07
22 Brett Butler	.75	.23
25 Dennis Cook	.25	.07
27 Mike Sharperson	.25	.07
28 Kal Daniels	.25	.07
29 Lenny Harris	.25	.07
30 Jose Offerman	.25	.07
31 Jim Neidlinger	.25	.07
33 Eddie Murray	1.25	.35
35 Jim Gott	.25	.07
36 Mike Morgan	.25	.07
38 Jose Gonzalez	.25	.07
40 Barry Lyons	.25	.07
44 Darryl Strawberry	.50	.15
45 Kevin Gross	.25	.07
46 Mike Hartley	.25	.07
48 Ramon Martinez	.50	.15
49 Tim Belcher	.25	.07
50 Jay Howell	.25	.07
52 Tim Crews	.25	.07
54 John Candelaria	.25	.07
55 Orel Hershiser	.50	.15
NNO Ben Hines CO	.50	.15
Ron Perranoski CO		
Mark Cresse CO		
Manny Mota CO		
Tommy Lasorda MG		
Joe Amalfitano CO		
Joe Ferguson CO		
Bill Russell CO		

1991 Dodgers Rini Postcards 2

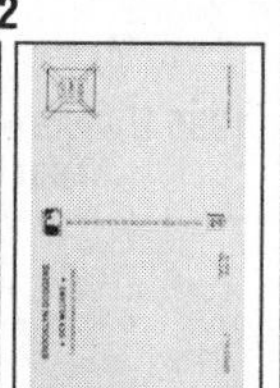

This set of 12 postcards measures 3 1/2" by 5 1/2" and showcases the Brooklyn Dodgers. On a blue background, the horizontal fronts feature color drawings by Susan Rini. The cards are numbered on the back as "X of 12."

	Nm-Mt	Ex-Mt
COMPLETE SET (12)	5.00	1.50
1 Charley Dressen MG	.50	.15
2 Johnny Roseboro	.50	.15
3 Eddie Stanky	.50	.15
4 Goodwin(Goody) Rosen	.25	.07
5 Ed Head	.25	.07
6 Dick Williams	.50	.15
7 Clarence(Bud) Podbielan	.25	.07
8 Erv Palica	.25	.07
9 Augie Galan	.25	.07
10 Billy Loes	.50	.15
11 Billy Cox	.50	.15
12 Phil Phifer	.25	.07

1991 Dodgers Rini Postcards 3

This set of 12 postcards measures 3 1/2" by 5 1/2" and showcases the Brooklyn Dodgers. On a blue background, the horizontal fronts feature color drawings by Susan Rini. The cards are numbered on the back as "X of 12."

	Nm-Mt	Ex-Mt
COMPLETE SET (12)	5.00	1.50
1 Joe Black	.50	.15
2 Jack Banta	.25	.07
3 Whitlow Wyatt	.25	.07
4 Gino Cimoli	.25	.07
5 Dolph Camilli	.50	.15
6 Dan Bankhead	.25	.07
7 Henry Behrman	.25	.07
8 Pete Reiser	.75	.23
9 Chris Van Cuyk	.25	.07
10 James(Junior) Gilliam	.75	.23
11 Don Zimmer	.50	.15
12 Ed Roebuck	.25	.07

1991 Dodgers Rini Postcards 4

This set of 12 postcards measures 3 1/2" by 5 1/2" and showcases the Brooklyn Dodgers. On a blue background, the horizontal fronts feature color drawings by Susan Rini. The cards are numbered on the back as "X of 12."

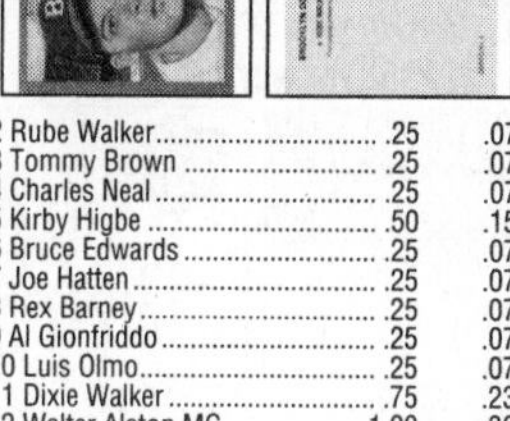

	Nm-Mt	Ex-Mt
COMPLETE SET (12)	5.00	1.50
1 Billy Herman	1.00	.30
2 Rube Walker	.25	.07
3 Tommy Brown	.25	.07
4 Charles Neal	.25	.07
5 Kirby Higbe	.50	.15
6 Bruce Edwards	.25	.07
7 Joe Hatten	.25	.07
8 Rex Barney	.25	.07
9 Al Gionfriddo	.25	.07
10 Luis Olmo	.25	.07
11 Dixie Walker	.75	.23
12 Walter Alston MG	1.00	.30

1991 Dodgers St. Vincent

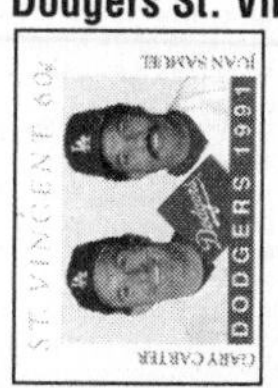

This 18-stamp set was issued by the government of the Caribbean Island of St. Vincent. The stamps were designed to be placed in a commemorative folder with the 1989 Dodgers team photo printed in the center section. Two players' photos appear on all of the player stamps. Manager and coaches share stamps as well. The stamps are unnumbered and checklisted below in alphabetical order according to the name of the player on the left of the stamp.

	Nm-Mt	Ex-Mt
COMPLETE SET (18)	10.00	3.00
1 Stan Javier	.50	.15
Alfredo Griffin		
2 Gary Carter	.75	.23
Juan Samuel		
3 Mike Scioscia	.50	.15
Chris Gwynn		
4 Bob Ojeda	.50	.15
Mitch Webster		
5 Dodger Stadium	.50	.15
6 Brett Butler	.50	.15
Mike Sharperson		
7 Joe Amalfitano CO	.50	.15
Ben Hines CO		
Manny Mota CO		
Ron Perranoski CO		
Mark Cresse CO		
Joe Ferguson CO		
Bill Russell CO		
8 Kal Daniels	.50	.15
Lenny Harris		
9 Dan Opperman	.50	.15
Jim Neidlinger		
Carlos Hernandez		
Henry Rodriguez		
Eric Karros		
Tom Goodwin		
10 Jose Offerman	.50	.15
Roger McDowell		
11 Eddie Murray	.75	.23
Jim Gott		
12 Mike Morgan	.50	.15
Dave Hansen		
13 Darryl Strawberry	.50	.15
Kevin Gross		
14 Tommy Lasorda MG	.75	.23
Jeff Hamilton		
15 Ramon Martinez	.75	.23
Tim Belcher		
16 Jay Howell	.50	.15
Tim Crews		
17 John Candelaria	.75	.23
Orel Hershiser		
18 Zak Shinall	.75	.23
Dennis Cook		
Mike Davis		
Greg Smith		
Mike James		
John Wetteland		

1992 Dodgers Mother's

The 1992 Mother's Cookies Los Angeles Dodgers set contains 28 standard size cards with rounded corners.

	Nm-Mt	Ex-Mt
COMPLETE SET (28)	10.00	3.00
1 Tom Lasorda MG	1.00	.30
2 Brett Butler	.75	.23
3 Tom Candiotti	.25	.07
4 Eric Davis	.75	.23
5 Lenny Harris	.25	.07
6 Orel Hershiser	.75	.23
7 Ramon Martinez	.50	.15
8 Jose Offerman	.25	.07
9 Mike Scioscia	.75	.23
10 Darryl Strawberry	.50	.15
11 Todd Benzinger	.25	.07
12 John Candelaria	.25	.07
13 Tim Crews	.25	.07
14 Kal Daniels	.25	.07
15 Jim Gott	.25	.07
16 Kevin Gross	.25	.07
17 Dave Hansen	.25	.07
18 Carlos Hernandez	.25	.07
19 Jay Howell	.25	.07
20 Stan Javier	.25	.07
21 Eric Karros	1.00	.30
22 Roger McDowell	.25	.07
23 Bob Ojeda	.25	.07
24 Juan Samuel	.25	.07
25 Mike Sharperson	.25	.07
26 Mitch Webster	.25	.07
27 Steve Wilson	.25	.07
28 Mark Cresse CO	.25	.07
Ron Perranoski CO		
Ben Hines CO		
Manny Mota CO		
Joe Amalfitano CO		
Joe Ferguson CO		
Ron Roenicke CO CL		

1992 Dodgers Police

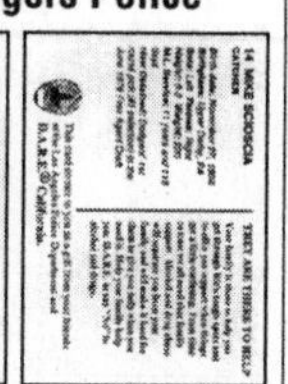

This 30-card standard size set was given out as a promotion at the ball park and was sponsored by the Los Angeles Police Department and D.A.R.E. California. The set, which commemorates the 30th anniversary of Dodger Stadium, features color action photos with rounded corners on a white card face with a navy blue stripe bordering the photos. The cards are skip-numbered by uniform number on the front and back.

	Nm-Mt	Ex-Mt
COMPLETE SET (30)	6.00	1.80
2 Tommy Lasorda MG	1.00	.30
3 Jeff Hamilton	.25	.07
5 Stan Javier	.25	.07
10 Juan Samuel	.25	.07
14 Mike Scioscia	.75	.23
15 Dave Hansen	.25	.07
17 Bob Ojeda	.25	.07
20 Mitch Webster	.25	.07
22 Brett Butler	.75	.23
23 Eric Karros	1.00	.30
27 Mike Sharperson	.25	.07
28 Kal Daniels	.25	.07
29 Lenny Harris	.25	.07
30 Jose Offerman	.25	.07
31 Roger McDowell	.25	.07
33 Eric Davis	.75	.23
35 Jim Gott	.25	.07
36 Todd Benzinger	.25	.07
38 Steve Wilson	.25	.07
41 Carlos Hernandez	.25	.07
44 Darryl Strawberry	.50	.15
46 Kevin Gross	.25	.07
48 Ramon Martinez	.50	.15
49 Tom Candiotti	.25	.07
50 Jay Howell	.25	.07
52 Tim Crews	.25	.07
54 John Candelaria	.25	.07
55 Orel Hershiser	.50	.15
57 Kip Gross	.25	.07
NNO Ben Hines CO	.50	.15
Ron Perranoski CO		
Tommy Lasorda MG		
Joe Amalfitano CO		
Ron Roenicke CO		
Joe Ferguson CO		
Manny Mota CO		
Mark Cresse CO		

1992 Dodgers Smokey

This set measures 3 1/2" by 5 1/2". The cards are numbered in various sequences but the last two numbers are always 92 since that was the year of issue.

	Nm-Mt	Ex-Mt
COMPLETE SET (30)	15.00	4.50
10092 Stan Javier	.50	.15
10192 Roger McDowell	.50	.15
10292 Jose Offerman	.50	.15
10392 Bob Ojeda	.50	.15
10492 Juan Samuel	.50	.15
10592 Mike Sharperson	.50	.15
10692 Mitch Webster	.50	.15
4192 Dodger Coaches	.50	.15
4292 Brett Butler	1.00	.30
4392 Eric Davis	1.00	.30
4492 Orel Hershiser	.75	.23
4592 Ramon Martinez	.75	.23
4692 Darryl Strawberry	.75	.23
4792 Tom Candiotti	.50	.15
4892 Jim Gott	.50	.15
4992 Eric Karros	1.50	.45
5092 Tom Lasorda MG	1.50	.45
5192 Mike Scioscia	1.00	.30
5292 Steve Wilson	.50	.15
5392 Dave Anderson	.50	.15
5492 Todd Benzinger	.50	.15
5592 John Candelaria	.50	.15
5692 Tim Crews	.50	.15
5792 Kal Daniels	.50	.15
5892 Kevin Gross	.50	.15
5992 Kip Gross	.50	.15
9692 Dave Hansen	.50	.15
9792 Lenny Harris	.50	.15
9892 Carlos Hernandez	.50	.15
9992 Jay Howell	.50	.15

1992 Dodgers Stamps Trak Auto

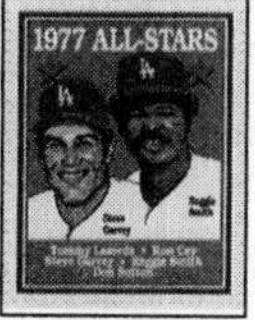

This 32-stamp set salutes the Los Angeles Dodgers All-Stars from 1962 through 1992. They were presented by Trak Auto and Valvoline. The stamps were designed to go into a folder making a frameable print. The stamps are listed below in chronological order according to their all-star years.

	Nm-Mt	Ex-Mt
COMPLETE SET (32)	10.00	3.00
1 Johnny Podres	.20	.06
John Roseboro		
2 Tommy Davis	.50	.15
Maury Wills		
3 Don Drysdale	.75	.23
4 Sandy Koufax	1.50	.45
5 Jim Lefebvre	.20	.06
Phil Regan		
6 Walter Alston MG	.50	.15
7 Tom Haller	.20	.06
8 Bill Singer	.20	.06
9 Bill Grabarkewitz	.20	.06
Claude Osteen		
10 Willie Davis	.30	.09
11 Don Sutton	.50	.15
12 Jim Brewer	.20	.06
Manny Mota		
13 Mike Marshall	.20	.06
Jimmy Wynn		
14 Ron Cey	.30	.09
Andy Messersmith		
15 Rick Rhoden	.20	.06
Bill Russell		
16 Steve Garvey	.50	.15
Reggie Smith		
17 Tommy John	.20	.06
Rick Monday		
18 Tommy Lasorda MG	.50	.15
19 Jerry Reuss	.30	.09
Bob Welch		
20 Burt Hooton	.20	.06
Davey Lopes		
21 Dusty Baker	.30	.09
Steve Howe		
22 Tommy Lasorda CO	.50	.15
23 Mike Marshall	.20	.06
24 Fernando Valenzuela	.30	.09
25 Steve Sax	.20	.06
26 Pedro Guerrero	.30	.09
27 Orel Hershiser	.50	.15
28 Jay Howell	.20	.06
Willie Randolph		
29 Ramon Martinez	.50	.15
Mike Scioscia		
30 Brett Butler	.30	.09
Mike Morgan		
Eddie Murray		
Juan Samuel		
Darryl Strawberry		
31 Mike Sharperson	.20	.06
32 Special Stamp	.20	.06

1993 Dodgers Mother's

The 1993 Mother's Cookies Dodgers set consists of 28 standard-size cards with rounded corners.

	Nm-Mt	Ex-Mt
COMPLETE SET (28)	15.00	4.50
1 Tommy Lasorda MG	1.00	.30
2 Eric Karros	1.00	.30
3 Brett Butler	.75	.23
4 Mike Piazza	8.00	2.40
5 Jose Offerman	.25	.07
6 Tim Wallach	.50	.15
7 Eric Davis	.50	.15
8 Darryl Strawberry	.50	.15
9 Jody Reed	.25	.07
10 Orel Hershiser	.75	.23
11 Tom Candiotti	.25	.07
12 Ramon Martinez	.50	.15
13 Lenny Harris	.25	.07
14 Mike Sharperson	.25	.07
15 Omar Daal	.75	.23
16 Pedro Martinez	4.00	1.20
17 Jim Gott	.25	.07
18 Carlos Hernandez	.25	.07
19 Kevin Gross	.25	.07
20 Cory Snyder	.25	.07
21 Todd Worrell	.50	.15
22 Mitch Webster	.25	.07
23 Steve Wilson	.25	.07
24 Dave Hansen	.25	.07
25 Roger McDowell	.25	.07
26 Pedro Astacio	.50	.15
27 Rick Trlicek	.25	.07
28 Joe Ferguson CO	.25	.07
Ben Hines CO		
Manny Mota CO		
Mark Cresse CO		
Ron Perranoski CO		
Joe Amalfitano CO		
Ron Roenicke CO CL		

1993 Dodgers Police

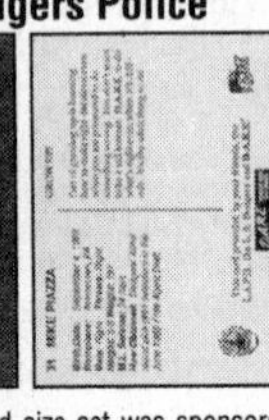

This 30-card standard size set was sponsored by the Los Angeles Police Department, the L.A. Dodgers, and D.A.R.E. Other than the uniform numbers on front and back, the cards are unnumbered and checklisted below in alphabetical order.

	Nm-Mt	Ex-Mt
COMPLETE SET (30)	8.00	2.40
1 Pedro Astacio	.75	.23
2 Brett Butler	.75	.23
3 Tom Candiotti	.25	.07
4 Eric Davis	.50	.15
5 Tom Goodwin	.50	.15
6 Jim Gott	.25	.07
7 Kevin Gross	.25	.07
8 Kip Gross	.25	.07
9 Dave Hansen	.25	.07
10 Lenny Harris	.25	.07
11 Carlos Hernandez	.25	.07
12 Orel Hershiser	.75	.23
13 Eric Karros	1.00	.30
14 Tommy Lasorda MG	1.00	.30
15 Pedro Martinez	2.00	.60
16 Ramon Martinez	.50	.15
17 Roger McDowell	.25	.07
18 Jose Offerman	.25	.07
19 Lance Parrish	.50	.15
20 Mike Piazza	3.00	.90
21 Jody Reed	.25	.07
22 Henry Rodriguez	.50	.15
23 Mike Sharperson	.25	.07
24 Cory Snyder	.25	.07
25 Darryl Strawberry	.50	.15
26 Tim Wallach	.50	.15
27 Mitch Webster	.25	.07
28 Steve Wilson	.25	.07
29 Todd Worrell	.50	.15
30 Joe Amalfitano CO	.50	.15
Ron Perranoski CO		
Ben Hines CO		
Manny Mota CO		
Mark Cresse CO		
Joe Ferguson CO		
Ron Roenicke CO		
Tommy Lasorda MG		

1993 Dodgers Stadium Club

This 30-card standard-size set features the 1993 Los Angeles Dodgers. The set was issued in hobby (plastic box) and retail (blister) form.

	Nm-Mt	Ex-Mt
COMP.FACT SET (30)	8.00	2.40
1 Darryl Strawberry	.25	.07
2 Pedro Martinez	1.50	.45
3 Jody Reed	.10	.03
4 Carlos Hernandez	.10	.03
5 Kevin Gross	.10	.03
6 Mike Piazza	3.00	.90
7 Jim Gott	.10	.03
8 Eric Karros	.50	.15
9 Mike Sharperson	.10	.03
10 Ramon Martinez	.25	.07
11 Tim Wallach	.10	.03
12 Pedro Astacio	.25	.07
13 Lenny Harris	.10	.03
14 Brett Butler	.25	.07
15 Raul Mondesi	.75	.23
16 Todd Worrell	.25	.07
17 Jose Offerman	.10	.03
18 Mitch Webster	.10	.03
19 Tom Candiotti	.10	.03
20 Eric Davis	.25	.07
21 Michael Moore	.10	.03
22 Billy Ashley	.10	.03
23 Orel Hershiser	.25	.07
24 Roger Cedeno	.75	.23
25 Roger McDowell	.10	.03
26 Mike James	.10	.03
27 Steve Wilson	.10	.03
28 Todd Hollandsworth	.25	.07
29 Cory Snyder	.10	.03
30 Todd Williams	.10	.03

1994 Dodgers Daily News

This 18-card set was issued by the Daily News and appeared on a page of their Sports section on certain dates. Originally a 25-card set was planned, but the baseball strike interfered. The cards feature large color action photos of the Los Angeles Dodgers which take up about 3/4 of the page with the pictured player's position and statistics, team schedule information, and the rules to a contest for Dodgers home game tickets taking up the rest of the page.

	Nm-Mt	Ex-Mt
COMPLETE SET (18)	25.00	7.50
1 Raul Mondesi	2.50	.75
2 Orel Hershiser	2.00	.60
3 Henry Rodriguez	1.00	.30
4 Tim Wallach	1.50	.45
5 Tom Candiotti	1.00	.30
6 Delino DeShields	1.50	.45
7 Ramon Martinez	1.50	.45
8 Brett Butler	2.00	.60
9 Kevin Gross	1.00	.30
10 Eric Karros	2.50	.75
11 Pedro Astacio	1.50	.45
12 Cory Snyder	1.00	.30
13 Todd Worrell	1.50	.45
14 Mike Piazza	5.00	1.50
15 Roger McDowell	1.00	.30
16 Chris Gwynn	1.00	.30
17 Jim Gott	1.00	.30
18 Mitch Webster	1.00	.30

1994 Dodgers Mother's

The 1994 Mother's Cookies Dodgers set consists of 28 standard-size cards with rounded corners. A blank slot for the player's autograph rounds out lthe back.

	Nm-Mt	Ex-Mt
COMPLETE SET (28)	15.00	4.50
1 Tommy Lasorda MG	1.00	.30
2 Mike Piazza	6.00	1.80
3 Delino DeShields	.50	.15
4 Eric Karros	.75	.23
5 Jose Offerman	.25	.07
6 Brett Butler	.75	.23
7 Orel Hershiser	.75	.23
8 Henry Rodriguez	.25	.07
9 Raul Mondesi	4.00	1.20
10 Tim Wallach	.50	.15
11 Ramon Martinez	.50	.15
12 Mitch Webster	.25	.07
13 Todd Worrell	.50	.15
14 Jeff Treadway	.25	.07
15 Tom Candiotti	.25	.07
16 Pedro Astacio	.50	.15
17 Chris Gwynn	.25	.07
18 Jim Gott	.25	.07
19 Omar Daal	.25	.07
20 Cory Snyder	.25	.07
21 Kevin Gross	.25	.07
22 Dave Hansen	.25	.07
23 Al Osuna	.50	.15
24 Darren Dreifort	.75	.23
25 Roger McDowell	.25	.07
26 Carlos Hernandez	.25	.07
27 Gary Wayne	.25	.07
28 Ron Perranoski CO	.25	.07
Joe Amalfitano CO		
Reggie Smith CO		
Joe Ferguson CO		
Bill Russell CO		
Mark Cresse CO CL		

1994 Dodgers Police

As part of an annual promotion, this 30-card standard-size set was given out at the home game vs. the Pirates on May 27, 1994. All fans in attendance were given a perforated, uncut sheet of the 30-card set. The set was also available as individual cards. The cards are unnumbered and checklisted below in alphabetical order.

	Nm-Mt	Ex-Mt
COMPLETE SET (30)	6.00	1.80
1 Billy Ashley	.25	.07
2 Pedro Astacio	.50	.15
3 Rafael Bournigal	.25	.07
4 Brett Butler	.75	.23
5 Tom Candiotti	.25	.07
6 Delino DeShields	.50	.15
7 Darren Dreifort	.50	.15
8 Jim Gott	.25	.07
9 Kevin Gross	.25	.07
10 Chris Gwynn	.25	.07
11 Dave Hansen	.25	.07
12 Carlos Hernandez	.25	.07
13 Orel Hershiser	.75	.23
14 Chan Ho Park	1.50	.45
15 Tommy Lasorda MG	1.00	.30
16 Eric Karros	.75	.23
17 Ramon Martinez	.50	.15
18 Roger McDowell	.25	.07
19 Raul Mondesi	1.00	.30
20 Jose Offerman	.25	.07
21 Mike Piazza	2.50	.75
22 Tom Prince	.25	.07
23 Henry Rodriguez	.25	.07
24 Cory Snyder	.25	.07
25 Jeff Treadway	.25	.07
26 Tim Wallach	.50	.15
27 Gary Wayne	.25	.07
28 Mitch Webster	.25	.07
29 Todd Worrell	.50	.15
30 Mark Cresse CO	.50	.15
Manny Mota CO		
Bill Russell CO		
Reggie Smith CO		
Joe Ferguson CO		
Ron Perranoski CO		
Tommy Lasorda MG		
Joe Amalfitano CO		

1995 Dodgers Mother's

The 1995 Mother's Cookies Los Angeles Dodgers set consists of 28 standard-size cards with rounded corners. A rookie year card of Hideo Nomo is in this set.

	Nm-Mt	Ex-Mt
COMPLETE SET (28)	15.00	4.50
1 Tommy Lasorda MG	1.00	.30
2 Mike Piazza	3.00	.90
3 Raul Mondesi	1.00	.30
4 Ramon Martinez	.50	.15
5 Eric Karros	.75	.23
6 Roberto Kelly	.25	.07
7 Tim Wallach	.50	.15
8 Jose Offerman	.25	.07
9 Delino DeShields	.50	.15
10 Dave Hansen	.25	.07
11 Pedro Astacio	.50	.15
12 Mitch Webster	.25	.07
13 Hideo Nomo	8.00	2.40
14 Billy Ashley	.25	.07
15 Chris Gwynn	.25	.07
16 Todd Hollandsworth	.50	.15
17 Omar Daal	.50	.15
18 Todd Worrell	.50	.15
19 Todd Williams	.25	.07
20 Carlos Hernandez	.25	.07
21 Tom Candiotti	.25	.07
22 Antonio Osuna	.50	.15
23 Ismael Valdes	.25	.07
24 Rudy Seanez	.25	.07
25 Joey Eischen	.25	.07
26 Greg Hansell	.25	.07
27 Rick Parker	.25	.07
28 Dave Wallace CO	.25	.07
Bill Russell CO		
Reggie Smith CO		
Joe Amalfitano CO		
Manny Mota CO		
Mark Cresse CO CL		

1995 Dodgers Police

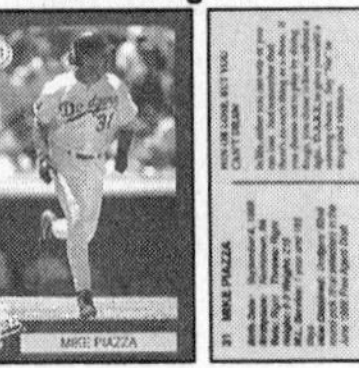

As part of an annual promotion, this 30-card standard-size set was given out at the home game vs. Atlanta on April 30, 1995. All fans in attendance were given a perforated, uncut sheet of this 30-card set. (40,785 sets were handed out.) The fronts feature color action player photos with blue borders. The team logo appears in the lower left, with the player's name inside a yellow bar next to it, while the player's uniform number is printed inside a baseball in the upper left corner. The backs carry player biography and a safety tip, along with the LAPD and D.A.R.E. logos. The cards are unnumbered and checklisted below in alphabetical order. The key card in this set is a rookie year card of international sensation Hideo Nomo.

	Nm-Mt	Ex-Mt
COMPLETE SET (30)	10.00	3.00
1 Billy Ashley	.25	.07
2 Pedro Astacio	.25	.07
3 Rafael Bournigal	.25	.07
4 Tom Candiotti	.25	.07
5 Ron Coomer	.25	.07
6 Omar Daal	.25	.07
7 Delino DeShields	.25	.07
8 Greg Hansell	.25	.07
9 Dave Hansen	.25	.07
10 Carlos Hernandez	.25	.07
11 Todd Hollandsworth	.50	.15
12 Eric Karros	1.00	.30
13 Tommy Lasorda MG	1.00	.30
14 Ramon Martinez	.50	.15
15 Raul Mondesi	1.00	.30
16 Hideo Nomo	5.00	1.50
17 Jose Offerman	.25	.07
18 Al Osuna	.50	.15
19 Antonio Osuna	.25	.07
20 Chan Ho Park	.50	.15
21 Mike Piazza	2.50	.75
22 Eddie Pye	.25	.07
23 Henry Rodriguez	.25	.07
24 Rudy Seanez	.25	.07
25 Jeff Treadway	.25	.07
26 Ismael Valdes	.25	.07
27 Tim Wallach	.50	.15
28 Todd Williams	.25	.07
29 Todd Worrell	.50	.15
30 Mark Cresse CO	.50	.15
Manny Mota CO		
Bill Russell CO		
Reggie Smith CO		
Tommy Lasorda MG		
Joe Amalfitano CO		
Dave Wallace CO		
Ralph Avila CO		

1995 Dodgers ROYs

Consisting of 14 standard-size cards, this team-issued boxed set features all 14 Dodger National League Rookie of the Year winners. The set was not sold but was made available to Dodger season ticket holders and preseason mail order customers. The cards are chromium-plated and feature on their fronts player action cutouts on colorful background designs. The words "Limited Edition," the year the player received the award, and his name are printed on bars superposed on the picture. The horizontal backs carry an oval-shaped portrait, biography, player profile, and statistics, all on a color background (red, green, turquoise, or purple) that varies from card to card. The cards are numbered on the back "X of 14."

	Nm-Mt	Ex-Mt
COMPLETE SET (14)	400.00	120.00
1 Jackie Robinson	120.00	36.00
2 Don Newcombe	30.00	9.00
3 Joe Black	15.00	4.50
4 Jim Gilliam	25.00	7.50
5 Frank Howard	25.00	7.50
6 Jim Lefebvre	15.00	4.50
7 Ted Sizemore	15.00	4.50
8 Rick Sutcliffe	15.00	4.50
9 Steve Howe	15.00	4.50
10 Fernando Valenzuela	30.00	9.00
11 Steve Sax	25.00	7.50
12 Eric Karros	30.00	9.00
13 Mike Piazza	100.00	30.00
14 Raul Mondesi	40.00	12.00

1995 Dodgers Rookie of the Year Pogs

Issued by the Los Angeles Dodgers along with the World Pog Federation, these Pogs feature the Dodgers who were the Rookie of the Year for the Dodgers either in Brooklyn or in Los Angeles. The pogs feature the player's name and photo on the front and the back has an interesting one-liner fact about the player along with his stats the year he won the award

	Nm-Mt	Ex-Mt
COMPLETE SET (14)	5.00	1.50
1 Jackie Robinson	1.50	.45
2 Don Newcombe	.75	.23
3 Joe Black	.25	.07
4 Jim Gilliam	.25	.07
5 Frank Howard	.25	.07
6 Jim Lefebvre	.10	.03
7 Ted Sizemore	.10	.03
8 Rick Sutcliffe	.25	.07
9 Steve Howe	.10	.03
10 Fernando Valenzuela	.75	.23
11 Steve Sax	.25	.07
12 Eric Karros	.50	.15
13 Mike Piazza	1.50	.45
14 Raul Mondesi	.25	.07

1996 Dodgers Fleer

These 20 standard-size cards feature the same design as the regular Fleer issue, except they are UV coated, use silver foil and are numbered "x of 20". The team set packs were available at retail locations and hobby shops in 10-card packs for a suggested retail price of $1.99.

	Nm-Mt	Ex-Mt
COMPLETE SET (20)	5.00	1.50
1 Mike Blowers	.10	.03
2 Brett Butler	.30	.09
3 Tom Candiotti	.10	.03
4 Roger Cedeno	.20	.06
5 Delino DeShields	.10	.03
6 Chad Fonville	.10	.03
7 Greg Gagne	.10	.03
8 Karim Garcia	.10	.03
9 Todd Hollandsworth	.10	.03
10 Eric Karros	.30	.09
11 Ramon Martinez	.20	.06
12 Raul Mondesi	.40	.12
13 Hideo Nomo	.75	.23
14 Antonio Osuna	.10	.03
15 Chan Ho Park	.20	.06
16 Mike Piazza	2.00	.60
17 Ismael Valdes	.10	.03
18 Todd Worrell	.20	.06
19 Logo card	.10	.03
20 Checklist	.10	.03

1996 Dodgers Mother's

This 28-card set consists of borderless posed color player portraits in stadium settings.

	Nm-Mt	Ex-Mt
COMPLETE SET (28)	12.00	3.60
1 Tommy Lasorda MG	1.00	.30
2 Mike Piazza	3.00	.90
3 Hideo Nomo	2.00	.60
4 Raul Mondesi	1.00	.30
5 Eric Karros	.75	.23
6 Delino DeShields	.50	.15
7 Greg Gagne	.25	.07
8 Brett Butler	.75	.23
9 Todd Hollandsworth	.50	.15
10 Mike Blowers	.25	.07
11 Ismael Valdes	.25	.07
12 Pedro Astacio	.50	.15
13 Billy Ashley	.25	.07
14 Tom Candiotti	.25	.07
15 Dave Hansen	.25	.07
16 Joey Eischen	.25	.07
17 Milt Thompson	.25	.07
18 Chan Ho Park	.50	.15
19 Antonio Osuna	.25	.07
20 Carlos Hernandez	.25	.07
21 Ramon Martinez	.50	.15
22 Scott Radinsky	.25	.07
23 Chad Fonville	.25	.07
24 Darren Hall	.25	.07
25 Todd Worrell	.50	.15
26 Mark Guthrie	.25	.07
27 Roger Cedeno	.50	.15
28 Joe Amalfitano CO	.25	.07
Mark Cresse CO		
Manny Mota CO		
Bill Russell CO		
Dave Wallace CO		
Reggie Smith CO CL		

1996 Dodgers Police

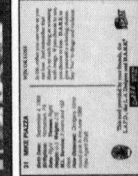

This 30-card set was distributed as a perforate[d] sheet. The fronts feature color action playe[r] photos in blue borders while the backs carr[y] player biography and a safety tip. The cards a[re] unnumbered and checklisted below i[n] alphabetical order.

	Nm-Mt	Ex-Mt
COMPLETE SET (30)	8.00	2.40
1 Billy Ashley	.10	.03
2 Pedro Astacio	.10	.03
3 Mike Blowers	.10	.03
4 Mike Busch	.10	.03
5 Brett Butler	.30	.09
6 Tom Candiotti	.10	.03
7 Roger Cedeno	.20	.06
8 Mark Cresse CO	.10	.03
Manny Mota CO		
Bill Russell CO		
Reggie Smith CO		
Tommy Lasorda MG		
Joe Amalfitano CO		
Dave Wallace CO		
9 John Cummings	.10	.03
10 Delino DeShields	.20	.06
11 Joey Eischen	.10	.03
12 Chad Fonville	.10	.03
13 Greg Gagne	.10	.03
14 Karim Garcia	.30	.09
15 Mark Guthrie	.10	.03
16 Darren Hall	.10	.03
17 Dave Hansen	.10	.03
18 Carlos Hernandez	.10	.03
19 Todd Hollandsworth	.10	.03
20 Garey Ingram	.10	.03
21 Eric Karros	.30	.09
22 Tommy Lasorda MG	.50	.15
23 Ramon Martinez	.20	.06
24 Raul Mondesi	.50	.15
25 Hideo Nomo	1.00	.30
26 Antonio Osuna	.10	.03
27 Mike Piazza	4.00	1.20
28 Milt Thompson	.10	.03
29 Ismael Valdes	.10	.03
30 Todd Worrell	.20	.06

1996 Dodgers Rookies of the Year

This standard-size card was issued as a on[e] card set premium to Los Angeles Dodg[er] season ticket holders. The card features the fi[ve] consecutive Rookie of the Years the Dodge[rs] had from 1992 through 1996. The fro[nt] features a head shot of all five players while t[he] back gives a quick stat line of how the play[ers] did in the year they won the honor.

	Nm-Mt	Ex-Mt
1 Eric Karros	5.00	1.50

Mike Piazza
Raul Mondesi
Hideo Nomo
Todd Hollandsworth

1997 Dodgers DWP Magnets

This five-card set features action color player photos printed on die-cut magnets. The magnets are unnumbered and checklisted below in alphabetical order.

	Nm-Mt	Ex-Mt
COMPLETE SET (5)	12.00	3.60
1 Todd Hollandsworth	1.00	.30
2 Eric Karros	3.00	.90
3 Raul Mondesi	3.00	.90
4 Hideo Nomo	4.00	1.20
5 Mike Piazza	6.00	1.80

1997 Dodgers Fan Appreciation

This three-card set features perforated color action photos of three Dodgers players distributed on a sheet measuring 8 1/2" by 11" that displayed savings on team merchandise. The backs of the player cards carry player information and questions and answers from about that player. The cards are unnumbered and checklisted below in alphabetical order.

	Nm-Mt	Ex-Mt
COMPLETE SET (3)	5.00	1.50
1 Hideo Nomo	1.50	.45
2 Chan Ho Park	1.00	.30
3 Mike Piazza	2.50	.75

1997 Dodgers Mothers

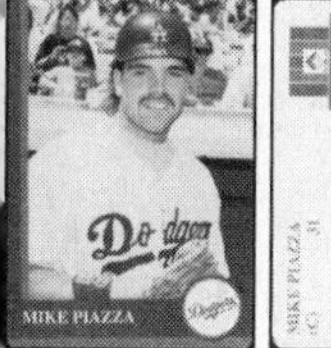

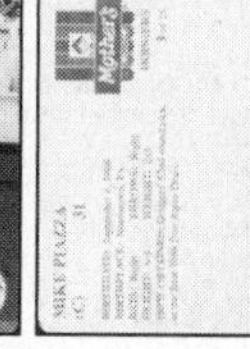

This 28-card set of the Los Angeles Dodgers sponsored by Mother's Cookies consists of posed color player photos with rounded corners.

	Nm-Mt	Ex-Mt
COMPLETE SET (28)	12.00	3.60
Bill Russell MG	.50	.15
Eric Karros	.75	.23
Mike Piazza	2.50	.75
Raul Mondesi	1.00	.30
Hideo Nomo	2.00	.60
Todd Hollandsworth	.25	.07
Greg Gagne	.25	.07
Brett Butler	.75	.23
Ramon Martinez	.50	.15
0 Todd Zeile	.50	.15
1 Ismael Valdes	.25	.07
2 Chip Hale	.25	.07
3 Tom Candiotti	.25	.07
4 Billy Ashley	.25	.07
5 Chan Ho Park	.75	.23
6 Wayne Kirby	.25	.07
7 Mark Guthrie	.25	.07
8 Juan Castro	.25	.07
9 Todd Worrell	.50	.15
0 Tom Prince	.25	.07
1 Scott Radinsky	.25	.07
2 Pedro Astacio	.50	.15
3 Wilton Guerrero	.25	.07
4 Darren Hall	.25	.07
5 Darren Dreifort	.25	.07
6 Nelson Liriano	.25	.07
7 Joe Amalfitano CO	.50	.15

Mark Cresse CO
Manny Mota CO
Mike Scioscia CO
Reggie Smith CO
Dave Wallace CO

3 Checklist	.25	.07

1997 Dodgers Police

This 30-card set features color action player photos in white borders. The backs carry biographical information and a safety tip. The cards are unnumbered and checklisted below in alphabetical order.

	Nm-Mt	Ex-Mt
COMPLETE SET (30)	8.00	2.40
1 Billy Ashley	.25	.07
2 Pedro Astacio	.50	.15
3 Brett Butler	.75	.23
4 Tom Candiotti	.25	.07
5 Juan Castro	.25	.07
6 Darren Dreifort	.25	.07
7 Chad Fonville	.25	.07
8 Greg Gagne	.25	.07
9 Karim Garcia	.50	.15
10 Wilton Guerrero	.25	.07
11 Mark Guthrie	.25	.07
12 Chip Hale	.25	.07
13 Darren Hall	.25	.07
14 Todd Hollandsworth	.25	.07
15 Eric Karros	.75	.23
16 Wayne Kirby	.25	.07
17 Nelson Liriano	.25	.07
18 Ramon Martinez	.50	.15
19 Raul Mondesi	1.00	.30
20 Hideo Nomo	2.00	.60
21 Antonio Osuna	.25	.07
22 Chan Ho Park	.50	.15
23 Mike Piazza	3.00	.90
24 Tom Prince	.25	.07
25 Scott Radinsky	.25	.07
26 Bill Russell MG	.50	.15
27 Ismael Valdes	.25	.07
28 Todd Worrell	.50	.15
29 Todd Zeile	.50	.15
30 Joe Amalfitano CO	.25	.07

Mark Cresse CO
Manny Mota CO
Mike Scioscia CO
Reggie Smith CO
Dave Wallace CO

1997 Dodgers Score

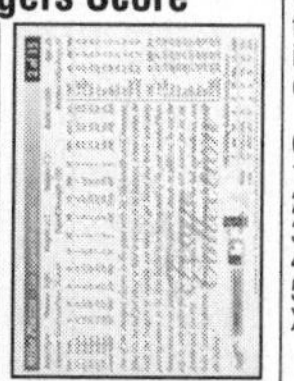

This 15-card set of the Los Angeles Dodgers was issued in five-card packs with a suggested retail price of $1.30 each. The fronts feature color player photos with special team specific color foil stamping. The backs carry player information. Only 100 cases were made for each team. Platinum parallel cards were inserted at a rate of 1:6, Premier parallel cards at a rate of 1:31.

	Nm-Mt	Ex-Mt
COMPLETE SET (15)	5.00	1.50
*PLATINUM: 5X BASIC CARDS		
*PREMIER: 20X BASIC CARDS		
1 Ismael Valdes	.25	.07
2 Mike Piazza	3.00	.90
3 Todd Hollandsworth	.25	.07
4 Delino DeShields	.50	.15
5 Chan Ho Park	.50	.15
6 Roger Cedeno	.50	.15
7 Raul Mondesi	1.00	.30
8 Darren Dreifort	.25	.07
9 Jim Bruske	.25	.07
10 Greg Gagne	.25	.07
11 Chad Curtis	.25	.07
12 Ramon Martinez	.50	.15
13 Brett Butler	.50	.15
14 Eric Karros	1.00	.30
15 Hideo Nomo	1.50	.45

1997 Dodgers Topps Rookies of the Year

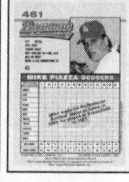

This six-card set honors five recent National League Rookies of the Year who have all been from the Los Angeles Dodgers. The fronts feature the player's rookie card reproduced on special foil board with the N.L. Rookie of the Year stamp. The backs carry player information. Jackie Robinson's 1952 Topps card with a Rookie of the Year designation has been reproduced to celebrate his being chosen as the very first Rookie of the Year recipient. The cards are listed below according to the year in which the player received the Rookie of the Year award.

	Nm-Mt	Ex-Mt
COMPLETE SET (6)	40.00	12.00
1 Jackie Robinson	15.00	4.50
2 Eric Karros	3.00	.90
3 Mike Piazza	12.00	3.60
4 Raul Mondesi	4.00	1.20
5 Hideo Nomo	5.00	1.50
6 Todd Hollandsworth	2.00	.60

1998 Dodgers Fan Appreciation

This three-card set features perforated color action photos of three Dodgers players distributed on a sheet measuring 8 1/2" by 11" that displayed savings on team merchandise. The backs of the player cards carry player information and questions and answers from "Doctor Baseball." The cards are unnumbered and checklisted below in alphabetical order.

	Nm-Mt	Ex-Mt
COMPLETE SET (4)	5.00	1.50
1 Comp Sheet	5.00	1.50
2 Eric Karros	2.00	.60
3 Raul Mondesi	2.50	.75
4 Gary Sheffield	2.50	.75

1998 Dodgers Kids Clubhouse

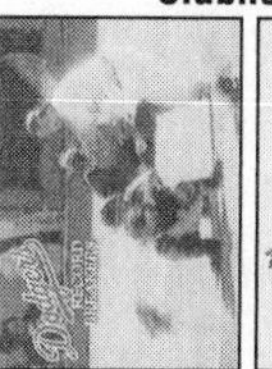

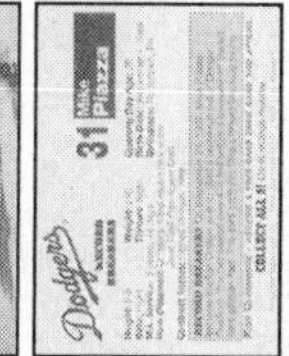

These five cards feature action shots from when various Dodger stars achieved a feat worth noting. The front feature footage from that event while the back has biographical information about the player as well as a description about the event and its significance.

	Nm-Mt	Ex-Mt
COMPLETE SET (5)	10.00	3.00
1 Eric Karros	2.50	.75
2 Raul Mondesi	1.50	.45
3 Ramon Martinez	1.50	.45
4 Hideo Nomo	3.00	.90
5 Mike Piazza	3.00	.90
XX Raul Mondesi	1.00	.30

Membership Card

1998 Dodgers Magnets

These four magnets were issued to honor the four players who were active with the Los Angeles Dodgers in 1998 who had appeared in an All-Star game while playing for the Dodgers at one time. Since the Magnets are unnumbered we have sequenced them in alphabetical order.

	Nm-Mt	Ex-Mt
COMPLETE SET (4)	6.00	1.80
1 Ramon Martinez	1.50	.45
2 Raul Mondesi	3.00	.90
3 Jeff Shaw	1.00	.30
4 Gary Sheffield	3.00	.90

1998 Dodgers Mother's

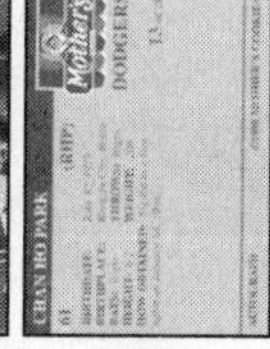

This 28-card set of the Los Angeles Dodgers sponsored by Mother's Cookies consists of posed color player photos with rounded corners.

	Nm-Mt	Ex-Mt
COMPLETE SET (28)	10.00	3.00
1 Glenn Hoffman MG	.25	.07
2 Eric Karros	1.00	.30
3 Bobby Bonilla	.50	.15
4 Raul Mondesi	1.00	.30
5 Gary Sheffield	1.00	.30
6 Ramon Martinez	.50	.15
7 Charles Johnson	.25	.07
8 Jose Vizcaino	.25	.07
9 Scott Radinsky	.25	.07
10 Jim Eisenreich	.25	.07
11 Ismael Valdes	.25	.07
12 Eric Young	.50	.15
13 Chan Ho Park	.50	.15
14 Roger Cedeno	.50	.15
15 Antonio Osuna	.25	.07
16 Dave Mlicki	.25	.07
17 Mark Guthrie	.25	.07
18 Juan Castro	.25	.07
19 Darren Dreifort	.25	.07
20 Tom Prince	.25	.07
21 Jeff Shaw	.50	.15
22 Alex Cora	.25	.07
23 Matt Luke	.25	.07
24 Darren Hall	.25	.07
25 Trenidad Hubbard	.25	.07
26 Jim Bruske	.25	.07
27 Tripp Cromer	.25	.07
28 Joe Amalfitano CO	.25	.07

Mickey Hatcher CO
Charlie Hough CO
Manny Mota CO
Mike Scioscia CO
John Shelby CO CL

1998 Dodgers Police

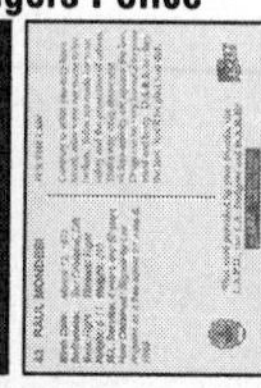

This 30 card standard-size set was issued by the LA Police department and featured members of the 1998 Dodgers Police set. The cards were also available in strips of six along with the purchase of a kids meal at Dodger Stadium. The cards are not numbered so we have sequenced them alphabetically.

	Nm-Mt	Ex-Mt
COMPLETE SET (30)	10.00	3.00
1 Jim Bruske	.25	.07
2 Juan Castro	.25	.07
3 Roger Cedeno	.50	.15
4 Tripp Cromer	.25	.07
5 Mike Devereaux	.25	.07
6 Darren Dreifort	.25	.07
7 Wilton Guerrero	.25	.07
8 Mark Guthrie	.25	.07
9 Darren Hall	.25	.07
10 Todd Hollandsworth	.25	.07
11 Thomas Howard	.25	.07
12 Trenidad Hubbard	.25	.07
13 Eric Karros	.75	.23
14 Paul Konerko	1.00	.30
15 Frank Lankford	.25	.07
16 Matt Luke	.25	.07
17 Ramon Martinez	.50	.15
18 Raul Mondesi	1.00	.30
19 Hideo Nomo	1.25	.35
20 Antonio Osuna	.25	.07
21 Chan Ho Park	.50	.15
22 Mike Piazza	2.00	.60
23 Tom Prince	.25	.07
24 Scott Radinsky	.25	.07
25 Bill Russell MG	.25	.07
26 Ismael Valdes	.25	.07
27 Jose Vizcaino	.25	.07
28 Eric Young	.50	.15
29 Todd Zeile	.50	.15
30 Joe Amalfitano CO	.25	.07

Mark Cresse CO
Glenn Gregson CO
Manny Mota CO
Mike Scioscia CO
Reggie Smith CO

1998 Dodgers Score

This 15-card set was issued in special retail packs and features color photos of the Los Angeles Dodgers team. The backs carry player information. A special platinum parallel set was also issued and randomly inserted in packs.

	Nm-Mt	Ex-Mt
COMPLETE SET (15)	8.00	2.40
*PLATINUM: 5X BASIC CARDS		
1 Hideo Nomo	1.25	.35
2 Mike Piazza	3.00	.90
3 Wilton Guerrero	.25	.07
4 Greg Gagne	.25	.07
5 Brett Butler	.50	.15
6 Todd Hollandsworth	.25	.07
7 Roger Cedeno	.50	.15
8 Chan Ho Park	.50	.15
9 Todd Worrell	.25	.07
10 Ramon Martinez	.50	.15
11 Ismael Valdes	.25	.07
12 Eric Karros	.75	.23
13 Raul Mondesi	.50	.15
14 Todd Zeile	.50	.15
15 Billy Ashley	.25	.07

1999 Dodgers Keebler

This 28 card standard-size set features members of the 1999 Los Angeles Dodgers. The borderless cards are similar to the old Mother Cookie sets and the players photo are in the top half with the the Dodgers Logo and player's name on the bottom in a combination of red, white and blue. The back has

biographical data. Similar to the old Mother's promotions, 20 different cards and eight cards of one number were handed out at a selected game and collectors were encouraged to trade for the missing numbers they needed.

	Nm-Mt	Ex-Mt
COMPLETE SET (28)	10.00	3.00
1 Davey Johnson MG	.50	.15
2 Eric Karros	.50	.15
3 Gary Sheffield	1.25	.35
4 Raul Mondesi	.50	.15
5 Kevin Brown	1.00	.30
6 Mark Grudzielanek	.25	.07
7 Todd Hollandsworth	.25	.07
8 Todd Hundley	.50	.15
9 Jeff Shaw	.50	.15
10 Pedro Borbon Jr.	.25	.07
11 Chan Ho Park	.50	.15
12 Jose Vizcaino	.25	.07
13 Devon White	.25	.07
14 Darren Dreifort	.25	.07
15 Osan Masaoka	.25	.07
16 Dave Hansen	.25	.07
17 Adrian Beltre	.75	.23
18 Ismael Valdes	.25	.07
19 Alan Mills	.25	.07
20 Eric Young	.50	.15
21 Mike Maddux	.25	.07
22 Carlos Perez	.25	.07
23 Tripp Cromer	.25	.07
24 Jamie Arnold	.25	.07
25 Angel Pena	.25	.07
26 Trenidad Hubbard	.25	.07
27 Doug Bochtler	.25	.07
28 Rick Dempsey CO	.25	.07

Claude Osteen CO
Rick Down CO
Manny Mota CO
Jim Tracy CO
Glenn Hoffman CO
John Shelby CO CL

1999 Dodger Kids

These three standard-size cards were originally issued as part of a three-card sheet. The fronts feature player drawings, similar to the 1953 Topps set design. The backs are written in a way similar the early 1950's Bowman sets. Since the cards are unnumbered, we have sequenced them in alphabetical order

	Nm-Mt	Ex-Mt
COMPLETE SET (3)	3.00	.90
1 Adrian Beltre	1.00	.30
2 Kevin Brown	1.00	.30
3 Eric Karros	1.00	.30

1999 Dodgers Police

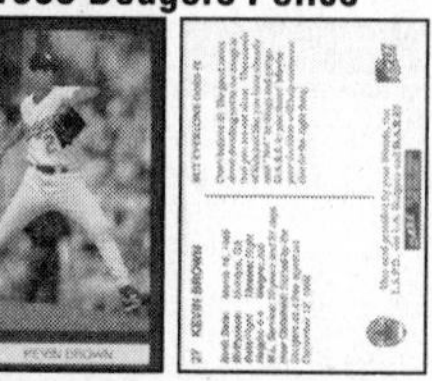

This set measures the standard-size when torn off the perforated strips it was issued on. Since the only numerical identification is the uniform number in the upper left corner, we have sequenced this set alphabetically.

	Nm-Mt	Ex-Mt
COMPLETE SET (30)	10.00	3.00
1 Adrian Beltre	.75	.23
2 Pedro Borbon	.25	.07
3 Kevin Brown	1.00	.30
4 Jacob Brumfield	.25	.07
5 Juan Castro	.25	.07
6 Tripp Cromer	.25	.07
7 Darren Dreifort	.25	.07
8 Mark Grudzielanek	.25	.07
9 Dave Hansen	.25	.07
10 Todd Hollandsworth	.25	.07
11 Todd Hundley	.50	.15
12 Davey Johnson MG	.50	.15
13 Eric Karros	.50	.15
14 Paul LoDuca	1.00	.30
15 Osan Masaoka	.25	.07
16 Alan Mills	.25	.07
17 Raul Mondesi	.50	.15
18 Antonio Osuna	.25	.07
19 Chan Ho Park	.50	.15
20 Angel Pena	.25	.07
21 Carlos Perez	.25	.07
22 Adam Riggs	.25	.07
23 Jeff Shaw	.50	.15
24 Gary Sheffield	1.00	.30
25 Ismael Valdes	.25	.07
26 Jose Vizcaino	.25	.07
27 Devon White	.25	.07

28 Rick Wilkins .25 .07
29 Eric Young .50 .15
30 Glenn Hoffman CO .25 .07
Rick Down CO
Rick Dempsey CO
Charlie Hough CO
Jim Tracy CO
Manny Mota CO

2000 Dodgers Keebler

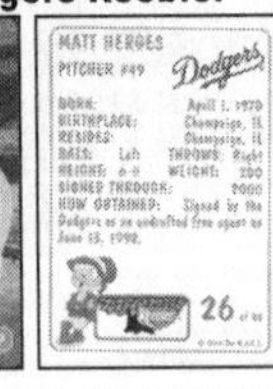

This 28 card standard-size set features members of the 2000 Los Angeles Dodgers and was issued in conjuction with Keebler foods. The front of the borderless cards have a player photo with the bottom devoted to the player's name, The Dodgers logo and the player's position. The back has vital stats.

	Nm-Mt	Ex-Mt
COMPLETE SET (28)	10.00	3.00
1 Davey Johnson MG	.50	.15
2 Eric Karros	.75	.23
3 Gary Sheffield	1.25	.35
4 Kevin Brown	1.00	.30
5 Shawn Green	1.25	.35
6 Mark Grudzielanek	.50	.15
7 Todd Hollandsworth	.25	.07
8 Todd Hundley	.50	.15
9 Jeff Shaw	.50	.15
10 Adrian Beltre	1.00	.30
11 Chan Ho Park	.50	.15
12 Jose Vizcaino	.25	.07
13 Devon White	.25	.07
14 Darren Dreifort	.25	.07
15 Onan Masaoka	.25	.07
16 Dave Hansen	.25	.07
17 Kevin Elster	.25	.07
18 Antonio Osuna	.25	.07
19 Geronimo Berroa	.25	.07
20 Orel Hershiser	.50	.15
21 Chad Krueter	.25	.07
22 Carlos Perez	.25	.07
23 F.P. Santangelo	.25	.07
24 Terry Adams	.25	.07
25 Alex Cora	.25	.07
26 Matt Herges	.25	.07
27 Mike Fetters	.25	.07
28 Rick Dempsey CO	.25	.07

Claude Osteen CO
Rick Down CO
Manny Mota CO
Jim Tracy CO
Glenn Hoffman CO
John Shelby CO

2000 Dodgers Kids

These three standard-size cards were originally issued as part of a three-card sheet. The fronts feature player portraits against a yellow background with "The Los Angeles Dodgers" on top and the player name on bottom with uniform number and position on the side. The backs combine to make a 2000 Dodger Team photo. Since the cards are unnumbered, we have sequenced them in alphabetical order.

	Nm-Mt	Ex-Mt
COMPLETE SET (3)	3.00	.90
1 Shawn Green	1.50	.45
2 Eric Karros	1.00	.30
3 Gary Sheffield	1.50	.45

2000 Dodgers Police

This 30 card standard-size set was issued by the L.A. Police Department and features members of the 2000 Los Angeles Dodgers. This set was issued in five strips of six cards each which were sequenced in alphabetical order. And since the cards are unnumbered except for uniform numbers, we have squenced this set in alphabetical order.

	Nm-Mt	Ex-Mt
COMPLETE SET (30)	10.00	3.00
1 Terry Adams	.25	.07
2 Adrian Beltre	.75	.23
3 Kevin Brown	.75	.23
4 Alex Cora	.25	.07
5 Darren Dreifort	.25	.07
6 Kevin Elster	.25	.07
7 Mike Fetters	.25	.07
8 Eric Gagne	.25	.07
9 Shawn Green	1.25	.35
10 Mark Grudzielanek	.50	.15
11 Dave Hansen	.25	.07
12 Orel Hershiser	.50	.15
13 Todd Hollandsworth	.25	.07
14 Todd Hundley	.50	.15
15 Eric Karros	.75	.23
16 Chad Kreuter	.25	.07
17 Paul Loduca	1.00	.30
18 Onan Masaoka	.25	.07
19 Alan Mills	.25	.07
20 Gregg Olson	.25	.07
21 Antonio Osuna	.25	.07
22 Chan Ho Park	.50	.15
23 Angel Pena	.25	.07
24 Carlos Perez	.25	.07
25 F.P. Santangelo	.25	.07
26 Jeff Shaw	.50	.15
27 Gary Sheffield	1.25	.35
28 Jose Vizcaino	.25	.07
29 Devon White	.25	.07
30 Rick Down CO	.25	.07

Manny Mota CO
Jim Tracy CO
Glenn Hoffman CO
Davey Johnson MG
John Shelby CO
Claude Osteen CO
Rick Dempsey CO

2001 Dodgers Fan Appreciation

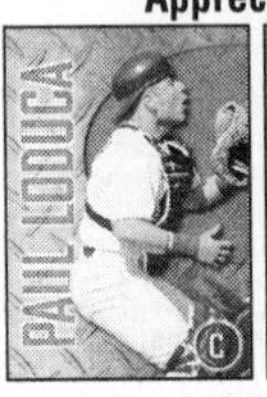

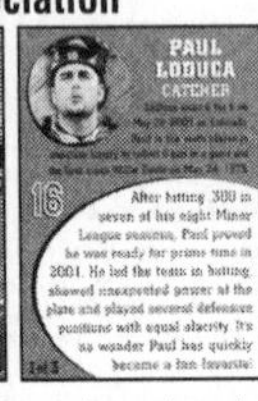

These three standard-size cards were issued on the bottom of a sheet promoting discounted Dodgers merchandise. The fronts have the player's name on the left with their photo on the right. The back of the card have a couple of blurbs about the player and what they mean to the Dodgers.

	Nm-Mt	Ex-Mt
COMPLETE SET	4.00	1.20
1 Paul LoDuca	1.50	.45
2 Chan Ho Park	1.00	.30
3 Gary Sheffield	1.50	.45

2001 Dodgers Keebler

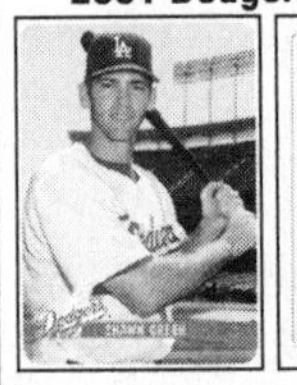

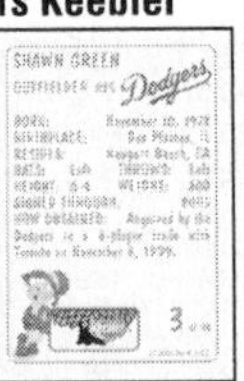

This 28 card standard-size set features the traditionally rounded corners which had been traditionally associated with Mother's Cookies sets. The packs were distributed at a game with 20 different cards and 8 duplicate cards of the same player which were designed to encourage trading to finish one's sets.

	Nm-Mt	Ex-Mt
COMPLETE SET	10.00	3.00
1 Jim Tracy MG	.25	.07
2 Eric Karros	.50	.15
3 Shawn Green	1.00	.30
4 Kevin Brown	1.00	.30
5 Gary Sheffield	1.25	.35
6 Mark Grudzielanek	.50	.15
7 Darren Dreifort	.25	.07
8 Dave Hansen	.25	.07
9 Jeff Shaw	.50	.15
10 Chad Kreuter	.25	.07
11 Chan Ho Park	.50	.15
12 Adrian Beltre	1.00	.30
13 Marquis Grissom	.50	.15
14 Alex Cora	.25	.07
15 Tom Goodwin	.25	.07
16 Gregg Olson	.25	.07
17 Andy Ashby	.25	.07
18 Paul LoDuca	1.00	.30
19 Luke Prokopec	.25	.07
20 Mike Fetters	.25	.07
21 Giovanni Carrara	.25	.07
22 Chris Donnels	.25	.07
23 Matt Herges	.25	.07
24 Jeff Reboulet	.25	.07
25 Terry Adams	.25	.07
26 Hiram Bocachica	.25	.07
27 Jesse Orosco	.50	.15
28 Travis Barbary CO	.25	.07

Jack Clark CO
Jim Colborn CO
Glenn Hoffman CO
Jim Lett CO
Manny Mota CO
Jim Riggleman CO
John Shelby CO

2001 Dodgers Police

This 30 card set (which measures the standard-size when removed from perforation), features members of the 2001 Los Angeles Dodgers. The fronts have blue borders with a player photo covering most of the card, and the player's name in yellow on the bottom. The horizontal backs have biographical information as well as a safety tip. Since these cards are unnumbered, we have sequenced them in alphabetical order.

	Nm-Mt	Ex-Mt
COMPLETE SET (30)	12.00	3.60
1 Terry Adams	.25	.07
2 Andy Ashby	.25	.07
3 Bruce Aven	.25	.07
4 Adrian Beltre	1.00	.30
5 Hiram Bocachica	.25	.07
6 Tim Bogar	.25	.07
7 Kevin Brown	1.00	.30
8 Alex Cora	.25	.07
9 Chris Donnels	.25	.07
10 Darren Dreifort	.25	.07
11 Mike Fetters	.25	.07
12 Eric Gagne	.25	.07
13 Tom Goodwin	.25	.07
14 Shawn Green	1.25	.35
15 Marquis Grissom	.50	.15
16 Mark Grudzielanek	.25	.07
17 Dave Hansen	.25	.07
18 Matt Herges	.25	.07
19 Eric Karros	.50	.15
20 Chad Kreuter	.25	.07
21 Paul LoDuca	1.00	.30
22 Onan Masaoka	.25	.07
23 Jose Nunez	.25	.07
24 Gregg Olson	.25	.07
25 Chan Ho Park	.50	.15
26 Angel Pena	.25	.07
27 Jeff Reboulet	.25	.07
28 Jeff Shaw	.50	.15
29 Gary Sheffield	1.25	.35
30 Jack Clark CO	.25	.07

Jim Lett CO
Jim Riggleman CO
Manny Mota CO
Jim Tracy MG
John Shelby CO
Glenn Hoffman CO
Jim Colborn CO
Travis Barbary CO

2001 Dodgers Upper Deck Collectibles

This 21 card standard-size set was issued in its own special box and featured members of the Los Angeles Dodgers. Card number 21, which measured 5 by 3 1/2" highlights some of the best moments in the Dodgers history. All cards in this set have an "LA" prefix.

	Nm-Mt	Ex-Mt
COMP.FACT SET (21)	12.00	3.60
LA1 Gary Sheffield	1.00	.30
LA2 Shawn Green	1.50	.45
LA3 Kevin Brown	1.00	.30
LA4 Adrian Beltre	.75	.23
LA5 Eric Karros	.75	.23
LA6 Darren Dreifort	.25	.07
LA7 Chan Ho Park	.50	.15
LA8 Alex Cora	.25	.07
LA9 Mark Grudzielanek	.25	.07
LA10 Paul LoDuca	1.00	.30
LA11 Dave Hansen	.25	.07
LA12 Tom Goodwin	.25	.07
LA13 Ramon Martinez	.25	.07
LA14 Luke Prokopec	.25	.07
LA15 Chad Krueter	.25	.07
LA16 Jeff Shaw	.50	.15
LA17 Erig Gagne	2.00	.60
LA18 Andy Ashby	.25	.07
LA19 F.P. Santangelo	.25	.07
LA20 Mike Fetters	.25	.07
LA21 Gary Sheffield	3.00	.90

Eric Karros
Kevin Brown
Adrian Beltre
Shawn Green
Darren Dreifort
Checklist
Card measures 5 by 3 1/2"

2002 Dodgers Keebler

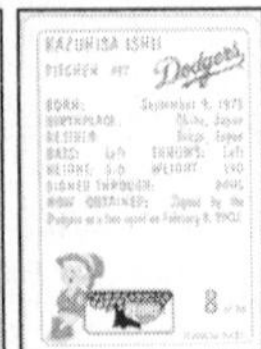

This 28-card standard-size set was issued at a Dodgers game during the 2002 season. These rounded-corner full-bleed cards have player portraits on the front and some biographical information about each player on the back.

	Nm-Mt	Ex-Mt
COMPLETE SET	12.00	3.60
1 Jim Tracy MG	.25	.07
2 Eric Karros	.50	.15
3 Shawn Green	1.25	.35
4 Kevin Brown	1.00	.30
5 Paul Lo Duca	1.00	.30
6 Mark Grudzielanek	.50	.15
7 Brian Jordan	.50	.15
8 Kazuhisa Ishii	1.50	.45
9 Dave Hansen	.25	.07
10 Chad Kreuter	.25	.07
11 Hideo Nomo	1.00	.30
12 Adrian Beltre	.75	.23
13 Marquis Grissom	.50	.15
14 Eric Gagne	1.25	.35
15 Odalis Perez	1.00	.30
16 Dave Roberts	.25	.07
17 Omar Daal	.25	.07
18 Alex Cora	.25	.07
19 Andy Ashby	.25	.07
20 Hiram Bocachica	.25	.07
21 Darren Dreifort	.25	.07
22 Jesse Orosco	.50	.15
23 Cesar Izturis	.25	.07
24 Terry Mulholland	.25	.07
25 Jeff Reboulet	.25	.07
26 Paul Quantrill	.50	.15
27 Giovanni Carrara	.25	.07
28 Jack Clark CO	.25	.07

Jim Colborn CO
Robert Flippo CO
Glenn Hoffman CO
Jim Lett CO
Manny Mota CO
Jim Riggleman CO
John Shelby CO

2002 Dodgers Police

When cut from sheets, this 30 card set measures the standard size. As has been the tradition the L.A. Police Department issues this set featuring members of the Los Angeles Dodgers. The cards have full color action photos surrounded by blue borders. The player's uniform number is located on the upper left corner while their name in set in yellow on the bottom. Since these cards are unnumbered, we have sequenced them in alphabetical order.

	Nm-Mt	Ex-Mt
COMPLETE SET	12.00	3.60
1 Andy Ashby	.25	.07
2 Adrian Beltre	.75	.23
3 Hiram Bocachica	.25	.07
4 Jeff Branson	.25	.07
5 Kevin Brown	1.00	.30
6 Giovanni Carrara	.25	.07
7 Alex Cora	.25	.07
8 Omar Daal	.25	.07
9 Darren Dreifort	.25	.07
10 Eric Gagne	1.50	.45
11 Shawn Green	1.50	.45
12 Marquis Grissom	.50	.15
13 Mark Grudzielanek	.50	.15
14 Dave Hansen	.25	.07
15 Phil Hiatt	.25	.07
16 Kazuhisa Ishii	3.00	.90
17 Cesar Izturis	.25	.07
18 Brian Jordan	.50	.15
19 Eric Karros	.75	.23
20 Mike Kinkade	.25	.07
21 Chad Kreuter	.25	.07
22 Paul LoDuca	1.00	.30
23 Terry Mulholland	.25	.07
24 Hideo Nomo	1.50	.45
25 Jesse Orosco	.50	.15
26 Odalis Perez	.75	.23
27 Paul Quantrill	.50	.15
28 Jeff Reboulet	.25	.07
29 Dave Roberts	.25	.07
30 Jim Tracy MG	.25	.07

Jack Clark CO
Jim Lett CO
Jim Riggleman CO
Manny Mota CO
John Shelby CO
Glenn Hoffman CO
Jim Colborn CO
Rob Flippo CO

2003 Dodgers Fan Appreciation

This three-card standard size set was issued at a late season Dodger game as a promotion to say thanks to the many fans who attended Dodger games in 2003. The full-color fronts feature the player's against a full-bleed border with their name, and uniform number in a pennant element. The back has biographical information as well as a brief informational blurb. Since these cards are unnumbered, we have sequenced them in alphabetical order.

	MINT	NRMT
COMPLETE SET (3)	5.00	2.20
1 Eric Gagne	2.50	1.10
2 Paul LoDuca	2.00	.90
3 Hideo Nomo	2.50	1.10

2003 Dodgers Keebler

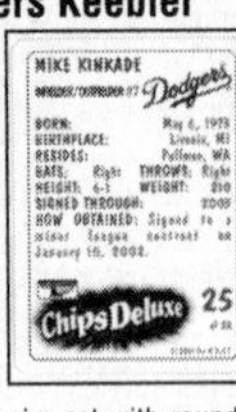

This 28 card standard-size set with rounded corners features members of the 2003 Los Angeles Dodgers. These cards were given away at a Dodgers game with each fan receiving 20 different cards and eight of the same card they could trade to finish their set.

	MINT	NRMT
COMPLETE SET (28)	12.00	5.50
1 Jim Tracy MG	.25	.11
2 Shawn Green	1.25	.55
3 Paul Lo Duca	1.00	.45
4 Kevin Brown	1.00	.45
5 Adrian Beltre	.75	.35
6 Eric Gagne	1.50	.70
7 Brian Jordan	.50	.23
8 Kazuhisa Ishii	1.00	.45
9 Fred McGriff	.75	.35
10 Dave Roberts	.25	.11
11 Hideo Nomo	1.25	.55
12 Alex Cora	.25	.11
13 Paul Quantrill	.50	.23
14 Darren Dreifort	.25	.11
15 Odalis Perez	.75	.35
16 Cesar Izturis	.25	.11
17 Todd Hundley	.25	.11
18 Daryle Ward	.25	.11
19 Paul Shuey	.25	.11
20 Guillermo Mota	.25	.11
21 Andy Ashby	.25	.11
22 Tom Martin	.25	.11
23 Jason Romano	.25	.11
24 Jolbert Cabrera	.25	.11
25 Mike Kinkade	.25	.11
26 Ron Coomer	.25	.11
27 David Ross	.25	.11
28 Jack Clark CO	.25	.11

Jim Colborn CO
Robert Flippo CO
Glenn Hoffman CO
Jim Lett CO
Manny Mota
Jim Rigglman CO
John Shelby CO

2003 Dodgers Police

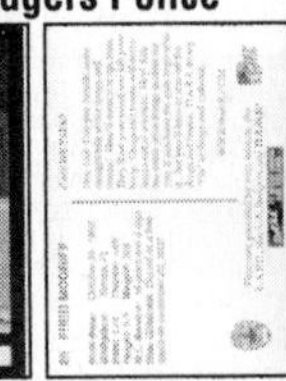

This 30-card set measures the standard-size when removed from the perforated sheet. The player photo's are surrounded by blue borders and his name is set in black ink against a yellow background. The player's uniform number is located in the upper left corner. The back has biographical information as well as a safety tip. Since the cards are not numbered we have sequenced them in alphabetical order.

	Nm-Mt	Ex-Mt
COMPLETE SET (30)	10.00	3.00
1 Victor Alvarez	.25	.07
2 Andy Ashby	.25	.07
3 Adrian Beltre	.75	.23
4 Troy Brohawn	.25	.07
5 Kevin Brown	1.00	.30
6 Jolbert Cabrera	.25	.07
7 Chin-Feng Chen	1.00	.30
8 Ron Coomer	.25	.07
9 Alex Cora	.25	.07
10 Darren Dreifort	.25	.07
11 Eric Gagne	1.50	.45
12 Shawn Green	1.25	.35
13 Chad Hermansen	.25	.07
14 Todd Hundley	.25	.07
15 Kazuhisa Ishii	1.25	.35
16 Cesar Izturis	.25	.07
17 Brian Jordan	.50	.15
18 Mike Kinkade	.25	.07
19 Paul Lo Duca	1.00	.30
20 Fred McGriff	.75	.23
21 Guillermo Mota	.25	.07
22 Hideo Nomo	1.25	.35
23 Odalis Perez	.75	.23
24 Paul Quantrill	.50	.1
25 Dave Roberts	.25	.07
26 David Ross	.25	.07
27 Wilkin Ruan	.25	.07
28 Paul Shuey	.25	.07
29 Daryle Ward	.25	.07
30 Jack Clark CO	.25	.07

Jim Lett CO
Jim Riggleman CO
Manny Mota CO
Jim Tracy MG
John Shelby CO
Glenn Hoffman CO
Jim Colborn CO
Rob Flippo CO

1955-62 Don Wingfield

This set of black and white and color postcards was first issued in 1955 and consists of three diffferent types. Type 1 postcards consist of Washington Senatos only and feature the player's name - Washington National copyright 1955 - Don Wingfield, Griffi

Stadium, Washington, D.C., at the base of the front. The type 2 postcards feature players from many teams and present the player's name on the back down the center of the card. The type 3 postcard is in color and consists of but one card (Killebrew). Multiple player poses of several of the Type 2 postcards exist. Cards 1-9 are Type 1 card, Cards 10-43 are Type 2 and Card 44 is Type 3.

	NM	Ex
COMPLETE SET (43)	500.00	250.00
1 Jim Busby	5.00	2.50
2 Charley Dressen MG	20.00	10.00
3 Ed Fitzgerald	20.00	10.00
4 Bob Porterfield	5.00	2.50
5 Roy Sievers	20.00	10.00
6 Chuck Stobbs	20.00	10.00
7 Dean Stone	20.00	10.00
8 Mickey Vernon	20.00	10.00
9 Eddie Yost	20.00	10.00
10 Ted Abernathy	5.00	2.50
11 Bob Allison (2)	5.00	2.50
12 Ernie Banks	25.00	12.50
13 Earl Battey	5.00	2.50
14 Norm Cash	10.00	5.00
15 Jim Coates	5.00	2.50
16 Rocky Colavito	15.00	7.50
17 Chuck Cottier	5.00	2.50
18 Bennie Daniels	5.00	2.50
19 Dan Dobbek	5.00	2.50
20 Nellie Fox	15.00	7.50
21 Jim Gentile	5.00	2.50
22 Gene Green	5.00	2.50
23 Steve Hamilton	5.00	2.50
24 Ken Hamlin	5.00	2.50
25 Rudy Hernandez	5.00	2.50
26 Ed Hobaugh	5.00	2.50
27 Elston Howard	15.00	7.50
28 Bob Johnson	5.00	2.50
29 Russ Kemmerer	5.00	2.50
30 Harmon Killebrew (3)	20.00	10.00
31 Dale Long	5.00	2.50
32 Mickey Mantle	50.00	25.00
33 Roger Maris	25.00	12.50
34 Willie Mays	30.00	15.00
35 Stan Musial	30.00	15.00
36 Claude Osteen	5.00	2.50
37 Ken Retzer	5.00	2.50
38 Brooks Robinson	20.00	10.00
39 Dick Rudolph	5.00	2.50
40 Dave Stenhouse	5.00	2.50
41 Jose Valdivielso	5.00	2.50
42 Gene Woodling	10.00	5.00
43 Bud Zipfel	5.00	2.50
44 Harmon Killebrew	20.00	10.00

1981 Donruss Test

These cards were issued in very limited quantities and were distributed as part of a test to see how collectors liked the original design for the 1981 Donruss set. According to published reports somewhere between 400 and 500 each of these cards were produced for this test. These were issued either seperately or as part of a three card strip

	Nm-Mt	Ex-Mt
COMPLETE SET (3)	40.00	16.00
1 George Brett	20.00	8.00
2 Reggie Jackson	20.00	8.00
3 Test Photo	1.00	.40
4 Uncut Strip	40.00	16.00

1981 Donruss

In 1981 Donruss launched itself into the baseball card market with a 600-card set. Wax packs contained 15 cards as well as a piece of gum. This would be the only year that Donruss was allowed to have any confectionary product in their packs. The standard-size cards are printed on thin stock and more than one pose exists for several popular players. Numerous errors of the first print run were later corrected by the company. These are marked P1 and P2 in our checklist below. According to published reports at the time, approximately 500 sets were made available in uncut sheet form. The key Rookie Cards in this set are Danny Ainge, Tim Raines, and Jeff Reardon.

	Nm-Mt	Ex-Mt
COMPLETE SET (605)	40.00	16.00
1 Ozzie Smith	3.00	1.20
2 Rollie Fingers	.25	.10
3 Rick Wise	.10	.04
4 Gene Richards	.10	.04
5 Alan Trammell	1.00	.40
6 Tom Brookens	.10	.04
7A Duffy Dyer P1	.25	.10
1980 batting average has decimal point		
7B Duffy Dyer P2	.10	.04
1980 batting average has no decimal point		
8 Mark Fidrych	1.00	.40
9 Dave Rozema	.10	.04
10 Ricky Peters	.10	.04
11 Mike Schmidt	2.50	1.00
12 Willie Stargell	.50	.20
13 Tim Foli	.10	.04
14 Manny Sanguillen	.25	.10
15 Grant Jackson	.10	.04
16 Eddie Solomon	.10	.04
17 Omar Moreno	.10	.04
18 Joe Morgan	.50	.20
19 Rafael Landestoy	.10	.04
20 Bruce Bochy	.10	.04
21 Joe Sambito	.10	.04
22 Manny Trillo	.10	.04
23A Dave Smith RC P1	.25	.10
Line box around stats is not complete		
23B Dave Smith RC P2	.25	.10
Box totally encloses stats at top		
24 Terry Puhl	.10	.04
25 Bump Wills	.10	.04
26A John Ellis P1 ERR	.50	.20
Danny Walton photo on front		
26B John Ellis P2 COR	.25	.10
27 Jim Kern	.10	.04
28 Richie Zisk	.10	.04
29 John Mayberry	.10	.04
30 Bob Davis	.10	.04
31 Jackson Todd	.10	.04
32 Alvis Woods	.10	.04
33 Steve Carlton	.25	.10
34 Lee Mazzilli	.10	.04
35 John Stearns	.10	.04
36 Roy Lee Jackson	.10	.04
37 Mike Scott	.25	.10
38 Lamar Johnson	.10	.04
39 Kevin Bell	.10	.04
40 Ed Farmer	.10	.04
41 Ross Baumgarten	.10	.04
42 Leo Sutherland	.10	.04
43 Dan Meyer	.10	.04
44 Ron Reed	.10	.04
45 Mario Mendoza	.10	.04
46 Rick Honeycutt	.10	.04
47 Glenn Abbott	.10	.04
48 Leon Roberts	.10	.04
49 Rod Carew	.50	.20
50 Bert Campaneris	.25	.10
51A T.Donahue P1 ERR	.25	.10
Name on front misspelled Donahue		
51B Tom Donohue P2 COR	.10	.04
52 Dave Frost	.10	.04
53 Ed Halicki	.10	.04
54 Dan Ford	.10	.04
55 Garry Maddox	.10	.04
56A Steve Garvey P1	.25	.10
Surpassed 25 HR		
56B Steve Garvey P2	.25	.10
Surpassed 21 HR		
57 Bill Russell	.25	.10
58 Don Sutton	1.00	.40
59 Reggie Smith	.25	.10
60 Rick Monday	.25	.10
61 Ray Knight	.25	.10
62 Johnny Bench	1.00	.40
63 Mario Soto	.10	.04
64 Doug Bair	.10	.04
65 George Foster	.25	.10
66 Jeff Burroughs	.10	.04
67 Keith Hernandez	.50	.20
68 Tom Herr	.25	.10
69 Bob Forsch	.10	.04
70 John Fulgham	.10	.04
71A Bobby Bonds P1 ERR	1.00	.40
986 lifetime HR		
71B Bobby Bonds P2 COR	.50	.20
326 lifetime HR		
72A Rennie Stennett P1	.25	.10
Breaking broke leg		
72B Rennie Stennett P2	.10	.04
Word "broke" deleted		
73 Joe Strain	.10	.04
74 Ed Whitson	.10	.04
75 Tom Griffin	.10	.04
76 Billy North	.10	.04
77 Gene Garber	.10	.04
78 Mike Hargrove	.25	.10
79 Dave Rosello	.10	.04
80 Ron Hassey	.10	.04
81 Sid Monge	.10	.04
82A J.Charboneau RC P1	1.00	.40
'78 highlights For some reason		
82B J.Charboneau RC P2	1.00	.40
Phrase "For some reason" deleted		
83 Cecil Cooper	.25	.10
84 Sal Bando	.25	.10
85 Moose Haas	.10	.04
86 Mike Caldwell	.10	.04
87A Larry Hisle P1	.25	.10
'77 highlights line ends with "28 RBI"		
87B Larry Hisle P2	.10	.04
Correct line "28 HR"		
88 Luis Gomez	.10	.04
89 Larry Parrish	.10	.04
90 Gary Carter	.50	.20
91 Bill Gullickson RC	.50	.20
92 Fred Norman	.10	.04
93 Tommy Hutton	.10	.04
94 Carl Yastrzemski	1.50	.60
95 Glenn Hoffman	.10	.04
96 Dennis Eckersley	.50	.20
97A Tom Burgmeier P1	.25	.10
ERR Throws: Right		
97B Tom Burgmeier P2	.10	.04
COR Throws: Left		
98 Win Remmerswaal	.10	.04
99 Bob Horner	.25	.10
100 George Brett	2.50	1.00
101 Dave Chalk	.10	.04
102 Dennis Leonard	.10	.04
103 Renie Martin	.10	.04
104 Amos Otis	.25	.10
105 Graig Nettles	.25	.10
106 Eric Soderholm	.10	.04
107 Tommy John	.50	.20
108 Tom Underwood	.10	.04
109 Lou Piniella	.25	.10
110 Mickey Klutts	.10	.04
111 Bobby Murcer	.25	.10
112 Eddie Murray	1.50	.60
113 Rick Dempsey	.25	.10
114 Scott McGregor	.10	.04
115 Ken Singleton	.25	.10
116 Gary Roenicke	.10	.04
117 Dave Revering	.10	.04
118 Mike Norris	.10	.04
119 Rickey Henderson	6.00	2.40
120 Mike Heath	.10	.04
121 Dave Cash	.10	.04
122 Randy Jones	.10	.04
123 Eric Rasmussen	.10	.04
124 Jerry Mumphrey	.10	.04
125 Richie Hebner	.10	.04
126 Mark Wagner	.10	.04
127 Jack Morris	.50	.20
128 Dan Petry	.10	.04
129 Bruce Robbins	.10	.04
130 Champ Summers	.10	.04
131 Pete Rose P1	3.00	1.20
Last line ends with see card 251		
131B Pete Rose P2	2.00	.80
Last line corrected see card 371		
132 Willie Stargell	.50	.20
133 Ed Ott	.10	.04
134 Jim Bibby	.10	.04
135 Bert Blyleven	.50	.20
136 Dave Parker	.25	.10
137 Bill Robinson	.25	.10
138 Enos Cabell	.10	.04
139 Dave Bergman	.10	.04
140 J.R. Richard	.25	.10
141 Ken Forsch	.10	.04
142 Larry Bowa UER	.25	.10
Shortshop on front		
143 Frank LaCorte UER	.10	.04
Photo actually Randy Niemann		
144 Denny Walling	.10	.04
145 Buddy Bell	.25	.10
146 Ferguson Jenkins	.25	.10
147 Danny Darwin	.10	.04
148 John Grubb	.10	.04
149 Alfredo Griffin	.10	.04
150 Jerry Garvin	.10	.04
151 Paul Mirabella	.10	.04
152 Rick Bosetti	.10	.04
153 Dick Ruthven	.10	.04
154 Frank Taveras	.10	.04
155 Craig Swan	.10	.04
156 Jeff Reardon RC	1.00	.40
157 Steve Henderson	.10	.04
158 Jim Morrison	.10	.04
159 Glenn Borgmann	.10	.04
160 LaMarr Hoyt RC	.25	.10
161 Rich Wortham	.10	.04
162 Thad Bosley	.10	.04
163 Julio Cruz	.10	.04
164A Del Unser P1	.25	.10
No "3B" heading		
164B Del Unser P2	.10	.04
Batting record on back corrected "3B"		
165 Jim Anderson	.10	.04
166 Jim Beattie	.10	.04
167 Shane Rawley	.10	.04
168 Joe Simpson	.10	.04
169 Rod Carew	.50	.20
170 Fred Patek	.10	.04
171 Frank Tanana	.25	.10
172 Alfredo Martinez	.10	.04
173 Chris Knapp	.10	.04
174 Joe Rudi	.25	.10
175 Greg Luzinski	.25	.10
176 Steve Garvey	.25	.10
177 Joe Ferguson	.10	.04
178 Bob Welch	.25	.10
179 Dusty Baker	.25	.10
180 Rudy Law	.10	.04
181 Dave Concepcion	.25	.10
182 Johnny Bench	1.00	.40
183 Mike LaCoss	.10	.04
184 Ken Griffey	.50	.20
185 Dave Collins	.10	.04
186 Brian Asselstine	.10	.04
187 Garry Templeton	.25	.10
188 Mike Phillips	.10	.04
189 Pete Vuckovich	.25	.10
190 John Urrea	.10	.04
191 Tony Scott	.10	.04
192 Darrell Evans	.25	.10
193 Milt May	.10	.04
194 Bob Knepper	.10	.04
195 Randy Moffitt	.10	.04
196 Larry Herndon	.10	.04
197 Rick Camp	.10	.04
198 Andre Thornton	.25	.10
199 Tom Veryzer	.10	.04
200 Gary Alexander	.10	.04
201 Rick Waits	.10	.04
202 Rick Manning	.10	.04
203 Paul Molitor	1.00	.40
204 Jim Gantner	.25	.10
205 Paul Mitchell	.10	.04
206 Reggie Cleveland	.10	.04
207 Sixto Lezcano	.10	.04
208 Bruce Benedict	.10	.04
209 Rodney Scott	.10	.04
210 John Tamargo	.10	.04
211 Bill Lee	.25	.10
212 Andre Dawson UER	.50	.20
Middle name Fernando should be Nolan		
213 Rowland Office	.10	.04
214 Carl Yastrzemski	1.50	.60
215 Jerry Remy	.10	.04
216 Mike Torrez	.10	.04
217 Skip Lockwood	.10	.04
218 Fred Lynn	.25	.10
219 Chris Chambliss	.25	.10
220 Willie Aikens	.25	.10
221 John Wathan	.10	.04
222 Dan Quisenberry	.25	.10
223 Willie Wilson	.25	.10
224 Clint Hurdle	.25	.10
225 Bob Watson	.25	.10
226 Jim Spencer	.10	.04
227 Ron Guidry	.25	.10
228 Reggie Jackson	.50	.20
229 Oscar Gamble	.10	.04
230 Jeff Cox	.10	.04
231 Luis Tiant	.25	.10
232 Rich Dauer	.10	.04
233 Dan Graham	.10	.04
234 Mike Flanagan	.25	.10
235 John Lowenstein	.10	.04
236 Benny Ayala	.10	.04
237 Wayne Gross	.10	.04
238 Rick Langford	.10	.04
239 Tony Armas	.25	.10
240A Bob Lacey P1 ERR	.50	.20
Name misspelled Lacy		
240B Bob Lacey P2 COR	.10	.04
241 Gene Tenace	.25	.10
242 Bob Shirley	.10	.04
243 Gary Lucas	.10	.04
244 Jerry Turner	.10	.04
245 John Wockenfuss	.10	.04
246 Stan Papi	.10	.04
247 Milt Wilcox	.10	.04
248 Dan Schatzeder	.10	.04
249 Steve Kemp	.10	.04
250 Jim Lentine	.10	.04
251 Pete Rose	3.00	1.20
252 Bill Madlock	.25	.10
253 Dale Berra	.10	.04
254 Kent Tekulve	.25	.10
255 Enrique Romo	.10	.04
256 Mike Easler	.10	.04
257 Chuck Tanner MG	.25	.10
258 Art Howe	.25	.10
259 Alan Ashby	.10	.04
260 Nolan Ryan	5.00	2.00
261A Vern Ruhle P1 ERR	.50	.20
Ken Forsch photo on front		
261B Vern Ruhle P2 COR	.25	.10
262 Bob Boone	.25	.10
263 Cesar Cedeno	.25	.10
264 Jeff Leonard	.25	.10
265 Pat Putnam	.10	.04
266 Jon Matlack	.10	.04
267 Dave Rajsich	.10	.04
268 Billy Sample	.10	.04
269 Damaso Garcia	.10	.04
270 Tom Buskey	.10	.04
271 Joey McLaughlin	.10	.04
272 Barry Bonnell	.10	.04
273 Tug McGraw	.25	.10
274 Mike Jorgensen	.10	.04
275 Pat Zachry	.10	.04
276 Neil Allen	.10	.04
277 Joel Youngblood	.10	.04
278 Greg Pryor	.10	.04
279 Britt Burns	.10	.04
280 Rich Dotson	.10	.04
281 Chet Lemon	.10	.04
282 Rusty Kuntz	.10	.04
283 Ted Cox	.10	.04
284 Sparky Lyle	.25	.10
285 Larry Cox	.10	.04
286 Floyd Bannister	.10	.04
287 Byron McLaughlin	.10	.04
288 Rodney Craig	.10	.04
289 Bobby Grich	.25	.10
290 Dickie Thon	.25	.10
291 Mark Clear	.10	.04
292 Dave Lemanczyk	.10	.04
293 Jason Thompson	.10	.04
294 Rick Miller	.10	.04
295 Lonnie Smith	.25	.10
296 Ron Cey	.25	.10
297 Steve Yeager	.25	.10
298 Bobby Castillo	.10	.04
299 Manny Mota	.25	.10
300 Jay Johnstone	.25	.10
301 Dan Driessen	.10	.04
302 Joe Nolan	.10	.04
303 Paul Householder	.10	.04
304 Harry Spilman	.10	.04
305 Cesar Geronimo	.10	.04
306A G.Mathews P1 ERR	.50	.20
Name misspelled		
306B G.Matthews P2 COR	.25	.10
307 Ken Reitz	.10	.04
308 Ted Simmons	.25	.10
309 John Littlefield	.10	.04
310 George Frazier	.10	.04
311 Dane Iorg	.10	.04
312 Mike Ivie	.10	.04
313 Dennis Littlejohn	.10	.04
314 Gary Lavelle	.10	.04
315 Jack Clark	.25	.10
316 Jim Wohlford	.10	.04
317 Rick Matula	.10	.04
318 Toby Harrah	.25	.10
319A D.Kuiper P1 ERR	.25	.10
Name misspelled		
319B D.Kuiper P2 COR	.10	.04
320 Len Barker	.10	.04
321 Victor Cruz	.10	.04
322 Dell Alston	.10	.04
323 Robin Yount	1.50	.60
324 Charlie Moore	.10	.04
325 Lary Sorensen	.10	.04
326A Gorman Thomas P1	.50	.20
2nd line on back: "30 HR mark 4th"		
326B Gorman Thomas P2	.25	.10
30 HR mark 3rd		
327 Bob Rodgers MG	.10	.04
328 Phil Niekro	.25	.10
329 Chris Speier	.10	.04
330A Steve Rodgers P1	.25	.10
ERR Name misspelled		
330B S.Rogers P2 COR	.10	.04
331 Woodie Fryman	.10	.04
332 Warren Cromartie	.10	.04
333 Jerry White	.10	.04
334 Tony Perez	.50	.20
335 Carlton Fisk	.50	.20
336 Dick Drago	.10	.04
337 Steve Renko	.10	.04
338 Jim Rice	.25	.10
339 Jerry Royster	.10	.04
340 Frank White	.25	.10
341 Jamie Quirk	.10	.04
342A P.Spittorff P1 ERR	.25	.10
Name misspelled		
342B Paul Splittorff P2 COR	.10	.04
343 Marty Pattin	.10	.04
344 Pete LaCock	.10	.04
345 Willie Randolph	.25	.10
346 Rick Cerone	.10	.04
347 Rich Gossage	.50	.20
348 Reggie Jackson	.50	.20
349 Ruppert Jones	.10	.04
350 Dave McKay	.10	.04
351 Yogi Berra CO	.50	.20
352 Doug DeCinces	.25	.10
353 Jim Palmer	.25	.10
354 Tippy Martinez	.10	.04
355 Al Bumbry	.25	.10
356 Earl Weaver MG	1.00	.40
357A Bob Picciolo P1 ERR	.25	.10
Name misspelled		
357B R.Picciolo P2 COR	.10	.04
358 Matt Keough	.10	.04
359 Dwayne Murphy	.10	.04
360 Brian Kingman	.10	.04
361 Bill Fahey	.10	.04
362 Steve Mura	.10	.04
363 Dennis Kinney	.10	.04
364 Dave Winfield	.50	.20
365 Lou Whitaker	.50	.20
366 Lance Parrish	.25	.10
367 Tim Corcoran	.10	.04
368 Pat Underwood	.10	.04
369 Al Cowens	.10	.04
370 Sparky Anderson MG	.25	.10
371 Pete Rose	3.00	1.20
372 Phil Garner	.25	.10
373 Steve Nicosia	.10	.04
374 John Candelaria	.25	.10
375 Don Robinson	.10	.04
376 Lee Lacy	.10	.04
377 John Milner	.10	.04
378 Craig Reynolds	.10	.04
379A Luis Pujols P1 ERR	.25	.10
Name misspelled Pujois		
379B Luis Pujols P2 COR	.10	.04
380 Joe Niekro	.25	.10
381 Joaquin Andujar	.25	.10
382 Keith Moreland	.25	.10
383 Jose Cruz	.25	.10
384 Bill Virdon MG	.10	.04
385 Jim Sundberg	.25	.10
386 Doc Medich	.10	.04
387 Al Oliver	.25	.10
388 Jim Norris	.10	.04
389 Bob Bailor	.10	.04
390 Ernie Whitt	.10	.04
391 Otto Velez	.10	.04
392 Roy Howell	.10	.04
393 Bob Walk RC	.25	.10
394 Doug Flynn	.10	.04
395 Pete Falcone	.10	.04
396 Tom Hausman	.10	.04
397 Elliott Maddox	.10	.04
398 Mike Squires	.10	.04
399 Marvis Foley	.10	.04
400 Steve Trout	.10	.04
401 Wayne Nordhagen	.10	.04
402 Tony LaRussa MG	.25	.10
403 Bruce Bochte	.10	.04
404 Bake McBride	.10	.04
405 Jerry Narron	.10	.04
406 Rob Dressler	.10	.04
407 Dave Heaverlo	.10	.04
408 Tom Paciorek	.25	.10
409 Carney Lansford	.25	.10
410 Brian Downing	.25	.10
411 Don Aase	.10	.04
412 Jim Barr	.10	.04
413 Don Baylor	.50	.20
414 Jim Fregosi MG	.10	.04
415 Dallas Green MG	.10	.04
416 Dave Lopes	.25	.10
417 Jerry Reuss	.25	.10
418 Rick Sutcliffe	.25	.10
419 Derrel Thomas	.10	.04
420 Tom Lasorda MG	1.00	.40
421 Charlie Leibrandt RC	.50	.20
422 Tom Seaver	.50	.20
423 Ron Oester	.10	.04
424 Junior Kennedy	.10	.04
425 Tom Seaver	.50	.20
426 Bobby Cox MG	.25	.10
427 Leon Durham	.25	.10
428 Terry Kennedy	.10	.04
429 Silvio Martinez	.10	.04
430 George Hendrick	.10	.04
431 Red Schoendienst MG	.50	.20
432 Johnnie LeMaster	.10	.04
433 Vida Blue	.25	.10
434 John Montefusco	.10	.04
435 Terry Whitfield	.10	.04
436 Dave Bristol MG	.10	.04
437 Dale Murphy	1.00	.40
438 Jerry Dybzinski	.10	.04
439 Jorge Orta	.10	.04
440 Wayne Garland	.10	.04
441 Miguel Dilone	.10	.04
442 Dave Garcia MG	.10	.04
443 Don Money	.10	.04
444A B.Martinez P1 ERR	.25	.10
Reverse negative		
444B Buck Martinez P2 COR	.10	.04
445 Jerry Augustine	.10	.04
446 Ben Oglivie	.25	.10
447 Jim Slaton	.10	.04
448 Doyle Alexander	.10	.04
449 Tony Bernazard	.10	.04
450 Scott Sanderson	.10	.04
451 David Palmer	.10	.04
452 Stan Bahnsen	.10	.04
453 Dick Williams MG	.10	.04
454 Rick Burleson	.10	.04
455 Gary Allenson	.10	.04
456 Bob Stanley	.10	.04
457A J. Tudor RC P1 ERR	.25	.10
Lifetime W-L 9.7		
457B J.Tudor RC P2 COR	.25	.10
Lifetime W-L 9-7		

458 Dwight Evans .50 .20
459 Glenn Hubbard .10 .04
460 U.L. Washington .10 .04
461 Larry Gura .10 .04
462 Rich Gale .10 .04
463 Hal McRae .25 .10
464 Jim Frey MG .10 .04
465 Bucky Dent .25 .10
466 Dennis Werth .10 .04
467 Ron Davis .10 .04
468 Reggie Jackson UER .50 .20
32 HR in 1970
should be 23
469 Bobby Brown .10 .04
470 Mike Davis .10 .04
471 Gaylord Perry .25 .10
472 Mark Belanger .25 .10
473 Jim Palmer .25 .10
474 Sammy Stewart .10 .04
475 Tim Stoddard .10 .04
476 Steve Stone .25 .10
477 Jeff Newman .10 .04
478 Steve McCatty .10 .04
479 Billy Martin MG .50 .20
480 Mitchell Page .10 .04
481 Steve Carlton CY .10 .04
482 Bill Buckner .25 .10
483A I.DeJesus P1 ERR .25 .10
Lifetime hits 702
483B I.DeJesus P2 COR .10 .04
Lifetime hits 642
484 Cliff Johnson .10 .04
485 Lenny Randle .10 .04
486 Larry Milbourne .10 .04
487 Roy Smalley .10 .04
488 John Castino .10 .04
489 Ron Jackson .10 .04
490A Dave Roberts P1 .25 .10
Career Highlights
Showed pop in
490B Dave Roberts P2 .10 .04
Declared himself
491 George Brett MVP 1.50 .60
492 Mike Cubbage .10 .04
493 Rob Wilfong .10 .04
494 Danny Goodwin .10 .04
495 Jose Morales .10 .04
496 Mickey Rivers .25 .10
497 Mike Edwards .10 .04
498 Mike Sadek .10 .04
499 Lenn Sakata .10 .04
500 Gene Michael MG .10 .04
501 Dave Roberts .10 .04
502 Steve Dillard .10 .04
503 Jim Essian .10 .04
504 Rance Mulliniks .10 .04
505 Darrell Porter .10 .04
506 Joe Torre MG .25 .10
507 Terry Crowley .10 .04
508 Bill Travers .10 .04
509 Nelson Norman .10 .04
510 Bob McClure .10 .04
511 Steve Howe .25 .10
512 Dave Rader .10 .04
513 Mick Kelleher .10 .04
514 Kiko Garcia .10 .04
515 Larry Biittner .10 .04
516A Willie Norwood P1 .25 .10
Career Highlights
Spent most of
516B Willie Norwood P2 .10 .04
Traded to Seattle
517 Bo Diaz .10 .04
518 Juan Beniquez .10 .04
519 Scot Thompson .10 .04
520 Jim Tracy RC .10 .04
521 Carlos Lezcano .10 .04
522 Joe Amalfitano MG .10 .04
523 Preston Hanna .10 .04
524A Ray Burris P1 .25 .10
Career Highlights
Went on ...
524B Ray Burris P2 .10 .04
Drafted by ...
525 Broderick Perkins .10 .04
526 Mickey Hatcher .25 .10
527 John Goryl MG .10 .04
528 Dick Davis .10 .04
529 Butch Wynegar .10 .04
530 Sal Butera .10 .04
531 Jerry Koosman .25 .10
532A Geoff Zahn P1 .25 .10
(Career Highlights
Was 2nd in
532B Geoff Zahn P2 .10 .04
Signed a 3 year
533 Dennis Martinez .50 .20
534 Gary Thomasson .10 .04
535 Steve Macko .10 .04
536 Jim Kaat .25 .10
537 George Brett 1.50 .60
Rod Carew
538 Tim Raines RC 2.00 .80
539 Keith Smith .10 .04
540 Ken Macha .10 .04
541 Burt Hooton .10 .04
542 Butch Hobson .10 .04
543 Bill Stein .10 .04
544 Dave Stapleton .10 .04
545 Bob Pate .10 .04
546 Doug Corbett .10 .04
547 Darrell Jackson .10 .04
548 Pete Redfern .10 .04
549 Roger Erickson .10 .04
550 Al Hrabosky .10 .04
551 Dick Tidrow .10 .04
552 Dave Ford .10 .04
553 Dave Kingman .50 .20
554A Mike Vail P1 .25 .10
Career Highlights
After two
554B Mike Vail P2 .10 .04
Traded to
555A Jerry Martin P1 .25 .10
Career Highlights
Overcame a
555B Jerry Martin P2 .10 .04
Traded to
556A Jesus Figueroa P1 .25 .10
Career Highlights
Had an
556B Jesus Figueroa P2 .10 .04
Traded to
557 Don Stanhouse .10 .04
558 Barry Foote .10 .04
559 Tim Blackwell .10 .04
560 Bruce Sutter .25 .10
561 Rick Reuschel .25 .10
562 Lynn McGlothen .10 .04
563A Bob Owchinko P1 .25 .10
Career Highlights
Traded to
563B Bob Owchinko P2 .10 .04
Involved in a
564 John Verhoeven .10 .04
565 Ken Landreaux .10 .04
566A Glen Adams P1 ERR .25 .10
Name misspelled
566B G. Adams P2 COR .10 .04
567 Hosken Powell .10 .04
568 Dick Noles .10 .04
569 Danny Ainge RC 2.00 .80
570 Bobby Mattick MG .10 .04
571 Joe Lefebvre .10 .04
572 Bobby Clark .10 .04
573 Dennis Lamp .10 .04
574 Randy Lerch .10 .04
575 Mookie Wilson RC .50 .20
576 Ron LeFlore .25 .10
577 Jim Dwyer .10 .04
578 Bill Castro .10 .04
579 Greg Minton .10 .04
580 Mark Littell .10 .04
581 Andy Hassler .10 .04
582 Dave Stieb .25 .10
583 Ken Oberkfell .10 .04
584 Larry Bradford .10 .04
585 Fred Stanley .10 .04
586 Bill Caudill .10 .04
587 Doug Capilla .10 .04
588 George Riley .10 .04
589 Willie Hernandez .25 .10
590 Mike Schmidt MVP 2.50 1.00
591 Steve Stone CY .10 .04
592 Rick Sofield .10 .04
593 Bombo Rivera .10 .04
594 Gary Ward .10 .04
595A Dave Edwards P1 .25 .10
Career Highlights
Sidelined the
595B Dave Edwards P2 .10 .04
Traded to
596 Mike Proly .10 .04
597 Tommy Boggs .10 .04
598 Greg Gross .10 .04
599 Elias Sosa .10 .04
600 Pat Kelly .10 .04
601A Checklist 1-120 P1 .25 .10
ERR Unnumbered
51 Donahue
601B Checklist 1-120 P2 .50 .20
COR Unnumbered
51 Donohue
602 Checklist 121-240 .25 .10
Unnumbered
603A CL 241-360 P1 .25 .10
ERR Unnumbered
306 Mathews
603B CL 241-360 P2 .25 .10
COR Unnumbered
306 Matthews
604A CL 361-480 P1 .25 .10
ERR Unnumbered
379 Pujois
604B CL 361-480 P2 .25 .10
COR Unnumbered
379 Pujols
605A CL 481-600 P1 .25 .10
ERR Unnumbered
566 Glen Adams
605B CL 481-600 P2 .25 .10
COR Unnumbered
566 Glenn Adams

1982 Donruss

The 1982 Donruss set contains 653 numbered standard-size cards and seven unnumbered checklists. The first 26 cards of this set are entitled Diamond Kings (DK) and feature the artwork of Dick Perez of Perez-Steele Galleries. The set was marketed with puzzle pieces in 15-card packs rather than with bubble gum. There are 63 pieces to the puzzle, which, when put together, make a collage of Babe Ruth entitled "Hall of Fame Diamond King." The card stock in this year's Donruss cards is considerably thicker than the 1981 cards. The seven unnumbered checklist cards are arbitrarily assigned numbers 654 through 660 and are listed at the end of the list below. Notable Rookie Cards in this set include Brett Butler, Cal Ripken Jr., Lee Smith and Dave Stewart.

Nm-Mt Ex-Mt
COMPLETE SET (660) 60.00 24.00
COMP.FACT.SET (660) 60.00 24.00
COMP.RUTH PUZZLE 10.00 4.00
1 Pete Rose DK 2.50 1.00
2 Gary Carter DK .20 .08
3 Steve Garvey DK .20 .08
4 Vida Blue DK .10 .04
5 Alan Trammell DK .40 .16
COR
5A Alan Trammel DK ERR .40 .16
(Name misspelled)
6 Len Barker DK .10 .04
7 Dwight Evans DK .40 .16
8 Rod Carew DK .40 .16
9 George Hendrick DK .20 .08
10 Phil Niekro DK .20 .08
11 Richie Zisk DK .10 .04
12 Dave Parker DK .20 .08
13 Nolan Ryan DK 4.00 1.60
14 Ivan DeJesus DK .10 .04
15 George Brett DK 2.00 .80
16 Tom Seaver DK .40 .16
17 Dave Kingman DK .20 .08
18 Dave Winfield DK .20 .08
19 Mike Norris DK .10 .04
20 Carlton Fisk DK .40 .16
21 Ozzie Smith DK 1.50 .60
22 Roy Smalley DK .20 .08
23 Buddy Bell DK .20 .08
24 Ken Singleton DK .10 .04
25 John Mayberry DK .10 .04
26 Gorman Thomas DK .20 .08
27 Earl Weaver MG .40 .16
28 Rollie Fingers .20 .08
29 Sparky Anderson MG .20 .08
30 Dennis Eckersley .40 .16
31 Dave Winfield .20 .08
32 Burt Hooton .10 .04
33 Rick Waits .10 .04
34 George Brett 2.00 .80
35 Steve McCatty .10 .04
36 Steve Rogers .10 .04
37 Bill Stein .10 .04
38 Steve Renko .10 .04
39 Mike Squires .10 .04
40 George Hendrick .10 .04
41 Bob Knepper .10 .04
42 Steve Carlton .20 .08
43 Larry Biittner .10 .04
44 Chris Welsh .10 .04
45 Steve Nicosia .10 .04
46 Jack Clark .20 .08
47 Chris Chambliss .20 .08
48 Ivan DeJesus .10 .04
49 Lee Mazzilli .10 .04
50 Julio Cruz .10 .04
51 Pete Redfern .10 .04
52 Dave Stieb .20 .08
53 Doug Corbett .10 .04
54 Jorge Bell RC .75 .30
55 Joe Simpson .10 .04
56 Rusty Staub .20 .08
57 Hector Cruz .10 .04
58 Claudell Washington .10 .04
59 Enrique Romo .10 .04
60 Gary Lavelle .10 .04
61 Tim Flannery .10 .04
62 Joe Nolan .10 .04
63 Larry Bowa .20 .08
64 Sixto Lezcano .10 .04
65 Joe Sambito .10 .04
66 Bruce Kison .10 .04
67 Wayne Nordhagen .10 .04
68 Woodie Fryman .10 .04
69 Billy Sample .10 .04
70 Amos Otis .20 .08
71 Matt Keough .10 .04
72 Toby Harrah .20 .08
73 Dave Righetti RC .75 .30
74 Carl Yastrzemski 1.25 .50
75 Bob Welch .20 .08
76 Alan Trammell COR .40 .16
76A Alan Trammel ERR .40 .16
(Name misspelled)
77 Rick Dempsey .20 .08
78 Paul Molitor .40 .16
79 Dennis Martinez .40 .16
80 Jim Slaton .10 .04
81 Champ Summers .10 .04
82 Carney Lansford .20 .08
83 Barry Foote .10 .04
84 Steve Garvey .20 .08
85 Rick Manning .10 .04
86 John Wathan .10 .04
87 Brian Kingman .10 .04
88 Andre Dawson UER .20 .08
(Middle name Fernando
should be Nolan)
89 Jim Kern .10 .04
90 Bobby Grich .20 .08
91 Bob Forsch .10 .04
92 Art Howe .10 .04
93 Marty Bystrom .10 .04
94 Ozzie Smith 1.50 .60
95 Dave Parker .20 .08
96 Doyle Alexander .10 .04
97 Al Hrabosky .10 .04
98 Frank Taveras .10 .04
99 Tim Blackwell .10 .04
100 Floyd Bannister .10 .04
101 Alfredo Griffin .10 .04
102 Dave Engle .10 .04
103 Mario Soto .10 .04
104 Ross Baumgarten .10 .04
105 Ken Singleton .20 .08
106 Ted Simmons .20 .08
107 Jack Morris .20 .08
108 Bob Watson .20 .08
109 Dwight Evans .40 .16
110 Tom Lasorda MG .40 .16
111 Bert Blyleven .40 .16
112 Dan Quisenberry .20 .08
113 Rickey Henderson 2.50 1.00
114 Gary Carter .40 .16
115 Brian Downing .10 .04
116 Al Oliver .20 .08
117 LaMarr Hoyt .10 .04
118 Cesar Cedeno .20 .08
119 Keith Moreland .10 .04
120 Bob Shirley .10 .04
121 Terry Kennedy .10 .04
122 Frank Pastore .10 .04
123 Gene Garber .10 .04
124 Tony Pena .20 .08
125 Allen Ripley .10 .04
126 Randy Martz .10 .04
127 Richie Zisk .10 .04
128 Mike Scott .20 .08
129 Lloyd Moseby .10 .04
130 Rob Wilfong .10 .04
131 Tim Stoddard .10 .04
132 Gorman Thomas .20 .08
133 Dan Petry .10 .04
134 Bob Stanley .10 .04
135 Lou Piniella .20 .08
136 Pedro Guerrero .20 .08
137 Len Barker .10 .04
138 Rich Gale .10 .04
139 Wayne Gross .10 .04
140 Tim Wallach RC .40 .16
141 Gene Mauch MG .10 .04
142 Doc Medich .10 .04
143 Tony Bernazard .10 .04
144 Bill Virdon MG .10 .04
145 John Littlefield .10 .04
146 Dave Bergman .10 .04
147 Dick Davis .10 .04
148 Tom Seaver .40 .16
149 Matt Sinatro .10 .04
150 Chuck Tanner MG .10 .04
151 Leon Durham .10 .04
152 Gene Tenace .20 .08
153 Al Bumbry .10 .04
154 Mark Brouhard .10 .04
155 Rick Peters .10 .04
156 Jerry Remy .10 .04
157 Rick Reuschel .20 .08
158 Steve Howe .10 .04
159 Alan Bannister .10 .04
160 U.L. Washington .10 .04
161 Rick Langford .10 .04
162 Bill Gullickson .10 .04
163 Mark Wagner .10 .04
164 Geoff Zahn .10 .04
165 Ron LeFlore .20 .08
166 Dane Iorg .10 .04
167 Joe Niekro .10 .04
168 Pete Rose 2.50 1.00
169 Dave Collins .10 .04
170 Rick Wise .10 .04
171 Jim Bibby .10 .04
172 Larry Herndon .10 .04
173 Bob Horner .20 .08
174 Steve Dillard .10 .04
175 Mookie Wilson .20 .08
176 Dan Meyer .10 .04
177 Fernando Arroyo .10 .04
178 Jackson Todd .10 .04
179 Darrell Jackson .10 .04
180 Alvis Woods .10 .04
181 Jim Anderson .10 .04
182 Dave Kingman .20 .08
183 Steve Henderson .10 .04
184 Brian Asselstine .10 .04
185 Rod Scurry .10 .04
186 Fred Breining .10 .04
187 Danny Boone .10 .04
188 Junior Kennedy .10 .04
189 Sparky Lyle .20 .08
190 Whitey Herzog MG .20 .08
191 Dave Smith .10 .04
192 Ed Ott .10 .04
193 Greg Luzinski .20 .08
194 Bill Lee .20 .08
195 Don Zimmer MG .10 .04
196 Hal McRae .20 .08
197 Mike Norris .10 .04
198 Duane Kuiper .10 .04
199 Rick Cerone .10 .04
200 Jim Rice .20 .08
201 Steve Yeager .10 .04
202 Tom Brookens .10 .04
203 Jose Morales .10 .04
204 Roy Howell .10 .04
205 Tippy Martinez .10 .04
206 Moose Haas .10 .04
207 Al Cowens .10 .04
208 Dave Stapleton .10 .04
209 Bucky Dent .20 .08
210 Ron Cey .20 .08
211 Jorge Orta .10 .04
212 Jamie Quirk .10 .04
213 Jeff Jones .10 .04
214 Tim Raines .75 .30
215 Jon Matlack .10 .04
216 Rod Carew .40 .16
217 Jim Kaat .20 .08
218 Joe Pittman .10 .04
219 Larry Christenson .10 .04
220 Juan Bonilla RC .10 .04
221 Mike Easler .10 .04
222 Vida Blue .20 .08
223 Rick Camp .10 .04
224 Mike Jorgensen .10 .04
225 Jody Davis .10 .04
226 Mike Parrott .10 .04
227 Jim Clancy .10 .04
228 Hosken Powell .10 .04
229 Tom Hume .10 .04
230 Britt Burns .10 .04
231 Jim Palmer .20 .08
232 Bob Rodgers MG .10 .04
233 Milt Wilcox .10 .04
234 Dave Revering .10 .04
235 Mike Torrez .10 .04
236 Robert Castillo .10 .04
237 Von Hayes .20 .08
238 Renie Martin .10 .04
239 Dwayne Murphy .10 .04
240 Rodney Scott .10 .04
241 Fred Patek .10 .04
242 Mickey Rivers .10 .04
243 Steve Trout .10 .04
244 Jose Cruz .20 .08
245 Manny Trillo .10 .04
246 Lary Sorensen .10 .04
247 Dave Edwards .10 .04
248 Dan Driessen .10 .04
249 Tommy Boggs .10 .04
250 Dale Berra .10 .04
251 Ed Whitson .10 .04
252 Lee Smith RC 2.00 .80
253 Tom Paciorek .20 .08
254 Pat Zachry .10 .04
255 Luis Leal .10 .04
256 John Castino .10 .04
257 Rich Dauer .10 .04
258 Cecil Cooper .20 .08
259 Dave Rozema .10 .04
260 John Tudor .10 .04
261 Jerry Mumphrey .10 .04
262 Jay Johnstone .20 .08
263 Bo Diaz .10 .04
264 Dennis Leonard .10 .04
265 Jim Spencer .10 .04
266 John Milner .10 .04
267 Don Aase .10 .04
268 Jim Sundberg .10 .04
269 Lamar Johnson .10 .04
270 Frank LaCorte .10 .04
271 Barry Evans .10 .04
272 Enos Cabell .10 .04
273 Del Unser .10 .04
274 George Foster .20 .08
275 Brett Butler RC 1.00 .40
276 Lee Lacy .10 .04
277 Ken Reitz .10 .04
278 Keith Hernandez .40 .16
279 Doug DeCinces .20 .08
280 Charlie Moore .10 .04
281 Lance Parrish .40 .16
282 Ralph Houk MG .20 .08
283 Rich Gossage .40 .16
284 Jerry Reuss .20 .08
285 Mike Stanton .10 .04
286 Frank White .20 .08
287 Bob Owchinko .10 .04
288 Scott Sanderson .10 .04
289 Bump Wills .10 .04
290 Dave Frost .10 .04
291 Chet Lemon .10 .04
292 Tito Landrum .10 .04
293 Vern Ruhle .10 .04
294 Mike Schmidt 2.00 .80
295 Sam Mejias .10 .04
296 Gary Lucas .10 .04
297 John Candelaria .10 .04
298 Jerry Martin .10 .04
299 Dale Murphy .75 .30
300 Mike Lum .10 .04
301 Tom Hausman .10 .04
302 Glenn Abbott .10 .04
303 Roger Erickson .10 .04
304 Otto Velez .10 .04
305 Danny Goodwin .10 .04
306 John Mayberry .10 .04
307 Lenny Randle .10 .04
308 Bob Bailor .10 .04
309 Jerry Morales .10 .04
310 Rufino Linares .10 .04
311 Kent Tekulve .20 .08
312 Joe Morgan .40 .16
313 John Urrea .10 .04
314 Paul Householder .10 .04
315 Garry Maddox .10 .04
316 Mike Ramsey .10 .04
317 Alan Ashby .10 .04
318 Bob Clark .10 .04
319 Tony LaRussa MG .20 .08
320 Charlie Lea .10 .04
321 Danny Darwin .10 .04
322 Cesar Geronimo .10 .04
323 Tom Underwood .10 .04
324 Andre Thornton .10 .04
325 Rudy May .10 .04
326 Frank Tanana .20 .08
327 Dave Lopes .20 .08
328 Richie Hebner .20 .08
329 Mike Flanagan .20 .08
330 Mike Caldwell .10 .04
331 Scott McGregor .10 .04
332 Jerry Augustine .10 .04
333 Stan Papi .10 .04
334 Rick Miller .10 .04
335 Graig Nettles .20 .08
336 Dusty Baker .40 .16
337 Dave Garcia MG .10 .04
338 Larry Gura .10 .04
339 Cliff Johnson .10 .04
340 Warren Cromartie .10 .04
341 Steve Comer .10 .04
342 Rick Burleson .10 .04
343 John Martin RC .10 .04
344 Craig Reynolds .10 .04
345 Mike Proly .10 .04
346 Ruppert Jones .10 .04
347 Omar Moreno .10 .04
348 Greg Minton .10 .04
349 Rick Mahler .10 .04
350 Alex Trevino .10 .04
351 Mike Krukow .10 .04
352A Shane Rawley ERR .40 .16
(Photo actually
Jim Anderson)
352B Shane Rawley COR .10 .04
353 Garth Iorg .10 .04
354 Pete Mackanin .10 .04
355 Paul Moskau .10 .04
356 Richard Dotson .10 .04
357 Steve Stone .20 .08
358 Larry Hisle .10 .04
359 Aurelio Lopez .10 .04
360 Oscar Gamble .10 .04
361 Tom Burgmeier .10 .04
362 Terry Forster .10 .04
363 Joe Charboneau .20 .08
364 Ken Brett .10 .04
365 Tony Armas .10 .04
366 Chris Speier .10 .04
367 Fred Lynn .20 .08
368 Buddy Bell .20 .08
369 Jim Essian .10 .04
370 Terry Puhl .10 .04
371 Greg Gross .10 .04
372 Bruce Sutter .20 .08
373 Joe Lefebvre .10 .04
374 Ray Knight .20 .08
375 Bruce Benedict .10 .04
376 Tim Foli .10 .04
377 Al Holland .10 .04
378 Ken Kravec .10 .04
379 Jeff Burroughs .10 .04
380 Pete Falcone .10 .04
381 Ernie Whitt .10 .04
382 Brad Havens .10 .04
383 Terry Crowley .10 .04
384 Don Money .10 .04
385 Dan Schatzeder .10 .04
386 Gary Allenson .10 .04
387 Yogi Berra CO .40 .16
388 Ken Landreaux .10 .04
389 Mike Hargrove .20 .08
390 Darryl Motley .10 .04
391 Dave McKay .10 .04
392 Stan Bahnsen .10 .04
393 Ken Forsch .10 .04
394 Mario Mendoza .10 .04
395 Jim Morrison .10 .04

396 Mike Ivie .10 .04
397 Broderick Perkins .10 .04
398 Darrell Evans .20 .08
399 Ron Reed .10 .04
400 Johnny Bench .75 .30
401 Steve Bedrosian RC .20 .08
402 Bill Robinson .10 .04
403 Bill Buckner .20 .08
404 Ken Oberkfell .10 .04
405 Cal Ripken RC 40.00 16.00
406 Jim Gantner .20 .08
407 Kirk Gibson .75 .30
408 Tony Perez .40 .16
409 Tommy John UER .40 .16
(Text says 52-56 as Yankee, should be 52-26)
410 Dave Stewart RC 1.00 .40
411 Dan Spillner .10 .04
412 Willie Aikens .10 .04
413 Mike Heath .10 .04
414 Ray Burris .10 .04
415 Leon Roberts .10 .04
416 Mike Witt .20 .08
417 Bob Molinaro .10 .04
418 Steve Braun .10 .04
419 Nolan Ryan UER 4.00 1.60
(Nisnumbering of Nolan's no-hitters on card back)
420 Tug McGraw .20 .08
421 Dave Concepcion .20 .08
422A Juan Eichelberger .40 .16
ERR (Photo actually Gary Lucas)
422B Juan Eichelberger .10 .04
COR
423 Rick Rhoden .10 .04
424 Frank Robinson MG .40 .16
425 Eddie Miller .10 .04
426 Bill Caudill .10 .04
427 Doug Flynn .10 .04
428 Larry Andersen UER .10 .04
(Misspelled Anderson on card front)
429 Al Williams .10 .04
430 Jerry Garvin .10 .04
431 Glenn Adams .10 .04
432 Barry Bonnell .10 .04
433 Jerry Narron .10 .04
434 John Stearns .10 .04
435 Mike Tyson .10 .04
436 Glenn Hubbard .10 .04
437 Eddie Solomon .10 .04
438 Jeff Leonard .10 .04
439 Randy Bass RC .10 .04
440 Mike LaCoss .10 .04
441 Gary Matthews .20 .08
442 Mark Littell .10 .04
443 Don Sutton .75 .30
444 John Harris .10 .04
445 Vada Pinson CO .20 .08
446 Elias Sosa .10 .04
447 Charlie Hough .20 .08
448 Willie Wilson .20 .08
449 Fred Stanley .10 .04
450 Tom Veryzer .10 .04
451 Ron Davis .10 .04
452 Mark Clear .10 .04
453 Bill Russell .10 .04
454 Lou Whitaker .20 .08
455 Dan Graham .10 .04
456 Reggie Cleveland .10 .04
457 Sammy Stewart .10 .04
458 Pete Vuckovich .10 .04
459 John Wockenfuss .10 .04
460 Glenn Hoffman .10 .04
461 Willie Randolph .20 .08
462 Fernando Valenzuela .75 .30
463 Ron Hassey .10 .04
464 Paul Splittorff .10 .04
465 Rob Picciolo .10 .04
466 Larry Parrish .10 .04
467 Johnny Grubb .10 .04
468 Dan Ford .10 .04
469 Silvio Martinez .10 .04
470 Kiko Garcia .10 .04
471 Bob Boone .20 .08
472 Luis Salazar .10 .04
473 Randy Niemann .10 .04
474 Tom Griffin .10 .04
475 Phil Niekro .20 .08
476 Hubie Brooks .20 .08
477 Dick Tidrow .10 .04
478 Jim Beattie .10 .04
479 Damaso Garcia .10 .04
480 Mickey Hatcher .10 .04
481 Joe Price .10 .04
482 Ed Farmer .10 .04
483 Eddie Murray .75 .30
484 Ben Oglivie .20 .08
485 Kevin Saucier .10 .04
486 Bobby Murcer .20 .08
487 Bill Campbell .10 .04
488 Reggie Smith .20 .08
489 Wayne Garland .10 .04
490 Jim Wright .10 .04
491 Billy Martin MG .20 .08
492 Jim Fanning MG .10 .04
493 Don Baylor .40 .16
494 Rick Honeycutt .10 .04
495 Carlton Fisk .40 .16
496 Denny Walling .10 .04
497 Bake McBride .10 .04
498 Darrell Porter .20 .08
499 Gene Richards .10 .04
500 Ron Oester .10 .04
501 Ken Dayley .10 .04
502 Jason Thompson .10 .04
503 Milt May .10 .04
504 Doug Bird .10 .04
505 Bruce Bochte .10 .04
506 Neil Allen .10 .04
507 Joey McLaughlin .10 .04
508 Butch Wynegar .10 .04
509 Gary Roenicke .10 .04
510 Robin Yount 1.25 .50
511 Dave Tobik .10 .04
512 Rich Gedman .20 .08
513 Gene Nelson .10 .04
514 Rick Monday .10 .04
515 Miguel Dilone .10 .04
516 Clint Hurdle .10 .04
517 Jeff Newman .10 .04
518 Grant Jackson .10 .04
519 Andy Hassler .10 .04
520 Pat Putnam .10 .04
521 Greg Pryor .10 .04
522 Tony Scott .10 .04
523 Steve Mura .10 .04
524 Johnnie LeMaster .10 .04
525 Dick Ruthven .10 .04
526 John McNamara MG .10 .04
527 Larry McWilliams .10 .04
528 Johnny Ray .20 .08
529 Pat Tabler .20 .08
530 Tom Herr .20 .08
531A SD Chicken RC .75 .30
ERR (Without TM)
531B San Diego Chicken .75 .30
COR (With TM)
532 Sal Butera .10 .04
533 Mike Griffin .10 .04
534 Kelvin Moore .10 .04
535 Reggie Jackson .40 .16
536 Ed Romero .10 .04
537 Derrel Thomas .10 .04
538 Mike O'Berry .10 .04
539 Jack O'Connor .10 .04
540 Bob Ojeda RC .40 .16
541 Roy Lee Jackson .10 .04
542 Lynn Jones .10 .04
543 Gaylord Perry .20 .08
544A Phil Garner ERR .40 .16
(Reverse negative)
544B Phil Garner COR .20 .08
545 Garry Templeton .10 .04
546 Rafael Ramirez .10 .04
547 Jeff Reardon .40 .16
548 Ron Guidry .20 .08
549 Tim Laudner .10 .04
550 John Henry Johnson .10 .04
551 Chris Bando .10 .04
552 Bobby Brown .10 .04
553 Larry Bradford .10 .04
554 Scott Fletcher RC .20 .08
555 Jerry Royster .10 .04
556 Shooty Babitt UER .10 .04
(Spelled Babbitt on front)
557 Kent Hrbek RC 1.00 .40
558 Ron Guidry .20 .08
Tommy John
559 Mark Bomback .10 .04
560 Julio Valdez .10 .04
561 Buck Martinez .10 .04
562 Mike A. Marshall .20 .08
563 Rennie Stennett .10 .04
564 Steve Crawford .10 .04
565 Bob Babcock .10 .04
566 Johnny Podres CO .20 .08
567 Paul Serna .10 .04
568 Harold Baines .75 .30
569 Dave LaRoche .10 .04
570 Lee May .20 .08
571 Gary Ward .10 .04
572 John Denny .10 .04
573 Roy Smalley .10 .04
574 Bob Brenly RC .40 .16
575 Reggie Jackson .20 .08
Dave Winfield
576 Luis Pujols .10 .04
577 Butch Hobson .10 .04
578 Harvey Kuenn MG .20 .08
579 Cal Ripken Sr. CO .20 .08
580 Juan Berenguer .10 .04
581 Benny Ayala .10 .04
582 Vance Law .10 .04
583 Rick Leach .10 .04
584 George Frazier .10 .04
585 Phillies Finest 1.50 .60
Pete Rose
Mike Schmidt
586 Joe Rudi .10 .04
587 Juan Beniquez .10 .04
588 Luis DeLeon .10 .04
589 Craig Swan .10 .04
590 Dave Chalk .10 .04
591 Billy Gardner MG .10 .04
592 Sal Bando .20 .08
593 Bert Campaneris .20 .08
594 Steve Kemp .10 .04
595A Randy Lerch ERR .40 .16
(Braves)
595B Randy Lerch COR .10 .04
(Brewers)
596 Bryan Clark RC .10 .04
597 Dave Ford .10 .04
598 Mike Scioscia .20 .08
599 John Lowenstein .10 .04
600 Rene Lachemann MG .10 .04
601 Mick Kelleher .10 .04
602 Ron Jackson .10 .04
603 Jerry Koosman .20 .08
604 Dave Goltz .10 .04
605 Ellis Valentine .10 .04
606 Lonnie Smith .10 .04
607 Joaquin Andujar .20 .08
608 Garry Hancock .10 .04
609 Jerry Turner .10 .04
610 Bob Bonner .10 .04
611 Jim Dwyer .10 .04
612 Terry Bulling .10 .04
613 Joel Youngblood .10 .04
614 Larry Milbourne .10 .04
615 Gene Roof UER .10 .04
(Name on front is Phil Roof)
616 Keith Drumwright .10 .04
617 Dave Rosello .10 .04
618 Rickey Keeton .10 .04
619 Dennis Lamp .10 .04
620 Sid Monge .10 .04
621 Jerry White .10 .04
622 Luis Aguayo .10 .04
623 Jamie Easterly .10 .04
624 Steve Sax RC .75 .30
625 Dave Roberts .10 .04
626 Rick Bosetti .10 .04
627 Terry Francona .40 .16
628 Tom Seaver .75 .30
Johnny Bench
629 Paul Mirabella .10 .04
630 Rance Mulliniks .10 .04
631 Kevin Hickey RC .10 .04
632 Reid Nichols .10 .04
633 Dave Geisel .10 .04
634 Ken Griffey .20 .08
635 Bob Lemon MG .75 .30
636 Orlando Sanchez .10 .04
637 Bill Almon .10 .04
638 Danny Ainge 1.00 .40
639 Willie Stargell .40 .16
640 Bob Sykes .10 .04
641 Ed Lynch .10 .04
642 John Ellis .10 .04
643 Ferguson Jenkins .20 .08
644 Lenn Sakata .10 .04
645 Julio Gonzalez .10 .04
646 Jesse Orosco .10 .04
647 Jerry Dybzinski .10 .04
648 Tommy Davis CO .20 .08
649 Ron Gardenhire RC .10 .04
650 Felipe Alou CO .20 .08
651 Harvey Haddix CO .20 .08
652 Willie Upshaw .10 .04
653 Bill Madlock .20 .08
654A DK Checklist 1-26 .40 .16
ERR (Unnumbered)
(With Trammel)
654B DK Checklist 1-26 .20 .08
COR (Unnumbered)
(With Trammell)
655 Checklist 27-130 .20 .08
(Unnumbered)
656 Checklist 131-234 .20 .08
(Unnumbered)
657 Checklist 235-338 .20 .08
(Unnumbered)
658 Checklist 339-442 .20 .08
(Unnumbered)
659 Checklist 443-544 .20 .08
(Unnumbered)
660 Checklist 545-653 .20 .08
(Unnumbered)

1983 Donruss

The 1983 Donruss baseball set leads off with a 26-card Diamond Kings (DK) series. Of the remaining 634 standard-size cards, two are combination cards, one portrays the San Diego Chicken, one shows the completed Ty Cobb puzzle, and seven are unnumbered checklist cards. The seven unnumbered checklist cards are arbitrarily assigned numbers 654 through 660 and are listed at the end of the list below. All cards measure the standard size. Card fronts feature full color photos around a framed white broder. Several printing variations are available but the complete set price below includes only the more common of each variation pair. Cards were issued in 15-card packs which included a three-piece Ty Cobb puzzle panel (21 different panels were needed to complete the puzzle). Notable Rookie Cards include Wade Boggs, Tony Gwynn and Ryne Sandberg.

	Nm-Mt	Ex-Mt
COMPLETE SET (660)	60.00	24.00
COMP.FACT.SET (660)	80.00	32.00
COMP.COBB PUZZLE	5.00	2.00

1 Fernando Valenzuela DK .40 .16
2 Rollie Fingers DK .40 .16
3 Reggie Jackson DK .40 .16
4 Jim Palmer DK .20 .08
5 Jack Morris DK .20 .08
6 George Foster DK .20 .08
7 Jim Sundberg DK .10 .04
8 Willie Stargell DK .20 .08
9 Dave Stieb DK .20 .08
10 Joe Niekro DK .20 .08
11 Rickey Henderson DK 1.50 .60
12 Dale Murphy DK .75 .30
13 Toby Harrah DK .10 .04
14 Bill Buckner DK .10 .04
15 Willie Wilson DK .10 .04
16 Steve Carlton DK .20 .08
17 Ron Guidry DK .20 .08
18 Steve Rogers DK .10 .04
19 Kent Hrbek DK .20 .08
20 Keith Hernandez DK .40 .16
21 Floyd Bannister DK .10 .04
22 Johnny Bench DK .75 .30
23 Britt Burns DK .10 .04
24 Joe Morgan DK .40 .16
25 Carl Yastrzemski DK .75 .30
26 Terry Kennedy DK .10 .04
27 Gary Roenicke .10 .04
28 Dwight Bernard .10 .04
29 Pat Underwood .10 .04
30 Gary Allenson .10 .04
31 Ron Guidry .20 .08
32 Burt Hooton .10 .04
33 Chris Bando .10 .04
34 Vida Blue .20 .08
35 Rickey Henderson 1.50 .60
36 Ray Burris .10 .04
37 John Butcher .10 .04
38 Don Aase .10 .04
39 Jerry Koosman .20 .08
40 Bruce Sutter .20 .08
41 Jose Cruz .20 .08
42 Pete Rose 2.50 1.00
43 Cesar Cedeno .20 .08
44 Floyd Chiffer .10 .04
45 Larry McWilliams .10 .04
46 Alan Fowlkes .10 .04
47 Dale Murphy .75 .30
48 Doug Bird .10 .04
49 Hubie Brooks .20 .08
50 Floyd Bannister .10 .04
51 Jack O'Connor .10 .04
52 Steve Senteney .10 .04
53 Gary Gaetti RC .75 .30
54 Damaso Garcia .10 .04
55 Gene Nelson .10 .04
56 Mookie Wilson .20 .08
57 Allen Ripley .10 .04
58 Bob Horner .10 .04
59 Tony Pena .10 .04
60 Gary Lavelle .10 .04
61 Tim Lollar .10 .04
62 Frank Pastore .10 .04
63 Garry Maddox .10 .04
64 Bob Forsch .10 .04
65 Harry Spilman .10 .04
66 Geoff Zahn .10 .04
67 Salome Barojas .10 .04
68 David Palmer .10 .04
69 Charlie Hough .20 .08
70 Dan Quisenberry .20 .08
71 Tony Armas .10 .04
72 Rick Sutcliffe .20 .08
73 Steve Balboni .10 .04
74 Jerry Remy .10 .04
75 Mike Scioscia .20 .08
76 John Wockenfuss .10 .04
77 Jim Palmer .20 .08
78 Rollie Fingers .20 .08
79 Joe Nolan .10 .04
80 Pete Vuckovich .10 .04
81 Rick Leach .10 .04
82 Rick Miller .10 .04
83 Graig Nettles .20 .08
84 Ron Cey .20 .08
85 Miguel Dilone .10 .04
86 John Wathan .10 .04
87 Kelvin Moore .10 .04
88A Byrn Smith ERR .20 .08
(Sic, Bryn)
88B Bryn Smith COR .40 .16
89 Dave Hostetler .10 .04
90 Rod Carew .40 .16
91 Lonnie Smith .10 .04
92 Bob Knepper .10 .04
93 Marty Bystrom .10 .04
94 Chris Welsh .10 .04
95 Jason Thompson .10 .04
96 Tom O'Malley .10 .04
97 Phil Niekro .20 .08
98 Neil Allen .10 .04
99 Bill Buckner .20 .08
100 Ed VandeBerg .10 .04
101 Jim Clancy .10 .04
102 Robert Castillo .10 .04
103 Bruce Berenyi .10 .04
104 Carlton Fisk .40 .16
105 Mike Flanagan .20 .08
106 Cecil Cooper .20 .08
107 Jack Morris .20 .08
108 Mike Morgan .10 .04
109 Luis Aponte .10 .04
110 Pedro Guerrero .20 .08
111 Len Barker .10 .04
112 Willie Wilson .20 .08
113 Dave Beard .10 .04
114 Mike Gates .10 .04
115 Reggie Jackson .40 .16
116 George Wright RC .10 .04
117 Vance Law .10 .04
118 Nolan Ryan 4.00 1.60
119 Mike Krukow .10 .04
120 Ozzie Smith 1.25 .50
121 Broderick Perkins .10 .04
122 Tom Seaver .40 .16
123 Chris Chambliss .20 .08
124 Chuck Tanner MG .10 .04
125 Johnnie LeMaster .10 .04
126 Mel Hall RC .20 .08
127 Bruce Bochte .10 .04
128 Charlie Puleo .10 .04
129 Luis Leal .10 .04
130 John Pacella .10 .04
131 Glenn Gulliver .10 .04
132 Don Money .10 .04
133 Dave Rozema .10 .04
134 Bruce Hurst .10 .04
135 Rudy May .10 .04
136 Tom Lasorda MG .40 .16
137 Dan Spillner UER .10 .04
(Photo actually Ed Whitson)
138 Jerry Martin .10 .04
139 Mike Norris .10 .04
140 Al Oliver .20 .08
141 Daryl Sconiers .10 .04
142 Lamar Johnson .10 .04
143 Harold Baines .75 .30
144 Alan Ashby .10 .04
145 Garry Templeton .10 .04
146 Al Holland .10 .04
147 Bo Diaz .10 .04
148 Dave Concepcion .20 .08
149 Rick Camp .10 .04
150 Jim Morrison .10 .04
151 Randy Martz .10 .04
152 Keith Hernandez .40 .16
153 John Lowenstein .10 .04
154 Mike Caldwell .10 .04
155 Milt Wilcox .10 .04
156 Rich Gedman .10 .04
157 Rich Gossage .40 .16
158 Jerry Reuss .20 .08
159 Ron Hassey .10 .04
160 Larry Gura .10 .04
161 Dwayne Murphy .10 .04
162 Woodie Fryman .10 .04
163 Steve Comer .10 .04
164 Ken Forsch .10 .04
165 Dennis Lamp .10 .04
166 David Green RC .10 .04
167 Terry Puhl .10 .04
168 Mike Schmidt 2.00 .80
(Wearing 37 rather than 20)
169 Eddie Milner .10 .04
170 John Curtis .10 .04
171 Don Robinson .10 .04
172 Rich Gale .10 .04
173 Steve Bedrosian .20 .08
174 Willie Hernandez .20 .08
175 Ron Gardenhire .10 .04
176 Jim Beattie .10 .04
177 Tim Laudner .10 .04
178 Buck Martinez .10 .04
179 Kent Hrbek .20 .08
180 Alfredo Griffin .10 .04
181 Larry Andersen .10 .04
182 Pete Falcone .10 .04
183 Jody Davis .10 .04
184 Glenn Hubbard .10 .04
185 Dale Berra .10 .04
186 Greg Minton .10 .04
187 Gary Lucas .10 .04
188 Dave Van Gorder .10 .04
189 Bob Dernier .10 .04
190 Willie McGee RC 1.50 .60
191 Dickie Thon .10 .04
192 Bob Boone .20 .08
193 Britt Burns .10 .04
194 Jeff Reardon .20 .08
195 Jon Matlack .10 .04
196 Don Slaught RC .40 .16
197 Fred Stanley .10 .04
198 Rick Manning .10 .04
199 Dave Righetti .20 .08
200 Dave Stapleton .10 .04
201 Steve Yeager .10 .04
202 Enos Cabell .10 .04
203 Sammy Stewart .10 .04
204 Moose Haas .10 .04
205 Lenn Sakata .10 .04
206 Charlie Moore .10 .04
207 Alan Trammell .40 .16
208 Jim Rice .20 .08
209 Roy Smalley .10 .04
210 Bill Russell .10 .04
211 Andre Thornton .10 .04
212 Willie Aikens .10 .04
213 Dave McKay .10 .04
214 Tim Blackwell .10 .04
215 Buddy Bell .20 .08
216 Doug DeCinces .20 .08
217 Tom Herr .20 .08
218 Frank LaCorte .10 .04
219 Steve Carlton .20 .08
220 Terry Kennedy .10 .04
221 Mike Easler .10 .04
222 Jack Clark .20 .08
223 Gene Garber .10 .04
224 Scott Holman .10 .04
225 Mike Proly .10 .04
226 Terry Bulling .10 .04
227 Jerry Garvin .10 .04
228 Ron Davis .10 .04
229 Tom Hume .10 .04
230 Marc Hill .10 .04
231 Dennis Martinez .20 .08
232 Jim Gantner .10 .04
233 Larry Pashnick .10 .04
234 Dave Collins .10 .04
235 Tom Burgmeier .10 .04
236 Ken Landreaux .10 .04
237 John Denny .10 .04
238 Hal McRae .20 .08
239 Matt Keough .10 .04
240 Doug Flynn .10 .04
241 Fred Lynn .20 .08
242 Billy Sample .10 .04
243 Tom Paciorek .20 .08
244 Joe Sambito .10 .04
245 Sid Monge .10 .04
246 Ken Oberkfell .10 .04
247 Joe Pittman UER .10 .04
(Photo actually Juan Eichelberger)
248 Mario Soto .10 .04
249 Claudell Washington .10 .04
250 Rick Rhoden .10 .04
251 Darrell Evans .20 .08
252 Steve Henderson .10 .04
253 Manny Castillo .10 .04
254 Craig Swan .10 .04
255 Joey McLaughlin .10 .04
256 Pete Redfern .10 .04
257 Ken Singleton .10 .04
258 Robin Yount 1.25 .50
259 Elias Sosa .10 .04
260 Bob Ojeda .10 .04
261 Bobby Murcer .20 .08
262 Candy Maldonado RC .20 .08
263 Rick Waits .10 .04
264 Greg Pryor .10 .04
265 Bob Owchinko .10 .04
266 Chris Speier .10 .04
267 Bruce Kison .10 .04
268 Mark Wagner .10 .04
269 Steve Kemp .10 .04
270 Phil Garner .20 .08
271 Gene Richards .10 .04
272 Renie Martin .10 .04
273 Dave Roberts .10 .04
274 Dan Driessen .10 .04
275 Rufino Linares .10 .04
276 Lee Lacy .10 .04
277 Ryne Sandberg RC 10.00 4.00
278 Darrell Porter .10 .04
279 Cal Ripken 6.00 2.40
280 Jamie Easterly .10 .04
281 Bill Fahey .10 .04
282 Glenn Hoffman .10 .04
283 Willie Randolph .20 .08
284 Fernando Valenzuela .40 .16
285 Alan Bannister .10 .04
286 Paul Splittorff .10 .04
287 Joe Rudi .10 .04
288 Bill Gullickson .10 .04
289 Danny Darwin .10 .04
290 Andy Hassler .10 .04
291 Ernesto Escarrega .10 .04
292 Steve Mura .10 .04
293 Tony Scott .10 .04
294 Manny Trillo .10 .04
295 Greg Harris .10 .04
296 Luis DeLeon .10 .04
297 Kent Tekulve .20 .08
298 Atlee Hammaker .10 .04

299 Bruce Benedict .10 .04
300 Fergie Jenkins .20 .08
301 Dave Kingman .40 .16
302 Bill Caudill .10 .04
303 John Castino .10 .04
304 Ernie Whitt .10 .04
305 Randy Johnson .10 .04
306 Garth Iorg .10 .04
307 Gaylord Perry .20 .08
308 Ed Lynch .10 .04
309 Keith Moreland .10 .04
310 Rafael Ramirez .10 .04
311 Bill Madlock .20 .08
312 Milt May .10 .04
313 John Montefusco .10 .04
314 Wayne Krenchicki .10 .04
315 George Vukovich .10 .04
316 Joaquin Andujar .10 .04
317 Craig Reynolds .10 .04
318 Rick Burleson .10 .04
319 Richard Dotson .10 .04
320 Steve Rogers .10 .04
321 Dave Schmidt .10 .04
322 Bud Black RC .20 .08
323 Jeff Burroughs .10 .04
324 Von Hayes .20 .08
325 Butch Wynegar .10 .04
326 Carl Yastrzemski 1.25 .50
327 Ron Roenicke .10 .04
328 Howard Johnson RC .75 .30
329 Rick Dempsey UER .20 .08
(Posing as a left-handed batter)
330A Jim Slaton .10 .04
(Bio printed black on white)
330B Jim Slaton .20 .08
(Bio printed black on yellow)
331 Benny Ayala .10 .04
332 Ted Simmons .20 .08
333 Lou Whitaker .20 .08
334 Chuck Rainey .10 .04
335 Lou Piniella .20 .08
336 Steve Sax .20 .08
337 Toby Harrah .10 .04
338 George Brett 2.00 .80
339 Dave Lopes .20 .08
340 Gary Carter .40 .16
341 John Grubb .10 .04
342 Tim Foli .10 .04
343 Jim Kaat .20 .08
344 Mike LaCoss .10 .04
345 Larry Christenson .10 .04
346 Juan Bonilla .10 .04
347 Omar Moreno .10 .04
348 Chili Davis .75 .30
349 Tommy Boggs .10 .04
350 Rusty Staub .20 .08
351 Bump Wills .10 .04
352 Rick Sweet .10 .04
353 Jim Gott RC .10 .04
354 Terry Felton .10 .04
355 Jim Kern .10 .04
356 Bill Almon UER .10 .04
(Expos/Mets in 1983, not Padres/Mets)
357 Tippy Martinez .10 .04
358 Roy Howell .10 .04
359 Dan Petry .10 .04
360 Jerry Mumphrey .10 .04
361 Mark Clear .10 .04
362 Mike Marshall .10 .04
363 Lary Sorensen .10 .04
364 Amos Otis .20 .08
365 Rick Langford .10 .04
366 Brad Mills .10 .04
367 Brian Downing .10 .04
368 Mike Richardt .10 .04
369 Aurelio Rodriguez .10 .04
370 Dave Smith .10 .04
371 Tug McGraw .20 .08
372 Doug Bair .10 .04
373 Ruppert Jones .10 .04
374 Alex Trevino .10 .04
375 Ken Dayley .10 .04
376 Rod Scurry .10 .04
377 Bob Brenly .10 .04
378 Scot Thompson .10 .04
379 Julio Cruz .10 .04
380 John Stearns .10 .04
381 Dale Murray .10 .04
382 Frank Viola RC .75 .30
383 Al Bumbry .10 .04
384 Ben Oglivie .10 .04
385 Dave Tobik .10 .04
386 Bob Stanley .10 .04
387 Andre Robertson .10 .04
388 Jorge Orta .10 .04
389 Ed Whitson .10 .04
390 Don Hood .10 .04
391 Tom Underwood .10 .04
392 Tim Wallach .20 .08
393 Steve Renko .10 .04
394 Mickey Rivers .10 .04
395 Greg Luzinski .20 .08
396 Art Howe .20 .08
397 Alan Wiggins .10 .04
398 Jim Barr .10 .04
399 Ivan DeJesus .10 .04
400 Tom Lawless .10 .04
401 Bob Walk .10 .04
402 Jimmy Smith .10 .04
403 Lee Smith .75 .30
404 George Hendrick .10 .04
405 Eddie Murray .75 .30
406 Marshall Edwards .10 .04
407 Lance Parrish .20 .08
408 Carney Lansford .20 .08
409 Dave Winfield .20 .08
410 Bob Welch .20 .08
411 Larry Milbourne .10 .04
412 Dennis Leonard .10 .04
413 Dan Meyer .10 .04
414 Charlie Lea .10 .04
415 Rick Honeycutt .10 .04
416 Mike Witt .10 .04
417 Steve Trout .10 .04
418 Glenn Brummer .10 .04
419 Denny Walling .10 .04
420 Gary Matthews .20 .08
421 Charlie Leibrandt UER .10 .04
(Liebrandt on front of card)
422 J.Eichelberger UER .10 .04
Photo actually Joe Pittman
423 Cecilio Guante UER .10 .04
(Listed as Matt on card)
424 Bill Laskey .10 .04
425 Jerry Royster .10 .04
426 Dickie Noles .10 .04
427 George Foster .20 .08
428 Mike Moore RC .20 .08
429 Gary Ward .10 .04
430 Barry Bonnell .10 .04
431 Ron Washington .10 .04
432 Rance Mulliniks .10 .04
433 Mike Stanton .10 .04
434 Jesse Orosco .10 .04
435 Larry Bowa .20 .08
436 Biff Pocoroba .10 .04
437 Johnny Ray .10 .04
438 Joe Morgan .40 .16
439 Eric Show .10 .04
440 Larry Biittner .10 .04
441 Greg Gross .10 .04
442 Gene Tenace .20 .08
443 Danny Heep .10 .04
444 Bobby Clark .10 .04
445 Kevin Hickey .10 .04
446 Scott Sanderson .10 .04
447 Frank Tanana .20 .08
448 Cesar Geronimo .10 .04
449 Jimmy Sexton .10 .04
450 Mike Hargrove .20 .08
451 Doyle Alexander .10 .04
452 Dwight Evans .20 .08
453 Terry Forster .10 .04
454 Tom Brookens .10 .04
455 Rich Dauer .10 .04
456 Rob Picciolo .10 .04
457 Terry Crowley .10 .04
458 Ned Yost .10 .04
459 Kirk Gibson .75 .30
460 Reid Nichols .10 .04
461 Oscar Gamble .10 .04
462 Dusty Baker .20 .08
463 Jack Perconte .10 .04
464 Frank White .20 .08
465 Mickey Klutts .10 .04
466 Warren Cromartie .10 .04
467 Larry Parrish .10 .04
468 Bobby Grich .20 .08
469 Dane Iorg .10 .04
470 Joe Niekro .20 .08
471 Ed Farmer .10 .04
472 Tim Flannery .10 .04
473 Dave Parker .20 .08
474 Jeff Leonard .10 .04
475 Al Hrabosky .10 .04
476 Ron Hodges .10 .04
477 Leon Durham .10 .04
478 Jim Essian .10 .04
479 Roy Lee Jackson .10 .04
480 Brad Havens .10 .04
481 Joe Price .10 .04
482 Tony Bernazard .10 .04
483 Scott McGregor .10 .04
484 Paul Molitor .40 .16
485 Mike Ivie .10 .04
486 Ken Griffey .20 .08
487 Dennis Eckersley .40 .16
488 Steve Garvey .20 .08
489 Mike Fischlin .10 .04
490 U.L. Washington .10 .04
491 Steve McCatty .10 .04
492 Roy Johnson .10 .04
493 Don Baylor .40 .16
494 Bobby Johnson .10 .04
495 Mike Squires .10 .04
496 Bert Roberge .10 .04
497 Dick Ruthven .10 .04
498 Tito Landrum .10 .04
499 Sixto Lezcano .10 .04
500 Johnny Bench .75 .30
501 Larry Whisenton .10 .04
502 Manny Sarmiento .10 .04
503 Fred Breining .10 .04
504 Bill Campbell .10 .04
505 Todd Cruz .10 .04
506 Bob Bailor .10 .04
507 Dave Stieb .20 .08
508 Al Williams .10 .04
509 Dan Ford .10 .04
510 Gorman Thomas .10 .04
511 Chet Lemon .10 .04
512 Mike Torrez .10 .04
513 Shane Rawley .10 .04
514 Mark Belanger .10 .04
515 Rodney Craig .10 .04
516 Onix Concepcion .10 .04
517 Mike Heath .10 .04
518 Andre Dawson UER .20 .08
(Middle name Fernando, should be Nolan)
519 Luis Sanchez .10 .04
520 Terry Bogener .10 .04
521 Rudy Law .10 .04
522 Ray Knight .20 .08
523 Joe Lefebvre .10 .04
524 Jim Wohlford .10 .04
525 Julio Franco RC 1.00 .40
526 Ron Oester .10 .04
527 Rick Mahler .10 .04
528 Steve Nicosia .10 .04
529 Junior Kennedy .10 .04
530A Whitey Herzog MG .20 .08
(Bio printed black on white)
530B Whitey Herzog MG .20 .08
(Bio printed black on yellow)
531A Don Sutton .75 .30
(Blue border on photo)
531B Don Sutton .75 .30
(Green border on photo)
532 Mark Brouhard .10 .04
533A S.Anderson MG .20 .08
Bio printed black on white
533B S.Anderson MG .20 .08
Bio printed black on yellow
534 Roger LaFrancois .10 .04
535 George Frazier .10 .04
536 Tom Niedenfuer .10 .04
537 Ed Glynn .10 .04
538 Lee May .20 .08
539 Bob Kearney .10 .04
540 Tim Raines .75 .30
541 Paul Mirabella .10 .04
542 Luis Tiant .20 .08
543 Ron LeFlore .10 .04
544 Dave LaPoint .10 .04
545 Randy Moffitt .10 .04
546 Luis Aguayo .10 .04
547 Brad Lesley .20 .08
548 Luis Salazar .10 .04
549 John Candelaria .10 .04
550 Dave Bergman .10 .04
551 Bob Watson .20 .08
552 Pat Tabler .10 .04
553 Brent Gaff .10 .04
554 Al Cowens .10 .04
555 Tom Brunansky .20 .08
556 Lloyd Moseby .10 .04
557A Pascual Perez ERR 2.00 .80
(Twins in glove)
557B Pascual Perez COR .20 .08
(Braves in glove)
558 Willie Upshaw .10 .04
559 Richie Zisk .10 .04
560 Pat Zachry .10 .04
561 Jay Johnstone .20 .08
562 Carlos Diaz RC .10 .04
563 John Tudor .10 .04
564 Frank Robinson MG .40 .16
565 Dave Edwards .10 .04
566 Paul Householder .10 .04
567 Ron Reed .10 .04
568 Mike Ramsey .10 .04
569 Kiko Garcia .10 .04
570 Tommy John .40 .16
571 Tony LaRussa MG .20 .08
572 Joel Youngblood .10 .04
573 Wayne Tolleson .10 .04
574 Keith Creel .10 .04
575 Billy Martin MG .20 .08
576 Jerry Dybzinski .10 .04
577 Rick Cerone .10 .04
578 Tony Perez .40 .16
579 Greg Brock .10 .04
580 Glenn Wilson .10 .04
581 Tim Stoddard .10 .04
582 Bob McClure .10 .04
583 Jim Dwyer .10 .04
584 Ed Romero .10 .04
585 Larry Herndon .10 .04
586 Wade Boggs RC 8.00 3.20
587 Jay Howell .10 .04
588 Dave Stewart .20 .08
589 Bert Blyleven .40 .16
590 Dick Howser MG .10 .04
591 Wayne Gross .10 .04
592 Terry Francona .10 .04
593 Don Werner .10 .04
594 Bill Stein .10 .04
595 Jesse Barfield .20 .08
596 Bob Molinaro .10 .04
597 Mike Vail .10 .04
598 Tony Gwynn RC 15.00 6.00
599 Gary Rajsich .10 .04
600 Jerry Ujdur .10 .04
601 Cliff Johnson .10 .04
602 Jerry White .10 .04
603 Bryan Clark .10 .04
604 Joe Ferguson .10 .04
605 Guy Sularz .10 .04
606A Ozzie Virgil .20 .08
(Green border on photo)
606B Ozzie Virgil .20 .08
(Orange border on photo)
607 Terry Harper .10 .04
608 Harvey Kuenn MG .10 .04
609 Jim Sundberg .20 .08
610 Willie Stargell .40 .16
611 Reggie Smith .20 .08
612 Rob Wilfong .10 .04
613 Joe Niekro .20 .08
Phil Niekro
614 Lee Elia MG .10 .04
615 Mickey Hatcher .10 .04
616 Jerry Hairston .10 .04
617 John Martin .10 .04
618 Wally Backman .10 .04
619 Storm Davis RC .10 .04
620 Alan Knicely .10 .04
621 John Stuper .10 .04
622 Matt Sinatro .10 .04
623 Geno Petralli .40 .16
624 Duane Walker .10 .04
625 Dick Williams MG .10 .04
626 Pat Corrales MG .10 .04
627 Vern Ruhle .10 .04
628 Joe Torre MG .20 .08
629 Anthony Johnson .10 .04
630 Steve Howe .10 .04
631 Gary Woods .10 .04
632 LaMarr Hoyt .20 .08
633 Steve Swisher .10 .04
634 Terry Leach .10 .04
635 Jeff Newman .10 .04
636 Brett Butler .75 .30
637 Gary Gray .10 .04
638 Lee Mazzilli .10 .04
639A Ron Jackson ERR 20.00 8.00
(A's in glove)
639B Ron Jackson COR .10 .04
(Angels in glove, red border on photo)
639C Ron Jackson COR .40 .16
(Angels in glove, green border on photo)
640 Juan Beniquez .10 .04
641 Dave Rucker .10 .04
642 Luis Pujols .10 .04
643 Rick Monday .10 .04
644 Hosken Powell .10 .04
645 The Chicken .75 .30
646 Dave Engle .10 .04
647 Dick Davis .10 .04
648 Frank Robinson .40 .16
Vida Blue
Joe Morgan
649 Al Chambers .10 .04
650 Jesus Vega .10 .04
651 Jeff Jones .10 .04
652 Marvis Foley .10 .04
653 Ty Cobb Puzzle Card .75 .30
654A Dick Perez/Diamond .40 .16
King Checklist 1-26
(Unnumbered) ERR
(Word "checklist" omitted from back)
654B Dick Perez/Diamond .40 .16
King Checklist 1-26
(Unnumbered) COR
(Word "checklist" is on back)
655 Checklist 27-130 .10 .04
(Unnumbered)
656 Checklist 131-234 .10 .04
(Unnumbered)
657 Checklist 235-338 .10 .04
(Unnumbered)
658 Checklist 339-442 .10 .04
(Unnumbered)
659 Checklist 443-544 .10 .04
(Unnumbered)
660 Checklist 545-653 .10 .04
(Unnumbered)

1983 Donruss Action All-Stars

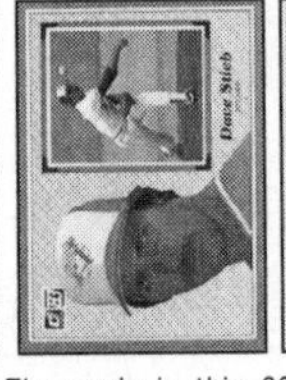
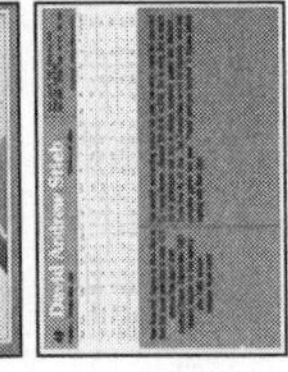

The cards in this 60-card set measure approximately 3 1/2" by 5". The 1983 Action All-Stars series depicts 60 major leaguers in a distinctive new style. A 63-piece Mickey Mantle puzzle (three pieces on one card per pack) was marketed as an insert premium; the complete puzzle card set is one of the more difficult of the Donruss insert puzzles.

	Nm-Mt	Ex-Mt
COMPLETE SET (60)	8.00	3.20
COMP.MANTLE PUZZLE	15.00	6.00
1 Eddie Murray	.60	.24
2 Dwight Evans	.10	.04
3A Reggie Jackson ERR (Red screen on back covers some stats)	3.00	1.20
3B Reggie Jackson COR	.50	.20
4 Greg Luzinski	.10	.04
5 Larry Herndon	.05	.02
6 Al Oliver	.10	.04
7 Bill Buckner	.10	.04
8 Jason Thompson	.05	.02
9 Andre Dawson	.40	.16
10 Greg Minton	.05	.02
11 Terry Kennedy	.05	.02
12 Phil Niekro	.40	.16
13 Willie Wilson	.05	.02
14 Johnny Bench	.50	.20
15 Ron Guidry	.10	.04
16 Hal McRae	.05	.02
17 Damaso Garcia	.05	.02
18 Gary Ward	.05	.02
19 Cecil Cooper	.10	.04
20 Keith Hernandez	.10	.04
21 Ron Cey	.10	.04
22 Rickey Henderson	.50	.20
23 Nolan Ryan	3.00	1.20
24 Steve Carlton	.40	.16
25 John Stearns	.05	.02
26 Jim Sundberg	.05	.02
27 Joaquin Andujar	.05	.02
28 Gaylord Perry	.30	.12
29 Jack Clark	.10	.04
30 Bill Madlock	.10	.04
31 Pete Rose	.75	.30
32 Mookie Wilson	.10	.04
33 Rollie Fingers	.30	.12
34 Lonnie Smith	.05	.02
35 Tony Pena	.05	.02
36 Dave Winfield	.40	.16
37 Tim Lollar	.05	.02
38 Rod Carew	.40	.16
39 Toby Harrah	.05	.02
40 Buddy Bell	.10	.04
41 Bruce Sutter	.10	.04
42 George Brett	1.25	.50
43 Carlton Fisk	.50	.20
44 Carl Yastrzemski	.50	.20
45 Dale Murphy	.30	.12
46 Bob Horner	.05	.02
47 Dave Concepcion	.10	.04
48 Dave Stieb	.05	.02
49 Kent Hrbek	.10	.04
50 Lance Parrish	.10	.04
51 Joe Niekro	.05	.02
52 Cal Ripken	3.00	1.20
53 Fernando Valenzuela	.10	.04
54 Richie Zisk	.05	.02
55 Leon Durham	.05	.02
56 Robin Yount	.50	.20
57 Mike Schmidt	.75	.30
58 Gary Carter	.50	.20
59 Fred Lynn	.05	.02
60 Checklist Card	.05	.02

1983 Donruss HOF Heroes

The cards in this 44-card set measure 2 1/2" by 3 1/2". Although it was issued with the same Mantle puzzle as the Action All Stars set, the Donruss Hall of Fame Heroes set is completely different in content and design. Of the 44 cards in the set, 42 are Dick Perez artwork portraying Hall of Fame members, while one card depicts the completed Mantle puzzle and the last card is a checklist. The red, white, and blue backs contain the card number and a short player biography. The cards were packaged eight cards plus one puzzle card (three pieces) for 30 cents in the summer of 1983.

	Nm-Mt	Ex-Mt
COMPLETE SET (44)	10.00	4.00
1 Ty Cobb	1.00	.40
2 Walter Johnson	.40	.16
3 Christy Mathewson	.40	.16
4 Josh Gibson	.40	.16
5 Honus Wagner	.75	.30
6 Jackie Robinson	1.25	.50
7 Mickey Mantle	2.50	1.00
8 Luke Appling	.05	.02
9 Ted Williams	1.00	.40
10 Johnny Mize	.15	.06
11 Satchel Paige	.40	.16
12 Lou Boudreau	.05	.02
13 Jimmie Foxx	.15	.06
14 Duke Snider	.40	.16
15 Monte Irvin	.15	.06
16 Hank Greenberg	.25	.10
17 Roberto Clemente	1.25	.50
18 Al Kaline	.40	.16
19 Frank Robinson	.40	.16
20 Joe Cronin	.15	.06
21 Burleigh Grimes	.05	.02
22 The Waner Brothers (Paul Waner, Lloyd Waner)	.05	.02
23 Grover Alexander	.15	.06
24 Yogi Berra	.40	.16
25 Cool Papa Bell	.15	.06
26 Bill Dickey	.15	.06
27 Cy Young	.25	.10
28 Charlie Gehringer	.05	.02
29 Dizzy Dean	.40	.16
30 Bob Lemon	.15	.06
31 Red Ruffing	.05	.02
32 Stan Musial	.75	.30
33 Carl Hubbell	.25	.10
34 Hank Aaron	.75	.30
35 John McGraw	.05	.02
36 Bob Feller	.40	.16
37 Casey Stengel	.40	.16
38 Ralph Kiner	.15	.06
39 Roy Campanella	.40	.16
40 Mel Ott	.15	.06
41 Robin Roberts	.15	.06
42 Early Wynn	.05	.02
43 Mantle Puzzle Card	2.50	1.00
44 Checklist Card	.05	.02

1984 Donruss

The 1984 Donruss set contains a total of 660 standard-size cards; however, only 658 are numbered. The first 26 cards in the set are again Diamond Kings (DK). A new feature, Rated Rookies (RR), was introduced with this set with Bill Madden's 20 selections comprising numbers 27 through 46. Two "Living Legend" cards designated A (featuring Gaylord Perry and Rollie Fingers) and B (featuring Johnny Bench and Carl Yastrzemski) were issued as bonus cards in wax packs, but were not issued in the factory sets sold to hobby dealers. The seven unnumbered checklist cards are arbitrarily assigned numbers 652 through 658 and are listed at the end of the list below. The attractive card front designs changed considerably from the previous two years. And this set has since grown in stature to be recognized as one of the finest produced in the 1980's. The backs contain statistics and are printed in green and black ink. The cards were distributed with a 3-piece puzzle panel of Duke Snider. There are no extra variation cards included in the complete set price below. The variation cards apparently resulted from a different printing for the factory sets as the Darling and Stenhouse no number variations as well as the Perez-Steele errors were corrected in the factory sets which were released later in the year. The Diamond King cards found in packs spelled Perez-Steele as Perez-Steel. Rookie Cards in this set include Joe Carter, Don Mattingly, Darryl Strawberry, and Andy Van Slyke. The Joe Carter card is almost never found well centered.

	Nm-Mt	Ex-Mt
COMPLETE SET (660)	120.00	47.50
COMP.FACT.SET (658)	150.00	60.00
COMP.SNIDER PUZZLE	5.00	2.00
1 Robin Yount DK COR	2.50	1.00
1A Robin Yount DK ERR	5.00	2.00
2 Dave Concepcion DK COR	1.50	.60

2A Dave Concepcion DK .75 .30
ERR (Perez Steel)
3 Dwayne Murphy DK .75 .30
COR
3A Dwayne Murphy DK .25 .10
ERR (Perez Steel)
4 John Castino DK COR .75 .30
4A John Castino DK ERR .25 .10
(Perez Steel)
5 Leon Durham DK COR .75 .30
5A Leon Durham DK ERR .25 .10
(Perez Steel)
6 Rusty Staub DK COR 1.50 .60
6A Rusty Staub DK ERR .75 .30
(Perez Steel)
7 Jack Clark DK COR .75 .30
7A Jack Clark DK ERR .75 .30
(Perez Steel)
8 Dave Dravecky DK .75 .30
COR
8A Dave Dravecky DK .75 .30
ERR (Perez Steel)
9 Al Oliver DK COR 1.50 .60
9A Al Oliver DK ERR .75 .30
(Perez Steel)
10 Dave Righetti DK .75 .30
COR
10A Dave Righetti DK .75 .30
ERR (Perez Steel)
11 Hal McRae DK COR 1.50 .60
11A Hal McRae DK ERR .75 .30
(Perez Steel)
12 Ray Knight DK COR .75 .30
12A Ray Knight DK ERR .75 .30
(Perez Steel)
13 Bruce Sutter DK COR 1.50 .60
13A Bruce Sutter DK ERR .75 .30
(Perez Steel)
14 Bob Horner DK COR .75 .30
14A Bob Horner DK ERR .75 .30
(Perez Steel)
15 Lance Parrish DK 1.50 .60
COR
15A Lance Parrish DK .75 .30
ERR (Perez Steel)
16 Matt Young DK COR .75 .30
16A Matt Young DK ERR .25 .10
(Perez Steel)
17 Fred Lynn DK COR .75 .30
17A Fred Lynn DK ERR .25 .10
(Perez Steel)
(A's logo on back
18 Ron Kittle DK COR .75 .30
18A Ron Kittle DK ERR .25 .10
(Perez Steel)
19 Jim Clancy DK COR .75 .30
19A Jim Clancy DK ERR .25 .10
(Perez Steel)
20 Bill Madlock DK COR 1.50 .60
20A Bill Madlock DK ERR .75 .30
(Perez Steel)
21 Larry Parrish DK .75 .30
COR
21A Larry Parrish DK .25 .10
ERR (Perez Steel)
22 Eddie Murray DK COR 3.00 1.20
22A Eddie Murray DK ERR 3.00 1.20
23 Mike Schmidt DK COR 5.00 2.00
23A M.Schmidt DK ERR 5.00 2.00
24 Pedro Guerrero DK .75 .30
COR
24A Pedro Guerrero DK .75 .30
ERR (Perez Steel)
25 Andre Thornton DK .75 .30
COR
25A Andre Thornton DK .75 .30
ERR (Perez Steel)
26 Wade Boggs DK COR 3.00 1.20
26A Wade Boggs DK ERR 2.50 1.00
27 Joel Skinner RR RC .25 .10
28 Tommy Dunbar RR RC .25 .10
29A M.Stenhouse RC RR .25 .10
ERR No number on back
29B Mike Stenhouse RR 3.00 1.20
COR Numbered on back
30A R.Darling RC RR ERR .75 .30
No number on back
30B Ron Darling RR COR 3.00 1.20
(Numbered on back)
31 Dion James RR RC .25 .10
32 Tony Fernandez RR RC 3.00 1.20
33 Angel Salazar RR RC .25 .10
34 K. McReynolds RR RC 1.50 .60
35 Dick Schofield RR RC .75 .30
36 Brad Komminsk RR RC .25 .10
37 Tim Teufel RR RC .25 .10
38 Doug Frobel RR RC .25 .10
39 Greg Gagne RR RC .75 .30
40 Mike Fuentes RR RC .25 .10
41 Joe Carter RR RC 10.00 4.00
42 Mike Brown RC RR .25 .10
(Angels OF)
43 Mike Jeffcoat RR RC .25 .10
44 Sid Fernandez RR RC 1.50 .60
45 Brian Dayett RR RC .25 .10
46 Chris Smith RR RC .25 .10
47 Eddie Murray 3.00 1.20
48 Robin Yount 5.00 2.00
49 Lance Parrish 1.50 .60
50 Jim Rice .75 .30
51 Dave Winfield .75 .30
52 Fernando Valenzuela .75 .30
53 George Brett 8.00 3.20
54 Rickey Henderson 5.00 2.00
55 Gary Carter 1.50 .60
56 Buddy Bell .75 .30
57 Reggie Jackson 1.50 .60
58 Harold Baines 3.00 1.20
59 Ozzie Smith 5.00 2.00
60 Nolan Ryan UER 15.00 6.00
(Text on back refers to 1972 as
the year he struck out 383;
the year was 1973)
61 Pete Rose 10.00 4.00
62 Ron Oester .25 .10
63 Steve Garvey .75 .30
64 Jason Thompson .25 .10
65 Jack Clark .75 .30
66 Dale Murphy 3.00 1.20
67 Leon Durham .25 .10
68 Darryl Strawberry RC 5.00 2.00
69 Richie Zisk .25 .10
70 Kent Hrbek .75 .30
71 Dave Stieb .25 .10
72 Ken Schrom .25 .10
73 George Bell .75 .30
74 John Moses .25 .10
75 Ed Lynch .25 .10
76 Chuck Rainey .25 .10
77 Biff Pocoroba .25 .10
78 Cecilio Guante .25 .10
79 Jim Barr .25 .10
80 Kurt Bevacqua .25 .10
81 Tom Foley .25 .10
82 Joe Lefebvre .25 .10
83 Andy Van Slyke RC 3.00 1.20
84 Bob Lillis MG .25 .10
85 Ricky Adams .25 .10
86 Jerry Hairston .25 .10
87 Bob James .25 .10
88 Joe Altobelli MG .25 .10
89 Ed Romero .25 .10
90 John Grubb .25 .10
91 John Henry Johnson .25 .10
92 Juan Espino .25 .10
93 Candy Maldonado .25 .10
94 Andre Thornton .25 .10
95 Onix Concepcion .25 .10
96 Donnie Hill UER .25 .10
(Listed as P,
should be 2B)
97 Andre Dawson UER .75 .30
(Wrong middle name,
should be Nolan)
98 Frank Tanana .75 .30
99 Curtis Wilkerson .25 .10
100 Larry Gura .25 .10
101 Dwayne Murphy .25 .10
102 Tom Brennan .25 .10
103 Dave Righetti .75 .30
104 Steve Sax .75 .30
105 Dan Petry .75 .30
106 Cal Ripken 20.00 8.00
107 Paul Molitor UER 1.50 .60
('83 stats should
say .270 BA, 608 AB,
and 164 hits)
108 Fred Lynn .75 .30
109 Neil Allen .25 .10
110 Joe Niekro .75 .30
111 Steve Carlton .75 .30
112 Terry Kennedy .25 .10
113 Bill Madlock .75 .30
114 Chili Davis 1.50 .60
115 Jim Gantner .25 .10
116 Tom Seaver 1.50 .60
117 Bill Buckner .75 .30
118 Bill Caudill .25 .10
119 Jim Clancy .25 .10
120 John Castino .25 .10
121 Dave Concepcion .75 .30
122 Greg Luzinski .75 .30
123 Mike Boddicker .25 .10
124 Pete Ladd .25 .10
125 Juan Berenguer .25 .10
126 John Montefusco .25 .10
127 Ed Jurak .25 .10
128 Tom Niedenfuer .25 .10
129 Bert Blyleven .75 .30
130 Bud Black .25 .10
131 Gorman Heimueller .25 .10
132 Dan Schatzeder .25 .10
133 Ron Jackson .25 .10
134 Tom Henke RC 1.50 .60
135 Kevin Hickey .25 .10
136 Mike Scott .75 .30
137 Bo Diaz .25 .10
138 Glenn Brummer .25 .10
139 Sid Monge .25 .10
140 Rich Gale .25 .10
141 Brett Butler 1.50 .60
142 Brian Harper RC .75 .30
143 John Rabb .25 .10
144 Gary Woods .25 .10
145 Pat Putnam .25 .10
146 Jim Acker .25 .10
147 Mickey Hatcher .25 .10
148 Todd Cruz .25 .10
149 Tom Tellmann .25 .10
150 John Wockenfuss .25 .10
151 Wade Boggs UER 8.00 3.20
1983 runs 10; should be 100
152 Don Baylor 1.50 .60
153 Bob Welch .25 .10
154 Alan Bannister .25 .10
155 Willie Aikens .25 .10
156 Jeff Burroughs .25 .10
157 Bryan Little .25 .10
158 Bob Boone .75 .30
159 Dave Hostetler .25 .10
160 Jerry Dybzinski .25 .10
161 Mike Madden .25 .10
162 Luis DeLeon .25 .10
163 Willie Hernandez .75 .30
164 Frank Pastore .25 .10
165 Rick Camp .25 .10
166 Lee Mazzilli .25 .10
167 Scot Thompson .25 .10
168 Bob Forsch .25 .10
169 Mike Flanagan .25 .10
170 Rick Manning .25 .10
171 Chet Lemon .25 .10
172 Jerry Remy .25 .10
173 Ron Guidry .75 .30
174 Pedro Guerrero .75 .30
175 Willie Wilson .75 .30
176 Carney Lansford .75 .30
177 Al Oliver .75 .30
178 Jim Sundberg .75 .30
179 Bobby Grich .75 .30
180 Rich Dotson .25 .10
181 Joaquin Andujar .25 .10
182 Jose Cruz .75 .30
183 Mike Schmidt 8.00 3.20
184 Gary Redus RC* .25 .10
185 Garry Templeton .25 .10
186 Tony Pena .25 .10
187 Greg Minton .25 .10
188 Phil Niekro .75 .30
189 Ferguson Jenkins .75 .30
190 Mookie Wilson .75 .30
191 Jim Beattie .25 .10
192 Gary Ward .75 .30
193 Jesse Barfield .75 .30
194 Pete Filson .25 .10
195 Roy Lee Jackson .25 .10
196 Rick Sweet .25 .10
197 Jesse Orosco .25 .10
198 Steve Lake .25 .10
199 Ken Dayley .25 .10
200 Manny Sarmiento .25 .10
201 Mark Davis .25 .10
202 Tim Flannery .25 .10
203 Bill Scherrer .25 .10
204 Al Holland .25 .10
205 Dave Von Ohlen .25 .10
206 Mike LaCoss .25 .10
207 Juan Beniquez .25 .10
208 Juan Agosto .25 .10
209 Bobby Ramos .25 .10
210 Al Bumbry .25 .10
211 Mark Brouhard .25 .10
212 Howard Bailey .25 .10
213 Bruce Hurst .25 .10
214 Bob Shirley .25 .10
215 Pat Zachry .25 .10
216 Julio Franco 1.50 .60
217 Mike Armstrong .25 .10
218 Dave Beard .25 .10
219 Steve Rogers .25 .10
220 John Butcher .25 .10
221 Mike Smithson .25 .10
222 Frank White .75 .30
223 Mike Heath .25 .10
224 Chris Bando .25 .10
225 Roy Smalley .25 .10
226 Dusty Baker .75 .30
227 Lou Whitaker .75 .30
228 John Lowenstein .25 .10
229 Ben Oglivie .25 .10
230 Doug DeCinces .25 .10
231 Lonnie Smith .25 .10
232 Ray Knight .75 .30
233 Gary Matthews .75 .30
234 Juan Bonilla .25 .10
235 Rod Scurry .25 .10
236 Atlee Hammaker .25 .10
237 Mike Caldwell .25 .10
238 Keith Hernandez 1.50 .60
239 Larry Bowa .75 .30
240 Tony Bernazard .25 .10
241 Damaso Garcia .25 .10
242 Tom Brunansky .75 .30
243 Dan Driessen .25 .10
244 Ron Kittle .25 .10
245 Tim Stoddard .25 .10
246 Bob L. Gibson RC .25 .10
(Brewers Pitcher)
247 Marty Castillo .25 .10
248 D.Mattingly RC UER 40.00 16.00
traiing on back
249 Jeff Newman .25 .10
250 Alejandro Pena RC* .75 .30
251 Toby Harrah .75 .30
252 Cesar Geronimo .25 .10
253 Tom Underwood .25 .10
254 Doug Flynn .25 .10
255 Andy Hassler .25 .10
256 Odell Jones .25 .10
257 Rudy Law .25 .10
258 Harry Spilman .25 .10
259 Marty Bystrom .25 .10
260 Dave Rucker .25 .10
261 Ruppert Jones .25 .10
262 Jeff R. Jones .25 .10
(Reds OF)
263 Gerald Perry .75 .30
264 Gene Tenace .75 .30
265 Brad Wellman .25 .10
266 Dickie Noles .25 .10
267 Jamie Allen .25 .10
268 Jim Gott .25 .10
269 Ron Davis .25 .10
270 Benny Ayala .25 .10
271 Ned Yost .25 .10
272 Dave Rozema .25 .10
273 Dave Stapleton .25 .10
274 Lou Piniella .75 .30
275 Jose Morales .25 .10
276 Broderick Perkins .25 .10
277 Butch Davis RC .25 .10
278 Tony Phillips RC 3.00 1.20
279 Jeff Reardon .75 .30
280 Ken Forsch .25 .10
281 Pete O'Brien RC* .75 .30
282 Tom Paciorek .75 .30
283 Frank LaCorte .25 .10
284 Tim Lollar .25 .10
285 Greg Gross .25 .10
286 Alex Trevino .25 .10
287 Gene Garber .25 .10
288 Dave Parker .75 .30
289 Lee Smith 3.00 1.20
290 Dave LaPoint .25 .10
291 John Shelby .25 .10
292 Charlie Moore .25 .10
293 Alan Trammell 1.50 .60
294 Tony Armas .25 .10
295 Shane Rawley .25 .10
296 Greg Brock .25 .10
297 Hal McRae .75 .30
298 Mike Davis .25 .10
299 Tim Raines 1.50 .60
300 Bucky Dent .75 .30
301 Tommy John 1.50 .60
302 Carlton Fisk 1.50 .60
303 Darrell Porter .25 .10
304 Dickie Thon .25 .10
305 Garry Maddox .75 .30
306 Cesar Cedeno .75 .30
307 Gary Lucas .25 .10
308 Johnny Ray .25 .10
309 Andy McGaffigan .25 .10
310 Claudell Washington .25 .10
311 Ryne Sandberg 12.00 4.80
312 George Foster .75 .30
313 Spike Owen RC .75 .30
314 Gary Gaetti 1.50 .60
315 Willie Upshaw .25 .10
316 Al Williams .25 .10
317 Jorge Orta .25 .10
318 Orlando Mercado .25 .10
319 Junior Ortiz .25 .10
320 Mike Proly .25 .10
321 Randy Johnson UER .25 .10
('72-'82 stats are
from Twins' Randy John-
son, '83 stats are from
Braves' Randy Johnson)
322 Jim Morrison .25 .10
323 Max Venable .25 .10
324 Tony Gwynn 12.00 4.80
325 Duane Walker .25 .10
326 Ozzie Virgil .25 .10
327 Jeff Lahti .25 .10
328 Bill Dawley .25 .10
329 Rob Wilfong .25 .10
330 Marc Hill .25 .10
331 Ray Burris .25 .10
332 Allan Ramirez .25 .10
333 Chuck Porter .25 .10
334 Wayne Krenchicki .25 .10
335 Gary Allenson .25 .10
336 Bobby Meacham .25 .10
337 Joe Beckwith .25 .10
338 Rick Sutcliffe .75 .30
339 Mark Huismann .25 .10
340 Tim Conroy .25 .10
341 Scott Sanderson .25 .10
342 Larry Biittner .25 .10
343 Dave Stewart .75 .30
344 Darryl Motley .25 .10
345 Chris Codiroli .25 .10
346 Rich Behenna .25 .10
347 Andre Robertson .25 .10
348 Mike Marshall .25 .10
349 Larry Herndon .75 .30
350 Rich Dauer .25 .10
351 Cecil Cooper .75 .30
352 Rod Carew 1.50 .60
353 Willie McGee 1.50 .60
354 Phil Garner .75 .30
355 Joe Morgan 1.50 .60
356 Luis Salazar .25 .10
357 John Candelaria .25 .10
358 Bill Laskey .25 .10
359 Bob McClure .25 .10
360 Dave Kingman 1.50 .60
361 Ron Cey .75 .30
362 Matt Young RC .25 .10
363 Lloyd Moseby .25 .10
364 Frank Viola 1.50 .60
365 Eddie Milner .25 .10
366 Floyd Bannister .25 .10
367 Dan Ford .25 .10
368 Moose Haas .25 .10
369 Doug Bair .25 .10
370 Ray Fontenot .25 .10
371 Luis Aponte .25 .10
372 Jack Fimple .25 .10
373 Neal Heaton .25 .10
374 Greg Pryor .25 .10
375 Wayne Gross .25 .10
376 Charlie Lea .25 .10
377 Steve Lubratich .25 .10
378 Jon Matlack .25 .10
379 Julio Cruz .25 .10
380 John Mizerock .25 .10
381 Kevin Gross RC .25 .10
382 Mike Ramsey .25 .10
383 Doug Gwosdz .25 .10
384 Kelly Paris .25 .10
385 Pete Falcone .25 .10
386 Milt May .25 .10
387 Fred Breining .25 .10
388 Craig Lefferts RC .25 .10
389 Steve Henderson .25 .10
390 Randy Moffitt .25 .10
391 Ron Washington .25 .10
392 Gary Roenicke .25 .10
393 Tom Candiotti RC 3.00 1.20
394 Larry Pashnick .25 .10
395 Dwight Evans .75 .30
396 Rich Gossage 1.50 .60
397 Derrel Thomas .25 .10
398 Juan Eichelberger .25 .10
399 Leon Roberts .25 .10
400 Dave Lopes .75 .30
401 Bill Gullickson .25 .10
402 Geoff Zahn .25 .10
403 Billy Sample .25 .10
404 Mike Squires .25 .10
405 Craig Reynolds .25 .10
406 Eric Show .25 .10
407 John Denny .25 .10
408 Dann Bilardello .25 .10
409 Bruce Benedict .25 .10
410 Kent Tekulve .75 .30
411 Mel Hall .75 .30
412 John Stuper .25 .10
413 Rick Dempsey .25 .10
414 Don Sutton 3.00 1.20
415 Jack Morris .75 .30
416 John Tudor .25 .10
417 Willie Randolph .75 .30
418 Jerry Reuss .25 .10
419 Don Slaught .75 .30
420 Steve McCatty .25 .10
421 Tim Wallach .75 .30
422 Larry Parrish .25 .10
423 Brian Downing .25 .10
424 Britt Burns .25 .10
425 David Green .25 .10
426 Jerry Mumphrey .25 .10
427 Ivan DeJesus .25 .10
428 Mario Soto .25 .10
429 Gene Richards .25 .10
430 Dale Berra .25 .10
431 Darrell Evans .75 .30
432 Glenn Hubbard .25 .10
433 Jody Davis .25 .10
434 Danny Heep .25 .10
435 Ed Nunez RC .25 .10
436 Bobby Castillo .25 .10
437 Ernie Whitt .25 .10
438 Scott Ullger .25 .10
439 Doyle Alexander .25 .10
440 Domingo Ramos .25 .10
441 Craig Swan .25 .10
442 Warren Brusstar .25 .10
443 Len Barker .25 .10
444 Mike Easler .25 .10
445 Renie Martin .25 .10
446 D.Rasmussen RC .25 .10
447 Ted Power .25 .10
448 Charles Hudson .25 .10
449 Danny Cox RC .25 .10
450 Kevin Bass .25 .10
451 Daryl Sconiers .25 .10
452 Scott Fletcher .25 .10
453 Bryn Smith .25 .10
454 Jim Dwyer .25 .10
455 Rob Picciolo .25 .10
456 Enos Cabell .25 .10
457 Dennis Boyd .75 .30
458 Butch Wynegar .25 .10
459 Burt Hooton .25 .10
460 Ron Hassey .25 .10
461 Danny Jackson RC 1.50 .60
462 Bob Kearney .25 .10
463 Terry Francona .25 .10
464 Wayne Tolleson .25 .10
465 Mickey Rivers .25 .10
466 John Wathan .25 .10
467 Bill Almon .25 .10
468 George Vukovich .25 .10
469 Steve Kemp .25 .10
470 Ken Landreaux .25 .10
471 Milt Wilcox .25 .10
472 Tippy Martinez .25 .10
473 Ted Simmons .75 .30
474 Tim Foli .25 .10
475 George Hendrick .25 .10
476 Terry Puhl .25 .10
477 Von Hayes .25 .10
478 Bobby Brown .25 .10
479 Lee Lacy .25 .10
480 Joel Youngblood .25 .10
481 Jim Slaton .25 .10
482 Mike Fitzgerald .25 .10
483 Keith Moreland .25 .10
484 Ron Roenicke .25 .10
485 Luis Leal .25 .10
486 Bryan Oelkers .25 .10
487 Bruce Berenyi .25 .10
488 LaMarr Hoyt .25 .10
489 Joe Nolan .25 .10
490 Marshall Edwards .25 .10
491 Mike Laga .75 .30
492 Rick Cerone .25 .10
493 Rick Miller UER .25 .10
(Listed as Mike
on card front)
494 Rick Honeycutt .25 .10
495 Mike Hargrove .75 .30
496 Joe Simpson .25 .10
497 Keith Atherton .25 .10
498 Chris Welsh .25 .10
499 Bruce Kison .25 .10
500 Bobby Johnson .25 .10
501 Jerry Koosman .75 .30
502 Frank DiPino .25 .10
503 Tony Perez 1.50 .60
504 Ken Oberkfell .25 .10
505 Mark Thurmond .25 .10
506 Joe Price .25 .10
507 Pascual Perez .25 .10
508 Marvell Wynne .25 .10
509 Mike Krukow .25 .10
510 Dick Ruthven .25 .10
511 Al Cowens .25 .10
512 Cliff Johnson .25 .10
513 Randy Bush .25 .10
514 Sammy Stewart .25 .10
515 Bill Schroeder .25 .10
516 Aurelio Lopez .75 .30
517 Mike G. Brown RC .25 .10
518 Graig Nettles .75 .30
519 Dave Sax .25 .10
520 Jerry Willard .25 .10
521 Paul Splittorff .25 .10
522 Tom Burgmeier .25 .10
523 Chris Speier .25 .10
524 Bobby Clark .25 .10
525 George Wright .25 .10
526 Dennis Lamp .25 .10
527 Tony Scott .25 .10
528 Ed Whitson .25 .10
529 Ron Reed .25 .10
530 Charlie Puleo .25 .10
531 Jerry Royster .25 .10
532 Don Robinson .25 .10
533 Steve Trout .25 .10
534 Bruce Sutter .75 .30
535 Bob Horner .25 .10
536 Pat Tabler .25 .10
537 Chris Chambliss .75 .30
538 Bob Ojeda .25 .10
539 Alan Ashby .25 .10
540 Jay Johnstone .75 .30
541 Bob Dernier .25 .10
542 Brook Jacoby .75 .30
543 U.L. Washington .25 .10
544 Danny Darwin .25 .10
545 Kiko Garcia .25 .10
546 Vance Law UER .25 .10
(Listed as P
on card front)
547 Tug McGraw .75 .30
548 Dave Smith .25 .10
549 Len Matuszek .25 .10
550 Tom Hume .25 .10
551 Dave Dravecky .75 .30
552 Rick Rhoden .25 .10
553 Duane Kuiper .25 .10
554 Rusty Staub .75 .30
555 Bill Campbell .25 .10
556 Mike Torrez .25 .10
557 Dave Henderson .75 .30
558 Len Whitehouse .25 .10
559 Barry Bonnell .25 .10
560 Rick Lysander .25 .10
561 Garth Iorg .25 .10
562 Bryan Clark .25 .10
563 Brian Giles .25 .10
564 Vern Ruhle .25 .10
565 Steve Bedrosian .25 .10
566 Larry McWilliams .25 .10
567 Jeff Leonard UER .25 .10
(Listed as P

on card front)
568 Alan Wiggins .25 .10
569 Jeff Russell RC .75 .30
570 Salome Barojas .25 .10
571 Dane Iorg .25 .10
572 Bob Knepper .25 .10
573 Gary Lavelle .25 .10
574 Gorman Thomas .25 .10
575 Manny Trillo .25 .10
576 Jim Palmer .75 .30
577 Dale Murray .25 .10
578 Tom Brookens .75 .30
579 Rich Gedman .25 .10
580 Bill Doran RC* .75 .30
581 Steve Yeager .25 .10
582 Dan Spillner .25 .10
583 Dan Quisenberry .25 .10
584 Rance Mulliniks .25 .10
585 Storm Davis .25 .10
586 Dave Schmidt .25 .10
587 Bill Russell .25 .10
588 Pat Sheridan .25 .10
589 Rafael Ramirez .25 .10
UER (A's on front)
590 Bud Anderson .25 .10
591 George Frazier .25 .10
592 Lee Tunnell .25 .10
593 Kirk Gibson 3.00 1.20
594 Scott McGregor .25 .10
595 Bob Bailor .25 .10
596 Tom Herr .75 .30
597 Luis Sanchez .25 .10
598 Dave Engle .25 .10
599 Craig McMurtry .25 .10
600 Carlos Diaz .25 .10
601 Tom O'Malley .25 .10
602 Nick Esasky .25 .10
603 Ron Hodges .25 .10
604 Ed VandeBerg .25 .10
605 Alfredo Griffin .25 .10
606 Glenn Hoffman .25 .10
607 Hubie Brooks .25 .10
608 Richard Barnes UER .25 .10
(Photo actually
Neal Heaton)
609 Greg Walker .75 .30
610 Ken Singleton .25 .10
611 Mark Clear .25 .10
612 Buck Martinez .25 .10
613 Ken Griffey .75 .30
614 Reid Nichols .25 .10
615 Doug Sisk .25 .10
616 Bob Brenly .25 .10
617 Joey McLaughlin .25 .10
618 Glenn Wilson .75 .30
619 Bob Stoddard .25 .10
620 Lenn Sakata UER .25 .10
(Listed as Len
on card front)
621 Mike Young RC .25 .10
622 John Stefero .25 .10
623 Carmelo Martinez .25 .10
624 Dave Bergman .25 .10
625 Runnin' Reds UER 3.00 1.20
(Sic, Redbirds)
David Green
Willie McGee
Lonnie Smith
Ozzie Smith
626 Rudy May .25 .10
627 Matt Keough .25 .10
628 Jose DeLeon RC .25 .10
629 Jim Essian .25 .10
630 Darnell Coles RC .25 .10
631 Mike Warren .25 .10
632 Del Crandall MG .25 .10
633 Dennis Martinez .75 .30
634 Mike Moore .75 .30
635 Lary Sorensen .25 .10
636 Ricky Nelson .25 .10
637 Omar Moreno .25 .10
638 Charlie Hough .75 .30
639 Dennis Eckersley 1.50 .60
640 Walt Terrell .25 .10
641 Denny Walling .25 .10
642 Dave Anderson RC .25 .10
643 Jose Oquendo RC .75 .30
644 Bob Stanley .25 .10
645 Dave Geisel .25 .10
646 Scott Garrelts .25 .10
647 Gary Pettis .25 .10
648 Duke Snider 1.50 .60
Puzzle Card
649 Johnnie LeMaster .25 .10
650 Dave Collins .25 .10
651 The Chicken 1.50 .60
652 DK Checklist 1-26 .75 .30
(Unnumbered)
653 Checklist 27-130 .25 .10
(Unnumbered)
654 Checklist 131-234 .25 .10
(Unnumbered)
655 Checklist 235-338 .25 .10
(Unnumbered)
656 Checklist 339-442 .25 .10
(Unnumbered)
657 Checklist 443-546 .25 .10
(Unnumbered)
658 Checklist 547-651 .25 .10
(Unnumbered)
A Living Legends A 2.50 1.00
Gaylord Perry
Rollie Fingers
B Living Legends B 5.00 2.00
Carl Yastrzemski
Johnny Bench

1984 Donruss Action All-Stars

The cards in this 60-card set measure approximately 3 1/2" by 5". For the second year in a row, Donruss issued a postcard-size card set. Unlike last year, when the fronts of the cards contained both an action and a portrait shot of the player, the fronts of this year's cards contain only an action photo. On the backs, the top section contains the card number and a full-color portrait of the player pictured on the front. The bottom half features the player's career statistics. The set was distributed with a 63-piece Ted Williams puzzle. This puzzle is the toughest of all the Donruss puzzles.

Nm-Mt Ex-Mt
COMPLETE SET (60) 8.00 3.20
COMP.WILLIAMS PUZZLE 25.00 10.00
1 Gary Lavelle .05 .02
2 Willie McGee .30 .12
3 Tony Pena .10 .04
4 Lou Whitaker .20 .08
5 Robin Yount .40 .16
6 Doug DeCinces .05 .02
7 John Castino .05 .02
8 Terry Kennedy .05 .02
9 Rickey Henderson 1.00 .40
10 Bob Horner .05 .02
11 Harold Baines .10 .04
12 Buddy Bell .10 .04
13 Fernando Valenzuela .10 .04
14 Nolan Ryan 2.50 1.00
15 Andre Thornton .05 .02
16 Gary Redus .05 .02
17 Pedro Guerrero .10 .04
18 Andre Dawson .30 .12
19 Dave Stieb .05 .02
20 Cal Ripken 2.50 1.00
21 Ken Griffey .10 .04
22 Wade Boggs 1.00 .40
23 Keith Hernandez .10 .04
24 Steve Carlton .50 .20
25 Hal McRae .05 .02
26 John Lowenstein .05 .02
27 Fred Lynn .10 .04
28 Bill Buckner .10 .04
29 Chris Chambliss .05 .02
30 Richie Zisk .05 .02
31 Jack Clark .10 .04
32 George Hendrick .05 .02
33 Bill Madlock .05 .02
34 Lance Parrish .20 .08
35 Paul Molitor .50 .20
36 Reggie Jackson .50 .20
37 Kent Hrbek .10 .04
38 Steve Garvey .10 .04
39 Carney Lansford .10 .04
40 Dale Murphy .30 .12
41 Greg Luzinski .10 .04
42 Larry Parrish .05 .02
43 Ryne Sandberg 1.25 .50
44 Dickie Thon .05 .02
45 Bert Blyleven .10 .04
46 Ron Oester .05 .02
47 Dusty Baker .10 .04
48 Steve Rogers .05 .02
49 Jim Clancy .05 .02
50 Eddie Murray .60 .24
51 Ron Guidry .10 .04
52 Jim Rice .10 .04
53 Tom Seaver .50 .20
54 Pete Rose .75 .30
55 George Brett 1.25 .50
56 Dan Quisenberry .05 .02
57 Mike Schmidt .60 .24
58 Ted Simmons .10 .04
59 Dave Righetti .05 .02
60 Checklist Card .05 .02

1984 Donruss Champions

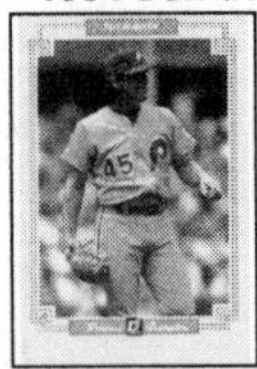

The cards in this 60-card set measure approximately 3 1/2" by 5". The 1984 Donruss Champions set is a hybrid photo/artwork issue. Grand Champions, listed GC in the checklist below, feature the artwork of Dick Perez of Perez-Steele Galleries. Current players in the set feature photographs. The theme of this postcard-size set features a Grand Champion and those current players that are directly behind him in a baseball statistical category, for example, Season Home Runs (1-7), Career Home Runs (8-13), Season Batting Average (14-19), Career Batting Average (20-25), Career Hits (26-30), Career Victories (31-36), Career Strikeouts (37-42), Most Valuable Players (43-49), World Series stars (50-54), and All-Star heroes (55-59). The cards were issued in cello packs with pieces of the Duke Snider puzzle.

Nm-Mt Ex-Mt
COMPLETE SET (60) 12.00 4.80
1 Babe Ruth GC 2.00 .80
2 George Foster .10 .04
3 Dave Kingman .10 .04
4 Jim Rice .10 .04
5 Gorman Thomas .05 .02
6 Ben Oglivie .05 .02
7 Jeff Burroughs .05 .02
8 Hank Aaron GC .75 .30
9 Reggie Jackson .50 .20
10 Carl Yastrzemski .50 .20
11 Mike Schmidt .60 .24
12 Graig Nettles .10 .04
13 Greg Luzinski .10 .04
14 Ted Williams GC 1.50 .60
15 George Brett 1.25 .50
16 Wade Boggs .50 .20
17 Hal McRae .05 .02
18 Bill Buckner .10 .04
19 Eddie Murray .60 .24
20 Rogers Hornsby GC .50 .20
21 Rod Carew .40 .16
22 Bill Madlock .10 .04
23 Lonnie Smith .05 .02
24 Cecil Cooper .10 .04
25 Ken Griffey .10 .04
26 Ty Cobb GC 1.00 .40
27 Pete Rose .75 .30
28 Rusty Staub .10 .04
29 Tony Perez .10 .04
30 Al Oliver .10 .04
31 Cy Young GC .50 .20
32 Gaylord Perry .40 .16
33 Ferguson Jenkins .40 .16
34 Phil Niekro .40 .16
35 Jim Palmer .40 .16
36 Tommy John .10 .04
37 Walter Johnson GC .50 .20
38 Steve Carlton .40 .16
39 Nolan Ryan 2.50 1.00
40 Tom Seaver .40 .16
41 Don Sutton .40 .16
42 Bert Blyleven .10 .04
43 Frank Robinson GC .40 .16
44 Joe Morgan .40 .16
45 Rollie Fingers .30 .12
46 Keith Hernandez .10 .04
47 Robin Yount .30 .12
48 Cal Ripken 2.50 1.00
49 Dale Murphy .30 .12
50 Mickey Mantle GC 3.00 1.20
51 Johnny Bench .50 .20
52 Carlton Fisk .50 .20
53 Tug McGraw .10 .04
54 Paul Molitor .50 .20
55 Carl Hubbell GC .30 .12
56 Steve Garvey .10 .04
57 Dave Parker .10 .04
58 Gary Carter .50 .20
59 Fred Lynn .10 .04
60 Checklist Card .05 .02

1985 Donruss

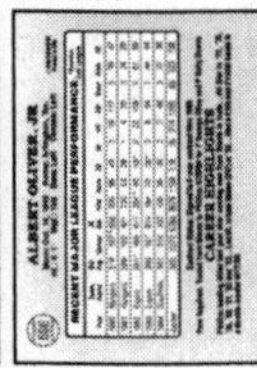

The 1985 Donruss set consists of 660 standard-size cards. Wax packs contained 15 cards and a Lou Gehrig puzzle panel. The fronts feature full color photos framed by jet black borders (making the cards condition sensitive). The first 26 cards of the set feature Diamond Kings (DK), for the fourth year in a row; the artwork on the Diamond Kings was again produced by the Perez-Steele Galleries. Cards 27-46 feature Rated Rookies (RR). The unnumbered checklist cards are arbitrarily numbered below as numbers 654 through 660. Rookie Cards in this set include Roger Clemens, Eric Davis, Shawon Dunston, Dwight Gooden, Orel Hershiser, Jimmy Key, Terry Pendleton, Kirby Puckett and Bret Saberhagen.

Nm-Mt Ex-Mt
COMPLETE SET (660) 60.00 24.00
COMP.FACT.SET (660) 100.00 40.00
COMP.GEHRIG PUZZLE 4.00 1.60
1 Ryne Sandberg DK 1.25 .50
2 Doug DeCinces DK .15 .06
3 Richard Dotson DK .15 .06
4 Bert Blyleven DK .15 .06
5 Lou Whitaker DK .40 .16
6 Dan Quisenberry DK .40 .16
7 Don Mattingly DK 2.50 1.00
8 Carney Lansford DK .15 .06
9 Frank Tanana DK .15 .06
10 Willie Upshaw DK .15 .06
11 C.Washington DK .15 .06
12 Mike Marshall DK .15 .06
13 Joaquin Andujar DK .15 .06
14 Cal Ripken DK 2.50 1.00
15 Jim Rice DK .40 .16
16 Don Sutton DK .40 .16
17 Frank Viola DK .15 .06
18 Alvin Davis DK .15 .06
19 Mario Soto DK .15 .06
20 Jose Cruz DK .15 .06
21 Charlie Lea DK .15 .06
22 Jesse Orosco DK .15 .06
23 Juan Samuel DK .15 .06
24 Tony Pena DK .15 .06
25 Tony Gwynn DK 1.25 .50
26 Bob Brenly DK .15 .06
27 Danny Tartabull RR RC 1.25 .50
28 Mike Bielecki RR .15 .06
29 Steve Lyons RR RC .40 .16
30 Jeff Reed RR .15 .06
31 Tony Brewer RR .15 .06
32 John Morris RR RC .15 .06
33 Daryl Boston RR RC .15 .06
34 Al Pulido RR .15 .06
35 Steve Kiefer RR .15 .06
36 Larry Sheets RR .15 .06
37 Scott Bradley RR .15 .06
38 Calvin Schiraldi RR .15 .06
39 S.Dunston RR RC .75 .30
40 Charlie Mitchell RR .15 .06
41 Billy Hatcher RR RC .75 .30
42 Russ Stephans RR .15 .06
43 Alejandro Sanchez RR .15 .06
44 Steve Jeltz RR .15 .06
45 Jim Traber RR .15 .06
46 Doug Loman RR .15 .06
47 Eddie Murray 1.25 .50
48 Robin Yount 2.00 .80
49 Lance Parrish .40 .16
50 Jim Rice .40 .16
51 Dave Winfield .40 .16
52 Fernando Valenzuela .40 .16
53 George Brett 3.00 1.20
54 Dave Kingman .40 .16
55 Gary Carter .75 .30
56 Buddy Bell .40 .16
57 Reggie Jackson .75 .30
58 Harold Baines .40 .16
59 Ozzie Smith 2.00 .80
60 Nolan Ryan UER 6.00 2.40
(Set strikeout record
in 1973, not 1972)
61 Mike Schmidt 3.00 1.20
62 Dave Parker .40 .16
63 Tony Gwynn 2.50 1.00
64 Tony Pena .15 .06
65 Jack Clark .40 .16
66 Dale Murphy 1.25 .50
67 Ryne Sandberg 2.50 1.00
68 Keith Hernandez .75 .30
69 Alvin Davis RC* .40 .16
70 Kent Hrbek .40 .16
71 Willie Upshaw .15 .06
72 Dave Engle .15 .06
73 Alfredo Griffin .15 .06
74A Jack Perconte .15 .06
(Career Highlights
takes four lines)
74B Jack Perconte .15 .06
(Career Highlights
takes three lines)
75 Jesse Orosco .15 .06
76 Jody Davis .15 .06
77 Bob Horner .15 .06
78 Larry McWilliams .15 .06
79 Joel Youngblood .15 .06
80 Alan Wiggins .15 .06
81 Ron Oester .15 .06
82 Ozzie Virgil .15 .06
83 Ricky Horton .15 .06
84 Bill Doran .15 .06
85 Rod Carew .75 .30
86 LaMarr Hoyt .15 .06
87 Tim Wallach .40 .16
88 Mike Flanagan .15 .06
89 Jim Sundberg .15 .06
90 Chet Lemon .15 .06
91 Bob Stanley .15 .06
92 Willie Randolph .40 .16
93 Bill Russell .15 .06
94 Julio Franco .75 .30
95 Dan Quisenberry .40 .16
96 Bill Caudill .15 .06
97 Bill Gullickson .15 .06
98 Danny Darwin .15 .06
99 Curtis Wilkerson .15 .06
100 Bud Black .15 .06
101 Tony Phillips .15 .06
102 Tony Bernazard .15 .06
103 Jay Howell .15 .06
104 Burt Hooton .15 .06
105 Milt Wilcox .15 .06
106 Rich Dauer .15 .06
107 Don Sutton 1.25 .50
108 Mike Witt .15 .06
109 Bruce Sutter .40 .16
110 Enos Cabell .15 .06
111 John Denny .15 .06
112 Dave Dravecky .40 .16
113 Marvell Wynne .15 .06
114 Johnnie LeMaster .15 .06
115 Chuck Porter .15 .06
116 John Gibbons .15 .06
117 Keith Moreland .15 .06
118 Darnell Coles .15 .06
119 Dennis Lamp .15 .06
120 Ron Davis .15 .06
121 Nick Esasky .15 .06
122 Vance Law .15 .06
123 Gary Roenicke .15 .06
124 Bill Schroeder .15 .06
125 Dave Rozema .15 .06
126 Bobby Meacham .15 .06
127 Marty Barrett .15 .06
128 R.J. Reynolds .15 .06
129 Ernie Camacho UER .15 .06
(Photo actually
Rich Thompson)
130 Jorge Orta .15 .06
131 Lary Sorensen .15 .06
132 Terry Francona .15 .06
133 Fred Lynn .40 .16
134 Bob Jones .15 .06
135 Jerry Hairston .15 .06
136 Kevin Bass .15 .06
137 Garry Maddox .15 .06
138 Dave LaPoint .15 .06
139 Kevin McReynolds .40 .16
140 Wayne Krenchicki .15 .06
141 Rafael Ramirez .15 .06
142 Rod Scurry .15 .06
143 Greg Minton .15 .06
144 Tim Stoddard .15 .06
145 Steve Henderson .15 .06
146 George Bell .40 .16
147 Dave Meier .15 .06
148 Sammy Stewart .15 .06
149 Mark Brouhard .15 .06
150 Larry Herndon .15 .06
151 Oil Can Boyd .15 .06
152 Brian Dayett .15 .06
153 Tom Niedenfuer .15 .06
154 Brook Jacoby .15 .06
155 Onix Concepcion .15 .06
156 Tim Conroy .15 .06
157 Joe Hesketh .15 .06
158 Brian Downing .15 .06
159 Tommy Dunbar .15 .06
160 Marc Hill .15 .06
161 Phil Garner .40 .16
162 Jerry Davis .15 .06
163 Bill Campbell .15 .06
164 John Franco RC 1.25 .50
165 Len Barker .15 .06
166 Benny Distefano .15 .06
167 George Frazier .15 .06
168 Tito Landrum .15 .06
169 Cal Ripken 5.00 2.00
170 Cecil Cooper .40 .16
171 Alan Trammell .75 .30
172 Wade Boggs 1.50 .60
173 Don Baylor .40 .16
174 Pedro Guerrero .40 .16
175 Frank White .40 .16
176 Rickey Henderson 1.50 .60
177 Charlie Lea .15 .06
178 Pete O'Brien .15 .06
179 Doug DeCinces .15 .06
180 Ron Kittle .15 .06
181 George Hendrick .15 .06
182 Joe Niekro .15 .06
183 Juan Samuel .15 .06
184 Mario Soto .15 .06
185 Rich Gossage .40 .16
186 Johnny Ray .15 .06
187 Bob Brenly .15 .06
188 Craig McMurtry .15 .06
189 Leon Durham .15 .06
190 Dwight Gooden RC 2.00 .80
191 Barry Bonnell .15 .06
192 Tim Teufel .15 .06
193 Dave Stieb .40 .16
194 Mickey Hatcher .15 .06
195 Jesse Barfield .15 .06
196 Al Cowens .15 .06
197 Hubie Brooks .15 .06
198 Steve Trout .15 .06
199 Glenn Hubbard .15 .06
200 Bill Madlock .40 .16
201 Jeff D. Robinson .15 .06
202 Eric Show .15 .06
203 Dave Concepcion .40 .16
204 Ivan DeJesus .15 .06
205 Neil Allen .15 .06
206 Jerry Mumphrey .15 .06
207 Mike C. Brown .15 .06
208 Carlton Fisk .75 .30
209 Bryn Smith .15 .06
210 Tippy Martinez .15 .06
211 Dion James .15 .06
212 Willie Hernandez .15 .06
213 Mike Easler .15 .06
214 Ron Guidry .40 .16
215 Rick Honeycutt .15 .06
216 Brett Butler .40 .16
217 Larry Gura .15 .06
218 Ray Burris .15 .06
219 Steve Rogers .15 .06
220 Frank Tanana UER .15 .06
(Bats Left listed
twice on card back)
221 Ned Yost .15 .06
222 B.Saberhagen RC UER 1.25 .50
18 career IP on back
223 Mike Davis .15 .06
224 Bert Blyleven .40 .16
225 Steve Kemp .15 .06
226 Jerry Reuss .15 .06
227 Darrell Evans UER .40 .16
(80 homers in 1980)
228 Wayne Gross .15 .06
229 Jim Gantner .15 .06
230 Bob Boone .40 .16
231 Lonnie Smith .15 .06
232 Frank DiPino .15 .06
233 Jerry Koosman .40 .16
234 Graig Nettles .40 .16
235 John Tudor .15 .06
236 John Rabb .15 .06
237 Rick Manning .15 .06
238 Mike Fitzgerald .15 .06
239 Gary Matthews .15 .06
240 Jim Presley .40 .16
241 Dave Collins .15 .06
242 Gary Gaetti .40 .16
243 Dann Bilardello .15 .06
244 Rudy Law .15 .06
245 John Lowenstein .15 .06
246 Tom Tellmann .15 .06
247 Howard Johnson .40 .16
248 Ray Fontenot .15 .06
249 Tony Armas .15 .06
250 Candy Maldonado .15 .06
251 Mike Jeffcoat .15 .06
252 Dane Iorg .15 .06
253 Bruce Bochte .15 .06
254 Pete Rose Expos 4.00 1.60
255 Don Aase .15 .06
256 George Wright .15 .06
257 Britt Burns .15 .06
258 Mike Scott .15 .06
259 Len Matuszek .15 .06
260 Dave Rucker .15 .06
261 Craig Lefferts .15 .06
262 Jay Tibbs .15 .06
263 Bruce Benedict .15 .06
264 Don Robinson .15 .06
265 Gary Lavelle .15 .06
266 Scott Sanderson .15 .06
267 Matt Young .15 .06
268 Ernie Whitt .15 .06
269 Houston Jimenez .15 .06
270 Ken Dixon .15 .06
271 Pete Ladd .15 .06
272 Juan Berenguer .15 .06
273 Roger Clemens RC 40.00 16.00
274 Rick Cerone .15 .06
275 Dave Anderson .15 .06
276 George Vukovich .15 .06
277 Greg Pryor .15 .06
278 Mike Warren .15 .06
279 Bob James .15 .06
280 Bobby Grich .40 .16
281 Mike Mason RC .15 .06
282 Ron Reed .15 .06
283 Alan Ashby .15 .06
284 Mark Thurmond .15 .06
285 Joe Lefebvre .15 .06
286 Ted Power .15 .06
287 Chris Chambliss .40 .16
288 Lee Tunnell .15 .06
289 Rich Bordi .15 .06
290 Glenn Brummer .15 .06
291 Mike Boddicker .15 .06
292 Rollie Fingers .40 .16
293 Lou Whitaker .40 .16
294 Dwight Evans .40 .16
295 Don Mattingly 5.00 2.00
296 Mike Marshall .15 .06
297 Willie Wilson .15 .06
298 Mike Heath .15 .06
299 Tim Raines .40 .16

300 Larry Parrish .15 .06
301 Geoff Zahn .15 .06
302 Rich Dotson .15 .06
303 David Green .15 .06
304 Jose Cruz .40 .16
305 Steve Carlton .40 .16
306 Gary Redus .15 .06
307 Steve Garvey .40 .16
308 Jose DeLeon .15 .06
309 Randy Lerch .15 .06
310 Claudell Washington .15 .06
311 Lee Smith .75 .30
312 Darryl Strawberry 1.25 .50
313 Jim Beattie .15 .06
314 John Butcher .15 .06
315 Damaso Garcia .15 .06
316 Mike Smithson .15 .06
317 Luis Leal .15 .06
318 Ken Phelps .15 .06
319 Wally Backman .15 .06
320 Ron Cey .40 .16
321 Brad Komminsk .15 .06
322 Jason Thompson .15 .06
323 Frank Williams .15 .06
324 Tim Lollar .15 .06
325 Eric Davis RC 2.00 .80
326 Von Hayes .15 .06
327 Andy Van Slyke .75 .30
328 Craig Reynolds .15 .06
329 Dick Schofield .15 .06
330 Scott Fletcher .15 .06
331 Jeff Reardon .40 .16
332 Rick Dempsey .15 .06
333 Ben Oglivie .15 .06
334 Dan Petry .15 .06
335 Jackie Gutierrez .15 .06
336 Dave Righetti .40 .16
337 Alejandro Pena .15 .06
338 Mel Hall .15 .06
339 Pat Sheridan .15 .06
340 Keith Atherton .15 .06
341 David Palmer .15 .06
342 Gary Ward .15 .06
343 Dave Stewart .40 .16
344 Mark Gubicza RC* .40 .16
345 Carney Lansford .40 .16
346 Jerry Willard .15 .06
347 Ken Griffey .40 .16
348 Franklin Stubbs .15 .06
349 Aurelio Lopez .15 .06
350 Al Bumbry .15 .06
351 Charlie Moore .15 .06
352 Luis Sanchez .15 .06
353 Darrell Porter .15 .06
354 Bill Dawley .15 .06
355 Charles Hudson .15 .06
356 Garry Templeton .15 .06
357 Cecilio Guante .15 .06
358 Jeff Leonard .15 .06
359 Paul Molitor .75 .30
360 Ron Gardenhire .15 .06
361 Larry Bowa .40 .16
362 Bob Kearney .15 .06
363 Garth Iorg .15 .06
364 Tom Brunansky .40 .16
365 Brad Gulden .15 .06
366 Greg Walker .15 .06
367 Mike Young .15 .06
368 Rick Waits .15 .06
369 Doug Bair .15 .06
370 Bob Shirley .15 .06
371 Bob Ojeda .15 .06
372 Bob Welch .15 .06
373 Neal Heaton .15 .06
374 Danny Jackson UER .15 .06
(Photo actually
Frank Wills)
375 Donnie Hill .15 .06
376 Mike Stenhouse .15 .06
377 Bruce Kison .15 .06
378 Wayne Tolleson .15 .06
379 Floyd Bannister .15 .06
380 Vern Ruhle .15 .06
381 Tim Corcoran .15 .06
382 Kurt Kepshire .15 .06
383 Bobby Brown .15 .06
384 Dave Van Gorder .15 .06
385 Rick Mahler .15 .06
386 Lee Mazzilli .15 .06
387 Bill Laskey .15 .06
388 Thad Bosley .15 .06
389 Al Chambers .15 .06
390 Tony Fernandez .40 .16
391 Ron Washington .15 .06
392 Bill Swaggerty .15 .06
393 Bob L. Gibson .15 .06
394 Marty Castillo .15 .06
395 Steve Crawford .15 .06
396 Clay Christiansen .15 .06
397 Bob Bailor .15 .06
398 Mike Hargrove .40 .16
399 Charlie Leibrandt .15 .06
400 Tom Burgmeier .15 .06
401 Razor Shines .15 .06
402 Rob Wilfong .15 .06
403 Tom Henke .40 .16
404 Al Jones .15 .06
405 Mike LaCoss .15 .06
406 Luis DeLeon .15 .06
407 Greg Gross .15 .06
408 Tom Hume .15 .06
409 Rick Camp .15 .06
410 Milt May .15 .06
411 Henry Cotto RC .15 .06
412 David Von Ohlen .15 .06
413 Scott McGregor .15 .06
414 Ted Simmons .40 .16
415 Jack Morris .40 .16
416 Bill Buckner .40 .16
417 Butch Wynegar .15 .06
418 Steve Sax .15 .06
419 Steve Balboni .15 .06
420 Dwayne Murphy .15 .06
421 Andre Dawson .40 .16
422 Charlie Hough .40 .16
423 Tommy John .75 .30
424A Tom Seaver ERR .75 .30
(Photo actually
Floyd Bannister)
424B Tom Seaver COR 10.00 4.00
425 Tom Herr .40 .16
426 Terry Puhl .15 .06
427 Al Holland .15 .06
428 Eddie Milner .15 .06
429 Terry Kennedy .15 .06
430 John Candelaria .15 .06
431 Manny Trillo .15 .06
432 Ken Oberkfell .15 .06
433 Rick Sutcliffe .40 .16
434 Ron Darling .40 .16
435 Spike Owen .15 .06
436 Frank Viola .40 .16
437 Lloyd Moseby .15 .06
438 Kirby Puckett RC 12.00 4.80
439 Jim Clancy .15 .06
440 Mike Moore .15 .06
441 Doug Sisk .15 .06
442 Dennis Eckersley .75 .30
443 Gerald Perry .15 .06
444 Dale Berra .15 .06
445 Dusty Baker .40 .16
446 Ed Whitson .15 .06
447 Cesar Cedeno .40 .16
448 Rick Schu .15 .06
449 Joaquin Andujar .15 .06
450 Mark Bailey .15 .06
451 Ron Romanick .15 .06
452 Julio Cruz .15 .06
453 Miguel Dilone .15 .06
454 Storm Davis .15 .06
455 Jaime Cocanower .15 .06
456 Barbaro Garbey .15 .06
457 Rich Gedman .15 .06
458 Phil Niekro .40 .16
459 Mike Scioscia .15 .06
460 Pat Tabler .15 .06
461 Darryl Motley .15 .06
462 Chris Codiroli .15 .06
463 Doug Flynn .15 .06
464 Billy Sample .15 .06
465 Mickey Rivers .15 .06
466 John Wathan .15 .06
467 Bill Krueger .15 .06
468 Andre Thornton .15 .06
469 Rex Hudler .15 .06
470 Sid Bream RC .40 .16
471 Kirk Gibson .40 .16
472 John Shelby .15 .06
473 Moose Haas .15 .06
474 Doug Corbett .15 .06
475 Willie McGee .40 .16
476 Bob Knepper .15 .06
477 Kevin Gross .15 .06
478 Carmelo Martinez .15 .06
479 Kent Tekulve .15 .06
480 Chili Davis .40 .16
481 Bobby Clark .15 .06
482 Mookie Wilson .40 .16
483 Dave Owen .15 .06
484 Ed Nunez .15 .06
485 Rance Mulliniks .15 .06
486 Ken Schrom .15 .06
487 Jeff Russell .15 .06
488 Tom Paciorek .40 .16
489 Dan Ford .15 .06
490 Mike Caldwell .15 .06
491 Scottie Earl .15 .06
492 Jose Rijo RC .75 .30
493 Bruce Hurst .15 .06
494 Ken Landreaux .15 .06
495 Mike Fischlin .15 .06
496 Don Slaught .15 .06
497 Steve McCatty .15 .06
498 Gary Lucas .15 .06
499 Gary Pettis .15 .06
500 Marvis Foley .15 .06
501 Mike Squires .15 .06
502 Jim Pankovits .15 .06
503 Luis Aguayo .15 .06
504 Ralph Citarella .15 .06
505 Bruce Bochy .15 .06
506 Bob Owchinko .15 .06
507 Pascual Perez .15 .06
508 Lee Lacy .15 .06
509 Atlee Hammaker .15 .06
510 Bob Dernier .15 .06
511 Ed VandeBerg .15 .06
512 Cliff Johnson .15 .06
513 Len Whitehouse .15 .06
514 Dennis Martinez .40 .16
515 Ed Romero .15 .06
516 Rusty Kuntz .15 .06
517 Rick Miller .15 .06
518 Dennis Rasmussen .15 .06
519 Steve Yeager .15 .06
520 Chris Bando .15 .06
521 U.L. Washington .15 .06
522 Curt Young .15 .06
523 Angel Salazar .15 .06
524 Curt Kaufman .15 .06
525 Odell Jones .15 .06
526 Juan Agosto .15 .06
527 Denny Walling .15 .06
528 Andy Hawkins .15 .06
529 Sixto Lezcano .15 .06
530 Skeeter Barnes RC .15 .06
531 Randy Johnson .15 .06
532 Jim Morrison .15 .06
533 Warren Brusstar .15 .06
534A J.Pendleton RC ERR 1.25 .50
Wrong first name
534B T.Pendleton RC COR 1.25 .50
535 Vic Rodriguez .15 .06
536 Bob McClure .15 .06
537 Dave Bergman .15 .06
538 Mark Clear .15 .06
539 Mike Pagliarulo .15 .06
540 Terry Whitfield .15 .06
541 Joe Beckwith .15 .06
542 Jeff Burroughs .15 .06
543 Dan Schatzeder .15 .06
544 Donnie Scott .15 .06
545 Jim Slaton .15 .06
546 Greg Luzinski .40 .16
547 Mark Salas .15 .06
548 Dave Smith .15 .06
549 John Wockenfuss .15 .06
550 Frank Pastore .15 .06
551 Tim Flannery .15 .06
552 Rick Rhoden .15 .06
553 Mark Davis .15 .06
554 Jeff Dedmon .15 .06
555 Gary Woods .15 .06
556 Danny Heep .15 .06
557 Mark Langston RC .75 .30
558 Darrell Brown .15 .06
559 Jimmy Key RC 1.25 .50
560 Rick Lysander .15 .06
561 Doyle Alexander .15 .06
562 Mike Stanton .15 .06
563 Sid Fernandez .40 .16
564 Richie Hebner .15 .06
565 Alex Trevino .15 .06
566 Brian Harper .15 .06
567 Dan Gladden RC .40 .16
568 Luis Salazar .15 .06
569 Tom Foley .15 .06
570 Larry Andersen .15 .06
571 Danny Cox .15 .06
572 Joe Sambito .15 .06
573 Juan Beniquez .15 .06
574 Joel Skinner .15 .06
575 Randy St.Claire .15 .06
576 Floyd Rayford .15 .06
577 Roy Howell .15 .06
578 John Grubb .15 .06
579 Ed Jurak .15 .06
580 John Montefusco .15 .06
581 Orel Hershiser RC 2.00 .80
582 Tom Waddell .15 .06
583 Mark Huismann .15 .06
584 Joe Morgan .75 .30
585 Jim Wohlford .15 .06
586 Dave Schmidt .15 .06
587 Jeff Kunkel .15 .06
588 Hal McRae .40 .16
589 Bill Almon .15 .06
590 Carmelo Castillo .15 .06
591 Omar Moreno .15 .06
592 Ken Howell .15 .06
593 Tom Brookens .15 .06
594 Joe Nolan .15 .06
595 Willie Lozado .15 .06
596 Tom Nieto .15 .06
597 Walt Terrell .15 .06
598 Al Oliver .40 .16
599 Shane Rawley .15 .06
600 Denny Gonzalez .15 .06
601 Mark Grant .15 .06
602 Mike Armstrong .15 .06
603 George Foster .40 .16
604 Dave Lopes .40 .16
605 Salome Barojas .15 .06
606 Roy Lee Jackson .15 .06
607 Pete Filson .15 .06
608 Duane Walker .15 .06
609 Glenn Wilson .15 .06
610 Rafael Santana .15 .06
611 Roy Smith .15 .06
612 Ruppert Jones .15 .06
613 Joe Cowley .15 .06
614 Al Nipper UER .15 .06
(Photo actually
Mike Brown)
615 Gene Nelson .15 .06
616 Joe Carter 1.25 .50
617 Ray Knight .15 .06
618 Chuck Rainey .15 .06
619 Dan Driessen .15 .06
620 Daryl Sconiers .15 .06
621 Bill Stein .15 .06
622 Roy Smalley .15 .06
623 Ed Lynch .15 .06
624 Jeff Stone .15 .06
625 Bruce Berenyi .15 .06
626 Kelvin Chapman .15 .06
627 Joe Price .15 .06
628 Steve Bedrosian .15 .06
629 Vic Mata .15 .06
630 Mike Krukow .15 .06
631 Phil Bradley .40 .16
632 Jim Gott .15 .06
633 Randy Bush .15 .06
634 Tom Browning RC .40 .16
635 Lou Gehrig 1.25 .50
Puzzle Card
636 Reid Nichols .15 .06
637 Dan Pasqua RC .40 .16
638 German Rivera .15 .06
639 Don Schulze .15 .06
640A Mike Jones .15 .06
(Career Highlights,
takes five lines)
640B Mike Jones .15 .06
(Career Highlights,
takes four lines)
641 Pete Rose 4.00 1.60
642 Wade Rowdon .15 .06
643 Jerry Narron .15 .06
644 Darrell Miller .15 .06
645 Tim Hulett RC .15 .06
646 Andy McGaffigan .15 .06
647 Kurt Bevacqua .15 .06
648 John Russell .15 .06
649 Ron Robinson .15 .06
650 Donnie Moore .15 .06
651A Two for the Title 2.00 .80
Dave Winfield
Don Mattingly
(Yellow letters)
651B Two for the Title 5.00 2.00
Dave Winfield
Don Mattingly
(White letters)
652 Tim Laudner .15 .06
653 Steve Farr RC .40 .16
654 DK Checklist 1-26 .15 .06
(Unnumbered)
655 Checklist 27-130 .15 .06
(Unnumbered)
656 Checklist 131-234 .15 .06
(Unnumbered)
657 Checklist 235-338 .15 .06
(Unnumbered)
658 Checklist 339-442 .15 .06
(Unnumbered)
659 Checklist 443-546 .15 .06
(Unnumbered)
660 Checklist 547-653 .15 .06
(Unnumbered)

1985 Donruss Wax Box Cards

The boxes of the 1985 Donruss regular issue baseball cards, in which the wax packs were contained, featured four standard-size cards, with backs. The complete set price of the regular issue set does not include these cards; they are considered a separate set. The cards and are styled the same as the regular Donruss cards. The cards are numbered but with the prefix PC before the number. The value of the panel uncut is slightly greater, perhaps by 25 percent greater, than the value of the individual cards cut up carefully.

	Nm-Mt	Ex-Mt
COMPLETE SET (4)	4.00	1.60
PC1 Dwight Gooden	1.00	.40
PC2 Ryne Sandberg	3.00	1.20
PC3 Ron Kittle	.25	.10
PUZ Lou Gehrig Puzzle Card	.75	.30

1985 Donruss Action All-Stars

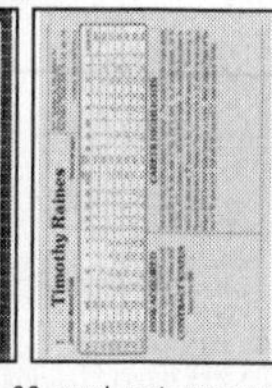

The cards in this 60-card set measure approximately 3 1/2" by 5". For the third year in a row, Donruss issued a set of Action All-Stars. This set features action photos on the obverse which also contains a portrait inset of the player. The backs, unlike the year before, do not contain a full color picture of the player but list, if space is available, full statistical data, biographical data, career highlights, and acquisition and contract status. The cards were issued with a Lou Gehrig puzzle card.

	Nm-Mt	Ex-Mt
COMPLETE SET (60)	8.00	3.20
1 Tim Raines	.10	.04
2 Jim Gantner	.05	.02
3 Mario Soto	.05	.02
4 Spike Owen	.05	.02
5 Lloyd Moseby	.05	.02
6 Damaso Garcia	.05	.02
7 Cal Ripken	2.50	1.00
8 Dan Quisenberry	.05	.02
9 Eddie Murray	.60	.24
10 Tony Pena	.10	.04
11 Buddy Bell	.10	.04
12 Dave Winfield	.40	.16
13 Ron Kittle	.05	.02
14 Rich Gossage	.10	.04
15 Dwight Evans	.10	.04
16 Alvin Davis	.05	.02
17 Mike Schmidt	.60	.24
18 Pascual Perez	.05	.02
19 Tony Gwynn	2.00	.80
20 Nolan Ryan	2.50	1.00
21 Robin Yount	.40	.16
22 Mike Marshall	.05	.02
23 Brett Butler	.10	.04
24 Ryne Sandberg	.75	.30
25 Dale Murphy	.30	.12
26 George Brett	1.25	.50
27 Jim Rice	.10	.04
28 Ozzie Smith	1.00	.40
29 Larry Parrish	.05	.02
30 Jack Clark	.10	.04
31 Manny Trillo	.05	.02
32 Dave Kingman	.20	.08
33 Geoff Zahn	.05	.02
34 Pedro Guerrero	.10	.04
35 Dave Parker	.10	.04
36 Rollie Fingers	.30	.12
37 Fernando Valenzuela	.20	.08
38 Wade Boggs	.50	.20
39 Reggie Jackson	.50	.20
40 Kent Hrbek	.10	.04
41 Keith Hernandez	.10	.04
42 Lou Whitaker	.10	.04
43 Tom Herr	.05	.02
44 Alan Trammell	.20	.08
45 Butch Wynegar	.05	.02
46 Leon Durham	.05	.02
47 Dwight Gooden	.50	.20
48 Don Mattingly	1.50	.60
49 Phil Niekro	.40	.16
50 Johnny Ray	.05	.02
51 Doug DeCinces	.05	.02
52 Willie Upshaw	.05	.02
53 Lance Parrish	.10	.04
54 Jody Davis	.05	.02
55 Steve Carlton	.40	.16
56 Juan Samuel	.50	.20
57 Gary Carter	.50	.20
58 Harold Baines	.30	.12
59 Eric Show	.05	.02
60 Checklist Card	.05	.02

1985 Donruss Highlights

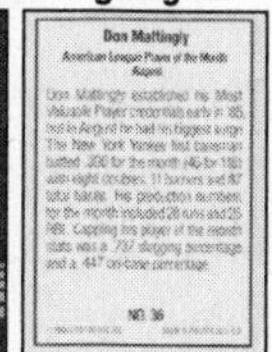

This 56-card standard-size set features the players and pitchers of the month for each league as well as a number of highlight cards commemorating the 1985 season. The Donruss Company dedicated the last two cards to their own selections for Rookies of the Year (ROY). This set proved to be more popular than the Donruss Company had predicted, as their first and only print run was exhausted before card dealers' initial orders were filled.

	Nm-Mt	Ex-Mt
COMP.FACT.SET (56)	15.00	6.00
1 Tom Seaver	.75	.30
2 Rollie Fingers	.50	.20
3 Mike Davis	.10	.04
4 Charlie Leibrandt	.10	.04
5 Dale Murphy	.50	.20
6 Fernando Valenzuela	.20	.08
7 Larry Bowa	.20	.08
8 Dave Concepcion	.20	.08
9 Tony Perez	.50	.20
10 Pete Rose	1.50	.60
11 George Brett	1.50	.60
12 Dave Stieb	.10	.04
13 Dave Parker	.20	.08
14 Andy Hawkins	.10	.04
15 Andy Hawkins	.10	.04
16 Von Hayes	.10	.04
17 Rickey Henderson	.75	.30
18 Jay Howell	.10	.04
19 Pedro Guerrero	.20	.08
20 John Tudor	.10	.04
21 Keith Hernandez Gary Carter	.50	.20
22 Nolan Ryan	5.00	2.00
23 LaMarr Hoyt	.10	.04
24 Oddibe McDowell	.10	.04
25 George Brett	1.50	.60
26 Bret Saberhagen	.50	.20
27 Keith Hernandez	.20	.08
28 Fernando Valenzuela	.20	.08
29 Willie McGee Vince Coleman	.20	.08
30 Tom Seaver	.50	.20
31 Rod Carew	.50	.20
32 Dwight Gooden	.75	.30
33 Dwight Gooden	.75	.30
34 Eddie Murray	.50	.20
35 Don Baylor	.20	.08
36 Don Mattingly	1.50	.60
37 Dave Righetti	.20	.08
38 Willie McGee	.20	.08
39 Shane Rawley	.10	.04
40 Pete Rose	1.50	.60
41 Andre Dawson	.50	.20
42 Rickey Henderson	.75	.30
43 Tom Browning	.20	.08
44 Don Mattingly	1.50	.60
45 Don Mattingly	1.50	.60
46 Charlie Leibrandt	.10	.04
47 Gary Carter	.30	.12
48 Dwight Gooden	.75	.30
49 Wade Boggs	.75	.30
50 Phil Niekro	.50	.20
51 Darrell Evans	.20	.08
52 Willie McGee	.30	.12
53 Dave Winfield	.50	.20
54 Vince Coleman	.20	.08
55 Ozzie Guillen	.50	.20
NNO Checklist Card	.10	.04

1985 Donruss HOF Sluggers

This eight-card set of Hall of Fame players features the artwork of resident Donruss artist Dick Perez. These oversized (3 1/2" by 6 1/2", blank backed cards actually form part of a box of gum distributed by the Donruss Company through supermarket type outlets. These cards are reminiscent of the Bazooka issues. The players in the set were ostensibly chosen based on their career slugging percentage. The cards themselves are numbered by (slugging percentage) rank. The boxes are also numbered on one of the white side tabs of the complete box; this completely different numbering system is not used.

	Nm-Mt	Ex-Mt
COMPLETE SET (8)	10.00	4.00
1 Babe Ruth	3.00	1.20
2 Ted Williams	2.00	.80
3 Lou Gehrig	2.00	.80
4 Johnny Mize	.50	.20
5 Stan Musial	.75	.30
6 Mickey Mantle	3.00	1.20
7 Hank Aaron	1.50	.60
8 Frank Robinson	.50	.20

1985 Donruss Super DK's

The cards in this 28-card set measure approximately 4 15/16 by 6 3/4". The 1985 Donruss Diamond Kings Supers set contains enlarged cards of the first 26 cards of the Donruss regular set of this year. In addition, the Diamond Kings checklist card, a card of artist Dick Perez and a Lou Gehrig puzzle card are included in the set. The set was the brainchild of the Perez-Steele Galleries and could be obtained via a write-in offer on the wrappers of the Donruss regular cards of this year. The Gehrig puzzle card is actually a 12-piece jigsaw puzzle. The back of the checklist card is blank; however, the Dick Perez card back gives a short history of Dick Perez and the Perez-Steele Galleries. The offer for obtaining this set was detailed on the wax pack wrappers; three wrappers plus $9.00 was required for this mail-in offer.

	Nm-Mt	Ex-Mt
COMPLETE SET (28)	12.00	4.80
1 Ryne Sandberg	2.00	.80

2 Doug DeCinces .25 .10
3 Richard Dotson .25 .10
4 Bert Blyleven .50 .20
5 Lou Whitaker .75 .30
6 Dan Quisenberry .25 .10
7 Don Mattingly 3.00 1.20
8 Carney Lansford .50 .20
9 Frank Tanana .25 .10
10 Willie Upshaw .25 .10
11 Claudell Washington .25 .10
12 Mike Marshall .25 .10
13 Joaquin Andujar .25 .10
14 Cal Ripken 5.00 2.00
15 Jim Rice .50 .20
16 Don Sutton 1.00 .40
17 Frank Viola .50 .20
18 Alvin Davis .25 .10
19 Mario Soto .25 .10
20 Jose Cruz .25 .10
21 Charlie Lea .25 .10
22 Jesse Orosco .50 .20
23 Juan Samuel .25 .10
24 Tony Pena .50 .20
25 Tony Gwynn 3.00 1.20
26 Bob Brenly .50 .20
NNO Checklist Card .25 .10
NNO Dick Perez .25 .10
(History of DK's)

1986 Donruss

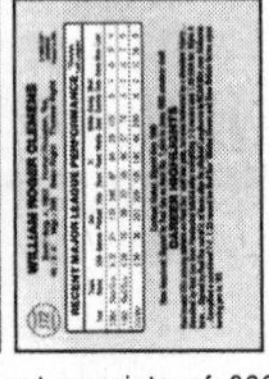

The 1986 Donruss set consists of 660 standard-size cards. Wax packs contained 15 cards plus a Hank Aaron puzzle panel. The card fronts feature blue borders, the standard team logo, player's name, position, and Donruss logo. The first 26 cards of the set are Diamond Kings (DK), for the fifth year in a row; the artwork on the Diamond Kings was again produced by the Perez-Steele Galleries. Cards 27-46 again feature Rated Rookies (RR). The unnumbered checklist cards are arbitrarily numbered below as numbers 654 through 660. Rookie Cards in this set include Jose Canseco, Darren Daulton, Len Dykstra, Cecil Fielder, Andres Galarraga, Fred McGriff and Paul O'Neill.

Nm-Mt Ex-Mt
COMPLETE SET (660) 50.00 20.00
COMP.FACT.SET (660) 50.00 20.00
COMP.AARON PUZZLE 2.00 .80
1 Kirk Gibson DK .25 .10
2 Rich Gossage DK .25 .10
3 Willie McGee DK .25 .10
4 George Bell DK .15 .06
5 Tony Armas DK .15 .06
6 Chili Davis DK .50 .20
7 Cecil Cooper DK .15 .06
8 Mike Boddicker DK .15 .06
9 Dave Lopes DK .25 .10
10 Bill Doran DK .15 .06
11 Bret Saberhagen DK .25 .10
12 Brett Butler DK .15 .06
13 Harold Baines DK .50 .20
14 Mike Davis DK .15 .06
15 Tony Perez DK .25 .10
16 Willie Randolph DK .15 .06
17 Bob Boone DK .15 .06
18 Orel Hershiser DK .25 .10
19 Johnny Ray DK .15 .06
20 Gary Ward DK .15 .06
21 Rick Mahler DK .15 .06
22 Phil Bradley DK .15 .06
23 Jerry Koosman DK .25 .10
24 Tom Brunansky DK .15 .06
25 Andre Dawson DK .15 .06
26 Dwight Gooden DK .75 .30
27 Kal Daniels RR .50 .20
28 Fred McGriff RR RC 10.00 4.00
29 Cory Snyder RR .15 .06
30 Jose Guzman RR RC .15 .06
31 Ty Gainey RC .15 .06
32 Johnny Abrego RC .15 .06
33A A.Galarraga RC RR 4.00 1.60
No accent
33B A.Galarraga RC RR 4.00 1.60
Accent over e
34 Dave Shipanoff RC .15 .06
35 M.McLemore RR RC 1.00 .40
36 Marty Clary RC .15 .06
37 Paul O'Neill RR RC 5.00 2.00
38 Danny Tartabull RR .25 .10
39 Jose Canseco RR RC 10.00 4.00
40 Juan Nieves RC .15 .06
41 Lance McCullers RC .15 .06
42 Rick Surhoff RC .15 .06
43 Todd Worrell RR RC .50 .20
44 Bob Kipper RC .15 .06
45 John Habyan RR RC .15 .06
46 Mike Woodard RC .15 .06
47 Mike Boddicker .15 .06
48 Robin Yount 1.25 .50
49 Lou Whitaker .25 .10
50 Oil Can Boyd .15 .06
51 Rickey Henderson .75 .30
52 Mike Marshall .15 .06
53 George Brett 2.00 .80
54 Dave Kingman .25 .10
55 Hubie Brooks .15 .06
56 Oddibe McDowell .15 .06
57 Doug DeCinces .15 .06
58 Britt Burns .15 .06
59 Ozzie Smith 1.25 .50
60 Jose Cruz .25 .10
61 Mike Schmidt 2.00 .80
62 Pete Rose 2.50 1.00
63 Steve Garvey .25 .10
64 Tony Pena .15 .06
65 Chili Davis .50 .20
66 Dale Murphy .75 .30
67 Ryne Sandberg 1.50 .60
68 Gary Carter .50 .20
69 Alvin Davis .15 .06
70 Kent Hrbek .25 .10
71 George Bell .25 .10
72 Kirby Puckett 2.00 .80
73 Lloyd Moseby .15 .06
74 Bob Kearney .15 .06
75 Dwight Gooden .75 .30
76 Gary Matthews .15 .06
77 Rick Mahler .15 .06
78 Benny Distefano .15 .06
79 Jeff Leonard .15 .06
80 Kevin McReynolds .25 .10
81 Ron Oester .15 .06
82 John Russell .15 .06
83 Tommy Herr .15 .06
84 Jerry Mumphrey .15 .06
85 Ron Romanick .15 .06
86 Daryl Boston .15 .06
87 Andre Dawson .25 .10
88 Eddie Murray .75 .30
89 Dion James .15 .06
90 Chet Lemon .15 .06
91 Bob Stanley .15 .06
92 Willie Randolph .25 .10
93 Mike Scioscia .15 .06
94 Tom Waddell .15 .06
95 Danny Jackson .15 .06
96 Mike Davis .15 .06
97 Mike Fitzgerald .15 .06
98 Gary Ward .15 .06
99 Pete O'Brien .15 .06
100 Bret Saberhagen .25 .10
101 Alfredo Griffin .15 .06
102 Brett Butler .25 .10
103 Ron Guidry .25 .10
104 Jerry Reuss .15 .06
105 Jack Morris .25 .10
106 Rick Dempsey .15 .06
107 Ray Burris .15 .06
108 Brian Downing .15 .06
109 Willie McGee .25 .10
110 Bill Doran .15 .06
111 Kent Tekulve .15 .06
112 Tony Gwynn 1.25 .50
113 Marvell Wynne .15 .06
114 David Green .15 .06
115 Jim Gantner .15 .06
116 George Foster .25 .10
117 Steve Trout .15 .06
118 Mark Langston .15 .06
119 Tony Fernandez .15 .06
120 John Butcher .15 .06
121 Ron Robinson .15 .06
122 Dan Spillner .15 .06
123 Mike Young .15 .06
124 Paul Molitor .50 .20
125 Kirk Gibson .25 .10
126 Ken Griffey .25 .10
127 Tony Armas .15 .06
128 Mariano Duncan RC* .50 .20
129 Pat Tabler .15 .06
130 Frank White .25 .10
131 Carney Lansford .25 .10
132 Vance Law .15 .06
133 Dick Schofield .15 .06
134 Wayne Tolleson .15 .06
135 Greg Walker .15 .06
136 Denny Walling .15 .06
137 Ozzie Virgil .15 .06
138 Ricky Horton .15 .06
139 LaMarr Hoyt .15 .06
140 Wayne Krenchicki .15 .06
141 Glenn Hubbard .15 .06
142 Cecilio Guante .15 .06
143 Mike Krukow .15 .06
144 Lee Smith .50 .20
145 Edwin Nunez .15 .06
146 Dave Stieb .15 .06
147 Mike Smithson .15 .06
148 Ken Dixon .15 .06
149 Danny Darwin .15 .06
150 Chris Pittaro .15 .06
151 Bill Buckner .25 .10
152 Mike Pagliarulo .15 .06
153 Bill Russell .15 .06
154 Brook Jacoby .15 .06
155 Pat Sheridan .15 .06
156 Mike Gallego RC .15 .06
157 Jim Wohlford .15 .06
158 Gary Pettis .15 .06
159 Toby Harrah .15 .06
160 Richard Dotson .15 .06
161 Bob Knepper .15 .06
162 Dave Dravecky .25 .10
163 Greg Gross .15 .06
164 Eric Davis .50 .20
165 Gerald Perry .15 .06
166 Rick Rhoden .15 .06
167 Keith Moreland .15 .06
168 Jack Clark .25 .10
169 Storm Davis .15 .06
170 Cecil Cooper .25 .10
171 Alan Trammell .50 .20
172 Roger Clemens 4.00 1.60
173 Don Mattingly 2.50 1.00
174 Pedro Guerrero .25 .10
175 Willie Wilson .15 .06
176 Dwayne Murphy .15 .06
177 Tim Raines .25 .10
178 Larry Parrish .15 .06
179 Mike Witt .15 .06
180 Harold Baines .50 .20
181 V.Coleman RC* UER 1.00 .40
BA 2.67 on back
182 Jeff Heathcock .15 .06
183 Steve Carlton .25 .10
184 Mario Soto .15 .06
185 Rich Gossage .25 .10
186 Johnny Ray .15 .06
187 Dan Gladden .15 .06
188 Bob Horner .15 .06
189 Rick Sutcliffe .25 .10
190 Keith Hernandez .25 .10
191 Phil Bradley .15 .06
192 Tom Brunansky .15 .06
193 Jesse Barfield .15 .06
194 Frank Viola .25 .10
195 Willie Upshaw .15 .06
196 Jim Beattie .15 .06
197 Darryl Strawberry .50 .20
198 Ron Cey .25 .10
199 Steve Bedrosian .15 .06
200 Steve Kemp .15 .06
201 Manny Trillo .15 .06
202 Garry Templeton .15 .06
203 Dave Parker .25 .10
204 John Denny .15 .06
205 Terry Pendleton .25 .10
206 Terry Puhl .15 .06
207 Bobby Grich .25 .10
208 Ozzie Guillen RC* .50 .20
209 Jeff Reardon .15 .06
210 Cal Ripken 3.00 1.20
211 Bill Schroeder .15 .06
212 Dan Petry .15 .06
213 Jim Rice .25 .10
214 Dave Righetti .15 .06
215 Fernando Valenzuela .25 .10
216 Julio Franco .25 .10
217 Darryl Motley .15 .06
218 Dave Collins .15 .06
219 Tim Wallach .15 .06
220 George Wright .15 .06
221 Tommy Dunbar .15 .06
222 Steve Balboni .15 .06
223 Jay Howell .15 .06
224 Joe Carter .75 .30
225 Ed Whitson .15 .06
226 Orel Hershiser .50 .20
227 Willie Hernandez .15 .06
228 Lee Lacy .15 .06
229 Rollie Fingers .25 .10
230 Bob Boone .25 .10
231 Joaquin Andujar .15 .06
232 Craig Reynolds .15 .06
233 Shane Rawley .15 .06
234 Eric Show .15 .06
235 Jose DeLeon .15 .06
236 Jose Uribe .15 .06
237 Moose Haas .15 .06
238 Wally Backman .15 .06
239 Dennis Eckersley .50 .20
240 Mike Moore .15 .06
241 Damaso Garcia .15 .06
242 Tim Teufel .15 .06
243 Dave Concepcion .25 .10
244 Floyd Bannister .15 .06
245 Fred Lynn .25 .10
246 Charlie Moore .15 .06
247 Walt Terrell .15 .06
248 Dave Winfield .25 .10
249 Dwight Evans .25 .10
250 Dennis Powell .15 .06
251 Andre Thornton .15 .06
252 Onix Concepcion .15 .06
253 Mike Heath .15 .06
254A David Palmer ERR .15 .06
(Position 2B)
254B David Palmer COR .50 .20
(Position P)
255 Donnie Moore .15 .06
256 Curtis Wilkerson .15 .06
257 Julio Cruz .15 .06
258 Nolan Ryan 4.00 1.60
259 Jeff Stone .15 .06
260 John Tudor .15 .06
261 Mark Thurmond .15 .06
262 Jay Tibbs .15 .06
263 Rafael Ramirez .15 .06
264 Larry McWilliams .15 .06
265 Mark Davis .15 .06
266 Bob Dernier .15 .06
267 Matt Young .15 .06
268 Jim Clancy .15 .06
269 Mickey Hatcher .15 .06
270 Sammy Stewart .15 .06
271 Bob L. Gibson .15 .06
272 Nelson Simmons .15 .06
273 Rich Gedman .15 .06
274 Butch Wynegar .15 .06
275 Ken Howell .15 .06
276 Mel Hall .15 .06
277 Jim Sundberg .15 .06
278 Chris Codiroli .15 .06
279 Herm Winningham .15 .06
280 Rod Carew .50 .20
281 Don Slaught .15 .06
282 Scott Fletcher .15 .06
283 Bill Dawley .15 .06
284 Andy Hawkins .15 .06
285 Glenn Wilson .15 .06
286 Nick Esasky .15 .06
287 Claudell Washington .15 .06
288 Lee Mazzilli .15 .06
289 Jody Davis .15 .06
290 Darrell Porter .25 .10
291 Scott McGregor .15 .06
292 Ted Simmons .25 .10
293 Aurelio Lopez .15 .06
294 Marty Barrett .15 .06
295 Dale Berra .15 .06
296 Greg Brock .15 .06
297 Charlie Leibrandt .15 .06
298 Bill Krueger .15 .06
299 Bryn Smith .15 .06
300 Burt Hooton .15 .06
301 Stu Cliburn .15 .06
302 Luis Salazar .15 .06
303 Ken Dayley .15 .06
304 Frank DiPino .15 .06
305 Von Hayes .15 .06
306 Gary Redus .15 .06
307 Craig Lefferts .15 .06
308 Sammy Khalifa .15 .06
309 Scott Garrelts .15 .06
310 Rick Cerone .15 .06
311 Shawon Dunston .25 .10
312 Howard Johnson .25 .10
313 Jim Presley .25 .10
314 Gary Gaetti .25 .10
315 Luis Leal .15 .06
316 Mark Salas .15 .06
317 Bill Caudill .15 .06
318 Dave Henderson .15 .06
319 Rafael Santana .15 .06
320 Leon Durham .15 .06
321 Bruce Sutter .25 .10
322 Jason Thompson .15 .06
323 Bob Brenly .15 .06
324 Carmelo Martinez .15 .06
325 Eddie Milner .15 .06
326 Juan Samuel .15 .06
327 Tom Nieto .15 .06
328 Dave Smith .15 .06
329 Urbano Lugo .15 .06
330 Joel Skinner .15 .06
331 Bill Gullickson .15 .06
332 Floyd Rayford .15 .06
333 Ben Oglivie .15 .06
334 Lance Parrish .25 .10
335 Jackie Gutierrez .15 .06
336 Dennis Rasmussen .15 .06
337 Terry Whitfield .15 .06
338 Neal Heaton .15 .06
339 Jorge Orta .15 .06
340 Donnie Hill .15 .06
341 Joe Hesketh .15 .06
342 Charlie Hough .25 .10
343 Dave Rozema .15 .06
344 Greg Pryor .15 .06
345 Mickey Tettleton RC .50 .20
346 George Vukovich .15 .06
347 Don Baylor .50 .20
348 Carlos Diaz .15 .06
349 Barbaro Garbey .15 .06
350 Larry Sheets .15 .06
351 Ted Higuera RC* .50 .20
352 Juan Beniquez .15 .06
353 Bob Forsch .15 .06
354 Mark Bailey .15 .06
355 Larry Andersen .15 .06
356 Terry Kennedy .15 .06
357 Don Robinson .15 .06
358 Jim Gott .15 .06
359 Earnie Riles .15 .06
360 John Christensen .15 .06
361 Ray Fontenot .15 .06
362 Spike Owen .15 .06
363 Jim Acker .15 .06
364 Ron Davis .15 .06
365 Tom Hume .15 .06
366 Carlton Fisk .50 .20
367 Nate Snell .15 .06
368 Rick Manning .15 .06
369 Darrell Evans .25 .10
370 Ron Hassey .15 .06
371 Wade Boggs .50 .20
372 Rick Honeycutt .15 .06
373 Chris Bando .15 .06
374 Bud Black .15 .06
375 Steve Henderson .15 .06
376 Charlie Lea .15 .06
377 Reggie Jackson .50 .20
378 Dave Schmidt .15 .06
379 Bob James .15 .06
380 Glenn Davis .25 .10
381 Tim Corcoran .15 .06
382 Danny Cox .15 .06
383 Tim Flannery .15 .06
384 Tom Browning .15 .06
385 Rick Camp .15 .06
386 Jim Morrison .15 .06
387 Dave LaPoint .15 .06
388 Dave Lopes .25 .10
389 Al Cowens .15 .06
390 Doyle Alexander .15 .06
391 Tim Laudner .15 .06
392 Don Aase .15 .06
393 Jaime Cocanower .15 .06
394 Randy O'Neal .15 .06
395 Mike Easler .15 .06
396 Scott Bradley .15 .06
397 Tom Niedenfuer .15 .06
398 Jerry Willard .15 .06
399 Lonnie Smith .15 .06
400 Bruce Bochte .15 .06
401 Terry Francona .15 .06
402 Jim Slaton .15 .06
403 Bill Stein .15 .06
404 Tim Hulett .15 .06
405 Alan Ashby .15 .06
406 Tim Stoddard .15 .06
407 Garry Maddox .15 .06
408 Ted Power .15 .06
409 Len Barker .15 .06
410 Denny Gonzalez .15 .06
411 George Frazier .15 .06
412 Andy Van Slyke .25 .10
413 Jim Dwyer .15 .06
414 Paul Householder .15 .06
415 Alejandro Sanchez .15 .06
416 Steve Crawford .15 .06
417 Dan Pasqua .15 .06
418 Enos Cabell .15 .06
419 Mike Jones .15 .06
420 Steve Kiefer .15 .06
421 Tim Burke .15 .06
422 Mike Mason .15 .06
423 Ruppert Jones .15 .06
424 Jerry Hairston .15 .06
425 Tito Landrum .15 .06
426 Jeff Calhoun .15 .06
427 Don Carman .15 .06
428 Tony Perez .50 .20
429 Jerry Davis .15 .06
430 Bob Walk .15 .06
431 Brad Wellman .15 .06
432 Terry Forster .15 .06
433 Billy Hatcher .15 .06
434 Clint Hurdle .15 .06
435 Ivan Calderon RC* .50 .20
436 Pete Filson .15 .06
437 Tom Henke .25 .10
438 Dave Engle .15 .06
439 Tom Filer .15 .06
440 Gorman Thomas .15 .06
441 Rick Aguilera RC .50 .20
442 Scott Sanderson .15 .06
443 Jeff Dedmon .15 .06
444 Joe Orsulak RC* .15 .06
445 Atlee Hammaker .15 .06
446 Jerry Royster .15 .06
447 Buddy Bell .25 .10
448 Dave Rucker .15 .06
449 Ivan DeJesus .15 .06
450 Jim Pankovits .15 .06
451 Jerry Narron .15 .06
452 Bryan Little .15 .06
453 Gary Lucas .15 .06
454 Dennis Martinez .25 .10
455 Ed Romero .15 .06
456 Bob Melvin .15 .06
457 Glenn Hoffman .15 .06
458 Bob Shirley .15 .06
459 Bob Welch .15 .06
460 Carmen Castillo .15 .06
461 Dave Leeper .15 .06
462 Tim Birtsas .15 .06
463 Randy St.Claire .15 .06
464 Chris Welsh .15 .06
465 Greg Harris .15 .06
466 Lynn Jones .15 .06
467 Dusty Baker .25 .10
468 Roy Smith .15 .06
469 Andre Robertson .15 .06
470 Ken Landreaux .15 .06
471 Dave Bergman .15 .06
472 Gary Roenicke .15 .06
473 Pete Vuckovich .15 .06
474 Kirk McCaskill RC .25 .10
475 Jeff Lahti .15 .06
476 Mike Scott .15 .06
477 Darren Daulton RC 1.50 .60
478 Graig Nettles .25 .10
479 Bill Almon .15 .06
480 Greg Minton .15 .06
481 Randy Ready .15 .06
482 Len Dykstra RC 1.50 .60
483 Thad Bosley .15 .06
484 Harold Reynolds RC 1.50 .60
485 Al Oliver .25 .10
486 Roy Smalley .15 .06
487 John Franco .75 .30
488 Juan Agosto .15 .06
489 Al Pardo .15 .06
490 Bill Wegman RC .15 .06
491 Frank Tanana .15 .06
492 Brian Fisher RC .15 .06
493 Mark Clear .15 .06
494 Len Matuszek .15 .06
495 Ramon Romero .15 .06
496 John Wathan .15 .06
497 Rob Picciolo .15 .06
498 U.L. Washington .15 .06
499 John Candelaria .15 .06
500 Duane Walker .15 .06
501 Gene Nelson .15 .06
502 John Mizerock .15 .06
503 Luis Aguayo .15 .06
504 Kurt Kepshire .15 .06
505 Ed Wojna .15 .06
506 Joe Price .15 .06
507 Milt Thompson RC .15 .06
508 Junior Ortiz .15 .06
509 Vida Blue .25 .10
510 Steve Engel .15 .06
511 Karl Best .15 .06
512 Cecil Fielder RC 1.50 .60
513 Frank Eufemia .15 .06
514 Tippy Martinez .15 .06
515 Billy Joe Robidoux .15 .06
516 Bill Scherrer .15 .06
517 Bruce Hurst .15 .06
518 Rich Bordi .15 .06
519 Steve Yeager .15 .06
520 Tony Bernazard .15 .06
521 Hal McRae .25 .10
522 Jose Rijo .15 .06
523 Mitch Webster .15 .06
524 Jack Howell .15 .06
525 Alan Bannister .15 .06
526 Ron Kittle .15 .06
527 Phil Garner .25 .10
528 Kurt Bevacqua .15 .06
529 Kevin Gross .15 .06
530 Bo Diaz .15 .06
531 Ken Oberkfell .15 .06
532 Rick Reuschel .15 .06
533 Ron Meridith .15 .06
534 Steve Braun .15 .06
535 Wayne Gross .15 .06
536 Ray Searage .15 .06
537 Tom Brookens .15 .06
538 Al Nipper .15 .06
539 Billy Sample .15 .06
540 Steve Sax .15 .06
541 Dan Quisenberry .15 .06
542 Tony Phillips .15 .06
543 Floyd Youmans .15 .06
544 Steve Buechele RC .50 .20
545 Craig Gerber .15 .06
546 Joe DeSa .15 .06
547 Brian Harper .15 .06
548 Kevin Bass .15 .06
549 Tom Foley .15 .06
550 Dave Van Gorder .15 .06
551 Bruce Bochy .15 .06
552 R.J. Reynolds .15 .06
553 Chris Brown .15 .06
554 Bruce Benedict .15 .06
555 Warren Brusstar .15 .06
556 Danny Heep .15 .06
557 Darnell Coles .15 .06
558 Greg Gagne .15 .06
559 Ernie Whitt .15 .06
560 Ron Washington .15 .06
561 Jimmy Key .75 .30
562 Billy Swift .15 .06
563 Ron Darling .15 .06
564 Dick Ruthven .15 .06
565 Zane Smith .15 .06
566 Sid Bream .15 .06
567A J.Youngblood ERR .15 .06
Position P
567B J.Youngblood COR .50 .20
Position IF
568 Mario Ramirez .15 .06
569 Tom Runnells .15 .06
570 Rick Schu .15 .06
571 Bill Campbell .15 .06
572 Dickie Thon .15 .06
573 Al Holland .15 .06
574 Reid Nichols .15 .06
575 Bert Roberge .15 .06
576 Mike Flanagan .15 .06
577 Tim Leary .15 .06
578 Mike Laga .15 .06
579 Steve Lyons .15 .06
580 Phil Niekro .25 .10
581 Gilberto Reyes .15 .06

582 Jamie Easterly .15 .06
583 Mark Gubicza .15 .06
584 Stan Javier RC .50 .20
585 Bill Laskey .15 .06
586 Jeff Russell .15 .06
587 Dickie Noles .15 .06
588 Steve Farr .15 .06
589 Steve Ontiveros RC .15 .06
590 Mike Hargrove .25 .10
591 Marty Bystrom .15 .06
592 Franklin Stubbs .15 .06
593 Larry Herndon .15 .06
594 Bill Swaggerty .15 .06
595 Carlos Ponce .15 .06
596 Pat Perry .15 .06
597 Ray Knight .25 .10
598 Steve Lombardozzi .15 .06
599 Brad Havens .15 .06
600 Pat Clements .15 .06
601 Joe Niekro .15 .06
602 Hank Aaron .75 .30
Puzzle Card
603 Dwayne Henry .15 .06
604 Mookie Wilson .25 .10
605 Buddy Biancalana .15 .06
606 Rance Mulliniks .15 .06
607 Alan Wiggins .15 .06
608 Joe Cowley .15 .06
609 Tom Seaver .50 .20
(Green borders on name)
609B Tom Seaver 2.00 .80
(Yellow borders on name)
610 Neil Allen .15 .06
611 Don Sutton .75 .30
612 Fred Toliver .15 .06
613 Jay Baller .15 .06
614 Marc Sullivan .15 .06
615 John Grubb .15 .06
616 Bruce Kison .15 .06
617 Bill Madlock .15 .06
618 Chris Chambliss .25 .10
619 Dave Stewart .25 .10
620 Tim Lollar .15 .06
621 Gary Lavelle .15 .06
622 Charles Hudson .15 .06
623 Joel Davis .15 .06
624 Joe Johnson .15 .06
625 Sid Fernandez .25 .10
626 Dennis Lamp .15 .06
627 Terry Harper .15 .06
628 Jack Lazorko .15 .06
629 Roger McDowell RC* .50 .20
630 Mark Funderburk .15 .06
631 Ed Lynch .15 .06
632 Rudy Law .15 .06
633 Roger Mason RC .15 .06
634 Mike Felder RC .15 .06
635 Ken Schrom .15 .06
636 Bob Ojeda .15 .06
637 Ed VandeBerg .15 .06
638 Bobby Meacham .15 .06
639 Cliff Johnson .15 .06
640 Garth Iorg .15 .06
641 Dan Driessen .15 .06
642 Mike Brown OF .15 .06
643 John Shelby .15 .06
644 Pete Rose RB .75 .30
645 Phil Niekro .25 .10
Joe Niekro
646 Jesse Orosco .15 .06
647 Billy Beane RC 1.00 .40
648 Cesar Cedeno .25 .10
649 Bert Blyleven .25 .10
650 Max Venable .15 .06
651 Vince Coleman .15 .06
Willie McGee
652 Calvin Schiraldi .15 .06
653 Pete Rose KING .75 .30
654 Dia. Kings CL 1-26 .15 .06
Unnumbered
655A CL 1: 27-130 .15 .06
(Unnumbered)
(45 Beane ERR)
655B CL 1: 27-130 .15 .06
(Unnumbered)
(45 Habyan COR)
656 CL 2: 131-234 .15 .06
(Unnumbered)
657 CL 3: 235-338 .15 .06
(Unnumbered)
658 CL 4: 339-442 .15 .06
(Unnumbered)
659 CL 5: 443-546 .15 .06
(Unnumbered)
660 CL 6: 547-653 .15 .06
(Unnumbered)

1986 Donruss Wax Box Cards

The cards in this four-card set measure the standard 2 1/2" by 3 1/2". Cards have essentially the same design as the 1986 Donruss regular issue set. The cards were printed on the bottoms of the regular issue wax pack boxes. The four cards (PC4 to PC6 plus a Hank Aaron puzzle card) are considered a separate set in their own right and are not typically included in a complete set of the regular issue 1986 Donruss cards. The value of the panel uncut is slightly greater, perhaps by 25 percent greater, than the value of the individual cards cut up carefully.

Nm-Mt Ex-Mt
COMPLETE SET (4) 1.00 .40
PC4 Kirk Gibson .40 .16
PC5 Willie Hernandez .10 .04
PC6 Doug DeCinces .10 .04
PUZ Hank Aaron .75 .30
Puzzle Card

1986 Donruss Rookies

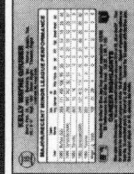

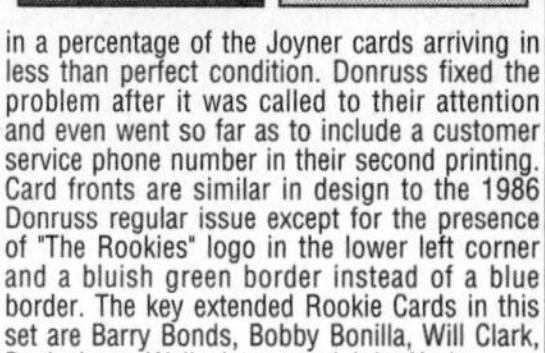

The 1986 Donruss "The Rookies" set features 56 full-color standard-size cards plus a 15-piece puzzle of Hank Aaron. The set was distributed through hobby dealers in a small green, cellophane wrapped factory box. Although the set was wrapped in cellophane, the top card was number one Joyner, resulting in a percentage of the Joyner cards arriving in less than perfect condition. Donruss fixed the problem after it was called to their attention and even went so far as to include a customer service phone number in their second printing. Card fronts are similar in design to the 1986 Donruss regular issue except for the presence of "The Rookies" logo in the lower left corner and a bluish green border instead of a blue border. The key extended Rookie Cards in this set are Barry Bonds, Bobby Bonilla, Will Clark, Bo Jackson, Wally Joyner and John Kruk.

Nm-Mt Ex-Mt
COMP.FACT.SET (56) 50.00 20.00
1 Wally Joyner XRC 1.00 .40
2 Tracy Jones .15 .06
3 Allan Anderson .15 .06
4 Ed Correa .15 .06
5 Reggie Williams .15 .06
6 Charlie Kerfeld .15 .06
7 Andres Galarraga 1.50 .60
8 Bob Tewksbury XRC .50 .20
9 Al Newman .15 .06
10 Andres Thomas .15 .06
11 Barry Bonds XRC 40.00 16.00
12 Juan Nieves .15 .06
13 Mark Eichhorn .15 .06
14 Dan Plesac XRC .50 .20
15 Cory Snyder .15 .06
16 Kelly Gruber .15 .06
17 Kevin Mitchell XRC 1.00 .40
18 Steve Lombardozzi .15 .06
19 Mitch Williams XRC .50 .20
20 John Cerutti .15 .06
21 Todd Worrell 1.00 .40
22 Jose Canseco 1.50 .60
23 Pete Incaviglia XRC .50 .20
24 Jose Guzman .15 .06
25 Scott Bailes .15 .06
26 Greg Mathews .15 .06
27 Eric King .15 .06
28 Paul Assenmacher .15 .06
29 Jeff Sellers .15 .06
30 Bobby Bonilla XRC 1.00 .40
31 Doug Drabek XRC 1.00 .40
32 Will Clark UER 2.00 .80
(Listed as throwing right, should be left) XRC
33 Bip Roberts XRC .50 .20
34 Jim Deshaies XRC .50 .20
35 Mike LaValliere XRC .50 .20
36 Scott Bankhead .15 .06
37 Dale Sveum .15 .06
38 Bo Jackson XRC 2.00 .80
39 Robby Thompson XRC .50 .20
40 Eric Plunk .15 .06
41 Bill Bathe .15 .06
42 John Kruk XRC 1.50 .60
43 Andy Allanson .15 .06
44 Mark Portugal XRC .50 .20
45 Danny Tartabull .25 .10
46 Bob Kipper .15 .06
47 Gene Walter .15 .06
48 Rey Quinones UER .15 .06
(Misspelled Quinonez)
49 Bobby Witt XRC .50 .20
50 Bill Mooneyham .15 .06
51 John Cangelosi .15 .06
52 Ruben Sierra XRC 1.50 .60
53 Rob Woodward .15 .06
54 Ed Hearn .15 .06
55 Joel McKeon .15 .06
56 Checklist 1-56 .15 .06

1986 Donruss All-Stars

The cards in this 60-card set measure approximately 3 1/2" by 5". Players featured were involved in the 1985 All-Star game played in Minnesota. Cards are very similar in design to the 1986 Donruss regular issue set. The backs give each player's All-Star game statistics and have an orange-yellow border.

Nm-Mt Ex-Mt
COMPLETE SET (60) 6.00 2.40
1 Tony Gwynn 1.25 .50
2 Tommy Herr .05 .02
3 Steve Garvey .20 .08
4 Dale Murphy .20 .08
5 Darryl Strawberry .10 .04
6 Graig Nettles .10 .04
7 Terry Kennedy .05 .02
8 Ozzie Smith .75 .30
9 LaMarr Hoyt .05 .02
10 Rickey Henderson .60 .24
11 Lou Whitaker .10 .04
12 George Brett 1.00 .40
13 Eddie Murray .50 .20
14 Cal Ripken 2.00 .80
15 Dave Winfield .30 .12
16 Jim Rice .10 .04
17 Carlton Fisk .30 .12
18 Jack Morris .10 .04
19 Jose Cruz .05 .02
20 Tim Raines .10 .04
21 Nolan Ryan 2.00 .80
22 Tony Pena .10 .04
23 Jack Clark .10 .04
24 Dave Parker .10 .04
25 Tim Wallach .05 .02
26 Ozzie Virgil .05 .02
27 Fernando Valenzuela .10 .04
28 Dwight Gooden .20 .08
29 Glenn Wilson .05 .02
30 Garry Templeton .05 .02
31 Goose Gossage .10 .04
32 Ryne Sandberg .50 .20
33 Jeff Reardon .05 .02
34 Pete Rose .50 .20
35 Scott Garrelts .05 .02
36 Willie McGee .10 .04
37 Ron Darling .05 .02
38 Dick Williams MG .05 .02
39 Paul Molitor .30 .12
40 Damaso Garcia .05 .02
41 Phil Bradley .05 .02
42 Dan Petry .05 .02
43 Willie Hernandez .05 .02
44 Tom Brunansky .05 .02
45 Alan Trammell .20 .08
46 Donnie Moore .05 .02
47 Wade Boggs .50 .20
48 Ernie Whitt .05 .02
49 Harold Baines .10 .04
50 Don Mattingly .75 .30
51 Gary Ward .05 .02
52 Bert Blyleven .10 .04
53 Jimmy Key .10 .04
54 Cecil Cooper .10 .04
55 Dave Stieb .05 .02
56 Rich Gedman .05 .02
57 Jay Howell .05 .02
58 Sparky Anderson MG .05 .02
59 Minn. Metrodome .05 .02
NNO Checklist Card .05 .02

1986 Donruss All-Star Box

The cards in this four-card set measure the standard size in spite of the fact that they form the bottom of the wax pack box for the larger Donruss All-Star cards. These box cards have essentially the same design as the 1986 Donruss regular issue set. The cards were printed on the bottoms of the Donruss All-Star (3 1/2" by 5") wax pack boxes. The four cards (PC7 to PC9 plus a Hank Aaron puzzle card) are considered a separate set in their own right and are not typically included in a complete set of the regular issue 1986 Donruss All-Star (or regular) cards. The value of the panel uncut is slightly greater, perhaps by 25 percent greater, than the value of the individual cards cut up carefully.

Nm-Mt Ex-Mt
COMPLETE SET (4) 2.00 .80
PC7 Wade Boggs 1.00 .40
PC8 Lee Smith .50 .20
PC9 Cecil Cooper .25 .10
PUZ Hank Aaron .75 .30
Puzzle Card

1986 Donruss Highlights

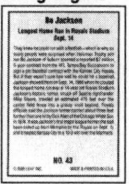

Donruss' second edition of Highlights was released late in 1986. These glossy-coated cards are standard size. Cards commemorate events during the 1986 season, as well as players and pitchers of the month from each league. The set was distributed in its own red, white, blue, and gold box along with a small Hank Aaron puzzle. Card fronts are similar to the regular 1986 Donruss issue except that the Highlights logo is positioned in the lower left-hand corner and the borders are in gold instead of blue. The backs are printed in black and gold on white card stock. A first year card of Jose Canseco highlights this set.

Nm-Mt Ex-Mt
COMP. FACT. SET (56) 5.00 2.00
1 Will Clark 1.00 .40
2 Jose Rijo .10 .04
3 George Brett .60 .24
4 Mike Schmidt .40 .16
5 Roger Clemens .75 .30
6 Roger Clemens .75 .30
7 Kirby Puckett .50 .20
8 Dwight Gooden .40 .16
9 Johnny Ray .10 .04
10 Mickey Mantle 1.00 .40
Reggie Jackson
11 Wade Boggs .25 .10
12 Don Aase .10 .04
13 Wade Boggs .25 .10
14 Jeff Reardon .10 .04
15 Hubie Brooks .10 .04
16 Don Sutton .40 .16
17 Roger Clemens .75 .30
18 Roger Clemens .75 .30
19 Kent Hrbek .15 .06
20 Rick Rhoden .10 .04
21 Kevin Bass .10 .04
22 Bob Horner .10 .04
23 Wally Joyner .40 .16
24 Darryl Strawberry .25 .10
25 Fernando Valenzuela .15 .06
26 Roger Clemens .75 .30
27 Jack Morris .15 .06
28 Scott Fletcher .10 .04
29 Todd Worrell .15 .06
30 Eric Davis .25 .10
31 Bert Blyleven .15 .06
32 Bobby Doerr .25 .10
33 Ernie Lombardi .15 .06
34 Willie McCovey .15 .06
35 Steve Carlton .15 .06
36 Mike Schmidt .40 .16
37 Juan Samuel .10 .04
38 Mike Witt .10 .04
39 Doug DeCinces .10 .04
40 Bill Gullickson .10 .04
41 Dale Murphy .40 .16
42 Joe Carter .40 .16
43 Bo Jackson 1.00 .40
44 Joe Cowley .10 .04
45 Jim Deshaies .10 .04
46 Mike Scott .10 .04
47 Bruce Hurst .10 .04
48 Don Mattingly .60 .24
49 Mike Krukow .10 .04
50 Steve Sax .10 .04
51 John Cangelosi .10 .04
52 Dave Righetti .10 .04
53 Don Mattingly .60 .24
54 Todd Worrell .15 .06
55 Jose Canseco 1.00 .40
56 Checklist Card .10 .04

1986 Donruss Pop-Ups

This set is the companion of the 1986 Donruss All-Star (60) set; as such it features the first 18 cards of that set (the All-Star starting line-ups) in a pop-up, die-cut type of card. These cards (measuring (2 1/2" X 5") can be "popped up" to feature a standing card showing the player in action in front of the Metrodome ballpark background. Although this set is unnumbered it is numbered in the same order as its companion set, presumably according to the respective batting orders of the starting line-ups. The first nine numbers below are National Leaguers and the last nine are American Leaguers. See also the Donruss All-Star checklist card which contains a checklist for the Pop-Ups as well.

Nm-Mt Ex-Mt
COMPLETE SET (18) 5.00 2.00
1 Tony Gwynn 1.50 .60
2 Tommy Herr .05 .02
3 Steve Garvey .20 .08
4 Dale Murphy .30 .12
5 Darryl Strawberry .10 .04
6 Graig Nettles .10 .04
7 Terry Kennedy .05 .02
8 Ozzie Smith 1.00 .40
9 LaMarr Hoyt .05 .02
10 Rickey Henderson .50 .20
11 Lou Whitaker .10 .04
12 George Brett 1.25 .50
13 Eddie Murray .60 .24
14 Cal Ripken 2.50 1.00
15 Dave Winfield .30 .12
16 Jim Rice .10 .04
17 Carlton Fisk .30 .12
18 Jack Morris .10 .04

1986 Donruss Super DK's

This 29-card set of large Diamond Kings features the full-color artwork of Dick Perez. The set could be obtained from Perez-Steele Galleries by sending three Donruss wrappers and $9.00. The cards measure 4 7/8" by 6 13/16" and are identical in design to the Diamond King cards in the Donruss regular issue.

Nm-Mt Ex-Mt
COMPLETE SET (27) 12.00 4.80
1 Kirk Gibson .50 .20
2 Goose Gossage .50 .20
3 Willie McGee .50 .20
4 George Bell .25 .10
5 Tony Armas .25 .10
6 Chili Davis .50 .20
7 Cecil Cooper .25 .10
8 Mike Boddicker .25 .10
9 Dave Lopes .25 .10
10 Bill Doran .25 .10
11 Bret Saberhagen .50 .20
12 Brett Butler .50 .20
13 Harold Baines .75 .30
14 Mike Davis .25 .10
15 Tony Perez 1.00 .40
16 Willie Randolph .50 .20
17 Bob Boone .50 .20
18 Orel Hershiser .75 .30
19 Johnny Ray .25 .10
20 Gary Ward .25 .10
21 Rick Mahler .25 .10
22 Phil Bradley .25 .10
23 Jerry Koosman .50 .20
24 Tom Brunansky .25 .10
25 Andre Dawson .75 .30
26 Dwight Gooden 1.00 .40
27 Pete Rose 2.50 1.00
King of Kings
NNO Checklist Card .25 .10
NNO Aaron Large Puzzle 1.00 .40

1987 Donruss

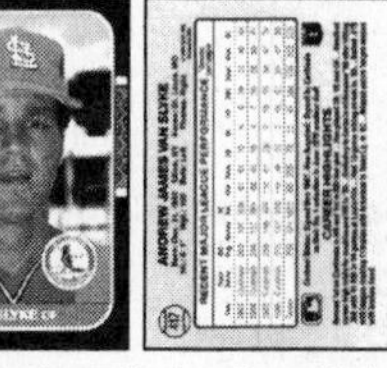
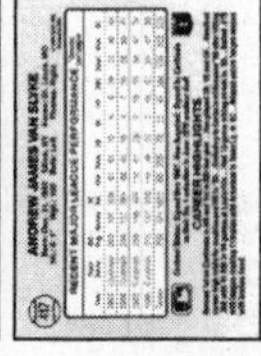

This set consists of 660 standard-size cards. Cards were primarily distributed in 15-card wax packs, rack packs and a factory set. All packs included a Roberto Clemente puzzle panel and the factory sets contained a complete puzzle.The regular-issue cards feature a black and gold border on the front. The backs of the cards in the factory sets are oriented differently than cards taken from wax packs, giving the appearance that one version or the other is upside down when sorting from the card backs. There are no premiums or discounts for either version. The popular Diamond King subset returns for the sixth consecutive year. Some of the Diamond King (1-26) selections are repeats from prior years; Perez-Steele Galleries had indicated in 1987 that a five-year rotation would be maintained in order to avoid depleting the pool of available worthy "kings" on some of the teams. The rich selection of Rookie Cards in this set include Barry Bonds, Bobby Bonilla, Kevin Brown, Will Clark, David Cone, Chuck Finley, Bo Jackson, Wally Joyner, Barry Larkin, Greg Maddux and Rafael Palmeiro.

Nm-Mt Ex-Mt
COMPLETE SET (660) 40.00 16.00
COMP.FACT.SET (660) 50.00 20.00
COMP.CLEMENTE PUZZLE 1.50 .60
1 Wally Joyner DK .40 .16
2 Roger Clemens DK .40 .16
3 Dale Murphy DK .40 .16
4 Darryl Strawberry DK .25 .10
5 Ozzie Smith DK .60 .24
6 Jose Canseco DK .50 .20
7 Charlie Hough DK .10 .04
8 Brook Jacoby DK .10 .04
9 Fred Lynn DK .15 .06
10 Rick Rhoden DK .10 .04
11 Chris Brown DK .10 .04
12 Von Hayes DK .10 .04
13 Jack Morris DK .15 .06
14A Kevin McReynolds DK .40 .16
ERR (Yellow strip missing on back)
14B Kevin McReynolds DK .10 .04
COR
15 George Brett DK 1.00 .40
16 Ted Higuera DK .10 .04
17 Hubie Brooks DK .10 .04
18 Mike Scott DK .10 .04
19 Kirby Puckett DK .25 .10
20 Dave Winfield DK .15 .06
21 Lloyd Moseby DK .10 .04
22A Eric Davis DK ERR .40 .16
(Yellow strip missing on back)
22B Eric Davis DK COR .15 .06
23 Jim Presley DK .10 .04
24 Keith Moreland DK .10 .04
25A Greg Walker DK ERR .40 .16
(Yellow strip missing on back)
25B Greg Walker DK COR .10 .04
26 Steve Sax DK .10 .04
27 DK Checklist 1-26 .10 .04
28 B.J. Surhoff RR RC .60 .24
29 Randy Myers RR RC .60 .24
30 Ken Gerhart RC .15 .06
31 Benito Santiago 1.00 .40
32 Greg Swindell RR RC .40 .16
33 Mike Birkbeck RC .15 .06
34 Terry Steinbach RR RC .40 .16
35 Bo Jackson RR RC 1.50 .60
36 Greg Maddux UER RC 10.00 4.00
middle name misspelled "Allen"
37 Jim Lindeman RC .15 .06
38 Devon White RR RC .60 .24
39 Eric Bell RC .15 .06
40 Willie Fraser RC .15 .06
41 Jerry Browne RR RC .15 .06
42 Chris James RR RC* .15 .06
43 Rafael Palmeiro RR RC 5.00 2.00
44 Pat Dodson RC .15 .06
45 Duane Ward RR RC* .40 .16
46 Mark McGwire RR 8.00 3.20
47 Bruce Fields UER RC .15 .06
(Photo actually Darnell Coles)
48 Eddie Murray .40 .16
49 Ted Higuera .10 .04
50 Kirk Gibson .15 .06
51 Oil Can Boyd .10 .04
52 Don Mattingly 1.25 .50
53 Pedro Guerrero .10 .04
54 George Brett 1.00 .40
55 Jose Rijo .10 .04
56 Tim Raines .15 .06
57 Ed Correa .10 .04
58 Mike Witt .10 .04
59 Greg Walker .10 .04
60 Ozzie Smith .60 .24
61 Glenn Davis .10 .04
62 Glenn Wilson .10 .04
63 Tom Browning .10 .04
64 Tony Gwynn .60 .24
65 R.J. Reynolds .10 .04
66 Will Clark RC 1.50 .60
67 Ozzie Virgil .10 .04
68 Rick Sutcliffe .15 .06
69 Gary Carter .25 .10
70 Mike Moore .10 .04
71 Bert Blyleven .15 .06
72 Tony Fernandez .10 .04
73 Kent Hrbek .15 .06
74 Lloyd Moseby .10 .04
75 Alvin Davis .10 .04
76 Keith Hernandez .25 .10
77 Ryne Sandberg .75 .30
78 Dale Murphy .40 .16
79 Sid Bream .10 .04
80 Chris Brown .10 .04
81 Steve Garvey .15 .06
82 Mario Soto .10 .04
83 Shane Rawley .10 .04
84 Willie McGee .15 .06
85 Jose Cruz .15 .06
86 Brian Downing .10 .04

1987 Donruss

87 Ozzie Guillen .10 .04
88 Hubie Brooks .10 .04
89 Cal Ripken 1.50 .60
90 Juan Nieves .10 .04
91 Lance Parrish .15 .06
92 Jim Rice .15 .06
93 Ron Guidry .15 .06
94 Fernando Valenzuela .15 .06
95 Andy Allanson .10 .04
96 Willie Wilson .15 .06
97 Jose Canseco 1.00 .40
98 Jeff Reardon .15 .06
99 Bobby Witt RC .40 .16
100 Checklist 28-133 .10 .04
101 Jose Guzman .10 .04
102 Steve Balboni .10 .04
103 Tony Phillips .10 .04
104 Brook Jacoby .10 .04
105 Dave Winfield .15 .06
106 Orel Hershiser .15 .06
107 Lou Whitaker .15 .06
108 Fred Lynn .15 .06
109 Bill Wegman .10 .04
110 Donnie Moore .10 .04
111 Jack Clark .15 .06
112 Bob Knepper .10 .04
113 Von Hayes .10 .04
114 Bip Roberts RC* .40 .16
115 Tony Pena .10 .04
116 Scott Garrelts .10 .04
117 Paul Molitor .25 .10
118 Darryl Strawberry .25 .10
119 Shawon Dunston .10 .04
120 Jim Presley .10 .04
121 Jesse Barfield .10 .04
122 Gary Gaetti .15 .06
123 Kurt Stillwell .10 .04
124 Joel Davis .10 .04
125 Mike Boddicker .10 .04
126 Robin Yount .60 .24
127 Alan Trammell .25 .10
128 Dave Righetti .10 .04
129 Dwight Evans .15 .06
130 Mike Scioscia .10 .04
131 Julio Franco .10 .04
132 Bret Saberhagen .15 .06
133 Mike Davis .10 .04
134 Joe Hesketh .10 .04
135 Wally Joyner RC .60 .24
136 Don Slaught .10 .04
137 Daryl Boston .10 .04
138 Nolan Ryan 2.00 .80
139 Mike Schmidt 1.00 .40
140 Tommy Herr .10 .04
141 Garry Templeton .10 .04
142 Kal Daniels .10 .04
143 Billy Sample .10 .04
144 Johnny Ray .10 .04
145 Rob Thompson RC* .40 .16
146 Bob Dernier .10 .04
147 Danny Tartabull .10 .04
148 Ernie Whitt .10 .04
149 Kirby Puckett .40 .16
150 Mike Young .10 .04
151 Ernest Riles .10 .04
152 Frank Tanana .10 .04
153 Rich Gedman .10 .04
154 Willie Randolph .15 .06
155 Bill Madlock .15 .06
156 Joe Carter .40 .16
157 Danny Jackson .10 .04
158 Carney Lansford .15 .06
159 Bryn Smith .10 .04
160 Gary Pettis .10 .04
161 Oddibe McDowell .10 .04
162 John Cangelosi .10 .04
163 Mike Scott .10 .04
164 Eric Show .10 .04
165 Juan Samuel .10 .04
166 Nick Esasky .10 .04
167 Zane Smith .10 .04
168 Mike C. Brown OF .10 .04
169 Keith Moreland .10 .04
170 John Tudor .10 .04
171 Ken Dixon .10 .04
172 Jim Gantner .10 .04
173 Jack Morris .15 .06
174 Bruce Hurst .10 .04
175 Dennis Rasmussen .10 .04
176 Mike Marshall .10 .04
177 Dan Quisenberry .10 .04
178 Eric Plunk .10 .04
179 Tim Wallach .10 .04
180 Steve Buechele .10 .04
181 Don Sutton .40 .16
182 Dave Schmidt .10 .04
183 Terry Pendleton .15 .06
184 Jim Deshaies RC * .15 .06
185 Steve Bedrosian .10 .04
186 Pete Rose 1.25 .50
187 Dave Dravecky .15 .06
188 Rick Reuschel .10 .04
189 Dan Gladden .10 .04
190 Rick Mahler .10 .04
191 Thad Bosley .10 .04
192 Ron Darling .10 .04
193 Matt Young .10 .04
194 Tom Brunansky .10 .04
195 Dave Stieb .10 .04
196 Frank Viola .10 .04
197 Tom Henke .10 .04
198 Karl Best .10 .04
199 Dwight Gooden .25 .10
200 Checklist 134-239 .10 .04
201 Steve Trout .10 .04
202 Rafael Ramirez .10 .04
203 Bob Walk .10 .04
204 Roger Mason .10 .04
205 Terry Kennedy .10 .04
206 Ron Oester .10 .04
207 John Russell .10 .04
208 Greg Mathews .10 .04
209 Charlie Kerfeld .10 .04
210 Reggie Jackson .25 .10
211 Floyd Bannister .10 .04
212 Vance Law .10 .04
213 Rich Bordi .10 .04
214 Dan Plesac .10 .04
215 Dave Collins .10 .04
216 Bob Stanley .10 .04
217 Joe Niekro .10 .04
218 Tom Niedenfuer .10 .04
219 Brett Butler .15 .06
220 Charlie Leibrandt .10 .04
221 Steve Ontiveros .10 .04
222 Tim Burke .10 .04
223 Curtis Wilkerson .10 .04
224 Pete Incaviglia RC * .40 .16
225 Lonnie Smith .10 .04
226 Chris Codiroli .10 .04
227 Scott Bailes .10 .04
228 Rickey Henderson .40 .16
229 Ken Howell .10 .04
230 Darnell Coles .10 .04
231 Don Aase .10 .04
232 Tim Leary .10 .04
233 Bob Boone .15 .06
234 Ricky Horton .10 .04
235 Mark Bailey .10 .04
236 Kevin Gross .10 .04
237 Lance McCullers .10 .04
238 Cecilio Guante .10 .04
239 Bob Melvin .10 .04
240 Billy Joe Robidoux .10 .04
241 Roger McDowell .10 .04
242 Leon Durham .10 .04
243 Ed Nunez .10 .04
244 Jimmy Key .15 .06
245 Mike Smithson .10 .04
246 Bo Diaz .10 .04
247 Carlton Fisk .25 .10
248 Larry Sheets .10 .04
249 Juan Castillo RC .15 .06
250 Eric King .10 .04
251 Doug Drabek RC .40 .16
252 Wade Boggs .25 .10
253 Mariano Duncan .10 .04
254 Pat Tabler .10 .04
255 Frank White .15 .06
256 Alfredo Griffin .10 .04
257 Floyd Youmans .10 .04
258 Rob Wilfong .10 .04
259 Pete O'Brien .10 .04
260 Tim Hulett .10 .04
261 Dickie Thon .10 .04
262 Darren Daulton .25 .10
263 Vince Coleman .10 .04
264 Andy Hawkins .10 .04
265 Eric Davis .25 .10
266 Andres Thomas .10 .04
267 Mike Diaz .10 .04
268 Chili Davis .25 .10
269 Jody Davis .10 .04
270 Phil Bradley .10 .04
271 George Bell .10 .04
272 Keith Atherton .10 .04
273 Storm Davis .10 .04
274 Rob Deer .10 .04
275 Walt Terrell .10 .04
276 Roger Clemens 1.00 .40
277 Mike Easler .10 .04
278 Steve Sax .10 .04
279 Andre Thornton .10 .04
280 Jim Sundberg .10 .04
281 Bill Bathe .10 .04
282 Jay Tibbs .10 .04
283 Dick Schofield .10 .04
284 Mike Mason .10 .04
285 Jerry Hairston .10 .04
286 Bill Doran .10 .04
287 Tim Flannery .10 .04
288 Gary Redus .10 .04
289 John Franco .15 .06
290 Paul Assenmacher .25 .10
291 Joe Orsulak .10 .04
292 Lee Smith .25 .10
293 Mike Laga .10 .04
294 Rick Dempsey .15 .06
295 Mike Felder .10 .04
296 Tom Brookens .10 .04
297 Al Nipper .10 .04
298 Mike Pagliarulo .10 .04
299 Franklin Stubbs .10 .04
300 Checklist 240-345 .10 .04
301 Steve Farr .10 .04
302 Bill Mooneyham .10 .04
303 Andres Galarraga .25 .10
304 Scott Fletcher .10 .04
305 Jack Howell .10 .04
306 Russ Morman .10 .04
307 Todd Worrell .15 .06
308 Dave Smith .10 .04
309 Jeff Stone .10 .04
310 Ron Robinson .10 .04
311 Bruce Bochy .10 .04
312 Jim Winn .10 .04
313 Mark Davis .10 .04
314 Jeff Dedmon .10 .04
315 Jamie Moyer RC 1.00 .40
316 Wally Backman .10 .04
317 Ken Phelps .10 .04
318 Steve Lombardozzi .10 .04
319 Rance Mulliniks .10 .04
320 Tim Laudner .10 .04
321 Mark Eichhorn .10 .04
322 Lee Guetterman .10 .04
323 Sid Fernandez .10 .04
324 Jerry Mumphrey .10 .04
325 David Palmer .10 .04
326 Bill Almon .10 .04
327 Candy Maldonado .10 .04
328 John Kruk RC .60 .24
329 John Denny .10 .04
330 Milt Thompson .10 .04
331 Mike LaValliere RC * .40 .16
332 Alan Ashby .10 .04
333 Doug Corbett .10 .04
334 Ron Karkovice RC .40 .16
335 Mitch Webster .10 .04
336 Lee Lacy .10 .04
337 Glenn Braggs RC .15 .06
338 Dwight Lowry .10 .04
339 Don Baylor .15 .06
340 Brian Fisher .10 .04
341 Reggie Williams .10 .04
342 Tom Candiotti .10 .04
343 Rudy Law .10 .04
344 Curt Young .10 .04
345 Mike Fitzgerald .10 .04
346 Ruben Sierra RC .60 .24
347 Mitch Williams RC * .40 .16
348 Jorge Orta .10 .04
349 Mickey Tettleton .10 .04
350 Ernie Camacho .10 .04
351 Ron Kittle .10 .04
352 Ken Landreaux .10 .04
353 Chet Lemon .10 .04
354 John Shelby .10 .04
355 Mark Clear .10 .04
356 Doug DeCinces .10 .04
357 Ken Dayley .10 .04
358 Phil Garner .10 .04
359 Steve Jeltz .10 .04
360 Ed Whitson .10 .04
361 Barry Bonds RC 15.00 6.00
362 Vida Blue .15 .06
363 Cecil Cooper .15 .06
364 Bob Ojeda .10 .04
365 Dennis Eckersley .25 .10
366 Mike Morgan .10 .04
367 Willie Upshaw .10 .04
368 Allan Anderson .10 .04
369 Bill Gullickson .10 .04
370 Bobby Thigpen RC .40 .16
371 Juan Beniquez .10 .04
372 Charlie Moore .10 .04
373 Dan Petry .10 .04
374 Rod Scurry .10 .04
375 Tom Seaver .25 .10
376 Ed VandeBerg .10 .04
377 Tony Bernazard .10 .04
378 Greg Pryor .10 .04
379 Dwayne Murphy .10 .04
380 Andy McGaffigan .10 .04
381 Kirk McCaskill .10 .04
382 Greg Harris .10 .04
383 Rich Dotson .10 .04
384 Craig Reynolds .10 .04
385 Greg Gross .10 .04
386 Tito Landrum .10 .04
387 Craig Lefferts .10 .04
388 Dave Parker .15 .06
389 Bob Horner .10 .04
390 Pat Clements .10 .04
391 Jeff Leonard .10 .04
392 Chris Speier .10 .04
393 John Moses .10 .04
394 Garth Iorg .10 .04
395 Greg Gagne .10 .04
396 Nate Snell .10 .04
397 Bryan Clutterbuck .10 .04
398 Darrell Evans .15 .06
399 Steve Crawford .10 .04
400 Checklist 346-451 .10 .04
401 Phil Lombardi .10 .04
402 Rick Honeycutt .10 .04
403 Ken Schrom .10 .04
404 Bud Black .10 .04
405 Donnie Hill .10 .04
406 Wayne Krenchicki .10 .04
407 Chuck Finley RC .60 .24
408 Toby Harrah .10 .04
409 Steve Lyons .10 .04
410 Kevin Bass .10 .04
411 Marvell Wynne .10 .04
412 Ron Roenicke .10 .04
413 Tracy Jones .10 .04
414 Gene Garber .10 .04
415 Mike Bielecki .10 .04
416 Frank DiPino .10 .04
417 Andy Van Slyke .15 .06
418 Jim Dwyer .10 .04
419 Ben Oglivie .10 .04
420 Dave Bergman .10 .04
421 Joe Sambito .10 .04
422 Bob Tewksbury RC * .40 .16
423 Len Matuszek .10 .04
424 Mike Kingery RC .15 .06
425 Dave Kingman .15 .06
426 Al Newman .10 .04
427 Gary Ward .10 .04
428 Ruppert Jones .10 .04
429 Harold Baines .15 .06
430 Pat Perry .10 .04
431 Terry Puhl .10 .04
432 Don Carman .10 .04
433 Eddie Milner .10 .04
434 LaMarr Hoyt .10 .04
435 Rick Rhoden .10 .04
436 Jose Uribe .10 .04
437 Ken Oberkfell .10 .04
438 Ron Davis .10 .04
439 Jesse Orosco .10 .04
440 Scott Bradley .10 .04
441 Randy Bush .10 .04
442 John Cerutti .10 .04
443 Roy Smalley .10 .04
444 Kelly Gruber .10 .04
445 Bob Kearney .10 .04
446 Ed Hearn .10 .04
447 Scott Sanderson .10 .04
448 Bruce Benedict .10 .04
449 Junior Ortiz .10 .04
450 Mike Aldrete .10 .04
451 Kevin McReynolds .10 .04
452 Rob Murphy .10 .04
453 Kent Tekulve .10 .04
454 Curt Ford .10 .04
455 Dave Lopes .15 .06
456 Bob Grich .15 .06
457 Jose DeLeon .10 .04
458 Andre Dawson .15 .06
459 Mike Flanagan .10 .04
460 Joey Meyer .10 .04
461 Chuck Cary .10 .04
462 Bill Buckner .15 .06
463 Bob Shirley .10 .04
464 Jeff Hamilton .10 .04
465 Phil Niekro .15 .06
466 Mark Gubicza .10 .04
467 Jerry Willard .10 .04
468 Bob Sebra .10 .04
469 Larry Parrish .10 .04
470 Charlie Hough .15 .06
471 Hal McRae .15 .06
472 Dave Leiper .10 .04
473 Mel Hall .10 .04
474 Dan Pasqua .10 .04
475 Bob Welch .10 .04
476 Johnny Grubb .10 .04
477 Jim Traber .10 .04
478 Chris Bosio RC .40 .16
479 Mark McLemore .15 .06
480 John Morris .10 .04
481 Billy Hatcher .10 .04
482 Dan Schatzeder .10 .04
483 Rich Gossage .15 .06
484 Jim Morrison .10 .04
485 Bob Brenly .10 .04
486 Bill Schroeder .10 .04
487 Mookie Wilson .15 .06
488 Dave Martinez RC .40 .16
489 Harold Reynolds .15 .06
490 Jeff Hearron .10 .04
491 Mickey Hatcher .10 .04
492 Barry Larkin RC 2.00 .80
493 Bob James .10 .04
494 John Habyan .10 .04
495 Jim Adduci .10 .04
496 Mike Heath .10 .04
497 Tim Stoddard .10 .04
498 Tony Armas .10 .04
499 Dennis Powell .10 .04
500 Checklist 452-557 .10 .04
501 Chris Bando .10 .04
502 David Cone RC 1.00 .40
503 Jay Howell .10 .04
504 Tom Foley .10 .04
505 Ray Chadwick .10 .04
506 Mike Loynd RC .10 .04
507 Neil Allen .10 .04
508 Danny Darwin .10 .04
509 Rick Schu .10 .04
510 Jose Oquendo .10 .04
511 Gene Walter .10 .04
512 Terry McGriff .10 .04
513 Ken Griffey .15 .06
514 Benny Distefano .10 .04
515 Terry Mulholland RC .40 .16
516 Ed Lynch .10 .04
517 Bill Swift .10 .04
518 Manny Lee .10 .04
519 Andre David .10 .04
520 Scott McGregor .10 .04
521 Rick Manning .10 .04
522 Willie Hernandez .10 .04
523 Marty Barrett .10 .04
524 Wayne Tolleson .10 .04
525 Jose Gonzalez RC .15 .06
526 Cory Snyder .10 .04
527 Buddy Biancalana .10 .04
528 Moose Haas .10 .04
529 Wilfredo Tejada .10 .04
530 Stu Cliburn .10 .04
531 Dale Mohorcic .10 .04
532 Ron Hassey .10 .04
533 Ty Gainey .10 .04
534 Jerry Royster .10 .04
535 Mike Maddux .10 .04
536 Ted Power .10 .04
537 Ted Simmons .15 .06
538 Rafael Belliard RC .40 .16
539 Chico Walker .10 .04
540 Bob Forsch .10 .04
541 John Stefero .10 .04
542 Dale Sveum .10 .04
543 Mark Thurmond .10 .04
544 Jeff Sellers .10 .04
545 Joel Skinner .10 .04
546 Alex Trevino .10 .04
547 Randy Kutcher .10 .04
548 Joaquin Andujar .10 .04
549 Casey Candaele .10 .04
550 Jeff Russell .10 .04
551 John Candelaria .10 .04
552 Joe Cowley .10 .04
553 Danny Cox .10 .04
554 Denny Walling .10 .04
555 Bruce Ruffin RC .15 .06
556 Buddy Bell .15 .06
557 Jimmy Jones RC .15 .06
558 Bobby Bonilla RC .60 .24
559 Jeff D. Robinson .10 .04
560 Ed Olwine .10 .04
561 Glenallen Hill RC .40 .16
562 Lee Mazzilli .10 .04
563 Mike G. Brown P .10 .04
564 George Frazier .10 .04
565 Mike Sharperson RC .15 .06
566 Mark Portugal RC * .15 .06
567 Rick Leach .10 .04
568 Mark Langston .10 .04
569 Rafael Santana .10 .04
570 Manny Trillo .10 .04
571 Cliff Speck .10 .04
572 Bob Kipper .10 .04
573 Kelly Downs RC .15 .06
574 Randy Asadoor .10 .04
575 Dave Magadan RC .40 .16
576 Marvin Freeman RC .15 .06
577 Jeff Lahti .10 .04
578 Jeff Calhoun .10 .04
579 Gus Polidor .10 .04
580 Gene Nelson .10 .04
581 Tim Teufel .10 .04
582 Odell Jones .10 .04
583 Mark Ryal .10 .04
584 Randy O'Neal .10 .04
585 Mike Greenwell RC .40 .16
586 Ray Knight .10 .04
587 Ralph Bryant .15 .06
588 Carmen Castillo .10 .04
589 Ed Wojna .10 .04
590 Stan Javier .10 .04
591 Jeff Musselman .10 .04
592 Mike Stanley RC .40 .16
593 Darrell Porter .10 .04
594 Drew Hall .10 .04
595 Rob Nelson .10 .04
596 Bryan Oelkers .10 .04
597 Scott Nielsen .10 .04
598 Brian Holton .10 .04
599 Kevin Mitchell RC * .60 .24
600 Checklist 558-660 .10 .04
601 Jackie Gutierrez .10 .04
602 Barry Jones .10 .04
603 Jerry Narron .10 .04
604 Steve Lake .10 .04
605 Jim Pankovits .10 .04
606 Ed Romero .10 .04
607 Dave LaPoint .10 .04
608 Don Robinson .10 .04
609 Mike Krukow .10 .04
610 Dave Valle RC ** .15 .06
611 Len Dykstra .25 .10
612 R.Clemente PUZ .50 .20
613 Mike Trujillo .10 .04
614 Damaso Garcia .10 .04
615 Neal Heaton .10 .04
616 Juan Berenguer .10 .04
617 Steve Carlton .15 .06
618 Gary Lucas .10 .04
619 Geno Petralli .10 .04
620 Rick Aguilera .15 .06
621 Fred McGriff .75 .30
622 Dave Henderson .10 .04
623 Dave Clark RC .15 .06
624 Angel Salazar .10 .04
625 Randy Hunt .10 .04
626 John Gibbons .10 .04
627 Kevin Brown RC 2.50 1.00
628 Bill Dawley .10 .04
629 Aurelio Lopez .10 .04
630 Charles Hudson .10 .04
631 Ray Soff .10 .04
632 Ray Hayward .10 .04
633 Spike Owen .10 .04
634 Glenn Hubbard .10 .04
635 Kevin Elster RC .40 .16
636 Mike LaCoss .10 .04
637 Dwayne Henry .10 .04
638 Rey Quinones .10 .04
639 Jim Clancy .10 .04
640 Larry Andersen .10 .04
641 Calvin Schiraldi .10 .04
642 Stan Jefferson .10 .04
643 Marc Sullivan .10 .04
644 Mark Grant .10 .04
645 Cliff Johnson .10 .04
646 Howard Johnson .10 .04
647 Dave Sax .10 .04
648 Dave Stewart .15 .06
649 Danny Heep .10 .04
650 Joe Johnson .10 .04
651 Bob Brower .10 .04
652 Rob Woodward .10 .04
653 John Mizerock .10 .04
654 Tim Pyznarski .10 .04
655 Luis Aquino .10 .04
656 Mickey Brantley .10 .04
657 Doyle Alexander .10 .04
658 Sammy Stewart .10 .04
659 Jim Acker .10 .04
660 Pete Ladd .10 .04

1987 Donruss Wax Box Cards

The cards in this four-card set measure the standard 2 1/2" by 3 1/2". Cards have essentially the same design as the 1987 Donruss regular issue set. The cards were printed on the bottoms of the regular issue wax pack boxes. The four cards (PC10 to PC12 plus a Roberto Clemente puzzle card) are considered a separate set in their own right and are not typically included in a complete set of the regular issue 1987 Donruss cards. The value of the panel uncut is slightly greater, perhaps by 25 percent greater, than the value of the individual cards cut up carefully.

	Nm-Mt	Ex-Mt
COMPLETE SET (4)	2.00	.80
PC10 Dale Murphy	.50	.20
PC11 Jeff Reardon	.25	.10
PC12 Jose Canseco	1.25	.50
PUZ Roberto Clemente (Puzzle Card)	.75	.30

1987 Donruss Rookies

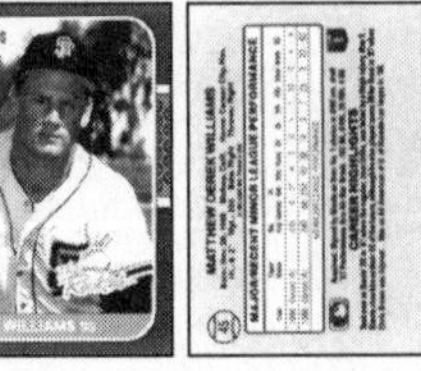

The 1987 Donruss "The Rookies" set features 56 full-color standard-size cards plus a 15-piece puzzle of Roberto Clemente. The set was distributed in factory set form packaged in a small green and black box through hobby dealers. Card fronts are similar in design to the 1987 Donruss regular issue except for the presence of "The Rookies" logo in the lower left corner and a green border instead of a black border. The key extended Rookie Cards in this set are Ellis Burks and Matt Williams. The second Donruss-issued cards of Greg Maddux and Rafael Palmeiro are also in this set. Because it's the first card in the set (of which came in a tightly-sealed cello wrap, the Mark McGwire card is quite condition sensitive.

	Nm-Mt	Ex-Mt
COMP.FACT.SET (56)	20.00	8.00
1 Mark McGwire	8.00	3.20
2 Eric Bell	.15	.06
3 Mark Williamson	.10	.04
4 Mike Greenwell	.40	.16
5 Ellis Burks XRC	.60	.24
6 DeWayne Buice	.10	.04
7 Mark McLemore	.25	.10
8 Devon White	.60	.24
9 Willie Fraser	.15	.06
10 Les Lancaster	.10	.04
11 Ken Williams XRC	.10	.04
12 Matt Nokes XRC	.40	.16
13 Jeff M. Robinson	.10	.04
14 Bo Jackson	1.00	.40
15 Kevin Seitzer XRC	.40	.16
16 Billy Ripken XRC	.40	.16
17 B.J. Surhoff	.60	.24
18 Chuck Crim	.10	.04
19 Mike Birkbeck	.15	.06
20 Chris Bosio	.40	.16
21 Les Straker	.10	.04
22 Mark Davidson	.10	.04
23 Gene Larkin XRC	.40	.16
24 Ken Gerhart	.10	.04
25 Luis Polonia XRC	.15	.06

26 Terry Steinbach .40 .16
27 Mickey Brantley .10 .04
28 Mike Stanley .40 .16
29 Jerry Browne .15 .06
30 Todd Benzinger XRC .40 .16
31 Fred McGriff 1.50 .60
32 Mike Henneman XRC .40 .16
33 Casey Candaele .10 .04
34 Dave Magadan .40 .16
35 David Cone 1.00 .40
36 Mike Jackson XRC .40 .16
37 John Mitchell XRC .15 .06
38 Mike Dunne .10 .04
39 John Smiley XRC .40 .16
40 Joe Magrane XRC .15 .06
41 Jim Lindeman .15 .06
42 Shane Mack .10 .04
43 Stan Jefferson .10 .04
44 Benito Santiago .50 .20
45 Matt Williams XRC 2.50 1.00
46 Dave Meads .10 .04
47 Rafael Palmeiro 5.00 2.00
48 Bill Long .10 .04
49 Bob Brower .10 .04
50 James Steels .10 .04
51 Paul Noce .10 .04
52 Greg Maddux 8.00 3.20
53 Jeff Musselman .10 .04
54 Brian Holton .10 .04
55 Chuck Jackson .10 .04
56 Checklist 1-56 .10 .04

1987 Donruss All-Stars

This 60-card set features cards measuring approximately 3 1/2" by 5". Card fronts are in full color with a black border. The card backs are printed in black and blue on white card stock. Cards are numbered on the back. Card backs feature statistical information about the player's performance in past All-Star games. The set was distributed in packs which also contained a Pop-Up.

	Nm-Mt	Ex-Mt
COMPLETE SET (60)	6.00	2.40
1 Wally Joyner	.30	.12
2 Dave Winfield	.30	.12
3 Lou Whitaker	.10	.04
4 Kirby Puckett	.75	.30
5 Cal Ripken	2.00	.80
6 Rickey Henderson	.50	.20
7 Wade Boggs	.50	.20
8 Roger Clemens	.75	.30
9 Lance Parrish	.10	.04
10 Dick Howser MG	.05	.02
11 Keith Hernandez	.10	.04
12 Darryl Strawberry	.10	.04
13 Ryne Sandberg	.50	.20
14 Dale Murphy	.30	.12
15 Ozzie Smith	.75	.30
16 Tony Gwynn	1.00	.40
17 Mike Schmidt	.50	.20
18 Dwight Gooden	.10	.04
19 Gary Carter	.50	.20
20 Whitey Herzog MG	.10	.04
21 Jose Canseco	.50	.20
22 John Franco	.10	.04
23 Jesse Barfield	.05	.02
24 Rick Rhoden	.05	.02
25 Harold Baines	.20	.08
26 Sid Fernandez	.05	.02
27 George Brett	1.00	.40
28 Steve Sax	.05	.02
29 Jim Presley	.05	.02
30 Dave Smith	.05	.02
31 Eddie Murray	.50	.20
32 Mike Scott	.05	.02
33 Don Mattingly	1.00	.40
34 Dave Parker	.10	.04
35 Tony Fernandez	.05	.02
36 Tim Raines	.20	.08
37 Brook Jacoby	.05	.02
38 Chili Davis	.10	.04
39 Rich Gedman	.05	.02
40 Kevin Bass	.05	.02
41 Frank White	.10	.04
42 Glenn Davis	.05	.02
43 Willie Hernandez	.05	.02
44 Chris Brown	.05	.02
45 Jim Rice	.10	.04
46 Tony Pena	.10	.04
47 Don Aase	.05	.02
48 Hubie Brooks	.05	.02
49 Charlie Hough	.05	.02
50 Jody Davis	.05	.02
51 Mike Witt	.05	.02
52 Jeff Reardon	.10	.04
53 Ken Schrom	.05	.02
54 Fernando Valenzuela	.10	.04
55 Dave Righetti	.05	.02
56 Shane Rawley	.05	.02
57 Ted Higuera	.05	.02
58 Mike Krukow	.05	.02
59 Lloyd Moseby	.05	.02
60 Checklist Card	.05	.02

1987 Donruss All-Star Box

The cards in this four-card set measure the standard 2 1/2" by 3 1/2" in spite of the fact that they form the bottom of the wax pack box for the larger Donruss All-Star cards. These box cards have essentially the same design as the 1987 Donruss regular issue set. The cards were printed on the bottoms of the Donruss All-Star (3 1/2" by 5") wax pack boxes. The four cards (PC13 to PC15 plus a Roberto Clemente puzzle card) are considered a separate set in their own right and are not typically included in a complete set of the 1987 Donruss All-Star (or regular) cards. The value of the panel uncut is slightly greater, perhaps by 25 percent greater, than the value of the individual cards cut up carefully.

	Nm-Mt	Ex-Mt
COMPLETE SET (4)	2.50	1.00
PC13 Mike Scott	.25	.10
PC14 Roger Clemens	1.25	.50
PC15 Mike Krukow	.25	.10
PUZ Roberto Clemente Puzzle Card	1.00	.40

1987 Donruss Highlights

Donruss' third (and last) edition of Highlights was released late in 1987. The cards are standard size and are glossy in appearance. Cards commemorate events during the 1987 season, as well as players and pitchers of the month from each league. The set was distributed in its own red, black, blue, and gold box along with a small Roberto Clemente puzzle. Card fronts are similar to the regular 1987 Donruss issue except that the Highlights logo is positioned in the lower right-hand corner and the borders are in blue instead of black. The backs are printed in black and gold on white card stock.

	Nm-Mt	Ex-Mt
COMP.FACT.SET (56)	12.00	4.80
1 Juan Nieves	.10	.04
2 Mike Schmidt	.40	.16
3 Eric Davis	.25	.10
4 Sid Fernandez	.10	.04
5 Brian Downing	.10	.04
6 Bret Saberhagen	.15	.06
7 Tim Raines	.15	.06
8 Eric Davis	.25	.10
9 Steve Bedrosian	.10	.04
10 Larry Parrish	.10	.04
11 Jim Clancy	.10	.04
12 Tony Gwynn UER	.40	.16
13 Orel Hershiser	.15	.06
14 Wade Boggs	.25	.10
15 Steve Ontiveros	.10	.04
16 Tim Raines	.15	.06
17 Don Mattingly	.75	.30
18 Ray Dandridge	.15	.06
19 Jim "Catfish" Hunter	.25	.10
20 Billy Williams	.15	.06
21 Bo Diaz	.10	.04
22 Floyd Youmans	.10	.04
23 Don Mattingly	.75	.30
24 Frank Viola	.10	.04
25 Bobby Witt	.15	.06
26 Kevin Seitzer	.40	.16
27 Mark McGwire	3.00	1.20
28 Andre Dawson	.15	.06
29 Paul Molitor	.25	.10
30 Kirby Puckett	.40	.16
31 Andre Dawson	.15	.06
32 Doug Drabek	.40	.16
33 Dwight Evans	.15	.06
34 Mark Langston	.10	.04
35 Wally Joyner	.40	.16
36 Vince Coleman	.10	.04
37 Eddie Murray	.40	.16
38 Cal Ripken	.75	.30
39 Fred McGriff Rob Ducey Ernie Whitt	.15	.06
40 Mark McGwire Jose Canseco	2.00	.80
41 Bob Boone	.15	.06
42 Darryl Strawberry	.25	.10
43 Howard Johnson	.10	.04
44 Wade Boggs	.25	.10
45 Benito Santiago	.50	.20
46 Mark McGwire	3.00	1.20
47 Kevin Seitzer	.40	.16
48 Don Mattingly	.75	.30
49 Darryl Strawberry	.25	.10
50 Pascual Perez	.10	.04
51 Alan Trammell	.25	.10
52 Doyle Alexander	.10	.04
53 Nolan Ryan	1.00	.40
54 Mark McGwire	3.00	1.20
55 Benito Santiago	.50	.20
56 Checklist 1-56	.10	.04

1987 Donruss Opening Day

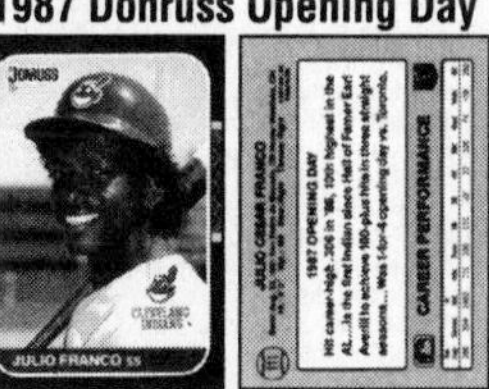

This innovative set of 272 standard-size cards features a card for each of the players in the starting line-ups of all the teams on Opening Day 1987. The set was packaged in a specially designed box. Cards are very similar in design to the 1987 regular Donruss issue except that these "OD" cards have a maroon border instead of a black border. Teams in the same city share a checklist card. A 15-piece puzzle of Roberto Clemente is also included with every complete set. The error on Barry Bonds (picturing Johnny Ray by mistake) was corrected very early in the press run; supposedly less than one percent of the sets have the error. Players in this set in their Rookie Card year include Will Clark, Bo Jackson, Wally Joyner and Barry Larkin.

	Nm-Mt	Ex-Mt
COMP.FACT. SET (272)	50.00	20.00
1 Doug DeCinces	.10	.04
2 Mike Witt	.10	.04
3 George Hendrick	.10	.04
4 Dick Schofield	.10	.04
5 Devon White	.60	.24
6 Butch Wynegar	.10	.04
7 Wally Joyner	.40	.16
8 Mark McLemore	.15	.06
9 Brian Downing	.10	.04
10 Gary Pettis	.10	.04
11 Bill Doran	.10	.04
12 Phil Garner	.15	.06
13 Jose Cruz	.15	.06
14 Kevin Bass	.10	.04
15 Mike Scott	.10	.04
16 Glenn Davis	.10	.04
17 Alan Ashby	.10	.04
18 Billy Hatcher	.10	.04
19 Craig Reynolds	.10	.04
20 Carney Lansford	.15	.06
21 Mike Davis	.10	.04
22 Reggie Jackson	.25	.10
23 Mickey Tettleton	.10	.04
24 Jose Canseco	1.00	.40
25 Rob Nelson	.10	.04
26 Tony Phillips	.10	.04
27 Dwayne Murphy	.10	.04
28 Alfredo Griffin	.10	.04
29 Curt Young	.10	.04
30 Willie Upshaw	.10	.04
31 Mike Sharperson	.15	.06
32 Rance Mulliniks	.10	.04
33 Ernie Whitt	.10	.04
34 Jesse Barfield	.10	.04
35 Tony Fernandez	.10	.04
36 Lloyd Moseby	.10	.04
37 Jimmy Key	.15	.06
38 Fred McGriff	.75	.30
39 George Bell	.10	.04
40 Dale Murphy	.40	.16
41 Rick Mahler	.10	.04
42 Ken Griffey	.15	.06
43 Andres Thomas	.10	.04
44 Dion James	.10	.04
45 Ozzie Virgil	.10	.04
46 Ken Oberkfell	.10	.04
47 Gary Roenicke	.10	.04
48 Glenn Hubbard	.10	.04
49 Bill Schroeder	.10	.04
50 Greg Brock	.10	.04
51 Billy Joe Robidoux	.10	.04
52 Glenn Braggs	.15	.06
53 Jim Gantner	.10	.04
54 Paul Molitor	.25	.10
55 Dale Sveum	.10	.04
56 Ted Higuera	.10	.04
57 Rob Deer	.10	.04
58 Robin Yount	.60	.24
59 Jim Lindeman	.15	.06
60 Vince Coleman	.10	.04
61 Tommy Herr	.10	.04
62 Terry Pendleton	.15	.06
63 John Tudor	.10	.04
64 Tony Pena	.10	.04
65 Ozzie Smith	.60	.24
66 Tito Landrum	.10	.04
67 Jack Clark	.15	.06
68 Bob Dernier	.10	.04
69 Rick Sutcliffe	.15	.06
70 Andre Dawson	.15	.06
71 Keith Moreland	.10	.04
72 Jody Davis	.10	.04
73 Brian Dayett	.10	.04
74 Leon Durham	.10	.04
75 Ryne Sandberg	.75	.30
76 Shawon Dunston	.10	.04
77 Mike Marshall	.10	.04
78 Bill Madlock	.15	.06
79 Orel Hershiser	.15	.06
80 Mike Ramsey	.10	.04
81 Ken Landreaux	.10	.04
82 Mike Scioscia	.10	.04
83 Franklin Stubbs	.10	.04
84 Mariano Duncan	.10	.04
85 Steve Sax	.10	.04
86 Mitch Webster	.10	.04
87 Reid Nichols	.10	.04
88 Tim Wallach	.10	.04
89 Floyd Youmans	.10	.04
90 Andres Galarraga	.25	.10
91 Hubie Brooks	.10	.04
92 Jeff Reed	.10	.04
93 Alonzo Powell	.10	.04
94 Vance Law	.10	.04
95 Bob Brenly	.10	.04
96 Will Clark	1.00	.40
97 Chili Davis	.25	.10
98 Mike Krukow	.10	.04
99 Jose Uribe	.10	.04
100 Chris Brown	.10	.04
101 Robby Thompson	.40	.16
102 Candy Maldonado	.10	.04
103 Jeff Leonard	.10	.04
104 Tom Candiotti	.10	.04
105 Chris Bando	.10	.04
106 Cory Snyder	.10	.04
107 Pat Tabler	.10	.04
108 Andre Thornton	.10	.04
109 Joe Carter	.40	.16
110 Tony Bernazard	.10	.04
111 Julio Franco	.15	.06
112 Brook Jacoby	.10	.04
113 Brett Butler	.15	.06
114 Donell Nixon	.10	.04
115 Alvin Davis	.10	.04
116 Mark Langston	.10	.04
117 Harold Reynolds	.15	.06
118 Ken Phelps	.10	.04
119 Mike Kingery	.15	.06
120 Dave Valle	.15	.06
121 Rey Quinones	.10	.04
122 Phil Bradley	.10	.04
123 Jim Presley	.10	.04
124 Keith Hernandez	.25	.10
125 Kevin McReynolds	.10	.04
126 Rafael Santana	.10	.04
127 Bob Ojeda	.10	.04
128 Darryl Strawberry	.25	.10
129 Mookie Wilson	.15	.06
130 Gary Carter	.25	.10
131 Tim Teufel	.10	.04
132 Howard Johnson	.10	.04
133 Cal Ripken	1.50	.60
134 Rick Burleson	.10	.04
135 Fred Lynn	.15	.06
136 Eddie Murray	.40	.16
137 Ray Knight	.10	.04
138 Alan Wiggins	.10	.04
139 John Shelby	.10	.04
140 Mike Boddicker	.10	.04
141 Ken Gerhart	.10	.04
142 Terry Kennedy	.10	.04
143 Steve Garvey	.15	.06
144 Marvell Wynne	.10	.04
145 Kevin Mitchell	.25	.10
146 Tony Gwynn	.60	.24
147 Joey Cora	.25	.10
148 Benito Santiago	.25	.10
149 Eric Show	.10	.04
150 Garry Templeton	.10	.04
151 Carmelo Martinez	.10	.04
152 Von Hayes	.10	.04
153 Lance Parrish	.15	.06
154 Milt Thompson	.10	.04
155 Mike Easler	.10	.04
156 Juan Samuel	.10	.04
157 Steve Jeltz	.10	.04
158 Glenn Wilson	.10	.04
159 Shane Rawley	.10	.04
160 Mike Schmidt	1.00	.40
161 Andy Van Slyke	.15	.06
162 Johnny Ray	.10	.04
163A Barry Bonds ERR (Photo actually Johnny Ray wearing a black shirt)	300.00	120.00
163B Barry Bonds COR	20.00	8.00
164 Junior Ortiz	.10	.04
165 Rafael Belliard	.40	.16
166 Bob Patterson	.10	.04
167 Bobby Bonilla	.40	.16
168 Sid Bream	.10	.04
169 Jim Morrison	.10	.04
170 Jerry Browne	.15	.06
171 Scott Fletcher	.10	.04
172 Ruben Sierra	.60	.24
173 Larry Parrish	.10	.04
174 Pete O'Brien	.10	.04
175 Pete Incaviglia	.40	.16
176 Don Slaught	.10	.04
177 Oddibe McDowell	.10	.04
178 Charlie Hough	.15	.06
179 Steve Buechele	.10	.04
180 Bob Stanley	.10	.04
181 Wade Boggs	.25	.10
182 Jim Rice	.15	.06
183 Bill Buckner	.15	.06
184 Dwight Evans	.15	.06
185 Spike Owen	.10	.04
186 Don Baylor	.15	.06
187 Marc Sullivan	.10	.04
188 Marty Barrett	.10	.04
189 Dave Henderson	.10	.04
190 Bo Diaz	.10	.04
191 Barry Larkin	2.00	.80
192 Kal Daniels	.15	.06
193 Terry Francona	.15	.06
194 Tom Browning	.10	.04
195 Ron Oester	.10	.04
196 Buddy Bell	.15	.06
197 Eric Davis	.25	.10
198 Dave Parker	.15	.06
199 Steve Balboni	.10	.04
200 Danny Tartabull	.10	.04
201 Ed Hearn	.10	.04
202 Buddy Biancalana	.10	.04
203 Danny Jackson	.10	.04
204 Frank White	.15	.06
205 Bo Jackson	1.00	.40
206 George Brett	1.00	.40
207 Kevin Seitzer	.40	.16
208 Willie Wilson	.15	.06
209 Orlando Mercado	.10	.04
210 Darrell Evans	.15	.06
211 Larry Herndon	.10	.04
212 Jack Morris	.15	.06
213 Chet Lemon	.10	.04
214 Mike Heath	.10	.04
215 Darnell Coles	.10	.04
216 Alan Trammell	.25	.10
217 Terry Harper	.10	.04
218 Lou Whitaker	.15	.06
219 Gary Gaetti	.15	.06
220 Tom Nieto	.10	.04
221 Kirby Puckett	.40	.16
222 Tom Brunansky	.10	.04
223 Greg Gagne	.10	.04
224 Dan Gladden	.10	.04
225 Mark Davidson	.10	.04
226 Bert Blyleven	.15	.06
227 Steve Lombardozzi	.10	.04
228 Kent Hrbek	.15	.06
229 Gary Redus	.10	.04
230 Ivan Calderon	.10	.04
231 Tim Hulett	.10	.04
232 Carlton Fisk	.25	.10
233 Greg Walker	.10	.04
234 Ron Karkovice	.40	.16
235 Ozzie Guillen	.10	.04
236 Harold Baines	.25	.10
237 Donnie Hill	.10	.04
238 Rich Dotson	.10	.04
239 Mike Pagliarulo	.10	.04
240 Joel Skinner	.10	.04
241 Don Mattingly	1.25	.50
242 Gary Ward	.10	.04
243 Dave Winfield	.15	.06
244 Dan Pasqua	.10	.04
245 Wayne Tolleson	.10	.04
246 Willie Randolph	.15	.06
247 Dennis Rasmussen	.10	.04
248 Rickey Henderson	.40	.16
249 Angels Logo	.05	.02
250 Astros Logo	.05	.02
251 A's Logo	.05	.02
252 Blue Jays Logo	.05	.02
253 Braves Logo	.05	.02
254 Brewers Logo	.05	.02
255 Cardinals Logo	.05	.02
256 Dodgers Logo	.05	.02
257 Expos Logo	.05	.02
258 Giants Logo	.05	.02
259 Indians Logo	.05	.02
260 Mariners Logo	.05	.02
261 Orioles Logo	.05	.02
262 Padres Logo	.05	.02
263 Phillies Logo	.05	.02
264 Pirates Logo	.05	.02
265 Rangers Logo	.05	.02
266 Red Sox Logo	.05	.02
267 Reds Logo	.05	.02
268 Royals Logo	.05	.02
269 Tigers Logo	.05	.02
270 Twins Logo	.05	.02
271 Chicago Logos	.05	.02
272 New York Logos	.05	.02

1987 Donruss Pop-Ups

This 20-card set features "fold-out" cards measuring approximately 2 1/2" X 5". Card fronts are in full color. Cards are unnumbered but are listed in the same order as the Donruss All-Stars on the All-Star checklist card. Card backs present essentially no information about the player. The set was distributed in packs which also contained All-Star cards (3 1/2" by 5").

	Nm-Mt	Ex-Mt
COMPLETE SET (20)	5.00	2.00
1 Wally Joyner	.30	.12
2 Dave Winfield	.40	.16
3 Lou Whitaker	.10	.04
4 Kirby Puckett	.75	.30
5 Cal Ripken	2.00	.80
6 Rickey Henderson	.50	.20
7 Wade Boggs	.50	.20
8 Roger Clemens	1.25	.50
9 Lance Parrish	.10	.04
10 Dick Howser MG	.05	.02
11 Keith Hernandez	.10	.04
12 Darryl Strawberry	.10	.04
13 Ryne Sandberg	.50	.20
14 Dale Murphy	.30	.12
15 Ozzie Smith	.75	.30
16 Tony Gwynn	1.00	.40
17 Mike Schmidt	.50	.20
18 Dwight Gooden	.20	.08
19 Gary Carter	.40	.16
20 Whitey Herzog MG	.10	.04

1987 Donruss Super DK's

This 28-card set was available through a mail-in offer detailed on the wax packs. The set was sent in return for $8.00 and three wrappers plus $1.50 postage and handling. The set features the popular Diamond King subseries in large (approximately 4 7/8" X 6 13/16") form. Dick Perez of Perez-Steele Galleries did the original artwork from which these cards were taken. The cards are essentially a large version of the Donruss regular issue Diamond Kings.

	Nm-Mt	Ex-Mt
COMPLETE SET (26)	12.00	4.80
1 Wally Joyner	1.50	.60
2 Roger Clemens	2.50	1.00
3 Dale Murphy	1.50	.60
4 Darryl Strawberry	.75	.30
5 Ozzie Smith	1.50	.60
6 Jose Canseco	2.50	1.00
7 Charlie Hough	.50	.20
8 Brook Jacoby	.50	.20
9 Fred Lynn	.75	.30
10 Rick Rhoden	.50	.20
11 Chris Brown	.50	.20
12 Von Hayes	.50	.20
13 Jack Morris	.75	.30
14 Kevin McReynolds	.50	.20
15 George Brett	3.00	1.20
16 Ted Higuera	.50	.20
17 Hubie Brooks	.50	.20
18 Mike Scott	.50	.20
19 Kirby Puckett	2.50	1.00
20 Dave Winfield	1.50	.60
21 Lloyd Moseby	.50	.20
22 Eric Davis	1.00	.40
23 Jim Presley	.50	.20
24 Keith Moreland	.50	.20
25 Greg Walker	.50	.20
26 Steve Sax	.50	.20
NNO Roberto Clemente Large Puzzle	1.50	.60
NNO DK Checklist 1-26	.50	.20

1988 Donruss

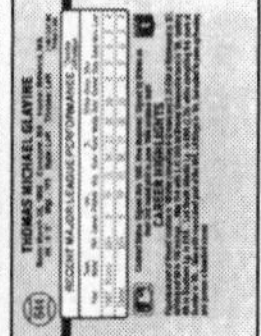

This set consists of 660 standard-size cards. For the seventh straight year, wax packs consisted of 15 cards plus a puzzle panel (featuring Stan Musial this time around). Cards were also distributed in rack packs and retail and hobby factory sets. Card fronts feature a distinctive black and blue border on the front. The card front border design pattern of the factory set card fronts is oriented differently from that of the regular wax pack cards. No premium or discount exists for either version. Subsets include Diamond Kings (1-27) and Rated Rookies (28-47). Cards marked as SP (short printed) from 648-660 are more difficult to find than the other 13 SP's in the lower 600s. These 26 cards listed as SP were apparently pulled from the printing sheet to make room for the 26 Bonus MVP cards. Six of the checklist cards were done two different ways to reflect the inclusion or exclusion of the Bonus MVP cards in the wax packs. In the checklist below, the A variations (for the checklist cards) are from the wax packs and the B variations are from the factory-collated sets. The key Rookie Cards in this set are Roberto Alomar, Jay Bell, Jay Buhner, Ellis Burks, Ken Caminiti, Tom Glavine, Mark Grace and Matt Williams. There was also a Kirby Puckett card issued as the package back of Donruss blister packs; it uses a different photo from both of Kirby's regular and Bonus MVP cards and is unnumbered on the back.

	Nm-Mt	Ex-Mt
COMPLETE SET (660)	10.00	4.00
COMP.FACT.SET (660)	15.00	6.00
COMMON CARD (1-660)	.05	.02
COMMON SP (648-660)	.07	.03
COMP.MUSIAL PUZZLE	1.00	.40
1 Mark McGwire DK	.75	.30
2 Tim Raines DK	.10	.04
3 Benito Santiago DK	.15	.06
4 Alan Trammell DK	.05	.02
5 Danny Tartabull DK	.05	.02
6 Ron Darling DK	.05	.02
7 Paul Molitor DK	.15	.06
8 Devon White DK	.05	.02
9 Andre Dawson DK	.05	.02
10 Julio Franco DK	.05	.02
11 Scott Fletcher DK	.05	.02
12 Tony Fernandez DK	.05	.02
13 Shane Rawley DK	.05	.02
14 Kal Daniels DK	.05	.02
15 Jack Clark DK	.10	.04
16 Dwight Evans DK	.10	.04
17 Tommy John DK	.05	.02
18 Andy Van Slyke DK	.05	.02
19 Gary Gaetti DK	.05	.02
20 Mark Langston DK	.05	.02
21 Will Clark DK	.20	.08
22 Glenn Hubbard DK	.05	.02
23 Billy Hatcher DK	.05	.02
24 Bob Welch DK	.05	.02
25 Ivan Calderon DK	.05	.02
26 Cal Ripken DK	.40	.16
27 DK Checklist 1-26	.05	.02
28 Mackey Sasser RR RC	.05	.02
29 Jeff Treadway RR RC	.05	.02
30 Mike Campbell RR	.05	.02
31 Lance Johnson RR RC	.20	.08
32 Nelson Liriano RR	.05	.02
33 Shawn Abner RR	.05	.02
34 Roberto Alomar RR RC	1.50	.60
35 Shawn Hillegas RR	.05	.02
36 Joey Meyer RR	.05	.02
37 Kevin Elster RR	.05	.02
38 Jose Lind RR RC	.05	.02
39 Kirt Manwaring RR RC	.05	.02
40 Mark Grace RR RC	1.50	.60
41 Jody Reed RR RC	.10	.04
42 John Farrell RR RC	.05	.02
43 Al Leiter RR RC	.50	.20
44 Gary Thurman RR	.05	.02
45 Vicente Palacios RR	.05	.02
46 Eddie Williams RR RC	.05	.02
47 Jack McDowell RR RC	.20	.08
48 Ken Dixon	.05	.02
49 Mike Birkbeck	.05	.02
50 Eric King	.05	.02
51 Roger Clemens	.50	.20
52 Pat Clements	.05	.02
53 Fernando Valenzuela	.10	.04
54 Mark Gubicza	.05	.02
55 Jay Howell	.05	.02
56 Floyd Youmans	.05	.02
57 Ed Correa	.05	.02
58 DeWayne Buice	.05	.02
59 Jose DeLeon	.05	.02
60 Danny Cox	.05	.02
61 Nolan Ryan	1.00	.40
62 Steve Bedrosian	.05	.02
63 Tom Browning	.05	.02
64 Mark Davis	.05	.02
65 R.J. Reynolds	.05	.02
66 Kevin Mitchell	.10	.04
67 Ken Oberkfell	.05	.02
68 Rick Sutcliffe	.10	.04
69 Dwight Gooden	.15	.06
70 Scott Bankhead	.05	.02
71 Bert Blyleven	.10	.04
72 Jimmy Key	.10	.04
73 Les Straker	.05	.02
74 Jim Clancy	.05	.02
75 Mike Moore	.05	.02
76 Ron Darling	.05	.02
77 Ed Lynch	.05	.02
78 Dale Murphy	.20	.08
79 Doug Drabek	.05	.02
80 Scott Garrelts	.05	.02
81 Ed Whitson	.05	.02
82 Rob Murphy	.05	.02
83 Shane Rawley	.05	.02
84 Greg Mathews	.05	.02
85 Jim Deshaies	.05	.02
86 Mike Witt	.05	.02
87 Donnie Hill	.05	.02
88 Jeff Reed	.05	.02
89 Mike Boddicker	.05	.02
90 Ted Higuera	.05	.02
91 Walt Terrell	.05	.02
92 Bob Stanley	.05	.02
93 Dave Righetti	.05	.02
94 Orel Hershiser	.10	.04
95 Chris Bando	.05	.02
96 Bret Saberhagen	.10	.04
97 Curt Young	.05	.02
98 Tim Burke	.05	.02
99 Charlie Hough	.10	.04
100A Checklist 28-137	.05	.02
100B Checklist 28-133	.05	.02
101 Bobby Witt	.05	.02
102 George Brett	.50	.20
103 Mickey Tettleton	.05	.02
104 Scott Bailes	.05	.02
105 Mike Pagliarulo	.05	.02
106 Mike Scioscia	.05	.02
107 Tom Brookens	.05	.02
108 Ray Knight	.05	.02
109 Dan Plesac	.05	.02
110 Wally Joyner	.15	.06
111 Bob Forsch	.05	.02
112 Mike Scott	.05	.02
113 Kevin Gross	.05	.02
114 Benito Santiago	.15	.06
115 Bob Kipper	.05	.02
116 Mike Krukow	.05	.02
117 Chris Bosio	.05	.02
118 Sid Fernandez	.05	.02
119 Jody Davis	.05	.02
120 Mike Morgan	.05	.02
121 Mark Eichhorn	.05	.02
122 Jeff Reardon	.10	.04
123 John Franco	.10	.04
124 Richard Dotson	.05	.02
125 Eric Bell	.05	.02
126 Juan Nieves	.05	.02
127 Jack Morris	.10	.04
128 Rick Rhoden	.05	.02
129 Rich Gedman	.05	.02
130 Ken Howell	.05	.02
131 Brook Jacoby	.05	.02
132 Danny Jackson	.05	.02
133 Gene Nelson	.05	.02
134 Neal Heaton	.05	.02
135 Willie Fraser	.05	.02
136 Jose Guzman	.05	.02
137 Ozzie Guillen	.05	.02
138 Bob Knepper	.05	.02
139 Mike Jackson RC*	.10	.04
140 Joe Magrane RC*	.05	.02
141 Jimmy Jones	.05	.02
142 Ted Power	.05	.02
143 Ozzie Virgil	.05	.02
144 Felix Fermin	.05	.02
145 Kelly Downs	.05	.02
146 Shawon Dunston	.05	.02
147 Scott Bradley	.05	.02
148 Dave Stieb	.05	.02
149 Frank Viola	.05	.02
150 Terry Kennedy	.05	.02
151 Bill Wegman	.05	.02
152 Matt Nokes RC*	.05	.02
153 Wade Boggs	.15	.06
154 Wayne Tolleson	.05	.02
155 Mariano Duncan	.05	.02
156 Julio Franco	.05	.02
157 Charlie Leibrandt	.05	.02
158 Terry Steinbach	.10	.04
159 Mike Fitzgerald	.05	.02
160 Jack Lazorko	.05	.02
161 Mitch Williams	.05	.02
162 Greg Walker	.05	.02
163 Alan Ashby	.05	.02
164 Tony Gwynn	.30	.12
165 Bruce Ruffin	.05	.02
166 Ron Robinson	.05	.02
167 Zane Smith	.05	.02
168 Junior Ortiz	.05	.02
169 Jamie Moyer	.20	.08
170 Tony Pena	.05	.02
171 Cal Ripken	.75	.30
172 B.J. Surhoff	.10	.04
173 Lou Whitaker	.10	.04
174 Ellis Burks RC	.40	.16
175 Ron Guidry	.05	.02
176 Steve Sax	.05	.02
177 Danny Tartabull	.05	.02
178 Carney Lansford	.10	.04
179 Casey Candaele	.05	.02
180 Scott Fletcher	.05	.02
181 Mark McLemore	.05	.02
182 Ivan Calderon	.05	.02
183 Jack Clark	.10	.04
184 Glenn Davis	.05	.02
185 Luis Aguayo	.05	.02
186 Bo Diaz	.05	.02
187 Stan Jefferson	.05	.02
188 Sid Bream	.05	.02
189 Bob Brenly	.05	.02
190 Dion James	.05	.02
191 Leon Durham	.05	.02
192 Jesse Orosco	.05	.02
193 Alvin Davis	.05	.02
194 Gary Gaetti	.10	.04
195 Fred McGriff	.20	.08
196 Steve Lombardozzi	.05	.02
197 Rance Mulliniks	.05	.02
198 Rey Quinones	.05	.02
199 Gary Carter	.15	.06
200A Checklist 138-247	.05	.02
200B Checklist 134-239	.05	.02
201 Keith Moreland	.05	.02
202 Ken Griffey	.10	.04
203 Tommy Gregg	.05	.02
204 Will Clark	.20	.08
205 John Kruk	.10	.04
206 Buddy Bell	.10	.04
207 Von Hayes	.05	.02
208 Tommy Herr	.05	.02
209 Craig Reynolds	.05	.02
210 Gary Pettis	.05	.02
211 Harold Baines	.10	.04
212 Vance Law	.05	.02
213 Ken Gerhart	.05	.02
214 Jim Gantner	.05	.02
215 Chet Lemon	.05	.02
216 Dwight Evans	.10	.04
217 Don Mattingly	.60	.24
218 Franklin Stubbs	.05	.02
219 Pat Tabler	.05	.02
220 Bo Jackson	.20	.08
221 Tony Phillips	.05	.02
222 Tim Wallach	.05	.02
223 Ruben Sierra	.05	.02
224 Steve Buechele	.05	.02
225 Frank White	.10	.04
226 Alfredo Griffin	.05	.02
227 Greg Swindell	.05	.02
228 Willie Randolph	.10	.04
229 Mike Marshall	.05	.02
230 Alan Trammell	.15	.06
231 Eddie Murray	.20	.08
232 Dale Sveum	.05	.02
233 Dick Schofield	.05	.02
234 Jose Oquendo	.05	.02
235 Bill Doran	.05	.02
236 Milt Thompson	.05	.02
237 Marvell Wynne	.05	.02
238 Bobby Bonilla	.10	.04
239 Chris Speier	.05	.02
240 Glenn Braggs	.05	.02
241 Wally Backman	.05	.02
242 Ryne Sandberg	.40	.16
243 Phil Bradley	.05	.02
244 Kelly Gruber	.05	.02
245 Tom Brunansky	.05	.02
246 Ron Oester	.05	.02
247 Bobby Thigpen	.05	.02
248 Fred Lynn	.05	.02
249 Paul Molitor	.15	.06
250 Darrell Evans	.10	.04
251 Gary Ward	.05	.02
252 Bruce Hurst	.05	.02
253 Bob Welch	.05	.02
254 Joe Carter	.20	.08
255 Willie Wilson	.05	.02
256 Mark McGwire	1.50	.60
257 Mitch Webster	.05	.02
258 Brian Downing	.05	.02
259 Mike Stanley	.10	.04
260 Carlton Fisk	.15	.06
261 Billy Hatcher	.05	.02
262 Glenn Wilson	.05	.02
263 Ozzie Smith	.30	.12
264 Randy Ready	.05	.02
265 Kurt Stillwell	.05	.02
266 David Palmer	.05	.02
267 Mike Diaz	.05	.02
268 Robby Thompson	.05	.02
269 Andre Dawson	.10	.04
270 Lee Guetterman	.05	.02
271 Willie Upshaw	.05	.02
272 Randy Bush	.05	.02
273 Larry Sheets	.05	.02
274 Rob Deer	.05	.02
275 Kirk Gibson	.10	.04
276 Marty Barrett	.05	.02
277 Rickey Henderson	.20	.08
278 Pedro Guerrero	.05	.02
279 Brett Butler	.10	.04
280 Kevin Seitzer	.10	.04
281 Mike Davis	.05	.02
282 Andres Galarraga	.10	.04
283 Devon White	.10	.04
284 Pete O'Brien	.05	.02
285 Jerry Hairston	.05	.02
286 Kevin Bass	.05	.02
287 Carmelo Martinez	.05	.02
288 Juan Samuel	.05	.02
289 Kal Daniels	.05	.02
290 Albert Hall	.05	.02
291 Andy Van Slyke	.10	.04
292 Lee Smith	.10	.04
293 Vince Coleman	.05	.02
294 Tom Niedenfuer	.05	.02
295 Robin Yount	.30	.12
296 Jeff M. Robinson	.05	.02
297 Todd Benzinger RC*	.05	.02
298 Dave Winfield	.10	.04
299 Mickey Hatcher	.05	.02
300A Checklist 248-357	.05	.02
300B Checklist 240-345	.05	.02
301 Bud Black	.05	.02
302 Jose Canseco	.20	.08
303 Tom Foley	.05	.02
304 Pete Incaviglia	.05	.02
305 Bob Boone	.10	.04
306 Bill Long	.05	.02
307 Willie McGee	.10	.04
308 Ken Caminiti RC	.40	.16
309 Darren Daulton	.10	.04
310 Tracy Jones	.05	.02
311 Greg Booker	.05	.02
312 Mike LaValliere	.05	.02
313 Chili Davis	.15	.06
314 Glenn Hubbard	.05	.02
315 Paul Noce	.05	.02
316 Keith Hernandez	.15	.06
317 Mark Langston	.05	.02
318 Keith Atherton	.05	.02
319 Tony Fernandez	.05	.02
320 Kent Hrbek	.10	.04
321 John Cerutti	.05	.02
322 Mike Kingery	.05	.02
323 Dave Magadan	.05	.02
324 Rafael Palmeiro	.40	.16
325 Jeff Dedmon	.05	.02
326 Barry Bonds	2.00	.80
327 Jeffrey Leonard	.05	.02
328 Tim Flannery	.05	.02
329 Dave Concepcion	.10	.04
330 Mike Schmidt	.50	.20
331 Bill Dawley	.05	.02
332 Larry Andersen	.05	.02
333 Jack Howell	.05	.02
334 Ken Williams RC	.05	.02
335 Bryn Smith	.05	.02
336 Bill Ripken RC*	.05	.02
337 Greg Brock	.05	.02
338 Mike Heath	.05	.02
339 Mike Greenwell	.05	.02
340 Claudell Washington	.05	.02
341 Jose Gonzalez	.05	.02
342 Mel Hall	.05	.02
343 Jim Eisenreich	.20	.08
344 Tony Bernazard	.05	.02
345 Tim Raines	.10	.04
346 Bob Brower	.05	.02
347 Larry Parrish	.05	.02
348 Thad Bosley	.05	.02
349 Dennis Eckersley	.10	.04
350 Cory Snyder	.05	.02
351 Rick Cerone	.05	.02
352 John Shelby	.05	.02
353 Larry Herndon	.05	.02
354 John Habyan	.05	.02
355 Chuck Crim	.05	.02
356 Gus Polidor	.05	.02
357 Ken Dayley	.05	.02
358 Danny Darwin	.05	.02
359 Lance Parrish	.05	.02
360 James Steels	.05	.02
361 Al Pedrique	.05	.02
362 Mike Aldrete	.05	.02
363 Juan Castillo	.05	.02
364 Len Dykstra	.10	.04
365 Luis Quinones	.05	.02
366 Jim Presley	.05	.02
367 Lloyd Moseby	.05	.02
368 Kirby Puckett	.20	.08
369 Eric Davis	.10	.04
370 Gary Redus	.05	.02
371 Dave Schmidt	.05	.02
372 Mark Clear	.05	.02
373 Dave Bergman	.05	.02
374 Charles Hudson	.05	.02
375 Calvin Schiraldi	.05	.02
376 Alex Trevino	.05	.02
377 Tom Candiotti	.05	.02
378 Steve Farr	.05	.02
379 Mike Gallego	.05	.02
380 Andy McGaffigan	.05	.02
381 Kirk McCaskill	.05	.02
382 Oddibe McDowell	.05	.02
383 Floyd Bannister	.05	.02
384 Denny Walling	.05	.02
385 Don Carman	.05	.02
386 Todd Worrell	.10	.04
387 Eric Show	.05	.02
388 Dave Parker	.10	.04
389 Rick Mahler	.05	.02
390 Mike Dunne	.05	.02
391 Candy Maldonado	.05	.02
392 Bob Dernier	.05	.02
393 Dave Valle	.05	.02
394 Ernie Whitt	.05	.02
395 Juan Berenguer	.05	.02
396 Mike Young	.05	.02
397 Mike Felder	.05	.02
398 Willie Hernandez	.05	.02
399 Jim Rice	.10	.04
400A Checklist 358-467	.05	.02
400B Checklist 346-451	.05	.02
401 Tommy John	.10	.04
402 Brian Holton	.05	.02
403 Carmen Castillo	.05	.02
404 Jamie Quirk	.05	.02
405 Dwayne Murphy	.05	.02
406 Jeff Parrett	.05	.02
407 Don Sutton	.20	.08
408 Jerry Browne	.05	.02
409 Jim Winn	.05	.02
410 Dave Smith	.05	.02
411 Shane Mack	.05	.02
412 Greg Gross	.05	.02
413 Nick Esasky	.05	.02
414 Damaso Garcia	.05	.02
415 Brian Fisher	.05	.02
416 Brian Dayett	.05	.02
417 Curt Ford	.05	.02
418 Mark Williamson	.05	.02
419 Bill Schroeder	.05	.02
420 Mike Henneman RC*	.10	.04
421 John Marzano	.05	.02
422 Ron Kittle	.05	.02
423 Matt Young	.05	.02
424 Steve Balboni	.05	.02
425 Luis Polonia RC*	.05	.02
426 Randy St.Claire	.05	.02
427 Greg Harris	.05	.02
428 Johnny Ray	.05	.02
429 Ray Searage	.05	.02
430 Ricky Horton	.05	.02
431 Gerald Young	.05	.02
432 Rick Schu	.05	.02
433 Paul O'Neill	.15	.06
434 Rich Gossage	.10	.04
435 John Cangelosi	.05	.02
436 Mike LaCoss	.05	.02
437 Gerald Perry	.05	.02
438 Dave Martinez	.05	.02
439 Darryl Strawberry	.15	.06
440 John Moses	.05	.02
441 Greg Gagne	.05	.02
442 Jesse Barfield	.05	.02
443 George Frazier	.05	.02
444 Garth Iorg	.05	.02
445 Ed Nunez	.05	.02
446 Rick Aguilera	.10	.04
447 Jerry Mumphrey	.05	.02
448 Rafael Ramirez	.05	.02
449 John Smiley RC*	.10	.04
450 Atlee Hammaker	.05	.02
451 Lance McCullers	.05	.02
452 Guy Hoffman	.05	.02
453 Chris James	.05	.02
454 Terry Pendleton	.10	.04
455 Dave Meads	.05	.02
456 Bill Buckner	.10	.04
457 John Pawlowski	.05	.02
458 Bob Sebra	.05	.02
459 Jim Dwyer	.05	.02
460 Jay Aldrich	.05	.02
461 Frank Tanana	.05	.02
462 Oil Can Boyd	.05	.02
463 Dan Pasqua	.05	.02
464 Tim Crews RC	.05	.02
465 Andy Allanson	.05	.02
466 Bill Pecota RC*	.05	.02
467 Steve Ontiveros	.05	.02
468 Hubie Brooks	.05	.02
469 Paul Kilgus	.05	.02
470 Dale Mohorcic	.05	.02
471 Dan Quisenberry	.05	.02
472 Dave Stewart	.10	.04
473 Dave Clark	.05	.02
474 Joel Skinner	.05	.02
475 Dave Anderson	.05	.02
476 Dan Petry	.05	.02
477 Carl Nichols	.05	.02
478 Ernest Riles	.05	.02
479 George Hendrick	.05	.02
480 John Morris	.05	.02
481 Manny Hernandez	.05	.02
482 Jeff Stone	.05	.02
483 Chris Brown	.05	.02
484 Mike Bielecki	.05	.02
485 Dave Dravecky	.10	.04
486 Rick Manning	.05	.02
487 Bill Almon	.05	.02
488 Jim Sundberg	.05	.02
489 Ken Phelps	.05	.02
490 Tom Henke	.05	.02
491 Dan Gladden	.05	.02
492 Barry Larkin	.20	.08
493 Fred Manrique	.05	.02
494 Mike Griffin	.05	.02
495 Mark Knudson	.05	.02
496 Bill Madlock	.10	.04
497 Tim Stoddard	.05	.02
498 Sam Horn RC	.05	.02
499 Tracy Woodson RC	.05	.02
500A Checklist 468-577	.05	.02
500B Checklist 452-557	.05	.02
501 Ken Schrom	.05	.02
502 Angel Salazar	.05	.02
503 Eric Plunk	.05	.02
504 Joe Hesketh	.05	.02
505 Greg Minton	.05	.02
506 Geno Petralli	.05	.02
507 Bob James	.05	.02
508 Robbie Wine	.05	.02
509 Jeff Calhoun	.05	.02
510 Steve Lake	.05	.02
511 Mark Grant	.05	.02
512 Frank Williams	.05	.02
513 Jeff Blauser RC	.20	.08
514 Bob Walk	.05	.02
515 Craig Lefferts	.05	.02
516 Manny Trillo	.05	.02
517 Jerry Reed	.05	.02
518 Rick Leach	.05	.02
519 Mark Davidson	.05	.02
520 Jeff Ballard	.05	.02
521 Dave Stapleton	.05	.02
522 Pat Sheridan	.05	.02
523 Al Nipper	.05	.02
524 Steve Trout	.05	.02
525 Jeff Hamilton	.05	.02
526 Tommy Hinzo	.05	.02
527 Lonnie Smith	.05	.02
528 Greg Cadaret	.05	.02
529 Bob McClure UER (Rob on front)	.05	.02
530 Chuck Finley	.15	.06
531 Jeff Russell	.05	.02
532 Steve Lyons	.05	.02
533 Terry Puhl	.05	.02
534 Eric Nolte	.05	.02
535 Kent Tekulve	.05	.02
536 Pat Pacillo	.05	.02
537 Charlie Puleo	.05	.02
538 Tom Prince	.05	.02
539 Greg Maddux	1.00	.40
540 Jim Lindeman	.05	.02
541 Pete Stanicek	.05	.02
542 Steve Kiefer	.05	.02
543A Jim Morrison ERR (No decimal before lifetime average)	.15	.06
543B Jim Morrison COR	.05	.02
544 Spike Owen	.05	.02
545 Jay Buhner RC	.50	.20
546 Mike Devereaux RC	.10	.04
547 Jerry Don Gleaton	.05	.02
548 Jose Rijo	.05	.02
549 Dennis Martinez	.10	.04
550 Mike Loynd	.05	.02
551 Darrell Miller	.05	.02
552 Dave LaPoint	.05	.02
553 John Tudor	.05	.02
554 Rocky Childress	.05	.02
555 Wally Ritchie	.05	.02
556 Terry McGriff	.05	.02
557 Dave Leiper	.05	.02
558 Jeff D. Robinson	.05	.02
559 Jose Uribe	.05	.02
560 Ted Simmons	.10	.04
561 Les Lancaster	.05	.02
562 Keith A. Miller RC	.05	.02
563 Harold Reynolds	.10	.04
564 Gene Larkin RC*	.05	.02
565 Cecil Fielder	.15	.06
566 Roy Smalley	.05	.02
567 Duane Ward	.05	.02
568 Bill Wilkinson	.05	.02
569 Howard Johnson	.05	.02
570 Frank DiPino	.05	.02
571 Pete Smith RC	.05	.02
572 Darnell Coles	.05	.02
573 Don Robinson	.05	.02
574 Rob Nelson UER (Career 0 RBI, but 1 RBI in '87)	.05	.02
575 Dennis Rasmussen	.05	.02
576 Steve Jeltz UER (Photo actually Juan Samuel; Samuel noted for one batting glove and black bat)	.05	.02
577 Tom Pagnozzi RC	.05	.02
578 Ty Gainey	.05	.02
579 Gary Lucas	.05	.02
580 Ron Hassey	.05	.02
581 Herm Winningham	.05	.02
582 Rene Gonzales RC	.05	.02
583 Brad Komminsk	.05	.02
584 Doyle Alexander	.05	.02
585 Jeff Sellers	.05	.02
586 Bill Gullickson	.05	.02
587 Tim Belcher	.10	.04
588 Doug Jones RC	.20	.08
589 Melido Perez RC	.05	.02
590 Rick Honeycutt	.05	.02
591 Pascual Perez	.05	.02
592 Curt Wilkerson	.05	.02
593 Steve Howe	.05	.02
594 John Davis	.05	.02
595 Storm Davis	.05	.02
596 Sammy Stewart	.05	.02
597 Neil Allen	.05	.02
598 Alejandro Pena	.05	.02
599 Mark Thurmond	.05	.02
600A Checklist 578-660 BC1-BC26	.05	.02
600B Checklist 558-660	.05	.02
601 Jose Mesa RC	.15	.06
602 Don August	.05	.02

603 Terry Leach SP .07 .03
604 Tom Newell .05 .02
605 Randall Byers SP .07 .03
606 Jim Gott .05 .02
607 Harry Spilman .05 .02
608 John Candelaria .05 .02
609 Mike Brumley .05 .02
610 Mickey Brantley .05 .02
611 Jose Nunez SP .07 .03
612 Tom Nieto .05 .02
613 Rick Reuschel .05 .02
614 Lee Mazzilli SP .07 .03
615 Scott Lusader .05 .02
616 Bobby Meacham .05 .02
617 Kevin McReynolds SP .07 .03
618 Gene Garber .05 .02
619 Barry Lyons SP .07 .03
620 Randy Myers .15 .06
621 Donnie Moore .05 .02
622 Domingo Ramos .05 .02
623 Ed Romero .05 .02
624 Greg Myers RC .05 .02
625 Ripken Family .40 .16
Cal Ripken Sr.
Cal Ripken Jr.
Billy Ripken
626 Pat Perry .05 .02
627 Andres Thomas SP .07 .03
628 Matt Williams SP RC .75 .30
629 Dave Hengel .05 .02
630 Jeff Musselman SP .07 .03
631 Tim Laudner .05 .02
632 Bob Ojeda SP .07 .03
633 Rafael Santana .05 .02
634 Wes Gardner .05 .02
635 Roberto Kelly RC SP .20 .08
636 Mike Flanagan SP .07 .03
637 Jay Bell RC .40 .16
638 Bob Melvin .05 .02
639 D.Berryhill RC UER .05 .02
Bats: Swithch
640 David Wells SP RC .75 .30
641 Stan Musial PUZ .20 .08
642 Doug Sisk .05 .02
643 Keith Hughes .05 .02
644 Tom Glavine RC 1.50 .60
645 Al Newman .05 .02
646 Scott Sanderson .05 .02
647 Scott Terry .05 .02
648 Tim Teufel SP .07 .03
649 Garry Templeton SP .07 .03
650 Manny Lee SP .07 .03
651 Roger McDowell SP .07 .03
652 Mookie Wilson SP .20 .08
653 David Cone SP .10 .04
654 Ron Gant SP RC .40 .16
655 Joe Price SP .07 .03
656 George Bell SP .10 .04
657 Gregg Jefferies SP RC .20 .08
658 T.Stottlemyre SP RC .20 .08
659 G.Berroa SP RC .25 .10
660 Jerry Royster SP .07 .03
XX Kirby Puckett 1.25 .50
Blister Pack

1988 Donruss Bonus MVP's

Numbered with the prefix "BC" for bonus card, this 26-card set featuring the most valuable player from each major league team was randomly inserted in the wax and rack packs. The cards are distinguished by the MVP logo in the upper left corner of the obverse, and cards BC14-BC26 are considered to be very slightly more difficult to find than cards BC1-BC13.

Nm-Mt Ex-Mt
COMPLETE SET (26) 3.00 1.20
BC1 Cal Ripken .75 .30
BC2 Eric Davis .10 .04
BC3 Paul Molitor .15 .06
BC4 Mike Schmidt .50 .20
BC5 Ivan Calderon .05 .02
BC6 Tony Gwynn .30 .12
BC7 Wade Boggs .15 .06
BC8 Andy Van Slyke .10 .04
BC9 Joe Carter .20 .08
BC10 Andre Dawson .10 .04
BC11 Alan Trammell .15 .06
BC12 Mike Scott .05 .02
BC13 Wally Joyner .15 .06
BC14 Dale Murphy SP .20 .08
BC15 Kirby Puckett SP .20 .08
BC16 Pedro Guerrero SP .05 .02
BC17 Kevin Seitzer SP .10 .04
BC18 Tim Raines SP .10 .04
BC19 George Bell SP .10 .04
BC20 D.Strawberry SP .15 .06
BC21 Don Mattingly SP .60 .24
BC22 Ozzie Smith SP .30 .12
BC23 Mark McGwire SP 1.50 .60
BC24 Will Clark SP .20 .08
BC25 Alvin Davis SP .05 .02
BC26 Ruben Sierra SP .05 .02

1988 Donruss Rookies

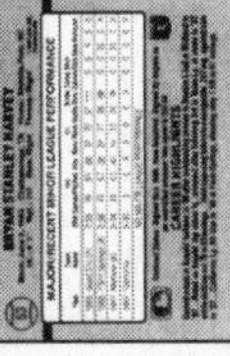

The 1988 Donruss "The Rookies" set features 56 standard-size full-color cards plus a 15-piece puzzle of Stan Musial. This set was distributed exclusively in factory set form in a small, cellophane-wrapped, green and black through hobby dealers. Card fronts are similar in design to the 1988 Donruss regular issue except for the presence of "The Rookies" logo in the lower right corner and a green and black border instead of a blue and black border on the fronts. Extended Rookie Cards in this set include Brady Anderson, Edgar Martinez, and Walt Weiss. Notable early cards were issued of Roberto Alomar, Mark Grace and Jay Buhner.

Nm-Mt Ex-Mt
COMP.FACT.SET (56) 10.00 4.00
1 Mark Grace 2.00 .80
2 Mike Campbell .15 .06
3 Todd Frohwirth .15 .06
4 Dave Stapleton .15 .06
5 Shawn Abner .15 .06
6 Jose Cecena .15 .06
7 Dave Gallagher .15 .06
8 Mark Parent .15 .06
9 Cecil Espy .15 .06
10 Pete Smith .15 .06
11 Jay Buhner 1.00 .40
12 Pat Borders XRC .30 .12
13 Doug Jennings .15 .06
14 Brady Anderson XRC 1.00 .40
15 Pete Stanicek .15 .06
16 Roberto Kelly .40 .16
17 Jeff Treadway .15 .06
18 Walt Weiss XRC* 1.00 .40
19 Paul Gibson .15 .06
20 Tim Crews .15 .06
21 Melido Perez .15 .06
22 Steve Peters .15 .06
23 Craig Worthington .15 .06
24 John Trautwein .15 .06
25 DeWayne Vaughn .15 .06
26 David Wells 1.50 .60
27 Al Leiter 1.00 .40
28 Tim Belcher .30 .12
29 Johnny Paredes .15 .06
30 Chris Sabo XRC .30 .12
31 Damon Berryhill .15 .06
32 Randy Milligan XRC* .15 .06
33 Gary Thurman .15 .06
34 Kevin Elster .15 .06
35 Roberto Alomar 5.00 2.00
36 E.Martinez UER XRC 2.00 .80
Photo actually
Edwin Nunez
37 Todd Stottlemyre .40 .16
38 Joey Meyer .15 .06
39 Carl Nichols .15 .06
40 Jack McDowell .60 .24
41 Jose Bautista XRC .15 .06
42 Sil Campusano .15 .06
43 John Dopson .15 .06
44 Jody Reed .30 .12
45 Darrin Jackson XRC* .15 .06
46 Mike Capel .15 .06
47 Ron Gant .75 .30
48 John Davis .15 .06
49 Kevin Coffman .15 .06
50 Cris Carpenter XRC .15 .06
51 Mackey Sasser .15 .06
52 Luis Alicea XRC .15 .06
53 Bryan Harvey XRC .30 .12
54 Steve Ellsworth .15 .06
55 Mike Macfarlane XRC .15 .06
56 Checklist 1-56 .15 .06

1988 Donruss All-Stars

This 64-card set features cards measures the standard size. Card fronts are in full color with a solid blue and black border. The card backs are printed in black and blue on white card stock. Cards are numbered on the back inside a blue star in the upper right hand corner. Card backs feature statistical information about the player's performance in past All-Star games. The set was distributed in packs which also contained a Pop-Up. The AL Checklist card number 32 has two uncorrected errors on it, Wade Boggs is erroneously listed as the AL Leftfielder and Dan Plesac is erroneously listed as being on the Tigers.

Nm-Mt Ex-Mt
COMPLETE SET (64) 8.00 3.20
1 Don Mattingly 1.00 .40
2 Dave Winfield .30 .12
3 Willie Randolph .10 .04
4 Rickey Henderson .50 .20
5 Cal Ripken 2.50 1.00
6 George Bell .05 .02
7 Wade Boggs .50 .20
8 Bret Saberhagen .10 .04
9 Terry Kennedy .05 .02
10 John McNamara MG .05 .02
11 Jay Howell .05 .02
12 Harold Baines .20 .08
13 Harold Reynolds .10 .04
14 Bruce Hurst .05 .02
15 Kirby Puckett 1.25 .50
16 Matt Nokes .05 .02
17 Pat Tabler .05 .02
18 Dan Plesac .05 .02
19 Mark McGwire 2.50 1.00
20 Mike Witt .05 .02
21 Larry Parrish .05 .02
22 Alan Trammell .20 .08
23 Dwight Evans .10 .04
24 Jack Morris .10 .04
25 Tony Fernandez .05 .02
26 Mark Langston .05 .02
27 Kevin Seitzer .10 .04
28 Tom Henke .05 .02
29 Dave Righetti .05 .02
30 Oakland Stadium .05 .02
31 Wade Boggs .50 .20
(Top AL Vote Getter)
32 AL Checklist UER .05 .02
33 Jack Clark .10 .04
34 Darryl Strawberry .10 .04
35 Ryne Sandberg .75 .30
36 Andre Dawson .30 .12
37 Ozzie Smith 1.00 .40
38 Eric Davis .10 .04
39 Mike Schmidt .75 .30
40 Mike Scott .05 .02
41 Gary Carter .50 .20
42 Davey Johnson MG .05 .02
43 Rick Sutcliffe .05 .02
44 Willie McGee .10 .04
45 Hubie Brooks .05 .02
46 Dale Murphy .30 .12
47 Bo Diaz .05 .02
48 Pedro Guerrero .05 .02
49 Keith Hernandez .10 .04
50 Ozzie Virgil UER .05 .02
(Phillies logo
on card back,
wrong birth year)
51 Tony Gwynn 1.25 .50
52 Rick Reuschel UER .05 .02
(Pirates logo
on card back)
53 John Franco .10 .04
54 Jeffrey Leonard .05 .02
55 Juan Samuel .05 .02
56 Orel Hershiser .10 .04
57 Tim Raines .10 .04
58 Sid Fernandez .05 .02
59 Tim Wallach .05 .02
60 Lee Smith .10 .04
61 Steve Bedrosian .05 .02
62 Tim Raines .10 .04
63 Ozzie Smith 1.00 .40
(Top NL Vote Getter)
64 NL Checklist .05 .02

1988 Donruss Baseball's Best

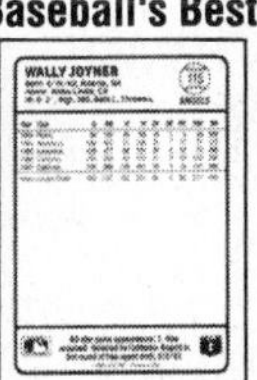

This innovative set of 336 standard-size cards was released by Donruss very late in the 1988 season to be sold in large national retail chains as a complete packaged set. The set was packaged in a specially designed box. Cards are very similar in design to the 1988 regular Donruss issue except that these cards have orange and black borders instead of blue and black borders. The set is also sometimes referred to as the Halloween set because of the orange box and design of the cards. Six (2 1/2" by 3 1/2") 15-piece puzzles of Stan Musial are also included with every complete set.

Nm-Mt Ex-Mt
COMP.FACT.SET (336) 25.00 10.00
1 Don Mattingly 1.00 .40
2 Ron Gant .50 .20
3 Bob Boone .20 .08
4 Mark Grace 1.50 .60
5 Andy Allanson .10 .04
6 Kal Daniels .10 .04
7 Floyd Bannister .10 .04
8 Alan Ashby .10 .04
9 Marty Barrett .10 .04
10 Tim Belcher .20 .08
11 Harold Baines .20 .08
12 Hubie Brooks .10 .04
13 Doyle Alexander .10 .04
14 Gary Carter .50 .20
15 Glenn Braggs .10 .04
16 Steve Bedrosian .10 .04
17 Barry Bonds 1.00 .40
18 Bert Blyleven .20 .08
19 Tom Brunansky .10 .04
20 John Candelaria .10 .04
21 Shawn Abner .10 .04
22 Jose Canseco .50 .20
23 Brett Butler .20 .08
24 Scott Bradley .10 .04
25 Ivan Calderon .10 .04
26 Rich Gossage .20 .08
27 Brian Downing .10 .04
28 Jim Rice .20 .08
29 Dion James .10 .04
30 Terry Kennedy .10 .04
31 George Bell .10 .04
32 Scott Fletcher .10 .04
33 Bobby Bonilla .20 .08
34 Tim Burke .10 .04
35 Darrell Evans .20 .08
36 Mike Davis .10 .04
37 Shawon Dunston .10 .04
38 Kevin Bass .10 .04
39 George Brett 1.25 .50
40 David Cone .40 .16
41 Ron Darling .10 .04
42 Roberto Alomar 2.00 .80
43 Dennis Eckersley .20 .08
44 Vince Coleman .10 .04
45 Sid Bream .10 .04
46 Gary Gaetti .20 .08
47 Phil Bradley .10 .04
48 Jim Clancy .10 .04
49 Jack Clark .20 .08
50 Mike Krukow .10 .04
51 Henry Cotto .10 .04
52 Rich Dotson .10 .04
53 Jim Gantner .10 .04
54 John Franco .20 .08
55 Pete Incaviglia .10 .04
56 Joe Carter .40 .16
57 Roger Clemens 1.00 .40
58 Gerald Perry .10 .04
59 Jack Howell .10 .04
60 Vance Law .10 .04
61 Jay Bell .50 .20
62 Eric Davis .20 .08
63 Gene Garber .20 .08
64 Glenn Davis .10 .04
65 Wade Boggs .50 .20
66 Kirk Gibson .20 .08
67 Carlton Fisk .50 .20
68 Casey Candaele .10 .04
69 Mike Heath .10 .04
70 Kevin Elster .10 .04
71 Greg Brock .10 .04
72 Don Carman .10 .04
73 Doug Drabek .20 .08
74 Greg Gagne .10 .04
75 Danny Cox .10 .04
76 Rickey Henderson .50 .20
77 Chris Brown .10 .04
78 Terry Steinbach .20 .08
79 Will Clark .50 .20
80 Mickey Brantley .10 .04
81 Ozzie Guillen .20 .08
82 Greg Maddux 1.25 .50
83 Kirk McCaskill .10 .04
84 Dwight Evans .20 .08
85 Ozzie Virgil .10 .04
86 Mike Morgan .10 .04
87 Tony Fernandez .20 .08
88 Jose Guzman .10 .04
89 Mike Dunne .10 .04
90 Andres Galarraga .40 .16
91 Mike Henneman .20 .08
92 Alfredo Griffin .10 .04
93 Rafael Palmeiro .75 .30
94 Jim Deshaies .10 .04
95 Mark Gubicza .10 .04
96 Dwight Gooden .20 .08
97 Howard Johnson .10 .04
98 Mark Davis .10 .04
99 Dave Stewart .20 .08
100 Joe Magrane .10 .04
101 Brian Fisher .10 .04
102 Kent Hrbek .20 .08
103 Kevin Gross .10 .04
104 Tom Henke .10 .04
105 Mike Pagliarulo .10 .04
106 Kelly Downs .10 .04
107 Alvin Davis .10 .04
108 Willie Randolph .20 .08
109 Rob Deer .10 .04
110 Bo Diaz .10 .04
111 Paul Kilgus .10 .04
112 Tom Candiotti .10 .04
113 Dale Murphy .40 .16
114 Rick Mahler .10 .04
115 Wally Joyner .30 .12
116 Ryne Sandberg .50 .20
117 John Farrell .10 .04
118 Nick Esasky .10 .04
119 Bo Jackson .40 .16
120 Bill Doran .10 .04
121 Ellis Burks .75 .30
122 Pedro Guerrero .10 .04
123 Dave LaPoint .10 .04
124 Neal Heaton .10 .04
125 Willie Hernandez .10 .04
126 Roger McDowell .10 .04
127 Ted Higuera .10 .04
128 Von Hayes .10 .04
129 Mike LaValliere .10 .04
130 Dan Gladden .10 .04
131 Willie McGee .20 .08
132 Al Leiter .50 .20
133 Mark Grant .10 .04
134 Bob Welch .10 .04
135 Dave Dravecky .20 .08
136 Mark Langston .10 .04
137 Dan Pasqua .10 .04
138 Rick Sutcliffe .10 .04
139 Dan Petry .10 .04
140 Rich Gedman .10 .04
141 Ken Griffey .10 .04
142 Eddie Murray .50 .20
143 Jimmy Key .20 .08
144 Dale Mohorcic .10 .04
145 Jose Lind .10 .04
146 Dennis Martinez .20 .08
147 Chet Lemon .10 .04
148 Orel Hershiser .20 .08
149 Dave Martinez .10 .04
150 Billy Hatcher .10 .04
151 Charlie Leibrandt .10 .04
152 Keith Hernandez .20 .08
153 Kevin McReynolds .10 .04
154 Tony Gwynn 1.00 .40
155 Stan Javier .10 .04
156 Tony Pena .20 .08
157 Andy Van Slyke .20 .08
158 Gene Larkin .10 .04
159 Chris James .10 .04
160 Fred McGriff .75 .30
161 Rick Rhoden .10 .04
162 Scott Garrelts .10 .04
163 Mike Campbell .10 .04
164 Dave Righetti .10 .04
165 Paul Molitor .50 .20
166 Danny Jackson .10 .04
167 Pete O'Brien .10 .04
168 Julio Franco .20 .08
169 Mark McGwire 2.00 .80
170 Zane Smith .10 .04
171 Johnny Ray .10 .04
172 Les Lancaster .10 .04
173 Mel Hall .10 .04
174 Tracy Jones .10 .04
175 Kevin Seitzer .20 .08
176 Bob Knepper .10 .04
177 Mike Greenwell .10 .04
178 Mike Marshall .10 .04
179 Melido Perez .10 .04
180 Tim Raines .20 .08
181 Jack Morris .20 .08
182 Darryl Strawberry .20 .08
183 Robin Yount .50 .20
184 Lance Parrish .10 .04
185 Darnell Coles .10 .04
186 Kirby Puckett .50 .20
187 Terry Pendleton .20 .08
188 Don Slaught .10 .04
189 Jimmy Jones .10 .04
190 Dave Parker .20 .08
191 Mike Aldrete .10 .04
192 Mike Moore .10 .04
193 Greg Walker .10 .04
194 Calvin Schiraldi .10 .04
195 Dick Schofield .10 .04
196 Jody Reed .20 .08
197 Pete Smith .10 .04
198 Cal Ripken 2.00 .80
199 Lloyd Moseby .10 .04
200 Ruben Sierra .20 .08
201 R.J. Reynolds .10 .04
202 Bryn Smith .10 .04
203 Gary Pettis .10 .04
204 Steve Sax .10 .04
205 Frank DiPino .10 .04
206 Mike Scott UER .10 .04
(1977 Jackson losses
say 1.10, should be 1)
207 Kurt Stillwell .10 .04
208 Mookie Wilson .20 .08
209 Lee Mazzilli .10 .04
210 Lance McCullers .10 .04
211 Rick Honeycutt .10 .04
212 John Tudor .10 .04
213 Jim Gott .10 .04
214 Frank Viola .10 .04
215 Juan Samuel .10 .04
216 Jesse Barfield .10 .04
217 Claudell Washington .10 .04
218 Rick Reuschel .10 .04
219 Jim Presley .10 .04
220 Tommy John .20 .08
221 Dan Plesac .10 .04
222 Barry Larkin .40 .16
223 Mike Stanley .10 .04
224 Cory Snyder .10 .04
225 Andre Dawson .40 .16
226 Ken Oberkfell .10 .04
227 Devon White .20 .08
228 Jamie Moyer .30 .12
229 Brook Jacoby .10 .04
230 Rob Murphy .10 .04
231 Bret Saberhagen .20 .08
232 Nolan Ryan 2.00 .80
233 Bruce Hurst .10 .04
234 Jesse Orosco .20 .08
235 Bobby Thigpen .10 .04
236 Pascual Perez .10 .04
237 Matt Nokes .20 .08
238 Bob Ojeda .10 .04
239 Joey Meyer .10 .04
240 Shane Rawley .10 .04
241 Jeff Robinson .10 .04
242 Jeff Reardon .20 .08
243 Ozzie Smith .40 .16
244 Dave Winfield .50 .20
245 John Kruk .20 .08
246 Carney Lansford .20 .08
247 Candy Maldonado .10 .04
248 Ken Phelps .10 .04
249 Ken Williams .20 .08
250 Al Nipper .10 .04
251 Mark McLemore .10 .04
252 Lee Smith .20 .08
253 Albert Hall .10 .04
254 Billy Ripken .10 .04
255 Kelly Gruber .10 .04
256 Charlie Hough .20 .08
257 John Smiley .20 .08
258 Tim Wallach .20 .08
259 Frank Tanana .20 .08
260 Mike Scioscia .20 .08
261 Damon Berryhill .10 .04
262 Dave Smith .20 .08
263 Willie Wilson .20 .08
264 Len Dykstra .20 .08
265 Randy Myers .30 .12
266 Keith Moreland .10 .04
267 Eric Plunk .10 .04
268 Todd Worrell .20 .08
269 Bob Walk .10 .04
270 Keith Atherton .10 .04
271 Mike Schmidt .50 .20
272 Mike Flanagan .10 .04
273 Rafael Santana .10 .04
274 Robby Thompson .20 .08
275 Rey Quinones .10 .04
276 Cecilio Guante .10 .04
277 B.J. Surhoff .30 .12
278 Chris Sabo .20 .08
279 Mitch Williams .10 .04
280 Greg Swindell .10 .04
281 Alan Trammell .30 .12
282 Storm Davis .10 .04
283 Chuck Finley .30 .12
284 Dave Stieb .20 .08
285 Scott Bailes .10 .04
286 Larry Sheets .10 .04
287 Danny Tartabull .10 .04
288 Checklist Card .10 .04
289 Todd Benzinger .10 .04
290 John Shelby .10 .04
291 Steve Lyons .20 .08
292 Mitch Webster .10 .04
293 Walt Terrell .10 .04
294 Pete Stanicek .10 .04
295 Chris Bosio .10 .04
296 Milt Thompson .10 .04
297 Fred Lynn .10 .04
298 Juan Berenguer .10 .04
299 Ken Dayley .10 .04
300 Joel Skinner .10 .04
301 Benito Santiago .20 .08
302 Ron Hassey .10 .04
303 Jose Uribe .10 .04
304 Harold Reynolds .20 .08
305 Dale Sveum .10 .04
306 Glenn Wilson .10 .04
307 Mike Witt .10 .04
308 Ron Robinson .10 .04
309 Denny Walling .10 .04
310 Joe Orsulak .10 .04
311 David Wells 1.50 .60
312 Steve Buechele .10 .04

313 Jose Oquendo .10 .04
314 Floyd Youmans .10 .04
315 Lou Whitaker .20 .08
316 Fernando Valenzuela .20 .08
317 Mike Boddicker .10 .04
318 Gerald Young .10 .04
319 Frank White .20 .08
320 Bill Wegman .10 .04
321 Tom Niedenfuer .10 .04
322 Ed Whitson .10 .04
323 Curt Young .10 .04
324 Greg Mathews .10 .04
325 Doug Jones .40 .16
326 Tommy Herr .10 .04
327 Kent Tekulve .10 .04
328 Rance Mulliniks .10 .04
329 Checklist Card .10 .04
330 Craig Lefferts .10 .04
331 Franklin Stubbs .10 .04
332 Rick Cerone .10 .04
333 Dave Schmidt .10 .04
334 Larry Parrish .10 .04
335 Tom Browning .10 .04
336 Checklist Card .10 .04

1988 Donruss Pop-Ups

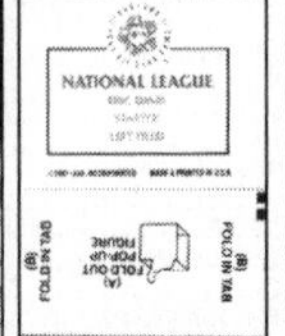

This 20-card set features "fold-out" cards measures the standard size. Card fronts are in full color. Cards are unnumbered but are listed in the same order as the Donruss All-Stars on the All-Star checklist card. Card backs present essentially no information about the player. The set was distributed in packs which also contained All-Star cards. In order to remain in mint condition, the cards should not be popped up.

Nm-Mt Ex-Mt
COMPLETE SET (20) 5.00 2.00
1 Don Mattingly 1.25 .50
2 Dave Winfield .40 .16
3 Willie Randolph .10 .04
4 Rickey Henderson .60 .24
5 Cal Ripken 2.00 .80
6 George Bell .05 .02
7 Wade Boggs .50 .20
8 Bret Saberhagen .10 .04
9 Terry Kennedy .05 .02
10 John McNamara MG .05 .02
11 Jack Clark .10 .04
12 Darryl Strawberry .10 .04
13 Ryne Sandberg .50 .20
14 Andre Dawson .30 .12
15 Ozzie Smith .75 .30
16 Eric Davis .10 .04
17 Mike Schmidt .50 .20
18 Mike Scott .05 .02
19 Gary Carter .40 .16
20 Davey Johnson MG .05 .02

1988 Donruss Super DK's

This 26-player card set was available through a mail-in offer detailed on the wax packs. The set was sent in return for 8.00 and three wrappers plus 1.50 postage and handling. The set features the popular Diamond King subseries in large (approximately 4 7/8" by 6 13/16") form. Dick Perez of Perez-Steele Galleries did another outstanding job on the artwork. The cards are essentially a large version of the Donruss regular issue Diamond Kings.

Nm-Mt Ex-Mt
COMPLETE SET (26) 15.00 6.00
1 Mark McGwire 4.00 1.60
2 Tim Raines .75 .30
3 Benito Santiago .75 .30
4 Alan Trammell 1.00 .40
5 Danny Tartabull .50 .20
6 Ron Darling .50 .20
7 Paul Molitor 2.00 .80
8 Devon White .75 .30
9 Andre Dawson 1.50 .60
10 Julio Franco .75 .30
11 Scott Fletcher .50 .20
12 Tony Fernandez .50 .20
13 Shane Rawley .50 .20
14 Kal Daniels .50 .20
15 Jack Clark .75 .30
16 Dwight Evans .75 .30
17 Tommy John .75 .30
18 Andy Van Slyke .50 .20
19 Gary Gaetti .75 .30
20 Mark Langston .50 .20
21 Will Clark 2.00 .80
22 Glenn Hubbard .50 .20
23 Billy Hatcher .50 .20
24 Bob Welch .50 .20
25 Ivan Calderon .50 .20
26 Cal Ripken 5.00 2.00

1989 Donruss

This set consists of 660 standard-size cards. The cards were primarily issued in 15-card wax packs, rack packs and hobby and retail factory sets. Each wax pack also contained a puzzle panel (featuring Warren Spahn this year). The cards feature a distinctive black side border with an alternating coating. Subsets include Diamond Kings (1-27) and Rated Rookies (28-47). There are two variations that occur throughout most of the set. On the card backs "Denotes Led League" can be found with one asterisk to the left or with an asterisk on each side. On the card fronts the horizontal lines on the left and right borders can be glossy or non-glossy. Since both of these variation types are relatively minor and seem equally common, there is no premium value for either type. Rather than short-printing 26 cards in order to make room for printing the Bonus MVP's this year, Donruss apparently chose to double print 106 cards. These double prints are listed below by DP. Rookie Cards in this set include Sandy Alomar Jr., Brady Anderson, Dante Bichette, Craig Biggio, Ken Griffey Jr., Randy Johnson, Curt Schilling, Gary Sheffield and John Smoltz. Similar to the 1988 Donruss set, a special card was issued on blister packs, and features the card number as "Bonus Card".

Nm-Mt Ex-Mt
COMPLETE SET (660) 25.00 10.00
COMP.FACT.SET (672) 30.00 12.00
COMP.SPAHN PUZZLE 1.00 .40
1 Mike Greenwell DK .05 .02
2 Bobby Bonilla DK DP .10 .04
3 Pete Incaviglia DK .05 .02
4 Chris Sabo DK DP .05 .02
5 Robin Yount DK .40 .16
6 Tony Gwynn DK DP .15 .06
7 Carlton Fisk DK UER .15 .06
(OF on back)
8 Cory Snyder DK .05 .02
9 David Cone DK UER .05 .02
("hurdlers")
10 Kevin Seitzer DK .05 .02
11 Rick Reuschel DK .05 .02
12 Johnny Ray DK .05 .02
13 Dave Schmidt DK .05 .02
14 Andres Galarraga DK .10 .04
15 Kirk Gibson DK .05 .02
16 Fred McGriff DK .10 .04
17 Mark Grace DK .25 .10
18 Jeff M. Robinson DK .05 .02
19 Vince Coleman DK DP .05 .02
20 Dave Henderson DK .05 .02
21 Harold Reynolds DK .10 .04
22 Gerald Perry DK .05 .02
23 Frank Viola DK .05 .02
24 Steve Bedrosian DK .05 .02
25 Glenn Davis DK .05 .02
26 Don Mattingly DK UER .30 .12
(Doesn't mention Don's previous DK in 1985)
27 DK Checklist 1-26 DP .05 .02
28 S.Alomar Jr. RR RC .40 .16
29 Steve Searcy RR .05 .02
30 Cameron Drew RR .05 .02
31 Gary Sheffield RR RC 1.50 .60
32 Erik Hanson RR RC .25 .10
33 Ken Griffey Jr. RR RC 8.00 3.20
34 Greg W. Harris RR RC .10 .04
35 Gregg Jefferies RR .10 .04
36 Luis Medina RR .05 .02
37 Carlos Quintana RR RC .10 .04
38 Felix Jose RR RC .10 .04
39 Cris Carpenter RR RC* .10 .04
40 Ron Jones RR .05 .02
41 Dave West RR RC .10 .04
42 R.Johnson RC RR UER 3.00 1.20
Card says born in 1964 he was born in 1963
43 Mike Harkey RR RC .10 .04
44 P.Harnisch RR DP RC .25 .10
45 Tom Gordon RR DP RC .25 .10
46 Gregg Olson RC RR DP .25 .10
47 Alex Sanchez RR DP .05 .02
48 Ruben Sierra .05 .02
49 Rafael Palmeiro .25 .10
50 Ron Gant .10 .04
51 Cal Ripken .75 .30
52 Wally Joyner .10 .04
53 Gary Carter .15 .06
54 Andy Van Slyke .10 .04
55 Robin Yount .40 .16
56 Pete Incaviglia .05 .02
57 Greg Brock .05 .02
58 Melido Perez .05 .02
59 Craig Lefferts .05 .02
60 Gary Pettis .05 .02
61 Danny Tartabull .05 .02
62 Guillermo Hernandez .05 .02
63 Ozzie Smith .40 .16
64 Gary Gaetti .10 .04
65 Mark Davis .05 .02
66 Lee Smith .10 .04
67 Dennis Eckersley .10 .04
68 Wade Boggs .15 .06
69 Mike Scott .05 .02
70 Fred McGriff .25 .10
71 Tom Browning .05 .02
72 Claudell Washington .05 .02
73 Mel Hall .05 .02
74 Don Mattingly .60 .24
75 Steve Bedrosian .05 .02
76 Juan Samuel .05 .02
77 Mike Scioscia .05 .02
78 Dave Righetti .05 .02
79 Alfredo Griffin .05 .02
80 Eric Davis UER .10 .04
(165 games in 1988, should be 135)
81 Juan Berenguer .05 .02
82 Todd Worrell .05 .02
83 Joe Carter .15 .06
84 Steve Sax .05 .02
85 Frank White .10 .04
86 John Kruk .10 .04
87 Rance Mulliniks .05 .02
88 Alan Ashby .05 .02
89 Charlie Leibrandt .05 .02
90 Frank Tanana .05 .02
91 Jose Canseco .25 .10
92 Barry Bonds 1.25 .50
93 Harold Reynolds .10 .04
94 Mark McLemore .05 .02
95 Mark McGwire 1.00 .40
96 Eddie Murray .25 .10
97 Tim Raines .10 .04
98 Robby Thompson .05 .02
99 Kevin McReynolds .05 .02
100 Checklist 28-137 .05 .02
101 Carlton Fisk .15 .06
102 Dave Martinez .05 .02
103 Glenn Braggs .05 .02
104 Dale Murphy .25 .10
105 Ryne Sandberg .40 .16
106 Dennis Martinez .10 .04
107 Pete O'Brien .05 .02
108 Dick Schofield .05 .02
109 Henry Cotto .05 .02
110 Mike Marshall .05 .02
111 Keith Moreland .05 .02
112 Tom Brunansky .05 .02
113 Kelly Gruber UER .05 .02
(Wrong birthdate)
114 Brook Jacoby .05 .02
115 Keith Brown .05 .02
116 Matt Nokes .05 .02
117 Keith Hernandez .15 .06
118 Bob Forsch .05 .02
119 Bert Blyleven UER .10 .04
(... 3000 strikeouts in 1987, should be 1986)
120 Willie Wilson .05 .02
121 Tommy Gregg .05 .02
122 Jim Rice .10 .04
123 Bob Knepper .05 .02
124 Danny Jackson .05 .02
125 Eric Plunk .05 .02
126 Brian Fisher .05 .02
127 Mike Pagliarulo .05 .02
128 Tony Gwynn .30 .12
129 Lance McCullers .05 .02
130 Andres Galarraga .10 .04
131 Jose Uribe .05 .02
132 Kirk Gibson UER .10 .04
(Wrong birthdate)
133 David Palmer .05 .02
134 R.J. Reynolds .05 .02
135 Greg Walker .05 .02
136 Kirk McCaskill UER .05 .02
(Wrong birthdate)
137 Shawon Dunston .05 .02
138 Andy Allanson .05 .02
139 Rob Murphy .05 .02
140 Mike Aldrete .05 .02
141 Terry Kennedy .05 .02
142 Scott Fletcher .05 .02
143 Steve Balboni .05 .02
144 Bret Saberhagen .10 .04
145 Ozzie Virgil .05 .02
146 Dale Sveum .05 .02
147 Darryl Strawberry .15 .06
148 Harold Baines .10 .04
149 George Bell .05 .02
150 Dave Parker .10 .04
151 Bobby Bonilla .10 .04
152 Mookie Wilson .10 .04
153 Ted Power .05 .02
154 Nolan Ryan 1.00 .40
155 Jeff Reardon .10 .04
156 Tim Wallach .05 .02
157 Jamie Moyer .10 .04
158 Rich Gossage .10 .04
159 Dave Winfield .10 .04
160 Von Hayes .05 .02
161 Willie McGee .10 .04
162 Rich Gedman .05 .02
163 Tony Pena .05 .02
164 Mike Morgan .05 .02
165 Charlie Hough .10 .04
166 Mike Stanley .05 .02
167 Andre Dawson .10 .04
168 Joe Boever .05 .02
169 Pete Stanicek .05 .02
170 Bob Boone .10 .04
171 Ron Darling .05 .02
172 Bob Walk .05 .02
173 Rob Deer .05 .02
174 Steve Buechele .05 .02
175 Ted Higuera .05 .02
176 Ozzie Guillen .05 .02
177 Candy Maldonado .05 .02
178 Doyle Alexander .05 .02
179 Mark Gubicza .05 .02
180 Alan Trammell .15 .06
181 Vince Coleman .05 .02
182 Kirby Puckett .25 .10
183 Chris Brown .05 .02
184 Marty Barrett .05 .02
185 Stan Javier .05 .02
186 Mike Greenwell .05 .02
187 Billy Hatcher .05 .02
188 Jimmy Key .10 .04
189 Nick Esasky .05 .02
190 Don Slaught .05 .02
191 Cory Snyder .05 .02
192 John Candelaria .05 .02
193 Mike Schmidt .50 .20
194 Kevin Gross .05 .02
195 John Tudor .05 .02
196 Neil Allen .05 .02
197 Orel Hershiser .10 .04
198 Kal Daniels .05 .02
199 Kent Hrbek .10 .04
200 Checklist 138-247 .05 .02
201 Joe Magrane .05 .02
202 Scott Bailes .05 .02
203 Tim Belcher .05 .02
204 George Brett .60 .24
205 Benito Santiago .10 .04
206 Tony Fernandez .05 .02
207 Gerald Young .05 .02
208 Bo Jackson .25 .10
209 Chet Lemon .05 .02
210 Storm Davis .05 .02
211 Doug Drabek .05 .02
212 Mickey Brantley UER .05 .02
(Photo actually Nelson Simmons)
213 Devon White .10 .04
214 Dave Stewart .10 .04
215 Dave Schmidt .05 .02
216 Bryn Smith .05 .02
217 Brett Butler .10 .04
218 Bob Ojeda .05 .02
219 Steve Rosenberg .05 .02
220 Hubie Brooks .05 .02
221 B.J. Surhoff .10 .04
222 Rick Mahler .05 .02
223 Rick Sutcliffe .10 .04
224 Neal Heaton .05 .02
225 Mitch Williams .05 .02
226 Chuck Finley .10 .04
227 Mark Langston .05 .02
228 Jesse Orosco .05 .02
229 Ed Whitson .05 .02
230 Terry Pendleton .10 .04
231 Lloyd Moseby .05 .02
232 Greg Swindell .05 .02
233 John Franco .10 .04
234 Jack Morris .10 .04
235 Howard Johnson .05 .02
236 Glenn Davis .05 .02
237 Frank Viola .05 .02
238 Kevin Seitzer .05 .02
239 Gerald Perry .05 .02
240 Dwight Evans .10 .04
241 Jim Deshaies .05 .02
242 Bo Diaz .05 .02
243 Carney Lansford .10 .04
244 Mike LaValliere .05 .02
245 Rickey Henderson .25 .10
246 Roberto Alomar .30 .12
247 Jimmy Jones .05 .02
248 Pascual Perez .05 .02
249 Will Clark .25 .10
250 Fernando Valenzuela .10 .04
251 Shane Rawley .05 .02
252 Sid Bream .05 .02
253 Steve Lyons .05 .02
254 Brian Downing .05 .02
255 Mark Grace .25 .10
256 Tom Candiotti .05 .02
257 Barry Larkin .25 .10
258 Mike Krukow .05 .02
259 Billy Ripken .05 .02
260 Cecilio Guante .05 .02
261 Scott Bradley .05 .02
262 Floyd Bannister .05 .02
263 Pete Smith .05 .02
264 Jim Gantner UER .05 .02
(Wrong birthdate)
265 Roger McDowell .05 .02
266 Bobby Thigpen .05 .02
267 Jim Clancy .05 .02
268 Terry Steinbach .10 .04
269 Mike Dunne .05 .02
270 Dwight Gooden .15 .06
271 Mike Heath .05 .02
272 Dave Smith .05 .02
273 Keith Atherton .05 .02
274 Tim Burke .05 .02
275 Damon Berryhill .05 .02
276 Vance Law .05 .02
277 Rich Dotson .05 .02
278 Lance Parrish .05 .02
279 Denny Walling .05 .02
280 Roger Clemens .50 .20
281 Greg Mathews .05 .02
282 Tom Niedenfuer .05 .02
283 Paul Kilgus .05 .02
284 Jose Guzman .05 .02
285 Calvin Schiraldi .05 .02
286 Charlie Puleo UER .05 .02
(Career ERA 4.24, should be 4.23)
287 Joe Orsulak .05 .02
288 Jack Howell .05 .02
289 Kevin Elster .05 .02
290 Jose Lind .05 .02
291 Paul Molitor .15 .06
292 Cecil Espy .05 .02
293 Bill Wegman .05 .02
294 Dan Pasqua .05 .02
295 Scott Garrelts UER .05 .02
(Wrong birthdate)
296 Walt Terrell .05 .02
297 Ed Hearn .05 .02
298 Lou Whitaker .10 .04
299 Ken Dayley .05 .02
300 Checklist 248-357 .05 .02
301 Tommy Herr .05 .02
302 Mike Brumley .05 .02
303 Ellis Burks .15 .06
304 Curt Young UER .05 .02
(Wrong birthdate)
305 Jody Reed .05 .02
306 Bill Doran .05 .02
307 David Wells .10 .04
308 Ron Robinson .05 .02
309 Rafael Santana .05 .02
310 Julio Franco .05 .02
311 Jack Clark .05 .02
312 Chris James .05 .02
313 Milt Thompson .05 .02
314 John Shelby .05 .02
315 Al Leiter .25 .10
316 Mike Davis .05 .02
317 Chris Sabo RC * .40 .16
318 Greg Gagne .05 .02
319 Jose Oquendo .05 .02
320 John Farrell .05 .02
321 Franklin Stubbs .05 .02
322 Kurt Stillwell .05 .02
323 Shawn Abner .05 .02
324 Mike Flanagan .05 .02
325 Kevin Bass .05 .02
326 Pat Tabler .05 .02
327 Mike Henneman .05 .02
328 Rick Honeycutt .05 .02
329 John Smiley .05 .02
330 Rey Quinones .05 .02
331 Johnny Ray .05 .02
332 Bob Welch .05 .02
333 Larry Sheets .05 .02
334 Jeff Parrett .05 .02
335 Rick Reuschel UER .05 .02
(For Don Robinson& should be Jeff)
336 Randy Myers .10 .04
337 Ken Williams .05 .02
338 Andy McGaffigan .05 .02
339 Joey Meyer .05 .02
340 Dion James .05 .02
341 Les Lancaster .05 .02
342 Tom Foley .05 .02
343 Geno Petralli .05 .02
344 Dan Petry .05 .02
345 Alvin Davis .05 .02
346 Mickey Hatcher .05 .02
347 Marvell Wynne .05 .02
348 Danny Cox .05 .02
349 Dave Stieb .05 .02
350 Jay Bell .15 .06
351 Jeff Treadway .05 .02
352 Luis Salazar .05 .02
353 Len Dykstra .10 .04
354 Juan Agosto .05 .02
355 Gene Larkin .05 .02
356 Steve Farr .05 .02
357 Paul Assenmacher .05 .02
358 Todd Benzinger .05 .02
359 Larry Andersen .05 .02
360 Paul O'Neill .15 .06
361 Ron Hassey .05 .02
362 Jim Gott .05 .02
363 Ken Phelps .05 .02
364 Tim Flannery .05 .02
365 Randy Ready .05 .02
366 Nelson Santovenia .05 .02
367 Kelly Downs .05 .02
368 Danny Heep .05 .02
369 Phil Bradley .05 .02
370 Jeff D. Robinson .05 .02
371 Ivan Calderon .05 .02
372 Mike Witt .05 .02
373 Greg Maddux .50 .20
374 Carmen Castillo .05 .02
375 Jose Rijo .05 .02
376 Joe Price .05 .02
377 Rene Gonzales .05 .02
378 Oddibe McDowell .05 .02
379 Jim Presley .05 .02
380 Brad Wellman .05 .02
381 Tom Glavine .25 .10
382 Dan Plesac .05 .02
383 Wally Backman .05 .02
384 Dave Gallagher .05 .02
385 Tom Henke .05 .02
386 Luis Polonia .05 .02
387 Junior Ortiz .05 .02
388 David Cone .10 .04
389 Dave Bergman .05 .02
390 Danny Darwin .05 .02
391 Dan Gladden .05 .02
392 John Dopson .05 .02
393 Frank DiPino .05 .02
394 Al Nipper .05 .02
395 Willie Randolph .10 .04
396 Don Carman .05 .02
397 Scott Terry .05 .02
398 Rick Cerone .05 .02
399 Tom Pagnozzi .05 .02
400 Checklist 358-467 .05 .02
401 Mickey Tettleton .05 .02
402 Curtis Wilkerson .05 .02
403 Jeff Russell .05 .02
404 Pat Perry .05 .02
405 Jose Alvarez RC .05 .02
406 Rick Schu .05 .02
407 Sherman Corbett .05 .02
408 Dave Magadan .05 .02
409 Bob Kipper .05 .02
410 Don August .05 .02
411 Bob Brower .05 .02
412 Chris Bosio .05 .02
413 Jerry Reuss .05 .02
414 Atlee Hammaker .05 .02
415 Jim Walewander .05 .02
416 Mike Macfarlane RC * .25 .10
417 Pat Sheridan .05 .02
418 Pedro Guerrero .05 .02
419 Allan Anderson .05 .02
420 Mark Parent .05 .02
421 Bob Stanley .05 .02
422 Mike Gallego .05 .02
423 Bruce Hurst .05 .02
424 Dave Meads .05 .02
425 Jesse Barfield .05 .02
426 Rob Dibble RC * .50 .20
427 Joel Skinner .05 .02
428 Ron Kittle .05 .02
429 Rick Rhoden .05 .02
430 Bob Dernier .05 .02
431 Steve Jeltz .05 .02
432 Rick Dempsey .05 .02
433 Roberto Kelly .10 .04
434 Dave Anderson .05 .02
435 Herm Winningham .05 .02
436 Al Newman .05 .02
437 Jose DeLeon .05 .02
438 Doug Jones .05 .02
439 Brian Holton .05 .02
440 Jeff Montgomery .10 .04
441 Dickie Thon .05 .02
442 Cecil Fielder .10 .04
443 John Fishel .05 .02
444 Jerry Don Gleaton .05 .02
445 Paul Gibson .05 .02
446 Walt Weiss .05 .02
447 Glenn Wilson .05 .02
448 Mike Moore .05 .02
449 Chili Davis .10 .04
450 Dave Henderson .05 .02
451 Jose Bautista RC .10 .04
452 Rex Hudler .05 .02
453 Bob Brenly .05 .02
454 Mackey Sasser .05 .02
455 Daryl Boston .05 .02
456 Mike R. Fitzgerald .05 .02
457 Jeffrey Leonard .05 .02
458 Bruce Sutter .05 .02
459 Mitch Webster .05 .02
460 Joe Hesketh .05 .02
461 Bobby Witt .05 .02
462 Stu Cliburn .05 .02
463 Scott Bankhead .05 .02
464 Ramon Martinez RC .25 .10
465 Dave Leiper .05 .02
466 Luis Alicea RC * .25 .10
467 John Cerutti .05 .02
468 Ron Washington .05 .02
469 Jeff Reed .05 .02
470 Jeff M. Robinson .05 .02
471 Sid Fernandez .05 .02
472 Terry Puhl .05 .02
473 Charlie Lea .05 .02

474 Israel Sanchez .05 .02
475 Bruce Benedict .05 .02
476 Oil Can Boyd .05 .02
477 Craig Reynolds .05 .02
478 Frank Williams .05 .02
479 Greg Cadaret .05 .02
480 Randy Kramer .05 .02
481 Dave Eiland .05 .02
482 Eric Show .05 .02
483 Garry Templeton .05 .02
484 Wallace Johnson .05 .02
485 Kevin Mitchell .10 .04
486 Tim Crews .05 .02
487 Mike Maddux .05 .02
488 Dave LaPoint .05 .02
489 Fred Manrique .05 .02
490 Greg Minton .05 .02
491 Doug Dascenzo UER .05 .02
(Photo actually
Damon Berryhill)
492 Willie Upshaw .05 .02
493 Jack Armstrong RC * .25 .10
494 Kirt Manwaring .05 .02
495 Jeff Ballard .05 .02
496 Jeff Kunkel .05 .02
497 Mike Campbell .05 .02
498 Gary Thurman .05 .02
499 Zane Smith .05 .02
500 Checklist 468-577 DP .05 .02
501 Mike Birkbeck .05 .02
502 Terry Leach .05 .02
503 Shawn Hillegas .05 .02
504 Manny Lee .05 .02
505 Doug Jennings .05 .02
506 Ken Oberkfell .05 .02
507 Tim Teufel .05 .02
508 Tom Brookens .05 .02
509 Rafael Ramirez .05 .02
510 Fred Toliver .05 .02
511 Brian Holman RC * .10 .04
512 Mike Bielecki .05 .02
513 Jeff Pico .05 .02
514 Charles Hudson .05 .02
515 Bruce Ruffin .05 .02
516 L.McWilliams UER .05 .02
New Richland, should
be North Richland
517 Jeff Sellers .05 .02
518 John Costello .05 .02
519 Brady Anderson RC .50 .20
520 Craig McMurtry .05 .02
521 Ray Hayward DP .05 .02
522 Drew Hall DP .05 .02
523 Mark Lemke DP RC .40 .16
524 Oswald Peraza DP .05 .02
525 Bryan Harvey DP RC * .25 .10
526 Rick Aguilera DP .10 .04
527 Tom Prince DP .05 .02
528 Mark Clear DP .05 .02
529 Jerry Browne DP .05 .02
530 Juan Castillo DP .05 .02
531 Jack McDowell DP .10 .04
532 Chris Speier DP .05 .02
533 Darrell Evans DP .10 .04
534 Luis Aquino DP .05 .02
535 Eric King DP .05 .02
536 Ken Hill DP RC .25 .10
537 Randy Bush DP .05 .02
538 Shane Mack DP .05 .02
539 Tom Bolton DP .05 .02
540 Gene Nelson DP .05 .02
541 Wes Gardner DP .05 .02
542 Ken Caminiti DP .10 .04
543 Duane Ward DP .05 .02
544 Norm Charlton DP RC .25 .10
545 Hal Morris DP RC .25 .10
546 Rich Yett DP .05 .02
547 H.Meulens DP RC .10 .04
548 Greg A. Harris DP .05 .02
549 Darren Daulton DP .10 .04
(Posing as right-
handed hitter)
550 Jeff Hamilton DP .05 .02
551 Luis Aguayo DP .05 .02
552 Tim Leary DP .05 .02
(Resembles M.Marshall)
553 Ron Oester DP .05 .02
554 S.Lombardozzi DP .05 .02
555 Tim Jones DP .05 .02
556 Bud Black DP .05 .02
557 Alejandro Pena DP .05 .02
558 Jose DeJesus DP .05 .02
559 D.Rasmussen DP .05 .02
560 Pat Borders DP RC* .25 .10
561 Craig Biggio DP RC .75 .30
562 Luis DeLosSantos DP .05 .02
563 Fred Lynn DP .05 .02
564 Todd Burns DP .05 .02
565 Felix Fermin DP .05 .02
566 Darnell Coles DP .05 .02
567 Willie Fraser DP .05 .02
568 Glenn Hubbard DP .05 .02
569 Craig Worthington DP .05 .02
570 Johnny Paredes DP .05 .02
571 Don Robinson DP .05 .02
572 Barry Lyons DP .05 .02
573 Bill Long DP .05 .02
574 Tracy Jones DP .05 .02
575 Juan Nieves DP .05 .02
576 Andres Thomas DP .05 .02
577 Rolando Roomes DP .05 .02
578 Luis Rivera UER DP .05 .02
(Wrong birthdate)
579 Chad Kreuter DP RC .25 .10
580 Tony Armas DP .05 .02
581 Jay Buhner .10 .04
582 Ricky Horton DP .05 .02
583 Andy Hawkins DP .05 .02
584 Sil Campusano .05 .02
585 Dave Clark .05 .02
586 Van Snider DP .05 .02
587 Todd Frohwirth DP .05 .02
588 W.Spahn DP PUZ .15 .06
589 William Brennan .05 .02
590 German Gonzalez .05 .02
591 Ernie Whitt DP .05 .02
592 Jeff Blauser .10 .04
593 Spike Owen DP .05 .02
594 Matt Williams .25 .10
595 Lloyd McClendon DP .05 .02
596 Steve Ontiveros .05 .02
597 Scott Medvin .05 .02
598 Hipolito Pena DP .05 .02
599 Jerald Clark DP RC .10 .04
600A CL 578-660 DP .05 .02
635 Kurt Schilling
600B CL 578-660 DP .05 .02
635 Curt Schilling;
MVP's not listed
on checklist card
600C CL 578-660 DP .05 .02
635 Curt Schilling;
MVP's listed
following 660
601 Carmelo Martinez DP .05 .02
602 Mike LaCoss .05 .02
603 Mike Devereaux .05 .02
604 Alex Madrid DP .05 .02
605 Gary Redus DP .05 .02
606 Lance Johnson .10 .04
607 Terry Clark DP .05 .02
608 Manny Trillo DP .05 .02
609 Scott Jordan RC .25 .10
610 Jay Howell DP .05 .02
611 Francisco Melendez .05 .02
612 Mike Boddicker .05 .02
613 Kevin Brown DP .25 .10
614 Dave Valle .05 .02
615 Tim Laudner DP .05 .02
616 Andy Nezelek UER .05 .02
(Wrong birthdate)
617 Chuck Crim .05 .02
618 Jack Savage DP .05 .02
619 Adam Peterson .05 .02
620 Todd Stottlemyre .15 .06
621 Lance Blankenship RC .10 .04
622 Miguel Garcia DP .05 .02
623 Keith A. Miller DP .05 .02
624 Ricky Jordan DP RC* .25 .10
625 Ernest Riles DP .05 .02
626 John Moses DP .05 .02
627 Nelson Liriano DP .05 .02
628 Mike Smithson DP .05 .02
629 Scott Sanderson .05 .02
630 Dale Mohorcic .05 .02
631 Marvin Freeman DP .05 .02
632 Mike Young DP .05 .02
633 Dennis Lamp .05 .02
634 Dante Bichette DP RC .40 .16
635 Curt Schilling DP RC 2.50 1.00
636 Scott May DP .05 .02
637 Mike Schooler .05 .02
638 Rick Leach .05 .02
639 Tom Lampkin UER .05 .02
(Throws Left, should
be Throws Right)
640 Brian Meyer .05 .02
641 Brian Harper .05 .02
642 John Smoltz RC 1.00 .40
643 Jose Canseco .10 .04
(40/40 Club)
644 Bill Schroeder .05 .02
645 Edgar Martinez .25 .10
646 Dennis Cook RC .25 .10
647 Barry Jones .05 .02
648 Orel Hershiser .10 .04
(59 and Counting)
649 Rod Nichols .05 .02
650 Jody Davis .05 .02
651 Bob Milacki .05 .02
652 Mike Jackson .05 .02
653 Derek Lilliquist RC .10 .04
654 Paul Mirabella .05 .02
655 Mike Diaz .05 .02
656 Jeff Musselman .05 .02
657 Jerry Reed .05 .02
658 Kevin Blankenship .05 .02
659 Wayne Tolleson .05 .02
660 Eric Hetzel .05 .02
BC Jose Canseco 2.00 .80
Blister Pack

1989 Donruss Bonus MVP's

Rather than short-printing 26 cards in order to make room for printing the Bonus MVP's this year, Donruss apparently chose to double print 106 cards. Numbered with the prefix "BC" for bonus card, the 26-card set featuring the most valuable player from each of the 26 teams was randomly inserted in the wax and rack packs. These cards are distinguished by the bold MVP logo in the upper background of the obverse, and the four doubleprinted cards are denoted by "DP" in the checklist below.

Nm-Mt Ex-Mt
COMPLETE SET (26) 1.50 .60
BC1 Kirby Puckett .25 .10
BC2 Mike Scott .05 .02
BC3 Joe Carter .15 .06
BC4 Orel Hershiser .10 .04
BC5 Jose Canseco .25 .10
BC6 Darryl Strawberry .15 .06
BC7 George Brett .60 .24
BC8 Andre Dawson .10 .04
BC9 Paul Molitor UER .15 .06
(Brewers logo missing
the word Milwaukee)
BC10 Andy Van Slyke .10 .04
BC11 Dave Winfield .10 .04
BC12 Kevin Gross .05 .02
BC13 Mike Greenwell .05 .02
BC14 Ozzie Smith .40 .16
BC15 Cal Ripken .75 .30
BC16 Andres Galarraga .10 .04
BC17 Alan Trammell .15 .06
BC18 Kal Daniels .05 .02
BC19 Fred McGriff .25 .10
BC20 Tony Gwynn .30 .12
BC21 Wally Joyner DP .10 .04
BC22 Will Clark DP .25 .10
BC23 Ozzie Guillen .05 .02
BC24 Gerald Perry DP .05 .02
BC25 Alvin Davis DP .05 .02
BC26 Ruben Sierra .05 .02

1989 Donruss Grand Slammers

The 1989 Donruss Grand Slammers set contains 12 standard-size cards. Each card in the set can be found with five different colored border combinations, but no color combination of borders appears to be scarcer than any other. The set includes cards for each player who hit one or more grand slams in 1988. The backs detail the players' grand slams. The cards were distributed one per cello pack as well as an insert (complete) set in each factory set.

Nm-Mt Ex-Mt
COMPLETE SET (12) 2.00 .80
1 Jose Canseco .25 .10
2 Mike Marshall .05 .02
3 Walt Weiss .05 .02
4 Kevin McReynolds .05 .02
5 Mike Greenwell .05 .02
6 Dave Winfield .10 .04
7 Mark McGwire 1.00 .40
8 Keith Hernandez .15 .06
9 Franklin Stubbs .05 .02
10 Danny Tartabull .05 .02
11 Jesse Barfield .05 .02
12 Ellis Burks .15 .06

1989 Donruss Rookies

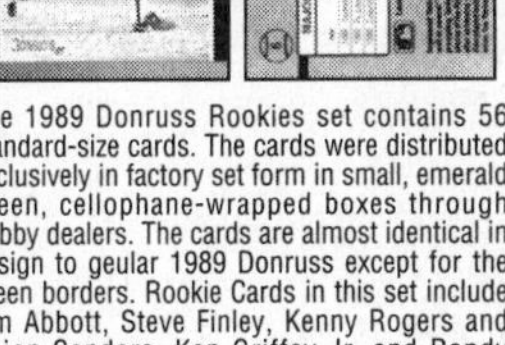

The 1989 Donruss Rookies set contains 56 standard-size cards. The cards were distributed exclusively in factory set form in small, emerald green, cellophane-wrapped boxes through hobby dealers. The cards are almost identical in design to geular 1989 Donruss except for the green borders. Rookie Cards in this set include Jim Abbott, Steve Finley, Kenny Rogers and Deion Sanders. Ken Griffey Jr. and Randy Johnson are also featured on a card within the set.

Nm-Mt Ex-Mt
COMP.FACT.SET (56) 15.00 6.00
1 Gary Sheffield 1.50 .60
2 Gregg Jefferies .10 .04
3 Ken Griffey Jr. 8.00 3.20
4 Tom Gordon .25 .10
5 Billy Spiers RC .25 .10
6 Deion Sanders RC .75 .30
7 Donn Pall .05 .02
8 Steve Carter .05 .02
9 Francisco Oliveras .05 .02
10 Steve Wilson RC .10 .04
11 Bob Geren RC .05 .02
12 Tony Castillo RC .10 .04
13 Kenny Rogers RC .50 .20
14 Carlos Martinez RC .10 .04
15 Edgar Martinez .25 .10
16 Jim Abbott RC .50 .20
17 Torey Lovullo RC .10 .04
18 Mark Carreon .05 .02
19 Geronimo Berroa .05 .02
20 Luis Medina .05 .02
21 Sandy Alomar Jr. .15 .06
22 Bob Milacki .05 .02
23 Joe Girardi RC .40 .16
24 German Gonzalez .05 .02
25 Craig Worthington .05 .02
26 Jerome Walton .25 .10
27 Gary Wayne .05 .02
28 Tim Jones .05 .02
29 Dante Bichette .15 .06
30 Alexis Infante .05 .02
31 Ken Hill .25 .10
32 Dwight Smith RC .25 .10
33 Luis de los Santos .05 .02
34 Eric Yelding .05 .02
35 Gregg Olson .25 .10
36 Phil Stephenson .05 .02
37 Ken Patterson .05 .02
38 Rick Wrona .05 .02
39 Mike Brumley .05 .02
40 Cris Carpenter .05 .02
41 Jeff Brantley RC .25 .10
42 Ron Jones .05 .02
43 Randy Johnson 3.00 1.20
44 Kevin Brown .25 .10
45 Ramon Martinez .10 .04
46 Greg W.Harris .05 .02
47 Steve Finley RC .50 .20
48 Randy Kramer .05 .02
49 Erik Hanson .10 .04
50 Matt Merullo .05 .02
51 Mike Devereaux .05 .02
52 Clay Parker .05 .02
53 Omar Vizquel RC .50 .20
54 Derek Lilliquist .05 .02
55 Junior Felix RC .10 .04
56 Checklist 1-56 .05 .02

1989 Donruss All-Stars

These All-Stars are standard size and very similar in design to the regular issue of 1989 Donruss. The set is distinguished by the presence of the respective League logos in the lower right corner of each obverse. The cards are numbered on the backs. The players chosen for the set are essentially the participants at the previous year's All-Star Game. Individual wax packs of All Stars (suggested retail price of 35 cents) contained one Pop-Up, five All-Star cards, and a Warren Spahn puzzle card.

Nm-Mt Ex-Mt
COMPLETE SET (64) 8.00 3.20
1 Mark McGwire 1.50 .60
2 Jose Canseco .50 .20
3 Paul Molitor .50 .20
4 Rickey Henderson .60 .24
5 Cal Ripken 2.00 .80
6 Dave Winfield .25 .10
7 Wade Boggs .25 .10
8 Frank Viola .05 .02
9 Terry Steinbach .10 .04
10 Tom Kelly MG .05 .02
11 George Brett 1.00 .40
12 Doyle Alexander .05 .02
13 Gary Gaetti .10 .04
14 Roger Clemens 1.00 .40
15 Mike Greenwell .05 .02
16 Dennis Eckersley .50 .20
17 Carney Lansford .10 .04
18 Mark Gubicza .05 .02
19 Tim Laudner .05 .02
20 Doug Jones .05 .02
21 Don Mattingly 1.00 .40
22 Dan Plesac .05 .02
23 Kirby Puckett .50 .20
24 Jeff Reardon .10 .04
25 Johnny Ray .05 .02
26 Jeff Russell .05 .02
27 Harold Reynolds .10 .04
28 Dave Stieb .05 .02
29 Kurt Stillwell .05 .02
30 Jose Canseco .10 .04
(Top AL Vote Getter)
31 Terry Steinbach .05 .02
(All-Star Game MVP)
32 AL Checklist 1-32 .05 .02
33 Will Clark .40 .16
34 Darryl Strawberry .10 .04
35 Ryne Sandberg 1.00 .40
36 Andre Dawson .20 .08
37 Ozzie Smith 1.00 .40
38 Vince Coleman .05 .02
39 Bobby Bonilla .05 .02
40 Dwight Gooden .10 .04
41 Gary Carter .40 .16
42 Whitey Herzog MG .05 .02
43 Shawon Dunston .05 .02
44 David Cone .15 .06
45 Andres Galarraga .20 .08
46 Mark Davis .05 .02
47 Barry Larkin .20 .08
48 Kevin Gross .05 .02
49 Vance Law .05 .02
50 Orel Hershiser .10 .04
51 Willie McGee .10 .04
52 Danny Jackson .05 .02
53 Rafael Palmeiro .40 .16
54 Bob Knepper .05 .02
55 Lance Parrish .05 .02
56 Greg Maddux 1.50 .60
57 Gerald Perry .05 .02
58 Bob Walk .05 .02
59 Chris Sabo .05 .02
60 Todd Worrell .05 .02
61 Andy Van Slyke .10 .04
62 Ozzie Smith .50 .20
(Top AL Vote Getter)
63 Riverfront Stadium .05 .02
64 NL Checklist 33-64 .05 .02

1989 Donruss Baseball's Best

The 1989 Donruss Baseball's Best set contains 336 standard-size glossy cards. The fronts are green and yellow, and the backs feature career highlight information. The backs are green, and feature vertically oriented career stats. The cards were distributed as a set in a blister pack through various retail and department store chains. The Sammy Sosa card in this set is the only major league licensed card issued of him in 1989. In addition, early cards of Ken Griffey Jr. and Randy Johnson are featured in this set.

Nm-Mt Ex-Mt
COMP.FACT.SET (336) 100.00 40.00
1 Don Mattingly 1.50 .60
2 Tom Glavine .60 .24
3 Bert Blyleven .25 .10
4 Andre Dawson .25 .10
5 Pete O'Brien .15 .06
6 Eric Davis .25 .10
7 George Brett 1.50 .60
8 Glenn Davis .15 .06
9 Ellis Burks .40 .16
10 Kirk Gibson .25 .10
11 Carlton Fisk .40 .16
12 Andres Galarraga .25 .10
13 Alan Trammell .40 .16
14 Dwight Gooden .40 .16
15 Paul Molitor .40 .16
16 Roger McDowell .15 .06
17 Doug Drabek .15 .06
18 Kent Hrbek .25 .10
19 Vince Coleman .15 .06
20 Steve Sax .15 .06
21 Roberto Alomar .75 .30
22 Carney Lansford .25 .10
23 Will Clark .60 .24
24 Alvin Davis .15 .06
25 Bobby Thigpen .15 .06
26 Ryne Sandberg 1.00 .40
27 Devon White .25 .10
28 Mike Greenwell .15 .06
29 Dale Murphy .60 .24
30 Jeff Ballard .15 .06
31 Kelly Gruber .15 .06
32 Julio Franco .25 .10
33 Bobby Bonilla .25 .10
34 Tim Wallach .15 .06
35 Lou Whitaker .25 .10
36 Jay Howell .15 .06
37 Greg Maddux 1.25 .50
38 Bill Doran .15 .06
39 Danny Tartabull .15 .06
40 Darryl Strawberry .40 .16
41 Ron Darling .15 .06
42 Tony Gwynn .75 .30
43 Mark McGwire 2.50 1.00
44 Ozzie Smith 1.00 .40
45 Andy Van Slyke .25 .10
46 Juan Berenguer .15 .06
47 Von Hayes .15 .06
48 Tony Fernandez .15 .06
49 Eric Plunk .15 .06
50 Ernest Riles .15 .06
51 Harold Reynolds .25 .10
52 Andy Hawkins .15 .06
53 Robin Yount 1.00 .40
54 Danny Jackson .15 .06
55 Nolan Ryan 2.50 1.00
56 Joe Carter .40 .16
57 Jose Canseco .60 .24
58 Jody Davis .15 .06
59 Lance Parrish .15 .06
60 Mitch Williams .15 .06
61 Brook Jacoby .15 .06
62 Tom Browning .15 .06
63 Kurt Stillwell .15 .06
64 Rafael Ramirez .15 .06
65 Roger Clemens 1.25 .50
66 Mike Scioscia .15 .06
67 Dave Gallagher .15 .06
68 Mark Langston .15 .06
69 Chet Lemon .15 .06
70 Kevin McReynolds .15 .06
71 Rob Deer .15 .06
72 Tommy Herr .15 .06
73 Barry Bonds 3.00 1.20
74 Frank Viola .15 .06
75 Pedro Guerrero .15 .06
76 Dave Righetti UER .15 .06
(ML total of 7
wins incorrect)
77 Bruce Hurst .15 .06
78 Rickey Henderson .60 .24
79 Robby Thompson .15 .06
80 Randy Johnson 8.00 3.20
81 Harold Baines .25 .10
82 Calvin Schiraldi .15 .06
83 Kirk McCaskill .15 .06
84 Lee Smith .25 .10
85 John Smoltz 2.00 .80
86 Mickey Tettleton .15 .06
87 Jimmy Key .25 .10
88 Rafael Palmeiro .60 .24
89 Sid Bream .15 .06
90 Dennis Martinez .25 .10
91 Frank Tanana .15 .06
92 Eddie Murray .60 .24
93 Shawon Dunston .15 .06
94 Mike Scott .15 .06
95 Bret Saberhagen .25 .10
96 David Cone .25 .10
97 Kevin Elster .15 .06
98 Jack Clark .15 .06
99 Dave Stewart .25 .10
100 Jose Oquendo .15 .06
101 Jose Lind .15 .06
102 Gary Gaetti .25 .10
103 Ricky Jordan .50 .20
104 Fred McGriff .60 .24
105 Don Slaught .15 .06
106 Jose Uribe .15 .06
107 Jeffrey Leonard .15 .06
108 Lee Guetterman .15 .06
109 Chris Bosio .15 .06
110 Barry Larkin .60 .24
111 Ruben Sierra .15 .06
112 Greg Swindell .15 .06
113 Gary Sheffield 3.00 1.20
114 Lonnie Smith .15 .06
115 Chili Davis .25 .10
116 Damon Berryhill .15 .06
117 Tom Candiotti .15 .06
118 Kal Daniels .15 .06
119 Mark Gubicza .15 .06
120 Jim Deshaies .15 .06
121 Dwight Evans .25 .10
122 Mike Morgan .15 .06
123 Dan Pasqua .15 .06
124 Bryn Smith .15 .06
125 Doyle Alexander .15 .06
126 Howard Johnson .15 .06
127 Chuck Crim .15 .06
128 Darren Daulton .25 .10
129 Jeff Robinson .15 .06
130 Kirby Puckett .60 .24
131 Joe Magrane .15 .06

132 Jesse Barfield .15 .06
133 Mark Davis UER .15 .06
(Photo actually
Dave Leiper)
134 Dennis Eckersley .25 .10
135 Mike Krukow .15 .06
136 Jay Buhner .25 .10
137 Ozzie Guillen .15 .06
138 Rick Sutcliffe .25 .10
139 Wally Joyner .25 .10
140 Wade Boggs .40 .16
141 Jeff Treadway .15 .06
142 Cal Ripken 2.00 .80
143 Dave Stieb .15 .06
144 Pete Incaviglia .15 .06
145 Bob Walk .15 .06
146 Nelson Santovenia .15 .06
147 Mike Heath .15 .06
148 Willie Randolph .25 .10
149 Paul Kilgus .15 .06
150 Billy Hatcher .15 .06
151 Steve Farr .15 .06
152 Gregg Jefferies .25 .10
153 Randy Myers .25 .10
154 Garry Templeton .15 .06
155 Walt Weiss .15 .06
156 Terry Pendleton .25 .10
157 John Smiley .15 .06
158 Greg Gagne .15 .06
159 Len Dykstra .25 .10
160 Nelson Liriano .15 .06
161 Alvaro Espinoza .15 .06
162 Rick Reuschel .15 .06
163 Omar Vizquel UER 1.00 .40
Photo actually
Darnell Coles
164 Clay Parker .15 .06
165 Dan Plesac .15 .06
166 John Franco .25 .10
167 Scott Fletcher .15 .06
168 Cory Snyder .15 .06
169 Bo Jackson .60 .24
170 Tommy Gregg .15 .06
171 Jim Abbott 1.00 .40
172 Jerome Walton .50 .20
173 Doug Jones .15 .06
174 Todd Benzinger .15 .06
175 Frank White .25 .10
176 Craig Biggio 2.00 .80
177 John Dopson .15 .06
178 Alfredo Griffin .15 .06
179 Melido Perez .15 .06
180 Tim Burke .15 .06
181 Matt Nokes .15 .06
182 Gary Carter .40 .16
183 Ted Higuera .15 .06
184 Ken Howell .15 .06
185 Rey Quinones .15 .06
186 Wally Backman .15 .06
187 Tom Brunansky .15 .06
188 Steve Balboni .15 .06
189 Marvell Wynne .15 .06
190 Dave Henderson .15 .06
191 Don Robinson .15 .06
192 Ken Griffey Jr. 20.00 8.00
193 Ivan Calderon .15 .06
194 Mike Bielecki .15 .06
195 Johnny Ray .15 .06
196 Rob Murphy .15 .06
197 Andres Thomas .15 .06
198 Phil Bradley .15 .06
199 Junior Felix .25 .10
200 Jeff Russell .15 .06
201 Mike LaValliere .15 .06
202 Kevin Gross .15 .06
203 Keith Moreland .15 .06
204 Mike Marshall .15 .06
205 Dwight Smith .50 .20
206 Jim Clancy .15 .06
207 Kevin Seitzer .15 .06
208 Keith Hernandez .40 .16
209 Bob Ojeda .15 .06
210 Ed Whitson .15 .06
211 Tony Phillips .15 .06
212 Milt Thompson .15 .06
213 Randy Kramer .15 .06
214 Randy Bush .15 .06
215 Randy Ready .15 .06
216 Duane Ward .15 .06
217 Jimmy Jones .15 .06
218 Scott Garrelts .15 .06
219 Scott Bankhead .15 .06
220 Lance McCullers .15 .06
221 B.J. Surhoff .25 .10
222 Chris Sabo .75 .30
223 Steve Buechele .15 .06
224 Joel Skinner .15 .06
225 Orel Hershiser .25 .10
226 Derek Lilliquist .25 .10
227 Claudell Washington .15 .06
228 Lloyd McClendon .15 .06
229 Felix Fermin .15 .06
230 Paul O'Neill .40 .16
231 Charlie Leibrandt .15 .06
232 Dave Smith .15 .06
233 Bob Stanley .15 .06
234 Tim Belcher .15 .06
235 Eric King .15 .06
236 Spike Owen .15 .06
237 Mike Henneman .15 .06
238 Juan Samuel .15 .06
239 Greg Brock .15 .06
240 John Kruk .25 .10
241 Glenn Wilson .15 .06
242 Jeff Reardon .25 .10
243 Todd Worrell .15 .06
244 Dave LaPoint .15 .06
245 Walt Terrell .15 .06
246 Mike Moore .15 .06
247 Kelly Downs .15 .06
248 Dave Valle .15 .06
249 Ron Kittle .15 .06
250 Steve Wilson .25 .10
251 Dick Schofield .15 .06
252 Marty Barrett .15 .06
253 Dion James .15 .06
254 Bob Milacki .15 .06
255 Ernie Whitt .15 .06
256 Kevin Brown .60 .24
257 R.J. Reynolds .15 .06
258 Tim Raines .25 .10
259 Frank Williams .15 .06
260 Jose Gonzalez .15 .06
261 Mitch Webster .15 .06
262 Ken Caminiti .25 .10
263 Bob Boone .25 .10
264 Dave Magadan .15 .06
265 Rick Aguilera .25 .10
266 Chris James .15 .06
267 Bob Welch .25 .10
268 Ken Dayley .15 .06
269 Junior Ortiz .15 .06
270 Allan Anderson .15 .06
271 Steve Jeltz .15 .06
272 George Bell .15 .06
273 Roberto Kelly .25 .10
274 Brett Butler .25 .10
275 Mike Schooler .25 .10
276 Ken Phelps .15 .06
277 Glenn Braggs .15 .06
278 Jose Rijo .15 .06
279 Bobby Witt .15 .06
280 Jerry Browne .15 .06
281 Kevin Mitchell .25 .10
282 Craig Worthington .15 .06
283 Greg Minton .15 .06
284 Nick Esasky .15 .06
285 John Farrell .15 .06
286 Rick Mahler .15 .06
287 Tom Gordon .50 .20
288 Gerald Young .15 .06
289 Jody Reed .15 .06
290 Jeff Hamilton .15 .06
291 Gerald Perry .15 .06
292 Hubie Brooks .15 .06
293 Bo Diaz .15 .06
294 Terry Puhl .15 .06
295 Jim Gantner .15 .06
296 Jeff Parrett .15 .06
297 Mike Boddicker .15 .06
298 Dan Gladden .15 .06
299 Tony Pena .15 .06
300 Checklist Card .15 .06
301 Tom Henke .15 .06
302 Pascual Perez .15 .06
303 Steve Bedrosian .15 .06
304 Ken Hill .50 .20
305 Jerry Reuss .15 .06
306 Jim Eisenreich .15 .06
307 Jack Howell .15 .06
308 Rick Cerone .15 .06
309 Tim Leary .15 .06
310 Joe Orsulak .15 .06
311 Jim Dwyer .15 .06
312 Geno Petralli .15 .06
313 Rick Honeycutt .15 .06
314 Tom Foley .15 .06
315 Kenny Rogers 1.00 .40
316 Mike Flanagan .15 .06
317 Bryan Harvey .15 .06
318 Billy Ripken .15 .06
319 Jeff Montgomery .25 .10
320 Erik Hanson .50 .20
321 Brian Downing .15 .06
322 Gregg Olson .50 .20
323 Terry Steinbach .25 .10
324 Sammy Sosa 40.00 16.00
325 Gene Harris .15 .06
326 Mike Devereaux .15 .06
327 Dennis Cook .50 .20
328 David Wells .25 .10
329 Checklist Card .15 .06
330 Kirt Manwaring .25 .10
331 Jim Presley .15 .06
332 Checklist Card .15 .06
333 Chuck Finley .25 .10
334 Rob Dibble 1.00 .40
335 Cecil Espy .15 .06
336 Dave Parker .25 .10

1989 Donruss Pop-Ups

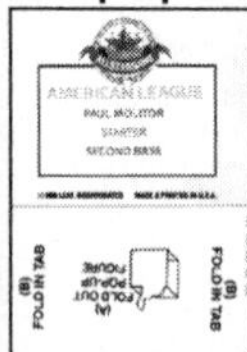

These Pop-Ups are borderless and standard size. The cards are unnumbered; however the All Star checklist card lists the same numbers as the All Star cards. Those numbers are used below for reference. The players chosen for the set are essentially the starting lineups for the previous year's All-Star Game. Individual wax packs of All Stars (suggested retail price of 35 cents) contained one Pop-Up, five All-Star cards and a puzzle card.

Nm-Mt Ex-Mt
COMPLETE SET (20) 5.00 2.00
1 Mark McGwire 2.50 1.00
2 Jose Canseco .50 .20
3 Paul Molitor .50 .20
4 Rickey Henderson 1.00 .40
5 Cal Ripken 3.00 1.20
6 Dave Winfield .50 .20
7 Wade Boggs .50 .20
8 Frank Viola .10 .04
9 Terry Steinbach .10 .04
10 Tom Kelly MG .10 .04
11 Will Clark .50 .20
34 Darryl Strawberry .20 .08
35 Ryne Sandberg 1.00 .40
36 Andre Dawson .40 .16
37 Ozzie Smith 1.00 .40
38 Vince Coleman .10 .04
39 Bobby Bonilla .20 .08
40 Dwight Gooden .20 .08
41 Gary Carter .50 .20
42 Whitey Herzog MG .10 .04

1989 Donruss Super DK's

This 26-player card set was available through a mail-in offer detailed on the wax packs. The set was sent in return for $8.00 and three wrappers plus $2.00 postage and handling. The set features the popular Diamond King subseries in large (approximately 4 7/8" X 6 13/16") form. Dick Perez of Perez-Steele Galleries did another outstanding job on the artwork. The cards are essentially a large version of the Donruss regular issue Diamond Kings.

Nm-Mt Ex-Mt
COMPLETE SET (26) 15.00 6.00
1 Mike Greenwell .10 .04
2 Bobby Bonilla .20 .08
3 Pete Incaviglia .10 .04
4 Chris Sabo .10 .04
5 Robin Yount .50 .20
6 Tony Gwynn 3.00 1.20
7 Carlton Fisk 2.50 1.00
8 Cory Snyder .10 .04
9 David Cone .30 .12
10 Kevin Seitzer .10 .04
11 Rick Reuschel .10 .04
12 Johnny Ray .10 .04
13 Dave Schmidt .10 .04
14 Andres Galarraga .40 .16
15 Kirk Gibson .20 .08
16 Fred McGriff 1.00 .40
17 Mark Grace 3.00 1.20
18 Jeff M. Robinson .10 .04
19 Vince Coleman .10 .04
20 Dave Henderson .10 .04
21 Harold Reynolds .20 .08
22 Gerald Perry .10 .04
23 Frank Viola .10 .04
24 Steve Bedrosian .10 .04
25 Glenn Davis .10 .04
26 Don Mattingly 3.00 1.20

1989 Donruss Traded

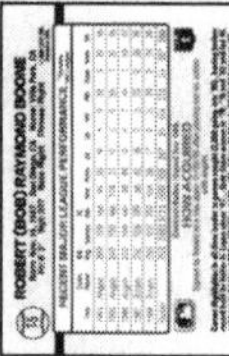

The 1989 Donruss Traded set contains 56 standard-size cards. The fronts have yellowish-orange borders; the backs are yellow and feature recent statistics. The cards were distributed as a boxed set. The set was never very popular with collectors since it included (as the name implies) only traded players rather than rookies. The cards are numbered with a "T" prefix.

Nm-Mt Ex-Mt
COMP.FACT.SET (56) 3.00 1.20
1 Jeffrey Leonard .10 .04
2 Jack Clark .20 .08
3 Kevin Gross .10 .04
4 Tommy Herr .10 .04
5 Bob Boone .20 .08
6 Rafael Palmeiro .50 .20
7 John Dopson .10 .04
8 Willie Randolph .20 .08
9 Chris Brown .10 .04
10 Wally Backman .10 .04
11 Steve Ontiveros .10 .04
12 Eddie Murray .50 .20
13 Lance McCullers .10 .04
14 Spike Owen .10 .04
15 Rob Murphy .10 .04
16 Pete O'Brien .10 .04
17 Ken Williams .10 .04
18 Nick Esasky .10 .04
19 Nolan Ryan 1.50 .60
20 Brian Holton .10 .04
21 Mike Moore .10 .04
22 Joel Skinner .10 .04
23 Steve Sax .10 .04
24 Rick Mahler .10 .04
25 Mike Aldrete .10 .04
26 Jesse Orosco .10 .04
27 Dave LaPoint .10 .04
28 Walt Terrell .10 .04
29 Eddie Williams .10 .04
30 Mike Devereaux .10 .04
31 Julio Franco .20 .08
32 Jim Clancy .10 .04
33 Felix Fermin .10 .04
34 Curt Wilkerson .10 .04
35 Bert Blyleven .20 .08
36 Mel Hall .10 .04
37 Eric King .10 .04
38 Mitch Williams .10 .04
39 Jamie Moyer .20 .08
40 Rick Rhoden .10 .04
41 Phil Bradley .10 .04
42 Paul Kilgus .10 .04
43 Milt Thompson .10 .04
44 Jerry Browne .10 .04
45 Bruce Hurst .10 .04
46 Claudell Washington .10 .04
47 Todd Benzinger .10 .04
48 Steve Balboni .10 .04
49 Oddibe McDowell .10 .04
50 Charles Hudson .10 .04
51 Ron Kittle .10 .04
52 Andy Hawkins .10 .04
53 Tom Brookens .10 .04
54 Tom Niedenfuer .10 .04
55 Jeff Parrett .10 .04
56 Checklist Card .10 .04

1990 Donruss Previews

The 1990 Donruss Previews set contains 12 standard-size cards. The bright red borders are exactly like the regular 1990 Donruss cards, but many of the photos are different. The horizontally oriented backs are plain white with career highlights in black lettering. Two cards were sent to each dealer in the Donruss dealer network thus making it quite difficult to put together a set.

Nm-Mt Ex-Mt
COMPLETE SET (12) 400.00 120.00
1 Todd Zeile 15.00 4.50
(Not shown as Rated
Rookie on front)
2 Ben McDonald 10.00 3.00
3 Bo Jackson 40.00 12.00
4 Will Clark 50.00 15.00
5 Dave Stewart 15.00 4.50
6 Kevin Mitchell 10.00 3.00
7 Nolan Ryan 200.00 60.00
8 Howard Johnson 10.00 3.00
9 Tony Gwynn 80.00 24.00
10 Jerome Walton 10.00 3.00
(Shown ready to bunt)
11 Wade Boggs 50.00 15.00
12 Kirby Puckett 50.00 15.00

1990 Donruss

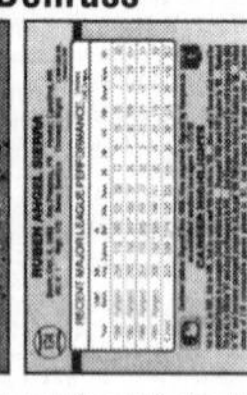

The 1990 Donruss set contains 716 standard-size cards. Cards were issued in wax packs and hobby and retail factory sets. The card fronts feature bright red borders. Subsets include Diamond Kings (1-27) and Rated Rookies (28-47). The set was the largest ever produced by Donruss, unfortunately it also had a large number of errors which were corrected after the cards were released. Most of these feature minor printing flaws and insignificant variations that collectors have found unworthy of price differentials. There are several double-printed cards indicated in our checklist with the set indicated with a "DP" coding. Rookie Cards of note include Juan Gonzalez, David Justice, John Olerud, Dean Palmer, Sammy Sosa, Larry Walker and Bernie Williams.

Nm-Mt Ex-Mt
COMPLETE SET (716) 15.00 4.50
COMP.FACT.SET (728) 15.00 4.50
COMP.YAZ PUZZLE 1.00 .30
1 Bo Jackson DK .15 .04
2 Steve Sax DK .05 .02
3A Ruben Sierra DK ERR .05 .02
(No small line on top
border on card back)
3B Ruben Sierra DK COR .05 .02
4 Ken Griffey Jr. DK .40 .12
5 Mickey Tettleton DK .05 .02
6 Dave Stewart DK .05 .02
7 Jim Deshaies DK DP .05 .02
8 John Smoltz DK .25 .07
9 Mike Bielecki DK .05 .02
10A Brian Downing DK .15 .04
ERR (Reverse neg-
ative on card front)
10B Brian Downing DK .05 .02
COR
11 Kevin Mitchell DK .05 .02
12 Kelly Gruber DK .05 .02
13 Joe Magrane DK .05 .02
14 John Franco DK .05 .02
15 Ozzie Guillen DK .05 .02
16 Lou Whitaker DK .05 .02
17 John Smiley DK .05 .02
18 Howard Johnson DK .05 .02
19 Willie Randolph DK .10 .03
20 Chris Bosio DK .05 .02
21 Tommy Herr DK DP .05 .02
22 Dan Gladden DK .05 .02
23 Ellis Burks DK .10 .03
24 Pete O'Brien DK .05 .02
25 Bryn Smith DK .05 .02
26 Ed Whitson DK DP .05 .02
27 DK Checklist 1-27 DP .05 .02
(Comments on Perez-
Steele on back)
28 Robin Ventura RR .25 .07
29 Todd Zeile RR .10 .03
30 Sandy Alomar Jr. .10 .03
31 Kent Mercker RR RC .25 .07
32 B.McDonald RC UER .25 .07
Middle name Benard
not Benjamin
33A J.Gonzalez RC ERR 2.00 .60
Reverse negative
33B J.Gonzalez COR RC 1.50 .45
34 Eric Anthony RR RC .10 .03
35 Mike Fetters RR RC .25 .07
36 Marquis Grissom RC .25 .07
37 Greg Vaughn RR .10 .03
38 Brian DuBois RC .10 .03
39 Steve Avery RR UER .05 .02
(Born in MI, not NJ)
40 Mark Gardner RR RC .10 .03
41 Andy Benes .10 .03
42 D.DeShields RR RC .25 .07
43 Scott Coolbaugh RC .10 .03
44 Pat Combs DP .05 .02
45 Alex Sanchez DP .05 .02
46 Kelly Mann DP RC .10 .03
47 Julio Machado DP RC .10 .03
48 Pete Incaviglia .05 .02
49 Shawon Dunston .05 .02
50 Jeff Treadway .05 .02
51 Jeff Ballard .05 .02
52 Claudell Washington .05 .02
53 Juan Samuel .05 .02
54 John Smiley .05 .02
55 Rob Deer .05 .02
56 Geno Petralli .05 .02
57 Chris Bosio .05 .02
58 Carlton Fisk .15 .04
59 Kirt Manwaring .05 .02
60 Chet Lemon .05 .02
61 Bo Jackson .25 .07
62 Doyle Alexander .05 .02
63 Pedro Guerrero .05 .02
64 Allan Anderson .05 .02
65 Greg W. Harris .05 .02
66 Mike Greenwell .05 .02
67 Walt Weiss .05 .02
68 Wade Boggs .15 .04
69 Jim Clancy .05 .02
70 Junior Felix .05 .02
71 Barry Larkin .25 .07
72 Dave LaPoint .05 .02
73 Joel Skinner .05 .02
74 Jesse Barfield .05 .02
75 Tommy Herr .05 .02
76 Ricky Jordan .05 .02
77 Eddie Murray .25 .07
78 Steve Sax .05 .02
79 Tim Belcher .05 .02
80 Danny Jackson .05 .02
81 Kent Hrbek .10 .03
82 Milt Thompson .05 .02
83 Brook Jacoby .05 .02
84 Mike Marshall .05 .02
85 Kevin Seitzer .05 .02
86 Tony Gwynn .30 .09
87 Dave Stieb .10 .03
88 Dave Smith .05 .02
89 Bret Saberhagen .10 .03
90 Alan Trammell .15 .04
91 Tony Phillips .05 .02
92 Doug Drabek .05 .02
93 Jeffrey Leonard .05 .02
94 Wally Joyner .10 .03
95 Carney Lansford .10 .03
96 Cal Ripken .75 .23
97 Andres Galarraga .10 .03
98 Kevin Mitchell .05 .02
99 Howard Johnson .05 .02
100A Checklist 28-129 .05 .02
100B Checklist 28-125 .05 .02
101 Melido Perez .05 .02
102 Spike Owen .05 .02
103 Paul Molitor .15 .04
104 Geronimo Berroa .05 .02
105 Ryne Sandberg .40 .12
106 Bryn Smith .05 .02
107 Steve Buechele .05 .02
108 Jim Abbott .15 .04
109 Alvin Davis .05 .02
110 Lee Smith .10 .03
111 Roberto Alomar .25 .07
112 Rick Reuschel .05 .02
113A Kelly Gruber ERR .05 .02
(Born 2/22)
113B Kelly Gruber COR .05 .02
(Born 2/26; corrected
in factory sets)
114 Joe Carter .10 .03
115 Jose Rijo .05 .02
116 Greg Minton .05 .02
117 Bob Ojeda .05 .02
118 Glenn Davis .05 .02
119 Jeff Reardon .10 .03
120 Kurt Stillwell .05 .02
121 John Smoltz .25 .07
122 Dwight Evans .10 .03
123 Eric Yelding .05 .02
124 John Franco .10 .03
125 Jose Canseco .25 .07
126 Barry Bonds .60 .18
127 Lee Guetterman .05 .02
128 Jack Clark .10 .03
129 Dave Valle .05 .02
130 Hubie Brooks .05 .02
131 Ernest Riles .05 .02
132 Mike Morgan .05 .02
133 Steve Jeltz .05 .02
134 Jeff D. Robinson .05 .02
135 Ozzie Guillen .05 .02
136 Chili Davis .10 .03
137 Mitch Webster .05 .02
138 Jerry Browne .05 .02
139 Bo Diaz .05 .02
140 Robby Thompson .05 .02
141 Craig Worthington .05 .02
142 Julio Franco .05 .02
143 Brian Holman .05 .02
144 George Brett .60 .18
145 Tom Glavine .15 .04
146 Robin Yount .40 .12
147 Gary Carter .15 .04
148 Ron Kittle .05 .02
149 Tony Fernandez .05 .02
150 Dave Stewart .10 .03
151 Gary Gaetti .10 .03
152 Kevin Elster .05 .02
153 Gerald Perry .05 .02
154 Jesse Orosco .05 .02
155 Wally Backman .05 .02
156 Dennis Martinez .10 .03
157 Rick Sutcliffe .10 .03
158 Greg Maddux .40 .12
159 Andy Hawkins .05 .02
160 John Kruk .10 .03
161 Jose Oquendo .05 .02
162 John Dopson .05 .02
163 Joe Magrane .05 .02
164 Bill Ripken .05 .02
165 Fred Manrique .05 .02
166 Nolan Ryan UER 1.00 .30
(Did not lead NL in
K's in '89 as he was
in AL in '89)
167 Damon Berryhill .05 .02
168 Dale Murphy .25 .07
169 Mickey Tettleton .05 .02
170A Kirk McCaskill ERR .05 .02
(Born 4/19)
170B Kirk McCaskill COR .05 .02
(Born 4/9; corrected
in factory sets)
171 Dwight Gooden .15 .04
172 Jose Lind .05 .02
173 B.J. Surhoff .10 .03
174 Ruben Sierra .05 .02
175 Dan Plesac .05 .02
176 Dan Pasqua .05 .02
177 Kelly Downs .05 .02
178 Matt Nokes .05 .02
179 Luis Aquino .05 .02
180 Frank Tanana .05 .02
181 Tony Pena .05 .02
182 Dan Gladden .05 .02
183 Bruce Hurst .05 .02
184 Roger Clemens .50 .15

185 Mark McGwire .60 .18
186 Rob Murphy .05 .02
187 Jim Deshaies .05 .02
188 Fred McGriff .25 .07
189 Rob Dibble .10 .03
190 Don Mattingly .60 .18
191 Felix Fermin .05 .02
192 Roberto Kelly .05 .02
193 Dennis Cook .05 .02
194 Darren Daulton .10 .03
195 Alfredo Griffin .05 .02
196 Eric Plunk .05 .02
197 Orel Hershiser .10 .03
198 Paul O'Neill .15 .04
199 Randy Bush .05 .02
200A Checklist 130-231 .05 .02
200B Checklist 126-223 .05 .02
201 Ozzie Smith .40 .12
202 Pete O'Brien .05 .02
203 Jay Howell .05 .02
204 Mark Gubicza .05 .02
205 Ed Whitson .05 .02
206 George Bell .05 .02
207 Mike Scott .05 .02
208 Charlie Leibrandt .05 .02
209 Mike Heath .05 .02
210 Dennis Eckersley .10 .03
211 Mike LaValliere .05 .02
212 Darnell Coles .05 .02
213 Lance Parrish .05 .02
214 Mike Moore .05 .02
215 Steve Finley .10 .03
216 Tim Raines .10 .03
217A Scott Garrelts ERR .05 .02
(Born 10/20)
217B Scott Garrelts COR .05 .02
(Born 10/30; corrected
in factory sets)
218 Kevin McReynolds .05 .02
219 Dave Gallagher .05 .02
220 Tim Wallach .05 .02
221 Chuck Crim .05 .02
222 Lonnie Smith .05 .02
223 Andre Dawson .10 .03
224 Nelson Santovenia .05 .02
225 Rafael Palmeiro .15 .04
226 Devon White .05 .02
227 Harold Reynolds .10 .03
228 Ellis Burks .15 .04
229 Mark Parent .05 .02
230 Will Clark .25 .07
231 Jimmy Key .10 .03
232 John Farrell .05 .02
233 Eric Davis .10 .03
234 Johnny Ray .05 .02
235 Darryl Strawberry .15 .04
236 Bill Doran .05 .02
237 Greg Gagne .05 .02
238 Jim Eisenreich .05 .02
239 Tommy Gregg .05 .02
240 Marty Barrett .05 .02
241 Rafael Ramirez .05 .02
242 Chris Sabo .05 .02
243 Dave Henderson .05 .02
244 Andy Van Slyke .10 .03
245 Alvaro Espinoza .05 .02
246 Garry Templeton .05 .02
247 Gene Harris .05 .02
248 Kevin Gross .05 .02
249 Brett Butler .10 .03
250 Willie Randolph .10 .03
251 Roger McDowell .05 .02
252 Rafael Belliard .05 .02
253 Steve Rosenberg .05 .02
254 Jack Howell .05 .02
255 Marvell Wynne .05 .02
256 Tom Candiotti .05 .02
257 Todd Benzinger .05 .02
258 Don Robinson .05 .02
259 Phil Bradley .05 .02
260 Cecil Espy .05 .02
261 Scott Bankhead .05 .02
262 Frank White .10 .03
263 Andres Thomas .05 .02
264 Glenn Braggs .05 .02
265 David Cone .10 .03
266 Bobby Thigpen .05 .02
267 Nelson Liriano .05 .02
268 Terry Steinbach .05 .02
269 Kirby Puckett UER .25 .07
(Back doesn't consider
Joe Torre's .363 in '71)
270 Gregg Jefferies .10 .03
271 Jeff Blauser .05 .02
272 Cory Snyder .05 .02
273 Roy Smith .05 .02
274 Tom Foley .05 .02
275 Mitch Williams .05 .02
276 Paul Kilgus .05 .02
277 Don Slaught .05 .02
278 Von Hayes .05 .02
279 Vince Coleman .05 .02
280 Mike Boddicker .05 .02
281 Ken Dayley .05 .02
282 Mike Devereaux .05 .02
283 Kenny Rogers .10 .03
284 Jeff Russell .05 .02
285 Jerome Walton .05 .02
286 Derek Lilliquist .05 .02
287 Joe Orsulak .05 .02
288 Dick Schofield .05 .02
289 Ron Darling .05 .02
290 Bobby Bonilla .10 .03
291 Jim Gantner .05 .02
292 Bobby Witt .05 .02
293 Greg Brock .05 .02
294 Ivan Calderon .05 .02
295 Steve Bedrosian .05 .02
296 Mike Henneman .05 .02
297 Tom Gordon .10 .03
298 Lou Whitaker .10 .03
299 Terry Pendleton .10 .03
300A Checklist 232-333 .05 .02
300B Checklist 224-321 .05 .02
301 Juan Berenguer .05 .02
302 Mark Davis .05 .02
303 Nick Esasky .05 .02
304 Rickey Henderson .25 .07
305 Rick Cerone .05 .02
306 Craig Biggio .15 .04
307 Duane Ward .05 .02
308 Tom Browning .05 .02
309 Walt Terrell .05 .02
310 Greg Swindell .05 .02
311 Dave Righetti .05 .02
312 Mike Maddux .05 .02
313 Len Dykstra .10 .03
314 Jose Gonzalez .05 .02
315 Steve Balboni .05 .02
316 Mike Scioscia .05 .02
317 Ron Oester .05 .02
318 Gary Wayne .05 .02
319 Todd Worrell .05 .02
320 Doug Jones .05 .02
321 Jeff Hamilton .05 .02
322 Danny Tartabull .05 .02
323 Chris James .05 .02
324 Mike Flanagan .05 .02
325 Gerald Young .05 .02
326 Bob Boone .10 .03
327 Frank Williams .05 .02
328 Dave Parker .10 .03
329 Sid Bream .05 .02
330 Mike Schooler .05 .02
331 Bert Blyleven .10 .03
332 Bob Welch .05 .02
333 Bob Milacki .05 .02
334 Tim Burke .05 .02
335 Jose Uribe .05 .02
336 Randy Myers .10 .03
337 Eric King .05 .02
338 Mark Langston .05 .02
339 Teddy Higuera .05 .02
340 Oddibe McDowell .05 .02
341 Lloyd McClendon .05 .02
342 Pascual Perez .05 .02
343 Kevin Brown UER .10 .03
(Signed is misspelled
as signeed on back)
344 Chuck Finley .10 .03
345 Erik Hanson .05 .02
346 Rich Gedman .05 .02
347 Bip Roberts .05 .02
348 Matt Williams .10 .03
349 Tom Henke .05 .02
350 Brad Komminsk .05 .02
351 Jeff Reed .05 .02
352 Brian Downing .05 .02
353 Frank Viola .05 .02
354 Terry Puhl .05 .02
355 Brian Harper .05 .02
356 Steve Farr .05 .02
357 Joe Boever .05 .02
358 Danny Heep .05 .02
359 Larry Andersen .05 .02
360 Rolando Roomes .05 .02
361 Mike Gallego .05 .02
362 Bob Kipper .05 .02
363 Clay Parker .05 .02
364 Mike Pagliarulo .05 .02
365 Ken Griffey Jr. UER .75 .23
(Signed through 1990,
should be 1991)
366 Rex Hudler .05 .02
367 Pat Sheridan .05 .02
368 Kirk Gibson .10 .03
369 Jeff Parrett .05 .02
370 Bob Walk .05 .02
371 Ken Patterson .05 .02
372 Bryan Harvey .05 .02
373 Mike Bielecki .05 .02
374 Tom Magrann .05 .02
375 Rick Mahler .05 .02
376 Craig Lefferts .05 .02
377 Gregg Olson .10 .03
378 Jamie Moyer .10 .03
379 Randy Johnson .40 .12
380 Jeff Montgomery .10 .03
381 Marty Clary .05 .02
382 Bill Spiers .05 .02
383 Dave Magadan .05 .02
384 Greg Hibbard RC .10 .03
385 Ernie Whitt .05 .02
386 Rick Honeycutt .05 .02
387 Dave West .05 .02
388 Keith Hernandez .15 .04
389 Jose Alvarez .05 .02
390 Joey Belle .25 .07
391 Rick Aguilera .10 .03
392 Mike Fitzgerald .05 .02
393 Dwight Smith .05 .02
394 Steve Wilson .05 .02
395 Bob Geren .05 .02
396 Randy Ready .05 .02
397 Ken Hill .10 .03
398 Jody Reed .05 .02
399 Tom Brunansky .05 .02
400A Checklist 334-435 .05 .02
400B Checklist 322-419 .05 .02
401 Rene Gonzales .05 .02
402 Harold Baines .10 .03
403 Cecilio Guante .05 .02
404 Joe Girardi .15 .04
405A Sergio Valdez ERR .05 .02
(Card front shows
black line crossing
S in Sergio)
405B Sergio Valdez COR .05 .02
406 Mark Williamson .05 .02
407 Glenn Hoffman .05 .02
408 Jeff Innis .05 .02
409 Randy Kramer .05 .02
410 Charlie O'Brien .05 .02
411 Charlie Hough .10 .03
412 Gus Polidor .05 .02
413 Ron Karkovice .05 .02
414 Trevor Wilson .05 .02
415 Kevin Ritz .05 .02
416 Gary Thurman .05 .02
417 Jeff M. Robinson .05 .02
418 Scott Terry .05 .02
419 Tim Laudner .05 .02
420 Dennis Rasmussen .05 .02
421 Luis Rivera .05 .02
422 Jim Corsi .05 .02
423 Dennis Lamp .05 .02
424 Ken Caminiti .10 .03
425 David Wells .10 .03
426 Norm Charlton .05 .02
427 Deion Sanders .25 .07
428 Dion James .05 .02
429 Chuck Cary .05 .02
430 Ken Howell .05 .02
431 Steve Lake .05 .02
432 Kal Daniels .05 .02
433 Lance McCullers .05 .02
434 Lenny Harris .05 .02
435 Scott Scudder .05 .02
436 Gene Larkin .05 .02
437 Dan Quisenberry .05 .02
438 Steve Olin RC .25 .07
439 Mickey Hatcher .05 .02
440 Willie Wilson .05 .02
441 Mark Grant .05 .02
442 Mookie Wilson .10 .03
443 Alex Trevino .05 .02
444 Pat Tabler .05 .02
445 Dave Bergman .05 .02
446 Todd Burns .05 .02
447 R.J. Reynolds .05 .02
448 Jay Buhner .10 .03
449 Lee Stevens .10 .03
450 Ron Hassey .05 .02
451 Bob Melvin .05 .02
452 Dave Martinez .05 .02
453 Greg Litton .05 .02
454 Mark Carreon .05 .02
455 Scott Fletcher .05 .02
456 Otis Nixon .05 .02
457 Tony Fossas .05 .02
458 John Russell .05 .02
459 Paul Assenmacher .05 .02
460 Zane Smith .05 .02
461 Jack Daugherty .05 .02
462 Rich Monteleone .05 .02
463 Greg Briley .05 .02
464 Mike Smithson .05 .02
465 Benito Santiago .10 .03
466 Jeff Brantley .05 .02
467 Jose Nunez .05 .02
468 Scott Bailes .05 .02
469 Ken Griffey Sr. .10 .03
470 Bob McClure .05 .02
471 Mackey Sasser .05 .02
472 Glenn Wilson .05 .02
473 Kevin Tapani RC .25 .07
474 Bill Buckner .05 .02
475 Ron Gant .10 .03
476 Kevin Romine .05 .02
477 Juan Agosto .05 .02
478 Herm Winningham .05 .02
479 Storm Davis .05 .02
480 Jeff King .05 .02
481 Kevin Mmahat .05 .02
482 Carmelo Martinez .05 .02
483 Omar Vizquel .25 .07
484 Jim Dwyer .05 .02
485 Bob Knepper .05 .02
486 Dave Anderson .05 .02
487 Ron Jones .05 .02
488 Jay Bell .10 .03
489 Sammy Sosa RC 8.00 2.40
490 Kent Anderson .05 .02
491 Domingo Ramos .05 .02
492 Dave Clark .05 .02
493 Tim Birtsas .05 .02
494 Ken Oberkfell .05 .02
495 Larry Sheets .05 .02
496 Jeff Kunkel .05 .02
497 Jim Presley .05 .02
498 Mike Macfarlane .05 .02
499 Pete Smith .05 .02
500A Checklist 436-537 DP .05 .02
500B Checklist 420-517 .05 .02
501 Gary Sheffield .25 .07
502 Terry Bross .05 .02
503 Jerry Kutzler .05 .02
504 Lloyd Moseby .05 .02
505 Curt Young .05 .02
506 Al Newman .05 .02
507 Keith Miller .05 .02
508 Mike Stanton RC .25 .07
509 Rich Yett .05 .02
510 Tim Drummond .05 .02
511 Joe Hesketh .05 .02
512 Rick Wrona .05 .02
513 Luis Salazar .05 .02
514 Hal Morris .05 .02
515 Terry Mulholland .05 .02
516 John Morris .05 .02
517 Carlos Quintana .05 .02
518 Frank DiPino .05 .02
519 Randy Milligan .05 .02
520 Chad Kreuter .05 .02
521 Mike Jeffcoat .05 .02
522 Mike Harkey .05 .02
523A Andy Nezelek ERR .05 .02
(Wrong birth year)
523B Andy Nezelek COR .15 .04
(Finally corrected
in factory sets)
524 Dave Schmidt .05 .02
525 Tony Armas .05 .02
526 Barry Lyons .05 .02
527 Rick Reed RC .25 .07
528 Jerry Reuss .05 .02
529 Dean Palmer RC .25 .07
530 Jeff Peterek .05 .02
531 Carlos Martinez .05 .02
532 Atlee Hammaker .05 .02
533 Mike Brumley .05 .02
534 Terry Leach .05 .02
535 Doug Strange .05 .02
536 Jose DeLeon .05 .02
537 Shane Rawley .05 .02
538 Joey Cora .10 .03
539 Eric Hetzel .05 .02
540 Gene Nelson .05 .02
541 Wes Gardner .05 .02
542 Mark Portugal .05 .02
543 Al Leiter .25 .07
544 Jack Armstrong .05 .02
545 Greg Cadaret .05 .02
546 Rod Nichols .05 .02
547 Luis Polonia .05 .02
548 Charlie Hayes .05 .02
549 Dickie Thon .05 .02
550 Tim Crews .05 .02
551 Dave Winfield .10 .03
552 Mike Davis .05 .02
553 Ron Robinson .05 .02
554 Carmen Castillo .05 .02
555 John Costello .05 .02
556 Bud Black .05 .02
557 Rick Dempsey .05 .02
558 Jim Acker .05 .02
559 Eric Show .05 .02
560 Pat Borders .05 .02
561 Danny Darwin .05 .02
562 Rick Luecken .05 .02
563 Edwin Nunez .05 .02
564 Felix Jose .05 .02
565 John Cangelosi .05 .02
566 Bill Swift .05 .02
567 Bill Schroeder .05 .02
568 Stan Javier .05 .02
569 Jim Traber .05 .02
570 Wallace Johnson .05 .02
571 Donell Nixon .05 .02
572 Sid Fernandez .05 .02
573 Lance Johnson .05 .02
574 Andy McGaffigan .05 .02
575 Mark Knudson .05 .02
576 Tommy Greene RC .10 .03
577 Mark Grace .15 .04
578 Larry Walker RC 1.00 .30
579 Mike Stanley .05 .02
580 Mike Witt DP .05 .02
581 Scott Bradley .05 .02
582 Greg A. Harris .05 .02
583A Kevin Hickey ERR .25 .07
583B Kevin Hickey COR .05 .02
584 Lee Mazzilli .05 .02
585 Jeff Pico .05 .02
586 Joe Oliver .05 .02
587 Willie Fraser DP .05 .02
588 Carl Yastrzemski .25 .07
Puzzle Card DP
589 Kevin Bass DP .05 .02
590 John Moses DP .05 .02
591 Tom Pagnozzi DP .05 .02
592 Tony Castillo DP .05 .02
593 Jerald Clark DP .05 .02
594 Dan Schatzeder .05 .02
595 Luis Quinones DP .05 .02
596 Pete Harnisch DP .05 .02
597 Gary Redus .05 .02
598 Mel Hall .05 .02
599 Rick Schu .05 .02
600A Checklist 538-639 .05 .02
600B Checklist 518-617 .05 .02
601 Mike Kingery DP .05 .02
602 Terry Kennedy DP .05 .02
603 Mike Sharperson DP .05 .02
604 Don Carman DP .05 .02
605 Jim Gott .05 .02
606 Donn Pall DP .05 .02
607 Rance Mulliniks .05 .02
608 Curt Wilkerson DP .05 .02
609 Mike Felder DP .05 .02
610 G.Hernandez DP .05 .02
611 Candy Maldonado DP .05 .02
612 Mark Thurmond DP .05 .02
613 Rick Leach DP .05 .02
614 Jerry Reed DP .05 .02
615 Franklin Stubbs .05 .02
616 Billy Hatcher DP .05 .02
617 Don August DP .05 .02
618 Tim Teufel .05 .02
619 Shawn Hillegas DP .05 .02
620 Manny Lee .05 .02
621 Gary Ward DP .05 .02
622 Mark Guthrie DP .05 .02
623 Jeff Musselman DP .05 .02
624 Mark Lemke DP .05 .02
625 Fernando Valenzuela .10 .03
626 Paul Sorrento DP RC .25 .07
627 Glenallen Hill DP .05 .02
628 Les Lancaster DP .05 .02
629 Vance Law DP .05 .02
630 Randy Velarde DP .05 .02
631 Todd Frohwirth DP .05 .02
632 Willie McGee .10 .03
633 Dennis Boyd DP .05 .02
634 Cris Carpenter DP .05 .02
635 Brian Holton .05 .02
636 Tracy Jones DP .05 .02
637A Terry Steinbach AS .05 .02
(Recent Major
League Performance)
637B Terry Steinbach AS .05 .02
(All-Star Game
Performance)
638 Brady Anderson .10 .03
639A Jack Morris ERR .10 .03
(Card front shows
black line crossing
J in Jack)
639B Jack Morris COR .10 .03
640 Jaime Navarro .05 .02
641 Darrin Jackson .05 .02
642 Mike Dyer RC .05 .02
643 Mike Schmidt .50 .15
644 Henry Cotto .05 .02
645 John Cerutti .05 .02
646 Francisco Cabrera .05 .02
647 Scott Sanderson .05 .02
648 Brian Meyer .05 .02
649 Ray Searage .05 .02
650A Bo Jackson AS .25 .07
(Recent Major
League Performance)
650B Bo Jackson AS .25 .07
(All-Star Game
Performance)
651 Steve Lyons .05 .02
652 Mike LaCoss .05 .02
653 Ted Power .05 .02
654A Howard Johnson AS .05 .02
(Recent Major
League Performance)
654B Howard Johnson AS .05 .02
(All-Star Game
Performance)
655 Mauro Gozzo .05 .02
656 Mike Blowers RC .10 .03
657 Paul Gibson .05 .02
658 Neal Heaton .05 .02
659 Nolan Ryan 5000K .50 .15
COR (Still an error as
Ryan did not lead AL
in K's in '75)
659A Nolan Ryan 5000K 1.50 .45
(665 King of
Kings back) ERR
660A Harold Baines AS .75 .23
(Black line through
star on front;
Recent Major
League Performance)
660B Harold Baines AS 1.00 .30
(Black line through
star on front;
All-Star Game
Performance)
660C Harold Baines AS .25 .07
(Black line behind
star on front;
Recent Major
League Performance)
660D Harold Baines AS .05 .02
(Black line behind
star on front;
All-Star Game
Performance)
661 Gary Pettis .05 .02
662 Clint Zavaras .05 .02
663A Rick Reuschel AS .05 .02
(Recent Major
League Performance)
663B Rick Reuschel AS .05 .02
(All-Star Game
Performance)
664 Alejandro Pena .05 .02
665 N.Ryan KING COR .50 .15
665A Nolan Ryan KING 1.50 .45
(659 5000 K
back) ERR
665C N.Ryan KING ERR .75 .23
No number on back
in factory sets
666 Ricky Horton .05 .02
667 Curt Schilling 1.00 .30
668 Bill Landrum .05 .02
669 Todd Stottlemyre .10 .03
670 Tim Leary .05 .02
671 John Wetteland .25 .07
672 Calvin Schiraldi .05 .02
673A Ruben Sierra AS .05 .02
(Recent Major
League Performance)
673B Ruben Sierra AS .05 .02
(All-Star Game
Performance)
674A Pedro Guerrero AS .05 .02
(Recent Major
League Performance)
674B Pedro Guerrero AS .05 .02
(All-Star Game
Performance)
675 Ken Phelps .05 .02
676A Cal Ripken AS .40 .12
(All-Star Game
Performance)
676B Cal Ripken AS .75 .23
(Recent Major
League Performance)
677 Denny Walling .05 .02
678 Goose Gossage .10 .03
679 Gary Mielke .05 .02
680 Bill Bathe .05 .02
681 Tom Lawless .05 .02
682 Xavier Hernandez RC .05 .02
683A Kirby Puckett AS .15 .04
(Recent Major
League Performance)
683B Kirby Puckett AS .15 .04
(All-Star Game
Performance)
684 Mariano Duncan .05 .02
685 Ramon Martinez .05 .02
686 Tim Jones .05 .02
687 Tom Filer .05 .02
688 Steve Lombardozzi .05 .02
689 Bernie Williams RC 1.00 .30
690 Chip Hale .05 .02
691 Beau Allred RC .05 .02
692A Ryne Sandberg AS .25 .07
(Recent Major
League Performance)
692B Ryne Sandberg AS .25 .07
(All-Star Game
Performance)
693 Jeff Huson RC .10 .03
694 Curt Ford .05 .02
695A Eric Davis AS .05 .02
(Recent Major
League Performance)
695B Eric Davis AS .05 .02
(All-Star Game
Performance)
696 Scott Lusader .05 .02
697A Mark McGwire AS .30 .09
(Recent Major
League Performance)
697B Mark McGwire AS .30 .09
(All-Star Game
Performance)
698 Steve Cummings RC .05 .02
699 George Canale .05 .02
700A Checklist 640-715 .25 .07
and BC1-BC26
700B Checklist 640-716 .10 .03
and BC1-BC26
700C Checklist 618-716 .05 .02
701A Julio Franco AS .05 .02
(Recent Major
League Performance)
701B Julio Franco AS .05 .02
(All-Star Game
Performance)
702 Dave Johnson (P) .05 .02
703A Dave Stewart AS .05 .02
(Recent Major
League Performance)
703B Dave Stewart AS .05 .02
(All-Star Game
Performance)
704 Dave Justice RC .50 .15
705 Tony Gwynn AS .15 .04

Card	Nm-Mt	Ex-Mt
(All-Star Game Performance)		
705A Tony Gwynn AS	.15	.04
(Recent Major League Performance)		
706 Greg Myers	.05	.02
707A Will Clark AS	.25	.07
(Recent Major League Performance)		
707B Will Clark AS	.25	.07
(All-Star Game Performance)		
708A Benito Santiago AS	.05	.02
(Recent Major League Performance)		
708B Benito Santiago AS	.05	.02
(All-Star Game Performance)		
709 Larry McWilliams	.05	.02
710A Ozzie Smith AS	.25	.07
(Recent Major League Performance)		
710B Ozzie Smith AS Perf	.25	.07
711 John Olerud RC	.50	.15
712A Wade Boggs AS	.10	.03
(Recent Major League Performance)		
712B Wade Boggs AS	.10	.03
(All-Star Game Performance)		
713 Gary Eave	.05	.02
714 Bob Tewksbury	.05	.02
715A Kevin Mitchell AS	.05	.02
(Recent Major League Performance)		
715B Kevin Mitchell AS	.05	.02
(All-Star Game Performance)		
716 B.Giamatti RC COMM	.25	.07
In Memoriam		

1990 Donruss Bonus MVP's

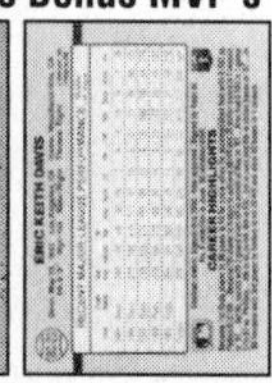

Numbered with the prefix "BC" for bonus card, a 26-card set featuring the most valuable player from each of the 26 teams was randomly inserted in all 1990 Donruss unopened pack formats. The factory sets were distributed without the Bonus Cards; thus there were again new checklist cards printed to reflect the exclusion of the Bonus Cards.

Card	Nm-Mt	Ex-Mt
COMPLETE SET (26)	1.50	.45
BC1 Bo Jackson	.25	.07
BC2 Howard Johnson	.05	.02
BC3 Dave Stewart	.10	.03
BC4 Tony Gwynn	.30	.09
BC5 Orel Hershiser	.10	.03
BC6 Pedro Guerrero	.05	.02
BC7 Tim Raines	.10	.03
BC8 Kirby Puckett	.25	.07
BC9 Alvin Davis	.05	.02
BC10 Ryne Sandberg	.40	.12
BC11 Kevin Mitchell	.05	.02
BC12A John Smoltz ERR	.15	.04
(Photo actually Tom Glavine)		
BC12B John Smoltz COR	.25	.07
BC13 George Bell	.05	.02
BC14 Julio Franco	.05	.02
BC15 Paul Molitor	.15	.04
BC16 Bobby Bonilla	.10	.03
BC17 Mike Greenwell	.05	.02
BC18 Cal Ripken	.75	.23
BC19 Carlton Fisk	.15	.04
BC20 Chili Davis	.10	.03
BC21 Glenn Davis	.05	.02
BC22 Steve Sax	.05	.02
BC23 Eric Davis DP	.10	.03
BC24 Greg Swindell DP	.05	.02
BC25 Von Hayes DP	.05	.02
BC26 Alan Trammell	.15	.04

1990 Donruss Grand Slammers

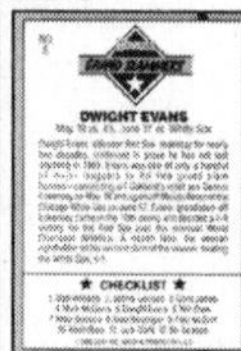

This 12-card standard size set was in the 1990 Donruss set as a special card deliniating each 55-card section of the 1990 Factory Set. This set honors those players who connected for grand slam homers during the 1989 season. The cards are in the 1990 Donruss design and the back describes the grand slam homer hit by each player.

Card	Nm-Mt	Ex-Mt
COMPLETE SET (12)	1.50	.45
1 Matt Williams	.10	.03
2 Jeffrey Leonard	.05	.02
3 Chris James	.05	.02
4 Mark McGwire	.60	.18
5 Dwight Evans	.10	.03
6 Will Clark	.25	.07
7 Mike Scioscia	.05	.02
8 Todd Benzinger	.05	.02
9 Fred McGriff	.25	.07
10 Kevin Bass	.05	.02
11 Jack Clark	.10	.03
12 Bo Jackson	.25	.07

1990 Donruss Rookies

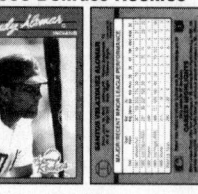

The 1990 Donruss Rookies set marked the fifth consecutive year that Donruss issued a boxed set at season's end honoring the best rookies of the season. This set, which used the 1990 Donruss design but featured a green border, was issued exclusively through the Donruss dealer network to hobby dealers. This 56-card, standard size set came in its own box and the words "The Rookies" are featured prominently on the front of the cards. There are no notable Rookie Cards in this set.

Card	Nm-Mt	Ex-Mt
COMP.FACT.SET (56)	2.00	.60
1 Sandy Alomar Jr. UER	.10	.03
(No stitches on base-ball on Donruss logo on card front)		
2 John Olerud	.50	.15
3 Pat Combs	.05	.02
4 Brian DuBois	.05	.02
5 Felix Jose	.05	.02
6 Delino DeShields	.25	.07
7 Mike Stanton	.05	.02
8 Mike Munoz	.05	.02
9 Craig Grebeck RC	.10	.03
10 Joe Kraemer	.05	.02
11 Jeff Huson	.05	.02
12 Bill Sampen	.05	.02
13 Brian Bohanon RC	.10	.03
14 Dave Justice	.50	.15
15 Robin Ventura	.25	.07
16 Greg Vaughn	.10	.03
17 Wayne Edwards	.05	.02
18 Shawn Boskie RC	.10	.03
19 Carlos Baerga RC	.25	.07
20 Mark Gardner	.05	.02
21 Kevin Appier	.25	.07
22 Mike Harkey	.05	.02
23 Tim Layana	.05	.02
24 Glenallen Hill	.05	.02
25 Jerry Kutzler	.05	.02
26 Mike Blowers	.10	.03
27 Scott Ruskin	.05	.02
28 Dana Kiecker	.05	.02
29 Willie Blair RC	.10	.03
30 Ben McDonald	.05	.02
31 Todd Zeile	.10	.03
32 Scott Coolbaugh	.05	.02
33 Xavier Hernandez	.05	.02
34 Mike Hartley	.05	.02
35 Kevin Tapani	.25	.07
36 Kevin Wickander	.05	.02
37 Carlos Hernandez RC	.25	.07
38 Brian Traxler RC	.10	.03
39 Marty Brown	.05	.02
40 Scott Radinsky RC	.10	.03
41 Julio Machado	.05	.02
42 Steve Avery	.05	.02
43 Mark Lemke	.05	.02
44 Alan Mills RC	.10	.03
45 Marquis Grissom	.25	.07
46 Greg Olson RC	.10	.03
47 Dave Hollins RC	.25	.07
48 Jerald Clark	.05	.02
49 Eric Anthony	.05	.02
50 Tim Drummond	.05	.02
51 John Burkett	.05	.02
52 Brent Knackert RC	.10	.03
53 Jeff Shaw	.05	.02
54 John Orton RC	.10	.03
55 Terry Shumpert	.05	.02
56 Checklist 1-56	.05	.02

1990 Donruss Aqueous Test

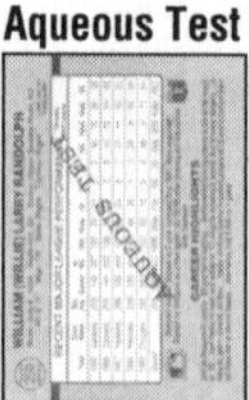

These cards are remarkably similar to the 1990 Donruss issue except that the words "Aqueous Test" are printed in black ink on the back. It is possible, but not confirmed that all cards may exist in this set. Any additions to this checklist is greatly appreciated.

Card	Nm-Mt	Ex-Mt
COMPLETE SET	1200.00	350.00
1 Bo Jackson DK	10.00	3.00
3 Ruben Sierra DK	6.00	1.80
6 Dave Stewart DK	5.00	1.50
9 Mike Bielecki DK	5.00	1.50
16 Lou Whitaker DK	6.00	1.80
18 Howard Johnson DK	5.00	1.50
22 Dan Gladden DK	5.00	1.50
30 Sandy Alomar Jr RR	5.00	1.50
32 Ben McDonald RR	5.00	1.50
33 Juan Gonzalez RR	25.00	7.50
34 Eric Anthony RR	5.00	1.50
35 Mike Fetters RR	5.00	1.50
48 Pete Incaviglia	5.00	1.50
51 Jeff Ballard	5.00	1.50
52 Claudell Washington	5.00	1.50
55 Rob Deer	5.00	1.50
56 Geno Petralli	5.00	1.50
57 Chris Bosio	5.00	1.50
60 Chet Lemon	5.00	1.50
65 Greg Harris	5.00	1.50
71 Barry Larkin	10.00	3.00
72 Dave LaPoint	5.00	1.50
77 Eddie Murray	15.00	4.50
78 Steve Sax	5.00	1.50
79 Tim Belcher	5.00	1.50
81 Kent Hrbek	6.00	1.80
83 Brook Jacoby	5.00	1.50
85 Kevin Seitzer	5.00	1.50
86 Tony Gwynn	20.00	6.00
89 Bret Saberhagen	6.00	1.80
91 Tony Phillips	5.00	1.50
93 Jeff Leonard	5.00	1.50
94 Wally Joyner	5.00	1.50
95 Carney Lansford	6.00	1.80
96 Cal Ripken Jr.	40.00	12.00
98 Kevin Mitchell	5.00	1.50
100 Checklist	5.00	1.50
102 Spike Owen	5.00	1.50
103 Paul Molitor	12.00	3.60
105 Ryne Sandberg	20.00	6.00
107 Steve Buechele	5.00	1.50
108 Jim Abbott	8.00	2.40
109 Alvin Davis	5.00	1.50
112 Rick Reuschel	6.00	1.80
114 Joe Carter	6.00	1.80
117 Bobby Ojeda	5.00	1.50
118 Glenn Davis	5.00	1.50
120 Kurt Stillwell	5.00	1.50
125 Jose Canseco	12.00	3.60
126 Barry Bonds	25.00	7.50
129 Dave Valle	5.00	1.50
132 Mike Morgan	5.00	1.50
134 Jeff Robinson	5.00	1.50
139 Bo Diaz	5.00	1.50
140 Robby Thompson	5.00	1.50
141 Craig Worthington	5.00	1.50
146 Robin Yount	12.00	3.60
147 Gary Carter	12.00	3.60
148 Ron Kittle	5.00	1.50
149 Tony Fernandez	6.00	1.80
154 Jesse Orosco	6.00	1.80
155 Wally Backman	5.00	1.50
158 Greg Maddux	25.00	7.50
162 John Dopson	5.00	1.50
164 Bill Ripken	5.00	1.50
165 Fred Manrique	5.00	1.50
166 Nolan Ryan	40.00	12.00
167 Damon Berryhill	5.00	1.50
168 Dale Murphy	10.00	3.00
169 Mickey Tettleton	5.00	1.50
170 Kirk McCaskill	5.00	1.50
171 Dwight Gooden	6.00	1.80
172 Jose Lind	5.00	1.50
173 B.J. Surhoff	6.00	1.80
174 Ruben Sierra	6.00	1.80
175 Dan Plesac	5.00	1.50
176 Dan Pasqua	5.00	1.50
177 Kelly Downs	5.00	1.50
178 Matt Nokes	5.00	1.50
179 Luis Aquino	5.00	1.50
180 Frank Tanana	6.00	1.80
181 Tony Pena	5.00	1.50
182 Dan Gladden	5.00	1.50
183 Bruce Hurst	5.00	1.50
184 Roger Clemens	20.00	6.00
185 Mark McGwire	30.00	9.00
186 Rob Murphy	5.00	1.50
187 Jim Deshaies	5.00	1.50
188 Fred McGriff	10.00	3.00
189 Rob Dibble	5.00	1.50
190 Don Mattingly	20.00	6.00
191 Felix Fermin	5.00	1.50
192 Roberto Kelly	5.00	1.50
193 Dennis Cook	5.00	1.50
194 Darren Daulton	5.00	1.50
195 Alfredo Griffin	5.00	1.50
196 Eric Plunk	5.00	1.50
197 Orel Hershiser	6.00	1.80
198 Paul O'Neill	8.00	2.40
199 Randy Bush	5.00	1.50
201 Ozzie Smith	15.00	4.50
202 Pete O'Brien	5.00	1.50
203 Jay Howell	5.00	1.50
204 Mark Gubicza	5.00	1.50
205 Ed Whitson	5.00	1.50
206 George Bell	5.00	1.50
207 Mike Scott	5.00	1.50
208 Charlie Liebrandt	5.00	1.50
209 Mike Heath	5.00	1.50
210 Dennis Eckersley	8.00	2.40
211 Mike LaVallilere	5.00	1.50
212 Darnell Coles	5.00	1.50
213 Lance Parrish	5.00	1.50
214 Mike Moore	5.00	1.50
215 Steve Finley	6.00	1.80
216 Tim Raines	6.00	1.80
217 Scott Garrelts	5.00	1.50
218 Kevin McReynolds	5.00	1.50
219 Dave Gallagher	5.00	1.50
220 Tim Wallach	5.00	1.50
221 Chuck Crim	5.00	1.50
222 Lonnie Smith	6.00	1.80
223 Andre Dawson	15.00	4.50
224 Nelson Santovenia	5.00	1.50
225 Rafael Palmeiro	10.00	3.00
226 Devon White	5.00	1.50
227 Harold Reynolds	6.00	1.80
228 Ellis Burks	6.00	1.80
229 Mark Parent	5.00	1.50
230 Will Clark	12.00	3.60
231 Jimmy Key	5.00	1.50
232 John Farrell	5.00	1.50
233 Eric Davis	6.00	1.80
234 Johnny Ray	5.00	1.50
235 Darryl Strawberry	6.00	1.80
236 Bill Doran	5.00	1.50
237 Greg Gagne	5.00	1.50
238 Jim Eisenreich	5.00	1.50
239 Tommy Gregg	5.00	1.50
240 Marty Barrett	5.00	1.50
241 Rafael Ramirez	5.00	1.50
242 Chris Sabo	5.00	1.50
243 Dave Henderson	5.00	1.50
245 Alvaro Espinoza	5.00	1.50
246 Garry Templeton	5.00	1.50
247 Gene Harris	5.00	1.50
248 Kevin Gross	5.00	1.50
249 Brett Butler	6.00	1.80
250 Willie Randolph	6.00	1.80
251 Roger McDowell	5.00	1.50
252 Rafael Belliard	5.00	1.50
253 Steve Rosenberg	5.00	1.50
254 Jack Howell	5.00	1.50
255 Marvell Wynne	5.00	1.50
256 Tom Candiotti	5.00	1.50
257 Todd Benzinger	5.00	1.50
258 Don Robinson	5.00	1.50
259 Phil Bradley	5.00	1.50
260 Cecil Espy	5.00	1.50
261 Scott Bankhead	5.00	1.50
262 Rafael Belliard	5.00	1.50
262 Frank White	6.00	1.80
263 Andres Thomas	5.00	1.50
264 Glenn Braggs	5.00	1.50
265 David Cone	8.00	2.40
266 Bobby Thigpen	5.00	1.50
267 Nelson Liriano	5.00	1.50
268 Terry Steinbach	5.00	1.50
269 Kirby Puckett	20.00	6.00
270 Gregg Jefferies	5.00	1.50
271 Jeff Blauser	5.00	1.50
272 Cory Snyder	5.00	1.50
273 Roy Smith	5.00	1.50
274 Tom Foley	5.00	1.50
275 Mitch Williams	5.00	1.50
276 Paul Kilgus	5.00	1.50
277 Don Slaught	5.00	1.50
278 Von Hayes	5.00	1.50
279 Vince Coleman	5.00	1.50
280 Mike Boddicker	5.00	1.50
281 Ken Dayley	5.00	1.50
282 Mike Devereaux	5.00	1.50
BC1 Bo Jackson MVP	10.00	3.00
BC3 Dave Stewart MVP	6.00	1.80
BC6 Pedro Guerrero MVP	6.00	1.80
BC7 Tim Raines MVP	6.00	1.80
BC8 Kirby Puckett MVP	20.00	6.00
BC9 Alvin Davis MVP	5.00	1.50

1990 Donruss Best AL

The 1990 Donruss Best of the American League set consists of 144 standard-size cards. This was Donruss' latest version of what had been titled the previous two years as Baseball's Best. In 1990, the sets were split into National and American League and marketed separately. The front design was similar to the regular issue Donruss set except for the front borders being blue while the backs have complete major and minor league statistics as compared to the regular Donruss cards which only cover the past five major-league seasons. An early Sammy Sosa card is featured within this set.

Card	Nm-Mt	Ex-Mt
COMP.FACT.SET (144)	40.00	12.00
1 Ken Griffey Jr.	1.25	.35
2 Bob Milacki	.15	.04
3 Mike Boddicker	.15	.04
4 Bert Blyleven	.20	.06
5 Carlton Fisk	.30	.09
6 Greg Swindell	.15	.04
7 Alan Trammell	.30	.09
8 Mark Davis	.15	.04
9 Chris Bosio	.15	.04
10 Gary Gaetti	.20	.06
11 Matt Nokes	.15	.04
12 Dennis Eckersley	.20	.06
13 Kevin Brown	.20	.06
14 Tom Henke	.15	.04
15 Mickey Tettleton	.15	.04
16 Jody Reed	.15	.04
17 Mark Langston	.15	.04
18 Melido Perez UER	.15	.04
(Listed as an Expo rather than White Sox)		
19 John Farrell	.15	.04
20 Tony Phillips	.15	.04
21 Bret Saberhagen	.20	.06
22 Robin Yount	.75	.23
23 Kirby Puckett	.50	.15
24 Steve Sax	.15	.04
25 Dave Stewart	.20	.06
26 Alvin Davis	.15	.04
27 Geno Petralli	.15	.04
28 Mookie Wilson	.20	.06
29 Jeff Ballard	.15	.04
30 Ellis Burks	.20	.06
31 Wally Joyner	.20	.06
32 Bobby Thigpen	.15	.04
33 Keith Hernandez	.30	.09
34 Jack Morris	.20	.06
35 George Brett	1.25	.35
36 Dan Plesac	.15	.04
37 Brian Harper	.15	.04
38 Don Mattingly	1.25	.35
39 Dave Henderson	.15	.04
40 Scott Bankhead UER	.15	.04
(Asheboro misspelled as Ashboro on card)		
41 Rafael Palmeiro	.30	.09
42 Jimmy Key	.20	.06
43 Gregg Olson	.15	.04
44 Tony Pena	.15	.04
45 Jack Howell	.15	.04
46 Eric King	.15	.04
47 Cory Snyder	.15	.04
48 Frank Tanana	.20	.06
49 Nolan Ryan	1.50	.45
50 Bob Boone	.20	.06
51 Dave Parker	.20	.06
52 Allan Anderson	.15	.04
53 Tim Leary	.15	.04
54 Mark McGwire	1.50	.45
55 Dave Valle	.15	.04
56 Fred McGriff	.30	.09
57 Cal Ripken	1.50	.45
58 Roger Clemens	1.00	.30
59 Lance Parrish	.20	.06
60 Robin Ventura	.50	.15
61 Doug Jones	.15	.04
62 Lloyd Moseby	.15	.04
63 Bo Jackson	.50	.15
64 Paul Molitor	.30	.09
65 Kent Hrbek	.20	.06
66 Mel Hall	.15	.04
67 Bob Welch	.20	.06
68 Erik Hanson	.15	.04
69 Harold Baines	.20	.06
70 Junior Felix	.15	.04
71 Craig Worthington	.15	.04
72 Jeff Reardon	.20	.06
73 Johnny Ray	.15	.04
74 Ozzie Guillen	.15	.04
75 Brook Jacoby	.15	.04
76 Chet Lemon	.15	.04
77 Mark Gubicza	.15	.04
78 B.J. Surhoff	.20	.06
79 Rick Aguilera	.20	.06
80 Pascual Perez	.15	.04
81 Jose Canseco	.50	.15
82 Mike Schooler	.15	.04
83 Jeff Huson	.15	.04
84 Kelly Gruber	.15	.04
85 Randy Milligan	.15	.04
86 Wade Boggs	.30	.09
87 Dave Winfield	.20	.06
88 Scott Fletcher	.15	.04
89 Tom Candiotti	.15	.04
90 Mike Heath	.15	.04
91 Kevin Seitzer	.15	.04
92 Ted Higuera	.15	.04
93 Kevin Tapani	.50	.15
94 Roberto Kelly	.15	.04
95 Walt Weiss	.15	.04
96 Checklist Card	.15	.04
97 Sandy Alomar Jr.	.20	.06
98 Pete O'Brien	.15	.04
99 Jeff Russell	.15	.04
100 John Olerud	1.50	.45
101 Pete Harnisch	.15	.04
102 Dwight Evans	.20	.06
103 Chuck Finley	.20	.06
104 Sammy Sosa	25.00	7.50
105 Mike Henneman	.15	.04
106 Kurt Stillwell	.15	.04
107 Greg Vaughn	.20	.06
108 Dan Gladden	.15	.04
109 Jesse Barfield	.15	.04
110 Willie Randolph	.20	.06
111 Randy Johnson	.60	.18
112 Julio Franco	.20	.06
113 Tony Fernandez	.15	.04
114 Ben McDonald	.15	.04
115 Mike Greenwell	.15	.04
116 Luis Polonia	.15	.04
117 Carney Lansford	.20	.06
118 Bud Black	.15	.04
119 Lou Whitaker	.20	.06
120 Jim Eisenreich	.15	.04
121 Gary Sheffield	.50	.15
122 Shane Mack	.15	.04
123 Alvaro Espinoza	.15	.04
124 Rickey Henderson	.50	.15
125 Jeffrey Leonard	.15	.04
126 Gary Pettis	.15	.04
127 Dave Stieb	.20	.06
128 Danny Tartabull	.15	.04
129 Joe Orsulak	.15	.04
130 Tom Brunansky	.15	.04
131 Dick Schofield	.15	.04
132 Candy Maldonado	.15	.04
133 Cecil Fielder	.20	.06
134 Terry Shumpert	.15	.04
135 Greg Gagne	.15	.04
136 Dave Righetti	.20	.06
137 Terry Steinbach	.15	.04
138 Harold Reynolds	.20	.06
139 George Bell	.15	.04
140 Carlos Quintana	.15	.04
141 Ivan Calderon	.15	.04
142 Greg Brock	.15	.04
143 Ruben Sierra	.15	.04
144 Checklist Card	.15	.04

1990 Donruss Best NL

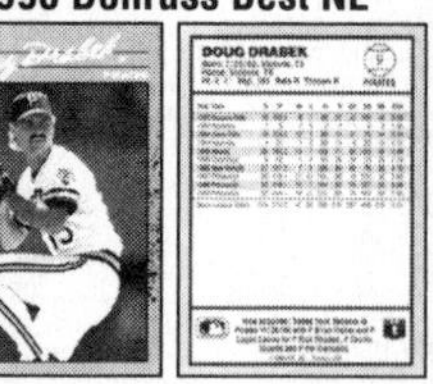

The 1990 Donruss Best of the National League set consists of 144 standard-size cards. This was Donruss' latest version of what had been titled the previous two years as Baseball's Best. In 1990, the sets were split into National and American League and marketed separately. The front design was similar to the regular issue Donruss set except for the front borders being blue while the backs have complete major and minor league statistics as compared to the regular Donruss cards which only cover the past five major-league seasons. An early Larry Walker card is featured within this set.

Card	Nm-Mt	Ex-Mt
COMP.FACT.SET (144)	8.00	2.40
1 Eric Davis	.20	.06
2 Tom Glavine	.30	.09
3 Mike Bielecki	.15	.04
4 Jim Deshaies	.15	.04
5 Mike Scioscia	.15	.04
6 Spike Owen	.15	.04
7 Dwight Gooden	.30	.09
8 Ricky Jordan	.15	.04
9 Doug Drabek	.15	.04
10 Bryn Smith	.15	.04
11 Tony Gwynn	.60	.18
12 John Burkett	.15	.04
13 Nick Esasky	.15	.04
14 Greg Maddux	.75	.23

15 Joe Oliver	.15	.04
16 Mike Scott	.15	.04
17 Tim Belcher	.15	.04
18 Kevin Gross	.15	.04
19 Howard Johnson	.15	.04
20 Darren Daulton	.20	.06
21 John Smiley	.15	.04
22 Ken Dayley	.15	.04
23 Craig Lefferts	.15	.04
24 Will Clark	.50	.15
25 Greg Olson	.15	.04
26 Ryne Sandberg	.60	.18
27 Tom Browning	.15	.04
28 Eric Anthony	.15	.04
29 Juan Samuel	.15	.04
30 Dennis Martinez	.20	.06
31 Kevin Elster	.15	.04
32 Tom Herr	.15	.04
33 Sid Bream	.15	.04
34 Terry Pendleton	.20	.06
35 Roberto Alomar	.50	.15
36 Kevin Bass	.15	.04
37 Jim Presley	.15	.04
38 Les Lancaster	.15	.04
39 Paul O'Neill	.30	.09
40 Dave Smith	.15	.04
41 Kirk Gibson	.20	.06
42 Tim Burke	.15	.04
43 David Cone	.20	.06
44 Ken Howell	.15	.04
45 Barry Bonds	1.25	.35
46 Joe Magrane	.15	.04
47 Andy Benes	.20	.06
48 Gary Carter	.30	.09
49 Pat Combs	.15	.04
50 John Smoltz	.50	.15
51 Mark Grace	.30	.09
52 Barry Larkin	.50	.15
53 Danny Darwin	.15	.04
54 Orel Hershiser	.20	.06
55 Tim Wallach	.15	.04
56 Dave Magadan	.15	.04
57 Roger McDowell	.15	.04
58 Bill Landrum	.15	.04
59 Jose DeLeon	.15	.04
60 Bip Roberts	.15	.04
61 Matt Williams	.20	.06
62 Dale Murphy	.50	.15
63 Dwight Smith	.15	.04
64 Chris Sabo	.15	.04
65 Glenn Davis	.15	.04
66 Jay Howell	.15	.04
67 Andres Galarraga	.20	.06
68 Frank Viola	.20	.06
69 John Kruk	.20	.06
70 Bobby Bonilla	.20	.06
71 Todd Zeile	.20	.06
72 Joe Carter	.20	.06
73 Robby Thompson	.15	.04
74 Jeff Blauser	.15	.04
75 Mitch Williams	.15	.04
76 Rob Dibble	.20	.06
77 Rafael Ramirez	.15	.04
78 Eddie Murray	.50	.15
79 Dave Martinez	.15	.04
80 Darryl Strawberry	.30	.09
81 Dickie Thon	.15	.04
82 Jose Lind	.15	.04
83 Ozzie Smith	.75	.23
84 Bruce Hurst	.15	.04
85 Kevin Mitchell	.15	.04
86 Lonnie Smith	.15	.04
87 Joe Girardi	.15	.04
88 Randy Myers	.20	.06
89 Craig Biggio	.30	.09
90 Fernando Valenzuela	.20	.06
91 Larry Walker	2.50	.75
92 John Franco	.20	.06
93 Dennis Cook	.15	.04
94 Bob Walk	.15	.04
95 Pedro Guerrero	.20	.06
96 Checklist Card	.15	.04
97 Andre Dawson	.20	.06
98 Ed Whitson	.15	.04
99 Steve Bedrosian	.15	.04
100 Oddibe McDowell	.15	.04
101 Todd Benzinger	.15	.04
102 Bill Doran	.15	.04
103 Alfredo Griffin	.15	.04
104 Tim Raines	.20	.06
105 Sid Fernandez	.15	.04
106 Charlie Hayes	.15	.04
107 Mike LaValliere	.15	.04
108 Jose Oquendo	.15	.04
109 Jack Clark	.20	.06
110 Scott Garrelts	.15	.04
111 Ron Gant	.20	.06
112 Shawon Dunston	.15	.04
113 Mariano Duncan	.15	.04
114 Eric Yelding	.15	.04
115 Hubie Brooks	.15	.04
116 Delino DeShields	.20	.06
117 Gregg Jefferies	.15	.04
118 Len Dykstra	.20	.06
119 Andy Van Slyke	.20	.06
120 Lee Smith	.20	.06
121 Benito Santiago	.20	.06
122 Jose Uribe	.15	.04
123 Jeff Treadway	.15	.04
124 Jerome Walton	.15	.04
125 Billy Hatcher	.15	.04
126 Ken Caminiti	.20	.06
127 Kal Daniels	.15	.04
128 Marquis Grissom	.50	.15
129 Kevin McReynolds	.15	.04
130 Wally Backman	.15	.04
131 Willie McGee	.20	.06
132 Terry Kennedy	.15	.04
133 Garry Templeton	.15	.04
134 Lloyd McClendon	.15	.04
135 Daryl Boston	.15	.04
136 Jay Bell	.20	.06
137 Mike Pagliarulo	.15	.04
138 Vince Coleman	.15	.04
139 Brett Butler	.20	.06
140 Von Hayes	.15	.04
141 Ramon Martinez	.15	.04
142 Jack Armstrong	.15	.04
143 Franklin Stubbs	.15	.04
144 Checklist Card	.15	.04

1990 Donruss Learning Series

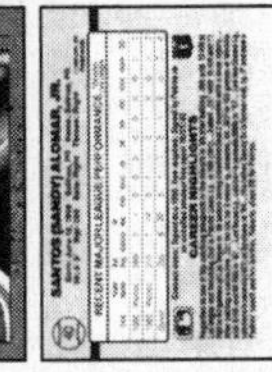

The 1990 Donruss Learning Series consists of 55 standard-size cards that served as part of an educational packet for elementary and middle school students. The cards were issued in two formats. Grades Three and Four received the cards, a historical timeline that relates events in baseball to major historical events, additional Donruss cards from wax packs, and a teacher's guide that focused on several academic subjects. Grades 5 through 8 received the cards, a teacher's guide designed for older students, and a 14-minute video shot at Chicago's Wrigley Field. The fronts feature color head shots of the players and bright red borders. The horizontally oriented backs are amber and present biography, statistics, and career highlights.

	Nm-Mt	Ex-Mt
COMPLETE SET (55)	30.00	9.00
1 George Brett DK	2.50	.75
2 Kevin Mitchell	.10	.03
3 Andy Van Slyke	.20	.06
4 Benito Santiago	.20	.06
5 Gary Carter	1.00	.30
6 Jose Canseco	1.25	.35
7 Rickey Henderson	1.25	.35
8 Ken Griffey Jr.	4.00	1.20
9 Ozzie Smith	2.50	.75
10 Dwight Gooden	.20	.06
11 Ryne Sandberg DK	2.50	.75
12 Don Mattingly	2.50	.75
13 Ozzie Guillen	.20	.06
14 Dave Righetti	.10	.03
15 Rick Dempsey	.10	.03
16 Tom Herr	.10	.03
17 Julio Franco	.20	.06
18 Von Hayes	.10	.03
19 Cal Ripken	5.00	1.50
20 Alan Trammell	.75	.23
21 Wade Boggs	1.00	.30
22 Glenn Davis	.10	.03
23 Will Clark	1.50	.45
24 Nolan Ryan	5.00	1.50
25 George Bell	.10	.03
26 Cecil Fielder	.50	.15
27 Gregg Olson	.10	.03
28 Tim Wallach	.10	.03
29 Ron Darling	.10	.03
30 Kelly Gruber	.10	.03
31 Shawn Boskie	.10	.03
32 Mike Greenwell	.10	.03
33 Dave Parker	.20	.06
34 Joe Magrane	.10	.03
35 Dave Stewart	.20	.06
36 Kent Hrbek	.20	.06
37 Robin Yount	1.00	.30
38 Bo Jackson	.50	.15
39 Fernando Valenzuela	.20	.06
40 Sandy Alomar Jr.	.20	.06
41 Lance Parrish	.10	.03
42 Candy Maldonado	.10	.03
43 Mike LaValliere	.10	.03
44 Jim Abbott	.20	.06
45 Edgar Martinez	.30	.09
46 Kirby Puckett	1.00	.30
47 Delino DeShields	.50	.15
48 Tony Gwynn	2.50	.75
49 Carlton Fisk	1.00	.30
50 Mike Scott	.10	.03
51 Barry Larkin	.75	.23
52 Andre Dawson	.50	.15
53 Tom Glavine	.75	.23
54 Tom Browning	.10	.03
55 Checklist Card	.10	.03

1990 Donruss Super DK's

This 26-player card set was available through a mail-in offer detailed on the wax packs. The set was sent in return for 10.00 and three wrappers plus 2.00 postage and handling. The set features the popular Donruss Diamond King subseries in large (approximately 4 7/8" by 6 13/16") form. Dick Perez of Perez-Steele Galleries did another outstanding job on the artwork. The cards are essentially a large version of the Donruss regular issue Diamond Kings. There is also a jumbo sized Ryan King of Kings card. Although not listed with the regular set; it is heavily sought after by Ryan collectors.

	Nm-Mt	Ex-Mt
COMPLETE SET (26)	25.00	7.50
1 Bo Jackson	1.00	.30
2 Steve Sax	.25	.07
3 Ruben Sierra	.50	.15
4 Ken Griffey Jr.	8.00	2.40
5 Mickey Tettleton	.50	.15
6 Dave Stewart	.50	.15
7 Jim Deshaies	.25	.07
8 John Smoltz	.75	.23
9 Mike Bielecki	.25	.07
10 Brian Downing	.25	.07
11 Kevin Mitchell	.25	.07
12 Kelly Gruber	.25	.07
13 Joe Magrane	.25	.07
14 John Franco	.50	.15
15 Ozzie Guillen	.25	.07
16 Lou Whitaker	.50	.15
17 John Smiley	.25	.07
18 Howard Johnson	.25	.07
19 Willie Randolph	.50	.15
20 Chris Bosio	.25	.07
21 Tommy Herr	.25	.07
22 Dan Gladden	.25	.07
23 Ellis Burks	.75	.23
24 Pete O'Brien	.25	.07
25 Bryn Smith	.25	.07
26 Ed Whitson	.25	.07
NNO Nolan Ryan King of Kings	15.00	4.50

1991 Donruss Previews

This 12-card standard-size set was issued by Donruss for hobby dealers as examples of what the 1991 Donruss cards would look like. These cards have the 1991 Donruss design on the front; the back merely says 1991 Preview card and identifies the player and the team.

	Nm-Mt	Ex-Mt
COMPLETE SET (12)	300.00	90.00
1 Dave Justice	15.00	4.50
2 Doug Drabek	5.00	1.50
3 Scott Chiamparino	5.00	1.50
4 Ken Griffey Jr.	60.00	18.00
5 Bob Welch	5.00	1.50
6 Tino Martinez	12.00	3.60
7 Nolan Ryan	80.00	24.00
8 Dwight Gooden	8.00	2.40
9 Ryne Sandberg	50.00	15.00
10 Barry Bonds	40.00	12.00
11 Jose Canseco	20.00	6.00
12 Eddie Murray	20.00	6.00

1991 Donruss

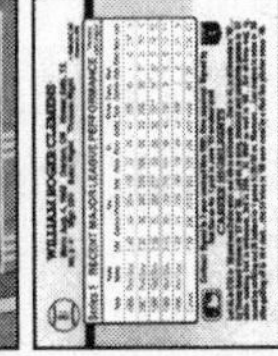

The 1991 Donruss set was issued in two series of 386 and 384 for a total of 770 standard-size cards. This set marked the first time Donruss issued cards in multiple series. The second series was issued approximately three months after the first series was issued. Cards were issued in wax packs and factory sets. As a separate promotion, wax packs were also given away with six and 12-packs of Coke and Diet Coke. First series cards feature blue borders and second series green borders with some stripes and the players name in white against a red background. Subsets include Diamond Kings (1-27), Rated Rookies (28-47/413-432), AL All-Stars (48-56), MVP's (387-412) and NL All-Stars (433-441). There were also special cards to honor the award winners and the heroes of the World Series. On cards 60, 70, 127, 182, 239, 294, 355, 368, and 377, the border stripes are red and yellow. There are no notable Rookie Cards in this set.

	Nm-Mt	Ex-Mt
COMPLETE SET (770)	8.00	2.40
COMP.FACT.w/LEAF PREV	10.00	3.00
COMP.FACT.w/STUD. PREV	10.00	3.00
COMP.STARGELL PUZZLE	1.00	.30
1 Dave Stieb DK	.05	.02
2 Craig Biggio DK	.10	.03
3 Cecil Fielder DK	.05	.02
4 Barry Bonds DK	.30	.09
5 Barry Larkin DK	.10	.03
6 Dave Parker DK	.05	.02
7 Len Dykstra DK	.05	.02
8 Bobby Thigpen DK	.05	.02
9 Roger Clemens DK	.25	.07
10 Ron Gant DK UER (No trademark on team logo on back)	.10	.03
11 Delino DeShields DK	.05	.02
12 R.Alomar DK UER No trademark on team logo on back	.10	.03
13 Sandy Alomar Jr. DK	.05	.02
14 R.Sandberg DK UER Was DK in '85, not '83 as shown	.25	.07
15 Ramon Martinez DK	.05	.02
16 Edgar Martinez DK	.15	.04
17 Dave Magadan DK	.05	.02
18 Matt Williams DK	.05	.02
19 Rafael Palmeiro DK UER (No trademark on team logo on back)	.10	.03
20 Bob Welch DK	.05	.02
21 Dave Righetti DK	.05	.02
22 Brian Harper DK	.05	.02
23 Gregg Olson DK	.05	.02
24 Kurt Stillwell DK	.05	.02
25 P.Guerrero DK UER No trademark on team logo on back	.05	.02
26 Chuck Finley DK UER (No trademark on team logo on back)	.05	.02
27 DK Checklist 1-27	.05	.02
28 Tino Martinez RR	.15	.04
29 Mark Lewis RR	.05	.02
30 Bernard Gilkey RR	.05	.02
31 Hensley Meulens RR	.05	.02
32 Derek Bell RR	.10	.03
33 Jose Offerman RR	.05	.02
34 Terry Bross RR	.05	.02
35 Leo Gomez RR	.05	.02
36 Derrick May RR	.05	.02
37 Kevin Morton RR	.05	.02
38 Moises Alou RR	.10	.03
39 Julio Valera RR	.05	.02
40 Milt Cuyler RR	.05	.02
41 Phil Plantier RR RC	.05	.02
42 Scott Chiamparino RR	.05	.02
43 Ray Lankford RR	.05	.02
44 Mickey Morandini RR	.05	.02
45 Dave Hansen RR	.05	.02
46 Kevin Belcher RR	.05	.02
47 Darrin Fletcher RR	.05	.02
48 Steve Sax AS	.05	.02
49 Ken Griffey Jr. AS	.25	.07
50A J.Canseco AS ERR Team in stat box should be AL, not A's	.10	.03
50B J.Canseco AS COR	.25	.07
51 Sandy Alomar Jr. AS	.05	.02
52 Cal Ripken AS	.40	.12
53 Rickey Henderson AS	.15	.04
54 Bob Welch AS	.05	.02
55 Wade Boggs AS	.10	.03
56 Mark McGwire AS	.30	.09
57A Jack McDowell ERR (Career stats do not include 1990)	.25	.07
57B Jack McDowell COR (Career stats do not include 1990)	.50	.15
58 Jose Lind	.05	.02
59 Alex Fernandez	.05	.02
60 Pat Combs	.05	.02
61 Mike Walker	.05	.02
62 Juan Samuel	.05	.02
63 Mike Blowers UER (Last line has aseball, not baseball)	.05	.02
64 Mark Guthrie	.05	.02
65 Mark Salas	.05	.02
66 Tim Jones	.05	.02
67 Tim Leary	.05	.02
68 Andres Galarraga	.10	.03
69 Bob Milacki	.05	.02
70 Tim Belcher	.05	.02
71 Todd Zeile	.05	.02
72 Jerome Walton	.05	.02
73 Kevin Seitzer	.05	.02
74 Jerald Clark	.05	.02
75 John Smoltz UER (Born in Detroit, not Warren)	.15	.04
76 Mike Henneman	.05	.02
77 Ken Griffey Jr.	.50	.15
78 Jim Abbott	.15	.04
79 Gregg Jefferies	.05	.02
80 Kevin Reimer	.05	.02
81 Roger Clemens	.50	.15
82 Mike Fitzgerald	.05	.02
83 Bruce Hurst UER (Middle name is Lee, not Vee)	.05	.02
84 Eric Davis	.10	.03
85 Paul Molitor	.15	.04
86 Will Clark	.25	.07
87 Mike Bielecki	.05	.02
88 Bret Saberhagen	.10	.03
89 Nolan Ryan	1.00	.30
90 Bobby Thigpen	.05	.02
91 Dickie Thon	.05	.02
92 Duane Ward	.05	.02
93 Luis Polonia	.05	.02
94 Terry Kennedy	.05	.02
95 Kent Hrbek	.10	.03
96 Danny Jackson	.05	.02
97 Sid Fernandez	.05	.02
98 Jimmy Key	.10	.03
99 Franklin Stubbs	.05	.02
100 Checklist 28-103	.05	.02
101 R.J. Reynolds	.05	.02
102 Dave Stewart	.10	.03
103 Dan Pasqua	.05	.02
104 Dan Plesac	.05	.02
105 Mark McGwire	.60	.18
106 John Farrell	.05	.02
107 Don Mattingly	.60	.18
108 Carlton Fisk	.15	.04
109 Ken Oberkfell	.05	.02
110 Darrel Akerfelds	.05	.02
111 Gregg Olson	.05	.02
112 Mike Scioscia	.05	.02
113 Bryn Smith	.05	.02
114 Bob Geren	.05	.02
115 Tom Candiotti	.05	.02
116 Kevin Tapani	.05	.02
117 Jeff Treadway	.05	.02
118 Alan Trammell	.15	.04
119 Pete O'Brien (Blue shading goes through stats)	.05	.02
120 Joel Skinner	.05	.02
121 Mike LaValliere	.05	.02
122 Dwight Evans	.10	.03
123 Jody Reed	.05	.02
124 Lee Guetterman	.05	.02
125 Tim Burke	.05	.02
126 Dave Johnson	.05	.02
127 Fernando Valenzuela (Lower large stripe in yellow instead of blue) UER	.10	.03
128 Jose DeLeon	.05	.02
129 Andre Dawson	.10	.03
130 Gerald Perry	.05	.02
131 Greg W. Harris	.05	.02
132 Tom Glavine	.15	.04
133 Lance McCullers	.05	.02
134 Randy Johnson	.30	.09
135 Lance Parrish UER (Born in McKeesport, not Clairton)	.10	.03
136 Mackey Sasser	.05	.02
137 Geno Petralli	.05	.02
138 Dennis Lamp	.05	.02
139 Dennis Martinez	.10	.03
140 Mike Pagliarulo	.05	.02
141 Hal Morris	.05	.02
142 Dave Parker	.10	.03
143 Brett Butler	.10	.03
144 Paul Assenmacher	.05	.02
145 Mark Gubicza	.05	.02
146 Charlie Hough	.10	.03
147 Sammy Sosa	.50	.15
148 Randy Ready	.05	.02
149 Kelly Gruber	.05	.02
150 Devon White	.05	.02
151 Gary Carter	.15	.04
152 Gene Larkin	.05	.02
153 Chris Sabo	.05	.02
154 David Cone	.10	.03
155 Todd Stottlemyre	.05	.02
156 Glenn Wilson	.05	.02
157 Bob Walk	.05	.02
158 Mike Gallego	.05	.02
159 Greg Hibbard	.05	.02
160 Chris Bosio	.05	.02
161 Mike Moore	.05	.02
162 Jerry Browne UER (Born Christiansted, should be St. Croix)	.05	.02
163 Steve Sax UER (No asterisk next to his 1989 At Bats)	.05	.02
164 Melido Perez	.05	.02
165 Danny Darwin	.05	.02
166 Roger McDowell	.05	.02
167 Bill Ripken	.05	.02
168 Mike Sharperson	.05	.02
169 Lee Smith	.10	.03
170 Matt Nokes	.05	.02
171 Jesse Orosco	.05	.02
172 Rick Aguilera	.10	.03
173 Jim Presley	.05	.02
174 Lou Whitaker	.10	.03
175 Harold Reynolds	.10	.03
176 Brook Jacoby	.05	.02
177 Wally Backman	.05	.02
178 Wade Boggs	.15	.04
179 Chuck Cary (Comma after DOB, not on other cards)	.05	.02
180 Tom Foley	.05	.02
181 Pete Harnisch	.05	.02
182 Mike Morgan	.05	.02
183 Bob Tewksbury	.05	.02
184 Joe Girardi	.05	.02
185 Storm Davis	.05	.02
186 Ed Whitson	.05	.02
187 Steve Avery UER (Born in New Jersey, should be Michigan)	.05	.02
188 Lloyd Moseby	.05	.02
189 Scott Bankhead	.05	.02
190 Mark Langston	.05	.02
191 Kevin McReynolds	.05	.02
192 Julio Franco	.10	.03
193 John Dopson	.05	.02
194 Dennis Boyd	.05	.02
195 Bip Roberts	.05	.02
196 Billy Hatcher	.05	.02
197 Edgar Diaz	.05	.02
198 Greg Litton	.05	.02
199 Mark Grace	.15	.04
200 Checklist 104-179	.05	.02
201 George Brett	.60	.18
202 Jeff Russell	.05	.02
203 Ivan Calderon	.05	.02
204 Ken Howell	.05	.02
205 Tom Henke	.05	.02
206 Bryan Harvey	.05	.02
207 Steve Bedrosian	.05	.02
208 Al Newman	.05	.02
209 Randy Myers	.05	.02
210 Daryl Boston	.05	.02
211 Manny Lee	.05	.02
212 Dave Smith	.05	.02
213 Don Slaught	.05	.02
214 Walt Weiss	.05	.02
215 Donn Pall	.05	.02
216 Jaime Navarro	.05	.02
217 Willie Randolph	.10	.03
218 Rudy Seanez	.05	.02
219 Jim Leyritz	.05	.02
220 Ron Karkovice	.05	.02
221 Ken Caminiti	.10	.03
222 Von Hayes	.05	.02
223 Cal Ripken	.75	.23
224 Lenny Harris	.05	.02
225 Milt Thompson	.05	.02
226 Alvaro Espinoza	.05	.02
227 Chris James	.05	.02
228 Dan Gladden	.05	.02
229 Jeff Blauser	.05	.02
230 Mike Heath	.05	.02
231 Omar Vizquel	.10	.03
232 Doug Jones	.05	.02
233 Jeff King	.05	.02
234 Luis Rivera	.05	.02
235 Ellis Burks	.10	.03
236 Greg Cadaret	.05	.02
237 Dave Martinez	.05	.02
238 Mark Williamson	.05	.02
239 Stan Javier	.05	.02
240 Ozzie Smith	.40	.12
241 Shawn Boskie	.05	.02
242 Tom Gordon	.05	.02
243 Tony Gwynn	.30	.09
244 Tommy Gregg	.05	.02
245 Jeff M. Robinson	.05	.02
246 Keith Comstock	.05	.02
247 Jack Howell	.05	.02
248 Keith Miller	.05	.02
249 Bobby Witt	.05	.02
250 Rob Murphy UER (Shown as on Reds in '89 in stats, should be Red Sox)	.05	.02
251 Spike Owen	.05	.02
252 Garry Templeton	.05	.02
253 Glenn Braggs	.05	.02
254 Ron Robinson	.05	.02
255 Kevin Mitchell	.05	.02
256 Les Lancaster	.05	.02
257 Mel Stottlemyre Jr.	.05	.02
258 Kenny Rogers UER (IP listed as 171, should be 172)	.10	.03
259 Lance Johnson	.05	.02
260 John Kruk	.10	.03
261 Fred McGriff	.15	.04
262 Dick Schofield	.05	.02
263 Trevor Wilson	.05	.02
264 David West	.05	.02
265 Scott Scudder	.05	.02
266 Dwight Gooden	.15	.04
267 Willie Blair	.05	.02
268 Mark Portugal	.05	.02
269 Doug Drabek	.05	.02
270 Dennis Eckersley	.10	.03
271 Eric King	.05	.02
272 Robin Yount	.40	.12
273 Carney Lansford	.10	.03
274 Carlos Baerga	.05	.02

275 Dave Righetti .10 .03
276 Scott Fletcher .05 .02
277 Eric Yelding .05 .02
278 Charlie Hayes .05 .02
279 Jeff Ballard .05 .02
280 Orel Hershiser .10 .03
281 Jose Oquendo .05 .02
282 Mike Witt .05 .02
283 Mitch Webster .05 .02
284 Greg Gagne .05 .02
285 Greg Olson .05 .02
286 Tony Phillips UER .05 .02
(Born 4/15
should be 4/25)
287 Scott Bradley .05 .02
288 Cory Snyder UER .05 .02
(In text, led is repeated
Inglewood is misspelled as Englewood)
289 Jay Bell UER .10 .03
(Born in Pensacola,
not Eglin AFB)
290 Kevin Romine .05 .02
291 Jeff D. Robinson .05 .02
292 Steve Frey UER .05 .02
(Bats left,
should be right)
293 Craig Worthington .05 .02
294 Tim Crews .05 .02
295 Joe Magrane .05 .02
296 Hector Villanueva .05 .02
297 Terry Shumpert .05 .02
298 Joe Carter .10 .03
299 Kent Mercker UER .05 .02
(IP listed as 53,
should be 52)
300 Checklist 180-255 .05 .02
301 Chet Lemon .05 .02
302 Mike Schooler .05 .02
303 Dante Bichette .10 .03
304 Kevin Elster .05 .02
305 Jeff Huson .05 .02
306 Greg A. Harris .05 .02
307 Marquis Grissom UER .05 .02
(Middle name Deon,
should be Dean)
308 Calvin Schiraldi .05 .02
309 Mariano Duncan .05 .02
310 Bill Spiers .05 .02
311 Scott Garrelts .05 .02
312 Mitch Williams .05 .02
313 Mike Macfarlane .05 .02
314 Kevin Brown .10 .03
315 Robin Ventura .10 .03
316 Darren Daulton .10 .03
317 Pat Borders .05 .02
318 Mark Eichhorn .05 .02
319 Jeff Brantley .05 .02
320 Shane Mack .05 .02
321 Rob Dibble .10 .03
322 John Franco .10 .03
323 Junior Felix .05 .02
324 Casey Candaele .05 .02
325 Bobby Bonilla .10 .03
326 Dave Henderson .05 .02
327 Wayne Edwards .05 .02
328 Mark Knudson .05 .02
329 Terry Steinbach .05 .02
330 Colby Ward UER .05 .02
(No comma between
city and state)
331 Oscar Azocar .05 .02
332 Scott Radinsky .05 .02
333 Eric Anthony .05 .02
334 Steve Lake .05 .02
335 Bob Melvin .05 .02
336 Kal Daniels .05 .02
337 Tom Pagnozzi .05 .02
338 Alan Mills .05 .02
339 Steve Olin .05 .02
340 Juan Berenguer .05 .02
341 Francisco Cabrera .05 .02
342 Dave Bergman .05 .02
343 Henry Cotto .05 .02
344 Sergio Valdez .05 .02
345 Bob Patterson .05 .02
346 John Marzano .05 .02
347 Dana Kiecker .05 .02
348 Dion James .05 .02
349 Hubie Brooks .05 .02
350 Bill Landrum .05 .02
351 Bill Sampen .05 .02
352 Greg Briley .05 .02
353 Paul Gibson .05 .02
354 Dave Eiland .05 .02
355 Steve Finley .10 .03
356 Bob Boone .10 .03
357 Steve Buechele .05 .02
358 Chris Hoiles .05 .02
359 Larry Walker .25 .07
360 Frank DiPino .05 .02
361 Mark Grant .05 .02
362 Dave Magadan .05 .02
363 Robby Thompson .05 .02
364 Lonnie Smith .05 .02
365 Steve Farr .05 .02
366 Dave Valle .05 .02
367 Tim Naehring .05 .02
368 Jim Acker .05 .02
369 Jeff Reardon UER .10 .03
(Born in Pittsfield,
not Dalton)
370 Tim Teufel .05 .02
371 Juan Gonzalez .25 .07
372 Luis Salazar .05 .02
373 Rick Honeycutt .05 .02
374 Greg Maddux .40 .12
375 Jose Uribe UER .05 .02
(Middle name Elta,
should be Alta)
376 Donnie Hill .05 .02
377 Don Carman .05 .02
378 Craig Grebeck .05 .02
379 Willie Fraser .05 .02
380 Glenallen Hill .05 .02
381 Joe Oliver .05 .02
382 Randy Bush .05 .02
383 Alex Cole .05 .02
384 Norm Charlton .05 .02
385 Gene Nelson .05 .02
386 Checklist 256-331 .05 .02
387 R. Henderson MVP .15 .04
388 Lance Parrish MVP .05 .02
389 Fred McGriff MVP .10 .03
390 Dave Parker MVP .05 .02
391 C. Maldonado MVP .05 .02
392 Ken Griffey Jr. MVP .25 .07
393 Gregg Olson MVP .05 .02
394 Rafael Palmeiro MVP .10 .03
395 Roger Clemens MVP .25 .07
396 George Brett MVP .25 .07
397 Cecil Fielder MVP .05 .02
398 Brian Harper MVP .05 .02
UER Major
League Performance,
should be Career
399 Bobby Thigpen MVP .05 .02
400 Roberto Kelly MVP .05 .02
UER (Second Base on
front and OF on back)
401 Danny Darwin MVP .05 .02
402 Dave Justice MVP .05 .02
403 Lee Smith MVP .05 .02
404 Ryne Sandberg MVP .25 .07
405 Eddie Murray MVP .15 .04
406 Tim Wallach MVP .05 .02
407 Kevin Mitchell MVP .05 .02
408 D. Strawberry MVP .10 .03
409 Joe Carter MVP .05 .02
410 Len Dykstra MVP .05 .02
411 Doug Drabek MVP .05 .02
412 Chris Sabo MVP .05 .02
413 Paul Marak RR .05 .02
414 Tim McIntosh RR .05 .02
415 Brian Barnes RR .05 .02
416 Eric Gunderson RR .05 .02
417 Mike Gardiner RR .05 .02
418 Steve Carter RR .05 .02
419 Gerald Alexander RR .05 .02
420 Rich Garces RR RC .05 .02
421 Chuck Knoblauch RR .10 .03
422 Scott Aldred RR .05 .02
423 W.Chamberlain RR RC .05 .02
424 Lance Dickson RR RC .05 .02
425 Greg Colbrunn RR RC .10 .03
426 Rich DeLucia RR UER .05 .02
(Misspelled Delucia
on card)
427 Jeff Conine RR RC .50 .15
428 Steve Decker RR .05 .02
429 Turner Ward RR RC .10 .03
430 Mo Vaughn RR .10 .03
431 Steve Chitren RR .05 .02
432 Mike Benjamin RR .05 .02
433 Ryne Sandberg AS .25 .07
434 Len Dykstra AS .05 .02
435 Andre Dawson AS .05 .02
436A Mike Scioscia AS .05 .02
(White star by name)
436B Mike Scioscia AS .05 .02
(Yellow star by name)
437 Ozzie Smith AS .25 .07
438 Kevin Mitchell AS .05 .02
439 Jack Armstrong AS .05 .02
440 Chris Sabo AS .05 .02
441 Will Clark AS .10 .03
442 Mel Hall .05 .02
443 Mark Gardner .05 .02
444 Mike Devereaux .05 .02
445 Kirk Gibson .10 .03
446 Terry Pendleton .10 .03
447 Mike Harkey .05 .02
448 Jim Eisenreich .05 .02
449 Benito Santiago .10 .03
450 Oddibe McDowell .05 .02
451 Cecil Fielder .10 .03
452 Ken Griffey Sr. .10 .03
453 Bert Blyleven .10 .03
454 Howard Johnson .05 .02
455 Monty Fariss UER .05 .02
(Misspelled Farris
on card)
456 Tony Pena .05 .02
457 Tim Raines .10 .03
458 Dennis Rasmussen .05 .02
459 Luis Quinones .05 .02
460 B.J. Surhoff .10 .03
461 Ernest Riles .05 .02
462 Rick Sutcliffe .10 .03
463 Danny Tartabull .05 .02
464 Pete Incaviglia .05 .02
465 Carlos Martinez .05 .02
466 Ricky Jordan .05 .02
467 John Cerutti .05 .02
468 Dave Winfield .10 .03
469 Francisco Oliveras .05 .02
470 Roy Smith .05 .02
471 Barry Larkin .25 .07
472 Ron Darling .05 .02
473 David Wells .10 .03
474 Glenn Davis .05 .02
475 Neal Heaton .05 .02
476 Ron Hassey .05 .02
477 Frank Thomas .25 .07
478 Greg Vaughn .10 .03
479 Todd Burns .05 .02
480 Candy Maldonado .05 .02
481 Dave LaPoint .05 .02
482 Alvin Davis .05 .02
483 Mike Scott .05 .02
484 Dale Murphy .25 .07
485 Ben McDonald .05 .02
486 Jay Howell .05 .02
487 Vince Coleman .05 .02
488 Alfredo Griffin .05 .02
489 Sandy Alomar Jr. .05 .02
490 Kirby Puckett .25 .07
491 Andres Thomas .05 .02
492 Jack Morris .10 .03
493 Matt Young .05 .02
494 Greg Myers .05 .02
495 Barry Bonds .60 .18
496 Scott Cooper UER .05 .02
(No BA for 1990
and career)
497 Dan Schatzeder .05 .02
498 Jesse Barfield .05 .02
499 Jerry Goff .05 .02
500 Checklist 332-408 .05 .02
501 Anthony Telford .05 .02
502 Eddie Murray .25 .07
503 Omar Olivares RC .10 .03
504 Ryne Sandberg .40 .12
505 Jeff Montgomery .05 .02
506 Mark Parent .05 .02
507 Ron Gant .10 .03
508 Frank Tanana .05 .02
509 Jay Buhner .10 .03
510 Max Venable .05 .02
511 Wally Whitehurst .05 .02
512 Gary Pettis .05 .02
513 Tom Brunansky .05 .02
514 Tim Wallach .05 .02
515 Craig Lefferts .05 .02
516 Tim Layana .05 .02
517 Darryl Hamilton .05 .02
518 Rick Reuschel .05 .02
519 Steve Wilson .05 .02
520 Kurt Stillwell .05 .02
521 Rafael Palmeiro .15 .04
522 Ken Patterson .05 .02
523 Len Dykstra .10 .03
524 Tony Fernandez .05 .02
525 Kent Anderson .05 .02
526 Mark Leonard .05 .02
527 Allan Anderson .05 .02
528 Tom Browning .05 .02
529 Frank Viola .10 .03
530 John Olerud .10 .03
531 Juan Agosto .05 .02
532 Zane Smith .05 .02
533 Scott Sanderson .05 .02
534 Barry Jones .05 .02
535 Mike Felder .05 .02
536 Jose Canseco .25 .07
537 Felix Fermin .05 .02
538 Roberto Kelly .05 .02
539 Brian Holman .05 .02
540 Mark Davidson .05 .02
541 Terry Mulholland .05 .02
542 Randy Milligan .05 .02
543 Jose Gonzalez .05 .02
544 Craig Wilson .05 .02
545 Mike Hartley .05 .02
546 Greg Swindell .05 .02
547 Gary Gaetti .10 .03
548 Dave Justice .10 .03
549 Steve Searcy .05 .02
550 Erik Hanson .05 .02
551 Dave Stieb .05 .02
552 Andy Van Slyke .10 .03
553 Mike Greenwell .05 .02
554 Kevin Maas .05 .02
555 Delino DeShields .10 .03
556 Curt Schilling .15 .04
557 Ramon Martinez .05 .02
558 Pedro Guerrero .10 .03
559 Dwight Smith .05 .02
560 Mark Davis .05 .02
561 Shawn Abner .05 .02
562 Charlie Leibrandt .05 .02
563 John Shelby .05 .02
564 Bill Swift .05 .02
565 Mike Fetters .05 .02
566 Alejandro Pena .05 .02
567 Ruben Sierra .05 .02
568 Carlos Quintana .05 .02
569 Kevin Gross .05 .02
570 Derek Lilliquist .05 .02
571 Jack Armstrong .05 .02
572 Greg Brock .05 .02
573 Mike Kingery .05 .02
574 Greg Smith .05 .02
575 Brian McRae RC .10 .03
576 Jack Daugherty .05 .02
577 Ozzie Guillen .05 .02
578 Joe Boever .05 .02
579 Luis Sojo .05 .02
580 Chili Davis .10 .03
581 Don Robinson .05 .02
582 Brian Harper .05 .02
583 Paul O'Neill .15 .04
584 Bob Ojeda .05 .02
585 Mookie Wilson .10 .03
586 Rafael Ramirez .05 .02
587 Gary Redus .05 .02
588 Jamie Quirk .05 .02
589 Shawn Hillegas .05 .02
590 Tom Edens .05 .02
591 Joe Klink .05 .02
592 Charles Nagy .05 .02
593 Eric Plunk .05 .02
594 Tracy Jones .05 .02
595 Craig Biggio .15 .04
596 Jose DeJesus .05 .02
597 Mickey Tettleton .05 .02
598 Chris Gwynn .05 .02
599 Rex Hudler .05 .02
600 Checklist 409-506 .05 .02
601 Jim Gott .05 .02
602 Jeff Manto .05 .02
603 Nelson Liriano .05 .02
604 Mark Lemke .05 .02
605 Clay Parker .05 .02
606 Edgar Martinez .15 .04
607 Mark Whiten .05 .02
608 Ted Power .05 .02
609 Tom Bolton .05 .02
610 Tom Herr .05 .02
611 Andy Hawkins UER .05 .02
Pitched No-Hitter
on 7/1, not 7/2
612 Scott Ruskin .05 .02
613 Ron Kittle .05 .02
614 John Wetteland .10 .03
615 Mike Perez RC .05 .02
616 Dave Clark .05 .02
617 Brent Mayne .05 .02
618 Jack Clark .10 .03
619 Marvin Freeman .05 .02
620 Edwin Nunez .05 .02
621 Russ Swan .05 .02
622 Johnny Ray .05 .02
623 Charlie O'Brien .05 .02
624 Joe Bitker .05 .02
625 Mike Marshall .05 .02
626 Otis Nixon .05 .02
627 Andy Benes .05 .02
628 Ron Oester .05 .02
629 Ted Higuera .05 .02
630 Kevin Bass .05 .02
631 Damon Berryhill .05 .02
632 Bo Jackson .25 .07
633 Brad Arnsberg .05 .02
634 Jerry Willard .05 .02
635 Tommy Greene .05 .02
636 Bob MacDonald .05 .02
637 Kirk McCaskill .05 .02
638 John Burkett .05 .02
639 Paul Abbott RC .10 .03
640 Todd Benzinger .05 .02
641 Todd Hundley .05 .02
642 George Bell .05 .02
643 Javier Ortiz .05 .02
644 Sid Bream .05 .02
645 Bob Welch .05 .02
646 Phil Bradley .05 .02
647 Bill Krueger .05 .02
648 Rickey Henderson .25 .07
649 Kevin Wickander .05 .02
650 Steve Balboni .05 .02
651 Gene Harris .05 .02
652 Jim Deshaies .05 .02
653 Jason Grimsley .05 .02
654 Joe Orsulak .05 .02
655 Jim Poole .05 .02
656 Felix Jose .05 .02
657 Denis Cook .05 .02
658 Tom Brookens .05 .02
659 Junior Ortiz .05 .02
660 Jeff Parrett .05 .02
661 Jerry Don Gleaton .05 .02
662 Brent Knackert .05 .02
663 Rance Mulliniks .05 .02
664 John Smiley .05 .02
665 Larry Andersen .05 .02
666 Willie McGee .10 .03
667 Chris Nabholz .05 .02
668 Brady Anderson .10 .03
669 D.Holmes UER RC .10 .03
19 CG's, should be 0
670 Ken Hill .05 .02
671 Gary Varsho .05 .02
672 Bill Pecota .05 .02
673 Fred Lynn .05 .02
674 Kevin D. Brown .05 .02
675 Dan Petry .05 .02
676 Mike Jackson .05 .02
677 Wally Joyner .10 .03
678 Danny Jackson .05 .02
679 Bill Haselman .05 .02
680 Mike Boddicker .05 .02
681 Mel Rojas .05 .02
682 Roberto Alomar .25 .07
683 Dave Justice ROY .05 .02
684 Chuck Crim .05 .02
685 Matt Williams .10 .03
686 Shawon Dunston .05 .02
687 Jeff Schulz .05 .02
688 John Barfield .05 .02
689 Gerald Young .05 .02
690 Luis Gonzalez RC 1.25 .35
691 Frank Wills .05 .02
692 Chuck Finley .10 .03
693 S.Alomar Jr. ROY .05 .02
694 Tim Drummond .05 .02
695 Herm Winningham .05 .02
696 Darryl Strawberry .15 .04
697 Al Leiter .10 .03
698 Karl Rhodes .05 .02
699 Stan Belinda .05 .02
700 Checklist 507-604 .05 .02
701 Lance Blankenship .05 .02
702 Willie Stargell PUZ .15 .04
703 Jim Gantner .05 .02
704 Reggie Harris .05 .02
705 Rob Ducey .05 .02
706 Tim Hulett .05 .02
707 Atlee Hammaker .05 .02
708 Xavier Hernandez .05 .02
709 Chuck McElroy .05 .02
710 John Mitchell .05 .02
711 Carlos Hernandez .05 .02
712 Geronimo Pena .05 .02
713 Jim Neidlinger .05 .02
714 John Orton .05 .02
715 Terry Leach .05 .02
716 Mike Stanton .05 .02
717 Walt Terrell .05 .02
718 Luis Aquino .05 .02
719 Bud Black .05 .02
Blue Jays uniform,
but Giants logo
720 Bob Kipper .05 .02
721 Jeff Gray .05 .02
722 Jose Rijo .05 .02
723 Curt Young .05 .02
724 Jose Vizcaino .05 .02
725 Randy Tomlin RC .05 .02
726 Junior Noboa .05 .02
727 Bob Welch CY .05 .02
728 Gary Ward .05 .02
729 Rob Deer .05 .02
(Brewers uniform,
but Tigers logo)
730 David Segui .05 .02
731 Mark Carreon .05 .02
732 Vicente Palacios .05 .02
733 Sam Horn .05 .02
734 Howard Farmer .05 .02
735 Ken Dayley .05 .02
(Cardinals uniform,
but Blue Jays logo)
736 Kelly Mann .05 .02
737 Joe Grahe RC .05 .02
738 Kelly Downs .05 .02
739 Jimmy Kremers .05 .02
740 Kevin Appier .10 .03
741 Jeff Reed .05 .02
742 Jose Rijo WS .05 .02
743 Dave Rohde .05 .02
744 Len Dykstra .15 .04
Dale Murphy
UER (No '91 Donruss
logo on card front)
745 Paul Sorrento .05 .02
746 Thomas Howard .05 .02
747 Matt Stark .05 .02
748 Harold Baines .10 .03
749 Doug Dascenzo .05 .02
750 Doug Drabek CY .05 .02
751 Gary Sheffield .10 .03
752 Terry Lee .05 .02
753 Jim Vatcher .05 .02
754 Lee Stevens .05 .02
755 Randy Veres .05 .02
756 Bill Doran .05 .02
757 Gary Wayne .05 .02
758 Pedro Munoz RC .05 .02
759 Chris Hammond .05 .02
760 Checklist 605-702 .05 .02
761 R.Henderson MVP .15 .04
762 Barry Bonds MVP .30 .09
763 Billy Hatcher WS .05 .02
UER (Line 13, on
should be one)
764 Julio Machado .05 .02
765 Jose Mesa .05 .02
766 Willie Randolph WS .05 .02
767 Scott Erickson .05 .02
768 Travis Fryman .10 .03
769 Rich Rodriguez .05 .02
770 Checklist 703-770 .05 .02
and BC1-BC22

1991 Donruss Bonus Cards

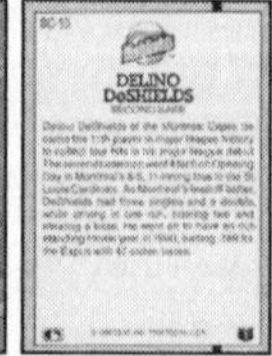

These bonus cards are standard size and were randomly inserted in Donruss packs and highlight outstanding player achievements, the first ten in the first series and the remaining 12 in the second series picking up in time beginning with Valenzuela's no-hitter and continuing until the end of the season.

Nm-Mt Ex-Mt
COMPLETE SET (22) 1.50 .45
BC1 Mark Langston .05 .02
Mike Witt
BC2 Randy Johnson .30 .09
BC3 Nolan Ryan 1.00 .30
No-Hitter
BC4 Dave Stewart .10 .03
BC5 Cecil Fielder .10 .03
BC6 Carlton Fisk .15 .04
BC7 Ryne Sandberg .40 .12
BC8 Gary Carter .15 .04
BC9 Mark McGwire .60 .18
Home Run Milestone
(Back says First
BC10 Bo Jackson .25 .07
BC11 Fernando Valenzuela .10 .03
BC12A Andy Hawkins ERR .05 .02
Pitcher
BC12B Andy Hawkins COR .05 .02
No Hits White Sox
BC13 Melido Perez .05 .02
BC14 T.Mulholland UER .05 .02
Charlie Hayes is
called Chris Hayes
BC15 Nolan Ryan 1.00 .30
300th Win
BC16 Delino DeShields .10 .03
BC17 Cal Ripken .75 .23
BC18 Eddie Murray .25 .07
BC19 George Brett .60 .18
BC20 Bobby Thigpen .05 .02
BC21 Dave Stieb .05 .02
BC22 Willie McGee .10 .03

1991 Donruss Elite

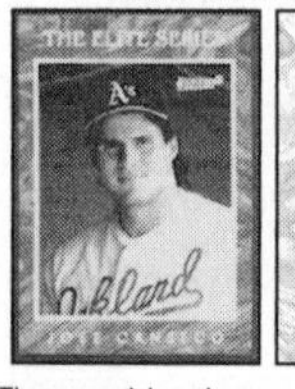

These special cards were randomly inserted in the 1991 Donruss first and second series wax packs. These cards marked the beginning of an eight-year run of Elite inserts. Production was limited to a maximum of 10,000 serial-numbered cards for each card in the Elite series, and lesser production for the Sandberg Signature (5,000) and Ryan Legend (7,500) cards. This was the first time that mainstream insert cards were ever serial numbered allowing for verifiable proof of print runs. The regular Elite cards are photos enclosed in a bronze marble borders which surround an evenly squared photo of the players. The Sandberg Signature card has a green marble border and is signed in a blue sharpie. The Nolan Ryan Legend card is a Dick Perez drawing with silver borders. The cards are all numbered on the back, 1 out of 10,000, etc.

Nm-Mt Ex-Mt
1 Barry Bonds 80.00 24.00
2 George Brett 60.00 18.00
3 Jose Canseco 40.00 12.00
4 Andre Dawson 20.00 6.00
5 Doug Drabek 20.00 6.00
6 Cecil Fielder 20.00 6.00
7 Rickey Henderson 40.00 12.00
8 Matt Williams 20.00 6.00
L1 Nolan Ryan (Legend) 100.00 30.00
S1 Ryne Sandberg 120.00 36.00
(Signature Series)

1991 Donruss Grand Slammers

This 14-card standard-size set commemorates players who hit grand slams in 1990. They were distributed in complete set form within factory sets in addition to being seeded at a rate of one per cello pack.

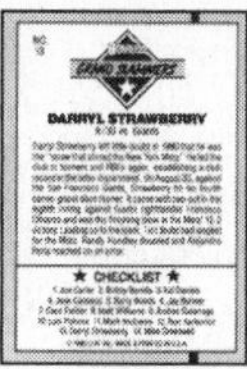

	Nm-Mt	Ex-Mt
COMPLETE SET (14)	2.00	.60
1 Joe Carter	.10	.03
2 Bobby Bonilla	.10	.03
3 Kal Daniels	.05	.02
4 Jose Canseco	.25	.07
5 Barry Bonds	.60	.18
6 Jay Buhner	.10	.03
7 Cecil Fielder	.10	.03
8 Matt Williams	.10	.03
9 Andres Galarraga	.10	.03
10 Luis Polonia	.05	.02
11 Mark McGwire	.60	.18
12 Ron Karkovice	.05	.02
13 Darryl Strawberry UER (Todd Hundley is called Randy)	.15	.04
14 Mike Greenwell	.05	.02

1991 Donruss Rookies

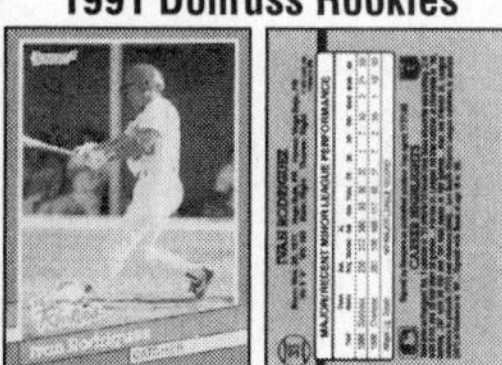

The 56-card 1991 Donruss Rookies set was issued exclusively in factory set form through hobby dealers. The cards measure the standard size and a mini puzzle featuring Hall of Famer Willie Stargell was included with the set. The fronts feature color action player photos, with white and red borders. Rookie Cards include Jeff Bagwell and Ivan Rodriguez.

	Nm-Mt	Ex-Mt
COMP.FACT.SET (56)	5.00	1.50
1 Pat Kelly RC	.05	.02
2 Rich DeLucia	.05	.02
3 Wes Chamberlain	.05	.02
4 Scott Leius	.05	.02
5 Darryl Kile	.10	.03
6 Milt Cuyler	.05	.02
7 Todd Van Poppel RC	.05	.02
8 Ray Lankford	.05	.02
9 Brian R. Hunter RC	.10	.03
10 Tony Perezchica	.05	.02
11 Ced Landrum	.05	.02
12 Dave Burba RC	.10	.03
13 Ramon Garcia	.05	.02
14 Ed Sprague	.05	.02
15 Warren Newson	.05	.02
16 Paul Faries	.05	.02
17 Luis Gonzalez	1.00	.30
18 Charles Nagy	.05	.02
19 Chris Hammond	.05	.02
20 Frank Castillo RC	.10	.03
21 Pedro Munoz	.05	.02
22 Orlando Merced RC	.05	.02
23 Jose Melendez	.05	.02
24 Kirk Dressendorfer RC	.05	.02
25 Heathcliff Slocumb RC	.10	.03
26 Doug Simons	.05	.02
27 Mike Timlin RC	.10	.03
28 Jeff Fassero RC	.10	.03
29 Mark Leiter RC	.05	.02
30 Jeff Bagwell RC	1.50	.45
31 Brian McRae	.10	.03
32 Mark Whiten	.05	.02
33 Ivan Rodriguez RC	2.00	.60
34 Wade Taylor	.05	.02
35 Darren Lewis	.05	.02
36 Mo Vaughn	.10	.03
37 Mike Remlinger	.05	.02
38 Rick Wilkins RC	.05	.02
39 Chuck Knoblauch	.10	.03
40 Kevin Morton	.05	.02
41 Carlos Rodriguez	.05	.02
42 Mark Lewis	.05	.02
43 Brent Mayne	.05	.02
44 Chris Haney RC	.05	.02
45 Denis Boucher RC	.05	.02
46 Mike Gardiner	.05	.02
47 Jeff Johnson	.05	.02
48 Dean Palmer	.10	.03
49 Chuck McElroy	.05	.02
50 Chris Jones RC	.05	.02
51 Scott Kamieniecki RC	.05	.02
52 Al Osuna RC	.05	.02
53 Rusty Meacham RC	.05	.02
54 Chito Martinez	.05	.02
55 Reggie Jefferson	.05	.02
56 Checklist 1-56	.05	.02

1991 Donruss Super DK's

For the seventh consecutive year Donruss issued a card set featuring the players used in the current year's Diamond King subset in a larger size, approximately 5" X 7". The set again featured the art work of famed sports artist Dick Perez and was available through a postpaid mail-in offer detailed on the 1991 Donruss wax packs involving $14.00 and three wax wrappers.

	Nm-Mt	Ex-Mt
COMPLETE SET (26)	30.00	9.00
1 Dave Stieb	.75	.23
2 Craig Biggio	2.00	.60
3 Cecil Fielder	.75	.23
4 Barry Bonds	5.00	1.50
5 Barry Larkin	1.50	.45
6 Dave Parker	.75	.23
7 Len Dykstra	.75	.23
8 Bobby Thigpen	.50	.15
9 Roger Clemens	5.00	1.50
10 Ron Gant	.75	.23
11 Delino DeShields	.75	.23
12 Roberto Alomar	1.50	.45
13 Sandy Alomar Jr.	.75	.23
14 Ryne Sandberg	5.00	1.50
15 Ramon Martinez	.75	.23
16 Edgar Martinez	1.00	.30
17 Dave Magadan	.50	.15
18 Matt Williams	1.00	.30
19 Rafael Palmeiro	1.50	.45
20 Bob Welch	.50	.15
21 Dave Righetti	.50	.15
22 Brian Harper	.50	.15
23 Gregg Olson	.50	.15
24 Kurt Stillwell	.50	.15
25 Pedro Guerrero	.50	.15
26 Chuck Finley	.75	.23

1992 Donruss Previews

This 12-card preview set was available only to Donruss dealers. The standard-size cards feature the same glossy color player photos on the fronts and player information on the backs as the regular series issue. The statistics only go through the 1990 season. Only the numbering of the cards on the back is different.

	Nm-Mt	Ex-Mt
COMPLETE SET (12)	200.00	60.00
1 Wade Boggs	15.00	4.50
2 Barry Bonds	25.00	7.50
3 Will Clark	15.00	4.50
4 Andre Dawson	12.00	3.60
5 Dennis Eckersley	10.00	3.00
6 Robin Ventura	8.00	2.40
7 Ken Griffey Jr.	40.00	12.00
8 Kelly Gruber	5.00	1.50
9 Ryan Klesko	10.00	3.00
10 Cal Ripken	50.00	15.00
11 Nolan Ryan	50.00	15.00
12 Todd Van Poppel	5.00	1.50

1992 Donruss

The 1992 Donruss set contains 784 standard-size cards issued in two separate series of 396. Cards were issued in first and second series foil wrapped packs in addition to hobby and retail factory sets. One of 21 different puzzle panels featuring Hall of Famer Rod Carew was inserted into each pack. The basic card design features glossy color player photos with white borders. Two-toned blue stripes overlay the top and bottom of the picture. Subsets include Rated Rookies (1-20, 397-421], All-Stars (21-30/422-431) and Highlights (33, 94, 154, 215, 276, 434, 495, 555, 616, 677). The only notable Rookie Card in the set features Scott Brosius.

	Nm-Mt	Ex-Mt
COMPLETE SET (784)	10.00	3.00
COMP.HOBBY SET (788)	10.00	3.00
COMP.RETAIL SET (788)	10.00	3.00
COMP. SERIES 1 (396)	5.00	1.50
COMP. SERIES 2 (388)	5.00	1.50
COMP.CAREW PUZZLE	1.00	.30
1 Mark Wohlers RR	.05	.02
2 Wil Cordero RR	.05	.02
3 Kyle Abbott RR	.05	.02
4 Dave Nilsson RR	.05	.02
5 Kenny Lofton RR	.25	.07
6 Luis Mercedes RR	.05	.02
7 Roger Salkeld RR	.05	.02
8 Eddie Zosky RR	.05	.02
9 Todd Van Poppel RR	.05	.02
10 Frank Seminara RR RC	.10	.03
11 Andy Ashby RR	.05	.02
12 Reggie Jefferson RR	.05	.02
13 Ryan Klesko RR	.10	.03
14 Carlos Garcia RR	.05	.02
15 John Ramos RR	.05	.02
16 Eric Karros RR	.10	.03
17 Patrick Lennon RR	.05	.02
18 E.Taubensee RR RC	.25	.07
19 Roberto Hernandez RR	.05	.02
20 D.J. Dozier RR	.05	.02
21 Dave Henderson AS	.05	.02
22 Cal Ripken AS	.40	.12
23 Wade Boggs AS	.10	.03
24 Ken Griffey Jr. AS	.25	.07
25 Jack Morris AS	.05	.02
26 Danny Tartabull AS	.05	.02
27 Cecil Fielder AS	.05	.02
28 Roberto Alomar AS	.10	.03
29 Sandy Alomar Jr. AS	.05	.02
30 Rickey Henderson AS	.15	.04
31 Ken Hill	.05	.02
32 John Habyan	.05	.02
33 Otis Nixon HL	.05	.02
34 Tim Wallach	.05	.02
35 Cal Ripken	.75	.23
36 Gary Carter	.15	.04
37 Juan Agosto	.05	.02
38 Doug Dascenzo	.05	.02
39 Kirk Gibson	.10	.03
40 Benito Santiago	.10	.03
41 Otis Nixon	.05	.02
42 Andy Allanson	.05	.02
43 Brian Holman	.05	.02
44 Dick Schofield	.05	.02
45 Dave Magadan	.05	.02
46 Rafael Palmeiro	.15	.04
47 Jody Reed	.05	.02
48 Ivan Calderon	.05	.02
49 Greg W. Harris	.05	.02
50 Chris Sabo	.05	.02
51 Paul Molitor	.15	.04
52 Robby Thompson	.05	.02
53 Dave Smith	.05	.02
54 Mark Davis	.05	.02
55 Kevin Brown	.10	.03
56 Donn Pall	.05	.02
57 Len Dykstra	.10	.03
58 Roberto Alomar	.25	.07
59 Jeff D. Robinson	.05	.02
60 Willie McGee	.10	.03
61 Jay Buhner	.10	.03
62 Mike Pagliarulo	.05	.02
63 Paul O'Neill	.15	.04
64 Hubie Brooks	.05	.02
65 Kelly Gruber	.05	.02
66 Ken Caminiti	.10	.03
67 Gary Redus	.05	.02
68 Harold Baines	.10	.03
69 Charlie Hough	.10	.03
70 B.J. Surhoff	.10	.03
71 Walt Weiss	.05	.02
72 Shawn Hillegas	.05	.02
73 Roberto Kelly	.05	.02
74 Jeff Ballard	.05	.02
75 Craig Biggio	.15	.04
76 Pat Combs	.05	.02
77 Jeff M. Robinson	.05	.02
78 Tim Belcher	.05	.02
79 Cris Carpenter	.05	.02
80 Checklist 1-79	.05	.02
81 Steve Avery	.05	.02
82 Chris James	.05	.02
83 Brian Harper	.05	.02
84 Charlie Leibrandt	.05	.02
85 Mickey Tettleton	.05	.02
86 Pete O'Brien	.05	.02
87 Danny Darwin	.05	.02
88 Bob Walk	.05	.02
89 Jeff Reardon	.10	.03
90 Bobby Rose	.05	.02
91 Danny Jackson	.05	.02
92 John Morris	.05	.02
93 Bud Black	.05	.02
94 Tommy Greene HL	.05	.02
95 Rick Aguilera	.10	.03
96 Gary Gaetti	.10	.03
97 David Cone	.10	.03
98 John Olerud	.10	.03
99 Joel Skinner	.05	.02
100 Jay Bell	.10	.03
101 Bob Milacki	.05	.02
102 Norm Charlton	.05	.02
103 Chuck Crim	.05	.02
104 Terry Steinbach	.05	.02
105 Juan Samuel	.05	.02
106 Steve Howe	.05	.02
107 Rafael Belliard	.05	.02
108 Joey Cora	.05	.02
109 Tommy Greene	.05	.02
110 Gregg Olson	.05	.02
111 Frank Tanana	.05	.02
112 Lee Smith	.10	.03
113 Greg A. Harris	.05	.02
114 Dwayne Henry	.05	.02
115 Chili Davis	.10	.03
116 Kent Mercker	.05	.02
117 Brian Barnes	.05	.02
118 Rich DeLucia	.05	.02
119 Andre Dawson	.10	.03
120 Carlos Baerga	.05	.02
121 Mike LaValliere	.05	.02
122 Jeff Gray	.05	.02
123 Bruce Hurst	.05	.02
124 Alvin Davis	.05	.02
125 John Candelaria	.05	.02
126 Matt Nokes	.05	.02
127 George Bell	.05	.02
128 Bret Saberhagen	.10	.03
129 Jeff Russell	.05	.02
130 Jim Abbott	.15	.04
131 Bill Gullickson	.05	.02
132 Todd Zeile	.05	.02
133 Dave Winfield	.10	.03
134 Wally Whitehurst	.05	.02
135 Matt Williams	.10	.03
136 Tom Browning	.05	.02
137 Marquis Grissom	.05	.02
138 Erik Hanson	.05	.02
139 Rob Dibble	.10	.03
140 Don August	.05	.02
141 Tom Henke	.05	.02
142 Dan Pasqua	.05	.02
143 George Brett	.60	.18
144 Jerald Clark	.05	.02
145 Robin Ventura	.10	.03
146 Dale Murphy	.25	.07
147 Dennis Eckersley	.10	.03
148 Eric Yelding	.05	.02
149 Mario Diaz	.05	.02
150 Casey Candaele	.05	.02
151 Steve Olin	.05	.02
152 Luis Salazar	.05	.02
153 Kevin Maas	.05	.02
154 Nolan Ryan HL	.50	.15
155 Barry Jones	.05	.02
156 Chris Hoiles	.05	.02
157 Bob Ojeda	.05	.02
158 Pedro Guerrero	.10	.03
159 Paul Assenmacher	.05	.02
160 Checklist 80-157	.05	.02
161 Mike Macfarlane	.05	.02
162 Craig Lefferts	.05	.02
163 Brian Hunter	.05	.02
164 Alan Trammell	.15	.04
165 Ken Griffey Jr.	.40	.12
166 Lance Parrish	.10	.03
167 Brian Downing	.05	.02
168 John Barfield	.05	.02
169 Jack Clark	.10	.03
170 Chris Nabholz	.05	.02
171 Tim Teufel	.05	.02
172 Chris Hammond	.05	.02
173 Robin Yount	.40	.12
174 Dave Righetti	.10	.03
175 Joe Girardi	.05	.02
176 Mike Boddicker	.05	.02
177 Dean Palmer	.10	.03
178 Greg Hibbard	.05	.02
179 Randy Ready	.05	.02
180 Devon White	.05	.02
181 Mark Eichhorn	.05	.02
182 Mike Felder	.05	.02
183 Joe Klink	.05	.02
184 Steve Bedrosian	.05	.02
185 Barry Larkin	.25	.07
186 John Franco	.10	.03
187 Ed Sprague	.05	.02
188 Mark Portugal	.05	.02
189 Jose Lind	.05	.02
190 Bob Welch	.05	.02
191 Alex Fernandez	.05	.02
192 Gary Sheffield	.10	.03
193 Rickey Henderson	.25	.07
194 Rod Nichols	.05	.02
195 Scott Kamieniecki	.05	.02
196 Mike Flanagan	.05	.02
197 Steve Finley	.10	.03
198 Darren Daulton	.10	.03
199 Leo Gomez	.05	.02
200 Mike Morgan	.05	.02
201 Bob Tewksbury	.05	.02
202 Sid Bream	.05	.02
203 Sandy Alomar Jr.	.05	.02
204 Greg Gagne	.05	.02
205 Juan Berenguer	.05	.02
206 Cecil Fielder	.10	.03
207 Randy Johnson	.25	.07
208 Tony Pena	.05	.02
209 Doug Drabek	.05	.02
210 Wade Boggs	.15	.04
211 Bryan Harvey	.05	.02
212 Jose Vizcaino	.05	.02
213 Alonzo Powell	.05	.02
214 Will Clark	.25	.07
215 Rickey Henderson HL	.15	.04
216 Jack Morris	.10	.03
217 Junior Felix	.05	.02
218 Vince Coleman	.05	.02
219 Jimmy Key	.10	.03
220 Alex Cole	.05	.02
221 Bill Landrum	.05	.02
222 Randy Milligan	.05	.02
223 Jose Rijo	.05	.02
224 Greg Vaughn	.10	.03
225 Dave Stewart	.10	.03
226 Lenny Harris	.05	.02
227 Scott Sanderson	.05	.02
228 Jeff Blauser	.05	.02
229 Ozzie Guillen	.05	.02
230 John Kruk	.10	.03
231 Bob Melvin	.05	.02
232 Milt Cuyler	.05	.02
233 Felix Jose	.05	.02
234 Ellis Burks	.10	.03
235 Pete Harnisch	.05	.02
236 Kevin Tapani	.05	.02
237 Terry Pendleton	.10	.03
238 Mark Gardner	.05	.02
239 Harold Reynolds	.10	.03
240 Checklist 158-237	.05	.02
241 Mike Harkey	.05	.02
242 Felix Fermin	.05	.02
243 Barry Bonds	.60	.18
244 Roger Clemens	.50	.15
245 Dennis Rasmussen	.05	.02
246 Jose DeLeon	.05	.02
247 Orel Hershiser	.10	.03
248 Mel Hall	.05	.02
249 Rick Wilkins	.05	.02
250 Tom Gordon	.05	.02
251 Kevin Reimer	.05	.02
252 Luis Polonia	.05	.02
253 Mike Henneman	.05	.02
254 Tom Pagnozzi	.05	.02
255 Chuck Finley	.10	.03
256 Mackey Sasser	.05	.02
257 John Burkett	.05	.02
258 Hal Morris	.05	.02
259 Larry Walker	.15	.04
260 Bill Swift	.05	.02
261 Joe Oliver	.05	.02
262 Julio Machado	.05	.02
263 Todd Stottlemyre	.05	.02
264 Matt Merullo	.05	.02
265 Brent Mayne	.05	.02
266 Thomas Howard	.05	.02
267 Lance Johnson	.05	.02
268 Terry Mulholland	.05	.02
269 Rick Honeycutt	.05	.02
270 Luis Gonzalez	.15	.04
271 Jose Guzman	.05	.02
272 Jimmy Jones	.05	.02
273 Mark Lewis	.05	.02
274 Rene Gonzales	.05	.02
275 Jeff Johnson	.05	.02
276 Dennis Martinez HL	.05	.02
277 Delino DeShields	.05	.02
278 Sam Horn	.05	.02
279 Kevin Gross	.05	.02
280 Jose Oquendo	.05	.02
281 Mark Grace	.15	.04
282 Mark Gubicza	.05	.02
283 Fred McGriff	.15	.04
284 Ron Gant	.10	.03
285 Lou Whitaker	.10	.03
286 Edgar Martinez	.15	.04
287 Ron Tingley	.05	.02
288 Kevin McReynolds	.05	.02
289 Ivan Rodriguez	.25	.07
290 Mike Gardiner	.05	.02
291 Chris Haney	.05	.02
292 Darrin Jackson	.05	.02
293 Bill Doran	.05	.02
294 Ted Higuera	.05	.02
295 Jeff Brantley	.05	.02
296 Les Lancaster	.05	.02
297 Jim Eisenreich	.05	.02
298 Ruben Sierra	.05	.02
299 Scott Radinsky	.05	.02
300 Jose DeJesus	.05	.02
301 Mike Timlin	.05	.02
302 Luis Sojo	.05	.02
303 Kelly Downs	.05	.02
304 Scott Bankhead	.05	.02
305 Pedro Munoz	.05	.02
306 Scott Scudder	.05	.02
307 Kevin Elster	.05	.02
308 Duane Ward	.05	.02
309 Darryl Kile	.10	.03
310 Orlando Merced	.05	.02
311 Dave Henderson	.05	.02
312 Tim Raines	.10	.03
313 Mark Lee	.05	.02
314 Mike Gallego	.05	.02
315 Charles Nagy	.05	.02
316 Jesse Barfield	.05	.02
317 Todd Frohwirth	.05	.02
318 Al Osuna	.05	.02
319 Darrin Fletcher	.05	.02
320 Checklist 238-316	.05	.02
321 David Segui	.05	.02
322 Stan Javier	.05	.02
323 Bryn Smith	.05	.02
324 Jeff Treadway	.05	.02
325 Mark Whiten	.05	.02
326 Kent Hrbek	.10	.03
327 Dave Justice	.10	.03
328 Tony Phillips	.05	.02
329 Rob Murphy	.05	.02
330 Kevin Morton	.05	.02
331 John Smiley	.05	.02
332 Luis Rivera	.05	.02
333 Wally Joyner	.10	.03
334 Heathcliff Slocumb	.05	.02
335 Rick Cerone	.05	.02
336 Mike Remlinger	.05	.02
337 Mike Moore	.05	.02
338 Lloyd McClendon	.05	.02
339 Al Newman	.05	.02
340 Kirk McCaskill	.05	.02
341 Howard Johnson	.05	.02
342 Greg Myers	.05	.02
343 Kal Daniels	.05	.02
344 Bernie Williams	.15	.04
345 Shane Mack	.05	.02
346 Gary Thurman	.05	.02
347 Dante Bichette	.10	.03
348 Mark McGwire	.60	.18
349 Travis Fryman	.10	.03
350 Ray Lankford	.05	.02
351 Mike Jeffcoat	.05	.02
352 Jack McDowell	.05	.02
353 Mitch Williams	.05	.02
354 Mike Devereaux	.05	.02
355 Andres Galarraga	.10	.03
356 Henry Cotto	.05	.02
357 Scott Bailes	.05	.02
358 Jeff Bagwell	.25	.07
359 Scott Leius	.05	.02
360 Zane Smith	.05	.02
361 Bill Pecota	.05	.02
362 Tony Fernandez	.05	.02
363 Glenn Braggs	.05	.02
364 Bill Spiers	.05	.02
365 Vicente Palacios	.05	.02
366 Tim Burke	.05	.02
367 Randy Tomlin	.05	.02
368 Kenny Rogers	.10	.03
369 Brett Butler	.10	.03
370 Pat Kelly	.05	.02
371 Bip Roberts	.05	.02
372 Gregg Jefferies	.05	.02
373 Kevin Bass	.05	.02
374 Ron Karkovice	.05	.02
375 Paul Gibson	.05	.02
376 Bernard Gilkey	.05	.02
377 Dave Gallagher	.05	.02
378 Bill Wegman	.05	.02
379 Pat Borders	.05	.02
380 Ed Whitson	.05	.02
381 Gilberto Reyes	.05	.02
382 Russ Swan	.05	.02
383 Andy Van Slyke	.10	.03
384 Wes Chamberlain	.05	.02
385 Steve Chitren	.05	.02
386 Greg Olson	.05	.02
387 Brian McRae	.05	.02
388 Rich Rodriguez	.05	.02
389 Steve Decker	.05	.02
390 Chuck Knoblauch	.10	.03
391 Bobby Witt	.05	.02
392 Eddie Murray	.25	.07
393 Juan Gonzalez	.25	.07
394 Scott Ruskin	.05	.02
395 Jay Howell	.05	.02
396 Checklist 317-396	.05	.02
397 Royce Clayton RR	.05	.02
398 John Jaha RR RC	.25	.07
399 Dan Wilson RR	.05	.02
400 Archie Corbin RR	.05	.02
401 Barry Manuel RR	.05	.02
402 Kim Batiste RR	.05	.02
403 Pat Mahomes RR RC	.25	.07
404 Dave Fleming RR	.05	.02
405 Jeff Juden RR	.05	.02
406 Jim Thome RR	.25	.07
407 Sam Militello RR	.05	.02
408 Jeff Nelson RR RC	.25	.07
409 Anthony Young RR	.05	.02
410 Tino Martinez RR	.15	.04
411 Jeff Mutis RR	.05	.02
412 Rey Sanchez RR RC	.25	.07
413 Chris Gardner RR	.05	.02
414 John Vander Wal RR	.05	.02
415 Reggie Sanders RR	.10	.03
416 Brian Williams RR RC	.10	.03
417 Mo Sanford RR	.05	.02
418 D.Weathers RR RC	.10	.03
419 Hector Fajardo RR RC	.10	.03
420 Steve Foster RR	.05	.02
421 Lance Dickson RR	.05	.02
422 Andre Dawson AS	.05	.02
423 Ozzie Smith AS	.25	.07
424 Chris Sabo AS	.05	.02
425 Tony Gwynn AS	.15	.04
426 Tom Glavine AS	.10	.03
427 Bobby Bonilla AS	.05	.02
428 Will Clark AS	.10	.03
429 Ryne Sandberg AS	.25	.07
430 Benito Santiago AS	.05	.02
431 Ivan Calderon AS	.05	.02
432 Ozzie Smith	.40	.12
433 Tim Leary	.05	.02
434 Bret Saberhagen HL	.05	.02
435 Mel Rojas	.05	.02
436 Ben McDonald	.05	.02
437 Tim Crews	.05	.02

438 Rex Hudler .05 .02
439 Chico Walker .05 .02
440 Kurt Stillwell .05 .02
441 Tony Gwynn .30 .09
442 John Smoltz .15 .04
443 Lloyd Moseby .05 .02
444 Mike Schooler .05 .02
445 Joe Grahe .05 .02
446 Dwight Gooden .15 .04
447 Oil Can Boyd .05 .02
448 John Marzano .05 .02
449 Bret Barberie .05 .02
450 Mike Maddux .05 .02
451 Jeff Reed .05 .02
452 Dale Sveum .05 .02
453 Jose Uribe .05 .02
454 Bob Scanlan .05 .02
455 Kevin Appier .10 .03
456 Jeff Huson .05 .02
457 Ken Patterson .05 .02
458 Ricky Jordan .05 .02
459 Tom Candiotti .05 .02
460 Lee Stevens .05 .02
461 Rod Beck RC .25 .07
462 Dave Valle .05 .02
463 Scott Erickson .05 .02
464 Chris Jones .05 .02
465 Mark Carreon .05 .02
466 Rob Ducey .05 .02
467 Jim Corsi .05 .02
468 Jeff King .05 .02
469 Curt Young .05 .02
470 Bo Jackson .25 .07
471 Chris Bosio .05 .02
472 Jamie Quirk .05 .02
473 Jesse Orosco .05 .02
474 Alvaro Espinoza .05 .02
475 Joe Orsulak .05 .02
476 Checklist 397-477 .05 .02
477 Gerald Young .05 .02
478 Wally Backman .05 .02
479 Juan Bell .05 .02
480 Mike Scioscia .05 .02
481 Omar Olivares .05 .02
482 Francisco Cabrera .05 .02
483 Greg Swindell UER .05 .02
(Shown on Indians, but listed on Reds)
484 Terry Leach .05 .02
485 Tommy Gregg .05 .02
486 Scott Aldred .05 .02
487 Greg Briley .05 .02
488 Phil Plantier .05 .02
489 Curtis Wilkerson .05 .02
490 Tom Brunansky .05 .02
491 Mike Fetters .05 .02
492 Frank Castillo .05 .02
493 Joe Boever .05 .02
494 Kirt Manwaring .05 .02
495 Wilson Alvarez HL .05 .02
496 Gene Larkin .05 .02
497 Gary DiSarcina .05 .02
498 Frank Viola .10 .03
499 Manuel Lee .05 .02
500 Albert Belle .10 .03
501 Stan Belinda .05 .02
502 Dwight Evans .10 .03
503 Eric Davis .10 .03
504 Darren Holmes .05 .02
505 Mike Bordick .05 .02
506 Dave Hansen .05 .02
507 Lee Guetterman .05 .02
508 Keith Mitchell .05 .02
509 Melido Perez .05 .02
510 Dickie Thon .05 .02
511 Mark Williamson .05 .02
512 Mark Salas .05 .02
513 Milt Thompson .05 .02
514 Mo Vaughn .10 .03
515 Jim Deshaies .05 .02
516 Rich Garces .05 .02
517 Lonnie Smith .05 .02
518 Spike Owen .05 .02
519 Tracy Jones .05 .02
520 Greg Maddux .40 .12
521 Carlos Martinez .05 .02
522 Neal Heaton .05 .02
523 Mike Greenwell .05 .02
524 Andy Benes .05 .02
525 Jeff Schaefer UER .05 .02
(Photo actually Tino Martinez)
526 Mike Sharperson .05 .02
527 Wade Taylor .05 .02
528 Jerome Walton .05 .02
529 Storm Davis .05 .02
530 Jose Hernandez RC .40 .12
531 Mark Langston .05 .02
532 Rob Deer .05 .02
533 Geronimo Pena .05 .02
534 Juan Guzman .05 .02
535 Pete Schourek .05 .02
536 Todd Benzinger .05 .02
537 Billy Hatcher .05 .02
538 Tom Foley .05 .02
539 Dave Cochrane .05 .02
540 Mariano Duncan .05 .02
541 Edwin Nunez .05 .02
542 Rance Mulliniks .05 .02
543 Carlton Fisk .15 .04
544 Luis Aquino .05 .02
545 Ricky Bones .05 .02
546 Craig Grebeck .05 .02
547 Charlie Hayes .05 .02
548 Jose Canseco .25 .07
549 Andujar Cedeno .05 .02
550 Geno Petralli .05 .02
551 Javier Ortiz .05 .02
552 Rudy Seanez .05 .02
553 Rich Gedman .05 .02
554 Eric Plunk .05 .02
555 Nolan Ryan HL .40 .12
(With Rich Gossage)
556 Checklist 478-555 .05 .02
557 Greg Colbrunn .05 .02
558 Chito Martinez .05 .02
559 Darryl Strawberry .15 .04
560 Luis Alicea .05 .02
561 Dwight Smith .05 .02
562 Terry Shumpert .05 .02
563 Jim Vatcher .05 .02
564 Deion Sanders .15 .04
565 Walt Terrell .05 .02
566 Dave Burba .05 .02
567 Dave Howard .05 .02
568 Todd Hundley .05 .02
569 Jack Daugherty .05 .02
570 Scott Cooper .05 .02
571 Bill Sampen .05 .02
572 Jose Melendez .05 .02
573 Freddie Benavides .05 .02
574 Jim Gantner .05 .02
575 Trevor Wilson .05 .02
576 Ryne Sandberg .40 .12
577 Kevin Seitzer .05 .02
578 Gerald Alexander .05 .02
579 Mike Huff .05 .02
580 Von Hayes .05 .02
581 Derek Bell .10 .03
582 Mike Stanley .05 .02
583 Kevin Mitchell .05 .02
584 Mike Jackson .05 .02
585 Dan Gladden .05 .02
586 Ted Power UER .05 .02
(Wrong year given for signing with Reds)
587 Jeff Innis .05 .02
588 Bob MacDonald .05 .02
589 Jose Tolentino .05 .02
590 Bob Patterson .05 .02
591 Scott Brosius RC .50 .15
592 Frank Thomas .25 .07
593 Darryl Hamilton .05 .02
594 Kirk Dressendorfer .05 .02
595 Jeff Shaw .05 .02
596 Don Mattingly .60 .18
597 Glenn Davis .05 .02
598 Andy Mota .05 .02
599 Jason Grimsley .05 .02
600 Jim Poole .05 .02
601 Jim Gott .05 .02
602 Stan Royer .05 .02
603 Marvin Freeman .05 .02
604 Denis Boucher .05 .02
605 Denny Neagle .10 .03
606 Mark Lemke .05 .02
607 Jerry Don Gleaton .05 .02
608 Brent Knackert .05 .02
609 Carlos Quintana .05 .02
610 Bobby Bonilla .10 .03
611 Joe Hesketh .05 .02
612 Daryl Boston .05 .02
613 Shawon Dunston .05 .02
614 Danny Cox .05 .02
615 Darren Lewis .05 .02
616 Braves No-Hitter UER .05 .02
Kent Mercker
(Misspelled Merker on card front)
Alejandro Pena
Mark Wohlers
617 Kirby Puckett .25 .07
618 Franklin Stubbs .05 .02
619 Chris Donnels .05 .02
620 David Wells UER .10 .03
(Career Highlights in black not red)
621 Mike Aldrete .05 .02
622 Bob Kipper .05 .02
623 Anthony Telford .05 .02
624 Randy Myers .05 .02
625 Willie Randolph .10 .03
626 Joe Slusarski .05 .02
627 John Wetteland .10 .03
628 Greg Cadaret .05 .02
629 Tom Glavine .15 .04
630 Wilson Alvarez .05 .02
631 Wally Ritchie .05 .02
632 Mike Mussina .25 .07
633 Mark Leiter .05 .02
634 Gerald Perry .05 .02
635 Matt Young .05 .02
636 Checklist 556-635 .05 .02
637 Scott Hemond .05 .02
638 David West .05 .02
639 Jim Clancy .05 .02
640 Doug Platt UER .05 .02
(Not born in 1955 as on card; incorrect info on How Acquired)
641 Omar Vizquel .10 .03
642 Rick Sutcliffe .10 .03
643 Glenallen Hill .05 .02
644 Gary Varsho .05 .02
645 Tony Fossas .05 .02
646 Jack Howell .05 .02
647 Jim Campanis .05 .02
648 Chris Gwynn .05 .02
649 Jim Leyritz .05 .02
650 Chuck McElroy .05 .02
651 Sean Berry .05 .02
652 Donald Harris .05 .02
653 Don Slaught .05 .02
654 Rusty Meacham .05 .02
655 Scott Terry .05 .02
656 Ramon Martinez .05 .02
657 Keith Miller .05 .02
658 Ramon Garcia .05 .02
659 Milt Hill .05 .02
660 Steve Frey .05 .02
661 Bob McClure .05 .02
662 Ced Landrum .05 .02
663 Doug Henry RC .10 .03
664 Candy Maldonado .05 .02
665 Carl Willis .05 .02
666 Jeff Montgomery .05 .02
667 Craig Shipley .05 .02
668 Warren Newson .05 .02
669 Mickey Morandini .05 .02
670 Brook Jacoby .05 .02
671 Ryan Bowen .05 .02
672 Bill Krueger .05 .02
673 Rob Mallicoat .05 .02
674 Doug Jones .05 .02
675 Scott Livingstone .05 .02
676 Danny Tartabull .05 .02
677 Joe Carter HL .05 .02
678 Cecil Espy .05 .02
679 Randy Velarde .05 .02
680 Bruce Ruffin .05 .02
681 Ted Wood .05 .02
682 Dan Plesac .05 .02
683 Eric Bullock .05 .02
684 Junior Ortiz .05 .02
685 Dave Hollins .05 .02
686 Dennis Martinez .10 .03
687 Larry Andersen .05 .02
688 Doug Simons .05 .02
689 Tim Spehr .05 .02
690 Calvin Jones .05 .02
691 Mark Guthrie .05 .02
692 Alfredo Griffin .05 .02
693 Joe Carter .10 .03
694 Terry Mathews .05 .02
695 Pascual Perez .05 .02
696 Gene Nelson .05 .02
697 Gerald Williams .05 .02
698 Chris Cron .05 .02
699 Steve Buechele .05 .02
700 Paul McClellan .05 .02
701 Jim Lindeman .05 .02
702 Francisco Oliveras .05 .02
703 Rob Maurer .05 .02
704 Pat Hentgen .05 .02
705 Jaime Navarro .05 .02
706 Mike Magnante RC .10 .03
707 Nolan Ryan 1.00 .30
708 Bobby Thigpen .05 .02
709 John Cerutti .05 .02
710 Steve Wilson .05 .02
711 Hensley Meulens .05 .02
712 Rheal Cormier .05 .02
713 Scott Bradley .05 .02
714 Mitch Webster .05 .02
715 Roger Mason .05 .02
716 Checklist 636-716 .05 .02
717 Jeff Fassero .05 .02
718 Cal Eldred .05 .02
719 Sid Fernandez .05 .02
720 Bob Zupcic RC .10 .03
721 Jose Offerman .05 .02
722 Cliff Brantley .05 .02
723 Ron Darling .05 .02
724 Dave Stieb .05 .02
725 Hector Villanueva .05 .02
726 Mike Hartley .05 .02
727 Arthur Rhodes .05 .02
728 Randy Bush .05 .02
729 Steve Sax .05 .02
730 Dave Otto .05 .02
731 John Wehner .05 .02
732 Dave Martinez .05 .02
733 Ruben Amaro .05 .02
734 Billy Ripken .05 .02
735 Steve Farr .05 .02
736 Shawn Abner .05 .02
737 Gil Heredia RC .25 .07
738 Ron Jones .05 .02
739 Tony Castillo .05 .02
740 Sammy Sosa .40 .12
741 Julio Franco .10 .03
742 Tim Naehring .05 .02
743 Steve Wapnick .05 .02
744 Craig Wilson .05 .02
745 Darrin Chapin .05 .02
746 Chris George .05 .02
747 Mike Simms .05 .02
748 Rosario Rodriguez .05 .02
749 Skeeter Barnes .05 .02
750 Roger McDowell .05 .02
751 Dann Howitt .05 .02
752 Paul Sorrento .05 .02
753 Braulio Castillo .05 .02
754 Yorkis Perez .05 .02
755 Willie Fraser .05 .02
756 Jeremy Hernandez RC .10 .03
757 Curt Schilling .15 .04
758 Steve Lyons .05 .02
759 Dave Anderson .05 .02
760 Willie Banks .05 .02
761 Mark Leonard .05 .02
762 Jack Armstrong .05 .02
(Listed on Indians, but shown on Reds)
763 Scott Servais .05 .02
764 Ray Stephens .05 .02
765 Junior Noboa .05 .02
766 Jim Olander .05 .02
767 Joe Magrane .05 .02
768 Lance Blankenship .05 .02
769 Mike Humphreys .05 .02
770 Jarvis Brown .05 .02
771 Damon Berryhill .05 .02
772 Alejandro Pena .05 .02
773 Jose Mesa .05 .02
774 Gary Cooper .05 .02
775 Carney Lansford .10 .03
776 Mike Bielecki .05 .02
Shown on Cubs, but listed on Braves
777 Charlie O'Brien .05 .02
778 Carlos Hernandez .05 .02
779 Howard Farmer .05 .02
780 Mike Stanton .05 .02
781 Reggie Harris .05 .02
782 Xavier Hernandez .05 .02
783 Bryan Hickerson RC .10 .03
784 Checklist 717-784 and BC1-BC8 .05 .02

1992 Donruss Bonus Cards

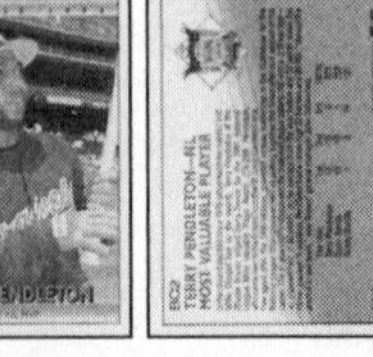

The 1992 Donruss Bonus Cards set contains eight standard-size. The cards are numbered on the back and checklisted below accordingly. The cards were randomly inserted in foil packs of 1992 Donruss baseball cards.

	Nm-Mt	Ex-Mt
COMPLETE SET (8)	2.00	.60
BC1 Cal Ripken MVP	.75	.23
BC2 Terry Pendleton MVP	.10	.03
BC3 Roger Clemens CY	.50	.15
BC4 Tom Glavine CY	.15	.04
BC5 C.Knoblauch ROY	.10	.03
BC6 Jeff Bagwell ROY	.25	.07
BC7 Colorado Rockies	.05	.02
BC8 Florida Marlins	.05	.02

1992 Donruss Diamond Kings

These standard-size cards were randomly inserted in 1992 Donruss I foil packs (cards 1-13 and the checklist only) and in 1992 Donruss II foil packs (cards 14-26). The decision at the time to transform the popular Diamond King subset into an limieted distribution insert set created notable groups of supporters and dissenters. The attractive fronts feature player portraits by noted sports artist Dick Perez. The words "Donruss Diamond Kings" are superimposed at the card top in a gold-trimmed blue and black banner, with the player's name in a similarly designed black stripe at the card bottom. A very limited amount of 5" by 7" cards were produced. These issues were never formally released but these cards were intended to be premiums in retail products.

	Nm-Mt	Ex-Mt
COMPLETE SET (27)	20.00	6.00
COMPLETE SERIES 1 (14)	16.00	4.80
COMPLETE SERIES 2 (13)	4.00	1.20
DK1 Paul Molitor	1.25	.35
DK2 Will Clark	2.00	.60
DK3 Joe Carter	.75	.23
DK4 Julio Franco	.75	.23
DK5 Cal Ripken	6.00	1.80
DK6 Dave Justice	.75	.23
DK7 George Bell	.40	.12
DK8 Frank Thomas	2.00	.60
DK9 Wade Boggs	1.25	.35
DK10 Scott Sanderson	.40	.12
DK11 Jeff Bagwell	2.00	.60
DK12 John Kruk	.75	.23
DK13 Felix Jose	.40	.12
DK14 Harold Baines	.75	.23
DK15 Dwight Gooden	1.25	.35
DK16 Brian McRae	.40	.12
DK17 Jay Bell	.75	.23
DK18 Brett Butler	.75	.23
DK19 Hal Morris	.40	.12
DK20 Mark Langston	.40	.12
DK21 Scott Erickson	.40	.12
DK22 Randy Johnson	2.00	.60
DK23 Greg Swindell	.40	.12
DK24 Dennis Martinez	.75	.23
DK25 Tony Phillips	.40	.12
DK26 Fred McGriff	1.25	.35
DK27 Checklist 1-26 DP (Dick Perez)	.40	.12

1992 Donruss Elite

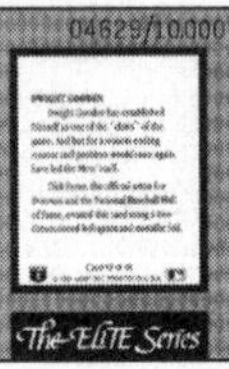

These cards were random inserts in 1992 Donruss first and second series foil packs. Like the previous year, the cards were indidvidually numbered of 10,000. Card fronts feature dramatic prismatic borders encasing a full color action or posed shot of the player. The numbering of the set is essentially a continuation of the series started the year before. Only 5,000 Ripken Signature Series cards were printed and only 7,500 Henderson Legends cards were printed. The complete set price does not include cards L2 and S2.

	Nm-Mt	Ex-Mt
9 Wade Boggs	25.00	7.50
10 Joe Carter	15.00	4.50
11 Will Clark	40.00	12.00
12 Dwight Gooden	25.00	7.50
13 Ken Griffey Jr.	40.00	12.00
14 Tony Gwynn	30.00	9.00
15 Howard Johnson	15.00	4.50
16 Terry Pendleton	15.00	4.50
17 Kirby Puckett	25.00	7.50
18 Frank Thomas	25.00	7.50
L2 Rickey Henderson (Legend Series)	25.00	7.50
S2 Cal Ripken (Signature Series)	200.00	60.00

1992 Donruss Update

Four cards from this 22-card standard-size set were included in each retail factory set. Card design is identical to regular issue 1992 Donruss cards except for the U-prefixed numbering on back. Card numbers U1-U6 are Rated Rookie cards, while card numbers U7-U9 are Highlights cards. A tough early Kenny Lofton card, his first as a member of the Cleveland Indians, highlights this set.

	Nm-Mt	Ex-Mt
COMPLETE SET (22)	50.00	15.00
U1 Pat Listach RR	1.50	.45
U2 Andy Stankiewicz RR	1.00	.30
U3 Brian Jordan RR	4.00	1.20
U4 Dan Walters RR	1.00	.30
U5 Chad Curtis RR	1.50	.45
U6 Kenny Lofton RR	1.50	.45
U7 Mark McGwire HL	10.00	3.00
U8 Eddie Murray HL	4.00	1.20
U9 Jeff Reardon HL	1.50	.45
U10 Frank Viola	1.50	.45
U11 Gary Sheffield	1.50	.45
U12 George Bell	1.00	.30
U13 Rick Sutcliffe	1.50	.45
U14 Wally Joyner	1.50	.45
U15 Kevin Seitzer	1.00	.30
U16 Bill Krueger	1.00	.30
U17 Danny Tartabull	1.00	.30
U18 Dave Winfield	1.50	.45
U19 Gary Carter	2.50	.75
U20 Bobby Bonilla	1.50	.45
U21 Cory Snyder	1.00	.30
U22 Bill Swift	1.00	.30

1992 Donruss Rookies

After six years of issuing "The Rookies" as a 56-card boxed set, Donruss expanded it to a 132-card standard-size set and distributed the cards in hobby and retail foil packs. The card design is the same as the 1992 Donruss regular issue except that the two-tone blue color bars have been replaced by green, as in the previous six Donruss Rookies sets. The cards are arranged in alphabetical order and numbered on the back. Rookie Cards in this set include Jeff Kent, Manny Ramirez and Eric Young. In addition an early card of Pedro Martinez is featured.

	Nm-Mt	Ex-Mt
COMPLETE SET (132)	10.00	3.00
1 Kyle Abbott	.05	.02
2 Troy Afenir	.05	.02
3 Rich Amaral RC	.10	.03
4 Ruben Amaro	.05	.02
5 Billy Ashley RC	.10	.03
6 Pedro Astacio RC	.25	.07
7 Jim Austin	.05	.02
8 Robert Ayrault	.05	.02
9 Kevin Baez	.05	.02
10 Esteban Beltre	.05	.02
11 Brian Bohanon	.05	.02
12 Kent Bottenfield RC	.25	.07
13 Jeff Branson	.05	.02
14 Brad Brink	.05	.02
15 John Briscoe	.05	.02
16 Doug Brocail RC	.10	.03
17 Rico Brogna	.05	.02
18 J.T. Bruett	.05	.02
19 Jacob Brumfield	.05	.02
20 Jim Bullinger	.05	.02
21 Kevin Campbell	.05	.02
22 Pedro Castellano RC	.10	.03
23 Mike Christopher	.05	.02
24 Archi Cianfrocco RC	.10	.03
25 Mark Clark RC	.10	.03
26 Craig Colbert	.05	.02
27 Victor Cole	.05	.02
28 Steve Cooke RC	.10	.03
29 Tim Costo	.05	.02
30 Chad Curtis RC	.25	.07
31 Doug Davis	.05	.02
32 Gary DiSarcina	.05	.02
33 John Doherty RC	.10	.03
34 Mike Draper	.05	.02
35 Monty Fariss	.05	.02
36 Bien Figueroa	.05	.02
37 John Flaherty	.05	.02
38 Tim Fortugno	.05	.02
39 Eric Fox RC	.10	.03
40 Jeff Frye RC	.10	.03
41 Ramon Garcia	.05	.02
42 Brent Gates RC	.10	.03
43 Tom Goodwin	.05	.02
44 Buddy Groom RC	.10	.03
45 Jeff Grotewold	.05	.02
46 Juan Guerrero	.05	.02
47 Johnny Guzman RC	.10	.03
48 Shawn Hare RC	.10	.03
49 Ryan Hawblitzel RC	.10	.03
50 Bert Heffernan	.05	.02
51 Butch Henry	.05	.02
52 Cesar Hernandez RC	.10	.03
53 Vince Horsman	.05	.02
54 Steve Hosey	.05	.02
55 Pat Howell	.05	.02
56 Peter Hoy	.05	.02
57 Jonathan Hurst RC	.10	.03
58 Mark Hutton RC	.10	.03
59 Shawn Jeter RC	.10	.03
60 Joel Johnston	.05	.02
61 Jeff Kent RC	1.00	.30
62 Kurt Knudsen RC	.10	.03
63 Kevin Koslofski	.05	.02
64 Danny Leon	.05	.02
65 Jesse Levis	.05	.02
66 Tom Marsh	.05	.02
67 Ed Martel	.05	.02
68 Al Martin RC	.25	.07

Card	Nm-Mt	Ex-Mt
69 Pedro Martinez	2.00	.60
70 Derrick May	.05	.02
71 Matt Maysey	.05	.02
72 Russ McGinnis	.05	.02
73 Tim McIntosh	.05	.02
74 Jim McNamara	.05	.02
75 Jeff McNeely	.05	.02
76 Rusty Meacham	.05	.02
77 Tony Menendez	.05	.02
78 Henry Mercedes	.05	.02
79 Paul Miller	.05	.02
80 Joe Millette	.05	.02
81 Blas Minor	.05	.02
82 Dennis Moeller	.05	.02
83 Raul Mondesi	.25	.07
84 Rob Natal	.05	.02
85 Troy Neel RC	.10	.03
86 David Nied RC	.10	.03
87 Jerry Nielson	.05	.02
88 Donovan Osborne	.05	.02
89 John Patterson RC	.10	.03
90 Roger Pavlik RC	.10	.03
91 Dan Peltier	.05	.02
92 Jim Pena	.05	.02
93 William Pennyfeather	.05	.02
94 Mike Perez	.05	.02
95 Hipolito Pichardo RC	.10	.03
96 Greg Pirkl RC	.10	.03
97 Harvey Pulliam	.05	.02
98 Manny Ramirez RC	2.50	.75
99 Pat Rapp RC	.10	.03
100 Jeff Reboulet	.05	.02
101 Darren Reed	.05	.02
102 Shane Reynolds RC	.25	.07
103 Bill Risley	.05	.02
104 Ben Rivera	.05	.02
105 Henry Rodriguez	.05	.02
106 Rico Rossy	.05	.02
107 Johnny Ruffin	.05	.02
108 Steve Scarsone	.05	.02
109 Tim Scott	.05	.02
110 Steve Shifflett	.05	.02
111 Dave Silvestri	.05	.02
112 Matt Stairs RC	.25	.07
113 William Suero	.05	.02
114 Jeff Tackett	.05	.02
115 Eddie Taubensee	.10	.03
116 Rick Trlicek RC	.10	.03
117 Scooter Tucker	.05	.02
118 Shane Turner	.05	.02
119 Julio Valera	.05	.02
120 Paul Wagner RC	.10	.03
121 Tim Wakefield RC	.50	.15
122 Mike Walker	.05	.02
123 Bruce Walton	.05	.02
124 Lenny Webster	.05	.02
125 Bob Wickman	.05	.02
126 Mike Williams RC	.25	.07
127 Kerry Woodson	.05	.02
128 Eric Young RC	.25	.07
129 Kevin Young RC	.25	.07
130 Pete Young	.05	.02
131 Checklist 1-66	.05	.02
132 Checklist 67-132	.05	.02

1992 Donruss Rookies Phenoms

This 20-card standard size set features a selection young prospects. The first twelve cards were randomly inserted into 1992 Donruss The Rookies 12-card foil packs. The last eight were inserted one per 1992 Donruss Rookies 30-card jumbo pack. Each glossy card front features a black border surrounding a full color photo and gold foil type. One of only three MLB-licensed cards of Mike Piazza issued in 1992 is featured within this set.

	Nm-Mt	Ex-Mt
COMP.FOIL SET (12)	30.00	9.00
COMP.JUMBO SET (8)	10.00	3.00
COMM.FOIL (BC1-BC12)	1.00	.30
COMMON (BC13-BC20)	1.00	.30
BC1 Moises Alou	1.50	.45
BC2 Bret Boone	1.50	.45
BC3 Jeff Conine	1.50	.45
BC4 Dave Fleming	1.00	.30
BC5 Tyler Green	1.00	.30
BC6 Eric Karros	1.50	.45
BC7 Pat Listach	1.50	.45
BC8 Kenny Lofton	1.50	.45
BC9 Mike Piazza	20.00	6.00
BC10 Tim Salmon	1.50	.45
BC11 Andy Stankiewicz	1.00	.30
BC12 Dan Walters	1.00	.30
BC13 Ramon Caraballo	1.00	.30
BC14 Brian Jordan	2.00	.60
BC15 Ryan Klesko	1.50	.45
BC16 Sam Militello	1.00	.30
BC17 Frank Seminara	1.00	.30
BC18 Salomon Torres	1.00	.30
BC19 John Valentin	1.50	.45
BC20 Wil Cordero	1.00	.30

1992 Donruss Coke Ryan

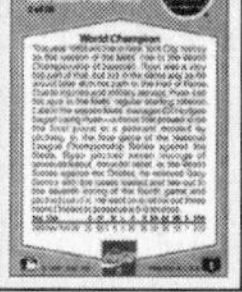

This 26-card standard-size set was produced by Donruss to commemorate each year of Ryan's professional baseball career. Both sides of the card bear the Coca-Cola logo, and four-card cello packs with one Ryan card and three regular issue 1992 Donruss cards were inserted in 12-can packs of Coca-Cola classic, caffeine-free Coca-Cola classic, diet Coke, caffeine-free diet Coke, Sprite, and diet Sprite. An offer on the back panel of specially marked Coca-Cola multi-packs (and the labels of two-liter bottles) made available boxed factory sets through a mail-in offer for 8.95 and UPC symbols from multi-pack wraps of Coca-Cola products. The promotion ran from April to June and covered nearly 90 percent of the country. The cards are numbered on the back in chronolgical order; each year Nolan is pictured with his then-current team, New York Mets (NYM), California Angels (CA), Houston Astros (HA), Texas Rangers (TR).

	Nm-Mt	Ex-Mt
COMPLETE SET (26)	10.00	3.00
COMMON CARD (1-26)	.50	.15

1992 Donruss Cracker Jack I

This 36-card set is the first of two series produced by Donruss for Cracker Jack, and the micro cards were protected by a paper sleeve and inserted into specially marked boxes of Cracker Jack. A side panel listed all 36 players in series I. The micro cards measure approximately 1 1/4" by 1 3/4". The front design is the same as the Donruss regular issue cards, only different color player photos are displayed. The backs, however, have a completely different design than the regular issue Donruss cards; they are horizontally oriented and present biography, major league pitching (or batting) record, and brief career summary inside navy blue borders. The cards are numbered on the back. On the paper sleeve was a mail-in offer for a mini card album with six top loading plastic pages for 4.95 per album.

	Nm-Mt	Ex-Mt
COMPLETE SET (36)	10.00	3.00
1 Dennis Eckersley	.50	.15
2 Jeff Bagwell	1.00	.30
3 Jim Abbott	.10	.03
4 Steve Avery	.05	.02
5 Kelly Gruber	.05	.02
6 Ozzie Smith	1.00	.30
7 Lance Dickson	.05	.02
8 Robin Yount	.50	.15
9 Brett Butler	.10	.03
10 Sandy Alomar Jr.	.10	.03
11 Travis Fryman	.10	.03
12 Ken Griffey Jr.	2.00	.60
13 Cal Ripken	2.50	.75
14 Will Clark	.25	.07
15 Nolan Ryan	2.50	.75
16 Tony Gwynn	1.00	.30
17 Roger Clemens	1.25	.35
18 Wes Chamberlain	.05	.02
19 Barry Larkin	.20	.06
20 Brian McRae	.05	.02
21 Marquis Grissom	.10	.03
22 Cecil Fielder	.10	.03
23 Dwight Gooden	.10	.03
24 Chuck Knoblauch	.20	.06
25 Jose Canseco	.50	.15
26 Terry Pendleton	.05	.02
27 Ivan Rodriguez	1.00	.30
28 Ryne Sandberg	.50	.15
29 Kent Hrbek	.10	.03
30 Ramon Martinez	.10	.03
31 Todd Zeile	.10	.03
32 Hal Morris	.05	.02
33 Robin Ventura	.20	.06
34 Doug Drabek	.05	.02
35 Frank Thomas	.50	.15
36 Don Mattingly	1.25	.35

1992 Donruss Cracker Jack II

This 36-card set is the second of two series produced by Donruss for Cracker Jack. The mini cards were protected by a paper sleeve and inserted into specially marked boxes of Cracker Jacks. A side panel listed all 36 players in series II. The micro cards measure 1 1/4" by 1 3/4". The front design is the same as the Donruss regular issue cards, only different color player photos are displayed. The backs, however, have a completely different design than the regular issue Donruss cards; they are horizontally oriented and present biography, major league pitching (or batting) record, and brief career summary inside red borders. The cards are numbered on the back. On the paper sleeve was a mail-in offer for a mini card album with six top loading plastic pages for 4.95 per album.

	Nm-Mt	Ex-Mt
COMPLETE SET (36)	6.00	1.80
1 Craig Biggio	.15	.04
2 Tom Glavine	.10	.03
3 David Justice	.25	.07
4 Lee Smith	.10	.03
5 Mark Grace	.25	.07
6 George Bell	.05	.02
7 Darryl Strawberry	.10	.03
8 Eric Davis	.10	.03
9 Ivan Calderon	.05	.02
10 Royce Clayton	.05	.02
11 Matt Williams	.15	.04
12 Fred McGriff	.15	.04
13 Len Dykstra	.10	.03
14 Barry Bonds	1.00	.30
15 Reggie Sanders	.10	.03
16 Chris Sabo	.05	.02
17 Howard Johnson	.05	.02
18 Bobby Bonilla	.05	.02
19 Rickey Henderson	.75	.23
20 Mark Langston	.05	.02
21 Joe Carter	.10	.03
22 Paul Molitor	.50	.15
23 Glenallen Hill	.05	.02
24 Edgar Martinez	.15	.04
25 Gregg Olson	.05	.02
26 Ruben Sierra	.10	.03
27 Julio Franco	.10	.03
28 Phil Plantier	.05	.02
29 Wade Boggs	.40	.12
30 George Brett	1.00	.30
31 Alan Trammell	.15	.04
32 Kirby Puckett	.50	.15
33 Scott Erickson	.05	.02
34 Matt Nokes	.05	.02
35 Danny Tartabull	.05	.02
36 Jack McDowell	.05	.02

1992 Donruss McDonald's

This 33-card standard-size set was produced by Donruss for distribution by McDonald's Restaurants in the Toronto area. For 39 cents with the purchase of any sandwich or breakfast entree, the collector received a four-card pack featuring three cards from the MVP series and one card from the Blue Jays Gold series. A player from each MLB team is represented in the numbered 26-card MVP subset. Checklist cards were also randomly inserted throughout the foil packs. In addition, 1,000 packs included a randomly inserted prize card. By filling it out, answering the question and sending it to the address on the card, the winner received one of 1,000 numbered cards autographed by Roberto Alomar. The cards have the same design as the regular issue cards, with color action photos bordered in white and accented by blue stripes above and below the picture. One difference is an MVP logo with the McDonald's "Golden Arches" trademark on the front. The backs present a head shot, biography, recent major league performance statistics, career highlights and the card number ("X of 26"). Again, the McDonald's "Golden Arches" trademark appears on the back alongside the other logos. One card from the six-card gold subset (of Toronto Blue Jays) was included in each 1992 Donruss McDonald's MVP four-card foil pack. The gold card fronts feature full-bleed color player photos accented by goil foil stamping. The gold cards are listed below with a "G" prefix below for reference& although a "G" prefix does not appear anywhere on the cards. The player's name appears in a dark blue bar that overlays the bottom gold foil border stripe. In a horizontal format, the backs carry biography, contract status information, recent major league performance statistics and career highlights. As with the MVP series, the McDonald's "Golden Arches" trademark adorns both sides of the card.

	Nm-Mt	Ex-Mt
COMPLETE SET (33)	15.00	4.50
COMMON CARD (1-26)	.10	.03
COMMON BJ (G1-G6)	.50	.15
1 Cal Ripken	2.50	.75
2 Frank Thomas	.50	.15
3 George Brett	1.25	.35
4 Roberto Kelly	.10	.03
5 Nolan Ryan	2.50	.75
6 Ryne Sandberg	.75	.23
7 Darryl Strawberry	.20	.06
8 Len Dykstra	.20	.06
9 Fred McGriff	.30	.09
10 Roger Clemens	1.25	.35
11 Sandy Alomar Jr.	.20	.06
12 Robin Yount	.50	.15
13 Jose Canseco	.75	.23
14 Jimmy Key	.20	.06
15 Barry Larkin	.40	.12
16 Dennis Martinez	.20	.06
17 Andy Van Slyke	.20	.06
18 Will Clark	.50	.15
19 Mark Langston	.10	.03
20 Cecil Fielder	.20	.06
21 Kirby Puckett	.50	.15
22 Ken Griffey Jr.	2.00	.60
23 David Justice	.40	.12
24 Jeff Bagwell	1.00	.30
25 Howard Johnson	.10	.03
26 Ozzie Smith	.75	.23
G1 Roberto Alomar	2.00	.60
G2 Joe Carter	.75	.23
G3 Kelly Gruber	.50	.15
G4 Jack Morris	.75	.23
G5 Tom Henke	.50	.15
G6 Devon White	.50	.15
GAU Roberto Alomar AU	40.00	12.00
NNO Checklist Card SP	.10	.03

1992 Donruss Super DK's

These cards are larger (5" by 7") versions of the 1992 Donruss Diamond King insert set. Although not formally available in 1992, a decent number have entered the secondary market in recent years making them more accessible in the hobby.

	Nm-Mt	Ex-Mt
COMPLETE SET (27)	600.00	180.00
COMPLETE SERIES 1 (14)	500.00	150.00
COMPLETE SERIES 2 (13)	100.00	30.00
DK1 Paul Molitor	30.00	9.00
DK2 Will Clark	30.00	9.00
DK3 Joe Carter	10.00	3.00
DK4 Julio Franco	8.00	2.40
DK5 Cal Ripken	150.00	45.00
DK6 Dave Justice	12.00	3.60
DK7 George Bell	8.00	2.40
DK8 Frank Thomas	50.00	15.00
DK9 Wade Boggs	40.00	12.00
DK10 Scott Sanderson	8.00	2.40
DK11 Jeff Bagwell	60.00	18.00
DK12 John Kruk	10.00	3.00
DK13 Felix Jose	8.00	2.40
DK14 Harold Baines	12.00	3.60
DK15 Dwight Gooden	10.00	3.00
DK16 Brian McRae	8.00	2.40
DK17 Jay Bell	8.00	2.40
DK18 Brett Butler	10.00	3.00
DK19 Hal Morris	8.00	2.40
DK20 Mark Langston	8.00	2.40
DK21 Scott Erickson	8.00	2.40
DK22 Randy Johnson	40.00	12.00
DK23 Greg Swindell	8.00	2.40
DK24 Dennis Martinez	10.00	3.00
DK25 Tony Phillips	8.00	2.40
DK26 Fred McGriff	12.00	3.60
DK27 Checklist 1-26 DP (Dick Perez)	8.00	2.40

1993 Donruss Previews

This 22-card standard-size set was issued by Donruss for hobby dealers to preview the 1993 Donruss regular issue series. The cards feature glossy color player photos with white borders on the fronts. The team logo appears in a diamond at the lower left corner, while the player's name appears in a bar that extends to the right. Both the diamond and bar are team-color coded. The top half of the back has a color close-up photo; the bottom half presents biography and recent major league statistics. In addition, one of these cards wer sent to each Donruss Club member. Also, George Brett has a card in this set but not in the 1993 regular Donruss set.

	Nm-Mt	Ex-Mt
COMPLETE SET (22)	80.00	24.00
1 Tom Glavine	4.00	1.20
2 Ryne Sandberg	8.00	2.40
3 Barry Larkin	4.00	1.20
4 Jeff Bagwell	6.00	1.80
5 Eric Karros	1.50	.45
6 Larry Walker	1.50	.45
7 Eddie Murray	5.00	1.50
8 Darren Daulton	1.50	.45
9 Andy Van Slyke	1.50	.45
10 Gary Sheffield	4.00	1.20
11 Will Clark	5.00	1.50
12 Cal Ripken	15.00	4.50
13 Roger Clemens	10.00	3.00
14 Frank Thomas	5.00	1.50
15 Cecil Fielder	1.50	.45
16 George Brett	8.00	2.40
17 Robin Yount	2.50	.75
18 Don Mattingly	8.00	2.40
19 Dennis Eckersley	1.50	.45
20 Ken Griffey Jr.	12.00	3.60
21 Jose Canseco	4.00	1.20
22 Roberto Alomar	4.00	1.20

1993 Donruss

The 792-card 1993 Donruss set was issued in two series, each with 396 standard-size cards. Cards were distributed in foil packs. The basic card fronts feature glossy color action photos with white borders. At the bottom of the picture, the team logo appears in a team color-coded diamond with the player's name in a color-coded bar extending to the right. A Rated Rookies (RR) subset, sprinkled throughout the set, spotlights 20 young prospects. There are no key Rookie Cards in this set.

	Nm-Mt	Ex-Mt
COMPLETE SET (792)	30.00	9.00
COMP.SERIES 1 (396)	15.00	4.50
COMP.SERIES 2 (396)	15.00	4.50
1 Craig Lefferts	.10	.03
2 Kent Mercker	.10	.03
3 Phil Plantier	.10	.03
4 Alex Arias	.10	.03
5 Julio Valera	.10	.03
6 Dan Wilson	.20	.06
7 Frank Thomas	.50	.15
8 Eric Anthony	.10	.03
9 Derek Lilliquist	.10	.03
10 Rafael Bournigal	.10	.03
11 Manny Alexander RR	.10	.03
12 Bret Barberie	.10	.03
13 Mickey Tettleton	.10	.03
14 Anthony Young	.10	.03
15 Tim Spehr	.10	.03
16 Bob Ayrault	.10	.03
17 Bill Wegman	.10	.03
18 Jay Bell	.20	.06
19 Rick Aguilera	.10	.03
20 Todd Zeile	.10	.03
21 Steve Farr	.10	.03
22 Andy Benes	.10	.03
23 Lance Blankenship	.10	.03
24 Ted Wood	.10	.03
25 Omar Vizquel	.20	.06
26 Steve Avery	.10	.03
27 Brian Bohanon	.10	.03
28 Rick Wilkins	.10	.03
29 Devon White	.10	.03
30 Bobby Ayala RC	.10	.03
31 Leo Gomez	.10	.03
32 Mike Simms	.10	.03
33 Ellis Burks	.20	.06
34 Steve Wilson	.10	.03
35 Jim Abbott	.30	.09
36 Tim Wallach	.10	.03
37 Wilson Alvarez	.10	.03
38 Daryl Boston	.10	.03
39 Sandy Alomar Jr.	.10	.03
40 Mitch Williams	.10	.03
41 Rico Brogna	.10	.03
42 Gary Varsho	.10	.03
43 Kevin Appier	.20	.06
44 Eric Wedge RR RC	.10	.03
45 Dante Bichette	.20	.06
46 Jose Oquendo	.10	.03
47 Mike Trombley	.10	.03
48 Dan Walters	.10	.03
49 Gerald Williams	.10	.03
50 Bud Black	.10	.03
51 Bobby Witt	.10	.03
52 Mark Davis	.10	.03
53 Shawn Barton RC	.10	.03
54 Paul Assenmacher	.10	.03
55 Kevin Reimer	.10	.03
56 Billy Ashley RR	.10	.03
57 Eddie Zosky	.10	.03
58 Chris Sabo	.10	.03
59 Billy Ripken	.10	.03
60 Scooter Tucker	.10	.03
61 Tim Wakefield RR	.20	.06
62 Mitch Webster	.10	.03
63 Jack Clark	.20	.06
64 Mark Gardner	.10	.03
65 Lee Stevens	.10	.03
66 Todd Hundley	.10	.03
67 Bobby Thigpen	.10	.03
68 Dave Hollins	.10	.03
69 Jack Armstrong	.10	.03
70 Alex Cole	.10	.03
71 Mark Carreon	.10	.03
72 Todd Worrell	.10	.03
73 Steve Shifflett	.10	.03
74 Jerald Clark	.10	.03
75 Paul Molitor	.30	.09
76 Larry Carter RC	.10	.03
77 Rich Rowland RR	.10	.03
78 Damon Berryhill	.10	.03
79 Willie Banks	.10	.03
80 Hector Villanueva	.10	.03
81 Mike Gallego	.10	.03
82 Tim Belcher	.10	.03
83 Mike Bordick	.10	.03
84 Craig Biggio	.30	.09
85 Lance Parrish	.20	.06
86 Brett Butler	.20	.06
87 Mike Timlin	.10	.03
88 Brian Barnes	.10	.03
89 Brady Anderson	.20	.06
90 D.J. Dozier	.10	.03
91 Frank Viola	.20	.06
92 Darren Daulton	.20	.06
93 Chad Curtis	.10	.03
94 Zane Smith	.10	.03
95 George Bell	.10	.03
96 Rex Hudler	.10	.03
97 Mark Whiten	.10	.03
98 Tim Teufel	.10	.03
99 Kevin Ritz	.10	.03
100 Jeff Brantley	.10	.03
101 Jeff Conine	.20	.06
102 Vinny Castilla	.20	.06
103 Greg Vaughn	.20	.06
104 Steve Buechele	.10	.03
105 Darren Reed	.10	.03
106 Bip Roberts	.10	.03
107 John Habyan	.10	.03
108 Scott Servais	.10	.03
109 Walt Weiss	.10	.03
110 J.T. Snow RR RC	.50	.15
111 Jay Buhner	.20	.06
112 Darryl Strawberry	.30	.09
113 Roger Pavlik	.10	.03
114 Chris Nabholz	.10	.03
115 Pat Borders	.10	.03
116 Pat Howell	.10	.03
117 Gregg Olson	.10	.03
118 Curt Schilling	.30	.09
119 Roger Clemens	1.00	.30
120 Victor Cole	.10	.03
121 Gary DiSarcina	.10	.03
122 Gary Carter CL Kirt Manwaring	.20	.06
123 Steve Sax	.10	.03
124 Chuck Carr	.10	.03
125 Mark Lewis	.10	.03
126 Tony Gwynn	.60	.18
127 Travis Fryman	.20	.06
128 Dave Burba	.10	.03
129 Wally Joyner	.20	.06
130 John Smoltz	.30	.09
131 Cal Eldred	.10	.03
132 Roberto Alomar CL Devon White	.20	.06
133 Arthur Rhodes	.10	.03
134 Jeff Blauser	.10	.03
135 Scott Cooper	.10	.03
136 Doug Strange	.10	.03
137 Luis Sojo	.10	.03
138 Jeff Branson	.10	.03
139 Alex Fernandez	.10	.03
140 Ken Caminiti	.20	.06
141 Charles Nagy	.10	.03
142 Tom Candiotti	.10	.03

143 Willie Greene RR .10 .03
144 John Vander Wal .10 .03
145 Kurt Knudsen .10 .03
146 John Franco .20 .06
147 Eddie Pierce RC .10 .03
148 Kim Batiste .10 .03
149 Darren Holmes .10 .03
150 Steve Cooke .10 .03
151 Terry Jorgensen .10 .03
152 Mark Clark .10 .03
153 Randy Velarde .10 .03
154 Greg W. Harris .10 .03
155 Kevin Campbell .10 .03
156 John Burkett .10 .03
157 Kevin Mitchell .10 .03
158 Deion Sanders .30 .09
159 Jose Canseco .50 .15
160 Jeff Hartsock .10 .03
161 Tom Quinlan RC .10 .03
162 Tim Pugh RC .10 .03
163 Glenn Davis .10 .03
164 Shane Reynolds .10 .03
165 Jody Reed .10 .03
166 Mike Sharperson .10 .03
167 Scott Lewis .10 .03
168 Dennis Martinez .20 .06
169 Scott Radinsky .10 .03
170 Dave Gallagher .10 .03
171 Jim Thome .50 .15
172 Terry Mulholland .10 .03
173 Milt Cuyler .10 .03
174 Bob Patterson .10 .03
175 Jeff Montgomery .10 .03
176 Tim Salmon RR .30 .09
177 Franklin Stubbs .10 .03
178 Donovan Osborne .10 .03
179 Jeff Reboulet .10 .03
180 Jeremy Hernandez .10 .03
181 Charlie Hayes .10 .03
182 Matt Williams .20 .06
183 Mike Raczka .10 .03
184 Francisco Cabrera .10 .03
185 Rich DeLucia .10 .03
186 Sammy Sosa .75 .23
187 Ivan Rodriguez .50 .15
188 Bret Boone RR .30 .09
189 Juan Guzman .10 .03
190 Tom Browning .10 .03
191 Randy Milligan .10 .03
192 Steve Finley .20 .06
193 John Patterson RR .10 .03
194 Kip Gross .10 .03
195 Tony Fossas .10 .03
196 Ivan Calderon .10 .03
197 Junior Felix .10 .03
198 Pete Schourek .10 .03
199 Craig Grebeck .10 .03
200 Juan Bell .10 .03
201 Glenallen Hill .10 .03
202 Danny Jackson .10 .03
203 John Kiely .10 .03
204 Bob Tewksbury .10 .03
205 Kevin Koslofski .10 .03
206 Craig Shipley .10 .03
207 John Jaha .10 .03
208 Royce Clayton .10 .03
209 Mike Piazza RR 1.25 .35
210 Ron Gant .20 .06
211 Scott Erickson .10 .03
212 Doug Dascenzo .10 .03
213 Andy Stankiewicz .10 .03
214 Geronimo Berroa .10 .03
215 Dennis Eckersley .20 .06
216 Al Osuna .10 .03
217 Tino Martinez .30 .09
218 Henry Rodriguez .10 .03
219 Ed Sprague .10 .03
220 Ken Hill .10 .03
221 Chito Martinez .10 .03
222 Bret Saberhagen .20 .06
223 Mike Greenwell .10 .03
224 Mickey Morandini .10 .03
225 Chuck Finley .20 .06
226 Denny Neagle .20 .06
227 Kirk McCaskill .10 .03
228 Rheal Cormier .10 .03
229 Paul Sorrento .10 .03
230 Darrin Jackson .10 .03
231 Rob Deer .10 .03
232 Bill Swift .10 .03
233 Kevin McReynolds .10 .03
234 Terry Pendleton .20 .06
235 Dave Nilsson .10 .03
236 Chuck McElroy .10 .03
237 Derek Parks .10 .03
238 Norm Charlton .10 .03
239 Matt Nokes .10 .03
240 Juan Guerrero .10 .03
241 Jeff Parrett .10 .03
242 Ryan Thompson RR .10 .03
243 Dave Fleming .10 .03
244 Dave Hansen .10 .03
245 Monty Fariss .10 .03
246 Archi Cianfrocco .10 .03
247 Pat Hentgen .10 .03
248 Bill Pecota .10 .03
249 Ben McDonald .10 .03
250 Cliff Brantley .10 .03
251 John Valentin .10 .03
252 Jeff King .10 .03
253 Reggie Williams .10 .03
254 Damon Berryhill CL .10 .03
Alex Arias
255 Ozzie Guillen .10 .03
256 Mike Perez .10 .03
257 Thomas Howard .10 .03
258 Kurt Stillwell .10 .03
259 Mike Henneman .10 .03
260 Steve Decker .10 .03
261 Brent Mayne .10 .03
262 Otis Nixon .10 .03
263 Mark Kiefer .10 .03
264 Don Mattingly CL .30 .09
Mike Bordick)
265 Richie Lewis RC .10 .03
266 Pat Gomez RC .10 .03
267 Scott Taylor .10 .03
268 Shawon Dunston .10 .03
269 Greg Myers .10 .03
270 Tim Costo .10 .03
271 Greg Hibbard .10 .03
272 Pete Harnisch .10 .03
273 Dave Mlicki .10 .03
274 Orel Hershiser .20 .06
275 Sean Berry RR .10 .03
276 Doug Simons .10 .03
277 John Doherty .10 .03
278 Eddie Murray .50 .15
279 Chris Haney .10 .03
280 Stan Javier .10 .03
281 Jaime Navarro .10 .03
282 Orlando Merced .10 .03
283 Kent Hrbek .20 .06
284 Bernard Gilkey .10 .03
285 Russ Springer .10 .03
286 Mike Maddux .10 .03
287 Eric Fox .10 .03
288 Mark Leonard .10 .03
289 Tim Leary .10 .03
290 Brian Hunter .10 .03
291 Donald Harris .10 .03
292 Bob Scanlan .10 .03
293 Turner Ward .10 .03
294 Hal Morris .10 .03
295 Jimmy Poole .10 .03
296 Doug Jones .10 .03
297 Tony Pena .10 .03
298 Ramon Martinez .10 .03
299 Tim Fortugno .10 .03
300 Marquis Grissom .10 .03
301 Lance Johnson .10 .03
302 Jeff Kent .50 .15
303 Reggie Jefferson .10 .03
304 Wes Chamberlain .10 .03
305 Shawn Hare .10 .03
306 Mike LaValliere .10 .03
307 Gregg Jefferies .10 .03
308 Troy Neel RR .10 .03
309 Pat Listach .10 .03
310 Geronimo Pena .10 .03
311 Pedro Munoz .10 .03
312 Guillermo Velasquez .10 .03
313 Roberto Kelly .10 .03
314 Mike Jackson .10 .03
315 Rickey Henderson .50 .15
316 Mark Lemke .10 .03
317 Erik Hanson .10 .03
318 Derrick May .10 .03
319 Geno Petralli .10 .03
320 Melvin Nieves RR .10 .03
321 Doug Linton .10 .03
322 Rob Dibble .20 .06
323 Chris Hoiles .10 .03
324 Jimmy Jones .10 .03
325 Dave Staton RR .10 .03
326 Pedro Martinez 1.00 .30
327 Paul Quantrill .10 .03
328 Greg Colbrunn .10 .03
329 Hilly Hathaway RC .10 .03
330 Jeff Innis .10 .03
331 Ron Karkovice .10 .03
332 Keith Shepherd RC .10 .03
333 Alan Embree .10 .03
334 Paul Wagner .10 .03
335 Dave Haas .10 .03
336 Ozzie Canseco .10 .03
337 Bill Sampen .10 .03
338 Rich Rodriguez .10 .03
339 Dean Palmer .20 .06
340 Greg Litton .10 .03
341 Jim Tatum RR RC .10 .03
342 Todd Haney RC .10 .03
343 Larry Casian .10 .03
344 Ryne Sandberg .75 .23
345 Sterling Hitchcock RC .20 .06
346 Chris Hammond .10 .03
347 Vince Horsman .10 .03
348 Butch Henry .10 .03
349 Dann Howitt .10 .03
350 Roger McDowell .10 .03
351 Jack Morris .20 .06
352 Bill Krueger .10 .03
353 Cris Colon .10 .03
354 Joe Vitko .10 .03
355 Willie McGee .20 .06
356 Jay Baller .10 .03
357 Pat Mahomes .10 .03
358 Roger Mason .10 .03
359 Jerry Nielsen .10 .03
360 Tom Pagnozzi .10 .03
361 Kevin Baez .10 .03
362 Tim Scott .10 .03
363 Domingo Martinez RC .10 .03
364 Kirt Manwaring .10 .03
365 Rafael Palmeiro .30 .09
366 Ray Lankford .10 .03
367 Tim McIntosh .10 .03
368 Jessie Hollins .10 .03
369 Scott Leius .10 .03
370 Bill Doran .10 .03
371 Sam Militello .10 .03
372 Ryan Bowen .10 .03
373 Dave Henderson .10 .03
374 Dan Smith RR .10 .03
375 Steve Reed RR RC .10 .03
376 Jose Offerman .10 .03
377 Kevin Brown .20 .06
378 Darrin Fletcher .10 .03
379 Duane Ward .10 .03
380 Wayne Kirby RR .10 .03
381 Steve Scarsone .10 .03
382 Mariano Duncan .10 .03
383 Ken Ryan RC .10 .03
384 Lloyd McClendon .10 .03
385 Brian Holman .10 .03
386 Braulio Castillo .10 .03
387 Danny Leon .10 .03
388 Omar Olivares .10 .03
389 Kevin Wickander .10 .03
390 Fred McGriff .30 .09
391 Phil Clark .10 .03
392 Darren Lewis .10 .03
393 Phil Hiatt .10 .03
394 Mike Morgan .10 .03
395 Shane Mack .10 .03
396 Dennis Eckersley CL .20 .06
Art Kusnyer CO
397 David Segui .10 .03
398 Rafael Belliard .10 .03
399 Tim Naehring .10 .03
400 Frank Castillo .10 .03
401 Joe Grahe .10 .03
402 Reggie Sanders .20 .06
403 Roberto Hernandez .10 .03
404 Luis Gonzalez .20 .06
405 Carlos Baerga .10 .03
406 Carlos Hernandez .10 .03
407 Pedro Astacio RR .10 .03
408 Mel Rojas .10 .03
409 Scott Livingstone .10 .03
410 Chico Walker .10 .03
411 Brian McRae .10 .03
412 Ben Rivera .10 .03
413 Ricky Bones .10 .03
414 Andy Van Slyke .20 .06
415 Chuck Knoblauch .20 .06
416 Luis Alicea .10 .03
417 Bob Wickman .10 .03
418 Doug Brocail .10 .03
419 Scott Brosius .20 .06
420 Rod Beck .10 .03
421 Edgar Martinez .30 .09
422 Ryan Klesko .20 .06
423 Nolan Ryan 2.00 .60
424 Rey Sanchez .10 .03
425 Roberto Alomar .50 .15
426 Barry Larkin .50 .15
427 Mike Mussina .50 .15
428 Jeff Bagwell .30 .09
429 Mo Vaughn .20 .06
430 Eric Karros .20 .06
431 John Orton .10 .03
432 Wil Cordero .10 .03
433 Jack McDowell .10 .03
434 Howard Johnson .10 .03
435 Albert Belle .20 .06
436 John Kruk .20 .06
437 Skeeter Barnes .10 .03
438 Don Slaught .10 .03
439 Rusty Meacham .10 .03
440 Tim Laker RR RC .10 .03
441 Robin Yount .75 .23
442 Brian Jordan .20 .06
443 Kevin Tapani .10 .03
444 Gary Sheffield .20 .06
445 Rich Monteleone .10 .03
446 Will Clark .50 .15
447 Jerry Browne .10 .03
448 Jeff Treadway .10 .03
449 Mike Schooler .10 .03
450 Mike Harkey .10 .03
451 Julio Franco .20 .06
452 Kevin Young RR .20 .06
453 Kelly Gruber .10 .03
454 Jose Rijo .10 .03
455 Mike Devereaux .10 .03
456 Andujar Cedeno .10 .03
457 Damion Easley RR .10 .03
458 Kevin Gross .10 .03
459 Matt Young .10 .03
460 Matt Stairs .10 .03
461 Luis Polonia .10 .03
462 Dwight Gooden .30 .09
463 Warren Newson .10 .03
464 Jose DeLeon .10 .03
465 Jose Mesa .10 .03
466 Danny Cox .10 .03
467 Dan Gladden .10 .03
468 Gerald Perry .10 .03
469 Mike Boddicker .10 .03
470 Jeff Gardner .10 .03
471 Doug Henry .10 .03
472 Mike Benjamin .10 .03
473 Dan Peltier RR .10 .03
474 Mike Stanton .10 .03
475 John Smiley .10 .03
476 Dwight Smith .10 .03
477 Jim Leyritz .10 .03
478 Dwayne Henry .10 .03
479 Mark McGwire 1.25 .35
480 Pete Incaviglia .10 .03
481 Dave Cochrane .10 .03
482 Eric Davis .20 .06
483 John Olerud .20 .06
484 Kent Bottenfield .10 .03
485 Mark McLemore .10 .03
486 Dave Magadan .10 .03
487 John Marzano .10 .03
488 Ruben Amaro .10 .03
489 Rob Ducey .10 .03
490 Stan Belinda .10 .03
491 Dan Pasqua .10 .03
492 Joe Magrane .10 .03
493 Brook Jacoby .10 .03
494 Gene Harris .10 .03
495 Mark Leiter .10 .03
496 Bryan Hickerson .10 .03
497 Tom Gordon .10 .03
498 Pete Smith .10 .03
499 Chris Bosio .10 .03
500 Shawn Boskie .10 .03
501 Dave West .10 .03
502 Milt Hill .10 .03
503 Pat Kelly .10 .03
504 Joe Boever .10 .03
505 Terry Steinbach .10 .03
506 Butch Huskey RR .10 .03
507 David Valle .10 .03
508 Mike Scioscia .10 .03
509 Kenny Rogers .20 .06
510 Moises Alou .20 .06
511 David Wells .20 .06
512 Mackey Sasser .10 .03
513 Todd Frohwirth .10 .03
514 Ricky Jordan .10 .03
515 Mike Gardiner .10 .03
516 Gary Redus .10 .03
517 Gary Gaetti .20 .06
518 Checklist .10 .03
519 Carlton Fisk .30 .09
520 Ozzie Smith .75 .23
521 Rod Nichols .10 .03
522 Benito Santiago .20 .06
523 Bill Gullickson .10 .03
524 Robby Thompson .10 .03
525 Mike Macfarlane .10 .03
526 Sid Bream .10 .03
527 Darryl Hamilton .10 .03
528 Checklist .10 .03
529 Jeff Tackett .10 .03
530 Greg Olson .10 .03
531 Bob Zupcic .10 .03
532 Mark Grace .30 .09
533 Steve Frey .10 .03
534 Dave Martinez .10 .03
535 Robin Ventura .20 .06
536 Casey Candaele .10 .03
537 Kenny Lofton .20 .06
538 Jay Howell .10 .03
539 Fern.Ramsey RR RC .10 .03
540 Larry Walker .30 .09
541 Cecil Fielder .20 .06
542 Lee Guetterman .10 .03
543 Keith Miller .10 .03
544 Len Dykstra .20 .06
545 B.J. Surhoff .20 .06
546 Bob Walk .10 .03
547 Brian Harper .10 .03
548 Lee Smith .20 .06
549 Danny Tartabull .10 .03
550 Frank Seminara .10 .03
551 Henry Mercedes .10 .03
552 Dave Righetti .20 .06
553 Ken Griffey Jr. .75 .23
554 Tom Glavine .30 .09
555 Juan Gonzalez .50 .15
556 Jim Bullinger .10 .03
557 Derek Bell .10 .03
558 Cesar Hernandez .10 .03
559 Cal Ripken 1.50 .45
560 Eddie Taubensee .10 .03
561 John Flaherty .10 .03
562 Todd Benzinger .10 .03
563 Hubie Brooks .10 .03
564 Delino DeShields .10 .03
565 Tim Raines .20 .06
566 Sid Fernandez .10 .03
567 Steve Olin .10 .03
568 Tommy Greene .10 .03
569 Buddy Groom .10 .03
570 Randy Tomlin .10 .03
571 Hipolito Pichardo .10 .03
572 Rene Arocha RR RC .20 .06
573 Mike Fetters .10 .03
574 Felix Jose .10 .03
575 Gene Larkin .10 .03
576 Bruce Hurst .10 .03
577 Bernie Williams .30 .09
578 Trevor Wilson .10 .03
579 Bob Welch .10 .03
580 David Justice .20 .06
581 Randy Johnson .50 .15
582 Jose Vizcaino .10 .03
583 Jeff Huson .10 .03
584 Rob Maurer RR .10 .03
585 Todd Stottlemyre .10 .03
586 Joe Oliver .10 .03
587 Bob Milacki .10 .03
588 Rob Murphy .10 .03
589 Greg Pirkl RR .10 .03
590 Lenny Harris .10 .03
591 Luis Rivera .10 .03
592 John Wetteland .20 .06
593 Mark Langston .10 .03
594 Bobby Bonilla .20 .06
595 Esteban Beltre .10 .03
596 Mike Hartley .10 .03
597 Felix Fermin .10 .03
598 Carlos Garcia .10 .03
599 Frank Tanana .10 .03
600 Pedro Guerrero .20 .06
601 Terry Shumpert .10 .03
602 Wally Whitehurst .10 .03
603 Kevin Seitzer .10 .03
604 Chris James .10 .03
605 Greg Gohr RR .10 .03
606 Mark Wohlers .10 .03
607 Kirby Puckett .50 .15
608 Greg Maddux .75 .23
609 Don Mattingly 1.25 .35
610 Greg Cadaret .10 .03
611 Dave Stewart .20 .06
612 Mark Portugal .10 .03
613 Pete O'Brien .10 .03
614 Bob Ojeda .10 .03
615 Joe Carter .20 .06
616 Pete Young .10 .03
617 Sam Horn .10 .03
618 Vince Coleman .10 .03
619 Wade Boggs .30 .09
620 Todd Pratt RC .20 .06
621 Ron Tingley .10 .03
622 Doug Drabek .10 .03
623 Scott Hemond .10 .03
624 Tim Jones .10 .03
625 Dennis Cook .10 .03
626 Jose Melendez .10 .03
627 Mike Munoz .10 .03
628 Jim Pena .10 .03
629 Gary Thurman .10 .03
630 Charlie Leibrandt .10 .03
631 Scott Fletcher .10 .03
632 Andre Dawson .20 .06
633 Greg Gagne .10 .03
634 Greg Swindell .10 .03
635 Kevin Maas .10 .03
636 Xavier Hernandez .10 .03
637 Ruben Sierra .10 .03
638 Dmitri Young RR .20 .06
639 Harold Reynolds .20 .06
640 Tom Goodwin .10 .03
641 Todd Burns .10 .03
642 Jeff Fassero .10 .03
643 Dave Winfield .20 .06
644 Willie Randolph .20 .06
645 Luis Mercedes .10 .03
646 Dale Murphy .50 .15
647 Danny Darwin .10 .03
648 Dennis Moeller .10 .03
649 Chuck Crim .10 .03
650 Checklist .10 .03
651 Shawn Abner .10 .03
652 Tracy Woodson .10 .03
653 Scott Scudder .10 .03
654 Tom Lampkin .10 .03
655 Alan Trammell .30 .09
656 Cory Snyder .10 .03
657 Chris Gwynn .10 .03
658 Lonnie Smith .10 .03
659 Jim Austin .10 .03
660 Rob Picciolo CL .10 .03
661 Tim Hulett .10 .03
662 Marvin Freeman .10 .03
663 Greg A. Harris .10 .03
664 Heathcliff Slocumb .10 .03
665 Mike Butcher .10 .03
666 Steve Foster .10 .03
667 Donn Pall .10 .03
668 Darryl Kile .20 .06
669 Jesse Levis .10 .03
670 Jim Gott .10 .03
671 Mark Hutton RR .10 .03
672 Brian Drahman .10 .03
673 Chad Kreuter .10 .03
674 Tony Fernandez .10 .03
675 Jose Lind .10 .03
676 Kyle Abbott .10 .03
677 Dan Plesac .10 .03
678 Barry Bonds 1.25 .35
679 Chili Davis .20 .06
680 Stan Royer .10 .03
681 Scott Kamieniecki .10 .03
682 Carlos Martinez .10 .03
683 Mike Moore .10 .03
684 Candy Maldonado .10 .03
685 Jeff Nelson .10 .03
686 Lou Whitaker .20 .06
687 Jose Guzman .10 .03
688 Manuel Lee .10 .03
689 Bob MacDonald .10 .03
690 Scott Bankhead .10 .03
691 Alan Mills .10 .03
692 Brian Williams .10 .03
693 Tom Brunansky .10 .03
694 Lenny Webster .10 .03
695 Greg Briley .10 .03
696 Paul O'Neill .30 .09
697 Joey Cora .10 .03
698 Charlie O'Brien .10 .03
699 Junior Ortiz .10 .03
700 Ron Darling .10 .03
701 Tony Phillips .10 .03
702 William Pennyfeather .10 .03
703 Mark Gubicza .10 .03
704 Steve Hosey RR .10 .03
705 Henry Cotto .10 .03
706 David Hulse RC .10 .03
707 Mike Pagliarulo .10 .03
708 Dave Stieb .10 .03
709 Melido Perez .10 .03
710 Jimmy Key .20 .06
711 Jeff Russell .10 .03
712 David Cone .20 .06
713 Russ Swan .10 .03
714 Mark Guthrie .10 .03
715 Checklist .10 .03
716 Al Martin RR .10 .03
717 Randy Knorr .10 .03
718 Mike Stanley .10 .03
719 Rick Sutcliffe .20 .06
720 Terry Leach .10 .03
721 Chipper Jones RR .50 .15
722 Jim Eisenreich .10 .03
723 Tom Henke .10 .03
724 Jeff Frye .10 .03
725 Harold Baines .20 .06
726 Scott Sanderson .10 .03
727 Tom Foley .10 .03
728 Bryan Harvey .10 .03
729 Tom Edens .10 .03
730 Eric Young .10 .03
731 Dave Weathers .10 .03
732 Spike Owen .10 .03
733 Scott Aldred .10 .03
734 Cris Carpenter .10 .03
735 Dion James .10 .03
736 Joe Girardi .10 .03
737 Nigel Wilson RR .10 .03
738 Scott Chiamparino .10 .03
739 Jeff Reardon .20 .06
740 Willie Blair .10 .03
741 Jim Corsi .10 .03
742 Ken Patterson .10 .03
743 Andy Ashby .10 .03
744 Rob Natal .10 .03
745 Kevin Bass .10 .03
746 Freddie Benavides .10 .03
747 Chris Donnels .10 .03
748 Kerry Woodson .10 .03
749 Calvin Jones .10 .03
750 Gary Scott .10 .03
751 Joe Orsulak .10 .03
752 Armando Reynoso .10 .03
753 Monty Fariss .10 .03
754 Billy Hatcher .10 .03
755 Denis Boucher .10 .03
756 Walt Weiss .10 .03
757 Mike Fitzgerald .10 .03
758 Rudy Seanez .10 .03
759 Bret Barberie .10 .03
760 Mo Sanford .10 .03
761 Pedro Castellano .10 .03
762 Chuck Carr .10 .03
763 Steve Howe .10 .03
764 Andres Galarraga .20 .06
765 Jeff Conine .20 .06
766 Ted Power .10 .03
767 Butch Henry .10 .03
768 Steve Decker .10 .03
769 Storm Davis .10 .03
770 Vinny Castilla .20 .06
771 Junior Felix .10 .03
772 Walt Terrell .10 .03
773 Brad Ausmus .10 .03
774 Jamie McAndrew .10 .03
775 Milt Thompson .10 .03
776 Charlie Hayes .10 .03
777 Jack Armstrong .10 .03
778 Dennis Rasmussen .10 .03
779 Darren Holmes .10 .03
780 Alex Arias .10 .03
781 Randy Bush .10 .03
782 Javy Lopez .30 .09
783 Dante Bichette .20 .06
784 John Johnstone RC .10 .03
785 Rene Gonzales .10 .03
786 Alex Cole .10 .03
787 Jeromy Burnitz RR .20 .06
788 Michael Huff .10 .03
789 Anthony Telford .10 .03
790 Jerald Clark .10 .03
791 Joel Johnston .10 .03
792 David Nied RR .10 .03

1993 Donruss Diamond Kings

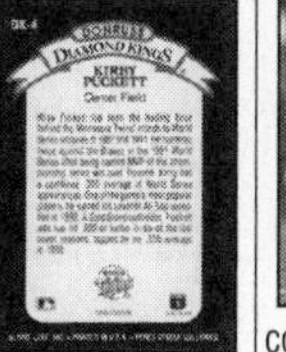

These standard-size cards, commemorating Donruss' annual selection of the games top players, were randomly inserted in 1993 Donruss packs. The first 15 cards were available in the first series of the 1993 Donruss and cards 16-31 were inserted with the second series. The cards are gold-foil stamped and feature player portraits by noted sports artist Dick Perez. Card numbers 27-28 honor the first draft picks of the new Florida Marlins and Colorado Rockies franchises. Collectors 16 years of age and younger could enter Donruss' Diamond King contest by writing an essay of 75 words or less explaining who their favorite Diamond King player was and why. Winners were awarded one of 30 framed watercolors at the National Convention, held in Chicago, July 22-25, 1993.

	Nm-Mt	Ex-Mt
COMPLETE SET (31)	30.00	9.00
COMPLETE SERIES 1 (15)	20.00	6.00
COMPLETE SERIES 2 (16)	10.00	3.00
DK1 Ken Griffey Jr.	5.00	1.50
DK2 Ryne Sandberg	5.00	1.50
DK3 Roger Clemens	6.00	1.80
DK4 Kirby Puckett	3.00	.90
DK5 Bill Swift	.60	.18
DK6 Larry Walker	2.00	.60
DK7 Juan Gonzalez	3.00	.90
DK8 Wally Joyner	1.25	.35
DK9 Andy Van Slyke	1.25	.35
DK10 Robin Ventura	1.25	.35
DK11 Bip Roberts	.60	.18
DK12 Roberto Kelly	.60	.18
DK13 Carlos Baerga	.60	.18
DK14 Orel Hershiser	1.25	.35
DK15 Cecil Fielder	1.25	.35
DK16 Robin Yount	5.00	1.50
DK17 Darren Daulton	1.25	.35
DK18 Mark McGwire	8.00	2.40
DK19 Tom Glavine	2.00	.60
DK20 Roberto Alomar	3.00	.90
DK21 Gary Sheffield	1.25	.35
DK22 Bob Tewksbury	.60	.18
DK23 Brady Anderson	1.25	.35
DK24 Craig Biggio	2.00	.60
DK25 Eddie Murray	3.00	.90
DK26 Luis Polonia	.60	.18
DK27 Nigel Wilson	.60	.18
DK28 David Nied	.60	.18
DK29 Pat Listach ROY	.60	.18
DK30 Eric Karros ROY	1.25	.35
DK31 Checklist 1-31	1.00	.30

1993 Donruss Elite

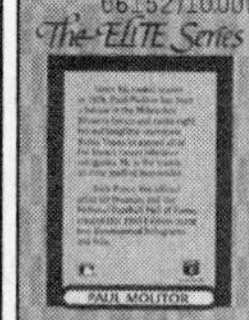

The numbering on the 1993 Elite cards follows consecutively after that of the 1992 Elite series cards, and each of the 10,000 Elite cards is serially numbered. Cards 19-27 were random inserts in 1993 Donruss series I foil packs while cards 28-36 were inserted in series II packs. The backs of the Elite cards also carry the serial number ("X" of 10,000) as well as the card number. The Signature Series Will Clark card was randomly inserted in 1993 Donruss foil packs; he personally autographed 5,000 cards. Featuring a Dick Perez portrait, the ten thousand Legends Series cards honor Robin Yount for his 3,000th hit achievement.

	Nm-Mt	Ex-Mt
9 Fred McGriff	15.00	4.50
0 Ryne Sandberg	40.00	12.00
1 Eddie Murray	25.00	7.50
2 Paul Molitor	15.00	4.50
3 Barry Larkin	25.00	7.50
4 Don Mattingly	50.00	15.00
5 Dennis Eckersley	15.00	4.50
6 Roberto Alomar	25.00	7.50
7 Edgar Martinez	15.00	4.50
8 Gary Sheffield	15.00	4.50
9 Darren Daulton	15.00	4.50
0 Larry Walker	15.00	4.50
1 Barry Bonds	50.00	15.00
2 Andy Van Slyke	15.00	4.50
3 Mark McGwire	50.00	15.00
4 Cecil Fielder	15.00	4.50
5 Dave Winfield	15.00	4.50
6 Juan Gonzalez	25.00	7.50
3 Robin Yount (Legend Series)	25.00	7.50
3 Will Clark AU (Signature Series)	50.00	15.00

1993 Donruss Long Ball Leaders

andomly inserted in 26-card magazine istributor packs (1-9 in series I and 10-18 in eries II), these standard-size cards feature ome of MLB's outstanding sluggers.

	Nm-Mt	Ex-Mt
OMPLETE SET (18)	60.00	18.00
COMPLETE SERIES 1 (9)	30.00	9.00
COMPLETE SERIES 2 (9)	30.00	9.00
LL1 Rob Deer	1.00	.30
LL2 Fred McGriff	3.00	.90
LL3 Albert Belle	2.00	.60
LL4 Mark McGwire	12.00	3.60
LL5 David Justice	2.00	.60
LL6 Jose Canseco	5.00	1.50
LL7 Kent Hrbek	2.00	.60
LL8 Roberto Alomar	5.00	1.50
LL9 Ken Griffey Jr.	8.00	2.40
LL10 Frank Thomas	5.00	1.50
LL11 Darryl Strawberry	3.00	.90
LL12 Felix Jose	1.00	.30
LL13 Cecil Fielder	2.00	.60
LL14 Juan Gonzalez	5.00	1.50
LL15 Ryne Sandberg	8.00	2.40
LL16 Gary Sheffield	2.00	.60
LL17 Jeff Bagwell	3.00	.90
LL18 Larry Walker	3.00	.90

1993 Donruss MVPs

These twenty-six standard size MVP cards were issued 13 cards in each series, and they were inserted one per 23-card jumbo packs.

	Nm-Mt	Ex-Mt
COMPLETE SET (26)	30.00	9.00
COMPLETE SERIES 1 (13)	10.00	3.00
COMPLETE SERIES 2 (13)	20.00	6.00
1 Luis Polonia	.40	.12
2 Frank Thomas	2.00	.60
3 George Brett	5.00	1.50
4 Paul Molitor	1.25	.35
5 Don Mattingly	5.00	1.50
6 Roberto Alomar	2.00	.60
7 Terry Pendleton	.75	.23
8 Eric Karros	.75	.23
9 Larry Walker	1.25	.35
10 Eddie Murray	2.00	.60
11 Darren Daulton	.75	.23
12 Ray Lankford	.40	.12
13 Will Clark	2.00	.60
14 Cal Ripken	6.00	1.80
15 Roger Clemens	4.00	1.20
16 Carlos Baerga	.40	.12
17 Cecil Fielder	.75	.23
18 Kirby Puckett	2.00	.60
19 Mark McGwire	5.00	1.50
20 Ken Griffey Jr.	3.00	.90
21 Juan Gonzalez	2.00	.60
22 Ryne Sandberg	3.00	.90
23 Bip Roberts	.40	.12
24 Jeff Bagwell	1.25	.35
25 Barry Bonds	5.00	1.50
26 Gary Sheffield	.75	.23

1993 Donruss Spirit of the Game

These 20 standard-size cards were randomly inserted in 1993 Donruss packs and packed approximately two per box. Cards 1-10 were first-series inserts, and cards 11-20 were second-series inserts. The fronts feature borderless glossy color action player photos.

	Nm-Mt	Ex-Mt
COMPLETE SET (20)	20.00	6.00
COMPLETE SERIES 1 (10)	8.00	2.40
COMPLETE SERIES 2 (10)	12.00	3.60
SG1 Mike Bordick Turning Two	.50	.15
SG2 Dave Justice Play at the Plate	1.00	.30
SG3 Roberto Alomar In There	2.50	.75
SG4 Dennis Eckersley Pumped	1.00	.30
SG5 Juan Gonzalez and Jose Canseco Dynamic Duo	2.50	.75
SG6 George Bell and Frank Thomas ... Gone	2.50	.75
SG7 Wade Boggs and Luis Polonia Safe or Out	1.50	.45
SG8 Will Clark The Thrill	2.50	.75
SG9 Bip Roberts Safe at Home	.50	.15
SG10 Cecil Fielder Rob Deer Mickey Tettleton Thirty 3	.50	.15
SG11 Kenny Lofton Bag Bandit	1.00	.30
SG12 Gary Sheffield Fred McGriff Back to Back	2.50	.75
SG13 Greg Gagne Barry Larkin	.50	.15
SG14 Ryne Sandberg The Ball Stops Here	4.00	1.20
SG15 Carlos Baerga Gary Gaetti Over the Top	.50	.15
SG16 Danny Tartabull At the Wall	.50	.15
SG17 Brady Anderson Head First	1.00	.30
SG18 Frank Thomas Big Hurt	2.50	.75
SG19 Kevin Gross No Hitter	.50	.15
SG20 Robin Yount 3,000 Hits	4.00	1.20

1993 Donruss Elite Dominators

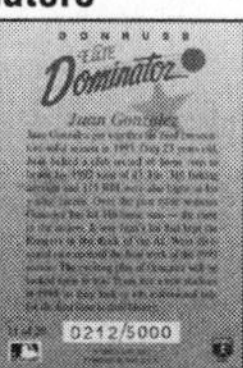

In a series of programs broadcast Dec. 8-13, 1993, on the Shop at Home cable network, viewers were offered the opportunity to purchase a factory-sealed box of either 1993 Donruss I or II, which included one Elite Dominator card produced especially for the promotion. The set retailed for 99.00 plus 6.00 for postage and handling. 5,000 serial-numbered sets were produced and half of the cards for Nolan Ryan, Juan Gonzalez, Paul Molitor, and Don Mattingly were signed by the player. The entire print run of 100,000 cards were reportedly purchased by the Shop at Home network and were to be offered periodically over the network. The production number, out of a total of 5,000 produced, is shown at the bottom.

	Nm-Mt	Ex-Mt
COMP.UNSIG. SET (20)	300.00	90.00
1 Ryne Sandberg	20.00	6.00
2 Fred McGriff	6.00	1.80
3 Greg Maddux	25.00	7.50
4 Ron Gant	5.00	1.50
5 David Justice	8.00	2.40
6 Don Mattingly	20.00	6.00
7 Tim Salmon	12.00	3.60
8 Mike Piazza	40.00	12.00
9 John Olerud	5.00	1.50
10 Nolan Ryan	40.00	12.00
11 Juan Gonzalez	8.00	2.40
12 Ken Griffey Jr.	20.00	6.00
13 Frank Thomas	12.00	3.60
14 Tom Glavine	6.00	1.80
15 George Brett	20.00	6.00
16 Barry Bonds	20.00	6.00
17 Albert Belle	5.00	1.50
18 Paul Molitor	8.00	2.40
19 Cal Ripken	40.00	12.00
20 Roberto Alomar	8.00	2.40
AU6 Don Mattingly AU	50.00	15.00
AU10 Nolan Ryan AU	100.00	30.00
AU11 Juan Gonzalez AU	25.00	7.50
AU18 Paul Molitor AU	30.00	9.00

1993 Donruss Elite Supers

Sequentially numbered one through 5,000, these 20 oversized cards measure approximately 3 1/2" by 5" and have wide prismatic foil borders with an inner gray borders. The Elite Update set features all the players found in the regular Elite set, plus Nolan Ryan and Frank Thomas, whose cards replace numbers 19 and 20 from the earlier release, and an updated card of Barry Bonds in his Giants uniform. The backs carry the production number and the card number.

	Nm-Mt	Ex-Mt
COMPLETE SET (20)	150.00	45.00
1 Fred McGriff	5.00	1.50
2 Ryne Sandberg	10.00	3.00
3 Eddie Murray	8.00	2.40
4 Paul Molitor	10.00	3.00
5 Barry Larkin	8.00	2.40
6 Don Mattingly	12.00	3.60
7 Dennis Eckersley	3.00	.90
8 Roberto Alomar	8.00	2.40
9 Edgar Martinez	3.00	.90
10 Gary Sheffield	5.00	1.50
11 Darren Daulton	3.00	.90
12 Larry Walker	3.00	.90
13 Barry Bonds	12.00	3.60
14 Andy Van Slyke	1.50	.45
15 Mark McGwire	20.00	6.00
16 Cecil Fielder	3.00	.90
17 Dave Winfield	5.00	1.50
18 Juan Gonzalez	8.00	2.40
19 Frank Thomas	10.00	3.00
20 Nolan Ryan	25.00	7.50

1993 Donruss Masters of the Game

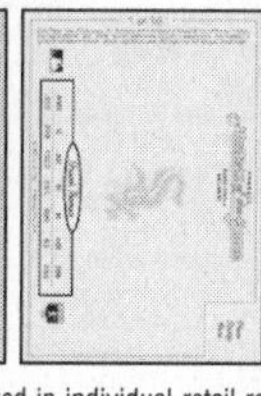

These cards were issued in individual retail re-packs, and also were included in special 18-pack boxes of 1993 Donruss second series. The cards were originally available only at retail outlets such as WalMart along with a foil pack of 1993 Donruss. These 16 postcards measure approximately 3 1/2" by 5" and feature the work of artist Dick Perez on their fronts.

	Nm-Mt	Ex-Mt
COMPLETE SET (16)	40.00	12.00
1 Frank Thomas	3.00	.90
2 Nolan Ryan	10.00	3.00
3 Gary Sheffield	3.00	.90
4 Fred McGriff	2.00	.60
5 Ryne Sandberg	4.00	1.20
6 Cal Ripken	10.00	3.00
7 Jose Canseco	2.50	.75
8 Ken Griffey Jr.	6.00	1.80
9 Will Clark	2.50	.75
10 Roberto Alomar	2.50	.75
11 Juan Gonzalez	3.00	.90
12 David Justice	2.50	.75
13 Kirby Puckett	3.00	.90
14 Barry Bonds	5.00	1.50
15 Robin Yount	3.00	.90
16 Deion Sanders	2.00	.60

1994 Donruss Promos

These 12 standard-size promo cards feature borderless color player action shots on their fronts. The player's name and position appear in gold foil within a team color-coded stripe near the bottom. His team logo appears within a black rectangle framed by a team color near the bottom. The set name and year, stamped in gold foil, also appear in this rectangle. Most of the backs are horizontal, and feature another borderless color player action photo. A black rectangle framed by a team color appears on one side and carries the player's name, team, uniform number, and biography. The player's 1992 stats appear within ghosted stripes near the bottom. The disclaimer "Promotional Sample" is printed diagonally across both sides of the cards. The cards are numbered on the back. Reportedly each of Leaf/Donruss' hobby accounts (roughly 3,000) received one complete 11-card promo set (including one but not both Special Edition cards) with their 1994 Donruss order form. Moreover, 42 different retail broker accounts also received five to ten complete 11-card promo sets for their presentations. From this information, it appears that approximately 3,500 11-card promo sets were printed. Each hobby account received one of two Special Edition promos, either Barry Bonds or Frank Thomas.

	Nm-Mt	Ex-Mt
COMPLETE SET (12)	60.00	18.00
COMMON CARD (1-10)	1.00	.30
COMMON SP	15.00	4.50
1 Barry Bonds	6.00	1.80
1SE Barry Bonds SP	20.00	6.00
2 Darren Daulton	1.00	.30
3 John Olerud	1.00	.30
4 Frank Thomas	4.00	1.20
4SE Frank Thomas SP	15.00	4.50
5 Mike Piazza	6.00	1.80
6 Tim Salmon	1.00	.30
7 Ken Griffey Jr.	10.00	3.00
8 Fred McGriff	1.50	.45
9 Don Mattingly	5.00	1.50
10 Gary Sheffield	2.50	.75

1994 Donruss

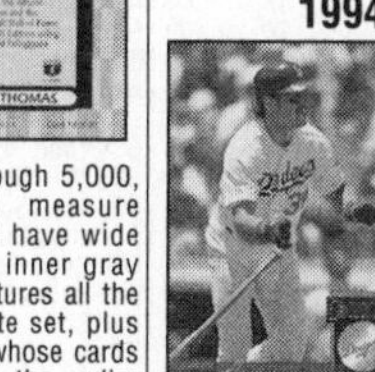

The 1994 Donruss set was issued in two separate series of 330 standard-size cards for a total of 660. Cards were issued in foil wrapped packs. The fronts feature borderless color player action photos on front. There are no notable Rookie Cards in this set.

	Nm-Mt	Ex-Mt
COMPLETE SET (660)	30.00	9.00
COMP.SERIES 1 (330)	15.00	4.50
COMP.SERIES 2 (330)	15.00	4.50
1 Nolan Ryan	4.00	1.20
2 Mike Piazza	1.50	.45
3 Moises Alou	.30	.09
4 Ken Griffey Jr.	1.25	.35
5 Gary Sheffield	.30	.09
6 Roberto Alomar	.75	.23
7 John Kruk	.30	.09
8 Gregg Olson	.15	.04
9 Gregg Jefferies	.15	.04
10 Tony Gwynn	1.00	.30
11 Chad Curtis	.15	.04
12 Craig Biggio	.50	.15
13 John Burkett	.15	.04
14 Carlos Baerga	.15	.04
15 Robin Yount	1.25	.35
16 Dennis Eckersley	.30	.09
17 Dwight Gooden	.50	.15
18 Ryne Sandberg	1.25	.35
19 Rickey Henderson	.75	.23
20 Jack McDowell	.15	.04
21 Jay Bell	.30	.09
22 Kevin Brown	.30	.09
23 Robin Ventura	.30	.09
24 Paul Molitor	.50	.15
25 David Justice	.30	.09
26 Rafael Palmeiro	.50	.15
27 Cecil Fielder	.30	.09
28 Chuck Knoblauch	.30	.09
29 Dave Hollins	.15	.04
30 Jimmy Key	.30	.09
31 Mark Langston	.15	.04
32 Darryl Kile	.30	.09
33 Ruben Sierra	.15	.04
34 Ron Gant	.30	.09
35 Ozzie Smith	1.25	.35
36 Wade Boggs	.50	.15
37 Marquis Grissom	.15	.04
38 Will Clark	.75	.23
39 Kenny Lofton	.30	.09
40 Cal Ripken	2.50	.75
41 Steve Avery	.15	.04
42 Mo Vaughn	.30	.09
43 Brian McRae	.15	.04
44 Mickey Tettleton	.15	.04
45 Barry Larkin	.75	.23
46 Charlie Hayes	.15	.04
47 Kevin Appier	.30	.09
48 Robby Thompson	.15	.04
49 Juan Gonzalez	.75	.23
50 Paul O'Neill	.50	.15
51 Marcos Armas	.15	.04
52 Mike Butcher	.15	.04
53 Ken Caminiti	.30	.09
54 Pat Borders	.15	.04
55 Pedro Munoz	.15	.04
56 Tim Belcher	.15	.04
57 Paul Assenmacher	.15	.04
58 Damon Berryhill	.15	.04
59 Ricky Bones	.15	.04
60 Rene Arocha	.15	.04
61 Shawn Boskie	.15	.04
62 Pedro Astacio	.15	.04
63 Frank Bolick	.15	.04
64 Bud Black	.15	.04
65 Sandy Alomar Jr.	.15	.04
66 Rich Amaral	.15	.04
67 Luis Aquino	.15	.04
68 Kevin Baez	.15	.04
69 Mike Devereaux	.15	.04
70 Andy Ashby	.15	.04
71 Larry Andersen	.15	.04
72 Steve Cooke	.15	.04
73 Mario Diaz	.15	.04
74 Rob Deer	.15	.04
75 Bobby Ayala	.15	.04
76 Freddie Benavides	.15	.04
77 Stan Belinda	.15	.04
78 John Doherty	.15	.04
79 Willie Banks	.15	.04
80 Spike Owen	.15	.04
81 Mike Bordick	.15	.04
82 Chili Davis	.30	.09
83 Luis Gonzalez	.30	.09
84 Ed Sprague	.15	.04
85 Jeff Reboulet	.15	.04
86 Jason Bere	.15	.04
87 Mark Hutton	.15	.04
88 Jeff Blauser	.15	.04
89 Cal Eldred	.15	.04
90 Bernard Gilkey	.15	.04
91 Frank Castillo	.15	.04
92 Jim Gott	.15	.04
93 Greg Colbrunn	.15	.04
94 Jeff Brantley	.15	.04
95 Jeremy Hernandez	.15	.04
96 Norm Charlton	.15	.04
97 Alex Arias	.15	.04
98 John Franco	.30	.09
99 Chris Hoiles	.15	.04
100 Brad Ausmus	.15	.04
101 Wes Chamberlain	.15	.04
102 Mark Dewey	.15	.04
103 Benji Gil	.15	.04
104 John Dopson	.15	.04
105 John Smiley	.15	.04
106 David Nied	.15	.04
107 George Brett	2.00	.60
108 Kirk Gibson	.30	.09
109 Larry Casian	.15	.04
110 Ryne Sandberg CL	.75	.23
111 Brent Gates	.15	.04
112 Damion Easley	.15	.04
113 Pete Harnisch	.15	.04
114 Danny Cox	.15	.04
115 Kevin Tapani	.15	.04
116 Roberto Hernandez	.15	.04
117 Domingo Jean	.15	.04
118 Sid Bream	.15	.04
119 Doug Henry	.15	.04
120 Omar Olivares	.15	.04
121 Mike Harkey	.15	.04
122 Carlos Hernandez	.15	.04
123 Jeff Fassero	.15	.04
124 Dave Burba	.15	.04
125 Wayne Kirby	.15	.04
126 John Cummings	.15	.04
127 Bret Barberie	.15	.04
128 Todd Hundley	.15	.04
129 Tim Hulett	.15	.04
130 Phil Clark	.15	.04
131 Danny Jackson	.15	.04
132 Tom Foley	.15	.04
133 Donald Harris	.15	.04
134 Scott Fletcher	.15	.04
135 Johnny Ruffin	.15	.04
136 Jerald Clark	.15	.04
137 Billy Brewer	.15	.04
138 Dan Gladden	.15	.04
139 Eddie Guardado	.30	.09
140 Cal Ripken CL	.75	.23
141 Scott Hemond	.15	.04
142 Steve Frey	.15	.04
143 Xavier Hernandez	.15	.04

144 Mark Eichhorn .15 .04
145 Ellis Burks .30 .09
146 Jim Leyritz .15 .04
147 Mark Lemke .15 .04
148 Pat Listach .15 .04
149 Donovan Osborne .15 .04
150 Glenallen Hill .15 .04
151 Orel Hershiser .30 .09
152 Darrin Fletcher .15 .04
153 Royce Clayton .15 .04
154 Derek Lilliquist .15 .04
155 Mike Felder .15 .04
156 Jeff Conine .30 .09
157 Ryan Thompson .15 .04
158 Ben McDonald .15 .04
159 Ricky Gutierrez .15 .04
160 Terry Mulholland .15 .04
161 Carlos Garcia .15 .04
162 Tom Henke .15 .04
163 Mike Greenwell .15 .04
164 Thomas Howard .15 .04
165 Joe Girardi .15 .04
166 Hubie Brooks .15 .04
167 Greg Gohr .15 .04
168 Chip Hale .15 .04
169 Rick Honeycutt .15 .04
170 Hilly Hathaway .15 .04
171 Todd Jones .15 .04
172 Tony Fernandez .15 .04
173 Bo Jackson .75 .23
174 Bobby Munoz .15 .04
175 Greg McMichael .15 .04
176 Graeme Lloyd .15 .04
177 Tom Pagnozzi .15 .04
178 Derrick May .15 .04
179 Pedro Martinez .75 .23
180 Ken Hill .15 .04
181 Bryan Hickerson .15 .04
182 Jose Mesa .15 .04
183 Dave Fleming .15 .04
184 Henry Cotto .15 .04
185 Jeff Kent .30 .09
186 Mark McLemore .15 .04
187 Trevor Hoffman .30 .09
188 Todd Pratt .15 .04
189 Blas Minor .15 .04
190 Charlie Leibrandt .15 .04
191 Tony Pena .15 .04
192 Larry Luebbers RC .15 .04
193 Greg W. Harris .15 .04
194 David Cone .30 .09
195 Bill Gullickson .15 .04
196 Brian Harper .15 .04
197 Steve Karsay .15 .04
198 Greg Myers .15 .04
199 Mark Portugal .15 .04
200 Pat Hentgen .15 .04
201 Mike LaValliere .15 .04
202 Mike Stanley .15 .04
203 Kent Mercker .15 .04
204 Dave Nilsson .15 .04
205 Erik Pappas .15 .04
206 Mike Morgan .15 .04
207 Roger McDowell .15 .04
208 Mike Lansing .15 .04
209 Kirt Manwaring .15 .04
210 Randy Milligan .15 .04
211 Erik Hanson .15 .04
212 Orestes Destrade .15 .04
213 Mike Maddux .15 .04
214 Alan Mills .15 .04
215 Tim Mauser .15 .04
216 Ben Rivera .15 .04
217 Don Slaught .15 .04
218 Bob Patterson .15 .04
219 Carlos Quintana .15 .04
220 Tim Raines CL .15 .04
221 Hal Morris .15 .04
222 Darren Holmes .15 .04
223 Chris Gwynn .15 .04
224 Chad Kreuter .15 .04
225 Mike Hartley .15 .04
226 Scott Lydy .15 .04
227 Eduardo Perez .15 .04
228 Greg Swindell .15 .04
229 Al Leiter .30 .09
230 Scott Radinsky .15 .04
231 Bob Wickman .15 .04
232 Otis Nixon .15 .04
233 Kevin Reimer .15 .04
234 Geronimo Pena .15 .04
235 Kevin Roberson .15 .04
236 Jody Reed .15 .04
237 Kirk Rueter .30 .09
238 Willie McGee .30 .09
239 Charles Nagy .15 .04
240 Tim Leary .15 .04
241 Carl Everett .30 .09
242 Charlie O'Brien .15 .04
243 Mike Pagliarulo .15 .04
244 Kerry Taylor .15 .04
245 Kevin Stocker .15 .04
246 Joel Johnston .15 .04
247 Geno Petralli .15 .04
248 Jeff Russell .15 .04
249 Joe Oliver .15 .04
250 Roberto Mejia .15 .04
251 Chris Haney .15 .04
252 Bill Krueger .15 .04
253 Shane Mack .15 .04
254 Terry Steinbach .15 .04
255 Luis Polonia .15 .04
256 Eddie Taubensee .15 .04
257 Dave Stewart .30 .09
258 Tim Raines .30 .09
259 Bernie Williams .50 .15
260 John Smoltz .50 .15
261 Kevin Seitzer .15 .04
262 Bob Tewksbury .15 .04
263 Bob Scanlan .15 .04
264 Henry Rodriguez .15 .04
265 Tim Scott .15 .04
266 Scott Sanderson .15 .04
267 Eric Plunk .15 .04
268 Edgar Martinez .50 .15
269 Charlie Hough .30 .09
270 Joe Orsulak .15 .04
271 Harold Reynolds .30 .09
272 Tim Teufel .15 .04
273 Bobby Thigpen .15 .04
274 Randy Tomlin .15 .04
275 Gary Redus .15 .04
276 Ken Ryan .15 .04
277 Tim Pugh .15 .04
278 Jayhawk Owens .15 .04
279 Phil Hiatt .15 .04
280 Alan Trammell .50 .15
281 Dave McCarty .15 .04
282 Bob Welch .15 .04
283 J.T. Snow .30 .09
284 Brian Williams .15 .04
285 Devon White .15 .04
286 Steve Sax .15 .04
287 Tony Tarasco .15 .04
288 Bill Spiers .15 .04
289 Allen Watson .15 .04
290 Rickey Henderson CL .50 .15
291 Jose Vizcaino .15 .04
292 Darryl Strawberry .50 .15
293 John Wetteland .30 .09
294 Bill Swift .15 .04
295 Jeff Treadway .15 .04
296 Tino Martinez .50 .15
297 Richie Lewis .15 .04
298 Bret Saberhagen .30 .09
299 Arthur Rhodes .15 .04
300 Guillermo Velasquez .15 .04
301 Milt Thompson .15 .04
302 Doug Strange .15 .04
303 Aaron Sele .15 .04
304 Bip Roberts .15 .04
305 Bruce Ruffin .15 .04
306 Jose Lind .15 .04
307 David Wells .30 .09
308 Bobby Witt .15 .04
309 Mark Wohlers .15 .04
310 B.J. Surhoff .30 .09
311 Mark Whiten .15 .04
312 Turk Wendell .15 .04
313 Raul Mondesi .30 .09
314 Brian Turang RC .15 .04
315 Chris Hammond .15 .04
316 Tim Bogar .15 .04
317 Brad Pennington .15 .04
318 Tim Worrell .15 .04
319 Mitch Williams .15 .04
320 Rondell White .30 .09
321 Frank Viola .30 .09
322 Manny Ramirez .50 .15
323 Gary Wayne .15 .04
324 Mike Macfarlane .15 .04
325 Russ Springer .15 .04
326 Tim Wallach .15 .04
327 Salomon Torres .15 .04
328 Omar Vizquel .30 .09
329 Andy Tomberlin RC .15 .04
330 Chris Sabo .15 .04
331 Mike Mussina .75 .23
332 Andy Benes .15 .04
333 Darren Daulton .30 .09
334 Orlando Merced .15 .04
335 Mark McGwire 2.00 .60
336 Dave Winfield .30 .09
337 Sammy Sosa 1.25 .35
338 Eric Karros .30 .09
339 Greg Vaughn .30 .09
340 Don Mattingly 2.00 .60
341 Frank Thomas .75 .23
342 Fred McGriff .50 .15
343 Kirby Puckett .75 .23
344 Roberto Kelly .15 .04
345 Wally Joyner .30 .09
346 Andres Galarraga .30 .09
347 Bobby Bonilla .30 .09
348 Benito Santiago .30 .09
349 Barry Bonds 2.00 .60
350 Delino DeShields .15 .04
351 Albert Belle .30 .09
352 Randy Johnson .75 .23
353 Tim Salmon .50 .15
354 John Olerud .30 .09
355 Dean Palmer .30 .09
356 Roger Clemens 1.50 .45
357 Jim Abbott .50 .15
358 Mark Grace .50 .15
359 Ozzie Guillen .15 .04
360 Lou Whitaker .30 .09
361 Jose Rijo .15 .04
362 Jeff Montgomery .15 .04
363 Chuck Finley .30 .09
364 Tom Glavine .50 .15
365 Jeff Bagwell .50 .15
366 Joe Carter .30 .09
367 Ray Lankford .15 .04
368 Ramon Martinez .15 .04
369 Jay Buhner .30 .09
370 Matt Williams .30 .09
371 Larry Walker .50 .15
372 Jose Canseco .75 .23
373 Lenny Dykstra .30 .09
374 Bryan Harvey .15 .04
375 Andy Van Slyke .30 .09
376 Ivan Rodriguez .75 .23
377 Kevin Mitchell .15 .04
378 Travis Fryman .30 .09
379 Duane Ward .15 .04
380 Greg Maddux 1.25 .35
381 Scott Servais .15 .04
382 Greg Olson .15 .04
383 Rey Sanchez .15 .04
384 Tom Kramer .15 .04
385 David Valle .15 .04
386 Eddie Murray .75 .23
387 Kevin Higgins .15 .04
388 Dan Wilson .15 .04
389 Todd Frohwirth .15 .04
390 Gerald Williams .15 .04
391 Hipolito Pichardo .15 .04
392 Pat Meares .15 .04
393 Luis Lopez .15 .04
394 Ricky Jordan .15 .04
395 Bob Walk .15 .04
396 Sid Fernandez .15 .04
397 Todd Worrell .15 .04
398 Darryl Hamilton .15 .04
399 Randy Myers .15 .04
400 Rod Brewer .15 .04
401 Lance Blankenship .15 .04
402 Steve Finley .30 .09
403 Phil Leftwich RC .15 .04
404 Juan Guzman .15 .04
405 Anthony Young .15 .04
406 Jeff Gardner .15 .04
407 Ryan Bowen .15 .04
408 Fernando Valenzuela .30 .09
409 David West .15 .04
410 Kenny Rogers .30 .09
411 Bob Zupcic .15 .04
412 Eric Young .15 .04
413 Bret Boone .30 .09
414 Danny Tartabull .15 .04
415 Bob MacDonald .15 .04
416 Ron Karkovice .15 .04
417 Scott Cooper .15 .04
418 Dante Bichette .30 .09
419 Tripp Cromer .15 .04
420 Billy Ashley .15 .04
421 Roger Smithberg .15 .04
422 Dennis Martinez .30 .09
423 Mike Blowers .15 .04
424 Darren Lewis .15 .04
425 Junior Ortiz .15 .04
426 Butch Huskey .15 .04
427 Jimmy Poole .15 .04
428 Walt Weiss .15 .04
429 Scott Bankhead .15 .04
430 Deion Sanders .50 .15
431 Scott Bullett .15 .04
432 Jeff Huson .15 .04
433 Tyler Green .15 .04
434 Billy Hatcher .15 .04
435 Bob Hamelin .15 .04
436 Reggie Sanders .30 .09
437 Scott Erickson .15 .04
438 Steve Reed .15 .04
439 Randy Velarde .15 .04
440 Tony Gwynn CL .50 .15
441 Terry Leach .15 .04
442 Danny Bautista .15 .04
443 Kent Hrbek .30 .09
444 Rick Wilkins .15 .04
445 Tony Phillips .15 .04
446 Dion James .15 .04
447 Joey Cora .15 .04
448 Andre Dawson .30 .09
449 Pedro Castellano .15 .04
450 Tom Gordon .15 .04
451 Rob Dibble .30 .09
452 Ron Darling .15 .04
453 Chipper Jones .75 .23
454 Joe Grahe .15 .04
455 Domingo Cedeno .15 .04
456 Tom Edens .15 .04
457 Mitch Webster .15 .04
458 Jose Bautista .15 .04
459 Troy O'Leary .15 .04
460 Todd Zeile .15 .04
461 Sean Berry .15 .04
462 Brad Holman RC .15 .04
463 Dave Martinez .15 .04
464 Mark Lewis .15 .04
465 Paul Carey .15 .04
466 Jack Armstrong .15 .04
467 David Telgheder .15 .04
468 Gene Harris .15 .04
469 Danny Darwin .15 .04
470 Kim Batiste .15 .04
471 Tim Wakefield .30 .09
472 Craig Lefferts .15 .04
473 Jacob Brumfield .15 .04
474 Lance Painter .15 .04
475 Milt Cuyler .15 .04
476 Melido Perez .15 .04
477 Derek Parks .15 .04
478 Gary DiSarcina .15 .04
479 Steve Bedrosian .15 .04
480 Eric Anthony .15 .04
481 Julio Franco .30 .09
482 Tommy Greene .15 .04
483 Pat Kelly .15 .04
484 Nate Minchey .15 .04
485 William Pennyfeather .15 .04
486 Harold Baines .30 .09
487 Howard Johnson .15 .04
488 Angel Miranda .15 .04
489 Scott Sanders .15 .04
490 Shawon Dunston .15 .04
491 Mel Rojas .15 .04
492 Jeff Nelson .15 .04
493 Archi Cianfrocco .15 .04
494 Al Martin .15 .04
495 Mike Gallego .15 .04
496 Mike Henneman .15 .04
497 Armando Reynoso .15 .04
498 Mickey Morandini .15 .04
499 Rick Renteria .15 .04
500 Rick Sutcliffe .30 .09
501 Bobby Jones .15 .04
502 Gary Gaetti .30 .09
503 Rick Aguilera .15 .04
504 Todd Stottlemyre .15 .04
505 Mike Mohler .15 .04
506 Mike Stanton .15 .04
507 Jose Guzman .15 .04
508 Kevin Rogers .15 .04
509 Chuck Carr .15 .04
510 Chris Jones .15 .04
511 Brent Mayne .15 .04
512 Greg Harris .15 .04
513 Dave Henderson .15 .04
514 Eric Hillman .15 .04
515 Dan Peltier .15 .04
516 Craig Shipley .15 .04
517 John Valentin .15 .04
518 Wilson Alvarez .15 .04
519 Andujar Cedeno .15 .04
520 Troy Neel .15 .04
521 Tom Candiotti .15 .04
522 Matt Mieske .15 .04
523 Jim Thome .75 .23
524 Lou Frazier .15 .04
525 Mike Jackson .15 .04
526 Pedro Martinez RC .15 .04
527 Roger Pavlik .15 .04
528 Kent Bottenfield .15 .04
529 Felix Jose .15 .04
530 Mark Guthrie .15 .04
531 Steve Farr .15 .04
532 Craig Paquette .15 .04
533 Doug Jones .15 .04
534 Luis Alicea .15 .04
535 Cory Snyder .15 .04
536 Paul Sorrento .15 .04
537 Nigel Wilson .15 .04
538 Jeff King .15 .04
539 Willie Greene .15 .04
540 Kirk McCaskill .15 .04
541 Al Osuna .15 .04
542 Greg Hibbard .15 .04
543 Brett Butler .30 .09
544 Jose Valentin .15 .04
545 Wil Cordero .15 .04
546 Chris Bosio .15 .04
547 Jamie Moyer .30 .09
548 Jim Eisenreich .15 .04
549 Vinny Castilla .30 .09
550 Dave Winfield CL .15 .04
551 John Roper .15 .04
552 Lance Johnson .15 .04
553 Scott Kamieniecki .15 .04
554 Mike Moore .15 .04
555 Steve Buechele .15 .04
556 Terry Pendleton .30 .09
557 Todd Van Poppel .15 .04
558 Rob Butler .15 .04
559 Zane Smith .15 .04
560 David Hulse .15 .04
561 Tim Costo .15 .04
562 John Habyan .15 .04
563 Terry Jorgensen .15 .04
564 Matt Nokes .15 .04
565 Kevin McReynolds .15 .04
566 Phil Plantier .15 .04
567 Chris Turner .15 .04
568 Carlos Delgado .50 .15
569 John Jaha .15 .04
570 Dwight Smith .15 .04
571 John Vander Wal .15 .04
572 Trevor Wilson .15 .04
573 Felix Fermin .15 .04
574 Marc Newfield .15 .04
575 Jeromy Burnitz .30 .09
576 Leo Gomez .15 .04
577 Curt Schilling .50 .15
578 Kevin Young .15 .04
579 Jerry Spradlin RC .15 .04
580 Curt Leskanic .15 .04
581 Carl Willis .15 .04
582 Alex Fernandez .15 .04
583 Mark Holzemer .15 .04
584 Domingo Martinez .15 .04
585 Pete Smith .15 .04
586 Brian Jordan .30 .09
587 Kevin Gross .15 .04
588 J.R. Phillips .15 .04
589 Chris Nabholz .15 .04
590 Bill Wertz .15 .04
591 Derek Bell .15 .04
592 Brady Anderson .30 .09
593 Matt Turner .15 .04
594 Pete Incaviglia .15 .04
595 Greg Gagne .15 .04
596 John Flaherty .15 .04
597 Scott Livingstone .15 .04
598 Rod Bolton .15 .04
599 Mike Perez .15 .04
600 Roger Clemens CL .75 .23
601 Tony Castillo .15 .04
602 Henry Mercedes .15 .04
603 Mike Fetters .15 .04
604 Rod Beck .15 .04
605 Damon Buford .15 .04
606 Matt Whiteside .15 .04
607 Shawn Green .75 .23
608 Midre Cummings .15 .04
609 Jeff McNeely .15 .04
610 Danny Sheaffer .15 .04
611 Paul Wagner .15 .04
612 Torey Lovullo .15 .04
613 Javier Lopez .30 .09
614 Mariano Duncan .15 .04
615 Doug Brocail .15 .04
616 Dave Hansen .15 .04
617 Ryan Klesko .30 .09
618 Eric Davis .30 .09
619 Scott Ruffcorn .15 .04
620 Mike Trombley .15 .04
621 Jaime Navarro .15 .04
622 Rheal Cormier .15 .04
623 Jose Offerman .15 .04
624 David Segui .15 .04
625 Robb Nen .30 .09
626 Dave Gallagher .15 .04
627 Julian Tavarez RC .30 .09
628 Chris Gomez .15 .04
629 Jeffrey Hammonds .15 .04
630 Scott Brosius .30 .09
631 Willie Blair .15 .04
632 Doug Drabek .15 .04
633 Bill Wegman .15 .04
634 Jeff McKnight .15 .04
635 Rich Rodriguez .15 .04
636 Steve Trachsel .15 .04
637 Buddy Groom .15 .04
638 Sterling Hitchcock .15 .04
639 Chuck McElroy .15 .04
640 Rene Gonzales .15 .04
641 Dan Plesac .15 .04
642 Jeff Branson .15 .04
643 Darrell Whitmore .15 .04
644 Paul Quantrill .15 .04
645 Rich Rowland .15 .04
646 Curtis Pride RC .30 .09
647 Erik Plantenberg RC .15 .04
648 Albie Lopez .15 .04
649 Rich Batchelor RC .15 .04
650 Lee Smith .30 .09
651 Cliff Floyd .30 .09
652 Pete Schourek .15 .04
653 Reggie Jefferson .15 .04
654 Bill Haselman .15 .04
655 Steve Hosey .15 .04
656 Mark Clark .15 .04
657 Mark Davis .15 .04
658 Dave Magadan .15 .04
659 Candy Maldonado .15 .04
660 Mark Langston CL .15 .04

1994 Donruss Special Edition

Issued in two series of 50 cards, this 100-card standard-size set of 1994 Donruss Special Edition represents a Gold edition parallel of the best players in the game. The first 50 cards correspond to cards 1-50 in the first series, while the second 50 cards correspond to cards 331-380 in the second series. The cards were issued one per pack or two per jumbo pack.

Nm-Mt Ex-Mt
*STARS: .75X TO 2X BASIC CARDS ...

1994 Donruss Anniversary '84

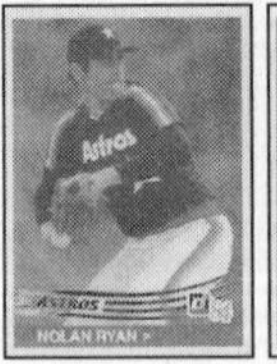

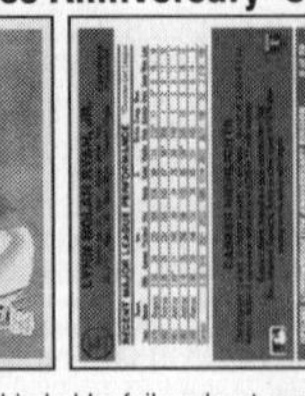

Randomly inserted in hobby foil packs at a rate of one in 12, this ten-card standard-size se reproduces selected cards from the 1984 Donruss baseball set. The cards feature white bordered color player photos on their fronts The cards are numbered on the back at the bottom right as "X of 10," and also carry the numbers from the original 1984 set at the upper left.

Nm-Mt Ex-Mt
COMPLETE SET (10) 60.00 18.00
1 Joe Carter 2.00 .60
2 Robin Yount 8.00 2.40
3 George Brett 12.00 3.60
4 Rickey Henderson 5.00 1.50
5 Nolan Ryan 25.00 7.50
6 Cal Ripken 15.00 4.50
7 Wade Boggs UER 3.00 .90
1983 runs 10, should be 100
8 Don Mattingly 12.00 3.60
9 Ryne Sandberg 8.00 2.40
10 Tony Gwynn 6.00 1.80

1994 Donruss Award Winner Jumbos

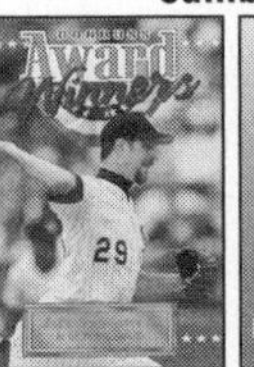

This 10-card set was issued one per jumbo fo and Canadian foil boxes and spotlights player that won various awards in 1993. Cards 1- were included in first series boxes and 6-1 with the second series. The cards measur approximately 3 1/2" by 5". Ten-thousand c each card were produced. Card fronts are full bleed with a color player photo and the Awar Winner logo at the top. The backs ar individually numbered out of 10,000.

Nm-Mt Ex-Mt
COMPLETE SET (10) 80.00 24.00
COMPLETE SERIES 1 (5) 60.00 18.00
COMPLETE SERIES 2 (5) 20.00 6.00
1 Barry Bonds MVP 20.00 6.00
2 Greg Maddux CY 12.00 3.60
3 Mike Piazza ROY 15.00 4.50
4 Barry Bonds HR King 20.00 6.00
5 Kirby Puckett AS MVP 8.00 2.40
6 Frank Thomas MVP 8.00 2.40
7 Jack McDowell CY 1.50 .45
8 Tim Salmon ROY 5.00 1.50
9 Juan Gonzalez HR King 8.00 2.40
10 Paul Molitor WS MVP 6.00 1.80

1994 Donruss Diamond Kings

This 30-card standard-size set was split in tw series. Cards 1-14 and 29 were random inserted in first series packs, while cards 15-2 and 30 were inserted in second series pack With each series, the insertion rate was one nine. The fronts feature full-bleed playe portraits by noted sports artist Dick Perez. Th cards are numbered on the back with the pref DK.

Nm-Mt Ex-M
COMPLETE SET (30) 50.00 15.0
*JUMBO DK's: .75X TO 2X BASIC DK'S
ONE JUMBO DK PER RETAIL BOX ......
DK1 Barry Bonds 6.00 1.8
DK2 Mo Vaughn 1.00 .3
DK3 Steve Avery .50 .1
DK4 Tim Salmon 1.50 .4
DK5 Rick Wilkins .50 .1
DK6 Brian Harper .50 .1
DK7 Andres Galarraga 1.00 .3
DK8 Albert Belle 1.00 .3
DK9 John Kruk 1.00 .3
DK10 Ivan Rodriguez 2.50 .7
DK11 Tony Gwynn 3.00 .9
DK12 Brian McRae .50 .1
DK13 Bobby Bonilla 1.00 .3
DK14 Ken Griffey Jr. 4.00 1.2
DK15 Mike Piazza 5.00 1.5
DK16 Don Mattingly 6.00 1.8
DK17 Barry Larkin 2.50 .7
DK18 Ruben Sierra .50 .1

DK19 Orlando Merced .50 .15
DK20 Greg Vaughn 1.00 .30
DK21 Gregg Jefferies .50 .15
DK22 Cecil Fielder 1.00 .30
DK23 Moises Alou 1.00 .30
DK24 John Olerud 1.00 .30
DK25 Gary Sheffield 1.00 .30
DK26 Mike Mussina 2.50 .75
DK27 Jeff Bagwell 1.50 .45
DK28 Frank Thomas 2.50 .75
DK29 Dave Winfield 1.00 .30
DK30 Checklist .50 .15

1994 Donruss Dominators

This 20-card, standard-size set was randomly inserted in all packs at a rate of one in 12. The 10 series 1 cards feature the top home run hitters of the '90s, while the 10 series 2 cards depict the decade's batting average leaders.

Nm-Mt Ex-Mt
COMP.SER.1 SET (10) 20.00 6.00
COMP.SER.2 SET (10) 20.00 6.00
*JUMBOS: .75X TO 2X BASIC DOM....
ONE JUMBO DOMINATOR PER HOBBY BOX
A1 Cecil Fielder 1.00 .30
A2 Barry Bonds 6.00 1.80
A3 Fred McGriff 1.50 .45
A4 Matt Williams 1.00 .30
A5 Joe Carter 1.00 .30
A6 Juan Gonzalez 2.50 .75
A7 Jose Canseco 2.50 .75
A8 Ron Gant 1.00 .30
A9 Ken Griffey Jr. 4.00 1.20
A10 Mark McGwire 6.00 1.80
B1 Tony Gwynn 3.00 .90
B2 Frank Thomas 2.50 .75
B3 Paul Molitor 1.50 .45
B4 Edgar Martinez 1.50 .45
B5 Kirby Puckett 2.50 .75
B6 Ken Griffey Jr. 4.00 1.20
B7 Barry Bonds 6.00 1.80
B8 Willie McGee 1.00 .30
B9 Lenny Dykstra 1.00 .30
B10 John Kruk 1.00 .30

1994 Donruss Elite

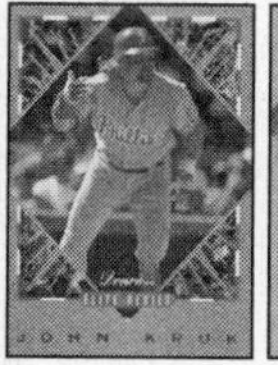

This 12-card set was issued in two series of six. Using a continued numbering system from previous years, cards 37-42 were randomly inserted in first series foil packs with cards 43-48 a second series offering. The cards measure the standard size. Only 10,000 of each card were produced. .

Nm-Mt Ex-Mt
COMPLETE SET (12) 140.00 42.50
COMPLETE SERIES 1 (6) 60.00 18.00
COMPLETE SERIES 2 (6) 80.00 24.00
37 Frank Thomas 10.00 3.00
38 Tony Gwynn 15.00 4.50
39 Tim Salmon 10.00 3.00
40 Albert Belle 10.00 3.00
41 John Kruk 10.00 3.00
42 Juan Gonzalez 10.00 3.00
43 John Olerud 10.00 3.00
44 Barry Bonds 30.00 9.00
45 Ken Griffey Jr. 20.00 6.00
46 Mike Piazza 20.00 6.00
47 Jack McDowell 10.00 3.00
48 Andres Galarraga 10.00 3.00

1994 Donruss Long Ball Leaders

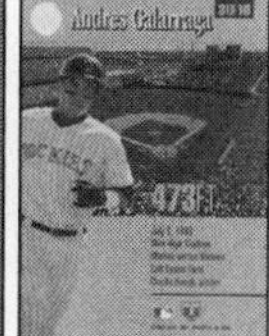

Inserted in second series hobby foil packs at a rate of one in 12, this 10-card standard-size set features some of top home run hitters and the distance of their longest home run of 1993.

Nm-Mt Ex-Mt
COMPLETE SET (10) 30.00 9.00
1 Cecil Fielder 1.50 .45
2 Dean Palmer 1.50 .45
3 Andres Galarraga 1.50 .45
4 Bo Jackson 4.00 1.20
5 Ken Griffey Jr. 6.00 1.80
6 David Justice 1.50 .45
7 Mike Piazza 8.00 2.40
8 Frank Thomas 4.00 1.20
9 Barry Bonds 10.00 3.00
10 Juan Gonzalez 4.00 1.20

1994 Donruss MVPs

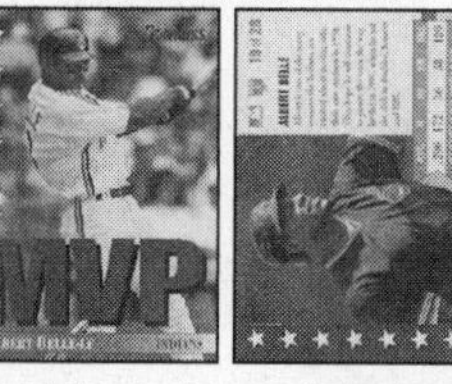

Inserted at a rate of one per first and second series jumbo pack, this 28-card standard-size set was split into two series of 14; one player for each team. The first 14 are of National League players with the latter group being American Leaguers. Full-bleed card fronts feature an action photo of the player with "MVP" in large red (American League) or blue (National) letters at the bottom. The player's name and, for Amercian League player cards only, team name are beneath the "MVP".

Nm-Mt Ex-Mt
COMPLETE SET (28) 60.00 18.00
COMPLETE SERIES 1 (14) 15.00 4.50
COMPLETE SERIES 2 (14) 50.00 15.00
1 David Justice 1.50 .45
2 Mark Grace 2.50 .75
3 Jose Rijo .75 .23
4 Andres Galarraga 1.50 .45
5 Bryan Harvey .75 .23
6 Jeff Bagwell 2.50 .75
7 Mike Piazza 8.00 2.40
8 Moises Alou 1.50 .45
9 Bobby Bonilla 1.50 .45
10 Len Dykstra 1.50 .45
11 Jeff King .75 .23
12 Gregg Jefferies .75 .23
13 Tony Gwynn 5.00 1.50
14 Barry Bonds 10.00 3.00
15 Cal Ripken Jr. 12.00 3.60
16 Mo Vaughn 1.50 .45
17 Tim Salmon 2.50 .75
18 Frank Thomas 4.00 1.20
19 Albert Belle 1.50 .45
20 Cecil Fielder 1.50 .45
21 Wally Joyner 1.50 .45
22 Greg Vaughn 1.50 .45
23 Kirby Puckett 4.00 1.20
24 Don Mattingly 10.00 3.00
25 Ruben Sierra .75 .23
26 Ken Griffey Jr. 6.00 1.80
27 Juan Gonzalez 4.00 1.20
28 John Olerud 1.50 .45

1994 Donruss Spirit of the Game

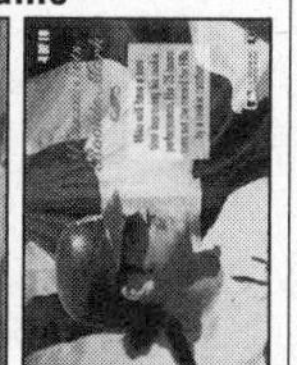

This ten card set features a selction of the games top stars. Cards 1-5 were randomly inserted in first-series magazine jumbo packs and cards 6-10 in second series magazine jumbo packs.

Nm-Mt Ex-Mt
COMPLETE SERIES 1 (5) 25.00 7.50
COMPLETE SERIES 2 (5) 20.00 6.00
*JUMBOS: .75X TO 2X BASIC SOG ....
ONE JUMBO SPIRIT PER MAG.JUMBO BOX
1 John Olerud 2.00 .60
2 Barry Bonds 12.00 3.60
3 Ken Griffey Jr. 8.00 2.40
4 Mike Piazza 10.00 3.00
5 Juan Gonzalez 5.00 1.50
6 Frank Thomas 5.00 1.50
7 Tim Salmon 3.00 .90
8 David Justice 2.00 .60
9 Don Mattingly 12.00 3.60
10 Lenny Dykstra 2.00 .60

1995 Donruss

The 1995 Donruss set consists of 550 standard-size cards. The first series had 330 cards while 220 cards comprised the second series. The fronts feature borderless color action player photos. A second, smaller color player photo in a homeplate shape with team color-coded borders appears in the lower left corner. There are no key Rookie Cards in this set. To preview the product prior to it's public release, Donruss printed up additional quantities of cards 5, 8, 20, 42, 55, 275, 331 and 340 and mailed them to dealers and hobby media.

Nm-Mt Ex-Mt
COMPLETE SET (550) 30.00 9.00
COMP.SERIES 1 (330) 20.00 6.00
COMP.SERIES 2 (220) 10.00 3.00
1 David Justice .30 .09
2 Rene Arocha .15 .04
3 Sandy Alomar Jr. .15 .04
4 Luis Lopez .15 .04
5 Mike Piazza 1.25 .35
6 Bobby Jones .15 .04
7 Damion Easley .15 .04
8 Barry Bonds 2.00 .60
9 Mike Mussina .75 .23
10 Kevin Seitzer .15 .04
11 John Smiley .15 .04
12 Wm.VanLandingham .15 .04
13 Ron Darling .15 .04
14 Walt Weiss .15 .04
15 Mike Lansing .15 .04
16 Allen Watson .15 .04
17 Aaron Sele .15 .04
18 Randy Johnson .75 .23
19 Dean Palmer .30 .09
20 Jeff Bagwell .50 .15
21 Curt Schilling .50 .15
22 Darrell Whitmore .15 .04
23 Steve Trachsel .15 .04
24 Dan Wilson .15 .04
25 Steve Finley .30 .09
26 Bret Boone .30 .09
27 Charles Johnson .30 .09
28 Mike Stanton .15 .04
29 Ismael Valdes .15 .04
30 Salomon Torres .15 .04
31 Eric Anthony .15 .04
32 Spike Owen .15 .04
33 Joey Cora .15 .04
34 Robert Eenhoorn .15 .04
35 Rick White .15 .04
36 Omar Vizquel .30 .09
37 Carlos Delgado .30 .09
38 Eddie Williams .15 .04
39 Shawon Dunston .15 .04
40 Darrin Fletcher .15 .04
41 Leo Gomez .15 .04
42 Juan Gonzalez .75 .23
43 Luis Alicea .15 .04
44 Ken Ryan .15 .04
45 Lou Whitaker .30 .09
46 Mike Blowers .15 .04
47 Willie Blair .15 .04
48 Todd Van Poppel .15 .04
49 Roberto Alomar .75 .23
50 Ozzie Smith 1.25 .35
51 Sterling Hitchcock .15 .04
52 Mo Vaughn .30 .09
53 Rick Aguilera .15 .04
54 Kent Mercker .15 .04
55 Don Mattingly 2.00 .60
56 Bob Scanlan .15 .04
57 Wilson Alvarez .15 .04
58 Jose Mesa .15 .04
59 Scott Kamieniecki .15 .04
60 Todd Jones .15 .04
61 John Kruk .30 .09
62 Mike Stanley .15 .04
63 Tino Martinez .50 .15
64 Eddie Zambrano .15 .04
65 Todd Hundley .15 .04
66 Jamie Moyer .30 .09
67 Rich Amaral .15 .04
68 Jose Valentin .15 .04
69 Alex Gonzalez .15 .04
70 Kurt Abbott .15 .04
71 Delino DeShields .15 .04
72 Brian Anderson .15 .04
73 John Vander Wal .15 .04
74 Turner Ward .15 .04
75 Tim Raines .30 .09
76 Mark Acre .15 .04
77 Jose Offerman .15 .04
78 Jimmy Key .30 .09
79 Mark Whiten .15 .04
80 Mark Gubicza .15 .04
81 Darren Hall .15 .04
82 Travis Fryman .30 .09
83 Cal Ripken 2.50 .75
84 Geronimo Berroa .15 .04
85 Bret Barberie .15 .04
86 Andy Ashby .15 .04
87 Steve Avery .15 .04
88 Rich Becker .15 .04
89 John Valentin .15 .04
90 Glenallen Hill .15 .04
91 Carlos Garcia .15 .04
92 Dennis Martinez .30 .09
93 Pat Kelly .15 .04
94 Orlando Miller .15 .04
95 Felix Jose .15 .04
96 Mike Kingery .15 .04
97 Jeff Kent .30 .09
98 Pete Incaviglia .15 .04
99 Chad Curtis .15 .04
100 Thomas Howard .15 .04
101 Hector Carrasco .15 .04
102 Tom Pagnozzi .15 .04
103 Danny Tartabull .15 .04
104 Donnie Elliott .15 .04
105 Danny Jackson .15 .04
106 Steve Dunn .15 .04
107 Roger Salkeld .15 .04
108 Jeff King .15 .04
109 Cecil Fielder .30 .09
110 Paul Molitor CL .30 .09
111 Denny Neagle .30 .09
112 Troy Neel .15 .04
113 Rod Beck .15 .04
114 Alex Rodriguez 2.00 .60
115 Joey Eischen .15 .04
116 Tom Candiotti .15 .04
117 Ray McDavid .15 .04
118 Vince Coleman .15 .04
119 Pete Harnisch .15 .04
120 David Nied .15 .04
121 Pat Rapp .15 .04
122 Sammy Sosa 1.25 .35
123 Steve Reed .15 .04
124 Jose Oliva .15 .04
125 Ricky Bottalico .15 .04
126 Jose DeLeon .15 .04
127 Pat Hentgen .15 .04
128 Will Clark .75 .23
129 Mark Dewey .15 .04
130 Greg Vaughn .30 .09
131 Darren Dreifort .15 .04
132 Ed Sprague .15 .04
133 Lee Smith .30 .09
134 Charles Nagy .15 .04
135 Phil Plantier .15 .04
136 Jason Jacome .15 .04
137 Jose Lima .15 .04
138 J.R. Phillips .15 .04
139 J.T. Snow .30 .09
140 Michael Huff .15 .04
141 Billy Brewer .15 .04
142 Jeromy Burnitz .30 .09
143 Ricky Bones .15 .04
144 Carlos Rodriguez .15 .04
145 Luis Gonzalez .30 .09
146 Mark Lemke .15 .04
147 Al Martin .15 .04
148 Mike Bordick .15 .04
149 Robb Nen .30 .09
150 Wil Cordero .15 .04
151 Edgar Martinez .50 .15
152 Gerald Williams .15 .04
153 Esteban Beltre .15 .04
154 Mike Moore .15 .04
155 Mark Langston .15 .04
156 Mark Clark .15 .04
157 Bobby Ayala .15 .04
158 Rick Wilkins .15 .04
159 Bobby Munoz .15 .04
160 Brett Butler CL .15 .04
161 Scott Erickson .15 .04
162 Paul Molitor .50 .15
163 Jon Lieber .15 .04
164 Jason Grimsley .15 .04
165 Norberto Martin .15 .04
166 Javier Lopez .30 .09
167 Brian McRae .15 .04
168 Gary Sheffield .30 .09
169 Marcus Moore .15 .04
170 John Hudek .15 .04
171 Kelly Stinnett .15 .04
172 Chris Gomez .15 .04
173 Rey Sanchez .15 .04
174 Juan Guzman .15 .04
175 Chan Ho Park .30 .09
176 Terry Shumpert .15 .04
177 Steve Ontiveros .15 .04
178 Brad Ausmus .15 .04
179 Tim Davis .15 .04
180 Billy Ashley .15 .04
181 Vinny Castilla .30 .09
182 Bill Spiers .15 .04
183 Randy Knorr .15 .04
184 Brian Hunter .15 .04
185 Pat Meares .15 .04
186 Steve Buechele .15 .04
187 Kirt Manwaring .15 .04
188 Tim Naehring .15 .04
189 Matt Mieske .15 .04
190 Josias Manzanillo .15 .04
191 Greg McMichael .15 .04
192 Chuck Carr .15 .04
193 Midre Cummings .15 .04
194 Darryl Strawberry .50 .15
195 Greg Gagne .15 .04
196 Steve Cooke .15 .04
197 Woody Williams .15 .04
198 Ron Karkovice .15 .04
199 Phil Leftwich .15 .04
200 Jim Thome .75 .23
201 Brady Anderson .30 .09
202 Pedro A.Martinez .15 .04
203 Steve Karsay .15 .04
204 Reggie Sanders .30 .09
205 Bill Risley .15 .04
206 Jay Bell .30 .09
207 Kevin Brown .30 .09
208 Tim Scott .15 .04
209 Lenny Dykstra .30 .09
210 Willie Greene .15 .04
211 Jim Eisenreich .15 .04
212 Cliff Floyd .30 .09
213 Otis Nixon .15 .04
214 Eduardo Perez .15 .04
215 Manuel Lee .15 .04
216 Armando Benitez .30 .09
217 Dave McCarty .15 .04
218 Scott Livingstone .15 .04
219 Chad Kreuter .15 .04
220 Don Mattingly CL 1.00 .30
221 Brian Jordan .30 .09
222 Matt Whiteside .15 .04
223 Jim Edmonds .30 .09
224 Tony Gwynn 1.00 .30
225 Jose Lind .15 .04
226 Marvin Freeman .15 .04
227 Ken Hill .15 .04
228 David Hulse .15 .04
229 Joe Hesketh .15 .04
230 Roberto Petagine .15 .04
231 Jeffrey Hammonds .15 .04
232 John Jaha .15 .04
233 John Burkett .15 .04
234 Hal Morris .15 .04
235 Tony Castillo .15 .04
236 Ryan Bowen .15 .04
237 Wayne Kirby .15 .04
238 Brent Mayne .15 .04
239 Jim Bullinger .15 .04
240 Mike Lieberthal .30 .09
241 Barry Larkin .75 .23
242 David Segui .15 .04
243 Jose Bautista .15 .04
244 Hector Fajardo .15 .04
245 Orel Hershiser .30 .09
246 James Mouton .15 .04
247 Scott Leius .15 .04
248 Tom Glavine .50 .15
249 Danny Bautista .15 .04
250 Jose Mercedes .15 .04
251 Marquis Grissom .15 .04
252 Charlie Hayes .15 .04
253 Ryan Klesko .30 .09
254 Vicente Palacios .15 .04
255 Matias Carrillo .15 .04
256 Gary DiSarcina .15 .04
257 Kirk Gibson .30 .09
258 Garey Ingram .15 .04
259 Alex Fernandez .15 .04
260 John Mabry .15 .04
261 Chris Howard .15 .04
262 Miguel Jimenez .15 .04
263 Heathcliff Slocumb .15 .04
264 Albert Belle .30 .09
265 Dave Clark .15 .04
266 Joe Orsulak .15 .04
267 Joey Hamilton .15 .04
268 Mark Portugal .15 .04
269 Kevin Tapani .15 .04
270 Sid Fernandez .15 .04
271 Steve Dreyer .15 .04
272 Denny Hocking .15 .04
273 Troy O'Leary .15 .04
274 Milt Cuyler .15 .04
275 Frank Thomas .75 .23
276 Jorge Fabregas .15 .04
277 Mike Gallego .15 .04
278 Mickey Morandini .15 .04
279 Roberto Hernandez .15 .04
280 Henry Rodriguez .15 .04
281 Garret Anderson .30 .09
282 Bob Wickman .15 .04
283 Gar Finnvold .15 .04
284 Paul O'Neill .50 .15
285 Royce Clayton .15 .04
286 Chuck Knoblauch .30 .09
287 Johnny Ruffin .15 .04
288 Dave Nilsson .15 .04
289 David Cone .30 .09
290 Chuck McElroy .15 .04
291 Kevin Stocker .15 .04
292 Jose Rijo .15 .04
293 Sean Berry .15 .04
294 Ozzie Guillen .15 .04
295 Chris Hoiles .15 .04
296 Kevin Foster .15 .04
297 Jeff Frye .15 .04
298 Lance Johnson .15 .04
299 Mike Kelly .15 .04
300 Ellis Burks .30 .09
301 Roberto Kelly .15 .04
302 Dante Bichette .30 .09
303 Alvaro Espinoza .15 .04
304 Alex Cole .15 .04
305 Rickey Henderson .75 .23
306 Dave Weathers .15 .04
307 Shane Reynolds .15 .04
308 Bobby Bonilla .30 .09
309 Junior Felix .15 .04
310 Jeff Fassero .15 .04
311 Darren Lewis .15 .04
312 John Doherty .15 .04
313 Scott Servais .15 .04
314 Rick Helling .15 .04
315 Pedro Martinez .75 .23
316 Wes Chamberlain .15 .04
317 Bryan Eversgerd .15 .04
318 Trevor Hoffman .30 .09
319 John Patterson .15 .04
320 Matt Walbeck .15 .04
321 Jeff Montgomery .15 .04
322 Mel Rojas .15 .04
323 Eddie Taubensee .15 .04
324 Ray Lankford .15 .04
325 Jose Vizcaino .15 .04
326 Carlos Baerga .15 .04
327 Jack Voigt .15 .04
328 Julio Franco .30 .09
329 Brent Gates .15 .04
330 Kirby Puckett CL .50 .15
331 Greg Maddux 1.25 .35
332 Jason Bere .15 .04
333 Bill Wegman .15 .04
334 Tuffy Rhodes .15 .04
335 Kevin Young .15 .04
336 Andy Benes .15 .04
337 Pedro Astacio .15 .04
338 Reggie Jefferson .15 .04
339 Tim Belcher .15 .04
340 Ken Griffey Jr. 1.25 .35
341 Mariano Duncan .15 .04
342 Andres Galarraga .30 .09
343 Rondell White .30 .09
344 Cory Bailey .15 .04
345 Bryan Harvey .15 .04
346 John Franco .30 .09
347 Greg Swindell .15 .04
348 David West .15 .04
349 Fred McGriff .50 .15
350 Jose Canseco .75 .23
351 Orlando Merced .15 .04
352 Rheal Cormier .15 .04
353 Carlos Pulido .15 .04
354 Terry Steinbach .15 .04
355 Wade Boggs .50 .15
356 B.J. Surhoff .30 .09
357 Rafael Palmeiro .50 .15
358 Anthony Young .15 .04
359 Tom Brunansky .15 .04
360 Todd Stottlemyre .15 .04
361 Chris Turner .15 .04
362 Joe Boever .15 .04
363 Jeff Blauser .15 .04
364 Derek Bell .15 .04
365 Matt Williams .30 .09
366 Jeremy Hernandez .15 .04
367 Joe Girardi .15 .04
368 Mike Devereaux .15 .04
369 Jim Abbott .50 .15
370 Manny Ramirez .30 .09
371 Kenny Lofton .30 .09
372 Mark Smith .15 .04
373 Dave Fleming .15 .04
374 Dave Stewart .30 .09
375 Roger Pavlik .15 .04
376 Hipolito Pichardo .15 .04
377 Bill Taylor .15 .04
378 Robin Ventura .30 .09
379 Bernard Gilkey .15 .04
380 Kirby Puckett .75 .23
381 Steve Howe .15 .04
382 Devon White .30 .09
383 Roberto Mejia .15 .04
384 Darrin Jackson .15 .04
385 Mike Morgan .15 .04
386 Rusty Meacham .15 .04
387 Bill Swift .15 .04
388 Lou Frazier .15 .04
389 Andy Van Slyke .30 .09
390 Brett Butler .30 .09
391 Bobby Witt .15 .04
392 Jeff Conine .30 .09
393 Tim Hyers .15 .04
394 Terry Pendleton .30 .09

Card	Nm-Mt	Ex-Mt
395 Ricky Jordan	.15	.04
396 Eric Plunk	.15	.04
397 Melido Perez	.15	.04
398 Darryl Kile	.30	.09
399 Mark McLemore	.15	.04
400 Greg W.Harris	.15	.04
401 Jim Leyritz	.15	.04
402 Doug Strange	.15	.04
403 Tim Salmon	.50	.15
404 Terry Mulholland	.15	.04
405 Robby Thompson	.15	.04
406 Ruben Sierra	.15	.04
407 Tony Phillips	.15	.04
408 Moises Alou	.30	.09
409 Felix Fermin	.15	.04
410 Pat Listach	.15	.04
411 Kevin Bass	.15	.04
412 Ben McDonald	.15	.04
413 Scott Cooper	.15	.04
414 Jody Reed	.15	.04
415 Deion Sanders	.50	.15
416 Ricky Gutierrez	.15	.04
417 Gregg Jefferies	.15	.04
418 Jack McDowell	.15	.04
419 Al Leiter	.30	.09
420 Tony Longmire	.15	.04
421 Paul Wagner	.15	.04
422 Geronimo Pena	.15	.04
423 Ivan Rodriguez	.75	.23
424 Kevin Gross	.15	.04
425 Kirk McCaskill	.15	.04
426 Greg Myers	.15	.04
427 Roger Clemens	1.50	.45
428 Chris Hammond	.15	.04
429 Randy Myers	.15	.04
430 Roger Mason	.15	.04
431 Bret Saberhagen	.30	.09
432 Jeff Reboulet	.15	.04
433 John Olerud	.30	.09
434 Bill Gullickson	.15	.04
435 Eddie Murray	.75	.23
436 Pedro Munoz	.15	.04
437 Charlie O'Brien	.15	.04
438 Jeff Nelson	.15	.04
439 Mike Macfarlane	.15	.04
440 Don Mattingly CL	1.00	.30
441 Derrick May	.15	.04
442 John Roper	.15	.04
443 Darryl Hamilton	.15	.04
444 Dan Miceli	.15	.04
445 Tony Eusebio	.15	.04
446 Jerry Browne	.15	.04
447 Wally Joyner	.30	.09
448 Brian Harper	.15	.04
449 Scott Fletcher	.15	.04
450 Bip Roberts	.15	.04
451 Pete Smith	.15	.04
452 Chili Davis	.30	.09
453 Dave Hollins	.15	.04
454 Tony Pena	.15	.04
455 Butch Henry	.15	.04
456 Craig Biggio	.50	.15
457 Zane Smith	.15	.04
458 Ryan Thompson	.15	.04
459 Mike Jackson	.15	.04
460 Mark McGwire	2.00	.60
461 John Smoltz	.50	.15
462 Steve Scarsone	.15	.04
463 Greg Colbrunn	.15	.04
464 Shawn Green	.30	.09
465 David Wells	.30	.09
466 Jose Hernandez	.15	.04
467 Chip Hale	.15	.04
468 Tony Tarasco	.15	.04
469 Kevin Mitchell	.15	.04
470 Billy Hatcher	.15	.04
471 Jay Buhner	.30	.09
472 Ken Caminiti	.30	.09
473 Tom Henke	.15	.04
474 Todd Worrell	.15	.04
475 Mark Eichhorn	.15	.04
476 Bruce Ruffin	.15	.04
477 Chuck Finley	.30	.09
478 Marc Newfield	.15	.04
479 Paul Shuey	.15	.04
480 Bob Tewksbury	.15	.04
481 Ramon J.Martinez	.15	.04
482 Melvin Nieves	.15	.04
483 Todd Zeile	.15	.04
484 Benito Santiago	.30	.09
485 Stan Javier	.15	.04
486 Kirk Rueter	.15	.04
487 Andre Dawson	.30	.09
488 Eric Karros	.30	.09
489 Dave Magadan	.15	.04
490 Joe Carter CL	.15	.04
491 Randy Velarde	.15	.04
492 Larry Walker	.50	.15
493 Cris Carpenter	.15	.04
494 Tom Gordon	.15	.04
495 Dave Burba	.15	.04
496 Darren Bragg	.15	.04
497 Darren Daulton	.30	.09
498 Don Slaught	.15	.04
499 Pat Borders	.15	.04
500 Lenny Harris	.15	.04
501 Joe Ausanio	.15	.04
502 Alan Trammell	.50	.15
503 Mike Fetters	.15	.04
504 Scott Ruffcorn	.15	.04
505 Rich Rowland	.15	.04
506 Juan Samuel	.15	.04
507 Bo Jackson	.75	.23
508 Jeff Branson	.15	.04
509 Bernie Williams	.50	.15
510 Paul Sorrento	.15	.04
511 Dennis Eckersley	.30	.09
512 Pat Mahomes	.15	.04
513 Rusty Greer	.30	.09
514 Luis Polonia	.15	.04
515 Willie Banks	.15	.04
516 John Wetteland	.30	.09
517 Mike LaValliere	.15	.04
518 Tommy Greene	.15	.04
519 Mark Grace	.50	.15
520 Bob Hamelin	.15	.04
521 Scott Sanderson	.15	.04
522 Joe Carter	.30	.09
523 Jeff Brantley	.15	.04
524 Andrew Lorraine	.15	.04
525 Rico Brogna	.15	.04
526 Shane Mack	.15	.04
527 Mark Wohlers	.15	.04
528 Scott Sanders	.15	.04
529 Chris Bosio	.15	.04
530 Andujar Cedeno	.15	.04
531 Kenny Rogers	.30	.09
532 Doug Drabek	.15	.04
533 Curt Leskanic	.15	.04
534 Craig Shipley	.15	.04
535 Craig Grebeck	.15	.04
536 Cal Eldred	.15	.04
537 Mickey Tettleton	.15	.04
538 Harold Baines	.30	.09
539 Tim Wallach	.15	.04
540 Damon Buford	.15	.04
541 Lenny Webster	.15	.04
542 Kevin Appier	.30	.09
543 Raul Mondesi	.30	.09
544 Eric Young	.15	.04
545 Russ Davis	.15	.04
546 Mike Benjamin	.15	.04
547 Mike Greenwell	.15	.04
548 Scott Brosius	.30	.09
549 Brian Dorsett	.15	.04
550 Chili Davis CL	.15	.04

1995 Donruss Press Proofs

Parallel to the basic Donruss set, the Press Proofs are distinguished by the player's name, team name and Donruss logo being done in gold foil on front. The words "Press Proof are also in gold at the top. The first 2,000 cards of the production run were stamped as such (though not serial numbered) and inserted at a rate of one in every 20 first series hobby and retail packs, 1:24 second series hobby and retail packs, 1:18 jumbo packs and 1:24 magazine packs.

	Nm-Mt	Ex-Mt
*STARS: 6X TO 15X BASIC CARDS		

1995 Donruss All-Stars

This 18-card standard-size set was randomly inserted into retail packs. The first series has the nine 1994 American League starters while the second series honored the National League starters. The cards are numbered in the upper right with either an "AL-X" or an "NL-X."

	Nm-Mt	Ex-Mt
COMPLETE SET (18)	150.00	45.00
COMPLETE SERIES 1 (9)	90.00	27.00
COMPLETE SERIES 2 (9)	60.00	18.00
AL1 Jimmy Key	3.00	.90
AL2 Ivan Rodriguez	8.00	2.40
AL3 Frank Thomas	8.00	2.40
AL4 Roberto Alomar	8.00	2.40
AL5 Wade Boggs	5.00	1.50
AL6 Cal Ripken	25.00	7.50
AL7 Joe Carter	3.00	.90
AL8 Ken Griffey Jr.	12.00	3.60
AL9 Kirby Puckett	8.00	2.40
NL1 Greg Maddux	12.00	3.60
NL2 Mike Piazza	12.00	3.60
NL3 Gregg Jefferies	1.50	.45
NL4 Mariano Duncan	1.50	.45
NL5 Matt Williams	3.00	.90
NL6 Ozzie Smith	12.00	3.60
NL7 Barry Bonds	20.00	6.00
NL8 Tony Gwynn	10.00	3.00
NL9 David Justice	3.00	.90

1995 Donruss Bomb Squad

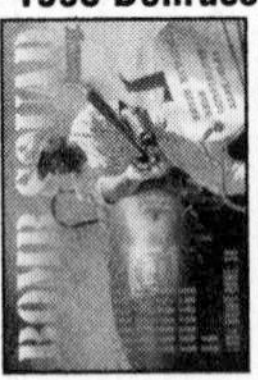

Randomly inserted one in every 24 retail packs and one in every 16 magazine packs, this set features the top six home run hitters in the National and American League. These cards were only included in first series packs. Each of the six cards shows a different slugger on the either side of the card.

	Nm-Mt	Ex-Mt
COMPLETE SET (6)	12.00	3.60
1 Ken Griffey	3.00	.90
Matt Williams		
2 Frank Thomas	2.00	.60
Jeff Bagwell		
3 Albert Belle	5.00	1.50
Barry Bonds		
4 Jose Canseco	2.00	.60
Fred McGriff		
5 Cecil Fielder	.75	.23
Andres Galarraga		
6 Joe Carter	.75	.23
Kevin Mitchell		

1995 Donruss Diamond Kings

The 1995 Donruss Diamond King set consists of 29 standard-size cards that were randomly inserted in packs. The fronts feature water color player portraits by noted sports artist Dick Perez. The player's name and "Diamond Kings" are in gold foil. The backs have a dark blue border with a player photo and text. The cards are numbered on back with a DK prefix.

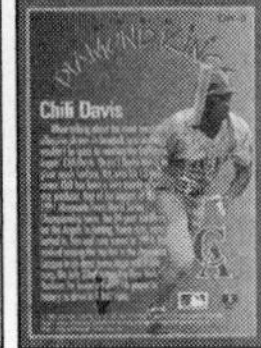

	Nm-Mt	Ex-Mt
COMPLETE SET (29)	50.00	15.00
COMPLETE SERIES 1 (14)	20.00	6.00
COMPLETE SERIES 2 (15)	30.00	9.00
DK1 Frank Thomas	3.00	.90
DK2 Jeff Bagwell	2.00	.60
DK3 Chili Davis	1.25	.35
DK4 Dante Bichette	1.25	.35
DK5 Ruben Sierra	.60	.18
DK6 Jeff Conine	1.25	.35
DK7 Paul O'Neill	2.00	.60
DK8 Bobby Bonilla	1.25	.35
DK9 Joe Carter	1.25	.35
DK10 Moises Alou	1.25	.35
DK11 Kenny Lofton	1.25	.35
DK12 Matt Williams	1.25	.35
DK13 Kevin Seitzer	.60	.18
DK14 Sammy Sosa	5.00	1.50
DK15 Scott Cooper	.60	.18
DK16 Raul Mondesi	1.25	.35
DK17 Will Clark	3.00	.90
DK18 Lenny Dykstra	1.25	.35
DK19 Kirby Puckett	3.00	.90
DK20 Hal Morris	.60	.18
DK21 Travis Fryman	1.25	.35
DK22 Greg Maddux	5.00	1.50
DK23 Rafael Palmeiro	2.00	.60
DK24 Tony Gwynn	4.00	1.20
DK25 David Cone	1.25	.35
DK26 Al Martin	.60	.18
DK27 Ken Griffey Jr.	5.00	1.50
DK28 Gregg Jefferies	.60	.18
DK29 Checklist	.60	.18

1995 Donruss Dominators

This nine-card standard-size set was randomly inserted in second series hobby packs. Each of these cards features three of the leading players at each position. The horizontal fronts have photos of all three players and identify only their last name. The words "remove protective film" cover a significant portion of the fronts as well. The cards are numbered in the upper right corner as "X" of 9.

	Nm-Mt	Ex-Mt
COMPLETE SET (9)	25.00	7.50
1 David Cone	3.00	.90
Mike Mussina		
Greg Maddux		
2 Ivan Rodriguez	3.00	.90
Mike Piazza		
Darren Daulton		
3 Fred McGriff	2.00	.60
Frank Thomas		
Jeff Bagwell		
4 Roberto Alomar	2.00	.60
Carlos Baerga		
Craig Biggio		
5 Robin Ventura	.75	.23
Travis Fryman		
Matt Williams		
6 Cal Ripken	6.00	1.80
Barry Larkin		
Wil Cordero		
7 Albert Belle	5.00	1.50
Barry Bonds		
Moises Alou		
8 Ken Griffey	3.00	.90
Kenny Lofton		
Marquis Grissom		
9 Kirby Puckett	2.50	.75
Paul O'Neill		
Tony Gwynn		

1995 Donruss Elite

Randomly inserted one in every 210 Series 1 and 2 packs, this set consists of 12 standard-size cards that are numbered (49-60) based on where the previous year's set left off. The fronts contain an action photo surrounded by a marble border. Silver holographic foil borders the card on all four sides. Limited to 10,000, the backs are individually numbered, contain a small photo and write-up.

	Nm-Mt	Ex-Mt
COMPLETE SET (12)	200.00	60.00
COMPLETE SERIES 1 (6)	100.00	30.00
COMPLETE SERIES 2 (6)	100.00	30.00
49 Jeff Bagwell	12.00	3.60
50 Paul O'Neill	12.00	3.60
51 Greg Maddux	25.00	7.50
52 Mike Piazza	25.00	7.50
53 Matt Williams	12.00	3.60
54 Ken Griffey	25.00	7.50
55 Frank Thomas	15.00	4.50
56 Barry Bonds	40.00	12.00
57 Kirby Puckett	15.00	4.50
58 Fred McGriff	12.00	3.60
59 Jose Canseco	15.00	4.50
60 Albert Belle	12.00	3.60

1995 Donruss Long Ball Leaders

Inserted one in every 24 series one hobby packs, this set features eight top home run hitters.

	Nm-Mt	Ex-Mt
COMPLETE SET (8)	20.00	6.00
1 Frank Thomas	2.50	.75
2 Fred McGriff	1.50	.45
3 Ken Griffey	4.00	1.20
4 Matt Williams	1.00	.30
5 Mike Piazza	4.00	1.20
6 Jose Canseco	2.50	.75
7 Barry Bonds	6.00	1.80
8 Jeff Bagwell	1.50	.45

1995 Donruss Mound Marvels

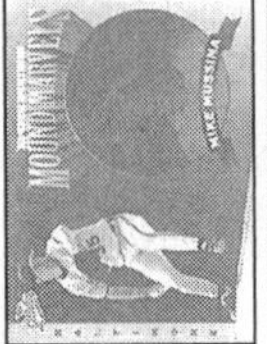

This eight-card standard-size set was randomly inserted into second series magazine jumbo and retail packs at a rate of one every 16 packs. This set features eight of the leading major league starters.

	Nm-Mt	Ex-Mt
COMPLETE SET (8)	20.00	6.00
1 Greg Maddux	6.00	1.80
2 David Cone	1.50	.45
3 Mike Mussina	4.00	1.20
4 Bret Saberhagen	1.50	.45
5 Jimmy Key	1.50	.45
6 Doug Drabek	.75	.23
7 Randy Johnson	4.00	1.20
8 Jason Bere	.75	.23

1995 Donruss Top of the Order

This 360-card standard-size set was distributed as a Major League Baseball Card Game. The cards were packaged in 80-card starter decks with other cards available in booster packs. The fronts carry player action photos with the player's name, team, position, and other player information needed to play the game. The green backs carry the card logo. The first 180 cards feature players in the American League with the National League represented by the second 180 cards. The cards are unnumbered and checklisted below in alphabetical order within each team. There are three levels of scarcity for these cards; common, uncommon and rare. All cards have been given either a designation of C (for common), U (for uncommon) or R (for rare).

	Nm-Mt	Ex-Mt
COMPLETE SET (360)	400.00	120.00
COMMON CARD (1-360)	.10	.03
COMMON UNCOM. (1-360)	.50	.15
COMMON RARE (1-360)	1.00	.30
1 Brady Anderson C	.20	.06
2 Harold Baines U	.75	.23
3 Bret Barberie U	.50	.15
4 Armando Benitez C	.20	.06
5 Bobby Bonilla U	.50	.15
6 Scott Erickson C	.10	.03
7 Leo Gomez C	.10	.03
8 Curtis Goodwin R	1.00	.30
9 Jeffrey Hammonds C	.20	.06
10 Chris Hoiles C	.10	.03
11 Doug Jones C	.10	.03
12 Ben McDonald U	.50	.15
13 Mike Mussina U	2.00	.60
14 Rafael Palmeiro R	2.50	.75
15 Cal Ripken Jr. R	30.00	9.00
16 Rick Aguilera C	.20	.06
17 Luis Alicea C	.10	.03
18 Jose Canseco U	2.00	.60
19 Roger Clemens C	1.25	.35
20 Mike Greenwell U	.50	.15
21 Erik Hanson C	.10	.03
22 Mike Macfarlane C	.10	.03
23 Tim Naehring R	1.00	.30
24 Troy O'Leary U	.50	.15
25 Ken Ryan C	.10	.03
26 Aaron Sele C	.75	.23
27 Lee Tinsley U	.50	.15
28 John Valentin R	1.00	.30
29 Mo Vaughn R	1.00	.30
30 Jim Abbott C	.20	.06
31 Mike Butcher C	.10	.03
32 Chili Davis R	1.50	.45
33 Gary DiSarcina R	1.00	.30
34 Damion Easley C	.10	.03
35 Jim Edmonds R	2.50	.75
36 Chuck Finley U	.75	.23
37 Mark Langston C	.10	.03
38 Greg Myers C	.10	.03
39 Spike Owen C	.10	.03
40 Troy Percival R	1.50	.45
41 Tony Phillips U	.50	.15
42 Tim Salmon R	2.00	.60
43 Lee Smith R	1.50	.45
44 J.T. Snow U	.75	.23
45 Jason Bere C	.10	.03
46 Mike Devereaux U	.50	.15
47 Ray Durham C	.75	.23
48 Alex Fernandez C	.10	.03
49 Ozzie Guillen R	1.50	.45
50 Roberto Hernandez C	.20	.06
51 Lance Johnson U	.50	.15
52 Ron Karkovice C	.10	.03
53 Tim Raines U	.75	.23
54 Frank Thomas R	6.00	1.80
55 Robin Ventura U	1.50	.45
56 Sandy Alomar R	1.50	.45
57 Carlos Baerga R	1.00	.30
58 Albert Belle R	1.50	.45
59 Kenny Lofton R	2.00	.60
60 Dennis Martinez C	.20	.06
61 Jose Mesa U	.50	.15
62 Eddie Murray R	2.50	.75
63 Charles Nagy C	.20	.06
64 Tony Pena C	.20	.06
65 Eric Plunk R	1.00	.30
66 Manny Ramirez R	6.00	1.80
67 Paul Sorrento C	.10	.03
68 Jim Thome R	2.50	.75
69 Omar Vizquel C	.20	.06
70 Danny Bautista C	.10	.03
71 Joe Boever C	.10	.03
72 Chad Curtis C	.10	.03
73 Cecil Fielder U	.75	.23
74 John Flaherty U	.50	.15
75 Travis Fryman U	.75	.23
76 Kirk Gibson C	.20	.06
77 Chris Gomez C	.10	.03
78 Mike Henneman R	1.00	.30
79 Bob Higginson C	.75	.23
80 Alan Trammell U	1.00	.30
81 Lou Whitaker R	1.50	.45
82 Kevin Appier R	1.50	.45
83 Billy Brewer C	.10	.03
84 Vince Coleman R	1.00	.30
85 Gary Gaetti C	.20	.06
86 Greg Gagne C	.10	.03
87 Tom Goodwin R	1.00	.30
88 Tom Gordon C	.20	.06
89 Mark Gubicza C	.10	.03
90 Bob Hamelin C	.10	.03
91 Phil Hiatt C	.10	.03
92 Wally Joyner R	1.00	.30
93 Brent Mayne C	.10	.03
94 Jeff Montgomery C	.10	.03
95 Ricky Bones C	.10	.03
96 Mike Fetters C	.10	.03
97 Darryl Hamilton C	.10	.03
98 Pat Listach C	.10	.03
99 Matt Mieske C	.10	.03
100 Dave Nilsson C	.10	.03
101 Joe Oliver U	.50	.15
102 Kevin Seitzer U	.50	.15
103 B.J. Surhoff U	.75	.23
104 Jose Valentin C	.10	.03
105 Greg Vaughn C	.20	.06
106 Bill Wegman C	.10	.03
107 Alex Cole U	.50	.15
108 Marty Cordova C	.20	.06
109 Chuck Knoblauch R	1.50	.45
110 Scott Leius C	.10	.03
111 Pat Meares C	.10	.03
112 Pedro Munoz C	.10	.03
113 Kirby Puckett R	15.00	4.50
114 Scott Stahoviak C	.10	.03
115 Mike Trombley C	.10	.03
116 Matt Walbeck C	.10	.03
117 Wade Boggs R	5.00	1.50
118 David Cone U	1.00	.30
119 Tony Fernandez C	.20	.06
120 Don Mattingly R	15.00	4.50
121 Jack McDowell C	.10	.03
122 Paul O'Neill U	.75	.23
123 Melido Perez C	.10	.03
124 Luis Polonia C	.10	.03
125 Ruben Sierra C	.20	.06
126 Mike Stanley C	.10	.03
127 Randy Velarde C	.10	.03
128 John Wetteland R	1.50	.45
129 Bob Wickman C	.10	.03
130 Bernie Williams C	.40	.12
131 Gerald Williams C	.10	.03
132 Geronimo Berroa C	.10	.03
133 Mike Bordick U	.50	.15
134 Scott Brosius C	.20	.06
135 Dennis Eckersley C	.50	.15
136 Brent Gates C	.10	.03
137 Rickey Henderson U	3.00	.90
138 Stan Javier C	.10	.03
139 Mark McGwire R	25.00	7.50
140 Steve Ontiveros U	.50	.15
141 Terry Steinbach C	.10	.03
142 Todd Stottlemyre R	1.00	.30
143 Danny Tartabull C	.10	.03
144 Bobby Ayala R	1.00	.30
145 Andy Benes U	.50	.15
146 Mike Blowers C	.10	.03
147 Jay Buhner U	.75	.23
148 Joey Cora U	.50	.15
149 Alex Diaz C	.10	.03
150 Ken Griffey Jr. R	15.00	4.50
151 Randy Johnson R	4.00	1.20
152 Edgar Martinez R	2.00	.60
153 Tino Martinez U	1.00	.30
154 Bill Risley R	1.00	.30

155 Alex Rodriguez C 3.00 .90
156 Dan Wilson C .10 .03
157 Will Clark R 2.50 .75
158 Jeff Frye U .50 .15
159 Benji Gil C .10 .03
160 Juan Gonzalez C .75 .23
161 Rusty Greer C .20 .06
162 Mark McLemore R 1.00 .30
163 Otis Nixon U .50 .15
164 Dean Palmer R 1.50 .45
165 Ivan Rodriguez R 8.00 2.40
166 Kenny Rogers C .20 .06
167 Jeff Russell C .10 .03
168 Mickey Tettleton C .10 .03
169 Bob Tewksbury C .10 .03
170 Bobby Witt C .10 .03
171 Roberto Alomar R 2.50 .75
172 Joe Carter R 1.50 .45
173 Alex Gonzalez C .10 .03
174 Candy Maldonado C .10 .03
175 Paul Molitor C .50 .15
176 John Olerud C .20 .06
177 Lance Parrish C .20 .06
178 Ed Sprague C .10 .03
179 Devon White C .10 .03
180 Woody Williams C .10 .03
181 Steve Avery C .10 .03
182 Jeff Blauser C .10 .03
183 Tom Glavine U 1.50 .45
184 Marquis Grissom R 1.00 .30
185 Chipper Jones C 1.50 .45
186 David Justice R 2.50 .75
187 Ryan Klesko U .75 .23
188 Mark Lemke C .10 .03
189 Javy Lopez C .40 .12
190 Greg Maddux R 20.00 6.00
191 Fred McGriff R 2.00 .60
192 Greg McMichael U .50 .15
193 John Smoltz R 1.50 .45
194 Mark Wohlers R 1.00 .30
195 Jim Bullinger U .50 .15
196 Shawon Dunston R 1.00 .30
197 Kevin Foster C .10 .03
198 Luis Gonzalez C .50 .15
199 Mark Grace R 2.50 .75
200 Brian McRae R 1.00 .30
201 Randy Myers R 1.50 .45
202 Jaime Navarro U .50 .15
203 Rey Sanchez U .50 .15
204 Scott Servais C .10 .03
205 Sammy Sosa R 15.00 4.50
206 Steve Trachsel U .75 .23
207 Todd Zeile C .20 .06
208 Bret Boone R 2.00 .60
209 Jeff Branson U .50 .15
210 Jeff Brantley R 1.50 .45
211 Hector Carrasco C .10 .03
212 Ron Gant R 1.50 .45
213 Lenny Harris C .10 .03
214 Barry Larkin R 2.50 .75
215 Darren Lewis C .10 .03
216 Hal Morris C .10 .03
217 Mark Portugal C .10 .03
218 Jose Rijo U .50 .15
219 Reggie Sanders R 1.50 .45
220 Pete Schourek U .50 .15
221 John Smiley C .10 .03
222 Eddie Taubensee C .10 .03
223 David Wells C .30 .09
224 Jason Bates C .10 .03
225 Dante Bichette R 1.50 .45
226 Vinny Castilla U .75 .23
227 Andres Galarraga R 2.50 .75
228 Joe Girardi U .50 .15
229 Mike Kingery C .10 .03
230 Steve Reed R 1.00 .30
231 Bruce Ruffin U .50 .15
232 Bret Saberhagen U .50 .15
233 Bill Swift C .10 .03
234 Larry Walker R 1.50 .45
235 Walt Weiss C .10 .03
236 Eric Young C .10 .03
237 Kurt Abbott C .10 .03
238 John Burkett C .20 .06
239 Chuck Carr C .10 .03
240 Greg Colbrunn C .10 .03
241 Jeff Conine R 1.00 .30
242 Andre Dawson C .40 .12
243 Chris Hammond R 1.00 .30
244 Charles Johnson C .20 .06
245 Robb Nen C .20 .06
246 Terry Pendleton U .75 .23
247 Gary Sheffield R 3.00 .90
248 Quilvio Veras C .10 .03
249 Jeff Bagwell U 3.00 .90
250 Derek Bell R 1.00 .30
251 Craig Biggio U 1.00 .30
252 Doug Drabek C .10 .03
253 Tony Eusebio U .50 .15
254 John Hudek C .10 .03
255 Brian L. Hunter U .50 .15
256 Todd Jones R 1.50 .45
257 Dave Magadan U .50 .15
258 Orlando Miller C .10 .03
259 James Mouton C .10 .03
260 Shane Reynolds C .10 .03
261 Greg Swindell C .10 .03
262 Billy Ashley C .10 .03
263 Tom Candiotti U .50 .15
264 Delino DeShields C .20 .06
265 Eric Karros R 1.50 .45
266 Roberto Kelly C .10 .03
267 Ramon Martinez C .20 .06
268 Raul Mondesi R 1.50 .45
269 Hideo Nomo R 30.00 9.00
270 Jose Offerman U .50 .15
271 Mike Piazza R 20.00 6.00
272 Kevin Tapani C .10 .03
273 Ismael Valdes U .50 .15
274 Tim Wallach C .10 .03
275 Todd Worrell R 1.00 .30
276 Moises Alou R 1.50 .45
277 Sean Berry U .50 .15
278 Wil Cordero U .50 .15
279 Jeff Fassero C .10 .03
280 Darrin Fletcher C .10 .03
281 Mike Lansing C .10 .03
282 Pedro Martinez R 6.00 1.80
283 Carlos Perez U .50 .15
284 Mel Rojas U .50 .15
285 Tim Scott R 1.00 .30
286 David Segui U .75 .23
287 Tony Tarasco U .50 .15
288 Rondell White C .20 .06
289 Rico Brogna C .10 .03
290 Brett Butler C .20 .06
291 John Franco C .20 .06
292 Pete Harnisch C .10 .03
293 Todd Hundley C .20 .06
294 Bobby Jones C .10 .03
295 Jeff Kent C .40 .12
296 Joe Orsulak U .50 .15
297 Ryan Thompson U .50 .15
298 Jose Vizcaino C .10 .03
299 Ricky Bottalico U .50 .15
300 Darren Daulton C .20 .06
301 Mariano Duncan U .50 .15
302 Lenny Dykstra U .75 .23
303 Jim Eisenreich U .75 .23
304 Tyler Green U .50 .15
305 Charlie Hayes U .50 .15
306 Dave Hollins C .10 .03
307 Gregg Jefferies C .10 .03
308 Mickey Morandini U .50 .15
309 Curt Schilling R 3.00 .90
310 Heathcliff Slocumb U .50 .15
311 Kevin Stocker C .10 .03
312 Jay Bell C .10 .03
313 Jacob Brumfield C .10 .03
314 Dave Clark U .50 .15
315 Carlos Garcia C .10 .03
316 Mark Johnson C .10 .03
317 Jeff King C .10 .03
318 Nelson Liriano U .50 .15
319 Al Martin U .50 .15
320 Orlando Merced U .50 .15
321 Dan Miceli U .50 .15
322 Denny Neagle C .20 .06
323 Mark Parent C .10 .03
324 Dan Plesac R 1.00 .30
325 Scott Cooper C .10 .03
326 Bernard Gilkey R 1.00 .30
327 Tom Henke R 1.00 .30
328 Ken Hill C .10 .03
329 Danny Jackson C .10 .03
330 Brian Jordan R 1.50 .45
331 Ray Lankford U .75 .23
332 John Mabry U .50 .15
333 Jose Oquendo C .10 .03
334 Tom Pagnozzi C .10 .03
335 Ozzie Smith U 4.00 1.20
336 Andy Ashby U .50 .15
337 Brad Ausmus U .50 .15
338 Ken Caminiti U .75 .23
339 Andujar Cedeno C .10 .03
340 Steve Finley R 1.50 .45
341 Tony Gwynn R 15.00 4.50
342 Joey Hamilton C .10 .03
343 Trevor Hoffman C .20 .06
344 Jody Reed C .10 .03
345 Bip Roberts R 1.00 .30
346 Eddie Williams C .10 .03
347 Rod Beck U .75 .23
348 Mike Benjamin U .50 .15
349 Barry Bonds R 15.00 4.50
350 Royce Clayton C .10 .03
351 Glenallen Hill C .10 .03
352 Kirt Manwaring C .10 .03
353 Terry Mulholland C .10 .03
354 John Patterson C .10 .03
355 J.R. Phillips C .10 .03
356 Deion Sanders R 1.50 .45
357 Steve Scarsone U .50 .15
358 Robby Thompson C .10 .03
359 W.VanLandingham C .10 .03
360 Matt Williams R 2.00 .60

1996 Donruss Samples

This eight-card standard-size set was issued to preview the 1996 Donruss series. The fronts feature full-bleed color action photos. The player's number, position, team name and team logo are printed on a silver foil square at the bottom center. The horizontal backs carry a second color photo, biography, and career statistics. The disclaimer "PROMOTIONAL SAMPLE" is stamped diagonally across both sides of the cards.

	Nm-Mt	Ex-Mt
COMPLETE SET (8)	15.00	4.50
1 Frank Thomas	1.25	.35
2 Barry Bonds	2.50	.75
3 Hideo Nomo	1.00	.30
4 Ken Griffey Jr.	3.00	.90
5 Cal Ripken	5.00	1.50
6 Manny Ramirez	1.25	.35
7 Mike Piazza	3.00	.90
8 Greg Maddux	2.50	.75

1996 Donruss

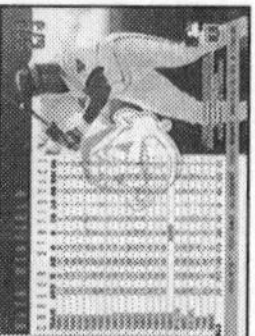

The 1996 Donruss set was issued in two series of 330 and 220 cards respectively, for a total of 550. The 12-card packs had a suggested retail price of $1.79. The full-bleed fronts feature full-color action photos with the player's name is in white ink in the upper right. The horizontal backs feature season and career stats, text, vital stats and another photo. Rookie Cards in this set include Mike Cameron.

	Nm-Mt	Ex-Mt
COMPLETE SET (550)	40.00	12.00
COMP.SERIES 1 (330)	25.00	7.50
COMP.SERIES 2 (220)	15.00	4.50
1 Frank Thomas	.75	.23
2 Jason Bates	.30	.09
3 Steve Sparks	.30	.09

4 Scott Servais .30 .09
5 Angelo Encarnacion RC .30 .09
6 Scott Sanders .30 .09
7 Billy Ashley .30 .09
8 Alex Rodriguez 1.50 .45
9 Sean Bergman .30 .09
10 Brad Radke .30 .09
11 Andy Van Slyke .30 .09
12 Joe Girardi .30 .09
13 Mark Grudzielanek .30 .09
14 Rick Aguilera .30 .09
15 Randy Veres .30 .09
16 Tim Bogar .30 .09
17 Dave Veres .30 .09
18 Kevin Stocker .30 .09
19 Marquis Grissom .30 .09
20 Will Clark .75 .23
21 Jay Bell .30 .09
22 Allen Battle .30 .09
23 Frank Rodriguez .30 .09
24 Terry Steinbach .30 .09
25 Gerald Williams .30 .09
26 Sid Roberson .30 .09
27 Greg Zaun .30 .09
28 Ozzie Timmons .30 .09
29 Vaughn Eshelman .30 .09
30 Ed Sprague .30 .09
31 Gary DiSarcina .30 .09
32 Joe Boever .30 .09
33 Steve Avery .30 .09
34 Brad Ausmus .30 .09
35 Kirt Manwaring .30 .09
36 Gary Sheffield .30 .09
37 Jason Bere .30 .09
38 Jeff Manto .30 .09
39 David Cone .30 .09
40 Manny Ramirez .30 .09
41 Sandy Alomar Jr. .30 .09
42 Curtis Goodwin .30 .09
43 Tino Martinez .50 .15
44 Woody Williams .30 .09
45 Dean Palmer .30 .09
46 Hipolito Pichardo .30 .09
47 Jason Giambi .75 .23
48 Lance Johnson .30 .09
49 Bernard Gilkey .30 .09
50 Kirby Puckett .75 .23
51 Tony Fernandez .30 .09
52 Alex Gonzalez .30 .09
53 Bret Saberhagen .30 .09
54 Lyle Mouton .30 .09
55 Brian McRae .30 .09
56 Mark Gubicza .30 .09
57 Sergio Valdez .30 .09
58 Darrin Fletcher .30 .09
59 Steve Parris .30 .09
60 Johnny Damon .30 .09
61 Rickey Henderson .75 .23
62 Darrell Whitmore .30 .09
63 Roberto Petagine .30 .09
64 Trenidad Hubbard .30 .09
65 Heathcliff Slocumb .30 .09
66 Steve Finley .30 .09
67 Mariano Rivera .50 .15
68 Brian L.Hunter .30 .09
69 Jamie Moyer .30 .09
70 Ellis Burks .30 .09
71 Pat Kelly .30 .09
72 Mickey Tettleton .30 .09
73 Garret Anderson .30 .09
74 Andy Pettitte .50 .15
75 Glenallen Hill .30 .09
76 Brent Gates .30 .09
77 Lou Whitaker .30 .09
78 David Segui .30 .09
79 Dan Wilson .30 .09
80 Pat Listach .30 .09
81 Jeff Bagwell .50 .15
82 Ben McDonald .30 .09
83 John Valentin .30 .09
84 John Jaha .30 .09
85 Pete Schourek .30 .09
86 Bryce Florie .30 .09
87 Brian Jordan .30 .09
88 Ron Karkovice .30 .09
89 Al Leiter .30 .09
90 Tony Longmire .30 .09
91 Nelson Liriano .30 .09
92 David Bell .30 .09
93 Kevin Gross .30 .09
94 Tom Candiotti .30 .09
95 Dave Martinez .30 .09
96 Greg Myers .30 .09
97 Rheal Cormier .30 .09
98 Chris Hammond .30 .09
99 Randy Myers .30 .09
100 Bill Pulsipher .30 .09
101 Jason Isringhausen .30 .09
102 Dave Stevens .30 .09
103 Roberto Alomar .75 .23
104 Bob Higginson .30 .09
105 Eddie Murray .75 .23
106 Matt Walbeck .30 .09
107 Mark Wohlers .30 .09
108 Jeff Nelson .30 .09
109 Tom Goodwin .30 .09
110 Cal Ripken CL 1.25 .35
111 Rey Sanchez .30 .09
112 Hector Carrasco .30 .09
113 B.J. Surhoff .30 .09
114 Dan Miceli .30 .09
115 Dean Hartgraves .30 .09
116 John Burkett .30 .09
117 Gary Gaetti .30 .09
118 Ricky Bones .30 .09
119 Mike Macfarlane .30 .09
120 Bip Roberts .30 .09
121 Dave Mlicki .30 .09
122 Chili Davis .30 .09
123 Mark Whiten .30 .09
124 Herbert Perry .30 .09
125 Butch Henry .30 .09
126 Derek Bell .30 .09
127 Al Martin .30 .09
128 John Franco .30 .09
129 W. VanLandingham .30 .09
130 Mike Bordick .30 .09
131 Mike Mordecai .30 .09
132 Robby Thompson .30 .09
133 Greg Colbrunn .30 .09
134 Domingo Cedeno .30 .09
135 Chad Curtis .30 .09
136 Jose Hernandez .30 .09
137 Scott Klingenbeck .30 .09
138 Ryan Klesko .30 .09
139 John Smiley .30 .09
140 Charlie Hayes .30 .09
141 Jay Buhner .30 .09
142 Doug Drabek .30 .09
143 Roger Pavlik .30 .09
144 Todd Worrell .30 .09
145 Cal Ripken 2.50 .75
146 Steve Reed .30 .09
147 Chuck Finley .30 .09
148 Mike Blowers .30 .09
149 Orel Hershiser .30 .09
150 Allen Watson .30 .09
151 Ramon Martinez .30 .09
152 Melvin Nieves .30 .09
153 Tripp Cromer .30 .09
154 Yorkis Perez .30 .09
155 Stan Javier .30 .09
156 Mel Rojas .30 .09
157 Aaron Sele .30 .09
158 Eric Karros .30 .09
159 Robb Nen .30 .09
160 Raul Mondesi .30 .09
161 John Wetteland .30 .09
162 Tim Scott .30 .09
163 Kenny Rogers .30 .09
164 Melvin Bunch .30 .09
165 Rod Beck .30 .09
166 Andy Benes .30 .09
167 Lenny Dykstra .30 .09
168 Orlando Merced .30 .09
169 Tomas Perez .30 .09
170 Xavier Hernandez .30 .09
171 Ruben Sierra .30 .09
172 Alan Trammell .50 .15
173 Mike Fetters .30 .09
174 Wilson Alvarez .30 .09
175 Erik Hanson .30 .09
176 Travis Fryman .30 .09
177 Jim Abbott .50 .15
178 Bret Boone .30 .09
179 Sterling Hitchcock .30 .09
180 Pat Mahomes .30 .09
181 Mark Acre .30 .09
182 Charles Nagy .30 .09
183 Rusty Greer .30 .09
184 Mike Stanley .30 .09
185 Jim Bullinger .30 .09
186 Shane Andrews .30 .09
187 Brian Keyser .30 .09
188 Tyler Green .30 .09
189 Mark Grace .50 .15
190 Bob Hamelin .30 .09
191 Luis Ortiz .30 .09
192 Joe Carter .30 .09
193 Eddie Taubensee .30 .09
194 Brian Anderson .30 .09
195 Edgardo Alfonzo .30 .09
196 Pedro Munoz .30 .09
197 David Justice .30 .09
198 Trevor Hoffman .30 .09
199 Bobby Ayala .30 .09
200 Tony Eusebio .30 .09
201 Jeff Russell .30 .09
202 Mike Hampton .30 .09
203 Walt Weiss .30 .09
204 Joey Hamilton .30 .09
205 Roberto Hernandez .30 .09
206 Greg Vaughn .30 .09
207 Felipe Lira .30 .09
208 Harold Baines .30 .09
209 Tim Wallach .30 .09
210 Manny Alexander .30 .09
211 Tim Laker .30 .09
212 Chris Haney .30 .09
213 Brian Maxcy .30 .09
214 Eric Young .30 .09
215 Darryl Strawberry .50 .15
216 Barry Bonds 2.00 .60
217 Tim Naehring .30 .09
218 Scott Brosius .30 .09
219 Reggie Sanders .30 .09
220 Eddie Murray CL .50 .15
221 Luis Alicea .30 .09
222 Albert Belle .30 .09
223 Benji Gil .30 .09
224 Dante Bichette .30 .09
225 Bobby Bonilla .30 .09
226 Todd Stottlemyre .30 .09
227 Jim Edmonds .30 .09
228 Todd Jones .30 .09
229 Shawn Green .30 .09
230 Javier Lopez .30 .09
231 Ariel Prieto .30 .09
232 Tony Phillips .30 .09
233 James Mouton .30 .09
234 Jose Oquendo .30 .09
235 Royce Clayton .30 .09
236 Chuck Carr .30 .09
237 Doug Jones .30 .09
238 Mark McLemore .30 .09
239 Bill Swift .30 .09
240 Scott Leius .30 .09
241 Russ Davis .30 .09
242 Ray Durham .30 .09
243 Matt Mieske .30 .09
244 Brent Mayne .30 .09
245 Thomas Howard .30 .09
246 Troy O'Leary .30 .09
247 Jacob Brumfield .30 .09
248 Mickey Morandini .30 .09
249 Todd Hundley .30 .09
250 Chris Bosio .30 .09
251 Omar Vizquel .30 .09
252 Mike Lansing .30 .09
253 John Mabry .30 .09
254 Mike Perez .30 .09
255 Delino DeShields .30 .09
256 Wil Cordero .30 .09
257 Mike James .30 .09
258 Todd Van Poppel .30 .09
259 Joey Cora .30 .09
260 Andre Dawson .30 .09
261 Jerry DiPoto .30 .09
262 Rick Krivda .30 .09
263 Glenn Dishman .30 .09
264 Mike Mimbs .30 .09
265 John Ericks .30 .09
266 Jose Canseco .75 .23
267 Jeff Branson .30 .09
268 Curt Leskanic .30 .09
269 Jon Nunnally .30 .09
270 Scott Stahoviak .30 .09
271 Jeff Montgomery .30 .09
272 Hal Morris .30 .09
273 Esteban Loaiza .30 .09
274 Rico Brogna .30 .09
275 Dave Winfield .30 .09
276 J.R. Phillips .30 .09
277 Todd Zeile .30 .09
278 Tom Pagnozzi .30 .09
279 Mark Lemke .30 .09
280 Dave Magadan .30 .09
281 Greg McMichael .30 .09
282 Mike Morgan .30 .09
283 Moises Alou .30 .09
284 Dennis Martinez .30 .09
285 Jeff Kent .30 .09
286 Mark Johnson .30 .09
287 Darren Lewis .30 .09
288 Brad Clontz .30 .09
289 Chad Fonville .30 .09
290 Paul Sorrento .30 .09
291 Lee Smith .30 .09
292 Tom Glavine .50 .15
293 Antonio Osuna .30 .09
294 Kevin Foster .30 .09
295 Sandy Martinez .30 .09
296 Mark Leiter .30 .09
297 Julian Tavarez .30 .09
298 Mike Kelly .30 .09
299 Joe Oliver .30 .09
300 John Flaherty .30 .09
301 Don Mattingly 2.00 .60
302 Pat Meares .30 .09
303 John Doherty .30 .09
304 Joe Vitiello .30 .09
305 Vinny Castilla .30 .09
306 Jeff Brantley .30 .09
307 Mike Greenwell .30 .09
308 Midre Cummings .30 .09
309 Curt Schilling .50 .15
310 Ken Caminiti .30 .09
311 Scott Erickson .30 .09
312 Carl Everett .30 .09
313 Charles Johnson .30 .09
314 Alex Diaz .30 .09
315 Jose Mesa .30 .09
316 Mark Carreon .30 .09
317 Carlos Perez .30 .09
318 Ismael Valdes .30 .09
319 Frank Castillo .30 .09
320 Tom Henke .30 .09
321 Spike Owen .30 .09
322 Joe Orsulak .30 .09
323 Paul Menhart .30 .09
324 Pedro Borbon .30 .09
325 Paul Molitor CL .30 .09
326 Jeff Cirillo .30 .09
327 Edwin Hurtado .30 .09
328 Orlando Miller .30 .09
329 Steve Ontiveros .30 .09
330 Kirby Puckett CL .50 .15
331 Scott Bullett .30 .09
332 Andres Galarraga .30 .09
333 Cal Eldred .30 .09
334 Sammy Sosa 1.25 .35
335 Don Slaught .30 .09
336 Jody Reed .30 .09
337 Roger Cedeno .30 .09
338 Ken Griffey Jr. 1.25 .35
339 Todd Hollandsworth .30 .09
340 Mike Trombley .30 .09
341 Gregg Jefferies .30 .09
342 Larry Walker .50 .15
343 Pedro Martinez .75 .23
344 Dwayne Hosey .30 .09
345 Terry Pendleton .30 .09
346 Pete Harnisch .30 .09
347 Tony Castillo .30 .09
348 Paul Quantrill .30 .09
349 Fred McGriff .50 .15
350 Ivan Rodriguez .75 .23
351 Butch Huskey .30 .09
352 Ozzie Smith 1.25 .35
353 Marty Cordova .30 .09
354 John Wasdin .30 .09
355 Wade Boggs .50 .15
356 Dave Nilsson .30 .09
357 Rafael Palmeiro .50 .15
358 Luis Gonzalez .30 .09
359 Reggie Jefferson .30 .09
360 Carlos Delgado .30 .09
361 Orlando Palmeiro .30 .09
362 Chris Gomez .30 .09
363 John Smoltz .50 .15
364 Marc Newfield .30 .09
365 Matt Williams .30 .09
366 Jesus Tavarez .30 .09
367 Bruce Ruffin .30 .09
368 Sean Berry .30 .09
369 Randy Velarde .30 .09
370 Tony Pena .30 .09
371 Jim Thome .75 .23
372 Jeffrey Hammonds .30 .09
373 Bob Wolcott .30 .09
374 Juan Guzman .30 .09
375 Juan Gonzalez .75 .23
376 Michael Tucker .30 .09
377 Doug Johns .30 .09
378 Mike Cameron RC 1.50 .45
379 Ray Lankford .30 .09
380 Jose Parra .30 .09
381 Jimmy Key .30 .09
382 John Olerud .30 .09
383 Kevin Ritz .30 .09
384 Tim Raines .30 .09
385 Rich Amaral .30 .09
386 Keith Lockhart .30 .09
387 Steve Scarsone .30 .09
388 Cliff Floyd .30 .09
389 Rich Aude .30 .09
390 Hideo Nomo .75 .23
391 Geronimo Berroa .30 .09
392 Pat Rapp .30 .09
393 Dustin Hermanson .30 .09

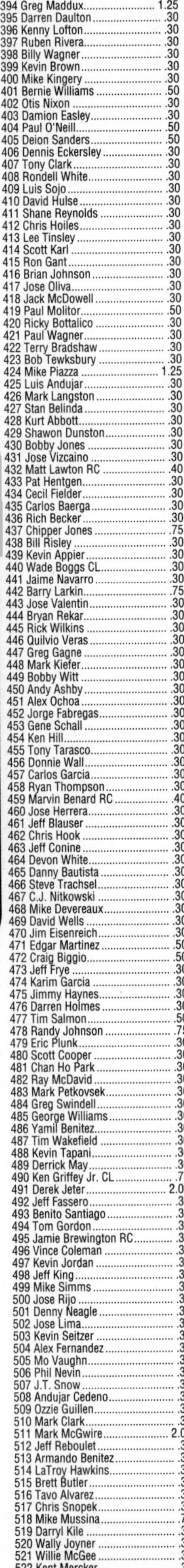

394 Greg Maddux 1.25 .35
395 Darren Daulton .30 .09
396 Kenny Lofton .30 .09
397 Ruben Rivera .30 .09
398 Billy Wagner .30 .09
399 Kevin Brown .30 .09
400 Mike Kingery .30 .09
401 Bernie Williams .50 .15
402 Otis Nixon .30 .09
403 Damion Easley .30 .09
404 Paul O'Neill .50 .15
405 Deion Sanders .50 .15
406 Dennis Eckersley .30 .09
407 Tony Clark .30 .09
408 Rondell White .30 .09
409 Luis Sojo .30 .09
410 David Hulse .30 .09
411 Shane Reynolds .30 .09
412 Chris Hoiles .30 .09
413 Lee Tinsley .30 .09
414 Scott Karl .30 .09
415 Ron Gant .30 .09
416 Brian Johnson .30 .09
417 Jose Oliva .30 .09
418 Jack McDowell .30 .09
419 Paul Molitor .50 .15
420 Ricky Bottalico .30 .09
421 Paul Wagner .30 .09
422 Terry Bradshaw .30 .09
423 Bob Tewksbury .30 .09
424 Mike Piazza 1.25 .35
425 Luis Andujar .30 .09
426 Mark Langston .30 .09
427 Stan Belinda .30 .09
428 Kurt Abbott .30 .09
429 Shawon Dunston .30 .09
430 Bobby Jones .30 .09
431 Jose Vizcaino .30 .09
432 Matt Lawton RC .40 .12
433 Pat Hentgen .30 .09
434 Cecil Fielder .30 .09
435 Carlos Baerga .30 .09
436 Rich Becker .30 .09
437 Chipper Jones .75 .23
438 Bill Risley .30 .09
439 Kevin Appier .30 .09
440 Wade Boggs CL .30 .09
441 Jaime Navarro .30 .09
442 Barry Larkin .75 .23
443 Jose Valentin .30 .09
444 Bryan Rekar .30 .09
445 Rick Wilkins .30 .09
446 Quilvio Veras .30 .09
447 Greg Gagne .30 .09
448 Mark Kiefer .30 .09
449 Bobby Witt .30 .09
450 Andy Ashby .30 .09
451 Alex Ochoa .30 .09
452 Jorge Fabregas .30 .09
453 Gene Schall .30 .09
454 Ken Hill .30 .09
455 Tony Tarasco .30 .09
456 Donnie Wall .30 .09
457 Carlos Garcia .30 .09
458 Ryan Thompson .30 .09
459 Marvin Benard RC .40 .12
460 Jose Herrera .30 .09
461 Jeff Blauser .30 .09
462 Chris Hook .30 .09
463 Jeff Conine .30 .09
464 Devon White .30 .09
465 Danny Bautista .30 .09
466 Steve Trachsel .30 .09
467 C.J. Nitkowski .30 .09
468 Mike Devereaux .30 .09
469 David Wells .30 .09
470 Jim Eisenreich .30 .09
471 Edgar Martinez .50 .15
472 Craig Biggio .50 .15
473 Jeff Frye .30 .09
474 Karim Garcia .30 .09
475 Jimmy Haynes .30 .09
476 Darren Holmes .30 .09
477 Tim Salmon .50 .15
478 Randy Johnson .75 .23
479 Eric Plunk .30 .09
480 Scott Cooper .30 .09
481 Chan Ho Park .30 .09
482 Ray McDavid .30 .09
483 Mark Petkovsek .30 .09
484 Greg Swindell .30 .09
485 George Williams .30 .09
486 Yamil Benitez .30 .09
487 Tim Wakefield .30 .09
488 Kevin Tapani .30 .09
489 Derrick May .30 .09
490 Ken Griffey Jr. CL .75 .23
491 Derek Jeter 2.00 .60
492 Jeff Fassero .30 .09
493 Benito Santiago .30 .09
494 Tom Gordon .30 .09
495 Jamie Brewington RC .30 .09
496 Vince Coleman .30 .09
497 Kevin Jordan .30 .09
498 Jeff King .30 .09
499 Mike Simms .30 .09
500 Jose Rijo .30 .09
501 Denny Neagle .30 .09
502 Jose Lima .30 .09
503 Kevin Seitzer .30 .09
504 Alex Fernandez .30 .09
505 Mo Vaughn .30 .09
506 Phil Nevin .30 .09
507 J.T. Snow .30 .09
508 Andujar Cedeno .30 .09
509 Ozzie Guillen .30 .09
510 Mark Clark .30 .09
511 Mark McGwire 2.00 .60
512 Jeff Reboulet .30 .09
513 Armando Benitez .30 .09
514 LaTroy Hawkins .30 .09
515 Brett Butler .30 .09
516 Tavo Alvarez .30 .09
517 Chris Snopek .30 .09
518 Mike Mussina .75 .23
519 Darryl Kile .30 .09
520 Wally Joyner .30 .09
521 Willie McGee .30 .09
522 Kent Mercker .30 .09
523 Mike Jackson .30 .09
524 Troy Percival .30 .09
525 Tony Gwynn 1.00 .30
526 Ron Coomer .30 .09
527 Darryl Hamilton .30 .09
528 Phil Plantier .30 .09
529 Norm Charlton .30 .09
530 Craig Paquette .30 .09
531 Dave Burba .30 .09
532 Mike Henneman .30 .09
533 Terrell Wade .30 .09
534 Eddie Williams .30 .09
535 Robin Ventura .30 .09
536 Chuck Knoblauch .30 .09
537 Les Norman .30 .09
538 Brady Anderson .30 .09
539 Roger Clemens 1.50 .45
540 Mark Portugal .30 .09
541 Mike Matheny .30 .09
542 Jeff Parrett .30 .09
543 Roberto Kelly .30 .09
544 Damon Buford .30 .09
545 Chad Ogea .30 .09
546 Jose Offerman .30 .09
547 Brian Barber .30 .09
548 Danny Tartabull .30 .09
549 Duane Singleton .30 .09
550 Tony Gwynn CL .50 .15

1996 Donruss Press Proofs

Randomly inserted at a rate of one in 12 first series packs and one in 10 second series packs, these cards parallel the regular Donruss issue. Even though they are not sequentially numbered, production on these cards were limited to 2,000 cards. Each card is noted as being a Press Proof in gold foil on the front.

Nm-Mt Ex-Mt
*STARS: 6X TO 15X BASIC CARDS
*ROOKIES: 4X TO 10X BASIC CARDS

1996 Donruss Diamond Kings

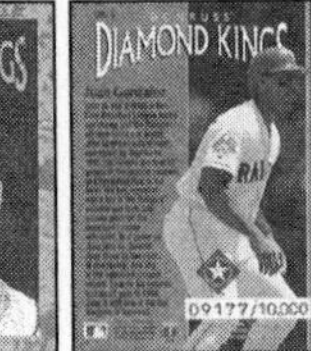

These 31 standard-size cards were randomly inserted into packs and issued in two series of 14 and 17 cards. They were inserted in first series packs at a ratio of approximately one every 60 packs. Second series cards were inserted one every 30 packs. The cards are sequentially numbered in the back lower right as "X" of 10,000. The fronts feature player portraits by noted sports artist Dick Perez. These cards are gold-foil stamped and the portraits are surrounded by gold-foil borders. The backs feature text about the player as well as a player photo. The cards are numbered on the back with a "DK" prefix.

Nm-Mt Ex-Mt
COMPLETE SET (31) 250.00 75.00
COMPLETE SERIES 1 (14) 150.00 45.00
COMPLETE SERIES 2 (17) 100.00 30.00
1 Frank Thomas 12.00 3.60
2 Mo Vaughn 5.00 1.50
3 Manny Ramirez 5.00 1.50
4 Mark McGwire 30.00 9.00
5 Juan Gonzalez 12.00 3.60
6 Roberto Alomar 12.00 3.60
7 Tim Salmon 8.00 2.40
8 Barry Bonds 30.00 9.00
9 Tony Gwynn 15.00 4.50
10 Reggie Sanders 5.00 1.50
11 Larry Walker 8.00 2.40
12 Pedro Martinez 12.00 3.60
13 Jeff King 5.00 1.50
14 Mark Grace 8.00 2.40
15 Greg Maddux 15.00 4.50
16 Don Mattingly 25.00 7.50
17 Gregg Jefferies 4.00 1.20
18 Chad Curtis 4.00 1.20
19 Jason Isringhausen 4.00 1.20
20 B.J. Surhoff 4.00 1.20
21 Jeff Conine 4.00 1.20
22 Kirby Puckett 10.00 3.00
23 Derek Bell 4.00 1.20
24 Wally Joyner 4.00 1.20
25 Brian Jordan 4.00 1.20
26 Edgar Martinez 6.00 1.80
27 Hideo Nomo 10.00 3.00
28 Mike Mussina 10.00 3.00
29 Eddie Murray 10.00 3.00
30 Cal Ripken 30.00 9.00
31 Checklist 4.00 1.20

1996 Donruss Elite

Randomly inserted approximately one in Donruss packs, this 12-card standard-size set is continuously numbered (61-72) from the previous year. First series cards were inserted one every 40 packs. Second series cards were inserted one every 75 packs. The fronts contain an action photo surrounded by a silver border. Limited to 10,000 and sequentially numbered, the backs contain a small photo and write up.

Nm-Mt Ex-Mt
COMPLETE SET (12) 110.00 33.00
COMPLETE SERIES 1 (6) 50.00 15.00
COMPLETE SERIES 2 (6) 60.00 18.00
61 Cal Ripken 30.00 9.00
62 Hideo Nomo 10.00 3.00
63 Reggie Sanders 4.00 1.20
64 Mo Vaughn 4.00 1.20
65 Tim Salmon 6.00 1.80
66 Chipper Jones 10.00 3.00
67 Manny Ramirez 4.00 1.20
68 Greg Maddux 15.00 4.50
69 Frank Thomas 10.00 3.00
70 Ken Griffey Jr. 15.00 4.50
71 Dante Bichette 4.00 1.20
72 Tony Gwynn 12.00 3.60

1996 Donruss Freeze Frame

Randomly inserted in second series packs at a rate of one in 60, this eight-card standard-size set features the top hitters and pitchers in baseball. Just 5,000 of each card were produced and sequentially numbered.

Nm-Mt Ex-Mt
COMPLETE SET (8) 100.00 30.00
1 Frank Thomas 10.00 3.00
2 Ken Griffey Jr. 15.00 4.50
3 Cal Ripken 30.00 9.00
4 Hideo Nomo 10.00 3.00
5 Greg Maddux 15.00 4.50
6 Albert Belle 4.00 1.20
7 Chipper Jones 10.00 3.00
8 Mike Piazza 15.00 4.50

1996 Donruss Hit List

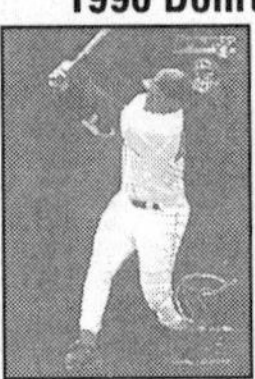

This 16-card standard-size set was randomly inserted in 97 Donruss and salutes the most consistent hitters in the game. The first series cards were inserted one every 105 packs while the second series cards were inserted one every 60 packs. The cards are sequentially numbered out of 10,000.

Nm-Mt Ex-Mt
COMPLETE SET (16) 100.00 30.00
COMPLETE SERIES 1 (8) 60.00 18.00
COMPLETE SERIES 2 (8) 40.00 12.00
1 Tony Gwynn 8.00 2.40
2 Ken Griffey Jr. 10.00 3.00
3 Will Clark 6.00 1.80
4 Mike Piazza 10.00 3.00
5 Carlos Baerga 2.50 .75
6 Mo Vaughn 2.50 .75
7 Mark Grace 4.00 1.20
8 Kirby Puckett 6.00 1.80
9 Frank Thomas 6.00 1.80
10 Barry Bonds 15.00 4.50
11 Jeff Bagwell 4.00 1.20
12 Edgar Martinez 4.00 1.20
13 Tim Salmon 4.00 1.20
14 Wade Boggs 4.00 1.20
15 Don Mattingly 15.00 4.50
16 Eddie Murray 6.00 1.80

1996 Donruss Long Ball Leaders

This eight-card standard-size set was randomly inserted into series one retail packs. They were inserted at a rate of approximately one in every 96 packs. The cards are sequentially numbered out of 5,000. The set highlights eight top sluggers and their farthest home run distance of 1995. The fronts feature a player photo set against a silver-foil background.

Nm-Mt Ex-Mt
COMPLETE SET (8) 120.00 36.00
1 Barry Bonds 30.00 9.00
2 Ryan Klesko 5.00 1.50
3 Mark McGwire 30.00 9.00
4 Raul Mondesi 5.00 1.50
5 Cecil Fielder 5.00 1.50
6 Ken Griffey Jr. 20.00 6.00
7 Larry Walker 8.00 2.40
8 Frank Thomas 12.00 3.60

1996 Donruss Power Alley

This ten-card standard-size set was randomly inserted into series one hobby packs. They were inserted at a rate of approximately one in every 92 packs. These cards are all sequentially numbered out of 5,000.

Nm-Mt Ex-Mt
COMPLETE SET (10) 80.00 24.00
*DC'S: 1.25X TO 3X BASIC POWER ALLEY

DC SER.1 ODDS 1:920 HOBBY
DC PRINT RUN 500 SERIAL #'d SETS
1 Frank Thomas 12.00 3.60
2 Barry Bonds 30.00 9.00
3 Reggie Sanders 5.00 1.50
4 Albert Belle 5.00 1.50
5 Tim Salmon 8.00 2.40
6 Dante Bichette 5.00 1.50
7 Mo Vaughn 5.00 1.50
8 Jim Edmonds 5.00 1.50
9 Manny Ramirez 5.00 1.50
10 Ken Griffey Jr. 20.00 6.00

1996 Donruss Pure Power

Randomly inserted in retail and magazine packs only at a rate of one in eight, this eight-card set features color action player photos of eight of the most powerful players in Major League baseball.

Nm-Mt Ex-Mt
COMPLETE SET (8) 80.00 24.00
1 Raul Mondesi 5.00 1.50
2 Barry Bonds 30.00 9.00
3 Albert Belle 5.00 1.50
4 Frank Thomas 12.00 3.60
5 Mike Piazza 20.00 6.00
6 Dante Bichette 5.00 1.50
7 Manny Ramirez 5.00 1.50
8 Mo Vaughn 5.00 1.50

1996 Donruss Round Trippers

Randomly inserted in second series hobby packs at a rate of one in 55, this 10-card standard-size set honors ten of Baseball's top homerun hitters. Just 5,000 of each card were produced and consecutively numbered.

Nm-Mt Ex-Mt
COMPLETE SET (10) 80.00 24.00
1 Albert Belle 4.00 1.20
2 Barry Bonds 25.00 7.50
3 Jeff Bagwell 6.00 1.80
4 Tim Salmon 6.00 1.80
5 Mo Vaughn 4.00 1.20
6 Ken Griffey Jr. 15.00 4.50
7 Mike Piazza 15.00 4.50
8 Cal Ripken 30.00 9.00
9 Frank Thomas 10.00 3.00
10 Dante Bichette 4.00 1.20

1996 Donruss Showdown

This eight-card standard-size set was randomly inserted in series one packs at a rate of one in every 105 packs. These cards feature one top hitter and one top pitcher from each league. The cards are sequentially numbered out of 10,000.

Nm-Mt Ex-Mt
COMPLETE SET (8) 100.00 30.00
1 Frank Thomas 8.00 2.40
Hideo Nomo
2 Barry Bonds 20.00 6.00
Randy Johnson
3 Greg Maddux 12.00 3.60
Ken Griffey Jr.
4 Roger Clemens 10.00 3.00
Tony Gwynn
5 Mike Piazza 12.00 3.60
Mike Mussina
6 Cal Ripken 25.00 7.50
Pedro J.Martinez
7 Tim Wakefield 3.00 .90
Matt Williams
8 Manny Ramirez 3.00 .90
Carlos Perez

1997 Donruss

The 1997 Donruss set was issued in two separate series of 270 and 180 cards

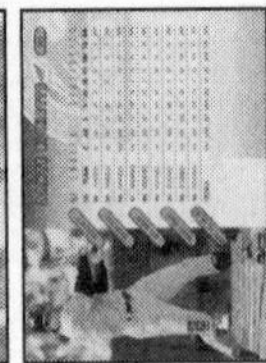

respectively. Both first series and Update cards were distributed in 10-card packs carrying a suggested retail price of $1.99 each. Card fronts feature color action player photos while the backs carry another color player photo with player information and career statistics. The following subsets are included within the set: Checklists (267-270/448-450), Rookies (353-397), Hit List (398-422), King of the Hill (423-437) and Interleague Showdown (438-447). Rookie Cards in this set include Jose Cruz Jr., Brian Giles and Hideki Irabu.

Nm-Mt Ex-Mt
COMPLETE SET (450) 50.00 15.00
COMP. SERIES 1 (270) 25.00 7.50
COMPLETE UPDATE (180) 25.00 7.50
1 Juan Gonzalez .75 .23
2 Jim Edmonds .30 .09
3 Tony Gwynn 1.00 .30
4 Andres Galarraga .30 .09
5 Joe Carter .30 .09
6 Raul Mondesi .30 .09
7 Greg Maddux 1.25 .35
8 Travis Fryman .30 .09
9 Brian Jordan .30 .09
10 Henry Rodriguez .30 .09
11 Manny Ramirez .30 .09
12 Mark McGwire 2.00 .60
13 Marc Newfield .30 .09
14 Craig Biggio .50 .15
15 Sammy Sosa 1.25 .35
16 Brady Anderson .30 .09
17 Wade Boggs .50 .15
18 Charles Johnson .30 .09
19 Matt Williams .30 .09
20 Denny Neagle .30 .09
21 Ken Griffey Jr. 1.25 .35
22 Robin Ventura .30 .09
23 Barry Larkin .75 .23
24 Todd Zeile .30 .09
25 Chuck Knoblauch .30 .09
26 Todd Hundley .30 .09
27 Roger Clemens 1.50 .45
28 Michael Tucker .30 .09
29 Rondell White .30 .09
30 Osvaldo Fernandez .30 .09
31 Ivan Rodriguez .75 .23
32 Alex Fernandez .30 .09
33 Jason Isringhausen .30 .09
34 Chipper Jones .75 .23
35 Paul O'Neill .50 .15
36 Hideo Nomo .75 .23
37 Roberto Alomar .75 .23
38 Derek Bell .30 .09
39 Paul Molitor .50 .15
40 Andy Benes .30 .09
41 Steve Trachsel .30 .09
42 J.T. Snow .30 .09
43 Jason Kendall .30 .09
44 Alex Rodriguez 1.25 .35
45 Joey Hamilton .30 .09
46 Carlos Delgado .30 .09
47 Jason Giambi .75 .23
48 Larry Walker .50 .15
49 Derek Jeter 2.00 .60
50 Kenny Lofton .30 .09
51 Devon White .30 .09
52 Matt Mieske .30 .09
53 Melvin Nieves .30 .09
54 Jose Canseco .75 .23
55 Tino Martinez .50 .15
56 Rafael Palmeiro .50 .15
57 Edgardo Alfonzo .30 .09
58 Jay Buhner .30 .09
59 Shane Reynolds .30 .09
60 Steve Finley .30 .09
61 Bobby Higginson .30 .09
62 Dean Palmer .30 .09
63 Terry Pendleton .30 .09
64 Marquis Grissom .30 .09
65 Mike Stanley .30 .09
66 Moises Alou .30 .09
67 Ray Lankford .30 .09
68 Marty Cordova .30 .09
69 John Olerud .30 .09
70 David Cone .30 .09
71 Benito Santiago .30 .09
72 Ryne Sandberg 1.25 .35
73 Rickey Henderson .75 .23
74 Roger Cedeno .30 .09
75 Wilson Alvarez .30 .09
76 Tim Salmon .50 .15
77 Orlando Merced .30 .09
78 Vinny Castilla .30 .09
79 Ismael Valdes .30 .09
80 Dante Bichette .30 .09
81 Kevin Brown .30 .09
82 Andy Pettitte .50 .15
83 Scott Stahoviak .30 .09
84 Mickey Tettleton .30 .09
85 Jack McDowell .30 .09
86 Tom Glavine .50 .15
87 Gregg Jefferies .30 .09
88 Chili Davis .30 .09
89 Randy Johnson .75 .23
90 John Mabry .30 .09
91 Billy Wagner .30 .09
92 Jeff Cirillo .30 .09
93 Trevor Hoffman .30 .09
94 Juan Guzman .30 .09
95 Geronimo Berroa .30 .09
96 Bernard Gilkey .30 .09
97 Danny Tartabull .30 .09
98 Johnny Damon .30 .09
99 Charlie Hayes .30 .09
100 Reggie Sanders .30 .09
101 Robby Thompson .30 .09
102 Bobby Bonilla .30 .09

103 Reggie Jefferson .30 .09
104 John Smoltz .50 .15
105 Jim Thome .75 .23
106 Ruben Rivera .30 .09
107 Darren Oliver .30 .09
108 Mo Vaughn .30 .09
109 Roger Pavlik .30 .09
110 Terry Steinbach .30 .09
111 Jermaine Dye .30 .09
112 Mark Grudzielanek .30 .09
113 Rick Aguilera .30 .09
114 Jamey Wright .30 .09
115 Eddie Murray .75 .23
116 Brian L. Hunter .30 .09
117 Hal Morris .30 .09
118 Tom Pagnozzi .30 .09
119 Mike Mussina .75 .23
120 Mark Grace .50 .15
121 Cal Ripken 2.50 .75
122 Tom Goodwin .30 .09
123 Paul Sorrento .30 .09
124 Jay Bell .30 .09
125 Todd Hollandsworth .30 .09
126 Edgar Martinez .50 .15
127 George Arias .30 .09
128 Greg Vaughn .30 .09
129 Roberto Hernandez .30 .09
130 Delino DeShields .30 .09
131 Bill Pulsipher .30 .09
132 Joey Cora .30 .09
133 Mariano Rivera .50 .15
134 Mike Piazza 1.25 .35
135 Carlos Baerga .30 .09
136 Jose Mesa .30 .09
137 Will Clark .75 .23
138 Frank Thomas .75 .23
139 John Wetteland .30 .09
140 Shawn Estes .30 .09
141 Garret Anderson .30 .09
142 Andre Dawson .30 .09
143 Eddie Taubensee .30 .09
144 Ryan Klesko .30 .09
145 Rocky Coppinger .30 .09
146 Jeff Bagwell .50 .15
147 Donovan Osborne .30 .09
148 Greg Myers .30 .09
149 Brant Brown .30 .09
150 Kevin Elster .30 .09
151 Bob Wells .30 .09
152 Wally Joyner .30 .09
153 Rico Brogna .30 .09
154 Dwight Gooden .50 .15
155 Jermaine Allensworth .30 .09
156 Ray Durham .30 .09
157 Cecil Fielder .30 .09
158 John Burkett .30 .09
159 Gary Sheffield .30 .09
160 Albert Belle .30 .09
161 Tomas Perez .30 .09
162 David Doster .30 .09
163 John Valentin .30 .09
164 Danny Graves .30 .09
165 Jose Paniagua .30 .09
166 Brian Giles RC 1.50 .45
167 Barry Bonds 2.00 .60
168 Sterling Hitchcock .30 .09
169 Bernie Williams .50 .15
170 Fred McGriff .50 .15
171 George Williams .30 .09
172 Amaury Telemaco .30 .09
173 Ken Caminiti .30 .09
174 Ron Gant .30 .09
175 Dave Justice .30 .09
176 James Baldwin .30 .09
177 Pat Hentgen .30 .09
178 Ben McDonald .30 .09
179 Tim Naehring .30 .09
180 Jim Eisenreich .30 .09
181 Ken Hill .30 .09
182 Paul Wilson .30 .09
183 Marvin Benard .30 .09
184 Alan Benes .30 .09
185 Ellis Burks .30 .09
186 Scott Servais .30 .09
187 David Segui .30 .09
188 Scott Brosius .30 .09
189 Jose Offerman .30 .09
190 Eric Davis .30 .09
191 Brett Butler .30 .09
192 Curtis Pride .30 .09
193 Yamil Benitez .30 .09
194 Chan Ho Park .30 .09
195 Bret Boone .30 .09
196 Omar Vizquel .30 .09
197 Orlando Miller .30 .09
198 Ramon Martinez .30 .09
199 Harold Baines .30 .09
200 Eric Young .30 .09
201 Fernando Vina .30 .09
202 Alex Gonzalez .30 .09
203 Fernando Valenzuela .30 .09
204 Steve Avery .30 .09
205 Ernie Young .30 .09
206 Kevin Appier .30 .09
207 Randy Myers .30 .09
208 Jeff Suppan .30 .09
209 James Mouton .30 .09
210 Russ Davis .30 .09
211 Al Martin .30 .09
212 Troy Percival .30 .09
213 Al Leiter .30 .09
214 Dennis Eckersley .30 .09
215 Mark Johnson .30 .09
216 Eric Karros .30 .09
217 Royce Clayton .30 .09
218 Tony Phillips .30 .09
219 Tim Wakefield .30 .09
220 Alan Trammell .50 .15
221 Eduardo Perez .30 .09
222 Butch Huskey .30 .09
223 Tim Belcher .30 .09
224 Jamie Moyer .30 .09
225 F.P. Santangelo .30 .09
226 Rusty Greer .30 .09
227 Jeff Brantley .30 .09
228 Mark Langston .30 .09
229 Ray Montgomery .30 .09
230 Rich Becker .30 .09
231 Ozzie Smith 1.25 .35
232 Rey Ordonez .30 .09
233 Ricky Otero .30 .09
234 Mike Cameron .30 .09
235 Mike Sweeney .30 .09
236 Mark Lewis .30 .09
237 Luis Gonzalez .30 .09
238 Marcus Jensen .30 .09
239 Ed Sprague .30 .09
240 Jose Valentin .30 .09
241 Jeff Frye .30 .09
242 Charles Nagy .30 .09
243 Carlos Garcia .30 .09
244 Mike Hampton .30 .09
245 B.J. Surhoff .30 .09
246 Wilton Guerrero .30 .09
247 Frank Rodriguez .30 .09
248 Gary Gaetti .30 .09
249 Lance Johnson .30 .09
250 Darren Bragg .30 .09
251 Darryl Hamilton .30 .09
252 John Jaha .30 .09
253 Craig Paquette .30 .09
254 Jaime Navarro .30 .09
255 Shawon Dunston .30 .09
256 Mark Loretta .30 .09
257 Tim Belk .30 .09
258 Jeff Darwin .30 .09
259 Ruben Sierra .30 .09
260 Chuck Finley .30 .09
261 Darryl Strawberry .50 .15
262 Shannon Stewart .30 .09
263 Pedro Martinez .75 .23
264 Neifi Perez .30 .09
265 Jeff Conine .30 .09
266 Orel Hershiser .30 .09
267 Eddie Murray CL .50 .15
268 Paul Molitor CL .30 .09
269 Barry Bonds CL .75 .23
270 Mark McGwire CL 1.00 .30
271 Matt Williams .30 .09
272 Todd Zeile .30 .09
273 Roger Clemens 1.50 .45
274 Michael Tucker .30 .09
275 J.T. Snow .30 .09
276 Kenny Lofton .30 .09
277 Jose Canseco .75 .23
278 Marquis Grissom .30 .09
279 Moises Alou .30 .09
280 Benito Santiago .30 .09
281 Willie McGee .30 .09
282 Chili Davis .30 .09
283 Ron Coomer .30 .09
284 Orlando Merced .30 .09
285 Delino DeShields .30 .09
286 John Wetteland .30 .09
287 Darren Daulton .30 .09
288 Lee Stevens .30 .09
289 Albert Belle .30 .09
290 Sterling Hitchcock .30 .09
291 David Justice .30 .09
292 Eric Davis .30 .09
293 Brian Hunter .30 .09
294 Darryl Hamilton .30 .09
295 Steve Avery .30 .09
296 Joe Vitiello .30 .09
297 Jaime Navarro .30 .09
298 Eddie Murray .75 .23
299 Randy Myers .30 .09
300 Francisco Cordova .30 .09
301 Javier Lopez .30 .09
302 Geronimo Berroa .30 .09
303 Jeffrey Hammonds .30 .09
304 Deion Sanders .50 .15
305 Jeff Fassero .30 .09
306 Curt Schilling .50 .15
307 Robb Nen .30 .09
308 Mark McLemore .30 .09
309 Jimmy Key .30 .09
310 Quilvio Veras .30 .09
311 Bip Roberts .30 .09
312 Esteban Loaiza .30 .09
313 Andy Ashby .30 .09
314 Sandy Alomar Jr. .30 .09
315 Shawn Green .30 .09
316 Luis Castillo .30 .09
317 Benji Gil .30 .09
318 Otis Nixon .30 .09
319 Aaron Sele .30 .09
320 Brad Ausmus .30 .09
321 Troy O'Leary .30 .09
322 Terrell Wade .30 .09
323 Jeff King .30 .09
324 Kevin Seitzer .30 .09
325 Mark Wohlers .30 .09
326 Edgar Renteria .30 .09
327 Dan Wilson .30 .09
328 Brian McRae .30 .09
329 Rod Beck .30 .09
330 Julio Franco .30 .09
331 Dave Nilsson .30 .09
332 Glenallen Hill .30 .09
333 Kevin Elster .30 .09
334 Joe Girardi .30 .09
335 David Wells .30 .09
336 Jeff Blauser .30 .09
337 Darryl Kile .30 .09
338 Jeff Kent .30 .09
339 Jim Leyritz .30 .09
340 Todd Stottlemyre .30 .09
341 Tony Clark .30 .09
342 Chris Hoiles .30 .09
343 Mike Lieberthal .30 .09
344 Matt Lawton .30 .09
345 Alex Ochoa .30 .09
346 Chris Snopek .30 .09
347 Rudy Pemberton .30 .09
348 Eric Owens .30 .09
349 Joe Randa .30 .09
350 John Olerud .30 .09
351 Steve Karsay .30 .09
352 Mark Whiten .30 .09
353 Bob Abreu .30 .09
354 Bartolo Colon .30 .09
355 Vladimir Guerrero .75 .23
356 Darin Erstad .30 .09
357 Scott Rolen .50 .15
358 Andruw Jones .30 .09
359 Scott Spiezio .30 .09
360 Karim Garcia .30 .09
361 Hideki Irabu RC .40 .12
362 Nomar Garciaparra 1.25 .35
363 Dmitri Young .30 .09
364 Bubba Trammell RC .40 .12
365 Kevin Orie .30 .09
366 Jose Rosado .30 .09
367 Jose Guillen .30 .09
368 Brooks Kieschnick .30 .09
369 Pokey Reese .30 .09
370 Glendon Rusch .30 .09
371 Jason Dickson .30 .09
372 Todd Walker .30 .09
373 Justin Thompson .30 .09
374 Todd Greene .30 .09
375 Jeff Suppan .30 .09
376 Trey Beamon .30 .09
377 Damon Mashore .30 .09
378 Wendell Magee .30 .09
379 S. Hasegawa RC .75 .23
380 Bill Mueller RC 2.00 .60
381 Chris Widger .30 .09
382 Tony Graffanino .30 .09
383 Derrek Lee .30 .09
384 Brian Moehler .30 .09
385 Quinton McCracken .30 .09
386 Matt Morris .30 .09
387 Marvin Benard .30 .09
388 Deivi Cruz RC .40 .12
389 Javier Valentin .30 .09
390 Todd Dunwoody .30 .09
391 Derrick Gibson .30 .09
392 Raul Casanova .30 .09
393 George Arias .30 .09
394 Tony Womack RC .40 .12
395 Antone Williamson .30 .09
396 Jose Cruz Jr. RC 1.25 .35
397 Desi Relaford .30 .09
398 Frank Thomas HIT .50 .15
399 Ken Griffey Jr. HIT .75 .23
400 Cal Ripken HIT 1.25 .35
401 Chipper Jones HIT .50 .15
402 Mike Piazza HIT .75 .23
403 Gary Sheffield HIT .30 .09
404 Alex Rodriguez HIT .75 .23
405 Wade Boggs HIT .30 .09
406 Juan Gonzalez HIT .50 .15
407 Tony Gwynn HIT .50 .15
408 Edgar Martinez HIT .30 .09
409 Jeff Bagwell HIT .30 .09
410 Larry Walker HIT .30 .09
411 Kenny Lofton HIT .30 .09
412 Manny Ramirez HIT .30 .09
413 Mark McGwire HIT 1.00 .30
414 Roberto Alomar HIT .30 .09
415 Derek Jeter HIT 1.00 .30
416 Brady Anderson HIT .30 .09
417 Paul Molitor HIT .30 .09
418 Dante Bichette HIT .30 .09
419 Jim Edmonds HIT .30 .09
420 Mo Vaughn HIT .30 .09
421 Barry Bonds HIT .75 .23
422 Rusty Greer HIT .30 .09
423 Greg Maddux KING .75 .23
424 Andy Pettitte KING .30 .09
425 John Smoltz KING .30 .09
426 Randy Johnson KING .50 .15
427 Hideo Nomo KING .30 .09
428 Roger Clemens KING .75 .23
429 Tom Glavine KING .30 .09
430 Pat Hentgen KING .30 .09
431 Kevin Brown KING .30 .09
432 Mike Mussina KING .50 .15
433 Alex Fernandez KING .30 .09
434 Kevin Appier KING .30 .09
435 David Cone KING .30 .09
436 Jeff Fassero KING .30 .09
437 John Wetteland KING .30 .09
438 Barry Bonds IS .75 .23
Ivan Rodriguez
439 Ken Griffey Jr. IS .75 .23
Andres Galarraga
440 Fred McGriff IS .30 .09
Rafael Palmeiro
441 Barry Larkin IS .30 .09
Jim Thome
442 Sammy Sosa IS .75 .23
Albert Belle
443 Bernie Williams IS .30 .09
Todd Hundley
444 Chuck Knoblauch IS .30 .09
Brian Jordan
445 Mo Vaughn IS .30 .09
Jeff Conine
446 Ken Caminiti IS .30 .09
Jason Giambi
447 Raul Mondesi IS .30 .09
Tim Salmon
448 Cal Ripken CL 1.25 .35
449 Greg Maddux CL .75 .23
450 Ken Griffey Jr. CL .75 .23

1997 Donruss Gold Press Proofs

Randomly inserted in first series at a rate of 1:32 and Update packs at an approximate rate of 1:64, cards from this 450-card set are a die-cut parallel rendition of the more common Silver Press Proof cards. Gold foil stamping further distinguishes them from the Silver Press Proofs. Only 500 gold sets were printed though they are not serial-numbered.

Nm-Mt Ex-Mt
*STARS: 10X TO 25X BASIC CARDS ..
*ROOKIES: 3X TO 8X BASIC CARDS ..

1997 Donruss Silver Press Proofs

Randomly inserted in first series packs at a rate of one in eight and Update packs at an approximate rate of one in 16, cards from this 450-card Silver foil set parallel the regular 1997 Donruss set. The silver foil stamped words, "Press Proof" down the front right-hand side of the card distinguish them from their regular issue counterparts. Only 2,000 of each card were produced though they are not serial numbered.

Nm-Mt Ex-Mt
*STARS: 4X TO 10X BASIC CARDS ....
*ROOKIES: 1.25X TO .3X BASIC CARDS

1997 Donruss Armed and Dangerous

Randomly inserted in hobby packs at a rate of one in 58 packs, this 15-card set features the League's hottest arms in the game. The fronts carry color action player photos with foil printing. The backs display player information and a color player head portrait at the end of a ribbon representing a medal. Only 5,000 of this set were produced and are sequentially numbered.

	Nm-Mt	Ex-Mt
COMPLETE SET (15)	120.00	36.00
1 Ken Griffey Jr.	10.00	3.00
2 Raul Mondesi	2.50	.75
3 Chipper Jones	6.00	1.80
4 Ivan Rodriguez	6.00	1.80
5 Randy Johnson	6.00	1.80
6 Alex Rodriguez	10.00	3.00
7 Larry Walker	4.00	1.20
8 Cal Ripken	20.00	6.00
9 Kenny Lofton	2.50	.75
10 Barry Bonds	15.00	4.50
11 Derek Jeter	15.00	4.50
12 Charles Johnson	2.50	.75
13 Greg Maddux	10.00	3.00
14 Roberto Alomar	6.00	1.80
15 Barry Larkin	6.00	1.80

1997 Donruss Diamond Kings

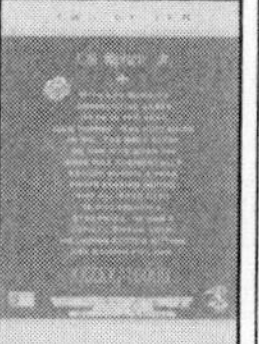

Randomly inserted in all first series packs at a rate of one in 45, this 10-card set commemorates the 15th anniversary of the annual art cards in Donruss baseball sets. Only 10,000 sets were produced each of which is sequentially numbered. Ten cards were printed with the number 1,982 representing the year the insert began and could be redeemed for an original piece of artwork by Diamond Kings artist Dan Gardiner. This was the first year Gardiner painted the Diamond King series.

	Nm-Mt	Ex-Mt
COMPLETE SET (10)	120.00	36.00
*CANVAS: 1.25X TO 3X BASIC DK'S ..		
CANVAS: RANDOM INS.IN SER.1 PACKS		
CANVAS PRINT RUN 500 SERIAL #'d SETS		
1 Ken Griffey Jr.	15.00	4.50
2 Cal Ripken	30.00	9.00
3 Mo Vaughn	4.00	1.20
4 Chuck Knoblauch	4.00	1.20
5 Jeff Bagwell	6.00	1.80
6 Henry Rodriguez	4.00	1.20
7 Mike Piazza	15.00	4.50
8 Ivan Rodriguez	10.00	3.00
9 Frank Thomas	10.00	3.00
10 Chipper Jones	10.00	3.00

1997 Donruss Dominators

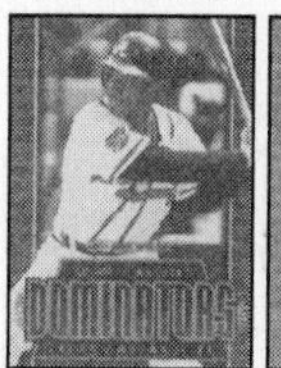
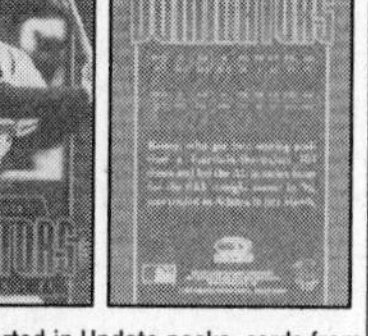

Randomly inserted in Update packs, cards from this 20-card set feature top stars with either incredible speed, awesome power, or unbelievable pitching ability. Card fronts feature red borders and silver foil stamping.

	Nm-Mt	Ex-Mt
COMPLETE SET (20)	80.00	24.00
1 Frank Thomas	4.00	1.20
2 Ken Griffey Jr.	6.00	1.80
3 Greg Maddux	6.00	1.80
4 Cal Ripken	12.00	3.60
5 Alex Rodriguez	6.00	1.80
6 Albert Belle	1.50	.45
7 Mark McGwire	10.00	3.00
8 Juan Gonzalez	4.00	1.20
9 Chipper Jones	4.00	1.20
10 Hideo Nomo	4.00	1.20
11 Roger Clemens	8.00	2.40
12 John Smoltz	2.50	.75
13 Mike Piazza	6.00	1.80
14 Sammy Sosa	6.00	1.80
15 Matt Williams	1.50	.45
16 Kenny Lofton	1.50	.45
17 Barry Larkin	4.00	1.20
18 Rafael Palmeiro	2.50	.75
19 Ken Caminiti	1.50	.45
20 Gary Sheffield	1.50	.45

1997 Donruss Elite Insert Promos

These 12 standard-size cards were issued by Pinnacle to promote their 1997 Donruss Elite Insert set. The fronts are the same as the regular 1997 Donruss Elite insert cards while the backs have a large sample card in black printed sideways on the card. The cards are also numbered promo/2500

	Nm-Mt	Ex-Mt
COMPLETE SET (12)	100.00	30.00
1 Frank Thomas	8.00	2.40
2 Paul Molitor	6.00	1.80
3 Sammy Sosa	10.00	3.00
4 Barry Bonds	10.00	3.00
5 Chipper Jones	10.00	3.00
6 Alex Rodriguez	15.00	4.50
7 Ken Griffey Jr.	10.00	3.00
8 Jeff Bagwell	6.00	1.80
9 Cal Ripken	20.00	6.00
10 Mo Vaughn	2.00	.60
11 Mike Piazza	15.00	4.50
12 Juan Gonzalez UER name mispelled as Gonzales	5.00	1.50

1997 Donruss Elite Inserts

Randomly inserted in all first series packs, this 12-card set honors perennial all-star players of the League. The fronts feature Micro-etched color action player photos, while the backs carry player information. Only 2,500 of this set were produced and are sequentially numbered.

	Nm-Mt	Ex-Mt
COMPLETE SET (12)	250.00	75.00
1 Frank Thomas	15.00	4.50
2 Paul Molitor	10.00	3.00
3 Sammy Sosa	25.00	7.50
4 Barry Bonds	40.00	12.00
5 Chipper Jones	15.00	4.50
6 Alex Rodriguez	25.00	7.50
7 Ken Griffey Jr.	25.00	7.50
8 Jeff Bagwell	10.00	3.00
9 Cal Ripken	50.00	15.00
10 Mo Vaughn	6.00	1.80
11 Mike Piazza	25.00	7.50
12 Juan Gonzalez UER name mispelled as Gonzales	15.00	4.50

1997 Donruss Franchise Features

Randomly inserted in Update hobby packs only at an approximate rate of 1:48, cards from this 15-card set feature color player photos on a unique "movie-poster" style, double-front card design. Each card highlights a superstar veteran on one side displaying a "Now Playing" banner, while the other side features a rookie prospect with a "Coming Attraction" banner. Each card is printed on an all foil card stock and serial numbered to 3,000.

	Nm-Mt	Ex-Mt
COMPLETE SET (15)	250.00	75.00
1 Ken Griffey Jr. Andruw Jones	15.00	4.50
2 Frank Thomas Darin Erstad	10.00	3.00
3 Alex Rodriguez Nomar Garciaparra	15.00	4.50
4 Chuck Knoblauch Wilton Guerrero	4.00	1.20
5 Juan Gonzalez Bubba Trammell	10.00	3.00
6 Chipper Jones Todd Walker	10.00	3.00
7 Barry Bonds Vladimir Guerrero	10.00	3.00
8 Mark McGwire Dmitri Young	25.00	7.50
9 Mike Piazza Mike Sweeney	15.00	4.50
10 Mo Vaughn Tony Clark	4.00	1.20
11 Gary Sheffield Jose Guillen	4.00	1.20
12 Kenny Lofton Shannon Stewart	4.00	1.20
13 Cal Ripken Scott Rolen	30.00	9.00
14 Derek Jeter Pokey Reese	25.00	7.50
15 Tony Gwynn Bob Abreu	12.00	3.60

1997 Donruss Longball Leaders

Randomly inserted in first series retail packs only, this 15-card set honors the league's most fearsome long-ball hitters. The fronts feature color action player photos and foil stamping. The backs carry player information.

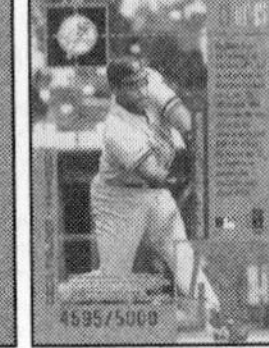

	Nm-Mt	Ex-Mt
COMPLETE SET (15)	80.00	24.00
1 Frank Thomas	6.00	1.80
2 Albert Belle	2.50	.75
3 Mo Vaughn	2.50	.75
4 Brady Anderson	2.50	.75
5 Greg Vaughn	2.50	.75
6 Ken Griffey Jr.	10.00	3.00
7 Jay Buhner	2.50	.75
8 Juan Gonzalez	6.00	1.80
9 Mike Piazza	10.00	3.00
10 Jeff Bagwell	4.00	1.20
11 Sammy Sosa	10.00	3.00
12 Mark McGwire	15.00	4.50
13 Cecil Fielder	2.50	.75
14 Ryan Klesko	2.50	.75
15 Jose Canseco	6.00	1.80

1997 Donruss Power Alley

This 24-card set features color images of some of the league's top hitters printed on a micro-etched, all-foil card stock with holographic foil stamping. Using a "fractured" printing structure, 12 players utilize a green finish and are numbered to 4,000. Eight players are printed on all blue finish and number to 2,000, with the last four players utilizing a gold finish and are numbered to 1,000.

	Nm-Mt	Ex-Mt
*GREEN DC's: 2X TO 5X BASIC GREEN		
*BLUE DC's: 1.25X TO 3X BASIC BLUE		
*GOLD DC's: .75X TO 2X BASIC GOLD		
DIE CUTS: RANDOM INS.IN UPDATE PACKS		
DIE CUTS PRINT RUN 250 SERIAL #'d SETS		
1 Frank Thomas G	15.00	4.50
2 Ken Griffey Jr. G	25.00	7.50
3 Cal Ripken G	50.00	15.00
4 Jeff Bagwell B	6.00	1.80
5 Mike Piazza B	15.00	4.50
6 Andruw Jones GR	2.50	.75
7 Alex Rodriguez G	25.00	7.50
8 Albert Belle GR	2.50	.75
9 Mo Vaughn GR	2.50	.75
10 Chipper Jones B	10.00	3.00
11 Juan Gonzalez B	10.00	3.00
12 Ken Caminiti GR	2.50	.75
13 Manny Ramirez GR	2.50	.75
14 Mark McGwire GR	15.00	4.50
15 Kenny Lofton B	4.00	1.20
16 Barry Bonds GR	15.00	4.50
17 Gary Sheffield GR	2.50	.75
18 Tony Gwynn GR	8.00	2.40
19 Vladimir Guerrero B	10.00	3.00
20 Ivan Rodriguez B	10.00	3.00
21 Paul Molitor B	6.00	1.80
22 Sammy Sosa GR	10.00	3.00
23 Matt Williams GR	2.50	.75
24 Derek Jeter GR	15.00	4.50

1997 Donruss Rated Rookies

Randomly inserted in all first series packs, this 30-card set honors the top rookie prospects as chosen by Donruss to be the most likely to succeed. The fronts feature color action player photos and silver foil printing. The backs carry a player portrait and player information.

	Nm-Mt	Ex-Mt
COMPLETE SET (30)	40.00	12.00
1 Jason Thompson	2.00	.60
2 LaTroy Hawkins	2.00	.60
3 Scott Rolen	3.00	.90
4 Trey Beamon	2.00	.60
5 Kimera Bartee	2.00	.60
6 Nerio Rodriguez	2.00	.60
7 Jeff D'Amico	2.00	.60
8 Quinton McCracken	2.00	.60
9 John Wasdin	2.00	.60
10 Robin Jennings	2.00	.60
11 Steve Gibralter	2.00	.60
12 Tyler Houston	2.00	.60
13 Tony Clark	2.00	.60
14 Ugueth Urbina	2.00	.60
15 Karim Garcia	2.00	.60
16 Raul Casanova	2.00	.60
17 Brooks Kieschnick	2.00	.60
18 Luis Castillo	2.00	.60
19 Edgar Renteria	2.00	.60
20 Andruw Jones	2.00	.60
21 Chad Mottola	2.00	.60
22 Mac Suzuki	2.00	.60
23 Justin Thompson	2.00	.60
24 Darin Erstad	2.00	.60
25 Todd Walker	2.00	.60
26 Todd Greene	2.00	.60
27 Vladimir Guerrero	5.00	1.50
28 Darren Dreifort	2.00	.60
29 John Burke	2.00	.60
30 Damon Mashore	2.00	.60

1997 Donruss Ripken The Only Way I Know

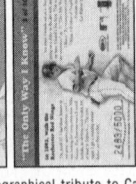

This special autobiographical tribute to Cal Ripken Jr. delivers a one-of-a-kind inside look at the modern day "Iron Man." Cards from this ten card set are printed on all foil card stock with foil stamping, utilizing exclusive photography and excerpts from his book. The first nine cards in the set were randomly seeded into packs of Donruss Update at an approximate rate of 1:24. Card number 10 was available exclusively in his book, "The Only Way I Know." Ripken autographed 2,131 of these number 10 cards and they were randomly inserted into the books. Because of it's separate distribution, card number 10 is not commonly included in complete sets, thus the mainstream set is considered complete with cards 1-9. Only 5,000 of each 1-9 card were produced, each of which are sequentially numbered on back.

	Nm-Mt	Ex-Mt
COMPLETE SET (9)	100.00	30.00
COMMON CARD (1-9)	12.00	3.60
COMMON CARD (10)	20.00	6.00
10A Cal Ripken AU/2131	200.00	60.00
distributed exclusively with book		

1997 Donruss Rocket Launchers

Randomly inserted in first series magazine packs only, this 15-card set honers baseball's top power hitters. The fronts feature color player photos, while the backs carry player information. Only 5,000 sets were produced and all are sequentially numbered.

	Nm-Mt	Ex-Mt
COMPLETE SET (15)	80.00	24.00
1 Frank Thomas	6.00	1.80
2 Albert Belle	2.50	.75
3 Chipper Jones	6.00	1.80
4 Mike Piazza	10.00	3.00
5 Mo Vaughn	2.50	.75
6 Juan Gonzalez	6.00	1.80
7 Fred McGriff	4.00	1.20
8 Jeff Bagwell	4.00	1.20
9 Matt Williams	2.50	.75
10 Gary Sheffield	2.50	.75
11 Barry Bonds	15.00	4.50
12 Manny Ramirez	2.50	.75
13 Henry Rodriguez	2.50	.75
14 Jason Giambi	6.00	1.80
15 Cal Ripken	20.00	6.00

1997 Donruss Rookie Diamond Kings

Randomly inserted in Update packs at an approximate rate of 1:24, cards from this 10-card set feature color portraits of some of the season's hottest rookie prospects in gold borders. Only 9,500 of each card were printed and are sequentially numbered. Please note that the numbering of each card runs to 10,000, but the first 500 of each card were Canvas parallels.

	Nm-Mt	Ex-Mt
COMPLETE SET (10)	60.00	18.00
*CANVAS: 1.25X TO 3X BASIC DK'S		
CANVAS PRINT RUN 500 SERIAL #'d SETS		
RANDOM INSERTS IN UPDATE PACKS		
1 Andruw Jones	4.00	1.20
2 Vladimir Guerrero	10.00	3.00
3 Scott Rolen	6.00	1.80
4 Todd Walker	4.00	1.20
5 Bartolo Colon	4.00	1.20
6 Jose Guillen	4.00	1.20
7 Nomar Garciaparra	15.00	4.50
8 Darin Erstad	4.00	1.20
9 Dmitri Young	4.00	1.20
10 Wilton Guerrero	4.00	1.20

1997 Donruss Update Ripken Info Card

This one-card set was inserted as the top card in prepackaged 1997 Donruss Update 14-card blister packs priced at $2.99 a package. The front features a borderless color action photo of Cal Ripken Jr. The back displays information about Donruss Update base and insert sets.

	Nm-Mt	Ex-Mt
1 Cal Ripken Jr.	3.00	.90

1998 Donruss

The 1998 Donruss set was issued in two series (series one numbers 1-170, series two numbers 171-420) and was distributed in 10-card packs with a suggested retail price of $1.99. The fronts feature color player photos with player information on the backs. The set contains the topical subsets: Fan Club (156-165), Hit List (346-375), The Untouchables (376-385), Spirit of the Game (386-415) and Checklists (416-420). Each Fan Club card carried instructions on how the fan could vote for their favorite players to be included in the 1998 Donruss Update set. Rookie Cards include Kevin Millwood and Magglio Ordonez. Sadly, after an eighteen year run, this was the last Donruss set to be issued due to card manufacturer Pinnacle's bankruptcy in 1998. In 2001, however, Donruss/Playoff procuured a license to produce baseball cards and the Donruss brand was reinstituted after a two year break.

	Nm-Mt	Ex-Mt
COMPLETE SET (420)	50.00	15.00
COMP.SERIES 1 (170)	20.00	6.00
COMPLETE UPDATE (250)	30.00	9.00
1 Paul Molitor	.40	.12
2 Juan Gonzalez	.60	.18
3 Darryl Kile	.25	.07
4 Randy Johnson	.60	.18
5 Tom Glavine	.40	.12
6 Pat Hentgen	.25	.07
7 David Justice	.25	.07
8 Kevin Brown	.40	.12
9 Mike Mussina	.60	.18
10 Ken Caminiti	.25	.07
11 Todd Hundley	.25	.07
12 Frank Thomas	.60	.18
13 Ray Lankford	.25	.07
14 Justin Thompson	.25	.07
15 Jason Dickson	.25	.07
16 Kenny Lofton	.25	.07
17 Ivan Rodriguez	.60	.18
18 Pedro Martinez	.60	.18
19 Brady Anderson	.25	.07
20 Barry Larkin	.60	.18
21 Chipper Jones	.60	.18
22 Tony Gwynn	.75	.23
23 Roger Clemens	1.25	.35
24 Sandy Alomar Jr.	.25	.07
25 Tino Martinez	.40	.12
26 Jeff Bagwell	.40	.12
27 Shawn Estes	.25	.07
28 Ken Griffey Jr.	1.00	.30
29 Javier Lopez	.25	.07
30 Denny Neagle	.25	.07
31 Mike Piazza	1.00	.30
32 Andres Galarraga	.25	.07
33 Larry Walker	.40	.12
34 Alex Rodriguez	1.00	.30
35 Greg Maddux	1.00	.30
36 Albert Belle	.25	.07
37 Barry Bonds	1.50	.45
38 Mo Vaughn	.25	.07
39 Kevin Appier	.25	.07
40 Wade Boggs	.40	.12
41 Garret Anderson	.25	.07
42 Jeffrey Hammonds	.25	.07
43 Marquis Grissom	.25	.07
44 Jim Edmonds	.25	.07
45 Brian Jordan	.25	.07
46 Raul Mondesi	.25	.07
47 John Valentin	.25	.07
48 Brad Radke	.25	.07
49 Ismael Valdes	.25	.07
50 Matt Stairs	.25	.07
51 Matt Williams	.25	.07
52 Reggie Jefferson	.25	.07
53 Alan Benes	.25	.07
54 Charles Johnson	.25	.07
55 Chuck Knoblauch	.25	.07
56 Edgar Martinez	.40	.12
57 Nomar Garciaparra	1.00	.30
58 Craig Biggio	.40	.12
59 Bernie Williams	.40	.12
60 David Cone	.25	.07
61 Cal Ripken	2.00	.60
62 Mark McGwire	1.50	.45
63 Roberto Alomar	.60	.18
64 Fred McGriff	.40	.12
65 Eric Karros	.25	.07
66 Robin Ventura	.25	.07
67 Darin Erstad	.25	.07
68 Michael Tucker	.25	.07
69 Jim Thome	.60	.18
70 Mark Grace	.40	.12
71 Lou Collier	.25	.07
72 Karim Garcia	.25	.07
73 Alex Fernandez	.25	.07
74 J.T. Snow	.25	.07
75 Reggie Sanders	.25	.07
76 John Smoltz	.40	.12
77 Tim Salmon	.40	.12
78 Paul O'Neill	.40	.12
79 Vinny Castilla	.25	.07
80 Rafael Palmeiro	.40	.12
81 Jaret Wright	.25	.07
82 Jay Buhner	.25	.07
83 Brett Butler	.25	.07
84 Todd Greene	.25	.07
85 Scott Rolen	.40	.12
86 Sammy Sosa	1.00	.30
87 Jason Giambi	.60	.18
88 Carlos Delgado	.25	.07
89 Deion Sanders	.40	.12
90 Wilton Guerrero	.25	.07
91 Andy Pettitte	.40	.12
92 Brian Giles	.25	.07
93 Dmitri Young	.25	.07
94 Ron Coomer	.25	.07
95 Mike Cameron	.25	.07
96 Edgardo Alfonzo	.25	.07
97 Jimmy Key	.25	.07
98 Ryan Klesko	.25	.07
99 Andy Benes	.25	.07
100 Derek Jeter	1.50	.45
101 Jeff Fassero	.25	.07
102 Neifi Perez	.25	.07
103 Hideo Nomo	.60	.18
104 Andruw Jones	.25	.07
105 Todd Helton	.40	.12
106 Livan Hernandez	.25	.07
107 Brett Tomko	.25	.07
108 Shannon Stewart	.25	.07
109 Bartolo Colon	.25	.07
110 Matt Morris	.25	.07
111 Miguel Tejada	.40	.12
112 Pokey Reese	.25	.07
113 Fernando Tatis	.25	.07
114 Todd Dunwoody	.25	.07
115 Jose Cruz Jr.	.25	.07
116 Chan Ho Park	.25	.07
117 Kevin Young	.25	.07
118 Rickey Henderson	.60	.18
119 Hideki Irabu	.25	.07
120 Francisco Cordova	.25	.07
121 Al Martin	.25	.07
122 Tony Clark	.25	.07
123 Curt Schilling	.40	.12
124 Rusty Greer	.25	.07
125 Jose Canseco	.60	.18
126 Edgar Renteria	.25	.07
127 Todd Walker	.25	.07
128 Wally Joyner	.25	.07
129 Bill Mueller	.25	.07
130 Jose Guillen	.25	.07
131 Manny Ramirez	.25	.07
132 Bobby Higginson	.25	.07
133 Kevin Orie	.25	.07
134 Will Clark	.60	.18
135 Dave Nilsson	.25	.07
136 Jason Kendall	.25	.07
137 Ivan Cruz	.25	.07
138 Gary Sheffield	.25	.07
139 Bubba Trammell	.25	.07
140 Vladimir Guerrero	.60	.18
141 Dennis Reyes	.25	.07
142 Bobby Bonilla	.25	.07
143 Ruben Rivera	.25	.07
144 Ben Grieve	.25	.07
145 Moises Alou	.25	.07
146 Tony Womack	.25	.07
147 Eric Young	.25	.07
148 Paul Konerko	.25	.07
149 Dante Bichette	.25	.07
150 Joe Carter	.25	.07
151 Rondell White	.25	.07
152 Chris Holt	.25	.07
153 Shawn Green	.25	.07
154 Mark Grudzielanek	.25	.07
UER back rudzielanek		
155 Jermaine Dye	.25	.07
156 Ken Griffey Jr. FC	.60	.18
157 Frank Thomas FC	.40	.12
158 Chipper Jones FC	.40	.12
159 Mike Piazza FC	.60	.18
160 Cal Ripken FC	1.00	.30
161 Greg Maddux FC	.60	.18
162 Juan Gonzalez FC	.40	.12
163 Alex Rodriguez FC	.60	.18
164 Mark McGwire FC	.75	.23
165 Derek Jeter FC	.75	.23
166 Larry Walker CL	.25	.07
167 Tony Gwynn CL	.40	.12
168 Tino Martinez CL	.25	.07
169 Scott Rolen CL	.25	.07
170 Nomar Garciaparra CL	.60	.18
171 Mike Sweeney	.25	.07
172 Dustin Hermanson	.25	.07
173 Darren Dreifort	.25	.07
174 Ron Gant	.25	.07
175 Todd Hollandsworth	.25	.07
176 John Jaha	.25	.07
177 Kerry Wood	.60	.18
178 Chris Stynes	.25	.07
179 Kevin Elster	.25	.07
180 Derek Bell	.25	.07
181 Darryl Strawberry	.40	.12
182 Damion Easley	.25	.07
183 Jeff Cirillo	.25	.07
184 John Thomson	.25	.07
185 Dan Wilson	.25	.07
186 Jay Bell	.25	.07
187 Bernard Gilkey	.25	.07
188 Marc Valdes	.25	.07
189 Ramon Martinez	.25	.07
190 Charles Nagy	.25	.07
191 Derek Lowe	.25	.07
192 Andy Benes	.25	.07
193 Delino DeShields	.25	.07
194 Ryan Jackson RC	.25	.07
195 Kenny Lofton	.25	.07
196 Chuck Knoblauch	.25	.07
197 Andres Galarraga	.25	.07
198 Jose Canseco	.60	.18
199 John Olerud	.25	.07
200 Lance Johnson	.25	.07
201 Darryl Kile	.25	.07
202 Luis Castillo	.25	.07
203 Joe Carter	.25	.07
204 Dennis Eckersley	.25	.07
205 Steve Finley	.25	.07
206 Esteban Loaiza	.25	.07
207 R.Christenson RC UER	.25	.07
birthdate says 1988		
208 Deivi Cruz	.25	.07
209 Mariano Rivera	.40	.12
210 Mike Judd RC	.40	.12
211 Billy Wagner	.25	.07
212 Scott Spiezio	.25	.07
213 Russ Davis	.25	.07
214 Jeff Suppan	.25	.07
215 Doug Glanville	.25	.07
216 Dmitri Young	.25	.07
217 Rey Ordonez	.25	.07
218 Cecil Fielder	.25	.07
219 Masato Yoshii RC	.60	.18
220 Raul Casanova	.25	.07
221 Rolando Arrojo RC	.40	.12
222 Ellis Burks	.25	.07
223 Butch Huskey	.25	.07
224 Brian Hunter	.25	.07
225 Marquis Grissom	.25	.07
226 Kevin Brown	.40	.12
227 Joe Randa	.25	.07
228 Henry Rodriguez	.25	.07
229 Omar Vizquel	.25	.07
230 Fred McGriff	.40	.12
231 Matt Williams	.25	.07
232 Moises Alou	.25	.07
233 Travis Fryman	.25	.07
234 Wade Boggs	.40	.12
235 Pedro Martinez	.60	.18
236 Rickey Henderson	.60	.18
237 Bubba Trammell	.25	.07
238 Mike Caruso	.25	.07
239 Wilson Alvarez	.25	.07
240 Geronimo Berroa	.25	.07
241 Eric Milton	.25	.07
242 Scott Erickson	.25	.07
243 Todd Erdos RC	.25	.07
244 Bobby Hughes	.25	.07
245 Dave Hollins	.25	.07
246 Dean Palmer	.25	.07
247 Carlos Baerga	.25	.07
248 Jose Silva	.25	.07
249 Jose Cabrera RC	.25	.07
250 Tom Evans	.25	.07
251 Marty Cordova	.25	.07
252 Hanley Frias RC	.25	.07
253 Javier Valentin	.25	.07
254 Mario Valdez	.25	.07
255 Joey Cora	.25	.07
256 Mike Lansing	.25	.07
257 Jeff Kent	.25	.07
258 Dave Dellucci RC	.40	.12
259 Curtis King RC	.25	.07
260 David Segui	.25	.07
261 Royce Clayton	.25	.07
262 Jeff Blauser	.25	.07
263 Manny Aybar RC	.25	.07
264 Mike Cather RC	.25	.07
265 Todd Zeile	.25	.07
266 Richard Hidalgo	.25	.07
267 Dante Powell	.25	.07
268 Mike DeJean RC	.25	.07
269 Ken Cloude	.25	.07
270 Danny Klassen	.25	.07
271 Sean Casey	.25	.07
272 A.J. Hinch	.25	.07
273 Rich Butler RC	.25	.07
274 Ben Ford RC	.25	.07
275 Billy McMillon	.25	.07
276 Wilson Delgado	.25	.07
277 Orlando Cabrera	.25	.07
278 Geoff Jenkins	.25	.07
279 Enrique Wilson	.25	.07
280 Derrek Lee	.25	.07
281 Marc Pisciotta RC	.25	.07
282 Abraham Nunez	.25	.07
283 Aaron Boone	.25	.07
284 Brad Fullmer	.25	.07
285 Rob Stanifer RC	.25	.07
286 Preston Wilson	.25	.07
287 Greg Norton	.25	.07
288 Bobby Smith	.25	.07
289 Josh Booty	.25	.07
290 Russell Branyan	.25	.07
291 Jeremi Gonzalez	.25	.07
292 Michael Coleman	.25	.07
293 Cliff Politte	.25	.07
294 Eric Ludwick	.25	.07
295 Rafael Medina	.25	.07
296 Jason Varitek	.25	.07
297 Ron Wright	.25	.07
298 Mark Kotsay	.25	.07
299 David Ortiz	.25	.07
300 Frank Catalanotto RC	.60	.18
301 Robinson Checo	.25	.07
302 Kevin Millwood RC	1.50	.45
303 Jacob Cruz	.25	.07
304 Javier Vazquez	.25	.07
305 Magglio Ordonez RC	1.50	.45
306 Kevin Witt	.25	.07
307 Derrick Gibson	.25	.07
308 Shane Monahan	.25	.07
309 Brian Rose	.25	.07
310 Bobby Estalella	.25	.07
311 Felix Heredia	.25	.07
312 Desi Relaford	.25	.07
313 Esteban Yan RC	.40	.12
314 Ricky Ledee	.25	.07
315 Steve Woodard	.25	.07
316 Pat Watkins	.25	.07
317 Damian Moss	.25	.07
318 Bob Abreu	.25	.07
319 Jeff Abbott	.25	.07
320 Miguel Cairo	.25	.07
321 Rigo Beltran RC	.25	.07
322 Tony Saunders	.25	.07
323 Randall Simon	.25	.07
324 Hiram Bocachica	.25	.07
325 Richie Sexson	.25	.07
326 Karim Garcia	.25	.07

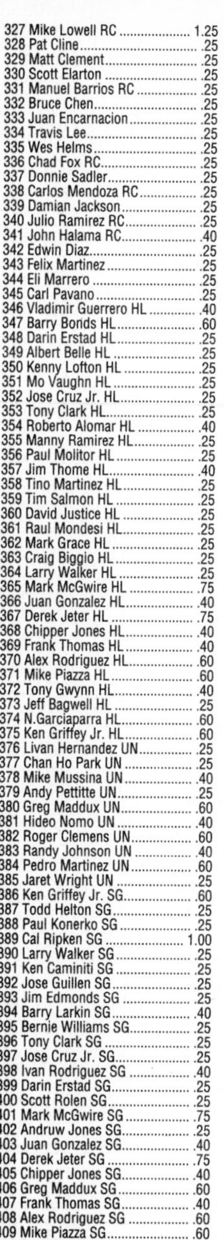
327 Mike Lowell RC .... 1.25 .35
328 Pat Cline............................... .25 .07
329 Matt Clement.......................... .25 .07
330 Scott Elarton .... .25 .07
331 Manuel Barrios RC .... .25 .07
332 Bruce Chen............................. .25 .07
333 Juan Encarnacion .... .25 .07
334 Travis Lee................................ .25 .07
335 Wes Helms .... .25 .07
336 Chad Fox RC........................... .25 .07
337 Donnie Sadler......................... .25 .07
338 Carlos Mendoza RC .... .25 .07
339 Damian Jackson .... .25 .07
340 Julio Ramirez RC .... .25 .07
341 John Halama RC .... .40 .12
342 Edwin Diaz.............................. .25 .07
343 Felix Martinez .... .25 .07
344 Eli Marrero .... .25 .07
345 Carl Pavano .... .25 .07
346 Vladimir Guerrero HL .... .40 .12
347 Barry Bonds HL....................... .60 .18
348 Darin Erstad HL...................... .25 .07
349 Albert Belle HL .... .25 .07
350 Kenny Lofton HL .... .25 .07
351 Mo Vaughn HL .... .25 .07
352 Jose Cruz Jr. HL..................... .25 .07
353 Tony Clark HL.......................... .25 .07
354 Roberto Alomar HL .... .40 .12
355 Manny Ramirez HL.................. .25 .07
356 Paul Molitor HL .... .25 .07
357 Jim Thome HL.......................... .40 .12
358 Tino Martinez HL..................... .25 .07
359 Tim Salmon HL .... .25 .07
360 David Justice HL .... .25 .07
361 Raul Mondesi HL..................... .25 .07
362 Mark Grace HL .... .25 .07
363 Craig Biggio HL .... .25 .07
364 Larry Walker HL .... .25 .07
365 Mark McGwire HL .... .75 .23
366 Juan Gonzalez HL................... .40 .12
367 Derek Jeter HL .... .75 .23
368 Chipper Jones HL.................... .40 .12
369 Frank Thomas HL.................... .40 .12
370 Alex Rodriguez HL.................. .60 .18
371 Mike Piazza HL .... .60 .18
372 Tony Gwynn HL....................... .40 .12
373 Jeff Bagwell HL .... .25 .07
374 N.Garciaparra HL.................... .60 .18
375 Ken Griffey Jr. HL................... .60 .18
376 Livan Hernandez UN............... .25 .07
377 Chan Ho Park UN .... .25 .07
378 Mike Mussina UN.................... .40 .12
379 Andy Pettitte UN..................... .25 .07
380 Greg Maddux UN.................... .60 .18
381 Hideo Nomo UN .... .40 .12
382 Roger Clemens UN................. .60 .18
383 Randy Johnson UN .... .40 .12
384 Pedro Martinez UN................. .60 .18
385 Jaret Wright UN .... .25 .07
386 Ken Griffey Jr. SG.................. .60 .18
387 Todd Helton SG...................... .25 .07
388 Paul Konerko SG .... .25 .07
389 Cal Ripken SG .... 1.00 .30
390 Larry Walker SG .... .25 .07
391 Ken Caminiti SG .... .25 .07
392 Jose Guillen SG...................... .25 .07
393 Jim Edmonds SG .... .25 .07
394 Barry Larkin SG...................... .40 .12
395 Bernie Williams SG................ .25 .07
396 Tony Clark SG .... .25 .07
397 Jose Cruz Jr. SG.................... .25 .07
398 Ivan Rodriguez SG .... .40 .12
399 Darin Erstad SG..................... .25 .07
400 Scott Rolen SG....................... .25 .07
401 Mark McGwire SG .... .75 .23
402 Andruw Jones SG.................. .25 .07
403 Juan Gonzalez SG.................. .40 .12
404 Derek Jeter SG .... .75 .23
405 Chipper Jones SG.................. .40 .12
406 Greg Maddux SG .... .60 .18
407 Frank Thomas SG.................. .40 .12
408 Alex Rodriguez SG .... .60 .18
409 Mike Piazza SG...................... .60 .18
410 Tony Gwynn SG .... .40 .12
411 Jeff Bagwell SG .... .25 .07
412 N.Garciaparra SG .... .60 .18
413 Hideo Nomo SG .... .40 .12
414 Barry Bonds SG...................... .60 .18
415 Ben Grieve SG .... .25 .07
416 Barry Bonds CL .... .60 .18
417 Mark McGwire CL.................... .75 .23
418 Roger Clemens CL .... .60 .18
419 Livan Hernandez CL .... .25 .07
420 Ken Griffey Jr. CL................... .60 .18

1998 Donruss Gold Press Proofs

This 420-card set is a limited production, die-cut parallel version of the regular base set. Card fronts are highlighted by a gold foil treatment. Each card is numbered on back as "1 of 500."

Nm-Mt Ex-Mt
*STARS: 10X TO 25X BASIC CARDS ..
*ROOKIES: 5X TO 12X BASIC CARDS

1998 Donruss Silver Press Proofs

Randomly inserted in packs, this 420-card set is a limited parallel version of the base set printed on silver foil board. Each card is numbered on back as "1 of 1500" produced.

Nm-Mt Ex-Mt
*STARS: 2.5X TO 12X BASIC CARDS .
*ROOKIES: 3X TO 6X BASIC CARDS ..

1998 Donruss Crusade Green

This 100-card set features a selection of the league's top stars. Cards were randomly inserted into three products as follows: 40 players into 1998 Donruss, 30 into 1998 Leaf, and 30 into 1998 Donruss Update. The fronts feature color player photos printed with Limited "refractive" technology. The backs carry player information. Only 250 of each of these Green cards were produced and sequentially numbered. Cards are designated below with a D, L or U suffix to denote their original

distribution within Donruss, Leaf or Donruss Update packs. All of the "Call to Arms" (sic CTA) subset cards were mistakenly printed without numbers. Corrected copies were never made.

Nm-Mt Ex-Mt
D SUFFIX ON DONRUSS DISTRIBUTION
L SUFFIX ON LEAF DISTRIBUTION .....
U SUFFIX ON DON.UPDATE DISTRIBUTION
ALL CTA CARDS ARE UNNUMBERED ERRORS
1 Tim Salmon U 25.00 7.50
2 Garret Anderson U 15.00 4.50
3 Jim Edmonds CTA L............... 15.00 4.50
4 Darin Erstad CTA L................. 15.00 4.50
5 Jason Dickson D 15.00 4.50
6 Todd Greene D 15.00 4.50
7 Roberto Alomar CTA 25.00 7.50
8 Cal Ripken D.......................... 80.00 24.00
9 Rafael Palmeiro CTA U 25.00 7.50
10 Brady Anderson U 15.00 4.50
11 Mike Mussina L..................... 25.00 7.50
12 Mo Vaughn CTA 15.00 4.50
13 Nomar Garciaparra D 40.00 12.00
14 Frank Thomas CTA U............ 25.00 7.50
15 Albert Belle CTA L 15.00 4.50
16 Mike Cameron D................... 15.00 4.50
17 Robin Ventura U.................... 15.00 4.50
18 Manny Ramirez L 15.00 4.50
19 Jim Thome CTA L.................. 25.00 7.50
20 Sandy Alomar Jr. D 15.00 4.50
21 David Justice D 15.00 4.50
22 Matt Williams U..................... 15.00 4.50
23 Tony Clark U.......................... 15.00 4.50
24 Bubba Trammell L................. 15.00 4.50
25 Justin Thompson D............... 15.00 4.50
26 Bobby Higginson L................ 15.00 4.50
27 Kevin Appier D 15.00 4.50
28 Paul Molitor L........................ 25.00 7.50
29 C.Knoblauch CTA U 15.00 4.50
30 Todd Walker L....................... 15.00 4.50
31 Bernie Williams U.................. 25.00 7.50
32 Derek Jeter CTA U 60.00 18.00
33 Tino Martinez D..................... 25.00 7.50
34 Andy Pettitte L....................... 25.00 7.50
35 Wade Boggs CTA L 25.00 7.50
36 Hideki Irabu D 15.00 4.50
37 Jose Canseco D.................... 25.00 7.50
38 Jason Giambi U..................... 25.00 7.50
39 Ken Griffey Jr. D.................... 40.00 12.00
40 Alex Rodriguez CTA L........... 40.00 12.00
41 Randy Johnson L 25.00 7.50
42 Edgar Martinez D.................. 25.00 7.50
43 Jay Buhner CTA U 15.00 4.50
44 Juan Gonzalez CTA U 25.00 7.50
45 Will Clark D 40.00 12.00
46 Ivan Rodriguez L 25.00 7.50
47 Rusty Greer D........................ 15.00 4.50
48 Roger Clemens L.................. 50.00 15.00
49 Carlos Delgado U 15.00 4.50
50 Shawn Green D 15.00 4.50
51 Jose Cruz Jr. D...................... 15.00 4.50
52 Kenny Lofton D 15.00 4.50
53 Chipper Jones D................... 25.00 7.50
54 Andruw Jones CTA L............ 15.00 4.50
55 Greg Maddux U 40.00 12.00
56 John Smoltz CTA L............... 25.00 7.50
57 Tom Glavine U....................... 25.00 7.50
58 Javier Lopez L 15.00 4.50
59 Fred McGriff L 25.00 7.50
60 Mark Grace U 25.00 7.50
61 Sammy Sosa CTA U 40.00 12.00
62 Kevin Orie D 15.00 4.50
63 Barry Larkin CTA U............... 25.00 7.50
64 Pokey Reese L...................... 15.00 4.50
65 Deion Sanders D 25.00 7.50
66 Andres Galarraga L............... 15.00 4.50
67 Larry Walker D 25.00 7.50
68 Dante Bichette CTA D 15.00 4.50
69 Neifi Perez U......................... 15.00 4.50
70 Eric Young L.......................... 15.00 4.50
71 Todd Helton D 25.00 7.50
72 Gary Sheffield CTA U............ 15.00 4.50
73 Moises Alou L 15.00 4.50
74 Bobby Bonilla D.................... 15.00 4.50
75 Kevin Brown D 25.00 7.50
76 Ben Grieve L.......................... 15.00 4.50
77 Jeff Bagwell CTA U 25.00 7.50
78 Craig Biggio D 25.00 7.50
79 Mike Piazza L 40.00 12.00
80 Raul Mondesi U..................... 15.00 4.50
81 Hideo Nomo CTA U 25.00 7.50
82 Wilton Guerrero D 15.00 4.50
83 Rondell White CTA U............ 15.00 4.50
84 V.Guerrero CTA U.................. 25.00 7.50
85 Pedro Martinez D 25.00 7.50
86 Edgardo Alfonzo D 15.00 4.50
87 Todd Hundley CTA U 15.00 4.50
88 Scott Rolen D........................ 25.00 7.50
89 Francisco Cordova D 15.00 4.50
90 Jose Guillen D 15.00 4.50
91 Jason Kendall L..................... 15.00 4.50
92 Ray Lankford D 15.00 4.50
93 Mark McGwire CTA D 60.00 18.00
94 Matt Morris D......................... 15.00 4.50
95 Alan Benes L 15.00 4.50
96 Brian Jordan CTA U.............. 15.00 4.50
97 Tony Gwynn L........................ 30.00 9.00
98 Ken Caminiti CTA L 15.00 4.50
99 Barry Bonds CTA U 60.00 18.00
100 Shawn Estes D 15.00 4.50

1998 Donruss Crusade Purple

Randomly inserted in packs of Donruss, Donruss Update and Leaf, cards from this set are a parallel version of the Donruss Crusade Green set. Only 100 of each card were produced each of which is sequentially numbered on back.

Nm-Mt Ex-Mt
*PURPLE: .75X TO 2X GREEN CRUSADE

1998 Donruss Diamond Kings

Randomly inserted in packs, this 20-card set features color player portraits of some of the greatest names in baseball. Only 9,500 sets were produced and are sequentially numbered. The first 500 of each card were printed on actual canvas card stock. In addition, a Frank Thomas sample card was created as a promo for the 1998 Donruss 1 product. The card was sent to all wholesale accounts along with the order forms for the product. The large "SAMPLE" stamp across the back of the card makes it easy to differentiate from Thomas' standard 1998 Diamond King insert card.

Nm-Mt Ex-Mt
COMPLETE SET (20)............... 100.00 30.00
*CANVAS: 1.25X TO 3X BASIC DIAM.KINGS
CANVAS: RANDOM INSERTS IN PACKS
CANVAS PRINT RUN 500 SERIAL #'d SETS
1 Cal Ripken 20.00 6.00
2 Greg Maddux......................... 10.00 3.00
3 Ivan Rodriguez 6.00 1.80
4 Tony Gwynn 8.00 2.40
5 Paul Molitor............................. 4.00 1.20
6 Kenny Lofton .... 2.50 .75
7 Andy Pettitte........................... 4.00 1.20
8 Darin Erstad .... 2.50 .75
9 Randy Johnson 6.00 1.80
10 Derek Jeter......................... 15.00 4.50
11 Hideo Nomo 6.00 1.80
12 David Justice........................ 2.50 .75
13 Bernie Williams 4.00 1.20
14 Roger Clemens.................... 12.00 3.60
15 Barry Larkin.......................... 6.00 1.80
16 Andruw Jones .... 2.50 .75
17 Mike Piazza 10.00 3.00
18 Frank Thomas 6.00 1.80
19 Alex Rodriguez 10.00 3.00
20 Ken Griffey Jr. 10.00 3.00
S20 Frank Thomas .... 2.00 .60
Sample

1998 Donruss Dominators

Randomly inserted in update packs, this 30-card set is an insert to the Donruss base set. The holographic foil-stamped fronts feature color action photos surrounded by an orange background. The featured player's team name sits in the upper right corner and the Donruss logo sits in the upper left corner.

Nm-Mt Ex-Mt
COMPLETE SET (30).............. 120.00 36.00
1 Roger Clemens........................ 8.00 2.40
2 Tony Clark............................... 1.50 .45
3 Darin Erstad .... 1.50 .45
4 Jeff Bagwell............................. 2.50 .75
5 Ken Griffey Jr 6.00 1.80
6 Andruw Jones .... 1.50 .45
7 Juan Gonzalez 4.00 1.20
8 Ivan Rodriguez 4.00 1.20
9 Randy Johnson 4.00 1.20
10 Tino Martinez .... 2.50 .75
11 Mark McGwire..................... 10.00 3.00
12 Chuck Knoblauch .... 1.50 .45
13 Jim Thome 4.00 1.20
14 Alex Rodriguez 6.00 1.80
15 Hideo Nomo 4.00 1.20
16 Jose Cruz Jr. .... 1.50 .45
17 Chipper Jones 4.00 1.20
18 Tony Gwynn 5.00 1.50
19 Barry Bonds 10.00 3.00
20 Mo Vaughn........................... 1.50 .45
21 Cal Ripken 12.00 3.60
22 Greg Maddux........................ 6.00 1.80
23 Manny Ramirez .... 1.50 .45
24 Andres Galarraga.................. 1.50 .45
25 Vladimir Guerrero.................. 4.00 1.20
26 Albert Belle........................... 1.50 .45
27 Nomar Garciaparra................ 6.00 1.80
28 Kenny Lofton......................... 1.50 .45
29 Mike Piazza 6.00 1.80
30 Frank Thomas 4.00 1.20

1998 Donruss Elite Inserts

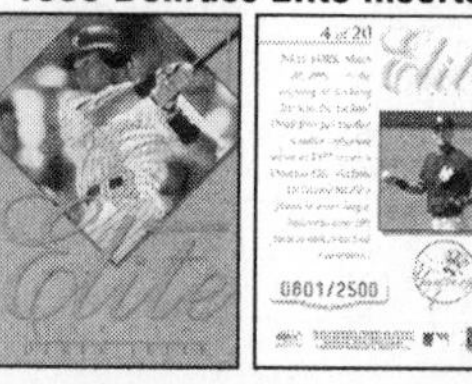

Continuing the popular tradition begun in 1991, Donruss again inserted Elite cards in their packs. These cards which have the work "Elite" written in big cursive letters on the bottom and a small player photo, were serially numbered to 2500 and has the "cream of the crop" of the baseball players. This set was designed to be the last time Donruss would issue Elite cards ending the succsessful eight year run. It's interesting to note that unlike previous Elite inserts, the 1998 cards were not numbered in continuation of the Elite run.

Nm-Mt Ex-Mt
COMPLETE SET (20).............. 300.00 90.00
1 Jeff Bagwell............................. 8.00 2.40
2 Andruw Jones 5.00 1.50
3 Ken Griffey Jr. 20.00 6.00
4 Derek Jeter........................... 30.00 9.00
5 Juan Gonzalez 12.00 3.60
6 Mark McGwire...................... 30.00 9.00
7 Ivan Rodriguez..................... 12.00 3.60
8 Paul Molitor............................ 8.00 2.40
9 Hideo Nomo 12.00 3.60
10 Mo Vaughn........................... 5.00 1.50
11 Chipper Jones 12.00 3.60
12 Nomar Garciaparra............. 20.00 6.00
13 Mike Piazza 20.00 6.00
14 Frank Thomas 12.00 3.60
15 Greg Maddux...................... 20.00 6.00
16 Cal Ripken 40.00 12.00
17 Alex Rodriguez 20.00 6.00
18 Jose Cruz Jr. 5.00 1.50
19 Barry Bonds 30.00 9.00
20 Tony Gwynn 15.00 4.50

1998 Donruss FANtasy Team

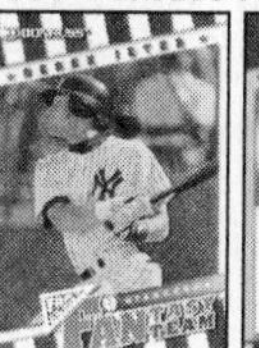

Randomly inserted in update packs, this 20-card set features the leading votegetters from the on-line Fan Club. The top vote-getters make up the 1st team FANtasy Team and are sequentially numbered to 1750. The reamining players make up the 2nd team FANtasy Team and are sequentially numbered to 3750. The fronts carry color action photos surrounded by a red, white, and blue star-studded background. Cards number 1-10 feature members from the first team while cards numbered from 11-20 feature members of the second team.

Nm-Mt Ex-Mt
COMPLETE SET (20).............. 150.00 45.00
*1ST TEAM DC's: 1X TO 2.5X BASIC FANTASY
*2ND TEAM DIE CUTS: 1.5X TO 4X BASIC FANTASY..
DIE CUTS PRINT RUN 250 SERIAL #'d SETS
RANDOM INSERTS IN UPDATE PACKS
1 Frank Thomas 10.00 3.00
2 Ken Griffey Jr. 15.00 4.50
3 Cal Ripken............................ 30.00 9.00
4 Jose Cruz Jr. 4.00 1.20
5 Travis Lee............................... 4.00 1.20
6 Greg Maddux....................... 15.00 4.50
7 Alex Rodriguez 15.00 4.50
8 Mark McGwire...................... 25.00 7.50
9 Chipper Jones 10.00 3.00
10 Andruw Jones 4.00 1.20
11 Mike Piazza 10.00 3.00
12 Tony Gwynn 8.00 2.40
13 Larry Walker.......................... 4.00 1.20
14 Nomar Garciaparra............. 10.00 3.00
15 Jaret Wright .... 2.50 .75
16 Livan Hernandez................... 2.50 .75
17 Roger Clemens.................... 12.00 3.60
18 Derek Jeter......................... 15.00 4.50
19 Scott Rolen 4.00 1.20
20 Jeff Bagwell.......................... 4.00 1.20

1998 Donruss Longball Leaders

Randomly inserted in first series packs, this 24-card set features color photos of the top sluggers in baseball printed on micro-etched cards. Only 5000 of each card were produced and are sequentially numbered.

Nm-Mt Ex-Mt
COMPLETE SET (24).............. 120.00 36.00
1 Ken Griffey Jr. 10.00 3.00
2 Mark McGwire...................... 15.00 4.50
3 Tino Martinez 4.00 1.20
4 Barry Bonds 15.00 4.50
5 Frank Thomas 6.00 1.80
6 Albert Belle........................... 2.50 .75
7 Mike Piazza 10.00 3.00
8 Chipper Jones 6.00 1.80
9 Vladimir Guerrero.................. 6.00 1.80
10 Matt Williams....................... 2.50 .75
11 Sammy Sosa...................... 10.00 3.00
12 Tim Salmon.......................... 4.00 1.20
13 Raul Mondesi .... 2.50 .75
14 Jeff Bagwell.......................... 4.00 1.20
15 Mo Vaughn........................... 2.50 .75
16 Manny Ramirez .... 2.50 .75
17 Jim Thome 6.00 1.80
18 Jim Edmonds .... 2.50 .75
19 Tony Clark............................ 2.50 .75
20 Nomar Garciaparra............. 10.00 3.00
21 Juan Gonzalez 6.00 1.80
22 Scott Rolen 4.00 1.20
23 Larry Walker......................... 4.00 1.20
24 Andres Galarraga.................. 2.50 .75

1998 Donruss MLB 99

This 20 card set was inserted into both Donruss Update and Studio packs. These cards feature 20 of the leading Baseball players and were widely available because of the insertion into both of the aforementioned brands.

Nm-Mt Ex-Mt
COMPLETE SET (20)................ 10.00 3.00
1 Cal Ripken.............................. 2.00 .60
2 Nomar Garciaparra................. 1.00 .30
3 Barry Bonds .... 1.50 .45
4 Mike Mussina.......................... .60 .18
5 Pedro Martinez........................ .60 .18
6 Derek Jeter............................ 1.50 .45
7 Andruw Jones .... .25 .07
8 Kenny Lofton............................ .25 .07
9 Gary Sheffield.......................... .25 .07
10 Raul Mondesi .... .25 .07
11 Jeff Bagwell............................ .40 .12
12 Tim Salmon............................ .40 .12
13 Tom Glavine .... .40 .12
14 Ben Grieve.............................. .25 .07
15 Matt Williams .... .25 .07
16 Juan Gonzalez .... .60 .18
17 Mark McGwire...................... 1.50 .45
18 Bernie Williams .... .40 .12
19 Andres Galarraga.................... .25 .07
20 Jose Cruz Jr. .... .25 .07

1998 Donruss Production Line On-Base

Randomly inserted in first series pre-priced packs only, this 20-card set features color player images printed on holographic board with green highlights. Each card is sequentially numbered according to the player's on-base percentage. Print runs for each card is matched with the player's 1997 on-base percentage and is listed individually below after each player's name in our checklist.

Nm-Mt Ex-Mt
COMPLETE SET (20).............. 600.00 180.00
1 Frank Thomas/456 .... 20.00 6.00
2 Edgar Martinez/456.............. 12.00 3.60
3 Roberto Alomar/390.............. 20.00 6.00
4 Chuck Knoblauch/390 .... 8.00 2.40
5 Mike Piazza/431 .... 30.00 9.00
6 Barry Larkin/440 .... 20.00 6.00
7 Kenny Lofton/409................... 8.00 2.40
8 Jeff Bagwell/425.................... 12.00 3.60
9 Barry Bonds/446 .... 50.00 15.00
10 Rusty Greer/405.................... 8.00 2.40
11 Gary Sheffield/424................. 8.00 2.40
12 Mark McGwire/393.............. 50.00 15.00
13 Chipper Jones/371 .... 20.00 6.00
14 Tony Gwynn/409................. 25.00 7.50
15 Craig Biggio/415 .... 12.00 3.60
16 Mo Vaughn/420 .... 8.00 2.40
17 Bernie Williams/408 .... 12.00 3.60
18 Ken Griffey Jr./382 .... 30.00 9.00
19 Brady Anderson/393 .... 8.00 2.40
20 Derek Jeter/370................... 50.00 15.00

1998 Donruss Production Line Power Index

Randomly inserted in first series hobby packs only, this 20-card set features color player images printed on holographic board with blue highlights. Each card is sequentially numbered according to the player's power index. Print runs for each card is matched with the player's 1997 power index percentage and is listed individually below after each player's name in our checklist.

Nm-Mt Ex-Mt
COMPLETE SET (20).............. 400.00 120.00
1 Frank Thomas/1067 .... 10.00 3.00
2 Mark McGwire/1039.............. 25.00 7.50
3 Barry Bonds/1031 .... 25.00 7.50
4 Jeff Bagwell/1017.................... 6.00 1.80
5 Ken Griffey Jr./1028 .... 15.00 4.50
6 Alex Rodriguez/846............... 15.00 4.50
7 Chipper Jones/850................ 10.00 3.00
8 Mike Piazza/1070 .... 15.00 4.50

9 Mo Vaughn/980 .... 4.00 1.20
10 Brady Anderson/863 .... 4.00 1.20
11 Manny Ramirez/953 .... 4.00 1.20
12 Albert Belle/823 .... 4.00 1.20
13 Jim Thome/1001 .... 10.00 3.00
14 Bernie Williams/952 .... 6.00 1.80
15 Scott Rolen/846 .... 6.00 1.80
16 Vladimir Guerrero/833 .... 10.00 3.00
17 Larry Walker/1172 .... 6.00 1.80
18 David Justice/1013 .... 4.00 1.20
19 Tino Martinez/948 .... 6.00 1.80
20 Tony Gwynn/957 .... 12.00 3.60

1998 Donruss Production Line Slugging

Randomly inserted in first series retail packs only, this 20-card set features color player images printed on holographic board with red highlights. Each card is sequentially numbered according to the player's slugging percentage and is detailed specifically in our checklist.

	Nm-Mt	Ex-Mt
COMPLETE SET (20)	600.00	180.00
1 Mark McGwire/646	40.00	12.00
2 Ken Griffey Jr./646	25.00	7.50
3 Andres Galarraga/585	6.00	1.80
4 Barry Bonds/585	40.00	12.00
5 Juan Gonzalez/589	15.00	4.50
6 Mike Piazza/638	25.00	7.50
7 Jeff Bagwell/592	10.00	3.00
8 Manny Ramirez/538	6.00	1.80
9 Jim Thome/579	15.00	4.50
10 Mo Vaughn/560	6.00	1.80
11 Larry Walker/720	10.00	3.00
12 Tino Martinez/577	10.00	3.00
13 Frank Thomas/611	15.00	4.50
14 Tim Salmon/517	10.00	3.00
15 Raul Mondesi/541	6.00	1.80
16 Alex Rodriguez/496	25.00	7.50
17 Nomar Garciaparra/534	25.00	7.50
18 Jose Cruz Jr./499	6.00	1.80
19 Tony Clark/500	6.00	1.80
20 Cal Ripken/402	50.00	15.00

1998 Donruss Rated Rookies

Randomly inserted in packs, this 30-card set features color action photos of some of the top rookie prospects as chosen by Donruss to be the most likely to succeed. The backs carry player information.

	Nm-Mt	Ex-Mt
COMPLETE SET (30)	40.00	12.00
*MEDALISTS: 2.5X TO 6X BASIC RR..		
MEDALIST PRINT RUN 250 SETS.......		
RANDOM INSERTS IN PACKS		
1 Mark Kotsay	2.00	.60
2 Neifi Perez	2.00	.60
3 Paul Konerko	2.00	.60
4 Jose Cruz Jr.	2.00	.60
5 Hideki Irabu	2.00	.60
6 Mike Cameron	2.00	.60
7 Jeff Suppan	2.00	.60
8 Kevin Orie	2.00	.60
9 Pokey Reese	2.00	.60
10 Todd Dunwoody	2.00	.60
11 Miguel Tejada	3.00	.90
12 Jose Guillen	2.00	.60
13 Bartolo Colon	2.00	.60
14 Derrek Lee	2.00	.60
15 Antone Williamson	2.00	.60
16 Wilton Guerrero	2.00	.60
17 Jaret Wright	2.00	.60
18 Todd Helton	3.00	.90
19 Shannon Stewart	2.00	.60
20 Nomar Garciaparra	8.00	2.40
21 Brett Tomko	2.00	.60
22 Fernando Tatis	2.00	.60
23 Raul Ibanez	2.00	.60
24 Dennis Reyes	2.00	.60
25 Bobby Estalella	2.00	.60
26 Lou Collier	2.00	.60
27 Bubba Trammell	2.00	.60
28 Ben Grieve	2.00	.60
29 Ivan Cruz	2.00	.60
30 Karim Garcia	2.00	.60

1998 Donruss Rookie Diamond Kings

These cards were randomly inserted in Donruss Update packs. This 12-card set is an insert to the Donruss base set. The set is sequentially numbered to 10,000. The fronts feature head and shoulder color prints surrounded by a four-sided border of the top young prospects in today's MLB.

	Nm-Mt	Ex-Mt
COMPLETE SET (12)	30.00	9.00
*CANVAS: 1.25X TO 3X BASIC ROOK.DK'S		
CANVAS PRINT RUN 500 SERIAL #'d SETS		
RANDOM INSERTS IN UPDATE PACKS		
1 Travis Lee	4.00	1.20
2 Fernando Tatis	4.00	1.20
3 Livan Hernandez	4.00	1.20
4 Todd Helton	6.00	1.80
5 Derrek Lee	4.00	1.20
6 Jaret Wright	4.00	1.20
7 Ben Grieve	4.00	1.20
8 Paul Konerko	4.00	1.20
9 Jose Cruz Jr.	4.00	1.20
10 Mark Kotsay	4.00	1.20
11 Todd Greene	4.00	1.20
12 Brad Fullmer	4.00	1.20

1998 Donruss Signature Series Previews

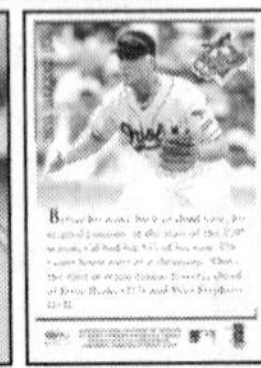

Twenty-nine of these 34 cards were randomly inserted into Donruss Update packs. These 29 cards were previewing the then-upcoming 1998 Donruss Signature Series set. Each player signed a slightly different amount of cards so we have put the amount of cards signed next to the players name in our checklist. The five additional cards (Alou, Casey, Jenkins, Jeter and Wilson) were never intended for public release. It's believed that four players (all except Jeter) signed 100 or more cards but failed to return their cards to the manufacturer (Pinnacle Brands) in time for the Donruss Update packout. Apparently, the cards were stored in Pinnacle's card vault, but an unknown amount of each card made their way into the secondary market during Pinnacle's bankruptcy proceeding when Playoff Inc. bought the holdings. It's believed that a handful of the Jeter cards were erroneously sent to Jeter in his 1998 Donruss Signature card agreement (red, green and blue cards for a separate brand). Jeter simply signed all of the cards and sent them back to the manufacturer.

	Nm-Mt	Ex-Mt
1 Sandy Alomar Jr./96	40.00	12.00
2 Moises Alou	50.00	15.00
3 Andy Benes/135	40.00	12.00
4 Russell Branyan/188	40.00	12.00
5 Sean Casey	50.00	15.00
6 Tony Clark/188	40.00	12.00
7 Juan Encarnacion/193	40.00	12.00
8 Brad Fullmer/396	20.00	6.00
9 Juan Gonzalez/108	100.00	30.00
10 Ben Grieve/100	40.00	12.00
11 Todd Helton/101	80.00	24.00
12 Richard Hidalgo/380	30.00	9.00
13 A.J. Hinch/400	20.00	6.00
14 Damian Jackson/15		
15 Geoff Jenkins	150.00	45.00
16 Derek Jeter SP		
17 Chipper Jones/112	120.00	36.00
18 Chuck Knoblauch/98	50.00	15.00
19 Travis Lee/101	40.00	12.00
20 Mike Lowell/450	30.00	9.00
21 Greg Maddux/92	300.00	90.00
22 Kevin Millwood/395	25.00	7.50
23 Magglio Ordonez/420	50.00	15.00
24 David Ortiz/393	40.00	12.00
25 Rafael Palmeiro/107	100.00	30.00
26 Cal Ripken/22		
27 Alex Rodriguez/23		
28 Curt Schilling/100	80.00	24.00
29 Randall Simon/380	20.00	6.00
30 Fernando Tatis/400	20.00	6.00
31 Miguel Tejada/375	40.00	12.00
32 Robin Ventura/95	50.00	15.00
33 Dan Wilson	40.00	12.00
34 Kerry Wood/373	60.00	18.00

1998 Donruss Days

As a special mid-season promotion, Donruss/Leaf distributed these special Donruss Days cards to selected hobby shops in fourteen different areas of the nation. To obtain these cards, collectors had to redeem a special exchange card of which was handed out at local ballparks upon entrance into the stadium. Each hobby shop was supplied with a complete selection of all fourteen players, but received larger supplies of their local stars. Collectors were free to choose any player they wished until supplies ran out. The cards are somewhat similar in design to standard 1998 Donruss but have been upgraded with 20 point cardboard stock and foil fronts. According to Donruss representatives, no more than 10,000 of any of these cards were produced.

	Nm-Mt	Ex-Mt
COMPLETE SET (14)	15.00	4.50
1 Frank Thomas	.75	.23
2 Tony Clark	.25	.07
3 Ivan Rodriguez	.75	.23
4 David Justice	.25	.07
5 Nomar Garciaparra	2.00	.60
6 Mark McGwire	2.50	.75
7 Travis Lee	.25	.07
8 Cal Ripken	3.00	.90
9 Jeff Bagwell	.75	.23
10 Barry Bonds	1.50	.45
11 Ken Griffey Jr.	2.00	.60
12 Derek Jeter	3.00	.90
13 Raul Mondesi	.25	.07
14 Greg Maddux	2.00	.60

2001 Donruss

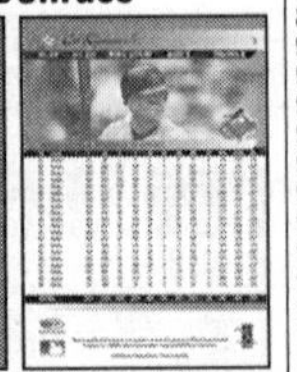

The 2001 Donruss product was released in early May, 2001. The 220-card base set was broken into tiers as follows: Base Veterans (1-150), short-printed Rated Rookies (151-200) serial numbered to 2001, and Fan Club cards (201-220) inserted approximatley one per box. Exchange cards with a redemption deadline of May 1st, 2003 was seeded into packs for card 156 Albert Pujols and 159 Ben Sheets. Each pack contained five cards, and a one card retro pack. Packs carried a suggested retail price of $1.99. Please note that 1999 Retro packs were inserted in Hobby packs, while 2000 Retro packs were inserted into Retail packs. One in every 720 packs contained an exchange card good for a complete set of 2001 Donruss Baseball's Best. One in every 72 packs contained and exchange card good for a complete set of 2001 Donruss the Rookies. The redemption deadline for both exchange cards was January 20th, 2002. The original exchange deadline was November 1st, 2001 but the manufacturer lengthened the redemption period.

	Nm-Mt	Ex-Mt
COMP.SET w/o SP's (150)	25.00	7.50
COMMON CARD (1-150)	.30	.09
COMMON (151-200)	8.00	2.40
COMMON (201-220)	3.00	.90
1 Alex Rodriguez	1.25	.35
2 Barry Bonds	2.00	.60
3 Cal Ripken	2.50	.75
4 Chipper Jones	.75	.23
5 Derek Jeter	2.00	.60
6 Troy Glaus	.50	.15
7 Frank Thomas	.75	.23
8 Greg Maddux	1.25	.35
9 Ivan Rodriguez	.75	.23
10 Jeff Bagwell	.50	.15
11 Jose Canseco	.75	.23
12 Todd Helton	.50	.15
13 Ken Griffey Jr.	1.25	.35
14 Manny Ramirez	.30	.09
15 Mark McGwire	2.00	.60
16 Mike Piazza	1.25	.35
17 Nomar Garciaparra	1.25	.35
18 Pedro Martinez	.75	.23
19 Randy Johnson	.75	.23
20 Rick Ankiel	.30	.09
21 Rickey Henderson	.75	.23
22 Roger Clemens	1.50	.45
23 Sammy Sosa	1.25	.35
24 Tony Gwynn	1.00	.30
25 Vladimir Guerrero	.75	.23
26 Eric Davis	.30	.09
27 Roberto Alomar	.30	.09
28 Mark Mulder	.30	.09
29 Pat Burrell	.30	.09
30 Harold Baines	.30	.09
31 Carlos Delgado	.30	.09
32 J.D. Drew	.30	.09
33 Jim Edmonds	.30	.09
34 Darin Erstad	.30	.09
35 Jason Giambi	.75	.23
36 Tom Glavine	.50	.15
37 Juan Gonzalez	.75	.23
38 Mark Grace	.50	.15
39 Shawn Green	.30	.09
40 Tim Hudson	.30	.09
41 Andruw Jones	.30	.09
42 David Justice	.30	.09
43 Jeff Kent	.30	.09
44 Barry Larkin	.75	.23
45 Pokey Reese	.30	.09
46 Mike Mussina	.75	.23
47 Hideo Nomo	.75	.23
48 Rafael Palmeiro	.50	.15
49 Adam Piatt	.30	.09
50 Scott Rolen	.50	.15
51 Gary Sheffield	.30	.09
52 Bernie Williams	.50	.15
53 Bob Abreu	.30	.09
54 Edgardo Alfonzo	.30	.09
55 Jermaine Clark RC	.50	.15
56 Albert Belle	.30	.09
57 Craig Biggio	.50	.15
58 Andres Galarraga	.30	.09
59 Edgar Martinez	.50	.15
60 Fred McGriff	.50	.15
61 Magglio Ordonez	.30	.09
62 Jim Thome	.75	.23
63 Matt Williams	.30	.09
64 Kerry Wood	.75	.23
65 Moises Alou	.30	.09
66 Brady Anderson	.30	.09
67 Garret Anderson	.30	.09
68 Tony Armas Jr.	.30	.09
69 Tony Batista	.30	.09
70 Jose Cruz Jr.	.30	.09
71 Carlos Beltran	.30	.09
72 Adrian Beltre	.30	.09
73 Kris Benson	.30	.09
74 Lance Berkman	.30	.09
75 Kevin Brown	.30	.09
76 Jay Buhner	.30	.09
77 Jeromy Burnitz	.30	.09
78 Ken Caminiti	.30	.09
79 Sean Casey	.30	.09
80 Luis Castillo	.30	.09
81 Eric Chavez	.30	.09
82 Jeff Cirillo	.30	.09
83 Bartolo Colon	.30	.09
84 David Cone	.30	.09
85 Freddy Garcia	.30	.09
86 Johnny Damon	.30	.09
87 Ray Durham	.30	.09
88 Jermaine Dye	.30	.09
89 Juan Encarnacion	.30	.09
90 Terrence Long	.30	.09
91 Carl Everett	.30	.09
92 Steve Finley	.30	.09
93 Cliff Floyd	.30	.09
94 Brad Fullmer	.30	.09
95 Brian Giles	.30	.09
96 Luis Gonzalez	.30	.09
97 Rusty Greer	.30	.09
98 Jeffrey Hammonds	.30	.09
99 Mike Hampton	.30	.09
100 Orlando Hernandez	.30	.09
101 Richard Hidalgo	.30	.09
102 Geoff Jenkins	.30	.09
103 Jacque Jones	.30	.09
104 Brian Jordan	.30	.09
105 Gabe Kapler	.30	.09
106 Eric Karros	.30	.09
107 Jason Kendall	.30	.09
108 Adam Kennedy	.30	.09
109 Byung-Hyun Kim	.30	.09
110 Ryan Klesko	.30	.09
111 Chuck Knoblauch	.30	.09
112 Paul Konerko	.30	.09
113 Carlos Lee	.30	.09
114 Kenny Lofton	.30	.09
115 Javy Lopez	.30	.09
116 Tino Martinez	.50	.15
117 Ruben Mateo	.30	.09
118 Kevin Millwood	.30	.09
119 Ben Molina	.30	.09
120 Raul Mondesi	.30	.09
121 Trot Nixon	.50	.15
122 John Olerud	.30	.09
123 Paul O'Neill	.50	.15
124 Chan Ho Park	.30	.09
125 Andy Pettitte	.50	.15
126 Jorge Posada	.50	.15
127 Mark Quinn	.30	.09
128 Aramis Ramirez	.30	.09
129 Mariano Rivera	.50	.15
130 Tim Salmon	.50	.15
131 Curt Schilling	.50	.15
132 Richie Sexson	.30	.09
133 John Smoltz	.50	.15
134 J.T. Snow	.30	.09
135 Jay Payton	.30	.09
136 Shannon Stewart	.30	.09
137 B.J. Surhoff	.30	.09
138 Mike Sweeney	.30	.09
139 Fernando Tatis	.30	.09
140 Miguel Tejada	.30	.09
141 Jason Varitek	.30	.09
142 Greg Vaughn	.30	.09
143 Mo Vaughn	.30	.09
144 Robin Ventura UER Listed as playing for Yankees last 2 years Also Bat and Throw information is wrong	.30	.09
145 Jose Vidro	.30	.09
146 Omar Vizquel	.30	.09
147 Larry Walker	.50	.15
148 David Wells	.30	.09
149 Rondell White	.30	.09
150 Preston Wilson	.30	.09
151 Brent Abernathy RR	8.00	2.40
152 Cory Aldridge RR RC	8.00	2.40
153 Gene Altman RR RC	8.00	2.40
154 Josh Beckett RR	10.00	3.00
155 W. Betemit RR RC	8.00	2.40
156 A.Pujols RR/500 RC	200.00	60.00
157 Joe Crede RR	8.00	2.40
158 Jack Cust RR	8.00	2.40
159 Ben Sheets RR/500	150.00	45.00
160 Alex Escobar RR	8.00	2.40
161 A. Hernandez RR RC	8.00	2.40
162 Pedro Feliz RR	8.00	2.40
163 Nate Frese RR RC	8.00	2.40
164 Carlos Garcia RR RC	8.00	2.40
165 Marcus Giles RR	8.00	2.40
166 Alexis Gomez RR RC	8.00	2.40
167 Jason Hart RR	8.00	2.40
168 Eric Hinske RR RC	10.00	3.00
169 Cesar Izturis RR	8.00	2.40
170 Nick Johnson RR	8.00	2.40
171 Mike Young RR	10.00	3.00
172 B. Lawrence RR RC	8.00	2.40
173 Steve Lomasney RR	8.00	2.40
174 Nick Maness RR	8.00	2.40
175 Jose Mieses RR RC	8.00	2.40
176 Greg Miller RR RC	8.00	2.40
177 Eric Munson RR	8.00	2.40
178 Xavier Nady RR	8.00	2.40
179 Blaine Neal RR RC	8.00	2.40
180 Abraham Nunez RR	8.00	2.40
181 Jose Ortiz RR	8.00	2.40
182 Jeremy Owens RR RC	8.00	2.40
183 Pablo Ozuna RR	8.00	2.40
184 Corey Patterson RR	8.00	2.40
185 Carlos Pena RR	8.00	2.40
186 Wily Mo Pena RR	8.00	2.40
187 Timo Perez RR	8.00	2.40
188 A. Pettyjohn RR RC	8.00	2.40
189 Luis Rivas RR	8.00	2.40
190 J. Melian RR RC	8.00	2.40
191 Wilken Ruan RR RC	8.00	2.40
192 D. Sanchez RR RC	8.00	2.40
193 Alfonso Soriano RR	10.00	3.00
194 Rafael Soriano RR RC	15.00	4.50
195 Ichiro Suzuki RR RC	50.00	15.00
196 Billy Sylvester RR RC	8.00	2.40
197 Juan Uribe RR RC	8.00	2.40
198 Eric Valent RR	8.00	2.40
199 C.Valderrama RR RC	8.00	2.40
200 Matt White RR RC	8.00	2.40
201 Alex Rodriguez FC	6.00	1.80
202 Barry Bonds FC	10.00	3.00
203 Cal Ripken FC	12.00	3.60
204 Chipper Jones FC	4.00	1.20
205 Derek Jeter FC	10.00	3.00
206 Troy Glaus FC	3.00	.90
207 Frank Thomas FC	4.00	1.20
208 Greg Maddux FC	6.00	1.80
209 Ivan Rodriguez FC	4.00	1.20
210 Jeff Bagwell FC	3.00	.90
211 Todd Helton FC	3.00	.90
212 Ken Griffey Jr. FC	6.00	1.80
213 Manny Ramirez FC	3.00	.90
214 Mark McGwire FC	10.00	3.00
215 Mike Piazza FC	6.00	1.80
216 Pedro Martinez FC	4.00	1.20
217 Sammy Sosa FC	6.00	1.80
218 Tony Gwynn FC	5.00	1.50
219 Vladimir Guerrero FC	4.00	1.20
220 Nomar Garciaparra FC	6.00	1.80
NNO BB Best Coupon	2.00	.60
NNO The Rookies Coupon	.50	.15

2001 Donruss Stat Line Career

Randomly inserted into 2001 Donruss packs, this 220-card insert parallels the 2001 Donruss base set. Each card is individually serial numbered to a career stat of the given players. Please note that the print runs are listed in our checklist. Exchange cards for Albert Pujols and Ben Sheets with a redemption deadline of May 1st, 2003 were seeded into packs. A special autographed version of Albert Pujols' Stat Line Career card was printed in response to an error in production whereby more Stat Line Career Pujols exchange cards were seeded into packs than the 154 copies intended for release. To honor their commitment to collectors redeeming the exchange card, Donruss had Pujols sign a special non-serial numbered version of the card and sent it out to collectors redeeming the exchange card. Cards with a print run of 25 or fewer are not priced due to market scarcity.

	Nm-Mt	Ex-Mt
*1-150 P/R b/wn 251-400: 2.5X TO 6X		
*1-150 P/R b/wn 201-250: 2.5X TO 6X		
*1-150 P/R b/wn 151-200: 3X TO 8X..		
*1-150 P/R b/wn 121-150: 3X TO 8X..		
*1-150 P/R b/wn 81-120: 4X TO 10X..		
*1-150 P/R b/wn 66-80: 5X TO 12X....		
*1-150 P/R b/wn 51-65: 6X TO 15X....		
*1-150 P/R b/wn 36-50: 8X TO 20X....		
*1-150 P/R b/wn 26-35: 10X TO 25X..		
*201-220 P/R b/wn 251-400 .5X TO 1.2X		
*201-220 P/R b/wn 201-250 .5X TO 1.2X		
*201-220 P/R b/wn 151-200 .6X TO 1.5X		
*201-220 P/R b/wn 121-150 .6X TO 1.5X		
*201-220 P/R b/wn 81-120 .75X TO 2X		
*201-220 P/R b/wn 36-50 1.5X TO 4X		
151 B. Abernathy RR/22		
152 Cory Aldridge RR/33	12.00	3.60
153 Gene Altman RR/351	2.00	.60
154 Josh Beckett RR/212	2.50	.75
155 Wilson Betemit RR/15		
156 Albert Pujols RR/154	200.00	60.00
156B Albert Pujols RR AU		
157 Joe Crede RR/357	2.00	.60
158 Jack Cust RR/66	6.00	1.80
159 Ben Sheets RR/159	25.00	7.50
160 Alex Escobar RR/45	10.00	3.00
161 A. Hernandez RR/86	5.00	1.50
162 Pedro Feliz RR/286	2.00	.60
163 Nate Frese RR/119	5.00	1.50
164 Carlos Garcia RR/106	5.00	1.50
165 Marcus Giles RR/320	2.00	.60
166 Alexis Gomez RR/34	12.00	3.60
167 Jason Hart RR/303	2.00	.60
168 Eric Hinske RR/332	4.00	1.20
169 Cesar Izturis RR/60	8.00	2.40
170 Nick Johnson RR/308	2.00	.60
171 Mike Young RR/37	10.00	3.00
172 B. Lawrence RR/281	2.00	.60
173 S. Lomasney RR/229	2.50	.75
174 Nick Maness RR/25		
175 Jose Mieses RR/265	2.00	.60
176 Greg Miller RR/328	2.00	.60
177 Eric Munson RR/3		
178 Xavier Nady RR/1		
179 Blaine Neal RR/296	2.00	.60
180 A. Nunez RR/38	10.00	3.00
181 Jose Ortiz RR/7		
182 J. Owens RR/273	2.00	.60
183 Pablo Ozuna RR/333	2.00	.60
184 Corey Patterson RR/11		
185 Carlos Pena RR/52	8.00	2.40
186 Wily Mo Pena RR/114	5.00	1.50
187 Timo Perez RR/49	10.00	3.00
188 A. Pettyjohn RR/20		
189 Luis Rivas RR/310	2.00	.60
190 J. Melian RR/26	12.00	3.60
191 Wilken Ruan RR/215	2.50	.75
192 D. Sanchez RR/19		
193 A. Soriano RR/50	10.00	3.00
194 Rafael Soriano RR/13		
195 Ichiro Suzuki RR/106	120.00	36.00
196 Billy Sylvester RR/11		
197 Juan Uribe RR/157	3.00	.90
198 Eric Valent RR/342	2.00	.60
199 Carlos Valderrama RR/13		
200 Matt White RR/31	12.00	3.60

2001 Donruss Stat Line Season

Randomly inserted into 2001 Donruss packs, this 220-card insert parallels the 2001 Donruss base set. Each card is individually serial numbered to a season stat of the given players. Please note that the print runs are listed in our checklist. Exchange cards for Albert Pujols and Ben Sheets with a redemption deadline of May 1st, 2003 were seeded into packs. Autographed versions of Pujols and Sheets were made available due to an error in production whereby more than the stated amount of Stat Line Season cards for each player were produced. To honor their commitment to collectors - Donruss contracted with the two athletes to sign special non-serial numbered versions of their Stat Line Season card and sent them out to collectors that redeemed the exchange cards. Cards with a print run of 25 or fewer are not priced due to market scarcity.

Nm-Mt Ex-Mt
*1-150 P/R b/wn 151-200: 3X TO 8X..
*1-150 P/R b/wn 121-150: 3X TO 8X..
*1-150 P/R b/wn 81-120: 4X TO 10X..
*1-150 P/R b/wn 66-80: 5X TO 12X....
*1-150 P/R b/wn 51-65: 6X TO 15X....
*1-150 P/R b/wn 36-50: 8X TO 20X....
*1-150 P/R b/wn 26-35: 10X TO 25X..
*201-220 P/R b/wn 151-200 .6X TO 1.5X
*201-220 P/R b/wn 121-150 .6X TO 1.5X
*201-220 P/R b/wn 81-120 .75X TO 2X
*201-220 P/R b/wn 66-80 1X TO 2.5X
*201-220 P/R b/wn 36-50 1.5X TO 4X
*201-220 P/R b/wn 26-35 2X TO 5X...
151 B. Abernathy RR/130 4.00 1.20
152 Cory Aldridge RR/100 5.00 1.50
153 Gene Altman RR/6
154 Josh Beckett RR/61 8.00 2.40
155 Wilson Betemit RR/89 5.00 1.50
156 Albert Pujols RR/17
156B Albert Pujols RR AU 375.00 110.00
157 Joe Crede RR/5
158 Jack Cust RR/131 4.00 1.20
159 Ben Sheets RR/8
159B Ben Sheets RR AU 80.00 24.00
160 Alex Escobar RR/126 4.00 1.20
161 Adrian Hernandez RR/8
162 Pedro Feliz RR/2
163 Nate Frese RR/126 4.00 1.20
164 Carlos Garcia RR/14
165 Marcus Giles RR/133 4.00 1.20
166 Alexis Gomez RR/117 5.00 1.50
167 Jason Hart RR/31 12.00 3.60
168 Eric Hinske RR/20
169 Cesar Izturis RR/95 5.00 1.50
170 Nick Johnson RR/145 4.00 1.20
171 Mike Young RR/155 3.00 .90
172 B. Lawrence RR/165 3.00 .90
173 Steve Lomasney RR/8
174 Nick Maness RR/127 4.00 1.20
175 Jose Mieses RR/17
176 Greg Miller RR/10
177 Eric Munson RR/1
178 Xavier Nady RR/1
179 Blaine Neal RR/65 8.00 2.40
180 A. Nunez RR/51 8.00 2.40
181 Jose Ortiz RR/2
182 Jeremy Owens RR/16
183 Pablo Ozuna RR/8
184 Corey Patterson RR/2
185 Carlos Pena RR/117 5.00 1.50
186 Wily Mo Pena RR/10
187 Timo Perez RR/14
188 A. Pettyjohn RR/68 6.00 1.80
189 Luis Rivas RR/18
190 J. Melian RR/73 6.00 1.80
191 Wilken Ruan RR/165 3.00 .90
192 D.Sanchez RR/121 4.00 1.20
193 Alfonso Soriano RR/2
194 Rafael Soriano RR/90 25.00 7.50
195 Ichiro Suzuki RR/153 100.00 30.00
196 Billy Sylvester RR/16
197 Juan Uribe RR/22
198 Eric Valent RR/22
199 C.Valderrama RR/137 4.00 1.20
200 Matt White RR/126 4.00 1.20

2001 Donruss 1999 Retro

Inserted into hobby packs at one per hobby pack, this 100-card insert features cards that Donruss would have released in 1999 had they been producing baseball cards at the time. The set is broken into tiers as follows: Base Veterans (1-80), and Short-printed Prospects (81-100) serial numbered to 1999. Please note that these cards have a 2001 copyright, thus, are listed under the 2001 products.

Nm-Mt Ex-Mt
COMPLETE SET (100) 150.00 45.00
COMP.SET w/o SP's (80) 50.00 15.00
COMMON CARD (1-80) .60 .18
COMMON CARD (81-100) 5.00 1.50
1 Ken Griffey Jr. 2.50 .75
2 Nomar Garciaparra 2.50 .75
3 Alex Rodriguez 2.50 .75
4 Mark McGwire 4.00 1.20
5 Sammy Sosa 2.50 .75
6 Chipper Jones 1.50 .45
7 Mike Piazza 2.50 .75
8 Barry Larkin 1.50 .45
9 Andruw Jones .60 .18
10 Albert Belle .60 .18
11 Jeff Bagwell 1.00 .30
12 Tony Gwynn 2.00 .60
13 Manny Ramirez .60 .18
14 Mo Vaughn .60 .18
15 Barry Bonds 4.00 1.20
16 Frank Thomas 1.50 .45
17 Vladimir Guerrero 1.50 .45
18 Derek Jeter 4.00 1.20
19 Randy Johnson 1.50 .45
20 Greg Maddux 2.50 .75
21 Pedro Martinez 1.50 .45
22 Cal Ripken 5.00 1.50
23 Ivan Rodriguez 1.50 .45
24 Matt Williams .60 .18
25 Javy Lopez .60 .18
26 Tim Salmon 1.00 .30
27 Raul Mondesi .60 .18
28 Todd Helton 1.00 .30
29 Magglio Ordonez .60 .18
30 Sean Casey .60 .18
31 Jeromy Burnitz .60 .18
32 Jeff Kent .60 .18
33 Jim Edmonds .60 .18
34 Jim Thome 1.50 .45
35 Dante Bichette .60 .18
36 Larry Walker 1.00 .30
37 Will Clark 1.50 .45
38 Omar Vizquel .60 .18
39 Mike Mussina 1.50 .45
40 Eric Karros .60 .18
41 Kenny Lofton .60 .18
42 David Justice .60 .18
43 Craig Biggio 1.00 .30
44 J.D. Drew .60 .18
45 Rickey Henderson 1.50 .45
46 Bernie Williams 1.00 .30
47 Brian Giles .60 .18
48 Paul O'Neill 1.00 .30
49 Orlando Hernandez .60 .18
50 Jason Giambi 1.50 .45
51 Curt Schilling 1.00 .30
52 Scott Rolen 1.00 .30
53 Mark Grace 1.00 .30
54 Moises Alou .60 .18
55 Jason Kendall .60 .18
56 Ray Lankford .60 .18
57 Kerry Wood 1.50 .45
58 Gary Sheffield .60 .18
59 Ruben Mateo .60 .18
60 Darin Erstad .60 .18
61 Troy Glaus 1.00 .30
62 Jose Canseco 1.50 .45
63 Wade Boggs 1.00 .30
64 Tom Glavine 1.00 .30
65 Gabe Kapler .60 .18
66 Juan Gonzalez 1.50 .45
67 Rafael Palmeiro 1.00 .30
68 Richie Sexson .60 .18
69 Carl Everett .60 .18
70 David Wells .60 .18
71 Carlos Delgado .60 .18
72 Eric Davis .60 .18
73 Shawn Green .60 .18
74 Andres Galarraga .60 .18
75 Edgar Martinez 1.00 .30
76 Roberto Alomar 1.50 .45
77 John Olerud .60 .18
78 Luis Gonzalez .60 .18
79 Kevin Brown .60 .18
80 Roger Clemens 3.00 .90
81 Josh Beckett SP 8.00 2.40
82 Alfonso Soriano SP 8.00 2.40
83 Alex Escobar SP 5.00 1.50
84 Pat Burrell SP 5.00 1.50
85 Eric Chavez SP 5.00 1.50
86 Erubiel Durazo SP 5.00 1.50
87 Abraham Nunez SP 5.00 1.50
88 Carlos Pena SP 5.00 1.50
89 Nick Johnson SP 5.00 1.50
90 Eric Munson SP 5.00 1.50
91 Corey Patterson SP 5.00 1.50
92 Wily Mo Pena SP 5.00 1.50
93 Rafael Furcal SP 5.00 1.50
94 Eric Valent SP 5.00 1.50
95 Mark Mulder SP 5.00 1.50
96 Chad Hutchinson SP 5.00 1.50
97 Freddy Garcia SP 5.00 1.50
98 Tim Hudson SP 5.00 1.50
99 Rick Ankiel SP 5.00 1.50
100 Kip Wells SP 5.00 1.50

2001 Donruss 1999 Retro Stat Line Career

Randomly inserted into 1999 Retro packs, this 100-card insert parallels the 1999 Retro base set. Each card is individually serial numbered to a career stat of the given players. Please note that the print runs are listed in our checklist. Cards with a print run of 25 or fewer are not priced due to market scarcity.

Nm-Mt Ex-Mt
*1-80 P/R b/wn 251-400: 1.25X TO 3X
*1-80 P/R b/wn 201-250: 1.25X TO 3X
*1-80 P/R b/wn 151-200: 1.5X TO 4X.
*1-80 P/R b/wn 121-150: 1.5X TO 4X.
*1-80 P/R b/wn 81-120: 2X TO 5X....
*1-80 P/R b/wn 66-80: 2.5X TO 6X....
*1-80 P/R b/wn 51-65: 3X TO 8X......
*1-80 P/R b/wn 36-50: 4X TO 10X.....
*1-80 P/R b/wn 26-35: 5X TO 12X.....
81 Josh Beckett/13
82 Alfonso Soriano/113 4.00 1.20
83 Alex Escobar/181 2.50 .75
84 Pat Burrell/303 2.00 .60
85 Eric Chavez/314 2.00 .60
86 Erubiel Durazo/147 3.00 .90
87 Abraham Nunez/106 4.00 1.20
88 Carlos Pena/46 8.00 2.40
89 Nick Johnson/259 2.00 .60
90 Eric Munson/392 2.00 .60
91 Corey Patterson/117 4.00 1.20
92 Wily Mo Pena/247 2.00 .60
93 Rafael Furcal/137 3.00 .90
94 Eric Valent/53 6.00 1.80
95 Mark Mulder/340 2.00 .60
96 Chad Hutchinson/2
97 Freddy Garcia/397 2.00 .60
98 Tim Hudson/17
99 Rick Ankiel/222 2.00 .60
100 Kip Wells/371 2.00 .60

2001 Donruss 1999 Retro Stat Line Season

Randomly inserted into 1999 Retro packs, this 100-card insert parallels the 1999 Retro base set. Each card is individually serial numbered to a season stat of the given players. Please note that the print runs are listed in our checklist. Cards issued to a stated print run of 25 or fewer are not priced due to market scarcity.

Nm-Mt Ex-Mt
*1-80 P/R b/wn 251-400: 1.25X TO 3X
*1-80 P/R b/wn 201-250: 1.25X TO 3X
*1-80 P/R b/wn 151-200: 1.5X TO 4X.
*1-80 P/R b/wn 121-150: 1.5X TO 4X.
*1-80 P/R b/wn 81-120: 2X TO 5X......
*1-80 P/R b/wn 66-80: 2.5X TO 6X.....
*1-80 P/R b/wn 51-65: 3X TO 8X.....
*1-80 P/R b/wn 36-50: 4X TO 10X.....
*1-80 P/R b/wn 26-35: 5X TO 12X.....
81 Josh Beckett/178 2.50 .75
82 Alfonso Soriano/7
83 Alex Escobar/27 10.00 3.00
84 Pat Burrell/7
85 Eric Chavez/33 10.00 3.00
86 Erubiel Durazo/19
87 Abraham Nunez/95 4.00 1.20
88 Carlos Pena/319 2.00 .60
89 Nick Johnson/17
90 Eric Munson/16
91 Corey Patterson/22
92 Wily Mo Pena/7
93 Rafael Furcal/88 4.00 1.20
94 Eric Valent/13
95 Mark Mulder/113 4.00 1.20
96 Chad Hutchinson/51 6.00 1.80
97 Freddy Garcia/10
98 Tim Hudson/152 2.50 .75
99 Rick Ankiel/12
100 Kip Wells/135 2.50 .75

2001 Donruss 1999 Retro Diamond Kings

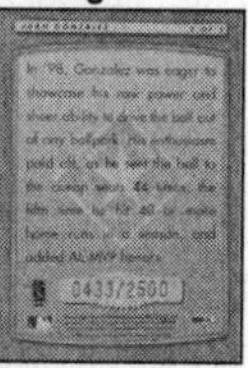

Randomly inserted into 1999 Retro packs, this 5-card insert set features the "Diamond King" cards that Donruss would have produced had they been producing baseball cards in 1999. Each card is individually serial numbered to 2500.

Nm-Mt Ex-Mt
COMPLETE SET (5) 60.00 18.00
*STUDIO: .75X TO 2X BASIC RETRO DK
STUDIO PRINT RUN 250 SERIAL #'d SETS
RANDOM INSERTS IN 1999 RETRO PACKS
1 Scott Rolen 10.00 3.00
2 Sammy Sosa 12.00 3.60
3 Juan Gonzalez 10.00 3.00
4 Ken Griffey Jr. 12.00 3.60
5 Derek Jeter 20.00 6.00

2001 Donruss 2000 Retro

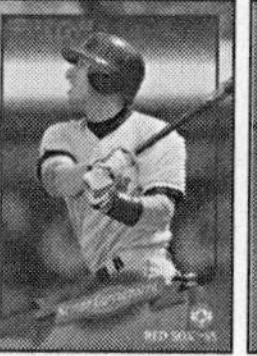

Inserted into retail packs at one per retail pack, this 100-card insert features cards that Donruss would have released in 2000 had they been producing baseball cards at the time. The set is broken into tiers as follows: Base Veterans (1-80), and Short-printed Prospects (81-100) serial numbered to 2000. Please note that these cards have a 2001 copyright, thus, are listed under the 2001 products. Exchange cards originally intended for number 82 C.C. Sabathia and number 95 Ben Sheets were both issued in packs with an expiration date of 05/01/03. Since that time, we've learned that the actual redeemed card number 95 features Ichiro Suzuki. It's not known at this time exactly which player was featured on the exchange card number 82.

Nm-Mt Ex-Mt
COMPLETE SET (100) 250.00 75.00
COMP.SET w/o SP's (80) 80.00 24.00
COMMON CARD (1-80) .60 .18
COMMON CARD (81-100) 5.00 1.50
SP * 82/95 WERE AVAIL.ONLY VIA MAIL
1 Vladimir Guerrero 1.50 .45
2 Alex Rodriguez 2.50 .75
3 Ken Griffey Jr. 2.50 .75
4 Nomar Garciaparra 2.50 .75
5 Mike Piazza 2.50 .75
6 Mark McGwire 4.00 1.20
7 Sammy Sosa 2.50 .75
8 Chipper Jones 1.50 .45
9 Jim Edmonds .60 .18
10 Tony Gwynn 2.00 .60
11 Andruw Jones .60 .18
12 Albert Belle .60 .18
13 Jeff Bagwell 1.00 .30
14 Manny Ramirez .60 .18
15 Mo Vaughn .60 .18
16 Barry Bonds 4.00 1.20
17 Frank Thomas 1.50 .45
18 Ivan Rodriguez 1.50 .45
19 Derek Jeter 4.00 1.20
20 Randy Johnson 1.50 .45
21 Greg Maddux 2.50 .75
22 Pedro Martinez 1.50 .45
23 Cal Ripken 5.00 1.50
24 Mark Grace 1.00 .30
25 Javy Lopez .60 .18
26 Ray Durham .60 .18
27 Todd Helton 1.00 .30
28 Magglio Ordonez .60 .18
29 Sean Casey .60 .18
30 Darin Erstad .60 .18
31 Barry Larkin 1.50 .45
32 Will Clark 1.50 .45
33 Jim Thome 1.50 .45
34 Dante Bichette .60 .18
35 Larry Walker 1.00 .30
36 Ken Caminiti .60 .18
37 Omar Vizquel .60 .18
38 Miguel Tejada .60 .18
39 Eric Karros .60 .18
40 Gary Sheffield .60 .18
41 Jeff Cirillo .60 .18
42 Rondell White .60 .18
43 Rickey Henderson 1.50 .45
44 Bernie Williams 1.00 .30
45 Brian Giles .60 .18
46 Paul O'Neill 1.00 .30
47 Orlando Hernandez .60 .18
48 Ben Grieve .60 .18
49 Jason Giambi 1.50 .45
50 Curt Schilling 1.00 .30
51 Scott Rolen 1.00 .30
52 Bobby Abreu .60 .18
53 Jason Kendall .60 .18
54 Fernando Tatis .60 .18
55 Jeff Kent .60 .18
56 Mike Mussina 1.50 .45
57 Troy Glaus 1.00 .30
58 Jose Canseco 1.50 .45
59 Wade Boggs 1.00 .30
60 Fred McGriff .60 .18
61 Juan Gonzalez 1.50 .45
62 Rafael Palmeiro 1.00 .30
63 Rusty Greer .60 .18
64 Carl Everett .60 .18
65 David Wells .60 .18
66 Carlos Delgado .60 .18
67 Shawn Green .60 .18
68 David Justice .60 .18
69 Edgar Martinez 1.00 .30
70 Andres Galarraga .60 .18
71 Roberto Alomar 1.50 .45
72 Jermaine Dye .60 .18
73 John Olerud .60 .18
74 Luis Gonzalez .60 .18
75 Craig Biggio 1.00 .30
76 Kevin Millwood .60 .18
77 Kevin Brown .60 .18
78 John Smoltz 1.00 .30
79 Roger Clemens 3.00 .90
80 Mike Hampton .60 .18
81 Tomas De La Rosa SP 5.00 1.50
82 TBD EXCH SP *
83 Ryan Christenson SP 5.00 1.50
84 Pedro Feliz SP 5.00 1.50
85 Jose Ortiz SP 5.00 1.50
86 Xavier Nady SP 5.00 1.50
87 Julio Zuleta SP 5.00 1.50
88 Jason Hart SP 5.00 1.50
89 Keith Ginter SP 5.00 1.50
90 Brent Abernathy SP 5.00 1.50
91 Timo Perez SP 5.00 1.50
92 Juan Pierre SP 5.00 1.50
93 Tike Redman SP 5.00 1.50
94 Mike Lamb SP 5.00 1.50
95 Ichiro Suzuki SP * 50.00 15.00
96 Kazuhiro Sasaki SP 5.00 1.50
97 Barry Zito SP 10.00 3.00
98 Adam Bernero SP 5.00 1.50
99 Chad Durbin SP 5.00 1.50
100 Matt Ginter SP 5.00 1.50

2001 Donruss 2000 Retro Stat Line Career

Randomly inserted into 2000 Retro packs, this 100-card insert parallels the 2000 Retro base set. Each card is individually serial numbered to a career stat of the given players. Please note that the print runs are listed in our checklist. Cards issued to a stated print run of 25 or fewer are not priced due to market scarcity. Exchange cards were seeded into packs for cards 82 and 95. These cards were originally intended to be redeemed for C.C. Sabathia and Ben Sheets. It's since been discovered that Ichiro Suzuki cards were actually redeemed for card 95.

Nm-Mt Ex-Mt
*1-80 P/R b/wn 251-400: 1.25X TO 3X
*1-80 P/R b/wn 201-250: 1.25X TO 3X
*1-80 P/R b/wn 151-200: 1.25X TO 3X
*1-80 P/R b/wn 121-150: 1.5X TO 4X.
*1-80 P/R b/wn 81-120: 1.5X TO 4X...
*1-80 P/R b/wn 66-80: 2X TO 5X.......
*1-80 P/R b/wn 51-65: 2.5X TO 6X.....
*1-80 P/R b/wn 36-50: 3X TO 8X.......
*1-80 P/R b/wn 26-35: 4X TO 10X.......
81 Tomas De La Rosa/76 5.00 1.50
82 C.C. Sabathia/6
83 Ryan Christenson/9
84 Pedro Feliz/45 6.00 1.80
85 Jose Ortiz/90 4.00 1.20
86 Xavier Nady/175 2.50 .75
87 Julio Zuleta/295 2.00 .60
88 Jason Hart/19
89 Keith Ginter/188 2.50 .75
90 Brent Abernathy/254 2.00 .60
91 Timo Perez/5
92 Juan Pierre/104 4.00 1.20
93 Tike Redman/151 2.50 .75
94 Mike Lamb/240 2.00 .60
95 Ichiro Suzuki/159 25.00 7.50
96 Kazuhiro Sasaki/229 2.00 .60
97 Barry Zito/6
98 Adam Bernero/254 2.00 .60
99 Chad Durbin/3
100 Matt Ginter/300 2.00 .60

2001 Donruss 2000 Retro Stat Line Season

Randomly inserted into 2000 Retro packs, this 100-card insert parallels the 2000 Retro base set. Each card is individually serial numbered to a season stat of the given players. Please note that the print runs are listed in our checklist. Cards printed to a stated print run of 25 or fewer are not printed due to market scarcity. Exchange cards were seeded into packs for cards 82 and 95. These cards were originally intended to be redeemed for C.C. Sabathia and Ben Sheets. It's since been discovered that Ichiro Suzuki cards were actually redeemed for card 95.

Nm-Mt Ex-Mt
*1-80 P/R b/wn 251-400: 1.25X TO 3X
*1-80 P/R b/wn 201-250: 1.25X TO 3X
*1-80 P/R b/wn 151-200: 1.5X TO 4X.
*1-80 P/R b/wn 121-150: 1.5X TO 4X.
*1-80 P/R b/wn 81-120: 2X TO 5X.....
*1-80 P/R b/wn 66-80: 2.5X TO 6X.....
*1-80 P/R b/wn 51-65: 3X TO 8X.....
*1-80 P/R b/wn 36-50: 4X TO 10X.....
*1-80 P/R b/wn 26-35: 5X TO 12X.....
81 Tomas De La Rosa/122 2.50 .75
82 C.C. Sabathia/76 25.00 7.50
83 Ryan Christenson/56 6.00 1.80
84 Pedro Feliz/13
85 Jose Ortiz/107 4.00 1.20
86 Xavier Nady/23
87 Julio Zuleta/21
88 Jason Hart/168 2.50 .75
89 Keith Ginter/13
90 Brent Abernathy/168 2.50 .75
91 Timo Perez/4
92 Juan Pierre/187 2.50 .75
93 Tike Redman/143 2.50 .75
94 Mike Lamb/177 2.50 .75
95 Ichiro Suzuki/8
96 Kazuhiro Sasaki/34 10.00 3.00
97 Barry Zito/97 4.00 1.20
98 Adam Bernero/80 5.00 1.50
99 Chad Durbin/3
100 Matt Ginter/66 5.00 1.50

2001 Donruss 2000 Retro Diamond Kings

Randomly inserted into 2000 Retro packs, this 5-card insert set features the "Diamond King" cards that Donruss would have produced had they been producing baseball cards in 2000. Each card is individually serial numbered to 2500. Card backs carry a "DK" prefix.

Nm-Mt Ex-Mt
COMPLETE SET (5) 60.00 18.00
*STUDIO: .75X TO 2X BASIC RETRO DK
RANDOM IN 2000 RETRO RETAIL PACKS
STUDIO PRINT RUN 250 SERIAL #'d SETS
DK1 Frank Thomas 10.00 3.00
DK2 Greg Maddux 12.00 3.60
DK3 Alex Rodriguez 12.00 3.60
DK4 Jeff Bagwell 10.00 3.00
DK5 Manny Ramirez 10.00 3.00

2001 Donruss 2000 Retro Diamond Kings Studio Series Autograph

An exchange card for an Alex Rodriguez autograph with a redemption deadline of May 1st, 2003 was randomly inserted in 2001 Donruss retro 2000 retail packs. The card is a signed version of A-Rod's basic Diamond King Studio Series insert and only 50 serial numbered copies were produced.

Nm-Mt Ex-Mt
DK3 Alex Rodriguez 250.00 75.00

2001 Donruss All-Time Diamond Kings

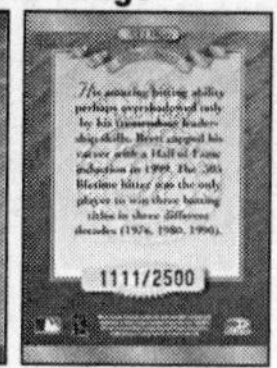

Randomly inserted into 2001 Donruss packs, this 10-card insert features some of the greatest players to have ever grace the front of a "Diamond Kings" card. Card backs carry a "ATDK" prefix. There were 2500 serial numbered sets produced. The Willie Mays and Hank Aaron cards both packed out as exchange cards with a redemption deadline of May 1st, 2003. The Mays card was originally intended to be card number ATDK-9 within this set, but was erroneously numbered ATDK-1 (the same number as the Frank Robinson card) when it was sent out by Donruss. Thus, this set has two card #1's and no card #9.

Nm-Mt Ex-Mt
COMPLETE SET (10) 150.00 45.00
*STUDIO: 1X TO 2.5X BASIC ALL-TIME DK
STUDIO PRINT RUN 200 SERIAL #'d SETS
STUDIO CARDS ARE SERIAL #'d 51-250
ATDK1 Willie Mays 25.00 7.50
ATDK1 Frank Robinson 10.00 3.00
ATDK2 Harmon Killebrew 12.00 3.60
ATDK3 Mike Schmidt 20.00 6.00
ATDK4 Reggie Jackson 10.00 3.00
ATDK5 Nolan Ryan 40.00 12.00
ATDK6 George Brett 25.00 7.50
ATDK7 Tom Seaver 10.00 3.00
ATDK8 Hank Aaron 25.00 7.50
ATDK10 Stan Musial 20.00 6.00

2001 Donruss All-Time Diamond Kings Autograph

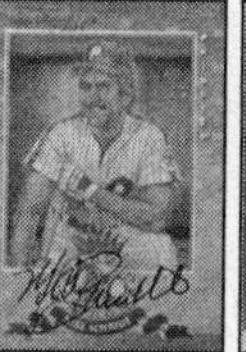
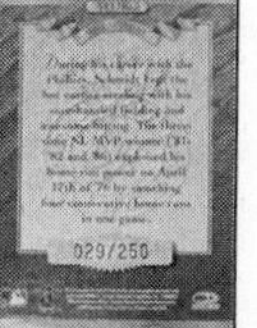

Randomly inserted into 2001 Donruss packs, this 10-card insert is a complete autographed parallel of the 2001 Donruss All-Time Diamond

Kings. Card backs carry a "ATDK" prefix. Please note that the first 50 of the All-Time Diamond Kings were autographed. Exchange cards with a redemption deadline of May 1st, 2003 were seeded into packs for Hank Aaron, Willie Mays and Nolan Ryan.

	Nm-Mt	Ex-Mt
ATDK1 Willie Mays		
ATDK1 Frank Robinson	80.00	24.00
ATDK2 Harmon Killebrew	120.00	36.00
ATDK3 Mike Schmidt	200.00	60.00
ATDK4 Reggie Jackson	120.00	36.00
ATDK5 Nolan Ryan	250.00	75.00
ATDK6 George Brett	250.00	75.00
ATDK7 Tom Seaver	100.00	30.00
ATDK8 Hank Aaron	250.00	75.00
ATDK10 Stan Musial	150.00	45.00

2001 Donruss Anniversary Originals Autograph

Each of these BGS graded cards were randomly inserted as box-toppers in boxes of 2001 Donruss. Unfortunately, exchange cards with a redemption deadline of May 1st, 2003 were seeded into packs for almost the entire set. Of the twelve cards featured in the set - only autograph cards for Tony Gwynn, David Justice and Ryne Sandberg actually made their way into packs. Since each card was signed to a different print run, we have included that information in our checklist.

	Nm-Mt	Ex-Mt
82-405 Cal Ripken/23		
83-277 Ryne Sandberg/24		
83-279 Cal Ripken/2		
83-586 Wade Boggs/25		
83-598 Tony Gwynn/24		
84-248 Don Mattingly/25		
87-36 Greg Maddux/25		
87-43 Rafael Palmeiro/250	80.00	24.00
87-361 Barry Bonds/25		
88-34 Roberto Alomar/250	80.00	24.00
88-644 Tom Glavine/250	80.00	24.00
89-42 Randy Johnson/25		
90-704 David Justice/24		

2001 Donruss Bat Kings

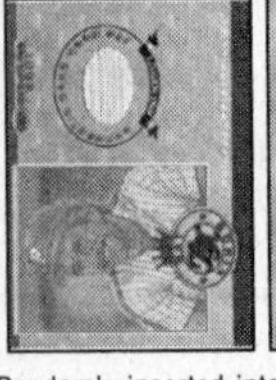

Randomly inserted into packs, this 10-card insert features swatches of actual game-used bat. Card backs carry a "BK" prefix. Each card is individually serial numbered to 200. An exchange card with a redemption deadline of May 1st, 2003 was seeded into packs for Hank Aaron.

	Nm-Mt	Ex-Mt
BK1 Ivan Rodriguez	25.00	7.50
BK2 Tony Gwynn	40.00	12.00
BK3 Barry Bonds	80.00	24.00
BK4 Todd Helton	25.00	7.50
BK5 Troy Glaus	25.00	7.50
BK6 Mike Schmidt	60.00	18.00
BK7 Reggie Jackson	25.00	7.50
BK8 Harmon Killebrew	25.00	7.50
BK9 Frank Robinson	25.00	7.50
BK10 Hank Aaron	100.00	30.00

2001 Donruss Bat Kings Autograph

Randomly inserted into packs, this 10-card insert features swatches of actual game-used bat, as well as, an autograph from the depicted player. Card backs carry a "BK" prefix. Each card is individually serial numbered to 50. Exchange cards with a redemption deadline of May 1st, 2003 were seeded into packs for Barry Bonds, Troy Glaus, Todd Helton and Ivan Rodriguez. Unfortunately, Donruss was not able to get Barry Bonds to sign his Bat King cards - thus a non-autographed version of Bonds' card was sent out to collectors. Bonds did, however, agree to sign 100 of his vintage Donruss cards (1988 - 25 copies, 1989 -25 copies and 1990 - 50 copies). These 100 cards were stamped with a "Recollection Collection" logo and sent out to collectors - along with the unsigned Bonds Bat King card.

	Nm-Mt	Ex-Mt
BK1 Ivan Rodriguez	150.00	45.00
BK2 Tony Gwynn	150.00	45.00
BK3 B.Bonds NO AU Bat	50.00	15.00
BK4 Todd Helton	120.00	36.00
BK5 Troy Glaus	120.00	36.00
BK6 Mike Schmidt	200.00	60.00
BK7 Reggie Jackson	150.00	45.00
BK8 Harmon Killebrew	150.00	45.00
BK9 Frank Robinson	120.00	36.00
BK10 Hank Aaron	250.00	75.00

2001 Donruss Diamond Kings Hawaii Promos

This card was given out to people who attended the 2001 Kit Young Hawaii Trade Conference. The card is gold-bordered and stamped with "Hawaii 2001" in gold lettering on the card front. Card back carries a "DK" prefix.

	Nm-Mt	Ex-Mt
HDK1 Alex Rodriguez Does not have "Sample" stamp on card back	10.00	3.00
HDK1 Alex Rodriguez Has "Sample" stamped on back and "2001 Hawaii" stamp on card front.	10.00	3.00
HDK1 Alex Rodriguez Has neither the "Hawaii 2001" stamp or "Sample" stamp on front.	200.00	60.00

2001 Donruss Diamond Kings

Randomly inserted into 2001 Donruss packs, this 20-card insert features players that are leaders on and off the baseball field. Card backs carry a "DK" prefix. Each card is individually serial numbered to 2500.

	Nm-Mt	Ex-Mt
COMPLETE SET (20)	250.00	75.00
*STUDIO: .75X TO 2X BASIC DK		
STUDIO NO AU PLAYER PRINT 250 #'d SETS		
STUDIO AU PLAYER PRINT 200 #'d SETS		
RANDOM INSERTS IN PACKS		
DK1 Alex Rodriguez	12.00	3.60
DK2 Cal Ripken	25.00	7.50
DK3 Mark McGwire	20.00	6.00
DK4 Ken Griffey Jr.	12.00	3.60
DK5 Derek Jeter	20.00	6.00
DK6 Nomar Garciaparra	12.00	3.60
DK7 Mike Piazza	12.00	3.60
DK8 Roger Clemens	15.00	4.50
DK9 Greg Maddux	12.00	3.60
DK10 Chipper Jones	10.00	3.00
DK11 Tony Gwynn	10.00	3.00
DK12 Barry Bonds	20.00	6.00
DK13 Sammy Sosa	12.00	3.60
DK14 Vladimir Guerrero	10.00	3.00
DK15 Frank Thomas	10.00	3.00
DK16 Troy Glaus	10.00	3.00
DK17 Todd Helton	10.00	3.00
DK18 Ivan Rodriguez	10.00	3.00
DK19 Pedro Martinez	10.00	3.00
DK20 Carlos Delgado	10.00	3.00

2001 Donruss Diamond Kings Studio Series Autograph

Randomly inserted into 2001 Donruss packs, this 11-card insert is a partial parallel of the 2001 Diamond Kings insert. Each of these autographed cards were serial numbered to 50. Exchange cards with a redemption deadline of May 1st, 2003 were seeded into packs for Barry Bonds, Roger Clemens, Troy Glaus, Vladimir Guerrero, Todd Helton, Chipper Jones, Alex Rodriguez and Ivan Rodriguez.

	Nm-Mt	Ex-Mt
DK1 Alex Rodriguez	200.00	60.00
DK2 Cal Ripken	300.00	90.00
DK8 Roger Clemens	200.00	60.00
DK9 Greg Maddux	200.00	60.00
DK10 Chipper Jones	120.00	36.00
DK11 Tony Gwynn	150.00	45.00
DK12 Barry Bonds		
DK14 Vladimir Guerrero	120.00	36.00
DK16 Troy Glaus	100.00	30.00
DK17 Todd Helton	100.00	30.00
DK18 I. Rodriguez EXCH	120.00	36.00

2001 Donruss Diamond Kings Reprints

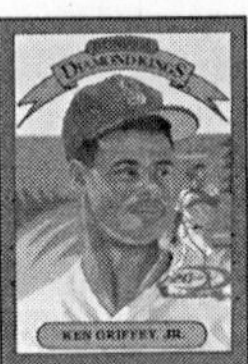

Randomly inserted into 2001 Donruss packs, this 20-card insert features reprints of past "Diamond King" cards. Card backs carry a "DKR" prefix. Print runs are listed in our checklist. An exchange card with a redemption deadline of May 1st, 2003 was seeded into packs for Will Clark.

	Nm-Mt	Ex-Mt
COMPLETE SET (20)	200.00	60.00
DKR1 Rod Carew/1982	10.00	3.00
DKR2 Nolan Ryan/1982	25.00	7.50
DKR3 Tom Seaver/1982	10.00	3.00
DKR4 Carlton Fisk/1982	10.00	3.00
DKR5 R.Jackson/1983	10.00	3.00
DKR6 S. Carlton/1983	10.00	3.00
DKR7 Johnny Bench/1983	10.00	3.00
DKR8 Joe Morgan/1983	10.00	3.00
DKR9 Mike Schmidt/1984	20.00	6.00
DKR10 Wade Boggs/1984	10.00	3.00
DKR11 Cal Ripken/1985	25.00	7.50
DKR12 Tony Gwynn/1985	12.00	3.60
DKR13 A.Dawson/1986	10.00	3.00
DKR14 Ozzie Smith/1987	15.00	4.50
DKR15 George Brett/1987	25.00	7.50
DKR16 D.Winfield/1987	10.00	3.00
DKR17 Paul Molitor/1988	10.00	3.00
DKR18 Will Clark/1988	15.00	4.50
DKR19 Robin Yount/1989	15.00	4.50
DKR20 K.Griffey Jr./1989	15.00	4.50

2001 Donruss Diamond Kings Reprints Autographs

Randomly inserted into 2001 Donruss packs, this 20-card insert features autographed reprints of past "Diamond King" cards. Card backs carry a "DKR" prefix. Print runs are listed below. Exchange cards with a redemption deadline of May 1st, 2003 were seeded into packs for Wade Boggs, Rod Carew, Steve Carlton, Will Clark, Andre Dawson, Carlton Fisk, Cal Ripken, Nolan Ryan, Ozzie Smith, Dave Winfield and Robin Yount. Ken Griffey Jr. had a card issued serial #'d of 89 copies but he was the only player featured in the set to not sign any of his cards.

	Nm-Mt	Ex-Mt
DKR1 Rod Carew/82	80.00	24.00
DKR2 Nolan Ryan/82	200.00	60.00
DKR3 Tom Seaver/82	80.00	24.00
DKR4 Carlton Fisk/82	80.00	24.00
DKR5 Reggie Jackson/83	100.00	30.00
DKR6 Steve Carlton/83	80.00	24.00
DKR7 Johnny Bench/83	100.00	30.00
DKR8 Joe Morgan/83	60.00	18.00
DKR9 Mike Schmidt/84	175.00	52.50
DKR10 Wade Boggs/84	80.00	24.00
DKR11 Cal Ripken/85	250.00	75.00
DKR12 Tony Gwynn/85	120.00	36.00
DKR13 Andre Dawson/86	60.00	18.00
DKR14 Ozzie Smith/87	100.00	30.00
DKR15 George Brett/87	150.00	45.00
DKR16 Dave Winfield/87	80.00	24.00
DKR17 Paul Molitor/88	80.00	24.00
DKR18 Will Clark/88	120.00	36.00
DKR19 Robin Yount/89	100.00	30.00
DKR20 Ken Griffey Jr. NO AU/89	50.00	15.00

2001 Donruss Elite Series

Randomly inserted into 2001 Donruss packs, this 20-card insert features many of the Major Leagues elite players. Card backs carry an "ES" prefix. Each card is individually serial numbered to 2500.

	Nm-Mt	Ex-Mt
COMPLETE SET (20)	150.00	45.00
*DOMINATORS: 6X TO 15X BASIC ELITE		
DOMINATORS PRINT RUN 25 SERIAL #'d SETS		
RANDOM INSERTS IN PACKS		
ES1 Vladimir Guerrero	5.00	1.50
ES2 Cal Ripken	15.00	4.50
ES3 Greg Maddux	8.00	2.40
ES4 Alex Rodriguez	8.00	2.40
ES5 Barry Bonds	12.00	3.60
ES6 Chipper Jones	5.00	1.50
ES7 Derek Jeter	12.00	3.60
ES8 Ivan Rodriguez	5.00	1.50
ES9 Ken Griffey Jr.	8.00	2.40
ES10 Mark McGwire	12.00	3.60
ES11 Mike Piazza	8.00	2.40
ES12 Nomar Garciaparra	8.00	2.40
ES13 Pedro Martinez	5.00	1.50
ES14 Randy Johnson	5.00	1.50
ES15 Roger Clemens	10.00	3.00
ES16 Sammy Sosa	8.00	2.40
ES17 Tony Gwynn	6.00	1.80
ES18 Darin Erstad	4.00	1.20
ES19 Andruw Jones	4.00	1.20
ES20 Bernie Williams	4.00	1.20

2001 Donruss Jersey Kings

Randomly inserted into packs, this 10-card insert features swatches of actual game-used jerseys. Card backs carry a "JK" prefix. Each card is individually serial numbered to 250. Chipper Jones and Ozzie Smith were available only via mail redemption. Exchange cards with a redemption deadline of May 1st, 2003 for "to be determined" players were seeded originally into packs and many months passed before Chipper Jones and Ozzie Smith were revealed as the players that would be used to fulfill these cards.

	Nm-Mt	Ex-Mt
JK1 Vladimir Guerrero	25.00	7.50
JK2 Cal Ripken	120.00	36.00
JK3 Greg Maddux	50.00	15.00
JK4 Chipper Jones	25.00	7.50
JK5 Roger Clemens	60.00	18.00
JK6 George Brett	60.00	18.00
JK7 Tom Seaver	25.00	7.50
JK8 Nolan Ryan	120.00	36.00
JK9 Stan Musial	60.00	18.00
JK10 Ozzie Smith	40.00	12.00

2001 Donruss Jersey Kings Autograph

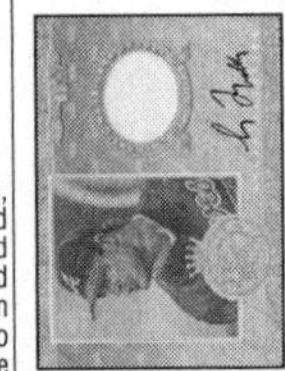

Randomly inserted into packs, this 10-card insert features swatches of actual game-used jerseys, as well as, an autograph from the depicted player. Card backs carry a "JK" prefix. Each card is individually serial numbered to 50. The following players players did not return their cards in time for inclusion in packs: Vladimir Guerrero, Cal Ripken, Chipper Jones, Roger Clemens, Nolan Ryan and Ozzie Smith. Exchange cards with a redemption deadline of May 1st, 2003 were seeded into packs for these players.

	Nm-Mt	Ex-Mt
JK1 Vladimir Guerrero	150.00	45.00
JK2 Cal Ripken	300.00	90.00
JK3 Greg Maddux	200.00	60.00
JK4 Chipper Jones	150.00	45.00
JK5 Roger Clemens	200.00	60.00
JK6 George Brett	250.00	75.00
JK7 Tom Seaver	120.00	36.00
JK8 Nolan Ryan	250.00	75.00
JK9 Stan Musial	200.00	60.00
JK10 Ozzie Smith	200.00	60.00

2001 Donruss Longball Leaders

Randomly inserted into packs, this 20-card insert features some of the Major Leagues top power hitters. Card backs carry a "LL" prefix. Each card is individually serial numbered to 1000.

	Nm-Mt	Ex-Mt
COMPLETE SET (20)	150.00	45.00
LL1 Vladimir Guerrero	8.00	2.40
LL2 Alex Rodriguez	12.00	3.60
LL3 Barry Bonds	20.00	6.00
LL4 Troy Glaus	5.00	1.50
LL5 Frank Thomas	8.00	2.40
LL6 Jeff Bagwell	5.00	1.50
LL7 Todd Helton	5.00	1.50
LL8 Ken Griffey Jr.	12.00	3.60
LL9 Manny Ramirez	4.00	1.20
LL10 Mike Piazza	12.00	3.60
LL11 Sammy Sosa	12.00	3.60
LL12 Carlos Delgado	4.00	1.20
LL13 Jim Edmonds	4.00	1.20
LL14 Jason Giambi	8.00	2.40
LL15 David Justice	4.00	1.20
LL16 Rafael Palmeiro	5.00	1.50
LL17 Gary Sheffield	4.00	1.20
LL18 Jim Thome	8.00	2.40
LL19 Tony Batista	4.00	1.20
LL20 Richard Hidalgo	4.00	1.20

2001 Donruss Production Line

Randomly inserted into packs, this 60-card insert features some of the Major League's most feared hitters. Card backs carry a "PL" prefix. Each card is individually serial numbered to one of three offensive categories: OBP, SLG, and PI. Print runs are listed in our checklist.

	Nm-Mt	Ex-Mt
COMPLETE SET (60)	400.00	120.00
COMMON SLG (21-40)	3.00	.90
COMMON PI (41-60)	2.50	.75
*DIE CUT OBP 1-20: .75X TO 2X BASIC PL		
*DIE CUT SLG 21-40: 1X TO 2.5X BASIC PL		
*DIE CUT PI 41-60: 1.25X TO 3X BASIC PL		
DIE CUT PRINT RUN 100 SERIAL #'d SETS		
PL1 J.Giambi OBP/476	10.00	3.00
PL2 C.Delgado OBP/470	4.00	1.20
PL3 Todd Helton OBP/463	6.00	1.80
PL4 M.Ramirez OBP/457	4.00	1.20
PL5 Barry Bonds OBP/440	25.00	7.50
PL6 G.Sheffield OBP/438	4.00	1.20
PL7 F.Thomas OBP/436	10.00	3.00
PL8 N.Garciaparra OBP/434	15.00	4.50
PL9 Brian Giles OBP/432	4.00	1.20
PL10 E.Alfonzo OBP/425	4.00	1.20
PL11 Jeff Kent OBP/424	4.00	1.20
PL12 J.Bagwell OBP/424	6.00	1.80
PL13 E.Martinez OBP/423	6.00	1.80
PL14 A.Rodriguez OBP/420	15.00	4.50
PL15 L.Castillo OBP/418	4.00	1.20
PL16 Will Clark OBP/418	10.00	3.00
PL17 J.Posada OBP/417	6.00	1.80
PL18 Derek Jeter OBP/416	25.00	7.50
PL19 Bob Abreu OBP/416	4.00	1.20
PL20 M.Alou OBP/416	4.00	1.20
PL21 T.Helton SLG/698	5.00	1.50
PL22 M.Ramirez SLG/697	3.00	.90
PL23 B.Bonds SLG/688	20.00	6.00
PL24 C.Delgado SLG/664	3.00	.90
PL25 V.Guerrero SLG/664	8.00	2.40
PL26 J.Giambi SLG/647	8.00	2.40
PL27 G.Sheffield SLG/643	3.00	.90
PL28 R.Hidalgo SLG/636	3.00	.90
PL29 S. Sosa SLG/634	12.00	3.60
PL30 F. Thomas SLG/625	8.00	2.40
PL31 M. Alou SLG/623	3.00	.90
PL32 J.Bagwell SLG/615	5.00	1.50
PL33 M. Piazza SLG/614	12.00	3.60
PL34 A. Rodriguez SLG/606	12.00	3.60
PL35 Troy Glaus SLG/604	5.00	1.50
PL36 N.Garciaparra SLG/599	12.00	3.60
PL37 Jeff Kent SLG/596	3.00	.90
PL38 Brian Giles SLG/594	3.00	.90
PL39 G. Jenkins SLG/588	3.00	.90
PL40 Carl Everett SLG/587	3.00	.90
PL41 Todd Helton PI/1161	4.00	1.20
PL42 M. Ramirez PI/1154	2.50	.75
PL43 C. Delgado PI/1134	2.50	.75
PL44 Barry Bonds PI/1128	15.00	4.50
PL45 J.Giambi PI/1123	6.00	1.80
PL46 G.Sheffield PI/1081	2.50	.75
PL47 V.Guerrero PI/1074	6.00	1.80
PL48 F.Thomas PI/1061	6.00	1.80
PL49 S.Sosa PI/1040	10.00	3.00
PL50 Moises Alou PI/1039	2.50	.75
PL51 Jeff Bagwell PI/1039	4.00	1.20
PL52 N.Garciaparra PI/1033	10.00	3.00
PL53 R.Hidalgo PI/1027	2.50	.75
PL54 A.Rodriguez PI/1026	10.00	3.00
PL55 Brian Giles PI/1026	2.50	.75
PL56 Jeff Kent PI/1020	2.50	.75
PL57 Mike Piazza PI/1012	10.00	3.00
PL58 Troy Glaus PI/1008	4.00	1.20
PL59 E.Martinez PI/1002	4.00	1.20
PL60 J.Edmonds PI/994	4.00	1.20

2001 Donruss Recollection Autographs

Two different players signed cards for this program. Barry Bonds and Alex Rodriguez each signed 100 total cards. The Rodriguez card were randomly inserted in packs as exchange cards and the Bonds cards were issued as concessionary cards for collectors that redeemed a Bat Kings Autograph Bonds. According to representatives at Donruss Bonds refused to sign the memorabilia ba cards, but did approve signing these Recollection buybacks. The exchange deadline for the Rodriguez cards was May 1st, 2003 The Rodriguez exchange cards that went into packs were numbered RC1-RC4, but the actual autograph cards are not numbered as such. For simplicity's sake we have kept the original RC1 RC4 checklisting.

	Nm-Mt	Ex-Mt
BB1 Barry Bonds 88/25		
BB2 Barry Bonds 89/25		
BB3 Barry Bonds 90/50		
RC1 Alex Rodriguez 97 Don Hit/10		
RC2 Alex Rodriguez 98 Don/20		

Card	Nm-Mt	Ex-Mt
RC3 Alex Rodriguez 01 Retro/30	150.00	45.00
RC4 Alex Rodriguez 01 Don/40	150.00	45.00

2001 Donruss Rookie Reprints

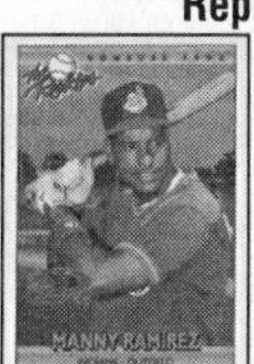

Randomly inserted into packs, this 40-card insert features reprinted Donruss rookie cards from the 80's-90s. Card backs carry a "RR" prefix. Please note that there was an error in production, and there are two number 39's, no number 40. Print runs are listed in our checklist.

	Nm-Mt	Ex-Mt
COMPLETE SET (40)	300.00	90.00
RR1 Cal Ripken/1982	25.00	7.50
RR2 Wade Boggs/1983	5.00	1.50
RR3 Tony Gwynn/1983	12.00	3.60
RR4 Ryne Sandberg/1983	15.00	4.50
RR5 Don Mattingly/1984	25.00	7.50
RR6 Joe Carter/1984	5.00	1.50
RR7 Roger Clemens/1985	20.00	6.00
RR8 Kirby Puckett/1985	8.00	2.40
RR9 Orel Hershiser/1985	5.00	1.50
RR10 A.Galarraga/1986	5.00	1.50
RR11 Jose Canseco/1986	8.00	2.40
RR12 Fred McGriff/1986	5.00	1.50
RR13 Paul O'Neill/1986	5.00	1.50
RR14 Mark McGwire/1987	20.00	6.00
RR15 Barry Bonds/1987	20.00	6.00
RR16 Kevin Brown/1987	5.00	1.50
RR17 David Cone/1987	5.00	1.50
RR18 R.Palmeiro/1987	5.00	1.50
RR19 Barry Larkin/1987	8.00	2.40
RR20 Bo Jackson/1987	8.00	2.40
RR21 Greg Maddux/1987	12.00	3.60
RR22 R. Alomar/1988	8.00	2.40
RR23 Mark Grace/1988	5.00	1.50
RR24 David Wells/1988	5.00	1.50
RR25 Tom Glavine/1988	5.00	1.50
RR26 Matt Williams/1988	5.00	1.50
RR27 Ken Griffey Jr./1989	12.00	3.60
RR28 R. Johnson/1989	8.00	2.40
RR29 Gary Sheffield/1989	5.00	1.50
RR30 Craig Biggio/1989	5.00	1.50
RR31 Curt Schilling/1989	5.00	1.50
RR32 Larry Walker/1990	5.00	1.50
RR33 B. Williams/1990	5.00	1.50
RR34 Sammy Sosa/1990	12.00	3.60
RR35 Juan Gonzalez/1990	8.00	2.40
RR36 David Justice/1990	5.00	1.50
RR37 I.Rodriguez/1991	8.00	2.40
RR38 Jeff Bagwell/1991	5.00	1.50
RR39 Jeff Kent/1992 UER Should have been RR40	5.00	1.50
RR39 M.Ramirez/1991	5.00	1.50

2001 Donruss Rookie Reprints Autograph

Randomly inserted into packs, this 26-card skip-numbered insert features autographed reprinted Donruss rookie cards from the 80's-90s. Card backs carry a "RR" prefix. Print runs are listed in our checklist. Nearly all of these cards packed out in the form of exchange cards - of which carried a May 1st, 2003 redemption deadline. Only autograph cards for Joe Carter, Tony Gwynn, David Justice, Greg Maddux and Ryne Sandberg actually made it into packs. Card RR24 was originally announced as a 1988 Donruss David Wells Reprint (with a print run of 88 copies) but due to contractual problems with the athlete the manufacturer substituted Diamondbacks outfielder Luis Gonzalez (reprinting 91 copies of his 1991 Donruss the Rookies RC).

	Nm-Mt	Ex-Mt
RR1 Cal Ripken/82	200.00	60.00
RR2 W.Boggs/83 EXCH	60.00	18.00
RR3 Tony Gwynn/83	100.00	30.00
RR4 Ryne Sandberg/83	150.00	45.00
RR5 D.Mattingly/84 EXCH	150.00	45.00
RR6 Joe Carter/84	40.00	12.00
RR7 R.Clemens/85 EXCH	150.00	45.00
RR8 K.Puckett/85 EXCH	80.00	24.00
RR9 O.Hershiser/85 EXCH	60.00	18.00
RR10 A.Galarraga/86 EXCH	40.00	12.00
RR15 B.Bonds/87 EXCH	250.00	75.00
RR16 K. Brown/87 EXCH	40.00	12.00
RR17 D.Cone/87 EXCH	40.00	12.00
RR18 R.Palmeiro/87 EXCH	80.00	24.00
RR20 B.Jackson/87 EXCH	120.00	36.00
RR21 Greg Maddux/87	150.00	45.00
RR22 R.Alomar/88 EXCH	80.00	24.00
RR24 D.Wells/88 EXCH	40.00	12.00
RR25 T.Glavine/88 EXCH	80.00	24.00
RR28 R.Johnson/89 EXCH	120.00	36.00
RR29 G.Sheffield/89 EXCH	60.00	18.00
RR31 C.Schilling/89 EXCH	60.00	18.00
RR35 J.Gonzalez/90 EXCH	80.00	24.00
RR36 David Justice/90	40.00	12.00
RR37 I.Rodriguez/91 EXCH	80.00	24.00
RR39 M.Ramirez/92 EXCH	60.00	18.00

2001 Donruss Rookies

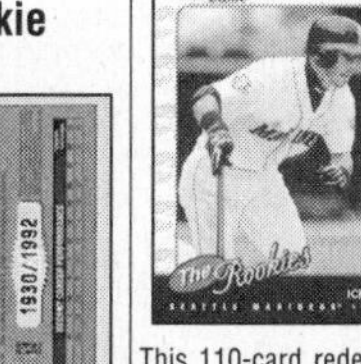
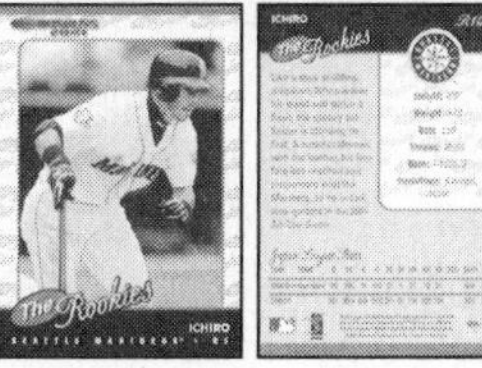

This 110-card redemption set was issued via coupons in the 2001 Donruss product. The coupons were issued in packs at a rate of 1:72 and were good for a complete factory sealed set of 2001 Donruss the Rookies. Collector's were to send the coupon along with $24.99 to Playoff by January 20th, 2002. The set also came with one additional Diamond King card (106-110).

	Nm-Mt	Ex-Mt
COMP.FACT.SET (106)	60.00	18.00
COMP.SET w/o SP's (105)	50.00	15.00
R1 Adam Dunn	.40	.12
R2 Ryan Drese RC	.40	.12
R3 Bud Smith RC	.40	.12
R4 Tsuyoshi Shinjo RC	1.50	.45
R5 Roy Oswalt	.75	.23
R6 Wilmy Caceres RC	.40	.12
R7 Willie Harris RC	.40	.12
R8 Andres Torres RC	.40	.12
R9 Brandon Knight RC	.40	.12
R10 Horacio Ramirez RC	1.25	.35
R11 Benito Baez RC	.40	.12
R12 Jeremy Affeldt RC	1.25	.35
R13 Ryan Jensen RC	.40	.12
R14 Casey Fossum RC	.40	.12
R15 Ramon Vazquez RC	.40	.12
R16 Dustan Mohr RC	.40	.12
R17 Saul Rivera RC	.40	.12
R18 Zach Day RC	.75	.23
R19 Erik Hiljus RC	.40	.12
R20 Cesar Crespo RC	.40	.12
R21 Wilson Guzman RC	.40	.12
R22 Travis Hafner RC	2.00	.60
R23 Grant Balfour RC	.40	.12
R24 Johnny Estrada RC	.75	.23
R25 Morgan Ensberg RC	1.50	.45
R26 Jack Wilson RC	.40	.12
R27 Aubrey Huff	.40	.12
R28 Endy Chavez RC	.40	.12
R29 Delvin James RC	.40	.12
R30 Michael Cuddyer	.40	.12
R31 Jason Michaels RC	.40	.12
R32 Martin Vargas RC	.40	.12
R33 Donaldo Mendez RC	.40	.12
R34 Jorge Julio RC	.40	.12
R35 T.Spooneybarger RC	.40	.12
R36 Kurt Ainsworth	.40	.12
R37 Josh Fogg RC	.40	.12
R38 Brian Reith RC	.40	.12
R39 Rick Bauer RC	.40	.12
R40 Tim Redding	.40	.12
R41 Erick Almonte RC	.40	.12
R42 Juan A.Pena RC	.40	.12
R43 Ken Harvey	.40	.12
R44 David Brous RC	.40	.12
R45 Kevin Olsen RC	.40	.12
R46 Henry Mateo RC	.40	.12
R47 Nick Neugebauer	.40	.12
R48 Mike Penney RC	.40	.12
R49 Jay Gibbons RC	1.50	.45
R50 Tim Christman RC	.40	.12
R51 B.Duckworth RC	.40	.12
R52 Brett Jodie RC	.40	.12
R53 Christian Parker RC	.40	.12
R54 Carlos Hernandez	.40	.12
R55 Brandon Larson RC	.40	.12
R56 Nick Punto RC	.40	.12
R57 Elpidio Guzman RC	.40	.12
R58 Joe Beimel RC	.40	.12
R59 Junior Spivey RC	1.25	.35
R60 Will Ohman RC	.40	.12
R61 Brandon Lyon RC	.40	.12
R62 Stubby Clapp RC	.40	.12
R63 J.Duchscherer RC	.40	.12
R64 Jimmy Rollins	.40	.12
R65 David Williams RC	.40	.12
R66 Craig Monroe RC	.40	.12
R67 Jose Acevedo RC	.40	.12
R68 Jason Jennings	.40	.12
R69 Josh Phelps	.40	.12
R70 Brian Roberts RC	.40	.12
R71 Claudio Vargas RC	.40	.12
R72 Adam Johnson	.40	.12
R73 Bart Miadich RC	.40	.12
R74 Juan Rivera	.40	.12
R75 Brad Voyles RC	.40	.12
R76 Nate Cornejo	.40	.12
R77 Juan Moreno RC	.40	.12
R78 Brian Rogers RC	.40	.12
R79 R.Rodriguez RC	.40	.12
R80 Geronimo Gil RC	.40	.12
R81 Joe Kennedy RC	.40	.12
R82 Kevin Joseph RC	.40	.12
R83 Josue Perez RC	.40	.12
R84 Victor Zambrano RC	.75	.23
R85 Josh Towers RC	.40	.12
R86 Mike Rivera RC	.40	.12
R87 Mark Prior RC	25.00	7.50
R88 Juan Cruz RC	.40	.12
R89 Dewon Brazelton RC	.75	.23
R90 Angel Berroa RC	2.50	.75
R91 Mark Teixeira RC	6.00	1.80
R92 Cody Ransom RC	.40	.12
R93 Angel Santos RC	.40	.12
R94 Corky Miller RC	.40	.12
R95 Brandon Berger RC	.40	.12
R96 Corey Patterson UPD	.40	.12
R97 A. Pujols UPD UER Homers and RBI Stats wrong	25.00	7.50
R98 Josh Beckett UPD	.75	.23
R99 C.C. Sabathia UPD	.40	.12
R100 A. Soriano UPD	.75	.23
R101 Ben Sheets UPD	.40	.12
R102 Rafael Soriano UPD	2.00	.60
R103 Wilson Betemit UPD	.40	.12
R104 Ichiro Suzuki UPD	10.00	3.00
R105 Jose Ortiz UPD	.40	.12

2001 Donruss Rookies Diamond Kings

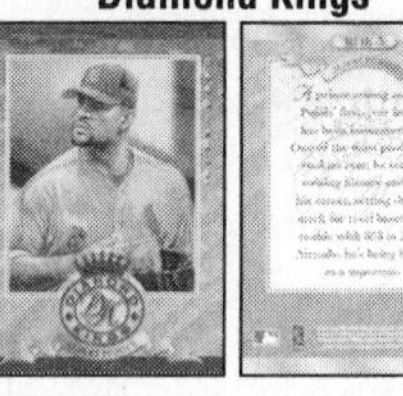

Inserted one per Donruss Rookies set, these five cards feature some of the leading 2001 rookies in a special Diamond King format.

	Nm-Mt	Ex-Mt
COMPLETE SET (5)	60.00	18.00
RDK-1 C.C. Sabathia DK	8.00	2.40
RDK-2 T.Shinjo DK	10.00	3.00
RDK-3 Albert Pujols DK	25.00	7.50
RDK-4 Roy Oswalt DK	10.00	3.00
RDK-5 Ichiro Suzuki DK	15.00	4.50

2002 Donruss Samples

Issued one per sealed copy of Beckett Baseball Card Monthly issue number 204, this is a partial parallel to the 2002 Leaf Set. Only the first 150 cards of this set were issued in this format.

Nm-Mt Ex-Mt

*SAMPLES: 1.5X TO 4X BASIC CARDS
ONE PER SEALED BBCM 204
*GOLD SAMPLES: 1.5X TO 4X LISTED PRICE

2002 Donruss

This 220 card set was issued in four card packs which had an SRP of $1.99 per pack and were issued 24 to a box and 20 boxes to a case. Cards numbered 151-200 featured leading rookie prospect and were inserted at stated odds of one in four. Card numbered 201-220 were Fan Club subset cards and were inserted at stated odds of one in eight.

	Nm-Mt	Ex-Mt
COMPLETE SET (220)	150.00	45.00
COMP.SET w/o SP'S (150)	25.00	7.50
COMMON CARD (1-150)	.30	.09
COMMON CARD (151-200)	3.00	.90
COMMON CARD (201-220)	2.00	.60
1 Alex Rodriguez	1.25	.35
2 Barry Bonds	2.00	.60
3 Derek Jeter	2.00	.60
4 Robert Fick	.30	.09
5 Juan Pierre	.30	.09
6 Torii Hunter	.30	.09
7 Todd Helton	.50	.15
8 Cal Ripken	2.50	.75
9 Manny Ramirez	.30	.09
10 Johnny Damon	.30	.09
11 Mike Piazza	1.25	.35
12 Nomar Garciaparra	1.25	.35
13 Pedro Martinez	.75	.23
14 Brian Giles	.30	.09
15 Albert Pujols	1.50	.45
16 Roger Clemens	1.50	.45
17 Sammy Sosa	1.25	.35
18 Vladimir Guerrero	.75	.23
19 Tony Gwynn	1.00	.30
20 Pat Burrell	.30	.09
21 Carlos Delgado	.30	.09
22 Tino Martinez	.50	.15
23 Jim Edmonds	.30	.09
24 Jason Giambi	.75	.23
25 Tom Glavine	.50	.15
26 Mark Grace	.50	.15
27 Tony Armas Jr.	.30	.09
28 Andruw Jones	.30	.09
29 Ben Sheets	.30	.09
30 Jeff Kent	.30	.09
31 Barry Larkin	.75	.23
32 Joe Mays	.30	.09
33 Mike Mussina	.75	.23
34 Hideo Nomo	.75	.23
35 Rafael Palmeiro	.50	.15
36 Scott Brosius	.30	.09
37 Scott Rolen	.50	.15
38 Gary Sheffield	.30	.09
39 Bernie Williams	.50	.15
40 Bob Abreu	.30	.09
41 Edgardo Alfonzo	.30	.09
42 C.C. Sabathia	.30	.09
43 Jeremy Giambi	.30	.09
44 Craig Biggio	.50	.15
45 Andres Galarraga	.30	.09
46 Edgar Martinez	.50	.15
47 Fred McGriff	.50	.15
48 Magglio Ordonez	.30	.09
49 Jim Thome	.75	.23
50 Matt Williams	.30	.09
51 Kerry Wood	.75	.23
52 Moises Alou	.30	.09
53 Brady Anderson	.30	.09
54 Garret Anderson	.30	.09
55 Juan Gonzalez	.75	.23
56 Bret Boone	.30	.09
57 Jose Cruz Jr.	.30	.09
58 Carlos Beltran	.30	.09
59 Adrian Beltre	.30	.09
60 Joe Kennedy	.30	.09
61 Lance Berkman	.30	.09
62 Kevin Brown	.30	.09
63 Tim Hudson	.30	.09
64 Jeromy Burnitz	.30	.09
65 Jarrod Washburn	.30	.09
66 Sean Casey	.30	.09
67 Eric Chavez	.30	.09
68 Bartolo Colon	.30	.09
69 Freddy Garcia	.30	.09
70 Jermaine Dye	.30	.09
71 Terrence Long	.30	.09
72 Cliff Floyd	.30	.09
73 Luis Gonzalez	.30	.09
74 Ichiro Suzuki	1.25	.35
75 Mike Hampton	.30	.09
76 Richard Hidalgo	.30	.09
77 Geoff Jenkins	.30	.09
78 Gabe Kapler	.30	.09
79 Ken Griffey Jr.	1.25	.35
80 Jason Kendall	.30	.09
81 Josh Towers	.30	.09
82 Ryan Klesko	.30	.09
83 Paul Konerko	.30	.09
84 Carlos Lee	.30	.09
85 Kenny Lofton	.30	.09
86 Josh Beckett	.50	.15
87 Raul Mondesi	.30	.09
88 Trot Nixon	.50	.15
89 John Olerud	.30	.09
90 Paul O'Neill	.50	.15
91 Chan Ho Park	.30	.09
92 Andy Pettitte	.50	.15
93 Jorge Posada	.50	.15
94 Mark Quinn	.30	.09
95 Aramis Ramirez	.30	.09
96 Curt Schilling	.50	.15
97 Richie Sexson	.30	.09
98 John Smoltz	.50	.15
99 Wilson Betemit	.30	.09
100 Shannon Stewart	.30	.09
101 Alfonso Soriano	.50	.15
102 Mike Sweeney	.30	.09
103 Miguel Tejada	.30	.09
104 Greg Vaughn	.30	.09
105 Robin Ventura	.30	.09
106 Jose Vidro	.30	.09
107 Larry Walker	.50	.15
108 Preston Wilson	.30	.09
109 Corey Patterson	.30	.09
110 Mark Mulder	.30	.09
111 Tony Clark	.30	.09
112 Roy Oswalt	.30	.09
113 Jimmy Rollins	.30	.09
114 Kazuhiro Sasaki	.30	.09
115 Barry Zito	.50	.15
116 Javier Vazquez	.30	.09
117 Mike Cameron	.30	.09
118 Phil Nevin	.30	.09
119 Bud Smith	.30	.09
120 Cristian Guzman	.30	.09
121 Al Leiter	.30	.09
122 Brad Radke	.30	.09
123 Bobby Higginson	.30	.09
124 Robert Person	.30	.09
125 Adam Dunn	.30	.09
126 Ben Grieve	.30	.09
127 Rafael Furcal	.30	.09
128 Jay Gibbons	.30	.09
129 Paul LoDuca	.30	.09
130 Wade Miller	.30	.09
131 Tsuyoshi Shinjo	.30	.09
132 Eric Milton	.30	.09
133 Rickey Henderson	.75	.23
134 Roberto Alomar	.75	.23
135 Darin Erstad	.30	.09
136 J.D. Drew	.30	.09
137 Shawn Green	.30	.09
138 Randy Johnson	.75	.23
139 Austin Kearns	.30	.09
140 Jose Canseco	.75	.23
141 Jeff Bagwell	.50	.15
142 Greg Maddux	1.25	.35
143 Mark Buehrle	.30	.09
144 Ivan Rodriguez	.75	.23
145 Frank Thomas	.75	.23
146 Rich Aurilia	.30	.09
147 Troy Glaus	.50	.15
148 Ryan Dempster	.30	.09
149 Chipper Jones	.75	.23
150 Matt Morris	.30	.09
151 Marlon Byrd RR	3.00	.90
152 Ben Howard RR RC	3.00	.90
153 Brandon Backe RR RC	3.00	.90
154 Jorge De La Rosa RR RC	3.00	.90
155 Corky Miller RR	3.00	.90
156 Dennis Tankersley RR	3.00	.90
157 Kyle Kane RR RC	3.00	.90
158 Justin Duchscherer RR	3.00	.90
159 Brian Mallette RR RC	3.00	.90
160 Chris Baker RR RC	3.00	.90
161 Jason Lane RR	3.00	.90
162 Hee Seop Choi RR	3.00	.90
163 Juan Cruz RR	3.00	.90
164 Rodrigo Rosario RR RC	3.00	.90
165 Matt Guerrier RR	3.00	.90
166 Anderson Machado RR RC	3.00	.90
167 Geronimo Gil RR	3.00	.90
168 Dewon Brazelton RR	3.00	.90
169 Mark Prior RR	15.00	4.50
170 Bill Hall RR	3.00	.90
171 Jorge Padilla RR RC	3.00	.90
172 Jose Cueto RR	3.00	.90
173 Allan Simpson RR RC	3.00	.90
174 Doug Devore RR RC	3.00	.90
175 Josh Pearce RR	3.00	.90
176 Angel Berroa RR	3.00	.90
177 Steve Bechler RR RC	3.00	.90
178 Antonio Perez RR	3.00	.90
179 Mark Teixeira RR	4.00	1.20
180 Erick Almonte RR	3.00	.90
181 Orlando Hudson RR	3.00	.90
182 Michael Rivera RR	3.00	.90
183 Raul Chavez RR RC	3.00	.90
184 Juan Pena RR	3.00	.90
185 Travis Hughes RR RC	3.00	.90
186 Ryan Ludwick RR	3.00	.90
187 Ed Rogers RR	3.00	.90
188 Andy Pratt RR RC	3.00	.90
189 Nick Neugebauer RR	3.00	.90
190 Tom Shearn RR RC	3.00	.90
191 Eric Cyr RR	3.00	.90
192 Victor Martinez RR	3.00	.90
193 Brandon Berger RR	3.00	.90
194 Erik Bedard RR	3.00	.90
195 Fernando Rodney RR	3.00	.90
196 Joe Thurston RR	3.00	.90
197 John Buck RR	3.00	.90
198 Jeff Deardorff RR	3.00	.90
199 Ryan Jamison RR	3.00	.90
200 Alfredo Amezaga RR	3.00	.90
201 Luis Gonzalez FC	2.00	.60
202 Roger Clemens FC	5.00	1.50
203 Barry Zito FC	2.00	.60
204 Bud Smith FC	2.00	.60
205 Magglio Ordonez FC	2.00	.60
206 Kerry Wood FC	2.50	.75
207 Freddy Garcia FC	2.00	.60
208 Adam Dunn FC	2.00	.60
209 Curt Schilling FC	2.00	.60
210 Lance Berkman FC	2.00	.60
211 Rafael Palmeiro FC	2.00	.60
212 Ichiro Suzuki FC	5.00	1.50
213 Bob Abreu FC	2.00	.60
214 Mark Mulder FC	2.00	.60
215 Roy Oswalt FC	2.00	.60
216 Mike Sweeney FC	2.00	.60
217 Paul LoDuca FC	2.00	.60
218 Aramis Ramirez FC	2.00	.60
219 Randy Johnson FC	2.50	.75
220 Albert Pujols FC	5.00	1.50

2002 Donruss Autographs

Inserted randomly in packs, these 19 cards feature signatures of players in the Fan Club subset. Since the cards have different stated print runs, we have listed those print runs in our checklist. Cards with a print run of 25 or fewer are not priced due to market scarcity.

	Nm-Mt	Ex-Mt
201 Luis Gonzalez FC/25		
202 Roger Clemens FC/25		
203 Barry Zito FC/200	40.00	12.00
204 Bud Smith FC/200	25.00	7.50
205 Magglio Ordonez FC/200	25.00	7.50
206 Kerry Wood FC/200	40.00	12.00
207 Freddy Garcia FC/200	25.00	7.50
208 Adam Dunn FC/200	40.00	12.00
209 Curt Schilling FC/25		
210 Lance Berkman FC/175	25.00	7.50
211 Rafael Palmeiro FC/25		
213 Bob Abreu FC/200	25.00	7.50
214 Mark Mulder FC/200	25.00	7.50
215 Roy Oswalt FC/200	25.00	7.50
216 Mike Sweeney FC/200	25.00	7.50
217 Paul LoDuca FC/200	25.00	7.50
218 Aramis Ramirez FC/200	25.00	7.50
219 Randy Johnson FC/10		
220 Albert Pujols FC/200	120.00	36.00

2002 Donruss Stat Line Career

Randomly inserted into packs, this is a parallel to the basic Donruss set. These cards feature cards printed on foil-board with silver holo-foil stamping. Each card has a stated print run to a unique career stat. Please note that is a card has a stated print run of 15 or less, no pricing is provided.

Nm-Mt Ex-Mt

*1-150 P/R b/wn 251-400: 2.5X TO 6X
*1-150 P/R b/wn 201-250: 2.5X TO 6X
*1-150 P/R b/wn 151-200: 3X TO 8X..
*1-150 P/R b/wn 121-150: 3X TO 8X..
*1-150 P/R b/wn 81-120: 4X TO 10X..
*1-150 P/R b/wn 66-80: 5X TO 12X....
*1-150 P/R b/wn 51-65: 6X TO 15X....
*1-150 P/R b/wn 36-50: 8X TO 20X....
*201-220 P/R b/wn 251-400 .5X TO 1.2X
*201-220 P/R b/wn 201-250 .6X TO 1.5X
*201-220 P/R b/wn 151-200 .75X TO 2X
*201-220 P/R b/wn 121-150 1X TO 2.5X
*201-220 P/R b/wn 51-65 2X TO 5X...

	Nm-Mt	Ex-Mt
151 Marlon Byrd RR/232	2.50	.75
152 Ben Howard RR/283	2.00	.60
153 Brandon Backe RR/94	5.00	1.50
154 Jorge De La Rosa RR/54	8.00	2.40
155 Corky Miller RR/184	3.00	.90
156 Dennis Tankersley RR/253	2.00	.60
157 Kyle Kane RR/179	3.00	.90
158 Justin Duchscherer RR/11		
159 Brian Mallette RR/273	2.00	.60
160 Chris Baker RR/270	2.00	.60
161 Jason Lane RR/302	2.00	.60
162 Hee Seop Choi RR/286	2.00	.60
163 Juan Cruz RR/322	2.00	.60
164 Rodrigo Rosario RR/313	2.00	.60
165 Matt Guerrier RR/280	2.00	.60
166 Anderson Machado RR/252	2.00	.60
167 Geronimo Gil RR/293	2.00	.60
168 Dewon Brazelton RR/335	2.00	.60
169 Mark Prior RR/303	10.00	3.00
170 Bill Hall RR/373	2.00	.60
171 Jorge Padilla RR/273	2.00	.60
172 Jose Cueto RR/156	3.00	.90
173 Allan Simpson RR/204	2.50	.75
174 Doug Devore RR/287	2.00	.60
175 Josh Pearce RR/315	2.00	.60
176 Angel Berroa RR/268	2.00	.60
177 Steve Bechler RR/25		
178 Antonio Perez RR/143	4.00	1.20
179 Mark Teixeira RR/165	5.00	1.50
180 Erick Almonte RR/4		
181 Orlando Hudson RR/283	2.00	.60
182 Michael Rivera RR/333	2.00	.60
183 Raul Chavez RR/253	2.00	.60
184 Juan Pena RR/293	2.00	.60
185 Travis Hughes RR/174	3.00	.90

186 Ryan Ludwick RR/264......... 2.00 .60
187 Ed Rogers RR/270............... 2.00 .60
188 Andy Pratt RR/203............... 2.50 .75
189 Nick Neugebauer RR/11..............
190 Tom Shearn RR/251............. 2.00 .60
191 Eric Cyr RR/161................. 3.00 .90
192 Victor Martinez RR/305........ 2.00 .60
193 Brandon Berger RR/313....... 2.00 .60
194 Erik Bedard RR/279............. 2.00 .60
195 Fernando Rodney RR/309.... 2.00 .60
196 Joe Thurston RR/284........... 2.00 .60
197 John Buck RR/271.............. 2.00 .60
198 Jeff Deardorff RR/201.......... 2.50 .75
199 Ryan Jamison RR/273.......... 2.00 .60
200 Alfredo Amezaga RR/290..... 2.00 .60

2002 Donruss Stat Line Season

Randomly inserted into packs, this is a parallel to the basic Donruss set. These cards feature cards printed on foil-board with silver holo-foil stamping. Each card has a stated print run to a unique seasonal stat. Please note that is a card has a stated print run of 15 or less, no pricing is provided.

Nm-Mt Ex-Mt
*1-150 P/R b/wn 151-200: 3X TO 8X..
*1-150 P/R b/wn 121-150: 3X TO 8X..
*1-150 P/R b/wn 81-120: 4X TO 10X..
*1-150 P/R b/wn 66-80: 5X TO 12X....
*1-150 P/R b/wn 51-65: 6X TO 15X....
*1-150 P/R b/wn 36-50: 8X TO 20X....
*1-150 P/R b/wn 26-35: 10X TO 25X..
*201-220 P/R b/wn 81-120 1.25X TO 3X
*201-220 P/R b/wn 66-80 1.5X TO 4X
*201-220 P/R b/wn 51-65 2X TO 5X...
*201-220 P/R b/wn 36-50 2.5X TO 6X
*201-220 P/R b/wn 26-35 3X TO 8X...
151 Marlon Byrd RR/89............ 5.00 1.50
152 Ben Howard RR/29............ 12.00 3.60
153 Brandon Backe RR/39......... 10.00 3.00
154 Jorge De La Rosa RR/32.... 12.00 3.60
155 Corky Miller RR/7..................
156 Dennis Tankersley RR/30... 12.00 3.60
157 Kyle Kane RR/75............... 6.00 1.80
158 Justin Duchscherer RR/20..........
159 Brian Mallette RR/94.......... 5.00 1.50
160 Chris Baker RR/121........... 4.00 1.20
161 Jason Lane RR/38.............. 10.00 3.00
162 Hee Seop Choi RR/45......... 10.00 3.00
163 Juan Cruz RR/39............... 10.00 3.00
164 Rodrigo Rosario RR/131...... 4.00 1.20
165 Matt Guerrier RR/118.......... 5.00 1.50
166 Anderson Machado RR/36. 10.00 3.00
167 Geronimo Gil RR/17....................
168 Dewon Brazelton RR/13..............
169 Mark Prior RR/14......................
170 Bill Hall RR/65.................... 8.00 2.40
171 Jorge Padilla RR/66........... 6.00 1.80
172 Jose Cueto RR/62............... 8.00 2.40
173 Allan Simpson RR/77.......... 6.00 1.80
174 Doug Devore RR/74............ 6.00 1.80
175 Josh Pearce RR/132............ 4.00 1.20
176 Angel Berroa RR/63............ 8.00 2.40
177 Steve Bechler RR/135.......... 4.00 1.20
178 Antonio Perez RR/143.......... 4.00 1.20
179 Mark Teixeira RR/20....................
180 Erick Almonte RR/8.....................
181 Orlando Hudson RR/79........ 6.00 1.80
182 Michael Rivera RR/4....................
183 Raul Chavez RR/5.......................
184 Juan Pena RR/106.............. 5.00 1.50
185 Travis Hughes RR/86........... 5.00 1.50
186 Ryan Ludwick RR/103.......... 5.00 1.50
187 Ed Rogers RR/54................ 8.00 2.40
188 Andy Pratt RR/132.............. 4.00 1.20
189 Nick Neugebauer RR/5..................
190 Tom Shearn RR/136............. 4.00 1.20
191 Eric Cyr RR/131................. 4.00 1.20
192 Victor Martinez RR/57.......... 8.00 2.40
193 Brandon Berger RR/16..................
194 Erik Bedard RR/137............. 4.00 1.20
195 Fernando Rodney RR/52...... 8.00 2.40
196 Joe Thurston RR/46........... 10.00 3.00
197 John Buck RR/73................ 6.00 1.80
198 Jeff Deardorff RR/100.......... 5.00 1.50
199 Ryan Jamison RR/95............ 5.00 1.50
200 Alfredo Amezaga RR/37..... 10.00 3.00

2002 Donruss All-Time Diamond Kings

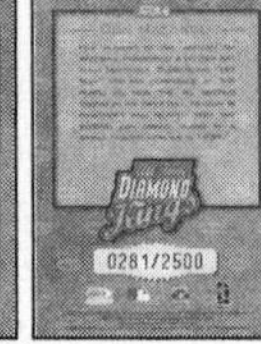

Randomly inserted in packs, these 10 cards feature legendary baseball superstars reproduced on conventional stock with bronze foil. These cards have a stated print run of 2,500 copies.

Nm-Mt Ex-Mt
*STUDIO: 1X TO 2.5X BASIC ALL-TIME DK
STUDIO PRINT RUN 250 SERIAL #'d SETS
1 Ted Williams UER............. 25.00 7.50
Rogers Hornsby also won the triple crown twice
2 Cal Ripken.......................... 30.00 9.00
3 Lou Gehrig.......................... 15.00 4.50
4 Babe Ruth.......................... 25.00 7.50
5 Roberto Clemente................ 20.00 6.00
6 Don Mattingly...................... 25.00 7.50
7 Kirby Puckett...................... 10.00 3.00
8 Stan Musial........................ 15.00 4.50
9 Yogi Berra.......................... 10.00 3.00
10 Ernie Banks...................... 10.00 3.00

2002 Donruss Bat Kings

Randomly inserted in packs, these five cards feature a mix of active and retired superstars

along with a sliver of each player's game-used bat. The active players have a stated print run of 250 copies while the retired players have a stated print run of 125 copies.

Nm-Mt Ex-Mt
*STUDIO 1-3: .75X TO 2X BASIC BAT KING
STUDIO 1-3 PRINT RUN 50 SERIAL #'d SETS
STUDIO 4-5 PRINT RUN 25 SERIAL #'d SETS
RANDOM INSERTS IN PACKS...........
1 Jason Giambi....................... 25.00 7.50
2 Alex Rodriguez..................... 25.00 7.50
3 Mike Piazza......................... 25.00 7.50
4 Roberto Clemente/125........ 100.00 30.00
5 Babe Ruth/125................... 200.00 60.00

2002 Donruss Diamond Kings Inserts

Randomly inserted in packs, these 20 cards feature leading players with silver foil stamping and stated sequential serial numbering to 2500.

Nm-Mt Ex-Mt
*STUDIO: .75X TO 2X BASIC DK'S.....
STUDIO PRINT RUN 250 SERIAL #'d SETS
RANDOM INSERTS IN PACKS...........
1 Nomar Garciaparra.............. 12.00 3.60
2 Shawn Green...................... 10.00 3.00
3 Randy Johnson.................... 10.00 3.00
4 Derek Jeter........................ 20.00 6.00
5 Carlos Delgado................... 10.00 3.00
6 Roger Clemens.................... 15.00 4.50
7 Jeff Bagwell........................ 10.00 3.00
8 Vladimir Guerrero................ 10.00 3.00
9 Luis Gonzalez...................... 10.00 3.00
10 Mike Piazza...................... 12.00 3.60
11 Ichiro Suzuki..................... 12.00 3.60
12 Pedro Martinez.................. 10.00 3.00
13 Todd Helton...................... 10.00 3.00
14 Sammy Sosa..................... 12.00 3.60
15 Ivan Rodriguez................... 10.00 3.00
16 Barry Bonds...................... 20.00 6.00
17 Albert Pujols...................... 15.00 4.50
18 Jim Thome......................... 10.00 3.00
19 Alex Rodriguez................... 12.00 3.60
20 Jason Giambi..................... 10.00 3.00

2002 Donruss Elite Series

Randomly inserted in packs, these 20 cards feature some of today's most storied performers. These cards are printed on metalized film board and are sequentially numbered to 2,500.

Nm-Mt Ex-Mt
1 Barry Bonds........................ 12.00 3.60
2 Lance Berkman..................... 4.00 1.20
3 Jason Giambi....................... 5.00 1.50
4 Nomar Garciaparra.............. 8.00 2.40
5 Curt Schilling...................... 4.00 1.20
6 Vladimir Guerrero................. 5.00 1.50
7 Shawn Green....................... 4.00 1.20
8 Jeff Bagwell......................... 4.00 1.20
9 Troy Glaus.......................... 4.00 1.20
10 Manny Ramirez.................. 4.00 1.20
11 Eric Chavez....................... 4.00 1.20
12 Carlos Delgado.................. 4.00 1.20
13 Mike Sweeney.................... 4.00 1.20
14 Todd Helton....................... 4.00 1.20
15 Luis Gonzalez..................... 4.00 1.20
16 Enos Slaughter LGD............ 4.00 1.20
17 Frank Robinson LGD........... 4.00 1.20
18 Bob Gibson LGD................. 4.00 1.20
19 Warren Spahn LGD............. 4.00 1.20
20 Whitey Ford LGD................ 4.00 1.20

2002 Donruss Elite Series Signatures

Randomly inserted in packs, these 18 cards feature players who signed cards for the 2002 Donruss Elite product. These cards have different print runs and we have notated that information in our checklist.

Nm-Mt Ex-Mt
2 Lance Berkman/25.........................
3 Jason Giambi/25...........................
4 Nomar Garciaparra/25...................
5 Curt Schilling/25...........................
6 Vladimir Guerrero/25.....................
7 Shawn Green/25............................
8 Jeff Bagwell/25.............................
9 Troy Glaus/25...............................
10 Manny Ramirez/25.......................
11 Eric Chavez/25............................
13 Mike Sweeney/25.........................
14 Todd Helton/25............................
15 Luis Gonzalez/25.........................
16 Enos Slaughter LGD/250...... 40.00 12.00
17 Frank Robinson LGD/250..... 40.00 12.00
18 Bob Gibson LGD/250.......... 40.00 12.00
19 Warren Spahn LGD/250....... 60.00 18.00
20 Whitey Ford LGD/250.......... 40.00 12.00

2002 Donruss Jersey Kings

Randomly inserted in packs, these 15 cards feature game-worn jersey swatches of a mix all-time greats and active superstars. The active players have a stated prinrt run of 250 serial numbered sets while the retired players have a stated print run of 125 sets.

Nm-Mt Ex-Mt
*STUDIO 1-12: .75X TO 2X BASIC JSY KINGS
STUDIO 1-12 PRINT RUN 50 SERIAL #'d SETS
STUDIO 13-15 PRINT RUN 25 SERIAL #'d SETS..............................
STUDIO 13-15 TOO SCARCE TO PRICE
RANDOM INSERTS IN PACKS..........
1 Alex Rodriguez.................... 25.00 7.50
2 Jason Giambi...................... 25.00 7.50
3 Carlos Delgado................... 15.00 4.50
4 Barry Bonds....................... 40.00 12.00
5 Randy Johnson................... 25.00 7.50
6 Jim Thome......................... 25.00 7.50
7 Shawn Green..................... 15.00 4.50
8 Pedro Martinez................... 25.00 7.50
9 Jeff Bagwell....................... 25.00 7.50
10 Vladimir Guerrero.............. 25.00 7.50
11 Ivan Rodriguez.................. 25.00 7.50
12 Nomar Garciaparra............ 25.00 7.50
13 Don Mattingly/125............. 60.00 18.00
14 Ted Williams/125............. 150.00 45.00
15 Lou Gehrig/125............... 200.00 60.00

2002 Donruss Longball Leaders

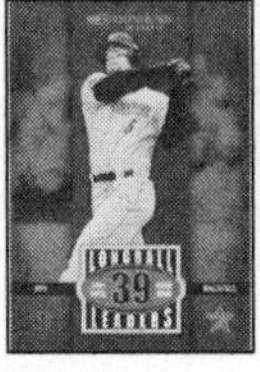

Randomly inserted in packs, these 20 cards feature the majors most powerful hitters and they are featured on metalized film board and have a stated print run of 1,000 sequentially numbered sets.

Nm-Mt Ex-Mt
1 Barry Bonds....................... 20.00 6.00
2 Sammy Sosa...................... 12.00 3.60
3 Luis Gonzalez..................... 4.00 1.20
4 Alex Rodriguez................... 12.00 3.60
5 Shawn Green...................... 4.00 1.20
6 Todd Helton....................... 5.00 1.50
7 Jim Thome......................... 8.00 2.40
8 Rafael Palmeiro.................. 5.00 1.50
9 Richie Sexson..................... 4.00 1.20
10 Troy Glaus........................ 5.00 1.50
11 Manny Ramirez.................. 4.00 1.20
12 Phil Nevin......................... 4.00 1.20
13 Jeff Bagwell...................... 5.00 1.50
14 Carlos Delgado.................. 4.00 1.20
15 Jason Giambi..................... 8.00 2.40
16 Chipper Jones.................... 8.00 2.40
17 Larry Walker...................... 5.00 1.50
18 Albert Pujols.................... 15.00 4.50
19 Brian Giles........................ 4.00 1.20
20 Bret Boone........................ 4.00 1.20

2002 Donruss Production Line

Randomly inserted in packs, these 60 cards feature the msot productive sluggers in three categories: On-Base Percentage, Slugging Percentage and OPS. Cards numbered 1-20 feature On-Base Percentage, while cards numbered 21-40 feature Slugging Percentage and cards numbered 41-60 feature OPS. Since all the cards have different stated print runs, we have listed that information next to the card in our checklist.

Nm-Mt Ex-Mt
COMMON OBP (1-20)............... 4.00 1.20
COMMON SLG (21-40).............. 3.00 .90
COMMON OPS (41-60).............. 2.50 .75
*DIE CUT OBP 1-20: .75X TO 2X BASIC PL
*DIE CUT SLG 21-40: 1X TO 2.5X BASIC PL
*DIE CUT OPS 41-60: 1.25X TO 3X BASIC PL
DIE CUT PRINT RUN 100 SERIAL #'d SETS
DC's ARE 1ST 100 #'d OF EACH PLAYER
RANDOM INSERTS IN PACKS..........
1 Barry Bonds OBP/415........... 25.00 7.50
2 Jason Giambi OBP/377.......... 10.00 3.00
3 Larry Walker OBP/349............ 6.00 1.80
4 Sammy Sosa OBP/337........... 15.00 4.50
5 Todd Helton OBP/332............. 6.00 1.80
6 Lance Berkman OBP/330......... 4.00 1.20
7 Luis Gonzalez OBP/329........... 4.00 1.20
8 Chipper Jones OBP/327......... 10.00 3.00
9 Edgar Martinez OBP/323......... 6.00 1.80
10 Gary Sheffield OBP/317.......... 4.00 1.20
11 Jim Thome OBP/316............ 10.00 3.00
12 Roberto Alomar OBP/315..... 10.00 3.00
13 J.D. Drew OBP/314................ 4.00 1.20
14 Jim Edmonds OBP/310........... 4.00 1.20
15 Carlos Delgado OBP/308........ 4.00 1.20
16 Manny Ramirez OBP/305....... 4.00 1.20
17 Brian Giles OBP/304.............. 4.00 1.20
18 Albert Pujols OBP/303.......... 20.00 6.00
19 John Olerud OBP/301............ 4.00 1.20
20 Alex Rodriguez OBP/299...... 15.00 4.50
21 Barry Bonds SLG/763.......... 20.00 6.00
22 Sammy Sosa SLG/637.......... 12.00 3.60
23 Luis Gonzalez SLG/588........... 3.00 .90
24 Todd Helton SLG/585............. 5.00 1.50
25 Larry Walker SLG/562............ 5.00 1.50
26 Jason Giambi SLG/560........... 8.00 2.40
27 Jim Thome SLG/524............... 8.00 2.40
28 Alex Rodriguez SLG/522....... 12.00 3.60
29 Lance Berkman SLG/520......... 3.00 .90
30 J.D. Drew SLG/513................. 3.00 .90
31 Albert Pujols SLG/510.......... 15.00 4.50
32 Manny Ramirez SLG/509........ 3.00 .90
33 Chipper Jones SLG/505.......... 8.00 2.40
34 Shawn Green SLG/498............ 3.00 .90
35 Brian Giles SLG/490............... 3.00 .90
36 Juan Gonzalez SLG/490.......... 8.00 2.40
37 Phil Nevin SLG/488................ 3.00 .90
38 Gary Sheffield SLG/483.......... 3.00 .90
39 Bret Boone SLG/478............... 3.00 .90
40 Cliff Floyd SLG/478................ 3.00 .90
41 Barry Bonds OPS/1278......... 15.00 4.50
42 Sammy Sosa OPS/1074........ 10.00 3.00
43 Jason Giambi OPS/1037......... 6.00 1.80
44 Todd Helton OPS/1017........... 4.00 1.20
45 Luis Gonzalez OPS/1017......... 2.50 .75
46 Larry Walker OPS/1011........... 4.00 1.20
47 Lance Berkman OPS/950......... 2.50 .75
48 Jim Thome OPS/940............... 6.00 1.80
49 Chipper Jones OPS/932.......... 6.00 1.80
50 J.D. Drew OPS/927................. 2.50 .75
51 Alex Rodriguez OPS/921....... 10.00 3.00
52 Manny Ramirez OPS/914........ 2.50 .75
53 Albert Pujols OPS/913........... 12.00 3.60
54 Gary Sheffield OPS/900.......... 2.50 .75
55 Brian Giles OPS/894............... 2.50 .75
56 Phil Nevin OPS/876................ 2.50 .75
57 Jim Edmonds OPS/874........... 2.50 .75
58 Shawn Green OPS/870........... 2.50 .75
59 Cliff Floyd OPS/868................ 2.50 .75
60 Edgar Martinez OPS/866......... 4.00 1.20

2002 Donruss Recollection Autographs

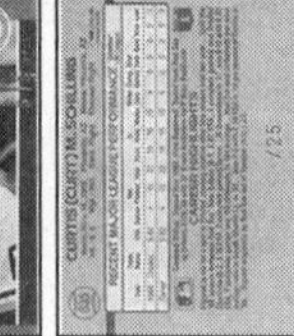

Randomly inserted in packs, these 47 cards feature players who signed repurchased copies of their original cards for inclusion in the 2002 Donruss set. Since each player signed a different amount of cards, we have noted that information in our checklist. Please note that due to market scarcity, not all cards can be priced.

Nm-Mt Ex-Mt
8 Gary Carter 87/100............... 40.00 12.00
9 Gary Carter 89/100............... 40.00 12.00
11 Joe Carter 87/45........................
13 Andre Dawson 81/50...................
14 Andre Dawson 83/50...................
16 Andre Dawson 87/45...................
17 Dennis Eckersley 81/45...............
24 Steve Garvey 87/75............. 40.00 12.00
46 Tom Seaver 87/60.......................
47 Don Sutton 87/200.............. 25.00 7.50

2002 Donruss Rookie Year Materials Bats

Randomly inserted into packs, these four cards feature a sliver of a game-used bat from the player's rookie season which includes silver holo-foil and are sequentially numbered a stated print run of 250 sequentially numbered sets.

Nm-Mt Ex-Mt
1 Barry Bonds........................ 60.00 18.00
2 Cal Ripken.......................... 80.00 24.00
3 Kirby Puckett...................... 40.00 12.00
4 Johnny Bench..................... 40.00 12.00

2002 Donruss Rookie Year Materials Bats ERA

These cards parallel the "Rookie Year Material Bats" insert set. These cards have gold holo-foil and have a stated print run sequentially numbered to the player's debut year. Since those years are all different, we have notated that information in our checklist.

Nm-Mt Ex-Mt
1 Barry Bonds/86.................. 120.00 36.00
2 Cal Ripken/81.................... 150.00 45.00
3 Kirby Puckett/84.................. 80.00 24.00
4 Johnny Bench/68.................. 80.00 24.00

2002 Donruss Rookie Year Materials Jersey

Randomly inserted into packs, these four cards feature a swatch of a game-used jersey from the player's rookie season which includes silver holo-foil and are sequentially numbered a stated print run of either 250 or 50 sequentially numbered sets. The active players have the print run of 250 while the retired players have the print run of 50 sets.

Nm-Mt Ex-Mt
1 Nomar Garciaparra.............. 50.00 15.00
2 Randy Johnson.................... 40.00 12.00
3 Ivan Rodriguez.................... 40.00 12.00
4 Vladimir Guerrero................. 40.00 12.00
5 Stan Musial/50.............................
6 Yogi Berra/50.................... 100.00 30.00

2002 Donruss Rookie Year Materials Jersey Numbers

These cards parallel the "Rookie Year Material Jerseys" insert set. These cards have gold holo-foil and have a stated print run sequentially numbered to the player's jersey number his rookie season. We have notated that specific stated print information in our checklist.

Nm-Mt Ex-Mt
1 Nomar Garciaparra/5......................
2 Randy Johnson/51.........................
3 Ivan Rodriguez/7..........................
4 Vladimir Guerrero/27.....................
5 Stan Musial/6...............................
6 Yogi Berra/35...............................

2002 Donruss Rookies

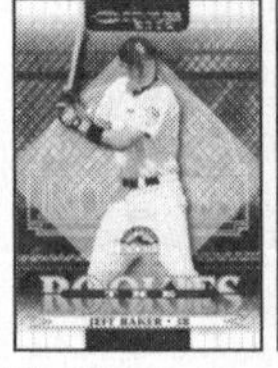

This 110 card set was released in December, 2002. These cards were issued in five card packs which came 24 packs to a box and 16 boxes to a case with an SRP of $3.29 per pack. This set features the top rookies and prospects of the 2002 season.

Nm-Mt Ex-Mt
COMPLETE SET (110)............. 25.00 7.50
1 Kazuhisa Ishii RC.................. 1.50 .45
2 P.J. Bevis RC........................ .40 .12
3 Jason Simontacchi RC............ .40 .12
4 John Lackey.......................... .25 .07
5 Travis Driskill RC................... .40 .12
6 Carl Sadler RC....................... .40 .12
7 Tim Kalita RC......................... .40 .12
8 Nelson Castro RC................... .40 .12
9 Francis Beltran RC................. .40 .12
10 So Taguchi RC..................... .60 .18
11 Ryan Bukvich RC.................. .40 .12
12 Brian Fitzgerald RC............... .40 .12
13 Kevin Frederick RC............... .40 .12
14 Chone Figgins RC................. .40 .12
15 Marlon Byrd......................... .40 .12
16 Ron Calloway RC.................. .40 .12
17 Jason Lane........................... .25 .07
18 Satoru Komiyama RC............ .40 .12
19 John Ennis RC...................... .40 .12
20 Juan Brito RC....................... .40 .12
21 Gustavo Chacin RC............... .40 .12
22 Josh Bard RC....................... .40 .12
23 Brett Myers.......................... .40 .12
24 Mike Smith RC...................... .40 .12
25 Eric Hinske.......................... .25 .07
26 Jake Peavy.......................... .40 .12
27 Todd Donovan RC................. .40 .12
28 Luis Ugueto RC.................... .40 .12
29 Corey Thurman RC............... .40 .12
30 Takahito Nomura RC............. .40 .12
31 Andy Shibilo RC................... .40 .12
32 Mike Crudale RC................... .40 .12
33 Earl Snyder RC.................... .40 .12
34 Brian Tallet RC..................... .60 .18
35 Miguel Asencio RC................ .40 .12
36 Felix Escalona RC................. .40 .12

Card	Nm-Mt	Ex-Mt
37 Drew Henson	.40	.12
38 Steve Kent RC	.40	.12
39 Rene Reyes RC	.40	.12
40 Edwin Almonte RC	.40	.12
41 Chris Snelling RC	1.25	.35
42 Franklyn German RC	.40	.12
43 Jeriome Robertson RC	.40	.12
44 Colin Young RC	.40	.12
45 Jeremy Lambert RC	.40	.12
46 Kirk Saarloos RC	.40	.12
47 Matt Childers RC	.40	.12
48 Justin Wayne	.25	.07
49 Jose Valverde RC	.60	.18
50 Wily Mo Pena	.25	.07
51 Victor Alvarez RC	.40	.12
52 Julius Matos RC	.40	.12
53 Aaron Cook RC	.40	.12
54 Jeff Austin RC	.40	.12
55 Adrian Burnside RC	.40	.12
56 Brandon Puffer RC	.40	.12
57 Jeremy Hill RC	.40	.12
58 Jaime Cerda RC	.40	.12
59 Aaron Guiel RC	.40	.12
60 Ron Chiavacci	.25	.07
61 Kevin Cash RC	.40	.12
62 Elio Serrano RC	.40	.12
63 Julio Mateo RC	.40	.12
64 Cam Esslinger RC	.40	.12
65 Ken Huckaby RC	.40	.12
66 Will Nieves RC	.40	.12
67 Luis Martinez RC	.40	.12
68 Scotty Layfield RC	.40	.12
69 Jeremy Guthrie RC	1.50	.45
70 Hansel Izquierdo RC	.40	.12
71 Shane Nance RC	.40	.12
72 Jeff Baker RC	1.50	.45
73 Cliff Bartosh RC	.40	.12
74 Mitch Wylie RC	.40	.12
75 Oliver Perez RC	.60	.18
76 Matt Thornton RC	.40	.12
77 John Foster RC	.40	.12
78 Joe Borchard	.40	.12
79 Eric Junge RC	.40	.12
80 Jorge Sosa RC	.40	.12
81 Runelvys Hernandez RC	.40	.12
82 Kevin Mench	.25	.07
83 Ben Kozlowski RC	.40	.12
84 Trey Hodges RC	.40	.12
85 Reed Johnson RC	.60	.18
86 Eric Eckenstahler RC	.40	.12
87 Franklin Nunez RC	.40	.12
88 Victor Martinez	.40	.12
89 Kevin Gryboski RC	.40	.12
90 Jason Jennings	.25	.07
91 Jim Rushford RC	.40	.12
92 Jeremy Ward RC	.40	.12
93 Adam Walker RC	.40	.12
94 Freddy Sanchez RC	.40	.12
95 Wilson Valdez RC	.40	.12
96 Lee Gardner RC	.40	.12
97 Eric Good RC	.40	.12
98 Hank Blalock	.75	.23
99 Mark Corey RC	.40	.12
100 Jason Davis RC	1.00	.30
101 Mike Gonzalez RC	.40	.12
102 David Ross RC	.40	.12
103 Tyler Yates RC	1.00	.30
104 Cliff Lee RC	1.00	.30
105 Mike Moriarty RC	.40	.12
106 Josh Hancock RC	.40	.12
107 Jason Beverlin RC	.40	.12
108 Clay Condrey RC	.40	.12
109 Shawn Sedlacek RC	.40	.12
110 Sean Burroughs	.40	.12

2002 Donruss Rookies Autographs

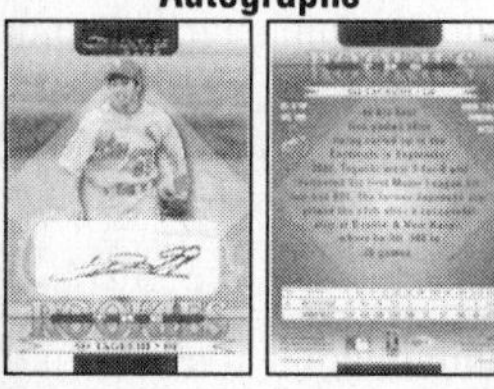

Randomly inserted into packs, this is a partial parallel to the Donruss Rookies set. Each players signed between 15 and 100 cards for insertion in this product and cards with a stated print run of 25 or fewer are not priced due to market scarcity.

Card	Nm-Mt	Ex-Mt
1 Kazuhisa Ishii/25		
2 P.J. Bevis/50	25.00	7.50
7 Tim Kalita/25		
9 Francis Beltran/100	15.00	4.50
10 So Taguchi/15		
13 Kevin Frederick/100	15.00	4.50
14 Chone Figgins/100	15.00	4.50
15 Marlon Byrd/100	15.00	4.50
17 Jason Lane/100	15.00	4.50
18 Satoru Komiyama/25		
19 John Ennis/100	15.00	4.50
22 Josh Bard/100	15.00	4.50
25 Eric Hinske/100	15.00	4.50
28 Luis Ugueto/100	15.00	4.50
29 Corey Thurman/100	15.00	4.50
30 Takahito Nomura/100	40.00	12.00
33 Earl Snyder/100	15.00	4.50
34 Brian Tallet/100	20.00	6.00
36 Felix Escalona/25		
37 Drew Henson/50	40.00	12.00
39 Rene Reyes/50	25.00	7.50
40 Edwin Almonte/50	25.00	7.50
41 Chris Snelling/50		
42 Franklyn German/100	15.00	4.50
45 Jeremy Lambert/100	15.00	4.50
46 Kirk Saarloos/50	15.00	4.50
47 Matt Childers/100	15.00	4.50
50 Wily Mo Pena/100	15.00	4.50
51 Victor Alvarez/100	15.00	4.50
61 Kevin Cash/100	15.00	4.50
62 Elio Serrano/100	15.00	4.50
64 Cam Esslinger/100	15.00	4.50
69 Jeremy Guthrie/100	40.00	12.00
71 Shane Nance/100	15.00	4.50
72 Jeff Baker/100	40.00	12.00
75 Oliver Perez/25		
76 Matt Thornton/100	15.00	4.50
78 Joe Borchard/100	15.00	4.50
79 Eric Junge/25		
82 Kevin Mench/100	15.00	4.50
83 Ben Kozlowski/100	15.00	4.50
84 Trey Hodges/100	15.00	4.50
85 Reed Johnson/100	20.00	6.00
88 Victor Martinez/100	15.00	4.50
90 Jason Jennings/100	15.00	4.50
95 Wilson Valdez/100	15.00	4.50
97 Eric Good/100	15.00	4.50
98 Hank Blalock/100	25.00	7.50
104 Cliff Lee/100	40.00	12.00
110 Sean Burroughs/50	25.00	7.50

2002 Donruss Rookies Crusade

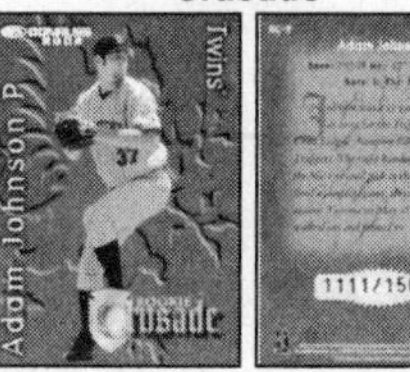

Randomly inserted into packs, these 50 cards, which were printed on metalized holo-foil board, were printed to a stated print run of 1500 serial numbered sets.

Card	Nm-Mt	Ex-Mt
1 Corky Miller	4.00	1.20
2 Jack Cust	4.00	1.20
3 Erik Bedard	4.00	1.20
4 Andres Torres	4.00	1.20
5 Geronimo Gil	4.00	1.20
6 Rafael Soriano	4.00	1.20
7 Johnny Estrada	4.00	1.20
8 Steve Bechler	4.00	1.20
9 Adam Johnson	4.00	1.20
10 So Taguchi	4.00	1.20
11 Dee Brown	4.00	1.20
12 Kevin Frederick	4.00	1.20
13 Allan Simpson	4.00	1.20
14 Ricardo Rodriguez	4.00	1.20
15 Jason Hart	4.00	1.20
16 Matt Childers	4.00	1.20
17 Jason Jennings	4.00	1.20
18 Anderson Machado	4.00	1.20
19 Fernando Rodney	4.00	1.20
20 Brandon Larson	4.00	1.20
21 Satoru Komiyama	4.00	1.20
22 Francis Beltran	4.00	1.20
23 Joe Thurston	4.00	1.20
24 Josh Pearce	4.00	1.20
25 Carlos Hernandez	4.00	1.20
26 Ben Howard	4.00	1.20
27 Wilson Valdez	4.00	1.20
28 Victor Alvarez	4.00	1.20
29 Cesar Izturis	4.00	1.20
30 Endy Chavez	4.00	1.20
31 Michael Cuddyer	4.00	1.20
32 Bobby Hill	4.00	1.20
33 Willie Harris	4.00	1.20
34 Joe Crede	4.00	1.20
35 Jorge Padilla	4.00	1.20
36 Brandon Backe	4.00	1.20
37 Franklyn German	4.00	1.20
38 Xavier Nady	4.00	1.20
39 Raul Chavez	4.00	1.20
40 Shane Nance	4.00	1.20
41 Brandon Claussen	5.00	1.50
42 Tom Shearn	4.00	1.20
43 Freddy Sanchez	4.00	1.20
44 Chone Figgins	4.00	1.20
45 Cliff Lee	5.00	1.50
46 Brian Mallette	4.00	1.20
47 Mike Rivera	4.00	1.20
48 Elio Serrano	4.00	1.20
49 Rodrigo Rosario	4.00	1.20
50 Earl Snyder	4.00	1.20

2002 Donruss Rookies Crusade Autographs

These 49 cards basically parallel the Rookies Crusade set. These cards were issued to a stated print run of anywhere from 15 to 500 sets. Cards with a print run of 25 or fewer are not priced due to market scarcity.

Card	Nm-Mt	Ex-Mt
COMMON CARD p/r 300+	10.00	3.00
COMMON ROOKIE p/r 300+	10.00	3.00
COMMON CARD p/r 150-250	10.00	3.00
COMMON CARD p/r 100	15.00	4.50
1 Corky Miller/500	10.00	3.00
2 Jack Cust/500	10.00	3.00
3 Erik Bedard/100	15.00	4.50
4 Andres Torres/500	10.00	3.00
5 Geronimo Gil/500	10.00	3.00
6 Rafael Soriano/500	10.00	3.00
7 Johnny Estrada/400	10.00	3.00
8 Steve Bechler/500	10.00	3.00
9 Adam Johnson/500	10.00	3.00
10 So Taguchi/15		
11 Dee Brown/500	10.00	3.00
12 Kevin Frederick/150	10.00	3.00
13 Allan Simpson/150	10.00	3.00
14 Ricardo Rodriguez/500	10.00	3.00
15 Jason Hart/500	10.00	3.00
16 Matt Childers/150	10.00	3.00
17 Jason Jennings/500	10.00	3.00
18 Anderson Machado/500	10.00	3.00
19 Fernando Rodney/500	10.00	3.00
20 Brandon Larson/400	10.00	3.00
21 Satoru Komiyama/25		
22 Francis Beltran/500	10.00	3.00
23 Joe Thurston/500	10.00	3.00
24 Josh Pearce/500	10.00	3.00
25 Carlos Hernandez/500	10.00	3.00
26 Ben Howard/500	10.00	3.00
27 Wilson Valdez/500	10.00	3.00
28 Victor Alvarez/500	10.00	3.00
29 Cesar Izturis/500	10.00	3.00
30 Endy Chavez/500	10.00	3.00
31 Michael Cuddyer/375	10.00	3.00
32 Bobby Hill/250	10.00	3.00
33 Willie Harris/300	10.00	3.00
34 Joe Crede/100	15.00	4.50
35 Jorge Padilla/475	10.00	3.00
36 Brandon Backe/350	10.00	3.00
37 Franklyn German/500	10.00	3.00
38 Xavier Nady/500	10.00	3.00
39 Raul Chavez/500	10.00	3.00
40 Shane Nance/500	10.00	3.00
41 Brandon Claussen/150	15.00	4.50
42 Tom Shearn/500	10.00	3.00
44 Chone Figgins/500	10.00	3.00
45 Cliff Lee/500	15.00	4.50
46 Brian Mallette/150	10.00	3.00
47 Mike Rivera/400	10.00	3.00
48 Elio Serrano/500	10.00	3.00
49 Rodrigo Rosario/100	15.00	4.50
50 Earl Snyder/100	15.00	4.50

2002 Donruss Rookies Phenoms

Randomly inserted into packs, these 25 cards, which are set on shimmering double rainbow holo-foil board were sequentially numbered to 1000 serial numbered sets.

Card	Nm-Mt	Ex-Mt
1 Kazuhisa Ishii	8.00	2.40
2 Eric Hinske	5.00	1.50
3 Jason Lane	5.00	1.50
4 Victor Martinez	5.00	1.50
5 Mark Prior	12.00	3.60
6 Antonio Perez	5.00	1.50
7 John Buck	5.00	1.50
8 Joe Borchard	5.00	1.50
9 Alexis Gomez	5.00	1.50
10 Sean Burroughs	5.00	1.50
11 Carlos Pena	5.00	1.50
12 Bill Hall	5.00	1.50
13 Alfredo Amezaga	5.00	1.50
14 Ed Rogers	5.00	1.50
15 Mark Teixeira	8.00	2.40
16 Chris Snelling	8.00	2.40
17 Nick Johnson	5.00	1.50
18 Angel Berroa	5.00	1.50
19 Orlando Hudson	5.00	1.50
20 Drew Henson	5.00	1.50
21 Austin Kearns	5.00	1.50
22 Dewon Brazelton	5.00	1.50
23 Dennis Tankersley	5.00	1.50
24 Josh Beckett	5.00	1.50
25 Marlon Byrd	5.00	1.50

2002 Donruss Rookies Phenoms Autographs

These cards parallel the Phenoms insert set. Each of these cards were issued to a stated print run of between 25 and 500 signed copies. As the Ishii was produced to a stated print run of 25 sets, no pricing is provided for that card.

Card	Nm-Mt	Ex-Mt
COMMON CARD p/r 300+	10.00	3.00
COMMON CARD p/r 150-250	10.00	3.00
1 Kazuhisa Ishii/25		
2 Eric Hinske/500	10.00	3.00
3 Jason Lane/500	10.00	3.00
4 Victor Martinez/225	15.00	4.50
5 Mark Prior/100	120.00	36.00
6 Antonio Perez/500	10.00	3.00
7 John Buck/100	15.00	4.50
8 Joe Borchard/100	15.00	4.50
9 Alexis Gomez/400	10.00	3.00
10 Sean Burroughs/150	15.00	4.50
11 Carlos Pena/150	10.00	3.00
12 Bill Hall/200	10.00	3.00
13 Alfredo Amezaga/500	10.00	3.00
14 Ed Rogers/500	10.00	3.00
15 Mark Teixeira/100	25.00	7.50
16 Chris Snelling/100	25.00	7.50
17 Nick Johnson/250	15.00	4.50
18 Angel Berroa/500	15.00	4.50
19 Orlando Hudson/400	10.00	3.00
20 Drew Henson/500	25.00	7.50
21 Austin Kearns/75	15.00	4.50
22 Dewon Brazelton/350	10.00	3.00
23 Dennis Tankersley/100	15.00	4.50
24 Josh Beckett/125	40.00	12.00
25 Marlon Byrd/500	15.00	4.50

2002 Donruss Rookies Recollection Autographs

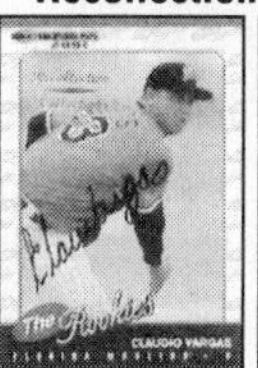

Randomly inserted into packs, these 55 cards feature cards from the 2001 and 2002 Donruss Rookie set which were "bought-back" by Donruss/Playoff for inclusion in this product. These cards were then signed by the player. Due to market scarcity, no pricing is provided for these cards.

Card	Nm-Mt	Ex-Mt
1 Jeremy Affeldt 01 DR/25		
2 Alfredo Amezaga 02 DN/24		
3 Erik Bedard 02 DN/20		
4 Angel Berroa 01 DR/50		
5 Angel Berroa 02 DN/6		
6 Dewon Brazelton 01 DR Black/25		
7 Dewon Brazelton 01 DR Blue/23		
8 Dewon Brazelton 02 DN/10		
9 Juan Cruz 01 DR/25		
10 Jorge De La Rosa 02 DN/20		
11 Brandon Duckworth 01 DR Black/25		
12 Brandon Duckworth 01 DR Blue/25		
13 Mark Ellis 02 DK/5		
14 Pedro Feliz 01 DN/55		
15 Pedro Feliz 01 DN SLC/1		
16 Pedro Feliz 01 DN SLS/1		
17 Pedro Feliz 01 DN R00 SLC/1		
18 Pedro Feliz 01 DN R00 SLS/1		
19 Casey Fossum 01 DR/49		
20 Jay Gibbons 02 DR Black/20		
21 Jay Gibbons 01 DR Blue/28		
22 Travis Hafner 01 DR/49		
23 Bill Hall 02 DN/20		
24 Aubrey Huff 01 DR/19		
25 Kazuhisa Ishii 02 DK/5		
26 Cesar Izturis 01 DN/45		
27 Cesar Izturis 01 DN SLC/1		
28 Cesar Izturis 01 DN SLS/1		
29 Jason Jennings 01 DR/15		
30 Brett Jodie 01 DR Black/27		
31 Brett Jodie 01 DR Blue/31		
32 Jason Lane 02 DN/1		
33 Nick Maness 01 DN/50		
34 Victor Martinez 01 ELI/25		
35 Donaldo Mendez 01 DR/17		
36 Corky Miller 01 DR/45		
37 Craig Monroe 01 DR/73		
38 Roy Oswalt 01 DR Black/1		
39 Roy Oswalt 01 DR Blue/49		
40 Adam Pettyjohn 01 DN/55		
41 Mark Prior 01 DR Black/1		
42 Mark Prior 01 DR Blue/22		
43 Brian Reith 01 DR/15		
44 Saul Rivera 01 DR/51		
45 C.C. Sabathia 01 DR/15		
46 Alfonso Soriano 01 DR/15		
47 Rafael Soriano 01 DR/99		
48 So Taguchi 02 DK/5		
49 Mark Teixeira 01 DR/50		
50 Mark Teixeira 02 DN/1		
51 Mark Teixeira 02 DK/5		
52 Claudio Vargas 01 DR/98		
53 Martin Vargas 01 DR/97		
54 Ramon Vazquez 01 DR/100		
55 Brad Voyles 01 DR/25		

2003 Donruss Samples

Issued as a one per in an issue of Beckett Baseball Card Monthly, these cards previewed the 2003 Donruss set. These cards have the word sample printed in silver on the back.

Nm-Mt Ex-Mt

*SAMPLES: 1.5X TO 4X BASIC CARDS
ONE PER BBCM MAGAZINE

2003 Donruss Samples Gold

These cards were randomly inserted into issues of Beckett Baseball Card Monthly. These cards have the word sample printed in gold on the back and comprise 10 percent of the total run of magazines printed.

Nm-Mt Ex-Mt

*GOLD SAMPLE: 4X TO 10X BASIC
RANDOM IN BBCM MAGAZINES
GOLD STATED 10% OF TOTAL PRINT RUN

2003 Donruss

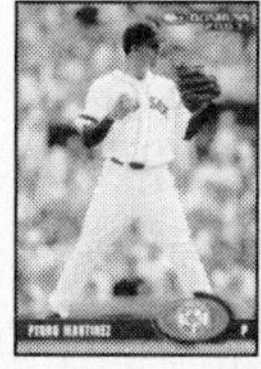

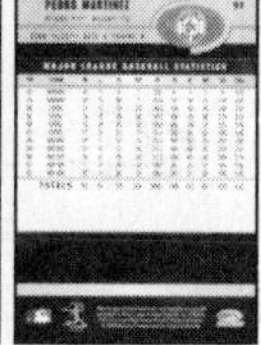

This 400 card set was released in December, 2002. The set was issued in 13 card packs with an SRP of $2.29 which were packed 24 packs to a box and 20 boxes to a case. Subsets in this set include cards numbered Diamond Kings (1-20) and Rated Rookies (21-70). For the first time since Donruss/Playoff returned to card production, this was a baseball set without short printed base cards.

Card	Nm-Mt	Ex-Mt
COMPLETE SET (400)	50.00	15.00
COMMON CARD (71-400)	.30	.09
COMMON CARD (1-20)	.50	.15
COMMON CARD (21-70)	.50	.15
1 Vladimir Guerrero DK	.75	.23
2 Derek Jeter DK	2.00	.60
3 Adam Dunn DK	.50	.15
4 Greg Maddux DK	1.25	.35
5 Lance Berkman DK	.50	.15
6 Ichiro Suzuki DK	1.25	.35
7 Mike Piazza DK	1.25	.35
8 Alex Rodriguez DK	1.25	.35
9 Tom Glavine DK	.50	.15
10 Randy Johnson DK	.75	.23
11 Nomar Garciaparra DK	1.25	.35
12 Jason Giambi DK	.75	.23
13 Sammy Sosa DK	1.25	.35
14 Barry Zito DK	.50	.15
15 Chipper Jones DK	.75	.23
16 Magglio Ordonez DK	.50	.15
17 Larry Walker DK	.50	.15
18 Alfonso Soriano DK	.50	.15
19 Curt Schilling DK	.50	.15
20 Barry Bonds DK	2.00	.60
21 Joe Borchard RR	.50	.15
22 Chris Snelling RR	.50	.15
23 Brian Tallet RR	.50	.15
24 Cliff Lee RR	.50	.15
25 Freddy Sanchez RR	.50	.15
26 Chone Figgins RR	.50	.15
27 Kevin Cash RR	.50	.15
28 Josh Bard RR	.50	.15
29 Jeriome Robertson RR	.50	.15
30 Jeremy Hill RR	.50	.15
31 Shane Nance RR	.50	.15
32 Jake Peavy RR	.50	.15
33 Trey Hodges RR	.50	.15
34 Eric Eckenstahler RR	.50	.15
35 Jim Rushford RR	.50	.15
36 Oliver Perez RR	.50	.15
37 Kirk Saarloos RR	.50	.15
38 Hank Blalock RR	.75	.23
39 Francisco Rodriguez RR	.50	.15
40 Runelvys Hernandez RR	.50	.15
41 Aaron Cook RR	.50	.15
42 Josh Hancock RR	.50	.15
43 P.J. Bevis RR	.50	.15
44 Jon Adkins RR	.50	.15
45 Tim Kalita RR	.50	.15
46 Nelson Castro RR	.50	.15
47 Colin Young RR	.50	.15
48 Adrian Burnside RR	.50	.15
49 Luis Martinez RR	.50	.15
50 Pete Zamora RR	.50	.15
51 Todd Donovan RR	.50	.15
52 Jeremy Ward RR	.50	.15
53 Wilson Valdez RR	.50	.15
54 Eric Good RR	.50	.15
55 Jeff Baker RR	.50	.15
56 Mitch Wylie RR	.50	.15
57 Ron Calloway RR	.50	.15
58 Jose Valverde RR	.50	.15
59 Jason Davis RR	.50	.15
60 Scotty Layfield RR	.50	.15
61 Matt Thornton RR	.50	.15
62 Adam Walker RR	.50	.15
63 Gustavo Chacin RR	.50	.15
64 Ron Chiavacci RR	.50	.15
65 Wiki Nieves RR	.50	.15
66 Cliff Bartosh RR	.50	.15
67 Mike Gonzalez RR	.50	.15
68 Justin Wayne RR	.50	.15
69 Eric Junge RR	.50	.15
70 Ben Kozlowski RR	.50	.15
71 Darin Erstad	.30	.09
72 Garret Anderson	.30	.09
73 Troy Glaus	.50	.15
74 David Eckstein	.30	.09
75 Adam Kennedy	.30	.09
76 Kevin Appier	.30	.09
77 Jarrod Washburn	.30	.09
78 Scott Spiezio	.30	.09
79 Tim Salmon	.50	.15
80 Ramon Ortiz	.30	.09
81 Bengie Molina	.30	.09
82 Brad Fullmer	.30	.09
83 Troy Percival	.30	.09
84 David Segui	.30	.09
85 Jay Gibbons	.30	.09
86 Tony Batista	.30	.09
87 Scott Erickson	.30	.09
88 Jeff Conine	.30	.09
89 Melvin Mora	.30	.09
90 Buddy Groom	.30	.09
91 Rodrigo Lopez	.30	.09
92 Marty Cordova	.30	.09
93 Geronimo Gil	.30	.09
94 Kenny Lofton	.30	.09
95 Shea Hillenbrand	.30	.09
96 Manny Ramirez	.30	.09
97 Pedro Martinez	.75	.23
98 Nomar Garciaparra	1.25	.35
99 Rickey Henderson	.75	.23
100 Johnny Damon	.30	.09
101 Trot Nixon	.50	.15
102 Derek Lowe	.30	.09
103 Hee Seop Choi	.30	.09
104 Mark Teixeira	.50	.15
105 Tim Wakefield	.30	.09
106 Jason Varitek	.30	.09
107 Frank Thomas	.75	.23
108 Joe Crede	.30	.09
109 Magglio Ordonez	.30	.09
110 Ray Durham	.30	.09
111 Mark Buehrle	.30	.09
112 Paul Konerko	.30	.09
113 Jose Valentin	.30	.09
114 Carlos Lee	.30	.09
115 Royce Clayton	.30	.09
116 C.C. Sabathia	.30	.09
117 Ellis Burks	.30	.09
118 Omar Vizquel	.30	.09
119 Jim Thome	.75	.23
120 Matt Lawton	.30	.09
121 Travis Fryman	.30	.09
122 Earl Snyder	.30	.09
123 Ricky Gutierrez	.30	.09
124 Einar Diaz	.30	.09
125 Danys Baez	.30	.09
126 Robert Fick	.30	.09
127 Bobby Higginson	.30	.09
128 Steve Sparks	.30	.09

129 Mike Rivera .30 .09
130 Wendell Magee .30 .09
131 Randall Simon .30 .09
132 Carlos Pena .30 .09
133 Mark Redman .30 .09
134 Juan Acevedo .30 .09
135 Mike Sweeney .30 .09
136 Aaron Guiel .30 .09
137 Carlos Beltran .30 .09
138 Joe Randa .30 .09
139 Paul Byrd .30 .09
140 Shawn Sedlacek .30 .09
141 Raul Ibanez .30 .09
142 Michael Tucker .30 .09
143 Torii Hunter .30 .09
144 Jacque Jones .30 .09
145 David Ortiz .30 .09
146 Corey Koskie .30 .09
147 Brad Radke .30 .09
148 Doug Mientkiewicz .30 .09
149 A.J. Pierzynski .30 .09
150 Dustan Mohr .30 .09
151 Michael Cuddyer .30 .09
152 Eddie Guardado .30 .09
153 Cristian Guzman .30 .09
154 Derek Jeter 2.00 .60
155 Bernie Williams .50 .15
156 Roger Clemens 1.50 .45
157 Mike Mussina .75 .23
158 Jorge Posada .50 .15
159 Alfonso Soriano .50 .15
160 Jason Giambi .75 .23
161 Robin Ventura .30 .09
162 Andy Pettitte .50 .15
163 David Wells .30 .09
164 Nick Johnson .30 .09
165 Jeff Weaver .30 .09
166 Raul Mondesi .30 .09
167 Rondell White .30 .09
168 Tim Hudson .30 .09
169 Barry Zito .50 .15
170 Mark Mulder .30 .09
171 Miguel Tejada .30 .09
172 Eric Chavez .30 .09
173 Billy Koch .30 .09
174 Jermaine Dye .30 .09
175 Scott Hatteberg .30 .09
176 Terrence Long .30 .09
177 David Justice .30 .09
178 Ramon Hernandez .30 .09
179 Ted Lilly .30 .09
180 Ichiro Suzuki 1.25 .35
181 Edgar Martinez .50 .15
182 Mike Cameron .30 .09
183 John Olerud .30 .09
184 Bret Boone .30 .09
185 Dan Wilson .30 .09
186 Freddy Garcia .30 .09
187 Jamie Moyer .30 .09
188 Carlos Guillen .30 .09
189 Ruben Sierra .30 .09
190 Kazuhiro Sasaki .30 .09
191 Mark McLemore .30 .09
192 John Halama .30 .09
193 Joel Pineiro .30 .09
194 Jeff Cirillo .30 .09
195 Rafael Soriano .30 .09
196 Ben Grieve .30 .09
197 Aubrey Huff .30 .09
198 Steve Cox .30 .09
199 Toby Hall .30 .09
200 Randy Winn .30 .09
201 Brent Abernathy .30 .09
202 Chris Gomez .30 .09
203 John Flaherty .30 .09
204 Paul Wilson .30 .09
205 Chan Ho Park .30 .09
206 Alex Rodriguez 1.25 .35
207 Juan Gonzalez .75 .23
208 Rafael Palmeiro .50 .15
209 Ivan Rodriguez .75 .23
210 Rusty Greer .30 .09
211 Kenny Rogers .30 .09
212 Ismael Valdes .30 .09
213 Frank Catalanotto .30 .09
214 Hank Blalock .50 .15
215 Michael Young .30 .09
216 Kevin Mench .30 .09
217 Herbert Perry .30 .09
218 Gabe Kapler .30 .09
219 Carlos Delgado .30 .09
220 Shannon Stewart .30 .09
221 Eric Hinske .30 .09
222 Roy Halladay .30 .09
223 Felipe Lopez .30 .09
224 Vernon Wells .30 .09
225 Josh Phelps .30 .09
226 Jose Cruz .30 .09
227 Curt Schilling .50 .15
228 Randy Johnson .75 .23
229 Luis Gonzalez .30 .09
230 Mark Grace .50 .15
231 Junior Spivey .30 .09
232 Tony Womack .30 .09
233 Matt Williams .30 .09
234 Steve Finley .30 .09
235 Byung-Hyun Kim .30 .09
236 Craig Counsell .30 .09
237 Greg Maddux 1.25 .35
238 Tom Glavine .50 .15
239 John Smoltz .50 .15
240 Chipper Jones .75 .23
241 Gary Sheffield .30 .09
242 Andruw Jones .30 .09
243 Vinny Castilla .30 .09
244 Damian Moss .30 .09
245 Rafael Furcal .30 .09
246 Javy Lopez .30 .09
247 Kevin Millwood .30 .09
248 Kerry Wood .75 .23
249 Fred McGriff .50 .15
250 Sammy Sosa 1.25 .35
251 Alex Gonzalez .30 .09
252 Corey Patterson .30 .09
253 Moises Alou .30 .09
254 Juan Cruz .30 .09
255 Jon Lieber .30 .09
256 Matt Clement .30 .09
257 Mark Prior 1.50 .45
258 Ken Griffey Jr. 1.25 .35
259 Barry Larkin .75 .23
260 Adam Dunn .30 .09
261 Sean Casey .30 .09
262 Jose Rijo .30 .09
263 Elmer Dessens .30 .09
264 Austin Kearns .30 .09
265 Corky Miller .30 .09
266 Todd Walker .30 .09
267 Chris Reitsma .30 .09
268 Ryan Dempster .30 .09
269 Aaron Boone .30 .09
270 Danny Graves .30 .09
271 Brandon Larson .30 .09
272 Larry Walker .50 .15
273 Todd Helton .50 .15
274 Juan Uribe .30 .09
275 Juan Pierre .30 .09
276 Mike Hampton .30 .09
277 Todd Zeile .30 .09
278 Todd Hollandsworth .30 .09
279 Jason Jennings .30 .09
280 Josh Beckett .50 .15
281 Mike Lowell .30 .09
282 Derrek Lee .30 .09
283 A.J. Burnett .30 .09
284 Luis Castillo .30 .09
285 Tim Raines .30 .09
286 Preston Wilson .30 .09
287 Juan Encarnacion .30 .09
288 Charles Johnson .30 .09
289 Jeff Bagwell .50 .15
290 Craig Biggio .50 .15
291 Lance Berkman .30 .09
292 Daryle Ward .30 .09
293 Roy Oswalt .30 .09
294 Richard Hidalgo .30 .09
295 Octavio Dotel .30 .09
296 Wade Miller .30 .09
297 Julio Lugo .30 .09
298 Billy Wagner .30 .09
299 Shawn Green .30 .09
300 Adrian Beltre .30 .09
301 Paul Lo Duca .30 .09
302 Eric Karros .30 .09
303 Kevin Brown .30 .09
304 Hideo Nomo .75 .23
305 Odalis Perez .30 .09
306 Eric Gagne .50 .15
307 Brian Jordan .30 .09
308 Cesar Izturis .30 .09
309 Mark Grudzielanek .30 .09
310 Kazuhisa Ishii .30 .09
311 Geoff Jenkins .30 .09
312 Richie Sexson .30 .09
313 Jose Hernandez .30 .09
314 Ben Sheets .30 .09
315 Ruben Quevedo .30 .09
316 Jeffrey Hammonds .30 .09
317 Alex Sanchez .30 .09
318 Eric Young .30 .09
319 Takahito Nomura .30 .09
320 Vladimir Guerrero .75 .23
321 Jose Vidro .30 .09
322 Orlando Cabrera .30 .09
323 Michael Barrett .30 .09
324 Javier Vazquez .30 .09
325 Tony Armas Jr. .30 .09
326 Andres Galarraga .30 .09
327 Tomo Ohka .30 .09
328 Bartolo Colon .30 .09
329 Fernando Tatis .30 .09
330 Brad Wilkerson .30 .09
331 Masato Yoshii .30 .09
332 Mike Piazza 1.25 .35
333 Jeromy Burnitz .30 .09
334 Roberto Alomar .75 .23
335 Mo Vaughn .30 .09
336 Al Leiter .30 .09
337 Pedro Astacio .30 .09
338 Edgardo Alfonzo .30 .09
339 Armando Benitez .30 .09
340 Timo Perez .30 .09
341 Jay Payton .30 .09
342 Roger Cedeno .30 .09
343 Rey Ordonez .30 .09
344 Steve Trachsel .30 .09
345 Satoru Komiyama .30 .09
346 Scott Rolen .50 .15
347 Pat Burrell .30 .09
348 Bobby Abreu .30 .09
349 Mike Lieberthal .30 .09
350 Brandon Duckworth .30 .09
351 Jimmy Rollins .30 .09
352 Marlon Anderson .30 .09
353 Travis Lee .30 .09
354 Vicente Padilla .30 .09
355 Randy Wolf .30 .09
356 Jason Kendall .30 .09
357 Brian Giles .30 .09
358 Aramis Ramirez .30 .09
359 Pokey Reese .30 .09
360 Kip Wells .30 .09
361 Josh Fogg .30 .09
362 Mike Williams .30 .09
363 Jack Wilson .30 .09
364 Craig Wilson .30 .09
365 Kevin Young .30 .09
366 Ryan Klesko .30 .09
367 Phil Nevin .30 .09
368 Brian Lawrence .30 .09
369 Mark Kotsay .30 .09
370 Brett Tomko .30 .09
371 Trevor Hoffman .30 .09
372 Deivi Cruz .30 .09
373 Bubba Trammell .30 .09
374 Sean Burroughs .30 .09
375 Barry Bonds 2.00 .60
376 Jeff Kent .30 .09
377 Rich Aurilia .30 .09
378 Tsuyoshi Shinjo .30 .09
379 Benito Santiago .30 .09
380 Kirk Rueter .30 .09
381 Livan Hernandez .30 .09
382 Russ Ortiz .30 .09
383 David Bell .30 .09
384 Jason Schmidt .30 .09
385 Reggie Sanders .30 .09
386 J.T. Snow .30 .09
387 Robb Nen .30 .09
388 Ryan Jensen .30 .09
389 Jim Edmonds .30 .09
390 J.D. Drew .30 .09
391 Albert Pujols 1.50 .45
392 Fernando Vina .30 .09
393 Tino Martinez .50 .15
394 Edgar Renteria .30 .09
395 Matt Morris .30 .09
396 Woody Williams .30 .09
397 Jason Isringhausen .30 .09
398 Placido Polanco .30 .09
399 Eli Marrero .30 .09
400 Jason Simontacchi .30 .09

2003 Donruss Chicago Collection

These cards were distributed in March 2003 at the Chicago Sportsfest at the Donruss-Playoff corporate booth. Any collector that opened three Donruss/Playoff packs at the Donruss booth received one of these cards as a redemption for the wrappers. Only five serial-numbered sets were produced, thus the cards are too scarce to price. They can be easily identified by the large silver-foil "Chicago Collection" logo and serial-numbering stamped on the front of each card.

Nm-Mt Ex-Mt
DISTRIBUTED AT CHICAGO SPORTSFEST
STATED PRINT RUN 5 SERIAL #'d SETS
NO PRICING DUE TO SCARCITY

2003 Donruss Stat Line Career

Randomly inserted into packs, this is a parallel to the 2003 Donruss set. Each card is printed to a number matching some career statistic and the cards are serial numbered to that amount. For those cards with a print run of 25 or fewer, no pricing is provided due to market scarcity.

Nm-Mt Ex-Mt
*STAT LINE 1-20: 2.5X TO 6X BASIC
*21-70 P/R b/wn 251-400: 1.25X TO 3X
*21-70 P/R b/wn 201-250: 1.25X TO 3X
*21-70 P/R b/wn 151-200 1.5X TO 4X
*21-70 P/R b/wn 121-150: 2X TO 5X
*21-70 P/R b/wn 81-120: 2.5X TO 6X
*21-70 P/R b/wn 51-65: 4X TO 10X
*21-70 P/R b/wn 36-50: 5X TO 12X
*21-70 P/R b/wn 26-35: 6X TO 15X
*71-400 P/R b/wn 251-400: 2.5X TO 6X
*71-400 P/R b/wn 201-250: 2.5X TO 6X
*71-400 P/R b/wn 151-200 3X TO 8X
*71-400 P/R b/wn 121-150: 3X TO 8X
*71-400 P/R b/wn 81-120: 4X TO 10X
*71-400 P/R b/wn 66-80: 5X TO 12X
*71-400 P/R b/wn 51-65: 6X TO 15X
*71-400 P/R b/wn 36-50: 8X TO 20X
*71-400 P/R b/wn 26-35: 10X TO 25X
RANDOM INSERTS IN PACKS
SEE BECKETT.COM FOR FOR PRINT RUNS
NO PRICING ON QTY OF 25 OR LESS.

2003 Donruss Stat Line Season

Randomly inserted into packs, this is a parallel to the 2003 Donruss set. Each card is printed to a number matching some seasonal statistic and the cards are serial numbered to that amount. For those cards with a print run of 25 or fewer, no pricing is provided due to market scarcity.

Nm-Mt Ex-Mt
*1-20 P/R b/wn 121-150 3X TO 8X
*1-20 P/R b/wn 81-120 4X TO 10X
*1-20 P/R b/wn 66-80 5X TO 12X
*1-20 P/R b/wn 51-65 6X TO 15X
*1-20 P/R b/wn 36-50 8X TO 20X
*1-20 P/R b/wn 26-35 10X TO 25X
*21-70 P/R b/wn 81-120 2.5X TO 6X
*21-70 P/R b/wn 66-80 3X TO 8X
*21-70 P/R b/wn 51-65 4X TO 10X
*21-70 P/R b/wn 36-50 5X TO 12X
*21-70 P/R b/wn 26-35 6X TO 15X
*71-400 P/R b/wn 81-120 4X TO 10X
*71-400 P/R b/wn 66-80 5X TO 12X
*71-400 P/R b/wn 51-65 6X TO 15X
*71-400 P/R b/wn 36-50 8X TO 20X
*71-400 P/R b/wn 26-35 10X TO 25X
RANDOM INSERTS IN PACKS
SEE BECKETT.COM FOR PRINT RUNS
NO PRICING ON QTY OF 25 OR LESS.

2003 Donruss All-Stars

Issued at a stated rate of one in 12 retail packs, these 10 cards feature players who are projected to be mainstays on the All-Star team.

	Nm-Mt	Ex-Mt
1 Ichiro Suzuki	5.00	1.50
2 Alex Rodriguez	5.00	1.50
3 Nomar Garciaparra	5.00	1.50
4 Derek Jeter	8.00	2.40
5 Manny Ramirez	3.00	.90
6 Barry Bonds	8.00	2.40
7 Adam Dunn	3.00	.90
8 Mike Piazza	5.00	1.50
9 Sammy Sosa	5.00	1.50
10 Todd Helton	3.00	.90

2003 Donruss Anniversary 1983

Issued at a stated rate of one in 12, this 20 card set features players who were among the most important players of that era. These cards use the 1983 Donruss design and photos.

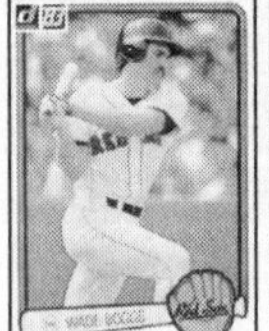

	Nm-Mt	Ex-Mt
1 Dale Murphy	3.00	.90
2 Jim Palmer	3.00	.90
3 Nolan Ryan	8.00	2.40
4 Ozzie Smith	5.00	1.50
5 Tom Seaver	3.00	.90
6 Mike Schmidt	6.00	1.80
7 Steve Carlton	3.00	.90
8 Robin Yount	5.00	1.50
9 Ryne Sandberg	5.00	1.50
10 Cal Ripken	10.00	3.00
11 Fernando Valenzuela	3.00	.90
12 Andre Dawson	3.00	.90
13 George Brett	8.00	2.40
14 Eddie Murray	3.00	.90
15 Dave Winfield	3.00	.90
16 Johnny Bench	3.00	.90
17 Wade Boggs	3.00	.90
18 Tony Gwynn	6.00	1.80
19 San Diego Chicken	3.00	.90
20 Ty Cobb	5.00	1.50

2003 Donruss Bat Kings

Randomly inserted into packs, these 20 cards feature a game bat chip long with a reproduction of a previously used Diamond King card. Cards numbered 1 through 10 have a stated print run of 250 serial numbered sets while cards numbered 11 through 20 have a stated print run of 100 serial numbered sets.

Nm-Mt Ex-Mt
1-10 PRINT RUN 250 SERIAL #'d SETS
11-20 PRINT RUN 100 SERIAL #'d SETS
*STUDIO 1-10: .75X TO 2X BASIC BAT KING
STUDIO 1-10 PRINT RUN 50 SERIAL #'d SETS
STUDIO 11-20 PRINT RUN 25 SERIAL #'d SETS
STUDIO 11-20 NO PRICING DUE TO SCARCITY
RANDOM INSERTS IN PACKS

	Nm-Mt	Ex-Mt
1 Scott Rolen 99 DK/250	20.00	6.00
2 Frank Thomas 00 DK/250	20.00	6.00
3 Chipper Jones 01 DK/250	20.00	6.00
4 Ivan Rodriguez 01 DK/250	20.00	6.00
5 Stan Musial 01 ATDK/100	50.00	15.00
6 Nomar Garciaparra 02 DK/250	25.00	7.50
7 Vladimir Guerrero 03 DK/250	20.00	6.00
8 Adam Dunn 03 DK/250	15.00	4.50
9 Lance Berkman 03 DK/250	15.00	4.50
10 Magglio Ordonez 03 DK/250	15.00	4.50
11 Ernie Banks 02 ATDK/50		
12 Manny Ramirez 95 DK/100	20.00	6.00
13 Mike Piazza 94 DK/100	40.00	12.00
14 Alex Rodriguez 97 DK/100	40.00	12.00
15 Todd Helton 97 RDK/100	25.00	7.50
16 Andre Dawson 85 DK/100	20.00	6.00
17 Cal Ripken 87 DK/100	80.00	24.00
18 Tony Gwynn 88 DK/100	30.00	9.00
19 Don Mattingly 02 ATDK/100	60.00	18.00
20 Ryne Sandberg 90 DK/100	60.00	18.00

2003 Donruss Diamond Kings Inserts

Randomly inserted into packs, these cards parallel the first 20 cards of the regular Donruss set except they are serial numbered to a stated print run of 2500 serial numbered sets. These cards can be easily seperated from the cards inserted into the regular packs as they were printed with a foil stamp.

Nm-Mt Ex-Mt
*STUDIO: .75X TO 2X BASIC DK
STUDIO PRINT RUN 250 SERIAL #'d SETS
RANDOM INSERTS IN PACKS

	Nm-Mt	Ex-Mt
1 Vladimir Guerrero	10.00	3.00
2 Derek Jeter	20.00	6.00
3 Adam Dunn	10.00	3.00
4 Greg Maddux	12.00	3.60
5 Lance Berkman	10.00	3.00
6 Ichiro Suzuki	12.00	3.60
7 Mike Piazza	12.00	3.60
8 Alex Rodriguez	12.00	3.60
9 Tom Glavine	10.00	3.00
10 Randy Johnson	10.00	3.00
11 Nomar Garciaparra	12.00	3.60
12 Jason Giambi	10.00	3.00
13 Sammy Sosa	12.00	3.60
14 Barry Zito	10.00	3.00
15 Chipper Jones	10.00	3.00
16 Magglio Ordonez	10.00	3.00
17 Larry Walker	10.00	3.00
18 Alfonso Soriano	10.00	3.00
19 Curt Schilling	10.00	3.00
20 Barry Bonds	20.00	6.00

2003 Donruss Elite Series

Randomly inserted into packs, this 15 card set, which is issued on metalized film board, features the elite 15 players in baseball. These cards were issued to a stated print run of 2500 serial numbered sets.

Nm-Mt Ex-Mt
DOMINATORS PR.RUN 25 SERIAL #'d SETS
DOMINATORS NO PRICE DUE TO SCARCITY
RANDOM INSERTS IN PACKS

	Nm-Mt	Ex-Mt
1 Alex Rodriguez	8.00	2.40
2 Barry Bonds	12.00	3.60
3 Ichiro Suzuki	8.00	2.40
4 Vladimir Guerrero	5.00	1.50
5 Randy Johnson	5.00	1.50
6 Pedro Martinez	5.00	1.50
7 Adam Dunn	4.00	1.20
8 Sammy Sosa	8.00	2.40
9 Jim Edmonds	4.00	1.20
10 Greg Maddux	8.00	2.40
11 Kazuhisa Ishii	4.00	1.20
12 Jason Giambi	5.00	1.50
13 Nomar Garciaparra	8.00	2.40
14 Tom Glavine	4.00	1.20
15 Todd Helton	4.00	1.20

2003 Donruss Gamers

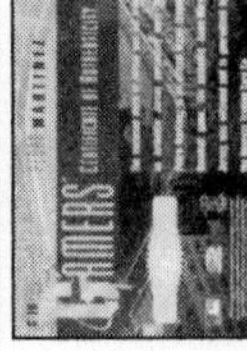

Randomly inserted in DLP (Donruss/Leaf/Playoff) rookie packs, these 50 cards have game-worn memorabilia swatches of the featured players.

MINT NRMT
STATED PRINT RUN 500 SERIAL #'d SETS
*JSY NUM: .6X TO 1.5X BASIC
JSY NUM PRINT RUN 100 SERIAL #'d SETS
*POSITION: .6X TO 1.5X BASIC
POSITION PRINT RUN 150 SERIAL #'d SETS
PRIME PRINT RUN 25 SERIAL #'d SETS
NO PRIME PRICING DUE TO SCARCITY
REWARDS PRINT RUN 10 SERIAL #'d SETS
NO REWARDS PRICING DUE TO SCARCITY
RANDOM INSERTS IN DLP R/T PACKS

	MINT	NRMT
1 Nomar Garciaparra	15.00	6.75
2 Alex Rodriguez	10.00	4.50
3 Mike Piazza	10.00	4.50
4 Greg Maddux	10.00	4.50
5 Roger Clemens	15.00	6.75
6 Sammy Sosa	15.00	6.75
7 Randy Johnson	10.00	4.50
8 Albert Pujols	15.00	6.75
9 Alfonso Soriano	10.00	4.50
10 Chipper Jones	10.00	4.50
11 Mark Prior	15.00	6.75
12 Hideo Nomo	10.00	4.50
13 Adam Dunn	8.00	3.60
14 Juan Gonzalez	10.00	4.50
15 Vladimir Guerrero	10.00	4.50
16 Pedro Martinez	10.00	4.50
17 Jim Thome	10.00	4.50
18 Brandon Webb	15.00	6.75
19 Mike Mussina	10.00	4.50
20 Mark Teixeira	10.00	4.50
21 Barry Larkin	10.00	4.50
22 Ivan Rodriguez	10.00	4.50
23 Hank Blalock	10.00	4.50
24 Rafael Palmeiro	10.00	4.50
25 Curt Schilling	10.00	4.50
26 Troy Glaus	10.00	4.50
27 Bernie Williams	10.00	4.50
28 Scott Rolen	10.00	4.50
29 Torii Hunter	8.00	3.60
30 Nick Johnson	8.00	3.60
31 Kazuhisa Ishii	8.00	3.60
32 Shawn Green	8.00	3.60
33 Jeff Bagwell	10.00	4.50
34 Lance Berkman	8.00	3.60
35 Roy Oswalt	8.00	3.60
36 Kerry Wood	10.00	4.50
37 Todd Helton	10.00	4.50
38 Manny Ramirez	8.00	3.60
39 Andruw Jones	8.00	3.60
40 Frank Thomas	10.00	4.50
41 Gary Sheffield	8.00	3.60
42 Magglio Ordonez	8.00	3.60
43 Mike Sweeney	8.00	3.60
44 Carlos Beltran	8.00	3.60
45 Richie Sexson	8.00	3.60
46 Jeff Kent	8.00	3.60
47 Carlos Delgado	8.00	3.60
48 Vernon Wells	8.00	3.60
49 Dontrelle Willis	10.00	4.50
50 Jae Weong Seo	8.00	3.60

2003 Donruss Gamers Autographs

MINT NRMT
RANDOM INSERTS IN DLP R/T PACKS
PRINT RUNS B/WN 5-50 COPIES PER
NO PRICING ON QTY OF 25 OR LESS.
2 Alex Rodriguez/5

3 Mike Piazza/5
4 Greg Maddux/5
5 Roger Clemens/5
7 Randy Johnson/5
8 Albert Pujols/5
9 Alfonso Soriano/5
10 Chipper Jones/10
11 Mark Prior/25
12 Hideo Nomo/5
13 Adam Dunn/25
14 Juan Gonzalez/25
15 Vladimir Guerrero/5
16 Pedro Martinez/5
18 Brandon Webb/25
19 Mike Mussina/5
20 Mark Teixeira/50 40.00 18.00
22 Ivan Rodriguez/5
23 Hank Blalock/50 40.00 18.00
24 Rafael Palmeiro/10
25 Curt Schilling/25
26 Troy Glaus/25
27 Bernie Williams/5
28 Scott Rolen/25
29 Torii Hunter/50 30.00 13.50
30 Nick Johnson/25
31 Kazuhisa Ishii/5
32 Shawn Green/5
33 Jeff Bagwell/5
34 Lance Berkman/10
35 Roy Oswalt/50 30.00 13.50
36 Kerry Wood/25
37 Todd Helton/10
39 Andruw Jones/25
40 Frank Thomas/10
41 Gary Sheffield/25
42 Magglio Ordonez/25
43 Mike Sweeney/50 30.00 13.50
44 Carlos Beltran/25
45 Richie Sexson/25
46 Jeff Kent/12
48 Vernon Wells/30 40.00 18.00
49 Dontrelle Willis/50 50.00 22.00
50 Jae Weong Seo/50 60.00 27.00

2003 Donruss Jersey Kings

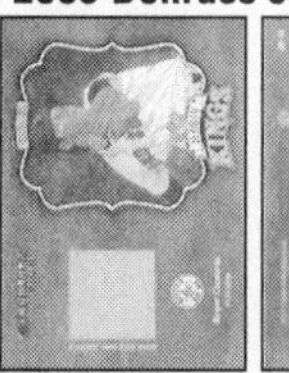

Randomly inserted into packs, this set features cards which parallel previously issued Diamond King cards along with a game-worn jersey swatch. Cards were printed to a stated print run of either 100 or 250 serial numbered cards and we have put that information next to the player's name in our checklist.

Nm-Mt Ex-Mt
*STUDIO 1-10: .75X TO 2X BASIC JSY KINGS
STUDIO 1-10 PRINT RUN 50 SERIAL #'d SETS
STUDIO 11-20 PRINT RUN 25 SERIAL #'d SETS
STUDIO 11-20 NO PRICE DUE TO SCARCITY
RANDOM INSERTS IN PACKS
1 Juan Gonzalez 99 DK/250 15.00 4.50
2 Greg Maddux 00 DK/250 20.00 6.00
3 Nomar Garciaparra 01 DK/250 25.00 7.50
4 Troy Glaus 01 DK/250 15.00 4.50
5 Reggie Jackson 01 ATDK/100 25.00 7.50
6 Alex Rodriguez 01 DK/250 25.00 7.50
7 Alfonso Soriano 03 DK/250 15.00 4.50
8 Curt Schilling 03 DK/250 15.00 4.50
9 Vladimir Guerrero 03 DK/250 15.00 4.50
10 Adam Dunn 03 DK/250 15.00 4.50
11 Mark Grace 88 DK/100 25.00 7.50
12 Roger Clemens 90 DK/100 40.00 12.00
13 Jeff Bagwell 91 DK/100 25.00 7.50
14 Tom Glavine 92 DK/100 25.00 7.50
15 Mike Piazza 94 DK/100 30.00 9.00
16 Rod Carew 82 DK/100 25.00 7.50
17 Rickey Henderson 82 DK/100 25.00 7.50
18 Mike Schmidt 83 DK/100 40.00 12.00
19 Cal Ripken 85 DK/100 80.00 24.00
20 Dale Murphy 86 DK/100 25.00 7.50

2003 Donruss Longball Leaders

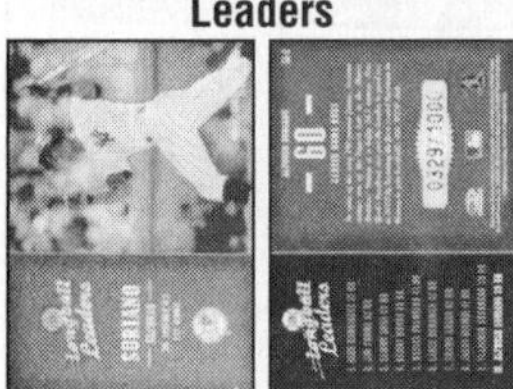

Randomly inserted into packs, these 10 cards, honoring some of the leading home run hitters, were printed on metalized film board and were issued to a stated print run of 1000 serial numbered sets.

Nm-Mt Ex-Mt
*SEASON SUM: 1.5X TO 4X BASIC LL
SEASON PRINT RUN BASED ON 02 HR'S
RANDOM INSERTS IN PACKS
1 Alex Rodriguez 12.00 3.60
2 Alfonso Soriano 5.00 1.50
3 Rafael Palmeiro 5.00 1.50
4 Jim Thome 8.00 2.40
5 Jason Giambi 8.00 2.40
6 Sammy Sosa 12.00 3.60
7 Barry Bonds 20.00 6.00
8 Lance Berkman 5.00 1.50
9 Shawn Green 5.00 1.50
10 Vladimir Guerrero 8.00 2.40

2003 Donruss Production Line

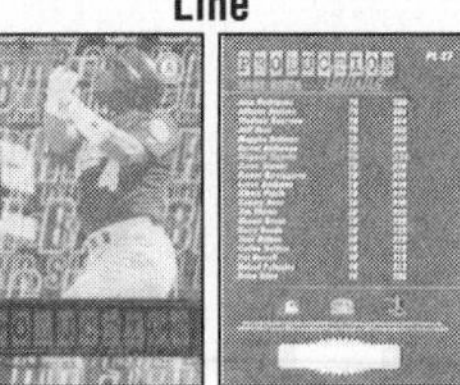

Randomly inserted into packs, these 30 cards feature players who excel in either on base percentage, slugging percentage, batting average or total bases. Each card is printed on metalized film board and was issued to that player's statistical information.

Nm-Mt Ex-Mt
*DIE CUT OPS: 1.25X TO 3X BASIC PL
*DIE CUT OBP/SLG: 1X TO 2.5X BASIC PL
*DIE CUT AVG/TB: .75X TO 2X BASIC PL
DIE CUT PRINT RUN 100 SERIAL #'d SETS
RANDOM INSERTS IN PACKS
1 Alex Rodriguez OPS/1015 10.00 3.00
2 Jim Thome OPS/1122 6.00 1.80
3 Lance Berkman OPS/982 2.50 .75
4 Barry Bonds OPS/1381 15.00 4.50
5 Sammy Sosa OPS/993 10.00 3.00
6 Vladimir Guerrero OPS/1010 6.00 1.80
7 Barry Bonds OBP/582 20.00 6.00
8 Jason Giambi OBP/435 8.00 2.40
9 Vladimir Guerrero OBP/417 8.00 2.40
10 Adam Dunn OBP/400 3.00 .90
11 Chipper Jones OBP/435 8.00 2.40
12 Todd Helton OBP/429 5.00 1.50
13 Rafael Palmeiro SLG/571 5.00 1.50
14 Sammy Sosa SLG/594 12.00 3.60
15 Alex Rodriguez SLG/623 12.00 3.60
16 Larry Walker SLG/602 5.00 1.50
17 Lance Berkman SLG/578 3.00 .90
18 Alfonso Soriano SLG/547 5.00 1.50
19 Ichiro Suzuki AVG/321 15.00 4.50
20 Mike Sweeney AVG/340 4.00 1.20
21 Manny Ramirez AVG/349 4.00 1.20
22 Larry Walker AVG/338 6.00 1.80
23 Barry Bonds AVG/370 25.00 7.50
24 Jim Edmonds AVG/311 4.00 1.20
25 Alfonso Soriano TB/381 6.00 1.80
26 Jason Giambi TB/335 10.00 3.00
27 Miguel Tejada TB/336 4.00 1.20
28 Brian Giles TB/309 4.00 1.20
29 Vladimir Guerrero TB/364 10.00 3.00
30 Pat Burrell TB/319 4.00 1.20

2003 Donruss Timber and Threads

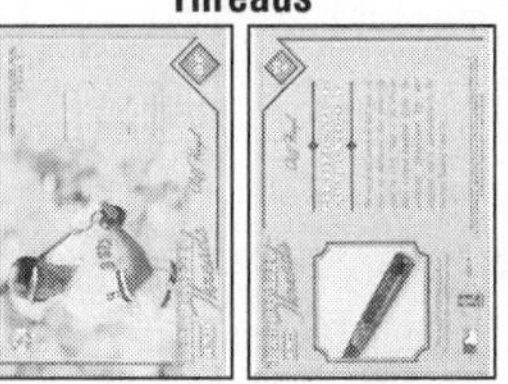

Randomly inserted into packs, these 50 cards feature either a game-used jersey swatch or a game-use bat chip of the featured player. Since these cards have different stated print runs we have put that information next to the player's name in our checklist.

Nm-Mt Ex-Mt
1 Al Kaline Bat/125 25.00 7.50
2 Alex Rodriguez Bat/350 20.00 6.00
3 Carlos Delgado Bat/250 10.00 3.00
4 Cliff Floyd Bat/250 10.00 3.00
5 Eddie Mathews Bat/125 25.00 7.50
6 Edgar Martinez Bat/125 25.00 7.50
7 Ernie Banks Bat/50 40.00 12.00
8 Ivan Rodriguez Bat/125 25.00 7.50
9 J.D. Drew Bat/125 15.00 4.50
10 Jorge Posada Bat/300 15.00 4.50
11 Lou Brock Bat/125 25.00 7.50
12 Mike Piazza Bat/125 25.00 7.50
13 Mike Schmidt Bat/125 60.00 18.00
14 Reggie Jackson Bat/125 25.00 7.50
15 Rickey Henderson Bat/125 25.00 7.50
16 Robin Yount Bat/125 40.00 12.00
17 Rod Carew Bat/125 25.00 7.50
18 Scott Rolen Bat/125 25.00 7.50
19 Shawn Green Bat/200 10.00 3.00
20 Willie Stargell Bat/125 25.00 7.50
21 Alex Rodriguez Jsy/175 30.00 9.00
22 Andruw Jones Jsy/275 10.00 3.00
23 Brooks Robinson Jsy/150 25.00 7.50
24 Chipper Jones Jsy/150 25.00 7.50
25 Greg Maddux Jsy/175 20.00 6.00
26 Hideo Nomo Jsy/300 40.00 12.00
27 Ivan Rodriguez Jsy/225 15.00 4.50
28 Jack Morris Jsy/150 15.00 4.50
29 J.D. Drew Jsy/150 15.00 4.50
30 Jeff Bagwell Jsy/500 15.00 4.50
31 Jim Thome Jsy/200 15.00 4.50
32 John Smoltz Jsy/175 15.00 4.50
33 John Olerud Jsy/450 10.00 3.00
34 Kerry Wood Jsy/200 15.00 4.50
35 Harmon Killebrew Jsy/50
36 Larry Walker Jsy/500 15.00 4.50
37 Magglio Ordonez Jsy/150 15.00 4.50
38 Manny Ramirez Jsy/500 10.00 3.00
39 Mike Piazza Jsy/300 15.00 4.50
40 Mike Sweeney Jsy/200 10.00 3.00
41 Nomar Garciaparra Jsy/200 25.00 7.50
42 Paul Konerko Jsy/500 10.00 3.00
43 Pedro Martinez Jsy/175 15.00 4.50
44 Randy Johnson Jsy/175 15.00 4.50
45 Roger Clemens Jsy/350 25.00 7.50
46 Shawn Green Jsy/250 10.00 3.00
47 Todd Helton Jsy/175 15.00 4.50
48 Tom Glavine Jsy/225 15.00 4.50
49 Tony Gwynn Jsy/150 25.00 7.50
50 Vladimir Guerrero Jsy/450 15.00 4.50

2003 Donruss Rookies

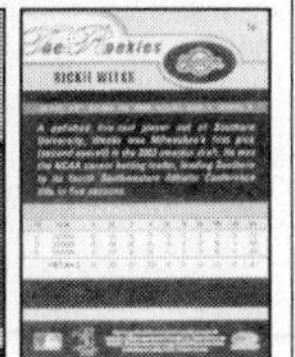

This 65-card set was released in December, 2003. This set was issued as part of the DLP (Donruss/Leaf/Playoff) Rookie Update product in which many of the products issued earlier in the year had Rookie Cards added. Each pack, contained eight cards and were sold at an $5 SRP with 24 packs in a box and 12 boxes in a case. In this Rookies set, cards 1-60 feature Rookie Cards while cards numbered 61-65 feature some of the most important players who changed teams during the 2003 season. As mentioned cards from the following DLP products were inserted into these packs: Donruss, Donruss Champions, Donruss Classics, Donruss Diamond Kings, Donruss Elite, Donruss Signature, Donruss Team Heroes, Leaf, Leaf Certified Materials, Leaf Limited, Playoff Absolute Memorabilia, Playoff Prestige and Studio.

MINT NRMT
COMPLETE SET (65) 20.00 9.00
COMMON CARD (1-65) .20 .09
COMMON RC .25 .11
1 Jeremy Bonderman RC .60 .25
2 Adam Loewen RC 1.25 .55
3 Dan Haren RC .60 .25
4 Jose Contreras RC 1.00 .45
5 Hideki Matsui RC 2.00 .90
6 Arnie Munoz RC .25 .11
7 Miguel Cabrera .75 .35
8 Andrew Brown RC .25 .11
9 Josh Hall RC .40 .18
10 Josh Stewart RC .25 .11
11 Clint Barmes RC .40 .18
12 Luis Ayala RC .25 .11
13 Brandon Webb RC 1.25 .55
14 Greg Aquino RC .25 .11
15 Chien-Ming Wang RC 1.00 .45
16 Rickie Weeks RC 2.50 1.10
17 Edgar Gonzalez RC .25 .11
18 Dontrelle Willis .50 .23
19 Bo Hart RC 1.00 .45
20 Rosman Garcia RC .25 .11
21 Jeremy Griffiths RC .40 .18
22 Craig Brazell RC .40 .18
23 Daniel Cabrera RC .25 .11
24 Fernando Cabrera RC .25 .11
25 Terrmel Sledge RC .40 .18
26 Ramon Nivar RC .50 .23
27 Rob Hammock RC .40 .18
28 Francisco Rosario RC .25 .11
29 Cory Stewart RC .25 .11
30 Felix Sanchez RC .25 .11
31 Jorge Cordova RC .25 .11
32 Rocco Baldelli .75 .35
33 Beau Kemp RC .25 .11
34 Mike Nakamura RC .25 .11
35 Rett Johnson RC .40 .18
36 Guillermo Quiroz RC .75 .35
37 Hong-Chih Kuo RC .50 .23
38 Ian Ferguson RC .25 .11
39 Franklin Perez RC .25 .11
40 Tim Olson RC .40 .18
41 Jerome Williams .20 .09
42 Rich Fischer RC .25 .11
43 Phil Seibel RC .25 .11
44 Aaron Looper RC .25 .11
45 Jae Weong Seo .20 .09
46 Chad Gaudin RC .25 .11
47 Matt Kata RC .50 .23
48 Ryan Wagner RC .75 .35
49 Michel Hernandez RC .25 .11
50 Diegomar Markwell RC .25 .11
51 Doug Waechter RC .40 .18
52 Mike Nicolas RC .25 .11
53 Prentice Redman RC .25 .11
54 Shane Bazzell RC .25 .11
55 Delmon Young RC 3.00 1.35
56 Brian Stokes RC .25 .11
57 Matt Bruback RC .25 .11
58 Nook Logan RC .25 .11
59 Oscar Villarreal RC .25 .11
60 Pete LaForest RC .40 .18
61 Shea Hillenbrand .20 .09
62 Aramis Ramirez .20 .09
63 Aaron Boone .20 .09
64 Roberto Alomar .50 .23
65 Rickey Henderson .50 .23

2003 Donruss Rookies Autographs

MINT NRMT
RANDOM INSERTS IN DLP R/T PACKS
PRINT RUNS B/WN 10-1000 COPIES PER
NO PRICING ON QTY OF 25 OR LESS.
1 Jeremy Bonderman/50 30.00 13.50
2 Adam Loewen/500 30.00 13.50
3 Dan Haren/100 20.00 9.00
4 Jose Contreras/100 40.00 18.00
6 Arnie Munoz/584 10.00 4.50
7 Miguel Cabrera/50 60.00 27.00

8 Andrew Brown/584 10.00 4.50
9 Josh Hall/1000 15.00 6.75
10 Josh Stewart/300 10.00 4.50
11 Clint Barmes/129 15.00 6.75
12 Luis Ayala/1000 10.00 4.50
13 Brandon Webb/100 40.00 18.00
14 Greg Aquino/1000 10.00 4.50
15 Chien-Ming Wang/100 40.00 18.00
16 Rickie Weeks/10
17 Edgar Gonzalez/400 10.00 4.50
18 Dontrelle Willis/25
19 Bo Hart/150 40.00 18.00
20 Rosman Garcia/250 10.00 4.50
21 Jeremy Griffiths/812 15.00 6.75
22 Craig Brazell/205 15.00 6.75
23 Daniel Cabrera/383 10.00 4.50
24 Fernando Cabrera/1000 10.00 4.50
25 Terrmel Sledge/250 15.00 6.75
26 Ramon Nivar/100 20.00 9.00
27 Rob Hammock/201 15.00 6.75
28 Francisco Rosario/25
29 Cory Stewart/1000 10.00 4.50
30 Felix Sanchez/1000 10.00 4.50
31 Jorge Cordova/1000 10.00 4.50
32 Rocco Baldelli/25
33 Beau Kemp/1000 10.00 4.50
34 Mike Nakamura/1000 10.00 4.50
35 Rett Johnson/1000 15.00 6.75
36 Guillermo Quiroz/90 25.00 11.00
37 Hong-Chih Kuo/50 40.00 18.00
38 Ian Ferguson/1000 10.00 4.50
39 Franklin Perez/1000 10.00 4.50
40 Tim Olson/150 15.00 6.75
41 Jerome Williams/50 25.00 11.00
42 Rich Fischer/734 10.00 4.50
43 Phil Seibel/1000 10.00 4.50
44 Aaron Looper/513 10.00 4.50
45 Jae Weong Seo/50 50.00 22.00
46 Chad Gaudin/19
47 Matt Kata/203 20.00 9.00
48 Ryan Wagner/100 25.00 11.00
49 Michel Hernandez/41
50 Diegomar Markwell/1000 10.00 4.50
51 Doug Waechter/583 15.00 6.75
52 Mike Nicolas/1000 10.00 4.50
53 Prentice Redman/425 10.00 4.50
54 Shane Bazzell/1000 10.00 4.50
55 Delmon Young/75 80.00 36.00
56 Brian Stokes/1000 10.00 4.50
57 Matt Bruback/513 10.00 4.50
58 Nook Logan/150 10.00 4.50
59 Oscar Villarreal/150 10.00 4.50
60 Pete LaForest/250 15.00 6.75

2003 Donruss Rookies Stat Line Career

MINT NRMT
*SLC P/R b/wn 201+: 4X TO 10X
*SLC P/R b/wn 121-200: 5X TO 12X
*SLC P/R b/wn 81-120: 6X TO 15X
*SLC P/R b/wn 66-80: 8X TO 20X
*SLC P/R b/wn 51-65: 10X TO 25X
*SLC RC's P/R b/wn 201+: 4X TO 10X
*SLC RC's P/R b/wn 121-200: 4X TO 10X
*SLC RC's P/R b/wn 81-120: 4X TO 10X
*SLC RC's P/R b/wn 66-80: 5X TO 12X
*SLC RC's P/R b/wn 51-65: 5X TO 12X
*SLC RC's P/R b/wn 36-50: 6X TO 15X
*SLC RC's P/R b/wn 26-35: 8X TO 20X
RANDOM INSERTS IN DLP R/T PACKS
PRINT RUNS B/WN 1-245 COPIES PER
NO PRICING ON QTY OF 25 OR LESS.

2003 Donruss Rookies Stat Line Season

MINT NRMT
*SLS P/R b/wn 201+: 4X TO 10X
*SLS P/R b/wn 121-200: 5X TO 12X
*SLS P/R b/wn 66-80: 8X TO 20X
*SLS P/R b/wn 36-50: 12.5X TO 30X
*SLS P/R b/wn 26-35: 15X TO 10X
*SLS RC's P/R b/wn 81-120: 4X TO 10X
*SLS RC's P/R b/wn 66-80: 5X TO 12X
*SLS RC's P/R b/wn 51-65: 5X TO 12X
*SLS RC's P/R b/wn 36-50: 6X TO 15X
*SLS RC's P/R b/wn 26-35: 8X TO 20X
RANDOM INSERTS IN PACKS
PRINT RUNS B/WN 1-130 COPIES PER
NO PRICING ON QTY OF 25 OR LESS.

2003 Donruss Rookies Recollection Autographs

MINT NRMT
RANDOM INSERTS IN DLP R/T PACKS
PRINT RUNS B/WN 1-75 COPIES PER
NO PRICING ON QTY OF 5 OR LESS
1 Sandy Alomar Jr. 89 DR/2
2 Sandy Alomar Jr. 90 Black/5
3 Sandy Alomar Jr. 90 Blue/5
4 Jay Buhner 88 DR/5
5 Jose Canseco 86/1
6 Sid Fernandez 84/5
7 Jack McDowell 88/75 25.00 11.00
8 Paul O'Neill 86/5
9 Gary Sheffield 89/5
10 Ruben Sierra 86 DR/1
11 J.T. Snow 93/5
12 Robby Thompson 86 DR/5
13 Matt Williams 87 DR/5

2003 Donruss Atlantic City National

Collectors who opened a speficied number of Donruss/Playoff Packs at the 2003 Atlantic City National Convention were able to receive one of these cards which had a special Atlantic City Logo stamped on the front and were serial numbered to five on the back. Please note that due to market scarcity, no pricing is provided

MINT NRMT
PRINT RUN 5 SERIAL #'d SETS

2004 Donruss

This 400-card standard-size set was released in November, 2003. This set was issued in 10 card packs with an $1.99 SRP and those cards came 24 packs to a box and 16 boxes to a case. Please note the following subsets were issued as part of this product: Diamond King (1-25); Rated Rookies (26-70) and Team Checklists (371-400).

MINT NRMT
COMPLETE SET (400) 150.00 70.00
COMP.SET w/o SP's (300) 25.00 11.00
COMMON CARD (71-370) .30 .14
COMMON CARD (1-25/371-400) 1.00 .45
COMMON CARD (26-70) 3.00 1.35
1 Derek Jeter DK 4.00 1.80
2 Greg Maddux DK 2.50 1.10
3 Albert Pujols DK 3.00 1.35
4 Ichiro Suzuki DK 2.50 1.10
5 Alex Rodriguez DK 2.50 1.10
6 Roger Clemens DK 3.00 1.35
7 Andruw Jones DK 1.00 .45
8 Barry Bonds DK 4.00 1.80
9 Jeff Bagwell DK 1.00 .45
10 Randy Johnson DK 1.50 .70
11 Scott Rolen DK 1.00 .45
12 Lance Berkman DK 1.00 .45
13 Barry Zito DK 1.00 .45
14 Manny Ramirez DK 1.00 .45
15 Carlos Delgado DK 1.00 .45
16 Alfonso Soriano DK 1.00 .45
17 Todd Helton DK 1.00 .45
18 Mike Mussina DK 1.50 .70
19 Austin Kearns DK 1.00 .45
20 Nomar Garciaparra DK 2.50 1.10
21 Chipper Jones DK 1.50 .70
22 Mark Prior DK 3.00 1.35
23 Jim Thome DK 1.50 .70
24 Vladimir Guerrero DK 1.50 .70
25 Pedro Martinez DK 1.50 .70
26 Sergio Mitre RR 3.00 1.35
27 Adam Loewen RR 3.00 1.35
28 Alfredo Gonzalez RR 3.00 1.35
29 Miguel Ojeda RR 3.00 1.35
30 Rosman Garcia RR 3.00 1.35
31 Arnie Munoz RR 3.00 1.35
32 Andrew Brown RR 3.00 1.35
33 Josh Hall RR 3.00 1.35
34 Josh Stewart RR 3.00 1.35
35 Clint Barmes RR 3.00 1.35
36 Brandon Webb RR 3.00 1.35
37 Chien-Ming Wang RR 3.00 1.35
38 Edgar Gonzalez RR 3.00 1.35
39 Alejandro Machado RR 3.00 1.35
40 Jeremy Griffiths RR 3.00 1.35
41 Craig Brazell RR 3.00 1.35
42 Daniel Cabrera RR 3.00 1.35
43 Francisco Cabrera RR 3.00 1.35
44 Terrmel Sledge RR 3.00 1.35
45 Rob Hammock RR 3.00 1.35
46 Francisco Rosario RR 3.00 1.35
47 Francisco Cruceta RR 3.00 1.35
48 Rett Johnson RR 3.00 1.35
49 Guillermo Quiroz RR 3.00 1.35
50 Hong-Chih Kuo RR 3.00 1.35
51 Ian Ferguson RR 3.00 1.35
52 Tim Olson RR 3.00 1.35
53 Todd Wellemeyer RR 3.00 1.35
54 Rich Fischer RR 3.00 1.35
55 Phil Seibel RR 3.00 1.35
56 Joe Valentine RR 3.00 1.35
57 Matt Kata RR 3.00 1.35
58 Michael Hessman RR 3.00 1.35
59 Michel Hernandez RR 3.00 1.35
60 Doug Waechter RR 3.00 1.35
61 Prentice Redman RR 3.00 1.35
62 Nook Logan RR 3.00 1.35
63 Oscar Villarreal RR 3.00 1.35
64 Pete LaForest RR 3.00 1.35
65 Matt Bruback RR 3.00 1.35
66 Dan Haren RR 3.00 1.35
67 Greg Aquino RR 3.00 1.35
68 Lew Ford RR 3.00 1.35
69 Jeff Duncan RR 3.00 1.35
70 Ryan Wagner RR 3.00 1.35
71 Bengie Molina .30 .14
72 Brad Fullmer .30 .14
73 Darin Erstad .30 .14
74 David Eckstein .30 .14
75 Garret Anderson .30 .14
76 Jarrod Washburn .30 .14
77 Kevin Appier .30 .14
78 Scott Spiezio .30 .14
79 Tim Salmon .50 .23
80 Troy Glaus .50 .23

81 Troy Percival .30 .14
82 Jason Johnson .30 .14
83 Jay Gibbons .30 .14
84 Melvin Mora .30 .14
85 Sidney Ponson .30 .14
86 Tony Batista .30 .14
87 Bill Mueller .30 .14
88 Byung-Hyun Kim .30 .14
89 David Ortiz .30 .14
90 Derek Lowe .30 .14
91 Johnny Damon .30 .14
92 Casey Fossum .30 .14
93 Manny Ramirez .30 .14
94 Nomar Garciaparra 1.25 .55
95 Pedro Martinez .75 .35
96 Todd Walker .30 .14
97 Trot Nixon .50 .23
98 Bartolo Colon .30 .14
99 Carlos Lee .30 .14
100 D'Angelo Jimenez .30 .14
101 Esteban Loaiza .30 .14
102 Frank Thomas .75 .35
103 Joe Crede .30 .14
104 Jose Valentin .30 .14
105 Magglio Ordonez .30 .14
106 Mark Buehrle .30 .14
107 Paul Konerko .30 .14
108 Brandon Phillips .30 .14
109 C.C Sabathia .30 .14
110 Ellis Burks .30 .14
111 Jeremy Guthrie .30 .14
112 Josh Bard .30 .14
113 Matt Lawton .30 .14
114 Milton Bradley .30 .14
115 Omar Vizquel .30 .14
116 Travis Hafner .30 .14
117 Bobby Higginson .30 .14
118 Carlos Pena .30 .14
119 Dmitri Young .30 .14
120 Eric Munson .30 .14
121 Jeremy Bonderman .30 .14
122 Nate Cornejo .30 .14
123 Omar Infante .30 .14
124 Ramon Santiago .30 .14
125 Angel Berroa .30 .14
126 Carlos Beltran .30 .14
127 Desi Relaford .30 .14
128 Jeremy Affeldt .30 .14
129 Joe Randa .30 .14
130 Ken Harvey .30 .14
131 Mike MacDougal .30 .14
132 Michael Tucker .30 .14
133 Mike Sweeney .30 .14
134 Raul Ibanez .30 .14
135 Runelvys Hernandez .30 .14
136 A.J. Pierzynski .30 .14
137 Brad Radke .30 .14
138 Corey Koskie .30 .14
139 Cristian Guzman .30 .14
140 Doug Mientkiewicz .30 .14
141 Dustan Mohr .30 .14
142 Jacque Jones .30 .14
143 Kenny Rogers .30 .14
144 Bobby Kielty .30 .14
145 Kyle Lohse .30 .14
146 Luis Rivas .30 .14
147 Torii Hunter .30 .14
148 Alfonso Soriano .50 .23
149 Andy Pettitte .50 .23
150 Bernie Williams .50 .23
151 David Wells .30 .14
152 Derek Jeter 2.00 .90
153 Hideki Matsui 1.25 .55
154 Jason Giambi .75 .35
155 Jorge Posada .50 .23
156 Jose Contreras .30 .14
157 Mike Mussina .75 .35
158 Nick Johnson .30 .14
159 Robin Ventura .30 .14
160 Roger Clemens 1.50 .70
161 Barry Zito .50 .23
162 Chris Singleton .30 .14
163 Eric Byrnes .30 .14
164 Eric Chavez .30 .14
165 Erubiel Durazo .30 .14
166 Keith Foulke .30 .14
167 Mark Ellis .30 .14
168 Miguel Tejada .30 .14
169 Mark Mulder .30 .14
170 Ramon Hernandez .30 .14
171 Ted Lilly .30 .14
172 Terrence Long .30 .14
173 Tim Hudson .30 .14
174 Bret Boone .30 .14
175 Carlos Guillen .30 .14
176 Dan Wilson .30 .14
177 Edgar Martinez .50 .23
178 Freddy Garcia .30 .14
179 Gil Meche .30 .14
180 Ichiro Suzuki 1.25 .55
181 Jamie Moyer .30 .14
182 Joel Pineiro .30 .14
183 John Olerud .30 .14
184 Mike Cameron .30 .14
185 Randy Winn .30 .14
186 Ryan Franklin .30 .14
187 Kazuhiro Sasaki .30 .14
188 Aubrey Huff .30 .14
189 Carl Crawford .30 .14
190 Joe Kennedy .30 .14
191 Marlon Anderson .30 .14
192 Rey Ordonez .30 .14
193 Rocco Baldelli .75 .35
194 Toby Hall .30 .14
195 Travis Lee .30 .14
196 Alex Rodriguez 1.25 .55
197 Carl Everett .30 .14
198 Chan Ho Park .30 .14
199 Einar Diaz .30 .14
200 Hank Blalock .30 .14
201 Ismael Valdes .30 .14
202 Juan Gonzalez .75 .35
203 Mark Teixeira .30 .14
204 Mike Young .30 .14
205 Rafael Palmeiro .50 .23
206 Carlos Delgado .30 .14
207 Kelvim Escobar .30 .14
208 Eric Hinske .30 .14
209 Frank Catalanotto .30 .14
210 Josh Phelps .30 .14
211 Orlando Hudson .30 .14
212 Roy Halladay .30 .14
213 Shannon Stewart .30 .14
214 Vernon Wells .30 .14
215 Carlos Baerga .30 .14
216 Curt Schilling .50 .23
217 Junior Spivey .30 .14
218 Luis Gonzalez .30 .14
219 Lyle Overbay .30 .14
220 Mark Grace .50 .23
221 Matt Williams .30 .14
222 Randy Johnson .75 .35
223 Shea Hillenbrand .30 .14
224 Steve Finley .30 .14
225 Andruw Jones .30 .14
226 Chipper Jones .75 .35
227 Gary Sheffield .30 .14
228 Greg Maddux 1.25 .55
229 Javy Lopez .30 .14
230 John Smoltz .50 .23
231 Marcus Giles .30 .14
232 Mike Hampton .30 .14
233 Rafael Furcal .30 .14
234 Robert Fick .30 .14
235 Russ Ortiz .30 .14
236 Alex Gonzalez .30 .14
237 Carlos Zambrano .30 .14
238 Corey Patterson .30 .14
239 Hee Seop Choi .30 .14
240 Kerry Wood .75 .35
241 Mark Bellhorn .30 .14
242 Mark Prior 1.50 .70
243 Moises Alou .30 .14
244 Sammy Sosa 1.25 .55
245 Aaron Boone .30 .14
246 Adam Dunn .30 .14
247 Austin Kearns .30 .14
248 Barry Larkin .75 .35
249 Felipe Lopez .30 .14
250 Jose Guillen .30 .14
251 Ken Griffey Jr. 1.25 .55
252 Jason LaRue .30 .14
253 Scott Williamson .30 .14
254 Sean Casey .30 .14
255 Shawn Chacon .30 .14
256 Chris Stynes .30 .14
257 Jason Jennings .30 .14
258 Jay Payton .30 .14
259 Jose Hernandez .30 .14
260 Larry Walker .50 .23
261 Preston Wilson .30 .14
262 Ronnie Belliard .30 .14
263 Todd Helton .50 .23
264 A.J. Burnett .30 .14
265 Alex Gonzalez .30 .14
266 Brad Penny .30 .14
267 Derrek Lee .30 .14
268 Ivan Rodriguez .75 .35
269 Josh Beckett .50 .23
270 Juan Encarnacion .30 .14
271 Juan Pierre .30 .14
272 Luis Castillo .30 .14
273 Mike Lowell .30 .14
274 Todd Hollandsworth .30 .14
275 Billy Wagner .30 .14
276 Brad Ausmus .30 .14
277 Craig Biggio .50 .23
278 Jeff Bagwell .50 .23
279 Jeff Kent .30 .14
280 Lance Berkman .30 .14
281 Richard Hidalgo .30 .14
282 Roy Oswalt .30 .14
283 Wade Miller .30 .14
284 Adrian Beltre .30 .14
285 Brian Jordan .30 .14
286 Cesar Izturis .30 .14
287 Dave Roberts .30 .14
288 Eric Gagne .50 .23
289 Fred McGriff .50 .23
290 Hideo Nomo .75 .35
291 Kazuhisa Ishii .30 .14
292 Kevin Brown .30 .14
293 Paul Lo Duca .30 .14
294 Shawn Green .30 .14
295 Ben Sheets .30 .14
296 Geoff Jenkins .30 .14
297 Rey Sanchez .30 .14
298 Richie Sexson .30 .14
299 Wes Helms .30 .14
300 Brad Wilkerson .30 .14
301 Claudio Vargas .30 .14
302 Endy Chavez .30 .14
303 Fernando Tatis .30 .14
304 Javier Vazquez .30 .14
305 Jose Vidro .30 .14
306 Michael Barrett .30 .14
307 Orlando Cabrera .30 .14
308 Tony Armas Jr. .30 .14
309 Vladimir Guerrero .75 .35
310 Zach Day .30 .14
311 Al Leiter .30 .14
312 Cliff Floyd .30 .14
313 Jae Weong Seo .30 .14
314 Jeromy Burnitz .30 .14
315 Mike Piazza 1.25 .55
316 Mo Vaughn .30 .14
317 Roberto Alomar .75 .35
318 Roger Cedeno .30 .14
319 Tom Glavine .50 .23
320 Jose Reyes .50 .23
321 Bobby Abreu .30 .14
322 Brett Myers .30 .14
323 David Bell .30 .14
324 Jim Thome .75 .35
325 Jimmy Rollins .30 .14
326 Kevin Millwood .30 .14
327 Marlon Byrd .30 .14
328 Mike Lieberthal .30 .14
329 Pat Burrell .30 .14
330 Randy Wolf .30 .14
331 Aramis Ramirez .30 .14
332 Brian Giles .30 .14
333 Jason Kendall .30 .14
334 Kenny Lofton .30 .14
335 Kip Wells .30 .14
336 Kris Benson .30 .14
337 Randall Simon .30 .14
338 Reggie Sanders .30 .14
339 Albert Pujols 1.50 .70
340 Edgar Renteria .30 .14
341 Fernando Vina .30 .14
342 J.D. Drew .30 .14
343 Jim Edmonds .30 .14
344 Matt Morris .30 .14
345 Mike Matheny .30 .14
346 Scott Rolen .50 .23
347 Tino Martinez .50 .23
348 Woody Williams .30 .14
349 Brian Lawrence .30 .14
350 Mark Kotsay .30 .14
351 Mark Loretta .30 .14
352 Ramon Vazquez .30 .14
353 Rondell White .30 .14
354 Ryan Klesko .30 .14
355 Sean Burroughs .30 .14
356 Trevor Hoffman .30 .14
357 Xavier Nady .30 .14
358 Andres Galarraga .30 .14
359 Barry Bonds 2.00 .90
360 Benito Santiago .30 .14
361 Deivi Cruz .30 .14
362 Edgardo Alfonzo .30 .14
363 J.T. Snow .30 .14
364 Jason Schmidt .30 .14
365 Kirk Rueter .30 .14
366 Kurt Ainsworth .30 .14
367 Marquis Grissom .30 .14
368 Ray Durham .30 .14
369 Rich Aurilia .30 .14
370 Tim Worrell .30 .14
371 Troy Glaus TC 1.00 .45
372 Melvin Mora TC 1.00 .45
373 Nomar Garciaparra TC 2.50 1.10
374 Magglio Ordonez TC 1.00 .45
375 Omar Vizquel TC 1.00 .45
376 Dmitri Young TC 1.00 .45
377 Mike Sweeney TC 1.00 .45
378 Torii Hunter TC 1.00 .45
379 Derek Jeter TC 4.00 1.80
380 Barry Zito TC 1.00 .45
381 Ichiro Suzuki TC 2.50 1.10
382 Rocco Baldelli TC 1.50 .70
383 Alex Rodriguez TC 2.50 1.10
384 Carlos Delgado TC 1.00 .45
385 Randy Johnson TC 1.50 .70
386 Greg Maddux TC 2.50 1.10
387 Sammy Sosa TC 2.50 1.10
388 Ken Griffey Jr. TC 2.50 1.10
389 Todd Helton TC 1.00 .45
390 Ivan Rodriguez TC 1.50 .70
391 Jeff Bagwell TC 1.00 .45
392 Hideo Nomo TC 1.50 .70
393 Richie Sexson TC 1.00 .45
394 Vladimir Guerrero TC 1.50 .70
395 Mike Piazza TC 2.50 1.10
396 Jim Thome TC 1.50 .70
397 Jason Kendall TC 1.00 .45
398 Albert Pujols TC 3.00 1.35
399 Ryan Klesko TC 1.00 .45
400 Barry Bonds TC 4.00 1.80

2004 Donruss Autographs

MINT NRMT
RANDOM INSERTS IN PACKS
#'d CARD PRINTS B/WN 5-141 COPIES PER
NO PRICING ON QTY OF 12 OR LESS.
51 Ian Ferguson 10.00 4.50
73 Darin Erstad/5
106 Mark Buehrle/141 15.00 6.75
112 Josh Bard 10.00 4.50
123 Omar Infante 10.00 4.50
172 Terrence Long 10.00 4.50
188 Aubrey Huff/143 15.00 6.75
194 Toby Hall 10.00 4.50
217 Junior Spivey/132 10.00 4.50
234 Robert Fick 10.00 4.50
312 Cliff Floyd/12
349 Brian Lawrence 10.00 4.50

2004 Donruss Press Proofs Black

MINT NRMT
RANDOM INSERTS IN PACKS
STATED PRINT RUN 10 SERIAL #'d SETS
NO PRICING DUE TO SCARCITY

2004 Donruss Press Proofs Blue

MINT NRMT
*PP BLUE 71-370: 4X TO 10X BASIC
*PP BLUE 1-25/371-400: 2X TO 5X BASIC
*PP BLUE 26-70: .5X TO 1.2X BASIC .
RANDOM INSERTS IN RETAIL PACKS
STATED PRINT RUN 100 SERIAL #'d SETS

2004 Donruss Press Proofs Gold

MINT NRMT
RANDOM INSERTS IN RETAIL PACKS
STATED PRINT RUN 25 SERIAL #'d SETS
NO PRICING DUE TO SCARCITY

2004 Donruss Press Proofs Red

MINT NRMT
*PP RED 71-370: 2.5X TO 6X BASIC
*PP RED 1-25/371-400: 1.25X TO 3X BASIC
*PP RED 26-70: .4X TO 1X BASIC
STATED ODDS 1:12 RETAIL

2004 Donruss Stat Line Career

MINT NRMT
*71-370 P/R b/wn 200-443 2.5X TO 6X
*71-370 P/R b/wn 121-200: 3X TO 8X
*71-370 P/R b/wn 81-120: 4X TO 10X
*71-370 P/R b/wn 66-80: 5X TO 12X
*71-370 P/R b/wn 51-65: 6X TO 15X
*71-370 P/R b/wn 36-50: 8X TO 20X
*71-370 P/R b/wn 26-35: 10X TO 25X
*1-25/371-400 P/R b/wn 200-500: 1.25X TO 3X
*1-25/371-400 P/R b/wn 121-200: 1.5X TO 4X
*1-25/371-400 P/R b/wn 81-120: 2X TO 5X
*1-25/371-400 P/R b/wn 66-80: 2.5X TO 6X
*1-25/371-400 P/R b/wn 51-65: 3X TO 8X
*1-25/371-400 P/R b/wn 36-50: 4X TO 10X
*1-25/371-400 P/R b/wn 26-35: 5X TO 12X
*26-70 P/R b/wn 200-491: .5X TO 1.2X
*26-70 P/R b/wn 121-200: .6X TO 1.5X
*26-70 P/R b/wn 81-120: .75X TO 2X.
*26-70 P/R b/wn 66-80: 1X TO 2.5X
*26-70 P/R b/wn 51-65: 1.25X TO 3X.
*26-70 P/R b/wn 36-50: 1.5X TO 4X
*26-70 P/R b/wn 26-35: 2X TO 5X
RANDOM INSERTS IN PACKS
PRINT RUNS B/WN 6-500 COPIES PER
NO PRICING ON QTY OF 25 OR LESS.

2004 Donruss Stat Line Season

MINT NRMT
*71-370 P/R b/wn 121-193: 3X TO 8X
*71-370 P/R b/wn 81-120: 4X TO 10X
*71-370 P/R b/wn 66-80: 5X TO 12X
*71-370 P/R b/wn 51-65: 6X TO 15X
*71-370 P/R b/wn 36-50: 8X TO 20X
*71-370 P/R b/wn 26-35: 10X TO 25X
*1-25/371-400 P/R b/wn 201-225: 1.25X TO 3X
*1-25/371-400 P/R b/wn 121-200: 1.5X TO 4X
*1-25/371-400 P/R b/wn 81-120: 2X TO 5X
*1-25/371-400 P/R b/wn 66-80: 2.5X TO 6X
*1-25/371-400 P/R b/wn 51-65: 3X TO 8X
*1-25/371-400 P/R b/wn 36-50: 4X TO 10X
*1-25/371-400 P/R b/wn 26-35: 5X TO 12X
*26-70 P/R b/wn 201-261: .5X TO 1.2X
*26-70 P/R b/wn 121-200: .6X TO 1.5X
*26-70 P/R b/wn 81-120: .75X TO 2X.
*26-70 P/R b/wn 66-80: 1X TO 2.5X
*26-70 P/R b/wn 51-65: 1.25X TO 3X.
*26-70 P/R b/wn 36-50: 1.5X TO 4X
*26-70 P/R b/wn 26-35: 2X TO 5X
RANDOM INSERTS IN PACKS
PRINT RUNS B/WN 1-261 COPIES PER
NO PRICING ON QTY OF 25 OR LESS.

2004 Donruss All-Stars American League

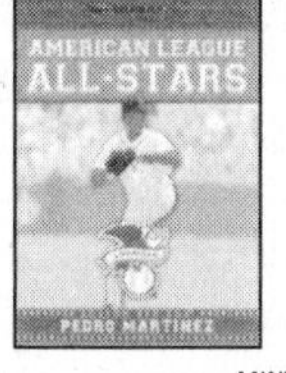

MINT NRMT
STATED PRINT RUN 1000 SERIAL #'d SETS
*BLACK: .6X TO 1.5X BASIC
BLACK PRINT RUN 250 SERIAL #'d SETS
RANDOM INSERTS IN PACKS
1 Alex Rodriguez 8.00 3.60
2 Roger Clemens 10.00 4.50
3 Ichiro Suzuki 8.00 3.60
4 Barry Zito 3.00 1.35
5 Garret Anderson 3.00 1.35
6 Derek Jeter 12.00 5.50
7 Manny Ramirez 3.00 1.35
8 Pedro Martinez 5.00 2.20
9 Alfonso Soriano 3.00 1.35
10 Carlos Delgado 3.00 1.35

2004 Donruss All-Stars National League

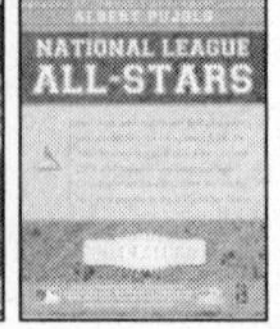

MINT NRMT
STATED PRINT RUN 1000 SERIAL #'d SETS
*BLACK: .6X TO 1.5X BASIC
BLACK PRINT RUN 250 SERIAL #'d SETS
RANDOM INSERTS IN PACKS
1 Barry Bonds 12.00 5.50
2 Andruw Jones 3.00 1.35
3 Scott Rolen 3.00 1.35
4 Austin Kearns 3.00 1.35
5 Mark Prior 10.00 4.50
6 Vladimir Guerrero 5.00 2.20
7 Jeff Bagwell 3.00 1.35
8 Mike Piazza 8.00 3.60
9 Albert Pujols 10.00 4.50
10 Randy Johnson 5.00 2.20

2004 Donruss Bat Kings

MINT NRMT
1-4 PRINT RUN 250 SERIAL #'d SETS
5-8 PRINT RUN 100 SERIAL #'d SETS
*STUDIO 1-4: .75X TO 2X BASIC
STUDIO 1-4 PRINT RUN 50 SERIAL #'d SETS
STUDIO 5-8 PRINT RUN 25 SERIAL #'d SETS
STUDIO 5-8 NO PRICING DUE TO SCARCITY
RANDOM INSERTS IN PACKS
1 Alex Rodriguez 03 20.00 9.00
2 Albert Pujols 03 25.00 11.00
3 Chipper Jones 03 15.00 6.75
4 Lance Berkman 03 10.00 4.50
5 Cal Ripken 88 80.00 36.00
6 George Brett 87 50.00 22.00
7 Don Mattingly 89 50.00 22.00
8 Roberto Clemente 02 100.00 45.00

2004 Donruss Craftsmen

MINT NRMT
STATED PRINT RUN 2000 SERIAL #'d SETS
*BLACK: 1X TO 2.5X BASIC
BLACK PRINT RUN 275 SERIAL #'d SETS
*MASTER: 1.25X TO 3X BASIC
MASTER PRINT RUN 150 SERIAL #'d SETS
RANDOM INSERTS IN PACKS
1 Alex Rodriguez 5.00 2.20
2 Mark Prior 6.00 2.70
3 Ichiro Suzuki 5.00 2.20
4 Barry Bonds 8.00 3.60
5 Ken Griffey Jr. 5.00 2.20
6 Alfonso Soriano 2.00 .90
7 Mike Piazza 5.00 2.20
8 Chipper Jones 3.00 1.35
9 Derek Jeter 8.00 3.60
10 Randy Johnson 3.00 1.35
11 Sammy Sosa 5.00 2.20
12 Roger Clemens 6.00 2.70
13 Nomar Garciaparra 5.00 2.20
14 Greg Maddux 5.00 2.20
15 Albert Pujols 6.00 2.70

2004 Donruss Diamond Kings Inserts

MINT NRMT
STATED PRINT RUN 2000 SERIAL #'d SETS
*BLACK: .75X TO 2X BASIC
BLACK PRINT RUN 100 SERIAL #'d SETS
*STUDIO: .6X TO 1.5X BASIC
STUDIO PRINT RUN 250 SERIAL #'d SETS
RANDOM INSERTS IN PACKS
1 Derek Jeter 15.00 6.75
2 Greg Maddux 10.00 4.50
3 Albert Pujols 12.00 5.50
4 Ichiro Suzuki 10.00 4.50
5 Alex Rodriguez 10.00 4.50
6 Roger Clemens 12.00 5.50
7 Andruw Jones 8.00 3.60
8 Barry Bonds 15.00 6.75
9 Jeff Bagwell 8.00 3.60
10 Randy Johnson 8.00 3.60
11 Scott Rolen 8.00 3.60
12 Lance Berkman 8.00 3.60
13 Barry Zito 8.00 3.60
14 Manny Ramirez 8.00 3.60
15 Carlos Delgado 8.00 3.60
16 Alfonso Soriano 8.00 3.60
17 Todd Helton 8.00 3.60
18 Mike Mussina 8.00 3.60
19 Austin Kearns 8.00 3.60
20 Nomar Garciaparra 10.00 4.50
21 Chipper Jones 8.00 3.60
22 Mark Prior 12.00 5.50
23 Jim Thome 8.00 3.60
24 Vladimir Guerrero 8.00 3.60
25 Pedro Martinez 8.00 3.60

2004 Donruss Elite Series

MINT NRMT
RANDOM INSERTS IN PACKS
STATED PRINT RUN 1500 SERIAL #'d SETS
*BLACK: 1X TO 2.5X BASIC
BLACK PRINT RUN 150 SERIAL #'d SETS
DOMINATORS PRINT 25 SERIAL #'d SETS
DOMINATORS NO PRICE DUE TO SCARCITY
RANDOM INSERTS IN PACKS
1 Albert Pujols 10.00 4.50
2 Barry Zito 3.00 1.35
3 Gary Sheffield 3.00 1.35
4 Mike Mussina 5.00 2.20
5 Lance Berkman 3.00 1.35

6 Alfonso Soriano 3.00 1.35
7 Randy Johnson 5.00 2.20
8 Nomar Garciaparra 8.00 3.60
9 Austin Kearns 3.00 1.35
10 Manny Ramirez 3.00 1.35
11 Mark Prior 10.00 4.50
12 Alex Rodriguez 8.00 3.60
13 Derek Jeter 12.00 5.50
14 Barry Bonds 12.00 5.50
15 Roger Clemens 10.00 4.50

2004 Donruss Inside View

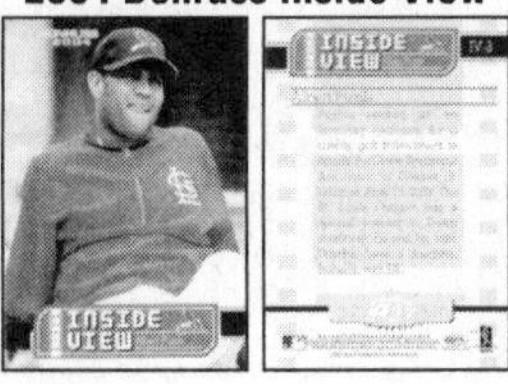

MINT NRMT
RANDOM INSERTS IN PACKS
STATED PRINT RUN 1250 SERIAL #'d SETS
1 Derek Jeter 10.00 4.50
2 Greg Maddux 6.00 2.70
3 Albert Pujols 8.00 3.60
4 Ichiro Suzuki 6.00 2.70
5 Alex Rodriguez 6.00 2.70
6 Roger Clemens 8.00 3.60
7 Andruw Jones 2.50 1.10
8 Barry Bonds 10.00 4.50
9 Jeff Bagwell 2.50 1.10
10 Randy Johnson 4.00 1.80
11 Scott Rolen 2.50 1.10
12 Lance Berkman 2.50 1.10
13 Barry Zito 2.50 1.10
14 Manny Ramirez 2.50 1.10
15 Carlos Delgado 2.50 1.10
16 Alfonso Soriano 2.50 1.10
17 Todd Helton 2.50 1.10
18 Mike Mussina 4.00 1.80
19 Austin Kearns 2.50 1.10
20 Nomar Garciaparra 6.00 2.70
21 Chipper Jones 4.00 1.80
22 Mark Prior 8.00 3.60
23 Jim Thome 4.00 1.80
24 Vladimir Guerrero 4.00 1.80
25 Pedro Martinez 4.00 1.80

2004 Donruss Jersey Kings

MINT NRMT
1-6 PRINT RUN 250 SERIAL #'d SETS
7-12 PRINT RUN 100 SERIAL #'d SETS
*STUDIO 1-6: .75X TO 2X BASIC JSY KINGS
STUDIO 1-6 PRINT RUN 50 SERIAL #'d SETS
STUDIO 7-12 PRINT RUN 25 SERIAL #'d SETS
STUDIO 7-12 NO PRICING DUE TO SCARCITY
RANDOM INSERTS IN PACKS
1 Alfonso Soriano 03 15.00 6.75
2 Sammy Sosa 03 20.00 9.00
3 Roger Clemens 03 25.00 11.00
4 Nomar Garciaparra 03 20.00 9.00
5 Mark Prior 03 25.00 11.00
6 Vladimir Guerrero 03 15.00 6.75
7 Don Mattingly 89 50.00 22.00
8 Roberto Clemente 02 100.00 45.00
9 George Brett 87 50.00 22.00
10 Nolan Ryan 01 50.00 22.00
11 Cal Ripken 01 80.00 36.00
12 Mike Schmidt 01 40.00 18.00

2004 Donruss Longball Leaders

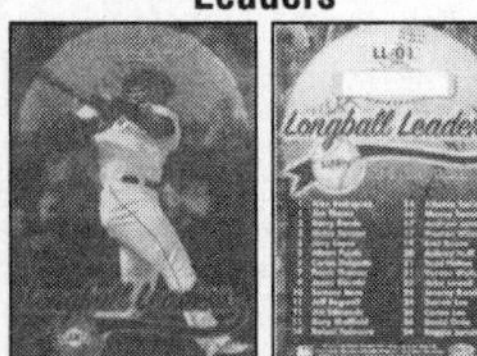

MINT NRMT
STATED PRINT RUN 1500 SERIAL #'d SETS
*BLACK: .75X TO 2X BASIC LL
BLACK PRINT RUN 250 SERIAL #'d SETS
*DIE CUT: 1.25X TO 3X BASIC LL
DIE CUT PRINT RUN 50 SERIAL #'d SETS
RANDOM INSERTS IN PACKS
1 Barry Bonds 10.00 4.50
2 Alfonso Soriano 2.50 1.10
3 Adam Dunn 2.50 1.10
4 Alex Rodriguez 6.00 2.70
5 Jim Thome 4.00 1.80
6 Garret Anderson 2.50 1.10
7 Juan Gonzalez 4.00 1.80
8 Jeff Bagwell 2.50 1.10
9 Gary Sheffield 2.50 1.10
10 Sammy Sosa 6.00 2.70

2004 Donruss Mound Marvels

MINT NRMT
STATED PRINT RUN 750 SERIAL #'d SETS
*BLACK: .75X TO 2X BASIC MM
BLACK PRINT RUN 175 SERIAL #'d SETS
RANDOM INSERTS IN PACKS

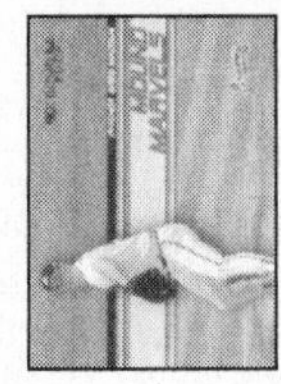

1 Mark Prior 10.00 4.50
2 Curt Schilling 3.00 1.35
3 Mike Mussina 5.00 2.20
4 Kevin Brown 3.00 1.35
5 Pedro Martinez 5.00 2.20
6 Mark Mulder 3.00 1.35
7 Kerry Wood 5.00 2.20
8 Greg Maddux 8.00 3.60
9 Kevin Millwood 3.00 1.35
10 Barry Zito 3.00 1.35
11 Roger Clemens 10.00 4.50
12 Randy Johnson 5.00 2.20
13 Hideo Nomo 5.00 2.20
14 Tim Hudson 3.00 1.35
15 Tom Glavine 3.00 1.35

2004 Donruss Power Alley Red

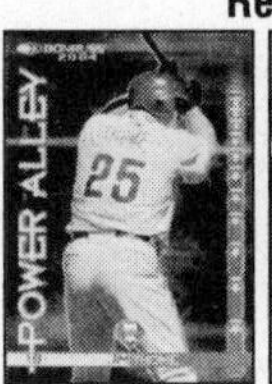

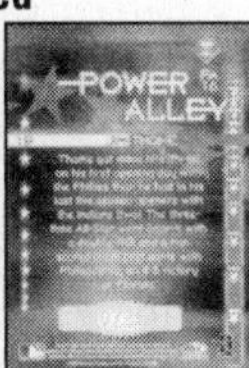

MINT NRMT
STATED PRINT RUN 2500 SERIAL #'d SETS
BLACK DC PRINT RUN 1 SERIAL #'d SET
BLACK DC NO PRICING DUE TO SCARCITY
*BLUE: .6X TO 1.5X BASIC RED
BLUE PRINT RUN 1000 SERIAL #'d SETS
*BLUE DC: 1.25X TO 3X BASIC RED
BLUE DC PRINT RUN 100 SERIAL #'d SETS
GREEN PRINT RUN 25 SERIAL #'d SETS
GREEN NO PRICING DUE TO SCARCITY
GREEN DC 5 SERIAL #'d SETS
GREEN DC NO PRICING DUE TO SCARCITY
*PURPLE: 1X TO 2.5X BASIC RED
PURPLE PRINT RUN 250 SERIAL #'d SETS
PURPLE DC PRINT RUN 25 SERIAL #'d SETS
PURPLE DC NO PRICING DUE TO SCARCITY
*RED DC: 1X TO 2.5X BASIC RED
RED DC PRINT RUN 250 SERIAL #'d SETS
*YELLOW: 1.25X TO 3X BASIC RED
YELLOW PRINT RUN 100 SERIAL #'d SETS
YELLOW DC PRINT RUN 10 SERIAL #'d SETS
YELLOW DC NO PRICING DUE TO SCARCITY
RANDOM INSERTS IN PACKS
1 Albert Pujols 6.00 2.70
2 Mike Piazza 5.00 2.20
3 Carlos Delgado 2.00 .90
4 Barry Bonds 8.00 3.60
5 Jim Edmonds 2.00 .90
6 Nomar Garciaparra 5.00 2.20
7 Alfonso Soriano 2.00 .90
8 Alex Rodriguez 5.00 2.20
9 Lance Berkman 2.00 .90
10 Scott Rolen 2.00 .90
11 Manny Ramirez 2.00 .90
12 Rafael Palmeiro 2.00 .90
13 Sammy Sosa 5.00 2.20
14 Adam Dunn 2.00 .90
15 Andruw Jones 2.00 .90
16 Jim Thome 3.00 1.35
17 Jason Giambi 3.00 1.35
18 Jeff Bagwell 2.00 .90
19 Juan Gonzalez 3.00 1.35
20 Austin Kearns 2.00 .90

2004 Donruss Production Line Average

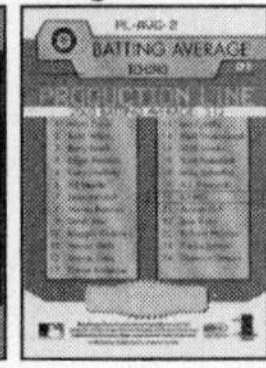

MINT NRMT
PRINT RUNS B/WN 300-359 COPIES PER
*BLACK: .75X TO 2X BASIC AVG
BLACK PRINT RUN 35 SERIAL #'d SETS
*DIE CUT: .5X TO 1.2X BASIC AVG
DIE CUT PRINT RUN 100 SERIAL #'d SETS
RANDOM INSERTS IN PACKS
1 Gary Sheffield/330 5.00 2.20
2 Ichiro Suzuki/312 12.00 5.50
3 Todd Helton/358 5.00 2.20
4 Manny Ramirez/325 5.00 2.20
5 Garret Anderson/315 5.00 2.20
6 Barry Bonds/341 20.00 9.00
7 Albert Pujols/359 15.00 6.75
8 Derek Jeter/324 20.00 9.00
9 Nomar Garciaparra/301 12.00 5.50
10 Hank Blalock/300 5.00 2.20

2004 Donruss Production Line OBP

MINT NRMT
PRINT RUNS B/WN 396-529 COPIES PER
*BLACK: 1X TO 2.5X BASIC OBP
BLACK PRINT RUN 40 SERIAL #'d SETS
*DIE CUT: .6X TO 1.5X BASIC OBP

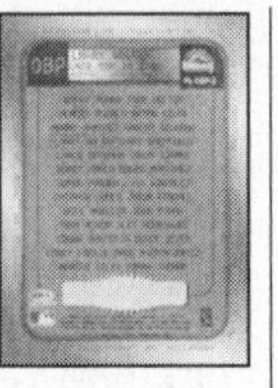

DIE CUT PRINT RUN 100 SERIAL #'d SETS
RANDOM INSERTS IN PACKS
1 Todd Helton/458 4.00 1.80
2 Albert Pujols/439 12.00 5.50
3 Larry Walker/422 4.00 1.80
4 Barry Bonds/529 15.00 6.75
5 Chipper Jones/402 6.00 2.70
6 Manny Ramirez/427 4.00 1.80
7 Gary Sheffield/419 4.00 1.80
8 Lance Berkman/412 4.00 1.80
9 Alex Rodriguez/396 10.00 4.50
10 Jason Giambi/412 6.00 2.70

2004 Donruss Production Line OPS

MINT NRMT
PRINT RUNS B/WN 910-1278 COPIES PER
*BLACK: .75X TO 2X BASIC OPS
BLACK PRINT RUN 125 SERIAL #'d SETS
*DIE CUT: .75X TO 2X BASIC OPS
DIE CUT PRINT RUN 100 SERIAL #'d SETS
RANDOM INSERTS IN PACKS
1 Albert Pujols/1106 10.00 4.50
2 Barry Bonds/1278 12.00 5.50
3 Gary Sheffield/1023 3.00 1.35
4 Todd Helton/1088 3.00 1.35
5 Scott Rolen/910 3.00 1.35
6 Manny Ramirez/1014 3.00 1.35
7 Alex Rodriguez/995 8.00 3.60
8 Jim Thome/958 5.00 2.20
9 Jason Giambi/939 5.00 2.20
10 Frank Thomas/952 5.00 2.20

2004 Donruss Production Line Slugging

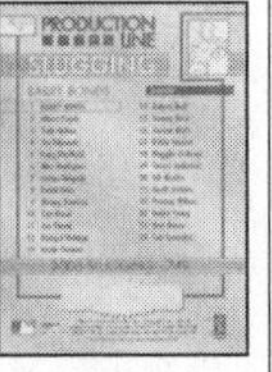

MINT NRMT
PRINT RUNS B/WN 541-749 COPIES PER
*BLACK: .75X TO 2X BASIC SLG
BLACK PRINT RUN 75 SERIAL #'d SETS
*DIE CUT: .6X TO 1.5X BASIC SLG
DIE CUT PRINT RUN 100 SERIAL #'d SETS
RANDOM INSERTS IN PACKS
1 Alex Rodriguez/600 10.00 4.50
2 Frank Thomas/562 6.00 2.70
3 Garret Anderson/541 4.00 1.80
4 Albert Pujols/667 12.00 5.50
5 Sammy Sosa/553 10.00 4.50
6 Gary Sheffield/604 4.00 1.80
7 Manny Ramirez/587 4.00 1.80
8 Jim Edmonds/617 4.00 1.80
9 Barry Bonds/749 15.00 6.75
10 Todd Helton/630 4.00 1.80

2004 Donruss Recollection Autographs

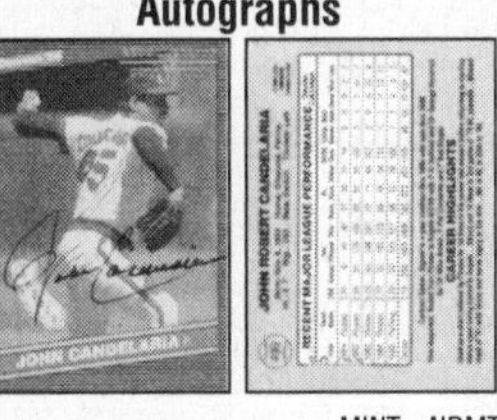

MINT NRMT
RANDOM INSERTS IN PACKS
PRINT RUNS B/WN 1-100 COPIES PER
NO PRICING ON QTY OF 50 OR LESS.
27 John Candelaria 88 Black/83 15.00 6.75
39 Jack Clark 87/67 20.00 9.00
40 Jack Clark 88/75 15.00 6.75
69 Sid Fernandez 86/52 20.00 9.00
72 Sid Fernandez 88/58 20.00 9.00
83 George Foster 83/50
84 George Foster 84/70 20.00 9.00
85 George Foster 85/50
86 George Foster 86/83 15.00 6.75
91 Cliff Lee 03/100 10.00 4.50
92 Terrence Long 01/90 15.00 6.75
93 Melvin Mora 03/50
100 Jesse Orosco 86 Blue/65 15.00 6.75
102 Jesse Orosco 87 Blue/90 10.00 4.50
115 Jose Vidro 01/89 15.00 6.75

2004 Donruss Timber and Threads

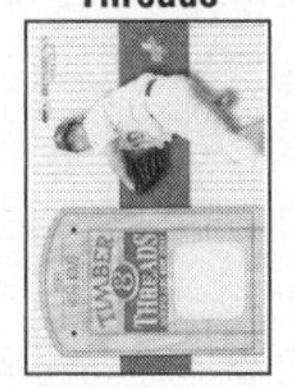

MINT NRMT
STATED ODDS 1:40
*STUDIO: .75X TO 2X BASIC TT
STUDIO RANDOM INSERTS IN PACKS
STUDIO PRINT RUN 50 SERIAL #'d SETS
1 Adam Dunn Jsy 8.00 3.60
2 Alex Rodriguez Blue Jsy 15.00 6.75
3 Alex Rodriguez White Jsy 15.00 6.75
4 Andruw Jones Jsy 8.00 3.60
5 Austin Kearns Jsy 8.00 3.60
6 Carlos Beltran Jsy 8.00 3.60
7 Carlos Lee Jsy 8.00 3.60
8 Frank Thomas Jsy 10.00 4.50
9 Greg Maddux Jsy 10.00 4.50
10 Hideo Nomo Jsy 10.00 4.50
11 Jeff Bagwell Jsy 10.00 4.50
12 Lance Berkman Jsy 8.00 3.60
13 Magglio Ordonez Jsy 8.00 3.60
14 Mike Sweeney Jsy 8.00 3.60
15 Randy Johnson Jsy 10.00 4.50
16 Rocco Baldelli Jsy 10.00 4.50
17 Roger Clemens Jsy 15.00 6.75
18 Sammy Sosa Jsy 15.00 6.75
19 Shawn Green Jsy 8.00 3.60
20 Tom Glavine Jsy 10.00 4.50
21 Adam Dunn Bat 8.00 3.60
22 Andruw Jones Bat 8.00 3.60
23 Bobby Abreu Bat 8.00 3.60
24 Hank Blalock Bat 8.00 3.60
25 Ivan Rodriguez Bat 10.00 4.50
26 Jim Edmonds Bat 8.00 3.60
27 Josh Phelps Bat 8.00 3.60
28 Juan Gonzalez Bat 10.00 4.50
29 Lance Berkman Bat 8.00 3.60
30 Larry Walker Bat 10.00 4.50
31 Magglio Ordonez Bat 8.00 3.60
32 Manny Ramirez Bat 8.00 3.60
33 Mike Piazza Bat 10.00 4.50
34 Nomar Garciaparra Bat 15.00 6.75
35 Paul Lo Duca Bat 8.00 3.60
36 Roberto Alomar Bat 10.00 4.50
37 Rocco Baldelli Bat 10.00 4.50
38 Sammy Sosa Bat 15.00 6.75
39 Vernon Wells Bat 8.00 3.60
40 Vladimir Guerrero Bat 10.00 4.50

2004 Donruss Timber and Threads Autographs

MINT NRMT
RANDOM INSERTS IN PACKS
PRINT RUNS B/WN 5-50 COPIES PER
NO PRICING ON QTY OF 34 OR LESS.
2 Alex Rodriguez Blue Jsy/5
5 Austin Kearns Jsy/19
6 Carlos Beltran Jsy/34
7 Carlos Lee Jsy/25
8 Frank Thomas Jsy/5
9 Greg Maddux Jsy/5
10 Hideo Nomo Jsy/5
11 Jeff Bagwell Jsy/5
12 Lance Berkman Jsy/5
13 Magglio Ordonez Jsy/30
14 Mike Sweeney Jsy/25
17 Roger Clemens Jsy/5
19 Shawn Green Jsy/5
20 Tom Glavine Jsy/5
21 Adam Dunn Bat/5
22 Andruw Jones Bat/5
23 Bobby Abreu Bat/50 25.00 11.00
24 Hank Blalock Bat/50 40.00 18.00
25 Ivan Rodriguez Bat/7
26 Jim Edmonds Bat/5
27 Josh Phelps Bat/50 25.00 11.00
28 Juan Gonzalez Bat/5
31 Magglio Ordonez Bat/30
32 Manny Ramirez Bat/5
35 Paul Lo Duca Bat/50 25.00 11.00
36 Roberto Alomar Bat/10
37 Rocco Baldelli Bat/15
40 Vladimir Guerrero Bat/50 60.00 27.00

2004 Donruss-Playoff Hawaii Fans of the Game Gandolfini

These cards, which were issued to select attendees of the 2004 Hawaii Trade Conference feature Sopranos star James Gandolfini. The cards were issued to promote the 2004 Donruss/Playoff initiative of having celebrity signatures within their 2004 products.

Nm-Mt Ex-Mt
ISSUED AT HAWAII TRADE SHOW
FG1 James Gandolfini/300
FG1A James Gandolfini AU/50

2001 Donruss Baseball's Best Bronze

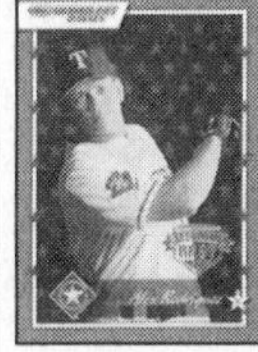

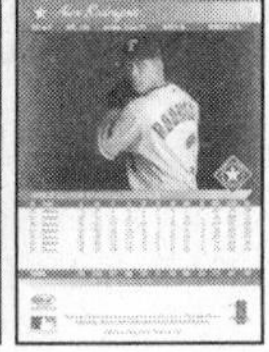

These 220 cards were available via a coupon randomly seeded into 2001 Donruss baseball packs at stated odds of 1:720. Consumers that pulled the Baseball's Best coupon (or bought it off the secondary market) then had to mail it into Donruss along with a check or money order for $105 prior to the January 20th, 2002 deadline to receive a factory sealed set 330-card set (of which contained the 220-card Baseball's Best set plus the 110-card Baseball's Best "The Rookies" set. The consumer did not know upon mailing in the coupon whether he or she would be receiving the Bronze, Silver or Gold version of the set of which were disseminated randomly. The 330 cards are glossy-coated parallels of the 220-card basic 2001 Donruss set and the 110-card 2001 Donruss the Rookies set. Only 999 serial-numbered Bronze sets were created, with each card carrying serial-numbering on back and Bronze foil accents on front.

Nm-Mt Ex-Mt
COMP.FACT.SET (330) 200.00 60.00
*STARS 1-150: 2X TO 5X BASIC CARDS
*ROOKIES 151-200: .2X TO .5X BASIC
*FAN CLUB 201-220: .5X TO 1.2X BASIC

2001 Donruss Baseball's Best Bronze Rookies

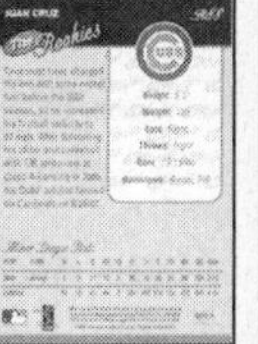

Issued as a redemption "update" set to the basic 2001 Donruss set, these 105 cards were available via a coupon which could be mailed into Donruss. There were only 999 bronze sets produced.

Nm-Mt Ex-Mt
*BRONZE: .75X TO 2X BASIC ROOKIES

2001 Donruss Baseball's Best Bronze Rookies Diamond Kings

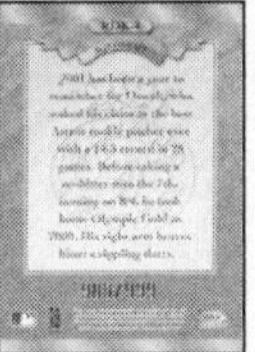

Inserted one per Donruss Baseball's Best Bronze, these five cards parallel the Donruss Rookies Diamond Kings.

Nm-Mt Ex-Mt
*BRONZE DK's: .6X TO 1.5X BASIC DK's

2001 Donruss Baseball's Best Gold

These 220 cards were available via a coupon randomly seeded into 2001 Donruss baseball packs at stated odds of 1:720. Consumers that pulled the Baseball's Best coupon (or bought it off the secondary market) then had to mail it into Donruss along with a check or money order for $105 prior to the January 20th, 2002 deadline to receive a factory sealed set 330-card set (of which contained the 220-card Baseball's Best set plus the 110-card Baseball's Best "The Rookies" set. The consumer did not know upon mailing in the coupon whether he or she would be receiving the Bronze, Silver or Gold version of the set of which were disseminated randomly. The 330 cards are glossy-coated parallels of the 220-card basic 2001 Donruss set and the 110-card 2001 Donruss the Rookies set. Only 99 serial-numbered Gold sets were created, with each card carrying serial-numbering on back and Gold foil accents on front.

Nm-Mt Ex-Mt
COMP.FACT.SET (330) 800.00 240.00
*STARS 1-150: 5X TO 12X BASIC CARDS
*ROOKIES 151-200: .5X TO 1.2X BASIC
*FAN CLUB 201-220: 1.25X TO 3X BASIC

2001 Donruss Baseball's Best Gold Rookies

Issued as a redemption "update" set to the basic 2001 Donruss set, these 105 cards were available via a coupon which could be mailed into Donruss for these 110 cards. There were only 99 gold sets produced.

Nm-Mt Ex-Mt
*GOLD: 2.5X TO 6X BASIC ROOKIES..

2001 Donruss Baseball's Best Gold Rookies Diamond Kings

Inserted one per Donruss Baseball's Best Gold set, these five card parallel the Donruss Rookies Diamond Kings set.

Nm-Mt Ex-Mt
*GOLD DK'S: 1.25X TO 3X BASIC DK'S

2001 Donruss Baseball's Best Silver

These 220 cards were available via a coupon randomly seeded into 2001 Donruss baseball packs at stated odds of 1:720. Consumers that pulled the Baseball's Best coupon (or bought it off the secondary market) then had to mail it into Donruss along with a check or money order for $105 prior to the January 20th, 2002 deadline to receive a factory sealed set 330-card set (of which contained the 220-card Baseball's Best set plus the 110-card Baseball's Best "The Rookies" set. The consumer did not know upon mailing in the coupon whether he or she would be receiving the Bronze, Silver or Gold version of the set of which were disseminated randomly. The 330 cards are glossy-coated parallels of the 220-card basic 2001 Donruss set and the 110-card 2001 Donruss the Rookies set. Only 499 serial-numbered Silver sets were created, with each card carrying serial-numbering on back and Silver foil accents on front.

Nm-Mt Ex-Mt
COMP.FACT.SET (330) 300.00 90.00
*STARS 1-150: 3X TO 8X BASIC CARDS
*ROOKIES 151-200: .3X TO .8X BASIC
*FAN CLUB 201-220: .75X TO 2X BASIC

2001 Donruss Baseball's Best Silver Rookies

Issued as a redemption "update" set to the basic 2001 Donruss set, these 105 cards were available via a coupon which could be mailed into Donruss for these 110 cards. There were only 499 silver sets produced.

Nm-Mt Ex-Mt
*SILVER: 1.25X TO 3X BASIC ROOKIES

2001 Donruss Baseball's Best Silver Rookies Diamond Kings

Inserted one per Donruss Baseball's Best Silver set, these five cards parallel the Donruss Rookies Diamond Kings set. These cards were issued to a stated print run of 499 serial numbered sets.

Nm-Mt Ex-Mt
*SILVER DK'S: .75X TO 2X BASIC DK'S

2002 Donruss Best of Fan Club

This 325-card set was distributed in two separate series. The standard hobby-only product, containing cards 1-300 of the base set, was released in late December 2001, and features a 300-card base set that was broken into tiers as follows: 200 Base Veterans, 60 Rookies/Prospects (numbered to 1350), and 40 Fan Club cards (numbered to 2025). Please note that a few of the players autographed a portion of their cards. Thus, cumulative print runs are listed in our checklist for these cards. Cards U201-U225 were distributed exclusively within hobby packs of 2002 Donruss the Rookies in mid-December, 2002. These twenty-five update cards are all serial numbered of 1,350 and feature a selection of prospects. Though odds per pack were never released by the manufacturer, we estimate the cards were seeded at a rate of 1:17. Please note, these update cards were originally intended to be numbered as 301-325 for the checklist, but were erroneously numbered 201-225. We've added a "U" prefix to the update card numbers to avoid confusion within our checklist.

Nm-Mt Ex-Mt
COMP.SET w/o SP's (200) 40.00 12.00
COMMON CARD (1-200) .50 .15
COMMON (201-260) 5.00 1.50
COMMON (261-300) 5.00 1.50
1 Alex Rodriguez 2.00 .60
2 Pedro Martinez 1.25 .35
3 Vladimir Guerrero 1.25 .35
4 Jim Edmonds .50 .15
5 Derek Jeter 3.00 .90
6 Johnny Damon .50 .15
7 Rafael Furcal .50 .15
8 Cal Ripken 4.00 1.20
9 Brad Radke .50 .15
10 Bret Boone .50 .15
11 Pat Burrell .50 .15
12 Roy Oswalt .50 .15
13 Cliff Floyd .50 .15
14 Robin Ventura .50 .15
15 Frank Thomas 1.25 .35
16 Mariano Rivera .75 .23
17 Paul LoDuca .50 .15
18 Geoff Jenkins .50 .15
19 Tony Gwynn 1.50 .45
20 Chipper Jones 1.25 .35
21 Eric Chavez .50 .15
22 Kerry Wood 1.25 .35
23 Jorge Posada .75 .23
24 J.D. Drew .50 .15
25 Garret Anderson .50 .15
26 Javier Vazquez .50 .15
27 Kenny Lofton .50 .15
28 Mike Mussina 1.25 .35
29 Paul Konerko .50 .15
30 Bernie Williams .75 .23
31 Eric Milton .50 .15
32 Craig Wilson .50 .15
33 Paul O'Neill .75 .23
34 Dmitri Young .50 .15
35 Andres Galarraga .50 .15
36 Gary Sheffield .50 .15
37 Ben Grieve .50 .15
38 Scott Rolen .75 .23
39 Mark Grace .75 .23
40 Albert Pujols 2.50 .75
41 Barry Zito .75 .23
42 Edgar Martinez .75 .23
43 Jarrod Washburn .50 .15
44 Juan Pierre .50 .15
45 Mark Buehrle .50 .15
46 Larry Walker .75 .23
47 Trot Nixon .75 .23
48 Wade Miller .50 .15
49 Robert Fick .50 .15
50 Sean Casey .50 .15
51 Joe Mays .50 .15
52 Brad Fullmer .50 .15
53 Chan Ho Park .50 .15
54 Carlos Delgado .50 .15
55 Phil Nevin .50 .15
56 Mike Cameron .50 .15
57 Raul Mondesi .50 .15
58 Roberto Alomar 1.25 .35
59 Ryan Klesko .50 .15
60 Andruw Jones .50 .15
61 Gabe Kapler .50 .15
62 Darin Erstad .50 .15
63 Cristian Guzman .50 .15
64 Kazuhiro Sasaki .50 .15
65 Doug Mientkiewicz .50 .15
66 Sammy Sosa 2.00 .60
67 Mike Hampton .50 .15
68 Rickey Henderson 1.25 .35
69 Mark Mulder .50 .15
70 Jeff Conine .50 .15
71 Freddy Garcia .50 .15
72 Ivan Rodriguez 1.25 .35
73 Terrence Long .50 .15
74 Adam Dunn .50 .15
75 Moises Alou .50 .15
76 Todd Helton .75 .23
77 Preston Wilson .50 .15
78 Roger Cedeno .50 .15
79 Tony Armas .50 .15
80 Manny Ramirez .50 .15
81 Jose Vidro .50 .15
82 Randy Johnson 1.25 .35
83 Richie Sexson .50 .15
84 Troy Glaus .75 .23
85 Kevin Brown .50 .15
86 Woody Williams .50 .15
87 Adrian Beltre .50 .15
88 Brian Giles .50 .15
89 Jermaine Dye .50 .15
90 Craig Biggio .75 .23
91 Richard Hidalgo .50 .15
92 Magglio Ordonez .50 .15
93 Al Leiter .50 .15
94 Jeff Kent .50 .15
95 Curt Schilling .75 .23
96 Tim Hudson .50 .15
97 Fred McGriff UER .75 .23
120 Homers for the Cubs in 2001
98 Barry Larkin 1.25 .35
99 Jim Thome 1.25 .35
100 Tom Glavine .75 .23
101 Alfonso Soriano .75 .23
102 Jamie Moyer .50 .15
103 Vinny Castilla .50 .15
104 Rich Aurilia .50 .15
105 Matt Morris .50 .15
106 Rafael Palmeiro .75 .23
107 Joe Crede .50 .15
108 Barry Bonds 3.00 .90
109 Robert Person .50 .15
110 Nomar Garciaparra 2.00 .60
111 Brandon Duckworth .50 .15
112 Russ Ortiz .50 .15
113 Jeff Weaver .50 .15
114 Carlos Beltran .50 .15
115 Ellis Burks .50 .15
116 Jeremy Giambi .50 .15
117 Carlos Lee .50 .15
118 Ken Griffey Jr. 2.00 .60
119 Torii Hunter .50 .15
120 Andy Pettitte .75 .23
121 Jose Canseco 1.25 .35
122 Charles Johnson .50 .15
123 Nick Johnson .50 .15
124 Luis Gonzalez .50 .15
125 Rondell White .50 .15
126 Miguel Tejada .50 .15
127 Jose Cruz Jr. .50 .15
128 Brent Abernathy .50 .15
129 Scott Brosius .50 .15
130 Jon Lieber .50 .15
131 John Smoltz .75 .23
132 Mike Sweeney .50 .15
133 Shannon Stewart .50 .15
134 Derrek Lee .50 .15
135 Brian Jordan .50 .15
136 Rusty Greer .50 .15
137 Mike Piazza 2.00 .60
138 Billy Wagner .50 .15
139 Shawn Green .50 .15
140 Orlando Cabrera .50 .15
141 Jeff Bagwell .75 .23
142 Aaron Sele .50 .15
143 Hideo Nomo 1.25 .35
144 Marlon Anderson .50 .15
145 Todd Walker .50 .15
146 Bobby Higginson .50 .15
147 Ichiro Suzuki 2.00 .60
148 Juan Uribe .50 .15
149 Jason Kendall .50 .15
150 Mark Quinn .50 .15
151 Ben Sheets .50 .15
152 Paul Abbott .50 .15
153 Aubrey Huff .50 .15
154 Greg Maddux 2.00 .60
155 Darryl Kile .50 .15
156 John Burkett .50 .15
157 Juan Gonzalez 1.25 .35
158 Javy Lopez .50 .15
159 Aramis Ramirez .50 .15
160 Lance Berkman .50 .15
161 David Cone .50 .15
162 Edgar Renteria .50 .15
163 Roger Clemens 2.50 .75
164 Frank Catalanotto .50 .15
165 Bartolo Colon .50 .15
166 Mark McGwire 3.00 .90
167 Jay Gibbons .50 .15
168 Tony Clark .50 .15
169 Tsuyoshi Shinjo .50 .15
170 Brad Penny .50 .15
171 Marcus Giles .50 .15
172 Matt Williams .50 .15
173 Bud Smith .50 .15
174 Tino Martinez .75 .23
175 Ryan Dempster .50 .15
176 Jimmy Rollins .50 .15
177 Edgardo Alfonzo .50 .15
178 Jason Giambi 1.25 .35
179 Aaron Boone .50 .15
180 Ray Durham .50 .15
181 Mike Lowell .50 .15
182 Jose Ortiz .50 .15
183 Johnny Estrada .50 .15
184 Shane Reynolds .50 .15
185 Joe Kennedy .50 .15
186 Corey Patterson .50 .15
187 Jeromy Burnitz .50 .15
188 C.C. Sabathia .50 .15
189 Kevin Millar .50 .15
190 Omar Vizquel .50 .15
191 John Olerud .50 .15
192 Dee Brown .50 .15
193 Kip Wells .50 .15
194 A.J. Burnett .50 .15
195 Josh Towers .50 .15
196 Jason Varitek .50 .15
197 Jason Isringhausen .50 .15
198 Fernando Vina .50 .15
199 Ramon Ortiz .50 .15
200 Bobby Abreu .50 .15
201 Willie Harris/850 5.00 1.50
202 Angel Santos/1350 5.00 1.50
203 Corky Miller/850 5.00 1.50
204 Michael Rivera/1350 5.00 1.50
205 J.Duchscherer/850 5.00 1.50
206 Rick Bauer/1350 5.00 1.50
207 Angel Berroa/1250 UER 5.00 1.50
Berroa is a shortstop, pitching stats used
208 Juan Cruz/1175 5.00 1.50
209 Dewon Brazelton/1298 5.00 1.50
210 Mark Prior/925 15.00 4.50
211 Mark Teixeira/925 8.00 2.40
212 Geronimo Gil/1350 5.00 1.50
213 Casey Fossum/1250 5.00 1.50
214 Ken Harvey/1350 5.00 1.50
215 M. Cuddyer/1298 5.00 1.50
216 Wilson Betemit/850 5.00 1.50
217 David Brous/850 5.00 1.50
218 Juan A. Pena/1162 5.00 1.50
219 Travis Hafner/975 5.00 1.50
220 Erick Almonte/1350 5.00 1.50
221 M. Ensberg/1298 5.00 1.50
222 Martin Vargas/850 5.00 1.50
223 Brandon Berger/850 5.00 1.50
224 Zach Day/850 5.00 1.50
225 Brad Voyles/850 5.00 1.50
226 Jeremy Affeldt/1100 5.00 1.50
227 N.Neugebauer/1125 5.00 1.50
228 Tim Redding/850 5.00 1.50
229 Adam Johnson/925 5.00 1.50
230 D.DeVore/1050 RC 5.00 1.50
231 Cody Ransom/850 5.00 1.50
232 Marlon Byrd/875 5.00 1.50
233 Delvin James/975 5.00 1.50
234 Eric Munson/1025 5.00 1.50
235 D. Tankersley/850 5.00 1.50
236 Josh Beckett/1325 8.00 2.40
237 Bill Hall/900 5.00 1.50
238 Kevin Olsen/1025 5.00 1.50
239 F. Beltran/1350 RC 5.00 1.50
240 Antonio Perez/825 5.00 1.50
241 Orlando Hudson/825 5.00 1.50
242 A.Machado/1350 RC 5.00 1.50
243 Tom Shearn/1350 RC 5.00 1.50
244 B. Mallette/1350 RC 5.00 1.50
245 Raul Chavez/1350 RC 5.00 1.50
246 Andy Pratt/1350 RC 5.00 1.50
247 J. De La Rosa/1350 RC 5.00 1.50
248 Jeff Deardorff/875 5.00 1.50
249 Ben Howard/1350 RC 5.00 1.50
250 B. Backe/1350 RC 5.00 1.50
251 Ed Rogers/950 5.00 1.50
252 T.Hughes/1350 RC 5.00 1.50
253 R.Rosario/1350 RC 5.00 1.50
254 A. Amezaga/1350 5.00 1.50
255 Jorge Padilla/900 RC 5.00 1.50
256 Victor Martinez/1350 5.00 1.50
257 S. Bechler/1350 RC 5.00 1.50
258 Chris Baker/1350 RC 5.00 1.50
259 Ryan Jamison/1350 5.00 1.50
260 A.Simpson/875 RC 5.00 1.50
261 A.Rodriguez FC/2000 8.00 2.40
262 V.Guerrero FC/2025 5.00 1.50
263 Bud Smith FC/2002 5.00 1.50
264 M.Tejada FC/2025 5.00 1.50
265 Craig Biggio FC/2010 5.00 1.50
266 L.Gonzalez FC/2010 5.00 1.50
267 I.Rodriguez FC/2025 5.00 1.50
268 C.C. Sabathia FC/2000 5.00 1.50
269 Jeff Bagwell FC/2010 5.00 1.50
270 A. Ramirez FC/2025 5.00 1.50
271 Bob Abreu FC/2025 5.00 1.50
272 Rich Aurilia FC/2000 5.00 1.50
273 J. Giambi FC/2025 5.00 1.50
274 R. Henderson FC/2025 5.00 1.50
275 Wade Miller FC/2002 5.00 1.50
276 A. Jones FC/2025 5.00 1.50
277 Troy Glaus FC/2025 5.00 1.50
278 Roy Oswalt FC/1950 5.00 1.50
279 Tony Gwynn FC/2000 6.00 1.80
280 Adam Dunn FC/2000 5.00 1.50
281 Larry Walker FC/2025 5.00 1.50
282 J.Canseco FC/2025 5.00 1.50
283 Todd Helton FC/2025 5.00 1.50
284 L.Berkman FC/2010 5.00 1.50
285 Cal Ripken FC/2010 15.00 4.50
286 Albert Pujols FC/2000 10.00 3.00
287 A.Soriano FC/2000 5.00 1.50
288 Mark Mulder FC/2025 5.00 1.50
289 M.Hampton FC/2025 5.00 1.50
290 A.Galarraga FC/2000 5.00 1.50
291 Barry Bonds FC/2025 12.00 3.60
292 Ben Sheets FC/2010 5.00 1.50
293 Ichiro Suzuki FC/2025 8.00 2.40
294 J.D. Drew FC/2000 5.00 1.50
295 Jose Ortiz FC/2025 5.00 1.50
296 Kerry Wood FC/2010 5.00 1.50
297 M.McGwire FC/2025 12.00 3.60
298 M.Sweeney FC/2025 5.00 1.50
299 Pat Burrell FC/2025 5.00 1.50
300 Tim Hudson FC/2000 5.00 1.50
U201 Kirk Saarloos RC 5.00 1.50
U202 Oliver Perez RC 8.00 2.40
U203 So Taguchi RC 8.00 2.40
U204 Runelvys Hernandez RC 5.00 1.50
U205 Freddy Sanchez RC 5.00 1.50
U206 Cliff Lee RC 8.00 2.40
U207 Kazuhisa Ishii RC 10.00 3.00
U208 Kevin Cash RC 5.00 1.50
U209 Trey Hodges RC 5.00 1.50
U210 Wilson Valdez RC 5.00 1.50
U211 Satoru Komiyama RC 5.00 1.50
U212 Luis Ugueto RC 5.00 1.50
U213 Joe Borchard 5.00 1.50
U214 Brian Tallet RC 8.00 2.40
U215 Jeriome Robertson RC 5.00 1.50
U216 Eric Junge RC 5.00 1.50
U217 Aaron Cook RC 5.00 1.50
U218 Jason Simontacchi RC 5.00 1.50
U219 Miguel Asencio RC 5.00 1.50
U220 Josh Bard RC 5.00 1.50
U221 Earl Snyder RC 5.00 1.50
U222 Felix Escalona RC 5.00 1.50
U223 Rene Reyes RC 5.00 1.50
U224 Chone Figgins RC 5.00 1.50
U225 Chris Snelling RC 8.00 2.40

2002 Donruss Best of Fan Club Autographs

Cards checklisted between 200-300 were inserted randomly in hobby packs. Cards checklisted U201-U225 were inserted into hobby packs of 2002 Donruss the Rookies. These cards feature autographed foil stickers from some of the rookies in the 2002 Best of Fan Club product. The actual autograph print runs are listed explicitly in our checklist.

Nm-Mt Ex-Mt
201 Willie Harris/500 10.00 3.00
203 Corky Miller/500 10.00 3.00
205 J.Duchscherer/500 10.00 3.00
207 Angel Berroa/100 15.00 4.50
208 Juan Cruz/175 10.00 3.00
209 Dewon Brazelton/52 20.00 6.00
210 Mark Prior/425 100.00 30.00
211 Mark Teixeira/425 25.00 7.50
213 Casey Fossum/100 15.00 4.50
215 Michael Cuddyer/52 20.00 6.00
216 Wilson Betemit/500 10.00 3.00
217 David Brous/500 10.00 3.00
218 Juan A. Pena/188 10.00 3.00
219 Travis Hafner/375 15.00 4.50
221 Morgan Ensberg/52 25.00 7.50
222 Martin Vargas/500 10.00 3.00
223 Brandon Berger/500 10.00 3.00
224 Zach Day/500 10.00 3.00
225 Brad Voyles/500 10.00 3.00
226 Jeremy Affeldt/250 10.00 3.00
227 Nick Neugebauer/225 10.00 3.00
228 Tim Redding/500 10.00 3.00
229 Adam Johnson/425 10.00 3.00
230 Doug DeVore/300 15.00 4.50
231 Cody Ransom/500 10.00 3.00
232 Marlon Byrd/475 15.00 4.50
233 Delvin James/375 10.00 3.00
234 Eric Munson/325 10.00 3.00
235 D.Tankersley/500 10.00 3.00
236 Josh Beckett/25
237 Bill Hall/450 10.00 3.00
238 Kevin Olsen/325 10.00 3.00
240 Antonio Perez/525 10.00 3.00
241 Orlando Hudson/525 10.00 3.00
248 Jeff Deardorff/475 10.00 3.00
251 Ed Rogers/400 10.00 3.00
255 Jorge Padilla/450 15.00 4.50
260 Allan Simpson/475 15.00 4.50
261 Alex Rodriguez FC/25
262 Vladimir Guerrero FC/25
263 Bud Smith FC/23
265 Craig Biggio FC/15
266 Luis Gonzalez FC/15
267 Ivan Rodriguez FC/TBD
268 C.C. Sabathia FC/25
269 Jeff Bagwell FC/15
270 Aramis Ramirez FC/TBD
272 Rich Aurilia FC/25
275 Wade Miller FC/23
277 Troy Glaus FC/25
278 Roy Oswalt FC/75
279 Tony Gwynn FC/25
280 Adam Dunn FC/25
284 Lance Berkman FC/15
285 Cal Ripken FC/15
286 Albert Pujols FC/25
287 Alfonso Soriano FC/25
290 Andres Galarraga FC/25
292 Ben Sheets FC/15
294 J.D. Drew FC/25
296 Kerry Wood FC/15
300 Tim Hudson FC/25
U201 Kirk Saarloos/100 15.00 4.50
U202 Oliver Perez/25
U203 So Taguchi/10
U206 Cliff Lee/50
U207 Kazuhisa Ishii/15
U208 Kevin Cash/50 15.00 4.50
U209 Trey Hodges/100 15.00 4.50
U210 Wilson Valdez/50 15.00 4.50
U211 Satoru Komiyama/25
U212 Luis Ugueto/75 15.00 4.50
U213 Joe Borchard/50 25.00 7.50
U214 Brian Tallet/50 25.00 7.50
U216 Eric Junge/25
U220 Josh Bard/50 15.00 4.50
U221 Earl Snyder/100 15.00 4.50
U222 Felix Escalona/25
U223 Rene Reyes/50 15.00 4.50
U224 Chone Figgins/100 15.00 4.50
U225 Chris Snelling/50

2002 Donruss Best of Fan Club Spotlight

Randomly inserted into hobby packs, this 325-card set is a complete parallel of the 2001 Donruss Best of Fan Club set featured on a special metalized film board. Each card is also individually serial numbered to 100.

Nm-Mt Ex-Mt
*DC 1-200: 5X TO 12X BASIC CARDS
*DC 261-300: 1.25X TO 3X BASIC CARDS
143 Hideo Nomo 30.00 9.00
U201 Kirk Saarloos 6.00 1.80
U202 Oliver Perez 10.00 3.00
U203 So Taguchi 10.00 3.00
U204 Runelvys Hernandez 6.00 1.80
U205 Freddy Sanchez 6.00 1.80
U206 Cliff Lee 15.00 4.50
U207 Kazuhisa Ishii 25.00 7.50
U208 Kevin Cash 6.00 1.80
U209 Trey Hodges 6.00 1.80
U210 Wilson Valdez 6.00 1.80
U211 Satoru Komiyama 6.00 1.80
U212 Luis Ugueto 6.00 1.80
U213 Joe Borchard 6.00 1.80
U214 Brian Tallet 10.00 3.00
U215 Jeriome Robertson 6.00 1.80
U216 Eric Junge 6.00 1.80
U217 Aaron Cook 6.00 1.80
U218 Jason Simontacchi 6.00 1.80
U219 Miguel Asencio 6.00 1.80
U220 Josh Bard 6.00 1.80
U221 Earl Snyder 6.00 1.80
U222 Felix Escalona 6.00 1.80
U223 Rene Reyes 6.00 1.80
U224 Chone Figgins 6.00 1.80
U225 Chris Snelling 15.00 4.50

2002 Donruss Best of Fan Club Artists

Randomly inserted in packs, these cards feature some of the leading pitchers in baseball. A few pitchers signed a few cards for this so the exact print runs are listed in our checklist.

Nm-Mt Ex-Mt
A1 Pedro Martinez/285 10.00 3.00
A2 Curt Schilling/285 6.00 1.80
A3 Kevin Brown/275 5.00 1.50
A4 Tim Hudson/275 5.00 1.50
A5 Kerry Wood/285 10.00 3.00
A6 Barry Zito/200 6.00 1.80
A7 Hideo Nomo 25.00 7.50
A8 Randy Johnson/285 10.00 3.00
A9 Greg Maddux/285 15.00 4.50
A10 Roger Clemens/285 20.00 6.00
A11 Kazuhiro Sasaki 5.00 1.50
A12 Joe Mays 5.00 1.50
A13 Mark Mulder 5.00 1.50
A14 Javier Vazquez 5.00 1.50

2002 Donruss Best of Fan Club Artists Autographs

Inserted randomly in packs, these 10 cards parallel the Artist insert set. These 10 pitchers each signed some cards for this product.

Nm-Mt Ex-Mt
A1 Pedro Martinez/15
A2 Curt Schilling/15
A3 Kevin Brown/25
A4 Tim Hudson/25

A5 Kerry Wood/15
A6 Barry Zito/100 50.00 15.00
A8 Randy Johnson/15
A9 Greg Maddux/15
A10 Roger Clemens/15

2002 Donruss Best of Fan Club Master Artists

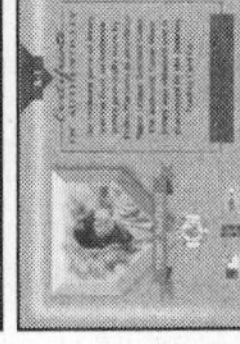

Inserted randomly into packs, these 14 cards feature some of the leading pitchers in baseball. These cards are all serial numbered to 150 and have a piece of a game jersey swatch on them.

	Nm-Mt	Ex-Mt
A1 Pedro Martinez	25.00	7.50
A2 Curt Schilling	25.00	7.50
A3 Kevin Brown	15.00	4.50
A4 Tim Hudson	15.00	4.50
A5 Kerry Wood	25.00	7.50
A6 Barry Zito	25.00	7.50
A7 Hideo Nomo	60.00	18.00
A8 Randy Johnson	25.00	7.50
A9 Greg Maddux	25.00	7.50
A10 Roger Clemens	40.00	12.00
A11 Kazuhiro Sasaki	15.00	4.50
A12 Joe Mays	15.00	4.50
A13 Mark Mulder	15.00	4.50
A14 Javier Vazquez	15.00	4.50

2002 Donruss Best of Fan Club Craftsmen

Randomly inserted into packs, these 18 cards honor some of the leading hitters in baseball. A few of these players signed cards for this product so exact print runs for each of these cards are listed in our checklist.

	Nm-Mt	Ex-Mt
C1 Ichiro Suzuki/300	15.00	4.50
C2 Todd Helton/285	6.00	1.80
C3 Manny Ramirez/285	5.00	1.50
C4 Luis Gonzalez/285	5.00	1.50
C5 Roberto Alomar/285	10.00	3.00
C6 Moises Alou/275	5.00	1.50
C7 Darin Erstad/275	5.00	1.50
C8 Mike Piazza/300	15.00	4.50
C9 Edgar Martinez/285	6.00	1.80
C10 V. Guerrero/275	10.00	3.00
C11 Juan Gonzalez/285	10.00	3.00
C12 N. Garciaparra/285	15.00	4.50
C13 Tony Gwynn/285	12.00	3.60
C14 Jeff Bagwell/285	6.00	1.80
C15 Albert Pujols/275	20.00	6.00
C16 Larry Walker/300	6.00	1.80
C17 Paul LoDuca/200	5.00	1.50
C18 Lance Berkman/300	5.00	1.50

2002 Donruss Best of Fan Club Craftsmen Autographs

Inserted randomly in packs, these 14 cards parallel the Craftsman insert set. These 14 hitters each signed some cards for this product.

	Nm-Mt	Ex-Mt
C2 Todd Helton/15		
C3 Manny Ramirez/15		
C4 Luis Gonzalez/15		
C5 Roberto Alomar/15		
C6 Moises Alou/25		
C7 Darin Erstad/25		
C9 Edgar Martinez/15		
C10 Vladimir Guerrero/25		
C11 Juan Gonzalez/15		
C12 Nomar Garciaparra/15		
C13 Tony Gwynn/15		
C14 Jeff Bagwell/15		
C15 Albert Pujols/25		
C17 Paul LoDuca/100	25.00	7.50

2002 Donruss Best of Fan Club Master Craftsmen

Randomly inserted into packs, these 18 cards parallel the Craftsmen set. The difference is that a piece of a game bat is now part of each card and these cards are serial numbered to 150 unless noted in our checklist.

	Nm-Mt	Ex-Mt
C1 Ichiro Suzuki Ball/51	100.00	30.00
C2 Todd Helton	25.00	7.50
C3 Manny Ramirez	15.00	4.50
C4 Luis Gonzalez	15.00	4.50
C5 Roberto Alomar	25.00	7.50
C6 Moises Alou	15.00	4.50
C7 Darin Erstad	15.00	4.50
C8 Mike Piazza	25.00	7.50
C9 Edgar Martinez	25.00	7.50
C10 Vladimir Guerrero	25.00	7.50
C11 Juan Gonzalez	25.00	7.50
C12 Nomar Garciaparra	40.00	12.00
C13 Tony Gwynn/175	30.00	9.00
C14 Jeff Bagwell	25.00	7.50
C15 Albert Pujols/175	40.00	12.00
C16 Larry Walker/175	25.00	7.50
C17 Paul LoDuca/175	15.00	4.50
C18 Lance Berkman	15.00	4.50

2002 Donruss Best of Fan Club Double Features

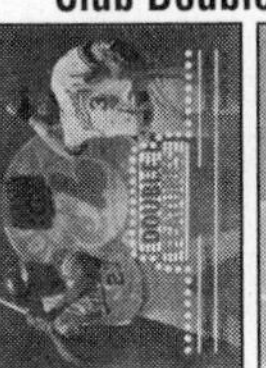

Randomly inserted into packs, these 10 cards feature teammates and are serial numbered to 125.

	Nm-Mt	Ex-Mt
DF-1 Larry Walker Todd Helton	15.00	4.50
DF-2 Vladimir Guerrero Jose Vidro	15.00	4.50
DF-3 Jason Giambi Jeremy Giambi	15.00	4.50
DF-4 Manny Ramirez Nomar Garciaparra	30.00	9.00
DF-5 Troy Glaus Darin Erstad	15.00	4.50
DF-6 Shawn Green Paul LoDuca	15.00	4.50
DF-7 Jeff Bagwell Craig Biggio	15.00	4.50
DF-8 Pedro Martinez Hideo Nomo	25.00	7.50
DF-9 Randy Johnson Curt Schilling	15.00	4.50
DF-10 Chipper Jones Andruw Jones	15.00	4.50

2002 Donruss Best of Fan Club Double Features Lumber

Randomly inserted into packs, these 10 cards parallel the Double Features set and feature game bat pieces on them.

	Nm-Mt	Ex-Mt
DF-1 Larry Walker Todd Helton	40.00	12.00
DF-2 Vladimir Guerrero Jose Vidro	40.00	12.00
DF-3 Jason Giambi Jeremy Giambi	40.00	12.00
DF-4 Manny Ramirez Nomar Garciaparra	80.00	24.00
DF-5 Troy Glaus Darin Erstad	40.00	12.00
DF-6 Shawn Green Paul LoDuca	40.00	12.00
DF-7 Jeff Bagwell Craig Biggio	40.00	12.00
DF-8 Pedro Martinez Hideo Nomo	80.00	24.00
DF-9 Randy Johnson Curt Schilling Glove	40.00	12.00
DF-10 Chipper Jones Andruw Jones	40.00	12.00

2002 Donruss Best of Fan Club Franchise Features

Inserted randomly into packs, these 40 cards feature some of the leading players in baseball. A few players signed cards for this product so the explicit print runs for each card is listed in our checklist.

	Nm-Mt	Ex-Mt
FF-1 Cliff Floyd/300	5.00	1.50
FF-2 Mike Piazza/300	15.00	4.50
FF-3 Cal Ripken/275	40.00	12.00
FF-4 Mike Sweeney/300	5.00	1.50
FF-5 Curt Schilling/275	6.00	1.80
FF-6 Aramis Ramirez/200	5.00	1.50
FF-7 V. Guerrero/275	10.00	3.00
FF-8 Andruw Jones/300	5.00	1.50
FF-9 Tim Hudson/250	5.00	1.50
FF-10 Bernie Williams/275	6.00	1.80
FF-11 Pedro Martinez/285	10.00	3.00
FF-12 Roberto Alomar/285	10.00	3.00
FF-13 Joe Mays/225	5.00	1.50
FF-14 Jason Giambi/300	10.00	3.00
FF-15 Kazuhiro Sasaki/300	5.00	1.50
FF-16 M. Ordonez/300	5.00	1.50
FF-17 N. Garciaparra/285	15.00	4.50
FF-18 Juan Gonzalez/275	10.00	3.00
FF-19 Carlos Beltran/200	5.00	1.50
FF-20 Javier Vazquez/275	5.00	1.50
FF-21 Miguel Tejada/300	5.00	1.50
FF-22 Luis Gonzalez/285	5.00	1.50
FF-23 Greg Maddux/285	15.00	4.50
FF-24 Rafael Palmeiro/275	6.00	1.80
FF-25 Freddy Garcia/200	5.00	1.50
FF-26 Barry Zito/200	6.00	1.80
FF-27 Paul LoDuca/200	5.00	1.50
FF-28 Robert Fick/200	5.00	1.50
FF-29 Roger Clemens/285	20.00	6.00
FF-30 Eric Chavez/250	5.00	1.50
FF-31 Ivan Rodriguez/285	10.00	3.00
FF-32 Chipper Jones/300	10.00	3.00
FF-33 Kerry Wood/285	10.00	3.00
FF-34 Randy Johnson/285	10.00	3.00
FF-35 Alex Rodriguez/285	15.00	4.50
FF-36 Manny Ramirez/275	5.00	1.50
FF-37 Mark Buehrle/200	5.00	1.50
FF-38 Mark Mulder/300	5.00	1.50
FF-39 Ichiro Suzuki/300	15.00	4.50
FF-40 Troy Glaus/275	6.00	1.80

2002 Donruss Best of Fan Club Franchise Features Autographs

Randomly inserted in packs, these 29 cards parallel the Franchise Features insert set and feature autographs of these players. Specific print runs of how many cards were signed are listed in our checklist.

	Nm-Mt	Ex-Mt
FF-3 Cal Ripken/25		
FF-5 Curt Schilling/25		
FF-6 Aramis Ramirez/100	25.00	7.50
FF-7 Vladimir Guerrero/25		
FF-9 Tim Hudson/50		
FF-10 Bernie Williams/25		
FF-11 Pedro Martinez/15		
FF-12 Roberto Alomar/15		
FF-13 Joe Mays/75	25.00	7.50
FF-17 Nomar Garciaparra/15		
FF-18 Juan Gonzalez/25		
FF-19 Carlos Beltran/100	25.00	7.50
FF-20 Javier Vazquez/25		
FF-22 Luis Gonzalez/15		
FF-23 Greg Maddux/15		
FF-24 Rafael Palmeiro/25		
FF-25 Freddy Garcia/100	25.00	7.50
FF-26 Barry Zito/100	60.00	18.00
FF-27 Paul LoDuca/100	25.00	7.50
FF-28 Robert Fick/100	25.00	7.50
FF-29 Roger Clemens/15		
FF-30 Eric Chavez/50		
FF-31 Ivan Rodriguez/15		
FF-33 Kerry Wood/15		
FF-34 Randy Johnson/15		
FF-35 Alex Rodriguez/15		
FF-36 Manny Ramirez/25		
FF-37 Mark Buehrle/100	25.00	7.50
FF-40 Troy Glaus/25		

2002 Donruss Best of Fan Club Franchise Features Materials

Randomly inserted in packs, these 40 cards parallel the Franchise Features insert set. These cards all feature a different piece of memorabilia on them. Most cards have a stated print run of 150 serial numbered set except for a few cards which we explicity list the print run in our checklist.

	Nm-Mt	Ex-Mt
FF-1 Cliff Floyd Jsy	15.00	4.50
FF-2 Mike Piazza Jsy	25.00	7.50
FF-3 Cal Ripken Jsy	80.00	24.00
FF-4 Mike Sweeney Jsy	15.00	4.50
FF-5 C. Schilling Jsy/175	25.00	7.50
FF-6 Aramis Ramirez Jsy	15.00	4.50
FF-7 V. Guerrero Jsy	25.00	7.50
FF-8 A.Jones Jsy/175	15.00	4.50
FF-9 Tim Hudson Jsy	15.00	4.50
FF-10 Bernie Williams Jsy	25.00	7.50
FF-11 Pedro Martinez Jsy	25.00	7.50
FF-12 Roberto Alomar Jsy	25.00	7.50
FF-13 Joe Mays Jsy	15.00	4.50
FF-14 Jason Giambi Jsy	25.00	7.50
FF-15 Kazuhiro Sasaki Jsy	15.00	4.50
FF-16 M.Ordonez Jsy	15.00	4.50
FF-17 N. Garciaparra Jsy	40.00	12.00
FF-18 Juan Gonzalez Jsy	25.00	7.50
FF-19 Carlos Beltran Jsy	15.00	4.50
FF-20 Javier Vazquez Jsy	15.00	4.50
FF-21 Miguel Tejada Jsy	15.00	4.50
FF-22 Luis Gonzalez Jsy	15.00	4.50
FF-23 G. Maddux Jsy/175	25.00	7.50
FF-24 Rafael Palmeiro Jsy	25.00	7.50
FF-25 Freddy Garcia Jsy	15.00	4.50
FF-26 Barry Zito Jsy	25.00	7.50
FF-27 Paul LoDuca Jsy	15.00	4.50
FF-28 Robert Fick Jsy	15.00	4.50
FF-29 R. Clemens Jsy/175	50.00	15.00
FF-30 Eric Chavez Bat	15.00	4.50
FF-31 Ivan Rodriguez Jsy	25.00	7.50
FF-32 Chipper Jones Jsy	25.00	7.50
FF-33 Kerry Wood Jsy	25.00	7.50
FF-34 Randy Johnson Jsy	25.00	7.50
FF-35 Alex Rodriguez Jsy	40.00	12.00
FF-36 Manny Ramirez Jsy	15.00	4.50
FF-37 Mark Buehrle Jsy	15.00	4.50
FF-38 Mark Mulder Jsy	15.00	4.50
FF-39 I. Suzuki Ball/51	100.00	30.00
FF-40 Troy Glaus Jsy	25.00	7.50

2002 Donruss Best of Fan Club League Leaders

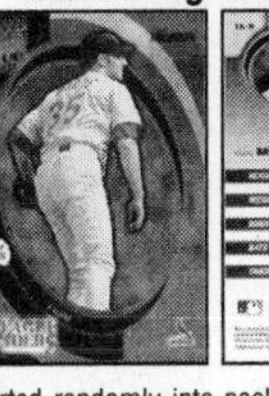

Inserted randomly into packs, these 45 cards feature league leaders in important statistical categories. While 300 of each card was produced, a few players signed some cards so the explicit print runs of these cards are listed in our checklist.

	Nm-Mt	Ex-Mt
LL-1 Roger Clemens Wins/275	20.00	6.00
LL-2 Curt Schilling Wins/275	6.00	1.80
LL-3 Matt Morris Wins/300	5.00	1.50
LL-4 Randy Johnson Wins/285	10.00	3.00
LL-5 Mark Mulder Wins/200	5.00	1.50
LL-6 Curt Schilling ERA/275	6.00	1.80
LL-7 Mike Mussina ERA/275	10.00	3.00
LL-8 Joe Mays ERA/275	5.00	1.50
LL-9 Matt Morris ERA/300	5.00	1.50
LL-10 Tim Hudson ERA/250	5.00	1.50
LL-11 Mark Buehrle ERA/200	5.00	1.50
LL-12 Greg Maddux ERA/275	15.00	4.50
LL-13 Freddy Garcia ERA/200	5.00	1.50
LL-14 Randy Johnson ERA/275	10.00	3.00
LL-15 Curt Schilling K's/275	6.00	1.80
LL-16 Chan Ho Park K's/285	5.00	1.50
LL-17 Roger Clemens K's/285	20.00	6.00
LL-18 Mike Mussina K's/285	10.00	3.00
LL-19 Javier Vazquez K's/200	5.00	1.50
LL-20 Kerry Wood K's/270	10.00	3.00
LL-21 Randy Johnson K's/285	10.00	3.00
LL-22 Barry Zito K's/200	6.00	1.80
LL-23 Hideo Nomo K's/300	25.00	7.50
LL-24 Ichiro Suzuki Hits/300	15.00	4.50
LL-25 Todd Helton Hits/275	6.00	1.80
LL-26 Albert Pujols Hits/200	20.00	6.00
LL-27 Alex Rodriguez Hits/285	15.00	4.50
LL-28 Shannon Stewart Hits/200	5.00	1.50
LL-29 Luis Gonzalez Hits/285	5.00	1.50
LL-30 Alex Rodriguez HR/285	15.00	4.50
LL-31 Barry Bonds HR/300	25.00	7.50
LL-32 Sammy Sosa HR/300	15.00	4.50
LL-33 Luis Gonzalez HR/285	5.00	1.50
LL-34 Todd Helton HR/275	6.00	1.80
LL-35 Jim Thome HR/300	10.00	3.00
LL-36 Shawn Green HR/285	5.00	1.50
LL-37 Jeff Bagwell RBI/285	6.00	1.80
LL-38 Todd Helton RBI/285	6.00	1.80
LL-39 Luis Gonzalez RBI/285	5.00	1.50
LL-40 Lance Berkman RBI/300	5.00	1.50
LL-41 Juan Gonzalez RBI/275	10.00	3.00
LL-42 Larry Walker Avg/300	6.00	1.80
LL-43 Ichiro Suzuki Avg/300	15.00	4.50
LL-44 Lance Berkman 2B's/300	5.00	1.50
LL-45 Todd Helton 2B's/285	6.00	1.80

2002 Donruss Best of Fan Club League Leaders Autographs

Randomly inserted into packs, these 34 cards parallel the League Leader insert set and feature autographs from the featured players. The amount of cards each player is listed explicity in our checklist.

	Nm-Mt	Ex-Mt
LL-1 Roger Clemens Wins/25		
LL-2 Curt Schilling Wins/25		
LL-4 Randy Johnson Wins/15		
LL-5 Mark Mulder Wins/100	25.00	7.50
LL-6 Curt Schilling ERA/25		
LL-7 Mike Mussina ERA/25		
LL-8 Joe Mays ERA/25		
LL-10 Tim Hudson ERA/50		
LL-11 Mark Buehrle ERA/100	25.00	7.50
LL-12 Greg Maddux ERA/25		
LL-13 Freddy Garcia ERA/100	25.00	7.50
LL-14 Randy Johnson ERA/25		
LL-15 Curt Schilling K's/25		
LL-16 Chan Ho Park K's/15		
LL-17 Roger Clemens K's/15		
LL-18 Mike Mussina K's/15		
LL-19 Javier Vazquez K's/100	25.00	7.50
LL-20 Kerry Wood K's/30		
LL-21 Randy Johnson K's/15		
LL-22 Barry Zito K's/100		
LL-25 Todd Helton Hits/25		
LL-26 Albert Pujols Hits/100	100.00	30.00
LL-27 Alex Rodriguez Hits/15		
LL-28 Shannon Stewart Hits/100	25.00	7.50
LL-29 Luis Gonzalez Hits/15		
LL-30 Alex Rodriguez HR/15		
LL-33 Luis Gonzalez HR/15		
LL-34 Todd Helton HR/25		
LL-36 Shawn Green HR/15		
LL-37 Jeff Bagwell RBI/15		
LL-38 Todd Helton RBI/15		
LL-39 Luis Gonzalez RBI/15		
LL-41 Juan Gonzalez RBI/25		
LL-45 Todd Helton 2B's/15		

2002 Donruss Best of Fan Club League Leaders Materials

Inserted randomly into packs, these 43 cards parallel the League Leaders insert set and featue a piece of memorabilia on them. Each card is printed to a different amount and that print run is listed explicity in our checklist.

	Nm-Mt	Ex-Mt
LL-1 Roger Clemens Wins Jsy/175	50.00	15.00
LL-2 Curt Schilling	25.00	7.50

	Nm-Mt	Ex-Mt
Wins Jsy/150		
LL-4 Randy Johnson Wins Jsy/175	25.00	7.50
LL-5 Mark Mulder Wins Jsy/175	15.00	4.50
LL-6 Curt Schilling ERA Shoe/150	25.00	7.50
LL-7 Mike Mussina ERA Shoe/50	60.00	18.00
LL-8 Joe Mays ERA Jsy/175	15.00	4.50
LL-10 Tim Hudson ERA Jsy/175	15.00	4.50
LL-11 Mark Buehrle ERA Jsy/175	15.00	4.50
LL-12 Greg Maddux ERA Jsy/175	25.00	7.50
LL-13 Freddy Garcia ERA Jsy/175	15.00	4.50
LL-14 Randy Johnson ERA Jsy/175	25.00	7.50
LL-15 Curt Schilling K's Jsy/150	25.00	7.50
LL-16 Chan Ho Park K's Jsy/175	15.00	4.50
LL-17 Roger Clemens K's Jsy/175	50.00	15.00
LL-18 Mike Mussina K's Shoe/50	60.00	18.00
LL-19 Javier Vazquez K's Jsy/175	15.00	4.50
LL-20 Kerry Wood K's Jsy/175	25.00	7.50
LL-21 Randy Johnson K's Jsy/175	25.00	7.50
LL-22 Barry Zito K's Jsy/175	25.00	7.50
LL-23 Hideo Nomo K's Jsy/175	80.00	24.00
LL-24 Ichiro Suzuki Hits Ball/51	100.00	30.00
LL-25 Todd Helton Hits Jsy/175	25.00	7.50
LL-26 Albert Pujols Hits Jsy/175	40.00	12.00
LL-27 Alex Rodriguez Hits Jsy/150	40.00	12.00
LL-28 Shan Stewart Hits Jsy/175	15.00	4.50
LL-29 Luis Gonzalez Hits Jsy/150	15.00	4.50
LL-30 Alex Rodriguez HR Jsy/150	40.00	12.00
LL-31 Barry Bonds HR Jsy/175	50.00	15.00
LL-32 Sammy Sosa HR Jsy/150	40.00	12.00
LL-33 Luis Gonzalez HR Jsy/150	15.00	4.50
LL-34 Todd Helton HR Jsy/175	25.00	7.50
LL-35 Jim Thome HR Jsy/175	25.00	7.50
LL-36 Shawn Green HR Jsy/175	15.00	4.50
LL-37 Jeff Bagwell RBI Jsy/150	25.00	7.50
LL-38 Todd Helton RBI Jsy/175	25.00	7.50
LL-39 Luis Gonzalez RBI Jsy/150	15.00	4.50
LL-40 Lance Berkman RBI Jsy/175	15.00	4.50
LL-41 Juan Gonzalez RBI Jsy/150	25.00	7.50
LL-42 Larry Walker Avg Jsy/175	25.00	7.50
LL-43 Ichiro Suzuki Avg Ball/51	100.00	30.00
LL-44 Lance Berkman 2B's Jsy/175	15.00	4.50
LL-45 Todd Helton 2B's Jsy/175	25.00	7.50

2002 Donruss Best of Fan Club Pure Power

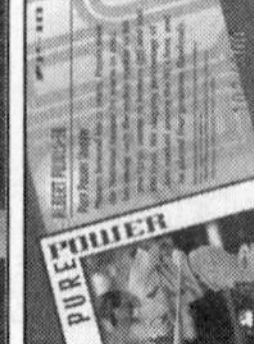

Inserted randomly into packs, these 18 cards feature some of the leading power hitters in baseball. Each card is serial numbered to 300 but a few players signed cards so those cards specific print runs are listed in our checklist.

	Nm-Mt	Ex-Mt
PP-1 Sammy Sosa	15.00	4.50
PP-2 Lance Berkman	5.00	1.50
PP-3 Chipper Jones	10.00	3.00
PP-4 Troy Glaus/275	6.00	1.80
PP-5 Barry Bonds	25.00	7.50
PP-6 Todd Helton/275	6.00	1.80
PP-7 Manny Ramirez/285	5.00	1.50
PP-8 Jason Giambi	10.00	3.00
PP-9 Juan Gonzalez/285	10.00	3.00
PP-10 Albert Pujols/275	20.00	6.00
PP-11 Jim Thome	10.00	3.00
PP-12 Mike Piazza	15.00	4.50
PP-13 Frank Thomas/275	10.00	3.00
PP-14 Richie Sexson/200	5.00	1.50
PP-15 Jeff Bagwell/285	6.00	1.80
PP-16 R.Palmeiro/275	6.00	1.80
PP-17 Luis Gonzalez/285	5.00	1.50
PP-18 Shawn Green	5.00	1.50

2002 Donruss Best of Fan Club Pure Power Autographs

Randomly inserted in packs, these 10 cards parallel the Pure Power insert set and feature

autographs of the featured player. Specific print runs are listed in our checklist.

	Nm-Mt	Ex-Mt
PP-4 Troy Glaus/25		
PP-6 Todd Helton/25		
PP-7 Manny Ramirez/15		
PP-9 Juan Gonzalez/15		
PP-10 Albert Pujols/25		
PP-13 Frank Thomas/25		
PP-14 Richie Sexson/100	25.00	7.50
PP-15 Jeff Bagwell/15		
PP-16 Rafael Palmeiro/25		
PP-17 Luis Gonzalez/15		

2002 Donruss Best of Fan Club Pure Power Masters

Randomly inserted in packs, these 18 cards parallel the Pure Power insert set and also has a memorabilia piece on each card. These cards are all serial numbered to 150.

	Nm-Mt	Ex-Mt
PP-1 Sammy Sosa	40.00	12.00
PP-2 Lance Berkman	15.00	4.50
PP-3 Chipper Jones	25.00	7.50
PP-4 Troy Glaus	25.00	7.50
PP-5 Barry Bonds	60.00	18.00
PP-6 Todd Helton	25.00	7.50
PP-7 Manny Ramirez	15.00	4.50
PP-8 Jason Giambi	25.00	7.50
PP-9 Juan Gonzalez	25.00	7.50
PP-10 Albert Pujols	40.00	12.00
PP-11 Jim Thome	25.00	7.50
PP-12 Mike Piazza	25.00	7.50
PP-13 Frank Thomas	25.00	7.50
PP-14 Richie Sexson	15.00	4.50
PP-15 Jeff Bagwell	25.00	7.50
PP-16 Rafael Palmeiro	25.00	7.50
PP-17 Luis Gonzalez	15.00	4.50
PP-18 Shawn Green	15.00	4.50

2002 Donruss Best of Fan Club Records

Inserted randomly into packs, these five cards feature players who reached important milestones in 2001. Each card is serial numbered to 300.

	Nm-Mt	Ex-Mt
R1 Barry Bonds HR	25.00	7.50
R2 Barry Bonds BB	25.00	7.50
R3 Barry Bonds SLUG	25.00	7.50
R4 R. Henderson Runs	15.00	4.50
R5 Rickey Henderson Hits	15.00	4.50

2002 Donruss Best of Fan Club Records Game Bat

Randomly inserted into hobby packs, these five cards parallel the Records insert set and features a game bat piece on each card. Each card is serial numbered to 150.

	Nm-Mt	Ex-Mt
R1 Barry Bonds HR	50.00	15.00
R2 Barry Bonds BB	50.00	15.00
R3 Barry Bonds SLUG	50.00	15.00
R4 R.Henderson Runs	40.00	12.00
R5 Rickey Henderson Hits	40.00	12.00

2003 Donruss Champions Samples

These cards, which parallel the basic Donruss Champions cards, were inserted into Beckett Baseball Collector magazines at a stated rate of one per magazine. Please note that the word sample was printed in silver on the back and that is how a collector can tell the difference between the regular Champions cards and the Samples.

Nm-Mt Ex-Mt

*SAMPLES: 1.5X TO 4X BASIC

2003 Donruss Champions

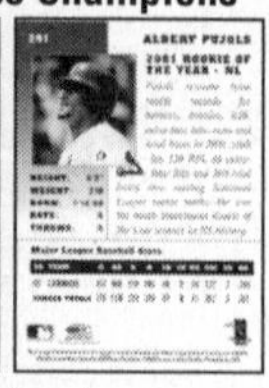

This 309 card set was issued in two separate releases. The primary Donruss Champions product - containing cards 1-301 within the basic set - was released in April, 2003. The set was issued in eight card packs with an $5 SRP. These packs were issued in 24 pack boxes which came 20 boxes to a case. This primary set was originally supposed to be capped at 300 cards but a late addition of Hideki Matsui (card number 301) brought the complete set to 301 cards. In December, 2003, eight additional cards (302-309) were seeded within packs of DLP Rookies and Traded.

	Nm-Mt	Ex-Mt
COMP.LO SET (301)	50.00	15.00
COMP.UPDATE SET (8)	8.00	2.40
COMMON CARD (302-309)	.50	.15
1 Adam Kennedy	.30	.09
2 Alfredo Amezaga	.30	.09
3 Chone Figgins	.30	.09
4 Darin Erstad	.50	.15
5 David Eckstein	.30	.09
6 Garret Anderson	.50	.15
7 Jarrod Washburn	.50	.15
8 Nolan Ryan Angels	3.00	.90
9 Tim Salmon	.75	.23
10 Troy Glaus	.75	.23
11 Troy Percival	.50	.15
12 Curt Schilling	.75	.23
13 Junior Spivey	.30	.09
14 Luis Gonzalez	.50	.15
15 Mark Grace	.75	.23
16 Randy Johnson	1.25	.35
17 Steve Finley	.50	.15
18 Andruw Jones	.50	.15
19 Chipper Jones	1.25	.35
20 Dale Murphy	1.25	.35
21 Gary Sheffield	.50	.15
22 Greg Maddux	2.00	.60
23 John Smoltz	.75	.23
24 Andy Pratt	.30	.09
25 Adam LaRoche	.75	.23
26 Trey Hodges	.30	.09
27 Warren Spahn	.75	.23
28 Cal Ripken	4.00	1.20
29 Ed Rogers	.30	.09
30 Brian Roberts	.30	.09
31 Geronimo Gil	.30	.09
32 Jay Gibbons	.50	.15
33 Josh Towers	.30	.09
34 Casey Fossum	.30	.09
35 Cliff Floyd	.50	.15
36 Derek Lowe	.50	.15
37 Fred Lynn	.50	.15
38 Freddy Sanchez	.30	.09
39 Manny Ramirez	.50	.15
40 Nomar Garciaparra	2.00	.60
41 Pedro Martinez	1.25	.35
42 Rickey Henderson	1.25	.35
43 Shea Hillenbrand	.50	.15
44 Trot Nixon	.75	.23
45 Bobby Hill	.30	.09
46 Corey Patterson	.50	.15
47 Fred McGriff	.75	.23
48 Hee Seop Choi	.50	.15
49 Juan Cruz	.30	.09
50 Kerry Wood	1.25	.35
51 Mark Prior	2.50	.75
52 Moises Alou	.50	.15
53 Nic Jackson	.30	.09
54 Ryne Sandberg	2.50	.75
55 Sammy Sosa	2.00	.60
56 Carlos Lee	.50	.15
57 Corwin Malone	.30	.09
58 Frank Thomas	1.25	.35
59 Joe Borchard	.50	.15
60 Joe Crede	.30	.09
61 Magglio Ordonez	.50	.15
62 Mark Buehrle	.50	.15
63 Paul Konerko	.50	.15
64 Tim Hummel	.30	.09
65 Jon Adkins	.30	.09
66 Adam Dunn	.50	.15
67 Austin Kearns	.50	.15
68 Barry Larkin	1.25	.35
69 Jose Acevedo	.30	.09
70 Corky Miller	.30	.09
71 Eric Davis	.50	.15
72 Ken Griffey Jr.	2.00	.60
73 Sean Casey	.50	.15
74 Wily Mo Pena	.30	.09
75 Bob Feller	.75	.23
76 Brian Tallet	.30	.09
77 C.C. Sabathia	.50	.15
78 Cliff Lee	.50	.15
79 Earl Snyder	.30	.09
80 Ellis Burks	.50	.15
81 Jeremy Guthrie	.30	.09
82 Travis Hafner	.50	.15
83 Luis Garcia	.30	.09
84 Omar Vizquel	.50	.15
85 Ricardo Rodriguez	.30	.09
86 Ryan Church	.30	.09
87 Victor Martinez	.50	.15
88 Brandon Phillips	.30	.09
89 Jack Cust	.30	.09
90 Jason Jennings	.30	.09
91 Jeff Baker	.30	.09
92 Garrett Atkins	.50	.15
93 Juan Uribe	.30	.09
94 Larry Walker	.75	.23
95 Rene Reyes	.30	.09
96 Todd Helton	.75	.23
97 Alan Trammell	.50	.15
98 Fernando Rodney	.30	.09
99 Carlos Pena	.30	.09
100 Jack Morris	.50	.15
101 Bobby Higginson	.50	.15
102 Mike Maroth	.30	.09
103 Robert Fick	.50	.15
104 Jesus Medrano	.30	.09
105 Josh Beckett	.75	.23
106 Luis Castillo	.50	.15
107 Mike Lowell	.50	.15
108 Juan Pierre	.50	.15
109 Josh Wilson	.30	.09
110 Tim Redding	.30	.09
111 Carlos Hernandez	.30	.09
112 Craig Biggio	.75	.23
113 Henri Stanley	.30	.09
114 Jason Lane	.30	.09
115 Jeff Bagwell	.75	.23
116 John Buck	.30	.09
117 Kirk Saarloos	.30	.09
118 Lance Berkman	.50	.15
119 Nolan Ryan Astros	3.00	.90
120 Richard Hidalgo	.50	.15
121 Rodrigo Rosario	.30	.09
122 Roy Oswalt	.50	.15
123 Tommy Whiteman	.30	.09
124 Wade Miller	.50	.15
125 Alexis Gomez	.30	.09
126 Angel Berroa	.50	.15
127 Brandon Berger	.30	.09
128 Carlos Beltran	.50	.15
129 George Brett	3.00	.90
130 Jimmy Gobble	.50	.15
131 Dee Brown	.30	.09
132 Mike Sweeney	.50	.15
133 Raul Ibanez	.30	.09
134 Runelvys Hernandez	.30	.09
135 Adrian Beltre	.50	.15
136 Brian Jordan	.50	.15
137 Cesar Izturis	.30	.09
138 Victor Alvarez	.30	.09
139 Hideo Nomo	1.25	.35
140 Joe Thurston	.30	.09
141 Kazuhisa Ishii	.50	.15
142 Kevin Brown	.50	.15
143 Odalis Perez	.30	.09
144 Paul Lo Duca	.50	.15
145 Shawn Green	.50	.15
146 Ben Sheets	.50	.15
147 Bill Hall	.30	.09
148 Nick Neugebauer	.30	.09
149 Richie Sexson	.50	.15
150 Robin Yount	2.00	.60
151 Shane Nance	.30	.09
152 Takahito Nomura	.30	.09
153 A.J. Pierzynski	.50	.15
154 Joe Mays	.30	.09
155 Kirby Puckett	1.25	.35
156 Adam Johnson	.30	.09
157 Rob Bowen	.30	.09
158 Torii Hunter	.50	.15
159 Andres Galarraga	.50	.15
160 Endy Chavez	.30	.09
161 Javier Vazquez	.50	.15
162 Jose Vidro	.50	.15
163 Vladimir Guerrero	1.25	.35
164 Dwight Gooden	.75	.23
165 Mike Piazza	2.00	.60
166 Roberto Alomar	1.25	.35
167 Tom Glavine	.75	.23
168 Alfonso Soriano	.75	.23
169 Bernie Williams	.75	.23
170 Brandon Claussen	.50	.15
171 Derek Jeter	3.00	.90
172 Don Mattingly	3.00	.90
173 Drew Henson	.50	.15
174 Jason Giambi	1.25	.35
175 Joe Torre MG	.75	.23
176 Jorge Posada	.75	.23
177 Mike Mussina	1.25	.35
178 Nick Johnson	.50	.15
179 Roger Clemens	2.50	.75
180 Whitey Ford	.75	.23
181 Adam Morrissey	.30	.09
182 Barry Zito	.75	.23
183 David Justice	.50	.15
184 Eric Chavez	.50	.15
185 Jermaine Dye	.50	.15
186 Mark Mulder	.50	.15
187 Miguel Tejada	.50	.15
188 Reggie Jackson	.75	.23
189 Terrence Long	.50	.15
190 Tim Hudson	.50	.15
191 Anderson Machado	.30	.09
192 Bobby Abreu	.50	.15
193 Brandon Duckworth	.30	.09
194 Jim Thome	1.25	.35
195 Eric Junge	.30	.09
196 Jeremy Giambi	.30	.09
197 Johnny Estrada	.30	.09
198 Jorge Padilla	.30	.09
199 Marlon Byrd	.50	.15
200 Mike Schmidt	2.50	.75
201 Pat Burrell	.50	.15
202 Steve Carlton	.50	.15
203 Aramis Ramirez	.50	.15
204 Brian Giles	.50	.15
205 Carlos Rivera	.30	.09
206 Craig Wilson	.30	.09
207 Dave Williams	.30	.09
208 Jack Wilson	.30	.09
209 Jose Castillo	.50	.15
210 Kip Wells	.30	.09
211 Roberto Clemente	3.00	.90
212 Walter Young	.30	.09
213 Ben Howard	.30	.09
214 Brian Lawrence	.30	.09
215 Cliff Bartosh	.30	.09
216 Dennis Tankersley	.30	.09
217 Oliver Perez	.30	.09
218 Phil Nevin	.50	.15
219 Ryan Klesko	.50	.15
220 Sean Burroughs	.50	.15
221 Tony Gwynn	1.50	.45
222 Xavier Nady	.30	.09
223 Mike Rivera	.30	.09
224 Barry Bonds	3.00	.90
225 Benito Santiago	.50	.15
226 Jason Schmidt	.50	.15
227 Jeff Kent	.50	.15
228 Kenny Lofton	.50	.15
229 Rich Aurilia	.50	.15
230 Robb Nen	.50	.15
231 Tsuyoshi Shinjo	.50	.15
232 Bret Boone	.50	.15
233 Chris Snelling	.50	.15
234 Edgar Martinez	.75	.23
235 Freddy Garcia	.50	.15
236 Ichiro Suzuki	2.00	.60
237 John Olerud	.50	.15
238 Kazuhiro Sasaki	.50	.15
239 Mike Cameron	.50	.15
240 Rafael Soriano	.30	.09
241 Albert Pujols	2.50	.75
242 J.D. Drew	.50	.15
243 Jim Edmonds	.50	.15
244 Ozzie Smith	2.00	.60
245 Scott Rolen	.75	.23
246 So Taguchi	.50	.15
247 Stan Musial	2.00	.60
248 Antonio Perez	.30	.09
249 Aubrey Huff	.50	.15
250 Dewon Brazelton	.30	.09
251 Delvin James	.30	.09
252 Joe Kennedy	.30	.09
253 Toby Hall	.30	.09
254 Alex Rodriguez	2.00	.60
255 Ben Kozlowski	.30	.09
256 Gerald Laird	.30	.09
257 Hank Blalock	.75	.23
258 Ivan Rodriguez	1.25	.35
259 Juan Gonzalez	1.25	.35
260 Kevin Mench	.30	.09
261 Mario Ramos	.30	.09
262 Mark Teixeira	.75	.23
263 Nolan Ryan Rangers	3.00	.90
264 Rafael Palmeiro	.75	.23
265 Alexis Rios	2.00	.60
266 Carlos Delgado	.50	.15
267 Eric Hinske	.30	.09
268 Josh Phelps	.30	.09
269 Kevin Cash	.30	.09
270 Orlando Hudson	.30	.09
271 Roy Halladay	.50	.15
272 Shannon Stewart	.50	.15
273 Vernon Wells	.50	.15
274 Vinny Chulk	.30	.09
275 Jason Anderson	.30	.09
276 Craig Brazell RC	.60	.18
277 Termel Sledge RC	.60	.18
278 Ryan Cameron RC	.40	.12
279 Clint Barmes RC	.60	.18
280 Jhonny Peralta RC	.40	.12
281 Todd Wellemeyer RC	.60	.18
282 John Leicester RC	.40	.12
283 Brandon Webb RC	3.00	.90
284 Tim Olson RC	.60	.18
285 Matt Kata RC	1.00	.30
286 Rob Hammock RC	.60	.18
287 Pete LaForest RC	.60	.18
288 Nook Logan RC	.40	.12
289 Prentice Redman RC	.40	.12
290 Joe Valentine RC	.40	.12
291 Jose Contreras RC	2.50	.75
292 Josh Stewart RC	.40	.12
293 Mike Nicolas RC	.40	.12
294 Marshall McDougall	.30	.09
295 Travis Chapman	.30	.09
296 Jose Morban	.30	.09
297 Michael Hessman RC	.40	.12
298 Buddy Hernandez RC	.40	.12
299 Shane Victorino RC	.40	.12
300 Jason Dubois	.50	.15
301 Hideki Matsui RC	4.00	1.20
302 Ryan Wagner RC	.75	.23
303 Adam Loewen RC	1.25	.35
304 Chien-Ming Wang RC	1.00	.30
305 Hong-Chih Kuo RC	.50	.15
306 Delmon Young RC	3.00	.90
307 Dan Haren RC	.60	.18
308 Rickie Weeks RC	2.50	.75
309 Ramon Nivar RC	1.00	.30

2003 Donruss Champions Autographs

Cards checklisted 1-300 from this set were randomly inserted into Donruss Champions packs. Cards 302-309 were randomly inserted into packs of DLP Rookies and Traded. These cards were issued to different stated print runs and we have notated that information next to the player's name in our checklist. Please note that for cards with stated print runs of 45 or fewer cards we have not priced these cards due to market scarcity.

	Nm-Mt	Ex-Mt
2 Alfredo Amezaga/325	10.00	3.00
3 Chone Figgins/375	15.00	4.50
4 Darin Erstad/9		
8 Nolan Ryan Angels/4		
10 Troy Glaus/20		
12 Curt Schilling/5		
13 Junior Spivey/45	15.00	4.50
14 Luis Gonzalez/5		
18 Andruw Jones/20		
19 Chipper Jones/10		
20 Dale Murphy/20		
21 Gary Sheffield/10		
24 Andy Pratt/475	10.00	3.00
25 Adam LaRoche/400	25.00	7.50
26 Trey Hodges/305	10.00	3.00
28 Cal Ripken/5		
29 Ed Rogers/305	10.00	3.00
30 Brian Roberts/500	10.00	3.00
31 Geronimo Gil/150	10.00	3.00
32 Jay Gibbons/475	15.00	4.50
33 Josh Towers/500	10.00	3.00

34 Casey Fossum/160 10.00 3.00
35 Cliff Floyd/70 25.00 7.50
37 Fred Lynn/80 40.00 12.00
38 Freddy Sanchez/400 10.00 3.00
39 Manny Ramirez/5
40 Nomar Garciaparra/5
41 Pedro Martinez/5
42 Rickey Henderson/5
45 Bobby Hill/5
46 Corey Patterson/100 25.00 7.50
49 Juan Cruz/250 10.00 3.00
50 Kerry Wood/20
51 Mark Prior/50 120.00 36.00
53 Nic Jackson/100 15.00 4.50
56 Carlos Lee/25
57 Corwin Malone/400 10.00 3.00
58 Frank Thomas/5
59 Joe Borchard/215 15.00 4.50
60 Joe Crede/5
61 Magglio Ordonez/25
62 Mark Buehrle/15
64 Tim Hummel/400 10.00 3.00
65 Jon Adkins/400 10.00 3.00
66 Adam Dunn/100 40.00 12.00
67 Austin Kearns/50 25.00 7.50
68 Barry Larkin/9
69 Jose Acevedo/315 10.00 3.00
70 Corky Miller/295 10.00 3.00
71 Eric Davis/45 40.00 12.00
73 Sean Casey/10
74 Wily Mo Pena/450 10.00 3.00
75 Bob Feller/20
76 Brian Tallet/250 10.00 3.00
77 C.C. Sabathia/25
78 Cliff Lee/330 15.00 4.50
79 Earl Snyder/225 10.00 3.00
81 Jeremy Guthrie/400 10.00 3.00
83 Luis Garcia/395 10.00 3.00
86 Ryan Church/395 10.00 3.00
87 Victor Martinez/250 15.00 4.50
88 Brandon Phillips/375 10.00 3.00
89 Jack Cust/498 10.00 3.00
90 Jason Jennings/375 10.00 3.00
91 Jeff Baker/400 10.00 3.00
92 Garrett Atkins/400 15.00 4.50
95 Rene Reyes/350 10.00 3.00
96 Todd Helton/5
97 Alan Trammell/25
98 Fernando Rodney/500 10.00 3.00
100 Jack Morris/50 40.00 12.00
102 Mike Maroth/400 10.00 3.00
103 Robert Fick/15
104 Jesus Medrano/500 10.00 3.00
105 Josh Beckett/14
109 Josh Wilson/400 10.00 3.00
110 Tim Redding/375 10.00 3.00
111 Carlos Hernandez/250 10.00 3.00
112 Craig Biggio/20
113 Henri Stanley/390 10.00 3.00
114 Jason Lane/250 10.00 3.00
117 Kirk Saarloos/149 10.00 3.00
118 Lance Berkman/10
119 Nolan Ryan Astros/4
120 Richard Hidalgo/120 15.00 4.50
121 Rodrigo Rosario/500 10.00 3.00
122 Roy Oswalt/100 25.00 7.50
123 Tommy Whiteman/375 10.00 3.00
124 Wade Miller/125 10.00 3.00
126 Angel Berroa/400 15.00 4.50
127 Brandon Berger/325 10.00 3.00
128 Carlos Beltran/10
129 George Brett/9
130 Jimmy Gobble/400 15.00 4.50
131 Dee Brown/500 10.00 3.00
132 Mike Sweeney/45 25.00 7.50
134 Runelvys Hernandez/400 10.00 3.00
135 Adrian Beltre/20
138 Victor Alvarez/308 10.00 3.00
141 Kazuhisa Ishii/20
142 Kevin Brown/30
144 Paul Lo Duca/45 25.00 7.50
145 Shawn Green/5
146 Ben Sheets/50 25.00 7.50
147 Bill Hall/450 10.00 3.00
148 Nick Neugebauer/375 10.00 3.00
149 Richie Sexson/25
150 Robin Yount/5
151 Shane Nance/150 10.00 3.00
152 Takahito Nomura/50 50.00 15.00
153 A.J. Pierzynski/250 15.00 4.50
154 Joe Mays/5
155 Kirby Puckett/10
156 Adam Johnson/500 10.00 3.00
157 Rob Bowen/375 10.00 3.00
158 Torii Hunter/45 25.00 7.50
159 Andres Galarraga/25
160 Endy Chavez/280 10.00 3.00
161 Javier Vazquez/50 25.00 7.50
162 Jose Vidro/45 25.00 7.50
163 Vladimir Guerrero/20
164 Dwight Gooden/45 60.00 18.00
166 Roberto Alomar/15
167 Tom Glavine/15
168 Alfonso Soriano/10
169 Bernie Williams/10
170 Brandon Claussen/475 15.00 4.50
172 Don Mattingly/20
173 Drew Henson/20
175 Joe Torre/20
177 Mike Mussina/5
178 Nick Johnson/500 15.00 4.50
179 Roger Clemens/5
180 Whitey Ford/10
181 Adam Morrissey/395 10.00 3.00
182 Barry Zito/25
183 David Justice/10
184 Eric Chavez/10
185 Jermaine Dye/125 15.00 4.50
186 Mark Mulder/25
187 Miguel Tejada/15
188 Reggie Jackson/9
189 Terrence Long/250 15.00 4.50
190 Tim Hudson/25
191 Anderson Machado/500 10.00 3.00
192 Bobby Abreu/25
193 Brandon Duckworth/100 15.00 4.50
194 Jim Thome/15
195 Eric Junge/279 10.00 3.00
196 Jeremy Giambi/195 10.00 3.00
198 Jorge Padilla/11
199 Marlon Byrd/10
200 Mike Schmidt/20
202 Steve Carlton/25
203 Aramis Ramirez/20
204 Brian Giles/25
205 Carlos Rivera/400 10.00 3.00
206 Craig Wilson/245 10.00 3.00
207 Dave Williams/265 10.00 3.00
208 Jack Wilson/500 10.00 3.00
209 Jose Castillo/400 15.00 4.50
210 Kip Wells/500 10.00 3.00
212 Walter Young/400 10.00 3.00
213 Ben Howard/500 10.00 3.00
214 Brian Lawrence/500 10.00 3.00
215 Cliff Bartosh/400 10.00 3.00
216 Dennis Tankersley/25
217 Oliver Perez/5
219 Ryan Klesko/20
220 Sean Burroughs/19
221 Tony Gwynn/15
222 Xavier Nady/250 10.00 3.00
223 Mike Rivera/90 15.00 4.50
228 Kenny Lofton/25
233 Chris Snelling/200 15.00 4.50
234 Edgar Martinez/20
235 Freddy Garcia/10
240 Rafael Soriano/500 10.00 3.00
241 Albert Pujols/10
242 J.D. Drew/5
243 Jim Edmonds/10
244 Ozzie Smith/20
245 Scott Rolen/10
246 So Taguchi/10
247 Stan Musial/15
248 Antonio Perez/500 10.00 3.00
249 Aubrey Huff/475 15.00 4.50
250 Dewon Brazelton/50 15.00 4.50
251 Delvin James/400 10.00 3.00
252 Joe Kennedy/250 10.00 3.00
253 Toby Hall/500 10.00 3.00
254 Alex Rodriguez/5
255 Ben Kozlowski/400 10.00 3.00
256 Gerald Laird/450 10.00 3.00
257 Hank Blalock/50 40.00 12.00
258 Ivan Rodriguez/5
259 Juan Gonzalez/20
260 Kevin Mench/475 10.00 3.00
261 Mario Ramos/475 10.00 3.00
262 Mark Teixeira/40 40.00 12.00
263 Nolan Ryan Rangers/4
264 Rafael Palmeiro/5
265 Alexis Rios/400 30.00 9.00
267 Eric Hinske/390 10.00 3.00
268 Josh Phelps/5
269 Kevin Cash/375 10.00 3.00
272 Shannon Stewart/25
274 Vinny Chulk/100 15.00 4.50
275 Jason Anderson/493 25.00 7.50
277 Terrmel Sledge/500 15.00 4.50
278 Ryan Cameron/475 10.00 3.00
279 Clint Barmes/475 15.00 4.50
280 Jhonny Peralta/500 10.00 3.00
281 Todd Wellemeyer/477 15.00 4.50
282 John Leicester/480 10.00 3.00
283 Brandon Webb/500 30.00 9.00
284 Tim Olson/500 15.00 4.50
285 Matt Kata/487 15.00 4.50
286 Rob Hammock/486 15.00 4.50
287 Pete LaForest/500 15.00 4.50
288 Nook Logan/500 10.00 3.00
289 Prentice Redman/488 10.00 3.00
290 Joe Valentine/475 10.00 3.00
291 Jose Contreras/100 40.00 12.00
292 Josh Stewart/485 10.00 3.00
293 Mike Nicolas/500 10.00 3.00
295 Travis Chapman/100 15.00 4.50
296 Jose Morban/475 10.00 3.00
297 Michael Hessman/500 10.00 3.00
298 Buddy Hernandez/500 10.00 3.00
299 Shane Victorino/480 10.00 3.00
300 Jason Dubois/480 15.00 4.50
302 Ryan Wagner/100 25.00 7.50
303 Adam Loewen/100 40.00 12.00
304 Chien-Ming Wang/100 40.00 12.00
305 Hong-Chih Kuo/100 30.00 9.00
306 Delmon Young/25
307 Dan Haren/100 20.00 6.00
308 Rickie Weeks/10
309 Ramon Nivar/100 20.00 6.00

2003 Donruss Champions Autographs Notation

Randomly inserted into packs, these 65 cards feature not only an authentic autograph of the featured player but a notation under their signature. Please note, card 303, Adam Loewen, was distributed within packs of DLP Rookies and Traded. Since the players signed different amounts of cards, we have notated the print run next to the player's name in our checklist. Since none of these cards were issued to stated print run of more than 25 copies, no pricing is provided due to market scarcity.

Nm-Mt Ex-Mt
4 Darin Erstad/1
8 Nolan Ryan/3
13 Junior Spivey/5
32 Jay Gibbons/25
35 Cliff Floyd/1
59 Joe Borchard/10
62 Mark Buehrle/10
68 Barry Larkin/1
70 Corky Miller/5
71 Eric Davis/5
75 Bob Feller/5
79 Earl Snyder/1
83 Luis Garcia/5
86 Ryan Church/5
88 Brandon Phillips/25
89 Jack Cust/2
90 Jason Jennings/25
103 Robert Fick/10
105 Josh Beckett/1
110 Tim Redding/25
113 Henri Stanley/10
117 Kirk Saarloos/1
120 Richard Hidalgo/5
123 Tommy Whiteman/24
129 George Brett/1
132 Mike Sweeney/5
144 Paul Lo Duca/5
148 Nick Neugebauer/25
157 Rob Bowen/25
158 Torii Hunter/25
162 Jose Vidro/5
167 Tom Glavine/5
170 Brandon Claussen/24
173 Drew Henson/5
181 Adam Morrissey/5
188 Reggie Jackson/1
189 Terrence Long/5
190 Tim Hudson/5
196 Jeremy Giambi/5
203 Aramis Ramirez/5
205 Carlos Rivera/25
219 Ryan Klesko/5
220 Sean Burroughs/1
234 Edgar Martinez/5
246 So Taguchi/5
249 Aubrey Huff/25
260 Kevin Mench/25
261 Mario Ramos/25
262 Mark Teixeira/10
267 Eric Hinske/10
269 Kevin Cash/25
275 Jason Anderson/7
278 Ryan Cameron/25
279 Clint Barmes/25
281 Todd Wellemeyer/23
282 Jon Leicester/20
285 Matt Kata/13
286 Rob Hammock/14
289 Prentice Redman/12
290 Joe Valentine/25
292 Josh Stewart/15
296 Jose Morban/25
299 Shane Victorino/20
300 Jason Dubois/20
303 Adam Loewen/10

2003 Donruss Champions Metalized

Randomly inserted into packs, this is a parallel to the Donruss Champions set. Cards 302-309 were randomly seeded within packs of DLP Rookies and Traded. These cards were issued with a special metalized film board and were issued to a stated print run of 100 serial numbered sets.

Nm-Mt Ex-Mt
*METALIZED ACTIVE 1-301: 4X TO 10X
*METALIZED RETIRED 1-301: 8X TO 20X
*METALIZED RC'S 1-301: 1.5X TO 4X
*METALIZED RC'S 302-309: 4X TO 10X

2003 Donruss Champions Call to the Hall

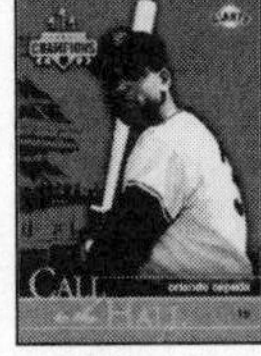

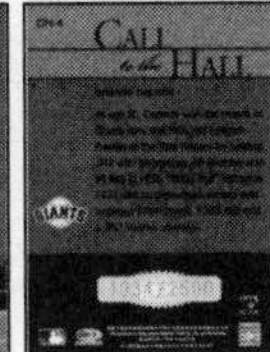

Randomly inserted into packs, these 10 cards feature players who have already been elected to the Hall of Fame. These cards were issued to a stated print run of 2500 serial numbered sets.

Nm-Mt Ex-Mt
HOLO-FOIL PRINT RUN 25 #'d SETS..
NO HOLO-FOIL PRICING DUE TO SCARCITY
*METALIZED: 2.5X TO 6X BASIC CALL
METALIZED PRINT RUN 100 #'d SETS
1 Nolan Ryan 10.00 3.00
2 Tom Seaver 5.00 1.50
3 Phil Rizzuto 5.00 1.50
4 Orlando Cepeda 3.00 .90
5 Al Kaline 5.00 1.50
6 Hoyt Wilhelm 3.00 .90
7 Luis Aparicio 3.00 .90
8 Billy Williams 3.00 .90
9 Jim Palmer 3.00 .90
10 Mike Schmidt 8.00 2.40

2003 Donruss Champions Call to the Hall Autographs

Randomly inserted into packs, these 10 cards parallel the Call to the Hall insert set. These cards feature an authentic autograph of the player featured in the set. Please note, that since Donruss/Playoff use stickers for their autographs, they were able to feature Hoyt Wilhelm who had passed away the previous year.

Nm-Mt Ex-Mt
1 Nolan Ryan/10
2 Tom Seaver/10
3 Phil Rizzuto/25
4 Orlando Cepeda/25
5 Al Kaline/25
6 Hoyt Wilhelm/25
7 Luis Aparicio/25
8 Billy Williams/25
9 Jim Palmer/25
10 Mike Schmidt/10

2003 Donruss Champions Grand Champions

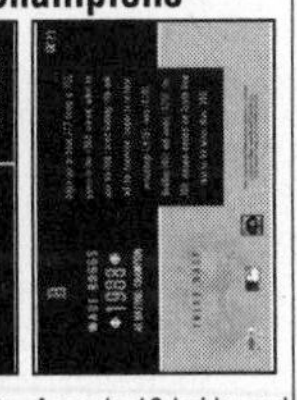

Issued at a stated rate of one in 18 hobby and one in 23 retail, this 25 card sets features a mix of Hall of Famers as well as guaranteed HOFers among active players.

Nm-Mt Ex-Mt
HOLO-FOIL RANDOM INSERTS IN PACKS
HOLO-FOIL PRINT RUN 25 #'d SETS..
NO HOLO-FOIL PRICING DUE TO SCARCITY
*METALIZED: 2X TO 5X BASIC GRAND
METALIZED RANDOM INSERTS IN PACKS
METALIZED PRINT RUN 100 SERIAL #'d SETS
1 Stan Musial 8.00 2.40
2 Bob Feller 5.00 1.50
3 Reggie Jackson 5.00 1.50
4 George Brett 12.00 3.60
5 Jim Palmer 3.00 .90
6 Harmon Killebrew 5.00 1.50
7 Ernie Banks 5.00 1.50
8 Frank Robinson 5.00 1.50
9 Greg Maddux 8.00 2.40
10 Whitey Ford 5.00 1.50
11 Bob Gibson 5.00 1.50
12 Mike Schmidt 10.00 3.00
13 Nolan Ryan 12.00 3.60
14 Warren Spahn 5.00 1.50
15 Rod Carew 5.00 1.50
16 Hoyt Wilhelm 3.00 .90
17 Duke Snider 5.00 1.50
18 Tom Seaver 5.00 1.50
19 Steve Carlton 3.00 .90
20 Yogi Berra 5.00 1.50
21 Cal Ripken 15.00 4.50
22 Tony Gwynn 6.00 1.80
23 Wade Boggs 5.00 1.50
24 Rickey Henderson 5.00 1.50
25 Roger Clemens 10.00 3.00

2003 Donruss Champions Statistical Champs

Inserted at a stated rate of one in 10 hobby and one in 23 retail, this 30 card set features a mix of active and retired players who have led the league in various offensive categories.

Nm-Mt Ex-Mt
1 Alex Rodriguez 6.00 1.80
2 Alfonso Soriano 4.00 1.20
3 Curt Schilling 4.00 1.20
4 Eddie Mathews 5.00 1.50
5 Fred Lynn 3.00 .90
6 Harmon Killebrew 5.00 1.50
7 Hideo Nomo 4.00 1.20
8 Jim Thome 4.00 1.20
9 Kirby Puckett 4.00 1.20
10 Luis Gonzalez 3.00 .90
11 Manny Ramirez 3.00 .90
12 Jason Giambi 4.00 1.20
13 Mike Schmidt 10.00 3.00
14 Nomar Garciaparra 6.00 1.80
15 Lou Brock 5.00 1.50
16 Randy Johnson 4.00 1.20
17 Reggie Jackson 5.00 1.50
18 Rickey Henderson 4.00 1.20
19 Roberto Clemente 12.00 3.60
20 Barry Zito 4.00 1.20
21 Todd Helton 4.00 1.20
22 Tom Seaver 5.00 1.50
23 Tony Gwynn 6.00 1.80
24 Torii Hunter 3.00 .90
25 Troy Glaus 4.00 1.20
26 Wade Boggs 5.00 1.50
27 Rod Carew 5.00 1.50
28 Juan Gonzalez 4.00 1.20
29 Sammy Sosa 6.00 1.80
30 Warren Spahn 5.00 1.50

2003 Donruss Champions Statistical Champs Materials

Randomly inserted into packs, this is a parallel to the Statistical Champs insert set. These cards basically feature game-used jersey pieces and were issued to different print runs. We have notated that print run information next to the player's name in our checklist.

Nm-Mt Ex-Mt
1 Alex Rodriguez Jsy/250 25.00 7.50
2 Alfonso Soriano Jsy/25
3 Curt Schilling Jsy/225 15.00 4.50

4 Eddie Mathews Jsy/200 25.00 7.50
5 Fred Lynn Jsy/50 40.00 12.00
6 Harmon Killebrew Jsy/250 25.00 7.50
7 Hideo Nomo Jsy/110 60.00 18.00
8 Jim Thome Jsy/250 15.00 4.50
9 Kirby Puckett Jsy/250 25.00 7.50
10 Luis Gonzalez Jsy/250 10.00 3.00
11 Manny Ramirez Jsy/155 10.00 3.00
12 Jason Giambi Jsy/250 15.00 4.50
13 Mike Schmidt Jsy/250 40.00 12.00
14 Nomar Garciaparra Jsy/99 40.00 12.00
15 Lou Brock Jsy/250 25.00 7.50
16 Randy Johnson Jsy/100 25.00 7.50
17 Reggie Jackson Jsy/200 25.00 7.50
18 Rickey Henderson Jsy/184 15.00 4.50
19 Roberto Clemente Jsy/64
20 Barry Zito Jsy/100 25.00 7.50
21 Todd Helton Jsy/250 15.00 4.50
22 Tom Seaver Jsy/100 40.00 12.00
23 Tony Gwynn Jsy/250 25.00 7.50
24 Torii Hunter Jsy/250 10.00 3.00
25 Troy Glaus Jsy/125 25.00 7.50
26 Wade Boggs Jsy/250 25.00 7.50
27 Rod Carew Hat/150 25.00 7.50
28 Juan Gonzalez Jsy/250 15.00 4.50
29 Sammy Sosa Jsy/250 25.00 7.50
30 Warren Spahn Jsy/150 25.00 7.50

2003 Donruss Champions Team Colors

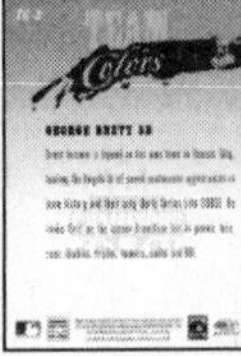

Issued at a stated rate of one in 10 hobby and one in 23 retail, these 30 cards feature star players from a team set against background colors of the teams colors.

Nm-Mt Ex-Mt
1 Miguel Tejada 3.00 .90
2 Mike Schmidt 10.00 3.00
3 George Brett 12.00 3.60
4 Magglio Ordonez 3.00 .90
5 Ryne Sandberg 10.00 3.00
6 Adam Dunn 3.00 .90
7 Mark Prior 8.00 2.40
8 Tony Gwynn 6.00 1.80
9 Troy Glaus 4.00 1.20
10 Stan Musial 8.00 2.40
11 Kirby Puckett 4.00 1.20
12 Don Mattingly 12.00 3.60
13 Bobby Abreu 3.00 .90
14 Ichiro Suzuki 6.00 1.80
15 Cal Ripken 15.00 4.50
16 Chipper Jones 4.00 1.20
17 Carlos Beltran 3.00 .90
18 Alfonso Soriano 4.00 1.20
19 Albert Pujols 8.00 2.40
20 Andruw Jones 3.00 .90
21 Bernie Williams 4.00 1.20
22 Todd Helton 4.00 1.20
23 Roberto Clemente 12.00 3.60
24 Jim Thome 4.00 1.20
25 Carlos Delgado 3.00 .90
26 Derek Jeter 10.00 3.00
27 Garret Anderson 3.00 .90
28 Nomar Garciaparra 6.00 1.80
29 Torii Hunter 3.00 .90
30 Vladimir Guerrero 4.00 1.20

2003 Donruss Champions Team Colors Materials

Randomly inserted in packs, this is a parallel to the Team Colors insert set. These cards feature a memorabilia piece associated with the player's career. Since each card is serial numbered to a different amount, we have notated that information next to the player's name in our checklist.

Nm-Mt Ex-Mt
1 Miguel Tejada Jsy/50 20.00 6.00
2 Mike Schmidt Jsy/200 40.00 12.00
3 George Brett Jsy/200 50.00 15.00
4 Magglio Ordonez Jsy/100 15.00 4.50
5 Ryne Sandberg Jsy/200 40.00 12.00
6 Adam Dunn Jsy/44 20.00 6.00
7 Mark Prior Jsy/200 30.00 9.00
8 Tony Gwynn Jsy/200 20.00 6.00
9 Troy Glaus Jsy/200 15.00 4.50
10 Stan Musial Jsy/200 40.00 12.00
11 Kirby Puckett Jsy/200 25.00 7.50
12 Don Mattingly Jsy/200 60.00 18.00
13 Bobby Abreu Jsy/200 10.00 3.00
14 Ichiro Suzuki Base/200 25.00 7.50

15 Cal Ripken Jsy/200 ... 60.00 18.00
16 Chipper Jones Jsy/200 ... 15.00 4.50
17 Carlos Beltran Jsy/200 ... 10.00 3.00
18 Alfonso Soriano Jsy/25 ...
19 Albert Pujols Base/200 ... 15.00 4.50
20 Andruw Jones Jsy/200 ... 10.00 3.00
21 Bernie Williams Jsy/200 ... 15.00 4.50
22 Todd Helton Jsy/200 ... 15.00 4.50
23 Roberto Clemente Jsy/200 . 100.00 30.00
24 Jim Thome Jsy/200 ... 15.00 4.50
25 Carlos Delgado Jsy/200 ... 10.00 3.00
26 Derek Jeter Base/200 ... 25.00 7.50
27 Garret Anderson Jsy/50 ... 20.00 6.00
28 Nomar Garciaparra Jsy/200 . 25.00 7.50
29 Torii Hunter Jsy/200 ... 10.00 3.00
30 Vladimir Guerrero Jsy/200 ... 15.00 4.50

2003 Donruss Champions Total Game

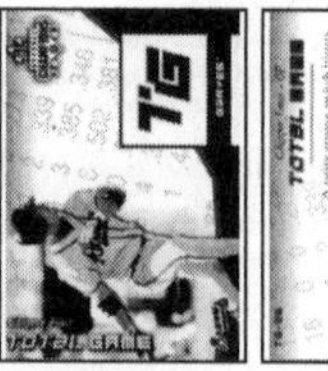

Inserted at a stated rate of one in nine hobby and one in 12 retail, these 40 cards feature position players who have well-rounded games.

Nm-Mt Ex-Mt
1 Vladimir Guerrero ... 4.00 1.20
2 Nomar Garciaparra ... 6.00 1.80
3 Magglio Ordonez ... 3.00 .90
4 Garret Anderson ... 3.00 .90
5 Derek Jeter ... 10.00 3.00
6 Jim Thome ... 4.00 1.20
7 Torii Hunter ... 3.00 .90
8 Todd Helton ... 4.00 1.20
9 Andruw Jones ... 3.00 .90
10 Alfonso Soriano ... 4.00 1.20
11 Luis Gonzalez ... 3.00 .90
12 Manny Ramirez ... 3.00 .90
13 Paul Konerko ... 3.00 .90
14 Alex Rodriguez ... 6.00 1.80
15 Carlos Beltran ... 3.00 .90
16 Bernie Williams ... 4.00 1.20
17 Barry Bonds ... 10.00 3.00
18 Miguel Tejada ... 3.00 .90
19 Jason Giambi ... 4.00 1.20
20 Ichiro Suzuki ... 6.00 1.80
21 Ivan Rodriguez ... 4.00 1.20
22 Rafael Palmeiro ... 4.00 1.20
23 Carlos Delgado ... 3.00 .90
24 Vernon Wells ... 3.00 .90
25 Sammy Sosa ... 6.00 1.80
26 Chipper Jones ... 4.00 1.20
27 Adam Dunn ... 3.00 .90
28 Larry Walker ... 4.00 1.20
29 Shawn Green ... 3.00 .90
30 Richie Sexson ... 3.00 .90
31 Jose Vidro ... 3.00 .90
32 Mike Piazza ... 6.00 1.80
33 Roberto Alomar ... 4.00 1.20
34 Bobby Abreu ... 3.00 .90
35 Pat Burrell ... 3.00 .90
36 Brian Giles ... 3.00 .90
37 Albert Pujols ... 8.00 2.40
38 Lance Berkman ... 3.00 .90
39 Ryan Klesko ... 3.00 .90
40 Jeff Kent ... 3.00 .90

2003 Donruss Champions Total Game Materials

Randomly inserted into packs, this is a parallel to the Total Game insert set. Each player has a game-used swatch of some item attached to their career. Since each card is serial numbered to a differing amount of cards, we have notated that information next to the player's name in our checklist.

Nm-Mt Ex-Mt
1 Vladimir Guerrero Jsy/200 ... 15.00 4.50
2 Nomar Garciaparra Jsy/200 ... 25.00 7.50
3 Magglio Ordonez Jsy/100 ... 15.00 4.50
4 Garret Anderson Jsy/50 ... 20.00 6.00
5 Derek Jeter Base/200 ... 25.00 7.50
6 Jim Thome Jsy/200 ... 15.00 4.50
7 Torii Hunter Jsy/200 ... 10.00 3.00
8 Todd Helton Jsy/200 ... 15.00 4.50
9 Andruw Jones Jsy/200 ... 10.00 3.00
10 Alfonso Soriano Jsy/25 ...
11 Luis Gonzalez Jsy/200 ... 10.00 3.00
12 Manny Ramirez Jsy/200 ... 10.00 3.00
13 Paul Konerko Jsy/200 ... 10.00 3.00
14 Alex Rodriguez Jsy/200 ... 25.00 7.50
15 Carlos Beltran Jsy/200 ... 10.00 3.00
16 Bernie Williams Jsy/200 ... 15.00 4.50
17 Barry Bonds Base/200 ... 25.00 7.50
18 Miguel Tejada Jsy/50 ... 20.00 6.00
19 Jason Giambi Base/200 ... 15.00 4.50
20 Ichiro Suzuki Base/200 ... 25.00 7.50
21 Ivan Rodriguez Jsy/100 ... 25.00 7.50
22 Rafael Palmeiro Jsy/200 ... 15.00 4.50
23 Carlos Delgado Jsy/200 ... 10.00 3.00
24 Vernon Wells Jsy/200 ... 10.00 3.00
25 Sammy Sosa Jsy/200 ... 25.00 7.50
26 Chipper Jones Jsy/200 ... 15.00 4.50
27 Adam Dunn Jsy/44 ... 20.00 6.00
28 Larry Walker Jsy/200 ... 15.00 4.50
29 Shawn Green Jsy/100 ... 15.00 4.50
30 Richie Sexson Jsy/200 ... 10.00 3.00
31 Jose Vidro Jsy/200 ... 10.00 3.00
32 Mike Piazza Jsy/50 ... 80.00 24.00
33 Roberto Alomar Jsy/100 ... 25.00 7.50
34 Bobby Abreu Jsy/200 ... 10.00 3.00
35 Pat Burrell Jsy/200 ... 10.00 3.00
36 Brian Giles Jsy/200 ... 10.00 3.00
37 Albert Pujols Base/200 ... 15.00 4.50
38 Lance Berkman Jsy/50 ... 20.00 6.00
39 Ryan Klesko Jsy/200 ... 10.00 3.00
40 Jeff Kent Jsy/200 ... 10.00 3.00

2003 Donruss Champions World Series Champs Samples

Randomly inserted into Beckett Baseball Collector magazines, these cards parallel the World Series Champs insert set. These cards were issued to a stated print run of 40 sets and are notated by the word "Sample" printed on the back.

Nm-Mt Ex-Mt
RANDOM INSERTS IN BBCM MAGAZINES
STATED PRINT RUN 40 SETS ...
*GOLD: 1.5X TO 4X BASIC SAMPLES
GOLD STATED PRINT RUN 10 SETS ..

2003 Donruss Champions World Series Champs

Randomly inserted into packs, this 15 card set honors key members of the 2002 Anaheim Angels. These cards were issued to a stated print run of 2,002 serial numbered sets.

Nm-Mt Ex-Mt
HOLO-FOIL PRINT RUN 25 #'d SETS..
NO HOLO-FOIL PRICING DUE TO SCARCITY
*METALIZED: 1.25X TO 3X BASIC WS
METALIZED PRINT RUN 100 #'d SETS
1 Troy Glaus ... 5.00 1.50
2 Jarrod Washburn ... 3.00 .90
3 Darin Erstad ... 3.00 .90
4 Troy Percival ... 3.00 .90
5 David Eckstein ... 3.00 .90
6 Francisco Rodriguez ... 3.00 .90
7 Garret Anderson ... 3.00 .90
8 John Lackey ... 3.00 .90
9 Tim Salmon ... 5.00 1.50
10 Chone Figgins ... 3.00 .90
11 Adam Kennedy ... 3.00 .90
12 Scott Spiezio ... 3.00 .90
13 Ben Molina ... 3.00 .90
14 Brad Fullmer ... 3.00 .90
15 Troy Glaus MVP ... 5.00 1.50

2003 Donruss Champions Atlantic City National

Collectors who opened a set number of Champions packs at the 2003 Atlantic City National were rewarded with a card from that set with a special Atlantic City National Logo on the front and serial numbering to five on the back. Due to market scarcity, no pricing is provided for these cards.

MINT NRMT
PRINT RUN 5 SERIAL #'d SETS ...

2001 Donruss Class of 2001 Samples

Inserted one per sealed Beckett Baseball Card Monthly issue number 203, these 100 cards preview veterans from the then-upcoming 2001 Donruss Class of 2001 set. Each card has the word Sample stamped on the back in silver foil.

Nm-Mt Ex-Mt
*STARS: 1.5X TO 4X BASIC CARDS ...
*GOLD: 1.5X TO 4X BASIC SAMPLES
GOLD: 10% OF THE TOTAL PRINT RUN

2001 Donruss Class of 2001

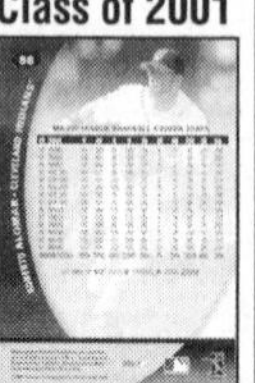

This product was released in mid-December 2001, and featured a 300-card base set that was broken into tiers as follows: 100 Base Veterans, 100 Rookies/Prospects serial numbered to 1875, and an additional 100 Rookies/Prospects serial numbered to 625. Each pack contained three cards, and carried a suggested retail price of $3.99. Due to an error in printing, two different players were checklisted as card 252 (John Buck and Adam Johnson) - thus, a total of 301 cards exist for the set, though it's numbering runs from 1-300. Both Buck and Johnson's cards are serial numbered "of 625" on back.

Nm-Mt Ex-Mt
COMP.SET w/o SP's (100) ... 25.00 7.50
COMMON CARD (1-100) ... .40 .12
COMMON (101-200) ... 4.00 1.20
COMMON (201-300) ... 6.00 1.80
1 Alex Rodriguez ... 1.50 .45
2 Barry Bonds ... 2.50 .75
3 Vladimir Guerrero ... 1.00 .30
4 Jim Edmonds ... .40 .12
5 Derek Jeter ... 2.50 .75
6 Jose Canseco ... 1.00 .30
7 Rafael Furcal ... .40 .12
8 Cal Ripken ... 3.00 .90
9 Brad Radke ... .40 .12
10 Miguel Tejada ... .40 .12
11 Pat Burrell ... .40 .12
12 Ken Griffey Jr. ... 1.50 .45
13 Cliff Floyd ... .40 .12
14 Luis Gonzalez ... .40 .12
15 Frank Thomas ... 1.00 .30
16 Mike Sweeney ... .40 .12
17 Paul LoDuca ... .40 .12
18 Lance Berkman ... .40 .12
19 Tony Gwynn ... 1.25 .35
20 Chipper Jones ... 1.00 .30
21 Eric Chavez ... .40 .12
22 Kerry Wood ... 1.00 .30
23 Jorge Posada ... .60 .18
24 J.D. Drew ... .40 .12
25 Garret Anderson ... .40 .12
26 Mike Piazza ... 1.50 .45
27 Kenny Lofton ... .40 .12
28 Mike Mussina ... 1.00 .30
29 Paul Konerko ... .40 .12
30 Bernie Williams ... .60 .18
31 Eric Milton ... .40 .12
32 Shawn Green ... .40 .12
33 Paul O'Neill ... .60 .18
34 Juan Gonzalez ... 1.00 .30
35 Andres Galarraga ... .40 .12
36 Gary Sheffield ... .40 .12
37 Ben Grieve ... .40 .12
38 Scott Rolen ... .60 .18
39 Mark Grace ... .60 .18
40 Hideo Nomo ... 1.00 .30
41 Barry Zito ... 1.00 .30
42 Edgar Martinez ... .60 .18
43 Jarrod Washburn ... .40 .12
44 Greg Maddux ... 1.50 .45
45 Mark Buehrle ... .40 .12
46 Larry Walker ... .60 .18
47 Trot Nixon ... .60 .18
48 Nomar Garciaparra ... 1.50 .45
49 Robert Fick ... .40 .12
50 Sean Casey ... .40 .12
51 Joe Mays ... .40 .12
52 Roger Clemens ... 2.00 .60
53 Chan Ho Park ... .40 .12
54 Carlos Delgado ... .40 .12
55 Phil Nevin ... .40 .12
56 Jason Giambi ... 1.00 .30
57 Raul Mondesi ... .40 .12
58 Roberto Alomar ... 1.00 .30
59 Ryan Klesko ... .40 .12
60 Andruw Jones ... .40 .12
61 Gabe Kapler ... .40 .12
62 Darin Erstad ... .40 .12
63 Cristian Guzman ... .40 .12
64 Kazuhiro Sasaki ... .40 .12
65 Doug Mientkiewicz ... .40 .12
66 Sammy Sosa ... 1.50 .45
67 Mike Hampton ... .40 .12
68 Rickey Henderson ... 1.00 .30
69 Mark Mulder ... .40 .12
70 Mark McGwire ... 2.50 .75
71 Freddy Garcia ... .40 .12
72 Ivan Rodriguez ... 1.00 .30
73 Terrence Long ... .40 .12
74 Jeff Bagwell ... .60 .18
75 Moises Alou ... .40 .12
76 Todd Helton ... .60 .18
77 Preston Wilson ... .40 .12
78 Pedro Martinez ... 1.00 .30
79 Bobby Abreu ... .40 .12
80 Manny Ramirez ... .40 .12
81 Jose Vidro ... .40 .12
82 Randy Johnson ... 1.00 .30
83 Richie Sexson ... .40 .12
84 Troy Glaus ... .60 .18
85 Kevin Brown ... .40 .12
86 Carlos Lee ... .40 .12
87 Adrian Beltre ... .40 .12
88 Brian Giles ... .40 .12
89 Jermaine Dye ... .40 .12
90 Craig Biggio ... .60 .18
91 Richard Hidalgo ... .40 .12
92 Magglio Ordonez ... .40 .12
93 Aramis Ramirez ... .40 .12
94 Jeff Kent ... .40 .12
95 Curt Schilling ... .60 .18
96 Tim Hudson ... .40 .12
97 Fred McGriff ... .60 .18
98 Barry Larkin ... 1.00 .30
99 Jim Thome ... 1.00 .30
100 Tom Glavine ... .60 .18
101 S.Douglass/1875 RC ... 4.00 1.20
102 R.MacKowiak/1875 RC ... 4.00 1.20
103 J.Fikac/1875 RC ... 4.00 1.20
104 Henry Mateo/1875 RC ... 4.00 1.20
105 G. Gil/1875 RC ... 4.00 1.20
106 R. Vazquez/1875 RC ... 4.00 1.20
107 P. Santana/1875 RC ... 4.00 1.20
108 Ryan Jensen/1875 RC ... 4.00 1.20
109 Paul Phillips/1625 RC ... 4.00 1.20
110 Saul Rivera/1875 RC ... 4.00 1.20
111 Larry Bigbie/1875 ... 4.00 1.20
112 Josh Phelps/1875 ... 4.00 1.20
113 Justin Kaye/1875 RC ... 4.00 1.20
114 Kris Keller/1625 RC ... 4.00 1.20
115 Adam Bernero/1625 ... 4.00 1.20
116 V.Zambrano/1875 RC ... 6.00 1.80
117 Felipe Lopez/1875 ... 4.00 1.20
118 B.Roberts/1875 RC ... 4.00 1.20
119 Kurt Ainsworth/1875 ... 4.00 1.20
120 G.Perez/1625 RC ... 4.00 1.20
121 W.Guzman/1875 RC ... 4.00 1.20
122 D.Lewis/1875 RC ... 4.00 1.20
123 Nate Teut/1625 RC ... 4.00 1.20
124 M. Vargas/1625 RC ... 4.00 1.20
125 Brandon Inge/1875 ... 4.00 1.20
126 T. Phelps/1875 RC ... 4.00 1.20
127 Les Walrond/1625 RC ... 4.00 1.20
128 J. Atchley/1875 RC ... 4.00 1.20
129 S. Clapp/1875 RC ... 4.00 1.20
130 Bret Prinz/1875 RC ... 4.00 1.20
131 Bert Snow/1875 RC ... 4.00 1.20
132 Joe Crede/1625 ... 4.00 1.20
133 Nick Punto/1875 RC ... 4.00 1.20
134 C. Hernandez/1875 ... 4.00 1.20
135 Ken Vining/1875 RC ... 4.00 1.20
136 Luis Pineda/1875 RC ... 4.00 1.20
137 W. Abreu/1625 RC ... 4.00 1.20
138 Matt Ginter/1625 ... 4.00 1.20
139 Jason Smith/1875 RC ... 4.00 1.20
140 Gene Altman/1625 RC ... 4.00 1.20
141 B. Rogers/1875 RC ... 4.00 1.20
142 M.Cuddyer/1625 ... 4.00 1.20
143 Mike Penney/1625 RC ... 4.00 1.20
144 S.Podsednik/1875 RC ... 15.00 4.50
145 Esix Snead/1625 RC ... 4.00 1.20
146 S.Watkins/1875 RC ... 4.00 1.20
147 O.Woodards/1625 RC ... 4.00 1.20
148 J.Deardorff/1775 RC ... 4.00 1.20
149 Eric Cyr/1875 RC ... 4.00 1.20
150 Blaine Neal/1625 RC ... 4.00 1.20
151 Ben Sheets/1875 ... 4.00 1.20
152 S.Stewart/1875 RC ... 4.00 1.20
153 M.Koplove/1875 RC ... 4.00 1.20
154 Kyle Lohse/1875 RC ... 6.00 1.80
155 F. Rodney/1875 RC ... 4.00 1.20
156 Aubrey Huff/1625 ... 4.00 1.20
157 Pablo Ozuna/1625 ... 4.00 1.20
158 Bill Ortega/1625 RC ... 4.00 1.20
159 Toby Hall/1875 ... 4.00 1.20
160 Kevin Olsen/1625 RC ... 4.00 1.20
161 Will Ohman/1625 RC ... 4.00 1.20
162 Nate Cornejo/1875 ... 4.00 1.20
163 Jack Cust/1625 ... 4.00 1.20
164 Juan Rivera/1875 ... 4.00 1.20
165 J. Riggan/1875 RC ... 4.00 1.20
166 D.Mohr/1875 RC ... 4.00 1.20
167 Doug Nickle/1875 RC ... 4.00 1.20
168 C.Monroe/1625 RC ... 4.00 1.20
169 Jason Jennings/1625 ... 4.00 1.20
170 Bart Miadich/1875 RC ... 4.00 1.20
171 Luis Rivas/1625 ... 4.00 1.20
172 T. Christman/1875 RC ... 4.00 1.20
173 L. Hudson/1625 RC ... 4.00 1.20
174 Brett Jodie/1875 RC ... 4.00 1.20
175 Jorge Julio/1875 RC ... 4.00 1.20
176 David Espinosa/1625 ... 4.00 1.20
177 Mike Maroth/1625 RC ... 4.00 1.20
178 Keith Ginter/1625 ... 4.00 1.20
179 J. Moreno/1875 RC ... 4.00 1.20
180 B. Knight/1875 RC ... 4.00 1.20
181 Steve Lomasney/1625 ... 4.00 1.20
182 J. Grabow/1625 RC ... 4.00 1.20
183 Steve Green/1875 RC ... 4.00 1.20
185 Bob File/1875 RC ... 4.00 1.20
186 Brent Abernathy/1625 ... 4.00 1.20
187 M.Ensberg/1875 RC ... 8.00 2.40
188 Wily Mo Pena/1625 ... 4.00 1.20
189 Ken Harvey/1875 ... 4.00 1.20
190 Josh Pearce/1875 RC ... 4.00 1.20
191 Cesar Izturis/1625 ... 4.00 1.20
192 Eric Hinske/1625 RC ... 6.00 1.80
193 Joe Beimel/1875 RC ... 4.00 1.20
194 Timo Perez/1775 ... 4.00 1.20
195 Troy Mattes/1875 RC ... 4.00 1.20
196 Eric Valent/1625 ... 4.00 1.20
197 Ed Rogers/1875 RC ... 4.00 1.20
198 G.Balfour/1875 RC ... 4.00 1.20
199 Benito Baez/1875 RC ... 4.00 1.20
200 Vernon Wells/1875 ... 4.00 1.20
201 J.Kennedy PH/525 RC ... 6.00 1.80
202 W.Betemit PH/525 RC ... 6.00 1.80
203 C.Parker PH/525 RC ... 6.00 1.80
204 J.Gibbons PH/525 RC ... 12.00 3.60
205 C.Garcia PH/425 RC ... 6.00 1.80
206 J.Wilson PH/525 RC ... 6.00 1.80
207 J.Estrada PH/425 RC ... 10.00 3.00
208 W.Ruan PH/425 RC ... 6.00 1.80
209 B.Duckworth PH/525 RC ... 6.00 1.80
210 W.Harris PH/625 RC ... 6.00 1.80
211 M.Byrd PH/525 RC ... 25.00 7.50
212 C.C. Sabathia PH/600 ... 6.00 1.80
213 D.Tankersley PH/525 RC ... 6.00 1.80
214 B.Larson PH/425 RC ... 6.00 1.80
215 A.Gomez PH/425 RC ... 6.00 1.80
216 Bill Hall PH/525 RC ... 6.00 1.80
217 A.Perez PH/525 RC ... 6.00 1.80
218 J.Affeldt PH/425 RC ... 10.00 3.00
219 J.Spivey PH/625 RC ... 10.00 3.00
220 C.Fossum PH/425 RC ... 6.00 1.80
221 B.Lyon PH/625 RC ... 6.00 1.80
222 A.Santos PH/625 RC ... 6.00 1.80
223 L.Davis PH/625 RC ... 6.00 1.80
224 Zach Day PH/425 RC ... 10.00 3.00
225 D.Williams PH/425 RC ... 6.00 1.80
226 C.Crespo PH/625 RC ... 6.00 1.80
227 J.Acevedo PH/425 RC ... 6.00 1.80
228 T.Hafner PH/625 RC ... 15.00 4.50
229 O.Hudson PH/525 RC ... 10.00 3.00
230 J.Mieses PH/425 RC ... 6.00 1.80
231 R.Rodriguez PH/425 RC ... 6.00 1.80
232 A.Soriano PH/525 ... 10.00 3.00
233 Jason Hart PH/525 ... 6.00 1.80
234 E.Chavez PH/425 RC ... 6.00 1.80
235 D.James PH/525 RC ... 6.00 1.80
236 R.Drese PH/625 RC ... 6.00 1.80
237 J.Owens PH/425 RC ... 6.00 1.80
238 B.Voyles PH/425 RC ... 6.00 1.80
239 Nate Frese PH/425 RC ... 6.00 1.80
240 Josh Beckett PH/600 ... 10.00 3.00
241 Roy Oswalt PH/525 ... 10.00 3.00
242 J.Uribe PH/475 RC ... 6.00 1.80
243 C.Aldridge PH/425 RC ... 6.00 1.80
244 Adam Dunn PH/525 ... 6.00 1.80
245 Bud Smith PH/525 RC ... 6.00 1.80
246 A.Hernandez PH/525 RC ... 6.00 1.80
247 M.Guerrier PH/625 RC ... 6.00 1.80
248 J.Rollins PH/625 ... 6.00 1.80
249 W.Caceres PH/425 RC ... 6.00 1.80
250 J.Michaels PH/425 RC ... 6.00 1.80
251 I.Suzuki PH/625 RC ... 40.00 12.00
252 John Buck PH/525 RC ... 10.00 3.00
252 Adam Johnson PH/625 ... 6.00 1.80
253 A.Torres PH/525 RC ... 6.00 1.80
254 A.Amezaga PH/625 RC ... 10.00 3.00
255 C.Miller PH/525 RC ... 6.00 1.80
256 R.Soriano PH/425 RC ... 15.00 4.50
257 D.Mendez PH/425 RC ... 6.00 1.80
258 V.Martinez PH/625 RC ... 40.00 12.00
259 C.Patterson PH/525 ... 6.00 1.80
260 H.Ramirez PH/425 RC ... 10.00 3.00
261 E.Guzman PH/425 RC ... 6.00 1.80
262 Juan Diaz PH/425 RC ... 6.00 1.80
263 M.Rivera PH/625 RC ... 6.00 1.80
264 B.Lawrence PH/425 RC ... 6.00 1.80
265 J.Perez PH/425 RC ... 6.00 1.80
266 J.Nunez PH/425 RC ... 6.00 1.80
267 E.Bedard PH/625 RC ... 10.00 3.00
268 A.Pujols PH/525 RC ... 80.00 24.00
269 D.Sanchez PH/425 RC ... 6.00 1.80
270 C.Ransom PH/625 RC ... 6.00 1.80
271 G.Miller PH/425 RC ... 6.00 1.80
272 A.Pettyjohn PH/425 RC ... 6.00 1.80
273 T.Shinjo PH/625 RC ... 12.00 3.60
274 C.Vargas PH/425 RC ... 6.00 1.80
275 J.Duchscherer PH/625 RC ... 6.00 1.80
276 Tim Spooneybarger PH/625 RC ... 6.00 1.80
277 R.Bauer PH/625 RC ... 6.00 1.80
278 Josh Fogg PH/625 RC ... 6.00 1.80
279 B.Reith PH/425 RC ... 6.00 1.80
280 S.MacRae PH/625 RC ... 6.00 1.80
281 R.Ludwick PH/625 RC ... 6.00 1.80
282 E.Almonte PH/625 RC ... 6.00 1.80
283 J.Towers PH/525 RC ... 6.00 1.80
284 J. A.Pena PH/625 RC ... 6.00 1.80
285 D. Brous PH/425 RC ... 6.00 1.80
286 Erik Hiljus PH/625 RC ... 6.00 1.80
287 N.Neugebauer PH/525 ... 6.00 1.80
288 J.Melian PH/625 RC ... 6.00 1.80
289 B.Sylvester PH/425 RC ... 6.00 1.80
290 Carlos Valderrama PH/425 RC ... 6.00 1.80
291 J.Cueto PH/625 RC ... 6.00 1.80
292 M.White PH/425 RC ... 6.00 1.80
293 N.Maness PH/425 RC ... 6.00 1.80
294 J.Lane PH/625 RC ... 10.00 3.00
295 B.Berger PH/625 RC ... 6.00 1.80
296 A.Berroa PH/525 RC ... 15.00 4.50
297 Juan Cruz PH/525 RC ... 6.00 1.80
298 D.Brazelton PH/525 RC ... 10.00 3.00
299 M.Prior PH/525 RC ... 80.00 24.00
300 M.Teixeira PH/525 RC ... 40.00 12.00

2001 Donruss Class of 2001 First Class

Randomly inserted into packs, this 284-card skip-numbered set parallels the Donruss Class of 2001 base set. Each card was produced with a special holographic foil. Please note that a few of the players were short-printed and are marked accordingly. Cards 1-100 were serial numbered to 100, while cards 101-300 were serial numbered to 50.

Nm-Mt Ex-Mt
*1ST CLASS 1-100: 6X TO 15X BASIC
*1ST CLASS 101-200: .75X TO 2X BASIC
*1ST CLASS 201-300: .5X TO 1.2X BASIC
1 Alex Rodriguez SP/75 ... 25.00 7.50
3 Vladimir Guerrero SP/75 ... 15.00 4.50
10 Miguel Tejada SP/25 ...
14 Luis Gonzalez SP/75 ... 6.00 1.80
15 Frank Thomas SP/75 ... 15.00 4.50
18 Lance Berkman SP/75 ... 6.00 1.80
20 Chipper Jones SP/75 ... 15.00 4.50
22 Kerry Wood SP/75 ... 15.00 4.50
24 J.D. Drew SP/75 ... 6.00 1.80
27 Kenny Lofton SP/75 ... 6.00 1.80
28 Mike Mussina SP/75 ... 15.00 4.50
30 Bernie Williams SP/75 ... 10.00 3.00
32 Shawn Green SP/85 ... 6.00 1.80
34 Juan Gonzalez SP/75 ... 15.00 4.50
35 Andres Galarraga SP/75 ... 6.00 1.80
36 Gary Sheffield SP/75 ... 6.00 1.80
38 Scott Rolen SP/75 ... 10.00 3.00
44 Greg Maddux SP/75 ... 25.00 7.50
48 Nomar Garciaparra SP/85 ... 25.00 7.50
52 Roger Clemens SP/75 ... 30.00 9.00
53 Chan Ho Park SP/85 ... 6.00 1.80
58 Roberto Alomar SP/85 ... 15.00 4.50
59 Ryan Klesko SP/50 ... 6.00 1.80
62 Darin Erstad SP/75 ... 6.00 1.80
72 Ivan Rodriguez SP/75 ... 15.00 4.50
74 Jeff Bagwell SP/85 ... 10.00 3.00
75 Moises Alou SP/75 ... 6.00 1.80
76 Todd Helton SP/75 ... 10.00 3.00
78 Pedro Martinez SP/85 ... 15.00 4.50
80 Manny Ramirez SP/85 ... 6.00 1.80
82 Randy Johnson SP/85 ... 15.00 4.50
85 Kevin Brown SP/75 ... 6.00 1.80
88 Brian Giles SP/75 ... 6.00 1.80
90 Craig Biggio SP/85 ... 10.00 3.00
95 Curt Schilling SP/75 ... 10.00 3.00
98 Barry Larkin SP/85 ... 15.00 4.50
100 Tom Glavine SP/75 ... 10.00 3.00

2001 Donruss Class of 2001 First Class Autographs

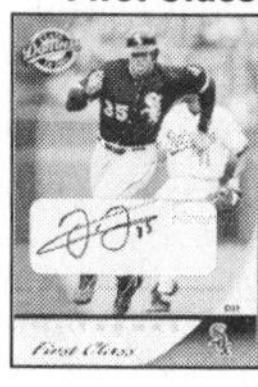
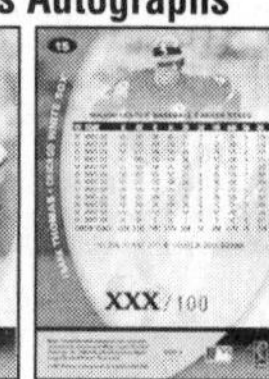

Randomly inserted into packs, this 53-card skip-numbered insert features authentic autographs from some of the hottest players in Major League Baseball. Individual print runs are listed in our checklist.

Nm-Mt Ex-Mt
1 Alex Rodriguez/25 ...
3 Vladimir Guerrero/25 ...
10 Miguel Tejada/75 ... 25.00 7.50
14 Luis Gonzalez/25 ...
15 Frank Thomas/25 ...
17 Paul LoDuca/100 ... 25.00 7.50
18 Lance Berkman/25 ...
20 Chipper Jones/25 ...
21 Eric Chavez/100 ... 25.00 7.50
22 Kerry Wood/25 ...
24 J.D. Drew/25 ...
27 Kenny Lofton/25 ...
28 Mike Mussina/25 ...
30 Bernie Williams/25 ...
32 Shawn Green/15 ...
34 Juan Gonzalez/25 ...

35 Andres Galarraga/25
36 Gary Sheffield/25
38 Scott Rolen/25
41 Barry Zito/100 40.00 12.00
44 Greg Maddux/25
45 Mark Buehrle/100 25.00 7.50
48 Nomar Garciaparra/15
49 Robert Fick/100 25.00 7.50
50 Sean Casey/100 25.00 7.50
51 Joe Mays/100 25.00 7.50
52 Roger Clemens/25
53 Chan Ho Park/15
58 Roberto Alomar/15
59 Ryan Klesko/50
62 Darin Erstad/25
69 Mark Mulder/100 25.00 7.50
72 Ivan Rodriguez/25
73 Terrence Long/100 25.00 7.50
74 Jeff Bagwell/15
75 Moises Alou/25
76 Todd Helton/25
78 Pedro Martinez/15
80 Manny Ramirez/15
81 Jose Vidro/100 25.00 7.50
82 Randy Johnson/15
83 Richie Sexson/100 25.00 7.50
84 Troy Glaus/100 40.00 12.00
85 Kevin Brown/25
88 Brian Giles/25
89 Jermaine Dye/100 25.00 7.50
90 Craig Biggio/15
91 Richard Hidalgo/100 25.00 7.50
93 Aramis Ramirez/100 25.00 7.50
95 Curt Schilling/25
96 Tim Hudson/100 25.00 7.50
98 Barry Larkin/15
100 Tom Glavine/25

2001 Donruss Class of 2001 Rookie Autographs

Randomly inserted into packs, this 109-card insert features authentic autographs from some of the hottest young talent in the Minor Leagues. Individual print runs are listed in our checklist.

Nm-Mt Ex-Mt
109 Paul Phillips/250 10.00 3.00
114 Kris Keller/250 10.00 3.00
115 Adam Bernero/250 10.00 3.00
120 George Perez/250 10.00 3.00
123 Nate Teut/250 10.00 3.00
124 Martin Vargas/250 10.00 3.00
127 Les Walrond/250 10.00 3.00
132 Joe Crede/250 10.00 3.00
137 Winston Abreu/250 10.00 3.00
138 Matt Ginter/250 10.00 3.00
140 Gene Altman/250 10.00 3.00
142 Michael Cuddyer/250 10.00 3.00
143 Mike Penney/250 10.00 3.00
145 Esix Snead/250 10.00 3.00
147 O.Woodards/250 10.00 3.00
148 Jeff Deardorff/100 10.00 3.00
150 Blaine Neal/250 10.00 3.00
156 Aubrey Huff/250 10.00 3.00
157 Pablo Ozuna/250 10.00 3.00
158 Bill Ortega/250 10.00 3.00
160 Kevin Olsen/250 10.00 3.00
161 Will Ohman/250 10.00 3.00
163 Jack Cust/250 10.00 3.00
168 Craig Monroe/250 10.00 3.00
169 Jason Jennings/250 10.00 3.00
171 Luis Rivas/250 10.00 3.00
173 Luke Hudson/250 10.00 3.00
176 David Espinosa/250 10.00 3.00
177 Mike Maroth/250 10.00 3.00
178 Keith Ginter/250 10.00 3.00
181 Steve Lomasney/250 10.00 3.00
182 John Grabow/250 10.00 3.00
184 Jason Karnuth/250 10.00 3.00
186 Brent Abernathy/250 10.00 3.00
188 Wily Mo Pena/250 10.00 3.00
191 Cesar Izturis/250 10.00 3.00
192 Eric Hinske/250 20.00 6.00
194 Timo Perez/100 15.00 4.50
196 Eric Valent/250 10.00 3.00
201 Joe Kennedy PH/100 15.00 4.50
202 W.Betemit PH/100 25.00 7.50
203 C.Parker PH/100 15.00 4.50
204 Jay Gibbons PH/100 40.00 12.00
205 Carlos Garcia PH/200 10.00 3.00
206 Jack Wilson PH/100 15.00 4.50
207 J.Estrada PH/200 15.00 4.50
208 Wilkin Ruan PH/200 10.00 3.00
209 B.Duckworth PH/100 25.00 7.50
211 Marlon Byrd PH/100 60.00 18.00
212 C.C. Sabathia PH/25
213 D.Tankersley PH/100 25.00 7.50
214 B.Larson PH/200 10.00 3.00
215 Alexis Gomez PH/200 10.00 3.00
216 Bill Hall PH/100 15.00 4.50
217 Antonio Perez PH/100 25.00 7.50
218 J. Affeldt PH/200 20.00 6.00
220 C. Fossum PH/200 10.00 3.00
224 Zach Day PH/200 15.00 4.50
225 D. Williams PH/200 10.00 3.00
227 Jose Acevedo PH/200 10.00 3.00
229 O.Hudson PH/100 25.00 7.50
230 Jose Mieses PH/200 10.00 3.00
231 Ric Rodriguez PH/200 10.00 3.00
232 A. Soriano PH/100 50.00 15.00
233 Jason Hart PH/100 15.00 4.50
234 Endy Chavez PH/200 10.00 3.00
235 Delvin James PH/100 15.00 4.50
237 J. Owens PH/200 10.00 3.00
238 Brad Voyles PH/200 10.00 3.00
239 Nate Frese PH/200 10.00 3.00
240 Josh Beckett PH/25
241 Roy Oswalt PH/100 30.00 9.00
242 Juan Uribe PH/150 10.00 3.00
243 Cory Aldridge PH/200 10.00 3.00
244 Adam Dunn PH/100 30.00 9.00
245 Bud Smith PH/100 15.00 4.50
246 A.Hernandez PH/100 15.00 4.50
249 W. Caceres PH/200 10.00 3.00
250 J.Michaels PH/200 10.00 3.00
252 John Buck PH/100 25.00 7.50
253 Andres Torres PH/100 15.00 4.50
255 Corky Miller PH/100 15.00 4.50
256 R. Soriano PH/200 30.00 9.00
257 D. Mendez PH/200 10.00 3.00
259 C.Patterson PH/100 25.00 7.50
260 H.Ramirez PH/200 20.00 6.00
261 E.Guzman PH/200 10.00 3.00
262 Juan Diaz PH/200 10.00 3.00
264 B.Lawrence PH/200 10.00 3.00
265 Josue Perez PH/200 10.00 3.00
266 Jose Nunez PH/200 10.00 3.00
268 Albert Pujols PH/100 400.00 120.00
269 D.Sanchez PH/200 10.00 3.00
271 Greg Miller PH/200 10.00 3.00
272 A.Pettyjohn PH/200 10.00 3.00
274 C.Vargas PH/200 10.00 3.00
279 Brian Reith PH/200 10.00 3.00
283 Josh Towers PH/100 15.00 4.50
285 David Brous PH/200 10.00 3.00
287 N.Neugebauer PH/100 15.00 4.50
289 Billy Sylvester PH/200 10.00 3.00
290 C.Valderrama PH/200 10.00 3.00
292 Matt White PH/200 10.00 3.00
293 Nick Maness PH/200 10.00 3.00
296 Angel Berroa PH/100 40.00 12.00
297 Juan Cruz PH/100 25.00 7.50
298 D.Brazelton PH/100 30.00 9.00
299 Mark Prior PH/100 300.00 90.00
300 Mark Teixeira PH/100 150.00 45.00

2001 Donruss Class of 2001 Aces

Randomly inserted into packs at one in 30, this 20-card insert features baseball's most prized pitchers. Card backs carry an "A" prefix.

Nm-Mt Ex-Mt
COMPLETE SET (20) 100.00 30.00
A1 Roger Clemens 12.00 3.60
A2 Randy Johnson 6.00 1.80
A3 Freddy Garcia 5.00 1.50
A4 Greg Maddux 10.00 3.00
A5 Tim Hudson 5.00 1.50
A6 Curt Schilling 5.00 1.50
A7 Mark Buehrle 5.00 1.50
A8 Matt Morris 5.00 1.50
A9 Joe Mays 5.00 1.50
A10 Javier Vazquez 5.00 1.50
A11 Mark Mulder 5.00 1.50
A12 Wade Miller 5.00 1.50
A13 Barry Zito 6.00 1.80
A14 Pedro Martinez 6.00 1.80
A15 Al Leiter 5.00 1.50
A16 Chan Ho Park 5.00 1.50
A17 John Burkett 5.00 1.50
A18 C.C. Sabathia 5.00 1.50
A19 Jamie Moyer 5.00 1.50
A20 Mike Mussina 6.00 1.80

2001 Donruss Class of 2001 Diamond Aces

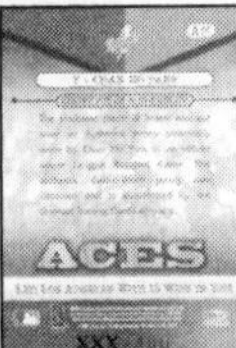

This 19-card set is a parallel to the more common Aces insert card. Randomly inserted into packs at an unspecified ratio, each Diamond Aces card features a swatch of game-used memorabilia. All cards utilize jersey swatches except card number A20 Mike Mussina of whom has a Hat swatch instead. Card number A8 was intended to feature Matt Morris, but the card was pulled from the set due to complications in obtaining game-used equipment featuring Morris.

Nm-Mt Ex-Mt
A1 Roger Clemens/200 40.00 12.00
A2 Randy Johnson/750 15.00 4.50
A3 Freddy Garcia/350 10.00 3.00
A4 Greg Maddux/750 25.00 7.50
A5 Tim Hudson/550 10.00 3.00
A6 Curt Schilling/525 15.00 4.50
A7 Mark Buehrle/750 10.00 3.00
A8 Does Not Exist
A9 Joe Mays/750 10.00 3.00
A10 Javier Vazquez/500 10.00 3.00
A11 Mark Mulder/300 10.00 3.00
A12 Wade Miller/525 10.00 3.00
A13 Barry Zito/550 15.00 4.50
A14 Pedro Martinez/550 15.00 4.50
A15 Al Leiter/525 10.00 3.00
A16 Chan Ho Park/400 10.00 3.00
A17 John Burkett/700 10.00 3.00
A18 C.C. Sabathia/550 10.00 3.00
A19 Jamie Moyer/700 10.00 3.00
A20 Mike Mussina Hat/75

2001 Donruss Class of 2001 BobbleHead

Each box of Donruss Class of 2001 featured one randomly inserted BobbleHead Doll. There were 2000 of each regular doll produced, and 1000 of each ROY doll.

Nm-Mt Ex-Mt
1 Ichiro Suzuki 40.00 12.00
2 Cal Ripken 40.00 12.00
3 Derek Jeter 30.00 9.00
4 Mark McGwire 40.00 12.00
5 Albert Pujols 40.00 12.00
6 Ken Griffey Jr. 20.00 6.00
7 Nomar Garciaparra 20.00 6.00
8 Mike Piazza 20.00 6.00
9 Alex Rodriguez 20.00 6.00
10 Manny Ramirez 15.00 4.50
11 Tsuyoshi Shinjo 15.00 4.50
12 Hideo Nomo 15.00 4.50
13 Chipper Jones 15.00 4.50
14 Sammy Sosa 20.00 6.00
15 Roger Clemens 25.00 7.50
16 Tony Gwynn 15.00 4.50
17 Barry Bonds 30.00 9.00
18 Kazuhiro Sasaki 15.00 4.50
19 Pedro Martinez 15.00 4.50
20 Jeff Bagwell 15.00 4.50
21 Ichiro Suzuki ROY 50.00 15.00
22 Albert Pujols ROY 40.00 12.00

2001 Donruss Class of 2001 BobbleHead Cards

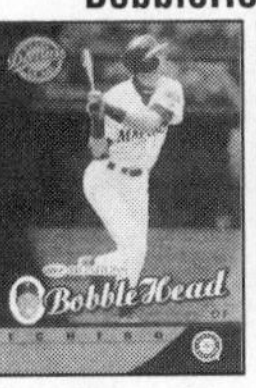

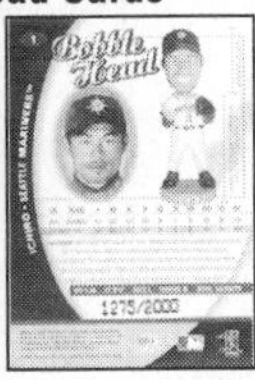

The cards were inserted in with the 2001 Donruss BobbleHead dolls, the 22-card set features some of baseball's most prized players. Please note that there were only 2000 of each card product, except for the two ROY cards numbered to 1000 each.

Nm-Mt Ex-Mt
COMPLETE SET (22) 200.00 60.00
1 Ichiro Suzuki 20.00 6.00
2 Cal Ripken 20.00 6.00
3 Derek Jeter 15.00 4.50
4 Mark McGwire 20.00 6.00
5 Albert Pujols 20.00 6.00
6 Ken Griffey Jr. 10.00 3.00
7 Nomar Garciaparra 10.00 3.00
8 Mike Piazza 10.00 3.00
9 Alex Rodriguez 10.00 3.00
10 Manny Ramirez 8.00 2.40
11 Tsuyoshi Shinjo 8.00 2.40
12 Hideo Nomo 10.00 3.00
13 Chipper Jones 8.00 2.40
14 Sammy Sosa 10.00 3.00
15 Roger Clemens 12.00 3.60
16 Tony Gwynn 8.00 2.40
17 Barry Bonds 15.00 4.50
18 Kazuhiro Sasaki 8.00 2.40
19 Pedro Martinez 8.00 2.40
20 Jeff Bagwell 8.00 2.40
21 Ichiro Suzuki ROY 25.00 7.50
22 Albert Pujols ROY 25.00 7.50

2001 Donruss Class of 2001 Crusade

Randomly inserted into packs, this 50-card insert features players on a mission. Card backs carry a "C" prefix. Individual print runs are listed in our checklist.

Nm-Mt Ex-Mt
C-1 Roger Clemens/275 25.00 7.50
C-2 Luis Gonzalez/275 8.00 2.40
C-3 Troy Glaus/275 8.00 2.40
C-4 Freddy Garcia/300 8.00 2.40
C-5 Sean Casey/285 8.00 2.40
C-6 Bobby Abreu/300 8.00 2.40
C-7 Matt Morris/300 8.00 2.40
C-8 Cal Ripken/275 40.00 12.00
C-9 Miguel Tejada/285 8.00 2.40
C-10 V.Guerrero/275 12.00 3.60
C-11 Mark Buehrle/100 8.00 2.40
C-12 Mike Sweeney/300 8.00 2.40
C-13 Ivan Rodriguez/275 12.00 3.60
C-14 Jeff Bagwell/275 8.00 2.40
C-15 Joe Mays/250 8.00 2.40
C-16 Cliff Floyd/300 8.00 2.40
C-17 Lance Berkman/300 8.00 2.40
C-18 Aramis Ramirez/100 8.00 2.40
C-19 Tony Gwynn/300 15.00 4.50
C-20 S.Stewart/100 8.00 2.40
C-21 Todd Helton/275 8.00 2.40
C-22 Chipper Jones/275 12.00 3.60
C-23 Javier Vazquez/100 8.00 2.40
C-24 Shawn Green/275 8.00 2.40
C-25 Barry Bonds/300 30.00 9.00
C-26 Albert Pujols/250 40.00 12.00
C-27 Wilson Betemit/100 8.00 2.40
C-28 C.C. Sabathia/290 8.00 2.40
C-29 Roy Oswalt/100 8.00 2.40
C-30 Johnny Estrada/100 8.00 2.40
C-31 Nick Johnson/100 8.00 2.40
C-32 Aubrey Huff/100 8.00 2.40
C-33 Corey Patterson/200 8.00 2.40
C-34 Jay Gibbons/100 10.00 3.00
C-35 Marcus Giles/100 8.00 2.40
C-36 Juan Cruz/100 8.00 2.40
C-37 Tsuyoshi Shinjo/300 12.00 3.60
C-38 Ben Sheets/285 8.00 2.40
C-39 Bud Smith/100 8.00 2.40
C-40 Alex Escobar/100 8.00 2.40
C-41 Joe Kennedy/100 8.00 2.40
C-42 Alexis Gomez/100 8.00 2.40
C-43 Jimmy Rollins/300 8.00 2.40
C-44 Josh Towers/100 8.00 2.40
C-45 Joe Crede/100 8.00 2.40
C-46 B.Duckworth/100 8.00 2.40
C-47 Ichiro Suzuki/300 40.00 12.00
C-48 Jose Ortiz/100 8.00 2.40
C-49 Casey Fossum/100 8.00 2.40
C-50 Adam Dunn/200 8.00 2.40

2001 Donruss Class of 2001 Crusade Autographs

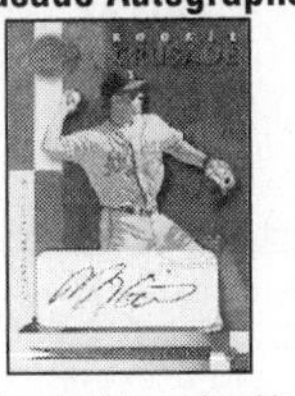

Randomly inserted into packs, this 39-card insert features authentic autographs from veterans like Cal Ripken and Chipper Jones. Card backs carry a "C" prefix. Individual print runs are listed in our checklist.

Nm-Mt Ex-Mt
C-1 Roger Clemens/25
C-2 Luis Gonzalez/25
C-3 Troy Glaus/25
C-5 Sean Casey/15
C-8 Cal Ripken/25
C-9 Miguel Tejada/15
C-10 Vladimir Guerrero/25
C-11 Mark Buehrle/200 15.00 4.50
C-13 Ivan Rodriguez/25
C-14 Jeff Bagwell/25
C-15 Joe Mays/50
C-18 Aramis Ramirez/200 15.00 4.50
C-20 S. Stewart/200 15.00 4.50
C-21 Todd Helton/25
C-22 Chipper Jones/25
C-23 Javier Vazquez/200 20.00 6.00
C-24 Shawn Green/25
C-26 Albert Pujols/50 350.00 105.00
C-27 Wilson Betemit/200 15.00 4.50
C-28 C.C. Sabathia/10
C-29 Roy Oswalt/200 20.00 6.00
C-30 Johnny Estrada/200 20.00 6.00
C-31 Nick Johnson/200 15.00 4.50
C-32 Aubrey Huff/200 15.00 4.50
C-33 Corey Patterson/100 15.00 4.50
C-34 Jay Gibbons/200 25.00 7.50
C-35 Marcus Giles/200 15.00 4.50
C-36 Juan Cruz/200 15.00 4.50
C-38 Ben Sheets/15
C-39 Bud Smith/200 15.00 4.50
C-40 Alex Escobar/200 15.00 4.50
C-41 Joe Kennedy/200 15.00 4.50
C-42 Alexis Gomez/200 15.00 4.50
C-44 Josh Towers/200 15.00 4.50
C-45 Joe Crede/200 15.00 4.50
C-46 B. Duckworth/200 15.00 4.50
C-48 Jose Ortiz/200 15.00 4.50
C-49 Casey Fossum/200 15.00 4.50
C-50 Adam Dunn/100 20.00 6.00

2001 Donruss Class of 2001 Dominators

Randomly inserted into packs at one in 20, this 30-card insert features players that dominate their opponents. Card backs carry a "DM" prefix.

Nm-Mt Ex-Mt
COMPLETE SET (30) 150.00 45.00
DM-1 Manny Ramirez 5.00 1.50
DM-2 Lance Berkman 5.00 1.50
DM-3 Juan Gonzalez 6.00 1.80
DM-4 Albert Pujols 25.00 7.50
DM-5 Jason Giambi 6.00 1.80
DM-6 Mike Sweeney 5.00 1.50
DM-7 Rafael Palmeiro 5.00 1.50
DM-8 Luis Gonzalez 5.00 1.50
DM-9 Ichiro Suzuki 15.00 4.50
DM-10 Cliff Floyd 5.00 1.50
DM-11 Roberto Alomar 6.00 1.80
DM-12 Paul LoDuca 5.00 1.50
DM-13 Shannon Stewart 5.00 1.50
DM-14 Barry Bonds 15.00 4.50
DM-15 Larry Walker 5.00 1.50
DM-16 Shawn Green 5.00 1.50
DM-17 Moises Alou 5.00 1.50
DM-18 Cal Ripken 20.00 6.00
DM-19 Brian Giles 5.00 1.50
DM-20 Magglio Ordonez 5.00 1.50
DM-21 Jose Vidro 5.00 1.50
DM-22 Edgar Martinez 5.00 1.50
DM-23 Aramis Ramirez 5.00 1.50
DM-24 Tony Gwynn 8.00 2.40
DM-25 Richie Sexson 5.00 1.50
DM-26 Todd Helton 5.00 1.50
DM-27 Garret Anderson 5.00 1.50
DM-28 Chipper Jones 6.00 1.80
DM-29 Troy Glaus 5.00 1.50
DM-30 Jeff Bagwell 5.00 1.50

2001 Donruss Class of 2001 Diamond Dominators

Randomly inserted into packs, this 30-card insert is a complete parallel of the Donruss Class of 2001 Dominators insert each featuring a game-used piece of memorabilia. Card backs carry a "DM" prefix. Individual print runs are listed below.

Nm-Mt Ex-Mt
DM-1 Manny Ramirez Bat/725 10.00 3.00
DM-2 Lance Berkman Bat/725 10.00 3.00
DM-3 Juan Gonzalez Bat/500 15.00 4.50
DM-4 Albert Pujols Bat/125 80.00 24.00
DM-5 Jason Giambi Bat/250 15.00 4.50
DM-6 Mike Sweeney Jsy/325 10.00 3.00
DM-7 Rafael Palmeiro Bat/550 15.00 4.50
DM-8 Luis Gonzalez Bat/725 10.00 3.00
DM-9 Ichiro Suzuki Ball/50
DM-10 Cliff Floyd Jsy/725 10.00 3.00
DM-11 Roberto Alomar Bat/200 15.00 4.50
DM-12 Paul LoDuca Jsy/600 10.00 3.00
DM-13 Shannon Stewart Bat/725 10.00 3.00
DM-14 Barry Bonds Bat/250 40.00 12.00
DM-15 Larry Walker Bat/500 15.00 4.50
DM-16 Shawn Green Bat/500 10.00 3.00
DM-17 Moises Alou Bat/550 10.00 3.00
DM-18 Cal Ripken Bat/250 60.00 18.00
DM-19 Brian Giles Bat/725 10.00 3.00
DM-20 Magglio Ordonez Bat/725 10.00 3.00
DM-21 Jose Vidro Jsy/725 10.00 3.00
DM-22 Edgar Martinez Jsy/200 15.00 4.50
DM-23 Aramis Ramirez Bat/200 10.00 3.00
DM-24 Tony Gwynn Bat/500 15.00 4.50
DM-25 Richie Sexson Bat/725 10.00 3.00
DM-26 Todd Helton Bat/725 15.00 4.50
DM-27 Garret Anderson Bat/725 10.00 3.00
DM-28 Chipper Jones Bat/725 15.00 4.50
DM-29 Troy Glaus Jsy/200 15.00 4.50
DM-30 Jeff Bagwell Jsy/325 15.00 4.50

2001 Donruss Class of 2001 Rewards

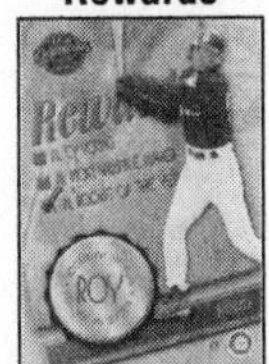

Randomly inserted into packs at one in 212, this 10-card insert features award winning players. Card backs carry a "RW" prefix.

Nm-Mt Ex-Mt
RW-1 Jason Giambi MVP 15.00 4.50
RW-2 Ichiro Suzuki MVP 30.00 9.00
RW-3 Roger Clemens CY 30.00 9.00
RW-4 Freddy Garcia CY 10.00 3.00
RW-5 Ichiro Suzuki ROY 30.00 9.00
RW-6 Albert Pujols ROY 40.00 12.00
RW-7 Barry Bonds MVP 30.00 9.00
RW-8 Albert Pujols MVP 40.00 12.00
RW-9 Randy Johnson CY 15.00 4.50
RW-10 Matt Morris CY 10.00 3.00

2001 Donruss Class of 2001 Final Rewards

Randomly inserted into packs, this nine-card insert is a partial parallel of the Donruss Class

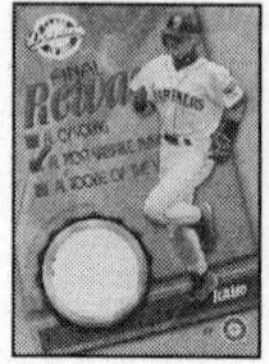
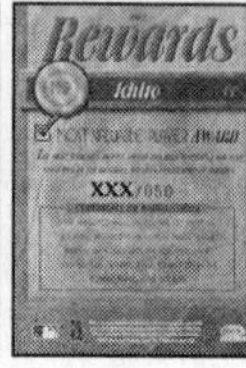

of 2001 Rewards insert. Each card includes a a swatch of game-used memorabilia. Individual print runs are listed below.

	Nm-Mt	Ex-Mt
RW-1 Jason Giambi MVP Jsy/250	25.00	7.50
RW-2 Ichiro Suzuki MVP Ball/50	120.00	36.00
RW-3 Roger Clemens CY Jsy/200	40.00	12.00
RW-4 Freddy Garcia CY Jsy/250	15.00	4.50
RW-5 Ichiro Suzuki ROY Ball/50	120.00	36.00
RW-6 Albert Pujols ROY Bat/125	80.00	24.00
RW-7 Barry Bonds MVP Jsy/200	50.00	15.00
RW-8 Albert Pujols MVP Bat/125	80.00	24.00
RW-9 Randy Johnson CY Jsy/250	25.00	7.50

2001 Donruss Class of 2001 Rookie Team

Randomly inserted into packs at one in 83, this 15-card insert features top rookies from the 2001 season. Card backs carry a "RT" prefix.

	Nm-Mt	Ex-Mt
COMPLETE SET (15)	150.00	45.00
RT1 Jay Gibbons	8.00	2.40
RT2 Alfonso Soriano	8.00	2.40
RT3 Jimmy Rollins	5.00	1.50
RT4 Wilson Betemit	5.00	1.50
RT5 Albert Pujols	40.00	12.00
RT6 Johnny Estrada	8.00	2.40
RT7 Ichiro Suzuki	25.00	7.50
RT8 Tsuyoshi Shinjo	8.00	2.40
RT9 Adam Dunn	5.00	1.50
RT10 C.C. Sabathia	5.00	1.50
RT11 Ben Sheets	5.00	1.50
RT12 Roy Oswalt	8.00	2.40
RT13 Bud Smith	5.00	1.50
RT14 Josh Towers	5.00	1.50
RT15 Juan Cruz	5.00	1.50

2001 Donruss Class of 2001 Rookie Team Materials

Randomly inserted into packs, this 15-card insert is a parallel of the Donruss Class of 2001 Rookie Team insert. Each card contains a swatch of game-used memorabilia. Individual print runs are listed in our checklist.

	Nm-Mt	Ex-Mt
RT1 Jay Gibbons Btg Glv/100	20.00	6.00
RT2 Alfonso Soriano Btg Glv/100		
RT3 J.Rollins Jsy/200	10.00	3.00
RT4 Wilson Betemit Hat/100	15.00	4.50
RT5 Albert Pujols Bat/100	80.00	24.00
RT6 Johnny Estrada Shoes/100	20.00	6.00
RT7 Ichiro Suzuki Ball/50		
RT8 T.Shinjo Shoes/200	15.00	4.50
RT9 Adam Dunn Bat/200	10.00	3.00
RT10 C.C. Sabathia Jsy/200	10.00	3.00
RT11 Ben Sheets Bat/200	10.00	3.00
RT12 Roy Oswalt Btg Glv/50	25.00	7.50
RT13 Bud Smith Jsy/250	10.00	3.00
RT14 J.Towers Pants/200	10.00	3.00
RT15 Juan Cruz Jsy/200	10.00	3.00

2001 Donruss Class of 2001 Yearbook

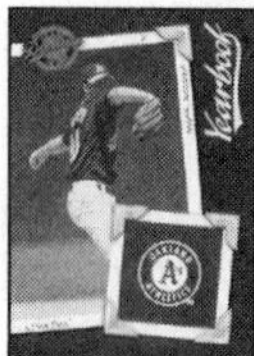

Randomly inserted into packs at one in 24, this 25-card insert features players that had outstanding seasons in 2001. Card backs carry a "YB" prefix.

	Nm-Mt	Ex-Mt
COMPLETE SET (25)	150.00	45.00
YB-1 Barry Bonds	15.00	4.50
YB-2 Mark Mulder	4.00	1.20
YB-3 Luis Gonzalez	4.00	1.20
YB-4 Lance Berkman	4.00	1.20
YB-5 Matt Morris	4.00	1.20
YB-6 Roy Oswalt	4.00	1.20
YB-7 Todd Helton	4.00	1.20
YB-8 Tsuyoshi Shinjo	6.00	1.80
YB-9 C.C. Sabathia	4.00	1.20
YB-10 Curt Schilling	4.00	1.20
YB-11 Rickey Henderson	6.00	1.80
YB-12 Jamie Moyer	4.00	1.20
YB-13 Shawn Green	4.00	1.20
YB-14 Randy Johnson	6.00	1.80
YB-15 Jim Thome	6.00	1.80
YB-16 Larry Walker	4.00	1.20
YB-17 Jimmy Rollins	4.00	1.20
YB-18 Kazuhiro Sasaki	4.00	1.20
YB-19 Hideo Nomo	6.00	1.80
YB-20 Roger Clemens	12.00	3.60
YB-21 Bud Smith	4.00	1.20
YB-22 Ichiro Suzuki	15.00	4.50
YB-23 Albert Pujols	15.00	4.50
YB-24 Cal Ripken	20.00	6.00
YB-25 Tony Gwynn	8.00	2.40

2001 Donruss Class of 2001 Scrapbook

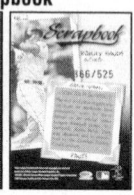

Randomly inserted into packs, this 24-card insert is a partial parallel of the Donruss Class of 2001 Yearbook insert. Each card contains a swatch of game-used memorabilia. Individual print runs are listed below.

	Nm-Mt	Ex-Mt
SB-1 B.Bonds Pants/525	25.00	7.50
SB-2 Mark Mulder/500	10.00	3.00
SB-3 Luis Gonzalez/500	10.00	3.00
SB-4 Lance Berkman/525	10.00	3.00
SB-5 Does Not Exist		
SB-6 Roy Oswalt/150	15.00	4.50
SB-7 Todd Helton/525	15.00	4.50
SB-8 Tsuyoshi Shinjo/75	25.00	7.50
SB-9 C.C. Sabathia/500	10.00	3.00
SB-10 Curt Schilling/525	15.00	4.50
SB-11 R.Henderson Bat/200	15.00	4.50
SB-12 Jamie Moyer/500	10.00	3.00
SB-13 Shawn Green/525	10.00	3.00
SB-14 R.Johnson/500	15.00	4.50
SB-15 Jim Thome/400	15.00	4.50
SB-16 Larry Walker/500	15.00	4.50
SB-17 Jimmy Rollins Base/25		
SB-18 K.Sasaki/500	10.00	3.00
SB-19 Hideo Nomo/150	50.00	15.00
SB-20 Roger Clemens/475	25.00	7.50
SB-21 Bud Smith/525	10.00	3.00
SB-22 Ichiro Suzuki Ball/75	80.00	24.00
SB-23 A.Pujols Bat/150	50.00	15.00
SB-24 Cal Ripken/525	40.00	12.00
SB-25 T.Gwynn Pants/500	15.00	4.50

2001 Donruss Classics

This 200-card set was distributed in six-card packs with a suggested retail price of $11.99. The set features color photos of stars of the game from the past, present, and future highlighted with silver tint and foil. Cards 101-150 display color photos of rookies and are sequentially numbered to 585. Cards 151-200 consisting of retired players are sequentailly numbered to 1755 and are highlighted with gold tint and foil. Cards 162 (Sandy Koufax LGD) and 185 (Robin Roberts LGD) were not intended for public release but a handful of copies made their way into packs despite the manufacturers efforts to physically pull them from the production process. Due to their scarcity, the set is considered complete at 198 cards and pricing is unavailable on them individually.

	Nm-Mt	Ex-Mt
COMP.SET w/o SP's (100)	25.00	7.50
COMMON CARD (1-100)	.60	.18
COMMON (101-150)	8.00	2.40
COMMON (151-200)	4.00	1.20
1 Alex Rodriguez	2.50	.75
2 Barry Bonds	4.00	1.20
3 Cal Ripken	5.00	1.50
4 Chipper Jones	1.50	.45
5 Derek Jeter	4.00	1.20
6 Troy Glaus	1.00	.30
7 Frank Thomas	1.50	.45
8 Greg Maddux	2.50	.75
9 Ivan Rodriguez	1.50	.45
10 Jeff Bagwell	1.00	.30
11 Cliff Floyd	.60	.18
12 Todd Helton	1.00	.30
13 Ken Griffey Jr.	2.50	.75
14 Manny Ramirez	.60	.18
15 Mark McGwire	4.00	1.20
16 Mike Piazza	2.50	.75
17 Nomar Garciaparra	2.50	.75
18 Pedro Martinez	1.50	.45
19 Randy Johnson	1.50	.45
20 Rick Ankiel	.60	.18
21 Rickey Henderson	1.50	.45
22 Roger Clemens	3.00	.90
23 Sammy Sosa	2.50	.75
24 Tony Gwynn	2.00	.60
25 Vladimir Guerrero	1.50	.45
26 Kazuhiro Sasaki	.60	.18
27 Roberto Alomar	1.50	.45
28 Barry Zito	1.50	.45
29 Pat Burrell	.60	.18
30 Harold Baines	.60	.18
31 Carlos Delgado	.60	.18
32 J.D. Drew	.60	.18
33 Jim Edmonds	.60	.18
34 Darin Erstad	.60	.18
35 Jason Giambi	1.50	.45
36 Tom Glavine	1.00	.30
37 Juan Gonzalez	1.50	.45
38 Mark Grace	1.00	.30
39 Shawn Green	.60	.18
40 Tim Hudson	.60	.18
41 Andruw Jones	.60	.18
42 Jeff Kent	.60	.18
43 Barry Larkin	1.50	.45
44 Rafael Furcal	.60	.18
45 Mike Mussina	1.50	.45
46 Hideo Nomo	1.50	.45
47 Rafael Palmeiro	1.00	.30
48 Scott Rolen	1.00	.30
49 Gary Sheffield	.60	.18
50 Bernie Williams	1.00	.30
51 Bob Abreu	.60	.18
52 Edgardo Alfonzo	.60	.18
53 Edgar Martinez	1.00	.30
54 Magglio Ordonez	.60	.18
55 Kerry Wood	1.50	.45
56 Adrian Beltre	.60	.18
57 Lance Berkman	.60	.18
58 Kevin Brown	.60	.18
59 Sean Casey	.60	.18
60 Eric Chavez	.60	.18
61 Bartolo Colon	.60	.18
62 Johnny Damon	.60	.18
63 Jermaine Dye	.60	.18
64 Juan Encarnacion	.60	.18
65 Carl Everett	.60	.18
66 Brian Giles	.60	.18
67 Mike Hampton	.60	.18
68 Richard Hidalgo	.60	.18
69 Geoff Jenkins	.60	.18
70 Jacque Jones	.60	.18
71 Jason Kendall	.60	.18
72 Ryan Klesko	.60	.18
73 Chan Ho Park	.60	.18
74 Richie Sexson	.60	.18
75 Mike Sweeney	.60	.18
76 Fernando Tatis	.60	.18
77 Miguel Tejada	.60	.18
78 Jose Vidro	.60	.18
79 Larry Walker	1.00	.30
80 Preston Wilson	.60	.18
81 Craig Biggio	1.00	.30
82 Fred McGriff	1.00	.30
83 Jim Thome	1.50	.45
84 Garret Anderson	.60	.18
85 Russell Branyan	.60	.18
86 Tony Batista	.60	.18
87 Terrence Long	.60	.18
88 Brad Fullmer	.60	.18
89 Rusty Greer	.60	.18
90 Orlando Hernandez	.60	.18
91 Gabe Kapler	.60	.18
92 Paul Konerko	.60	.18
93 Carlos Lee	.60	.18
94 Kenny Lofton	.60	.18
95 Raul Mondesi	.60	.18
96 Jorge Posada	1.00	.30
97 Tim Salmon	1.00	.30
98 Greg Vaughn	.60	.18
99 Mo Vaughn	.60	.18
100 Omar Vizquel	.60	.18
101 Aubrey Huff SP	8.00	2.40
102 Jimmy Rollins SP	8.00	2.40
103 Cory Aldridge SP RC	8.00	2.40
104 Wilmy Caceres SP RC	8.00	2.40
105 Josh Beckett SP	10.00	3.00
106 Wilson Betemit SP RC	8.00	2.40
107 Timo Perez SP	8.00	2.40
108 Albert Pujols SP RC	80.00	24.00
109 Bud Smith SP RC	8.00	2.40
110 Jack Wilson SP RC	8.00	2.40
111 Alex Escobar SP	8.00	2.40
112 J. Estrada SP RC	10.00	3.00
113 Pedro Feliz SP	8.00	2.40
114 Nate Frese SP RC	8.00	2.40
115 Carlos Garcia SP RC	8.00	2.40
116 Brandon Larson SP RC	8.00	2.40
117 Alexis Gomez SP RC	8.00	2.40
118 Jason Hart SP	8.00	2.40
119 Adam Dunn SP	8.00	2.40
120 Marcus Giles SP	8.00	2.40
121 C. Parker SP RC	8.00	2.40
122 J.Melian SP RC	8.00	2.40
123 Endy Chavez SP RC	8.00	2.40
124 A.Hernandez SP RC	8.00	2.40
125 Joe Kennedy SP RC	8.00	2.40
126 Jose Mieses SP RC	8.00	2.40
127 C.C. Sabathia SP	8.00	2.40
128 Eric Munson SP	8.00	2.40
129 Xavier Nady SP	8.00	2.40
130 H. Ramirez SP RC	10.00	3.00
131 Abraham Nunez SP	8.00	2.40
132 Jose Ortiz SP	8.00	2.40
133 Jeremy Owens SP RC	8.00	2.40
134 Claudio Vargas SP RC	8.00	2.40
135 Corey Patterson SP	8.00	2.40
136 Andres Torres SP RC	8.00	2.40
137 Ben Sheets SP	8.00	2.40
138 Joe Crede SP	8.00	2.40
139 A.Pettyjohn SP RC	8.00	2.40
140 E.Guzman SP RC	8.00	2.40
141 Jay Gibbons SP RC	15.00	4.50
142 Wilkin Ruan SP RC	8.00	2.40
143 Tsuyoshi Shinjo SP RC	15.00	4.50
144 Alfonso Soriano SP	10.00	3.00
145 Nick Johnson SP	8.00	2.40
146 Ichiro Suzuki SP RC	60.00	18.00
147 Juan Uribe SP RC	8.00	2.40
148 Jack Cust SP	8.00	2.40
149 C.Valderrama SP RC	8.00	2.40
150 Matt White SP RC	8.00	2.40
151 Hank Aaron LGD	10.00	3.00
152 Ernie Banks LGD	5.00	1.50
153 Johnny Bench LGD	5.00	1.50
154 George Brett LGD	12.00	3.60
155 Lou Brock LGD	5.00	1.50
156 Rod Carew LGD	5.00	1.50
157 Steve Carlton LGD	4.00	1.20
158 Bob Feller LGD	5.00	1.50
159 Bob Gibson LGD	5.00	1.50
160 Reggie Jackson LGD	5.00	1.50
161 Al Kaline LGD	5.00	1.50
162 Sandy Koufax LGD SP		
163 Don Mattingly LGD	12.00	3.60
164 Willie Mays LGD	10.00	3.00
165 Willie McCovey LGD	4.00	1.20
166 Joe Morgan LGD	4.00	1.20
167 Stan Musial LGD	8.00	2.40
168 Jim Palmer LGD	4.00	1.20
169 Brooks Robinson LGD	5.00	1.50
170 Frank Robinson LGD	5.00	1.50
171 Nolan Ryan LGD	12.00	3.60
172 Mike Schmidt LGD	10.00	3.00
173 Tom Seaver LGD	5.00	1.50
174 Warren Spahn LGD	5.00	1.50
175 Robin Yount LGD	8.00	2.40
176 Wade Boggs LGD	5.00	1.50
177 Ty Cobb LGD	8.00	2.40
178 Lou Gehrig LGD	10.00	3.00
179 Luis Aparicio LGD	4.00	1.20
180 Babe Ruth LGD	15.00	4.50
181 Ryne Sandberg LGD	10.00	3.00
182 Yogi Berra LGD	5.00	1.50
183 R.Clemente LGD	12.00	3.60
184 Eddie Murray LGD	5.00	1.50
185 Robin Roberts LGD SP		
186 Duke Snider LGD	5.00	1.50
187 Orlando Cepeda LGD	4.00	1.20
188 Billy Williams LGD	4.00	1.20
189 Juan Marichal LGD	4.00	1.20
190 Harmon Killebrew LGD	5.00	1.50
191 Kirby Puckett LGD	5.00	1.50
192 Carlton Fisk LGD	5.00	1.50
193 Dave Winfield LGD	4.00	1.20
194 Whitey Ford LGD	5.00	1.50
195 Paul Molitor LGD	5.00	1.50
196 Tony Perez LGD	4.00	1.20
197 Ozzie Smith LGD	8.00	2.40
198 Ralph Kiner LGD	5.00	1.50
199 Fergie Jenkins LGD	4.00	1.20
200 Phil Rizzuto LGD	5.00	1.50

2001 Donruss Classics Significant Signatures

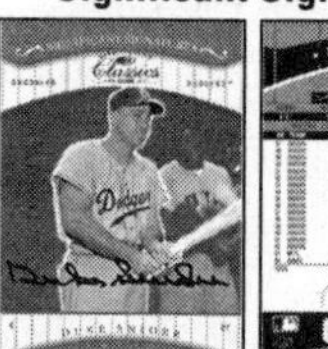
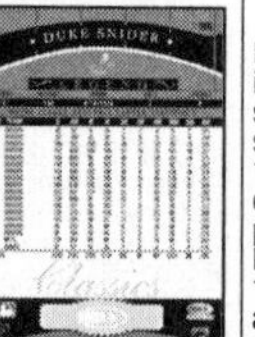

Randomly inserted into packs at the rate of one in 18, this 83-card set is a partial parallel version of the base set. Each card is autographed and displays a rookie/prospect or retired player with platinum tint and holographic foil. Please note, the following cards packed out as redemption cards with an expiration date of September 10th, 2003: Hank Aaron, Luis Aparicio, Ernie Banks, Josh Beckett, Yogi Berra, Rod Carew, Steve Carlton, Orlando Cepeda, Adam Dunn, Johnny Estrada, Bob Feller, Carlton Fisk, Whitey Ford, Bob Gibson, Reggie Jackson, Nick Johnson, Juan Marichal, Willie Mays, Paul Molitor, Joe Morgan, Eddie Murray, Jim Palmer, Corey Patterson, Tony Perez, Kirby Puckett, Phil Rizzuto, Brooks Robinson, Frank Robinson, Nolan Ryan (Astros), C.C. Sabathia, Ryne Sandberg, Ron Santo, Mike Schmidt, Ben Sheets, Ozzie Smith, Billy Williams, Dave Winfield and Robin Yount. Exchange card 162 was originally intended to feature Sandy Koufax but in late 2002 representatives at Donruss switched the redemption to a Nolan Ryan Mets card (Ryan's basic card 171 in the set pictures him as a member of the Texas Rangers). In addition, exchange card 185 was originally intended to feature Robin Roberts but the redemption was switched in late 2002 to Ron Santo.

	Nm-Mt	Ex-Mt
101 Aubrey Huff	15.00	4.50
103 Cory Aldridge	15.00	4.50
105 Josh Beckett SP	40.00	12.00
106 Wilson Betemit	15.00	4.50
107 Timo Perez	10.00	3.00
108 Albert Pujols	250.00	75.00
110 Jack Wilson	15.00	4.50
111 Alex Escobar	10.00	3.00
112 Johnny Estrada	15.00	4.50
113 Pedro Feliz	10.00	3.00
114 Nate Frese	15.00	4.50
115 Carlos Garcia	15.00	4.50
116 Brandon Larson	15.00	4.50
118 Jason Hart	10.00	3.00
119 Adam Dunn SP	25.00	7.50
120 Marcus Giles	15.00	4.50
121 Christian Parker	10.00	3.00
126 Jose Mieses	15.00	4.50
127 C.C.Sabathia SP	20.00	6.00
129 Xavier Nady	15.00	4.50
130 Horacio Ramirez	20.00	6.00
131 Abraham Nunez	10.00	3.00
132 Jose Ortiz	10.00	3.00
133 Jeremy Owens	15.00	4.50
134 Claudio Vargas	15.00	4.50
135 Corey Patterson SP	20.00	6.00
136 Andres Torres	15.00	4.50
137 Ben Sheets SP	40.00	12.00
138 Joe Crede	10.00	3.00
139 Adam Pettyjohn	15.00	4.50
140 Elpidio Guzman	15.00	4.50
141 Jay Gibbons	20.00	6.00
142 Wilkin Ruan	15.00	4.50
144 Alfonso Soriano SP	50.00	15.00
145 Nick Johnson SP	20.00	6.00
147 Juan Uribe	15.00	4.50
149 Carlos Valderrama	15.00	4.50
151 Hank Aaron SP	150.00	45.00
152 Ernie Banks	40.00	12.00
153 Johnny Bench SP		
154 George Brett SP	150.00	45.00
155 Lou Brock	25.00	7.50
156 Rod Carew	25.00	7.50
157 Steve Carlton	25.00	7.50
158 Bob Feller	25.00	7.50
159 Bob Gibson	25.00	7.50
160 Reggie Jackson SP		
161 Al Kaline	50.00	15.00
162 Nolan Ryan Astros SP	150.00	45.00
163 Don Mattingly	100.00	30.00
164 Willie Mays SP	150.00	45.00
165 Willie McCovey	25.00	7.50
166 Joe Morgan	20.00	6.00
167 Stan Musial SP	100.00	30.00
168 Jim Palmer	20.00	6.00
169 B. Robinson EXCH	40.00	12.00
170 Frank Robinson	25.00	7.50
171 Nolan Ryan Rangers SP	150.00	45.00
172 Mike Schmidt	80.00	24.00
173 Tom Seaver	25.00	7.50
174 Warren Spahn	40.00	12.00
175 Robin Yount SP	120.00	36.00
176 Wade Boggs SP	80.00	24.00
179 Luis Aparicio	20.00	6.00
181 Ryne Sandberg	80.00	24.00
182 Yogi Berra	40.00	12.00
184 Eddie Murray	60.00	18.00
185 Ron Santo	25.00	7.50
186 Duke Snider	25.00	7.50
187 Orlando Cepeda	20.00	6.00
188 Billy Williams	20.00	6.00
189 Juan Marichal	20.00	6.00
190 Harmon Killebrew	40.00	12.00
191 Kirby Puckett SP	100.00	30.00
192 Carlton Fisk	25.00	7.50
193 Dave Winfield SP	80.00	24.00
194 Whitey Ford	25.00	7.50
195 Paul Molitor SP	80.00	24.00
196 Tony Perez	20.00	6.00
197 Ozzie Smith SP	120.00	36.00
198 Ralph Kiner	25.00	7.50
199 Fergie Jenkins	20.00	6.00
200 Phil Rizzuto	40.00	12.00

2001 Donruss Classics Timeless Tributes

Randomly inserted in packs, this 198-card set is a parallel version of the base set featuring silver or gold holo-foil highlights. The cards are sequentially numbered to 100. Cards 162 and 185 are believed to not exist. It's likely the cards were printed, but due to contractual problems with the featured athletes (Sandy Koufax for card 162 and Robin Roberts for card 185), the manufacturer made the effort to pull and destroy all copies found within the print run during the packout process. A handful of copies of the basic versions of these cards have been confirmed to exist, but given the fact that 1755 of each of those were originally printed versus only 100 of the Timeless Tribute parallels, the likelihood of the parallels sneaking into packs is far slimmer.

Nm-Mt Ex-Mt

*TRIBUTE 1-100: 2.5X TO 6X BASIC ..
*TRIBUTE 101-150: .5X TO 1.2X BASIC
*TRIBUTE 151-200: 1.25X TO 3X BASIC

2001 Donruss Classics Benchmarks

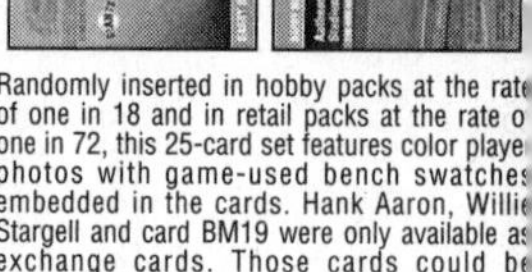

Randomly inserted in hobby packs at the rate of one in 18 and in retail packs at the rate of one in 72, this 25-card set features color player photos with game-used bench swatches embedded in the cards. Hank Aaron, Willie Stargell and card BM19 were only available as exchange cards. Those cards could be redeemed until September 10, 2003.

	Nm-Mt	Ex-Mt
BM1 Todd Helton	15.00	4.50
BM2 Roberto Clemente	50.00	15.00
BM3 Mark McGwire	40.00	12.00
BM4 Barry Bonds	30.00	9.00
BM5 Bob Gibson	15.00	4.50
BM6 Ken Griffey Jr.	20.00	6.00
BM7 Frank Robinson	15.00	4.50
BM8 Greg Maddux	20.00	6.00
BM9 Reggie Jackson	15.00	4.50
BM10 Sammy Sosa	20.00	6.00
BM11 Willie Stargell		
BM12 Vladimir Guerrero	15.00	4.50
BM13 Johnny Bench	15.00	4.50
BM14 Tony Gwynn	15.00	4.50
BM15 Mike Schmidt	25.00	7.50
BM16 Ivan Rodriguez	15.00	4.50
BM17 Jeff Bagwell	15.00	4.50
BM18 Cal Ripken	40.00	12.00
BM19 TBD		
BM20 Kirby Puckett	15.00	4.50
BM21 Frank Thomas	15.00	4.50
BM22 Joe Morgan	10.00	3.00
BM23 Mike Piazza	20.00	6.00
BM24 Hank Aaron		
BM25 Andruw Jones	10.00	3.00

2001 Donruss Classics Benchmarks Autographs

Randomly inserted in packs, this nine-card set is a partial parallel autographed version of the regular insert set. No autographed cards were seeded into packs. Rather, exchange cards with a redemption deadline of September 10th, 2003 were inserted in their place.

	Nm-Mt	Ex-Mt
BM5 Bob Gibson		
BM7 Frank Robinson		
BM9 Reggie Jackson		
BM12 Vladimir Guerrero		
BM13 Johnny Bench		
BM15 Mike Schmidt		
BM20 Kirby Puckett		
BM22 Joe Morgan		
BM25 Andruw Jones		

2001 Donruss Classics Combos

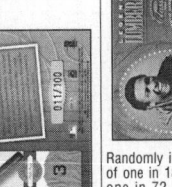

Randomly inserted in packs, this 45-card set features color action photos of baseball legends. Some cards consist of one player while others display a pairing of two great players. Each card has two or four swatches of game-worn/used memorabilia. One player cards are sequentially numbered to 100 while two player cards are sequentially numbered to 50. The following cards were issued in packs as exchange cards with a redemption deadline of September 10th, 2003: Hank Aaron, Ernie Banks, Wade Boggs, Lou Brock, Steve Carlton, Andre Dawson, Don Mattingly, Jackie Robinson, Ryne Sandberg, Willie Stargell and Billy Williams. In addition, the following dual-player cards packed out as exchange cards (with the same redemption deadline as detailed above): Banks/Williams, Carlton/Schmidt, Clemente/Stargell, Dawson/Sandberg, Mattingly/Boggs, Musial/Brock and Robinson/Snider.

	Nm-Mt	Ex-Mt
1 R.Clemente/100	150.00	45.00
2 Willie Stargell/100	50.00	15.00
3 Babe Ruth/100	800.00	240.00
4 Lou Gehrig/100	600.00	180.00
5 Hank Aaron/100	150.00	45.00
6 Eddie Mathews/100	50.00	15.00
7 Johnny Bench/100	50.00	15.00
8 Joe Morgan/100	25.00	7.50
9 Robin Yount/100	50.00	15.00
10 Paul Molitor/100	50.00	15.00
11 S.Carlton/85 EXCH	25.00	7.50
12 Mike Schmidt/85	100.00	30.00
13 Stan Musial/100	120.00	36.00
14 Lou Brock/100	50.00	15.00
15 Yogi Berra/100	50.00	15.00
16 Phil Rizzuto/100	50.00	15.00
17 Ernie Banks/85	50.00	15.00
18 B. Williams/85 EXCH	25.00	7.50
19 Don Mattingly/100	100.00	30.00
20 Wade Boggs/100	50.00	15.00
21 Jackie Robinson/100		
22 Duke Snider/100	50.00	15.00
23 Frank Robinson/85	50.00	15.00
24 Brooks Robinson/85	50.00	15.00
25 Orlando Cepeda/100	25.00	7.50
26 Willie McCovey/100	25.00	7.50
27 Ryne Sandberg/100	100.00	30.00
28 Andre Dawson/100	25.00	7.50
29 H.Killebrew/100	50.00	15.00
30 Rod Carew/100	50.00	15.00
31 Roberto Clemente	250.00	75.00
Willie Stargell/50		
32 Babe Ruth	1200.00	350.00
Lou Gehrig		
33 Hank Aaron		
Eddie Mathews		
34 Johnny Bench	120.00	36.00
Joe Morgan		
35 Robin Yount	150.00	45.00
Paul Molitor		
36 Steve Carlton	250.00	75.00
Mike Schmidt/40		
37 Stan Musial	250.00	75.00
Lou Brock/50		
38 Yogi Berra	150.00	45.00
Phil Rizzuto/50		
39 Ernie Banks	120.00	36.00
Billy Williams/40		
40 Don Mattingly		
Wade Boggs/50		
41 Jackie Robinson Jacket-Jsy	200.00	60.00
Duke Snider Bat-Jsy/50		
42 Brooks Robinson	120.00	36.00
Frank Robinson		
43 Orlando Cepeda	60.00	18.00
Willie McCovey/50		
44 Andre Dawson		
Ryne Sandberg/50		
45 Harmon Killebrew	120.00	36.00
Rod Carew		

2001 Donruss Classics Combos Autograph

Randomly inserted in packs, this nine-card set is a partial parallel autographed version of the regular insert set. No autographed cards were seeded into packs. Rather, exchange cards with a redemption deadline of September 10th, 2003 were seeded in their place. Each actual single-player autograph card is serial numbered to 15 copies and dual-player card serial numbered to 10 copies.

	Nm-Mt	Ex-Mt
CC11 Steve Carlton/15		
CC12 Mike Schmidt/15		
CC17 Ernie Banks/15		
CC18 Billy Williams/15		
CC23 Frank Robinson/15		
CC24 Brooks Robinson/15		
CC36 Steve Carlton		
Mike Schmidt		
CC39 Ernie Banks		
Billy Williams		
CC42 Brooks Robinson		
Frank Robinson		

2001 Donruss Classics Legendary Lumberjacks

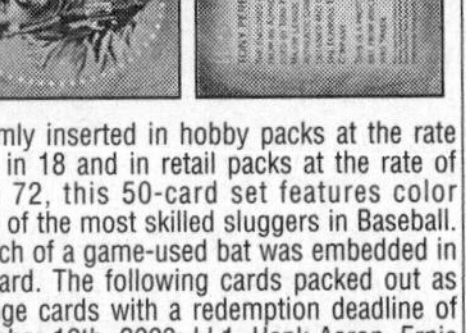

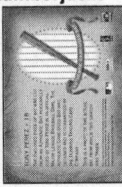

Randomly inserted in hobby packs at the rate of one in 18 and in retail packs at the rate of one in 72, this 50-card set features color photos of the most skilled sluggers in Baseball. A swatch of a game-used bat was embedded in each card. The following cards packed out as exchange cards with a redemption deadline of September 10th, 2003: LL1, Hank Aaron, Ernie Banks, Nellie Fox, Jimmie Foxx, Rogers Hornsby, Roger Maris, Willie Stargell and Ted Williams.

	Nm-Mt	Ex-Mt
LL1 TBD SP		
LL2 Chipper Jones	20.00	6.00
LL3 Rogers Hornsby SP		
LL4 Nellie Fox		
LL5 Ivan Rodriguez	20.00	6.00
LL6 Jimmie Foxx SP		
LL7 Hank Aaron	50.00	15.00
LL8 Yogi Berra	20.00	6.00
LL9 Ernie Banks SP		
LL10 George Brett	40.00	12.00
LL11 Ty Cobb SP	200.00	60.00
LL12 R. Clemente SP	120.00	36.00
LL13 Carlton Fisk	15.00	4.50
LL14 Reggie Jackson	15.00	4.50
LL15 Al Kaline	20.00	6.00
LL16 Harmon Killebrew	20.00	6.00
LL17 Ralph Kiner	15.00	4.50
LL18 Roger Maris SP		
LL19 Eddie Mathews	20.00	6.00
LL20 Ted Williams SP		
LL21 Willie McCovey	10.00	3.00
LL22 Eddie Murray	20.00	6.00
LL23 Joe Morgan SP	15.00	4.50
LL24 Frank Robinson	15.00	4.50
LL25 Tony Perez	10.00	3.00
LL26 Mike Schmidt	50.00	15.00
LL27 Ryne Sandberg	50.00	15.00
LL28 Duke Snider SP	25.00	7.50
LL29 Willie Stargell		
LL30 Billy Williams	10.00	3.00
LL31 Dave Winfield	10.00	3.00
LL32 Robin Yount	25.00	7.50
LL33 Barry Bonds	30.00	9.00
LL34 Stan Musial SP	50.00	15.00
LL35 Johnny Bench SP	30.00	9.00
LL36 Orlando Cepeda	10.00	3.00
LL37 Todd Helton	15.00	4.50
LL38 Frank Thomas	20.00	6.00
LL39 Juan Gonzalez	20.00	6.00
LL40 Cal Ripken	50.00	15.00
LL41 Rafael Palmeiro	15.00	4.50
LL42 Troy Glaus SP	25.00	7.50
LL43 Vladimir Guerrero	20.00	6.00
LL44 Paul Molitor	15.00	4.50
LL45 Tony Gwynn	15.00	4.50
LL46 Rod Carew	15.00	4.50
LL47 Lou Brock	15.00	4.50
LL48 Wade Boggs	15.00	4.50
LL49 Babe Ruth SP	300.00	90.00
LL50 Lou Gehrig SP	200.00	60.00

2001 Donruss Classics Stadium Stars

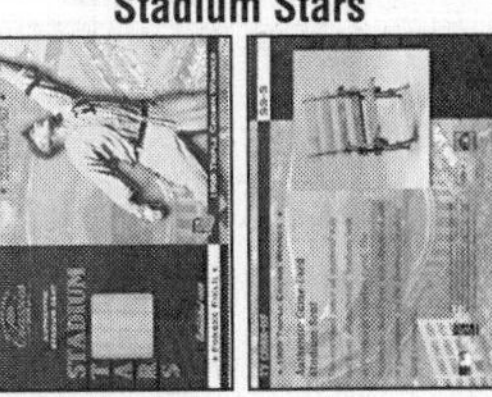

Randomly inserted in hobby packs at the rate of one in 18 and in retail packs at the rate of one in 72, this 25-card set features color action player photos with swatches of stadium seats taken from some of the most heralded ballparks embedded in the cards. An exchange card with a redemption deadline of September 10th, 2003 was seeded into packs for Honus Wagner's card.

	Nm-Mt	Ex-Mt
SS1 Babe Ruth SP	80.00	24.00
SS2 Cal Ripken	25.00	7.50
SS3 Brooks Robinson	10.00	3.00
SS4 Tony Gwynn SP	15.00	4.50
SS5 Ty Cobb	40.00	12.00
SS6 Vladimir Guerrero SP	15.00	4.50
SS7 Lou Gehrig SP	50.00	15.00
SS8 Nomar Garciaparra	15.00	4.50
SS9 Sammy Sosa SP	15.00	4.50
SS10 Reggie Jackson SP	15.00	4.50
SS11 Alex Rodriguez	15.00	4.50
SS12 Derek Jeter	25.00	7.50
SS13 Willie McCovey SP	10.00	3.00
SS14 Mark McGwire	25.00	7.50
SS15 Chipper Jones	10.00	3.00
SS16 H. Wagner EXCH	25.00	7.50
SS17 Ken Griffey Jr.	15.00	4.50
SS18 Frank Robinson	10.00	3.00
SS19 Barry Bonds SP	25.00	7.50
SS20 Yogi Berra SP	15.00	4.50
SS21 Mike Piazza SP	15.00	4.50
SS22 Roger Clemens	15.00	4.50
SS23 Duke Snider SP	15.00	4.50
SS24 Frank Thomas	10.00	3.00
SS25 Andruw Jones	8.00	2.40

2001 Donruss Classics Timeless Treasures

Randomly inserted in hobby packs at the rate of one in 420, and in retail packs at the rate of one in 1680, this five-card set features pictures of great players with swatches of memorabilia from five famous events in baseball history.

	Nm-Mt	Ex-Mt
TT1 M. McGwire Ball SP	200.00	60.00
TT2 Babe Ruth Seat	80.00	24.00
TT3 H. Killebrew Bat SP	50.00	15.00
TT4 Derek Jeter Base	50.00	15.00
TT5 Barry Bonds Ball SP	120.00	36.00

2002 Donruss Classics Samples

This partial parallel to the Donruss Classics set was issued as inserts in Beckett Baseball Card Monthly issue number 209. Only the first 100 cards of this set were created for this project.

Nm-Mt Ex-Mt

*SAMPLES: .75X TO 2X BASIC CARDS
*GOLD: 1.5X TO 4X BASIC SAMPLES

2002 Donruss Classics

This 200 card standard-size was issued in June, 2002. An additional 25 update cards were seeded into Donruss the Rookies packs distributed in December, 2002. The basic set was released in six card packs which came in two nine-pack mini boxes per full box. The full boxes were issued four boxes to a case and had an SRP of $6 per pack. Cards 1-100 feature veteran active players, while cards 101-150 feature rookies and prospects and cards 151-200 feature retired greats. Cards numbered 101-200 were all printed to a stated print run of 1500 sets and were released two cards per mini-box (or 4 per full box of 18 packs). Update cards 201-225 were also serial-numbered to 1500.

	Nm-Mt	Ex-Mt
COMP.SET w/o SP's (100)	25.00	7.50
COMMON CARD (1-100)	.60	.18
COMMON (101-150/201-225)	4.00	1.20
COMMON CARD (151-200)	4.00	1.20
1 Alex Rodriguez	2.50	.75
2 Barry Bonds	4.00	1.20
3 C.C. Sabathia	.60	.18
4 Chipper Jones	1.50	.45
5 Derek Jeter	4.00	1.20
6 Troy Glaus	1.00	.30
7 Frank Thomas	1.50	.45
8 Greg Maddux	2.50	.75
9 Ivan Rodriguez	1.50	.45
10 Jeff Bagwell	1.00	.30
11 Mark Buehrle	.60	.18
12 Todd Helton	1.00	.30
13 Ken Griffey Jr.	2.50	.75
14 Manny Ramirez	.60	.18
15 Brad Penny	.60	.18
16 Mike Piazza	2.50	.75
17 Nomar Garciaparra	2.50	.75
18 Pedro Martinez	1.50	.45
19 Randy Johnson	1.50	.45
20 Bud Smith	.60	.18
21 Rickey Henderson	1.50	.45
22 Roger Clemens	3.00	.90
23 Sammy Sosa	2.50	.75
24 Brandon Duckworth	.60	.18
25 Vladimir Guerrero	1.50	.45
26 Kazuhiro Sasaki	.60	.18
27 Roberto Alomar	1.50	.45
28 Barry Zito	1.00	.30
29 Rich Aurilia	.60	.18
30 Ben Sheets	.60	.18
31 Carlos Delgado	.60	.18
32 J.D. Drew	.60	.18
33 Jermaine Dye	.60	.18
34 Darin Erstad	.60	.18
35 Jason Giambi	1.50	.45
36 Tom Glavine	1.00	.30
37 Juan Gonzalez	1.50	.45
38 Luis Gonzalez	.60	.18
39 Shawn Green	.60	.18
40 Tim Hudson	.60	.18
41 Andruw Jones	.60	.18
42 Shannon Stewart	.60	.18
43 Barry Larkin	1.50	.45
44 Wade Miller	.60	.18
45 Mike Mussina	1.50	.45
46 Hideo Nomo	1.50	.45
47 Rafael Palmeiro	1.00	.30
48 Scott Rolen	1.00	.30
49 Gary Sheffield	.60	.18
50 Bernie Williams	1.00	.30
51 Bob Abreu	.60	.18
52 Javier Vazquez	.60	.18
53 Edgar Martinez	1.00	.30
54 Magglio Ordonez	.60	.18
55 Kerry Wood	1.50	.45
56 Adrian Beltre	.60	.18
57 Lance Berkman	.60	.18
58 Kevin Brown	.60	.18
59 Sean Casey	.60	.18
60 Eric Chavez	.60	.18
61 Robert Person	.60	.18
62 Jeremy Giambi	.60	.18
63 Freddy Garcia	.60	.18
64 Alfonso Soriano	1.00	.30
65 Doug Davis	.60	.18
66 Brian Giles	.60	.18
67 Moises Alou	.60	.18
68 Richard Hidalgo	.60	.18
69 Paul LoDuca	.60	.18
70 Aramis Ramirez	.60	.18
71 Andres Galarraga	.60	.18
72 Ryan Klesko	.60	.18
73 Chan Ho Park	.60	.18
74 Richie Sexson	.60	.18
75 Mike Sweeney	.60	.18
76 Aubrey Huff	.60	.18
77 Miguel Tejada	.60	.18
78 Jose Vidro	.60	.18
79 Larry Walker	1.00	.30
80 Roy Oswalt	.60	.18
81 Craig Biggio	1.00	.30
82 Juan Pierre	.60	.18
83 Jim Thome	1.50	.45
84 Josh Towers	.60	.18
85 Alex Escobar	.60	.18
86 Cliff Floyd	.60	.18
87 Terrence Long	.60	.18
88 Curt Schilling	1.00	.30
89 Carlos Beltran	.60	.18
90 Albert Pujols	3.00	.90
91 Gabe Kapler	.60	.18
92 Mark Mulder	.60	.18
93 Carlos Lee	.60	.18
94 Robert Fick	.60	.18
95 Raul Mondesi	.60	.18
96 Ichiro Suzuki	2.50	.75
97 Adam Dunn	.60	.18
98 Corey Patterson	.60	.18
99 Tsuyoshi Shinjo	.60	.18
100 Joe Mays	.60	.18
101 Juan Cruz ROO	4.00	1.20
102 Marlon Byrd ROO	4.00	1.20
103 Luis Garcia ROO	4.00	1.20
104 Jorge Padilla ROO RC	4.00	1.20
105 Dennis Tankersley ROO	4.00	1.20
106 Josh Pearce ROO	4.00	1.20
107 Ramon Vazquez ROO	4.00	1.20
108 Chris Baker ROO RC	4.00	1.20
109 Eric Cyr ROO	4.00	1.20
110 Reed Johnson ROO RC	5.00	1.50
111 Ryan Jamison ROO	4.00	1.20
112 Antonio Perez ROO	4.00	1.20
113 Satoru Komiyama ROO RC	4.00	1.20
114 Austin Kearns ROO	4.00	1.20
115 Juan Pena ROO	4.00	1.20
116 Orlando Hudson ROO	4.00	1.20
117 Kazuhisa Ishii ROO RC	8.00	2.40
118 Erik Bedard ROO	4.00	1.20
119 Luis Ugueto ROO RC	4.00	1.20
120 Ben Howard ROO RC	4.00	1.20
121 Morgan Ensberg ROO	4.00	1.20
122 Doug Devore ROO RC	4.00	1.20
123 Josh Phelps ROO	4.00	1.20
124 Angel Berroa ROO	4.00	1.20
125 Ed Rogers ROO	4.00	1.20
126 Takahito Nomura ROO RC	4.00	1.20
127 John Ennis ROO RC	4.00	1.20
128 Bill Hall ROO	4.00	1.20
129 Dewon Brazelton ROO	4.00	1.20
130 Hank Blalock ROO	5.00	1.50
131 So Taguchi ROO RC	5.00	1.50
132 Jorge De La Rosa ROO RC	4.00	1.20
133 Matt Thornton ROO RC	4.00	1.20
134 Brandon Backe ROO RC	4.00	1.20
135 Jeff Deardorff ROO	4.00	1.20
136 Steve Smyth ROO	4.00	1.20
137 An. Machado ROO RC	4.00	1.20
138 John Buck ROO	4.00	1.20
139 Mark Prior ROO	10.00	3.00
140 Sean Burroughs ROO	4.00	1.20
141 Alex Herrera ROO	4.00	1.20
142 Francis Beltran ROO RC	4.00	1.20
143 Jason Romano ROO	4.00	1.20
144 Michael Cuddyer ROO	4.00	1.20
145 Steve Bechler ROO RC	4.00	1.20
146 Alfredo Amezaga ROO	4.00	1.20
147 Ryan Ludwick ROO	4.00	1.20
148 Martin Vargas ROO	4.00	1.20
149 Allan Simpson ROO RC	4.00	1.20
150 Mark Teixeira ROO	5.00	1.50
151 Dale Murphy LGD	5.00	1.50
152 Ernie Banks LGD	5.00	1.50
153 Johnny Bench LGD	5.00	1.50
154 George Brett LGD	10.00	3.00
155 Lou Brock LGD	5.00	1.50
156 Rod Carew LGD	5.00	1.50
157 Steve Carlton LGD	4.00	1.20
158 Joe Torre LGD	5.00	1.50
159 Dennis Eckersley LGD	4.00	1.20
160 Reggie Jackson LGD	5.00	1.50
161 Al Kaline LGD	5.00	1.50
162 Dave Parker LGD	4.00	1.20
163 Don Mattingly LGD	10.00	3.00
164 Tony Gwynn LGD	5.00	1.50
165 Willie McCovey LGD	4.00	1.20
166 Joe Morgan LGD	4.00	1.20
167 Stan Musial LGD	6.00	1.80
168 Jim Palmer LGD	4.00	1.20
169 Brooks Robinson LGD	5.00	1.50
170 Bo Jackson LGD	5.00	1.50
171 Nolan Ryan LGD	10.00	3.00
172 Mike Schmidt LGD	8.00	2.40
173 Tom Seaver LGD	5.00	1.50
174 Cal Ripken LGD	12.00	3.60
175 Robin Yount LGD	6.00	1.80
176 Wade Boggs LGD	5.00	1.50
177 Gary Carter LGD	5.00	1.50
178 Ron Santo LGD	5.00	1.50
179 Luis Aparicio LGD	4.00	1.20
180 Bobby Doerr LGD	5.00	1.50
181 Ryne Sandberg LGD	8.00	2.40
182 Yogi Berra LGD	5.00	1.50
183 Will Clark LGD	5.00	1.50
184 Eddie Murray LGD	5.00	1.50
185 Andre Dawson LGD	4.00	1.20
186 Duke Snider LGD	5.00	1.50
187 Orlando Cepeda LGD	4.00	1.20
188 Billy Williams LGD	4.00	1.20
189 Juan Marichal LGD	4.00	1.20
190 Harmon Killebrew LGD	5.00	1.50
191 Kirby Puckett LGD	5.00	1.50
192 Carlton Fisk LGD	5.00	1.50
193 Dave Winfield LGD	4.00	1.20
194 Alan Trammell LGD	5.00	1.50
195 Paul Molitor LGD	5.00	1.50
196 Tony Perez LGD	4.00	1.20
197 Ozzie Smith LGD	6.00	1.80
198 Ralph Kiner LGD	4.00	1.20
199 Fergie Jenkins LGD	4.00	1.20
200 Phil Rizzuto LGD	5.00	1.50
201 Oliver Perez ROO RC	5.00	1.50
202 Aaron Cook ROO RC	4.00	1.20
203 Eric Junge ROO RC	4.00	1.20
204 Freddy Sanchez ROO RC	4.00	1.20
205 Cliff Lee ROO RC	5.00	1.50
206 Run. Hernandez ROO RC	4.00	1.20
207 Chone Figgins ROO RC	4.00	1.20
208 Rodrigo Rosario ROO RC	4.00	1.20
209 Kevin Cash ROO RC	4.00	1.20
210 Josh Bard ROO RC	4.00	1.20
211 Felix Escalona ROO RC	4.00	1.20
212 Jer. Robertson ROO RC	4.00	1.20
213 J. Simontacchi ROO RC	4.00	1.20
214 Shane Nance ROO RC	4.00	1.20
215 Ben Kozlowski ROO RC	4.00	1.20
216 Brian Tallet ROO RC	5.00	1.50
217 Earl Snyder ROO RC	4.00	1.20
218 Andy Pratt ROO RC	4.00	1.20
219 Trey Hodges ROO RC	4.00	1.20
220 Kirk Saarloos ROO RC	4.00	1.20
221 Rene Reyes ROO RC	4.00	1.20
222 Joe Borchard ROO RC	4.00	1.20
223 Wilson Valdez ROO RC	4.00	1.20
224 Miguel Asencio ROO RC	4.00	1.20
225 Chris Snelling ROO RC	6.00	1.80

2002 Donruss Classics Significant Signatures

Cards checklisted 1-200 were randomly inserted in basic Donruss Classics packs. Cards 201-225 were randomly inserted in 2002 Donruss the Rookies packs in mid-December, 2002. This is a 202-card, skip-numbered, partial parallel to the Donruss Classics set. Each card has an autographed foil sticker attached to it and since each card has a different stated print run, we have notated that information next to the player's name. Cards with a print run of 25 or less are not priced due to market scarcity. A few signed signed cards were issued in "personal" form if the number of the signature had something important to their career.

	Nm-Mt	Ex-Mt
1 Alex Rodriguez/15		
3 C.C. Sabathia/20		
4 Chipper Jones/15		
6 Troy Glaus/25		
7 Frank Thomas/15		
8 Greg Maddux/15		
9 Ivan Rodriguez/15		
10 Jeff Bagwell/15		
11 Mark Buehrle/25		
12 Todd Helton/15		
14 Manny Ramirez/15		
15 Brad Penny/25		
17 Nomar Garciaparra/15		
18 Pedro Martinez/15		
20 Bud Smith/25		
21 Rickey Henderson/15		
22 Roger Clemens/15		
24 Brandon Duckworth/25		
25 Vladimir Guerrero/25		
27 Roberto Alomar/15		
28 Barry Zito/25		
29 Rich Aurilia/25		
30 Ben Sheets/25		
32 J.D. Drew/15		
33 Jermaine Dye/25		
34 Darin Erstad/15		
35 Jason Giambi/15		
36 Tom Glavine/15		

37 Juan Gonzalez/15
38 Luis Gonzalez/15
40 Tim Hudson/25
41 Andruw Jones/15
42 Shannon Stewart/25
43 Barry Larkin/15
44 Wade Miller/25
45 Mike Mussina/15
47 Rafael Palmeiro/15
48 Scott Rolen/15
49 Gary Sheffield/15
50 Bernie Williams/15
51 Bobby Abreu/25
52 Javier Vazquez/25
53 Edgar Martinez/25
55 Kerry Wood/15
56 Adrian Beltre/25
57 Lance Berkman/25
58 Kevin Brown/15
59 Sean Casey/20
60 Eric Chavez/25
61 Robert Person/25
62 Jeremy Giambi/25
63 Freddy Garcia/25
64 Alfonso Soriano/25
65 Doug Davis/25
66 Brian Giles/13
67 Moises Alou/15
68 Richard Hidalgo/25
69 Paul LoDuca/25
70 Aramis Ramirez/25
71 Andres Galarraga/15
72 Ryan Klesko/20
74 Richie Sexson/25
75 Mike Sweeney/25
76 Aubrey Huff/25
77 Miguel Tejada/25
78 Jose Vidro/25
80 Roy Oswalt/25
81 Craig Biggio/15
82 Juan Pierre/25
84 Josh Towers/25
85 Alex Escobar/25
86 Cliff Floyd/25
87 Terrence Long/25
88 Curt Schilling/15
89 Carlos Beltran/25
90 Albert Pujols/25
91 Gabe Kapler/25
92 Mark Mulder/25
93 Carlos Lee/25
94 Robert Fick/25
97 Adam Dunn/6
98 Corey Patterson/25
100 Joe Mays/25
101 Juan Cruz ROO/400 10.00 3.00
102 Marlon Byrd ROO/500 15.00 4.50
103 Luis Garcia ROO/500 10.00 3.00
104 Jorge Padilla ROO/500 10.00 3.00
105 Dennis Tankersley ROO/250 15.00 4.50
106 Josh Pearce ROO/500 10.00 3.00
107 Ramon Vazquez ROO/500 10.00 3.00
108 Chris Baker ROO/500 10.00 3.00
109 Eric Cyr ROO/500 10.00 3.00
110 Reed Johnson ROO/500 15.00 4.50
111 Ryan Jamison ROO/500 10.00 3.00
112 Antonio Perez ROO/500 10.00 3.00
113 Satoru Komiyama ROO/50
114 Austin Kearns ROO/500 15.00 4.50
115 Juan Pena ROO/500 10.00 3.00
116 Orlando Hudson ROO/400 10.00 3.00
117 Kazuhisa Ishii ROO/50
118 Erik Bedard ROO/500 10.00 3.00
119 Luis Ugueto ROO/250 15.00 4.50
120 Ben Howard ROO/500 10.00 3.00
121 Morgan Ensberg ROO/500 15.00 4.50
122 Doug Devore ROO/500 10.00 3.00
123 Josh Phelps ROO/500 10.00 3.00
124 Angel Berroa ROO/500 15.00 4.50
125 Ed Rogers ROO/500 10.00 3.00
126 Takahito Nomura ROO/25
127 John Ennis ROO/500 10.00 3.00
128 Bill Hall ROO/400 10.00 3.00
129 Dewon Brazelton ROO/400 10.00 3.00
130 Hank Blalock ROO/100 25.00 7.50
131 So Taguchi ROO/150 40.00 12.00
132 Jorge De La Rosa ROO/500 10.00 3.00
133 Matt Thornton ROO/500 10.00 3.00
134 Brandon Backe ROO/500 10.00 3.00
135 Jeff Deardorff ROO/500 10.00 3.00
136 Steve Smyth ROO/400 10.00 3.00
137 Anderson Machado ROO/500 10.00 3.00
138 John Buck ROO/500 10.00 3.00
139 Mark Prior ROO/250 100.00 30.00
140 Sean Burroughs ROO/50 25.00 7.50
141 Alex Herrera ROO/500 10.00 3.00
142 Francis Beltran ROO/500 10.00 3.00
143 Jason Romano ROO/500 10.00 3.00
144 Michael Cuddyer ROO/400 10.00 3.00
145 Steve Bechler ROO/500 10.00 3.00
146 Alfredo Amezaga ROO/500 10.00 3.00
147 Ryan Ludwick ROO/500 10.00 3.00
148 Martin Vargas ROO/500 10.00 3.00
149 Allan Simpson ROO/500 10.00 3.00
150 Mark Teixeira ROO/200 25.00 7.50
151 Dale Murphy LGD/25
152 Ernie Banks LGD/25
153 Johnny Bench LGD/25
154 George Brett LGD/25
155 Lou Brock LGD/100 40.00 12.00
156 Rod Carew LGD/25
157 Steve Carlton LGD/125 40.00 12.00
158 Joe Torre LGD/25
159 Dennis Eckersley LGD/500 15.00 4.50
160 Reggie Jackson LGD/25
161 Al Kaline LGD/125 50.00 15.00
162 Dave Parker LGD/500 15.00 4.50
163 Don Mattingly LGD/50 120.00 36.00
164 Tony Gwynn LGD/25
165 Willie McCovey LGD/25
166 Joe Morgan LGD/25
167 Stan Musial LGD/25
168 Jim Palmer LGD/125 25.00 7.50
169 Brooks Robinson LGD/125 50.00 15.00
170 Bo Jackson LGD/25
171 Nolan Ryan LGD/25
172 Mike Schmidt LGD/25
173 Tom Seaver LGD/25
174 Cal Ripken LGD/25
175 Robin Yount LGD/25
176 Wade Boggs LGD/25
177 Gary Carter LGD/150 30.00 9.00
178 Ron Santo LGD/500 25.00 7.50
179 Luis Aparicio LGD/400 15.00 4.50
180 Bobby Doerr LGD/500 15.00 4.50
181 Ryne Sandberg LGD/25
182 Yogi Berra LGD/25
183 Will Clark LGD/50
184 Eddie Murray LGD/25
185 Andre Dawson LGD/200 20.00 6.00
186 Duke Snider LGD/25
187 Orlando Cepeda LGD/125 25.00 7.50
188 Billy Williams LGD/200 20.00 6.00
189 Juan Marichal LGD/500 15.00 4.50
190 Harmon Killebrew LGD/100 50.00 15.00
191 Kirby Puckett LGD/25
192 Carlton Fisk LGD/25
193 Dave Winfield LGD/25
194 Alan Trammell LGD/200 30.00 9.00
195 Paul Molitor LGD/25
196 Tony Perez LGD/150 20.00 6.00
197 Ozzie Smith LGD/25
198 Ralph Kiner LGD/125 25.00 7.50
199 Fergie Jenkins LGD/200 20.00 6.00
200 Phil Rizzuto LGD/125 40.00 12.00
201 Oliver Perez ROO/50 25.00 7.50
203 Eric Junge ROO/50 15.00 4.50
205 Cliff Lee ROO/100 40.00 12.00
207 Chone Figgins ROO/100 15.00 4.50
208 Rodrigo Rosario ROO/250 15.00 4.50
209 Kevin Cash ROO/100 15.00 4.50
210 Josh Bard ROO/100 15.00 4.50
211 Felix Escalona ROO/25
214 Shane Nance ROO/200 15.00 4.50
215 Ben Kozlowski ROO/200 15.00 4.50
216 Brian Tallet ROO/100 20.00 6.00
217 Earl Snyder ROO/100 15.00 4.50
218 Andy Pratt ROO/250 15.00 4.50
219 Trey Hodges ROO/250 15.00 4.50
220 Kirk Saarloos ROO/100 15.00 4.50
221 Rene Reyes ROO/50 15.00 4.50
222 Joe Borchard ROO/100 15.00 4.50
223 Wilson Valdez ROO/100 15.00 4.50
225 Chris Snelling ROO/100 40.00 12.00

2002 Donruss Classics Timeless Tributes

Cards 1-200 were randomly inserted in Donruss Classics packs and cards 201-225 in Donruss the Rookies packs. This is a parallel to the Donruss Classics set. The set is issued to a stated print run of 100 serial-numbered sets.

Nm-Mt Ex-Mt
*TRIBUTE 1-100: 2.5X TO 6X BASIC
*TRIB.101-150/201-225: .6X TO 1.5X BASIC
*TRIB.151-200: 1.25X TO 3X BASIC

101 Juan Cruz ROO 6.00 1.80
102 Marlon Byrd ROO 6.00 1.80
103 Luis Garcia ROO 6.00 1.80
104 Jorge Padilla ROO 6.00 1.80
105 Dennis Tankersley ROO 6.00 1.80
106 Josh Pearce ROO 6.00 1.80
107 Ramon Vazquez ROO 6.00 1.80
108 Chris Baker ROO 6.00 1.80
109 Eric Cyr ROO 6.00 1.80
110 Reed Johnson ROO 8.00 2.40
111 Ryan Jamison ROO 6.00 1.80
112 Antonio Perez ROO 6.00 1.80
113 Satoru Komiyama ROO 6.00 1.80
114 Austin Kearns ROO 6.00 1.80
115 Juan Pena ROO 6.00 1.80
116 Orlando Hudson ROO 6.00 1.80
117 Kazuhisa Ishii ROO 12.00 3.60
118 Erik Bedard ROO 6.00 1.80
119 Luis Ugueto ROO 6.00 1.80
120 Ben Howard ROO 6.00 1.80
121 Morgan Ensberg ROO 6.00 1.80
122 Doug Devore ROO 6.00 1.80
123 Josh Phelps ROO 6.00 1.80
124 Angel Berroa ROO 6.00 1.80
125 Ed Rogers ROO 6.00 1.80
126 Takahito Nomura ROO 6.00 1.80
127 John Ennis ROO 6.00 1.80
128 Bill Hall ROO 6.00 1.80
129 Dewon Brazelton ROO 6.00 1.80
130 Hank Blalock ROO 8.00 2.40
131 So Taguchi ROO 8.00 2.40
132 Jorge De La Rosa ROO 6.00 1.80
133 Matt Thornton ROO 6.00 1.80
134 Brandon Backe ROO 6.00 1.80
135 Jeff Deardorff ROO 6.00 1.80
136 Steve Smyth ROO 6.00 1.80
137 Anderson Machado ROO 6.00 1.80
138 John Buck ROO 6.00 1.80
139 Mark Prior ROO 15.00 4.50
140 Sean Burroughs ROO 6.00 1.80
141 Alex Herrera ROO 6.00 1.80
142 Francis Beltran ROO 6.00 1.80
143 Jason Romano ROO 6.00 1.80
144 Michael Cuddyer ROO 6.00 1.80
145 Steve Bechler ROO 6.00 1.80
146 Alfredo Amezaga ROO 6.00 1.80
147 Ryan Ludwick ROO 6.00 1.80
148 Martin Vargas ROO 6.00 1.80
149 Allan Simpson ROO 6.00 1.80
150 Mark Teixeira ROO 8.00 2.40
201 Oliver Perez ROO 8.00 2.40
202 Aaron Cook ROO 6.00 1.80
203 Eric Junge ROO 6.00 1.80
204 Freddy Sanchez ROO 6.00 1.80
205 Cliff Lee ROO 8.00 2.40
206 Runelvys Hernandez ROO 6.00 1.80
207 Chone Figgins ROO 6.00 1.80
208 Rodrigo Rosario ROO 6.00 1.80
209 Kevin Cash ROO 6.00 1.80
210 Josh Bard ROO 6.00 1.80
211 Felix Escalona ROO 6.00 1.80
212 Jeriome Robertson ROO 6.00 1.80
213 Jason Simontacchi ROO 6.00 1.80
214 Shane Nance ROO 6.00 1.80
215 Ben Kozlowski ROO 6.00 1.80
216 Brian Tallet ROO 8.00 2.40
217 Earl Snyder ROO 6.00 1.80
218 Andy Pratt ROO 6.00 1.80
219 Trey Hodges ROO 6.00 1.80
220 Kirk Saarloos ROO 6.00 1.80
221 Rene Reyes ROO 6.00 1.80
222 Joe Borchard ROO 6.00 1.80
223 Wilson Valdez ROO 6.00 1.80
224 Miguel Asencio ROO 6.00 1.80
225 Chris Snelling ROO 10.00 3.00

2002 Donruss Classics Classic Combos

Randomly inserted in packs, each of these 20 cards features two game-used pieces on them. Since each card is printed to a stated print run of 25 or less (which we have notated in our checklist), no pricing is provided for these cards.

Nm-Mt Ex-Mt
1 Eddie Murray Jsy
Cal Ripken Jsy/25
2 George Brett Jsy
Bo Jackson Jsy/25
3 Ted Williams Bat
Jimmie Foxx Bat/25
4 Nolan Ryan Jsy
Steve Carlton Jsy/25
5 Mel Ott Jsy
Babe Ruth Jsy/15
6 Nolan Ryan Jsy
George Brett Jsy/25
7 Babe Ruth Bat
Ty Cobb Bat/15
8 Jackie Robinson Jsy
Duke Snider Jsy/15
9 Nolan Ryan Jsy
George Brett Jsy
Robin Yount Jsy
Orlando Cepeda Jsy/25
10 Rickey Henderson Bat
Ty Cobb Bat/25
11 Ted Williams Jsy
Tony Gwynn Jsy/15
12 Tony Gwynn Bat
Rickey Henderson Bat/25
13 Ty Cobb Bat
Tony Gwynn Bat/25
14 Dave Parker Jsy
Willie Stargell Jsy/25
15 Ted Williams Bat
Ty Cobb Bat/25
16 Jimmie Foxx Bat
Lou Gehrig Bat/15
17 Catfish Hunter Jsy
Reggie Jackson Jsy/25
18 Ted Williams Bat
Ty Cobb Bat
Jimmie Foxx Bat
Lou Gehrig Bat/15
19 Bobby Doerr Jsy
Ted Williams Jsy/15
20 Mike Schmidt Jsy
George Brett Jsy/25

2002 Donruss Classics Classic Singles

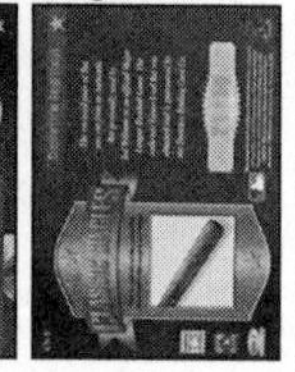

Randomly inserted into packs, these 30 cards feature both a veteran great as well as a game-used memorabilia piece. As these cards have varying print runs, we have notated that information next to the player's name as well as the information as to what memorabilia piece is used.

Nm-Mt Ex-Mt
1 Cal Ripken Jsy/100 80.00 24.00
2 Eddie Murray Jsy/100 25.00 7.50
3 George Brett Jsy/100 40.00 12.00
4 Bo Jackson Jsy/100 25.00 7.50
5 Ted Williams Bat/50 150.00 45.00
6 Jimmie Foxx Sox Bat/50 80.00 24.00
7 Steve Carlton Jsy/50 25.00 7.50
8 Reg Jackson Yanks Jsy/100 25.00 7.50
9 Mel Ott Jsy/50 80.00 24.00
10 Catfish Hunter Jsy/100 25.00 7.50
11 Nolan Ryan Jsy/100 60.00 18.00
12 Rickey Henderson Jsy /100 25.00 7.50
13 Robin Yount Jsy/100 25.00 7.50
14 Orlando Cepeda Jsy/100 15.00 4.50
15 Ty Cobb Bat/50 150.00 45.00
16 Babe Ruth Bat/50 300.00 90.00
17 Dave Parker Jsy/100 15.00 4.50
18 Willie Stargell Jsy/100 25.00 7.50
19 Ernie Banks Bat/100 25.00 7.50
20 Mike Schmidt Jsy/100 50.00 15.00
21 Duke Snider Jsy/50 40.00 12.00
22 Jackie Robinson Jsy/50 100.00 30.00
23 Rickey Henderson Bat/100 25.00 7.50
24 Dale Murphy Bat/100 25.00 7.50
25 Lou Gehrig Bat/50 200.00 60.00
26 Jimmie Foxx A's Bat/50 80.00 24.00
27 Reggie Jackson A's Jsy/100 25.00 7.50
28 Tony Gwynn Bat/100 40.00 12.00
29 Bobby Doerr Jsy/100 15.00 4.50
30 Joe Torre Jsy/100 25.00 7.50

2002 Donruss Classics Legendary Hats

Randomly inserted into packs, this five-card set features not only a retired great but a game-

worn swatch of a cap. Each card was printed to a stated print run of 50 serial numbered sets.

Nm-Mt Ex-Mt
1 Don Mattingly 150.00 45.00
2 George Brett 150.00 45.00
3 Wade Boggs 50.00 15.00
4 Reggie Jackson 50.00 15.00
5 Ryne Sandberg 120.00 36.00

2002 Donruss Classics Legendary Leather

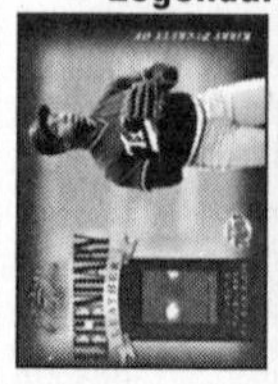

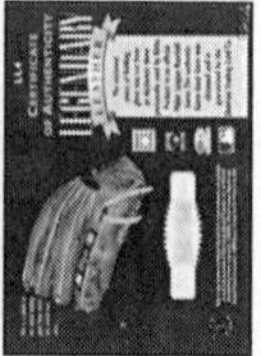

Randomly inserted into packs, this five-card set features not only a retired great but a game-worn swatch of a glove. Each card was printed to a stated print run of 50 serial numbered sets.

Nm-Mt Ex-Mt
1 Don Mattingly Btg Glv 150.00 45.00
2 Wade Boggs Btg Glv 50.00 15.00
3 Tony Gwynn Fld Glv 100.00 30.00
4 Kirby Puckett Fld Glv 80.00 24.00
5 Mike Schmidt Fld Glv 120.00 36.00

2002 Donruss Classics Legendary Lumberjacks

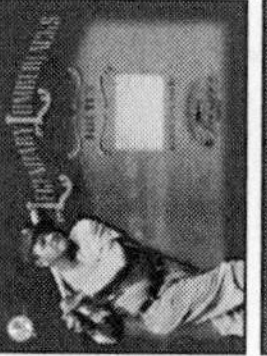

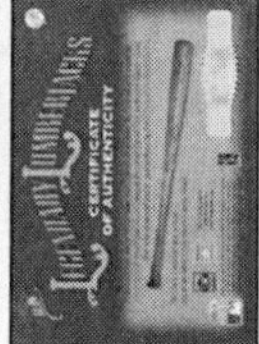

Randomly inserted in packs, this 35 card set features great players of the past along with a game-used bat piece. Since this set was printed to different amounts of cards printed, we have notated the stated print run information next to the player's name.

Nm-Mt Ex-Mt
1 Don Mattingly/500 25.00 7.50
2 George Brett/400 25.00 7.50
3 Stan Musial/100 50.00 15.00
4 Lou Gehrig/50 200.00 60.00
5 Mike Piazza/500 15.00 4.50
6 Mel Ott/50 80.00 24.00
7 Ted Williams/50 150.00 45.00
8 Bo Jackson/500 15.00 4.50
9 Kirby Puckett/500 15.00 4.50
10 Rafael Palmeiro/500 15.00 4.50
11 Andre Dawson/500 10.00 3.00
12 Ozzie Smith/500 15.00 4.50
13 Paul Molitor/500 15.00 4.50
14 Babe Ruth/50 300.00 90.00
15 Carlton Fisk/500 15.00 4.50
16 Rickey Henderson/500 15.00 4.50
17 Gary Carter/500 15.00 4.50
18 Cal Ripken/100 60.00 18.00
19 Eddie Mathews/100 25.00 7.50
20 Luis Aparicio/500 10.00 3.00
21 Al Kaline/100 25.00 7.50
22 Eddie Murray/500 15.00 4.50
23 Yogi Berra/100 25.00 7.50
24 Alex Rodriguez/500 15.00 4.50
25 Tony Gwynn/500 15.00 4.50
26 Roberto Clemente/100 100.00 30.00
27 Mike Schmidt/400 25.00 7.50
28 Reggie Jackson/500 15.00 4.50
29 Ryne Sandberg/500 25.00 7.50
30 Joe Morgan/400 10.00 3.00
31 Joe Torre/500 15.00 4.50
32 Gary Sheffield/500 10.00 3.00
33 Nomar Garciaparra/500 15.00 4.50
34 Jeff Bagwell/500 15.00 4.50
35 Manny Ramirez/500 10.00 3.00

2002 Donruss Classics Legendary Spikes

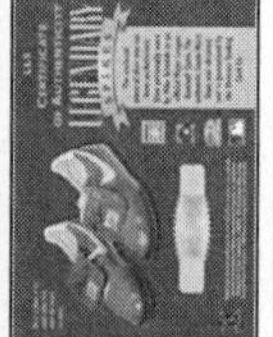

Randomly inserted into packs, this five-card set features not only a retired great but a game-worn piece of a pair of spikes. Each card was printed to a stated print run of 50 serial numbered sets.

Nm-Mt Ex-Mt
1 Don Mattingly 150.00 45.00
2 Eddie Murray 60.00 18.00
3 Paul Molitor 50.00 15.00
4 Harmon Killebrew 60.00 18.00
5 Mike Schmidt 120.00 36.00

2002 Donruss Classics New Millenium Classics

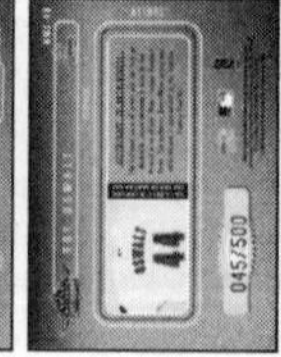

Randomly inserted into packs, these 60 cards feature both an active star as well as a game-used memorabilia piece. As these cards have varying print runs, we have notated that information next to the player's name as well as the information as to what memorabilia piece is used. The Ishii and Taguchi jersey cards were not ready as Donruss went to press and those cards were issued as exchange cards with an deadline of June 1, 2004 to redeem those cards.

Nm-Mt Ex-Mt
*MULTI-COLOR PATCH: 1.25X TO 3X BASIC
1 Curt Schilling Jsy/500 15.00 4.50
2 Vladimir Guerrero Jsy/100 25.00 7.50
3 Jim Thome Jsy/500 15.00 4.50
4 Troy Glaus Jsy/400 15.00 4.50
5 Ivan Rodriguez Jsy/200 20.00 6.00
6 Todd Helton Jsy/400 15.00 4.50
7 Sean Casey Jsy/500 10.00 3.00
8 Scott Rolen Jsy/475 15.00 4.50
9 Ken Griffey Jr. Base/150 15.00 4.50
10 Hideo Nomo Jsy/100 40.00 12.00
11 Tom Glavine Jsy/350 15.00 4.50
12 Pedro Martinez Jsy/100 25.00 7.50
13 Cliff Floyd Jsy/500 10.00 3.00
14 Shawn Green Jsy/125 20.00 6.00
15 Rafael Palmeiro Jsy/250 15.00 4.50
16 Luis Gonzalez Jsy/100 20.00 6.00
17 Lance Berkman Jsy/100 20.00 6.00
18 Frank Thomas Jsy/500 15.00 4.50
19 Randy Johnson Jsy/400 15.00 4.50
20 Moises Alou Jsy/500 10.00 3.00
21 Chipper Jones Jsy/500 15.00 4.50
22 Larry Walker Jsy/300 15.00 4.50
23 Mike Sweeney Jsy/500 10.00 3.00
24 Juan Gonzalez Jsy/300 15.00 4.50
25 Roger Clemens Jsy/100 25.00 7.50
26 Albert Pujols Base/300 15.00 4.50
27 Magglio Ordonez Jsy/500 10.00 3.00
28 Alex Rodriguez Jsy/400 15.00 4.50
29 Jeff Bagwell Jsy/125 25.00 7.50
30 Kazuhiro Sasaki Jsy/500 10.00 3.00
31 Barry Larkin Jsy/300 15.00 4.50
32 Andruw Jones Jsy/350 10.00 3.00
33 Kerry Wood Jsy/200 20.00 6.00
34 Rickey Henderson Jsy/100 25.00 7.50
35 Greg Maddux Jsy/100 25.00 7.50
36 Brian Giles Jsy/400 10.00 3.00
37 Craig Biggio Jsy/100 25.00 7.50
38 Roberto Alomar Jsy/400 15.00 4.50
39 Mike Piazza Jsy/400 15.00 4.50
40 Bernie Williams Jsy/100 25.00 7.50
41 Ichiro Suzuki Ball/150 40.00 12.00
42 Kenny Lofton Jsy/450 10.00 3.00
43 Mark Mulder Jsy/500 10.00 3.00
44 Kazuhisa Ishii Jsy/100 EXCH 25.00 7.50
45 Darin Erstad Jsy/500 10.00 3.00
46 Jose Vidro Jsy/500 10.00 3.00
47 Miguel Tejada Jsy/475 10.00 3.00
48 Roy Oswalt Jsy/500 10.00 3.00
49 So Taguchi Jsy/100 EXCH 25.00 7.50
50 Barry Zito Jsy/500 15.00 4.50
51 Manny Ramirez Jsy/400 10.00 3.00
52 Nomar Garciaparra Jsy/400 15.00 4.50
53 C.C. Sabathia Jsy/500 10.00 3.00
54 Carlos Delgado Jsy/500 10.00 3.00
55 Gary Sheffield Jsy/500 10.00 3.00
56 J.D. Drew Jsy/500 10.00 3.00
57 Barry Bonds Ball/150 40.00 12.00
58 Derek Jeter Ball/150 40.00 12.00
59 Edgar Martinez Jsy/400 15.00 4.50
60 Sammy Sosa Ball/150 25.00 7.50

2002 Donruss Classics Timeless Treasures

Randomly inserted into packs, these 17 cards feature all-time greats along with key pieces of their memorabilia. These cards have different print runs which we have put next to their names. Those cards with a stated print run of 25 or less are not priced due to market scarcity.

Nm-Mt Ex-Mt
1 Ted Williams .406 Avg Jsy/25
2 Ted Williams The Kid Jsy/10
3 Ted Williams Ballgame Jsy/10
4 Ted Williams Splinter Jsy/10
5 Ted Williams Crown Bat/42 150.00 45.00
6 Ted Williams Crown Bat/47 150.00 45.00
7 Ted Williams MVP Bat/46 150.00 45.00
8 Ted Williams MVP Bat/49 150.00 45.00
9 Ted Williams Jsy/9
10 Cal Ripken Iron Man Jsy/98 80.00 24.00
11 Cal Ripken ROY Jsy/82 100.00 30.00
12 Cal Ripken MVP Jsy/83 100.00 30.00

13 Cal Ripken MVP Jsy/91 100.00 30.00
14 Cal Ripken
Lou Gehrig Jsy/25
15 Cal Ripken 2131 Jsy/25
16 Cal Ripken 3000 Hits Jsy/25
17 Cal Ripken Jsy/8

2003 Donruss Classics Samples

Inserted at a stated rate of one per sealed Beckett Baseball Collector Magazine, these cards parallel the basic Donruss Classic cards and can be differentiated by the word "Sample" printed in silver on the back.

Nm-Mt Ex-Mt
*SAMPLES: 1.5X TO 4X BASIC CARDS
ONE PER SEALED BBC MAGAZINE
*GOLD: 1.5X TO 4X BASIC SAMPLES

2003 Donruss Classics

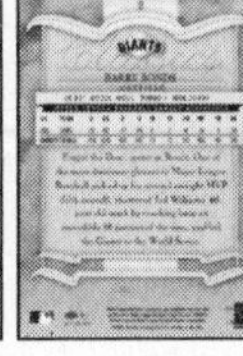

This 211-card set was released in two separate series. The primary Donruss Classics product - containing cards 1-200 from the basic set - was released in April, 2003. This set was issued in seven-card packs with an $6 SRP which were packed 18 to a box and 12 boxes to a case. Cards 201-211 were randomly seeded within packs of DLP Rookies and Traded of which was distributed in December, 2003. The first 100 cards feature active veterans, while cards 101-150 feature retired legends and cards 151-211 feature rookies and leading prospects. Please note that cards 101-200 were issued at a stated rate of one in nine and were issued to a stated print run of 1500 serial numbered sets. Cards 201-211 were serial-numbered to 1000 copies each.

Nm-Mt Ex-Mt
COMP.LO SET w/o SP's (100) 25.00 7.50
COMMON CARD (1-100) .60 .18
COMMON CARD (101-150) 4.00 1.20
COMMON CARD (151-200) 4.00 1.20
COIMMON CARD (201-211) 4.00 1.20
1 Troy Glaus 1.00 .30
2 Barry Bonds 4.00 1.20
3 Miguel Tejada .60 .18
4 Randy Johnson 1.50 .45
5 Eric Hinske .60 .18
6 Barry Zito 1.00 .30
7 Jason Jennings .60 .18
8 Derek Jeter 4.00 1.20
9 Vladimir Guerrero 1.50 .45
10 Corey Patterson .60 .18
11 Manny Ramirez .60 .18
12 Edgar Martinez 1.00 .30
13 Roy Oswalt .60 .18
14 Andruw Jones .60 .18
15 Alex Rodriguez 2.50 .75
16 Mark Mulder .60 .18
17 Kazuhisa Ishii .60 .18
18 Gary Sheffield .60 .18
19 Jay Gibbons .60 .18
20 Roberto Alomar 1.50 .45
21 A.J. Pierzynski .60 .18
22 Eric Chavez .60 .18
23 Roger Clemens 3.00 .90
24 C.C. Sabathia .60 .18
25 Jose Vidro .60 .18
26 Shannon Stewart .60 .18
27 Mark Teixeira 1.00 .30
28 Joe Thurston .60 .18
29 Josh Beckett 1.00 .30
30 Jeff Bagwell 1.00 .30
31 Geronimo Gil .60 .18
32 Curt Schilling 1.00 .30
33 Frank Thomas 1.50 .45
34 Lance Berkman .60 .18
35 Adam Dunn .60 .18
36 Christian Parker .60 .18
37 Jim Thome 1.50 .45
38 Shawn Green .60 .18
39 Drew Henson .60 .18
40 Chipper Jones 1.50 .45
41 Kevin Mench .60 .18
42 Hideo Nomo 1.50 .45
43 Andres Galarraga .60 .18
44 Doug Davis .60 .18
45 Mark Prior 3.00 .90
46 Sean Casey .60 .18
47 Magglio Ordonez .60 .18
48 Tom Glavine 1.00 .30
49 Marlon Byrd .60 .18
50 Albert Pujols 3.00 .90
51 Mark Buehrle .60 .18
52 Aramis Ramirez .60 .18
53 Pat Burrell .60 .18
54 Craig Biggio 1.00 .30
55 Alfonso Soriano 1.00 .30
56 Kerry Wood 1.50 .45
57 Wade Miller .60 .18
58 Hank Blalock 1.00 .30
59 Cliff Floyd .60 .18
60 Jason Giambi 1.50 .45
61 Carlos Beltran .60 .18
62 Brian Roberts .60 .18
63 Paul Lo Duca .60 .18
64 Tim Redding .60 .18
65 Sammy Sosa 2.50 .75
66 Joe Borchard .60 .18
67 Ryan Klesko .60 .18
68 Richie Sexson .60 .18
69 Carlos Lee .60 .18
70 Rickey Henderson 1.50 .45
71 Brian Tallet .60 .18
72 Luis Gonzalez .60 .18
73 Satoru Komiyama .60 .18
74 Tim Hudson .60 .18
75 Ken Griffey Jr. 2.50 .75
76 Adam Johnson .60 .18
77 Bobby Abreu .60 .18
78 Adrian Beltre .60 .18
79 Rafael Palmeiro 1.00 .30
80 Ichiro Suzuki 2.50 .75
81 Kenny Lofton .60 .18
82 Brian Giles .60 .18
83 Barry Larkin 1.50 .45
84 Robert Fick .60 .18
85 Ben Sheets .60 .18
86 Scott Rolen 1.00 .30
87 Nomar Garciaparra 2.50 .75
88 Brandon Phillips .60 .18
89 Ben Kozlowski .60 .18
90 Bernie Williams 1.00 .30
91 Pedro Martinez 1.50 .45
92 Todd Helton 1.00 .30
93 Jermaine Dye .60 .18
94 Carlos Delgado .60 .18
95 Mike Piazza 2.50 .75
96 Junior Spivey .60 .18
97 Torii Hunter .60 .18
98 Mike Sweeney .60 .18
99 Ivan Rodriguez 1.50 .45
100 Greg Maddux 2.50 .75
101 Ernie Banks LGD 5.00 1.50
102 Steve Garvey LGD 4.00 1.20
103 George Brett LGD 10.00 3.00
104 Lou Brock LGD 5.00 1.50
105 Hoyt Wilhelm LGD 4.00 1.20
106 Steve Carlton LGD 4.00 1.20
107 Joe Torre LGD 5.00 1.50
108 Dennis Eckersley LGD 4.00 1.20
109 Reggie Jackson LGD 5.00 1.50
110 Al Kaline LGD 5.00 1.50
111 Harold Reynolds LGD 4.00 1.20
112 Don Mattingly LGD 10.00 3.00
113 Tony Gwynn LGD 5.00 1.50
114 Willie McCovey LGD 4.00 1.20
115 Joe Morgan LGD 4.00 1.20
116 Stan Musial LGD 6.00 1.80
117 Jim Palmer LGD 4.00 1.20
118 Brooks Robinson LGD 5.00 1.50
119 Don Sutton LGD 4.00 1.20
120 Nolan Ryan LGD 10.00 3.00
121 Mike Schmidt LGD 8.00 2.40
122 Tom Seaver LGD 5.00 1.50
123 Cal Ripken LGD 12.00 3.60
124 Robin Yount LGD 6.00 1.80
125 Bob Feller LGD 5.00 1.50
126 Joe Carter LGD 4.00 1.20
127 Jack Morris LGD 4.00 1.20
128 Luis Aparicio LGD 4.00 1.20
129 Bobby Doerr LGD 4.00 1.20
130 Dave Parker LGD 4.00 1.20
131 Yogi Berra LGD 5.00 1.50
132 Will Clark LGD 5.00 1.50
133 Fred Lynn LGD 4.00 1.20
134 Andre Dawson LGD 4.00 1.20
135 Duke Snider LGD 5.00 1.50
136 Orlando Cepeda LGD 4.00 1.20
137 Billy Williams LGD 4.00 1.20
138 Dale Murphy LGD 5.00 1.50
139 Harmon Killebrew LGD 5.00 1.50
140 Kirby Puckett LGD 5.00 1.50
141 Carlton Fisk LGD 5.00 1.50
142 Eric Davis LGD 4.00 1.20
143 Alan Trammell LGD 5.00 1.50
144 Paul Molitor LGD 5.00 1.50
145 Jose Canseco LGD 5.00 1.50
146 Ozzie Smith LGD 6.00 1.80
147 Ralph Kiner LGD 4.00 1.20
148 Dwight Gooden LGD 5.00 1.50
149 Phil Rizzuto LGD 5.00 1.50
150 Lenny Dykstra LGD 4.00 1.20
151 Adam LaRoche ROO 5.00 1.50
152 Tim Hummel ROO 4.00 1.20
153 Matt Kata ROO RC 5.00 1.50
154 Jeff Baker ROO 4.00 1.20
155 Josh Stewart ROO RC 4.00 1.20
156 Marshall McDougall ROO 4.00 1.20
157 Jhonny Peralta ROO RC 4.00 1.20
158 Mike Nicolas ROO RC 4.00 1.20
159 Jeremy Guthrie ROO 4.00 1.20
160 Craig Brazell ROO RC 5.00 1.50
161 Joe Valentine ROO RC 4.00 1.20
162 Buddy Hernandez ROO RC 4.00 1.20
163 Freddy Sanchez ROO 4.00 1.20
164 Shane Victorino ROO RC 4.00 1.20
165 Corwin Malone ROO 4.00 1.20
166 Jason Dubois ROO 4.00 1.20
167 Josh Wilson ROO 4.00 1.20
168 Tim Olson ROO RC 5.00 1.50
169 Cliff Bartosh ROO 4.00 1.20
170 Michael Hessman ROO RC 4.00 1.20
171 Ryan Church ROO 4.00 1.20
172 Garrett Atkins ROO 4.00 1.20
173 Jose Morban ROO 4.00 1.20
174 Ryan Cameron ROO RC 4.00 1.20
175 Todd Wellemeyer ROO RC 5.00 1.50
176 Travis Chapman ROO 4.00 1.20
177 Jason Anderson ROO 4.00 1.20
178 Adam Morrissey ROO 4.00 1.20
179 Jose Contreras ROO RC 6.00 1.80
180 Nic Jackson ROO 4.00 1.20
181 Rob Hammock ROO RC 5.00 1.50
182 Carlos Rivera ROO 4.00 1.20
183 Vinny Chulk ROO 4.00 1.20
184 Pete LaForest ROO RC 5.00 1.50
185 Jon Leicester ROO RC 4.00 1.20
186 Terrmel Sledge ROO RC 5.00 1.50
187 Jose Castillo ROO 4.00 1.20
188 Gerald Laird ROO 4.00 1.20
189 Nook Logan ROO RC 4.00 1.20
190 Clint Barmes ROO RC 5.00 1.50
191 Jesus Medrano ROO 4.00 1.20
192 Henri Stanley ROO 4.00 1.20
193 Hideki Matsui ROO RC 15.00 4.50
194 Walter Young ROO 4.00 1.20
195 Jon Adkins ROO 4.00 1.20
196 Tommy Whiteman ROO 4.00 1.20
197 Rob Bowen ROO 4.00 1.20
198 Brandon Webb ROO RC 8.00 2.40
199 Prentice Redman ROO RC 4.00 1.20
200 Jimmy Gobble ROO 4.00 1.20
201 Jeremy Bonderman ROO RC 5.00 1.50
202 Adam Loewen ROO RC 8.00 2.40
203 Chien-Ming Wang ROO RC 6.00 1.80
204 Hong-Chih Kuo ROO RC 5.00 1.50
205 Ryan Wagner ROO RC 5.00 1.50
206 Dan Haren ROO RC 5.00 1.50
207 Dontrelle Willis ROO 5.00 1.50
208 Rickie Weeks ROO RC 15.00 4.50
209 Ramon Nivar ROO RC 5.00 1.50
210 Chad Gaudin ROO RC 4.00 1.20
211 Delmon Young ROO RC 15.00 4.50

2003 Donruss Classics Significant Signatures

Randomly inserted into packs, this is an almost complete parallel to the basic set. Please note, cards 201-211 were randomly inserted within packs of DLP Rookies and Traded. Each of the these cards feature an authentic "sticker" autograph of the featured player on them. Please note that these players signed a different amount of cards ranging between 5-500 copies per and that information is next to the player's name in our checklist. Please note that if the print run is 25 or fewer, no pricing is provided due to market scarcity. Also please note that Hoyt Wilhelm, since he had signed stickers, is able to have signed cards in this set despite having passed on the previous year.

Nm-Mt Ex-Mt
1 Troy Glaus/10
3 Miguel Tejada/5
5 Eric Hinske/250 10.00 3.00
6 Barry Zito/25
7 Jason Jennings/250 10.00 3.00
9 Vladimir Guerrero/5
10 Corey Patterson/100 25.00 7.50
11 Manny Ramirez/5
12 Edgar Martinez/20
13 Roy Oswalt/100 25.00 7.50
14 Andruw Jones/10
15 Alex Rodriguez/5
16 Mark Mulder/100 40.00 12.00
17 Kazuhisa Ishii/5
18 Gary Sheffield/5
19 Jay Gibbons/250 15.00 4.50
20 Roberto Alomar/5
21 A.J. Pierzynski/75 25.00 7.50
22 Eric Chavez/20
23 Roger Clemens/5
24 C.C. Sabathia/5
25 Jose Vidro/75 25.00 7.50
26 Shannon Stewart/25
27 Mark Teixeira/50 40.00 12.00
29 Josh Beckett/5
31 Geronimo Gil/50 15.00 4.50
32 Curt Schilling/5
33 Frank Thomas/5
34 Lance Berkman/5
35 Adam Dunn/100 40.00 12.00
36 Christian Parker/250 10.00 3.00
37 Jim Thome/5
38 Shawn Green/5
39 Drew Henson/100 40.00 12.00
40 Chipper Jones/5
41 Kevin Mench/250 10.00 3.00
43 Andres Galarraga/5
44 Doug Davis/15
45 Mark Prior/50 120.00 36.00
46 Sean Casey/5
47 Magglio Ordonez/5
48 Tom Glavine/10
49 Marlon Byrd/10
50 Albert Pujols/10
51 Mark Buehrle/25
52 Aramis Ramirez/10
53 Pat Burrell/10
54 Craig Biggio/5
55 Alfonso Soriano/5
56 Kerry Wood/15
57 Wade Miller/200 10.00 3.00
58 Hank Blalock/50 40.00 12.00
59 Cliff Floyd/20
61 Carlos Beltran/20
62 Brian Roberts/250 10.00 3.00
63 Paul Lo Duca/100 25.00 7.50
64 Tim Redding/250 10.00 3.00
66 Joe Borchard/100 25.00 7.50
67 Ryan Klesko/20
68 Richie Sexson/20
69 Carlos Lee/25
70 Rickey Henderson/5
71 Brian Tallet/25
72 Luis Gonzalez/5
73 Satoru Komiyama/124 25.00 7.50
74 Tim Hudson/20
76 Adam Johnson/200 10.00 3.00
77 Bobby Abreu/10
78 Adrian Beltre/10
79 Rafael Palmeiro/5
81 Kenny Lofton/5
82 Brian Giles/25
83 Barry Larkin/5
84 Robert Fick/50 25.00 7.50
85 Ben Sheets/20
86 Scott Rolen/5
88 Brandon Phillips/250 10.00 3.00
89 Ben Kozlowski/150 10.00 3.00
90 Bernie Williams/5
91 Pedro Martinez/5
92 Todd Helton/5
93 Jermaine Dye/100 25.00 7.50
96 Junior Spivey/100 15.00 4.50
97 Torii Hunter/50 25.00 7.50
98 Mike Sweeney/25
99 Ivan Rodriguez/5
100 Greg Maddux/5
101 Ernie Banks LGD/5
102 Steve Garvey LGD/100 25.00 7.50
103 George Brett LGD/5
104 Lou Brock LGD/20
105 Hoyt Wilhelm LGD/25
106 Steve Carlton LGD/20
107 Joe Torre LGD/5
108 Dennis Eckersley LGD/50 40.00 12.00
109 Reggie Jackson LGD/5
110 Al Kaline LGD/20
111 Harold Reynolds LGD/50 40.00 12.00
112 Don Mattingly LGD/15
113 Tony Gwynn LGD/5
114 Willie McCovey LGD/5
115 Joe Morgan LGD/5
116 Stan Musial LGD/5
117 Jim Palmer LGD/20
118 Brooks Robinson LGD/20

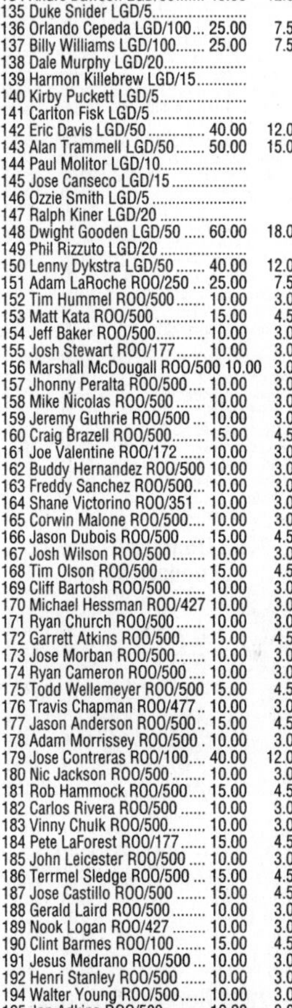

119 Don Sutton LGD/100 25.00 7.50
120 Nolan Ryan LGD/50 200.00 60.00
121 Mike Schmidt LGD/15
122 Tom Seaver LGD/5
123 Cal Ripken LGD/50 250.00 75.00
124 Robin Yount LGD/5
125 Bob Feller LGD/25
126 Joe Carter LGD/100 25.00 7.50
127 Jack Morris LGD/100 25.00 7.50
128 Luis Aparicio LGD/50 40.00 12.00
129 Bobby Doerr LGD/25
130 Dave Parker LGD/10
131 Yogi Berra LGD/10
132 Will Clark LGD/20
133 Fred Lynn LGD/50 40.00 12.00
134 Andre Dawson LGD/50 40.00 12.00
135 Duke Snider LGD/5
136 Orlando Cepeda LGD/100 25.00 7.50
137 Billy Williams LGD/100 25.00 7.50
138 Dale Murphy LGD/20
139 Harmon Killebrew LGD/15
140 Kirby Puckett LGD/5
141 Carlton Fisk LGD/5
142 Eric Davis LGD/50 40.00 12.00
143 Alan Trammell LGD/50 50.00 15.00
144 Paul Molitor LGD/10
145 Jose Canseco LGD/15
146 Ozzie Smith LGD/5
147 Ralph Kiner LGD/20
148 Dwight Gooden LGD/50 60.00 18.00
149 Phil Rizzuto LGD/20
150 Lenny Dykstra LGD/50 40.00 12.00
151 Adam LaRoche ROO/250 25.00 7.50
152 Tim Hummel ROO/500 10.00 3.00
153 Matt Kata ROO/500 15.00 4.50
154 Jeff Baker ROO/500 10.00 3.00
155 Josh Stewart ROO/177 10.00 3.00
156 Marshall McDougall ROO/500 10.00 3.00
157 Jhonny Peralta ROO/500 10.00 3.00
158 Mike Nicolas ROO/500 10.00 3.00
159 Jeremy Guthrie ROO/500 10.00 3.00
160 Craig Brazell ROO/500 15.00 4.50
161 Joe Valentine ROO/172 10.00 3.00
162 Buddy Hernandez ROO/500 10.00 3.00
163 Freddy Sanchez ROO/500 10.00 3.00
164 Shane Victorino ROO/351 10.00 3.00
165 Corwin Malone ROO/500 10.00 3.00
166 Jason Dubois ROO/500 15.00 4.50
167 Josh Wilson ROO/500 10.00 3.00
168 Tim Olson ROO/500 15.00 4.50
169 Cliff Bartosh ROO/500 10.00 3.00
170 Michael Hessman ROO/427 10.00 3.00
171 Ryan Church ROO/500 10.00 3.00
172 Garrett Atkins ROO/500 15.00 4.50
173 Jose Morban ROO/500 10.00 3.00
174 Ryan Cameron ROO/500 10.00 3.00
175 Todd Wellemeyer ROO/500 15.00 4.50
176 Travis Chapman ROO/477 10.00 3.00
177 Jason Anderson ROO/500 15.00 4.50
178 Adam Morrissey ROO/500 10.00 3.00
179 Jose Contreras ROO/100 40.00 12.00
180 Nic Jackson ROO/500 10.00 3.00
181 Rob Hammock ROO/500 15.00 4.50
182 Carlos Rivera ROO/500 10.00 3.00
183 Vinny Chulk ROO/500 10.00 3.00
184 Pete LaForest ROO/177 15.00 4.50
185 John Leicester ROO/500 10.00 3.00
186 Terrmel Sledge ROO/500 15.00 4.50
187 Jose Castillo ROO/500 15.00 4.50
188 Gerald Laird ROO/500 10.00 3.00
189 Nook Logan ROO/427 10.00 3.00
190 Clint Barmes ROO/100 15.00 4.50
191 Jesus Medrano ROO/500 10.00 3.00
192 Henri Stanley ROO/500 10.00 3.00
194 Walter Young ROO/500 10.00 3.00
195 Jon Adkins ROO/500 10.00 3.00
196 Tommy Whiteman ROO/500 10.00 3.00
197 Rob Bowen ROO/500 10.00 3.00
198 Brandon Webb ROO/500 30.00 9.00
199 Prentice Redman ROO/127 10.00 3.00
200 Jimmy Gobble ROO/500 15.00 4.50
201 Jeremy Bonderman ROO/100 20.00 6.00
202 Adam Loewen ROO/100 40.00 12.00
203 Chien-Ming Wang ROO/50 60.00 18.00
204 Hong-Chih Kuo ROO/25
205 Ryan Wagner ROO/100 25.00 7.50
206 Dan Haren ROO/100 20.00 6.00
207 Dontrelle Willis ROO/25
208 Rickie Weeks ROO/10
209 Ramon Nivar ROO/100 20.00 6.00
210 Chad Gaudin ROO/25
211 Delmon Young ROO/25

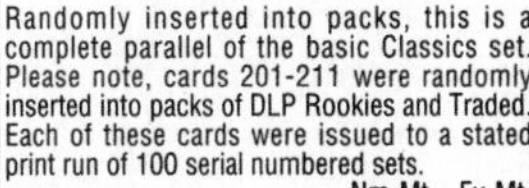

2003 Donruss Classics Timeless Tributes

Randomly inserted into packs, this is a complete parallel of the basic Classics set. Please note, cards 201-211 were randomly inserted into packs of DLP Rookies and Traded. Each of these cards were issued to a stated print run of 100 serial numbered sets.

Nm-Mt Ex-Mt
*TRIBUTE 1-100: 2.5X TO 6X BASIC
*TRIB.101-150: 1.25X TO 3X BASIC
*TRIBUTE 151-200: .6X TO 1.5X BASIC
*TRIBUTE 201-211: .6X TO 1.5X BASIC

2003 Donruss Classics Classic Combos

Randomly inserted in packs, this 15 card set features two players along with game-used memorabilia of each player. We have noted the

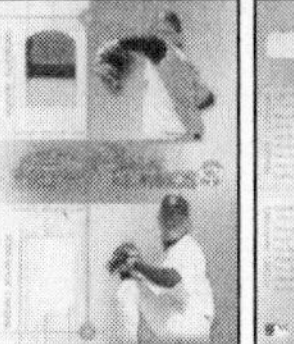

print run information next to the player's name in our checklist. Please note that if a card has a stated print run of 25 or fewer we have not priced the card due to market scarcity.

Nm-Mt Ex-Mt
1 Babe Ruth Jsy 800.00 240.00
Lou Gehrig Jsy/50
2 Jackie Robinson Jsy 100.00 30.00
Pee Wee Reese Jsy/50
3 Bobby Doerr Jsy
Fred Lynn Jsy/25
4 Honus Wagner Seat 200.00 60.00
Roberto Clemente Jsy/50
5 Kirby Puckett Jsy
Torri Hunter Jsy/25
6 Ryne Sandberg Jsy
Sammy Sosa Jsy/25
7 Hideo Nomo Jsy
Kazuhisa Ishii Jsy/25
8 Mike Schmidt Jsy
Steve Carlton Jsy/25
9 Paul Molitor Jsy
Robin Yount Jsy/25
10 Duke Snider Jsy
Mike Piazza Jsy/25
11 Al Kaline Jsy
Ty Cobb Bat/25
12 Don Mattingly Jsy
Jason Giambi Jsy/25
13 Ozzie Smith Jsy
Stan Musial Jsy/25
14 Pedro Martinez Jsy
Roger Clemens Jsy/25
15 Thurman Munson Jsy
Yogi Berra Jsy/25

2003 Donruss Classics Classic Singles

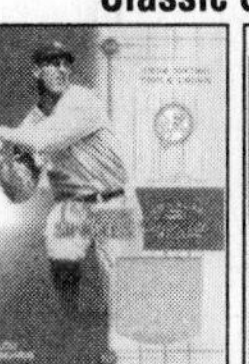
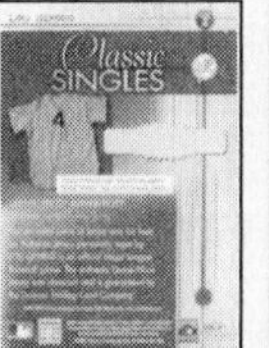

Randomly inserted into packs, this 30-card set features a mix of active and retired players along with a memorabilia piece about that player. We have noted the stated print run information next to the player's name in our checklist and if a card was issued to a stated print run of 25 or fewer, there is no pricing due to market scarcity.

Nm-Mt Ex-Mt
1 Babe Ruth Jsy/100 350.00 105.00
2 Lou Gehrig Jsy/80 250.00 75.00
3 Jackie Robinson Jsy/80 100.00 30.00
4 Pee Wee Reese Jsy/25
5 Bobby Doerr Jsy/100 20.00 6.00
6 Fred Lynn Jsy/100 20.00 6.00
7 Honus Wagner Seat/100 50.00 15.00
8 Roberto Clemente Jsy/80 120.00 36.00
9 Kirby Puckett Jsy/100 40.00 12.00
10 Torii Hunter Jsy/100 15.00 4.50
11 Sammy Sosa Jsy/100 25.00 7.50
12 Ryne Sandberg Jsy/100 60.00 18.00
13 Hideo Nomo Jsy/50 120.00 36.00
14 Kazuhisa Ishii Jsy/50 25.00 7.50
15 Mike Schmidt Jsy/100 60.00 18.00
16 Steve Carlton Jsy/100 20.00 6.00
17 Robin Yount Jsy/100 40.00 12.00
18 Paul Molitor Jsy/100 25.00 7.50
19 Mike Piazza Jsy/100 25.00 7.50
20 Duke Snider Jsy/50 40.00 12.00
21 Al Kaline Jsy/50 60.00 18.00
22 Ty Cobb Bat/25
23 Don Mattingly Jsy/100 60.00 18.00
24 Jason Giambi Jsy/100 25.00 7.50
25 Stan Musial Jsy/25
26 Ozzie Smith Jsy/100 40.00 12.00
27 Roger Clemens Jsy/100 30.00 9.00
28 Pedro Martinez Jsy/100 25.00 7.50
29 Thurman Munson Jsy/50 60.00 18.00
30 Yogi Berra Jsy/25

2003 Donruss Classics Dress Code

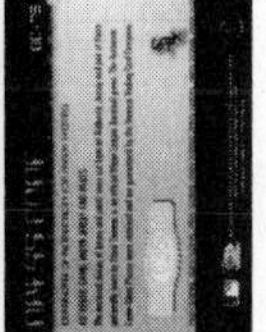

Randomly inserted into pack, this 75-card set features anywhere from one to four swatches of game-worn/used materials. Each card was issued to different quantities and we have notated that information next to the card in our checklist.

Nm-Mt Ex-Mt
1 Roger Clemens Yanks Jsy/500 15.00 4.50
2 Miguel Tejada Bat-Hat-Jsy/250 20.00 6.00
3 Vladimir Guerrero Jsy/425 10.00 3.00

4 Kazuhisa Ishii Jsy/250 10.00 3.00
5 Chipper Jones Jsy/425 10.00 3.00
6 Troy Glaus Jsy/425 10.00 3.00
7 Rafael Palmeiro Jsy/425 10.00 3.00
8 R.Henderson R.Sox Jsy/250 20.00 6.00
9 Pedro Martinez Jsy/425 10.00 3.00
10 Andruw Jones Jsy/425 8.00 2.40
11 Nomar Garciaparra Jsy/500 15.00 4.50
12 Carlos Delgado Jsy/500 8.00 2.40
13 R.Hend Padres Hat-Jsy/250 30.00 9.00
14 Kerry Wood Hat-Jsy/250 30.00 9.00
15 Lance Berkman Hat-Jsy/50 30.00 9.00
16 Tony Gwynn 80.00 24.00
Hat-Jsy-Pants-Shoe/100
17 Mark Mulder Jsy/425 8.00 2.40
18 Jim Thome Jsy/500 10.00 3.00
19 Mike Piazza Jsy/500 15.00 4.50
20 Mike Mussina Jsy/500 10.00 3.00
21 Luis Gonzalez Jsy/500 8.00 2.40
22 Ryan Klesko Jsy/500 8.00 2.40
23 Richie Sexson Jsy/500 8.00 2.40
24 Curt Schilling Jsy/200 15.00 4.50
25 Alex Rodriguez Rgr Jsy/500 15.00 4.50
26 Bernie Williams Jsy/425 10.00 3.00
27 Cal Ripken Jsy/500 40.00 12.00
28 C.C. Sabathia Jsy/500 8.00 2.40
29 Mike Piazza Bat-Jsy/200 40.00 12.00
30 R.Hend Mets Hat-Jsy/250 30.00 9.00
31 Torii Hunter Jsy/425 8.00 2.40
32 Mark Teixeira Jsy/425 10.00 3.00
33 Dale Murphy Bat-Jsy/300 30.00 9.00
34 Todd Helton Jsy/425 10.00 3.00
35 Eric Chavez Jsy/425 8.00 2.40
36 Vernon Wells Jsy/425 8.00 2.40
37 Jeff Bagwell Hat-Jsy/100 30.00 9.00
38 Nick Johnson Jsy/425 8.00 2.40
39 Tim Hudson Hat-Jsy/250 20.00 6.00
40 Shawn Green Jsy/425 8.00 2.40
41 Mark Buehrle Jsy/500 8.00 2.40
42 Garret Anderson Jsy/100 15.00 4.50
43 Alex Rodriguez M's Jsy/500 15.00 4.50
44 Jason Giambi Jsy/500 10.00 3.00
45 Carlos Beltran Jsy/500 8.00 2.40
46 Adam Dunn Hat-Jsy/100 25.00 7.50
47 Jorge Posada Jsy/425 10.00 3.00
48 Roy Oswalt Hat-Jsy/200 20.00 6.00
49 Rich Aurilia Jsy/500 8.00 2.40
50 Jason Jennings 20.00 6.00
Bat-Hat-Jsy-Shoe/250
51 Mark Prior 80.00 24.00
Fld Glv-Hat-Jsy-Shoe/250
52 Jim Edmonds Jsy/500 8.00 2.40
53 Fred McGriff Jsy/500 10.00 3.00
54 A.Soriano Jsy-Shoe/100 20.00 6.00
55 Jeff Kent Jsy/425 8.00 2.40
56 Hideo Nomo R.Sox Jsy/200 40.00 12.00
57 Manny Ramirez Jsy/425 8.00 2.40
58 Jose Canseco Bat-Jsy/350 30.00 9.00
59 Magglio Ordonez Jsy/500 8.00 2.40
60 Alan Trammell Bat-Jsy/250 20.00 6.00
61 Bobby Abreu Jsy/500 8.00 2.40
62 Rickey Henderson 30.00 9.00
A's Hat-Jsy/200
63 Josh Beckett Jsy/500 10.00 3.00
64 Barry Larkin Jsy/500 10.00 3.00
65 Randy Johnson Jsy/200 20.00 6.00
66 Juan Gonzalez Jsy/500 10.00 3.00
67 Barry Zito Hat-Jsy/125 30.00 9.00
68 Roger Clemens R.Sox Jsy/500 15.00 4.50
69 R.Henderson M's Hat-Jsy/100 40.00 12.00
70 Hideo Nomo Mets Jsy/100 60.00 18.00
71 Paul Konerko Jsy/400 8.00 2.40
72 Pat Burrell Jsy/100 15.00 4.50
73 Frank Thomas Jsy-Pants/500 30.00 9.00
74 Sammy Sosa Jsy/500 15.00 4.50
75 Greg Maddux Btg Glv-Jsy/50 80.00 24.00

2003 Donruss Classics Legendary Hats

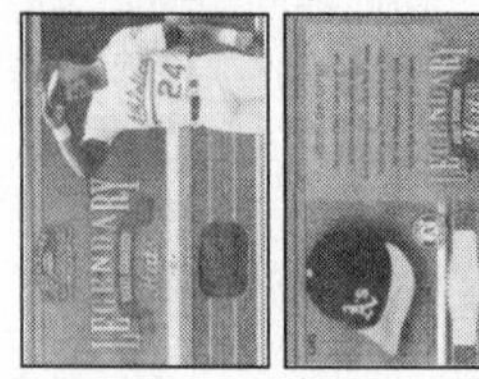

Randomly inserted in packs, this five-card set features a game-worn hat swatch of the featured player. The Roberto Clemente card was issued to a stated print run of 80 serial numbered sets.

	Nm-Mt	Ex-Mt
1 Roberto Clemente/80	100.00	30.00
2 Kirby Puckett	60.00	18.00
3 Mike Schmidt	120.00	36.00
4 Tony Gwynn	100.00	30.00
5 Rickey Henderson	60.00	18.00

2003 Donruss Classics Legendary Leather

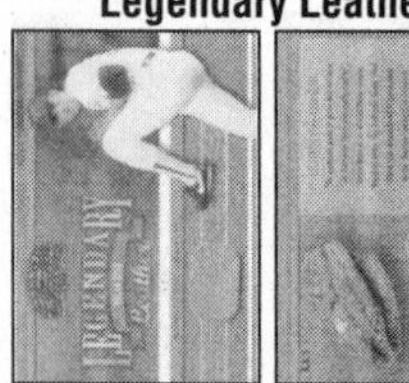

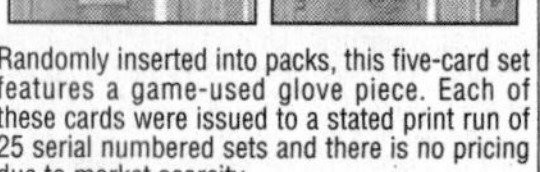

Randomly inserted into packs, this five-card set features a game-used glove piece. Each of these cards were issued to a stated print run of 25 serial numbered sets and there is no pricing due to market scarcity.

	Nm-Mt	Ex-Mt
1 Nolan Ryan Fld Glv/80	120.00	36.00
2 Jimmie Foxx Fld Glv		
3 Steve Carlton Fld Glv		
4 Don Mattingly Btg Glv		
5 Mike Schmidt Btg Glv		

2003 Donruss Classics Legendary Lumberjacks

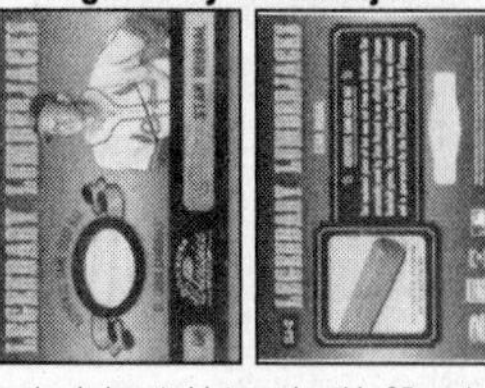

Randomly inserted into packs, this 35-card set feature retired players along with a game-used bat swatch. These cards were issued to different stated print runs and we have notated that information next to their name in our checklist. Please note that for cards with a stated print run of 25 or fewer, there is no pricing due to market scarcity.

	Nm-Mt	Ex-Mt
1 Babe Ruth/100	200.00	60.00
2 Lou Gehrig/80	150.00	45.00
3 George Brett/250	30.00	9.00
4 Duke Snider/250	25.00	7.50
5 Roberto Clemente/25		
6 Ryne Sandberg/400	30.00	9.00
7 Robin Yount/300	20.00	6.00
8 Harmon Killebrew/250	25.00	7.50
9 Al Kaline/250	25.00	7.50
10 Eddie Mathews/225	25.00	7.50
11 Brooks Robinson/400	20.00	6.00
12 Stan Musial/11		
13 Kirby Puckett/375	20.00	6.00
14 Jose Canseco/400	20.00	6.00
15 Nellie Fox/325	20.00	6.00
16 Don Mattingly/400	40.00	12.00
17 Joe Torre/250	15.00	4.50
18 Cal Ripken/250	50.00	15.00
19 Richie Ashburn/250	25.00	7.50
20 Mike Schmidt/250	30.00	9.00
21 Dale Murphy/250	25.00	7.50
22 Thurman Munson/400	20.00	6.00
23 Tony Gwynn/400	20.00	6.00
24 Orlando Cepeda/225	15.00	4.50
25 Ty Cobb/25		
26 Paul Molitor/325	20.00	6.00
27 Ralph Kiner/200	15.00	4.50
28 Frank Robinson/225	25.00	7.50
29 Yogi Berra/50	60.00	18.00
30 Reggie Jackson/375	20.00	6.00
31 Rod Carew/325	20.00	6.00
32 Carlton Fisk/325	20.00	6.00
33 Rogers Hornsby/50	80.00	24.00
34 Mel Ott/125	40.00	12.00
35 Jimmie Foxx/50	80.00	24.00

2003 Donruss Classics Legendary Spikes

Randomly inserted into packs, this five-card set featureds game-used spike pieces of the featured players. These cards were issued to a stated print run of 50 serial numbered sets.

	Nm-Mt	Ex-Mt
1 Kirby Puckett	60.00	18.00
2 Tony Gwynn	100.00	30.00
3 Don Mattingly	150.00	45.00
4 Frank Robinson	50.00	15.00
5 Gary Carter	50.00	15.00

2003 Donruss Classics Legends of the Fall

Randomly inserted into packs, this 10 card set featured players who were stars of at least one World Series they played in. Each of these cards were issued to a stated print run of 2500 serial numbered sets.

	Nm-Mt	Ex-Mt
1 Reggie Jackson	4.00	1.20
2 Duke Snider	4.00	1.20
3 Roberto Clemente	12.00	3.60
4 Mel Ott	5.00	1.50
5 Yogi Berra	5.00	1.50
6 Jackie Robinson	6.00	1.80
7 Enos Slaughter	4.00	1.20
8 Willie Stargell	4.00	1.20
9 Bobby Doerr	4.00	1.20
10 Thurman Munson	6.00	1.80

2003 Donruss Classics Legends of the Fall Fabrics

Randomly inserted into packs, this is a parallel to the Legends of the Fall insert set. Each of these cards features a game-worn/used memorabilia swatch sequentially numbered to varying quantities. Please note that we have put that stated print run information next to the player's name in our checklist and if the print run is 25 or fewer, no pricing is provided due to market scarcity.

	Nm-Mt	Ex-Mt
1 Reggie Jackson/100	25.00	7.50
2 Duke Snider/25		
3 Roberto Clemente/50	150.00	45.00
4 Mel Ott/25		
5 Yogi Berra/15		
6 Jackie Robinson/50	100.00	30.00
7 Enos Slaughter/25		
8 Willie Stargell/100	25.00	7.50
9 Bobby Doerr/100	20.00	6.00
10 Thurman Munson/25		

2003 Donruss Classics Membership

Randomly inserted into packs, this 15-card set feature members of some of the most prestigious stat groups. Each of these cards were issued to a stated print run of 2500 serial numbered sets.

	Nm-Mt	Ex-Mt
1 Babe Ruth	15.00	4.50
2 Steve Carlton	4.00	1.20
3 Honus Wagner	8.00	2.40
4 Warren Spahn	4.00	1.20
5 Eddie Mathews	5.00	1.50
6 Nolan Ryan	12.00	3.60
7 Rogers Hornsby	4.00	1.20
8 Ernie Banks	5.00	1.50
9 Harmon Killebrew	5.00	1.50
10 Tom Seaver	4.00	1.20
11 Jimmie Foxx	5.00	1.50
12 Ty Cobb	8.00	2.40
13 Frank Robinson	4.00	1.20
14 Mel Ott	5.00	1.50
15 Lou Gehrig	10.00	3.00

2003 Donruss Classics Membership VIP Memorabilia

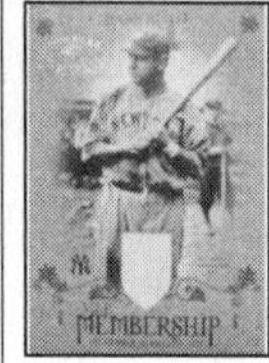

Randomly inserted in packs, this is a parallel to the Membership insert set. Each of these cards feature a game worn/used memorabilia swatch. Each of these cards were issued to a varying sequential numbering and we have put that information next to the player's name in our checklist. Please note that if a card has a print run of 25 or fewer, no pricing is provided due to market scarcity.

	Nm-Mt	Ex-Mt
1 Babe Ruth Bat/29		
2 Steve Carlton Jsy/81	25.00	7.50
3 Honus Wagner Seat/14		
4 Warren Spahn Jsy/61	50.00	15.00
5 Eddie Mathews Bat/67	60.00	18.00
6 Nolan Ryan Jsy/80	100.00	30.00
7 Rogers Hornsby Bat/31		
8 Ernie Banks Jsy/70	60.00	18.00
9 Harmon Killebrew Jsy/71	60.00	18.00
10 Tom Seaver Jsy/81	40.00	12.00
11 Jimmie Foxx Bat/40	80.00	24.00
12 Ty Cobb Bat/21		
13 Frank Robinson Jsy/71	50.00	15.00
14 Mel Ott Jsy/45	80.00	24.00
15 Lou Gehrig Bat/31		

2003 Donruss Classics Timeless Treasures

Randomly inserted into packs, these five cards featured some of the game's most legendary players along with two swatches of game-worn/used material sequentially numbered to varying quantities. Please note that for cards with stated print runs of 25 or fewer, no pricing is provided due to market scarcity.

	Nm-Mt	Ex-Mt
1 Stan Musial Jsy	150.00	45.00
Tony Gwynn Jsy/50		
2 Alex Rodriguez Jsy		
Cal Ripken Jsy/25		
3 Roberto Clemente Jsy	150.00	45.00
Vladimir Guerrero Jsy/50		
4 Ernie Banks Jsy		
Sammy Sosa Jsy/25		
5 Don Mattingly Jsy	150.00	45.00
Jason Giambi Jsy/50		

2003 Donruss Classics Atlantic City National

Collectors who opened a stated number of Donruss Classic packs at the Donruss booth at the Atlantic City National were rewarded with these cards. The fronts of these cards had a special Atlantic City embossed logo while the backs show serial numbering to five.

MINT NRMT

PRINT RUN 5 SERIAL #'d SETS

2004 Donruss Classics

This 213-card set was released in April, 2004. The set was issued in six card packs with an $6 SRP which came 18 packs to a box and 14 boxes to a case. The first 150 cards in this set are active veterans while cards 151-175 and 206-211 featured retired greats and cards number 176-205 feature leading prospects. All those cards were printed to a print run of 1999 serial numbered sets. The set closes with three cards featuring leading players who switched teams in the off-season and those cards were issued at a stated rate of one in 18.

	Nm-Mt	Ex-Mt
COMP.SET w/o SP's (153)	25.00	7.50
COMMON CARD (1-150)	.60	.18
COMMON (151-180/206-210)	4.00	1.20
COMMON CARD (181-205)	4.00	1.20
COMMON CARD (211-213)	1.00	.30
1 Albert Pujols	3.00	.90
2 Derek Jeter	4.00	1.20
3 Hank Blalock	.60	.18
4 Shannon Stewart	.60	.18
5 Jason Giambi	1.50	.45
6 Carlos Lee	.60	.18
7 Trot Nixon	1.00	.30
8 Bret Boone	.60	.18
9 Mark Mulder	.60	.18
10 Mariano Rivera	1.00	.30
11 Scott Podsednik	1.50	.45
12 Jim Edmonds	.60	.18
13 Mike Lowell	.60	.18
14 Robin Ventura	.60	.18
15 Brian Giles	.60	.18
16 Jose Vidro	.60	.18
17 Manny Ramirez	.60	.18
18 Alex Rodriguez Rgr	2.50	.75
19 Carlos Beltran	.60	.18
20 Hideki Matsui	2.50	.75
21 Johan Santana	.60	.18
22 Richie Sexson	.60	.18
23 Chipper Jones	1.50	.45
24 Steve Finley	.60	.18
25 Mark Prior	3.00	.90
26 Alexis Rios	1.00	.30
27 Rafael Palmeiro	1.00	.30
28 Jorge Posada	1.00	.30
29 Barry Zito	1.00	.30
30 Jamie Moyer	.60	.18
31 Preston Wilson	.60	.18
32 Miguel Cabrera	1.50	.45
33 Pedro Martinez	1.50	.45
34 Curt Schilling	1.00	.30
35 Hee Seop Choi	.60	.18
36 Dontrelle Willis	.60	.18
37 Rafael Soriano	.60	.18
38 Richard Fischer	.60	.18
39 Brian Tallet	.60	.18
40 Jose Castillo	.60	.18
41 Wade Miller	.60	.18
42 Jose Contreras	.60	.18
43 Runelvys Hernandez	.60	.18
44 Joe Borchard	.60	.18
45 Kazuhisa Ishii	.60	.18
46 Jose Reyes	1.00	.30
47 Adam Dunn	.60	.18
48 Randy Johnson	1.50	.45
49 Brandon Phillips	.60	.18
50 Scott Rolen	1.00	.30
51 Ken Griffey Jr.	2.50	.75
52 Tom Glavine	1.00	.30
53 Cliff Lee	.60	.18
54 Chien-Ming Wang	.60	.18
55 Roy Oswalt	.60	.18
56 Austin Kearns	.60	.18
57 Jhonny Peralta	.60	.18
58 Greg Maddux Braves	2.50	.75
59 Mark Grace	1.00	.30
60 Jae Weong Seo	.60	.18
61 Nic Jackson	.60	.18
62 Roger Clemens	3.00	.90
63 Jimmy Gobble	.60	.18
64 Travis Hafner	.60	.18
65 Paul Konerko	.60	.18
66 Jerome Williams	.60	.18
67 Ryan Klesko	.60	.18
68 Alexis Gomez	.60	.18
69 Omar Vizquel	.60	.18
70 Zach Day	.60	.18
71 Rickey Henderson	1.50	.45
72 Morgan Ensberg	.60	.18
73 Josh Beckett	1.00	.30
74 Garrett Atkins	.60	.18
75 Sean Casey	.60	.18
76 Julio Franco	.60	.18
77 Lyle Overbay	.60	.18
78 Josh Phelps	.60	.18
79 Juan Gonzalez	1.50	.45
80 Rich Harden	.60	.18
81 Bernie Williams	1.00	.30
82 Torii Hunter	.60	.18
83 Angel Berroa	.60	.18
84 Jody Gerut	.60	.18
85 Roberto Alomar	1.50	.45
86 Byung-Hyun Kim	.60	.18
87 Jay Gibbons	.60	.18
88 Chone Figgins	.60	.18
89 Fred McGriff	1.00	.30
90 Rich Aurilia	.60	.18
91 Xavier Nady	.60	.18
92 Marlon Byrd	.60	.18
93 Mike Piazza	2.50	.75
94 Vladimir Guerrero	1.50	.45
95 Shawn Green	.60	.18
96 Jeff Kent	.60	.18
97 Ivan Rodriguez	1.50	.45
98 Jay Payton	.60	.18
99 Barry Larkin	1.50	.45
100 Mike Sweeney	.60	.18
101 Adrian Beltre	.60	.18
102 Robby Hammock	.60	.18
103 Orlando Hudson	.60	.18
104 Mark Teixeira	.60	.18
105 Hong-Chih Kuo	.60	.18
106 Eric Chavez	.60	.18
107 Nick Johnson	.60	.18
108 Jacque Jones	.60	.18
109 Ken Harvey	.60	.18
110 Aramis Ramirez	.60	.18
111 Victor Martinez	.60	.18
112 Joe Crede	.60	.18
113 Jason Varitek	.60	.18
114 Troy Glaus	1.00	.30
115 Billy Wagner	.60	.18
116 Kerry Wood	1.50	.45
117 Hideo Nomo	1.50	.45
118 Brandon Webb	.60	.18
119 Craig Biggio	1.00	.30
120 Orlando Cabrera	.60	.18
121 Sammy Sosa	2.50	.75
122 Bobby Abreu	.60	.18
123 Andruw Jones	.60	.18
124 Jeff Bagwell	1.00	.30
125 Jim Thome	1.50	.45
126 Javy Lopez	.60	.18
127 Luis Castillo	.60	.18
128 Todd Helton	1.00	.30
129 Roy Halladay	.60	.18
130 Mike Mussina	1.50	.45
131 Eric Byrnes	.60	.18
132 Eric Hinske	.60	.18
133 Nomar Garciaparra	2.50	.75
134 Edgar Martinez	1.00	.30
135 Rocco Baldelli	1.50	.45
136 Miguel Tejada	.60	.18
137 Alfonso Soriano Yanks	1.00	.30
138 Carlos Delgado	.60	.18
139 Rafael Furcal	.60	.18
140 Ichiro Suzuki	2.50	.75
141 Aubrey Huff	.60	.18
142 Garret Anderson	.60	.18
143 Vernon Wells	.60	.18
144 Magglio Ordonez	.60	.18
145 Brett Myers	.60	.18
146 Luis Gonzalez	.60	.18
147 Lance Berkman	.60	.18
148 Frank Thomas	1.50	.45
149 Gary Sheffield	.60	.18
150 Tim Hudson	.60	.18
151 Duke Snider LGD	5.00	1.50
152 Carl Yastrzemski LGD	6.00	1.80
153 Whitey Ford LGD	5.00	1.50
154 Cal Ripken LGD	12.00	3.60
155 Dwight Gooden LGD	5.00	1.50
156 Warren Spahn LGD	5.00	1.50
157 Bob Gibson LGD	5.00	1.50
158 Don Mattingly LGD	10.00	3.00
159 Jack Morris LGD	4.00	1.20
160 Jim Bunning LGD	5.00	1.50
161 Fergie Jenkins LGD	4.00	1.20
162 Brooks Robinson LGD	5.00	1.50
163 George Kell LGD	4.00	1.20
164 Darryl Strawberry LGD	5.00	1.50
165 Robin Roberts LGD	4.00	1.20
166 Monte Irvin LGD	4.00	1.20
167 Ernie Banks LGD	5.00	1.50
168 Wade Boggs LGD	5.00	1.50
169 Gaylord Perry LGD	4.00	1.20
170 Keith Hernandez LGD	5.00	1.50
171 Lou Brock LGD	5.00	1.50
172 Frank Robinson LGD	4.00	1.20
173 Nolan Ryan LGD	10.00	3.00
174 Stan Musial LGD	6.00	1.80
175 Eddie Murray LGD	5.00	1.50
176 Byron Gettis ROO	4.00	1.20
177 Merkin Valdez ROO RC	8.00	2.40
178 Rickie Weeks ROO	5.00	1.50
179 Akinori Otsuka ROO RC	5.00	1.50
180 Brian Bruney ROO	4.00	1.20
181 Freddy Guzman ROO RC	4.00	1.20
182 Brendan Harris ROO	4.00	1.20
183 John Gall ROO RC	4.00	1.20
184 Jason Kubel ROO	4.00	1.20
185 Delmon Young ROO	5.00	1.50
186 Ryan Howard ROO UER	4.00	1.20
Stat headers are for a pitcher		
187 Adam Loewen ROO	4.00	1.20
188 J.D. Durbin ROO	4.00	1.20
189 Dan Haren ROO	4.00	1.20
190 Dustin McGowan ROO	4.00	1.20
191 Chad Gaudin ROO	4.00	1.20
192 Preston Larrison ROO	4.00	1.20
193 Ramon Nivar ROO	4.00	1.20
194 Ronald Belisario ROO RC	4.00	1.20
195 Mike Gosling ROO RC	4.00	1.20
196 Kevin Youkilis ROO	4.00	1.20
197 Ryan Wagner ROO	4.00	1.20
198 Bubba Nelson ROO	4.00	1.20
199 Edwin Jackson ROO	5.00	1.50
200 Chris Burke ROO	4.00	1.20
201 Carlos Hines ROO RC	4.00	1.20

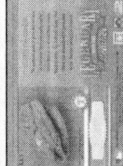

202 Greg Dobbs ROO RC 4.00 1.20
203 Jamie Brown ROO RC 4.00 1.20
204 Dave Crouthers ROO RC 4.00 1.20
205 Ian Snell ROO RC 5.00 1.50
206 Gary Carter LGD 5.00 1.50
207 Dale Murphy LGD 5.00 1.50
208 Ryne Sandberg LGD 8.00 2.40
209 Phil Niekro LGD 4.00 1.20
210 Don Sutton LGD 4.00 1.20
211 Alex Rodriguez Yanks SP 8.00 2.40
212 Alfonso Soriano Rgr SP 1.50 .45
213 Greg Maddux Cubs SP 4.00 1.20

2004 Donruss Classics Significant Signatures Green

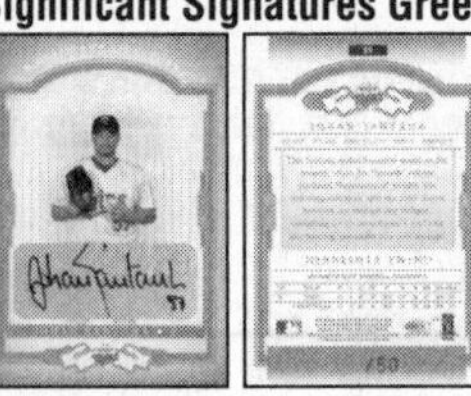

Nm-Mt Ex-Mt
RANDOM INSERTS IN PACKS
PRINT RUNS B/WN 1-100 COPIES PER
NO PRICING ON QTY OF 15 OR LESS.
3 Hank Blalock/25 40.00 12.00
4 Shannon Stewart/50 20.00 6.00
6 Carlos Lee/10
7 Trot Nixon/25 40.00 12.00
9 Mark Mulder/10
10 Mariano Rivera/5
12 Jim Edmonds/10
13 Mike Lowell/25 25.00 7.50
14 Robin Ventura/25 25.00 7.50
16 Jose Vidro/10
17 Manny Ramirez/5
18 Alex Rodriguez Rgr/1
19 Carlos Beltran/25 40.00 12.00
21 Johan Santana/50 30.00 9.00
22 Richie Sexson/5
23 Chipper Jones/1
24 Steve Finley/25 40.00 12.00
25 Mark Prior/5
26 Alexis Rios/100 25.00 7.50
27 Rafael Palmeiro/10
28 Jorge Posada/10
29 Barry Zito/10
30 Jamie Moyer/5
32 Miguel Cabrera/50 50.00 15.00
33 Pedro Martinez/1
34 Curt Schilling/1
36 Dontrelle Willis/25 40.00 12.00
37 Rafael Soriano/100 10.00 3.00
38 Richard Fischer/100 10.00 3.00
39 Brian Tallet/100 10.00 3.00
40 Jose Castillo/100 10.00 3.00
41 Wade Miller/25 25.00 7.50
42 Jose Contreras/10
43 Runelvys Hernandez/20 20.00 6.00
44 Joe Borchard/50 15.00 4.50
47 Adam Dunn/25 40.00 12.00
48 Randy Johnson/1
49 Brandon Phillips/50 15.00 4.50
50 Scott Rolen/10
52 Tom Glavine/5
53 Cliff Lee/50 15.00 4.50
54 Chien-Ming Wang/50 30.00 9.00
55 Roy Oswalt/10
56 Austin Kearns/10
57 Jhonny Peralta/100 10.00 3.00
58 Greg Maddux Braves/1
59 Mark Grace/5
60 Jae Weong Seo/50 30.00 9.00
61 Nic Jackson/100 10.00 3.00
62 Roger Clemens/1
63 Jimmy Gobble/45 15.00 4.50
64 Travis Hafner/50 20.00 6.00
65 Paul Konerko/10
66 Jerome Williams/50 50.00 15.00
67 Ryan Klesko/5
68 Alexis Gomez/50 15.00 4.50
70 Zach Day/50 15.00 4.50
72 Morgan Ensberg/50 20.00 6.00
73 Josh Beckett/5
74 Garrett Atkins/99 10.00 3.00
75 Sean Casey/10
76 Julio Franco/10
77 Lyle Overbay/100 10.00 3.00
78 Josh Phelps/25 20.00 6.00
79 Juan Gonzalez/25 60.00 18.00
80 Rich Harden/50 20.00 6.00
82 Torii Hunter/10
83 Angel Berroa/5
84 Jody Gerut/50 30.00 9.00
85 Roberto Alomar/5
87 Jay Gibbons/50 20.00 6.00
88 Chone Figgins/50 15.00 4.50
89 Fred McGriff/5
90 Rich Aurilia/10
91 Xavier Nady/5
92 Marlon Byrd/10
93 Mike Piazza/1
94 Vladimir Guerrero/5
95 Shawn Green/1
97 Ivan Rodriguez/5
98 Jay Payton/50 15.00 4.50
99 Barry Larkin/25 60.00 18.00
100 Mike Sweeney/1
101 Adrian Beltre/5
102 Robby Hammock/50 15.00 4.50
103 Orlando Hudson/50 15.00 4.50
104 Mark Teixeira/10
105 Hong-Chih Kuo/50 30.00 9.00
106 Eric Chavez/25 25.00 7.50
107 Nick Johnson/10
108 Jacque Jones/50 20.00 6.00
109 Ken Harvey/100 10.00 3.00
110 Aramis Ramirez/50 20.00 6.00
111 Victor Martinez/50 20.00 6.00
112 Joe Crede/50 15.00 4.50
113 Jason Varitek/25 60.00 18.00
114 Troy Glaus/10
116 Kerry Wood/5
117 Hideo Nomo/1
118 Brandon Webb/25 25.00 7.50
119 Craig Biggio/10
120 Orlando Cabrera/10
121 Sammy Sosa/21 200.00 60.00
122 Bobby Abreu/10
123 Andruw Jones/10
124 Jeff Bagwell/5
127 Luis Castillo/25 25.00 7.50
128 Todd Helton/1
130 Mike Mussina/1
131 Eric Byrnes/10
132 Eric Hinske/10
134 Edgar Martinez/25 60.00 18.00
135 Rocco Baldelli/10
136 Miguel Tejada/5
141 Aubrey Huff/5
142 Garret Anderson/5
143 Vernon Wells/10
144 Magglio Ordonez/10
145 Brett Myers/50 20.00 6.00
147 Lance Berkman/5
148 Frank Thomas/5
149 Gary Sheffield/25 40.00 12.00
150 Tim Hudson/10
151 Duke Snider LGD/25 50.00 15.00
152 Carl Yastrzemski LGD/5
153 Whitey Ford LGD/25 50.00 15.00
154 Cal Ripken LGD/5
155 Dwight Gooden LGD/50 40.00 12.00
156 Warren Spahn LGD/10
157 Bob Gibson LGD/5
158 Don Mattingly LGD/25 150.00 45.00
159 Jack Morris LGD/50 15.00 4.50
160 Jim Bunning LGD/25 50.00 15.00
161 Fergie Jenkins LGD/50 25.00 7.50
162 Brooks Robinson LGD/10
163 George Kell LGD/50 25.00 7.50
164 Darryl Strawberry LGD/50 40.00 12.00
165 Robin Roberts LGD/25 50.00 15.00
166 Monte Irvin LGD/25 30.00 9.00
167 Ernie Banks LGD/25 80.00 24.00
168 Wade Boggs LGD/25 80.00 24.00
169 Gaylord Perry LGD/50 15.00 4.50
170 Keith Hernandez LGD/50 40.00 12.00
171 Lou Brock LGD/10
172 Frank Robinson LGD/25 50.00 15.00
173 Nolan Ryan LGD/25 150.00 45.00
174 Stan Musial LGD/25 100.00 30.00
175 Eddie Murray LGD/25 100.00 30.00
176 Byron Gettis ROO/100 10.00 3.00
177 Merkin Valdez ROO/100 40.00 12.00
178 Rickie Weeks ROO/25 80.00 24.00
180 Brian Bruney ROO/100 10.00 3.00
181 Freddy Guzman ROO/100 10.00 3.00
182 Brendan Harris ROO/100 10.00 3.00
183 John Gall ROO/100 10.00 3.00
184 Jason Kubel ROO/100 10.00 3.00
185 Delmon Young ROO/100 50.00 15.00
186 Ryan Howard ROO/100 10.00 3.00
187 Adam Loewen ROO/100 25.00 7.50
188 J.D. Durbin ROO/100 15.00 4.50
189 Dan Haren ROO/100 15.00 4.50
190 Dustin McGowan ROO/100 15.00 4.50
191 Chad Gaudin ROO/100 10.00 3.00
192 Preston Larrison ROO/100 10.00 3.00
193 Ramon Nivar ROO/100 10.00 3.00
195 Mike Gosling ROO/100 10.00 3.00
196 Kevin Youkilis ROO/100 25.00 7.50
197 Ryan Wagner ROO/100 15.00 4.50
198 Bubba Nelson ROO/100 15.00 4.50
199 Edwin Jackson ROO/100 25.00 7.50
200 Chris Burke ROO/100 10.00 3.00
201 Carlos Hines ROO/100 10.00 3.00
202 Greg Dobbs ROO/50 15.00 4.50
203 Jamie Brown ROO/100 10.00 3.00
204 Dave Crouthers ROO/100
205 Ian Snell ROO/100 25.00 7.50
206 Gary Carter LGD/50 40.00 12.00
207 Dale Murphy LGD/50 40.00 12.00
208 Ryne Sandberg LGD/50 80.00 24.00
209 Phil Niekro LGD/50 40.00 12.00
210 Don Sutton LGD/50 25.00 7.50
211 Alex Rodriguez Yanks/1
213 Greg Maddux Cubs/1

2004 Donruss Classics Significant Signatures Platinum

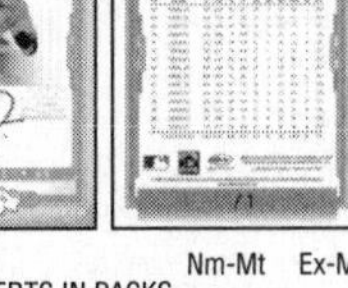

Nm-Mt Ex-Mt
RANDOM INSERTS IN PACKS
STATED PRINT RUN 1 SERIAL #'d SET
NO PRICING DUE TO SCARCITY

2004 Donruss Classics Significant Signatures Red

Nm-Mt Ex-Mt
RANDOM INSERTS IN PACKS
PRINT RUNS B/WN 1-250 COPIES PER
NO PRICING ON QTY OF 15 OR LESS
3 Hank Blalock/50 30.00 9.00
4 Shannon Stewart/100 15.00 4.50
6 Carlos Lee/25 25.00 7.50
7 Trot Nixon/25 30.00 9.00
9 Mark Mulder/25 40.00 12.00
10 Mariano Rivera/5
12 Jim Edmonds/25 25.00 7.50
13 Mike Lowell/50 20.00 6.00
14 Robin Ventura/50 20.00 6.00
16 Jose Vidro/25 25.00 7.50
17 Manny Ramirez/5
18 Alex Rodriguez Rgr/5
19 Carlos Beltran/25 40.00 12.00
21 Johan Santana/100 25.00 7.50
22 Richie Sexson/10
23 Chipper Jones/5
24 Steve Finley/100 25.00 7.50
25 Mark Prior/10
26 Alexis Rios/250 25.00 7.50
27 Rafael Palmeiro/25 100.00 30.00
28 Jorge Posada/25 60.00 18.00
29 Barry Zito/10
30 Jamie Moyer/5
32 Miguel Cabrera/100 40.00 12.00
33 Pedro Martinez/5
34 Curt Schilling/5
36 Dontrelle Willis/100 25.00 7.50
37 Rafael Soriano/250 10.00 3.00
38 Richard Fischer/250 10.00 3.00
39 Brian Tallet/250 10.00 3.00
40 Jose Castillo/250 10.00 3.00
41 Wade Miller/92 15.00 4.50
42 Jose Contreras/25 40.00 12.00
43 Runelvys Hernandez/50 15.00 4.50
44 Joe Borchard/250 10.00 3.00
47 Adam Dunn/25 40.00 12.00
48 Randy Johnson/3
49 Brandon Phillips/70 10.00 3.00
50 Scott Rolen/25 40.00 12.00
52 Tom Glavine/10
53 Cliff Lee/100 10.00 3.00
54 Chien-Ming Wang/250 25.00 7.50
55 Roy Oswalt/25 40.00 12.00
56 Austin Kearns/25 25.00 7.50
57 Jhonny Peralta/250 10.00 3.00
58 Greg Maddux Braves/5
59 Mark Grace/5
60 Jae Weong Seo/100 25.00 7.50
61 Nic Jackson/250 10.00 3.00
62 Roger Clemens/1
63 Jimmy Gobble/200 10.00 3.00
64 Travis Hafner/100 15.00 4.50
65 Paul Konerko/25 25.00 7.50
66 Jerome Williams/250 40.00 12.00
67 Ryan Klesko/5
68 Alexis Gomez/100 10.00 3.00
70 Zach Day/100 10.00 3.00
72 Morgan Ensberg/100 15.00 4.50
73 Josh Beckett/5
74 Garrett Atkins/245 10.00 3.00
75 Sean Casey/10
76 Julio Franco/25 40.00 12.00
77 Lyle Overbay/250 10.00 3.00
78 Josh Phelps/50 15.00 4.50
79 Juan Gonzalez/25 60.00 18.00
80 Rich Harden/150 15.00 4.50
82 Torii Hunter/25 25.00 7.50
83 Angel Berroa/10
84 Jody Gerut/100 25.00 7.50
85 Roberto Alomar/10
87 Jay Gibbons/100 15.00 4.50
88 Chone Figgins/100 10.00 3.00
89 Fred McGriff/5
90 Rich Aurilia/25 25.00 7.50
91 Xavier Nady/10
92 Marlon Byrd/25 20.00 6.00
93 Mike Piazza/10
94 Vladimir Guerrero/10
95 Shawn Green/1
97 Ivan Rodriguez/10
98 Jay Payton/100 10.00 3.00
99 Barry Larkin/25 60.00 18.00
100 Mike Sweeney/1
101 Adrian Beltre/5
102 Robby Hammock/150 10.00 3.00
103 Orlando Hudson/100 10.00 3.00
104 Mark Teixeira/10
105 Hong-Chih Kuo/100 25.00 7.50
106 Eric Chavez/25 25.00 7.50
107 Nick Johnson/25 25.00 7.50
108 Jacque Jones/100 15.00 4.50
109 Ken Harvey/250 10.00 3.00
110 Aramis Ramirez/100 15.00 4.50
111 Victor Martinez/99 15.00 4.50
112 Joe Crede/250 10.00 3.00
113 Jason Varitek/50 50.00 15.00
114 Troy Glaus/25 40.00 12.00
116 Kerry Wood/10
117 Hideo Nomo/1
118 Brandon Webb/50 20.00 6.00
119 Craig Biggio/25 40.00 12.00
120 Orlando Cabrera/50 15.00 4.50
121 Sammy Sosa/25 200.00 60.00
122 Bobby Abreu/25 25.00 7.50
123 Andruw Jones/25 40.00 12.00
124 Jeff Bagwell/25 80.00 24.00
127 Luis Castillo/50 20.00 6.00
128 Todd Helton/5
130 Mike Mussina/5
131 Eric Byrnes/25 20.00 6.00
132 Eric Hinske/25 20.00 6.00
134 Edgar Martinez/50 50.00 15.00
135 Rocco Baldelli/25 60.00 18.00
136 Miguel Tejada/5
141 Aubrey Huff/5
142 Garret Anderson/5
143 Vernon Wells/25 25.00 7.50
144 Magglio Ordonez/25 40.00 12.00
145 Brett Myers/100 15.00 4.50
147 Lance Berkman/5
148 Frank Thomas/5
149 Gary Sheffield/50 30.00 9.00
150 Tim Hudson/25 40.00 12.00
151 Duke Snider LGD/50 40.00 12.00
152 Carl Yastrzemski LGD/10
153 Whitey Ford LGD/50 40.00 12.00
154 Cal Ripken LGD/10
155 Dwight Gooden LGD/100 25.00 7.50
156 Warren Spahn LGD/25 80.00 24.00
157 Bob Gibson LGD/15
158 Don Mattingly LGD/25 150.00 45.00
159 Jack Morris LGD/100 15.00 4.50
160 Jim Bunning LGD/100 25.00 7.50
161 Fergie Jenkins LGD/100 20.00 6.00
162 Brooks Robinson LGD/20. 120.00 36.00
163 George Kell LGD/100 20.00 6.00
164 Darryl Strawberry LGD/100 25.00 7.50
165 Robin Roberts LGD/100 25.00 7.50
166 Monte Irvin LGD/100 20.00 6.00
167 Ernie Banks LGD/50 60.00 18.00
168 Wade Boggs LGD/50 60.00 18.00
169 Gaylord Perry LGD/100 15.00 4.50
170 Keith Hernandez LGD/100 25.00 7.50
171 Lou Brock LGD/25 50.00 15.00
172 Frank Robinson LGD/50 40.00 12.00
173 Nolan Ryan LGD/50 120.00 36.00
174 Stan Musial LGD/50 80.00 24.00
175 Eddie Murray LGD/50 80.00 24.00
176 Byron Gettis ROO/250 10.00 3.00
177 Merkin Valdez ROO/250 30.00 9.00
178 Rickie Weeks ROO/50 60.00 18.00
180 Brian Bruney ROO/250 10.00 3.00
181 Freddy Guzman ROO/250 10.00 3.00
182 Brendan Harris ROO/250 10.00 3.00
183 John Gall ROO/250 10.00 3.00
184 Jason Kubel ROO/250 10.00 3.00
185 Delmon Young ROO/100 40.00 12.00
186 Ryan Howard ROO/250 10.00 3.00
187 Adam Loewen ROO/250 25.00 7.50
188 J.D. Durbin ROO/250 15.00 4.50
189 Dan Haren ROO/250 15.00 4.50
190 Dustin McGowan ROO/250 15.00 4.50
191 Chad Gaudin ROO/250 10.00 3.00
192 Preston Larrison ROO/250. 10.00 3.00
193 Ramon Nivar ROO/250 10.00 3.00
195 Mike Gosling ROO/250 10.00 3.00
196 Kevin Youkilis ROO/250 25.00 7.50
197 Ryan Wagner ROO/250 15.00 4.50
198 Bubba Nelson ROO/250 15.00 4.50
199 Edwin Jackson ROO/250 25.00 7.50
200 Chris Burke ROO/250 10.00 3.00
201 Carlos Hines ROO/250 10.00 3.00
202 Greg Dobbs ROO/100 10.00 3.00
203 Jamie Brown ROO/250 10.00 3.00
204 Dave Crouthers ROO/250 10.00 3.00
205 Ian Snell ROO/250 15.00 4.50
206 Gary Carter LGD/100 25.00 7.50
207 Dale Murphy LGD/50 40.00 12.00
208 Ryne Sandberg LGD/25 100.00 30.00
209 Phil Niekro LGD/100 25.00 7.50
210 Don Sutton LGD/100 20.00 6.00
211 Alex Rodriguez Yanks/5
213 Greg Maddux Cubs/5

2004 Donruss Classics Timeless Tributes Green

Nm-Mt Ex-Mt
*GREEN 1-150: 3X TO 8X BASIC
*GREEN 151-175/206-210: 1.5X TO 4X BASIC
*GREEN 176-205: .75X TO 2X BASIC
*GREEN 211-213: 2X TO 5X BASIC
RANDOM INSERTS IN PACKS
STATED PRINT RUN 50 SERIAL #'d SETS

2004 Donruss Classics Timeless Tributes Platinum

Nm-Mt Ex-Mt
RANDOM INSERTS IN PACKS
STATED PRINT RUN 1 SERIAL #'d SET
NO PRICING DUE TO SCARCITY

2004 Donruss Classics Timeless Tributes Red

Nm-Mt Ex-Mt
*RED 1-150: 2.5X TO 6X BASIC
*RED 151-175/206-210: 1.25X TO 3X BASIC
*RED 176-205: .6X TO 1.5X BASIC
*RED 211-213: 1.5X TO 4X BASIC
RANDOM INSERTS IN PACKS
STATED PRINT RUN 100 SERIAL #'d SETS

2004 Donruss Classics Classic Combos Bat

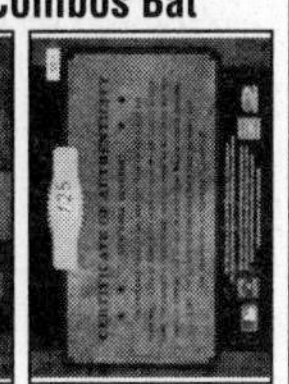

Nm-Mt Ex-Mt
RANDOM INSERTS IN PACKS
PRINT RUNS B/WN 25-50 COPIES PER
ALL CARDS FEATURE BAT-BAT COMBOS
1 Babe Ruth
Lou Gehrig/25
2 Roy Campanella 40.00 12.00
Pee Wee Reese/50
3 Ted Williams 200.00 60.00
Carl Yastrzemski/25
4 Roberto Clemente 150.00 45.00
Willie Stargell/25
5 Eddie Murray 80.00 24.00
Cal Ripken/50
6 Roger Maris 100.00 30.00
Yogi Berra/25
10 Nolan Ryan 50.00 15.00
Rod Carew/50
11 Don Mattingly 60.00 18.00
Rickey Henderson/50
15 Robin Yount 60.00 18.00
Paul Molitor/50
16 Mark Grace 40.00 12.00
Sammy Sosa/50
17 Ted Williams 150.00 45.00
Bobby Doerr/25
18 Reggie Jackson 40.00 12.00
Rod Carew/50

2004 Donruss Classics Classic Combos Jersey

Nm-Mt Ex-Mt
PRINT RUNS B/WN
NO PRICING ON QTY OF 10 OR LESS.
PRIME PRINT RUN 1 SERIAL #'d SET
NO PRIME PRICING DUE TO SCARCITY
RANDOM INSERTS IN PACKS
ALL ARE JSY-JSY COMBOS UNLESS NOTED
1 Babe Ruth Pants
Lou Gehrig Pants/15
2 Roy Campanella Pants 50.00 15.00
Pee Wee Reese/25
3 Ted Williams 300.00 90.00
Carl Yastrzemski/15
4 Roberto Clemente 150.00 45.00
Willie Stargell/25
5 Eddie Murray 120.00 36.00
Cal Ripken/25
6 Roger Maris 100.00 30.00
Yogi Berra/25
7 Stan Musial
Bob Gibson/10
8 Whitey Ford 50.00 15.00
Yogi Berra/25
9 Marty Marion 60.00 18.00
Stan Musial/25
10 Nolan Ryan 60.00 18.00
Rod Carew/25
11 Don Mattingly 60.00 18.00
Rickey Henderson/50
12 Jack Morris 40.00 12.00
Alan Trammell/50
13 Whitey Ford 50.00 15.00
Phil Rizzuto/25
14 Marty Marion 40.00 12.00
Red Schoendienst/25
15 Robin Yount 60.00 18.00
Paul Molitor/50
16 Mark Grace 40.00 12.00
Sammy Sosa/50
17 Ted Williams 250.00 75.00
Bobby Doerr/15
18 Reggie Jackson 40.00 12.00
Rod Carew/50

2004 Donruss Classics Classic Combos Quad

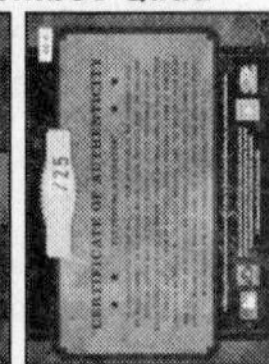

Nm-Mt Ex-Mt
NO PRICING ON QTY OF 5 OR LESS
PRIME PRINT RUN 1 SERIAL #'d SET
NO PRIME PRICING DUE TO SCARCITY
RANDOM INSERTS IN PACKS
1 Babe Ruth Bat-Pants
Lou Gehrig Bat-Pants/5
2 Roy Campanella Bat-Pants 100.00 30.00
Pee Wee Reese Bat-Jsy/25
3 Ted Williams Bat-Jsy 400.00 120.00
Carl Yastrzemski Bat-Jsy/15
4 Roberto Clemente Bat-Jsy 300.00 90.00
Willie Stargell Bat-Jsy/25
5 Eddie Murray Bat-Jsy 200.00 60.00
Cal Ripken Bat-Jsy/25
6 Roger Maris Bat-Jsy 250.00 75.00
Yogi Berra Bat-Jsy/15
10 Nolan Ryan Bat-Jsy 120.00 36.00
Rod Carew Bat-Jsy/25
11 Don Mattingly Bat-Jsy 150.00 45.00
Rickey Henderson Bat-Jsy/25
15 Robin Yount Bat-Jsy 120.00 36.00
Paul Molitor Bat-Jsy/25
16 Mark Grace Bat-Jsy 100.00 30.00
Sammy Sosa Bat-Jsy/25
17 Ted Williams Bat-Jsy 300.00 90.00
Bobby Doerr Bat-Jsy/15
18 Reggie Jackson Bat-Jsy 80.00 24.00
Rod Carew Bat-Jsy/25

2004 Donruss Classics Classic Singles Bat

Nm-Mt Ex-Mt
RANDOM INSERTS IN PACKS
PRINT RUNS B/WN 10-50 COPIES PER
NO PRICING ON QTY OF 10 OR LESS.
1 Babe Ruth/15 400.00 120.00
2 Nolan Ryan/10
3 Stan Musial/25 50.00 15.00
4 Ted Williams/25 150.00 45.00
5 Lou Gehrig/50 150.00 45.00
6 Eddie Murray/50 30.00 9.00

7 Roy Campanella/50 30.00 9.00
8 Robin Yount/50 30.00 9.00
9 Roberto Clemente/25 100.00 30.00
10 Don Mattingly/50 50.00 15.00
12 Carl Yastrzemski/50 40.00 12.00
13 Mark Grace/50 25.00 7.50
15 Rickey Henderson/50 30.00 9.00
16 Reggie Jackson/50 25.00 7.50
17 Pee Wee Reese/50 25.00 7.50
20 Roger Maris/25 60.00 18.00
21 Cal Ripken/50 80.00 24.00
23 Willie Stargell/50 25.00 7.50
24 Paul Molitor/50 25.00 7.50
26 Alan Trammell/50 25.00 7.50
27 Sammy Sosa/50 25.00 7.50
28 Bobby Doerr/50 15.00 4.50
29 Rod Carew/50 25.00 7.50
30 Yogi Berra/25 40.00 12.00
32 George Brett/50 50.00 15.00

2004 Donruss Classics Classic Singles Jersey

Nm-Mt Ex-Mt
PRINT RUNS B/WN 10-100 COPIES PER
NO PRICING ON QTY FO 10 OR LESS.
PRIME PRINT RUN 1 SERIAL #'d SET
NO PRIME PRICING DUE TO SCARCITY
RANDOM INSERTS IN PACKS
1 Babe Ruth Pants/10
2 Nolan Ryan/50 50.00 15.00
3 Stan Musial/15 60.00 18.00
4 Ted Williams/10
5 Lou Gehrig Pants/10
6 Eddie Murray/100 20.00 6.00
7 Roy Campanella Pants/50 30.00 9.00
8 Robin Yount/100 25.00 7.50
9 Roberto Clemente/25 120.00 36.00
10 Don Mattingly/100 40.00 12.00
11 Bob Gibson/15 40.00 12.00
12 Carl Yastrzemski/50 40.00 12.00
13 Mark Grace/25 30.00 9.00
14 Jack Morris/100 10.00 3.00
15 Rickey Henderson/25 40.00 12.00
16 Reggie Jackson/50 25.00 7.50
17 Pee Wee Reese/25 30.00 9.00
18 Marty Marion/100 10.00 3.00
19 Tommy John/100 10.00 3.00
20 Roger Maris/25 60.00 18.00
21 Cal Ripken/25 120.00 36.00
22 Red Schoendienst/25 20.00 6.00
23 Willie Stargell/100 15.00 4.50
24 Paul Molitor/100 15.00 4.50
25 Whitey Ford/50 25.00 7.50
26 Alan Trammell/100 15.00 4.50
27 Sammy Sosa/50 25.00 7.50
28 Bobby Doerr/50 15.00 4.50
29 Rod Carew/100 15.00 4.50
30 Yogi Berra/15 50.00 15.00
31 Phil Rizzuto/25 30.00 9.00
32 George Brett/25 60.00 18.00

2004 Donruss Classics Classic Singles Jersey-Bat

Nm-Mt Ex-Mt
PRINT RUNS B/WN 5-25 COPIES PER
NO PRICING ON QTY OF 10 OR LESS.
PRIME PRINT RUN 1 SERIAL #'d SET
NO PRIME PRICING DUE TO SCARCITY
RANDOM INSERTS IN PACKS
ALL ARE JSY-BAT COMBOS UNLESS NOTED
1 Babe Ruth Pants/5
2 Nolan Ryan/25 60.00 18.00
3 Stan Musial/15 80.00 24.00
4 Ted Williams/10
5 Lou Gehrig Pants/10
6 Eddie Murray/25 50.00 15.00
7 Roy Campanella Pants/25 50.00 15.00
8 Robin Yount/25 60.00 18.00
9 Roberto Clemente/25 200.00 60.00
10 Don Mattingly/25 80.00 24.00
12 Carl Yastrzemski/25 60.00 18.00
13 Mark Grace/25 40.00 12.00
15 Rickey Henderson/25 50.00 15.00
16 Reggie Jackson/25 40.00 12.00
17 Pee Wee Reese/25 40.00 12.00
20 Roger Maris/15 120.00 36.00
21 Cal Ripken/25 150.00 45.00
23 Willie Stargell/25 40.00 12.00
24 Paul Molitor/25 40.00 12.00
26 Alan Trammell/25 40.00 12.00
27 Sammy Sosa/25 50.00 15.00
28 Bobby Doerr/25 25.00 7.50
29 Rod Carew/25 40.00 12.00
30 Yogi Berra/15 60.00 18.00
32 George Brett/25 80.00 24.00

2004 Donruss Classics Dress Code Bat

Nm-Mt Ex-Mt
STATED PRINT RUN 50 SERIAL #'d SETS
S.STEWART PRINT 10 SERIAL #'d CARDS
*DC COMBO MTRL: .5X TO 1.2X BASIC
DC COMBO MTRL PRINT 50 SERIAL #'d SETS
DC COMBO MTRL STEWART 10 #'d CARDS
RANDOM INSERTS IN PACKS
NO S.STEWART PRICING DUE TO SCARCITY
1 Derek Jeter 40.00 12.00
2 Kerry Wood 15.00 4.50
3 Nomar Garciaparra 20.00 6.00
4 Jacque Jones 10.00 3.00
5 Mark Teixeira 10.00 3.00
6 Troy Glaus 15.00 4.50
7 Todd Helton 15.00 4.50
8 Miguel Tejada 10.00 3.00
9 Mike Piazza 20.00 6.00
11 Mike Sweeney 10.00 3.00
12 Albert Pujols 25.00 7.50
13 Rickey Henderson 15.00 4.50
14 Chipper Jones 15.00 4.50
15 Don Mattingly 50.00 15.00
16 Shawn Green 10.00 3.00
17 Mark Grace 15.00 4.50
18 Jason Giambi 15.00 4.50
19 Barry Zito 15.00 4.50
20 Sammy Sosa 20.00 6.00
22 Rafael Palmeiro 15.00 4.50
23 Frank Thomas 15.00 4.50
24 Manny Ramirez 10.00 3.00
25 Mike Mussina 15.00 4.50
26 Magglio Ordonez 10.00 3.00
27 Rocco Baldelli 15.00 4.50
28 Andruw Jones 10.00 3.00
29 Torii Hunter 10.00 3.00
30 Ivan Rodriguez 15.00 4.50
31 Jeff Bagwell 15.00 4.50
32 Mark Mulder 10.00 3.00
33 Trot Nixon 15.00 4.50
34 Cal Ripken 80.00 24.00
35 Dontrelle Willis 10.00 3.00
36 Hank Blalock 10.00 3.00
37 Brandon Webb 10.00 3.00
38 Miguel Cabrera 15.00 4.50
39 Hideo Nomo 15.00 4.50
40 Shannon Stewart/10
41 Tim Hudson 10.00 3.00
42 Pedro Martinez 15.00 4.50
43 Hee Seop Choi 10.00 3.00
44 Randy Johnson 15.00 4.50
45 Tony Gwynn 25.00 7.50
46 Mark Prior 25.00 7.50
47 Eric Chavez 10.00 3.00
48 Alex Rodriguez 15.00 4.50
50 Alfonso Soriano 15.00 4.50

2004 Donruss Classics Dress Code Combos Signature

Nm-Mt Ex-Mt
PRINT RUNS B/WN 1-25 COPIES PER
NO PRICING ON QTY OF 10 OR LESS.
PRIME PRINT RUN 1 SERIAL #'d SET
NO PRIME PRICING DUE TO SCARCITY
RANDOM INSERTS IN PACKS
2 Kerry Wood Jsy/5
4 Jacque Jones Jsy/25 40.00 12.00
5 Mark Teixeira Jsy/5
6 Troy Glaus Jsy/5
7 Todd Helton Jsy/5
8 Miguel Tejada Jsy/5
9 Mike Piazza Jsy/5
11 Mike Sweeney Jsy/5
13 Rickey Henderson Jsy/5
14 Chipper Jones Jsy/5
15 Don Mattingly Jsy/5
16 Shawn Green Jsy/1
17 Mark Grace Jsy/5
19 Barry Zito Jsy/5
20 Sammy Sosa Jsy/5
21 Jay Gibbons Jsy/25 40.00 12.00
22 Rafael Palmeiro Jsy/5
23 Frank Thomas Jsy/5
25 Mike Mussina Jsy/5
26 Magglio Ordonez Jsy/5
27 Rocco Baldelli Jsy/10
28 Andruw Jones Jsy/5
29 Torii Hunter Jsy/10
30 Ivan Rodriguez Jsy/5
31 Jeff Bagwell Jsy/5
32 Mark Mulder Jsy/25 40.00 12.00
33 Trot Nixon Jsy/25 60.00 18.00
34 Cal Ripken Jsy/5
35 Dontrelle Willis Jsy/25 60.00 18.00
36 Hank Blalock Jsy/10
37 Brandon Webb Jsy/10
38 Miguel Cabrera Jsy/25 100.00 30.00
39 Hideo Nomo Jsy/5
40 Shannon Stewart Jsy/25 40.00 12.00
41 Tim Hudson Jsy/10
42 Pedro Martinez Jsy/5
44 Randy Johnson Jsy/5
45 Tony Gwynn Jsy/5
46 Mark Prior Jsy/10
47 Eric Chavez Jsy/10
48 Alex Rodriguez Jsy/5
49 Johan Santana Jsy/25 60.00 18.00

2004 Donruss Classics Dress Code Jersey

Nm-Mt Ex-Mt
STATED PRINT RUN 100 SERIAL #'d SETS
RIPKEN PRINT RUN 25 SERIAL #'d CARDS
*NUMBER: .4X TO 1X BASIC
*NUMBER RIPKEN: .15X TO .4X BASIC RIPKEN
NUMBER PRINT RUN 100 SERIAL #'d SETS
*PRIME: 1.5X TO 4X BASIC
*PRIME MATTINGLY: .75X TO 2X BASIC MATT
*PRIME RIPKEN: .6X TO 1.2X BASIC RIPKEN
PRIME PRINT RUN 25 SERIAL #'d SETS
PRIME SORIANO PRINT 12 #'d CARDS
NO PRIME SORIANO PRICING AVAILABLE
RANDOM INSERTS IN PACKS
1 Derek Jeter 30.00 9.00
2 Kerry Wood 10.00 3.00
3 Nomar Garciaparra 15.00 4.50
4 Jacque Jones 8.00 2.40
5 Mark Teixeira 8.00 2.40
6 Troy Glaus 10.00 3.00
7 Todd Helton 10.00 3.00
8 Miguel Tejada 8.00 2.40
9 Mike Piazza 15.00 4.50
11 Mike Sweeney 8.00 2.40
12 Albert Pujols 20.00 6.00
13 Rickey Henderson 10.00 3.00
14 Chipper Jones 10.00 3.00
15 Don Mattingly 40.00 12.00
16 Shawn Green 8.00 2.40
17 Mark Grace 10.00 3.00
18 Jason Giambi 10.00 3.00
19 Barry Zito 10.00 3.00
20 Sammy Sosa 15.00 4.50
21 Jay Gibbons 8.00 2.40
22 Rafael Palmeiro 10.00 3.00
23 Frank Thomas 10.00 3.00
24 Manny Ramirez 8.00 2.40
25 Mike Mussina 10.00 3.00
26 Magglio Ordonez 8.00 2.40
27 Rocco Baldelli 10.00 3.00
28 Andruw Jones 8.00 2.40
29 Torii Hunter 8.00 2.40
30 Ivan Rodriguez 10.00 3.00
31 Jeff Bagwell 10.00 3.00
32 Mark Mulder 8.00 2.40
33 Trot Nixon 10.00 3.00
34 Cal Ripken/25 120.00 36.00
35 Dontrelle Willis 8.00 2.40
36 Hank Blalock 8.00 2.40
37 Brandon Webb 8.00 2.40
38 Miguel Cabrera 10.00 3.00
39 Hideo Nomo 10.00 3.00
40 Shannon Stewart 8.00 2.40
41 Tim Hudson 8.00 2.40
42 Pedro Martinez 10.00 3.00
43 Hee Seop Choi 8.00 2.40
44 Randy Johnson 10.00 3.00
45 Tony Gwynn 20.00 6.00
46 Mark Prior 20.00 6.00
47 Eric Chavez 8.00 2.40
48 Alex Rodriguez 10.00 3.00
49 Johan Santana 8.00 2.40
50 Alfonso Soriano 10.00 3.00

2004 Donruss Classics Famous Foursomes

Nm-Mt Ex-Mt
RANDOM INSERTS IN PACKS
STATED PRINT RUN 99 SERIAL #'d SETS
1 Roy Campanella 25.00 7.50
Pee Wee Reese
Jackie Robinson
Duke Snider
2 Stan Musial 25.00 7.50
Bob Gibson
Red Schoendienst
Ken Boyer

2004 Donruss Classics Famous Foursomes Jersey

Nm-Mt Ex-Mt
STATED PRINT RUN 10 SERIAL #'d SETS
PRIME PRINT RUN 1 SERIAL #'d SET
NO PRIME PRICING DUE TO SCARCITY
RANDOM INSERTS IN PACKS
ALL ARE QUAD JSY CARDS UNLESS NOTED
1 Roy Campanella Pants
Pee Wee Reese
Jackie Robinson
Duke Snider
2 Stan Musial
Bob Gibson
Red Schoendienst
Ken Boyer

2004 Donruss Classics Legendary Hats Material

Nm-Mt Ex-Mt
RANDOM INSERTS IN PACKS
PRINT RUNS B/WN 5-25 COPIES PER
NO PRICING ON QTY OF 10 OR LESS.
1 Tony Gwynn/10
2 Mike Schmidt/25 80.00 24.00
6 George Brett/25 80.00 24.00
14 Cal Ripken/25 150.00 45.00
16 Kirby Puckett/25 50.00 15.00
20 Reggie Jackson Yanks/25 40.00 12.00
21 Roberto Clemente/5
22 Ernie Banks/25 50.00 15.00
29 Dave Winfield/25 25.00 7.50
40 Wade Boggs/25 40.00 12.00
42 Rickey Henderson A's/25 50.00 15.00
49 Reggie Jackson Angels/25 40.00 12.00
51 Rafael Palmeiro/25 40.00 12.00
52 Sammy Sosa/25 40.00 12.00
55 Steve Carlton/25 25.00 7.50
56 Rod Carew Angels/25 40.00 12.00
60 R.Henderson Angels/25 50.00 15.00

2004 Donruss Classics Legendary Jackets Material

Nm-Mt Ex-Mt
RANDOM INSERTS IN PACKS
STATED PRINT RUN 100 SERIAL #'d SETS
2 Mike Schmidt 40.00 12.00
8 Reggie Jackson A's 15.00 4.50
17 Don Mattingly 40.00 12.00
32 Gary Carter 15.00 4.50
54 Nolan Ryan 50.00 15.00
56 Rod Carew Angels 15.00 4.50

2004 Donruss Classics Legendary Jerseys Material

Nm-Mt Ex-Mt
PRINT RUNS B/WN 5-50 COPIES PER
NO PRICING ON QTY OF 10 OR LESS.
PRIME PRINT RUN 1 SERIAL #'d SET
NO PRIME PRICING DUE TO SCARCITY
RANDOM INSERTS IN PACKS
1 Tony Gwynn/50 25.00 7.50
2 Mike Schmidt/25 60.00 18.00
3 Johnny Bench/50 25.00 7.50
4 Roger Maris Yanks/10
5 Ted Williams/10
6 George Brett/25 60.00 18.00
7 Carlton Fisk/50 25.00 7.50
8 Reggie Jackson A's/25 30.00 9.00
9 Joe Morgan/25 20.00 6.00
10 Bo Jackson/25 40.00 12.00
11 Stan Musial/10
12 Andre Dawson/50 15.00 4.50
13 R.Henderson Yanks/25 40.00 12.00
14 Cal Ripken/25 120.00 36.00
15 Dale Murphy/25 30.00 9.00
16 Kirby Puckett/50 30.00 9.00
17 Don Mattingly/50 50.00 15.00
18 Brooks Robinson/50 30.00 9.00
19 Orlando Cepeda/50 15.00 4.50
20 Reggie Jackson Yanks/25 30.00 9.00
21 Roberto Clemente/25 120.00 36.00
22 Ernie Banks/10
23 Frank Robinson/50 15.00 4.50
24 Harmon Killebrew/50 30.00 9.00
25 Willie Stargell/50 25.00 7.50
26 Al Kaline/15 50.00 15.00
27 Carl Yastrzemski/50 40.00 12.00
28 Duke Snider/10
29 Dave Winfield/50 15.00 4.50
30 Eddie Murray/50 30.00 9.00
31 Eddie Mathews/25 40.00 12.00
32 Gary Carter/50 25.00 7.50
33 Rod Carew Twins/25 30.00 9.00
35 Mel Ott/10
36 Paul Molitor/50 25.00 7.50
37 Thurman Munson/15 50.00 15.00
39 Robin Yount/50 30.00 9.00
40 Wade Boggs/50 25.00 7.50
41 Jackie Robinson/5
42 Rickey Henderson A's/25 40.00 12.00
44 Yogi Berra/15 50.00 15.00
46 Luis Aparicio/50 15.00 4.50
47 Phil Rizzuto/25 30.00 9.00
48 Roger Maris A's/25 60.00 18.00
49 Reggie Jackson Angels/50 25.00 7.50
50 Lou Gehrig/5
51 Rafael Palmeiro/50 25.00 7.50
52 Sammy Sosa/50 25.00 7.50
53 Roger Clemens/50 30.00 9.00
54 Nolan Ryan/50 50.00 15.00
55 Steve Carlton/50 15.00 4.50
56 Rod Carew Angels/50 25.00 7.50
57 Whitey Ford/25 30.00 9.00
59 Babe Ruth/5

2004 Donruss Classics Legendary Jerseys Material Number

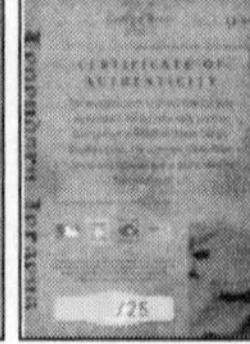

Nm-Mt Ex-Mt
*NUMBER p/r 50: .4X TO 1X BASIC p/r 50
*NUMBER p/r 25: .5X TO 1.2X BASIC p/r 50
*NUMBER p/r 25: .4X TO 1X BASIC p/r 25
*NUMBER p/r 15: .5X TO 1.2X BASIC p/r 25
*NUMBER p/r 15: .4X TO 1X BASIC p/r 15
RANDOM INSERTS IN PACKS
PRINT RUNS B/WN 3-50 COPIES PER
NO PRICNG ON QTY OF 10 OR LESS
45 Roy Campanella Pants/25 40.00 12.00
58 Fergie Jenkins Pants/25 20.00 6.00

2004 Donruss Classics Legendary Leather Material

Nm-Mt Ex-Mt
RANDOM INSERTS IN PACKS
PRINT RUNS B/WN 5-25 COPIES PER
NO PRICING ON QTY OF 10 OR LESS.
1 Tony Gwynn Fld Glv/10
2 Mike Schmidt Fld Glv/10
16 Kirby Puckett Fld Glv/25 50.00 15.00
17 Don Mattingly Btg Glv/10
29 Dave Winfield Fld Glv/10
32 Gary Carter Fld Glv/25 40.00 12.00
34 Jimmie Foxx Fld Glv/10
51 Rafael Palmeiro Fld Glv/25 40.00 12.00
52 Sammy Sosa Btg Glv/25 60.00 18.00
54 Nolan Ryan Fld Glv/5
55 Steve Carlton Fld Glv/25 25.00 7.50
58 Fergie Jenkins Fld Glv/25 25.00 7.50

2004 Donruss Classics Legendary Lumberjacks

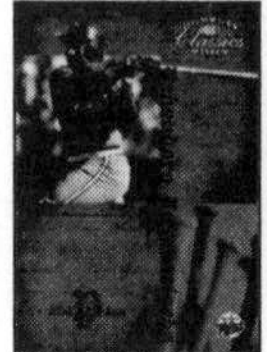
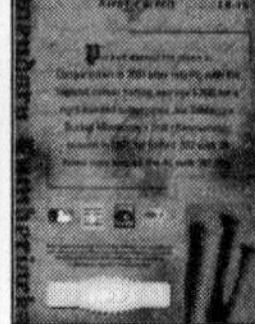

Nm-Mt Ex-Mt
STATED PRINT RUN 1000 SERIAL #'d SETS
*HATS: 1.5X TO 4X LUMBERJACKS
HATS PRINT RUN 50 SERIAL #'d SETS
*JACKETS: 1.5X TO 4X LUMBERJACKS
JACKET PRINT RUN 50 SERIAL #'d SETS
*JERSEYS: .6X TO 1.5X LUMBERJACKS
JERSEY PRINT RUN 500 SERIAL #'d SETS
*LEATHER: 1.2X TO 3X LUMBERJACKS
LEATHER PRINT RUN 100 SERIAL #'d SETS
*PANTS: 1.5X TO 4X LUMBERJACKS
PANTS PRINT RUN 50 SERIAL #'d SETS
*SPIKES: 1.25X TO 3X LUMBERJACKS
SPIKES PRINT RUN 100 SERIAL #'d SETS
RANDOM INSERTS IN PACKS
1 Tony Gwynn 5.00 1.50
2 Mike Schmidt 8.00 2.40
3 Johnny Bench 4.00 1.20
4 Roger Maris Yanks 6.00 1.80
5 Ted Williams 10.00 3.00
6 George Brett 10.00 3.00
7 Carlton Fisk 4.00 1.20
8 Reggie Jackson A's 4.00 1.20
9 Joe Morgan 2.50 .75
10 Bo Jackson 4.00 1.20
11 Stan Musial 6.00 1.80
12 Andre Dawson 2.50 .75
13 Rickey Henderson Yanks 4.00 1.20
14 Cal Ripken 12.00 3.60
15 Dale Murphy 4.00 1.20
16 Kirby Puckett 4.00 1.20
17 Don Mattingly 10.00 3.00
18 Brooks Robinson 4.00 1.20
19 Orlando Cepeda 2.50 .75
20 Reggie Jackson Yanks 4.00 1.20
21 Roberto Clemente 10.00 3.00

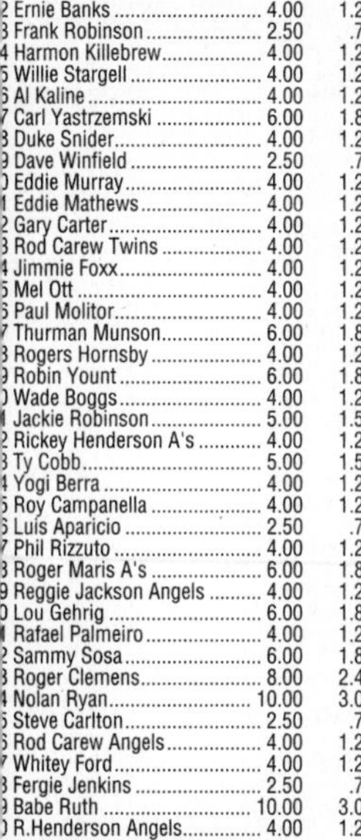

2 Ernie Banks 4.00 1.20
3 Frank Robinson 2.50 .75
4 Harmon Killebrew 4.00 1.20
5 Willie Stargell 4.00 1.20
6 Al Kaline 4.00 1.20
7 Carl Yastrzemski 6.00 1.80
8 Duke Snider 4.00 1.20
9 Dave Winfield 2.50 .75
0 Eddie Murray 4.00 1.20
1 Eddie Mathews 4.00 1.20
2 Gary Carter 4.00 1.20
3 Rod Carew Twins 4.00 1.20
4 Jimmie Foxx 4.00 1.20
5 Mel Ott 4.00 1.20
6 Paul Molitor 4.00 1.20
7 Thurman Munson 6.00 1.80
8 Rogers Hornsby 4.00 1.20
9 Robin Yount 6.00 1.80
0 Wade Boggs 4.00 1.20
1 Jackie Robinson 5.00 1.50
2 Rickey Henderson A's 4.00 1.20
3 Ty Cobb 5.00 1.50
4 Yogi Berra 4.00 1.20
5 Roy Campanella 4.00 1.20
6 Luis Aparicio 2.50 .75
7 Phil Rizzuto 4.00 1.20
8 Roger Maris A's 6.00 1.80
9 Reggie Jackson Angels 4.00 1.20
0 Lou Gehrig 6.00 1.80
1 Rafael Palmeiro 4.00 1.20
2 Sammy Sosa 6.00 1.80
3 Roger Clemens 8.00 2.40
4 Nolan Ryan 10.00 3.00
5 Steve Carlton 2.50 .75
6 Rod Carew Angels 4.00 1.20
7 Whitey Ford 4.00 1.20
8 Fergie Jenkins 2.50 .75
9 Babe Ruth 10.00 3.00
0 R.Henderson Angels 4.00 1.20

2004 Donruss Classics Legendary Lumberjacks Material

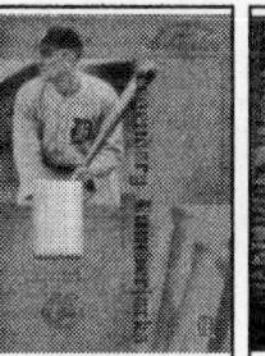

Nm-Mt Ex-Mt
ANDOM INSERTS IN PACKS
RINT RUNS B/WN 10-100 COPIES PER
O PRICING ON QTY OF 10 OR LESS.
Tony Gwynn/100 20.00 6.00
Mike Schmidt/100 20.00 6.00
Johnny Bench/100 15.00 4.50
Roger Maris Yanks/25 60.00 18.00
Ted Williams/25 150.00 45.00
George Brett/100 40.00 12.00
Carlton Fisk/100 15.00 4.50
Reggie Jackson A's/100 15.00 4.50
Joe Morgan/100 10.00 3.00
0 Bo Jackson/100 20.00 6.00
1 Stan Musial/25 50.00 15.00
2 Andre Dawson/100 10.00 3.00
3 R.Henderson Yanks/100 20.00 6.00
4 Cal Ripken/100 50.00 15.00
5 Dale Murphy/100 15.00 4.50
6 Kirby Puckett/100 20.00 6.00
7 Don Mattingly/100 40.00 12.00
8 Brooks Robinson/100 20.00 6.00
9 Orlando Cepeda/100 10.00 3.00
0 Reggie Jackson Yanks/100 15.00 4.50
1 Roberto Clemente/25 100.00 30.00
2 Ernie Banks/100 20.00 6.00
3 Frank Robinson/100 10.00 3.00
4 Harmon Killebrew/100 20.00 6.00
5 Willie Stargell/100 15.00 4.50
6 Al Kaline/100 20.00 6.00
7 Carl Yastrzemski/100 30.00 9.00
8 Duke Snider/10
9 Dave Winfield/100 10.00 3.00
0 Eddie Murray/100 20.00 6.00
1 Eddie Mathews/50 30.00 9.00
2 Gary Carter/100 15.00 4.50
3 Rod Carew Twins/100 15.00 4.50
4 Jimmie Foxx/10
5 Mel Ott/25 40.00 12.00
6 Paul Molitor/100 15.00 4.50
7 Thurman Munson/50 25.00 7.50
8 Rogers Hornsby/25 80.00 24.00
9 Robin Yount/100 25.00 7.50
0 Wade Boggs/100 15.00 4.50
2 Rickey Henderson A's/50 30.00 9.00
3 Ty Cobb/10
4 Yogi Berra/25 40.00 12.00
5 Roy Campanella/25 40.00 12.00
6 Luis Aparicio/100 10.00 3.00
8 Roger Maris A's/25 60.00 18.00
9 Reggie Jackson Angels/100 15.00 4.50
0 Lou Gehrig/25 200.00 60.00
1 Rafael Palmeiro/100 15.00 4.50
2 Sammy Sosa/100 15.00 4.50
6 Rod Carew Angels/100 15.00 4.50
9 Babe Ruth/10
0 R.Henderson Angels/100 20.00 6.00

2004 Donruss Classics Legendary Pants Material

Nm-Mt Ex-Mt
ANDOM INSERTS IN PACKS
RINT RUNS B/WN 3-50 COPIES PER
O PRICING ON QTY OF 10 OR LESS.
Tony Gwynn/25 40.00 12.00
2 Andre Dawson/25 20.00 6.00
4 Harmon Killebrew/50 30.00 9.00
6 Al Kaline/50 30.00 9.00
5 Mel Ott/10
3 Ty Cobb/5
5 Roy Campanella/25 40.00 12.00
6 Luis Aparicio/50 15.00 4.50

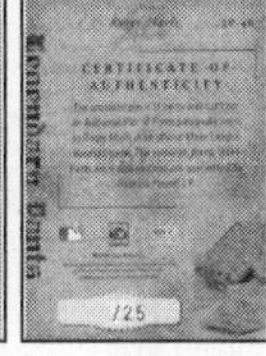

47 Phil Rizzuto/50 25.00 7.50
48 Roger Maris A's/25 60.00 18.00
50 Lou Gehrig/4
51 Rafael Palmeiro/25 30.00 9.00
56 Rod Carew Angels/50 25.00 7.50
57 Whitey Ford/25 30.00 9.00
58 Fergie Jenkins/25 20.00 6.00
59 Babe Ruth/3

2004 Donruss Classics Legendary Spikes Material

Nm-Mt Ex-Mt
RANDOM INSERTS IN PACKS
NO PRICING ON QTY OF 10 OR LESS.
13 R.Henderson Yanks/25 50.00 15.00
17 Don Mattingly/50 80.00 24.00
29 Dave Winfield/50 20.00 6.00
42 Rickey Henderson A's/25 50.00 15.00
51 Rafael Palmeiro/25 40.00 12.00
52 Sammy Sosa/50 40.00 12.00
56 Rod Carew Angels/10
60 R.Henderson Angels/25 50.00 15.00

2004 Donruss Classics Membership

Nm-Mt Ex-Mt
RANDOM INSERTS IN PACKS
STATED PRINT RUN 2499 SERIAL #'d SETS
1 Stan Musial 5.00 1.50
2 Ted Williams 8.00 2.40
3 Early Wynn 2.00 .60
4 Roberto Clemente 8.00 2.40
5 Al Kaline 3.00 .90
6 Bob Gibson 3.00 .90
7 Lou Brock 3.00 .90
8 Carl Yastrzemski 5.00 1.50
9 Gaylord Perry 2.00 .60
10 Fergie Jenkins 2.00 .60
11 Steve Carlton 2.00 .60
12 Reggie Jackson 3.00 .90
13 Rod Carew 3.00 .90
14 Bert Blyleven 2.00 .60
15 Mike Schmidt 6.00 1.80
16 Nolan Ryan 8.00 2.40
17 Robin Yount 5.00 1.50
18 George Brett 8.00 2.40
19 Eddie Murray 3.00 .90
20 Tony Gwynn 4.00 1.20
21 Cal Ripken 10.00 3.00
22 Randy Johnson 3.00 .90
23 Sammy Sosa 5.00 1.50
24 Rafael Palmeiro 3.00 .90
25 Roger Clemens 6.00 1.80

2004 Donruss Classics Membership VIP Bat

Nm-Mt Ex-Mt
RANDOM INSERTS IN PACKS
PRINT RUNS B/WN 10-25 COPIES PER
NO PRICING ON QTY OF 10 OR LESS.
1 Stan Musial/25 50.00 15.00
2 Ted Williams/25 150.00 45.00
4 Roberto Clemente/25 100.00 30.00
5 Al Kaline/25 40.00 12.00
7 Lou Brock/25 30.00 9.00
8 Carl Yastrzemski/25 50.00 15.00
11 Steve Carlton/25 20.00 6.00
12 Reggie Jackson/25 30.00 9.00
13 Rod Carew/25 30.00 9.00
15 Mike Schmidt/25 60.00 18.00
16 Nolan Ryan/10
17 Robin Yount/25 40.00 12.00
18 George Brett/10
19 Eddie Murray/25 40.00 12.00
20 Tony Gwynn/25 40.00 12.00
21 Cal Ripken/10
22 Randy Johnson/25 40.00 12.00
23 Sammy Sosa/25 40.00 12.00
24 Rafael Palmeiro/25 30.00 9.00
25 Roger Clemens/25 40.00 12.00

2004 Donruss Classics Membership VIP Combos Material

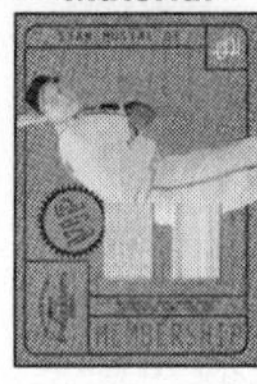

Nm-Mt Ex-Mt
PRINT RUNS B/WN 9-25 COPIES PER
NO PRICING ON QTY OF 10 OR LESS.
PRIME PRINT RUN 1 SERIAL #'d SET
NO PRIME PRICING DUE TO SCARCITY
RANDOM INSERTS IN PACKS
1 Stan Musial Bat-Jsy/15 80.00 24.00
2 Ted Williams Bat-Jsy/9
4 Rob Clemente Bat-Jsy/25 200.00 60.00
5 Al Kaline Bat-Pants/25 50.00 15.00
7 Lou Brock Bat-Jsy/10
8 Carl Yastrzemski Bat-Jsy/25 60.00 18.00
10 F.Jenkins Fld Glv-Pants/25 25.00 7.50
11 Steve Carlton Bat-Jsy/25 25.00 7.50
12 Reggie Jackson Bat-Jsy/25 40.00 12.00
13 Rod Carew Bat-Pants/25 40.00 12.00
15 Mike Schmidt Bat-Jsy/25 60.00 18.00
16 Nolan Ryan Bat-Jsy/25 60.00 18.00
17 Robin Yount Bat-Jsy/25 60.00 18.00
18 George Brett Bat-Jsy/25 80.00 24.00
19 Eddie Murray Bat-Jsy/25 50.00 15.00
20 Tony Gwynn Bat-Jsy/25 60.00 18.00
21 Cal Ripken Bat-Jsy/25 150.00 45.00
22 Randy Johnson Bat-Jsy/25 50.00 15.00
23 Sammy Sosa Bat-Jsy/25 50.00 15.00
24 Rafael Palmeiro Bat-Jsy/25 40.00 12.00
25 Roger Clemens Bat-Jsy/25 50.00 15.00

2004 Donruss Classics Membership VIP Combos Signature

Nm-Mt Ex-Mt
PRINT RUNS B/WN 1-50 COPIES PER
NO PRICING ON QTY OF 5 OR LESS...
PRIME PRINT RUN 1 SERIAL #'d SET
NO PRIME PRICING DUE TO SCARCITY
RANDOM INSERTS IN PACKS
1 Stan Musial Jsy/5
5 Al Kaline Pants/25 120.00 36.00
6 Bob Gibson Jsy/5
7 Lou Brock Jsy/5
8 Carl Yastrzemski Jsy/5
9 Gaylord Perry Jsy/50 25.00 7.50
10 Fergie Jenkins Pants/50 40.00 12.00
11 Steve Carlton Jsy/25 80.00 24.00
12 Reggie Jackson Jsy/5
13 Rod Carew Pants/5
14 Bert Blyleven Jsy/50 25.00 7.50
16 Nolan Ryan Jsy/5
17 Robin Yount Jsy/5
18 George Brett Jsy/5
19 Eddie Murray Jsy/5
20 Tony Gwynn Jsy/5
21 Cal Ripken Jsy/5
22 Randy Johnson Jsy/5
23 Sammy Sosa Jsy/5
24 Rafael Palmeiro Jsy/5
25 Roger Clemens Jsy/1

2004 Donruss Classics Membership VIP Jersey

Nm-Mt Ex-Mt
PRINT RUNS B/WN 9-25 COPIES PER
NO PRICING ON QTY OF 10 OR LESS.
PRIME PRINT RUN 1 SERIAL #'d SET
NO PRIME PRICING DUE TO SCARCITY
RANDOM INSERTS IN PACKS
1 Stan Musial/15 60.00 18.00
2 Ted Williams/9
3 Early Wynn/10
4 Roberto Clemente/25 120.00 36.00
5 Al Kaline Pants/25 40.00 12.00
6 Bob Gibson/10
7 Lou Brock/10
8 Carl Yastrzemski/25 50.00 15.00
9 Gaylord Perry/25 20.00 6.00
10 Fergie Jenkins Pants/25 20.00 6.00
11 Steve Carlton/25 20.00 6.00
12 Reggie Jackson/25 30.00 9.00
13 Rod Carew/25 30.00 9.00
14 Bert Blyleven/25 20.00 6.00
15 Mike Schmidt/25 60.00 18.00
16 Nolan Ryan/25 60.00 18.00
17 Robin Yount/25 40.00 12.00
18 George Brett/25 60.00 18.00
19 Eddie Murray/25 40.00 12.00
20 Tony Gwynn/25 40.00 12.00
21 Cal Ripken/25 120.00 36.00
22 Randy Johnson/25 40.00 12.00
23 Sammy Sosa/25 40.00 12.00
24 Rafael Palmeiro/25 30.00 9.00
25 Roger Clemens/25 40.00 12.00

2004 Donruss Classics Membership VIP Signatures

Nm-Mt Ex-Mt
RANDOM INSERTS IN PACKS
PRINT RUNS B/WN 1-50 COPIES PER
NO PRICING ON QTY OF 5 OR LESS...
1 Stan Musial/5
5 Al Kaline/20 80.00 24.00
6 Bob Gibson/5
7 Lou Brock/5
8 Carl Yastrzemski/5
9 Gaylord Perry/50 15.00 4.50
10 Fergie Jenkins/50 25.00 7.50
11 Steve Carlton/20 50.00 15.00
12 Reggie Jackson/5
13 Rod Carew/5
14 Bert Blyleven/50 15.00 4.50
16 Nolan Ryan/5
17 Robin Yount/5
18 George Brett/5
19 Eddie Murray/5
20 Tony Gwynn/5
21 Cal Ripken/5
22 Randy Johnson/5
23 Sammy Sosa/5
24 Rafael Palmeiro/5
25 Roger Clemens/1

2004 Donruss Classics October Heroes

Nm-Mt Ex-Mt
RANDOM INSERTS IN PACKS
STATED PRINT RUN 2499 SERIAL #'d SETS
1 Reggie Jackson 3.00 .90
2 Bob Gibson 3.00 .90
3 Carlton Fisk 3.00 .90
4 Whitey Ford 3.00 .90
5 George Brett 8.00 2.40
6 Roberto Clemente 8.00 2.40
7 Roy Campanella 3.00 .90
8 Babe Ruth 8.00 2.40

2004 Donruss Classics October Heroes Bat

Nm-Mt Ex-Mt
RANDOM INSERTS IN PACKS
PRINT RUNS B/WN 10-25 COPIES PER
NO PRICING OON QTY OF 10 OR LESS
1 Reggie Jackson/25 30.00 9.00
3 Carlton Fisk/25 30.00 9.00
5 George Brett/10
6 Roberto Clemente/25 100.00 30.00
7 Roy Campanella/25 40.00 12.00
8 Babe Ruth/10

2004 Donruss Classics October Heroes Combos Material

Nm-Mt Ex-Mt
PRINT RUNS B/WN 3-25 COPIES PER
NO PRICING ON QTY OF 5 OR LESS...
PRIME PRINT RUN 1 SERIAL #'d SET
NO PRIME PRICING DUE TO SCARCITY
RANDOM INSERTS IN PACKS
1 Reggie Jackson Bat-Hat/25 40.00 12.00
3 Carlton Fisk Bat-Jsy/25 40.00 12.00
5 George Brett Bat-Jsy/25 80.00 24.00
6 Roberto Clemente Bat-Jsy/5
7 R.Campanella Bat-Pants/25 50.00 15.00
8 Babe Ruth Bat-Pants/3

2004 Donruss Classics October Heroes Combos Signature

Nm-Mt Ex-Mt
PRINT RUNS B/WN 5-50 COPIES PER
NO PRICING ON QTY OF 5 OR LESS...
PRIME PRINT RUN 1 SERIAL #'d SET
NO PRIME PRICING DUE TO SCARCITY
RANDOM INSERTS IN PACKS
1 Reggie Jackson Bat/5
2 Bob Gibson Jsy/5
3 Carlton Fisk Jsy/5
4 Whitey Ford Jsy/50 60.00 18.00
5 George Brett Jsy/5

2004 Donruss Classics October Heroes Fabric

Nm-Mt Ex-Mt
PRINT RUNS B/WN 5-25 COPIES PER
NO PRICING ON QTY OF 5 OR LESS...
PRIME PRINT RUN 1 SERIAL #'d SET
NO PRIME PRICING DUE TO SCARCITY
RANDOM INSERTS IN PACKS
2 Bob Gibson Jsy/15 40.00 12.00
3 Carlton Fisk Jsy/25 30.00 9.00
4 Whitey Ford Jsy/25 30.00 9.00
5 George Brett Jsy/25 60.00 18.00
6 Roberto Clemente Jsy/5
7 Roy Campanella Pants/25 40.00 12.00
8 Babe Ruth Pants/5

2004 Donruss Classics October Heroes Signature

Nm-Mt Ex-Mt
RANDOM INSERTS IN PACKS
PRINT RUNS B/WN 5-50 COPIES PER
NO PRICING ON QTY OF 5 OR LESS...
1 Reggie Jackson/5
2 Bob Gibson/5
3 Carlton Fisk/5
4 Whitey Ford/50 40.00 12.00
5 George Brett/5

2004 Donruss Classics Team Colors Bat

Nm-Mt Ex-Mt
RANDOM INSERTS IN PACKS
PRINT RUNS B/WN 10-50 COPIES PER
NO PRICING ON QTY OF 10 OR LESS.
2 Steve Garvey/50 15.00 4.50
3 Eric Davis/25 30.00 9.00
4 Al Oliver/50 10.00 3.00
5 Nolan Ryan/10
6 Bobby Doerr/25 20.00 6.00
7 Paul Molitor/50 25.00 7.50
8 Dale Murphy/50 25.00 7.50
11 Jose Canseco/50 30.00 9.00
12 Jim Rice/50 25.00 7.50
13 Will Clark/50 50.00 15.00
14 Alan Trammell/50 25.00 7.50
16 Dwight Evans/50 25.00 7.50
18 Dave Parker Pirates/25 20.00 6.00
21 Andre Dawson Expos/50 15.00 4.50
22 Darryl Strawberry Dgr/50 25.00 7.50
23 George Foster/50 10.00 3.00
26 Bo Jackson/50 30.00 9.00
27 Cal Ripken/50 80.00 24.00
28 Deion Sanders/25 30.00 9.00
29 Don Mattingly/50 50.00 15.00
30 Mark Grace/50 25.00 7.50
31 Fred Lynn/50 10.00 3.00
33 Ernie Banks/25 40.00 12.00
34 Gary Carter/50 25.00 7.50
35 Roger Maris/25 60.00 18.00
36 Ron Santo/50 25.00 7.50
38 Tony Gwynn/50 25.00 7.50
40 Red Schoendienst/25 20.00 6.00
41 Steve Carlton/25 20.00 6.00
42 Wade Boggs/25 30.00 9.00
44 Luis Aparicio/25 20.00 6.00
46 Andre Dawson Cubs/25 20.00 6.00
48 Darryl Strawberry Mets/50 25.00 7.50
49 Dave Parker Reds/50 15.00 4.50

2004 Donruss Classics Team Colors Combos Material

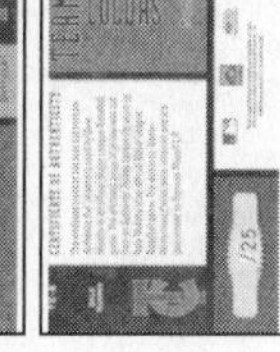

Nm-Mt Ex-Mt
STATED PRINT RUN 25 SERIAL #'d SETS
MARIS PRINT RUN 10 SERIAL #'d CARDS
NO MARIS PRICING DUE TO SCARCITY
PRIME PRINT RUN 1 SERIAL #'d SET
NO PRIME PRICING DUE TO SCARCITY
RANDOM INSERTS IN PACKS
2 Steve Garvey Bat-Jsy 25.00 7.50
3 Eric Davis Bat-Jsy 40.00 12.00
5 Nolan Ryan Bat-Jsy 60.00 18.00
6 Bobby Doerr Bat-Jsy 25.00 7.50
7 Paul Molitor Bat-Jsy 40.00 12.00
8 Dale Murphy Bat-Jsy 40.00 12.00
11 Jose Canseco Bat-Jsy 50.00 15.00
12 Jim Rice Bat-Jsy 40.00 12.00
13 Will Clark Bat-Jsy 80.00 24.00
14 Alan Trammell Bat-Jsy 40.00 12.00
16 Dwight Evans Bat-Jsy 40.00 12.00
18 Dave Parker Pirates Bat-Jsy 25.00 7.50
21 Andre Dawson Expos Bat-Jsy 25.00 7.50
22 Darryl Strawberry Dgr Bat-Jsy 40.00 12.00
23 George Foster Bat-Jsy 20.00 6.00
26 Bo Jackson Bat-Jsy 50.00 15.00
27 Cal Ripken Bat-Jsy 150.00 45.00
28 Deion Sanders Bat-Jsy 40.00 12.00
29 Don Mattingly Bat-Jsy 80.00 24.00
30 Mark Grace Bat-Jsy 40.00 12.00
33 Ernie Banks Bat-Jsy 50.00 15.00
34 Gary Carter Bat-Jacket 40.00 12.00

Card	Nm-Mt	Ex-Mt
35 Roger Maris Bat-Jsy/10		
38 Tony Gwynn Bat-Jsy	60.00	18.00
40 Red Schoendienst Bat-Jsy	25.00	7.50
41 Steve Carlton Bat-Jsy	25.00	7.50
42 Wade Boggs Bat-Jsy	40.00	12.00
44 Luis Aparicio Bat-Jsy	25.00	7.50
46 Andre Dawson Cubs Bat-Jsy	25.00	7.50
48 D.Strawberry Mets Bat-Jsy	40.00	12.00
49 Dave Parker Reds Bat-Jsy	25.00	7.50

2004 Donruss Classics Team Colors Combos Signature

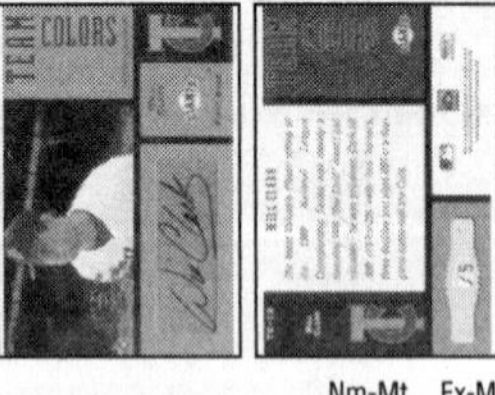

PRINT RUNS B/WN 2-100 COPIES PER
NO PRICING ON QTY OF 10 OR LESS.
PRIME PRINT RUN 1 SERIAL #'d SET
NO PRIME PRICING DUE TO SCARCITY
RANDOM INSERTS IN PACKS

Card	Nm-Mt	Ex-Mt
1 L.Dykstra Mets Fld Glv/100	25.00	7.50
2 Steve Garvey Jsy/100	25.00	7.50
3 Eric Davis Jsy/100	40.00	12.00
4 Al Oliver Bat/100	25.00	7.50
5 Nolan Ryan Jsy/5		
6 Bobby Doerr Jsy/100	25.00	7.50
7 Paul Molitor Jsy/10		
8 Dale Murphy Jsy/10		
9 Harold Baines Jsy/100	40.00	12.00
10 Dwight Gooden Jsy/100	40.00	12.00
11 Jose Canseco Jsy/10		
12 Jim Rice Jsy/100	40.00	12.00
13 Will Clark Jsy/10		
14 Alan Trammell Jsy/100	40.00	12.00
15 Lee Smith Jsy/100	25.00	7.50
16 Dwight Evans Jsy/100	40.00	12.00
17 Tony Oliva Jsy/100	25.00	7.50
18 Dave Parker Pirates Jsy/100	25.00	7.50
19 Jack Morris Jsy/100	25.00	7.50
20 Luis Tiant Jsy/100	25.00	7.50
21 Andre Dawson Expos Jsy/50	40.00	12.00
22 D.Strawberry Dgr Jsy/100	40.00	12.00
23 George Foster Jsy/100	25.00	7.50
24 Marty Marion Jsy/100	25.00	7.50
25 Dennis Eckersley Jsy/100	40.00	12.00
26 Bo Jackson Jsy/10		
27 Cal Ripken Jsy/5		
28 Deion Sanders Jsy/5		
29 Don Mattingly Jacket/10		
30 Mark Grace Jsy/10		
31 Fred Lynn Jsy/100	25.00	7.50
32 Enos Slaughter Jsy/2		
33 Ernie Banks Jsy/25	120.00	36.00
34 Gary Carter Jacket/50	60.00	18.00
36 Ron Santo Bat/25	50.00	15.00
37 Keith Hernandez Jsy/25	80.00	24.00
38 Tony Gwynn Jsy/5		
39 Jim Palmer Jsy/50	40.00	12.00
40 Red Schoendienst Jsy/100	25.00	7.50
41 Steve Carlton Jsy/50	60.00	18.00
42 Wade Boggs Jsy/5		
43 Tommy John Jsy/100	25.00	7.50
44 Luis Aparicio Jsy/100	25.00	7.50
45 Bob Feller Jsy/100	40.00	12.00
46 Andre Dawson Cubs Jsy/50	40.00	12.00
47 Bert Blyleven Jsy/100	25.00	7.50
48 D.Strawberry Mets Jsy/100	40.00	12.00
49 Dave Parker Reds Jsy/100	25.00	7.50
50 L.Dykstra Phils Btg Glv/30	50.00	15.00

2004 Donruss Classics Team Colors Jersey

PRINT RUNS B/WN 10-100 COPIES PER
NO PRICING ON QTY OF 10 OR LESS.
PRIME PRINT RUN 1 SERIAL #'d SET
NO PRIME PRICING DUE TO SCARCITY
RANDOM INSERTS IN PACKS

Card	Nm-Mt	Ex-Mt
1 L.Dykstra Mets Fld Glv/25	20.00	6.00
2 Steve Garvey/100	10.00	3.00
3 Eric Davis/25	30.00	9.00
5 Nolan Ryan/50	50.00	15.00
6 Bobby Doerr/25	20.00	6.00
7 Paul Molitor/100	15.00	4.50
8 Dale Murphy/50	25.00	7.50
9 Harold Baines/100	15.00	4.50
10 Dwight Gooden/50	25.00	7.50
11 Jose Canseco/100	20.00	6.00
12 Jim Rice/100	15.00	4.50
13 Will Clark/50	50.00	15.00
14 Alan Trammell/100	15.00	4.50
15 Lee Smith/100	10.00	3.00
16 Dwight Evans/50	25.00	7.50
17 Tony Oliva/100	10.00	3.00
18 Dave Parker Pirates/25	20.00	6.00
19 Jack Morris/100	10.00	3.00
20 Luis Tiant/100	10.00	3.00
21 Andre Dawson Expos/100	10.00	3.00
22 Darryl Strawberry Dgr/100	15.00	4.50
23 George Foster/100	10.00	3.00
24 Marty Marion/50	15.00	4.50
25 Dennis Eckersley/100	10.00	3.00
26 Bo Jackson/50	30.00	9.00
27 Cal Ripken/100	50.00	15.00
28 Deion Sanders/50	25.00	7.50
29 Don Mattingly Jacket/100	40.00	12.00
30 Mark Grace/50	25.00	7.50
31 Fred Lynn/50	15.00	4.50
32 Enos Slaughter/10		
33 Ernie Banks/25	40.00	12.00
34 Gary Carter Jacket/100	15.00	4.50
35 Roger Maris/10		
37 Keith Hernandez/25	30.00	9.00
38 Tony Gwynn/50	25.00	7.50
39 Jim Palmer/25	20.00	6.00
40 Red Schoendienst/25	20.00	6.00
41 Steve Carlton/25	20.00	6.00
42 Wade Boggs/25	30.00	9.00
43 Tommy John/100	10.00	3.00
44 Luis Aparicio/25	20.00	6.00
45 Bob Feller/10		
46 Andre Dawson Cubs/25	20.00	6.00
47 Bert Blyleven/100	10.00	3.00
48 Darryl Strawberry Mets/100	15.00	4.50
49 Dave Parker Reds/100	10.00	3.00

2004 Donruss Classics Team Colors Signatures

RANDOM INSERTS IN PACKS
PRINT RUNS B/WN 1-50 COPIES PER
NO PRICING ON QTY OF 10 OR LESS.

Card	Nm-Mt	Ex-Mt
1 Len Dykstra Mets/50	25.00	7.50
2 Steve Garvey/50	25.00	7.50
3 Eric Davis/50	40.00	12.00
4 Al Oliver/50	15.00	4.50
5 Nolan Ryan/5		
6 Bobby Doerr/50	25.00	7.50
7 Paul Molitor/5		
8 Dale Murphy/5		
9 Harold Baines/50	40.00	12.00
10 Dwight Gooden/50	40.00	12.00
11 Jose Canseco/5		
12 Jim Rice/50	40.00	12.00
13 Will Clark/5		
14 Alan Trammell/50	40.00	12.00
15 Lee Smith/50	25.00	7.50
16 Dwight Evans/50	40.00	12.00
17 Tony Oliva/50	25.00	7.50
18 Dave Parker Pirates/50	25.00	7.50
19 Jack Morris/50	15.00	4.50
20 Luis Tiant/50	15.00	4.50
21 Andre Dawson Expos/25	30.00	9.00
22 Darryl Strawberry Dgr/50	40.00	12.00
23 George Foster/50	15.00	4.50
24 Marty Marion/50	25.00	7.50
25 Dennis Eckersley/50	40.00	12.00
26 Bo Jackson/5		
27 Cal Ripken/5		
28 Deion Sanders/5		
29 Don Mattingly/5		
30 Mark Grace/5		
31 Fred Lynn/50	15.00	4.50
32 Enos Slaughter/1		
33 Ernie Banks/10		
34 Gary Carter/20	50.00	15.00
36 Ron Santo/10		
37 Keith Hernandez/25	50.00	15.00
38 Tony Gwynn/5		
39 Jim Palmer/20	30.00	9.00
40 Red Schoendienst/50	25.00	7.50
41 Steve Carlton/20	50.00	15.00
42 Wade Boggs/5		
43 Tommy John/50	15.00	4.50
44 Luis Aparicio/50	25.00	7.50
45 Bob Feller/50	40.00	12.00
46 Andre Dawson Cubs/25	30.00	9.00
47 Bert Blyleven/50	15.00	4.50
48 Darryl Strawberry Mets/50	40.00	12.00
49 Dave Parker Reds/50	25.00	7.50
50 Len Dykstra Phils/50	25.00	7.50

2004 Donruss Classics Timeless Triples

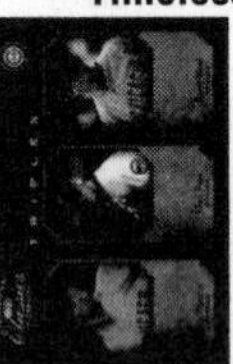

RANDOM INSERTS IN PACKS
STATED PRINT RUN 500 SERIAL #'d SETS

Card	Nm-Mt	Ex-Mt
1 Ted Williams Carl Yastrzemski Carlton Fisk	15.00	4.50
2 Lou Gehrig Roger Maris Thurman Munson	10.00	3.00
3 Brooks Robinson Frank Robinson Cal Ripken	15.00	4.50
4 Roger Clemens Andy Pettitte Roy Oswalt	8.00	2.40
5 Greg Maddux Mark Prior Kerry Wood	10.00	3.00
6 Alex Rodriguez Derek Jeter Gary Sheffield	15.00	4.50

2004 Donruss Classics Timeless Triples Bat

RANDOM INSERTS IN PACKS

Card	Nm-Mt	Ex-Mt
1 Ted Williams Carl Yastrzemski Carlton Fisk	250.00	75.00
2 Lou Gehrig Roger Maris Thurman Munson	300.00	90.00
3 Brooks Robinson Frank Robinson Cal Ripken	175.00	52.50

2004 Donruss Classics Timeless Triples Jersey

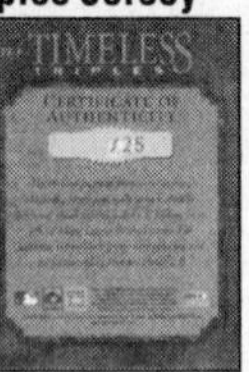

PRINT RUNS B/WN 10-25 COPIES PER
NO PRICING ON QTY OF 10 OR LESS.
ALL ARE JSY SWATCHES UNLESS NOTED
GEHRIG IS PANTS SWATCH
PRIME PRINT RUN 1 SERIAL #'d SET
NO PRIME PRICING DUE TO SCARCITY
RANDOM INSERTS IN PACKS

Card	Nm-Mt	Ex-Mt
1 Ted Williams Carl Yastrzemski Carlton Fisk/10		
2 Lou Gehrig Pants Roger Maris Thurman Munson/10		
3 Brooks Robinson Frank Robinson Cal Ripken/25	200.00	60.00

1998 Donruss Collections Samples

This 200 card standard-size set was issued one per dealer order form or one per media release to herald the release of the 1998 Donruss Prized Collections set. The cards are similar to the regular 1998 Donruss Prized Collections except the backs have the word "Sample" printed on them in big capital black letters.

Card	Nm-Mt	Ex-Mt
COMPLETE SET (200)	1200.00	350.00
1 Paul Molitor	12.00	3.60
2 Juan Gonzalez	10.00	3.00
3 Darryl Kile	2.00	.60
4 Randy Johnson	15.00	4.50
5 Tom Glavine	8.00	2.40
6 Pat Hentgen	2.00	.60
7 David Justice	4.00	1.20
8 Kevin Brown	6.00	1.80
9 Mike Mussina	8.00	2.40
10 Ken Caminiti	4.00	1.20
11 Todd Hundley	4.00	1.20
12 Frank Thomas	12.00	3.60
13 Ray Lankford	4.00	1.20
14 Justin Thompson	2.00	.60
15 Jason Dickson	2.00	.60
16 Kenny Lofton	6.00	1.80
17 Ivan Rodriguez	12.00	3.60
18 Pedro Martinez	12.00	3.60
19 Brady Anderson	4.00	1.20
20 Barry Larkin	8.00	2.40
21 Chipper Jones	25.00	7.50
22 Tony Gwynn	20.00	6.00
23 Roger Clemens	20.00	6.00
24 Sandy Alomar Jr.	4.00	1.20
25 Tino Martinez	4.00	1.20
26 Jeff Bagwell	12.00	3.60
27 Shawn Estes	2.00	.60
28 Ken Griffey Jr.	30.00	9.00
29 Javier Lopez	4.00	1.20
30 Denny Neagle	2.00	.60
31 Mike Piazza	25.00	7.50
32 Andres Galarraga	8.00	2.40
33 Larry Walker	4.00	1.20
34 Alex Rodriguez	25.00	7.50
35 Greg Maddux	25.00	7.50
36 Albert Belle	4.00	1.20
37 Barry Bonds	20.00	6.00
38 Mo Vaughn	2.00	.60
39 Kevin Appier	4.00	1.20
40 Wade Boggs	12.00	3.60
41 Garret Anderson	4.00	1.20
42 Jeffrey Hammonds	2.00	.60
43 Marquis Grissom	4.00	1.20
44 Jim Edmonds	8.00	2.40
45 Brian Jordan	4.00	1.20
46 Raul Mondesi	4.00	1.20
47 John Valentin	2.00	.60
48 Brad Radke	4.00	1.20
49 Ismael Valdes	2.00	.60
50 Matt Stairs	2.00	.60
51 Matt Williams	6.00	1.80
52 Reggie Jefferson	2.00	.60
53 Alan Benes	2.00	.60
54 Charles Johnson	2.00	.60
55 Chuck Knoblauch	4.00	1.20
56 Edgar Martinez	6.00	1.80
57 Nomar Garciaparra	25.00	7.50
58 Craig Biggio	6.00	1.80
59 Bernie Williams	8.00	2.40
60 David Cone	6.00	1.80
61 Cal Ripken	40.00	12.00
62 Mark McGwire	30.00	9.00
63 Roberto Alomar	8.00	2.40
64 Fred McGriff	6.00	1.80
65 Eric Karros	4.00	1.20
66 Robin Ventura	4.00	1.20
67 Darin Erstad	8.00	2.40
68 Michael Tucker	2.00	.60
69 Jim Thome	8.00	2.40
70 Mark Grace	8.00	2.40
71 Lou Collier	2.00	.60
72 Karim Garcia	6.00	1.80
73 Alex Fernandez	2.00	.60
74 J.T. Snow	4.00	1.20
75 Reggie Sanders	4.00	1.20
76 John Smoltz	4.00	1.20
77 Tim Salmon	6.00	1.80
78 Paul O'Neill	4.00	1.20
79 Vinny Castilla	4.00	1.20
80 Rafael Palmeiro	8.00	2.40
81 Jaret Wright	2.00	.60
82 Jay Buhner	4.00	1.20
83 Brett Butler	4.00	1.20
84 Todd Greene	2.00	.60
85 Scott Rolen	8.00	2.40
86 Sammy Sosa	20.00	6.00
87 Jason Giambi	10.00	3.00
88 Carlos Delgado	8.00	2.40
89 Deion Sanders	4.00	1.20
90 Wilton Guerrero	2.00	.60
91 Andy Pettitte	4.00	1.20
92 Brian Giles	6.00	1.80
93 Dmitri Young	4.00	1.20
94 Ron Coomer	2.00	.60
95 Mike Cameron	4.00	1.20
96 Edgardo Alfonzo	8.00	2.40
97 Jimmy Key	2.00	.60
98 Ryan Klesko	4.00	1.20
99 Andy Benes	2.00	.60
100 Derek Jeter	40.00	12.00
101 Jeff Fassero	2.00	.60
102 Neifi Perez	2.00	.60
103 Hideo Nomo	25.00	7.50
104 Andruw Jones	8.00	2.40
105 Todd Helton	12.00	3.60
106 Livan Hernandez	2.00	.60
107 Brett Tomko	2.00	.60
108 Shannon Stewart	4.00	1.20
109 Bartolo Colon	4.00	1.20
110 Matt Morris	6.00	1.80
111 Miguel Tejada	10.00	3.00
112 Pokey Reese	2.00	.60
113 Fernando Tatis	4.00	1.20
114 Todd Dunwoody	2.00	.60
115 Jose Cruz Jr.	4.00	1.20
116 Chan Ho Park	4.00	1.20
117 Kevin Young	2.00	.60
118 Rickey Henderson	20.00	6.00
119 Hideki Irabu	2.00	.60
120 Francisco Cordova	2.00	.60
121 Al Martin	2.00	.60
122 Tony Clark	2.00	.60
123 Curt Schilling	10.00	3.00
124 Rusty Greer	4.00	1.20
125 Jose Canseco	12.00	3.60
126 Edgar Renteria	6.00	1.80
127 Todd Walker	4.00	1.20
128 Wally Joyner	4.00	1.20
129 Bill Mueller	6.00	1.80
130 Jose Guillen	6.00	1.80
131 Manny Ramirez	12.00	3.60
132 Bobby Higginson	4.00	1.20
133 Kevin Orie	2.00	.60
134 Will Clark	15.00	4.50
135 Dave Nilsson	2.00	.60
136 Jason Kendall	4.00	1.20
137 Ivan Cruz	2.00	.60
138 Gary Sheffield	10.00	3.00
139 Bubba Trammell	2.00	.60
140 Vladimir Guerrero	15.00	4.50
141 Dennis Reyes	2.00	.60
142 Bobby Bonilla	2.00	.60
143 Ruben Rivera	2.00	.60
144 Ben Grieve	4.00	1.20
145 Moises Alou	4.00	1.20
146 Tony Womack	2.00	.60
147 Eric Young	2.00	.60
148 Paul Konerko	4.00	1.20
149 Dante Bichette	4.00	1.20
150 Joe Carter	4.00	1.20
151 Rondell White	4.00	1.20
152 Chris Holt	2.00	.60
153 Shawn Green	8.00	2.40
154 Mark Grudzielanek	2.00	.60
155 Jermaine Dye	4.00	1.20
156 Ken Griffey Jr. FC	15.00	4.50
157 Frank Thomas FC	8.00	2.40
158 Chipper Jones FC	8.00	2.40
159 Mike Piazza FC	15.00	4.50
160 Cal Ripken FC	20.00	6.00
161 Greg Maddux FC	10.00	3.00
162 Juan Gonzalez FC	4.00	1.20
163 Alex Rodriguez FC	12.00	3.60
164 Mark McGwire FC	15.00	4.50
165 Derek Jeter FC	20.00	6.00
166 Larry Walker CL	4.00	1.20
167 Tony Gwynn CL	10.00	3.00
168 Tino Martinez CL	2.00	.60
169 Scott Rolen CL	6.00	1.80
170 Nomar Garciaparra CL	12.00	3.60
171 Mark Kotsay RR	4.00	1.20
172 Neifi Perez RR	2.00	.60
173 Paul Konerko RR	4.00	1.20
174 Jose Cruz RR	4.00	1.20
175 Hideki Irabu RR	2.00	.60
176 Mike Cameron RR	4.00	1.20
177 Jeff Suppan RR	2.00	.60
178 Kevin Orie RR	2.00	.60
179 Pokey Reese RR	2.00	.60
180 Todd Dunwoody RR	2.00	.60
181 Miguel Tejada RR	10.00	3.00
182 Jose Guillen RR	6.00	1.80
183 Bartolo Colon RR	8.00	2.40
184 Derrek Lee RR	2.00	.60
185 A.Williamson RR	2.00	.60
186 Wilton Guerrero RR	2.00	.60
187 Jaret Wright RR	2.00	.60
188 Todd Helton RR	12.00	3.60
189 Shannon Stewart RR	4.00	1.20
190 N.Garciaparra RR	30.00	9.00
191 Brett Tomko RR	2.00	.60
192 Fernando Tatis RR	4.00	1.20
193 Raul Ibanez RR	4.00	1.20
194 Dennis Reyes RR	2.00	.60
195 Bobby Estalella RR	2.00	.60
196 Lou Collier RR	2.00	.60
197 Bubba Trammell RR	2.00	.60
198 Ben Grieve RR	4.00	1.20
199 Ivan Cruz RR	2.00	.60
200 Karim Garcia RR	6.00	1.80

1998 Donruss Collections Donruss

The Donruss Collections set was issued in one series totalling 200 cards and inserted at a rate of two cards per pack. The five-card packs retailed for $4.99 each. The set contains the subsets: Fan Club (156-165), Rated Rookie (176-205), and Checklists (166-170). The fronts feature color action photography surrounded by a background of blue and silver stars.

Card	Nm-Mt	Ex-Mt
COMPLETE SET (200)	120.00	36.00
1 Paul Molitor	1.00	.3
2 Juan Gonzalez	1.50	.4
3 Darryl Kile	.60	.1
4 Randy Johnson	1.50	.4
5 Tom Glavine	1.00	.3
6 Pat Hentgen	.40	.1
7 David Justice	.60	.1
8 Kevin Brown	1.00	.3
9 Mike Mussina	1.50	.4
10 Ken Caminiti	.60	.1
11 Todd Hundley	.40	.1
12 Frank Thomas	1.50	.4
13 Ray Lankford	.40	.1
14 Justin Thompson	.40	.1
15 Jason Dickson	.40	.1
16 Kenny Lofton	.60	.1
17 Ivan Rodriguez	1.50	.4
18 Pedro Martinez	1.50	.4
19 Brady Anderson	.60	.1
20 Barry Larkin	1.50	.4
21 Chipper Jones	1.50	.4
22 Tony Gwynn	2.00	.6
23 Roger Clemens	3.00	.9
24 Sandy Alomar Jr.	.40	.1
25 Tino Martinez	1.00	.3
26 Jeff Bagwell	1.00	.3
27 Shawn Estes	.40	.1
28 Ken Griffey Jr.	2.50	.7
29 Javier Lopez	.60	.1
30 Denny Neagle	.40	.1
31 Mike Piazza	2.50	.7
32 Andres Galarraga	.60	.1
33 Larry Walker	1.00	.3
34 Alex Rodriguez	2.50	.7
35 Greg Maddux	2.50	.7
36 Albert Belle	.60	.1
37 Barry Bonds	4.00	1.2
38 Mo Vaughn	.60	.1
39 Kevin Appier	.60	.1
40 Wade Boggs	1.00	.3
41 Garret Anderson	.60	.1
42 Jeffrey Hammonds	.40	.1
43 Marquis Grissom	.40	.1
44 Jim Edmonds	.60	.1
45 Brian Jordan	.60	.1
46 Raul Mondesi	.60	.1
47 John Valentin	.40	.1
48 Brad Radke	.60	.1
49 Ismael Valdes	.40	.1
50 Matt Stairs	.40	.1
51 Matt Williams	.60	.1
52 Reggie Jefferson	.40	.1
53 Alan Benes	.40	.1
54 Charles Johnson	.60	.1
55 Chuck Knoblauch	.60	.1
56 Edgar Martinez	1.00	.3
57 Nomar Garciaparra	2.50	.7
58 Craig Biggio	1.00	.3
59 Bernie Williams	1.00	.3
60 David Cone	.60	.1
61 Cal Ripken	5.00	1.5
62 Mark McGwire	4.00	1.2
63 Roberto Alomar	1.50	.4
64 Fred McGriff	1.00	.3
65 Eric Karros	.60	.1
66 Robin Ventura	.60	.1
67 Darin Erstad	.60	.1
68 Michael Tucker	.40	.1
69 Jim Thome	1.50	.4
70 Mark Grace	1.00	.3
71 Lou Collier	.40	.1
72 Karim Garcia	.40	.1
73 Alex Fernandez	.40	.1
74 J.T. Snow	.60	.1
75 Reggie Sanders	.60	.1
76 John Smoltz	1.00	.3
77 Tim Salmon	1.00	.3
78 Paul O'Neill	1.00	.3
79 Vinny Castilla	.60	.1
80 Rafael Palmeiro	1.00	.3
81 Jaret Wright	.40	.1
82 Jay Buhner	.60	.1
83 Brett Butler	.60	.1
84 Todd Greene	.40	.1
85 Scott Rolen	1.00	.3
86 Sammy Sosa	2.50	.7
87 Jason Giambi	1.50	.4
88 Carlos Delgado	.60	.1
89 Deion Sanders	1.00	.3
90 Wilton Guerrero	.40	.1
91 Andy Pettitte	1.00	.3
92 Brian Giles	.60	.1
93 Dmitri Young	.60	.1
94 Ron Coomer	.40	.1
95 Mike Cameron	.60	.1
96 Edgardo Alfonzo	.60	.1
97 Jimmy Key	.60	.1
98 Ryan Klesko	.60	.1
99 Andy Benes	.40	.1
100 Derek Jeter	4.00	1.2
101 Jeff Fassero	.40	.1
102 Neifi Perez	.40	.1
103 Hideo Nomo	1.50	.4
104 Andruw Jones	.60	.1
105 Todd Helton	1.00	.3
106 Livan Hernandez	.40	.1
107 Brett Tomko	.40	.1
108 Shannon Stewart	.60	.1
109 Bartolo Colon	.60	.1
110 Matt Morris	.60	.1
111 Miguel Tejada	1.00	.3
112 Pokey Reese	.40	.1
113 Fernando Tatis	.40	.1
114 Todd Dunwoody	.40	.1
115 Jose Cruz Jr.	.60	.1
116 Chan Ho Park	.60	.1
117 Kevin Young	.60	.1
118 Rickey Henderson	1.50	.4

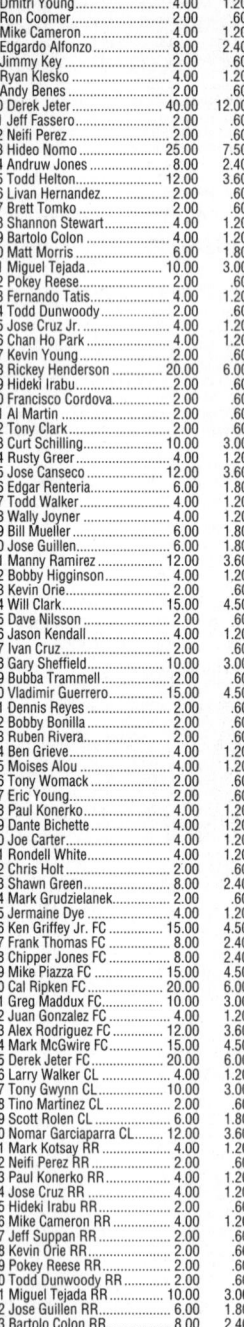

119 Hideki Irabu .40 .12
120 Francisco Cordova .40 .12
121 Al Martin .40 .12
122 Tony Clark .40 .12
123 Curt Schilling 1.00 .30
124 Rusty Greer .60 .18
125 Jose Canseco 1.50 .45
126 Edgar Renteria .60 .18
127 Todd Walker .60 .18
128 Wally Joyner .60 .18
129 Bill Mueller .60 .18
130 Jose Guillen .40 .12
131 Manny Ramirez .60 .18
132 Bobby Higginson .60 .18
133 Kevin Orie .40 .12
134 Will Clark 1.50 .45
135 Dave Nilsson .40 .12
136 Jason Kendall .60 .18
137 Ivan Cruz .40 .12
138 Gary Sheffield .60 .18
139 Bubba Trammell .40 .12
140 Vladimir Guerrero 1.50 .45
141 Dennis Reyes .40 .12
142 Bobby Bonilla .60 .18
143 Ruben Rivera .40 .12
144 Ben Grieve .40 .12
145 Moises Alou .60 .18
146 Tony Womack .40 .12
147 Eric Young .40 .12
148 Paul Konerko .60 .18
149 Dante Bichette .60 .18
150 Joe Carter .60 .18
151 Rondell White .60 .18
152 Chris Holt .40 .12
153 Shawn Green .60 .18
154 Mark Grudzielanek .40 .12
155 Jermaine Dye .60 .18
156 Ken Griffey Jr. FC 1.50 .45
157 Frank Thomas FC 1.00 .30
158 Chipper Jones FC 1.00 .30
159 Mike Piazza FC 1.50 .45
160 Cal Ripken FC 2.50 .75
161 Greg Maddux FC 1.50 .45
162 Juan Gonzalez FC 1.00 .30
163 Alex Rodriguez FC 1.50 .45
164 Mark McGwire FC 2.00 .60
165 Derek Jeter FC 2.00 .60
166 Larry Walker CL .60 .18
167 Tony Gwynn CL 1.00 .30
168 Tino Martinez CL .60 .18
169 Scott Rolen CL .60 .18
170 Nomar Garciaparra CL 1.50 .45
176 Mark Kotsay RR .40 .12
177 Neifi Perez RR .40 .12
178 Paul Konerko RR .60 .18
179 Jose Cruz Jr. RR .60 .18
180 Hideki Irabu RR .40 .12
181 Mike Cameron RR .60 .18
182 Jeff Suppan RR .40 .12
183 Kevin Orie RR .40 .12
184 Pokey Reese RR .40 .12
185 Todd Dunwoody RR .40 .12
186 Miguel Tejada RR 1.00 .30
187 Jose Guillen RR .40 .12
188 Bartolo Colon RR .60 .18
189 Derrek Lee RR .60 .18
190 A.Williamson RR .40 .12
191 Wilton Guerrero RR .40 .12
192 Jaret Wright RR .40 .12
193 Todd Helton RR 1.00 .30
194 Shannon Stewart RR .60 .18
195 N.Garciaparra RR 2.50 .75
196 Brett Tomko RR .40 .12
197 Fernando Tatis RR .40 .12
198 Raul Ibanez RR .40 .12
199 Dennis Reyes RR .40 .12
200 Bobby Estalella RR .40 .12
201 Lou Collier RR .40 .12
202 Bubba Trammell RR .40 .12
203 Ben Grieve RR .40 .12
204 Ivan Cruz RR .40 .12
205 Karim Garcia RR .40 .12

1998 Donruss Collections Elite

These cards were issued one card per Donruss Collection pack. These cards parallel the Donruss Elite set and have the same checklist and subsets as the regular Donruss cards.

Nm-Mt Ex-Mt
401 Ken Griffey Jr. 4.00 1.20
402 Frank Thomas 2.50 .75
403 Alex Rodriguez 4.00 1.20
404 Mike Piazza 4.00 1.20
405 Greg Maddux 4.00 1.20
406 Cal Ripken 8.00 2.40
407 Chipper Jones 2.50 .75
408 Derek Jeter 6.00 1.80
409 Tony Gwynn 3.00 .90
410 Andruw Jones 1.00 .30
411 Juan Gonzalez 2.50 .75
412 Jeff Bagwell 1.50 .45
413 Mark McGwire 6.00 1.80
414 Roger Clemens 5.00 1.50
415 Albert Belle 1.00 .30
416 Barry Bonds 6.00 1.80
417 Kenny Lofton 1.00 .30
418 Ivan Rodriguez 2.50 .75
419 Manny Ramirez 1.00 .30
420 Jim Thome 2.50 .75
421 Chuck Knoblauch 1.00 .30
422 Paul Molitor 1.50 .45
423 Barry Larkin 2.50 .75
424 Andy Pettitte 1.50 .45
425 John Smoltz 1.50 .45
426 Randy Johnson 2.50 .75
427 Bernie Williams 1.50 .45
428 Larry Walker 1.50 .45
429 Mo Vaughn 1.00 .30
430 Bobby Higginson 1.00 .30
431 Edgardo Alfonzo 1.00 .30
432 Justin Thompson .60 .18
433 Jeff Suppan .60 .18
434 Roberto Alomar 2.50 .75
435 Hideo Nomo 2.50 .75
436 Rusty Greer 1.00 .30
437 Tim Salmon 1.50 .45
438 Jim Edmonds 1.00 .30
439 Gary Sheffield 1.00 .30
440 Ken Caminiti 1.00 .30
441 Sammy Sosa 4.00 1.20
442 Tony Womack .60 .18
443 Matt Williams 1.00 .30
444 Andres Galarraga 1.00 .30
445 Garret Anderson 1.00 .30
446 Rafael Palmeiro 1.50 .45
447 Mike Mussina 2.50 .75
448 Craig Biggio 1.50 .45
449 Wade Boggs 1.50 .45
450 Tom Glavine 1.50 .45
451 Jason Giambi 2.50 .75
452 Will Clark 2.50 .75
453 David Justice 1.00 .30
454 Sandy Alomar Jr. .60 .18
455 Edgar Martinez 1.50 .45
456 Brady Anderson 1.00 .30
457 Eric Young .60 .18
458 Ray Lankford .60 .18
459 Kevin Brown 1.50 .45
460 Raul Mondesi 1.00 .30
461 Bobby Bonilla 1.00 .30
462 Javier Lopez 1.00 .30
463 Fred McGriff 1.50 .45
464 Rondell White 1.00 .30
465 Todd Hundley .60 .18
466 Mark Grace 1.50 .45
467 Alan Benes .60 .18
468 Jeff Abbott .60 .18
469 Bob Abreu 1.00 .30
470 Deion Sanders 1.00 .30
471 Tino Martinez 1.50 .45
472 Shannon Stewart 1.00 .30
473 Homer Bush .60 .18
474 Carlos Delgado 1.00 .30
475 Raul Ibanez .60 .18
476 Hideki Irabu .60 .18
477 Jose Cruz Jr. 1.00 .30
478 Tony Clark 1.00 .30
479 Wilton Guerrero .60 .18
480 Vladimir Guerrero 2.50 .75
481 Scott Rolen 1.50 .45
482 Nomar Garciaparra 4.00 1.20
483 Darin Erstad 1.00 .30
484 Chan Ho Park 1.00 .30
485 Mike Cameron 1.00 .30
486 Todd Walker 1.00 .30
487 Todd Dunwoody .60 .18
488 Neifi Perez .60 .18
489 Brett Tomko .60 .18
490 Jose Guillen .60 .18
491 Matt Morris 1.00 .30
492 Bartolo Colon 1.00 .30
493 Jaret Wright .60 .18
494 Shawn Estes .60 .18
495 Livan Hernandez .60 .18
496 Bobby Estalella .60 .18
497 Ben Grieve .60 .18
498 Paul Konerko 1.00 .30
499 David Ortiz 1.00 .30
500 Todd Helton 1.50 .45
501 Juan Encarnacion .60 .18
502 Bubba Trammell .60 .18
503 Miguel Tejada 1.50 .45
504 Jacob Cruz .60 .18
505 Todd Greene .60 .18
506 Kevin Orie .60 .18
507 Mark Kotsay .60 .18
508 Fernando Tatis .60 .18
509 Jay Payton .60 .18
510 Pokey Reese .60 .18
511 Derrek Lee 1.00 .30
512 Richard Hidalgo 1.00 .30
513 Ricky Ledee .60 .18
514 Lou Collier .60 .18
515 Ruben Rivera .60 .18
516 Shawn Green 1.00 .30
517 Moises Alou 1.00 .30
518 Ken Griffey Jr. GEN 2.50 .75
519 Frank Thomas GEN 1.50 .45
520 Alex Rodriguez GEN 2.50 .75
521 Mike Piazza GEN 2.50 .75
522 Greg Maddux GEN 2.50 .75
523 Cal Ripken GEN 4.00 1.20
524 Chipper Jones GEN 1.50 .45
525 Derek Jeter GEN 3.00 .90
526 Tony Gwynn GEN 1.50 .45
527 Andruw Jones GEN .60 .18
528 Juan Gonzalez GEN 1.50 .45
529 Jeff Bagwell GEN 1.00 .30
530 Mark McGwire GEN 3.00 .90
531 Roger Clemens GEN 2.50 .75
532 Albert Belle GEN .60 .18
533 Barry Bonds GEN 2.50 .75
534 Kenny Lofton GEN .60 .18
535 Ivan Rodriguez GEN 1.50 .45
536 Manny Ramirez GEN 1.00 .30
537 Jim Thome GEN 1.50 .45
538 C.Knoblauch GEN .60 .18
539 Paul Molitor GEN 1.00 .30
540 Barry Larkin GEN 1.50 .45
541 Mo Vaughn GEN .60 .18
542 Hideki Irabu GEN .60 .18
543 Jose Cruz Jr. GEN .60 .18
544 Tony Clark GEN .60 .18
545 V.Guerrero GEN 1.50 .45
546 Scott Rolen GEN 1.00 .30
547 N.Garciaparra GEN 2.50 .75
548 Nomar Garciaparra CL 2.50 .75
549 Larry Walker CL 1.00 .30
550 Tino Martinez CL 1.00 .30

1998 Donruss Collections Leaf

The Donruss Collections Leaf set contains 200 cards and inserted at a rate of two cards per pack. The set contains the subsets: Curtain Calls (347-356), Gold Leaf Stars (357-376), Gold Leaf Rookies (377-396), and Checklists (397-399).

Nm-Mt Ex-Mt
201 Rusty Greer .75 .23
202 Tino Martinez 1.25 .35
203 Bobby Bonilla .75 .23
204 Jason Giambi 2.00 .60
205 Matt Morris .75 .23
206 Craig Counsell .50 .15
207 Reggie Jefferson .50 .15
208 Brian Rose .50 .15
209 Ruben Rivera .50 .15
210 Shawn Estes .50 .15
211 Tony Gwynn 2.50 .75
212 Jeff Abbott .50 .15
213 Jose Cruz Jr. .75 .23
214 Francisco Cordova .50 .15
215 Ryan Klesko .75 .23
216 Tim Salmon 1.25 .35
217 Brett Tomko .50 .15
218 Matt Williams .75 .23
219 Joe Carter .75 .23
220 Harold Baines .75 .23
221 Gary Sheffield .75 .23
222 Charles Johnson .75 .23
223 Aaron Boone .75 .23
224 Eddie Murray 2.00 .60
225 Matt Stairs .50 .15
226 David Cone .75 .23
227 Jon Nunnally .50 .15
228 Chris Stynes .50 .15
229 Enrique Wilson .50 .15
230 Randy Johnson 2.00 .60
231 Garret Anderson .75 .23
232 Manny Ramirez .75 .23
233 Jeff Suppan .50 .15
234 Rickey Henderson 2.00 .60
235 Scott Spiezio .50 .15
236 Rondell White .75 .23
237 Todd Greene .50 .15
238 Delino DeShields .50 .15
239 Kevin Brown 1.25 .35
240 Chili Davis .75 .23
241 Jimmy Key .75 .23
242 Mike Mussina 2.00 .60
243 Joe Randa .50 .15
244 Chan Ho Park .75 .23
245 Brad Radke .75 .23
246 Geronimo Berroa .50 .15
247 Wade Boggs 1.25 .35
248 Kevin Appier .75 .23
249 Moises Alou .75 .23
250 David Justice .75 .23
251 Ivan Rodriguez 2.00 .60
252 J.T. Snow .75 .23
253 Brian Giles .75 .23
254 Will Clark 2.00 .60
255 Justin Thompson .50 .15
256 Javier Lopez .75 .23
257 Hideki Irabu .50 .15
258 Mark Grudzielanek .50 .15
259 Abraham Nunez .50 .15
260 Todd Hollandsworth .50 .15
261 Jay Bell .75 .23
262 Nomar Garciaparra 3.00 .90
263 Vinny Castilla .75 .23
264 Lou Collier .50 .15
265 Kevin Orie .50 .15
266 John Valentin .50 .15
267 Robin Ventura .75 .23
268 Denny Neagle .50 .15
269 Tony Womack .50 .15
270 Dennis Reyes .50 .15
271 Wally Joyner .75 .23
272 Kevin Brown 1.25 .35
273 Ray Durham .75 .23
274 Mike Cameron .75 .23
275 Dante Bichette .75 .23
276 Jose Guillen .50 .15
277 Carlos Delgado .75 .23
278 Paul Molitor 1.25 .35
279 Jason Kendall .75 .23
280 Mark Bellhorn .50 .15
281 Damian Jackson .50 .15
282 Bill Mueller .75 .23
283 Kevin Young .75 .23
284 Curt Schilling 1.25 .35
285 Jeffrey Hammonds .50 .15
286 Sandy Alomar Jr. .50 .15
287 Bartolo Colon .75 .23
288 Wilton Guerrero .50 .15
289 Bernie Williams 1.25 .35
290 Deion Sanders 1.25 .35
291 Mike Piazza 3.00 .90
292 Butch Huskey .50 .15
293 Edgardo Alfonzo .75 .23
294 Alan Benes .50 .15
295 Craig Biggio 1.25 .35
296 Mark Grace 1.25 .35
297 Shawn Green .75 .23
298 Derrek Lee .75 .23
299 Ken Griffey Jr. 3.00 .90
300 Tim Raines .75 .23
301 Pokey Reese .50 .15
302 Lee Stevens .50 .15
303 Shannon Stewart .75 .23
304 John Smoltz 1.25 .35
305 Frank Thomas 2.00 .60
306 Jeff Fassero .50 .15
307 Jay Buhner .75 .23
308 Jose Canseco 2.00 .60
309 Omar Vizquel .75 .23
310 Travis Fryman .75 .23
311 Dave Nilsson .50 .15
312 John Olerud .75 .23
313 Larry Walker 1.25 .35
314 Jim Edmonds .75 .23
315 Bobby Higginson .75 .23
316 Todd Hundley .50 .15
317 Paul O'Neill 1.25 .35
318 Bip Roberts .50 .15
319 Ismael Valdes .50 .15
320 Pedro Martinez 2.00 .60
321 Jeff Cirillo .50 .15
322 Andy Benes .50 .15
323 Bobby Jones .50 .15
324 Brian Hunter .50 .15
325 Darryl Kile .75 .23
326 Pat Hentgen .50 .15
327 Marquis Grissom .50 .15
328 Eric Davis .75 .23
329 Chipper Jones 2.00 .60
330 Edgar Martinez 1.25 .35
331 Andy Pettitte 1.25 .35
332 Cal Ripken 6.00 1.80
333 Scott Rolen 1.25 .35
334 Ron Coomer .50 .15
335 Luis Castillo .75 .23
336 Fred McGriff 1.25 .35
337 Neifi Perez .50 .15
338 Eric Karros .75 .23
339 Alex Fernandez .50 .15
340 Jason Dickson .50 .15
341 Lance Johnson .50 .15
342 Ray Lankford .50 .15
343 Sammy Sosa 3.00 .90
344 Eric Young .50 .15
345 Bubba Trammell .50 .15
346 Todd Walker .75 .23
347 Mo Vaughn CC .50 .15
348 Jeff Bagwell CC .75 .23
349 Kenny Lofton CC .50 .15
350 Raul Mondesi CC .50 .15
351 Mike Piazza CC 2.00 .60
352 Chipper Jones CC 1.25 .35
353 Larry Walker CC .75 .23
354 Greg Maddux CC 2.00 .60
355 Ken Griffey Jr. CC 2.00 .60
356 Frank Thomas CC 1.25 .35
357 Darin Erstad GLS .50 .15
358 Roberto Alomar GLS 1.25 .35
359 Albert Belle GLS .50 .15
360 Jim Thome GLS 1.25 .35
361 Tony Clark GLS .50 .15
362 Chuck Knoblauch GLS .50 .15
363 Derek Jeter GLS 2.50 .75
364 Alex Rodriguez GLS 2.00 .60
365 Tony Gwynn GLS 1.25 .35
366 Roger Clemens GLS 2.00 .60
367 Barry Larkin GLS 1.25 .35
368 Andres Galarraga GLS .50 .15
369 V.Guerrero GLS 1.25 .35
370 Mark McGwire GLS 2.50 .75
371 Barry Bonds GLS 2.00 .60
372 Juan Gonzalez GLS 1.25 .35
373 Andruw Jones GLS .50 .15
374 Paul Molitor GLS .75 .23
375 Hideo Nomo GLS 1.25 .35
376 Cal Ripken GLS 3.00 .90
377 Brad Fullmer GLR .50 .15
378 Jaret Wright GLR .50 .15
379 Bobby Estalella GLR .50 .15
380 Ben Grieve GLR .50 .15
381 Paul Konerko GLR .75 .23
382 David Ortiz GLR .75 .23
383 Todd Helton GLR 1.25 .35
384 J.Encarnacion GLR .50 .15
385 Miguel Tejada GLR 1.25 .35
386 Jacob Cruz GLR .50 .15
387 Mark Kotsay GLR .50 .15
388 Fernando Tatis GLR .50 .15
389 Ricky Ledee GLR .50 .15
390 Richard Hidalgo GLR .75 .23
391 Richie Sexson GLR .75 .23
392 Luis Ordaz GLR .50 .15
393 Eli Marrero GLR .50 .15
394 Livan Hernandez GLR .50 .15
395 Homer Bush GLR .50 .15
396 Raul Ibanez GLR .50 .15
397 Nomar Garciaparra CL 2.00 .60
398 Scott Rolen CL .75 .23
399 Jose Cruz Jr. CL .50 .15
400 Al Martin .50 .15

1998 Donruss Collections Preferred

These cards, which parallel the regular Donruss Preferred set were issued one every two packs. According to published reports, less than 1400 sets were produced. Again, the checklist matches the regular Donruss Preferred set.

Nm-Mt Ex-Mt
551 Ken Griffey Jr. EX 12.00 3.60
552 Frank Thomas EX 8.00 2.40
553 Cal Ripken EX 25.00 7.50
554 Alex Rodriguez EX 12.00 3.60
555 Greg Maddux EX 12.00 3.60
556 Mike Piazza EX 12.00 3.60
557 Chipper Jones EX 8.00 2.40
558 Tony Gwynn FB 10.00 3.00
559 Derek Jeter FB 20.00 6.00
560 Jeff Bagwell EX 5.00 1.50
561 Juan Gonzalez EX 8.00 2.40
562 Nomar Garciaparra EX 12.00 3.60
563 Andruw Jones FB 3.00 .90
564 Hideo Nomo FB 8.00 2.40
565 Roger Clemens FB 15.00 4.50
566 Mark McGwire FB 20.00 6.00
567 Scott Rolen FB 5.00 1.50
568 Vladimir Guerrero FB 8.00 2.40
569 Barry Bonds FB 20.00 6.00
570 Darin Erstad FB 3.00 .90
571 Albert Belle FB 3.00 .90
572 Kenny Lofton FB 3.00 .90
573 Mo Vaughn FB 3.00 .90
574 Tony Clark FB 2.00 .60
575 Ivan Rodriguez FB 8.00 2.40
576 Larry Walker CB 5.00 1.50
577 Eddie Murray CB 8.00 2.40
578 Andy Pettitte CB 5.00 1.50
579 Roberto Alomar CB 8.00 2.40
580 Randy Johnson CB 8.00 2.40
581 Manny Ramirez CB 3.00 .90
582 Paul Molitor FB 5.00 1.50
583 Mike Mussina CB 8.00 2.40
584 Jim Thome FB 8.00 2.40
585 Tino Martinez CB 5.00 1.50
586 Gary Sheffield CB 3.00 .90
587 Chuck Knoblauch CB 3.00 .90
588 Bernie Williams CB 5.00 1.50
589 Tim Salmon CB 5.00 1.50
590 Sammy Sosa CB 12.00 3.60
591 Wade Boggs CB 5.00 1.50
592 Will Clark GS 8.00 2.40
593 Andres Galarraga CB 3.00 .90
594 Raul Mondesi CB 3.00 .90
595 Rickey Henderson GS 8.00 2.40
596 Jose Canseco GS 8.00 2.40
597 Pedro Martinez GS 8.00 2.40
598 Jay Buhner GS 3.00 .90
599 Ryan Klesko GS 3.00 .90
600 Barry Larkin CB 8.00 2.40
601 Charles Johnson GS 3.00 .90
602 Tom Glavine GS 5.00 1.50
603 Edgar Martinez CB 5.00 1.50
604 Fred McGriff GS 5.00 1.50
605 Moises Alou ME 3.00 .90
606 Dante Bichette GS 3.00 .90
607 Jim Edmonds CB 3.00 .90
608 Mark Grace ME 5.00 1.50
609 Chan Ho Park ME 3.00 .90
610 Justin Thompson ME 2.00 .60
611 John Smoltz ME 5.00 1.50
612 Craig Biggio CB 5.00 1.50
613 Ken Caminiti ME 3.00 .90
614 Deion Sanders ME 5.00 1.50
615 Carlos Delgado GS 3.00 .90
616 David Justice CB 3.00 .90
617 J.T. Snow GS 3.00 .90
618 Jason Giambi CB 8.00 2.40
619 Garret Anderson ME 3.00 .90
620 Rondell White ME 3.00 .90
621 Matt Williams ME 3.00 .90
622 Brady Anderson ME 3.00 .90
623 Eric Karros GS 3.00 .90
624 Javier Lopez GS 3.00 .90
625 Pat Hentgen GS 2.00 .60
626 Todd Hundley GS 2.00 .60
627 Ray Lankford GS 2.00 .60
628 Denny Neagle GS 2.00 .60
629 Henry Rodriguez GS 2.00 .60
630 Sandy Alomar Jr. ME 2.00 .60
631 Rafael Palmeiro ME 5.00 1.50
632 Robin Ventura GS 3.00 .90
633 John Olerud GS 3.00 .90
634 Omar Vizquel GS 3.00 .90
635 Joe Randa GS 2.00 .60
636 Lance Johnson GS 2.00 .60
637 Kevin Brown GS 5.00 1.50
638 Curt Schilling GS 5.00 1.50
639 Ismael Valdes GS 2.00 .60
640 Francisco Cordova GS 2.00 .60
641 David Cone GS 3.00 .90
642 Paul O'Neill GS 5.00 1.50
643 Jimmy Key GS 3.00 .90
644 Brad Radke GS 3.00 .90
645 Kevin Appier GS 3.00 .90
646 Al Martin GS 2.00 .60
647 Rusty Greer ME 3.00 .90
648 Reggie Jefferson GS 2.00 .60
649 Ron Coomer GS 2.00 .60
650 Vinny Castilla GS 3.00 .90
651 Bobby Bonilla ME 3.00 .90
652 Eric Young GS 2.00 .60
653 Tony Womack GS 2.00 .60
654 Jason Kendall GS 3.00 .90
655 Jeff Suppan GS 2.00 .60
656 Shawn Estes ME 2.00 .60
657 Shawn Green GS 3.00 .90
658 Edgardo Alfonzo ME 3.00 .90
659 Alan Benes ME 2.00 .60
660 Bobby Higginson GS 3.00 .90
661 Mark Grudzielanek GS 2.00 .60
662 Wilton Guerrero GS 2.00 .60
663 Todd Greene ME 2.00 .60
664 Pokey Reese GS 2.00 .60
665 Jose Guillen CB 2.00 .60
666 Neifi Perez ME 2.00 .60
667 Luis Castillo GS 3.00 .90
668 Edgar Renteria GS 3.00 .90
669 Karim Garcia GS 2.00 .60
670 Butch Huskey GS 2.00 .60
671 Michael Tucker GS 2.00 .60
672 Jason Dickson GS 2.00 .60
673 Todd Walker ME 3.00 .90
674 Brian Jordan GS 3.00 .90
675 Joe Carter GS 3.00 .90
676 Matt Morris ME 3.00 .90
677 Brett Tomko ME 2.00 .60
678 Mike Cameron CB 3.00 .90
679 Russ Davis GS 2.00 .60
680 Shannon Stewart ME 3.00 .90
681 Kevin Orie GS 2.00 .60
682 Scott Spiezio GS 2.00 .60
683 Brian Giles GS 3.00 .90
684 Raul Casanova GS 2.00 .60
685 Jose Cruz Jr. CB 3.00 .90
686 Hideki Irabu GS 2.00 .60
687 Bubba Trammell GS 2.00 .60
688 Richard Hidalgo CB 3.00 .90
689 Paul Konerko GS 3.00 .90
690 Todd Helton FB 5.00 1.50
691 Miguel Tejada CB 5.00 1.50
692 Fernando Tatis ME 2.00 .60
693 Ben Grieve FB 2.00 .60
694 Travis Lee FB 2.00 .60
695 Mark Kotsay CB 2.00 .60
696 Eli Marrero ME 2.00 .60
697 David Ortiz CB 3.00 .90
698 Juan Encarnacion ME 2.00 .60
699 Jaret Wright ME 2.00 .60

700 Livan Hernandez CB 2.00 .60
701 Ruben Rivera GS 2.00 .60
702 Brad Fullmer ME 2.00 .60
703 Dennis Reyes GS 2.00 .60
704 Enrique Wilson ME 2.00 .60
705 Todd Dunwoody ME 2.00 .60
706 Derrick Gibson ME 2.00 .60
707 Aaron Boone ME 3.00 .90
708 Ron Wright ME 2.00 .60
709 Preston Wilson ME 3.00 .90
710 Abraham Nunez GS 2.00 .60
711 Shane Monahan GS 2.00 .60
712 Carl Pavano GS 2.00 .60
713 Derrek Lee GS 3.00 .90
714 Jeff Abbott GS 2.00 .60
715 Wes Helms ME 2.00 .60
716 Brian Rose GS 2.00 .60
717 Bobby Estalella GS 2.00 .60
718 Ken Griffey Jr. PP GS 8.00 2.40
719 Frank Thomas PP GS 5.00 1.50
720 Cal Ripken PP GS 12.00 3.60
721 Alex Rodriguez PP GS 8.00 2.40
722 Greg Maddux PP GS 8.00 2.40
723 Mike Piazza PP GS 8.00 2.40
724 Chipper Jones PP GS 5.00 1.50
725 Tony Gwynn PP GS 5.00 1.50
726 Derek Jeter PP GS 10.00 3.00
727 Jeff Bagwell PP GS 3.00 .90
728 Juan Gonzalez PP GS 5.00 1.50
729 N. Garciaparra PP GS 8.00 2.40
730 Andruw Jones PP GS 2.00 .60
731 Hideo Nomo PP GS 5.00 1.50
732 R.Clemens PP GS 8.00 2.40
733 Mark McGwire PP GS 10.00 3.00
734 Scott Rolen PP GS 3.00 .90
735 Barry Bonds PP GS 8.00 2.40
736 Darin Erstad PP GS 2.00 .60
737 Mo Vaughn PP GS 2.00 .60
738 Ivan Rodriguez PP GS 8.00 2.40
739 Larry Walker PP ME 3.00 .90
740 Andy Pettitte PP GS 3.00 .90
741 R.Johnson PP ME 5.00 1.50
742 Paul Molitor PP GS 3.00 .90
743 Jim Thome PP GS 5.00 1.50
744 Tino Martinez PP ME 3.00 .90
745 Gary Sheffield PP GS 2.00 .60
746 Albert Belle PP GS 2.00 .60
747 Jose Cruz Jr. PP GS 2.00 .60
748 Todd Helton CL GS 3.00 .90
749 Ben Grieve CL GS 2.00 .60
750 Paul Konerko CL GS 2.00 .60

1998 Donruss Prized Collections Donruss

These cards parallel the 1998 Donruss set. According to published reports, less than 560 sets were produced.

Nm-Mt Ex-Mt
*STARS: 1.25X TO 3X BASIC DONRUSS COLL.

1998 Donruss Prized Collections Elite

These cards parallel the already paralleled Donruss Elite set. According to published reports, less than 220 sets were produced.

Nm-Mt Ex-Mt
*STARS: 1.5X TO 4X BASIC ELITE COLL.

1998 Donruss Prized Collections Leaf

These cards parallel the already parallelled Leaf set. According to published reports, less than 400 sets were produced.

Nm-Mt Ex-Mt
*STARS: 1.25X TO 3X BASIC LEAF COLL.

1998 Donruss Prized Collections Preferred

These cards parallel the already parallelled Donruss Preferred set. According to published reports, less than 55 sets were produced.

Nm-Mt Ex-Mt
*STARS: 1.25X TO 3X BASIC PREF.COLL.

1997 Donruss Elite

The 1997 Donruss Elite set was issued in one series totalling 150 cards. The product was distributed exclusively to hobby dealers around February, 1997. Each foil-wrapped pack contained eight cards and carried a suggested retail price of $3.49. Player selection was limited to the top stars (plus three player checklist cards) and card design is very similar to the Donruss Elite hockey set that was released one year earlier. Strangely enough, the backs only provide career statistics neglecting statistics from the previous season.

Nm-Mt Ex-Mt
COMPLETE SET (150) 25.00 7.50
1 Juan Gonzalez 1.00 .30
2 Alex Rodriguez 1.50 .45
3 Frank Thomas 1.00 .30
4 Greg Maddux 1.50 .45
5 Ken Griffey Jr. 1.50 .45
6 Cal Ripken 3.00 .90
7 Mike Piazza 1.50 .45
8 Chipper Jones 1.00 .30
9 Albert Belle .40 .12
10 Andruw Jones .40 .12
11 Vladimir Guerrero 1.00 .30
12 Mo Vaughn .40 .12
UER front Gonzales
13 Ivan Rodriguez 1.00 .30
14 Andy Pettitte .60 .18
15 Tony Gwynn 1.25 .35
16 Barry Bonds 2.50 .75
17 Jeff Bagwell .60 .18
18 Manny Ramirez .40 .12
19 Kenny Lofton .40 .12
20 Roberto Alomar 1.00 .30
21 Mark McGwire 2.50 .75
22 Ryan Klesko .40 .12
23 Tim Salmon .60 .18
24 Derek Jeter 2.50 .75
25 Eddie Murray 1.00 .30
26 Jermaine Dye .40 .12
27 Ruben Rivera .40 .12
28 Jim Edmonds .40 .12
29 Mike Mussina 1.00 .30
30 Randy Johnson 1.00 .30
31 Sammy Sosa 1.50 .45
32 Hideo Nomo 1.00 .30
33 Chuck Knoblauch .40 .12
34 Paul Molitor .60 .18
35 Rafael Palmeiro .60 .18
36 Brady Anderson .40 .12
37 Will Clark 1.00 .30
38 Craig Biggio .60 .18
39 Jason Giambi 1.00 .30
40 Roger Clemens 2.00 .60
41 Jay Buhner .40 .12
42 Edgar Martinez .60 .18
43 Gary Sheffield .40 .12
44 Fred McGriff .60 .18
45 Bobby Bonilla .40 .12
46 Tom Glavine .60 .18
47 Wade Boggs .60 .18
48 Jeff Conine .40 .12
49 John Smoltz .60 .18
50 Jim Thome 1.00 .30
51 Billy Wagner .40 .12
52 Jose Canseco 1.00 .30
53 Javy Lopez .40 .12
54 Cecil Fielder .40 .12
55 Garret Anderson .40 .12
56 Alex Ochoa .40 .12
57 Scott Rolen .60 .18
58 Darin Erstad .40 .12
59 Rey Ordonez .40 .12
60 Dante Bichette .40 .12
61 Joe Carter .40 .12
62 Moises Alou .40 .12
63 Jason Isringhausen .40 .12
64 Karim Garcia .40 .12
65 Brian Jordan .40 .12
66 Ruben Sierra .40 .12
67 Todd Hollandsworth .40 .12
68 Paul Wilson .40 .12
69 Ernie Young .40 .12
70 Ryne Sandberg 1.50 .45
71 Raul Mondesi .40 .12
72 George Arias .40 .12
73 Ray Durham .40 .12
74 Dean Palmer .40 .12
75 Shawn Green .40 .12
76 Eric Young .40 .12
77 Jason Kendall .40 .12
78 Greg Vaughn .40 .12
79 Terrell Wade .40 .12
80 Bill Pulsipher .40 .12
81 Bobby Higginson .40 .12
82 Mark Grudzielanek .40 .12
83 Ken Caminiti .40 .12
84 Todd Greene .40 .12
85 Carlos Delgado .40 .12
86 Mark Grace .60 .18
87 Rondell White .40 .12
88 Barry Larkin 1.00 .30
89 J.T. Snow .40 .12
90 Alex Gonzalez .40 .12
91 Raul Casanova .40 .12
92 Marc Newfield .40 .12
93 Jermaine Allensworth .40 .12
94 John Mabry .40 .12
95 Kirby Puckett 1.00 .30
96 Travis Fryman .40 .12
97 Kevin Brown .40 .12
98 Andres Galarraga .40 .12
99 Marty Cordova .40 .12
100 Henry Rodriguez .40 .12
101 Sterling Hitchcock .40 .12
102 Trey Beamon .40 .12
103 Brett Butler .40 .12
104 Rickey Henderson 1.00 .30
105 Tino Martinez .60 .18
106 Kevin Appier .40 .12
107 Brian Hunter .40 .12
108 Eric Karros .40 .12
109 Andre Dawson .40 .12
110 Darryl Strawberry .60 .18
111 James Baldwin .40 .12
112 Chad Mottola .40 .12
113 Dave Nilsson .40 .12
114 Carlos Baerga .40 .12
115 Chan Ho Park .40 .12
116 John Jaha .40 .12
117 Alan Benes .40 .12
118 Mariano Rivera .60 .18
119 Ellis Burks .40 .12
120 Tony Clark .40 .12
121 Todd Walker .40 .12
122 Dwight Gooden .60 .18
123 Ugueth Urbina .40 .12
124 David Cone .40 .12
125 Ozzie Smith 1.50 .45
126 Kimera Bartee .40 .12
127 Rusty Greer .40 .12
128 Pat Hentgen .40 .12
129 Charles Johnson .40 .12
130 Quinton McCracken .40 .12
131 Troy Percival .40 .12
132 Shane Reynolds .40 .12
133 Charles Nagy .40 .12
134 Tom Goodwin .40 .12
135 Ron Gant .40 .12
136 Dan Wilson .40 .12
137 Matt Williams .40 .12
138 LaTroy Hawkins .40 .12
139 Kevin Seitzer .40 .12
140 Michael Tucker .40 .12
141 Todd Hundley .40 .12
142 Alex Fernandez .40 .12
143 Marquis Grissom .40 .12
144 Steve Finley .40 .12
145 Curtis Pride .40 .12
146 Derek Bell .40 .12
147 Butch Huskey .40 .12
148 Dwight Gooden CL .40 .12
149 Al Leiter CL .40 .12
150 Hideo Nomo CL .40 .12

1997 Donruss Elite Gold Stars

Randomly seeded into one in every nine packs, cards from this set parallel the 150-card base issue. The distinctive gold foil fronts easily differentiate them from their silver-foiled base-issue brethren. The following cards were erroneously printed with a silver (rather than gold) logo on front: 6, 15, 25, 32, 42, 47, 57, 60, 69 and 70. Corrected gold logo versions of these cards do exist but are in far shorter supply though secondary market trading values remain similar to general indifference at this time. The set is considered complete with the erroneous silver logo cards.

Nm-Mt Ex-Mt
*STARS: 4X TO 10X BASIC CARDS ....

1997 Donruss Elite Leather and Lumber

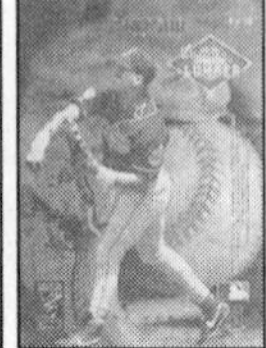

This ten-card insert set features color action veteran player photos printed on two unique materials. The fronts display a player image on real wood card stock with the end of a baseball bat as background. The backs carry another player photo printed on genuine leather card stock with a baseball and glove as background. Only 500 of each card was produced and are sequentially numbered.

Nm-Mt Ex-Mt
COMPLETE SET (10) 300.00 90.00
1 Ken Griffey Jr. 40.00 12.00
2 Alex Rodriguez 40.00 12.00
3 Frank Thomas 25.00 7.50
4 Chipper Jones 25.00 7.50
5 Ivan Rodriguez 25.00 7.50
6 Cal Ripken 80.00 24.00
7 Barry Bonds 60.00 18.00
8 Chuck Knoblauch 10.00 3.00
9 Manny Ramirez 10.00 3.00
10 Mark McGwire 60.00 18.00

1997 Donruss Elite Passing the Torch

This 12-card insert set features eight players on four double-sided cards. A color portrait of a superstar veteran is displayed on one side with a gold foil background, and a portrait of a rising young star is printed on the flipside. Each of the eight players also has his own card to round out the 12-card set. Only 1500 of this set were produced and are sequentially numbered. However, only 1,350 of each card are available without autographs.

Nm-Mt Ex-Mt
COMPLETE SET (12) 250.00 75.00
1 Cal Ripken 40.00 12.00
2 Alex Rodriguez 20.00 6.00
3 Cal Ripken 50.00 15.00
Alex Rodriguez
4 Kirby Puckett 12.00 3.60
5 Andruw Jones 5.00 1.50
6 Kirby Puckett 10.00 3.00
Andruw Jones
7 Cecil Fielder 5.00 1.50
8 Frank Thomas 12.00 3.60
9 Cecil Fielder 10.00 3.00
Frank Thomas
10 Ozzie Smith 20.00 6.00
11 Derek Jeter 30.00 9.00
12 Ozzie Smith 30.00 9.00
Derek Jeter

1997 Donruss Elite Passing the Torch Autographs

This 12-card set consists of the first 150 sets of the regular "Passing the Torch" set with each card displaying an authentic player autograph. The set features a double front design which captures eight of the league's top superstars, alternating one of four different megastars on the flipside. An individual card for each of the eight players rounds out the set. Each set is sequentially numbered to 150.

Nm-Mt Ex-Mt
1 Cal Ripken 250.00 75.00
2 Alex Rodriguez 200.00 60.00
3 Cal Ripken 600.00 180.00
Alex Rodriguez
4 Kirby Puckett 80.00 24.00
5 Andruw Jones 50.00 15.00
6 Kirby Puckett 100.00 30.00
Andruw Jones
7 Cecil Fielder 30.00 9.00
8 Frank Thomas 80.00 24.00
9 Cecil Fielder 80.00 24.00
Frank Thomas
10 Ozzie Smith 150.00 45.00
11 Derek Jeter 200.00 60.00
12 Ozzie Smith 300.00 90.00
Derek Jeter

1997 Donruss Elite Turn of the Century

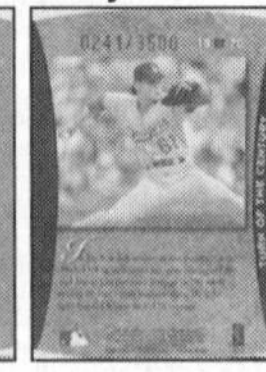

This 20-card set showcases the stars of the next millennium and features a color player image on a silver-and-black background. The backs display another player photo with a short paragraph about the player. Only 3,500 of this set were produced and are sequentially numbered.

Nm-Mt Ex-Mt
COMPLETE SET (20) 120.00 36.00
*DIE CUTS: 1.25X TO 3X BASIC TURN CENT.
DC STATED PRINT RUN 500 SERIAL #'d SETS
RANDOM INSERTS IN PACKS ....
1 Alex Rodriguez 15.00 4.50
2 Andruw Jones 4.00 1.20
3 Chipper Jones 10.00 3.00
4 Todd Walker 4.00 1.20
5 Scott Rolen 6.00 1.80
6 Trey Beamon 4.00 1.20
7 Derek Jeter 25.00 7.50
8 Darin Erstad 4.00 1.20
9 Tony Clark 4.00 1.20
10 Todd Greene 4.00 1.20
11 Jason Giambi 10.00 3.00
12 Justin Thompson 4.00 1.20
13 Ernie Young 4.00 1.20
14 Jason Kendall 4.00 1.20
15 Alex Ochoa 4.00 1.20
16 Brooks Kieschnick 4.00 1.20
17 Bobby Higginson 4.00 1.20
18 Ruben Rivera 4.00 1.20
19 Chan Ho Park 4.00 1.20
20 Chad Mottola 4.00 1.20
P5 Scott Rolen Promo 2.00 .60
P7 Derek Jeter Promo 3.00 .90

1998 Donruss Elite

The 1998 Donruss Elite set was issued in one series totalling 150 cards and distributed in five-card packs with a suggested retail price of $3.99. The fronts feature color player action photos. The backs carry player information. The set contains the topical subset: Generations (118-147). A special embossed Frank Thomas autograph card (parallel to basic issue card number two, except, of course, for Thomas' signature) was available to lucky collectors who pulled a Back to the Future Frank Thomas/David Ortiz card serial numbered between 1 and 100 and redeemed it to Donruss/Leaf.

Nm-Mt Ex-Mt
COMPLETE SET (150) 25.00 7.50
1 Ken Griffey Jr. 1.25 .35
2 Frank Thomas .75 .23
3 Alex Rodriguez 1.25 .35
4 Mike Piazza 1.25 .35
5 Greg Maddux 1.25 .35
6 Cal Ripken 2.50 .75
7 Chipper Jones .75 .23
8 Derek Jeter 2.00 .60
9 Tony Gwynn 1.00 .30
10 Andruw Jones .30 .09
11 Juan Gonzalez .75 .23
12 Jeff Bagwell .50 .15
13 Mark McGwire 2.00 .60
14 Roger Clemens 1.50 .45
15 Albert Belle .30 .09
16 Barry Bonds 2.00 .60
17 Kenny Lofton .30 .09
18 Ivan Rodriguez .75 .23
19 Manny Ramirez .30 .09
20 Jim Thome .75 .23
21 Chuck Knoblauch .30 .09
22 Paul Molitor .50 .15
23 Barry Larkin .75 .23
24 Andy Pettitte .50 .15
25 John Smoltz .50 .15
26 Randy Johnson .75 .23
27 Bernie Williams .50 .15
28 Larry Walker .50 .15
29 Mo Vaughn .30 .09
30 Bobby Higginson .30 .09
31 Edgardo Alfonzo .30 .09
32 Justin Thompson .30 .09
33 Jeff Suppan .30 .09
34 Roberto Alomar .75 .23
35 Hideo Nomo .75 .23
36 Rusty Greer .30 .09
37 Tim Salmon .50 .15
38 Jim Edmonds .30 .09
39 Gary Sheffield .30 .09
40 Ken Caminiti .30 .09
41 Sammy Sosa 1.25 .35
42 Tony Womack .30 .09
43 Matt Williams .30 .09
44 Andres Galarraga .30 .09
45 Garret Anderson .30 .09
46 Rafael Palmeiro .50 .15
47 Mike Mussina .75 .23
48 Craig Biggio .50 .15
49 Wade Boggs .50 .15
50 Tom Glavine .50 .15
51 Jason Giambi .75 .23
52 Will Clark .75 .23
53 David Justice .30 .09
54 Sandy Alomar Jr. .30 .09
55 Edgar Martinez .50 .15
56 Brady Anderson .30 .09
57 Eric Young .30 .09
58 Ray Lankford .30 .09
59 Kevin Brown .50 .15
60 Raul Mondesi .30 .09
61 Bobby Bonilla .30 .09
62 Javier Lopez .30 .09
63 Fred McGriff .50 .15
64 Rondell White .30 .09
65 Todd Hundley .30 .09
66 Mark Grace .50 .15
67 Alan Benes .30 .09
68 Jeff Abbott .30 .09
69 Bob Abreu .30 .09
70 Deion Sanders .50 .15
71 Tino Martinez .50 .15
72 Shannon Stewart .30 .09
73 Homer Bush .30 .09
74 Carlos Delgado .30 .09
75 Raul Ibanez .30 .09
76 Hideki Irabu .30 .09
77 Jose Cruz Jr. .30 .09
78 Tony Clark .30 .09
79 Wilton Guerrero .30 .09
80 Vladimir Guerrero .75 .23
81 Scott Rolen .50 .15
82 Nomar Garciaparra 1.25 .35
83 Darin Erstad .30 .09
84 Chan Ho Park .30 .09
85 Mike Cameron .30 .09
86 Todd Walker .30 .09
87 Todd Dunwoody .30 .09
88 Neifi Perez .30 .09
89 Brett Tomko .30 .09
90 Jose Guillen .30 .09
91 Matt Morris .30 .09
92 Bartolo Colon .30 .09
93 Jaret Wright .30 .09
94 Shawn Estes .30 .09
95 Livan Hernandez .30 .09
96 Bobby Estalella .30 .09
97 Ben Grieve .30 .09
98 Paul Konerko .30 .09
99 David Ortiz .30 .09
100 Todd Helton .50 .15
101 Juan Encarnacion .30 .09
102 Bubba Trammell .30 .09
103 Miguel Tejada .50 .15
104 Jacob Cruz .30 .09
105 Todd Greene .30 .09
106 Kevin Orie .30 .09
107 Mark Kotsay .30 .09
108 Fernando Tatis .30 .09
109 Jay Payton .30 .09
110 Pokey Reese .30 .09
111 Derrek Lee .30 .09
112 Richard Hidalgo .30 .09
113 Ricky Ledee .30 .09
UER front Rickey
114 Lou Collier .30 .09
115 Ruben Rivera .30 .09
116 Shawn Green .30 .09
117 Moises Alou .30 .09
118 Ken Griffey Jr. GEN .75 .23
119 Frank Thomas GEN .50 .15
120 Alex Rodriguez GEN .75 .23
121 Mike Piazza GEN .75 .23
122 Greg Maddux GEN .75 .23
123 Cal Ripken GEN 1.25 .35
124 Chipper Jones GEN .50 .15
125 Derek Jeter GEN 1.00 .30
126 Tony Gwynn GEN .50 .15
127 Andruw Jones GEN .30 .09
128 Juan Gonzalez GEN .50 .15
129 Jeff Bagwell GEN .30 .09
130 Mark McGwire GEN 1.00 .30
131 Roger Clemens GEN .75 .23
132 Albert Belle GEN .30 .09
133 Barry Bonds GEN .75 .23
134 Kenny Lofton GEN .30 .09
135 Ivan Rodriguez GEN .50 .15
136 Manny Ramirez GEN .30 .09
137 Jim Thome GEN .50 .15
138 C.Knoblauch GEN .30 .09
139 Paul Molitor GEN .30 .09
140 Barry Larkin GEN .50 .15
141 Mo Vaughn GEN .30 .09
142 Hideki Irabu GEN .30 .09
143 Jose Cruz Jr. GEN .30 .09
144 Tony Clark GEN .30 .09
145 V.Guerrero GEN .50 .15
146 Scott Rolen GEN .30 .09
147 N.Garciaparra GEN .75 .23
148 Nomar Garciaparra CL .75 .23
149 Larry Walker CL .30 .09
150 Tino Martinez CL .30 .09
AU2 F.Thomas AUTO/100 80.00 24.00

1998 Donruss Elite Aspirations

Randomly inserted in packs, this 150-card set is parallel to the base set. Only 750 of this set were produced and are sequentially numbered.

Nm-Mt Ex-Mt
*STARS: 3X TO 8X BASIC CARDS......

1998 Donruss Elite Status

Randomly inserted in packs, this 150-card set is parallel to the base set. Only 100 of this set were produced and are serially numbered.

Nm-Mt Ex-Mt
*STARS: 10X TO 25X BASIC CARDS..

1998 Donruss Elite Back to the Future

Randomly inserted in packs, this eight-card set is double-sided and features color images of top veteran and new players on a tile background. Only 1,500 of each card were produced and sequentially numbered.

Nm-Mt Ex-Mt
COMPLETE SET (8)................ 120.00 36.00
1 Cal Ripken.............................. 30.00 9.00
Paul Konerko
2 Jeff Bagwell............................. 6.00 1.80
Todd Helton
3 Eddie Mathews........................ 10.00 3.00
Chipper Jones
4 Juan Gonzalez......................... 10.00 3.00
Ben Grieve
5 Hank Aaron............................. 20.00 6.00
Jose Cruz Jr.
6 Frank Thomas......................... 10.00 3.00
David Ortiz
1-100
7 Nolan Ryan............................. 40.00 12.00
Greg Maddux
8 Alex Rodriguez....................... 15.00 4.50
Nomar Garciaparra

1998 Donruss Elite Back to the Future Autographs

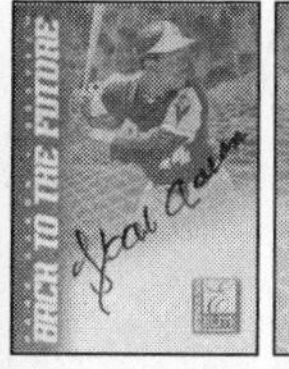

Randomly inserted in packs, this seven-card set is a parallel version of the regular 1998 Donruss Elite Back to the Future insert set and contains the first 100 cards of the regular set signed by both pictured players. Card number six does not exist. Cal Ripken did not sign card number 1 along with Paul Konerko. Ripken eventually signed 200 separate cards. One hundred special redemptions (rather bland black and white text-based cards) were issued for the Ripken card and randomly seeded into packs. In addition, lucky collectors that pulled one of the first 100 serial numbered Back to the Future Konerko autograph cards could exchange it for a Ripken autograph AND still receive their Konerko autograph back. The first 100 of each card were autographed by both players pictured on the card. There is no autographed card number six. Due to problems in obtaining Frank Thomas' autograph prior to the shipping deadline for the parallel signed Back to the Future cards, the manufacturer was forced to make the first 100 serial numbered cards of card number 6 a redemption for a special Frank Thomas autographed card (a basic 1998 Donruss Elite Thomas card, embossed with a special stamp and signed by Thomas on front). Due to Pinnacle's bankruptcy, the exchange program was abruptly halted in late 1998. Prior to this, the serial numbered 1-100 Thomas/Ortiz cards traded for as much as $300. After this date, the premiums disappeared entirely.

Nm-Mt Ex-Mt
1A Cal Ripken........................... 40.00 12.00
Paul Konerko Redeemed/100
Redeemed card signed only by Konerko
1B C. Ripken AU/200................. 200.00 60.00
Redeemed card signed only by Ripken
2 Jeff Bagwell......................... 150.00 45.00
Todd Helton
3 Eddie Mathews..................... 250.00 75.00
Chipper Jones
4 Juan Gonzalez...................... 150.00 45.00
Ben Grieve
5 Hank Aaron.......................... 200.00 60.00
Jose Cruz Jr.
7 Nolan Ryan......................... 1200.00 350.00
Greg Maddux
8 Alex Rodriguez.................... 600.00 180.00
Nomar Garciaparra

1998 Donruss Elite Craftsmen

Randomly inserted in packs, this 30-card set features color photos of players who are the best at what they do. Only 3,500 of this set were produced and are sequentially numbered.

Nm-Mt Ex-Mt
COMPLETE SET (30)............. 150.00 45.00
*MASTER: 2.5X TO 6X BASIC CRAFTSMEN
MASTER PRINT RUN 100 SERIAL #'d SETS
RANDOM INSERTS IN PACKS ....

1 Ken Griffey Jr. 10.00 3.00
2 Frank Thomas 6.00 1.80
3 Alex Rodriguez 10.00 3.00
4 Cal Ripken 20.00 6.00
5 Greg Maddux......................... 10.00 3.00
6 Mike Piazza 10.00 3.00
7 Chipper Jones 6.00 1.80
8 Derek Jeter........................... 15.00 4.50
9 Tony Gwynn 8.00 2.40
10 Nomar Garciaparra.............. 10.00 3.00
11 Scott Rolen 4.00 1.20
12 Jose Cruz Jr. .... 2.50 .75
13 Tony Clark............................ 2.50 .75
14 Vladimir Guerrero................. 6.00 1.80
15 Todd Helton.......................... 4.00 1.20
16 Ben Grieve .... 2.50 .75
17 Andruw Jones .... 2.50 .75
18 Jeff Bagwell 4.00 1.20
19 Mark McGwire...................... 15.00 4.50
20 Juan Gonzalez 6.00 1.80
21 Roger Clemens..................... 12.00 3.60
22 Albert Belle.......................... 2.50 .75
23 Barry Bonds 15.00 4.50
24 Kenny Lofton........................ 2.50 .75
25 Ivan Rodriguez 6.00 1.80
26 Paul Molitor.......................... 4.00 1.20
27 Barry Larkin UER.................. 6.00 1.80
His team was midentified as the Cardinals
28 Mo Vaughn.......................... 2.50 .75
29 Larry Walker........................ 4.00 1.20
30 Tino Martinez 4.00 1.20

1998 Donruss Elite Prime Numbers Samples

Promotional samples were created for all 36 Prime Numbers inserts and distributed one per wholesale dealer order form. The cards are identical to regular Prime Numbers inserts except for the large "SAMPLE" text running diagonally across the backs and lack of serial numbering.

Nm-Mt Ex-Mt
COMPLETE SET (36).............. 350.00 105.00
1A Ken Griffey Jr. 2................ 12.00 3.60
1B Ken Griffey Jr. 9................ 12.00 3.60
1C Ken Griffey Jr. 4................ 12.00 3.60
2A Frank Thomas 4.................. 6.00 1.80
2B Frank Thomas 5.................. 6.00 1.80
2C Frank Thomas 6.................. 6.00 1.80
3A Mark McGwire 3................. 15.00 4.50
3B Mark McGwire 8................. 15.00 4.50
3C Mark McGwire 7................. 15.00 4.50
4A Cal Ripken 5....................... 20.00 6.00
4B Cal Ripken 1....................... 20.00 6.00
4C Cal Ripken 7....................... 20.00 6.00
5A Mike Piazza 5...................... 15.00 4.50
5B Mike Piazza 7...................... 15.00 4.50
5C Mike Piazza 6...................... 15.00 4.50
6A Chipper Jones 4.................. 10.00 3.00
6B Chipper Jones 8.................. 10.00 3.00
6C Chipper Jones 9.................. 10.00 3.00
7A Tony Gwynn 3..................... 10.00 3.00
7B Tony Gwynn 7..................... 10.00 3.00
7C Tony Gwynn 2..................... 10.00 3.00
8A Barry Bonds 3...................... 10.00 3.00
8B Barry Bonds 7...................... 10.00 3.00
8C Barry Bonds 4...................... 10.00 3.00
9A Jeff Bagwell 4...................... 6.00 1.80
9B Jeff Bagwell 2...................... 6.00 1.80
9C Jeff Bagwell 5...................... 6.00 1.80
10A Juan Gonzalez 5................ 5.00 1.50
10B Juan Gonzalez 8................ 5.00 1.50
10C Juan Gonzalez 9................ 5.00 1.50
11A Alex Rodriguez 5............... 15.00 4.50
11B Alex Rodriguez 3............... 15.00 4.50
11C Alex Rodriguez 4............... 15.00 4.50
12A Kenny Lofton 3................... 4.00 1.20
12B Kenny Lofton 5................... 4.00 1.20
12C Kenny Lofton 4................... 4.00 1.20

1998 Donruss Elite Prime Numbers

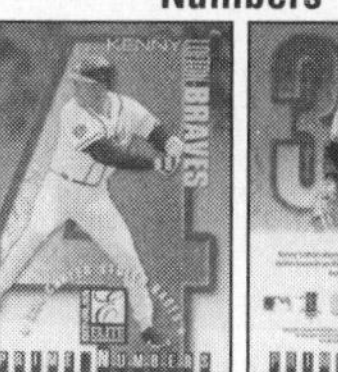

Randomly inserted in packs, this 36-card set features three cards each of 12 top players in the league printed with three different numerical backgrounds (of which form a statistical benchmark when placed together). The total number of each card produced depended on the player's particular statistic. Print runs are included below in parentheses at the end of each card description.

Nm-Mt Ex-Mt
1A Ken Griffey Jr. 2 (94).......... 50.00 15.00
1B Ken Griffey Jr. 9 (204)........ 25.00 7.50
1C Ken Griffey Jr. 4 (290)........ 20.00 6.00
2A Frank Thomas 4 (56)........... 40.00 12.00
2B Frank Thomas 5 (406)......... 10.00 3.00
2C Frank Thomas 6 (450)......... 10.00 3.00
3A Mark McGwire 3 (87).......... 100.00 30.00
3B Mark McGwire 8 (307)......... 40.00 12.00
3C Mark McGwire 7 (380)......... 40.00 12.00
4A Cal Ripken 5 (17).............. 400.00 120.00
4B Cal Ripken 1 (507).............. 30.00 9.00
4C Cal Ripken 7 (510).............. 30.00 9.00
5A Mike Piazza 5 (76)............... 50.00 15.00
5B Mike Piazza 7 (506)............. 15.00 4.50
5C Mike Piazza 6 (570)............. 15.00 4.50
6A Chipper Jones 4 (89).......... 30.00 9.00
6B Chipper Jones 8 (409)........ 10.00 3.00
6C Chipper Jones 9 (480)........ 10.00 3.00
7A Tony Gwynn 3 (72).............. 40.00 12.00
7B Tony Gwynn 7 (302)............ 15.00 4.50
7C Tony Gwynn 2 (370)............ 15.00 4.50
8A Barry Bonds 3 (74).............. 80.00 24.00
8B Barry Bonds 7 (304)............ 30.00 9.00
8C Barry Bonds 4 (370)............ 30.00 9.00
9A Jeff Bagwell 4 (25).............. 60.00 18.00
9B Jeff Bagwell 2 (405)............ 6.00 1.80
9C Jeff Bagwell 5 (420)............ 6.00 1.80
10A Juan Gonzalez 5 (89)........ 25.00 7.50
10B J.Gonzalez 8 (509)........... 10.00 3.00
10C J.Gonzalez 9 (580)........... 10.00 3.00
11A Alex Rodriguez 5 (34)........ 80.00 24.00
11B A.Rodriguez 3 (504)........... 15.00 4.50
11C A.Rodriguez 4 (530)........... 15.00 4.50
12A Kenny Lofton 3 (54)........... 20.00 6.00
12B Kenny Lofton 5 (304).......... 5.00 1.50
12C Kenny Lofton 4 (350).......... 5.00 1.50

1998 Donruss Elite Prime Numbers Die Cuts

Randomly inserted in packs, this 36-card set is a die-cut parallel version to the regular Donruss Elite Prime Numbers set. Print runs are included below in parentheses at the end of each card description. Cards printed in quantites of 10 or less are identified in the checklist but not priced below.

Nm-Mt Ex-Mt
1A Ken Griffey Jr. 2 (200)......... 25.00 7.50
1B Ken Griffey Jr. 9 (90).......... 50.00 15.00
1C Ken Griffey Jr. 4 (4)...................
2A Frank Thomas 4 (400)......... 10.00 3.00
2B Frank Thomas 5 (50).......... 40.00 12.00
2C Frank Thomas 6 (6)...................
3A Mark McGwire 3 (300)......... 40.00 12.00
3B Mark McGwire 8 (80)......... 100.00 30.00
3C Mark McGwire 7 (7)...................
4A Cal Ripken 5 (500)............... 30.00 9.00
4B Cal Ripken 1 (10)...................
4C Cal Ripken 7 (7).....................
5A Mike Piazza 5 (500)............. 15.00 4.50
5B Mike Piazza 7 (70).............. 50.00 15.00
5C Mike Piazza 6 (6)...................
6A Chipper Jones 4 (400)......... 10.00 3.00
6B Chipper Jones 8 (80)........... 30.00 9.00
7A Tony Gwynn 3 (300)............ 15.00 4.50
7B Tony Gwynn 7 (70).............. 40.00 12.00
7C Tony Gwynn 2 (2)...................
8A Barry Bonds 3 (300)............ 30.00 9.00
8B Barry Bonds 7 (70)............. 80.00 24.00
8C Barry Bonds 4 (4)...................
9A Jeff Bagwell 4 (400).............. 6.00 1.80
9B Jeff Bagwell 2 (20).............. 80.00 24.00
9C Jeff Bagwell 5 (5)...................
10A J.Gonzalez 5 (500)............ 10.00 3.00
10B Juan Gonzalez 8 (80)........ 25.00 7.50
10C Juan Gonzalez 9 (9)...................
11A A.Rodriguez 5 (500)........... 15.00 4.50
11B Alex Rodriguez 3 (30)........ 100.00 30.00
11C Alex Rodriguez 4 (4)...................
12A Kenny Lofton 3 (300)........... 5.00 1.50
12B Kenny Lofton 5 (50)........... 20.00 6.00
12C Kenny Lofton 4 (4)...................

2001 Donruss Elite

This 200-card hobby only set was distributed in May, 2001 in five-card packs with a suggested retail price of $3.99 and features color photos of some of Baseball's finest players and hot rookies. The low series rookie cards are sequentially numbered to 1000 with the first 100 labeled "Turn of the Century." Cards 201-250 were issued as exchange coupons for unspecified rookies and prospects and randomly seeded into packs at a rate of 1:14. Specific players for each exchange card were announced on Donruss' website in late October, 2001 (and about 15 players were dropped and updated with new players about a month later). The deadline to redeem the coupons was originally 11/01/01 but it was extended to January 20th, 2002. Each coupon carried a cost of $5.99 to redeem. In April of 2002 representatives at Donruss-Playoff released explicit quantities for each of these exchange cards, of which ranged from as few as 377 to as many as 556. All of these cards are actually serial-numbered "XXX/1000" on back but were mailed out in non-sequential order, thus cards serial-numbered as high as 900/1000 etc are in existence but it doesn't mean that 900+ copies were distributed. When the January 20th deadline passed, according to representatives at Donruss-Playoff, the remaining cards were destroyed. Please see our checklist for specific quantities of each card produced.

Nm-Mt Ex-Mt
COMP.SET w/o SP's (150)......... 40.00 12.00
COMMON CARD (1-150).............. .50 .15
COMMON (151-200).................. 10.00 3.00
COMMON CARD (201-250)......... 10.00 3.00
1 Alex Rodriguez........................ 2.00 .60
2 Barry Bonds .... 3.00 .90
3 Cal Ripken.............................. 4.00 1.20
4 Chipper Jones .... 1.25 .35
5 Derek Jeter............................. 3.00 .90
6 Troy Glaus.............................. .75 .23
7 Frank Thomas .... 1.25 .35
8 Greg Maddux......................... 2.00 .60
9 Ivan Rodriguez .... 1.25 .35
10 Jeff Bagwell .... .75 .23
11 Jose Canseco .... 1.25 .35
12 Todd Helton.......................... .75 .23
13 Ken Griffey Jr. .... 2.00 .60
14 Manny Ramirez .... .50 .15
15 Mark McGwire...................... 3.00 .90
16 Mike Piazza .... 2.00 .60
17 Nomar Garciaparra............... 2.00 .60
18 Pedro Martinez .... 1.25 .35
19 Randy Johnson .... 1.25 .35
20 Rick Ankiel .... .50 .15
21 Rickey Henderson .... 1.25 .35
22 Roger Clemens..................... 2.50 .75
23 Sammy Sosa .... 2.00 .60
24 Tony Gwynn .... 1.50 .45
25 Vladimir Guerrero................. 1.25 .35
26 Eric Davis.............................. .50 .15
27 Roberto Alomar .... 1.25 .35
28 Mark Mulder.......................... .50 .15
29 Pat Burrell .... .50 .15
30 Harold Baines .... .50 .15
31 Carlos Delgado .... .50 .15
32 J.D. Drew .... .50 .15
33 Jim Edmonds .... .50 .15
34 Darin Erstad .... .50 .15
35 Jason Giambi .... 1.25 .35
36 Tom Glavine .... .75 .23
37 Juan Gonzalez .... 1.25 .35
38 Mark Grace............................. .75 .23
39 Shawn Green .... .50 .15
40 Tim Hudson............................. .50 .15
41 Andruw Jones .... .50 .15
42 David Justice .... .50 .15
43 Jeff Kent.................................. .50 .15
44 Barry Larkin........................... 1.25 .35
45 Pokey Reese........................... .50 .15
46 Mike Mussina......................... 1.25 .35
47 Hideo Nomo .... 1.25 .35
48 Rafael Palmeiro .... .75 .23
49 Adam Piatt .... .50 .15
50 Scott Rolen .... .75 .23
51 Gary Sheffield......................... .50 .15
52 Bernie Williams .... .75 .23
53 Bob Abreu .... .50 .15
54 Edgardo Alfonzo .... .50 .15
55 Jermaine Clark RC.................. .75 .23
56 Albert Belle............................. .50 .15
57 Craig Biggio............................ .75 .23
58 Andres Galarraga.................... .50 .15
59 Edgar Martinez .... .75 .23
60 Fred McGriff .... .75 .23
61 Magglio Ordonez..................... .50 .15
62 Jim Thome .... 1.25 .35
63 Matt Williams .... .50 .15
64 Kerry Wood .... 1.25 .35
65 Moises Alou .... .50 .15
66 Brady Anderson....................... .50 .15
67 Garret Anderson...................... .50 .15
68 Tony Armas Jr. .... .50 .15
69 Tony Batista .... .50 .15
70 Jose Cruz Jr. .... .50 .15
71 Carlos Beltran.......................... .50 .15
72 Adrian Beltre .... .50 .15
73 Kris Benson.............................. .50 .15
74 Lance Berkman .... .50 .15
75 Kevin Brown .... .50 .15
76 Jay Buhner .... .50 .15
77 Jeromy Burnitz......................... .50 .15
78 Ken Caminiti............................ .50 .15
79 Sean Casey.............................. .50 .15
80 Luis Castillo............................. .50 .15
81 Eric Chavez.............................. .50 .15
82 Jeff Cirillo .... .50 .15
83 Bartolo Colon .... .50 .15
84 David Cone.............................. .50 .15
85 Freddy Garcia .... .50 .15
86 Johnny Damon.......................... .50 .15
87 Ray Durham .... .50 .15
88 Jermaine Dye .... .50 .15
89 Juan Encarnacion...................... .50 .15
90 Terrence Long .... .50 .15
91 Carl Everett.............................. .50 .15
92 Steve Finley.............................. .50 .15
93 Cliff Floyd .... .50 .15
94 Brad Fullmer............................. .50 .15
95 Brian Giles................................ .50 .15
96 Luis Gonzalez .... .50 .15
97 Rusty Greer............................... .50 .15
98 Jeffrey Hammonds.................... .50 .15
99 Mike Hampton........................... .50 .15
100 Orlando Hernandez.................. .50 .15
101 Richard Hidalgo....................... .50 .15
102 Geoff Jenkins .... .50 .15
103 Jacque Jones .... .50 .15
104 Brian Jordan............................ .50 .15
105 Gabe Kapler............................ .50 .15
106 Eric Karros .... .50 .15
107 Jason Kendall.......................... .50 .15
108 Adam Kennedy .... .50 .15
109 Byung-Hyun Kim...................... .50 .15
110 Ryan Klesko .... .50 .15
111 Chuck Knoblauch .... .50 .15
112 Paul Konerko........................... .50 .15
113 Carlos Lee .... .50 .15
114 Kenny Lofton............................ .50 .15
115 Javy Lopez .... .50 .15
116 Tino Martinez .... .75 .23
117 Ruben Mateo............................ .50 .15
118 Kevin Millwood......................... .50 .15
119 Ben Molina .... .50 .15
120 Raul Mondesi .... .50 .15
121 Trot Nixon .... .75 .23
122 John Olerud.............................. .50 .15
123 Paul O'Neill............................... .75 .23
124 Chan Ho Park .... .50 .15
125 Andy Pettitte............................. .75 .23
126 Jorge Posada .... .75 .23
127 Mark Quinn .... .50 .15
128 Aramis Ramirez........................ .50 .15
129 Mariano Rivera......................... .75 .23
130 Tim Salmon.............................. .75 .23
131 Curt Schilling............................ .75 .23
132 Richie Sexson .... .50 .15
133 John Smoltz.............................. .75 .23
134 J.T. Snow .... .50 .15
135 Jay Payton................................ .50 .15
136 Shannon Stewart...................... .50 .15
137 B.J. Surhoff.............................. .50 .15
138 Mike Sweeney .... .50 .15
139 Fernando Tatis.......................... .50 .15
140 Miguel Tejada........................... .50 .15
141 Jason Varitek............................ .50 .15
142 Greg Vaughn .... .50 .15
143 Mo Vaughn............................... .50 .15
144 Robin Ventura UER .... .50 .15
Listed as playing for Yankees last 2 years,
Also Bat and Throw information is wrong
145 Jose Vidro .... .50 .15
146 Omar Vizquel............................ .50 .15
147 Larry Walker............................. .75 .23
148 David Wells .... .50 .15
149 Rondell White........................... .50 .15
150 Preston Wilson.......................... .50 .15
151 Brent Abernathy SP............. 10.00 3.00
152 Cory Aldridge SP RC........... 10.00 3.00
153 Gene Altman SP RC............ 10.00 3.00
154 Josh Beckett SP 15.00 4.50
155 Wilson Betemit SP RC......... 10.00 3.00
156 Albert Pujols SP RC.......... 250.00 75.00
157 Joe Crede SP...................... 10.00 3.00
158 Jack Cust SP 10.00 3.00
159 Ben Sheets SP.................... 10.00 3.00
160 Alex Escobar SP 10.00 3.00
161 A. Hernandez SP RC............ 10.00 3.00
162 Pedro Feliz SP 10.00 3.00
163 Nate Frese SP RC 10.00 3.00
164 Carlos Garcia SP RC............ 10.00 3.00
165 Marcus Giles SP.................. 10.00 3.00
166 Alexis Gomez SP RC 10.00 3.00
167 Jason Hart SP 10.00 3.00
168 Aubrey Huff SP 10.00 3.00
169 Cesar Izturis SP.................. 10.00 3.00
170 Nick Johnson SP.................. 10.00 3.00
171 Jack Wilson SP RC.............. 10.00 3.00
172 B.Lawrence SP RC 10.00 3.00
173 C. Parker SP RC.................. 10.00 3.00
174 Nick Maness SP RC............. 10.00 3.00
175 Jose Mieses SP RC 10.00 3.00
176 Greg Miller SP RC................ 10.00 3.00
177 Eric Munson SP 10.00 3.00
178 Xavier Nady SP.................... 10.00 3.00
179 Blaine Neal SP RC 10.00 3.00
180 Abraham Nunez SP 10.00 3.00
181 Jose Ortiz SP....................... 10.00 3.00
182 Jeremy Owens SP RC 10.00 3.00
183 Jay Gibbons SP RC 15.00 4.50
184 Corey Patterson SP 10.00 3.00
185 Carlos Pena SP.................... 10.00 3.00
186 C.C. Sabathia SP 10.00 3.00
187 Timo Perez SP..................... 10.00 3.00
188 A. Pettyjohn SP RC 10.00 3.00
189 D. Mendez SP RC................ 10.00 3.00
190 J. Melian SP RC 10.00 3.00
191 Wilkin Ruan SP RC.............. 10.00 3.00
192 D. Sanchez SP RC 10.00 3.00
193 Alfonso Soriano SP.............. 15.00 4.50
194 Rafael Soriano SP RC.......... 20.00 6.00
195 Ichiro Suzuki SP RC............ 80.00 24.00
196 Billy Sylvester SP RC........... 10.00 3.00
197 Juan Uribe SP RC................ 10.00 3.00
198 T. Shinjo SP RC................... 15.00 4.50
199 C. Valderrama SP RC 10.00 3.00
200 Matt White SP RC 10.00 3.00
201 Adam Dunn/468................... 10.00 3.00
202 Joe Kennedy/465 XRC......... 10.00 3.00
203 Mike Rivera/427 XRC 10.00 3.00
204 Erick Almonte/401 XRC........ 10.00 3.00
205 Bran Duckworth EXCH 10.00 3.00
206 Victor Martinez/410 XRC...... 60.00 18.00
207 Rick Bauer/390 XRC............. 10.00 3.00
208 Jeff Deardorff/396 XRC 10.00 3.00
209 Antonio Perez/448 XRC........ 10.00 3.00
210 Bill Hall/404 XRC.................. 10.00 3.00
211 D. Tankersley EXCH............. 10.00 3.00
212 Jeremy Affeldt/386 XRC 40.00 12.00
213 Junior Spivey/377 XRC 25.00 7.50
214 Casey Fossum/393 XRC....... 10.00 3.00
215 Brandon Lyon/402 XRC........ 10.00 3.00
216 Angel Santos/408 XRC......... 10.00 3.00
217 Cody Ransom/404 XRC 10.00 3.00
218 Jason Lane/424 XRC 15.00 4.50
219 David Williams/408 XRC 10.00 3.00
220 Alex Herrera/405 XRC 10.00 3.00
221 Ryan Drese/378 XRC........... 10.00 3.00
222 Travis Hafner/419 XRC........ 40.00 12.00
223 Bud Smith/468 XRC............. 10.00 3.00
224 Johnny Estrada/415 XRC 15.00 4.50
225 R. Rodriguez EXCH.............. 10.00 3.00
226 Brandon Berger/428 XRC..... 10.00 3.00
227 Claudio Vargas/395 XRC 10.00 3.00
228 Luis Garcia/438 XRC........... 10.00 3.00
229 Marlon Byrd/452 XRC 60.00 18.00
230 Hee Seop Choi/479 XRC...... 80.00 24.00
231 Corky Miller/431 XRC.......... 10.00 3.00
232 J. Duchscherer EXCH.......... 10.00 3.00
233 T. Spooneybarger EXCH...... 10.00 3.00
234 Roy Oswalt/427.................... 15.00 4.50
235 Willie Harris/418 XRC.......... 10.00 3.00
236 Josh Towers/437 XRC 10.00 3.00
237 Juan A.Pena/400 XRC 10.00 3.00
238 A. Amezaga EXCH............... 15.00 4.50
239 Geronimo Gil/396 XRC 10.00 3.00
240 Juan Cruz/489 XRC 10.00 3.00
241 Ed Rogers/429 XRC 10.00 3.00
242 Joe Thurston/420 XRC 25.00 7.50
243 O.Hudson EXCH 15.00 4.50
244 John Buck/416 XRC 15.00 4.50
245 Martin Vargas/400 XRC........ 10.00 3.00
246 David Brous/399 XRC........... 10.00 3.00
247 D. Brazelton EXCH............... 15.00 4.50
248 Mark Prior/556 XRC 250.00 75.00
249 Angel Berroa/420 XRC 40.00 12.00
250 Mark Teixeira/543 XRC...... 100.00 30.00

2001 Donruss Elite Aspirations

Randomly inserted in packs at the rate of one in 62, this 200-card set is a parallel version of the base set printed on holo-foil board with red foil and red tint. Each card was sequentially numbered to the remaining number after subtracting the player's jersey number from

100. Cards with a print run of 25 or fewer are not priced due to market scarcity.

	Nm-Mt	Ex-Mt
*1-150 PRINT RUN b/wn 81-100: 6X TO 15X		
*1-150 PRINT RUN b/wn 66-80: 8X TO 20X		
*1-150 PRINT RUN b/wn 51-65: 10X TO 25X		
*1-150 PRINT RUN b/wn 36-50: 12.5X TO 30X		
*1-150 PRINT RUN b/wn 26-35: 15X TO 40X		
COMMON (151-200) p/r 81-100	4.00	1.20
MINOR 151-200 p/r 81-100	6.00	1.80
UNLISTED 151-200 p/r 81-100	15.00	4.50
MINOR 151-200 p/r 66-80	8.00	2.40
SEMISTARS 151-200 p/r 66-80	12.00	3.60
UNLISTED 151-200 p/r 66-80	20.00	6.00
MINOR 151-200 p/r 51-65	10.00	3.00
UNLISTED 151-200 p/r 51-65	25.00	7.50
COMMON (151-200) p/r 36-50	8.00	2.40
MINOR 151-200 p/r 36-50	12.00	3.60
SEMISTARS 151-200 p/r 36-50	20.00	6.00
UNLISTED 151-200 p/r 36-50	30.00	9.00
COMMON (151-200) p/r 26-35	10.00	3.00
MINOR 151-200 p/r 26-35	15.00	4.50
UNLISTED 151-200 p/r 26-35	40.00	12.00
UNLISTED 151-200 p/r 21-25	50.00	15.00
MINOR 151-200 p/r 16-20	25.00	7.50
RANDOM INSERTS IN PACKS		
SEE BECKETT.COM FOR PRINT RUNS		
PRINTS b/wn 1-15 TOO SCARCE TO PRICE		
RC'S OF 25 OR LESS TOO SCARCE TO PRICE		

2001 Donruss Elite Status

Randomly inserted in packs at the rate of one in 163, this 200-card set is a parallel version of the base set printed on holo-foil board with gold foil and gold tint. Each card is sequentially numbered to the player's jersey number. Cards issued to a stated print run of 25 or fewer are not priced due to market scarcity.

	Nm-Mt	Ex-Mt
*1-150 PRINT RUN b/wn 81-100: 6X TO 15X		
*1-150 PRINT RUN b/wn 66-80: 8X TO 20X		
*1-150 PRINT RUN b/wn 51-65: 10X TO 25X		
*1-150 PRINT RUN b/wn 36-50: 12.5X TO 30X		
*1-150 PRINT RUN b/wn 26-35: 15X TO 40X		
*1-150 PRINT RUN b/wn 21-25: 20X TO 50X		
*1-150 PRINT RUN b/wn 16-20: 25X TO 60X		
MINOR 151-200 p/r 81-100	6.00	1.80
COMMON (151-200) p/r 66-80	5.00	1.50
MINOR 151-200 p/r 66-80	8.00	2.40
UNLISTED 151-200 p/r 66-80	20.00	6.00
COMMON (151-200) p/r 51-65	6.00	1.80
MINOR 151-200 p/r 51-65	10.00	3.00
SEMISTARS 151-200 p/r 51-65	15.00	4.50
UNLISTED 151-200 p/r 51-65	25.00	7.50
MINOR 151-200 p/r 36-50	12.00	3.60
SEMISTARS 151-200 p/r 36-50	20.00	6.00
MINOR 151-200 p/r 21-25	20.00	6.00
UNLISTED 151-200 p/r 21-25	50.00	15.00
MINOR 151-200 p/r 16-20	25.00	7.50
SEMISTARS 151-200 p/r 16-20	40.00	12.00
UNLISTED 151-200 p/r 16-20	60.00	18.00
RANDOM INSERTS IN PACKS		
SEE BECKETT.COM FOR PRINT RUNS		
PRINTS b/wn 1-15 TOO SCARCE TO PRICE		

2001 Donruss Elite Extra Edition Autographs

These certified autograph cards were made available as a compensation by Donruss-Playoff to collectors for autograph exchange cards that the manufacturer was unable to fulfill in the 2001 season. Each card is serial-numbered of 100 on front. Unlike most Donruss-Playoff autograph cards from 2001, the athletes signed the actual card rather than signing a sticker (of which was then affixed to the card at a later date). The cards first started to appear on the secondary market in April, 2002 but are catalogued as 2001 cards to avoid confusion for collectors looking to reference them.

	Nm-Mt	Ex-Mt
234 Roy Oswalt	40.00	12.00
238 Alfredo Amezaga	20.00	6.00
241 Ed Rogers	20.00	6.00

2001 Donruss Elite Turn of the Century Autographs

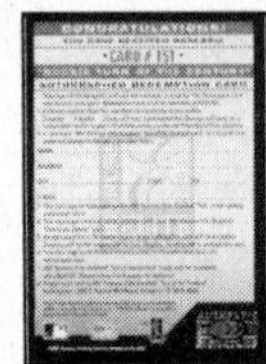

Randomly inserted in packs, these 50 cards feature prospects who signed their cards for the Donruss Elite product. Each card had a stated print run of 100 sets though they are cumulatively serial-numbered to 1000 (only the first 100 numbered copies of each card Turn of the Century Autographs - the last 900 numbered copies of each card are basic Elite cards). Some players did not return their cards in time for inclusion in the product and these cards had an redemption deadline of May 1, 2003. Cards number 195 and 198 at first were not believed to exist, but subsequently were issued without autographs.

	Nm-Mt	Ex-Mt
151 Brent Abernathy	15.00	4.50
152 Cory Aldridge	15.00	4.50
153 Gene Altman	15.00	4.50
154 Josh Beckett	100.00	30.00
155 Wilson Betemit	25.00	7.50
156 Albert Pujols	600.00	180.00
157 Joe Crede	15.00	4.50
158 Jack Cust	15.00	4.50
159 Ben Sheets	25.00	7.50
160 Alex Escobar	15.00	4.50
161 Adrian Hernandez	15.00	4.50
162 Pedro Feliz	15.00	4.50
163 Nate Frese	15.00	4.50
164 Carlos Garcia	15.00	4.50
165 Marcus Giles	25.00	7.50
166 Alexis Gomez	15.00	4.50
167 Jason Hart	15.00	4.50
168 Aubrey Huff	25.00	7.50
169 Cesar Izturis	15.00	4.50
170 Nick Johnson	25.00	7.50
171 Jack Wilson	15.00	4.50
172 Brian Lawrence	15.00	4.50
173 Christian Parker	15.00	4.50
174 Nick Maness	15.00	4.50
175 Jose Mieses	15.00	4.50
176 Greg Miller	15.00	4.50
177 Eric Munson	15.00	4.50
178 Xavier Nady	25.00	7.50
179 Blaine Neal	15.00	4.50
180 Abraham Nunez	15.00	4.50
181 Jose Ortiz	15.00	4.50
182 Jeremy Owens	15.00	4.50
183 Jay Gibbons	40.00	12.00
184 Corey Patterson	25.00	7.50
185 Carlos Pena	15.00	4.50
186 C.C. Sabathia	25.00	7.50
187 Timo Perez	15.00	4.50
188 Adam Pettyjohn	15.00	4.50
189 Donaldo Mendez	15.00	4.50
190 Jackson Melian	15.00	4.50
191 Wilkin Ruan	15.00	4.50
192 Duaner Sanchez	15.00	4.50
193 Alfonso Soriano	100.00	30.00
194 Rafael Soriano	50.00	15.00
195 Ichiro Suzuki NO AU		
196 Billy Sylvester	15.00	4.50
197 Juan Uribe	15.00	4.50
198 Tsuyoshi Shinjo NO AU		
199 Carlos Valderrama	15.00	4.50
200 Matt White	15.00	4.50

2001 Donruss Elite Back 2 Back Jacks

Randomly inserted in packs, this double-sided 45-card set features color photos of one or two players with game-used bat pieces embedded in the cards. Cards with single players are sequentially numbered to 100 while those with doubles were numbered to 50. Exchange cards with a redemption deadline of May 1st, 2003 were seeded into packs for Eddie Mathews, Frank Thomas, Mathews/Glaus combo and F.Robinson/Thomas combo.

	Nm-Mt	Ex-Mt
BB1 Ernie Banks SP/75	40.00	12.00
BB2 Ryne Sandberg SP/75	100.00	30.00
BB3 Babe Ruth	200.00	60.00
BB4 Lou Gehrig	200.00	60.00
BB5 Eddie Mathews	40.00	12.00
BB6 Troy Glaus SP/50	50.00	15.00
BB7 Don Mattingly SP/50	120.00	36.00
BB8 Todd Helton	40.00	12.00
BB9 Wade Boggs	40.00	12.00
BB10 Tony Gwynn	40.00	12.00
BB11 Robin Yount	40.00	12.00
BB12 Paul Molitor SP/50	50.00	15.00
BB13 Mike Schmidt SP/50	100.00	30.00
BB14 Scott Rolen SP/75	40.00	12.00
BB15 Reggie Jackson	40.00	12.00
BB16 Dave Winfield	25.00	7.50
BB17 J. Bench SP/50	50.00	15.00
BB18 Joe Morgan	25.00	7.50
BB19 B. Robinson SP/50	50.00	15.00
BB20 Cal Ripken	100.00	30.00
BB21 Ty Cobb	120.00	36.00
BB22 Al Kaline SP/50	50.00	15.00
BB23 F. Robinson SP/50	50.00	15.00
BB24 Frank Thomas	40.00	12.00
BB25 Roberto Clemente	120.00	36.00
BB26 V. Guerrero SP/50	50.00	15.00
BB27 H.Killebrew SP/50	50.00	15.00
BB28 Kirby Puckett	40.00	12.00
BB29 Yogi Berra SP/75	50.00	15.00
BB30 Phil Rizzuto SP/75	50.00	15.00
BB31 Ernie Banks	150.00	45.00
Ryne Sandberg		
BB32 Babe Ruth	800.00	240.00
Lou Gehrig		
BB33 Eddie Mathews	100.00	30.00
Troy Glaus		
BB34 Don Mattingly	120.00	36.00
Todd Helton		
BB35 Wade Boggs	120.00	36.00
Tony Gwynn		
BB36 Robin Yount	100.00	30.00
Paul Molitor		
BB37 Mike Schmidt	150.00	45.00
Scott Rolen		
BB38 Reggie Jackson	60.00	18.00
Dave Winfield		
BB39 Johnny Bench	100.00	30.00
Joe Morgan		
BB40 Brooks Robinson	200.00	60.00
Cal Ripken		
BB41 Ty Cobb	200.00	60.00
Al Kaline		
BB42 Frank Robinson	100.00	30.00
Frank Thomas		
BB43 Roberto Clemente	150.00	45.00
Vladimir Guerrero		
BB44 Harmon Killebrew	100.00	30.00
Kirby Puckett		
BB45 Yogi Berra		
Phil Rizzuto		

2001 Donruss Elite Back 2 Back Jacks Autograph

Randomly inserted in packs, this 16-card set is a partial parallel autographed version of the regular insert set. Almost every card in the set packed out as an exchange card with a redemption deadline of May 1st, 2003. Only Johnny Bench, Al Kaline and Harmon Killebrew signed cards in time to be seeded directly into packs. Cards with a print run of 25 copies are not priced due to scarcity.

	Nm-Mt	Ex-Mt
BB1 Ernie Banks/25		
BB2 Ryne Sandberg/25		
BB6 Troy Glaus/50	100.00	30.00
BB7 Don Mattingly/50	300.00	90.00
BB12 Paul Molitor/50	100.00	30.00
BB13 Mike Schmidt/50	200.00	60.00
BB14 Scott Rolen/25		
BB17 Johnny Bench/50	150.00	45.00
BB19 Brooks Robinson/50	150.00	45.00
BB22 Al Kaline/50	200.00	60.00
BB23 Frank Robinson/50	100.00	30.00
BB26 Vladimir Guerrero/50	150.00	45.00
BB27 Harmon Killebrew/50	150.00	45.00
BB29 Yogi Berra/25		
BB30 Phil Rizzuto/25		
BB45 Yogi Berra		
Phil Rizzuto		

2001 Donruss Elite Passing the Torch

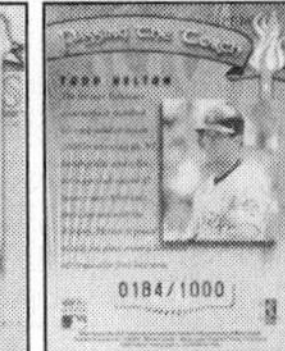

Randomly inserted in packs, this 24-card set features color action photos of legendary players and up-and-coming phenoms printed on holo-foil board. Cards with single players were sequentially numbered to 1000 while those with two players were numbered to 500.

	Nm-Mt	Ex-Mt
COMPLETE SET (24)	500.00	150.00
PT1 Stan Musial	12.00	3.60
PT2 Tony Gwynn	10.00	3.00
PT3 Willie Mays	15.00	4.50
PT4 Barry Bonds	20.00	6.00
PT5 Mike Schmidt	15.00	4.50
PT6 Scott Rolen	5.00	1.50
PT7 Cal Ripken	25.00	7.50
PT8 Alex Rodriguez	12.00	3.60
PT9 Hank Aaron	15.00	4.50
PT10 Andruw Jones	5.00	1.50
PT11 Nolan Ryan	20.00	6.00
PT12 Pedro Martinez	8.00	2.40
PT13 Wade Boggs	5.00	1.50
PT14 Nomar Garciaparra	12.00	3.60
PT15 Don Mattingly	20.00	6.00
PT16 Todd Helton	5.00	1.50
PT17 Stan Musial	20.00	6.00
Tony Gwynn		
PT18 Willie Mays	25.00	7.50
Barry Bonds		
PT19 Mike Schmidt	20.00	6.00
Scott Rolen		
PT20 Cal Ripken	40.00	12.00
Alex Rodriguez		
PT21 Hank Aaron	25.00	7.50
Andruw Jones		
PT22 Nolan Ryan	30.00	9.00
Pedro Martinez		
PT23 Wade Boggs	20.00	6.00
Nomar Garciaparra		
PT24 Don Mattingly	30.00	9.00
Todd Helton		

2001 Donruss Elite Passing the Torch Autographs

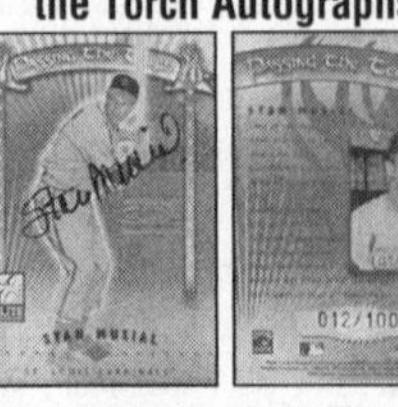

Randomly inserted in packs, this 22-card set is a partial autographed parallel version of the regular insert set printed on double-sided holo-foil board. Cards with single players were sequentially numbered to 100 while those with dual players were numbered to 50. Nearly all of these cards were not available in time for insertion into packs and collectors had until May 1st, 2003 to redeem them. Wade Boggs, Todd Helton, Stan Musial and Nolan Ryan were the only players to return their cards in time for them to be seeded into packs. Cards PT22, PT23 and PT24 were actually 2001 Donruss Elite football exchange cards that were erroneously placed into baseball packs. To honor their commitment to collectors that pulled these cards - the manufacturer created three additional dual autograph baseball cards. These cards are tagged in our checklist with an "FB" status to indicate their origin. The set contains two separate cards numbered PT22 because of this same football snafu - whereby it's theorized that the baseball was originally intended to be complete at 22 cards. The three additional football exchange cards expanded the set to 25 cards and also created two separate PT22 cards.

	Nm-Mt	Ex-Mt
PT1 Stan Musial	150.00	45.00
PT2 Tony Gwynn	100.00	30.00
PT3 Willie Mays	200.00	60.00
PT4 Barry Bonds	250.00	75.00
PT5 Mike Schmidt	150.00	45.00
PT6 Scott Rolen	50.00	15.00
PT7 Cal Ripken	200.00	60.00
PT8 Alex Rodriguez	150.00	45.00
PT9 Hank Aaron	200.00	60.00
PT10 Andruw Jones	50.00	15.00
PT11 Nolan Ryan	200.00	60.00
PT12 P.Martinez EXCH	100.00	30.00
PT13 Wade Boggs	50.00	15.00
PT14 N.Garciaparra EXCH	150.00	45.00
PT15 Don Mattingly	150.00	45.00
PT16 Todd Helton	50.00	15.00
PT17 Stan Musial	200.00	60.00
Tony Gwynn		
PT18 Willie Mays	800.00	240.00
Barry Bonds		
PT19 Mike Schmidt	200.00	60.00
Scott Rolen		
PT20 Cal Ripken	600.00	180.00
Alex Rodriguez		
PT21 Hank Aaron	250.00	75.00
Andruw Jones		
PT22A Nolan Ryan	500.00	150.00
Roger Clemens FB		
PT22B Nolan Ryan	400.00	120.00
Pedro Martinez BB		
PT23 Wade Boggs	250.00	75.00
Nomar Garciaparra FB		
PT24 Don Mattingly	250.00	75.00
Todd Helton FB		

2001 Donruss Elite Primary Colors Red

Randomly inserted in packs, this 40-card set features color action player images with the initials "PC" on a red background. The cards are sequentially numbered to 975. A die-cut holo-foil parallel version of this set was produced and sequentially numbered to 25. A Blue parallel version numbered to 200 and a Yellow one numbered to 25 were also printed. Holo-foil, die-cut parallel versions of both of these sets were produced with the Blue sequentially numbered to 50 and the Yellow to 75.

	Nm-Mt	Ex-Mt
COMPLETE SET (40)	400.00	120.00
*BLUE: .6X TO 1.5X BASIC RED		
BLUE PRINT RUN 200 SERIAL #'d SETS		
*BLUE DIE CUT: 1.25X TO 3X BASIC RED		
BLUE DC PRINT RUN 50 SERIAL #'d SETS		
*RED DIE CUT: 2X TO 5X BASIC RED.		
RED DC PRINT RUN 25 SERIAL #'d SETS		
*YELLOW: 2X TO 5X BASIC RED		
YELLOW PRINT RUN 25 SERIAL #'d SETS		
*YELLOW DIE CUT: 1X TO 2.5X BASIC RED		
YELLOW DC PRINT RUN 75 SERIAL #'d SETS		
RANDOM INSERTS IN PACKS		
PC1 Alex Rodriguez	15.00	4.50
PC2 Barry Bonds	20.00	6.00
PC3 Cal Ripken	30.00	9.00
PC4 Chipper Jones	10.00	3.00
PC5 Derek Jeter	25.00	7.50
PC6 Troy Glaus	6.00	1.80
PC7 Frank Thomas	10.00	3.00
PC8 Greg Maddux	15.00	4.50
PC9 Ivan Rodriguez	10.00	3.00
PC10 Jeff Bagwell	6.00	1.80
PC11 Todd Helton	6.00	1.80
PC12 Ken Griffey Jr.	15.00	4.50
PC13 Manny Ramirez	5.00	1.50
PC14 Mark McGwire	25.00	7.50
PC15 Mike Piazza	15.00	4.50
PC16 Nomar Garciaparra	15.00	4.50
PC17 Pedro Martinez	10.00	3.00
PC18 Randy Johnson	10.00	3.00
PC19 Rick Ankiel	5.00	1.50
PC20 Roger Clemens	20.00	6.00
PC21 Sammy Sosa	15.00	4.50
PC22 Tony Gwynn	12.00	3.60
PC23 Vladimir Guerrero	10.00	3.00
PC24 Carlos Delgado	5.00	1.50
PC25 Jason Giambi	10.00	3.00
PC26 Andruw Jones	5.00	1.50
PC27 Bernie Williams	6.00	1.80
PC28 Roberto Alomar	10.00	3.00
PC29 Shawn Green	5.00	1.50
PC30 Barry Larkin	10.00	3.00
PC31 Scott Rolen	6.00	1.80
PC32 Gary Sheffield	5.00	1.50
PC33 Rafael Palmeiro	6.00	1.80
PC34 Albert Belle	5.00	1.50
PC35 Magglio Ordonez	5.00	1.50
PC36 Jim Thome	10.00	3.00
PC37 Jim Edmonds	5.00	1.50
PC38 Darin Erstad	5.00	1.50
PC39 Kris Benson	5.00	1.50
PC40 Sean Casey	5.00	1.50

2001 Donruss Elite Prime Numbers

Randomly inserted in packs at the rate of one in 84, this 30-card set features color action images of 10 stellar performers. Each player has three cards highlighted by a single digit from his high average. The cards are sequentially numbered to the base total of the digit displayed.

	Nm-Mt	Ex-Mt
PN-1A Alex Rodriguez/300	20.00	6.00
PN-1B Alex Rodriguez/50	50.00	15.00
PN-1C Alex Rodriguez/8		
PN-2A Ken Griffey Jr./400	20.00	6.00
PN-2B Ken Griffey Jr./30	60.00	18.00
PN-2C Ken Griffey Jr./8		
PN-3A Mark McGwire/500	30.00	9.00
PN-3B Mark McGwire/50	80.00	24.00
PN-3C Mark McGwire/4		
PN-4A Cal Ripken/400	40.00	12.00
PN-4B Cal Ripken/10		
PN-4C Cal Ripken/7		
PN-5A Derek Jeter/300	30.00	9.00
PN-5B Derek Jeter/20	150.00	45.00
PN-5C Derek Jeter/2		
PN-6A Mike Piazza/300	20.00	6.00
PN-6B Mike Piazza/60	40.00	12.00
PN-6C Mike Piazza/2		
PN-7A N.Garciaparra/300	20.00	6.00
PN-7B N.Garciaparra/70	30.00	9.00
PN-7C Nomar Garciaparra/2		
PN-8A Sammy Sosa/300	20.00	6.00
PN-8B Sammy Sosa/80	30.00	9.00
PN-8C Sammy Sosa/6		
PN-9A V.Guerrero/300	12.00	3.60
PN-9B V.Guerrero/40	30.00	9.00
PN-9C Vladimir Guerrero/5		
PN-10A Tony Gwynn/300	15.00	4.50
PN-10B Tony Gwynn/90	20.00	6.00
PN-10C Tony Gwynn/4		

2001 Donruss Elite Throwback Threads

Randomly inserted into packs, this 45-card set features past and present greats with swatches of game-worn jerseys displayed on the cards. Cards with single players are sequentially numbered to 100 while those with doubles are numbered to 50. Exchange cards with a redemption deadline of May 1st, 2003 were seeded into packs for Ernie Banks, Lou Brock, Pedro Martinez, Ozzie Smith and Frank Thomas. In addition, exchange cards packed out for the following dual-player cards: Brock/Ozzie, Banks/Sandberg F.Robinson/Thomas and Clemens/Pedro. Pricing is not available for cards with a print run of 25 copies due to scarcity.

	Nm-Mt	Ex-Mt
TT1 Stan Musial SP/75	80.00	24.00
TT2 Tony Gwynn SP/75	50.00	15.00
TT3 Willie McCovey	40.00	12.00
TT4 Barry Bonds	80.00	24.00
TT5 Babe Ruth	300.00	90.00
TT6 Lou Gehrig	300.00	90.00
TT7 Mike Schmidt SP/75	80.00	24.00
TT8 Scott Rolen	40.00	12.00
TT9 H.Killebrew SP/75	40.00	12.00
TT10 Kirby Puckett	40.00	12.00
TT11 Al Kaline SP/75	40.00	12.00
TT12 Eddie Mathews	40.00	12.00
TT13 Hank Aaron SP/75	80.00	24.00
TT14 Andruw Jones SP/50	30.00	9.00
TT15 Lou Brock	40.00	12.00
TT16 Ozzie Smith	40.00	12.00
TT17 E.Banks SP/TBD		
TT18 Ryne Sandberg	80.00	24.00
TT19 Roberto Clemente	120.00	36.00
TT20 V. Guerrero SP/50	50.00	15.00
TT21 F.Robinson SP/50	50.00	15.00
TT22 Frank Thomas	40.00	12.00
TT23 B.Robinson SP/50	50.00	15.00
TT24 Cal Ripken	100.00	30.00
TT25 Roger Clemens	50.00	15.00
TT26 Pedro Martinez	40.00	12.00
TT27 Reggie Jackson	40.00	12.00
TT28 Dave Winfield	25.00	7.50
TT29 Don Mattingly SP/50	120.00	36.00
TT30 Todd Helton	40.00	12.00
TT32 Willie McCovey	150.00	45.00
Barry Bonds		
TT33 Babe Ruth	800.00	240.00
Lou Gehrig		
TT34 Mike Schmidt		
Scott Rolen SP/25		
TT35 Harmon Killebrew	100.00	30.00
Kirby Puckett		
TT36 Al Kaline	100.00	30.00
Eddie Mathews		
TT37 Hank Aaron	120.00	36.00
Andruw Jones		
TT38 Lou Brock	100.00	30.00
Ozzie Smith		

TT39 Ernie Banks ....
Ryne Sandberg SP/25
TT40 Roberto Clemente 120.00 36.00
Vladimir Guerrero
TT41 Frank Robinson............. 100.00 30.00
Frank Thomas
TT42 Brooks Robinson........... 150.00 45.00
Cal Ripken
TT43 Roger Clemens.............. 120.00 36.00
Pedro Martinez
TT44 Reggie Jackson.............. 60.00 18.00
Dave Winfield
TT45 Don Mattingly................ 120.00 36.00
Todd Helton

2001 Donruss Elite Throwback Threads Autographs

Randomly inserted in packs, this 15-card set is a partial parallel autographed version of the regular insert set. Exchange cards with a May 1st, 2003 redemption deadline were seeded into packs for almost the entire set. Only Al Kaline, Harmon Killebrew and Stan Musial managed to return their cards in time for packout. 2001 Donruss Elite football exchange cards were erroneously seeded into baseball packs for cards TT21 and TT22. Those cards have an "FB" tag added to their listing to denote their origins. The quantity for Ernie Banks signed cards was never revealed by the manufacturer.

Nm-Mt Ex-Mt
TT1 Stan Musial/25.............................
TT2 Tony Gwynn/25...........................
TT7 Mike Schmidt/25..........................
TT9 Harmon Killebrew/25....................
TT11 Al Kaline/25...............................
TT13 Hank Aaron/25...........................
TT14 Andruw Jones/50........... 100.00 30.00
TT17 Ernie Banks/TBD........................
TT20 Vladimir Guerrero/50....... 150.00 45.00
TT21 Frank Robinson/50 FB...............
TT22 Frank Thomas/50 FB.................
TT23 Brooks Robinson/50 .... 150.00 45.00
TT29 Don Mattingly/50........... 250.00 75.00
TT31 Stan Musial
Tony Gwynn/50
TT34 Mike Schmidt...........................
Scott Rolen/25
TT39 Ernie Banks ....
Ryne Sandberg/25

2001 Donruss Elite Title Waves

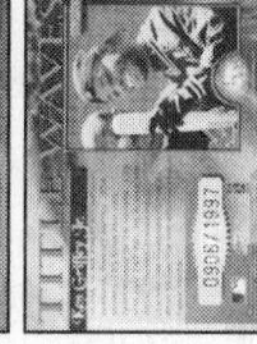

Randomly inserted in packs, this 30-card set features the game's most decorated performers highlighted in five different title-winning categories and sequentially numbered to the year they won the title.

Nm-Mt Ex-Mt
COMPLETE SET (30)............... 250.00 75.00
*HOLO: 1.5X TO 4X BASIC WAVES ....
HOLO-FOIL PRINT RUN 100 SERIAL #'d SETS
RANDOM INSERTS IN PACKS ....
TW1 Tony Gwynn/1994.............. 8.00 2.40
TW2 Todd Helton/2000.............. 4.00 1.20
TW3 N.Garciaparra/2000........... 10.00 3.00
TW4 Frank Thomas/1997........... 6.00 1.80
TW5 Alex Rodriguez/1996.......... 10.00 3.00
TW6 Jeff Bagwell/1994 .... 4.00 1.20
TW7 Mark McGwire/1998 .... 15.00 4.50
TW8 Sammy Sosa/2000............ 10.00 3.00
TW9 Ken Griffey Jr./1997.......... 10.00 3.00
TW10 Albert Belle/1995 .... 3.00 .90
TW11 Barry Bonds/1993............ 15.00 4.50
TW12 Jose Canseco/1991.......... 6.00 1.80
TW13 M.Ramirez/1999 .... 3.00 .90
TW14 Sammy Sosa/1998.......... 10.00 3.00
TW15 A.Galarraga/1996............ 3.00 .90
TW16 Todd Helton/2000............ 4.00 1.20
TW17 Ken Griffey Jr./1997......... 10.00 3.00
TW18 Jeff Bagwell/1994 .... 4.00 1.20
TW19 Mike Piazza/1995............ 10.00 3.00
TW20 A.Rodriguez/1995............ 10.00 3.00
TW21 Jason Giambi/2000.......... 6.00 1.80
TW22 I.Rodriguez/1999............ 6.00 1.80
TW23 Greg Maddux/1997 .... 10.00 3.00
TW24 P.Martinez/1994.............. 6.00 1.80
TW25 Derek Jeter/2000 .... 15.00 4.50
TW26 B.Williams/1998............. 4.00 1.20
TW27 R.Clemens/1999 .... 12.00 3.60
TW28 Chipper Jones/1995......... 6.00 1.80
TW29 M.McGwire/1997 .... 15.00 4.50
TW30 Cal Ripken/1983............. 20.00 6.00

2002 Donruss Elite Samples

Issued one per sealed copy of Beckett Baseball Card Monthly issue number 207, this is a partial parallel to the 2002 Donruss Elite Set. Only the first 100 cards of this set were issued in this format.

Nm-Mt Ex-Mt
*SAMPLES: 1.5X TO 4X BASIC CARDS
ONE PER SEALED BBCM 207 ....
*GOLD: 4X TO 10X BASIC SAMPLES .
GOLD 10% OF PRESS RUN ....

2002 Donruss Elite Samples Gold

Randomly inserted in sealed copies of Beckett Baseball Card Monthly issue number 207, this is a partial parallel to the 2002 Donruss Elite set. These cards which say "Sample" in gold, are 10 percent of the total print run of the 2002 Donruss Elite Sample set.

Nm-Mt Ex-Mt
*GOLD: 4X TO 10X BASIC CARDS......
RANDOM INSERTS IN SEALED BBCM 207
TEN PERCENT OF PRINT RUN IS GOLD

2002 Donruss Elite

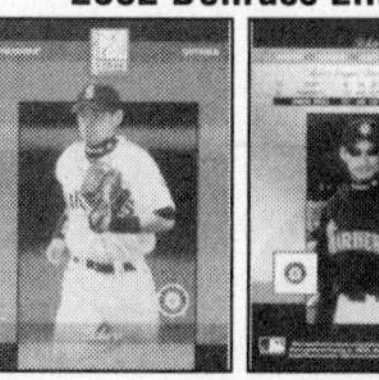

This 268-card set highlights baseball's premier performers. The standard-size set is made up of 100 veteran players, 50 STAR veteran subset cards and 50 rookie players. The fronts feature full color action shots. The STAR subset cards (101-150) were seeded into packs at a rate of 1:10. The rookie cards (151-200) are sequentially numbered to 1500 but only 1350 of each were actually produced. The first 150 of each rookie card is die-cut and labeled "Turn of the Century" with varying quantities of some autographed. These cards were issued in 5 card packs with a $3.99 SRP which came 20 packs to a box and 20 boxes to a case. Cards 256, 263 and 267-271 were never released.

Nm-Mt Ex-Mt
COMP.LO SET w/o SP's (100) .. 20.00 6.00
COMMON CARD (1-100)............. .40 .12
COMMON CARD (101-150)......... 4.00 1.20
COMMON CARD (151-200)......... 5.00 1.50
COMMON CARD (201-275)......... 8.00 2.40
1 Vladimir Guerrero.................... 1.00 .30
2 Bernie Williams......................... .60 .18
3 Ichiro Suzuki.......................... 1.50 .45
4 Roger Clemens....................... 2.00 .60
5 Greg Maddux......................... 1.50 .45
6 Fred McGriff.............................. .60 .18
7 Jermaine Dye .... .40 .12
8 Ken Griffey Jr. .... 1.50 .45
9 Todd Helton.............................. .60 .18
10 Torii Hunter .... .40 .12
11 Pat Burrell .... .40 .12
12 Chipper Jones .... 1.00 .30
13 Ivan Rodriguez .... 1.00 .30
14 Roy Oswalt.............................. .40 .12
15 Shannon Stewart..................... .40 .12
16 Magglio Ordonez .... .40 .12
17 Lance Berkman .... .40 .12
18 Mark Mulder............................ .40 .12
19 Al Leiter.................................. .40 .12
20 Sammy Sosa......................... 1.50 .45
21 Scott Rolen .... .60 .18
22 Aramis Ramirez........................ .40 .12
23 Alfonso Soriano........................ .60 .18
24 Phil Nevin................................. .40 .12
25 Barry Bonds .... 2.50 .75
26 Joe Mays.................................. .40 .12
27 Jeff Kent................................... .40 .12
28 Mark Quinn .... .40 .12
29 Adrian Beltre .... .40 .12
30 Freddy Garcia .... .40 .12
31 Pedro Martinez .... 1.00 .30
32 Darryl Kile .... .40 .12
33 Mike Cameron.......................... .40 .12
34 Frank Catalanotto .... .40 .12
35 Jose Vidro .... .40 .12
36 Jim Thome .... 1.00 .30
37 Javy Lopez .... .40 .12
38 Paul Konerko............................ .40 .12
39 Jeff Bagwell.............................. .60 .18
40 Curt Schilling........................... .60 .18
41 Miguel Tejada.......................... .40 .12
42 Jim Edmonds .... .40 .12
43 Ellis Burks .... .40 .12
44 Mark Grace.............................. .60 .18
45 Robb Nen .... .40 .12
46 Jeff Conine .... .40 .12
47 Derek Jeter.......................... 2.50 .75
48 Mike Lowell .... .40 .12
49 Javier Vazquez......................... .40 .12
50 Manny Ramirez .... .40 .12
51 Bartolo Colon .... .40 .12
52 Carlos Beltran.......................... .40 .12
53 Tim Hudson............................. .40 .12
54 Rafael Palmeiro .... .60 .18
55 Jimmy Rollins .... .40 .12
56 Andruw Jones .... .40 .12
57 Orlando Cabrera .... .40 .12
58 Dean Palmer............................. .40 .12
59 Bret Boone .... .40 .12
60 Carlos Febles............................ .40 .12
61 Ben Grieve................................ .40 .12
62 Richie Sexson .... .40 .12
63 Alex Rodriguez .... 1.50 .45
64 Juan Pierre............................... .40 .12
65 Bobby Higginson...................... .40 .12
66 Barry Zito .... .60 .18
67 Raul Mondesi .... .40 .12
68 Albert Pujols .... 2.00 .60
69 Omar Vizquel........................... .40 .12
70 Bobby Abreu .... .40 .12
71 Corey Koskie .... .40 .12
72 Tom Glavine............................. .60 .18
73 Paul LoDuca............................. .40 .12
74 Terrence Long.......................... .40 .12
75 Matt Morris .... .40 .12
76 Andy Pettitte............................. .60 .18
77 Rich Aurilia.............................. .40 .12
78 Todd Walker............................. .40 .12
79 John Olerud UER....................... .40 .12
Career Header stats are those for a pitcher
80 Mike Sweeney .... .40 .12
81 Ray Durham .... .40 .12
82 Fernando Vina .... .40 .12
83 Nomar Garciaparra................ 1.50 .45
84 Mariano Rivera.......................... .60 .18
85 Mike Piazza .... 1.50 .45
86 Mark Buehrle............................ .40 .12
87 Adam Dunn .... .40 .12
88 Luis Gonzalez........................... .40 .12
89 Richard Hidalgo........................ .40 .12
90 Brad Radke............................... .40 .12
91 Russ Ortiz .... .40 .12
92 Brian Giles................................ .40 .12
93 Billy Wagner............................. .40 .12
94 Cliff Floyd .... .40 .12
95 Eric Milton................................ .40 .12
96 Bud Smith................................. .40 .12
97 Wade Miller.............................. .40 .12
98 Jon Lieber .... .40 .12
99 Derrek Lee................................ .40 .12
100 Jose Cruz Jr............................. .40 .12
101 Dmitri Young STAR.............. 4.00 1.20
102 Mo Vaughn STAR................ 4.00 1.20
103 Tino Martinez STAR 5.00 1.50
104 Larry Walker STAR.............. 5.00 1.50
105 Chuck Knoblauch STAR 4.00 1.20
106 Troy Glaus STAR.................. 5.00 1.50
107 Jason Giambi STAR.............. 8.00 2.40
108 Travis Fryman STAR............. 4.00 1.20
109 Josh Beckett STAR................ 5.00 1.50
110 Edgar Martinez STAR 5.00 1.50
111 Tim Salmon STAR................ 5.00 1.50
112 C.C. Sabathia STAR.............. 4.00 1.20
113 Randy Johnson STAR 8.00 2.40
114 Juan Gonzalez STAR............. 8.00 2.40
115 Carlos Delgado STAR............ 4.00 1.20
116 Hideo Nomo STAR 8.00 2.40
117 Kerry Wood STAR 8.00 2.40
118 Brian Jordan STAR................ 4.00 1.20
119 Carlos Pena STAR 4.00 1.20
120 Roger Cedeno STAR.............. 4.00 1.20
121 Chan Ho Park STAR 4.00 1.20
122 Rafael Furcal STAR.............. 4.00 1.20
123 Frank Thomas STAR.............. 8.00 2.40
124 Mike Mussina STAR.............. 8.00 2.40
125 Rickey Henderson STAR 8.00 2.40
126 Sean Casey STAR.................. 4.00 1.20
127 Barry Larkin STAR................ 8.00 2.40
128 Kazuhiro Sasaki STAR........... 4.00 1.20
129 Moises Alou STAR 4.00 1.20
130 Jeff Cirillo STAR.................. 4.00 1.20
131 Jason Kendall STAR.............. 4.00 1.20
132 Gary Sheffield STAR............. 4.00 1.20
133 Ryan Klesko STAR 4.00 1.20
134 Kevin Brown STAR 4.00 1.20
135 Darin Erstad STAR................ 4.00 1.20
136 Roberto Alomar STAR........... 8.00 2.40
137 Brad Fullmer STAR............... 4.00 1.20
138 Eric Chavez STAR................. 4.00 1.20
139 Ben Sheets STAR.................. 4.00 1.20
140 Trot Nixon STAR 5.00 1.50
141 Garret Anderson STAR........... 4.00 1.20
142 Shawn Green STAR............... 4.00 1.20
143 Troy Percival STAR 4.00 1.20
144 Craig Biggio STAR................ 5.00 1.50
145 Jorge Posada STAR 5.00 1.50
146 J.D. Drew STAR.................... 4.00 1.20
147 Johnny Damon STAR............. 4.00 1.20
148 Jeromy Burnitz STAR............ 4.00 1.20
149 Robin Ventura STAR 4.00 1.20
150 Aaron Sele STAR.................. 4.00 1.20
151 Cam Esslinger ROO RC 5.00 1.50
152 Ben Howard ROO RC............ 5.00 1.50
153 Brandon Backe ROO RC 5.00 1.50
154 Jorge De La Rosa ROO RC.... 5.00 1.50
155 Austin Kearns ROO............... 5.00 1.50
156 Carlos Zambrano ROO 5.00 1.50
157 Kyle Kane ROO RC 5.00 1.50
158 So Taguchi ROO RC.............. 8.00 2.40
159 Brian Mallette ROO RC 5.00 1.50
160 Brett Jodie ROO.................... 5.00 1.50
161 Elio Serrano ROO RC............ 5.00 1.50
162 Joe Thurston ROO.................. 5.00 1.50
163 Kevin Olsen ROO.................. 5.00 1.50
164 Rodrigo Rosario ROO RC....... 5.00 1.50
165 Matt Guerrier ROO................ 5.00 1.50
166 And. Machado ROO RC......... 5.00 1.50
167 Bert Snow ROO.................... 5.00 1.50
168 Franklyn German ROO RC..... 5.00 1.50
169 Brandon Claussen ROO.......... 8.00 2.40
170 Jason Romano ROO............... 5.00 1.50
171 Jorge Padilla ROO RC 5.00 1.50
172 Jose Cueto ROO 5.00 1.50
173 Allan Simpson ROO RC 5.00 1.50
174 Doug Devore ROO RC........... 5.00 1.50
175 Justin Duchscherer ROO......... 5.00 1.50
176 Josh Pearce ROO................... 5.00 1.50
177 Steve Bechler ROO RC.......... 5.00 1.50
178 Josh Phelps ROO 5.00 1.50
179 Juan Diaz ROO 5.00 1.50
180 Victor Alvarez ROO RC 5.00 1.50
181 Ramon Vazquez ROO 5.00 1.50
182 Mike Rivera ROO.................. 5.00 1.50
183 Kazuhisa Ishii ROO RC 10.00 3.00
184 Henry Mateo ROO 5.00 1.50
185 Travis Hughes ROO RC 5.00 1.50
186 Zach Day ROO...................... 5.00 1.50
187 Brad Voyles ROO.................. 5.00 1.50
188 Sean Douglass ROO 5.00 1.50
189 Nick Neugebauer ROO........... 5.00 1.50
190 Tom Shearn ROO RC............. 5.00 1.50
191 Eric Cyr ROO 5.00 1.50
192 Adam Johnson ROO 5.00 1.50
193 Michael Cuddyer ROO 5.00 1.50
194 Erik Bedard ROO 5.00 1.50
195 Mark Ellis ROO..................... 5.00 1.50
196 Carlos Hernandez ROO.......... 5.00 1.50
197 Deivis Santos ROO 5.00 1.50
198 Morgan Ensberg ROO 5.00 1.50
199 Ryan Jamison ROO 5.00 1.50
200 Cody Ransom ROO 5.00 1.50
201 Chris Snelling ROO RC 15.00 4.50
202 Satoru Komiyama ROO RC.... 8.00 2.40
203 Jas. Simontacchi ROO RC...... 8.00 2.40
204 Tim Kalita ROO RC 8.00 2.40
205 Run. Hernandez ROO RC.... 20.00 6.00
206 Kirk Saarloos ROO RC.......... 8.00 2.40
207 Aaron Cook ROO RC 8.00 2.40
208 Luis Ugueto ROO RC............ 8.00 2.40
209 Gustavo Chacin ROO RC 8.00 2.40
210 Francis Beltran ROO RC 8.00 2.40
211 Takahito Nomura ROO RC..... 8.00 2.40
212 Oliver Perez ROO RC.......... 10.00 3.00
213 Miguel Asencio ROO RC....... 8.00 2.40
214 Rene Reyes ROO RC 8.00 2.40
215 Jeff Baker ROO RC 30.00 9.00
216 Jon Adkins ROO RC 8.00 2.40
217 Carlos Rivera ROO RC........ 10.00 3.00
218 Corey Thurman ROO RC 8.00 2.40
219 Earl Snyder ROO RC 8.00 2.40
220 Felix Escalona ROO RC......... 8.00 2.40
221 Jeremy Guthrie ROO RC...... 30.00 9.00
222 Josh Hancock ROO RC 8.00 2.40
223 Ben Kozlowski ROO RC........ 8.00 2.40
224 Eric Good ROO RC 8.00 2.40
225 Eric Junge ROO RC 8.00 2.40
226 Andy Pratt ROO RC 8.00 2.40
227 Matt Thornton ROO RC 8.00 2.40
228 Jorge Sosa ROO RC.............. 8.00 2.40
229 Mike Smith ROO RC............. 8.00 2.40
230 Mitch Wylie ROO RC 8.00 2.40
231 John Ennis ROO RC 8.00 2.40
232 Reed Johnson ROO RC 10.00 3.00
233 Joe Borchard ROO 8.00 2.40
234 Ron Calloway ROO RC 8.00 2.40
235 Brian Tallet ROO RC 10.00 3.00
236 Chris Baker ROO RC............ 8.00 2.40
237 Cliff Lee ROO RC............... 15.00 4.50
238 Matt Childers ROO RC.......... 8.00 2.40
239 Freddy Sanchez ROO RC....... 8.00 2.40
240 Chone Figgins ROO RC 8.00 2.40
241 Kevin Cash ROO RC............. 8.00 2.40
242 Josh Bard ROO RC 8.00 2.40
243 Jer. Robertson ROO RC 8.00 2.40
244 Jeremy Hill ROO RC............. 8.00 2.40
245 Shane Nance ROO RC........... 8.00 2.40
246 Wes Obermueller ROO RC.... 8.00 2.40
247 Trey Hodges ROO RC........... 8.00 2.40
248 Eric Eckenstahler ROO RC.... 8.00 2.40
249 Jim Rushford ROO RC 8.00 2.40
250 Jose Castillo ROO RC 50.00 15.00
251 Garrett Atkins ROO RC 15.00 4.50
252 Alexis Rios ROO RC 150.00 45.00
253 Ryan Church ROO RC 10.00 3.00
254 Jimmy Gobble ROO RC 15.00 4.50
255 Corwin Malone ROO RC 8.00 2.40
256 Does Not Exist.............................
257 Nic Jackson ROO RC............. 8.00 2.40
258 Tommy Whiteman ROO RC 15.00 4.50
259 Mario Ramos ROO RC........... 8.00 2.40
260 Rob Bowen ROO RC............. 8.00 2.40
261 Josh Wilson ROO RC 8.00 2.40
262 Tim Hummel ROO RC 8.00 2.40
263 Does Not Exist.............................
264 Gerald Laird ROO RC......... 20.00 6.00
265 Vinny Chulk ROO RC 8.00 2.40
266 Jesus Medrano ROO RC........ 8.00 2.40
267 Does Not Exist.............................
268 Does Not Exist.............................
269 Does Not Exist.............................
270 Does Not Exist.............................
271 Does Not Exist.............................
272 Adam LaRoche ROO RC..... 60.00 18.00
273 Adam Morrissey ROO RC..... 8.00 2.40
274 Henri Stanley ROO RC........ 10.00 3.00
275 Walter Young ROO RC 20.00 6.00

2002 Donruss Elite Aspirations

Randomly inserted into packs, this 200-card set is a parallel to the base set. The cards are standard-size and die-cut on holo-foil board with blue tint and blue foil stamping sequentially numbered to the featured player's jersey number. Due to market scarcity, cards with a print run of less than 25 are not priced.

Nm-Mt Ex-Mt
*1-100 PRINT RUN b/wn 26-35 15X TO 40X
*1-100 PRINT RUN b/wn 36-50 12.5X TO 30X
*1-100 PRINT RUN b/wn 51-65 10X TO 25X
*1-100 PRINT RUN b/wn 66-80 8X TO 20X
*101-150 PRINT RUN b/wn 26-35 2X TO 5X
*101-150 PRINT RUN b/wn 36-50 1.5X TO 4X
*101-150 PRINT RUN b/wn 51-65 1.25X TO 3X
UNLISTED 151-200 p/r 81-99... 15.00 4.50
COMMON (151-200) p/r 66-80... 8.00 2.40
SEMIS 151-200 p/r 66-80......... 12.00 3.60
UNLISTED 151-200 p/r 66-80... 20.00 6.00
COMMON (151-200) p/r 51-65 . 10.00 3.00
SEMIS 151-200 p/r 51-65......... 15.00 4.50
UNLISTED 151-200 p/r 51-65... 25.00 7.50
COMMON (151-200) p/r 36-50 . 12.00 3.60
SEMIS 151-200 p/r 36-50......... 20.00 6.00
UNLISTED 151-200 p/r 36-50... 30.00 9.00
COMMON (151-200) p/r 26-35 . 15.00 4.50
SEMIS 151-200 p/r 26-35......... 25.00 7.50
UNLISTED 151-200 p/r 26-35... 40.00 12.00
RANDOM INSERTS IN PACKS ....
SEE BECKETT.COM FOR PRINT RUNS
NO PRICING ON QUANTITIES OF 25 OR LESS

2002 Donruss Elite Status

Randomly inserted into packs, this 200-card set is a parallel to the base set. The cards are die-cut on holo-foil board with platinum tint and platinum foil stamping sequentially numbered to the remaining number out of 100 as reduced from the Donruss Elite Aspirations parallel (of which was serial numbered to the featured player's jersey number). We have listed the stated print run next to the player's name in our checklist. Cards with a stated print run of 25 or fewer are not printed due to market scarcity.

Nm-Mt Ex-Mt
*1-100 PRINT RUN b/wn 36-50 12.5X TO 30X
*1-100 PRINT RUN b/wn 51-65 10X TO 25X
*1-100 PRINT RUN b/wn 66-80 8X TO 20X
*1-100 PRINT RUN b/wn 81-98 6X TO 15X
*101-150 PRINT RUN b/wn 36-50 1.5X TO 4X
*101-150 PRINT RUN b/wn 51-65 1.25X TO 3X
*101-150 PRINT RUN b/wn 66-80 1X TO 2.5X
*101-150 PRINT RUN b/wn 81-99 .75X TO 2X
COMMON (151-200) p/r 81-99 ... 6.00 1.80
SEMIS 151-200 p/r 81-99......... 10.00 3.00
UNLISTED 151-200 p/r 81-99... 15.00 4.50
COMMON (151-200) p/r 66-80 ... 8.00 2.40
SEMIS 151-200 p/r 66-80......... 12.00 3.60
UNLISTED 151-200 p/r 66-80... 20.00 6.00
COMMON (151-200) p/r 51-65 . 10.00 3.00
SEMIS 151-200 p/r 51-65......... 15.00 4.50
UNLISTED 151-200 p/r 51-65... 25.00 7.50
COMMON (151-200) p/r 36-50 . 12.00 3.60
SEMIS 151-200 p/r 36-50......... 20.00 6.00
UNLISTED 151-200 p/r 36-50... 30.00 9.00
COMMON (151-200) p/r 26-35 . 15.00 4.50
SEMIS 151-200 p/r 26-35......... 25.00 7.50
UNLISTED 151-200 p/r 26-35... 40.00 12.00
RANDOM INSERTS IN PACKS ....
SEE BECKETT.COM FOR PRINT RUNS
NO PRICING ON QUANTITIES OF 25 OR LESS

2002 Donruss Elite Turn of the Century

Randomly inserted in packs of Elite and Donruss the Rookies, these 71 cards partially parallel the prospect cards in 2002 Donruss Elite. Cards checklisted between 151-200 were distributed in Elite packs and 201-275 in Donruss the Rookies packs. The Turn of the Century parallels are easily identified from basic issue cards by their rounded corners. It's important to note that Turn of the Century cards were cumulatively serial-numbered, intermingling the basic Elite cards and the Turn of the Century Autograph cards. For example, card 201 Chris Snelling features serial numbering to 1000. The first 100 numbered copies were devoted to the Turn of the Century sets with Snelling signing cards "1 of 1000" through "50 of 1000". The last 900 numbered cards are his basic Elite Rookie Card. Some players signed all of their Turn of the Century cards and others signed none. We have notated the stated print run next to the player's name in our checklist and cards with a print run of less than 25 are not priced due to market scarcity.

Nm-Mt Ex-Mt
154 Jorge De La Rosa/50.......... 10.00 3.00
156 Carlos Zambrano/50........... 10.00 3.00
157 Kyle Kane/50 .... 10.00 3.00
158 So Taguchi/25...........................
159 Brian Mallette/50............... 10.00 3.00
160 Brett Jodie/50.................... 10.00 3.00
165 Matt Guerrier/50................ 10.00 3.00
168 Franklyn German/50........... 10.00 3.00
169 Brandon Claussen/50......... 25.00 7.50
171 Jorge Padilla/50 .... 10.00 3.00
172 Jose Cueto/50 .... 10.00 3.00
176 Josh Pearce/50.................. 10.00 3.00
177 Steve Bechler/50 .... 10.00 3.00
178 Josh Phelps/50 .... 10.00 3.00
180 Victor Alvarez/50............... 10.00 3.00
182 Michael Rivera/50 .... 15.00 4.50
183 Kazuhisa Ishii/125 .... 25.00 7.50
184 Henry Mateo/50................. 15.00 4.50
186 Zach Day/50 .... 15.00 4.50
189 Nick Neugebauer/100......... 10.00 3.00
192 Adam Johnson/125 .... 10.00 3.00
193 Michael Cuddyer/50 .... 15.00 4.50
195 Mark Ellis/25.............................
196 Carlos Hernandez/150......... 10.00 3.00
198 Morgan Ensberg/50............ 15.00 4.50
200 Cody Ransom/150.............. 10.00 3.00
201 Chris Snelling/50................ 40.00 12.00
202 Satoru Komiyama/75.......... 15.00 4.50
203 Jason Simontacchi/75.......... 15.00 4.50
204 Tim Kalita/100 .... 10.00 3.00
205 Runelvys Hernandez/100..... 25.00 7.50
206 Kirk Saarloos/50................ 15.00 4.50
207 Aaron Cook/100 .... 10.00 3.00
208 Luis Ugueto/75.................. 15.00 4.50
209 Gustavo Chacin/75 .... 15.00 4.50
210 Francis Beltran/75.............. 15.00 4.50
211 Takahito Nomura/75........... 15.00 4.50
212 Oliver Perez/75.................. 20.00 6.00
213 Miguel Asencio/75.............. 15.00 4.50
214 Rene Reyes/75................... 15.00 4.50
218 Corey Thurman/75 .... 15.00 4.50
219 Earl Snyder/75................... 15.00 4.50
220 Felix Escalona/75............... 15.00 4.50
222 Josh Hancock/100.............. 10.00 3.00
225 Eric Junge/75..................... 15.00 4.50
226 Andy Pratt/75 .... 15.00 4.50
227 Matt Thornton/75 .... 15.00 4.50
228 Jorge Sosa/100.................. 10.00 3.00
229 Mike Smith/100.................. 10.00 3.00
230 Mitch Wylie/100 .... 10.00 3.00
231 John Ennis/75.................... 15.00 4.50
232 Reed Johnson/75................ 20.00 6.00
233 Joe Borchard/75................. 15.00 4.50
234 Ron Calloway/100 .... 10.00 3.00
235 Brian Tallet/75 .... 20.00 6.00
236 Chris Baker/75................... 15.00 4.50
237 Cliff Lee/75....................... 30.00 9.00
238 Matt Childers/75................ 15.00 4.50
239 Freddy Sanchez/100........... 10.00 3.00
242 Josh Bard/75..................... 15.00 4.50
243 Jeriome Robertson/100...... 10.00 3.00
244 Jeremy Hill/100 .... 10.00 3.00
245 Shane Nance/75 .... 15.00 4.50
246 Wes Obermueller/100 .... 10.00 3.00
248 Eric Eckenstahler/100......... 10.00 3.00
249 Jim Rushford/100............... 10.00 3.00
250 Jose Castillo/100.............. 100.00 30.00
252 Alexis Rios/100 .... 250.00 75.00
257 Nic Jackson/100................. 10.00 3.00
265 Vinny Chulk/100................ 10.00 3.00
275 Walter Young/100.............. 30.00 9.00

2002 Donruss Elite Turn of the Century Autographs

Randomly inserted into packs of Elite and Donruss the Rookies, these 95 cards basically parallel the prospect cards in 2002 Donruss Elite. Cards 151-200 were distributed in Elite packs and cards 201-275 in Donruss the Rookies. These cards are all signed by the featured player and we have notated the stated print run information next to the player's name

in our checklist. Please note, the cards are serial numbered cumulatively out of 1,500 for cards 151-200 and 1,000 for cards 201-275 - intermingling the basic issue Elite set, the Turn of the Century parallel die cuts and the Turn of the Century Autographs. Actual print runs for the autographs are listed below.

	Nm-Mt	Ex-Mt
151 Cam Esslinger/150	15.00	4.50
152 Ben Howard/150	15.00	4.50
153 Brandon Backe/150	15.00	4.50
154 Jorge De La Rosa/100	15.00	4.50
155 Austin Kearns/150	15.00	4.50
156 Carlos Zambrano/100	25.00	7.50
157 Kyle Kane/100	15.00	4.50
158 So Taguchi/125	25.00	7.50
159 Brian Mallette/100	15.00	4.50
160 Brett Jodie/100	15.00	4.50
161 Elio Serrano/150	15.00	4.50
162 Joe Thurston/150	15.00	4.50
163 Kevin Olsen/150	15.00	4.50
164 Rodrigo Rosario/150	15.00	4.50
165 Matt Guerrier/100	15.00	4.50
166 Anderson Machado/150	15.00	4.50
167 Bert Snow/150	15.00	4.50
168 Franklyn German/100	15.00	4.50
169 Brandon Claussen/100	40.00	12.00
170 Jason Romano/150	15.00	4.50
171 Jorge Padilla/100	15.00	4.50
172 Jose Cueto/100	15.00	4.50
173 Allan Simpson/150	15.00	4.50
174 Doug Devore/150	15.00	4.50
175 Justin Duchscherer/150	15.00	4.50
176 Josh Pearce/100	15.00	4.50
177 Steve Bechler/100	15.00	4.50
178 Josh Phelps/100	15.00	4.50
179 Juan Diaz/150	15.00	4.50
180 Victor Alvarez/100	15.00	4.50
181 Ramon Vazquez/150	15.00	4.50
182 Michael Rivera/100	15.00	4.50
183 Kazuhisa Ishii/25		
184 Henry Mateo/100	15.00	4.50
185 Travis Hughes/150	15.00	4.50
186 Zach Day/100	15.00	4.50
187 Brad Voyles/150	15.00	4.50
188 Sean Douglass/150	15.00	4.50
189 Nick Neugebauer/50	25.00	7.50
190 Tom Shearn/150	15.00	4.50
191 Eric Cyr/150	15.00	4.50
192 Adam Johnson/25		
193 Michael Cuddyer/100	15.00	4.50
194 Erik Bedard/150	15.00	4.50
195 Mark Ellis/125	15.00	4.50
197 Deivis Santos/150	15.00	4.50
198 Morgan Ensberg/100	15.00	4.50
199 Ryan Jamison/150	15.00	4.50
201 Chris Snelling/50	40.00	12.00
202 Satoru Komiyama/25		
204 Tim Kalita/25		
206 Kirk Saarloos/50	25.00	7.50
208 Luis Ugueto/25		
210 Francis Beltran/25		
211 Takahito Nomura/25		
212 Oliver Perez/25		
214 Rene Reyes/25		
215 Jeff Baker/100	60.00	18.00
216 Jon Adkins/100	15.00	4.50
217 Carlos Rivera/100	25.00	7.50
218 Corey Thurman/25		
219 Earl Snyder/25		
220 Felix Escalona/25		
221 Jeremy Guthrie/100	60.00	18.00
223 Ben Kozlowski/100	15.00	4.50
224 Eric Good/100	15.00	4.50
225 Eric Junge/25		
226 Andy Pratt/25		
227 Matt Thornton/25		
231 John Ennis/25		
232 Reed Johnson/25		
233 Joe Borchard/25		
235 Brian Tallet/25		
236 Chris Baker/25		
237 Cliff Lee/25		
238 Matt Childers/25		
240 Chone Figgins/100	15.00	4.50
241 Kevin Cash/100	15.00	4.50
242 Josh Bard/25		
245 Shane Nance/25		
247 Trey Hodges/100	15.00	4.50
251 Garrett Atkins/100	30.00	9.00
253 Ryan Church/100	25.00	7.50
254 Jimmy Gobble/100	40.00	12.00
255 Corwin Malone/100	15.00	4.50
258 Tommy Whiteman/100	40.00	12.00
259 Mario Ramos/100	15.00	4.50
260 Rob Bowen/100	15.00	4.50
261 Josh Wilson/100	15.00	4.50
262 Tim Hummel/100	15.00	4.50
264 Gerald Laird/100	50.00	15.00
266 Jesus Medrano/100	15.00	4.50
272 Adam LaRoche/100	200.00	60.00
273 Adam Morrissey/100	15.00	4.50
274 Henri Stanley/100	25.00	7.50

2002 Donruss Elite All-Star Salutes

Randomly inserted into packs, this 25-card insert set spotlights on the most heralded players. The fronts of the standard-size cards feature full color action shots set on metalized film board with foil and is sequentially numbered to the year the featured player shined in the All-Star Game.

	Nm-Mt	Ex-Mt
COMPLETE SET (25)	150.00	45.00

*CENTURY: 1.25X TO 3X BASIC AS SALUTE

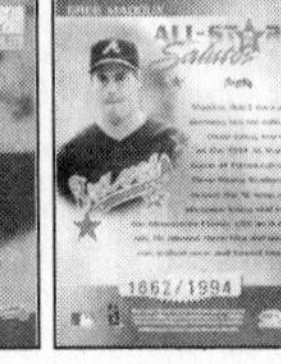

CENTURY PRINT RUN 100 SERIAL #'d SETS

1 Ichiro Suzuki/2001	10.00	3.00
2 Tony Gwynn/2001	8.00	2.40
3 Magglio Ordonez/2001	4.00	1.20
4 Cal Ripken/2001	20.00	6.00
5 Roger Clemens/1998	12.00	3.60
6 Kazuhiro Sasaki/2001	4.00	1.20
7 Freddy Garcia/2001	4.00	1.20
8 Luis Gonzalez/2001	4.00	1.20
9 Lance Berkman/2001	4.00	1.20
10 Derek Jeter/2000	15.00	4.50
11 Chipper Jones/2000	6.00	1.80
12 Randy Johnson/2000	6.00	1.80
13 Andruw Jones/2000	4.00	1.20
14 Pedro Martinez/1999	6.00	1.80
15 Jim Thome/1999	6.00	1.80
16 Rafael Palmeiro/1999	4.00	1.20
17 Barry Larkin/1999	6.00	1.80
18 Ivan Rodriguez/1998	6.00	1.80
19 Omar Vizquel/1998	4.00	1.20
20 Edgar Martinez/1997	4.00	1.20
21 Larry Walker/1997	4.00	1.20
22 Javy Lopez/1997	4.00	1.20
23 Mariano Rivera/1997	4.00	1.20
24 Frank Thomas/1995	6.00	1.80
25 Greg Maddux/1994	10.00	3.00

2002 Donruss Elite Back 2 Back Jacks

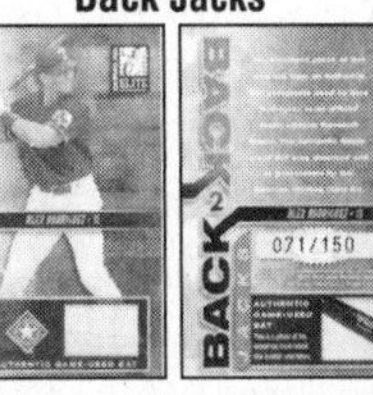

Randomly inserted into pack, this 30-card insert set showcases both retired and present-day stars. The standard-size fronts are full color action shots that are featured with one or two swatches of game-used bats. Cards featuring one player have a stated print run of 150 sets while cards featuring two players have a stated print run of 75 sets.

	Nm-Mt	Ex-Mt
1 Ivan Rodriguez / Alex Rodriguez	60.00	18.00
2 Kirby Puckett / Dave Winfield	50.00	15.00
3 Ted Williams / Nomar Garciaparra	150.00	45.00
4 Jeff Bagwell / Craig Biggio	50.00	15.00
5 Eddie Murray / Cal Ripken	120.00	36.00
6 Andruw Jones / Chipper Jones	50.00	15.00
7 Roberto Clemente / Willie Stargell	120.00	36.00
8 Lou Gehrig / Don Mattingly	200.00	60.00
9 Larry Walker / Todd Helton	50.00	15.00
10 Manny Ramirez / Trot Nixon	50.00	15.00
11 Ivan Rodriguez	25.00	7.50
12 Alex Rodriguez	40.00	12.00
13 Kirby Puckett	40.00	12.00
14 Dave Winfield	25.00	7.50
15 Ted Williams	120.00	36.00
16 Nomar Garciaparra	40.00	12.00
17 Jeff Bagwell	25.00	7.50
18 Craig Biggio	25.00	7.50
19 Eddie Murray	40.00	12.00
20 Cal Ripken	80.00	24.00
21 Andruw Jones	15.00	4.50
22 Chipper Jones	25.00	7.50
23 Roberto Clemente	100.00	30.00
24 Willie Stargell	25.00	7.50
25 Lou Gehrig	180.00	55.00
26 Don Mattingly	80.00	24.00
27 Larry Walker	25.00	7.50
28 Todd Helton	25.00	7.50
29 Manny Ramirez	15.00	4.50
30 Trot Nixon	25.00	7.50

2002 Donruss Elite Back to the Future

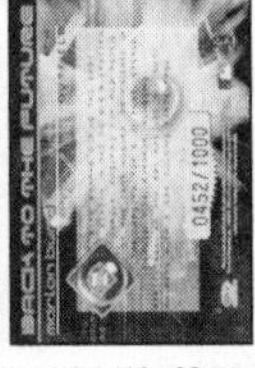

Randomly inserted into packs, this 22-card insert set matches both current and future stars on the fronts and backs respectively. The standard-size card fronts/backs feature full color action shots on metalized film board. 500 serial-numbered copies of each dual-player card were produced and 1000 serial-numbered copies of each single-player card were produced. Card number 6 was originally intended to feature Cardinals rookie So Taguchi paired up with Jim Edmonds and card number 20 was to feature Taguchi by himself, but both cards were pulled from the set before production was finalized, thus this set is complete at 22 cards. Cards featuring one player had a stated print run of 1000 sets and cards featuring two players had a stated print run of 500 sets.

	Nm-Mt	Ex-Mt
1 Scott Rolen / Marlon Byrd	6.00	1.80
2 Joe Crede / Frank Thomas	10.00	3.00
3 Lance Berkman / Jeff Bagwell	6.00	1.80
4 Marcus Giles / Chipper Jones	10.00	3.00
5 Shawn Green / Paul LoDuca	6.00	1.80
7 Kerry Wood / Juan Cruz	10.00	3.00
8 Vladimir Guerrero / Orlando Cabrera	10.00	3.00
9 Scott Rolen	4.00	1.20
10 Marlon Byrd	4.00	1.20
11 Frank Thomas	6.00	1.80
12 Joe Crede	4.00	1.20
13 Jeff Bagwell	4.00	1.20
14 Lance Berkman	4.00	1.20
15 Chipper Jones	6.00	1.80
16 Marcus Giles	4.00	1.20
17 Shawn Green	4.00	1.20
18 Paul LoDuca	4.00	1.20
19 Jim Edmonds	4.00	1.20
21 Kerry Wood	6.00	1.80
22 Juan Cruz	4.00	1.20
23 Vladimir Guerrero	6.00	1.80
24 Orlando Cabrera	4.00	1.20

2002 Donruss Elite Back to the Future Threads

Randomly inserted into packs, this 24-card insert set is a parallel to Donruss Elite Back to the Future. It matches both current and future stars on the fronts and backs respectively. The standard-size card fronts/backs feature full color action shots on metalized film board. The fronts differ by offering one or two swatches of game-worn jerseys. Autograph exchange cards for the Edmonds/Taguchi dual card and So Taguchi's stand alone card were seeded into packs. Please note that only Taguchi was contracted to sign the Edmonds/Taguchi combo card. Both cards had a redemption deadline of October 10th, 2003. Cards featuring one player had a stated print run of 100 sets and cards featuring two players have a stated print run of 50 sets.

	Nm-Mt	Ex-Mt
1 Scott Rolen Jsy / Marlon Byrd Jsy	40.00	12.00
2 Frank Thomas Jsy / Joe Crede Hat	50.00	15.00
3 Jeff Bagwell Jsy / Lance Berkman Jsy	40.00	12.00
4 Chipper Jones Jsy / Marcus Giles Jsy	50.00	15.00
5 Shawn Green Jsy / Paul LoDuca Jsy	40.00	12.00
6 So Taguchi Jsy AU / Jim Edmonds Jsy EXCH	60.00	18.00
7 Kerry Wood Jsy / Juan Cruz Jsy	50.00	15.00
8 Vladimir Guerrero Jsy / Orlando Cabrera Jsy	50.00	15.00
9 Scott Rolen	25.00	7.50
10 Marlon Byrd	15.00	4.50
11 Frank Thomas	40.00	12.00
12 Joe Crede Shoes	15.00	4.50
13 Jeff Bagwell	25.00	7.50
14 Lance Berkman	15.00	4.50
15 Chipper Jones	40.00	12.00
16 Marcus Giles	15.00	4.50
17 Shawn Green	15.00	4.50
18 Paul LoDuca	15.00	4.50
19 Jim Edmonds	15.00	4.50
20 So Taguchi AU EXCH	50.00	15.00
21 Kerry Wood	40.00	12.00
22 Juan Cruz	15.00	4.50
23 Vladimir Guerrero	40.00	12.00
24 Orlando Cabrera	15.00	4.50

2002 Donruss Elite Career Best

Randomly inserted into packs, this 40-card insert set spotlights on players who established career statistical highs in 2001. Each card is serial numbered to a specific statistical achievement and the cards were randomly seeded into packs. The standard-size card fronts feature color action shots on metalized film board with silver holo-foil stamping. Cards with a stated print run of less than 25 copies are not priced due to market scarcity.

	Nm-Mt	Ex-Mt
1 Albert Pujols OPS/1013	12.00	3.60
2 Alex Rodriguez HR/52	25.00	7.50
3 Alex Rodriguez RBI/135	20.00	6.00
4 Andruw Jones RBI/104	8.00	2.40
5 Barry Bonds HR/73	40.00	12.00
6 Barry Bonds OPS/1379	15.00	4.50
7 Barry Bonds BB/177	30.00	9.00
8 C.C. Sabathia K/171	8.00	2.40
9 Carlos Beltran OPS/876	4.00	1.20
10 Chipper Jones BA/330	8.00	2.40
11 Derek Jeter SB/900	15.00	4.50
12 Eric Chavez RBI/114	8.00	2.40
13 Frank Catalanotto BA/330	5.00	1.50
14 Ichiro Suzuki OPS/838	10.00	3.00
15 Ichiro Suzuki RUN/127	20.00	6.00
16 Ichiro Suzuki 3B/8		
17 J.D. Drew HR/27	30.00	9.00
18 J.D. Drew OPS/1027	4.00	1.20
19 Jason Giambi SLG/660	6.00	1.80
20 Jim Thome HR/49	50.00	15.00
21 Jim Thome SLG/624	6.00	1.80
22 Jorge Posada RBI/95	15.00	4.50
23 Jose Cruz Jr. SLG/856	4.00	1.20
24 Kazuhiro Sasaki SV/45	30.00	9.00
25 Kerry Wood ERA/336	8.00	2.40
26 Lance Berkman OPS/1050	4.00	1.20
27 Magglio Ordonez OB/382	5.00	1.50
28 Mark Mulder ERA/345	5.00	1.50
29 Pat Burrell HR/27	30.00	9.00
30 Pat Burrell SLG/469	5.00	1.50
31 Randy Johnson K/372	8.00	2.40
32 Randy Johnson WIN/21		
33 Richie Sexson SLG/547	4.00	1.20
34 Roberto Alomar OPS/956	6.00	1.80
35 Sammy Sosa RBI/160	20.00	6.00
36 Sammy Sosa OPS/1174	10.00	3.00
37 Shawn Green RBI/125	8.00	2.40
38 Tsuyoshi Shinjo RUN/10		
39 Trot Nixon HIT/150	8.00	2.40
40 Troy Glaus RBI/108	8.00	2.40

2002 Donruss Elite Passing the Torch

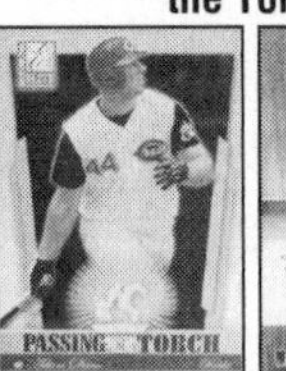

Randomly inserted into packs, this 24-card insert set presents baseball legends and rising stars on double-sided holo-foil board. The front/back of these standard-size cards feature color photos of the players. 500 serial-numbered copies of each dual-player card were produced. 1000 serial-numbered copies of single player card were produced.

	Nm-Mt	Ex-Mt
COMPLETE SET (24)	250.00	75.00
1 Fergie Jenkins / Mark Prior	12.00	3.60
2 Nolan Ryan / Roy Oswalt	30.00	9.00
3 Ozzie Smith / J.D. Drew	15.00	4.50
4 George Brett / Carlos Beltran	25.00	7.50
5 Kirby Puckett / Michael Cuddyer	10.00	3.00
6 Johnny Bench / Adam Dunn	10.00	3.00
7 Duke Snider / Paul LoDuca	10.00	3.00
8 Tony Gwynn / Xavier Nady	15.00	4.50
9 Fergie Jenkins	5.00	1.50
10 Mark Prior	12.00	3.60
11 Nolan Ryan	20.00	6.00
12 Roy Oswalt	5.00	1.50
13 Ozzie Smith	12.00	3.60
14 J.D. Drew	5.00	1.50
15 George Brett	20.00	6.00
16 Carlos Beltran	5.00	1.50
17 Kirby Puckett	8.00	2.40
18 Michael Cuddyer	5.00	1.50
19 Johnny Bench	8.00	2.40
20 Adam Dunn	5.00	1.50
21 Duke Snider	5.00	1.50
22 Paul LoDuca	5.00	1.50
23 Tony Gwynn	10.00	3.00
24 Xavier Nady	5.00	1.50

2002 Donruss Elite Passing the Torch Autographs

Randomly inserted into packs, this 24-card autograph set is a parallel to the Donruss Elite Passing the Torch insert set. It presents baseball legends and rising stars on double-sided holo-foil board. The front/back of these standard-size cards also feature color photos of the players, but differ by using color highlight overlays. We have notated the stated print runs next to the player's name in our checklist.

	Nm-Mt	Ex-Mt
1 Fergie Jenkins / Mark Prior/50	150.00	45.00
2 Nolan Ryan / Roy Oswalt/50	200.00	60.00
3 Ozzie Smith / J.D. Drew/50	150.00	45.00
4 George Brett / Carlos Beltran/25		
5 Kirby Puckett / Michael Cuddyer/50	120.00	36.00
6 Johnny Bench / Adam Dunn/50	120.00	36.00
7 Duke Snider / Paul LoDuca/50	120.00	36.00
8 Tony Gwynn / Xavier Nady/50	150.00	45.00
9 Fergie Jenkins/50	50.00	15.00
10 Mark Prior/100	120.00	36.00
11 Nolan Ryan/100	150.00	45.00
12 Roy Oswalt/100	40.00	12.00
13 Ozzie Smith/25		
14 J.D. Drew/100	25.00	7.50
15 George Brett/25		
16 Carlos Beltran/100	25.00	7.50
17 Kirby Puckett/25		
18 Michael Cuddyer/100	25.00	7.50
19 Johnny Bench/100	60.00	18.00
20 Adam Dunn/50	60.00	18.00
21 Duke Snider/100	40.00	12.00
22 Paul LoDuca/100	25.00	7.50
23 Tony Gwynn/100	80.00	24.00
24 Xavier Nady/100	25.00	7.50

2002 Donruss Elite Recollection Autographs

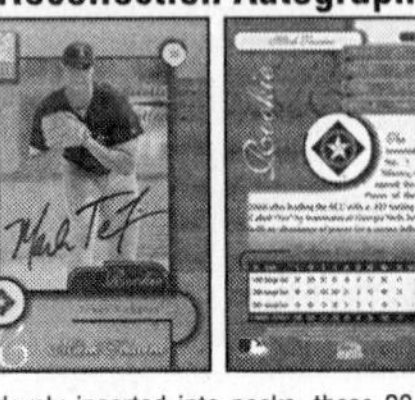

Randomly inserted into packs, these 23 cards featured signed copies of the player's 2001 Donruss Elite card. We have notated the stated print run next to the player's name and cards with a stated print run of 25 or less are not priced due to market scarcity.

	Nm-Mt	Ex-Mt
1 Jeremy Affeldt 01/25		
2 Alfredo Amezaga 01/50	20.00	6.00
3 Angel Berroa 01/25		
4 Dewon Brazelton 01/25		
5 John Buck 01/25		
6 Marlon Byrd 01/25		
7 Juan Cruz 01/25		
8 Brandon Duckworth 01/10		
9 Brandon Duckworth 01/15		
10 Casey Fossum 01/25		
11 Luis Garcia 01/25		
12 Tony Gwynn 01/10		
13 Bill Hall 01/25		
14 Orlando Hudson 01/50	20.00	6.00
15 Ryan Klesko 01/5		
16 Jason Lane 01/24		
17 Corky Miller 01/25		
18 Roy Oswalt 01/25		
19 Antonio Perez 01/50	20.00	6.00
20 Mark Prior 01/25		
21 Mike Rivera 01/50	20.00	6.00
22 Mark Teixeira 01/25		
23 Claudio Vargas 01/50	20.00	6.00
24 Martin Vargas 01/50	20.00	6.00

2002 Donruss Elite Throwback Threads

Randomly inserted into packs, this 64-card insert set offers standard-size cards that display one or two swatches of game-used jerseys from retired legends or current stars. The card front/back features a white border background with color action shots. Card number 28 (intended to be a Rickey Henderson Red Sox card) does not exist in unsigned form. The legendary speedster signed all 100 copies produced and this card can be referenced in the Throwback Threads Autographs parallel set. Cards featuring one player have a stated print run of 100 sets while cards featuring two players have a stated print run of 50 sets.

	Nm-Mt	Ex-Mt
1 Ted Williams / Manny Ramirez	120.00	36.00
2 Carlton Fisk / Mike Piazza	80.00	24.00
3 Bo Jackson / George Brett	120.00	36.00
4 Curt Schilling / Randy Johnson	60.00	18.00
5 Don Mattingly / Lou Gehrig	300.00	90.00
6 Bernie Williams / Dave Winfield	60.00	18.00
7 Rickey Henderson / Ricky Henderson	60.00	18.00
8 Robin Yount / Paul Molitor	100.00	30.00
9 Stan Musial / J.D. Drew	120.00	36.00
10 Andre Dawson / Ryne Sandberg	100.00	30.00
11 Babe Ruth	400.00	120.00

Reggie Jackson
12 Brooks Robinson 120.00 36.00
Cal Ripken
13 Ted Williams 150.00 45.00
Nomar Garciaparra
14 Jackie Robinson 100.00 30.00
Shawn Green
15 Cal Ripken 120.00 36.00
Tony Gwynn
16 Ted Williams 120.00 36.00
17 Manny Ramirez 20.00 6.00
18 Carlton Fisk Red Sox 40.00 12.00
19 Mike Piazza 25.00 7.50
20 Bo Jackson 40.00 12.00
21 George Brett 60.00 18.00
22 Curt Schilling 25.00 7.50
23 Randy Johnson 25.00 7.50
24 Don Mattingly 60.00 18.00
25 Lou Gehrig 250.00 75.00
26 Bernie Williams 25.00 7.50
27 Dave Winfield 40.00 12.00
29 Rickey Henderson Mariners . 25.00 7.50
30 Robin Yount 40.00 12.00
31 Paul Molitor 40.00 12.00
32 Stan Musial 80.00 24.00
33 J.D. Drew 20.00 6.00
34 Andre Dawson 40.00 12.00
35 Ryne Sandberg 60.00 18.00
36 Babe Ruth 300.00 90.00
37 Reggie Jackson 40.00 12.00
38 Brooks Robinson 40.00 12.00
39 Cal Ripken Running 100.00 30.00
40 Nomar Garciaparra ....
41 Jackie Robinson 100.00 30.00
42 Shawn Green 20.00 6.00
43 Pedro Martinez Grey 25.00 7.50
44 Nolan Ryan Astros 100.00 30.00
45 Kazuhiro Sasaki 20.00 6.00
46 Tony Gwynn 40.00 12.00
47 Carlton Fisk White Sox 40.00 12.00
48 Cal Ripken Batting 100.00 30.00
49 Rod Carew Angels 40.00 12.00
50 Nolan Ryan Rangers 100.00 30.00
51 Alex Rodriguez 40.00 12.00
52 Greg Maddux 25.00 7.50
53 Pedro Martinez White 25.00 7.50
54 Rickey Henderson Padres 25.00 7.50
55 Rod Carew Twins 40.00 12.00
56 Roberto Clemente 100.00 30.00
57 Hideo Nomo 50.00 15.00
58 Rickey Henderson Mets 25.00 7.50
59 Dave Parker 40.00 12.00
60 Eddie Mathews 40.00 12.00
61 Eddie Murray 40.00 12.00
62 Nolan Ryan Angels 100.00 30.00
63 Tom Seaver 40.00 12.00
64 Roger Clemens 60.00 18.00
65 Rickey Henderson A's 25.00 7.50

2002 Donruss Elite Throwback Threads Autographs

Randomly inserted in packs, these cards partially parallel the Throwback Threads insert set. Other than the Rickey Henderson card, all these cards have stated print runs of 25 or less and we have notated that information in our checklist. Also, due to market scarcity, no pricing is provided for these cards.

Nm-Mt Ex-Mt
17 Manny Ramirez/10
18 Carlton Fisk Red Sox/15
20 Bo Jackson/10
21 George Brett/5
22 Curt Schilling/10
24 Don Mattingly/20
26 Bernie Williams/5
27 Dave Winfield/10
28 R.Henderson/100 EXCH 200.00 60.00
30 Robin Yount/10
31 Paul Molitor/15
32 Stan Musial/10
33 J.D. Drew/25
34 Andre Dawson/15
35 Ryne Sandberg/20
37 Reggie Jackson/10
43 Pedro Martinez/10
44 Nolan Ryan Astros/10
46 Tony Gwynn/10
47 Carlton Fisk White Sox/10
49 Rod Carew Angels/10
50 Nolan Ryan Rangers/10
51 Alex Rodriguez/10
52 Greg Maddux/10
55 Rod Carew Twins/10
59 Dave Parker/25
61 Eddie Murray/10
62 Nolan Ryan Angels/10
63 Tom Seaver/15

2003 Donruss Elite

This 200 card set was released in June, 2003. The first 180 cards consist of veterans while the final 20 cards are either rookies or leading prospects. This product was issued in five card packs which came 20 packs to a box and 20 boxes to a case with an $5 SRP. The final 20 cards consists of rookies and leading prospects, which were randomly inserted into packs and printed to a stated print run of 1750 serial numbered sets.

Nm-Mt Ex-Mt
COMP.SET w/o SP's (180) 20.00 6.00
COMMON CARD (1-180) .... .40 .12
COMMON CARD (181-200) 4.00 1.20
1 Darin Erstad .40 .12
2 David Eckstein .40 .12
3 Garret Anderson .40 .12
4 Jarrod Washburn .40 .12
5 Tim Salmon .60 .18
6 Troy Glaus .60 .18
7 Marty Cordova .40 .12
8 Melvin Mora .40 .12
9 Rodrigo Lopez .40 .12
10 Tony Batista .40 .12
11 Derek Lowe .40 .12
12 Johnny Damon .40 .12
13 Manny Ramirez .40 .12
14 Nomar Garciaparra 1.50 .45
15 Pedro Martinez 1.00 .30
16 Shea Hillenbrand .40 .12
17 Carlos Lee .40 .12
18 Joe Crede .40 .12
19 Frank Thomas 1.00 .30
20 Magglio Ordonez .40 .12
21 Mark Buehrle .40 .12
22 Paul Konerko .40 .12
23 C.C. Sabathia .40 .12
24 Ellis Burks .40 .12
25 Omar Vizquel .40 .12
26 Brian Tallet .40 .12
27 Bobby Higginson .40 .12
28 Carlos Pena .40 .12
29 Mark Redman .40 .12
30 Steve Sparks .40 .12
31 Carlos Beltran .40 .12
32 Joe Randa .40 .12
33 Mike Sweeney .40 .12
34 Raul Ibanez .40 .12
35 Runelvys Hernandez .40 .12
36 Brad Radke .40 .12
37 Corey Koskie .40 .12
38 Cristian Guzman .40 .12
39 David Ortiz .40 .12
40 Doug Mientkiewicz .40 .12
41 Jacque Jones .40 .12
42 Torii Hunter .40 .12
43 Alfonso Soriano .60 .18
44 Andy Pettitte .60 .18
45 Bernie Williams .60 .18
46 David Wells .40 .12
47 Derek Jeter 2.50 .75
48 Jason Giambi 1.00 .30
49 Jeff Weaver .40 .12
50 Jorge Posada .60 .18
51 Mike Mussina 1.00 .30
52 Roger Clemens 2.00 .60
53 Barry Zito .60 .18
54 Eric Chavez .40 .12
55 Jermaine Dye .40 .12
56 Mark Mulder .40 .12
57 Miguel Tejada .40 .12
58 Tim Hudson .40 .12
59 Bret Boone .40 .12
60 Chris Snelling .40 .12
61 Edgar Martinez .60 .18
62 Freddy Garcia .40 .12
63 Ichiro Suzuki 1.50 .45
64 Jamie Moyer .40 .12
65 John Olerud .40 .12
66 Kazuhiro Sasaki .40 .12
67 Aubrey Huff .40 .12
68 Joe Kennedy .40 .12
69 Paul Wilson .40 .12
70 Alex Rodriguez 1.50 .45
71 Chan Ho Park .40 .12
72 Hank Blalock .60 .18
73 Juan Gonzalez 1.00 .30
74 Kevin Mench .40 .12
75 Rafael Palmeiro .60 .18
76 Carlos Delgado .40 .12
77 Eric Hinske .40 .12
78 Josh Phelps .40 .12
79 Roy Halladay .40 .12
80 Shannon Stewart .40 .12
81 Vernon Wells .40 .12
82 Curt Schilling .60 .18
83 Junior Spivey .40 .12
84 Luis Gonzalez .40 .12
85 Mark Grace .60 .18
86 Randy Johnson 1.00 .30
87 Steve Finley .40 .12
88 Andruw Jones .40 .12
89 Chipper Jones 1.00 .30
90 Gary Sheffield .40 .12
91 Greg Maddux 1.50 .45
92 John Smoltz .60 .18
93 Corey Patterson .40 .12
94 Kerry Wood 1.00 .30
95 Mark Prior 2.00 .60
96 Moises Alou .40 .12
97 Sammy Sosa 1.50 .45
98 Adam Dunn .40 .12
99 Austin Kearns .40 .12
100 Barry Larkin 1.00 .30
101 Ken Griffey Jr. 1.50 .45
102 Sean Casey .40 .12
103 Jason Jennings .40 .12
104 Jay Payton .40 .12
105 Larry Walker .60 .18
106 Todd Helton .60 .18
107 A.J. Burnett .40 .12
108 Josh Beckett .60 .18
109 Juan Encarnacion .40 .12
110 Mike Lowell .40 .12
111 Craig Biggio .60 .18
112 Daryle Ward .40 .12
113 Jeff Bagwell .60 .18
114 Lance Berkman .40 .12
115 Roy Oswalt .40 .12
116 Jason Lane .40 .12
117 Adrian Beltre .40 .12
118 Hideo Nomo 1.00 .30
119 Kazuhisa Ishii .40 .12
120 Kevin Brown .40 .12
121 Odalis Perez .40 .12
122 Paul Lo Duca .40 .12
123 Shawn Green .40 .12
124 Ben Sheets .40 .12
125 Jeffrey Hammonds .40 .12
126 Jose Hernandez .40 .12
127 Richie Sexson .40 .12
128 Bartolo Colon .40 .12
129 Brad Wilkerson .40 .12
130 Javier Vazquez .40 .12
131 Jose Vidro .40 .12
132 Michael Barrett .40 .12
133 Vladimir Guerrero 1.00 .30
134 Al Leiter .40 .12
135 Mike Piazza 1.50 .45
136 Mo Vaughn .40 .12
137 Pedro Astacio .40 .12
138 Roberto Alomar 1.00 .30
139 Pat Burrell .40 .12
140 Vicente Padilla .40 .12
141 Jimmy Rollins .40 .12
142 Bobby Abreu .40 .12
143 Marlon Byrd .40 .12
144 Brian Giles .40 .12
145 Jason Kendall .40 .12
146 Aramis Ramirez .40 .12
147 Josh Fogg .40 .12
148 Ryan Klesko .40 .12
149 Phil Nevin .40 .12
150 Sean Burroughs .40 .12
151 Mark Kotsay .40 .12
152 Barry Bonds 2.50 .75
153 Damian Moss .40 .12
154 Jason Schmidt .40 .12
155 Benito Santiago .40 .12
156 Rich Aurilia .40 .12
157 Scott Rolen .60 .18
158 J.D. Drew .40 .12
159 Jim Edmonds .40 .12
160 Matt Morris .40 .12
161 Tino Martinez .60 .18
162 Albert Pujols 2.00 .60
163 Russ Ortiz .40 .12
164 Rey Ordonez .40 .12
165 Paul Byrd .40 .12
166 Kenny Lofton .40 .12
167 Kenny Rogers .40 .12
168 Rickey Henderson 1.00 .30
169 Fred McGriff .60 .18
170 Charles Johnson .40 .12
171 Mike Hampton .40 .12
172 Jim Thome 1.00 .30
173 Travis Hafner .40 .12
174 Ivan Rodriguez 1.00 .30
175 Ray Durham .40 .12
176 Jeremy Giambi .40 .12
177 Jeff Kent .40 .12
178 Cliff Floyd .40 .12
179 Kevin Millwood .40 .12
180 Tom Glavine .60 .18
181 Hideki Matsui ROO RC 15.00 4.50
182 Jose Contreras ROO RC 6.00 1.80
183 Terrmel Sledge ROO RC 5.00 1.50
184 Lew Ford ROO RC 5.00 1.50
185 Jhonny Peralta ROO RC 4.00 1.20
186 Alexis Rios ROO 10.00 3.00
187 Jeff Baker ROO 4.00 1.20
188 Jeremy Guthrie ROO 4.00 1.20
189 Jose Castillo ROO 4.00 1.20
190 Garrett Atkins ROO 4.00 1.20
191 Jer. Bonderman ROO RC 5.00 1.50
192 Adam LaRoche ROO 5.00 1.50
193 Vinny Chulk ROO 4.00 1.20
194 Walter Young ROO 4.00 1.20
195 Jimmy Gobble ROO 4.00 1.20
196 Prentice Redman ROO RC 4.00 1.20
197 Jason Anderson ROO 4.00 1.20
198 Nic Jackson ROO 4.00 1.20
199 Travis Chapman ROO 4.00 1.20
200 Shane Victorino ROO RC 4.00 1.20

2003 Donruss Elite Aspirations

Nm-Mt Ex-Mt
*1-180 PRINT RUN b/wn 36-50 12.5X TO 30X
*1-180 PRINT RUN b/wn 51-65: 10X TO 25X
*1-180 PRINT RUN b/wn 66-80 8X TO 20X
*1-180 PRINT RUN b/wn 81-99 6X TO 15X
COMMON (181-200) p/r 81-99 .. 6.00 1.80
SEMIS 181-200 p/r 81-99 .... 10.00 3.00
COMMON (181-200) p/r 51-65 . 10.00 3.00
SEMIS 181-200 p/r 51-65 .... 15.00 4.50
COMMON (181-200) p/r 36-50 . 10.00 3.00
COMMON (181-200) p/r 26-35 . 12.00 3.60
SEMIS 181-200 p/r 26-35 .... 20.00 6.00
RANDOM INSERTS IN PACKS
SEE BECKETT.COM FOR PRINT RUNS
NO PRICING ON QTY OF 25 OR LESS.

2003 Donruss Elite Aspirations Gold

Nm-Mt Ex-Mt
RANDOM INSERTS IN PACKS
STATED PRINT RUN 1 SERIAL #'d SET
NO PRICING DUE TO SCARCITY

2003 Donruss Elite Status

Nm-Mt Ex-Mt
*1-180 PRINT RUN b/wn 26-35: 15X TO 40X
*1-180 PRINT RUN b/wn 36-50: 12.5X TO 30X
*1-180 PRINT RUN b/wn 51-65: 10X TO 25X
*1-180 PRINT RUN b/wn 66-80: 8X TO 20X
*1-180 PRINT RUN b/wn 81-99: 6X TO 15X
COMMON (181-200) p/r 66-80 .. 8.00 2.40
COMMON (181-200) p/r 51-65 . 10.00 3.00
COMMON (181-200) p/r 36-50 . 10.00 3.00
RANDOM INSERTS IN PACKS
NO PRICING ON QTY OF 25 OR LESS.

2003 Donruss Elite Status Gold

Nm-Mt Ex-Mt
RANDOM INSERTS IN PACKS
STATED PRINT RUN 24 SERIAL #'d SETS
NO PRICING DUE TO SCARCITY

2003 Donruss Elite Turn of the Century Autographs

Randomly inserted into packs, this is a partial parallel to the Donruss Elite set and features just the rookie cards with the exception of Hideki Matsui who was under an exclusive contract to Upper Deck. These cards are signed by the player and were issued to a stated print run of 50 serial numbered sets.

Nm-Mt Ex-Mt
182 Jose Contreras ROO 50.00 15.00
183 Terrmel Sledge ROO 25.00 7.50
184 Lew Ford ROO 25.00 7.50
185 Jhonny Peralta ROO 15.00 4.50
186 Alexis Rios ROO 60.00 18.00
187 Jeff Baker ROO 15.00 4.50
188 Jeremy Guthrie ROO 15.00 4.50
189 Jose Castillo ROO 25.00 7.50
190 Garrett Atkins ROO 25.00 7.50
191 Jeremy Bonderman ROO 40.00 12.00
192 Adam LaRoche ROO 40.00 12.00
193 Vinny Chulk ROO 15.00 4.50
194 Walter Young ROO 15.00 4.50
195 Jimmy Gobble ROO 25.00 7.50
196 Prentice Redman ROO 15.00 4.50
197 Jason Anderson ROO 15.00 4.50
198 Nic Jackson ROO 15.00 4.50
199 Travis Chapman ROO 15.00 4.50
200 Shane Victorino ROO 15.00 4.50

2003 Donruss Elite All-Time Career Best

Nm-Mt Ex-Mt
STATED ODDS 1:9
*PARALLEL 1-25 p/r 211-239: 1X TO 2.5X
*PARALLEL 1-25 p/r 105-140: 1.25X TO 3X
*PARALLEL 1-25 p/r 53-60: 2X TO 5X
*PARALLEL 1-25 p/r 39-49: 2.5X TO 6X
*PARALLEL 1-25 p/r 29-31: 3X TO 8X
*PARALLEL 26-50 p/r 130-137: 1X TO 2.5X
*PARALLEL 26-50 p/r 55-66: 1.5X TO 4X
*PARALLEL 26-50 p/r 37-49: 2X TO 5X
*PARALLEL 26-50 p/r 35: 2.5X TO 6X
PARALLEL RANDOM INSERTS IN PACKS
PARALLEL PRINTS B/WN 1-393 COPIES PER
NO PARALLEL PRICING ON QTY OF 25 OR LESS
1 Babe Ruth 12.00 3.60
2 Ty Cobb 8.00 2.40
3 Jackie Robinson 5.00 1.50
4 Lou Gehrig 8.00 2.40
5 Thurman Munson 5.00 1.50
6 Nolan Ryan 12.00 3.60
7 Mike Schmidt 8.00 2.40
8 Don Mattingly 10.00 3.00
9 Yogi Berra 4.00 1.20
10 Rod Carew 3.00 .90
11 Reggie Jackson 4.00 1.20
12 Al Kaline 4.00 1.20
13 Harmon Killebrew 4.00 1.20
14 Eddie Mathews 4.00 1.20
15 Stan Musial 6.00 1.80
16 Jim Palmer 3.00 .90
17 Phil Rizzuto 3.00 .90
18 Brooks Robinson 4.00 1.20
19 Tom Seaver 3.00 .90
20 Robin Yount 6.00 1.80
21 Carlton Fisk 3.00 .90
22 Dale Murphy 4.00 1.20
23 Cal Ripken 12.00 3.60
24 Tony Gwynn 5.00 1.50
25 Andre Dawson 3.00 .90
26 Derek Jeter 10.00 3.00
27 Ken Griffey Jr. 6.00 1.80
28 Albert Pujols 8.00 2.40
29 Sammy Sosa 6.00 1.80
30 Jason Giambi 4.00 1.20
31 Randy Johnson 4.00 1.20
32 Greg Maddux 6.00 1.80
33 Rickey Henderson 4.00 1.20
34 Pedro Martinez 4.00 1.20
35 Jeff Bagwell 3.00 .90
36 Alex Rodriguez 6.00 1.80
37 Vladimir Guerrero 4.00 1.20
38 Chipper Jones 4.00 1.20
39 Shawn Green 3.00 .90
40 Tom Glavine 3.00 .90
41 Curt Schilling 3.00 .90
42 Todd Helton 3.00 .90
43 Roger Clemens 8.00 2.40
44 Lance Berkman 3.00 .90
45 Nomar Garciaparra 6.00 1.80

2003 Donruss Elite All-Time Career Best Materials

Randomly inserted into packs, this is a parallel to the All-Time Career Best insert set. Each of these cards feature not only the player but also a piece of game-used memorabilia from their career. We have printed what type of material

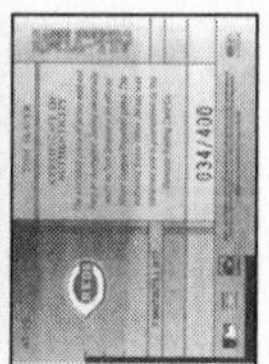

as well as the stated print run next to the player's name in our checklist. Please note that for cards with a stated print run of 25 or fewer, there is no pricing due to market scarcity.

Nm-Mt Ex-Mt
*MULTI-COLOR PATCH: 1.5X TO 4X HI COL
1 Babe Ruth Bat/25
2 Ty Cobb Bat/25
3 Jackie Robinson Jkt/50 80.00 24.00
4 Lou Gehrig Bat/100 150.00 45.00
5 Thurman Munson Bat/200 25.00 7.50
6 Nolan Ryan Jkt/400 50.00 15.00
7 Mike Schmidt Jkt/400 40.00 12.00
8 Don Mattingly Hat/250 50.00 15.00
9 Yogi Berra Bat/100 30.00 9.00
10 Rod Carew Bat/400 15.00 4.50
11 Reggie Jackson Bat/400 15.00 4.50
12 Al Kaline Bat/400 20.00 6.00
13 Harmon Killebrew Pants/400 20.00 6.00
14 Eddie Mathews Bat/200 25.00 7.50
15 Stan Musial Bat/100 50.00 15.00
16 Jim Palmer Jsy/200 20.00 6.00
17 Phil Rizzuto Bat/400 15.00 4.50
18 Brooks Robinson Bat/400 20.00 6.00
19 Tom Seaver Jsy/400 15.00 4.50
20 Robin Yount Bat/400 20.00 6.00
21 Carlton Fisk Bat/400 15.00 4.50
22 Dale Murphy Bat/400 20.00 6.00
23 Cal Ripken Bat/400 40.00 12.00
24 Tony Gwynn Pants/400 15.00 4.50
25 Andre Dawson Bat/400 10.00 3.00
26 Derek Jeter Base/400 20.00 6.00
27 Ken Griffey Jr. Base/400 15.00 4.50
28 Albert Pujols Base/400 15.00 4.50
29 Sammy Sosa Bat/400 15.00 4.50
30 Jason Giambi Bat/400 10.00 3.00
31 Randy Johnson Jsy/400 10.00 3.00
32 Greg Maddux Jsy/400 10.00 3.00
33 Rickey Henderson Bat/400 10.00 3.00
34 Pedro Martinez Jsy/400 10.00 3.00
35 Jeff Bagwell Pants/400 10.00 3.00
36 Alex Rodriguez Bat/400 15.00 4.50
37 Vladimir Guerrero Bat/400 10.00 3.00
38 Chipper Jones Bat/400 10.00 3.00
39 Shawn Green Bat/400 8.00 2.40
40 Tom Glavine Jsy/400 10.00 3.00
41 Curt Schilling Jsy/400 10.00 3.00
42 Todd Helton Bat/400 10.00 3.00
43 Roger Clemens Jsy/400 20.00 6.00
44 Lance Berkman Bat/400 8.00 2.40
45 Nomar Garciaparra Bat/400 15.00 4.50

2003 Donruss Elite All-Time Career Best Materials Parallel

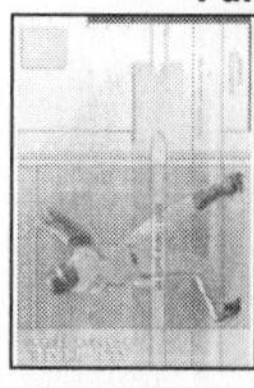
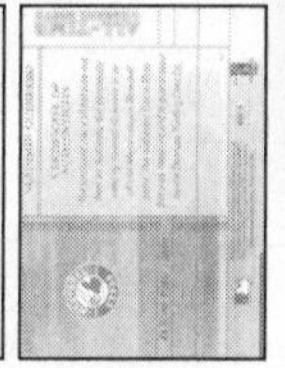

Nm-Mt Ex-Mt
RANDOM INSERTS IN PACKS
PRINT RUNS B/WN 1-393 COPIES PER
NO PRICING ON QTY OF 25 OR LESS.
1 Babe Ruth Bat/60 150.00 45.00
2 Ty Cobb Bat/24
3 Jackie Robinson Jkt/19
4 Lou Gehrig Bat/49 150.00 45.00
5 Thurman Munson Bat/105 40.00 12.00
6 Nolan Ryan Jkt/22
7 Mike Schmidt Jkt/48 80.00 24.00
8 Don Mattingly Hat/53 100.00 30.00
9 Yogi Berra Bat/30 80.00 24.00
10 Rod Carew Bat/239 15.00 4.50
11 Reggie Jackson Bat/39 40.00 12.00
12 Al Kaline Bat/29 80.00 24.00
13 Harmon Killebrew Pants/140 30.00 9.00
14 Eddie Mathews Bat/31 80.00 24.00
15 Stan Musial Bat/33 100.00 30.00
16 Jim Palmer Jsy/23
17 Phil Rizzuto Bat/10
18 Brooks Robinson Bat/118 30.00 9.00
19 Tom Seaver Jsy/7
20 Robin Yount Bat/49 60.00 18.00
21 Carlton Fisk Bat/107 25.00 7.50
22 Dale Murphy Bat/44 60.00 18.00
23 Cal Ripken Bat/211 50.00 15.00
24 Tony Gwynn Pants/220 20.00 6.00
25 Andre Dawson Bat/49 25.00 7.50
26 Derek Jeter Base/24
27 Ken Griffey Jr. Base/56 40.00 12.00
28 Albert Pujols Base/37 50.00 15.00
29 Sammy Sosa Bat/66 50.00 15.00
30 Jason Giambi Bat/137 20.00 6.00
31 Randy Johnson Jsy/12
32 Greg Maddux Jsy/20
33 Rickey Henderson Bat/130 20.00 6.00
34 Pedro Martinez Jsy/23
35 Jeff Bagwell Pants/47 25.00 7.50
36 Alex Rodriguez Bat/393 15.00 4.50
37 Vladimir Guerrero Bat/44 40.00 12.00
38 Chipper Jones Bat/45 40.00 12.00
39 Shawn Green Bat/49 25.00 7.50
40 Tom Glavine Jsy/22
41 Curt Schilling Jsy/35 25.00 7.50
42 Todd Helton Bat/59 25.00 7.50
43 Roger Clemens Jsy/1

44 Lance Berkman Bat/55 .... 25.00 7.50
45 Nomar Garciaparra Bat/35.... 80.00 24.00

2003 Donruss Elite Back to Back Jacks

Randomly inserted into packs, these 50 cards feature game use bat pieces on them. These cards were issued to different print runs depending on what the card number is and we have notated that information in our headers to this set.

Nm-Mt Ex-Mt
1-25 PRINT RUN 250 SERIAL #'d SETS
26-35 PRINT RUN 125 SERIAL #'d SETS
36-40 PRINT RUN 100 SERIAL #'d SETS
41-45 PRINT RUN 75 SERIAL #'d SETS
46-50 PRINT RUN 50 SERIAL #'d SETS
1 Adam Dunn 8.00 2.40
2 Alex Rodriguez 15.00 4.50
3 Alfonso Soriano..................... 10.00 3.00
4 Andruw Jones 8.00 2.40
5 Chipper Jones 10.00 3.00
6 Jason Giambi 10.00 3.00
7 Jeff Bagwell........................... 10.00 3.00
8 Jim Thome 10.00 3.00
9 Juan Gonzalez 10.00 3.00
10 Lance Berkman 8.00 2.40
11 Magglio Ordonez.................... 8.00 2.40
12 Manny Ramirez 8.00 2.40
13 Miguel Tejada......................... 8.00 2.40
14 Mike Piazza 15.00 4.50
15 Nomar Garciaparra.............. 15.00 4.50
16 Rafael Palmeiro 10.00 3.00
17 Rickey Henderson 10.00 3.00
18 Sammy Sosa 15.00 4.50
19 Scott Rolen 10.00 3.00
20 Shawn Green.......................... 8.00 2.40
21 Todd Helton.......................... 10.00 3.00
22 Vladimir Guerrero................ 10.00 3.00
23 Ivan Rodriguez 10.00 3.00
24 Eric Chavez............................ 8.00 2.40
25 Larry Walker......................... 10.00 3.00
26 Garret Anderson.................. 20.00 6.00
Troy Glaus
27 Adam Dunn 20.00 6.00
Austin Kearns
28 Alex Rodriguez 30.00 9.00
Rafael Palmeiro
29 Miguel Tejada....................... 20.00 6.00
Eric Chavez
30 Magglio Ordonez.................. 25.00 7.50
Frank Thomas
31 Lance Berkman 20.00 6.00
Jeff Bagwell
32 Nomar Garciaparra.............. 40.00 12.00
Manny Ramirez
33 Vladimir Guerrero................ 25.00 7.50
Jose Vidro
34 Mike Piazza 25.00 7.50
Roberto Alomar
35 Todd Helton.......................... 20.00 6.00
Larry Walker
36 Babe Ruth 150.00 45.00
37 Cal Ripken 80.00 24.00
38 Don Mattingly........................ 60.00 18.00
39 Kirby Puckett........................ 25.00 7.50
40 Roberto Clemente 100.00 30.00
41 Alfonso Soriano.................... 40.00 12.00
Phil Rizzuto
42 Sammy Sosa......................... 60.00 18.00
Andre Dawson
43 Ozzie Smith 60.00 18.00
Scott Rolen
44 Don Mattingly........................ 80.00 24.00
Jason Giambi
45 Rickey Henderson............... 150.00 45.00
Ty Cobb
46 Joe Morgan........................... 60.00 18.00
Johnny Bench
47 Cal Ripken 150.00 45.00
Brooks Robinson
48 George Brett....................... 150.00 45.00
Bo Jackson
49 Babe Ruth 500.00 150.00
Lou Gehrig
50 Yogi Berra 80.00 24.00
Thurman Munson

2003 Donruss Elite Back to the Future

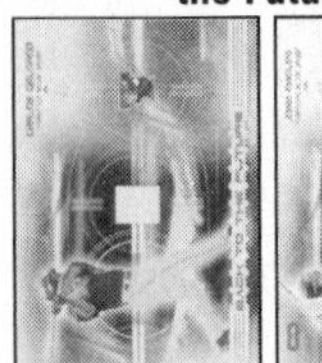
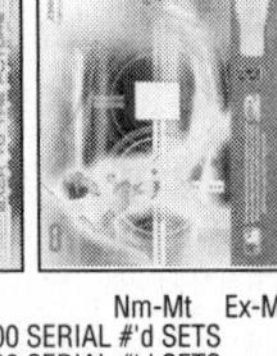

Nm-Mt Ex-Mt
1-10 PRINT RUN 1000 SERIAL #'d SETS
11-15 PRINT RUN 500 SERIAL #'d SETS
RANDOM INSERTS IN PACKS ....
1 Kerry Wood 5.00 1.50
2 Mark Prior............................. 10.00 3.00
3 Magglio Ordonez..................... 4.00 1.20
4 Joe Borchard 4.00 1.20
5 Lance Berkman 4.00 1.20
6 Jason Lane.............................. 4.00 1.20
7 Rafael Palmeiro 4.00 1.20
8 Mark Teixeira.......................... 4.00 1.20
9 Carlos Delgado........................ 4.00 1.20
10 Josh Phelps........................... 4.00 1.20
11 Kerry Wood 15.00 4.50
Mark Prior
12 Magglio Ordonez.................... 6.00 1.80
Joe Borchard
13 Lance Berkman 6.00 1.80
Jason Lane
14 Rafael Palmeiro 6.00 1.80
Mark Teixeira
15 Carlos Delgado....................... 6.00 1.80
John Phelps

2003 Donruss Elite Back to the Future Threads

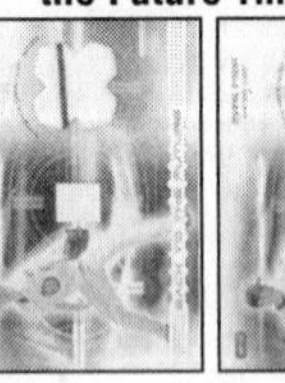
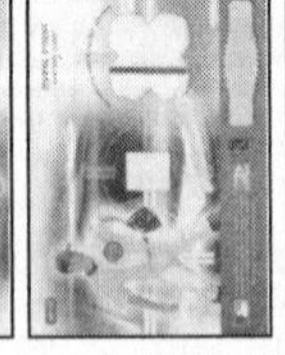

Nm-Mt Ex-Mt
*MULTI-COLOR PATCH: .75X TO 2X HI COL
1-10 PRINT RUN 250 SERIAL #'d SETS
11-15 PRINT RUN 125 SERIAL #'d SETS
RANDOM INSERTS IN PACKS ....
1 Kerry Wood 15.00 4.50
2 Mark Prior............................. 30.00 9.00
3 Magglio Ordonez...................... 8.00 2.40
4 Joe Borchard 8.00 2.40
5 Lance Berkman 8.00 2.40
6 Jason Lane............................... 8.00 2.40
7 Rafael Palmeiro 10.00 3.00
8 Mark Teixeira......................... 10.00 3.00
9 Carlos Delgado......................... 8.00 2.40
10 Josh Phelps............................ 8.00 2.40
11 Kerry Wood 50.00 15.00
Mark Prior
12 Magglio Ordonez.................. 15.00 4.50
Joe Borchard
13 Lance Berkman 15.00 4.50
Jason Lane
14 Rafael Palmeiro 15.00 4.50
Mark Teixeira
15 Carlos Delgado..................... 15.00 4.50
John Phelps

2003 Donruss Elite Career Bests

Nm-Mt Ex-Mt
RANDOM INSERTS IN PACKS ....
PRINT RUNS B/WN 4-417 COPIES PER
NO PRICING ON QTY OF 25 OR LESS.
1 Randy Johnson WIN/24 ....
2 Curt Schilling WIN/23....................
3 Garret Anderson 2B/56.......... 10.00 3.00
4 Andruw Jones BB/83............. 10.00 3.00
5 Kerry Wood CG/4 ....
6 Magglio Ordonez HR/38 .... 12.00 3.60
7 Magglio Ordonez RBI/135 .... 6.00 1.80
8 Adam Dunn HR/26 .... 15.00 4.50
9 Roy Oswalt WIN/19.........................
10 Lance Berkman HR/42 .... 12.00 3.60
11 Lance Berkman RBI/128......... 6.00 1.80
12 Shawn Green OBP/385........... 5.00 1.50
13 Alfonso Soriano HR/39.......... 12.00 3.60
14 Alfonso Soriano AVG/300........ 5.00 1.50
15 Jason Giambi RUN/120......... 10.00 3.00
16 Derek Jeter SB/32 .... 60.00 18.00
17 Vladimir Guerrero SB/40...... 20.00 6.00
18 Vladimir Guerrero OBP/417.... 8.00 2.40
19 Barry Zito WIN/23 ....
20 Miguel Tejada HR/34............ 15.00 4.50
21 Barry Bonds BB/198............. 25.00 7.50
22 Barry Bonds AVG/370 .... 20.00 6.00
23 Ichiro Suzuki OBP/388 .... 12.00 3.60
24 Alex Rodriguez HR/57 .... 30.00 9.00
25 Alex Rodriguez RBI/142 .... 20.00 6.00

2003 Donruss Elite Career Bests Materials

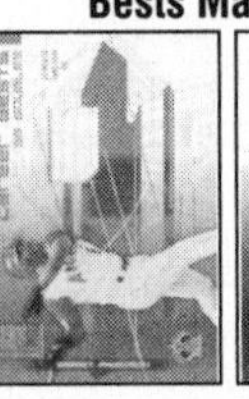

Nm-Mt Ex-Mt
RANDOM INSERTS IN PACKS ....
STATED PRINT RUN 500 SERIAL #'d SETS
1 Randy Johnson WIN Jsy........ 10.00 3.00
2 Curt Schilling WIN Jsy.......... 10.00 3.00
3 Garret Anderson 2B Bat........... 8.00 2.40
4 Andruw Jones BB Bat.............. 8.00 2.40
5 Kerry Wood CG Shoe 15.00 4.50
6 Magglio Ordonez HR Bat.......... 8.00 2.40
7 Magglio Ordonez RBI Bat......... 8.00 2.40
8 Adam Dunn HR Bat 8.00 2.40
9 Roy Oswalt WIN Jsy................. 8.00 2.40
10 Lance Berkman HR Bat 8.00 2.40
11 Lance Berkman RBI Bat.......... 8.00 2.40
12 Shawn Green OBP Bat............ 8.00 2.40
13 Alfonso Soriano HR Bat....... 10.00 3.00
14 Alfonso Soriano AVG Bat...... 10.00 3.00
15 Jason Giambi RUN Bat.......... 10.00 3.00
16 Derek Jeter SB Base 20.00 6.00
17 Vladimir Guerrero SB Bat...... 10.00 3.00
18 Vladimir Guerrero OBP Bat... 10.00 3.00
19 Barry Zito WIN Jsy 10.00 3.00
20 Miguel Tejada HR Bat 8.00 2.40
21 Barry Bonds BB Base 20.00 6.00
22 Barry Bonds AVG Base 20.00 6.00
23 Ichiro Suzuki OBP Base........ 20.00 6.00
24 Alex Rodriguez HR Jsy 15.00 4.50
25 Alex Rodriguez RBI Jsy 15.00 4.50

2003 Donruss Elite Career Bests Materials Autographs

Nm-Mt Ex-Mt
RANDOM INSERTS IN PACKS ....
PRINT RUNS B/WN 5-250 COPIES PER
NO PRICING ON QTY OF 25 OR LESS.
2 Curt Schilling WIN Jsy/5..................
3 Garret Anderson 2B Bat/75 .... 50.00 15.00
4 Andruw Jones BB Bat/10..................
5 Kerry Wood CG Shoe/15.................
6 Magglio Ordonez HR Bat/10............
7 Magglio Ordonez RBI Bat/10...........
8 Adam Dunn HR Bat/100.......... 60.00 18.00
9 Roy Oswalt WIN Jsy/250........ 40.00 12.00
10 Lance Berkman HR Bat/25 ....
11 Lance Berkman RBI Bat/25 ....
13 Alfonso Soriano HR Bat/5 ....
14 Alfonso Soriano AVG Bat/5 ....
17 Vlad Guerrero SB Bat/50 .... 100.00 30.00
18 Vlad Guerrero OBP Bat/50.. 100.00 30.00
19 Barry Zito WIN Jsy/75........... 80.00 24.00
20 Miguel Tejada HR Bat/25...............
24 Alex Rodriguez HR Jsy/5...............
25 Alex Rodriguez RBI Jsy/5..............

2003 Donruss Elite Highlights

Nm-Mt Ex-Mt
RANDOM INSERTS IN PACKS ....
STATED PRINT RUN 500 SERIAL #'d SETS
1 Sammy Sosa 500 HR 12.00 3.60
2 Rafael Palmeiro 500 HR........... 8.00 2.40
3 Hideki Matsui Debut.............. 15.00 4.50
4 Jose Contreras Debut.............. 8.00 2.40
5 Kevin Millwood No-Hit 5.00 1.50

2003 Donruss Elite Highlights Autographs

Nm-Mt Ex-Mt
RANDOM INSERTS IN PACKS ....
STATED PRINT RUN 50 SERIAL #'d SETS
2 Rafael Palmeiro 500 HR 100.00 30.00
4 Jose Contreras Debut............. 60.00 18.00

2003 Donruss Elite Passing the Torch

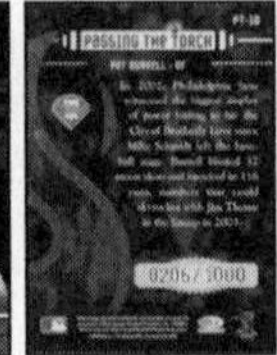

Nm-Mt Ex-Mt
1-10 PRINT RUN 1000 SERIAL #'d SETS
11-15 PRINT RUN 500 SERIAL #'d SETS
RANDOM INSERTS IN PACKS ....
1 Stan Musial 10.00 3.00
2 Jim Edmonds 4.00 1.20
3 Dale Murphy............................. 6.00 1.80
4 Andruw Jones 4.00 1.20
5 Roger Clemens........................ 12.00 3.60
6 Mark Prior 12.00 3.60
7 Tom Seaver 6.00 1.80
8 Tom Glavine 6.00 1.80
9 Mike Schmidt.......................... 12.00 3.60
10 Pat Burrell 4.00 1.20
11 Stan Musial 15.00 4.50
Jim Edmonds
12 Dale Murphy.......................... 10.00 3.00
Andruw Jones
13 Roger Clemens...................... 20.00 6.00
Mark Prior
14 Tom Seaver 10.00 3.00
Tom Glavine
15 Mike Schmidt........................ 20.00 6.00
Pat Burrell

2003 Donruss Elite Passing the Torch Autographs

Randomly inserted into packs, these cards feature the continuation of the popular Passing the Torch Autograph insert set. The first 10 cards feature individual autographs while the final five cards feature dual autographs of the players.

Nm-Mt Ex-Mt
1-10 PRINT RUN 50 SERIAL #'d SETS
11-15 PRINT RUN 25 SERIAL #'d SETS
NO 11-15 PRICING DUE TO SCARCITY
RANDOM INSERTS IN PACKS ....
1 Stan Musial 120.00 36.00
2 Jim Edmonds 50.00 15.00
3 Dale Murphy.......................... 80.00 24.00
4 Andruw Jones 80.00 24.00
5 Roger Clemens.................... 200.00 60.00
6 Mark Prior 150.00 45.00
7 Tom Seaver 80.00 24.00
8 Tom Glavine 80.00 24.00
9 Mike Schmidt...................... 150.00 45.00
10 Pat Burrell 50.00 15.00
11 Stan Musial ....
Jim Edmonds
12 Dale Murphy.............................
Andruw Jones
13 Roger Clemens..........................
Mark Prior
14 Tom Seaver ....
Tom Glavine
15 Mike Schmidt.............................
Pat Burrell

2003 Donruss Elite Recollection Autographs

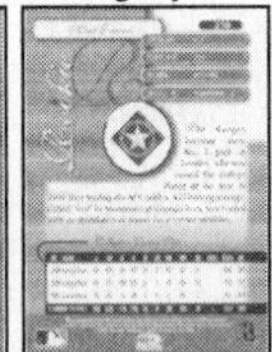

Randomly inserted into packs, these 65 cards feature cards prepared for previous Donruss Elite products and they feature both autographs and a recollection collection stamp on all the cards. Please note that we have notated the stated print run next to the player's name and specific card in our checklist. For cards with print runs of 25 or fewer, no pricing is available due to market scarcity.

Nm-Mt Ex-Mt
1 Jeremy Affeldt 01/75............. 40.00 12.00
2 Erick Almonte 01/75............. 20.00 6.00
3 Jeff Bagwell 02/1.......................
4 Adrian Beltre 02/36 .... 40.00 12.00
5 Adrian Beltre 02 Asp/5..............
6 Adrian Beltre 02 Sta/3...............
7 Brandon Berger 01/83............ 20.00 6.00
8 Angel Berroa 01/28 .... 60.00 18.00
9 John Buck 01/25.........................
10 Mark Buehrle 02/23...................
11 Marlon Byrd 01/24 ....
12 Jose Castillo 02/23....................
13 Jeff Deardorff 01/53............. 25.00 7.50
14 Ryan Drese 01/100.............. 20.00 6.00
15 J.D. Drew 01/15 ....
16 J.D. Drew 02/10 ....
17 J.D. Drew 02 CB/5.....................
18 Jim Edmonds 01/15....................
19 Jim Edmonds 02/5......................
20 Jim Edmonds 02 BTF/5..............
21 Luis Garcia 01/28 .... 40.00 12.00
22 Geronimo Gil 01/75............. 20.00 6.00
23 Mark Grace 02/2........................
24 Shawn Green 01/2......................
25 Shawn Green 02/2......................
26 Shawn Green 02 BTF/2...............
27 Shawn Green 02 CB/2................
28 Travis Hafner 01 Black/52 .... 40.00 12.00
29 Travis Hafner 01 Blue/23............
30 Bill Hall 01/27 .... 40.00 12.00
31 Orlando Hudson 01 Black/12.......
32 Orlando Hudson 01 Blue /13 ......
33 Tim Hudson 01/25 ....
34 Tim Hudson 02/25 ....
35 Gerald Laird 02/46 .... 30.00 9.00
36 Jason Lane 01/27................. 40.00 12.00
37 Adam LaRoche 02/25.................
38 Cliff Lee 01/25...........................
39 Kenny Lofton 01/25....................
40 Greg Maddux 01/5 ....
41 Greg Maddux 01 TW/5...............
42 Greg Maddux 02/10 ....
43 Greg Maddux 02 AS/5................
44 Victor Martinez 01/52........... 60.00 18.00
45 Corky Miller 01/25.....................
46 Roy Oswalt 01 Black/61 .... 40.00 12.00
47 Roy Oswalt 01 Blue/9................
48 Roy Oswalt 02/24.......................
49 Mark Prior 01/10........................
50 Mike Rivera 01/3 ....
51 Ricardo Rodriguez 01/75 ..... 20.00 6.00
52 Freddy Sanchez 02/25...............
53 Gary Sheffield 01/25..................
54 Gary Sheffield 02/14...................
55 Bud Smith 01/50 .... 30.00 9.00
56 Bud Smith 02/28 .... 40.00 12.00
57 Chris Snelling 02/25..................
58 Junior Spivey 01/45 .... 50.00 15.00
59 Tim Spooneybarger 01/100.. 20.00 6.00
60 Shannon Stewart 01/24.............
61 Shannon Stewart 02/35......... 40.00 12.00
62 Dennis Tankersley 01/15 ....
63 Mark Teixeira 01/19 ....
64 Claudio Vargas 01/51 .... 25.00 7.50
65 Martin Vargas 01/10..................

2003 Donruss Elite Throwback Threads

Randomly inserted into packs, these 100 cards feature not only the player's featured but also a game-worn uniform piece from during their career. Please note that the final 10 cards in the checklist feature either two different pieces from a player's career or two pieces from players who have something in common.

Nm-Mt Ex-Mt
1-45 PRINT RUN 250 SERIAL #'d SETS
46-75 PRINT RUN 125 SERIAL #'d SETS
76-90 PRINT RUN 100 SERIAL #'d SETS
91-95 PRINT RUN 75 SERIAL #'d SETS
96-100 PRINT RUN 50 SERIAL #'d SETS
*MULTI-COLOR PATCH: .75X TO 2X HI COL
1 Randy Johnson D'backs......... 10.00 3.00
2 Randy Johnson M's 10.00 3.00
3 Roger Clemens Yanks 25.00 7.50
4 Roger Clemens Red Sox 25.00 7.50
5 Manny Ramirez 8.00 2.40
6 Greg Maddux......................... 15.00 4.50
7 Jason Giambi Yanks.............. 10.00 3.00
8 Jason Giambi A's 10.00 3.00
9 Alex Rodriguez Rgr 15.00 4.50
10 Alex Rodriguez M's 15.00 4.50
11 Miguel Tejada........................ 8.00 2.40
12 Alfonso Soriano................... 10.00 3.00
13 Nomar Garciaparra.............. 15.00 4.50
14 Pedro Martinez Red Sox....... 10.00 3.00
15 Pedro Martinez Expos 10.00 3.00
16 Andruw Jones 8.00 2.40
17 Chipper Jones 10.00 3.00
18 Barry Zito............................. 10.00 3.00
19 Mark Mulder........................... 8.00 2.40
20 Lance Berkman 8.00 2.40
21 Magglio Ordonez..................... 8.00 2.40
22 Mike Piazza Mets.................. 15.00 4.50
23 Mike Piazza Dodgers 15.00 4.50
24 Rickey Henderson Padres 10.00 3.00
25 Rickey Henderson Mets 10.00 3.00
26 Rickey Henderson M's 10.00 3.00
27 Sammy Sosa......................... 15.00 4.50
28 Shawn Green.......................... 8.00 2.40
29 Troy Glaus............................ 10.00 3.00
30 Vladimir Guerrero................. 10.00 3.00
31 Adam Dunn 8.00 2.40
32 Jeff Bagwell.......................... 10.00 3.00
33 Curt Schilling....................... 10.00 3.00
34 Hideo Nomo Dodgers........... 40.00 12.00
35 Hideo Nomo Red Sox........... 40.00 12.00
36 Hideo Nomo Mets 40.00 12.00
37 Kerry Wood 10.00 3.00
38 Mark Prior............................ 25.00 7.50
39 Roberto Alomar.................... 10.00 3.00
40 Todd Helton......................... 10.00 3.00
41 Jim Thome 10.00 3.00
42 Rafael Palmeiro 10.00 3.00
43 Juan Gonzalez 10.00 3.00
44 Vernon Wells.......................... 8.00 2.40
45 Torii Hunter............................ 8.00 2.40
46 Randy Johnson D'backs........ 25.00 7.50
Randy Johnson M's
47 Roger Clemens Yankees....... 50.00 15.00
Roger Clemens Red Sox
48 Jason Giambi Yankees 25.00 7.50
Jason Giambi A's
49 Alex Rodriguez Rangers....... 40.00 12.00
Alex Rodriguez M's
50 Pedro Martinez Red Sox....... 25.00 7.50
Pedro Martinez Expos
51 Mike Piazza Mets................. 40.00 12.00
Mike Piazza Dodgers
52 Rickey Henderson A's 25.00 7.50
Rickey Henderson M's
53 Rickey Henderson Padres 25.00 7.50
Rickey Henderson Mets
54 Rickey Henderson Angels..... 25.00 7.50
Rickey Henderson Padres
55 Hideo Nomo Dodgers........... 50.00 15.00
Hideo Nomo Red Sox
56 Randy Johnson D'backs....... 25.00 7.50
Randy Johnson Expos
57 Randy Johnson 25.00 7.50
Curt Schilling
58 Alfonso Soriano.................... 25.00 7.50
Jason Giambi
59 Barry Zito 25.00 7.50
Mark Mulder
60 Andruw Jones 25.00 7.50
Chipper Jones
61 Greg Maddux........................ 60.00 18.00
Tom Glavine
62 Lance Berkman 25.00 7.50
Jeff Bagwell
63 Roger Clemens..................... 50.00 15.00
Mark Prior
64 Alex Rodriguez 30.00 9.00
Rafael Palmeiro
65 Jim Thome 25.00 7.50

Roberto Alomar
66 Mike Piazza 25.00 7.50
Roberto Alomar
67 Sammy Sosa 40.00 12.00
Mark Grace
68 Todd Helton 25.00 7.50
Larry Walker
69 Adam Dunn 20.00 6.00
Austin Kearns
70 Alex Rodriguez 25.00 7.50
Ivan Rodriguez
71 Bobby Abreu 20.00 6.00
Marlon Byrd
72 Miguel Tejada 20.00 6.00
Eric Chavez
73 Greg Maddux 40.00 12.00
John Smoltz
74 Kerry Wood 10.00 3.00
Mark Prior
75 Barry Zito 25.00 7.50
Tim Hudson
76 Babe Ruth 400.00 120.00
77 Ty Cobb 120.00 36.00
78 Jackie Robinson 100.00 30.00
79 Lou Gehrig 150.00 45.00
80 Thurman Munson 50.00 15.00
81 Nolan Ryan Astros 50.00 15.00
82 Don Mattingly 50.00 15.00
83 Mike Schmidt 40.00 12.00
84 Reggie Jackson 25.00 7.50
85 George Brett 50.00 15.00
86 Cal Ripken 60.00 18.00
87 Tony Gwynn 25.00 7.50
88 Yogi Berra 25.00 7.50
89 Stan Musial 50.00 15.00
90 Jim Palmer 20.00 6.00
91 Thurman Munson 60.00 18.00
Jorge Posada
92 Dale Murphy 60.00 18.00
Chipper Jones
93 Don Mattingly 100.00 30.00
Jason Giambi
94 Andre Dawson 60.00 18.00
Sammy Sosa
95 Nolan Ryan 120.00 36.00
Mark Prior
96 Babe Ruth ....
Lou Gehrig
97 Tom Seaver 60.00 18.00
Joe Morgan
98 Harmon Killebrew 60.00 18.00
Rod Carew
99 Nolan Ryan Rangers 120.00 36.00
Nolan Ryan Angels
100 Reggie Jackson Yankees 60.00 18.00
Reggie Jackson A's

2003 Donruss Elite Throwback Threads Autographs

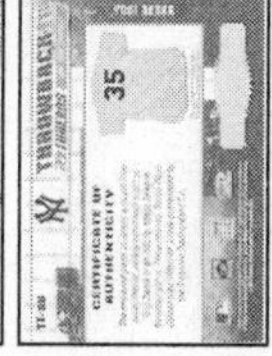

Randomly inserted into packs, this is a quasi-parallel to the Throwback Threads insert set. These cards were signed by the player featured and issued to stated print runs of between five and 75 copies per. Please note that if a player signed 25 or fewer copies, there is no pricing due to market scarcity.

Nm-Mt Ex-Mt
3 Roger Clemens Yanks/15 ....
4 Roger Clemens Red Sox/5 ....
6 Greg Maddux/5 ....
9 Alex Rodriguez Rgr/5 ....
10 Alex Rodriguez M's/5 ....
12 Alfonso Soriano/5 ....
14 Pedro Martinez Red Sox/5 ....
15 Pedro Martinez Expos/5 ....
16 Andruw Jones/25 ....
17 Chipper Jones/20 ....
18 Barry Zito/25 ....
19 Mark Mulder/10 ....
20 Lance Berkman/25 ....
21 Magglio Ordonez/15 ....
24 Rickey Henderson Padres/10 ....
25 Rickey Henderson Mets/5 ....
26 Rickey Henderson M's/5 ....
27 Sammy Sosa/15 ....
29 Troy Glaus/15 ....
30 Vladimir Guerrero/50 .... 100.00 30.00
31 Adam Dunn/50 .... 100.00 30.00
37 Kerry Wood/50 .... 100.00 30.00
38 Mark Prior/75 .... 150.00 45.00
39 Roberto Alomar/50 .... 100.00 30.00
40 Todd Helton/15 ....
41 Jim Thome/25 ....
45 Torii Hunter/25 ....
81 Nolan Ryan Angels/25 ....
82 Don Mattingly/25 ....
83 Mike Schmidt/25 ....
84 Reggie Jackson/25 ....
85 George Brett/15 ....
86 Cal Ripken/15 ....
87 Tony Gwynn/25 ....
88 Yogi Berra/25 ....
89 Stan Musial/25 ....
90 Jim Palmer/25 ....

2003 Donruss Elite Throwback Threads Prime

Nm-Mt Ex-Mt
1-45 PRINT RUN 25 SERIAL #'d SETS
46-75 PRINT RUN 15 SERIAL #'d SETS
76-95 PRINT RUN 10 SERIAL #'d SETS
96-100 PRINT RUN 5 SERIAL #'d SETS

2003 Donruss Elite Extra Edition

These cards were also inserted as part of the overall DLP Rookie/Traded Packs. Each of these cards feature Rookie Cards and are all issued to a stated print run of 900 serial numbered sets. Please note that cards numbered 42, 51, 54 and 56 do not exist for this set.

MINT NRMT
1 Adam Loewen RC 12.00 5.50
2 Brandon Webb RC 12.00 5.50
3 Chien-Ming Wang RC 10.00 4.50
4 Hong-Chih Kuo RC 6.00 2.70
5 Clint Barmes RC 6.00 2.70
6 Guillermo Quiroz RC 8.00 3.60
7 Edgar Gonzalez RC 5.00 2.20
8 Todd Wellemeyer RC 6.00 2.70
9 Alfredo Gonzalez RC 5.00 2.20
10 Craig Brazell RC 6.00 2.70
11 Tim Olson RC 6.00 2.70
12 Rich Fischer RC 5.00 2.20
13 Daniel Cabrera RC 5.00 2.20
14 Francisco Rosario RC 5.00 2.20
15 Francisco Cruceta RC 5.00 2.20
16 Alejandro Machado RC 5.00 2.20
17 Andrew Brown RC 5.00 2.20
18 Rob Hammock RC 6.00 2.70
19 Arnie Munoz RC 5.00 2.20
20 Felix Sanchez RC 5.00 2.20
21 Nook Logan RC 5.00 2.20
22 Cory Stewart RC 5.00 2.20
23 Michel Hernandez RC 5.00 2.20
24 Rett Johnson RC 6.00 2.70
25 Josh Hall RC 6.00 2.70
26 Doug Waechter RC 6.00 2.70
27 Matt Kata RC 6.00 2.70
28 Dan Haren RC 6.00 2.70
29 Dontrelle Willis 6.00 2.70
30 Ramon Nivar RC 6.00 2.70
31 Chad Gaudin RC 5.00 2.20
32 Rickie Weeks RC 25.00 11.00
33 Ryan Wagner RC 8.00 3.60
34 Kevin Correia RC 5.00 2.20
35 Bo Hart RC 10.00 4.50
36 Oscar Villarreal RC 5.00 2.20
37 Josh Willingham RC 8.00 3.60
38 Jeff Duncan RC 6.00 2.70
39 David DeJesus RC 6.00 2.70
40 Dustin McGowan RC 6.00 2.70
41 Preston Larrison RC 6.00 2.70
42 Does Not Exist ....
43 Kevin Youkilis RC 15.00 6.75
44 Bubba Nelson RC 6.00 2.70
45 Chris Burke RC 6.00 2.70
46 J.D. Durbin RC 6.00 2.70
47 Ryan Howard RC 6.00 2.70
48 Jason Kubel RC 6.00 2.70
49 Brendan Harris RC 6.00 2.70
50 Brian Bruney RC 6.00 2.70
51 Does Not Exist ....
52 Byron Gettis RC 5.00 2.20
53 Edwin Jackson RC 15.00 6.75
54 Does Not Exist ....
55 Daniel Garcia RC 5.00 2.20
56 Does Not Exist ....
57 Chad Cordero RC 5.00 2.20
58 Delmon Young RC 30.00 13.50

2003 Donruss Elite Extra Edition Aspirations

MINT NRMT
*ASP P/R b/wn 51-65: 1X TO 2.5X
*ASP RC's P/R b/wn 81-120: .6X TO 1.5X
*ASP RC's P/R b/wn 66-80: .75X TO 2X
*ASP RC's P/R b/wn 51-65: .75X TO 2X
*ASP RC's P/R b/wn 36-50: 1X TO 2.5X
*ASP RC's P/R b/wn 26-35: 1.25X TO 3X
RANDOM INSERTS IN DLP R/T PACKS
PRINT RUNS B/WN 24-98 COPIES PER
NO PRICING ON QTY OF 25 OR LESS.
CARDS 42/51/54/56 DO NOT EXIST ...

2003 Donruss Elite Extra Edition Aspirations Gold

MINT NRMT
RANDOM INSERTS IN DLP R/T PACKS
STATED PRINT RUN 1 SERIAL #'d SET
NO PRICING DUE TO SCARCITY ....
CARDS 42/51/54/56 DO NOT EXIST ...

2003 Donruss Elite Extra Edition Status

MINT NRMT
*STATUS P/R b/wn 26-35: 1.5X TO 4X
*STATUS RC's P/R b/wn 66-80: .75X TO 2X
*STATUS RC's P/R b/wn 51-65: .75X TO 2X
*STATUS RC's P/R b/wn 36-50: 1X TO 2.5X
*STATUS RC's P/R b/wn 26-35: 1.25X TO 3X
RANDOM INSERTS IN DLP R/T PACKS
PRINT RUNS B/WN 2-76 COPIES PER
NO PRICING ON QTY OF 25 OR LESS.
CARDS 42/51/54/56 DO NOT EXIST ...

2003 Donruss Elite Extra Edition Status Gold

MINT NRMT
RANDOM INSERTS IN DLP R/T PACKS
STATED PRINT RUN 24 SERIAL #'d SETS
NO PRICING DUE TO SCARCITY ....
CARDS 42/51/54/56 DO NOT EXIST ...

2003 Donruss Elite Extra Edition Turn of the Century

MINT NRMT
*TOC P/R b/wn 66-80: .75X TO 2X .....
*TOC RC's P/R b/wn 66-80: .75X TO 2X
RANDOM INSERTS IN DLP R/T PACKS
PRINT RUNS B/WN 75-100 COPIES PER

2003 Donruss Elite Extra Edition Turn of the Century Autographs

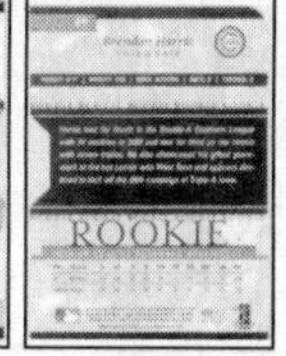

MINT NRMT
RANDOM INSERTS IN DLP R/T PACKS
STATED PRINT RUN 100 SERIAL #'d SETS
CARDS 29/32/34 PRINT RUN 25 #'d SETS
NO PRICING ON QTY OF 25 OR LESS.
1 Adam Loewen 60.00 27.00
2 Brandon Webb 40.00 18.00
3 Chien-Ming Wang 60.00 27.00
4 Hong-Chih Kuo 40.00 18.00
5 Clint Barmes 15.00 6.75
6 Guillermo Quiroz 25.00 11.00
7 Edgar Gonzalez 10.00 4.50
8 Todd Wellemeyer 15.00 6.75
9 Alfredo Gonzalez 10.00 4.50
10 Craig Brazell 15.00 6.75
11 Tim Olson 15.00 6.75
12 Rich Fischer 10.00 4.50
13 Daniel Cabrera 10.00 4.50
14 Francisco Rosario 10.00 4.50
15 Francisco Cruceta 10.00 4.50
16 Alejandro Machado 10.00 4.50
17 Andrew Brown 10.00 4.50
18 Rob Hammock 15.00 6.75
19 Arnie Munoz 10.00 4.50
20 Felix Sanchez 10.00 4.50
21 Nook Logan 10.00 4.50
22 Cory Stewart 10.00 4.50
23 Michel Hernandez 10.00 4.50
24 Rett Johnson 15.00 6.75
25 Josh Hall 15.00 6.75
26 Doug Waechter 15.00 6.75
27 Matt Kata 20.00 9.00
28 Dan Haren 20.00 9.00
29 Dontrelle Willis/25 ....
30 Ramon Nivar 20.00 9.00
31 Chad Gaudin 10.00 4.50
32 Rickie Weeks/25 ....
33 Ryan Wagner 30.00 13.50
34 Kevin Correia/25 ....
35 Bo Hart 40.00 18.00
36 Oscar Villarreal 10.00 4.50
37 Josh Willingham 25.00 11.00
38 Jeff Duncan 15.00 6.75
40 Dustin McGowan 20.00 9.00
41 Preston Larrison 10.00 4.50
43 Kevin Youkilis 50.00 22.00
44 Bubba Nelson 25.00 11.00
45 Chris Burke 15.00 6.75
46 J.D. Durbin 20.00 9.00
47 Ryan Howard 30.00 13.50
48 Jason Kubel 15.00 6.75
49 Brendan Harris 15.00 6.75
50 Brian Bruney 15.00 6.75
52 Byron Gettis 10.00 4.50
53 Edwin Jackson 80.00 36.00
55 Daniel Garcia 10.00 4.50
58 Delmon Young 120.00 55.00

2003 Donruss Elite Atlantic City National

Collectors who opened Donruss Elite product while at the Donruss corporate booth at the 2003 Atlantic City National were eligible to receive these specially produced cards. The fronts of these cards have special stamping with the Atlantic City National logo and the backs are serially numbered to a stated print run of five copies. Due to market scarcity, no pricing is provided for these cards.

MINT NRMT
PRINT RUN 5 SERIAL #'d SETS ....

2002 Donruss Fan Club

This 325 card set was issued in two separate series. The basic Fan Club product was released in early January 2002 and featured a 300-card base set that was broken into tiers as follows: 200 Base Veterans, and 60 Prospects/Rookies, and 40 Fan Club cards. Each pack contained seven cards and carried a suggested retail pre printed price of $1.29. The 60 prospects/rookie cards were seeded into packs at a stated rate of one in four packs. Cards U201-U225, featuring a selection of prospects, were issued exclusivley in retail packs of 2002 Donruss the Rookies in mid-December 2002 at a rate of 1:4. These update cards were intended to be numbered 301-325 but due to an error in production were actually numbered 201-225. To avoid confusion in the checklist, we've added a "U" prefix to these twenty-five update cards.

Nm-Mt Ex-Mt
COMP.SET w/o SP's (240) 40.00 12.00
COMMON (1-200/261-300) .... .30 .09
COMMON (201-260/U201-U225) 2.00 .60
1 Alex Rodriguez .... 1.25 .35
2 Pedro Martinez .... .75 .23
3 Vladimir Guerrero .... .75 .23
4 Jim Edmonds .... .30 .09
5 Derek Jeter .... 2.00 .60
6 Johnny Damon .... .30 .09
7 Rafael Furcal .... .30 .09
8 Cal Ripken .... 2.50 .75
9 Brad Radke .... .30 .09
10 Bret Boone .... .30 .09
11 Pat Burrell .... .30 .09
12 Roy Oswalt .... .30 .09
13 Cliff Floyd .... .30 .09
14 Robin Ventura .... .30 .09
15 Frank Thomas .... .75 .23
16 Mariano Rivera .... .50 .15
17 Paul LoDuca .... .30 .09
18 Geoff Jenkins .... .30 .09
19 Tony Gwynn .... 1.00 .30
20 Chipper Jones .... .75 .23
21 Eric Chavez .... .30 .09
22 Kerry Wood .... .75 .23
23 Jorge Posada .... .50 .15
24 J.D. Drew .... .30 .09
25 Garret Anderson .... .30 .09
26 Javier Vazquez .... .30 .09
27 Kenny Lofton .... .30 .09
28 Mike Mussina .... .75 .23
29 Paul Konerko .... .30 .09
30 Bernie Williams .... .50 .15
31 Eric Milton .... .30 .09
32 Craig Wilson .... .30 .09
33 Paul O'Neill .... .50 .15
34 Dmitri Young .... .30 .09
35 Andres Galarraga .... .30 .09
36 Gary Sheffield .... .30 .09
37 Ben Grieve .... .30 .09
38 Scott Rolen .... .50 .15
39 Mark Grace .... .50 .15
40 Albert Pujols .... 1.50 .45
41 Barry Zito .... .50 .15
42 Edgar Martinez .... .50 .15
43 Jarrod Washburn .... .30 .09
44 Juan Pierre .... .30 .09
45 Mark Buehrle .... .30 .09
46 Larry Walker .... .50 .15
47 Trot Nixon .... .50 .15
48 Wade Miller .... .30 .09
49 Robert Fick .... .30 .09
50 Sean Casey .... .30 .09
51 Joe Mays .... .30 .09
52 Brad Fullmer .... .30 .09
53 Chan Ho Park .... .30 .09
54 Carlos Delgado .... .30 .09
55 Phil Nevin .... .30 .09
56 Mike Cameron .... .30 .09
57 Raul Mondesi .... .30 .09
58 Roberto Alomar .... .75 .23
59 Ryan Klesko .... .30 .09
60 Andruw Jones .... .30 .09
61 Gabe Kapler .... .30 .09
62 Darin Erstad .... .30 .09
63 Cristian Guzman .... .30 .09
64 Kazuhiro Sasaki .... .30 .09
65 Doug Mientkiewicz .... .30 .09
66 Sammy Sosa .... 1.25 .35
67 Mike Hampton .... .30 .09
68 Rickey Henderson .... .75 .23
69 Mark Mulder .... .30 .09
70 Jeff Conine .... .30 .09
71 Freddy Garcia .... .30 .09
72 Ivan Rodriguez .... .75 .23
73 Terrence Long .... .30 .09
74 Adam Dunn .... .30 .09
75 Moises Alou .... .30 .09
76 Todd Helton .... .50 .15
77 Preston Wilson .... .30 .09
78 Roger Cedeno .... .30 .09
79 Tony Armas Jr. .... .30 .09
80 Manny Ramirez .... .30 .09
81 Jose Vidro .... .30 .09
82 Randy Johnson .... .75 .23
83 Richie Sexson .... .30 .09
84 Troy Glaus .... .50 .15
85 Kevin Brown .... .30 .09
86 Woody Williams .... .30 .09
87 Adrian Beltre .... .30 .09
88 Brian Giles .... .30 .09
89 Jermaine Dye .... .30 .09
90 Craig Biggio .... .50 .15
91 Richard Hidalgo .... .30 .09
92 Maggio Ordonez .... .30 .09
93 Al Leiter .... .30 .09
94 Jeff Kent .... .30 .09
95 Curt Schilling .... .50 .15
96 Tim Hudson .... .30 .09
97 Fred McGriff .... .50 .15
98 Barry Larkin .... .75 .23
99 Jim Thome .... .75 .23
100 Tom Glavine .... .50 .15
101 Alfonso Soriano .... .50 .15
102 Jamie Moyer .... .30 .09
103 Vinny Castilla .... .30 .09
104 Rich Aurilia .... .30 .09
105 Matt Morris .... .30 .09
106 Rafael Palmeiro .... .50 .15
107 Joe Crede .... .30 .09
108 Barry Bonds .... 2.00 .60
109 Robert Person .... .30 .09
110 Nomar Garciaparra .... 1.25 .35
111 Brandon Duckworth .... .30 .09
112 Russ Ortiz .... .30 .09
113 Jeff Weaver .... .30 .09
114 Carlos Beltran .... .30 .09
115 Ellis Burks .... .30 .09
116 Jeremy Giambi .... .30 .09
117 Carlos Lee .... .30 .09
118 Ken Griffey Jr. .... 1.25 .35
119 Torii Hunter .... .30 .09
120 Andy Pettitte .... .50 .15
121 Jose Canseco .... .75 .23
122 Charles Johnson .... .30 .09
123 Nick Johnson .... .30 .09
124 Luis Gonzalez .... .30 .09
125 Rondell White .... .30 .09
126 Miguel Tejada .... .30 .09
127 Jose Cruz Jr. .... .30 .09
128 Brent Abernathy .... .30 .09
129 Scott Brosius .... .30 .09
130 Jon Lieber .... .30 .09
131 John Smoltz .... .50 .15
132 Mike Sweeney .... .30 .09
133 Shannon Stewart .... .30 .09
134 Derrek Lee .... .30 .09
135 Brian Jordan .... .30 .09
136 Rusty Greer .... .30 .09
137 Mike Piazza .... 1.25 .35
138 Billy Wagner .... .30 .09
139 Shawn Green .... .30 .09
140 Orlando Cabrera .... .30 .09
141 Jeff Bagwell .... .50 .15
142 Aaron Sele .... .30 .09
143 Hideo Nomo .... .75 .23
144 Marlon Anderson .... .30 .09
145 Todd Walker .... .30 .09
146 Bobby Higginson .... .30 .09
147 Ichiro Suzuki .... 1.25 .35
148 Juan Uribe .... .30 .09
149 Jason Kendall .... .30 .09
150 Mark Quinn .... .30 .09
151 Ben Sheets .... .30 .09
152 Paul Abbott .... .30 .09
153 Aubrey Huff .... .30 .09
154 Greg Maddux .... 1.25 .35
155 Darryl Kile .... .30 .09
156 John Burkett .... .30 .09
157 Juan Gonzalez .... .75 .23
158 Javy Lopez .... .30 .09
159 Aramis Ramirez .... .30 .09
160 Lance Berkman .... .30 .09
161 David Cone .... .30 .09
162 Edgar Renteria .... .30 .09
163 Roger Clemens .... 1.50 .45
164 Frank Catalanotto .... .30 .09
165 Bartolo Colon .... .30 .09
166 Mark McGwire .... 2.00 .60
167 Jay Gibbons .... .30 .09
168 Tony Clark .... .30 .09
169 Tsuyoshi Shinjo .... .30 .09
170 Brad Penny .... .30 .09
171 Marcus Giles .... .30 .09
172 Matt Williams .... .30 .09
173 Bud Smith .... .30 .09
174 Tino Martinez .... .50 .15
175 Ryan Dempster .... .30 .09
176 Jimmy Rollins .... .30 .09
177 Edgardo Alfonzo .... .30 .09
178 Jason Giambi .... .75 .23
179 Aaron Boone .... .30 .09
180 Ray Durham .... .30 .09
181 Mike Lowell .... .30 .09
182 Jose Ortiz .... .30 .09
183 Johnny Estrada .... .30 .09
184 Shane Reynolds .... .30 .09
185 Joe Kennedy .... .30 .09
186 Corey Patterson .... .30 .09
187 Jeromy Burnitz .... .30 .09
188 C.C. Sabathia .... .30 .09
189 Kevin Millar .... .30 .09
190 Omar Vizquel .... .30 .09
191 John Olerud .... .30 .09
192 Dee Brown .... .30 .09
193 Kip Wells .... .30 .09
194 A.J. Burnett .... .30 .09
195 Josh Towers .... .30 .09
196 Jason Varitek .... .30 .09
197 Jason Isringhausen .... .30 .09
198 Fernando Vina .... .30 .09
199 Ramon Ortiz .... .30 .09
200 Bobby Abreu .... .30 .09
201 Willie Harris .... 2.00 .60
202 Angel Santos .... 2.00 .60
203 Corky Miller .... 2.00 .60
204 Michael Rivera .... 2.00 .60
205 Justin Duchscherer .... 2.00 .60
206 Rick Bauer .... 2.00 .60
207 Angel Berroa .... 2.00 .60
208 Juan Cruz .... 2.00 .60
209 Dewon Brazelton .... 2.00 .60
210 Mark Prior 8.00 2.40
211 Mark Teixeira .... 3.00 .90
212 Geronimo Gil .... 2.00 .60
213 Casey Fossum .... 2.00 .60
214 Ken Harvey .... 2.00 .60
215 Michael Cuddyer .... 2.00 .60
216 Wilson Betemit .... 2.00 .60
217 David Brous .... 2.00 .60
218 Juan A. Pena .... 2.00 .60
219 Travis Hafner .... 2.00 .60
220 Erick Almonte .... 2.00 .60
221 Morgan Ensberg .... 2.00 .60
222 Martin Vargas .... 2.00 .60
223 Brandon Berger .... 2.00 .60
224 Zach Day .... 2.00 .60
225 Brad Voyles .... 2.00 .60
226 Jeremy Affeldt .... 2.00 .60
227 Nick Neugebauer .... 2.00 .60
228 Tim Redding .... 2.00 .60
229 Adam Johnson .... 2.00 .60
230 Doug DeVore RC .... 2.00 .60
231 Cody Ransom .... 2.00 .60
232 Marlon Byrd .... 2.00 .60
233 Delvin James .... 2.00 .60
234 Eric Munson .... 2.00 .60
235 Dennis Tankersley .... 2.00 .60
236 Josh Beckett .... 3.00 .90
237 Bill Hall .... 2.00 .60
238 Kevin Olsen .... 2.00 .60
239 Francis Beltran RC .... 2.00 .60
240 Antonio Perez .... 2.00 .60
241 Orlando Hudson .... 2.00 .60
242 Anderson Machado RC .... 2.00 .60
243 Tom Shearn RC .... 2.00 .60
244 Brian Mallette RC .... 2.00 .60
245 Raul Chavez RC .... 2.00 .60
246 Andy Pratt RC .... 2.00 .60
247 Jorge De La Rosa RC .... 2.00 .60
248 Jeff Deardorff .... 2.00 .60
249 Ben Howard RC .... 2.00 .60
250 Brandon Backe RC .... 2.00 .60
251 Ed Rogers .... 2.00 .60
252 Travis Hughes RC .... 2.00 .60
253 Rodrigo Rosario RC .... 2.00 .60

254 Alfredo Amezaga 2.00 .60
255 Jorge Padilla RC 2.00 .60
256 Victor Martinez 2.00 .60
257 Steve Bechler RC 2.00 .60
258 Chris Baker RC 2.00 .60
259 Ryan Jamison 2.00 .60
260 Allan Simpson RC 2.00 .60
261 Alex Rodriguez FC 1.25 .35
262 Vladimir Guerrero FC .75 .23
263 Bud Smith FC .30 .09
264 Miguel Tejada FC .30 .09
265 Craig Biggio FC .50 .15
266 Luis Gonzalez FC .30 .09
267 Ivan Rodriguez FC .75 .23
268 C.C. Sabathia FC .30 .09
269 Jeff Bagwell FC .50 .15
270 Aramis Ramirez FC .30 .09
271 Bob Abreu FC .30 .09
272 Rich Aurilia FC .30 .09
273 Jason Giambi FC .75 .23
274 Rickey Henderson FC .75 .23
275 Wade Miller FC .30 .09
276 Andruw Jones FC .30 .09
277 Troy Glaus FC .50 .15
278 Roy Oswalt FC .30 .09
279 Tony Gwynn FC 1.00 .30
280 Adam Dunn FC .30 .09
281 Larry Walker FC .50 .15
282 Jose Canseco FC .75 .23
283 Todd Helton FC .50 .15
284 Lance Berkman FC .30 .09
285 Cal Ripken FC UER 2.50 .75
Wrong birthdate
286 Albert Pujols FC 1.50 .45
287 Alfonso Soriano FC .50 .15
288 Mark Mulder FC .30 .09
289 Mike Hampton FC .30 .09
290 Andres Galarraga FC .30 .09
291 Barry Bonds FC 2.00 .60
292 Ben Sheets FC .30 .09
293 Ichiro Suzuki FC 1.25 .35
294 J.D. Drew FC .30 .09
295 Jose Ortiz FC .30 .09
296 Kerry Wood FC .75 .23
297 Mark McGwire FC 2.00 .60
298 Mike Sweeney FC .30 .09
299 Pat Burrell FC .30 .09
300 Tim Hudson FC .30 .09
U201 Kirk Saarloos RC 2.00 .60
U202 Oliver Perez RC 3.00 .90
U203 So Taguchi RC 3.00 .90
U204 Runelvys Hernandez RC 2.00 .60
U205 Freddy Sanchez RC 2.00 .60
U206 Cliff Lee RC 3.00 .90
U207 Kazuhisa Ishii RC 4.00 1.20
U208 Kevin Cash RC 2.00 .60
U209 Trey Hodges RC 2.00 .60
U210 Wilson Valdez RC 2.00 .60
U211 Satoru Komiyama RC 2.00 .60
U212 Luis Ugueto RC 2.00 .60
U213 Joe Borchard 2.00 .60
U214 Brian Tallet RC 3.00 .90
U215 Jeriome Robertson RC 2.00 .60
U216 Eric Junge RC 2.00 .60
U217 Aaron Cook RC 2.00 .60
U218 Jason Simontacchi RC 2.00 .60
U219 Miguel Asencio RC 2.00 .60
U220 Josh Bard RC 2.00 .60
U221 Earl Snyder RC 2.00 .60
U222 Felix Escalona RC 2.00 .60
U223 Rene Reyes RC 2.00 .60
U224 Chone Figgins RC 2.00 .60
U225 Chris Snelling RC 3.00 .90

2002 Donruss Fan Club Autographs

Randomly inserted into packs of Fan Club and Donruss the Rookies (retail-only), this 53-card insert features authentic autographs from 2001 draft picks and Major League prospects. Individual print runs are listed below.

Nm-Mt Ex-Mt
201 Willie Harris/200
203 Corky Miller/200
205 Justin Duchscherer/200
207 Angel Berroa/175
208 Juan Cruz/25
209 Dewon Brazelton/175
210 Mark Prior/175
211 Mark Teixeira/175
215 Michael Cuddyer/200
216 Wilson Betemit/200
217 David Brous/200
219 Travis Hafner/125
220 Erick Almonte/200
221 Morgan Ensberg/200
222 Martin Vargas/200
223 Brandon Berger/200
224 Zach Day/200
225 Brad Voyles/200
226 Jeremy Affeldt/100
227 Nick Neugebauer/125
228 Tim Redding/200
229 Adam Johnson/125
231 Cody Ransom/200
232 Marlon Byrd/125
233 Delvin James/175
234 Eric Munson/175
235 Dennis Tankersley/200
237 Bill Hall/200
238 Kevin Olsen/175
240 Antonio Perez/175
241 Orlando Hudson/175
248 Jeff Deardorff/225
255 Jorge Padilla/150
260 Allan Simpson/225
U201 Kirk Saarloos/100
U202 Oliver Perez/25
U203 So Taguchi/10
U206 Cliff Lee/50
U207 Kazuhisa Ishii/10
U208 Kevin Cash/50
U209 Trey Hodges/100
U210 Wilson Valdez/50
U211 Satoru Komiyama/25
U212 Luis Ugueto/50
U213 Joe Borchard/50
U214 Brian Tallet/50
U216 Eric Junge/25
U220 Josh Bard/50
U221 Earl Snyder/100
U222 Felix Escalona/25
U223 Rene Reyes/50
U224 Chone Figgins/100
U225 Chris Snelling/50

2002 Donruss Fan Club Credits

This is a parallel set for the Donruss Fan Club set. Cards 1-300 were randomly inserted into Fan Club retail packs and U201-U225 into retail packs of Donruss the Rookies. These cards are all serial numbered to 100.

Nm-Mt Ex-Mt
*STARS 1-200/261-300: 8X TO 20X BASIC
*PROSPECTS 201-260: 1.5X TO 4X BASIC

2002 Donruss Fan Club Die-Cuts

Randomly inserted into retail packs at one in four, this 200-card die-cut set is a partial parallel of the 2001 Donruss Fan Club base set. The parallel set excludes the last 100 cards from the basic Fan Club issue.

Nm-Mt Ex-Mt
*DIE CUTS 1-200: 1.5X TO 4X BASIC.

2002 Donruss Fan Club Artists

Inserted into retail packs at stated odds of one in 172, these 14 cards feature some of the leading pitchers in baseball.

Nm-Mt Ex-Mt
*ARTISTS: .4X TO 1X HOBBY INSERTS

2002 Donruss Fan Club Craftsmen

Inserted into retail packs at stated odds of one in 134, these 18 cards feature some of the leading hitters in baseball.

Nm-Mt Ex-Mt
*CRAFTSMEN: .4X TO 1X HOBBY INSERTS

2002 Donruss Fan Club Double Features

Inserted into retail packs at stated odds of one in 240, these 10 cards feature teammates from 10 teams.

Nm-Mt Ex-Mt
*DOUB.FEAT: .4X TO 1X HOBBY INSERTS

2002 Donruss Fan Club Franchise Features

Inserted into retail packs at stated odds of one in 60, these 40 cards featue a mix of veterans and young players who are the stars of their teams.

Nm-Mt Ex-Mt
*FRAN.FEAT: .4X TO 1X HOBBY INSERTS

2002 Donruss Fan Club League Leaders

Inserted into retail packs at stated odds of one in 54, these 45 cards feature players who were among the majors best in important statistical categories.

Nm-Mt Ex-Mt
*LEADERS: .4X TO 1X HOBBY INSERTS

2002 Donruss Fan Club Pure Power

Inserted into retail packs at stated odds of one in 134, these 18 cards feature some of the leading power hitters in baseball.

Nm-Mt Ex-Mt
*POWER: .4X TO 1X HOBBY INSERTS

2002 Donruss Fan Club Records

Randomly inserted in packs, these five cards feature players who would set important records in 2001.

Nm-Mt Ex-Mt
*RECORDS: .4X TO 1X HOBBY INSERTS

1997 Donruss Limited

The 1997 Donruss Limited set was issued in one series totalling 200 cards and distributed in five-card packs with a suggested retail price of $4.99. The set is divided into four unique subsets: Counterparts, Double Team, Star Factor and Unlimited Potential/Talent. The Counterparts subset features 100 double-sided cards with full-bleed photos of two star players who play the same position. The Double Team subset displays color action photos of two star teammates back-to-back on 40 double-sided cards. The Star Factor subset highlights 40 superstars with a different photo of the same player on each side of the card plus unique player statistics. The Unlimited Potential/Talent subset features double-front cards with color photo matchups of a veteran and a rookie. Less than 1100 of each Unlimited Potential/Talent card was produced. Judging from case breakdowns provided to us from dealers in the field, the odds appear to be as follows: Double Team 1:6, Star Factor 1:24 and Unlimited Potential/Talent 1:36.

Nm-Mt Ex-Mt
COMP.COUNTER (100) 25.00 7.50
COMMON COUNTERPART .30 .09
COMMON DOUBLE TEAM 2.00 .60
COMMON STAR FACTOR 4.00 1.20
COMMON UNLIMITED 3.00 .90
1 Ken Griffey Jr. C 1.25 .35
Rondell White
2 Greg Maddux C 1.25 .35
David Cone
3 Gary Sheffield D 2.00 .60
Moises Alou
4 Frank Thomas S 6.00 1.80
5 Cal Ripken C 2.50 .75
Kevin Orie
6 Vladimir Guerrero U 12.00 3.60
Barry Bonds
7 Eddie Murray C .75 .23
Reggie Jefferson
8 Manny Ramirez D 2.00 .60
Marquis Grissom
9 Mike Piazza S 10.00 3.00
10 Barry Larkin C .75 .23
Rey Ordonez
11 Jeff Bagwell C .50 .15
Eric Karros
12 Chuck Knoblauch C .30 .09
Ray Durham
13 Alex Rodriguez C 1.25 .35
Edgar Renteria
14 Matt Williams C .30 .09
Vinny Castilla
15 Todd Hollandsworth C .30 .09
Bob Abreu
16 John Smoltz C .75 .23
Pedro Martinez
17 Jose Canseco C .75 .23
Chili Davis
18 Jose Cruz Jr. U 8.00 2.40
Ken Griffey Jr.
19 Ken Griffey Jr. S 10.00 3.00
20 Paul Molitor C .50 .15
John Olerud
21 Roberto Alomar C .30 .09
Luis Castillo
22 Derek Jeter C 1.50 .45
Lou Collier
23 Chipper Jones C .75 .23
Robin Ventura
24 Gary Sheffield C .30 .09
Ron Gant
25 Ramon Martinez C .30 .09
Bobby Jones
26 Mike Piazza D 5.00 1.50
Raul Mondesi
27 Darin Erstad U 5.00 1.50
Jeff Bagwell
28 Ivan Rodriguez S .75 .23
29 J.T.Snow C .30 .09
Kevin Young
30 Ryne Sandberg C 1.25 .35
Julio Franco
31 Travis Fryman C .30 .09
Chris Snopek
32 Wade Boggs C .50 .15
Russ Davis
33 Brooks Kieschnick C .30 .09
Marty Cordova
34 Andy Pettitte C .50 .15
Denny Neagle
35 Paul Molitor D 3.00 .90
Matt Lawton
36 Scott Rolen U 15.00 4.50
Cal Ripken
37 Cal Ripken S 20.00 6.00
38 Jim Thome C .75 .23
Dave Nilsson
39 Tony Womack RC C .30 .09
Carlos Baerga
40 Nomar Garciaparra C 1.25 .35
Mark Grudzielanek
41 Todd Greene C .30 .09
Chris Widger
42 Deion Sanders C .50 .15
Bernard Gilkey
43 Hideo Nomo C .75 .23
Charles Nagy
44 Ivan Rodriguez D 3.00 .90
Rusty Greer
45 Todd Walker U 5.00 1.50
Chipper Jones
46 Greg Maddux S 10.00 3.00
47 Mo Vaughn C .30 .09
Cecil Fielder
48 Craig Biggio C .50 .15
Scott Spiezio
49 Pokey Reese C .30 .09
Jeff Blauser
50 Ken Caminiti C .30 .09
Joe Randa
51 Albert Belle C .30 .09
Shawn Green
52 Randy Johnson C .75 .23
Jason Dickson
53 Hideo Nomo D 3.00 .90
Chan Ho Park
54 Scott Spiezio U 3.00 .90
Chuck Knoblauch
55 Chipper Jones S 6.00 1.80
56 Tino Martinez C .50 .15
Ryan McGuire
57 Eric Young C .30 .09
Wilton Guerrero
58 Ron Coomer C .30 .09
Dave Hollins
59 Sammy Sosa C 1.25 .35
Angel Echevarria
60 Dennis Reyes RC C .30 .09
Jimmy Key
61 Barry Larkin D 3.00 .90
Deion Sanders
62 Wilton Guerrero U 5.00 1.50
Roberto Alomar
63 Albert Belle S 4.00 1.20
64 Mark McGwire C 2.00 .60
Andre Galarraga
65 Edgar Martinez C .50 .15
Todd Walker
66 Steve Finley C .30 .09
Rich Becker
67 Tom Glavine C .50 .15
Andy Ashby
68 Sammy Sosa D 6.00 1.80
Ryne Sandberg
69 Nomar Garciaparra U 8.00 2.40
Alex Rodriguez
70 Jeff Bagwell S 6.00 1.80
71 Darin Erstad C .50 .15
Mark Grace
72 Scott Rolen C .50 .15
Edgardo Alfonzo
73 Kenny Lofton C .30 .09
Lance Johnson
74 Joey Hamilton C .30 .09
Brett Tomko
75 Eddie Murray D 3.00 .90
Tim Salmon
76 Dmitri Young U 3.00 .90
Mo Vaughn
77 Juan Gonzalez S 6.00 1.80
78 Frank Thomas C .75 .23
Tony Clark
79 Shannon Stewart C .30 .09
Bip Roberts
80 Shawn Estes C .30 .09
Alex Fernandez
81 John Smoltz D 3.00 .90
Javier Lopez
82 Todd Greene U 8.00 2.40
Mike Piazza
83 Derek Jeter S 15.00 4.50
84 Dmitri Young C .30 .09
Antone Williamson
85 Rickey Henderson C .75 .23
Darryl Hamilton
86 Billy Wagner C .30 .09
Dennis Eckersley
87 Larry Walker D 3.00 .90
Eric Young
88 Mark Kotsay RC U 5.00 1.50
Juan Gonzalez
89 Barry Bonds S 15.00 4.50
90 Will Clark C .75 .23
Jeff Conine
91 Tony Gwynn C 1.00 .30
Brett Butler
92 John Wetteland C .30 .09
Rod Beck
93 Bernie Williams D 3.00 .90
Tony Martinez
94 Andruw Jones U 3.00 .90
Kenny Lofton
95 Mo Vaughn S 4.00 1.20
96 Joe Carter C .30 .09
Derrek Lee
97 John Mabry C .30 .09
F.P. Santangelo
98 Esteban Loaiza C .30 .09
Wilson Alvarez
99 Matt Williams D 2.00 .60
David Justice
100 Derrek Lee U 5.00 1.50
Frank Thomas
101 Mark McGwire S 15.00 4.50
102 Fred McGriff C .50 .15
Paul Sorrento
103 J.Allensworth C .50 .15
Bernie Williams
104 Ismael Valdes C .30 .09
Chris Holt
105 Fred McGriff D 3.00 .90
Ryan Klesko
106 Tony Clark U 12.00 3.60
Mark McGwire
107 Tony Gwynn S 8.00 2.40
108 Jeffrey Hammonds C .30 .09
Ellis Burks
109 Shane Reynolds C .30 .09
Andy Benes
110 Roger Clemens D 6.00 1.80
Carlos Delgado
111 Karim Garcia U 3.00 .90
Albert Belle
112 Paul Molitor S 6.00 1.80
113 Trey Beamon C .30 .09
Eric Owens
114 Curt Schilling C .50 .15
Darryl Kile
115 Tom Glavine D 3.00 .90
Michael Tucker
116 Pokey Reese U 12.00 3.60
Derek Jeter
117 Manny Ramirez S 4.00 1.20
118 Juan Gonzalez C .75 .23
Brant Brown
119 Juan Guzman C .30 .09
Francisco Cordova
120 Randy Johnson D 3.00 .90
Edgar Martinez
121 Hideki Irabu U 8.00 2.40
Greg Maddux
122 Alex Rodriguez S 10.00 3.00
123 Barry Bonds C 2.00 .60
Quinton McCracken
124 Roger Clemens C 1.50 .45
Andy Benes
125 Wade Boggs D 3.00 .90
Paul O'Neill
126 Mike Cameron U 5.00 1.50
Larry Walker
127 Gary Sheffield S 4.00 1.20
128 Andruw Jones C .30 .09
Raul Mondesi
129 Brady Anderson C .30 .09
Terrell Wade
130 Brady Anderson D 3.00 .90
Rafael Palmeiro
131 Neifi Perez U 5.00 1.50
Barry Larkin
132 Ken Caminiti S 4.00 1.20
133 Larry Walker C .50 .15
Rusty Greer
134 Mariano Rivera C .50 .15
Mark Wohlers
135 Hideki Irabu RC D 3.00 .90
Andy Pettitte
136 Jose Guillen U 6.00 1.80
Tony Gwynn
137 Hideo Nomo S 6.00 1.80
138 Vladimir Guerrero C .75 .23
Jim Edmonds
139 Justin Thompson C .30 .09
Dwight Gooden
140 Andres Galarraga D 2.00 .60
Dante Bichette
141 Kenny Lofton S 4.00 1.20
142 Tim Salmon C .30 .09
Manny Ramirez
143 Kevin Brown C .30 .09
Matt Morris
144 Craig Biggio D 3.00 .90
Bob Abreu
145 Roberto Alomar S 6.00 1.80
146 Jose Guillen C .30 .09
Brian Jordan
147 Bartolo Colon C .30 .09
Kevin Appier
148 Ray Lankford D 2.00 .60
Brian Jordan
149 Chuck Knoblauch S 4.00 1.20
150 Henry Rodriguez C .30 .09
Ray Lankford
151 Jaret Wright RC C .30 .09
Ben McDonald
152 Bobby Bonilla D 2.00 .60
Kevin Brown
153 Barry Larkin S 6.00 1.80
154 David Justice C .30 .09
Reggie Sanders
155 Mike Mussina C .75 .23
Ken Hill
156 Mark Grace D 3.00 .90
Brooks Kieschnick
157 Jim Thome S 6.00 1.80
158 Michael Tucker C .30 .09
Curtis Goodwin
159 Jeff Suppan C .30 .09
Jeff Fassero
160 Mike Mussina D 3.00 .90
Jeffrey Hammonds
161 John Smoltz S 6.00 1.80
162 Moises Alou C .30 .09
Eric Davis
163 Sandy Alomar Jr. C .30 .09
Dan Wilson
164 Rondell White D 2.00 .60
Henry Rodriguez
165 Roger Clemens S 12.00 3.60
166 Brady Anderson C .30 .09
Al Martin
167 Jason Kendall C .30 .09
Charles Johnson
168 Jason Giambi D 3.00 .90
Jose Canseco
169 Larry Walker S 6.00 1.80
170 Jay Buhner C .30 .09
Geronimo Berroa
171 Ivan Rodriguez C .75 .23
Mike Sweeney
172 Kevin Appier D 2.00 .60
Jose Rosado
173 Bernie Williams S 6.00 1.80
174 Todd Dunwoody C 1.50 .45
Brian Giles RC
175 Javier Lopez C .30 .09
Scott Hatteberg
176 John Jaha D 2.00 .60
Jeff Cirillo
177 Andy Pettitte S 6.00 1.80
178 Dante Bichette C .30 .09
Butch Huskey
179 Raul Casanova C .30 .09
Todd Hundley
180 Jim Edmonds D 2.00 .60
Garrett Anderson
181 Deion Sanders S 6.00 1.80
182 Ryan Klesko C .50 .15
Paul O'Neill
183 Joe Carter D 2.00 .60
Pat Hentgen
184 Brady Anderson S 4.00 1.20
185 Carlos Delgado C .30 .09
Wally Joyner
186 Jermaine Dye D 2.00 .60
Johnny Damon
187 Randy Johnson S 6.00 1.80
188 Todd Hundley D 2.00 .60
Carlos Baerga
189 Tom Glavine S 6.00 1.80
190 Damon Mashore D 2.00 .60
Jason McDonald
191 Wade Boggs S 6.00 1.80
192 Al Martin D 2.00 .60
Jason Kendall
193 Matt Williams S 4.00 1.20
194 Will Clark D 3.00 .90
Dean Palmer
195 Sammy Sosa S 10.00 3.00
196 Jose Cruz Jr. RC D 4.00 1.20
Jay Buhner
197 Eddie Murray S 6.00 1.80
198 Darin Erstad D 2.00 .60
Jason Dickson
199 Fred McGriff S 6.00 1.80
200 Bubba Trammell RC D 2.00 .60
Bobby Higginson
S4 Frank Thomas Sample

1997 Donruss Limited Exposure

Randomly inserted in packs, this 200-card set is parallel to the base set and was printed using Holographic Poly-Chromium technology on both sides. The set is designated by an exclusive"Limited Exposure" stamp. Less than 40 of the "Star Factor" subsets exist.

Nm-Mt Ex-Mt
*COUNTER.STARS: 2.5X TO 6X BASIC CARDS
*COUNTER.ROOKIES: .75X TO 2X BASIC
*DOUBLE TEAM: 1.5X TO 4X BASIC CARDS
*STAR FACTOR: 1X TO 2.5X BASIC CARDS
*UNLIMITED: 1.25X TO 3X BASIC CARDS

1997 Donruss Limited Exposure Non-Glossy

Randomly inserted in packs, this 100-card double-sided set is a partial parallel version of

the base counterparts subset. The cards were actually the result of an error at the printing plant whereby the holographic poly-chromium technology of the normal exposure was left off.
Nm-Mt Ex-Mt
*NON-GLOSSY: .1X TO .25X BASIC CARDS

1997 Donruss Limited Fabric of the Game

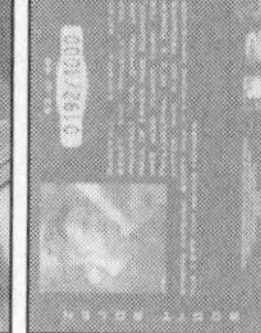

Randomly inserted in packs at a rate of 1:20, cards from this 69-card multi-fractured chase set highlights color player photos using three different technologies, each of which represents a different statistical category: Canvas (Stolen Bases), Leather (Doubles), and Wood (Homeruns). Five more levels cross the sections and are sequentially numbered: Legendary Material (numbered to 100), Hall of Fame Material (numbered to 250), Superstar Material (numbered to 500), Star Material (numbered to 750), and Major League Material (numbered to 1000)

	Nm-Mt	Ex-Mt
COMPLETE SET (69)	1000.00	300.00
1 Cal Ripken HF	80.00	24.00
2 Tony Gwynn SS	40.00	12.00
3 Ivan Rodriguez S	15.00	4.50
4 Rickey Henderson L	40.00	12.00
5 Ken Griffey Jr. SS	50.00	15.00
6 Chipper Jones ML	12.00	3.60
7 Sammy Sosa S	30.00	9.00
8 Wade Boggs HF	15.00	4.50
9 Manny Ramirez ML	5.00	1.50
10 Barry Bonds HF	60.00	18.00
11 Mike Piazza S	30.00	9.00
12 Rondell White ML	5.00	1.50
13 Albert Belle S	6.00	1.80
14 Tony Clark ML	3.00	.90
15 Edgar Martinez SS	12.00	3.60
16 Deion Sanders S	10.00	3.00
17 Juan Gonzalez SS	20.00	6.00
18 Nomar Garciaparra ML	30.00	9.00
19 Rafael Palmeiro SS	12.00	3.60
20 Dave Justice S	6.00	1.80
21 Bob Abreu ML	5.00	1.50
22 Paul Molitor L	25.00	7.50
23 Vladimir Guerrero ML	12.00	3.60
24 Chuck Knoblauch SS	8.00	2.40
25 Tony Gwynn HF	30.00	9.00
26 Darin Erstad ML	5.00	1.50
27 Mark McGwire HF	60.00	18.00
28 Larry Walker S	10.00	3.00
29 Gary Sheffield S	6.00	1.80
30 Jose Cruz Jr. ML	15.00	4.50
31 Kenny Lofton HF	10.00	3.00
32 Andres Galarraga SS	8.00	2.40
33 Raul Mondesi ML	5.00	1.50
34 Eddie Murray L	40.00	12.00
35 Tino Martinez ML	8.00	2.40
36 Todd Walker ML	5.00	1.50
37 Frank Thomas SS	20.00	6.00
38 Ken Caminiti S	6.00	1.80
39 Pokey Reese ML	3.00	.90
40 Barry Bonds HF	60.00	18.00
41 Barry Larkin SS	20.00	6.00
42 Bernie Williams S	10.00	3.00
43 Cal Ripken HF	80.00	24.00
44 Bobby Bonilla SS	8.00	2.40
45 Ken Griffey Jr. S	30.00	9.00
46 Tim Salmon S	10.00	3.00
47 Ryne Sandberg HF	50.00	15.00
48 Rusty Greer ML	5.00	1.50
49 Matt Williams SS	8.00	2.40
50 Eric Young S	4.00	1.20
51 Andruw Jones ML	5.00	1.50
52 Jeff Bagwell S	10.00	3.00
53 Wilton Guerrero ML	3.00	.90
54 Fred McGriff HF	15.00	4.50
55 Jose Guillen ML	5.00	1.50
56 Brady Anderson SS	8.00	2.40
57 Mo Vaughn S	6.00	1.80
58 Craig Biggio SS	12.00	3.60
59 Dmitri Young ML	5.00	1.50
60 Frank Thomas S	15.00	4.50
61 Derek Jeter ML	40.00	12.00
62 Albert Belle SS	8.00	2.40
63 Scott Rolen ML	8.00	2.40
64 Roberto Alomar HF	25.00	7.50
65 Jeff Bagwell S	10.00	3.00
66 Mark Grace SS	12.00	3.60
67 Gary Sheffield S	6.00	1.80
68 Joe Carter HF	10.00	3.00
69 Jim Thome ML	12.00	3.60

1998 Donruss Limited Exposure Sample

his lone Frank Thomas card was distributed to holesale dealer and retail accounts just prior o Pinnacle's bankruptcy in late-Summer, 1998. he card was intended to preview the 1998 onruss Limited brand, a product that was ever printed. In all likelihood, the card would ave been a parallel version of Thomas' Star Factor Exposure insert, except for the large "SAMPLE" text running diagonally across the back.

	Nm-Mt	Ex-Mt
S Frank Thomas S	3.00	.90

2002 Donruss Originals Samples

Issued one per sealed copy of Beckett Baseball Card Monthly 212, these cards parallel 100 assorted cards in the 2002 Originals set. Each card has the word "Sample" notated on the back.
Nm-Mt Ex-Mt
*SAMPLES: 1.5X TO 4X BASIC..........
ONE PER SEALED BBCM 212 ....
*GOLD:1.5X TO 4X BASIC SAMPLES .
GOLD: 10% OF TOTAL PRINT RUN.....

2002 Donruss Originals

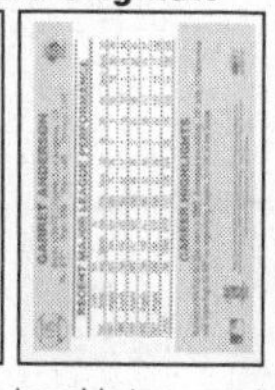

This 425 card set was issued in two separate series. The Donruss Originals product, containing cards 1-400, was released in September, 2002. This product was issued in five card packs which were seeded 24 packs to a box and 20 boxes to a case with each pack having a suggested retail price of $3. Fifty cards in this set were printed to a quantity of approximately 20 percent fewer than the other 350 cards in this set. All 50 cards are tagged as SP's in our checklist. This set was issued in the styles of the 1982, 1984, 1986 and 1988 Donruss sets but featured active 2002 players. The "style year" of the card is listed next to the player's name in our checklist. In addition, puzzle pieces featuring the late Ted Williams were randomly inserted into packs. Cards 401-425 were randomly seeded into hobby and retail packs of 2002 Donruss the Rookies (of which was released in mid-December 2002) at the following ratios: hobby 1:3, retail 1:4. These update cards feature a selection of prospects.

	Nm-Mt	Ex-Mt
COMP.LOW SET (400)	200.00	60.00
COMP.UPDATE SET (25)	25.00	7.50
COMMON CARD (1-400)	.40	.12
COMMON SP	1.00	.30
COMMON CARD (401-425)	.75	.23
COMP.WILLIAMS PUZZLE (63)	40.00	12.00
1 So Taguchi 82 RR RC	1.00	.30
2 Allan Simpson 82 RR RC	.60	.18
3 Brian Mallette 82 RR RC	.60	.18
4 Ben Howard 82 RR RC	.60	.18
5 Kazuhisa Ishii 82 RR RC	2.50	.75
6 Francis Beltran 82 RR RC	.60	.18
7 Jorge Padilla 82 RR RC	.60	.18
8 Brandon Puffer 82 RR RC	.60	.18
9 Oliver Perez 82 RR RC	1.00	.30
10 Kirk Saarloos 82 RR RC	.60	.18
11 Travis Driskill 82 RR RC	.60	.18
12 Jeremy Lambert 82 RR RC	.60	.18
13 John Foster 82 RR RC	.60	.18
14 Steve Kent 82 RR RC	.60	.18
15 Shawn Sedlacek 82 RR RC	.60	.18
16 Alex Rodriguez 82	1.50	.45
17 Lance Berkman 82	.40	.12
18 Kevin Brown 82	.40	.12
19 Garret Anderson 82	.40	.12
20 Bobby Abreu 82	.40	.12
21 Richard Hidalgo 82	.40	.12
22 Matt Morris 82	.40	.12
23 Manny Ramirez 82 SP	1.00	.30
24 Derek Jeter 82	2.50	.75
25 Kerry Wood 82	1.00	.30
26 Mark Grace 82	.60	.18
27 Edgar Martinez 82	.60	.18
28 Nomar Garciaparra 82	1.50	.45
29 Roberto Alomar 82 SP	2.00	.60
30 Jason Giambi 82	1.00	.30
31 Juan Gonzalez 82 SP	2.00	.60
32 Albert Pujols 82	2.00	.60
33 Juan Cruz 82	.40	.12
34 Troy Glaus 82	.60	.18
35 Greg Maddux 82	1.50	.45
36 Adam Dunn 82 SP	1.00	.30
37 J.D. Drew 82	.40	.12
38 Tsuyoshi Shinjo 82	.40	.12
39 Vladimir Guerrero 82	1.00	.30
40 Barry Bonds 82	2.50	.75
41 Carlos Delgado 82	.40	.12
42 Ken Griffey Jr. 82	1.50	.45
43 Carlos Pena 82	.40	.12
44 Jeff Kent 82	.40	.12
45 Roger Clemens 82 SP	4.00	1.20
46 Frank Thomas 82	1.00	.30
47 Larry Walker 82	.60	.18
48 Pedro Martinez 82	1.00	.30
49 Moises Alou 82	.40	.12
50 Andruw Jones 82 SP	1.00	.30
51 Luis Gonzalez 82	.40	.12
52 Adrian Beltre 82	.40	.12
53 Bobby Hill 82	.40	.12
54 Roy Oswalt 82	.40	.12
55 Tim Hudson 82	.40	.12
56 Trot Nixon 82	.60	.18
57 Jeff Bagwell 82	.60	.18
58 Bernie Williams 82	.60	.18
59 Maggio Ordonez 82 SP	1.00	.30
60 Bartolo Colon 82	.40	.12
61 Shawn Green 82	.40	.12
62 Mark Buehrle 82	.40	.12
63 Sean Casey 82	.40	.12
64 Rickey Henderson 82	1.00	.30
65 Aramis Ramirez 82 SP	1.00	.30
66 Ichiro Suzuki 82	1.50	.45
67 Cliff Floyd 82	.40	.12
68 Darin Erstad 82	.40	.12
69 Paul LoDuca 82	.40	.12
70 Ivan Rodriguez 82	1.00	.30
71 Mo Vaughn 82	.40	.12
72 Todd Helton 82 SP	1.50	.45
73 Raul Mondesi 82	.40	.12
74 Sammy Sosa 82	1.50	.45
75 Cristian Guzman 82	.40	.12
76 Jimmy Rollins 82	.40	.12
77 Hideo Nomo 82	1.00	.30
78 C.C. Sabathia 82	.40	.12
79 Wade Miller 82	.40	.12
80 Drew Henson 82 SP	1.00	.30
81 Chipper Jones 82	1.00	.30
82 Miguel Tejada 82	.40	.12
83 Freddy Garcia 82	.40	.12
84 Richie Sexson 82	.40	.12
85 Robin Ventura 82	.40	.12
86 Jose Vidro 82	.40	.12
87 Rich Aurilla 82	.40	.12
88 Scott Rolen 82	.60	.18
89 Carlos Beltran 82	.40	.12
90 Austin Kearns 82 SP	1.00	.30
91 Kazuhiro Sasaki 82	.40	.12
92 Carlos Hernandez 82	.40	.12
93 Randy Johnson 82	1.00	.30
94 Jim Thome 82	1.00	.30
95 Curt Schilling 82	.60	.18
96 Alfonso Soriano 82 SP	1.50	.45
97 Barry Larkin 82	1.00	.30
98 Rafael Palmeiro 82	.60	.18
99 Tom Glavine 82	.60	.18
100 Barry Zito 82	.60	.18
101 Craig Biggio 82	.60	.18
102 Mike Piazza 82	1.50	.45
103 Ben Sheets 82	.40	.12
104 Mark Mulder 82	.40	.12
105 Mike Mussina 82	1.00	.30
106 Jim Edmonds 82	.40	.12
107 Paul Konerko 82	.40	.12
108 Pat Burrell 82	.40	.12
109 Chan Ho Park 82	.40	.12
110 Mike Sweeney 82	.40	.12
111 Phil Nevin 82	.40	.12
112 Brian Giles 82	.40	.12
113 Eric Chavez 82 SP	1.00	.30
114 Corey Patterson 82	.40	.12
115 Gary Sheffield 82	.40	.12
116 Kazuhisa Ishii 84 RR RC	2.50	.75
117 Kyle Kane 84 RR RC	.60	.18
118 Eric Junge 84 RR RC	.60	.18
119 Luis Ugueto 84 RR RC	.60	.18
120 Cam Esslinger 84 RR RC	.60	.18
121 Earl Snyder 84 RR RC	.60	.18
122 Oliver Perez 84 RR RC	1.00	.30
123 Victor Alvarez 84 RR RC	.60	.18
124 Tom Shearn 84 RR RC	.60	.18
125 Corey Thurman 84 RR RC	.60	.18
126 Satoru Komiyama 84 RR RC	.60	.18
127 Hansel Izquierdo 84 RR RC	.60	.18
128 Elio Serrano 84 RR RC	.60	.18
129 Mike Crudale 84 RR RC	.60	.18
130 Chris Snelling 84 RR RC	2.00	.60
131 Nomar Garciaparra 84	1.50	.45
132 Roger Clemens 84	2.00	.60
133 Hank Blalock 84	1.00	.30
134 Eric Chavez 84	.40	.12
135 Corey Patterson 84	.40	.12
136 Richie Sexson 84	.40	.12
137 Freddy Garcia 84	.40	.12
138 Miguel Tejada 84	.40	.12
139 Alex Rodriguez 84 SP	3.00	.90
140 Adrian Beltre 84	.40	.12
141 Bobby Abreu 84	.40	.12
142 Bret Boone 84	.40	.12
143 Tim Hudson 84	.40	.12
144 Roy Oswalt 84	.40	.12
145 Derek Jeter 84	2.50	.75
146 Rich Aurilla 84	.40	.12
147 Mark Grace 84	.60	.18
148 Kerry Wood 84 SP	2.00	.60
149 Geronimo Gil 84	.40	.12
150 Mark Buehrle 84	.40	.12
151 Jim Edmonds 84	.40	.12
152 Ichiro Suzuki 84	1.50	.45
153 Juan Gonzalez 84	1.00	.30
154 Darin Erstad 84	.40	.12
155 Barry Bonds 84 SP	5.00	1.50
156 Greg Maddux 84	1.50	.45
157 Adam Dunn 84	.40	.12
158 Todd Helton 84	.60	.18
159 Roberto Alomar 84	1.00	.30
160 Sammy Sosa 84	1.50	.45
161 Sean Burroughs 84	.40	.12
162 Albert Pujols 84	2.00	.60
163 Carlos Delgado 84	.40	.12
164 Frank Thomas 84	1.00	.30
165 Ken Griffey Jr. 84	1.50	.45
166 Jason Giambi 84 SP	2.00	.60
167 Chipper Jones 84	1.00	.30
168 Ivan Rodriguez 84	1.00	.30
169 Pedro Martinez 84 SP	2.00	.60
170 Gary Sheffield 84	.40	.12
171 Andruw Jones 84	.40	.12
172 Luis Gonzalez 84 SP	1.00	.30
173 Raul Mondesi 84	.40	.12
174 Jose Vidro 84	.40	.12
175 Garret Anderson 84 SP	1.00	.30
176 Scott Rolen 84	.60	.18
177 Kazuhiro Sasaki 84	.40	.12
178 Jeff Bagwell 84	.60	.18
179 Manny Ramirez 84	.40	.12
180 Jim Thome 84	1.00	.30
181 Ben Sheets 84	.40	.12
182 Randy Johnson 84	1.00	.30
183 Lance Berkman 84	.40	.12
184 Shawn Green 84	.40	.12
185 Rickey Henderson 84 SP	2.00	.60
186 Edgar Martinez 84	.60	.18
187 Barry Larkin 84	1.00	.30
188 Bernie Williams 84	.60	.18
189 Luis Aparicio 84	.40	.12
190 Troy Glaus 84 SP	1.50	.45
191 Mike Mussina 84	1.00	.30
192 Pee Wee Reese 84	.60	.18
193 Craig Biggio 84	.60	.18
194 Vladimir Guerrero 84	1.00	.30
195 J.D. Drew 84	.40	.12
196 Jeff Kent 84	.40	.12
197 Dewon Brazelton 84	.40	.12
198 Tsuyoshi Shinjo 84 SP	1.00	.30
199 Sean Casey 84	.40	.12
200 Hideo Nomo 84	1.00	.30
201 C.C. Sabathia 84	.40	.12
202 Larry Walker 84	.60	.18
203 Mark Teixeira 84	1.00	.30
204 Mike Sweeney 84 SP	1.00	.30
205 Moises Alou 84	.40	.12
206 Mark Prior 84	2.00	.60
207 Javier Vazquez 84	.40	.12
208 Phil Nevin 84 SP	1.00	.30
209 Harmon Killebrew 84	1.00	.30
210 Brian Giles 84	.40	.12
211 Carlos Beltran 84	.40	.12
212 Don Drysdale 84	1.00	.30
213 Matt Morris 84	.40	.12
214 Trot Nixon 84	.60	.18
215 Magglio Ordonez 84	.40	.12
216 Curt Schilling 84 SP	1.50	.45
217 Mark Mulder 84	.40	.12
218 Alfonso Soriano 84	.60	.18
219 Rafael Palmeiro 84 SP	1.50	.45
220 Tom Glavine 84	.60	.18
221 Barry Zito 84	.60	.18
222 Mike Piazza 84	1.50	.45
223 Bartolo Colon 84	.40	.12
224 Cliff Floyd 84	.40	.12
225 Paul LoDuca 84 SP	1.00	.30
226 Cristian Guzman 84	.40	.12
227 Mo Vaughn 84	.40	.12
228 Aramis Ramirez 84	.40	.12
229 Pat Burrell 84	.40	.12
230 Chan Ho Park 84	.40	.12
231 Satoru Komiyama 86 RR RC	.60	.18
232 Brandon Backe 86 RR RC	.60	.18
233 Anderson Machado 86 RR RC	.60	.18
234 Doug Devore 86 RR RC	.60	.18
235 Steve Bechler 86 RR RC	.60	.18
236 John Ennis 86 RR RC	.60	.18
237 Rodrigo Rosario 86 RR RC	.60	.18
238 Jorge Sosa 86 RR RC	.60	.18
239 Ken Huckaby 86 RR RC	.60	.18
240 Mike Moriarty 86 RR RC	.60	.18
241 Kirk Saarloos 86 RR RC	.60	.18
242 Kevin Frederick 86 RR RC	.60	.18
243 Aaron Guiel 86 RR RC	.60	.18
244 Jose Rodriguez 86 RR RC	.60	.18
245 So Taguchi 86 RR RC	1.00	.30
246 Albert Pujols 86	2.00	.60
247 Derek Jeter 86	2.50	.75
248 Brian Giles 86	.40	.12
249 Mike Cameron 86	.40	.12
250 Josh Beckett 86	.60	.18
251 Ken Griffey Jr. 86 SP	3.00	.90
252 Aramis Ramirez 86	.40	.12
253 Miguel Tejada 86	.40	.12
254 Carlos Delgado 86	.40	.12
255 Pedro Martinez 86	1.00	.30
256 Raul Mondesi 86	.40	.12
257 Roger Clemens 86	2.00	.60
258 Gary Sheffield 86	.40	.12
259 Jose Vidro 86 SP	1.00	.30
260 Alex Rodriguez 86	1.50	.45
261 Larry Walker 86	.60	.18
262 Mark Mulder 86	.40	.12
263 Scott Rolen 86	.60	.18
264 Tim Hudson 86	.40	.12
265 Manny Ramirez 86	.40	.12
266 Rich Aurilla 86	.40	.12
267 Roy Oswalt 86	.40	.12
268 Mark Grace 86	.60	.18
269 Lance Berkman 86 SP	1.00	.30
270 Nomar Garciaparra 86 SP	3.00	.90
271 Barry Bonds 86	2.50	.75
272 Ryan Klesko 86	.40	.12
273 Ichiro Suzuki 86	1.50	.45
274 Shawn Green 86	.40	.12
275 Darin Erstad 86	.40	.12
276 Bernie Williams 86	.60	.18
277 Greg Maddux 86 SP	3.00	.90
278 Eric Hinske 86	.40	.12
279 Randy Johnson 86	1.00	.30
280 Todd Helton 86	.60	.18
281 Sammy Sosa 86 SP	3.00	.90
282 Nick Johnson 86	.40	.12
283 Jose Cruz Jr. 86	.40	.12
284 Frank Thomas 86	1.00	.30
285 Tsuyoshi Shinjo 86	.40	.12
286 Troy Glaus 86	.60	.18
287 Jason Giambi 86	1.00	.30
288 Chipper Jones 86 SP	2.00	.60
289 Roberto Alomar 86	1.00	.30
290 Bobby Hill 86	.40	.12
291 Garret Anderson 86	.40	.12
292 Andruw Jones 86	.40	.12
293 Luis Gonzalez 86	.40	.12
294 Mike Mussina 86	1.00	.30
295 Ivan Rodriguez 86 SP	2.00	.60
296 Barry Larkin 86	1.00	.30
297 Kazuhiro Sasaki 86	.40	.12
298 Alfonso Soriano 86	.60	.18
299 Jeff Bagwell 86 SP	1.50	.45
300 Bobby Abreu 86	.40	.12
301 Ben Sheets 86	.40	.12
302 Curt Schilling 86	.60	.18
303 Jim Thome 86	1.00	.30
304 Kerry Wood 86	1.00	.30
305 Mark Buehrle 86 SP	1.00	.30
306 Rickey Henderson 86	1.00	.30
307 Rafael Palmeiro 86	.60	.18
308 Jim Edmonds 86	.40	.12
309 Mike Piazza 86	1.50	.45
310 Edgar Martinez 86	.60	.18
311 Tom Glavine 86	.60	.18
312 Adrian Beltre 86	.40	.12
313 Adam Dunn 86	.40	.12
314 Craig Biggio 86	.60	.18
315 Vladimir Guerrero 86 SP	2.00	.60
316 Bret Boone 86	.40	.12
317 Hideo Nomo 86 SP	2.00	.60
318 Jeff Kent 86	.40	.12
319 Juan Gonzalez 86	1.00	.30
320 Sean Casey 86	.40	.12
321 C.C. Sabathia 86	.40	.12
322 J.D. Drew 86	.40	.12
323 Torii Hunter 86 SP	1.00	.30
324 Chan Ho Park 86	.40	.12
325 Mike Sweeney 86	.40	.12
326 Javier Vazquez 86	.40	.12
327 Jorge Posada 86	.60	.18
328 Barry Zito 86	.60	.18
329 Willie McCovey 86	.40	.12
330 Kevin Brown 86	.40	.12
331 Mo Vaughn 86	.40	.12
332 Carlos Beltran 86	.40	.12
333 Bobby Doerr 86	.40	.12
334 Matt Morris 86	.40	.12
335 Trot Nixon 86 SP	1.50	.45
336 Magglio Ordonez 86	.40	.12
337 Paul LoDuca 86	.40	.12
338 Phil Nevin 86	.40	.12
339 Eric Chavez 86	.40	.12
340 Corey Patterson 86	.40	.12
341 Richie Sexson 86	.40	.12
342 Pat Burrell 86 SP	1.00	.30
343 Freddy Garcia 86	.40	.12
344 Bartolo Colon 86	.40	.12
345 Cliff Floyd 86	.40	.12
346 Deivis Santos 88 RR	.60	.18
347 Felix Escalona 88 RR RC	.60	.18
348 Miguel Asencio 88 RR RC	.60	.18
349 Takahito Nomura 88 RR RC	.60	.18
350 Jorge Padilla 88 RR RC	.60	.18
351 Torii Hunter 88	.40	.12
352 Ichiro Suzuki 88	1.50	.45
353 Jay Gibbons 88	.40	.12
354 Alfonso Soriano 88	.60	.18
355 Mark Buehrle 88	.40	.12
356 Shawn Green 88 SP	1.00	.30
357 Barry Larkin 88	1.00	.30
358 Josh Fogg 88	.40	.12
359 Shannon Stewart 88	.40	.12
360 Andruw Jones 88	.40	.12
361 Juan Gonzalez 88	1.00	.30
362 Ken Griffey Jr. 88	1.50	.45
363 Tim Hudson 88	.40	.12
364 Roy Oswalt 88 SP	1.00	.30
365 Carlos Delgado 88	.40	.12
366 Albert Pujols 88 SP	4.00	1.20
367 Willie Stargell 88	.60	.18
368 Roger Clemens 88	2.00	.60
369 Luis Gonzalez 88	.40	.12
370 Barry Zito 88	.60	.18
371 Alex Rodriguez 88	1.50	.45
372 Troy Glaus 88	.60	.18
373 Vladimir Guerrero 88	1.00	.30
374 Jeff Bagwell 88	.60	.18
375 Randy Johnson 88	1.00	.30
376 Manny Ramirez 88	.40	.12
377 Derek Jeter 88 SP	5.00	1.50
378 C.C. Sabathia 88	.40	.12
379 Rickey Henderson 88	1.00	.30
380 J.D. Drew 88 SP	1.00	.30
381 Nomar Garciaparra 88	1.50	.45
382 Darin Erstad 88	.40	.12
383 Ben Sheets 88	.40	.12
384 Frank Thomas 88	1.00	.30
385 Barry Bonds 88	2.50	.75
386 Pedro Martinez 88	1.00	.30
387 Mark Mulder 88	.40	.12
388 Greg Maddux 88	1.50	.45
389 Todd Helton 88	.60	.18
390 Lance Berkman 88	.40	.12
391 Sammy Sosa 88	1.50	.45
392 Mike Piazza 88 SP	3.00	.90
393 Chipper Jones 88	1.00	.30
394 Adam Dunn 88	.40	.12
395 Jason Giambi 88	1.00	.30
396 Eric Chavez 88	.40	.12
397 Bobby Abreu 88	.40	.12
398 Aramis Ramirez 88	.40	.12
399 Paul LoDuca 88	.40	.12
400 Miguel Tejada 88	.40	.12
401 Runelvys Hernandez 82 RC	.75	.23
402 Wilson Valdez 82 RC	.75	.23
403 Brian Tallet 82 RC	1.25	.35
404 Chone Figgins 82 RC	.75	.23
405 Jeriome Robertson 82 RC	.75	.23
406 Shane Nance 84 RC	.75	.23
407 Aaron Cook 84 RC	.75	.23
408 Trey Hodges 84 RC	.75	.23
409 Matt Childers 84 RC	.75	.23
410 Mitch Wylie 84 RC	.75	.23
411 Rene Reyes 84 RC	.75	.23
412 Mike Smith 84 RC	.75	.23
413 Jason Simontacchi 84 RC	.60	.18
414 Luis Martinez 84 RC	.75	.23
415 Kevin Cash 84 RC	.75	.23
416 Todd Donovan 86 RC	.75	.23
417 Scotty Layfield 86 RC	.75	.23
418 Joe Borchard 86	.75	.23
419 Adrian Burnside 86 RC	.75	.23
420 Ben Kozlowski 86 RC	.75	.23
421 Clay Condrey 88 RC	.75	.23
422 Cliff Lee 88 RC	2.00	.60
423 Josh Bard 88 RC	.75	.23
424 Freddy Sanchez 88 RC	.75	.23
425 Ron Calloway 88 RC	.75	.23

2002 Donruss Originals Aqueous

Randomly inserted in packs, these cards which are known as the Aqueous cards are actually "glossy" in nature and parallel the entire 2002 Donruss Originals set.
Nm-Mt Ex-Mt
*AQUEOUS: 3X TO 8X BASIC...
*AQUEOUS: 1.5X TO 4X BASIC SP's ..
*AQUEOUS: 1.25X TO 3X BASIC RC's

2002 Donruss Originals All-Stars

Inserted at stated odds of one one in 120 retail, this 25 car of the leading active player the greats of the 1980's.

	Nm-Mt	Ex-Mt
1 George Brett	12.00	3.60
2 Rickey Henderson	5.00	1.50
3 Mike Schmidt	12.00	3.60
4 Vladimir Guerrero	5.00	1.50
5 Tony Gwynn	8.00	2.40
6 Curt Schilling	5.00	1.50
7 Don Mattingly	15.00	4.50
8 Roberto Alomar	5.00	1.50
9 Cal Ripken	20.00	6.00
10 Carlton Fisk	5.00	1.50
11 Roger Clemens	10.00	3.00
12 Jeff Bagwell	5.00	1.50
13 Kirby Puckett	5.00	1.50
14 Nolan Ryan	15.00	4.50
15 Ryne Sandberg	12.00	3.60
16 Ivan Rodriguez	5.00	1.50
17 Sammy Sosa	8.00	2.40
18 Greg Maddux	8.00	2.40
19 Alex Rodriguez	8.00	2.40
20 Todd Helton	5.00	1.50
21 Randy Johnson	5.00	1.50
22 Troy Glaus	5.00	1.50
23 Ichiro Suzuki	8.00	2.40
24 Barry Bonds	12.00	3.60
25 Derek Jeter	12.00	3.60

2002 Donruss Originals Box Bottoms

Issued at the bottom of each Donruss Originals box was this four card blank-backed set featuring a design from each of the 1980's even years that Donruss produced cards during.

	Nm-Mt	Ex-Mt
COMPLETE SET (4)	2.00	.60
NNO Kazuhisa Ishii 82	.50	.15
NNO Nomar Garciaparra 84	.50	.15
NNO Roger Clemens 86	.50	.15
NNO Mike Piazza 88	.50	.15

2002 Donruss Originals Champions

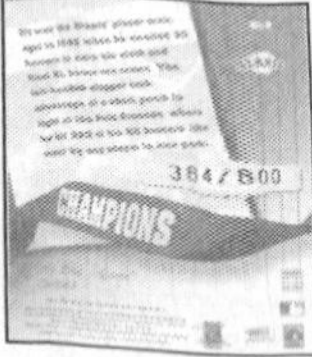

Randomly inserted in packs this 25 card set was issued to a stated print run of 800 serial numbered sets and featured a mix of the best players of today along with some all time greats.

	Nm-Mt	Ex-Mt
1 Nolan Ryan	20.00	6.00
2 George Brett	15.00	4.50
3 Edgar Martinez	8.00	2.40
4 Mike Schmidt	15.00	4.50
5 Randy Johnson	8.00	2.40
6 Tony Gwynn	10.00	3.00
7 John Smoltz	8.00	2.40
8 Roger Clemens	15.00	4.50
9 Mel Ott	8.00	2.40
10 Todd Helton	8.00	2.40
11 Bernie Williams	8.00	2.40
12 Troy Glaus	8.00	2.40
13 Steve Carlton	8.00	2.40
14 Ryne Sandberg	15.00	4.50
15 Ted Williams UER	15.00	4.50
Williams played in the AL, card says NL		
16 Alex Rodriguez M's	12.00	3.60
17 Lou Boudreau	8.00	2.40
18 Luis Gonzalez	8.00	2.40
19 Rickey Henderson	8.00	2.40
20 Jose Canseco	8.00	2.40
21 Stan Musial	10.00	3.00
22 Randy Johnson	8.00	2.40
23 Don Mattingly	20.00	6.00
24 Nomar Garciaparra	12.00	3.60
25 Wade Boggs	8.00	2.40

2002 Donruss Originals Champions Materials

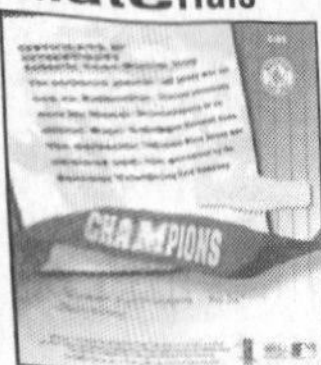

Randomly inserted in packs, this parallel to the Champions insert set features game-used jersey swatches of the featured player. Since the cards have different print runs, we have notated that information next to the player's name in our checklist.

	Nm-Mt	Ex-Mt
/78	80.00	24.00
[illegible]		
[illegible]	25.00	7.50
[illegible]	60.00	18.00
[illegible]		7.50
[illegible]		7.50
[illegible]		[illegible]
[illegible]		[illegible]
[illegible]		7.50
[illegible]		7.50
[illegible]		7.50
[illegible]		4.50
[illegible]		18.00
[illegible]		12.00

in 30 hobby and
set features a mix
as well as some of

265
KETT.COM
OM

	Nm-Mt	Ex-Mt
17 Lou Boudreau/44	25.00	7.50
18 Luis Gonzalez/99	15.00	4.50
19 Rickey Henderson/82	25.00	7.50
20 Jose Canseco/88		
21 Stan Musial/50		
22 Randy Johnson/88	25.00	7.50
23 Don Mattingly/84	80.00	24.00
24 Nomar Garciaparra/100	40.00	12.00
25 Wade Boggs/88	25.00	7.50

2002 Donruss Originals Embossed Notation

Randomly inserted in packs, these 97 cards represent cards which were "bought back" by Donruss/Playoff. Each card have not only an "embossing" on the front but also an "inscription" which indicated that it was purchased for this product. In addition, these cards were not serial numbered so we are using the stated print runs in our checklist provided by the company. Please note that each card has a stated print run of one copy so no pricing is provided.

	Nm-Mt	Ex-Mt
1 Yogi Berra 1982 HOF		
2 Wade Boggs 1986 AS		
3 George Brett 1982 AS		
4 George Brett 1982 HOF		
5 George Brett 1984 AS		
6 George Brett 1984 HOF		
7 George Brett 1986 AS		
8 George Brett 1986 HOF		
9 George Brett 1986 HL HOF		
10 George Brett 1988 AS		
11 George Brett 1988 HOF		
12 Rod Carew 1982 AS		
13 Rod Carew 1982 HOF		
14 Rod Carew 1984 HOF		
15 Rod Carew 1986 HOF		
16 Steve Carlton 1982 AS		
17 Steve Carlton 1982 CY		
18 Steve Carlton 1982 HOF		
19 Steve Carlton 1984 HOF		
20 Gary Carter 1982 AS		
21 Gary Carter 1984 AS		
22 Gary Carter 1984 AS MVP		
23 Gary Carter 1986 AS		
24 Roger Clemens 1986 AS		
25 Andre Dawson 1982 AS		
26 Carlton Fisk 1982 AS		
27 Carlton Fisk 1982 HOF		
28 Carlton Fisk 1984 HOF		
29 Carlton Fisk 1986 HOF		
30 Tony Gwynn 1986 AS		
31 Rickey Henderson 1982 AS		
32 Rickey Henderson 1984 AS		
33 Rickey Henderson 1986 AS		
34 Rickey Henderson 1988 AS		
35 Reggie Jackson 1984 AS		
36 Reggie Jackson 1984 HOF		
37 Reggie Jackson 1986 HOF		
38 Fergie Jenkins 1982 HOF		
39 Ferguson Jenkins 1984 HOF		
40 Fred Lynn 1982 AS		
41 Greg Maddux 1988 AS		
42 Don Mattingly 1986 AS		
43 Don Mattingly 1988 AS		
44 Paul Molitor 1982 HOF		
45 Paul Molitor 1984 HOF		
46 Paul Molitor 1986 HOF		
47 Dale Murphy 1982 AS		
48 Dale Murphy 1982 MVP		
49 Dale Murphy 1984 AS		
50 Dale Murphy 1986 AS		
51 Eddie Murray 1982 AS		
52 Eddie Murray 1982 HOF		
53 Eddie Murray 1984 AS		
54 Eddie Murray 1984 HOF		
55 Eddie Murray 1986 AS		
56 Eddie Murray 1986 HOF		
57 Phil Niekro 1982 AS		
58 Phil Niekro 1982 HOF		
59 Phil Niekro 1984 HOF		
60 Phil Niekro 1986 HOF		
61 Jim Palmer 1982 HOF		
62 Jim Palmer 1984 HOF		
63 Dave Parker 1986 AS		
64 Kirby Puckett 1986 AS		
65 Kirby Puckett 1986 HOF		
66 Kirby Puckett 1986 HL HOF		
67 Kirby Puckett 1988 AS		
68 Cal Ripken 1984 AS		
69 Cal Ripken 1986 AS		
70 Cal Ripken 1986 AS		
71 Cal Ripken 1988 AS		
72 Nolan Ryan 1986 HOF		
73 Ryne Sandberg 1986 AS		
74 Mike Schmidt 1984 HOF		
75 Mike Schmidt 1986 AS		
76 Mike Schmidt 1986 HOF		
77 Mike Schmidt 1986 HL HOF #4		
78 Mike Schmidt 1986 HL HOF #36		
79 Mike Schmidt 1988 HOF		
80 Tom Seaver 1984 HOF		
81 Tom Seaver 1986 HOF		
82 Ozzie Smith 1984 AS		
83 Ozzie Smith 1984 HOF		
84 Ozzie Smith 1986 AS		
85 Ozzie Smith 1986 HOF		
86 Willie Stargell 1982 HOF		
87 Dave Winfield 1982 HOF		
88 Dave Winfield 1982 HOF		
89 Dave Winfield 1984 AS		
90 Dave Winfield 1984 HOF		
91 Dave Winfield 1986 AS		
92 Dave Winfield 1986 HOF		
93 Robin Yount 1982 AS		
94 Robin Yount 1982 HOF		
95 Robin Yount 1982 MVP		
96 Robin Yount 1984 HOF		
97 Robin Yount 1986 HOF		

2002 Donruss Originals Gamers

Randomly inserted into packs, these 50 cards feature a mix of players along with a game-used jersey swatch of the featured player. Since players have varying print runs, we have

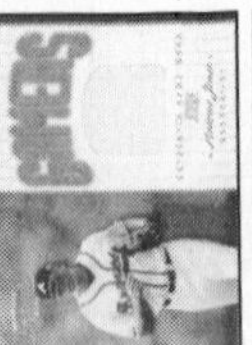

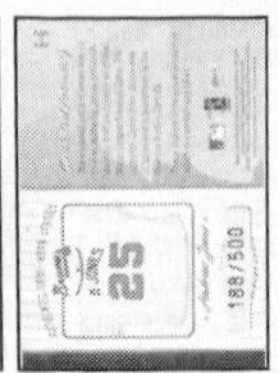

notated that information next to their name in our checklist.

	Nm-Mt	Ex-Mt
1 Alfonso Soriano/400	15.00	4.50
2 Shawn Green/500	10.00	3.00
3 Curt Schilling/250	20.00	6.00
4 Hideo Nomo Red Sox/100	80.00	24.00
5 Toby Hall/500	10.00	3.00
6 Andruw Jones/500	10.00	3.00
7 Cliff Floyd/500	10.00	3.00
8 Mark Ellis/500	10.00	3.00
9 Gabe Kapler/500	10.00	3.00
10 Andres Galarraga/500	10.00	3.00
11 Freddy Garcia/500	10.00	3.00
12 Tsuyoshi Shinjo/200	15.00	4.50
13 Robin Ventura/500	10.00	3.00
14 Paul LoDuca/500	10.00	3.00
15 Manny Ramirez/500	10.00	3.00
16 Garret Anderson/250	15.00	4.50
17 Joe Kennedy/500	10.00	3.00
18 Roger Clemens/500	20.00	6.00
19 Gary Sheffield/500	10.00	3.00
20 Vernon Wells/500	10.00	3.00
21 Matt Guerrier/500		
22 Hideo Nomo Dodgers/100	80.00	24.00
23 Tim Hudson/500	10.00	3.00
24 Larry Bigbie/500	10.00	3.00
25 Larry Walker/500	15.00	4.50
26 Ryan Ludwick/500		
27 John Olerud/500	10.00	3.00
28 Chipper Jones/500	15.00	4.50
29 Tony Gwynn/500	15.00	4.50
30 Juan Gonzalez/500	15.00	4.50
31 Jacque Jones/500	10.00	3.00
32 Frank Thomas/500	15.00	4.50
33 Luis Gonzalez/500	10.00	3.00
34 Geoff Jenkins/500	10.00	3.00
35 J.D. Drew/500	10.00	3.00
36 Edgardo Alfonzo/500	10.00	3.00
37 Todd Helton/500	15.00	4.50
38 Brad Penny/500	10.00	3.00
39 Robert Fick/500	10.00	3.00
40 Will Clark/500	15.00	4.50
41 Tony Armas Jr./500	10.00	3.00
42 Nick Johnson/400	10.00	3.00
43 Ben Grieve/500	10.00	3.00
44 Vladimir Guerrero/500	15.00	4.50
45 Jason Jennings/500	10.00	3.00
46 Carlos Lee/500	10.00	3.00
47 Carlos Delgado/500	10.00	3.00
48 Chan Ho Park/500	10.00	3.00
49 Juan Diaz/500	10.00	3.00
50 Alex Rodriguez M's/400	20.00	6.00

2002 Donruss Originals Hit List

Randomly inserted into packs, this 20 card set features some of the leading hitters in Baseball and these cards are printed to a stated print run of 1500 serial numbered sets.

	Nm-Mt	Ex-Mt
1 Ichiro Suzuki	6.00	1.80
2 Shawn Green	4.00	1.20
3 Alex Rodriguez	6.00	1.80
4 Nomar Garciaparra	6.00	1.80
5 Derek Jeter	10.00	3.00
6 Barry Bonds	10.00	3.00
7 Mike Piazza	6.00	1.80
8 Albert Pujols	8.00	2.40
9 Chipper Jones	4.00	1.20
10 Sammy Sosa	6.00	1.80
11 Rickey Henderson	4.00	1.20
12 Frank Thomas	4.00	1.20
13 Jeff Bagwell	4.00	1.20
14 Vladimir Guerrero	4.00	1.20
15 Todd Helton	4.00	1.20
16 Adam Dunn	4.00	1.20
17 Rafael Palmeiro	4.00	1.20
18 Manny Ramirez	4.00	1.20
19 Lance Berkman	4.00	1.20
20 Jason Giambi A's	4.00	1.20

2002 Donruss Originals Hit List Total Bases

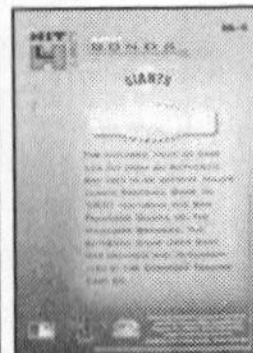

Randomly inserted into packs, this is a parallel of the Hit List insert set. Each card features a game-used piece and we have notated what type of memorabilia next to the player's name in our checklist.

	Nm-Mt	Ex-Mt
1 Ichiro Suzuki Base/316	25.00	7.50
2 Shawn Green Bat/370	15.00	4.50
3 Alex Rodriguez Rgr Bat/393	20.00	6.00
4 Nomar Garciaparra Bat/365	15.00	4.50
5 Derek Jeter Base/346	25.00	7.50
6 Barry Bonds Base/411	25.00	7.50
7 Mike Piazza Dodgers Bat/355	15.00	4.50
8 Albert Pujols Base/360	15.00	4.50
9 Chipper Jones Bat/359	15.00	4.50
10 Sammy Sosa Base/425	15.00	4.50
11 Rickey Henderson Bat/285	15.00	4.50
12 Frank Thomas Bat/364	15.00	4.50
13 Jeff Bagwell Bat/363	15.00	4.50
14 Vladimir Guerrero Bat/379	15.00	4.50
15 Todd Helton Bat/405	15.00	4.50
16 Adam Dunn Bat/141	15.00	4.50
17 Rafael Palmeiro Bat/356	15.00	4.50
18 Manny Ramirez Bat/346	15.00	4.50
19 Lance Berkman Bat/358	15.00	4.50
20 Jason Giambi A's Base/343	15.00	4.50

2002 Donruss Originals Making History

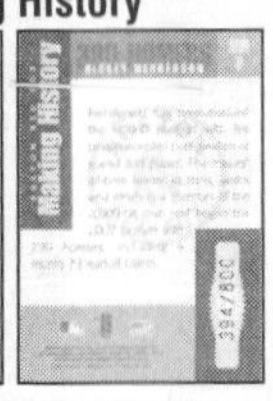

Randomly inserted into packs, this 10 card set features players on the verge of either setting records or achieving important milestones in baseball history. Each of these cards were issued to a stated print run of 800 serial numbered sets.

	Nm-Mt	Ex-Mt
1 Rafael Palmeiro	8.00	2.40
2 Roger Clemens	15.00	4.50
3 Greg Maddux	12.00	3.60
4 Randy Johnson	8.00	2.40
5 Barry Bonds	20.00	6.00
6 Mike Piazza	12.00	3.60
7 Roberto Alomar	8.00	2.40
8 Rickey Henderson	8.00	2.40
9 Sammy Sosa	12.00	3.60
10 Tom Glavine	8.00	2.40

2002 Donruss Originals Making History Materials

Randomly inserted into packs, these 10 cards parallel the Making History insert set. Each card features a game-used memorabilia piece and were issued to a stated print run of 100 serial numbered sets.

	Nm-Mt	Ex-Mt
1 Rafael Palmeiro Jsy	25.00	7.50
2 Roger Clemens Jsy	40.00	12.00
3 Greg Maddux Jsy	25.00	7.50
4 Randy Johnson Jsy	25.00	7.50
5 Barry Bonds Base	40.00	12.00
6 Mike Piazza Jsy	25.00	7.50
7 Roberto Alomar Jsy	25.00	7.50
8 Rickey Henderson Jsy	25.00	7.50
9 Sammy Sosa Base	25.00	7.50
10 Tom Glavine Jsy	25.00	7.50

2002 Donruss Originals Mound Marvels

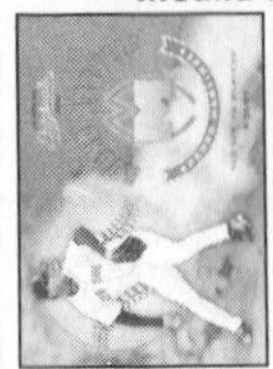

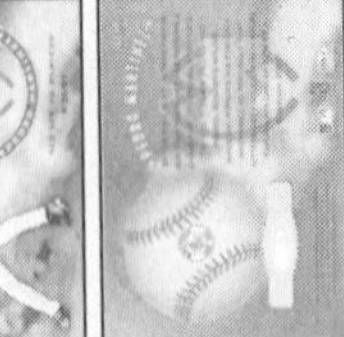

Inserted into packs at stated odds of one in 40 hobby and one in 72 retail, these 15 cards feature some of the leading pitchers in the game. Roger Clemens has two cards in this set.

	Nm-Mt	Ex-Mt
1 Roger Clemens 8/20/01	8.00	2.40
2 Matt Morris	4.00	1.20
3 Pedro Martinez	4.00	1.20
4 Randy Johnson	4.00	1.20
5 Wade Miller	4.00	1.20
6 Tim Hudson	4.00	1.20
7 Mike Mussina	4.00	1.20
8 C.C. Sabathia	4.00	1.20
9 Kazuhiro Sasaki	4.00	1.20
10 Curt Schilling	4.00	1.20
11 Hideo Nomo	4.00	1.20
12 Roger Clemens 10/30/01	8.00	2.40
13 Mark Buehrle	4.00	1.20
14 Barry Zito	4.00	1.20
15 Roy Oswalt	4.00	1.20

2002 Donruss Originals Mound Marvels High Heat

Randomly inserted into packs, this is a parallel of the Mound Marvels insert set. These cards

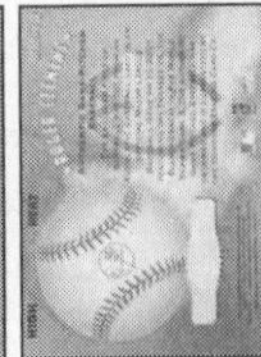

all feature pieces of game-used balls on them are are issued to a stated print run of 100 serial numbered sets.

	Nm-Mt	Ex-Mt
1 Roger Clemens 8/20/01	50.00	15.00
2 Matt Morris	20.00	6.00
3 Pedro Martinez	25.00	7.50
4 Randy Johnson	25.00	7.50
5 Wade Miller	20.00	6.00
6 Tim Hudson	20.00	6.00
7 Mike Mussina	25.00	7.50
8 C.C. Sabathia	20.00	6.00
9 Kazuhiro Sasaki	20.00	6.00
10 Curt Schilling	25.00	7.50
11 Hideo Nomo	80.00	24.00
12 Roger Clemens 10/30/01	50.00	15.00
13 Mark Buehrle	20.00	6.00
14 Barry Zito	25.00	7.50
15 Roy Oswalt	20.00	6.00

2002 Donruss Originals Nifty Fifty Bats

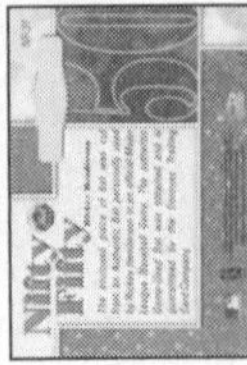

Randomly inserted into packs, these fifty cards feature game-used bat pieces and are issued to a stated print run of 50 serial numbered sets.

	Nm-Mt	Ex-Mt
1 Alex Rodriguez Rangers	50.00	15.00
2 Kerry Wood	25.00	7.50
3 Ivan Rodriguez	25.00	7.50
4 Geronimo Gil	12.00	3.60
5 Vladimir Guerrero	25.00	7.50
6 Corky Miller	12.00	3.60
7 Todd Helton	25.00	7.50
8 Rickey Henderson Padres	25.00	7.50
9 Andruw Jones	20.00	6.00
10 Barry Bonds Ball	60.00	18.00
11 Tom Glavine	25.00	7.50
12 Mark Teixeira	25.00	7.50
13 Mike Piazza Mets	50.00	15.00
14 Austin Kearns	20.00	6.00
15 Rickey Henderson M's	25.00	7.50
16 Derek Jeter Ball	50.00	15.00
17 Barry Larkin	25.00	7.50
18 Jeff Bagwell	25.00	7.50
19 Bernie Williams	25.00	7.50
20 Frank Thomas	25.00	7.50
21 Lance Berkman	20.00	6.00
22 Marlon Byrd	20.00	6.00
23 Randy Johnson	25.00	7.50
24 Ichiro Suzuki Ball	80.00	24.00
25 Darin Erstad	20.00	6.00
26 Jason Lane	12.00	3.60
27 Roberto Alomar	25.00	7.50
28 Ken Griffey Jr. Ball		
29 Tsuyoshi Shinjo	20.00	6.00
30 Pedro Martinez	25.00	7.50
31 Rickey Henderson Mets	25.00	7.50
32 Albert Pujols Ball	40.00	12.00
33 Nomar Garciaparra	50.00	15.00
34 Troy Glaus	25.00	7.50
35 Chipper Jones	25.00	7.50
36 Adam Dunn	20.00	6.00
37 Jason Giambi Ball		
38 Greg Maddux	50.00	15.00
39 Mike Piazza Dodgers	50.00	15.00
40 So Taguchi	25.00	7.50
41 Manny Ramirez	20.00	6.00
42 Scott Rolen	25.00	7.50
43 Sammy Sosa Ball	40.00	12.00
44 Shawn Green	20.00	6.00
45 Rickey Henderson Red Sox	25.00	7.50
46 Alex Rodriguez M's	50.00	15.00
47 Hideo Nomo Red Sox	100.00	30.00
48 Kazuhisa Ishii	25.00	7.50
49 Luis Gonzalez	20.00	6.00
50 Jim Thome	25.00	7.50

2002 Donruss Originals Nifty Fifty Combos

Randomly inserted into packs, these fifty card feature game-used bat and jersey pieces an are issued to a stated print run of 50 seria numbered sets. A few cards feature other type of memorabilia and we have notated tha information next to the player's name in ou checklist.

	Nm-Mt	Ex-Mt
1 Alex Rodriguez Rangers	80.00	24.0
2 Kerry Wood	40.00	12.0
3 Ivan Rodriguez	40.00	12.0

4 Geronimo Gil 20.00 6.00
5 Vladimir Guerrero 40.00 12.00
6 Corky Miller 20.00 6.00
7 Todd Helton 40.00 12.00
8 Rickey Henderson Padres 40.00 12.00
9 Andruw Jones 30.00 9.00
10 Barry Bonds Base/Ball 100.00 30.00
11 Tom Glavine 40.00 12.00
12 Mark Teixeira 40.00 12.00
13 Mike Piazza Mets 80.00 24.00
14 Austin Kearns 30.00 9.00
15 Rickey Henderson M's 40.00 12.00
16 Derek Jeter Base/Ball 80.00 24.00
17 Barry Larkin 40.00 12.00
18 Jeff Bagwell 40.00 12.00
19 Bernie Williams 40.00 12.00
20 Frank Thomas 40.00 12.00
21 Lance Berkman 30.00 9.00
22 Marlon Byrd 30.00 9.00
23 Randy Johnson 40.00 12.00
24 Ichiro Suzuki Base/Ball
25 Darin Erstad 30.00 9.00
26 Jason Lane 20.00 6.00
27 Roberto Alomar 40.00 12.00
28 Ken Griffey Jr. Base/Ball 50.00 15.00
29 Tsuyoshi Shinjo 30.00 9.00
30 Pedro Martinez 40.00 12.00
31 Rickey Henderson Mets 40.00 12.00
32 Albert Pujols Base/Ball
33 Nomar Garciaparra 80.00 24.00
34 Troy Glaus 40.00 12.00
35 Chipper Jones 40.00 12.00
36 Adam Dunn 30.00 9.00
37 Jason Giambi Base/Ball 40.00 12.00
38 Greg Maddux 80.00 24.00
39 Mike Piazza Dodgers 80.00 24.00
40 So Taguchi 40.00 12.00
41 Manny Ramirez 30.00 9.00
42 Scott Rolen 40.00 12.00
43 Sammy Sosa Base/Ball
44 Shawn Green 30.00 9.00
45 Rickey Henderson Red Sox 40.00 12.00
46 Alex Rodriguez M's 80.00 24.00
47 Hideo Nomo Red Sox
48 Kazuhisa Ishii 40.00 12.00
49 Luis Gonzalez 30.00 9.00
50 Jim Thome 40.00 12.00

2002 Donruss Originals Nifty Fifty Jerseys

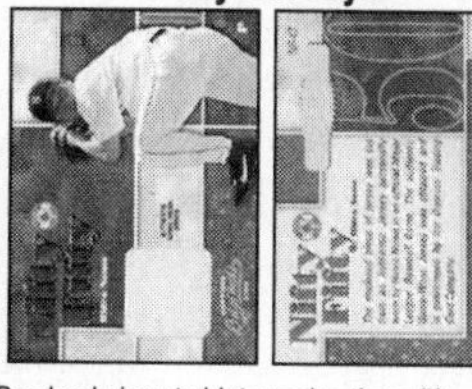

Randomly inserted into packs, these fifty cards feature game-used jersey pieces and are issued to a stated print run of 50 serial numbered sets.

Nm-Mt Ex-Mt
1 Alex Rodriguez Rangers
2 Kerry Wood 25.00 7.50
3 Ivan Rodriguez 25.00 7.50
4 Geronimo Gil 12.00 3.60
5 Vladimir Guerrero 25.00 7.50
6 Corky Miller 12.00 3.60
7 Todd Helton 25.00 7.50
8 Rickey Henderson Padres 25.00 7.50
9 Andruw Jones 20.00 6.00
10 Barry Bonds Base
11 Tom Glavine 25.00 7.50
12 Mark Teixeira 25.00 7.50
13 Mike Piazza Mets 50.00 15.00
14 Austin Kearns 20.00 6.00
15 Rickey Henderson M's 25.00 7.50
16 Derek Jeter Base 50.00 15.00
17 Barry Larkin 25.00 7.50
18 Jeff Bagwell 25.00 7.50
19 Bernie Williams 25.00 7.50
20 Frank Thomas 25.00 7.50
21 Lance Berkman 20.00 6.00
22 Marlon Byrd 20.00 6.00
23 Randy Johnson 25.00 7.50
24 Ichiro Suzuki Base 80.00 24.00
25 Darin Erstad 20.00 6.00
26 Jason Lane 12.00 3.60
27 Roberto Alomar 25.00 7.50
28 Ken Griffey Jr. Base 30.00 9.00
29 Tsuyoshi Shinjo 20.00 6.00
30 Pedro Martinez 25.00 7.50
31 Rickey Henderson Mets 25.00 7.50
32 Albert Pujols Base 40.00 12.00
33 Nomar Garciaparra 50.00 15.00
34 Troy Glaus 25.00 7.50
35 Chipper Jones 25.00 7.50
36 Adam Dunn 20.00 6.00
37 Jason Giambi Base
38 Greg Maddux
39 Mike Piazza Dodgers 50.00 15.00
40 So Taguchi 25.00 7.50
41 Manny Ramirez 20.00 6.00
42 Scott Rolen 25.00 7.50
43 Sammy Sosa Base
44 Shawn Green 20.00 6.00
45 Rickey Henderson Red Sox 25.00 7.50
46 Alex Rodriguez M's 50.00 15.00
47 Hideo Nomo Red Sox 100.00 30.00
48 Kazuhisa Ishii 25.00 7.50
49 Luis Gonzalez 20.00 6.00
50 Jim Thome 25.00 7.50

2002 Donruss Originals On The Record

Randomly inserted into packs, this 15 card sets feature players and some of their most famous accomplishments. These cards were issued to a stated print run of 800 serial numbered sets.

Nm-Mt Ex-Mt
1 Ty Cobb HR 9 10.00 3.00
2 Jimmie Foxx 8.00 2.40
3 Lou Gehrig 15.00 4.50

4 Dale Murphy 20.00 6.00
5 Steve Carlton 8.00 2.40
6 Randy Johnson 8.00 2.40
7 Greg Maddux 12.00 3.60
8 Roger Clemens 15.00 4.50
9 Yogi Berra 8.00 2.40
10 Don Mattingly 20.00 6.00
11 Rickey Henderson 8.00 2.40
12 Stan Musial 10.00 3.00
13 Jackie Robinson 10.00 3.00
14 Roberto Clemente 40.00 12.00
15 Mike Schmidt 15.00 4.50

2002 Donruss Originals On The Record Materials

Randomly inserted into packs, these cards parallel the On the Record insert set and each of these cards feature a game-used memorabilia piece. Each card has a stated print run to a year in which they either accomplished an important feat or won a major award and we have notated that information in our checklist.

Nm-Mt Ex-Mt
1 Ty Cobb Bat/9
2 Jimmie Foxx Bat/33
3 Lou Gehrig Jsy/34
4 Dale Murphy Jsy/83 15.00 4.50
5 Steve Carlton Jsy/72 15.00 4.50
6 Randy Johnson Jsy/100 15.00 4.50
7 Greg Maddux Jsy/93 20.00 6.00
8 Roger Clemens Jsy/87 25.00 7.50
9 Yogi Berra Jsy/51 15.00 4.50
10 Don Mattingly Jsy/85 40.00 12.00
11 Rickey Henderson Jsy/90 15.00 4.50
12 Stan Musial Jsy/43
13 Jackie Robinson Jsy/49
14 Roberto Clemente Jsy/66 100.00 30.00
15 Mike Schmidt Jsy/80 40.00 12.00

2002 Donruss Originals Power Alley

Randomly inserted into packs, these 15 cards feature some of the leading power hitters of 2002 along with some of the best power hitters of Donruss' early years. Each card was issued to a stated print run of 1500 serial numbered sets.

Nm-Mt Ex-Mt
*DIE CUTS: 1.25X TO 3X BASIC ALLEY
DIE CUT PRINT RUN 100 SERIAL #'d SETS
1 Barry Bonds 10.00 3.00
2 Sammy Sosa 6.00 1.80
3 Lance Berkman 4.00 1.20
4 Luis Gonzalez 4.00 1.20
5 Alex Rodriguez 6.00 1.80
6 Troy Glaus 4.00 1.20
7 Vladimir Guerrero 4.00 1.20
8 Jason Giambi 4.00 1.20
9 Mike Piazza 6.00 1.80
10 Todd Helton 4.00 1.20
11 Mike Schmidt 8.00 2.40
12 Don Mattingly 10.00 3.00
13 Andre Dawson 4.00 1.20
14 Reggie Jackson 4.00 1.20
15 Dale Murphy 10.00 3.00

2002 Donruss Originals Recollection Autographs Notation

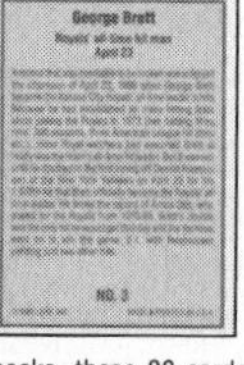

Randomly inserted into packs, these 88 cards feature original Donruss cards "bought back" for insertion into 2002 Donruss Originals packs. Each card has a "recollection" logo as well as an inscription. Since each of these cards have a stated print run of one copy, there is no pricing provided due to scarcity.

Nm-Mt Ex-Mt
1 Johnny Bench 82 HOF
2 Wade Boggs 86 AS
3 George Brett 82 AS
4 George Brett 82 HOF
5 George Brett 84 AS
6 George Brett 84 HOF
7 George Brett 86 AS
8 George Brett 86 HOF
9 George Brett 88 AS
10 George Brett 88 HOF
11 Jose Canseco 86 AS
12 Jose Canseco 88 AS
13 Jose Canseco 88 MVP
14 Rod Carew 82 AS
15 Rod Carew 84 HOF
16 Steve Carlton 82 CY
17 Steve Carlton 84 HOF
18 Steve Carlton 86 HOF
19 Carlton Fisk 82 AS
20 Carlton Fisk 82 HOF
21 Carlton Fisk 84 HOF
22 Carlton Fisk 86 HOF
23 Steve Garvey 84 AS
24 Tony Gwynn 84 AS
25 Tony Gwynn 86 AS
26 Rickey Henderson 88 AS
27 Reggie Jackson 82 HOF
28 Reggie Jackson 82 MVP
29 Reggie Jackson 84 AS
30 Reggie Jackson 84 HOF
31 Reggie Jackson 86 HOF
32 Fergie Jenkins 82 HOF
33 Fergie Jenkins 84 HOF
34 Fred Lynn 82 AS
35 Greg Maddux 88 AS
36 Greg Maddux 88 AS
37 Don Mattingly 84 AS
38 Don Mattingly 86 AS
39 Don Mattingly 88 AS
40 Don Mattingly 88 AS
41 Paul Molitor 82 HOF
42 Paul Molitor 84 HOF
43 Paul Molitor 86 HOF
44 Paul Molitor 88 HOF
45 Joe Morgan 82 HOF
46 Joe Morgan 84 HOF
47 Jack Morris 84 AS
48 Jim Palmer 82 HOF
49 Jim Palmer 84 HOF
50 Dave Parker 86 AS
51 Tony Perez 82 HOF
52 Tony Perez 84 HOF
53 Tony Perez 86 HOF
54 Kirby Puckett 86 AS
55 Kirby Puckett 86 HOF
56 Kirby Puckett 88 MVP AS
57 Nolan Ryan 82 HOF
58 Nolan Ryan 84 HOF
59 Nolan Ryan 86 HOF
60 Nolan Ryan 88 HOF
61 Ryne Sandberg 84 AS
62 Ryne Sandberg 84 HOF
63 Ryne Sandberg 84 MVP
64 Ryne Sandberg 86 AS
65 Ryne Sandberg 86 HOF
66 Mike Schmidt 82 AS
67 Mike Schmidt 82 HOF
68 Mike Schmidt 84 AS
69 Mike Schmidt 84 HOF
70 Mike Schmidt 86 AS
71 Mike Schmidt 86 HOF
72 Mike Schmidt 86 MVP
73 Mike Schmidt 86 HL #4 MVP
74 Mike Schmidt 86 HL #36 MVP
75 Mike Schmidt 88 HOF
76 Tom Seaver 82 HOF
77 Tom Seaver 86 HOF
78 Don Sutton 82 HOF
79 Don Sutton 84 HOF
80 Don Sutton 86 HOF
81 Alan Trammell 84 AS
82 Alan Trammell 88 AS
83 Dave Winfield 82 AS
84 Dave Winfield 82 HOF
85 Dave Winfield 84 AS
86 Dave Winfield 84 HOF
87 Dave Winfield 86 AS
88 Dave Winfield 86 HOF

2002 Donruss Originals Signature Marks

Randomly inserted into packs, these 50 cards feature signed cards. Since these cards have some varying stated print run information, we have notated that information next to their name in our checklist.

Nm-Mt Ex-Mt
1 Kazuhisa Ishii/50
2 Eric Hinske/200 10.00 3.00
3 Cesar Izturis/200 10.00 3.00
4 Roy Oswalt/100 20.00 6.00
5 Jack Cust/200 10.00 3.00
6 Nick Johnson/200 15.00 4.50
7 Jason Hart/200 10.00 3.00
8 Mark Prior/100 80.00 24.00
9 Luis Garcia/200 10.00 3.00
10 Jay Gibbons/200 15.00 4.50
11 Corky Miller/200 10.00 3.00
12 Antonio Perez/100 15.00 4.50
13 Andres Torres/200 10.00 3.00
14 Brandon Claussen/200 25.00 7.50
15 Ed Rogers/200 10.00 3.00
16 Jorge Padilla/200 10.00 3.00
17 Francis Beltran/200 10.00 3.00
18 Kip Wells/200 10.00 3.00
19 Ryan Ludwick/200 10.00 3.00
20 Juan Cruz/100
21 Juan Diaz/200 10.00 3.00
22 Marcus Giles/200 15.00 4.50
23 Joe Kennedy/200 10.00 3.00
24 Wade Miller/100 20.00 6.00
25 Corey Patterson/100 20.00 6.00
26 Angel Berroa/200 15.00 4.50
27 Ricardo Rodriguez/200 10.00 3.00
28 Toby Hall/200 10.00 3.00
29 Carlos Pena/50 20.00 6.00
30 Jason Jennings/200 10.00 3.00
31 Rafael Soriano/200 15.00 4.50
32 Marlon Byrd/100 15.00 4.50
33 Rodrigo Rosario/200 10.00 3.00
34 Rick Ankiel/200
35 Brent Abernathy/200 10.00 3.00
36 Bill Hall/200 10.00 3.00
37 Fernando Rodney/200
38 Josh Pearce/200 10.00 3.00
39 Brian Lawrence/200 10.00 3.00
40 Tim Redding/200 10.00 3.00
41 Matt Guerrier/200
42 Jeremy Giambi/200 10.00 3.00
43 Victor Martinez/200 15.00 4.50
44 Hank Blalock/50 40.00 12.00
45 Larry Bigbie/200
46 Geronimo Gil/200 10.00 3.00
47 So Taguchi/50 40.00 12.00
48 Austin Kearns/200 15.00 4.50
49 Alfonso Soriano/50 50.00 15.00
50 Jose Ortiz/100

2002 Donruss Originals What If 1978

Issued as part of the What If series which were inserted at an overall rate of one in 12 hobby and one in 24 retail. These cards feature players active in 1978 along with what their cards could have looked like if Donruss had been producing cards at that time.

Nm-Mt Ex-Mt
1 Paul Molitor RR 8.00 2.40
2 Alan Trammell RR 8.00 2.40
3 Ozzie Smith RR 15.00 4.50
4 George Brett 15.00 4.50
5 Johnny Bench 10.00 3.00
6 Rod Carew 8.00 2.40
7 Carlton Fisk 8.00 2.40
8 Reggie Jackson 8.00 2.40
9 Dale Murphy 15.00 4.50
10 Joe Morgan 5.00 1.50
11 Eddie Murray 20.00 6.00
12 Jim Palmer 5.00 1.50
13 Tom Seaver 8.00 2.40
14 Willie Stargell 8.00 2.40
15 Dave Winfield 5.00 1.50
16 Dave Parker 5.00 1.50
17 Mike Schmidt 15.00 4.50
18 Eddie Mathews 10.00 3.00
19 Lou Brock 8.00 2.40
20 Willie McCovey 5.00 1.50
21 Andre Dawson 5.00 1.50
22 Dennis Eckersley 5.00 1.50
23 Robin Yount 10.00 3.00
24 Nolan Ryan 15.00 4.50
25 Steve Carlton 5.00 1.50
26 Paul Molitor 8.00 2.40
27 Ozzie Smith 10.00 3.00

2002 Donruss Originals What If 1980

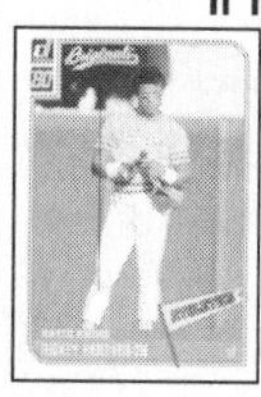

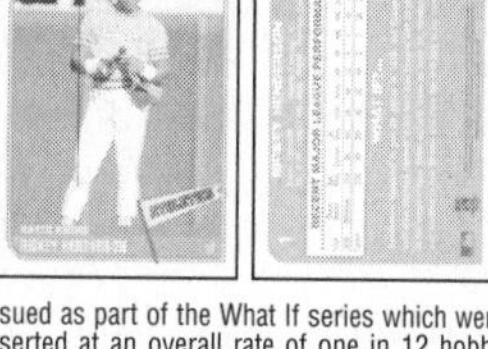

Issued as part of the What If series which were inserted at an overall rate of one in 12 hobby and one in 24 retail. These cards feature players active in 1980 along with what their cards could have looked like if Donruss had been producing cards at that time.

Nm-Mt Ex-Mt
1 Rickey Henderson RR 10.00 3.00
2 Johnny Bench 10.00 3.00
3 George Brett 15.00 4.50
4 Steve Carlton 5.00 1.50
5 Rod Carew 8.00 2.40
6 Gary Carter 8.00 2.40
7 Carlton Fisk 8.00 2.40
8 Reggie Jackson 8.00 2.40
9 Dave Parker 5.00 1.50
10 Dale Murphy 15.00 4.50
11 Paul Molitor 8.00 2.40
12 Mike Schmidt 15.00 4.50
13 Alan Trammell 8.00 2.40
14 Dave Winfield 5.00 1.50
15 Robin Yount 10.00 3.00
16 Joe Morgan 5.00 1.50
17 Jim Palmer 5.00 1.50
18 Nolan Ryan 15.00 4.50
19 Tom Seaver 8.00 2.40
20 Ozzie Smith 10.00 3.00
21 Willie McCovey 5.00 1.50
22 Andre Dawson 5.00 1.50
23 Eddie Murray 10.00 3.00
24 Al Kaline 10.00 3.00
25 Duke Snider 8.00 2.40

2002 Donruss Originals What If Rookies

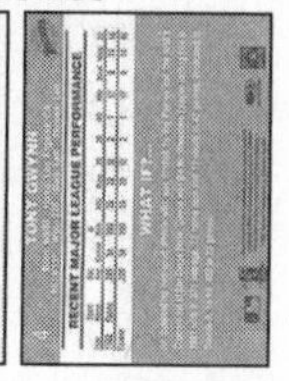

Issued as part of the What If series which were inserted at an overall rate of one in 12 hobby and one in 24 retail. These cards feature players active in the 1980's along with what their cards would have looked like if Donruss had made a card of the featured player that year.

Nm-Mt Ex-Mt
1 Wade Boggs 82 RR 8.00 2.40
2 Ryne Sandberg 82 RR 15.00 4.50
3 Cal Ripken 82 RR 25.00 7.50
4 Tony Gwynn 82 10.00 3.00
5 Don Mattingly 82 25.00 7.50
6 Wade Boggs 82 8.00 2.40
7 Roger Clemens 84 RR 15.00 4.50
8 Kirby Puckett 84 RR 10.00 3.00
9 Eric Davis 84 RR 5.00 1.50
10 Dwight Gooden 84 RR 8.00 2.40
11 Eric Davis 84 5.00 1.50
12 Roger Clemens 84 15.00 4.50
13 Kirby Puckett 84 10.00 3.00
14 Dwight Gooden 84 8.00 2.40
15 Barry Bonds 86 RR 15.00 4.50
16 Will Clark 86 10.00 3.00
17 Barry Larkin 86 10.00 3.00
18 Greg Maddux 86 15.00 4.50
19 Rafael Palmeiro 86 8.00 2.40
20 Craig Biggio 88 8.00 2.40
21 Gary Sheffield 88 5.00 1.50
22 Randy Johnson 88 10.00 3.00
23 Curt Schilling 88 8.00 2.40

1997 Donruss Preferred

The 1997 Donruss Preferred set was issued in one series totalling 200 cards and distributed in five-card packs with a suggested retail of $4.99. The set features color player photos on an all-foil, micro-etched card stock. The set is divided into 100 bronze (5:1 insert odds), 60 silver (1:3), 30 gold (1:12), and 10 platinum (1:48) cards. Notable Rookie Cards include Brian Giles (silver).

Nm-Mt Ex-Mt
COMP.BRONZE SET (100) 25.00 7.50
1 Frank Thomas P 15.00 4.50
2 Ken Griffey Jr. P 20.00 6.00
3 Cecil Fielder B .40 .12
4 Chuck Knoblauch G 4.00 1.20
5 Garret Anderson B .40 .12
6 Greg Maddux P 20.00 6.00
7 Matt Williams S 2.00 .60
8 Marquis Grissom S 2.00 .60
9 Jason Isringhausen B .40 .12
10 Larry Walker S 3.00 .90
11 Charles Nagy B .40 .12
12 Dan Wilson B .40 .12
13 Albert Belle G 4.00 1.20
14 Javier Lopez B .40 .12
15 David Cone B .40 .12
16 Bernard Gilkey B .40 .12
17 Andres Galarraga S 2.00 .60
18 Bill Pulsipher B .40 .12
19 Alex Fernandez B .40 .12
20 Andy Pettitte S 3.00 .90
21 Mark Grudzielanek B .40 .12
22 Juan Gonzalez P 15.00 4.50
23 Reggie Sanders B .40 .12
24 Kenny Lofton G 4.00 1.20
25 Andy Ashby B .40 .12
26 John Wetteland B .40 .12
27 Bobby Bonilla B .40 .12
28 Hideo Nomo G 10.00 3.00
29 Joe Carter B .40 .12
30 Jose Canseco B 1.00 .30
31 Ellis Burks B .40 .12
32 Edgar Martinez S 3.00 .90
33 Chan Ho Park B .40 .12
34 Dave Justice B .40 .12
35 Carlos Delgado B .40 .12
36 Jeff Cirillo S 2.00 .60
37 Charles Johnson B .40 .12
38 Manny Ramirez G 4.00 1.20
39 Greg Vaughn B .40 .12
40 Henry Rodriguez B .40 .12
41 Darryl Strawberry B .60 .18
42 Jim Thome G 10.00 3.00
43 Ryan Klesko S 2.00 .60
44 Ruben Sierra B .40 .12
45 Brian Jordan G 4.00 1.20
46 Tony Gwynn P 15.00 4.50
47 Rafael Palmeiro G 6.00 1.80
48 Dante Bichette S 2.00 .60
49 Ivan Rodriguez G 1.00 .30
50 Mark McGwire G 25.00 7.50
51 Tim Salmon S 3.00 .90
52 Roger Clemens B 2.00 .60
53 Matt Lawton B .40 .12

54 Wade Boggs S 3.00 .90
55 Travis Fryman B .40 .12
56 Bobby Higginson S 2.00 .60
57 John Jaha S 2.00 .60
58 Rondell White S 2.00 .60
59 Tom Glavine S 3.00 .90
60 Eddie Murray S 5.00 1.50
61 Vinny Castilla B .40 .12
62 Todd Hundley B .40 .12
63 Jay Buhner S 2.00 .60
64 Paul O'Neill B .60 .18
65 Steve Finley B .40 .12
66 Kevin Appier B .40 .12
67 Ray Durham B .40 .12
68 Dave Nilsson B .40 .12
69 Jeff Bagwell G 6.00 1.80
70 Al Martin S 2.00 .60
71 Paul Molitor G 6.00 1.80
72 Kevin Brown S 2.00 .60
73 Ron Gant B .40 .12
74 Dwight Gooden B .60 .18
75 Quinton McCracken B .40 .12
76 Rusty Greer S 2.00 .60
77 Juan Guzman B .40 .12
78 Fred McGriff S 3.00 .90
79 Tino Martinez B .60 .18
80 Ray Lankford B .40 .12
81 Ken Caminiti G 4.00 1.20
82 James Baldwin B .40 .12
83 Jermaine Dye G 4.00 1.20
84 Mark Grace S 3.00 .90
85 Pat Hentgen S 2.00 .60
86 Jason Giambi S 5.00 1.50
87 Brian Hunter B .40 .12
88 Andy Benes B .40 .12
89 Jose Rosado B .40 .12
90 Shawn Green B .40 .12
91 Jason Kendall B .40 .12
92 Alex Rodriguez P 20.00 6.00
93 Chipper Jones P 15.00 4.50
94 Barry Bonds G 25.00 7.50
95 Brady Anderson G 4.00 1.20
96 Ryne Sandberg S 8.00 2.40
97 Lance Johnson B .40 .12
98 Cal Ripken P 40.00 12.00
99 Craig Biggio S 6.00 1.80
100 Dean Palmer B .40 .12
101 Gary Sheffield G 4.00 1.20
102 Johnny Damon B .40 .12
103 Mo Vaughn G 4.00 1.20
104 Randy Johnson S 5.00 1.50
105 Raul Mondesi S 2.00 .60
106 Roberto Alomar G 10.00 3.00
107 Mike Piazza P 20.00 6.00
108 Rey Ordonez B .40 .12
109 Barry Larkin G 10.00 3.00
110 Tony Clark S 2.00 .60
111 Bernie Williams S 3.00 .90
112 John Smoltz G 6.00 1.80
113 Moises Alou B .40 .12
114 Will Clark B 1.00 .30
115 Sammy Sosa G 15.00 4.50
116 Jim Edmonds S 2.00 .60
117 Jeff Conine B .40 .12
118 Joey Hamilton B .40 .12
119 Todd Hollandsworth B .40 .12
120 Troy Percival B .40 .12
121 Paul Wilson B .40 .12
122 Ken Hill B .40 .12
123 Mariano Rivera S 3.00 .90
124 Eric Karros B .40 .12
125 Derek Jeter G 25.00 7.50
126 Eric Young S .40 .12
127 John Mabry B .40 .12
128 Gregg Jefferies B .40 .12
129 Ismael Valdes S 2.00 .60
130 Marty Cordova B .40 .12
131 Omar Vizquel B .40 .12
132 Mike Mussina S 5.00 1.50
133 Darin Erstad B .40 .12
134 Edgar Renteria S 2.00 .60
135 Billy Wagner B .40 .12
136 Alex Ochoa B .40 .12
137 Luis Castillo B .40 .12
138 Rocky Coppinger B .40 .12
139 Mike Sweeney B .40 .12
140 Michael Tucker B .40 .12
141 Chris Snopek B .40 .12
142 Dmitri Young S 2.00 .60
143 Andruw Jones P 15.00 4.50
144 Mike Cameron S 2.00 .60
145 Brant Brown B .40 .12
146 Todd Walker G 4.00 1.20
147 Nomar Garciaparra G 15.00 4.50
148 Glendon Rusch B .40 .12
149 Karim Garcia S 2.00 .60
150 Bubba Trammell S RC 2.00 .60
151 Todd Greene B .40 .12
152 Wilton Guerrero G 4.00 1.20
153 Scott Spiezio B .40 .12
154 Brooks Kieschnick B .40 .12
155 Vladimir Guerrero G 10.00 3.00
156 Brian Giles S RC 8.00 2.40
157 Pokey Reese B .40 .12
158 Jason Dickson G 4.00 1.20
159 Kevin Orie S 4.00 1.20
160 Scott Rolen G 6.00 1.80
161 Bartolo Colon S 2.00 .60
162 Shannon Stewart G 4.00 1.20
163 Wendell Magee B .40 .12
164 Jose Guillen S 2.00 .60
165 Bob Abreu S 2.00 .60
166 Deivi Cruz B RC .40 .12
167 Alex Rodriguez NT B 1.50 .45
168 Frank Thomas NT B 1.00 .30
169 Cal Ripken NT B 3.00 .90
170 Chipper Jones NT B 1.00 .30
171 Mike Piazza NT B 1.50 .45
172 Tony Gwynn NT S 6.00 1.80
173 Juan Gonzalez NT B 1.00 .30
174 Kenny Lofton NT S 2.00 .60
175 Ken Griffey Jr. NT B 1.50 .45
176 Mark McGwire NT B 2.50 .75
177 Jeff Bagwell NT B .60 .18
178 Paul Molitor NT S 3.00 .90
179 Andruw Jones NT B .40 .12
180 Manny Ramirez NT S 2.00 .60
181 Ken Caminiti NT S 2.00 .60
182 Barry Bonds NT B 2.50 .75
183 Mo Vaughn NT B .40 .12
184 Derek Jeter NT B 2.50 .75
185 Barry Larkin NT S 5.00 1.50
186 Ivan Rodriguez NT B 1.00 .30
187 Albert Belle NT S 2.00 .60
188 John Smoltz NT S 3.00 .90
189 C.Knoblauch NT S 2.00 .60
190 Brian Jordan NT S 2.00 .60
191 Gary Sheffield NT S 2.00 .60
192 Jim Thome NT S 5.00 1.50
193 Brady Anderson NT S 2.00 .60
194 Hideo Nomo NT S 5.00 1.50
195 Sammy Sosa NT S 8.00 2.40
196 Greg Maddux NT B 1.50 .45
197 V.Guerrero CL B 1.00 .30
198 Scott Rolen CL B .60 .18
199 Todd Walker CL B .40 .12
200 N.Garciaparra CL B 1.25 .35

1997 Donruss Preferred Cut to the Chase

These die cut cards parallel their more common non-die cut siblings. The set is broken into four different groupings by color and scarcity. Pack odds for the different colored subsets become more difficult in this way: Bronze is the easiest, then Silver, Gold and Platinum being the hardest to pull.

Nm-Mt Ex-Mt
*BRONZE STARS: 3X TO 8X BASIC...
*SILVER STARS: 1.5X TO 4X BASIC...
*SILVER ROOKIES: .6X TO 1.5X BASIC
*GOLD STARS: 1X TO 2.5X BASIC CARDS
*PLAT.STARS: 1X TO 2.5X BASIC CARDS

1997 Donruss Preferred Precious Metals

Randomly inserted in packs, this 25-card set is a partial parallel version of the regular set printed on actual silver, gold, or platinum. No more than 100 of each card was produced.

Nm-Mt Ex-Mt
COMPLETE SET (25)
1 Frank Thomas P 50.00 15.00
2 Ken Griffey Jr. P 80.00 24.00
3 Greg Maddux P 80.00 24.00
4 Albert Belle G 30.00 9.00
5 Juan Gonzalez P 50.00 15.00
6 Kenny Lofton G 30.00 9.00
7 Tony Gwynn P 60.00 18.00
8 Ivan Rodriguez G 50.00 15.00
9 Mark McGwire G 120.00 36.00
10 Matt Williams S 30.00 9.00
11 Wade Boggs S 40.00 12.00
12 Eddie Murray S 50.00 15.00
13 Jeff Bagwell G 40.00 12.00
14 Ken Caminiti G 30.00 9.00
15 Alex Rodriguez P 80.00 24.00
16 Chipper Jones P 50.00 15.00
17 Barry Bonds G 120.00 36.00
18 Cal Ripken P 150.00 45.00
19 Mo Vaughn G 30.00 9.00
20 Mike Piazza P 80.00 24.00
21 Derek Jeter G 120.00 36.00
22 Bernie Williams S 40.00 12.00
23 Andruw Jones P 30.00 9.00
24 Vladimir Guerrero G 50.00 15.00
25 Jose Guillen S 30.00 9.00

1997 Donruss Preferred Staremasters Samples

Promotional samples of Staremasters inserts were distributed within wholesale dealer order forms prior to the products release (one card per order). The Samples parallel the regular Staremasters inserts except for the bold "SAMPLE" text running diagonally across both front and back of the card. In addition, Sample cards are numbered as "PROMO/1500" on back rather than the typical serial numbering of the true insert cards. Please see the multiplier provided below for values on the singles.

Nm-Mt Ex-Mt
COMPLETE SET (20) 40.00 12.00
1 Alex Rodriguez 3.00 .90
2 Frank Thomas 1.25 .35
3 Chipper Jones 2.50 .75
4 Cal Ripken 5.00 1.50
5 Mike Piazza 4.00 1.20
6 Juan Gonzalez 1.00 .30
7 Derek Jeter 5.00 1.50
8 Jeff Bagwell 1.25 .35
9 Ken Griffey Jr. 3.00 .90
10 Tony Gwynn 2.50 .75
11 Barry Bonds 2.50 .75
12 Albert Belle .50 .15
13 Greg Maddux 2.50 .75
14 Mark McGwire 4.00 1.20
15 Ken Caminiti .50 .15
16 Hideo Nomo 1.00 .30
17 Gary Sheffield 1.25 .35
18 Andruw Jones 1.50 .45
19 Mo Vaughn .50 .15
20 Ivan Rodriguez 1.25 .35

1997 Donruss Preferred Staremasters

Randomly inserted in packs, this 20-card set features up-close face photos of superstar players printed on all-foil card stock and accented with holographic foil stamping. Each card is sequentially numbered out of 1,500.

Nm-Mt Ex-Mt
1 Alex Rodriguez 12.00 3.60
2 Frank Thomas 8.00 2.40

3 Chipper Jones 8.00 2.40
4 Cal Ripken 25.00 7.50
5 Mike Piazza 12.00 3.60
6 Juan Gonzalez 8.00 2.40
7 Derek Jeter 20.00 6.00
8 Jeff Bagwell 5.00 1.50
9 Ken Griffey Jr. 12.00 3.60
10 Tony Gwynn 10.00 3.00
11 Barry Bonds 20.00 6.00
12 Albert Belle 4.00 1.20
13 Greg Maddux 12.00 3.60
14 Mark McGwire 20.00 6.00
15 Ken Caminiti 4.00 1.20
16 Hideo Nomo 8.00 2.40
17 Gary Sheffield 4.00 1.20
18 Andruw Jones 4.00 1.20
19 Mo Vaughn 4.00 1.20
20 Ivan Rodriguez 8.00 2.40

1997 Donruss Preferred Tin Packs

Each pack of Donruss Preferred Baseball cards comes in one of 25 different player tins. These 25 tins come packed in hobby only, sequentially numbered display tins. Less than 1,200 of each Hobby-Only Display Master Tins were produced with each featuring one of 25 star players. The tins are unnumbered and checklisted below alphabetically.

Nm-Mt Ex-Mt
COMPLETE SET (25) 20.00 6.00
*GOLD PACKS: 4X TO 10X BASIC PACKS
ONE GOLD PACK PER BOX
GOLD PACKS: 1200 SERIAL #'d SETS
*BLUE BOXES: 3X TO 8X BASIC PACKS
BLUE BOXES: 1200 SERIAL #'d SETS
*GOLD BOXES: 8X TO 20X BASIC PACKS
GOLD BOXES: 299 SERIAL #'d SETS..
PRICES BELOW REFER TO OPENED PACKS
1 Jeff Bagwell .30 .09
2 Albert Belle .25 .07
3 Barry Bonds 1.50 .45
4 Roger Clemens 1.25 .35
5 Juan Gonzalez .50 .15
6 Ken Griffey Jr. 1.00 .30
7 Tony Gwynn .75 .23
8 Derek Jeter 1.50 .45
9 Andruw Jones .25 .07
10 Chipper Jones .50 .15
11 Kenny Lofton .25 .07
12 Greg Maddux 1.00 .30
13 Mark McGwire 1.50 .45
14 Hideo Nomo .50 .15
15 Mike Piazza 1.00 .30
16 Manny Ramirez .25 .07
17 Cal Ripken 2.00 .60
18 Alex Rodriguez 1.00 .30
19 Ivan Rodriguez .50 .15
20 Ryne Sandberg 1.00 .30
21 Gary Sheffield .25 .07
22 John Smoltz .30 .09
23 Sammy Sosa 1.00 .30
24 Frank Thomas .50 .15
25 Mo Vaughn .25 .07

1997 Donruss Preferred X-Ponential Power

Randomly inserted in packs, this 20-card set features color player action photos of two of the best hitters from 10 of the hottest teams in the league printed on die-cut thick plastic card stock with gold holographic foil treatment. When the cards of both superstar teammates are placed side-by-side, their cards form a complete "X." Only 3,000 of each card was produced and sequentially numbered.

Nm-Mt Ex-Mt
COMPLETE SET (20) 200.00 60.00
1A Manny Ramirez 3.00 .90
1B Jim Thome 8.00 2.40
2A Paul Molitor 5.00 1.50
2B Chuck Knoblauch 3.00 .90
3A Ivan Rodriguez 8.00 2.40
3B Juan Gonzalez 8.00 2.40
4A Albert Belle 3.00 .90
4B Frank Thomas 8.00 2.40
5A Roberto Alomar 8.00 2.40
5B Cal Ripken 30.00 9.00
6A Tim Salmon 5.00 1.50
6B Jim Edmonds 3.00 .90
7A Ken Griffey Jr. 15.00 4.50
7B Alex Rodriguez 15.00 4.50
8A Chipper Jones 8.00 2.40
8B Andruw Jones 3.00 .90
9A Mike Piazza 15.00 4.50
9B Raul Mondesi 3.00 .90
10A Tony Gwynn 12.00 3.60
10B Ken Caminiti 3.00 .90

1997 Donruss Preferred Tins Fanfest

This 25-tin set was given out at the 1997 Fanfest and is parallel to the Donruss Preferred Tin Packs set. The difference is found in the gold trim on the tin.

Nm-Mt Ex-Mt
COMPLETE SET (25) 40.00 12.00
1 Jeff Bagwell 1.25 .35
2 Albert Belle .50 .15
3 Barry Bonds 2.50 .75
4 Roger Clemens 2.50 .75
5 Juan Gonzalez 1.25 .35
6 Ken Griffey Jr. 3.00 .90
7 Tony Gwynn 2.50 .75
8 Derek Jeter 5.00 1.50
9 Andruw Jones 1.50 .45
10 Chipper Jones 2.50 .75
11 Kenny Lofton .75 .23
12 Greg Maddux 3.00 .90
13 Mark McGwire 4.00 1.20
14 Hideo Nomo 1.25 .35
15 Mike Piazza 3.00 .90
16 Manny Ramirez 1.25 .35
17 Cal Ripken 5.00 1.50
18 Alex Rodriguez 3.00 .90
19 Ivan Rodriguez 1.25 .35
20 Ryne Sandberg 1.50 .45
21 Gary Sheffield 1.00 .30
22 John Smoltz .50 .15
23 Sammy Sosa 2.50 .75
24 Frank Thomas 1.25 .35
25 Mo Vaughn .50 .15

1998 Donruss Preferred

The Donruss Preferred set was issued in one series totalling 200 cards and distributed in five-card packs with a suggested retail price of $4.99. The fronts feature color player photos on micro-etched backgrounds with specially micro-etched borders unique to each color. The set is fractured into varying levels of scarcity as follows: 10 Executive Suite cards with an insertion rate of 1:65, 20 Field Box cards inserted 1:23, 30 Club Level cards inserted 1:12, 40 Mezzanine cards inserted 1:6, and 100 Grand Stand cards inserted four or five per pack.

Nm-Mt Ex-Mt
COMP.GS (100) 25.00 7.50
COMMON GRAND STAND .30 .09
COMP.MEZZANINE (40) 60.00 18.00
COMMON MEZZANINE 2.00 .60
COMP.CLUB LEVEL (30) 100.00 30.00
COMMON CLUB LEVEL 3.00 .90
COMP.FIELD BOX (20) 150.00 45.00
COMMON FIELD BOX 4.00 1.20
COMP.EXEC.SUITE (10) 150.00 45.00
COMMON EXEC.SUITE 10.00 3.00
1 Ken Griffey Jr. EX 15.00 4.50
2 Frank Thomas EX 10.00 3.00
3 Cal Ripken EX 30.00 9.00
4 Alex Rodriguez EX 15.00 4.50
5 Greg Maddux EX 15.00 4.50
6 Mike Piazza EX 15.00 4.50
7 Chipper Jones EX 10.00 3.00
8 Tony Gwynn FB 12.00 3.60
9 Derek Jeter FB 25.00 7.50
10 Jeff Bagwell EX 10.00 3.00
11 Juan Gonzalez EX 10.00 3.00
12 Nomar Garciaparra EX 15.00 4.50
13 Andruw Jones FB 4.00 1.20
14 Hideo Nomo FB 10.00 3.00
15 Roger Clemens FB 20.00 6.00
16 Mark McGwire FB 25.00 7.50
17 Scott Rolen FB 6.00 1.80
18 Vladimir Guerrero FB 10.00 3.00
19 Barry Bonds FB 25.00 7.50
20 Darin Erstad FB 4.00 1.20
21 Albert Belle FB 4.00 1.20
22 Kenny Lofton FB 4.00 1.20
23 Mo Vaughn FB 4.00 1.20
24 Tony Clark FB 4.00 1.20
25 Ivan Rodriguez FB 10.00 3.00
26 Larry Walker CB 5.00 1.50
27 Eddie Murray CB 8.00 2.40
28 Andy Pettitte CB 5.00 1.50
29 Roberto Alomar CB 8.00 2.40
30 Randy Johnson CB 8.00 2.40
31 Manny Ramirez CB 3.00 .90
32 Paul Molitor FB 6.00 1.80
33 Mike Mussina CB 8.00 2.40
34 Jim Thome FB 10.00 3.00
35 Tino Martinez CB 5.00 1.50
36 Gary Sheffield CB 3.00 .90
37 Chuck Knoblauch CB 3.00 .90
38 Bernie Williams CB 5.00 1.50
39 Tim Salmon CB 5.00 1.50
40 Sammy Sosa CB 12.00 3.60
41 Wade Boggs ME 3.00 .90
42 Will Clark GS .75 .23
43 Andres Galarraga CB 3.00 .90
44 Raul Mondesi CB 3.00 .90
45 Rickey Henderson GS .75 .23
46 Jose Canseco GS .75 .23
47 Pedro Martinez GS .75 .23
48 Jay Buhner GS .30 .09
49 Ryan Klesko GS .30 .09
50 Barry Larkin CB 8.00 2.40
51 Charles Johnson GS .30 .09
52 Tom Glavine GS .50 .15
53 Edgar Martinez CB 5.00 1.50
54 Fred McGriff GS .50 .15
55 Moises Alou ME 2.00 .60
56 Dante Bichette GS .30 .09
57 Jim Edmonds CB 3.00 .90
58 Mark Grace ME 3.00 .90
59 Chan Ho Park ME 2.00 .60
60 Justin Thompson ME 2.00 .60
61 John Smoltz ME 3.00 .90
62 Craig Biggio CB 5.00 1.50
63 Ken Caminiti ME 2.00 .60
64 Deion Sanders ME 3.00 .90
65 Carlos Delgado GS .30 .09
66 David Justice CB 3.00 .90
67 J.T. Snow GS .30 .09
68 Jason Giambi CB 8.00 2.40
69 Garret Anderson ME 2.00 .60
70 Rondell White ME 2.00 .60
71 Matt Williams ME 2.00 .60
72 Brady Anderson ME 2.00 .60
73 Eric Karros GS .30 .09
74 Javier Lopez GS .30 .09
75 Pat Hentgen GS .30 .09
76 Todd Hundley GS .30 .09
77 Ray Lankford GS .30 .09
78 Denny Neagle GS .30 .09
79 Henry Rodriguez GS .30 .09
80 Sandy Alomar Jr. ME 2.00 .60
81 Rafael Palmeiro ME 3.00 .90
82 Robin Ventura GS .30 .09
83 John Olerud GS .30 .09
84 Omar Vizquel GS .30 .09
85 Joe Randa GS .30 .09
86 Lance Johnson GS .30 .09
87 Kevin Brown GS .50 .15
88 Curt Schilling GS .50 .15
89 Ismael Valdes GS .30 .09
90 Francisco Cordova GS .30 .09
91 David Cone GS .30 .09
92 Paul O'Neill GS .50 .15
93 Jimmy Key GS .30 .09
94 Brad Radke GS .30 .09
95 Kevin Appier GS .30 .09
96 Al Martin GS .30 .09
97 Rusty Greer ME 2.00 .60
98 Reggie Jefferson GS .30 .09
99 Ron Coomer GS .30 .09
100 Vinny Castilla GS .30 .09
101 Bobby Bonilla ME 2.00 .60
102 Eric Young GS .30 .09
103 Tony Womack GS .30 .09
104 Jason Kendall GS .30 .09
105 Jeff Suppan GS .30 .09
106 Shawn Estes ME 2.00 .60
107 Shawn Green GS .30 .09
108 Edgardo Alfonzo ME 2.00 .60
109 Alan Benes ME 2.00 .60
110 Bobby Higginson GS .30 .09
111 Mark Grudzielanek GS .30 .09
112 Wilton Guerrero GS .30 .09
113 Todd Greene ME 2.00 .60
114 Pokey Reese GS .30 .09
115 Jose Guillen CB 3.00 .90
116 Neifi Perez ME 2.00 .60
117 Luis Castillo GS .30 .09
118 Edgar Renteria GS .30 .09
119 Karim Garcia GS .30 .09
120 Butch Huskey GS .30 .09
121 Michael Tucker GS .30 .09
122 Jason Dickson GS .30 .09
123 Todd Walker ME 2.00 .60
124 Brian Jordan GS .30 .09
125 Joe Carter GS .30 .09
126 Matt Morris ME 2.00 .60
127 Brett Tomko ME 2.00 .60
128 Mike Cameron CB 3.00 .90
129 Russ Davis GS .30 .09
130 Shannon Stewart ME 2.00 .60
131 Kevin Orie GS .30 .09
132 Scott Spiezio GS .30 .09
133 Brian Giles GS .30 .09
134 Raul Casanova GS .30 .09
135 Jose Cruz Jr. CB 3.00 .90
136 Hideki Irabu GS .30 .09
137 Bubba Trammell GS .30 .09
138 Richard Hidalgo CB 3.00 .90
139 Paul Konerko CB 3.00 .90
140 Todd Helton FB 6.00 1.80
141 Miguel Tejada CB 5.00 1.50
142 Fernando Tatis ME 2.00 .60
143 Ben Grieve FB 4.00 1.20
144 Travis Lee FB 4.00 1.20
145 Mark Kotsay CB 3.00 .90
146 Eli Marrero ME 2.00 .60
147 David Ortiz CB 3.00 .90
148 Juan Encarnacion ME 2.00 .60
149 Jaret Wright ME 2.00 .60
150 Livan Hernandez CB 3.00 .90
151 Ruben Rivera GS .30 .09
152 Brad Fullmer ME 2.00 .60
153 Dennis Reyes GS .30 .09
154 Enrique Wilson ME 2.00 .60
155 Todd Dunwoody ME 2.00 .60
156 Derrick Gibson ME 2.00 .60
157 Aaron Boone ME 2.00 .60
158 Ron Wright ME 2.00 .60
159 Preston Wilson ME 2.00 .60
160 Abraham Nunez GS .30 .09
161 Shane Monahan GS .30 .09
162 Carl Pavano GS .30 .09
163 Derrek Lee GS .30 .09
164 Jeff Abbott GS .30 .09
165 Wes Helms ME 2.00 .60
166 Brian Rose GS .30 .09
167 Bobby Estalella GS .30 .09

168 Ken Griffey Jr. PP GS 1.25 .35
169 Frank Thomas PP GS .75 .23
170 Cal Ripken PP GS 2.50 .75
171 Alex Rodriguez PP GS 1.25 .35
172 Greg Maddux PP GS 1.25 .35
173 Mike Piazza PP GS 1.25 .35
174 Chipper Jones PP GS .75 .23
175 Tony Gwynn PP GS .50 .15
176 Derek Jeter PP GS 2.00 .60
177 Jeff Bagwell PP GS .50 .15
178 Juan Gonzalez PP GS .75 .23
179 N. Garciaparra PP GS 1.25 .35
180 Andruw Jones PP GS .30 .09
181 Hideo Nomo PP GS .75 .23
182 R.Clemens PP GS 1.50 .45
183 Mark McGwire PP GS 2.00 .60
184 Scott Rolen PP GS .50 .15
185 Barry Bonds PP GS 2.00 .60
186 Darin Erstad PP GS .30 .09
187 Mo Vaughn PP GS .30 .09
188 Ivan Rodriguez PP GS .75 .23
189 Larry Walker PP ME 3.00 .90
190 Andy Pettitte PP GS .50 .15
191 R.Johnson PP ME 5.00 1.50
192 Paul Molitor PP GS .50 .15
193 Jim Thome PP GS .75 .23
194 Tino Martinez PP ME 3.00 .90
195 Gary Sheffield PP GS .30 .09
196 Albert Belle PP GS .30 .09
197 Jose Cruz Jr. PP GS .30 .09
198 Todd Helton CL GS .30 .09
199 Ben Grieve CL GS .30 .09
200 Paul Konerko CL GS .30 .09

1998 Donruss Preferred Seating

This 200-card set is a die-cut parallel version of the base set with each setion having a unique die-cut shape and printed to varying levels of scarcity.

Nm-Mt Ex-Mt
*GRAND STAND: 4X TO 10X BASIC CARDS
*MEZZANINE: .75X TO 2X BASIC CARDS
*CLUB LEVEL: .75X TO 2X BASIC CARDS
*FIELD BOX STARS: .75X TO 2X BASIC CARDS
*EXEC.SUITE STARS: .75X TO 2X BASIC CARDS

1998 Donruss Preferred Great X-Pectations Samples

These cards were distributed to dealers (one per wholesale order form) to preview the upcoming 1998 Donruss Preferred release. The cards are parallel to the regular-issue Great X-Pectations inserts except for the text "SAMPLE" running across the back and lack of serial numbering.

Nm-Mt Ex-Mt
COMPLETE SET (26) 200.00 60.00
1 Jeff Bagwell 6.00 1.80
Travis Lee
2 Jose Cruz Jr. 20.00 6.00
Ken Griffey Jr.
3 Larry Walker 2.00 .60
Ben Grieve
4 FrankThomas 10.00 3.00
Todd Helton
5 Jim Thome 2.50 .75
Paul Konerko
6 Alex Rodriguez 15.00 4.50
Miguel Tejada
7 Greg Maddux 12.00 3.60
Livan Hernandez
8 Roger Clemens 10.00 3.00
Jaret Wright
9 Albert Belle 2.50 .75
Juan Encarnacion
10 Mo Vaughn 2.00 .60
David Ortiz
11 Manny Ramirez 6.00 1.80
Mark Kotsay
12 Tim Salmon 2.00 .60
Brad Fullmer UER
misspelled Fulmer
13 Cal Ripken 20.00 6.00
Fernando Tatis
14 Hideo Nomo 10.00 3.00
Hideki Irabu
15 Mike Piazza 15.00 4.50
Todd Greene
16 Gary Sheffield 5.00 1.50
Ricardo Hidalgo
17 Paul Molitor 6.00 1.80
Darin Erstad
18 Ivan Rodriguez 6.00 1.80
Eli Marrero
19 Ken Caminiti 2.00 .60
Todd Walker
20 Tony Gwynn 10.00 3.00
Jose Guillen
21 Derek Jeter 20.00 6.00
Nomar Garciaparra
22 Chipper Jones 12.00 3.60
Scott Rolen
23 Juan Gonzalez 5.00 1.50
Andruw Jones
24 Barry Bonds 8.00 2.40
Vladimir Guerrero
25 Mark McGwire 20.00 6.00
Tony Clark
26 Bernie Williams 5.00 1.50
Mike Cameron

1998 Donruss Preferred Great X-Pectations

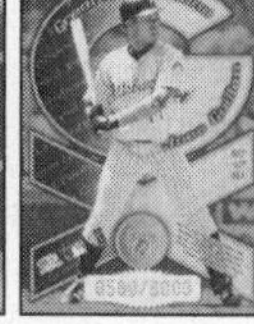

Randomly inserted in packs, this 26-card set features double-sided cards with color photos of a veteran on one side and a young star on the other. Only 2700 sequentially numbered regular sets were produced.

Nm-Mt Ex-Mt
COMPLETE SET (26) 250.00 75.00
*DIE CUTS: .75X TO 2X BASIC X-PECTATION
DIE CUT PRINT RUN 300 SERIAL #'d SETS
RANDOM INSERTS IN PACKS
1 Jeff Bagwell 5.00 1.50
Travis Lee
2 Jose Cruz Jr. 12.00 3.60
Ken Griffey Jr.
3 Larry Walker 5.00 1.50
Ben Grieve
4 Frank Thomas 8.00 2.40
Todd Helton
5 Jim Thome 8.00 2.40
Paul Konerko
6 Alex Rodriguez 12.00 3.60
Miguel Tejada
7 Greg Maddux 12.00 3.60
Livan Hernandez
8 Roger Clemens 15.00 4.50
Jaret Wright
9 Albert Belle 3.00 .90
Juan Encarnacion
10 Mo Vaughn 3.00 .90
David Ortiz
11 Manny Ramirez 3.00 .90
Mark Kotsay
12 Tim Salmon 5.00 1.50
Brad Fullmer UER
misspelled Fulmer
13 Cal Ripken 25.00 7.50
Fernando Tatis
14 Hideo Nomo 8.00 2.40
Hideki Irabu
15 Mike Piazza 12.00 3.60
Todd Greene
16 Gary Sheffield 3.00 .90
Richard Hidalgo
17 Paul Molitor 5.00 1.50
Darin Erstad
18 Ivan Rodriguez 8.00 2.40
Eli Marrero
19 Ken Caminiti 3.00 .90
Todd Walker
20 Tony Gwynn 10.00 3.00
Jose Guillen
21 Deter Jeter 20.00 6.00
Nomar Garciaparra
22 Chipper Jones 8.00 2.40
Scott Rolen
23 Juan Gonzalez 8.00 2.40
Andruw Jones
24 Barry Bonds 20.00 6.00
Vladimir Guerrero
25 Mark McGwire 20.00 6.00
Tony Clark
26 Bernie Williams 5.00 1.50
Mike Cameron

1998 Donruss Preferred Precious Metals

Randomly inserted in packs, this 30-card set is a partial parallel version of the base set and features the base cards of 30 of the top players printed on card sock made using real Silver, Gold, or Platinum. Only 50 of each card was produced.

Nm-Mt Ex-Mt
1 Ken Griffey Jr. 80.00 24.00
2 Frank Thomas 50.00 15.00
3 Cal Ripken 150.00 45.00
4 Alex Rodriguez 80.00 24.00
5 Greg Maddux 80.00 24.00
6 Mike Piazza 80.00 24.00
7 Chipper Jones 50.00 15.00
8 Tony Gwynn 60.00 18.00
9 Derek Jeter 120.00 36.00
10 Jeff Bagwell 40.00 12.00
11 Juan Gonzalez 50.00 15.00
12 Nomar Garciaparra 80.00 24.00
13 Andruw Jones 25.00 7.50
14 Hideo Nomo 50.00 15.00
15 Roger Clemens 100.00 30.00
16 Mark McGwire 120.00 36.00
17 Scott Rolen 40.00 12.00
18 Barry Bonds 120.00 36.00
19 Darin Erstad 25.00 7.50
20 Kenny Lofton 25.00 7.50
21 Mo Vaughn 25.00 7.50
22 Ivan Rodriguez 50.00 15.00
23 Randy Johnson 50.00 15.00
24 Paul Molitor 40.00 12.00
25 Jose Cruz Jr. 25.00 7.50
26 Paul Konerko 25.00 7.50
27 Todd Helton 40.00 12.00
28 Ben Grieve 25.00 7.50
29 Travis Lee 25.00 7.50
30 Mark Kotsay 25.00 7.50

1998 Donruss Preferred Tin Packs

Each pack of Donruss Preferred Baseball cards comes in one of 24 different player tins. These 24 tins come packed within the large hobby only tins. Retail packaging features special double-wide tins that mix-and-match the different players.

Nm-Mt Ex-Mt
COMPLETE SET (24) 15.00 4.50
*GOLD PACKS: 8X TO 20X BASIC PACKS

GOLD PACKS: RANDOM INSERTS IN BOXES
GOLD PACK PRINT RUN 199 SERIAL #'d SETS
*SILVER PACKS: 3X TO 8X BASIC PACKS
SILVER PACK RANDOM INSERTS IN BOXES
SILVER PACK PR.RUN 999 SERIAL #'d SETS
*GREEN BOXES: 3X TO 8X BASIC PACKS
GREEN BOX PRINT RUN 999 SERIAL #'d SETS
*GOLD BOXES: 8X TO 20X BASIC PACKS
GOLD BOX PRINT RUN 199 SERIAL #'d SETS
PRICES BELOW ARE FOR OPEN GREEN PACKS
1 Todd Helton .40 .12
2 Ben Grieve .25 .07
3 Cal Ripken 2.00 .60
4 Alex Rodriguez 1.00 .30
5 Greg Maddux 1.00 .30
6 Mike Piazza 1.00 .30
7 Chipper Jones .60 .18
8 Travis Lee .25 .07
9 Derek Jeter 1.50 .45
10 Jeff Bagwell .40 .12
11 Juan Gonzalez .60 .18
12 Mark McGwire 1.50 .45
13 Hideo Nomo .60 .18
14 Roger Clemens 1.25 .35
15 Andruw Jones .25 .07
16 Paul Molitor .40 .12
17 Vladimir Guerrero .60 .18
18 Jose Cruz Jr. .25 .07
19 Nomar Garciaparra PH 1.00 .30
20 Scott Rolen PH .40 .12
21 Ken Griffey Jr. PH 1.00 .30
22 Larry Walker PH .40 .12
23 Frank Thomas PH .60 .18
24 Tony Gwynn PH .75 .23

1998 Donruss Preferred Tin Packs Double-Wide

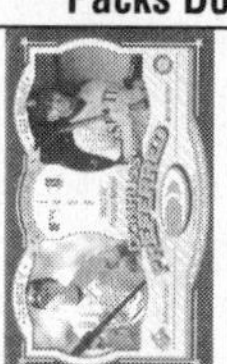

Available only in retail outlets, these special "Double-Wide" blue tin packs contained five cards per pack and carried a $5.99 SRP. The checklist and player images used are identical to that of the green hobby Tin Packs, but the retail Double-Wide packs paired up two players at a time.

Nm-Mt Ex-Mt
COMPLETE SET (12) 25.00 7.50
1 Todd Helton .75 .23
Ben Grieve
2 Cal Ripken 3.00 .90
Alex Rodriguez
3 Greg Maddux 1.25 .35
Mike Piazza
4 Chipper Jones 1.00 .30
Travis Lee
5 Derek Jeter 2.50 .75
Jeff Bagwell
6 Juan Gonzalez 2.50 .75
Mark McGwire
7 Hideo Nomo 2.00 .60
Roger Clemens
8 Andruw Jones .75 .23
Paul Molitor
9 Vladimir Guerrero 1.00 .30
Jose Cruz Jr.
10 Nomar Garciaparra 1.50 .45
Scott Rolen PH
11 Ken Griffey Jr. 1.50 .45
Larry Walker PH
12 Frank Thomas 1.25 .35
Tony Gwynn PH

1998 Donruss Preferred Title Waves

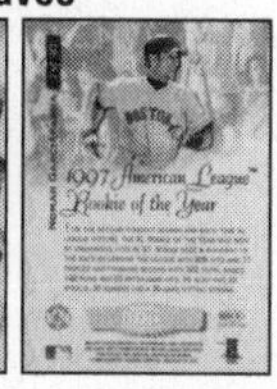

Randomly inserted in packs, this 30-card set features color photos of players who have won various titles in 1993, '95, '96, and '97. The cards are die-cut so as to link up with cards commemorating awards won from the same year or type of title and are printed on platic card stock. The cards are sequentially numbered to the year in which the title was won.

Nm-Mt Ex-Mt
COMPLETE SET (30) 300.00 90.00
1 Nomar Garciaparra 20.00 6.00
97 AL ROY
2 Scott Rolen 8.00 2.40
97 NL ROY
3 Roger Clemens 25.00 7.50
97 AL Cy Young
4 Gary Sheffield 5.00 1.50
97 World Series
5 Jeff Bagwell 8.00 2.40
97 Wildcard
6 Cal Ripken 40.00 12.00
97 AL East Penn.
7 Frank Thomas 12.00 3.60
97 AL Batting
8 Ken Griffey Jr. 20.00 6.00
97 AL HR
9 Larry Walker 8.00 2.40
97 NL HR
10 Derek Jeter 30.00 9.00
96 AL ROY
11 Juan Gonzalez 12.00 3.60
96 AL MVP
12 Bernie Williams 8.00 2.40
96 ALCS MVP
13 Andruw Jones 5.00 1.50
96 NLCS
14 Andy Pettitte 8.00 2.40
96 World Series
15 Ivan Rodriguez 12.00 3.60
96 AL West Penn.
16 Alex Rodriguez 20.00 6.00
96 AL Batting
17 Mark McGwire 30.00 9.00
96 AL HR
18 Andres Galarraga 5.00 1.50
96 NL HR
19 Hideo Nomo 12.00 3.60
95 ROY
20 Mo Vaughn 5.00 1.50
95 AL MVP
21 Randy Johnson 12.00 3.60
95 AL Cy Young
22 Chipper Jones 12.00 3.60
95 World Series
23 Greg Maddux 20.00 6.00
95 World Series
24 Manny Ramirez 5.00 1.50
95 ALCS
25 Tony Gwynn 15.00 4.50
95 NL Batting
26 Albert Belle 5.00 1.50
95 AL HR
27 Kenny Lofton 5.00 1.50
95 AL SB
28 Mike Piazza 20.00 6.00
93 NL ROY
29 Paul Molitor 8.00 2.40
93 World Series
30 Barry Bonds 30.00 9.00
93 NL HR

1997 Donruss Signature

Distributed in five-card packs with one authentic autographed card per pack, this 100-card set was issued in two series. However, these regular cards were issued with both series and one could make sets from either series. These packs carried a suggested retail price of $14.99. The fronts feature color player photos with player information on the backs. The only Rookie Cards of note in this set are Jose Cruz Jr. and Mark Kotsay.

Nm-Mt Ex-Mt
COMPLETE SET (100) 50.00 15.00
1 Mark McGwire 3.00 .90
2 Kenny Lofton .50 .15
3 Tony Gwynn 1.50 .45
4 Tony Clark .50 .15
5 Tim Salmon .75 .23
6 Ken Griffey Jr. 2.00 .60
7 Mike Piazza 2.00 .60
8 Greg Maddux 2.00 .60
9 Roberto Alomar 1.25 .35
10 Andres Galarraga .50 .15
11 Roger Clemens 2.50 .75
12 Bernie Williams .75 .23
13 Rondell White .50 .15
14 Kevin Appier .50 .15
15 Ray Lankford .50 .15
16 Frank Thomas 1.25 .35
17 Will Clark 1.25 .35
18 Chipper Jones 1.25 .35
19 Jeff Bagwell .75 .23
20 Manny Ramirez .50 .15
21 Ryne Sandberg 2.00 .60
22 Paul Molitor .75 .23
23 Gary Sheffield .50 .15
24 Jim Edmonds .50 .15
25 Barry Larkin 1.25 .35
26 Rafael Palmeiro .75 .23
27 Alan Benes .50 .15
28 Dave Justice .50 .15
29 Randy Johnson 1.25 .35
30 Barry Bonds 3.00 .90
31 Mo Vaughn .50 .15
32 Michael Tucker .50 .15
33 Larry Walker .75 .23
34 Tino Martinez .75 .23
35 Jose Guillen .50 .15
36 Carlos Delgado .50 .15
37 Jason Dickson .50 .15
38 Tom Glavine .75 .23
39 Raul Mondesi .50 .15
40 Jose Cruz Jr. RC 2.00 .60
41 Johnny Damon .50 .15
42 Mark Grace .75 .23
43 Juan Gonzalez 1.25 .35
44 Vladimir Guerrero 1.25 .35
45 Kevin Brown .50 .15
46 Justin Thompson .50 .15
47 Eric Young .50 .15
48 Ron Coomer .50 .15
49 Mark Kotsay RC .50 .15
50 Scott Rolen .75 .23
51 Derek Jeter 3.00 .90
52 Jim Thome 1.25 .35
53 Fred McGriff .75 .23
54 Albert Belle .50 .15
55 Garret Anderson .50 .15
56 Wilton Guerrero .50 .15
57 Jose Canseco 1.25 .35
58 Cal Ripken 4.00 1.20
59 Sammy Sosa 2.00 .60
60 Dmitri Young .50 .15
61 Alex Rodriguez 2.00 .60
62 Javier Lopez .50 .15
63 Sandy Alomar Jr. .50 .15
64 Joe Carter .50 .15
65 Dante Bichette .50 .15
66 Al Martin .50 .15
67 Darin Erstad .50 .15
68 Pokey Reese .50 .15
69 Brady Anderson .50 .15
70 Andruw Jones .50 .15
71 Ivan Rodriguez 1.25 .35
72 Nomar Garciaparra 2.00 .60
73 Moises Alou .50 .15
74 Andy Pettitte .75 .23
75 Jay Buhner .50 .15
76 Craig Biggio .75 .23
77 Wade Boggs .75 .23
78 Shawn Estes .50 .15
79 Neifi Perez .50 .15
80 Rusty Greer .50 .15
81 Pedro Martinez 1.25 .35
82 Mike Mussina 1.25 .35
83 Jason Giambi 1.25 .35
84 Hideo Nomo 1.25 .35
85 Todd Hundley .50 .15
86 Deion Sanders .75 .23
87 Mike Cameron .50 .15
88 Bobby Bonilla .50 .15
89 Todd Greene .50 .15
90 Kevin Orie .50 .15
91 Ken Caminiti .50 .15
92 Chuck Knoblauch .50 .15
93 Matt Morris .50 .15
94 Matt Williams .50 .15
95 Pat Hentgen .50 .15
96 John Smoltz .75 .23
97 Edgar Martinez .75 .23
98 Jason Kendall .50 .15
99 Ken Griffey Jr. CL 1.25 .35
100 Frank Thomas CL .75 .23

1997 Donruss Signature Platinum Press Proofs

Randomly inserted in packs, this set is a holo foil parallel version of the base set. Only 150 of this set were produced. Each card is numbered "1 of 150" on the back. Some cards were mistakenly printed with the "1 of 150 backs" but did not have the platinum press proof front. These cards are valued at approximately the same price as the values below.

Nm-Mt Ex-Mt
*STARS: 10X TO 25X BASIC CARDS..
*ROOKIES: 4X TO 10X BASIC CARDS

1997 Donruss Signature Autographs

Inserted one per pack, this 117-card set features color player autographed photos. The first 100 cards each player signed were blue, sequentially numbered to 100, and designated as "Century Marks." The next 100 cards signed were green, sequentially numbered 101-1100, and designated as "Millenium Marks." Player autographs surpassing 1100 were red and were not numbered. Some autographed signature cards were not available at first and were designated by blank-backed redemption cards which could be redeemed by mail for the player's autograph card. The cards are checklisted below in alphabetical order. Asterisk cards were found in both Series A and B. Print runs for how many cards each player signed is noted next to the players name. Exchange cards for Raul Mondesi and Edgar Renteria were seeded into packs. Notable cards of players in their Rookie Card seasons include Brian Giles and Miguel Tejada. The Miguel Tejada card was signed in either black or blue ink. At this time, there is no price differential for either version of this card.

Nm-Mt Ex-Mt
1 Jeff Abbott/3900 4.00 1.20
2 Bob Abreu/3900 10.00 3.00
3 Edgardo Alfonzo/3900 10.00 3.00
4 Roberto Alomar/150 * 80.00 24.00
5 Sandy Alomar Jr./1400 6.00 1.80
6 Moises Alou/900 15.00 4.50
7 Garret Anderson/3900 15.00 4.50
8 Andy Ashby/3900 4.00 1.20
9 Trey Beamon/3900 4.00 1.20
10 Alan Benes/3900 4.00 1.20
11 Geronimo Berroa/3900 4.00 1.20
12 Wade Boggs/150 * 120.00 36.00
13 Kevin Brown C/3900 4.00 1.20
14 Brett Butler/1400 15.00 4.50
15 Mike Cameron/3900 10.00 3.00
16 Giovanni Carrara/2900 4.00 1.20
17 Luis Castillo/3900 10.00 3.00
18 Tony Clark/3900 4.00 1.20
19 Will Clark/1400 25.00 7.50
20 Lou Collier/3900 4.00 1.20
21 Bartolo Colon/3900 10.00 3.00
22 Ron Coomer/3900 4.00 1.20

23 Marty Cordova/3900	4.00	1.20
24 Jacob Cruz/3900 *	4.00	1.20
25 Jose Cruz Jr./900 *	15.00	4.50
26 Russ Davis/3900	4.00	1.20
27 Jason Dickson/3900	4.00	1.20
28 Todd Dunwoody/3900	4.00	1.20
29 Jermaine Dye/3900	10.00	3.00
30 Jim Edmonds/3900	15.00	4.50
31 Darin Erstad/900 *	15.00	4.50
32 Bobby Estalella/3900	4.00	1.20
33 Shawn Estes/3900	4.00	1.20
34 Jeff Fassero/3900	4.00	1.20
35 Andres Galarraga/900	15.00	4.50
36 Karim Garcia/3900	4.00	1.20
37 Derrick Gibson/3900	4.00	1.20
38 Brian Giles/3900	15.00	4.50
39 Tom Glavine/150	80.00	24.00
40 Rick Gorecki/900	6.00	1.80
41 Shawn Green/1900	15.00	4.50
42 Todd Greene/3900	4.00	1.20
43 Rusty Greer/3900	10.00	3.00
44 Ben Grieve/3900	4.00	1.20
45 M.Grudzielanek/3900	4.00	1.20
46 V.Guerrero/1900 *	25.00	7.50
47 Wilton Guerrero/2150	4.00	1.20
48 Jose Guillen/2900	10.00	3.00
49 J.Hammonds/2150	4.00	1.20
50 Todd Helton/1400	25.00	7.50
51 T.Hollandsworth/2900	4.00	1.20
52 Trenidad Hubbard/900	6.00	1.80
53 Todd Hundley/1400	6.00	1.80
54 Bobby Jones/3900	4.00	1.20
55 Brian Jordan/1400	15.00	4.50
56 David Justice/900	15.00	4.50
57 Eric Karros/650	15.00	4.50
58 Jason Kendall/3900	10.00	3.00
59 Jimmy Key/3900	15.00	4.50
60 B.Kieschnick/3900	4.00	1.20
61 Ryan Klesko/225	30.00	9.00
62 Paul Konerko/3900	10.00	3.00
63 Mark Kotsay/2400	8.00	2.40
64 Ray Lankford/3900	4.00	1.20
65 Barry Larkin/150 *	80.00	24.00
66 Derrek Lee/3900	10.00	3.00
67 Esteban Loaiza/3900	10.00	3.00
68 Javier Lopez/1400	15.00	4.50
69 Edgar Martinez/150 *	80.00	24.00
70 Pedro Martinez/900	60.00	18.00
71 Rafael Medina/3900	4.00	1.20
72 Raul Mondesi/650	15.00	4.50
73 Matt Morris/3900	15.00	4.50
74 Paul O'Neill/900	25.00	7.50
75 Kevin Orie/3900	4.00	1.20
76 David Ortiz/3900	15.00	4.50
77 Rafael Palmeiro/900	40.00	12.00
78 Jay Payton/3900	4.00	1.20
79 Neifi Perez/3900	4.00	1.20
80 Manny Ramirez/900	25.00	7.50
81 Joe Randa/3900	4.00	1.20
82 Pokey Reese/3900	4.00	1.20
83 Edgar Renteria SP	25.00	7.50
84 Dennis Reyes/3900	4.00	1.20
85 Henry Rodriguez/3900	4.00	1.20
86 Scott Rolen/1900 *	15.00	4.50
87 Kirk Rueter/2900	10.00	3.00
88 Ryne Sandberg/400	80.00	24.00
89 Dwight Smith/2900	4.00	1.20
90 J.T. Snow/900	15.00	4.50
91 Scott Spiezio/3900	4.00	1.20
92 Shannon Stewart/2900	10.00	3.00
93 Jeff Suppan/1900	4.00	1.20
94 Mike Sweeney/3900	15.00	4.50
95 Miguel Tejada/3900	25.00	7.50
96 Justin Thompson/2400	4.00	1.20
97 Brett Tomko/3900	4.00	1.20
98 Bubba Trammell/3900	8.00	2.40
99 Michael Tucker/3900	4.00	1.20
100 Javier Valentin/3900	4.00	1.20
101 Mo Vaughn/150 *	30.00	9.00
102 Robin Ventura/1400	15.00	4.50
103 Terrell Wade/3900	4.00	1.20
104 Billy Wagner/3900	15.00	4.50
105 Larry Walker/900	50.00	15.00
106 Todd Walker/2400	10.00	3.00
107 Rondell White/3900	10.00	3.00
108 Kevin Wickander/900	4.00	1.20
109 Chris Widger/3900	4.00	1.20
110 Matt Williams/150 *	30.00	9.00
111 A.Williamson/3900	4.00	1.20
112 Dan Wilson/3900	4.00	1.20
113 Tony Womack/3900	8.00	2.40
114 Jaret Wright/3900	4.00	1.20
115 Dmitri Young/3900	10.00	3.00
116 Eric Young/3900	4.00	1.20
117 Kevin Young/3900	4.00	1.20
NNO F.Thomas Sample	2.00	.60
Fascimile Autograph		

1997 Donruss Signature Autographs Century

Randomly inserted in packs, this set, identified with blue card fronts, features the first 100 cards signed by each player. The cards are sequentially numbered. Raul Mondesi, Eddie Murray, Edgar Renteria and Jim Thome were seeded in packs as exchange cards. The cards are checklisted below in alphabetical order. A number of Nomar Garciaparra Century marks were lost or destroyed during packaging and only 62 of these cards were inserted into packs.

	Nm-Mt	Ex-Mt
1 Jeff Abbott	25.00	7.50
2 Bob Abreu	40.00	12.00
3 Edgardo Alfonzo	40.00	12.00
4 Roberto Alomar *	100.00	30.00
5 Sandy Alomar Jr.	25.00	7.50
6 Moises Alou	40.00	12.00
7 Garret Anderson	80.00	24.00
8 Andy Ashby	25.00	7.50
9 Jeff Bagwell	120.00	36.00
10 Trey Beamon	25.00	7.50
11 Albert Belle	40.00	12.00
12 Alan Benes	25.00	7.50
13 Geronimo Berroa	25.00	7.50
14 Wade Boggs *	100.00	30.00
15 Barry Bonds	250.00	75.00
16 Bobby Bonilla *	40.00	12.00
17 Kevin Brown	80.00	24.00
18 Kevin Brown C	25.00	7.50
19 Jay Buhner	80.00	24.00
20 Brett Butler	40.00	12.00
21 Mike Cameron	40.00	12.00
22 Giovanni Carrara	25.00	7.50
23 Luis Castillo	40.00	12.00
24 Tony Clark	25.00	7.50
25 Will Clark	120.00	36.00
26 Roger Clemens *	250.00	75.00
27 Lou Collier	25.00	7.50
28 Bartolo Colon	40.00	12.00
29 Ron Coomer	25.00	7.50
30 Marty Cordova	25.00	7.50
31 Jacob Cruz *	25.00	7.50
32 Jose Cruz Jr. *	60.00	18.00
33 Russ Davis	25.00	7.50
34 Jason Dickson	25.00	7.50
35 Todd Dunwoody	25.00	7.50
36 Jermaine Dye	40.00	12.00
37 Jim Edmonds	80.00	24.00
38 Darin Erstad *	40.00	12.00
39 Bobby Estalella	25.00	7.50
40 Shawn Estes	25.00	7.50
41 Jeff Fassero	25.00	7.50
42 Andres Galarraga	40.00	12.00
43 Karim Garcia	25.00	7.50
44 N. Garciaparra SP62 *	250.00	75.00
45 Derrick Gibson	25.00	7.50
46 Brian Giles	60.00	18.00
47 Tom Glavine	100.00	30.00
48 Juan Gonzalez	100.00	30.00
49 Rick Gorecki	25.00	7.50
50 Shawn Green	80.00	24.00
51 Todd Greene	25.00	7.50
52 Rusty Greer	40.00	12.00
53 Ben Grieve	25.00	7.50
54 Mark Grudzielanek	25.00	7.50
55 Vladimir Guerrero *	100.00	30.00
56 Wilton Guerrero	25.00	7.50
57 Jose Guillen	40.00	12.00
58 Tony Gwynn *	150.00	45.00
59 Jeffrey Hammonds	25.00	7.50
60 Todd Helton	100.00	30.00
61 Todd Hollandsworth	25.00	7.50
62 Trenidad Hubbard	25.00	7.50
63 Todd Hundley	25.00	7.50
64 Derek Jeter *	250.00	75.00
65 Andruw Jones *	80.00	24.00
66 Bobby Jones	25.00	7.50
67 Chipper Jones *	120.00	36.00
68 Brian Jordan	40.00	12.00
69 David Justice	40.00	12.00
70 Eric Karros	40.00	12.00
71 Jason Kendall	40.00	12.00
72 Jimmy Key	80.00	24.00
73 Brooks Kieschnick	25.00	7.50
74 Ryan Klesko	40.00	12.00
75 Chuck Knoblauch *	40.00	12.00
76 Paul Konerko	40.00	12.00
77 Mark Kotsay	25.00	7.50
78 Ray Lankford	25.00	7.50
79 Barry Larkin *	100.00	30.00
80 Derrek Lee	40.00	12.00
81 Esteban Loaiza	40.00	12.00
82 Javier Lopez	40.00	12.00
83 Greg Maddux *	200.00	60.00
84 Edgar Martinez *	100.00	30.00
85 Pedro Martinez	120.00	36.00
86 Tino Martinez *	100.00	30.00
87 Rafael Medina	25.00	7.50
88 Raul Mondesi	40.00	12.00
89 Matt Morris	80.00	24.00
90 Eddie Murray EXCH*	120.00	36.00
91 Mike Mussina	100.00	30.00
92 Paul O'Neill	80.00	24.00
93 Kevin Orie	25.00	7.50
94 David Ortiz	80.00	24.00
95 Rafael Palmeiro	100.00	30.00
96 Jay Payton	25.00	7.50
97 Neifi Perez	25.00	7.50
98 Andy Pettitte *	100.00	30.00
99 Manny Ramirez	80.00	24.00
100 Joe Randa	25.00	7.50
101 Pokey Reese	25.00	7.50
102 Edgar Renteria	40.00	12.00
103 Dennis Reyes	25.00	7.50
104 Cal Ripken	250.00	75.00
105 Alex Rodriguez	250.00	75.00
106 Henry Rodriguez	25.00	7.50
107 Ivan Rodriguez	100.00	30.00
108 Scott Rolen *	80.00	24.00
109 Kirk Rueter	40.00	12.00
110 Ryne Sandberg	150.00	45.00
111 Gary Sheffield *	80.00	24.00
112 Dwight Smith	25.00	7.50
113 J.T. Snow	40.00	12.00
114 Scott Spiezio	25.00	7.50
115 Shannon Stewart	40.00	12.00
116 Jeff Suppan	25.00	7.50
117 Mike Sweeney	80.00	24.00
118 Miguel Tejada	100.00	30.00
119 Frank Thomas	100.00	30.00
120 Jim Thome	100.00	30.00
121 Justin Thompson	25.00	7.50
122 Brett Tomko	25.00	7.50
123 Bubba Trammell	25.00	7.50
124 Michael Tucker	25.00	7.50
125 Javier Valentin	25.00	7.50
126 Mo Vaughn *	40.00	12.00
127 Robin Ventura	40.00	12.00
128 Terrell Wade	25.00	7.50
129 Billy Wagner	80.00	24.00
130 Larry Walker	120.00	36.00
131 Todd Walker	40.00	12.00
132 Rondell White	40.00	12.00
133 Kevin Wickander	25.00	7.50
134 Chris Widger	25.00	7.50
135 Bernie Williams	100.00	30.00
136 Matt Williams *	40.00	12.00
137 Antone Williamson	25.00	7.50
138 Dan Wilson	25.00	7.50
139 Tony Womack	40.00	12.00
140 Jaret Wright	25.00	7.50
141 Dmitri Young	40.00	12.00
142 Eric Young	25.00	7.50
143 Kevin Young	25.00	7.50

1997 Donruss Signature Autographs Millennium

Randomly inserted in packs, this set, identified with green card fronts, features the second group of 100 cards signed by each player. The cards are sequentially numbered 101-1,100 (except for some shortprinted cards in quantities of 400, 650 or 900) and are checklisted in alphabetical order. It has been noted that there are some cards in circulation that lack serial numbering. Edgar Renteria was seeded into packs as an exchange card and has been verified by representatives at Donruss as being a short-print. Eddie Murray, Raul Mondesi and Jim Thome were also exchange cards.

	Nm-Mt	Ex-Mt
1 Jeff Abbott	8.00	2.40
2 Bob Abreu	15.00	4.50
3 Edgardo Alfonzo	15.00	4.50
4 Roberto Alomar *	40.00	12.00
5 Sandy Alomar Jr.	8.00	2.40
6 Moises Alou	15.00	4.50
7 Garret Anderson	25.00	7.50
8 Andy Ashby	8.00	2.40
9 Jeff Bagwell/400	80.00	24.00
10 Trey Beamon	8.00	2.40
11 Albert Belle/400	40.00	12.00
12 Alan Benes	8.00	2.40
13 Geronimo Berroa	8.00	2.40
14 Wade Boggs *	40.00	12.00
15 Barry Bonds/400	175.00	52.50
16 Bobby Bonilla/900 *	15.00	4.50
17 Kevin Brown/900	25.00	7.50
18 Kevin Brown C	8.00	2.40
19 Jay Buhner/900	25.00	7.50
20 Brett Butler	15.00	4.50
21 Mike Cameron	15.00	4.50
22 Giovanni Carrara	8.00	2.40
23 Luis Castillo	15.00	4.50
24 Tony Clark	8.00	2.40
25 Will Clark	40.00	12.00
26 Roger Clemens/400 *	150.00	45.00
27 Lou Collier	8.00	2.40
28 Bartolo Colon	15.00	4.50
29 Ron Coomer	8.00	2.40
30 Marty Cordova	8.00	2.40
31 Jacob Cruz	8.00	2.40
32 Jose Cruz Jr. *	25.00	7.50
33 Russ Davis	8.00	2.40
34 Jason Dickson	8.00	2.40
35 Todd Dunwoody	8.00	2.40
36 Jermaine Dye	15.00	4.50
37 Jim Edmonds	25.00	7.50
38 Darin Erstad *	15.00	4.50
39 Bobby Estalella	8.00	2.40
40 Shawn Estes	8.00	2.40
41 Jeff Fassero	8.00	2.40
42 Andres Galarraga	15.00	4.50
43 Karim Garcia	8.00	2.40
44 N.Garciaparra/650 *	150.00	45.00
45 Derrick Gibson	8.00	2.40
46 Brian Giles	25.00	7.50
47 Tom Glavine	40.00	12.00
48 Juan Gonzalez/900	40.00	12.00
49 Rick Gorecki	8.00	2.40
50 Shawn Green	25.00	7.50
51 Todd Greene	8.00	2.40
52 Rusty Greer	15.00	4.50
53 Ben Grieve	8.00	2.40
54 Mark Grudzielanek	8.00	2.40
55 Vladimir Guerrero *	40.00	12.00
56 Wilton Guerrero	8.00	2.40
57 Jose Guillen	15.00	4.50
58 Tony Gwynn/900 *	50.00	15.00
59 Jeffrey Hammonds	8.00	2.40
60 Todd Helton	40.00	12.00
61 Todd Hundley	8.00	2.40
62 Todd Hollandsworth	8.00	2.40
63 Trenidad Hubbard	8.00	2.40
64 Derek Jeter/400 *	150.00	45.00
65 Andruw Jones/900 *	25.00	7.50
66 Bobby Jones	8.00	2.40
67 Chipper Jones/900 *	40.00	12.00
68 Brian Jordan	15.00	4.50
69 David Justice	15.00	4.50
70 Eric Karros	15.00	4.50
71 Jason Kendall	15.00	4.50
72 Jimmy Key	25.00	7.50
73 Brooks Kieschnick	8.00	2.40
74 Ryan Klesko	15.00	4.50
75 C.Knoblauch/900 *	15.00	4.50
76 Paul Konerko	15.00	4.50
77 Mark Kotsay	10.00	3.00
78 Ray Lankford	8.00	2.40
79 Barry Larkin *	40.00	12.00
80 Derrek Lee	15.00	4.50
81 Esteban Loaiza	15.00	4.50
82 Javier Lopez	15.00	4.50
83 Greg Maddux/400 *	120.00	36.00
84 Edgar Martinez *	40.00	12.00
85 Pedro Martinez	60.00	18.00
86 Tino Martinez/900 *	40.00	12.00
87 Rafael Medina	8.00	2.40
88 Raul Mondesi	15.00	4.50
89 Matt Morris	25.00	7.50
90 Eddie Murray/900 *	50.00	15.00
91 Mike Mussina/900	40.00	12.00
92 Paul O'Neill	25.00	7.50
93 Kevin Orie	8.00	2.40
94 David Ortiz	25.00	7.50
95 Rafael Palmeiro	40.00	12.00
96 Jay Payton	8.00	2.40
97 Neifi Perez	8.00	2.40
98 Andy Pettitte/900 *	40.00	12.00
99 Manny Ramirez	25.00	7.50
100 Joe Randa	8.00	2.40
101 Pokey Reese	8.00	2.40
102 Edgar Renteria SP	60.00	18.00
103 Dennis Reyes	8.00	2.40
104 Cal Ripken/400	150.00	45.00
105 Alex Rodriguez/400	150.00	45.00
106 Henry Rodriguez	8.00	2.40
107 Ivan Rodriguez/900	40.00	12.00
108 Scott Rolen *	25.00	7.50
109 Kirk Rueter	15.00	4.50
110 Ryne Sandberg	60.00	18.00
111 Gary Sheffield/400 *	40.00	12.00
112 Dwight Smith	8.00	2.40
113 J.T. Snow	15.00	4.50
114 Scott Spiezio	8.00	2.40
115 Shannon Stewart	15.00	4.50
116 Jeff Suppan	8.00	2.40
117 Mike Sweeney	25.00	7.50
118 Miguel Tejada	40.00	12.00
119 Frank Thomas/400	80.00	24.00
120 Jim Thome/900	40.00	12.00
121 Justin Thompson	8.00	2.40
122 Brett Tomko	8.00	2.40
123 Bubba Trammell	10.00	3.00
124 Michael Tucker	8.00	2.40
125 Javier Valentin	8.00	2.40
126 Mo Vaughn *	15.00	4.50
127 Robin Ventura	15.00	4.50
128 Terrell Wade	8.00	2.40
129 Billy Wagner	25.00	7.50
130 Larry Walker	50.00	15.00
131 Todd Walker	15.00	4.50
132 Rondell White	15.00	4.50
133 Kevin Wickander	8.00	2.40
134 Chris Widger	8.00	2.40
135 Bernie Williams/400	80.00	24.00
136 Matt Williams *	15.00	4.50
137 Antone Williamson	8.00	2.40
138 Dan Wilson	8.00	2.40
139 Tony Womack	10.00	3.00
140 Jaret Wright	8.00	2.40
141 Dmitri Young	15.00	4.50
142 Eric Young	8.00	2.40
143 Kevin Young	8.00	2.40

1997 Donruss Signature Notable Nicknames

Randomly inserted in packs, this 10-card set features photos of players with notable nicknames. Only 200 of this serial numbered set were produced. The cards are unnumbered and checklisted in alphabetical order. Roger Clemens signed a good deal of his cards without using his "Rocket" nickname. In addition, some Frank Thomas cards have been seen signed without "The Big Hurt" nickname. There is no difference in value between the two versions.

	Nm-Mt	Ex-Mt
1 Ernie Banks	150.00	45.00
Mr. Cub		
2 Tony Clark	60.00	18.00
The Tiger		
3 Roger Clemens	450.00	135.00
The Rocket		
4 Reggie Jackson	150.00	45.00
Mr. October		
5 Randy Johnson	350.00	105.00
The Big Unit		
6 Stan Musial	200.00	60.00
The Man		
7 Ivan Rodriguez	150.00	45.00
Pudge		
8 Frank Thomas	150.00	45.00
The Big Hurt		
9 Mo Vaughn	80.00	24.00
The Hit Dog		
10 Billy Wagner	120.00	36.00
The Kid		

1997 Donruss Signature Significant Signatures

Randomly inserted in packs, this 22-card set features photos with autographs of legendary Hall of Fame players. Only 2000 of each card was produced and serially numbered. The cards are checklisted below in alphabetical order. Reggie Jackson signed his cards in 2 different color inks. The cards he signed in silver are in shorter supply and are valued higher.

	Nm-Mt	Ex-Mt
1 Ernie Banks	40.00	12.00
2 Johnny Bench	40.00	12.00
3 Yogi Berra	40.00	12.00
4 George Brett	60.00	18.00
5 Lou Brock	40.00	12.00
6 Rod Carew	40.00	12.00
7 Steve Carlton	40.00	12.00
8 Larry Doby	80.00	24.00
9 Carlton Fisk	40.00	12.00
10 Bob Gibson	40.00	12.00
11 Reggie Jackson	40.00	12.00
11A R.Jackson Silver Ink	120.00	36.00
12 Al Kaline	40.00	12.00
13 Harmon Killebrew	40.00	12.00
14 Don Mattingly	50.00	15.00
15 Stan Musial	50.00	15.00
16 Jim Palmer	25.00	7.50
17 Brooks Robinson	40.00	12.00
18 Frank Robinson	25.00	7.50
19 Mike Schmidt	50.00	15.00
20 Tom Seaver	40.00	12.00
21 Duke Snider	40.00	12.00
22 Carl Yastrzemski	50.00	15.00

1998 Donruss Signature

The 140-card 1998 Donruss Signature set was distributed in five-card packs with one authentic autographed card per pack and a suggested retail price of $14.99. The fronts feature color action player photos in white borders. The backs carry player information and career statistics. Due to Pinnacle's bankruptcy, these cards were later released by Playoff. This set was released in very late December, 1998. Notable Rookie Cards in this set include J.D. Drew, Troy Glaus, Orlando Hernandez, Gabe Kapler, Kevin Millwood and Magglio Ordonez.

	Nm-Mt	Ex-Mt
COMPLETE SET (140)	50.00	15.00
1 David Justice	.40	.12
2 Derek Jeter	2.50	.75
3 Nomar Garciaparra	1.50	.45
4 Ryan Klesko	.40	.12
5 Jeff Bagwell	.60	.18
6 Dante Bichette	.40	.12
7 Ivan Rodriguez	1.00	.30
8 Albert Belle	.40	.12
9 Cal Ripken	3.00	.90
10 Craig Biggio	.60	.18
11 Barry Larkin	1.00	.30
12 Jose Guillen	.40	.12
13 Will Clark	1.00	.30
14 J.T. Snow	.40	.12
15 Chuck Knoblauch	.40	.12
16 Todd Walker	.40	.12
17 Scott Rolen	.60	.18
18 Rickey Henderson	1.00	.30
19 Juan Gonzalez	1.00	.30
20 Justin Thompson	.40	.12
21 Roger Clemens	2.00	.60
22 Ray Lankford	.40	.12
23 Jose Cruz Jr.	.40	.12
24 Ken Griffey Jr.	1.50	.45
25 Andruw Jones	.40	.12
26 Darin Erstad	.40	.12
27 Jim Thome	1.00	.30
28 Wade Boggs	.60	.18
29 Ken Caminiti	.40	.12
30 Todd Hundley	.40	.12
31 Mike Piazza	1.50	.45
32 Sammy Sosa	1.50	.45
33 Larry Walker	.60	.18
34 Matt Williams	.40	.12
35 Frank Thomas	1.00	.30
36 Gary Sheffield	.40	.12
37 Alex Rodriguez	1.50	.45
38 Hideo Nomo	1.00	.30
39 Kenny Lofton	.40	.12
40 John Smoltz	.60	.18
41 Mo Vaughn	.40	.12
42 Edgar Martinez	.60	.18
43 Paul Molitor	.60	.18
44 Rafael Palmeiro	.60	.18
45 Barry Bonds	2.50	.75
46 Vladimir Guerrero	1.00	.30
47 Carlos Delgado	.40	.12
48 Bobby Higginson	.40	.12
49 Greg Maddux	1.50	.45
50 Jim Edmonds	.40	.12
51 Randy Johnson	1.00	.30
52 Mark McGwire	2.50	.75
53 Rondell White	.40	.12
54 Raul Mondesi	.40	.12
55 Manny Ramirez	.40	.12
56 Pedro Martinez	1.00	.30
57 Tim Salmon	.60	.18
58 Moises Alou	.40	.12
59 Fred McGriff	.60	.18
60 Garret Anderson	.40	.12
61 Sandy Alomar Jr.	.40	.12
62 Chan Ho Park	.40	.12
63 Mark Kotsay	.40	.12
64 Mike Mussina	1.00	.30
65 Tom Glavine	.60	.18
66 Tony Clark	.40	.12
67 Mark Grace	.60	.18
68 Tony Gwynn	1.25	.35
69 Tino Martinez	.60	.18
70 Kevin Brown	.60	.18
71 Todd Greene	.40	.12
72 Andy Pettitte	.60	.18
73 Livan Hernandez	.40	.12
74 Curt Schilling	.60	.18
75 Andres Galarraga	.40	.12
76 Rusty Greer	.40	.12
77 Jay Buhner	.40	.12
78 Bobby Bonilla	.40	.12
79 Chipper Jones	1.00	.30
80 Eric Young	.40	.12
81 Jason Giambi	1.00	.30
82 Javy Lopez	.40	.12

83 Roberto Alomar 1.00 .30
84 Bernie Williams .60 .18
85 A.J. Hinch .40 .12
86 Kerry Wood 1.00 .30
87 Juan Encarnacion .40 .12
88 Brad Fullmer .40 .12
89 Ben Grieve .40 .12
90 Magglio Ordonez RC 8.00 2.40
91 Todd Helton .60 .18
92 Richard Hidalgo .40 .12
93 Paul Konerko .40 .12
94 Aramis Ramirez .40 .12
95 Ricky Ledee .40 .12
96 Derrek Lee .40 .12
97 Travis Lee .40 .12
98 Matt Anderson RC .60 .18
99 Jaret Wright .40 .12
100 David Ortiz .40 .12
101 Carl Pavano .40 .12
102 O.Hernandez RC 2.00 .60
103 Fernando Tatis .40 .12
104 Miguel Tejada .60 .18
105 Rolando Arrojo RC .60 .18
106 Kevin Millwood RC 3.00 .90
107 Ken Griffey Jr. CL 1.00 .30
108 Frank Thomas CL .60 .18
109 Cal Ripken CL 1.50 .45
110 Greg Maddux CL 1.00 .30
111 John Olerud .40 .12
112 David Cone .40 .12
113 Vinny Castilla .40 .12
114 Jason Kendall .40 .12
115 Brian Jordan .40 .12
116 Hideki Irabu .40 .12
117 Bartolo Colon .40 .12
118 Greg Vaughn .40 .12
119 David Segui .40 .12
120 Bruce Chen .40 .12
121 Julio Ramirez RC .40 .12
122 Troy Glaus RC 10.00 3.00
123 Jeremy Giambi RC .60 .18
124 Ryan Minor RC .40 .12
125 Richie Sexson .40 .12
126 Dermal Brown .40 .12
127 Adrian Beltre .40 .12
128 Eric Chavez .60 .18
129 J.D. Drew RC 8.00 2.40
130 Gabe Kapler RC 1.00 .30
131 Masato Yoshii RC 1.00 .30
132 Mike Lowell RC 4.00 1.20
133 Jim Parque RC .60 .18
134 Roy Halladay .40 .12
135 Carlos Lee RC 2.00 .60
136 Jin Ho Cho RC .40 .12
137 Michael Barrett .40 .12
138 F.Seguignol RC .40 .12
139 Odalis Perez RC UER 1.00 .30
Back pictures John Rocker
140 Mark McGwire CL 1.25 .35

1998 Donruss Signature Proofs

Randomly inserted in packs, this 140-card set is a holo-foil treated parallel version of the base set. Only 150 sets were produced and numbered "1 of 150."

Nm-Mt Ex-Mt
*STARS: 6X TO 15X BASIC CARDS ....
*ROOKIES: 2X TO 5X BASIC CARDS ..

1998 Donruss Signature Autographs

Inserted one per pack, this 98-card set features color action player images on a red foil background with the player's autograph in the lower portion of the card. The numbers following the player's name in our checklist indicate how many cards that player signed. The first 100 cards signed by each player are blue, sequentially-numbered and designated as "Century Marks." The next 1,000 signed are green, sequentially numbered and designated as "Millennium Marks." The cards are unnumbered and checklisted below in alphabetical order. An unnumbered Travis Lee sample card was distributed many months prior to the product's release. It's important to note that sample card features a facsimile autograph of Lee's.

Nm-Mt Ex-Mt
1 Roberto Alomar/150 40.00 12.00
2 Sandy Alomar Jr./700 10.00 3.00
3 Moises Alou/900 20.00 6.00
4 Gabe Alvarez/2900 4.00 1.20
5 Wilson Alvarez/1600 4.00 1.20
6 Jay Bell/1500 10.00 3.00
7 Adrian Beltre/1900 10.00 3.00
8 Andy Benes/2600 4.00 1.20
9 Aaron Boone/3400 25.00 7.50
10 Russell Branyan/1650 4.00 1.20
11 Orlando Cabrera/3100 4.00 1.20
12 Mike Cameron/1150 10.00 3.00
13 Joe Carter/400 20.00 6.00
14 Sean Casey/2275 10.00 3.00
15 Bruce Chen/150 15.00 4.50
16 Tony Clark/2275 4.00 1.20
17 Will Clark/1400 25.00 7.50
18 Matt Clement/1400 10.00 3.00
19 Pat Cline/1400 4.00 1.20
20 Ken Cloude/3400 4.00 1.20
21 Michael Coleman/2800 4.00 1.20
22 David Cone/25
23 Jeff Conine/1400 10.00 3.00
24 Jacob Cruz/3200 4.00 1.20
25 Russ Davis/3500 4.00 1.20
26 Jason Dickson/1400 4.00 1.20
27 Todd Dunwoody/3500 4.00 1.20
28 Juan Encarnacion/3400 4.00 1.20
29 Darin Erstad/700 20.00 6.00
30 Bobby Estalella/3400 4.00 1.20
31 Jeff Fassero/3400 4.00 1.20
32 John Franco/1800 10.00 3.00
33 Brad Fullmer/3100 4.00 1.20
34 Jason Giambi/3100 40.00 12.00
35 Derrick Gibson/1200 4.00 1.20
36 Todd Greene/1400 4.00 1.20
37 Ben Grieve/1400 4.00 1.20
38 M.Grudzielanek/3200 4.00 1.20
39 V.Guerrero/2100 40.00 12.00
40 Wilton Guerrero/1900 4.00 1.20
41 Jose Guillen/2400 4.00 1.20
42 Todd Helton/1300 25.00 7.50
43 Richard Hidalgo/3400 10.00 3.00
44 A.J. Hinch/2900 4.00 1.20
45 Butch Huskey/1900 4.00 1.20
46 Raul Ibanez/3300 4.00 1.20
47 Damian Jackson/900 10.00 3.00
48 Geoff Jenkins/3100 10.00 3.00
49 Eric Karros/650 20.00 6.00
50 Ryan Klesko/400 20.00 6.00
51 Mark Kotsay/3600 4.00 1.20
52 Ricky Ledee/2200 4.00 1.20
53 Derrek Lee/3400 10.00 3.00
54 Travis Lee/150 15.00 4.50
55 Javier Lopez/650 20.00 6.00
56 Mike Lowell/3500 15.00 4.50
57 Greg Maddux/12
58 Eli Marrero/3400 4.00 1.20
59 Al Martin/1300 4.00 1.20
60 Rafael Medina/1400 4.00 1.20
61 Scott Morgan/900 10.00 3.00
62 Abraham Nunez/3500 4.00 1.20
63 Paul O'Neill/1000 25.00 7.50
64 Luis Ordaz/2700 4.00 1.20
65 Magglio Ordonez/3200 25.00 7.50
66 Kevin Orie/1350 4.00 1.20
67 David Ortiz/3400 15.00 4.50
68 Rafael Palmeiro/1000 40.00 12.00
69 Carl Pavano/2600 10.00 3.00
70 Neifi Perez/3300 4.00 1.20
71 Dante Powell/3050 4.00 1.20
72 Aramis Ramirez/2800 10.00 3.00
73 Mariano Rivera/900 50.00 15.00
74 Felix Rodriguez/1400 4.00 1.20
75 Henry Rodriguez/3400 4.00 1.20
76 Scott Rolen/1900 25.00 7.50
77 Brian Rose/1400 4.00 1.20
78 Curt Schilling/900 30.00 9.00
79 Richie Sexson/3500 10.00 3.00
80 Randall Simon/3500 4.00 1.20
81 J.T. Snow/400 20.00 6.00
82 Jeff Suppan/1400 4.00 1.20
83 Fernando Tatis/3900 4.00 1.20
84 Miguel Tejada/3800 25.00 7.50
85 Brett Tomko/3400 4.00 1.20
86 Bubba Trammell/3900 4.00 1.20
87 Ismael Valdes/1900 4.00 1.20
88 Robin Ventura/1400 10.00 3.00
89 Billy Wagner/3900 25.00 7.50
90 Todd Walker/1900 10.00 3.00
91 Daryle Ward/400 10.00 3.00
92 Rondell White/3400 10.00 3.00
93 A.Williamson/3350 4.00 1.20
94 Dan Wilson/2400 4.00 1.20
95 Enrique Wilson/3400 4.00 1.20
96 Preston Wilson/2100 10.00 3.00
97 Tony Womack/3500 4.00 1.20
98 Kerry Wood/3400 40.00 12.00
NNO Travis Lee Sample 1.00 .30
Facsimile Autograph

1998 Donruss Signature Autographs Century

Randomly inserted in packs, this 122-card set is a sequentially numbered, blue parallel version of the Signature Autographs insert set and features the first 100 cards signed by each pictured player. The cards are unnumbered and checklisted in alphabetical order.

Nm-Mt Ex-Mt
1 Roberto Alomar 100.00 30.00
2 Sandy Alomar Jr. 25.00 7.50
3 Moises Alou 40.00 12.00
4 Gabe Alvarez 25.00 7.50
5 Wilson Alvarez 25.00 7.50
6 Brady Anderson 40.00 12.00
7 Jay Bell 40.00 12.00
8 Albert Belle 40.00 12.00
9 Adrian Beltre 40.00 12.00
10 Andy Benes 25.00 7.50
11 Wade Boggs 100.00 30.00
12 Barry Bonds 300.00 90.00
13 Aaron Boone 80.00 24.00
14 Russell Branyan 25.00 7.50
15 Jay Buhner 80.00 24.00
16 Ellis Burks 40.00 12.00
17 Orlando Cabrera 25.00 7.50
18 Mike Cameron 40.00 12.00
19 Ken Caminiti 40.00 12.00
20 Joe Carter 40.00 12.00
21 Sean Casey 40.00 12.00
22 Bruce Chen 25.00 7.50
23 Tony Clark 25.00 7.50
24 Will Clark 100.00 30.00
25 Roger Clemens 200.00 60.00
26 Matt Clement 40.00 12.00
27 Pat Cline 25.00 7.50
28 Ken Cloude 25.00 7.50
29 Michael Coleman 25.00 7.50
30 David Cone 40.00 12.00
31 Jeff Conine 40.00 12.00
32 Jacob Cruz 25.00 7.50
33 Jose Cruz Jr. 40.00 12.00
34 Russ Davis 25.00 7.50
35 Jason Dickson 25.00 7.50
36 Todd Dunwoody 25.00 7.50
37 Scott Elarton 25.00 7.50
38 Darin Erstad 40.00 12.00
39 Bobby Estalella 25.00 7.50
40 Jeff Fassero 25.00 7.50
41 John Franco 40.00 12.00
42 Brad Fullmer 25.00 7.50
43 Andres Galarraga 40.00 12.00
44 Nomar Garciaparra 200.00 60.00
45 Jason Giambi 100.00 30.00
46 Derrick Gibson 25.00 7.50
47 Tom Glavine 100.00 30.00
48 Juan Gonzalez 100.00 30.00
49 Todd Greene 25.00 7.50
50 Ben Grieve 25.00 7.50
51 Mark Grudzielanek 25.00 7.50
52 Vladimir Guerrero 100.00 30.00
53 Wilton Guerrero 25.00 7.50
54 Jose Guillen 25.00 7.50
55 Tony Gwynn 120.00 36.00
56 Todd Helton 80.00 24.00
57 Richard Hidalgo 40.00 12.00
58 A.J. Hinch 25.00 7.50
59 Butch Huskey 25.00 7.50
60 Raul Ibanez 25.00 7.50
61 Damian Jackson 25.00 7.50
62 Geoff Jenkins 40.00 12.00
63 Derek Jeter 250.00 75.00
64 Randy Johnson 150.00 45.00
65 Chipper Jones 120.00 36.00
66 Eric Karros/50 40.00 12.00
67 Ryan Klesko 40.00 12.00
68 Chuck Knoblauch 40.00 12.00
69 Mark Kotsay 25.00 7.50
70 Ricky Ledee 25.00 7.50
71 Derrek Lee 40.00 12.00
72 Travis Lee 25.00 7.50
73 Javier Lopez 40.00 12.00
74 Mike Lowell 50.00 15.00
75 Greg Maddux 200.00 60.00
76 Eli Marrero 25.00 7.50
77 Al Martin 25.00 7.50
78 Rafael Medina 25.00 7.50
79 Paul Molitor 80.00 24.00
80 Scott Morgan 25.00 7.50
81 Mike Mussina 100.00 30.00
82 Abraham Nunez 25.00 7.50
83 Paul O'Neill 80.00 24.00
84 Luis Ordaz 25.00 7.50
85 Magglio Ordonez 80.00 24.00
86 Kevin Orie 25.00 7.50
87 David Ortiz 60.00 18.00
88 Rafael Palmeiro 100.00 30.00
89 Carl Pavano 40.00 12.00
90 Neifi Perez 25.00 7.50
91 Andy Pettitte 100.00 30.00
92 Aramis Ramirez 40.00 12.00
93 Cal Ripken 250.00 75.00
94 Mariano Rivera 120.00 36.00
95 Alex Rodriguez 200.00 60.00
96 Felix Rodriguez 25.00 7.50
97 Henry Rodriguez 25.00 7.50
98 Ivan Rodriguez 100.00 30.00
99 Scott Rolen 80.00 24.00
100 Brian Rose 25.00 7.50
101 Curt Schilling 80.00 24.00
102 Richie Sexson 40.00 12.00
103 Randall Simon 25.00 7.50
104 J.T. Snow 40.00 12.00
105 Darryl Strawberry 100.00 30.00
106 Jeff Suppan 25.00 7.50
107 Fernando Tatis 25.00 7.50
108 Brett Tomko 25.00 7.50
109 Bubba Trammell 25.00 7.50
110 Ismael Valdes 25.00 7.50
111 Robin Ventura 40.00 12.00
112 Billy Wagner 80.00 24.00
113 Todd Walker 40.00 12.00
114 Daryle Ward 25.00 7.50
115 Rondell White 40.00 12.00
116 Matt Williams/80 40.00 12.00
117 Antone Williamson 25.00 7.50
118 Dan Wilson 25.00 7.50
119 Enrique Wilson 25.00 7.50
120 Preston Wilson 40.00 12.00
121 Tony Womack 25.00 7.50
122 Kerry Wood 100.00 30.00

1998 Donruss Signature Autographs Millennium

Randomly inserted in packs, this 125-card set is a sequentially numbered, green foil parallel version of the Signature Autographs insert set and features the next 1,000 cards signed by each pictured player after the initial 100. In numerous cases, players signed less than 1,000 cards. Print runs for these short-prints are specified after the player's name in the checklist. The cards are unnumbered and checklisted below in alphabetical order.

Nm-Mt Ex-Mt
1 Roberto Alomar 40.00 12.00
2 Sandy Alomar Jr. 8.00 2.40
3 Moises Alou 15.00 4.50
4 Gabe Alvarez 8.00 2.40
5 Wilson Alvarez 8.00 2.40
6 Brady Anderson/800 15.00 4.50
7 Jay Bell 15.00 4.50
8 Albert Belle/400 40.00 12.00
9 Adrian Beltre 15.00 4.50
10 Andy Benes 8.00 2.40
11 Wade Boggs/900 40.00 12.00
12 Barry Bonds/400 175.00 52.50
13 Aaron Boone 25.00 7.50
14 Russell Branyan 8.00 2.40
15 Jay Buhner/400 60.00 18.00
16 Ellis Burks/900 15.00 4.50
17 Orlando Cabrera 8.00 2.40
18 Mike Cameron 15.00 4.50
19 Ken Caminiti/900 15.00 4.50
20 Joe Carter 15.00 4.50
21 Sean Casey 15.00 4.50
22 Bruce Chen 8.00 2.40
23 Tony Clark 8.00 2.40
24 Will Clark 40.00 12.00
25 Roger Clemens/400 100.00 30.00
26 Matt Clement/900 15.00 4.50
27 Pat Cline 8.00 2.40
28 Ken Cloude 8.00 2.40
29 Michael Coleman 8.00 2.40
30 David Cone 15.00 4.50
31 Jeff Conine 15.00 4.50
32 Jacob Cruz 8.00 2.40
33 Jose Cruz Jr./850 15.00 4.50
34 Russ Davis/950 8.00 2.40
35 Jason Dickson/950 8.00 2.40
36 Todd Dunwoody 8.00 2.40
37 Scott Elarton/900 8.00 2.40
38 Juan Encarnacion 8.00 2.40
39 Darin Erstad 15.00 4.50
40 Bobby Estalella 8.00 2.40
41 Jeff Fassero 8.00 2.40
42 John Franco/950 15.00 4.50
43 Brad Fullmer 8.00 2.40
44 Andres Galarraga/900 15.00 4.50
45 Nomar Garciaparra/400 120.00 36.00
46 Jason Giambi 40.00 12.00
47 Derrick Gibson 8.00 2.40
48 Tom Glavine/700 40.00 12.00
49 Juan Gonzalez 40.00 12.00
50 Todd Greene 8.00 2.40
51 Ben Grieve 8.00 2.40
52 Mark Grudzielanek 8.00 2.40
53 Vladimir Guerrero 40.00 12.00
54 Wilton Guerrero 8.00 2.40
55 Jose Guillen 8.00 2.40
56 Tony Gwynn/900 50.00 15.00
57 Todd Helton 25.00 7.50
58 Richard Hidalgo 15.00 4.50
59 A.J. Hinch 8.00 2.40
60 Butch Huskey 8.00 2.40
61 Raul Ibanez 8.00 2.40
62 Damian Jackson 8.00 2.40
63 Geoff Jenkins 15.00 4.50
64 Derek Jeter/400 150.00 45.00
65 Randy Johnson/800 80.00 24.00
66 Chipper Jones/900 40.00 12.00
67 Eric Karros 15.00 4.50
68 Ryan Klesko 15.00 4.50
69 Chuck Knoblauch/900 15.00 4.50
70 Mark Kotsay 8.00 2.40
71 Ricky Ledee 8.00 2.40
72 Derrek Lee 15.00 4.50
73 Travis Lee 8.00 2.40
74 Javier Lopez/800 15.00 4.50
75 Mike Lowell 25.00 7.50
76 Greg Maddux/400 100.00 30.00
77 Eli Marrero 8.00 2.40
78 Al Martin/950 8.00 2.40
79 Rafael Medina/850 8.00 2.40
80 Paul Molitor/900 25.00 7.50
81 Scott Morgan 8.00 2.40
82 Mike Mussina/900 40.00 12.00
83 Abraham Nunez 8.00 2.40
84 Paul O'Neill/900 25.00 7.50
85 Luis Ordaz 8.00 2.40
86 Magglio Ordonez 40.00 12.00
87 Kevin Orie 8.00 2.40
88 David Ortiz 20.00 6.00
89 Rafael Palmeiro/900 40.00 12.00
90 Carl Pavano 15.00 4.50
91 Neifi Perez 8.00 2.40
92 Andy Pettitte/900 40.00 12.00
93 Dante Powell/950 8.00 2.40
94 Aramis Ramirez 15.00 4.50
95 Cal Ripken/375 150.00 45.00
96 Mariano Rivera 50.00 15.00
97 Alex Rodriguez/350 120.00 36.00
98 Felix Rodriguez 8.00 2.40
99 Henry Rodriguez 8.00 2.40
100 Ivan Rodriguez 50.00 15.00
101 Scott Rolen 25.00 7.50
102 Brian Rose 8.00 2.40
103 Curt Schilling 25.00 7.50
104 Richie Sexson 15.00 4.50
105 Randall Simon 8.00 2.40
106 J.T. Snow 15.00 4.50
107 Darryl Strawberry/900 50.00 15.00
108 Jeff Suppan 8.00 2.40
109 Fernando Tatis 8.00 2.40
110 Miguel Tejada 25.00 7.50
111 Brett Tomko 8.00 2.40
112 Bubba Trammell 8.00 2.40
113 Ismael Valdes 8.00 2.40
114 Robin Ventura 15.00 4.50
115 Billy Wagner/900 25.00 7.50
116 Todd Walker 15.00 4.50
117 Daryle Ward 8.00 2.40
118 Rondell White 15.00 4.50
119 Matt Williams/820 15.00 4.50
120 Antone Williamson 8.00 2.40
121 Dan Wilson 8.00 2.40
122 Enrique Wilson 8.00 2.40
123 Preston Wilson/400 40.00 12.00
124 Tony Womack 8.00 2.40
125 Kerry Wood 40.00 12.00

1998 Donruss Signature Significant Signatures

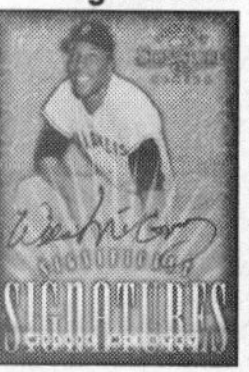

Randomly inserted in packs, this 18-card set features color photos with autographs of some of baseball's all-time great players. Only 2,000 of this sequentially-numbered set were produced. Sandy Koufax was on the original checklist but his cards were not returned in time for the pack out. Thus, officials at Donruss made the Billy Williams card an exchange card. Each collector that pulled a Billy Williams card could send it in to Donruss for a Koufax card. In addition, the signed Williams card was sent back too. Special exchange cards were created for Nolan Ryan and Ozzie Smith. The cards were randomly seeded into packs and then redeemed to Donruss for the real autograph cards. The exchange deadline for cards R1-R3 was December 31st, 1999.

Nm-Mt Ex-Mt
1 Ernie Banks 40.00 12.00
2 Yogi Berra 40.00 12.00
3 George Brett 60.00 18.00
4 Catfish Hunter 50.00 15.00
5 Al Kaline 40.00 12.00
6 Harmon Killebrew 40.00 12.00
7 Ralph Kiner 25.00 7.50
9 Eddie Mathews 50.00 15.00
10 Don Mattingly 60.00 18.00
11 Willie McCovey 25.00 7.50
12 Stan Musial 50.00 15.00
13 Phil Rizzuto SP/1000 50.00 15.00
14 N.Ryan EXCH 15.00 4.50
15 O.Smith EXCH 5.00 1.50
16 Duke Snider 25.00 7.50
17 Don Sutton 25.00 7.50
18 Billy Williams 25.00 7.50
18A B.Williams Redeemed 5.00 1.50
R1 Nolan Ryan 100.00 30.00
R2 Ozzie Smith 40.00 12.00
R3 Sandy Koufax 250.00 75.00

2001 Donruss Signature

This 311 card set was issued 25 cards to a "gift" box. The 25 card boxes had a SRP of $49.99 per box and the boxes were issued eight to a mini case. Cards numbered from 111 through 165 were inserted at an approximate rate of one per box and were serial numbered to 330. Cards numbered 166 to 311 were issued at an approximate rate of two per box and were serial numbered to 800.

Nm-Mt Ex-Mt
COMP.SET w/o SP'S (110) 50.00 15.00
COMMON CARD (1-110) 1.00 .30
COMMON (111-165) 15.00 4.50
COMMON (166-311) 8.00 2.40
1 Alex Rodriguez 4.00 1.20
2 Barry Bonds 6.00 1.80
3 Cal Ripken 8.00 2.40
4 Chipper Jones 2.50 .75
5 Derek Jeter 6.00 1.80
6 Troy Glaus 1.50 .45
7 Frank Thomas 2.50 .75
8 Greg Maddux 4.00 1.20
9 Ivan Rodriguez 2.50 .75
10 Jeff Bagwell 1.50 .45
11 John Olerud 1.00 .30
12 Todd Helton 1.50 .45
13 Ken Griffey Jr. 4.00 1.20
14 Manny Ramirez 1.00 .30
15 Mark McGwire 6.00 1.80
16 Mike Piazza 4.00 1.20
17 Nomar Garciaparra 4.00 1.20
18 Moises Alou 1.00 .30
19 Aramis Ramirez 1.00 .30
20 Curt Schilling 1.50 .45
21 Pat Burrell 1.00 .30
22 Doug Mientkiewicz 1.00 .30
23 Carlos Delgado 1.00 .30
24 J.D. Drew 1.00 .30
25 Cliff Floyd 1.00 .30
26 Freddy Garcia 1.00 .30
27 Roberto Alomar 2.50 .75
28 Barry Zito 2.50 .75
29 Juan Encarnacion 1.00 .30
30 Paul Konerko 1.00 .30
31 Mark Mulder 1.00 .30
32 Andy Pettitte 1.50 .45
33 Jim Edmonds 1.00 .30
34 Darin Erstad 1.00 .30
35 Jason Giambi 2.50 .75
36 Tom Glavine 1.50 .45
37 Juan Gonzalez 2.50 .75
38 Fred McGriff 1.50 .45
39 Shawn Green 1.00 .30
40 Tim Hudson 1.00 .30
41 Andruw Jones 1.00 .30
42 Jeff Kent 1.00 .30
43 Barry Larkin 2.50 .75
44 Brad Radke 1.00 .30
45 Mike Mussina 2.50 .75
46 Hideo Nomo 2.50 .75
47 Rafael Palmeiro 1.50 .45
48 Scott Rolen 1.50 .45
49 Gary Sheffield 1.00 .30
50 Bernie Williams 1.50 .45
51 Bob Abreu 1.00 .30
52 Edgardo Alfonzo 1.00 .30
53 Edgar Martinez 1.50 .45
54 Magglio Ordonez 1.00 .30
55 Kerry Wood 2.50 .75
56 Adrian Beltre 1.00 .30
57 Lance Berkman 1.00 .30
58 Kevin Brown 2.50 .75
59 Sean Casey 1.00 .30
60 Eric Chavez 1.00 .30
61 Bartolo Colon 1.00 .30
62 Sammy Sosa 4.00 1.20

2001 Donruss Signature

63 Jermaine Dye 1.00 .30
64 Tony Gwynn 3.00 .90
65 Carl Everett 1.00 .30
66 Brian Giles 1.00 .30
67 Mike Hampton 1.00 .30
68 Richard Hidalgo 1.00 .30
69 Geoff Jenkins 1.00 .30
70 Tony Clark 1.00 .30
71 Roger Clemens 5.00 1.50
72 Ryan Klesko 1.00 .30
73 Chan Ho Park 1.00 .30
74 Richie Sexson 1.00 .30
75 Mike Sweeney 1.00 .30
76 Kazuhiro Sasaki 1.00 .30
77 Miguel Tejada 1.00 .30
78 Jose Vidro 1.00 .30
79 Larry Walker 1.50 .45
80 Preston Wilson 1.00 .30
81 Craig Biggio 1.50 .45
82 Andres Galarraga 1.00 .30
83 Jim Thome 2.50 .75
84 Vladimir Guerrero 2.50 .75
85 Rafael Furcal 1.00 .30
86 Cristian Guzman 1.00 .30
87 Terrence Long 1.00 .30
88 Bret Boone 1.00 .30
89 Wade Miller 1.00 .30
90 Eric Milton 1.00 .30
91 Gabe Kapler 1.00 .30
92 Johnny Damon 1.00 .30
93 Carlos Lee 1.00 .30
94 Kenny Lofton 1.00 .30
95 Raul Mondesi 1.00 .30
96 Jorge Posada 1.50 .45
97 Mark Grace 1.50 .45
98 Robert Fick 1.00 .30
99 Joe Mays 1.00 .30
100 Aaron Sele 1.00 .30
101 Ben Grieve 1.00 .30
102 Luis Gonzalez 1.00 .30
103 Ray Durham 1.00 .30
104 Mark Quinn 1.00 .30
105 Jose Canseco 2.50 .75
106 David Justice 1.00 .30
107 Pedro Martinez 2.50 .75
108 Randy Johnson 2.50 .75
109 Phil Nevin 1.00 .30
110 Rickey Henderson 2.50 .75
111 Alex Escobar AU 15.00 4.50
112 J.Estrada AU RC 25.00 7.50
113 Pedro Feliz AU 15.00 4.50
114 Nate Frese AU RC 15.00 4.50
115 R. Rodriguez AU RC 15.00 4.50
116 B.Larson AU RC 15.00 4.50
117 Alexis Gomez AU RC 15.00 4.50
118 Jason Hart AU 15.00 4.50
119 C.C. Sabathia AU 15.00 4.50
120 Endy Chavez AU RC 15.00 4.50
121 C.Parker AU RC 15.00 4.50
122 Jackson Melian RC 8.00 2.40
123 Joe Kennedy AU RC 15.00 4.50
124 A.Hernandez AU RC 15.00 4.50
125 Cesar Izturis AU 15.00 4.50
126 Jose Mieses AU RC 15.00 4.50
127 Roy Oswalt AU 25.00 7.50
128 Eric Munson AU 15.00 4.50
129 Xavier Nady AU 15.00 4.50
130 H.Ramirez AU RC 40.00 12.00
131 Abraham Nunez AU 15.00 4.50
132 Jose Ortiz AU 15.00 4.50
133 Jeremy Owens AU RC 15.00 4.50
134 Claudio Vargas AU RC 15.00 4.50
135 Corey Patterson AU 25.00 7.50
136 Carlos Pena 8.00 2.40
137 Bud Smith AU RC 15.00 4.50
138 Adam Dunn AU 1.50 .45
139 A.Pettyjohn AU RC 15.00 4.50
140 E.Guzman AU RC 15.00 4.50
141 Jay Gibbons AU RC 25.00 7.50
142 Wilkin Ruan AU RC 15.00 4.50
143 Tsuyoshi Shinjo RC 12.00 3.60
144 Alfonso Soriano AU 50.00 15.00
145 Marcus Giles AU 15.00 4.50
146 Ichiro Suzuki RC 80.00 24.00
147 Juan Uribe AU RC 15.00 4.50
148 David Williams AU RC 15.00 4.50
149 C. Valderrama AU RC 15.00 4.50
150 Matt White AU RC 15.00 4.50
151 Albert Pujols AU RC 350.00 105.00
152 D.Mendez AU RC 15.00 4.50
153 Cory Aldridge AU RC 15.00 4.50
154 B. Duckworth AU RC 15.00 4.50
155 Josh Beckett AU 40.00 12.00
156 W.Betemit AU RC 15.00 4.50
157 Ben Sheets AU 15.00 4.50
158 Andres Torres AU RC 15.00 4.50
159 Aubrey Huff AU 15.00 4.50
160 Jack Wilson AU RC 15.00 4.50
161 Rafael Soriano AU RC 50.00 15.00
162 Nick Johnson AU 15.00 4.50
163 Carlos Garcia AU RC 15.00 4.50
164 Josh Towers AU RC 15.00 4.50
165 J.Michaels AU RC 15.00 4.50
166 Ryan Drese RC 8.00 2.40
167 Dewon Brazelton RC 10.00 3.00
168 Kevin Olsen RC 8.00 2.40
169 Benito Baez RC 8.00 2.40
170 Mark Prior RC 80.00 24.00
171 Wilmy Caceres RC 8.00 2.40
172 Mark Teixeira RC 40.00 12.00
173 Willie Harris RC 8.00 2.40
174 Mike Koplove RC 8.00 2.40
175 Brandon Knight RC 8.00 2.40
176 John Grabow RC 8.00 2.40
177 Jeremy Affeldt RC 10.00 3.00
178 Brandon Inge 8.00 2.40
179 Casey Fossum RC 8.00 2.40
180 Scott Stewart RC 8.00 2.40
181 Luke Hudson RC 8.00 2.40
182 Ken Vining RC 8.00 2.40
183 Toby Hall 8.00 2.40
184 Eric Knott RC 8.00 2.40
185 Kris Foster RC 8.00 2.40
186 David Brous RC 8.00 2.40
187 Roy Smith RC 8.00 2.40
188 Grant Balfour RC 8.00 2.40
189 Jeremy Fikac RC 8.00 2.40
190 Morgan Ensberg RC 12.00 3.60
191 Ryan Freel RC 8.00 2.40
192 Ryan Jensen RC 8.00 2.40
193 Lance Davis RC 8.00 2.40
194 Delvin James RC 8.00 2.40
195 Timo Perez 8.00 2.40
196 Michael Cuddyer 8.00 2.40
197 Bob File RC 8.00 2.40
198 Martin Vargas RC 8.00 2.40
199 Kris Keller RC 8.00 2.40
200 T.Spooneybarger RC 8.00 2.40
201 Adam Everett 8.00 2.40
202 Josh Fogg RC 8.00 2.40
203 Kip Wells 8.00 2.40
204 Rick Bauer RC 8.00 2.40
205 Brent Abernathy 8.00 2.40
206 Erick Almonte RC 8.00 2.40
207 Pedro Santana RC 8.00 2.40
208 Ken Harvey 8.00 2.40
209 Jerrod Riggan RC 8.00 2.40
210 Nick Punto RC 8.00 2.40
211 Steve Green RC 8.00 2.40
212 Nick Neugebauer 8.00 2.40
213 Chris George 8.00 2.40
214 Mike Penney RC 8.00 2.40
215 Bret Prinz RC 8.00 2.40
216 Tim Christman RC 8.00 2.40
217 Sean Douglass RC 8.00 2.40
218 Brett Jodie RC 8.00 2.40
219 Juan Diaz RC 8.00 2.40
220 Carlos Hernandez 8.00 2.40
221 Alex Cintron 8.00 2.40
222 Juan Cruz RC 8.00 2.40
223 Larry Bigbie 8.00 2.40
224 Junior Spivey RC 10.00 3.00
225 Luis Rivas 8.00 2.40
226 Brandon Lyon RC 8.00 2.40
227 Tony Cogan RC 8.00 2.40
228 J.Duchscherer RC 8.00 2.40
229 Tike Redman 8.00 2.40
230 Jimmy Rollins 8.00 2.40
231 Scott Podsednik RC 30.00 9.00
232 Jose Acevedo RC 8.00 2.40
233 Luis Pineda RC 8.00 2.40
234 Josh Phelps 8.00 2.40
235 Paul Phillips RC 8.00 2.40
236 Brian Roberts RC 8.00 2.40
237 O.Woodards RC 8.00 2.40
238 Bart Miadich RC 8.00 2.40
239 Les Walrond RC 8.00 2.40
240 Brad Voyles RC 8.00 2.40
241 Joe Crede 8.00 2.40
242 Juan Moreno RC 8.00 2.40
243 Matt Ginter 8.00 2.40
244 Brian Rogers RC 8.00 2.40
245 Pablo Ozuna 8.00 2.40
246 Geronimo Gil RC 8.00 2.40
247 Mike Maroth RC 8.00 2.40
248 Josue Perez RC 8.00 2.40
249 Dee Brown 8.00 2.40
250 Victor Zambrano RC 10.00 3.00
251 Nick Maness RC 8.00 2.40
252 Kyle Lohse RC 10.00 3.00
253 Greg Miller RC 8.00 2.40
254 Henry Mateo RC 8.00 2.40
255 Duaner Sanchez RC 8.00 2.40
256 Rob MacKowiak RC 8.00 2.40
257 Steve Lomasney 8.00 2.40
258 Angel Santos RC 8.00 2.40
259 Winston Abreu RC 8.00 2.40
260 Brandon Berger RC 8.00 2.40
261 Tomas De La Rosa 8.00 2.40
262 Ramon Vazquez RC 8.00 2.40
263 Mickey Callaway RC 8.00 2.40
264 Corky Miller RC 8.00 2.40
265 Keith Ginter 8.00 2.40
266 Cody Ransom RC 8.00 2.40
267 Doug Nickle RC 8.00 2.40
268 Derrick Lewis RC 8.00 2.40
269 Eric Hinske RC 10.00 3.00
270 Travis Phelps RC 8.00 2.40
271 Eric Valent 8.00 2.40
272 Michael Rivera RC 8.00 2.40
273 Esix Snead RC 8.00 2.40
274 Troy Mattes RC 8.00 2.40
275 Jermaine Clark RC 8.00 2.40
276 Nate Cornejo 8.00 2.40
277 George Perez RC 8.00 2.40
278 Juan Rivera 8.00 2.40
279 Justin Atchley RC 8.00 2.40
280 Adam Johnson 8.00 2.40
281 Gene Altman RC 8.00 2.40
282 Jason Jennings 8.00 2.40
283 Scott MacRae RC 8.00 2.40
284 Craig Monroe RC 8.00 2.40
285 Bert Snow RC 8.00 2.40
286 Stubby Clapp RC 8.00 2.40
287 Jack Cust 8.00 2.40
288 Will Ohman RC 8.00 2.40
289 Wily Mo Pena 8.00 2.40
290 Joe Beimel RC 8.00 2.40
291 Jason Karnuth RC 8.00 2.40
292 Bill Ortega RC 8.00 2.40
293 Nate Teut RC 8.00 2.40
294 Erik Hiljus RC 8.00 2.40
295 Jason Smith RC 8.00 2.40
296 Juan A.Pena RC 8.00 2.40
297 David Espinosa 8.00 2.40
298 Tim Redding 8.00 2.40
299 Brian Lawrence RC 8.00 2.40
300 Brian Reith RC 8.00 2.40
301 Chad Durbin 8.00 2.40
302 Kurt Ainsworth 8.00 2.40
303 Blaine Neal RC 8.00 2.40
304 Jorge Julio RC 8.00 2.40
305 Adam Bernero 8.00 2.40
306 Travis Hafner RC 10.00 3.00
307 Dustan Mohr RC 8.00 2.40
308 Cesar Crespo RC 8.00 2.40
309 Billy Sylvester RC 8.00 2.40
310 Zach Day RC 10.00 3.00
311 Angel Berroa RC 15.00 4.50

2001 Donruss Signature Proofs

Randomly inserted in gift boxes, these 311 cards parallel the Donruss Signature set. Cards numbered 1-110 were issued to a print run of 175 sets while cards numbered 111-311 were issued to a print run of 25 sets. Please note that all cards numbered between 111 and 165 were autographed in addition to a few other scattered cards throughout the set. Due to

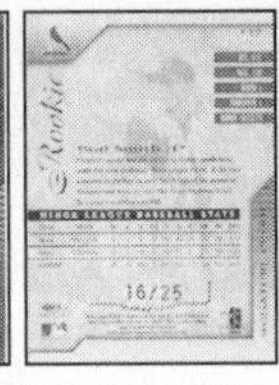

market scarcity, no pricing is provided for cards numbered 111-311.

Nm-Mt Ex-Mt
*PROOFS 1-110: 1.5X TO 4X BASIC...
111 Alex Escobar AU
112 Johnny Estrada AU
113 Pedro Feliz AU
114 Nate Frese AU
115 Ricardo Rodriguez AU
116 Brandon Larson AU
117 Alexis Gomez AU
118 Jason Hart AU
119 C.C. Sabathia AU
120 Endy Chavez AU
121 Christian Parker AU
122 Jackson Melian
123 Joe Kennedy AU
124 Adrian Hernandez AU
125 Cesar Izturis AU
126 Jose Mieses AU
127 Roy Oswalt AU
128 Eric Munson AU
129 Xavier Nady AU
130 Horacio Ramirez AU
131 Abraham Nunez AU
132 Jose Ortiz AU
133 Jeremy Owens AU
134 Claudio Vargas AU
135 Corey Patterson AU
136 Carlos Pena AU
137 Bud Smith AU
138 Adam Dunn AU
139 Adam Pettyjohn AU
140 Elpidio Guzman AU
141 Jay Gibbons AU
142 Wilkin Ruan AU
143 Tsuyoshi Shinjo
144 Alfonso Soriano AU
145 Marcus Giles AU
146 Ichiro Suzuki
147 Juan Uribe AU
148 David Williams AU
149 Carlos Valderrama AU
150 Matt White AU
151 Albert Pujols AU
152 Donaldo Mendez AU
153 Cory Aldridge AU
154 Brandon Duckworth AU
155 Josh Beckett AU
156 Wilson Betemit AU
157 Ben Sheets AU
158 Andres Torres AU
159 Aubrey Huff AU
160 Jack Wilson AU
161 Rafael Soriano AU
162 Nick Johnson AU
163 Carlos Garcia AU
164 Josh Towers AU
165 Jason Michaels AU
167 Dewon Brazelton AU
172 Mark Teixeira AU
179 Casey Fossum AU
194 Delvin James AU
196 Michael Cuddyer AU
222 Juan Cruz AU
241 Joe Crede AU
249 Dee Brown AU
265 Keith Ginter AU
269 Eric Hinske AU
271 Eric Valent AU
280 Adam Johnson AU
282 Jason Jennings AU
287 Jack Cust AU
289 Wily Mo Pena AU
297 David Espinosa AU
311 Angel Berroa AU

2001 Donruss Signature Award Winning Signatures

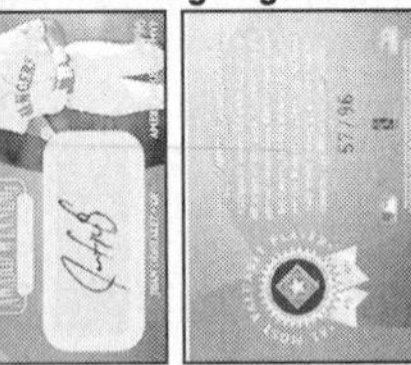

Randomly inserted in gift boxes, these cards feature signature from various players who won awards and the cards have stated print runs to that year they won an award. Please see our checklist for specific print run information.

Nm-Mt Ex-Mt
1 Jeff Bagwell/94 100.00 30.00
2 Carlos Beltran/99 25.00 7.50
3 Johnny Bench/68 100.00 30.00
4 Yogi Berra/55 60.00 18.00
5 Craig Biggio/97 50.00 15.00
6 Barry Bonds/93 200.00 60.00
7 Rod Carew/77 80.00 24.00
8 Orlando Cepeda/67 30.00 9.00
9 Andre Dawson/77 30.00 9.00
10 D.Eckersley CY/92 30.00 9.00
11 D.Eckersley MVP/92 30.00 9.00
12 Whitey Ford/61 60.00 18.00
13 Jason Giambi/100 60.00 18.00
14 Bob Gibson/68 50.00 15.00
15 Juan Gonzalez/96 40.00 12.00
16 Orel Hershiser/88 40.00 12.00
17 Al Kaline/67 100.00 30.00
18 Fred Lynn/75 MVP 30.00 9.00
19 Fred Lynn/75 ROY 30.00 9.00
20 Jim Palmer/76 30.00 9.00
21 Cal Ripken/83 150.00 45.00
22 Phil Rizzuto/50 50.00 15.00
23 Brooks Robinson/64 60.00 18.00
24 Scott Rolen/97 40.00 12.00
25 Ryne Sandberg/84 120.00 36.00
26 Warren Spahn/57 60.00 18.00
27 Frank Thomas/94 40.00 12.00
28 Billy Williams/61 30.00 9.00
29 Kerry Wood/98 40.00 12.00
30 Robin Yount/89 80.00 24.00

2001 Donruss Signature Award Winning Signatures Masters Series

Randomly inserted in gift boxes, these cards feature various award winners who signed cards relating to various awards they won during their career.

Nm-Mt Ex-Mt
1 Jeff Bagwell
2 Carlos Beltran 20.00 6.00
3 Johnny Bench
4 Yogi Berra
5 Craig Biggio 50.00 15.00
6 Barry Bonds
7 Rod Carew
8 Orlando Cepeda 20.00 6.00
9 Andre Dawson 20.00 6.00
10 Dennis Eckersley CY 20.00 6.00
11 Dennis Eckersley MVP 20.00 6.00
12 Whitey Ford 80.00 24.00
13 Jason Giambi
14 Bob Gibson 40.00 12.00
15 Juan Gonzalez
16 Orel Hershiser 100.00 30.00
17 Al Kaline 80.00 24.00
18 Fred Lynn MVP 20.00 6.00
19 Fred Lynn ROY 20.00 6.00
20 Jim Palmer 20.00 6.00
21 Cal Ripken
22 Phil Rizzuto 40.00 12.00
23 Brooks Robinson 50.00 15.00
24 Scott Rolen 50.00 15.00
25 Ryne Sandberg
26 Warren Spahn 50.00 15.00
27 Frank Thomas
28 Billy Williams 20.00 6.00
29 Kerry Wood 50.00 15.00
30 Robin Yount

2001 Donruss Signature Century Marks

Randomly inserted in gift boxes, these 48 cards feature signed cards of the featured players to various amounts. Please see our checklist to get the specific information on how many cards each player signed for this part of the promotion.

Nm-Mt Ex-Mt
1 Brent Abernathy/184 10.00 3.00
2 Roberto Alomar/102 60.00 18.00
3 Rick Ankiel/119 10.00 3.00
4 Lance Berkman/121 15.00 4.50
5 Mark Buehrle/224 15.00 4.50
6 Wilmy Caceres/194 10.00 3.00
7 Eric Chavez/170 15.00 4.50
8 Joe Crede/154 10.00 3.00
9 Jack Cust/178 10.00 3.00
10 B. Duckworth/183 15.00 4.50
11 David Espinosa/199 10.00 3.00
12 Johnny Estrada/198 15.00 4.50
13 Pedro Feliz/180 10.00 3.00
14 Robert Fick/232 15.00 4.50
15 Cliff Floyd/146 15.00 4.50
16 Casey Fossum/100 15.00 4.50
17 Jay Gibbons/175 25.00 7.50
18 Keith Ginter/163 10.00 3.00
19 Troy Glaus/144 25.00 7.50
20 Luis Gonzalez/101 15.00 4.50
21 Vladimir Guerrero/187 40.00 12.00
22 Richard Hidalgo/173 15.00 4.50
23 Tim Hudson/145 25.00 7.50
24 Adam Johnson/130 10.00 3.00
25 Gabe Kapler/150 10.00 3.00
26 Joe Kennedy/219 15.00 4.50
27 Ryan Klesko/176 15.00 4.50
28 Carlos Lee/179 15.00 4.50
29 Terrence Long/180 15.00 4.50
30 Edgar Martinez/110 40.00 12.00
31 Joe Mays/209 10.00 3.00
32 Greg Miller/194 10.00 3.00
33 Wade Miller/180 15.00 4.50
34 Mark Mulder/203 25.00 7.50
35 Xavier Nady/180 15.00 4.50
36 Magglio Ordonez/104 15.00 4.50
37 Jose Ortiz/187 10.00 3.00
38 Roy Oswalt/192 25.00 7.50
39 Wily Mo Pena/203 10.00 3.00
40 Brad Penny/198 10.00 3.00
41 Aramis Ramirez/241 15.00 4.50
42 Luis Rivas/163 10.00 3.00
43 Alex Rodriguez/110 150.00 45.00
44 Scott Rolen/106 25.00 7.50
45 Mike Sweeney/99 15.00 4.50
46 Eric Valent/163 10.00 3.00
47 Kip Wells/223 10.00 3.00
48 Kerry Wood/109 40.00 12.00

2001 Donruss Signature Century Marks Masters Series

Randomly inserted in packs, these cards were signed by the players.

Nm-Mt Ex-Mt
1 Brent Abernathy 10.00 3.00
2 Roberto Alomar 80.00 24.00
3 Rick Ankiel 10.00 3.00
4 Lance Berkman 15.00 4.50
5 Mark Buehrle 15.00 4.50
6 Wilmy Caceres 10.00 3.00
7 Eric Chavez 15.00 4.50
8 Joe Crede 10.00 3.00
9 Jack Cust 10.00 3.00
10 Brandon Duckworth 15.00 4.50
11 David Espinosa 10.00 3.00
12 Johnny Estrada 15.00 4.50
13 Pedro Feliz 10.00 3.00
14 Robert Fick 15.00 4.50
15 Cliff Floyd 15.00 4.50
16 Casey Fossum 15.00 4.50
17 Jay Gibbons 25.00 7.50
18 Keith Ginter 10.00 3.00
19 Troy Glaus 80.00 24.00
20 Luis Gonzalez
21 Vladimir Guerrero
22 Richard Hidalgo 15.00 4.50
23 Tim Hudson 25.00 7.50
24 Adam Johnson 10.00 3.00
25 Gabe Kapler 10.00 3.00
26 Joe Kennedy 15.00 4.50
27 Ryan Klesko 15.00 4.50
28 Carlos Lee 15.00 4.50
29 Terrence Long 15.00 4.50
30 Edgar Martinez 40.00 12.00
31 Joe Mays 10.00 3.00
32 Greg Miller 10.00 3.00
33 Wade Miller 15.00 4.50
34 Mark Mulder 25.00 7.50
35 Xavier Nady 15.00 4.50
36 Magglio Ordonez 15.00 4.50
37 Jose Ortiz 10.00 3.00
38 Roy Oswalt 25.00 7.50
39 Wily Mo Pena 10.00 3.00
40 Brad Penny 10.00 3.00
41 Aramis Ramirez 15.00 4.50
42 Luis Rivas 10.00 3.00
43 Alex Rodriguez
44 Scott Rolen
45 Mike Sweeney 15.00 4.50
46 Eric Valent 10.00 3.00
47 Kip Wells 10.00 3.00
48 Kerry Wood

2001 Donruss Signature Milestone Marks

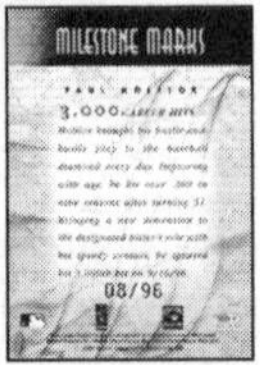

Randomly inserted in gift boxes, these 36 cards feature players autographs on a card related to specific highlights from each player's career. Since each player signed a different number of cards, please see our checklist for more detailed information on how many of each card was signed.

Nm-Mt Ex-Mt
1 Ernie Banks/285 50.00 15.00
2 Yogi Berra/120 60.00 18.00
3 Wade Boggs/98 120.00 36.00
4 Barry Bonds/55 200.00 60.00
5 G. Brett 3000 Hits/27
6 George Brett 1500 RBI/23
7 Lou Brock/83 30.00 9.00
8 Rod Carew/110 50.00 15.00
9 Steve Carlton/75 50.00 15.00
10 Gary Carter/213 30.00 9.00
11 Bobby Doerr/192 20.00 6.00
12 Bob Feller/202 30.00 9.00
13 Whitey Ford/186 30.00 9.00
14 Steve Garvey/175 20.00 6.00
15 Tony Gwynn/99 60.00 18.00
16 Fergie Jenkins/149 20.00 6.00
17 Al Kaline/149 60.00 18.00
18 Harmon Killebrew/127 50.00 15.00
19 Ralph Kiner/105 20.00 6.00
20 Willie McCovey/20
21 Paul Molitor/96 60.00 18.00
22 E. Murray 3000 Hits/46 150.00 45.00
23 Eddie Murray 1500 RBI/17
24 Stan Musial/109 100.00 30.00
25 Phil Niekro/300 20.00 6.00
26 Tony Perez/146 20.00 6.00
27 Cal Ripken/25
28 Frank Robinson/136 30.00 9.00
29 M. Schmidt 500 HR/40
30 Mike Schmidt 1500 RBI/23

Card	Nm-Mt	Ex-Mt
31 Enos Slaughter/117	30.00	9.00
32 Warren Spahn/300	50.00	15.00
33 Alan Trammell/154	50.00	15.00
34 Hoyt Wilhelm/227	20.00	6.00
35 D.Winfield Padres/31		
36 Dave Winfield Yankees/15		

2001 Donruss Signature Milestone Marks Masters Series

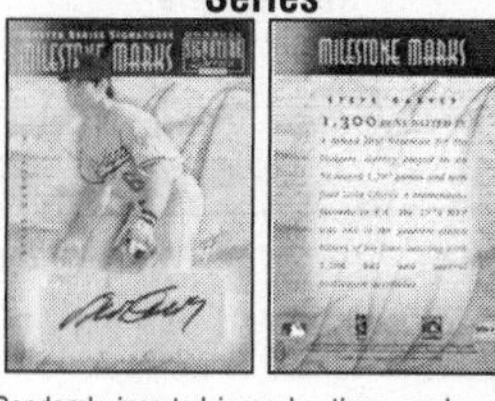

Randomly inserted in packs, these cards were signed by the players. Card number one does not exist for this set.

Card	Nm-Mt	Ex-Mt
1 Does Not Exist		
2 Yogi Berra		
3 Wade Boggs		
4 Barry Bonds		
5 George Brett 3000 Hits		
6 George Brett 1500 RBI		
7 Lou Brock	30.00	9.00
8 Rod Carew		
9 Steve Carlton	60.00	18.00
10 Gary Carter	30.00	9.00
11 Bobby Doerr	20.00	6.00
12 Bob Feller	30.00	9.00
13 Whitey Ford	80.00	24.00
14 Steve Garvey	20.00	6.00
15 Tony Gwynn		
16 Fergie Jenkins	20.00	6.00
17 Al Kaline	100.00	30.00
18 Harmon Killebrew	80.00	24.00
19 Ralph Kiner	20.00	6.00
20 Willie McCovey		
21 Paul Molitor	120.00	36.00
22 Eddie Murray 3000 Hits		
23 Eddie Murray 1500 RBI		
24 Stan Musial		
25 Phil Niekro	20.00	6.00
26 Tony Perez	20.00	6.00
27 Cal Ripken		
28 Frank Robinson	30.00	9.00
29 Mike Schmidt 500 HR		
30 Mike Schmidt 1500 RBI		
31 Enos Slaughter	30.00	9.00
32 Warren Spahn		
33 Alan Trammell	30.00	9.00
34 Hoyt Wilhelm	20.00	6.00
35 Dave Winfield Padres		
36 Dave Winfield Yankees		

2001 Donruss Signature Notable Nicknames

Randomly inserted in gift boxes, these 18 cards feature players along with their nickname. Each player signed 100 of these cards for inclusion in this product.

Card	Nm-Mt	Ex-Mt
1 Ernie Banks	100.00	30.00
Mr. Cub		
2 Orlando Cepeda	60.00	18.00
Baby Bull		
3 Will Clark	250.00	75.00
The Thrill		
4 Roger Clemens	350.00	105.00
The Rocket		
5 Andre Dawson	60.00	18.00
The Hawk		
6 Bob Feller	100.00	30.00
Rapid Robert		
7 Carlton Fisk	100.00	30.00
Pudge		
8 Andres Galarraga	60.00	18.00
Big Cat		
9 Luis Gonzalez	60.00	18.00
4		
10 Reggie Jackson	100.00	30.00
Mr. October		
11 Harmon Killebrew	100.00	30.00
Killer		
12 Stan Musial	150.00	45.00
The Man		
13 Brooks Robinson	100.00	30.00
Hoover		
14 Nolan Ryan	300.00	90.00
The Express		
15 Ryne Sandberg	250.00	75.00
Ryno		
16 Enos Slaughter	100.00	30.00
Country		
17 Duke Snider	100.00	30.00
4		
18 Frank Thomas	150.00	45.00
MVP		

2001 Donruss Signature Notable Nicknames Masters Series

Randomly inserted into gift boxes, these 18 cards featured signed cards of star players along with their nicknames.

Card	Nm-Mt	Ex-Mt
1 Ernie Banks	150.00	45.00
Mr. Cub		
2 Orlando Cepeda	100.00	30.00
Baby Bull		
3 Will Clark	250.00	75.00
The Thrill		
4 Roger Clemens		
The Rocket		
5 Andre Dawson	100.00	30.00
The Hawk		
6 Bob Feller	150.00	45.00
Rapid Robert		
7 Carlton Fisk	150.00	45.00
Pudge		
8 Andres Galarraga	100.00	30.00
Big Cat		
9 Luis Gonzalez	100.00	30.00
4		
10 Reggie Jackson		
Mr. October		
11 Harmon Killebrew	150.00	45.00
Killer		
12 Stan Musial		
The Man		
13 Brooks Robinson	150.00	45.00
Hoover		
14 Nolan Ryan	500.00	150.00
The Express		
15 Ryne Sandberg	400.00	120.00
Rhino		
16 Enos Slaughter	150.00	45.00
Country		
17 Duke Snider		
4		
18 Frank Thomas		
MVP		

2001 Donruss Signature Stats

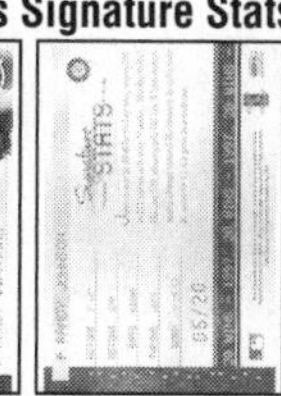

Randomly inserted into gift boxes, these 52 cards feature players who signed cards relating to a key stat in their career. Since each card is signed to a different amount, please see our checklist for specific information about each card.

Card	Nm-Mt	Ex-Mt
1 Roberto Alomar/120	60.00	18.00
2 Moises Alou/124	15.00	4.50
3 Luis Aparicio/313	15.00	4.50
4 Lance Berkman/297	15.00	4.50
5 Wade Boggs/51	150.00	45.00
6 Lou Brock/118	25.00	7.50
7 Gary Carter/32		
8 Joe Carter/121	15.00	4.50
9 Sean Casey/103	15.00	4.50
10 Darin Erstad/100	15.00	4.50
11 Bob Feller/26		
12 Cliff Floyd/45	25.00	7.50
13 Whitey Ford/72	60.00	18.00
14 Andres Galarraga/150	15.00	4.50
15 Bob Gibson/112	25.00	7.50
16 Brian Giles/123	15.00	4.50
17 Troy Glaus/102	25.00	7.50
18 Luis Gonzalez/114	15.00	4.50
19 Vladimir Guerrero/131	40.00	12.00
20 Tony Gwynn/17		
21 Richard Hidalgo/314	15.00	4.50
22 Bo Jackson/32		
23 Fergie Jenkins/25		
24 Randy Johnson/20		
25 Al Kaline/128	60.00	18.00
26 Gabe Kapler/302	10.00	3.00
27 Ralph Kiner/54	40.00	12.00
28 Ryan Klesko/23		
29 Carlos Lee/261	15.00	4.50
30 Kenny Lofton/210	15.00	4.50
31 Edgar Martinez/145	40.00	12.00
32 Joe Mays/115	10.00	3.00
33 Paul Molitor/41	80.00	24.00
34 Mark Mulder/88	40.00	12.00
35 Phil Niekro/23		
36 Magglio Ordonez/126	15.00	4.50
37 Rafael Palmeiro/47	60.00	18.00
38 Jim Palmer/23		
39 Chan Ho Park/18		
40 Kirby Puckett/31		
41 Manny Ramirez/45	80.00	24.00
42 Alex Rodriguez/132	150.00	45.00
43 Ivan Rodriguez/113	40.00	12.00
44 Curt Schilling/15		
45 Tom Seaver/25		
46 Shannon Stewart/319	15.00	4.50
47 Mike Sweeney/144	15.00	4.50
48 Miguel Tejada/115	15.00	4.50
49 Joe Torre/230	40.00	12.00
50 Javier Vazquez/405	25.00	7.50
51 Jose Vidro/330	15.00	4.50
52 Hoyt Wilhelm/243	15.00	4.50

2001 Donruss Signature Stats Masters Series

Randomly inserted into gift boxes, these 52 cards featured signed cards of star players

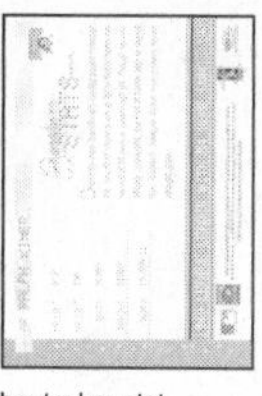

along with information about a key stat.

Card	Nm-Mt	Ex-Mt
1 Roberto Alomar	100.00	30.00
2 Moises Alou	15.00	4.50
3 Luis Aparicio	15.00	4.50
4 Lance Berkman	15.00	4.50
5 Wade Boggs		
6 Lou Brock	80.00	24.00
7 Gary Carter	50.00	15.00
8 Joe Carter	25.00	7.50
9 Sean Casey	15.00	4.50
10 Darin Erstad	60.00	18.00
11 Bob Feller	25.00	7.50
12 Cliff Floyd	15.00	4.50
13 Whitey Ford	80.00	24.00
14 Andres Galarraga	60.00	18.00
15 Bob Gibson	50.00	15.00
16 Brian Giles	15.00	4.50
17 Troy Glaus	60.00	18.00
18 Luis Gonzalez		
19 Vladimir Guerrero		
20 Tony Gwynn		
21 Richard Hidalgo	15.00	4.50
22 Bo Jackson	120.00	36.00
23 Fergie Jenkins	25.00	7.50
24 Randy Johnson		
25 Al Kaline	80.00	24.00
26 Gabe Kapler	10.00	3.00
27 Ralph Kiner	25.00	7.50
28 Ryan Klesko	15.00	4.50
29 Carlos Lee	15.00	4.50
30 Kenny Lofton	25.00	7.50
31 Edgar Martinez	50.00	15.00
32 Joe Mays	10.00	3.00
33 Paul Molitor		
34 Mark Mulder	25.00	7.50
35 Phil Niekro	15.00	4.50
36 Magglio Ordonez	15.00	4.50
37 Rafael Palmeiro		
38 Jim Palmer	40.00	12.00
39 Chan Ho Park	200.00	60.00
40 Kirby Puckett		
41 Manny Ramirez		
42 Alex Rodriguez		
43 Ivan Rodriguez		
44 Curt Schilling	60.00	18.00
45 Tom Seaver		
46 Shannon Stewart	15.00	4.50
47 Mike Sweeney	15.00	4.50
48 Miguel Tejada	15.00	4.50
49 Joe Torre	100.00	30.00
50 Javier Vazquez	25.00	7.50
51 Jose Vidro	15.00	4.50
52 Hoyt Wilhelm		

2001 Donruss Signature Team Trademarks

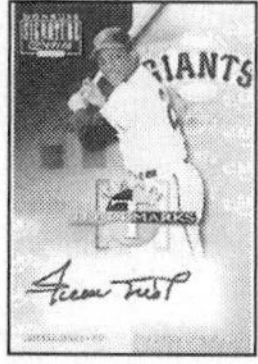

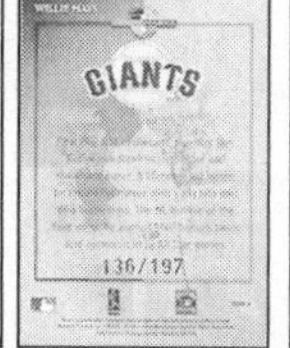

Randomly inserted into gift boxes, these 58 cards feature signed cards of a player as well as information about the team they played for. Since each player signed a different amount of cards for this promotion, we have included detailed information in our checklist.

Card	Nm-Mt	Ex-Mt
1 Rick Ankiel/179	20.00	6.00
2 Ernie Banks/180	60.00	18.00
3 Johnny Bench/20		
4 Yogi Berra/124	60.00	18.00
5 Wade Boggs/89	120.00	36.00
6 Barry Bonds/77	200.00	60.00
7 Lou Brock/29		
8 Steve Carlton/174	30.00	9.00
9 Sean Casey/123	20.00	6.00
10 Orlando Cepeda/100	20.00	6.00
11 Roger Clemens RS/30		
12 Roger Clemens Yankees/21		
13 Andre Dawson/176	20.00	6.00
14 Bobby Doerr/193	30.00	9.00
15 Whitey Ford/94	50.00	15.00
16 Does Not Exist		
17 Steve Garvey/182	20.00	6.00
18 Bob Gibson/98	40.00	12.00
19 Juan Gonzalez/70	100.00	30.00
20 Shawn Green/109	20.00	6.00
21 Orel Hershiser/210	50.00	15.00
22 Reggie Jackson/73	80.00	24.00
23 Fergie Jenkins/213	20.00	6.00
24 Chipper Jones/74	80.00	24.00
25 Pedro Martinez/27		
26 Don Mattingly/72	150.00	45.00
27 Willie Mays/197	150.00	45.00
28 Willie McCovey/26	80.00	24.00
29 Joe Morgan/33		
30 Eddie Murray/45	120.00	36.00
31 Stan Musial/65	150.00	45.00
32 Mike Mussina Balt./85	80.00	24.00
33 M.Mussina Yanks/95	80.00	24.00
34 Phil Niekro/187	20.00	6.00
35 Rafael Palmeiro/99	50.00	15.00
36 Jim Palmer/142	20.00	6.00
37 Tony Perez/73	20.00	6.00
38 Manny Ramirez/57	60.00	18.00
39 Cal Ripken/47	300.00	90.00
40 Phil Rizzuto/98	50.00	15.00
41 Brooks Robinson/146	40.00	12.00
42 F.Robinson Orioles/118	30.00	9.00
43 F.Robinson Reds/116	30.00	9.00
44 Alex Rodriguez/100	150.00	45.00
45 Ivan Rodriguez/62	80.00	24.00
46 Scott Rolen/39		
47 Nolan Ryan/153	150.00	45.00
48 Ryne Sandberg/52	150.00	45.00
49 Curt Schilling/63	40.00	12.00
50 Mike Schmidt/107	100.00	30.00
51 Tom Seaver/25		
52 Gary Sheffield/194	30.00	9.00
53 Enos Slaughter/215	30.00	9.00
54 Duke Snider/47	80.00	24.00
55 Warren Spahn/140	40.00	12.00
56 Joe Torre/90	60.00	18.00
57 Billy Williams/194	20.00	6.00
58 Kerry Wood/52	60.00	18.00

2001 Donruss Signature Team Trademarks Masters Series

Randomly inserted into gift boxes, these 56 cards featured signed cards of star players along with information about the team they played for. Card number 27 does not exist in this set.

Card	Nm-Mt	Ex-Mt
1 Rick Ankiel		
2 Does Not Exist		
3 Johnny Bench		
4 Yogi Berra		
5 Wade Boggs		
6 Barry Bonds		
7 Lou Brock		
8 Steve Carlton	60.00	18.00
9 Sean Casey		
10 Orlando Cepeda	15.00	4.50
11 Roger Clemens Red Sox		
12 Roger Clemens Yankees		
13 Andre Dawson	15.00	4.50
14 Bobby Doerr	15.00	4.50
15 Whitey Ford		
16 Nomar Garciaparra	250.00	75.00
17 Steve Garvey	15.00	4.50
18 Bob Gibson	60.00	18.00
19 Juan Gonzalez		
20 Shawn Green		
21 Orel Hershiser	100.00	30.00
22 Reggie Jackson		
23 Fergie Jenkins	15.00	4.50
24 Chipper Jones		
25 Pedro Martinez		
26 Don Mattingly	200.00	60.00
27 Does Not Exist		
28 Willie McCovey		
29 Joe Morgan		
30 Eddie Murray		
31 Stan Musial		
32 Mike Mussina Orioles		
33 Mike Mussina Yankees		
34 Phil Niekro	15.00	4.50
35 Rafael Palmeiro		
36 Jim Palmer	25.00	7.50
37 Tony Perez	15.00	4.50
38 Manny Ramirez		
39 Cal Ripken		
40 Phil Rizzuto	50.00	15.00
41 Brooks Robinson	80.00	24.00
42 Frank Robinson Orioles	80.00	24.00
43 Frank Robinson Reds		
44 Alex Rodriguez		
45 Ivan Rodriguez		
46 Scott Rolen		
47 Nolan Ryan	250.00	75.00
48 Ryne Sandberg		
49 Curt Schilling	40.00	12.00
50 Mike Schmidt		
51 Tom Seaver	60.00	18.00
52 Gary Sheffield	25.00	7.50
53 Enos Slaughter	20.00	6.00
54 Duke Snider		
55 Warren Spahn	50.00	15.00
56 Joe Torre		
57 Billy Williams	15.00	4.50
58 Kerry Wood		

2001-02 Donruss Signature Hawaii

These cards are exact parallels to the standard 2001 Donruss Signature cards except for the foil "2002 Hawaii Trade Conference" logo stamped on front. In addition, each card was serial numbered on front as follows: cards 1-110 - "X/25" and cards 112-306 - "X/10". Though numbered up to card 306, the set is actually composed of a skip-numbered selection of 227 different subjects. The cards were distributed in cello-wrapped sealed black boxes and given at a rate of one per attendee at the 2002 Hawaii Trade Conference Meet the Industry event at the Playoff presentation area. Attendees actually received either a football box (containing Playoff Contenders cards) or one of these baseball boxes. Each baseball box contained several basic cards plus one autograph card.

112-306 NO PRICING DUE TO SCARCITY
ONE BOX PER MEET INDUSTRY ATTENDEE

Card	Nm-Mt	Ex-Mt
1 Alex Rodriguez	20.00	6.00
2 Barry Bonds	25.00	7.50
3 Cal Ripken	30.00	9.00
4 Chipper Jones	12.00	3.60
5 Derek Jeter	30.00	9.00
6 Troy Glaus	6.00	1.80
7 Frank Thomas	6.00	1.80
8 Greg Maddux	20.00	6.00
9 Ivan Rodriguez	6.00	1.80
10 Jeff Bagwell	6.00	1.80
11 John Olerud	4.00	1.20
12 Todd Helton	6.00	1.80
13 Ken Griffey Jr.	15.00	4.50
14 Manny Ramirez	6.00	1.80
15 Mark McGwire	25.00	7.50
16 Mike Piazza	15.00	4.50
17 Nomar Garciaparra	20.00	6.00
18 Moises Alou	4.00	1.20
19 Aramis Ramirez	4.00	1.20
20 Curt Schilling	6.00	1.80
21 Pat Burrell	6.00	1.80
22 Doug Mientkiewicz	4.00	1.20
23 Carlos Delgado	4.00	1.20
24 J.D. Drew	4.00	1.20
25 Cliff Floyd	4.00	1.20
26 Freddy Garcia	4.00	1.20
27 Roberto Alomar	10.00	3.00
28 Barry Zito	10.00	3.00
29 Juan Encarnacion	4.00	1.20
30 Paul Konerko	4.00	1.20
31 Mark Mulder	4.00	1.20
32 Andy Pettitte	6.00	1.80
33 Jim Edmonds	4.00	1.20
34 Darin Erstad	6.00	1.80
35 Jason Giambi	10.00	3.00
36 Tom Glavine	10.00	3.00
37 Juan Gonzalez	10.00	3.00
38 Fred McGriff	6.00	1.80
39 Shawn Green	6.00	1.80
40 Tim Hudson	4.00	1.20
41 Andruw Jones	6.00	1.80
42 Jeff Kent	4.00	1.20
43 Barry Larkin	10.00	3.00
44 Brad Radke	4.00	1.20
45 Mike Mussina	10.00	3.00
46 Hideo Nomo	10.00	3.00
47 Rafael Palmeiro	6.00	1.80
48 Scott Rolen	6.00	1.80
49 Gary Sheffield	4.00	1.20
50 Bernie Williams	6.00	1.80
51 Bob Abreu	4.00	1.20
52 Edgardo Alfonzo	4.00	1.20
53 Edgar Martinez	6.00	1.80
54 Magglio Ordonez	4.00	1.20
55 Kerry Wood	6.00	1.80
56 Adrian Beltre	4.00	1.20
57 Lance Berkman	6.00	1.80
58 Kevin Brown	10.00	3.00
59 Sean Casey	4.00	1.20
60 Eric Chavez	4.00	1.20
61 Bartolo Colon	4.00	1.20
62 Sammy Sosa	15.00	4.50
63 Jermaine Dye	4.00	1.20
64 Tony Gwynn	15.00	4.50
65 Carl Everett	4.00	1.20
66 Brian Giles	4.00	1.20
67 Mike Hampton	4.00	1.20
68 Richard Hidalgo	4.00	1.20
69 Geoff Jenkins	4.00	1.20
70 Tony Clark	4.00	1.20
71 Roger Clemens	20.00	6.00
72 Ryan Klesko	4.00	1.20
73 Chan Ho Park	4.00	1.20
74 Richie Sexson	4.00	1.20
75 Mike Sweeney	4.00	1.20
76 Kazuhiro Sasaki	6.00	1.80
77 Miguel Tejada	4.00	1.20
78 Jose Vidro	4.00	1.20
79 Larry Walker	6.00	1.80
80 Preston Wilson	4.00	1.20
81 Craig Biggio	6.00	1.80
82 Andres Galarraga	4.00	1.20
83 Jim Thome	10.00	3.00
84 Vladimir Guerrero	10.00	3.00
85 Rafael Furcal	4.00	1.20
86 Cristian Guzman	4.00	1.20
87 Terrence Long	4.00	1.20
88 Bret Boone	4.00	1.20
89 Wade Miller	4.00	1.20
90 Eric Milton	4.00	1.20
91 Gabe Kapler	4.00	1.20
92 Johnny Damon	4.00	1.20
93 Carlos Lee	4.00	1.20
94 Kenny Lofton	4.00	1.20
95 Raul Mondesi	4.00	1.20
96 Jorge Posada	6.00	1.80
97 Mark Grace	10.00	3.00
98 Robert Fick	4.00	1.20
99 Joe Mays	4.00	1.20
100 Aaron Sele	4.00	1.20
101 Ben Grieve	4.00	1.20
102 Luis Gonzalez	4.00	1.20
103 Ray Durham	4.00	1.20
104 Mark Quinn	4.00	1.20
105 Jose Canseco	10.00	3.00
106 David Justice	4.00	1.20
107 Pedro Martinez	10.00	3.00
108 Randy Johnson	15.00	4.50
109 Phil Nevin	4.00	1.20
110 Rickey Henderson	15.00	4.50
112 Johnny Estrada		
114 Nate Frese		
115 Ricardo Rodriguez		
116 Brandon Larson		
117 Alexis Gomez		
118 Jason Hart		
119 C.C. Sabathia		
120 Endy Chavez		
121 Christian Parker		
122 Jackson Melian		
123 Joe Kennedy		
124 Adrian Hernandez		
126 Jose Mieses		
127 Roy Oswalt		
129 Xavier Nady		
130 Horacio Ramirez		
133 Jeremy Owens		
134 Claudio Vargas		
136 Carlos Pena		
137 Bud Smith		
138 Adam Dunn		
139 Adam Pettyjohn		
140 Elpidio Guzman		
141 Jay Gibbons		

142 Wilken Ruan
143 Tsuyoshi Shinjo
144 Alfonso Soriano
146 Ichiro Suzuki
147 Juan Uribe
148 David Williams
149 Carlos Valderrama
150 Matt White
151 Albert Pujols
152 Donaldo Mendez
153 Cory Aldridge
154 Brandon Duckworth
155 Josh Beckett
156 Wilson Betemit
157 Ben Sheets
158 Andres Torres
160 Jack Wilson
161 Rafael Soriano
162 Nick Johnson
163 Carlos Garcia
164 Josh Towers
165 Jason Michaels
166 Ryan Drese
167 Dewon Brazelton
168 Kevin Olsen
169 Benito Baez
170 Mark Prior
171 Wilmy Caceres
172 Mark Teixeira
173 Willie Harris
174 Mike Koplove
175 Brandon Knight
176 John Grabow
177 Jeremy Affeldt
179 Casey Fossum
180 Scott Stewart
181 Luke Hudson
182 Ken Vining
184 Eric Knott
185 Kris Foster
186 David Brous
187 Roy Smith
188 Grant Balfour
189 Jeremy Fikac
190 Morgan Ensberg
191 Ryan Freel
192 Ryan Jensen
193 Lance Davis
194 Delvin James
197 Bob File
198 Martin Vargas
199 Kris Keller
200 Tim Spooneybarger
202 Josh Fogg
204 Rick Bauer
206 Erick Almonte
207 Pedro Santana
209 Jerrod Riggan
210 Nick Punto
211 Steve Green
212 Nick Neugebauer
214 Mike Penney
215 Bret Prinz
216 Tim Christman
217 Sean Douglass
218 Brett Jodie
219 Juan Diaz
222 Juan Cruz
224 Junior Spivey
226 Brandon Lyon
227 Tony Cogan
228 Justin Duchscherer
231 Scott Podsednik
232 Jose Acevedo
233 Luis Pineda
235 Paul Phillips
236 Brian Roberts
237 Orlando Woodards
238 Bart Miadich
239 Les Walrond
240 Brad Voyles
242 Juan Moreno
244 Brian Rogers
246 Geronimo Gil
247 Mike Maroth
248 Josue Perez
251 Nick Maness
252 Kyle Lohse
262 Ramon Vazquez
269 Eric Hinske
284 Craig Monroe
298 Tim Redding
306 Travis Hafner

2001-02 Donruss Signature Hawaii Award Winning Signatures Master Series

These cards are exact parallels of the basic 2001 Donruss Signature autographed Master Series inserts except for the foil "2002 Hawaii Trade Conference" logo and serial numbering on front. The cards were distributed at a rate of one per sealed box at the Playoff presentation area for the Hawaii Trade Conference Meet the Industry event. Each attendee received either a sealed box of Playoff Contenders football cards or a sealed box of Donruss Signature baseball. The cards are too scarce to provide pricing, but have been checklisted alphabetically by each player's last name with specific print runs for each card.

Nm-Mt Ex-Mt

1 Carlos Beltran/10
2 Johnny Bench/1
3 Orlando Cepeda/5
4 Dennis Eckersley CY/5
5 Dennis Eckersley MVP/5
6 Whitey Ford/4
7 Jason Giambi/5
8 Bob Gibson/5
9 Tom Glavine/15
10 Orel Hershiser/5
11 Barry Larkin/15
12 Fred Lynn MVP/5
13 Fred Lynn ROY/5
14 Greg Maddux/1
15 Cal Ripken/1
16 Phil Rizzuto/3
17 Ryne Sandberg/3
18 Warren Spahn5
19 Kerry Wood/5

2001-02 Donruss Signature Hawaii Century Marks Master Series

These cards are exact parallels of the basic 2001 Donruss Signature autographed Master Series inserts except for the foil "2002 Hawaii Trade Conference" logo and serial numbering on front. The cards were distributed at a rate of one per sealed box at the Playoff presentation area for the Hawaii Trade Conference Meet the Industry event. Each attendee received either a sealed box of Playoff Contenders football cards or a sealed box of Donruss Signature baseball. The cards are too scarce to provide pricing, but have been checklisted alphabetically by each player's last name with specific print runs for each card.

Nm-Mt Ex-Mt

1 Bobby Abreu/5
2 Roberto Alomar/5
3 Eric Chavez/5
4 J.D. Drew/5
5 Troy Glaus/5
6 Luis Gonzalez/1
7 Vladimir Guerrero/5
8 Todd Helton/10
9 Andruw Jones/10
10 Mark Mulder/1
11 Xavier Nady/1
12 Roy Oswalt/1
13 Alex Rodriguez/5
14 Scott Rolen/5
15 Miguel Tejada/5

2001-02 Donruss Signature Hawaii Milestone Marks Master Series

These cards are exact parallels of the basic 2001 Donruss Signature autographed Master Series inserts except for the foil "2002 Hawaii Trade Conference" logo and serial numbering on front. The cards were distributed at a rate of one per sealed box at the Playoff presentation area for the Hawaii Trade Conference Meet the Industry event. Each attendee received either a sealed box of Playoff Contenders football cards or a sealed box of Donruss Signature baseball. The cards are too scarce to provide pricing, but have been checklisted alphabetically by each player's last name with specific print runs for each card.

Nm-Mt Ex-Mt

1 Yogi Berra/1
2 Wade Boggs/1
3 George Brett/1
4 Rod Carew/1
5 Bobby Doerr/1
6 Bob Feller/1
7 Whitey Ford/1
8 Steve Garvey/1
9 Tony Gwynn/1
10 Fergie Jenkins/1
11 Ralph Kiner/1
12 Paul Molitor/1
13 Stan Musial/1
14 Mike Schmidt HR/1
15 Mike Schmidt RBI/1
16 Tom Seaver/1
17 Enos Slaughter/1
18 Warren Spahn/1
19 Don Sutton/1
20 Alan Trammell/1
21 Hoyt Wilhelm/1
22 Dave Winfield Padres/1
23 Dave Winfield Yankees/1

2001-02 Donruss Signature Hawaii Notable Nicknames Master Series

These cards are exact parallels of the basic 2001 Donruss Signature autographed Master Series inserts except for the foil "2002 Hawaii Trade Conference" logo and serial numbering on front. The cards were distributed at a rate of one per sealed box at the Playoff presentation area for the Hawaii Trade Conference Meet the Industry event. Each attendee received either a sealed box of Playoff Contenders football cards or a sealed box of Donruss Signature baseball. The cards are too scarce to provide pricing, but have been checklisted alphabetically by each player's last name with specific print runs for each card.

Nm-Mt Ex-Mt

1 Orlando Cepeda/4
2 Roger Clemens/15
3 Andre Dawson/1
4 Carlton Fisk/1
5 Andres Galarraga/1
6 Luis Gonzalez/1
7 Harmon Killebrew/1
8 Greg Maddux/20
9 Stan Musial/1
10 Phil Rizzuto/20
11 Enos Slaughter/1
12 Frank Thomas/1

2001-02 Donruss Signature Hawaii Stats Master Series

These cards are exact parallels of the basic 2001 Donruss Signature autographed Master Series inserts except for the foil "2002 Hawaii Trade Conference" logo and serial numbering on front. The cards were distributed at a rate of one per sealed box at the Playoff presentation area for the Hawaii Trade Conference Meet the Industry event. Each attendee received either a sealed box of Playoff Contenders football cards or a sealed box of Donruss Signature baseball. The cards are too scarce to provide pricing, but have been checklisted with specific print runs for each card.

Nm-Mt Ex-Mt

1 Bob Abreu/5
2 Luis Aparicio/1
3 Lance Berkman/1
4 Wade Boggs/1
5 Gary Carter/1
6 Joe Carter/1
7 Whitey Ford/1
8 Luis Gonzalez/1
9 Vladimir Guerrero/1
10 Todd Helton/10
11 Bo Jackson/1
12 Fergie Jenkins/1
13 Andruw Jones/15
14 Edgar Martinez/1
15 Kirby Puckett/1
16 Manny Ramirez/1
17 Alex Rodriguez/1
18 Ivan Rodriguez/1
19 Miguel Tejada/1
20 Joe Torre/1

2001-02 Donruss Signature Hawaii Team Trademarks Master Series

These cards are exact parallels of the basic 2001 Donruss Signature autographed Master Series inserts except for the foil "2002 Hawaii Trade Conference" logo and serial numbering on front. The cards were distributed at a rate of one per sealed box at the Playoff presentation area for the Hawaii Trade Conference Meet the Industry event. Each attendee received either a sealed box of Playoff Contenders football cards or a sealed box of Donruss Signature baseball. The cards are too scarce to provide pricing, but have been checklisted with specific print runs for each card.

Nm-Mt Ex-Mt

1 Andruw Jones/5
2 Barry Larkin/5
3 Bernie Williams/1
4 Bob Gibson/1
5 Bobby Doerr/1
6 Brooks Robinson/1
7 Cal Ripken/1
8 Chipper Jones/3
9 Don Mattingly/1
10 Eddie Murray/1
11 Enos Slaughter/1
12 Joe Torre/1
13 Johnny Bench/1
14 Lou Brock/1
15 Manny Ramirez/1
16 Mike Mussina Orioles/1
17 Mike Mussina Yankees/1
18 Nolan Ryan/1
19 Orel Hershiser/1
20 Phil Rizzuto/1
21 Reggie Jackson/1
22 Roger Clemens Red Sox/1
23 Roger Clemens Yankees/1
24 Ryne Sandberg/1
25 Steve Carlton/1
26 Steve Garvey/1
27 Tom Glavine/5
28 Wade Boggs/1
29 Whitey Ford/1
30 Yogi Berra/1

2003 Donruss Signature

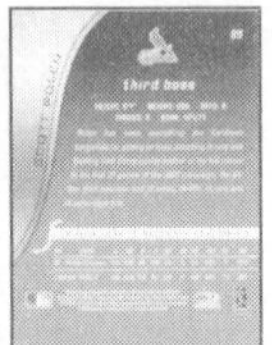

This 150 card set was released in August, 2003. This set was issued in four card packs issued in a special "box". These pack/boxes had a $50 SRP. Cards numbered 1-100 feature veterans in team alphabetical order while cards numbered 111 through 150 feature rookies. Unlike most Donruss/Playoff products, these rookie cards were not shortprinted.

	MINT	NRMT
COMMON CARD (1-100)	1.00	.45
COMMON CARD (101-150)	1.00	.45
1 Garret Anderson	1.00	.45
2 Tim Salmon	1.50	.70
3 Troy Glaus	1.50	.70
4 Curt Schilling	1.50	.70
5 Luis Gonzalez	1.00	.45
6 Mark Grace	1.50	.70
7 Matt Williams	1.00	.45
8 Randy Johnson	2.50	1.10
9 Andruw Jones	1.00	.45
10 Chipper Jones	2.50	1.10
11 Gary Sheffield	1.00	.45
12 Greg Maddux	4.00	1.80
13 Johnny Damon	1.00	.45
14 Manny Ramirez	1.00	.45
15 Nomar Garciaparra	4.00	1.80
16 Pedro Martinez	2.50	1.10
17 Corey Patterson	1.00	.45
18 Kerry Wood	2.50	1.10
19 Mark Prior	5.00	2.20
20 Sammy Sosa	4.00	1.80
21 Bartolo Colon	1.00	.45
22 Frank Thomas	2.50	1.10
23 Magglio Ordonez	1.00	.45
24 Paul Konerko	1.00	.45
25 Adam Dunn	1.00	.45
26 Austin Kearns	1.00	.45
27 Barry Larkin	2.50	1.10
28 Ken Griffey Jr.	4.00	1.80
29 C.C. Sabathia	1.00	.45
30 Omar Vizquel	1.00	.45
31 Larry Walker	1.50	.70
32 Todd Helton	1.50	.70
33 Ivan Rodriguez	2.50	1.10
34 Josh Beckett	1.50	.70
35 Craig Biggio	1.50	.70
36 Jeff Bagwell	1.50	.70
37 Jeff Kent	1.00	.45
38 Lance Berkman	1.00	.45
39 Richard Hidalgo	1.00	.45
40 Roy Oswalt	1.00	.45
41 Carlos Beltran	1.00	.45
42 Mike Sweeney	1.00	.45
43 Runelvys Hernandez	1.00	.45
44 Hideo Nomo	2.50	1.10
45 Kazuhisa Ishii	1.00	.45
46 Paul Lo Duca	1.00	.45
47 Shawn Green	1.00	.45
48 Ben Sheets	1.00	.45
49 Richie Sexson	1.00	.45
50 A.J. Pierzynski	1.00	.45
51 Torii Hunter	1.00	.45
52 Javier Vazquez	1.00	.45
53 Jose Vidro	1.00	.45
54 Vladimir Guerrero	2.50	1.10
55 Cliff Floyd	1.00	.45
56 David Cone	1.00	.45
57 Mike Piazza	4.00	1.80
58 Roberto Alomar	2.50	1.10
59 Tom Glavine	1.50	.70
60 Alfonso Soriano	1.50	.70
61 Derek Jeter	6.00	2.70
62 Drew Henson	1.00	.45
63 Jason Giambi	2.50	1.10
64 Mike Mussina	2.50	1.10
65 Nick Johnson	1.00	.45
66 Roger Clemens	5.00	2.20
67 Barry Zito	1.50	.70
68 Eric Chavez	1.00	.45
69 Mark Mulder	1.00	.45
70 Miguel Tejada	1.00	.45
71 Tim Hudson	1.00	.45
72 Bobby Abreu	1.00	.45
73 Jim Thome	2.50	1.10
74 Kevin Millwood	1.00	.45
75 Pat Burrell	1.00	.45
76 Brian Giles	1.00	.45
77 Jason Kendall	1.00	.45
78 Kenny Lofton	1.00	.45
79 Phil Nevin	1.00	.45
80 Ryan Klesko	1.00	.45
81 Andres Galarraga	1.00	.45
82 Barry Bonds	6.00	2.70
83 Rich Aurilia	1.00	.45
84 Edgar Martinez	1.50	.70
85 Freddy Garcia	1.00	.45
86 Ichiro Suzuki	4.00	1.80
87 Albert Pujols	5.00	2.20
88 Jim Edmonds	1.00	.45
89 Scott Rolen	1.50	.70
90 So Taguchi	1.00	.45
91 Rocco Baldelli	4.00	1.80
92 Alex Rodriguez	4.00	1.80
93 Hank Blalock	1.50	.70
94 Juan Gonzalez	2.50	1.10
95 Mark Teixeira	1.50	.70
96 Rafael Palmeiro	1.50	.70
97 Carlos Delgado	1.00	.45
98 Eric Hinske	1.00	.45
99 Roy Halladay	1.00	.45
100 Vernon Wells	1.00	.45
101 Hideki Matsui ROO RC	12.00	5.50
102 Jose Contreras ROO RC	5.00	2.20
103 Jer. Bonderman ROO RC	3.00	1.35
104 Bernie Castro ROO RC	1.00	.45
105 Alfredo Gonzalez ROO RC	1.00	.45
106 Arnie Munoz ROO RC	1.00	.45
107 Andrew Brown ROO RC	1.00	.45
108 Josh Hall ROO RC	1.50	.70
109 Josh Stewart ROO RC	1.00	.45
110 Clint Barmes ROO RC	1.50	.70
111 Brandon Webb ROO RC	6.00	2.70
112 Chien-Ming Wang ROO RC	5.00	2.20
113 Edgar Gonzalez ROO RC	1.00	.45
114 Al. Machado ROO RC	1.00	.45
115 Jeremy Griffiths ROO RC	1.50	.70
116 Craig Brazell ROO RC	1.50	.70
117 Shane Bazzell ROO RC	1.00	.45
118 Fernando Cabrera ROO RC	1.00	.45
119 Terrmel Sledge ROO RC	1.50	.70
120 Rob Hammock ROO RC	1.50	.70
121 Francisco Rosario ROO RC	1.00	.45
122 Francisco Cruceta ROO RC	1.00	.45
123 Rett Johnson ROO RC	1.50	.70
124 Guillermo Quiroz ROO RC	4.00	1.80
125 Hong-Chih Kuo ROO RC	2.50	1.10
126 Ian Ferguson ROO RC	1.00	.45
127 Tim Olson ROO RC	1.50	.70
128 Todd Wellemeyer ROO RC	1.50	.70
129 Rich Fischer ROO RC	1.00	.45
130 Phil Seibel ROO RC	1.00	.45
131 Joe Valentine ROO RC	1.00	.45
132 Matt Kata ROO RC	2.50	1.10
133 Michael Hessman ROO RC	1.00	.45
134 Michel Hernandez ROO RC	1.00	.45
135 Doug Waechter ROO RC	1.50	.70
136 Prentice Redman ROO RC	1.00	.45
137 Nook Logan ROO RC	1.00	.45
138 Oscar Villarreal ROO RC	1.00	.45
139 Pete LaForest ROO RC	1.50	.70
140 Matt Bruback ROO RC	1.00	.45
141 Dontrelle Willis ROO	2.50	1.10
142 Greg Aquino ROO RC	1.00	.45
143 Lew Ford ROO RC	1.50	.70
144 Jeff Duncan ROO RC	1.50	.70
145 Dan Haren ROO RC	3.00	1.35
146 Miguel Ojeda ROO RC	1.00	.45
147 Rosman Garcia ROO RC	1.00	.45
148 Felix Sanchez ROO RC	1.00	.45
149 Jon Leicester ROO RC	1.00	.45
150 Roger Deago ROO RC	1.00	.45

2003 Donruss Signature Century Proofs

MINT NRMT

*CENTURY 1-100: 2X TO 5X BASIC
*CENTURY 101-150: 1X TO 2.5X BASIC
RANDOM INSERTS IN PACKS
STATED PRINT RUN 100 SERIAL #'d SETS

2003 Donruss Signature Decade Proofs

MINT NRMT

RANDOM INSERTS IN PACKS
STATED PRINT RUN 10 SERIAL #'d SETS
NO PRICING DUE TO SCARCITY

2003 Donruss Signature Autographs

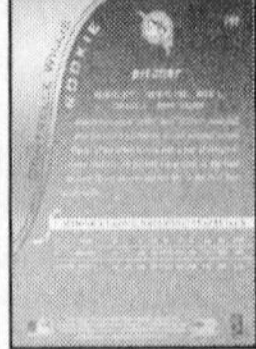

Randomly inserted into packs; these 50 cards parallel the basic set and feature autographs of the featured players. The first 47 of these cards (checklisted from 1-102) are not serial numbered but we are giving print run information in our checklist provided by Donruss/Playoff. Cards 151-153 were distributed as random inserts within packs of DLP Rookies and Traded and each is serial numbered to 200. No pricing is provided for cards with print runs of 28 or fewer due to scarcity.

	MINT	NRMT
1 Garret Anderson	15.00	6.75
6 Mark Grace SP/141	50.00	22.00
7 Matt Williams	15.00	6.75
8 Randy Johnson SP/50	80.00	36.00
10 Chipper Jones SP/50	60.00	27.00
12 Greg Maddux SP/25		
14 Manny Ramirez SP/50	40.00	18.00
16 Pedro Martinez SP/5		
27 Barry Larkin SP/159	40.00	18.00
32 Todd Helton SP/5		
33 Ivan Rodriguez SP/50	50.00	22.00
36 Jeff Bagwell SP/25		
38 Lance Berkman SP/75	25.00	11.00
39 Richard Hidalgo	15.00	6.75
40 Roy Oswalt SP/150	15.00	6.75
42 Mike Sweeney	15.00	6.75
44 Hideo Nomo SP/25		
45 Kazuhisa Ishii SP/25		
50 A.J. Pierzynski	15.00	6.75
51 Torii Hunter	15.00	6.75
53 Jose Vidro	10.00	4.50
54 Vladimir Guerrero	25.00	11.00
55 Cliff Floyd	15.00	6.75
56 David Cone SP/35	25.00	11.00
57 Mike Piazza SP/5		
58 Roberto Alomar SP/50	50.00	22.00
62 Drew Henson SP/28		
64 Mike Mussina SP/5		
65 Nick Johnson	15.00	6.75
67 Barry Zito SP/150	25.00	11.00
68 Eric Chavez	15.00	6.75
69 Mark Mulder SP/50	25.00	11.00
72 Bobby Abreu	15.00	6.75
78 Kenny Lofton SP/229	15.00	6.75
80 Ryan Klesko SP/150	15.00	6.75
81 Andres Galarraga	15.00	6.75
83 Rich Aurilia SP/122	15.00	6.75
84 Edgar Martinez	25.00	11.00
88 Jim Edmonds SP/25		
89 Scott Rolen SP/200	25.00	11.00
90 So Taguchi SP/220	15.00	6.75
92 Alex Rodriguez SP/25		
95 Mark Teixeira SP/150	25.00	11.00
96 Rafael Palmeiro SP/25		
100 Vernon Wells	15.00	6.75
102 Jose Contreras ROO	25.00	11.00
141 D.Willis ROO SP/150	25.00	11.00
151 Delmon Young ROO	60.00	27.00
152 Rickie Weeks ROO	60.00	27.00
153 Edwin Jackson ROO	40.00	18.00

2003 Donruss Signature Autographs Century

1-RANDOM INSERTS IN PACKS
151-154 RANDOM IN DLP R/T PACKS
1-102 PRINT RUN 100 SERIAL #'d SETS
151-154 PRINT RUN 21 SERIAL #'d SETS
NO PRICING ON QTY OF 25 OR LESS.
CARD 154 IS NOT SIGNED

	MINT	NRMT
1 Garret Anderson	25.00	11.00
7 Matt Williams	25.00	11.00
27 Barry Larkin	50.00	22.00
39 Richard Hidalgo	25.00	11.00
42 Mike Sweeney	25.00	11.00
50 A.J. Pierzynski	25.00	11.00
51 Torii Hunter	25.00	11.00
53 Jose Vidro	25.00	11.00
54 Vladimir Guerrero	40.00	18.00
55 Cliff Floyd	25.00	11.00
62 Drew Henson	40.00	18.00
65 Nick Johnson	25.00	11.00
69 Mark Mulder	25.00	11.00
72 Bobby Abreu	25.00	11.00
78 Kenny Lofton	25.00	11.00
81 Andres Galarraga	25.00	11.00
84 Edgar Martinez	40.00	18.00
89 Scott Rolen	40.00	18.00
90 So Taguchi	25.00	11.00
100 Vernon Wells	25.00	11.00
102 Jose Contreras ROO	40.00	18.00
151 Delmon Young ROO		
152 Rickie Weeks ROO		
153 Edwin Jackson ROO		

2003 Donruss Signature Autographs Decade

MINT NRMT

1-102 RANDOM INSERTS IN PACKS
151-154 RANDOM IN DLP R/T PACKS
STATED PRINT RUN 10 SERIAL #'d SETS

NO PRICING DUE TO SCARCITY.........
CARD 154 IS NOT SIGNED ....

2003 Donruss Signature Autographs Notations

Randomly inserted into packs, these cards feature not only authentic autographs from the featured player but also a special "notation" next to their name in the checklist. Since each card has a different print run we have put that information next to the card in our checklist. Please note that for cards with print runs of 30 or fewer, no pricing is provided.

	MINT	NRMT
1A Garret Anderson #16/75.......	25.00	11.00
1B Garret Anderson 7-27-94/45	30.00	13.50
1C Garret Anderson WSC 02/75	25.00	11.00
6 Mark Grace Amazing/5....................		
7A Matt Williams #9/250...........	15.00	6.75
7B Matt Williams 01 WS/50......	30.00	13.50
10A Chipper Jones 96-01 AS/25.........		
10B Chipper Jones MVP 99/25...........		
32 Todd Helton 02 AS/15..................		
33 Ivan Rodriguez #7/5......................		
36 Jeff Bagwell Baggy/5.....................		
38A Lance Berkman #17/15................		
38B Lance Berkman #22/5..................		
38C Lance Berkman #27/1..................		
38D Lance Berkman 02/1....................		
38E Lance Berkman Rice Owls/5.........		
38F Lance Berkman Rice Univ./5.........		
38G Lance Berkman William/1............		
40 Roy Oswalt #44/25........................		
45 Kazuhisa Ishii #17/35...........	50.00	22.00
50 A.J. Pierzynski 02 AS/200....	15.00	6.75
51A Torii Hunter 02 AS/25.................		
51B Torii Hunter #48/20.....................		
53A Jose Vidro #3/40................	20.00	9.00
53B Jose Vidro AS 00/15....................		
53C Jose Vidro 2X AS/6......................		
55 Cliff Floyd #30/5...........................		
57A Mike Piazza #31/5.......................		
57B Mike Piazza ROY 93/1..................		
62A Drew Henson UM #7/2..................		
62B Drew Henson QB #7/24................		
62C Drew Henson DH #7/73......	40.00	18.00
68A Eric Chavez #3/50..............	30.00	13.50
68B Eric Chavez Chavy/25..................		
69 Mark Mulder MSU/30.....................		
78 Kenny Lofton #7/150............	15.00	6.75
80 Ryan Klesko #30/75.............	25.00	11.00
83 Rich Aurilia #35/61..............	20.00	9.00
84A Edgar Martinez #11/250.....	25.00	11.00
84B E.Martinez BT 92-95/60.....	50.00	22.00
92A Alex Rodriguez #3/5.....................		
92B Alex Rodriguez WCS 93/5............		
92C Alex Rodriguez Westminster/1.....		
96 Rafael Palmeiro 500 HR/25............		
100 Vernon Wells #10/75..........	25.00	11.00

2003 Donruss Signature Autographs Notations Century

	MINT	NRMT
RANDOM INSERTS IN PACKS............		
STATED PRINT RUN 100 SERIAL #'d SETS		
1A Garret Anderson #16...........	25.00	11.00
1B Garret Anderson 7-27-94.....	25.00	11.00
7A Matt Williams #9.................	25.00	11.00
7B Matt Williams 01 WS...........	25.00	11.00
50 A.J. Pierzynski 02 AS...........	25.00	11.00
68A Eric Chavez #3..................	25.00	11.00
78 Kenny Lofton #7..................	25.00	11.00
84A Edgar Martinez #11...........	40.00	18.00

2003 Donruss Signature Autographs Notations Decade

	MINT	NRMT
RANDOM INSERTS IN PACKS............		
STATED PRINT RUN 10 SERIAL #'d SETS		
NO PRICING DUE TO SCARCITY.........		

2003 Donruss Signature Cuts

Randomly inserted into packs, these 15 cards feature "cut" signatures from the featured player. Each of these cards have different print runs and we have notated that print run information in our checklist. Please note for cards with 25 or fewer copies, no pricing is provided.

	MINT	NRMT
4 Curt Schilling/7..............................		
8 Randy Johnson/40.................	80.00	36.00
10 Chipper Jones/9............................		
33 Ivan Rodriguez/122.............	40.00	18.00
54 Vladimir Guerrero/34...........	50.00	22.00
58 Roberto Alomar/100............	40.00	18.00
59 Tom Glavine/9...............................		
64 Mike Mussina/82.................	50.00	22.00
66 Roger Clemens/9............................		
73 Jim Thome/127....................	40.00	18.00
80 Ryan Klesko/35..................	30.00	13.50
81 Andres Galarraga/51...........	30.00	13.50
89 Scott Rolen/36....................	50.00	22.00
94 Juan Gonzalez/9............................		
96 Rafael Palmeiro/13........................		

2003 Donruss Signature Cuts Decade

	MINT	NRMT
RANDOM INSERTS IN PACKS............		
STATED PRINT RUN 10 SERIAL #'d SETS		
NO PRICING DUE TO SCARCITY.........		

2003 Donruss Signature Authentic Cuts

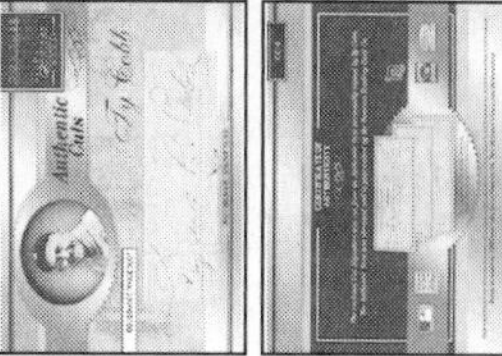

Randomly inserted into packs, these three cards feature cut signatures of the most legendary players in baseball history. We have notated the print run next to the player's name in our checklist and due to market scarcity, no pricing is provided for these cards.

	MINT	NRMT
1 Ty Cobb/3......................................		
2 Babe Ruth/1....................................		
3 Lou Gehrig/1...................................		

2003 Donruss Signature INKredible Three

Randomly inserted into packs, these five cards feature three signatures on each card from players with a common team allegiance. Each of these cards were issued to a stated print run of 50 serial numbered sets.

	MINT	NRMT
1 Barry Zito Mark Mulder Tim Hudson	400.00	180.00
2 Greg Maddux Chipper Jones Andruw Jones	500.00	220.00
3 Kerry Wood Mark Prior Ernie Banks	500.00	220.00
4 Kirby Puckett Harmon Killebrew Torii Hunter	250.00	110.00
5 Vladimir Guerrero Jose Vidro Javier Vazquez	150.00	70.00

2003 Donruss Signature INKredible Four

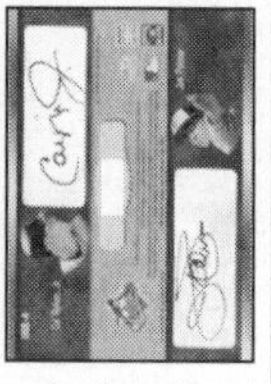

Randomly inserted into packs, these 10 cards feature four signatures from players with a common team allegiance. Each of these cards were issued to a stated print run of 25 serial numbered sets and no pricing is provided due to market scarcity.

	MINT	NRMT
1 Jeff Bagwell Craig Biggio Lance Berkman Roy Oswalt		
2 Mike Schmidt Steve Carlton Pat Burrell Jim Thome		
3 Carlos Lee Magglio Ordonez Frank Thomas Mark Buehrle		
4 Brooks Robinson Frank Robinson Cal Ripken Jim Palmer		
5 Pedro Martinez Manny Ramirez Rickey Henderson Bobby Doerr		
6 Mike Sweeney Carlos Beltran Bo Jackson George Brett		
7 Randy Johnson Curt Schilling Mark Grace Junior Spivey		
8 Dwight Gooden Lenny Dykstra Tom Glavine Roberto Alomar		
9 Alex Rodriguez Rafael Palmeiro Nolan Ryan Ferguson Jenkins		
10 Roberto Alomar Joe Carter Ryan Klesko Tony Gwynn		

2003 Donruss Signature INKredible Six

Randomly inserted into packs, these five cards feature six signatures on each card with a common thread tying together all the players. Each of these cards were issued to a stated print run of 10 serial numbered sets and no pricing is provided due to market scarcity.

	MINT	NRMT
1 Adam Dunn Tom Seaver Johnny Bench Austin Kearns Joe Morgan Barry Larkin		
2 Albert Pujols Stan Musial Jim Edmonds Scott Rolen Lou Brock Ozzie Smith		
3 Andre Dawson Ernie Banks Mark Prior Ryne Sandberg Kerry Wood Mark Grace		
4 Yogi Berra Whitey Ford Rickey Henderson Don Mattingly Phil Rizzuto Reggie Jackson		
5 Alex Rodriguez Roger Clemens Hideo Nomo George Brett Don Mattingly Nolan Ryan		

2003 Donruss Signature Legends of Summer

Randomly inserted into packs, these 40 cards feature some of the best retired players. Each of these cards were issued to a stated print run of 250 serial numbered sets.

	MINT	NRMT
*CENTURY: .6X TO 1.5X BASIC..........		
CENTURY PRINT RUN 100 SERIAL #'d SETS		
DECADE PRINT RUN 10 SERIAL #'d SETS		
NO DECADE PRICING DUE TO SCARCITY		
RANDOM INSERTS IN PACKS............		
1 Al Kaline..	8.00	3.60
2 Alan Trammell................................	5.00	2.20
3 Andre Dawson................................	5.00	2.20
4 Babe Ruth.....................................	15.00	6.75
5 Billy Williams..................................	5.00	2.20
6 Bo Jackson.....................................	8.00	3.60
7 Bob Feller.......................................	5.00	2.20
8 Bobby Doerr...................................	5.00	2.20
9 Brooks Robinson............................	8.00	3.60
10 Dale Murphy..................................	8.00	3.60
11 Dennis Eckersley..........................	5.00	2.20
12 Don Mattingly..............................	15.00	6.75
13 Duke Snider..................................	5.00	2.20
14 Eric Davis.....................................	5.00	2.20
15 Frank Robinson............................	5.00	2.20
16 Fred Lynn.....................................	5.00	2.20
17 Gary Carter...................................	5.00	2.20
18 Harmon Killebrew.........................	8.00	3.60
19 Jack Morris...................................	5.00	2.20
20 Jim Palmer....................................	5.00	2.20
21 Jim Abbott....................................	5.00	2.20
22 Joe Morgan...................................	5.00	2.20
23 Joe Torre.......................................	5.00	2.20
24 Johnny Bench...............................	8.00	3.60
25 Jose Canseco...............................	8.00	3.60
26 Kirby Puckett................................	8.00	3.60
27 Lenny Dykstra..............................	5.00	2.20
28 Lou Brock.....................................	5.00	2.20
29 Ralph Kiner...................................	5.00	2.20
30 Mike Schmidt...............................	12.00	5.50
31 Nolan Ryan Rgr............................	15.00	6.75
32 Nolan Ryan Angels.......................	15.00	6.75
33 Orel Hershiser..............................	5.00	2.20
34 Phil Rizzuto...................................	5.00	2.20
35 Orlando Cepeda............................	5.00	2.20
36 Ryne Sandberg.............................	12.00	5.50
37 Stan Musial...................................	10.00	4.50
38 Steve Garvey.................................	5.00	2.20
39 Tony Perez.....................................	5.00	2.20
40 Ty Cobb..	10.00	4.50

2003 Donruss Signature Legends of Summer Autographs

Randomly inserted into packs, this is a partial parallel of the Legends of Summer set. A few cards were issued in smaller quantities and we have notated that information (as provided by Donruss/Playoff) in our checklist.

	MINT	NRMT
1 Al Kaline.......................................	25.00	11.00
2 Alan Trammell...............................	15.00	6.75
3 Andre Dawson...............................	15.00	6.75
5 Billy Williams.................................	15.00	6.75
6 Bo Jackson SP/100.......................	60.00	27.00
7 Bob Feller......................................	25.00	11.00
8 Bobby Doerr..................................	15.00	6.75
9 Brooks Robinson...........................	25.00	11.00
10 Dale Murphy SP/75....................	40.00	18.00
11 Dennis Eckersley.........................	15.00	6.75
12 Don Mattingly SP/50..................	100.00	45.00
13 Duke Snider SP/225...................	25.00	11.00
14 Eric Davis....................................	15.00	6.75
15 Frank Robinson...........................	15.00	6.75
16 Fred Lynn....................................	15.00	6.75
17 Gary Carter..................................	15.00	6.75
18 Harmon Killebrew SP/171..........	25.00	11.00
19 Jack Morris..................................	15.00	6.75
20 Jim Palmer...................................	15.00	6.75
21 Jim Abbott....................................	15.00	6.75
22 Joe Morgan SP/125.....................	25.00	11.00
23 Joe Torre......................................	15.00	6.75
24 Johnny Bench SP/75...................	40.00	18.00
25 Jose Canseco SP/75...................	40.00	18.00
26 Kirby Puckett SP/75....................	50.00	22.00
27 Lenny Dykstra..............................	15.00	6.75
28 Lou Brock.....................................	25.00	11.00
29 Ralph Kiner...................................	15.00	6.75
30 Mike Schmidt SP/75....................	80.00	36.00
31 Nolan Ryan Rgr SP/75................	150.00	70.00
33 Orel Hershiser..............................	25.00	11.00
34 Phil Rizzuto..................................	25.00	11.00
35 Orlando Cepeda...........................	15.00	6.75
36 Ryne Sandberg SP/75.................	80.00	36.00
37 Stan Musial SP/200.....................	60.00	27.00
38 Steve Garvey................................	15.00	6.75
39 Tony Perez....................................	15.00	6.75

2003 Donruss Signature Legends of Summer Autographs Century

	MINT	NRMT
RANDOM INSERTS IN PACKS............		
STATED PRINT RUN 100 SERIAL #'d SETS		
1 Al Kaline.......................................	40.00	18.00
2 Alan Trammell...............................	25.00	11.00
3 Andre Dawson...............................	25.00	11.00
5 Billy Williams................................	25.00	11.00
6 Bo Jackson....................................	60.00	27.00
7 Bob Feller......................................	40.00	18.00
8 Bobby Doerr..................................	25.00	11.00
9 Brooks Robinson...........................	40.00	18.00
11 Dennis Eckersley.........................	25.00	11.00
12 Don Mattingly..............................	80.00	36.00
14 Eric Davis.....................................	25.00	11.00
15 Frank Robinson............................	25.00	11.00
16 Fred Lynn.....................................	25.00	11.00
17 Gary Carter..................................	25.00	11.00
19 Jack Morris...................................	25.00	11.00
20 Jim Palmer....................................	25.00	11.00
21 Jim Abbott....................................	25.00	11.00
23 Joe Torre.......................................	25.00	11.00
27 Lenny Dykstra..............................	25.00	11.00
28 Lou Brock.....................................	40.00	18.00
29 Ralph Kiner...................................	25.00	11.00
33 Orel Hershiser..............................	80.00	36.00
34 Phil Rizzuto..................................	40.00	18.00
35 Orlando Cepeda...........................	25.00	11.00
36 Ryne Sandberg.............................	80.00	36.00
37 Stan Musial...................................	80.00	36.00
38 Steve Garvey................................	25.00	11.00
39 Tony Perez....................................	25.00	11.00

2003 Donruss Signature Legends of Summer Autographs Decade

	MINT	NRMT
RANDOM INSERTS IN PACKS............		
STATED PRINT RUN 10 SERIAL #'d SETS		
NO PRICING DUE TO SCARCITY.........		

2003 Donruss Signature Legends of Summer Autographs Notations

This parallel to the Legends of Summer insert set features not only authentic autographs from some of the featured players but also special notations added by the player. Since there are varying print runs on these cards we have provided that information next to the player's name in our checklist. Please note that cards with a print run of 25 or fewer are not priced due to market scarcity.

	MINT	NRMT
1A Al Kaline #6/200..................	25.00	11.00
1B Al Kaline HOF '80/200..........	25.00	11.00
1C Al Kaline Mr. Tiger/200........	25.00	11.00
2 A.Trammell 84 WS MVP/250.	15.00	6.75
3A Andre Dawson #8/165.........	15.00	6.75
3B Andre Dawson 87 MVP/250.	15.00	6.75
5B Billy Williams 61 ROY/250...	15.00	6.75
5C Billy Williams 87 HOF/150....	15.00	6.75
7A Bob Feller #19/250..............	25.00	11.00
7B Bob Feller HOF 62/250.........	25.00	11.00
7C Bob Feller Triple Crown/200...........		
8A Bobby Doerr #1/250.............	15.00	6.75
8B Bobby Doerr HOF 86/250.....	15.00	6.75
8C Bobby Doerr MVP 44/250....	15.00	6.75
9A B.Robinson 64 MVP/150......	25.00	11.00
9B B.Robinson 70 WS MVP/50.	50.00	22.00
10A Dale Murphy MVP 82/50....	50.00	22.00
10B Dale Murphy MVP 83/50....	50.00	22.00
11A D.Eckersley 92 CY/250.......	15.00	6.75
11B D.Eckersley 92 CY-MVP/250	15.00	6.75
11C D.Eckersley 92 MVP/250....	15.00	6.75
13 Duke Snider HOF 80/25.................		
14A Eric Davis #44/250.............	15.00	6.75
14B Eric Davis 87 AS/150.........	15.00	6.75
14C Eric Davis 90 WS/200........	15.00	6.75
16A Fred Lynn 75 MVP-ROY/240	15.00	6.75
16B Fred Lynn 75-83 AS/250....	15.00	6.75
17 Gary Carter The Kid/5.....................		
18A H.Killebrew #3/75...............	40.00	18.00
18B H.Killebrew 69 MVP/50......	50.00	22.00
18C H.Killebrew 573 HR/50.......	50.00	22.00
18D H.Killebrew HOF 84/125.....	40.00	18.00
19A J.Morris 91 WS MVP/250..	15.00	6.75
19B Jack Morris 92 WS/250.....	15.00	6.75
20A Jim Palmer 73 CY/190.......	15.00	6.75
20B Jim Palmer 75 CY/140.......	15.00	6.75
20C Jim Palmer 76 CY/50.........	30.00	13.50
21A Jim Abbott 4-8-89/200.......	15.00	6.75
21B Jim Abbott 9-4-93/100.......	25.00	11.00
21C Jim Abbott 6-15-99/75.......	25.00	11.00
21D Jim Abbott U of Mich/50....	30.00	13.50
21E Jim Abbott Yanks/25....................		
24A Johnny Bench #5/20....................		
24B Johnny Bench HOF/1...................		
24C Johnny Bench HOF 89/5.............		
24D Johnny Bench MVP 70/1.............		
24E Johnny Bench MVP 72/1.............		
27 Lenny Dykstra 86 WS/226....	15.00	6.75
28A Lou Brock SB 938/25..................		
28B Lou Brock HOF 85/50.........	50.00	22.00
29A Ralph Kiner #4/150............	15.00	6.75
29B Ralph Kiner 48-53 AS/25............		
29C Ralph Kiner HOF/200.........	15.00	6.75
29D Ralph Kiner HOF 75/100....	25.00	11.00
31 Nolan Ryan Rgr 5714 SO/25.........		
35A O.Cepeda Baby Bull/75.......	50.00	22.00
35B O.Cepeda MVP 67/40.........	30.00	13.50
35C O.Cepeda 58 ROY/40.........	30.00	13.50
35D O.Cepeda 67 WS/40...........	30.00	13.50
35E O.Cepeda 68 WS/40...........	30.00	13.50
36A Ryne Sandberg #23/5..................		
36B Ryne Sandberg Cubs/20..............		
36C Ryne Sandberg 84 MVP/25.........		
38A Steve Garvey #6/150..........	15.00	6.75
38B Steve Garvey 74 MVP/25............		
38C Steve Garvey 78 AS MVP/50	30.00	13.50
38D Steve Garvey 81 WS/75.....	25.00	11.00
39A Tony Perez #24/250..........	15.00	6.75
39B Tony Perez HOF 02/175.....	15.00	6.75
39C Tony Perez WS 75/125......	25.00	11.00
39D Tony Perez WS 76/75........	25.00	11.00

2003 Donruss Signature Legends of Summer Autographs Notations Century

	MINT	NRMT
RANDOM INSERTS IN PACKS............		
STATED PRINT RUN 100 SERIAL #'d SETS		
1A Al Kaline #6........................	40.00	18.00
1B Al Kaline HOF 80................	40.00	18.00
1C Al Kaline Mr. Tiger..............	40.00	18.00
2 Alan Trammell 84 WS MVP....	25.00	11.00
3A Andre Dawson #8................	25.00	11.00
3B Andre Dawson 87 MVP........	25.00	11.00
5A Billy Williams #26...............	25.00	11.00
5B Billy Williams 61 ROY..........	25.00	11.00
5C Billy Williams 87 HOF..........	25.00	11.00
7A Bob Feller #19....................	40.00	18.00
7B Bob Feller HOF 62...............	40.00	18.00
7C Bob Feller Triple Crown........	40.00	18.00
8A Bobby Doerr #1..................	25.00	11.00
8B Bobby Doerr HOF 86...........	25.00	11.00
8C Bobby Doerr MVP 44..........	25.00	11.00
11A Dennis Eckersley 92 CY.....	25.00	11.00
11B D.Eckersley 92 CY-MVP.....	25.00	11.00
11C Dennis Eckersley 92 MVP..	25.00	11.00
14A Eric Davis #44...................	25.00	11.00
14B Eric Davis 87 AS...............	25.00	11.00
14C Eric Davis 90 WS..............	25.00	11.00
16A Fred Lynn 75 MVP-ROY.....	25.00	11.00
16B Fred Lynn 75-83 AS..........	25.00	11.00
19A Jack Morris 91 WS MVP....	25.00	11.00
19B Jack Morris 92 WS............	25.00	11.00
20A Jim Palmer 73 CY..............	25.00	11.00
20B Jim Palmer 75 CY..............	25.00	11.00
20C Jim Palmer 76 CY..............	25.00	11.00
21A Jim Abbott 4-8-89..............	25.00	11.00
21B Jim Abbott 9-4-93..............	25.00	11.00
21C Jim Abbott 6-15-99............	25.00	11.00
21D Jim Abbott U of Mich.........	25.00	11.00
21E Jim Abbott Yanks..............	25.00	11.00
27 Lenny Dykstra 86 WS..........	25.00	11.00
29A Ralph Kiner #4..................	25.00	11.00
29B Ralph Kiner 48-53 AS........	25.00	11.00
29C Ralph Kiner HOF...............	25.00	11.00
29D Ralph Kiner HOF 75..........	25.00	11.00
38A Steve Garvey #6...............	25.00	11.00
38B Steve Garvey 74 MVP........	25.00	11.00
38C Steve Garvey 78 AS MVP...	25.00	11.00
38D Steve Garvey 81 WS.........	25.00	11.00
39A Tony Perez #24.................	25.00	11.00
39B Tony Perez HOF 02............	25.00	11.00
39C Tony Perez WS 75.............	25.00	11.00
39D Tony Perez WS 76.............	25.00	11.00

2003 Donruss Signature Legends of Summer Autographs Notations Decade

	MINT	NRMT
RANDOM INSERTS IN PACKS............		
STATED PRINT RUN 10 SERIAL #'d SETS		
NO PRICING DUE TO SCARCITY.........		

2003 Donruss Signature Notable Nicknames

Randomly inserted into packs, these 20 cards players who are commonly known by a nickname. Each of these cards were issued to a stated print run of 750 serial numbered sets.

*CENTURY: .6X TO 1.5X BASIC
CENTURY PRINT RUN 100 SERIAL #'d SETS
DECADE PRINT RUN 10 SERIAL #'d SETS
NO DECADE PRICING DUE TO SCARCITY
RANDOM INSERTS IN PACKS

	MINT	NRMT
1 Andre Dawson	5.00	2.20
2 Torii Hunter	5.00	2.20
3 Brooks Robinson	6.00	2.70
4 Carlton Fisk	5.00	2.20
5 Mike Mussina	6.00	2.70
6 Don Mattingly	15.00	6.75
7 Duke Snider	5.00	2.20
8 Eric Davis	5.00	2.20
9 Frank Thomas	6.00	2.70
10 Randy Johnson	6.00	2.70
11 Lenny Dykstra	5.00	2.20
12 Ivan Rodriguez	6.00	2.70
13 Nolan Ryan	15.00	6.75
14 Phil Rizzuto	5.00	2.20
15 Reggie Jackson	5.00	2.20
16 Roger Clemens	12.00	5.50
17 Ryne Sandberg	12.00	5.50
18 Stan Musial	10.00	4.50
19 Luis Gonzalez	5.00	2.20
20 Will Clark	6.00	2.70

2003 Donruss Signature Notable Nicknames Century

MINT NRMT
RANDOM INSERTS IN PACKS
STATED PRINT RUN 100 SERIAL #'d SETS

2003 Donruss Signature Notable Nicknames Decade

MINT NRMT
STATED PRINT RUN 10 SERIAL #'d SETS
NO PRICING DUE TO SCARCITY

2003 Donruss Signature Notable Nicknames Autographs

Randomly inserted in packs, these cards parallel the regular Notable Nickname set but also include an authentic autograph from the featured player as well as his nickname. Most of these cards were issued to a stated print run of 100 copies but a few were issued in smaller quantities and that information is notated in our checklist. For those cards with a print run of 25 or fewer, no pricing is provided due to market scarcity.

	MINT	NRMT
1 Andre Dawson	50.00	22.00
2 Torii Hunter	50.00	22.00
3 Brooks Robinson	80.00	36.00
4 Carlton Fisk	80.00	36.00
5 Mike Mussina	100.00	45.00
6 Don Mattingly	150.00	70.00
7 Duke Snider	80.00	36.00
8 Eric Davis/40	80.00	36.00
9 Frank Thomas	100.00	45.00
10 Randy Johnson	150.00	70.00
11 Lenny Dykstra	30.00	13.50
12 Ivan Rodriguez/75	80.00	36.00
13 Nolan Ryan/15		
14 Phil Rizzuto	80.00	36.00
15 Reggie Jackson	80.00	36.00
16 Roger Clemens	200.00	90.00
17 Ryne Sandberg	100.00	45.00
18 Stan Musial	120.00	55.00
19 Luis Gonzalez	50.00	22.00
20 Will Clark	80.00	36.00

2003 Donruss Signature Notable Nicknames Autographs Decade

MINT NRMT
RANDOM INSERTS IN PACKS
STATED PRINT RUN 10 SERIAL #'d SETS
NO PRICING DUE TO SCARCITY

2003 Donruss Signature Player Collection Autographs

Randomly inserted in packs, these cards feature authentic autographs on "player collection" cards. Since each of these cards were issued to a different print run, we have notated that information next to the player's name in our checklist.

	MINT	NRMT
1 Roberto Alomar/75	40.00	18.00
2 Adrian Beltre/104	15.00	6.75
3 Lance Berkman/50	30.00	13.50
4 Craig Biggio Btg/26		
5 Craig Biggio Fldg/26		
6 Joe Borchard/53	30.00	13.50
7 Roger Clemens Pitch/9		
8 Roger Clemens Stretch/4		
9 J.D. Drew/52	30.00	13.50
10 Jim Edmonds/52	30.00	13.50
11 Tony Gwynn/11		
12 Todd Helton/50	50.00	22.00
13 Jason Jennings/49	20.00	9.00
14 Andruw Jones Away/25		
15 Andruw Jones Home/25		
16 Chipper Jones/51	60.00	27.00
17 Paul Konerko/26		
18 Paul Lo Duca/227	15.00	6.75
19 Magglio Ordonez/102	25.00	11.00
20 Roy Oswalt/10		
21 Rafael Palmeiro/25		
22 Mark Prior/27	120.00	55.00
23 Cal Ripken/22		
24 Alex Rodriguez M's/24		
25 Alex Rodriguez Rgr/25		
26 Ivan Rodriguez/52	50.00	22.00
27 Richie Sexson/50	30.00	13.50
28 Alfonso Soriano/11		
29A Matt Williams/19		
29B Matt Williams/483	15.00	6.75

2003 Donruss Signature Team Trademarks

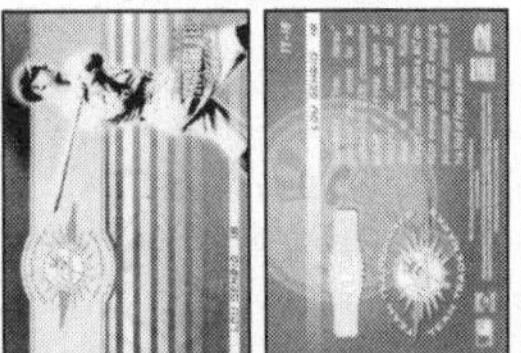

Randomly inserted into packs, these cards feature the term "team trademark" on the card. Each of these cards were issued to a stated print run of 500 serial numbered sets.

*CENTURY: .75X TO 2X BASIC
CENTURY PRINT RUN 100 SERIAL #'d SETS
DECADE PRINT RUN 10 SERIAL #'d SETS
NO DECADE PRICING DUE TO SCARCITY
RANDOM INSERTS IN PACKS

	MINT	NRMT
1 Adam Dunn	4.00	1.80
2 Andre Dawson	4.00	1.80
3 Babe Ruth	12.00	5.50
4 Barry Bonds	12.00	5.50
5 Brooks Robinson	5.00	2.20
6 Cal Ripken	15.00	6.75
7 Derek Jeter	12.00	5.50
8 Don Mattingly	12.00	5.50
9 Frank Robinson	4.00	1.80
10 Fred Lynn	4.00	1.80
11 Gary Carter	4.00	1.80
12 George Brett	12.00	5.50
13 Greg Maddux	8.00	3.60
14 Ichiro Suzuki	8.00	3.60
15 Jim Palmer	4.00	1.80
16 Jose Contreras	8.00	3.60
17 Kerry Wood	5.00	2.20
18 Lou Gehrig	8.00	3.60
19 Magglio Ordonez	4.00	1.80
20 Mark Grace	4.00	1.80
21 Mike Schmidt	10.00	4.50
22 Nolan Ryan Rgr	12.00	5.50
23 Nolan Ryan Astros	12.00	5.50
24 Reggie Jackson	4.00	1.80
25 Rickey Henderson	5.00	2.20
26 Roberto Clemente	10.00	4.50
27 Roger Clemens Sox	10.00	4.50
28 Roger Clemens Yanks	10.00	4.50
29 Ryne Sandberg	10.00	4.50
30 Sammy Sosa	8.00	3.60
31 Stan Musial	8.00	3.60
32 Steve Carlton	4.00	1.80
33 Tim Hudson	4.00	1.80
34 Tom Glavine	4.00	1.80
35 Tom Seaver	4.00	1.80
36 Tony Gwynn	6.00	2.70
37 Torii Hunter	4.00	1.80
38 Ty Cobb	8.00	3.60
39 Vladimir Guerrero	5.00	2.20
40 Will Clark	5.00	2.20

2003 Donruss Signature Team Trademarks Decade

MINT NRMT
STATED PRINT RUN 10 SERIAL #'d SETS
NO PRICING DUE TO SCARCITY

2003 Donruss Signature Team Trademarks Autographs

Randomly inserted into packs, these cards partially parallel the Team Trademark insert set. Each of these cards feature an authentic autograph from the featured player. Since there are some different print runs we have notated that information in our checklist next to the player's name. For those cards with print runs of 25 or fewer, no pricing is provided due to market scarcity.

	MINT	NRMT
1 Adam Dunn/50	50.00	22.00
2 Andre Dawson/250	15.00	6.75
5 Brooks Robinson/250	25.00	11.00
6 Cal Ripken/50	200.00	90.00
8 Don Mattingly/75	100.00	45.00
10 Fred Lynn/250	15.00	6.75
11 Gary Carter/250	15.00	6.75
12 George Brett/50	120.00	55.00
13 Greg Maddux/50	120.00	55.00
16 Jose Contreras/250	25.00	11.00
17 Kerry Wood/50	50.00	22.00
19 Magglio Ordonez/75	25.00	11.00
20 Mark Grace/25		
23 Nolan Ryan Astros/50	150.00	70.00
24 Reggie Jackson/75	40.00	18.00
25 Rickey Henderson/50	120.00	55.00
27 Roger Clemens Sox/50	150.00	70.00
28 Roger Clemens Yanks/50	150.00	70.00
29 Ryne Sandberg/100	80.00	36.00
31 Stan Musial/200	60.00	27.00
32 Steve Carlton/150	25.00	11.00
33 Tim Hudson/100	50.00	22.00
34 Tom Glavine/50	50.00	22.00
35 Tom Seaver/50	50.00	22.00
36 Tony Gwynn/50	80.00	36.00
37 Torii Hunter/250	15.00	6.75
39 Vladimir Guerrero/250	25.00	11.00
40 Will Clark/125	40.00	18.00

2003 Donruss Signature Team Trademarks Autographs Century

RANDOM INSERTS IN PACKS
STATED PRINT RUN 100 SERIAL #'d SETS

	MINT	NRMT
1 Andre Dawson	25.00	11.00
5 Brooks Robinson	40.00	18.00
9 Frank Robinson	25.00	11.00
10 Fred Lynn	25.00	11.00
11 Gary Carter	25.00	11.00
15 Jim Palmer	25.00	11.00
16 Jose Contreras	40.00	18.00
20 Mark Grace	60.00	27.00
29 Ryne Sandberg	80.00	36.00
31 Stan Musial	80.00	36.00
32 Steve Carlton	40.00	18.00
34 Tom Glavine	40.00	18.00
37 Torii Hunter	25.00	11.00
39 Vladimir Guerrero	40.00	18.00

2003 Donruss Signature Team Trademarks Autographs Decade

MINT NRMT
RANDOM INSERTS IN PACKS
STATED PRINT RUN 10 SERIAL #'d SETS
NO PRICING DUE TO SCARCITY

2003 Donruss Signature Team Trademarks Autographs Notations

Randomly inserted into packs, these cards feature not only authentic autographs from the featured player as well as a special notation added to that autographs. Each of these cards have varying print runs and we have added that information in our checklist next to the player's name. For those cards with a stated print run of 25 or fewer copies, no pricing is provided due to market scarcity.

	MINT	NRMT
2A Andre Dawson #10/250	15.00	6.75
2B Andre Dawson ROY 77/150	15.00	6.75
5A B.Robinson 64 MVP/75	50.00	22.00
5B B.Robinson 70 WS MVP/125	40.00	18.00
10A Fred Lynn 75-83 AS/50	30.00	13.50
11 Gary Carter The Kid/25		
12 George Brett #5/25		
15A Jim Palmer 73 CY/32	30.00	13.50
15B Jim Palmer 75 CY/128	25.00	11.00
15C Jim Palmer 76 CY/150	15.00	6.75
17 Kerry Wood ROY 98/25		
24A Reggie Jackson #44/5		
24B Reggie Jackson 99/20		
29A Ryne Sandberg #23/40	120.00	55.00
29B Ryne Sandberg Cubs/5		
29C Ryne Sandberg 84 MVP/55	100.00	45.00
32A Steve Carlton 72 CY/50	50.00	22.00
32B Steve Carlton 77 CY/50	50.00	22.00
32C Steve Carlton 80 CY/50	50.00	22.00
32D Steve Carlton 82 CY/50	50.00	22.00
33A Tim Hudson Black Angus/5		
33B Tim Hudson Huddy/50	60.00	27.00
37A Torii Hunter #48/20		
40A Will Clark 89 MVP/52	80.00	36.00
40B Will Clark 89 WS/52	80.00	36.00

2003 Donruss Signature Team Trademarks Autographs Notations Century

RANDOM INSERTS IN PACKS
STATED PRINT RUN 100 SERIAL #'d SETS

	MINT	NRMT
2A Andre Dawson #10	25.00	11.00
2B Andre Dawson ROY 77	25.00	11.00
10A Fred Lynn 75-83 AS	25.00	11.00
10B Fred Lynn 75 MVP-ROY	25.00	11.00
15A Jim Palmer 73 CY	25.00	11.00
15B Jim Palmer 75 CY	25.00	11.00
15C Jim Palmer 76 CY	25.00	11.00

2003 Donruss Signature Team Trademarks Autographs Notations Decade

MINT NRMT
RANDOM INSERTS IN PACKS
STATED PRINT RUN 10 SERIAL #'d SETS
NO PRICING DUE TO SCARCITY

2002 Donruss Super Estrellas

This 150 card set was officially released in Fall, 2002. The cards were issued in seven card packs which came 24 packs to a box and 12 boxes to a case with a SRP of $1.99 per pack. This set is the first major "Spanish Billingual" Baseball set issued since Pacific surrendered their Baseball license. The first 100 cards in this set featured veteran players while the final 50 cards featured rookies and prospects. Those final fifty cards were issued at a stated rate of one in four.

	Nm-Mt	Ex-Mt
COMP.SET w/o SP's (100)	40.00	12.00
COMMON CARD (1-100)	.40	.12
COMMON CARD (101-150)	2.00	.60
1 Darin Erstad	.40	.12
2 Tim Salmon	.60	.18
3 Troy Glaus	.60	.18
4 Curt Schilling	.60	.18
5 Luis Gonzalez	.40	.12
6 Mark Grace	.60	.18
7 Randy Johnson	1.00	.30
8 Andruw Jones	.40	.12
9 Chipper Jones	1.00	.30
10 Greg Maddux	1.50	.45
11 Javy Lopez	.40	.12
12 Tom Glavine	.60	.18
13 Manny Ramirez	.40	.12
14 Nomar Garciaparra	1.50	.45
15 Pedro Martinez	1.00	.30
16 Trot Nixon	.60	.18
17 Fred McGriff	.60	.18
18 Sammy Sosa	1.50	.45
19 Kerry Wood	1.00	.30
20 Moises Alou	.40	.12
21 Frank Thomas	1.00	.30
22 Magglio Ordonez	.40	.12
23 Adam Dunn	.40	.12
24 Barry Larkin	1.00	.30
25 Juan Encarnacion	.40	.12
26 Ken Griffey Jr.	1.50	.45
27 Sean Casey	.40	.12
28 C.C. Sabathia	.40	.12
29 Jim Thome	1.00	.30
30 Omar Vizquel	.40	.12
31 Larry Walker	.60	.18
32 Mike Hampton	.40	.12
33 Todd Helton	.60	.18
34 Bobby Higginson	.40	.12
35 Charles Johnson	.40	.12
36 Craig Biggio	.60	.18
37 Jeff Bagwell	.60	.18
38 Lance Berkman	.40	.12
39 Carlos Beltran	.40	.12
40 Mike Sweeney	.40	.12
41 Adrian Beltre	.40	.12
42 Gary Sheffield	.40	.12
43 Hideo Nomo	1.00	.30
44 Kevin Brown	.40	.12
45 Shawn Green	.40	.12
46 Ben Sheets	.40	.12
47 Richie Sexson	.40	.12
48 Brad Radke	.40	.12
49 Javier Vazquez	.40	.12
50 Jose Vidro	.40	.12
51 Vladimir Guerrero	1.00	.30
52 Mike Piazza	1.50	.45
53 Roberto Alomar	1.00	.30
54 Alfonso Soriano	.60	.18
55 Bernie Williams	.60	.18
56 Derek Jeter	2.50	.75
57 Jason Giambi	1.00	.30
58 Jorge Posada	.60	.18
59 Mariano Rivera	.60	.18
60 Mike Mussina	1.00	.30
61 Orlando Hernandez	.40	.12
62 Roger Clemens	2.00	.60
63 Barry Zito	.60	.18
64 Eric Chavez	.40	.12
65 Jermaine Dye	.40	.12
66 Mark Mulder	.40	.12
67 Miguel Tejada	.40	.12
68 Tim Hudson	.40	.12
69 Bobby Abreu	.40	.12
70 Pat Burrell	.40	.12
71 Scott Rolen	.60	.18
72 Brian Giles	.40	.12
73 Jason Kendall	.40	.12
74 Phil Nevin	.40	.12
75 Rickey Henderson	1.00	.30
76 Ryan Klesko	.40	.12
77 Andres Galarraga	.40	.12
78 Barry Bonds	2.50	.75
79 Tsuyoshi Shinjo	.40	.12
80 Jeff Kent	.40	.12
81 Bret Boone	.40	.12
82 Edgar Martinez	.60	.18
83 Freddy Garcia	.40	.12
84 Ichiro Suzuki	1.50	.45
85 Kazuhiro Sasaki	.40	.12
86 John Olerud	.40	.12
87 Albert Pujols	2.00	.60
88 Bud Smith	.40	.12
89 J.D. Drew	.40	.12
90 Jim Edmonds	.40	.12
91 Matt Morris	.40	.12
92 Greg Vaughn	.40	.12
93 Alex Rodriguez	1.50	.45
94 Chan Ho Park	.40	.12
95 Ivan Rodriguez	1.00	.30
96 Juan Gonzalez	1.00	.30
97 Rafael Palmeiro	.60	.18
98 Carlos Delgado	.40	.12
99 Raul Mondesi	.40	.12
100 Shannon Stewart	.40	.12
101 Marlon Byrd NV	2.00	.60
102 Alex Herrera NV	2.00	.60
103 Brandon Backe NV	2.00	.60
104 Jorge De La Rosa NV RC	2.00	.60
105 Corky Miller NV	2.00	.60
106 Dennis Tankersley NV	2.00	.60
107 Kyle Kane NV RC	2.00	.60
108 Justin Duchscherer NV	2.00	.60
109 Brian Mallette NV RC	2.00	.60
110 Eric Hinske NV	2.00	.60
111 Jason Lane NV	2.00	.60
112 Hee Seop Choi NV	2.50	.75
113 Juan Cruz NV	2.00	.60
114 Rodrigo Rosario NV RC	2.00	.60
115 Matt Guerrier NV	2.00	.60
116 Anderson Machado NV RC	2.00	.60
117 Geronimo Gil NV	2.00	.60
118 Dewon Brazelton NV	2.00	.60
119 Mark Prior NV	8.00	2.40
120 Bill Hall NV	2.00	.60
121 Jorge Padilla NV RC	2.00	.60
122 Josh Pearce NV	2.00	.60
123 Allan Simpson NV RC	2.00	.60
124 Doug Devore NV RC	2.00	.60
125 Luis Garcia NV	2.00	.60
126 Angel Berroa NV	2.00	.60
127 Steve Bechler NV RC	2.00	.60
128 Antonio Perez NV	2.00	.60
129 Mark Teixeira NV	3.00	.90
130 Mark Ellis NV	2.00	.60
131 Michael Cuddyer NV	2.00	.60
132 Mike Rivera NV	2.00	.60
133 Raul Chavez NV RC	2.00	.60
134 Juan Pena NV	2.00	.60
135 Austin Kearns NV	2.00	.60
136 Ryan Ludwick NV	2.00	.60
137 Eddie Rogers NV	2.00	.60
138 Wilson Betemit NV	2.00	.60
139 Nick Neugebauer NV	2.00	.60
140 Tom Shearn NV RC	2.00	.60
141 Eric Cyr NV	2.00	.60
142 Victor Martinez NV	2.00	.60
143 Brandon Berger NV	2.00	.60
144 Erik Bedard NV	2.00	.60
145 Franklyn German NV RC	2.00	.60
146 Joe Thurston NV	2.00	.60
147 John Buck NV	2.00	.60
148 Jeff Deardorff NV	2.00	.60
149 Ryan Jamison NV	2.00	.60
150 Alfredo Amezaga NV	2.00	.60

2002 Donruss Super Estrellas Estrellas

Issued at stated odds of one in 12, these five cards featured leading hitters of "Spanish" heritage.

	Nm-Mt	Ex-Mt
COMPLETE SET (5)	10.00	3.00
1 Alex Rodriguez	3.00	.90
2 Ivan Rodriguez	2.00	.60
3 Vladimir Guerrero	2.00	.60
4 Sammy Sosa	3.00	.90
5 Nomar Garciaparra	3.00	.90

2002 Donruss Super Estrellas Nacion De Origen

Issued at stated odds of one in four, these 20 cards featured some of the leading players who have a Spanish heritage.

	Nm-Mt	Ex-Mt
COMPLETE SET (20)	25.00	7.50
1 Livan Hernandez	1.50	.45
2 Albert Pujols	4.00	1.20
3 Ivan Rodriguez	2.00	.60
4 Mariano Rivera	1.50	.45
5 Richard Hidalgo	1.50	.45
6 Eric Chavez	1.50	.45
7 Vinny Castilla	1.50	.45
8 Geronimo Gil	1.50	.45

9 Elmer Dessens 1.50 .45
10 Ismael Valdes 1.50 .45
11 Edgar Renteria 1.50 .45
12 Rafael Palmeiro 1.50 .45
13 Luis Gonzalez 1.50 .45
14 Orlando Hernandez 1.50 .45
15 Vladimir Guerrero 2.00 .60
16 Manny Ramirez 1.50 .45
17 Sammy Sosa 3.00 .90
18 Vicente Padilla 1.50 .45
19 Roberto Alomar 2.00 .60
20 Bernie Williams 1.50 .45

2002 Donruss Super Estrellas Poder De Cuadrangular

Issued at stated odds of one in six, these 15 cards feature some of the leading hitters in baseball.

Nm-Mt Ex-Mt
COMPLETE SET (15) 25.00 7.50
1 Sammy Sosa 4.00 1.20
2 Juan Gonzalez 2.50 .75
3 Carlos Delgado 2.00 .60
4 Todd Helton 2.00 .60
5 Alex Rodriguez 4.00 1.20
6 Troy Glaus 2.00 .60
7 Manny Ramirez 2.00 .60
8 Vladimir Guerrero 2.50 .75
9 Jim Thome 2.50 .75
10 Luis Gonzalez 2.00 .60
11 Shawn Green 2.00 .60
12 Barry Bonds 6.00 1.80
13 Larry Walker 2.00 .60
14 Jeff Bagwell 2.00 .60
15 Rafael Palmeiro 2.00 .60

2002 Donruss Super Estrellas Posters De Jugadores

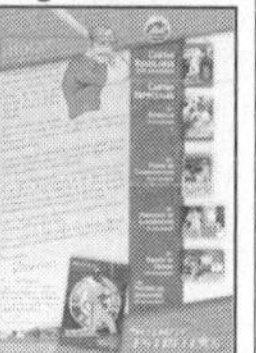

Issued at stated odds of one per pack, these 25 "posters" feature some of the leading players in baseball. It should be noted that due to the way these posters must be inserted into packs, every one will have some fold lines.

Nm-Mt Ex-Mt
COMPLETE SET (25) 20.00 6.00
1 Roberto Alomar .50 .15
2 Jeff Bagwell .50 .15
3 Barry Bonds 2.50 .75
4 Roger Clemens 2.00 .60
5 Carlos Delgado .50 .15
6 Nomar Garciaparra 1.50 .45
7 Jason Giambi .50 .15
8 Juan Gonzalez .50 .15
9 Ken Griffey Jr. 1.50 .45
10 Vladimir Guerrero .50 .15
11 Tony Gwynn 1.25 .35
12 Derek Jeter 2.50 .75
13 Randy Johnson .50 .15
14 Chipper Jones .50 .15
15 Greg Maddux 1.50 .45
16 Pedro Martinez .50 .15
17 Mike Piazza 1.50 .45
18 Albert Pujols 2.00 .60
19 Manny Ramirez .50 .15
20 Cal Ripken 3.00 .90
21 Alex Rodriguez 1.50 .45
22 Ivan Rodriguez .50 .15
23 Sammy Sosa 1.50 .45
24 Ichiro Suzuki 1.50 .45
25 Frank Thomas .50 .15

2002 Donruss Super Estrellas Precision De Lanzamiento

Issued at stated odds of one in 12, these five cards feature some of the leading pitchers in baseball.

Nm-Mt Ex-Mt
COMPLETE SET (5) 10.00 3.00
1 Pedro Martinez 2.00 .60
2 Greg Maddux 3.00 .90
3 Randy Johnson 2.00 .60
4 Roger Clemens 4.00 1.20
5 Curt Schilling 1.50 .45

2003 Donruss Team Heroes Samples

Issued one per Beckett Baseball Card Magazine, these cards were issued to preview the Donruss Team Heroes set. These cards can be differentiated by the word "sample" printed in silver on the back.

Nm-Mt Ex-Mt
*SAMPLES: 1.5X TO 4X BASIC CARDS

2003 Donruss Team Heroes Samples Gold

Randomly inserted into Beckett Baseball Card Magazines, this is a parallel to the Team Heroes Samples set. These cards can be noted by the word "Sample" printed in gold on the back.

Nm-Mt Ex-Mt
*GOLD SAMPLES: 4X TO 10X BASIC CARDS

2003 Donruss Team Heroes

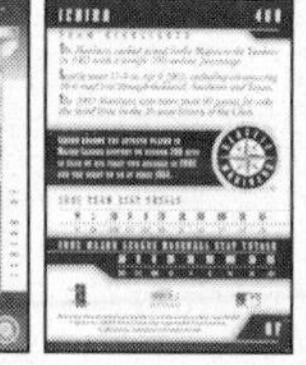

This 548 card set was distributed in two separate series. The primary Team Heroes product - containing cards 1-540 from the basic set - was released very late in December, 2002. These cards were issued in 13 card packs with an SRP of $3 per pack. This product was issued in 24 pack boxes which came 20 boxes to a case. Several great players, were issued as members of two or more different teams. Update cards 541-548 were distributed as commonly available cards within packs of 2003 DLP Rookies and Traded of which was released in December, 2003. Due to a problem in production, these update cards feature a glossy sheen, differentiating them from the remaining 540 cards within the basic set. Furthermore, they may be confused with the Team Heroes Glossy parallel cards of which were issued as random inserts in basic Team Heroes packs.

Nm-Mt Ex-Mt
COMP.LO SET (540) 80.00 24.00
COMP.UPDATE SET (8) 8.00 2.40
COMMON CARD (541-548) .60 .18
1 Adam Kennedy .30 .09
2 Steve Green .30 .09
3 Rod Carew Angels .75 .23
4 Alfredo Amezaga .30 .09
5 Reggie Jackson Angels .75 .23
6 Jarrod Washburn .30 .09
7 Nolan Ryan Angels 3.00 .90
8 Tim Salmon .50 .15
9 Garret Anderson .30 .09
10 Darin Erstad .30 .09
11 Elpidio Guzman .30 .09
12 David Eckstein .30 .09
13 Troy Percival .30 .09
14 Troy Glaus .50 .15
15 Doug Devore .30 .09
16 Tony Womack .30 .09
17 Matt Williams .30 .09
18 Junior Spivey .30 .09
19 Mark Grace .50 .15
20 Curt Schilling .50 .15
21 Erubiel Durazo .30 .09
22 Craig Counsell .30 .09
23 Byung-Hyun Kim .30 .09
24 Randy Johnson D'backs .75 .23
25 Luis Gonzalez .30 .09
26 John Smoltz .50 .15
27 Tim Spooneybarger .30 .09
28 Dale Murphy 1.25 .35
29 Warren Spahn .75 .23
30 Jason Marquis .30 .09
31 Kevin Millwood .30 .09
32 Javy Lopez .30 .09
33 Vinny Castilla .30 .09
34 Julio Franco .30 .09
35 Trey Hodges .30 .09
36 Chipper Jones .75 .23
37 Gary Sheffield .30 .09
38 Billy Sylvester .30 .09
39 Tom Glavine .50 .15
40 Rafael Furcal .30 .09
41 Cory Aldridge .30 .09
42 Greg Maddux Braves 1.25 .35
43 John Ennis .30 .09
44 Wes Helms .30 .09
45 Horacio Ramirez .30 .09
46 Derrick Lewis .30 .09
47 Marcus Giles .30 .09
48 Eddie Mathews 1.25 .35
49 Wilson Betemit .30 .09
50 Andruw Jones .30 .09
51 Josh Towers .30 .09
52 Ed Rogers .30 .09
53 Kris Foster .30 .09
54 Brooks Robinson 1.25 .35
55 Cal Ripken 4.00 1.20
56 Brian Roberts .30 .09
57 Luis Rivera .30 .09
58 Rodrigo Lopez .30 .09
59 Geronimo Gil .30 .09
60 Erik Bedard .30 .09
61 Jim Palmer .50 .15
62 Jay Gibbons .30 .09
63 Travis Driskill .30 .09
64 Larry Bigbie .30 .09
65 Eddie Murray 1.25 .35
66 Hoyt Wilhelm .50 .15
67 Bobby Doerr .50 .15
68 Pedro Martinez .75 .23
69 Roger Clemens Red Sox 1.50 .45
70 Nomar Garciaparra 1.50 .45
71 Trot Nixon .50 .15
72 Dennis Eckersley Red Sox .50 .15
73 John Burkett .30 .09
74 Tim Wakefield .30 .09
75 Wade Boggs Red Sox .75 .23
76 Cliff Floyd .30 .09
77 Casey Fossum .30 .09
78 Johnny Damon .30 .09
79 Fred Lynn .50 .15
80 Rickey Henderson Red Sox .75 .23
81 Juan Diaz .30 .09
82 Manny Ramirez .30 .09
83 Carlton Fisk Red Sox .75 .23
84 Jorge De La Rosa .30 .09
85 Shea Hillenbrand .30 .09
86 Derek Lowe .30 .09
87 Jason Varitek .30 .09
88 Carlos Baerga .30 .09
89 Freddy Sanchez .30 .09
90 Ugueth Urbina .30 .09
91 Rey Sanchez .30 .09
92 Josh Hancock .30 .09
93 Tony Clark .30 .09
94 Dustin Hermanson .30 .09
95 Ryne Sandberg 2.50 .75
96 Fred McGriff .50 .15
97 Alex Gonzalez .30 .09
98 Mark Bellhorn .30 .09
99 Fergie Jenkins .50 .15
100 Jon Lieber .30 .09
101 Francis Beltran .30 .09
102 Greg Maddux Cubs 1.25 .35
103 Nate Frese .30 .09
104 Andre Dawson Cubs .75 .23
105 Carlos Zambrano .30 .09
106 Steve Smyth .30 .09
107 Ernie Banks 1.25 .35
108 Will Ohman .30 .09
109 Kerry Wood .75 .23
110 Bobby Hill .30 .09
111 Moises Alou .30 .09
112 Hee Seop Choi .30 .09
113 Corey Patterson .30 .09
114 Sammy Sosa 1.25 .35
115 Mark Prior 1.50 .45
116 Juan Cruz .30 .09
117 Ron Santo .75 .23
118 Billy Williams .50 .15
119 Antonio Alfonseca .30 .09
120 Matt Clement .30 .09
121 Carlton Fisk White Sox .75 .23
122 Joe Crede .30 .09
123 Magglio Ordonez .30 .09
124 Frank Thomas .75 .23
125 Joe Borchard .30 .09
126 Royce Clayton .30 .09
127 Luis Aparicio .50 .15
128 Willie Harris .30 .09
129 Kyle Kane .30 .09
130 Paul Konerko .30 .09
131 Matt Ginter .30 .09
132 Carlos Lee .30 .09
133 Mark Buehrle .30 .09
134 Adam Dunn .30 .09
135 Eric Davis .50 .15
136 Johnny Bench 1.25 .35
137 Joe Morgan .50 .15
138 Austin Kearns .30 .09
139 Barry Larkin .75 .23
140 Ken Griffey Jr. Reds 1.25 .35
141 Luis Pineda .30 .09
142 Corky Miller .30 .09
143 Brandon Larson .30 .09
144 Wily Mo Pena .30 .09
145 Lance Davis .30 .09
146 Tom Seaver Reds .75 .23
147 Luke Hudson .30 .09
148 Sean Casey .30 .09
149 Tony Perez .50 .15
150 Todd Walker .30 .09
151 Aaron Boone .30 .09
152 Jose Rijo .30 .09
153 Ryan Dempster .30 .09
154 Danny Graves .30 .09
155 Matt Lawton .30 .09
156 Cliff Lee 2.00 .60
157 Ryan Drese .30 .09
158 Danys Baez .30 .09
159 Einar Diaz .30 .09
160 Milton Bradley .30 .09
161 Earl Snyder .30 .09
162 Ellis Burks .30 .09
163 Lou Boudreau .50 .15
164 Bob Feller .75 .23
165 Ricardo Rodriguez .30 .09
166 Victor Martinez .30 .09
167 Alex Herrera .30 .09
168 Omar Vizquel .30 .09
169 David Elder .30 .09
170 C.C. Sabathia .30 .09
171 Alex Escobar .30 .09
172 Brian Tallet .30 .09
173 Jim Thome .75 .23
174 Rene Reyes .30 .09
175 Juan Uribe .30 .09
176 Jason Romano .30 .09
177 Juan Pierre .30 .09
178 Jason Jennings .30 .09
179 Jose Ortiz .30 .09
180 Larry Walker .50 .15
181 Cam Esslinger .30 .09
182 Todd Helton .50 .15
183 Aaron Cook .30 .09
184 Jack Cust .30 .09
185 Jack Morris Tigers .50 .15
186 Mike Rivera .30 .09
187 Bobby Higginson .30 .09
188 Fernando Rodney .30 .09
189 Al Kaline 1.25 .35
190 Carlos Pena .30 .09
191 Alan Trammell .75 .23
192 Mike Maroth .30 .09
193 Adam Pettyjohn .30 .09
194 David Espinosa .30 .09
195 Adam Bernero .30 .09
196 Franklyn German .30 .09
197 Robert Fick .30 .09
198 Andres Torres .30 .09
199 Luis Castillo .30 .09
200 Preston Wilson .30 .09
201 Pablo Ozuna .30 .09
202 Brad Penny .30 .09
203 Josh Beckett .50 .15
204 Charles Johnson .30 .09
205 Wilson Valdez .30 .09
206 A.J. Burnett .30 .09
207 Abraham Nunez .30 .09
208 Mike Lowell .30 .09
209 Jose Cueto .30 .09
210 Jeriome Robertson .30 .09
211 Jeff Bagwell .50 .15
212 Kirk Saarloos .30 .09
213 Craig Biggio .50 .15
214 Rodrigo Rosario .30 .09
215 Roy Oswalt .30 .09
216 John Buck .30 .09
217 Tim Redding .30 .09
218 Morgan Ensberg .30 .09
219 Richard Hidalgo .30 .09
220 Wade Miller .30 .09
221 Lance Berkman .30 .09
222 Raul Chavez .30 .09
223 Carlos Hernandez .30 .09
224 Greg Miller .30 .09
225 Tom Shearn .30 .09
226 Jason Lane .30 .09
227 Nolan Ryan Astros 3.00 .90
228 Billy Wagner .30 .09
229 Octavio Dotel .30 .09
230 Shane Reynolds .30 .09
231 Julio Lugo .30 .09
232 Daryle Ward .30 .09
233 Mike Sweeney .30 .09
234 Angel Berroa .30 .09
235 George Brett 3.00 .90
236 Brad Voyles .30 .09
237 Brandon Berger .30 .09
238 Chad Durbin .30 .09
239 Alexis Gomez .30 .09
240 Jeremy Affeldt .30 .09
241 Bo Jackson 1.25 .35
242 Dee Brown .30 .09
243 Tony Cogan .30 .09
244 Carlos Beltran .30 .09
245 Joe Randa .30 .09
246 Pee Wee Reese .75 .23
247 Andy Ashby .30 .09
248 Cesar Izturis .30 .09
249 Duke Snider .75 .23
250 Mark Grudzielanek .30 .09
251 Chin-Feng Chen .30 .09
252 Brian Jordan .30 .09
253 Steve Garvey .50 .15
254 Odalis Perez .30 .09
255 Hideo Nomo .75 .23
256 Kevin Brown .30 .09
257 Eric Karros .30 .09
258 Joe Thurston .30 .09
259 Carlos Garcia .30 .09
260 Shawn Green .30 .09
261 Paul Lo Duca .30 .09
262 Kazuhisa Ishii .30 .09
263 Victor Alvarez .30 .09
264 Eric Gagne .50 .15
265 Don Sutton .50 .15
266 Orel Hershiser .50 .15
267 Dave Roberts .30 .09
268 Adrian Beltre .30 .09
269 Don Drysdale 1.25 .35
270 Jackie Robinson 1.50 .45
271 Tyler Houston .30 .09
272 Omar Daal .30 .09
273 Marquis Grissom .30 .09
274 Paul Quantrill .30 .09
275 Paul Molitor .75 .23
276 Jose Hernandez .30 .09
277 Takahito Nomura .30 .09
278 Nick Neugebauer .30 .09
279 Jose Mieses .30 .09
280 Richie Sexson .30 .09
281 Matt Childers .30 .09
282 Bill Hall .30 .09
283 Ben Sheets .30 .09
284 Brian Mallette .30 .09
285 Geoff Jenkins .30 .09
286 Robin Yount 2.00 .60
287 Jeff Deardorff .30 .09
288 Luis Rivas .30 .09
289 Harmon Killebrew 1.25 .35
290 Michael Cuddyer .30 .09
291 Torii Hunter .30 .09
292 Kevin Frederick .30 .09
293 Adam Johnson .30 .09
294 Jack Morris Twins .50 .15
295 Rod Carew Twins .75 .23
296 Kirby Puckett 1.25 .35
297 Joe Mays .30 .09
298 Jacque Jones .30 .09
299 Cristian Guzman .30 .09
300 Kyle Lohse .30 .09
301 Eric Milton .30 .09
302 Brad Radke .30 .09
303 Doug Mientkiewicz .30 .09
304 Corey Koskie .30 .09
305 Jose Vidro .30 .09
306 Claudio Vargas .30 .09
307 Gary Carter Expos .75 .23
308 Andre Dawson Expos .75 .23
309 Henry Mateo .30 .09
310 Andres Galarraga .30 .09
311 Zach Day .30 .09
312 Bartolo Colon .30 .09
313 Endy Chavez .30 .09
314 Javier Vazquez .30 .09
315 Michael Barrett .30 .09
316 Vladimir Guerrero .75 .23
317 Orlando Cabrera .30 .09
318 Al Leiter .30 .09
319 Timo Perez .30 .09
320 Rey Ordonez .30 .09
321 Gary Carter .75 .23
322 Armando Benitez .30 .09
323 Dwight Gooden .75 .23
324 Pedro Astacio .30 .09
325 Roberto Alomar .75 .23
326 Edgardo Alfonzo .30 .09
327 Nolan Ryan Mets 3.00 .90
328 Mo Vaughn .30 .09
329 Ryan Jamison .30 .09
330 Satoru Komiyama .30 .09
331 Mike Piazza 1.25 .35
332 Tom Seaver Mets .75 .23
333 Jorge Posada .50 .15
334 Derek Jeter 2.00 .60
335 Babe Ruth 3.00 .90
336 Lou Gehrig 2.00 .60
337 Andy Pettitte .50 .15
338 Mariano Rivera .50 .15
339 Robin Ventura .30 .09
340 Yogi Berra 1.25 .35
341 Phil Rizzuto .75 .23
342 Bernie Williams .50 .15
343 Alfonso Soriano .50 .15
344 Drew Henson .30 .09
345 Erick Almonte .30 .09
346 Rondell White .30 .09
347 Christian Parker .30 .09
348 Joe Torre MG Yankees .75 .23
349 Nick Johnson .30 .09
350 Raul Mondesi .30 .09
351 Brandon Claussen .30 .09
352 Reggie Jackson Yankees .75 .23
353 Roger Clemens Yankees 1.50 .45
354 Don Mattingly 3.00 .90
355 Jason Giambi .75 .23
356 Adrian Hernandez .30 .09
357 Jeff Weaver .30 .09
358 Mike Mussina .75 .23
359 Brett Jodie .30 .09
360 David Wells .30 .09
361 Enos Slaughter Yankees .50 .15
362 Whitey Ford .75 .23
363 Eric Chavez .30 .09
364 Miguel Tejada .30 .09
365 Barry Zito .50 .15
366 Bert Snow .30 .09
367 Rickey Henderson A's .75 .23
368 Juan Pena .30 .09
369 Terrence Long .30 .09
370 Dennis Eckersley A's .50 .15
371 Mark Ellis .30 .09
372 Tim Hudson .30 .09
373 Jose Canseco 1.25 .35
374 Reggie Jackson A's .75 .23
375 Mark Mulder .30 .09
376 David Justice .30 .09
377 Jermaine Dye .30 .09
378 Brett Myers .30 .09
379 Lenny Dykstra .50 .15
380 Vicente Padilla .30 .09
381 Bobby Abreu .30 .09
382 Pat Burrell .30 .09
383 Jorge Padilla .30 .09
384 Jeremy Giambi .30 .09
385 Mike Lieberthal .30 .09
386 Anderson Machado .30 .09
387 Marlon Byrd .30 .09
388 Bud Smith .30 .09
389 Eric Valent .30 .09
390 Elio Serrano .30 .09
391 Jimmy Rollins .30 .09
392 Brandon Duckworth .30 .09
393 Robin Roberts .50 .15
394 Marlon Anderson .30 .09
395 Robert Person .30 .09
396 Johnny Estrada .30 .09
397 Mike Schmidt 3.00 .90
398 Eric Junge .30 .09
399 Jason Michaels .30 .09
400 Steve Carlton .50 .15
401 Placido Polanco .30 .09
402 John Grabow .30 .09
403 Tomas De La Rosa .30 .09
404 Tike Redman .30 .09
405 Willie Stargell .75 .23
406 Dave Williams .30 .09
407 John Candelaria .30 .09
408 Jack Wilson .30 .09
409 Matt Guerrier .30 .09
410 Jason Kendall .30 .09
411 Josh Fogg .30 .09
412 Aramis Ramirez .30 .09
413 Dave Parker .50 .15
414 Roberto Clemente 2.50 .75
415 Kip Wells .30 .09
416 Brian Giles .30 .09
417 Honus Wagner 1.25 .35
418 Ramon Vazquez .30 .09
419 Oliver Perez .30 .09
420 Ryan Klesko .30 .09
421 Brian Lawrence .30 .09
422 Ben Howard .30 .09
423 Ozzie Smith Padres 2.00 .60
424 Dennis Tankersley .30 .09
425 Tony Gwynn 1.00 .30
426 Sean Burroughs .30 .09
427 Xavier Nady .30 .09
428 Phil Nevin .30 .09
429 Trevor Hoffman .30 .09
430 Jake Peavy .30 .09
431 Cody Ransom .30 .09
432 Kenny Lofton .30 .09
433 Mel Ott .75 .23
434 Tsuyoshi Shinjo .30 .09
435 Deivis Santos .30 .09
436 Rich Aurilia .30 .09
437 Will Clark Giants 1.25 .35
438 Pedro Feliz .30 .09
439 J.T. Snow .30 .09
440 Robb Nen .30 .09
441 Carlos Valderrama .30 .09
442 Willie McCovey .50 .15
443 Jeff Kent .30 .09
444 Orlando Cepeda .50 .15
445 Barry Bonds 2.00 .60
446 Alex Rodriguez M's 1.25 .35
447 Allan Simpson .30 .09
448 Antonio Perez .30 .09
449 Edgar Martinez .50 .15
450 Freddy Garcia .30 .09
451 Chris Snelling .30 .09
452 Matt Thornton .30 .09
453 Kazuhiro Sasaki .30 .09
454 Harold Reynolds .50 .15
455 Randy Johnson M's .75 .23
456 Bret Boone .30 .09
457 Rafael Soriano .30 .09
458 Luis Ugueto .30 .09
459 Ken Griffey Jr. M's 1.25 .35
460 Ichiro Suzuki 1.25 .35
461 Jamie Moyer .30 .09
462 Joel Pineiro .30 .09
463 Jeff Cirillo .30 .09
464 John Olerud .30 .09
465 Mike Cameron .30 .09
466 Ruben Sierra .30 .09

467 Mark McLemore .30 .09
468 Carlos Guillen .30 .09
469 Dan Wilson .30 .09
470 Shigetoshi Hasegawa .30 .09
471 Ben Davis .30 .09
472 Ozzie Smith Cards 2.00 .60
473 Matt Morris .30 .09
474 Edgar Renteria .30 .09
475 Les Walrond .30 .09
476 Albert Pujols 1.50 .45
477 Stan Musial 2.00 .60
478 J.D. Drew .30 .09
479 Josh Pearce .30 .09
480 Enos Slaughter Cards .50 .15
481 Jason Simontacchi .30 .09
482 Jeremy Lambert .30 .09
483 Tino Martinez .50 .15
484 Rogers Hornsby 1.25 .35
485 Rick Ankiel .30 .09
486 Jim Edmonds .30 .09
487 Scott Rolen .50 .15
488 Kevin Joseph .30 .09
489 Fernando Vina .30 .09
490 Jason Isringhausen .30 .09
491 Lou Brock .75 .23
492 Joe Torre Cards .75 .23
493 Bob Gibson .75 .23
494 Chuck Finley .30 .09
495 So Taguchi .30 .09
496 Ben Grieve .30 .09
497 Toby Hall .30 .09
498 Brent Abernathy .30 .09
499 Brandon Backe .30 .09
500 Felix Escalona .30 .09
501 Matt White .30 .09
502 Randy Winn .30 .09
503 Carl Crawford .30 .09
504 Dewon Brazelton .30 .09
505 Joe Kennedy .30 .09
506 Wade Boggs D-Rays .75 .23
507 Aubrey Huff .30 .09
508 Alex Rodriguez Rangers 1.25 .35
509 Ivan Rodriguez .75 .23
510 Will Clark Rangers 1.25 .35
511 Hank Blalock .50 .15
512 Travis Hughes .30 .09
513 Travis Hafner .30 .09
514 Ryan Ludwick .30 .09
515 Doug Davis .30 .09
516 Juan Gonzalez .75 .23
517 Jason Hart .30 .09
518 Mark Teixeira .50 .15
519 Nolan Ryan Rangers 3.00 .90
520 Rafael Palmeiro .50 .15
521 Kevin Mench .30 .09
522 Chan Ho Park .30 .09
523 Kenny Rogers .30 .09
524 Rusty Greer .30 .09
525 Michael Young .30 .09
526 Carlos Delgado .30 .09
527 Vernon Wells .30 .09
528 Orlando Hudson .30 .09
529 Shannon Stewart .30 .09
530 Joe Carter .50 .15
531 Chris Baker .30 .09
532 Eric Hinske .30 .09
533 Corey Thurman .30 .09
534 Josh Phelps .30 .09
535 Reed Johnson .30 .09
536 Brian Bowles .30 .09
537 Roy Halladay .30 .09
538 Jose Cruz Jr. .30 .09
539 Kelvim Escobar .30 .09
540 Chris Carpenter .30 .09
541 Rickie Weeks RC 2.50 .75
542 Hideki Matsui RC 2.00 .60
543 Ramon Nivar RC 1.00 .30
544 Adam Loewen RC 1.25 .35
545 Brandon Webb RC 1.25 .35
546 Dan Haren RC .60 .18
547 Delmon Young RC 3.00 .90
548 Ryan Wagner RC .75 .23

2003 Donruss Team Heroes Autographs

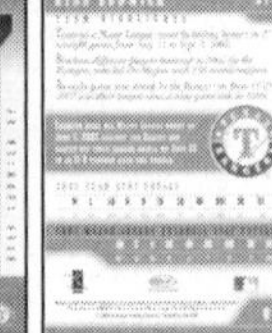

Randomly inserted into packs, this is a partial parallel to the Team Heroes set. Cards 541-548 were randomly seeded into packs of DLP Rookies and Traded. Each player signed a different amount of cards for this set and that information is noted next to the player's name in our checklist. It's important to note, though the manufacturer did publicly release print runs for all cards within this set, only those cards prtoduced in quantities of 100 or fewer copies actually carry foil serial-numbering on front. For those cards with a stated print run of 25 or fewer, no pricing is provided due to market scarcity. This set includes the first ever certified autographs for ESPN announcer Harold Reynolds and pitcher John Candelaria.

Nm-Mt Ex-Mt

2 Steve Green/25
3 Rod Carew Angels/10
4 Alfredo Amezaga/250 10.00 3.00
5 Reggie Jackson Angels/5
7 Nolan Ryan Angels/10
10 Darin Erstad/5
11 Elpidio Guzman/100 15.00 4.50
14 Troy Glaus/15
15 Doug Devore/122 15.00 4.50
20 Curt Schilling/5
25 Luis Gonzalez/5
28 Dale Murphy/15
35 Trey Hodges/250 10.00 3.00
36 Chipper Jones/10
37 Gary Sheffield/10
38 Billy Sylvester/250 10.00 3.00
39 Tom Glavine/15
41 Cory Aldridge/250 10.00 3.00
42 Greg Maddux Braves/5
43 John Ennis/25
45 Horacio Ramirez/200 10.00 3.00
46 Derrick Lewis/250 10.00 3.00
47 Marcus Giles/200 15.00 4.50
49 Wilson Betemit/75 15.00 4.50
50 Andruw Jones/15
51 Josh Towers/110 15.00 4.50
52 Ed Rogers/250 10.00 3.00
53 Kris Foster/250 10.00 3.00
54 Brooks Robinson/20
55 Cal Ripken/5
56 Brian Roberts/250 10.00 3.00
57 Luis Rivera/25
59 Geronimo Gil/60 15.00 4.50
60 Erik Bedard/250 10.00 3.00
61 Jim Palmer/5
62 Jay Gibbons/181 15.00 4.50
64 Larry Bigbie/100 15.00 4.50
65 Eddie Murray/10
66 Hoyt Wilhelm/25
67 Bobby Doerr/25
68 Pedro Martinez/5
69 Roger Clemens Red Sox/10
70 Nomar Garciaparra/10
72 Dennis Eckersley Red Sox/25
75 Wade Boggs Red Sox/10
76 Cliff Floyd/25
77 Casey Fossum/250 10.00 3.00
79 Fred Lynn/50 25.00 7.50
80 Rickey Henderson Red Sox/10
81 Juan Diaz/250 10.00 3.00
82 Manny Ramirez/5
83 Carlton Fisk Red Sox/5
84 Jorge De La Rosa/250 10.00 3.00
95 Ryne Sandberg/15
99 Fergie Jenkins/50 25.00 7.50
101 Francis Beltran/250 10.00 3.00
102 Greg Maddux Cubs/5
103 Nate Frese/250 10.00 3.00
104 Andre Dawson Cubs/25
105 Carlos Zambrano/150 25.00 7.50
106 Steve Smyth/25
107 Ernie Banks/15
108 Will Ohman/50 15.00 4.50
109 Bobby Hill/150 10.00 3.00
113 Corey Patterson/25
115 Mark Prior/50 120.00 36.00
116 Juan Cruz/50 15.00 4.50
117 Ron Santo/25
118 Billy Williams/10
121 Carlton Fisk White Sox/5
122 Joe Crede/250 10.00 3.00
123 Magglio Ordonez/25
124 Frank Thomas/5
125 Joe Borchard/250 15.00 4.50
127 Luis Aparicio/50 25.00 7.50
128 Willie Harris/129 15.00 4.50
129 Kyle Kane/100 15.00 4.50
131 Matt Ginter/250 10.00 3.00
132 Carlos Lee/50 25.00 7.50
133 Mark Buehrle/50 25.00 7.50
134 Adam Dunn/25
135 Eric Davis/75 25.00 7.50
136 Johnny Bench/10
137 Joe Morgan/15
138 Austin Kearns/71 25.00 7.50
139 Barry Larkin/15
141 Luis Pineda/25
142 Corky Miller/250 10.00 3.00
143 Brandon Larson/143 10.00 3.00
144 Wily Mo Pena/250 10.00 3.00
146 Tom Seaver Reds/15
147 Luke Hudson/50 15.00 4.50
148 Sean Casey/25
149 Tony Perez/50 25.00 7.50
156 Cliff Lee/250 15.00 4.50
161 Earl Snyder/250 10.00 3.00
165 Ricardo Rodriguez/250 10.00 3.00
166 Victor Martinez/200 15.00 4.50
167 Alex Herrera/250 10.00 3.00
170 C.C. Sabathia/20
171 Alex Escobar/125 15.00 4.50
172 Brian Tallet/250 10.00 3.00
173 Jim Thome/15
174 Rene Reyes/250 10.00 3.00
175 Juan Uribe/33
176 Jason Romano/50 15.00 4.50
177 Juan Pierre/66 25.00 7.50
178 Jason Jennings/250 10.00 3.00
179 Jose Ortiz/250 10.00 3.00
181 Cam Esslinger/250 10.00 3.00
182 Todd Helton/10
184 Jack Cust/250 10.00 3.00
185 Jack Morris Tigers/50 25.00 7.50
186 Mike Rivera/250 10.00 3.00
188 Fernando Rodney/250 10.00 3.00
189 Al Kaline/15
190 Carlos Pena/96 15.00 4.50
191 Alan Trammell/25
192 Mike Maroth/250 10.00 3.00
193 Adam Pettyjohn/250 10.00 3.00
194 David Espinosa/250 10.00 3.00
195 Adam Bernero/250 10.00 3.00
196 Franklyn German/250 10.00 3.00
197 Robert Fick/50 25.00 7.50
198 Andres Torres/250 10.00 3.00
201 Pablo Ozuna/250 10.00 3.00
203 Josh Beckett/20
205 Wilson Valdez/250 10.00 3.00
207 Abraham Nunez/250 10.00 3.00
209 Jose Cueto/25
211 Jeff Bagwell/10
212 Kirk Saarloos/250 10.00 3.00
213 Craig Biggio/10
214 Rodrigo Rosario/250 10.00 3.00
215 Roy Oswalt/50 25.00 7.50
216 John Buck/25
217 Tim Redding/250 10.00 3.00
218 Morgan Ensberg/250 10.00 3.00
219 Richard Hidalgo/100 25.00 7.50
220 Wade Miller/200 15.00 4.50
221 Lance Berkman/25
222 Raul Chavez/125 25.00 7.50
223 Carlos Hernandez/250 10.00 3.00
224 Greg Miller/90 15.00 4.50
225 Tom Shearn/25
226 Jason Lane/250 10.00 3.00
227 Nolan Ryan Astros/10
233 Mike Sweeney/25
234 Angel Berroa/200 15.00 4.50
235 George Brett/10
236 Brad Voyles/200 10.00 3.00
237 Brandon Berger/250 10.00 3.00
238 Chad Durbin/250 10.00 3.00
239 Alexis Gomez/165 10.00 3.00
240 Jeremy Affeldt/250 10.00 3.00
241 Bo Jackson/5
242 Dee Brown/50 15.00 4.50
243 Tony Cogan/250 10.00 3.00
244 Carlos Beltran/25
248 Cesar Izturis/200 10.00 3.00
249 Duke Snider/5
253 Steve Garvey/75 40.00 12.00
256 Kevin Brown/15
258 Joe Thurston/108 15.00 4.50
259 Carlos Garcia/100 15.00 4.50
260 Shawn Green/10
261 Paul Lo Duca/50 25.00 7.50
262 Kazuhisa Ishii/15
263 Victor Alvarez/250 10.00 3.00
265 Don Sutton/50 25.00 7.50
266 Orel Hershiser/15
268 Adrian Beltre/25
275 Paul Molitor/10
277 Takahito Nomura/100 40.00 12.00
278 Nick Neugebauer/25
279 Jose Mieses/50 15.00 4.50
280 Richie Sexson/5
281 Matt Childers/50 15.00 4.50
283 Ben Sheets/100 25.00 7.50
284 Brian Mallette/250 10.00 3.00
286 Robin Yount/15
287 Jeff Deardorff/100 15.00 4.50
288 Luis Rivas/200 15.00 4.50
289 Harmon Killebrew/15
290 Michael Cuddyer/250 10.00 3.00
291 Torii Hunter/100 25.00 7.50
292 Kevin Frederick/25
293 Adam Johnson/25
294 Jack Morris Twins/50 25.00 7.50
295 Rod Carew Twins/10
296 Kirby Puckett/10
297 Joe Mays/5
305 Jose Vidro/50 25.00 7.50
306 Claudio Vargas/150 10.00 3.00
307 Gary Carter Expos/20
308 Andre Dawson Expos/25
309 Henry Mateo/250 10.00 3.00
310 Andres Galarraga 15
311 Zach Day/250 10.00 3.00
313 Endy Chavez/250 10.00 3.00
314 Javier Vazquez/50 25.00 7.50
316 Vladimir Guerrero/15
319 Timo Perez/29
321 Gary Carter/20
323 Dwight Gooden/75
325 Roberto Alomar/15
327 Nolan Ryan Mets/10
329 Ryan Jamison/25
330 Satoru Komiyama/25
332 Tom Seaver Mets/15
340 Yogi Berra/15
341 Phil Rizzuto/15
342 Bernie Williams/10
343 Alfonso Soriano/25
344 Drew Henson/50 40.00 12.00
345 Erick Almonte/250 10.00 3.00
347 Christian Parker/200 10.00 3.00
348 Joe Torre Yankees/5
351 Brandon Claussen/250 15.00 4.50
352 Reggie Jackson Yankees/5
353 Roger Clemens Yankees/10
354 Don Mattingly/15
356 Adrian Hernandez/200 10.00 3.00
358 Mike Mussina/5
359 Brett Jodie/250 10.00 3.00
363 Eric Chavez/25
364 Miguel Tejada/20
365 Barry Zito/25
366 Bert Snow/250 10.00 3.00
367 Rickey Henderson A's/10
368 Juan Pena/250 10.00 3.00
369 Terrence Long/25
370 Dennis Eckersley A's/25
371 Mark Ellis/150 10.00 3.00
372 Tim Hudson/15
373 Jose Canseco/15
374 Reggie Jackson A's/5
375 Mark Mulder/25
376 David Justice/5
377 Jermaine Dye/15
379 Lenny Dykstra/75 25.00 7.50
381 Bobby Abreu/20
383 Jorge Padilla/250 10.00 3.00
384 Jeremy Giambi/100 15.00 4.50
386 Anderson Machado/250 10.00 3.00
387 Marlon Byrd/200 15.00 4.50
388 Bud Smith/125 15.00 4.50
389 Eric Valent/100 15.00 4.50
390 Elio Serrano/250 10.00 3.00
392 Brandon Duckworth/100 15.00 4.50
395 Robert Person/100 15.00 4.50
396 Johnny Estrada/209 10.00 3.00
397 Mike Schmidt/10
398 Eric Junge/250 10.00 3.00
399 Jason Michaels/221 10.00 3.00
400 Steve Carlton/20
402 John Grabow/250 10.00 3.00
403 Tomas De La Rosa/25
404 Tike Redman/25
406 Dave Williams/250 10.00 3.00
407 John Candelaria/100 25.00 7.50
408 Jack Wilson/250 10.00 3.00
409 Matt Guerrier/200 10.00 3.00
412 Aramis Ramirez/50 25.00 7.50
413 Dave Parker/50 25.00 7.50
415 Kip Wells/250 10.00 3.00
416 Brian Giles/25
418 Ramon Vazquez/200 10.00 3.00
419 Oliver Perez/150 10.00 3.00
420 Ryan Klesko/15
421 Brian Lawrence/250 10.00 3.00
422 Ben Howard/250 10.00 3.00
423 Ozzie Smith Padres/15
425 Tony Gwynn/15
426 Sean Burroughs/25
427 Xavier Nady/50 15.00 4.50
431 Cody Ransom/100 15.00 4.50
432 Kenny Lofton/15
435 Deivis Santos/100 15.00 4.50
436 Rich Aurilia/5
437 Will Clark Giants/10
438 Pedro Feliz/50 15.00 4.50
441 Carlos Valderrama/250 10.00 3.00
442 Willie McCovey/15
444 Orlando Cepeda/25
446 Alex Rodriguez M's/5
447 Allan Simpson/250 10.00 3.00
448 Antonio Perez/250 10.00 3.00
449 Edgar Martinez/15
450 Freddy Garcia/5
451 Chris Snelling/100 25.00 7.50
452 Matt Thornton/200 10.00 3.00
454 Harold Reynolds/100 25.00 7.50
457 Rafael Soriano/250 10.00 3.00
458 Luis Ugueto/50 15.00 4.50
472 Ozzie Smith Cards/15
475 Les Walrond/50 15.00 4.50
476 Albert Pujols/15
477 Stan Musial/15
478 J.D. Drew/10
479 Josh Pearce/200 10.00 3.00
482 Jeremy Lambert/25
485 Rick Ankiel/15
487 Scott Rolen/15
491 Lou Brock/15
492 Joe Torre Cards/10
497 Toby Hall/200 10.00 3.00
498 Brent Abernathy/250 10.00 3.00
499 Brandon Backe/250 10.00 3.00
500 Felix Escalona/50 15.00 4.50
501 Matt White/25
504 Dewon Brazelton/100 15.00 4.50
505 Joe Kennedy/200 10.00 3.00
506 Wade Boggs D-Rays/10
507 Aubrey Huff/100 25.00 7.50
508 Alex Rodriguez Rangers/5
509 Ivan Rodriguez/5
510 Will Clark Rangers/15
511 Hank Blalock/25
512 Travis Hughes/200 10.00 3.00
513 Travis Hafner/10
514 Ryan Ludwick/250 10.00 3.00
515 Doug Davis/250 10.00 3.00
516 Juan Gonzalez/5
517 Jason Hart/123 15.00 4.50
518 Mark Teixeira/50 40.00 12.00
519 Nolan Ryan Rangers/10
520 Rafael Palmeiro/10
521 Kevin Mench/250 10.00 3.00
528 Orlando Hudson/120 15.00 4.50
529 Shannon Stewart/25
530 Joe Carter/20
531 Chris Baker/200 10.00 3.00
532 Eric Hinske/200 10.00 3.00
533 Corey Thurman/250 10.00 3.00
534 Josh Phelps/150 10.00 3.00
535 Reed Johnson/250 10.00 3.00
536 Brian Bowles/250 10.00 3.00
541 Rickie Weeks/10
543 Ramon Nivar/100 20.00 6.00
544 Adam Loewen/100 40.00 12.00
545 Brandon Webb/100 40.00 12.00
546 Dan Haren/100 20.00 6.00
547 Delmon Young/25
548 Ryan Wagner/100 25.00 7.50

2003 Donruss Team Heroes Autographs Hawaii

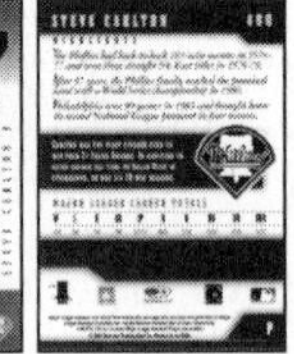

These cards were issued as an random insert in the special Hawaii Trade Conference box. Every box contained either an autograph card or a team timeline thread card. These cards were printed to a stated print run of one serial numbered set and no pricing is available due to market scarcity.

Nm-Mt Ex-Mt

3 Rod Carew
5 Reggie Jackson
7 Nolan Ryan
14 Troy Glaus
18 Junior Spivey
20 Curt Schilling
25 Luis Gonzalez
28 Dale Murphy
36 Chipper Jones
39 Tom Glavine
42 Greg Maddux
50 Andruw Jones
54 Brooks Robinson
55 Cal Ripken Jr.
61 Jim Palmer
65 Eddie Murray
66 Hoyt Wilhelm
67 Bobby Doerr
68 Pedro Martinez
69 Roger Clemens
70 Nomar Garciaparra
75 Wade Boggs
79 Rickey Henderson
82 Manny Ramirez
83 Carlton Fisk
95 Ryne Sandberg
99 Fergie Jenkins
102 Greg Maddux
104 Andre Dawson
107 Ernie Banks
109 Kerry Wood
115 Mark Prior
117 Ron Santo
121 Carlton Fisk
124 Frank Thomas
125 Joe Borchard
127 Luis Aparicio
134 Adam Dunn
136 Johnny Bench
137 Joe Morgan
146 Tom Seaver
173 Jim Thome
182 Todd Helton
189 Al Kaline
191 Alan Trammell
203 Josh Beckett
215 Roy Oswalt
221 Lance Berkman
227 Nolan Ryan
235 George Brett
241 Bo Jackson
249 Duke Snider
260 Shawn Green
262 Kazuhisa Ishii
275 Paul Molitor
286 Robin Yount
289 Harmon Killebrew
291 Torii Hunter
295 Rod Carew
296 Kirby Puckett
316 Vladimir Guerrero
321 Gary Carter
323 Dwight Gooden
327 Nolan Ryan
332 Tom Seaver
340 Yogi Berra
341 Phil Rizzuto
342 Bernie Williams
343 Alfonso Soriano
344 Drew Henson
348 Joe Torre
352 Reggie Jackson
353 Roger Clemens
354 Don Mattingly
358 Mike Mussina
363 Eric Chavez
364 Miguel Tejada
365 Barry Zito
367 Rickey Henderson
373 Jose Canseco
374 Reggie Jackson
397 Mike Schmidt
400 Steve Carlton
423 Ozzie Smith
425 Tony Gwynn
442 Willie McCovey
444 Orlando Cepeda
446 Alex Rodriguez
472 Ozzie Smith
476 Albert Pujols
477 Stan Musial
487 Scott Rolen
491 Lou Brock
506 Wade Boggs
508 Alex Rodriguez
509 Ivan Rodriguez
518 Mark Teixeira
519 Nolan Ryan
520 Rafael Palmeiro
532 Eric Hinske

2003 Donruss Team Heroes Chicago Collection

These cards were distributed in March 2003 at the Chicago Sportsfest at the Donruss-Playoff corporate booth. A collector who opened three packs of this product at the Donruss/Playoff booth received one of these cards as a redemption for the wrappers. Only five serial-numbered sets were produced, thus the cards are too scarce to price. They can be easily identified by the large gold-foil "Chicago Collection" logo and serial-numbering stamped on the front of each card.

Nm-Mt Ex-Mt

DISRIBUTED AT CHICAGO SPORTSFEST
STATED PRINT RUN 5 SERIAL #'d SETS
NO PRICING DUE TO SCARCITY

2003 Donruss Team Heroes Glossy

Issued one per pack, this is a parallel to the Donruss Team Heroes set. These cards can be differentiated from the regular cards as the fronts have a glossy sheen.

Nm-Mt Ex-Mt

* ACTIVE PLAYERS: 1.25X TO 3X BASIC
*RETIRED PLAYERS: 2X TO 5X BASIC

2003 Donruss Team Heroes Stat Line

Randomly inserted in packs, this is a parallel to the Donruss Team Heroes set. Cards 541-548 were randomly inserted into packs of DLP Rookies and Traded. Each card is sequentially numbered to a different quantity depending on the stat involved in producing the card. If the card was issued to a stated print run of 25 or fewer for a player active at time of issue or 36 or fewer for a player retired at time of issue, we are not providing pricing due to market scarcity.

Nm-Mt Ex-Mt

*ACTIVE P/R b/wn 201-250: 5X TO 12X
*ACTIVE P/R b/wn 151-200: 6X TO 15X
*ACTIVE P/R b/wn 121-150: 8X TO 20X
*ACTIVE P/R b/wn 81-120: 10X TO 25X
*ACTIVE P/R b/wn 66-80: 12.5X TO 30X
*ACTIVE P/R b/wn 51-65: 15X TO 40X
*ACTIVE P/R b/wn 36-50: 20X TO 50X
*ACTIVE P/R b/wn 26-35: 25X TO 60X
*RETIRED P/R b/wn 201-250: 3X TO 8X
*RETIRED P/R b/wn 151-200: 4X TO 10X
*RETIRED P/R b/wn 121-150: 5X TO 12X
*RETIRED P/R b/wn 81-120: 6X TO 15X
*RETIRED P/R b/wn 66-80: 10X TO 25X
*RETIRED P/R b/wn 51-65: 8X TO 20X
*RETIRED P/R b/wn 36-50: 12.5X TO 30X
*RC's P/R b/wn 36-50: 6X TO 15X
*RC's P/R b/wn 26-35: 8X TO 20X
541-548 RANDOM IN DLP R/T PACKS
1 Adam Kennedy/148 6.00 1.80
2 Steve Green/4
3 Rod Carew Angels/38 25.00 7.50
4 Alfredo Amezaga/7

5 Reggie Jackson Angels/39 ..... 25.00 7.50
6 Jarrod Washburn/139 ..... 6.00 1.80
7 Nolan Ryan Angels/61 ..... 80.00 24.00
8 Tim Salmon/138 ..... 10.00 3.00
9 Garret Anderson/123 ..... 6.00 1.80
10 Darin Erstad/177 ..... 5.00 1.50
11 Elpidio Guzman/112 ..... 8.00 2.40
12 David Eckstein/178 ..... 5.00 1.50
13 Troy Percival/68 ..... 10.00 3.00
14 Troy Glaus/111 ..... 12.00 3.60
15 Doug Devore/114 ..... 8.00 2.40
16 Tony Womack/160 ..... 5.00 1.50
17 Matt Williams/56 ..... 12.00 3.60
18 Junior Spivey/162 ..... 5.00 1.50
19 Mark Grace/75 ..... 15.00 4.50
20 Curt Schilling/23 .....
21 Erubiel Durazo/58 ..... 12.00 3.60
22 Craig Counsell/123 ..... 6.00 1.80
23 Byung-Hyun Kim/92 ..... 8.00 2.40
24 Randy Johnson D'backs/24 .....
25 Luis Gonzalez/151 ..... 5.00 1.50
26 John Smoltz/85 ..... 12.00 3.60
27 Tim Spooneybarger/51 ..... 12.00 3.60
28 Dale Murphy/39 ..... 40.00 12.00
29 Warren Spahn/63 ..... 20.00 6.00
30 Jason Marquis/84 ..... 8.00 2.40
31 Kevin Millwood/178 ..... 5.00 1.50
32 Javy Lopez/81 ..... 8.00 2.40
33 Vinny Castilla/126 ..... 6.00 1.80
34 Julio Franco/96 ..... 8.00 2.40
35 Trey Hodges/6 .....
36 Chipper Jones/100 ..... 20.00 6.00
37 Gary Sheffield/84 ..... 8.00 2.40
38 Billy Sylvester/53 ..... 12.00 3.60
39 Tom Glavine/127 ..... 10.00 3.00
40 Rafael Furcal/175 ..... 5.00 1.50
41 Cory Aldridge/17 .....
42 Greg Maddux Braves/118 ..... 30.00 9.00
43 John Ennis/1 .....
44 Wes Helms/51 ..... 12.00 3.60
45 Horacio Ramirez/69 ..... 10.00 3.00
46 Derrick Lewis/61 ..... 12.00 3.60
47 Marcus Giles/49 ..... 15.00 4.50
48 Eddie Mathews/47 ..... 40.00 12.00
49 Wilson Betemit/89 ..... 8.00 2.40
50 Andruw Jones/148 ..... 6.00 1.80
51 Josh Towers/13 .....
52 Ed Rogers/5 .....
53 Kris Foster/14 .....
54 Brooks Robinson/16 .....
55 Cal Ripken/44 ..... 120.00 36.00
56 Brian Roberts/29 ..... 20.00 6.00
57 Luis Rivera/1 .....
58 Rodrigo Lopez/136 ..... 6.00 1.80
59 Geronimo Gil/98 ..... 8.00 2.40
60 Erik Bedard/1 .....
61 Jim Palmer/20 .....
62 Jay Gibbons/121 ..... 6.00 1.80
63 Travis Driskill/78 ..... 10.00 3.00
64 Larry Bigbie/3 .....
65 Eddie Murray/124 ..... 15.00 4.50
66 Hoyt Wilhelm/143 ..... 6.00 1.80
67 Bobby Doerr/27 .....
68 Pedro Martinez/20 .....
69 Roger Clemens Red Sox/20 .....
70 Nomar Garciaparra/24 .....
71 Trot Nixon/136 ..... 10.00 3.00
72 Dennis Eckersley Red Sox/20 .....
73 John Burkett/124 ..... 6.00 1.80
74 Tim Wakefield/134 ..... 6.00 1.80
75 Wade Boggs Red Sox/24 .....
76 Cliff Floyd/150 ..... 6.00 1.80
77 Casey Fossum/101 ..... 8.00 2.40
78 Johnny Damon/178 ..... 5.00 1.50
79 Fred Lynn/16 .....
80 Rickey Henderson Red Sox/8 .....
81 Juan Diaz/2 .....
82 Manny Ramirez/107 ..... 8.00 2.40
83 Carlton Fisk Red Sox/22 .....
84 Jorge De La Rosa/110 ..... 8.00 2.40
85 Shea Hillenbrand/186 ..... 5.00 1.50
86 Derek Lowe/21 .....
87 Jason Varitek/124 ..... 6.00 1.80
88 Carlos Baerga/52 ..... 12.00 3.60
89 Freddy Sanchez/3 .....
90 Ugueth Urbina/71 ..... 10.00 3.00
91 Rey Sanchez/102 ..... 8.00 2.40
92 Josh Hancock/6 .....
93 Tony Clark/57 ..... 12.00 3.60
94 Dustin Hermanson/13 .....
95 Ryne Sandberg/123 ..... 30.00 9.00
96 Fred McGriff/143 ..... 10.00 3.00
97 Alex Gonzalez/127 ..... 6.00 1.80
98 Mark Bellhorn/115 ..... 8.00 2.40
99 Fergie Jenkins/20 .....
100 Jon Lieber/87 ..... 8.00 2.40
101 Francis Beltran/11 .....
102 Greg Maddux Cubs/20 .....
103 Nate Frese/24 .....
104 Andre Dawson Cubs/49 ..... 25.00 7.50
105 Carlos Zambrano/93 ..... 8.00 2.40
106 Steve Smyth/16 .....
107 Ernie Banks/143 ..... 15.00 4.50
108 Will Ohman/12 .....
109 Kerry Wood/12 .....
110 Bobby Hill/20 .....
111 Moises Alou/133 ..... 6.00 1.80
112 Hee Seop Choi/9 .....
113 Corey Patterson/150 ..... 6.00 1.80
114 Sammy Sosa/49 ..... 60.00 18.00
115 Mark Prior/6 .....
116 Juan Cruz/81 ..... 8.00 2.40
117 Ron Santo/5 .....
118 Billy Williams/137 ..... 6.00 1.80
119 Antonio Alfonseca/61 ..... 12.00 3.60
120 Matt Clement/215 ..... 4.00 1.20
121 Carlton Fisk White Sox/107 12.00 3.60
122 Joe Crede/57 ..... 12.00 3.60
123 Magglio Ordonez/38 ..... 15.00 4.50
124 Frank Thomas/132 ..... 15.00 4.50
125 Joe Borchard/5 .....
126 Royce Clayton/86 ..... 8.00 2.40
127 Luis Aparicio/92 ..... 8.00 2.40
128 Willie Harris/14 .....
129 Kyle Kane/9 .....
130 Paul Konerko/173 ..... 5.00 1.50
131 Matt Ginter/37 ..... 15.00 4.50
132 Carlos Lee/130 ..... 6.00 1.80
133 Mark Buehrle/19 .....
134 Adam Dunn/26 ..... 20.00 6.00
135 Eric Davis/27 ..... 30.00 9.00
136 Johnny Bench/40 ..... 40.00 12.00
137 Joe Morgan/17 .....
138 Austin Kearns/13 .....
139 Barry Larkin/114 ..... 15.00 4.50
140 Ken Griffey Jr. Reds/52 ..... 50.00 15.00
141 Luis Pineda/31 ..... 20.00 6.00
142 Corky Miller/29 ..... 20.00 6.00
143 Brandon Larson/14 .....
144 Wily Mo Pena/4 .....
145 Lance Davis/78 ..... 10.00 3.00
146 Tom Seaver Reds/61 ..... 20.00 6.00
147 Luke Hudson/7 .....
148 Sean Casey/111 ..... 8.00 2.40
149 Tony Perez/79 ..... 10.00 3.00
150 Todd Walker/183 ..... 5.00 1.50
151 Aaron Boone/146 ..... 6.00 1.80
152 Jose Rijo/38 ..... 15.00 4.50
153 Ryan Dempster/151 ..... 5.00 1.50
154 Danny Graves/58 ..... 12.00 3.60
155 Matt Lawton/98 ..... 8.00 2.40
156 Cliff Lee/6 .....
157 Ryan Drese/102 ..... 8.00 2.40
158 Danys Baez/130 ..... 6.00 1.80
159 Einar Diaz/66 ..... 10.00 3.00
160 Milton Bradley/81 ..... 8.00 2.40
161 Earl Snyder/11 .....
162 Ellis Burks/156 ..... 5.00 1.50
163 Lou Boudreau/46 ..... 15.00 4.50
164 Bob Feller/27 .....
165 Ricardo Rodriguez/24 .....
166 Victor Martinez/9 .....
167 Alex Herrera/5 .....
168 Omar Vizquel/160 ..... 5.00 1.50
169 David Elder/23 .....
170 C.C. Sabathia/149 ..... 6.00 1.80
171 Alex Escobar/10 .....
172 Brian Tallet/5 .....
173 Jim Thome/52 ..... 30.00 9.00
174 Rene Reyes/133 ..... 6.00 1.80
175 Juan Uribe/136 ..... 6.00 1.80
176 Jason Romano/23 .....
177 Juan Pierre/170 ..... 5.00 1.50
178 Jason Jennings/16 .....
179 Jose Ortiz/48 ..... 15.00 4.50
180 Larry Walker/26 ..... 30.00 9.00
181 Cam Esslinger/29 ..... 20.00 6.00
182 Todd Helton/30 ..... 30.00 9.00
183 Aaron Cook/14 .....
184 Jack Cust/11 .....
185 Jack Morris Tigers/17 .....
186 Mike Rivera/30 ..... 20.00 6.00
187 Bobby Higginson/125 ..... 6.00 1.80
188 Fernando Rodney/10 .....
189 Al Kaline/137 ..... 15.00 4.50
190 Carlos Pena/96 ..... 8.00 2.40
191 Alan Trammell/55 ..... 20.00 6.00
192 Mike Maroth/58 ..... 12.00 3.60
193 Adam Pettyjohn/40 ..... 15.00 4.50
194 David Espinosa/90 ..... 8.00 2.40
195 Adam Bernero/69 ..... 10.00 3.00
196 Franklyn German/6 .....
197 Robert Fick/150 ..... 6.00 1.80
198 Andres Torres/14 .....
199 Luis Castillo/185 ..... 5.00 1.50
200 Preston Wilson/124 ..... 6.00 1.80
201 Pablo Ozuna/13 .....
202 Brad Penny/93 ..... 8.00 2.40
203 Josh Beckett/6 .....
204 Charles Johnson/53 ..... 12.00 3.60
205 Wilson Valdez/98 ..... 8.00 2.40
206 A.J. Burnett/203 ..... 4.00 1.20
207 Abraham Nunez/2 .....
208 Mike Lowell/165 ..... 5.00 1.50
209 Jose Cueto/47 ..... 15.00 4.50
210 Jeriome Robertson/6 .....
211 Jeff Bagwell/31 ..... 30.00 9.00
212 Kirk Saarloos/54 ..... 12.00 3.60
213 Craig Biggio/15 .....
214 Rodrigo Rosario/94 ..... 8.00 2.40
215 Roy Oswalt/19 .....
216 John Buck/118 ..... 8.00 2.40
217 Tim Redding/63 ..... 12.00 3.60
218 Morgan Ensberg/32 ..... 20.00 6.00
219 Richard Hidalgo/91 ..... 8.00 2.40
220 Wade Miller/144 ..... 6.00 1.80
221 Lance Berkman/42 ..... 15.00 4.50
222 Raul Chavez/1 .....
223 Carlos Hernandez/93 ..... 8.00 2.40
224 Greg Miller/51 ..... 12.00 3.60
225 Tom Shearn/80 ..... 10.00 3.00
226 Jason Lane/20 .....
227 Nolan Ryan Astros/38 ..... 100.00 30.00
228 Billy Wagner/88 ..... 8.00 2.40
229 Octavio Dotel/118 ..... 8.00 2.40
230 Shane Reynolds/47 ..... 15.00 4.50
231 Julio Lugo/84 ..... 8.00 2.40
232 Daryle Ward/125 ..... 6.00 1.80
233 Mike Sweeney/160 ..... 5.00 1.50
234 Angel Berroa/17 .....
235 George Brett/45 ..... 100.00 30.00
236 Brad Voyles/26 ..... 20.00 6.00
237 Brandon Berger/27 ..... 20.00 6.00
238 Chad Durbin/5 .....
239 Alexis Gomez/2 .....
240 Jeremy Affeldt/67 ..... 10.00 3.00
241 Bo Jackson/32 .....
242 Dee Brown/12 .....
243 Tony Cogan/62 ..... 12.00 3.60
244 Carlos Beltran/174 ..... 5.00 1.50
245 Joe Randa/155 ..... 5.00 1.50
246 Pee Wee Reese/33 .....
247 Andy Ashby/107 ..... 8.00 2.40
248 Cesar Izturis/102 ..... 8.00 2.40
249 Duke Snider/136 ..... 10.00 3.00
250 Mark Grudzielanek/145 ..... 6.00 1.80
251 Chin-Feng Chen/1 .....
252 Brian Jordan/134 ..... 6.00 1.80
253 Steve Garvey/115 ..... 8.00 2.40
254 Odalis Perez/155 ..... 5.00 1.50
255 Hideo Nomo/16 .....
256 Kevin Brown/58 ..... 12.00 3.60
257 Eric Karros/142 ..... 6.00 1.80
258 Joe Thurston/6 .....
259 Carlos Garcia/9 .....
260 Shawn Green/42 ..... 15.00 4.50
261 Paul Lo Duca/163 ..... 5.00 1.50
262 Kazuhisa Ishii/14 .....
263 Victor Alvarez/7 .....
264 Eric Gagne/114 ..... 12.00 3.60
265 Don Sutton/21 .....
266 Orel Hershiser/59 ..... 12.00 3.60
267 Dave Roberts/117 ..... 8.00 2.40
268 Adrian Beltre/151 ..... 5.00 1.50
269 Don Drysdale/58 ..... 30.00 9.00
270 Jackie Robinson/39 ..... 50.00 15.00
271 Tyler Houston/90 ..... 8.00 2.40
272 Omar Daal/105 ..... 8.00 2.40
273 Marquis Grissom/95 ..... 8.00 2.40
274 Paul Quantrill/53 ..... 12.00 3.60
275 Paul Molitor/114 ..... 12.00 3.60
276 Jose Hernandez/151 ..... 5.00 1.50
277 Takahito Nomura/9 .....
278 Nick Neugebauer/47 ..... 15.00 4.50
279 Jose Mieses/55 ..... 12.00 3.60
280 Richie Sexson/102 ..... 8.00 2.40
281 Matt Childers/6 .....
282 Bill Hall/7 .....
283 Ben Sheets/170 ..... 5.00 1.50
284 Brian Mallette/5 .....
285 Geoff Jenkins/59 ..... 12.00 3.60
286 Robin Yount/29 .....
287 Jeff Deardorff/108 ..... 8.00 2.40
288 Luis Rivas/81 ..... 8.00 2.40
289 Harmon Killebrew/44 ..... 40.00 12.00
290 Michael Cuddyer/29 ..... 20.00 6.00
291 Torii Hunter/29 ..... 20.00 6.00
292 Kevin Frederick/5 .....
293 Adam Johnson/112 ..... 8.00 2.40
294 Jack Morris Twins/18 .....
295 Rod Carew Twins/128 ..... 10.00 3.00
296 Kirby Puckett/31 .....
297 Joe Mays/38 ..... 15.00 4.50
298 Jacque Jones/173 ..... 5.00 1.50
299 Cristian Guzman/170 ..... 5.00 1.50
300 Kyle Lohse/124 ..... 6.00 1.80
301 Eric Milton/121 ..... 6.00 1.80
302 Brad Radke/62 ..... 12.00 3.60
303 Doug Mientkiewicz/122 ..... 6.00 1.80
304 Corey Koskie/131 ..... 6.00 1.80
305 Jose Vidro/19 .....
306 Claudio Vargas/95 ..... 8.00 2.40
307 Gary Carter Expos/105 ..... 12.00 3.60
308 Andre Dawson Expos/107 .. 12.00 3.60
309 Henry Mateo/4 .....
310 Andres Galarraga/76 ..... 10.00 3.00
311 Zach Day/25 .....
312 Bartolo Colon/149 ..... 6.00 1.80
313 Endy Chavez/37 ..... 15.00 4.50
314 Javier Vazquez/179 ..... 5.00 1.50
315 Michael Barrett/99 ..... 8.00 2.40
316 Vladimir Guerrero/39 ..... 40.00 12.00
317 Orlando Cabrera/148 ..... 6.00 1.80
318 Al Leiter/172 ..... 5.00 1.50
319 Timo Perez/131 ..... 6.00 1.80
320 Rey Ordonez/117 ..... 8.00 2.40
321 Gary Carter/105 ..... 12.00 3.60
322 Armando Benitez/79 ..... 10.00 3.00
323 Dwight Gooden/24 .....
324 Pedro Astacio/152 ..... 5.00 1.50
325 Roberto Alomar/11 .....
326 Edgardo Alfonzo/151 ..... 5.00 1.50
327 Nolan Ryan Mets/92 ..... 50.00 15.00
328 Mo Vaughn/126 ..... 6.00 1.80
329 Ryan Jamison/90 ..... 8.00 2.40
330 Satoru Komiyama/33 ..... 20.00 6.00
331 Mike Piazza/33 ..... 80.00 24.00
332 Tom Seaver Mets/25 .....
333 Jorge Posada/20 .....
334 Derek Jeter/18 .....
335 Babe Ruth/60 ..... 80.00 24.00
336 Lou Gehrig/23 .....
337 Andy Pettitte/97 ..... 12.00 3.60
338 Mariano Rivera/45 ..... 25.00 7.50
339 Robin Ventura/115 ..... 8.00 2.40
340 Yogi Berra/30 .....
341 Phil Rizzuto/36 ..... 25.00 7.50
342 Bernie Williams/19 .....
343 Alfonso Soriano/39 ..... 25.00 7.50
344 Drew Henson/1 .....
345 Erick Almonte/97 ..... 8.00 2.40
346 Rondell White/109 ..... 8.00 2.40
347 Christian Parker/1 .....
348 Joe Torre Yankees/103 ..... 12.00 3.60
349 Nick Johnson/15 .....
350 Raul Mondesi/65 ..... 12.00 3.60
351 Brandon Claussen/73 ..... 10.00 3.00
352 Reggie Jackson Yankees/5 .....
353 Roger Clemens Yankees/13 .....
354 Don Mattingly/53 ..... 80.00 24.00
355 Jason Giambi/41 ..... 40.00 12.00
356 Adrian Hernandez/9 .....
357 Jeff Weaver/132 ..... 6.00 1.80
358 Mike Mussina/18 .....
359 Brett Jodie/14 .....
360 David Wells/137 ..... 6.00 1.80
361 Enos Slaughter Yankees/148 6.00 1.80
362 Whitey Ford/25 .....
363 Eric Chavez/161 ..... 5.00 1.50
364 Miguel Tejada/34 ..... 20.00 6.00
365 Barry Zito/23 .....
366 Bert Snow/54 ..... 12.00 3.60
367 Rickey Henderson A's/108 . 20.00 6.00
368 Juan Pena/34 ..... 20.00 6.00
369 Terrence Long/141 ..... 6.00 1.80
370 Dennis Eckersley A's/33 .....
371 Mark Ellis/94 ..... 8.00 2.40
372 Tim Hudson/15 .....
373 Jose Canseco/100 ..... 20.00 6.00
374 Reggie Jackson A's/117 ..... 12.00 3.60
375 Mark Mulder/19 .....
376 David Justice/106 ..... 8.00 2.40
377 Jermaine Dye/123 ..... 6.00 1.80
378 Brett Myers/34 ..... 20.00 6.00
379 Lenny Dykstra/19 .....
380 Vicente Padilla/128 ..... 6.00 1.80
381 Bobby Abreu/20 .....
382 Pat Burrell/37 ..... 15.00 4.50
383 Jorge Padilla/124 ..... 6.00 1.80
384 Jeremy Giambi/81 ..... 8.00 2.40
385 Mike Lieberthal/133 ..... 6.00 1.80
386 Anderson Machado/113 ..... 8.00 2.40
387 Marlon Byrd/8 .....
388 Bud Smith/22 .....
389 Eric Valent/2 .....
390 Elio Serrano/45 ..... 15.00 4.50
391 Jimmy Rollins/156 ..... 5.00 1.50
392 Brandon Duckworth 167 ..... 5.00 1.50
393 Robin Roberts/28 ..... 30.00 9.00
394 Marlon Anderson 139 ..... 6.00 1.80
395 Robert Person/61 ..... 12.00 3.60
396 Johnny Estrada/2 .....
397 Mike Schmidt/30 .....
398 Eric Junge/11 .....
399 Jason Michaels/28 ..... 20.00 6.00
400 Steve Carlton/20 .....
401 Placido Polanco/158 ..... 5.00 1.50
402 John Grabow/97 ..... 8.00 2.40
403 Tomas De La Rosa/78 ..... 10.00 3.00
404 Tike Redman/84 ..... 8.00 2.40
405 Willie Stargell/48 ..... 25.00 7.50
406 Dave Williams/33 ..... 20.00 6.00
407 John Candelaria/177 ..... 3.00 .90
408 Jack Wilson/133 ..... 6.00 1.80
409 Matt Guerrier/130 ..... 6.00 1.80
410 Jason Kendall/154 ..... 5.00 1.50
411 Josh Fogg/113 ..... 8.00 2.40
412 Aramis Ramirez/122 ..... 6.00 1.80
413 Dave Parker/125 ..... 5.00 1.50
414 Roberto Clemente/29 .....
415 Kip Wells/134 ..... 6.00 1.80
416 Brian Giles/148 ..... 6.00 1.80
417 Honus Wagner/61 ..... 30.00 9.00
418 Ramon Vazquez/116 ..... 8.00 2.40
419 Oliver Perez/94 ..... 8.00 2.40
420 Ryan Klesko/162 ..... 5.00 1.50
421 Brian Lawrence/149 ..... 6.00 1.80
422 Ben Howard/10 .....
423 Ozzie Smith Padres/40 ..... 60.00 18.00
424 Dennis Tankersley/39 ..... 15.00 4.50
425 Tony Gwynn/49 ..... 30.00 9.00
426 Sean Burroughs/52 ..... 12.00 3.60
427 Xavier Nady/136 ..... 6.00 1.80
428 Phil Nevin/116 ..... 8.00 2.40
429 Trevor Hoffman/69 ..... 10.00 3.00
430 Jake Peavy/90 ..... 8.00 2.40
431 Cody Ransom/2 .....
432 Kenny Lofton/139 ..... 6.00 1.80
433 Mel Ott/151 ..... 8.00 2.40
434 Tsuyoshi Shinjo/86 ..... 8.00 2.40
435 Deivis Santos/152 ..... 5.00 1.50
436 Rich Aurilia/138 ..... 6.00 1.80
437 Will Clark Giants/116 ..... 20.00 6.00
438 Pedro Feliz/37 ..... 15.00 4.50
439 J.T. Snow/104 ..... 8.00 2.40
440 Robb Nen/81 ..... 8.00 2.40
441 Carlos Valderrama/127 ..... 6.00 1.80
442 Willie McCovey/126 ..... 6.00 1.80
443 Jeff Kent/37 ..... 15.00 4.50
444 Orlando Cepeda/96 ..... 8.00 2.40
445 Barry Bonds/46 ..... 100.00 30.00
446 Alex Rodriguez M's/46 ..... 60.00 18.00
447 Allan Simpson/99 ..... 8.00 2.40
448 Antonio Perez/62 ..... 12.00 3.60
449 Edgar Martinez/91 ..... 12.00 3.60
450 Freddy Garcia/181 ..... 5.00 1.50
451 Chris Snelling/4 .....
452 Matt Thornton/44 ..... 15.00 4.50
453 Kazuhiro Sasaki/73 ..... 10.00 3.00
454 Harold Reynolds/60 ..... 12.00 3.60
455 Randy Johnson M's/53 ..... 30.00 9.00
456 Bret Boone/169 ..... 5.00 1.50
457 Rafael Soriano/32 ..... 20.00 6.00
458 Luis Ugueto/19 .....
459 Ken Griffey Jr. M's/56 ..... 50.00 15.00
460 Ichiro Suzuki/51 ..... 50.00 15.00
461 Jamie Moyer/147 ..... 6.00 1.80
462 Joel Pineiro/136 ..... 6.00 1.80
463 Jeff Cirillo/121 ..... 6.00 1.80
464 John Olerud/166 ..... 5.00 1.50
465 Mike Cameron/130 ..... 6.00 1.80
466 Ruben Sierra/113 ..... 8.00 2.40
467 Mark McLemore/91 ..... 8.00 2.40
468 Carlos Guillen/124 ..... 6.00 1.80
469 Dan Wilson /106 ..... 8.00 2.40
470 Shigetoshi Hasegawa/39 ..... 15.00 4.50
471 Ben Davis/59 ..... 12.00 3.60
472 Ozzie Smith Cards/57 ..... 50.00 15.00
473 Matt Morris/171 ..... 5.00 1.50
474 Edgar Renteria/166 ..... 5.00 1.50
475 Les Walrond/142 ..... 6.00 1.80
476 Albert Pujols/34 ..... 100.00 30.00
477 Stan Musial/31 .....
478 J.D. Drew/107 ..... 8.00 2.40
479 Josh Pearce/1 .....
480 Enos Slaughter Cards/130 ..... 6.00 1.80
481 Jason Simontacchi/72 ..... 10.00 3.00
482 Jeremy Lambert/21 .....
483 Tino Martinez/134 ..... 10.00 3.00
484 Rogers Hornsby/42 ..... 40.00 12.00
485 Rick Ankiel/27 ..... 20.00 6.00
486 Jim Edmonds/148 ..... 6.00 1.80
487 Scott Rolen/14 .....
488 Kevin Joseph/2 .....
489 Fernando Vina/168 ..... 5.00 1.50
490 Jason Isringhausen/68 ..... 10.00 3.00
491 Lou Brock/52 ..... 20.00 6.00
492 Joe Torre Cards/100 ..... 12.00 3.60
493 Bob Gibson/22 .....
494 Chuck Finley/174 ..... 5.00 1.50
495 So Taguchi/6 .....
496 Ben Grieve/121 ..... 6.00 1.80
497 Toby Hall/85 ..... 8.00 2.40
498 Brent Abernathy/112 ..... 8.00 2.40
499 Brandon Backe/6 .....
500 Felix Escalona/34 ..... 20.00 6.00
501 Matt White/58 ..... 12.00 3.60
502 Randy Winn/181 ..... 5.00 1.50
503 Carl Crawford/67 ..... 10.00 3.00
504 Dewon Brazelton/5 .....
505 Joe Kennedy/109 ..... 8.00 2.40
506 Wade Boggs D-Rays/60 ..... 20.00 6.00
507 Aubrey Huff/142 ..... 6.00 1.80
508 Alex Rodriguez Rangers/57 50.00 15.00
509 Ivan Rodriguez/19 .....
510 Will Clark Rangers/102 ..... 20.00 6.00
511 Hank Blalock/31 ..... 30.00 9.00
512 Travis Hughes/137 ..... 6.00 1.80
513 Travis Hafner/15 .....
514 Ryan Ludwick/19 .....
515 Doug Davis/28 ..... 20.00 6.00
516 Juan Gonzalez/78 ..... 25.00 7.50
517 Jason Hart/4 .....
518 Mark Teixeira/69 ..... 15.00 4.50
519 Nolan Ryan Rangers/51 ..... 80.00 24.00
520 Rafael Palmeiro/43 ..... 25.00 7.50
521 Kevin Mench/95 ..... 8.00 2.40
522 Chan Ho Park/9 .....
523 Kenny Rogers/107 ..... 8.00 2.40
524 Rusty Greer/59 ..... 12.00 3.60
525 Michael Young/150 ..... 6.00 1.80
526 Carlos Delgado/33 ..... 20.00 6.00
527 Vernon Wells/167 ..... 5.00 1.50
528 Orlando Hudson/53 ..... 12.00 3.60
529 Shannon Stewart/175 ..... 5.00 1.50
530 Joe Carter/121 ..... 6.00 1.80
531 Chris Baker/42 ..... 15.00 4.50
532 Eric Hinske/24 .....
533 Corey Thurman/56 ..... 12.00 3.60
534 Josh Phelps/82 ..... 8.00 2.40
535 Reed Johnson/46 ..... 15.00 4.50
536 Brian Bowles/19 .....
537 Roy Halladay/168 ..... 5.00 1.50
538 Jose Cruz Jr./114 ..... 8.00 2.40
539 Kelvim Escobar/85 ..... 8.00 2.40
540 Chris Carpenter/45 ..... 15.00 4.50
541 Rickie Weeks/27 .....
542 Hideki Matsui/50 ..... 50.00 15.00
543 Ramon Nivar/39 ..... 10.00 3.00
544 Adam Loewen/25 .....
545 Brandon Webb/10 .....
546 Dan Haren/10 .....
547 Delmon Young/7 .....
548 Ryan Wagner/15 .....

2003 Donruss Team Heroes Timeline Threads

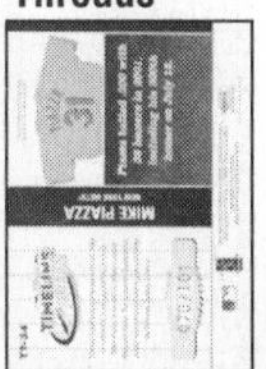

Randomly inserted into packs, these 50 cards feature game-used jersey swatches from a mix of active and retired players. These cards are serial numbered to some year which matches an important year in the player's career.

Nm-Mt Ex-Mt
1 Bobby Doerr/39 ..... 30.00 9.00
2 Phil Rizzuto/47 ..... 50.00 15.00
3 Yogi Berra/47 ..... 60.00 18.00
4 Pee Wee Reese/58 ..... 30.00 9.00
5 Stan Musial/42 .....
6 Al Kaline/64 ..... 50.00 15.00
7 Orlando Cepeda/65 ..... 25.00 7.50
8 Eddie Mathews/66 ..... 50.00 15.00
9 Lou Brock/66 ..... 30.00 9.00
10 Juan Marichal/67 ..... 25.00 7.50
11 Ernie Banks/68 ..... 50.00 15.00
12 Willie Stargell/68 ..... 30.00 9.00
13 Jim Palmer/69 ..... 25.00 7.50
14 Luis Aparicio/69 ..... 25.00 7.50
15 Tom Seaver/69 ..... 30.00 9.00
16 Harmon Killebrew/71 ..... 50.00 15.00
17 Joe Morgan/74 ..... 25.00 7.50
18 Brooks Robinson/76 ..... 50.00 15.00
19 Mike Schmidt/81 ..... 80.00 24.00
20 Willie McCovey/77 ..... 25.00 7.50
21 Robin Yount/78 ..... 50.00 15.00
22 Reggie Jackson/79 ..... 30.00 9.00
23 Rod Carew/85 ..... 50.00 15.00
24 Nolan Ryan/91 ..... 100.00 30.00
25 Tony Gwynn/98 ..... 30.00 9.00
26 Alex Rodriguez/100 ..... 40.00 12.00
27 Carlos Delgado/101 ..... 20.00 6.00
28 Lance Berkman/102 ..... 20.00 6.00
29 Randy Johnson/100 ..... 30.00 9.00
30 Josh Beckett/101 ..... 25.00 7.50
31 Eric Davis/89 ..... 25.00 7.50
32 Todd Helton/100 ..... 25.00 7.50
33 Jose Canseco/89 ..... 50.00 15.00
34 Mike Piazza/101 ..... 40.00 12.00
35 Fred Lynn/75 ..... 25.00 7.50
36 Mike Sweeney/101 ..... 20.00 6.00
37 Miguel Tejada/101 ..... 20.00 6.00
38 Curt Schilling/101 ..... 25.00 7.50
39 Dale Murphy/87 ..... 50.00 15.00
40 Jim Thome/101 ..... 30.00 9.00
41 Adam Dunn/102 ..... 20.00 6.00
42 Nomar Garciaparra/100 ..... 40.00 12.00
43 Vladimir Guerrero/100 ..... 30.00 9.00
44 Alfonso Soriano/102 ..... 25.00 7.50
45 Wade Boggs/90 ..... 30.00 9.00
46 Randy Johnson/89 ..... 30.00 9.00
47 Hal Newhouser/55 ..... 25.00 7.50
48 Chipper Jones/93 ..... 30.00 9.00
49 Andruw Jones/96 ..... 20.00 6.00
50 Frank Thomas/94 ..... 30.00 9.00

2003 Donruss Team Heroes Atlantic City National

Collectors attending the 2003 Atlantic City National who opened Donruss Product while at their corporate booth were able to receive these specially produced cards. These cards parallel the regular Team Heroes set but have a special Atlantic City National embossing on the front and were printed to a stated print run of five serial numbers which is visible on the back. Due to market scarcity, no pricing is provided for these cards.

MINT NRMT
PRINT RUN 5 SERIAL #'d SETS.........

1997 Donruss Team Sets

This 165-card set features color action player photos from eleven Major League teams printed on specially treated card stock with team color matching foil stamping. The set was distributed in five-card packs with a suggested retail price of $1.99. The Indians and Angels packs were sold exclusively at the respective ballparks during their home games. Due to manufacturing problems, Russ Davis (supposed to be #144) and Bernie Williams (supposed to be #131) were never printed, thus the set is complete at 163 cards.

	Nm-Mt	Ex-Mt
COMP.ANGELS (1-15)	2.00	.60
COMP.BRAVES (16-30)	5.00	1.50
COMP.ORIOLES (31-45)	3.00	.90
COMP.RED SOX (46-60)	3.00	.90
COMP.W.SOX (61-75)	3.00	.90
COMP.INDIANS (76-90)	5.00	1.50
COMP.ROCKIES (91-105)	2.50	.75
COMP.LA (106-120)	3.00	.90
COMP.NYY (121-135)	5.00	1.50
COMP.SEATTLE (136-150)	5.00	1.50
COMP.CARDS (151-165)	2.00	.60
1 Jim Edmonds	.25	.07
2 Tim Salmon	.40	.12
3 Tony Phillips	.15	.04
4 Garret Anderson	.25	.07
5 Troy Percival	.25	.07
6 Mark Langston	.15	.04
7 Chuck Finley	.25	.07
8 Eddie Murray	.60	.18
9 Jim Leyritz	.15	.04
10 Darin Erstad	.25	.07
11 Jason Dickson	.15	.04
12 Allen Watson	.15	.04
13 Shigetoshi Hasegawa	.60	.18
14 Dave Hollins	.15	.04
15 Gary DiSarcina	.15	.04
16 Greg Maddux	1.25	.35
17 Denny Neagle	.15	.04
18 Chipper Jones	.60	.18
19 Tom Glavine	.40	.12
20 John Smoltz	.40	.12
21 Ryan Klesko	.25	.07
22 Fred McGriff	.40	.12
23 Michael Tucker	.15	.04
24 Kenny Lofton	.25	.07
25 Javier Lopez	.25	.07
26 Mark Wohlers	.15	.04
27 Jeff Blauser	.15	.04
28 Andruw Jones	.25	.07
29 Tony Graffanino	.15	.04
30 Terrell Wade	.15	.04
31 Brady Anderson	.25	.07
32 Roberto Alomar	.60	.18
33 Rafael Palmeiro	.40	.12
34 Mike Mussina	.60	.18
35 Cal Ripken	2.50	.75
36 Rocky Coppinger	.15	.04
37 Randy Myers	.25	.07
38 B.J. Surhoff	.25	.07
39 Eric Davis	.25	.07
40 Armando Benitez	.25	.07
41 Jeffrey Hammonds	.15	.04
42 Jimmy Key	.25	.07
43 Chris Hoiles	.15	.04
44 Mike Bordick	.25	.07
45 Pete Incaviglia	.15	.04
46 Mike Stanley	.15	.04
47 Reggie Jefferson	.15	.04
48 Mo Vaughn	.25	.07
49 John Valentin	.15	.04
50 Tim Naehring	.15	.04
51 Jeff Suppan	.15	.04
52 Tim Wakefield	.25	.07
53 Jeff Frye	.15	.04
54 Darren Bragg	.15	.04
55 Steve Avery	.15	.04
56 Shane Mack	.15	.04
57 Aaron Sele	.15	.04
58 Troy O'Leary	.15	.04
59 Rudy Pemberton	.15	.04
60 Nomar Garciaparra	1.25	.35
61 Robin Ventura	.25	.07
62 Wilson Alvarez	.15	.04
63 Roberto Hernandez	.15	.04
64 Frank Thomas	.60	.18
65 Ray Durham	.25	.07
66 James Baldwin	.15	.04
67 Harold Baines	.25	.07
68 Doug Drabek	.15	.04
69 Mike Cameron	.25	.07
70 Albert Belle	.25	.07
71 Jaime Navarro	.15	.04
72 Chris Snopek	.15	.04
73 Lyle Mouton	.15	.04
74 Dave Martinez	.15	.04
75 Ozzie Guillen	.15	.04
76 Manny Ramirez	.25	.07
77 Jack McDowell	.15	.04
78 Jim Thome	.60	.18
79 Jose Mesa	.15	.04
80 Brian Giles	1.00	.30
81 Omar Vizquel	.25	.07
82 Charles Nagy	.15	.04
83 Orel Hershiser	.25	.07
84 Matt Williams	.25	.07
85 Marquis Grissom	.15	.04
86 David Justice	.25	.07
87 Sandy Alomar Jr.	.15	.04
88 Kevin Seitzer	.15	.04
89 Julio Franco	.25	.07
90 Bartolo Colon	.25	.07
91 Andres Galarraga	.25	.07
92 Larry Walker	.40	.12
93 Vinny Castilla	.25	.07
94 Dante Bichette	.25	.07
95 Jamey Wright	.15	.04
96 Ellis Burks	.25	.07
97 Eric Young	.15	.04
98 Neifi Perez	.15	.04
99 Quinton McCracken	.15	.04
100 Bruce Ruffin	.15	.04
101 Walt Weiss	.15	.04
102 Roger Bailey	.15	.04
103 Jeff Reed	.15	.04
104 Bill Swift	.15	.04
105 Kirt Manwaring	.15	.04
106 Raul Mondesi	.25	.07
107 Hideo Nomo	.60	.18
108 Roger Cedeno	.15	.04
109 Ismael Valdes	.15	.04
110 Todd Hollandsworth	.15	.04
111 Mike Piazza	1.25	.35
112 Brett Butler	.25	.07
113 Chan Ho Park	.25	.07
114 Ramon Martinez	.15	.04
115 Eric Karros	.25	.07
116 Wilton Guerrero	.15	.04
117 Todd Zeile	.25	.07
118 Karim Garcia	.15	.04
119 Greg Gagne	.15	.04
120 Darren Dreifort	.15	.04
121 Wade Boggs	.40	.12
122 Paul O'Neill	.40	.12
123 Derek Jeter	2.00	.60
124 Tino Martinez	.40	.12
125 David Cone	.25	.07
126 Andy Pettitte	.40	.12
127 Charlie Hayes	.15	.04
128 Mariano Rivera	.40	.12
129 Dwight Gooden	.40	.12
130 Cecil Fielder	.25	.07
132 Darryl Strawberry	.40	.12
133 Joe Girardi	.15	.04
134 David Wells	.25	.07
135 Hideki Irabu	.25	.07
136 Ken Griffey Jr.	1.25	.35
137 Alex Rodriguez	1.25	.35
138 Jay Buhner	.25	.07
139 Randy Johnson	.60	.18
140 Paul Sorrento	.15	.04
141 Edgar Martinez	.40	.12
142 Joey Cora	.15	.04
143 Bob Wells	.15	.04
145 Jamie Moyer	.25	.07
146 Jeff Fassero	.15	.04
147 Dan Wilson	.15	.04
148 Jose Cruz Jr.	1.00	.30
149 Scott Sanders	.15	.04
150 Rich Amaral	.15	.04
151 Brian Jordan	.25	.07
152 Andy Benes	.15	.04
153 Ray Lankford	.15	.04
154 John Mabry	.15	.04
155 Tom Pagnozzi	.15	.04
156 Ron Gant	.25	.07
157 Alan Benes	.15	.04
158 Dennis Eckersley	.25	.07
159 Royce Clayton	.15	.04
160 Todd Stottlemyre	.15	.04
161 Gary Gaetti	.25	.07
162 Willie McGee	.25	.07
163 Delino DeShields	.15	.04
164 Dmitri Young	.25	.07
165 Matt Morris	.25	.07

1997 Donruss Team Sets Pennant Edition

Randomly inserted at an approximate rate of one in every six packs, cards from this 163-card set parallel the Donruss Team Sets base set and displays red and gold foil treatment.

Nm-Mt Ex-Mt

*STARS: 8X TO 20X BASIC CARDS
*ROOKIES: 4X TO 10X BASIC CARDS

1997 Donruss Team Sets MVP's

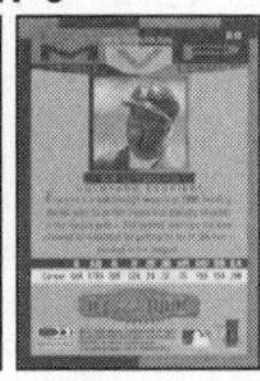

Randomly inserted in packs at an approximate rate of 1:36, this 18-card set features color action player photos printed on microetched foil with foil stamping. Only 1,000 sets were produced and all of the cards are sequentially numbered on back.

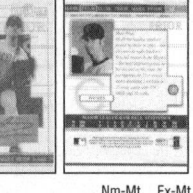

	Nm-Mt	Ex-Mt
COMPLETE SET (18)	300.00	90.00
1 Ivan Rodriguez	10.00	3.00
2 Mike Piazza	20.00	6.00
3 Frank Thomas	10.00	3.00
4 Jeff Bagwell	6.00	1.80
5 Chuck Knoblauch	5.00	1.50
6 Eric Young	5.00	1.50
7 Alex Rodriguez	25.00	7.50
8 Barry Larkin	10.00	3.00
9 Cal Ripken	40.00	12.00
10 Chipper Jones	10.00	3.00
11 Albert Belle	5.00	1.50
12 Barry Bonds	30.00	9.00
13 Ken Griffey Jr.	20.00	6.00
14 Kenny Lofton	5.00	1.50
15 Juan Gonzalez	10.00	3.00
16 Larry Walker	6.00	1.80
17 Roger Clemens	25.00	7.50
18 Greg Maddux	20.00	6.00

2004 Donruss Timelines

This 50-card set was released in January, 2004. These cards were issued in five-card packs with an $50 SRP which came four packs to a box and eight boxes to a case.

	Nm-Mt	Ex-Mt
COMPLETE SET (50)	50.00	15.00
1 Adam Dunn	2.00	.60
2 Albert Pujols	6.00	1.80
3 Alex Rodriguez	5.00	1.50
4 Alfonso Soriano	2.00	.60
5 Andruw Jones	2.00	.60
6 Austin Kearns	2.00	.60
7 Miguel Cabrera	3.00	.90
8 Barry Zito	2.00	.60
9 Carlos Beltran	2.00	.60
10 Carlos Delgado	2.00	.60
11 Chipper Jones	3.00	.90
12 Curt Schilling	2.00	.60
13 Derek Jeter	8.00	2.40
14 Frank Thomas	3.00	.90
15 Garret Anderson	2.00	.60
16 Gary Sheffield	2.00	.60
17 Greg Maddux	5.00	1.50
18 Hank Blalock	2.00	.60
19 Hideki Matsui	5.00	1.50
20 Hideo Nomo	3.00	.90
21 Ichiro Suzuki	5.00	1.50
22 Ivan Rodriguez	3.00	.90
23 Jason Giambi	3.00	.90
24 Jeff Bagwell	2.00	.60
25 Jim Thome	3.00	.90
26 Juan Gonzalez	3.00	.90
27 Ken Griffey Jr.	5.00	1.50
28 Kevin Brown	2.00	.60
29 Kerry Wood	3.00	.90
30 Lance Berkman	2.00	.60
31 Magglio Ordonez	2.00	.60
32 Manny Ramirez	2.00	.60
33 Mark Prior	6.00	1.80
34 Mike Mussina	3.00	.90
35 Mike Piazza	5.00	1.50
36 Nomar Garciaparra	5.00	1.50
37 Pedro Martinez	3.00	.90
38 Rafael Palmeiro	2.00	.60
39 Randy Johnson	3.00	.90
40 Richie Sexson	2.00	.60
41 Roger Clemens	6.00	1.80
42 Roy Halladay	2.00	.60
43 Sammy Sosa	5.00	1.50
44 Scott Rolen	2.00	.60
45 Shawn Green	2.00	.60
46 Tim Hudson	2.00	.60
47 Todd Helton	2.00	.60
48 Torii Hunter	2.00	.60
49 Clayton Wells	2.00	.60
50 Vladimir Guerrero	3.00	.90

2004 Donruss Timelines Gold

Nm-Mt Ex-Mt

*GOLD: 2.5X TO 6X BASIC
RANDOM INSERTS IN PACKS
STATED PRINT RUN 25 SERIAL #'d SETS

2004 Donruss Timelines Platinum

Nm-Mt Ex-Mt

RANDOM INSERTS IN PACKS
STATED PRINT RUN 1 SERIAL #'d SET
NO PRICING DUE TO SCARCITY

2004 Donruss Timelines Silver

Nm-Mt Ex-Mt

*SILVER: 1X TO 2.5X BASIC
RANDOM INSERTS IN PACKS
STATED PRINT RUN 100 SERIAL #'d SETS

2004 Donruss Timelines Autograph Gold

Nm-Mt Ex-Mt

STATED PRINT RUN 25 SERIAL #'d SETS
PLATINUM PRINT RUN 1 SERIAL #'d SET
NO PLATINUM PRICING DUE TO SCARCITY
RANDOM INSERTS IN PACKS

	Nm-Mt	Ex-Mt
1 Adam Dunn	50.00	15.00
7 Miguel Cabrera	80.00	24.00
9 Carlos Beltran	40.00	12.00
15 Garret Anderson	40.00	12.00
18 Hank Blalock	50.00	15.00
22 Ivan Rodriguez	80.00	24.00
26 Juan Gonzalez	80.00	24.00
31 Magglio Ordonez	50.00	15.00
33 Mark Prior	150.00	45.00
44 Scott Rolen	50.00	15.00
48 Torii Hunter	40.00	12.00
49 Vernon Wells	40.00	12.00
50 Vladimir Guerrero	80.00	24.00

2004 Donruss Timelines Material

Nm-Mt Ex-Mt

STATED ODDS 1:2
*COMBO: 1X TO 2.5X BASIC
*COMBO: .5X TO 1.2X BASIC SP
COMBO PRINT RUN 125 SERIAL #'d SETS
COMBOS FEATURE BAT-JSY SWATCHES
*PRIME: 1X TO 2.5X BASIC
PRIME PRINT RUN 125 SERIAL #'d SETS
PRIME M.CABRERA PRINT 10 #'d CARDS
NO PRIME M.CABRERA PRICING AVAIL.

	Nm-Mt	Ex-Mt
1 Adam Dunn Jsy	8.00	2.40
2 Albert Pujols Jsy	15.00	4.50
3 Alex Rodriguez Jsy	15.00	4.50
4 Alfonso Soriano Jsy	10.00	3.00
5 Andruw Jones Jsy	8.00	2.40
7 Miguel Cabrera Jsy SP	20.00	6.00
10 Carlos Delgado Jsy	8.00	2.40
11 Chipper Jones Jsy	10.00	3.00
14 Frank Thomas Jsy	10.00	3.00
17 Greg Maddux Jsy	10.00	3.00
20 Hideo Nomo Jsy	15.00	4.50
22 Ivan Rodriguez Bat	10.00	3.00
23 Jason Giambi Bat	10.00	3.00
24 Jeff Bagwell Bat	10.00	3.00
25 Jim Thome Jsy	10.00	3.00
26 Juan Gonzalez Bat	10.00	3.00
30 Lance Berkman Jsy	8.00	2.40
33 Mark Prior Jsy	20.00	6.00
35 Mike Piazza Jsy	10.00	3.00
36 Nomar Garciaparra Jsy	15.00	4.50
37 Pedro Martinez Jsy	10.00	3.00
39 Randy Johnson Jsy	10.00	3.00
41 Roger Clemens Jsy	15.00	4.50
43 Sammy Sosa Jsy	15.00	4.50
45 Shawn Green Jsy	8.00	2.40
47 Todd Helton Jsy	10.00	3.00
49 Vernon Wells Jsy	8.00	2.40

2004 Donruss Timelines Material Autograph

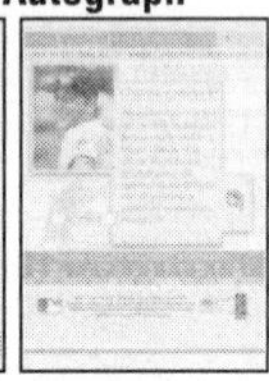

Nm-Mt Ex-Mt

PRINT RUNS B/WN 1-50 COPIES PER
NO PRICING ON QTY OF 5 OR LESS
PRIME PRINT RUN 1 SERIAL #'d SET
NO PRIME PRICING DUE TO SCARCITY
RANDOM INSERTS IN PACKS

	Nm-Mt	Ex-Mt
1 Adam Dunn Jsy/5		
2 Albert Pujols Jsy/5		
3 Alex Rodriguez Jsy/5		
4 Alfonso Soriano Jsy/1		
5 Andruw Jones Jsy/5		
7 Miguel Cabrera Bat/25	100.00	30.00
11 Chipper Jones Jsy/5		
14 Frank Thomas Jsy/5		
17 Greg Maddux Jsy/5		
20 Hideo Nomo Jsy/5		
22 Ivan Rodriguez Bat/25	120.00	36.00
24 Jeff Bagwell Bat/5		
26 Juan Gonzalez Bat/5		
30 Lance Berkman Jsy/5		
33 Mark Prior Jsy/50	150.00	45.00
35 Mike Piazza Jsy/5		
39 Randy Johnson Jsy/5		
41 Roger Clemens Jsy/5		
45 Shawn Green Jsy/5		
49 Vernon Wells Jsy/50	40.00	12.00

2004 Donruss Timelines Boys of Summer

Nm-Mt Ex-Mt

STATED PRINT RUN 250 SERIAL #'d SETS
*GOLD: 2X TO 5X BASIC
GOLD PRINT RUN 25 SERIAL #'d SETS
PLATINUM 1 SERIAL #'d SET
NO PLATINUM PRICING DUE TO SCARCITY
*SILVER: .6X TO 1.5X BASIC
SILVER PRINT RUN 100 SERIAL #'d SETS
RANDOM INSERTS IN PACKS

	Nm-Mt	Ex-Mt
1 Alan Trammell	5.00	1.50
2 Marty Marion	5.00	1.50
3 Andre Dawson	5.00	1.50
4 Bo Jackson	8.00	2.40
5 Cal Ripken	20.00	6.00
6 Steve Garvey	5.00	1.50
7 Dale Murphy	8.00	2.40
8 Darren Daulton	5.00	1.50
9 Darryl Strawberry	8.00	2.40
10 Dave Parker	5.00	1.50
11 Doc Gooden	5.00	1.50
12 Don Mattingly	15.00	4.50
13 Eric Davis	5.00	1.50
14 Dwight Evans	5.00	1.50
15 Fred Lynn	5.00	1.50
16 Graig Nettles	5.00	1.50
17 Jay Buhner	5.00	1.50
18 Jim Rice	5.00	1.50
19 Jose Canseco	8.00	2.40
20 Keith Hernandez	5.00	1.50
21 Rickey Henderson	8.00	2.40
22 Jack Morris	5.00	1.50
23 Tony Gwynn	10.00	3.00
24 Vida Blue	5.00	1.50
25 Will Clark	15.00	4.50

2004 Donruss Timelines Boys of Summer Autograph

Nm-Mt Ex-Mt

PLATINUM PRINT RUN 1 SERIAL #'d SET
NO PLATINUM PRICING DUE TO SCARCITY

RANDOM INSERTS IN PACKS

	Nm-Mt	Ex-Mt
2 Marty Marion	15.00	4.50
3 Andre Dawson	15.00	4.50
6 Steve Garvey	15.00	4.50
8 Darren Daulton	15.00	4.50
9 Darryl Strawberry	20.00	6.00
10 Dave Parker	15.00	4.50
11 Doc Gooden	15.00	4.50
13 Eric Davis	15.00	4.50
15 Fred Lynn	15.00	4.50
16 Graig Nettles	15.00	4.50
17 Jay Buhner	15.00	4.50
20 Keith Hernandez	15.00	4.50
22 Jack Morris	15.00	4.50
24 Vida Blue	15.00	4.50

2004 Donruss Timelines Boys of Summer Autograph Gold

Nm-Mt Ex-Mt

*GOLD: 1X TO 2.5X BASIC BOYS AUTO
RANDOM INSERTS IN PACKS
STATED PRINT RUN 25 SERIAL #'d SETS

	Nm-Mt	Ex-Mt
1 Alan Trammell	50.00	15.00
12 Don Mattingly	120.00	36.00
14 Dwight Evans	50.00	15.00
18 Jim Rice	50.00	15.00
25 Will Clark	150.00	45.00

2004 Donruss Timelines Boys of Summer Autograph Silver

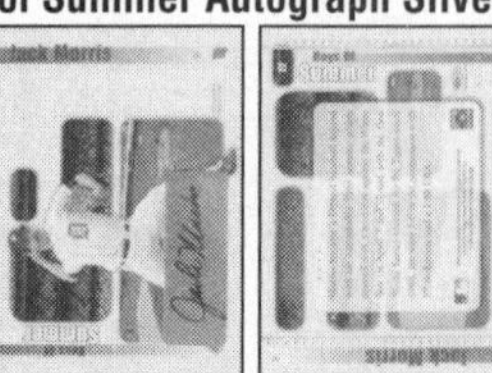

Nm-Mt Ex-Mt

*SILVER: .6X TO 1.5X BASIC BOYS AUTO
RANDOM INSERTS IN PACKS
STATED PRINT RUN 100 SERIAL #'d SETS

2004 Donruss Timelines Boys of Summer Material

Nm-Mt Ex-Mt

*COMBO: 1X TO 2.5X BASIC
COMBO PRINT RUN 100 SERIAL #'d SETS
MOST COMBOS ARE BAT-JSY SWATCHES
*PRIME: 1X TO 2.5X BASIC
PRIME PRINT RUN 100 SERIAL #'d SETS
RANDOM INSERTS IN PACKS

	Nm-Mt	Ex-Mt
3 Andre Dawson Jsy	8.00	2.40
4 Bo Jackson Jsy	15.00	4.50
5 Cal Ripken Jsy	40.00	12.00
7 Dale Murphy Bat	15.00	4.50
9 Darryl Strawberry Jsy	15.00	4.50
11 Doc Gooden Jsy	10.00	3.00
12 Don Mattingly Jacket	20.00	6.00
19 Jose Canseco Bat	15.00	4.50
21 Rickey Henderson Jsy	15.00	4.50
22 Jack Morris Jsy	8.00	2.40
23 Tony Gwynn Jsy	15.00	4.50
25 Will Clark Jsy	15.00	4.50

2004 Donruss Timelines Boys of Summer Material Autograph

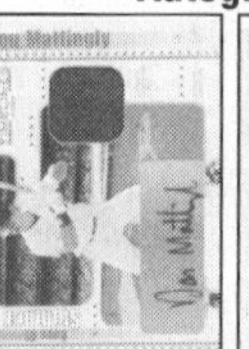

Nm-Mt Ex-Mt

PRINT RUNS B/WN 5-150 COPIES PER

NO PRICING ON QTY OF 10 OR LESS.
PRIME PRINT RUN 1 SERIAL #'d SET
NO PRIME PRICING DUE TO SCARCITY
RANDOM INSERTS IN PACKS
3 Andre Dawson Jsy/50 40.00 12.00
4 Bo Jackson Jsy/5
5 Cal Ripken Jsy/5
7 Dale Murphy Bat/10
9 Darryl Strawberry Jsy/150 50.00 15.00
11 Doc Gooden Jsy/100 40.00 12.00
12 Don Mattingly Jacket/25 150.00 45.00
19 Jose Canseco Bat/5
21 Rickey Henderson Jsy/5
22 Jack Morris Jsy/150 25.00 7.50
23 Tony Gwynn Jsy/10
25 Will Clark Jsy/15

2004 Donruss Timelines Call to the Hall

Nm-Mt Ex-Mt
STATED PRINT RUN 250 SERIAL #'d SETS
*GOLD: 2X TO 5X BASIC
GOLD PRINT RUN 25 SERIAL #'d SETS
PLATINUM PRINT RUN 1 SERIAL #'d SET
NO PLATINUM PRICING DUE TO SCARCITY
*SILVER: .6X TO 1.5X BASIC
SILVER PRINT RUN 100 SERIAL #'d SETS
RANDOM INSERTS IN PACKS
1 Babe Ruth 15.00 4.50
2 Billy Williams 5.00 1.50
3 Bob Feller 5.00 1.50
4 Bobby Doerr 5.00 1.50
5 Carlton Fisk 5.00 1.50
6 Gary Carter 5.00 1.50
7 George Brett 15.00 4.50
8 Carl Yastrzemski 10.00 3.00
9 Harmon Killebrew 8.00 2.40
10 Jim Palmer 5.00 1.50
11 Joe Morgan 5.00 1.50
12 Johnny Bench 8.00 2.40
13 Kirby Puckett 8.00 2.40
14 Gaylord Perry 5.00 1.50
15 Mike Schmidt 12.00 3.60
16 Nolan Ryan 15.00 4.50
17 Ozzie Smith 10.00 3.00
18 Phil Rizzuto 5.00 1.50
19 Reggie Jackson 5.00 1.50
20 Roberto Clemente 15.00 4.50
21 Robin Yount 10.00 3.00
22 Rod Carew 5.00 1.50
23 Rollie Fingers 5.00 1.50
24 Steve Carlton 5.00 1.50
25 Tom Seaver 5.00 1.50

2004 Donruss Timelines Call to the Hall Autograph

Nm-Mt Ex-Mt
PLATINUM PRINT RUN 1 SERIAL #'d SET
NO PLATINUM PRICING DUE TO SCARCITY
RANDOM INSERTS IN PACKS
3 Bob Feller 20.00 6.00
4 Bobby Doerr 15.00 4.50
14 Gaylord Perry 15.00 4.50
23 Rollie Fingers 15.00 4.50

2004 Donruss Timelines Call to the Hall Autograph Gold

Nm-Mt Ex-Mt
*GOLD: 1X TO 2.5X BASIC CALL AUTO
RANDOM INSERTS IN PACKS
STATED PRINT RUN 25 SERIAL #'d SETS
2 Billy Williams 40.00 12.00
6 Gary Carter 50.00 15.00
10 Jim Palmer 40.00 12.00
18 Phil Rizzuto 60.00 18.00
24 Steve Carlton 50.00 15.00

2004 Donruss Timelines Call to the Hall Autograph Silver

Nm-Mt Ex-Mt
*SILVER: .6X TO 1.5X BASIC CALL AUTO
RANDOM INSERTS IN PACKS

STATED PRINT RUN 100 SERIAL #'d SETS
3 Bob Feller 40.00 12.00

2004 Donruss Timelines Call to the Hall Material

Nm-Mt Ex-Mt
CLEMENTE PRINT RUN 100 #'d CARDS
B.RUTH PRINT RUN 50 #'d CARDS
ALL OTHER CARDS ARE NOT SERIAL #'d
*COMBO: 1X TO 2.5X BASIC
COMBO PRINT RUN 125 SERIAL #'d SETS
MOST COMBOS ARE BAT-JSY SWATCHES
RANDOM INSERTS IN PACKS
1 Babe Ruth Jsy/50 800.00 240.00
4 Bobby Doerr Bat 8.00 2.40
6 Gary Carter Jacket 10.00 3.00
7 George Brett Bat 20.00 6.00
8 Carl Yastrzemski Bat 20.00 6.00
13 Kirby Puckett Bat 15.00 4.50
15 Mike Schmidt Bat 20.00 6.00
16 Nolan Ryan Jsy 20.00 6.00
17 Ozzie Smith Bat 15.00 4.50
19 Reggie Jackson Bat 10.00 3.00
20 Roberto Clemente Bat/100 60.00 18.00

2004 Donruss Timelines Call to the Hall Material Autograph

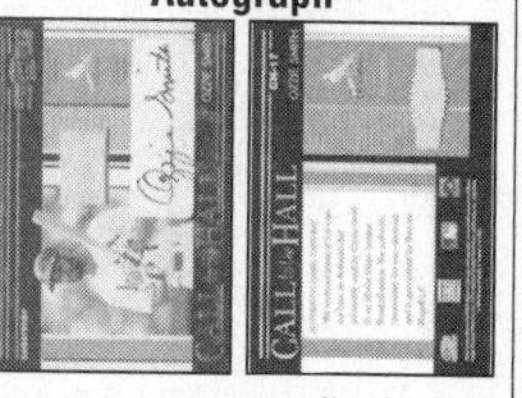

Nm-Mt Ex-Mt
RANDOM INSERTS IN PACKS
PRINT RUNS B/WN 5-100 COPIES PER
NO PRICING ON QTY OF 5 OR LESS
4 Bobby Doerr Bat/100 30.00 9.00
6 Gary Carter Jacket/25 60.00 18.00
7 George Brett Bat/5
8 Carl Yastrzemski Bat/5
13 Kirby Puckett Bat/5
16 Nolan Ryan Jsy/5
17 Ozzie Smith Bat/5
19 Reggie Jackson Bat/25 80.00 24.00

2004 Donruss Timelines Recollection Autographs

Issued at a stated rate of one in two, this set features an astounding 1576 cards procured by Donruss/Playoff from hobby sources as "buy-back" cards feature many of the best players of the 80's, 90's and the present time who signed copies of these cards in a quantity from anywhere from 1 to 225 of the featured cards. Each of these cards have a recollection autograph embossing on the front and stated serial numbering on the back. Please note that for cards issued to a stated print run of 15 or fewer that no pricing is provided.

Nm-Mt Ex-Mt
1 Sandy Alomar Jr. 89/25 20.00 6.00
2 Sandy Alomar Jr. 90 Black/5
3 Sandy Alomar Jr. 90 Blue/13
4 Sandy Alomar Jr. 90 DR/5
5 Sandy Alomar Jr. 91 Black/15
5A Sandy Alomar Jr. 91 Blue/5
6 San Alomar Jr. 91 AS Black/32 20.00 6.00
7 Sandy Alomar Jr. 91 AS Blue/13
8 Sandy Alomar Jr. 91 DK Black/15
9 Sandy Alomar Jr. 91 DK Blue/10
10 Sandy Alomar Jr. 91 ROY Black/8
11 Sandy Alomar Jr. 91 ROY Blue/15
12 Sandy Alomar Jr. 92 Black/20 20.00 6.00
13 Sandy Alomar Jr. 92 Blue/14
14 Sandy Alomar Jr. 92 AS Black/13
15 Sandy Alomar Jr. 92 AS Blue/11
16 Sandy Alomar Jr. 93 Black/14
17 Sandy Alomar Jr. 93 Blue/7
18 Sandy Alomar Jr. 94/15
19 Sandy Alomar Jr. 95/5
20 Sandy Alomar Jr. 96/14
21 Sandy Alomar Jr. 97/16 25.00 7.50
22 Sandy Alomar Jr. 97 PP/1
23 Sandy Alomar Jr. 98 Black/18 25.00 7.50
24 Sandy Alomar Jr. 98 Blue/2
25 Sandy Alomar Jr. 98 PP/3
26 Rich Aurilia 02/10
27 Rich Aurilia 03/10
28 Wally Backman 83/38 15.00 4.50
29 Wally Backman 85/97 15.00 4.50
30 Wally Backman 86/67 15.00 4.50
31 Wally Backman 87/38 15.00 4.50
32 Wally Backman 88/190 15.00 4.50
33 Wally Backman 89/30 20.00 6.00
34 Wally Backman 89 BB/1
35 Wally Backman 89 TR/2
36 Wally Backman 90/74 15.00 4.50
37 Wally Backman 91/79 15.00 4.50
38 Wally Backman 92/59 15.00 4.50
39 Jeff Bagwell 92/1
40 Jeff Bagwell 93 MVP/1
41 Jeff Bagwell 00 Retro DK/2
42 Jeff Bagwell 02/1
43 Jeff Bagwell 03/1
44 Harold Baines 82 Black/15
45 Harold Baines 82 Blue/15
46 Harold Baines 83 Black/8
47 Harold Baines 83 Blue/20 50.00 15.00
48 Harold Baines 84 Black/20 50.00 15.00
49 Harold Baines 84 Blue/10
50 Harold Baines 85 Black/1
51 Harold Baines 85 Blue/10
52 Harold Baines 86 Black/5
53 Harold Baines 86 Blue/2
54 Harold Baines 86 DK Black/32 50.00 15.00
55 Harold Baines 86 DK Blue/14
56 Harold Baines 87 Blue/59 30.00 9.00
57 Harold Baines 87 Black/7
58 Harold Baines 88 Black/1
59 Harold Baines 88 Blue/26 50.00 15.00
60 Harold Baines 88 AS/2
61 Harold Baines 88 BB/1
62 Harold Baines 89 Black/33 50.00 15.00
63 Harold Baines 89 Blue/39 40.00 12.00
64 Harold Baines 90 Black/1
65 Harold Baines 90 Blue/28 50.00 15.00
66 Harold Baines 90 AS/19 60.00 18.00
67 Harold Baines 91/6
68 Harold Baines 92 Black/7
69 Harold Baines 92 Blue/17 60.00 18.00
70 Harold Baines 93/9
71 Harold Baines 94/9
72 Harold Baines 95/3
73 Harold Baines 96/3
74 Harold Baines 97/11
75 Harold Baines 97 GPP/1
76 Harold Baines 01/5
77 Dusty Baker 81/36 25.00 7.50
78 Dusty Baker 82/20 30.00 9.00
79 Dusty Baker 83/36 25.00 7.50
80 Dusty Baker 84/37 25.00 7.50
81 Dusty Baker 85/30 30.00 9.00
82 Dusty Baker 86/35 30.00 9.00
83 Jesse Barfield 83/42 15.00 4.50
84 Jesse Barfield 84/63 15.00 4.50
85 Jesse Barfield 85/88 15.00 4.50
86 Jesse Barfield 86/41 15.00 4.50
87 Jesse Barfield 87/61 15.00 4.50
88 Jesse Barfield 88/42 15.00 4.50
89 Jesse Barfield 88 BB/1
90 Jesse Barfield 89/41 15.00 4.50
91 Jesse Barfield 90/42 15.00 4.50
92 Jesse Barfield 91 Black/2
93 Jesse Barfield 91 Blue/27 20.00 6.00
94 Jesse Barfield 92 Black/1
95 Jesse Barfield 92 Blue/28 20.00 6.00
96 Don Baylor 81 Black/30 20.00 6.00
97 Don Baylor 81 Blue/47 15.00 4.50
98 Don Baylor 82 Black/27 20.00 6.00
99 Don Baylor 82 Blue/56 15.00 4.50
100 Don Baylor 83 Black/23 20.00 6.00
101 Don Baylor 83 Blue/23 20.00 6.00
102 Don Baylor 84 Black/15
103 Don Baylor 84 Blue/12
104 Don Baylor 85 Black/20 20.00 6.00
105 Don Baylor 85 Blue/4
106 Don Baylor 86 Black/42 15.00 4.50
107 Don Baylor 86 Blue/28 20.00 6.00
108 Don Baylor 87 Black/28 20.00 6.00
109 Don Baylor 87 Blue/37 15.00 4.50
110 Josh Beckett 99 Retro/3
111 Josh Beckett 02/1
112 Josh Beckett 03/1
113 Carlos Beltran 01/56 20.00 6.00
114 Carlos Beltran 02/34 30.00 9.00
115 Adrian Beltre 01/5
116 Adrian Beltre 02/5
117 Adrian Beltre 03/3
118 Johnny Bench 81 #62/5
119 Johnny Bench 81 #182/1
120 Johnny Bench 82/15
121 Johnny Bench 82 w/Seaver/4
122 Johnny Bench 83/6
123 Kris Benson 01/104 15.00 4.50
124 Kris Benson 01 SLC/6
125 Yogi Berra 82/5
126 Craig Biggio 89/5
127 Craig Biggio 90/1
128 Craig Biggio 91/1
129 Vida Blue 81/5
130 Vida Blue 82/26 20.00 6.00
131 Vida Blue 82 DK/16 25.00 7.50
132 Vida Blue 83/26 20.00 6.00
133 Vida Blue 83 MVP/20 20.00 6.00
134 Vida Blue 86/51 15.00 4.50
135 Vida Blue 87/28 20.00 6.00
136 Bert Blyleven 81 Black/14
137 Bert Blyleven 81 Blue/3
138 Bert Blyleven 82 Black/5
139 Bert Blyleven 82 Blue/12
140 Bert Blyleven 83 Black/4
141 Bert Blyleven 83 Blue/1
142 Bert Blyleven 84 Black/6
143 Bert Blyleven 84 Blue/23 20.00 6.00
144 Bert Blyleven 85 Black/52 15.00 4.50
145 Bert Blyleven 85 Blue/4
146 Bert Blyleven 85 DK Black/5
147 Bert Blyleven 85 DK Blue/40 15.00 4.50
148 Bert Blyleven 86 Black/5
149 Bert Blyleven 86 Blue/1
150 Bert Blyleven 87 Black/32 20.00 6.00
151 Bert Blyleven 87 Blue/2
152 Bert Blyleven 88 Black/15
153 Bert Blyleven 88 Blue/101 15.00 4.50
154 Bert Blyleven 88 BB Black/3
155 Bert Blyleven 88 BB Blue/1
156 Bert Blyleven 89 Black/39 15.00 4.50
157 Bert Blyleven 89 Blue/2
158 Bert Blyleven 89 BB/1
159 Bert Blyleven 90 Black/57 15.00 4.50
160 Bert Blyleven 90 Blue/2
161 Bert Blyleven 91 Black/52 15.00 4.50
162 Bert Blyleven 91 Blue/10
163 Wade Boggs 83/7
164 Wade Boggs 84/1
165 Wade Boggs 85/3
166 Wade Boggs 85 HL/1
167 Wade Boggs 86/2
168 Wade Boggs 87/1
169 Wade Boggs 87 HL #14/1
170 Wade Boggs 87 HL #44/1
171 Wade Boggs 88/1
172 Wade Boggs 88 AS #31/1
173 Wade Boggs 88 AS #7/1
174 Wade Boggs 88 BB/1
175 Wade Boggs 88 MVP/1
176 Wade Boggs 89/1
177 Wade Boggs 90/1
178 Wade Boggs 90 AS/1
179 Wade Boggs 90 BB/1
180 Wade Boggs 91/1
181 Wade Boggs 91 AS/1
182 Wade Boggs 92/1
183 Wade Boggs 92 AS/1
184 Wade Boggs 93/1
185 Wade Boggs 94/2
186 Wade Boggs 94 SE/2
187 Wade Boggs 95/3
188 Wade Boggs 96/4
189 Wade Boggs 97/10
190 Wade Boggs 97 HIT/9
191 Wade Boggs 98/13
192 Wade Boggs 99 Retro/1
193 Wade Boggs 00 Retro/1
194 Wade Boggs 01 RR/1
195 George Brett 82/1
196 George Brett 84/1
197 George Brett 86 HL/1
198 George Brett 87 DK/1
199 George Brett 88 BB/1
200 Bill Buckner 81/25 30.00 9.00
201 Bill Buckner 82/25 30.00 9.00
202 Bill Buckner 83/25 30.00 9.00
203 Bill Buckner 83 DK/33 30.00 9.00
204 Bill Buckner 84/25 30.00 9.00
205 Bill Buckner 85 Black/21 30.00 9.00
206 Bill Buckner 85 Blue/4
207 Bill Buckner 86/25 30.00 9.00
208 Bill Buckner 87/25 30.00 9.00
209 Bill Buckner 88 Black/24 30.00 9.00
210 Bill Buckner 88 Blue/1
211 Bill Buckner 90 Black/2
212 Bill Buckner 90 Blue/23 30.00 9.00
213 Jay Buhner 88/15
214 Jay Buhner 88 DR/5
215 Jay Buhner 89/11
216 Jay Buhner 90/14
217 Jay Buhner 91/14
218 Jay Buhner 91 GS/1
219 Jay Buhner 92/19 60.00 18.00
220 Jay Buhner 93/20 50.00 15.00
221 Jay Buhner 94/16 60.00 18.00
222 Jay Buhner 95/3
223 Jay Buhner 96/4
224 Jay Buhner 97/19 60.00 18.00
225 Jay Buhner 98/18 60.00 18.00
226 Jay Buhner 98 SPP/4
227 Jay Buhner 01/5
228 Marlon Byrd 02/28 30.00 9.00
229 Jose Canseco 86/4
230 Jose Canseco 87/5
231 Jose Canseco 87 DK/16 80.00 24.00
232 Jose Canseco 88/18 80.00 24.00
233 Jose Canseco 88 BB/1
234 Jose Canseco 89/4
235 Jose Canseco 89 40-40/17 80.00 24.00
236 Jose Canseco 89 GS/3
237 Jose Canseco 89 MVP/4
238 Jose Canseco 90/12
239 Jose Canseco 91/3
240 Jose Canseco 91 AS/7
241 Jose Canseco 92/13
242 Jose Canseco 93/18 80.00 24.00
243 Jose Canseco 94/1
244 Jose Canseco 94 LL/1
245 Jose Canseco 95/8
246 Jose Canseco 96/1
247 Jose Canseco 97 #54/6
248 Jose Canseco 97 #277/2
249 Jose Canseco 98/2
250 Jose Canseco 98 SPP/1
251 Rod Carew 81 #49/5
252 Rod Carew 81 #169/3
253 Rod Carew 81 w/Brett/1
254 Rod Carew 82/3
255 Rod Carew 82 DK/2
256 Rod Carew 83/4
257 Rod Carew 84/5
258 Rod Carew 85/2
259 Rod Carew 86/2
260 Steve Carlton 81/29 50.00 15.00
261 Steve Carlton 81 CY/30 50.00 15.00
262 Steve Carlton 82/30 50.00 15.00
263 Steve Carlton 83/57 30.00 9.00
264 Steve Carlton 83 DK/25 50.00 15.00
265 Steve Carlton 84/3
266 Steve Carlton 85/48 40.00 12.00
267 Steve Carlton 86/15
268 Steve Carlton 87/7
269 Steve Carlton 03 A83/1
270 Gary Carter 81/27 50.00 15.00
271 Gary Carter 82/36 40.00 12.00
272 Gary Carter 82 DK/16 60.00 18.00
273 Gary Carter 83/42 40.00 12.00
274 Gary Carter 84/13
275 Gary Carter 85/19 60.00 18.00
276 Gary Carter 86/61 30.00 9.00
277 Gary Carter 87/75 30.00 9.00
278 Gary Carter 88/47 40.00 12.00
279 Gary Carter 88 BB/1
280 Gary Carter 89 Black/16 60.00 18.00
281 Gary Carter 89 Blue/15
282 Gary Carter 89 BB/1
283 Gary Carter 90 Black/1
284 Gary Carter 90 Blue/12
285 Gary Carter 91/26 50.00 15.00
286 Gary Carter 91 HL Black/1
287 Gary Carter 91 HL Blue/21
288 Gary Carter 92 Black/12
289 Gary Carter 92 Blue/4
290 Gary Carter 93 CL/19 60.00 18.00
291 Jack Clark 84 DK/17 40.00 12.00
292 Jack Clark 88 DK/67 20.00 6.00
293 Will Clark 87/10
294 Will Clark 88/3
295 Will Clark 88 BB/1
296 Will Clark 88 DK/2
297 Will Clark 89/5
298 Will Clark 89 AS/2
299 Will Clark 89 GS/1
300 Will Clark 89 MVP/4
301 Will Clark 90/4
302 Will Clark 91/3
303 Will Clark 92/6
304 Will Clark 94/1
305 Will Clark 95/1
306 Will Clark 96/1
307 Will Clark 99 Retro/2
308 Will Clark 00 Retro/4
309 Roger Clemens 86/1
310 Roger Clemens 86 HL #5/1
311 Roger Clemens 86 HL #6/1
312 Roger Clemens 86 HL #17/1
313 Roger Clemens 86 HL #18/1
314 Roger Clemens 86 HL #26/1
315 Roger Clemens 87/1
316 Roger Clemens 88/1
317 Roger Clemens 88 BB/1
318 Roger Clemens 89/1
319 Roger Clemens 90/1
320 Roger Clemens 91/1
321 Roger Clemens 91 MVP/1
322 Roger Clemens 92/1
323 Roger Clemens 95/1
324 Roger Clemens 98 SPP/1
325 Roger Clemens 99 Retro/2
326 Roger Clemens 00 Retro/1
327 Roger Clemens 01/1
328 Roger Clemens 02/1
329 Jose Cruz Sr. 81/39 15.00 4.50
330 Jose Cruz Sr. 82/50 15.00 4.50
331 Jose Cruz Sr. 83/50 15.00 4.50
332 Jose Cruz Sr. 84/50 15.00 4.50
333 Jose Cruz Sr. 85/49 15.00 4.50
334 Jose Cruz Sr. 86/50 15.00 4.50
335 Jose Cruz Sr. 87/57 15.00 4.50
336 Darren Daulton 86/24 30.00 9.00
337 Darren Daulton 87 Black/32 30.00 9.00
338 Darren Daulton 87 Blue/68 20.00 6.00
339 Darren Daulton 88 Black/21 30.00 9.00
340 Darren Daulton 88 Blue/18 40.00 12.00
341 Darren Daulton 89 Black/30 30.00 9.00
342 Darren Daulton 89 Blue/104 15.00 4.50
343 Darren Daulton 90/2
344 Darren Daulton 91/7
345 Darren Daulton 92 Black/7
346 Darren Daulton 92 Blue/1
347 Darren Daulton 93 Black/10
348 Darren Daulton 93 Blue/23 30.00 9.00
349 Darren Daulton 93 DK/1
350 Darren Daulton 94/10
351 Darren Daulton 96/12
352 Darren Daulton 97/3
353 Darren Daulton 97 SPP/1
354 Alvin Davis 85 DK/1
355 Eric Davis 85/4
356 Eric Davis 86/5
357 Eric Davis 87/62 20.00 6.00
358 Eric Davis 87 DK COR Black/2
359 E.Davis 87 DK COR Blue/39 25.00 7.50
360 Eric Davis 87 DK ERR/6
361 Eric Davis 87 HL/1
362 Eric Davis 88/80 20.00 6.00
363 Eric Davis 88 AS/1
364 Eric Davis 88 BB/1
365 Eric Davis 88 MVP/36 25.00 7.50
366 Eric Davis 89/71 20.00 6.00
367 Eric Davis 90/42 25.00 7.50
368 Eric Davis 90 AS/41 25.00 7.50
369 Eric Davis 91/66 20.00 6.00
370 Eric Davis 91 BC/102 15.00 4.50
371 Eric Davis 92/49 25.00 7.50
372 Eric Davis 93/20 30.00 9.00
373 Eric Davis 94/44 25.00 7.50
374 Eric Davis 97 #190/40 25.00 7.50
375 Eric Davis 97 #292/30 30.00 9.00
376 Eric Davis 99 Retro/95 15.00 4.50
377 Eric Davis 01/122 15.00 4.50
378 Eric Davis 01 SLS/6
379 Andre Dawson 81/25 30.00 9.00
380 Andre Dawson 82 Black/20
381 Andre Dawson 82 Blue/4
382 Andre Dawson 83 Black/20 30.00 9.00
383 Andre Dawson 83 Blue/4
384 Andre Dawson 84 Black/33 30.00 9.00
385 Andre Dawson 84 Blue/1
386 Andre Dawson 85 Black/17 40.00 12.00
387 Andre Dawson 85 Blue/14
388 Andre Dawson 86 Black/29 30.00 9.00
389 Andre Dawson 86 Blue/10
390 A.Dawson 86 DK Black/34 30.00 9.00
391 A.Dawson 86 DK Blue/19 40.00 12.00
392 Andre Dawson 87 Black/19 40.00 12.00
393 Andre Dawson 87 Blue/18 40.00 12.00
394 Andre Dawson 87 HL #28/10
395 Andre Dawson 87 HL #31/10
396 Andre Dawson 88 Black/20 30.00 9.00
397 Andre Dawson 88 Blue/1
398 Andre Dawson 88 AS/5
399 Andre Dawson 88 BB/1
400 A.Dawson 88 DK Black/35 30.00 9.00
401 A.Dawson 88 DK Blue/30 30.00 9.00
402 Andre Dawson 88 MVP/19 40.00 12.00
403 Andre Dawson 89 Black/20 30.00 9.00
404 Andre Dawson 89 Blue/10
405 Andre Dawson 89 BB/1
406 A.Dawson 89 MVP Black/20 30.00 9.00
407 Andre Dawson 89 MVP Blue/1
408 Andre Dawson 90 Black/18 40.00 12.00

409 Andre Dawson 90 Blue/2
410 Andre Dawson 91/20 30.00 9.00
411 A.Dawson 91 AS Black/20 30.00 9.00
412 Andre Dawson 91 AS Blue/1
413 Andre Dawson 92 Blue/30 30.00 9.00
414 Andre Dawson 92 AS Black/12
415 Andre Dawson 92 AS Blue/9
416 Andre Dawson 93/19 40.00 12.00
417 Andre Dawson 94/10
418 Andre Dawson 95/20
419 Andre Dawson 96/15
420 Andre Dawson 97/18 40.00 12.00
421 Lenny Dykstra 86/17 40.00 12.00
422 Lenny Dykstra 87/80 20.00 6.00
423 Lenny Dykstra 88/88 15.00 4.50
424 Lenny Dykstra 88 BB/1
425 Lenny Dykstra 89/71 20.00 6.00
426 Lenny Dykstra 89 BB/1
427 Lenny Dykstra 90/51 20.00 6.00
428 Lenny Dykstra 91/43 25.00 7.50
429 Lenny Dykstra 91 AS/37 25.00 7.50
430 Lenny Dykstra 91 DK/23
431 Lenny Dykstra 91 MVP/21 30.00 9.00
432 Lenny Dykstra 91 w/Murphy/5
433 Lenny Dykstra 92/64 20.00 6.00
434 Lenny Dykstra 93/32 30.00 9.00
435 Lenny Dykstra 94/21 30.00 9.00
436 Lenny Dykstra 95/25 30.00 9.00
437 Jim Edmonds 95/2
438 Jim Edmonds 97/7
439 Jim Edmonds 97 HIT/3
440 Jim Edmonds 98/1
441 Jim Edmonds 98 GPP SG/1
442 Jim Edmonds 98 SPP/1
443 Jim Edmonds 98 SPP SG/1
444 Jim Edmonds 99 Retro/25 30.00 9.00
445 Jim Edmonds 00 Retro/25 30.00 9.00
446 Jim Edmonds 01/25 30.00 9.00
447 Jim Edmonds 02/6
448 Dwight Evans 81/36 25.00 7.50
449 Dwight Evans 82/16 40.00 12.00
450 Dwight Evans 82 DK/4
451 Dwight Evans 83/42 25.00 7.50
452 Dwight Evans 84/16 40.00 12.00
453 Dwight Evans 85/29 30.00 9.00
454 Dwight Evans 86/28 30.00 9.00
455 Dwight Evans 87/25 30.00 9.00
456 Dwight Evans 87 HL/10
457 Dwight Evans 88/25 30.00 9.00
458 Dwight Evans 88 BB/1
459 Dwight Evans 88 DK/30 30.00 9.00
460 Dwight Evans 89/16 40.00 12.00
461 Dwight Evans 91/4
462 Dwight Evans 92/7
463 Sid Fernandez 84/8
464 Sid Fernandez 85/1
465 Sid Fernandez 87/30 30.00 9.00
466 Sid Fernandez 88/56 20.00 6.00
467 Sid Fernandez 89/26 30.00 9.00
468 Sid Fernandez 90/1
469 Sid Fernandez 91/14
470 Sid Fernandez 92/8
471 Sid Fernandez 93/4
472 Sid Fernandez 94/8
473 Sid Fernandez 95/4
474 Rollie Fingers 81/56 20.00 6.00
475 Rollie Fingers 82/42 25.00 7.50
476 Rollie Fingers 83/62 20.00 6.00
477 Rollie Fingers 83 DK/24 30.00 9.00
478 Rollie Fingers 85/34 30.00 9.00
479 Rollie Fingers 86/43 25.00 7.50
480 Carlton Fisk 82 DK/11
481 Carlton Fisk 83/3
482 Carlton Fisk 85/1
483 Carlton Fisk 87/4
484 George Foster 83 DK/10
485 John Franco 85/37 15.00 4.50
486 John Franco 86/41 15.00 4.50
487 John Franco 87/112 15.00 4.50
488 John Franco 88/225 15.00 4.50
489 John Franco 88 BB/1
490 John Franco 89/83 15.00 4.50
491 John Franco 90/50 15.00 4.50
492 John Franco 90 DK/57 15.00 4.50
493 John Franco 91/72 15.00 4.50
494 John Franco 92/66 15.00 4.50
495 John Franco 93/64 15.00 4.50
496 John Franco 94/21 20.00 6.00
497 John Franco 95/19 25.00 7.50
498 John Franco 96/25 20.00 6.00
499 Julio Franco 83/14
500 Julio Franco 84/15
501 Julio Franco 85/30 30.00 9.00
502 Julio Franco 86/46 25.00 7.50
503 Julio Franco 87/59 20.00 6.00
504 Julio Franco 88/122 15.00 4.50
505 Julio Franco 88 BB/1
506 Julio Franco 88 DK/75 15.00 4.50
507 Julio Franco 89/48 25.00 7.50
508 Julio Franco 90/46 25.00 7.50
509 Julio Franco 90 AS/26 30.00 9.00
510 Julio Franco 90 MVP/1
511 Julio Franco 91/62 20.00 6.00
512 Julio Franco 92/38 25.00 7.50
513 Julio Franco 93/33 30.00 9.00
514 Julio Franco 94/18
515 Julio Franco 95/21 30.00 9.00
516 Julio Franco 97/14
517 Freddy Garcia 01/50 25.00 7.50
518 Freddy Garcia 01 SLC/1
519 Freddy Garcia 01 SLS/1
520 Freddy Garcia 02/27 30.00 9.00
521 Freddy Garcia 03/25 30.00 9.00
522 Jay Gibbons 01 DR/50 25.00 7.50
523 Jay Gibbons 02/3
524 Jay Gibbons 03/24 30.00 9.00
525 Juan Gonzalez 90/10
526 Juan Gonzalez 90 RevNeg/5
527 D.Gooden 85/31 60.00 18.00
528 D.Gooden 86/9
529 D.Gooden 86 DK/28 50.00 15.00
530 D.Gooden 87 Black/9
531 D.Gooden 87 Blue/99 25.00 7.50
532 D.Gooden 88 Black/27 50.00 15.00
533 D.Gooden 88 Blue/121 25.00 7.50
534 D.Gooden 88 BB/2
535 D.Gooden 89 Black/48 40.00 12.00
536 D.Gooden 89 Blue/49 40.00 12.00
537 D.Gooden 89 AS/1
538 D.Gooden 90 Black/2
539 D.Gooden 90 Blue/87 25.00 7.50
540 D.Gooden 91 Black/12
541 D.Gooden 91 Blue/71 30.00 9.00
542 D.Gooden 92 Black/23 50.00 15.00
543 D.Gooden 92 Blue/6
544 D.Gooden 93 Black/12
545 D.Gooden 93 Blue/12
546 D.Gooden 94 Black/3
547 D.Gooden 94 Blue/20 50.00 15.00
548 D.Gooden 97 Black/16 60.00 18.00
549 D.Gooden 97 Blue/4
550 Mark Grace 88/5
551 Mark Grace 90/1
552 Mark Grace 91/1
553 Mark Grace 92/1
554 Mark Grace 99 Retro/1
555 Mark Grace 01/1
556 Mark Grace 02/1
557 Mark Grace 03/1
558 Bobby Grich 81/88 15.00 4.50
559 Bobby Grich 82/88 15.00 4.50
560 Bobby Grich 83/70 15.00 4.50
561 Bobby Grich 84/73 15.00 4.50
562 Bobby Grich 85/84 15.00 4.50
563 Bobby Grich 86/67 15.00 4.50
564 Bobby Grich 87/90 15.00 4.50
565 Tony Gwynn 83/8
566 Todd Helton 99 Retro/6
567 Todd Helton 00 Retro/1
568 Todd Helton 01/2
569 Todd Helton 01 DK/2
570 Todd Helton 01 FC/2
571 Todd Helton 01 LL/2
572 Todd Helton 01 LLDC/1
573 Todd Helton 01 PL #3/1
574 Todd Helton 01 PL #21/1
575 Todd Helton 02/7
576 Rickey Henderson 82/1
577 Rickey Henderson 83/3
578 Rickey Henderson 85/2
579 Rickey Henderson 85 HL #17/1
580 Rickey Henderson 85 HL #42/1
581 Rickey Henderson 88/1
582 Rickey Henderson 88 AS/2
583 Rickey Henderson 88 BB/1
584 Rickey Henderson 89/3
585 Rickey Henderson 90/1
586 Rickey Henderson 91/1
587 Rickey Henderson 91 AS/2
588 Rickey Henderson 91 AW/1
589 Rickey Henderson 91 MVP/2
590 Rickey Henderson 92/1
591 Rickey Henderson 92 AS/2
592 Rickey Henderson 92 HL/2
593 Rickey Henderson 93/2
594 Rickey Henderson 94/1
595 Rickey Henderson 94 SE/1
596 Rickey Henderson 95/2
597 Rickey Henderson 96/1
598 Rickey Henderson 98/1
599 Rickey Henderson 00 Retro/1
600 Rickey Henderson 01/1
601 Keith Hernandez 81/19 60.00 18.00
602 Keith Hernandez 82/36 40.00 12.00
603 Keith Hernandez 83/39 40.00 12.00
604 Keith Hernandez 83 DK/25 50.00 15.00
605 Keith Hernandez 84/36 40.00 12.00
606 Keith Hernandez 85/80 30.00 9.00
607 Keith Hernandez 86/66 30.00 9.00
608 Keith Hernandez 87/123 25.00 7.50
609 Keith Hernandez 88 Black/91 25.00 7.50
610 Keith Hernandez 88 Blue/74 30.00 9.00
611 Keith Hernandez 88 BB/1
612 Keith Hernandez 89/76 30.00 9.00
613 Keith Hernandez 89 BB/1
614 Keith Hernandez 89 GS Green/2
615 Keith Hernandez 89 GS Purple/4
616 Keith Hernandez 89 GS Black/1
617 Keith Hernandez 90/87 25.00 7.50
618 Eric Hinske 03/20 20.00 6.00
619 Eric Hinske 04/1
620 Charlie Hough 82/60 15.00 4.50
621 Charlie Hough 83/56 15.00 4.50
622 Charlie Hough 84/79 15.00 4.50
623 Charlie Hough 85/69 15.00 4.50
624 Charlie Hough 86/58 15.00 4.50
625 Charlie Hough 87/150 15.00 4.50
626 Charlie Hough 87 DK/81 15.00 4.50
627 Charlie Hough 88/184 15.00 4.50
628 Charlie Hough 88 BB/1
629 Charlie Hough 89/51 15.00 4.50
630 Charlie Hough 90/45 15.00 4.50
631 Charlie Hough 91/88 15.00 4.50
632 Charlie Hough 92/55 15.00 4.50
633 Charlie Hough 94/19 25.00 7.50
634 Art Howe 81/43 15.00 4.50
635 Art Howe 82 Black/37 15.00 4.50
636 Art Howe 82 Blue/57 15.00 4.50
637 Art Howe 83 Black/20 20.00 6.00
638 Art Howe 83 Blue/54 15.00 4.50
639 Tim Hudson 01/2
640 Tim Hudson 02/13
641 Tim Hudson 03/39 40.00 12.00
642 Aubrey Huff 04/3
643 Bo Jackson 86 DR/3
644 Bo Jackson 86 HL/3
645 Bo Jackson 90 DK/1
646 Bo Jackson 92/1
647 Fergie Jenkins 81/21 30.00 9.00
648 Fergie Jenkins 82/57 20.00 6.00
649 Fergie Jenkins 83/29 30.00 9.00
650 Fergie Jenkins 84/45 25.00 7.50
651 Tommy John 81 Black/15
652 Tommy John 81 Blue/6
653 Tommy John 82 Black/15
654 Tommy John 82 Blue/23 20.00 6.00
655 Tommy John 82 w/Guidry/11
656 Tommy John 83 Black/4
657 Tommy John 83 Blue/35 20.00 6.00
658 Tommy John 84 Black/15
659 Tommy John 84 Blue/31 20.00 6.00
660 Tommy John 85 Black/19 25.00 7.50
661 Tommy John 85 Blue/25 20.00 6.00
662 Tommy John 88 Black/66 15.00 4.50
663 Tommy John 88 Blue/25 20.00 6.00
664 Tommy John 88 DK Blue/50 15.00 4.50
665 Howard Johnson 83/28 20.00 6.00
666 Howard Johnson 85/29 20.00 6.00
667 Howard Johnson 86/24 20.00 6.00
668 Howard Johnson 87 Black/1
669 Howard Johnson 87 Blue/24 20.00 6.00
670 Howard Johnson 87 HL/9
671 Howard Johnson 88/25 20.00 6.00
672 Howard Johnson 89/25 20.00 6.00
673 Howard Johnson 90/25 20.00 6.00
674 Howard Johnson 90 AS/28 20.00 6.00
675 Howard Johnson 90 MVP/24 20.00 6.00
676 Howard Johnson 91/25 20.00 6.00
677 Howard Johnson 92 Black/26 20.00 6.00
678 Howard Johnson 92 Blue/4
679 Howard Johnson 93/17 25.00 7.50
680 Howard Johnson 94/24 20.00 6.00
681 Nick Johnson 99 Retro/53 20.00 6.00
682 Nick Johnson 99 Retro SLC/2
683 Nick Johnson 99 Retro SLS/2
684 Nick Johnson 01/55 20.00 6.00
685 Nick Johnson 01 SLC/2
686 Nick Johnson 01 SLS/2
687 Randy Johnson 89/1
688 Randy Johnson 90/1
689 Randy Johnson 91/1
690 Randy Johnson 92/1
691 Randy Johnson 95/1
692 Randy Johnson 96/1
693 Randy Johnson 99 Retro/1
694 Randy Johnson 01/1
695 Randy Johnson 02/1
696 Randy Johnson 03/1
697 Andruw Jones 99 Retro/10
698 Chipper Jones 96/2
699 Chipper Jones 99 Retro/2
700 Chipper Jones 00 Retro/2
701 Chipper Jones 01/2
702 Chipper Jones 01 DK/2
703 Chipper Jones 02/1
704 Dave Justice 90/24 50.00 15.00
705 Dave Justice 91/3
706 Dave Justice 91 MVP/9
707 Dave Justice 91 ROY/9
708 Dave Justice 92/8
709 Dave Justice 93/8
710 Dave Justice 94/16 60.00 18.00
711 Dave Justice 95/10
712 Dave Justice 96/3
713 Dave Justice 97 #175/2
714 Dave Justice 97 #291/4
715 Dave Justice 97 GPP #291/1
716 Dave Justice 97 SPP #175/2
717 Dave Justice 97 TSPE/2
718 Dave Justice 98/2
719 Dave Justice 98 GPP/1
720 Dave Justice 98 SPP/2
721 Dave Justice 99 Retro/10
722 Dave Justice 00 Retro/10
723 Dave Justice 01/25 50.00 15.00
724 Austin Kearns 02/14
725 Austin Kearns 03 Black/48 25.00 7.50
726 Austin Kearns 03 Blue/2
727 Jimmy Key 85/8
728 Jimmy Key 86/54 30.00 9.00
729 Jimmy Key 87/92 25.00 7.50
730 Jimmy Key 87 OD/3
731 Jimmy Key 88/74 30.00 9.00
732 Jimmy Key 89/64 30.00 9.00
733 Jimmy Key 90/42 40.00 12.00
734 Jimmy Key 91/20 50.00 15.00
735 Jimmy Key 92/38 40.00 12.00
736 Jimmy Key 93/23 50.00 15.00
737 Jimmy Key 94/19 60.00 18.00
738 Jimmy Key 94 SE/1
739 Jimmy Key 95/17 60.00 18.00
740 Jimmy Key 96/31 50.00 15.00
741 Jimmy Key 97/16 60.00 18.00
742 Jimmy Key 98/2
743 Carney Lansford 81 Black/87 15.00 4.50
744 Carney Lansford 81 Blue/9
745 Carney Lansford 82 Black/36 15.00 4.50
746 Carney Lansford 82 Blue/23 20.00 6.00
747 Carney Lansford 83 Black/10
748 Carney Lansford 83 Blue/29 20.00 6.00
749 Carney Lansford 84 Black/9
750 Carney Lansford 84 Blue/12
751 Carney Lansford 85/21 20.00 6.00
752 Carney Lansford 86/54 15.00 4.50
753 Carney Lansford 87/76 15.00 4.50
754 Carney Lansford 88 BB/1
755 Carney Lansford 88 Black/2
756 Carney Lansford 88 Blue/66 15.00 4.50
757 Carney Lansford 89/17 25.00 7.50
758 Carney Lansford 90/3
759 Carney Lansford 91/19 25.00 7.50
760 Carney Lansford 92/6
761 Carlos Lee 01/110 15.00 4.50
762 Carlos Lee 01 SLS/2
763 Carlos Lee 02/6
764 Kenny Lofton 92/1
765 Greg Luzinski 81 Black/15
766 Greg Luzinski 81 Blue/72 20.00 6.00
767 Greg Luzinski 82/67 25.00 7.50
768 Greg Luzinski 83/52 20.00 6.00
769 Greg Luzinski 84/43 25.00 7.50
770 Greg Luzinski 85/44 25.00 7.50
771 Fred Lynn 81 Black/43 25.00 7.50
772 Fred Lynn 81 Blue/23 30.00 9.00
773 Fred Lynn 82 Black/17 40.00 12.00
774 Fred Lynn 82 Blue/37 25.00 7.50
775 Fred Lynn 83 Black/1
776 Fred Lynn 83 Blue/42 25.00 7.50
777 Fred Lynn 84 Blue/25 30.00 9.00
778 Fred Lynn 84 Black/9
779 Fred Lynn 84 DK/21 30.00 9.00
780 Fred Lynn 85 Black/5
781 Fred Lynn 85 Blue/28 30.00 9.00
782 Fred Lynn 86 Black/43 25.00 7.50
783 Fred Lynn 86 Blue/8
784 Fred Lynn 87 Black/38 25.00 7.50
785 Fred Lynn 87 Blue/25 30.00 9.00
786 Fred Lynn 87 DK/82 15.00 4.50
787 Fred Lynn 88 Black/30 30.00 9.00
788 Fred Lynn 88 Blue/14
789 Fred Lynn 88 BB/1
790 Fred Lynn 89 Black/5
791 Fred Lynn 89 Blue/50 25.00 7.50
792 Fred Lynn 91/18 40.00 12.00
793 Greg Maddux 87/4
794 Greg Maddux 87 DR/5
795 Greg Maddux 88/1
796 Greg Maddux 89/1
797 Greg Maddux 90/1
798 Greg Maddux 91/1
799 Greg Maddux 92/1
800 Greg Maddux 93/1
801 Greg Maddux 94/1
802 Greg Maddux 95/1
803 Greg Maddux 96/1
804 Greg Maddux 98/1
805 Greg Maddux 98 DOM/1
806 Greg Maddux 99 Retro/1
807 Greg Maddux 00 Retro DK/1
808 Greg Maddux 01/1
809 Greg Maddux 01 DK/1
810 Greg Maddux 02/1
811 Greg Maddux 03 DK/1
812 Edgar Martinez 89/39 50.00 15.00
813 Edgar Martinez 91 DK/7
814 Edgar Martinez 92/9
815 Edgar Martinez 93/10
816 Edgar Martinez 94/3
817 Edgar Martinez 96/13
818 Edgar Martinez 97/3
819 Edgar Martinez 98/3
820 Edgar Martinez 99 Retro/42 50.00 15.00
821 Edgar Martinez 00 Retro/43 50.00 15.00
822 Edgar Martinez 01/58 50.00 15.00
823 Edgar Martinez 02/25 60.00 18.00
824 Pedro Martinez 92 DR/2
825 Pedro Martinez 93/1
826 Pedro Martinez 95/1
827 Pedro Martinez 96/1
828 Pedro Martinez 98/1
829 Pedro Martinez 01/1
830 Pedro Martinez 01 DK/1
831 Pedro Martinez 01 FC/1
832 Gary Matthews Sr. 81 COR/14
833 Gary Matthews Sr. 81 ERR/7
834 Gary Matthews Sr. 82/76 15.00 4.50
835 Gary Matthews Sr. 83/52 15.00 4.50
836 G.Matthews Sr. 84 Black/49 15.00 4.50
837 Gary Matthews Sr. 84 Blue/11
838 Gary Matthews Sr. 85/45 15.00 4.50
839 Gary Matthews Sr. 86/54 15.00 4.50
840 Don Mattingly 85/1
841 Don Mattingly 86/3
842 Don Mattingly 87/2
843 Don Mattingly 87 HL #17/5
844 Don Mattingly 87 HL #23/5
845 Don Mattingly 88/2
846 Don Mattingly 88 BB/1
847 Don Mattingly 88 MVP/2
848 Don Mattingly 89/2
849 Don Mattingly 90/2
850 Don Mattingly 91/2
851 Don Mattingly 92/2
852 Don Mattingly 93/3
853 Don Mattingly 94/5
854 Don Mattingly 95/3
855 Don Mattingly 95 CL/1
856 Jack McDowell 88/213 15.00 4.50
857 Jack McDowell 89/114 15.00 4.50
858 Jack McDowell 91/19 40.00 12.00
859 Jack McDowell 92/26 30.00 9.00
860 Jack McDowell 93/11
861 Jack McDowell 94/8
862 Jack McDowell 94 SE/3
863 Jack McDowell 95/5
864 Jack McDowell 96/17 40.00 12.00
865 Jack McDowell 97/6
866 Jack McDowell 97 SPP/1
867 Fred McGriff 86/20
868 Fred McGriff 88/1
869 Fred McGriff 89 DK/3
870 Fred McGriff 90/1
871 Fred McGriff 91/1
872 Fred McGriff 91 MVP/2
873 Fred McGriff 92/1
874 Fred McGriff 93/1
875 Fred McGriff 93 SOG/1
876 Fred McGriff 94/1
877 Fred McGriff 94 DOM/1
878 Fred McGriff 97/1
879 Fred McGriff 97 SPP/1
880 Fred McGriff 98 #64/1
881 Fred McGriff 98 GPP #64/1
882 Fred McGriff 98 SPP #230/1
883 Fred McGriff 00 Retro/1
884 Fred McGriff 01/1
885 Paul Molitor 81/6
886 Paul Molitor 82/5
887 Paul Molitor 83/9
888 Paul Molitor 84/2
889 Paul Molitor 85/4
890 Paul Molitor 86/6
891 Paul Molitor 87/1
892 Paul Molitor 87 HL/2
893 Paul Molitor 88/4
894 Paul Molitor 88 BB/1
895 Paul Molitor 88 DK/7
896 Paul Molitor 88 MVP/2
897 Paul Molitor 89/4
898 Paul Molitor 89 MVP/2
899 Paul Molitor 90/1
900 Paul Molitor 90 MVP/3
901 Paul Molitor 91/1
902 Paul Molitor 92/2
903 Paul Molitor 92 DK/1
904 Paul Molitor 93/2
905 Paul Molitor 94/2
906 Paul Molitor 94 SE/2
907 Paul Molitor 95/2
908 Paul Molitor 96 CL/1
909 Paul Molitor 96 CL/1
910 Paul Molitor 97/4
911 Paul Molitor 97 CL/1
912 Paul Molitor 97 HIT/2
913 Paul Molitor 98/6
914 Paul Molitor 98 HIT/1
915 Joe Morgan 81/7
916 Joe Morgan 82/6
917 Joe Morgan 82 DK/15
918 Joe Morgan 83/1
919 Joe Morgan 83 w/F.Rob/4
920 Joe Morgan 84/2
921 Joe Morgan 85/10
922 Jack Morris 81/31 30.00 9.00
923 Jack Morris 82/56 20.00 6.00
924 Jack Morris 83/48 25.00 7.50
925 Jack Morris 83 DK/14
926 Jack Morris 84/36 25.00 7.50
927 Jack Morris 85/42 25.00 7.50
928 Jack Morris 86/45 25.00 7.50
929 Jack Morris 87/123 15.00 4.50
930 Jack Morris 87 DK/106 15.00 4.50
931 Jack Morris 88/139 15.00 4.50
932 Jack Morris 88 AS/6
933 Jack Morris 88 BB/1
934 Jack Morris 89/107 15.00 4.50
935 Jack Morris 90/71 20.00 6.00
936 Jack Morris 91/34 30.00 9.00
937 Jack Morris 92/59 20.00 6.00
938 Jack Morris 92 AS/40 25.00 7.50
939 Jack Morris 93/78 20.00 6.00
940 Jamie Moyer 87/50 25.00 7.50
941 Jamie Moyer 88/24 30.00 9.00
942 Jamie Moyer 88 BB/1
943 Jamie Moyer 89/44 25.00 7.50
944 Jamie Moyer 90/35 30.00 9.00
945 Jamie Moyer 94/19 40.00 12.00
946 Jamie Moyer 95/29 30.00 9.00
947 Jamie Moyer 96/16 40.00 12.00
948 Jamie Moyer 97/11
949 Jamie Moyer 03/21 30.00 9.00
950 Dale Murphy 81 Black/21 60.00 18.00
951 Dale Murphy 81 Blue/14
952 Dale Murphy 82/9
953 Dale Murphy 83 Black/2
954 Dale Murphy 83 Blue/24 60.00 18.00
955 Dale Murphy 83 DK Black/1
956 Dale Murphy 83 DK Blue/11
957 Dale Murphy 84 Black/3
958 Dale Murphy 84 Blue/11
959 Dale Murphy 85 Black/8
960 Dale Murphy 85 Blue/13
961 Dale Murphy 86 Black/1
962 Dale Murphy 86 Blue/10
963 Dale Murphy 87 Black/2
964 Dale Murphy 87 Blue/37 50.00 15.00
965 Dale Murphy 87 DK Black/5
966 Dale Murphy 87 DK Blue/64 50.00 15.00
967 Dale Murphy 88 Black/3
968 Dale Murphy 88 Blue/40 50.00 15.00
969 Dale Murphy 88 AS Black/1
970 Dale Murphy 88 AS Blue/1
971 Dale Murphy 88 BB/1
972 Dale Murphy 88 MVP Black/2
973 Dale Murphy 88 MVP Blue/18
974 Dale Murphy 89 Black/5
975 Dale Murphy 89 Blue/40 50.00 15.00
976 Dale Murphy 90 Black/4
977 Dale Murphy 90 Blue/15
978 Dale Murphy 91 Black/2
979 Dale Murphy 91 Blue/4
980 Dale Murphy 92 Black/17 80.00 24.00
981 Dale Murphy 92 Blue/4
982 Dale Murphy 93 Black/12
983 Dale Murphy 93 Blue/3
984 Eddie Murray 81 Black/1
985 Eddie Murray 81 Blue/1
986 Eddie Murray 82/2
987 Eddie Murray 83/2
988 Eddie Murray 85/2
989 Eddie Murray 86 Black/1
990 Eddie Murray 86 Blue/1
991 Eddie Murray 87/2
992 Eddie Murray 87 HL/1
993 Eddie Murray 88/2
994 Eddie Murray 89/2
995 Eddie Murray 90/2
996 Eddie Murray 91 Black/1
997 Eddie Murray 91 Blue/1
998 Eddie Murray 91 BC Black/1
999 Eddie Murray 91 BC Blue/1
1000 Eddie Murray 91 MVP/2
1001 Eddie Murray 92/2
1002 Eddie Murray 93 Black/1
1003 Eddie Murray 93 Blue/1
1004 Eddie Murray 94/1
1005 Eddie Murray 95/2
1006 Stan Musial 01 ATDK/1
1007 Mike Mussina 95/3
1008 Mike Mussina 99 Retro/5
1009 Mike Mussina 00 Retro/5
1010 Mike Mussina 01/5
1011 Mike Mussina 02/5
1012 Graig Nettles 81 Black/6
1013 Graig Nettles 81 Blue/6
1014 Graig Nettles 82 Black/15
1015 Graig Nettles 82 Blue/27 30.00 9.00
1016 Graig Nettles 83 Black/15
1017 Graig Nettles 83 Blue/48 25.00 7.50
1018 Graig Nettles 84 Black/37 25.00 7.50
1019 Graig Nettles 84 Blue/13
1020 Graig Nettles 85 Black/23 30.00 9.00
1021 Graig Nettles 85 Blue/10
1022 Graig Nettles 86 Black/41 25.00 7.50
1023 Graig Nettles 86 Blue/11
1024 Phil Niekro 81/13
1025 Phil Niekro 82/15
1026 Phil Niekro 83/15
1027 Phil Niekro 83 w/Joe/2
1028 Phil Niekro 84/10
1029 Phil Niekro 85/9
1030 Phil Niekro 86/10
1031 Phil Niekro 86 w/Joe/10
1032 Phil Niekro 87/8
1033 Trot Nixon 01/110 25.00 7.50
1034 Trot Nixon 02/27 50.00 15.00
1035 Trot Nixon 03/25 50.00 15.00
1036 Al Oliver 81/65 15.00 4.50
1037 Al Oliver 82/60 15.00 4.50
1038 Al Oliver 83/49 15.00 4.50
1039 Al Oliver 84 Black/61 15.00 4.50
1040 Al Oliver 84 Blue/1
1041 Al Oliver 84 DK/29 20.00 6.00
1042 Al Oliver 85/55 15.00 4.50
1043 Al Oliver 86/58 15.00 4.50
1044 Paul O'Neill 86/21 50.00 15.00
1045 Paul O'Neill 88/1
1046 Paul O'Neill 89/15
1047 Paul O'Neill 91/10
1048 Paul O'Neill 92/3
1049 Paul O'Neill 93/2
1050 Paul O'Neill 96 GPP/3
1051 Paul O'Neill 99 Retro/10
1052 Paul O'Neill 00 Retro/12
1053 Paul O'Neill 01/29 50.00 15.00
1054 Paul O'Neill 02/29 50.00 15.00
1055 M.Ordonez 99 Retro/25 60.00 18.00
1056 M.Ordonez 00 Retro/25 60.00 18.00
1057 Magglio Ordonez 01/25 60.00 18.00
1058 Maggio Ordonez 02/25 60.00 18.00
1059 Jesse Orosco 85 DK Black/4
1060 Jesse Orosco 85 DK Blue/25 20.00 6.00
1061 Roy Oswalt 01 DR/30 30.00 9.00
1062 Roy Oswalt 02/11
1063 Roy Oswalt 02 FC/1

1064 Roy Oswalt 03/31 30.00 9.00
1065 Amos Otis 81/43 25.00 7.50
1066 Amos Otis 82/52 20.00 6.00
1067 Amos Otis 83/41 25.00 7.50
1068 Rafael Palmeiro 87/35 100.00 30.00
1069 Rafael Palmeiro 89/2
1070 Rafael Palmeiro 90/1
1071 Rafael Palmeiro 91/1
1072 Rafael Palmeiro 91 MVP/2
1073 Rafael Palmeiro 92/5
1074 Rafael Palmeiro 96/1
1075 Rafael Palmeiro 01/1
1076 Jim Palmer 81 #353 Black/11
1077 Jim Palmer 81 #353 Blue/11
1078 J.Palmer 81 #473 Black/16 40.00 12.00
1079 J.Palmer 81 #473 Blue/19 40.00 12.00
1080 Jim Palmer 82/49 25.00 7.50
1081 Jim Palmer 83/6
1082 Jim Palmer 83 DK/20
1083 Jim Palmer 84/17 40.00 12.00
1084 Dave Parker 81/18
1085 Dave Parker 82/31 30.00 9.00
1086 Dave Parker 83/39 25.00 7.50
1087 Dave Parker 84 Black/21 30.00 9.00
1088 Dave Parker 84 Blue/18 40.00 12.00
1089 Dave Parker 85 Black/1
1090 Dave Parker 85 Blue/19 40.00 12.00
1091 Dave Parker 86 Black/5
1092 Dave Parker 86 Blue/23 30.00 9.00
1093 Dave Parker 87 Black/66 20.00 6.00
1094 Dave Parker 87 Blue/11
1095 Dave Parker 88/85 15.00 4.50
1096 Dave Parker 89/21 30.00 9.00
1097 Dave Parker 90 Black/8
1098 Dave Parker 90 Blue/18 40.00 12.00
1099 Dave Parker 91/15
1100 Dave Parker 91 MVP/20 30.00 9.00
1101 Tony Pena 82/61 15.00 4.50
1102 Tony Pena 83/51 15.00 4.50
1103 Tony Pena 84/45 15.00 4.50
1104 Tony Pena 85/22 20.00 6.00
1105 Tony Pena 86/29 20.00 6.00
1106 Tony Pena 87/69 15.00 4.50
1107 Tony Pena 88/46 15.00 4.50
1108 Tony Pena 88 BB/1
1109 Tony Pena 89/36 15.00 4.50
1110 Tony Pena 90/16 25.00 7.50
1111 Tony Pena 91/17 25.00 7.50
1112 Tony Pena 92/30 20.00 6.00
1113 Tony Pena 93/43 15.00 4.50
1114 Tony Pena 94/8
1115 Tony Pena 95/3
1116 Tony Pena 96/11
1117 Tony Pena 96 GPP/1
1118 Terry Pendleton 85 COR/6
1119 Terry Pendleton 85 ERR/16 25.00 7.50
1120 Terry Pendleton 86/48 15.00 4.50
1121 Terry Pendleton 87/53 15.00 4.50
1122 Terry Pendleton 88/58 15.00 4.50
1123 Terry Pendleton 88 BB/1
1124 Terry Pendleton 89/54 15.00 4.50
1125 Terry Pendleton 90/60 15.00 4.50
1126 Terry Pendleton 91 Black/3
1127 Terry Pendleton 91 Blue/36 15.00 4.50
1128 Terry Pendleton 92/18 25.00 7.50
1129 Terry Pendleton 92 BC/4
1130 Terry Pendleton 93/43 15.00 4.50
1131 Terry Pendleton 94/27
1132 Terry Pendleton 95/13
1133 Terry Pendleton 96/17 25.00 7.50
1134 Terry Pendleton 97/21 20.00 6.00
1135 Gaylord Perry 81/91 15.00 4.50
1136 Gaylord Perry 82/79 20.00 6.00
1137 Gaylord Perry 83/55 20.00 6.00
1138 Jorge Posada 01/109 60.00 18.00
1139 Jorge Posada 01 PL/5
1140 Jorge Posada 01 PLDC/1
1141 Jorge Posada 02/4
1142 Kirby Puckett 85/8
1143 Kirby Puckett 87/21 80.00 24.00
1143 Harold Reynolds 86/32 30.00 9.00
1145 Harold Reynolds 87/65 20.00 6.00
1146 Harold Reynolds 88/65 20.00 6.00
1147 Harold Reynolds 89/22 30.00 9.00
1148 Harold Reynolds 89 BB/1
1149 Harold Reynolds 89 DK/12
1150 Harold Reynolds 90/4
1151 Harold Reynolds 91/13
1152 Harold Reynolds 92/26 30.00 9.00
1153 Harold Reynolds 93/16 40.00 12.00
1154 Harold Reynolds 94/6
1155 Jim Rice 81/13
1156 Jim Rice 82 Black/23 50.00 15.00
1157 Jim Rice 82 Blue/7
1158 Jim Rice 83/25 50.00 15.00
1159 Jim Rice 84/20 50.00 15.00
1160 Jim Rice 85/17 60.00 18.00
1161 Jim Rice 85 DK Black/23 50.00 15.00
1162 Jim Rice 85 DK Blue/2
1163 Jim Rice 86/28 30.00 9.00
1164 Jim Rice 87 Black/6
1165 Jim Rice 87 Blue/18 60.00 18.00
1166 Jim Rice 88/25 50.00 15.00
1167 Jim Rice 88 BB/1
1168 Jim Rice 89/12
1169 Cal Ripken 84/1
1170 Cal Ripken 85 DK/2
1171 Cal Ripken 86/1
1172 Cal Ripken 87/1
1173 Cal Ripken 87 HL/1
1174 Cal Ripken 88/1
1175 Cal Ripken 88 BC/1
1176 Cal Ripken 88 DK/2
1177 Cal Ripken 89/1
1178 Cal Ripken 90/1
1179 Cal Ripken 90 AS/1
1180 Cal Ripken 91/1
1181 Cal Ripken 91 AS/1
1182 Cal Ripken 92/1
1183 Cal Ripken 92 AS/1
1184 Cal Ripken 93 MVP/1
1185 Cal Ripken 99 Retro/1
1186 Cal Ripken 00 Retro/1
1187 Cal Ripken 01/1
1188 Cal Ripken 01 DK/1
1189 Cal Ripken 02/1
1190 Mariano Rivera 96/1
1191 Mariano Rivera 97/9
1192 M.Rivera 01 Black/27 100.00 30.00
1193 Mariano Rivera 01 Blue/23 100.00 30.00
1194 Frank Robinson 82/47 40.00 12.00
1195 Frank Robinson 83/36 40.00 12.00
1196 Frank Robinson 83 w/Morgan/10
1197 Frank Robinson 01 ATDK/1
1198 Alex Rodriguez 95/6
1199 Alex Rodriguez 97/1
1200 Alex Rodriguez 98/2
1201 Alex Rodriguez 98 FC/6
1202 Alex Rodriguez 98 HL/1
1203 Alex Rodriguez 99 Retro/1
1204 Alex Rodriguez 00 Retro/1
1205 Alex Rodriguez 00 Retro DK/1
1206 Alex Rodriguez 01/1
1207 Alex Rodriguez 01 DKSS/1
1208 Alex Rodriguez 02/1
1209 Ivan Rodriguez 91 DR/3
1210 Ivan Rodriguez 92/14
1211 Ivan Rodriguez 93/28 80.00 24.00
1212 Ivan Rodriguez 94/5
1213 Ivan Rodriguez 94 SE/3
1214 Ivan Rodriguez 95/2
1215 Ivan Rodriguez 96/16 120.00 36.00
1216 Ivan Rodriguez 97/5
1217 Ivan Rodriguez 98/2
1218 Ivan Rodriguez 98 SPP SG/1
1219 Ivan Rodriguez 99 Retro/10
1220 Ivan Rodriguez 99 Retro SLC/3
1221 Ivan Rodriguez 00 Retro/5
1222 Ivan Rodriguez 00 Retro SLC/3
1223 Ivan Rodriguez 01/5
1224 Ivan Rodriguez 01 DK/2
1225 Ivan Rodriguez 01 DKS/3
1226 Ivan Rodriguez 01 FC/5
1227 Ivan Rodriguez 01 RR/3
1228 Ivan Rodriguez 01 SLC/3
1229 Ivan Rodriguez 02/4
1230 Scott Rolen 98 SPP/1
1231 Scott Rolen 99 Retro/3
1232 Scott Rolen 99 Retro DK/3
1233 Scott Rolen 00 Retro/3
1234 Scott Rolen 01/2
1235 Scott Rolen 02/1
1236 Scott Rolen 03/1
1237 Nolan Ryan 83/2
1238 Nolan Ryan 85/3
1239 Nolan Ryan 86/2
1240 Nolan Ryan 87/5
1241 Nolan Ryan 87 HL/7
1242 Nolan Ryan 88/2
1243 Nolan Ryan 89/4
1244 Nolan Ryan 90/25 200.00 60.00
1245 Nolan Ryan 92/1
1246 Nolan Ryan 92 HL/1
1247 Nolan Ryan 92 HL w/Gossage/1
1248 Nolan Ryan 01 ATDK/1
1249 Ryne Sandberg 89/15
1249A Ryne Sandberg 89 Black/1
1250 Deion Sanders 89 DR/3
1251 Deion Sanders 90/4
1252 Deion Sanders 92/11
1253 Curt Schilling 89/67 50.00 15.00
1254 Richie Sexson 99 Retro/30 30.00 9.00
1255 Richie Sexson 01/30 30.00 9.00
1256 Richie Sexson 02/29 30.00 9.00
1257 Gary Sheffield 89/19 100.00 30.00
1258 Gary Sheffield 89 DR/10
1259 Gary Sheffield 90/1
1260 Gary Sheffield 91/2
1261 Gary Sheffield 92/1
1262 Gary Sheffield 94/2
1263 Gary Sheffield 96/1
1264 Gary Sheffield 99 Retro/2
1265 Gary Sheffield 00 Retro/1
1266 Gary Sheffield 02/1
1267 Ruben Sierra 86 DR/4
1268 Ruben Sierra 87 Black/121 15.00 4.50
1269 Ruben Sierra 87 Blue/101 15.00 4.50
1270 Ruben Sierra 88 Black/18. 25.00 7.50
1271 Ruben Sierra 88 Blue/2
1272 Ruben Sierra 88 BB/1
1273 Ruben Sierra 88 MVP Black/12
1274 Ruben Sierra 88 MVP Blue/1
1275 Ruben Sierra 89/9
1276 R.Sierra 89 MVP Black/26 20.00 6.00
1277 Ruben Sierra 89 MVP Blue/3
1278 Ruben Sierra 91 Black/1
1279 Ruben Sierra 91 Blue/7
1280 Ruben Sierra 92/15
1281 Ruben Sierra 93 Black/1
1282 Ruben Sierra 93 Blue/6
1283 Ruben Sierra 94/4
1284 Ruben Sierra 95 DK/1
1285 Ruben Sierra 97 Black/9
1286 Ruben Sierra 97 Blue/2
1287 Lee Smith 83/9
1288 Duke Snider 84/26 50.00 15.00
1289 J.T. Snow 93 Black/34 20.00 6.00
1290 J.T. Snow 93 Blue/3
1291 J.T. Snow 94/1
1292 J.T. Snow 95 Black/1
1293 J.T. Snow 95 Blue/13
1294 J.T. Snow 96 Black/6
1295 J.T. Snow 96 Blue/19 25.00 7.50
1296 J.T. Snow 97 #42 Black/2
1297 J.T. Snow 97 #42 Blue/21 20.00 6.00
1298 J.T. Snow 97 #275 Black/4
1299 J.T. Snow 97 #275 Blue/13
1300 J.T. Snow 98 Black/19 25.00 7.50
1301 J.T. Snow 98 Blue/2
1302 J.T. Snow 98 SPP Black/1
1303 J.T. Snow 98 SPP Blue/1
1304 J.T. Snow 01 Black/81 15.00 4.50
1305 J.T. Snow 01 Blue/19 25.00 7.50
1306 J.T. Snow 03 Black/7
1307 J.T. Snow 03 Blue/2
1308 Sammy Sosa 90/15
1309 Sammy Sosa 91/4
1310 Sammy Sosa 92/2
1311 Sammy Sosa 93/1
1312 Sammy Sosa 95/4
1313 Sammy Sosa 96/2
1314 Sammy Sosa 99 Retro/3
1315 Sammy Sosa 00 Retro/2
1316 Sammy Sosa 01/3
1317 Sammy Sosa 01 PL/1
1318 Sammy Sosa 01 RR/1
1319 Sammy Sosa 02/2
1320 Warren Spahn 89/1
1321 Junior Spivey 03/20 20.00 6.00
1322 Terry Steinbach 87/22 20.00 6.00
1323 Terry Steinbach 87 DR/1
1324 Terry Steinbach 88/41
1325 Terry Steinbach 88 BB/1
1326 Terry Steinbach 89/34 20.00 6.00
1327 Terry Steinbach 90/30 20.00 6.00
1328 Terry Steinbach 90 AS/10
1329 Terry Steinbach 91/11
1330 Terry Steinbach 92 Black/6
1331 Terry Steinbach 92 Blue/10
1332 Terry Steinbach 93 Black/3
1333 Terry Steinbach 93 Blue/11
1334 Terry Steinbach 94 Black/1
1335 Terry Steinbach 94 Blue/5
1336 Terry Steinbach 95/3
1337 Terry Steinbach 96/4
1338 Terry Steinbach 96 GPP/5
1339 Terry Steinbach 97 Black/8
1340 Terry Steinbach 97 Blue/13
1341 Shannon Stewart 01/108 15.00 4.50
1342 Shannon Stewart 02/36 25.00 7.50
1343 Shannon Stewart 03/36 25.00 7.50
1344 Dave Stieb 81/3
1345 Dave Stieb 82/15
1346 Dave Stieb 83/24
1347 Dave Stieb 83 DK/9
1348 Dave Stieb 84/30 30.00 9.00
1349 Dave Stieb 85/19 40.00 12.00
1350 Dave Stieb 86/23 30.00 9.00
1351 Dave Stieb 87/99 15.00 4.50
1352 Dave Stieb 88/51 20.00 6.00
1353 Dave Stieb 88 BB/1
1354 Dave Stieb 89/36 25.00 7.50
1355 Dave Stieb 89 BB/1
1356 Dave Stieb 90/29 30.00 9.00
1357 Dave Stieb 91/10
1358 Dave Stieb 91 DK/17 40.00 12.00
1359 Dave Stieb 91 HL/3
1360 Dave Stieb 92/13
1361 Dave Stieb 93/12
1362 Darryl Strawberry 84/13
1363 Darryl Strawberry 85/30 50.00 15.00
1364 Darryl Strawberry 86/11
1365 Darryl Strawberry 86 HL/9
1366 Darryl Strawberry 87/83 25.00 7.50
1367 Darryl Strawberry 87 DK/81 25.00 7.50
1368 Darryl Strawberry 87 HL #42/10
1369 Darryl Strawberry 87 HL #49/11
1370 Darryl Strawberry 88/71 30.00 9.00
1371 Darryl Strawberry 88 AS/9
1372 Darryl Strawberry 88 BB/1
1373 D.Strawberry 88 MVP/38 40.00 12.00
1374 Darryl Strawberry 89/67 30.00 9.00
1375 Darryl Strawberry 89 BB/2
1376 D.Strawberry 89 MVP/63 30.00 9.00
1377 Darryl Strawberry 90/84 25.00 7.50
1378 Darryl Strawberry 91/33 50.00 15.00
1379 Darryl Strawberry 91 GS Blue/1
1380 Darryl Strawberry 91 GS Green/4
1381 D.Strawberry 91 MVP/33 50.00 15.00
1382 Darryl Strawberry 92/23 50.00 15.00
1383 Darryl Strawberry 92 McD/2
1384 Darryl Strawberry 93/41 40.00 12.00
1385 Darryl Strawberry 94/9
1386 Darryl Strawberry 95/22 50.00 15.00
1387 Darryl Strawberry 96/8
1388 Darryl Strawberry 97/36 40.00 12.00
1389 Darryl Strawberry 97 PP/1
1390 Darryl Strawberry 98/8
1391 Darryl Strawberry 98 GPP/1
1392 Darryl Strawberry 98 SPP/1
1393 B.J. Surhoff 87/108 15.00 4.50
1394 B.J. Surhoff 87 DR/15
1395 B.J. Surhoff 88/69 15.00 4.50
1396 B.J. Surhoff 88 BB/1
1397 B.J. Surhoff 89/44 15.00 4.50
1398 B.J. Surhoff 90/3
1399 B.J. Surhoff 91/13
1400 B.J. Surhoff 92/21 20.00 6.00
1401 B.J. Surhoff 93/10
1402 B.J. Surhoff 95/1
1403 B.J. Surhoff 97/2
1404 B.J. Surhoff 01/92 15.00 4.50
1405 B.J. Surhoff 01 SLS/9
1406 Frank Thomas 91/1
1407 Frank Thomas 92/1
1408 Frank Thomas 93/2
1409 Frank Thomas 93 SOG/1
1410 Frank Thomas 94/2
1411 Frank Thomas 94 SE/1
1412 Frank Thomas 95/1
1413 Frank Thomas 97/2
1414 Frank Thomas 98/1
1415 Frank Thomas 98 FC/2
1416 Frank Thomas 99 Retro/1
1417 Frank Thomas 00 Retro/1
1418 Frank Thomas 01/1
1419 Frank Thomas 01 LL/1
1420 Frank Thomas 02/1
1421 Gorman Thomas 81 Black/26
1422 Gorman Thomas 81 Blue/12
1423 G.Thomas 82 Black/35 15.00 4.50
1424 Gorman Thomas 82 Blue/30 20.00 6.00
1425 G.Thomas 83 Black/28 20.00 6.00
1426 Gorman Thomas 83 Blue/34 20.00 6.00
1427 G.Thomas 84 Black/33 20.00 6.00
1428 Gorman Thomas 84 Blue/37 15.00 4.50
1429 G.Thomas 86 Black/27 20.00 6.00
1430 Gorman Thomas 86 Blue/31 20.00 6.00
1431 Robby Thompson 86 DR/10
1432 Robby Thompson 87/36 15.00 4.50
1433 Robby Thompson 88 BB/1
1434 R.Thompson 88 Black/77 15.00 4.50
1435 R.Thompson 88 Blue/62 15.00 4.50
1436 Robby Thompson 89/57 15.00 4.50
1437 Robby Thompson 90/65 15.00 4.50
1438 Robby Thompson 91/46 15.00 4.50
1439 Robby Thompson 92/25 20.00 6.00
1440 Robby Thompson 93/17 25.00 7.50
1441 Robby Thompson 94/20 20.00 6.00
1442 Robby Thompson 95/14
1443 Robby Thompson 96/21 20.00 6.00
1444 Robby Thompson 97/27 20.00 6.00
1445 Luis Tiant 81/3
1446 Luis Tiant 83/27 20.00 6.00
1447 Alan Trammell 81/5
1448 Alan Trammell 82 COR/8
1449 Alan Trammell 82 ERR/11
1450 A.Trammell 82 DK COR/21 50.00 15.00
1451 Alan Trammell 82 DK ERR/4
1452 Alan Trammell 83 Black/21 50.00 15.00
1453 Alan Trammell 83 Blue/1
1454 Alan Trammell 84/6
1455 Alan Trammell 85/2
1456 Alan Trammell 86/15
1457 Alan Trammell 87 Black/38 40.00 12.00
1458 Alan Trammell 87 Blue/10
1459 Alan Trammell 87 HL/10
1460 Alan Trammell 88/89 25.00 7.50
1461 Alan Trammell 88 BB/1
1462 Alan Trammell 88 DK/77 30.00 9.00
1463 Alan Trammell 88 MVP/18 60.00 18.00
1464 Alan Trammell 89 Black/9
1465 Alan Trammell 89 Blue/13
1466 A.Tram 89 MVP Black/20 50.00 15.00
1467 Alan Trammell 89 MVP Blue/11
1468 Alan Trammell 90/1
1469 Alan Trammell 90 MVP/2
1470 Alan Trammell 91/12
1471 Alan Trammell 92/13
1472 Alan Trammell 93/16 60.00 18.00
1473 Alan Trammell 94 Black/1
1474 Alan Trammell 94 Blue/3
1475 Alan Trammell 95/1
1476 Alan Trammell 97/7
1477 Jason Varitek 01/110 25.00 7.50
1478 Robin Ventura 90/5
1479 Robin Ventura 90 DR/2
1480 Robin Ventura 91/17 40.00 12.00
1481 Robin Ventura 92/18 40.00 12.00
1482 Robin Ventura 93/9
1483 Robin Ventura 96 PP/1
1484 Robin Ventura 97/1
1485 Robin Ventura 98 SPP/3
1486 Robin Ventura 01/34 30.00 9.00
1487 Robin Ventura 02/34 30.00 9.00
1488 Frank White 81/5
1489 Frank White 82/24 20.00 6.00
1490 Frank White 83/25 20.00 6.00
1491 Frank White 84/28
1492 Frank White 85/11
1493 Frank White 86/15
1494 Frank White 87/15
1495 Frank White 88/47 15.00 4.50
1496 Frank White 88 BB/1
1497 Frank White 89/23 20.00 6.00
1498 Frank White 90/3
1499 Bernie Williams 90/5
1500 Matt Williams 87 DR/9
1501 Matt Williams 88/78 25.00 7.50
1502 Matt Williams 89/38 40.00 12.00
1503 Matt Williams 90/5
1504 Matt Williams 91/4
1505 Matt Williams 91 DK/10
1506 Matt Williams 91 GS/2
1507 Matt Williams 92/19 60.00 18.00
1508 Matt Williams 93/24 50.00 15.00
1509 Matt Williams 94/2
1510 Matt Williams 95/21 50.00 15.00
1511 Matt Williams 96/3
1512 Matt Williams 97 #19/10
1513 Matt Williams 97 #271/6
1514 Matt Williams 97 PP #19/2
1515 Matt Williams 98/2
1516 Matt Williams 99 Retro/50 40.00 12.00
1517 Matt Williams 01/35 50.00 15.00
1518 Matt Williams 02/28 50.00 15.00
1519 Mookie Wilson 81/50
1520 Mookie Wilson 82/39 25.00 7.50
1521 Mookie Wilson 83/24 30.00 9.00
1522 Mookie Wilson 84/26 30.00 9.00
1523 Mookie Wilson 85/50 25.00 7.50
1524 Mookie Wilson 86/40 25.00 7.50
1525 Mookie Wilson 87/35 30.00 9.00
1526 Mookie Wilson 88/4
1527 Mookie Wilson 88 BB/1
1528 Mookie Wilson 89/28 30.00 9.00
1529 Mookie Wilson 90/20 30.00 9.00
1530 Mookie Wilson 91/25 30.00 9.00
1531 Dave Winfield 81/5
1532 Dave Winfield 82/4
1533 Dave Winfield 82 DK/4
1534 Dave Winfield 82 w/Reggie/3
1535 Dave Winfield 83/3
1536 Dave Winfield 84/2
1537 Dave Winfield 85/3
1538 Dave Winfield 86/2
1539 Dave Winfield 87/2
1540 Dave Winfield 87 DK/2
1541 Dave Winfield 88/2
1542 Dave Winfield 88 AS/2
1543 Dave Winfield 88 BB/1
1544 Dave Winfield 89/2
1545 Dave Winfield 89 AS/2
1546 Dave Winfield 89 BC/2
1547 Dave Winfield 89 GS/2
1548 Dave Winfield 90/2
1549 Dave Winfield 91/2
1550 Dave Winfield 92/4
1551 Dave Winfield 93/2
1552 Carl Yastrzemski 81 #94/2
1553 Carl Yastrzemski 81 #214/3
1554 Carl Yastrzemski 82/3
1555 Carl Yastrzemski 83/3
1556 Carl Yastrzemski 83 DK/3
1557 Carl Yastrzemski 90/4
1558 Robin Yount 82/3
1559 Robin Yount 83/3
1560 Robin Yount 84/2
1561 Robin Yount 84 DK/2
1562 Robin Yount 85/3
1563 Robin Yount 86/2
1564 Robin Yount 87/1
1565 Robin Yount 88/2
1566 Robin Yount 88 BB/1
1567 Robin Yount 89/1
1568 Robin Yount 89 DK/3
1569 Robin Yount 90/3
1570 Robin Yount 91/2
1571 Robin Yount 92/3
1572 Robin Yount 93/1
1573 Robin Yount 94/1
1574 Barry Zito 02/4
1575 Barry Zito 03/25 60.00 18.00
1576 Barry Zito 03 DK/5

1997 Donruss VxP 1.0

The 1997 Donruss VxP 1.0 set was issued in one series totalling 50 cards. The cards were distributed 10 to a pack with one CD trading

card and feature a small player action photo with a head shot. When tilted slightly, the card changes to another photo of the same player beside a disc photo.

	Nm-Mt	Ex-Mt
COMPLETE SET (50)	25.00	7.50
1 Darin Erstad	.50	.15
2 Jim Thome	.40	.12
3 Alex Rodriguez	1.25	.35
4 Greg Maddux	1.25	.35
5 Scott Rolen	.40	.12
6 Roberto Alomar	.40	.12
7 Tony Clark	.10	.03
8 Randy Johnson	.50	.15
9 Sammy Sosa	1.00	.30
10 Jose Guillen	.25	.07
11 Cal Ripken	2.00	.60
12 Paul Molitor	.40	.12
13 Jose Cruz Jr.	.75	.23
14 Barry Larkin	.40	.12
15 Ken Caminiti	.15	.04
16 Rafael Palmeiro	.40	.12
17 Chuck Knoblauch	.15	.04
18 Juan Gonzalez	.50	.15
19 Larry Walker	.15	.04
20 Tony Gwynn	1.00	.30
21 Brady Anderson	.15	.04
22 Derek Jeter	2.00	.60
23 Rusty Greer	.15	.04
24 Gary Sheffield	.50	.15
25 Barry Bonds	1.00	.30
26 Mo Vaughn	.10	.03
27 Tino Martinez	.15	.04
28 Ivan Rodriguez	.50	.15
29 Jeff Bagwell	.50	.15
30 Tim Salmon	.40	.12
31 Nomar Garciaparra	1.25	.35
32 Bernie Williams	.40	.12
33 Kenny Lofton	.25	.07
34 Mike Piazza	1.25	.35
35 Jim Edmonds	.40	.12
36 Frank Thomas	.75	.23
37 Andy Pettitte	.25	.07
38 Andruw Jones	1.00	.30
39 Raul Mondesi	.25	.07
40 John Smoltz	.15	.04
41 Albert Belle	.15	.04
42 Mark McGwire	1.50	.45
43 Chipper Jones	1.00	.30
44 Hideo Nomo	.40	.12
45 David Justice	.40	.12
46 Manny Ramirez	.50	.15
47 Ken Griffey Jr.	1.50	.45
48 Roger Clemens	1.00	.30
49 Vladimir Guerrero	1.00	.30
50 Ryne Sandberg	.50	.15

1997 Donruss VxP 1.0 CD Roms

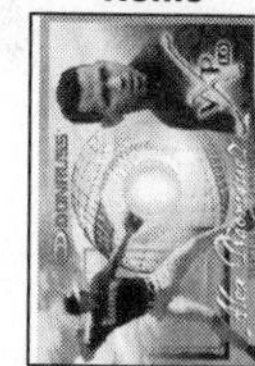

This set features six collectible CD-ROM trading cards shaped and styled like an actual trading card. Each CD was distributed in a pack with ten regular VxP 1.0 cards and features personal and career player information, batting and fielding strategies, video highlights, and an interactive baseball trivia game. When all six were collected and added to a hard drive, a special screen saver with an interactive desktop game was unlocked. The cards are listed below in alphabetical order.

	Nm-Mt	Ex-Mt
COMPLETE SET (6)	30.00	9.00
1 Ken Griffey Jr.	5.00	1.50
2 Greg Maddux	5.00	1.50
3 Mike Piazza	5.00	1.50
4 Cal Ripken	5.00	1.50
5 Alex Rodriguez	5.00	1.50
6 Frank Thomas	5.00	1.50

1953-55 Dormand

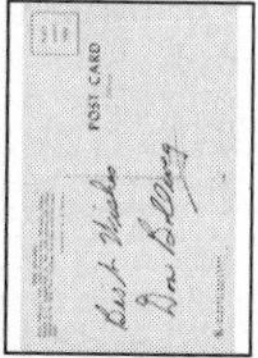

One of the most attractive and popular postcards ever issued are the full color postcards of Louis Dormand, which were issued as premiums by the Mason Candy Company. The cards are numbered on the reverse in the line which seperates the address portion from the message portion of the postcards. Two variations of the McDougald, Collins and Sain exist. Rizzuto and Mantle also exist in a 6" by 9" postcard, and a 9" by 12"

postcard also exists. The Hodges card is quite scarce.

	NM	Ex
COMPLETE SET	3000.00	1500.00
101 Phil Rizzuto	50.00	25.00
101A Phil Rizzuto Straight Sig at top	50.00	25.00
101B Phil Rizzuto Straight Sig at top; smaller	50.00	25.00
101C Phil Rizzuto Signature at an angle	40.00	20.00
101D Phil Rizzuto Jumbo 6 by 9	120.00	60.00
102 Yogi Berra	80.00	40.00
103 Ed Lopat	25.00	12.50
104A Hank Bauer Large Sig	40.00	20.00
104B Hank Bauer Smaller Signature	40.00	20.00
105A Joe Collins Patch on Sleeve Signature on Top	20.00	10.00
105B Joe Collins Patch on Sleeve Signature at Bottom	40.00	20.00
105C Joe Collins No Patch on Sleeve Signature at top	40.00	20.00
105D Joe Collins No Patch on Sleeve Signature on Bottom	40.00	20.00
106 Ralph Houk	25.00	12.50
107 Bill Miller	20.00	10.00
108 Ray Scarborough	20.00	10.00
109 Allie Reynolds	25.00	12.50
110 Gil McDougald Large Signature	25.00	12.50
110A Gil McDougald Small Signature Variation	40.00	20.00
111 Mickey Mantle Batting Left	120.00	60.00
111A Mickey Mantle Bat on Shoulder	200.00	100.00
111B Mickey Mantle Jumbo 6 by 9	300.00	150.00
111C Mickey Mantle Jumbo 9 by 12	300.00	150.00
112 Johnny Mize	80.00	40.00
113A Casey Stengel MG Signature on Top	80.00	40.00
113B Casey Stengel Signature on Bottom	80.00	40.00
114A Bobby Shantz Signature on Top	20.00	10.00
114B Bobby Shantz Signature at an angle	20.00	10.00
115 Whitey Ford	80.00	40.00
116 Johnny Sain Pitching	25.00	12.50
116A Johnny Sain Winding Up	100.00	50.00
117 Jim McDonald	20.00	10.00
118 Gene Woodling	25.00	12.50
119 Charlie Silvera	20.00	10.00
120 Don Bollweg	20.00	10.00
121 Billy Pierce	25.00	12.50
122 Chico Carrasquel	25.00	12.50
123 Willie Miranda	25.00	12.50
124 Carl Erskine	50.00	25.00
125 Roy Campanella	150.00	75.00
126 Jerry Coleman	25.00	12.50
127 Pee Wee Reese	80.00	40.00
128 Carl Furillo	40.00	20.00
129 Gil Hodges SP	500.00	250.00
130 Billy Martin	50.00	25.00
132 Irv Noren	20.00	10.00
133 Enos Slaughter	80.00	40.00
134 Tom Gorman	20.00	10.00
135 Eddie Robinson	20.00	10.00
136 Frank Crosetti CO	50.00	25.00
138 Jim Konstanty	100.00	50.00
139 Elston Howard	120.00	60.00
140 Bill Skowron	40.00	20.00

1986 Dorman's Cheese

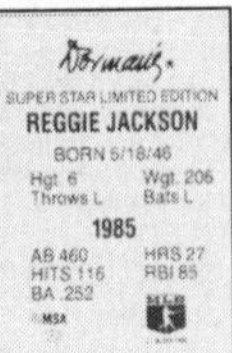

This 20-card set was issued in panels of two cards. The individual cards measure approximately 1 1/2" by 2" whereas the panels measure 3" by 2". Team logos have been removed from the photos as these cards were not licensed by Major League Baseball (team owners). The backs contain a minimum of information.

	Nm-Mt	Ex-Mt
COMPLETE PANEL SET	20.00	8.00
COMPLETE SET	10.00	4.00
COMMON PAIR	.25	.10
1 George Brett	2.50	1.00
2 Jack Morris	.50	.20
3 Gary Carter	1.25	.50
4 Cal Ripken	5.00	2.00
5 Dwight Gooden	.75	.30
6 Kent Hrbek	.25	.10
7 Rickey Henderson	1.50	.60
8 Mike Schmidt	1.50	.60
9 Keith Hernandez	.50	.20
10 Dale Murphy	1.00	.40
11 Reggie Jackson	1.50	.60
12 Eddie Murray	1.50	.60
13 Don Mattingly	3.00	1.20
14 Ryne Sandberg	2.50	1.00
15 Willie McGee	.50	.20
16 Robin Yount	.75	.30
17 Rick Sutcliffe	.25	.10
18 Wade Boggs	1.25	.50
19 Dave Winfield	1.25	.50
20 Jim Rice	.50	.20

1941 Double Play R330

The cards in this 75-card set measure approximately 2 1/2" by 3 1/8" was a blank-backed issue distributed by Gum Products. It consists of 75 numbered cards (two consecutive numbers per card), each depicting two players in sepia tone photographs. Cards 81-100 contain action poses, and the last 50 numbers of the set are slightly harder to find. Cards that have been cut in half to form "singles" have a greatly reduced value. These cards have a value from five to ten percent of the uncut strips and are very difficult to sell. The player on the left has an odd number and the other player has an even number. We are using only the odd numbers to identify these panels. Each penny pack contained two cards and they were issued 100 packs to a box.

	Ex-Mt	VG
COMPLETE SET (150)	5000.00	2500.00
COMMON PAIRS (1-100)	25.00	12.50
COMMON (101-150)	30.00	15.00
WRAPPER (1-CENT)	500.00	250.00
1 Larry French Vance Page	60.00	30.00
3 Billy Herman Stan Hack	50.00	25.00
5 Lonny Frey Johnny VanderMeer	40.00	20.00
7 Paul Derringer Bucky Walters	40.00	20.00
9 Frank McCormick Billy Werber	25.00	12.50
11 Johnny Ripple Ernie Lombardi	50.00	25.00
13 Alex Kampouris Whitlow Wyatt	25.00	12.50
15 Mickey Owen Paul Waner	50.00	25.00
17 Cookie Lavagetto Pete Reiser	30.00	15.00
19 James Wasdell Dolph Camilli	30.00	15.00
21 Dixie Walker Joe Medwick	50.00	25.00
23 Pee Wee Reese Kirby Higbe	200.00	100.00
25 Harry Danning Cliff Melton	25.00	12.50
27 Harry Gumbert Burgess Whitehead	25.00	12.50
29 Joe Orengo Joe Moore	25.00	12.50
31 Mel Ott Norman Young	100.00	50.00
33 Lee Handley Arky Vaughan	50.00	25.00
35 Bob Klinger Stanley Brown	25.00	12.50
37 Terry Moore Gus Mancuso	30.00	15.00
39 Johnny Mize Enos Slaughter	150.00	75.00
41 Johnny Cooney Sibby Sisti	25.00	12.50
43 Max West Carvel Rowell	25.00	12.50
45 Danny Litwhiler Merrill May	25.00	12.50
47 Frank Hayes Al Brancato	25.00	12.50
49 Bob Johnson Bill Nagel	30.00	15.00
51 Bobo Newsom Hank Greenberg	100.00	50.00
53 Barney McCosky Charlie Gehringer	75.00	38.00
55 Mike Higgins Dick Bartell	30.00	15.00
57 Ted Williams Jim Tabor	500.00	250.00
59 Joe Cronin Jimmy Foxx	200.00	100.00
61 Lefty Gomez Phil Rizzuto	250.00	125.00
63 Joe DiMaggio Charlie Keller	750.00	375.00
65 Red Rolfe Bill Dickey	100.00	50.00
67 Joe Gordon Red Ruffing	100.00	50.00
69 Mike Tresh Luke Appling	60.00	30.00
71 Moose Solters Johnny Rigney	25.00	12.50
73 Buddy Myer Ben Chapman	30.00	15.00
75 Cecil Travis George Case	30.00	15.00
77 Joe Krakauskas Bob Feller	125.00	60.00
79 Ken Keltner Hal Trosky	30.00	15.00
81 Ted Williams Joe Cronin	600.00	300.00
83 Joe Gordon Charlie Keller	40.00	20.00
85 Hank Greenberg Red Ruffing	200.00	100.00
87 Hal Trosky George Case	30.00	15.00
89 Mel Ott Burgess Whitehead	100.00	50.00
91 Harry Danning Harry Gumbert	25.00	12.50
93 Norman Young Cliff Melton	25.00	12.50
95 Jimmy Ripple Bucky Walters	30.00	15.00
97 Stan Hack Bob Klinger	30.00	15.00
99 Johnny Mize Dan Litwhiler	75.00	38.00
101 Dom Dallesandro Augie Galan	30.00	15.00
103 Bill Lee Phil Cavarretta	40.00	20.00
105 Lefty Grove Bobby Doerr	150.00	75.00
107 Frank Pytlak Dom DiMaggio	60.00	30.00
109 Jerry Priddy Johnny Murphy	40.00	20.00
111 Tommy Henrich Marius Russo	50.00	25.00
113 Frank Crosetti Johnny Sturm	50.00	25.00
115 Ival Goodman Myron McCormick	30.00	15.00
117 Eddie Joost Ernie Koy	30.00	15.00
119 Lloyd Waner Hank Majeski	60.00	30.00
121 Buddy Hassett Eugene Moore	30.00	15.00
123 Nick Etten Johnny Rizzo	30.00	15.00
125 Sam Chapman Wally Moses	30.00	15.00
127 Johnny Babich Dick Siebert	30.00	15.00
129 Nelson Potter Benny McCoy	30.00	15.00
131 Clarence Campbell Lou Boudreau	75.00	38.00
133 Rollie Hemsley Mel Harder	40.00	20.00
135 Gerald Walker Joe Heving	30.00	15.00
137 Johnny Rucker Ace Adams	30.00	15.00
139 Morris Arnovich Carl Hubbell	90.00	45.00
141 Lew Riggs Leo Durocher	75.00	38.00
143 Fred Fitzsimmons Joe Vosmik	30.00	15.00
145 Frank Crespi Jim Brown	30.00	15.00
147 Don Heffner Harlond Clift	30.00	15.00
149 Debs Garms Elbie Fletcher	40.00	20.00

1950 Drake's

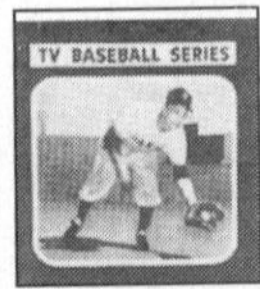

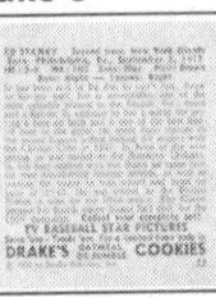

The cards in this 36-card set measure approximately 2 1/2" by 2 1/2". The 1950 Drake's Cookies set contains numbered black and white cards. The players are pictured inside a simulated television screen and the caption "TV Baseball Series" appears on the cards. The players selected for this set show a heavy representation of players from New York teams. The catalog designation for this set is D358.

	NM	Ex
COMPLETE SET (36)	7000.00	3500.00
1 Preacher Roe	100.00	50.00
2 Clint Hartung	80.00	40.00
3 Earl Torgeson	80.00	40.00
4 Lou Brissie	80.00	40.00
5 Duke Snider	400.00	200.00
6 Roy Campanella	500.00	250.00
7 Sheldon Jones	80.00	40.00
8 Whitey Lockman	80.00	40.00
9 Bobby Thomson	100.00	50.00
10 Dick Sisler	80.00	40.00
11 Gil Hodges	200.00	100.00
12 Eddie Waitkus	80.00	40.00
13 Bobby Doerr	150.00	75.00
14 Warren Spahn	300.00	150.00
15 Buddy Kerr	80.00	40.00
16 Sid Gordon	80.00	40.00
17 Willard Marshall	80.00	40.00
18 Carl Furillo	100.00	50.00
19 Pee Wee Reese	300.00	150.00
20 Alvin Dark	100.00	50.00
21 Del Ennis	100.00	50.00
22 Ed Stanky	100.00	50.00
23 Tom Henrich	120.00	60.00
24 Yogi Berra	400.00	200.00
25 Phil Rizzuto	200.00	100.00
26 Jerry Coleman	100.00	50.00
27 Joe Page	100.00	50.00
28 Allie Reynolds	100.00	50.00
29 Ray Scarborough	80.00	40.00
30 Birdie Tebbetts	80.00	40.00
31 Maurice McDermott	80.00	40.00
32 Johnny Pesky	100.00	50.00
33 Dom DiMaggio	120.00	60.00
34 Vern Stephens	100.00	50.00
35 Bob Elliott	100.00	50.00
36 Enos Slaughter	200.00	100.00

1981 Drake's

The cards in this 33-card set measure 2 1/2" by 3 1/2". The 1981 Drake's Bakeries set contains National and American League stars. Produced in conjunction with Topps and released to the public in Drake's Cakes, this set features red frames for American League players and blue frames for National League players. A Drake's Cakes logo with the words "Big Hitters" appears on the lower front of each card. The backs are quite similar to the 1981 Topps backs but contain the Drake's logo, a different card number, and a short paragraph entitled "What Makes a Big Hitter" at the top of the card.

	Nm-Mt	Ex-Mt
COMPLETE SET (33)	6.00	2.40
1 Carl Yastrzemski	.50	.20
2 Rod Carew	.50	.20
3 Pete Rose	.75	.30
4 Dave Parker	.10	.04
5 George Brett	2.00	.80
6 Eddie Murray	1.25	.50
7 Mike Schmidt	1.00	.40
8 Jim Rice	.15	.06
9 Fred Lynn	.10	.04
10 Reggie Jackson	.50	.20
11 Steve Garvey	.20	.08
12 Ken Singleton	.05	.02
13 Bill Buckner	.10	.04
14 Dave Winfield	.75	.30
15 Jack Clark	.10	.04
16 Cecil Cooper	.10	.04
17 Bob Horner	.05	.02
18 George Foster	.10	.04
19 Dave Kingman	.10	.04
20 Cesar Cedeno	.10	.04
21 Joe Charboneau	.20	.08
22 George Hendrick	.05	.02
23 Gary Carter	.50	.20
24 Al Oliver	.10	.04
25 Bruce Bochte	.05	.02
26 Jerry Mumphrey	.05	.02
27 Steve Kemp	.05	.02
28 Bob Watson	.10	.04
29 John Castino	.05	.02
30 Tony Armas	.05	.02
31 John Mayberry	.05	.02
32 Carlton Fisk	.50	.20
33 Lee Mazzilli	.05	.02

1982 Drake's

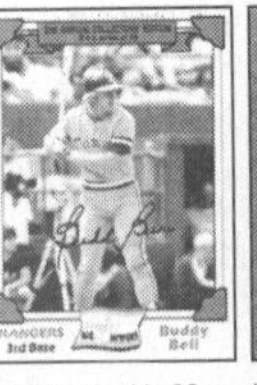

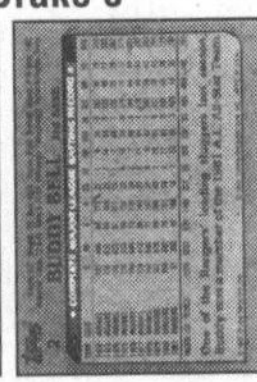

The cards in this 33-card set measure 2 1/2" by 3 1/2". The 1982 Drake's Big Hitters series cards each has the title "2nd Annual Collectors' Edition" in a ribbon design at the top of the picture area. Each color player photo has "photo mount" designs in the corners, red for the AL and green for the NL. The reverses are green and blue, the same as the regular 1982 Topps format, and the photos are larger than those of the previous year. Of the 33 hitters featured, 19 represent the National League. There are 21 returnees from the 1981 set and only one photo, that of Kennedy, is the same as that appearing in the regular Topps issue. The Drake's logo appears centered in the bottom border on the obverse. This set's card numbering is essentially in alphabetical order by the player's name.

	Nm-Mt	Ex-Mt
COMPLETE SET (33)	6.00	2.40
1 Tony Armas	.05	.02
2 Buddy Bell	.10	.04
3 Johnny Bench	.50	.20
4 George Brett	1.50	.60
5 Bill Buckner	.10	.04
6 Rod Carew	.30	.12
7 Gary Carter	.40	.16
8 Jack Clark	.10	.04
9 Cecil Cooper	.10	.04
10 Jose Cruz	.10	.04
11 Dwight Evans	.15	.06
12 Carlton Fisk	.40	.16
13 George Foster	.10	.04
14 Steve Garvey	.20	.08
15 Kirk Gibson	.20	.08
16 Mike Hargrove	.10	.04
17 George Hendrick	.05	.02
18 Bob Horner	.05	.02
19 Reggie Jackson	.40	.16
20 Terry Kennedy	.05	.02
21 Dave Kingman	.10	.04
22 Greg Luzinski	.10	.04
23 Bill Madlock	.05	.02
24 John Mayberry	.05	.02
25 Eddie Murray	.75	.30
26 Graig Nettles	.10	.04
27 Jim Rice	.10	.04
28 Pete Rose	.75	.30
29 Mike Schmidt	.75	.30
30 Ken Singleton	.05	.02
31 Dave Winfield	.50	.20
32 Butch Wynegar	.05	.02
33 Richie Zisk	.05	.02

1983 Drake's

The cards in this 33-card series measure 2 1/2" by 3 1/2". For the third year in a row, Drake's Cakes, in conjunction with Topps, issued a set entitled Big Hitters. The fronts appear very similar to those of the previous two years with slight variations on the framelines and player identification sections. The backs are the same as the Topps backs of this year except for the card number and the Drake's logo. This set's card numbering is essentially in alphabetical order by the player's name.

	Nm-Mt	Ex-Mt
COMPLETE SET (33)	6.00	2.40
1 Don Baylor	.10	.04
2 Bill Buckner	.10	.04
3 Rod Carew	.40	.16
4 Gary Carter	.40	.16
5 Jack Clark	.10	.04
6 Cecil Cooper	.05	.02
7 Dwight Evans	.15	.06
8 George Foster	.10	.04
9 Pedro Guerrero	.05	.02
10 George Hendrick	.05	.02
11 Bob Horner	.05	.02
12 Reggie Jackson	.50	.20
13 Steve Kemp	.05	.02
14 Dave Kingman	.10	.04
15 Bill Madlock	.05	.02
16 Gary Matthews	.05	.02
17 Hal McRae	.05	.02
18 Dale Murphy	.40	.16
19 Eddie Murray	.75	.30
20 Ben Oglivie	.05	.02
21 Al Oliver	.10	.04
22 Jim Rice	.10	.04
23 Cal Ripken	3.00	1.20
24 Pete Rose	.50	.20
25 Mike Schmidt	.50	.20
26 Ken Singleton	.05	.02
27 Gorman Thomas	.05	.02
28 Jason Thompson	.05	.02
29 Mookie Wilson	.10	.04
30 Willie Wilson	.05	.02
31 Dave Winfield	.50	.20
32 Carl Yastrzemski	.50	.20
33 Robin Yount	.40	.16

1984 Drake's

The cards in this 33-card set measure 2 1/2" by 3 1/2". The Fourth Annual Collectors Edition of baseball cards produced by Drake's Cakes in conjunction with Topps continued this now annual set entitled Big Hitters. As in previous years, the front contains a frameline in which the title of the set, the Drake's logo, and the player's name, his team, and position appear. The cards all feature the player in a batting action pose. While the cards fronts are different from the Topps fronts of this year, the backs differ only in the card number and the use of the Drake's logo instead of the Topps logo. This set's card numbering is essentially in alphabetical order by the player's name.

	Nm-Mt	Ex-Mt
COMPLETE SET (33)	6.00	2.40
1 Don Baylor	.10	.04
2 Wade Boggs	1.00	.40
3 George Brett	1.25	.50
4 Bill Buckner	.10	.04
5 Rod Carew	.30	.12
6 Gary Carter	.40	.16
7 Ron Cey	.10	.04
8 Cecil Cooper	.10	.04
9 Andre Dawson	.20	.08
10 Steve Garvey	.10	.04
11 Pedro Guerrero	.05	.02
12 George Hendrick	.05	.02
13 Keith Hernandez	.10	.04
14 Bob Horner	.05	.02
15 Reggie Jackson	.40	.16
16 Steve Kemp	.05	.02
17 Ron Kittle	.05	.02
18 Greg Luzinski	.10	.04
19 Fred Lynn	.10	.04
20 Bill Madlock	.10	.04
21 Gary Matthews	.05	.02
22 Dale Murphy	.30	.12
23 Eddie Murray	.75	.30
24 Al Oliver	.10	.04
25 Jim Rice	.10	.04
26 Cal Ripken	3.00	1.20
27 Pete Rose	.50	.20
28 Mike Schmidt	.50	.20
29 Darryl Strawberry	.20	.08
30 Alan Trammell	.20	.08
31 Mookie Wilson	.05	.02
32 Dave Winfield	.50	.20
33 Robin Yount	.40	.16

1985 Drake's

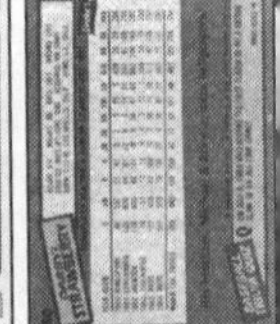

The cards in this 44-card set measure 2 1/2" b 3 1/2". The Fifth Annual Collectors Edition c baseball cards produced by Drake's Cakes i conjunction with Topps continued thi apparently annual set with a new twist, for th first time, 11 pitchers were included. The "Bi Hitters" are numbered 1-33 and the pitchers ar r right corner of the backs of the cards. The mplete set could be obtained directly from e company by sending 2.95 with four proofs purchase.

	Nm-Mt	Ex-Mt
MP.FACT. SET (44)	8.00	3.20
MPLETE SET (44)	8.00	3.20
MMON CARD (1-33)	.05	.02
MMON CARD (34-44)	.10	.04
ony Armas	.05	.02
arold Baines	.15	.06
on Baylor	.10	.04
eorge Brett	1.00	.40
ary Carter	.40	.16
on Cey	.10	.04
ose Cruz	.10	.04
lvin Davis	.05	.02
hili Davis	.10	.04
Dwight Evans	.10	.04
Steve Garvey	.10	.04
Kirk Gibson	.15	.06
Pedro Guerrero	.05	.02
Tony Gwynn	2.00	.80
Keith Hernandez	.10	.04
Kent Hrbek	.10	.04
Reggie Jackson	.50	.20
Gary Matthews	.05	.02
Don Mattingly	1.50	.60
Dale Murphy	.20	.08
Eddie Murray	.50	.20
Dave Parker	.10	.04
Lance Parrish	.10	.04
Tim Raines	.10	.04
Jim Rice	.10	.04
Cal Ripken	2.50	1.00
Juan Samuel	.05	.02
Ryne Sandberg	1.00	.40
Mike Schmidt	.50	.20
Darryl Strawberry	.10	.04
Alan Trammell	.15	.06
Dave Winfield	.50	.20
Robin Yount	.20	.08
Mike Boddicker	.10	.04
Steve Carlton	.50	.20
Dwight Gooden	.25	.10
Willie Hernandez	.10	.04
Mark Langston	.15	.06
Dan Quisenberry	.10	.04
Dave Righetti	.10	.04
Tom Seaver	.50	.20
Bob Stanley	.10	.04
Rick Sutcliffe	.10	.04
Bruce Sutter	.15	.06

1986 Drake's

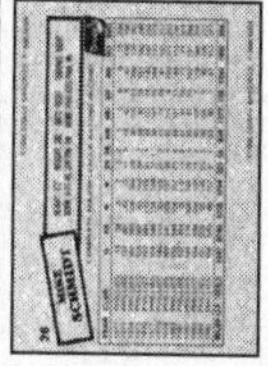

set of 37 cards was distributed as back els of various Drake's snack products. Each vidual card measures 2 1/2" by 3 1/2". Each cially marked package features two, three, our cards on the back. The set is easily gnized by the Drake's logo and "6th Annual ector's Edition" at the top of the obverse. s are numbered on the front and the back. s below are coded based on the product n which they appeared, for example, Apple (AP), Cherry Pies (CP), Chocolate Donut tes (CDD), Coffee Cake Jr. (CCJ), Creme rtcakes (CS), Devil Dogs (DD), Fudge wnies (FUD), Funny Bones (FB), Peanut er Squares (PBS), Powdered Sugar Donut tes (PSDD), Ring Ding Jr. (RDJ), Sunny dles (SD), Swiss Rolls (SR), Yankee dles (YD), and Yodels (Y). The last nine s are pitchers. Complete panels would be ed approximately 50 percent higher than ndividual card prices listed below.

	Nm-Mt	Ex-Mt
PLETE SET (37)	80.00	32.00
ry Carter Y	1.50	.60
ight Evans Y	.50	.20
ggie Jackson SR	3.00	1.20
ve Parker SR	.50	.20
ckey Henderson FB	4.00	1.60
dro Guerrero FB	.50	.20
n Mattingly YD	8.00	3.20
ke Marshall YD	.25	.10
th Moreland YD	.25	.10
eith Hernandez CS	.50	.20
al Ripken CS	15.00	6.00
ale Murphy RDJ	1.00	.40
m Rice RDJ	.50	.20
eorge Brett CCJ	8.00	3.20
m Raines CCJ	.50	.20
arryl Strawberry DD	.50	.20
ll Buckner DD	.50	.20
ave Winfield AP	2.50	1.00
yne Sandberg AP	6.00	2.40
teve Balboni AP	.25	.10
ommy Herr AP	.25	.10
ete Rose CP	3.00	1.20
illie McGee CP	1.00	.40
arold Baines CP	.75	.30
ddie Murray CP	3.00	1.20
ike Schmidt SD/FUD	4.00	1.60
ade Boggs SD/FUD	5.00	2.00
rk Gibson SD/FUD	.50	.20
et Saberhagen PBS	.50	.20
hn Tudor PBS	.25	.10
el Hershiser PBS	.50	.20
on Guidry CDD	.50	.20
olan Ryan CDD	15.00	6.00
ave Stieb CDD	.25	.10
wight Gooden SDD	.50	.20
rn.Valenzuela SDD	.50	.20
m Browning SDD	.25	.10

1987 Drake's

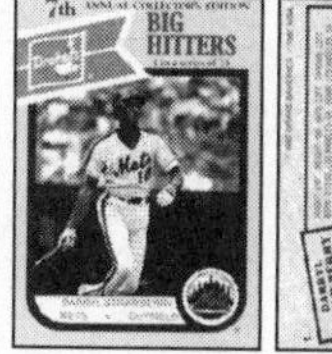

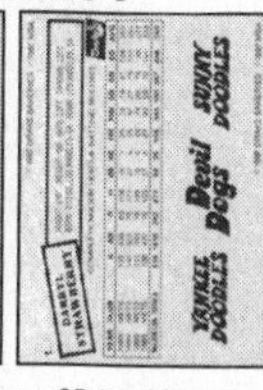

This 33-card set features 25 top hitters and eight top pitchers. Cards were printed in groups of two, three, or four on the backs of Drake's bakery products. Individual cards measure 2 1/2" by 3 1/2" and tout the 7th annual edition. Card backs feature year-by-year season statistics. The cards are numbered such that the pitchers are listed numerically last, e.g., top hitters 1-25 and pitchers 26-33). Complete panels would be valued approximately 50 percent higher than the individual card prices listed below.

	Nm-Mt	Ex-Mt
COMPLETE SET (33)	80.00	32.00
1 Darryl Strawberry	.50	.20
2 Wally Joyner	.75	.30
3 Von Hayes	.25	.10
4 Jose Canseco	4.00	1.60
5 Dave Winfield	3.00	1.20
6 Cal Ripken	15.00	6.00
7 Keith Moreland	.25	.10
8 Don Mattingly	8.00	3.20
9 Willie McGee	.50	.20
10 Keith Hernandez	.50	.20
11 Tony Gwynn	8.00	3.20
12 Rickey Henderson	5.00	2.00
13 Dale Murphy	1.00	.40
14 George Brett	8.00	3.20
15 Jim Rice	.50	.20
16 Wade Boggs	4.00	1.60
17 Kevin Bass	.25	.10
18 Dave Parker	.50	.20
19 Kirby Puckett	3.00	1.20
20 Gary Carter	1.00	.40
21 Ryne Sandberg	3.00	1.20
22 Harold Baines	.75	.30
23 Mike Schmidt	3.00	1.20
24 Eddie Murray	3.00	1.20
25 Steve Sax	.25	.10
26 Dwight Gooden	.50	.20
27 Jack Morris	.50	.20
28 Ron Darling	.25	.10
29 Fernando Valenzuela	.50	.20
30 John Tudor	.25	.10
31 Roger Clemens	10.00	4.00
32 Nolan Ryan	15.00	6.00
33 Mike Scott	.25	.10

1988 Drake's

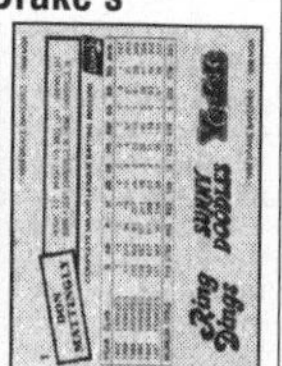

This 33-card set features 27 top hitters and six top pitchers. Cards were printed in groups of two, three, or four on the backs of Drake's bakery products. Individual cards measure approximately 2 1/2" by 3 1/2" and tout the 8th annual edition. Card backs feature year-by-year season statistics. The cards are numbered such that the pitchers are listed numerically last, e.g., top hitters 1-27 and pitchers 28-33). The product affiliations are as follows, 1-2 Ring Dings, 3-4 Devil Dogs, 5-6 Coffee Cakes, 7-9 Yankee Doodles, 10-11 Funny Bones, 12-14 Fudge Brownies, 15-18 Cherry Pies, 19-21 Sunny Doodles, 22-24 Powdered Sugar Donuts, 25-27 Chocolate Donuts, 28-29 Yodels, and 30-33 Apple Pies. Complete panels would be valued approximately 50 percent higher than the individual card prices listed below.

	Nm-Mt	Ex-Mt
COMPLETE SET (33)	100.00	40.00
1 Don Mattingly	10.00	4.00
2 Tim Raines	.50	.20
3 Darryl Strawberry	.50	.20
4 Wade Boggs	5.00	2.00
5 Keith Hernandez	.50	.20
6 Mark McGwire	15.00	6.00
7 Rickey Henderson	8.00	3.20
8 Mike Schmidt	4.00	1.60
9 Dwight Evans	.50	.20
10 Gary Carter	3.00	1.20
11 Paul Molitor	5.00	2.00
12 Dave Winfield	4.00	1.60
13 Alan Trammell	.75	.30
14 Tony Gwynn	10.00	4.00
15 Dale Murphy	1.00	.40
16 Andre Dawson	1.00	.40
17 Von Hayes	.25	.10
18 Willie Randolph	.50	.20
19 Kirby Puckett	3.00	1.20
20 Juan Samuel	.25	.10
21 Eddie Murray	4.00	1.60
22 George Bell	.25	.10
23 Larry Sheets	.25	.10
24 Eric Davis	.50	.20
25 Cal Ripken	20.00	8.00
26 Pedro Guerrero	.25	.10
27 Will Clark	8.00	3.20
28 Dwight Gooden	.50	.20
29 Frank Viola	.25	.10
30 Roger Clemens	10.00	4.00
31 Rick Sutcliffe	.25	.10
32 Jack Morris	.50	.20
33 John Tudor	.25	.10

1894 Duke Cabinets N142

These four cabinets were produced by W.H. Duke. These color cabinets measure approximately 6" X 9 1/2" and a portrait takes up almost the entire card. The player is identified on the bottom.

	Ex-Mt	VG
COMPLETE SET (4)	25000.00	12500.00
1 George Davis	8000.00	4000.00
2 Ed Delahanty	8000.00	4000.00
3 Billy Nash	4000.00	2000.00
4 Wilbert Robinson	8000.00	4000.00

2002 J.D. Drew

This one card set was issued in 2002 and features a photo of J.D. Drew on the front along with religious testimony by Drew on the back.

	MINT	NRMT
1 J.D. Drew	1.00	.45

1893 Duke Talk of the Diamond N135

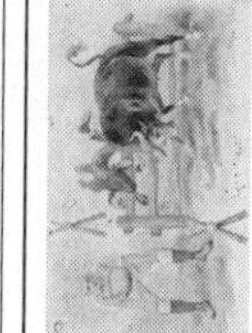

The 25 cards in Duke's Talk of the Diamond set feature a humorous situation placed alongside a baseball design. Since the reverse lists the manufacturer as a branch of the American Tobacco Company, it is thought that this set was issued about 1893. A list of the 25 titles appears on the back of each card. Most of the baseball designs are similar to those appearing in the Buchner Gold Coin set (N284).

	Ex-Mt	VG
COMPLETE SET (25)	2500.00	1250.00
COMMON CARD (1-25)	100.00	50.00

1987 DuPont

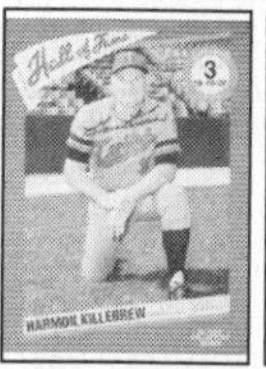

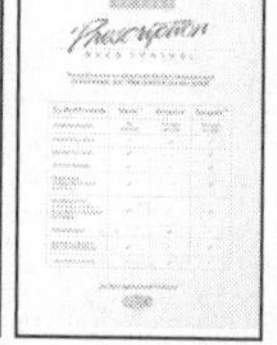

This 8 1/2" by 11" large size cards features Hall of Famers. The front is a posed shot from near the end of his career and the back features information about various DuPont products. It is possible there might be more players so any additions are appreciated.

	Nm-Mt	Ex-Mt
COMPLETE SET (2)	10.00	4.00
1 Harmon Killebrew	10.00	4.00
2 Willie Mays	15.00	6.00

1993 Duracell Power Players I

This 24-card standard-size set was divided into six packs with four cards and one Duracell Official Order Form in each pack. One pack was free with a purchase of Duracell Saver Pack or could be ordered with proof of purchase of several other Duracell products.

	Nm-Mt	Ex-Mt
COMPLETE SET (24)	3.00	.90
1 Roger Clemens	.50	.15
2 Frank Thomas	.30	.09
3 Andre Dawson	.15	.04
4 Orel Hershiser	.10	.03
5 Kirby Puckett	.30	.09
6 Edgar Martinez	.15	.04
7 Craig Biggio	.15	.04
8 Terry Pendleton	.05	.02
9 Mark McGwire	.75	.23
10 Dave Stewart	.10	.03
11 Ozzie Smith	.50	.15
12 Doug Drabek	.05	.02
13 Dwight Gooden	.10	.03
14 Tony Gwynn	.50	.15
15 Carlos Baerga	.05	.02
16 Robin Yount	.25	.07
17 Barry Bonds	.50	.15
18 Bip Roberts	.05	.02
19 Don Mattingly	.50	.15
20 Nolan Ryan	1.00	.30
21 Tom Glavine	.25	.07
22 Will Clark	.25	.07
23 Cecil Fielder	.10	.03
24 Dave Winfield	.25	.07

1993 Duracell Power Players II

This 24-card standard-size set was divided into six packs with four cards and one Duracell Official Order Form in each pack. One pack was free with a purchase of a Duracell Saver Pack or could be ordered with proof of purchase of several other Duracell products.

	Nm-Mt	Ex-Mt
COMPLETE SET (24)	3.00	.90
1 Cal Ripken	1.00	.30
2 Melido Perez	.05	.02
3 John Kruk	.10	.03
4 Charlie Hayes	.05	.02
5 George Brett	.50	.15
6 Ruben Sierra	.10	.03
7 Deion Sanders	.15	.04
8 Andy Van Slyke	.05	.02
9 Fred McGriff	.15	.04
10 Benito Santiago	.05	.02
11 Charles Nagy	.05	.02
12 Greg Maddux	.60	.18
13 Ryne Sandberg	.50	.15
14 Dennis Martinez	.10	.03
15 Ken Griffey Jr.	.60	.18
16 Jim Abbott	.10	.03
17 Barry Larkin	.25	.07
18 Gary Sheffield	.25	.07
19 Jose Canseco	.30	.09
20 Jack McDowell	.05	.02
21 Darryl Strawberry	.05	.02
22 Delino DeShields	.05	.02
23 Dennis Eckersley	.10	.03
24 Paul Molitor	.25	.07

1914 E and S Publishing

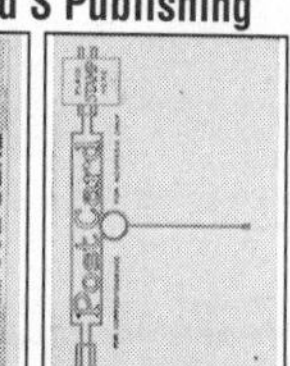

These ornate styled postcards produced by the E and S Pub. Co. of Chicago in 1914 are extremely rare. This bluetone cards have a closeup head and shoulders caraciture of the player surrounded by cartoon vignettes of his career done by an obviously gifted cartoonist, possibly from one of the Chicago newspapers. The art is signed T.S. Several additions were made in the past couple years; there are probably others as well; any further additions to this checklist are greatly appreciated.

	Ex-Mt	VG
COMPLETE SET	4000.00	2000.00
1 Joe Benz	400.00	200.00
2 Ty Cobb	1200.00	600.00
3 Miller Huggins	400.00	200.00
4 Joe Jackson	1000.00	500.00
5 James Lavender	400.00	200.00
6 Frank Schulte	400.00	200.00
7 Art Wilson	400.00	200.00

1911 E94

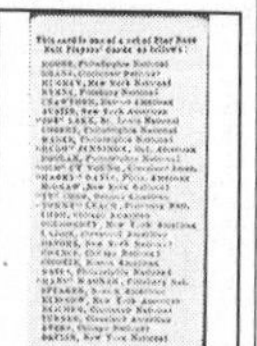

The cards in this 30-card set measure 1 1/2" by 2 3/4". The E94 format, like that of E93, consists of tinted, black and white photos on solid color backgrounds (seven colors seen; each player seen in more than one color). Issued in 1911, cards from this set may be found with advertising overstamps covering the gray print checklist on the back (begins with Moore). Some blank backs have been found, and the set is identical to M131.

	Ex-Mt	VG
COMPLETE SET (30)	8000.00	4000.00
1 Jimmy Austin	120.00	60.00
2 Johnny Bates	120.00	60.00
3 Bob Bescher	120.00	60.00
4 Bobby Byrne	120.00	60.00
5 Frank Chance	400.00	200.00
6 Eddie Cicotte	250.00	125.00
7 Ty Cobb	2000.00	1000.00
8 Sam Crawford	250.00	125.00
9 Harry Davis	120.00	60.00
10 Art Devlin	120.00	60.00
11 Josh Devore	120.00	60.00
12 Mickey Doolan	120.00	60.00
13 Patsy Dougherty	120.00	60.00
14 Johnny Evers	250.00	125.00
15 Eddie Grant	120.00	60.00
16 Hugh Jennings	250.00	125.00
17 Red Kleinow	120.00	60.00
18 Napoleon Lajoie	600.00	300.00
19 Joe Lake	120.00	60.00
20 Tommy Leach	150.00	75.00
21 Hans Lobert	120.00	60.00
22 Harry Lord	120.00	60.00
23 Sherry Magee	150.00	75.00
24 John McGraw MG	250.00	125.00
25 Earl Moore	120.00	60.00
26 Red Murray	120.00	60.00
27 Tris Speaker	600.00	300.00
28 Terry Turner	120.00	60.00
29 Honus Wagner	1000.00	500.00
30 Cy Young	600.00	300.00

1910 E98

The cards in this 30-card set measure 1 1/2" by 2 3/4". E98 is an anonymous set with more similarities to Standard Caramel issues than to Briggs. Most players are found with four different background colors and the brown print checklist (starts with "1. Christy Mathewson") has been alphabetized below. The set was issued in 1910.

	Ex-Mt	VG
COMPLETE SET (30)	8000.00	4000.00
1 Chief Bender	200.00	100.00
2 Roger Bresnahan	200.00	100.00
3 Al Bridwell	100.00	50.00
4 Miner Brown	200.00	100.00
5 Frank Chance	200.00	100.00
6 Hal Chase	150.00	75.00
7 Fred Clarke	200.00	100.00
8 Ty Cobb	2000.00	1000.00
9 Eddie Collins	200.00	100.00
10 Jack Coombs	120.00	60.00
11 Bill Dahlen	150.00	75.00
12 Harry Davis	100.00	50.00
13 Red Dooin	100.00	50.00
14 Johnny Evers	200.00	100.00
15 Russ Ford	100.00	50.00
16 Hugh Jennings	200.00	100.00
17 Johnny Kling	100.00	50.00
18 Nap Lajoie	400.00	200.00
19 Connie Mack MG	200.00	100.00
20 Christy Mathewson	600.00	300.00
21 John McGraw MG	200.00	100.00
22 Larry McLean	100.00	50.00
23 Chief Meyers	120.00	60.00
24 George Mullin	120.00	60.00
25 Fred Tenney	100.00	50.00
26 Joe Tinker	350.00	180.00
27 Hippo Vaughn	100.00	50.00
28 Honus Wagner	600.00	300.00
29 Ed Walsh	200.00	100.00
30 Cy Young	400.00	200.00

1910 E101

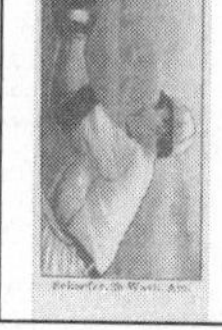

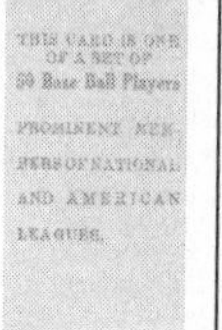

The cards in this 50-card set measure 1 1/2" by 2 3/4". The "Prominent Members of National and American Leagues" portrayed in E101 are identical to the line drawings of E92 and E105. The set was distributed about 1910. The set issuer is not mentioned anywhere on the cards. The complete set price includes all variation cards listed in the checklist below.

	Ex-Mt	VG
COMPLETE SET (50)	10000.00	5000.00
1 Jack Barry	100.00	50.00
2 Harry Bemis	100.00	50.00
3A Chief Bender (white cap)	200.00	100.00
3B Chief Bender (striped cap)	200.00	100.00
4 Bill Bergen	100.00	50.00
5 Bob Bescher	100.00	50.00
6 Al Bridwell	100.00	50.00
7 Doc Casey	100.00	50.00
8 Frank Chance	200.00	100.00
9 Hal Chase	150.00	75.00
10 Ty Cobb	2000.00	1000.00
11 Eddie Collins	300.00	150.00
12 Sam Crawford	200.00	100.00
13 Harry Davis	100.00	50.00
14 Art Devlin	100.00	50.00
15 Bill Donovan	100.00	50.00
16 Red Dooin	100.00	50.00

1910 E101

17 Mickey Doolan 100.00 50.00
18 Patsy Dougherty 100.00 50.00
19A Larry Doyle 120.00 60.00
(batting)
19B Larry Doyle 120.00 60.00
(throwing)
20 Johnny Evers 200.00 100.00
21 George Gibson 100.00 50.00
22 Topsy Hartsel 100.00 50.00
23 Fred Jacklitsch 100.00 50.00
24 Hugh Jennings 200.00 100.00
25 Red Kleinow 100.00 50.00
26 Otto Knabe 100.00 50.00
27 John Knight 100.00 50.00
28 Nap Lajoie 400.00 200.00
29 Hans Lobert 100.00 50.00
30 Sherry Magee 120.00 60.00
31 Christy Mathewson 600.00 300.00
32 John McGraw 300.00 150.00
33 Larry McLean 100.00 50.00
34A J.B. Miller 100.00 50.00
(batting)
34B J.B. Miller 100.00 50.00
(fielding)
35 Danny Murphy 100.00 50.00
36 Bill O'Hara 100.00 50.00
37 Germany Schaefer 120.00 60.00
38 Admiral Schlei 100.00 50.00
39 Boss Schmidt 100.00 50.00
40 Johnny Seigle 100.00 50.00
(sic, Siegle)
41 Dave Shean 100.00 50.00
42 Frank Smith 100.00 50.00
43 Joe Tinker 200.00 100.00
44A Honus Wagner 600.00 300.00
(batting)
44B Honus Wagner 600.00 300.00
(throwing)
45 Cy Young 400.00 200.00
46 Heine Zimmerman 100.00 50.00

1910 E102

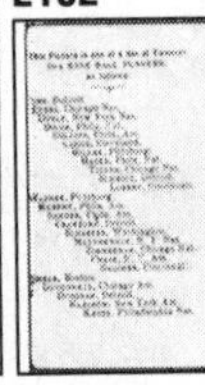

The cards in this 29-card set measure 1 1/2" by 2 3/4". The player poses in E102 are identical to those in E92. The reverse of each card carries an angled checklist (Begins with "COBB, Detroit") printed in black. Smith is not listed, and two poses exist for Doyle, Miller and Wagner. The set was issued circa 1910. The complete set price includes all variation cards listed in the checklist below.

Ex-Mt VG
COMPLETE SET (29) 7000.00 3500.00
1 Chief Bender 200.00 100.00
2 Bob Bescher 100.00 50.00
3 Hal Chase 150.00 75.00
4 Ty Cobb 2000.00 1000.00
5 Eddie Collins 200.00 100.00
6 Sam Crawford 200.00 100.00
7 Bill Donovan 100.00 50.00
8 Red Dooin 100.00 50.00
9 Patsy Dougherty 100.00 50.00
10A Larry Doyle 125.00 60.00
(batting)
10B Larry Doyle 125.00 60.00
(throwing)
11 Johnny Evers 200.00 100.00
12 Red Kleinow 100.00 50.00
13 Otto Knabe 100.00 50.00
14 Nap Lajoie 400.00 200.00
15 Hans Lobert 100.00 50.00
16 Sherry Magee 125.00 60.00
17 Christy Mathewson 600.00 300.00
18A J.B. Miller 100.00 50.00
(batting)
18B J.B. Miller 500.00 250.00
(fielding)
19 Danny Murphy 100.00 50.00
20 Germany Schaefer 125.00 60.00
21 Boss Schmidt 100.00 50.00
22 Boss Schmidt 100.00 50.00
Sic, Spelled as Smith
23 Dave Shean 100.00 50.00
24 Joe Tinker 200.00 100.00
25A Honus Wagner 600.00 300.00
(batting)
25B Honus Wagner 600.00 300.00
(throwing)
26 Heinie Zimmerman 100.00 50.00

1922 E120

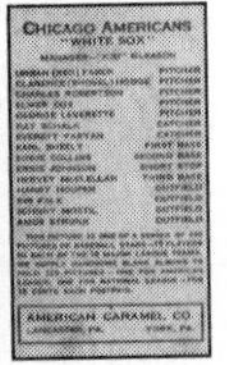

The cards in this 240-card set measure 2" by 3 1/2". The 1922 E120 set was issued by American Caramels and contains unnumbered cards which are numbered here alphabetically within team for convenience. The order of teams is alphabeticallly within league: Boston AL (1-15), Chicago AL (16-30), Cleveland (31-45), Detroit (46-60), New York AL (61-75), Philadelphia AL (76-90), St. Louis AL (91-105), Washington (106-120), Boston NL (121-135), Brooklyn (136-150), Chicago NL (151-165), Cincinnati (166-180), New York NL (181-195), Philadelphia NL (196-210), Pittsburgh (211-225) and St. Louis NL (226-240). This set is one of the most popular of the E card sets.

Ex-Mt VG
COMPLETE SET (240) 12000.00 6000.00
1 George Burns 40.00 20.00
2 John Collins 40.00 20.00
3 Joe Dugan 50.00 25.00
4 Joe Harris 40.00 20.00
5 Bennie Karr 40.00 20.00
6 Nemo Leibold 40.00 20.00
7 Michael Menosky 40.00 20.00
8 Elmer Myers 40.00 20.00
9 Herb Pennock 80.00 40.00
10 Clarke Pittenger 40.00 20.00
11 Derrill Pratt 40.00 20.00
12 John Quinn 50.00 25.00
13 Muddy Ruel 40.00 20.00
14 Elmer Smith 40.00 20.00
15 Al Walters 40.00 20.00
16 Eddie Collins 120.00 60.00
17 Elmer Cox 40.00 20.00
18 Urban Faber 80.00 40.00
19 Bib Falk 40.00 20.00
20 Clarence Hodge 40.00 20.00
21 Harry Hooper 80.00 40.00
22 Ernie Johnson 40.00 20.00
23 Horace Leverette 40.00 20.00
24 Harvey McClellan 40.00 20.00
25 Johnny Mostil 40.00 20.00
26 Charles Robertson 40.00 20.00
27 Ray Schalk 80.00 40.00
28 Earl Sheely 40.00 20.00
29 Amos Strunk 40.00 20.00
30 Clarence Yaryan 40.00 20.00
31 Jim Bagby 40.00 20.00
32 Stan Coveleskie 80.00 40.00
33 Harry Gardner 40.00 20.00
34 Jack Graney 40.00 20.00
35 Charles Jamieson 40.00 20.00
36 John Mails 40.00 20.00
37 Stuffy McInnis 50.00 25.00
38 Leslie Nunamaker 40.00 20.00
39 Steve O'Neill 50.00 25.00
40 Joe Sewell 80.00 40.00
41 Allen Sothoron 40.00 20.00
42 Tris Speaker 200.00 100.00
43 George Uhle 40.00 20.00
44 Bill Wambsganss 50.00 25.00
45 Joe Wood 60.00 30.00
46 John Bassler 40.00 20.00
47 Lu Blue 40.00 20.00
48 Ty Cobb 600.00 300.00
49 Bert Cole 40.00 20.00
50 George Cutshaw 40.00 20.00
51 George Dauss 40.00 20.00
52 Howard Ehmke 50.00 25.00
53 Ira Flagstead 40.00 20.00
54 Harry Heilmann 80.00 40.00
55 Sylvester Johnson 40.00 20.00
56 Bob Jones 40.00 20.00
57 Herman Pillette 40.00 20.00
58 Emory Rigney 40.00 20.00
59 Bob Veach 40.00 20.00
60 Charles Woodall 40.00 20.00
61 Frank Baker 80.00 40.00
62 Joe Bush 50.00 25.00
63 Al DeVormer 40.00 20.00
64 Waite Hoyt 80.00 40.00
65 Sam Jones 50.00 25.00
66 Carl Mays 50.00 25.00
67 Michael McNally 40.00 20.00
68 Bob Meusel 60.00 30.00
69 Elmer Miller 40.00 20.00
70 Wally Pipp 50.00 25.00
71 Babe Ruth 800.00 400.00
72 Wallie Schang 40.00 20.00
73 Everett Scott 50.00 25.00
74 Bob Shawkey 50.00 25.00
75 Aaron Ward 40.00 20.00
76 Frank Calloway 40.00 20.00
77 Jimmy Dykes 60.00 30.00
78 Alfred Fuhrman 40.00 20.00
79 Chick Galloway 40.00 20.00
80 Bryan Harris 40.00 20.00
81 Robert Hasty 40.00 20.00
82 Joe Hauser 40.00 20.00
83 W.F.(Doc) Johnston 40.00 20.00
84 Bing Miller 40.00 20.00
85 Roy Moore 40.00 20.00
86 Roleine Naylor 40.00 20.00
87 Cy Perkins 40.00 20.00
88 Ed Rommel 50.00 25.00
89 Clarence Walker 40.00 20.00
Tillie
90 Frank Welch 40.00 20.00
91 William Bayne 40.00 20.00
92 Pat Collins 40.00 20.00
93 David Danforth 40.00 20.00
94 Frank Davis 40.00 20.00
95 Francis Ellerbe 40.00 20.00
96 Walter Gerber 40.00 20.00
97 Will Jacobson 40.00 20.00
98 Marty McManus 40.00 20.00
99 Hank Severeid 40.00 20.00
100 Urban Shocker 50.00 25.00
101 Charles Shorten 40.00 20.00
102 George Sisler 120.00 60.00
103 John Tobin 40.00 20.00
104 Elam Van Gilder 40.00 20.00
105 Ken Williams 50.00 25.00
106 Henry Courtney 40.00 20.00
107 Edward Gharrity 40.00 20.00
108 Goose Goslin 80.00 40.00
109 Stanley Harris 80.00 40.00
110 Walter Johnson 250.00 125.00
111 Joe Judge 40.00 20.00
112 Clyde Milan 40.00 20.00
113 George Mogridge 40.00 20.00
114 Roger Peckinpaugh 50.00 25.00
115 Tom Phillips 40.00 20.00
116 Val Picinich 40.00 20.00
117 Sam Rice 80.00 40.00
118 Howard Shanks 40.00 20.00
119 Earl Smith 40.00 20.00
120 Tom Zachary 40.00 20.00
121 Walter Barbare 40.00 20.00
122 Norman Boeckel 40.00 20.00
123 Walton Cruise 40.00 20.00
124 Dana Fillingim 40.00 20.00
125 Horace Ford 40.00 20.00
126 Hank Gowdy 50.00 25.00
127 Walter Holke 40.00 20.00
128 Larry Kopf 40.00 20.00
129 Rube Marquard 80.00 40.00
130 Hugh McQuillan 40.00 20.00
131 Joe Oeschger 40.00 20.00
132 George O'Neil 40.00 20.00
133 Roy Powell 40.00 20.00
134 Billy Southworth 50.00 25.00
135 John Watson 40.00 20.00
136 Leon Cadore 40.00 20.00
137 Samuel Crane 40.00 20.00
138 Hank DeBerry 40.00 20.00
139 Tom Griffith 40.00 20.00
140 Burleigh Grimes 80.00 40.00
141 Bernard Hungling 40.00 20.00
142 Jimmy Johnston 40.00 20.00
143 Al Mamaux 40.00 20.00
144 Clarence Mitchell 40.00 20.00
145 Hy Myers 40.00 20.00
146 Ivan Olson 40.00 20.00
147 Dutch Reuther 50.00 25.00
148 Ray Schmandt 40.00 20.00
149 Sherrod Smith 40.00 20.00
150 Zach Wheat 80.00 40.00
151 Victor Aldridge 40.00 20.00
152 Grover C. Alexander 120.00 60.00
153 Tyrus Barber 40.00 20.00
154 Marty Callaghan 40.00 20.00
155 Virgil Cheeves 40.00 20.00
156 Max Flack 40.00 20.00
157 Oscar Grimes 40.00 20.00
158 Gabby Hartnett 80.00 40.00
159 Charles Hollocher 40.00 20.00
160 Percy Jones 40.00 20.00
161 Johnny Kelleher 40.00 20.00
162 Martin Krug 40.00 20.00
163 Hack Miller 40.00 20.00
164 Bob O'Farrell 50.00 25.00
165 Arnold Statz 40.00 20.00
166 Sammy Bohne 40.00 20.00
167 George Burns 40.00 20.00
168 James Caveney 40.00 20.00
169 Jake Daubert 50.00 25.00
170 Pete Donohue 40.00 20.00
171 Pat Duncan 40.00 20.00
172 John Gillespie 40.00 20.00
173 Gene Hargrave 40.00 20.00
Bubbles
174 Dolph Luque 50.00 25.00
175 Cliff Markle 40.00 20.00
176 Greasy Neale 50.00 25.00
177 Ralph Pinelli 50.00 25.00
178 Eppa Rixey 80.00 40.00
179 Ed Roush 80.00 40.00
180 Ivy Wingo 40.00 20.00
181 Dave Bancroft 80.00 40.00
182 Jesse Barnes 40.00 20.00
183 Bill Cunningham 40.00 20.00
184 Phil Douglas 40.00 20.00
185 Frankie Frisch 120.00 60.00
186 Heine Groh 50.00 25.00
187 George Kelly 80.00 40.00
188 Emil Meusel 50.00 25.00
189 Art Nehf 40.00 20.00
190 John Rawlings 40.00 20.00
191 Ralph Shinners 40.00 20.00
192 Earl Smith 40.00 20.00
193 Frank Snyder 40.00 20.00
194 Fred Toney 40.00 20.00
195 Ross (Pep) Young 80.00 40.00
(sic, Youngs)
196 Walter Betts 40.00 20.00
197 Art Fletcher 40.00 20.00
198 Walter Henline 40.00 20.00
199 Wilbur Hubbell 50.00 25.00
200 Lee King 40.00 20.00
201 Roy Leslie 40.00 20.00
202 Henry Meadows 40.00 20.00
203 Frank Parkinson 40.00 20.00
204 Jack Peters 40.00 20.00
205 Joseph Rapp 40.00 20.00
206 James Ring 40.00 20.00
207 Colonel Snover 40.00 20.00
208 Curtis Walker 40.00 20.00
209 Cy Williams 50.00 25.00
210 Russel Wrightstone 40.00 20.00
211 Babe Adams 60.00 30.00
212 Clyde Barnhart 40.00 20.00
213 Carlson Bigbee 40.00 20.00
214 Max Carey 80.00 40.00
215 Wilbur Cooper 40.00 20.00
216 Charles Glazner 40.00 20.00
217 Johnny Gooch 40.00 20.00
218 Charlie Grimm 50.00 25.00
219 Earl Hamilton 40.00 20.00
220 Rabbit Maranville 80.00 40.00
221 John L. Mokan 40.00 20.00
222 John Morrison 40.00 20.00
223 Walter Schmidt 40.00 20.00
224 James Tierney 40.00 20.00
225 Pie Traynor 80.00 40.00
226 Edward Ainsmith 40.00 20.00
227 Vern Clemons 40.00 20.00
228 William Doak 40.00 20.00
229 John Fournier 40.00 20.00
230 Jesse Haines 80.00 40.00
231 Cliff Heathcoate 40.00 20.00
232 Rogers Hornsby 200.00 100.00
233 John Lavan 40.00 20.00
234 Austin McHenry 40.00 20.00
235 Wil Pertice 40.00 20.00
236 Joe Schultz 40.00 20.00
237 William Sherdel 40.00 20.00
238 Jack Smith 40.00 20.00
239 Milton Stock 40.00 20.00
240 George Torporcer 40.00 20.00

1921-22 E121 Series of 120

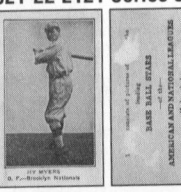

The cards in this set measure 2" by 3 1/2". Many of the photos which appear in the "Series of 80" are duplicated in the so-called "Series of 120". As noted above, the variations in titling and photos have run the known number of cards past the original statement of length and collectors should expect to encounter additions to both E121 lists in the future. The cards have been alphabetized and numbered in the checklist below. The complete set price includes all variation cards listed in the checklist below.

Ex-Mt VG
COMPLETE SET (136) 10000.00 5000.00
1 Babe Adams 40.00 20.00
2 Grover C. Alexander 120.00 60.00
3 Jim Bagby 30.00 15.00
4 Dave Bancroft 60.00 30.00
5 Turner Barber 30.00 15.00
6A Carlson Bigbee 30.00 15.00
6B Carlson Bigbee 30.00 15.00
6C Corson L. Bigbee 30.00 15.00
6D L. Bigbee 30.00 15.00
7 Joe Bush 40.00 20.00
8 Max Carey 60.00 30.00
9 Cecil Causey 30.00 15.00
10A Ty Cobb 600.00 300.00
batting
10B Ty Cobb 600.00 300.00
throwing
11 Eddie Collins 60.00 30.00
12 A. Wilbur Cooper 30.00 15.00
13 Stan Coveleskie 60.00 30.00
14 Dave Danforth 30.00 15.00
15 Jake Daubert 40.00 20.00
16 George Dauss 30.00 15.00
17 Dixie Davis 30.00 15.00
18 Al DeVormer 30.00 15.00
19 William Doak 30.00 15.00
20 Phil Douglas 30.00 15.00
21 Urban Faber 60.00 30.00
22 Bib Falk 30.00 15.00
23 Chick Fewster 30.00 15.00
24 Max Flack 30.00 15.00
25 Ira Flagstead 30.00 15.00
26 Frankie Frisch 100.00 50.00
27 Larry Gardner 30.00 15.00
28 Alexander Gaston 30.00 15.00
29 E.P. Gharrity 30.00 15.00
30 George Gibson 30.00 15.00
31 Whitey Glazner 30.00 15.00
32 Kid Gleason MG 40.00 20.00
33 Hank Gowdy 40.00 20.00
34 John Graney 30.00 15.00
35 Tom Griffith 30.00 15.00
36 Charlie Grimm 40.00 20.00
37 Heinie Groh 40.00 20.00
38 Jesse Haines 60.00 30.00
39 Harry Harper 30.00 15.00
40A Harry Heilman 60.00 30.00
40B Harry Heilmann 60.00 30.00
41 Clarence Hodge 30.00 15.00
42A Walter Holke 30.00 15.00
portrait
42B Walter Holke 30.00 15.00
throwing
43 Charles Hollocher 30.00 15.00
44 Harry Hooper 60.00 30.00
45 Rogers Hornsby 120.00 60.00
46 Waite Hoyt 60.00 30.00
47 Miller Huggins MG 60.00 30.00
48 Walter Johnson 300.00 150.00
49 Joe Judge 30.00 15.00
50 George Kelly 60.00 30.00
51 Dick Kerr 40.00 20.00
52 P.J. Kilduff 30.00 15.00
53A Bill Killifer 30.00 15.00
bat on shoulder
53B Bill Killifer 30.00 15.00
throwing
54 John Lavan 30.00 15.00
55 Walter Mails 30.00 15.00
56 Rabbit Maranville 60.00 30.00
57 Elwood Martin 30.00 15.00
58 Carl Mays 40.00 20.00
59 John J. McGraw MG 100.00 50.00
60 Jack McInnis 40.00 20.00
61 M.J. McNally 30.00 15.00
62 Emil Meusel 30.00 15.00
63 Bob Meusel 50.00 25.00
64 Clyde Milan 40.00 20.00
65 Elmer Miller 30.00 15.00
66 Otto Miller 30.00 15.00
67 Johnny Mostil 30.00 15.00
68 Eddie Mulligan 30.00 15.00
69A Hy Myers 30.00 15.00
69B Hy Myers 30.00 15.00
70 Greasy Neale 50.00 25.00
71 Art Nehf 30.00 15.00
72 Leslie Nunamaker 30.00 15.00
73 Joe Oeschger 30.00 15.00
74 Charley O'Leary CO 30.00 15.00
75 Steve O'Neill 40.00 20.00
76 Del Pratt 30.00 15.00
77 John Rawlings 30.00 15.00
78 Sam Rice 60.00 30.00
79A Eppa J. Rixey 60.00 30.00
79B Eppa Rixey 60.00 30.00
80 Wilbert Robinson MG 60.00 30.00
81 Tom Rogers 30.00 15.00
82A Ed Rommel 40.00 20.00
82B Ed Rounnel 40.00 20.00
83 Ed Roush 60.00 30.00
84 Muddy Ruel 30.00 15.00
85 Walter Ruether 40.00 20.00
86A Babe Ruth 800.00 400.00
three pictures
86B Babe Ruth 1000.00 500.00
three pictures
86C Babe Ruth 800.00 400.00
holding bird
86D Babe Ruth 1000.00 500.00
holding bird
86E Babe Ruth 800.00 400.00
holding ball in right hand
87 Bill Ryan 30.00 15.00
88A Ray Schalk 60.00 30.00
catching
88B Ray Schalk 60.00 30.00
bunting
89 Wally Schang 30.00 15.00
90 Ferd Schupp 30.00 15.00
91 Everett Scott 40.00 20.0
92 Joe Sewell 60.00 30.0
93 Bob Shawkey 40.00 20.0
94 Pat Shea 30.00 15.0
95 Earl Sheely 30.00 15.0
96 Urban Shocker 40.00 20.0
97A George Sisler 100.00 50.0
batting
97B George Sisler 100.00 50.0
throwing
98 Earl Smith 30.00 15.0
99 Elmer Smith 30.00 15.0
100 Frank Snyder 30.00 15.0
101 Billy Southworth 40.00 20.0
102A Tris Speaker 120.00 60.0
large projection
102B Tris Speaker 120.00 60.0
small projection
103A Milton Stock 30.00 15.0
103B Milton Stock 30.00 15.0
104 Amos Strunk 30.00 15.0
105 Zeb Terry 30.00 15.0
106 Fred Toney 30.00 15.0
107 George Torporcer 30.00 15.0
108 Bob Veach 30.00 15.0
109 Oscar Vitt 30.00 15.0
110 Curtis Walker 30.00 15.0
111 Bill Wambsganss 40.00 20.0
112 Aaron Ward 30.00 15.0
113 Zach Wheat 60.00 30.0
114A George Whitted 30.00 15.0
Brooklyn
114B George Whitted 30.00 15.0
Pittsburgh
115 Fred Williams 40.00 20.0
116 Ivy Wingo 30.00 15.0
117 Ross Young 60.00 30.0
sic, Youngs

1921-22 E121 Series of 80

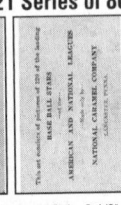

The cards in this set measure 2" by 3 1/2". E121 sets contain many errors, misspelli[ngs] and minor variations in titles and photos, wh[ich] accounts for the difficulty in collecting [an] entire set. Many photos were taken from E[...] and a fine screen is apparent on the cards. American Caramel Co. marketed this black [and] white issue about 1922. Many locali[zed] advertising reverses have been found, a[nd] these cards more properly belong to the[ir] classification than to E121. The cards h[ave] been alphabetized and numbered in [the] checklist below. The complete set p[rice] includes all variation cards listed in [the] checklist below.

Ex-Mt
COMPLETE SET (134) 10000.00 5000
1A Grover C. Alexander 120.00 60
1B Grover C. Alexander 100.00 50
2 Jim Bagby 30.00 15
3A Frank Baker 60.00 30
3B Frank Baker 60.00 30
4A Dave Bancroft 60.00 30
batting
4B Dave Bancroft 60.00 30
fielding
5 Ping Bodie 30.00 15
6 George Burns 30.00 15
7 Geo. J. Burns 30.00 15
8 Owen Bush 30.00 15
9A Max Carey 60.00 30
batting
9B Max Carey 60.00 30
hands on hips
10 Cecil Causey 30.00 15
11A Ty Cobb Mgr. 600.00 300
11B Ty Cobb Manager 600.00 300
12 Eddie Collins 60.00 30
13 Rip Collins 30.00 15
14 Jake Daubert 40.00 20
15 George Dauss 30.00 15
16A Charles Deal 30.00 15
dark uniform
16B Charles Deal 30.00 1
light uniform
17 William Doak 30.00 1
18 Bill Donovan 30.00 1
19 Phil Douglas 30.00 1
20A Johnny Evers Manager 60.00 3
20B Johnny Evers Mgr. 60.00 3
21A Urban Faber 60.00 3
dark uniform
21B Urban Faber 60.00 3
white uniform
22 Wm. Fewster 30.00 1
23 Eddie Foster 30.00 1
24 Frankie Frisch 100.00 5
25 Larry Gardner 30.00 1
26 Alexander Gaston 30.00 1
27 Kid Gleason MG 40.00 2
28 Mike Gonzalez 30.00 1
29 Hank Gowdy 40.00 2
30 John Graney 30.00 1
31 Tom Griffith 30.00 1
32 Heinie Groh 40.00 2
33 Harry Harper 30.00 1
34 Harry Heilmann 60.00 3
35A Walter Holke 30.00 1
portrait
35B Walter Holke 30.00 1
throwing
36 Charles Hollacher 30.00 1
37 Harry Hooper 60.00
38 Rogers Hornsby 120.00
39 Waite Hoyt 60.00
40 Miller Huggins MG 60.00

41 Baby Doll Jacobson	30.00	15.00
42 Hugh Jennings MG	60.00	30.00
43A Walter Johnson	300.00	150.00
throwing		
43B Walter Johnson	300.00	150.00
arms at chest		
44 James Johnston	30.00	15.00
45 Joe Judge	30.00	15.00
46 George Kelly	60.00	30.00
47 Dick Kerr	40.00	20.00
48 Pete Kilduff	30.00	15.00
49A Bill Killefer	30.00	15.00
49B Bill Killifer	30.00	15.00
50 John Lavan	30.00	15.00
51 Nemo Leibold	30.00	15.00
52 Duffy Lewis	30.00	15.00
53 Al Mamaux	30.00	15.00
54 Rabbit Maranville	60.00	30.00
55A Carl May	40.00	20.00
(sic, Mays)		
55B Carl Mays	40.00	20.00
56 John McGraw MG	100.00	50.00
57 Snuffy McInnis	40.00	20.00
58 M.J. McNally	30.00	15.00
59 Emil Muesel	30.00	15.00
60 Bob Meusel	50.00	25.00
61 Clyde Milan	40.00	20.00
62 Elmer Miller	30.00	15.00
63 Otto Miller	30.00	15.00
64 Guy Morton	30.00	15.00
65 Eddie Murphy	30.00	15.00
66 Hy Myers	30.00	15.00
67 Art Nehf	30.00	15.00
68 Steve O'Neill	30.00	15.00
69A Roger Peckinbaugh	40.00	20.00
sic		
69B Roger Peckinpaugh	40.00	20.00
70 Jeff Pfeffer	30.00	15.00
Brooklyn		
71 Jeff Pfeffer	30.00	15.00
St. Louis NL		
72 Wally Pipp	40.00	20.00
73 Jack Quinn	30.00	15.00
74 John Rawlings	30.00	15.00
75 Sam Rice	60.00	30.00
76 Eppa Rixey	60.00	30.00
77 Wilburt Robinson MG	60.00	30.00
78 Tom Rogers	30.00	15.00
79 Robert Roth	30.00	15.00
80 Bill Ryan	30.00	15.00
81 Ed Roush	60.00	30.00
82A Babe Ruth	800.00	400.00
Babe Ruth		
82B Babe Ruth	1000.00	500.00
Babe is in parentheses "Babe"		
82C Babe Ruth	800.00	400.00
George Ruth		
83A Slim Sallee	30.00	15.00
ball in hand		
83B Slim Sallee	30.00	15.00
no ball		
84 Ray Schalk	60.00	30.00
85 Walter Schang	30.00	15.00
86A Ferd Schupp	30.00	15.00
86B Fred Schupp	30.00	15.00
87 Everett Scott	30.00	15.00
88 Hank Severeid	30.00	15.00
89 Bob Shawkey	40.00	20.00
90A Pat Shea	30.00	15.00
90B Pat Shea	30.00	15.00
91A George Sisler	100.00	50.00
batting		
91B George Sisler	100.00	50.00
throwing		
92 Earl Smith	30.00	15.00
93 Frank Snyder	30.00	15.00
94A Tris Speaker Manager	120.00	60.00
94B Tris Speaker Mgr.	120.00	60.00
95 Milton Stock	30.00	15.00
96 Amos Strunk	30.00	15.00
97 Zeb Terry	30.00	15.00
98 Chester Thomas	30.00	15.00
99A Fred Toney	30.00	15.00
foot up		
99B Fred Toney	30.00	15.00
both feet down		
100 George Tyler	30.00	15.00
101A Jim Vaughn	30.00	15.00
plain uniform		
101B Jim Vaughn	30.00	15.00
striped uniform		
102A Bob Veach	30.00	15.00
arm raised		
102B Bob Veach	30.00	15.00
folded arms		
103 Oscar Vitt	30.00	15.00
104 Bill Wambsganss	40.00	20.00
105 Aaron Ward	30.00	15.00
106 Zach Wheat	60.00	30.00
107 George Whitted	30.00	15.00
108 Fred Williams	40.00	20.00
109 Ivy Wingo	30.00	15.00
110 Joe Wood	50.00	25.00
111 Pep Young	30.00	15.00

1910 E-Unc. Orange Bordered Strip Cards

This unusual card set features black-and-white pictures surrounded by a thin orange border and measures approximately 1 5/8" by 2 5/8". These orange bordered cards apparently were part of a box of candy. Only 24 cards are checklisted below, but the box indicates that there are 144 in the whole set. Any known additions to the checklist would be welcomed.

	Ex-Mt	VG
COMPLETE SET	3500.00	1800.00
Pittsburgh Pirates TP	50.00	25.00
Detroit Tigers TP	50.00	25.00
Bill Bergen	50.00	25.00
Bill Carrigan	50.00	25.00
Hal Chase	100.00	50.00
Fred Clarke UER	150.00	75.00
(misspelled Clark)		
Ty Cobb	1200.00	600.00
Sam Crawford	150.00	75.00
Lou Criger	50.00	25.00
0 Mickey Doolan	50.00	25.00
1 George Gibson	50.00	25.00

12 Frank LaPorte	50.00	25.00
13 Nap Lajoie	300.00	150.00
14 Harry Lord	50.00	25.00
15 Christy Mathewson	300.00	150.00
16 John McGraw MG	150.00	75.00
17 Dots Miller	50.00	25.00
18 George Mullin	50.00	25.00
19 Eddie Plank	150.00	75.00
20 Tris Speaker	250.00	125.00
21 Jake Stahl	50.00	25.00
22 Heinie Wagner	50.00	25.00
23 Honus Wagner	400.00	200.00
24 Jack Warhop	50.00	25.00

1995 Eagle Ballpark Legends

Upper Deck produced this nine-card standard-size set as part of a promotion for Eagle Ballpark Style Peanuts. The set could be obtained by sending in a cash register receipt as evidence for the purchase of two cans Eagle Ballpark Style Peanuts (11 oz. or larger) and $1.00 to cover shipping and handling. The fronts freature full-bleed sepia-toned player photos. The sponsor logo appears in the upper left corner, the Upper Deck logo in the lower left, and the player's name across the bottom. The backs present player profile and career highlights. Some card sets contained randomly inserted autographed Harmon Killebrew cards.

	Nm-Mt	Ex-Mt
COMPLETE SET (9)	10.00	3.00
1 Nolan Ryan	5.00	1.50
2 Reggie Jackson	2.00	.60
3 Tom Seaver	2.00	.60
4 Harmon Killebrew	.75	.23
5 Ted Williams	4.00	1.20
6 Whitey Ford	2.00	.60
7 Al Kaline	1.50	.45
8 Willie Stargell	.75	.23
9 Bob Gibson	.75	.23
S4 Harmon Killebrew AU	25.00	7.50

1889 Edgerton R. Williams Game

The cards measure 2 7/16" by 3 1/2" and have green tinted backs and was issued as part of a parlor game. Each card features two players on the front -- therefore 38 players in total are featured in the set. Only the cards with Baseball players are included in this checklist.

	Ex-Mt	VG
COMPLETE SET (19)	7000.00	3500.00
1 Cap Anson	600.00	300.00
Buck Ewing		
2 Dan Brouthers	500.00	250.00
Arlie Latham		
3 Charlie Buffington	300.00	150.00
Bob Carruthers		
4 Fred Carroll	300.00	150.00
Hick Carpenter		
5 Roger Connor	600.00	300.00
Charles Comiskey		
6 Pop Corkhill	300.00	150.00
Jim Fogarty		
7 John Clarkson	600.00	300.00
Tim Keefe		
8 Jerry Denny	300.00	150.00
Mike Tiernan		
9 Dave Foutz	500.00	250.00
King Kelly		
10 Pud Galvin	500.00	250.00
Dave Orr		
11 Jack Glasscock	400.00	200.00
Tommy Tucker		
12 Mike Griffin	300.00	150.00
Ed McKean		
13 Dummy Hoy	400.00	200.00
John Reilly		
14 Arthur Irwin	300.00	150.00
Ned Williamson		
15 Silver King	300.00	150.00
John Tener		
16 Al Myers	300.00	150.00
Cub Stricker		
17 Fred Pfeffer	300.00	150.00
Jimmy Wolf		
18 Toad Ramsey	300.00	150.00
Gus Weyhing		
19 Mickey Ward	300.00	150.00
Curt Welch		

1994 El Sid Pogs

Titled "Limited Edition El Sid." Blank-backed white milk cap-types. Foil on fronts; measure about 1 5/8" in diameter. No other ID markings.

	Nm-Mt	Ex-Mt
COMPLETE SET (5)	1.00	.30
COMMON CARD (1-5)	.25	.07

1990 Elite Senior League

The 1990 Elite Senior Pro League Set was a 126-card standard-size set issued after the

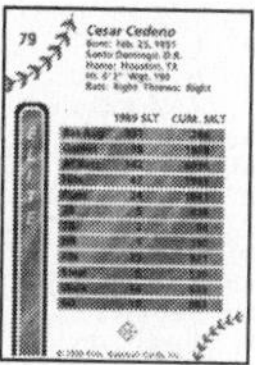

conclusion of the first Senior League season. The card stock was essentially the same type of card stock used by Upper Deck. The set featured full-color fronts and had complete Senior League stats on the back. It has been reported that there were 5,000 cases of these cards produced. Prior to the debut of the set, Elite also passed out (to prospective dealers) two promo cards for the set, Earl Weaver (numbered 120 rather than 91) and Mike Easler (numbered 1 rather than 19).

	Nm-Mt	Ex-Mt
COMPLETE SET (126)	5.00	1.50
1 Curt Flood COMM	.25	.07
2 Bob Tolan	.05	.02
3 Dick Bosman	.05	.02
4 Ivan DeJesus	.05	.02
5 Dock Ellis	.10	.03
6 Roy Howell	.05	.02
7 Lamar Johnson	.05	.02
8 Steve Kemp	.05	.02
9 Ken Landreaux	.05	.02
10 Randy Lerch	.05	.02
11 Jon Matlack	.05	.02
12 Gary Rajsich	.05	.02
13 Lenny Randle	.05	.02
14 Elias Sosa	.05	.02
15 Ozzie Virgil	.05	.02
16 Milt Wilcox	.05	.02
17 Steve Henderson 3X	.05	.02
18 Ray Burris	.05	.02
19 Mike Easler	.05	.02
20 Juan Eichelberger	.05	.02
21 Rollie Fingers	.50	.15
22 Toby Harrah	.05	.02
23 Randy Johnson	.05	.02
24 Dave Kingman	.25	.07
25 Lee Lacy	.05	.02
26 Tito Landrum	.05	.02
27 Paul Mirabella	.05	.02
28 Mickey Rivers	.10	.03
29 Rodney Scott	.05	.02
30 Tim Stoddard	.05	.02
31 Ron Washington	.05	.02
32 Jerry White	.05	.02
33 Dick Williams MG	.10	.03
34 Clete Boyer MG	.05	.02
35 Steve Dillard	.05	.02
36 Garth Iorg	.05	.02
37 Bruce Kison	.05	.02
38 Wayne Krenchicki	.05	.02
39 Ron LeFlore	.10	.03
40 Tippy Martinez	.05	.02
41 Omar Moreno	.05	.02
42 Jim Morrison	.05	.02
43 Graig Nettles	.15	.04
44 Jim Nettles	.05	.02
45 Wayne Nordhagen	.05	.02
46 Al Oliver	.15	.04
47 Jerry Royster	.05	.02
48 Sammy Stewart	.05	.02
49 Randy Bass	.05	.02
50 Vida Blue	.15	.04
51 Bruce Bochy	.05	.02
52 Doug Corbett	.05	.02
53 Jose Cruz	.10	.03
54 Jamie Easterly	.05	.02
55 Pete Falcone	.05	.02
56 Bob Galasso	.05	.02
57 Johnny Grubb	.05	.02
58 Bake McBride	.05	.02
59 Dyar Miller	.05	.02
60 Tom Paciorek	.10	.03
61 Ken Reitz	.05	.02
62 U.L. Washington	.05	.02
63 Alan Ashby	.05	.02
64 Pat Dobson	.05	.02
65 Doug Bird	.05	.02
66 Marty Castillo	.05	.02
67 Dan Driessen	.05	.02
68 Wayne Garland	.05	.02
69 Tim Ireland	.05	.02
70 Ron Jackson	.05	.02
71 Bobby Jones	.05	.02
72 Dennis Leonard	.05	.02
73 Rick Manning	.05	.02
74 Amos Otis	.10	.03
75 Pat Putnam	.05	.02
76 Eric Rasmussen	.05	.02
77 Paul Blair	.05	.02
78 Bert Campaneris	.10	.03
79 Cesar Cedeno	.10	.03
80 Ed Figueroa	.05	.02
81 Ross Grimsley	.05	.02
82 George Hendrick	.05	.02
83 Cliff Johnson	.05	.02
84 Mike Kekich	.05	.02
85 Rafael Landestoy	.05	.02
86 Larry Milbourne	.05	.02
87 Bobby Molinaro	.05	.02
88 Sid Monge	.05	.02
89 Rennie Stennett	.05	.02
90 Derrell Thomas	.05	.02
91 Earl Weaver MG	.50	.15
92 Gary Allenson	.05	.02
93 Pedro Borbon	.05	.02
94 Al Bumbry	.05	.02
95 Bill Campbell	.05	.02
96 Bernie Carbo	.05	.02
97 Fergie Jenkins	.50	.15
98 Pete LaCock	.05	.02
99 Bill Lee	.10	.03
100 Tommy McMillan	.05	.02
101 Joe Pittman	.05	.02
102 Gene Richards	.05	.02
103 Leon Roberts	.05	.02
104 Tony Scott	.05	.02
105 Doug Simunic	.05	.02
106 Rick Wise	.05	.02
107 Willie Aikens	.05	.02
108 Juan Beniquez	.05	.02
109 Bobby Bonds	.15	.04
110 Sergio Ferrer	.05	.02
111 Chuck Ficks	.05	.02
112 George Foster	.15	.04
113 Dave Hilton	.05	.02
114 Al Holland	.05	.02
115 Clint Hurdle	.05	.02
116 Bill Madlock	.15	.04
117 Steve Ontiveros	.05	.02
118 Roy Thomas	.05	.02
119 Luis Tiant	.15	.04
120 Walt Williams	.05	.02
121 Vida Blue	.15	.04
122 Bobby Bonds	.25	.07
123 Rollie Fingers	.50	.15
124 George Foster	.15	.04
125 Fergie Jenkins	.50	.15
126 Dave Kingman	.25	.07

1995 Emotion

This 200-card standard-size set was produced by Fleer/SkyBox. The first-year brand has double-thick card stock with borderless fronts. Card fronts and backs are either horizontal or vertical. On the front of each player card is a theme such as Class (Cal Ripken) and Confident (Barry Bonds). The backs have two player photos, '94 stats and career numbers. The checklist is arranged alphabetically by team with AL preceding NL. Notable Rookie Cards include Hideo Nomo.

	Nm-Mt	Ex-Mt
COMPLETE SET (200)	40.00	12.00
1 Brady Anderson	.40	.12
2 Kevin Brown	.40	.12
3 Curtis Goodwin	.20	.06
4 Jeffrey Hammonds	.20	.06
5 Ben McDonald	.20	.06
6 Mike Mussina	1.00	.30
7 Rafael Palmeiro	.60	.18
8 Cal Ripken Jr.	3.00	.90
9 Jose Canseco	1.00	.30
10 Roger Clemens	2.00	.60
11 Vaughn Eshelman	.20	.06
12 Mike Greenwell	.20	.06
13 Erik Hanson	.20	.06
14 Tim Naehring	.20	.06
15 Aaron Sele	.20	.06
16 John Valentin	.20	.06
17 Mo Vaughn	.40	.12
18 Chili Davis	.40	.12
19 Gary DiSarcina	.20	.06
20 Chuck Finley	.40	.12
21 Tim Salmon	.60	.18
22 Lee Smith	.40	.12
23 J.T. Snow	.40	.12
24 Jim Abbott	.60	.18
25 Jason Bere	.20	.06
26 Ray Durham	.40	.12
27 Ozzie Guillen	.20	.06
28 Tim Raines	.40	.12
29 Frank Thomas	1.00	.30
30 Robin Ventura	.40	.12
31 Carlos Baerga	.20	.06
32 Albert Belle	.40	.12
33 Orel Hershiser	.40	.12
34 Kenny Lofton	.40	.12
35 Dennis Martinez	.40	.12
36 Eddie Murray	1.00	.30
37 Manny Ramirez	.40	.12
38 Julian Tavarez	.20	.06
39 Jim Thome	1.00	.30
40 Dave Winfield	.40	.12
41 Chad Curtis	.20	.06
42 Cecil Fielder	.40	.12
43 Travis Fryman	.40	.12
44 Kirk Gibson	.40	.12
45 Bobby Higginson RC	1.00	.30
46 Alan Trammell	.60	.18
47 Lou Whitaker	.40	.12
48 Kevin Appier	.40	.12
49 Gary Gaetti	.40	.12
50 Jeff Montgomery	.20	.06
51 Jon Nunnally	.20	.06
52 Ricky Bones	.20	.06
53 Cal Eldred	.20	.06
54 Joe Oliver	.20	.06
55 Kevin Seitzer	.20	.06
56 Marty Cordova	.20	.06
57 Chuck Knoblauch	.40	.12
58 Kirby Puckett	1.00	.30
59 Wade Boggs	.60	.18
60 Derek Jeter	2.50	.75
61 Jimmy Key	.40	.12
62 Don Mattingly	2.50	.75
63 Jack McDowell	.20	.06
64 Paul O'Neill	.60	.18
65 Andy Pettitte	.60	.18
66 Ruben Rivera	.20	.06
67 Mike Stanley	.20	.06
68 John Wetteland	.40	.12
69 Geronimo Berroa	.20	.06
70 Dennis Eckersley	.40	.12
71 Rickey Henderson	1.00	.30
72 Mark McGwire	2.50	.75
73 Steve Ontiveros	.20	.06
74 Ruben Sierra	.20	.06
75 Terry Steinbach	.20	.06
76 Jay Buhner	.40	.12
77 Ken Griffey Jr.	1.50	.45
78 Randy Johnson	1.00	.30
79 Edgar Martinez	.60	.18
80 Tino Martinez	.60	.18
81 Marc Newfield	.20	.06
82 Alex Rodriguez	2.50	.75
83 Will Clark	1.00	.30
84 Benji Gil	.20	.06
85 Juan Gonzalez	1.00	.30
86 Rusty Greer	.40	.12
87 Dean Palmer	.40	.12
88 Ivan Rodriguez	1.00	.30
89 Kenny Rogers	.40	.12
90 Roberto Alomar	1.00	.30
91 Joe Carter	.40	.12
92 David Cone	.40	.12
93 Alex Gonzalez	.20	.06
94 Shawn Green	.40	.12
95 Pat Hentgen	.20	.06
96 Paul Molitor	.60	.18
97 John Olerud	.40	.12
98 Devon White	.40	.12
99 Steve Avery	.20	.06
100 Tom Glavine	.60	.18
101 Marquis Grissom	.20	.06
102 Chipper Jones	1.00	.30
103 David Justice	.40	.12
104 Ryan Klesko	.40	.12
105 Javier Lopez	.40	.12
106 Greg Maddux	1.50	.45
107 Fred McGriff	.60	.18
108 John Smoltz	.60	.18
109 Shawon Dunston	.20	.06
110 Mark Grace	.60	.18
111 Brian McRae	.20	.06
112 Randy Myers	.20	.06
113 Sammy Sosa	1.50	.45
114 Steve Trachsel	.20	.06
115 Bret Boone	.40	.12
116 Ron Gant	.40	.12
117 Barry Larkin	1.00	.30
118 Deion Sanders	.60	.18
119 Reggie Sanders	.40	.12
120 Pete Schourek	.20	.06
121 John Smiley	.20	.06
122 Jason Bates	.20	.06
123 Dante Bichette	.40	.12
124 Vinny Castilla	.40	.12
125 Andres Galarraga	.40	.12
126 Larry Walker	.60	.18
127 Greg Colbrunn	.20	.06
128 Jeff Conine	.40	.12
129 Andre Dawson	.40	.12
130 Chris Hammond	.20	.06
131 Charles Johnson	.40	.12
132 Gary Sheffield	.40	.12
133 Quilvio Veras	.20	.06
134 Jeff Bagwell	.60	.18
135 Derek Bell	.20	.06
136 Craig Biggio	.60	.18
137 Jim Dougherty RC	.20	.06
138 John Hudek	.20	.06
139 Orlando Miller	.20	.06
140 Phil Plantier	.20	.06
141 Eric Karros	.40	.12
142 Ramon Martinez	.20	.06
143 Raul Mondesi	.40	.12
144 Hideo Nomo RC	2.00	.60
145 Mike Piazza	1.50	.45
146 Ismael Valdes	.20	.06
147 Todd Worrell	.20	.06
148 Moises Alou	.40	.12
149 Yamil Benitez RC	.20	.06
150 Wil Cordero	.20	.06
151 Jeff Fassero	.20	.06
152 Cliff Floyd	.40	.12
153 Pedro Martinez	1.00	.30
154 Carlos Perez RC	.40	.12
155 Tony Tarasco	.20	.06
156 Rondell White	.40	.12
157 Edgardo Alfonzo	.40	.12
158 Bobby Bonilla	.40	.12
159 Rico Brogna	.20	.06
160 Bobby Jones	.20	.06
161 Bill Pulsipher	.20	.06
162 Bret Saberhagen	.40	.12
163 Ricky Bottalico	.20	.06
164 Darren Daulton	.40	.12
165 Lenny Dykstra	.40	.12
166 Charlie Hayes	.20	.06
167 Dave Hollins	.20	.06
168 Gregg Jefferies	.20	.06
169 Michael Mimbs RC	.20	.06
170 Curt Schilling	.60	.18
171 Heathcliff Slocumb	.20	.06
172 Jay Bell	.40	.12
173 Micah Franklin RC	.20	.06
174 Mark Johnson RC	.40	.12
175 Jeff King	.20	.06
176 Al Martin	.20	.06
177 Dan Miceli	.20	.06
178 Denny Neagle	.40	.12
179 Bernard Gilkey	.20	.06
180 Ken Hill	.20	.06
181 Brian Jordan	.40	.12
182 Ray Lankford	.20	.06
183 Ozzie Smith	1.50	.45
184 Andy Benes	.20	.06
185 Ken Caminiti	.40	.12
186 Steve Finley	.40	.12
187 Tony Gwynn	1.25	.35
188 Joey Hamilton	.20	.06
189 Melvin Nieves	.20	.06
190 Scott Sanders	.20	.06
191 Rod Beck	.20	.06
192 Barry Bonds	2.50	.75
193 Royce Clayton	.20	.06
194 Glenallen Hill	.20	.06
195 Darren Lewis	.20	.06
196 Mark Portugal	.20	.06
197 Matt Williams	.40	.12
198 Checklist 1-82	.20	.06
199 Checklist 83-162	.20	.06
200 CL 163-200/Inserts	.20	.06
P8 Cal Ripken Promo	2.00	.60

1995 Emotion Masters

The theme of this 10-card standard-size set is the showcasing of players that come through in the clutch. Randomly inserted at a rate of one in eight packs, a player photo is superimposed over a larger photo that is ghosted in a color emblematic of that team. The player's name

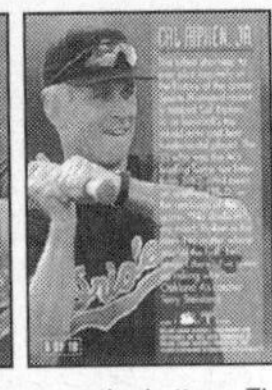

and the Emotion logo are at the bottom. The backs have a photo to the left and text to the right. Both sides of the card are shaded in the color scheme of the player's team.

	Nm-Mt	Ex-Mt
COMPLETE SET (10)	40.00	12.00
1 Barry Bonds	8.00	2.40
2 Juan Gonzalez	3.00	.90
3 Ken Griffey Jr.	5.00	1.50
4 Tony Gwynn	4.00	1.20
5 Kenny Lofton	1.25	.35
6 Greg Maddux	5.00	1.50
7 Raul Mondesi	1.25	.35
8 Cal Ripken	10.00	3.00
9 Frank Thomas	3.00	.90
10 Matt Williams	1.25	.35

1995 Emotion N-Tense

Randomly inserted at a rate of one in 37 packs, this 12-card standard-size set features fronts that have a player photo surrounded by a swirling color scheme and a large holographic "N" in the background. The backs feature a like color scheme with text and player photo.

	Nm-Mt	Ex-Mt
COMPLETE SET (12)	100.00	30.00
1 Jeff Bagwell	5.00	1.50
2 Albert Belle	3.00	.90
3 Barry Bonds	20.00	6.00
4 Cecil Fielder	3.00	.90
5 Ron Gant	3.00	.90
6 Ken Griffey Jr.	12.00	3.60
7 Mark McGwire	20.00	6.00
8 Mike Piazza	12.00	3.60
9 Manny Ramirez	3.00	.90
10 Frank Thomas	8.00	2.40
11 Mo Vaughn	3.00	.90
12 Matt Williams	3.00	.90

1995 Emotion Ripken

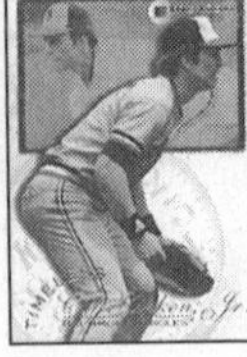

This 15-card Cal Ripken standard-size set features great moments from the career of the Baltimore Orioles' great. Inserted at a rate of one in 12 packs, cards 1-10 feature moments actually selected by the record-breaking shortstop. Referred to as "Timeless", an action photo of Ripken is superimposed over a silver background that includes a watch and another photo at the top. The backs elaborate on the event or events which Cal selected. This text is superimposed over a large photo. A five-card mail-in set (described on wrapper) was also made available. The expiration was 3/1/96.

	Nm-Mt	Ex-Mt
COMPLETE SET (10)	40.00	12.00
COMMON CARD (1-10)	5.00	1.50
COMMON MAIL (11-15)	5.00	1.50

1995 Emotion Rookies

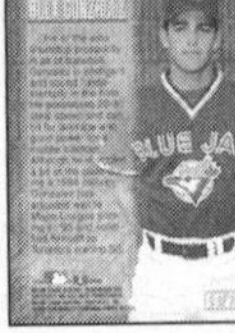

This 10-card standard-size set was inserted at a rate of one in five packs. Card fronts feature an action photo superimposed over background that is in a color consistent with that of the team's. The backs have a player photo and a write-up.

	Nm-Mt	Ex-Mt
COMPLETE SET (10)	25.00	7.50
1 Edgardo Alfonzo	1.00	.30
2 Jason Bates	1.00	.30
3 Marty Cordova	1.00	.30
4 Ray Durham	1.00	.30
5 Alex Gonzalez	1.00	.30
6 Shawn Green	1.00	.30
7 Charles Johnson	1.00	.30
8 Chipper Jones	2.00	.60
9 Hideo Nomo	4.00	1.20
10 Alex Rodriguez	8.00	2.40

1996 Emotion-XL

The 1996 Emotion-XL set (produced by Fleer/SkyBox) was issued in one series totalling 300 standard-size cards. The seven-card packs retailed for $4.99 each. The fronts feature a color action player photo with either a blue, green or maroon frame and the player's name and team printed in a foil-stamped medallion. A descriptive term describing the player completes the front. The backs carry player information and statistics. The cards are grouped alphabetically by team with AL preceding NL. A Manny Ramirez promo card was distributed to dealers and hobby media to preview the set.

	Nm-Mt	Ex-Mt
COMPLETE SET (300)	60.00	18.00
1 Roberto Alomar	2.00	.60
2 Brady Anderson	.75	.23
3 Bobby Bonilla	.75	.23
4 Jeffrey Hammonds	.75	.23
5 Chris Hoiles	.75	.23
6 Mike Mussina	2.00	.60
7 Randy Myers	.75	.23
8 Rafael Palmeiro	1.25	.35
9 Cal Ripken	6.00	1.80
10 B.J. Surhoff	.75	.23
11 Jose Canseco	2.00	.60
12 Roger Clemens	4.00	1.20
13 Wil Cordero	.75	.23
14 Mike Greenwell	.75	.23
15 Dwayne Hosey	.75	.23
16 Tim Naehring	.75	.23
17 Troy O'Leary	.75	.23
18 Mike Stanley	.75	.23
19 John Valentin	.75	.23
20 Mo Vaughn	.75	.23
21 Jim Abbott	1.25	.35
22 Garret Anderson	.75	.23
23 George Arias	.75	.23
24 Chili Davis	.75	.23
25 Jim Edmonds	.75	.23
26 Chuck Finley	.75	.23
27 Todd Greene	.75	.23
28 Mark Langston	.75	.23
29 Troy Percival	.75	.23
30 Tim Salmon	1.25	.35
31 Lee Smith	.75	.23
32 J.T. Snow	.75	.23
33 Harold Baines	.75	.23
34 Jason Bere	.75	.23
35 Ray Durham	.75	.23
36 Alex Fernandez	.75	.23
37 Ozzie Guillen	.75	.23
38 Darren Lewis	.75	.23
39 Lyle Mouton	.75	.23
40 Tony Phillips	.75	.23
41 Danny Tartabull	.75	.23
42 Frank Thomas	2.00	.60
43 Robin Ventura	.75	.23
44 Sandy Alomar Jr.	.75	.23
45 Carlos Baerga	.75	.23
46 Albert Belle	.75	.23
47 Julio Franco	.75	.23
48 Orel Hershiser	.75	.23
49 Kenny Lofton	.75	.23
50 Dennis Martinez	.75	.23
51 Jack McDowell	.75	.23
52 Jose Mesa	.75	.23
53 Eddie Murray	2.00	.60
54 Charles Nagy	.75	.23
55 Manny Ramirez	.75	.23
56 Jim Thome	2.00	.60
57 Omar Vizquel	.75	.23
58 Chad Curtis	.75	.23
59 Cecil Fielder	.75	.23
60 Travis Fryman	.75	.23
61 Chris Gomez	.75	.23
62 Felipe Lira	.75	.23
63 Alan Trammell	1.25	.35
64 Kevin Appier	.75	.23
65 Johnny Damon	.75	.23
66 Tom Goodwin	.75	.23
67 Mark Gubicza	.75	.23
68 Jeff Montgomery	.75	.23
69 Jon Nunnally	.75	.23
70 Bip Roberts	.75	.23
71 Ricky Bones	.75	.23
72 Chuck Carr	.75	.23
73 John Jaha	.75	.23
74 Ben McDonald	.75	.23
75 Matt Mieske	.75	.23
76 Dave Nilsson	.75	.23
77 Kevin Seitzer	.75	.23
78 Greg Vaughn	.75	.23
79 Rick Aguilera	.75	.23
80 Marty Cordova	.75	.23
81 Roberto Kelly	.75	.23
82 Chuck Knoblauch	.75	.23
83 Pat Meares	.75	.23
84 Paul Molitor	1.25	.35
85 Kirby Puckett	2.00	.60
86 Brad Radke	.75	.23
87 Wade Boggs	1.25	.35
88 David Cone	.75	.23
89 Dwight Gooden	1.25	.35
90 Derek Jeter	5.00	1.50
91 Tino Martinez	1.25	.35
92 Paul O'Neill	1.25	.35
93 Andy Pettitte	1.25	.35
94 Tim Raines	.75	.23
95 Ruben Rivera	.75	.23
96 Kenny Rogers	.75	.23
97 Ruben Sierra	.75	.23
98 John Wetteland	.75	.23
99 Bernie Williams	1.25	.35
100 Allen Battle	.75	.23
101 Geronimo Berroa	.75	.23
102 Brent Gates	.75	.23
103 Doug Johns	.75	.23
104 Mark McGwire	5.00	1.50
105 Pedro Munoz	.75	.23
106 Ariel Prieto	.75	.23
107 Terry Steinbach	.75	.23
108 Todd Van Poppel	.75	.23
109 Chris Bosio	.75	.23
110 Jay Buhner	.75	.23
111 Joey Cora	.75	.23
112 Russ Davis	.75	.23
113 Ken Griffey Jr.	3.00	.90
114 Sterling Hitchcock	.75	.23
115 Randy Johnson	2.00	.60
116 Edgar Martinez	1.25	.35
117 Alex Rodriguez	4.00	1.20
118 Paul Sorrento	.75	.23
119 Dan Wilson	.75	.23
120 Will Clark	2.00	.60
121 Juan Gonzalez	2.00	.60
122 Rusty Greer	.75	.23
123 Kevin Gross	.75	.23
124 Ken Hill	.75	.23
125 Dean Palmer	.75	.23
126 Roger Pavlik	.75	.23
127 Ivan Rodriguez	2.00	.60
128 Mickey Tettleton	.75	.23
129 Joe Carter	.75	.23
130 Carlos Delgado	.75	.23
131 Alex Gonzalez	.75	.23
132 Shawn Green	.75	.23
133 Erik Hanson	.75	.23
134 Pat Hentgen	.75	.23
135 Otis Nixon	.75	.23
136 John Olerud	.75	.23
137 Ed Sprague	.75	.23
138 Steve Avery	.75	.23
139 Jermaine Dye	.75	.23
140 Tom Glavine	1.25	.35
141 Marquis Grissom	.75	.23
142 Chipper Jones	2.00	.60
143 David Justice	.75	.23
144 Ryan Klesko	.75	.23
145 Javier Lopez	.75	.23
146 Greg Maddux	3.00	.90
147 Fred McGriff	1.25	.35
148 Jason Schmidt	.75	.23
149 John Smoltz	1.25	.35
150 Mark Wohlers	.75	.23
151 Jim Bullinger	.75	.23
152 Frank Castillo	.75	.23
153 Kevin Foster	.75	.23
154 Luis Gonzalez	.75	.23
155 Mark Grace	1.25	.35
156 Brian McRae	.75	.23
157 Jaime Navarro	.75	.23
158 Rey Sanchez	.75	.23
159 Ryne Sandberg	3.00	.90
160 Sammy Sosa	3.00	.90
161 Bret Boone	.75	.23
162 Jeff Brantley	.75	.23
163 Vince Coleman	.75	.23
164 Steve Gibralter	.75	.23
165 Barry Larkin	2.00	.60
166 Hal Morris	.75	.23
167 Mark Portugal	.75	.23
168 Reggie Sanders	.75	.23
169 Pete Schourek	.75	.23
170 John Smiley	.75	.23
171 Jason Bates	.75	.23
172 Dante Bichette	.75	.23
173 Ellis Burks	.75	.23
174 Vinny Castilla	.75	.23
175 Andres Galarraga	.75	.23
176 Kevin Ritz	.75	.23
177 Bill Swift	.75	.23
178 Larry Walker	1.25	.35
179 Walt Weiss	.75	.23
180 Eric Young	.75	.23
181 Kurt Abbott	.75	.23
182 Kevin Brown	.75	.23
183 John Burkett	.75	.23
184 Greg Colbrunn	.75	.23
185 Jeff Conine	.75	.23
186 Chris Hammond	.75	.23
187 Charles Johnson	.75	.23
188 Terry Pendleton	.75	.23
189 Pat Rapp	.75	.23
190 Gary Sheffield	.75	.23
191 Quilvio Veras	.75	.23
192 Devon White	.75	.23
193 Jeff Bagwell	1.25	.35
194 Derek Bell	.75	.23
195 Sean Berry	.75	.23
196 Craig Biggio	1.25	.35
197 Doug Drabek	.75	.23
198 Tony Eusebio	.75	.23
199 Mike Hampton	.75	.23
200 Brian L.Hunter	.75	.23
201 Derrick May	.75	.23
202 Orlando Miller	.75	.23
203 Shane Reynolds	.75	.23
204 Mike Blowers	.75	.23
205 Tom Candiotti	.75	.23
206 Delino DeShields	.75	.23
207 Greg Gagne	.75	.23
208 Karim Garcia	.75	.23
209 Todd Hollandsworth	.75	.23
210 Eric Karros	.75	.23
211 Ramon Martinez	.75	.23
212 Raul Mondesi	.75	.23
213 Hideo Nomo	2.00	.60
214 Chan Ho Park	.75	.23
215 Mike Piazza	3.00	.90
216 Ismael Valdes	.75	.23
217 Todd Worrell	.75	.23
218 Moises Alou	.75	.23
219 Yamil Benitez	.75	.23
220 Jeff Fassero	.75	.23
221 Darrin Fletcher	.75	.23
222 Cliff Floyd	.75	.23
223 Pedro Martinez	2.00	.60
224 Carlos Perez	.75	.23
225 Mel Rojas	.75	.23
226 David Segui	.75	.23
227 Rondell White	.75	.23
228 Rico Brogna	.75	.23
229 Carl Everett	.75	.23
230 John Franco	.75	.23
231 Bernard Gilkey	.75	.23
232 Todd Hundley	.75	.23
233 Jason Isringhausen	.75	.23
234 Lance Johnson	.75	.23
235 Bobby Jones	.75	.23
236 Jeff Kent	.75	.23
237 Rey Ordonez	.75	.23
238 Bill Pulsipher	.75	.23
239 Jose Vizcaino	.75	.23
240 Paul Wilson	.75	.23
241 Ricky Bottalico	.75	.23
242 Darren Daulton	.75	.23
243 Lenny Dykstra	.75	.23
244 Jim Eisenreich	.75	.23
245 Sid Fernandez	.75	.23
246 Gregg Jefferies	.75	.23
247 Mickey Morandini	.75	.23
248 Benito Santiago	.75	.23
249 Curt Schilling	1.25	.35
250 Mark Whiten	.75	.23
251 Todd Zeile	.75	.23
252 Jay Bell	.75	.23
253 Carlos Garcia	.75	.23
254 Charlie Hayes	.75	.23
255 Jason Kendall	.75	.23
256 Jeff King	.75	.23
257 Al Martin	.75	.23
258 Orlando Merced	.75	.23
259 Dan Miceli	.75	.23
260 Denny Neagle	.75	.23
261 Alan Benes	.75	.23
262 Andy Benes	.75	.23
263 Royce Clayton	.75	.23
264 Dennis Eckersley	.75	.23
265 Gary Gaetti	.75	.23
266 Ron Gant	.75	.23
267 Brian Jordan	.75	.23
268 Ray Lankford	.75	.23
269 John Mabry	.75	.23
270 Tom Pagnozzi	.75	.23
271 Ozzie Smith	3.00	.90
272 Todd Stottlemyre	.75	.23
273 Andy Ashby	.75	.23
274 Brad Ausmus	.75	.23
275 Ken Caminiti	.75	.23
276 Steve Finley	.75	.23
277 Tony Gwynn	2.50	.75
278 Joey Hamilton	.75	.23
279 Rickey Henderson	2.00	.60
280 Trevor Hoffman	.75	.23
281 Wally Joyner	.75	.23
282 Jody Reed	.75	.23
283 Bob Tewksbury	.75	.23
284 Fernando Valenzuela	.75	.23
285 Rod Beck	.75	.23
286 Barry Bonds	5.00	1.50
287 Mark Carreon	.75	.23
288 Shawn Dunston	.75	.23
289 O.Fernandez RC	.75	.23
290 Glenallen Hill	.75	.23
291 Stan Javier	.75	.23
292 Mark Leiter	.75	.23
293 Kirt Manwaring	.75	.23
294 Robby Thompson	.75	.23
295 W.VanLandingham	.75	.23
296 Allen Watson	.75	.23
297 Matt Williams	.75	.23
298 Checklist	.75	.23
299 Checklist	.75	.23
300 Checklist	.75	.23
P55 Manny Ramirez Promo	.75	.23

1996 Emotion-XL D-Fense

Randomly inserted in packs at a rate of one in four, this 10-card set showcases outstanding defensive players. The fronts feature a color action player cut-out on a sepia portait background with silver foil print and border. The backs carry information about the player on another sepia portrait background.

	Nm-Mt	Ex-Mt
COMPLETE SET (10)	25.00	7.50
1 Roberto Alomar	2.50	.75
2 Barry Bonds	6.00	1.80
3 Mark Grace	1.50	.45
4 Ken Griffey Jr.	4.00	1.20
5 Kenny Lofton	1.00	.30
6 Greg Maddux	4.00	1.20
7 Raul Mondesi	1.00	.30
8 Cal Ripken	8.00	2.40
9 Ivan Rodriguez	2.50	.75
10 Matt Williams	1.00	.30

1996 Emotion-XL Legion of Boom

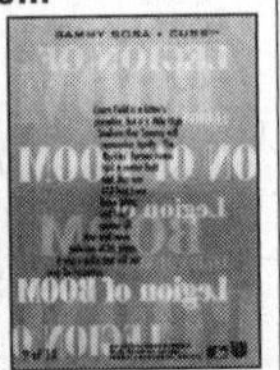

Randomly inserted in packs at a rate of one in 36, this 12-card set features the game's big hitters on cards with translucent card backs. The fronts carry a color action player cut-out with silver foil print.

	Nm-Mt	Ex-Mt
COMPLETE SET (12)	150.00	45.00
1 Albert Belle	5.00	1.50
2 Barry Bonds	30.00	9.00
3 Juan Gonzalez	12.00	3.60
4 Ken Griffey Jr.	20.00	6.00
5 Mark McGwire	30.00	9.00
6 Mike Piazza	20.00	6.00
7 Manny Ramirez	5.00	1.50
8 Tim Salmon	8.00	2.40
9 Sammy Sosa	20.00	6.00
10 Frank Thomas	12.00	3.60
11 Mo Vaughn	5.00	1.50
12 Matt Williams	5.00	1.50

1996 Emotion-XL N-Tense

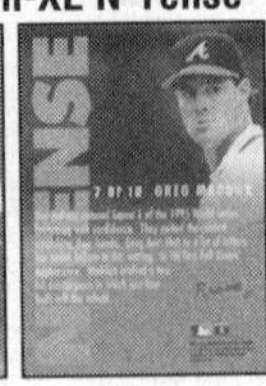

Randomly inserted in packs at a rate of one in 12, this 10-card set highlights top-clutch performers on special, front N-shaped die-cut cards. The backs carry information about the player on a player portrait background.

	Nm-Mt	Ex-Mt
COMPLETE SET (10)	60.00	18.00
1 Albert Belle	2.00	.60
2 Barry Bonds	12.00	3.60
3 Jose Canseco	5.00	1.50
4 Ken Griffey Jr.	8.00	2.40
5 Tony Gwynn	6.00	1.80
6 Randy Johnson	5.00	1.50
7 Greg Maddux	8.00	2.40
8 Cal Ripken	15.00	4.50
9 Frank Thomas	5.00	1.50
10 Matt Williams	2.00	.60

1996 Emotion-XL Rare Breed

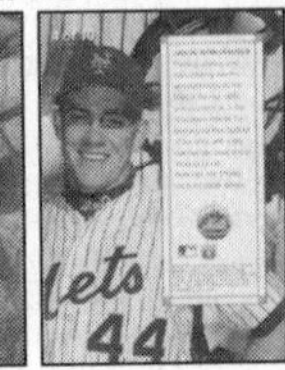

Randomly inserted in packs at a rate of one in 100, this 10-card set showcases young stars on lenticular cards. The fronts feature color action player cut-outs on a baseball graphics background. The backs carry player information over a color player portrait.

	Nm-Mt	Ex-Mt
COMPLETE SET (10)	120.00	36.00
1 Garret Anderson	10.00	3.00
2 Marty Cordova	8.00	2.40
3 Brian L.Hunter	8.00	2.40
4 Jason Isringhausen	10.00	3.00
5 Charles Johnson	10.00	3.00
6 Chipper Jones	25.00	7.50
7 Raul Mondesi	10.00	3.00
8 Hideo Nomo	25.00	7.50
9 Manny Ramirez	10.00	3.00
10 Rondell White	10.00	3.00

2001 eTopps

One of the more unique products of the yea 2001 made its long-awaited debut (afte months of technical setbacks) in mid September. eTopps was distributed an marketed in a manner unlike any other brand c cards before them. The only place they wer initially offered for sale was at the eTopp website (www.eTopps.com). Starting in lat September on a weekly basis - and for abou three months, Topps released IPO's (aka Initia Player Offerings) on a handful of cards to th point where all 150 eTopps baseball cards wer available. A pre-determined number of share were given for each player based upon Topp estimation of popularity (a.k.a. they offere 10,000 Ichiro's and only 4,000 Rafael Furcal's Price per card during IPO status typical ranged from $3.50 per card to $9.50 per card again based on popularity. The one week IP period was the only time these cards were eve offered for sale by Topps and most important Topps only printed the exact amount of carc that were ordered during that window of tim Thus, even though Topps had offered 4,0C shares of Jeff Bagwell, only 485 copies we ordered - thus that's all they produce Consumers had the option to have their carc held by Topps whereby they cou automatically trade them to other collecto (much like one would buy and sell stocks) c the eTopps "floor" - a special section of eB created for this product, or have the ca mailed to them ($6.95 for the first card and cents for each additional).

	Nm-Mt	Ex-M
1 Nomar Garciaparra/1315		
2 Chipper Jones/674		
3 Jeff Bagwell/485		
4 Randy Johnson/1499		
7 Adam Dunn/4197		

8 J.D. Drew/767
9 Larry Walker/420
10 Edgardo Alfonzo/338
11 Lance Berkman/595
12 Tony Gwynn/828
13 Andruw Jones/908
15 Troy Glaus/862
17 Sammy Sosa/2487
21 Darin Erstad/664
22 Barry Bonds/1567
27 Derek Jeter/1041
29 Curt Schilling/2125
30 Roberto Alomar/448
31 Luis Gonzalez/1104
32 Jimmy Rollins/1307
34 Joe Crede/1050
39 Sean Casey/537
46 Alex Rodriguez/2212
47 Tom Glavine/437
50 Jose Ortiz/738
51 Cal Ripken/2201
52 Bob Abreu/677
55 Alex Escobar/931
56 Ivan Rodriguez/698
59 Jeff Kent/452
62 Rick Ankiel/752
65 Craig Biggio/410
66 Carlos Delgado/398
68 Greg Maddux/1031
69 Kerry Wood/1056
71 Todd Helton/978
72 Mariano Rivera/824
73 Jason Kendall/672
75 Scott Rolen/498
76 Kazuhiro Sasaki/5000
77 Roy Oswalt/915
78 C.C. Sabathia/1974
3 Brian Giles/400
7 Rafael Furcal/646
8 Mike Mussina/793
9 Gary Sheffield/359
2 Mark McGwire/2908
4 Tsuyoshi Shinjo/3000
9 Jose Vidro/443
00 Ichiro Suzuki/10000 20.00 6.00
05 Manny Ramirez/1074
09 Juan Gonzalez/558
12 Ken Griffey Jr./2398
14 Tim Hudson/663
15 Nick Johnson/1217
18 Jason Giambi/897
22 Rafael Palmeiro/464
24 V. Guerrero/854
25 Vernon Wells/349
27 Roger Clemens/1462
28 Frank Thomas/834
29 Carlos Beltran/489
30 Pat Burrell/1253
31 Pedro Martinez/1038
32 Mike Piazza/1379
35 Luis Montanez/5000
40 Sean Burroughs/5000
41 Barry Zito/843
42 Bobby Bradley/5000
43 Albert Pujols/5000 40.00 12.00
44 Ben Sheets/1713
45 Alfonso Soriano/1699
46 Josh Hamilton/5000
47 Eric Munson/5000
50 Mark Mulder/4335

2002 eTopps

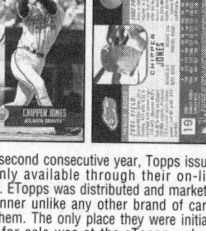

r the second consecutive year, Topps issued set only available through their on-line rvices. ETopps was distributed and marketed a manner unlike any other brand of cards fore them. The only place they were initially fered for sale was at the eTopps website ww.eTopps.com). Starting with the ginning of the 2002 season and continuing rough the 2002 All-Star break these cards re made available on a weekly basis. A pre-termined number of shares (ranging from as w as 2,000 to as many as 6,000) were given each player based upon Topps estimation of pularity. For 2002, your "portfolio" could crease if the players in the set met certain atistical goals for the season. Price per card ring IPO status typically ranged from proximately $4 per card to $9 per card - ain based on popularity. The one week IPO riod was the only time these cards were ever ered for sale by Topps and most importantly pps only printed the exact amount of cards at were ordered during that window of time. ese print runs are displayed in our checklist. nsumers had the option to have their cards ld by Topps, whereby they could tomatically sell them or buy more to and m other collectors (much like one would buy d sell stocks) on the eTopps "floor" - a ecial section of eBay created for this product, have the card mailed to them ($6.95 for the t card and 85 cents for each additional).

Nm-Mt Ex-Mt

chiro Suzuki/9477
ason Giambi/5142
oberto Alomar/2711
ret Boone/2000
rank Catalanotto/2000
lex Rodriguez/6393
im Thome/2927
oby Hall/2000
roy Glaus/4323
Derek Jeter/8000
Alfonso Soriano/5000
Eric Chavez/4334

13 Preston Wilson/2000
14 Bernie Williams/4436
15 Larry Walker/2546
16 Todd Helton/3430
17 Moises Alou/2856
18 Lance Berkman/5000
19 Chipper Jones/4734
20 Andruw Jones/4849
21 Barry Bonds/6658
22 Sammy Sosa/8000
23 Luis Gonzalez/2671
24 Shawn Green/4438
25 Jeff Bagwell/3359
26 Albert Pujols/5531
27 Rafael Palmeiro/2700
28 Jimmy Rollins/5000
29 Vladimir Guerrero/6000
30 Jeff Kent/3000
31 Ken Griffey Jr./4569
32 Magglio Ordonez/4000
33 Mike Piazza/4202
34 Pedro Martinez/6000
35 Mark Mulder/4000
36 Roger Clemens/4567
37 Freddy Garcia/4986
38 Tim Hudson/2000
39 Mike Mussina/3708
40 Joe Mays/3000
41 Barry Zito/3590
42 Jermaine Dye/2693
43 Mariano Rivera/3709
44 Randy Johnson/6211
45 Curt Schilling/5190
46 Greg Maddux/4008
47 Javier Vazquez/3000
48 Kerry Wood/3346
49 Wilson Betemit/2377
50 Adam Dunn/6000
51 Josh Beckett/5000
52 Paul LoDuca/3998
53 Ben Sheets/3842
54 Eric Valent/5000
55 Brian Giles/2000
56 Mo Vaughn/2772
57 C.C. Sabathia/2525
58 Nick Johnson/5000
59 Miguel Tejada/4000
60 Carlos Delgado/3604
61 Tsuyoshi Shinjo/3000
62 Juan Gonzalez/2361
63 Mike Sweeney/3173
64 Ivan Rodriguez/3000
65 Bud Smith/3000
66 Brandon Duckworth/2000
67 Xavier Nady/4000
68 D'Angelo Jimenez/1725
69 Roy Oswalt/3523
70 J.D. Drew/3195
71 Cliff Floyd/3725
72 Kevin Brown/3000
73 Gary Sheffield/3593
74 Aramis Ramirez/3000
75 Nomar Garciaparra/5090
76 Phil Nevin/2348
77 Juan Cruz/4000
78 Hideo Nomo/2857
79 Chris George/3000
80 Matt Morris/3000
81 Corey Patterson/4000
82 Joel Pineiro/4776
83 Mark Buehrle/3000
84 Shannon Stewart/1992
85 Kazuhisa Sasaki/4000
86 Carlos Pena/4000
87 Brad Penny/3000
88 Rich Aurilia/2795
89 Wade Miller/4000
90 Tim Raines Jr./5000
91 Kazuhisa Ishii/6000
92 Hank Blalock/5000
93 So Taguchi/5000
94 Mark Prior/5000
95 Rickey Henderson/4013
96 Austin Kearns/6000
97 Tom Glavine/3000
98 Manny Ramirez/4905
99 Shea Hillenbrand/4000
100 Junior Spivey/5000
101 Derek Lowe/4911
102 Torii Hunter/4000
103 Juan Rivera/4000
104 Eric Hinske/5000
105 Bobby Hill/3000
106 Rafael Soriano/4000
107 Jim Edmonds/3851

2003 eTopps

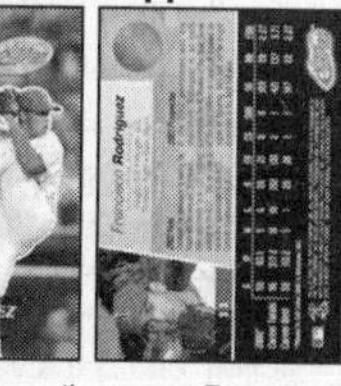

For the third consecutive season, Topps issued cards through their eTopps network. The distribution of these cards began in March, 2003. These cards were printed to match the amount of orders received and were available at an original cost of between $4 and $9.50. Please note, card 117 was never issued - thus, though the set is numbered 1-123 only 122 cards were produced.

Nm-Mt Ex-Mt

1 Troy Glaus
2 Manny Ramirez
3 Magglio Ordonez
4 Jim Thome
5 Torii Hunter
6 Jason Giambi
7 Tim Hudson
8 Ichiro Suzuki
9 Aubrey Huff
10 Alex Rodriguez
11 Francisco Rodriguez
12 Joe Borchard
13 Mark Teixeira
14 Marlon Byrd
15 Carlos Delgado
16 Tom Glavine
17 Curt Schilling
18 Mark Prior
19 Ken Griffey Jr.
20 Todd Helton
21 Jeff Bagwell
22 Shawn Green
23 Vladimir Guerrero
24 Roberto Alomar
25 Brian Giles
26 Barry Bonds
27 Albert Pujols
28 Nomar Garciaparra
29 Alfonso Soriano
30 Barry Zito
31 Edgar Martinez
32 Ivan Rodriguez
33 Greg Maddux
34 Sammy Sosa
35 Austin Kearns
36 Craig Biggio
37 Mike Piazza
38 Andruw Jones
39 Jeff Kent
40 Roy Oswalt
41 Miguel Tejada
42 Derek Jeter
43 Pedro Martinez
44 Jarrod Washburn
45 Randy Johnson
46 Bernie Williams
47 Chipper Jones
48 Gary Sheffield
49 Larry Walker
50 Lance Berkman
51 Garret Anderson
52 Jason Schmidt
53 Rodrigo Lopez
54 Oliver Perez
55 Derek Lowe
56 Vicente Padilla
57 Paul Konerko
58 Bartolo Colon
59 Omar Vizquel
60 Adam Dunn
61 Carlos Pena
62 Richie Sexson
63 Paul Byrd
64 Eric Gagne
65 Brad Radke
66 A.J. Burnett
67 Brandon Phillips
68 Mike Hampton
69 Tim Salmon
70 Roger Clemens
71 Jake Peavy
72 Pat Burrell
73 Ben Sheets
74 Fred McGriff
75 John Smoltz
76 Josh Phelps
77 John Olerud
78 Eric Chavez
79 Jeff Weaver
80 Scott Rolen
81 Carl Crawford
82 Rafael Palmeiro
83 Roy Halladay
84 Josh Beckett
85 Jorge Posada
86 Mark Mulder
87 Eric Milton
88 Angel Berroa
89 Jason Lane
90 Kerry Wood
91 Brad Wilkerson
92 Orlando Hudson
93 Mike Mussina
94 Hee Seop Choi
95 Chris Snelling
96 Tomo Ohka
97 Andy Pettitte
98 Drew Henson
99 Chin-Feng Chen
100 Jason Jennings
101 Hideki Matsui
102 Jose Contreras
103 Rocco Baldelli
104 Jeremy Bonderman
105 Jesse Foppert
106 Randy Wolf
107 Kevin Millwood
108 Eric Byrnes
109 Edgar Renteria
110 Jose Reyes
111 Dontrelle Willis
112 Mike Lowell
113 Jerome Williams
114 Esteban Loaiza
115 Gil Meche
116 Ty Wigginton
117 Does Not Exist
118 Brett Myers
119 Miguel Cabrera
120 Brandon Webb
121 Aaron Heilman
122 Rich Harden
123 Morgan Ensberg

2002 eTopps Classic

Distribution started in mid July, 2002 for this set with two new cards being offered each Monday. The first 20 cards checklisted (1-20) were issued in 2002. Cards numbered from 21 and above were issued in 2003. All of the cards, however, share a similar design. 4000 copies of each card were initially offered, though the cards were printed to order, thus final quantities produced fluctuated based on demand.

Nm-Mt Ex-Mt

1 Babe Ruth
2 Tom Seaver
3 Honus Wagner
4 Warren Spahn
5 Frank Robinson
6 Whitey Ford
7 Bob Gibson
8 Reggie Jackson
9 Joe Morgan
10 Harmon Killebrew
11 Eddie Mathews
12 Willie Mays
13 Brooks Robinson
14 Ty Cobb
15 Carl Yastrzemski
16 Jackie Robinson
17 Mike Schmidt
18 Nolan Ryan
19 Duke Snider
20 Stan Musial
24 Lou Brock
26 Bob Feller
31 Lou Gehrig
32 Johnny Bench

2002 eTopps Event Series *

Issued sporadically throughout the Baseball season, these cards honor leading historical events of the 2002 Baseball season. Please note that the stated print run for each card is listed next to the featured player in our checklist.

Nm-Mt Ex-Mt

1 Mike Cameron 4 HR's/5000
2 Shawn Green 4 HR's/5000
3 Oakland A's Winning Streak/5000
4 Greg Maddux 15 Years/15 Wins/4000

2003 eTopps Event Series *

Issued sporadically throughout the Baseball season, these cards honor leading historical events of the 2003 Baseball season.

Nm-Mt Ex-Mt

9 Rafael Palmeiro
500 Homers
10 Roger Clemens
300 Wins
11 Barry Bonds

1949 Eureka Stamps

This set features National League players only. Apparently the promotion was not successful enough to warrant continuing on to do the American League, even though it was pre-announced in the back of the stamp album. Album is available to house the stamps. The album measures 7 1/2" by 9 1/4" whereas the individual stamps measure approximately 1 1/2" by 2". The stamps are numbered and are in full color. The album and stamp numbering is organized by teams (and alphabetically within teams), e.g., Boston Braves (3-27), Brooklyn Dodgers (28-51), Chicago Cubs (52-75), Cincinnati Reds (76-100), New York Giants (101-126), Philadelphia Phillies (127-151), Pittsburgh Pirates (152-176) and St. Louis Cardinals (177-200). At the bottom of the stamp the player's name is given in a narrow yellow strip.

	NM	Ex
COMPLETE SET (200)	1000.00	500.00
1 Happy Chandler COMM	10.00	5.00
2 Ford Frick PRES	10.00	5.00
3 Johnny Antonelli	4.00	2.00
4 Red Barrett	3.00	1.50
5 Clint Conaster	3.00	1.50
6 Alvin Dark	6.00	3.00
7 Bob Elliott	4.00	2.00
8 Glenn Elliott	3.00	1.50
9 Elbie Fletcher	3.00	1.50
10 Bob Hall	3.00	1.50
11 Jeff Heath	3.00	1.50
12 Bobby Hogue	3.00	1.50
13 Tommy Holmes	4.00	2.00
14 Al Lakeman	3.00	1.50
15 Phil Masi	3.00	1.50
16 Nelson Potter	3.00	1.50
17 Pete Reiser	6.00	3.00
18 Rick Rickert	3.00	1.50
19 Connie Ryan	3.00	1.50
20 Jim Russell	3.00	1.50
21 Johnny Sain	6.00	3.00
22 Bill Salkeld	3.00	1.50
23 Sibby Sisti	3.00	1.50
24 Billy Southworth MG	3.00	1.50
25 Warren Spahn	30.00	15.00
26 Eddie Stanky	5.00	2.50
27 Bill Voiselle	3.00	1.50
28 Jack Banta	3.00	1.50
29 Rex Barney	4.00	2.00
30 Ralph Branca	6.00	3.00
31 Tommy Brown	3.00	1.50
32 Roy Campanella	40.00	20.00
33 Billy Cox	4.00	2.00
34 Bruce Edwards	3.00	1.50
35 Carl Furillo	10.00	5.00
36 Joe Hatten	3.00	1.50
37 Gene Hermanski	3.00	1.50
38 Gil Hodges	20.00	10.00
39 Johnny Jorgensen	3.00	1.50
40 Lefty Martin	3.00	1.50
41 Mike McCormick	3.00	1.50
42 Eddie Miksis	3.00	1.50
43 Paul Minner	3.00	1.50
44 Sam Narron	3.00	1.50
45 Don Newcombe	10.00	5.00
46 Jake Pitler CO	3.00	1.50
47 Pee Wee Reese	30.00	15.00
48 Jackie Robinson	60.00	30.00
49 Burt Shotton MG	3.00	1.50
50 Duke Snider	40.00	20.00
51 Dick Whitman	3.00	1.50
52 Smoky Burgess	4.00	2.00
53 Phil Cavarretta	4.00	2.00
54 Bob Chipman	3.00	1.50
55 Walt Dubiel	3.00	1.50
56 Hank Edwards	3.00	1.50
57 Frankie Gustine	3.00	1.50
58 Hal Jeffcoat	3.00	1.50
59 Emil Kush	3.00	1.50
60 Doyle Lade	3.00	1.50
61 Dutch Leonard	3.00	1.50
62 Peanuts Lowrey	3.00	1.50
63 Gene Mauch	5.00	2.50
64 Cal McLish	3.00	1.50
65 Rube Novotney	3.00	1.50
66 Andy Pafko	4.00	2.00
67 Bob Ramazzotti	3.00	1.50
68 Herman Reich	3.00	1.50
69 Bob Rush	3.00	1.50
70 Johnny Schmitz	3.00	1.50
71 Bob Scheffing	3.00	1.50
72 Roy Smalley	4.00	2.00
73 Emil Verban	3.00	1.50
74 Al Walker	3.00	1.50
75 Harry Walker	4.00	2.00
76 Bobby Adams	3.00	1.50
77 Ewell Blackwell	5.00	2.50
78 Jimmy Bloodworth	3.00	1.50
79 Walker Cooper	3.00	1.50
80 Tony Cuccinello	3.00	1.50
81 Jess Dobernick	3.00	1.50
82 Eddie Erautt	3.00	1.50
83 Frank Fanovich	3.00	1.50
84 Howie Fox	3.00	1.50
85 Grady Hatton	3.00	1.50
86 Homer Howell	3.00	1.50
87 Ted Kluszewski	10.00	5.00
88 Danny Litwhiler	3.00	1.50
89 Everett Lively	3.00	1.50
90 Lloyd Merriman	3.00	1.50
91 Phil Page	3.00	1.50
92 Kent Peterson	3.00	1.50
93 Ken Raffensberger	3.00	1.50
94 Luke Sewell CO	4.00	2.00
95 Virgil Stallcup	3.00	1.50
96 John Vander Meer	6.00	3.00
97 Bucky Walters MG	5.00	2.50
98 Herman Wehmeier	3.00	1.50
99 Johnny Wyrostek	3.00	1.50
100 Benny Zientara	3.00	1.50
101 Hank Behrman	3.00	1.50
102 Leo Durocher MG	10.00	5.00
103 Augie Galan	3.00	1.50
104 Sid Gordon	3.00	1.50
105 Bert Haas	3.00	1.50
106 Andy Hansen	3.00	1.50
107 Clint Hartung	4.00	2.00
108 Kirby Higbe	3.00	1.50
109 George Hausman	3.00	1.50
110 Larry Jansen	4.00	2.00
111 Sheldon Jones	3.00	1.50
112 Monte Kennedy	3.00	1.50
113 Buddy Kerr	3.00	1.50
114 Dave Koslo	3.00	1.50
115 Joe Lafata	3.00	1.50
116 Whitey Lockman	4.00	2.00
117 Jack Lohrke	3.00	1.50
118 Willard Marshall	3.00	1.50
119 Bill Milne	3.00	1.50
120 Johnny Mize	20.00	10.00
121 Don Mueller	5.00	2.50
122 Ray Mueller	3.00	1.50
123 Bill Rigney	4.00	2.00
124 Bobby Thomson	6.00	3.00
125 Sam Webb	3.00	1.50
126 Wes Westrum	4.00	2.00
127 Richie Ashburn	20.00	10.00
128 Bennie Bengough CO	3.00	1.50
129 Charlie Bicknell	3.00	1.50
130 Buddy Blattner	3.00	1.50
131 Hank Borowy	3.00	1.50
132 Ralph Caballero	3.00	1.50
133 Blix Donnelly	3.00	1.50
134 Del Ennis	4.00	2.00
135 Granville Hamner	4.00	2.00
136 Ken Heintzelman	3.00	1.50
137 Stan Hollmig	3.00	1.50
138 Willie Jones	3.00	1.50
139 Jim Konstanty	5.00	2.50
140 Stan Lopata	3.00	1.50
141 Jackie Mayo	3.00	1.50
142 Bill Nicholson	4.00	2.00
143 Robin Roberts	20.00	10.00
144 Schoolboy Rowe	5.00	2.50
145 Eddie Sawyer MG	4.00	2.00
146 Andy Seminick	3.00	1.50
147 Ken Silvestri	3.00	1.50
148 Curt Simmons	5.00	2.50
149 Dick Sisler	4.00	2.00
150 Ken Trinkle	3.00	1.50
151 Eddie Waitkus	4.00	2.00
152 Romanus Basgall	3.00	1.50
153 Eddie Bockman	3.00	1.50
154 Ernie Bonham	3.00	1.50
155 Hugh Casey	4.00	2.00
156 Pete Castiglione	3.00	1.50
157 Cliff Chambers	3.00	1.50
158 Murry Dickson	3.00	1.50
159 Ed Fitzgerald	3.00	1.50
160 Les Fleming	3.00	1.50
161 Hal Gregg	3.00	1.50
162 Goldie Holt	3.00	1.50
163 Johnny Hopp	4.00	2.00
164 Ralph Kiner	20.00	10.00
165 Vic Lombardi	3.00	1.50
166 Clyde McCullough	3.00	1.50

167 Bill Meyer MG 4.00 2.00
168 Danny Murtaugh 4.00 2.00
169 Barnacle Bill Posedel 3.00 1.50
170 Elmer Riddle 3.00 1.50
171 Stan Rojek 3.00 1.50
172 Rip Sewell 4.00 2.00
173 Eddie Stevens 3.00 1.50
174 Dixie Walker 4.00 2.00
175 Bill Werle 3.00 1.50
176 Wally Westlake 3.00 1.50
177 Bill Baker 3.00 1.50
178 Al Brazle 3.00 1.50
179 Harry Brecheen 4.00 2.00
180 Chuck Diering 3.00 1.50
181 Eddie Dyer MG 4.00 2.00
182 Joe Garagiola 20.00 10.00
183 Tom Glaviano 3.00 1.50
184 Jim Hearn 3.00 1.50
185 Ken Johnson 3.00 1.50
186 Nippy Jones 3.00 1.50
187 Ed Kazak 3.00 1.50
188 Lou Klein 3.00 1.50
189 Marty Marion 15.00 7.50
190 George Munger 3.00 1.50
191 Stan Musial 50.00 25.00
192 Spike Nelson 3.00 1.50
193 Howie Pollet 3.00 1.50
194 Bill Reeder 3.00 1.50
195 Del Rice 3.00 1.50
196 Ed Sauer 3.00 1.50
197 Red Schoendienst 15.00 7.50
198 Enos Slaughter 20.00 10.00
199 Ted Wilks 3.00 1.50
200 Ray Yochim 3.00 1.50
XX Album

1997 E-X2000

This 100-card set (produced by Fleer/SkyBox) was distributed in two-card foil packs with a suggested retail price of $3.99. An oversized Alex Rodriguez card shipped in its own holder was mailed to dealers who ordered E-X 2000 cases. They are numbered out of 3,000 and priced below. Also priced below is the redemption card for a baseball signed by Rodriguez. 100 of these cards were produced and the redemption deadline was May 1, 1998.

Nm-Mt Ex-Mt
COMPLETE SET (100) 80.00 24.00
1 Jim Edmonds .75 .23
2 Darin Erstad .75 .23
3 Eddie Murray 2.00 .60
4 Roberto Alomar 2.00 .60
5 Brady Anderson .75 .23
6 Mike Mussina 2.00 .60
7 Rafael Palmeiro 1.25 .35
8 Cal Ripken 6.00 1.80
9 Steve Avery .75 .23
10 Nomar Garciaparra 3.00 .90
11 Mo Vaughn .75 .23
12 Albert Belle .75 .23
13 Mike Cameron .75 .23
14 Ray Durham .75 .23
15 Frank Thomas 2.00 .60
16 Robin Ventura .75 .23
17 Manny Ramirez .75 .23
18 Jim Thome 2.00 .60
19 Matt Williams .75 .23
20 Tony Clark .75 .23
21 Travis Fryman .75 .23
22 Bob Higginson .75 .23
23 Kevin Appier .75 .23
24 Johnny Damon .75 .23
25 Jermaine Dye .75 .23
26 Jeff Cirillo .75 .23
27 Ben McDonald .75 .23
28 Chuck Knoblauch .75 .23
29 Paul Molitor 1.25 .35
30 Todd Walker .75 .23
31 Wade Boggs 1.25 .35
32 Cecil Fielder .75 .23
33 Derek Jeter 5.00 1.50
34 Andy Pettitte 1.25 .35
35 Ruben Rivera .75 .23
36 Bernie Williams 1.25 .35
37 Jose Canseco 2.00 .60
38 Mark McGwire 5.00 1.50
39 Jay Buhner .75 .23
40 Ken Griffey Jr. 3.00 .90
41 Randy Johnson 2.00 .60
42 Edgar Martinez 1.25 .35
43 Alex Rodriguez 3.00 .90
44 Dan Wilson .75 .23
45 Will Clark 2.00 .60
46 Juan Gonzalez 2.00 .60
47 Ivan Rodriguez 2.00 .60
48 Joe Carter .75 .23
49 Roger Clemens 4.00 1.20
50 Juan Guzman .75 .23
51 Pat Hentgen .75 .23
52 Tom Glavine 1.25 .35
53 Andruw Jones .75 .23
54 Chipper Jones 2.00 .60
55 Ryan Klesko .75 .23
56 Kenny Lofton .75 .23
57 Greg Maddux 3.00 .90
58 Fred McGriff 1.25 .35
59 John Smoltz 1.25 .35
60 Mark Wohlers .75 .23
61 Mark Grace 1.25 .35
62 Ryne Sandberg 3.00 .90
63 Sammy Sosa 3.00 .90
64 Barry Larkin 2.00 .60
65 Deion Sanders 1.25 .35
66 Reggie Sanders .75 .23
67 Dante Bichette .75 .23
68 Ellis Burks .75 .23
69 Andres Galarraga .75 .23
70 Moises Alou .75 .23
71 Kevin Brown .75 .23
72 Cliff Floyd .75 .23
73 Edgar Renteria .75 .23
74 Gary Sheffield .75 .23
75 Bob Abreu .75 .23
76 Jeff Bagwell 1.25 .35
77 Craig Biggio 1.25 .35
78 Todd Hollandsworth .75 .23
79 Eric Karros .75 .23
80 Raul Mondesi .75 .23
81 Hideo Nomo 2.00 .60
82 Mike Piazza 3.00 .90
83 Vladimir Guerrero 2.00 .60
84 Henry Rodriguez .75 .23
85 Todd Hundley .75 .23
86 Alex Ochoa .75 .23
87 Rey Ordonez .75 .23
88 Gregg Jefferies .75 .23
89 Scott Rolen 1.25 .35
90 Jermaine Allensworth .75 .23
91 Jason Kendall .75 .23
92 Ken Caminiti .75 .23
93 Tony Gwynn 2.50 .75
94 Rickey Henderson 2.00 .60
95 Barry Bonds 5.00 1.50
96 J.T. Snow .75 .23
97 Dennis Eckersley .75 .23
98 Ron Gant .75 .23
99 Brian Jordan .75 .23
100 Ray Lankford .75 .23
101 Checklist .75 .23
102 Checklist .75 .23
P43 Alex Rodriguez 1.50 .45
Three card promo strip
S43 Alex Rodriguez 10.00 3.00
Mailed to Dealers who ordered Cases
Card is numbered out of 3,000
NNO Alex Rodriguez 100.00 30.00
Ball Exch 100 produced

1997 E-X2000 Credentials

Randomly inserted in packs at the approximate rate of one in 60, this 100-card set is parallel to the base set with an etched holofoil border. The stated print run was less than 299 sets.

Nm-Mt Ex-Mt
*STARS: 3X TO 8X BASIC CARDS

1997 E-X2000 Essential Credentials

Randomly inserted in packs at the rate of one in 200, this 100-card set is parallel to the base set with an etched refractive holographic foil border. Less than 99 sets were produced and are sequentially numbered.

Nm-Mt Ex-Mt
*STARS: 8X TO 20X BASIC CARDS

1997 E-X2000 A Cut Above

Randomly inserted in packs at the rate of one in 288, this 10-card set features color images of "power hitters" on a holographic foil, die-cut sawblade background.

Nm-Mt Ex-Mt
COMPLETE SET (10) 250.00 75.00
1 Frank Thomas 20.00 6.00
2 Ken Griffey Jr. 30.00 9.00
3 Alex Rodriguez 30.00 9.00
4 Albert Belle 8.00 2.40
5 Juan Gonzalez 20.00 6.00
6 Mark McGwire 50.00 15.00
7 Mo Vaughn 8.00 2.40
8 Manny Ramirez 8.00 2.40
9 Barry Bonds 50.00 15.00
10 Fred McGriff 12.00 3.60

1997 E-X2000 Emerald Autographs

This six-card set features autographed color player photos of some of the hottest young stars in baseball. In addition to an authentic black-ink autograph, each card is embossed with a SkyBox logo about the size of a quarter. These cards were obtained by exchanging a redemption card by mail before the May 1, 1998, deadline.

Nm-Mt Ex-Mt
*EXCH.CARDS: .1X TO .25X BASIC AUTO
2 Darin Erstad 15.00 4.50
30 Todd Walker 15.00 4.50
43 Alex Rodriguez 120.00 36.00
78 Todd Hollandsworth 15.00 4.50
86 Alex Ochoa 15.00 4.50
89 Scott Rolen 25.00 7.50

1997 E-X2000 Hall or Nothing

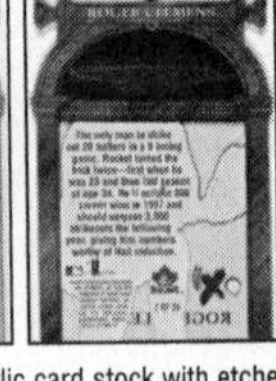

Randomly inserted in packs at the rate of one in 20, this 20-card set features color images of future Cooperstown Hall of Fame candidates printed on 30-pt. acrylic card stock with etched cooper foil borders and gold foil stamping.

Nm-Mt Ex-Mt
COMPLETE SET (20) 120.00 36.00
1 Frank Thomas 5.00 1.50
2 Ken Griffey Jr. 8.00 2.40
3 Eddie Murray 5.00 1.50
4 Cal Ripken 15.00 4.50
5 Ryne Sandberg 8.00 2.40
6 Wade Boggs 3.00 .90
7 Roger Clemens 10.00 3.00
8 Tony Gwynn 6.00 1.80
9 Alex Rodriguez 8.00 2.40
10 Mark McGwire 12.00 3.60
11 Barry Bonds 12.00 3.60
12 Greg Maddux 8.00 2.40
13 Juan Gonzalez 5.00 1.50
14 Albert Belle 2.00 .60
15 Mike Piazza 8.00 2.40
16 Jeff Bagwell 3.00 .90
17 Dennis Eckersley 2.00 .60
18 Mo Vaughn 2.00 .60
19 Roberto Alomar 5.00 1.50
20 Kenny Lofton 2.00 .60

1997 E-X2000 Star Date 2000

Randomly inserted in packs at the rate of one in nine, this 15-card set features color images of young star players printed on holographic foil with swirls of spot glitter coating.

Nm-Mt Ex-Mt
COMPLETE SET (15) 30.00 9.00
1 Alex Rodriguez 5.00 1.50
2 Andruw Jones 1.25 .35
3 Andy Pettitte 2.00 .60
4 Brooks Kieschnick 1.25 .35
5 Chipper Jones 3.00 .90
6 Darin Erstad 1.25 .35
7 Derek Jeter 8.00 2.40
8 Jason Kendall 1.25 .35
9 Jermaine Dye 1.25 .35
10 Neifi Perez 1.25 .35
11 Scott Rolen 2.00 .60
12 Todd Hollandsworth 1.25 .35
13 Todd Walker 1.25 .35
14 Tony Clark 1.25 .35
15 Vladimir Guerrero 3.00 .90

1998 E-X2001 Rodriguez Hawaii XIII Promo

This card was distributed to industry leaders at the 13th Annual Hawaii Trade Show in late February, 1998. It previewed the upcoming 1998 E-X2001 baseball release. A small gold foil "Hawaii XIII" stamp with a palm tree on the left-hand side of the card front distinguishes the card. According to informed sources, Fleer/SkyBox produced approximately 200 of these cards.

Nm-Mt Ex-Mt
NNO Alex Rodriguez 25.00 7.50

1998 E-X2001

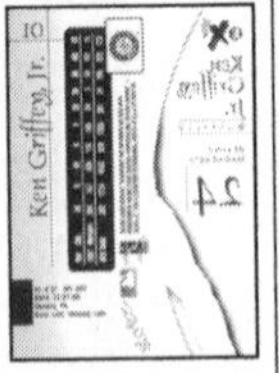

The 1998 E-X2001 set (made by Fleer/SkyBox) was issued in one series totalling 100 cards and distributed exclusively to hobby outlets. Cards were issued in two-card packs carrying a $3.99 suggested retail price. The cards are stunningly attractive, featuring full color action shots printed on clear acetate stock with sparkling foil backgrounds. An unnumbered Kerry Wood exchange card was randomly seeded into 1 in every 50 packs (the same pull rate as any other basic issue card). Unlike the acetate stock basic cards, this Wood exchange card was printed on paper stock and could be redeemed until March 31st, 1999 for a real E-X2001 acetate stock Wood card (number 101). In addition, an Alex Rodriguez sample card was issued a few months prior to the product's release. This sample card was distributed to dealers and hobby media to preview the upcoming release. The card is identical to a standard Alex Rodriguex E-X2001 except for the text "PROMOTIONAL SAMPLE" printed diagonally across the card back. There are no key Rookie Cards in this set.

Nm-Mt Ex-Mt
COMPLETE SET (100) 80.00 24.00
1 Alex Rodriguez 3.00 .90
2 Barry Bonds 5.00 1.50
3 Greg Maddux 3.00 .90
4 Roger Clemens 4.00 1.20
5 Juan Gonzalez 2.00 .60
6 Chipper Jones 2.00 .60
7 Derek Jeter 5.00 1.50
8 Frank Thomas 2.00 .60
9 Cal Ripken 6.00 1.80
10 Ken Griffey Jr. 3.00 .90
11 Mark McGwire 5.00 1.50
12 Hideo Nomo 2.00 .60
13 Tony Gwynn 2.50 .75
14 Ivan Rodriguez 2.00 .60
15 Mike Piazza 3.00 .90
16 Roberto Alomar 2.00 .60
17 Jeff Bagwell 1.25 .35
18 Andruw Jones .75 .23
19 Albert Belle .75 .23
20 Mo Vaughn .75 .23
21 Kenny Lofton .75 .23
22 Gary Sheffield .75 .23
23 Tony Clark .50 .15
24 Mike Mussina 2.00 .60
25 Barry Larkin 2.00 .60
26 Moises Alou .75 .23
27 Brady Anderson .75 .23
28 Andy Pettitte 1.25 .35
29 Sammy Sosa 3.00 .90
30 Raul Mondesi .75 .23
31 Andres Galarraga .75 .23
32 Chuck Knoblauch .75 .23
33 Jim Thome 2.00 .60
34 Craig Biggio 1.25 .35
35 Jay Buhner .75 .23
36 Rafael Palmeiro 1.25 .35
37 Curt Schilling 1.25 .35
38 Tino Martinez 1.25 .35
39 Pedro Martinez 2.00 .60
40 Jose Canseco 2.00 .60
41 Jeff Cirillo .50 .15
42 Dean Palmer .75 .23
43 Tim Salmon 1.25 .35
44 Jason Giambi 2.00 .60
45 Bobby Higginson .75 .23
46 Jim Edmonds .75 .23
47 David Justice .75 .23
48 John Olerud .75 .23
49 Ray Lankford .50 .15
50 Al Martin .50 .15
51 Mike Lieberthal .75 .23
52 Henry Rodriguez .50 .15
53 Edgar Renteria .75 .23
54 Eric Karros .75 .23
55 Marquis Grissom .50 .15
56 Wilson Alvarez .50 .15
57 Darryl Kile .75 .23
58 Jeff King .50 .15
59 Shawn Estes .50 .15
60 Tony Womack .50 .15
61 Willie Greene .50 .15
62 Ken Caminiti .75 .23
63 Vinny Castilla .75 .23
64 Mark Grace 1.25 .35
65 Ryan Klesko .75 .23
66 Robin Ventura .75 .23
67 Todd Hundley .75 .23
68 Travis Fryman .75 .23
69 Edgar Martinez 1.25 .35
70 Matt Williams .75 .23
71 Paul Molitor 1.25 .35
72 Kevin Brown 1.25 .35
73 Randy Johnson 2.00 .60
74 Bernie Williams 1.25 .35
75 Manny Ramirez .75 .23
76 Fred McGriff 1.25 .35
77 Tom Glavine 1.25 .35
78 Carlos Delgado .75 .23
79 Larry Walker 1.25 .35
80 Hideki Irabu .50 .15
81 Ryan McGuire .50 .15
82 Justin Thompson .50 .15
83 Kevin Orie .50 .15
84 Jon Nunnally .50 .15
85 Mark Kotsay .50 .15
86 Todd Walker .75 .23
87 Jason Dickson .50 .15
88 Fernando Tatis .50 .15
89 Karim Garcia .50 .15
90 Ricky Ledee .50 .15
91 Paul Konerko .75 .23
92 Jaret Wright .75 .23
93 Darin Erstad .75 .23
94 Livan Hernandez .50 .15
95 Nomar Garciaparra 3.00 .90
96 Jose Cruz Jr. .75 .23
97 Scott Rolen 1.25 .35
98 Ben Grieve .50 .15
99 Vladimir Guerrero 2.00 .60
100 Travis Lee .50 .15
101 K.Wood Redemption 5.00 1.50
NNO Kerry Wood EXCH 2.50 .75
NNO A.Rodriguez Sample 1.50 .45

1998 E-X2001 Essential Credentials Future

These cards were randomly inserted in E-X2001 packs. For this parallel version, the amount of cards produced is inverse to the card number. Each card is individually serial numbered on the lower edge of the card back. For conveniece, the amount of each player produced is listed next to their listing. Cards between 76 and 100 are not priced due to scarcity.

Nm-Mt Ex-Mt
1 Alex Rodriguez (100) 60.00 18.00
2 Barry Bonds (99) 100.00 30.00
3 Greg Maddux (98) 60.00 18.00
4 Roger Clemens (97) 80.00 24.00
5 Juan Gonzalez (96) 40.00 12.00
6 Chipper Jones (95) 40.00 12.00
7 Derek Jeter (94) 100.00 30.00
8 Frank Thomas (93) 40.00 12.00
9 Cal Ripken (92) 120.00 36.00
10 Ken Griffey Jr. (91) 60.00 18.00
11 Mark McGwire (90) 100.00 30.00
12 Hideo Nomo (89) 40.00 12.00
13 Tony Gwynn (88) 50.00 15.00
14 Ivan Rodriguez (87) 40.00 12.00
15 Mike Piazza (86) 60.00 18.00
16 Roberto Alomar (85) 40.00 12.00
17 Jeff Bagwell (84) 25.00 7.50
18 Andruw Jones (83) 25.00 7.50
19 Albert Belle (82) 25.00 7.50
20 Mo Vaughn (81) 25.00 7.50
21 Kenny Lofton (80) 25.00 7.50
22 Gary Sheffield (79) 25.00 7.50
23 Tony Clark (78) 15.00 4.50
24 Mike Mussina (77) 40.00 12.00
25 Barry Larkin (76) 40.00 12.00
26 Moises Alou (75) 25.00 7.50
27 Brady Anderson (74) 25.00 7.50
28 Andy Pettitte (73) 25.00 7.50
29 Sammy Sosa (72) 60.00 18.00
30 Raul Mondesi (71) 25.00 7.50
31 Andres Galarraga (70) 25.00 7.50
32 Chuck Knoblauch (69) 20.00 6.00
33 Jim Thome (68) 50.00 15.00
34 Craig Biggio (67) 30.00 9.00
35 Jay Buhner (66) 20.00 6.00
36 Rafael Palmeiro (65) 30.00 9.00
37 Curt Schilling (64) 30.00 9.00
38 Tino Martinez (63) 30.00 9.00
39 Pedro Martinez (62) 50.00 15.00
40 Jose Canseco (61) 50.00 15.00
41 Jeff Cirillo (60) 12.00 3.60
42 Dean Palmer (59) 20.00 6.00
43 Tim Salmon (58) 30.00 9.00
44 Jason Giambi (57) 50.00 15.00
45 Bobby Higginson (56) 20.00 6.00
46 Jim Edmonds (55) 20.00 6.00
47 David Justice (54) 20.00 6.00
48 John Olerud (53) 20.00 6.00
49 Ray Lankford (52) 12.00 3.60
50 Al Martin (51) 12.00 3.60
51 Mike Lieberthal (50) 25.00 7.50
52 Henry Rodriguez (49) 15.00 4.50
53 Edgar Renteria (48) 25.00 7.50
54 Eric Karros (47) 25.00 7.50
55 Marquis Grissom (46) 15.00 4.50
56 Wilson Alvarez (45) 15.00 4.50
57 Darryl Kile (44) 25.00 7.50
58 Jeff King (43) 15.00 4.50
59 Shawn Estes (42) 15.00 4.50
60 Tony Womack (41) 15.00 4.50
61 Willie Greene (40) 15.00 4.50
62 Ken Caminiti (39) 25.00 7.50
63 Vinny Castilla (38) 25.00 7.50
64 Mark Grace (37) 40.00 12.00
65 Ryan Klesko (36) 25.00 7.50
66 Robin Ventura (35) 40.00 12.00
67 Todd Hundley (34) 30.00 9.00
68 Travis Fryman (33) 40.00 12.00
69 Edgar Martinez (32) 50.00 15.00
70 Matt Williams (31) 40.00 12.00
71 Paul Molitor (30) 50.00 15.00
72 Kevin Brown (29) 50.00 15.00
73 Randy Johnson (28) 80.00 24.00
74 Bernie Williams (27) 50.00 15.00
75 Manny Ramirez (26) 40.00 12.00
76 Fred McGriff (25)
77 Tom Glavine (24)
78 Carlos Delgado (23)
79 Larry Walker (22)
80 Hideki Irabu (21)
81 Ryan McGuire (20)
82 Justin Thompson (19)
83 Kevin Orie (18)
84 Jon Nunnally (17)
85 Mark Kotsay (16)
86 Todd Walker (15)
87 Jason Dickson (14)
88 Fernando Tatis (13)
89 Karim Garcia (12)
90 Ricky Ledee (11)
91 Paul Konerko (10)
92 Jaret Wright (9)
93 Darin Erstad (8)
94 Livan Hernandez (7)
95 Nomar Garciaparra (6)
96 Jose Cruz Jr. (5)
97 Scott Rolen (4)
98 Ben Grieve (3)
99 Vladimir Guerrero (2)
100 Travis Lee (1)

1998 E-X2001 Essential Credentials Now

These cards were randomly inserted in X2001 packs. For this parallel version, t amount of cards produced is equal to their ca number. Each card in individually ser numbered on the lower edge of the card ba Again like in the Essential Credentials Futu we have put the amount of cards produced ne to the players name. Cards numbered betwe 1 and 25 are not priced due to scarcity.

Nm-Mt Ex-M
1 Alex Rodriguez (1)
2 Barry Bonds (2)
3 Greg Maddux (3)
4 Roger Clemens (4)
5 Juan Gonzalez (5)
6 Chipper Jones (6)
7 Derek Jeter (7)
8 Frank Thomas (8)
9 Cal Ripken (9)
10 Ken Griffey Jr. (10)
11 Mark McGwire (11)
12 Hideo Nomo (12)
13 Tony Gwynn (13)
14 Ivan Rodriguez (14)
15 Mike Piazza (15)
16 Roberto Alomar (16)
17 Jeff Bagwell (17)
18 Andruw Jones (18)
19 Albert Belle (19)
20 Mo Vaughn (20)
21 Kenny Lofton (21)
22 Gary Sheffield (22)
23 Tony Clark (23)
24 Mike Mussina (24)
25 Barry Larkin (25)
26 Moises Alou (26) 40.00 12.
27 Brady Anderson (27) 40.00 12.
28 Andy Pettitte (28) 50.00 15.
29 Sammy Sosa (29) 120.00 36.
30 Raul Mondesi (30) 40.00 12.

31 Andres Galarraga (31) 40.00 12.00
32 Chuck Knoblauch (32) 40.00 12.00
33 Jim Thome (33) 60.00 18.00
34 Craig Biggio (34) 50.00 15.00
35 Jay Buhner (35) 40.00 12.00
36 Rafael Palmeiro (36) 40.00 12.00
37 Curt Schilling (37) 40.00 12.00
38 Tino Martinez (38) 40.00 12.00
39 Pedro Martinez (39) 50.00 15.00
40 Jose Canseco (40) 50.00 15.00
41 Jeff Cirillo (41) 15.00 4.50
42 Dean Palmer (42) 25.00 7.50
43 Tim Salmon (43) 40.00 12.00
44 Jason Giambi (44) 50.00 15.00
45 Bobby Higginson (45) 25.00 7.50
46 Jim Edmonds (46) 25.00 7.50
47 David Justice (47) 25.00 7.50
48 John Olerud (48) 25.00 7.50
49 Ray Lankford (49) 15.00 4.50
50 Al Martin (50) 15.00 4.50
51 Mike Lieberthal (51) 20.00 6.00
52 Henry Rodriguez (52) 12.00 3.60
53 Edgar Renteria (53) 20.00 6.00
54 Eric Karros (54) 20.00 6.00
55 Marquis Grissom (55) 12.00 3.60
56 Wilson Alvarez (56) 12.00 3.60
57 Darryl Kile (57) 20.00 6.00
58 Jeff King (58) 12.00 3.60
59 Shawn Estes (59) 12.00 3.60
60 Tony Womack (60) 12.00 3.60
61 Willie Greene (61) 12.00 3.60
62 Ken Caminiti (62) 20.00 6.00
63 Vinny Castilla (63) 20.00 6.00
64 Mark Grace (64) 25.00 7.50
65 Ryan Klesko (65) 20.00 6.00
66 Robin Ventura (66) 20.00 6.00
67 Todd Hundley (67) 12.00 3.60
68 Travis Fryman (68) 20.00 6.00
69 Edgar Martinez (69) 25.00 7.50
70 Matt Williams (70) 20.00 6.00
71 Paul Molitor (71) 25.00 7.50
72 Kevin Brown (72) 25.00 7.50
73 Randy Johnson (73) 40.00 12.00
74 Bernie Williams (74) 25.00 7.50
75 Manny Ramirez (75) 25.00 7.50
76 Fred McGriff (76) 25.00 7.50
77 Tom Glavine (77) 25.00 7.50
78 Carlos Delgado (78) 15.00 4.50
79 Larry Walker (79) 25.00 7.50
80 Hideki Irabu (80) 10.00 3.00
81 Ryan McGuire (81) 10.00 3.00
82 Justin Thompson (82) 10.00 3.00
83 Kevin Orie (83) 10.00 3.00
84 Jon Nunnally (84) 10.00 3.00
85 Mark Kotsay (85) 10.00 3.00
86 Todd Walker (86) 15.00 4.50
87 Jason Dickson (87) 10.00 3.00
88 Fernando Tatis (88) 10.00 3.00
89 Karim Garcia (89) 10.00 3.00
90 Ricky Ledee (90) 10.00 3.00
91 Paul Konerko (91) 15.00 4.50
92 Jaret Wright (92) 10.00 3.00
93 Darin Erstad (93) 15.00 4.50
94 Livan Hernandez (94) 10.00 3.00
95 N.Garciaparra (95) 60.00 18.00
96 Jose Cruz Jr. (96) 15.00 4.50
97 Scott Rolen (97) 25.00 7.50
98 Ben Grieve (98) 10.00 3.00
99 Vladimir Guerrero (99) 40.00 12.00
100 Travis Lee (100) 10.00 3.00

1998 E-X2001 Cheap Seat Treats

Randomly inserted in packs at a rate of one in 24, this 20-card set is an insert to the SkyBox E-X2001 brand. Each die-cut card is shaped like a folding chair with silver foil stamping and features a color player photo of some of today's greatest sluggers.

	Nm-Mt	Ex-Mt
COMPLETE SET (20)	100.00	30.00
1 Frank Thomas	8.00	2.40
2 Ken Griffey Jr.	12.00	3.60
3 Mark McGwire	20.00	6.00
4 Tino Martinez	5.00	1.50
5 Larry Walker	5.00	1.50
6 Juan Gonzalez	8.00	2.40
7 Mike Piazza	12.00	3.60
8 Jeff Bagwell	5.00	1.50
9 Tony Clark	2.00	.60
10 Albert Belle	3.00	.90
11 Andres Galarraga	3.00	.90
12 Jim Thome	8.00	2.40
13 Mo Vaughn	3.00	.90
14 Barry Bonds	20.00	6.00
15 Vladimir Guerrero	8.00	2.40
16 Scott Rolen	5.00	1.50
17 Travis Lee	2.00	.60
18 David Justice	3.00	.90
19 Jose Cruz Jr.	3.00	.90
20 Andruw Jones	3.00	.90

1998 E-X2001 Destination Cooperstown

Randomly inserted in packs at a rate of one in 720, this 15-card set is an insert to the SkyBox E-X2001 brand. Each card is designed to resemble a luggage destination tag including a piece of string tied to a hole at the top of each card and honors future Hall-of Famers with color player photos. The cards also provide the featured player's name, team, and position.

	Nm-Mt	Ex-Mt
COMPLETE SET (15)	500.00	150.00
1 Alex Rodriguez	40.00	12.00
2 Frank Thomas	25.00	7.50
3 Cal Ripken	80.00	24.00
4 Roger Clemens	50.00	15.00
5 Greg Maddux	40.00	12.00
6 Chipper Jones	25.00	7.50
7 Ken Griffey Jr.	40.00	12.00
8 Mark McGwire	60.00	18.00
9 Tony Gwynn	30.00	9.00
10 Mike Piazza	40.00	12.00
11 Jeff Bagwell	15.00	4.50
12 Jose Cruz Jr.	10.00	3.00
13 Derek Jeter	60.00	18.00
14 Hideo Nomo	40.00	12.00
15 Ivan Rodriguez	25.00	7.50

1998 E-X2001 Signature 2001

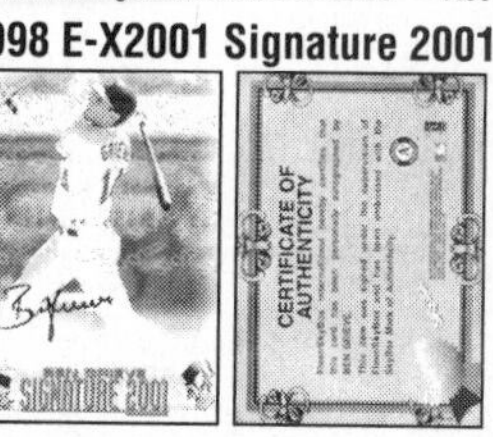

Randomly inserted in packs at a rate of one in 60, this 17-card set is an insert to the SkyBox E-X2001 brand. The exclusive insert features color action photos and autographs signed by some of MLB's brightest young stars.

	Nm-Mt	Ex-Mt
1 Ricky Ledee	5.00	1.50
2 Derrick Gibson	5.00	1.50
3 Mark Kotsay	5.00	1.50
4 Kevin Millwood	20.00	6.00
5 Brad Fullmer	5.00	1.50
6 Todd Walker	10.00	3.00
7 Ben Grieve	5.00	1.50
8 Tony Clark	5.00	1.50
9 Jaret Wright	5.00	1.50
10 Randall Simon	5.00	1.50
11 Paul Konerko	10.00	3.00
12 Todd Helton	25.00	7.50
13 David Ortiz	15.00	4.50
14 Alex Gonzalez	5.00	1.50
15 Bobby Estalella	5.00	1.50
16 Alex Rodriguez SP	120.00	36.00
17 Mike Lowell	25.00	7.50

1998 E-X2001 Star Date 2001

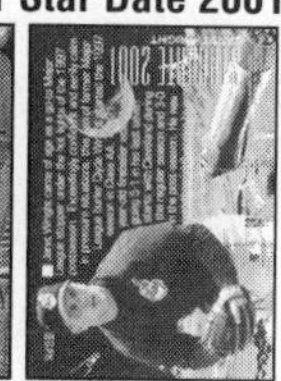

Randomly inserted in packs at a rate of one in 12, this 15-card set is an insert to the SkyBox E-X2001 brand. The fronts feature a background of space-age graphics and gold-foil stamping on plastic stock. The color action photos showcase some of the hottest up-and-coming stars in the MLB.

	Nm-Mt	Ex-Mt
COMPLETE SET (15)	15.00	4.50
1 Travis Lee	1.00	.30
2 Jose Cruz Jr.	1.00	.30
3 Paul Konerko	1.00	.30
4 Bobby Estalella	1.00	.30
5 Magglio Ordonez	4.00	1.20
6 Juan Encarnacion	1.00	.30
7 Richard Hidalgo	1.00	.30
8 Abraham Nunez	1.00	.30
9 Sean Casey	1.00	.30
10 Todd Helton	1.50	.45
11 Brad Fullmer	1.00	.30
12 Ben Grieve	1.00	.30
13 Livan Hernandez	1.00	.30
14 Jaret Wright	1.00	.30
15 Todd Dunwoody	1.00	.30

1999 E-X Century

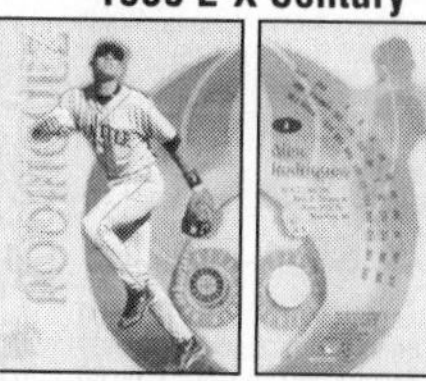

This 120-card set features color action player photos silhouetted on extra thick transparent plastic card stock. Each pack contained three cards and carried a suggested retail price of $5.99. The set contains a 30-card Rookie short-printed subset (91-120) with an insertion rate of 1:2 packs. A promotional sample card featuring Ben Grieve was distributed to dealer accounts and hobby media shortly before the product's national release. This card can be easily identified by the "PROMOTIONAL SAMPLE" text running across the back. Notable Rookie Cards include Pat Burrell.

	Nm-Mt	Ex-Mt
COMPLETE SET (120)	80.00	24.00
COMP.SET w/o SP's (90)	40.00	12.00
COMMON CARD (1-90)	.50	.15
COMMON SP (91-120)	1.00	.30
1 Scott Rolen	1.25	.35
2 Nomar Garciaparra	3.00	.90
3 Mike Piazza	3.00	.90
4 Tony Gwynn	2.50	.75
5 Sammy Sosa	3.00	.90
6 Alex Rodriguez	3.00	.90
7 Vladimir Guerrero	2.00	.60
8 Chipper Jones	2.00	.60
9 Derek Jeter	5.00	1.50
10 Kerry Wood	2.00	.60
11 Juan Gonzalez	2.00	.60
12 Frank Thomas	2.00	.60
13 Mo Vaughn	.75	.23
14 Greg Maddux	3.00	.90
15 Jeff Bagwell	1.25	.35
16 Mark McGwire	5.00	1.50
17 Ken Griffey Jr.	3.00	.90
18 Roger Clemens	4.00	1.20
19 Cal Ripken	6.00	1.80
20 Travis Lee	.50	.15
21 Todd Helton	1.25	.35
22 Darin Erstad	.75	.23
23 Pedro Martinez	2.00	.60
24 Barry Bonds	5.00	.45
25 Andruw Jones	.75	.23
26 Larry Walker	1.25	.35
27 Albert Belle	.75	.23
28 Ivan Rodriguez	2.00	.60
29 Magglio Ordonez	.75	.23
30 Andres Galarraga	.75	.23
31 Mike Mussina	2.00	.60
32 Randy Johnson	2.00	.60
33 Tom Glavine	1.25	.35
34 Barry Larkin	2.00	.60
35 Jim Thome	2.00	.60
36 Gary Sheffield	.75	.23
37 Bernie Williams	1.25	.35
38 Carlos Delgado	.75	.23
39 Rafael Palmeiro	1.25	.35
40 Edgar Renteria	.75	.23
41 Brad Fullmer	.50	.15
42 David Wells	.75	.23
43 Dante Bichette	.75	.23
44 Jaret Wright	.50	.15
45 Ricky Ledee	.50	.15
46 Ray Lankford	.50	.15
47 Mark Grace	1.25	.35
48 Jeff Cirillo	.50	.15
49 Rondell White	.75	.23
50 Jeromy Burnitz	.75	.23
51 Sean Casey	.75	.23
52 Rolando Arrojo	.50	.15
53 Jason Giambi	2.00	.60
54 John Olerud	.75	.23
55 Will Clark	2.00	.60
56 Raul Mondesi	.75	.23
57 Scott Brosius	.75	.23
58 Bartolo Colon	.75	.23
59 Steve Finley	.75	.23
60 Javy Lopez	.75	.23
61 Tim Salmon	1.25	.35
62 Roberto Alomar	2.00	.60
63 Vinny Castilla	.75	.23
64 Craig Biggio	1.25	.35
65 Jose Guillen	.50	.15
66 Greg Vaughn	.75	.23
67 Jose Canseco	2.00	.60
68 Shawn Green	.75	.23
69 Curt Schilling	1.25	.35
70 Orlando Hernandez	.75	.23
71 Jose Cruz Jr.	.75	.23
72 Alex Gonzalez	.50	.15
73 Tino Martinez	1.25	.35
74 Todd Hundley	.50	.15
75 Brian Giles	.75	.23
76 Cliff Floyd	.75	.23
77 Paul O'Neill	1.25	.35
78 Ken Caminiti	.75	.23
79 Ron Gant	.75	.23
80 Juan Encarnacion	.50	.15
81 Ben Grieve	.50	.15
82 Brian Jordan	.75	.23
83 Rickey Henderson	2.00	.60
84 Tony Clark	.50	.15
85 Shannon Stewart	.75	.23
86 Robin Ventura	.75	.23
87 Todd Walker	.75	.23
88 Kevin Brown	1.25	.35
89 Moises Alou	.75	.23
90 Manny Ramirez	.75	.23
91 Gabe Alvarez SP	1.00	.30
92 Jeremy Giambi SP	1.00	.30
93 Adrian Beltre SP	1.00	.30
94 George Lombard SP	1.00	.30
95 Ryan Minor SP	1.00	.30
96 Kevin Witt SP	1.00	.30
97 Scott Hunter SP RC	1.00	.30
98 Carlos Guillen SP	1.00	.30
99 Derrick Gibson SP	1.00	.30
100 Trot Nixon SP	1.00	.30
101 Troy Glaus SP	1.00	.25
102 Armando Rios SP	1.00	.30
103 Preston Wilson SP	1.00	.30
104 Pat Burrell SP RC	5.00	1.50
105 J.D. Drew SP	1.00	.30
106 Bruce Chen SP	1.00	.30
107 Matt Clement SP	1.00	.30
108 Carlos Beltran SP	1.00	.30
109 Carlos Febles SP	1.00	.30
110 Rob Fick SP	1.00	.30
111 Russell Branyan SP	1.00	.30
112 R.Brown SP RC	1.00	.30
113 Corey Koskie SP	1.00	.30
114 M.Encarnacion SP RC	1.00	.30
115 Peter Tucci SP	1.00	.30
116 Eric Chavez SP	1.00	.30
117 Gabe Kapler SP	1.00	.30
118 Marlon Anderson SP	1.00	.30
119 A.J. Burnett SP RC	1.50	.45
120 Ryan Bradley SP	1.00	.30
P81 Ben Grieve Sample	1.00	.30

1999 E-X Century Essential Credentials Future

Randomly inserted into packs, this 120-card set is a sequentially numbered gold foil parallel version of the E-X Century base set. The print run for each card follows the player's name in the checklist below.

	Nm-Mt	Ex-Mt
1 Scott Rolen (120)	20.00	6.00
2 N.Garciaparra (119)	50.00	15.00
3 Mike Piazza (118)	50.00	15.00
4 Tony Gwynn (117)	40.00	12.00
5 Sammy Sosa (116)	50.00	15.00
6 Alex Rodriguez (115)	50.00	15.00
7 Vladimir Guerrero (114)	20.00	6.00
8 Chipper Jones (113)	20.00	6.00
9 Derek Jeter (112)	80.00	24.00
10 Kerry Wood (111)	20.00	6.00
11 Juan Gonzalez (110)	20.00	6.00
12 Frank Thomas (109)	20.00	6.00
13 Mo Vaughn (108)	15.00	4.50
14 Greg Maddux (107)	50.00	15.00
15 Jeff Bagwell (106)	20.00	6.00
16 Mark McGwire (105)	80.00	24.00
17 Ken Griffey Jr. (104)	50.00	15.00
18 Roger Clemens (103)	60.00	18.00
19 Cal Ripken (102)	100.00	30.00
20 Travis Lee (101)	12.00	3.60
21 Todd Helton (100)	20.00	6.00
22 Darin Erstad (99)	12.00	3.60
23 Pedro Martinez (98)	30.00	9.00
24 Barry Bonds (97)	100.00	30.00
25 Andruw Jones (96)	12.00	3.60
26 Larry Walker (95)	20.00	6.00
27 Albert Belle (94)	12.00	3.60
28 Ivan Rodriguez (93)	30.00	9.00
29 Magglio Ordonez (92)	12.00	3.60
30 Andres Galarraga (91)	12.00	3.60
31 Mike Mussina (90)	30.00	9.00
32 Randy Johnson (89)	30.00	9.00
33 Tom Glavine (88)	20.00	6.00
34 Barry Larkin (87)	30.00	9.00
35 Jim Thome (86)	30.00	9.00
36 Gary Sheffield (85)	12.00	3.60
37 Bernie Williams (84)	20.00	6.00
38 Carlos Delgado (83)	12.00	3.60
39 Rafael Palmeiro (82)	20.00	6.00
40 Edgar Renteria (81)	12.00	3.60
41 Brad Fullmer (80)	10.00	3.00
42 David Wells (79)	12.00	3.60
43 Dante Bichette (78)	12.00	3.60
44 Jaret Wright (77)	10.00	3.00
45 Ricky Ledee (76)	10.00	3.00
46 Ray Lankford (75)	10.00	3.00
47 Mark Grace (74)	20.00	6.00
48 Jeff Cirillo (73)	10.00	3.00
49 Rondell White (72)	12.00	3.60
50 Jeromy Burnitz (71)	12.00	3.60
51 Sean Casey (70)	15.00	4.50
52 Rolando Arrojo (69)	12.00	3.60
53 Jason Giambi (68)	40.00	12.00
54 John Olerud (67)	15.00	4.50
55 Will Clark (66)	40.00	12.00
56 Raul Mondesi (65)	15.00	4.50
57 Scott Brosius (64)	15.00	3.70
58 Bartolo Colon (63)	15.00	4.50
59 Steve Finley (62)	15.00	4.50
60 Javy Lopez (61)	15.00	4.50
61 Tim Salmon (60)	25.00	7.50
62 Roberto Alomar (59)	40.00	12.00
63 Vinny Castilla (58)	15.00	4.50
64 Craig Biggio (57)	25.00	7.50
65 Jose Guillen (56)	12.00	3.60
66 Greg Vaughn (55)	15.00	4.50
67 Jose Canseco (54)	40.00	12.00
68 Shawn Green (53)	15.00	4.50
69 Curt Schilling (52)	25.00	7.50
70 O.Hernandez (51)	15.00	4.50
71 Jose Cruz Jr. (50)	15.00	4.50
72 Alex Gonzalez (49)	12.00	3.60
73 Tino Martinez (48)	30.00	9.00
74 Todd Hundley (47)	12.00	3.60
75 Brian Giles (46)	20.00	6.00
76 Cliff Floyd (45)	20.00	6.00
77 Paul O'Neill (44)	30.00	9.00
78 Ken Caminiti (43)	20.00	6.00
79 Ron Gant (42)	20.00	6.00
80 Juan Encarnacion (41)	12.00	3.60
81 Ben Grieve (40)	12.00	3.60
82 Brian Jordan (39)	20.00	6.00
83 Rickey Henderson (38)	50.00	15.00
84 Tony Clark (37)	12.00	3.60
85 Shannon Stewart (36)	20.00	6.00
86 Robin Ventura (35)	25.00	7.50
87 Todd Walker (34)	25.00	7.50
88 Kevin Brown (33)	40.00	12.00
89 Moises Alou (32)	25.00	7.50
90 Manny Ramirez (31)	25.00	7.50
91 Gabe Alvarez (30)	15.00	4.50
92 Jeremy Giambi (29)	15.00	4.50
93 Adrian Beltre (28)	25.00	7.50
94 George Lombard (27)	15.00	4.50
95 Ryan Minor (26)	15.00	4.50
96 Kevin Witt (25)		
97 Scott Hunter (24)		
98 Carlos Guillen (23)		
99 Derrick Gibson (22)		
100 Trot Nixon (21)		
101 Troy Glaus (20)		
102 Armando Rios (19)		
103 Preston Wilson (18)		
104 Pat Burrell (17)		
105 J.D. Drew (16)		
106 Bruce Chen (15)		
107 Matt Clement (14)		
108 Carlos Beltran (13)		
109 Carlos Febles (12)		
110 Rob Fick (11)		
111 Russell Branyan (10)		
112 Roosevelt Brown (9)		
113 Corey Koskie (8)		
114 Mario Encarnacion (7)		
115 Peter Tucci (6)		
116 Eric Chavez (5)		
117 Gabe Kapler (4)		
118 Marlon Anderson (3)		
119 A.J. Burnett (2)		
120 Ryan Bradley (1)		

1999 E-X Century Essential Credentials Now

Randomly inserted into packs, this 120-card set is a silver foil parallel version of the E-X Century base set. Each card is sequentially numbered to the pictured player's card number and follows the player's name in the checklist below.

	Nm-Mt	Ex-Mt
1 Scott Rolen (1)		
2 Nomar Garciaparra (2)		
3 Mike Piazza (3)		
4 Tony Gwynn (4)		
5 Sammy Sosa (5)		
6 Alex Rodriguez (6)		
7 Vladimir Guerrero (7)		
8 Chipper Jones (8)		
9 Derek Jeter (9)		
10 Kerry Wood (10)		
11 Juan Gonzalez (11)		
12 Frank Thomas (12)		
13 Mo Vaughn (13)		
14 Greg Maddux (14)		
15 Jeff Bagwell (15)		
16 Mark McGwire (16)		
17 Ken Griffey Jr. (17)		
18 Roger Clemens (18)		
19 Cal Ripken (19)		
20 Travis Lee (20)		
21 Todd Helton (21)		
22 Darin Erstad (22)		
23 Pedro Martinez (23)		
24 Barry Bonds (24)		
25 Andruw Jones (25)		
26 Larry Walker (26)	50.00	15.00
27 Albert Belle (27)	40.00	12.00
28 Ivan Rodriguez (28)	60.00	18.00
29 Magglio Ordonez (29)	40.00	12.00
30 Andres Galarraga (30)	40.00	12.00
31 Mike Mussina (31)	60.00	18.00
32 Randy Johnson (32)	60.00	18.00
33 Tom Glavine (33)	50.00	15.00
34 Barry Larkin (34)	60.00	18.00
35 Jim Thome (35)	60.00	18.00
36 Gary Sheffield (36)	20.00	6.00
37 Bernie Williams (37)	30.00	9.00
38 Carlos Delgado (38)	20.00	16.00
39 Rafael Palmeiro (39)	30.00	9.00
40 Edgar Renteria (40)	20.00	6.00
41 Brad Fullmer (41)	12.00	3.60
42 David Wells (42)	20.00	6.00
43 Dante Bichette (43)	20.00	6.00
44 Jaret Wright (44)	12.00	3.60
45 Ricky Ledee (45)	12.00	3.60
46 Ray Lankford (46)	12.00	3.60
47 Mark Grace (47)	30.00	9.00
48 Jeff Cirillo (48)	12.00	3.60
49 Rondell White (49)	20.00	6.00
50 Jeromy Burnitz (50)	20.00	6.00
51 Sean Casey (51)	15.00	4.50
52 Rolando Arrojo (52)	12.00	3.60
53 Jason Giambi (53)	40.00	12.00
54 John Olerud (54)	15.00	4.50
55 Will Clark (55)	40.00	12.00
56 Raul Mondesi (56)	15.00	4.50
57 Scott Brosius (57)	15.00	4.50
58 Bartolo Colon (58)	15.00	4.50
59 Steve Finley (59)	15.00	4.50
60 Javy Lopez (60)	15.00	4.50
61 Tim Salmon (61)	25.00	7.50
62 Roberto Alomar (62)	40.00	12.00
63 Vinny Castilla (63)	15.00	4.50
64 Craig Biggio (64)	25.00	7.50
65 Jose Guillen (65)	12.00	3.60
66 Greg Vaughn (66)	15.00	4.50
67 Jose Canseco (67)	40.00	12.00
68 Shawn Green (68)	15.00	4.50
69 Curt Schilling (69)	25.00	7.50
70 O.Hernandez (70)	15.00	4.50
71 Jose Cruz Jr. (71)	12.00	3.60
72 Alex Gonzalez (72)	10.00	3.00
73 Tino Martinez (73)	20.00	6.00
74 Todd Hundley (74)	10.00	3.00
75 Brian Giles (75)	12.00	3.60
76 Cliff Floyd (76)	12.00	3.60
77 Paul O'Neill (77)	20.00	6.00
78 Ken Caminiti (78)	12.00	3.60
79 Ron Gant (79)	12.00	3.60
80 Juan Encarnacion (80)	10.00	3.00
81 Ben Grieve (81)	10.00	3.00
82 Brian Jordan (82)	12.00	3.60
83 Rickey Henderson (83)	30.00	9.00
84 Tony Clark (84)	10.00	3.00
85 Shannon Stewart (85)	12.00	3.60
86 Robin Ventura (86)	12.00	3.60
87 Todd Walker (87)	12.00	3.60
88 Kevin Brown (88)	20.00	6.00
89 Moises Alou (89)	12.00	3.60
90 Manny Ramirez (90)	12.00	3.60
91 Gabe Alvarez (91)	10.00	3.00
92 Jeremy Giambi (92)	10.00	3.00
93 Adrian Beltre (93)	12.00	3.60
94 George Lombard (94)	10.00	3.00
95 Ryan Minor (95)	10.00	3.00
96 Kevin Witt (96)	10.00	3.00
97 Scott Hunter (97)	10.00	3.00
98 Carlos Guillen (98)	10.00	3.00
99 Derrick Gibson (99)	10.00	3.00
100 Trot Nixon (100)	20.00	6.00
101 Troy Glaus (101)	15.00	4.50
102 Armando Rios (102)	6.00	1.80
103 Preston Wilson (103)	10.00	3.00
104 Pat Burrell (104)	60.00	18.00
105 J.D. Drew (105)	10.00	3.00
106 Bruce Chen (106)	6.00	1.80
107 Matt Clement (107)	10.00	3.00
108 Carlos Beltran (108)	10.00	3.00
109 Carlos Febles (109)	6.00	6.00
110 Rob Fick (110)	10.00	3.00
111 Russell Branyan (111)	6.00	1.80
112 R.Brown (112)	10.00	3.00
113 Corey Koskie (113)	10.00	3.00
114 M.Encarnacion (114)	6.00	1.80
115 Peter Tucci (115)	6.00	1.80
116 Eric Chavez (116)	10.00	3.00
117 Gabe Kapler (117)	6.00	1.80
118 M.Anderson (118)	6.00	1.80
119 A.J. Burnett (119)	25.00	7.50
120 Ryan Bradley (120)	6.00	1.80

1999 E-X Century Authen-Kicks

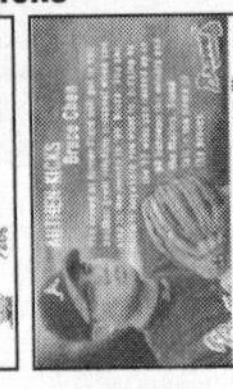

Randomly inserted into packs, this nine-card set features color cut-outs of top young players with swatches of their game-worn shoes embedded in the cards beside black-and-white head shots of the players in the background. The print run for each card follows the player's name in our checklist.

	Nm-Mt	Ex-Mt
1 J.D. Drew/160	25.00	7.50
2 Travis Lee/175	15.00	4.50
3 Kevin Millwood/165	25.00	7.50
4 Bruce Chen/205	15.00	4.50
5 Troy Glaus/205	40.00	12.00
6 Todd Helton/205	40.00	12.00
7 Ricky Ledee/180	15.00	4.50
8 Scott Rolen/205	40.00	12.00
9 Jeremy Giambi/205	15.00	4.50
B1 J.D. Drew Black AU/8		
R1 J.D. Drew Red AU/8		

1999 E-X Century E-X Quisite

Randomly inserted into packs at the rate of one in 18, this 15-card set features color cut-outs of top young players printed on cards with an unique interior die-cut design.

	Nm-Mt	Ex-Mt
COMPLETE SET (15)	40.00	12.00
1 Troy Glaus	1.50	.45
2 J.D. Drew	1.50	.45
3 Pat Burrell	6.00	1.80
4 Russell Branyan	1.50	.45
5 Kerry Wood	6.00	1.80
6 Eric Chavez	1.50	.45
7 Ben Grieve	1.50	.45
8 Gabe Kapler	1.50	.45
9 Adrian Beltre	1.50	.45
10 Todd Helton	4.00	1.20
11 Roosevelt Brown	1.50	.45
12 Marlon Anderson	1.50	.45
13 Jeremy Giambi	1.50	.45
14 Magglio Ordonez	2.50	.75
15 Travis Lee	1.50	.23

1999 E-X Century Favorites for Fenway '99

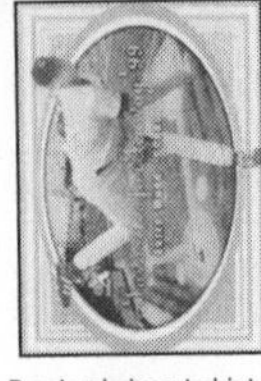

Randomly inserted into packs at the rate of one in 36, this 20-card set features color cut-outs of All-Star Game starters silhouetted in front of The Green Monster, Fenway Park.

	Nm-Mt	Ex-Mt
COMPLETE SET (20)	300.00	90.00
1 Mo Vaughn	4.00	1.20
2 Nomar Garciaparra	15.00	4.50
3 Frank Thomas	10.00	3.00
4 Ken Griffey Jr.	15.00	4.50
5 Roger Clemens	20.00	6.00
6 Alex Rodriguez	15.00	4.50
7 Derek Jeter	25.00	7.50
8 Juan Gonzalez	10.00	3.00
9 Cal Ripken	30.00	9.00
10 Ivan Rodriguez	10.00	3.00
11 J.D. Drew	5.00	1.50
12 Barry Bonds	25.00	7.50
13 Tony Gwynn	12.00	3.60
14 Vladimir Guerrero	10.00	3.00
15 Chipper Jones	10.00	3.00
16 Kerry Wood	10.00	3.00
17 Mike Piazza	15.00	4.50
18 Sammy Sosa	15.00	4.50
19 Scott Rolen	6.00	1.80
20 Mark McGwire	25.00	7.50

1999 E-X Century Milestones of the Century

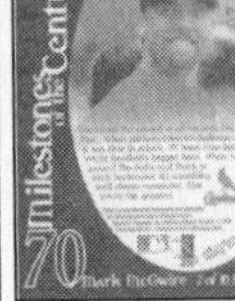

Randomly inserted into packs, this 10-card set features color action photos of players with top statistical performances from the 1998 season printed on a multi-layered card design. Each card is sequentially numbered to the pictured player's 1998 statistical performance and follows the player's name in our checklist.

	Nm-Mt	Ex-Mt
1 Kerry Wood/20		
2 Mark McGwire/70	120.00	36.00
3 Sammy Sosa/66	60.00	18.00
4 Ken Griffey Jr./350	30.00	9.00
5 Roger Clemens/98	60.00	18.00
6 Cal Ripken/17		
7 Alex Rodriguez/40	80.00	24.00
8 Barry Bonds/400	40.00	12.00
9 N.Y. Yankees/114	80.00	24.00
10 Travis Lee/98	5.00	1.50

2000 E-X

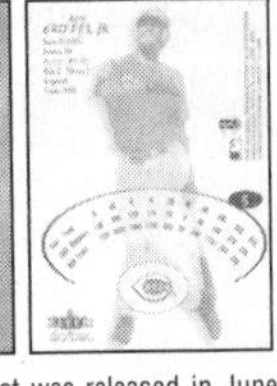

The 2000 E-X product was released in June, 2000 as a 90-card set. The set featured 60-player cards and 30-short printed prospect cards. Each of the prospect cards were individually serial numbered to 3499. Each pack contained three cards and carried a suggested retail price of $3.99.

	Nm-Mt	Ex-Mt
COMPLETE SET (90)	100.00	30.00
COMP.SET w/o SP's (60)	20.00	6.00
COMMON CARD (1-60)	.40	.12
COMMON PROS (61-90)	4.00	1.20
1 Alex Rodriguez	1.50	.45
2 Jeff Bagwell	.60	.18
3 Mike Piazza	1.50	.45
4 Tony Gwynn	1.25	.35
5 Ken Griffey Jr.	1.50	.45
6 Juan Gonzalez	1.00	.30
7 Vladimir Guerrero	1.00	.30
8 Cal Ripken	3.00	.90
9 Mo Vaughn	.40	.12
10 Chipper Jones	1.00	.30
11 Derek Jeter	2.50	.75
12 Nomar Garciaparra	1.50	.45
13 Mark McGwire	2.50	.75
14 Sammy Sosa	1.50	.45
15 Pedro Martinez	1.00	.30
16 Greg Maddux	1.50	.45
17 Frank Thomas	1.00	.30
18 Shawn Green	.40	.12
19 Carlos Beltran	.40	.12
20 Roger Clemens	2.00	.60
21 Randy Johnson	1.00	.30
22 Bernie Williams	.60	.18
23 Carlos Delgado	.40	.12
24 Manny Ramirez	.40	.12
25 Freddy Garcia	.40	.12
26 Barry Bonds	2.50	.75
27 Tim Hudson	.60	.18
28 Larry Walker	.60	.18
29 Raul Mondesi	.40	.12
30 Ivan Rodriguez	1.00	.30
31 Magglio Ordonez	.40	.12
32 Scott Rolen	.60	.18
33 Mike Mussina	1.00	.30
34 J.D. Drew	.40	.12
35 Tom Glavine	.60	.18
36 Barry Larkin	1.00	.30
37 Jim Thome	1.00	.30
38 Erubiel Durazo	.40	.12
39 Curt Schilling	.60	.18
40 Orlando Hernandez	.40	.12
41 Rafael Palmeiro	.60	.18
42 Gabe Kapler	.40	.12
43 Mark Grace	.60	.18
44 Jeff Cirillo	.40	.12
45 Jeromy Burnitz	.40	.12
46 Sean Casey	.40	.12
47 Kevin Millwood	.40	.12
48 Vinny Castilla	.40	.12
49 Jose Canseco	1.00	.30
50 Roberto Alomar	1.00	.30
51 Craig Biggio	.60	.18
52 Preston Wilson	.40	.12
53 Jeff Weaver	.40	.12
54 Robin Ventura	.40	.12
55 Ben Grieve	.40	.12
56 Troy Glaus	.60	.18
57 Jacque Jones	.40	.12
58 Brian Giles	.40	.12
59 Kevin Brown	.40	.12
60 Todd Helton	.60	.18
61 Ben Petrick PROS	4.00	1.20
62 C.Hermansen PROS	4.00	1.20
63 Kevin Barker PROS	4.00	1.20
64 Matt LeCroy PROS	4.00	1.20
65 Brad Penny PROS	4.00	1.20
66 D.T. Cromer PROS	4.00	1.20
67 Steve Lomasney PROS	4.00	1.20
68 Cole Liniak PROS	4.00	1.20
69 B.J. Ryan PROS	4.00	1.20
70 Wilton Veras PROS	4.00	1.20
71 A.McNeal PROS RC	4.00	1.20
72 Nick Johnson PROS	4.00	1.20
73 Adam Piatt PROS	4.00	1.20
74 Adam Kennedy PROS	4.00	1.20
75 Cesar King PROS	4.00	1.20
76 Peter Bergeron PROS	4.00	1.20
77 Rob Bell PROS	4.00	1.20
78 Wily Pena PROS	4.00	1.20
79 Ruben Mateo PROS	4.00	1.20
80 Kip Wells PROS	4.00	1.20
81 Alex Escobar PROS	4.00	1.20
82 Danys Baez PROS RC	5.00	1.50
83 Travis Dawkins PROS	4.00	1.20
84 Mark Quinn PROS	4.00	1.20
85 Jimmy Anderson PROS	4.00	1.20
86 Rick Ankiel PROS	4.00	1.20
87 Alfonso Soriano PROS	5.00	1.50
88 Pat Burrell PROS	5.00	1.50
89 Eric Munson PROS	4.00	1.20
90 Josh Beckett PROS	6.00	1.80

2000 E-X Essential Credentials Future

Randomly inserted into packs, this 90-card insert is a complete parallel of the E-X base set. Print runs for each of these cards are provided after the player's name in our checklist.

	Nm-Mt	Ex-Mt
1 Alex Rodriguez (60)	80.00	24.00
2 Jeff Bagwell (59)	30.00	9.00
3 Mike Piazza (58)	80.00	24.00
4 Tony Gwynn (57)	60.00	18.00
5 Ken Griffey Jr. (56)	80.00	24.00
6 Juan Gonzalez (55)	40.00	12.00
7 Vladimir Guerrero (54)	40.00	12.00
8 Cal Ripken (53)	150.00	45.00
9 Mo Vaughn (52)	30.00	9.00
10 Chipper Jones (51)	40.00	12.00
11 Derek Jeter (50)	120.00	36.00
12 N.Garciaparra (49)	80.00	24.00
13 Mark McGwire (48)	120.00	36.00
14 Sammy Sosa (47)	80.00	24.00
15 Pedro Martinez (46)	40.00	12.00
16 Greg Maddux (45)	80.00	24.00
17 Frank Thomas (44)	40.00	12.00
18 Shawn Green (43)	20.00	6.00
19 Carlos Beltran (42)	20.00	6.00
20 Roger Clemens (41)	100.00	30.00
21 Randy Johnson (40)	40.00	12.00
22 Bernie Williams (39)	40.00	12.00
23 Carlos Delgado (38)	20.00	6.00
24 Manny Ramirez (37)	20.00	6.00
25 Freddy Garcia (36)	20.00	6.00
26 Barry Bonds (35)	150.00	45.00
27 Tim Hudson (34)	50.00	15.00
28 Larry Walker (33)	50.00	15.00
29 Raul Mondesi (32)	40.00	12.00
30 Ivan Rodriguez (31)	60.00	18.00
31 Magglio Ordonez (30)	40.00	12.00
32 Scott Rolen (29)	50.00	15.00
33 Mike Mussina (28)	60.00	18.00
34 J.D. Drew (27)	40.00	12.00
35 Tom Glavine (26)	50.00	15.00
36 Barry Larkin (25)		
37 Jim Thome (24)		
38 Erubiel Durazo (23)		
39 Curt Schilling (22)		
40 O.Hernandez (21)		
41 Rafael Palmeiro (20)		
42 Gabe Kapler (19)		
43 Mark Grace (18)		
44 Jeff Cirillo (17)		
45 Jeromy Burnitz (16)		
46 Sean Casey (15)		
47 Kevin Millwood (14)		
48 Vinny Castilla (13)		
49 Jose Canseco (12)		
50 Roberto Alomar (11)		
51 Craig Biggio (10)		
52 Preston Wilson (9)		
53 Jeff Weaver (8)		
54 Robin Ventura (7)		
55 Ben Grieve (6)		
56 Troy Glaus (5)		
57 Jacque Jones (4)		
58 Brian Giles (3)		
59 Kevin Brown (2)		
60 Todd Helton (1)		
61 Ben Petrick (30)	25.00	7.50
62 Chad Hermansen (29)	25.00	7.50
63 Kevin Barker (28)	25.00	7.50
64 Matt LeCroy (27)	25.00	7.50
65 Brad Penny (26)	25.00	7.50
66 D.T. Cromer (25)		
67 Steve Lomasney (24)		
68 Cole Liniak (23)		
69 B.J. Ryan (22)		
70 Wilton Veras (21)		
71 Aaron McNeal (20)		
72 Nick Johnson (19)		
73 Adam Piatt (18)		
74 Adam Kennedy (17)		
75 Cesar King (16)		
76 Peter Bergeron (15)		
77 Rob Bell (14)		
78 Wily Pena (13)		
79 Ruben Mateo (12)		
80 Kip Wells (11)		
81 Alex Escobar (10)		
82 Danys Baez (9)		
83 Travis Dawkins (8)		
84 Mark Quinn (7)		
85 Jimmy Anderson (6)		
86 Rick Ankiel (5)		
87 Alfonso Soriano (4)		
88 Pat Burrell (3)		
89 Eric Munson (2)		
90 Josh Beckett (1)		

2000 E-X Essential Credentials Now

Randomly inserted into packs, this 90-card insert is a complete parallel of the E-X base set. Print runs for each of these cards are provided after the player's name in our checklist.

	Nm-Mt	Ex-Mt
1 Alex Rodriguez (1)		
2 Jeff Bagwell (2)		
3 Mike Piazza (3)		
4 Tony Gwynn (4)		
5 Ken Griffey Jr. (5)		
6 Juan Gonzalez (6)		
7 Vladimir Guerrero (7)		
8 Cal Ripken (8)		
9 Mo Vaughn (9)		
10 Chipper Jones (10)		
11 Derek Jeter (11)		
12 Nomar Garciaparra (12)		
13 Mark McGwire (13)		
14 Sammy Sosa (14)		
15 Pedro Martinez (15)		
16 Greg Maddux (16)		
17 Frank Thomas (17)		
18 Shawn Green (18)		
19 Carlos Beltran (19)		
20 Roger Clemens (20)		
21 Randy Johnson (21)		
22 Bernie Williams (22)		
23 Carlos Delgado (23)		
24 Manny Ramirez (24)		
25 Freddy Garcia (25)		
26 Barry Bonds (26)	150.00	45.00
27 Tim Hudson (27)	50.00	15.00
28 Larry Walker (28)	50.00	15.00
29 Raul Mondesi (29)	40.00	12.00
30 Ivan Rodriguez (30)	60.00	18.00
31 Magglio Ordonez (31)	40.00	12.00
32 Scott Rolen (32)	50.00	15.00
33 Mike Mussina (33)	60.00	18.00
34 J.D. Drew (34)	40.00	12.00
35 Tom Glavine (35)	50.00	15.00
36 Barry Larkin (36)	50.00	15.00
37 Jim Thome (37)	50.00	15.00
38 Erubiel Durazo (38)	20.00	6.00
39 Curt Schilling (39)	30.00	9.00
40 O.Hernandez (40)	25.00	7.50
41 Rafael Palmeiro (41)	30.00	9.00
42 Gabe Kapler (42)	20.00	6.00
43 Mark Grace (43)	30.00	9.00
44 Jeff Cirillo (44)	20.00	6.00
45 Jeromy Burnitz (45)	25.00	7.50
46 Sean Casey (46)	25.00	7.50
47 Kevin Millwood (47)	25.00	7.50
48 Vinny Castilla (48)	25.00	7.50
49 Jose Canseco (49)	50.00	15.00
50 Roberto Alomar (50)	50.00	15.00
51 Craig Biggio (51)	25.00	7.50
52 Preston Wilson (52)	20.00	6.00
53 Jeff Weaver (53)	15.00	4.50
54 Robin Ventura (54)	20.00	6.00
55 Ben Grieve (55)	15.00	4.50
56 Troy Glaus (56)	25.00	7.50
57 Jacque Jones (57)	20.00	6.00
58 Brian Giles (58)	20.00	6.00
59 Kevin Brown (59)	25.00	7.50
60 Todd Helton (60)	25.00	7.50
61 Ben Petrick (1)		
62 Chad Hermansen (2)		
63 Kevin Barker (3)		
64 Matt LeCroy (4)		
65 Brad Penny (5)		
66 D.T. Cromer (6)		
67 Steve Lomasney (7)		
68 Cole Liniak (8)		
69 B.J. Ryan (9)		
70 Wilton Veras (10)		
71 Aaron McNeal (11)		
72 Nick Johnson (12)		
73 Adam Piatt (13)		
74 Adam Kennedy (14)		
75 Cesar King (15)		
76 Peter Bergeron (16)		
77 Rob Bell (17)		
78 Wily Pena (18)		
79 Ruben Mateo (19)		
80 Kip Wells (20)		
81 Alex Escobar (21)		
82 Danys Baez (22)		
83 Travis Dawkins (23)		
84 Mark Quinn (24)		
85 Jimmy Anderson (25)		
86 Rick Ankiel (26)	50.00	15.00
87 Alfonso Soriano (27)	60.00	18.00
88 Pat Burrell (28)	60.00	18.00
89 Eric Munson (29)	50.00	15.00
90 Josh Beckett (30)	60.00	18.00

2000 E-X E-Xceptional Red

Randomly inserted into packs, this 15-card insert features some of the hottest major league ballplayers. Each card is individually numbered to 1999. Card backs carry a "XC" prefix.

	Nm-Mt	Ex-Mt
COMPLETE SET (15)	150.00	45.00
*BLUE: 1.25X TO 3X RED		
BLUE PRINT RUN 250 SERIAL #'d SETS		
*GREEN: .6X TO 1.5X RED		
GREEN PRINT RUN 999 SERIAL #'d SETS		
RANDOM INSERTS IN PACKS		
XC1 Ken Griffey Jr.	10.00	3.00
XC2 Derek Jeter	15.00	4.50
XC3 Nomar Garciaparra	10.00	3.00
XC4 Mark McGwire	15.00	4.50
XC5 Sammy Sosa	10.00	3.00
XC6 Mike Piazza	10.00	3.00
XC7 Alex Rodriguez	10.00	3.00
XC8 Cal Ripken	20.00	6.00
XC9 Chipper Jones	6.00	1.80
XC10 Pedro Martinez	6.00	1.80
XC11 Jeff Bagwell	4.00	1.20
XC12 Greg Maddux	10.00	3.00
XC13 Roger Clemens	12.00	3.60
XC14 Tony Gwynn	8.00	2.40
XC15 Frank Thomas	6.00	1.80

2000 E-X E-Xciting

Randomly inserted into packs at one in 24, this 10-card insert set features some of the most exciting players in modern major league baseball. Card backs carry a "XT" prefix.

	Nm-Mt	Ex-Mt
COMPLETE SET (10)	60.00	18.00
XT1 Mark McGwire	10.00	3.00
XT2 Ken Griffey Jr.	6.00	1.80
XT3 Randy Johnson	4.00	1.20
XT4 Sammy Sosa	6.00	1.80
XT5 Manny Ramirez	1.50	.45
XT6 Jose Canseco	4.00	1.20
XT7 Derek Jeter	10.00	3.00
XT8 Scott Rolen	2.50	.75
XT9 Juan Gonzalez	4.00	1.20
XT10 Barry Bonds	10.00	3.00

2000 E-X E-Xplosive

Randomly inserted into packs, this 20-card set features some of the most explosive players in major league baseball. Each card is individually serial numbered to 2499. Card backs carry a "XP" prefix.

	Nm-Mt	Ex-Mt
COMPLETE SET (20)	200.00	60.00
XP1 Tony Gwynn	8.00	2.40
XP2 Alex Rodriguez	10.00	3.00
XP3 Pedro Martinez	4.00	1.20
XP4 Sammy Sosa	10.00	3.00
XP5 Cal Ripken	20.00	6.00
XP6 Adam Piatt	2.00	.60
XP7 Pat Burrell	2.50	.75
XP8 J.D. Drew	4.00	1.20
XP9 Mike Piazza	10.00	3.00
XP10 Shawn Green	4.00	1.20
XP11 Troy Glaus	2.50	.75
XP12 Randy Johnson	4.00	1.20
XP13 Juan Gonzalez	4.00	1.20
XP14 Chipper Jones	4.00	1.20
XP15 Ivan Rodriguez	4.00	1.20
XP16 Nomar Garciaparra	10.00	3.00
XP17 Ken Griffey Jr.	10.00	3.00
XP18 Nick Johnson	2.00	.60
XP19 Mark McGwire	15.00	4.50
XP20 Frank Thomas	4.00	1.20

2000 E-X Generation E-X

Randomly inserted into packs at one in eight, this15-card insert set features some of the hottest young talent in major league baseball. Card backs carry a "GX" prefix.

	Nm-Mt	Ex-Mt
COMPLETE SET (15)	50.00	15.00
GX1 Rick Ankiel	1.50	.45
GX2 Josh Beckett	4.00	1.20
GX3 Carlos Beltran	1.50	.45
GX4 Pat Burrell	2.00	.60
GX5 Freddy Garcia	1.50	.45
GX6 Alex Rodriguez	6.00	1.80
GX7 Derek Jeter	10.00	3.00
GX8 Tim Hudson	2.00	.60
GX9 Shawn Green	3.00	.90
GX10 Eric Munson	3.00	.90
GX11 Adam Piatt	1.50	.45
GX12 Adam Kennedy	1.50	.45
GX13 Nick Johnson	1.50	.45
GX14 Alfonso Soriano	3.00	.90
GX15 Nomar Garciaparra	6.00	1.80

2000 E-X Genuine Coverage

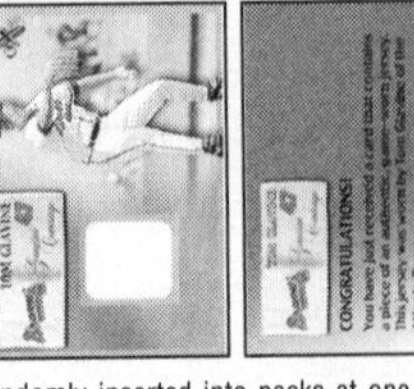

Randomly inserted into packs at one in 144 this 10-card insert set features swatches from actual game-used jerseys. Cards are numbered based on each player's actual uniform number

	Nm-Mt	Ex-Mt
2 Derek Jeter	40.00	12.00
3 Alex Rodriguez	25.00	7.50
8 Cal Ripken	40.00	12.00
10 Chipper Jones	15.00	4.50
11 Edgar Martinez	15.00	4.50
25 Barry Bonds	40.00	12.00
43 Raul Mondesi	10.00	3.00
47 Tom Glavine	15.00	4.50
52 Tim Hudson	15.00	4.50

2001 E-X

The 2001 E-X product was released in mi[d] May, 2001, and featured a 130-card base s[et] that was broken into tiers as follows: Bas[e] Veterans (1-100), and Rookies/Prospects (10[1]

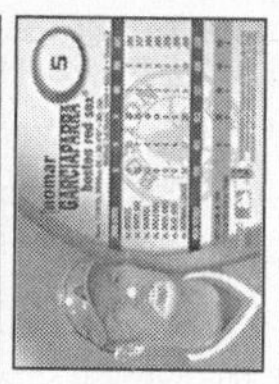

130) (individually serial numbered). Each pack contained 5 cards, and carried a suggested retail price of $4.99. An additional ten cards (131-140) featuring a selection of top prospects was distributed in late December, 2001 within Fleer Platinum RC packs. Each of these cards is serial-numbered to 499 copies.

	Nm-Mt	Ex-Mt
COMP.SET w/o SP's (100)	25.00	7.50
COMMON CARD (1-100)	.50	.15
COMMON (101-130)	8.00	2.40
COMMON (131-140)	15.00	4.50
1 Jason Kendall	.50	.15
2 Derek Jeter	3.00	.90
3 Greg Vaughn	.50	.15
4 Eric Chavez	.50	.15
5 Nomar Garciaparra	2.00	.60
6 Roberto Alomar	1.25	.35
7 Barry Larkin	1.25	.35
8 Matt Lawton	.50	.15
9 Larry Walker	.75	.23
10 Chipper Jones	1.25	.35
11 Scott Rolen	.75	.23
12 Carlos Lee	.50	.15
13 Adrian Beltre	.50	.15
14 Ben Grieve	.50	.15
15 Mike Sweeney	.50	.15
16 John Olerud	.50	.15
17 Gabe Kapler	.50	.15
18 Brian Giles	.50	.15
19 Luis Gonzalez	.50	.15
20 Sammy Sosa	2.00	.60
21 Roger Clemens	2.50	.75
22 Vladimir Guerrero	1.25	.35
23 Ken Griffey Jr.	2.00	.60
24 Mark McGwire	3.00	.90
25 Orlando Hernandez	.50	.15
26 Shannon Stewart	.50	.15
27 Fred McGriff	.75	.23
28 Lance Berkman	.50	.15
29 Carlos Delgado	.50	.15
30 Mike Piazza	2.00	.60
31 Juan Encarnacion	.50	.15
32 David Justice	.50	.15
33 Greg Maddux	2.00	.60
34 Frank Thomas	1.25	.35
35 Jason Giambi	1.25	.35
36 Ruben Mateo	.50	.15
37 Todd Helton	.75	.23
38 Jim Edmonds	.50	.15
39 Steve Finley	.50	.15
40 Tom Glavine	.75	.23
41 Mo Vaughn	.50	.15
42 Phil Nevin	.50	.15
43 Richie Sexson	.50	.15
44 Craig Biggio	.75	.23
45 Kerry Wood	1.25	.35
46 Pat Burrell	.50	.15
47 Edgar Martinez	.75	.23
48 Jim Thome	1.25	.35
49 Jeff Bagwell	.75	.23
50 Bernie Williams	.75	.23
51 Andruw Jones	.50	.15
52 Gary Sheffield	.50	.15
53 Johnny Damon	.50	.15
54 Rondell White	.50	.15
55 J.D. Drew	.50	.15
56 Tony Batista	.50	.15
57 Paul Konerko	.50	.15
58 Rafael Palmeiro	.75	.23
59 Cal Ripken	4.00	1.20
60 Darin Erstad	.50	.15
61 Ivan Rodriguez	1.25	.35
62 Barry Bonds	3.00	.90
63 Edgardo Alfonzo	.50	.15
64 Ellis Burks	.50	.15
65 Mike Lieberthal	.50	.15
66 Robin Ventura	.50	.15
67 Richard Hidalgo	.50	.15
68 Magglio Ordonez	.50	.15
69 Kazuhiro Sasaki	.50	.15
70 Miguel Tejada	.50	.15
71 David Wells	.50	.15
72 Troy Glaus	.75	.23
73 Jose Vidro	.50	.15
74 Shawn Green	.50	.15
75 Barry Zito	1.25	.35
76 Jermaine Dye	.50	.15
77 Geoff Jenkins	.50	.15
78 Jeff Kent	.50	.15
79 Al Leiter	.50	.15
80 Deivi Cruz	.50	.15
81 Eric Karros	.50	.15
82 Albert Belle	.50	.15
83 Pedro Martinez	1.25	.35
84 Raul Mondesi	.50	.15
85 Preston Wilson	.50	.15
86 Rafael Furcal	.50	.15
87 Rick Ankiel	.50	.15
88 Randy Johnson	1.25	.35
89 Kevin Brown	.50	.15
90 Sean Casey	.50	.15
91 Mike Mussina	1.25	.35
92 Alex Rodriguez	2.00	.60
93 Andres Galarraga	.50	.15
94 Juan Gonzalez	1.25	.35
95 Manny Ramirez	.50	.15
96 Mark Grace	.75	.23
97 Carl Everett	.50	.15
98 Tony Gwynn	1.50	.45
99 Mike Hampton	.50	.15
100 Ken Caminiti	.50	.15
101 Jason Hart/1749	8.00	2.40
102 Corey Patterson/1199	8.00	2.40
103 Timo Perez/1999	8.00	2.40
104 Marcus Giles/1999	8.00	2.40
105 I. Suzuki/1999 RC	60.00	18.00
106 Aubrey Huff/1499	8.00	2.40
107 Joe Crede/1999	8.00	2.40
108 Larry Barnes/1499	8.00	2.40
109 Esix Snead/1999 RC	8.00	2.40
110 Kenny Kelly/2249	8.00	2.40
111 Justin Miller/2249	8.00	2.40
112 Jack Cust/1999	8.00	2.40
113 Xavier Nady/999	8.00	2.40
114 Eric Munson/1499	8.00	2.40
115 E. Guzman/1749 RC	8.00	2.40
116 Juan Pierre/2189	8.00	2.40
117 W. Abreu/1749 RC	8.00	2.40
118 Keith Ginter/1999	8.00	2.40
119 Jace Brewer/2699	8.00	2.40
120 P. Crawford/2249	8.00	2.40
121 Jason Tyner/2249	8.00	2.40
122 Tike Redman/1999	8.00	2.40
123 John Riedling/2499	8.00	2.40
124 Jose Ortiz/1499	8.00	2.40
125 O. Mairena/2499	8.00	2.40
126 Eric Byrnes/2249	8.00	2.40
127 Brian Cole/999	8.00	2.40
128 Adam Piatt/2249	8.00	2.40
129 Nate Rolison/2499	8.00	2.40
130 Keith McDonald/2249	8.00	2.40
131 Albert Pujols/499 RC	80.00	24.00
132 Bud Smith/499 RC	15.00	4.50
133 T.Shinjo/499 RC	20.00	6.00
134 W.Betemit/499 RC	15.00	4.50
135 A.Hernandez/499 RC	15.00	4.50
136 J.Melian/499 RC	15.00	4.50
137 Jay Gibbons/499 RC	20.00	6.00
138 J.Estrada/499 RC	20.00	6.00
139 M.Ensberg/499 RC	25.00	7.50
140 Drew Henson/499 RC	25.00	7.50
NNO Derek Jeter Base Inks AU/500	150.00	45.00
MM2 Derek Jeter Monumental Moments	12.00	3.60
NNO Derek Jeter Monumental Moments AU/96	120.00	36.00

2001 E-X Prospect Autographs

Randomly inserted into packs, this 29-card insert is actually an autographed parallel of cards 101-130 in the 2001 E-X base set (with exception of card 105). Please note that the print runs are listed below for each card.

	Nm-Mt	Ex-Mt
101 Jason Hart/250 EXCH	15.00	4.50
102 Corey Patterson/800	20.00	6.00
103 Timo Perez/1000	15.00	4.50
104 Marcus Giles/500	20.00	6.00
106 Aubrey Huff/500	20.00	6.00
107 Joe Crede/500	15.00	4.50
108 Larry Barnes/500	15.00	4.50
109 Esix Snead/500	20.00	6.00
110 Kenny Kelly/250	15.00	4.50
111 Justin Miller/250	15.00	4.50
112 Jack Cust/1000	15.00	4.50
113 Xavier Nady/1000	20.00	6.00
114 Eric Munson/1500	15.00	4.50
115 Elpidio Guzman/250	20.00	6.00
116 Juan Pierre/810	20.00	6.00
117 Winston Abreu/250	15.00	4.50
118 Keith Ginter/500	15.00	4.50
119 Jace Brewer/300	15.00	4.50
120 Paxton Crawford/250	15.00	4.50
121 Jason Tyner/250	15.00	4.50
122 Tike Redman/250	15.00	4.50
123 John Riedling/500	15.00	4.50
124 Jose Ortiz/500	15.00	4.50
125 Oswaldo Mairena/500	15.00	4.50
126 Eric Byrnes/250	15.00	4.50
127 Brian Cole/2000	20.00	6.00
128 Adam Piatt/250	15.00	4.50
129 Nate Rolison/500	15.00	4.50
130 Keith McDonald/250	15.00	4.50

2001 E-X Essential Credentials

Randomly inserted into packs, this 130-card insert is a complete parallel of the 2001 E-X base set. Please note that cards 1-100 are individually serial numbered to 299, while cards 101-130 are serial numbered to 29.

	Nm-Mt	Ex-Mt
COMMON CARD (1-100)	5.00	1.50
*STARS 1-100: 5X TO 12X BASIC CARDS		
COMMON (101-130)	20.00	6.00

2001 E-X Behind the Numbers Game Jersey

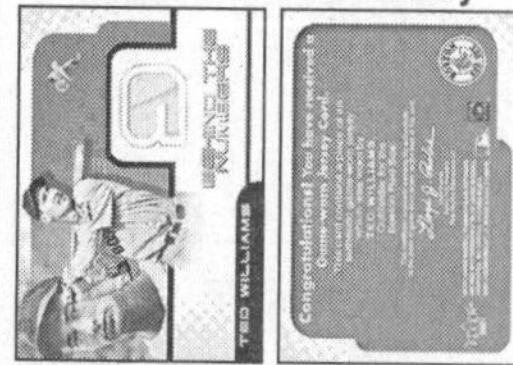

Randomly inserted into packs at one in 33, this 44-card insert features game used jersey swatches for some of the greatest players of all-time. Card backs carry a "BH" prefix.

	Nm-Mt	Ex-Mt
BH1 Johnny Bench	15.00	4.50
BH2 Wade Boggs	15.00	4.50
BH3 George Brett	25.00	7.50
BH4 Lou Brock	15.00	4.50
BH5 Rollie Fingers	10.00	3.00
BH6 Carlton Fisk	15.00	4.50
BH7 Reggie Jackson	15.00	4.50
BH8 Al Kaline	15.00	4.50
BH9 Willie Mays		
BH10 Willie McCovey	10.00	3.00
BH11 Paul Molitor	15.00	4.50
BH12 Eddie Murray	15.00	4.50
BH13 Jim Palmer	10.00	3.00
BH14 Ozzie Smith	15.00	4.50
BH15 Nolan Ryan	50.00	15.00
BH16 Mike Schmidt	25.00	7.50
BH17 Tom Seaver	15.00	4.50
BH18 Dave Winfield	10.00	3.00
BH19 Ted Williams	100.00	30.00
BH20 Robin Yount	15.00	4.50
BH21 Brady Anderson	10.00	3.00
BH22 Rick Ankiel	10.00	3.00
BH23 Albert Belle	10.00	3.00
BH24 Adrian Beltre	10.00	3.00
BH25 Barry Bonds	40.00	12.00
BH26 Eric Chavez	10.00	3.00
BH27 J.D. Drew	10.00	3.00
BH28 Darin Erstad	10.00	3.00
BH29 Troy Glaus	15.00	4.50
BH30 Mark Grace	15.00	4.50
BH31 Ben Grieve	10.00	3.00
BH32 Tony Gwynn	20.00	6.00
BH33 Todd Helton	15.00	4.50
BH34 Derek Jeter	40.00	12.00
BH35 Jeff Kent	10.00	3.00
BH36 Jason Kendall	10.00	3.00
BH37 Greg Maddux	20.00	6.00
BH38 John Olerud	10.00	3.00
BH39 Cal Ripken	40.00	12.00
BH40 Chipper Jones	15.00	4.50
BH41 John Smoltz	15.00	4.50
BH42 Frank Thomas	15.00	4.50
BH43 Robin Ventura	10.00	3.00
BH44 Bernie Williams	15.00	4.50

2001 E-X Behind the Numbers Game Jersey Autograph

Randomly inserted into packs, this 42-card insert is a partial parallel of the 2001 E-X Behind the Numbers insert. Each card in this set is autographed, and the stated print run for each card is listed below for your convenience.

	Nm-Mt	Ex-Mt
1 Brady Anderson/9		
2 Rick Ankiel/66	40.00	12.00
3 Albert Belle/88	50.00	15.00
4 Adrian Beltre/29	50.00	15.00
5 Johnny Bench/5		
6 Wade Boggs/26	200.00	60.00
7 Barry Bonds/25		
8 George Brett/5		
9 Lou Brock/20		
10 Eric Chavez/3		
11 J.D. Drew/7		
12 Darin Erstad/17		
13 Rollie Fingers/34	100.00	30.00
14 Carlton Fisk/27	200.00	60.00
15 Troy Glaus/25		
16 Mark Grace/17		
17 Ben Grieve/14		
18 Tony Gwynn/19		
19 Todd Helton/17		
20 Reggie Jackson/44	150.00	45.00
21 Derek Jeter/2		
22 Chipper Jones/10		
23 Al Kaline/6		
24 Jason Kendall/18		
25 Jeff Kent/21		
26 Greg Maddux/31	300.00	90.00
27 Willie McCovey/44	100.00	30.00
28 Paul Molitor/4		
29 Eddie Murray/33	200.00	60.00
30 John Olerud/5		
31 Jim Palmer/22		
32 Cal Ripken/8		
33 Nolan Ryan/34	500.00	150.00
34 Mike Schmidt/20		
35 Tom Seaver/41	150.00	45.00
36 Ozzie Smith/1		
37 John Smoltz/29	120.00	36.00
38 Frank Thomas/35	150.00	45.00
39 Robin Ventura/4		
40 Bernie Williams/51	150.00	45.00
41 Dave Winfield/31	150.00	45.00
42 Robin Yount/19		

2001 E-X Extra Innings

Randomly inserted into retail packs at one in 20, this 10-card insert features players that keep on going long after 9-innings. Card backs carry an "XI" prefix.

	Nm-Mt	Ex-Mt
COMPLETE SET (10)	100.00	30.00
XI1 Mark McGwire	12.00	3.60
XI2 Sammy Sosa	8.00	2.40
XI3 Chipper Jones	5.00	1.50
XI4 Mike Piazza	8.00	2.40
XI5 Cal Ripken	15.00	4.50
XI6 Ken Griffey Jr.	8.00	2.40
XI7 Alex Rodriguez	8.00	2.40
XI8 Vladimir Guerrero	5.00	1.50
XI9 Nomar Garciaparra	8.00	2.40
XI10 Derek Jeter	12.00	3.60

2001 E-X Wall of Fame

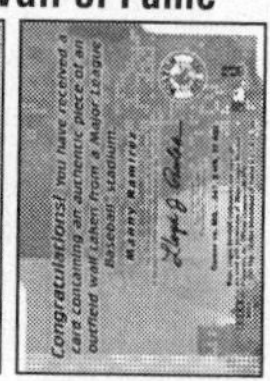

Randomly inserted into packs at one in 24, this 30-card insert features swatches of the outfield walls used in Major League ballparks. Please note that the cards are not numbered, and are listed below in alphabetical order for convenience.

	Nm-Mt	Ex-Mt
1 Jeff Bagwell	10.00	3.00
2 Barry Bonds	25.00	7.50
3 Pat Burrell	8.00	2.40
4 Roger Clemens	15.00	4.50
5 Nomar Garciaparra	15.00	4.50
6 Jason Giambi	10.00	3.00
7 Troy Glaus	10.00	3.00
8 Juan Gonzalez	10.00	3.00
9 Ken Griffey Jr.	15.00	4.50
10 Vladimir Guerrero	10.00	3.00
11 Tony Gwynn	15.00	4.50
12 Todd Helton	10.00	3.00
13 Geoff Jenkins	8.00	2.40
14 Derek Jeter	25.00	7.50
15 Andruw Jones	8.00	2.40
16 Chipper Jones	10.00	3.00
17 Jason Kendall	8.00	2.40
18 Greg Maddux	10.00	3.00
19 Pedro Martinez	10.00	3.00
20 Mark McGwire	40.00	12.00
21 Paul Molitor	10.00	3.00
22 Mike Piazza	10.00	3.00
23 Manny Ramirez	8.00	2.40
24 Cal Ripken	40.00	12.00
25 Alex Rodriguez	15.00	4.50
26 Ivan Rodriguez	10.00	3.00
27 Scott Rolen	10.00	3.00
28 Sammy Sosa	15.00	4.50
29 Frank Thomas	10.00	3.00
30 Robin Yount	10.00	3.00

2002 E-X

This 139 card set was issued in May, 2002. It was released in four card packs which came 24 packs to a box and four boxes to a case. The price for hobby packs (which had many more inserts) was $5 per pack and the retail packs were $3 per pack. The first 100 cards featured veterans while the last 40 cards featured rookies and prospects. Cards numbered 101 through 125 were printed to specific serial numbers while cards numbered 126-140 were issued at a stated rate of one in 24 hobby or retail packs. Though the set is checklisted 1-140, card 133 does not exist. It was originally intended to feature Yankees prospect Drew Henson, but Fleer's exclusive contract with the ballplayer expired two weeks prior to the release of E-X.

	Nm-Mt	Ex-Mt
COMP.SET w/o SP's (100)	25.00	7.50
COMMON CARD (1-100)	.50	.15
COMMON CARD (101-120)	5.00	1.50
COMMON CARD (121-125)	5.00	1.50
COMMON CARD (126-140)	5.00	1.50
1 Alex Rodriguez	2.00	.60
2 Albert Pujols	2.50	.75
3 Ken Griffey Jr.	2.00	.60
4 Vladimir Guerrero	1.25	.35
5 Sammy Sosa	2.00	.60
6 Ichiro Suzuki	2.00	.60
7 Jorge Posada	.75	.23
8 Matt Williams	.50	.15
9 Adrian Beltre	.50	.15
10 Pat Burrell	.50	.15
11 Roger Cedeno	.50	.15
12 Tony Clark	.50	.15
13 Steve Finley	.50	.15
14 Rafael Furcal	.50	.15
15 Rickey Henderson	1.25	.35
16 Richard Hidalgo	.50	.15
17 Jason Kendall	.50	.15
18 Tino Martinez	.75	.23
19 Scott Rolen	.75	.23
20 Shannon Stewart	.50	.15
21 Jose Vidro	.50	.15
22 Preston Wilson	.50	.15
23 Raul Mondesi	.50	.15
24 Lance Berkman	.50	.15
25 Rick Ankiel	.50	.15
26 Kevin Brown	.50	.15
27 Jeromy Burnitz	.50	.15
28 Jeff Cirillo	.50	.15
29 Carl Everett	.50	.15
30 Eric Chavez	.50	.15
31 Freddy Garcia	.50	.15
32 Mark Grace	.75	.23
33 David Justice	.50	.15
34 Fred McGriff	.75	.23
35 Mike Mussina	1.25	.35
36 John Olerud	.50	.15
37 Magglio Ordonez	.50	.15
38 Curt Schilling	.75	.23
39 Aaron Sele	.50	.15
40 Robin Ventura	.50	.15
41 Adam Dunn	.50	.15
42 Jeff Bagwell	.75	.23
43 Barry Bonds	3.00	.90
44 Roger Clemens	2.50	.75
45 Cliff Floyd	.50	.15
46 Jason Giambi	1.25	.35
47 Juan Gonzalez	1.25	.35
48 Luis Gonzalez	.50	.15
49 Cristian Guzman	.50	.15
50 Todd Helton	.75	.23
51 Derek Jeter	3.00	.90
52 Rafael Palmeiro	.75	.23
53 Mike Sweeney	.50	.15
54 Ben Grieve	.50	.15
55 Phil Nevin	.50	.15
56 Mike Piazza	2.00	.60
57 Moises Alou	.50	.15
58 Ivan Rodriguez	1.25	.35
59 Manny Ramirez	.50	.15
60 Brian Giles	.50	.15
61 Jim Thome	1.25	.35
62 Larry Walker	.75	.23
63 Bobby Abreu	.50	.15
64 Troy Glaus	.75	.23
65 Garret Anderson	.50	.15
66 Roberto Alomar	1.25	.35
67 Bret Boone	.50	.15
68 Marty Cordova	.50	.15
69 Craig Biggio	.75	.23
70 Omar Vizquel	.50	.15
71 Jermaine Dye	.50	.15
72 Darin Erstad	.50	.15
73 Carlos Delgado	.50	.15
74 Nomar Garciaparra	2.00	.60
75 Greg Maddux	2.00	.60
76 Tom Glavine	.75	.23
77 Frank Thomas	1.25	.35
78 Shawn Green	.50	.15
79 Bobby Higginson	.50	.15
80 Jeff Kent	.50	.15
81 Chuck Knoblauch	.50	.15
82 Paul Konerko	.50	.15
83 Carlos Lee	.50	.15
84 Jon Lieber	.50	.15
85 Paul LoDuca	.50	.15
86 Mike Lowell	.50	.15
87 Edgar Martinez	.75	.23
88 Doug Mientkiewicz	.50	.15
89 Pedro Martinez	1.25	.35
90 Randy Johnson	1.25	.35
91 Aramis Ramirez	.50	.15
92 J.D. Drew	.50	.15
93 Chris Richard	.50	.15
94 Jimmy Rollins	.50	.15
95 Ryan Klesko	.50	.15
96 Gary Sheffield	.50	.15
97 Chipper Jones	1.25	.35
98 Greg Vaughn	.50	.15
99 Mo Vaughn	.50	.15
100 Bernie Williams	.75	.23
101 John Foster NT/2999 RC	5.00	1.50
102 J. DeLaRosa NT/2999 RC	5.00	1.50
103 Ed. Almonte NT/2999 RC	5.00	1.50
104 Chris Booker NT/2999 RC	5.00	1.50
105 Victor Alvarez NT/2999 RC	5.00	1.50
106 Cliff Bartosh NT/2999 RC	5.00	1.50
107 Felix Escalona NT/2999 RC	5.00	1.50
108 C. Thurman NT/2999 RC	5.00	1.50
109 Kazuhisa Ishii NT/2999 RC	10.00	3.00
110 Mig. Asencio NT/2999 RC	5.00	1.50
111 P.J. Bevis NT/2499 RC	5.00	1.50
112 Gus. Chacin NT/2499 RC	5.00	1.50
113 Steve Kent NT/2499 RC	5.00	1.50
114 Tak. Nomura NT/2499 RC	5.00	1.50
115 Adam Walker NT/2499 RC	5.00	1.50
116 So Taguchi NT/2499 RC	8.00	2.40
117 Reed Johnson NT/2499 RC	8.00	2.40
118 Rod Rosario NT/2499 RC	5.00	1.50
119 Luis Martinez NT/2499 RC	5.00	1.50
120 Sat Komiyama NT/2499 RC	5.00	1.50
121 Sean Burroughs NT/1999	5.00	1.50
122 Hank Blalock NT/1999	8.00	2.40
123 Marlon Byrd NT/1999	5.00	1.50
124 Nick Johnson NT/1999	5.00	1.50
125 Mark Teixeira NT/1999	8.00	2.40
126 David Espinosa NT	5.00	1.50
127 Adrian Burnside NT RC	5.00	1.50
128 Mark Corey NT RC	5.00	1.50
129 Matt Thornton NT RC	5.00	1.50
130 Dane Sardinha NT	5.00	1.50
131 Juan Rivera NT	5.00	1.50
132 Austin Kearns NT	5.00	1.50
133 Does Not Exist		
134 Ben Broussard NT	5.00	1.50
135 Orlando Hudson NT	5.00	1.50
136 Carlos Pena NT	5.00	1.50
137 Kenny Kelly NT	5.00	1.50
138 Bill Hall NT	5.00	1.50
139 Ron Chiavacci NT	5.00	1.50
140 Mark Prior NT	15.00	4.50

2002 E-X Essential Credentials Future

Randomly inserted in packs, these 125 cards have two distinct patterns of serial numbering. Cards numbered 1 through 60 are inversely numbered and have a game used piece on them while cards numbered 61 through 125 are also inversley numbered.

	Nm-Mt	Ex-Mt
1 Alex Rodriguez Jsy/60	60.00	18.00
2 Albert Pujols Base/59	60.00	18.00
3 Ken Griffey Jr. Base/58	60.00	18.00
4 Vladimir Guerrero Base/57	40.00	12.00
5 Sammy Sosa Base/56	60.00	18.00
6 Ichiro Suzuki Base/55		
7 Jorge Posada Bat/54	30.00	9.00
8 Matt Williams Bat/53	25.00	7.50
9 Adrian Beltre Bat/52	25.00	7.50
10 Pat Burrell Bat/51	25.00	7.50

11 Roger Cedeno Bat/50 25.00 7.50
12 Tony Clark Bat/49 25.00 7.50
13 Steve Finley Bat/48 30.00 9.00
14 Rafael Furcal Bat/47 30.00 9.00
15 Rickey Henderson Bat/46 50.00 15.00
16 Richard Hidalgo Bat/45 30.00 9.00
17 Jason Kendall Bat/44 30.00 9.00
18 Tino Martinez Bat/43 40.00 12.00
19 Scott Rolen Bat/42 40.00 12.00
20 Shannon Stewart Bat/41 30.00 9.00
21 Jose Vidro Bat/40 30.00 9.00
22 Preston Wilson Bat/39 30.00 9.00
23 Raul Mondesi Bat/38 30.00 9.00
24 Lance Berkman Bat/37 30.00 9.00
25 Rick Ankiel Jsy/36 25.00 7.50
26 Kevin Brown Jsy/35 40.00 12.00
27 Jeromy Burnitz Bat/34 40.00 12.00
28 Jeff Cirillo Jsy/33 30.00 9.00
29 Carl Everett Jsy/32 40.00 12.00
30 Eric Chavez Bat/31 40.00 12.00
31 Freddy Garcia Jsy/30 40.00 12.00
32 Mark Grace Jsy/29 50.00 15.00
33 David Justice Jsy/28 40.00 12.00
34 Fred McGriff Jsy/27 50.00 15.00
35 Mike Mussina Jsy/26
36 John Olerud Jsy/25
37 Magglio Ordonez Jsy/24
38 Curt Schilling Jsy/23
39 Aaron Sele Jsy/22
40 Robin Ventura Jsy/21
41 Adam Dunn Bat/20
42 Jeff Bagwell Jsy/19
43 Barry Bonds Pants/18
44 Roger Clemens Bat/17
45 Cliff Floyd Bat/16
46 Jason Giambi Base/15
47 Juan Gonzalez Jsy/14
48 Luis Gonzalez Base/13
49 Cristian Guzman Bat/12
50 Todd Helton Base/11
51 Derek Jeter Bat/10
52 Rafael Palmeiro Bat/9
53 Mike Sweeney Bat/8
54 Ben Grieve Jsy/7
55 Phil Nevin Bat/6
56 Mike Piazza Base/5
57 Moises Alou Bat/4
58 Ivan Rodriguez Jsy/3
59 Manny Ramirez Base/2
60 Brian Giles Bat/1
61 Jim Thome/125 20.00 6.00
62 Larry Walker/124 12.00 3.60
63 Bobby Abreu/123 8.00 2.40
64 Troy Glaus/122 12.00 3.60
65 Garret Anderson/121 8.00 2.40
66 Roberto Alomar/120 20.00 6.00
67 Bret Boone/119 8.00 2.40
68 Marty Cordova/118 8.00 2.40
69 Craig Biggio/117 12.00 3.60
70 Omar Vizquel/116 8.00 2.40
71 Jermaine Dye/115 8.00 2.40
72 Darin Erstad/114 8.00 2.40
73 Carlos Delgado/113 8.00 2.40
74 Nomar Garciaparra/112 30.00 9.00
75 Greg Maddux/111 30.00 9.00
76 Tom Glavine/110 12.00 3.60
77 Frank Thomas/109 20.00 6.00
78 Shawn Green/108 8.00 2.40
79 Bobby Higginson/107 8.00 2.40
80 Jeff Kent/106 8.00 2.40
81 Chuck Knoblauch/105 8.00 2.40
82 Paul Konerko/104 8.00 2.40
83 Carlos Lee/103 8.00 2.40
84 Jon Lieber/102 8.00 2.40
85 Paul LoDuca/101 8.00 2.40
86 Mike Lowell/100 8.00 2.40
87 Edgar Martinez/99 12.00 3.60
88 Doug Mientkiewicz/98 8.00 2.40
89 Pedro Martinez/97 20.00 6.00
90 Randy Johnson/96 20.00 6.00
91 Aramis Ramirez/95 8.00 2.40
92 J.D. Drew/94 8.00 2.40
93 Chris Richard/93 8.00 2.40
94 Jimmy Rollins/92 8.00 2.40
95 Ryan Klesko/91 8.00 2.40
96 Gary Sheffield/90 8.00 2.40
97 Chipper Jones/89 20.00 6.00
98 Greg Vaughn/88 8.00 2.40
99 Mo Vaughn/87 8.00 2.40
100 Bernie Williams/86 12.00 3.60
101 John Foster NT/85 8.00 2.40
102 Jorge De La Rosa NT/84 8.00 2.40
103 Edwin Almonte NT/83 8.00 2.40
104 Chris Booker NT/82 8.00 2.40
105 Victor Alvarez NT/81 8.00 2.40
106 Cliff Bartosh NT/80 10.00 3.00
107 Felix Escalona NT/79 10.00 3.00
108 Corey Thurman NT/78 10.00 3.00
109 Kazuhisa Ishii NT/77 25.00 7.50
110 Miguel Asencio NT/76 10.00 3.00
111 P.J. Bevis NT/75 10.00 3.00
112 Gustavo Chacin NT/74 10.00 3.00
113 Steve Kent NT/73 10.00 3.00
114 Takahito Nomura NT/72 10.00 3.00
115 Adam Walker NT/71 10.00 3.00
116 So Taguchi NT/70 15.00 4.50
117 Reed Johnson NT/69 15.00 4.50
118 Rodrigo Rosario NT/68 10.00 3.00
119 Luis Martinez NT/67 10.00 3.00
120 Satoru Komiyama NT/66 10.00 3.00
121 Sean Burroughs NT/65 12.00 3.60
122 Hank Blalock NT/64 30.00 9.00
123 Marlon Byrd NT/63 12.00 3.60
124 Nick Johnson NT/62 12.00 3.60
125 Mark Teixeira NT/61 30.00 9.00

2002 E-X Essential Credentials Now

Randomly inserted in packs, these 125 cards are printed to a stated print run matching their card number. In addition, the first 60 cards of the set have a game-used piece mounted to the card.

Nm-Mt Ex-Mt
1 Alex Rodriguez Jsy/1
2 Albert Pujols Base/2
3 Ken Griffey Jr. Base/3
4 Vladimir Guerrero Base/4
5 Sammy Sosa Base/5
6 Ichiro Suzuki Base/6
7 Jorge Posada Bat/7
8 Matt Williams Bat/8
9 Adrian Beltre Bat/9
10 Pat Burrell Bat/10
11 Roger Cedeno Bat/11
12 Tony Clark Bat/12
13 Steve Finley Bat/13
14 Rafael Furcal Bat/14
15 Rickey Henderson Bat/15
16 Richard Hidalgo Bat/16
17 Jason Kendall Bat/17
18 Tino Martinez Bat/18
19 Scott Rolen Bat/19
20 Shannon Stewart Bat/20
21 Jose Vidro Bat/21
22 Preston Wilson Bat/22
23 Raul Mondesi Bat/23
24 Lance Berkman Bat/24
25 Rick Ankiel Jsy/25
26 Kevin Brown Jsy/26 40.00 12.00
27 Jeromy Burnitz Bat/27 40.00 12.00
28 Jeff Cirillo Jsy/28 30.00 9.00
29 Carl Everett Jsy/29 40.00 12.00
30 Eric Chavez Bat/30 40.00 12.00
31 Freddy Garcia Jsy/31 40.00 12.00
32 Mark Grace Jsy/32 50.00 15.00
33 David Justice Jsy/33 40.00 12.00
34 Fred McGriff Jsy/34 50.00 15.00
35 Mike Mussina Jsy/35
36 John Olerud Jsy/36 30.00 9.00
37 Magglio Ordonez Jsy/37 30.00 9.00
38 Curt Schilling Jsy/38 40.00 12.00
39 Aaron Sele Jsy/39 25.00 7.50
40 Robin Ventura Jsy/40 30.00 9.00
41 Adam Dunn Bat/41 30.00 9.00
42 Jeff Bagwell Jsy/42 40.00 12.00
43 Barry Bonds Pants/43 120.00 36.00
44 Roger Clemens Bat/44 100.00 30.00
45 Cliff Floyd Bat/45 30.00 9.00
46 Jason Giambi Base/46 50.00 15.00
47 Juan Gonzalez Jsy/47 50.00 15.00
48 Luis Gonzalez Base/48 30.00 9.00
49 Cristian Guzman Bat/49 30.00 9.00
50 Todd Helton Base/50 40.00 12.00
51 Derek Jeter Bat/51 120.00 36.00
52 Rafael Palmeiro Bat/52 30.00 9.00
53 Mike Sweeney Bat/53 25.00 7.50
54 Ben Grieve Jsy/54 20.00 6.00
55 Phil Nevin Bat/55 25.00 7.50
56 Mike Piazza Base/56 60.00 18.00
57 Moises Alou Bat/57 25.00 7.50
58 Ivan Rodriguez Jsy/58 40.00 12.00
59 Manny Ramirez Base/59 25.00 7.50
60 Brian Giles Bat/60 25.00 7.50
61 Jim Thome/61 30.00 9.00
62 Larry Walker/62 20.00 6.00
63 Bobby Abreu/63 12.00 3.60
64 Troy Glaus/64 20.00 6.00
65 Garret Anderson/65 12.00 3.60
66 Roberto Alomar/66 25.00 7.50
67 Bret Boone/67 10.00 3.00
68 Marty Cordova/68 10.00 3.00
69 Craig Biggio/69 15.00 4.50
70 Omar Vizquel/70 10.00 3.00
71 Jermaine Dye/71 10.00 3.00
72 Darin Erstad/72 10.00 3.00
73 Carlos Delgado/73 10.00 3.00
74 Nomar Garciaparra/74 40.00 12.00
75 Greg Maddux/75 40.00 12.00
76 Tom Glavine/76 15.00 4.50
77 Frank Thomas/77 25.00 7.50
78 Shawn Green/78 10.00 3.00
79 Bobby Higginson/79 10.00 3.00
80 Jeff Kent/80 10.00 3.00
81 Chuck Knoblauch/81 8.00 2.40
82 Paul Konerko/82 8.00 2.40
83 Carlos Lee/83 8.00 2.40
84 Jon Lieber/84 8.00 2.40
85 Paul LoDuca/85 8.00 2.40
86 Mike Lowell/86 8.00 2.40
87 Edgar Martinez/87 12.00 3.60
88 Doug Mientkiewicz/88 8.00 2.40
89 Pedro Martinez/89 20.00 6.00
90 Randy Johnson/90 20.00 6.00
91 Aramis Ramirez/91 8.00 2.40
92 J.D. Drew/92 8.00 2.40
93 Chris Richard/93 8.00 2.40
94 Jimmy Rollins/94 8.00 2.40
95 Ryan Klesko/95 8.00 2.40
96 Gary Sheffield/96 8.00 2.40
97 Chipper Jones/97 20.00 6.00
98 Greg Vaughn/98 8.00 2.40
99 Mo Vaughn/99 8.00 2.40
100 Bernie Williams/100 12.00 3.60
101 John Foster NT/101 8.00 2.40
102 Jorge De La Rosa NT/102 8.00 2.40
103 Edwin Almonte NT/103 8.00 2.40
104 Chris Booker NT/104 8.00 2.40
105 Victor Alvarez NT/105 8.00 2.40
106 Cliff Bartosh NT/106 8.00 2.40
107 Felix Escalona NT/107 8.00 2.40
108 Corey Thurman NT/108 8.00 2.40
109 Kazuhisa Ishii NT/109 25.00 7.50
110 Miguel Asencio NT/110 8.00 2.40
111 P.J. Bevis NT/111 8.00 2.40
112 Gustavo Chacin NT/112 8.00 2.40
113 Steve Kent NT/113 8.00 2.40
114 Takahito Nomura NT/114 8.00 2.40
115 Adam Walker NT/115 8.00 2.40
116 So Taguchi NT/116 12.00 3.60
117 Reed Johnson NT/117 12.00 3.60
118 Rodrigo Rosario NT/118 8.00 2.40
119 Luis Martinez NT/119 8.00 2.40
120 Satoru Komiyama NT/120 8.00 2.40
121 Sean Burroughs NT/121 8.00 2.40
122 Hank Blalock NT/122 20.00 6.00
123 Marlon Byrd NT/123 8.00 2.40
124 Nick Johnson NT/124 8.00 2.40
125 Mark Teixeira NT/125 20.00 6.00

2002 E-X Behind the Numbers

Inserted at stated odds of one in eight hobby and one in 12 retail, these 35 cards pays tribute to special numbers for hitters and pitchers.

Nm-Mt Ex-Mt
COMPLETE SET (35) 120.00 36.00
1 Ichiro Suzuki 6.00 1.80
2 Jason Giambi 4.00 1.20
3 Mike Piazza 6.00 1.80
4 Brian Giles 2.50 .75
5 Barry Bonds 10.00 3.00
6 Pedro Martinez 4.00 1.20
7 Nomar Garciaparra 6.00 1.80
8 Randy Johnson 4.00 1.20
9 Craig Biggio 2.50 .75
10 Manny Ramirez 2.50 .75
11 Mike Mussina 4.00 1.20
12 Kerry Wood 4.00 1.20
13 Jim Edmonds 2.50 .75
14 Ivan Rodriguez 4.00 1.20
15 Jeff Bagwell 2.50 .75
16 Roger Clemens 8.00 2.40
17 Chipper Jones 4.00 1.20
18 Shawn Green 2.50 .75
19 Albert Pujols 8.00 2.40
20 Andruw Jones 2.50 .75
21 Luis Gonzalez 2.50 .75
22 Todd Helton 2.50 .75
23 Jorge Posada 2.50 .75
24 Scott Rolen 2.50 .75
25 Ben Sheets 2.50 .75
26 Alfonso Soriano 2.50 .75
27 Greg Maddux 6.00 1.80
28 Gary Sheffield 2.50 .75
29 Barry Zito 2.50 .75
30 Alex Rodriguez 6.00 1.80
31 Larry Walker 2.50 .75
32 Derek Jeter 10.00 3.00
33 Ken Griffey Jr. 6.00 1.80
34 Vladimir Guerrero 4.00 1.20
35 Sammy Sosa 6.00 1.80

2002 E-X Behind the Numbers Game Jersey

This partial parallel, issued at a stated rate of one in 24 hobby packs and one in 130 retail packs, features not only the Behind the Numbers insert card but a swatch of game used memorabilia.

Nm-Mt Ex-Mt
1 Jeff Bagwell 15.00 4.50
2 Craig Biggio Jsy/Pants 15.00 4.50
3 Barry Bonds SP/50
4 Roger Clemens 25.00 7.50
5 Jim Edmonds 10.00 3.00
6 Brian Giles 10.00 3.00
7 Luis Gonzalez 10.00 3.00
8 Shawn Green 10.00 3.00
9 Todd Helton 15.00 4.50
10 Derek Jeter SP 40.00 12.00
11 Randy Johnson SP 15.00 4.50
12 Andruw Jones 10.00 3.00
13 Chipper Jones 15.00 4.50
14 Greg Maddux 15.00 4.50
15 Pedro Martinez 15.00 4.50
16 Mike Mussina 15.00 4.50
17 Mike Piazza Pants 15.00 4.50
18 Jorge Posada 15.00 4.50
19 Manny Ramirez 10.00 3.00
20 Alex Rodriguez 20.00 6.00
21 Ivan Rodriguez 15.00 4.50
22 Scott Rolen 15.00 4.50
23 Alfonso Soriano SP 15.00 4.50
24 Barry Zito 15.00 4.50

2002 E-X Behind the Numbers Game Jersey Dual

Randomly inserted in packs, these seven cards feature two swatches of jerseys from players who wear the same uniform number. These cards have a stated print run of 25 serial number sets and there is no pricing due to scarcity.

Nm-Mt Ex-Mt
1 Craig Biggio
Ivan Rodriguez
2 Barry Bonds
Andruw Jones
3 Jim Edmonds
Shawn Green
4 Brian Giles
Manny Ramirez
5 Greg Maddux
Mike Piazza
6 Scott Rolen
Todd Helton
7 Alfonso Soriano
Larry Walker

2002 E-X Barry Bonds 4X MVP

Randomly inserted in packs, these four cards have a stated print run to the years in which Barry Bonds won the MVP award.

Nm-Mt Ex-Mt
COMMON CARD (1-4) 10.00 3.00

2002 E-X Game Essentials

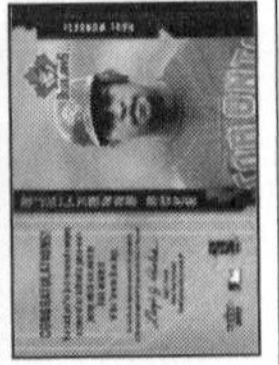

Randomly inserted in packs, these 35 cards feature players along with a piece of their game-used gear.

Nm-Mt Ex-Mt
*PATCH PREMIUM: 1.5X TO 3X LISTED PRICE
1 Carlos Beltran Jsy 10.00 3.00
2 Barry Bonds Btg Glv SP
3 Barry Bonds Wristband SP
4 Kevin Brown Pants 10.00 3.00
5 Jeromy Burnitz Jsy 10.00 3.00
6 Carlos Delgado Bat 10.00 3.00
7 Jason Hart Bat SP
8 Rickey Henderson Bat 15.00 4.50
9 Rickey Henderson Jsy 15.00 4.50
10 Drew Henson Bat 10.00 3.00
11 Drew Henson Cleat 10.00 3.00
12 Drew Henson Fld Glv 15.00 4.50
13 Derek Jeter Cleat 50.00 15.00
14 Jason Kendall Jsy 10.00 3.00
15 Jeff Kent Jsy SP
16 Barry Larkin Fld Glv 30.00 9.00
17 Javy Lopez Jsy 10.00 3.00
18 Raul Mondesi Btg Glv 15.00 4.50
19 Raul Mondesi Jsy 10.00 3.00
20 Rafael Palmeiro Bat 15.00 4.50
21 Rafael Palmeiro Pants 15.00 4.50
22 Adam Piatt Jsy 10.00 3.00
23 Brad Radke Jsy 10.00 3.00
24 Cal Ripken Jsy 40.00 12.00
25 Mariano Rivera Jsy 15.00 4.50
26 Alex Rodriguez Btg Glv 25.00 7.50
27 Alex Rodriguez Cleat SP
28 Ivan Rodriguez Cleat SP
29 Kazuhiro Sasaki Jsy 10.00 3.00
30 J.T. Snow Jsy SP
31 Mo Vaughn Jsy 10.00 3.00
32 Robin Ventura Btg Glv 15.00 4.50
33 Robin Ventura Jsy 10.00 3.00
34 Jose Vidro Jsy 10.00 3.00
35 Matt Williams Jsy 10.00 3.00

2002 E-X HardWear

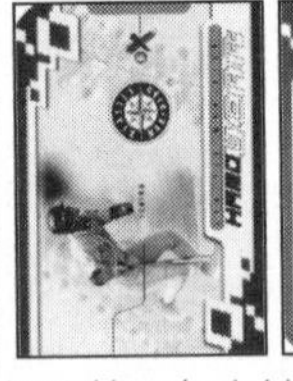

Inserted in packs at stated odds of one in 72 hobby and one in 216 retail, these 10 cards feature players who play the game with proper aggressiveness.

Nm-Mt Ex-Mt
COMPLETE SET (10) 100.00 30.00
1 Ivan Rodriguez 8.00 2.40
2 Mike Piazza 12.00 3.60
3 Derek Jeter 20.00 6.00
4 Barry Bonds 20.00 6.00
5 Todd Helton 8.00 2.40
6 Roberto Alomar 8.00 2.40
7 Albert Pujols 15.00 4.50
8 Ichiro Suzuki 12.00 3.60
9 Ken Griffey Jr. 12.00 3.60
10 Jason Giambi 8.00 2.40

2002 E-X Hit and Run

Inserted at stated odds of one in 12 hobby and one in 72 retail, these 30 cards feature players who do the best job of hitting a baseball.

Nm-Mt Ex-Mt
COMPLETE SET (30) 100.00 30.00
1 Adam Dunn 2.50 .75
2 Derek Jeter 10.00 3.00
3 Frank Thomas 4.00 1.20
4 Albert Pujols 8.00 2.40
5 J.D. Drew 2.50 .75
6 Richard Hidalgo 2.50 .75
7 John Olerud 2.50 .75
8 Roberto Alomar 4.00 1.20
9 Pat Burrell 2.50 .75
10 Darin Erstad 2.50 .75
11 Mark Grace 2.50 .75
12 Chipper Jones 4.00 1.20
13 Jose Vidro 2.50 .75
14 Cliff Floyd 2.50 .75
15 Mo Vaughn 2.50 .75
16 Nomar Garciaparra 6.00 1.80
17 Ivan Rodriguez 4.00 1.20
18 Luis Gonzalez 2.50 .75
19 Jason Giambi 4.00 1.20
20 Bernie Williams 2.50 .75
21 Mike Piazza 6.00 1.80
22 Barry Bonds 10.00 3.00
23 Jose Ortiz 2.50 .75
24 Magglio Ordonez 2.50 .75
25 Troy Glaus 2.50 .75
26 Alex Rodriguez 6.00 1.80
27 Ichiro Suzuki 6.00 1.80
28 Sammy Sosa 6.00 1.80
29 Ken Griffey Jr. 6.00 1.80
30 Vladimir Guerrero 4.00 1.20

2002 E-X Hit and Run Game Base

Inserted in packs at stated odds of one in 120 hobby and one in 360 retail, this 10-card partial parallel set to the Hit and Run set includes a game base piece.

Nm-Mt Ex-Mt
1 J.D. Drew 8.00 2.40
2 Adam Dunn 8.00 2.40
3 Jason Giambi 10.00 3.00
4 Troy Glaus 10.00 3.00
5 Ken Griffey Jr. 15.00 4.50
6 Vladimir Guerrero 10.00 3.00
7 Albert Pujols 15.00 4.50
8 Sammy Sosa 15.00 4.50
9 Ichiro Suzuki 15.00 4.50
10 Bernie Williams 10.00 3.00

2002 E-X Hit and Run Game Bat

Inserted in packs at a stated rate of one in 24 hobby and one in 130 retail packs, this 19-carc partial parallel set features not only players from the Hit and Run insert set but a game ba sliver attached to the card.

Nm-Mt Ex-Mt
1 Roberto Alomar 12.00 3.60
2 J.D. Drew 8.00 2.40
3 Darin Erstad 8.00 2.40
4 Cliff Floyd 8.00 2.40
5 Nomar Garciaparra 25.00 7.50
6 Luis Gonzalez 8.00 2.40
7 Richard Hidalgo 8.00 2.40
8 Derek Jeter 30.00 9.00
9 Chipper Jones 12.00 3.60
10 John Olerud 8.00 2.40
11 Magglio Ordonez 8.00 2.40
12 Jose Ortiz 8.00 2.40
13 Mike Piazza 15.00 4.50
14 Alex Rodriguez 20.00 6.00
15 Ivan Rodriguez 12.00 3.60
16 Frank Thomas 12.00 3.60
17 Mo Vaughn 8.00 2.40
18 Jose Vidro 8.00 2.40
19 Bernie Williams 12.00 3.60

2002 E-X Hit and Run Game Bat and Base

Inserted in packs at a stated rate of one in 24 hobby and one in 720 retail packs, these eig cards are a partial parallel to the Hit and Ru insert set. These cards feature both a piece of game bat and a base used by the feature players.

Nm-Mt Ex-M
1 Roberto Alomar 25.00 7.5
2 Barry Bonds SP
3 Nomar Garciaparra 40.00 12.0
4 Derek Jeter 50.00 15.0
5 Chipper Jones 25.00 7.5

6 Mike Piazza	30.00	9.00
7 Alex Rodriguez	40.00	12.00
8 Mo Vaughn	15.00	4.50

2002 E-X Derek Jeter 4X Champ

Randomly inserted in packs, these four cards honor the four years that Fleer representative Derek Jeter was on a World Series Champion. These cards have a stated print run of the season in which Jeter finished as a champion.

	Nm-Mt	Ex-Mt
COMMON CARD (1-4)	10.00	3.00

2003 E-X

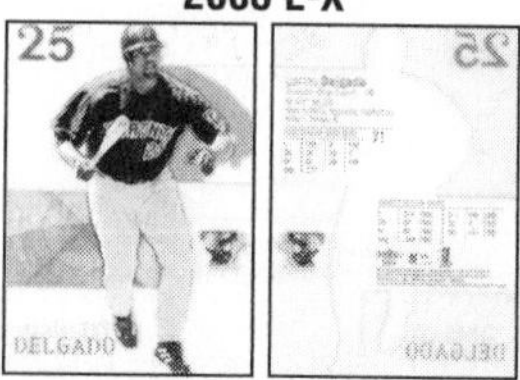

This 102 card set was issued in October, 2003. This set was issued in three card packs which had an $6 SRP and were issued 20 packs to a box and 12 boxes to a case. The first 72 cards featured common veterans while cards 73 through 82 feature shorter printed veterans and cards numbered 83 through 86 feature 2003 rookies and cards numbered 87 through 102 feature Rookie Cards of the player.

	MINT	NRMT
COMP.SET w/o SP's (72)	40.00	18.00
COMMON CARD (1-72)	.50	.23
COMMON CARD (73-82)	5.00	2.20
COMMON CARD (83-86)	5.00	2.20
COMMON CARD (87-102)	5.00	2.20
1 Troy Glaus	.75	.35
2 Darin Erstad	.50	.23
3 Garret Anderson	.50	.23
4 Curt Schilling	.75	.35
5 Randy Johnson	1.25	.55
6 Luis Gonzalez	.50	.23
7 Greg Maddux	2.00	.90
8 Chipper Jones	1.25	.55
9 Andruw Jones	.50	.23
10 Melvin Mora	.50	.23
11 Jay Gibbons	.50	.23
12 Nomar Garciaparra	2.00	.90
13 Pedro Martinez	1.25	.55
14 Manny Ramirez	.50	.23
15 Sammy Sosa	2.00	.90
16 Kerry Wood	1.25	.55
17 Magglio Ordonez	.50	.23
18 Frank Thomas	1.25	.55
19 Roberto Alomar	1.25	.55
20 Barry Larkin	1.25	.55
21 Adam Dunn	.50	.23
22 Austin Kearns	.50	.23
23 Omar Vizquel	.50	.23
24 Larry Walker	.75	.35
25 Todd Helton	.75	.35
26 Preston Wilson	.50	.23
27 Dmitri Young	.50	.23
28 Ivan Rodriguez	1.25	.55
29 Mike Lowell	.50	.23
30 Jeff Kent	.50	.23
31 Jeff Bagwell	.75	.35
32 Roy Oswalt	.50	.23
33 Craig Biggio	.75	.35
34 Mike Sweeney	.50	.23
35 Carlos Beltran	.50	.23
36 Shawn Green	.50	.23
37 Kazuhisa Ishii	.50	.23
38 Richie Sexson	.50	.23
39 Torii Hunter	.50	.23
40 Jacque Jones	.50	.23
41 Jose Vidro	.50	.23
42 Vladimir Guerrero	1.25	.55
43 Mike Piazza	2.00	.90
44 Tom Glavine	.75	.35
45 Roger Clemens	2.50	1.10
46 Jason Giambi	1.25	.55
47 Bernie Williams	.75	.35
48 Alfonso Soriano	.75	.35
49 Mike Mussina	1.25	.55
50 Barry Zito	.75	.35
51 Miguel Tejada	.50	.23
52 Eric Chavez	.50	.23
53 Eric Byrnes	.50	.23
54 Jim Thome	1.25	.55
55 Kevin Millwood	.50	.23
56 Brian Giles	.50	.23
57 Xavier Nady	.50	.23
58 Barry Bonds	3.00	1.35
59 Bret Boone	.50	.23
60 Edgar Martinez	.75	.35
61 Kazuhiro Sasaki	.50	.23
62 Edgar Renteria	.50	.23
63 J.D. Drew	.50	.23
64 Scott Rolen	.75	.35
65 Jim Edmonds	.50	.23
66 Aubrey Huff	.50	.23
67 Alex Rodriguez	2.00	.90
68 Juan Gonzalez	1.25	.55
69 Hank Blalock	.75	.35
70 Mark Teixeira	.75	.35
71 Carlos Delgado	.50	.23
72 Vernon Wells	.50	.23
73 Shea Hillenbrand SP	5.00	2.20
74 Gary Sheffield SP	5.00	2.20
75 Mark Prior SP	15.00	6.75
76 Ken Griffey Jr. SP	12.00	5.50
77 Lance Berkman SP	5.00	2.20
78 Hideo Nomo SP	15.00	6.75
79 Derek Jeter SP	20.00	9.00
80 Ichiro Suzuki SP	12.00	5.50
81 Albert Pujols SP	15.00	6.75
82 Rafael Palmeiro SP	8.00	3.60
83 Jose Reyes ROO SP	8.00	3.60
84 Rocco Baldelli ROO SP	10.00	4.50
85 Hee Seop Choi ROO SP	5.00	2.20
86 Dontrelle Willis ROO SP	8.00	3.60
87 Robb Hammock ROO SP RC	8.00	3.60
88 Brandon Webb ROO SP RC	12.00	5.50
89 Matt Kata ROO SP RC	8.00	3.60
90 T.Wellemeyer ROO SP RC	8.00	3.60
91 Fran Cruceta ROO SP RC	5.00	2.20
92 Clint Barmes ROO SP RC	8.00	3.60
93 Jer Bonderman ROO SP RC	8.00	3.60
94 David Matranga ROO SP RC	5.00	2.20
95 Ryan Wagner ROO SP RC	8.00	3.60
96 Jeremy Griffiths ROO SP RC	8.00	3.60
97 Hideki Matsui ROO SP RC	25.00	11.00
98 Jose Contreras ROO SP RC	10.00	4.50
99 C.Wang ROO SP RC	10.00	4.50
100 Bo Hart ROO SP RC	10.00	4.50
101 Danny Haren ROO SP RC	8.00	3.60
102 Rickie Weeks ROO SP RC	15.00	6.75

2003 E-X Essential Credentials Future

MINT NRMT

*EC FUTURE 1-22: 5X TO 12X BASIC
*EC FUTURE 23-52: 6X TO 15X BASIC
*EC FUTURE 53-67: 8X TO 20X BASIC
*EC FUTURE 68-72: 10X TO 25X BASIC
*EC FUTURE 73-77: 2X TO 5X BASIC
RANDOM INSERTS IN PACKS
PRINT RUNS B/WN 1-102 COPIES PER
78-102 NOT PRICED DUE TO SCARCITY

2003 E-X Essential Credentials Now

MINT NRMT

*EC NOW 26-30: 12.5X TO 30X BASIC
*EC NOW 31-35: 10X TO 25X BASIC
*EC NOW 36-50: 8X TO 20X BASIC
*EC NOW 51-72: 6X TO 15X BASIC
*EC NOW 73-80: 1X TO 2.5X BASIC
*EC NOW 81-82: .75X TO 2X BASIC
*EC NOW 83-102: 1X TO 2.5X BASIC
*EC NOW 83-102: 1X TO 2.5X BASIC RC'S
RANDOM INSERTS IN PACKS
PRINT RUNS B/WN 1-102 COPIES PER
1-25 NO PRICING DUE TO SCARCITY

2003 E-X Behind the Numbers

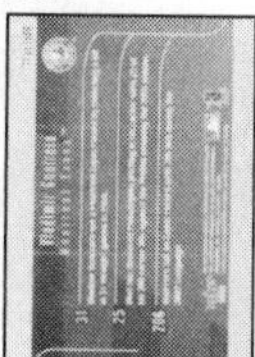

	MINT	NRMT
STATED ODDS 1:80		
1 Derek Jeter	20.00	9.00
2 Alex Rodriguez	12.00	5.50
3 Randy Johnson	8.00	3.60
4 Chipper Jones	8.00	3.60
5 Jim Thome	8.00	3.60
6 Alfonso Soriano	8.00	3.60
7 Adam Dunn	5.00	2.20
8 Nomar Garciaparra	12.00	5.50
9 Roger Clemens	15.00	6.75
10 Gary Sheffield	5.00	2.20
11 Vladimir Guerrero	8.00	3.60
12 Greg Maddux	12.00	5.50
13 Sammy Sosa	12.00	5.50
14 Mike Piazza	12.00	5.50
15 Troy Glaus	8.00	3.60

2003 E-X Behind the Numbers Game Jersey 500

MINT NRMT

PRINT RUN 500 SERIAL #'d SETS
*BTN 199: .5X TO 1.2X BTN 500
BTN 199 PRINT RUN 199 #'d SETS
*BTN 99 MULTI-PATCH: 1.25X TO 3X BTN 500
*BTN 99 ONE COLOR: .75X TO 2X BTN 500
BTN 99 PRINT RUN 99 #'d SETS
BTN 99 ARE MOSTLY PATCH CARDS.
RANDOM INSERTS IN PACKS

	MINT	NRMT
AD Adam Dunn	5.00	2.20
AR Alex Rodriguez	12.00	5.50
AS Alfonso Soriano	8.00	3.60
BM Brett Myers	5.00	2.20
BZ Barry Zito	8.00	3.60
CJ Chipper Jones	8.00	3.60
DJ Derek Jeter	20.00	9.00
DW Dontrelle Willis	8.00	3.60
GM Greg Maddux	10.00	4.50
GS Gary Sheffield	5.00	2.20
HB Hank Blalock	8.00	3.60
JT Jim Thome	8.00	3.60
LB Lance Berkman	5.00	2.20
MB Marlon Byrd	5.00	2.20
MP Mike Piazza	10.00	4.50
NG Nomar Garciaparra	12.00	5.50
RA Roberto Alomar	8.00	3.60
RB Rocco Baldelli	10.00	4.50
RC Roger Clemens	12.00	5.50
RJ Randy Johnson	8.00	3.60
RP Rafael Palmeiro	8.00	3.60
SS Sammy Sosa	12.00	5.50
TG Troy Glaus	8.00	3.60
TGL Tom Glavine	8.00	3.60
VG Vladimir Guerrero	8.00	3.60

2003 E-X Behind the Numbers Game Jersey Autographs

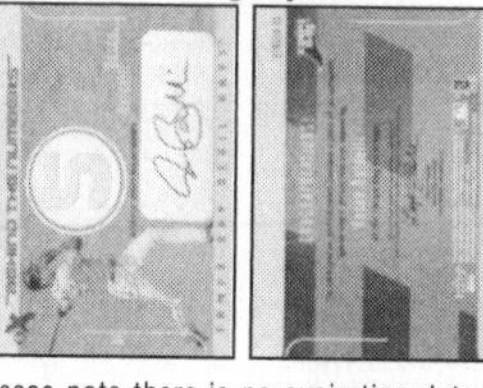

Please note there is no expiration date to redeem the Marlon Byrd autographs.

	MINT	NRMT
RANDOM INSERTS IN PACKS		
PRINT RUNS B/WN 5-35 COPIES PER		
DW Dontrelle Willis/35	60.00	27.00
HB Hank Blalock/9		
MB Marlon Byrd/29 EXCH	40.00	18.00
RB Rocco Baldelli/5		

2003 E-X Behind the Numbers Game Jersey Number

	MINT	NRMT
RANDOM INSERTS IN PACKS		
PRINT RUNS B/WN 2-75 COPIES PER		
NO PRICING ON QTY OF 25 OR LESS.		
AD Adam Dunn/44	20.00	9.00
AR Alex Rodriguez/3		
AS Alfonso Soriano/12		
BM Brett Myers/39	15.00	6.75
BZ Barry Zito/75	15.00	6.75
CJ Chipper Jones/10		
DJ Derek Jeter/2		
DW Dontrelle Willis/35	25.00	11.00
GM Greg Maddux/31	40.00	18.00
GS Gary Sheffield/11		
HB Hank Blalock/9		
JT Jim Thome/25		
LB Lance Berkman/17		
MB Marlon Byrd/29	20.00	9.00
MP Mike Piazza/31	40.00	18.00
NG Nomar Garciaparra/5		
RA Roberto Alomar/12		
RB Rocco Baldelli/5		
RC Roger Clemens/22		
RJ Randy Johnson/51	15.00	6.75
RP Rafael Palmeiro/25		
SS Sammy Sosa/21		
TG Troy Glaus/25		
TGL Tom Glavine/47	20.00	9.00
VG Vladimir Guerrero/27	25.00	11.00

2003 E-X Diamond Essentials

MINT NRMT

STATED ODDS 1:480
NO MORE THAN 30 SETS PRODUCED
PRINT RUN INFO PROVIDED BY FLEER
NO PRICING DUE TO SCARCITY
1 Randy Johnson
2 Ichiro Suzuki
3 Albert Pujols
4 Barry Bonds
5 Hideki Matsui
6 Derek Jeter
7 Chipper Jones
8 Sammy Sosa
9 Jeff Bagwell
10 Mike Piazza
11 Pedro Martinez
12 Mark Prior
13 Jason Giambi
14 Jose Reyes
15 Alfonso Soriano

2003 E-X Diamond Essentials Autographs

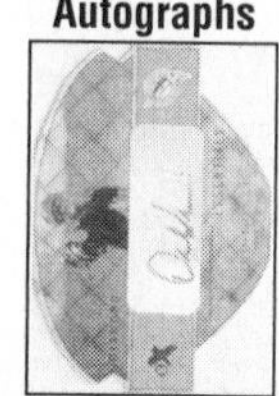

Please note there is no scheduled expiration date to redeem these Albert Pujols autographs.

	MINT	NRMT
RANDOM INSERTS IN PACKS		
PRINT RUNS B/WN 100-299 COPIES PER		
AP Albert Pujols/100 EXCH	150.00	70.00
DW Dontrelle Willis/265	25.00	11.00
RB Rocco Baldelli/299	40.00	18.00
RW Ryan Wagner/199	30.00	13.50

2003 E-X Diamond Essentials Game Jersey 345

MINT NRMT

STATED PRINT RUN 345 SERIAL #'d SETS
*DE 245: .5X TO 1.2X DE 345
DE 245 PRINT RUN 245 #'d SETS
*DE 145: .6X TO 1.5X DE 345
DE 145 PRINT RUN 145 #'d SETS
*DE 55 MULTI-PATCH: 1.25X TO 3X DE 345
*DE 55 ONE COLOR: 1X TO 2.5X DE 345
DE 55 PRINT RUN 55 #'d SETS
DE 55 ARE MOSTLY PATCH CARDS
DE 5 PRINT RUN 5 #'d SETS
NO DE 5 PRICING DUE TO SCARCITY

	MINT	NRMT
CJ Chipper Jones	8.00	3.60
DJ Derek Jeter	20.00	9.00
JB Jeff Bagwell	8.00	3.60
JG Jason Giambi	8.00	3.60
JR Jose Reyes	8.00	3.60
MP Mike Piazza	12.00	5.50
MP Mark Prior	15.00	6.75
PM Pedro Martinez	8.00	3.60
RJ Randy Johnson	8.00	3.60
SS Sammy Sosa	12.00	5.50

2003 E-X Emerald Essentials

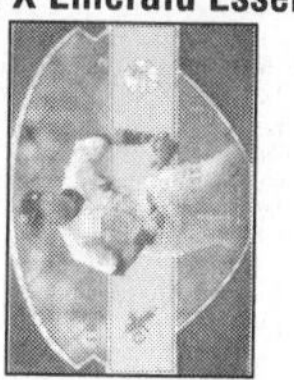

MINT NRMT

STATED ODDS 1:240
NO PRICING DUE TO SCARCITY
1 Austin Kearns
2 Alfonso Soriano
3 Miguel Tejada
4 Troy Glaus
5 Adam Dunn
6 Hideo Nomo
7 Kerry Wood
8 Nomar Garciaparra
9 Roger Clemens
10 Derek Jeter

2003 E-X Emerald Essentials Autographs

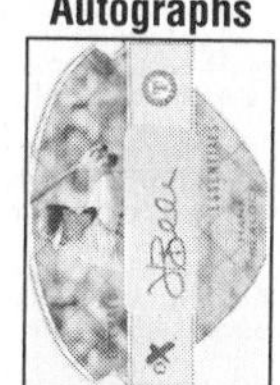

Please note that there is no expiration date to redeem the Marlon Byrd autographs.

	MINT	NRMT
RANDOM INSERTS IN PACKS		
PRINT RUNS B/WN 29-299 COPIES PER		
BW Brandon Webb/299	30.00	13.50
HB Hank Blalock/299	25.00	11.00
MB Marlon Byrd/29 EXCH		

2003 E-X Emerald Essentials Game Jersey 375

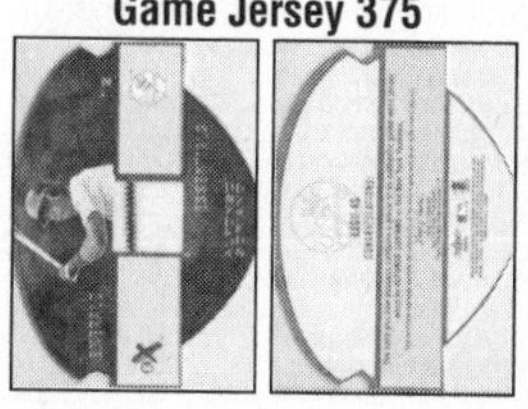

MINT NRMT

STATED PRINT RUN 375 SERIAL #'d SETS
*EE 250: .5X TO 1.2X EE 375
EE 250 PRINT RUN 250 #'d SETS
*EE 175: .6X TO 1.5X EE 375
EE 175 PRINT RUN 175 #'d SETS
*EE 60 SWATCH: 1X TO 2.5X EE 375
*EE 60 MULTI-PATCH: 1.25X TO 3X EE 375
EE 60 PRINT RUN 60 #'d SETS
ABOUT HALF OF EE 60'S ARE PATCH CARDS
EE 15 PRINT RUN 15 #'d SETS
NO EE 15 PRICING DUE TO SCARCITY

	MINT	NRMT
AD Adam Dunn	5.00	2.20
AK Austin Kearns	5.00	2.20
AR Alex Rodriguez	12.00	5.50
AS Alfonso Soriano	8.00	3.60
HN Hideo Nomo	15.00	6.75
KW Kerry Wood	8.00	3.60
MT Miguel Tejada	5.00	2.20
NG Nomar Garciaparra	12.00	5.50
RC Roger Clemens	12.00	5.50
TG Troy Glaus	8.00	3.60

2003 E-X X-tra Innings

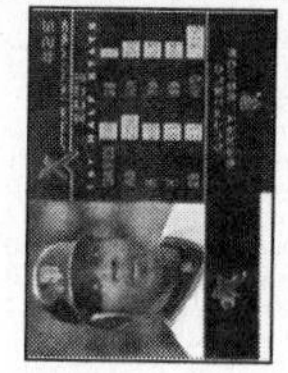

	MINT	NRMT
STATED ODDS 1:32		
1 Ichiro Suzuki	8.00	3.60
2 Albert Pujols	10.00	4.50
3 Barry Bonds	12.00	5.50
4 Jason Giambi	5.00	2.20
5 Pedro Martinez	5.00	2.20
6 Mark Prior	10.00	4.50
7 Derek Jeter	12.00	5.50
8 Curt Schilling	5.00	2.20
9 Jeff Bagwell	5.00	2.20
10 Alex Rodriguez	8.00	3.60

1921-24 Exhibits

Although the Exhibit Supply Company issued 64 cards in 1921 and 128 cards in each of the following three years, the category of 1921-24 was created because of the large number of pictures found repeated in all four years. Each exhibit card measures 3 3/8" by 5 3/8". The cards of 1921 are characterized by ornate hand-lettered names while the cards of 1922-24 have players' names hand-written in a plainer style. Also for 1921 cards, the abbreviation used for the junior circuit is "Am.L." In contrast, cards of the 1922-24 period have the American League abbreviated "A.L." All the cards in the 1921-24 category are black and white and have blank backs; some have white borders measuring approximately 3/16" in width. There is some mislabeling of pictures, incorrect assignment of proper names and many misspellings. Some of the cards have a horizontal (HOR) orientation.

	Ex-Mt	VG
COMPLETE SET (193)	5000.00	2500.00
1 Chas. B. Adams	25.00	12.50
2 Grover C. Alexander	40.00	20.00
3 James Bagby	20.00	10.00
4 J. Frank Baker	40.00	20.00
5 David Bancroft	40.00	20.00
6 Walter Barbare	20.00	10.00
7 Turner Barber	20.00	10.00
8 Clyde Barnhart	20.00	10.00
9 John Bassler	20.00	10.00
10 Carlson L. Bigbee	20.00	10.00
11 Ray Blades	20.00	10.00
12 Sam Bohne	20.00	10.00
13 James Bottomley	40.00	20.00
14 Geo. Burns (Cinn) portrait	20.00	10.00
15 Geo. J. Burns (New York NL)	20.00	10.00
16 George Burns (Boston AL)	20.00	10.00
17 George Burns (Cleveland)	20.00	10.00
18 Joe Bush	25.00	12.50
19 Owen Bush	20.00	10.00
20 Leon Cadore	20.00	10.00
21 Max G. Carey	40.00	20.00
22 Jim Caveney	20.00	10.00
23 Dan Clark	20.00	10.00
24 Ty R. Cobb	400.00	200.00
25 Eddie T. Collins	40.00	20.00
26 John Collins	20.00	10.00
27 Wilbur Cooper	20.00	10.00
28 Stanley Coveleskie sic, Coveleski	40.00	20.00
29 Walton E. Cruse sic, Cruise	20.00	10.00
30 George Cutshaw	20.00	10.00
31 Dave Danforth	20.00	10.00
32 Jacob E. Daubert	25.00	12.50
33 George Dauss	20.00	10.00
34 Charles A. Deal	20.00	10.00
35 Bill Doak (Brooklyn)	20.00	10.00
36 Bill Doak (St. Louis NL)	20.00	10.00
37 Joe Dugan (Boston AL)	25.00	12.50
38 Joe A. Dugan (New York AL)	25.00	12.50
39 Joe A. Dugan (Philadelphia AL)	25.00	12.50
40 Pat Duncan	20.00	10.00
41 James Dykes	25.00	12.50
42 Howard J. Ehmke (Boston AL)	25.00	12.50
43 Howard Ehmke (Detroit) (with border)	25.00	12.50
44 Wm. Evans (Umpire)	80.00	40.00

45 U.C. Red Faber 40.00 20.00
46 Bib Falk 20.00 10.00
47 Dana Fillingim 20.00 10.00
48 Ira Flagstead 20.00 10.00
(Boston AL)
49 A. Fletcher 20.00 10.00
50 J.F. Fournier 20.00 10.00
(Brooklyn)
51 J.F. Fournier 20.00 10.00
(St. Louis NL)
52 Howard Freigau 20.00 10.00
53 Frank F. Frisch 40.00 20.00
54 C.E. Galloway 20.00 10.00
55 W.L. Gardner 20.00 10.00
(Cleveland)
56 Joe Genewich 20.00 10.00
57 Wally Gerber 20.00 10.00
58 Mike Gonzales 20.00 10.00
59 H.M. "Hank" Gowdy 25.00 12.50
(Boston NL)
60 H.M. "Hank" Gowdy 25.00 12.50
(New York NL)
61 Burleigh A. Grimes 40.00 20.00
62 Ray Grimes 20.00 10.00
63 Charles Grimm 25.00 12.50
64 Heinie Groh 25.00 12.50
Cincinnati
65 Heinie Groh 25.00 12.50
New York NL
66 Jesse Haines 40.00 20.00
67 Chas. L. Hartnett 40.00 20.00
68 George Harper 20.00 10.00
69 Sam Harris 20.00 10.00
70 Slim Harris 20.00 10.00
71 Clifton Heathcote 20.00 10.00
72 Harry Heilmann 40.00 20.00
73 Andy High 20.00 10.00
74 George Hildebrand UMP 25.00 12.50
75 Walter L. Holke 20.00 10.00
Boston NL
76 Walter L. Holke 20.00 10.00
Philadelphia NL
77 Chas.J. Hollicher 20.00 10.00
sic, Hollocher
78 Rogers Hornsby 80.00 40.00
79 Wilbert Hubbell 20.00 10.00
80 Bill Jacobson 20.00 10.00
81 Charles D. Jamieson 20.00 10.00
82 E.R. Johnson 20.00 10.00
83 James H. Johnston 20.00 10.00
84 Walter P. Johnson 150.00 75.00
85 Sam P. Jones 20.00 10.00
86 Joe Judge 20.00 10.00
87 Willie Kamm 20.00 10.00
88 Tony Kaufman 20.00 10.00
89 George L. Kelly 40.00 20.00
90 Dick Kerr 25.00 12.50
91 William L. Killefer 20.00 10.00
92 Bill Klem UMP 80.00 40.00
93 Ed Konetchy 20.00 10.00
94 John "Doc" Lavan 20.00 10.00
95 Dudley Lee 20.00 10.00
96 Nemo Leibold 20.00 10.00
Boston AL
97 Nemo Leibold 20.00 10.00
Washington
with border
98 Adolph Luque 25.00 12.50
99 Walter Mails 20.00 10.00
100 Geo. Maisel 20.00 10.00
101 Walt. J. Maranville 40.00 20.00
102 W.C. (Wid) Matthews 20.00 10.00
103 Carl W. Mays 25.00 12.50
104 John McGraw 40.00 20.00
105 J. Stuffy McInnis 25.00 12.50
Boston AL
106 J. Stuffy McInnis 25.00 12.50
Boston NL
107 Lee Meadows 20.00 10.00
108 Clyde Milan 20.00 10.00
109 Ed (Bing) Miller 20.00 10.00
110 Hack Miller 20.00 10.00
111 George Moriarty UMP 25.00 12.50
112 Johnny Morrison 20.00 10.00
113 John A. Mostil 20.00 10.00
114 Robert Meusel 30.00 15.00
115 Harry Myers 20.00 10.00
116 Rollie C. Naylor 20.00 10.00
117 A. Earl Neale 25.00 12.50
118 Arthur Nehf 25.00 12.50
119 Joe Oeschger 20.00 10.00
120 Ivan M. Olson 20.00 10.00
121 Geo. O'Neil 20.00 10.00
122 S.F."Steve" O'Neil 25.00 12.50
sic, O'Neill
123 J.F. O'Neill 20.00 10.00
124 Ernest Padgett 20.00 10.00
125 Roger Peckinpaugh 25.00 12.50
New York AL
with border
126 Peckinpaugh 25.00 12.50
Washington
127 Ralph "Cy" Perkins 20.00 10.00
128 Val Picinich 20.00 10.00
Boston AL
129 Val Picinich 20.00 10.00
Washington
130 Bill Piercy 20.00 10.00
light background
131 Bill Piercy 20.00 10.00
dark background
132 Herman Pillett 20.00 10.00
133 Wally Pipp 25.00 12.50
134 Raymond R. Powell 20.00 10.00
light background
135 Raymond R. Powell 20.00 10.00
dark background
136 Del Pratt 20.00 10.00
Detroit
137 Derrill Pratt 20.00 10.00
Boston AL
138 Joe "Goldie" Rapp 20.00 10.00
139 Walter Reuther 20.00 10.00
140 Edgar S. Rice 40.00 20.00
141 Cy Rigler UMP 25.00 12.50
142 E. E. Rigney 20.00 10.00
143 Jimmy Ring 20.00 10.00
144 Eppa Rixey 40.00 20.00
145 Chas. Robertson 20.00 10.00
146 Eddie Rommel 25.00 12.50
147 Muddy Ruel 20.00 10.00
148 Babe Ruth 400.00 200.00
149 Babe Ruth 800.00 400.00
with border
150 J. H. Sand 20.00 10.00
151 Ray W. Schalk 40.00 20.00
152 Wallie Schang 25.00 12.50
153 Everett Scott 25.00 12.50
Boston AL
154 Everett Scott 25.00 12.50
New York AL
155 Harry Severeid 20.00 10.00
156 Joseph Sewell 40.00 20.00
157 H.S. Shanks 20.00 10.00
photo actually
Wally Schang
158 Earl Sheely 20.00 10.00
159 Urban Shocker 25.00 12.50
160 Al Simmons 40.00 20.00
161 George H. Sisler 40.00 20.00
162 Earl Smith 20.00 10.00
New York NL
with border
163 Earl Smith 20.00 10.00
New York NL
2/3 shot
164 Elmer Smith 20.00 10.00
Boston AL
165 Jack Smith 20.00 10.00
166 R.E. Smith 20.00 10.00
167 Sherrod Smith 20.00 10.00
Brooklyn
168 Sherrod Smith 20.00 10.00
Cleveland
169 Frank Snyder 20.00 10.00
170 Allan Sothoron 20.00 10.00
171 Tris Speaker 100.00 50.00
172 Arnold Statz 20.00 10.00
173 Casey Stengel 100.00 50.00
174 J.R. Stevenson 20.00 10.00
175 Milton Stock 20.00 10.00
176 James Tierney 20.00 10.00
Boston NL
177 James Tierney 20.00 10.00
Pittsburgh
178 John Tobin 20.00 10.00
179 George Toporcer 20.00 10.00
180 Robert Veach 20.00 10.00
181 Clar.(Tillie)Walker 20.00 10.00
182 Curtis Walker 20.00 10.00
183 Aaron Ward 20.00 10.00
184 Zack D. Wheat 40.00 20.00
185 Geo. B. Whitted 20.00 10.00
186 Cy Williams 20.00 10.00
187 Kenneth R. Williams 25.00 12.50
188 Ivy B. Wingo 20.00 10.00
189 Joe Wood 30.00 15.00
190 L. Woodall 20.00 10.00
191 Russell G.Wrightstone 20.00 10.00
192 Moses Yellowhorse 20.00 10.00
193 Ross Youngs 40.00 20.00

1925 Exhibits

The most dramatic change in the 1925 series from that of the preceding group was the printed legend which appeared for the first time in this printing. The subject's name, position, team and the line "(Made in U.S.A.)" appear on four separate lines in a bottom corner, enclosed in a small white box. The name of the player is printed in large capitals while the other lines are of a smaller type size. The cards are black and white, have plain backs and are unnumbered. Each exhibit card measures 3 3/8" by 5 3/8". There are 128 cards in the set and numerous misspellings exist. Note: the card marked "Robert Veach" does not picture that player, but is thought to contain a photo of Ernest Vache. A few of the cards are presented in a horizontal (HOR) format. Players are arranged below in alphabetical order by team: Boston NL 1-8, Brooklyn 9-16, Chicago 17-24, Cincinnati 25-32, New York 33-40, Philadelphia 41-48, Pittsburgh 49-56, St. Louis 57-64, Boston AL 65-72, Chicago 73-80, Cleveland 81-88, Detroit 89-96, New York 97-104, Philadelphia 105-112, St. Louis 113-120 and Washington 121-128.

Ex-Mt VG
COMPLETE SET (128) 8000.00 4000.00
1 David Bancroft 80.00 40.00
2 Jesse Barnes 50.00 25.00
3 Lawrence Benton 50.00 25.00
4 Maurice Burrus 50.00 25.00
5 Joseph Genewich 50.00 25.00
6 Frank Gibson 50.00 25.00
7 David Harris 50.00 25.00
8 George O'Neil 50.00 25.00
9 John H. Deberry 50.00 25.00
10 Art Decatur 50.00 25.00
11 Jacques F. Fournier 50.00 25.00
12 Burleigh A. Grimes 80.00 40.00
13 James H. Johnson 50.00 25.00
sic, Johnston
14 Milton J. Stock 50.00 25.00
15 A.C. Dazzy Vance 80.00 40.00
16 Zack Wheat 100.00 50.00
17 Sparky Adams 50.00 25.00
18 Grover C. Alexander 150.00 75.00
19 John Brooks 50.00 25.00
20 Howard Freigau 50.00 25.00
21 Charles Grimm 60.00 30.00
22 Leo Hartnett 80.00 40.00
23 Walter Maranville 80.00 40.00
24 A.J. Weis 50.00 25.00
25 Raymond Bressler 50.00 25.00
26 Hugh M. Critz 50.00 25.00
27 Peter Donohue 50.00 25.00
28 Charles Dressen 60.00 30.00
29 John (Stuffy) 60.00 30.00
McInnes (McInnis)
30 Eppa Rixey 80.00 40.00
31 Ed. Roush 100.00 50.00
32 Ivy Wingo 50.00 25.00
33 Frank Frisch 150.00 75.00
34 Heine Groh 60.00 30.00
35 Travis C. Jackson 80.00 40.00
36 Emil Meusel 50.00 25.00
37 Arthur Nehf 60.00 30.00
38 Frank Snyder 50.00 25.00
39 Wm. H. Southworth 60.00 30.00
40 William Terry 150.00 75.00
41 George Harper 50.00 25.00
42 Nelson Hawks 50.00 25.00
43 Walter Henline 50.00 25.00
44 Walter Holke 50.00 25.00
45 Wilbur Hubbell 50.00 25.00
46 John Mokan 50.00 25.00
47 John Sand 50.00 25.00
48 Fred Williams 50.00 25.00
49 Carson Bigbee 50.00 25.00
50 Max Carey 80.00 40.00
51 Hazen Cuyler 80.00 40.00
52 George Grantham 50.00 25.00
53 Ray Kremer 50.00 25.00
54 Earl Smith 50.00 25.00
55 Harold Traynor 100.00 50.00
56 Glenn Wright 50.00 25.00
57 Lester Bell HOR 50.00 25.00
58 Raymond Blates 50.00 25.00
sic, Blades
59 James Bottomly 80.00 40.00
sic, Bottomley
60 Max Flack 50.00 25.00
61 Rogers Hornsby 200.00 100.00
62 Clarence Mueller 50.00 25.00
63 William Sherdell 50.00 25.00
64 George Toporcer 50.00 25.00
65 Howard Ehmke 60.00 30.00
66 Ira Flagstead 50.00 25.00
67 I.Valentine Picinich 50.00 25.00
68 John Quinn 60.00 30.00
69 Red Ruffing 100.00 50.00
70 Philip Todt 50.00 25.00
71 Robert Veach 50.00 25.00
72 William Wambsganss 50.00 25.00
73 Eddie Collins 100.00 50.00
74 Bib Falk 50.00 25.00
75 Harry Hooper 100.00 50.00
76 Willie Kamm 50.00 25.00
77 I.M. Davis 50.00 25.00
78 Ray Shalk (Schalk) 80.00 40.00
79 Earl Sheely 50.00 25.00
80 Hollis Thurston 50.00 25.00
81 Wilson Fewster 50.00 25.00
82 Charles Jamieson 50.00 25.00
83 Walter Lutzke 50.00 25.00
84 Glenn Myatt 50.00 25.00
85 Joseph Sewell 80.00 40.00
86 Sherrod Smith 50.00 25.00
87 Tristram Speaker 200.00 100.00
88 Homer Summa 50.00 25.00
89 John Bassler 50.00 25.00
90 Tyrus Cobb 800.00 400.00
91 George Dauss 50.00 25.00
92 Harry Heilmann 100.00 50.00
93 Frank O'Rourke 50.00 25.00
94 Emory Rigney 50.00 25.00
95 Al Wings(Wingo) HOR 50.00 25.00
96 Larry Woodall 50.00 25.00
97 Henry L. Gehrig 800.00 400.00
98 Robert W. Muesel 60.00 30.00
sic, Meusel
99 Walter C. Pipp 80.00 40.00
100 Babe Ruth 1000.00 500.00
101 Walter H. Shang 60.00 30.00
sic, Schang
102 J.R. Shawkey 60.00 30.00
103 Urban J. Shocker 60.00 30.00
104 Aaron Ward 50.00 25.00
105 Max Bishop 50.00 25.00
106 James J. Dykes 60.00 30.00
107 Samuel Gray 50.00 25.00
108 Samuel Hale 50.00 25.00
109 Edmund(Bind) Miller 50.00 25.00
sic, Bing
110 Ralph Perkins 50.00 25.00
111 Edwin Rommel 60.00 30.00
112 Frank Welch 50.00 25.00
113 Walter Gerber 50.00 25.00
114 William Jacobson 50.00 25.00
115 Martin McManus 50.00 25.00
116 Henry Severid 50.00 25.00
sic, Severeid
117 George Sissler 150.00 75.00
sic, Sisler
118 John Tobin 50.00 25.00
119 Kenneth Williams 50.00 25.00
120 Ernest Wingard 50.00 25.00
121 Oswald Bluege 50.00 25.00
122 Stanley Coveleski 80.00 40.00
123 Leon Goslin 100.00 50.00
124 Stanley Harris 80.00 40.00
125 Walter Johnson 300.00 150.00
126 Joseph Judge 60.00 30.00
127 Earl McNeely 50.00 25.00
128 Harold Ruel 50.00 25.00

1926 Exhibits

The year 1926 marked the last of the 128-card sets produced by Exhibit Supply. Of this number, 70 cards are identical to those issued in 1925 but are easily identified because of the new blue-gray color introduced in 1926. Another 21 cards use 1925 pictures but contain the line "Ex. Sup. Co., U.S.A."; these are marked with an asterisk in the checklist below. The 37 photos new to this set have an unboxed legend and carry the new company line. Bischoff is incorrectly placed with Boston, N.L. (should be A.L.); the picture of Galloway is reversed; the photos of Hunnefield and Thomas are wrongly exchanged. Each exhibit card measures 3 3/8" by 5 3/8". Players are in alphabetical order by team: Boston NL 1-8, Brooklyn 9-16, Chicago 17-24, Cincinnati 25-32, New York 33-40, Philadelphia 41-48, Pittsburgh 49-56, St. Louis 57-64, Boston AL 65-72, Chicago 73-80, Cleveland 81-88, Detroit 89-96, New York 97-104, Philadelphia 105-112, St. Louis 113-120 and Washington 121-128.

Ex-Mt VG
COMPLETE SET (128) 8000.00 4000.00
1 Lawrence Benton 50.00 25.00
2 Andrew High 50.00 25.00
3 Maurice Burrus 50.00 25.00
4 David Bancroft 80.00 40.00
5 Joseph Genewich 50.00 25.00
6 Bernie F. Neis 50.00 25.00
7 Edward Taylor 50.00 25.00
8 John Taylor 50.00 25.00
9 John Butler 50.00 25.00
10 Jacques F. Furnier 50.00 25.00
(sic, Fournier) *
11 Burleigh A.Grimes 80.00 40.00
12 Wilson Fewster 50.00 25.00
13 Douglas McWeeny 50.00 25.00
14 George O'Neil 50.00 25.00
15 Walter Maranville 80.00 40.00
16 Zach Wheat 100.00 50.00
17 Sparky Adams 50.00 25.00
18 J. Fred Blake 50.00 25.00
19 James E. Cooney 50.00 25.00
20 Howard Freigau 50.00 25.00
21 Charles Grimm 60.00 30.00
22 Leo Hartnett 80.00 40.00
23 C.E. Heathcote 50.00 25.00
24 Joseph M. Munson 50.00 25.00
25 Raymond Bressler 50.00 25.00
26 Hugh M. Critz 50.00 25.00
27 Peter Donohue 50.00 25.00
28 Charles Dressen 60.00 30.00
29 Walter C. Pipp 60.00 30.00
30 Eppa Rixey 80.00 40.00
31 Ed. Roush 100.00 50.00
32 Ivy Wingo 50.00 25.00
33 Edward S. Farrell 50.00 25.00
34 Frank Frisch 150.00 75.00
35 Frank Snyder 50.00 25.00
36 Fredrick Lindstrom 100.00 50.00
(sic, Frederick) *
37 Hugh A.McQuillan 50.00 25.00
38 Emil Musel 50.00 25.00
(sic, Meusel)
39 James J. Ring 50.00 25.00
40 William Terry 150.00 75.00
41 John M. Bentley 50.00 25.00
42 Bernard Friberg 50.00 25.00
43 George Harper 50.00 25.00
44 Walter Henline 50.00 25.00
45 Clarence Huber 50.00 25.00
46 John Makan 50.00 25.00
(sic, Mokan)
47 John Sand 50.00 25.00
48 Russell Wrigtstone 50.00 25.00
(sic, Wrightstone) *
49 Carson Bigbee 50.00 25.00
50 Max Carey 80.00 40.00
51 Hazen Cuyler 80.00 40.00
52 George Grantham 50.00 25.00
53 Ray Kremer 50.00 25.00
54 Earl Smith 50.00 25.00
55 Harold Traynor 120.00 60.00
56 Glen Wright 50.00 25.00
57 Lester Bell 50.00 25.00
58 Raymond Blates 50.00 25.00
(sic, Blades)
59 James Bottomly 100.00 50.00
(sic, Bottomley)
60 Rogers Hornsby 175.00 90.00
61 Clarence Mueller 50.00 25.00
62 Robert O'Farrell 50.00 25.00
63 William Sherdell 50.00 25.00
64 George Torporcer 50.00 25.00
65 Ira Flagstead 50.00 25.00
66 Fred Haney 60.00 30.00
67 Ramon Herrera 50.00 25.00
68 John Quinn 60.00 30.00
69 Emory Rigney 50.00 25.00
70 Red Ruffing 100.00 50.00
71 Philip Todt 50.00 25.00
72 Fred Wingfield 50.00 25.00
73 Ted Blankenship 50.00 25.00
74 Eddie Collins 100.00 50.00
75 Bib Falk 50.00 25.00
76 Wm. Hunnefield 50.00 25.00
(sic, Tommy Thomas)
77 Willie Kamm 50.00 25.00
78 Ray Shalk (Schalk) 80.00 40.00
79 Earl Sheely 50.00 25.00
80 Hollis Thurston 50.00 25.00
81 Geo.H. Burns HOR 50.00 25.00
82 Walter Lutzke 50.00 25.00
83 Glenn Myatt 50.00 25.00
84 Joseph Sewell 80.00 40.00
85 Sherrod Smith 50.00 25.00
86 Tristram Speaker 200.00 100.00
87 Fred Spurgeon 50.00 25.00
88 Homer Summa 50.00 25.00
89 John Bassler 50.00 25.00
90 Lucerne Blue 50.00 25.00
(sic, Luzerne)
91 Tyrus Cobb 800.00 400.00
92 George Dauss 50.00 25.00
93 Harry Heilmann 100.00 50.00
94 Frank O'Rourke 50.00 25.00
95 Charles Gehringer 150.00 75.00
(batting)
96 John Warner 50.00 25.00
97 Patrick T.Collins 50.00 25.00
98 Earle Combs 100.00 50.00
99 Henry L. Gehrig 800.00 400.00
100 Tony Lazzeri 80.00 40.00
101 Robert W. Muesel 60.00 30.00
(sic, Meusel)
102 Babe Ruth 1000.00 500.00
103 J. R. Shawkey 60.00 30.00
104 Urban J. Shocker 60.00 30.00
105 Max Bishop 50.00 25.00
106 Joseph Galloway 50.00 25.00
107 James J. Dykes 60.00 30.00
108 Joseph Hauser 50.00 25.00
109 Edmund(Bind) Miller 50.00 25.00
sic, Bing
110 Ralph Perkins 50.00 25.00
111 Edwin Rommel 60.00 30.00
112 Wm. Wambsganss 50.00 25.00
113 Wm. Hargrave 50.00 25.00
114 William Jacobson 50.00 25.00
115 Martin McManus 50.00 25.00
116 Oscar Melillo 50.00 25.00
117 Walter Gerber 50.00 25.00
118 George Sissler 150.00 75.00
sic, Sisler
119 Kenneth Williams 50.00 25.00
120 Ernest Wingard 50.00 25.00
121 Oswald Bluege 50.00 25.00
122 Stanley Coveleski 80.00 40.00
123 Leon Goslin 80.00 40.00
124 Stanley Harris 80.00 40.00
125 Walter Johnson 300.00 150.00
126 Joseph Judge 50.00 25.00
127 Earl McNeely 50.00 25.00
128 Harold Ruel 50.00 25.00

1927 Exhibits

Two innovations characterize the 64-card set produced by Exhibit Supply Company for 1927. The first was a radical departure from the color scheme of previous sets marked by this year's light green hue. The second was the installation of the divided legend, whereby the player's name (all caps) and team were set in one corner, and the lines "Ex. Sup. Co., Chgo." and "Made in U.S.A." were set in the other. All the photos employed in this set were taken from the previous issues in 1925 and 1926, although 13 players appear with new teams. The usual misspellings and incorrect labeling of names and initials occurs throughout the set. Note: Genewich and Hunnefield have a different style of print, and Myatt is missing the right side of the legend. Each card measures 3 3/8" by 5 3/8". Players are listed in alphabetical order by team: Boston NL 1-4, Brooklyn 5-8, Chicago 9-12, Cincinnati 13-16, New York 17-20, Philadelphia 21-24, Pittsburgh 25-28, St. Louis 29-32, Boston AL 33-36, Chicago 37-40, Cleveland 41-44, Detroit 45-48, New York 49-52, Philadelphia 53-56, St. Louis 57-60, Washington 61-64.

Ex-Mt VG
COMPLETE SET (64) 3000.00 1500.00
1 David Bancroft 50.00 25.00
2 Joseph Genewich 25.00 12.50
3 Andrew High 25.00 12.50
4 J. Taylor 25.00 12.50
5 John Buttler (Butler) 25.00 12.50
6 Wilson Fewster 25.00 12.50
7 Burleigh A. Grimes 50.00 25.00
8 Walter Henline 25.00 12.50
9 Sparky Adams 25.00 12.50
10 Charles Grimm 30.00 15.00
11 Leo Hartnett 50.00 25.00
12 Clifton Heathcote 25.00 12.50
13 Raymond Bressler 25.00 12.50
14 Walter C. Pipp 40.00 20.00
15 Eppa Rixey 50.00 25.00
16 Ivy Wingo 25.00 12.50
17 John M. Bentley 25.00 12.50
18 George Harper 25.00 12.50
19 Rogers Hornsby 100.00 50.00
20 Fredrick Lindstrom 50.00 25.00
21 A.R. Decatur 25.00 12.50
22 John "Stuffy" McInnes 30.00 15.00
(sic, McInnis)
23 John Mokan 25.00 12.50
24 Russell Wrightstone 25.00 12.50
25 Hazen Cuyler 50.00 25.00
26 Ray Kremer 25.00 12.50
27 Earl Smith 25.00 12.50
28 Harold Traynor 50.00 25.00
29 Grover C. Alexander 80.00 40.00
30 James Bottomly 60.00 30.00
(sic, Bottomley)
31 Robert O'Farrell 25.00 12.50
32 Wm. H. Southworth 30.00 15.00
33 Ira Flagstead 25.00 12.50
34 Fred Haney 25.00 12.50
35 Philip Todt 25.00 12.50
36 Fred Wingfield 25.00 12.50
37 Fred Blankenship 25.00 12.50
(sic, Ted)
38 Wm. Hunnefield 25.00 12.50
(sic, Tommy Thomas)
39 Willie Kamm 25.00 12.50
40 Ray Schalk 50.00 25.00
41 Geo. H. Burns HOR 25.00 12.50
42 Walter Lutzke 25.00 12.50
43 Glenn Myatt 25.00 12.50
44 Bernie Neis 25.00 12.50
45 John Bassler 25.00 12.50
46 George Daus 25.00 12.50
(sic, Dauss)
47 Charles Gehringer 75.00 38.00
48 Harry Heilman 50.00 25.00
(sic, Heilmann)
49 Henry L. Gehrig 400.00 200.00
50 Tony Lazzeri 50.00 25.00
51 Robert W. Muesel 25.00 12.50
(sic, Meusel)
52 Babe Ruth 600.00 300.00
53 Tyrus Cobb 400.00 200.00
54 Eddie Collins 50.00 25.00
55 William Wambsganns 30.00 15.00
sic, Wambsganss
56 Zach Wheat 50.00 25.00
57 Wm. Hargrave 25.00 12.50
58 Kenneth Williams 30.00 15.00
59 George Sissler 80.00 40.00

sic, Sisler
60 Ernest Wingard 25.00 12.50
61 Leon Goslin 50.00 25.00
62 Walter Johnson 200.00 100.00
63 Harold Ruel 25.00 12.50
64 Tristam Speaker 100.00 50.00
sic, Tristram

1928 Exhibits

In contrast to the green color of the preceding year, the 64 Exhibit cards of 1928 are blue in color. Each card measures 3 3/8" by 5 3/8". They may be found with blank backs, or postcard backs containing a small premium offer clip-off in one corner. The use of the divided legend was continued, with the Roush card being unique in the set as it also cites his position. Of the 64 players in the set, 24 appear for the first time, while 12 of the holdovers show new poses. In addition, four players are shown with new team affiliations. The remaining 24 cards are identical to those issued in 1927 except for color. Once again, there is at least one mistaken identity and many misspellings and wrong names. A few of the cards are presented horizontally (HOR). Players are listed below in alphabetical order by team: Boston NL 1-4, Brooklyn 5-8, Chicago 9-12, Cincinnati 13-16, New York 17-20, Philadelphia 21-24, Pittsburgh 25-28, St. Louis 29-32, Boston AL 33-36, Chicago 37-40, Cleveland 41-44, Detroit 45-48, New York 49-52, Philadelphia 53-56, St. Louis 57-60 and Washington 61-64.

Ex-Mt VG
COMPLETE SET (64) 2500.00 1250.00
1 Edward Brown 25.00 12.50
2 Rogers Hornsby HOR 120.00 60.00
3 Robert Smith 25.00 12.50
4 John Taylor 25.00 12.50
5 David Bancroft 50.00 25.00
6 Max G. Carey 50.00 25.00
7 Charles R. Hargraves 25.00 12.50
8 Arthur "Dazzy" Vance 50.00 25.00
9 Woody English 25.00 12.50
10 Leo Hartnett 50.00 25.00
11 Charlie Root 25.00 12.50
12 L.R. (Hack) Wilson 80.00 40.00
13 Hugh M. Critz 25.00 12.50
14 Eugene Hargrave 25.00 12.50
15 Adolph Luque 30.00 15.00
16 William A. Zitzmann 25.00 12.50
17 Virgil Barnes 25.00 12.50
18 J. Francis Hogan 25.00 12.50
19 Fredrick Lindstrom 50.00 25.00
sic, Frederick
20 Edd. Roush, Outfield 50.00 25.00
21 Fred Leach 25.00 12.50
22 James Ring 25.00 12.50
23 Henry Sand HOR 25.00 12.50
24 Fred Williams 30.00 15.00
25 Ray Kremer 25.00 12.50
26 Earl Smith 25.00 12.50
27 Paul Waner 50.00 25.00
28 Glenn Wright 25.00 12.50
29 Grover C. Alexander 80.00 40.00
no emblem
30 Francis R. Blades 25.00 12.50
31 Frank Frisch 80.00 40.00
32 James Wilson 30.00 15.00
33 Ira Flagstead 25.00 12.50
34 Bryan "Slim" Harriss 25.00 12.50
35 Fred Hoffman 25.00 12.50
36 Philip Todt 25.00 12.50
37 Chalmer W. Cissell HOR 25.00 12.50
38 Bib Falk 25.00 12.50
39 Theodore Lyons 50.00 25.00
40 Harry McCurdy 25.00 12.50
41 Chas. Jamieson 25.00 12.50
42 Glenn Myatt 25.00 12.50
43 Joseph Sewell 50.00 25.00
44 Geo. Uhle 25.00 12.50
45 Robert Fothergill 25.00 12.50
46 Jack Tavener HOR 25.00 12.50
47 Earl G. Whitehill 25.00 12.50
48 Lawrence Woodall 25.00 12.50
49 Pat Collins 25.00 12.50
50 Lou Gehrig 400.00 200.00
51 Geo.H."Babe" Ruth 600.00 300.00
52 Urban J. Shocker 25.00 12.50
53 Gordon S. Cochrane 80.00 40.00
54 Howard Ehmke 30.00 15.00
55 Joseph Hauser 25.00 12.50
56 Al. Simmons 50.00 25.00
57 L.A. Blue 25.00 12.50
58 John Ogden 25.00 12.50
sic, Warren Ogden
59 Walter Shang 30.00 15.00
sic, Schang
60 Fred Schulte 25.00 12.50
61 Leon Goslin 50.00 25.00
62 Stanley Harris 50.00 25.00
63 Sam Jones 30.00 15.00
64 Harold Ruel 25.00 12.50

1929-30 Exhibits Four-in-One

The years 1929-30 marked the initial appearance of the Exhibit Company's famous "Four-In-One" design. Each of the 32 cards depict four players from one team, with a total of 128 players shown (eight from each of 16 major league teams). Each of these exhibit cards measures 3 3/8" by 5 3/8". The player's names and teams are located under each picture in dark blue or white print. All the reverses are post card style with the premium

clip-off across one corner. There are 11 color combinations known for the fronts. The backs may be uncolored, red (black/red front) or yellow (blue/yellow front). The card labeled "Babe Herman" actually depicts Jesse Petty. The catalog designation is W463-1.

EX-MT VG-E
COMPLETE SET (32) 2400.00 1100.00
1 Pat Collins 80.00 36.00
Joe Dugan
Edward Farrel
(sic, Farrell)
George Sisler
2 Lance Richbourg 50.00 22.00
Fred Maguire
Robert Smith
George Harper
3 D'Arcy Flowers 60.00 27.00
Arthur "Dazzy" Vance
Nick Cullop
Harvey Hendrick
4 Babe Herman 60.00 27.00
David Bancroft
John H. Deberry
Del L. Bisonette
(sic, Bissonette)
5A Gabby Hartnett 150.00 70.00
Clyde Beck
Hack Wilson
Rogers Hornsby
5B Clyde Beck
Gabby Hartnett
Hack Wilson
Rogers Hornsby
6 Charlie Root 60.00 27.00
Kiki Cuyler
Woody English
Charlie Grimm
7 Hugh Critz 60.00 27.00
Curt Walker
George L. Kelly
Val Picinich
8 Pid Purdy 50.00 22.00
Pinky Pittenger
Red Lucas
Hod Ford
9 Larry Benton 80.00 36.00
Melvin Ott
William Terry
Andrew Reese
10 Shanty Hogan 80.00 36.00
Travis Jackson
Jimmy Welsh
Fred Lindstrom
11 Frank O'Doul 50.00 22.00
Bernard Friberg
Fresco Thompson
Donald Hurst
12 Cy Williams 50.00 22.00
Pinky Whitney
Ray Benge
Les Sweetland
13 Earl J. Adams 60.00 27.00
Dick Bartell
Harold Traynor
Earl Sheely
14 Lloyd Waner 80.00 36.00
Bubbles Hargreaves
Ray Kremer
Paul Waner
15 Grover C. Alexander 100.00 45.00
James Wilson
Frank Frisch
James Bottomly
(sic, Bottomley)
16 Fred Haney 60.00 27.00
Chick Hafey
Taylor Douthit
Charlie Gilbert
(sic, Gelbert)
17 Johnnie Heving 60.00 27.00
Jack Rothrock
Red Ruffing
Bobby Reeves
18 Phil Todt 50.00 22.00
Hal Rhyne
Bill Regan
Doug Taitt
19 Chalmer Cissell 50.00 22.00
John W. Clancy
John L. Kerr
Willie Kamm
20 Alex Metzler 50.00 22.00
Alphonse Thomas
Carl Reynolds
Martin G. Autrey
(sic, Autry)
21 Lew Fonseca 60.00 27.00
Joe Sewell
Carl Lind
Jackie Tavener
22 Ken Holloway 60.00 27.00
Bibb A. Falk
Luke Sewell
Earl Averill
23 Dale Alexander 80.00 36.00
Marty McManus
Harry Rice
Charlie Gehringer
24 Merv Shea 60.00 27.00
George Uhle
Harry Heilman
(sic& Heilmann)
Nolen Richardson
25 Waite Hoyt 100.00 45.00
Anthony Lazzeri
Benny Bengough
Earle Coombs
(sic, Combs)
26 Mark Koenig 800.00 350.00
Geo.H."Babe" Ruth
Leo Durocher
Henry L. Gehrig
27 Jimmy Foxx 150.00 70.00
Gordon S. Cochrane
Robert M. Grove
George Haas
28 Homer Summa 50.00 22.00
James Dykes
Samuel Hale
Max Bishop
29 Heine Manush 60.00 27.00
Wally Shang
(sic, Schang)
Sam Gray
Red Kress
30 Oscar Melillo 50.00 22.00
Frank O'Rourke
sic, O'Rourke
Lu Blue
Fred Schulte
31 Leon Goslin 60.00 27.00
Oswald Bluege
Harold Ruel
Joseph Judge
32 Sam Rice 60.00 27.00
Jack Hayes
Sam P. Jones
Buddy M. Myer

1931-32 Exhibits Four-in-One

The collector should refer to the checklists when trying to determine the year of issue of any "Four-In-One" set because the checklist (showing the players as they are, appear in groups of four) and the card color will ultimately provide the right clues. Some of the colors of the previous issue -- black on green, orange, red or yellow, and blue on white -- are repeated in this series, but the 1931-32 cards are distinguishable by the combinations of players which appear. Each card measures 3 3/8" by 5 3/8". The backs contain a description of attainable "Free Prizes" for coupons. The backs also contain the clip-off premium coupon. There are numerous misspellings, as usual, in the set. The catalog designation for this set is W463-2.

Ex-Mt VG
COMPLETE SET (32) 4000.00 2000.00
1 Walter Maranville 120.00 60.00
Tom Zachary
Alfred Spohrer
Randolph Moore
2 Lance Richbourg 100.00 50.00
Fred Maguire
Earl Sheely
Walter Berger
3 D'Arcy Flowers 120.00 60.00
Arthur "Dazzy" Vance
Frank O'Doul
Fresco Thompson
4 Floyd C. Herman 100.00 50.00
Glenn Wright
Jack Quinn
Del L. Bissonette
5 Leo Hartnett 250.00 125.00
Riggs Stevenson
(sic, Stephenson)
L.R.(Hack) Wilson
Rogers Hornsby
6 Charlie Root 120.00 60.00
Hazen Cuyler
Woody English
Charlie Grimm
7 Les Durocher 150.00 75.00
(sic, Leo)
Curt Walker
Harry Heilmann
Nick Cullop
8 Wally Roettger 100.00 50.00
Johnny Gooch
Red Lucas
Hod Ford
9 Shanty Hogan 120.00 60.00
Travis Jackson
Hugh Critz
Fred Lindstrom
10 Robert O'Farrell 200.00 100.00
Melvin Ott
William Terry
Fred Fitzsimmons
11 Chuck Klein 120.00 60.00
Pinky Whitney
Ray Benge
Buzz Arlett
12 Harry McCurdy 100.00 50.00
Bernard Friberg
Richard Bartell
Donald Hurst
13 Adam Comorosky 120.00 60.00
Gus Suhr
Harold Traynor
Tommy Thevenow
14 Lloyd Waner 120.00 60.00
George Grantham
Ray Kremer
Paul Waner
15 Earl J. Adams 150.00 75.00
James Wilson
Frank Frisch
James Bottomly
(sic, Bottomley)
16 Bill Hallahan 120.00 60.00
Chick Hafey
Taylor Douthit
Charlie Gilbert
(sic& Gelbert)
17 Chas. Berry 100.00 50.00
Jack Rothrock
Bobby Reeves
Bobby . (R.E.) Reeves
18 Earl Webb 100.00 50.00
Hal Rhyne
Bill Sweeney
Danny MacFayden
19 Luke L. Appling 120.00 60.00
Ted Lyons
Chalmer W. Cissell
Willie Kamm
20 Smead Jolley 100.00 50.00
Lu Blue
Carl Reynolds
Henry Tate
21 William Hunnefield 100.00 50.00
Jonah Goldman
Ed Morgan
Wes Ferrell
22 Lew Fonseca 120.00 60.00
Bibb Falk
Luke Sewell
Earl Averill
23 Dale Alexander 120.00 60.00
Marty McManus
George Uhle
Charlie Gehringer
24 Wallie Schang 120.00 60.00
Liz Funk
Mark Koenig
Waite Hoyt
25 Bill Dickey 300.00 150.00
Anthony Lazzeri
Herb Pennock
Earl Coombs
(sic, Combs)
26 Lyn Lary 1200.00 600.00
Geo. H. Babe Ruth
James Reese
Henry L. Gehrig
27 John Boley 120.00 60.00
James Dykes
Bing. Miller
Al Simmons
28 Jimmy Foxx 200.00 100.00
Gordon S. Cochrane
Robert M. Grove
George Haas
29 Oscar Melillo 120.00 60.00
Frank O'Rourke
(sic, O'Rourke)
Leon Goslin
Fred Schulte
30 Lefty Stewart 120.00 60.00
Richard Farrell
(sic, Ferrell)
Sam Gray
Red Kress
31 Roy Spencer 120.00 60.00
Heine Manush
Joe Cronin
Fred Marberry
32 Ossie Bluege 120.00 60.00
Joe Judge
Sam Rice
Buddy Myer

1933 Exhibits Four-in-One

The physical dimensions of the cardboard sheet used by the Exhibit Supply Company in printing their card sets over the years allows the following correlation to be made when one establishes that 32 of the standard-sized cards (3 3/8" by 5 3/8") are printed per sheet. Sets of 128 cards are equal to four sheets, 64 cards to two sheets, 32 cards to one sheet and 16 cards to one-half sheet. Whether it was economics, the Depression, or simplicity of operation, something caused the company to change their set totals in a descending order since 1922 in 1933. The first of a series of 16-card sets was released. The fronts of these cards are black green, orange, red or yellow; the backs are blank. The catalog designation for this set is W463-3.

Ex-Mt VG
COMPLETE SET (16) 2400.00 1200.00
1 Lance Richbourg 80.00 40.00
Fred Maguire
Earl Sheely
Walter Berger
2 Vincent Lopez (Al) 120.00 60.00
Glenn Wright
Arthur Dazzy Vance
Frank O'Doul
3 Riggs Stephenson 80.00 40.00
Charlie Grimm
Woody English
Charlie Root
4 Taylor Douthit 100.00 50.00
George Grantham
Red Lucas
Chick Hafey
5 Fred Fitzsimmons 100.00 50.00
Hugh Critz
Fred Lindstrom
Robert O'Farrell
6 Chuck Klein 100.00 50.00
Ray Benge
Richard Bartell
Donald Hurst
7 Tom J. Thevenow 120.00 60.00
Paul Waner
Gus Suhr
Lloyd Waner
8 Earl J. Adams 120.00 60.00
Frank Frisch
Bill Halloran
Charlie Gelbert
9 Danny MacFayden 80.00 40.00
Earl Webb
Hal Rhyne
Charlie Berry
10 Charles Berry 100.00 50.00
Bob Seeds
Lu Blue
Ted Lyons
11 Wes Ferrell 100.00 50.00
Luke Sewell
Ed Morgan
Earl Averill
12 Muddy Ruel 120.00 60.00
George Uhle
Jonathon Stone
Charlie Gehringer
13 Babe Ruth 1200.00 600.00
Herb Pennock
Anthony Lazzeri
Bill Dickey
14 Mickey Cochrane 250.00 125.00
Jimmy Foxx
Al Simmons
Robert M. Grove
15 Richard Farrell 120.00 60.00
(sic, Ferrell)
Oscar Melillo
Leon Goslin
S. Grey
16 Heinie Manush 100.00 50.00
Firpo Marberry
Joe Judge
Roy Spencer

1934 Exhibits Four-in-One W463-4

The emergence of the bubble gum card producers in 1933-34 may have motivated Exhibit Supply to make a special effort to provide a "quality" set for 1934. The new 16-card series was printed in colors of blue, brown, olive green and violet -- all in softer tones than used in previous years. No less than 25 players appeared on cards for the first time, and another 16 were given entirely new poses. For the first time in the history of the Exhibit baseball series, there were no spelling errors. However, perfection is rarely attained in any endeavor, and the "bugaboo" of 1934 was the labeling of Al Lopez as Vincent Lopez (famous band leader and prognosticator). The cards have plain backs. Each card measures 3 3/8" by 5 3/8".

Ex-Mt VG
COMPLETE SET (16) 1800.00 900.00
1 Bill Urbansky 50.00 25.00
Ed Brandt
Walter Berger
Frank Hogan
2 Vincent Lopez (Al) 60.00 30.00
Glenn Wright
Sam Leslie
Leonard Koenecke
3 Chas. Klein 60.00 30.00
C.J. Grimm
Woody English
Lon Warneke
4 Ernie Lombardi 100.00 50.00
Tony Piet
Jimmy Bottomley
Chas. J. Hafey
5 Blondy Ryan 150.00 75.00
Bill Terry
Carl Hubbell
Mel Ott
6 Jimmy Wilson 50.00 25.00
Wesley Schulmerich
Richard Bartell
Donald Hurst
7 Tommy Thevenow 100.00 50.00
Paul Waner
Pie Traynor
Lloyd Waner
8 Pepper Martin 80.00 40.00
Frank Frisch
Bill Hallahan
John Rothrock
9 Lefty Grove 100.00 50.00
Roy Johnson
Bill Cissell
Rick Ferrell
10 Luke Appling 80.00 40.00
Al Simmons
Evar Swanson
George Earnshaw
11 Wes Ferrell 60.00 30.00
Frank Pytlak
Willie Kamm
Earl Averill
12 Mickey Cochrane 150.00 75.00
Goose Goslin
Fred Marberry
Charlie Gehringer
13 Babe Ruth 800.00 400.00
Lefty Gomez
Lou Gehrig
Bill Dickey
14 Slug Mahaffey 100.00 50.00
Jimmie Foxx

Card	Ex-Mt	VG
Doc Cramer		
Frank Higgins		
15 Irving Burns	50.00	25.00
Oscar Melillo		
Irving Hadley		
Rollie Hemsley		
16 Heine Manush	80.00	40.00
Alvin Crowder		
Joe Cronin		
Joe Kuhel		

1935 Exhibits Four-in-One W463-5

The year 1935 marked the return of the 16-card Exhibit series to a simple slate blue color. Babe Ruth appears with Boston, N.L., the last time his card would be made while he was playing, after being included in every Exhibit series since 1921. Of the 64 players pictured, 17 are shown for the first time, while 11 of the returnees are graced with new poses. The infamous "Vincent Lopez" card returns with this set, and the photo purportedly showing Tony Cuccinello is really that of George Puccinelli. The cards have plain backs. The cards measure 3 3/8" by 5 3/8".

	Ex-Mt	VG
COMPLETE SET (16)	2400.00	1200.00
1 Babe Ruth	800.00	400.00
Frank Hogan		
Walter Berger		
Ed Brandt		
2 Van Mungo	60.00	30.00
Vincent Lopez (Al)		
Dan Taylor		
Tony Cuccinello		
3 Chuck Klein	80.00	40.00
Charlie Grimm		
Lon Warneke		
Gabby Hartnett		
4 Ernie Lombardi	100.00	50.00
Paul Derringer		
Jimmy Bottomley		
Chick Hafey		
5 Hughie Critz	150.00	75.00
Bill Terry		
Carl Hubbell		
Mel Ott		
6 Jimmy Wilson	50.00	25.00
Phil Collins		
John "Blondy" Ryan		
George Watkins		
7 Paul Waner	100.00	50.00
Pie Traynor		
Guy Bush		
Floyd Vaughan		
8 Pepper Martin	250.00	125.00
Frank Frisch		
Jerome "Dizzy" Dean		
Paul Dean		
9 Lefty Grove	150.00	75.00
Billy Werber		
Joe Cronin		
Rick Ferrell		
10 Al Simmons	80.00	40.00
Jimmy Dykes		
Ted Lyons		
Henry Bonura		
11 Mel Harder	60.00	30.00
Hal Trosky		
Willie Kamm		
Earl Averill		
12 Mickey Cochrane	100.00	50.00
Goose Goslin		
Linwood Rowe		
(sic& Lynwood)		
Charlie Gehringer		
13 Tony Lazzeri	600.00	300.00
Lefty Gomez		
Lou Gehrig		
Bill Dickey		
14 Slug Mahaffey	80.00	40.00
Jimmy Foxx		
George Cramer		
Bob Johnson		
15 Irving Burns	50.00	25.00
Oscar Melillo		
Bobo Newson		
Rollie Hemsley		
16 Buddy Meyer (Myer)	60.00	30.00
Earl Whitehill		
Heinie Manush		
Fred Schulte		

1936 Exhibits Four-in-One W463-6

In 1936, the 16-card Exhibit set retained the "slate" or blue-gray color of the preceding year, but also added an olive green hue to the set. The cards are blank-backed, but for the first time since the "Four-In-One" design was introduced in 1929, a line reading "Ptd. in U.S.A." was placed in the bottom border on the obverse. The set contains 16 players making their debut in Exhibit cards, while nine holdovers have new poses. The photos of George Puccinelli was correctly identified and placed with Philadelphia, A.L. The cards measure 3 3/8" by 5 3/8".

	Ex-Mt	VG
COMPLETE SET (16)	1500.00	750.00
1 Bill Urbanski	50.00	25.00
Pinky Whitney		
Walter Berger		
Danny MacFayden		
2 Van Mungo	60.00	30.00
Stan Bordagaray		
Fred Lindstrom		
Dutch Brandt		
3 Billy Herman	80.00	40.00
Augie Galan		
Lon Warneke		
Gabby Hartnett		
4 Ernie Lombardi	60.00	30.00
Paul Derringer		
Babe Herman		
Alex Kampouris		
5 Gus. Mancuso	150.00	75.00
Bill Terry		
Carl Hubbell		
Mel Ott		
6 Jimmy Wilson	50.00	25.00
Curt Davis		
Dolph Camilli		
Johnny Moore		
7 Paul Waner	80.00	40.00
Pie Traynor		
Guy Bush		
Floyd Vaughan		
8 Joe "Ducky" Medwick	150.00	75.00
Frank Frisch		
Jerome "Dizzy" Dean		
Paul Dean		
9 Lefty Grove	150.00	75.00
Jimmy Foxx		
Joe Cronin		
Rick Ferrell		
10 Luke Appling	80.00	40.00
Jimmy Dykes		
Ted Lyons		
Henry Bonura		
11 Mel Harder	60.00	30.00
Hal Trosky		
Joe Vosmik		
Earl Averill		
12 Mickey Cochrane	150.00	75.00
Goose Goslin		
Linwood Rowe		
(sic& Lynwood)		
Charlie Gehringer		
13 Tony Lazzeri	600.00	300.00
Vernon Gomez		
Lou Gehrig		
Red Ruffing		
14 Charles Berry	50.00	25.00
George Puccinelli		
Frank Higgins		
Bob Johnson		
15 Harland Clift	50.00	25.00
Sammy West		
Paul Andrews		
Rollie Hemsley		
16 Buddy Meyer (Myer)	50.00	25.00
Earl Whitehill		
Ossie Bluege		
Bobo Newsom		

1937 Exhibits Four-in-One W463-7

It would appear that Exhibit Supply was merely "flip-flopping" color schemes during the three year period 1935-37. In 1935, the cards were blue-gray; in 1936, the cards were either blue-gray or green; in 1937, the cards appear in green only. As with the previous set, the name and team of each player is printed in two or three lines under his picture, the "Ptd. in U.S.A." line appears in the bottom border (missing on some cards) and the backs are blank. The catalog designation is W463-7

	Ex-Mt	VG
COMPLETE SET (16)	2000.00	1000.00
1 Bill Urbanski	80.00	40.00
Alfonso Lopez		
Walter Berger		
Danny MacFayden		
2 Van Mungo	60.00	30.00
Woody English		
Johnny Moore		
(Philadelphia NL)		
Gordon Phelps		
3 Billy Herman	80.00	40.00
Augie Galan		
Bill Lee		
Gabby Hartnett		
4 Ernie Lombardi	60.00	30.00
Paul Derringer		
Lew Riggs		
Phil Weintraub		
5 Gus Mancuso	120.00	60.00
Sam Leslie		
Carl Hubbell		
Mel Ott		
6 Pinky Whitney	60.00	30.00
Bucky Walters		
Dolph Camilli		
Johnny Moore		
7 Paul Waner	80.00	40.00
Gus Suhr		
Cy Blanton		
Floyd Vaughan		
8 Joe "Duck" Medwick	200.00	100.00
Lon Warneke		
Jerome "Dizzy" Dean		
Stuart Martin		
9 Lefty Grove	300.00	150.00
Jimmy Foxx		
Joe Cronin		
Rick Ferrell		
10 Luke Appling	60.00	30.00
Jimmy Dykes		
Vernon Kennedy		
Henry Bonura		
11 Bob Feller	200.00	100.00
Hal Trosky		
Frank Pytlak		
Earl Averill		
12 Mickey Cochrane	120.00	60.00
Goose Goslin		
Linwood Rowe		
Charlie Gehringer		
13 Tony Lazzeri	800.00	400.00
Vernon Gomez		
Lou Gehrig		
Joe DiMaggio		
14 Billy Weber	60.00	30.00
(sic, Werber)		
Harry Kelly		
(sic, Kelley)		
Wallace Moses		
Bob Johnson		
15 Harland Clift	60.00	30.00
Sammy West		
Oral Hildebrand		
Rollie Hemsley		
16 Buddy Meyer (Myer)	60.00	30.00
Jonathan Stone		
Joe Kuhel		
Bobo Newsom		

1938 Exhibits Four-in-One

The 1938 set of 16 cards demonstrated the fact that one consistent "quality" of Exhibit Supply sets is their inconsistency. For example, the card of Tony Cuccinello once again contains the photo of George Puccinelli, a mistake first made in 1935, corrected in 1936 and now made again in 1938. The set is also rife with name and spelling errors. Of the 64 players depicted, 12 are new arrivals and three are returnees with new poses. Another ten retained their 1937 photos but were designated new team affiliations. The cards have blank backs. The set was the last to employ the "Four-In-One" format. The catalog designation is W463-8. The cards measure 3 3/8" by 5 3/8".

	Ex-Mt	VG
COMPLETE SET (16)	2400.00	1200.00
1 Tony Cuccinello	80.00	40.00
(sic, Geo.Puccinelli)		
Roy Johnson		
Vince DiMaggio		
Danny MacFayden		
2 Van Mungo	80.00	40.00
Leo Durocher		
Dolph Camilli		
Gordon Phelps		
3 Billy Herman	250.00	125.00
Augie Galan		
Jerome "Dizzy" Dean		
Gabby Hartnett		
4 Dutch Lombardi	80.00	40.00
Paul Derringer		
Lew Riggs		
Ival Goodman		
5 Hank Leiber	150.00	75.00
Jim Ripple		
Carl Hubbell		
Mel Ott		
6 Pinky Whitney	80.00	40.00
Bucky Walters		
Chuck Klein		
Morris Arnovich		
7 Paul Waner	100.00	50.00
Gus Suhr		
Cy Blanton		
Floyd Vaughan		
8 Joe "Ducky" Medwick	100.00	50.00
Lon Warneke		
John Mize		
Stuart Martin		
9 Lefty Grove	150.00	75.00
Jimmy Foxx		
Joe Cronin		
Joe Vosmik		
10 Luke Appling	100.00	50.00
Luke Sewell		
Mike Kreevich		
Ted Lyons		
11 Bob Feller	150.00	75.00
Hal Trosky		
Odell Hale		
Earl Averill		
12 Hank Greenberg	150.00	75.00
Rudy York		
Tom Bridges		
Charlie Gehringer		
13 Bill Dickey	1000.00	500.00
Lefty Gomez		
Lou Gehrig		
Joe DiMaggio		
14 Billy Weber	80.00	40.00
sic, Werber		
Harry Kelly		
sic, Kelley		
Wallace Moses		
Bob Johnson		
15 Harland Clift	80.00	40.00
Sammy West		
Beau Bell		
Bobo Newsom		
16 Buddy Meyer (Myer)	80.00	40.00
Jonathan Stone		
Wes Ferrell		
Rick Ferrell		

1939-46 Exhibits Salutation

This collection of exhibit cards shares a common style: the "Personal Greeting" or "Salutation". The specific greeting varies from card to card -- "Yours truly, Best wishes, etc." -- as does the location of the exhibit identification (lower left, LL, or lower right, LR). Some players appear with different teams and there are occasional misspellings. Each card measures 3 3/8" by 5 3/8". The Bob Feller (Yours Truly), Andy Pafko (Yours Truly) and Ted Williams (Sincerely Yours) cards are relatively quite common as they were still being printed into the middle to late 1950s, i.e., basically until the end of their respective careers. The Jeff Heath small picture variation (26B) is differentiated by measuring the distance between the top of his cap and the top edge of the card; for the small picture variation that distance is approximately 5/8" whereas it is only 3/8" for 26A. There is some doubt about whether Camilli #6B exists. An Andy Pafko sincerely yours card is rumored to exist but has never been verified, while the 50B Pafko is a very tough card since it was printed only in 1960.

	Ex-Mt	VG
COMPLETE SET (84)	6000.00	3000.00
1A Luke Appling LL	25.00	12.50
Sincerely Yours		
1B Luke Appling LR	15.00	7.50
Sincerely Yours		
2 Earl Averill	800.00	400.00
Very Best Wishes		
3 Charles "Red" Barrett	5.00	2.50
Yours Truly		
4 Henry "Hank" Borowy	5.00	2.50
Sincerely Yours		
5 Lou Boudreau	8.00	4.00
Sincerely		
6A Adolf Camilli LL	25.00	12.50
Very Truly Yours		
6B Adolf Camilli LR	200.00	100.00
Very Truly Yours		
7 Phil Cavarretta	5.00	2.50
Cordially Yours		
8 Harland Clift	20.00	10.00
Very Truly Yours		
9 Tony Cuccinello	40.00	20.00
Very Best Wishes		
10 Dizzy Dean	100.00	50.00
Sincerely		
11 Paul Derringer	5.00	2.50
Yours Truly		
12A Bill Dickey LL	50.00	25.00
Cordially Yours		
12B Bill Dickey LR	50.00	25.00
Cordially Yours		
13 Joe DiMaggio	120.00	60.00
Cordially		
14 Bob Elliott	5.00	2.50
Truly Yours		
15A Bob Feller	120.00	60.00
Best Wishes		
(portrait)		
15B Bob Feller	15.00	7.50
Yours Truly		
(pitching pose)		
16 Dave Ferriss	5.00	2.50
Best of Luck		
17 Jimmy Foxx	200.00	100.00
Sincerely		
18 Lou Gehrig	2000.00	1000.00
Sincerely		
19 Charlie Gehringer	125.00	60.00
Yours Truly		
20 Lefty Gomez	200.00	100.00
Sincerely Yours		
21A Joe Gordon	25.00	12.50
(Cleveland)		
Sincerely		
21B Joe Gordon	5.00	2.50
(New York)		
Sincerely		
22A Hank Greenberg	35.00	17.50
Truly Yours		
22B Henry Greenberg	150.00	75.00
Very Truly Yours		
23 Robert Grove	125.00	60.00
Cordially Yours		
24 Gabby Hartnett	350.00	180.00
Cordially		
25 Buddy Hassett	25.00	12.50
Yours Truly		
26A Jeff Heath	25.00	12.50
Best Wishes		
26B Jeff Heath	5.00	2.50
(Small Picture)		
Best Wishes		
27 Kirby Higbe	25.00	12.50
Sincerely		
28A Tommy Holmes	200.00	100.00
Sincerely Yours		
28B Tommy Holmes	5.00	2.50
Yours Truly		
29 Carl Hubbell	100.00	50.00
Best Wishes		
30 Bob Johnson	25.00	12.50
Yours Truly		
31A Charles Keller LL	25.00	12.50
Best Wishes		
31B Charles Keller LR	10.00	5.00
Best Wishes		
32 Ken Keltner	50.00	25.00
Sincerly (sic)		
33 Chuck Klein	300.00	150.00
Yours Truly		
34 Mike Kreevich	250.00	125.00
Sincerely		
35 Joe Kuhel	5.00	2.50
Truly Yours		
36 Bill Lee	20.00	10.00
Cordially Yours		
37A Ernie Lombardi	400.00	200.00
(1/2 B) Cordially		
38B Ernie Lombardi	10.00	5.00
Cordially Yours		
39 Marty Marion	10.00	5.00
Best Wishes		
40 Merrill May	25.00	12.50
Best Wishes		
41A Frank McCormick LL	25.00	12.50
Sincerely		
41B Frank McCormick LR	5.00	2.50
Sincerely		
42A George McQuinn LL	25.00	12.50
Yours Truly		
42B George McQuinn LR	5.00	2.50
Yours Truly		
43 Joe Medwick	35.00	17.50
Very Best Wishes		
44A Johnny Mize LL	40.00	20.00
Yours Truly		
44B Johnny Mize LR	15.00	7.50
Yours Truly		
45 Hugh Mulcahy	25.00	12.50
Cordially		
46 Hal Newhouser	15.00	7.50
Best Wishes		
47 Louis (Buck) Newsom	25.00	12.50
Sincerely		
48 Buck Newson (sic)	300.00	150.00
Very Best Wishes		
49A Mel Ott LL	50.00	25.00
Sincerely Yours		
49B Mel Ott LR	40.00	20.00
Sincerely Yours		
50A Andy Pafko	5.00	2.50
Yours Truly		
50B Andy Pafko	35.00	17.50
Yours Truly		
(plain cap)		
51 Claude Passeau	5.00	2.50
Sincerely		
52A Howard Pollet LL	25.00	12.50
Best Wishes		
52B Howard Pollet LR	5.00	2.50
Best Wishes		
53A Pete Reiser LL	100.00	50.00
Truly Yours		
53B Pete Reiser LR	8.00	4.00
Truly Yours		
54 Johnny Rizzo	500.00	250.00
Sincerely Yours		
55 Glenn Russell	300.00	150.00
Sincerely		
56 George Stirnweiss	5.00	2.50
Yours Truly		
57 Cecil Travis	15.00	7.50
Best Wishes		
58 Paul Trout	5.00	2.50
Truly Yours		
59 Johnny Vander Meer	50.00	25.00
Cordially Yours		
60 Arky Vaughan	25.00	12.50
Best Wishes		
61A Fred "Dixie" Walker	5.00	2.50
(D on Hat)		
Yours Truly		
61B Fred "Dixie" Walker	65.00	32.00
Cap blanked out		
Yours Truly		
62 Bucky Walters	5.00	2.50
Sincerely Yours		
63 Lon Warneke	20.00	10.00
Very Truly Yours		
64A Ted Williams (9)	350.00	180.00
Sincerely		
64B Ted Williams	75.00	38.00
Sincerely Yours		
watch out for the illegal reprint; see set caption below		
65 Rudy York	5.00	2.50
Cordially		

1947-66 Exhibits

This grouping encompasses a wide time span but displays a common design. The following players have been illegally reprinted in mass quantities on a thinner-than-original cardboard which is also characterized by a dark gray back: Aaron, Ford, Fox, Hodges, Elston Howard, Mantle, Mays, Musial, Newcombe, Reese, Spahn, and Ted Williams. Each card measures 3 3/8" by 5 3/8". In the checklist below SIG refers to signature and SCR refers to script name on card. The abbreviations POR (portrait), BAT (batting), and FIE (fielding) are also used below. There are many levels of scarcity within this "set," essentially based on which year(s) the player's card was printed. The Mickey Mantle portrait card, for example, was only printed in 1966, the last year of production. Those scarce cards which were only produced one or two years are noted parenthetically below by the last two digits of the year(s) of issue. Cards which seem to be especially difficult to obtain are the ones produced only in 1966 which are the aforementioned Mantle Portrait, Ford, Kranepool, Richardson, Skowron (White Sox), Ward and Yastrzemski. Some leading exhibit experts believe that the salutation and these cards should be checklisted together because of the long printing history of some of the salutations.

EX-MT VG-E
COMPLETE SET (321) 6500.00 2900.00
1 Hank Aaron 40.00 18.00
(has been reprinted)
2A Joe Adcock SCR 5.00 2.20
2B Joe Adcock SIG 5.00 2.20
3 Max Alvis 66 .... 40.00 18.00
4A Johnny Antonelli 3.00 1.35
(Braves)
4B Johnny Antonelli 3.00 1.35
(Giants)
5A Luis Aparicio POR 6.00 2.70
5B Luis Aparicio BAT 64 .... 60.00 27.00
6 Luke Appling 6.00 2.70
7A Richie Ashburn 40.00 18.00
(Phillies)
7B Ritchie Ashburn 10.00 4.50
(sic, Richie)
7C Richie Ashburn 50.00 22.00
(Cubs) 61
8 Bob Aspromonte 64/66 .... 5.00 2.20
9 Toby Atwell 5.00 2.20
10A Ed Bailey 61 .... 10.00 4.50
(Cincinnati cap)
10B Ed Bailey (no cap) 3.00 1.35
11 Gene Baker 3.00 1.35
12A Ernie Banks SCR 30.00 13.50
12B Ernie Banks SIG 15.00 6.75
12C Ernie Banks POR 30.00 13.50
64/66
13 Steve Barber 64/66 .... 5.00 2.20
14 Earl Battey 64/66 .... 5.00 2.20
15 Matt Batts 6.00 2.70
16A Hank Bauer 5.00 2.20
(New York cap)
16B Hank Bauer 61 .... 30.00 13.50
(plain cap)
17 Frank Baumholtz 5.00 2.20
18 Gene Bearden 3.00 1.35
19 Joe Beggs 47 .... 20.00 9.00
20A Yogi Berra 10.00 4.50
20B Larry "Yogi" Berra 40.00 18.00
64/66
21 Steve Bilko 3.00 1.35
22A Ewell Blackwell 6.00 2.70
(foot up)
22B Ewell Blackwell POR 4.00 1.80
23A Don Blasingame 3.00 1.35
(St. Louis cap)
23B Don Blasingame 6.00 2.70
(plain cap)
24 Ken Boyer 64/66 .... 20.00 9.00
25 Ralph Branca 3.00 1.35
26 Jackie Brandt 61 .... 60.00 27.00
27 Harry Brecheen 3.00 1.35
28 Tom Brewer 61 .... 40.00 18.00
29 Lou Brissie 3.00 1.35
30 Bill Bruton 3.00 1.35
31A Lew Burdette 3.00 1.35
(side view)
31B Lew Burdette 25.00 11.00
(facing) 64
32 Johnny Callison 64/66 .... 6.00 2.70
33 Roy Campanella 40.00 18.00
34A Chico Carrasquel 5.00 2.20
(White Sox)
34B Chico Carrasquel 15.00 6.75
(plain cap)
35 George Case 47 .... 20.00 9.00
36 Hugh Casey 10.00 4.50
37 Norm Cash 64/66 .... 15.00 6.75
38A Orlando Cepeda POR 15.00 6.75
60/61
38B Orlando Cepeda BAT 15.00 6.75
64/66
39A Bob Cerv 60 .... 5.00 2.20
(A's uniform)
39B Bob Cerv 61 .... 40.00 18.00
(plain uniform)
40 Dean Chance 64/66 .... 5.00 2.20
41 Spud Chandler 47 .... 20.00 9.00
42 Tom Cheney 64/66 .... 5.00 2.20
43 Bubba Church 4.00 1.80
44 Roberto Clemente 100.00 45.00
45A Rocky Colavito POR 100.00 45.00
61
45B Rocky Colavito BAT 25.00 11.00
64/66
46 Choo Choo Coleman 64 .... 25.00 11.00
47 Gordy Coleman 66 .... 40.00 18.00
48 Jerry Coleman 3.00 1.35
49 Mort Cooper 47 .... 25.00 11.00
50 Walker Cooper 3.00 1.35
51 Roger Craig 64/66 .... 10.00 4.50
52 Delmar Crandall 3.00 1.35
53A Joe Cunningham POR 6.00 2.70
64/66
53B Joe Cunningham BAT 50.00 22.00
61
54 Guy Curtwright 47 .... 20.00 9.00
(sic, Curtright)
55 Bud Daley 61 .... 40.00 18.00
56A Alvin Dark 10.00 4.50
(Boston cap)
56B Alvin Dark 5.00 2.20
(New York cap)
56C Alvin Dark (Cubs) 60 .... 30.00 13.50
57 Murray Dickson 3.00 1.35
58 Bob Dillinger 10.00 4.50
59 Dom DiMaggio 10.00 4.50
60 Joe Dobson 3.00 1.35
61 Larry Doby 5.00 2.20
62 Bobby Doerr 10.00 4.50
63A Dick Donovan 5.00 2.20
(Braves, plain cap)
63B Dick Donovan 3.00 1.35
(White Sox)
64 Walter Dropo 3.00 1.35
65A Don Drysdale POR 40.00 18.00
60/61
65B Don Drysdale 64/66 .... 40.00 18.00
POR 1/2
66 Luke Easter 5.00 2.20
67 Bruce Edwards 10.00 4.50
68 Del Ennis 3.00 1.35
69 Al Evans 3.00 1.35
70 Walter Evers 3.00 1.35
71A Ferris Fain FIE 10.00 4.50
71B Ferris Fain POR 5.00 2.20
72 Dick Farrell 64/66 .... 5.00 2.20
73A Whitey Ford 10.00 4.50
(has been reprinted)
(no glove, throwing)
73B Whitey Ford POR 66 .... 300.00 135.00
73C Ed "Whitey" Ford 40.00 18.00
(glove on shoulder)
64/66
74 Dick Fowler 5.00 2.20
75 Nelson Fox 15.00 6.75
(has been reprinted)
76 Tito Francona 64/66 .... 5.00 2.20
77 Bob Friend 5.00 2.20
78 Carl Furillo 20.00 9.00
79 Augie Galan 20.00 9.00
80 Jim Gentile 64/66 .... 5.00 2.20
81 Tony Gonzalez 64/66 .... 5.00 2.20
82A Billy Goodman FIE 5.00 2.20
(fielding)
82B Billy Goodman BAT 20.00 9.00
60/61
83 Ted Greengrass 10.00 4.50
(sic, Jim)
84 Dick Groat 5.00 2.20
85 Steve Gromek 10.00 4.50
86 Johnny Groth 3.00 1.35
87 Orval Grove 47 .... 20.00 9.00
88A Frank Gustine 5.00 2.20
(Pirates)
88B Frank Gustine(Cubs) 5.00 2.20
89 Berthold Haas 20.00 9.00
90 Grady Hatton 5.00 2.20
91 Jim Hegan 3.00 1.35
92 Tommy Henrich 5.00 2.20
93 Ray Herbert 66 .... 40.00 18.00
94 Gene Hermanski 10.00 4.50
95 Whitey Herzog 60/61 .... 10.00 4.50
96 Kirby Higbe 47 .... 20.00 9.00
97 Chuck Hinton 64/66 .... 5.00 2.20
98 Don Hoak 64 .... 25.00 11.00
99A Gil Hodges 10.00 4.50
(Brooklyn cap)
(has been reprinted)
99B Gil Hodges 20.00 9.00
(Los Angeles cap)
100 Johnny Hopp 47 .... 20.00 9.00
101 Elston Howard 5.00 2.20
(has been reprinted)
102 Frank Howard 64/66 .... 15.00 6.75
103 Ken Hubbs 64 .... 100.00 45.00
104 Tex Hughson 47 .... 20.00 9.00
105 Fred Hutchinson 50 .... 10.00 4.50
106 Monte Irvin 10.00 4.50
107 Joey Jay 64/66 .... 5.00 2.20
108 Jackie Jensen 60 .... 50.00 22.00
109 Sam Jethroe 6.00 2.70
110 Bill Johnson 50 .... 6.00 2.70
111 Walter Judnich 47 .... 20.00 9.00
112A Al Kaline SCR 20.00 9.00
(kneeling)
112B Al Kaline SIG POR 15.00 6.75
113 George Kell 10.00 4.50
114 Charley Keller 10.00 4.50
115 Alex Kellner 3.00 1.35
116 Kenn Keltner 20.00 9.00
(sic, Ken)
117A Harmon Killebrew 40.00 18.00
pinstripes, batting)
60/61
117B Harmon Killibrew 50.00 22.00
(sic, Killebrew)
POR 66
117C Harmon Killebrew 25.00 11.00
(throwing) 64/66
118 Ellis Kinder 5.00 2.20
119 Ralph Kiner 10.00 4.50
120 Billy Klaus 60 .... 40.00 18.00
121A Ted Kluszewski(Reds) 20.00 9.00
121B Ted Kluszewski 20.00 9.00
(Pirates)
121C Ted Kluszewski 50.00 22.00
(plain uniform) 60/61
122 Don Kolloway 50 .... 10.00 4.50
123 Jim Konstanty 6.00 2.70
124 Sandy Koufax 64/66 .... 100.00 45.00
125 Ed Kranepool 66 .... 250.00 110.00
126A Tony Kubek 5.00 2.20
(dark background)
126B Tony Kubek 5.00 2.20
(light background)
127A Harvey Kuenn 60 .... 10.00 4.50
(Detroit)
127B Harvey Kuenn 61 .... 40.00 18.00
(plain uniform)
127C Harvey Kuenn 10.00 4.50
(San Francisco) 64/66
128 Whitey Kurowski 50 .... 20.00 9.00
129 Eddie Lake 47 .... 20.00 9.00
130 Jim Landis 64/66 .... 5.00 2.20
131 Don Larsen 5.00 2.20
132A Bob Lemon 6.00 2.70
(left arm not shown)
132B Bob Lemon 60.00 27.00
(left arm extended)
133 Buddy Lewis 47 .... 20.00 9.00
134 Johnny Lindell 50 .... 20.00 9.00
135 Phil Linz 66 .... 40.00 18.00
136 Don Lock 66 .... 40.00 18.00
137 Whitey Lockman 5.00 2.20
138 Johnny Logan 3.00 1.35
139A Dale Long (Pirates) 3.00 1.35
139B Dale Long (Cubs) 61 .... 40.00 18.00
140 Ed Lopat 5.00 2.20
141A Harry Lowery 10.00 4.50
(sic, Lowrey)
141B Harry Lowrey 5.00 2.20
142 Sal Maglie 5.00 2.20
143 Art Mahaffey 64/66 .... 5.00 2.20
144 Hank Majeski 3.00 1.35
145 Frank Malzone 4.00 1.80
146A Mickey Mantle 150.00 70.00
(batting to waist)
(white outline around
first letters in Mickey)
146B Mickey Mantle 250.00 110.00
(batting to waist)
(no white outline)
(has been reprinted)
146C Mickey Mantle 150.00 70.00
(batting full) 64/66
146D Mickey Mantle POR 600.00 275.00
66
147 Marty Marion 5.00 2.20
148 Roger Maris 64/66 .... 50.00 22.00
149 Willard Marshall 3.00 1.35
150A Ed Matthews SCR 15.00 6.75
(sic, Mathews)
150B Eddie Mathews SIG 25.00 11.00
151 Ed Mayo 5.00 2.20
152A Willie Mays 40.00 18.00
(New York)
(has been reprinted)
152B Willie Mays 40.00 18.00
(San Francisco)
153A Bill Mazeroski POR 12.00 5.50
60/61
153B Bill Mazeroski BAT 12.00 5.50
64/66
154 Ken McBride 64/66 .... 5.00 2.20
155A Barney McCaskey 25.00 11.00
(sic, McCosky)
155B Barney McCoskey 80.00 36.00
(sic, McCosky)
156 Lindy McDaniel 60/61 .... 5.00 2.20
157 Gil McDougald 5.00 2.20
158 Albert Mele 40.00 18.00
159 Sam Mele 10.00 4.50
160A Minnie Minoso 5.00 2.20
(White Sox)
160B Minnie Minoso 10.00 4.50
(Cleveland)
161 Dale Mitchell 3.00 1.35
162 Wally Moon 5.00 2.20
163 Don Mueller 25.00 11.00
164A Stan Musial 40.00 18.00
(three bats, kneeling)
(has been reprinted)
164B Stan Musial BAT 64 .... 150.00 70.00
165 Charles Neal 64 .... 25.00 11.00
166A Don Newcombe 10.00 4.50
(shaking hands)
166B Don Newcombe 5.00 2.20
(Brooklyn cap)
(has been reprinted)
166C Don Newcombe 15.00 6.75
(plain cap)
167 Hal Newhouser 10.00 4.50
168 Ron Northey 47 .... 25.00 11.00
169 Bill O'Dell 64/66 .... 5.00 2.20
170 Joe Page 50 .... 20.00 9.00
171 Satchel Paige 100.00 45.00
172 Milt Pappas 64/66 .... 5.00 2.20
173 Camilo Pascual 64/66 .... 5.00 2.20
174 Albie Pearson 66 .... 35.00 16.00
175 Johnny Pesky 3.00 1.35
176 Gary Peters 66 .... 35.00 16.00
177 Dave Philley 5.00 2.20
178 Billy Pierce 60/61 .... 5.00 2.20
179 Jimmy Piersall 66 .... 75.00 34.00
180 Vada Pinson 64/66 .... 15.00 6.75
181 Bob Porterfield 5.00 2.20
182 Boog Powell 66 .... 100.00 45.00
183 Vic Raschi 5.00 2.20
184A Harold "Peewee" Reese 15.00 6.75
(ball visible along
bottom border)
184B Harold "Peewee" Reese 15.00 6.75
(ball not visible)
(has been reprinted)
185 Del Rice 3.00 1.35
186 Bobby Richardson 66 .... 300.00 135.00
187A Phil Rizzuto 15.00 6.75
(small photo)
187B Phil Rizzuto 10.00 4.50
(larger photo)
188A Robin Roberts SIG 10.00 4.50
188B Robin Roberts SCR 12.00 5.50
189 Brooks Robinson 40.00 18.00
190 Eddie Robinson POR 5.00 2.20
191 Floyd Robinson 66 .... 40.00 18.00
192 Frankie Robinson 40.00 18.00
64/66
193 Jackie Robinson 60.00 27.00
194 Preacher Roe 5.00 2.20
195 Bob Rogers 66 .... 40.00 18.00
(sic, Rodgers)
196 Richard Rollins 66 .... 40.00 18.00
197 Pete Runnels 64 .... 25.00 11.00
198 John Sain 5.00 2.20
199 Ron Santo 64/66 .... 20.00 9.00
200 Henry Sauer 5.00 2.20
201A Carl Sawatski 3.00 1.35
(Milwaukee cap)
201B Carl Sawatski 3.00 1.35
(Philadelphia cap)
201C Carl Sawatski 61 .... 25.00 11.00
(plain cap)
202 Johnny Schmitz 6.00 2.70
203A Red Schoendeinst 25.00 11.00
(one foot shown
catching)
(sic, Schoendienst)
203B Red Schoendeinst 40.00 18.00
(both feet shown
catching)
(sic, Schoendienst)
203C Red Schoendinst BAT 10.00 4.50
(sic, Schoendienst)
204A Herb Score 10.00 4.50
(Cleveland cap)
204B Herb Score 61 .... 40.00 18.00
(plain cap)
205 Andy Seminick 5.00 2.20
206 Rip Sewell 47 .... 25.00 11.00
207 Norm Siebern 5.00 2.20
208A Roy Sievers 51 .... 50.00 22.00
(Browns)
208B Roy Sievers 5.00 2.20
(Senators)
dark background)
208C Roy Sievers 5.00 2.20
(Senators)
light background)
208D Roy Sievers 61 .... 35.00 16.00
(plain uniform)
209 Curt Simmons 5.00 2.20
210 Dick Sisler 5.00 2.20
211A Bill Skowron 5.00 2.20
(New York)
211B Bill "Moose" Skowron 250.00 110.00
(White Sox) 66
212 Enos Slaughter 10.00 4.50
213A Duke Snider 15.00 6.75
(Brooklyn)
213B Duke Snider 25.00 11.00
(Los Angeles)
214A Warren Spahn 10.00 4.50
(Boston)
(has been reprinted)
214B Warren Spahn 20.00 9.00
(Milwaukee)
215 Stanley Spence 20.00 9.00
216A Ed Stanky 5.00 2.20
(plain uniform)
216B Ed Stanky (Giants) 5.00 2.20
217A Vern Stephens 5.00 2.20
(Browns)
217B Vern Stephens 6.00 2.70
(Red Sox)
218 Ed Stewart 3.00 1.35
219 Snuffy Stirnweiss 25.00 11.00
220 George "Birdie" Tebbets 15.00 6.75
221A Frankie Thomas BAT 35.00 16.00
(Bob Skinner picture)
59
221B Frank Thomas (Cubs) 35.00 16.00
60/61
222 Lee Thomas 64/66 .... 5.00 2.20
223 Bobby Thomson 10.00 4.50
224A Earl Torgeson 3.00 1.35
(Braves)
224B Earl Torgeson 60/61 .... 5.00 2.20
(plain uniform)
225 Gus Triandos 60/61 .... 10.00 4.50
226 Virgil Trucks 5.00 2.20
227 Johnny Vandermeer 47 .... 50.00 22.00
228 Emil Verban 25.00 11.00
229A Mickey Vernon 3.00 1.35
(throwing)
229B Mickey Vernon BAT 3.00 1.35
230 Bill Voiselle 47 .... 25.00 11.00
231 Leon Wagner 64/66 .... 5.00 2.20
232A Eddie Waitkus BAT 5.00 2.20
(Cub uniform)
232B Eddie Waitkus BAT 5.00 2.20
(plain uniform)
232C Eddie Waitkus POR 40.00 18.00
(Phillies uniform)
233 Dick Wakefield 5.00 2.20
234 Harry Walker 50.00 22.00
235 Bucky Walters 10.00 4.50
236 Pete Ward 66 .... 200.00 90.00
237 Herman Wehmeier 3.00 1.35
238A Vic Wertz (Tigers) 3.00 1.35
238B Vic Wertz(Red Sox) 5.00 2.20
239 Wally Westlake 3.00 1.35
240 Wes Westrum 40.00 18.00
241 Billy Williams 64/66 .... 40.00 18.00
242 Maurice Wills 64/66 .... 20.00 9.00
243A Gene Woodling SCR 3.00 1.35
243B Gene Woodling SIG 5.00 2.20
244 Taffy Wright 47 .... 20.00 9.00
245 Carl Yastrzemski 66 .... 300.00 135.00
246 Al Zarilla 51 .... 10.00 4.50
247A Gus Zernial SCR 3.00 1.35
247B Gus Zernial SIG 5.00 2.20

1948 Exhibit Hall of Fame

This exhibit set, entitled "Baseball's Great Hall of Fame," consists of black and white photos on gray background. The pictures are framed on the sides by Greek columns and a short biography is printed at the bottom. The cards are blank backed. Twenty four of the cards were reissued in 1974 on extremely white stock. Each card measures 3 3/8" by 5 3/8".

NM Ex
COMPLETE SET (33) 600.00 300.00
1 G.C. Alexander 8.00 4.00
2 Roger Bresnahan 5.00 2.50
3 Frank Chance 6.00 3.00
4 Jack Chesbro 5.00 2.50
5 Fred Clarke 5.00 2.50
6 Ty Cobb 80.00 40.00
7 Mickey Cochrane 8.00 4.00
8 Eddie Collins 5.00 2.50
9 Hugh Duffy 5.00 2.50
10 Johnny Evers 6.00 3.00
11 Frankie Frisch 6.00 3.00
12 Lou Gehrig 80.00 40.00
13 Clark Griffith 5.00 2.50
14 Robert "Lefty" Grove 8.00 4.00
15 Rogers Hornsby 10.00 5.00
16 Carl Hubbell 6.00 3.00
17 Hughie Jennings 5.00 2.50
18 Walter Johnson 15.00 7.50
19 Willie Keeler 5.00 2.50
20 Nap Lajoie 10.00 5.00
21 Connie Mack 8.00 4.00
22 Christy Mathewson 15.00 7.50
23 John McGraw 10.00 5.00
24 Eddie Plank 6.00 3.00
25A Babe Ruth 50.00 25.00
(swinging)
25B Babe Ruth 300.00 150.00
(bats in front)
ten bats pose
26 George Sisler 6.00 3.00
27 Tris Speaker 10.00 5.00
28 Joe Tinker 6.00 3.00
29 Rube Waddell 5.00 2.50
30 Honus Wagner 15.00 7.50
31 Ed Walsh 5.00 2.50
32 Cy Young 10.00 5.00

1948-56 Exhibits Team

The cards found listed in this classification were not a separate issue from the individual player cards of the same period but have been assembled together in the Price Guide for emphasis. Each of these 1948-1956 Exhibit team cards was issued to honor the champions of the National and American Leagues, except for 1953, when none were printed. Reprints of these popular cards are known to exist. Each card measures 3 3/8" by 5 3/8".

NM Ex
COMPLETE SET (16) 800.00 400.00
1 1948 Boston Braves 25.00 12.50
2 1948 Cleveland Indians 30.00 15.00
3 1949 Brooklyn Dodgers 50.00 25.00
4 1949 New York Yankees 50.00 25.00
5 1950 Philadelphia 40.00 20.00
Phillies
6 1950 New York Yankees 50.00 25.00
7 1951 New York Giants 40.00 20.00
8 1951 New York Yankees 25.00 12.50
9 1952 Brooklyn Dodgers 50.00 25.00
10 1952 New York Yankees 50.00 25.00
11 1954 New York Giants 50.00 25.00
12 1954 Cleveland Indians 50.00 25.00
13 1955 Brooklyn Dodgers 200.00 100.00
14 1955 New York Yankees 100.00 50.00
15 1956 Brooklyn Dodgers 300.00 150.00
16 1956 New York Yankees 100.00 50.00

1953 Exhibits Canadian

This numbered, blank-backed set depicts both major league players (reprinted from American Exhibit sets) and International League Montreal Royals. The cards (3 1/4" by 5 1/4") are slightly smaller than regular Exhibit issues and are printed on gray stock. Numbers 1-32 are printed in green or wine-red color, while 33-64 are blue or reddish-brown. Cards 1-32 are numbered in a small& diamond-shaped white box at lower right; cards 33-64 have a large, hand-lettered number at upper right.

NM Ex
COMPLETE SET (64) 900.00 450.00
COMMON CARD (1-32) 6.00 3.00
COMMON CARD (33-64) 4.00 2.00
1 Preacher Roe 8.00 4.00
2 Luke Easter 6.00 3.00
3 Gene Bearden 6.00 3.00
4 Chico Carrasquel 6.00 3.00
5 Vic Raschi 8.00 4.00
6 Monte Irvin 12.00 6.00
7 Hank Sauer 6.00 3.00
8 Ralph Branca 8.00 4.00
9 Eddie Stanky 6.00 3.00
10 Sam Jethroe 6.00 3.00
11 Larry Doby 12.00 6.00
12 Hal Newhouser 12.00 6.00
13 Gil Hodges 20.00 10.00
14 Harry Brecheen 6.00 3.00
15 Ed Lopat 10.00 5.00
16 Don Newcombe 10.00 5.00
17 Bob Feller 40.00 20.00
18 Tommy Holmes 6.00 3.00
19 Jackie Robinson 120.00 60.00
20 Roy Campanella 60.00 30.00
21 Pee Wee Reese 30.00 15.00
22 Ralph Kiner 12.00 6.00
23 Dom DiMaggio 10.00 5.00
24 Bobby Doerr 12.00 6.00
25 Phil Rizzuto 25.00 12.50
26 Bob Elliott 6.00 3.00
27 Tom Henrich 8.00 4.00
28 Joe DiMaggio 200.00 100.00
29 Harry Lowery 6.00 3.00
30 Ted Williams 120.00 60.00
31 Bob Lemon 15.00 7.50
32 Warren Spahn 20.00 10.00
33 Don Hoak 6.00 3.00
34 Bob Alexander 4.00 2.00
35 John Simmons 4.00 2.00
36 Steve Lembo 4.00 2.00
37 Norman Larker 8.00 4.00
38 Bob Ludwick 4.00 2.00
39 Walter Moryn 6.00 3.00
40 Charlie Thompson 6.00 3.00
41 Ed Roebuck 6.00 3.00
42 Rose 4.00 2.00
43 Edmundo Amoros 8.00 4.00
44 Bob Milliken 6.00 3.00
45 Art Fabbro 4.00 2.00
46 Forrest Jacobs 6.00 3.00
47 Carmen Mauro 4.00 2.00
48 Walter Fiala 4.00 2.00
49 Rocky Nelson 4.00 2.00
50 Tom Lasorda 50.00 25.00
51 Ronnie Lee 4.00 2.00
52 Hampton Coleman 4.00 2.00
53 Frank Marchio 4.00 2.00
54 William Samson 4.00 2.00
55 Gil Mills 4.00 2.00
56 Al Ronning 4.00 2.00
57 Stan Musial 60.00 30.00
58 Walker Cooper 6.00 3.00
59 Mickey Vernon 8.00 4.00
60 Del Ennis 8.00 4.00

1953 Exhibits Canadian

Card	NM	Ex
61 Walter Alston MG	30.00	15.00
62 Dick Sisler	6.00	3.00
63 Billy Goodman	6.00	3.00
64 Alex Kellner	6.00	3.00

1960-61 Exhibits Wrigley HOF

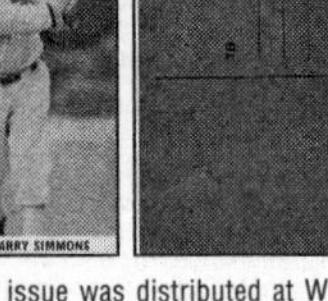

This Exhibit issue was distributed at Wrigley Field in Chicago in the early sixties. The set consists entirely of Hall of Famers, many of whom are depicted in their younger days. The set is complete at 24 cards and is interesting in that the full name of each respective Hall of famer is given on the front of the card. Card backs feature a postcard back on gray card stock. Each card measures 3 3/8" by 5 3/8".

	NM	Ex
COMPLETE SET (24)	300.00	120.00
1 Grover Cleveland Alexander	10.00	4.00
2 Cap Anson	10.00	4.00
3 Frank Baker	6.00	2.40
4 Roger Bresnahan	6.00	2.40
5 Mordecai Brown	6.00	2.40
6 Frank Chance	8.00	3.20
7 Tyrus Cobb	40.00	16.00
8 Eddie Collins	8.00	3.20
9 Jimmy Collins	6.00	2.40
10 Johnnie Evers	6.00	2.40
11 Lou Gehrig	40.00	16.00
12 Clark Griffith	6.00	2.40
13 Walter Johnson	20.00	8.00
14 Tony Lazzeri	6.00	2.40
15 Rabbit Maranville	6.00	2.40
16 Christy Mathewson	20.00	8.00
17 John McGraw	10.00	4.00
18 Melvin Ott	12.00	4.80
19 Herb Pennock	6.00	2.40
20 Babe Ruth	75.00	30.00
21 Al Simmons	6.00	2.40
22 Tris Speaker	12.00	4.80
23 Joe Tinker	6.00	2.40
24 Honus Wagner	20.00	8.00

1962 Exhibit Stat Back

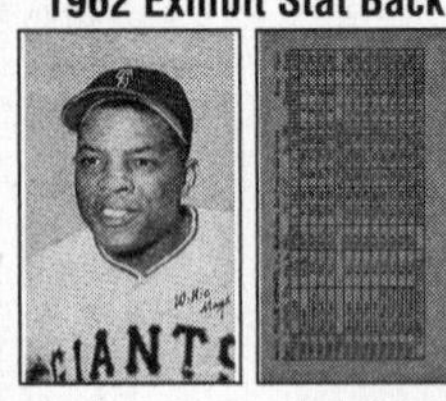

The 32-card sheet was a standard production feature of the Exhibit Supply Company, although, generally more than one sheet comprised a set. The 32-card set issued in 1962 thus amounted to one-half a normal printing, and is differentiated from other concurrent Exhibit issues by the inclusion of records, printed in black or red, on the reverse of each card. Each card measures 3 3/8" by 5 3/8". Backs printed in red ink are slightly more difficult to find but there is no difference in price.

	NM	Ex
COMPLETE SET (32)	500.00	200.00
1 Hank Aaron	40.00	16.00
2 Luis Aparicio	10.00	4.00
3 Ernie Banks	20.00	8.00
4 Yogi Berra	30.00	12.00
5 Ken Boyer	10.00	4.00
6 Lew Burdette	5.00	2.00
7 Norm Cash	10.00	4.00
8 Orlando Cepeda	10.00	4.00
9 Roberto Clemente	60.00	24.00
10 Rocky Colavito	20.00	8.00
11 Whitey Ford	20.00	8.00
12 Nellie Fox	10.00	4.00
13 Tito Francona	3.00	1.20
14 Jim Gentile	3.00	1.20
15 Dick Groat	5.00	2.00
16 Don Hoak	3.00	1.20
17 Al Kaline	20.00	8.00
18 Harmon Killebrew	15.00	6.00
19 Sandy Koufax	50.00	20.00
20 Jim Landis	3.00	1.20
21 Art Mahaffey	3.00	1.20
22 Frank Malzone	3.00	1.20
23 Mickey Mantle	150.00	60.00
24 Roger Maris	30.00	12.00
25 Eddie Mathews	20.00	8.00
26 Willie Mays	40.00	16.00
27 Wally Moon	3.00	1.20
28 Stan Musial	40.00	16.00
29 Milt Pappas	3.00	1.20
30 Vada Pinson	5.00	2.00
31 Norm Siebern	3.00	1.20
32 Warren Spahn	15.00	6.00

1963 Exhibit Stat Back

The 1963 Exhibit issue features 64 thick-stock cards with statistics printed in red on the backs. Each card measures 3 3/8" by 5 3/8". The set is quite similar to the set of the previous year -- but this set can be distinguished by the red print on the backs and the additional year of statistics.

	NM	Ex
COMPLETE SET (64)	600.00	240.00
1 Hank Aaron	40.00	16.00
2 Luis Aparicio	10.00	4.00
3 Bob Aspromonte	3.00	1.20
4 Ernie Banks	20.00	8.00
5 Steve Barber	3.00	1.20
6 Earl Battey	3.00	1.20
7 Yogi Berra	30.00	12.00
8 Ken Boyer	10.00	4.00
9 Lew Burdette	5.00	2.00
10 Johnny Callison	4.00	1.60
11 Norm Cash	10.00	4.00
12 Orlando Cepeda	10.00	4.00
13 Dean Chance	3.00	1.20
14 Tom Cheney	3.00	1.20
15 Roberto Clemente	60.00	24.00
16 Rocky Colavito	10.00	4.00
17 Choo Choo Coleman	5.00	2.00
18 Roger Craig	5.00	2.00
19 Joe Cunningham	5.00	2.00
20 Don Drysdale	15.00	6.00
21 Dick Farrell	3.00	1.20
22 Whitey Ford	20.00	8.00
23 Nellie Fox	10.00	4.00
24 Tito Francona	3.00	1.20
25 Jim Gentile	4.00	1.60
26 Tony Gonzales	3.00	1.20
27 Dick Groat	5.00	2.00
28 Ray Herbert	3.00	1.20
29 Chuck Hinton	3.00	1.20
30 Don Hoak	3.00	1.20
31 Frank Howard	6.00	2.40
32 Ken Hubbs	20.00	8.00
33 Joey Jay	3.00	1.20
34 Al Kaline	20.00	8.00
35 Harmon Killebrew	15.00	6.00
36 Sandy Koufax	50.00	20.00
37 Harvey Kuenn	5.00	2.00
38 Jim Landis	3.00	1.20
39 Art Mahaffey	3.00	1.20
40 Frank Malzone	4.00	1.60
41 Mickey Mantle	150.00	60.00
42 Roger Maris	40.00	16.00
43 Eddie Mathews	15.00	6.00
44 Willie Mays	40.00	16.00
45 Bill Mazeroski	10.00	4.00
46 Ken McBride	3.00	1.20
47 Wally Moon	4.00	1.60
48 Stan Musial	40.00	16.00
49 Charlie Neal	5.00	2.00
50 Billy O'Dell	3.00	1.20
51 Milt Pappas	3.00	1.20
52 Camilo Pascual	3.00	1.20
53 Jim Piersall	8.00	3.20
54 Vada Pinson	8.00	3.20
55 Brooks Robinson	25.00	10.00
56 Frank Robinson	20.00	8.00
57 Pete Runnels	3.00	1.20
58 Ron Santo	8.00	3.20
59 Norm Siebern	3.00	1.20
60 Warren Spahn	15.00	6.00
61 Lee Thomas	3.00	1.20
62 Leon Wagner	3.00	1.20
63 Billy Williams	15.00	6.00
64 Maury Wills	10.00	4.00

1969 Expos Fud's Photography

This blank-backed set was apparently issued by Bob Solon in the Chicago area. The black-and-white cards measure approximately 3 1/2" by 3" and feature Montreal Expos players of the 1969 season. The fronts carry action player photos with a white border. The player's name appears in a white bar in the lower right corner of the photo. The words "Compliments of" are printed in the upper border, while the words "Fud's Photography" appear in the lower border. The cards are unnumbered and checklisted below in alphabetical order.

	NM	Ex
COMPLETE SET (14)	20.00	8.00
1 Bob Bailey	1.25	.50
2 John Bateman	1.25	.50
3 Don Bosch	1.00	.40
4 Jim Grant	1.50	.60
5 Mack Jones	1.25	.50
6 Coco Laboy	1.25	.50
7 Dan McGinn	1.00	.40
8 Cal McLish CO	1.00	.40
9 Carl Morton	1.25	.50
10 Manny Mota	2.00	.80
11 Rusty Staub	5.00	2.00
12 Gary Sutherland	1.00	.40
13 Mike Wegener	1.00	.40
14 Floyd Wicker	1.00	.40

1969 Expos Postcards

These postcards were issued during the Expos debut season. More cards should exist so all additions to this list is appreciated. These postcards are sequenced by uniform number.

	NM	Ex
COMPLETE SET	10.00	4.00
18 Steve Renko	1.00	.40
19 Jerry Robertson	1.00	.40
22 Ron Fairly	2.00	.80
23 Jose Herrera	1.00	.40
25 Adolfo Phillips	1.00	.40
27 Gene Mauch MG	1.50	.60
28 Peanuts Lowrey CO	1.00	.40
30 Bob Oldis CO	1.00	.40
31 Jerry Zimmerman CO	1.00	.40

1970 Expos Postcards

These 16 Montreal Expos postcards measure approximately 3 1/2" by 5 1/2" and feature borderless posed color player photos on their fronts. The player's facsimile autograph appears near the bottom. The backs carry the player's name and bilingual position in black ink at the upper left. The cards are numbered on the back.

	NM	Ex
COMPLETE SET (16)	20.00	8.00
1 Roy Face	2.00	.80
2 Don Shaw	1.00	.40
3 Dan McGinn	1.00	.40
4 Bill Stoneman	1.50	.60
5 Mike Wegener	1.00	.40
6 Bob Bailey	1.50	.60
7 Gary Sutherland	1.00	.40
8 Coco Laboy	1.25	.50
9 Bobby Wine UER (Misspelled Boby on back)	1.25	.50
10 Mack Jones	1.25	.50
11 Rusty Staub	5.00	2.00
12 Don Bosch	1.00	.40
13 Larry Jaster	1.50	.60
14 John Bateman	1.25	.50
15 John Boccabella	1.25	.50
16 Ron Brand	1.00	.40

1971 Expos La Pizza Royale

Featuring members of the Montreal Expos, this set, like the Fud's set, is thought to have been issued by Bob Solon in the Chicago area. Printed on thick cardboard paper, the cards measure approximately 2 1/2" by 5". The fronts typically feature blue-tinted player photos on a dark blue background; however the set was also issued in at least three other colors: green, gold, and red. The words "La Pizza Royale" are printed in white letters above the photo, while the player's name and position in French appear under the photo. The backs are blank. The cards are unnumbered and checklisted below in alphabetical order.

	NM	Ex
COMPLETE SET (14)	25.00	10.00
1 Bob Bailey	3.00	1.20
2 John Boccabella	2.50	1.00
3 Ron Fairly	3.00	1.20
4 Jim Gosger	2.00	.80
5 Coco Laboy	2.50	1.00
6 Gene Mauch MG	3.00	1.20
7 Rich Nye	2.00	.80
8 John O'Donoghue	2.00	.80
9 Adolfo Phillips	2.00	.80
10 Howie Reed	2.00	.80
11 Marv Staehle	2.00	.80
12 Rusty Staub	8.00	3.20
13 Gary Sutherland	2.00	.80
14 Bobby Wine	2.50	1.00

1971 Expos Pro Stars

Printed in Canada by Pro Stars Publications, these 28 blank-backed postcards measure approximately 3 1/2" by 5 1/2" and feature white-bordered color player photos. The player's name appears as a facsimile autograph across the bottom of the photo. The postcards are unnumbered and checklisted below in alphabetical order.

	NM	Ex
COMPLETE SET (28)	60.00	24.00
1 Bob Bailey	3.00	1.20
2 John Bateman	2.50	1.00
3 John Boccabella	2.50	1.00
4 Ron Brand	2.00	.80
5 Boots Day	2.00	.80
6 Jim Fairey	2.00	.80
7 Ron Fairly	3.00	1.20
8 Jim Gosger	2.00	.80
9 Don Hahn	2.00	.80
10 Ron Hunt	3.00	1.20
11 Mack Jones	2.50	1.00
12 Coco Laboy	2.50	1.00
13 Mike Marshall	4.00	1.60
14 Clyde Mashore	2.00	.80
15 Gene Mauch MG	3.00	1.20
16 Dan McGinn	2.00	.80
17 Carl Morton	2.50	1.00
18 John O'Donoghue	2.00	.80
19 Adolfo Phillips	2.00	.80
20 Claude Raymond	2.50	1.00
21 Howie Reed	2.00	.80
22 Steve Renko	2.00	.80
23 Rusty Staub	8.00	3.20
24 Bill Stoneman	3.00	1.20
25 John Strohmayer	2.00	.80
26 Gary Sutherland	2.00	.80
27 Mike Wegener	2.00	.80
28 Bobby Wine	2.50	1.00

1972 Expos Matchbooks

These seven matchbooks, which measure 2 1/8" by 4 3/8" were issued by the Eddy Match Co. The fronts have a player photo while the backs have the home team schedule. Since these are unnumbered, we have sequenced them in alphabetical order.

	NM	Ex
COMPLETE SET	15.00	6.00
1 Boots Day	2.00	.80
2 Ron Fairly	2.50	1.00
3 Ron Hunt	2.00	.80
4 Steve Renko	2.00	.80
5 Rusty Staub	4.00	1.60
6 Bobby Wine	2.00	.80
7 Scoreboard (Honoring Ron Hunt's 50th Hit by Pitcher)	2.00	.80

1973 Expos Matchbooks

These seven matchbooks, which measure 2 1/8" by 4 3/8" were issued by the Eddy Match Co. The fronts have a player photo while the backs have the home team schedule. Since these are unnumbered, we have sequenced them in alphabetical order.

	NM	Ex
COMPLETE SET	12.00	4.80
1 Tim Foli	2.00	.80
2 Ron Hunt	2.00	.80
3 Mike Jorgensen	2.00	.80
4 Gene Mauch MG	2.00	.80
5 Balor Moore	2.00	.80
6 Ken Singleton	2.00	.80
7 Bill Stoneman (No-hitter congratulations)	2.50	1.00

1974 Expos Weston

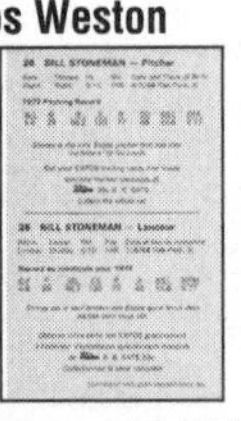

This ten-card set, featuring members of the Montreal Expos, measures approximately 3 1/2" by 5 1/2". The fronts have color player photos inside a thin white border with a facsimile autograph in black ink, and the player's name under the photo. The player's uniforms and caps have been airbrushed to remove the Expos insignia. The backs carry biography and statistics in English and French. The cards are unnumbered and checklisted below in alphabetical order. These cards were originally issued one to a package of Weston 39 cent baseball bats.

	NM	Ex
COMPLETE SET (10)	8.00	3.20
1 Bob Bailey	1.25	.50
2 John Boccabella	1.00	.40
3 Boots Day	.75	.30
4 Tim Foli	1.00	.40
5 Ron Hunt	1.25	.50
6 Mike Jorgensen	1.00	.40
7 Ernie McAnally	.75	.30
8 Steve Renko	.75	.30
9 Ken Singleton	2.00	.80
10 Bill Stoneman	1.50	.60

1975 Expos Postcards

This 39-card set of the Montreal Expos features player photos on postcard-size cards. The cards are unnumbered and checklisted below in alphabetical order.

	NM	Ex
COMPLETE SET (39)	20.00	8.00
1 Bob Bailey	.50	.20
2 Larry Biittner	.50	.20
3 Dennis Blair	.50	.20
4 Hal Breeden	.50	.20
5 Dave Bristol CO	.50	.20
6 Don Carrithers	.50	.20
7 Gary Carter	5.00	2.00
8 Rich Coggins	.50	.20
9 Nate Colbert	.50	.20
10 Don DeMola	.50	.20
11 Jim Dwyer	.50	.20
12 Tim Foli	.50	.20
13 Barry Foote	.50	.20
14 Pepe Frias	.50	.20
15 Woodie Fryman	.50	.20
16 Walt Hriniak	.50	.20
17 Mike Jorgensen	.50	.20
18 Jim Lyttle	.50	.20
19 Pete Mackanin	.50	.20
20 Pepe Mangual	.50	.20
21 Gene Mauch MG	.50	.20
22 Cal McLish CO	.50	.20
23 Dave McNally	.75	.30
24 John Montague	.50	.20
25 Jose Morales	.50	.20
26 Dale Murray	.50	.20
27 Larry Parrish	.50	.20
28 Steve Renko	.50	.20
29 Bombo Rivera	.50	.20
30 Steve Rogers	.50	.20
31 Pat Scanlon	.50	.20
32 Fred Scherman	.50	.20
33 Tony Scott	.50	.20
34 Duke Snider CO	1.50	.60
35 Don Stanhouse	.50	.20
36 Chuck Taylor	.50	.20
37 Dan Warthen	.50	.20
38 Jerry White	.50	.20
39 Jerry Zimmerman CO	.50	.20

1976 Expos Matchbooks

These seven matchbooks, which measure 2 1/8" by 4 3/8" were issued by the Eddy Match Co. The fronts have a player photo while the backs have the home team schedule. Since these are unnumbered, we have sequenced them in alphabetical order.

	NM	Ex
COMPLETE SET	12.00	4.80
1 Barry Foote	2.00	.80
2 Mike Jorgensen	2.00	.80
3 Pete Mackanin	2.00	.80
4 Dale Murray	2.00	.80
5 Larry Parrish	2.50	1.00
6 Steve Rogers	2.00	.80
7 Dan Warthen	2.00	.80

1976 Expos Postcards

This 31-card set of the Montreal Expos features player photos on postcard-size cards. The cards are unnumbered and checklisted below in alphabetical order.

	NM	Ex
COMPLETE SET (31)	15.00	6.00
1 Billy Adair CO	.50	.20
2 Larry Bearnarth CO	.50	.20
3 Don Carrithers	.50	.20
4 Gary Carter	4.00	1.60
5 Nate Colbert	.50	.20
6 Jim Cox	.50	.20
7 Larry Doby CO	1.50	.60
8 Jim Dwyer	.50	.20
9 Tim Foli	.50	.20
10 Barry Foote	.50	.20
11 Pepe Frias	.50	.20
12 Woodie Fryman	.50	.20
13 Wayne Granger	.50	.20
14 Mike Jorgensen	.50	.20
15 Clay Kirby	.50	.20
16 Karl Kuehl MG	.50	.20
17 Chip Lang	.50	.20
18 Jim Lyttle	.50	.20
19 Pepe Manguel	.50	.20
20 Pete MacKanin	.50	.20
21 Jose Morales	.50	.20
22 Dale Murray	.50	.20
23 Larry Parrish	1.50	.60
24 Ron Piche CO	.50	.20
25 Bombo Rivera	.50	.20
26 Steve Rogers	1.00	.40
27 Fred Scherman	.50	.20
28 Don Stanhouse	.50	.20
29 Ozzie Virgil CO	.50	.20
30 Dan Warthen	.50	.20
31 Jerry White	.50	.20

1976 Expos Redpath

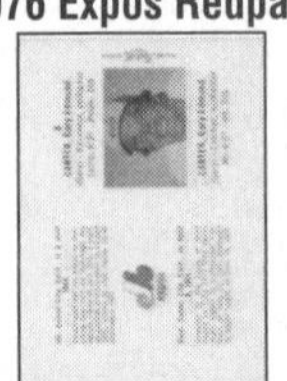

This set of 1976 Montreal Expos was issued by the Redpath Sugar company. The sheets measure approximately 3 1/4" by 10" and each sheet features four team members. The white fronts have a color head shot of the player on the right with the player's name and position printed above the photo in French and below the photo in English. To the left of the photo is brief biography and how they were acquired by Montreal Expos written in both French and English. The players are listed below in alphabetical order.

	NM	Ex
COMMON PLAYER (1-36)	25.00	10.00
1 Bill Adair CO	.75	.30
2 Larry Bearnarth CO	.75	.30
3 Don Carrithers	.75	.30
4 Gary Carter	4.00	1.60
5 Larry Doby CO	2.00	.80
6 Steve Dunning	.75	.30
7 Jim Dwyer	.75	.30
8 Tim Foli	.75	.30
9 Barry Foote	.75	.30
10 Pepe Frias	.75	.30
11 Woodie Fryman	.75	.30
12 Wayne Garrett	.75	.30
13 Wayne Granger	.75	.30
14 Mike Jorgensen	.75	.30
15 Joe Kerrigan	.75	.30
16 Clay Kirby	.75	.30
17 Karl Kuehl MG	.75	.30
18 Chip Lang	.75	.30
19 Jim Lyttle	.75	.30
20 Pete MacKanin	.75	.30
21 Jose Mangual	.75	.30
22 Jose Morales	.75	.30
23 Dale Murray	.75	.30
24 Larry Parrish	.75	.30
25 Ron Piche CO	.75	.30
26 Bombo Rivera	.75	.30
27 Steve Rogers	1.50	.60
28 Fred Scherman	.75	.30
29 Don Stanhouse	.75	.30
30 Chuck Taylor	.75	.30
31 Andre Thornton	1.00	.40
32 Del Unser	.75	.30
33 Ellis Valentine	1.00	.40
34 Ossie Virgil CO	1.50	.60

35 Dan Warthen	.75	.30
36 Jerry White	.75	.30

1977 Expos Postcards

These 39 postcards feature all sorts of people in the Expos orginization. This was not just issued as one set, but these postcards were continually printed during the season to account for new additions.

	NM	Ex
COMPLETE SET	25.00	10.00
1 Santo Alcala	.75	.30
2 Bill Atkinson	.75	.30
3 Bill Atkinson	.75	.30
(Tree in background)		
4 Stan Bahnsen	.75	.30
5 Tim Blackwell	.75	.30
6 Jim Brewer CO	.75	.30
7 Jackie Brown CO	.75	.30
8 Gary Carter	4.00	1.60
9 Dave Cash	.75	.30
10 Warren Cromartie	1.50	.60
11 Andre Dawson	5.00	2.00
12 Andre Dawson	5.00	2.00
(Wearing batting helmet)		
13 Barry Foote	.75	.30
14 Pepe Frias	.75	.30
15 Bill Gardner CO	.75	.30
16 Wayne Garrett	.75	.30
17 Gerald Hannahs	.75	.30
18 Mike Jorgensen	.75	.30
19 Joe Kerrigan	.75	.30
20 Pete Mackanin	.75	.30
21 Will McEnaney	.75	.30
22 Sam Mejias	.75	.30
23 Jose Morales	.75	.30
24 Larry Parrish	1.00	.40
25 Tony Perez	2.00	.80
26 Steve Rogers	1.00	.40
27 Dan Schatzeder	.75	.30
28 Chris Speier	.75	.30
29 Don Stanhouse	.75	.30
30 Jeff Terpko	.75	.30
31 Wayne Twitchell	.75	.30
32 Del Unser	.75	.30
33 Ellis Valentine	.75	.30
34 Mickey Vernon CO	1.00	.40
35 Ozzie Virgil CO	.75	.30
36 Tom Walker	.75	.30
37 Dan Warthen	.75	.30
38 Jerry White	.75	.30
39 Dick Williams MG	1.00	.40

1978 Expos Postcards

This 15-card set features a borerless front with the player's name and team in a box near the bottom. The player's position is also printed on the front in both French and English. Backs are blank. cards are aphabetically checklisted below.

	NM	Ex
COMPLETE SET (15)	15.00	6.00
1 Stan Bahnsen	.75	.30
2 Gary Carter	4.00	1.60
3 Andre Dawson	3.00	1.20
4 Hal Dues	.75	.30
5 Ross Grimsley	.75	.30
6 Fred Holdsworth	.75	.30
7 Darold Knowles	.75	.30
8 Rudy May	.75	.30
9 Stan Papi	.75	.30
10 Larry Parrish	1.00	.40
11 Bob Reece	.75	.30
12 Norm Sherry CO	.75	.30
13 Dan Schatzeder	.75	.30
14 Chris Speier	1.00	.40
15 Wayne Twitchell	.75	.30

1979 Expos Postcards

These postcards feature members from the Montreal Expos organization. These postcards are blankbacked and are borderless. The only identification is the player's name and billungual player information on the bottom.

	NM	Ex
COMPLETE SET (32)	25.00	10.00
1 Felipe Alou CO	1.50	.60
2 Stan Bahnsen	.75	.30
3 Tony Bernazard	.75	.30
4 Jim Brewer CO	.75	.30
5 Dave Cash	.75	.30
6 Warren Cromartie	1.00	.40
7 Andre Dawson	3.00	1.20
8 Duffy Dyer	.75	.30
9 Woodie Fryman	.75	.30
10 Mike Garman	.75	.30
11 Ed Herrmann	.75	.30
12 Tommy Hutton	.75	.30
13 Bill Lee	1.00	.40
With facial hair		
14 Bill Lee	1.00	.40
Clean-shaven		
15 Ken Macha	1.50	.60
16 Jim Mason	.75	.30
17 Pat Mullin CO	.75	.30
18 Dave Palmer	.75	.30
19 Tony Perez	2.00	.80
20 Vern Rapp CO	.75	.30
21 Steve Rogers	1.00	.40
22 Scott Sanderson	1.50	.60
23 Rodney Scott	.75	.30
number 3 on uniform		
24 Rodney Scott	.75	.30
number 19 on uniform		
25 Norm Sherry CO	.75	.30
26 Tony Solaita	.75	.30
27 Elias Sosa	.75	.30
28 Rusty Staub	2.00	.80
29 Ellis Valentine	1.00	.40
30 Ozzie Virgil CO	1.00	.40
31 Jerry White	.75	.30
32 Dick Williams MG	1.00	.40

1980 Expos Postcards

These postcards feature members of the 1980 Montreal Expos. These postcards are similar to those issued in the three previous seasons but they have no positions on them. These are all new photos that have red and blue shoulder striping. These cards are unnumbered so we have sequenced them in alphabetical order.

	NM	Ex
COMPLETE SET (35)	15.00	6.00
1 Bill Almon	.50	.20
2 Felipe Alou CO	1.00	.40
3 Stan Bahnsen	.50	.20
4 Tony Bernazard	.50	.20
5 Gary Carter	2.50	1.00
6 Galen Cisco CO	.50	.20
7 Warren Cromartie	.75	.30
8 Andre Dawson	2.00	.80
9 Woodie Fryman	.50	.20
10 Ross Grimsley	.50	.20
11 Bill Gullickson	.75	.30
12 Tommy Hutton	.50	.20
13 Charlie Lea	.50	.20
14 Bill Lee	.75	.30
15 Ron LeFlore	.50	.20
16 Ken Macha	.75	.30
17 Pat Mullin CO	.50	.20
18 Dale Murray	.50	.20
19 Fred Norman	.50	.20
20 Rowland Office	.50	.20
21 David Palmer	.50	.20
22 Larry Parrish	.50	.20
23 Bobby Ramos	.50	.20
24 Vern Rapp CO	.50	.20
25 Steve Rogers	.50	.20
26 Scott Sanderson	.50	.20
27 Rodney Scott	.50	.20
28 Norm Sherry CO	.50	.20
29 Elias Sosa	.50	.20
30 Chris Speier	.50	.20
31 John Tamargo	.50	.20
32 Ellis Valentine	.50	.20
33 Ozzie Virgil CO	.50	.20
34 Jerry White	.50	.20
35 Dick Williams MG	1.00	.40

1981 Expos Postcards

These postcards feature members of the 1981 Montreal Expos. These cards are unnumbered and we have sequenced them in alphabetical order. Many of the poses of the 1980 players were repeated. We have included only new players or players with different photos from the year before. Very early issues of Tim Raines, Jeff Reardon and Tim Wallach are included in this set.

	Nm-Mt	Ex-Mt
COMPLETE SET (16)	10.00	4.00
1 Steve Boros CO	.50	.20
2 Ray Burris	.50	.20
3 Charlie Lea	.50	.20
4 Bill Lee	.75	.30
5 Jerry Manuel	.75	.30
6 Willie Montanez	.50	.20
7 Ron McLain	.50	.20
8 Mike Phillips	.50	.20
9 Tim Raines	5.00	2.00
10 Bobby Ramos	.50	.20
11 Steve Ratzer	.50	.20
12 Jeff Reardon	2.50	1.00
13 Steve Rogers	.50	.20
14 Scott Sanderson	.50	.20
15 Chris Speier	.50	.20
16 Tim Wallach	1.50	.60

1982 Expos Hygrade Meats

The cards in this 24-card set measure approximately 2" by 3". This series depicting the Montreal Expos was distributed by the Hygrade company in Quebec Province, Canada. Single cello-packed cards are found in packages of Hygrade smoked sausages; each has a color photo of an Expo player, with his name and uniform number in a white panel at the base of the picture. The back, printed only in French, advertises a leatherette album designed to hold a complete set of cards. The card stock is actually thick paper rather than cardboard, and the edges are rounded. The cards are unnumbered and checklisted below in alphabetical order.

	Nm-Mt	Ex-Mt
COMPLETE SET (24)	40.00	16.00
1 Tim Blackwell	1.00	.40
2 Ray Burris	1.00	.40
3 Gary Carter	12.00	4.80
4 Warren Cromartie	2.00	.80
5 Andre Dawson	10.00	4.00
6 Jim Fanning MG	1.00	.40
7 Terry Francona	2.00	.80
8 Woodie Fryman	1.00	.40
9 Bill Gullickson	2.00	.80
10 Bob James	1.00	.40
11 Charlie Lea	1.00	.40
12 Brad Mills	1.00	.40
13 John Milner	1.00	.40
14 Dan Norman	1.00	.40
15 Al Oliver	2.50	1.00
16 Tim Raines	10.00	4.00
17 Jeff Reardon	4.00	1.60
18 Steve Rogers	1.50	.60
19 Scott Sanderson	1.00	.40
20 Bryn Smith	1.00	.40
21 Chris Speier	1.00	.40
22 Frank Taveras	1.00	.40
23 Tim Wallach	4.00	1.60
24 Jerry White	1.00	.40
xx0 Leatherette Album	8.00	3.20

1982 Expos Postcards

These postcards feature members of the 1982 Montreal Expos. These postcards are in the same style as used over the previous five years. The cards are unnumbered and we have sequenced them in alphabetical order.

	Nm-Mt	Ex-Mt
COMPLETE SET (43)	25.00	10.00
1 Tim Blackwell	.50	.20
2 Steve Boros CO	.50	.20
3 Ray Burris	.50	.20
4 Gary Carter	5.00	2.00
5 Galen Cisco CO	.50	.20
6 Warren Cromartie	.75	.30
7 Warren Cromartie	.75	.30
(Close-up)		
8 Andre Dawson	4.00	1.60
9 Billy DeMars CO	.50	.20
10 Jim Fanning MG	.50	.20
11 Doug Flynn	.50	.20
12 Terry Francona	1.00	.40
13 Woodie Fryman	.50	.20
14 Bob Gebhard CO	.50	.20
15 Bill Gullickson	.50	.20
16 Bob James	.50	.20
17 Roy Johnson	.50	.20
18 Wallace Johnson	.50	.20
19 Charlie Lea	.50	.20
20 Bill Lee	.75	.30
21 Bryan Little	.50	.20
22 Brad Mills	.50	.20
23 John Milner	.50	.20
24 Don Norman	.50	.20
25 Al Oliver	1.00	.40
(Portrait)		
26 Al Oliver	1.00	.40
(Bat on shoulder)		
27 Al Oliver	1.00	.40
(Bat on shoulder under stadium roof)		
28 Rowland Office	.50	.20
29 David Palmer	.50	.20
30 Mike Phillips	.50	.20
31 Tim Raines	4.00	1.60
32 Vern Rapp CO	.50	.20
33 Jeff Reardon	1.50	.60
34 Steve Rogers	.50	.20
35 Scott Sanderson	.50	.20
36 Dan Schatzeder	.50	.20
37 Rodney Scott	.50	.20
38 Bryn Smith	.50	.20
39 Chris Speier	.50	.20
40 Tim Wallach	3.00	1.20
41 Jerry White	.50	.20
42 Joel Youngblood	.50	.20
43 Frank Taveras	.50	.20

1982 Expos Zellers

Sponsored by Zellers Department Stores and subtitled "Baseball Pro Tips," the 60 standard-size cards comprising this set were originally distributed in 20 perforated three-card panels. The yellow-bordered fronts feature circular color player action shots circumscribed by red, white, and blue lines. The player's name appears in black lettering in the yellow margin below the photo. Below his name is a description in both English and French of the action depicted. The back carries the "Pro Tip" in English and French explaining the techniques used by the player pictured on the front. The cards are numbered on the front, and each card is marked "A," "B" or "C" next to its number, which denotes its location on the original three-card panel. Eleven players and one coach of the Montreal Expos are featured, each explaining a particular facet of baseball in the three card sequences which comprise a panel. Gary Carter (5), Cromartie (2), Dawson (3) and Francona (2) are pictured on multiple panels. The prices below are for intact three-card panels.

	Nm-Mt	Ex-Mt
COMPLETE SET (20)	20.00	8.00
1 Gary Carter	2.00	.80
(Catching position)		
2 Steve Rogers	.75	.30
(Pitching stance)		
3 Tim Raines	2.00	.80
(Sliding)		
4 Andre Dawson	2.00	.80
(Batting stance)		
5 Terry Francona	1.00	.40
(Contact hitting)		
6 Gary Carter	1.00	.40
(Fielding pop fouls)		
7 Warren Cromartie	.75	.30
(Fielding at 1B)		
8 Chris Speier	.75	.30
(Fielding at SS)		
9 Billy DeMars CO	.75	.30
(Signals)		
10 Andre Dawson	2.00	.80
(Batting)		
11 Terry Francona	1.00	.40
(Outfield throws)		
12 Woodie Fryman	.75	.30
(Holding runner)		
13 Gary Carter	2.00	.80
(Fielding low balls)		
14 Andre Dawson	2.00	.80
(Playing CF)		
15 Bill Gullickson	1.00	.40
(Slurve)		
16 Gary Carter	2.00	.80
(Catching stance)		
17 Scott Sanderson	.75	.30
(Fielding as a P)		
18 Warren Cromartie	.75	.30
(Handling bad throws)		
19 Gary Carter	2.00	.80
(Hitting stride)		
20 Ray Burris	.75	.30
(Holding runner)		

1983 Expos Postcards

These 39 blank-backed Expos postcards measure approximately 3 1/2" by 5 1/2" and feature posed color player photos that are borderless, except at the bottom, where a white margin carries the player's name in black lettering. The cards are unnumbered and checklisted below in alphabetical order.

	Nm-Mt	Ex-Mt
COMPLETE SET (39)	30.00	12.00
1 Tim Blackwell	1.00	.40
2 Ray Burris	1.00	.40
3 Gary Carter	5.00	2.00
4 Galen Cisco CO	1.00	.40
5 Warren Cromartie	1.25	.50
6 Terry Crowley	1.00	.40
7 Andre Dawson	3.00	1.20
8 Billy DeMars CO	1.00	.40
9 Doug Flynn	1.00	.40
10 Terry Francona	1.25	.50
11 Woodie Fryman	1.00	.40
12 Bill Gullickson	1.25	.50
13 Bob James	1.00	.40
14 Joe Kerrigan CO	1.00	.40
15 Charlie Lea	1.00	.40
16 Randy Lerch	1.00	.40
17 Bryan Little	1.00	.40
18 Ron McClain TR	1.00	.40
19 Brad Mills	1.00	.40
20 Al Oliver	2.00	.80
21 David Palmer	1.00	.40
22 Mike Phillips	1.00	.40
23 Tim Raines	3.00	1.20
24 Bobby Ramos	1.00	.40
25 Vern Rapp CO	1.00	.40
26 Jeff Reardon	2.50	1.00
27 Steve Rogers	1.50	.60
28 Scott Sanderson	1.00	.40
29 Dan Schatzeder	1.00	.40
30 Bryn Smith	1.00	.40
31 Chris Speier	1.00	.40
32 Mike Vail	1.00	.40
33 Bill Virdon MG	1.25	.50
34 Tim Wallach	2.00	.80
35 Chris Welsh	1.00	.40
36 Jerry White	1.00	.40
37 Tom Wieghaus	1.00	.40
38 Jim Wohlford	1.00	.40
39 Mel Wright CO	1.00	.40

1983 Expos Stuart

These 30 standard-size cards feature players of the Montreal Expos. The fronts carry white-bordered color player photos. The player's name and uniform number, along with the Montreal Expos' and Stuart's logo, appear within the broad white margin at the bottom. The plain back carries the player's bilingual biography and career highlights and features red and blue print on off-white card stock.

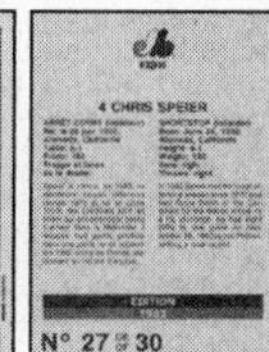

	Nm-Mt	Ex-Mt
COMPLETE SET (30)	10.00	4.00
1 Bill Virdon MG	.50	.20
2 Woodie Fryman	.25	.10
3 Vern Rapp CO	.25	.10
4 Andre Dawson	2.00	.80
5 Jeff Reardon	.75	.30
6 Al Oliver	.75	.30
7 Doug Flynn	.25	.10
8 Gary Carter	2.50	1.00
9 Tim Raines	2.00	.80
10 Steve Rogers	.50	.20
11 Billy DeMars CO	.25	.10
12 Tim Wallach	.75	.30
13 Galen Cisco CO	.25	.10
14 Terry Francona	.50	.20
15 Bill Gullickson	.25	.10
16 Ray Burris	.25	.10
17 Scott Sanderson	.25	.10
18 Warren Cromartie	.50	.20
19 Jerry White	.25	.10
20 Bobby Ramos	.25	.10
21 Jim Wohlford	.25	.10
22 Dan Schatzeder	.25	.10
23 Charlie Lea	.25	.10
24 Bryan Little UER	.25	.10
(Misspelled Brian)		
25 Mel Wright CO	.25	.10
26 Tim Blackwell	.25	.10
27 Chris Speier	.25	.10
28 Randy Lerch	.25	.10
29 Bryn Smith	.25	.10
30 Brad Mills	.25	.10

1984 Expos Postcards

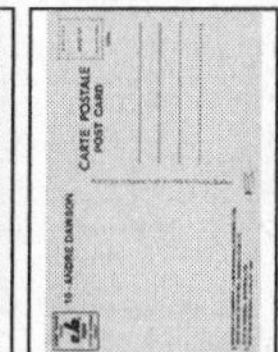

These 36 Expos postcards measure approximately 3 1/2" by 5 1/2" and feature borderless posed color player photos on their fronts. The backs carry the player's name and uniform number at the upper left. Some backs also carry the bilingual Expos' product license seal and trademarks on the left side. The rectangle for the stamp and the year of issue appear at the upper right. The postcards are unnumbered and checklisted below in alphabetical order.

	Nm-Mt	Ex-Mt
COMPLETE SET (36)	35.00	14.00
1 Felipe Alou CO	2.00	.80
2 Fred Breining	1.00	.40
3 Gary Carter	6.00	2.40
4 Galen Cisco CO	1.00	.40
5 Andre Dawson	5.00	2.00
6 Billy DeMars CO	1.00	.40
7 Miguel Dilone	1.00	.40
8 Doug Flynn	1.00	.40
9 Terry Francona	1.50	.60
10 Mike Fuentes	1.00	.40
11 Bill Gullickson	1.00	.40
12 Greg A. Harris	1.00	.40
13 Bob James	1.00	.40
14 Roy Johnson	1.00	.40
15 Joe Kerrigan CO	1.00	.40
16 Charlie Lea	1.00	.40
17 Bryan Little	1.00	.40
18 Gary Lucas	1.00	.40
19 Andy McGaffigan	1.00	.40
20 Russ Nixon CO	1.00	.40
21 David Palmer	1.00	.40
22 Tim Raines	5.00	2.00
23 Bobby Ramos	1.00	.40
24 Jeff Reardon	2.00	.80
25 Steve Rogers	1.00	.40
26 Pete Rose	8.00	3.20
27 Angel Salazar	1.00	.40
28 Dan Schatzeder	1.00	.40
29 Bryn Smith	1.00	.40
30 Chris Speier	1.00	.40
31 Mike Stenhouse	1.00	.40
32 Derrel Thomas	1.00	.40
33 Mike Vail	1.00	.40
34 Bill Virdon MG	1.50	.60
35 Tim Wallach	2.00	.80
36 Jim Wohlford	1.00	.40

1984 Expos Stuart

These 40 standard-size cards feature players of the Montreal Expos. The fronts carry white-bordered color player photos framed by a red line. The player's name and uniform number, along with the Montreal Expos' and Stuart's logo, appear within the broad white margin at the bottom. The white back is also framed by a red line and carries the player's bilingual biography and career highlights. The cards are numbered on the back. The first series of 20 cards was distributed from mid-April through June; the second series was distributed in July and August. After the completion of the promotion, the remainder of the first series cards were released to a few card dealers for distribution to the hobby. This set is distinguished from the previous year by the red border around the picture on the obverse. An album was also available for holding the cards; the album is gray, white, blue, and red and contains two-pocket plastic pages.

Nm-Mt Ex-Mt
COMPLETE SET (40) 20.00 8.00
COMMON CARD (1-20) .25 .10
COMMON CARD (21-40) .50 .20
1 Youppi (Mascot) .50 .20
2 Bill Virdon MG .50 .20
3 Billy DeMars CO .25 .10
4 Galen Cisco CO .25 .10
5 Russ Nixon CO .25 .10
6 Felipe Alou CO .75 .30
7 Dan Schatzeder .25 .10
8 Charlie Lea .25 .10
9 Roberto Ramos .25 .10
10 Bob James .25 .10
11 Andre Dawson 1.50 .60
12 Gary Lucas .25 .10
13 Jeff Reardon .50 .20
14 Tim Wallach .75 .30
15 Gary Carter 2.00 .80
16 Bill Gullickson .50 .20
17 Pete Rose 3.00 1.20
18 Terry Francona .75 .30
19 Steve Rogers .75 .30
20 Tim Raines 1.50 .60
21 Bryn Smith .50 .20
22 Greg A. Harris .50 .20
23 David Palmer .50 .20
24 Jim Wohlford .50 .20
25 Miguel Dilone .50 .20
26 Mike Stenhouse .50 .20
27 Chris Speier .50 .20
28 Derrel Thomas .50 .20
29 Doug Flynn .50 .20
30 Bryan Little .50 .20
31 Angel Salazar .50 .20
32 Mike Fuentes .50 .20
33 Joe Kerrigan CO .50 .20
34 Andy McGaffigan .50 .20
35 Fred Breining .50 .20
36 Gary Carter 1.50 .60
Andre Dawson
Tim Raines
Steve Rogers
37 Andre Dawson 1.50 .60
Tim Raines
38 Bill Virdon MG .75 .30
Felipe Alou CO
Galen Cisco CO
Billy DeMars CO
Joe Kerrigan CO
Russ Nixon CO
39 Expos Team Photo .75 .30
40 Checklist Card .75 .30
xx0 Album 3.00 1.20

1985 Expos Postcards

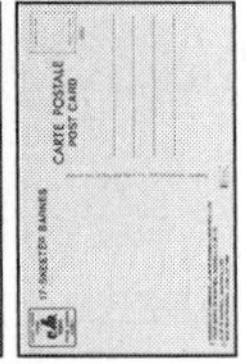

These 26 Expos postcards measure approximately 3 1/2" by 5 1/2" and feature borderless posed color player photos on their fronts. The backs carry the player's name and uniform number at the upper left. The bilingual Expos' product license seal and trademarks appear on the left side. The rectangle for the stamp and the year of issue appear at the upper right. The postcards are unnumbered and checklisted below in alphabetical order.

Nm-Mt Ex-Mt
COMPLETE SET (26) 12.00 4.80
1 Skeeter Barnes .50 .20
2 Larry Bearnarth CO .50 .20
3 Hubie Brooks .75 .30
4 Tim Burke .50 .20
5 Sal Butera .50 .20
6 Andre Dawson 2.50 1.00
7 Dan Driessen .50 .20
8 Mike Fitzgerald .50 .20
9 Ron Hansen CO .50 .20
10 Joe Hesketh .50 .20
11 Vance Law .50 .20
12 Mickey Mahler .50 .20
13 Al Newman .50 .20
14 Steve Nicosia .50 .20
15 Jack O'Connor UER .50 .20
(Misspelled O'Conner on back)
16 David Palmer .50 .20
17 Tim Raines 2.50 1.00
18 Rick Renick CO .50 .20
19 Bert Roberge .50 .20
20 Buck Rodgers MG .50 .20
21 Razor Shines .75 .30
22 Bryn Smith .50 .20
23 Randy St. Claire .50 .20
24 U.L. Washington .50 .20
25 Herm Winningham .50 .20
26 Youppi (Mascot) .75 .30

1986 Expos Greats TCMA

This 12-card standard-size set features some of the best Expos players from their first two decades. The fronts have player photos, their

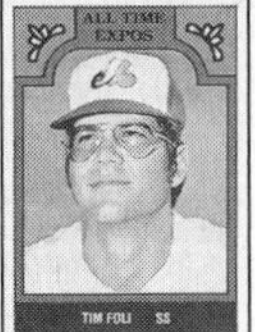

names and position. The backs have vital statistics as well as career statistics.

Nm-Mt Ex-Mt
COMPLETE SET (12) 3.00 1.20
1 Ron Fairly .50 .20
2 Dave Cash .25 .10
3 Tim Foli .25 .10
4 Bob Bailey .25 .10
5 Ken Singleton .25 .10
6 Ellis Valentine .25 .10
7 Rusty Staub .75 .30
8 John Bateman .25 .10
9 Steve Rogers .50 .20
10 Woodie Fryman .25 .10
11 Mike Marshall .25 .10
12 Jim Fanning MG .25 .10

1986 Expos Postcards

These postcards are very similar to the 85 Expos Postcards. These postcards feature no name box or fascimile autograph. The Expos logo and the player name are printed in blue. The cards are unnumbered and sequenced in alphabetical order. Andres Galarraga is featured in his Rookie Card year.

Nm-Mt Ex-Mt
COMPLETE SET (20) 8.00 3.20
1 Dann Bilardello .50 .20
2 Tim Burke .50 .20
3 Mike Fitzgerald .50 .20
4 Andres Galarraga 4.00 1.60
5 Joe Hesketh .50 .20
6 Wayne Krenchicki .50 .20
7 Ken Macha .75 .30
8 Andy McGaffigan .50 .20
9 Al Newman .50 .20
10 Tom Nieto .50 .20
11 Jeff Parrett .50 .20
12 George Riley .50 .20
13 Dan Schatzeder .50 .20
14 Bryn Smith .50 .20
15 Jason Thompson .50 .20
16 Jay Tibbs .50 .20
17 Tim Wallach 1.00 .40
18 Mitch Webster .50 .20
19 Bobby Winkles CO .50 .20
20 Floyd Youmans .50 .20

1986 Expos Provigo Panels

These 28 cards are found in lightly perforated panels of three (two player cards and an advertising card). The panel of three measures approximately 7 1/2" by 3 3/8", whereas each individual card measures 2 1/2" by 3 3/8". The fronts feature white-bordered color player action shots. The player's name and uniform number, along with the Provigo name and logo, appear within a yellow stripe across the bottom of the photo. The red, white, and blue Montreal Expos' logo appears at the top of the front. It also appears at the top of the white back, followed below by bilingual player biography and career highlights. An album was available to hold the cards; however in order to use the album, the cards had to be separated into individuals. The cards are attractive and the backs feature blue and red printing on a white card stock.

Nm-Mt Ex-Mt
COMPLETE SET (28) 8.00 3.20
1 Hubie Brooks .50 .20
2 Dann Bilardello .25 .10
3 Buck Rodgers MG .25 .10
4 Andy McGaffigan .25 .10
5 Mitch Webster .25 .10
6 Jim Wohlford .25 .10
7 Tim Raines 1.00 .40
8 Jay Tibbs .25 .10
9 Andre Dawson 1.00 .40
10 Andres Galarraga 2.00 .80
11 Tim Wallach .75 .30
12 Dan Schatzeder .25 .10
13 Jeff Reardon .75 .30
14 Joe Kerrigan CO .25 .10
Bobby Winkles CO
Larry Bearnarth CO
15 Jason Thompson .25 .10
16 Bert Roberge .25 .10
17 Tim Burke .25 .10
18 Al Newman .25 .10
19 Bryn Smith .25 .10
20 Wayne Krenchicki .25 .10
21 Joe Hesketh .25 .10
22 Herm Winningham .25 .10
23 Vance Law .25 .10
24 Floyd Youmans .25 .10
25 Jeff Parrett .25 .10
26 Mike Fitzgerald .25 .10
27 Youppi (Mascot) .50 .20
28 Rick Renick CO .25 .10
Ron Hansen CO
Ken Macha CO

1986 Expos Provigo Posters

These 12 blank-backed posters measure approximately 9" by 14 3/4", with the bottom 2 1/2" being a perforated strip carrying various Provigo coupons. The posters feature posed color photos of the Montreal Expos. These photos are borderless, except at the bottom, where a team color-coded border carries the player's name and uniform number, the Provigo and Expos logos, and the poster's number. The player's facsimile autograph appears across the photo. The backs are red and white or blue and blank.

Nm-Mt Ex-Mt
COMPLETE SET (12) 15.00 6.00
1 Tim Raines 2.00 .80
2 Bryn Smith 1.00 .40
3 Hubie Brooks 1.50 .60
4 Buck Rodgers MG 1.00 .40
5 Mitch Webster 1.00 .40
6 Joe Hesketh 1.00 .40
7 Mike Fitzgerald 1.00 .40
8 Andy McGaffigan 1.00 .40
9 Andre Dawson 2.50 1.00
10 Tim Wallach 2.00 .80
11 Jeff Reardon 2.00 .80
12 Vance Law 1.00 .40

1987 Expos Postcards

These 37 Montreal Expos postcards measure approximately 3 1/2" by 5 1/2" and feature borderless posed color player photos on their fronts. The backs are blank, except for the Expos logo and the player's name and uniform number printed in blue ink at the upper left. Otherwise, the postcards are unnumbered and so are checklisted below in alphabetical order.

Nm-Mt Ex-Mt
COMPLETE SET (37) 15.00 6.00
1 Larry Bearnarth CO .50 .20
2 Hubie Brooks .75 .30
3 Tim Burke .50 .20
4 Casey Candaele .50 .20
5 Dave Engle .50 .20
6 Mike Fitzgerald .50 .20
7 Tom Foley .50 .20
8 Andres Galarraga 2.50 1.00
9 Ron Hansen CO .50 .20
10 Neal Heaton .50 .20
11 Joe Hesketh .50 .20
12 Wallace Johnson .50 .20
13 Vance Law .50 .20
14 Bob McClure .50 .20
15 Andy McGaffigan .50 .20
16 Ken Macha .75 .30
17 Jackie Moore CO .50 .20
18 Reid Nichols .50 .20
19 Jeff Parrett .50 .20
20 Alonzo Powell .50 .20
21 Tim Raines 1.50 .60
22 Jeff Reed .50 .20
23 Luis Rivera .50 .20
24 Buck Rodgers MG .50 .20
25 Dan Schatzeder .50 .20
26 Bob Sebra .50 .20
27 Bryn Smith .50 .20
28 Lary Sorensen .50 .20
29 Randy St. Claire .50 .20
30 John Stefero .50 .20
31 Jay Tibbs .50 .20
32 Tim Wallach 1.00 .40
33 Mitch Webster .50 .20
34 Bobby Winkles CO .50 .20
35 Herman Winningham .50 .20
36 Floyd Youmans .50 .20
37 Youppi (Mascot) .75 .30

1988 Expos Postcards

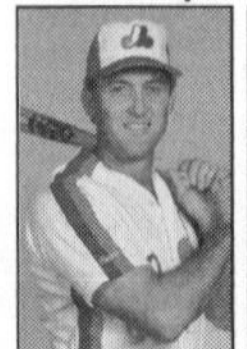

These postcards feature members of the 1988 Montreal Expos. They are similar in format to the 1987 Expos postcards. These cards are unnumbered and we have sequenced them in alphabetical order.

Nm-Mt Ex-Mt
COMPLETE SET (38) 12.00 4.80
1 Larry Bearnarth CO .50 .20
2 Hubie Brooks .75 .30
3 Tim Burke .50 .20
4 Casey Candaele .50 .20
5 Leonel Carrion CO .50 .20
6 John Dodson .50 .20
7 Dave Engle .50 .20
8 Mike Fitzgerald .50 .20
9 Tom Foley .50 .20
10 Andres Galarraga 2.50 1.00
11 Ron Hansen CO .50 .20
12 Neal Heaton .50 .20
13 Joe Hesketh .50 .20
14 Brian Holman .50 .20
15 Rex Hudler .75 .30
16 Wallace Johnson .50 .20
17 Tracy Jones .50 .20
18 Dave Martinez .75 .30
19 Dennis Martinez 1.00 .40
20 Bob McClure .50 .20
21 Andy McGaffigan .50 .20
22 Jackie Moore CO .50 .20
23 Graig Nettles 1.00 .40
24 Otis Nixon .50 .20
25 Jeff Parrett .50 .20
26 Pascual Perez .50 .20
27 Tim Raines 1.50 .60
28 Jeff Reed .50 .20
29 Luis Rivera .50 .20
30 Buck Rodgers MG .50 .20
31 Nelson Santovenia .50 .20
32 Bryn Smith .50 .20
33 Tim Wallach 1.00 .40
34 Mitch Webster .50 .20
35 Bobby Winkles CO .50 .20
36 Herm Winningham .50 .20
37 Floyd Youmans .50 .20
38 Youppi (Mascot) .50 .20

1989 Expos Postcards

These cards are very similar to the 1988 Expos Postcards. The cards are unnumbered and we have sequenced them in alphabetical order. Cy Young award winner Randy Johnson has a very early card in this set.

Nm-Mt Ex-Mt
COMPLETE SET (29) 20.00 8.00
1 Mike Aldrete .50 .20
2 Larry Bearnarth CO .50 .20
3 Hubie Brooks .75 .30
4 Tim Burke .50 .20
5 Mike Fitzgerald .50 .20
6 Tom Foley .50 .20
7 Steve Frey .50 .20
8 Andres Galarraga 2.00 .80
9 Damaso Garcia .50 .20
10 Brett Gideon .50 .20
11 Kevin Gross .50 .20
12 Ron Hansen CO .50 .20
13 Gene Harris .50 .20
14 Joe Hesketh .50 .20
15 Randy Johnson 15.00 6.00
16 Rafael Landestoy CO .50 .20
17 Mark Langston .75 .30
18 Ken Macha .75 .30
19 Dave Martinez .75 .30
20 Dennis Martinez 1.00 .40
21 Andy McGaffigan .50 .20
22 Jackie Moore CO .50 .20
23 Spike Owen .50 .20
24 Tim Raines 1.50 .60
25 Buck Rodgers MG .50 .20
26 Nelson Santovenia .50 .20
27 Bryn Smith .50 .20
28 Joe Sparks CO .50 .20
29 Tim Wallach 1.00 .40

1990 Expos Postcards

These postcards feature members of the 1990 Montreal Expos. Players featured early in their career include Delino DeShields, Marquis Grissom and Larry Walker. These cards are unnumbered are we have checklisted them in alphabetical order.

Nm-Mt Ex-Mt
COMPLETE SET (37) 30.00 9.00
1 Mike Aldrete .50 .15
2 Larry Bearnarth CO .50 .15
3 Dennis Boyd .50 .15
4 Tim Burke .50 .15
5 John Costello .50 .15
6 Delino DeShields 2.00 .60
7 Mike Fitzgerald .50 .15
8 Tom Foley .50 .15
9 Steve Frey .50 .15
10 Andres Galarraga 1.50 .45
11 Mark Gardner .50 .15
12 Brett Gideon .50 .15
13 Marquis Grissom 2.00 .60
14 Kevin Gross .50 .15
15 Drew Hall .50 .15
16 Tommy Harper CO .50 .15
17 Rex Hudler .75 .23
18 Jeff Huson .50 .15
19 Wallace Johnson .50 .15
20 Rafael Landestoy CO .50 .15
21 Ken Macha .75 .23
22 Dave Martinez .75 .23
23 Dennis Martinez 1.00 .30
24 Hal McRae CO .75 .23
25 Otis Nixon .50 .15
26 Junior Noboa .50 .15
27 Spike Owen .50 .15
28 Tim Raines 1.50 .45
29 Buck Rodgers MG .50 .15
30 Tom Runnells CO .50 .15
31 Bill Sampen .50 .15
32 Nelson Santovenia .50 .15
33 Dave Schmidt .50 .15
34 Zane Smith .50 .15
35 Rich Thompson .50 .15
36 Larry Walker 4.00 1.20
37 Tim Wallach 1.00 .30

1991 Expos Postcards

These postcards feature members of the 1991 Montreal Expos. They measure approximately 3 1/2" by 5 1/2" and feature borderless posed color player photos. The player's name appears in a lower corner. These cards are unnumbered and sequenced in alphabetical order.

Nm-Mt Ex-Mt
COMPLETE SET (22) 10.00 3.00
1 Brian Barnes .50 .15
2 Eric Bullock .50 .15
3 Ivan Calderon .50 .15
4 Mike Fitzgerald .50 .15
5 Tom Foley .50 .15
6 Steve Frey .50 .15
7 Andres Galarraga 2.00 .60
8 Mark Gardner .50 .15
9 Chris Haney .50 .15
10 Ron Hassey .50 .15
11 Barry Jones .50 .15
12 Rick Mahler .50 .15
13 Dave Martinez .50 .15
14 Dennis Martinez 1.00 .30
15 Chris Nabholz .50 .15
16 Junior Noboa .50 .15
17 Gilberto Reyes .50 .15
18 Mel Rojas .75 .23
19 Tom Runnells MG .50 .15
20 Scott Ruskin .50 .15
21 Nelson Santovenia .50 .15
22 Larry Walker 2.00 .60

1992 Expos Donruss Durivage

Featuring the Montreal Expos, the 26-card standard-size set was produced by Donruss for Durivage (a Canadian bread company). The fronts have posed color photos of the players without hats, framed by a gray inner border and a dark green outer border. The team logo, "Durivage" set name, and player information appear at the bottom of card front. In a horizontal format, the bilingual (English and French) backs carry biography and recent major league performance statistics, on a background of gray vertical stripes that fade to white as one moves down the card. The cards are numbered on the back, "No. X de/of 20." The complete set price does include all variations and the unnumbered checklist card.

Nm-Mt Ex-Mt
COMPLETE SET (26) 70.00 21.00
1 Bret Barberie 1.00 .30
2A Chris Haney 2.50 .75
2B Brian Barnes 5.00 1.50
3A Bill Sampen 1.00 .30
3B Phil Bradley 2.50 .75
4 Ivan Calderon 1.50 .45
5 Gary Carter 8.00 2.40
6 Delino DeShields 4.00 1.20
7 Jeff Fassero 2.00 .60
8 Darrin Fletcher 1.50 .45
9 Mark Gardner 1.00 .30
10 Marquis Grissom 4.00 1.20
11 Ken Hill 2.50 .75
12 Dennis Martinez 2.50 .75
13 Chris Nabholz 1.00 .30
14 Spike Owen 1.00 .30
15A Tom Runnells MG 2.00 .60
15B Felipe Alou MG 6.00 1.80
16A John Vander Wal 2.50 .75
16B Matt Stairs 6.00 1.80
17A Bill Landrum 1.00 .30
17B Dave Wainhouse 2.50 .75
18 Larry Walker 2.00 .60
19 Tim Wallach 3.00 .90
20 John Wetteland 3.00 .90
xx0 Album 5.00 1.50
NNO0 Checklist Card SP 5.00 1.50

1992 Expos Postcards

These postcards feature members of the 1992 Montreal Expos. They measure approximately 3 1/2" by 5 1/2" and feature borderless posed color player photos. The player's name appears in a lower corner. These postcards are unnumbered and checklisted below in alphabetical order.

Nm-Mt Ex-Mt
COMPLETE SET (32) 18.00 5.50
1 Felipe Alou MG 1.00 .30
2 Moises Alou 1.50 .45
3 Pierre Arsenault ANN .75 .23
4 Bret Barberie .50 .15
5 Eric Bullock .50 .15
6 Gary Carter 4.00 1.20
7 Ivan Calderon .50 .15
8 Rick Cerone .50 .15
9 Archi Cianfrocco .50 .15
10 Delino DeShields 1.00 .30
11 Jeff Fassero .50 .15
12 Darrin Fletcher .50 .15
13 Tom Foley .50 .15
14 Mark Gardner .50 .15
15 Marquis Grissom .75 .23
16 Chris Haney .50 .15
17 Tommy Harper CO .50 .15
18 Ken Hill .50 .15
19 Joe Kerrigan CO .50 .15
20 Bill Landrum .50 .15
21 Jerry Manuel CO .50 .15
22 Dennis Martinez 1.00 .30
23 Chris Nabholz .50 .15
24 Spike Owen .50 .15
25 Mel Rojas .50 .15
26 Tom Runnells MG .50 .15
27 Bill Sampen .50 .15

28 John Vander Wal .75 .23
29 Larry Walker 2.00 .60
30 Tim Wallach 1.00 .30
31 Jay Ward CO .50 .15
32 John Wetteland 1.00 .30

1993 Expos Donruss McDonald's

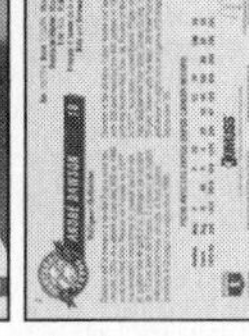

This 33-card set was produced by Donruss for McDonald's and commemorates the Montreal Expos' 25th year in baseball. The standard-size cards have fronts displaying full-bleed action pictures with the McDonald's logo at the top left. Across the bottom, the player's name and uniform number are printed on a blue stripe, with the silver-foil 25-year Expos' logo stamped to the left. The horizontal backs carry biography, statistics, and career summaries in both French and English on a beige background. The player's name and number appear near the top, printed in a dark blue stripe edged in red. The 25-year Expos' logo is displayed in the top left in red, white, and blue. The certified signed and numbered (out of 2,000) Felipe Alou card was reportedly inserted at a rate of one per case of 2,500 packs. The cards were distributed in four-card foil packs.

Nm-Mt Ex-Mt
COMPLETE SET (33) 10.00 3.00
1 Moises Alou .50 .15
2 Andre Dawson 1.00 .30
3 Delino DeShields .50 .15
4 Andres Galarraga 1.50 .45
5 Marquis Grissom .25 .07
6 Tim Raines 1.00 .30
7 Larry Walker 1.00 .30
8 Tim Wallach .10 .03
9 Ken Hill .10 .03
10 Dennis Martinez .25 .07
11 Jeff Reardon .25 .07
12 Gary Carter 1.50 .45
13 Dave Cash .10 .03
14 Warren Cromartie .25 .07
15 Mack Jones .10 .03
16 Al Oliver .50 .15
17 Larry Parrish .25 .07
18 Rodney Scott .10 .03
19 Ken Singleton .25 .07
20 Rusty Staub .50 .15
21 Ellis Valentine .10 .03
22 Woodie Fryman .10 .03
23 Charlie Lea .10 .03
24 Bill Lee .25 .07
25 Mike Marshall .25 .07
26 Claude Raymond .25 .07
27 Steve Renko .10 .03
28 Steve Rogers .25 .07
29 Bill Stoneman .25 .07
30 Gene Mauch MG .10 .03
31 Felipe Alou MG .25 .07
32 Buck Rodgers MG .10 .03
33 Checklist 1-32 .10 .03
AU0 Felipe Alou AU/2000 50.00 15.00
(Certified autograph)

1993 Expos Postcards Named

These postcards are similar to the 1992 Expos postcards. They are blank-backed and we have sequenced them in alphabetical order. All these postcards have a blue background except for Wil Cordero.

Nm-Mt Ex-Mt
COMPLETE SET (22) 10.00 3.00
1 Felipe Alou MG .75 .23
2 Moises Alou 1.00 .30
3 Brian Barnes .50 .15
4 Sean Berry .50 .15
5 Frank Bolick .50 .15
6 Kent Bottenfield .50 .15
7 Greg Colbrunn .50 .15
8 Wil Cordero .50 .15
9 Jeff Fassero .75 .23
10 Darrin Fletcher .50 .15
11 Lou Frazier .50 .15
12 Mark Gardner .50 .15
13 Tim Johnson CO .50 .15
14 Jimmy Jones .50 .15
15 Mike Lansing .50 .15
16 Tim McIntosh .50 .15
17 Chris Nabholz .50 .15
18 Luis Pujols CO .50 .15
19 Mel Rojas .50 .15
20 Jeff Shaw .75 .23
21 Tim Spehr .50 .15
22 Larry Walker 2.00 .60

1993 Expos Postcards

These cards have no border or player name on the front. Backs contain the Expos' logo and card number. The cards are checklisted aphabetically below.

Nm-Mt Ex-Mt
COMPLETE SET (7) 5.00 1.50
1 Moises Alou 1.00 .30
2 Archi Cianfrocco .50 .15
3 Wil Cordero .50 .15
4 Delino DeShields 1.00 .30
5 Dennis Martinez 1.00 .30
6 Mel Rojas .50 .15
7 Larry Walker 2.00 .60

1996 Expos Bookmarks

This six-card set of the Montreal Expos measures approximately 2 1/2" by 6 1/4". One

side features a color player portrait with personal statistics in English and a facsimile autograph. The other side displays the same color portrait with personal statistics in French and a facsimile autograph. The cards are unnumbered and checklisted below in alphabetical order.

Nm-Mt Ex-Mt
COMPLETE SET (6) 3.00 .90
1 Felipe Alou MG 1.00 .30
2 Shane Andrews .25 .07
3 Mark Grudzielanek 1.00 .30
4 Tim Scott .25 .07
5 David Segui .25 .07
6 Dave Veres .25 .07

1996 Expos Discs

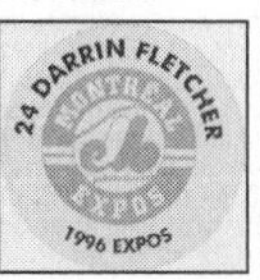

This 24-disc set consists of six 1 5/8" perforated discs on each of four larger discs with 6 3/8" diameters. The small discs carry color action player photos with the player name, jersey number and a faded team logo on the back. The center disc in each of the large discs is the team logo.

Nm-Mt Ex-Mt
COMPLETE SET (24) 5.00 1.50
1 Felipe Alou MG .25 .07
2 Moises Alou .50 .15
(Batting)
3 Moises Alou .50 .15
(Sliding into base)
4 Shane Andrews .10 .03
5 Derek Aucoin .10 .03
6 Rheal Cormier .10 .03
7 Jeff Fassero .10 .03
8 Darrin Fletcher .10 .03
9 Mark Grudzielanek .25 .07
(Batting)
10 Mark Grudzielanek .25 .07
(Fielding)
11 Mike Lansing .10 .03
12 Pedro Martinez 1.50 .45
(With glove at mouth)
13 Pedro Martinez 1.50 .45
(Pitching)
14 Carlos Perez .10 .03
15 Henry Rodriguez .10 .03
16 Mel Rojas .10 .03
17 Tim Scott .10 .03
18 David Segui .10 .03
(Ready to catch the ball)
19 David Segui .10 .03
(Catching the ball)
20 Tim Spehr .10 .03
21 Dave Veres .10 .03
22 Rondell White .75 .23
(Batting)
23 Rondell White .75 .23
(Running to base)
24 Youppi(Mascot) .25 .07

1999 Expos Postcards

These 3 1/2" by 5 1/2" blank backed postcards feature members of the 1999 Montreal Expos. Some of the poses were repeats of previous years so the only way to know that those players were issued in 1999 is by having a complete set. The postcards feature a player photo with the players name and uniform number in the lower left handed corner. We have sequenced this set in alphabetical order and notated new poses for 1999 but putting the word "NEW" next to the players name.

Nm-Mt Ex-Mt
COMPLETE SET 12.00 3.60
1 Felipe Alou MG .50 .15
2 Shane Andrews .25 .07
3 Pierre Arsenault CO .50 .15
4 Bobby Ayala NEW .25 .07
5 Michael Barrett NEW .50 .15
6 Miguel Batista .25 .07
7 Orlando Cabrera .25 .07
8 Darron Cox NEW .25 .07
9 Bobby Cuellar CO .25 .07
10 Brad Fullmer .50 .15
11 Gene Glynn CO NEW .25 .07
12 Vladimir Guerrero 3.00 .90
13 Wilton Guerrero .25 .07
14 Tommy Harper CO .25 .07
15 Bob Henley NEW .25 .07
16 Dustin Hermanson NEW .25 .07
17 Steve Kline NEW .25 .07
18 Pete Mackanin CO .25 .07
19 Manny Martinez NEW .25 .07
20 Ryan McGuire .25 .07
21 Orlando Merced NEW .25 .07
22 Mike Mordecai .25 .07
23 Guillermo Mota NEW .25 .07
24 James Mouton NEW .25 .07
25 Carl Pavano NEW .25 .07
26 Luis Pujols CO .25 .07
27 J.D. Smart NEW .25 .07
28 Dan Smith NEW .25 .07
29 Anthony Telford .25 .07
30 Mike Thurman .25 .07
31 Ugueth Urbina .50 .15
32 Javier Vazquez 1.50 .45
33 Jose Vidro 1.00 .30
34 Rondell White .50 .15
35 Chris Widger .25 .07
36 Youppi .50 .15
Mascot

2000 Expos Postcards

These postcards are very similar to the 1999 Expos issue. Many of these cards are either repeats of the 1999 pose or just have very slight cropping differences. Since these cards are unnumbered, we have sequenced them in alphabetical order.

Nm-Mt Ex-Mt
COMPLETE SET 20.00 6.00
1 Felipe Alou MG .75 .23
2 Tony Armas Jr. .75 .23
3 Brad Arnsberg CO .50 .15
4 Pierre Arseneault ANN .50 .15
5 Michael Barrett .50 .15
6 Peter Bergeron .50 .15
7 Geoff Blum .50 .15
8 Orlando Cabrera 1.00 .30
9 Bobby Cuellar CO .50 .15
10 Vladimir Guerrero 2.50 .75
11 Wilton Guerrero .50 .15
12 Dustin Hermansen .50 .15
13 Perry Hill CO .50 .15
14 Hideki Irabu .75 .23
15 Mike Johnson .50 .15
16 Terry Jones .50 .15
17 Steve Kline .50 .15
18 Felipe Lira .50 .15
19 Pete Mackanin CO .50 .15
20 Mike Mordecai .50 .15
21 Carl Pavano .50 .15
22 Luis Pujols CO .50 .15
23 Pat Roessler CO .50 .15
24 Fernando Seguignol .50 .15
25 Lee Stevens .50 .15
26 Scott Strickland .50 .15
27 Anthony Telford .50 .15
28 Mike Thurman .50 .15
29 Ugueth Urbina .75 .23
30 Javier Vazquez 2.00 .60
31 Jose Vidro 1.50 .45
32 Lenny Webster .50 .15
33 Rondell White .75 .23
34 Chris Widger .50 .15
35 Youppi .50 .15
Mascot

2001 Expos Team Issue

The 35-card set is 3 1/2" x 5 1/2" with blank backs. The cards are unnumbered and listed below in alphabetical order.

Nm-Mt Ex-Mt
COMPLETE SET (35) 12.00 3.60
1 Felipe Alou MG .50 .15
2 Tony Armas .50 .15
3 Michael Barrett .75 .23
4 Peter Bergeron .50 .15
5 Matt Blank .25 .07
6 Geoff Blum .25 .07
7 Milton Bradley .75 .23
8 Orlando Cabrera .25 .07
9 Tomas De La Rosa .25 .07
10 Vladimir Guerrero 2.00 .60
11 Hideki Irabu .25 .07
12 Mike Johnson .25 .07
13 Terry Jones .25 .07
14 Felipe Lira .25 .07
15 Graeme Lloyd .25 .07
16 Sandy Martinez .25 .07
17 Mike Mordecai .25 .07
18 Guillermo Mota .25 .07
19 Carl Pavano .25 .07
20 Chris Peters .25 .07
21 Tim Raines .75 .23
22 Britt Reames .25 .07
23 Brian Schneider .25 .07
24 Fernando Seguignol .25 .07
25 Mark Smith .25 .07
26 Lee Stevens .25 .07
27 Scott Strickland .25 .07
28 Fernando Tatis .25 .07
29 Anthony Telford .25 .07
30 Mike Thurman .25 .07
31 Andy Tracy .25 .07
32 Ugueth Urbina .50 .15
33 Javier Vazquez 1.50 .45
34 Jose Vidro 1.00 .30
35 Youppi! .75 .23

2003 Expos Donruss

This 59-card standard-size set was given away at an Expos game during the 2003 season. The fronts have the players photo surrounded by white borders. The Donruss 2003 logo is at the upper left while the player's name and position is set as white lettering against a blue background. The backs have biographical information, major league career statistics and

brief blurb about that player's highlights while an Expo.

Nm-Mt Ex-Mt
COMPLETE SET 25.00 7.50
1 Claude Raymond .25 .07
2 Javier Vazquez 1.50 .45
3 John Boccabella .25 .07
4 Bill Stoneman .25 .07
5 Carl Morton .25 .07
6 Ron Fairly .25 .07
7 Bob Bailey .25 .07
8 Steve Renko .25 .07
9 Mike Marshall .50 .15
10 Ron Hunt .25 .07
11 Ken Singleton .25 .07
12 Pedro Martinez 2.50 .75
13 Tim Foli .25 .07
14 Mike Jorgensen .25 .07
15 Steve Rogers .25 .07
16 Willie Davis .25 .07
17 Larry Parrish .25 .07
18 Jerry White .25 .07
19 Ellis Valentine .25 .07
20 Woodie Fryman .25 .07
21 Andre Dawson 1.00 .30
22 Warren Cromartie .50 .15
23 Vladimir Guerrero 2.00 .60
24 Tony Perez 1.00 .30
25 Chris Speier .25 .07
26 Dan Schatzeder .25 .07
27 Ross Grimsley .25 .07
28 Scott Sanderson .25 .07
29 Tim Wallach .50 .15
30 Dave Cash .25 .07
31 Bill Gullickson .25 .07
32 Tim Raines 1.00 .30
33 Rodney Scott .25 .07
34 Ron LeFlore .25 .07
35 Charlie Lea .25 .07
36 Bill Lee .25 .07
37 Jeff Reardon .50 .15
38 Bryn Smith .25 .07
39 Al Oliver .50 .15
40 Hubie Brooks .25 .07
41 Terry Francona .50 .15
42 Gary Carter 1.25 .35
43 Spike Owen .25 .07
44 Tim Burke .25 .07
45 Andres Galarraga 1.00 .30
46 Marquis Grissom .75 .23
47 Larry Walker 1.00 .30
48 Moises Alou .50 .15
49 Dennis Martinez .50 .15
50 Denis Boucher .25 .07
51 Rondell White .50 .15
52 Mel Rojas .25 .07
53 Henry Rodriguez .25 .07
54 David Segui .25 .07
55 Ugueth Urbina .50 .15
56 Jose Vidro 1.00 .30
57 Darrin Fletcher .25 .07
58 Orlando Cabrera .25 .07
59 John Wetteland .50 .15

2003 Expos Team Issue

These postcard-size blank-backed cards feature a player's portrait as well as the player's name on the left side of the card. Some of the cards were also issued in 2002 but we are including them as they were also issued as part of the 2003 set. Since these cards are not numbered, we have sequenced them in alphabetical order.

MINT NRMT
COMPLETE SET 25.00 11.00
1 Manny Acta .50 .23
2 Hector Almonte .50 .23
3 Tony Armas Jr. .75 .35
4 Luis Ayala .50 .23
5 Michael Barrett .75 .35
6 Rocky Biddle 1.00 .45
7 Orlando Cabrera 1.50 .70
8 Ron Calloway .50 .23
9 Jamey Carroll .50 .23
10 Endy Chavez .50 .23
11 Wil Cordero .50 .23
12 Zach Day .50 .23
13 Tim Drew .50 .23
14 Joey Eischen .50 .23
15 Vladimir Guerrero 2.50 1.10
16 Edward Guzman .50 .23
17 Livan Hernandez 1.00 .45
18 Orlando Hernandez .75 .35
19 Eric Knott .50 .23
20 Jeff Liefer .50 .23
21 Jose Macias .50 .23
22 Julio Manon .50 .23
23 Henry Mateo .50 .23
24 Tom McCraw CO .50 .23
25 Brad Mills CO .50 .23
26 Jerry Morales CO .50 .23
27 Bob Natal .50 .23
28 Tomo Ohka .75 .35
29 Claude Raymond ANN .50 .23
30 Britt Reames .50 .23
31 Frank Robinson MG 1.50 .70
32 Fernando Tatis .50 .23
33 T.J. Tucker .50 .23
34 Brian Schneider .50 .23
35 Dan Smith .50 .23
36 Randy St. Claire CO .50 .23
37 Scott Stewart .50 .23
38 Claudio Vargas .50 .23
39 Javier Vazquez 2.00 .90
40 Jose Vidro 1.50 .70
41 Joe Vitiello .50 .23
42 Brad Wilkerson .50 .23
43 Youppi .50 .23
Mascot

1960 El Roy Face Motel

This one-card set was actually a business card advertising the motel in Penn Run, Pennsylvania, which was owned by El Roy Face of the Pittsburgh Pirates. The front features a black-and-white autographed photo of the player. The back displays the motel information. The card measures approximately 2 1/8" by 3 1/2".

NM Ex
1 Roy Face 15.00 6.00

1922 Fan T231

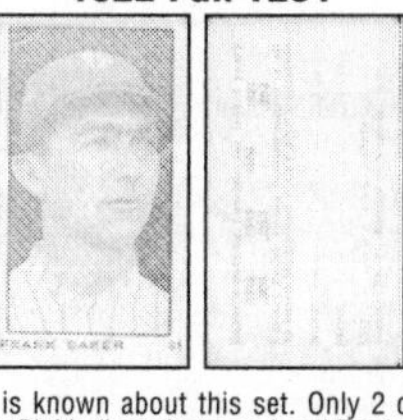

Little is known about this set. Only 2 cards, Carson Bigbie (in a photocopy) and Frank Baker have ever been discovered. The card has a sepia toned photo on the front and the back has batting information from the previous few seasons. Also on the back was a entry form for a contest, meaning these cards were probably sent back to the factory.

Ex-Mt VG
1 Carson Bigbee
61 Frank Baker 2000.00 1000.00

1906 Fan Craze AL WG2

These cards were distributed as part of a baseball game produced in 1906. The cards each measure approximately 2 1/2" by 3 1/2" and have rounded corners. The card fronts show a black and white cameo photo of the player, his name, his team and the game outcome associated with that particular card. The card backs are all the same, each showing "Art Series" and "Fan Craze" in dark blue and white. This set features only players from the American League. Since the cards are unnumbered, they are listed below in alphabetical order.

Ex-Mt VG
COMPLETE SET (51) 5000.00 2500.00
1 Nick Altrock 120.00 60.00
2 Jim Barrett 80.00 40.00
3 Harry Bay 80.00 40.00
4 Chief Bender 150.00 75.00
5 Bill Bernhardt 80.00 40.00
6 Bill Bradley 80.00 40.00
7 Jack Chesbro 150.00 75.00
8 Jimmy Collins 150.00 75.00
9 Sam Crawford 150.00 75.00
10 Lou Criger 80.00 40.00
11 Lave Cross 80.00 40.00
12 Monty Cross 80.00 40.00
13 Harry Davis 80.00 40.00
14 Bill Dineen 80.00 40.00
15 Pat Donovan 80.00 40.00
16 Pat Dougherty 80.00 40.00
17 Norman Elberfeld 80.00 40.00
18 Hobe Ferris 80.00 40.00
19 Elmer Flick 150.00 75.00
20 Buck Freeman 80.00 40.00
21 Fred Glade 80.00 40.00
22 Clark Griffith 150.00 75.00
23 Charles Hickman 80.00 40.00
24 William Holmes 80.00 40.00
25 Harry Howell 80.00 40.00
26 Frank Isbell 80.00 40.00
27 Albert Jacobson 80.00 40.00
28 Ban Johnson PRES 150.00 75.00
29 Fielder Jones 80.00 40.00
30 Adrian Joss 250.00 125.00
31 Willie Keeler 250.00 125.00
32 Nap Lajoie 300.00 150.00
33 Connie Mack MG 250.00 125.00
34 Jimmy McAleer 80.00 40.00
35 Jim McGuire 80.00 40.00
36 Earl Moore 80.00 40.00
37 George Mullen 100.00 50.00
38 Billy Owen 80.00 40.00
39 Fred Parent 80.00 40.00
40 Case Patten 80.00 40.00
41 Eddie Plank 250.00 125.00
42 Ossie Schreckengost 80.00 40.00
43 Jake Stahl 120.00 60.00
44 Fred Stone 80.00 40.00
45 William Sudhoff 80.00 40.00
46 Roy Turner 80.00 40.00
47 Rube Waddell 150.00 75.00
48 Bob Wallace 150.00 75.00
49 G. Harris White 80.00 40.00

50 George Winter 80.00 40.00
51 Cy Young 250.00 125.00

1906 Fan Craze NL WG3

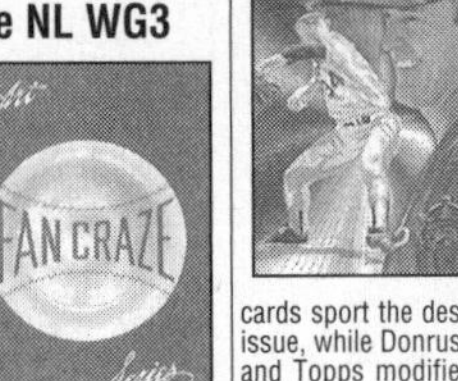

These cards were distributed as part of a baseball game produced in 1906. The game cost 50 cents upon issuance in 1906. The cards each measure approximately 2 1/2" by 3 1/2" and have rounded corners. The card fronts show a black and white cameo photo of the player, his name, his team, and the game outcome associated with that particular card. The card backs are all the same, each showing "Art Series" and "Fan Craze" in dark blue and white. This set features only players from the National League. Since the cards are unnumbered, they are listed below in alphabetical order.

	Ex-Mt	VG
COMPLETE SET (54)	4000.00	2000.00
1 Red Ames	80.00	40.00
2 Ginger Beaumont	80.00	40.00
3 Jake Beckley	150.00	75.00
4 Billy Bergen	80.00	40.00
5 Roger Bresnahan	150.00	75.00
6 George Brown	80.00	40.00
7 Mordacai Brown sic, Mordecai	150.00	75.00
8 Doc Casey	80.00	40.00
9 Frank Chance	150.00	75.00
10 Fred Clarke	150.00	75.00
11 Tommy Corcoran	80.00	40.00
12 Bill Dahlen	120.00	60.00
13 Mike Donlin	100.00	50.00
14 Charley Dooin	80.00	40.00
15 Mickey Doolin	80.00	40.00
16 Hugh Duffy	150.00	75.00
17 John E. Dunleavy	80.00	40.00
18 Bob Ewing	80.00	40.00
19 Chick Fraser	80.00	40.00
20 Ned Hanlon MG	120.00	60.00
21 Del Howard	80.00	40.00
22 Miller Huggins	150.00	75.00
23 Joe Kelley	150.00	75.00
24 John Kling	80.00	40.00
25 Tommy Leach	100.00	50.00
26 Harry Lumley	80.00	40.00
27 Carl Lundgren	80.00	40.00
28 Bill Maloney	80.00	40.00
29 Dan McGann	80.00	40.00
30 Joe McGinnity	150.00	75.00
31 John McGraw MG	150.00	75.00
32 Harry McIntire	80.00	40.00
33 Kid Nichols	150.00	75.00
34 Mike O'Neil	80.00	40.00
35 Orval Overall	80.00	40.00
36 Frank Pfeffer	80.00	40.00
37 Deacon Philippe	100.00	50.00
38 Charley Pittinger	80.00	40.00
39 Harry C. Pulliam PRES	80.00	40.00
40 Ed Reulbach	100.00	50.00
41 Claude Ritchey	80.00	40.00
42 Cy Seymour	80.00	40.00
43 Jim Sheckard	80.00	40.00
44 Jack Taylor	80.00	40.00
45 Dummy Taylor	80.00	40.00
46 Fred Tenney	80.00	40.00
47 Harry Theilman	80.00	40.00
48 Roy Thomas	80.00	40.00
49 Honus Wagner	400.00	200.00
50 Jake Weimer	80.00	40.00
51 Bob Wicker	80.00	40.00
52 Vic Willis	150.00	75.00
53 Lew Wiltsie	80.00	40.00
54 Irving Young	80.00	40.00

1994 FanFest Clemente

This standard-size redemption set was reportedly the brainchild of MLB's Ray Schulte, who obtained the cooperation of the five major baseball card manufacturers to each produce 15,000 special Roberto Clemente cards for the '94 All-Star FanFest in Pittsburgh, July 8-12. Each card was redeemable only at each manufacturer's booth for five wrappers of any '94 baseball product from that company. The undistributed cards were reportedly destroyed. It has been estimated that less than 10,000 of each card were distributed. All the cards are numbered on the back as "X of 5."

	Nm-Mt	Ex-Mt
COMPLETE SET (5)	80.00	24.00
COMMON CARD (1-5)	15.00	4.50
4 Roberto Clemente 1954 Topps Archives	20.00	6.00

1995 FanFest Ryan

Five MLB licensors produced one card each as part of a wrapper redemption program featuring Nolan Ryan for All-Star FanFest in Dallas in July. Pinnacle, Ultra, and Upper Deck

cards sport the design of the licensor's regular issue, while Donruss produced a special design and Topps modified Ryan's 1968 rookie card (shared with Jerry Koosman) to feature only Ryan. Again, Ray Schulte, promoter of the Pinnacle All-Star Fan Fest shows, was involved in the creation of this set. The cards are numbered on the back "X of 5."

	Nm-Mt	Ex-Mt
COMPLETE SET (5)	40.00	12.00
COMMON CARD (1-5)	10.00	3.00
1 Nolan Ryan 1995 Upper Deck	12.00	3.60
4 Nolan Ryan 1995 Ultra	12.00	3.60

1996 FanFest Carlton

These five standard-size cards marked the third straight year that a set of one player's cards were issued in conjunction with the annual All-Star Fan Fest. MLB's Ray Schulte, who originated the idea of these cards was again instrumental in arranging for the companies to issue these cards as part of a wrapper redemption program.

	Nm-Mt	Ex-Mt
COMPLETE SET (5)	25.00	7.50
COMMON CARD (1-5)	5.00	1.50
3 Steve Carlton Pinnacle	6.00	1.80
4 Steve Carlton 1965 Topps	6.00	1.80

1997 FanFest Jackie Robinson

These five cards marked the fourth straight year that a set of one player's cards were issued in conjunction with the annual All-Star Fan Fest. MLB's Ray Schulte, who originated the idea of these cards was again instrumental in arranging for the companies to issue these cards as part of a wrapper redemption program. Fleer/SkyBox also issued a Ultra Larry Doby card as part of the Fan Fest celebration. This card is priced below but not considered part of the Robinson set.

	Nm-Mt	Ex-Mt
COMPLETE SET (5)	25.00	7.50
COMMON CARD (1-5)	5.00	1.50
6 Larry Doby Fleer Ultra	5.00	1.50

1998 FanFest Brock

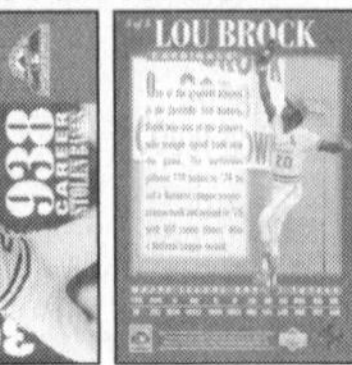

These five cards marked the fifth straight year that a set of one player's cards were issued in conjunction with the annual All-Star FanFest. This five-card set features Lou Brock's cards including a reprint of his Topps 1962 Rookie card. The cards were issued as part of a wrapper redemption program.

	Nm-Mt	Ex-Mt
COMPLETE SET (5)	20.00	6.00
COMMON CARD (1-5)	5.00	1.50
1 Lou Brock 1962 Topps	6.00	1.80

1999 FanFest Yastrzemski

This four-card standard-size set was issued as a wrapper redemption at the Baseball All-Star Fanfest held in Boston in July, 1999. Each major manufacturer issued a card of Carl Yastrzemski, who played more than 20 seasons for the Boston Red Sox. Only four cards were issued in 1999 due to Pinnacle's bankruptcy and subsequent leaving of the card producing business.

	Nm-Mt	Ex-Mt
COMPLETE SET (4)	20.00	6.00
COMMON CARD (1-4)	5.00	1.50
1 Carl Yastrzemski 1960 Topps	6.00	1.80

2000 FanFest Aaron

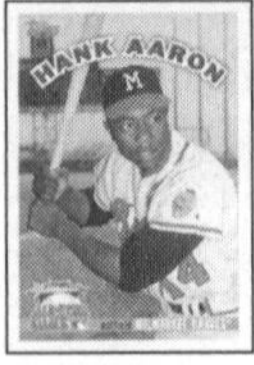

This four-card standard-size set was released at the 2000 Fan Fest in Atlanta in July, 2000. The set features Hank Aaron cards from four different card companies. Again, only four cards were issued a there were only four major manufacturers in 2000.

	Nm-Mt	Ex-Mt
COMPLETE SET (4)	15.00	4.50
COMMON CARD (1-4)	4.00	1.20

2000 FanFest Aaron Mastercard

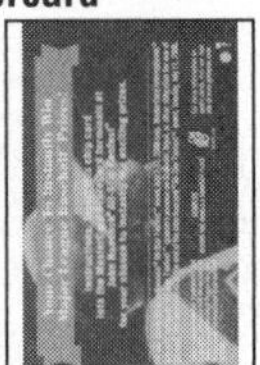

This one card MasterCard was used at Fan Fest as a promotion for giving away various prizes. A collector who had one of these cards needed to try three different machines to see if they had won a prize. Please note, these are not real credit cards.

	Nm-Mt	Ex-Mt
1 Hank Aaron	5.00	1.50

2002 FanFest

These eight standard-size cards were available through a wrapper redemption at the 2002 All-Star Fan Fest held in Milwaukee, Wisconsin. Each card company got to issue two cards for this promotion. The Sosa "refractor" style card was given away to lucky collectors who won prizes in "Pack Wars" at the Topps booth.

	Nm-Mt	Ex-Mt
COMPLETE SET (8)	15.00	4.50
1 Derek Jeter Fleer	5.00	1.50
2 Ichiro Suzuki Upper Deck	5.00	1.50
3 Sammy Sosa Finest	2.50	.75
3A Sammy Sosa REF Finest	15.00	4.50
4 Barry Bonds Studio	2.50	.75
5 Robin Yount Studio	1.00	.30
6 Geoff Jenkins Finest	.50	.15
7 Ben Sheets Upper Deck	.50	.15
8 Richie Sexson Fleer	.50	.15

2002 FanFest Memorabilia

These four cards were issued as special redemption cards at the 2002 FanFest. These cards featured a major superstar along with a base used in a game they played in. Each manufacturer got to use one player for this redemption.

	Nm-Mt	Ex-Mt
COMPLETE SET (4)	50.00	15.00
1 Barry Bonds Studio	10.00	3.00
2 Derek Jeter Fleer	20.00	6.00
3 Sammy Sosa Topps	10.00	3.00
4 Ichiro Suzuki Upper Deck	20.00	6.00

2003 Fanfest All-Star

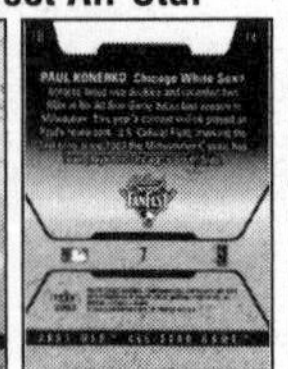

These eight standard-size cards were available through a redemption program at the 2003 All-Star Fan Fest held in Chicago, Illinois. Each card company got to issue two cards for this promotion. Each customer must open at least five premium packs from a given company in order to receive the card being redeemed by that company. Cards 1-4 were limited to just 2,000 and features a piece of a base from a Major League game that that player took part in. Sammy Sosa's is from April 1, 2002, the Cubs first game of the season vs. the Reds. Barry Bonds' memorablia card is from the 2002 NLCS vs. St. Louis.

	MINT	NRMT
COMPLETE SET	40.00	18.00
COMMON CARD	1.00	.45
COMMON MEMORABILIA CARD	8.00	3.60
1 Hideki Matsui Base Upper Deck	10.00	4.50
2 Barry Bonds Base Topps	10.00	4.50
3 Derek Jeter Base Fleer Authentix	10.00	4.50
4 Sammy Sosa Base Studio Masterstrokes	8.00	3.60
5 Frank Thomas Upper Deck	2.50	1.10
6 Bartolo Colon Topps	1.50	.70
7 Paul Konerko Fleer Authentix	1.50	.70
8 Magglio Ordonez Studio	2.00	.90

1939 Father and Son Shoes

These black and white blank-backed cards, which measure approximately 3" by 4" feature members of both Philadelphia area baseball teams. The fronts have a posed action shot with the player's name, position and team on the the bottom. Since these cards are unnumbered, we have sequenced them in alphabetical order.

	Ex-Mt	VG
COMPLETE SET	1500.00	750.00
1 Moe Arnovich	100.00	50.00
2 Earl Brucker	100.00	50.00
3 George Caster	100.00	50.00
4 Sam Chapman	120.00	60.00
5 Spud Davis	100.00	50.00
6 Joe Gantenbein	100.00	50.00
7 Bob Johnson	120.00	60.00
8 Chuck Klein	200.00	100.00
9 Herschel Martin	100.00	50.00
10 Pinky May	100.00	50.00
11 Wally Moses	120.00	60.00
12 Emmitt Mueller	100.00	50.00
13 Hugh Mulcahy	100.00	50.00
14 Skeeter Newsome	100.00	50.00
15 Claude Passeau	120.00	60.00
16 George Scharein	100.00	50.00
17 Dick Siebert	100.00	50.00

1910 Fatima Cigarettes Premiums

These 12 1/2" by 19" black and white blank-backed photos were issued by Fatima as a premium promotion. The player's photo takes up most of the card with a brief biography and advertisment for Fatima on the bottom. There may be additions to this checklist so any additional information is appreciated.

	Ex-Mt	VG
COMPLETE SET	6000.00	3000.00
15 Christy Mathewson	1500.00	750.00
22 Ty Cobb	3000.00	1500.00
51 Walter Johnson	2000.00	1000.00

1913 Fatima T200

The cards in this 16-card set measure approximately 2 5/8" by 5 13/16". The 1913 Fatima Cigarettes issue contains unnumbered glossy surface team cards. Both St. Louis team cards are considered difficult to obtain. A large 13" by 21" unnumbered, heavy cardboard parallel premium issue is also known to exist and is quite scarce. These unnumbered team cards are ordered below by team alphabetical order within league.

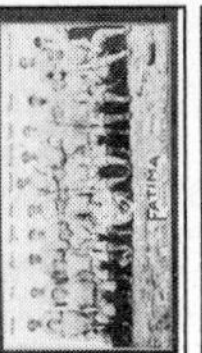

	Ex-Mt	VG
COMPLETE SET (16)	8000.00	4000.00
1 Boston Red Sox	400.00	200.00
2 Chicago White Sox	450.00	220.00
3 Cleveland Indians	800.00	400.00
4 Detroit Tigers	1000.00	500.00
5 New York Yankees	1000.00	500.00
6 Philadelphia Athletics	350.00	180.00
7 St. Louis Browns	800.00	400.00
8 Washington Senators	450.00	220.00
9 Boston Braves	450.00	220.00
10 Brooklyn Dodgers	350.00	180.00
11 Chicago Cubs	350.00	180.00
12 Cincinnati Reds	350.00	180.00
13 New York Giants	600.00	300.00
14 Philadelphia Phillies	350.00	180.00
15 Pittsburgh Pirates	450.00	220.00
16 St. Louis Cardinals	450.00	220.00

1914 Fatima Players T222

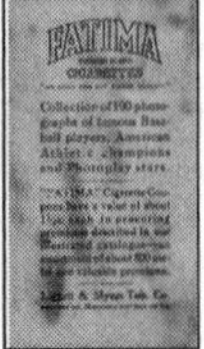

The cards in this 52-card set measure approximately 2 1/2" by 4 1/2" and are unnumbered. The cards are quite fragile on thin, brittle paper stock. The set was produced in 1914 by Liggett and Myers Tobacco Co. The players in the set have been alphabetized and numbered for reference in the checklist below.

	Ex-Mt	VG
COMPLETE SET (52)	3500.00	1800.00
1 Grover C. Alexander	250.00	125.00
2 Jimmy Archer	50.00	25.00
3 James Austin	60.00	30.00
4 Jack Barry	50.00	25.00
5 George Baumgardner	50.00	25.00
6 Rube Benton	50.00	25.00
7 Roger Bresnahan	100.00	50.00
8 Mordecai Brown	100.00	50.00
9 George J. Burns	50.00	25.00
10 Joe Bush	50.00	25.00
11 George Chalmers	50.00	25.00
12 Frank Chance	150.00	75.00
13 Albert Demaree	50.00	25.00
14 Arthur Fletcher	50.00	25.00
15 Earl Hamilton	50.00	25.00
16 John Henry	60.00	30.00
17 Byron Houck	50.00	25.00
18 Miller Huggins	100.00	50.00
19 Hugh Jennings MG	100.00	50.00
20 Walter Johnson	600.00	300.00
21 Ray Keating	50.00	25.00
22 John Lapp	50.00	25.00
23 Thomas Leach	50.00	25.00
24 Nemo Leibold	50.00	25.00
25 John Frank Lelivelt	50.00	25.00
26 Hans Lobert	60.00	30.00
27 Lee Magee	50.00	25.00
28 Sherry Magee	80.00	40.00
29 Fritz Maisel	50.00	25.00
30 Rube Marquard	100.00	50.00
31 George McBride	50.00	25.00
32 Stuffy McInnis	50.00	25.00
33 Larry McLean	50.00	25.00
34 Raymond Morgan	50.00	25.00
35 Eddie Murphy	50.00	25.00
36 Red Murray	50.00	25.00
37 Rube Oldring	60.00	30.00
38 William J. Orr	50.00	25.00
39 Hub Perdue	60.00	30.00
40 Arthur Phelan	50.00	25.00
41 Ed Reulbach	80.00	40.00
42 Vic Saier	50.00	25.00
43 Slim Sallee	50.00	25.00
44 Wally Schang	60.00	30.00
45 Frank Schulte	60.00	30.00
46 Jimmy Smith	50.00	25.00
47 Amos Strunk	50.00	25.00
48 Bill Sweeney	50.00	25.00
49 Lefty Tyler	60.00	30.00
50 Oscar Vitt	50.00	25.00
51 Ivy Wingo	50.00	25.00
52 Heinie Zimmerman	50.00	25.00

1982 FBI Discs

These discs were issued in Canada. These blank-backed circular white cutouts from the perforated bottoms of boxes of various FBI Foods' Bantam drinks measure approximately 2 7/8" in diameter and display black-and-white player head shots. Two players were featured on each box bottom. The player's name appears to the left of his photo; his team's name appears to the right. The cards are unnumbered and checklisted below in alphabetical order

	Nm-Mt	Ex-Mt
COMPLETE SET (32)	1200.00	475.00

*COMPLETE BOXES: 2X COMBINED PRICES

1 Don Baylor 20.00 8.00
2 Vida Blue 20.00 8.00
3 George Brett 120.00 47.50
4 Rod Carew 80.00 32.00
5 Steve Carlton 80.00 32.00
6 Gary Carter 80.00 32.00
7 Warren Cromartie 10.00 4.00
8 Andre Dawson 60.00 24.00
9 Rollie Fingers 40.00 16.00
10 Steve Garvey 50.00 20.00
11 Rich Gossage 30.00 12.00
12 Alfredo Griffin 10.00 4.00
13 Bill Gullickson 10.00 4.00
14 Steve Henderson 10.00 4.00
15 Keith Hernandez 20.00 8.00
16 Larry Hisle 10.00 4.00
17 John Mayberry 10.00 4.00
18 Al Oliver 20.00 8.00
19 Dave Parker 20.00 8.00
20 Tim Raines 40.00 16.00
21 Jim Rice 20.00 8.00
22 Steve Rogers 10.00 4.00
23 Pete Rose 100.00 40.00
24 Nolan Ryan 250.00 100.00
25 Mike Schmidt 100.00 40.00
26 Tom Seaver 80.00 32.00
27 Ken Singleton 10.00 4.00
28 Dave Stieb 10.00 4.00
29 Bruce Sutter 20.00 8.00
30 Garry Templeton 10.00 4.00
31 Ellis Valentine 10.00 4.00
32 Dave Winfield 80.00 32.00

1996-98 Fiesta Chips

These chips, issued over a two year period, featued various baseball players and themes. Since they are unnumbered, we have sequenced them alphabetically within groups which are arranged by date of issue

Nm-Mt Ex-Mt
COMPLETE SET 100.00 30.00
1 Ray Boone 5.00 1.50
Sports Edition
2 Mickey McDermott 5.00 1.50
Sports Edition
3 Duke Snider 15.00 4.50
Sports Edition
4 Ted Radcliffe 10.00 3.00
Negro League 3/97
5 Nap Gulley 6.00 1.80
Negro League 3/97
6 Marlon Duckett 6.00 1.80
Negro League 6/97
7 Tommy Henrich 10.00 3.00
6/97
8 Sam Jethroe 6.00 1.80
Negro League 6/97
9 Buck O'Neil 10.00 3.00
Negro League 9/97
10 Walt Dropo 5.00 1.50
ROY 1950 12/97
11 Lefty Mathis 5.00 1.50
Negro League 12/97
12 Ed Kranepool 6.00 1.80
1969 Mets 6/98
13 Amos Otis 6.00 1.80
1969 Mets 6/98
14 Ron Swoboda 6.00 1.80
1969 Mets 6/98
15 Pete Coscarat 5.00 1.50
Brooklyn Dodgers
9/98
16 Al Gionfriddo 5.00 1.50
Brooklyn Dodgers
9/98
17 Norm Sherry 5.00 1.50
Brooklyn Dodgers
9/98

1984 Fifth National Convention

These eight standard-size cards were given away at the 1984 5th Annual National Convention at the Aspen Hotel in Parsippany, N.J. August 9-12. Cards 1-5 below feature posed black-and-white player photos with white outer borders and brown inner borders. The player's name appears in white lettering within the brown margin below the photo. Cards 6-8 feature posed color player photos framed by a purple line and with green outer borders. Purple stars appear in the photos' upper corners. The player's name appears in white lettering in the bottom green margin. All the white backs carry the logo for the Fifth Annual National. All the players pictured were supposed to sign free autographs at the show. The cards are unnumbered and checklisted below in alphabetical order within each design type.

Nm-Mt Ex-Mt
COMPLETE SET (8) 2.50 1.00
1 Tom Gorman UMP .25 .10
2 Bud Harrelson .50 .20
3 Gene Hermanski .25 .10
4 Ed Lopat .25 .10
5 Bobby Thomson .75 .30
6 Joe Collins .25 .10
7 Larry Doby 1.50 .60
8 Willard Marshall .25 .10

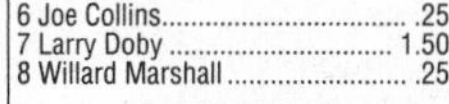

1984 Fifth National Convention Tickets

This 18-card set of 5th Annual National Convention Tickets measures approximately 2" by 5 1/2" and features black-and-white head photos of 1954 baseball players on an orange background. The player's name and team are printed in black below the photo. The convention was held in Parsippany, New Jersey, on August 9 through August 12 at the Aspen Hotel. The backs are blank. The tickets are checklisted below in alphabetical order.

Nm-Mt Ex-Mt
COMPLETE SET (18) 25.00 10.00
1 Hank Bauer 1.00 .40
2 Yogi Berra 2.00 .80
3 Alvin Dark .75 .30
4 Carl Erskine 1.00 .40
5 Carl Furillo 1.00 .40
6 Whitey Ford 2.00 .80
7 Bob Grim .50 .20
8 Gil Hodges 2.00 .80
9 Whitey Lockman .75 .30
10 Sal Maglie .50 .20
Johnny Antonelli
11 Mickey Mantle 7.50 3.00
12 Willie Mays 5.00 2.00
13 Pee Wee Reese 2.00 .80
14 Allie Reynolds 1.00 .40
15 Dusty Rhodes .50 .20
16 Jackie Robinson 4.00 1.60
17 Duke Snider 3.00 1.20
18 Hoyt Wilhelm 1.50 .60

1984 Fifth National Convention Uncut Sheet

This nine-card uncut sheet features players who would be signing at the 5th National Sports Card Convention. The players on the sheet are featured in black and white photos and the back is blank.

Nm-Mt Ex-Mt
1 Uncut Sheet 5.00 2.00
Bill Hands
Sal Yvars
Eddie Lopat
Hank Bowory
Bobby Hofman
Bobby Malkmus
Johnny Kucks
Allie Clark
Arturo Lopez

1993 Finest Promos

Topps gave 5,000 of these three-card promo standard-size sets to its dealer customers to promote the release of its 1993 Topps Baseball's Finest set. The standard-size cards have metallic finishes on their fronts and feature color player action photos. The words "Promotional Sample 1 of 5000" appears in red lettering superposed upon the player's biography on the back of the card. A limited amount of these cards were issued as refractors. They are valued as well.

Nm-Mt Ex-Mt
*REFRACTORS: 20X to 40X BASIC CARDS
88 Roberto Alomar 8.00 2.40
98 Don Mattingly AS 15.00 4.50
107 Nolan Ryan 30.00 9.00

1993 Finest

This 199-card standard-size single series set is widely recognized as one of the most important issues of the 1990's. The Finest brand was Topps first attempt at the super-premium card market. Production was announced at 4,000 cases and cards were distributed exclusively through hobby dealers in the fall of 1993. This was the first time in the history of the hobby that a major manufacturer publicly released production figures. Cards were issued in seven-card foil fin-wrapped packs that carried a suggested retail price of $3.99. The product was a smashing success upon release with pack prices immediately soaring well above suggested retail prices. The popularity of the product has continued to grow throughout the years as it's place in hobby lore is now well soldified. The cards have silver-blue metallic finishes on their fronts and feature color player action photos. The set's title appears at the top, and the player's name is shown at the bottom. J.T. Snow is the only Rookie Card of note in this set.

Nm-Mt Ex-Mt
COMPLETE SET (199) 120.00 36.00
1 David Justice 2.50 .75
2 Lou Whitaker 2.50 .75
3 Bryan Harvey 1.50 .45
4 Carlos Garcia 1.50 .45
5 Sid Fernandez 1.50 .45
6 Brett Butler 2.50 .75
7 Scott Cooper 1.50 .45
8 B.J. Surhoff 2.50 .75
9 Steve Finley 2.50 .75
10 Curt Schilling 4.00 1.20
11 Jeff Bagwell 4.00 1.20
12 Alex Cole 1.50 .45
13 John Olerud 2.50 .75
14 John Smiley 1.50 .45
15 Bip Roberts 1.50 .45
16 Albert Belle 2.50 .75
17 Duane Ward 1.50 .45
18 Alan Trammell 4.00 1.20
19 Andy Benes 1.50 .45
20 Reggie Sanders 2.50 .75
21 Todd Zeile 1.50 .45
22 Rick Aguilera 1.50 .45
23 Dave Hollins 1.50 .45
24 Jose Rijo 1.50 .45
25 Matt Williams 2.50 .75
26 Sandy Alomar Jr. 1.50 .45
27 Alex Fernandez 1.50 .45
28 Ozzie Smith 10.00 3.00
29 Ramon Martinez 1.50 .45
30 Bernie Williams 4.00 1.20
31 Gary Sheffield 2.50 .75
32 Eric Karros 2.50 .75
33 Frank Viola 2.50 .75
34 Kevin Young 2.50 .75
35 Ken Hill 1.50 .45
36 Tony Fernandez 1.50 .45
37 Tim Wakefield 2.50 .75
38 John Kruk 2.50 .75
39 Chris Sabo 1.50 .45
40 Marquis Grissom 1.50 .45
41 Glenn Davis 1.50 .45
42 Jeff Montgomery 1.50 .45
43 Kenny Lofton 2.50 .75
44 John Burkett 1.50 .45
45 Darryl Hamilton 1.50 .45
46 Jim Abbott 4.00 1.20
47 Ivan Rodriguez 6.00 1.80
48 Eric Young 1.50 .45
49 Mitch Williams 1.50 .45
50 Harold Reynolds 2.50 .75
51 Brian Harper 1.50 .45
52 Rafael Palmeiro 4.00 1.20
53 Bret Saberhagen 2.50 .75
54 Jeff Conine 2.50 .75
55 Ivan Calderon 1.50 .45
56 Juan Guzman 1.50 .45
57 Carlos Baerga 1.50 .45
58 Charles Nagy 1.50 .45
59 Wally Joyner 2.50 .75
60 Charlie Hayes 1.50 .45
61 Shane Mack 1.50 .45
62 Pete Harnisch 1.50 .45
63 George Brett 15.00 4.50
64 Lance Johnson 1.50 .45
65 Ben McDonald 1.50 .45
66 Bobby Bonilla 2.50 .75
67 Terry Steinbach 1.50 .45
68 Ron Gant 2.50 .75
69 Doug Jones 1.50 .45
70 Paul Molitor 4.00 1.20
71 Brady Anderson 2.50 .75
72 Chuck Finley 2.50 .75
73 Mark Grace 4.00 1.20
74 Mike Devereaux 1.50 .45
75 Tony Phillips 1.50 .45
76 Chuck Knoblauch 2.50 .75
77 Tony Gwynn 8.00 2.40
78 Kevin Appier 2.50 .75
79 Sammy Sosa 10.00 3.00
80 Mickey Tettleton 1.50 .45
81 Felix Jose 1.50 .45
82 Mark Langston 1.50 .45
83 Gregg Jefferies 1.50 .45
84 Andre Dawson AS 2.50 .75
85 Greg Maddux AS 10.00 3.00
86 Rickey Henderson AS 6.00 1.80
87 Tom Glavine AS 4.00 1.20
88 Roberto Alomar AS 6.00 1.80
89 Darryl Strawberry AS 4.00 1.20
90 Wade Boggs AS 4.00 1.20
91 Bo Jackson AS 6.00 1.80
92 Mark McGwire AS 15.00 4.50
93 Robin Ventura AS 2.50 .75
94 Joe Carter AS 2.50 .75
95 Lee Smith AS 2.50 .75
96 Cal Ripken AS 20.00 6.00
97 Larry Walker AS 4.00 1.20
98 Don Mattingly AS 15.00 4.50
99 Jose Canseco AS 6.00 1.80
100 Dennis Eckersley AS 2.50 .75
101 Terry Pendleton AS 2.50 .75
102 Frank Thomas AS 6.00 1.80
103 Barry Bonds AS 15.00 4.50
104 Roger Clemens AS 12.00 3.60
105 Ryne Sandberg AS 10.00 3.00
106 Fred McGriff AS 4.00 1.20
107 Nolan Ryan AS 25.00 7.50
108 Will Clark AS 6.00 1.80
109 Pat Listach AS 1.50 .45
110 Ken Griffey Jr. AS 10.00 3.00
111 Cecil Fielder AS 2.50 .75
112 Kirby Puckett AS 6.00 1.80
113 Dwight Gooden AS 4.00 1.20
114 Barry Larkin AS 6.00 1.80
115 David Cone AS 2.50 .75
116 Juan Gonzalez AS 6.00 1.80
117 Kent Hrbek 2.50 .75
118 Tim Wallach 1.50 .45
119 Craig Biggio 4.00 1.20
120 Roberto Kelly 1.50 .45
121 Gregg Olson 1.50 .45
122 Eddie Murray UER 6.00 1.80
122 career strikeouts
should be 1224
123 Wil Cordero 1.50 .45
124 Jay Buhner 2.50 .75
125 Carlton Fisk 4.00 1.20
126 Eric Davis 2.50 .75
127 Doug Drabek 1.50 .45
128 Ozzie Guillen 1.50 .45
129 John Wetteland 2.50 .75
130 Andres Galarraga 2.50 .75
131 Ken Caminiti 2.50 .75
132 Tom Candiotti 1.50 .45
133 Pat Borders 1.50 .45
134 Kevin Brown 2.50 .75
135 Travis Fryman 2.50 .75
136 Kevin Mitchell 1.50 .45
137 Greg Swindell 1.50 .45
138 Benito Santiago 2.50 .75
139 Reggie Jefferson 1.50 .45
140 Chris Bosio 1.50 .45
141 Deion Sanders 4.00 1.20
142 Scott Erickson 1.50 .45
143 Howard Johnson 1.50 .45
144 Orestes Destrade 1.50 .45
145 Jose Guzman 1.50 .45
146 Chad Curtis 1.50 .45
147 Cal Eldred 1.50 .45
148 Willie Greene 1.50 .45
149 Tommy Greene 1.50 .45
150 Erik Hanson 1.50 .45
151 Bob Welch 1.50 .45
152 John Jaha 1.50 .45
153 Harold Baines 2.50 .75
154 Randy Johnson 6.00 1.80
155 Al Martin 1.50 .45
156 J.T. Snow RC 6.00 1.80
157 Mike Mussina 6.00 1.80
158 Ruben Sierra 1.50 .45
159 Dean Palmer 2.50 .75
160 Steve Avery 1.50 .45
161 Julio Franco 2.50 .75
162 Dave Winfield 2.50 .75
163 Tim Salmon 4.00 1.20
164 Tom Henke 1.50 .45
165 Mo Vaughn 2.50 .75
166 John Smoltz 4.00 1.20
167 Danny Tartabull 1.50 .45
168 Delino DeShields 1.50 .45
169 Charlie Hough 2.50 .75
170 Paul O'Neill 4.00 1.20
171 Darren Daulton 2.50 .75
172 Jack McDowell 1.50 .45
173 Junior Felix 1.50 .45
174 Jimmy Key 2.50 .75
175 George Bell 1.50 .45
176 Mike Stanton 1.50 .45
177 Len Dykstra 2.50 .75
178 Norm Charlton 1.50 .45
179 Eric Anthony 1.50 .45
180 Rob Dibble 2.50 .75
181 Otis Nixon 1.50 .45
182 Randy Myers 1.50 .45
183 Tim Raines 2.50 .75
184 Orel Hershiser 2.50 .75
185 Andy Van Slyke 2.50 .75
186 Mike Lansing RC 2.50 .75
187 Ray Lankford 1.50 .45
188 Mike Morgan 1.50 .45
189 Moises Alou 2.50 .75
190 Edgar Martinez 4.00 1.20
191 John Franco 2.50 .75
192 Robin Yount 10.00 3.00
193 Bob Tewksbury 1.50 .45
194 Jay Bell 2.50 .75
195 Luis Gonzalez 2.50 .75
196 Dave Fleming 1.50 .45
197 Mike Greenwell 1.50 .45
198 David Nied 1.50 .45
199 Mike Piazza 15.00 4.50

1993 Finest Refractors

Randomly inserted in packs at a rate of one in 18, these 199 standard-size cards are identical to the regular-issue 1993 Topps Finest except that their fronts have been laminated with a plastic diffraction grating that gives the card a colorful 3-D appearance. Because of the known production numbers, these cards are believed to have a print run of 241 of each card. It is believed that there might be short printed cards in this set. Topps, however, has never publicly released any verification of shortprinted singles, but some of the singles are accepted as being tough to find due to poor regional distribution and hoarding. Due to their high value, these cards are extremely condition sensitive, with much attention paid to centering and minor scratches on the card fronts.

Nm-Mt Ex-Mt
COMMON CARD(1-199) 1.00 .45
28 Ozzie Smith 150.00 45.00
41 Glenn Davis* 250.00 75.00
47 Ivan Rodriguez * 200.00 60.00
63 George Brett 300.00 90.00
77 Tony Gwynn 200.00 60.00
79 Sammy Sosa * 300.00 90.00
81 Felix Jose* 200.00 60.00
85 Greg Maddux AS 250.00 75.00
88 Roberto Alomar AS 150.00 45.00
91 Bo Jackson AS 150.00 45.00
92 Mark McGwire AS 500.00 150.00
96 Cal Ripken AS 800.00 240.00
98 Don Mattingly AS 300.00 90.00
99 Jose Canseco AS ! 150.00 45.00
102 Frank Thomas AS 200.00 60.00
103 Barry Bonds AS 500.00 150.00
104 Roger Clemens AS 250.00 75.00
105 Ryne Sandberg AS 300.00 90.00
107 Nolan Ryan AS ! 800.00 240.00
108 Will Clark AS 150.00 45.00
110 Ken Griffey Jr. AS ! 400.00 120.00
112 Kirby Puckett AS 150.00 45.00
114 Barry Larkin AS 150.00 45.00
116 Juan Gonzalez AS * 400.00 120.00
122 Eddie Murray UER 150.00 45.00
122 career strikeouts
should be 1224
154 Randy Johnson 150.00 45.00
157 Mike Mussina 150.00 45.00
192 Robin Yount 150.00 45.00
199 Mike Piazza 250.00 75.00

1993 Finest Jumbos

These oversized (approximately 4" by 6") cards were inserted one per sealed box of 1993 Topps Finest packs and feature reproductions of 33 players from that set's All-Star subset (84-116). Some hobby dealers believe because of the known production numbers that slightly less than 1,500 of each of these cards were produced.

Nm-Mt Ex-Mt
COMPLETE SET (33) 500.00 150.00
*STARS: 1X TO 2.5X BASIC CARDS ...

1994 Finest Pre-Production

This 40-card preview standard-size set is identical in design to the basic Finest set. Cards were randomly inserted at a rate of one in 36 in second series Topps packs and three cards were issued with each Topps factory set. The card numbers on back correspond to those of the regular issue. The only way to distinguish between the preview and basic cards is "Pre-Production" in small red letters on back.

Nm-Mt Ex-Mt
COMPLETE SET (40) 150.00 45.00
22P Deion Sanders 12.00 3.60
23P Jose Offerman 5.00 1.50
26P Alex Fernandez 5.00 1.50
31P Steve Finley 8.00 2.40
35P Andres Galarraga 8.00 2.40
43P Reggie Sanders 8.00 2.40
47P Dave Hollins 5.00 1.50
52P David Cone 8.00 2.40
59P Dante Bichette 8.00 2.40
61P Orlando Merced 5.00 1.50
62P Brian McRae 5.00 1.50
66P Mike Mussina 20.00 6.00
76P Mike Stanley 5.00 1.50
78P Mark McGwire 50.00 15.00
79P Pat Listach 5.00 1.50
82P Dwight Gooden 12.00 3.60
84P Phil Plantier 5.00 1.50
90P Jeff Russell 5.00 1.50
92P Gregg Jefferies 5.00 1.50
93P Jose Guzman 5.00 1.50
100P John Smoltz 12.00 3.60
102P Jim Thome 20.00 6.00
121P Moises Alou 8.00 2.40
125P Devon White 5.00 1.50
126P Ivan Rodriguez 20.00 6.00
130P Dave Magadan 5.00 1.50
136P Ozzie Smith 30.00 9.00
141P Chris Hoiles 5.00 1.50
149P Jim Abbott 12.00 3.60
151P Bill Swift 5.00 1.50
154P Edgar Martinez 12.00 3.60
157P J.T. Snow 8.00 2.40
159P Alan Trammell 12.00 3.60
163P Roberto Kelly 5.00 1.50
166P Scott Erickson 5.00 1.50
168P Scott Cooper 5.00 1.50
169P Rod Beck 5.00 1.50
177P Dean Palmer 8.00 2.40
182P Todd Van Poppel 5.00 1.50
185P Paul Sorrento 5.00 1.50

1994 Finest

The 1994 Topps Finest baseball set consists of two series of 220 cards each, for a total of 440 standard-size cards. Each series includes 40 special design Finest cards: 20 top 1993 rookies (1-20), 20 top 1994 rookies (421-440) and 40 top veterans (201-240). It's believed that these subset cards are in slightly shorter supply than the basic issue cards, but the manufacturer has never confirmed this. These glossy and metallic cards have a color photo on front with green and gold borders. A color photo on back is accompanied by statistics and a "Finest Moment" note. Some series 2 packs contained either one or two series 1 cards. The only notable Rookie Card is Chan Ho Park.

Nm-Mt Ex-Mt
COMPLETE SET (440) 120.00 36.00
COMP. SERIES 1 (220) 60.00 18.00
COMP. SERIES 2 (220) 60.00 18.00
1 Mike Piazza FIN 6.00 1.80
2 Kevin Stocker FIN .75 .23
3 Greg McMichael FIN .75 .23
4 Jeff Conine FIN 1.25 .35
5 Rene Arocha FIN .75 .23
6 Aaron Sele FIN .75 .23
7 Brent Gates FIN .75 .23
8 Chuck Carr FIN .75 .23
9 Kirk Rueter FIN 1.25 .35
10 Mike Lansing FIN .75 .23
11 Al Martin FIN .75 .23
12 Jason Bere FIN .75 .23
13 Troy Neel FIN .75 .23
14 Armando Reynoso FIN .75 .23
15 Jeromy Burnitz FIN 1.25 .35
16 Rich Amaral FIN .75 .23
17 David McCarty FIN .75 .23
18 Tim Salmon FIN 2.00 .60
19 Steve Cooke FIN .75 .23
20 Wil Cordero FIN .75 .23
21 Kevin Tapani .75 .23
22 Deion Sanders 2.00 .60
23 Jose Offerman .75 .23

24 Mark Langston .75 .23
25 Ken Hill .75 .23
26 Alex Fernandez .75 .23
27 Jeff Blauser .75 .23
28 Royce Clayton .75 .23
29 Brad Ausmus .75 .23
30 Ryan Bowen .75 .23
31 Steve Finley 1.25 .35
32 Charlie Hayes .75 .23
33 Jeff Kent 1.25 .35
34 Mike Henneman .75 .23
35 Andres Galarraga 1.25 .35
36 Wayne Kirby .75 .23
37 Joe Oliver .75 .23
38 Terry Steinbach .75 .23
39 Ryan Thompson .75 .23
40 Luis Alicea .75 .23
41 Randy Velarde .75 .23
42 Bob Tewksbury .75 .23
43 Reggie Sanders 1.25 .35
44 Brian Williams .75 .23
45 Joe Orsulak .75 .23
46 Jose Lind .75 .23
47 Dave Hollins .75 .23
48 Graeme Lloyd .75 .23
49 Jim Gott .75 .23
50 Andre Dawson 1.25 .35
51 Steve Buechele .75 .23
52 David Cone 1.25 .35
53 Ricky Gutierrez .75 .23
54 Lance Johnson .75 .23
55 Tino Martinez 2.00 .60
56 Phil Hiatt .75 .23
57 Carlos Garcia .75 .23
58 Danny Darwin .75 .23
59 Dante Bichette 1.25 .35
60 Scott Kamieniecki .75 .23
61 Orlando Merced .75 .23
62 Brian McRae .75 .23
63 Pat Kelly .75 .23
64 Tom Henke .75 .23
65 Jeff King .75 .23
66 Mike Mussina 3.00 .90
67 Tim Pugh .75 .23
68 Robby Thompson .75 .23
69 Paul O'Neill 2.00 .60
70 Hal Morris .75 .23
71 Ron Karkovice .75 .23
72 Joe Girardi .75 .23
73 Eduardo Perez .75 .23
74 Raul Mondesi 1.25 .35
75 Mike Gallego .75 .23
76 Mike Stanley .75 .23
77 Kevin Roberson .75 .23
78 Mark McGwire 8.00 2.40
79 Pat Listach .75 .23
80 Eric Davis 1.25 .35
81 Mike Bordick .75 .23
82 Dwight Gooden 2.00 .60
83 Mike Moore .75 .23
84 Phil Plantier .75 .23
85 Darren Lewis .75 .23
86 Rick Wilkins .75 .23
87 Darryl Strawberry 2.00 .60
88 Rob Dibble 1.25 .35
89 Greg Vaughn 1.25 .35
90 Jeff Russell .75 .23
91 Mark Lewis .75 .23
92 Gregg Jefferies .75 .23
93 Jose Guzman .75 .23
94 Kenny Rogers 1.25 .35
95 Mark Lemke .75 .23
96 Mike Morgan .75 .23
97 Andujar Cedeno .75 .23
98 Orel Hershiser 1.25 .35
99 Greg Swindell .75 .23
100 John Smoltz 2.00 .60
101 Pedro A.Martinez RC .75 .23
102 Jim Thome 3.00 .90
103 David Segui .75 .23
104 Charles Nagy .75 .23
105 Shane Mack .75 .23
106 John Jaha .75 .23
107 Tom Candiotti .75 .23
108 David Wells 1.25 .35
109 Bobby Jones .75 .23
110 Bob Hamelin .75 .23
111 Bernard Gilkey .75 .23
112 Chili Davis 1.25 .35
113 Todd Stottlemyre .75 .23
114 Derek Bell .75 .23
115 Mark McLemore .75 .23
116 Mark Whiten .75 .23
117 Mike Devereaux .75 .23
118 Terry Pendleton 1.25 .35
119 Pat Meares .75 .23
120 Pete Harnisch .75 .23
121 Moises Alou 1.25 .35
122 Jay Buhner 1.25 .35
123 Wes Chamberlain .75 .23
124 Mike Perez .75 .23
125 Devon White .75 .23
126 Ivan Rodriguez 3.00 .90
127 Don Slaught .75 .23
128 John Valentin .75 .23
129 Jaime Navarro .75 .23
130 Dave Magadan .75 .23
131 Brady Anderson 1.25 .35
132 Juan Guzman .75 .23
133 John Wetteland 1.25 .35
134 Dave Stewart 1.25 .35
135 Scott Servais .75 .23
136 Ozzie Smith 5.00 1.50
137 Darrin Fletcher .75 .23
138 Jose Mesa .75 .23
139 Wilson Alvarez .75 .23
140 Pete Incaviglia .75 .23
141 Chris Hoiles .75 .23
142 Darryl Hamilton .75 .23
143 Chuck Finley 1.25 .35
144 Archi Cianfrocco .75 .23
145 Bill Wegman .75 .23
146 Joey Cora .75 .23
147 Darrell Whitmore .75 .23
148 David Hulse .75 .23
149 Jim Abbott 2.00 .60
150 Curt Schilling 2.00 .60
151 Bill Swift .75 .23
152 Tommy Greene .75 .23
153 Roberto Mejia .75 .23
154 Edgar Martinez 2.00 .60
155 Roger Pavlik .75 .23
156 Randy Tomlin .75 .23
157 J.T. Snow 1.25 .35
158 Bob Welch .75 .23
159 Alan Trammell 2.00 .60
160 Ed Sprague .75 .23
161 Ben McDonald .75 .23
162 Derrick May .75 .23
163 Roberto Kelly .75 .23
164 Bryan Harvey .75 .23
165 Ron Gant 1.25 .35
166 Scott Erickson .75 .23
167 Anthony Young .75 .23
168 Scott Cooper .75 .23
169 Rod Beck .75 .23
170 John Franco 1.25 .35
171 Gary DiSarcina .75 .23
172 Dave Fleming .75 .23
173 Wade Boggs 2.00 .60
174 Kevin Appier 1.25 .35
175 Jose Bautista .75 .23
176 Wally Joyner 1.25 .35
177 Dean Palmer 1.25 .35
178 Tony Phillips .75 .23
179 John Smiley .75 .23
180 Charlie Hough 1.25 .35
181 Scott Fletcher .75 .23
182 Todd Van Poppel .75 .23
183 Mike Blowers .75 .23
184 Willie McGee 1.25 .35
185 Paul Sorrento .75 .23
186 Eric Young .75 .23
187 Bret Barberie .75 .23
188 Manuel Lee .75 .23
189 Jeff Branson .75 .23
190 Jim Deshaies .75 .23
191 Ken Caminiti 1.25 .35
192 Tim Raines 1.25 .35
193 Joe Grahe .75 .23
194 Hipolito Pichardo .75 .23
195 Denny Neagle 1.25 .35
196 Jeff Gardner .75 .23
197 Mike Benjamin .75 .23
198 Milt Thompson .75 .23
199 Bruce Ruffin .75 .23
200 Chris Hammond UER .75 .23
(Back of card has Mariners; should be Marlins)
201 Tony Gwynn FIN 4.00 1.20
202 Robin Ventura FIN 1.25 .35
203 Frank Thomas FIN 3.00 .90
204 Kirby Puckett FIN 3.00 .90
205 Roberto Alomar FIN 3.00 .90
206 Dennis Eckersley FIN 1.25 .35
207 Joe Carter FIN 1.25 .35
208 Albert Belle FIN 1.25 .35
209 Greg Maddux FIN 5.00 1.50
210 Ryne Sandberg FIN 5.00 1.50
211 Juan Gonzalez FIN 3.00 .90
212 Jeff Bagwell FIN 2.00 .60
213 Randy Johnson FIN 3.00 .90
214 Matt Williams FIN 1.25 .35
215 Dave Winfield FIN 1.25 .35
216 Larry Walker FIN 2.00 .60
217 Roger Clemens FIN 6.00 1.80
218 Kenny Lofton FIN 1.25 .35
219 Cecil Fielder FIN 1.25 .35
220 Darren Daulton FIN 1.25 .35
221 John Olerud FIN 1.25 .35
222 Jose Canseco FIN 3.00 .90
223 Rickey Henderson FIN 3.00 .90
224 Fred McGriff FIN 2.00 .60
225 Gary Sheffield FIN 1.25 .35
226 Jack McDowell FIN .75 .23
227 Rafael Palmeiro FIN 2.00 .60
228 Travis Fryman FIN 1.25 .35
229 Marquis Grissom FIN .75 .23
230 Barry Bonds FIN 8.00 2.40
231 Carlos Baerga FIN .75 .23
232 Ken Griffey Jr. FIN 5.00 1.50
233 David Justice FIN 1.25 .35
234 Bobby Bonilla FIN 1.25 .35
235 Cal Ripken FIN 10.00 3.00
236 Sammy Sosa FIN 5.00 1.50
237 Len Dykstra FIN 1.25 .35
238 Will Clark FIN 3.00 .90
239 Paul Molitor FIN 2.00 .60
240 Barry Larkin FIN 3.00 .90
241 Bo Jackson 3.00 .90
242 Mitch Williams .75 .23
243 Ron Darling .75 .23
244 Darryl Kile 1.25 .35
245 Geronimo Berroa .75 .23
246 Gregg Olson .75 .23
247 Brian Harper .75 .23
248 Rheal Cormier .75 .23
249 Rey Sanchez .75 .23
250 Jeff Fassero .75 .23
251 Sandy Alomar Jr. 1.25 .35
252 Chris Bosio .75 .23
253 Andy Stankiewicz .75 .23
254 Harold Baines 1.25 .35
255 Andy Ashby .75 .23
256 Tyler Green .75 .23
257 Kevin Brown 1.25 .35
258 Mo Vaughn 1.25 .35
259 Mike Harkey .75 .23
260 Dave Henderson .75 .23
261 Kent Hrbek 1.25 .35
262 Darrin Jackson .75 .23
263 Bob Wickman .75 .23
264 Spike Owen .75 .23
265 Todd Jones .75 .23
266 Pat Borders .75 .23
267 Tom Glavine 2.00 .60
268 Dave Nilsson .75 .23
269 Rich Batchelor .75 .23
270 Delino DeShields .75 .23
271 Felix Fermin .75 .23
272 Orestes Destrade .75 .23
273 Mickey Morandini .75 .23
274 Otis Nixon .75 .23
275 Ellis Burks 1.25 .35
276 Greg Gagne .75 .23
277 John Doherty .75 .23
278 Julio Franco 1.25 .35
279 Bernie Williams 2.00 .60
280 Rick Aguilera .75 .23
281 Mickey Tettleton .75 .23
282 David Nied .75 .23
283 Johnny Ruffin .75 .23
284 Dan Wilson .75 .23
285 Omar Vizquel 1.25 .35
286 Willie Banks .75 .23
287 Erik Pappas .75 .23
288 Cal Eldred .75 .23
289 Bobby Witt .75 .23
290 Luis Gonzalez 1.25 .35
291 Greg Pirkl .75 .23
292 Alex Cole .75 .23
293 Ricky Bones .75 .23
294 Denis Boucher .75 .23
295 John Burkett .75 .23
296 Steve Trachsel .75 .23
297 Ricky Jordan .75 .23
298 Mark Dewey .75 .23
299 Jimmy Key 1.25 .35
300 Mike Macfarlane .75 .23
301 Tim Belcher .75 .23
302 Carlos Reyes .75 .23
303 Greg A. Harris .75 .23
304 Brian Anderson RC 1.25 .35
305 Terry Mulholland .75 .23
306 Felix Jose .75 .23
307 Darren Holmes .75 .23
308 Jose Rijo .75 .23
309 Paul Wagner .75 .23
310 Bob Scanlan .75 .23
311 Mike Jackson .75 .23
312 Jose Vizcaino .75 .23
313 Rob Butler .75 .23
314 Kevin Seitzer .75 .23
315 Geronimo Pena .75 .23
316 Hector Carrasco .75 .23
317 Eddie Murray 3.00 .90
318 Roger Salkeld .75 .23
319 Todd Hundley .75 .23
320 Danny Jackson .75 .23
321 Kevin Young .75 .23
322 Mike Greenwell .75 .23
323 Kevin Mitchell .75 .23
324 Chuck Knoblauch 1.25 .35
325 Danny Tartabull .75 .23
326 Vince Coleman .75 .23
327 Marvin Freeman .75 .23
328 Andy Benes .75 .23
329 Mike Kelly .75 .23
330 Karl Rhodes .75 .23
331 Allen Watson .75 .23
332 Damion Easley .75 .23
333 Reggie Jefferson .75 .23
334 Kevin McReynolds .75 .23
335 Arthur Rhodes .75 .23
336 Brian R. Hunter .75 .23
337 Tom Browning .75 .23
338 Pedro Munoz .75 .23
339 Billy Ripken .75 .23
340 Gene Harris .75 .23
341 Fernando Vina 2.00 .60
342 Sean Berry .75 .23
343 Pedro Astacio .75 .23
344 B.J. Surhoff 1.25 .35
345 Doug Drabek .75 .23
346 Jody Reed .75 .23
347 Ray Lankford .75 .23
348 Steve Farr .75 .23
349 Eric Anthony .75 .23
350 Pete Smith .75 .23
351 Lee Smith 1.25 .35
352 Mariano Duncan .75 .23
353 Doug Strange .75 .23
354 Tim Bogar .75 .23
355 Dave Weathers .75 .23
356 Eric Karros 1.25 .35
357 Randy Myers .75 .23
358 Chad Curtis .75 .23
359 Steve Avery .75 .23
360 Brian Jordan 1.25 .35
361 Tim Wallach .75 .23
362 Pedro Martinez 3.00 .90
363 Bip Roberts .75 .23
364 Lou Whitaker 1.25 .35
365 Luis Polonia .75 .23
366 Benito Santiago 1.25 .35
367 Brett Butler 1.25 .35
368 Shawon Dunston .75 .23
369 Kelly Stinnett RC .75 .23
370 Chris Turner .75 .23
371 Ruben Sierra .75 .23
372 Greg A. Harris .75 .23
373 Xavier Hernandez .75 .23
374 Howard Johnson .75 .23
375 Duane Ward .75 .23
376 Roberto Hernandez .75 .23
377 Scott Leius .75 .23
378 Dave Valle .75 .23
379 Sid Fernandez .75 .23
380 Doug Jones .75 .23
381 Zane Smith .75 .23
382 Craig Biggio 2.00 .60
383 Rick White RC .75 .23
384 Tom Pagnozzi .75 .23
385 Chris James .75 .23
386 Bret Boone 1.25 .35
387 Jeff Montgomery .75 .23
388 Chad Kreuter .75 .23
389 Greg Hibbard .75 .23
390 Mark Grace 2.00 .60
391 Phil Leftwich RC .75 .23
392 Don Mattingly 8.00 2.40
393 Ozzie Guillen .75 .23
394 Gary Gaetti 1.25 .35
395 Erik Hanson .75 .23
396 Scott Brosius 1.25 .35
397 Tom Gordon .75 .23
398 Bill Gullickson .75 .23
399 Matt Mieske .75 .23
400 Pat Hentgen .75 .23
401 Walt Weiss .75 .23
402 Greg Blosser .75 .23
403 Stan Javier .75 .23
404 Doug Henry .75 .23
405 Ramon Martinez .75 .23
406 Frank Viola 1.25 .35
407 Mike Hampton 1.25 .35
408 Andy Van Slyke 1.25 .35
409 Bobby Ayala .75 .23
410 Todd Zeile .75 .23
411 Jay Bell 1.25 .35
412 Dennis Martinez 1.25 .35
413 Mark Portugal .75 .23
414 Bobby Munoz .75 .23
415 Kirt Manwaring .75 .23
416 John Kruk 1.25 .35
417 Trevor Hoffman 1.25 .35
418 Chris Sabo .75 .23
419 Bret Saberhagen 1.25 .35
420 Chris Nabholz .75 .23
421 James Mouton FIN .75 .23
422 Tony Tarasco FIN .75 .23
423 Carlos Delgado FIN 2.00 .60
424 Rondell White FIN 1.25 .35
425 Javier Lopez FIN 1.25 .35
426 Chan Ho Park FIN RC 5.00 1.50
427 Cliff Floyd FIN 1.25 .35
428 Dave Staton FIN .75 .23
429 J.R. Phillips FIN .75 .23
430 Manny Ramirez FIN 2.00 .60
431 Kurt Abbott FIN RC 1.25 .35
432 Melvin Nieves FIN .75 .23
433 Alex Gonzalez FIN .75 .23
434 Rick Helling FIN .75 .23
435 Danny Bautista FIN .75 .23
436 Matt Walbeck FIN .75 .23
437 Ryan Klesko FIN 1.25 .35
438 Steve Karsay FIN .75 .23
439 Salomon Torres FIN .75 .23
440 Scott Ruffcorn FIN .75 .23

1994 Finest Refractors

The 1994 Topps Finest Refractors baseball set consists of two series of 220 cards each, for a total of 440 cards. These special cards were inserted at a rate of one in every nine packs. They are identical to the basic Finest card except for a more intense luster and 3-D appearance.

Nm-Mt Ex-Mt
*STARS: 2.5X TO 6X BASIC CARDS ...
*ROOKIES: 1.5X TO 4X BASIC CARDS

1994 Finest Jumbos

Inserted one per Finest box, this 80-card oversized set (3 1/2" by 5") was issued in two series of 40. Each of the 80 cards is identical in design to the special "Finest" cards from the basic Finest set except for the size. The "Finest" subset was designated to showcase top rookies, prospects and veterans. The card numbering is the same as the corresponding basic issue cards. Hence, the first series comprises of cards 1-20 and 201-220. The second series is cards 221-240 and 421-440.

Nm-Mt Ex-Mt
*JUMBOS: 1.25X TO 3X BASIC CARDS

1995 Finest

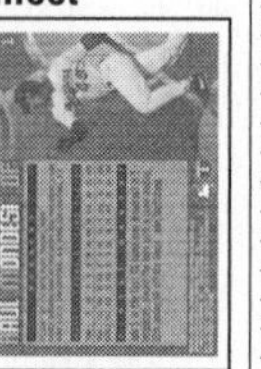

Consisting of 330 standard-size cards, this set (produced by Topps) was issued in series of 220 and 110. A protective film, designed to keep the card from scratching and to maintain original gloss, covers the front. With the Finest logo at the top, a silver baseball diamond design surrounded by green (field) form the background to an action photo. Horizontally designed backs have a photo to the right with statistical information to the left. A Finest Moment, or career highlight, is also included. Rookie Cards in this set include Bobby Higginson and Hideo Nomo.

Nm-Mt Ex-Mt
COMPLETE SET (330) 60.00 18.00
COMP. SERIES 1 (220) 50.00 15.00
COMP. SERIES 2 (110) 15.00 4.50
1 Raul Mondesi 1.00 .30
2 Kurt Abbott .50 .15
3 Chris Gomez .50 .15
4 Manny Ramirez 1.00 .30
5 Rondell White 1.00 .30
6 William VanLandingham .50 .15
7 Jon Lieber .50 .15
8 Ryan Klesko 1.00 .30
9 John Hudek .50 .15
10 Joey Hamilton .50 .15
11 Bob Hamelin .50 .15
12 Brian Anderson .50 .15
13 Mike Lieberthal 1.00 .30
14 Rico Brogna .50 .15
15 Rusty Greer 1.00 .30
16 Carlos Delgado 1.00 .30
17 Jim Edmonds 1.00 .30
18 Steve Trachsel .50 .15
19 Matt Walbeck .50 .15
20 Armando Benitez 1.00 .30
21 Steve Karsay .50 .15
22 Jose Oliva .50 .15
23 Cliff Floyd 1.00 .30
24 Kevin Foster .50 .15
25 Javier Lopez 1.00 .30
26 Jose Valentin .50 .15
27 James Mouton .50 .15
28 Hector Carrasco .50 .15
29 Orlando Miller .50 .15
30 Garret Anderson 1.00 .30
31 Marvin Freeman .50 .15
32 Brett Butler 1.00 .30
33 Roberto Kelly .50 .15
34 Rod Beck .50 .15
35 Jose Rijo .50 .15
36 Edgar Martinez 1.50 .45
37 Jim Thome 2.50 .75
38 Rick Wilkins .50 .15
39 Wally Joyner 1.00 .30
40 Wil Cordero .50 .15
41 Tommy Greene .50 .15
42 Travis Fryman 1.00 .30
43 Don Slaught .50 .15
44 Brady Anderson 1.00 .30
45 Matt Williams 1.00 .30
46 Rene Arocha .50 .15
47 Rickey Henderson 2.50 .75
48 Mike Mussina 2.50 .75
49 Greg McMichael .50 .15
50 Jody Reed .50 .15
51 Tino Martinez 1.50 .45
52 Dave Clark .50 .15
53 John Valentin .50 .15
54 Bret Boone 1.00 .30
55 Walt Weiss .50 .15
56 Kenny Lofton 1.00 .30
57 Scott Leius .50 .15
58 Eric Karros 1.00 .30
59 John Olerud 1.00 .30
60 Chris Hoiles .50 .15
61 Sandy Alomar Jr. .50 .15
62 Tim Wallach .50 .15
63 Cal Eldred .50 .15
64 Tom Glavine 1.50 .45
65 Mark Grace 1.50 .45
66 Rey Sanchez .50 .15
67 Bobby Ayala .50 .15
68 Dante Bichette 1.00 .30
69 Andres Galarraga 1.00 .30
70 Chuck Carr .50 .15
71 Bobby Witt .50 .15
72 Steve Avery .50 .15
73 Bobby Jones .50 .15
74 Delino DeShields .50 .15
75 Kevin Tapani .50 .15
76 Randy Johnson 2.50 .75
77 David Nied .50 .15
78 Pat Hentgen .50 .15
79 Tim Salmon 1.50 .45
80 Todd Zeile .50 .15
81 John Wetteland 1.00 .30
82 Albert Belle 1.00 .30
83 Ben McDonald .50 .15
84 Bobby Munoz .50 .15
85 Bip Roberts .50 .15
86 Mo Vaughn 1.00 .30
87 Chuck Finley 1.00 .30
88 Chuck Knoblauch 1.00 .30
89 Frank Thomas 2.50 .75
90 Danny Tartabull .50 .15
91 Dean Palmer 1.00 .30
92 Len Dykstra 1.00 .30
93 J.R. Phillips .50 .15
94 Tom Candiotti .50 .15
95 Marquis Grissom .50 .15
96 Barry Larkin 2.50 .75
97 Bryan Harvey .50 .15
98 David Justice 1.00 .30
99 David Cone 1.00 .30
100 Wade Boggs 1.50 .45
101 Jason Bere .50 .15
102 Hal Morris .50 .15
103 Fred McGriff 1.50 .45
104 Bobby Bonilla 1.00 .30
105 Jay Buhner 1.00 .30
106 Allen Watson .50 .15
107 Mickey Tettleton .50 .15
108 Kevin Appier 1.00 .30
109 Ivan Rodriguez 2.50 .75
110 Carlos Garcia .50 .15
111 Andy Benes .50 .15
112 Eddie Murray 2.50 .75
113 Mike Piazza 4.00 1.20
114 Greg Vaughn 1.00 .30
115 Paul Molitor 1.50 .45
116 Terry Steinbach .50 .15
117 Jeff Bagwell 1.50 .45
118 Ken Griffey Jr. 4.00 1.20
119 Gary Sheffield 1.00 .30
120 Cal Ripken 8.00 2.40
121 Jeff Kent 1.00 .30
122 Jay Bell 1.00 .30
123 Will Clark 2.50 .75
124 Cecil Fielder 1.00 .30
125 Alex Fernandez .50 .15
126 Don Mattingly 6.00 1.80
127 Reggie Sanders 1.00 .30
128 Moises Alou 1.00 .30
129 Craig Biggio 1.50 .45
130 Eddie Williams .50 .15
131 John Franco 1.00 .30
132 John Kruk 1.00 .30
133 Jeff King .50 .15
134 Royce Clayton .50 .15
135 Doug Drabek .50 .15
136 Ray Lankford .50 .15
137 Roberto Alomar 2.50 .75
138 Todd Hundley .50 .15
139 Alex Cole .50 .15
140 Shawon Dunston .50 .15
141 John Roper .50 .15
142 Mark Langston .50 .15
143 Tom Pagnozzi .50 .15
144 Wilson Alvarez .50 .15
145 Scott Cooper .50 .15
146 Kevin Mitchell .50 .15
147 Mark Whiten .50 .15
148 Jeff Conine 1.00 .30
149 Chili Davis 1.00 .30
150 Luis Gonzalez 1.00 .30
151 Juan Guzman .50 .15
152 Mike Greenwell .50 .15
153 Mike Henneman .50 .15
154 Rick Aguilera .50 .15
155 Dennis Eckersley 1.00 .30
156 Darrin Fletcher .50 .15
157 Darren Lewis .50 .15
158 Juan Gonzalez 2.50 .75
159 Dave Hollins .50 .15
160 Jimmy Key 1.00 .30
161 Roberto Hernandez .50 .15
162 Randy Myers .50 .15
163 Joe Carter 1.00 .30
164 Darren Daulton 1.00 .30
165 Mike Macfarlane .50 .15
166 Bret Saberhagen 1.00 .30
167 Kirby Puckett 2.50 .75
168 Lance Johnson .50 .15
169 Mark McGwire 6.00 1.80
170 Jose Canseco 2.50 .75
171 Mike Stanley .50 .15
172 Lee Smith 1.00 .30
173 Robin Ventura 1.00 .30
174 Greg Gagne .50 .15
175 Brian McRae .50 .15

176 Mike Bordick .50 .15
177 Rafael Palmeiro 1.50 .45
178 Kenny Rogers 1.00 .30
179 Chad Curtis .50 .15
180 Devon White 1.00 .30
181 Paul O'Neill 1.50 .45
182 Ken Caminiti 1.00 .30
183 Dave Nilsson .50 .15
184 Tim Naehring .50 .15
185 Roger Clemens 5.00 1.50
186 Otis Nixon .50 .15
187 Tim Raines 1.00 .30
188 Denny Martinez 1.00 .30
189 Pedro Martinez 2.50 .75
190 Jim Abbott 1.50 .45
191 Ryan Thompson .50 .15
192 Barry Bonds 6.00 1.80
193 Joe Girardi .50 .15
194 Steve Finley 1.00 .30
195 John Jaha .50 .15
196 Tony Gwynn 3.00 .90
197 Sammy Sosa 4.00 1.20
198 John Burkett .50 .15
199 Carlos Baerga .50 .15
200 Ramon Martinez .50 .15
201 Aaron Sele .50 .15
202 Eduardo Perez .50 .15
203 Alan Trammell 1.50 .45
204 Orlando Merced .50 .15
205 Deion Sanders 1.50 .45
206 Robb Nen 1.00 .30
207 Jack McDowell .50 .15
208 Ruben Sierra .50 .15
209 Bernie Williams 1.50 .45
210 Kevin Seitzer .50 .15
211 Charles Nagy .50 .15
212 Tony Phillips .50 .15
213 Greg Maddux 4.00 1.20
214 Jeff Montgomery .50 .15
215 Larry Walker 1.50 .45
216 Andy Van Slyke 1.00 .30
217 Ozzie Smith 4.00 1.20
218 Geronimo Pena .50 .15
219 Gregg Jefferies .50 .15
220 Lou Whitaker 1.00 .30
221 Chipper Jones 2.50 .75
222 Benji Gil .50 .15
223 Tony Phillips .50 .15
224 Trevor Wilson .50 .15
225 Tony Tarasco .50 .15
226 Roberto Petagine .50 .15
227 Mike Macfarlane .50 .15
228 Hideo Nomo RCUER 8.00 2.40
(In 3rd line agianst)
229 Mark McLemore .50 .15
230 Ron Gant 1.00 .30
231 Andujar Cedeno .50 .15
232 Mike Mimbs RC .50 .15
233 Jim Abbott 1.50 .45
234 Ricky Bones .50 .15
235 Marty Cordova .50 .15
236 Mark Johnson RC 1.00 .30
237 Marquis Grissom .50 .15
238 Tom Henke .50 .15
239 Terry Pendleton 1.00 .30
240 John Wetteland 1.00 .30
241 Lee Smith 1.00 .30
242 Jaime Navarro .50 .15
243 Luis Alicea .50 .15
244 Scott Cooper .50 .15
245 Gary Gaetti 1.00 .30
246 Edgardo Alfonzo UER 1.00 .30
(Incomplete career BA)
247 Brad Clontz .50 .15
248 Dave Mlicki .50 .15
249 Dave Winfield 1.00 .30
250 Mark Grudzielanek RC 1.50 .45
251 Alex Gonzalez .50 .15
252 Kevin Brown 1.00 .30
253 Esteban Loaiza 1.00 .30
254 Vaughn Eshelman .50 .15
255 Bill Swift .50 .15
256 Brian McRae .50 .15
257 Bobby Higginson RC 2.50 .75
258 Jack McDowell .50 .15
259 Scott Stahoviak .50 .15
260 Jon Nunnally .50 .15
261 Charlie Hayes .50 .15
262 Jacob Brumfield .50 .15
263 Chad Curtis .50 .15
264 Heathcliff Slocumb .50 .15
265 Mark Whiten .50 .15
266 Mickey Tettleton .50 .15
267 Jose Mesa .50 .15
268 Doug Jones .50 .15
269 Trevor Hoffman 1.00 .30
270 Paul Sorrento .50 .15
271 Shane Andrews .50 .15
272 Brett Butler 1.00 .30
273 Curtis Goodwin .50 .15
274 Larry Walker 1.50 .45
275 Phil Plantier .50 .15
276 Ken Hill .50 .15
277 Vinny Castilla UER 1.00 .30
Rockies spelled Rockie
278 Billy Ashley .50 .15
279 Derek Jeter 6.00 1.80
280 Bob Tewksbury .50 .15
281 Jose Offerman .50 .15
282 Glenallen Hill .50 .15
283 Tony Fernandez .50 .15
284 Mike Devereaux .50 .15
285 John Burkett .50 .15
286 Geronimo Berroa .50 .15
287 Quilvio Veras .50 .15
288 Jason Bates .50 .15
289 Lee Tinsley .50 .15
290 Derek Bell .50 .15
291 Jeff Fassero .50 .15
292 Ray Durham 1.00 .30
293 Chad Ogea .50 .15
294 Bill Pulsipher .50 .15
295 Phil Nevin 1.00 .30
296 Carlos Perez RC 1.00 .30
297 Roberto Kelly .50 .15
298 Tim Wakefield 1.00 .30
299 Jeff Manto .50 .15
300 Brian Hunter .50 .15
301 C.J. Nitkowski .50 .15
302 Dustin Hermanson .50 .15
303 John Mabry .50 .15
304 Orel Hershiser 1.00 .30
305 Ron Villone .50 .15
306 Sean Bergman .50 .15
307 Tom Goodwin .50 .15
308 Al Reyes .50 .15
309 Todd Stottlemyre .50 .15
310 Rich Becker .50 .15
311 Joey Cora .50 .15
312 Ed Sprague .50 .15
313 John Smoltz UER 1.50 .45
(3rd line; from spelled as form)
314 Frank Castillo .50 .15
315 Chris Hammond .50 .15
316 Ismael Valdes .50 .15
317 Pete Harnisch .50 .15
318 Bernard Gilkey .50 .15
319 John Kruk 1.00 .30
320 Marc Newfield .50 .15
321 Brian Johnson .50 .15
322 Mark Portugal .50 .15
323 David Hulse .50 .15
324 Luis Ortiz UER .50 .15
(Below spelled beloe)
325 Mike Benjamin .50 .15
326 Brian Jordan 1.00 .30
327 Shawn Green 1.00 .30
328 Joe Oliver .50 .15
329 Felipe Lira .50 .15
330 Andre Dawson 1.00 .30

1995 Finest Refractors

This set is a parallel to the basic Finest set, including the use of protective coating, the difference can be found in the refractive sheen. The cards were inserted at a rate of one in 12 packs.

Nm-Mt Ex-Mt
*STARS: 4X TO 10X BASIC CARDS
*ROOKIES: 3X TO 8X BASIC CARDS

1995 Finest Flame Throwers

Randomly inserted in first series packs at a rate of 1:48, this nine-card set showcases strikeout leaders who bring on the heat. With a protective coating, a player photo is superimposed over a fiery orange background.

	Nm-Mt	Ex-Mt
COMPLETE SET (9)	40.00	12.00
FT1 Jason Bere	3.00	.90
FT2 Roger Clemens	30.00	9.00
FT3 Juan Guzman	3.00	.90
FT4 John Hudek	3.00	.90
FT5 Randy Johnson	15.00	4.50
FT6 Pedro Martinez	15.00	4.50
FT7 Jose Rijo	3.00	.90
FT8 Bret Saberhagen	6.00	1.80
FT9 John Wetteland	6.00	1.80

1995 Finest Power Kings

Randomly inserted in series one packs at a rate of one in 24, Power Kings is an 18-card set highlighting top sluggers. With a protective coating, the fronts feature chromium technology that allows the player photo to be further enhanced as if to jump out from a blue lightning bolt background.

	Nm-Mt	Ex-Mt
COMPLETE SET (18)	150.00	45.00
PK1 Bob Hamelin	2.50	.75
PK2 Raul Mondesi	5.00	1.50
PK3 Ryan Klesko	5.00	1.50
PK4 Carlos Delgado	5.00	1.50
PK5 Manny Ramirez	5.00	1.50
PK6 Mike Piazza	20.00	6.00
PK7 Jeff Bagwell	8.00	2.40
PK8 Mo Vaughn	5.00	1.50
PK9 Frank Thomas	12.00	3.60
PK10 Ken Griffey Jr.	20.00	6.00
PK11 Albert Belle	5.00	1.50
PK12 Sammy Sosa	20.00	6.00
PK13 Dante Bichette	5.00	1.50
PK14 Gary Sheffield	5.00	1.50
PK15 Matt Williams	5.00	1.50
PK16 Fred McGriff	8.00	2.40
PK17 Barry Bonds	30.00	9.00
PK18 Cecil Fielder	5.00	1.50

1995 Finest Bronze

Available exclusively direct from Topps, this six-card set features 1994 league leaders. The fronts feature chromium metallized graphics, mounted on bronze and factory sealed in clear resin. The cards are numbered on the back "X of 6."

	Nm-Mt	Ex-Mt
COMPLETE SET (6)	80.00	24.00
1 Matt Williams	8.00	2.40
2 Tony Gwynn	25.00	7.50
3 Jeff Bagwell	15.00	4.50
4 Ken Griffey Jr.	30.00	9.00
5 Paul O'Neill	5.00	1.50
6 Frank Thomas	15.00	4.50

1996 Finest

The 1996 Finest set (produced by Topps) was issued in two series of 191 cards and 168 cards respectively, for a total of 359 cards. The six-card foil packs originally retailed for $5.00 each. A protective film, designed to keep the card from scratching and to maintain original gloss, covers the front. This product provides collectors with the opportunity to complete a number of sets within sets, each with a different degree of insertion. Each card is numbered twice to indicate the set count and the theme count. Series 1 set covers four distinct themes: Finest Phenoms, Finest Intimidators, Finest Gamers and Finest Sterling. Within the first three themes, some players will be common (bronze trim), some uncommon (silver) and some rare (gold). Finest Sterling consists of star players included within one of the other three themes, but featured with a new design and different photography. The breakdown for the player selection of common, uncommon and rare cards is completely random. There are 110 common, 55 uncommon (1:4 packs) and 25 rare cards (1:24 packs). Series 2 covers four distict themes also with common, uncommon and rare cards seeded at the same ratio. The four themes are: Finest Franchises which features 36 team leaders and bonafide superstars, Finest Additions which features 47 players who have switched teams in '96, Finest Prodigies which features 45 best up-and-coming players, and Finest Sterling with 39 top stars. In addition to the cards' special borders, each card will also have either "common," "uncommon", or "rare" written within the numbering box on the card backs to let collectors know which type of card they hold.

Nm-Mt Ex-Mt
COMP.BRONZE SER.1 (110) 25.00 7.50
COMP.BRONZE SER.2 (110) 25.00 7.50
COMMON BRONZE .50 .15
COMMON GOLD 5.00 1.50
COMMON SILVER 2.50 .75
B5 Roberto Hernandez B .50 .15
B8 Terry Pendleton B .50 .15
B12 Ken Caminiti B .50 .15
B15 Dan Miceli B .50 .15
B16 Chipper Jones B 1.25 .35
B17 John Wetteland B .50 .15
B19 Tim Naehring B .50 .15
B21 Eddie Murray B 1.25 .35
B23 Kevin Appier B .50 .15
B24 Ken Griffey Jr. B 2.00 .60
B26 Brian McRae B .50 .15
B27 Pedro Martinez B 1.25 .35
B28 Brian Jordan B .50 .15
B29 Mike Fetters B .50 .15
B30 Carlos Delgado B .50 .15
B31 Shane Reynolds B .50 .15
B32 Terry Steinbach B .50 .15
B34 Mark Leiter B .50 .15
B36 David Segui B .50 .15
B40 Fred McGriff B .75 .23
B44 Glenallen Hill B .50 .15
B45 Brady Anderson B .50 .15
B47 Jim Thome B 1.25 .35
B48 Frank Thomas B 1.25 .35
B49 Chuck Knoblauch B .50 .15
B50 Len Dykstra B .50 .15
B53 Tom Pagnozzi B .50 .15
B55 Ricky Bones B .50 .15
B56 David Justice B .50 .15
B57 Steve Avery B .50 .15
B58 Robby Thompson B .50 .15
B61 Tony Gwynn B 1.50 .45
B63 Denny Neagle B .50 .15
B67 Robin Ventura B .50 .15
B70 Kevin Seitzer B .50 .15
B71 Ramon Martinez B .50 .15
B75 Brian L.Hunter B .50 .15
B76 Alan Benes B .50 .15
B80 Ozzie Guillen B .50 .15
B82 Benji Gil B .50 .15
B85 Todd Hundley B .50 .15
B87 Pat Hentgen B .50 .15
B89 Chuck Finley B .50 .15
B92 Derek Jeter B 3.00 .90
B93 Paul O'Neill B .75 .23
B94 Darrin Fletcher B .50 .15
B96 Delino DeShields B .50 .15
B97 Tim Salmon B .75 .23
B98 John Olerud B .50 .15
B101 Tim Wakefield B .50 .15
B103 Dave Stevens B .50 .15
B104 Orlando Merced B .50 .15
B106 Jay Bell B .50 .15
B107 John Burkett B .50 .15
B108 Chris Hoiles B .50 .15
B110 Dave Nilsson B .50 .15
B111 Rod Beck B .50 .15
B113 Mike Piazza B 2.00 .60
B114 Mark Langston B .50 .15
B116 Rico Brogna B .50 .15
B118 Tom Goodwin B .50 .15
B119 Bryan Rekar B .50 .15
B120 David Cone B .50 .15
B122 Andy Pettitte B .75 .23
B123 Chili Davis B .50 .15
B124 John Smoltz B .75 .23
B125 H.Slocumb B .50 .15
B126 Dante Bichette B .50 .15
B128 Alex Gonzalez B .50 .15
B129 Jeff Montgomery B .50 .15
B131 Denny Martinez B .50 .15
B132 Mel Rojas B .50 .15
B133 Derek Bell B .50 .15
B134 Trevor Hoffman B .50 .15
B136 Darren Daulton B .50 .15
B137 Pete Schourek B .50 .15
B138 Phil Nevin B .50 .15
B139 Andres Galarraga B .50 .15
B140 Chad Fonville B .50 .15
B144 J.T. Snow B .50 .15
B146 Barry Bonds B 3.00 .90
B147 Orel Hershiser B .50 .15
B148 Quilvio Veras B .50 .15
B149 Will Clark B 1.25 .35
B150 Jose Rijo B .50 .15
B152 Travis Fryman B .50 .15
B154 Alex Fernandez B .50 .15
B155 Wade Boggs B .75 .23
B156 Troy Percival B .50 .15
B157 Moises Alou B .50 .15
B158 Javy Lopez B .50 .15
B159 Jason Giambi B 1.25 .35
B162 Mark McGwire B 3.00 .90
B163 Eric Karros B .50 .15
B166 Mickey Tettleton B .50 .15
B167 Barry Larkin B 1.25 .35
B169 Ruben Sierra B .50 .15
B170 Bill Swift B .50 .15
B172 Chad Curtis B .50 .15
B173 Dean Palmer B .50 .15
B175 Bobby Bonilla B .50 .15
B176 Greg Colbrunn B .50 .15
B177 Jose Mesa B .50 .15
B178 Mike Greenwell B .50 .15
B181 Doug Drabek B .50 .15
B183 Wilson Alvarez B .50 .15
B184 Marty Cordova B .50 .15
B185 Hal Morris B .50 .15
B187 Carlos Garcia B .50 .15
B190 Marquis Grissom B .50 .15
B193 Will Clark B 1.25 .35
B194 Paul Molitor B .75 .23
B195 Kenny Rogers B .50 .15
B196 Reggie Sanders B .50 .15
B199 Raul Mondesi B .50 .15
B200 Lance Johnson B .50 .15
B201 Alvin Morman B .50 .15
B203 Jack McDowell B .50 .15
B204 Randy Myers B .50 .15
B205 Harold Baines B .50 .15
B206 Marty Cordova B .50 .15
B207 Rich Hunter B RC .50 .15
B208 Al Leiter B .50 .15
B209 Greg Gagne B .50 .15
B210 Ben McDonald B .50 .15
B212 Terry Adams B .50 .15
B213 Paul Sorrento B .50 .15
B214 Albert Belle B .50 .15
B215 Mike Blowers B .50 .15
B216 Jim Edmonds B .50 .15
B217 Felipe Crespo B .50 .15
B219 Shawon Dunston B .50 .15
B220 Jimmy Haynes B .50 .15
B221 Jose Canseco B 1.25 .35
B222 Eric Davis B .50 .15
B224 Tim Raines B .50 .15
B225 Tony Phillips B .50 .15
B226 Charlie Hayes B .50 .15
B227 Eric Owens B .50 .15
B228 Roberto Alomar B 1.25 .35
B233 Kenny Lofton B .50 .15
B236 Mark McGwire B 3.00 .90
B237 Jay Buhner B .50 .15
B238 Craig Biggio B .75 .23
B240 Barry Bonds B 3.00 .90
B244 Ron Gant B .50 .15
B245 Paul Wilson B .50 .15
B246 T.Hollandsworth B .50 .15
B247 Todd Zeile B .50 .15
B248 David Justice B .50 .15
B250 Moises Alou B .50 .15
B251 Bob Wolcott B .50 .15
B252 David Wells B .50 .15
B253 Juan Gonzalez B 1.25 .35
B254 Andres Galarraga B .50 .15
B255 Dave Hollins B .50 .15
B257 Sammy Sosa B 2.00 .60
B258 Ivan Rodriguez B 1.25 .35
B259 Bip Roberts B .50 .15
B260 Tino Martinez B .75 .23
B262 Mike Stanley B .50 .15
B264 Butch Huskey B .50 .15
B265 Jeff Conine B .50 .15
B267 Mark Grace B .75 .23
B268 Jason Schmidt B .50 .15
B269 Otis Nixon B .50 .15
B271 Kirby Puckett B 1.25 .35
B273 Andy Benes B .50 .15
B275 Mike Piazza B 2.00 .60
B276 Rey Ordonez B .50 .15
B278 Gary Gaetti B .50 .15
B280 Robin Ventura B .50 .15
B281 Cal Ripken B 4.00 1.20
B282 Carlos Baerga B .50 .15
B283 Roger Cedeno B .50 .15
B285 Terrell Wade B .50 .15
B286 Kevin Brown B .50 .15
B287 Rafael Palmeiro B .75 .23
B288 Mo Vaughn B .50 .15
B292 Bob Tewksbury B .50 .15
B297 T.J. Mathews B .50 .15
B298 Manny Ramirez B .50 .15
B299 Jeff Bagwell B .75 .23
B301 Wade Boggs B .75 .23
B303 Steve Gibralter B .50 .15
B304 B.J. Surhoff B .50 .15
B306 Royce Clayton B .50 .15
B307 Sal Fasano B .50 .15
B309 Gary Sheffield B .50 .15
B310 Ken Hill B .50 .15
B311 Joe Girardi B .50 .15
B312 Matt Lawton B RC .50 .15
B314 Julio Franco B .50 .15
B315 Joe Carter B .50 .15
B316 Brooks Kieschnick B .50 .15
B318 H.Slocumb B .50 .15
B319 Barry Larkin B 1.25 .35
B320 Tony Gwynn B 1.50 .45
B322 Frank Thomas B 1.25 .35
B323 Edgar Martinez B .75 .23
B325 Henry Rodriguez B .50 .15
B326 Marvin Benard B RC .50 .15
B329 Ugueth Urbina B .50 .15
B331 Roger Salkeld B .50 .15
B332 Edgar Renteria B .50 .15
B333 Ryan Klesko B .50 .15
B334 Ray Lankford B .50 .15
B336 Justin Thompson B .50 .15
B339 Mark Clark B .50 .15
B340 Ruben Rivera B .50 .15
B342 Matt Williams B .50 .15
B343 F.Cordova B RC .50 .15
B344 Cecil Fielder B .50 .15
B348 Mark Grudzielanek B .50 .15
B349 Ron Coomer B .50 .15
B351 Rich Aurilia B RC 1.50 .45
B352 Jose Herrera B .50 .15
B356 Tony Clark B .50 .15
B358 Dan Naulty B .50 .15
B359 Checklist B .50 .15
G4 Marty Cordova G 5.00 1.50
G6 Tony Gwynn G 15.00 4.50
G9 Albert Belle G 5.00 1.50
G18 Kirby Puckett G 12.00 3.60
G20 Karim Garcia G 5.00 1.50
G25 Cal Ripken G 40.00 12.00
G33 Hideo Nomo G 12.00 3.60
G39 Ryne Sandberg G 20.00 6.00
G42 Jeff Bagwell G 4.00 1.20
G51 Jason Isringhausen G 5.00 1.50
G64 Mo Vaughn G 5.00 1.50
G66 Dante Bichette G 5.00 1.50
G74 Mark McGwire G 30.00 9.00
G81 Kenny Lofton G 5.00 1.50
G83 Jim Edmonds G 5.00 1.50
G90 Mike Mussina G 12.00 3.60
G100 Jeff Conine G 5.00 1.50
G102 Johnny Damon G 5.00 1.50
G105 Barry Bonds G 30.00 9.00
G117 Jose Canseco G 1.25 .35
G135 Ken Griffey Jr. G 20.00 6.00
G141 Chipper Jones G 12.00 3.60
G145 Greg Maddux G 20.00 6.00
G164 Jay Buhner G 5.00 1.50
G186 Frank Thomas G 12.00 3.60
G191 Checklist G 5.00 1.50
G192 Chipper Jones G 12.00 3.60
G197 Roberto Alomar G 12.00 3.60
G198 Dennis Eckersley G 5.00 1.50
G202 George Arias G 5.00 1.50
G232 Hideo Nomo G 12.00 3.60
G243 Chris Snopek G 5.00 1.50
G249 Tim Salmon G 8.00 2.40
G266 Matt Williams G 5.00 1.50
G270 Randy Johnson G 12.00 3.60
G279 Paul Molitor G 8.00 2.40
G290 Cecil Fielder G 5.00 1.50
G294 L.Hernandez G RC 8.00 2.40
G300 Marty Janzen G RC 5.00 1.50
G308 Ron Gant G 5.00 1.50
G321 Ryan Klesko G 5.00 1.50
G324 Jermaine Dye G 5.00 1.50
G330 Jason Giambi G 12.00 3.60
G335 Edgar Martinez G 8.00 2.40
G338 Rey Ordonez G 5.00 1.50
G347 Sammy Sosa G 20.00 6.00
G354 Juan Gonzalez G 12.00 3.60
G355 Craig Biggio G 8.00 2.40
S1 Greg Maddux S UER 10.00 3.00
95 stats listed as Mariners
S2 Bernie Williams S 4.00 1.20
S3 Ivan Rodriguez S 1.25 .35
S7 Barry Larkin S 6.00 1.80
S10 Ray Lankford S 2.50 .75
S11 Mike Piazza S 10.00 3.00
S13 Larry Walker S 4.00 1.20
S14 Matt Williams S 2.50 .75
S22 Tim Salmon S 4.00 1.20
S35 Edgar Martinez S 4.00 1.20
S37 Gregg Jefferies S 2.50 .75
S38 Bill Pulsipher S 2.50 .75
S41 Shawn Green S 2.50 .75
S43 Jim Abbott S 4.00 1.20
S46 Roger Clemens S 12.00 3.60
S52 Rondell White S 2.50 .75
S54 Dennis Eckersley S 2.50 .75
S59 Hideo Nomo S 6.00 1.80
S60 Gary Sheffield S 2.50 .75
S62 Will Clark S 6.00 1.80
S65 Bret Boone S 2.50 .75
S68 Rafael Palmeiro S 4.00 1.20
S69 Carlos Baerga S 2.50 .75
S72 Tom Glavine S 4.00 1.20
S73 Garret Anderson S 2.50 .75
S77 Randy Johnson S 6.00 1.80
S78 Jeff King S 2.50 .75
S79 Kirby Puckett S 6.00 1.80
S84 Cecil Fielder S 2.50 .75
S86 Reggie Sanders S 2.50 .75
S88 Ryan Klesko S 2.50 .75
S91 John Valentin S 2.50 .75
S95 Manny Ramirez S 2.50 .75
S99 Vinny Castilla S 2.50 .75
S109 Carlos Perez S 2.50 .75
S112 Craig Biggio S 4.00 1.20
S115 Juan Gonzalez S 6.00 1.80
S121 Ray Durham S 2.50 .75
S127 C.J. Nitkowski S 2.50 .75
S130 Raul Mondesi S 2.50 .75
S142 Lee Smith S 2.50 .75
S143 Joe Carter S 2.50 .75
S151 Mo Vaughn S 2.50 .75
S153 Frank Rodriguez S 2.50 .75
S160 Steve Finley S 2.50 .75
S161 Jeff Bagwell S .75 .23
S165 Cal Ripken S 20.00 6.00
S168 Lyle Mouton S 2.50 .75

S171 Sammy Sosa S 10.00 3.00
S174 John Franco S 2.50 .75
S179 Greg Vaughn S 2.50 .75
S180 Mark Wohlers S 2.50 .75
S182 Paul O'Neill S 4.00 1.20
S188 Albert Belle S 2.50 .75
S189 Mark Grace S 4.00 1.20
S211 Ernie Young S 2.50 .75
S218 Fred McGriff S 4.00 1.20
S223 Kimera Bartee S 2.50 .75
S229 Rickey Henderson S 6.00 1.80
S230 Sterling Hitchcock S 2.50 .75
S231 Bernard Gilkey S 2.50 .75
S234 Ryne Sandberg S 10.00 3.00
S235 Greg Maddux S 10.00 3.00
S239 Todd Stottlemyre S 2.50 .75
S241 Jason Kendall S 2.50 .75
S242 Paul O'Neill S 4.00 1.20
S256 Devon White S 2.50 .75
S261 Chuck Knoblauch S 2.50 .75
S263 Wally Joyner S 2.50 .75
S272 Andy Fox S 2.50 .75
S274 Sean Berry S 2.50 .75
S277 Benito Santiago S 2.50 .75
S284 Chad Mottola S 2.50 .75
S289 Dante Bichette S 2.50 .75
S292 Dwight Gooden S 4.00 1.20
S293 Kevin Mitchell S 2.50 .75
S295 Russ Davis S 2.50 .75
S296 Chan Ho Park S 2.50 .75
S302 Larry Walker S 4.00 1.20
S305 Ken Griffey Jr. S 10.00 3.00
S313 Billy Wagner S 2.50 .75
S317 Mike Grace S RC 2.50 .75
S327 Kenny Lofton S 2.50 .75
S328 Derek Bell S 2.50 .75
S337 Gary Sheffield S 2.50 .75
S341 Mark Grace S 4.00 1.20
S345 Andres Galarraga S 2.50 .75
S346 Brady Anderson S 2.50 .75
S350 Derek Jeter S 12.00 3.60
S353 Jay Buhner S 2.50 .75
S357 Tino Martinez S 4.00 1.20

1996 Finest Refractors

This 359-card set is parallel to the basic 1996 Finest set. The first 191 cards are parallel to the regular Series 1 with the second 168 cards parallel to regular Series 2. The word "refractor" is printed above the numbers on the card backs. The rate of insertion is one in 12 for a Bronze refractor (common), one in 48 for a Silver refractor (uncommon), and one in 288 for a Gold refractor (rare).

Nm-Mt Ex-Mt
*BRONZE STARS: 4X to 10X BASIC CARDS
*GOLD STARS: .75X to 2X BASIC CARDS
*SILVER STARS: 1.25X TO 3X BASIC CARDS

1996 Finest Landmark

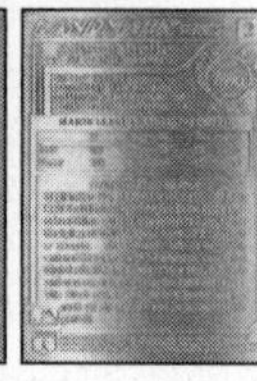

This four-card limited edition medallion set came with a Certificate of Authenticity and was produced by Topps. Only 2,000 sets were made. The fronts feature color action player photos on a gold ball and star metallic background. The backs carry player biographical and career information including batting records.

Nm-Mt Ex-Mt
COMPLETE SET (4) 100.00 30.00
1 Greg Maddux 30.00 9.00
2 Albert Belle 10.00 3.00
3 Cal Ripken 60.00 18.00
4 Eddie Murray 15.00 4.50

1997 Finest Promos

This five-card set features one promo card for each of the five themes found in the 1997 Finest Series I set. The fronts, backs, and card numbers are identical to the regular set with the exception of the words, "Promotional Sample Not for Resale" printed in red across the back. The cards are checklisted below according to their numbers in the regular set.

Nm-Mt Ex-Mt
COMPLETE SET (5) 8.00 2.40
1 Barry Bonds C 1.50 .45
15 Derek Jeter C 3.00 .90
30 Mark McGwire C 2.50 .75
143 Hideo Nomo U 1.00 .30
159 Jeff Bagwell R 1.50 .45

1997 Finest

The 1997 Finest set (produced by Topps) was issued in two series of 175 cards each and was distributed in six-card packs with a suggested retail price of $5.00. The fronts feature a borderless action player photo while the backs carry player information with another player photo. Series one is divided into five distinct themes: Finest Hurlers (top pitchers), Finest Blue Chips (up-and-coming future stars), Finest Power (long-ball hitters), Finest Warriors (superstar players), and Finest Masters (hottest players). Series two is also divided into five distinct themes: Finest Power (power hitters and pitchers), Finest Masters (top players), Finest Blue Chips (top new players), Finest Competitors (hottest players), and Finest Acquisitions (latest trades and new signings). All five themes of each series have common cards (1-100 and 176-275) designated with bronze trim, uncommon (101-150 and 276-325) with silver trim and an insertion rate of one in four for both series, and rare (151-175 and 326-350) with gold trim and an insertion rate of one in 24 for both series. The cards are numbered on the backs within the whole set and within the theme set. Notable Rookie Cards include Brian Giles.

Nm-Mt Ex-Mt
COMP.BRONZE SER.1 (100) 30.00 9.00
COMP.BRONZE SER.2 (100) 30.00 9.00
COM.BRON.(1-100/176-275) .50 .15
COMP.SILVER SER.1 (50) 120.00 36.00
COMP.SILVER SER.2 (50) 150.00 45.00
COM.SILV.(101-150/276-325) 2.00 .60
COMP.GOLD SER.1 (25) 300.00 90.00
COMP.GOLD SER.2 (25) 250.00 75.00
COM.GOLD (151-175/326-350) 5.00 1.50
1 Barry Bonds B 3.00 .90
2 Ryne Sandberg B 2.00 .60
3 Brian Jordan B .50 .15
4 Rocky Coppinger B .50 .15
5 Dante Bichette B UER .50 .15
Card is erroneously numbered 155
6 Al Martin B .50 .15
7 Charles Nagy B .50 .15
8 Otis Nixon B .50 .15
9 Mark Johnson B .50 .15
10 Jeff Bagwell B .75 .23
11 Ken Hill B .50 .15
12 Willie Adams B .50 .15
13 Raul Mondesi B .50 .15
14 Reggie Sanders B .50 .15
15 Derek Jeter B 3.00 .90
16 Jermaine Dye B .50 .15
17 Edgar Renteria B .50 .15
18 Travis Fryman B .50 .15
19 Roberto Hernandez B .50 .15
20 Sammy Sosa B 2.00 .60
21 Garret Anderson B .50 .15
22 Rey Ordonez B .50 .15
23 Glenallen Hill B .50 .15
24 Dave Nilsson B .50 .15
25 Kevin Brown B .50 .15
26 Brian McRae B .50 .15
27 Joey Hamilton B .50 .15
28 Jamey Wright B .50 .15
29 Frank Thomas B 1.25 .35
30 Mark McGwire B 3.00 .90
31 Ramon Martinez B .50 .15
32 Jaime Bluma B .50 .15
33 Frank Rodriguez B .50 .15
34 Andy Benes B .50 .15
35 Jay Buhner B .50 .15
36 Justin Thompson B .50 .15
37 Darin Erstad B .50 .15
38 Gregg Jefferies B .50 .15
39 Jeff D'Amico B .50 .15
40 Pedro Martinez B 1.25 .35
41 Nomar Garciaparra B 2.00 .60
42 Jose Valentin B .50 .15
43 Pat Hentgen B .50 .15
44 Will Clark B 1.25 .35
45 Bernie Williams B .75 .23
46 Luis Castillo B .50 .15
47 B.J. Surhoff B .50 .15
48 Greg Gagne B .50 .15
49 Pete Schourek B .50 .15
50 Mike Piazza B 2.00 .60
51 Dwight Gooden B .75 .23
52 Javy Lopez B .50 .15
53 Chuck Finley B .50 .15
54 James Baldwin B .50 .15
55 Jack McDowell B .50 .15
56 Royce Clayton B .50 .15
57 Carlos Delgado B .50 .15
58 Neifi Perez B .50 .15
59 Eddie Taubensee B .50 .15
60 Rafael Palmeiro B .75 .23
61 Marty Cordova B .50 .15
62 Wade Boggs B .75 .23
63 Rickey Henderson B 1.25 .35
64 Mike Hampton B .50 .15
65 Troy Percival B .50 .15
66 Barry Larkin B 1.25 .35
67 J.Allensworth B .50 .15
68 Mark Clark B .50 .15
69 Mike Lansing B .50 .15
70 Mark Grudzielanek B .50 .15
71 Todd Stottlemyre B .50 .15
72 Juan Guzman B .50 .15
73 John Burkett B .50 .15
74 Wilson Alvarez B .50 .15
75 Ellis Burks B .50 .15
76 Bobby Higginson B .50 .15
77 Ricky Bottalico B .50 .15
78 Omar Vizquel B .50 .15
79 Paul Sorrento B .50 .15
80 Denny Neagle B .50 .15
81 Roger Pavlik B .50 .15
82 Mike Lieberthal B .50 .15
83 Devon White B .50 .15
84 John Olerud B .50 .15
85 Kevin Appier B .50 .15
86 Joe Girardi B .50 .15
87 Paul O'Neill B .75 .23
88 Mike Sweeney B .50 .15
89 John Smiley B .50 .15
90 Ivan Rodriguez B 1.25 .35
91 Randy Myers B .50 .15
92 Bip Roberts B .50 .15
93 Jose Mesa B .50 .15
94 Paul Wilson B .50 .15
95 Mike Mussina B 1.25 .35
96 Ben McDonald B .50 .15
97 John Mabry B .50 .15
98 Tom Goodwin B .50 .15
99 Edgar Martinez B .75 .23
100 Andruw Jones B .50 .15
101 Jose Canseco S 5.00 1.50
102 Billy Wagner S 2.00 .60
103 Dante Bichette S 2.00 .60
104 Curt Schilling S 3.00 .90
105 Dean Palmer S 2.00 .60
106 Larry Walker S 3.00 .90
107 Bernie Williams S 3.00 .90
108 Chipper Jones S 5.00 1.50
109 Gary Sheffield S 2.00 .60
110 Randy Johnson S 5.00 1.50
111 Roberto Alomar S 5.00 1.50
112 Todd Walker S 2.00 .60
113 Sandy Alomar Jr. S 2.00 .60
114 John Jaha S 2.00 .60
115 Ken Caminiti S UER 2.00 .60
Card is numbered 135
116 Ryan Klesko S 2.00 .60
117 Mariano Rivera S 3.00 .90
118 Jason Giambi S 5.00 1.50
119 Lance Johnson S 2.00 .60
120 Robin Ventura S 2.00 .60
121 Todd Hollandsworth S 2.00 .60
122 Johnny Damon S 2.00 .60
123 W. VanLandingham S 2.00 .60
124 Jason Kendall S 2.00 .60
125 Vinny Castilla S 2.00 .60
126 Harold Baines S 2.00 .60
127 Joe Carter S 2.00 .60
128 Craig Biggio S 3.00 .90
129 Tony Clark S 2.00 .60
130 Ron Gant S 2.00 .60
131 David Segui S 2.00 .60
132 Steve Trachsel S 2.00 .60
133 Scott Rolen S 3.00 .90
134 Mike Stanley S 2.00 .60
135 Cal Ripken S 15.00 4.50
136 John Smoltz S 3.00 .90
137 Bobby Jones S 2.00 .60
138 Manny Ramirez S 2.00 .60
139 Ken Griffey Jr. S 8.00 2.40
140 Chuck Knoblauch S 2.00 .60
141 Mark Grace S 3.00 .90
142 Chris Snopek S 2.00 .60
143 Hideo Nomo S 5.00 1.50
144 Tim Salmon S 3.00 .90
145 David Cone S 2.00 .60
146 Eric Young S 2.00 .60
147 Jeff Brantley S 2.00 .60
148 Jim Thome S 5.00 1.50
149 Trevor Hoffman S 2.00 .60
150 Juan Gonzalez S 5.00 1.50
151 Mike Piazza G 20.00 6.00
152 Ivan Rodriguez G 12.00 3.60
153 Mo Vaughn G 5.00 1.50
154 Brady Anderson G 5.00 1.50
155 Mark McGwire G 30.00 9.00
156 Rafael Palmeiro G 8.00 2.40
157 Barry Larkin G 12.00 3.60
158 Greg Maddux G 20.00 6.00
159 Jeff Bagwell G 8.00 2.40
160 Frank Thomas G 12.00 3.60
161 Ken Caminiti G 5.00 1.50
162 Andruw Jones G 5.00 1.50
163 Dennis Eckersley G 5.00 1.50
164 Jeff Conine G 5.00 1.50
165 Jim Edmonds G 5.00 1.50
166 Derek Jeter G 30.00 9.00
167 Vladimir Guerrero G 12.00 3.60
168 Sammy Sosa G 20.00 6.00
169 Tony Gwynn G 15.00 4.50
170 Andres Galarraga G 5.00 1.50
171 Todd Hundley G 5.00 1.50
172 Jay Buhner G UER 5.00 1.50
Card is numbered 164
173 Paul Molitor G 8.00 2.40
174 Kenny Lofton G 5.00 1.50
175 Barry Bonds G 30.00 9.00
176 Gary Sheffield B .50 .15
177 Dmitri Young B .50 .15
178 Jay Bell B .50 .15
179 David Wells B .50 .15
180 Walt Weiss B .50 .15
181 Paul Molitor B .75 .23
182 Jose Guillen B .50 .15
183 Al Leiter B .50 .15
184 Mike Fetters B .50 .15
185 Mark Langston B .50 .15
186 Fred McGriff B .75 .23
187 Darrin Fletcher B .50 .15
188 Brant Brown B .50 .15
189 Geronimo Berroa B .50 .15
190 Jim Thome B 1.25 .35
191 Jose Vizcaino B .50 .15
192 Andy Ashby B .50 .15
193 Rusty Greer B .50 .15
194 Brian Hunter B .50 .15
195 Chris Hoiles B .50 .15
196 Orlando Merced B .50 .15
197 Brett Butler B .50 .15
198 Derek Bell B .50 .15
199 Bobby Bonilla B .50 .15
200 Alex Ochoa B .50 .15
201 Wally Joyner B .50 .15
202 Mo Vaughn B .50 .15
203 Doug Drabek B .50 .15
204 Tino Martinez B .75 .23
205 Roberto Alomar B 1.25 .35
206 Brian Giles B RC 3.00 .90
207 Todd Worrell B .50 .15
208 Alan Benes B .50 .15
209 Jim Leyritz B .50 .15
210 Darryl Hamilton B .50 .15
211 Jimmy Key B .50 .15
212 Juan Gonzalez B 1.25 .35
213 Vinny Castilla B .50 .15
214 Chuck Knoblauch B .50 .15
215 Tony Phillips B .50 .15
216 Jeff Cirillo B .50 .15
217 Carlos Garcia B .50 .15
218 Brooks Kieschnick B .50 .15
219 Marquis Grissom B .50 .15
220 Dan Wilson B .50 .15
221 Greg Vaughn B .50 .15
222 John Wetteland B .50 .15
223 Andres Galarraga B .50 .15
224 Ozzie Guillen B .50 .15
225 Kevin Elster B .50 .15
226 Bernard Gilkey B .50 .15
227 Mike Macfarlane B .50 .15
228 Heathcliff Slocumb B .50 .15
229 Wendell Magee Jr. B .50 .15
230 Carlos Baerga B .50 .15
231 Kevin Seitzer B .50 .15
232 Henry Rodriguez B .50 .15
233 Roger Clemens B 2.50 .75
234 Mark Wohlers B .50 .15
235 Eddie Murray B 1.25 .35
236 Todd Zeile B .50 .15
237 J.T. Snow B .50 .15
238 Ken Griffey Jr. B 2.00 .60
239 Sterling Hitchcock B .50 .15
240 Albert Belle B .50 .15
241 Terry Steinbach B .50 .15
242 Robb Nen B .50 .15
243 Mark McLemore B .50 .15
244 Jeff King B .50 .15
245 Tony Clark B .50 .15
246 Tim Salmon B .75 .23
247 Benito Santiago B .50 .15
248 Robin Ventura B .50 .15
249 Bubba Trammell B RC .50 .15
250 Chili Davis B .50 .15
251 John Valentin B .50 .15
252 Cal Ripken B 4.00 1.20
253 Matt Williams B .50 .15
254 Jeff Kent B .50 .15
255 Eric Karros B .50 .15
256 Ray Lankford B .50 .15
257 Ed Sprague B .50 .15
258 Shane Reynolds B .50 .15
259 Jaime Navarro B .50 .15
260 Eric Davis B .50 .15
261 Orel Hershiser B .50 .15
262 Mark Grace B .75 .23
263 Rod Beck B .50 .15
264 Ismael Valdes B .50 .15
265 Manny Ramirez B .50 .15
266 Ken Caminiti B .50 .15
267 Tim Naehring B .50 .15
268 Jose Rosado B .50 .15
269 Greg Colbrunn B .50 .15
270 Dean Palmer B .50 .15
271 David Justice B .50 .15
272 Scott Spiezio B .50 .15
273 Chipper Jones B 1.25 .35
274 Mel Rojas B .50 .15
275 Bartolo Colon B .50 .15
276 Darin Erstad S 2.00 .60
277 Sammy Sosa S 6.00 1.80
278 Rafael Palmeiro S 3.00 .90
279 Frank Thomas S 5.00 1.50
280 Ruben Rivera S 2.00 .60
281 Hal Morris S 2.00 .60
282 Jay Buhner S 2.00 .60
283 Kenny Lofton S 2.00 .60
284 Jose Canseco S 5.00 1.50
285 Alex Fernandez S 2.00 .60
286 Todd Helton S 5.00 1.50
287 Andy Pettitte S 3.00 .90
288 John Franco S 2.00 .60
289 Ivan Rodriguez S 5.00 1.50
290 Ellis Burks S 2.00 .60
291 Julio Franco S 2.00 .60
292 Mike Piazza S 8.00 2.40
293 Brian Jordan S 2.00 .60
294 Greg Maddux S 8.00 2.40
295 Bob Abreu S 2.00 .60
296 Rondell White S 2.00 .60
297 Moises Alou S 2.00 .60
298 Tony Gwynn S 6.00 1.80
299 Deion Sanders S 3.00 .90
300 Jeff Montgomery S 2.00 .60
301 Ray Durham S 2.00 .60
302 John Wasdin S 2.00 .60
303 Ryne Sandberg S 8.00 2.40
304 Delino DeShields S 2.00 .60
305 Mark McGwire S 12.00 3.60
306 Andruw Jones S 2.00 .60
307 Kevin Orie S 2.00 .60
308 Matt Williams S 2.00 .60
309 Karim Garcia S 2.00 .60
310 Derek Jeter S 12.00 3.60
311 Mo Vaughn S 2.00 .60
312 Brady Anderson S 2.00 .60
313 Barry Bonds S 12.00 3.60
314 Steve Finley S 2.00 .60
315 Vladimir Guerrero S 5.00 1.50
316 Matt Morris S 2.00 .60
317 Tom Glavine S 3.00 .90
318 Jeff Bagwell S 3.00 .90
319 Albert Belle S 2.00 .60
320 Hideki Irabu S RC 2.00 .60
321 Andres Galarraga S 2.00 .60
322 Cecil Fielder S 2.00 .60
323 Barry Larkin S 5.00 1.50
324 Todd Hundley S 2.00 .60
325 Fred McGriff S 3.00 .90
326 Gary Sheffield G 5.00 1.50
327 Craig Biggio G 8.00 2.40
328 Raul Mondesi G 5.00 1.50
329 Edgar Martinez G 8.00 2.40
330 Chipper Jones G 12.00 3.60
331 Bernie Williams G 8.00 2.40
332 Juan Gonzalez G 12.00 3.60
333 Ron Gant G 5.00 1.50
334 Cal Ripken G 40.00 12.00
335 Larry Walker G 8.00 2.40
336 Matt Williams G 5.00 1.50
337 Jose Cruz Jr. G RC 15.00 4.50
338 Joe Carter G 5.00 1.50
339 Wilton Guerrero G 5.00 1.50
340 Cecil Fielder G 5.00 1.50
341 Todd Walker G 5.00 1.50
342 Ken Griffey Jr. G 20.00 6.00
343 Ryan Klesko G 5.00 1.50
344 Roger Clemens G 25.00 7.50
345 Hideo Nomo G 12.00 3.60
346 Dante Bichette G 5.00 1.50
347 Albert Belle G 5.00 1.50
348 Randy Johnson G 12.00 3.60
349 Manny Ramirez G 5.00 1.50
350 John Smoltz G 8.00 2.40

1997 Finest Embossed

This 150-card set is parallel to regular set numbers 101-175 of Finest Series 1 and 276-350 of Finest Series 2. There is an embossed version of cards 101-150 and 276-325 with an insertion rate of one in 16 for each series. There is an embossed die-cut version of cards 151-175 and 326-350 with an insertion rate of one in 96 packs for each series.

Nm-Mt Ex-Mt
*SILV.STARS: .60X TO 1.5X BASIC CARD
*SILVER ROOKIES: .5X TO 1.25X BASIC
*GOLD STARS: .6X TO 1.5X BASIC CARD
*GOLD ROOKIES: .4X TO 1X BASIC CARD

1997 Finest Embossed Refractors

This 150-card set is a parallel version of the regular Finest Embossed set and is similar in design. The difference is found in the refractive quality of the cards.

Nm-Mt Ex-Mt
*SILVER STARS: 2.5X TO 6X BASIC CARDS
*SILVER ROOKIES: 2X TO 5X BASIC CARDS
*SER.1 GOLD STARS: 1.5X TO 4X BASIC
*SER.2 GOLD STARS: 1.5X TO 4X BASIC
*SER.2 GOLD RC'S: 1X TO 2.5X BASIC

1997 Finest Refractors

This 350-card set is parallel and similar in design to the regular Finest set. The distinction is in the refractive quality of the card. Cards 1-100 and 176-275 have an insertion rate of one in 12 in each series packs. Cards 101-150 and 276-325 have an insertion rate of one in 48 in each series packs. Cards 151-175 and 326-350 have an insertion rate of one in 288.

Nm-Mt Ex-Mt
*BRONZE STARS: 4X TO 10X BASIC CARD
*BRONZE RC'S: 1.25X TO 3X BASIC CARD
*SILVER STARS: 1.25X TO 3X BASIC CARD
*SILVER ROOKIES: 1X TO 2.5X BASIC CARD
*GOLD STARS: 1X TO 2.5X BASIC CARD
*GOLD ROOKIES: .6X TO 1.5X BASIC CARD

1998 Finest Pre-Production

These five cards tagged with a "PP" prefix were created so collectors and dealers could get an early look about the 1998 Finest set.

Nm-Mt Ex-Mt
COMPLETE SET (5) 12.00 3.60
PP1 Nomar Garciaparra 3.00 .90
PP2 Mark McGwire 3.00 .90
PP3 Ivan Rodriguez 1.50 .45
PP4 Ken Griffey Jr 3.00 .90
PP5 Roger Clemens 2.00 .60

1998 Finest

This 275-card set (produced by Topps) was distributed in first and second series six-card packs with a suggested retail price of $5. Series one contains cards 1-150 and series two contains cards 151-275. Each card features action color player photos printed on 26 pt. card stock with each postion identified by a different card design. The backs carry player information and career statistics.

Nm-Mt Ex-Mt
COMPLETE SET (275) 50.00 15.00
COMP.SERIES 1 (150) 25.00 7.50
COMP.SERIES 2 (125) 25.00 7.50
1 Larry Walker .60 .18
2 Andruw Jones .40 .12
3 Ramon Martinez .25 .07
4 Geronimo Berroa .25 .07
5 David Justice .40 .12
6 Rusty Greer .40 .12
7 Chad Ogea .25 .07
8 Tom Goodwin .25 .07
9 Tino Martinez .60 .18
10 Jose Guillen .25 .07
11 Jeffrey Hammonds .25 .07
12 Brian McRae .25 .07
13 Jeremi Gonzalez .25 .07
14 Craig Counsell .25 .07
15 Mike Piazza 1.50 .45
16 Greg Maddux 1.50 .45
17 Todd Greene .25 .07
18 Rondell White .40 .12
19 Kirk Rueter .25 .07
20 Tony Clark .25 .07
21 Brad Radke .40 .12
22 Jaret Wright .25 .07
23 Carlos Delgado .40 .12
24 Dustin Hermanson .25 .07
25 Gary Sheffield .40 .12
26 Jose Canseco 1.00 .30
27 Kevin Young .40 .12
28 David Wells .40 .12
29 Mariano Rivera .60 .18
30 Reggie Sanders .40 .12
31 Mike Cameron .40 .12
32 Bobby Witt .25 .07
33 Kevin Orie .25 .07
34 Royce Clayton .25 .07
35 Edgar Martinez .60 .18
36 Neifi Perez .25 .07
37 Kevin Appier .40 .12
38 Darryl Hamilton .25 .07
39 Michael Tucker .25 .07
40 Roger Clemens 2.00 .60
41 Carl Everett .40 .12
42 Mike Sweeney .40 .12
43 Pat Meares .25 .07
44 Brian Giles .40 .12
45 Matt Morris .40 .12
46 Jason Dickson .25 .07
47 Rich Loiselle RC .40 .12
48 Joe Girardi .25 .07
49 Steve Trachsel .25 .07
50 Ben Grieve .25 .07
51 Brian Johnson .25 .07
52 Hideki Irabu .25 .07
53 J.T. Snow .40 .12
54 Mike Hampton .40 .12
55 Dave Nilsson .25 .07

56 Alex Fernandez .25 .07
57 Brett Tomko .25 .07
58 Wally Joyner .40 .12
59 Kelvim Escobar .25 .07
60 Roberto Alomar 1.00 .30
61 Todd Jones .25 .07
62 Paul O'Neill .60 .18
63 Jamie Moyer .40 .12
64 Mark Wohlers .25 .07
65 Jose Cruz Jr. .40 .12
66 Troy Percival .40 .12
67 Rick Reed .25 .07
68 Will Clark 1.00 .30
69 Jamey Wright .25 .07
70 Mike Mussina 1.00 .30
71 David Cone .40 .12
72 Ryan Klesko .40 .12
73 Scott Hatteberg .25 .07
74 James Baldwin .25 .07
75 Tony Womack .25 .07
76 Carlos Perez .25 .07
77 Charles Nagy .25 .07
78 Jeromy Burnitz .40 .12
79 Shane Reynolds .25 .07
80 Cliff Floyd .40 .12
81 Jason Kendall .40 .12
82 Chad Curtis .25 .07
83 Matt Karchner .25 .07
84 Ricky Bottalico .25 .07
85 Sammy Sosa 1.50 .45
86 Javy Lopez .40 .12
87 Jeff Kent .40 .12
88 Shawn Green .40 .12
89 Joey Cora .25 .07
90 Tony Gwynn 1.25 .35
91 Bob Tewksbury .25 .07
92 Derek Jeter 2.50 .75
93 Eric Davis .40 .12
94 Jeff Fassero .25 .07
95 Denny Neagle .25 .07
96 Ismael Valdes .25 .07
97 Tim Salmon .60 .18
98 Mark Grudzielanek .25 .07
99 Curt Schilling .60 .18
100 Ken Griffey Jr. 1.50 .45
101 Edgardo Alfonzo .40 .12
102 Vinny Castilla .40 .12
103 Jose Rosado .25 .07
104 Scott Erickson .25 .07
105 Alan Benes .25 .07
106 Shannon Stewart .40 .12
107 Delino DeShields .25 .07
108 Mark Loretta .25 .07
109 Todd Hundley .25 .07
110 Chuck Knoblauch .40 .12
111 Todd Helton .60 .18
112 F.P. Santangelo .25 .07
113 Jeff Cirillo .25 .07
114 Omar Vizquel .40 .12
115 John Valentin .25 .07
116 Damion Easley .25 .07
117 Matt Lawton .25 .07
118 Jim Thome 1.00 .30
119 Sandy Alomar Jr. .25 .07
120 Albert Belle .40 .12
121 Chris Stynes .25 .07
122 Butch Huskey .25 .07
123 Shawn Estes .25 .07
124 Terry Adams .25 .07
125 Ivan Rodriguez 1.00 .30
126 Ron Gant .40 .12
127 John Mabry .25 .07
128 Jeff Shaw .25 .07
129 Jeff Montgomery .25 .07
130 Justin Thompson .25 .07
131 Livan Hernandez .25 .07
132 Ugueth Urbina .25 .07
133 Scott Servais .25 .07
134 Troy O'Leary .25 .07
135 Cal Ripken 3.00 .90
136 Quilvio Veras .25 .07
137 Pedro Astacio .25 .07
138 Willie Greene .25 .07
139 Lance Johnson .25 .07
140 Nomar Garciaparra 1.50 .45
141 Jose Offerman .25 .07
142 Scott Rolen .60 .18
143 Derek Bell .25 .07
144 Johnny Damon .40 .12
145 Mark McGwire 2.50 .75
146 Chan Ho Park .40 .12
147 Edgar Renteria .40 .12
148 Eric Young .25 .07
149 Craig Biggio .60 .18
150 Checklist (1-150) .25 .07
151 Frank Thomas 1.00 .30
152 John Wetteland .40 .12
153 Mike Lansing .25 .07
154 Pedro Martinez 1.00 .30
155 Rico Brogna .25 .07
156 Kevin Brown .60 .18
157 Alex Rodriguez 1.50 .45
158 Wade Boggs .60 .18
159 Richard Hidalgo .40 .12
160 Mark Grace .60 .18
161 Jose Mesa .25 .07
162 John Olerud .40 .12
163 Tim Belcher .25 .07
164 Chuck Finley .40 .12
165 Brian Hunter .40 .12
166 Joe Carter .40 .12
167 Stan Javier .25 .07
168 Jay Bell .40 .12
169 Ray Lankford .25 .07
170 John Smoltz .60 .18
171 Ed Sprague .25 .07
172 Jason Giambi 1.00 .30
173 Todd Walker .40 .12
174 Paul Konerko .40 .12
175 Rey Ordonez .25 .07
176 Dante Bichette .40 .12
177 Bernie Williams .60 .18
178 Jon Nunnally .25 .07
179 Rafael Palmeiro .60 .18
180 Jay Buhner .40 .12
181 Devon White .25 .07
182 Jeff D'Amico .25 .07
183 Walt Weiss .40 .12
184 Scott Spiezio .25 .07
185 Moises Alou .40 .12
186 Carlos Baerga .25 .07
187 Todd Zeile .40 .12
188 Gregg Jefferies .25 .07
189 Mo Vaughn .40 .12
190 Terry Steinbach .25 .07
191 Ray Durham .40 .12
192 Robin Ventura .40 .12
193 Jeff Reed .25 .07
194 Ken Caminiti .40 .12
195 Eric Karros .40 .12
196 Wilson Alvarez .25 .07
197 Gary Gaetti .40 .12
198 Andres Galarraga .40 .12
199 Alex Gonzalez .25 .07
200 Garret Anderson .40 .12
201 Andy Benes .25 .07
202 Harold Baines .40 .12
203 Ron Coomer .25 .07
204 Dean Palmer .40 .12
205 Reggie Jefferson .25 .07
206 John Burkett .25 .07
207 Jermaine Allensworth .25 .07
208 Bernard Gilkey .25 .07
209 Jeff Bagwell .60 .18
210 Kenny Lofton .40 .12
211 Bobby Jones .25 .07
212 Bartolo Colon .40 .12
213 Jim Edmonds .40 .12
214 Pat Hentgen .25 .07
215 Matt Williams .40 .12
216 Bob Abreu .40 .12
217 Jorge Posada .60 .18
218 Marty Cordova .25 .07
219 Ken Hill .25 .07
220 Steve Finley .40 .12
221 Jeff King .25 .07
222 Quinton McCracken .25 .07
223 Matt Stairs .25 .07
224 Darin Erstad .40 .12
225 Fred McGriff .60 .18
226 Marquis Grissom .25 .07
227 Doug Glanville .25 .07
228 Tom Glavine .60 .18
229 John Franco .40 .12
230 Darren Bragg .25 .07
231 Barry Larkin 1.00 .30
232 Trevor Hoffman .40 .12
233 Brady Anderson .40 .12
234 Al Martin .25 .07
235 B.J. Surhoff .40 .12
236 Ellis Burks .40 .12
237 Randy Johnson 1.00 .30
238 Mark Clark .25 .07
239 Tony Saunders .25 .07
240 Hideo Nomo 1.00 .30
241 Brad Fullmer .25 .07
242 Chipper Jones 1.00 .30
243 Jose Valentin .25 .07
244 Manny Ramirez .40 .12
245 Derrek Lee .40 .12
246 Jimmy Key .40 .12
247 Tim Naehring .25 .07
248 Bobby Higginson .40 .12
249 Charles Johnson .40 .12
250 Chili Davis .40 .12
251 Tom Gordon .25 .07
252 Mike Lieberthal .40 .12
253 Billy Wagner .40 .12
254 Juan Guzman .25 .07
255 Todd Stottlemyre .25 .07
256 Brian Jordan .40 .12
257 Barry Bonds 2.50 .75
258 Dan Wilson .25 .07
259 Paul Molitor .60 .18
260 Juan Gonzalez 1.00 .30
261 Francisco Cordova .25 .07
262 Cecil Fielder .40 .12
263 Travis Lee .25 .07
264 Kevin Tapani .25 .07
265 Raul Mondesi .40 .12
266 Travis Fryman .40 .12
267 Armando Benitez .25 .07
268 Pokey Reese .25 .07
269 Rick Aguilera .25 .07
270 Andy Pettitte .60 .18
271 Jose Vizcaino .25 .07
272 Kerry Wood 1.00 .30
273 Vladimir Guerrero 1.00 .30
274 John Smiley .25 .07
275 Checklist (151-275) .25 .07

1998 Finest No-Protectors

Randomly inserted in retail packs at the rate of one in two and one in every HTA pack, this 275-card set is parallel to the base set only without the Finest Protector covering and features double-sided Finest technology.

Nm-Mt Ex-Mt
COMPLETE SET (275) 350.00 105.00
COMP. SERIES 1 (150) 200.00 60.00
COMP. SERIES 2 (125) 150.00 45.00
*STARS: 2X TO 4X BASIC CARDS

1998 Finest Oversize

These sixteen 3" by 5" cards were inserted one every three hobby boxes. Though not actually on the cards, first series cards have been assigned an A prefix and second series a B prefix to clarify our listing. The cards are parallel to the regular Finest cards except numbering "of 8". They were issued as chiptoppers in the boxes.

Nm-Mt Ex-Mt
COMPLETE SERIES 1 (8) 120.00 36.00
COMPLETE SERIES 2 (8) 80.00 24.00
*REFRACTORS: .75X TO 2X BASIC OVERSIZE
REF.ODDS 1:6 HOBBY/HTA BOXES
A1 Mark McGwire 15.00 4.50
A2 Cal Ripken 20.00 6.00
A3 Nomar Garciaparra 10.00 3.00
A4 Mike Piazza 10.00 3.00
A5 Greg Maddux 10.00 3.00
A6 Jose Cruz Jr. 2.50 .75
A7 Roger Clemens 12.00 3.60
A8 Ken Griffey Jr. 10.00 3.00
B1 Frank Thomas 6.00 1.80
B2 Bernie Williams 4.00 1.20
B3 Randy Johnson 6.00 1.80
B4 Chipper Jones 6.00 1.80
B5 Manny Ramirez 2.50 .75
B6 Barry Bonds 15.00 4.50
B7 Juan Gonzalez 6.00 1.80
B8 Jeff Bagwell 4.00 1.20

1998 Finest Refractors

Randomly inserted in retail packs at the rate of one in 12 and in HTA packs at the rate of one in five, this 275-card set is parallel to the base set. The difference is found in the refractive quality of the card.

Nm-Mt Ex-Mt
*STARS: 5X TO 12X BASIC CARDS

1998 Finest Centurions

Randomly inserted in Series one hobby packs at a rate of 1:153 and Home Team Advantage packs at a rate of 1:71, cards from this 20-card set feature action color photos of top players who will lead the game into the next century. Each card is sequentially numbered on back to 500. Unfortunately, an unknown quantity of unnumbered Centurions made their way into the secondary market in 1999. It's believed that these cards were quality control extras. To further compound this situation, some unscrupulous parties attempted to serial-number the cards. The fake cards have flat gold foil numbering. The real cards have bright foil numbering.

Nm-Mt Ex-Mt
COMPLETE SET (20) 100.00 30.00
*REF: 2X TO 5X BASIC CENTURIONS.
SER.1 REF.ODDS 1:1020 HOBBY, 1:471 HTA
REFRACTOR PR.RUN 75 SERIAL #'d SETS
C1 Andruw Jones 2.00 .60
C2 Vladimir Guerrero 5.00 1.50
C3 Nomar Garciaparra 8.00 2.40
C4 Scott Rolen 3.00 .90
C5 Ken Griffey Jr. 8.00 2.40
C6 Jose Cruz Jr. 2.00 .60
C7 Barry Bonds 12.00 3.60
C8 Mark McGwire 12.00 3.60
C9 Juan Gonzalez 5.00 1.50
C10 Jeff Bagwell 3.00 .90
C11 Frank Thomas 5.00 1.50
C12 Paul Konerko 2.00 .60
C13 Alex Rodriguez 8.00 2.40
C14 Mike Piazza 8.00 2.40
C15 Travis Lee 1.25 .35
C16 Chipper Jones 5.00 1.50
C17 Larry Walker 3.00 .90
C18 Mo Vaughn 2.00 .60
C19 Livan Hernandez 1.25 .35
C20 Jaret Wright 1.25 .35

1998 Finest The Man

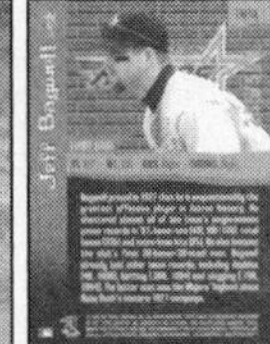

Randomly inserted in packs at a rate of one in 119, this 20-card set is an insert to the 1998 Finest base set. The entire set is sequentially numbered to 500.

Nm-Mt Ex-Mt
COMPLETE SET (20) 400.00 120.00
*REF: 1X TO 2.5X BASIC THE MAN
REF.SER.2 ODDS 1:793
REFRACTOR PR.RUN 75 SERIAL #'d SETS
TM1 Ken Griffey Jr. 25.00 7.50
TM2 Barry Bonds 40.00 12.00
TM3 Frank Thomas 15.00 4.50
TM4 Chipper Jones 15.00 4.50
TM5 Cal Ripken 50.00 15.00
TM6 Nomar Garciaparra 25.00 7.50
TM7 Mark McGwire 40.00 12.00
TM8 Mike Piazza 25.00 7.50
TM9 Derek Jeter 40.00 12.00
TM10 Alex Rodriguez 25.00 7.50
TM11 Jose Cruz Jr. 6.00 1.80
TM12 Larry Walker 10.00 3.00
TM13 Jeff Bagwell 10.00 3.00
TM14 Tony Gwynn 20.00 6.00
TM15 Travis Lee 4.00 1.20
TM16 Juan Gonzalez 15.00 4.50
TM17 Scott Rolen 10.00 3.00
TM18 Randy Johnson 15.00 4.50
TM19 Roger Clemens 30.00 9.00
TM20 Greg Maddux 25.00 7.50

1998 Finest Mystery Finest 1

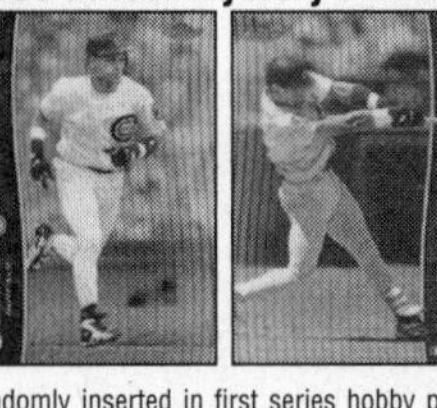

Randomly inserted in first series hobby packs at the rate of one in 36 and Home Team Advantage packs at the rate of one in 15, cards from this 50-card set feature color action photos of 20 top players on double-sided cards. Each player is matched with three different players on the opposite side or another photo of himself. Each side is covered with the Finest opaque protector.

Nm-Mt Ex-Mt
COMPLETE SET (50) 500.00 150.00
*REFRACTOR: 1X TO 2.5X BASIC MYSTERY
REF.SER.1 ODDS 1:144 HOBBY, 1:64 HTA
M1 Frank Thomas 15.00 4.50
Ken Griffey Jr.
M2 Frank Thomas 15.00 4.50
Mike Piazza
M3 Frank Thomas 25.00 7.50
Mark McGwire
M4 Frank Thomas 10.00 3.00
Frank Thomas
M5 Ken Griffey Jr. 15.00 4.50
Mike Piazza
M6 Ken Griffey Jr. 25.00 7.50
Mark McGwire
M7 Ken Griffey Jr. 15.00 4.50
Ken Griffey Jr.
M8 Mike Piazza 25.00 7.50
Mark McGwire
M9 Mike Piazza 20.00 6.00
Mike Piazza
M10 Mark McGwire 30.00 9.00
Mark McGwire
M11 Nomar Garciaparra 15.00 4.50
Jose Cruz Jr.
M12 Nomar Garciaparra 20.00 6.00
Derek Jeter
M13 Nomar Garciaparra 15.00 4.50
Andruw Jones
M14 Nomar Garciaparra 20.00 6.00
Nomar Garciaparra
M15 Jose Cruz Jr. 25.00 7.50
Derek Jeter
M16 Jose Cruz Jr. 4.00 1.20
Andruw Jones
M17 Jose Cruz Jr. 4.00 1.20
Jose Cruz Jr.
M18 Derek Jeter 25.00 7.50
Andruw Jones
M19 Derek Jeter 30.00 9.00
Derek Jeter
M20 Andruw Jones 4.00 1.20
Andruw Jones
M21 Cal Ripken 25.00 7.50
Tony Gwynn
M22 Cal Ripken 30.00 9.00
Barry Bonds
M23 Cal Ripken 30.00 9.00
Greg Maddux
M24 Cal Ripken 40.00 12.00
Cal Ripken
M25 Tony Gwynn 30.00 9.00
Barry Bonds
M26 Tony Gwynn 15.00 4.50
Greg Maddux
M27 Tony Gwynn 15.00 4.50
Tony Gwynn
M28 Barry Bonds 30.00 9.00
Greg Maddux
M29 Barry Bonds 30.00 9.00
Barry Bonds
M30 Greg Maddux 20.00 6.00
Greg Maddux
M31 Juan Gonzalez 10.00 3.00
Larry Walker
M32 Juan Gonzalez 10.00 3.00
Andres Galarraga
M33 Juan Gonzalez 10.00 3.00
Chipper Jones
M34 Juan Gonzalez 10.00 3.00
Juan Gonzalez
M35 Larry Walker 6.00 1.80
Andres Galarraga
M36 Larry Walker 10.00 3.00
Chipper Jones
M37 Larry Walker 6.00 1.80
Larry Walker
M38 Andres Galarraga 10.00 3.00
Chipper Jones
M39 Andres Galarraga 4.00 1.20
Andres Galarraga
M40 Chipper Jones 10.00 3.00
Chipper Jones
M41 Gary Sheffield 15.00 4.50
Sammy Sosa
M42 Gary Sheffield 6.00 1.80
Jeff Bagwell
M43 Gary Sheffield 6.00 1.80
Tino Martinez
M44 Gary Sheffield 4.00 1.20
Gary Sheffield
M45 Sammy Sosa 20.00 6.00
Jeff Bagwell
M46 Sammy Sosa 15.00 4.50
Tino Martinez
M47 Sammy Sosa 20.00 6.00
Sammy Sosa
M48 Jeff Bagwell 6.00 1.80
Tino Martinez
M49 Jeff Bagwell 6.00 1.80
Jeff Bagwell
M50 Tino Martinez 6.00 1.80
Tino Martinez

1998 Finest Mystery Finest 2

Randomly inserted in second series hobby packs at the rate of one in 36 and Home Team Advantage packs at the rate of one in 15, cards from this 50-card set feature color action photos of 20 top players on double-sided cards. Each player is matched with three different players on the opposite side or another photo of himself. Each side is covered with the Finest opaque protector.

Nm-Mt Ex-Mt
COMPLETE SET (40) 300.00 90.00
*REFRACTOR: 1X TO 2.5X BASIC MYSTERY
REF.SER.2 ODDS 1:144
M1 Nomar Garciaparra 15.00 4.50
Frank Thomas
M2 Nomar Garciaparra 15.00 4.50
Albert Belle
M3 Nomar Garciaparra 15.00 4.50
Scott Rolen
M4 Frank Thomas 10.00 3.00
Albert Belle
M5 Frank Thomas 10.00 3.00
Scott Rolen
M6 Albert Belle 6.00 1.80
Scott Rolen
M7 Ken Griffey Jr. 15.00 4.50
Jose Cruz Jr.
M8 Ken Griffey Jr. 15.00 4.50
Alex Rodriguez
M9 Ken Griffey Jr. 20.00 6.00
Roger Clemens
M10 Jose Cruz Jr. 15.00 4.50
Alex Rodriguez
M11 Jose Cruz Jr. 20.00 6.00
Roger Clemens
M12 Alex Rodriguez 15.00 4.50
Roger Clemens
M13 Mike Piazza 30.00 9.00
Barry Bonds
M14 Mike Piazza 25.00 7.50
Derek Jeter
M15 Mike Piazza 15.00 4.50
Bernie Williams
M16 Barry Bonds 30.00 9.00
Derek Jeter
M17 Barry Bonds 15.00 4.50
Bernie Williams
M18 Deter Jeter 25.00 7.50
Bernie Williams
M19 Mark McGwire 25.00 7.50
Jeff Bagwell
M20 Mark McGwire 25.00 7.50
Mo Vaughn
M21 Mark McGwire 25.00 7.50
Jim Thome
M22 Jeff Bagwell 6.00 1.80
Mo Vaughn
M23 Jeff Bagwell 10.00 3.00
Jim Thome
M24 Mo Vaughn 10.00 3.00
Jim Thome
M25 Juan Gonzalez 10.00 3.00
Travis Lee
M26 Juan Gonzalez 10.00 3.00
Ben Grieve
M27 Juan Gonzalez 10.00 3.00
Fred McGriff
M28 Travis Lee 4.00 1.20
Ben Grieve
M29 Travis Lee 6.00 1.80
Fred McGriff
M30 Ben Grieve 6.00 1.80
Fred McGriff
M31 Albert Belle 4.00 1.20
Albert Belle
M32 Scott Rolen 6.00 1.80
Scott Rolen
M33 Alex Rodriguez 20.00 6.00
Alex Rodriguez
M34 Roger Clemens 20.00 6.00
Roger Clemens
M35 Bernie Williams 6.00 1.80
Bernie Williams
M36 Mo Vaughn 4.00 1.20
Mo Vaughn
M37 Jim Thome 10.00 3.00
Jim Thome
M38 Travis Lee 4.00 1.20
Travis Lee
M39 Fred McGriff 6.00 1.80
Fred McGriff
M40 Ben Grieve 4.00 1.20
Ben Grieve

1998 Finest Mystery Finest Oversize

One of these three different cards was randomly seeded as chiptoppers (lying on top of the packs, but within the sealed box) at a rate of 1:6 series two Home Team Collector boxes. Besides the obvious difference in size, these cards are also numbered differently than the standard-sized cards, but beyond that they're essentially straight parallels of their standard sized siblings.

Nm-Mt Ex-Mt
COMPLETE SET (3) 40.00 12.00
SER.2 STATED ODDS 1:6 HTA BOXES
*REFRACTOR: .75X TO 2X OVERSIZE
SER.2 REF.STATED ODDS 1:12 HTA BOXES
1 Ken Griffey Jr. 10.00 3.00
Alex Rodriguez
2 Derek Jeter 15.00 4.50
Bernie Williams
3 Mark McGwire 15.00 4.50
Jeff Bagwell

1998 Finest Power Zone

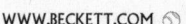

Randomly inserted in series one hobby packs at the rate of one in 72 and in series one Home

Team Advantage packs at the rate of one in 32, this 20-card set features color action photos of top players printed with new "Flop Inks" technology which actually changes the color of the card when it is held at different angles.

	Nm-Mt	Ex-Mt
COMPLETE SET (20)	200.00	60.00
P1 Ken Griffey Jr.	20.00	6.00
P2 Jeff Bagwell	8.00	2.40
P3 Jose Cruz Jr.	5.00	1.50
P4 Barry Bonds	30.00	9.00
P5 Mark McGwire	30.00	9.00
P6 Jim Thome	12.00	3.60
P7 Mo Vaughn	5.00	1.50
P8 Gary Sheffield	5.00	1.50
P9 Andres Galarraga	5.00	1.50
P10 Nomar Garciaparra	20.00	6.00
P11 Rafael Palmeiro	8.00	2.40
P12 Sammy Sosa	20.00	6.00
P13 Jay Buhner	5.00	1.50
P14 Tony Clark	3.00	.90
P15 Mike Piazza	20.00	6.00
P16 Larry Walker	8.00	2.40
P17 Albert Belle	5.00	1.50
P18 Tino Martinez	8.00	2.40
P19 Juan Gonzalez	12.00	3.60
P20 Frank Thomas	12.00	3.60

1998 Finest Stadium Stars

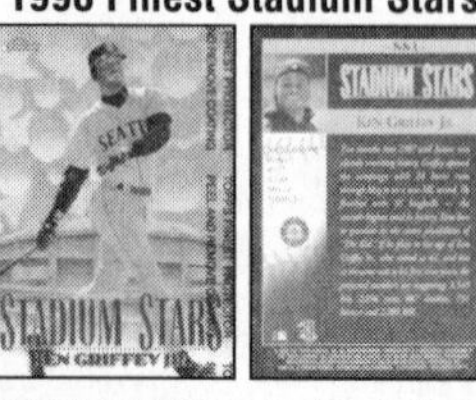

Randomly inserted in packs at a rate of one in 72, this 24-card set features a selection of the majors top hitters set against an attractive foil-glowing stadium background.

	Nm-Mt	Ex-Mt
COMPLETE SET (24)	300.00	90.00
SS1 Ken Griffey Jr.	20.00	6.00
SS2 Alex Rodriguez	20.00	6.00
SS3 Mo Vaughn	5.00	1.50
SS4 Nomar Garciaparra	20.00	6.00
SS5 Frank Thomas	12.00	3.60
SS6 Albert Belle	5.00	1.50
SS7 Derek Jeter	30.00	9.00
SS8 Chipper Jones	12.00	3.60
SS9 Cal Ripken	40.00	12.00
SS10 Jim Thome	12.00	3.60
SS11 Mike Piazza	20.00	6.00
SS12 Juan Gonzalez	12.00	3.60
SS13 Jeff Bagwell	8.00	2.40
SS14 Sammy Sosa	20.00	6.00
SS15 Jose Cruz Jr.	5.00	1.50
SS16 Gary Sheffield	5.00	1.50
SS17 Larry Walker	8.00	2.40
SS18 Tony Gwynn	15.00	4.50
SS19 Mark McGwire	30.00	9.00
SS20 Barry Bonds	30.00	9.00
SS21 Tino Martinez	8.00	2.40
SS22 Manny Ramirez	5.00	1.50
SS23 Ken Caminiti	5.00	1.50
SS24 Andres Galarraga	5.00	1.50

1999 Finest Pre-Production

This six-card set was issued to preview the 1999 Finest set. Six of the more popular players in baseball today were picked to represent the players in the set. The cards are numbered with a "PP" prefix.

	Nm-Mt	Ex-Mt
COMPLETE SET (6)	8.00	2.40
PP1 Darin Erstad	2.00	.60
PP2 Javy Lopez	2.00	.60
PP3 Vinny Castilla	1.00	.30
PP4 Jim Thome	1.50	.45
PP5 Tino Martinez	1.00	.30
PP6 Mark Grace	2.00	.60

1999 Finest

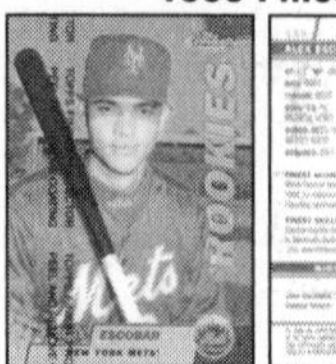

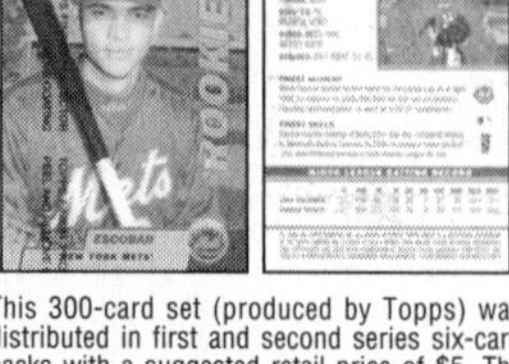

This 300-card set (produced by Topps) was distributed in first and second series six-card packs with a suggested retail price of $5. The fronts feature color action player photos printed on 27 pt. card stock using Chromium technology. The backs carry player information. The set includes the following subsets: Gems (101-120), Sensations (121-130) Rookies (131-150/277-299), Sterling (251-265) and Gamers (266-276). Card number 300 is a special Hank Aaron/Mark McGwire tribute. Cards numbered from 101 through 150 and 251 through 300 were short printed and seeded at a rate of one per hobby, one per retail and two per Home Team Advantage pack. Notable Rookie Cards include Pat Burrell, Sean Burroughs, Nick Johnson, Austin Kearns, Corey Patterson and Alfonso Soriano.

	Nm-Mt	Ex-Mt
COMPLETE SET (300)	100.00	30.00
COMP.SERIES 1 (150)	50.00	15.00
COMP.SERIES 2 (150)	50.00	15.00
COMP.SER.1 w/o SP's (100)	20.00	6.00
COMP.SER.2 w/o SP's (100)	20.00	6.00
COMMON (1-100/151-250)	.40	.12
COMMON (101-150/251-300)	.60	.18
1 Darin Erstad	.40	.12
2 Javy Lopez	.40	.12
3 Vinny Castilla	.40	.12
4 Jim Thome	1.00	.30
5 Tino Martinez	.60	.18
6 Mark Grace	.60	.18
7 Shawn Green	.40	.12
8 Dustin Hermanson	.40	.12
9 Kevin Young	.40	.12
10 Tony Clark	.40	.12
11 Scott Brosius	.40	.12
12 Craig Biggio	.60	.18
13 Brian McRae	.40	.12
14 Chan Ho Park	.40	.12
15 Manny Ramirez	.40	.12
16 Chipper Jones	1.00	.30
17 Rico Brogna	.40	.12
18 Quinton McCracken	.40	.12
19 J.T. Snow	.40	.12
20 Tony Gwynn	1.25	.35
21 Juan Guzman	.40	.12
22 John Valentin	.40	.12
23 Rick Helling	.40	.12
24 Sandy Alomar Jr.	.40	.12
25 Frank Thomas	1.00	.30
26 Jorge Posada	.60	.18
27 Dmitri Young	.40	.12
28 Rick Reed	.40	.12
29 Kevin Tapani	.40	.12
30 Troy Glaus	.60	.18
31 Kenny Rogers	.40	.12
32 Jeromy Burnitz	.40	.12
33 Mark Grudzielanek	.40	.12
34 Mike Mussina	1.00	.30
35 Scott Rolen	.60	.18
36 Neifi Perez	.40	.12
37 Brad Radke	.40	.12
38 Darryl Strawberry	.60	.18
39 Robb Nen	.40	.12
40 Moises Alou	.40	.12
41 Eric Young	.40	.12
42 Livan Hernandez	.40	.12
43 John Wetteland	.40	.12
44 Matt Lawton	.40	.12
45 Ben Grieve	.40	.12
46 Fernando Tatis	.40	.12
47 Travis Fryman	.40	.12
48 David Segui	.40	.12
49 Bob Abreu	.40	.12
50 Nomar Garciaparra	1.50	.45
51 Paul O'Neill	.60	.18
52 Jeff King	.40	.12
53 Francisco Cordova	.40	.12
54 John Olerud	.40	.12
55 Vladimir Guerrero	1.00	.30
56 Fernando Vina	.40	.12
57 Shane Reynolds	.40	.12
58 Chuck Finley	.40	.12
59 Rondell White	.40	.12
60 Greg Vaughn	.40	.12
61 Ryan Minor	.40	.12
62 Tom Gordon	.40	.12
63 Damion Easley	.40	.12
64 Ray Durham	.40	.12
65 Orlando Hernandez	.40	.12
66 Bartolo Colon	.40	.12
67 Jaret Wright	.40	.12
68 Royce Clayton	.40	.12
69 Tim Salmon	.60	.18
70 Mark McGwire	2.50	.75
71 Alex Gonzalez	.40	.12
72 Tom Glavine	.60	.18
73 David Justice	.40	.12
74 Omar Vizquel	.40	.12
75 Juan Gonzalez	1.00	.30
76 Bobby Higginson	.40	.12
77 Todd Walker	.40	.12
78 Dante Bichette	.40	.12
79 Kevin Millwood	.40	.12
80 Roger Clemens	2.00	.60
81 Kerry Wood	1.00	.30
82 Cal Ripken	3.00	.90
83 Jay Bell	.40	.12
84 Barry Bonds	2.50	.75
85 Alex Rodriguez	1.50	.45
86 Doug Glanville	.40	.12
87 Jason Kendall	.40	.12
88 Sean Casey	.40	.12
89 Aaron Sele	.40	.12
90 Derek Jeter	2.50	.75
91 Andy Ashby	.40	.12
92 Rusty Greer	.40	.12
93 Rod Beck	.40	.12
94 Matt Williams	.40	.12
95 Mike Piazza	1.50	.45
96 Wally Joyner	.40	.12
97 Barry Larkin	1.00	.30
98 Eric Milton	.40	.12
99 Gary Sheffield	.40	.12
100 Greg Maddux	1.50	.45
101 Ken Griffey Jr. GEM	2.50	.75
102 Frank Thomas GEM	1.50	.45
103 N.Garciaparra GEM	2.50	.75
104 Mark McGwire GEM	4.00	1.20
105 Alex Rodriguez GEM	2.50	.75
106 Tony Gwynn GEM	2.00	.60
107 Juan Gonzalez GEM	1.50	.45
108 Jeff Bagwell GEM	1.00	.30
109 Sammy Sosa GEM	2.50	.75
110 V.Guerrero GEM	1.50	.45
111 Roger Clemens GEM	3.00	.90
112 Barry Bonds GEM	4.00	1.20
113 Darin Erstad GEM	.60	.18
114 Mike Piazza GEM	2.50	.75
115 Derek Jeter GEM	4.00	1.20
116 Chipper Jones GEM	1.50	.45
117 Larry Walker GEM	1.00	.30
118 Scott Rolen GEM	1.00	.30
119 Cal Ripken GEM	5.00	1.50
120 Greg Maddux GEM	2.50	.75
121 Troy Glaus SENS	1.00	.30
122 Ben Grieve SENS	.60	.18
123 Ryan Minor SENS	.60	.18
124 Kerry Wood SENS	1.50	.45
125 Travis Lee SENS	.60	.18
126 Adrian Beltre SENS	.60	.18
127 Brad Fullmer SENS	.60	.18
128 Aramis Ramirez SENS	.60	.18
129 Eric Chavez SENS	.60	.18
130 Todd Helton SENS	1.00	.30
131 Pat Burrell RC	6.00	1.80
132 Ryan Mills RC	.60	.18
133 Austin Kearns RC	8.00	2.40
134 Josh McKinley RC	.60	.18
135 Adam Everett RC	.60	.18
136 Marlon Anderson	.60	.18
137 Bruce Chen	.60	.18
138 Matt Clement	.60	.18
139 Alex Gonzalez	.60	.18
140 Roy Halladay	.60	.18
141 Calvin Pickering	.60	.18
142 Randy Wolf	.60	.18
143 Ryan Anderson	.60	.18
144 Ruben Mateo	.60	.18
145 Alex Escobar RC	.60	.18
146 Jeremy Giambi	.60	.18
147 Lance Berkman	.60	.18
148 Michael Barrett	.60	.18
149 Preston Wilson	.60	.18
150 Gabe Kapler	.60	.18
151 Roger Clemens	2.00	.60
152 Jay Buhner	.40	.12
153 Brad Fullmer	.40	.12
154 Ray Lankford	.40	.12
155 Jim Edmonds	.40	.12
156 Jason Giambi	1.00	.30
157 Bret Boone	.40	.12
158 Jeff Cirillo	.40	.12
159 Rickey Henderson	1.00	.30
160 Edgar Martinez	.60	.18
161 Ron Gant	.40	.12
162 Mark Kotsay	.40	.12
163 Trevor Hoffman	.40	.12
164 Jason Schmidt	.40	.12
165 Brett Tomko	.40	.12
166 David Ortiz	.40	.12
167 Dean Palmer	.40	.12
168 Hideki Irabu	.40	.12
169 Mike Cameron	.40	.12
170 Pedro Martinez	1.00	.30
171 Tom Goodwin	.40	.12
172 Brian Hunter	.40	.12
173 Al Leiter	.40	.12
174 Charles Johnson	.40	.12
175 Curt Schilling	.60	.18
176 Robin Ventura	.40	.12
177 Travis Lee	.40	.12
178 Jeff Shaw	.40	.12
179 Ugueth Urbina	.40	.12
180 Roberto Alomar	1.00	.30
181 Cliff Floyd	.40	.12
182 Adrian Beltre	.40	.12
183 Tony Womack	.40	.12
184 Brian Jordan	.40	.12
185 Randy Johnson	1.00	.30
186 Mickey Morandini	.40	.12
187 Todd Hundley	.40	.12
188 Jose Valentin	.40	.12
189 Eric Davis	.40	.12
190 Ken Caminiti	.40	.12
191 David Wells	.40	.12
192 Ryan Klesko	.40	.12
193 Garret Anderson	.40	.12
194 Eric Karros	.40	.12
195 Ivan Rodriguez	1.00	.30
196 Aramis Ramirez	.40	.12
197 Mike Lieberthal	.40	.12
198 Will Clark	1.00	.30
199 Rey Ordonez	.40	.12
200 Ken Griffey Jr.	1.50	.45
201 Jose Guillen	.40	.12
202 Scott Erickson	.40	.12
203 Paul Konerko	.40	.12
204 Johnny Damon	.40	.12
205 Larry Walker	.60	.18
206 Denny Neagle	.40	.12
207 Jose Offerman	.40	.12
208 Andy Pettitte	.60	.18
209 Bobby Jones	.40	.12
210 Kevin Brown	.60	.18
211 John Smoltz	.60	.18
212 Henry Rodriguez	.40	.12
213 Tim Belcher	.40	.12
214 Carlos Delgado	.40	.12
215 Andruw Jones	.40	.12
216 Andy Benes	.40	.12
217 Fred McGriff	.60	.18
218 Edgar Renteria	.40	.12
219 Miguel Tejada	.40	.12
220 Bernie Williams	.60	.18
221 Justin Thompson	.40	.12
222 Marty Cordova	.40	.12
223 Delino DeShields	.40	.12
224 Ellis Burks	.40	.12
225 Kenny Lofton	.40	.12
226 Steve Finley	.40	.12
227 Eric Chavez	.40	.12
228 Jose Cruz Jr.	.40	.12
229 Marquis Grissom	.40	.12
230 Jeff Bagwell	.60	.18
231 Jose Canseco	1.00	.30
232 Edgardo Alfonzo	.40	.12
233 Richie Sexson	.40	.12
234 Jeff Kent	.40	.12
235 Rafael Palmeiro	.60	.18
236 David Cone	.40	.12
237 Gregg Jefferies	.40	.12
238 Mike Lansing	.40	.12
239 Mariano Rivera	.60	.18
240 Albert Belle	.40	.12
241 Chuck Knoblauch	.40	.12
242 Derek Bell	.40	.12
243 Pat Hentgen	.40	.12
244 Andres Galarraga	.40	.12
245 Mo Vaughn	.40	.12
246 Wade Boggs	.60	.18
247 Devon White	.40	.12
248 Todd Helton	.60	.18
249 Raul Mondesi	.40	.12
250 Sammy Sosa	1.50	.45
251 Nomar Garciaparra ST	2.50	.75
252 Mark McGwire ST	4.00	1.20
253 Alex Rodriguez ST	2.50	.75
254 Juan Gonzalez ST	1.50	.45
255 Vladimir Guerrero ST	1.50	.45
256 Ken Griffey Jr. ST	2.50	.75
257 Mike Piazza ST	2.50	.75
258 Derek Jeter ST	4.00	1.20
259 Albert Belle ST	.60	.18
260 Greg Vaughn ST	.60	.18
261 Sammy Sosa ST	2.50	.75
262 Greg Maddux ST	2.50	.75
263 Frank Thomas ST	1.50	.45
264 Mark Grace ST	1.00	.30
265 Ivan Rodriguez ST	1.50	.45
266 Roger Clemens GM	3.00	.90
267 Mo Vaughn GM	.60	.18
268 Jim Thome GM	1.50	.45
269 Darin Erstad GM	.60	.18
270 Chipper Jones GM	1.50	.45
271 Larry Walker GM	1.00	.30
272 Cal Ripken GM	5.00	1.50
273 Scott Rolen GM	1.00	.30
274 Randy Johnson GM	1.50	.45
275 Tony Gwynn GM	2.00	.60
276 Barry Bonds GM	4.00	1.20
277 Sean Burroughs RC	5.00	1.50
278 J.M. Gold RC	.60	.18
279 Carlos Lee	.60	.18
280 George Lombard	.60	.18
281 Carlos Beltran	.60	.18
282 Fernando Seguignol	.60	.18
283 Eric Chavez	.60	.18
284 Carlos Pena RC	1.50	.45
285 Corey Patterson RC	6.00	1.80
286 Alfonso Soriano RC	12.00	3.60
287 Nick Johnson RC	3.00	.90
288 Jorge Toca RC	.60	.18
289 A.J. Burnett RC	1.50	.45
290 Andy Brown RC	.60	.18
291 D.Mientkiewicz RC	2.00	.60
292 Bobby Seay RC	.60	.18
293 Chip Ambres RC	.60	.18
294 C.C. Sabathia RC	1.50	.45
295 Choo Freeman RC	.60	.18
296 Eric Valent RC	.60	.18
297 Matt Belisle RC	.60	.18
298 Jason Tyner RC	.60	.18
299 Masao Kida RC	.60	.18
300 Hank Aaron Mark McGwire	3.00	.90

1999 Finest Gold Refractors

This 300-card set is a die-cut gold foil parallel version of the base set. Only 100 serially numbered sets were produced. Cards were randomly inserted in hobby and retail packs. Series one packs were at the rate of one in 82 and HTA packs at a rate of one in 38. Series 2 packs were at the rate of one in 57 and HTA packs at a rate of one in 26.

Nm-Mt Ex-Mt
*STARS 1-100/151-250: 10X TO 25X BASIC
*STARS 101-150/251-300: 6X TO 15X BAS.
*ROOKIES: 4X TO 10X BASIC

1999 Finest Refractors

Randomly inserted in series one and two packs at the rate of one in 12 hobby/retail and one in five HTA, this 300-card set is a parallel version of the base set and is similar in design. The difference is found in the refractive quality of the card.

Nm-Mt Ex-Mt
*STARS 1-100/151-250: 3X TO 8X BASIC
*STARS 101-150/251-300: 2X TO 5X BASIC
*ROOKIES: 1.5X TO 4X BASIC

1999 Finest Aaron Award Contenders

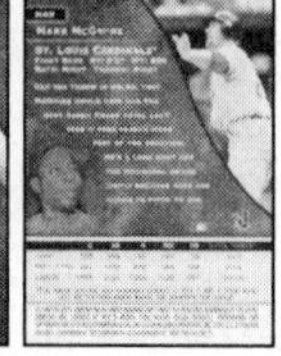

Randomly inserted into Series two packs at different rates depending on the player, this nine-card set features color action photos of players vying for the Hank Aaron Award.

	Nm-Mt	Ex-Mt
COMPLETE SET (9)	60.00	18.00
HA1 SER.2 ODDS 1:216, 1:108 HTA		
HA2 SER.2 ODDS 1:108, 1:54 HTA		
HA3 SER.2 ODDS 1:72, 1:36 HTA		
HA4 SER.2 ODDS 1:54, 1:27 HTA		
HA5 SER.2 ODDS 1:43, 1:21 HTA		
HA6 SER.2 ODDS 1:36, 1:18 HTA		
HA7 SER.2 ODDS 1:31, 1:15 HTA		
HA8 SER.2 ODDS 1:27, 1:13 HTA		
HA9 SER.2 ODDS 1:24, 1:12 HTA		
*REFRACTORS: 1.5X TO 4X BASIC AARON AW		
REF HA1 SER.2 ODDS 1:1728, 1:864 HTA		
REF HA2 SER.2 ODDS 1:864, 1:432 HTA		
REF HA3 SER.2 ODDS 1:576, 1:288 HTA		
REF HA4 SER.2 ODDS 1:432, 1:216 HTA		
REF HA5 SER.2 ODDS 1:344, 1:172 HTA		
REF HA6 SER.2 ODDS 1:288, 1:144 HTA		
REF HA7 SER.2 ODDS 1:248, 1:124 HTA		
REF HA8 SER.2 ODDS 1:216, 1:108 HTA		
REF HA9 SER.2 ODDS 1:192, 1:96 HTA		
HA1 Juan Gonzalez	8.00	2.40
HA2 Vladimir Guerrero	10.00	3.00
HA3 Nomar Garciaparra	12.00	3.60
HA4 Albert Belle	3.00	.90
HA5 Frank Thomas	5.00	1.50
HA6 Sammy Sosa	6.00	1.80
HA7 Alex Rodriguez	5.00	1.50
HA8 Ken Griffey Jr.	4.00	1.20
HA9 Mark McGwire	5.00	1.50

1999 Finest Complements

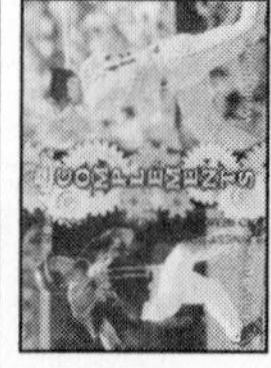

Randomly inserted into Series two packs at the rate of one in 56, this seven-card set features color action photos of 14 stars who complement each other's skills and share a common bond paired together on cards printed with advanced "Split Screen" technology which combines Refractor and Non-Refractor technology on the same card. Each card has three variations as follows: 1) Non-Refractor/Refractor, 2) Refractor/Non-Refractor, and 3) Refractor/Refractor.

	Nm-Mt	Ex-Mt
COMPLETE SET (7)	50.00	15.00
RIGHT/LEFT REF.VARIATIONS EQUAL VALUE		
*DUAL REF: 1.25X TO 3X BASIC COMP.		
DUAL REF.SER.2 ODDS 1:168, 1:81 HTA		
C1 Mike Piazza Ivan Rodriguez	6.00	1.80
C2 Tony Gwynn Wade Boggs	5.00	1.50
C3 Kerry Wood Roger Clemens	8.00	2.40
C4 Juan Gonzalez Sammy Sosa	6.00	1.80
C5 Derek Jeter Nomar Garciaparra	10.00	3.00
C6 Mark McGwire Frank Thomas	10.00	3.00
C7 Vladimir Guerrero Andruw Jones	4.00	1.20

1999 Finest Double Feature

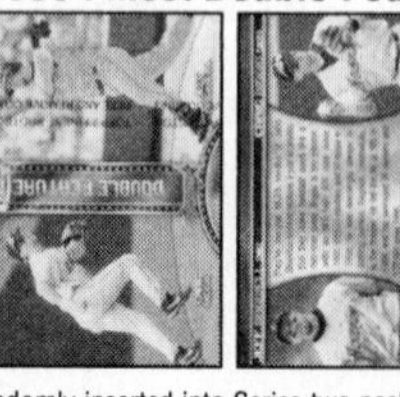

Randomly inserted into Series two packs at the rate of one in 56, this seven-card set features color photos of fourteen paired teammates printed on cards using Split Screen technology combining Refractor and Non-Refractor technology on the same card. There are three different versions of each card as follows: 1) Non-Refractor/Refractor, 2) Refractor/Non-Refractor, and 3) Refractor/Refractor.

	Nm-Mt	Ex-Mt
COMPLETE SET (7)	40.00	12.00
RIGHT/LEFT REF.VARIATIONS EQUAL VALUE		
*DUAL REF: 1.25X TO 3X BASIC DOUB.FEAT.		
*DUAL REF BURRELL: 1.25X TO 3X HI COLUMN		
DUAL REF.SER.2 ODDS 1:168, 1:81 HTA		
DF1 Ken Griffey Jr. Alex Rodriguez	6.00	1.80
DF2 Chipper Jones Andruw Jones	4.00	1.20
DF3 Darin Erstad Mo Vaughn	1.50	.45
DF4 Craig Biggio Jeff Bagwell	2.50	.75
DF5 Ben Grieve Eric Chavez	1.50	.45
DF6 Albert Belle Cal Ripken	12.00	3.60
DF7 Scott Rolen Pat Burrell	5.00	1.50

1999 Finest Franchise Records

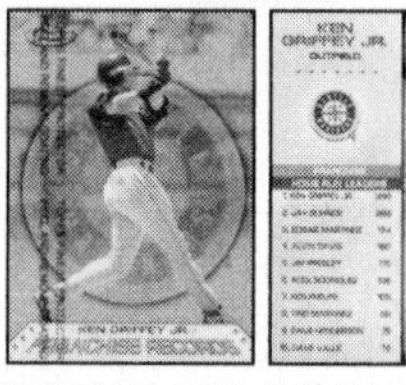

Randomly inserted into Series two packs at the rate of one in 129, this ten-card set features color action photos of all-time and single-season franchise statistic holders. A refractive parallel version of this set was also produced and inserted in Series two packs at the rate of one in 378.

	Nm-Mt	Ex-Mt
COMPLETE SET (10)	150.00	45.00
*REFRACTORS: .75X TO 2X BASIC FRAN.REC.		
REF.SER.2 ODDS 1:378, 1:189 HTA		
FR1 Frank Thomas	10.00	3.00
FR2 Ken Griffey Jr.	15.00	4.50
FR3 Mark McGwire	25.00	7.50
FR4 Juan Gonzalez	10.00	3.00
FR5 Nomar Garciaparra	15.00	4.50
FR6 Mike Piazza	15.00	4.50
FR7 Cal Ripken	30.00	9.00
FR8 Sammy Sosa	15.00	4.50
FR9 Barry Bonds	25.00	7.50
FR10 Tony Gwynn	12.00	3.60

1999 Finest Future's Finest

Randomly inserted into Series two packs at the rate of one in 171, this 10-card set features olor photos of top young stars printed on card tock using Refractive Finest technology. The ards are sequentially numbered to 500.

	Nm-Mt	Ex-Mt
COMPLETE SET (10)	100.00	30.00
F1 Pat Burrell	20.00	6.00
F2 Troy Glaus	10.00	3.00
F3 Eric Chavez	10.00	3.00
F4 Ryan Anderson	10.00	3.00
F5 Ruben Mateo	10.00	3.00
F6 Gabe Kapler	10.00	3.00
F7 Alex Gonzalez	10.00	3.00
F8 Michael Barrett	10.00	3.00
F9 Adrian Beltre	10.00	3.00
F10 Fernando Seguignol	10.00	3.00

1999 Finest Leading Indicators

Randomly inserted in Series one packs at the rate of one in 24, this 10-card set features color action photos highlighting the 1998 home run totals of superstar players and printed on cards using a heat-sensitvie, thermal-ink technology. When a collector touched the baseball field background in left, center, or right field, the heat from his finger revealed the pictured player's '98 home run totals in that direction.

	Nm-Mt	Ex-Mt
COMPLETE SET (10)	50.00	15.00
L1 Mark McGwire	10.00	3.00
L2 Sammy Sosa	6.00	1.80
L3 Ken Griffey Jr.	6.00	1.80
L4 Greg Vaughn	1.50	.45
L5 Albert Belle	1.50	.45
L6 Juan Gonzalez	4.00	1.20
L7 Andres Galarraga	1.50	.45
L8 Alex Rodriguez	6.00	1.80
L9 Barry Bonds	10.00	3.00
L10 Jeff Bagwell	2.50	.75

1999 Finest Milestones

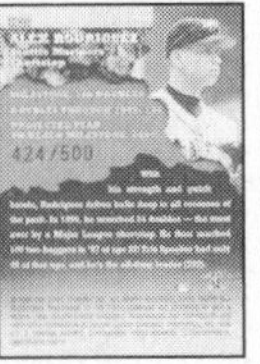

Randomly inserted into packs at the rate of one in 29, this 40-card set features color photos of players who have the highest statistics in four categories: Hits, Home Runs, RBI's and Doubles. The cards are printed with Refractor technology and sequentially numbered based on the category as follows: Hits to 3,000, Home Runs to 500, RBIs to 1,400, and Doubles to 500.

	Nm-Mt	Ex-Mt
M1 Tony Gwynn HIT	5.00	1.50
M2 Cal Ripken HIT	12.00	3.60
M3 Wade Boggs HIT	2.50	.75
M4 Ken Griffey Jr. HIT	6.00	1.80
M5 Frank Thomas HIT	4.00	1.20
M6 Barry Bonds HIT	10.00	3.00
M7 Travis Lee HIT	1.50	.45
M8 Alex Rodriguez HIT	6.00	1.80
M9 Derek Jeter HIT	10.00	3.00
M10 V.Guerrero HIT	4.00	1.20
M11 Mark McGwire HR	30.00	9.00
M12 Ken Griffey Jr. HR	20.00	6.00
M13 Vladimir Guerrero HR	12.00	3.60
M14 Alex Rodriguez HR	20.00	6.00
M15 Barry Bonds HR	30.00	9.00
M16 Sammy Sosa HR	20.00	6.00
M17 Albert Belle HR	5.00	1.50
M18 Frank Thomas HR	12.00	3.60
M19 Jose Canseco HR	12.00	3.60
M20 Mike Piazza HR	20.00	6.00
M21 Jeff Bagwell RBI	4.00	1.20
M22 Barry Bonds RBI	15.00	4.50
M23 Ken Griffey Jr. RBI	10.00	3.00
M24 Albert Belle RBI	2.50	.75
M25 Juan Gonzalez RBI	6.00	1.80
M26 Vinny Castilla RBI	2.50	.75
M27 Mark McGwire RBI	15.00	4.50
M28 Alex Rodriguez RBI	10.00	3.00
M29 N.Garciaparra RBI	10.00	3.00
M30 Frank Thomas RBI	6.00	1.80
M31 Barry Bonds 2B	30.00	9.00
M32 Albert Belle 2B	5.00	1.50
M33 Ben Grieve 2B	5.00	1.50
M34 Craig Biggio 2B	8.00	2.40
M35 Vladimir Guerrero 2B	12.00	3.60
M36 N.Garciaparra 2B	20.00	6.00
M37 Alex Rodriguez 2B	20.00	6.00
M38 Derek Jeter 2B	30.00	9.00
M39 Ken Griffey Jr. 2B	20.00	6.00
M40 Brad Fullmer 2B	5.00	1.50

1999 Finest Peel and Reveal Sparkle

Randomly inserted in Series one packs at the rate of one in 30, this 20-card set features color action player images on a sparkle background. This set was considered Common and the protective coating had to be peeled from the card front and back to reveal the level.

	Nm-Mt	Ex-Mt
COMPLETE SET (20)	120.00	36.00

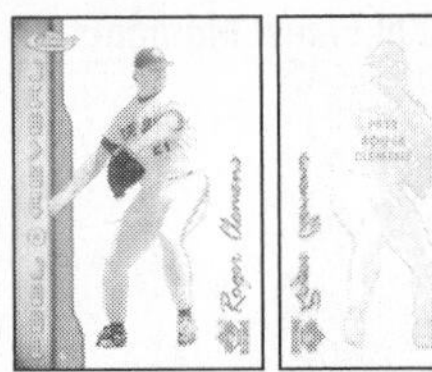

*HYPERPLAID: .6X TO 1.5X SPARKLE
HYPERPLAID SER.1 ODDS 1:60 H/R,1:30 HTA
*STADIUM STARS: 1.25X TO 3X SPARKLE
STAD.STAR SER.1 ODDS 1:120 H/R, 1:60 HTA

1 Kerry Wood	5.00	1.50
2 Mark McGwire	12.00	3.60
3 Sammy Sosa	8.00	2.40
4 Ken Griffey Jr.	8.00	2.40
5 Nomar Garciaparra	8.00	2.40
6 Greg Maddux	8.00	2.40
7 Derek Jeter	12.00	3.60
8 Andres Galarraga	2.00	.60
9 Alex Rodriguez	8.00	2.40
10 Frank Thomas	5.00	1.50
11 Roger Clemens	10.00	3.00
12 Juan Gonzalez	5.00	1.50
13 Ben Grieve	2.00	.60
14 Jeff Bagwell	3.00	.90
15 Todd Helton	3.00	.90
16 Chipper Jones	5.00	1.50
17 Barry Bonds	12.00	3.60
18 Travis Lee	2.00	.60
19 Vladimir Guerrero	5.00	1.50
20 Pat Burrell	6.00	1.80

1999 Finest Prominent Figures

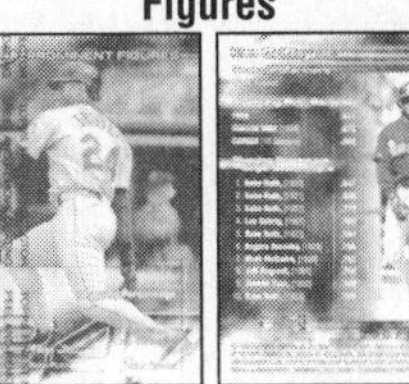

Randomly inserted in Series one packs with various insertion rates, this 50-card set features color action photos of ten superstars in each of five statistical categories and printed with refractor technology. The categories are: Home Runs (with an insertion rate of 1:1,749) and sequentially numbered to 70, Slugging Percentage (1:145) numbered to 847, Batting Average (1:289) numbered to 424, Runs Batted In (1:644) numbered to 190, and Total Bases (1:268) numbered to 457.

	Nm-Mt	Ex-Mt
COMPLETE SET (50)	1000.00	300.00
PF1 Mark McGwire HR	100.00	30.00
PF2 Sammy Sosa HR	60.00	18.00
PF3 Ken Griffey Jr. HR	60.00	18.00
PF4 Mike Piazza HR	60.00	18.00
PF5 Juan Gonzalez HR	40.00	12.00
PF6 Greg Vaughn HR	15.00	4.50
PF7 Alex Rodriguez HR	60.00	18.00
PF8 Manny Ramirez HR	15.00	4.50
PF9 Jeff Bagwell HR	25.00	7.50
PF10 Andres Galarraga HR	15.00	4.50
PF11 Mark McGwire SLG	20.00	6.00
PF12 Sammy Sosa SLG	12.00	3.60
PF13 Juan Gonzalez SLG	8.00	2.40
PF14 Ken Griffey Jr. SLG	12.00	3.60
PF15 Barry Bonds SLG	20.00	6.00
PF16 Greg Vaughn SLG	3.00	.90
PF17 Larry Walker SLG	5.00	1.50
PF18 A.Galarraga SLG	3.00	.90
PF19 Jeff Bagwell SLG	5.00	1.50
PF20 Albert Belle SLG	3.00	.90
PF21 Tony Gwynn BAT	20.00	6.00
PF22 Mike Piazza BAT	15.00	4.50
PF23 Larry Walker BAT	6.00	1.80
PF24 Alex Rodriguez BAT	15.00	4.50
PF25 John Olerud BAT	4.00	1.20
PF26 Frank Thomas BAT	10.00	3.00
PF27 Bernie Williams BAT	6.00	1.80
PF28 Chipper Jones BAT	10.00	3.00
PF29 Jim Thome BAT	10.00	3.00
PF30 Barry Bonds BAT	25.00	7.50
PF31 Juan Gonzalez RBI	15.00	4.50
PF32 Sammy Sosa RBI	25.00	7.50
PF33 Mark McGwire RBI	40.00	12.00
PF34 Albert Belle RBI	6.00	1.80
PF35 Ken Griffey Jr. RBI	25.00	7.50
PF36 Jeff Bagwell RBI	10.00	3.00
PF37 Chipper Jones RBI	15.00	4.50
PF38 Vinny Castilla RBI	6.00	1.80
PF39 Alex Rodriguez RBI	25.00	7.50
PF40 A.Galarraga RBI	6.00	1.80
PF41 Sammy Sosa TB	15.00	4.50
PF42 Mark McGwire TB	25.00	7.50
PF43 Albert Belle TB	4.00	1.20
PF44 Ken Griffey Jr. TB	15.00	4.50
PF45 Jeff Bagwell TB	6.00	1.80
PF46 Juan Gonzalez TB	10.00	3.00
PF47 Barry Bonds TB	25.00	7.50
PF48 V.Guerrero TB	10.00	3.00
PF49 Larry Walker TB	6.00	1.80
PF50 Alex Rodriguez TB	15.00	4.50

1999 Finest Split Screen

Randomly inserted in Series one packs at the rate of one in 28, this 14-card set features action color photos of two players paired together on the same card and printed using a special refractor and non-refractor technology. Each card was printed with right/left refractor variations.

	Nm-Mt	Ex-Mt
COMPLETE SET (14)	100.00	30.00

RIGHT/LEFT REF.VARIATIONS EQUAL VALUE
*DUAL REF: 1.25X TO 3X BASIC SCREEN

DUAL REF.SER.1 ODDS 1:82 H/R, 1:42 HTA

SS1 Mark McGwire Sammy Sosa	10.00	3.00
SS2 Ken Griffey Jr. Alex Rodriguez	6.00	1.80
SS3 Nomar Garciaparra Derek Jeter	10.00	3.00
SS4 Barry Bonds Albert Belle	10.00	3.00
SS5 Cal Ripken Tony Gwynn	12.00	3.60
SS6 Manny Ramirez Juan Gonzalez	1.50	.45
SS7 Frank Thomas Andres Galarraga	4.00	1.20
SS8 Scott Rolen Chipper Jones	4.00	1.20
SS9 Ivan Rodriguez Mike Piazza	6.00	1.80
SS10 Kerry Wood Roger Clemens	8.00	2.40
SS11 Greg Maddux Tom Glavine	6.00	1.80
SS12 Troy Glaus Eric Chavez	2.50	.75
SS13 Ben Grieve Todd Helton	2.50	.75
SS14 Travis Lee Pat Burrell	5.00	1.50

1999 Finest Team Finest Blue

Randomly inserted in Series one and Series two packs at the rate of one in 82 first series and one in 57 second series. Also distributed in HTA packs at a rate of one in 38 first series and one in 26 second series. This 20-card set features color action player images printed using prismatic Chromium technology with blue highlights and is sequentially numbered to 1500. Cards 1-10 were distributed in first series packs and 11-20 in second series packs.

	Nm-Mt	Ex-Mt
COMP.BLUE SET (20)	150.00	45.00

*BLUE REF: .75X TO 2X BASIC BLUE .
BLUE REF.SER.1 ODDS 1:816 HOB, 1:377 HTA
BLUE REF.SER.2 ODDS 1:571 HOB, 1:263 HTA
BLUE REF.PRINT RUN 150 SERIAL #'d SETS
*RED: .5X TO 1.2X BASIC BLUE
RED SER.2 ODDS 1:18 HTA
RED SER.1 ODDS 1:25 HTA
RED PRINT RUN 500 SERIAL #'d SETS
*RED REF: 2.5X TO 6X BASIC BLUE
RED REF.SER.1 ODDS 1:254 HTA
RED REF.SER.2 ODDS 1:184 HTA
RED REF.PRINT RUN 50 SERIAL #'d SETS
*GOLD: .6X TO 1.5X BASIC BLUE
GOLD SER.1 ODDS 1:51 HTA
GOLD SER.2 ODDS 1:37 HTA
GOLD PRINT RUN 250 SERIAL #'d SETS
*GOLD REF: 4X TO 10X BASIC BLUE..
GOLD REF.SER.1 ODDS 1:510 HTA
GOLD REF.SER.2 ODDS 1:369 HTA
GOLD REF.PRINT RUN 25 SERIAL #'d SETS

TF1 Greg Maddux	6.00	1.80
TF2 Mark McGwire	10.00	3.00
TF3 Sammy Sosa	6.00	1.80
TF4 Juan Gonzalez	4.00	1.20
TF5 Alex Rodriguez	6.00	1.80
TF6 Travis Lee	2.00	.60
TF7 Roger Clemens	8.00	2.40
TF8 Darin Erstad	2.00	.60
TF9 Todd Helton	2.50	.75
TF10 Mike Piazza	6.00	1.80
TF11 Kerry Wood	4.00	1.20
TF12 Ken Griffey Jr.	6.00	1.80
TF13 Frank Thomas	4.00	1.20
TF14 Jeff Bagwell	2.50	.75
TF15 Nomar Garciaparra	6.00	1.80
TF16 Derek Jeter	10.00	3.00
TF17 Chipper Jones	4.00	1.20
TF18 Barry Bonds	10.00	3.00
TF19 Tony Gwynn	5.00	1.50
TF20 Ben Grieve	2.00	.60

2000 Finest Pre-Production

This five card standard-size set was issued to preview what the 2000 Finest set would look like. It was issued to the dealers and hobby media on Topps' mailing list several weeks before the release of 2000 Finest. The cards can be differentiated from the regular Finest cards by the "PP" numbering on the back.

	Nm-Mt	Ex-Mt
COMPLETE SET (5)	6.00	1.80
PP1 Brian Jordan	.50	.15
PP2 Bernie Williams	1.00	.30
PP3 Pat Burrell	.50	.15
PP4 Corey Myers	.50	.15
PP5 Derek Jeter GEM	4.00	1.20

2000 Finest

Produced by Topps, the 2000 Finest Series one product was released in April, 2000 as a 147-card set. The Finest Series two product was released in July, 2000 as a 140-card set. Each hobby and retail pack contained six cards and carried a suggested retail price of $4.99. Each HTA pack contained 13 cards and carried a suggested retail price of $10.00. The set includes 179-player cards, 20 first series Rookie Cards (cards 101-120) each serial numbered to 2000 and 20 second series Rookie Cards (cards 247-266) each serial numbered to 3000, 15 Features subset cards (cards 121-135), 10 Counterparts subset cards (numbers 267-276), and 20 Gems subset cards (numbers 136-145 and 277-286). The set also includes two versions of card number 146 Ken Griffey Jr. wearing his Reds uniform (a portrait and action shot). Rookie Cards were seeded at a rate of 1:23 hobby/retail packs and 1:6 HTA packs. Features and Counterparts subset cards were inserted one every eight hobby and retail packs and one every three HTA packs. Gems subset cards were inserted one every 24 hobby and retail packs and one every nine HTA packs. Notable Rookie Cards include Rick Asadoorian and Bobby Bradley. Finally, 20 "Graded Gems" exchange cards were randomly seeded into packs (10 per series). The lucky handful of collectors that found these cards could send them into Topps for a complete Gems subset, each of which was professionally graded "Gem Mint 10" by PSA.

	Nm-Mt	Ex-Mt
COMP.SERIES 1 w/o SP's (100)	25.00	7.50
COMP.SERIES 2 w/o SP's (100)	25.00	7.50
COMMON (1-100/147-246)	.40	.12
COMMON (101-120)	5.00	1.50
COMMON (121-135)	1.50	.45
COMMON (136-145/277-286)	2.00	.60
COMMON (247-266)	5.00	1.50
COMMON (267-276)	1.00	.30
1 Nomar Garciaparra	1.50	.45
2 Chipper Jones	1.00	.30
3 Erubiel Durazo	.40	.12
4 Robin Ventura	.60	.18
5 Garret Anderson	.40	.12
6 Dean Palmer	.40	.12
7 Mariano Rivera	.60	.18
8 Rusty Greer	.40	.12
9 Jim Thome	1.00	.30
10 Jeff Bagwell	.60	.18
11 Jason Giambi	1.00	.30
12 Jeromy Burnitz	.40	.12
13 Mark Grace	.60	.18
14 Russ Ortiz	.40	.12
15 Kevin Brown	.60	.18
16 Kevin Millwood	.40	.12
17 Scott Williamson	.40	.12
18 Orlando Hernandez	.40	.12
19 Todd Walker	.40	.12
20 Carlos Beltran	.40	.12
21 Ruben Rivera	.40	.12
22 Curt Schilling	.60	.18
23 Brian Giles	.40	.12
24 Eric Karros	.40	.12
25 Preston Wilson	.40	.12
26 Al Leiter	.40	.12
27 Juan Encarnacion	.40	.12
28 Tim Salmon	.60	.18
29 B.J. Surhoff	.40	.12
30 Bernie Williams	.60	.18
31 Lee Stevens	.40	.12
32 Pokey Reese	.40	.12
33 Mike Sweeney	.40	.12
34 Corey Koskie	.40	.12
35 Roberto Alomar	1.00	.30
36 Tim Hudson	.60	.18
37 Tom Glavine	.60	.18
38 Jeff Kent	.40	.12
39 Mike Lieberthal	.40	.12
40 Barry Larkin	1.00	.30
41 Paul O'Neill	.60	.18
42 Rico Brogna	.40	.12
43 Brian Daubach	.40	.12
44 Rich Aurilia	.40	.12
45 Vladimir Guerrero	1.00	.30
46 Luis Castillo	.40	.12
47 Bartolo Colon	.40	.12
48 Kevin Appier	.40	.12
49 Mo Vaughn	.40	.12
50 Alex Rodriguez	1.50	.45
51 Randy Johnson	1.00	.30
52 Kris Benson	.40	.12
53 Tony Clark	.40	.12
54 Chad Allen	.40	.12
55 Larry Walker	.60	.18
56 Freddy Garcia	.40	.12
57 Paul Konerko	.40	.12
58 Edgardo Alfonzo	.40	.12
59 Brady Anderson	.40	.12
60 Derek Jeter	2.50	.75
61 John Smoltz	.60	.18
62 Doug Glanville	.40	.12
63 Shannon Stewart	.40	.12
64 Greg Maddux	1.50	.45
65 Mark McGwire	2.50	.75
66 Gary Sheffield	.40	.12
67 Kevin Young	.40	.12
68 Tony Gwynn	1.25	.35
69 Rey Ordonez	.40	.12
70 Cal Ripken	3.00	.90
71 Todd Helton	.60	.18
72 Brian Jordan	.40	.12
73 Jose Canseco	1.00	.30
74 Luis Gonzalez	.40	.12
75 Barry Bonds	2.50	.75
76 Jermaine Dye	.40	.12
77 Jose Offerman	.40	.12
78 Magglio Ordonez	.40	.12
79 Fred McGriff	.60	.18
80 Ivan Rodriguez	1.00	.30
81 Josh Hamilton	.40	.12
82 Vernon Wells	.40	.12
83 Mark Mulder	.60	.18
84 John Patterson	.40	.12
85 Nick Johnson	.40	.12
86 Pablo Ozuna	.40	.12
87 A.J. Burnett	.40	.12
88 Jack Cust	.40	.12
89 Adam Piatt	.40	.12
90 Rob Ryan	.40	.12
91 Sean Burroughs	.60	.18
92 D'Angelo Jimenez	.40	.12
93 Chad Hermansen	.40	.12
94 Robert Fick	.40	.12
95 Ruben Mateo	.40	.12
96 Alex Escobar	.40	.12
97 Wily Pena	.40	.12
98 Corey Patterson	.60	.18
99 Eric Munson	.40	.12
100 Pat Burrell	.60	.18
101 Michael Tejera RC	5.00	1.50
102 Bobby Bradley RC	5.00	1.50
103 Larry Bigbie RC	8.00	2.40
104 B.J. Garbe RC	5.00	1.50
105 Josh Kalinowski RC	5.00	1.50
106 Brett Myers RC	15.00	4.50
107 Chris Mears RC	5.00	1.50
108 Aaron Rowand RC	5.00	1.50
109 Corey Myers RC	5.00	1.50
110 John Sneed RC	5.00	1.50
111 Ryan Christianson RC	5.00	1.50
112 Kyle Snyder	5.00	1.50
113 Mike Paradis	5.00	1.50
114 Chance Caple RC	5.00	1.50
115 Ben Christensen RC	5.00	1.50
116 Brad Baker RC	5.00	1.50
117 Rob Purvis RC	5.00	1.50
118 Rick Asadoorian RC	5.00	1.50
119 Ruben Salazar RC	5.00	1.50
120 Julio Zuleta RC	5.00	1.50
121 Alex Rodriguez Ken Griffey Jr.	4.00	1.20
122 Nomar Garciaparra Derek Jeter	5.00	1.50
123 Mark Mcgwire Sammy Sosa	6.00	1.80
124 Randy Johnson Pedro Martinez	2.50	.75
125 Ivan Rodriguez Mike Piazza	4.00	1.20
126 Manny Ramirez Roberto Alomar	2.50	.75
127 Chipper Jones Andruw Jones	2.50	.75
128 Cal Ripken Tony Gwynn	8.00	2.40
129 Jeff Bagwell Craig Biggio	1.50	.45
130 Barry Bonds Vladimir Guerrero	6.00	1.80
131 Nick Johnson Alfonso Soriano	2.50	.75
132 Josh Hamilton Pat Burrell	5.00	1.50
133 Corey Patterson Ruben Mateo	1.50	.45
134 Larry Walker Todd Helton	1.50	.45
135 Rey Ordonez Edgardo Alfonzo	1.50	.45
136 Derek Jeter GEM	12.00	3.60
137 Alex Rodriguez GEM	8.00	2.40
138 Chipper Jones GEM	5.00	1.50
139 Mike Piazza GEM	8.00	2.40
140 Mark McGwire GEM	12.00	3.60
141 Ivan Rodriguez GEM	5.00	1.50
142 Cal Ripken GEM	15.00	4.50
143 V.Guerrero GEM	5.00	1.50
144 Randy Johnson GEM	5.00	1.50
145 Jeff Bagwell GEM	3.00	.90
146 K.Griffey Jr. ACTION	1.50	.45
146A Ken Griffey Jr. PORT	1.50	.45
147 Andruw Jones	.40	.12
148 Kerry Wood	1.00	.30
149 Jim Edmonds	.40	.12
150 Pedro Martinez	1.00	.30
151 Warren Morris	.40	.12
152 Trevor Hoffman	.40	.12
153 Ryan Klesko	.40	.12
154 Andy Pettitte	.60	.18
155 Frank Thomas	1.00	.30
156 Damion Easley	.40	.12
157 Cliff Floyd	.40	.12
158 Ben Davis	.40	.12
159 John Valentin	.40	.12
160 Rafael Palmeiro	.60	.18
161 Andy Ashby	.40	.12
162 J.D. Drew	.40	.12
163 Jay Bell	.40	.12
164 Adam Kennedy	.40	.12
165 Manny Ramirez	.40	.12
166 John Halama	.40	.12
167 Octavio Dotel	.40	.12
168 Darin Erstad	.40	.12
169 Jose Lima	.40	.12
170 Andres Galarraga	.40	.12
171 Scott Rolen	.60	.18
172 Delino DeShields	.40	.12
173 J.T. Snow	.40	.12
174 Tony Womack	.40	.12
175 John Olerud	.40	.12
176 Jason Kendall	.40	.12
177 Carlos Lee	.40	.12
178 Eric Milton	.40	.12
179 Jeff Cirillo	.40	.12
180 Gabe Kapler	.40	.12
181 Greg Vaughn	.40	.12
182 Denny Neagle	.40	.12
183 Tino Martinez	.60	.18
184 Doug Mientkiewicz	.40	.12
185 Juan Gonzalez	1.00	.30
186 Ellis Burks	.40	.12
187 Mike Hampton	.40	.12
188 Royce Clayton	.40	.12
189 Mike Mussina	1.00	.30
190 Carlos Delgado	.40	.12
191 Ben Grieve	.40	.12

192 Fernando Tatis .40 .12
193 Matt Williams .40 .12
194 Rondell White .40 .12
195 Shawn Green .40 .12
196 Hideki Irabu .40 .12
197 Troy Glaus .60 .18
198 Roger Cedeno .40 .12
199 Ray Lankford .40 .12
200 Sammy Sosa 1.50 .45
201 Kenny Lofton .40 .12
202 Edgar Martinez .60 .18
203 Mark Kotsay .40 .12
204 David Wells .40 .12
205 Craig Biggio .60 .18
206 Ray Durham .40 .12
207 Troy O'Leary .40 .12
208 Rickey Henderson 1.00 .30
209 Bob Abreu .40 .12
210 Neifi Perez .40 .12
211 Carlos Febles .40 .12
212 Chuck Knoblauch .40 .12
213 Moises Alou .40 .12
214 Omar Vizquel .40 .12
215 Vinny Castilla .40 .12
216 Javy Lopez .40 .12
217 Johnny Damon .40 .12
218 Roger Clemens 2.00 .60
219 Miguel Tejada .40 .12
220 Carl Everett .40 .12
221 Matt Lawton .40 .12
222 Albert Belle .40 .12
223 Adrian Beltre .40 .12
224 Dante Bichette .40 .12
225 Raul Mondesi .40 .12
226 Mike Piazza 1.50 .45
227 Brad Penny .40 .12
228 Kip Wells .40 .12
229 Adam Everett .40 .12
230 Eddie Yarnall .40 .12
231 Matt LeCroy .40 .12
232 Jason Tyner .40 .12
233 Rick Ankiel .40 .12
234 Lance Berkman .40 .12
235 Rafael Furcal .40 .12
236 Dee Brown .40 .12
237 Gookie Dawkins .40 .12
238 Eric Valent .40 .12
239 Peter Bergeron .40 .12
240 Alfonso Soriano 1.00 .30
241 Adam Dunn 1.00 .30
242 Jorge Toca .40 .12
243 Ryan Anderson .40 .12
244 Jason Dellaero .40 .12
245 Jason Grilli .40 .12
246 Milton Bradley .40 .12
247 Scott Downs RC 5.00 1.50
248 Keith Reed RC 5.00 1.50
249 Edgar Cruz RC 5.00 1.50
250 Wes Anderson RC 5.00 1.50
251 Lyle Overbay RC 6.00 1.80
252 Mike Lamb RC 5.00 1.50
253 Vince Faison RC 5.00 1.50
254 Chad Alexander 5.00 1.50
255 Chris Wakeland RC 5.00 1.50
256 Aaron McNeal RC 5.00 1.50
257 Tomo Ohka RC 5.00 1.50
258 Ty Howington RC 5.00 1.50
259 Javier Colina RC 5.00 1.50
260 Jason Jennings 5.00 1.50
261 Ramon Santiago RC 5.00 1.50
262 Johan Santana RC 20.00 6.00
263 Quincy Foster RC 5.00 1.50
264 Junior Brignac RC 5.00 1.50
265 Rico Washington RC 5.00 1.50
266 Scott Sobkowiak RC 5.00 1.50
267 Pedro Martinez 2.50 .75
Rick Ankiel
268 Manny Ramirez 2.50 .75
Vladimir Guerrero
269 A.J.Burnett 1.00 .30
Mark Mulder
270 Mike Piazza 4.00 1.20
Eric Munson
271 Josh Hamilton 1.00 .30
Corey Patterson
272 Ken Griffey Jr. 3.00 .90
Sammy Sosa
273 Derek Jeter 6.00 1.80
Alfonso Soriano
274 Mark McGwire 6.00 1.80
Pat Burrell
275 Chipper Jones 6.00 1.80
Cal Ripken
276 Nomar Garciaparra 4.00 1.20
Alex Rodriguez
277 Pedro Martinez GEM 5.00 1.50
278 Tony Gwynn GEM 6.00 1.80
279 Barry Bonds GEM 12.00 3.60
280 Juan Gonzalez GEM 5.00 1.50
281 Larry Walker GEM 3.00 .90
282 N.Garciaparra GEM 8.00 2.40
283 Ken Griffey Jr. GEM 8.00 2.40
284 Manny Ramirez GEM 2.00 .60
285 Shawn Green GEM 2.00 .60
286 Sammy Sosa GEM 8.00 2.40
NNO Graded Gems Ser.1 EXCH/10
NNO Graded Gems Ser.2 EXCH/10

2000 Finest Gold Refractors

Randomly inserted in packs, this 287-card set parallels the base set. The set includes 179-player cards, 40 Rookie Cards (numbers 101-120 and 247-266) each serial numbered to 100, 15 Features subset cards (numbers 121-135), 10 Counterparts subset cards (numbers 267-276), and 20 Gems subset cards (numbers 136-145 and 277-286). The set also includes two versions of card number 146 Ken Griffey Jr. wearing his Reds uniform (a portrait and action shot). Rookie/Veteran Cards were seeded at a rate of 1:240 hobby/retail packs and TBD HTA packs. Features and Counterparts subset cards were inserted one every 960 hobby and retail packs and one every 400 HTA packs. Gems subset cards were inserted one every 2880 hobby and retail packs and one every 1200 HTA packs. All cards are featured on gold die-cut technology.

Nm-Mt Ex-Mt
*STARS 1-100/146-246: &&20X TO &&50X BASIC
*ROOKIES 101-120: 1.5X TO 4X BASIC
*ROOKIES 247-260: 1.5X TO 4X BASIC
*FEATURES 121-135: 4X TO 10X BASIC
*GEMS 136-145/277-286: 4X TO 10X BASIC
*COUNTER 267-276: 4X TO 10X BASIC

2000 Finest Refractors

Randomly inserted in packs, this 146-card set parallels the base set. The set includes 179-player cards, 40 Rookie Cards (numbers 101-120 and 247-266) each serial numbered to 500, 15 Features subset cards (numbers 121-135), 10 Counterparts subset cards (numbers 267-276), and 20 Gems subset cards (numbers 136-145 and 277-286). The set also includes two versions of card number 146 Ken Griffey Jr. wearing his Reds uniform (a portrait and action shot). Rookie/Veteran Cards were seeded at a rate of 1:24 hobby/retail packs and 1:6 HTA packs. Features and Counterparts subset cards were inserted one every 96 hobby and retail packs and one every 40 HTA packs. Gems subset cards were inserted one every 288 hobby and retail packs and one every 120 HTA packs.

Nm-Mt Ex-Mt
*STARS 1-100/146-246: 6X TO 15X BASIC
*ROOKIES 101-120: .75X TO 2X BASIC
*FEATURES 121-135: 1.5X TO 4X BASIC
*GEMS 136-145/277-286: 1.5X TO 4X BASIC
*ROOKIES 247-266: .75X TO 2X BASIC RC'S
*COUNTER 267-276: 1.5X TO 4X BASIC

2000 Finest Gems Oversize

Randomly inserted as a "box-topper", this 20-card oversized set features some of the best players in major league baseball. Please note that cards 1-10 were inserted into series one boxes, and cards 11-20 were inserted into series two boxes.

Nm-Mt Ex-Mt
COMPLETE SERIES 1 (10) 60.00 18.00
COMPLETE SERIES 2 (10) 50.00 15.00
*REF: .4X TO 1X BASIC GEMS OVERSIZE
REFRACTORS ONE PER HTA CHIP-TOPPER
1 Derek Jeter 10.00 3.00
2 Alex Rodriguez 6.00 1.80
3 Chipper Jones 4.00 1.20
4 Mike Piazza 6.00 1.80
5 Mark McGwire 10.00 3.00
6 Ivan Rodriguez 4.00 1.20
7 Cal Ripken 12.00 3.60
8 Vladimir Guerrero 4.00 1.20
9 Randy Johnson 4.00 1.20
10 Jeff Bagwell 2.50 .75
11 Nomar Garciaparra 6.00 1.80
12 Ken Griffey Jr. 6.00 1.80
13 Manny Ramirez 1.50 .45
14 Shawn Green 1.50 .45
15 Sammy Sosa 6.00 1.80
16 Pedro Martinez 4.00 1.20
17 Tony Gwynn 5.00 1.50
18 Barry Bonds 10.00 3.00
19 Juan Gonzalez 4.00 1.20
20 Larry Walker 2.50 .75

2000 Finest Ballpark Bounties

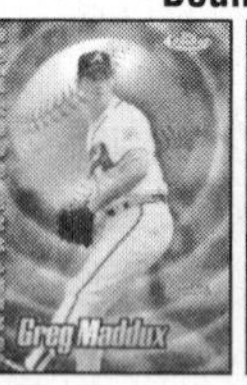
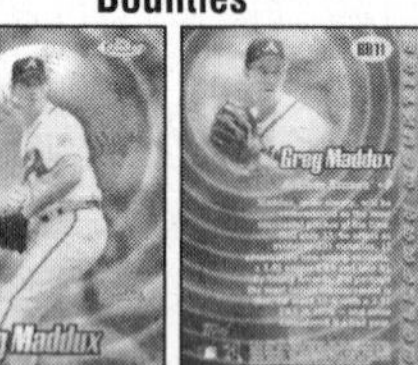

Randomly inserted into first and second series packs at one in 24 hobby/retail and 1:12 HTA, this insert set features 30 MLB players who are "wanted" for their pure talent. Card backs carry a "BB" prefix. Please note that cards 1-15 were inserted into series one packs, while cards 16-30 were inserted into series two packs.

Nm-Mt Ex-Mt
COMPLETE SERIES 1 (15) 80.00 24.00
COMPLETE SERIES 2 (15) 100.00 30.00
BB1 Chipper Jones 5.00 1.50
BB2 Mike Piazza 8.00 2.40
BB3 Vladimir Guerrero 5.00 1.50
BB4 Sammy Sosa 8.00 2.40
BB5 Nomar Garciaparra 8.00 2.40
BB6 Manny Ramirez 2.00 .60
BB7 Jeff Bagwell 3.00 .90
BB8 Scott Rolen 3.00 .90
BB9 Carlos Beltran 2.00 .60
BB10 Pedro Martinez 5.00 1.50
BB11 Greg Maddux 8.00 2.40
BB12 Josh Hamilton 2.00 .60
BB13 Adam Piatt 2.00 .60
BB14 Pat Burrell 3.00 .90
BB15 Alfonso Soriano 5.00 1.50
BB16 Alex Rodriguez 8.00 2.40
BB17 Derek Jeter 12.00 3.60
BB18 Cal Ripken 15.00 4.50
BB19 Larry Walker 3.00 .90
BB20 Barry Bonds 12.00 3.60
BB21 Ken Griffey Jr. 8.00 2.40
BB22 Mark McGwire 12.00 3.60
BB23 Ivan Rodriguez 5.00 1.50
BB24 Andruw Jones 2.00 .60
BB25 Todd Helton 3.00 .90
BB26 Randy Johnson 5.00 1.50
BB27 Ruben Mateo 2.00 .60
BB28 Corey Patterson 3.00 .90
BB29 Sean Burroughs 3.00 .90
BB30 Eric Munson 2.00 .60

2000 Finest Dream Cast

Randomly inserted into series two packs at one in 36 hobby/retail packs and one in 13 HTA packs, this 10-card insert features players that have skills people dream about having. Card backs carry a "DC" prefix.

Nm-Mt Ex-Mt
COMPLETE SET (10) 100.00 30.00
DC1 Mark McGwire 15.00 4.50
DC2 Roberto Alomar 6.00 1.80
DC3 Chipper Jones 6.00 1.80
DC4 Derek Jeter 15.00 4.50
DC5 Barry Bonds 15.00 4.50
DC6 Ken Griffey Jr. 10.00 3.00
DC7 Sammy Sosa 10.00 3.00
DC8 Mike Piazza 10.00 3.00
DC9 Pedro Martinez 6.00 1.80
DC10 Randy Johnson 6.00 1.80

2000 Finest For the Record

Randomly inserted in first series packs at a rate of 1:71 hobby or retail and 1:33 HTA, this insert set features 30 serial-numbered cards. Each player has three versions that are sequentially numbered to the distance of the left, center, and right field walls of their home ballpark. Card backs carry a "FR" prefix.

Nm-Mt Ex-Mt
COMPLETE SET (30) 800.00 240.00
FR1A Derek Jeter/318 30.00 9.00
FR1B Derek Jeter/408 30.00 9.00
FR1C Derek Jeter/314 30.00 9.00
FR2A Mark McGwire/330 30.00 9.00
FR2B Mark McGwire/402 30.00 9.00
FR2C Mark McGwire/330 30.00 9.00
FR3A Ken Griffey Jr./331 15.00 4.50
FR3B Ken Griffey Jr./405 15.00 4.50
FR3C Ken Griffey Jr./327 15.00 4.50
FR4A Alex Rodriguez/331 20.00 6.00
FR4B Alex Rodriguez/405 20.00 6.00
FR4C Alex Rodriguez/327 20.00 6.00
FR5A N.Garciaparra/310 15.00 4.50
FR5B N.Garciaparra/390 15.00 4.50
FR5C N.Garciaparra/302 15.00 4.50
FR6A Cal Ripken/333 40.00 12.00
FR6B Cal Ripken/410 40.00 12.00
FR6C Cal Ripken/318 40.00 12.00
FR7A Sammy Sosa/355 15.00 4.50
FR7B Sammy Sosa/400 15.00 4.50
FR7C Sammy Sosa/353 15.00 4.50
FR8A Manny Ramirez/325 10.00 3.00
FR8B Manny Ramirez/410 10.00 3.00
FR8C Manny Ramirez/325 10.00 3.00
FR9A Mike Piazza/338 15.00 4.50
FR9B Mike Piazza/410 15.00 4.50
FR9C Mike Piazza/338 15.00 4.50
FR10A Chipper Jones/335 10.00 3.00
FR10B Chipper Jones/401 10.00 3.00
FR10C Chipper Jones/330 10.00 3.00

2000 Finest Going the Distance

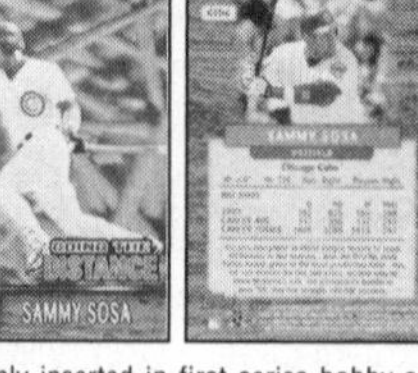

Randomly inserted in first series hobby and retail packs at one in 24 and HTA packs at a rate of one in 12, this 12-card insert set features some of the best hitters in major league baseball. Card backs carry a "GTD" prefix.

Nm-Mt Ex-Mt
COMPLETE SET (12) 80.00 24.00
GTD1 Tony Gwynn 5.00 1.50
GTD2 Alex Rodriguez 6.00 1.80
GTD3 Derek Jeter 10.00 3.00
GTD4 Chipper Jones 4.00 1.20
GTD5 Nomar Garciaparra 6.00 1.80
GTD6 Sammy Sosa 6.00 1.80
GTD7 Ken Griffey Jr. 6.00 1.80
GTD8 Vladimir Guerrero 4.00 1.20
GTD9 Mark McGwire 10.00 3.00
GTD10 Mike Piazza 6.00 1.80
GTD11 Manny Ramirez 1.50 .45
GTD12 Cal Ripken 12.00 3.60

2000 Finest Moments

Randomly inserted into series two hobby and retail packs at one in nine, and HTA packs at one in four, this four-card insert features great moments from the 1999 baseball season. Card backs carry a "FM" prefix.

Nm-Mt Ex-Mt
COMPLETE SET (4) 6.00 1.80
*REFRACTORS: .75X TO 2X BASIC MOMENTS
SER.2 REF.ODDS 1:20 H/R 1:9 HTA
FM1 Chipper Jones 1.50 .45
FM2 Ivan Rodriguez 1.50 .45
FM3 Tony Gwynn 2.00 .60
FM4 Wade Boggs 1.50 .45

2000 Finest Moments Refractors Autograph

Randomly inserted into series two hobby/retail packs at one in 425, and in HTA packs at one in 196, this four-card set is a complete parallel of the Finest Moments insert. This set is autographed by the player depicted on the card. Card backs carry a "FM" prefix.

Nm-Mt Ex-Mt
FM1 Chipper Jones 40.00 12.00
FM2 Ivan Rodriguez 40.00 12.00
FM3 Tony Gwynn 60.00 18.00
FM4 Wade Boggs 40.00 12.00

2001 Finest

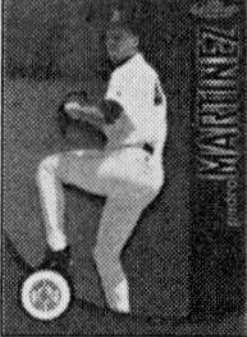
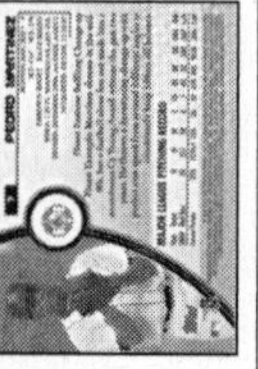

This 140-card set was distributed in six-card hobby packs with a suggested retail price of $6. Printed on 27 pt. card stock, the set features color action photos of 100 veteran players, 30 draft picks and prospects printed with the "Rookie Card" logo and sequentially numbered to 999, and 10 standout veterans sequentially numbered to 1999.

Nm-Mt Ex-Mt
COMP.SET w/o SP's 25.00 7.50
COMMON CARD (1-110) .40 .12
COMMON SP 10.00 3.00
COMMON (111-140) 10.00 3.00
1 Mike Piazza SP 20.00 6.00
2 Andruw Jones .40 .12
3 Jason Giambi 1.00 .30
4 Fred McGriff .60 .18
5 Vladimir Guerrero SP 1.00 .30
6 Adrian Gonzalez .40 .12
7 Pedro Martinez 1.00 .30
8 Mike Lieberthal .40 .12
9 Warren Morris .40 .12
10 Juan Gonzalez 1.00 .30
11 Jose Canseco 1.00 .30
12 Jose Valentin .40 .12
13 Jeff Cirillo .40 .12
14 Pokey Reese .40 .12
15 Scott Rolen .60 .18
16 Greg Maddux 1.50 .45
17 Carlos Delgado .40 .12
18 Rick Ankiel .40 .12
19 Steve Finley .40 .12
20 Shawn Green .40 .12
21 Orlando Cabrera .40 .12
22 Roberto Alomar 1.00 .30
23 John Olerud .40 .12
24 Albert Belle .40 .12
25 Edgardo Alfonzo .40 .12
26 Rafael Palmeiro .60 .18
27 Mike Sweeney .40 .12
28 Bernie Williams .60 .18
29 Larry Walker .60 .18
30 Barry Bonds SP 25.00 7.50
31 Orlando Hernandez .40 .12
32 Randy Johnson 1.00 .30
33 Shannon Stewart .40 .12
34 Mark Grace .60 .18
35 Alex Rodriguez SP 25.00 7.50
36 Tino Martinez .60 .18
37 Carlos Febles .40 .12
38 Al Leiter .40 .12
39 Omar Vizquel .40 .12
40 Chuck Knoblauch .40 .12
41 Tim Salmon .60 .18
42 Brian Jordan .40 .12
43 Edgar Renteria .40 .12
44 Preston Wilson .40 .12
45 Mariano Rivera .60 .18
46 Gabe Kapler .40 .12
47 Jason Kendall .40 .12
48 Rickey Henderson 1.00 .30
49 Luis Gonzalez .40 .12
50 Tom Glavine .60 .18
51 Jeromy Burnitz .40 .12
52 Garret Anderson .40 .12
53 Craig Biggio .60 .18
54 Vinny Castilla .40 .12
55 Jeff Kent .40 .12
56 Gary Sheffield .40 .12
57 Jorge Posada .60 .18
58 Sean Casey .40 .12
59 Johnny Damon .40 .12
60 Dean Palmer .40 .12
61 Todd Helton .60 .18
62 Barry Larkin 1.00 .30
63 Robin Ventura .40 .12
64 Kenny Lofton .40 .12
65 Sammy Sosa SP 15.00 4.50
66 Rafael Furcal .40 .12
67 Jay Bell .40 .12
68 J.T. Snow .40 .12
69 Jose Vidro .40 .12
70 Ivan Rodriguez 1.00 .30
71 Jermaine Dye .40 .12
72 Chipper Jones SP 10.00 3.00
73 Fernando Vina .40 .12
74 Ben Grieve .40 .12
75 Mark McGwire SP 25.00 7.50
76 Matt Williams .40 .12
77 Mark Grudzielanek .40 .12
78 Mike Hampton .40 .12
79 Brian Giles .40 .12
80 Tony Gwynn 1.25 .35
81 Carlos Beltran .40 .12
82 Ray Durham .40 .12
83 Brad Radke .40 .12
84 David Justice .40 .12
85 Frank Thomas 1.00 .30
86 Todd Zeile .40 .12
87 Pat Burrell .40 .12
88 Jim Thome 1.00 .30
89 Greg Vaughn .40 .12
90 Ken Griffey Jr. SP 15.00 4.50
91 Mike Mussina 1.00 .30
92 Magglio Ordonez .40 .12
93 Bob Abreu .40 .12
94 Alex Gonzalez .40 .12
95 Kevin Brown .40 .12
96 Jay Buhner .40 .12
97 Roger Clemens 2.00 .60
98 Nomar Garciaparra SP 15.00 4.50
99 Derrek Lee .40 .12
100 Derek Jeter SP 25.00 7.50
101 Adrian Beltre .40 .12
102 Geoff Jenkins .40 .12
103 Javy Lopez .40 .12
104 Raul Mondesi .40 .12
105 Troy Glaus .60 .18
106 Jeff Bagwell .60 .18
107 Eric Karros .40 .12
108 Mo Vaughn .40 .12
109 Cal Ripken 3.00 .90
110 Manny Ramirez .40 .12
111 Scott Heard PROS 10.00 3.00
112 L. Montanez PROS RC 10.00 3.00
113 Ben Diggins PROS 10.00 3.00
114 Shaun Boyd PROS RC 10.00 3.00
115 Sean Burnett PROS 10.00 3.00
116 Carmen Cali PROS RC 10.00 3.00
117 D.Thompson PROS 10.00 3.00
118 D.Parrish PROS RC 10.00 3.00
119 D.Rich PROS RC 10.00 3.00
120 Chad Petty PROS RC 10.00 3.00
121 S.Smyth PROS RC 10.00 3.00
122 John Lackey PROS 10.00 3.00
123 M.Galante PROS RC 10.00 3.00
124 D.Borrell PROS RC 10.00 3.00
125 Bob Keppel PROS RC 15.00 4.50
126 J.Wayne PROS RC 15.00 4.50
127 J.R. House PROS 10.00 3.00
128 Brian Sellier PROS RC 10.00 3.00
129 Dan Moylan PROS RC 10.00 3.00
130 Scott Pratt PROS RC 10.00 3.00
131 Victor Hall PROS RC 10.00 3.00
132 Joel Pineiro PROS 20.00 6.00
133 J.Axelson PROS RC 10.00 3.00
134 Jose Reyes PROS RC 80.00 24.00
135 G. Runser PROS RC 10.00 3.00
136 B. Hebson PROS RC 10.00 3.00
137 S.Serrano PROS RC 10.00 3.00
138 K. Joseph PROS RC 10.00 3.00
139 J. Richardson PROS RC 10.00 3.00
140 M. Fischer PROS RC 10.00 3.00

2001 Finest Refractors

This 140-card set is a parallel version of the base set and is distinguished by the refractive quality of the cards. The 100 veteran cards are sequentially numbered to 499, the 30 draft picks and prospects to 241, and the 10 standout veterans to 399.

Nm-Mt Ex-Mt
*1-110 REF: 4X TO 10X BASIC 1-110.
*SP REF: .5X TO 1.2X BASIC SP
*111-140 REF: .75X TO 2X BASIC 111-140

2001 Finest All-Stars

Randomly inserted in packs at the rate of one in five, this 10-card set features color photos of the preeminent players at their respective postions. A refractive parallel version of this insert set was also produced and inserted in packs at the rate of one in 20.

Nm-Mt Ex-Mt
COMPLETE SET (10) 60.00 18.00
*REF: 1X TO 2.5X BASIC ALL-STARS
REFRACTOR ODDS 1:40 HOBBY, 1:20 HTA

FAS1 Mark McGwire 10.00 3.00
FAS2 Derek Jeter 10.00 3.00
FAS3 Alex Rodriguez 6.00 1.80
FAS4 Chipper Jones 4.00 1.20
FAS5 Nomar Garciaparra 6.00 1.80
FAS6 Sammy Sosa 6.00 1.80
FAS7 Mike Piazza 6.00 1.80
FAS8 Barry Bonds 10.00 3.00
FAS9 Vladimir Guerrero 4.00 1.20
FAS10 Ken Griffey Jr. 6.00 1.80

2001 Finest Autographs

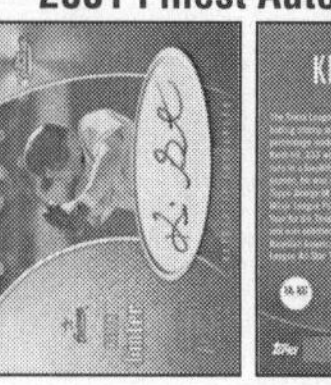

Randomly inserted in packs at the rate of one in 22, this 29-card set features autographed color photos of players who made the moments. All of these cards are refractors and carry the Topps "Certified Autograph" stamp and the Topps "Genuine Issue" sticker.

Nm-Mt Ex-Mt
FA-AG Adrian Gonzalez 15.00 4.50
FA-AH Adam Hyzdu 10.00 3.00
FA-AK Adam Kennedy 15.00 4.50
FA-AP Albert Pujols 250.00 75.00
FA-BD Ben Diggins 10.00 3.00
FA-BM Ben Molina 10.00 3.00
FA-BS Ben Sheets 15.00 4.50
FA-BZ Barry Zito 25.00 7.50
FA-BKC Brian Cole 15.00 4.50
FA-CD Chad Durham 10.00 3.00
FA-CP Carlos Pena 10.00 3.00
FA-DK Dave Krynzel 10.00 3.00
FA-DCP Corey Patterson 15.00 4.50
FA-JC Joe Crede 10.00 3.00
FA-JH Jason Hart 10.00 3.00
FA-JM Justin Morneau 25.00 7.50
FA-JO Jose Ortiz 10.00 3.00
FA-JP Jay Payton 10.00 3.00
FA-JHH Josh Hamilton 10.00 3.00
FA-JRH J.R. House 10.00 3.00
FA-KG Keith Ginter 10.00 3.00
FA-KM Kevin Mench 10.00 3.00
FA-MB Milton Bradley 15.00 4.50
FA-MQ Mark Quinn 10.00 3.00
FA-MR Mark Redman 10.00 3.00
FA-RF Rafael Furcal 15.00 4.50
FA-SB Sean Burnett 15.00 4.50
FA-TF Troy Farnsworth 15.00 4.50
FA-TL Terrence Long 15.00 4.50

2001 Finest Moments

Randomly inserted in packs at the rate of one in 12, this 25-card set features color photos of players involved in great moments from the 2000 season plus both active and retired 3000 Hit Club members. A refractive parallel version of this set was also produced with an insertion rate of 1:40.

Nm-Mt Ex-Mt
COMPLETE SET (25) 120.00 36.00
*REF: .75X TO 2X BASIC MOMENTS ..
REFRACTOR ODDS 1:40 HOBBY, 1:20 HTA
FM1 Pat Burrell 2.50 .75
FM2 Adam Kennedy 2.50 .75
FM3 Mike Lamb 2.50 .75
FM4 Rafael Furcal 2.50 .75
FM5 Terrence Long 2.50 .75
FM6 Jay Payton 2.50 .75
FM7 Mark Quinn 2.50 .75
FM8 Ben Molina 2.50 .75
FM9 Kazuhiro Sasaki 2.50 .75
FM10 Mark Redman 2.50 .75
FM11 Barry Bonds 15.00 4.50
FM12 Alex Rodriguez 10.00 3.00
FM13 Roger Clemens 12.00 3.60
FM14 Jim Edmonds 2.50 .75
FM15 Jason Giambi 6.00 1.80
FM16 Todd Helton 4.00 1.20
FM17 Troy Glaus 4.00 1.20
FM18 Carlos Delgado 2.50 .75
FM19 Darin Erstad 2.50 .75
FM20 Cal Ripken 20.00 6.00
FM21 Paul Molitor 4.00 1.20
FM22 Robin Yount 10.00 3.00
FM23 George Brett 15.00 4.50
FM24 Dave Winfield 2.50 .75
FM25 Eddie Murray 6.00 1.80

2001 Finest Moments Refractors Autograph

Randomly inserted in packs at the rate of one in 250, this 10-card set features autographed player photos with the Topps "Certified Autograph" stamp and the Topps "Genuine Issue" sticker printed on these refractive cards. Exchange cards with a redemption deadline of April 30, 2003 were seeded into packs for Cal Ripken, Eddie Murray and Robin Yount.

Nm-Mt Ex-Mt
FMA-BB Barry Bonds 175.00 52.50
FMA-CR Cal Ripken 200.00 60.00
FMA-DW Dave Winfield 40.00 12.00
FMA-EM Eddie Murray 60.00 18.00
FMA-GB George Brett 100.00 30.00
FMA-JG Jason Giambi 60.00 18.00
FMA-PM Paul Molitor 40.00 12.00
FMA-RY Robin Yount 60.00 18.00
FMA-TG Troy Glaus 40.00 12.00
FMA-TH Todd Helton 40.00 12.00

2001 Finest Origins

Randomly inserted in packs at the rate of one in seven, this 15-card set features some of today's best ballplayers who didn't make the 1993 Finest cut. These cards are printed in the 1993 classic Finest card design. A refractive parallel version of this set was also produced with an insertion rate of 1:40.

Nm-Mt Ex-Mt
COMPLETE SET (15) 40.00 12.00
*REF: 1X TO 2.5X BASIC ORIGINS ....
REFRACTOR ODDS 1:40 HOBBY, 1:20 HTA
FO1 Derek Jeter 12.00 3.60
FO2 Jason Kendall 2.00 .60
FO3 Jose Vidro 2.00 .60
FO4 Preston Wilson 2.00 .60
FO5 Jim Edmonds 2.00 .60
FO6 Vladimir Guerrero 5.00 1.50
FO7 Andruw Jones 2.00 .60
FO8 Scott Rolen 3.00 .90
FO9 Edgardo Alfonzo 2.00 .60
FO10 Mike Sweeney 2.00 .60
FO11 Alex Rodriguez 8.00 2.40
FO12 Jermaine Dye 2.00 .60
FO13 Charles Johnson 2.00 .60
FO14 Darren Dreifort 2.00 .60
FO15 Neifi Perez 2.00 .60

2002 Finest

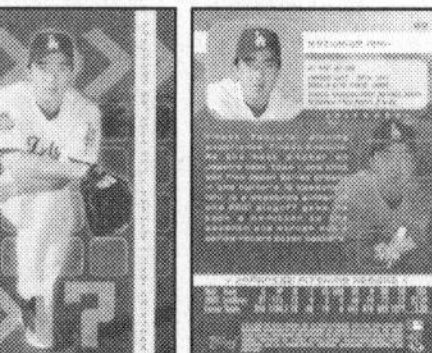

This 110 card set was issued in five card pack with an SRP of $6 per pack which were packed six per mini box with three mini boxes per full box and twelve boxes per case. Cards number 101 through 110 are Rookie Cards which were all autographed by the featured player. One of these autograph cards were inserted into each six pack mini box.

Nm-Mt Ex-Mt
COMP.SET w/o SP's (100) 25.00 7.50
COMMON CARD (1-100) .50 .15
COMMON CARD (101-110) 10.00 3.00
1 Mike Mussina 1.25 .35
2 Steve Sparks .50 .15
3 Randy Johnson 1.25 .35
4 Orlando Cabrera .50 .15
5 Jeff Kent .50 .15
6 Carlos Delgado .50 .15
7 Ivan Rodriguez 1.25 .35
8 Jose Cruz .50 .15
9 Jason Giambi 1.25 .35
10 Brad Penny .50 .15
11 Moises Alou .50 .15
12 Mike Piazza 2.00 .60
13 Ben Grieve .50 .15
14 Derek Jeter 3.00 .90
15 Roy Oswalt .50 .15
16 Pat Burrell .50 .15
17 Preston Wilson .50 .15
18 Kevin Brown .50 .15
19 Barry Bonds 3.00 .90
20 Phil Nevin .50 .15
21 Aramis Ramirez .50 .15
22 Carlos Beltran .50 .15
23 Chipper Jones 1.25 .35
24 Curt Schilling .75 .23
25 Jorge Posada .75 .23
26 Alfonso Soriano .75 .23
27 Cliff Floyd .50 .15
28 Rafael Palmeiro .75 .23
29 Terrence Long .50 .15
30 Ken Griffey Jr. 2.00 .60
31 Jason Kendall .50 .15
32 Jose Vidro .50 .15
33 Jermaine Dye .50 .15
34 Bobby Higginson .50 .15
35 Albert Pujols 2.50 .75
36 Miguel Tejada .50 .15
37 Jim Edmonds .50 .15
38 Barry Zito .75 .23
39 Jimmy Rollins .50 .15
40 Rafael Furcal .50 .15
41 Omar Vizquel .50 .15
42 Kazuhiro Sasaki .50 .15
43 Brian Giles .50 .15
44 Darin Erstad .50 .15
45 Mariano Rivera .75 .23
46 Troy Percival .50 .15
47 Mike Sweeney .50 .15
48 Vladimir Guerrero 1.25 .35
49 Troy Glaus .75 .23
50 So Taguchi RC 3.00 .90
51 Edgardo Alfonzo .50 .15
52 Roger Clemens 2.50 .75
53 Eric Chavez .50 .15
54 Alex Rodriguez 2.00 .60
55 Cristian Guzman .50 .15
56 Jeff Bagwell .75 .23
57 Bernie Williams .75 .23
58 Kerry Wood 1.25 .35
59 Ryan Klesko .50 .15
60 Ichiro Suzuki 2.00 .60
61 Larry Walker .75 .23
62 Nomar Garciaparra 2.00 .60
63 Craig Biggio .75 .23
64 J.D. Drew .50 .15
65 Juan Pierre .50 .15
66 Roberto Alomar 1.25 .35
67 Luis Gonzalez .50 .15
68 Bud Smith .50 .15
69 Magglio Ordonez .50 .15
70 Scott Rolen .75 .23
71 Tsuyoshi Shinjo .50 .15
72 Paul Konerko .50 .15
73 Garret Anderson .50 .15
74 Tim Hudson .50 .15
75 Adam Dunn .50 .15
76 Gary Sheffield .50 .15
77 Johnny Damon .50 .15
78 Todd Helton .75 .23
79 Geoff Jenkins .50 .15
80 Shawn Green .50 .15
81 C.C. Sabathia .50 .15
82 Kazuhisa Ishii RC UER 4.00 1.20
2001 ERA is incorrect
83 Rich Aurilia .50 .15
84 Mike Hampton .50 .15
85 Ben Sheets .50 .15
86 Andruw Jones .50 .15
87 Richie Sexson .50 .15
88 Jim Thome 1.25 .35
89 Sammy Sosa 2.00 .60
90 Greg Maddux 2.00 .60
91 Pedro Martinez 1.25 .35
92 Jeromy Burnitz .50 .15
93 Raul Mondesi .50 .15
94 Bret Boone .50 .15
95 Jerry Hairston .50 .15
96 Mike Rivera .50 .15
97 Juan Cruz .50 .15
98 Morgan Ensberg .50 .15
99 Nathan Haynes .50 .15
100 Xavier Nady .50 .15
101 Nic Jackson FY AU RC 10.00 3.00
102 Mauricio Lara FY AU RC 10.00 3.00
103 Freddy Sanchez FY AU RC 10.00 3.00
104 Clint Nageotte FY AU RC 15.00 4.50
105 Beltran Perez FY AU RC 10.00 3.00
106 Garrett Gentry FY AU RC 10.00 3.00
107 Chad Qualls FY AU RC 10.00 3.00
108 Jason Bay FY AU RC 30.00 9.00
109 Michael Hill FY AU RC 10.00 3.00
110 Brian Tallet FY AU RC 15.00 4.50

2002 Finest Refractors

Inserted in packs at stated odds of one in two mini boxes, these cards parallel the 2002 Finest set. These cards have the patented topps "refractor" sheen and have a stated print run of 499 serial numbered sets.

Nm-Mt Ex-Mt
*REFRACTORS 1-100: 2.5X TO 6X BASIC
*REF.RC'S 1-100: 1.5X TO 4X BASIC .
101 Nic Jackson FY 8.00 2.40
102 Mauricio Lara FY 8.00 2.40
103 Freddy Sanchez FY 8.00 2.40
104 Clint Nageotte FY 15.00 4.50
105 Beltran Perez FY 8.00 2.40
106 Garett Gentry FY 8.00 2.40
107 Chad Qualls FY 8.00 2.40
108 Jason Bay FY 25.00 7.50
109 Michael Hill FY 8.00 2.40
110 Brian Tallet FY 10.00 3.00

2002 Finest Xfractors

Inserted at a rate of one in three mini boxes, these cards parallel the Finest set. These cards have a uniquely patterned finest design and are printed to a stated print run of 299 serial numbered sets.

Nm-Mt Ex-Mt
*XRACTOR 1-100: 3X TO 8X BASIC ...
*XFRACT.RC'S 1-100: 2X TO 5X BASIC
*XFRACTOR 101-110: .5X TO 1.2X REFRACTOR

2002 Finest Xfractors Protectors

Inserted at a rate of one in seven mini boxes, these cards parallel the Finest set. These cards have a uniquely patterned finest design and were created with a "finest protector" and are printed to a stated print run of 99 serial numbered sets.

Nm-Mt Ex-Mt
*XF PROT. 1-100: 6X TO 15X BASIC ..
*XF PROT.RC'S 1-100: 4X TO 10X BASIC
*XF PROT 101-110: .75X TO 2X REFRACTOR

2002 Finest Bat Relics

Inserted at a stated rate of one in 12 mini boxes these 15 cards feature a bat slice from the featured player.

Nm-Mt Ex-Mt
FBR-AJ Andruw Jones 10.00 3.00
FBR-AP Albert Pujols 20.00 6.00
FBR-AR Alex Rodriguez 15.00 4.50
FBR-AS Alfonso Soriano 15.00 4.50
FBR-BB Barry Bonds 25.00 7.50
FBR-BO Bret Boone 10.00 3.00
FBR-BW Bernie Williams 15.00 4.50
FBR-CJ Chipper Jones 15.00 4.50
FBR-IR Ivan Rodriguez 15.00 4.50
FBR-LG Luis Gonzalez 10.00 3.00
FBR-MP Mike Piazza 15.00 4.50
FBR-NG Nomar Garciaparra 20.00 6.00
FBR-TG Tony Gwynn 15.00 4.50
FBR-TH Todd Helton 15.00 4.50
FBR-TS Tsuyoshi Shinjo 10.00 3.00

2002 Finest Jersey Relics

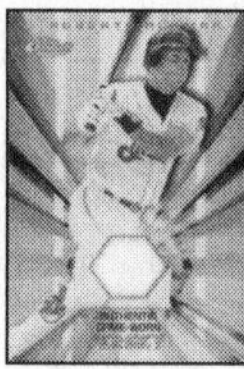

Inserted at a stated rate of one in four mini boxes, these 24 cards feature the player photo along with a game-used jersey swatch.

Nm-Mt Ex-Mt
FJR-AJ Andruw Jones 10.00 3.00
FJR-AR Alex Rodriguez 15.00 4.50
FJR-BB Barry Bonds 25.00 7.50
FJR-BO Bret Boone 10.00 3.00
FJR-CD Carlos Delgado 10.00 3.00
FJR-CJ Chipper Jones 15.00 4.50
FJR-CS Curt Schilling 15.00 4.50
FJR-FT Frank Thomas 15.00 4.50
FJR-GM Greg Maddux 15.00 4.50
FJR-HN Hideo Nomo 40.00 12.00
FJR-IR Ivan Rodriguez 15.00 4.50
FJR-JB Jeff Bagwell 15.00 4.50
FJR-LG Luis Gonzalez 10.00 3.00
FJR-LW Larry Walker 15.00 4.50
FJR-MG Mark Grace 15.00 4.50
FJR-MP Mike Piazza 15.00 4.50
FJR-PM Pedro Martinez 15.00 4.50
FJR-RA Roberto Alomar 15.00 4.50
FJR-RH Rickey Henderson 15.00 4.50
FJR-RP Rafael Palmeiro 15.00 4.50
FJR-SG Shawn Green 10.00 3.00
FJR-TG Tony Gwynn 15.00 4.50
FJR-TH Todd Helton 15.00 4.50
FJR-TS Tsuyoshi Shinjo 10.00 3.00

2002 Finest Moments Autographs

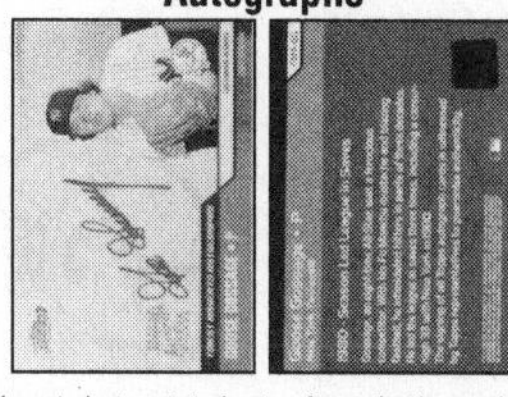

Inserted at a stated rate of one in three mini boxes, these cards feature leading retired players who signed cards honoring their greatest career moment.

Nm-Mt Ex-Mt
FMA-BG Bob Gibson 25.00 7.50
FMA-BR Bobby Richardson 25.00 7.50
FMA-BT Bobby Thomson 15.00 4.50
FMA-DL Don Larsen 15.00 4.50
FMA-DM Don Mattingly 80.00 24.00
FMA-FJ Fergie Jenkins 15.00 4.50
FMA-GG Goose Gossage 15.00 4.50
FMA-GP Gaylord Perry 15.00 4.50
FMA-JB Jim Bunning 25.00 7.50
FMA-JS Johnny Sain 15.00 4.50
FMA-LA Luis Aparicio 15.00 4.50
FMA-MS Mike Schmidt 80.00 24.00
FMA-RS Red Schoendienst 15.00 4.50
FMA-YB Yogi Berra 40.00 12.00
FMA-BRO Brooks Robinson 40.00 12.00

2003 Finest

This 110 card set was released in May, 2003. This product was issued in six pack mini-boxes with an SRP of $36. The first 100 cards are veterans while the final 10 cards featured autographed cards of leading rookies and prospects. Those cards (101-110) were issued at a stated rate of one in four mini boxes.

Nm-Mt Ex-Mt
COMP.SET w/o SP's (100) 25.00 7.50
COMMON CARD (1-100) .50 .15
COMMON CARD (101-110) 15.00 4.50
1 Sammy Sosa 2.00 .60
2 Paul Konerko .50 .15
3 Todd Helton .75 .23
4 Mike Lowell .50 .15
5 Lance Berkman .50 .15
6 Kazuhisa Ishii .50 .15
7 A.J. Pierzynski .50 .15
8 Jose Vidro .50 .15
9 Roberto Alomar 1.25 .35
10 Derek Jeter 3.00 .90
11 Barry Zito .75 .23
12 Jimmy Rollins .50 .15
13 Brian Giles .50 .15
14 Ryan Klesko .50 .15
15 Rich Aurilia .50 .15
16 Jim Edmonds .50 .15
17 Aubrey Huff .50 .15
18 Ivan Rodriguez 1.25 .35
19 Eric Hinske .50 .15
20 Barry Bonds 3.00 .90
21 Darin Erstad .50 .15
22 Curt Schilling .75 .23
23 Andruw Jones .50 .15
24 Jay Gibbons .50 .15
25 Nomar Garciaparra 2.00 .60
26 Kerry Wood 1.25 .35
27 Magglio Ordonez .50 .15
28 Austin Kearns .50 .15
29 Jason Jennings .50 .15
30 Jason Giambi 1.25 .35
31 Tim Hudson .50 .15
32 Edgar Martinez .75 .23
33 Carl Crawford .50 .15
34 Hee Seop Choi .50 .15
35 Vladimir Guerrero 1.25 .35
36 Jeff Kent .50 .15
37 John Smoltz .75 .23
38 Frank Thomas 1.25 .35
39 Cliff Floyd .50 .15
40 Mike Piazza 2.00 .60
41 Mark Prior 2.50 .75
42 Tim Salmon .75 .23
43 Shawn Green .50 .15
44 Bernie Williams .75 .23
45 Jim Thome 1.25 .35
46 John Olerud .50 .15
47 Orlando Hudson .50 .15
48 Mark Teixeira .75 .23
49 Gary Sheffield .50 .15
50 Ichiro Suzuki 2.00 .60
51 Tom Glavine .75 .23
52 Torii Hunter .50 .15
53 Craig Biggio .75 .23
54 Carlos Beltran .50 .15
55 Bartolo Colon .50 .15
56 Jorge Posada .75 .23
57 Pat Burrell .50 .15
58 Edgar Renteria .50 .15
59 Rafael Palmeiro .75 .23
60 Alfonso Soriano .75 .23
61 Brandon Phillips .50 .15
62 Luis Gonzalez .50 .15
63 Manny Ramirez .50 .15
64 Garret Anderson .50 .15
65 Ken Griffey Jr. 2.00 .60
66 A.J. Burnett .50 .15
67 Mike Sweeney .50 .15
68 Doug Mientkiewicz .50 .15
69 Eric Chavez .50 .15
70 Adam Dunn .50 .15
71 Shea Hillenbrand .50 .15
72 Troy Glaus .75 .23
73 Rodrigo Lopez .50 .15
74 Moises Alou .50 .15
75 Chipper Jones 1.25 .35
76 Bobby Abreu .50 .15
77 Mark Mulder .50 .15
78 Kevin Brown .50 .15
79 Josh Beckett .75 .23
80 Larry Walker .75 .23
81 Randy Johnson 1.25 .35
82 Greg Maddux 2.00 .60
83 Johnny Damon .50 .15
84 Omar Vizquel .50 .15
85 Jeff Bagwell .75 .23
86 Carlos Pena .50 .15
87 Roy Oswalt .50 .15
88 Richie Sexson .50 .15
89 Roger Clemens 2.50 .75
90 Miguel Tejada .50 .15
91 Vicente Padilla .50 .15
92 Phil Nevin .50 .15
93 Edgardo Alfonzo .50 .15
94 Bret Boone .50 .15
95 Albert Pujols 2.50 .75
96 Carlos Delgado .50 .15
97 Jose Contreras RC 2.50 .75
98 Scott Rolen .75 .23
99 Pedro Martinez 1.25 .35
100 Alex Rodriguez 2.00 .60
101 Adam LaRoche AU RC 20.00 6.00
102 Andy Marte AU RC 40.00 12.00
103 Daryl Clark AU RC 15.00 4.50
104 J.D. Durbin AU RC 15.00 4.50
105 Craig Brazell AU RC 15.00 4.50
106 Brian Burgamy AU RC 10.00 3.00
107 Tyler Johnson AU RC 10.00 3.00
108 Joey Gomes AU RC 10.00 3.00
109 Bryan Bullington AU RC 30.00 9.00
110 Byron Gettis AU RC 10.00 3.00

2003 Finest Refractors

This is a complete parallel of the basic Finest set. Cards numbered 1-100 were issued at a stated rate of one per mini-box and cards numbered 101-110 were issued at a stated rate of one every 34 mini-boxes.

Nm-Mt Ex-Mt
*REFRACTORS 1-100: 2X TO 5X BASIC
*REFRACTOR RC'S 1-100: 1.25X TO 3X BASIC
*REFRACTORS 101-110: .75X TO 2X BASIC

2003 Finest X-Fractors

Inserted at a stated rate of one in seven mini-boxes, this is a parallel to the Finest set. These cards were issued to a stated print run of 99 serial numbered sets.

Nm-Mt Ex-Mt
*X-FRACTORS 1-100: 6X TO 15X BASIC
*X-FRACTOR RC'S 1-100: 4X TO 10X BASIC
*X-FRACTORS 101-110: 1.25X TO 3X BASIC

2003 Finest Uncirculated Gold X-Fractors

Issued as a box topper for the big box which contained all the mini-boxes, this is a parallel to the basic set. These cards are sealed in plastic holders and were issued to a stated print run of 199 serial numbered sets.

Nm-Mt Ex-Mt

*GOLD X-F 1-100: 5X TO 12X BASIC..
*GOLD X-F RC'S 1-100: 3X TO 8X BASIC
*GOLD X-F 101-110: 1X TO 2.5X BASIC

2003 Finest Bat Relics

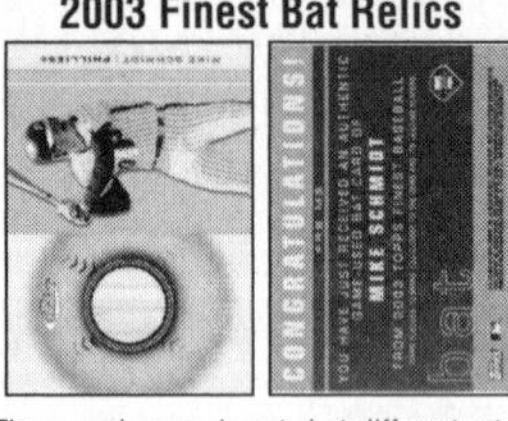

These cards were inserted at different rates depending on what group the bat relic belonged to. We have notated what group the player belonged to next to their name in our checklist.

GROUP A STATED ODDS 1:104 MINI-BOXES
GROUP B STATED ODDS 1:32 MINI-BOXES
GROUP C STATED ODDS 1:29 MINI-BOXES
GROUP D STATED ODDS 1:42 MINI-BOXES
GROUP E STATED ODDS 1:40 MINI-BOXES
GROUP F STATED ODDS 1:23 MINI-BOXES
GROUP G STATED ODDS 1:18 MINI-BOXES
GROUP H STATED ODDS 1:24 MINI-BOXES
GROUP I STATED ODDS 1:12 MINI-BOXES
GROUP J STATED ODDS 1:22 MINI-BOXES
GROUP K STATED ODDS 1:21 MINI-BOXES

	Nm-Mt	Ex-Mt
AD Adam Dunn H	8.00	2.40
AK Austin Kearns F	8.00	2.40
AP Albert Pujols I	15.00	4.50
AR Alex Rodriguez E	15.00	4.50
AS Alfonso Soriano H	10.00	3.00
BB Barry Bonds F	20.00	6.00
CJ Chipper Jones G	15.00	4.50
CR Cal Ripken B	40.00	12.00
DM Dale Murphy I	15.00	4.50
GM Greg Maddux F	15.00	4.50
IR Ivan Rodriguez G	15.00	4.50
JB Jeff Bagwell D	10.00	3.00
JT Jim Thome D	15.00	4.50
KP Kirby Puckett K	15.00	4.50
LB Lance Berkman C	8.00	2.40
MP Mike Piazza E	15.00	4.50
MR Manny Ramirez I	8.00	2.40
MS Mike Schmidt C	25.00	7.50
MT Miguel Tejada I	8.00	2.40
NG Nomar Garciaparra A	25.00	7.50
PM Paul Molitor C	15.00	4.50
RC Rod Carew K	10.00	3.00
RCL Roger Clemens J	15.00	4.50
RH Rickey Henderson B	15.00	4.50
RP Rafael Palmeiro J	10.00	3.00
TH Todd Helton B	10.00	3.00
WB Wade Boggs G	10.00	3.00

2003 Finest Moments Refractors Autographs

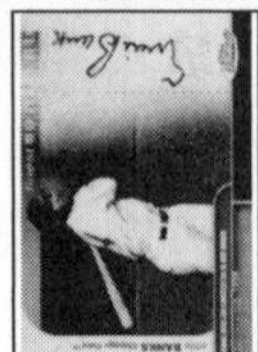

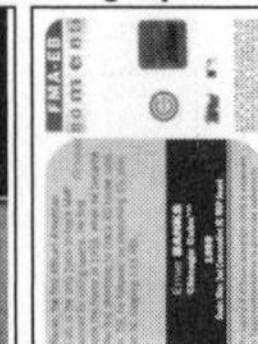

Inserted at different odds depening on whether the card was issued as part of group A or group B, this 12 card set features authentic signatures of baseball legends. Johnny Sain did not return his card in time for inclusion in this product and the exchange cards could be redeemed until April 30, 2005.

GROUP A STATED ODDS 1:113 MINI-BOXES
GROUP B STATED ODDS 1:5 MINI-BOXES
EXCHANGE DEADLINE 04/30/05........

	Nm-Mt	Ex-Mt
DL Don Larsen B	15.00	4.50
EB Ernie Banks A	60.00	18.00
GC Gary Carter B	25.00	7.50
GF George Foster B	15.00	4.50
GG Goose Gossage B	15.00	4.50
GP Gaylord Perry B	15.00	4.50
JP Jim Palmer B	15.00	4.50
JS Johnny Sain B EXCH	15.00	4.50
KH Keith Hernandez B	25.00	7.50
LB Lou Brock B	25.00	7.50
OC Orlando Cepeda B	15.00	4.50
PB Paul Blair B	15.00	4.50
WMA Willie Mays A	175.00	52.50

2003 Finest Uniform Relics

These 22 cards were inserted in different odds depending on what group the player belonged to. We have notated what group the player belonged to next to their name in our checklist.

GROUP A STATED ODDS 1:28 MINI-BOXES
GROUP B STATED ODDS 1:11 MINI-BOXES
GROUP C STATED ODDS 1:11 MINI-BOXES
GROUP D STATED ODDS 1:10 MINI-BOXES
GROUP E STATED ODDS 1:19 MINI-BOXES
GROUP F STATED ODDS 1:12 MINI-BOXES
GROUP G STATED ODDS 1:34 MINI-BOXES
GROUP H STATED ODDS 1:17 MINI-BOXES

	Nm-Mt	Ex-Mt
AD Adam Dunn B	8.00	2.40
AJ Andruw Jones H	8.00	2.40
AP Albert Pujols D	15.00	4.50
AR Alex Rodriguez F	15.00	4.50
AS Alfonso Soriano A	10.00	3.00
BB Barry Bonds D	20.00	6.00
CJ Chipper Jones B	15.00	4.50
CS Curt Schilling B	10.00	3.00
EC Eric Chavez B	8.00	2.40
GM Greg Maddux C	15.00	4.50
LG Luis Gonzalez D	8.00	2.40
LW Larry Walker C	10.00	3.00
MM Mark Mulder C	8.00	2.40
MP Mike Piazza C	15.00	4.50
MR Manny Ramirez E	8.00	2.40
MSW Mike Sweeney F	8.00	2.40
RJ Randy Johnson H	15.00	4.50
RO Roy Oswalt G	8.00	2.40
RP Rafael Palmeiro E	10.00	3.00
SS Sammy Sosa D	20.00	6.00
TH Todd Helton F	10.00	3.00
WM Willie Mays A	50.00	15.00

1951-52 Fischer Baking Labels

One of the popular "Bread for Energy" end-labels sets, these labels are found with blue, red and yellow backgrounds. Each bread label measures 2 3/4" by 2 3/4". They were distributed mainly in the northeast section of the country and there may be an album associated with the set. These labels are unnumbered and we have sequenced them in alphabetical order. The catalog designation is D290-3.

	NM	Ex
COMPLETE SET (32)	2000.00	1000.00
1 Vern Bickford	80.00	40.00
2 Ralph Branca	100.00	50.00
3 Harry Brecheen	80.00	40.00
4 Chico Carrasquel	80.00	40.00
5 Cliff Chambers	80.00	40.00
6 Hoot Evers	80.00	40.00
7 Ned Garver	80.00	40.00
8 Billy Goodman	80.00	40.00
9 Gil Hodges	150.00	75.00
10 Larry Jansen	80.00	40.00
11 Willie Jones	80.00	40.00
12 Eddie Joost	80.00	40.00
13 George Kell	150.00	75.00
14 Alex Kellner	80.00	40.00
15 Ted Kluszewski	120.00	60.00
16 Jim Konstanty	100.00	50.00
17 Bob Lemon	150.00	75.00
18 Cass Michaels	80.00	40.00
19 Johnny Mize	150.00	75.00
20 Irv Noren	80.00	40.00
21 Andy Pafko	80.00	40.00
22 Joe Page	100.00	50.00
23 Mel Parnell	100.00	50.00
24 Johnny Sain	120.00	60.00
25 Red Schoendienst	150.00	75.00
26 Roy Sievers	100.00	50.00
27 Roy Smalley	80.00	40.00
28 Herm Wehmeier	80.00	40.00
29 Bill Werle	80.00	40.00
30 Wes Westrum	80.00	40.00
31 Early Wynn	150.00	75.00
32 Gus Zernial	100.00	50.00

1993 Flair Promos

This eight-card standard-size set was issued to preview the design of the 1993 Flair series. These cards can be distinguished by triple zero on their backs; otherwise, they are identical to their regular issue counterparts. The cards are listed below in alphabetical order by player's last name. According to unverified reports, Fleer shredded a 5,000 count box of these cards to avoid potential difficulties with their liscening organizations.

	Nm-Mt	Ex-Mt
COMPLETE SET (8)	300.00	90.00
1 Will Clark	40.00	12.00
2 Darren Daulton	15.00	4.50
3 Andres Galarraga	20.00	6.00
4 Bryan Harvey	10.00	3.00
5 David Justice	20.00	6.00
6 Jody Reed	10.00	3.00
7 Nolan Ryan	150.00	45.00
8 Sammy Sosa	80.00	24.00

1993 Flair

This 300-card standard-size set represents Fleer's entrance into the super-premium category of trading cards. Cards were distributed exclusively in specially encased "hardpacks". The cards are made from heavy 24 point board card stock, with an additional three points of high-gloss laminate on each side, and feature full-bleed color fronts that sport two photos of each player, one superposed upon the other. The cards are numbered alphabetically within teams with National League preceding American league. There are no key Rookie Cards in this set.

	Nm-Mt	Ex-Mt
COMPLETE SET (300)	50.00	15.00
1 Steve Avery	.25	.07
2 Jeff Blauser	.25	.07
3 Ron Gant	.50	.15
4 Tom Glavine	.75	.23
5 David Justice	.50	.15
6 Mark Lemke	.25	.07
7 Greg Maddux	2.00	.60
8 Fred McGriff	.75	.23
9 Terry Pendleton	.50	.15
10 Deion Sanders	.75	.23
11 John Smoltz	.75	.23
12 Mike Stanton	.25	.07
13 Steve Buechele	.25	.07
14 Mark Grace	.75	.23
15 Greg Hibbard	.25	.07
16 Derrick May	.25	.07
17 Chuck McElroy	.25	.07
18 Mike Morgan	.25	.07
19 Randy Myers	.25	.07
20 Ryne Sandberg	2.00	.60
21 Dwight Smith	.25	.07
22 Sammy Sosa	2.00	.60
23 Jose Vizcaino	.25	.07
24 Tim Belcher	.25	.07
25 Rob Dibble	.50	.15
26 Roberto Kelly	.25	.07
27 Barry Larkin	1.25	.35
28 Kevin Mitchell	.25	.07
29 Hal Morris	.25	.07
30 Joe Oliver	.25	.07
31 Jose Rijo	.25	.07
32 Bip Roberts	.25	.07
33 Chris Sabo	.25	.07
34 Reggie Sanders	.50	.15
35 Dante Bichette	.50	.15
36 Willie Blair	.25	.07
37 Jerald Clark	.25	.07
38 Alex Cole	.25	.07
39 Andres Galarraga	.50	.15
40 Joe Girardi	.25	.07
41 Charlie Hayes	.25	.07
42 Chris Jones	.25	.07
43 David Nied	.25	.07
44 Eric Young	.25	.07
45 Alex Arias	.25	.07
46 Jack Armstrong	.25	.07
47 Bret Barberie	.25	.07
48 Chuck Carr	.25	.07
49 Jeff Conine	.50	.15
50 Orestes Destrade	.25	.07
51 Chris Hammond	.25	.07
52 Bryan Harvey	.25	.07
53 Benito Santiago	.50	.15
54 Gary Sheffield	.50	.15
55 Walt Weiss	.25	.07
56 Eric Anthony	.25	.07
57 Jeff Bagwell	.75	.23
58 Craig Biggio	.75	.23
59 Ken Caminiti	.50	.15
60 Andujar Cedeno	.25	.07
61 Doug Drabek	.25	.07
62 Steve Finley	.50	.15
63 Luis Gonzalez	.50	.15
64 Pete Harnisch	.25	.07
65 Doug Jones	.25	.07
66 Darryl Kile	.50	.15
67 Greg Swindell	.25	.07
68 Brett Butler	.50	.15
69 Jim Gott	.25	.07
70 Orel Hershiser	.50	.15
71 Eric Karros	.50	.15
72 Pedro Martinez	2.50	.75
73 Ramon Martinez	.25	.07
74 Roger McDowell	.25	.07
75 Mike Piazza	3.00	.90
76 Jody Reed	.25	.07
77 Tim Wallach	.25	.07
78 Moises Alou	.50	.15
79 Greg Colbrunn	.25	.07
80 Wil Cordero	.25	.07
81 Delino DeShields	.25	.07
82 Jeff Fassero	.25	.07
83 Marquis Grissom	.25	.07
84 Ken Hill	.25	.07
85 Mike Lansing RC	.50	.15
86 Dennis Martinez	.50	.15
87 Larry Walker	.75	.23
88 John Wetteland	.50	.15
89 Bobby Bonilla	.50	.15
90 Vince Coleman	.25	.07
91 Dwight Gooden	.75	.23
92 Todd Hundley	.25	.07
93 Howard Johnson	.25	.07
94 Eddie Murray	1.25	.35
95 Joe Orsulak	.25	.07
96 Bret Saberhagen	.50	.15
97 Darren Daulton	.50	.15
98 Mariano Duncan	.25	.07
99 Len Dykstra	.50	.15
100 Jim Eisenreich	.25	.07
101 Tommy Greene	.25	.07
102 Dave Hollins	.25	.07
103 Pete Incaviglia	.25	.07
104 Danny Jackson	.25	.07
105 John Kruk	.50	.15
106 Terry Mulholland	.25	.07
107 Curt Schilling	.75	.23
108 Mitch Williams	.25	.07
109 Stan Belinda	.25	.07
110 Jay Bell	.50	.15
111 Steve Cooke	.25	.07
112 Carlos Garcia	.25	.07
113 Jeff King	.25	.07
114 Al Martin	.25	.07
115 Orlando Merced	.25	.07
116 Don Slaught	.25	.07
117 Andy Van Slyke	.50	.15
118 Tim Wakefield	.50	.15
119 Rene Arocha RC	.50	.15
120 Bernard Gilkey	.25	.07
121 Gregg Jefferies	.25	.07
122 Ray Lankford	.25	.07
123 Donovan Osborne	.25	.07
124 Tom Pagnozzi	.25	.07
125 Erik Pappas	.25	.07
126 Geronimo Pena	.25	.07
127 Lee Smith	.50	.15
128 Ozzie Smith	2.00	.60
129 Bob Tewksbury	.25	.07
130 Mark Whiten	.25	.07
131 Derek Bell	.25	.07
132 Andy Benes	.25	.07
133 Tony Gwynn	1.50	.45
134 Gene Harris	.25	.07
135 Trevor Hoffman	.50	.15
136 Phil Plantier	.25	.07
137 Rod Beck	.25	.07
138 Barry Bonds	3.00	.90
139 John Burkett	.25	.07
140 Will Clark	1.25	.35
141 Royce Clayton	.25	.07
142 Mike Jackson	.25	.07
143 Darren Lewis	.25	.07
144 Kirt Manwaring	.25	.07
145 Willie McGee	.50	.15
146 Bill Swift	.25	.07
147 Robby Thompson	.25	.07
148 Matt Williams	.50	.15
149 Brady Anderson	.50	.15
150 Mike Devereaux	.25	.07
151 Chris Hoiles	.25	.07
152 Ben McDonald	.25	.07
153 Mark McLemore	.25	.07
154 Mike Mussina	1.25	.35
155 Gregg Olson	.25	.07
156 Harold Reynolds	.50	.15
157 Cal Ripken UER (Back refers to his games streak going into 1992; should be 1993) Also streak is spelled steak	4.00	1.20
158 Rick Sutcliffe	.50	.15
159 Fernando Valenzuela	.50	.15
160 Roger Clemens	2.50	.75
161 Scott Cooper	.25	.07
162 Andre Dawson	.50	.15
163 Scott Fletcher	.25	.07
164 Mike Greenwell	.25	.07
165 Greg A. Harris	.25	.07
166 Billy Hatcher	.25	.07
167 Jeff Russell	.25	.07
168 Mo Vaughn	.50	.15
169 Frank Viola	.50	.15
170 Chad Curtis	.25	.07
171 Chili Davis	.50	.15
172 Gary DiSarcina	.25	.07
173 Damion Easley	.25	.07
174 Chuck Finley	.50	.15
175 Mark Langston	.25	.07
176 Luis Polonia	.25	.07
177 Tim Salmon	.75	.23
178 Scott Sanderson	.25	.07
179 J.T.Snow RC	1.25	.35
180 Wilson Alvarez	.25	.07
181 Ellis Burks	.50	.15
182 Joey Cora	.25	.07
183 Alex Fernandez	.25	.07
184 Ozzie Guillen	.25	.07
185 Roberto Hernandez	.25	.07
186 Bo Jackson	1.25	.35
187 Lance Johnson	.25	.07
188 Jack McDowell	.25	.07
189 Frank Thomas	1.25	.35
190 Robin Ventura	.50	.15
191 Carlos Baerga	.25	.07
192 Albert Belle	.50	.15
193 Wayne Kirby	.25	.07
194 Derek Lilliquist	.25	.07
195 Kenny Lofton	.50	.15
196 Carlos Martinez	.25	.07
197 Jose Mesa	.25	.07
198 Eric Plunk	.25	.07
199 Paul Sorrento	.25	.07
200 John Doherty	.25	.07
201 Cecil Fielder	.50	.15
202 Travis Fryman	.50	.15
203 Kirk Gibson	.50	.15
204 Mike Henneman	.25	.07
205 Chad Kreuter	.25	.07
206 Scott Livingstone	.25	.07
207 Tony Phillips	.25	.07
208 Mickey Tettleton	.25	.07
209 Alan Trammell	.75	.23
210 David Wells	.50	.15
211 Lou Whitaker	.50	.15
212 Kevin Appier	.50	.15
213 George Brett	3.00	.90
214 David Cone	.50	.15
215 Tom Gordon	.25	.07
216 Phil Hiatt	.25	.07
217 Felix Jose	.25	.07
218 Wally Joyner	.50	.15
219 Jose Lind	.25	.07
220 Mike Macfarlane	.25	.07
221 Brian McRae	.25	.07
222 Jeff Montgomery	.25	.07
223 Cal Eldred	.25	.07
224 Darryl Hamilton	.25	.07
225 John Jaha	.25	.07
226 Pat Listach	.25	.07
227 Graeme Lloyd RC	.50	.15
228 Kevin Reimer	.25	.07
229 Bill Spiers	.25	.07
230 B.J. Surhoff	.50	.15
231 Greg Vaughn	.50	.15
232 Robin Yount	2.00	.60
233 Rick Aguilera	.25	.07
234 Jim Deshaies	.25	.07
235 Brian Harper	.25	.07
236 Kent Hrbek	.50	.15
237 Chuck Knoblauch	.50	.15
238 Shane Mack	.25	.07
239 David McCarty	.25	.07
240 Pedro Munoz	.25	.07
241 Mike Pagliarulo	.25	.07
242 Kirby Puckett	1.25	.35
243 Dave Winfield	.50	.15
244 Jim Abbott	.75	.23
245 Wade Boggs	.75	.23
246 Pat Kelly	.25	.07
247 Jimmy Key	.50	.15
248 Jim Leyritz	.25	.07
249 Don Mattingly	3.00	.90
250 Matt Nokes	.25	.07
251 Paul O'Neill	.75	.23
252 Mike Stanley	.25	.07
253 Danny Tartabull	.25	.07
254 Bob Wickman	.25	.07
255 Bernie Williams	.75	.23
256 Mike Bordick	.25	.07
257 Dennis Eckersley	.50	.15
258 Brent Gates	.25	.07
259 Rich Gossage	.50	.15
260 Rickey Henderson	1.25	.35
261 Mark McGwire	3.00	.90
262 Ruben Sierra	.25	.07
263 Terry Steinbach	.25	.07
264 Bob Welch	.25	.07
265 Bobby Witt	.25	.07
266 Rich Amaral	.25	.07
267 Chris Bosio	.25	.07
268 Jay Buhner	.50	.15
269 Norm Charlton	.25	.07
270 Ken Griffey Jr.	2.00	.60
271 Erik Hanson	.25	.07
272 Randy Johnson	1.25	.35
273 Edgar Martinez	.75	.23
274 Tino Martinez	.75	.23
275 Dave Valle	.25	.07
276 Omar Vizquel	.50	.15
277 Kevin Brown	.50	.15
278 Jose Canseco	1.25	.35
279 Julio Franco	.50	.15
280 Juan Gonzalez	1.25	.35
281 Tom Henke	.25	.07
282 David Hulse RC	.25	.07
283 Rafael Palmeiro	.75	.23
284 Dean Palmer	.50	.15
285 Ivan Rodriguez	1.25	.35
286 Nolan Ryan	5.00	1.50
287 Roberto Alomar	1.25	.35
288 Pat Borders	.25	.07
289 Joe Carter	.50	.15
290 Juan Guzman	.25	.07
291 Pat Hentgen	.25	.07
292 Paul Molitor	.75	.23
293 John Olerud	.50	.15
294 Ed Sprague	.25	.07
295 Dave Stewart	.50	.15
296 Duane Ward	.25	.07
297 Devon White	.25	.07
298 Checklist 1-100	.25	.07
299 Checklist 101-200	.25	.07
300 Checklist 201-300	.25	.07

1993 Flair Wave of the Future

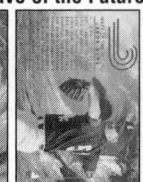

This 20-card standard-size limited edition insert set features a selction of top prospects. Cards were randomly seeded into1993 Flair packs. Each card is made of the same thick card stock as the regular-issue set and features full-bleed color player action photos on the fronts, with the Flair logo, player's name, and the "Wave of the Future" name and logo in gold foil, all superimposed upon an ocean breaker. A Rookie Year Jim Edmonds card is a highlight of this set.

	Nm-Mt	Ex-Mt
COMPLETE SET (20)	40.00	12.00
1 Jason Bere	1.00	.30
2 Jeromy Burnitz	2.00	.60
3 Russ Davis	2.00	.60
4 Jim Edmonds	4.00	1.20
5 Cliff Floyd	2.50	.75
6 Jeffrey Hammonds	1.00	.30
7 Trevor Hoffman	2.00	.60
8 Domingo Jean	1.00	.30
9 David McCarty	1.00	.30
10 Bobby Munoz	1.00	.30
11 Brad Pennington	1.00	.30
12 Mike Piazza	10.00	3.00
13 Manny Ramirez	4.00	1.20
14 John Roper	1.00	.30
15 Tim Salmon	2.50	.75
16 Aaron Sele	1.00	.30
17 Allen Watson	1.00	.30
18 Rondell White	2.00	.60
19 Darrell Whitmore UER (Nigel Wilson back)	1.00	.30
20 Nigel Wilson UER (Darrell Whitmore back)	1.00	.30

1994 Flair

For the second consecutive year Fleer issued their premium-level Flair brand. The set consists of 450 full bleed cards in two series of 250 and 200. The card stock is thicker than the traditional standard card. Card fronts feature two photos with the player's name and team name at the bottom in gold foil. The cards are grouped alphabetically by team within each league with AL preceding NL. Notable Rookie Cards include Chan Ho Park and Alex Rodriguez. An Aaron Sele promo card was distributed to dealers and hobby media to preview the product.

	Nm-Mt	Ex-Mt
COMPLETE SET (450)	80.00	24.00
COMP. SERIES 1 (250)	20.00	6.00
COMP. SERIES 2 (200)	60.00	18.00
1 Harold Baines	.50	.15
2 Jeffrey Hammonds	.25	.07
3 Chris Hoiles	.25	.07
4 Ben McDonald	.25	.07
5 Mark McLemore	.25	.07
6 Jamie Moyer	.50	.15
7 Jim Poole	.25	.07
8 Cal Ripken Jr.	4.00	1.20
9 Chris Sabo	.25	.07
10 Scott Bankhead	.25	.07
11 Scott Cooper	.25	.07
12 Danny Darwin	.25	.07
13 Andre Dawson	.50	.15
14 Billy Hatcher	.25	.07
15 Aaron Sele	.25	.07
16 John Valentin	.25	.07
17 Dave Valle	.25	.07
18 Mo Vaughn	.50	.15
19 Brian Anderson RC	.50	.15
20 Gary DiSarcina	.25	.07
21 Jim Edmonds	.75	.23
22 Chuck Finley	.50	.15
23 Bo Jackson	1.25	.35
24 Mark Leiter	.25	.07
25 Greg Myers	.25	.07
26 Eduardo Perez	.25	.07
27 Tim Salmon	.75	.23
28 Wilson Alvarez	.25	.07
29 Jason Bere	.25	.07
30 Alex Fernandez	.25	.07
31 Ozzie Guillen	.25	.07
32 Joe Hall RC	.25	.07
33 Darrin Jackson	.25	.07
34 Kirk McCaskill	.25	.07
35 Tim Raines	.50	.15
36 Frank Thomas	1.25	.35
37 Carlos Baerga	.25	.07
38 Albert Belle	.50	.15
39 Mark Clark	.25	.07
40 Wayne Kirby	.25	.07
41 Dennis Martinez	.50	.15
42 Charles Nagy	.25	.07
43 Manny Ramirez	.75	.23
44 Paul Sorrento	.25	.07
45 Jim Thome	1.25	.35
46 Eric Davis	.50	.15
47 John Doherty	.25	.07
48 Junior Felix	.25	.07
49 Cecil Fielder	.50	.15
50 Kirk Gibson	.50	.15
51 Mike Moore	.25	.07
52 Tony Phillips	.25	.07
53 Alan Trammell	.75	.23
54 Kevin Appier	.50	.15
55 Stan Belinda	.25	.07
56 Vince Coleman	.25	.07
57 Greg Gagne	.25	.07
58 Bob Hamelin	.25	.07
59 Dave Henderson	.25	.07
60 Wally Joyner	.50	.15
61 Mike Macfarlane	.25	.07
62 Jeff Montgomery	.25	.07
63 Ricky Bones	.25	.07
64 Jeff Bronkey	.25	.07
65 Alex Diaz RC	.25	.07
66 Cal Eldred	.25	.07
67 Darryl Hamilton	.25	.07
68 John Jaha	.25	.07
69 Mark Kiefer	.25	.07
70 Kevin Seitzer	.25	.07
71 Turner Ward	.25	.07
72 Rich Becker	.25	.07
73 Scott Erickson	.25	.07
74 Keith Garagozzo RC	.25	.07
75 Kent Hrbek	.50	.15
76 Scott Leius	.25	.07
77 Kirby Puckett	1.25	.35
78 Matt Walbeck	.25	.07
79 Dave Winfield	.50	.15
80 Mike Gallego	.25	.07
81 Xavier Hernandez	.25	.07
82 Jimmy Key	.50	.15
83 Jim Leyritz	.25	.07
84 Don Mattingly	3.00	.90
85 Matt Nokes	.25	.07
86 Paul O'Neill	.75	.23
87 Melido Perez	.25	.07
88 Danny Tartabull	.25	.07
89 Mike Bordick	.25	.07
90 Ron Darling	.25	.07
91 Dennis Eckersley	.50	.15
92 Stan Javier	.25	.07
93 Steve Karsay	.25	.07
94 Mark McGwire	3.00	.90
95 Troy Neel	.25	.07
96 Terry Steinbach	.25	.07
97 Bill Taylor RC	.50	.15
98 Eric Anthony	.25	.07
99 Chris Bosio	.25	.07
100 Tim Davis	.25	.07
101 Felix Fermin	.25	.07
102 Dave Fleming	.25	.07
103 Ken Griffey Jr.	2.00	.60
104 Greg Hibbard	.25	.07
105 Reggie Jefferson	.25	.07
106 Tino Martinez	.75	.23
107 Jack Armstrong	.25	.07
108 Will Clark	1.25	.35
109 Juan Gonzalez	1.25	.35
110 Rick Helling	.25	.07
111 Tom Henke	.25	.07
112 David Hulse	.25	.07
113 Manuel Lee	.25	.07
114 Doug Strange	.25	.07
115 Roberto Alomar	1.25	.35
116 Joe Carter	.50	.15
117 Carlos Delgado	.75	.23
118 Pat Hentgen	.25	.07
119 Paul Molitor	.75	.23
120 John Olerud	.50	.15
121 Dave Stewart	.50	.15
122 Todd Stottlemyre	.25	.07
123 Mike Timlin	.25	.07
124 Jeff Blauser	.25	.07
125 Tom Glavine	.75	.23
126 David Justice	.50	.15
127 Mike Kelly	.25	.07
128 Ryan Klesko	.50	.15
129 Javier Lopez	.50	.15
130 Greg Maddux	2.00	.60
131 Fred McGriff	.75	.23
132 Kent Mercker	.25	.07
133 Mark Wohlers	.25	.07
134 Willie Banks	.25	.07
135 Steve Buechele	.25	.07
136 Shawon Dunston	.25	.07
137 Jose Guzman	.25	.07
138 Glenallen Hill	.25	.07
139 Randy Myers	.25	.07
140 Karl Rhodes	.25	.07
141 Ryne Sandberg	2.00	.60
142 Steve Trachsel	.25	.07
143 Bret Boone	.50	.15
144 Tom Browning	.25	.07
145 Hector Carrasco	.25	.07
146 Barry Larkin	1.25	.35
147 Hal Morris	.25	.07
148 Jose Rijo	.25	.07
149 Reggie Sanders	.50	.15
150 John Smiley	.25	.07
151 Dante Bichette	.50	.15
152 Ellis Burks	.50	.15
153 Joe Girardi	.25	.07
154 Mike Harkey	.25	.07
155 Roberto Mejia	.25	.07
156 Marcus Moore	.25	.07
157 Armando Reynoso	.25	.07
158 Bruce Ruffin	.25	.07
159 Eric Young	.25	.07
160 Kurt Abbott RC	.50	.15
161 Jeff Conine	.50	.15
162 Orestes Destrade	.25	.07
163 Chris Hammond	.25	.07
164 Bryan Harvey	.25	.07
165 Dave Magadan	.25	.07
166 Gary Sheffield	.50	.15
167 David Weathers	.25	.07
168 Andujar Cedeno	.25	.07
169 Tom Edens	.25	.07
170 Luis Gonzalez	.50	.15
171 Pete Harnisch	.25	.07
172 Todd Jones	.25	.07
173 Darryl Kile	.50	.15
174 James Mouton	.25	.07
175 Scott Servais	.25	.07
176 Mitch Williams	.25	.07
177 Pedro Astacio	.25	.07
178 Orel Hershiser	.50	.15
179 Raul Mondesi	.50	.15
180 Jose Offerman	.25	.07
181 Chan Ho Park RC	1.50	.45
182 Mike Piazza	2.50	.75
183 Cory Snyder	.25	.07
184 Tim Wallach	.25	.07
185 Todd Worrell	.25	.07
186 Sean Berry	.25	.07
187 Wil Cordero	.25	.07
188 Darrin Fletcher	.25	.07
189 Cliff Floyd	.50	.15
190 Marquis Grissom	.25	.07
191 Rod Henderson	.25	.07
192 Ken Hill	.25	.07
193 Pedro Martinez	1.25	.35
194 Kirk Rueter	.50	.15
195 Jeromy Burnitz	.50	.15
196 John Franco	.50	.15
197 Dwight Gooden	.75	.23
198 Todd Hundley	.25	.07
199 Bobby Jones	.25	.07
200 Jeff Kent	.50	.15
201 Mike Maddux	.25	.07
202 Ryan Thompson	.25	.07
203 Jose Vizcaino	.25	.07
204 Darren Daulton	.50	.15
205 Lenny Dykstra	.50	.15
206 Jim Eisenreich	.25	.07
207 Dave Hollins	.25	.07
208 Danny Jackson	.25	.07
209 Doug Jones	.25	.07
210 Jeff Juden	.25	.07
211 Ben Rivera	.25	.07
212 Kevin Stocker	.25	.07
213 Milt Thompson	.25	.07
214 Jay Bell	.50	.15
215 Steve Cooke	.25	.07
216 Mark Dewey	.25	.07
217 Al Martin	.25	.07
218 Orlando Merced	.25	.07
219 Don Slaught	.25	.07
220 Zane Smith	.25	.07
221 Rick White RC	.25	.07
222 Kevin Young	.25	.07
223 Rene Arocha	.25	.07
224 Rheal Cormier	.25	.07
225 Brian Jordan	.50	.15
226 Ray Lankford	.50	.15
227 Mike Perez	.25	.07
228 Ozzie Smith	2.00	.60
229 Mark Whiten	.25	.07
230 Todd Zeile	.25	.07
231 Derek Bell	.25	.07
232 Archi Cianfrocco	.25	.07
233 Ricky Gutierrez	.25	.07
234 Trevor Hoffman	.50	.15
235 Phil Plantier	.25	.07
236 Dave Staton	.25	.07
237 Wally Whitehurst	.25	.07
238 Todd Benzinger	.25	.07
239 Barry Bonds	3.00	.90
240 John Burkett	.25	.07
241 Royce Clayton	.25	.07
242 Bryan Hickerson	.25	.07
243 Mike Jackson	.25	.07
244 Darren Lewis	.25	.07
245 Kirt Manwaring	.25	.07
246 Mark Portugal	.25	.07
247 Salomon Torres	.25	.07
248 Checklist	.25	.07
249 Checklist	.25	.07
250 Checklist	.25	.07
251 Brady Anderson	.50	.15
252 Mike Devereaux	.25	.07
253 Sid Fernandez	.25	.07
254 Leo Gomez	.25	.07
255 Mike Mussina	1.25	.35
256 Mike Oquist	.25	.07
257 Rafael Palmeiro	.75	.23
258 Lee Smith	.50	.15
259 Damon Berryhill	.25	.07
260 Wes Chamberlain	.25	.07
261 Roger Clemens	2.50	.75
262 Gar Finnvold RC	.25	.07
263 Mike Greenwell	.25	.07
264 Tim Naehring	.25	.07
265 Otis Nixon	.25	.07
266 Ken Ryan	.25	.07
267 Chad Curtis	.25	.07
268 Chili Davis	.50	.15
269 Damion Easley	.25	.07
270 Jorge Fabregas	.25	.07
271 Mark Langston	.25	.07
272 Phil Leftwich RC	.25	.07
273 Harold Reynolds	.50	.15
274 J.T. Snow	.50	.15
275 Joey Cora	.25	.07
276 Julio Franco	.50	.15
277 Roberto Hernandez	.25	.07
278 Lance Johnson	.25	.07
279 Ron Karkovice	.25	.07
280 Jack McDowell	.25	.07
281 Robin Ventura	.50	.15
282 Sandy Alomar Jr.	.25	.07
283 Kenny Lofton	.50	.15
284 Jose Mesa	.25	.07
285 Jack Morris	.50	.15
286 Eddie Murray	1.25	.35
287 Chad Ogea	.25	.07
288 Eric Plunk	.25	.07
289 Paul Shuey	.25	.07
290 Omar Vizquel	.50	.15
291 Danny Bautista	.25	.07
292 Travis Fryman	.50	.15
293 Greg Gohr	.25	.07
294 Chris Gomez	.25	.07
295 Mickey Tettleton	.25	.07
296 Lou Whitaker	.50	.15
297 David Cone	.50	.15
298 Gary Gaetti	.50	.15
299 Tom Gordon	.25	.07
300 Felix Jose	.25	.07
301 Jose Lind	.25	.07
302 Brian McRae	.25	.07
303 Mike Fetters	.25	.07
304 Brian Harper	.25	.07
305 Pat Listach	.25	.07
306 Matt Mieske	.25	.07
307 Dave Nilsson	.25	.07
308 Jody Reed	.25	.07
309 Greg Vaughn	.50	.15
310 Bill Wegman	.25	.07
311 Rick Aguilera	.25	.07
312 Alex Cole	.25	.07
313 Denny Hocking	.25	.07
314 Chuck Knoblauch	.50	.15
315 Shane Mack	.25	.07
316 Pat Meares	.25	.07
317 Kevin Tapani	.25	.07
318 Jim Abbott	.75	.23
319 Wade Boggs	.75	.23
320 Sterling Hitchcock	.25	.07
321 Pat Kelly	.25	.07
322 Terry Mulholland	.25	.07
323 Luis Polonia	.25	.07
324 Mike Stanley	.25	.07
325 Bob Wickman	.25	.07
326 Bernie Williams	.75	.23
327 Mark Acre RC	.25	.07
328 Geronimo Berroa	.25	.07
329 Scott Brosius	.50	.15
330 Brent Gates	.25	.07
331 Rickey Henderson	1.25	.35
332 Carlos Reyes RC	.25	.07
333 Ruben Sierra	.25	.07
334 Bobby Witt	.25	.07
335 Bobby Ayala	.25	.07
336 Jay Buhner	.50	.15
337 Randy Johnson	1.25	.35
338 Edgar Martinez	.75	.23
339 Bill Risley	.25	.07
340 Alex Rodriguez RC	40.00	12.00
341 Roger Salkeld	.25	.07
342 Dan Wilson	.25	.07
343 Kevin Brown	.50	.15
344 Jose Canseco	1.25	.35
345 Dean Palmer	.50	.15
346 Ivan Rodriguez	1.25	.35
347 Kenny Rogers	.50	.15
348 Pat Borders	.25	.07
349 Juan Guzman	.25	.07
350 Ed Sprague	.25	.07
351 Devon White	.25	.07
352 Steve Avery	.25	.07
353 Roberto Kelly	.25	.07
354 Mark Lemke	.25	.07
355 Greg McMichael	.25	.07
356 Terry Pendleton	.50	.15
357 John Smoltz	.75	.23
358 Mike Stanton	.25	.07
359 Tony Tarasco	.25	.07
360 Mark Grace	.75	.23
361 Derrick May	.25	.07
362 Rey Sanchez	.25	.07
363 Sammy Sosa	2.00	.60
364 Rick Wilkins	.25	.07
365 Jeff Brantley	.25	.07
366 Tony Fernandez	.25	.07
367 Chuck McElroy	.25	.07
368 Kevin Mitchell	.25	.07
369 John Roper	.25	.07
370 Johnny Ruffin	.25	.07
371 Deion Sanders	.75	.23
372 Marvin Freeman	.25	.07
373 Andres Galarraga	.50	.15
374 Charlie Hayes	.25	.07
375 Nelson Liriano	.25	.07
376 David Nied	.25	.07
377 Walt Weiss	.25	.07
378 Bret Barberie	.25	.07
379 Jerry Browne	.25	.07
380 Chuck Carr	.25	.07
381 Greg Colbrunn	.50	.15
382 Charlie Hough	.50	.15
383 Kurt Miller	.25	.07
384 Benito Santiago	.50	.15
385 Jeff Bagwell	.75	.23
386 Craig Biggio	.75	.23
387 Ken Caminiti	.50	.15
388 Doug Drabek	.25	.07
389 Steve Finley	.50	.15
390 John Hudek RC	.25	.07
391 Orlando Miller	.25	.07
392 Shane Reynolds	.25	.07
393 Brett Butler	.50	.15
394 Tom Candiotti	.25	.07
395 Delino DeShields	.25	.07
396 Kevin Gross	.25	.07
397 Eric Karros	.50	.15
398 Ramon Martinez	.25	.07
399 Henry Rodriguez	.25	.07
400 Moises Alou	.50	.15
401 Jeff Fassero	.25	.07
402 Mike Lansing	.25	.07
403 Mel Rojas	.25	.07
404 Larry Walker	.75	.23
405 John Wetteland	.50	.15
406 Gabe White	.25	.07
407 Bobby Bonilla	.50	.15
408 Josias Manzanillo	.25	.07
409 Bret Saberhagen	.50	.15
410 David Segui	.25	.07
411 Mariano Duncan	.25	.07
412 Tommy Greene	.25	.07
413 Billy Hatcher	.25	.07
414 Ricky Jordan	.25	.07
415 John Kruk	.50	.15
416 Bobby Munoz	.25	.07
417 Curt Schilling	.75	.23
418 Fernando Valenzuela	.50	.15
419 David West	.25	.07
420 Carlos Garcia	.25	.07
421 Brian Hunter	.25	.07
422 Jeff King	.25	.07
423 Jon Lieber	.25	.07
424 Ravelo Manzanillo	.25	.07
425 Denny Neagle	.50	.15
426 Andy Van Slyke	.50	.15
427 Bryan Eversgerd RC	.25	.07
428 Bernard Gilkey	.25	.07
429 Gregg Jefferies	.25	.07
430 Tom Pagnozzi	.25	.07
431 Bob Tewksbury	.25	.07
432 Allen Watson	.25	.07
433 Andy Ashby	.25	.07
434 Andy Benes	.25	.07
435 Donnie Elliott	.25	.07
436 Tony Gwynn	1.50	.45
437 Joey Hamilton	.25	.07
438 Tim Hyers RC	.25	.07
439 Luis Lopez	.25	.07
440 Bip Roberts	.25	.07
441 Scott Sanders	.25	.07
442 Rod Beck	.25	.07
443 Dave Burba	.25	.07
444 Darryl Strawberry	.75	.23
445 Bill Swift	.25	.07
446 Robby Thompson	.25	.07
447 B.VanLandingham RC	.25	.07
448 Matt Williams	.50	.15
449 Checklist	.25	.07
450 Checklist	.25	.07
P15 Aaron Sele Promo	1.00	.30

1994 Flair Hot Gloves

Randomly inserted in second series packs at a rate of one in 24, this set highlights 10 of the game's top players that also have outstanding defensive ability. The cards feature a special die-cut "glove" design with the player appearing within the glove. The back has a short write-up and a photo.

	Nm-Mt	Ex-Mt
COMPLETE SET (10)	120.00	36.00
1 Barry Bonds	25.00	7.50
2 Will Clark	10.00	3.00
3 Ken Griffey Jr.	15.00	4.50
4 Kenny Lofton	4.00	1.20
5 Greg Maddux	15.00	4.50
6 Don Mattingly	25.00	7.50
7 Kirby Puckett	10.00	3.00
8 Cal Ripken Jr.	30.00	9.00
9 Tim Salmon	6.00	1.80
10 Matt Williams	4.00	1.20

1994 Flair Hot Numbers

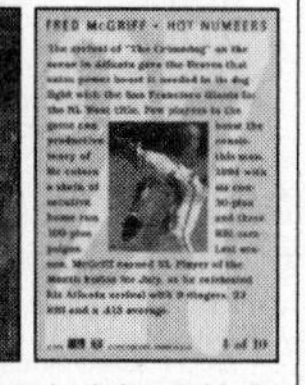

This 10-card set was randomly inserted in first series packs at a rate of one in 24. Metallic fronts feature a player photo with various numbers or statistics serving as background. The backs have a small photo centered in the middle surrounded by text highlighting achievements.

	Nm-Mt	Ex-Mt
COMPLETE SET (10)	80.00	24.00
1 Roberto Alomar	8.00	2.40
2 Carlos Baerga	1.50	.45
3 Will Clark	8.00	2.40
4 Fred McGriff	5.00	1.50
5 Paul Molitor	5.00	1.50
6 John Olerud	3.00	.90
7 Mike Piazza	15.00	4.50
8 Cal Ripken Jr.	25.00	7.50
9 Ryne Sandberg	12.00	3.60
10 Frank Thomas	8.00	2.40

1994 Flair Infield Power

Randomly inserted in second series packs at a rate of one in five, this 10-card standard-size set spotlights major league infielders who are power hitters. Card fronts feature a horizontal format with two photos of the player. The backs contain a short write-up with emphasis on power numbers and a small photo.

	Nm-Mt	Ex-Mt
COMPLETE SET (10)	15.00	4.50
1 Jeff Bagwell	1.25	.35
2 Will Clark	2.00	.60
3 Darren Daulton	.75	.23
4 Don Mattingly	5.00	1.50
5 Fred McGriff	1.25	.35
6 Rafael Palmeiro	1.25	.35
7 Mike Piazza	4.00	1.20
8 Cal Ripken Jr.	6.00	1.80
9 Frank Thomas	2.00	.60
10 Matt Williams	.75	.23

1994 Flair Outfield Power

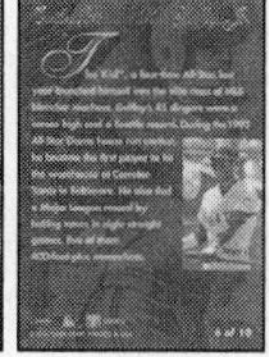

This 10-card standard-size set was randomly inserted in both first and second series packs at a rate of one in five. Two photos on the front feature the player fielding and hitting. The back contains a small photo and text.

	Nm-Mt	Ex-Mt
COMPLETE SET (10)	20.00	6.00
1 Albert Belle	1.00	.30
2 Barry Bonds	6.00	1.80
3 Joe Carter	1.00	.30
4 Lenny Dykstra	1.00	.30
5 Juan Gonzalez	2.50	.75
6 Ken Griffey Jr.	4.00	1.20
7 David Justice	1.00	.30
8 Kirby Puckett	2.50	.75
9 Tim Salmon	1.50	.45
10 Dave Winfield	1.00	.30

1994 Flair Wave of the Future

This 20-card standard-size set takes a look at potential big league stars. The cards were randomly inserted in packs at a rate of one in five -- the first 10 in series one, the second 10 in series two. The fronts and backs have the player superimposed over a wavy colored background. The front has the Wave of the Future logo and a paragraph or two about the player along with a photo on the back. This set is highlighted by an early Alex Rodriguez card.

	Nm-Mt	Ex-Mt
COMPLETE SER.1 (10)	15.00	4.50
COMPLETE SER.2 (10)	40.00	12.00
A1 Kurt Abbott	2.00	.60
A2 Carlos Delgado	2.50	.75
A3 Steve Karsay	1.00	.30
A4 Ryan Klesko	2.00	.60
A5 Javier Lopez	2.00	.60
A6 Raul Mondesi	2.00	.60
A7 James Mouton	1.00	.30
A8 Chan Ho Park	3.00	.90
A9 Dave Staton	1.00	.30
A10 Rick White	1.00	.30
B1 Mark Acre	1.00	.30
B2 Chris Gomez	1.00	.30
B3 Joey Hamilton	1.00	.30
B4 John Hudek	1.00	.30
B5 Jon Lieber	1.00	.30
B6 Matt Mieske	1.00	.30
B7 Orlando Miller	1.00	.30
B8 Alex Rodriguez	30.00	9.00
B9 Tony Tarasco	1.00	.30
B10 W.VanLandingham	1.00	.30

1995 Flair

This set (produced by Fleer) was issued in two series of 216 cards for a total of 432 standard-size cards. Horizontally designed fronts have a 100 percent etched foil surface containing two player photos. The backs feature a full-bleed photo with yearly statistics superimposed. The checklist is arranged alphabetically by league

with AL preceding NL. Rookie Cards include Bobby Higginson and Hideo Nomo.

	Nm-Mt	Ex-Mt
COMPLETE SET (432)	50.00	15.00
COMP. SERIES 1 (216)	30.00	9.00
COMP. SERIES 2 (216)	20.00	6.00
1 Brady Anderson	.50	.15
2 Harold Baines	.50	.15
3 Leo Gomez	.25	.07
4 Alan Mills	.25	.07
5 Jamie Moyer	.50	.15
6 Mike Mussina	1.25	.35
7 Mike Oquist	.25	.07
8 Arthur Rhodes	.25	.07
9 Cal Ripken Jr.	4.00	1.20
10 Roger Clemens	2.50	.75
11 Scott Cooper	.25	.07
12 Mike Greenwell	.25	.07
13 Aaron Sele	.25	.07
14 John Valentin	.25	.07
15 Mo Vaughn	.50	.15
16 Chad Curtis	.25	.07
17 Gary DiSarcina	.25	.07
18 Chuck Finley	.50	.15
19 Andrew Lorraine	.25	.07
20 Spike Owen	.25	.07
21 Tim Salmon	.75	.23
22 J.T. Snow	.50	.15
23 Wilson Alvarez	.25	.07
24 Jason Bere	.25	.07
25 Ozzie Guillen	.25	.07
26 Mike LaValliere	.25	.07
27 Frank Thomas	1.25	.35
28 Robin Ventura	.50	.15
29 Carlos Baerga	.25	.07
30 Albert Belle	.50	.15
31 Jason Grimsley	.25	.07
32 Dennis Martinez	.50	.15
33 Eddie Murray	1.25	.35
34 Charles Nagy	.25	.07
35 Manny Ramirez	.50	.15
36 Paul Sorrento	.25	.07
37 John Doherty	.25	.07
38 Cecil Fielder	.50	.15
39 Travis Fryman	.50	.15
40 Chris Gomez	.25	.07
41 Tony Phillips	.25	.07
42 Lou Whitaker	.50	.15
43 David Cone	.50	.15
44 Gary Gaetti	.50	.15
45 Mark Gubicza	.25	.07
46 Bob Hamelin	.25	.07
47 Wally Joyner	.50	.15
48 Rusty Meacham	.25	.07
49 Jeff Montgomery	.25	.07
50 Ricky Bones	.25	.07
51 Cal Eldred	.25	.07
52 Pat Listach	.25	.07
53 Matt Mieske	.25	.07
54 Dave Nilsson	.25	.07
55 Greg Vaughn	.50	.15
56 Bill Wegman	.25	.07
57 Chuck Knoblauch	.50	.15
58 Scott Leius	.25	.07
59 Pat Mahomes	.25	.07
60 Pat Meares	.25	.07
61 Pedro Munoz	.25	.07
62 Kirby Puckett	1.25	.35
63 Wade Boggs	.75	.23
64 Jimmy Key	.50	.15
65 Jim Leyritz	.25	.07
66 Don Mattingly	3.00	.90
67 Paul O'Neill	.75	.23
68 Melido Perez	.25	.07
69 Danny Tartabull	.25	.07
70 John Briscoe	.25	.07
71 Scott Brosius	.50	.15
72 Ron Darling	.25	.07
73 Brent Gates	.25	.07
74 Rickey Henderson	1.25	.35
75 Stan Javier	.25	.07
76 Mark McGwire	3.00	.90
77 Todd Van Poppel	.25	.07
78 Bobby Ayala	.25	.07
79 Mike Blowers	.25	.07
80 Jay Buhner	.50	.15
81 Ken Griffey Jr.	2.00	.60
82 Randy Johnson	1.25	.35
83 Tino Martinez	.75	.23
84 Jeff Nelson	.25	.07
85 Alex Rodriguez	3.00	.90
86 Will Clark	1.25	.35
87 Jeff Frye	.25	.07
88 Juan Gonzalez	1.25	.35
89 Rusty Greer	.50	.15
90 Darren Oliver	.25	.07
91 Dean Palmer	.50	.15
92 Ivan Rodriguez	1.25	.35
93 Matt Whiteside	.25	.07
94 Roberto Alomar	1.25	.35
95 Joe Carter	.50	.15
96 Tony Castillo	.25	.07
97 Juan Guzman	.25	.07
98 Pat Hentgen	.25	.07
99 Mike Huff	.25	.07
100 John Olerud	.50	.15
101 Woody Williams	.25	.07
102 Roberto Kelly	.25	.07
103 Ryan Klesko	.50	.15
104 Javier Lopez	.50	.15
105 Greg Maddux	2.00	.60
106 Fred McGriff	.75	.23
107 Jose Oliva	.25	.07
108 John Smoltz	.75	.23
109 Tony Tarasco	.25	.07
110 Mark Wohlers	.25	.07
111 Jim Bullinger	.25	.07
112 Shawon Dunston	.25	.07
113 Derrick May	.25	.07
114 Randy Myers	.25	.07
115 Karl Rhodes	.25	.07
116 Rey Sanchez	.25	.07
117 Steve Trachsel	.25	.07
118 Eddie Zambrano	.25	.07
119 Bret Boone	.50	.15
120 Brian Dorsett	.25	.07
121 Hal Morris	.25	.07
122 Jose Rijo	.25	.07
123 John Roper	.25	.07
124 Reggie Sanders	.50	.15
125 Pete Schourek	.25	.07
126 John Smiley	.25	.07
127 Ellis Burks	.50	.15
128 Vinny Castilla	.50	.15
129 Marvin Freeman	.25	.07
130 Andres Galarraga	.50	.15
131 Mike Munoz	.25	.07
132 David Nied	.25	.07
133 Bruce Ruffin	.25	.07
134 Walt Weiss	.25	.07
135 Eric Young	.25	.07
136 Greg Colbrunn	.25	.07
137 Jeff Conine	.50	.15
138 Jeremy Hernandez	.25	.07
139 Charles Johnson	.50	.15
140 Robb Nen	.50	.15
141 Gary Sheffield	.50	.15
142 Dave Weathers	.25	.07
143 Jeff Bagwell	.75	.23
144 Craig Biggio	.75	.23
145 Tony Eusebio	.25	.07
146 Luis Gonzalez	.50	.15
147 John Hudek	.25	.07
148 Darryl Kile	.50	.15
149 Dave Veres	.25	.07
150 Billy Ashley	.25	.07
151 Pedro Astacio	.25	.07
152 Rafael Bournigal	.25	.07
153 Delino DeShields	.25	.07
154 Raul Mondesi	.50	.15
155 Mike Piazza	2.00	.60
156 Rudy Seanez	.25	.07
157 Ismael Valdes	.25	.07
158 Tim Wallach	.25	.07
159 Todd Worrell	.25	.07
160 Moises Alou	.50	.15
161 Cliff Floyd	.50	.15
162 Gil Heredia	.25	.07
163 Mike Lansing	.25	.07
164 Pedro Martinez	1.25	.35
165 Kirk Rueter	.25	.07
166 Tim Scott	.25	.07
167 Jeff Shaw	.25	.07
168 Rondell White	.50	.15
169 Bobby Bonilla	.50	.15
170 Rico Brogna	.25	.07
171 Todd Hundley	.25	.07
172 Jeff Kent	.50	.15
173 Jim Lindeman	.25	.07
174 Joe Orsulak	.25	.07
175 Bret Saberhagen	.50	.15
176 Toby Borland	.25	.07
177 Darren Daulton	.50	.15
178 Lenny Dykstra	.50	.15
179 Jim Eisenreich	.25	.07
180 Tommy Greene	.25	.07
181 Tony Longmire	.25	.07
182 Bobby Munoz	.25	.07
183 Kevin Stocker	.25	.07
184 Jay Bell	.50	.15
185 Steve Cooke	.25	.07
186 Ravelo Manzanillo	.25	.07
187 Al Martin	.25	.07
188 Denny Neagle	.50	.15
189 Don Slaught	.25	.07
190 Paul Wagner	.25	.07
191 Rene Arocha	.25	.07
192 Bernard Gilkey	.25	.07
193 Jose Oquendo	.25	.07
194 Tom Pagnozzi	.25	.07
195 Ozzie Smith	2.00	.60
196 Allen Watson	.25	.07
197 Mark Whiten	.25	.07
198 Andy Ashby	.25	.07
199 Donnie Elliott	.25	.07
200 Bryce Florie	.25	.07
201 Tony Gwynn	1.50	.45
202 Trevor Hoffman	.50	.15
203 Brian Johnson	.25	.07
204 Tim Mauser	.25	.07
205 Bip Roberts	.25	.07
206 Rod Beck	.25	.07
207 Barry Bonds	3.00	.90
208 Royce Clayton	.25	.07
209 Darren Lewis	.25	.07
210 Mark Portugal	.25	.07
211 Kevin Rogers	.25	.07
212 W.VanLandingham	.25	.07
213 Matt Williams	.50	.15
214 Checklist	.25	.07
215 Checklist	.25	.07
216 Checklist	.25	.07
217 Bret Barberie	.25	.07
218 Armando Benitez	.50	.15
219 Kevin Brown	.50	.15
220 Sid Fernandez	.25	.07
221 Chris Hoiles	.25	.07
222 Doug Jones	.25	.07
223 Ben McDonald	.25	.07
224 Rafael Palmeiro	.75	.23
225 Andy Van Slyke	.50	.15
226 Jose Canseco	1.25	.35
227 Vaughn Eshelman	.25	.07
228 Mike Macfarlane	.25	.07
229 Tim Naehring	.25	.07
230 Frank Rodriguez	.25	.07
231 Lee Tinsley	.25	.07
232 Mark Whiten	.25	.07
233 Garret Anderson	.50	.15
234 Chili Davis	.50	.15
235 Jim Edmonds	.50	.15
236 Mark Langston	.25	.07
237 Troy Percival	.50	.15
238 Tony Phillips	.25	.07
239 Lee Smith	.50	.15
240 Jim Abbott	.75	.23
241 James Baldwin	.25	.07
242 Mike Devereaux	.25	.07
243 Ray Durham	.50	.15
244 Alex Fernandez	.25	.07
245 Roberto Hernandez	.25	.07
246 Lance Johnson	.25	.07
247 Ron Karkovice	.25	.07
248 Tim Raines	.50	.15
249 Sandy Alomar Jr.	.25	.07
250 Orel Hershiser	.50	.15
251 Julian Tavarez	.25	.07
252 Jim Thome	1.25	.35
253 Omar Vizquel	.50	.15
254 Dave Winfield	.50	.15
255 Chad Curtis	.25	.07
256 Kirk Gibson	.50	.15
257 Mike Henneman	.25	.07
258 Bob Higginson RC	1.25	.35
259 Felipe Lira	.25	.07
260 Rudy Pemberton	.25	.07
261 Alan Trammell	.75	.23
262 Kevin Appier	.50	.15
263 Pat Borders	.25	.07
264 Tom Gordon	.25	.07
265 Jose Lind	.25	.07
266 Jon Nunnally	.25	.07
267 Dilson Torres RC	.25	.07
268 Michael Tucker	.25	.07
269 Jeff Cirillo	.25	.07
270 Darryl Hamilton	.25	.07
271 David Hulse	.25	.07
272 Mark Kiefer	.25	.07
273 Graeme Lloyd	.25	.07
274 Joe Oliver	.25	.07
275 Al Reyes RC	.25	.07
276 Kevin Seitzer	.25	.07
277 Rick Aguilera	.25	.07
278 Marty Cordova	.25	.07
279 Scott Erickson	.25	.07
280 LaTroy Hawkins	.25	.07
281 Brad Radke RC	2.00	.60
282 Kevin Tapani	.25	.07
283 Tony Fernandez	.25	.07
284 Sterling Hitchcock	.25	.07
285 Pat Kelly	.25	.07
286 Jack McDowell	.25	.07
287 Andy Pettitte	.75	.23
288 Mike Stanley	.25	.07
289 John Wetteland	.50	.15
290 Bernie Williams	.75	.23
291 Mark Acre	.25	.07
292 Geronimo Berroa	.25	.07
293 Dennis Eckersley	.50	.15
294 Steve Ontiveros	.25	.07
295 Ruben Sierra	.25	.07
296 Terry Steinbach	.25	.07
297 Dave Stewart	.50	.15
298 Todd Stottlemyre	.25	.07
299 Darren Bragg	.25	.07
300 Joey Cora	.25	.07
301 Edgar Martinez	.75	.23
302 Bill Risley	.25	.07
303 Ron Villone	.25	.07
304 Dan Wilson	.25	.07
305 Benji Gil	.25	.07
306 Wilson Heredia	.25	.07
307 Mark McLemore	.25	.07
308 Otis Nixon	.25	.07
309 Kenny Rogers	.50	.15
310 Jeff Russell	.25	.07
311 Mickey Tettleton	.25	.07
312 Bob Tewksbury	.25	.07
313 David Cone	.50	.15
314 Carlos Delgado	.50	.15
315 Alex Gonzalez	.25	.07
316 Shawn Green	.50	.15
317 Paul Molitor	.75	.23
318 Ed Sprague	.25	.07
319 Devon White	.50	.15
320 Steve Avery	.25	.07
321 Jeff Blauser	.25	.07
322 Brad Clontz	.25	.07
323 Tom Glavine	.75	.23
324 Marquis Grissom	.25	.07
325 Chipper Jones	1.25	.35
326 David Justice	.50	.15
327 Mark Lemke	.25	.07
328 Kent Mercker	.25	.07
329 Jason Schmidt	1.50	.45
330 Steve Buechele	.25	.07
331 Kevin Foster	.25	.07
332 Mark Grace	.75	.23
333 Brian McRae	.25	.07
334 Sammy Sosa	2.00	.60
335 Ozzie Timmons	.25	.07
336 Rick Wilkins	.25	.07
337 Hector Carrasco	.25	.07
338 Ron Gant	.50	.15
339 Barry Larkin	1.25	.35
340 Deion Sanders	.75	.23
341 Benito Santiago	.50	.15
342 Roger Bailey	.25	.07
343 Jason Bates	.25	.07
344 Dante Bichette	.50	.15
345 Joe Girardi	.25	.07
346 Bill Swift	.25	.07
347 Mark Thompson	.25	.07
348 Larry Walker	.75	.23
349 Kurt Abbott	.25	.07
350 John Burkett	.25	.07
351 Chuck Carr	.25	.07
352 Andre Dawson	.50	.15
353 Chris Hammond	.25	.07
354 Charles Johnson	.50	.15
355 Terry Pendleton	.50	.15
356 Quilvio Veras	.25	.07
357 Derek Bell	.25	.07
358 Jim Dougherty RC	.25	.07
359 Doug Drabek	.25	.07
360 Todd Jones	.25	.07
361 Orlando Miller	.25	.07
362 James Mouton	.25	.07
363 Phil Plantier	.25	.07
364 Shane Reynolds	.25	.07
365 Todd Hollandsworth	.25	.07
366 Eric Karros	.50	.15
367 Ramon Martinez	.25	.07
368 Hideo Nomo RC	3.00	.90
369 Jose Offerman	.25	.07
370 Antonio Osuna	.25	.07
371 Todd Williams	.25	.07
372 Shane Andrews	.25	.07
373 Wil Cordero	.25	.07
374 Jeff Fassero	.25	.07
375 Darrin Fletcher	.25	.07
376 Mark Grudzielanek RC	.75	.23
377 Carlos Perez RC	.50	.15
378 Mel Rojas	.25	.07
379 Tony Tarasco	.25	.07
380 Edgardo Alfonzo	.50	.15
381 Brett Butler	.50	.15
382 Carl Everett	.50	.15
383 John Franco	.50	.15
384 Pete Harnisch	.25	.07
385 Bobby Jones	.25	.07
386 Dave Mlicki	.25	.07
387 Jose Vizcaino	.25	.07
388 Ricky Bottalico	.25	.07
389 Tyler Green	.25	.07
390 Charlie Hayes	.25	.07
391 Dave Hollins	.25	.07
392 Gregg Jefferies	.25	.07
393 Michael Mimbs RC	.25	.07
394 Mickey Morandini	.25	.07
395 Curt Schilling	.75	.23
396 Heathcliff Slocumb	.25	.07
397 J.Christiansen RC	.25	.07
398 Midre Cummings	.25	.07
399 Carlos Garcia	.25	.07
400 Mark Johnson RC	.50	.15
401 Jeff King	.25	.07
402 Jon Lieber	.25	.07
403 Esteban Loaiza	.50	.15
404 Orlando Merced	.25	.07
405 Gary Wilson RC	.25	.07
406 Scott Cooper	.25	.07
407 Tom Henke	.25	.07
408 Ken Hill	.25	.07
409 Danny Jackson	.25	.07
410 Brian Jordan	.50	.15
411 Ray Lankford	.25	.07
412 John Mabry	.25	.07
413 Todd Zeile	.25	.07
414 Andy Benes	.25	.07
415 Andres Berumen	.25	.07
416 Ken Caminiti	.50	.15
417 Andujar Cedeno	.25	.07
418 Steve Finley	.50	.15
419 Joey Hamilton	.25	.07
420 Dustin Hermanson	.25	.07
421 Melvin Nieves	.25	.07
422 Roberto Petagine	.25	.07
423 Eddie Williams	.25	.07
424 Glenallen Hill	.25	.07
425 Kirt Manwaring	.25	.07
426 Terry Mulholland	.25	.07
427 J.R. Phillips	.25	.07
428 Joe Rosselli	.25	.07
429 Robby Thompson	.25	.07
430 Checklist	.25	.07
431 Checklist	.25	.07
432 Checklist	.25	.07

1995 Flair Hot Gloves

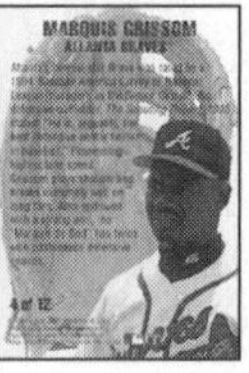

This 12-card standard-size set features players that are known for their defensive prowess. Randomly inserted in series two packs at a rate of one in 25, a player photo is superimposed over an embossed design of a bronze glove.

	Nm-Mt	Ex-Mt
COMPLETE SET (12)	80.00	24.00
1 Roberto Alomar	10.00	3.00
2 Barry Bonds	25.00	7.50
3 Ken Griffey Jr.	15.00	4.50
4 Marquis Grissom	2.00	.60
5 Barry Larkin	10.00	3.00
6 Darren Lewis	2.00	.60
7 Kenny Lofton	4.00	1.20
8 Don Mattingly	25.00	7.50
9 Cal Ripken	30.00	9.00
10 Ivan Rodriguez	10.00	3.00
11 Devon White	4.00	1.20
12 Matt Williams	4.00	1.20

1995 Flair Hot Numbers

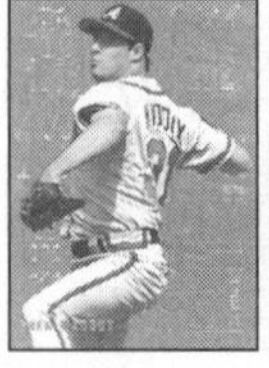

Randomly inserted in series one packs at a rate of one in nine, this 10-card standard-size set showcases top players. A player photo on front is superimposed over a gold background that contains player stats from 1994.

	Nm-Mt	Ex-Mt
COMPLETE SET (10)	50.00	15.00
1 Jeff Bagwell	2.50	.75
2 Albert Belle	1.50	.45
3 Barry Bonds	10.00	3.00
4 Ken Griffey Jr.	6.00	1.80
5 Kenny Lofton	4.00	1.20
6 Greg Maddux	6.00	1.80
7 Mike Piazza	6.00	1.80
8 Cal Ripken	12.00	3.60
9 Frank Thomas	4.00	1.20
10 Matt Williams	1.50	.45

1995 Flair Infield Power

Randomly inserted in second series packs at a rate of one in six, this 10-card standard-size set features sluggers that man the infield. A player photo on front is surrounded by multiple color schemes with a horizontal back offering a player photo and highlights.

	Nm-Mt	Ex-Mt
COMPLETE SET (10)	12.00	3.60
1 Jeff Bagwell	1.25	.35
2 Darren Daulton	.75	.23
3 Cecil Fielder	.75	.23
4 Andres Galarraga	.75	.23
5 Fred McGriff	1.25	.35
6 Rafael Palmeiro	1.25	.35
7 Mike Piazza	3.00	.90
8 Frank Thomas	2.00	.60
9 Mo Vaughn	.75	.23
10 Matt Williams	.75	.23

1995 Flair Outfield Power

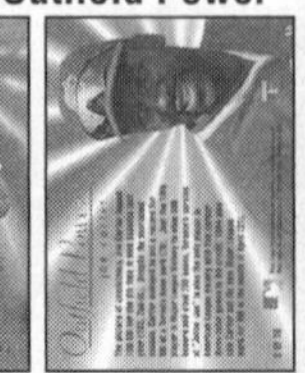

Randomly inserted in first series packs at a rate of one in six, this 10-card standard-size set features sluggers that patrol the outfield. A player photo on front is surrounded by multiple color schemes with a horizontal back offering a player photo and highlights.

	Nm-Mt	Ex-Mt
COMPLETE SET (10)	12.00	3.60
1 Albert Belle	.75	.23
2 Dante Bichette	.75	.23
3 Barry Bonds	5.00	1.50
4 Jose Canseco	2.00	.60
5 Joe Carter	.75	.23
6 Juan Gonzalez	2.00	.60
7 Ken Griffey Jr.	3.00	.90
8 Kirby Puckett	2.00	.60
9 Gary Sheffield	.75	.23
10 Ruben Sierra	.40	.12

1995 Flair Ripken

Titled "Enduring", this 10-card standard-size set is a tribute to Cal Ripken's career through the '94 season. Cards were randomly inserted in second series packs at a rate of one in 12. Full-bleed fronts have the set title in silver foil toward the bottom. The backs have a photo and a write-up on a specific achievement as selected by Cal. A five-card mail-in wrapper offer completes the set. The expiration date on this offer was March 1, 1996.

	Nm-Mt	Ex-Mt
COMPLETE SET (10)	80.00	24.00
COMMON CARD (1-10)	10.00	3.00
COMMON MAIL (11-15)	5.00	1.50

1995 Flair Today's Spotlight

This 12-card die-cut set was randomly inserted in first series packs at a rate of one in 25 packs. The upper portion of the player photo on front has the spotlight effect as the remainder of the photo is darkened.

	Nm-Mt	Ex-Mt
COMPLETE SET (12)	100.00	30.00
1 Jeff Bagwell	8.00	2.40
2 Jason Bere	2.50	.75
3 Cliff Floyd	5.00	1.50
4 Chuck Knoblauch	5.00	1.50
5 Kenny Lofton	12.00	3.60
6 Javier Lopez	5.00	1.50
7 Raul Mondesi	5.00	1.50
8 Mike Mussina	12.00	3.60
9 Mike Piazza	20.00	6.00
10 Manny Ramirez	5.00	1.50
11 Tim Salmon	8.00	2.40
12 Frank Thomas	12.00	3.60

1995 Flair Wave of the Future

Spotlighting 10 of the game's hottest young stars, cards were randomly inserted in second series packs at a rate of one in nine. An action

photo is superimposed over primarily a solid background save for the player's name, team and same name which appear several times.

	Nm-Mt	Ex-Mt
COMPLETE SET (10)	25.00	7.50
1 Jason Bates	1.00	.30
2 Armando Benitez	1.50	.45
3 Marty Cordova	1.00	.30
4 Ray Durham	1.50	.45
5 Vaughn Eshelman	1.00	.30
6 Carl Everett	1.50	.45
7 Shawn Green	1.50	.45
8 Dustin Hermanson	1.00	.30
9 Chipper Jones	4.00	1.20
10 Hideo Nomo	5.00	1.50

1996 Flair

Released in July, 1996, this 400-card set (produced by Fleer) was issued in one series and sold in seven-card packs at a suggested retail price of $4.99. Gold and Silver etched foil front variations exist for all cards. These color variations were printed in similar quantities and are valued equally. The fronts and backs each carry a color action player cut-out on a player portrait background with player statistics on the backs. The cards are grouped alphabetically within teams and checklisted below alphabetically according to teams for each league. Notable Rookie Cards include Tony Batista.

	Nm-Mt	Ex-Mt
COMPLETE SET (400)	100.00	30.00
1 Roberto Alomar	2.50	.75
2 Brady Anderson	1.00	.30
3 Bobby Bonilla	1.00	.30
4 Scott Erickson	1.00	.30
5 Jeffrey Hammonds	1.00	.30
6 Jimmy Haynes	1.00	.30
7 Chris Hoiles	1.00	.30
8 Kent Mercker	1.00	.30
9 Mike Mussina	2.50	.75
10 Randy Myers	1.00	.30
11 Rafael Palmeiro	1.50	.45
12 Cal Ripken	8.00	2.40
13 B.J. Surhoff	1.00	.30
14 David Wells	1.00	.30
15 Jose Canseco	2.50	.75
16 Roger Clemens	5.00	1.50
17 Wil Cordero	1.00	.30
18 Tom Gordon	1.00	.30
19 Mike Greenwell	1.00	.30
20 Dwayne Hosey	1.00	.30
21 Jose Malave	1.00	.30
22 Tim Naehring	1.00	.30
23 Troy O'Leary	1.00	.30
24 Aaron Sele	1.00	.30
25 Heathcliff Slocumb	1.00	.30
26 Mike Stanley	1.00	.30
27 Jeff Suppan	1.00	.30
28 John Valentin	1.00	.30
29 Mo Vaughn	1.00	.30
30 Tim Wakefield	1.00	.30
31 Jim Abbott	1.50	.45
32 Garret Anderson	1.00	.30
33 George Arias	1.00	.30
34 Chili Davis	1.00	.30
35 Gary DiSarcina	1.00	.30
36 Jim Edmonds	1.00	.30
37 Chuck Finley	1.00	.30
38 Todd Greene	1.00	.30
39 Mark Langston	1.00	.30
40 Troy Percival	1.00	.30
41 Tim Salmon	1.50	.45
42 Lee Smith	1.00	.30
43 J.T. Snow	1.00	.30
44 Randy Velarde	1.00	.30
45 Tim Wallach	1.00	.30
46 Wilson Alvarez	1.00	.30
47 Harold Baines	1.00	.30
48 Jason Bere	1.00	.30
49 Ray Durham	1.00	.30
50 Alex Fernandez	1.00	.30
51 Ozzie Guillen	1.00	.30
52 Roberto Hernandez	1.00	.30
53 Ron Karkovice	1.00	.30
54 Darren Lewis	1.00	.30
55 Lyle Mouton	1.00	.30
56 Tony Phillips	1.00	.30
57 Chris Snopek	1.00	.30
58 Kevin Tapani	1.00	.30
59 Danny Tartabull	1.00	.30
60 Frank Thomas	2.50	.75
61 Robin Ventura	1.00	.30
62 Sandy Alomar Jr.	1.00	.30
63 Carlos Baerga	1.00	.30
64 Albert Belle	1.00	.30
65 Julio Franco	1.00	.30
66 Orel Hershiser	1.00	.30
67 Kenny Lofton	1.00	.30
68 Dennis Martinez	1.00	.30
69 Jack McDowell	1.00	.30
70 Jose Mesa	1.00	.30
71 Eddie Murray	2.50	.75
72 Charles Nagy	1.00	.30
73 Tony Pena	1.00	.30
74 Manny Ramirez	1.00	.30
75 Julian Tavarez	1.00	.30
76 Jim Thome	2.50	.75
77 Omar Vizquel	1.00	.30
78 Chad Curtis	1.00	.30
79 Cecil Fielder	1.00	.30
80 Travis Fryman	1.00	.30
81 Chris Gomez	1.00	.30
82 Bob Higginson	1.00	.30
83 Mark Lewis	1.00	.30
84 Felipe Lira	1.00	.30
85 Alan Trammell	1.50	.45
86 Kevin Appier	1.00	.30
87 Johnny Damon	1.00	.30
88 Tom Goodwin	1.00	.30
89 Mark Gubicza	1.00	.30
90 Bob Hamelin	1.00	.30
91 Keith Lockhart	1.00	.30
92 Jeff Montgomery	1.00	.30
93 Jon Nunnally	1.00	.30
94 Bip Roberts	1.00	.30
95 Michael Tucker	1.00	.30
96 Joe Vitiello	1.00	.30
97 Ricky Bones	1.00	.30
98 Chuck Carr	1.00	.30
99 Jeff Cirillo	1.00	.30
100 Mike Fetters	1.00	.30
101 John Jaha	1.00	.30
102 Mike Matheny	1.00	.30
103 Ben McDonald	1.00	.30
104 Matt Mieske	1.00	.30
105 Dave Nilsson	1.00	.30
106 Kevin Seitzer	1.00	.30
107 Steve Sparks	1.00	.30
108 Jose Valentin	1.00	.30
109 Greg Vaughn	1.00	.30
110 Rick Aguilera	1.00	.30
111 Rich Becker	1.00	.30
112 Marty Cordova	1.00	.30
113 LaTroy Hawkins	1.00	.30
114 Dave Hollins	1.00	.30
115 Roberto Kelly	1.00	.30
116 Chuck Knoblauch	1.00	.30
117 Matt Lawton RC	1.00	.30
118 Pat Meares	1.00	.30
119 Paul Molitor	1.50	.45
120 Kirby Puckett	2.50	.75
121 Brad Radke	1.00	.30
122 Frank Rodriguez	1.00	.30
123 Scott Stahoviak	1.00	.30
124 Matt Walbeck	1.00	.30
125 Wade Boggs	1.50	.45
126 David Cone	1.00	.30
127 Joe Girardi	1.00	.30
128 Dwight Gooden	1.50	.45
129 Derek Jeter	6.00	1.80
130 Jimmy Key	1.00	.30
131 Jim Leyritz	1.00	.30
132 Tino Martinez	1.50	.45
133 Paul O'Neill	1.50	.45
134 Andy Pettitte	1.50	.45
135 Tim Raines	1.00	.30
136 Ruben Rivera	1.00	.30
137 Kenny Rogers	1.00	.30
138 Ruben Sierra	1.00	.30
139 John Wetteland	1.00	.30
140 Bernie Williams	1.50	.45
141 Tony Batista RC	5.00	1.50
142 Allen Battle	1.00	.30
143 Geronimo Berroa	1.00	.30
144 Mike Bordick	1.00	.30
145 Scott Brosius	1.00	.30
146 Steve Cox	1.00	.30
147 Brent Gates	1.00	.30
148 Jason Giambi	2.50	.75
149 Doug Johns	1.00	.30
150 Mark McGwire	6.00	1.80
151 Pedro Munoz	1.00	.30
152 Ariel Prieto	1.00	.30
153 Terry Steinbach	1.00	.30
154 Todd Van Poppel	1.00	.30
155 Bobby Ayala	1.00	.30
156 Chris Bosio	1.00	.30
157 Jay Buhner	1.00	.30
158 Joey Cora	1.00	.30
159 Russ Davis	1.00	.30
160 Ken Griffey Jr.	4.00	1.20
161 Sterling Hitchcock	1.00	.30
162 Randy Johnson	2.50	.75
163 Edgar Martinez	1.50	.45
164 Alex Rodriguez	5.00	1.50
165 Paul Sorrento	1.00	.30
166 Dan Wilson	1.00	.30
167 Will Clark	2.50	.75
168 Benji Gil	1.00	.30
169 Juan Gonzalez	2.50	.75
170 Rusty Greer	1.00	.30
171 Kevin Gross	1.00	.30
172 Darryl Hamilton	1.00	.30
173 Mike Henneman	1.00	.30
174 Ken Hill	1.00	.30
175 Mark McLemore	1.00	.30
176 Dean Palmer	1.00	.30
177 Roger Pavlik	1.00	.30
178 Ivan Rodriguez	2.50	.75
179 Mickey Tettleton	1.00	.30
180 Bobby Witt	1.00	.30
181 Joe Carter	1.00	.30
182 Felipe Crespo	1.00	.30
183 Alex Gonzalez	1.00	.30
184 Shawn Green	1.00	.30
185 Juan Guzman	1.00	.30
186 Erik Hanson	1.00	.30
187 Pat Hentgen	1.00	.30
188 Sandy Martinez	1.00	.30
189 Otis Nixon	1.00	.30
190 John Olerud	1.00	.30
191 Paul Quantrill	1.00	.30
192 Bill Risley	1.00	.30
193 Ed Sprague	1.00	.30
194 Steve Avery	1.00	.30
195 Jeff Blauser	1.00	.30
196 Brad Clontz	1.00	.30
197 Jermaine Dye	1.00	.30
198 Tom Glavine	1.50	.45
199 Marquis Grissom	1.00	.30
200 Chipper Jones	2.50	.75
201 David Justice	1.00	.30
202 Ryan Klesko	1.00	.30
203 Mark Lemke	1.00	.30
204 Javier Lopez	1.00	.30
205 Greg Maddux	4.00	1.20
206 Fred McGriff	1.50	.45
207 Greg McMichael	1.00	.30
208 Wonderful Monds RC	1.00	.30
209 Jason Schmidt	1.00	.30
210 John Smoltz	1.50	.45
211 Mark Wohlers	1.00	.30
212 Jim Bullinger	1.00	.30
213 Frank Castillo	1.00	.30
214 Kevin Foster	1.00	.30
215 Luis Gonzalez	1.00	.30
216 Mark Grace	1.50	.45
217 Robin Jennings	1.00	.30
218 Doug Jones	1.00	.30
219 Dave Magadan	1.00	.30
220 Brian McRae	1.00	.30
221 Jaime Navarro	1.00	.30
222 Rey Sanchez	1.00	.30
223 Ryne Sandberg	4.00	1.20
224 Scott Servais	1.00	.30
225 Sammy Sosa	4.00	1.20
226 Ozzie Timmons	1.00	.30
227 Bret Boone	1.00	.30
228 Jeff Branson	1.00	.30
229 Jeff Brantley	1.00	.30
230 Dave Burba	1.00	.30
231 Vince Coleman	1.00	.30
232 Steve Gibralter	1.00	.30
233 Mike Kelly	1.00	.30
234 Barry Larkin	2.50	.75
235 Hal Morris	1.00	.30
236 Mark Portugal	1.00	.30
237 Jose Rijo	1.00	.30
238 Reggie Sanders	1.00	.30
239 Pete Schourek	1.00	.30
240 John Smiley	1.00	.30
241 Eddie Taubensee	1.00	.30
242 Jason Bates	1.00	.30
243 Dante Bichette	1.00	.30
244 Ellis Burks	1.00	.30
245 Vinny Castilla	1.00	.30
246 Andres Galarraga	1.00	.30
247 Darren Holmes	1.00	.30
248 Curt Leskanic	1.00	.30
249 Steve Reed	1.00	.30
250 Kevin Ritz	1.00	.30
251 Bret Saberhagen	1.00	.30
252 Bill Swift	1.00	.30
253 Larry Walker	1.50	.45
254 Walt Weiss	1.00	.30
255 Eric Young	1.00	.30
256 Kurt Abbott	1.00	.30
257 Kevin Brown	1.00	.30
258 John Burkett	1.00	.30
259 Greg Colbrunn	1.00	.30
260 Jeff Conine	1.00	.30
261 Andre Dawson	1.00	.30
262 Chris Hammond	1.00	.30
263 Charles Johnson	1.00	.30
264 Al Leiter	1.00	.30
265 Robb Nen	1.00	.30
266 Terry Pendleton	1.00	.30
267 Pat Rapp	1.00	.30
268 Gary Sheffield	1.00	.30
269 Quilvio Veras	1.00	.30
270 Devon White	1.00	.30
271 Bob Abreu	1.00	.30
272 Jeff Bagwell	1.50	.45
273 Derek Bell	1.00	.30
274 Sean Berry	1.00	.30
275 Craig Biggio	1.50	.45
276 Doug Drabek	1.00	.30
277 Tony Eusebio	1.00	.30
278 Richard Hidalgo	1.00	.30
279 Brian L.Hunter	1.00	.30
280 Todd Jones	1.00	.30
281 Derrick May	1.00	.30
282 Orlando Miller	1.00	.30
283 James Mouton	1.00	.30
284 Shane Reynolds	1.00	.30
285 Greg Swindell	1.00	.30
286 Mike Blowers	1.00	.30
287 Brett Butler	1.00	.30
288 Tom Candiotti	1.00	.30
289 Roger Cedeno	1.00	.30
290 Delino DeShields	1.00	.30
291 Greg Gagne	1.00	.30
292 Karim Garcia	1.00	.30
293 Todd Hollandsworth	1.00	.30
294 Eric Karros	1.00	.30
295 Ramon Martinez	1.00	.30
296 Raul Mondesi	1.00	.30
297 Hideo Nomo	2.50	.75
298 Mike Piazza	4.00	1.20
299 Ismael Valdes	1.00	.30
300 Todd Worrell	1.00	.30
301 Moises Alou	1.00	.30
302 Shane Andrews	1.00	.30
303 Yamil Benitez	1.00	.30
304 Jeff Fassero	1.00	.30
305 Darrin Fletcher	1.00	.30
306 Cliff Floyd	1.00	.30
307 Mark Grudzielanek	1.00	.30
308 Mike Lansing	1.00	.30
309 Pedro Martinez	2.50	.75
310 Ryan McGuire	1.00	.30
311 Carlos Perez	1.00	.30
312 Mel Rojas	1.00	.30
313 David Segui	1.00	.30
314 Rondell White	1.00	.30
315 Edgardo Alfonzo	1.00	.30
316 Rico Brogna	1.00	.30
317 Carl Everett	1.00	.30
318 John Franco	1.00	.30
319 Bernard Gilkey	1.00	.30
320 Todd Hundley	1.00	.30
321 Jason Isringhausen	1.00	.30
322 Lance Johnson	1.00	.30
323 Bobby Jones	1.00	.30
324 Jeff Kent	1.00	.30
325 Rey Ordonez	1.00	.30
326 Bill Pulsipher	1.00	.30
327 Jose Vizcaino	1.00	.30
328 Paul Wilson	1.00	.30
329 Ricky Bottalico	1.00	.30
330 Darren Daulton	1.00	.30
331 David Doster	1.00	.30
332 Lenny Dykstra	1.00	.30
333 Jim Eisenreich	1.00	.30
334 Sid Fernandez	1.00	.30
335 Gregg Jefferies	1.00	.30
336 Mickey Morandini	1.00	.30
337 Benito Santiago	1.00	.30
338 Curt Schilling	1.50	.45
339 Kevin Stocker	1.00	.30
340 David West	1.00	.30
341 Mark Whiten	1.00	.30
342 Todd Zeile	1.00	.30
343 Jay Bell	1.00	.30
344 John Ericks	1.00	.30
345 Carlos Garcia	1.00	.30
346 Charlie Hayes	1.00	.30
347 Jason Kendall	1.00	.30
348 Jeff King	1.00	.30
349 Mike Kingery	1.00	.30
350 Al Martin	1.00	.30
351 Orlando Merced	1.00	.30
352 Dan Miceli	1.00	.30
353 Denny Neagle	1.00	.30
354 Alan Benes	1.00	.30
355 Andy Benes	1.00	.30
356 Royce Clayton	1.00	.30
357 Dennis Eckersley	1.00	.30
358 Gary Gaetti	1.00	.30
359 Ron Gant	1.00	.30
360 Brian Jordan	1.00	.30
361 Ray Lankford	1.00	.30
362 John Mabry	1.00	.30
363 T.J. Mathews	1.00	.30
364 Mike Morgan	1.00	.30
365 Donovan Osborne	1.00	.30
366 Tom Pagnozzi	1.00	.30
367 Ozzie Smith	4.00	1.20
368 Todd Stottlemyre	1.00	.30
369 Andy Ashby	1.00	.30
370 Brad Ausmus	1.00	.30
371 Ken Caminiti	1.00	.30
372 Andujar Cedeno	1.00	.30
373 Steve Finley	1.00	.30
374 Tony Gwynn	3.00	.90
375 Joey Hamilton	1.00	.30
376 Rickey Henderson	2.50	.75
377 Trevor Hoffman	1.00	.30
378 Wally Joyner	1.00	.30
379 Marc Newfield	1.00	.30
380 Jody Reed	1.00	.30
381 Bob Tewksbury	1.00	.30
382 Fernando Valenzuela	1.00	.30
383 Rod Beck	1.00	.30
384 Barry Bonds	6.00	1.80
385 Mark Carreon	1.00	.30
386 Shawon Dunston	1.00	.30
387 O.Fernandez RC	1.00	.30
388 Glenallen Hill	1.00	.30
389 Stan Javier	1.00	.30
390 Mark Leiter	1.00	.30
391 Kirt Manwaring	1.00	.30
392 Robby Thompson	1.00	.30
393 W.VanLandingham	1.00	.30
394 Allen Watson	1.00	.30
395 Matt Williams	1.00	.30
396 Checklist 1-92	1.00	.30
397 Checklist 93-180	1.00	.30
398 Checklist 181-272	1.00	.30
399 Checklist 273-365	1.00	.30
400 CL 366-400/Inserts	1.00	.30
P12 Cal Ripken Jr PROMO		

1996 Flair Diamond Cuts

Randomly inserted in packs at a rate of one in 20, this 12-card set showcases the game's greatest stars with rainbow holofoil and glitter coating on the card.

	Nm-Mt	Ex-Mt
COMPLETE SET (12)	100.00	30.00
1 Jeff Bagwell	4.00	1.20
2 Albert Belle	2.50	.75
3 Barry Bonds	15.00	4.50
4 Juan Gonzalez	6.00	1.80
5 Ken Griffey Jr.	10.00	3.00
6 Greg Maddux	10.00	3.00
7 Eddie Murray	6.00	1.80
8 Mike Piazza	10.00	3.00
9 Cal Ripken	20.00	6.00
10 Frank Thomas	6.00	1.80
11 Mo Vaughn	2.50	.75
12 Matt Williams	2.50	.75

1996 Flair Hot Gloves

Randomly inserted in hobby packs only at a rate of one in 90, this 10-card set is printed on special, thermo-embossed die-cut cards and spotlights the best defensive players.

	Nm-Mt	Ex-Mt
COMPLETE SET (10)	120.00	36.00
1 Roberto Alomar	15.00	4.50
2 Barry Bonds	40.00	12.00
3 Will Clark	15.00	4.50
4 Ken Griffey Jr.	25.00	7.50
5 Kenny Lofton	6.00	1.80
6 Greg Maddux	25.00	7.50
7 Mike Piazza	25.00	7.50
8 Cal Ripken	50.00	15.00
9 Ivan Rodriguez	15.00	4.50
10 Matt Williams	6.00	1.80

1996 Flair Powerline

Randomly inserted in packs at a rate of one in six, this 10-card set features baseball's leading power hitters. The fronts display a color action close-up player photo with a green overlay indicating his power. The backs carry a player portrait and a statement about the player's hitting power.

	Nm-Mt	Ex-Mt
COMPLETE SET (10)	30.00	9.00
1 Albert Belle	1.00	.30
2 Barry Bonds	6.00	1.80
3 Juan Gonzalez	2.50	.75
4 Ken Griffey Jr.	4.00	1.20
5 Mark McGwire	6.00	1.80
6 Mike Piazza	4.00	1.20
7 Manny Ramirez	1.00	.30
8 Sammy Sosa	4.00	1.20
9 Frank Thomas	2.50	.75
10 Matt Williams	1.00	.30

1996 Flair Wave of the Future

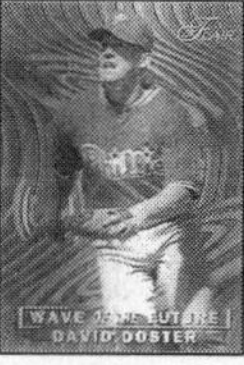

Randomly inserted in packs at a rate of one in 72, this 20-card set highlights the top 1996 rookies and prospects on lenticular cards.

	Nm-Mt	Ex-Mt
COMPLETE SET (20)	200.00	60.00
1 Bob Abreu	15.00	4.50
2 George Arias	10.00	3.00
3 Tony Batista	15.00	4.50
4 Alan Benes	10.00	3.00
5 Yamil Benitez	10.00	3.00
6 Steve Cox	10.00	3.00
7 David Doster	10.00	3.00
8 Jermaine Dye	15.00	4.50
9 Osvaldo Fernandez	10.00	3.00
10 Karim Garcia	10.00	3.00
11 Steve Gibralter	10.00	3.00
12 Todd Greene	10.00	3.00
13 Richard Hidalgo	15.00	4.50
14 Robin Jennings	10.00	3.00
15 Jason Kendall	15.00	4.50
16 Jose Malave	10.00	3.00
17 Wonderful Monds	10.00	3.00
18 Rey Ordonez	10.00	3.00
19 Ruben Rivera	10.00	3.00
20 Paul Wilson	10.00	3.00

2002 Flair

This 138 card set was issued in April, 2002. These cards were issued in five card packs which came 20 boxes to a case with a cost of $7 per pack. Each unopened box also contained a "Sweet Swatch" box topper. The last 38 cards in the set are are future fame cards featuring leading prospects in the game. These cards have a stated print run of 1750 serial numbered sets.

	Nm-Mt	Ex-Mt
COMP.SET w/o SP's (100)	25.00	7.50
COMMON CARD (1-100)	.50	.15
COMMON CARD (101-138)	5.00	1.50
1 Scott Rolen	.75	.23
2 Derek Jeter	3.00	.90
3 Sean Casey	.50	.15
4 Hideo Nomo	1.25	.35
5 Craig Biggio	.75	.23
6 Randy Johnson	1.25	.35
7 J.D. Drew	.50	.15
8 Greg Maddux	2.00	.60
9 Paul LoDuca	.50	.15
10 John Olerud	.50	.15
11 Barry Larkin	1.25	.35
12 Mark Grace	.75	.23
13 Jimmy Rollins	.50	.15
14 Todd Helton	.75	.23
15 Jim Edmonds	.50	.15
16 Roy Oswalt	.50	.15
17 Phil Nevin	.50	.15
18 Tim Salmon	.75	.23
19 Magglio Ordonez	.50	.15
20 Roger Clemens	2.50	.75
21 Raul Mondesi	.50	.15
22 Edgar Martinez	.75	.23
23 Pedro Martinez	1.25	.35
24 Edgardo Alfonzo	.50	.15

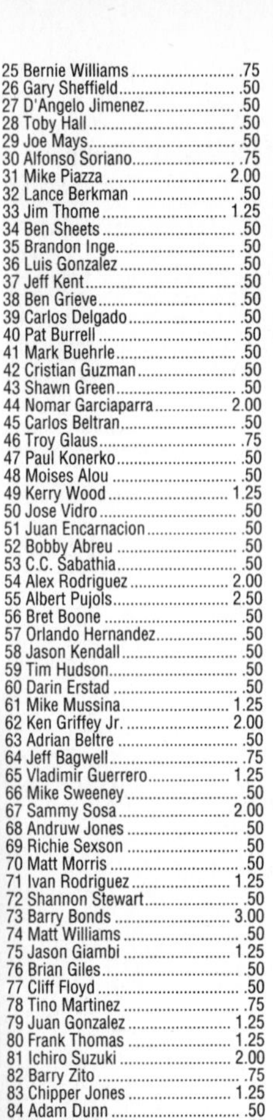

25 Bernie Williams .75 .23
26 Gary Sheffield .50 .15
27 D'Angelo Jimenez .50 .15
28 Toby Hall .50 .15
29 Joe Mays .50 .15
30 Alfonso Soriano .75 .23
31 Mike Piazza 2.00 .60
32 Lance Berkman .50 .15
33 Jim Thome 1.25 .35
34 Ben Sheets .50 .15
35 Brandon Inge .50 .15
36 Luis Gonzalez .50 .15
37 Jeff Kent .50 .15
38 Ben Grieve .50 .15
39 Carlos Delgado .50 .15
40 Pat Burrell .50 .15
41 Mark Buehrle .50 .15
42 Cristian Guzman .50 .15
43 Shawn Green .50 .15
44 Nomar Garciaparra 2.00 .60
45 Carlos Beltran .50 .15
46 Troy Glaus .75 .23
47 Paul Konerko .50 .15
48 Moises Alou .50 .15
49 Kerry Wood 1.25 .35
50 Jose Vidro .50 .15
51 Juan Encarnacion .50 .15
52 Bobby Abreu .50 .15
53 C.C. Sabathia .50 .15
54 Alex Rodriguez 2.00 .60
55 Albert Pujols 2.50 .75
56 Bret Boone .50 .15
57 Orlando Hernandez .50 .15
58 Jason Kendall .50 .15
59 Tim Hudson .50 .15
60 Darin Erstad .50 .15
61 Mike Mussina 1.25 .35
62 Ken Griffey Jr. 2.00 .60
63 Adrian Beltre .50 .15
64 Jeff Bagwell .75 .23
65 Vladimir Guerrero 1.25 .35
66 Mike Sweeney .50 .15
67 Sammy Sosa 2.00 .60
68 Andruw Jones .50 .15
69 Richie Sexson .50 .15
70 Matt Morris .50 .15
71 Ivan Rodriguez 1.25 .35
72 Shannon Stewart .50 .15
73 Barry Bonds 3.00 .90
74 Matt Williams .50 .15
75 Jason Giambi 1.25 .35
76 Brian Giles .50 .15
77 Cliff Floyd .50 .15
78 Tino Martinez .75 .23
79 Juan Gonzalez 1.25 .35
80 Frank Thomas 1.25 .35
81 Ichiro Suzuki 2.00 .60
82 Barry Zito .75 .23
83 Chipper Jones 1.25 .35
84 Adam Dunn .50 .15
85 Kazuhiro Sasaki .50 .15
86 Mark Quinn .50 .15
87 Rafael Palmeiro .75 .23
88 Jeromy Burnitz .50 .15
89 Curt Schilling .75 .23
90 Chris Richard .50 .15
91 Jon Lieber .50 .15
92 Doug Mientkiewicz .50 .15
93 Roberto Alomar 1.25 .35
94 Rich Aurilia .50 .15
95 Eric Chavez .50 .15
96 Larry Walker .75 .23
97 Manny Ramirez .50 .15
98 Tony Clark .50 .15
99 Tsuyoshi Shinjo .50 .15
100 Josh Beckett .75 .23
101 Dewon Brazelton FF 5.00 1.50
102 Jeremy Lambert FF RC 5.00 1.50
103 Andres Torres FF 5.00 1.50
104 Matt Childers FF RC 5.00 1.50
105 Wilson Betemit FF 5.00 1.50
106 Willie Harris FF 5.00 1.50
107 Drew Henson FF 5.00 1.50
108 Rafael Soriano FF 5.00 1.50
109 Carlos Valderrama FF 5.00 1.50
110 Victor Martinez FF 5.00 1.50
111 Juan Rivera FF 5.00 1.50
112 Felipe Lopez FF 5.00 1.50
113 Brandon Duckworth FF 5.00 1.50
114 Jeremy Owens FF 5.00 1.50
115 Aaron Cook FF RC 5.00 1.50
116 Derrick Lewis FF 5.00 1.50
117 Mark Teixeira FF 8.00 2.40
118 Ken Harvey FF 5.00 1.50
119 Tim Spooneybarger FF 5.00 1.50
120 Bill Hall FF 5.00 1.50
121 Adam Pettyjohn FF 5.00 1.50
122 Ramon Castro FF 5.00 1.50
123 Marlon Byrd FF 5.00 1.50
124 Matt White FF 5.00 1.50
125 Eric Cyr FF 5.00 1.50
126 Morgan Ensberg FF 5.00 1.50
127 Horacio Ramirez FF 5.00 1.50
128 Ron Calloway FF RC 5.00 1.50
129 Nick Punto FF 5.00 1.50
130 Joe Kennedy FF 5.00 1.50
131 So Taguchi FF RC 8.00 2.40
132 Austin Kearns FF 5.00 1.50
133 Mark Prior FF 15.00 4.50
134 Kazuhisa Ishii FF RC 10.00 3.00
135 Steve Torrealba FF 5.00 1.50
136 Adam Walker FF RC 5.00 1.50
137 Travis Hafner FF 5.00 1.50
138 Zach Day FF 5.00 1.50

2002 Flair Collection

Randomly inserted into packs, this is a parallel set to the basic Flair set. These cards are serial numbered to 175 for the lower number cards and to 50 for the future fame set.

Nm-Mt Ex-Mt
*COLLECTION 1-100: 3X TO 8X BASIC
*COLLECTION 101-138: 1X TO 2.5X BASIC

2002 Flair Jersey Heights

This 25-card set features game-used jersey swatches from a selection of major league stars. The cards were seeded into packs at a rate of 1:18 hobby and 1:100 retail. Though the

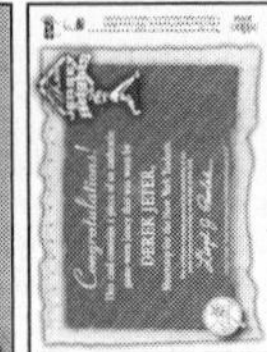

cards are not serial-numbered in any way, representatives at Fleer confirmed that the following players were produced in slightly lower quantities: Barry Bonds, Roger Clemens, J.D. Drew, Greg Maddux and Alex Rodriguez. In addition, based upon analysis of secondary market trading volume by our staff, the following cards are perceived to be in greater supply: Jeff Bagwell, Jim Edmonds, Randy Johnson, Chipper Jones, Ivan Rodriguez, Curt Schilling and Larry Walker.

Nm-Mt Ex-Mt
1 Edgardo Alfonzo 8.00 2.40
2 Jeff Bagwell * 8.00 2.40
3 Craig Biggio 8.00 2.40
4 Barry Bonds SP 25.00 7.50
5 Sean Casey 8.00 2.40
6 Roger Clemens SP 25.00 7.50
7 Carlos Delgado 8.00 2.40
8 J.D. Drew SP 8.00 2.40
9 Jim Edmonds * 8.00 2.40
10 Nomar Garciaparra 20.00 6.00
11 Shawn Green 8.00 2.40
12 Todd Helton 8.00 2.40
13 Derek Jeter * 25.00 7.50
14 Randy Johnson * 10.00 3.00
15 Chipper Jones * 10.00 3.00
16 Barry Larkin 10.00 3.00
17 Greg Maddux SP 15.00 4.50
18 Pedro Martinez 10.00 3.00
19 Rafael Palmeiro 8.00 2.40
20 Mike Piazza 15.00 4.50
21 Manny Ramirez 8.00 2.40
22 Alex Rodriguez SP 15.00 4.50
23 Ivan Rodriguez * 10.00 3.00
24 Curt Schilling * 8.00 2.40
25 Larry Walker * 8.00 2.40

2002 Flair Jersey Heights Dual Swatch

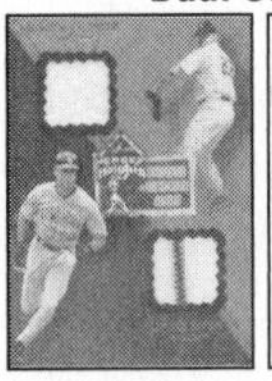

Randomly inserted in packs, these 12 cards features not only two players (usually teammates) with something in common but also a jersey swatch from each player featured. These cards have a stated print run of 100 serial numbered sets.

Nm-Mt Ex-Mt
1 Randy Johnson 40.00 12.00
Curt Schilling
2 Pedro Martinez 80.00 24.00
Nomar Garciaparra
3 Edgardo Alfonzo 40.00 12.00
Mike Piazza
4 Derek Jeter 100.00 30.00
Roger Clemens
5 Greg Maddux 40.00 12.00
Chipper Jones
6 Jim Edmonds 25.00 7.50
J.D. Drew
7 Jeff Bagwell 40.00 12.00
Craig Biggio
8 Rafael Palmeiro 40.00 12.00
Ivan Rodriguez
9 Carlos Delgado 25.00 7.50
Shawn Green
10 Todd Helton 40.00 12.00
Larry Walker
11 Sean Casey 40.00 12.00
Barry Larkin
12 Alex Rodriguez 40.00 12.00
Manny Ramirez

2002 Flair Jersey Heights Hot Numbers Patch

Randomly inserted into packs, these 24 cards feature a jersey patch from the featured player. These cards have a stated print run of 100 serial numbered sets.

Nm-Mt Ex-Mt
1 Edgardo Alfonzo 25.00 7.50
2 Jeff Bagwell 40.00 12.00
3 Craig Biggio 40.00 12.00
4 Sean Casey 25.00 7.50
5 Roger Clemens
6 Carlos Delgado 25.00 7.50
7 J.D. Drew 25.00 7.50
8 Jim Edmonds 25.00 7.50
9 Nomar Garciaparra 80.00 24.00
10 Shawn Green 25.00 7.50
11 Todd Helton 40.00 12.00
12 Derek Jeter 100.00 30.00
13 Randy Johnson 40.00 12.00
14 Chipper Jones 40.00 12.00
15 Barry Larkin 40.00 12.00
16 Greg Maddux 60.00 18.00
17 Pedro Martinez 40.00 12.00
18 Rafael Palmeiro 40.00 12.00
19 Mike Piazza 60.00 18.00
20 Manny Ramirez 25.00 7.50
21 Alex Rodriguez 60.00 18.00
22 Ivan Rodriguez 40.00 12.00
23 Curt Schilling 40.00 12.00
24 Larry Walker 40.00 12.00

2002 Flair Power Tools Bats

This 28-card set features game-used bat chips from a selection of major league stars. The cards were seeded into packs at a rate of 1:19 hobby and 1:123 retail. Though not serial-numbered, the following players were reported by Fleer as being short prints: Jeff Bagwell, Pat Burrell, J.D. Drew, Rafael Palmeiro, Scott Rolen, Reggie Sanders and Jim Thome. All of these cards are immeasurably tougher to pull from packs than others from this set. Please refer to our checklist for specific print run quantities on these short prints. In addition, based on market research by our staff, the following players appear to be in greater supply than other cards from this set: Bret Boone, Ivan Rodriguez and Tsuyoshi Shinjo.

Nm-Mt Ex-Mt
1 Roberto Alomar 10.00 3.00
2 Jeff Bagwell SP/150 15.00 4.50
3 Craig Biggio 8.00 2.40
4 Barry Bonds 20.00 6.00
5 Bret Boone * 8.00 2.40
6 Pat Burrell SP/225 15.00 4.50
7 Eric Chavez 8.00 2.40
8 J.D. Drew SP/150 15.00 4.50
9 Jim Edmonds 8.00 2.40
10 Juan Gonzalez 10.00 3.00
11 Luis Gonzalez 8.00 2.40
12 Shawn Green 8.00 2.40
13 Derek Jeter 20.00 6.00
14 Doug Mientkiewicz 8.00 2.40
15 Magglio Ordonez 8.00 2.40
16 Rafael Palmeiro SP/100 15.00 4.50
17 Mike Piazza 15.00 4.50
18 Alex Rodriguez 15.00 4.50
19 Ivan Rodriguez * 10.00 3.00
20 Scott Rolen SP/42
21 Reggie Sanders SP/120 15.00 4.50
22 Gary Sheffield 8.00 2.40
23 Tsuyoshi Shinjo * 8.00 2.40
24 Miguel Tejada 8.00 2.40
25 Frank Thomas 10.00 3.00
26 Jim Thome SP/225 15.00 4.50
27 Larry Walker 8.00 2.40
28 Bernie Williams 8.00 2.40

2002 Flair Power Tools Dual Bats

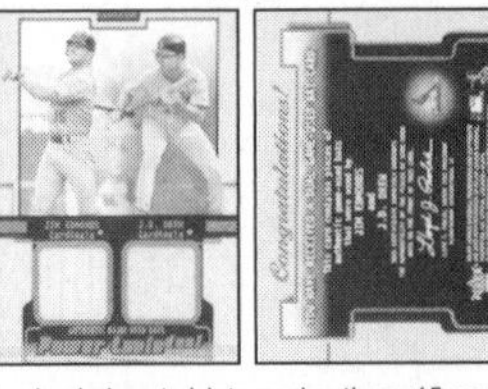

Randomly inserted into packs, these 15 cards feature not only two players but bat chips from each of the featured players. A few cards were issued in lesser quantity and we have notated those cards along with the stated print run in our checklist. Please note that these cards are not serial numbered.

Nm-Mt Ex-Mt
*GOLD: 1X TO 2.5X BASIC DUAL BAT
GOLD RANDOM INSERTS IN PACKS
GOLD PRINT RUN 50 SERIAL #'d SETS
GOLD CARDS 7 AND 13 DO NOT EXIST
1 Eric Chavez 15.00 4.50
Miguel Tejada
2 Barry Bonds 30.00 9.00
Tsuyoshi Shinjo
3 Jim Edmonds 15.00 4.50
J.D. Drew
4 Jeff Bagwell 25.00 7.50
Craig Biggio
5 Bernie Williams 40.00 12.00
Derek Jeter
6 Roberto Alomar 25.00 7.50
Mike Piazza
7 Sean Casey
Jim Thome SP/40
8 Pat Burrell 15.00 4.50
Scott Rolen
9 Gary Sheffield 15.00 4.50
Shawn Green
10 Ivan Rodriguez 25.00 7.50
Alex Rodriguez
11 Juan Gonzalez 20.00 6.00
Rafael Palmeiro
12 Magglio Ordonez 20.00 6.00
Frank Thomas
13 Larry Walker 15.00 4.50
Todd Helton SP/225
14 Luis Gonzalez 15.00 4.50
Reggie Sanders
15 Doug Mientkiewicz 15.00 4.50
Bret Boone

2002 Flair Sweet Swatch

Issued one per hobby box as a "box-topper", these cards feature a larger jersey swatch from the featured players. Each player was issued to a different print run and we have notated the stated print run in our checklist.

Nm-Mt Ex-Mt
1 Jeff Bagwell/490 15.00 4.50
2 Josh Beckett/500 15.00 4.50
3 Darin Erstad/525 15.00 4.50
4 Freddy Garcia/620 15.00 4.50

5 Brian Giles Pants/445 15.00 4.50
6 Juan Gonzalez/505 15.00 4.50
7 Mark Grace/795 15.00 4.50
8 Derek Jeter/525 50.00 15.00
9 Jason Kendall/990 15.00 4.50
10 Paul LoDuca/440 15.00 4.50
11 Greg Maddux/475 15.00 4.50
12 Magglio Ordonez/495 15.00 4.50
13 Rafael Palmeiro/535 15.00 4.50
14 Mike Piazza/1000 15.00 4.50
15 Alex Rodriguez/550 25.00 7.50
16 Ivan Rodriguez/475 15.00 4.50
17 Tim Salmon/465 15.00 4.50
18 Kazuhiro Sasaki/770 15.00 4.50
19 Alfonso Soriano/775 15.00 4.50
20 Larry Walker/430 15.00 4.50
21 Ted Williams/250 150.00 45.00

2002 Flair Sweet Swatch Bat Autograph

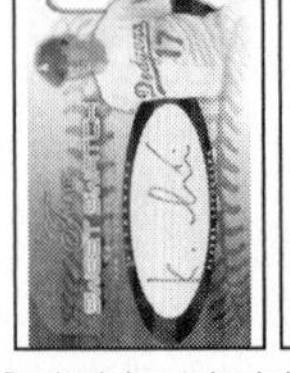

Randomly inserted as hobby box toppers, these cards feature not only a bat chip from the featured player but also an autograph. Each card was printed to a different amount and we have notated that stated print run information next to the player's name in our checklist. Some of the Drew Henson cards and all of the Derek Jeter cards were issued as exchange cards and those cards could be redeemed until April 30th, 2003.

Nm-Mt Ex-Mt
GOLD PARALLELS RANDOM BOX-TOPPERS
GOLD PRINT RUN 15 SERIAL #'d SETS
GOLD NOT PRICED DUE TO SCARCITY
1 Barry Bonds/35 250.00 75.00
2 Dewon Brazelton/185 20.00 6.00
3 Marlon Byrd/185 25.00 7.50
4 Ron Cey/285 25.00 7.50
5 David Espinosa/485 20.00 6.00
6 Drew Henson/785 40.00 12.00
7 Kazuhisa Ishii/335 50.00 15.00
8 Derek Jeter/375 150.00 45.00
9 Al Kaline/285 60.00 18.00
10 Don Mattingly/85 200.00 60.00
11 Paul Molitor/85 60.00 18.00
12 Dale Murphy/285 80.00 24.00
13 Tony Perez/115 25.00 7.50
14 Mark Prior/285 120.00 36.00
15 Albert Pujols/50
16 Brooks Robinson/185 60.00 18.00
17 Dane Sardinha/485 20.00 6.00
18 Ben Sheets/85 50.00 15.00
19 Ozzie Smith/185 100.00 30.00
20 So Taguchi/335 40.00 12.00
21 Mark Teixeira/185 40.00 12.00
22 Maury Wills/285 25.00 7.50

2002 Flair Sweet Swatch Patch

This 20-card over-sized set is a premium parallel version of the basic Sweet Swatch inserts. The cards were randomly seeded exclusively into hobby boxes as box-toppers. Unlike the basic cards, each of these parallels features a piece of jersey patch (often with very colorful pieces of the player's name or a team logo taken from their game used jersey). Each card was serial-numbered by hand. In general, between 50-80 copies of each card were produced, but please reference our checklist for specific quantities. Ted Williams (15 copies) and Derek Jeter (20 copies) are the scarcest cards in this set. Also, Pirates outfielder Brian Giles was the only player to have a basic Sweet Swatch card that was NOT featured in this Patch parallel because Fleer used a pair of his game-used pants for the basic card (thus no patch swatches were available).

Nm-Mt Ex-Mt
*PREMIUM PATCHES: 2X LISTED PRICES
1 OF 1 PARALLEL RANDOM BOX-TOPPER
NO 1 OF 1 PRICING DUE TO SCARCITY
1 Jeff Bagwell/45 100.00 30.00
2 Josh Beckett/60 100.00 30.00
3 Darin Erstad/50 80.00 24.00
4 Freddy Garcia/50 80.00 24.00
5 Juan Gonzalez/55 120.00 36.00
6 Mark Grace/75 100.00 30.00
7 Derek Jeter/20
8 Jason Kendall/120 60.00 18.00
9 Paul LoDuca/50 80.00 24.00
10 Greg Maddux/50 150.00 45.00
11 Magglio Ordonez/55 80.00 24.00
12 Rafael Palmeiro/60 100.00 30.00
13 Mike Piazza/95 150.00 45.00
14 Alex Rodriguez/50 150.00 45.00
15 Ivan Rodriguez/50 120.00 36.00
16 Tim Salmon/40 100.00 30.00
17 Kazuhiro Sasaki/80 80.00 24.00
18 Alfonso Soriano/35 120.00 36.00
19 Larry Walker/60 100.00 30.00
20 Ted Williams/15

2003 Flair

This 135 card set was issued in two separate releases. The primary Flair product was released in June, 2003. These cards were issued in five card packs with an $6 SRP which came 20 packs to a box and 12 boxes to a case. Cards numbered 1-90 feature veterans while cards numbered 91-125 feature rookies. The cards 91 through 125 were issued to a stated print run of 500 serial numbered sets. Cards 126-135 were randomly seeded into packs of Fleer Rookies and Greats of which was distributed in December, 2003. Each of these update cards featured a top prospect and was serial numbered to 500 copies.

Nm-Mt Ex-Mt
COMP.LO SET w/o SP's (90) 25.00 7.50
COMMON CARD (1-90) .50 .15
COMMON CARD (91-135) 8.00 2.40
1 Hideo Nomo 1.25 .35
2 Derek Jeter 3.00 .90
3 Junior Spivey .50 .15
4 Rich Aurilia .50 .15
5 Luis Gonzalez .50 .15
6 Sean Burroughs .50 .15
7 Pedro Martinez 1.25 .35
8 Randy Winn .50 .15
9 Carlos Delgado .50 .15
10 Pat Burrell .50 .15
11 Barry Larkin 1.25 .35
12 Roberto Alomar 1.25 .35
13 Tony Batista .50 .15
14 Barry Bonds 3.00 .90
15 Craig Biggio .75 .23
16 Ivan Rodriguez 1.25 .35
17 Javier Vazquez .50 .15
18 Joe Borchard .50 .15
19 Josh Phelps .50 .15
20 Omar Vizquel .50 .15
21 Tom Glavine .75 .23
22 Darin Erstad .50 .15
23 Hee Seop Choi .50 .15
24 Roger Clemens 2.50 .75
25 Michael Cuddyer .50 .15
26 Mike Sweeney .50 .15
27 Phil Nevin .50 .15
28 Torii Hunter .50 .15
29 Vladimir Guerrero 1.25 .35
30 Ellis Burks .50 .15
31 Jimmy Rollins .50 .15
32 Ken Griffey Jr. 2.00 .60
33 Magglio Ordonez .50 .15
34 Mark Prior 2.50 .75
35 Mike Lieberthal .50 .15
36 Jorge Posada .75 .23
37 Rodrigo Lopez .50 .15
38 Todd Helton .75 .23
39 Adam Kennedy .50 .15
40 Curt Schilling .75 .23
41 Jim Thome 1.25 .35
42 Josh Beckett .75 .23
43 Carlos Pena .50 .15
44 Jason Kendall .50 .15
45 Sammy Sosa 2.00 .60
46 Scott Rolen .75 .23
47 Alex Rodriguez 2.00 .60
48 Aubrey Huff .50 .15
49 Bobby Abreu .50 .15
50 Jeff Kent .50 .15
51 Joe Randa .50 .15
52 Lance Berkman .50 .15
53 Orlando Cabrera .50 .15
54 Richie Sexson .50 .15
55 Albert Pujols 2.00 .60
56 Alfonso Soriano .75 .23
57 Greg Maddux 2.00 .60
58 Jason Giambi 1.25 .35
59 Jeff Bagwell .75 .23
60 Kerry Wood 1.25 .35
61 Manny Ramirez .50 .15
62 Eric Chavez .50 .15
63 Preston Wilson .50 .15
64 Shawn Green .50 .15
65 Shea Hillenbrand .50 .15
66 Austin Kearns .50 .15
67 Cliff Floyd .50 .15
68 Edgardo Alfonzo .50 .15
69 J.D. Drew .50 .15
70 Larry Walker .75 .23
71 Mike Piazza 2.00 .60
72 Andruw Jones .50 .15
73 Ben Grieve .50 .15
74 Eric Hinske .50 .15
75 Geoff Jenkins .50 .15
76 Kazuhiro Sasaki .50 .15
77 Matt Morris .50 .15
78 Miguel Tejada .50 .15
79 Aramis Ramirez .50 .15
80 Troy Glaus .75 .23
81 Ichiro Suzuki 2.00 .60
82 Mark Teixeira .75 .23
83 Nomar Garciaparra 2.00 .60
84 Chipper Jones 1.25 .35
85 Frank Thomas 1.25 .35
86 Paul Lo Duca .50 .15
87 Bernie Williams .75 .23
88 Adam Dunn .50 .15
89 Randy Johnson 1.25 .35
90 Barry Zito .75 .23
91 Lew Ford FF RC 10.00 3.00
92 Joe Valentine FF RC 8.00 2.40
93 Jhonny Peralta FF RC 8.00 2.40
94 Hideki Matsui FF RC 25.00 7.50
95 Francisco Rosario FF RC 8.00 2.40
96 Adam LaRoche FF 10.00 3.00
97 Josh Hall FF RC 10.00 3.00
98 Chien-Ming Wang FF RC 10.00 3.00

99 Josh Willingham FF RC........ 10.00 3.00
100 Guillermo Quiroz FF RC...... 10.00 3.00
101 Terrmel Sledge FF RC......... 10.00 3.00
102 Prentice Redman FF RC......... 8.00 2.40
103 Matt Bruback FF RC............. 8.00 2.40
104 Alejandro Machado FF RC 8.00 2.40
105 Shane Victorino FF RC.......... 8.00 2.40
106 Chris Waters FF RC 8.00 2.40
107 Jose Contreras FF RC.......... 10.00 3.00
108 Pete LaForest FF RC 10.00 3.00
109 Nook Logan FF RC............... 8.00 2.40
110 Hector Luna FF RC 8.00 2.40
111 Daniel Cabrera FF RC........... 8.00 2.40
112 Matt Kata FF RC................ 10.00 3.00
113 Rontrez Johnson FF RC......... 8.00 2.40
114 Josh Stewart FF RC 8.00 2.40
115 Michael Hessman FF RC....... 8.00 2.40
116 Felix Sanchez FF RC 8.00 2.40
117 Michel Hernandez FF RC 8.00 2.40
118 Arnaldo Munoz FF RC........... 8.00 2.40
119 Ian Ferguson FF RC 8.00 2.40
120 Clint Barmes FF RC 10.00 3.00
121 Brian Stokes FF RC.............. 8.00 2.40
122 Craig Brazell FF RC............ 10.00 3.00
123 John Webb FF 8.00 2.40
124 Tim Olson FF RC 10.00 3.00
125 Jeremy Bonderman FF RC.. 10.00 3.00
126 Jeff Duncan RC 10.00 3.00
127 Rickie Weeks RC 25.00 7.50
128 Brandon Webb RC............... 15.00 4.50
129 Robby Hammock RC.......... 10.00 3.00
130 Jon Leicester RC.................. 8.00 2.40
131 Ryan Wagner RC................ 10.00 3.00
132 Bo Hart RC 10.00 3.00
133 Edwin Jackson RC.............. 20.00 6.00
134 Sergio Mitre RC.................. 10.00 3.00
135 Delmon Young RC............. 25.00 7.50

2003 Flair Collection Row 1

Nm-Mt Ex-Mt
*ROW 1 1-90: 2.5X TO 6X BASIC
*ROW 1 91-125: .4X TO 1X BASIC .....
RANDOM INSERTS IN PACKS ....
STATED PRINT RUN 150 SERIAL #'d SETS

2003 Flair Collection Row 2

Nm-Mt Ex-Mt
RANDOM INSERTS IN PACKS ....
STATED PRINT RUN 25 SERIAL #'d SETS
NO PRICING DUE TO SCARCITY.........

2003 Flair Diamond Cuts Jersey

ssued at a stated rate of one in 10, these 15 cards feature jersey swatches from some of baseball's leading players.

Nm-Mt Ex-Mt
STATED ODDS 1:10 ....
*GOLD: 1X TO 2.5X BASIC ....
GOLD RANDOM INSERTS IN PACKS ..
GOLD PRINT RUN 100 SERIAL #'d SETS
AR Alex Rodriguez 10.00 3.00
AS Alfonso Soriano 8.00 2.40
BZ Barry Zito 8.00 2.40
CJ Chipper Jones 8.00 2.40
DJ Derek Jeter........................ 15.00 4.50
GM Greg Maddux.................... 10.00 3.00
JD J.D. Drew............................ 5.00 1.50
MP Mike Piazza 10.00 3.00
PB Pat Burrell........................... 5.00 1.50
RA Roberto Alomar 8.00 2.40
RC Roger Clemens 10.00 3.00
RO Roy Oswalt.......................... 5.00 1.50
SR Scott Rolen.......................... 8.00 2.40
TG Troy Glaus 8.00 2.40
VG Vladimir Guerrero 8.00 2.40

2003 Flair Hot Numbers Patch

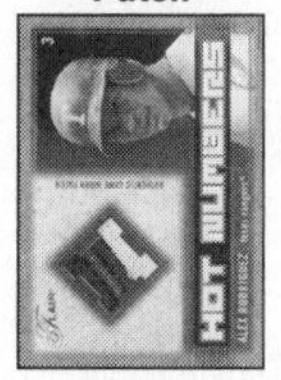

Randomly inserted into packs, these 15 cards feature game-used "patch pieces" from leading baseball players. Each of these cards were issued to a stated print run of 100 serial numbered sets.

Nm-Mt Ex-Mt
AR Alex Rodriguez 40.00 12.00
AS Alfonso Soriano 30.00 9.00
BZ Barry Zito 30.00 9.00
CJ Chipper Jones 30.00 9.00
DJ Derek Jeter........................ 60.00 18.00
GM Greg Maddux..................... 40.00 12.00
JD J.D. Drew 25.00 7.50
MP Mike Piazza 40.00 12.00
PB Pat Burrell........................... 25.00 7.50
RA Roberto Alomar 30.00 9.00
RC Roger Clemens ....
RO Roy Oswalt......................... 25.00 7.50
SR Scott Rolen......................... 30.00 9.00
TG Troy Glaus 30.00 9.00
VG Vladimir Guerrero 30.00 9.00

2003 Flair Hot Numbers Dual Patch

Randomly inserted into packs, these cards feature two "patch" swatches from leading baseball players. Each of these cards were issued to a stated print run of 25 serial numbered sets and no pricing is available due to market scarcity.

Nm-Mt Ex-Mt
ARVG Alex Rodriguez ....
Vladimir Guerrero
ASDJ Alfonso Soriano.........................
Derek Jeter
ASRA Alfonso Soriano ....
Roberto Alomar
CJPB Chipper Jones............................
Pat Burrell
DJAR Derek Jeter ....
Alex Rodriguez
JDSR J.D. Drew ....
Scott Rolen
PBJD Pat Burrell..................................
J.D. Drew
RAMP Roberto Alomar.........................
Mike Piazza
SRCJ Scott Rolen................................
Chipper Jones
VGMP Vladimir Guerrero.....................
Mike Piazza

2003 Flair Power Tools Bats

Randomly inserted into packs, these 18 cards feature game-used bat chips from leading players. Each of these cards were issued to a stated print run of 500 serial numbered sets.

Nm-Mt Ex-Mt
*GOLD: .6X TO 1.5X BASIC ....
GOLD PRINT RUN 100 SERIAL #'d SETS
RANDOM INSERTS IN PACKS ....
AD Adam Dunn 8.00 2.40
AJ Andruw Jones 8.00 2.40
AK Austin Kearns 8.00 2.40
AR Alex Rodriguez 15.00 4.50
AS Alfonso Soriano 10.00 3.00
BW Bernie Williams.................... 10.00 3.00
DJ Derek Jeter........................... 20.00 6.00
HSC Hee-Seop Choi 8.00 2.40
JB Jeff Bagwell.......................... 10.00 3.00
JGI Jason Giambi...................... 10.00 3.00
JGO Juan Gonzalez................... 10.00 3.00
JT Jim Thome 10.00 3.00
LB Lance Berkman 8.00 2.40
MP Mike Piazza 15.00 4.50
MT Miguel Tejada....................... 8.00 2.40
NG Nomar Garciaparra.............. 15.00 4.50
SR Scott Rolen.......................... 10.00 3.00
SS Sammy Sosa 15.00 4.50

2003 Flair Power Tools Dual Bats

Randomly inserted into packs, these cards feature two "game-used" bat chips of the featured players. Each of these cards were issued to a stated print run of 200 serial numbered sets.

Nm-Mt Ex-Mt
ADAK Adam Dunn 15.00 4.50
Austin Kearns
ARNG Alex Rodriguez............... 30.00 9.00
Nomar Garciaparra
DJAS Derek Jeter 40.00 12.00
Alfonso Soriano
JGBW Jason Giambi................. 20.00 6.00
Bernie Williams
JGMP Jason Giambi................. 25.00 7.50
Mike Piazza
JTSS Jim Thome 20.00 6.00
Sammy Sosa
LBJB Lance Berkman 20.00 6.00
Jeff Bagwell
MTAR Miguel Tejada 20.00 6.00
Alex Rodriguez
NBDJ Nomar Garciaparra.......... 40.00 12.00
Derek Jeter

2003 Flair Sweet Swatch Autos Jumbo

Randomly inserted in jumbo packs, these seven cards feature authentic autographs from

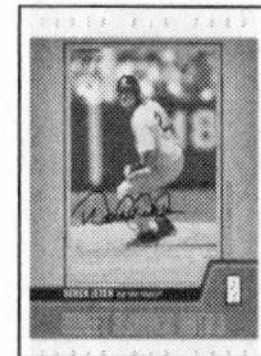

leading players. There are three different varieties of Derek Jeter autographs. Please note that we have put the stated serial numbered print run next to the player's name in our checklist.

Nm-Mt Ex-Mt
GOLD PRINT RUN 25 SERIAL #'d SETS
NO GOLD PRICING DUE TO SCARCITY
MASTERPIECE PRINT 1 SERIAL #'d SET
NO M'PIECE PRICING DUE TO SCARCITY
RANDOM INSERTS IN JUMBO PACKS
AD Adam Dunn/218 .... 50.00 15.00
DJ Derek Jeter/312................. 100.00 30.00
DJA Derek Jeter/30 ....
DJW Derek Jeter/50 ....
JB Jeff Bagwell/218.................. 50.00 15.00
RJ Randy Johnson/218............ 80.00 24.00
TG Troy Glaus/116 .... 50.00 15.00

2003 Flair Sweet Swatch Jersey

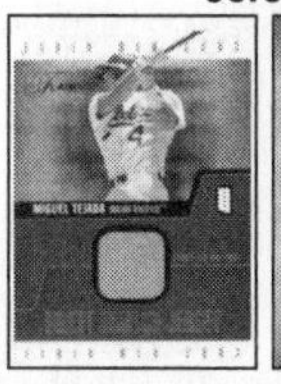

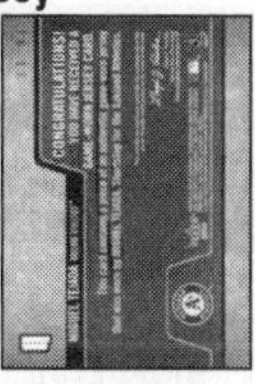

Randomly inserted into packs, these 18 cards feature game-used jersey swatches from some of baseball's star players.

Nm-Mt Ex-Mt
*JUMBO 50: 1X TO 2.5X BASIC.........
JUMBO 50 PRINT RUN 50 SERIAL #'d SETS
*JUMBO 150: .6X TO 1.5X BASIC.......
JUMBO 150 PRINT RUN 150 SERIAL #'d SETS
JUMBO MASTERPIECE 1 SERIAL #'d SET
NO JUMBO M'PIECE PRICING AVAILABLE
JUMBOS RANDOM IN JUMBO PACKS
SSAD Adam Dunn 8.00 2.40
SSAR Alex Rodriguez............... 15.00 4.50
SSAS Alfonso Soriano.............. 10.00 3.00
SSBW Bernie Williams 10.00 3.00
SSCJ Chipper Jones 10.00 3.00
SSDJ Derek Jeter 20.00 6.00
SSHN Hideo Nomo................... 15.00 4.50
SSJG Jason Giambi.................. 10.00 3.00
SSKS Kazuhiro Sasaki............... 8.00 2.40
SSLB Lance Berkman................. 8.00 2.40
SSMP Mark Prior 15.00 4.50
SSMT Miguel Tejada 8.00 2.40
SSNG Nomar Garciaparra.......... 15.00 4.50
SSPM Pedro Martinez 10.00 3.00
SSRC Roger Clemens............... 15.00 4.50
SSRJ Randy Johnson............... 10.00 3.00
SSSS Sammy Sosa 15.00 4.50
SSVG Vladimir Guerrero........... 10.00 3.00

2003 Flair Sweet Swatch Jersey Jumbo

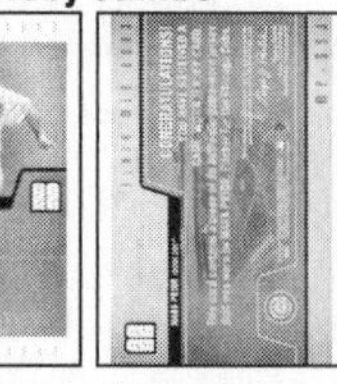

Inserted at a stated rate of one per jumbo pack, these 18 cards feature jersey swatches from some of baseball's leading players.

Nm-Mt Ex-Mt
ADSSJ Adam Dunn/1090 .... 10.00 3.00
ARSSJ Alex Rodriguez/55......... 40.00 12.00
ASSSJ Alfonso Soriano/57......... 25.00 7.50
BWSSJ Bernie Williams/1420 ... 10.00 3.00
CJSSJ Chipper Jones/80.......... 25.00 7.50
DJSSJ Derek Jeter/47 .... 50.00 15.00
HNSSJ Hideo Nomo/970........... 10.00 3.00
JGSSJ Jason Giambi/350.......... 15.00 4.50
KSSSJ Kazuhiro Sasaki/505...... 10.00 3.00
LBSSJ Lance Berkman/1465...... 10.00 3.00
MPSSJ Mark Prior/1195 .... 20.00 6.00
MTSSJ Miguel Tejada/518 .... 10.00 3.00
NGSSJ Nomar Garciaparra/727. 20.00 6.00
PMSSJ Pedro Martinez/1480 .... 10.00 3.00
RCSSJ Roger Clemens/97......... 30.00 9.00
RJSSJ Randy Johnson/274........ 15.00 4.50
SSSSJ Sammy Sosa/279 .... 20.00 6.00
VGSSJ Vladimir Guerrero/46..... 40.00 12.00

2003 Flair Sweet Swatch Jersey Dual Jumbo

Randomly inserted into jumbo packs, these eight cards feature two jersey swatches from some of baseball's leading players. Each of these cards were issued to a stated print run of 25 serial numbered sets and no pricing is available due to market scarcity.

Nm-Mt Ex-Mt
ADLB Adam Dunn ....
Lance Berkman
DJBW Derek Jeter ....
Bernie Williams

JGAS Jason Giambi.................................
Alfonso Soriano
KSHN Kazuhiro Sasaki ....
Hideo Nomo
MTAR Miguel Tejada ....
Alex Rodriguez
NMPM Nomar Garciaparra ....
Pedro Martinez
RJMP Randy Johnson.............................
Mark Prior
VGCJ Vladimir Guerrero ....
Chipper Jones

2003 Flair Sweet Swatch Patch

Randomly inserted into packs, these 18 cards feature patches from some of baseball's superstars. Each of these cards were issued to a stated print run of 50 serial numbered sets.

Nm-Mt Ex-Mt
SSPAD Adam Dunn ....
SSPAR Alex Rodriguez............. 50.00 15.00
SSPAS Alfonso Soriano 40.00 12.00
SSPBW Bernie Williams 40.00 12.00
SSPCJ Chipper Jones.............. 40.00 12.00
SSPDJ Derek Jeter 80.00 24.00
SSPHN Hideo Nomo 40.00 12.00
SSPJG Jason Giambi 40.00 12.00
SSPKS Kazuhiro Sasaki............ 30.00 9.00
SSPLB Lance Berkman............. 30.00 9.00
SSPMP Mark Prior.................... 60.00 18.00
SSPMT Miguel Tejada 30.00 9.00
SSPNG Nomar Garciaparra 50.00 15.00
SSPPM Pedro Martinez............. 40.00 12.00
SSPRC Roger Clemens 60.00 18.00
SSPRJ Randy Johnson 40.00 12.00
SSPSS Sammy Sosa 50.00 15.00
SSPVG Vladimir Guerrero 40.00 12.00

2003 Flair Sweet Swatch Patch Jumbo

Randomly inserted in jumbo packs, these 18 cards feature patch pieces of leading players. Each of these cards were produced to differing print runs and we have notated the print run next to the player's name in our checklist. If any card was issued to a stated print run of 25 or fewer cards, there is no pricing due to market scarcity.

Nm-Mt Ex-Mt
ADSSPE Adam Dunn/130.......... 30.00 9.00
ARSSPE Alex Rodriguez/298..... 50.00 15.00
ASSSPE Alfonso Soriano/28 ....
BWSSPE Bernie Williams/123... 40.00 12.00
CJSSPE Chipper Jones/284 ...... 30.00 9.00
DJSSPE Derek Jeter/35..........................
HNSSPE Hideo Nomo/114 .... 60.00 18.00
JGSSPE Jason Giambi/26 ....
KSSSPE Kazuhiro Sasaki/90...... 30.00 9.00
LBSSPE Lance Berkman/287 .... 25.00 7.50
MPSSPE Mark Prior/290........... 50.00 15.00
MTSSPE Miguel Tejada/183 ...... 25.00 7.50
NGSSPE Nomar Garciaparra/124 50.00 15.00
PMSSPE Pedro Martinez/185.... 30.00 9.00
RCSSPE Roger Clemens/1 ....
RJSSPE Randy Johnson/46 ...... 50.00 15.00
SSSSPE Sammy Sosa/190........ 50.00 15.00
VGSSPE Vladimir Guerrero/290 30.00 9.00

2003 Flair Wave of the Future Memorabilia

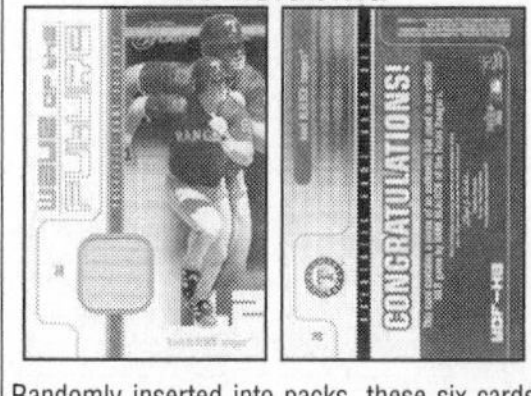

Randomly inserted into packs, these six cards feature not only some of the up and coming young prospects but also an game-used memorabilia piece. Each of these cards were issued to a stated print run of 500 serial numbered sets.

Nm-Mt Ex-Mt
*GOLD: .6X TO 1.5X BASIC ....
GOLD PRINT RUN 100 SERIAL #'d SETS
RANDOM INSERTS IN PACKS ....
AH Aubrey Huff Bat 8.00 2.40
AK Austin Kearns Jsy 8.00 2.40
CC Carl Crawford Bat.................. 8.00 2.40
HB Hank Blalock Bat.................. 10.00 3.00
JP Josh Phelps Jsy 8.00 2.40
SB Sean Burroughs Jsy............... 8.00 2.40

2003 Flair Greats

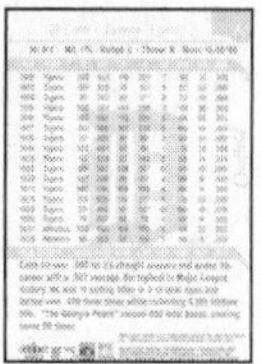

This 133 card set was released in December, 2002. These cards were issued in five card packs with an SRP of $6. These cards were issued in 20 pack boxes which came 12 boxes to a case. Cards numbered 96 through 133 were inserted four per special home team boxes which also had 20 packs in a box but only had 4 boxes to a case. A promo card of Al Kaline was also issued before the product was issued and we have placed that card at the end of our set listings.

Nm-Mt Ex-Mt
COMP.SET w/o SP's (95).......... 40.00 12.00
COMMON CARD (1-95).............. 1.00 .30
COMMON CARD (96-133)........... 5.00 1.50
1 Ozzie Smith 4.00 1.20
2 Red Schoendienst .... 1.00 .30
3 Harmon Killebrew..................... 2.50 .75
4 Ralph Kiner .... 1.00 .30
5 Johnny Bench .... 2.50 .75
6 Al Kaline .... 2.50 .75
7 Bobby Doerr............................. 1.00 .30
8 Cal Ripken................................ 8.00 2.40
9 Enos Slaughter......................... 1.00 .30
10 Phil Rizzuto .... 1.50 .45
11 Luis Aparicio .... 1.00 .30
12 Pee Wee Reese....................... 1.50 .45
13 Richie Ashburn........................ 1.50 .45
14 Ernie Banks .... 2.50 .75
15 Earl Weaver .... 1.00 .30
16 Whitey Ford............................ 1.50 .45
17 Brooks Robinson..................... 2.50 .75
18 Lou Boudreau.......................... 1.00 .30
19 Robin Yount 4.00 1.20
20 Mike Schmidt 5.00 1.50
21 Bob Lemon.............................. 1.00 .30
22 Stan Musial 4.00 1.20
23 Joe Morgan .... 1.00 .30
24 Early Wynn.............................. 1.00 .30
25 Willie Stargell .... 1.50 .45
26 Yogi Berra .... 2.50 .75
27 Juan Marichal.......................... 1.00 .30
28 Rick Ferrell .... 1.00 .30
29 Rod Carew............................... 1.50 .45
30 Jim Bunning............................ 1.00 .30
31 Ferguson Jenkins .... 1.00 .30
32 Steve Carlton........................... 1.00 .30
33 Larry Doby .... 1.00 .30
34 Nolan Ryan.............................. 6.00 1.80
35 Phil Niekro UER....................... 1.00 .30
Career win total in blurb is wrong
36 Billy Williams.......................... 1.00 .30
37 Hal Newhouser........................ 1.00 .30
38 Bob Feller .... 1.50 .45
39 Lou Brock................................ 1.50 .45
40 Monte Irvin.............................. 1.00 .30
41 Eddie Mathews .... 2.50 .75
42 Rollie Fingers .... 1.00 .30
43 Gaylord Perry .... 1.00 .30
44 Reggie Jackson........................ 1.50 .45
45 Bob Gibson .... 1.50 .45
46 Robin Roberts.......................... 1.50 .45
47 Tom Seaver .... 1.50 .45
48 Willie McCovey........................ 1.00 .30
49 Hoyt Wilhelm........................... 1.00 .30
50 George Kell.............................. 1.00 .30
51 Warren Spahn .... 1.50 .45
52 Catfish Hunter .... 1.50 .45
53 Dom DiMaggio .... 1.00 .30
54 Joe Medwick .... 1.00 .30
55 Johnny Pesky .... 1.00 .30
56 Steve Garvey .... 1.00 .30
57 Harry Heilmann .... 1.00 .30
58 Dave Winfield .... 1.00 .30
59 Andre Dawson.......................... 1.00 .30
60 Jimmie Foxx............................. 2.50 .75
61 Buddy Bell .... 1.00 .30
62 Gabby Hartnett .... 1.00 .30
63 Babe Ruth 8.00 2.40
64 Dizzy Dean............................... 1.50 .45
65 Hank Greenberg .... 2.50 .75
66 Don Drysdale........................... 2.50 .75
67 Gary Carter .... 1.50 .45
68 Wade Boggs............................. 1.50 .45
69 Tony Perez .... 1.00 .30
70 Mickey Cochrane...................... 1.50 .45
71 Bill Dickey .... 1.50 .45
72 George Brett............................ 6.00 1.80
73 Honus Wagner .... 2.50 .75
74 George Sisler........................... 1.00 .30
75 Walter Johnson........................ 2.50 .75
76 Ron Santo .... 1.50 .45
77 Roy Campanella .... 2.50 .75
78 Roger Maris 4.00 1.20
79 Kirby Puckett........................... 2.50 .75
80 Alan Trammell.......................... 1.50 .45
81 Don Mattingly........................... 6.00 1.80
82 Ty Cobb.................................... 3.00 .90
83 Lou Gehrig 5.00 1.50
84 Jackie Robinson....................... 3.00 .90
85 Billy Martin............................... 1.50 .45
86 Paul Molitor.............................. 1.50 .45
87 Duke Snider............................. 1.50 .45
88 Thurman Munson..................... 3.00 .90
89 Luke Appling .... 1.00 .30

Card	Nm-Mt	Ex-Mt
90 Ernie Lombardi	1.00	.30
91 Rube Waddell	1.00	.30
92 Travis Jackson	1.00	.30
93 Joe Sewell	1.00	.30
94 King Kelly	1.50	.45
95 Heinie Manush	1.00	.30
96 Bobby Doerr HT	5.00	1.50
97 Johnny Pesky HT	5.00	1.50
98 Wade Boggs HT	8.00	2.40
99 Tony Conigliaro HT	8.00	2.40
100 Carlton Fisk HT	8.00	2.40
101 Rico Petrocelli HT	5.00	1.50
102 Jim Rice HT	5.00	1.50
103 Al Lopez HT	5.00	1.50
104 Pee Wee Reese HT	8.00	2.40
105 Tommy Lasorda HT	5.00	1.50
106 Gil Hodges HT	8.00	2.40
107 Jackie Robinson HT	10.00	3.00
108 Duke Snider HT	8.00	2.40
109 Don Drysdale HT	8.00	2.40
110 Steve Garvey HT	5.00	1.50
111 Hoyt Wilhelm HT	5.00	1.50
112 Juan Marichal HT	5.00	1.50
113 Monte Irvin HT	5.00	1.50
114 Willie McCovey HT	5.00	1.50
115 Travis Jackson HT	5.00	1.50
116 Bobby Bonds HT	5.00	1.50
117 Orlando Cepeda HT	5.00	1.50
118 Whitey Ford HT	8.00	2.40
119 Phil Rizzuto HT	8.00	2.40
120 Reggie Jackson HT	8.00	2.40
121 Yogi Berra HT	8.00	2.40
122 Roger Maris HT	10.00	3.00
123 Don Mattingly HT	25.00	7.50
124 Babe Ruth HT	15.00	4.50
125 Dave Winfield HT	5.00	1.50
126 Bob Gibson HT	8.00	2.40
127 Enos Slaughter HT	5.00	1.50
128 Joe Medwick HT	5.00	1.50
129 Lou Brock HT	8.00	2.40
130 Ozzie Smith HT	10.00	3.00
131 Stan Musial HT	10.00	3.00
132 Steve Carlton HT	5.00	1.50
133 Dizzy Dean HT	8.00	2.40
P6 Al Kaline	2.00	.60
Promotional Sample		

2003 Flair Greats Ballpark Heroes

Issued at a stated rate of one in 10, these nine cards feature some of baseball's greatest players.

Card	Nm-Mt	Ex-Mt
1 Nolan Ryan	6.00	1.80
2 Babe Ruth	8.00	2.40
3 Honus Wagner	2.50	.75
4 Ty Cobb	4.00	1.20
5 Ernie Banks	2.50	.75
6 Mike Schmidt	5.00	1.50
7 Duke Snider	2.50	.75
8 Cal Ripken	8.00	2.40
9 Stan Musial	4.00	1.20

2003 Flair Greats Bat Rack Classics Quads

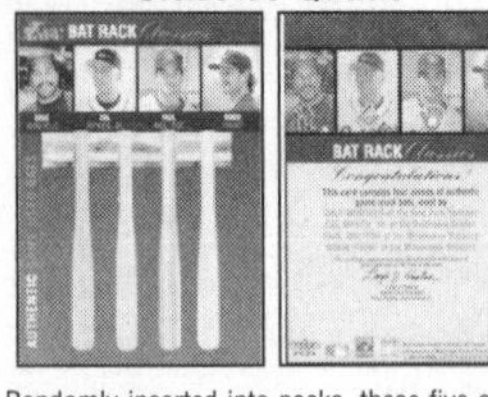

Randomly inserted into packs, these five cards feature game-used bat chips from four players all on the same card. These cards were issued to a stated print run of 150 serial numbered sets.

Card	Nm-Mt	Ex-Mt
1 Don Mattingly	120.00	36.00
Joe Morgan		
Cal Ripken		
Brooks Robinson		
2 Eddie Murray	60.00	18.00
Eddie Mathews		
Reggie Jackson		
Willie McCovey		
3 Tony Perez	80.00	24.00
Don Mattingly		
Hank Greenberg		
Willie Stargell		
4 Ryne Sandberg	60.00	18.00
Ron Santo		
Billy Williams		
Andre Dawson		
5 Dave Winfield	80.00	24.00
Cal Ripken		
Paul Molitor		
Robin Yount		

2003 Flair Greats Bat Rack Classics Trios

Randomly inserted into packs, these five cards feature game-used bat chips from three players all on the same card. These cards were issued to a stated print run of 300 serial numbered sets.

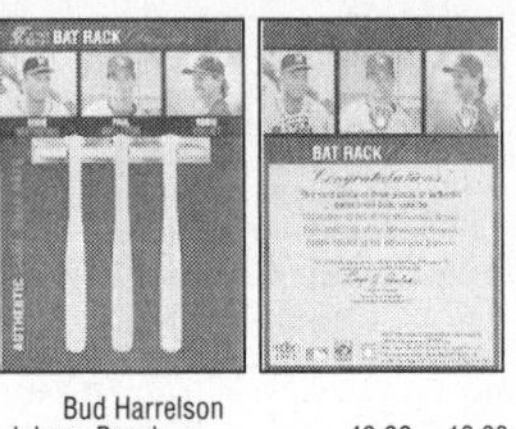

Card	Nm-Mt	Ex-Mt
1 Tommy Agee	25.00	7.50
Jerry Grote		
Bud Harrelson		
2 Johnny Bench	40.00	12.00
Joe Morgan		
Tony Perez		
3 Hank Greenberg	50.00	15.00
Harry Heilman		
George Kell		
4 Reggie Jackson	50.00	15.00
Don Mattingly		
Dave Winfield		
5 Eddie Mathews	50.00	15.00
Paul Molitor		
Robin Yount		
6 Eddie Murray	80.00	24.00
Cal Ripken		
Brooks Robinson		
7 Dave Parker	25.00	7.50
Willie Stargell		
8 Ryne Sandberg	50.00	15.00
Ron Santo		
Billy Williams		

2003 Flair Greats Classic Numbers

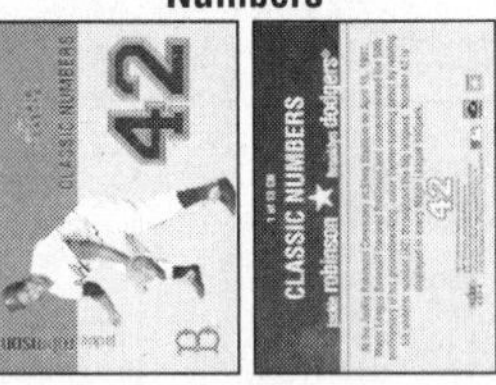

Inserted into packs at a stated rate of one in 20, these 13 cards feature some of the most famous uniform numbers ever.

Card	Nm-Mt	Ex-Mt
1 Jackie Robinson	8.00	2.40
2 Willie McCovey	4.00	1.20
3 Brooks Robinson	6.00	1.80
4 Reggie Jackson	4.00	1.20
5 Ozzie Smith	10.00	3.00
6 Johnny Bench	6.00	1.80
7 Yogi Berra	6.00	1.80
8 Cal Ripken	20.00	6.00
9 George Brett	15.00	4.50
10 Thurman Munson	8.00	2.40
11 Joe Morgan	4.00	1.20
12 Nolan Ryan	15.00	4.50
13 Steve Carlton	4.00	1.20

2003 Flair Greats Classic Numbers Game Used

Inserted at stated odds of one in 24 hobby packs and one in 27 home team packs, these 11 cards feature game-worn material from 11 of the players from the Classic Numbers set. A few players were issued in shorter supply and we have notated that information along with their announced print run information next to the player's name in our checklist.

Card	Nm-Mt	Ex-Mt
PATCH RANDOM INSERTS IN PACKS		
PATCH PRINT RUN 25 SERIAL #'d SETS		
NO PATCH PRICING DUE TO SCARCITY		
1 Johnny Bench Jsy	20.00	6.00
2 Yogi Berra Pants SP/75	25.00	7.50
3 George Brett Jsy	25.00	7.50
4 Steve Carlton Jsy	20.00	6.00
5 Willie McCovey Jsy SP/125	15.00	4.50
6 Joe Morgan Pants SP/200	15.00	4.50
7 Thurman Munson Pants	30.00	9.00
8 Cal Ripken Jsy	30.00	9.00
9 Nolan Ryan Jsy	50.00	15.00
10 Ryne Sandberg Jsy	25.00	7.50
11 Ozzie Smith Jsy	20.00	6.00

2003 Flair Greats Classic Numbers Game Used Dual

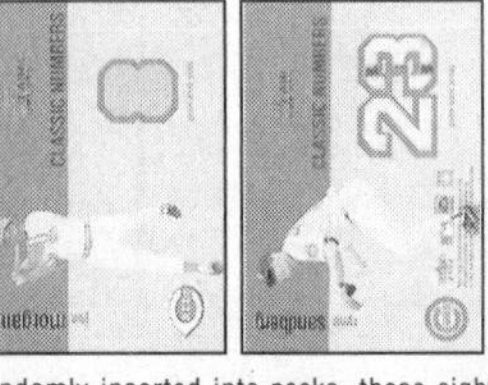

Randomly inserted into packs, these eight cards feature two players along with game-worn swatches of each of these players. Each of these cards was issued to a stated print run of 250 serial numbered sets.

Card	Nm-Mt	Ex-Mt
1 Johnny Bench Jsy	40.00	12.00
Thurman Munson Pants		
2 Yogi Berra Pants	40.00	12.00
Thurman Munson Pants		
3 Yogi Berra Pants	60.00	18.00
Cal Ripken Jsy		
4 George Brett Jsy	80.00	24.00
Nolan Ryan Jsy		
5 Willie McCovey Jsy	25.00	7.50
Johnny Bench Jsy		
6 Joe Morgan Pants	40.00	12.00
Ryne Sandberg Jsy		
7 Cal Ripken Pants	60.00	18.00
Ozzie Smith Jsy		
8 Nolan Ryan Jsy	60.00	18.00
Steve Carlton Jsy		

2003 Flair Greats Cut of History Autographs

Randomly inserted into packs, these cards feature authentic autographs of the featured player. These cards were issued to different print runs and we have notated that information in our checklist.

Card	Nm-Mt	Ex-Mt
1 Johnny Bench/161	60.00	18.00
2 Steve Carlton/506	25.00	7.50
3 Dom DiMaggio/402	50.00	15.00
4 Tony Kubek/161	50.00	15.00
5 Cal Ripken/155	175.00	52.50
6 Alan Trammell/211	25.00	7.50

2003 Flair Greats Cut of History Game Used

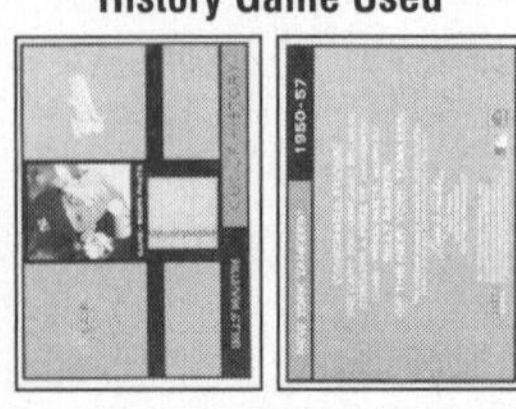

Issued at a stated rate of one in ten packs, these 27 cards feature game-used pieces of 27 of baseball's all time greats. A few players were issued in smaller quantity and we have notated that information along with their stated print run next to their name in our checklist.

Card	Nm-Mt	Ex-Mt
1 Luis Aparicio Jsy	8.00	2.40
2 Frank Baker Bat SP/50	50.00	15.00
3 Buddy Bell Bat	8.00	2.40
4 Wade Boggs Jsy SP/250	20.00	6.00
5 Steve Carlton Pants	8.00	2.40
6 Gary Carter Jsy	10.00	3.00
7 Dennis Eckersley Jsy	8.00	2.40
8 Hank Greenberg Bat SP/100	50.00	15.00
9 Catfish Hunter Jsy SP/200	20.00	6.00
10 Reggie Jackson Bat	10.00	3.00
11 Ferguson Jenkins Pants	8.00	2.40
12 Roger Maris Jsy SP/250	60.00	18.00
13 Billy Martin Pants	10.00	3.00
14 Willie McCovey Pants	8.00	2.40
15 Joe Medwick Bat	20.00	6.00
16 Eddie Murray Jsy	10.00	3.00
17 Graig Nettles Bat	8.00	2.40
18 Phil Niekro Pants	8.00	2.40
19 Paul O'Neill Jsy	10.00	3.00
20 Jim Palmer Pants	8.00	2.40
21 Kirby Puckett Bat	10.00	3.00
22 Cal Ripken Pants	25.00	7.50
23 Tom Seaver Pants	10.00	3.00
24A Alan Trammell Bat	10.00	3.00
24B Alan Trammell Jsy	10.00	3.00
25 Hoyt Wilhelm Jsy	8.00	2.40
26 Early Wynn Jsy	8.00	2.40

2003 Flair Greats of the Grain

Randomly inserted into packs, these nine cards feature all-time greats laser etched on to a wood swatch. These cards were issued to a stated print run of 50 serial numbered sets. Please note that these cards do not contain game-used wood on them.

Card	Nm-Mt	Ex-Mt
1 George Brett	150.00	45.00
2 Ty Cobb	100.00	30.00
3 Lou Gehrig	80.00	24.00
4 Eddie Mathews	100.00	30.00
5 Don Mattingly	150.00	45.00
6 Stan Musial	100.00	30.00
7 Cal Ripken	120.00	36.00
8 Babe Ruth	120.00	36.00
9 Mike Schmidt	100.00	30.00

2003 Flair Greats Hall of Fame Postmark

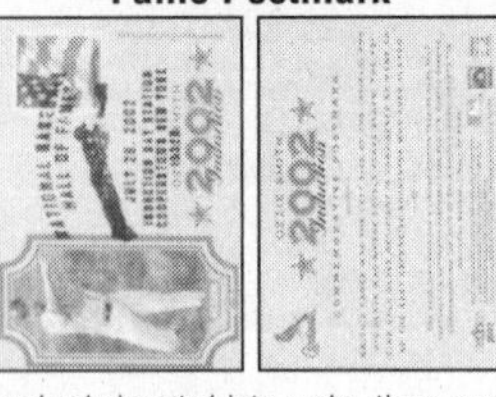

Randomly inserted into packs, these cards honor the day that Ozzie Smith was inducted into the Hall of Fame. Some of these cards were autographed and we have noted the print run for both of these cards in our checklist.

Card	Nm-Mt	Ex-Mt
1 Ozzie Smith/2002	25.00	7.50
2 Ozzie Smith AU/202	100.00	30.00

2003 Flair Greats Home Team Cuts Game Used

These cards were issued at an overall rate of one in 20 for both single or dual game used cards in the home team boxes. A few cards were issued in smaller quantities than the others and we have notated that information in our checklist.

Card	Nm-Mt	Ex-Mt
1 Wade Boggs Jsy SP/250	20.00	6.00
2 Bobby Bonds Bat	10.00	3.00
3 Carlton Fisk Jsy	15.00	4.50
4 Steve Garvey Jsy	10.00	3.00
5 Reggie Jackson Bat	15.00	4.50
6 Tom Lasorda Jsy SP/150	15.00	4.50
7 Juan Marichal Pants	10.00	3.00
8 Roger Maris Jsy SP/150	80.00	24.00
9 Billy Martin Pants	15.00	4.50
10 Willie McCovey Pants SP/200	15.00	4.50
11 Joe Medwick Bat SP/250	25.00	7.50
12 P.Reese Pants SP/75	20.00	6.00
13 Jim Rice Bat	10.00	3.00
14 R.Schoendienst Pants SP/200	15.00	4.50
15 Ozzie Smith Bat	20.00	6.00
16 Duke Snider Pants	15.00	4.50
17 Dave Winfield Bat	10.00	3.00

2003 Flair Greats Home Team Cuts Game Used Dual

These cards were issued at an overall rate of one in 20 for both single or dual game used cards in the home team boxes. A few cards were issued in smaller quantities than the others and we have notated that information in our checklist.

Card	Nm-Mt	Ex-Mt
1 Bobby Bonds Bat	40.00	12.00
Willie McCovey Pants/100		
2 Carlton Fisk Jsy	30.00	9.00
Jim Rice Bat/100		
3 Billy Martin Pants	30.00	9.00
Reggie Jackson Bat/175		
4 Pee Wee Reese Pants	30.00	9.00
Duke Snider Pants/100		
5 Red Schoendienst Pants	25.00	7.50
Joe Medwick Bat/125		

2003 Flair Greats Sweet Swatch Classic Bat

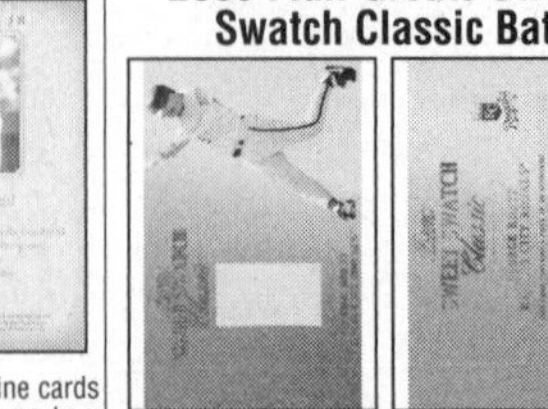

Randomly inserted into jumbo packs, these 12 cards feature game-used bat pieces of the featured players. Each player was issued to a different print run and we have notated that information in our checklist.

Card	Nm-Mt	Ex-Mt
1 Johnny Bench/175	25.00	7.50
2 George Brett/320	40.00	12.00
3 Jose Canseco/175	25.00	7.50
4 Orlando Cepeda/165	20.00	6.00
5 Andre Dawson/310	15.00	4.50
6 Reggie Jackson/155	25.00	7.50
7 Eddie Mathews/185	25.00	7.50
8 Don Mattingly/340	50.00	15.00
9 Willie McCovey/155	20.00	6.00
10 Kirby Puckett/165	25.00	7.50
11 Pee Wee Reese/165	25.00	7.50
12 Cal Ripken/305	50.00	15.00

2003 Flair Greats Sweet Swatch Classic Bat Image

These four cards partially parallel the sweet swatch classic bat insert set. Each of these cards were issued to a stated print run of less than 50 copies.

Card	Nm-Mt	Ex-Mt
1 Johnny Bench/36	80.00	24.00
2 Tony Kubek/35	60.00	18.00
3 Cal Ripken/42	150.00	45.00
4 Alan Trammell/44	60.00	18.00

2003 Flair Greats Sweet Swatch Classic Bat Image Autographs

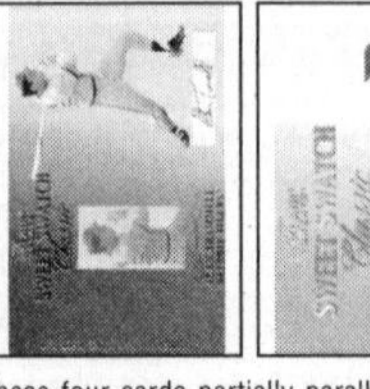

These four cards partially parallel the sweet swatch classic bat insert image set along with the player's autograph. Each of these cards were issued to a stated print run of 40 serial numbered sets.

Card	Nm-Mt	Ex-Mt
1 Johnny Bench		
2 Tony Kubek		
3 Cal Ripken		
4 Alan Trammell		

2003 Flair Greats Sweet Swatch Classic Jersey

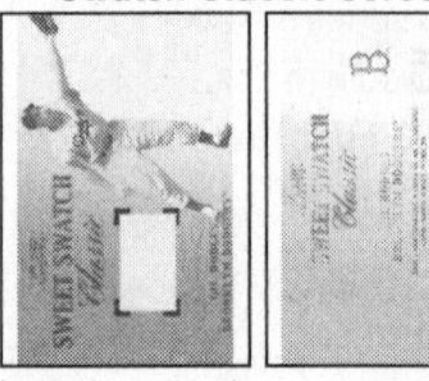

Randomly inserted into jumbo packs, these 72 cards feature game-used jersey swatches of the featured players. Each player was issued to a different print run and we have notated that information in our checklist.

Card	Nm-Mt	Ex-Mt
1 Johnny Bench Jsy/410	20.00	6.00
2 George Brett Jsy/384	40.00	12.00
3 Jose Canseco Jsy/1329	15.00	4.50
4 Jerry Coleman Jsy/528	20.00	6.00
5 Andre Dawson Jsy/335	20.00	6.00
6 Carlton Fisk Jsy/1200	15.00	4.50
7 Gil Hodges Jsy/545	20.00	6.00
8 Juan Marichal Jsy/385	20.00	6.00
9 Don Mattingly Jsy/880	40.00	12.00
10 Paul Molitor Jsy/592	20.00	6.00
11 Jim Palmer Jsy/335	20.00	6.00
12 Kirby Puckett Jsy/445	20.00	6.00
13 Cal Ripken Jsy/557	40.00	12.00
14 Nolan Ryan Jsy/590	50.00	15.00
15 Ryne Sandberg Jsy/374	30.00	9.00
17 Robin Yount Jsy/340	25.00	7.50
19 Tom Seaver Jsy/385	20.00	6.00

2003 Flair Greats Sweet Swatch Classic Patch

This 16 card set partially parallels the sweet swatch classic jersey set. Each of these cards feature a game-used patch piece and we have notated the stated print run in our checklist.

Card	Nm-Mt	Ex-Mt
PATCH MASTERPIECE PRINT RUN 1 #'d SET		
NO PATCH MP PRICING DUE TO SCARCITY		
1 Johnny Bench/59	80.00	24.00
2 George Brett/53	150.00	45.00
3 Jose Canseco/177	60.00	18.00
4 Jerry Coleman/37	50.00	15.00
5 Andre Dawson/58	50.00	15.00
6 Carlton Fisk/51	80.00	24.00
7 Juan Marichal/48	50.00	15.00
8 Don Mattingly/106	150.00	45.00
9 Paul Molitor/96	60.00	18.00
10 Jim Palmer/63	60.00	18.00
11 Kirby Puckett/72	80.00	24.00
12 Cal Ripken/69	150.00	45.00
13 Nolan Ryan/60	150.00	45.00
14 Ryne Sandberg/40	150.00	45.00
15 Tom Seaver/66	60.00	18.00
16 Robin Yount/66	100.00	30.00

1997 Flair Showcase Rodriguez Sample Strip

This three-card unperforated strip was distributed to dealers and hobby media a few

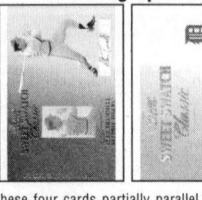

nonths prior to the release of 1997 Flair Showcase. The strip contains parallel versions of three different Alex Rodriguez cards later ssued in packs. The cards on this promotional strip are identical to the standard Rodriguez Flair Showcase cards except for the text "PROMOTIONAL SAMPLE" written diagonally across the front and back.

	Nm-Mt	Ex-Mt
NNO Alex Rodriguez Promo Strip	3.00	
Row 2, Row 1, Row 0		

1997 Flair Showcase Row 2

The 1997 Flair Showcase set (produced by Fleer) was issued in one series totalling 540 cards and was distributed in five-card packs with a suggested retail price of $4.99. Three groups of 60 cards were inserted at different rates: Cards numbered from one through 60 were inserted 1.5 cards per pack, cards numbered from 61 through 120 were inserted one every 1.5 packs and cards numbered from 1 through 120 were inserted at a rate of one per pack. This hobby exclusive set is divided into three 180-card sets (Row2/Style, Row1/Grace, and Row0/Showcase) and features holographic foil fronts with an action photo of the player silhouetted over a larger black-and-white head-shot image in the background. The thick card stock is laminated with a shiny glossy coating for a super-premium "feel." Also inserted one in every pack was a Million Dollar Moments card. Rookie Cards include Brian Giles. Finally, 25 serial-numbered Alex Rodriguez Emerald Exchange cards (good for a signed Rodriguez glove) were randomly seeded into packs. The card fronts were very similar in design to the regular Row 2 Rodriguez, except for green foil accents. The card back, however, consisted entirely of text explaining prize guidelines. The deadline to exchange the card was 8/1/98.

	Nm-Mt	Ex-Mt
COMPLETE SET (180)	80.00	24.00
COMMON CARD (1-60)	.50	.15
OMMON (61-120)	.75	.23
COMMON (121-180)	.60	.18
Andruw Jones	.50	.15
Derek Jeter	3.00	.90
Alex Rodriguez	2.00	.60
Paul Molitor	.75	.23
Jeff Bagwell	.75	.23
Scott Rolen	.75	.23
Kenny Lofton	.50	.15
Cal Ripken	4.00	1.20
Brady Anderson	.50	.15
0 Chipper Jones	2.00	.60
1 Todd Greene	.50	.15
2 Todd Walker	.50	.15
3 Billy Wagner	.50	.15
4 Craig Biggio	.75	.23
5 Kevin Orie	.50	.15
6 Hideo Nomo	1.25	.35
7 Kevin Appier	.50	.15
8 B.Trammell RC	.50	.15
9 Juan Gonzalez	1.25	.35
0 Randy Johnson	1.25	.35
1 Roger Clemens	2.50	.75
2 Johnny Damon	.50	.15
3 Ryne Sandberg	2.00	.60
4 Ken Griffey Jr.	2.00	.60
5 Barry Bonds	3.00	.90
6 Nomar Garciaparra	2.00	.60
7 Vladimir Guerrero	1.25	.35
8 Ron Gant	.50	.15
9 Joe Carter	.50	.15
0 Tim Salmon	.75	.23
1 Mike Piazza	2.00	.60
2 Barry Larkin	1.25	.35
3 Manny Ramirez	.50	.15
4 Sammy Sosa	2.00	.60
5 Frank Thomas	1.25	.35
6 Melvin Nieves	.50	.15
7 Tony Gwynn	1.50	.45
8 Gary Sheffield	.50	.15
9 Darin Erstad	.50	.15
0 Ken Caminiti	.50	.15
1 Jermaine Dye	.50	.15
2 Mo Vaughn	.50	.15
3 Raul Mondesi	.50	.15
4 Greg Maddux	2.00	.60
5 Chuck Knoblauch	.50	.15
6 Andy Pettitte	.75	.23
7 Deion Sanders	.75	.23
8 Albert Belle	.50	.15
9 Jamey Wright	.50	.15
0 Rey Ordonez	.50	.15
1 Bernie Williams	.75	.23
2 Mark McGwire	3.00	.90
3 Mike Mussina	1.25	.35
4 Bob Abreu	.50	.15
5 Reggie Sanders	.50	.15
6 Brian Jordan	.50	.15
7 Ivan Rodriguez	1.25	.35
8 Roberto Alomar	1.25	.35
9 Tim Naehring	.50	.15
0 Edgar Renteria	.50	.15
1 Dean Palmer	.75	.23
2 Benito Santiago	.75	.23
3 David Cone	.75	.23
4 Carlos Delgado	.75	.23
5 Brian Giles RC	2.00	.60
6 Alex Ochoa	.75	.23
7 Rondell White	.75	.23
8 Robin Ventura	.75	.23
9 Eric Karros	.75	.23
0 Jose Valentin	.75	.23
71 Rafael Palmeiro	1.25	.35
72 Chris Snopek	.75	.23
73 David Justice	.75	.23
74 Tom Glavine	1.25	.35
75 Rudy Pemberton	.75	.23
76 Larry Walker	.75	.23
77 Jim Thome	2.00	.60
78 Charles Johnson	.75	.23
79 Dante Powell	.75	.23
80 Derrek Lee	.75	.23
81 Jason Kendall	.75	.23
82 Todd Hollandsworth	.75	.23
83 Bernard Gilkey	.75	.23
84 Mel Rojas	.75	.23
85 Dmitri Young	.75	.23
86 Bret Boone	.75	.23
87 Pat Hentgen	.75	.23
88 Bobby Bonilla	.75	.23
89 John Wetteland	.75	.23
90 Todd Hundley	.75	.23
91 Wilton Guerrero	.75	.23
92 Geronimo Berroa	.75	.23
93 Al Martin	.75	.23
94 Danny Tartabull	.75	.23
95 Brian McRae	.75	.23
96 Steve Finley	.75	.23
97 Todd Stottlemyre	.75	.23
98 John Smoltz	1.25	.35
99 Matt Williams	.75	.23
100 Eddie Murray	2.00	.60
101 Henry Rodriguez	.75	.23
102 Marty Cordova	.75	.23
103 Juan Guzman	.75	.23
104 Chili Davis	.75	.23
105 Eric Young	.75	.23
106 Jeff Abbott	.75	.23
107 Shannon Stewart	.75	.23
108 Rocky Coppinger	.75	.23
109 Jose Canseco	1.25	.35
110 Dante Bichette	.75	.23
111 Dwight Gooden	1.25	.35
112 Scott Brosius	.75	.23
113 Steve Avery	.75	.23
114 Andres Galarraga	.75	.23
115 Sandy Alomar Jr.	.75	.23
116 Ray Lankford	.75	.23
117 Jorge Posada	1.25	.35
118 Ryan Klesko	.75	.23
119 Jay Buhner	.75	.23
120 Jose Guillen	.75	.23
121 Paul O'Neill	1.00	.30
122 Jimmy Key	.60	.18
123 Hal Morris	.60	.18
124 Travis Fryman	.60	.18
125 Jim Edmonds	.60	.18
126 Jeff Cirillo	.60	.18
127 Fred McGriff	1.00	.30
128 Alan Benes	.60	.18
129 Derek Bell	.60	.18
130 Tony Graffanino	.60	.18
131 Shawn Green	.60	.18
132 Denny Neagle	.60	.18
133 Alex Fernandez	.60	.18
134 Mickey Morandini	.60	.18
135 Royce Clayton	.60	.18
136 Jose Mesa	.60	.18
137 Edgar Martinez	1.00	.30
138 Curt Schilling	1.00	.30
139 Lance Johnson	.60	.18
140 Andy Benes	.60	.18
141 Charles Nagy	.60	.18
142 Mariano Rivera	1.00	.30
143 Mark Wohlers	.60	.18
144 Ken Hill	.60	.18
145 Jay Bell	.60	.18
146 Bob Higginson	.60	.18
147 Mark Grudzielanek	.60	.18
148 Ray Durham	.60	.18
149 John Olerud	.60	.18
150 Joey Hamilton	.60	.18
151 Trevor Hoffman	.60	.18
152 Dan Wilson	.60	.18
153 J.T. Snow	.60	.18
154 Marquis Grissom	.60	.18
155 Yamil Benitez	.60	.18
156 Rusty Greer	.60	.18
157 Darryl Kile	.60	.18
158 Ismael Valdes	.60	.18
159 Jeff Conine	.60	.18
160 Darren Daulton	.60	.18
161 Chan Ho Park	.60	.18
162 Troy Percival	.60	.18
163 Wade Boggs	.75	.23
164 Dave Nilsson	.60	.18
165 Vinny Castilla	.60	.18
166 Kevin Brown	.60	.18
167 Dennis Eckersley	.60	.18
168 Wendell Magee Jr.	.60	.18
169 John Jaha	.60	.18
170 Garret Anderson	.60	.18
171 Jason Giambi	1.50	.45
172 Mark Grace	1.00	.30
173 Tony Clark	.60	.18
174 Moises Alou	.60	.18
175 Brett Butler	.60	.18
176 Cecil Fielder	.60	.18
177 Chris Widger	.60	.18
178 Doug Drabek	.60	.18
179 Ellis Burks	.60	.18
180 S. Hasegawa RC	1.50	.45
NNO Alex Rodriguez Glove EXCH/25		

1997 Flair Showcase Row 1

Randomly inserted in packs at various rates: Cards number 1 through 60 at a rate of one in 2.5 packs, cards numbered 61 through 120 at one every two packs and cards numbered from 121 through 180 at a rate of one every three packs. This 180-card Grace set is parallel to the base Flair Showcase Row 2 (Style) set and features holographic foil fronts with an action photo of the player silhouetted over a larger color head-shot image in the background.

Nm-Mt Ex-Mt

*STARS 1-60: .75X TO 2X ROW 2
*STARS 61-120: .4X TO 1X ROW 2
*ROOKIES 61-120: .5X TO 1.25X ROW 2
*ROOKIES 61-120: .5X TO 1.25X ROW 2

1997 Flair Showcase Row 0

Randomly inserted in various rates depending on the card number: Cards numbered one through 60 were inserted one every 24 packs, cards numbered 61 through 120 at a rate of one per 12 and cards numbered 121 through 180 at a rate of one every five packs. This 180-card Showcase set is parallel to the base Flair Showcase Row 2 (Style) set and features holographic foil fronts with a head-shot image of the player silhouetted over a larger player action-shot in the background.

Nm-Mt Ex-Mt

*STARS 1-60: 4X TO 10X ROW 2
*STARS 61-120: 1.25X TO 3X ROW 2
*ROOKIES 61-120: 1.5X TO 4X ROW 2
*STARS 121-180: 1X TO 2.5X ROW 2

1997 Flair Showcase Legacy Collection Row 2

Randomly inserted in packs at a rate of one in 30 (cumulatively between all three rows of Legacy), this 180-card set is parallel to the regular set. Only 100 sequentially numbered sets were produced, each featuring an "alternate" player photo printed on a matte finish/foil stamped card.

Nm-Mt Ex-Mt

*LC ROW 2 1-60: 12.5X TO 30X BASIC
*LC ROW 2 61-120: 8X TO 20X BASIC
*LC ROW 2 RC'S 61-120: 6X TO 15X BASIC
*LC ROW 2 121-180: 10X TO 25X BASIC

1997 Flair Showcase Legacy Collection Row 1

Randomly inserted in packs at a rate of one in 30 (cumulatively between all three rows of Legacy), this 180-card set is parallel to the regular set. Only 100 sequentially numbered sets were produced, each featuring an "alternate" player photo printed on a matte finish/foil stamped card.

Nm-Mt Ex-Mt

*LC ROW 1 1-60: 12.5X TO 30X BASIC
*LC ROW 1 61-120: 8X TO 20X BASIC
*LC ROW 1 RC'S 61-120: 6X TO 15X BASIC
*LC ROW 1 121-180: 10X TO 25X BASIC

1997 Flair Showcase Legacy Collection Row 0

Randomly inserted in packs at a rate of one in 30 (cumulatively between all three rows of Legacy), this 180-card set is parallel to the regular set. Only 100 sequentially numbered sets were produced, each featuring an "alternate" player photo printed on a matte finish/foil stamped card.

Nm-Mt Ex-Mt

*LC ROW 0 1-60: 12.5X TO 30X BASIC
*LC ROW 0 61-120: 8X TO 20X BASIC
*LC ROW 0 RC'S 61-120: 6X TO 15X BASIC
*LC ROW 0 121-180: 10X TO 25X BASIC

1997 Flair Showcase Diamond Cuts

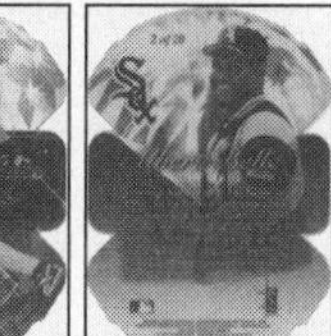

Randomly inserted in packs at a rate of one in 20, this 20-card set features color images of baseball's brightest stars silhouetted on a holofoil-stamped die-cut diamond-design background.

	Nm-Mt	Ex-Mt
COMPLETE SET (20)	150.00	45.00
1 Jeff Bagwell	4.00	1.20
2 Albert Belle	2.50	.75
3 Ken Caminiti	2.50	.75
4 Juan Gonzalez	6.00	1.80
5 Ken Griffey Jr.	10.00	3.00
6 Tony Gwynn	8.00	2.40
7 Todd Hundley	4.00	1.20
8 Andruw Jones	2.50	.75
9 Chipper Jones	10.00	3.00
10 Greg Maddux	10.00	3.00
11 Mark McGwire	15.00	4.50
12 Mike Piazza	10.00	3.00
13 Derek Jeter	15.00	4.50
14 Manny Ramirez	2.50	.75
15 Cal Ripken	20.00	6.00
16 Alex Rodriguez	10.00	3.00
17 Frank Thomas	6.00	1.80
18 Mo Vaughn	2.50	.75
19 Bernie Williams	4.00	1.20
20 Matt Williams	4.00	1.20

1997 Flair Showcase Hot Gloves

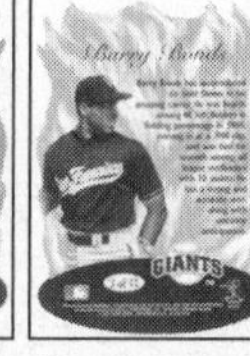

Randomly inserted in packs at a rate of one in 90, this 15-card set features color images of baseball's top glovemen silhouetted against a die-cut flame and glove background with temperature-sensitive inks.

	Nm-Mt	Ex-Mt
COMPLETE SET (15)	400.00	120.00
1 Roberto Alomar	20.00	6.00
2 Barry Bonds	50.00	15.00
3 Juan Gonzalez	20.00	6.00
4 Ken Griffey Jr.	30.00	9.00
5 Marquis Grissom	10.00	3.00
6 Derek Jeter	50.00	15.00
7 Chipper Jones	30.00	9.00
8 Barry Larkin	20.00	6.00
9 Kenny Lofton	8.00	2.40
10 Greg Maddux	30.00	9.00
11 Mike Piazza	30.00	9.00
12 Cal Ripken	60.00	18.00
13 Alex Rodriguez	30.00	9.00
14 Ivan Rodriguez	20.00	6.00
15 Frank Thomas	20.00	6.00

1997 Flair Showcase Wave of the Future

Randomly inserted in packs at a rate of one in four, this 27-card set features color images of top rookies silhouetted against a background of an embossed wave design with simulated sand.

	Nm-Mt	Ex-Mt
COMPLETE SET (27)	50.00	15.00
1 Todd Greene	1.00	.30
2 Andruw Jones	1.50	.45
3 Randall Simon	2.00	.60
4 Wady Almonte	1.00	.30
5 Pat Cline	1.00	.30
6 Jeff Abbott	1.00	.30
7 Justin Towle	1.00	.30
8 Richie Sexson	1.50	.45
9 Bubba Trammell	1.50	.45
10 Bob Abreu	1.50	.45
11 David Arias-Ortiz	4.00	1.20
12 Todd Walker	1.50	.45
13 Orlando Cabrera	1.50	.45
14 Vladimir Guerrero	3.00	.90
15 Ricky Ledee	1.50	.45
16 Jorge Posada	2.00	.60
17 Ruben Rivera	1.00	.30
18 Scott Spiezio	1.00	.30
19 Scott Rolen	2.00	.60
20 Emil Brown	1.00	.30
21 Jose Guillen	1.50	.45
22 T.J. Staton	1.00	.30
23 Eli Marrero	1.00	.30
24 Fernando Tatis	3.00	.90
25 Ryan Jones	1.00	.30
WF1 Hideki Irabu	1.50	.45
WF2 Jose Cruz Jr.	4.00	1.20

1998 Flair Showcase Ripken Sample Strip

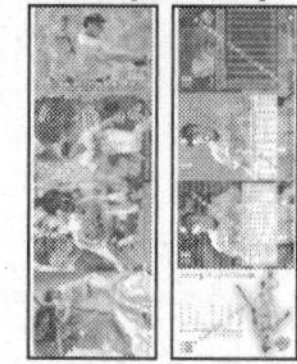

This four-card unperforated strip was distributed to dealers and hobby media a few months prior to the release of 1998 Flair Showcase. The strip contains parallel versions of four different Cal Ripken cards later issued in packs. The cards on this promotional strip are identical to the standard Ripken Flair Showcase cards except for the text "PROMOTIONAL SAMPLE" written diagonally across the front and back.

	Nm-Mt	Ex-Mt
NNO Cal Ripken Promo Strip	3.00	.90
Row 3 Cal Ripken Flair		
Row 2 Cal Ripken Style		
Row 1 Cal Ripken Grace		
Row 0 Cal Ripken Showcase		

1998 Flair Showcase Row 3

This set (produced by Fleer) was issued in five card packs which retailed for $4.99 per pack and were released in July, 1998. Each player was featured in four rows with Row 3 being the easiest to obtain from opening packs. This 120 card set features two photos of the player on the front. The Row 3 cards were inserted in different ratios depending on which numbers they are. The complete odds are listed below for each group of 30 cards. Cards numbered 1-30 were seeded one every 9/10th of a pack; cards numbered 31-60 were seeded one every 1.1 packs; cards numbered 61-90 were seeded one every 1.5 packs and cards 91-120 were seeded one every two packs. Rookie Cards include Maggio Ordonez.

	Nm-Mt	Ex-Mt
COMPLETE SET (120)	60.00	18.00
COMMON CARD (1-30)	.50	.15
COMMON CARD (31-60)	.50	.15
COMMON CARD (61-90)	.60	.18
COMMON CARD (91-120)	.75	.23
1 Ken Griffey Jr.	2.00	.60
2 Travis Lee	.50	.15
3 Frank Thomas	1.25	.35
4 Ben Grieve	.50	.15
5 Nomar Garciaparra	2.00	.60
6 Jose Cruz Jr.	.50	.15
7 Alex Rodriguez	2.00	.60
8 Cal Ripken	4.00	1.20
9 Mark McGwire	3.00	.90
10 Chipper Jones	1.25	.35
11 Paul Konerko	.50	.15
12 Todd Helton	.75	.23
13 Greg Maddux	2.00	.60
14 Derek Jeter	3.00	.90
15 Jaret Wright	.50	.15
16 Livan Hernandez	.50	.15
17 Mike Piazza	2.00	.60
18 Juan Encarnacion	.50	.15
19 Tony Gwynn	1.50	.45
20 Scott Rolen	.75	.23
21 Roger Clemens	2.50	.75
22 Tony Clark	.50	.15
23 Albert Belle	.50	.15
24 Mo Vaughn	.50	.15
25 Andruw Jones	.50	.15
26 Jason Dickson	.50	.15
27 Fernando Tatis	.50	.15
28 Ivan Rodriguez	1.25	.35
29 Ricky Ledee	.50	.15
30 Darin Erstad	.50	.15
31 Brian Rose	.50	.15
32 Magglio Ordonez RC	4.00	1.20
33 Larry Walker	.75	.23
34 Bobby Higginson	.50	.15
35 Chili Davis	.50	.15
36 Barry Bonds	3.00	.90
37 Vladimir Guerrero	1.25	.35
38 Jeff Bagwell	.75	.23
39 Kenny Lofton	.50	.15
40 Ryan Klesko	.50	.15
41 Mike Cameron	.50	.15
42 Charles Johnson	.50	.15
43 Andy Pettitte	.75	.23
44 Juan Gonzalez	1.25	.35
45 Tim Salmon	.75	.23
46 Hideki Irabu	.50	.15
47 Paul Molitor	.75	.23
48 Edgar Renteria	.50	.15
49 Manny Ramirez	.50	.15
50 Jim Edmonds	.50	.15
51 Bernie Williams	.75	.23
52 Roberto Alomar	1.25	.35
53 David Justice	.50	.15
54 Rey Ordonez	.50	.15
55 Ken Caminiti	.50	.15
56 Jose Guillen	.50	.15
57 Randy Johnson	1.25	.35
58 Brady Anderson	.50	.15
59 Hideo Nomo	1.25	.35
60 Tino Martinez	.75	.23
61 John Smoltz	1.00	.30
62 Joe Carter	.60	.18
63 Matt Williams	.60	.18
64 Robin Ventura	.60	.18
65 Barry Larkin	1.50	.45
66 Dante Bichette	.60	.18
67 Travis Fryman	.60	.18
68 Gary Sheffield	.60	.18
69 Eric Karros	.60	.18
70 Matt Stairs	.60	.18
71 Al Martin	.60	.18
72 Jay Buhner	.60	.18
73 Ray Lankford	.60	.18
74 Carlos Delgado	.60	.18
75 Edgardo Alfonzo	.60	.18
76 Rondell White	.60	.18
77 Chuck Knoblauch	.60	.18
78 Raul Mondesi	.60	.18
79 Johnny Damon	.60	.18
80 Matt Morris	.60	.18
81 Tom Glavine	1.00	.30
82 Kevin Brown	1.00	.30
83 Garret Anderson	.60	.18
84 Mike Mussina	1.50	.45
85 Pedro Martinez	1.50	.45
86 Craig Biggio	1.00	.30
87 Darryl Kile	.60	.18
88 Rafael Palmeiro	1.00	.30
89 Jim Thome	1.50	.45
90 Andres Galarraga	.60	.18
91 Sammy Sosa	3.00	.90
92 Willie Greene	.75	.23
93 Vinny Castilla	.75	.23
94 Justin Thompson	.75	.23
95 Jeff King	.75	.23
96 Jeff Cirillo	.75	.23
97 Mark Grudzielanek	.75	.23
98 Brad Radke	.75	.23
99 John Olerud	.75	.23
100 Curt Schilling	1.25	.35
101 Steve Finley	.75	.23
102 J.T. Snow	.75	.23
103 Edgar Martinez	1.25	.35
104 Wilson Alvarez	.75	.23
105 Rusty Greer	.75	.23
106 Pat Hentgen	.75	.23
107 David Cone	.75	.23
108 Fred McGriff	1.25	.35
109 Jason Giambi	2.00	.60
110 Tony Womack	.75	.23
111 Bernard Gilkey	.75	.23
112 Alan Benes	.75	.23
113 Mark Grace	1.25	.35
114 Reggie Sanders	.75	.23
115 Moises Alou	.75	.23
116 John Jaha	.75	.23
117 Henry Rodriguez	.75	.23
118 Dean Palmer	.75	.23
119 Mike Lieberthal	.75	.23
120 Shawn Estes	.75	.23

1998 Flair Showcase Row 2

These Row 2 cards are parallel to regular base set. Similar to the other rows there is different pull ratios for each group of 30 cards as follows. Cards numbered 1 through 30 are seeded one every two packs; cards numbered from 31 through 60 are seeded one every 2.5 packs; cards numbered from 61 through 90 are seeded one every four packs and cards numbered from 91-120 are seeded one every 3.5 packs.

	Nm-Mt	Ex-Mt
COMPLETE SET (120)	100.00	30.00

*STARS 1-30: .6X TO 1.5X ROW 3 .....
*STARS 31-60: .5X TO 1.25X ROW 3 .
*STARS 61-90: .6X TO 1.5X ROW 3 ...
*STARS 91-120: .5X TO 1.25X ROW 3

1998 Flair Showcase Row 1

These Row 1 cards are parallel to regular base set. Similar to the other rows there is different pull ratios for each group of 30 cards as follows. Cards numbered from 1 through 30 are inserted one every 16 packs; cards numbered from 31 through 60 are inserted one every 24 packs; cards numbered from 61 through 90 are inserted one every six packs and cards numbered from 91 through 120 are inserted one every 10 packs.

Nm-Mt Ex-Mt

*STARS 1-30: 2X TO 5X ROW 3 ....
*STARS 31-60: 2.5X TO 6X ROW 3 ....
*ROOKIES 31-60: 2.5X TO 6X ROW 3
*STARS 61-90: .75X TO 2X ROW 3 ....
*STARS 91-120: 1X TO 2.5X ROW 3 ..

1998 Flair Showcase Row 0

These Row 0 cards are parallel to regular base set. These cards are serial numbered and get more plentiful as they are numbered higher in the set. Serial numbering is as follows: Cards numbered from 1 through 30 are serial numbered to 250, cards numbered from 31 through 60 are serial numbered to 500, cards numbered from 61 through 90 are serial numbered to 1000 and cards numbered 91 through 120 are serial numbered to 2000.

Nm-Mt Ex-Mt

*STARS 1-30: 6X TO 15X ROW 3 ......
*STARS 31-60: 5X TO 12X ROW 3 .....
*ROOKIES 31-60: 5X TO 12X ROW 3 .
*STARS 61-90: 3X TO 8X ROW 3 ....
*STARS 91-120: 1.5X TO 4X ROW 3 ..

1998 Flair Showcase Legacy Collection Row 3

Yet another parallel version of the Flair Showcase set, these cards are serial numbered to 100 each.

Nm-Mt Ex-Mt

*STARS 1-30: 10X TO 25X BASIC ROW 3
*STARS 31-60: 10X TO 25X BASIC ROW 3
*ROOKIES 31-60: 8X TO 20X BASIC ROW 3
*STARS 61-90: 8X TO 20X ROW 3 .....
*STARS 91-120: 6X TO 15X BASIC ROW 3

1998 Flair Showcase Legacy Collection Row 2

Yet another parallel version of the Flair Showcase set, these cards are serial numbered to 100 each.

Nm-Mt Ex-Mt

*STARS 1-30: 10X TO 25X BASIC ROW 3
*STARS 31-60: 10X TO 25X BASIC ROW 3
*ROOKIES 31-60: 8X TO 20X BASIC ROW 2
*STARS 61-90: 8X TO 20X ROW 3 .....
*STARS 91-120: 6X TO 15X BASIC ROW 3

1998 Flair Showcase Legacy Collection Row 1

Yet another parallel version of the Flair Showcase set, these cards are serial numbered to 100 each.

Nm-Mt Ex-Mt

*STARS 1-30: 10X TO 25X BASIC ROW 3
*STARS 31-60: 10X TO 25X BASIC ROW 3
*ROOKIES 31-60: 8X TO 20X BASIC ROW 1
*STARS 61-90: 8X TO 20X ROW 3 .....
*STARS 91-120: 6X TO 15X BASIC ROW 3

1998 Flair Showcase Legacy Collection Row 0

Yet another parallel version of the Flair Showcase set, these cards are serial numbered to 100 each.

Nm-Mt Ex-Mt

*STARS 1-30: 10X TO 25X BASIC ROW 3
*STARS 31-60: 10X TO 25X BASIC ROW 3
*ROOKIES 31-60: 8X TO 20X BASIC ROW 3
*STARS 61-90: 8X TO 20X ROW 3 .....
*STARS 91-120: 6X TO 15X BASIC ROW 3

1998 Flair Showcase Perfect 10

Sequentially numbered to 10, this 10-card insert features color player photography using silk-screen technology. While no pricing is available due to scarcity, we provide a checklist for identification purposes.

	Nm-Mt	Ex-Mt
1 Ken Griffey Jr.		
2 Cal Ripken		
3 Frank Thomas		
4 Mike Piazza		
5 Greg Maddux		
6 Nomar Garciaparra		
7 Mark McGwire		
8 Scott Rolen		
9 Alex Rodriguez		
10 Roger Clemens		

1998 Flair Showcase Wave of the Future

Randomly inserted in packs at a rate of one in 20, this 12-card insert feature color action photography on cards filled with vegetable oil and sparkles in an attempt to mimic ocean waters.

	Nm-Mt	Ex-Mt
COMPLETE SET (12)	25.00	7.50
1 Travis Lee	2.00	.60
2 Todd Helton	3.00	.90
3 Ben Grieve	2.00	.60
4 Juan Encarnacion	2.00	.60
5 Brad Fullmer	2.00	.60
6 Ruben Rivera	2.00	.60
7 Paul Konerko	2.00	.60
8 Derrek Lee	2.00	.60
9 Mike Lowell	5.00	1.50
10 Maggio Ordonez	5.00	1.50
11 Rich Butler	2.00	.60
12 Eli Marrero	2.00	.60

1999 Flair Showcase Samples

These sample cards were distributed to dealers and hobby media as a complete set in a three-card clear cello-wrapped pack several weeks prior to the national release of 1999 Flair Showcase. Company spokesperson Scott Rolen was the only player featured. Each card is parallel to it's accompanying basic issue card except for the text "PROMOTIONAL SAMPLE" running diagonally across the front and back.

	Nm-Mt	Ex-Mt
COMPLETE SET (3)	3.00	.90
COMMON ROLEN (1-3)	1.00	.30

1999 Flair Showcase Row 3

This 144-card set was distributed in five-card packs with a suggested retail price of $4.99 and features two color player photos on the front with full rainbow holofoil, silver foil and embossing. This base set is considered the "Power" level. The set was broken into three separate tiers of 28 card subsets as follows: Cards numbered from 1 through 48 were seeded one every .9 packs; cards numbered 49 through 96 were seeded one every 1.1 packs and cards numbered 97 through 144 were seeded one every 1.2 packs. Rookie Cards include Pat Burrell.

	Nm-Mt	Ex-Mt
COMPLETE SET (144)	60.00	18.00
COMMON CARD (1-48)	.50	.15
COMMON CARD (49-96)	.50	.15
COMMON CARD (97-144)	.60	.18
1 Mark McGwire	3.00	.90
2 Sammy Sosa	2.00	.60
3 Ken Griffey Jr.	2.00	.60
4 Chipper Jones	1.25	.35
5 Ben Grieve	.50	.15
6 J.D. Drew	.50	.15
7 Jeff Bagwell	.75	.23
8 Cal Ripken	4.00	1.20
9 Tony Gwynn	1.50	.45
10 Nomar Garciaparra	2.00	.60
11 Travis Lee	.50	.15
12 Troy Glaus UER Spelled Tony on back	.75	.23
13 Mike Piazza	2.00	.60
14 Alex Rodriguez	2.00	.60
15 Kevin Brown	.75	.23
16 Darin Erstad	.50	.15
17 Scott Rolen	.75	.23
18 Micah Bowie RC	.50	.15
19 Juan Gonzalez	1.25	.35
20 Kerry Wood	1.25	.35
21 Roger Clemens	2.50	.75
22 Derek Jeter	3.00	.90
23 Pat Burrell RC	5.00	1.50
24 Tim Salmon	.75	.23
25 Barry Bonds	3.00	.90
26 Roosevelt Brown RC	.50	.15
27 Vladimir Guerrero	1.25	.35
28 Randy Johnson	1.25	.35
29 Mo Vaughn	.50	.15
30 Fernando Seguignol	.50	.15
31 Greg Maddux	2.00	.60
32 Tony Clark	.50	.15
33 Eric Chavez	.50	.15
34 Kris Benson	.50	.15
35 Frank Thomas	1.25	.35
36 Mario Encarnacion RC	.50	.15
37 Gabe Kapler	.50	.15
38 Jeremy Giambi	.50	.15
39 Peter Tucci	.50	.15
40 Manny Ramirez	.50	.15
41 Albert Belle	.50	.15
42 Warren Morris	.50	.15
43 Michael Barrett	.50	.15
44 Andruw Jones	.50	.15
45 Carlos Delgado	.50	.15
46 Jaret Wright	.50	.15
47 Juan Encarnacion	.50	.15
48 Scott Hunter RC	.50	.15
49 Tino Martinez	.75	.23
50 Craig Biggio	.75	.23
51 Jim Thome	1.25	.35
52 Vinny Castilla	.50	.15
53 Tom Glavine	.75	.23
54 Bob Higginson	.50	.15
55 Moises Alou	.50	.15
56 Robin Ventura	.50	.15
57 Bernie Williams	.75	.23
58 Pedro Martinez	1.25	.35
59 Greg Vaughn	.50	.15
60 Ray Lankford	.50	.15
61 Jose Canseco	1.25	.35
62 Ivan Rodriguez	1.25	.35
63 Shawn Green	.50	.15
64 Rafael Palmeiro	.75	.23
65 Ellis Burks	.50	.15
66 Jason Kendall	.50	.15
67 David Wells	.50	.15
68 Rondell White	.50	.15
69 Gary Sheffield	.50	.15
70 Ken Caminiti	.50	.15
71 Cliff Floyd	.50	.15
72 Larry Walker	.75	.23
73 Bartolo Colon	.50	.15
74 Barry Larkin	1.25	.35
75 Calvin Pickering	.50	.15
76 Jim Edmonds	.50	.15
77 Henry Rodriguez	.50	.15
78 Roberto Alomar	1.25	.35
79 Andres Galarraga	.50	.15
80 Richie Sexson	.50	.15
81 Todd Helton	.75	.23
82 Damion Easley	.50	.15
83 Livan Hernandez	.50	.15
84 Carlos Beltran	.50	.15
85 Todd Hundley	.50	.15
86 Todd Walker	.50	.15
87 Scott Brosius	.50	.15
88 Bob Abreu	.50	.15
89 Corey Koskie	.50	.15
90 Ruben Rivera	.50	.15
91 Edgar Renteria	.50	.15
92 Quinton McCracken	.50	.15
93 Bernard Gilkey	.50	.15
94 Shannon Stewart	.50	.15
95 Dustin Hermanson	.50	.15
96 Mike Caruso	.50	.15
97 Alex Gonzalez	.60	.18
98 Raul Mondesi	.60	.18
99 David Cone	.60	.18
100 Curt Schilling	1.00	.30
101 Brian Giles	.60	.18
102 Edgar Martinez	1.00	.30
103 Rolando Arrojo	.60	.18
104 Derek Bell	.60	.18
105 Denny Neagle	.60	.18
106 Marquis Grissom	.60	.18
107 Bret Boone	.60	.18
108 Mike Mussina	1.50	.45
109 John Smoltz	1.00	.30
110 Brett Tomko	.60	.18
111 David Justice	.60	.18
112 Andy Pettitte	1.00	.30
113 Eric Karros	.60	.18
114 Dante Bichette	.60	.18
115 Jeromy Burnitz	.60	.18
116 Paul Konerko	.60	.18
117 Steve Finley	.60	.18
118 Ricky Ledee	.60	.18
119 Edgardo Alfonzo	.60	.18
120 Dean Palmer	.60	.18
121 Rusty Greer	.60	.18
122 Luis Gonzalez	.60	.18
123 Randy Winn	.60	.18
124 Jeff Kent	.60	.18
125 Doug Glanville	.60	.18
126 Justin Thompson	.60	.18
127 Bret Saberhagen	.60	.18
128 Wade Boggs	1.00	.30
129 Al Leiter	.60	.18
130 Paul O'Neill	1.00	.30
131 Chan Ho Park	.60	.18
132 Johnny Damon	.60	.18
133 Darryl Kile	.60	.18
134 Reggie Sanders	.60	.18
135 Kevin Millwood	.60	.18
136 Charles Johnson	.60	.18
137 Ray Durham	.60	.18
138 Rico Brogna	.60	.18
139 Matt Williams	.60	.18
140 Sandy Alomar Jr.	.60	.18
141 Jeff Cirillo	.60	.18
142 Devon White	.60	.18
143 Andy Benes	.60	.18
144 Mike Stanley	.60	.18

1999 Flair Showcase Row 2

This 144-card set is parallel to the Row 1 or base set and features two action player photos with embossed jersey-like background printed on full rainbow holofoil cards. This set is called the "Passion" level. Seeding rates are as follows, cards numbered one through 48 are seeded one every three packs; cards numbered 49 through 96 are seeded one every 1.33 packs and cards numbered 97-144 are seeded one every two packs.

Nm-Mt Ex-Mt

COMPLETE SET (144) ....
*STARS 1-48: 1X TO 2.5X ROW 3 ......
*ROOKIES 1-48: 1.25X TO 3X ROW 3
*STARS 49-96: .5X TO 1.25X ROW 3 .
*STARS 97-144: .5X TO 1.25X ROW 3

1999 Flair Showcase Row 1

This 144-card set is parallel to the base set and features three photos of the same player on a plastic laminate individual numbered card. Cards 1-48 are serially numbered to 1500; Cards 49-96 to 3000; Cards 97-144 to 6000. This set is the "Showcase" level.

Nm-Mt Ex-Mt

*STARS 1-48: 4X TO 10X ROW 3 ....
*ROOKIES 1-48: 4X TO 10X ROW 3 ...
*STARS 49-96: 2.5X TO 6X ROW 3 ....
*STARS 97-144: 1.25X TO 3X ROW 3

1999 Flair Showcase Legacy Collection

Randomly inserted in packs, this set is a blue foil parallel version of the regular Flair Showcase set. Only 99 sequentially numbered sets were produced for each Row. Similar to the regular Showcase set, each player has three different cards. Therefore, in actuality, 297 cards of each player were produced.

Nm-Mt Ex-Mt

*STARS 1-48: 12.5X TO 25X ROW 3 ..
*ROOKIES 1-48: 7.5X TO 15X ROW 3
*STARS 49-96: 12.5X TO 25X ROW 3
*STARS 97-144: 10X TO 20X ROW 3 .

1999 Flair Showcase Masterpiece

Randomly inserted into packs, three versions of this 144-card set were created as exclusive one of one parallels. Only one of each card was printed with purple foil stamping on the fronts and "The Only 1 of 1 Masterpiece" printed on the backs. No pricing is available due to scarcity.

Nm-Mt Ex-Mt

PRINT RUN 1 SERIAL #'d SET FOR EACH ROW
NOT PRICED DUE TO SCARCITY ....

1999 Flair Showcase Measure of Greatness

Randomly inserted into packs, this 15-card set features color photos of superstars who are closing in on milestones of all-time great players. Only 500 serial-numbered cards were produced.

	Nm-Mt	Ex-Mt
COMPLETE SET (15)	400.00	120.00
1 Roger Clemens	30.00	9.00
2 Nomar Garciaparra	25.00	7.50
3 Juan Gonzalez	15.00	4.50
4 Ken Griffey Jr.	25.00	7.50
5 Vladimir Guerrero	15.00	4.50
6 Tony Gwynn	20.00	6.00
7 Derek Jeter	40.00	12.00
8 Chipper Jones	15.00	4.50
9 Mark McGwire	40.00	12.00
10 Mike Piazza	25.00	7.50
11 Manny Ramirez	6.00	1.80
12 Cal Ripken	50.00	15.00
13 Alex Rodriguez	25.00	7.50
14 Sammy Sosa	25.00	7.50
15 Frank Thomas	15.00	4.50

1999 Flair Showcase Wave of the Future

Randomly inserted into packs, this 15-card set features color photos of young stars. Each card is serially numbered to 1000.

	Nm-Mt	Ex-Mt
COMPLETE SET (15)	100.00	30.00
1 Kerry Wood	10.00	3.00
2 Ben Grieve	5.00	1.50
3 J.D. Drew	5.00	1.50
4 Juan Encarnacion	5.00	1.50
5 Travis Lee	5.00	1.50
6 Todd Helton	8.00	2.40
7 Troy Glaus	8.00	2.40
8 Ricky Ledee	5.00	1.50
9 Eric Chavez	5.00	1.50
10 Ben Davis	5.00	1.50
11 George Lombard	5.00	1.50
12 Jeremy Giambi	5.00	1.50
13 Roosevelt Brown	5.00	1.50
14 Pat Burrell	15.00	4.50
15 Preston Wilson	5.00	1.50

1959 Fleer Ted Williams

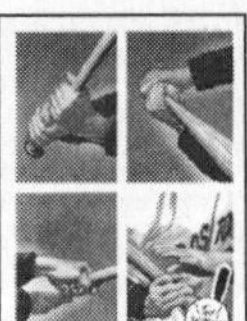

The cards in this 80-card set measure 2 1/2" by 3 1/2". The 1959 Fleer set, with a catalog designation of R418-1, portrays the life of Ted Williams. The wording of the wrapper, "Baseball's Greatest Series," has led to speculation that Fleer contemplated similar sets honoring other baseball immortals, but chose to develop instead the 1960 and 1961 issues. These packs contained either six or eight cards. The packs cost a nickel and were packed 24 to a box which were packed 24 to a case. Card number 68, which was withdrawn early in production, is considered scarce and has even been counterfeited; the fake has a rosy coloration and a cross-hatch pattern visible over the picture area. The card numbering is arranged essentially in chronological order.

	NM	Ex
COMPLETE SET (80)	1800.00	900.00
WRAPPER (6-CARD)	125.00	60.00
WRAPPER (8-CARD)	150.00	75.00
1 Ted Williams The Early Years Choosing up sides on the sandlots	100.00	50.00
2 Ted Williams Babe Ruth Meeting boyhood idol Babe Ruth	100.00	50.00
3 Ted Williams Practice Makes Perfect At place practicing on the sandlots	15.00	7.50
4 Ted Williams Learns Fine Points Sliding at Herbert Hoover High	12.00	6.00
5 Ted Williams Ted's Fame Spreads At plate at Herbert Hoover High	12.00	6.00
6 Ted Williams Ted Turns Pro Portrait San Diego Padres PCL League uniform)	20.00	10.00
7 Ted Williams From Mound to Plate At plate San Diego Padres, PCL	15.00	7.50
8 Ted Williams 1937 First Full Season Making a leaping catch	15.00	7.50
9 Ted Williams Eddie Collins First Step to Majors	18.00	9.00
10 Ted Williams Gunning as Pastime Wearing hunting gear, taking aim	12.00	6.00
11 Ted Williams Jimmie Foxx First Spring Training	35.00	17.50
12 Ted Williams Burning Up Minors Pitching for Minneapolis American Association	18.00	9.00
13 Ted Williams 1939 Shows Will Stay Follow-through	15.00	7.50
14 Ted Williams Outstanding Rookie '39 Follow-through	15.00	7.50
15 Ted Williams Licks Sophomore Jinx Sliding into third base for a triple	18.00	9.00
16 Ted Williams 1941 Greatest Year Follow-through at plate	15.00	7.50
17 Ted Williams How Ted Hit .400 Youthful Williams as he looked in '41	35.00	17.50
18 Ted Williams 1941 All Star Hero Crossing plate after home run	18.00	9.00
19 Ted Williams Wins Triple Crown Crossing plate at Fenway Park	15.00	7.50
20 Ted Williams On to Naval Training In training plane at Amherst College	15.00	7.50
21 Ted Williams Honors for Williams Receiving 1942 Sporting News POY	15.00	7.50
22 Ted Williams 1944 Ted Solos In cockpit at Pensacola, FL Navy Air Station	12.00	6.00
23 Ted Williams Williams Wins Wings Wearing Naval Aviation Cadet uniform	15.00	7.50
24 Ted Williams 1945 Sharpshooter Taking Naval eye test	12.00	6.00
25 Ted Williams 1945 Ted Discharged In cockpit, giving the thumbs up	15.00	7.50
26 Ted Williams Off to Flying Start In batters box spring training, 1946	15.00	7.50
27 Ted Williams 7/9/46 One Man Show Riding blooper pitch out of park	15.00	7.50
28 Ted Williams The Williams Shift Diagram of Cleveland Indians position shift to defense Williams	12.00	6.00
29 Ted Williams Ted Hits for Cycle Close-up of follow through	18.00	9.00
30 Ted Williams Beating Williams Shift	15.00	7.50

Crossing plate after home run
31 Ted Williams 18.00 9.00
Sox Lose Series
Sliding across plate
Sept. 14, 1946
32 Ted Williams 15.00 7.50
Joseph Cashman
Most Valuable Player
Receiving MVP Award
33 Ted Williams 12.00 6.00
Another Triple Crown
Famous Williams' Grip
34 Ted Williams 12.00 6.00
Runs Scored Record
Sliding into 2nd base
in 1947 AS Game
35 Ted Williams 15.00 7.50
Sox Miss Pennant
Checking weight on
new 36 oz. hickory bat
36 Ted Williams 15.00 7.50
Banner Year for Ted
Bunting down the
3rd base line
37 Ted Williams 15.00 7.50
1949 Sox Miss Again
Two moods: grim and determined
smiling and happy
38 Ted Williams 15.00 7.50
1949 Power Rampage
Full shot of his
batting follow through
39 Ted Williams 20.00 10.00
Joe Cronin
Eddie Collins
1950 Great Start
Signing $125,000 contract
40 Ted Williams 15.00 7.50
Ted Crashes into Wall
Making catch in
1950 All Star game
and crashing into wall
41 Ted WIlliams 12.00 6.00
1950 Ted Recovers
Recuperating from elbow operation
in hospital
42 Ted Williams 15.00 7.50
Tom Yawkey
Slowed by Injury
43 Ted Williams 15.00 7.50
Double Play Lead
Leaping high to
make great catch
44 Ted Williams 15.00 7.50
Back to Marines
Hanging up number 9
prior to leaving for Marines
45 Ted Williams 15.00 7.50
Farewell to Baseball
Honored at Fenway Park
prior to return to service
46 Ted Williams 12.00 6.00
Ready for Combat
Drawing jet pilot equipment
in Willow Grove
47 Ted Williams 12.00 6.00
Ted Crash Lands Jet
In flying gear
and jet he crash landed in
48 Ted Williams 18.00 9.00
Ford Frick
1953 Ted Returns
Throwing out 1st ball
at All-Star Game in Cincinnati
49 Ted Williams 15.00 7.50
Smash Return
Giving his arm
whirlpool treatment
50 Ted Williams 20.00 10.00
1954 Spring Injury
Full batting pose at plate
51 Ted Williams 12.00 6.00
Ted is Patched Up
In first workout after
fractured collar bone
52 Ted Williams 18.00 9.00
1954 Ted's Comeback
Hitting a home run
against Detroit
53 Ted Williams 15.00 7.50
Comeback is Success
Beating catcher's
tag at home plate
54 Ted Williams 15.00 7.50
Ted Hooks Big One
With prize catch
1235 lb. black marlin
55 Ted Williams 18.00 9.00
Joe Cronin
Retirement "No Go"
Returning from retirement
56 Ted Williams 15.00 7.50
2,000th Hit
8/11/55
57 Ted Williams 18.00 9.00
400th Homer
In locker room
58 Ted Williams 15.00 7.50
Williams Hits .388
Four-picture sequence
of his batting swing
59 Ted Williams 12.00 6.00
Hot September for Ted
Full shot of follow through
at plate
60 Ted Williams 15.00 7.50
More Records for Ted
Swinging and missing
61 Ted Williams 18.00 9.00
1957 Outfielder
Warming up prior
to ball game
62 Ted Williams 12.00 6.00
1958 Sixth Batting Title
Slamming pitch into stands
63 Ted Williams 75.00 38.00
Ted's All-Star Record
Portrait and facsimile autograph
64 Ted Williams 12.00 6.00
Barbara Williams
Daughter and Daddy
In uniform holding his daughter
65 Ted Williams 18.00 9.00
1958 August 30
Determination on face
connecting with ball
66 Ted Williams 12.00 6.00
1958 Powerhouse
Stance and follow through
in batters box
67 Ted Williams 40.00 20.00
Sam Snead
Two Famous Fishermen
testing fishing equipment
68 Ted Williams 700.00 350.00
Bucky Harris
Ted Signs for 1959 SP
signing contract
69 Ted Williams 15.00 7.50
A Future Ted Williams
With eager, young newcomer
70 Ted Williams 35.00 17.50
Jim Thorpe
at Sportsmen's Show
71 Ted Williams 12.00 6.00
Hitting Fund. 1
Proper gripping of
a baseball bat
72 Ted Williams 12.00 6.00
Hitting Fund. 2
Checking his swing
73 Ted Williams 12.00 6.00
Hitting Fund. 3
Stance and follow-through
74 Ted Williams 12.00 6.00
Here's How
Demonstrating in locker room
an aspect of hitting
75 Ted Williams 50.00 25.00
Eddie Collins
Babe Ruth
Williams' Value to Sox
76 Ted Williams 12.00 6.00
On Base Record
Awaiting intentional walk
to first base
77 Ted Williams 15.00 7.50
Ted Relaxes
Displaying bonefish
which he caught
78 Ted Williams 15.00 7.50
Rep. Joe Martin
Justice Earl Warren
Honors for Williams
Clark Griffith Memorial Award
79 Ted Williams 20.00 10.00
Where Ted Stands
Wielding giant eight foot bat
when honored as modern-day Paul
Bunyan
80 Ted Williams 35.00 17.50
Ted's Goals for 1959
Admiring his portrait

1960 Fleer

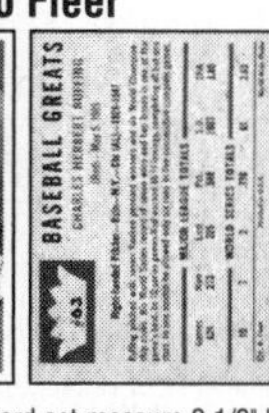

The cards in this 79-card set measure 2 1/2" by 3 1/2". The cards from the 1960 Fleer series of Baseball Greats are sometimes mistaken for 1930s cards by collectors not familiar with this set. The cards each contain a tinted photo of a baseball immortal, and were issued in one series. There are no known scarcities, although a number 80 card (Pepper Martin reverse with Eddie Collins, Joe Tinker or Lefty Grove obverse) exists (this is not considered part of the set). The catalog designation for 1960 Fleer is R418-2. The cards were printed on a 96-card sheet with 17 double prints. These are noted in the checklist below by DP. On the sheet the second Eddie Collins card is typically found in the number 80 position. According to correspondence sent from Fleers at the time -- no card 80 was issued because of contract problems. Some cards have been discovered with wrong backs. The cards were issued in nickel packs which were packed 24 to a box.

NM Ex
COMPLETE SET (79) 600.00 240.00
WRAPPER 100.00 40.00
1 Napoleon Lajoie DP 30.00 12.00
2 Christy Mathewson 15.00 6.00
3 Babe Ruth 100.00 40.00
4 Carl Hubbell 8.00 3.20
5 Grover C. Alexander 8.00 3.20
6 Walter Johnson DP 10.00 4.00
7 Chief Bender 4.00 1.60
8 Roger Bresnahan 4.00 1.60
9 Mordecai Brown 4.00 1.60
10 Tris Speaker 8.00 3.20
11 Arky Vaughan DP 4.00 1.60
12 Zach Wheat 4.00 1.60
13 George Sisler 4.00 1.60
14 Connie Mack 8.00 3.20
15 Clark Griffith 4.00 1.60
16 Lou Boudreau DP 8.00 3.20
17 Ernie Lombardi 4.00 1.60
18 Heinie Manush 4.00 1.60
19 Marty Marion 6.00 2.40
20 Eddie Collins DP 4.00 1.60
21 Rabbit Maranville DP 4.00 1.60
22 Joe Medwick 4.00 1.60
23 Ed Barrow 4.00 1.60
24 Mickey Cochrane 6.00 2.40
25 Jimmy Collins 4.00 1.60
26 Bob Feller DP 15.00 6.00
27 Luke Appling 6.00 2.40
28 Lou Gehrig 80.00 32.00
29 Gabby Hartnett 4.00 1.60
30 Chuck Klein 4.00 1.60
31 Tony Lazzeri DP 6.00 2.40
32 Al Simmons 4.00 1.60
33 Wilbert Robinson 4.00 1.60
34 Sam Rice 4.00 1.60
35 Herb Pennock 4.00 1.60
36 Mel Ott DP 8.00 3.20
37 Lefty O'Doul 4.00 1.60
38 Johnny Mize 8.00 3.20
39 Edmund(Bing) Miller 4.00 1.60
40 Joe Tinker 4.00 1.60
41 Frank Baker DP 4.00 1.60
42 Ty Cobb 60.00 24.00
43 Paul Derringer 4.00 1.60
44 Cap Anson 4.00 1.60
45 Jim Bottomley 4.00 1.60
46 Eddie Plank DP 4.00 1.60
47 Denton(Cy) Young 10.00 4.00
48 Hack Wilson 6.00 2.40
49 Ed Walsh UER 4.00 1.60
(Photo actually
Ed Walsh Jr.)
50 Frank Chance 4.00 1.60
51 Dazzy Vance DP 4.00 1.60
52 Bill Terry 6.00 2.40
53 Jimmie Foxx 10.00 4.00
54 Lefty Gomez 8.00 3.20
55 Branch Rickey 4.00 1.60
56 Ray Schalk DP 4.00 1.60
57 Johnny Evers 4.00 1.60
58 Charley Gehringer 6.00 2.40
59 Burleigh Grimes 4.00 1.60
60 Lefty Grove 8.00 3.20
61 Rube Waddell DP 4.00 1.60
62 John(Honus) Wagner 15.00 6.00
63 Red Ruffing 4.00 1.60
64 Kenesaw M. Landis 4.00 1.60
65 Harry Heilmann 4.00 1.60
66 John McGraw DP 4.00 1.60
67 Hughie Jennings 4.00 1.60
68 Hal Newhouser 6.00 2.40
69 Waite Hoyt 4.00 1.60
70 Bobo Newsom 4.00 1.60
71 Earl Averill DP 4.00 1.60
72 Ted Williams 80.00 32.00
73 Warren Giles 6.00 2.40
74 Ford Frick 6.00 2.40
75 Kiki Cuyler 4.00 1.60
76 Paul Waner DP 6.00 2.40
77 Pie Traynor 4.00 1.60
78 Lloyd Waner 4.00 1.60
79 Ralph Kiner 10.00 4.00
80A Pepper Martin SP 2500.00 1000.00
Eddie Collins
pictured on obverse
80B Pepper Martin SP 2000.00 800.00
Lefty Grove
pictured on obverse
80C Pepper Martin SP 2000.00 800.00
Joe Tinker on Front

1960 Fleer Stickers

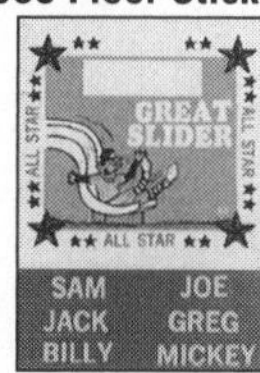

This 20-sticker set measures the standard size. The fronts feature a cartoon depicting the title of the card. The pictures are framed with red and black stars and the words "All Star" printed in blue. First names are printed below and are used to place in the blank box of each sticker to represent the person the sticker depicts. The stickers are unnumbered and checklisted below in alphabetical order.

NM Ex
COMPLETE SET (20) 50.00 20.00
COMMON CARD (1-20) 3.00 1.20

1961 Fleer

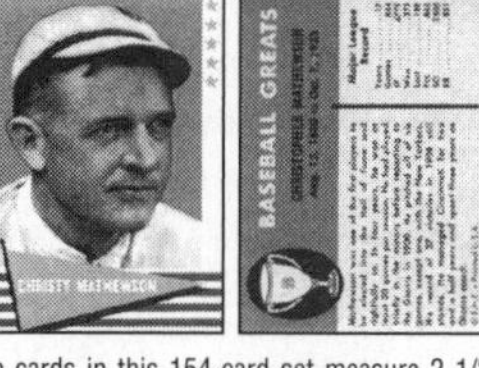

The cards in this 154-card set measure 2 1/2" by 3 1/2". In 1961, Fleer continued its Baseball Greats format by issuing this series of cards. The set was released in two distinct series, 1-88 and 89-154 (of which the latter is more difficult to obtain). The players within each series are conveniently numbered in alphabetical order. The catalog number for this set is F418-3. In each first series pack Fleer inserted a Major League team decal and a pennant sticker honoring past World Series winners. The cards were issued in nickel packs which were issued 24 to a box.

NM Ex
COMPLETE SET (154) 1200.00 475.00
COMMON CARD (1-88) 3.00 1.20
COMMON CARD (89-154) 8.00 3.20
WRAPPER (5-CENT) 100.00 40.00
1 Frank Baker CL 50.00 15.00
Ty Cobb
Zack Wheat
2 Grover C. Alexander 6.00 2.40
3 Nick Altrock 3.00 1.20
4 Cap Anson 4.00 1.60
5 Earl Averill 4.00 1.60
6 Frank Baker 4.00 1.60
7 Dave Bancroft 4.00 1.60
8 Chief Bender 4.00 1.60
9 Jim Bottomley 4.00 1.60
10 Roger Bresnahan 4.00 1.60
11 Mordecai Brown 4.00 1.60
12 Max Carey 4.00 1.60
13 Jack Chesbro 4.00 1.60
14 Ty Cobb 50.00 20.00
15 Mickey Cochrane 4.00 1.60
16 Eddie Collins 6.00 2.40
17 Earle Combs 4.00 1.60
18 Charles Comiskey 4.00 1.60
19 Kiki Cuyler 4.00 1.60
20 Paul Derringer 3.00 1.20
21 Howard Ehmke 3.00 1.20
22 Billy Evans 4.00 1.60
23 Johnny Evers 4.00 1.60
24 Urban Faber 4.00 1.60
25 Bob Feller 12.00 4.80
26 Wes Ferrell 3.00 1.20
27 Lew Fonseca 3.00 1.20
28 Jimmie Foxx 6.00 2.40
29 Ford Frick 3.00 1.20
30 Frankie Frisch 4.00 1.60
31 Lou Gehrig 80.00 32.00
32 Charley Gehringer 4.00 1.60
33 Warren Giles 3.00 1.20
34 Lefty Gomez 4.00 1.60
35 Goose Goslin 4.00 1.60
36 Clark Griffith 4.00 1.60
37 Burleigh Grimes 4.00 1.60
38 Lefty Grove 6.00 2.40
39 Chick Hafey 4.00 1.60
40 Jesse Haines 4.00 1.60
41 Gabby Hartnett 4.00 1.60
42 Harry Heilmann 4.00 1.60
43 Rogers Hornsby 6.00 2.40
44 Waite Hoyt 4.00 1.60
45 Carl Hubbell 6.00 2.40
46 Miller Huggins 4.00 1.60
47 Hughie Jennings 4.00 1.60
48 Ban Johnson 4.00 1.60
49 Walter Johnson 12.00 4.80
50 Ralph Kiner 6.00 2.40
51 Chuck Klein 4.00 1.60
52 Johnny Kling 3.00 1.20
53 Kenesaw M. Landis 4.00 1.60
54 Tony Lazzeri 4.00 1.60
55 Ernie Lombardi 4.00 1.60
56 Dolf Luque 3.00 1.20
57 Heinie Manush 4.00 1.60
58 Marty Marion 3.00 1.20
59 Christy Mathewson 12.00 4.80
60 John McGraw 4.00 1.60
61 Joe Medwick 4.00 1.60
62 Edmund(Bing) Miller 3.00 1.20
63 Johnny Mize 4.00 1.60
64 John Mostil 3.00 1.20
65 Art Nehf 3.00 1.20
66 Hal Newhouser 4.00 1.60
67 Bobo Newsom 3.00 1.20
68 Mel Ott 6.00 2.40
69 Allie Reynolds 3.00 1.20
70 Sam Rice 4.00 1.60
71 Eppa Rixey 4.00 1.60
72 Edd Roush 4.00 1.60
73 Schoolboy Rowe 3.00 1.20
74 Red Ruffing 4.00 1.60
75 Babe Ruth 125.00 50.00
76 Joe Sewell 4.00 1.60
77 Al Simmons 4.00 1.60
78 George Sisler 4.00 1.60
79 Tris Speaker 4.00 1.60
80 Fred Toney 3.00 1.20
81 Dazzy Vance 4.00 1.60
82 Hippo Vaughn 3.00 1.20
83 Ed Walsh 4.00 1.60
84 Lloyd Waner 4.00 1.60
85 Paul Waner 4.00 1.60
86 Zack Wheat 4.00 1.60
87 Hack Wilson 4.00 1.60
88 Jimmy Wilson 3.00 1.20
89 George Sisler CL 60.00 18.00
Pie Traynor
90 Babe Adams 8.00 3.20
91 Dale Alexander 8.00 3.20
92 Jim Bagby 8.00 3.20
93 Ossie Bluege 8.00 3.20
94 Lou Boudreau 10.00 4.00
95 Tommy Bridges 8.00 3.20
96 Donie Bush 8.00 3.20
97 Dolph Camilli 8.00 3.20
98 Frank Chance 10.00 4.00
99 Jimmy Collins 10.00 4.00
100 Stan Coveleskie 10.00 4.00
101 Hugh Critz 8.00 3.20
102 Alvin Crowder 8.00 3.20
103 Joe Dugan 8.00 3.20
104 Bibb Falk 8.00 3.20
105 Rick Ferrell 10.00 4.00
106 Art Fletcher 8.00 3.20
107 Dennis Galehouse 8.00 3.20
108 Chick Galloway 8.00 3.20
109 Mule Haas 8.00 3.20
110 Stan Hack 8.00 3.20
111 Bump Hadley 8.00 3.20
112 Billy Hamilton 10.00 4.00
113 Joe Hauser 8.00 3.20
114 Babe Herman 8.00 3.20
115 Travis Jackson 10.00 4.00
116 Eddie Joost 8.00 3.20
117 Addie Joss 10.00 4.00
118 Joe Judge 8.00 3.20
119 Joe Kuhel 8.00 3.20
120 Napoleon Lajoie 12.00 4.80
121 Dutch Leonard 8.00 3.20
122 Ted Lyons 10.00 4.00
123 Connie Mack 12.00 4.80
124 Rabbit Maranville 10.00 4.00
125 Fred Marberry 8.00 3.20
126 Joe McGinnity 10.00 4.00
127 Oscar Melillo 8.00 3.20
128 Ray Mueller 8.00 3.20
129 Kid Nichols 10.00 4.00
130 Lefty O'Doul 10.00 4.00
131 Bob O'Farrell 8.00 3.20
132 Roger Peckinpaugh 8.00 3.20
133 Herb Pennock 10.00 4.00
134 George Pipgras 8.00 3.20
135 Eddie Plank 10.00 4.00
136 Ray Schalk 10.00 4.00
137 Hal Schumacher 8.00 3.20
138 Luke Sewell 8.00 3.20
139 Bob Shawkey 8.00 3.20
140 Riggs Stephenson 8.00 3.20
141 Billy Sullivan 8.00 3.20
142 Bill Terry 12.00 4.80
143 Joe Tinker 10.00 4.00
144 Pie Traynor 10.00 4.00
145 Hal Trosky 8.00 3.20
146 George Uhle 8.00 3.20
147 Johnny VanderMeer 10.00 4.00
148 Arky Vaughan 10.00 4.00
149 Rube Waddell 10.00 4.00
150 Honus Wagner 50.00 20.00
151 Dixie Walker 8.00 3.20
152 Ted Williams 125.00 50.00
153 Cy Young 40.00 16.00
154 Ross Youngs 40.00 16.00

1963 Fleer

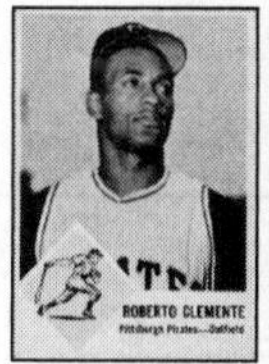

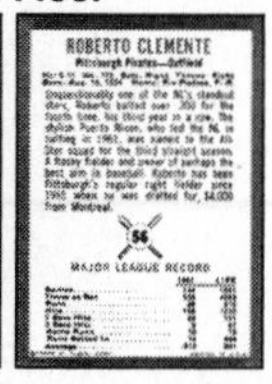

The Fleer set of current baseball players was marketed in 1963 in a gum card-style waxed wrapper package which contained a cherry cookie instead of gum. The five cent packs were packaged 24 to a box. The cards were printed in sheets of 66 with the scarce card of Joe Adcock (number 46) replaced by the unnumbered checklist card for the final press run. The complete set price includes the checklist card. The catalog designation for this set is R418-4. The key Rookie Card in this set is Maury Wills. The set is basically arranged numerically in alphabetical order by teams which are also in alphabetical order.

NM Ex
COMPLETE SET (67) 2000.00 800.00
WRAPPER (5-CENT) 100.00 40.00
1 Steve Barber 25.00 7.50
2 Ron Hansen 15.00 6.00
3 Milt Pappas 20.00 8.00
4 Brooks Robinson 100.00 40.00
5 Willie Mays 175.00 70.00
6 Lou Clinton 15.00 6.00
7 Bill Monbouquette 15.00 6.00
8 Carl Yastrzemski 100.00 40.00
9 Ray Herbert 15.00 6.00
10 Jim Landis 15.00 6.00
11 Dick Donovan 15.00 6.00
12 Tito Francona 15.00 6.00
13 Jerry Kindall 15.00 6.00
14 Frank Lary 20.00 8.00
15 Dick Howser 20.00 8.00
16 Jerry Lumpe 15.00 6.00
17 Norm Siebern 15.00 6.00
18 Don Lee 15.00 6.00
19 Albie Pearson 20.00 8.00
20 Bob Rodgers 20.00 8.00
21 Leon Wagner 15.00 6.00
22 Jim Kaat 25.00 10.00
23 Vic Power 20.00 8.00
24 Rich Rollins 20.00 8.00
25 Bobby Richardson 25.00 10.00
26 Ralph Terry 20.00 8.00
27 Tom Cheney 15.00 6.00
28 Chuck Cottier 15.00 6.00
29 Jimmy Piersall 20.00 8.00
30 Dave Stenhouse 15.00 6.00
31 Glen Hobbie 15.00 6.00
32 Ron Santo 25.00 10.00
33 Gene Freese 15.00 6.00
34 Vada Pinson 25.00 10.00
35 Bob Purkey 15.00 6.00
36 Joe Amalfitano 15.00 6.00
37 Bob Aspromonte 15.00 6.00
38 Dick Farrell 15.00 6.00
39 Al Spangler 15.00 6.00
40 Tommy Davis 20.00 8.00
41 Don Drysdale 80.00 32.00
42 Sandy Koufax 200.00 80.00
43 Maury Wills RC 100.00 40.00
44 Frank Bolling 15.00 6.00
45 Warren Spahn 80.00 32.00
46 Joe Adcock SP 150.00 60.00
47 Roger Craig 20.00 8.00
48 Al Jackson 20.00 8.00
49 Rod Kanehl 20.00 8.00
50 Ruben Amaro 15.00 6.00
51 Johnny Callison 20.00 8.00
52 Clay Dalrymple 15.00 6.00
53 Don Demeter 15.00 6.00
54 Art Mahaffey 15.00 6.00
55 Smoky Burgess 20.00 8.00
56 Roberto Clemente 175.00 70.00
57 Roy Face 20.00 8.00
58 Vern Law 20.00 8.00
59 Bill Mazeroski 30.00 12.00
60 Ken Boyer 25.00 10.00
61 Bob Gibson 80.00 32.00
62 Gene Oliver 15.00 6.00
63 Bill White 20.00 8.00
64 Orlando Cepeda 30.00 12.00
65 Jim Davenport 15.00 6.00
66 Billy O'Dell 25.00 7.50
NNO Checklist card 500.00 160.00

1966 Fleer AS Match Game

The 1966 Fleer All-Star Match Baseball Game set consists of 66 standard-size cards. The front of each card has nine rectangular boxes, one for each inning of a baseball game. These boxes are either blue (for American All Stars) or yellow (for National All Stars). In the lower right corner, a tie breaker rule is listed. When properly placed, the backs of all the cards form a composite black and white photo of Don Drysdale. The cards are numbered on the front.

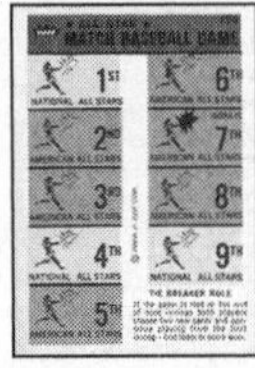

This is a rare instance where the set is worth much more than any individual part.

NM Ex
COMPLETE SET (66) 200.00 80.00
COMMON CARD (1-66) 2.50 1.00

1968-72 Fleer Cloth Stickers

This set was issued over a period of four years. This can be determined by the inclusion of the Seattle Pilots, who only played in 1969, as well as the Texas Rangers who did not move to Texas until 1972. This sticker set measures 2 1/2" by 3 1/4" and is comprised of two different types of stickers. The first group (1-24) are all the same design with the team city printed in a banner across the top and the official team logo in a circular design below. Both are designed to peel off. The second group (25-48) are of a different design with the team logo letter being the top portion and the city left off. The team name makes up the bottom section. Again, both are designed to be peeled off. The stickers are unnumbered and checklisted below in alphabetical order within each sticker type.

NM Ex
COMPLETE SET (48) 50.00 20.00
1 Atlanta Braves 1.25 .50
2 Baltimore Orioles 1.25 .50
3 Boston Red Sox 1.25 .50
4 California Angels 1.25 .50
5 Chicago Cubs 1.25 .50
6 Chicago White Sox 1.25 .50
7 Cincinnati Reds 1.25 .50
8 Cleveland Indians 1.25 .50
9 Detroit Tigers 1.25 .50
10 Houston Astros 1.25 .50
11 Kansas City Royals 1.25 .50
12 Los Angeles Dodgers 1.25 .50
13 Minnesota Twins 1.25 .50
14 Montreal Expos 1.25 .50
15 New York Mets 1.25 .50
16 New York Yankees 1.25 .50
17 Oakland A's 1.25 .50
18 Philadelphia Phillies 1.25 .50
19 Pittsburgh Pirates 1.25 .50
20 St. Louis Cardinals 1.25 .50
21 San Francisco Giants 1.25 .50
22 Seattle Pilots 2.00 .80
23 Texas Rangers 1.25 .50
24 Washington Senators 1.25 .50
25 California Angels 1.25 .50
26 Houston Astros 1.25 .50
27 Atlanta Braves 1.25 .50
28 St. Louis Cardinals 1.25 .50
29 Chicago Cubs 1.25 .50
30 Los Angeles Dodgers 1.25 .50
31 Montreal Expos 1.25 .50
32 San Francisco Giants 1.25 .50
33 Cleveland Indians 1.25 .50
34 New York Mets 1.25 .50
35 Oakland A's 1.25 .50
36 Baltimore Orioles 1.25 .50
37 Philadelphia Phillies 1.25 .50
38 Seattle Pilots 2.00 .80
39 Pittsburgh Pirates 1.25 .50
40 Texas Rangers 1.25 .50
41 Reds 1.25 .50
42 Red Sox 1.25 .50
43 Royals 1.25 .50
44 Senators 1.25 .50
45 Sox 1.25 .50
46 Tigers 1.25 .50
47 Twins 1.25 .50
48 Yankees 1.25 .50

1970 Fleer World Series

This set of 66 standard-size cards was distributed by Fleer. The cards are in crude color on the front with light blue printing on white card stock on the back. All the years are represented except for 1904 when no World Series was played. In the list below, the winning series team is listed first. The year of the Series on the obverse is inside a white baseball. The original art for the cards in this set was drawn by sports artist R.G. Laughlin.

NM Ex
COMPLETE SET (66) 150.00 60.00
1 1903 Red Sox/Pirates 1.50 .60
2 1905 Giants/A's 4.00 1.60
(Christy Mathewson)
3 1906 White Sox/Cubs 1.50 .60
4 1907 Cubs/Tigers 1.50 .60
5 1908 Cubs/Tigers 4.00 1.60
(Joe Tinker,
Johnny Evers,
and Frank Chance)
6 1909 Pirates/Tigers 6.00 2.40
(Honus Wagner
and Ty Cobb)
7 1910 A's/Cubs 2.50 1.00
(Chief Bender
and Jack Coombs)
8 1911 A's/Giants 2.50 1.00
(John McGraw)
9 1912 Red Sox/Giants 1.50 .60
10 1913 A's/Giants 1.50 .60
11 1914 Braves/A's 1.50 .60
12 1915 Red Sox/Phillies 8.00 3.20
(Babe Ruth)
13 1916 Red Sox/Dodgers 8.00 3.20
(Babe Ruth)
14 1917 White Sox/Giants 1.50 .60
15 1918 Red Sox/Cubs 1.50 .60
16 1919 Reds/White Sox 8.00 3.20
17 1920 Indians/Dodgers 2.50 1.00
(Stan Coveleski)
18 1921 Giants/Yankees 1.50 .60
(Commissioner Landis)
19 1922 Giants/Yankees 1.50 .60
20 1923 Yankees/Giants 8.00 3.20
(Babe Ruth)
21 1924 Senators/Giants 2.50 1.00
(John McGraw)
22 1925 Pirates/Senators 4.00 1.60
(Walter Johnson)
23 1926 Cardinals 2.50 1.00
Yankees
Grover C. Alexander
Tony Lazzeri
24 1927 Yankees/Pirates 1.50 .60
25 1928 Yankees 8.00 3.20
Cardinals
Babe Ruth
Lou Gehrig
26 1929 A's/Cubs 1.50 .60
27 1930 A's/Cardinals 1.50 .60
28 1931 Cardinals/A's 1.50 .60
(Pepper Martin)
29 1932 Yankees/Cubs 8.00 3.20
(Babe Ruth
and Lou Gehrig)
30 1933 Giants/Senators 2.50 1.00
(Mel Ott)
31 1934 Cardinals/Tigers 1.50 .60
32 1935 Tigers/Cubs 2.50 1.00
(Charlie Gehringer
and Tommy Bridges)
33 1936 Yankees/Giants 1.50 .60
34 1937 Yankees/Giants 2.50 1.00
(Carl Hubbell)
35 1938 Yankees/Cubs 6.00 2.40
(Lou Gehrig)
36 1939 Yankees/Reds 1.50 .60
37 1940 Reds/Tigers 1.50 .60
38 1941 Yankees/Dodgers 1.50 .60
39 1942 Cardinals 1.50 .60
Yankees
40 1943 Yankees 1.50 .60
Cardinals
41 1944 Cardinals/Browns 1.50 .60
42 1945 Tigers/Cubs 4.00 1.60
(Hank Greenberg)
43 1946 Cardinals 2.50 1.00
Red Sox
Enos Slaughter
44 1947 Yankees/Dodgers 1.50 .60
(Al Gionfriddo)
45 1948 Indians/Braves 1.50 .60
46 1949 Yankees/Dodgers 1.50 .60
(Allie Reynolds
and Preacher Roe)
47 1950 Yankees/Phillies 1.50 .60
48 1951 Yankees/Giants 1.50 .60
49 1952 Yankees/Dodgers 6.00 2.40
(Johnny Mize
and Duke Snider)
50 1953 Yankees/Dodgers 1.50 .60
(Carl Erskine)
51 1954 Giants/Indians 1.50 .60
(Johnny Antonelli)
52 1955 Dodgers/Yankees 1.50 .60
(Johnny Podres)
53 1956 Yankees/Dodgers 1.50 .60
54 1957 Braves/Yankees 1.50 .60
(Lew Burdette)
55 1958 Yankees/Braves 1.50 .60
(Bob Turley)
56 1959 Dodgers 1.50 .60
White Sox
Chuck Essegian
57 1960 Pirates/Yankees 1.50 .60
58 1961 Yankees/Reds 2.50 1.00
(Whitey Ford)
59 1962 Yankees/Giants 1.50 .60
60 1963 Dodgers/Yankees 1.50 .60
(Moose Skowron)
61 1964 Cardinals/Yankees 2.50 1.00
(Bobby Richardson)
62 1965 Dodgers/Twins 1.50 .60
63 1966 Orioles/Dodgers 1.50 .60
64 1967 Cardinals/Red Sox 1.50 .60
65 1968 Tigers/Cardinals 1.50 .60
66 1969 Mets/Orioles 2.50 1.00

1971 Fleer World Series

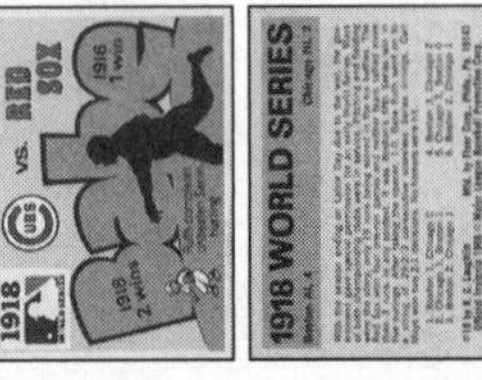

This set of 68 standard-size cards was distributed by Fleer. The cards are in crude color on the front with brown printing on white card stock on the back. All the years since 1903 are represented in this set including 1904, when no World Series was played. That year is represented by a card explaining why there was no World Series that year. In the list below, the winning series team is listed first. The year of the Series on the obverse is inside a white square over the official World Series logo.

NM Ex
COMPLETE SET (68) 125.00 50.00
1 1903 Red Sox/Pirates 4.00 1.60
(Cy Young)
2 1904 NO Series 2.50 1.00
(John McGraw)
3 1905 Giants/A's 4.00 1.60
(Christy Mathewson,
Chief Bender, and
Joe McGinnity)
4 1906 White Sox/Cubs 1.50 .60
5 1907 Cubs/Tigers 1.50 .60
6 1908 Cubs/Tigers 5.00 2.00
(Ty Cobb)
7 1909 Pirates/Tigers 1.50 .60
8 1910 A's/Cubs 2.50 1.00
(Eddie Collins)
9 1911 A's/Giants 2.50 1.00
(Home Run Baker)
10 1912 Red Sox/Giants 1.50 .60
11 1913 A's/Giants 4.00 1.60
(Christy Mathewson)
12 1914 Braves/A's 1.50 .60
13 1915 Red Sox/Phillies 2.50 1.00
(Grover Alexander)
14 1916 Red Sox/Dodgers 1.50 .60
15 1917 White Sox/Giants 2.50 1.00
(Red Faber)
16 1918 Red Sox/Cubs 8.00 3.20
(Babe Ruth)
17 1919 Reds/White Sox 8.00 3.20
18 1920 Indians/Dodgers 1.50 .60
19 1921 Giants/Yankees 2.50 1.00
(Waite Hoyt)
20 1922 Giants/Yankees 1.50 .60
21 1923 Yankees/Giants 2.50 1.00
(Herb Pennock)
22 1924 Senators/Giants 4.00 1.60
(Walter Johnson)
23 1925 Pirates/Senators 2.50 1.00
(Kiki Cuyler and
Walter Johnson)
24 1926 Cardinals 4.00 1.60
Yankees
Rogers Hornsby
25 1927 Yankees/Pirates 1.50 .60
26 1928 Yankees/Cardinals 5.00 2.00
(Lou Gehrig)
27 1929 A's/Cubs 1.50 .60
28 1930 A's/Cardinals 4.00 1.60
(Jimmie Foxx)
29 1931 Cardinals/A's 1.50 .60
(Pepper Martin)
30 1932 Yankees/Cubs 8.00 3.20
(Babe Ruth)
31 1933 Giants/Senators 2.50 1.00
(Carl Hubbell)
32 1934 Cardinals/Tigers 1.50 .60
33 1935 Tigers/Cubs 2.50 1.00
(Mickey Cochrane)
34 1936 Yankees/Giants 1.50 .60
(Red Rolfe)
35 1937 Yankees/Giants 2.50 1.00
(Tony Lazzeri)
36 1938 Yankees/Cubs 1.50 .60
37 1939 Yankees/Reds 1.50 .60
38 1940 Reds/Tigers 1.50 .60
39 1941 Yankees/Dodgers 1.50 .60
40 1942 Cardinals 1.50 .60
Yankees
41 1943 Yankees 1.50 .60
Cardinals
42 1944 Cardinals/Browns 1.50 .60
43 1945 Tigers/Cubs 4.00 1.60
(Hank Greenberg)
44 1946 Cardinals 2.50 1.00
Red Sox
Enos Slaughter
45 1947 Yankees/Dodgers 1.50 .60
46 1948 Indians/Braves 1.50 .60
47 1949 Yankees/Dodgers 1.50 .60
(Preacher Roe)
48 1950 Yankees/Phillies 1.50 .60
(Allie Reynolds)
49 1951 Yankees/Giants 1.50 .60
(Ed Lopat)
50 1952 Yankees/Dodgers 2.50 1.00
(Johnny Mize)
51 1953 Yankees/Dodgers 1.50 .60
52 1954 Giants/Indians 1.50 .60
53 1955 Dodgers/Yankees 2.50 1.00
(Duke Snider)
54 1956 Yankees/Dodgers 1.50 .60
55 1957 Braves/Yankees 1.50 .60
56 1958 Yankees/Braves 1.50 .60
(Hank Bauer)
57 1959 Dodgers/Wh.Sox 2.50 1.00
(Duke Snider)
58 1960 Pirates/Yankees 1.50 .60
59 1961 Yankees/Reds 2.50 1.00
(Whitey Ford)
60 1962 Yankees/Giants 1.50 .60
61 1963 Dodgers/Yankees 1.50 .60
62 1964 Cardinals 1.50 .60
Yankees
63 1965 Dodgers/Twins 1.50 .60
64 1966 Orioles/Dodgers 1.50 .60
65 1967 Cardinals/Red Sox 1.50 .60
66 1968 Tigers/Cardinals 1.50 .60
67 1969 Mets/Orioles 1.50 .60
68 1970 Orioles/Reds 2.50 1.00

1972 Fleer Famous Feats

This Fleer set of 40 cards features the artwork of sports artist R.G. Laughlin. The set is titled "Baseball's Famous Feats." The cards are numbered both on the front and back. The backs are printed in light blue on white card stock. The cards measure approximately 2 1/2" by 4". This set was licensed by Major League Baseball.

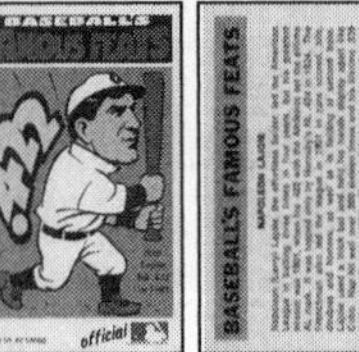

NM Ex
COMPLETE SET (40) 60.00 24.00
1 Joe McGinnity 1.50 .60
2 Rogers Hornsby 2.50 1.00
3 Christy Mathewson 5.00 2.00
4 Dazzy Vance 1.50 .60
5 Lou Gehrig 8.00 3.20
6 Jim Bottomley 1.50 .60
7 Johnny Evers 1.50 .60
8 Walter Johnson 5.00 2.00
9 Hack Wilson 1.50 .60
10 Wilbert Robinson 1.50 .60
11 Cy Young 2.50 1.00
12 Rudy York 1.00 .40
13 Grover C. Alexander 1.50 .60
14 Fred Toney and 1.00 .40
Hippo Vaughn
15 Ty Cobb 8.00 3.20
16 Jimmie Foxx 5.00 2.00
17 Hub Leonard 1.00 .40
18 Eddie Collins 1.50 .60
19 Joe Oeschger and 1.00 .40
Leon Cadore
20 Babe Ruth 10.00 4.00
21 Honus Wagner 2.50 1.00
22 Red Rolfe 1.00 .40
23 Ed Walsh 1.50 .60
24 Paul Waner 1.50 .60
25 Mel Ott 2.00 .80
26 Eddie Plank 1.50 .60
27 Sam Crawford 1.50 .60
28 Napoleon Lajoie 2.00 .80
29 Ed Reulbach 1.00 .40
30 Pinky Higgins 1.00 .40
31 Bill Klem 1.50 .60
32 Tris Speaker 2.00 .80
33 Hank Gowdy 1.00 .40
34 Lefty O'Doul 1.00 .40
35 Lloyd Waner 1.50 .60
36 Chuck Klein 1.50 .60
37 Deacon Phillippe 1.00 .40
38 Ed Delahanty 1.50 .60
39 Jack Chesbro 1.50 .60
40 Willie Keeler 1.50 .60

1973 Fleer Big Signs

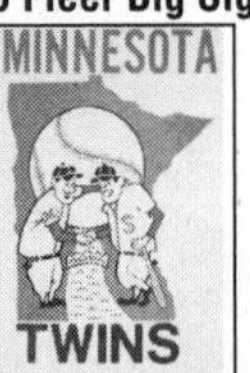

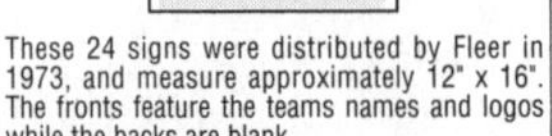

These 24 signs were distributed by Fleer in 1973, and measure approximately 12" x 16". The fronts feature the teams names and logos while the backs are blank.

NM Ex
COMPLETE SET (24) 40.00 16.00
1 Atlanta Braves 2.00 .80
2 Baltimore Orioles 2.00 .80
3 Boston Red Sox 2.00 .80
4 California Angels 2.00 .80
5 Chicago Cubs 2.00 .80
6 Chicago White Sox 2.00 .80
7 Cincinnati Reds 2.00 .80
8 Cleveland Indians 2.00 .80
9 Detroit Tigers 2.00 .80
10 Houston Astros 2.00 .80
11 Kansas City Royals 2.00 .80
12 Los Angeles Dodgers 2.00 .80
13 Milwaukee Brewers 2.00 .80
14 Minnesota Twins 2.00 .80
15 Montreal Expos 2.00 .80
16 New York Mets 2.00 .80
17 New York Yankees 2.00 .80
18 Oakland Athletics 2.00 .80
19 Philadelphia Phillies 2.00 .80
20 Pittsburgh Pirates 2.00 .80
21 San Diego Padres 2.00 .80
22 San Francisco Giants 2.00 .80
23 St. Louis Cardinals 2.00 .80
24 Texas Rangers 2.00 .80

1973 Fleer Wildest Days

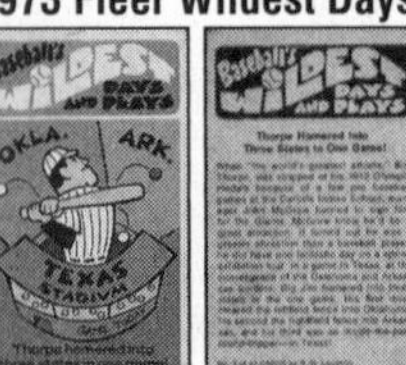

This Fleer set of 42 cards is titled "Baseball's Wildest Days and Plays" and features the artwork of sports artist R.G. Laughlin. The sets were available from Bob Laughlin for $3. The backs are printed in dark red on white card stock. The cards measure approximately 2 1/2" by 4". This set was not licensed by Major League Baseball.

NM Ex
COMPLETE SET (42) 50.00 20.00
1 Cubs and Phillies 2.00 .80
Score 49 Runs in Game
2 Frank Chance 1.50 .60
Five HBP's in One Day
3 Jim Thorpe 5.00 2.00
Homered into 3 States
4 Eddie Gaedel 2.50 1.00
Midget in Majors
5 Most Tied Game Ever 1.00 .40
6 Seven Errors in 1.00 .40
One Inning
7 Four 20-Game Winners 1.00 .40
But No Pennant
8 Dummy Hoy 2.00 .80
Umpires Signal Strikes
9 Fourteen Hits in 1.00 .40
One Inning
10 Yankees Not Shut Out 1.00 .40
For Two Years
11 Buck Weaver 2.50 1.00
17 Straight Fouls
12 George Sisler 1.50 .60
Greatest Thrill
Was as a Pitcher
13 Wrong-Way Baserunner 1.00 .40
14 Kiki Cuyler 1.50 .60
Sits Out Series
15 Grounder Climbed Wall 1.00 .40
16 Gabby Street 1.50 .60
Washington Monument
17 Mel Ott 4.00 1.60
Ejected Twice
18 Shortest Pitching 1.00 .40
Career
19 Three Homers in 1.00 .40
One Inning
20 Bill Byron 1.00 .40
Singing Umpire
21 Fred Clarke 1.50 .60
Walking Steal of Home
22 Christy Mathewson 4.00 1.60
373rd Win Discovered
23 Hitting Through the 1.00 .40
Unglaub Arc
24 Jim O'Rourke 1.00 .40
Catching at 52
25 Fired for Striking 1.00 .40
Out in Series
26 Eleven Run Inning 1.00 .40
on One Hit
27 58 Innings in 3 Days 1.00 .40
28 Homer on Warm-Up 1.00 .40
Pitch
29 Giants Win 26 Straight 1.00 .40
But Finish Fourth
30 Player Who Stole 1.00 .40
First Base
31 Ernie Shore 1.50 .60
Perfect Game
in Relief
32 Greatest Comeback 1.00 .40
33 All-Time Flash- 1.00 .40
In-The-Pan
34 Hub Pruett 2.50 1.00
Fanned Ruth
19 out of 31
35 Fixed Batting Race 4.00 1.60
Ty Cobb
Nap Lajoie
36 Wild-Pitch Rebound 1.00 .40
Play
37 17 Straight Scoring 1.00 .40
Innings
38 Wildest Opening Day 1.00 .40
39 Baseball's Strike One 1.00 .40
40 Opening Day No Hitter 1.00 .40
That Didn't Count
41 Jimmie Foxx 4.00 1.60
Six Straight Walks
in One Game
42 Entire Team Hit and 2.00 .80
Scored in Inning

1974 Fleer Baseball Firsts

This Fleer set of 42 cards is titled "Baseball Firsts" and features the artwork of sports artist R.G. Laughlin. The cards are numbered on the back. The backs are printed in black on gray card stock. The cards measure approximately 2 1/2" by 4". This set was not licensed by Major League Baseball.

NM Ex
COMPLETE SET (42) 25.00 10.00
COMMON CARD (1-42) .50 .20
5 Lou Gehrig 6.00 2.40
Four straight Homers

1975 Fleer Pioneers

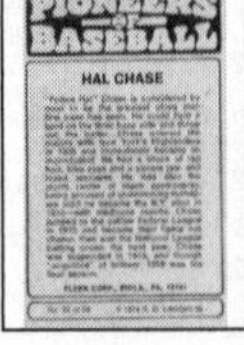

This 28-card set of brown and white sepia-toned photos of old timers is subtitled "Pioneers of Baseball. The graphics artwork was done by R.G. Laughlin. The cards measure approximately 2 1/2" X 4". The card backs are a narrative about the particular player.

NM Ex
COMPLETE SET (28) 40.00 16.00
1 Cap Anson 2.50 1.00

2 Harry Wright 1.50 .60
3 Buck Ewing 1.50 .60
4 Al G. Spalding 1.50 .60
5 Old Hoss Radbourn 1.50 .60
6 Dan Brouthers 1.50 .60
7 Roger Bresnahan 1.50 .60
8 Mike Kelly 1.50 .60
9 Ned Hanlon 1.50 .60
10 Ed Delahanty 1.50 .60
11 Pud Galvin 1.50 .60
12 Amos Rusie 1.50 .60
13 Tommy McCarthy 1.50 .60
14 Ty Cobb 8.00 3.20
15 John McGraw 1.50 .60
16 Home Run Baker 1.50 .60
17 Johnny Evers 1.50 .60
18 Nap Lajoie 2.00 .80
19 Cy Young 2.50 1.00
20 Eddie Collins 2.00 .80
21 John Glasscock 1.00 .40
22 Hal Chase 1.00 .40
23 Mordecai Brown 1.50 .60
24 Jake Daubert 1.00 .40
25 Mike Donlin 1.00 .40
26 John Clarkson 1.50 .60
27 Buck Herzog 1.00 .40
28 Art Nehf 1.00 .40

1981 Fleer

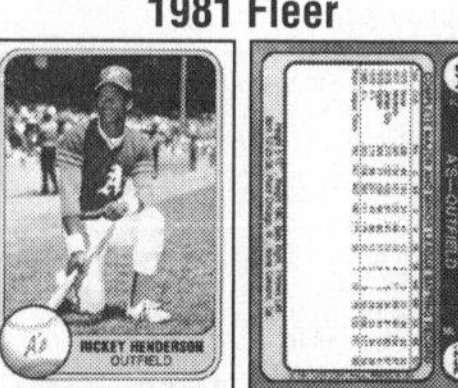

This issue of cards marks Fleer's first modern era entry into the current player baseball card market since 1963. Unopened packs contained 17 cards as well as a piece of gum. Unopened boxes contained 38 packs. As a matter of fact, the boxes actually told the retailer there was extra profit as they were charged as if there were 36 packs in the box. Cards are grouped in team order and teams are ordered based upon their standings from the 1980 season with the World Series champion Philadelphia Phillies starting off the set. Cards 638-660 feature specials and checklists. The cards of pitchers in this set erroneously show a heading (on the card backs) of "Batting Record" over their career pitching statistics. There were three distinct printings: the two following the primary run were designed to correct numerous errors. The variations caused by these multiple printings are noted in the checklist below (P1, P2, or P3). The Craig Nettles variation was corrected before the end of the first printing and thus is not included in the complete set consideration due to scarcity. The key Rookie Cards in this set are Danny Ainge, Harold Baines, Kirk Gibson, Jeff Reardon, and Fernando Valenzuela, whose first name was erroneously spelled Fernand on the card front.

Nm-Mt Ex-Mt
COMPLETE SET (660) 40.00 16.00
1 Pete Rose UER 3.00 1.20
270 hits in 63
should be 170
2 Larry Bowa .25 .10
3 Manny Trillo .10 .04
4 Bob Boone .25 .10
5 Mike Schmidt 2.50 1.00
See also 640A
6 Steve Carlton P1 .25 .10
Golden Arm
Back 1066 Cardinals
Number on back 6
6B Steve Carlton P2 1.50 .60
Pitcher of Year
Back 1066 Cardinals
6C Steve Carlton P3 2.00 .80
1966 Cardinals
7 Tug McGraw .25 .10
See 657A
8 Larry Christenson .10 .04
9 Bake McBride .10 .04
10 Greg Luzinski .25 .10
11 Ron Reed .10 .04
12 Dickie Noles .10 .04
13 Keith Moreland .25 .10
14 Bob Walk RC .25 .10
15 Lonnie Smith .25 .10
16 Dick Ruthven .10 .04
17 Sparky Lyle .25 .10
18 Greg Gross .10 .04
19 Garry Maddox .10 .04
20 Nino Espinosa .10 .04
21 George Vukovich .10 .04
22 John Vukovich .10 .04
23 Ramon Aviles .10 .04
24A Kevin Saucier P1 .10 .04
Name on back Ken
24B Kevin Saucier P2 .10 .04
Name on back Ken
24C Kevin Saucier P3 .50 .20
Name on back Kevin
25 Randy Lerch .10 .04
26 Del Unser .10 .04
27 Tim McCarver .50 .20
28 George Brett 2.50 1.00
See also 655A
29 Willie Wilson .25 .10
See also 653A
30 Paul Splittorff .10 .04
31 Dan Quisenberry .25 .10
32A Amos Otis P1 .25 .10
(Batting Pose
Outfield
32 on back
32B Amos Otis P2 .25 .10
Series Starter
483 on back
33 Steve Busby .10 .04
34 U.L. Washington .10 .04
35 Dave Chalk .10 .04
36 Darrell Porter .10 .04
37 Marty Pattin .10 .04
38 Larry Gura .10 .04
39 Renie Martin .10 .04
40 Rich Gale .10 .04
41A Hal McRae P1 .50 .20
(Royals on front
in black letters
41B Hal McRae P2 .25 .10
(Royals on front
in blue letters
42 Dennis Leonard .10 .04
43 Willie Aikens .10 .04
44 Frank White .25 .10
45 Clint Hurdle .10 .04
46 John Wathan .10 .04
47 Pete LaCock .10 .04
48 Rance Mulliniks .10 .04
49 Jeff Twitty .10 .04
50 Jamie Quirk .10 .04
51 Art Howe .25 .10
52 Ken Forsch .10 .04
53 Vern Ruhle .10 .04
54 Joe Niekro .25 .10
55 Frank LaCorte .10 .04
56 J.R. Richard .25 .10
57 Nolan Ryan 5.00 2.00
58 Enos Cabell .10 .04
59 Cesar Cedeno .25 .10
60 Jose Cruz .25 .10
61 Bill Virdon MG .10 .04
62 Terry Puhl .10 .04
63 Joaquin Andujar .25 .10
64 Alan Ashby .10 .04
65 Joe Sambito .10 .04
66 Denny Walling .10 .04
67 Jeff Leonard .25 .10
68 Luis Pujols .10 .04
69 Bruce Bochy .10 .04
70 Rafael Landestoy .10 .04
71 Dave Smith RC .25 .10
72 Danny Heep .10 .04
73 Julio Gonzalez .10 .04
74 Craig Reynolds .10 .04
75 Gary Woods .10 .04
76 Dave Bergman .10 .04
77 Randy Niemann .10 .04
78 Joe Morgan .50 .20
79 Reggie Jackson .50 .20
See also 650A
80 Bucky Dent .25 .10
81 Tommy John .50 .20
82 Luis Tiant .25 .10
83 Rick Cerone .10 .04
84 Dick Howser MG .25 .10
85 Lou Piniella .25 .10
86 Ron Davis .10 .04
87A Graig Nettles ERR 5.00 2.00
Name on back spelled Craig
87B Graig Nettles COR .25 .10
Graig
88 Ron Guidry .25 .10
89 Rich Gossage .50 .20
90 Rudy May .10 .04
91 Gaylord Perry .25 .10
92 Eric Soderholm .10 .04
93 Bob Watson .25 .10
94 Bobby Murcer .25 .10
95 Bobby Brown .10 .04
96 Jim Spencer .10 .04
97 Tom Underwood .10 .04
98 Oscar Gamble .10 .04
99 Johnny Oates .25 .10
100 Fred Stanley .10 .04
101 Ruppert Jones .10 .04
102 Dennis Werth .10 .04
103 Joe Lefebvre .10 .04
104 Brian Doyle .10 .04
105 Aurelio Rodriguez .10 .04
106 Doug Bird .10 .04
107 Mike Griffin RC .10 .04
108 Tim Lollar .10 .04
109 Willie Randolph .25 .10
110 Steve Garvey .25 .10
111 Reggie Smith .25 .10
112 Don Sutton 1.00 .40
113 Burt Hooton .10 .04
114A Dave Lopes P1 .50 .20
Small hand on back
114B Dave Lopes P2 .25 .10
No hand
115 Dusty Baker .50 .20
116 Tom Lasorda MG .25 .10
117 Bill Russell .25 .10
118 Jerry Reuss UER .25 .10
Home omitted
119 Terry Forster .10 .04
120A Bob Welch P1 .25 .10
(Name on back is Bob
120B Bob Welch P2 .50 .20
Name on back is Robert
121 Don Stanhouse .10 .04
122 Rick Monday .25 .10
123 Derrel Thomas .10 .04
124 Joe Ferguson .10 .04
125 Rick Sutcliffe .25 .10
126A Ron Cey P1 .50 .20
Small hand on back
126B Ron Cey P2 .25 .10
No hand
127 Dave Goltz .10 .04
128 Jay Johnstone .25 .10
129 Steve Yeager .10 .04
130 Gary Weiss .10 .04
131 Mike Scioscia RC 1.50 .60
132 Vic Davalillo .10 .04
133 Doug Rau .10 .04
134 Pepe Frias .10 .04
135 Mickey Hatcher .25 .10
136 Steve Howe .25 .10
137 Robert Castillo .10 .04
138 Gary Thomasson .10 .04
139 Rudy Law .10 .04
140 F.Valenzuela RC UER 2.00 .80
Misspelled Fernand on card
141 Manny Mota .25 .10
142 Gary Carter .50 .20
143 Steve Rogers .10 .04
144 Warren Cromartie .10 .04
145 Andre Dawson .50 .20
146 Larry Parrish .10 .04
147 Rowland Office .10 .04
148 Ellis Valentine .10 .04
149 Dick Williams MG .10 .04
150 Bill Gullickson RC .50 .20
151 Elias Sosa .10 .04
152 John Tamargo .10 .04
153 Chris Speier .10 .04
154 Ron LeFlore .25 .10
155 Rodney Scott .10 .04
156 Stan Bahnsen .10 .04
157 Bill Lee .25 .10
158 Fred Norman .10 .04
159 Woodie Fryman .10 .04
160 David Palmer .10 .04
161 Jerry White .10 .04
162 Roberto Ramos .10 .04
163 John D'Acquisto .10 .04
164 Tommy Hutton .10 .04
165 Charlie Lea .10 .04
166 Scott Sanderson .10 .04
167 Ken Macha .10 .04
168 Tony Bernazard .10 .04
169 Jim Palmer .25 .10
170 Steve Stone .25 .10
171 Mike Flanagan .25 .10
172 Al Bumbry .25 .10
173 Doug DeCinces .25 .10
174 Scott McGregor .10 .04
175 Mark Belanger .25 .10
176 Tim Stoddard .10 .04
177A Rick Dempsey P1 .50 .20
Small hand on front
177B Rick Dempsey P2 .25 .10
No hand
178 Earl Weaver MG 1.00 .40
179 Tippy Martinez .10 .04
180 Dennis Martinez .50 .20
181 Sammy Stewart .10 .04
182 Rich Dauer .10 .04
183 Lee May .25 .10
184 Eddie Murray 1.50 .60
185 Benny Ayala .10 .04
186 John Lowenstein .10 .04
187 Gary Roenicke .10 .04
188 Ken Singleton .25 .10
189 Dan Graham .10 .04
190 Terry Crowley .10 .04
191 Kiko Garcia .10 .04
192 Dave Ford .10 .04
193 Mark Corey .10 .04
194 Lenn Sakata .10 .04
195 Doug DeCinces .25 .10
196 Johnny Bench 1.00 .40
197 Dave Concepcion .25 .10
198 Ray Knight .25 .10
199 Ken Griffey .50 .20
200 Tom Seaver .50 .20
201 Dave Collins .10 .04
202A George Foster P1 .50 .20
Slugger
Number on back 216
202B George Foster P2 .50 .20
Slugger
Number on back 202
203 Junior Kennedy .10 .04
204 Frank Pastore .10 .04
205 Dan Driessen .10 .04
206 Hector Cruz .10 .04
207 Paul Moskau .10 .04
208 Charlie Leibrandt RC .50 .20
209 Harry Spilman .10 .04
210 Joe Price .10 .04
211 Tom Hume .10 .04
212 Joe Nolan .10 .04
213 Doug Bair .10 .04
214 Mario Soto .10 .04
215A Bill Bonham P1 .50 .20
(Small hand on back)
215B Bill Bonham P2 .10 .04
(No hand)
216 George Foster .25 .10
(See 202)
217 Paul Householder .10 .04
218 Ron Oester .10 .04
219 Sam Mejias .10 .04
220 Sheldon Burnside .10 .04
221 Carl Yastrzemski 1.50 .60
222 Jim Rice .25 .10
223 Fred Lynn .25 .10
224 Carlton Fisk .50 .20
225 Rick Burleson .10 .04
226 Dennis Eckersley .50 .20
227 Butch Hobson .10 .04
228 Tom Burgmeier .10 .04
229 Garry Hancock .10 .04
230 Don Zimmer MG .25 .10
231 Steve Renko .10 .04
232 Dwight Evans .50 .20
233 Mike Torrez .10 .04
234 Bob Stanley .10 .04
235 Jim Dwyer .10 .04
236 Dave Stapleton .10 .04
237 Glenn Hoffman .10 .04
238 Jerry Remy .10 .04
239 Dick Drago .10 .04
240 Bill Campbell .10 .04
241 Tony Perez .50 .20
242 Phil Niekro .25 .10
243 Dale Murphy 1.00 .40
244 Bob Horner .25 .10
245 Jeff Burroughs .10 .04
246 Rick Camp .10 .04
247 Bobby Cox MG .25 .10
248 Bruce Benedict .10 .04
249 Gene Garber .10 .04
250 Jerry Royster .10 .04
251A Gary Matthews P1 .50 .20
Small hand on back
251B Gary Matthews P2 .25 .10
No hand
252 Chris Chambliss .25 .10
253 Luis Gomez .10 .04
254 Bill Nahorodny .10 .04
255 Doyle Alexander .10 .04
256 Brian Asselstine .10 .04
257 Biff Pocoroba .10 .04
258 Mike Lum .10 .04
259 Charlie Spikes .10 .04
260 Glenn Hubbard .10 .04
261 Tommy Boggs .10 .04
262 Al Hrabosky UER .10 .04
Card lists him as 5' 1"
263 Rick Matula .10 .04
264 Preston Hanna .10 .04
265 Larry Bradford .10 .04
266 Rafael Ramirez .10 .04
267 Larry McWilliams .10 .04
268 Rod Carew .50 .20
269 Bobby Grich .25 .10
270 Carney Lansford .25 .10
271 Don Baylor .50 .20
272 Joe Rudi .25 .10
273 Dan Ford .10 .04
274 Jim Fregosi MG .10 .04
275 Dave Frost .10 .04
276 Frank Tanana .25 .10
277 Dickie Thon .25 .10
278 Jason Thompson .10 .04
279 Rick Miller .10 .04
280 Bert Campaneris .25 .10
281 Tom Donohue .10 .04
282 Brian Downing .25 .10
283 Fred Patek .10 .04
284 Bruce Kison .10 .04
285 Dave LaRoche .10 .04
286 Don Aase .10 .04
287 Jim Barr .10 .04
288 Alfredo Martinez .10 .04
289 Larry Harlow .10 .04
290 Andy Hassler .10 .04
291 Dave Kingman .50 .20
292 Bill Buckner .25 .10
293 Rick Reuschel .25 .10
294 Bruce Sutter .25 .10
295 Jerry Martin .10 .04
296 Scot Thompson .10 .04
297 Ivan DeJesus .10 .04
298 Steve Dillard .10 .04
299 Dick Tidrow .10 .04
300 Randy Martz .10 .04
301 Lenny Randle .10 .04
302 Lynn McGlothen .10 .04
303 Cliff Johnson .10 .04
304 Tim Blackwell .10 .04
305 Dennis Lamp .10 .04
306 Bill Caudill .10 .04
307 Carlos Lezcano .10 .04
308 Jim Tracy RC .10 .04
309 Doug Capilla UER .10 .04
Cubs on front but
Braves on back
310 Willie Hernandez .25 .10
311 Mike Vail .10 .04
312 Mike Krukow .10 .04
313 Barry Foote .10 .04
314 Larry Biittner .10 .04
315 Mike Tyson .10 .04
316 Lee Mazzilli .10 .04
317 John Stearns .10 .04
318 Alex Trevino .10 .04
319 Craig Swan .10 .04
320 Frank Taveras .10 .04
321 Steve Henderson .10 .04
322 Neil Allen .10 .04
323 Mark Bomback .10 .04
324 Mike Jorgensen .10 .04
325 Joe Torre MG .25 .10
326 Elliott Maddox .10 .04
327 Pete Falcone .10 .04
328 Ray Burris .10 .04
329 Claudell Washington .10 .04
330 Doug Flynn .10 .04
331 Joel Youngblood .10 .04
332 Bill Almon .10 .04
333 Tom Hausman .10 .04
334 Pat Zachry .10 .04
335 Jeff Reardon RC 1.00 .40
336 Wally Backman .25 .10
337 Dan Norman .10 .04
338 Jerry Morales .10 .04
339 Ed Farmer .10 .04
340 Bob Molinaro .10 .04
341 Todd Cruz .10 .04
342A Britt Burns P1 .50 .20
Small hand on front
342B Britt Burns P2 .25 .10
No hand
343 Kevin Bell .10 .04
344 Tony LaRussa MG .25 .10
345 Steve Trout .10 .04
346 Harold Baines RC 5.00 2.00
347 Richard Wortham .10 .04
348 Wayne Nordhagen .10 .04
349 Mike Squires .10 .04
350 Lamar Johnson .10 .04
351 Rickey Henderson 3.00 1.20
Most Stolen Bases AL
352 Francisco Barrios .10 .04
353 Thad Bosley .10 .04
354 Chet Lemon .10 .04
355 Bruce Kimm .10 .04
356 Richard Dotson .10 .04
357 Jim Morrison .10 .04
358 Mike Proly .10 .04
359 Greg Pryor .10 .04
360 Dave Parker .25 .10
361 Omar Moreno .10 .04
362A Kent Tekulve P1 .25 .10
Back 1071 Waterbury
and 1078 Pirates
362B Kent Tekulve P2 .25 .10
1971 Waterbury and
1978 Pirates
363 Willie Stargell .50 .20
364 Phil Garner .25 .10
365 Ed Ott .10 .04
366 Don Robinson .10 .04
367 Chuck Tanner MG .25 .10
368 Jim Rooker .10 .04
369 Dale Berra .10 .04
370 Jim Bibby .10 .04
371 Steve Nicosia .10 .04
372 Mike Easler .10 .04
373 Bill Robinson .25 .10
374 Lee Lacy .10 .04
375 John Candelaria .25 .10
376 Manny Sanguillen .25 .10
377 Rick Rhoden .10 .04
378 Grant Jackson .10 .04
379 Tim Foli .10 .04
380 Rod Scurry .10 .04
381 Bill Madlock .25 .10
382A Kurt Bevacqua .25 .10
P1 ERR
P on cap backwards
382B Kurt Bevacqua P2 .10 .04
COR
383 Bert Blyleven .50 .20
384 Eddie Solomon .10 .04
385 Enrique Romo .10 .04
386 John Milner .10 .04
387 Mike Hargrove .25 .10
388 Jorge Orta .10 .04
389 Toby Harrah .25 .10
390 Tom Veryzer .10 .04
391 Miguel Dilone .10 .04
392 Dan Spillner .10 .04
393 Jack Brohamer .10 .04
394 Wayne Garland .10 .04
395 Sid Monge .10 .04
396 Rick Waits .10 .04
397 Joe Charboneau RC 1.00 .40
398 Gary Alexander .10 .04
399 Jerry Dybzinski .10 .04
400 Mike Stanton .10 .04
401 Mike Paxton .10 .04
402 Gary Gray .10 .04
403 Rick Manning .10 .04
404 Bo Diaz .10 .04
405 Ron Hassey .10 .04
406 Ross Grimsley .10 .04
407 Victor Cruz .10 .04
408 Len Barker .10 .04
409 Bob Bailor .10 .04
410 Otto Velez .10 .04
411 Ernie Whitt .10 .04
412 Jim Clancy .10 .04
413 Barry Bonnell .10 .04
414 Dave Stieb .25 .10
415 Damaso Garcia .10 .04
416 John Mayberry .10 .04
417 Roy Howell .10 .04
418 Danny Ainge RC 2.00 .80
419A Jesse Jefferson P1 .10 .04
Back says Pirates
419B Jesse Jefferson P2 .10 .04
Back says Pirates
419C Jesse Jefferson P3 .50 .20
Back says Blue Jays
420 Joey McLaughlin .10 .04
421 Lloyd Moseby .25 .10
422 Alvis Woods .10 .04
423 Garth Iorg .10 .04
424 Doug Ault .10 .04
425 Ken Schrom .10 .04
426 Mike Willis .10 .04
427 Steve Braun .10 .04
428 Bob Davis .10 .04
429 Jerry Garvin .10 .04
430 Alfredo Griffin .10 .04
431 Bob Mattick MG .10 .04
432 Vida Blue .25 .10
433 Jack Clark .25 .10
434 Willie McCovey .25 .10
435 Mike Ivie .10 .04
436A Darrel Evans P1 ERR .50 .20
(Name on front Darrel
436B Darrell Evans P2 COR .50 .20
Name on front Darrell
437 Terry Whitfield .10 .04
438 Rennie Stennett .10 .04
439 John Montefusco .10 .04
440 Jim Wohlford .10 .04
441 Bill North .10 .04
442 Milt May .10 .04
443 Max Venable .10 .04
444 Ed Whitson .10 .04
445 Al Holland .10 .04
446 Randy Moffitt .10 .04
447 Bob Knepper .10 .04
448 Gary Lavelle .10 .04
449 Greg Minton .10 .04
450 Johnnie LeMaster .10 .04
451 Larry Herndon .10 .04
452 Rich Murray .10 .04
453 Joe Pettini .10 .04
454 Allen Ripley .10 .04
455 Dennis Littlejohn .10 .04
456 Tom Griffin .10 .04
457 Alan Hargesheimer .10 .04
458 Joe Strain .10 .04
459 Steve Kemp .10 .04
460 Sparky Anderson MG .25 .10
461 Alan Trammell 1.00 .40
462 Mark Fidrych 1.00 .40
463 Lou Whitaker .50 .20
464 Dave Rozema .10 .04
465 Milt Wilcox .10 .04
466 Champ Summers .10 .04
467 Lance Parrish .25 .10
468 Dan Petry .10 .04
469 Pat Underwood .10 .04
470 Rick Peters .10 .04
471 Al Cowens .10 .04
472 John Wockenfuss .10 .04
473 Tom Brookens .10 .04
474 Richie Hebner .10 .04
475 Jack Morris .50 .20
476 Jim Lentine .10 .04
477 Bruce Robbins .10 .04
478 Mark Wagner .10 .04
479 Tim Corcoran .10 .04
480A Stan Papi P1 .25 .10
Front as Pitcher
480B Stan Papi P2 .10 .04
Front as Shortstop
481 Kirk Gibson RC 2.00 .80
482 Dan Schatzeder .10 .04
483A Amos Otis P1 .25 .10
See card 32
483B Amos Otis P2 .25 .10
See card 32
484 Dave Winfield .50 .20
485 Rollie Fingers .25 .10
486 Gene Richards .10 .04
487 Randy Jones .10 .04
488 Ozzie Smith 3.00 1.20

489 Gene Tenace .25 .10
490 Bill Fahey .10 .04
491 John Curtis .10 .04
492 Dave Cash .10 .04
493A Tim Flannery P1 .25 .10
Batting right
493B Tim Flannery P2 .10 .04
Batting left
494 Jerry Mumphrey .10 .04
495 Bob Shirley .10 .04
496 Steve Mura .10 .04
497 Eric Rasmussen .10 .04
498 Broderick Perkins .10 .04
499 Barry Evans .10 .04
500 Chuck Baker .10 .04
501 Luis Salazar RC .10 .04
502 Gary Lucas .10 .04
503 Mike Armstrong .10 .04
504 Jerry Turner .10 .04
505 Dennis Kinney .10 .04
506 Willie Montanez UER .10 .04
Spelled Willy on card front
507 Gorman Thomas .25 .10
508 Ben Oglivie .25 .10
509 Larry Hisle .10 .04
510 Sal Bando .25 .10
511 Robin Yount 1.50 .60
512 Mike Caldwell .10 .04
513 Sixto Lezcano .10 .04
514A Bill Travers P1 ERR .25 .10
Jerry Augustine
with Augustine back
514B Bill Travers P2 COR .10 .04
515 Paul Molitor 1.00 .40
516 Moose Haas .10 .04
517 Bill Castro .10 .04
518 Jim Slaton .10 .04
519 Lary Sorensen .10 .04
520 Bob McClure .10 .04
521 Charlie Moore .10 .04
522 Jim Gantner .25 .10
523 Reggie Cleveland .10 .04
524 Don Money .10 .04
525 Bill Travers .10 .04
526 Buck Martinez .10 .04
527 Dick Davis .10 .04
528 Ted Simmons .25 .10
529 Garry Templeton .10 .04
530 Ken Reitz .10 .04
531 Tony Scott .10 .04
532 Ken Oberkfell .10 .04
533 Bob Sykes .10 .04
534 Keith Smith .10 .04
535 John Littlefield .10 .04
536 Jim Kaat .25 .10
537 Bob Forsch .10 .04
538 Mike Phillips .10 .04
539 Terry Landrum .10 .04
540 Leon Durham .25 .10
541 Terry Kennedy .10 .04
542 George Hendrick .10 .04
543 Dane Iorg .10 .04
544 Mark Littell .10 .04
545 Keith Hernandez .50 .20
546 Silvio Martinez .10 .04
547A Don Hood P1 ERR .25 .10
Pete Vuckovich
with Vuckovich back
547B Don Hood P2 COR .10 .04
548 Bobby Bonds .25 .10
549 Mike Ramsey RC .10 .04
550 Tom Herr .25 .10
551 Roy Smalley .10 .04
552 Jerry Koosman .25 .10
553 Ken Landreaux .10 .04
554 John Castino .10 .04
555 Doug Corbett .10 .04
556 Bombo Rivera .10 .04
557 Ron Jackson .10 .04
558 Butch Wynegar .10 .04
559 Hosken Powell .10 .04
560 Pete Redfern .10 .04
561 Roger Erickson .10 .04
562 Glenn Adams .10 .04
563 Rick Sofield .10 .04
564 Geoff Zahn .10 .04
565 Pete Mackanin .10 .04
566 Mike Cubbage .10 .04
567 Darrell Jackson .10 .04
568 Dave Edwards .10 .04
569 Rob Wilfong .10 .04
570 Sal Butera .10 .04
571 Jose Morales .10 .04
572 Rick Langford .10 .04
573 Mike Norris .10 .04
574 Rickey Henderson 6.00 2.40
575 Tony Armas .25 .10
576 Dave Revering .10 .04
577 Jeff Newman .10 .04
578 Bob Lacey .10 .04
579 Brian Kingman .10 .04
580 Mitchell Page .10 .04
581 Billy Martin MG .50 .20
582 Rob Picciolo .10 .04
583 Mike Heath .10 .04
584 Mickey Klutts .10 .04
585 Orlando Gonzalez .10 .04
586 Mike Davis .10 .04
587 Wayne Gross .10 .04
588 Matt Keough .10 .04
589 Steve McCatty .10 .04
590 Dwayne Murphy .10 .04
591 Mario Guerrero .10 .04
592 Dave McKay .10 .04
593 Jim Essian .10 .04
594 Dave Heaverlo .10 .04
595 Maury Wills MG .25 .10
596 Juan Beniquez .10 .04
597 Rodney Craig .10 .04
598 Jim Anderson .10 .04
599 Floyd Bannister .10 .04
600 Bruce Bochte .10 .04
601 Julio Cruz .10 .04
602 Ted Cox .10 .04
603 Dan Meyer .10 .04
604 Larry Cox .10 .04
605 Bill Stein .10 .04
606 Steve Garvey .25 .10
Most Hits NL
607 Dave Roberts .10 .04
608 Leon Roberts .10 .04
609 Reggie Walton .10 .04
610 Dave Edler .10 .04
611 Larry Milbourne .10 .04
612 Kim Allen .10 .04
613 Mario Mendoza .10 .04
614 Tom Paciorek .25 .10
615 Glenn Abbott .10 .04
616 Joe Simpson .10 .04
617 Mickey Rivers .25 .10
618 Jim Kern .10 .04
619 Jim Sundberg .25 .10
620 Richie Zisk .10 .04
621 Jon Matlack .10 .04
622 Ferguson Jenkins .25 .10
623 Pat Corrales MG .10 .04
624 Ed Figueroa .10 .04
625 Buddy Bell .25 .10
626 Al Oliver .25 .10
627 Doc Medich .10 .04
628 Bump Wills .10 .04
629 Rusty Staub .25 .10
630 Pat Putnam .10 .04
631 John Grubb .10 .04
632 Danny Darwin .10 .04
633 Ken Clay .10 .04
634 Jim Norris .10 .04
635 John Butcher .10 .04
636 Dave Roberts .10 .04
637 Billy Sample .10 .04
638 Carl Yastrzemski 1.50 .60
639 Cecil Cooper .25 .10
640 Mike Schmidt P1 2.50 1.00
Portrait
Third Base
number on back 5
640B Mike Schmidt P2 2.50 1.00
1980 Home Run King
640 on back
641A CL: Phils/Royals P1 .25 .10
41 is Hal McRae
641B CL: Phils/Royals P2 .25 .10
41 is Hal McRae
Double Threat
642 CL: Astros/Yankees .10 .04
643 CL: Expos/Dodgers .10 .04
644A CL: Reds/Orioles P1 .25 .10
202 is George Foster
Joe Nolan pitcher
should be catcher
644B CL: Reds/Orioles P2 .25 .10
202 is Foster Slugger
Joe Nolan pitcher
should be catcher
645 Pete Rose 1.50 .60
Larry Bowa
Mike Schmidt
Triple Threat P1
No number on back
645B Pete Rose 2.50 1.00
Larry Bowa
Mike Schmidt
Triple Threat P2
Back numbered 645
646 CL: Braves/Red Sox .10 .04
647 CL: Cubs/Angels .10 .04
648 CL: Mets/White Sox .10 .04
649 CL: Indians/Pirates .10 .04
650 Reggie Jackson .50 .20
Mr. Baseball P1
Number on back 79
650B Reggie Jackson .50 .20
Mr. Baseball P2
Number on back 650
651 CL: Giants/Blue Jays .10 .04
652A CL:Tigers/Padres P1 .25 .10
483 is listed
652B CL:Tigers/Padres P2 .25 .10
483 is deleted
653A Willie Wilson P1 .25 .10
Most Hits Most Runs
Number on back 29
653B Willie Wilson P2 .25 .10
Most Hits Most Runs
Number on back 653
654A Checklist Brewers .25 .10
Cards P1
514 Jerry Augustine
547 Pete Vuckovich
654B Checklist Brewers .25 .10
Cards P2
514 Billy Travers
547 Don Hood
655 George Brett P1 2.50 1.00
.390 Average
Number on back 28
655B George Brett P2 2.50 1.00
.390 Average
Number on back 655
656 CL:Twins/Oakland A's .25 .10
657A Tug McGraw P1 .25 .10
Game Saver
Number on back 7
657B Tug McGraw P2 .25 .10
Game Saver
Number on back 657
658 CL: Rangers/Mariners .10 .04
659A Checklist P1 .10 .04
of Special Cards
Last lines on front
Wilson Most Hits
659B Checklist P2 .10 .04
of Special Cards
Last lines on front
Otis Series Starter
660 Steve Carlton P1 .25 .10
Golden Arm
(Number on back 660
Back 1066 Cardinals
660B Steve Carlton P2 2.00 .80
Golden Arm
1966 Cardinals

1981 Fleer Sticker Cards

The stickers in this 128-sticker standard-size set were distributed in wax packs. The 1981 Fleer Baseball Star Stickers consist of numbered cards with peelable, full-color sticker fronts and three unnumbered checklists. The backs of the numbered player cards are the same as the 1981 Fleer regular issue cards except for the numbers, while the checklist cards (cards 126-128 below) have sticker fronts of Jackson (1-42), Brett (43-83), and Schmidt (84-125).

Nm-Mt Ex-Mt
COMPLETE SET (128) 30.00 12.00
1 Steve Garvey .50 .20
2 Ron LeFlore .10 .04
3 Ron Cey .15 .06
4 Dave Revering .10 .04
5 Tony Armas .10 .04
6 Mike Norris .10 .04
7 Steve Kemp .10 .04
8 Bruce Bochte .10 .04
9 Mike Schmidt 2.50 1.00
10 Scott McGregor .10 .04
11 Buddy Bell .15 .06
12 Carney Lansford .15 .06
13 Carl Yastrzemski 1.00 .40
14 Ben Oglivie .10 .04
15 Willie Stargell .50 .20
16 Cecil Cooper .15 .06
17 Gene Richards .10 .04
18 Jim Kern .10 .04
19 Jerry Koosman .15 .06
20 Larry Bowa .15 .06
21 Kent Tekulve .15 .06
22 Dan Driessen .10 .04
23 Phil Niekro .50 .20
24 Dan Quisenberry .15 .06
25 Dave Winfield 1.00 .40
26 Dave Parker .15 .06
27 Rick Langford .10 .04
28 Amos Otis .15 .06
29 Bill Buckner .15 .06
30 Al Bumbry .10 .04
31 Bake McBride .10 .04
32 Mickey Rivers .15 .06
33 Rick Burleson .10 .04
34 Dennis Eckersley .50 .20
35 Cesar Cedeno .15 .06
36 Enos Cabell .10 .04
37 Johnny Bench 1.00 .40
38 Robin Yount 1.00 .40
39 Mark Belanger .15 .06
40 Rod Carew .75 .30
41 George Foster .15 .06
42 Lee Mazzilli .10 .04
43 Pete Rose 2.00 .80
Larry Bowa
Mike Schmidt
44 J.R. Richard .10 .04
45 Lou Piniella .15 .06
46 Ken Landreaux .10 .04
47 Rollie Fingers .50 .20
48 Joaquin Andujar .15 .06
49 Tom Seaver 1.00 .40
50 Bobby Grich .15 .06
51 Jon Matlack .10 .04
52 Jack Clark .15 .06
53 Jim Rice .15 .06
54 Rickey Henderson 4.00 1.60
55 Roy Smalley .10 .04
56 Mike Flanagan .10 .04
57 Steve Rogers .10 .04
58 Carlton Fisk 1.50 .60
59 Don Sutton .50 .20
60 Ken Griffey .15 .06
61 Burt Hooton .10 .04
62 Dusty Baker .15 .06
63 Vida Blue .15 .06
64 Al Oliver .15 .06
65 Jim Bibby .10 .04
66 Tony Perez .30 .12
67 Davey Lopes .15 .06
68 Bill Russell .15 .06
69 Larry Parrish .10 .04
70 Garry Maddox .10 .04
71 Phil Garner .10 .04
72 Graig Nettles .20 .08
73 Gary Carter .75 .30
74 Pete Rose 1.50 .60
75 Greg Luzinski .15 .06
76 Ron Guidry .15 .06
77 Gorman Thomas .10 .04
78 Jose Cruz .15 .06
79 Bob Boone .15 .06
80 Bruce Sutter .15 .06
81 Chris Chambliss .15 .06
82 Paul Molitor 2.00 .80
83 Tug McGraw .15 .06
84 Ferguson Jenkins .30 .12
85 Steve Carlton .75 .30
86 Miguel Dilone .10 .04
87 Reggie Smith .15 .06
88 Rick Cerone .10 .04
89 Alan Trammell .50 .20
90 Doug DeCinces .10 .04
91 Sparky Lyle .15 .06
92 Warren Cromartie .10 .04
93 Rick Reuschel .15 .06
94 Larry Hisle .10 .04
95 Paul Splittorff .10 .04
96 Manny Trillo .10 .04
97 Frank White .15 .06
98 Fred Lynn .15 .06
99 Bob Horner .15 .06
100 Omar Moreno .10 .04
101 Dave Concepcion .15 .06
102 Larry Gura .10 .04
103 Ken Singleton .15 .06
104 Steve Stone .10 .04
105 Richie Zisk .15 .06
106 Willie Wilson .15 .06
107 Willie Randolph .15 .06
108 Nolan Ryan 8.00 3.20
109 Joe Morgan .75 .30
110 Bucky Dent .15 .06
111 Dave Kingman .20 .08
112 John Castino .10 .04
113 Joe Rudi .10 .04
114 Ed Farmer .10 .04
115 Reggie Jackson 1.00 .40
116 George Brett 3.00 1.20
117 Eddie Murray 2.00 .80
118 Rich Gossage .25 .10
119 Dale Murphy .75 .30
120 Ted Simmons .15 .06
121 Tommy John .25 .10
122 Don Baylor .20 .08
123 Andre Dawson .75 .30
124 Jim Palmer .75 .30
125 Garry Templeton .10 .04
126 Reggie Jackson CL 1 .50 .20
Unnumbered
127 George Brett CL 2 1.50 .60
Unnumbered
128 Mike Schmidt CL3 1.00 .40
Unnumbered

1982 Fleer

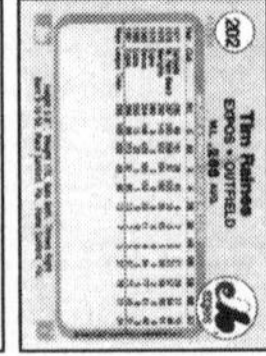

The 1982 Fleer set contains 660-card standard-size cards, of which are grouped in team order based upon standings from the previous season. Cards numbered 628 through 646 are special cards highlighting some of the stars and leaders of the 1981 season. The last 14 cards in the set (647-660) are checklist cards. The backs feature player statistics and a full-color team logo in the upper right-hand corner of each card. The complete set price below does not include any of the more valuable variation cards listed. Fleer was not allowed to insert bubble gum or other confectionary products into these packs; therefore logo stickers were included in these 15-card packs. Notable Rookie Cards in this set include Cal Ripken Jr., Lee Smith, and Dave Stewart.

Nm-Mt Ex-Mt
COMPLETE SET (660) 50.00 20.00
1 Dusty Baker .40 .16
2 Robert Castillo .10 .04
3 Ron Cey .20 .08
4 Terry Forster .10 .04
5 Steve Garvey .20 .08
6 Dave Goltz .10 .04
7 Pedro Guerrero .20 .08
8 Burt Hooton .10 .04
9 Steve Howe .10 .04
10 Jay Johnstone .20 .08
11 Ken Landreaux .10 .04
12 Dave Lopes .20 .08
13 Mike A. Marshall .20 .08
14 Bobby Mitchell .10 .04
15 Rick Monday .10 .04
16 Tom Niedenfuer .10 .04
17 Ted Power RC .10 .04
18 Jerry Reuss UER .20 .08
("Home:" omitted)
19 Ron Roenicke .10 .04
20 Bill Russell .10 .04
21 Steve Sax RC .75 .30
22 Mike Scioscia .20 .08
23 Reggie Smith .20 .08
24 Dave Stewart RC 1.00 .40
25 Rick Sutcliffe .20 .08
26 Derrel Thomas .10 .04
27 Fernando Valenzuela .75 .30
28 Bob Welch .20 .08
29 Steve Yeager .10 .04
30 Bobby Brown .10 .04
31 Rick Cerone .10 .04
32 Ron Davis .10 .04
33 Bucky Dent .20 .08
34 Barry Foote .10 .04
35 George Frazier .10 .04
36 Oscar Gamble .10 .04
37 Rich Gossage .40 .16
38 Ron Guidry .20 .08
39 Reggie Jackson .40 .16
40 Tommy John .40 .16
41 Rudy May .10 .04
42 Larry Milbourne .10 .04
43 Jerry Mumphrey .10 .04
44 Bobby Murcer .20 .08
45 Gene Nelson .10 .04
46 Graig Nettles .20 .08
47 Johnny Oates .20 .08
48 Lou Piniella .20 .08
49 Willie Randolph .20 .08
50 Rick Reuschel .20 .08
51 Dave Revering .10 .04
52 Dave Righetti RC .75 .30
53 Aurelio Rodriguez .10 .04
54 Bob Watson .20 .08
55 Dennis Werth .10 .04
56 Dave Winfield .20 .08
57 Johnny Bench .75 .30
58 Bruce Berenyi .10 .04
59 Larry Biittner .10 .04
60 Scott Brown .10 .04
61 Dave Collins .10 .04
62 Geoff Combe .10 .04
63 Dave Concepcion .20 .08
64 Dan Driessen .10 .04
65 Joe Edelen .10 .04
66 George Foster .20 .08
67 Ken Griffey .20 .08
68 Paul Householder .10 .04
69 Tom Hume .10 .04
70 Junior Kennedy .10 .04
71 Ray Knight .20 .08
72 Mike LaCoss .10 .04
73 Rafael Landestoy .10 .04
74 Charlie Leibrandt .10 .04
75 Sam Mejias .10 .04
76 Paul Moskau .10 .04
77 Joe Nolan .10 .04
78 Mike O'Berry .10 .04
79 Ron Oester .10 .04
80 Frank Pastore .10 .04
81 Joe Price .10 .04
82 Tom Seaver .40 .16
83 Mario Soto .10 .04
84 Mike Vail .10 .04
85 Tony Armas .10 .04
86 Shooty Babitt .10 .04
87 Dave Beard .10 .04
88 Rick Bosetti .10 .04
89 Keith Drumwright .10 .04
90 Wayne Gross .10 .04
91 Mike Heath .10 .04
92 Rickey Henderson 2.50 1.00
93 Cliff Johnson .10 .04
94 Jeff Jones .10 .04
95 Matt Keough .10 .04
96 Brian Kingman .10 .04
97 Mickey Klutts .10 .04
98 Rick Langford .10 .04
99 Steve McCatty .10 .04
100 Dave McKay .10 .04
101 Dwayne Murphy .10 .04
102 Jeff Newman .10 .04
103 Mike Norris .10 .04
104 Bob Owchinko .10 .04
105 Mitchell Page .10 .04
106 Rob Picciolo .10 .04
107 Jim Spencer .10 .04
108 Fred Stanley .10 .04
109 Tom Underwood .10 .04
110 Joaquin Andujar .20 .08
111 Steve Braun .10 .04
112 Bob Forsch .10 .04
113 George Hendrick .10 .04
114 Keith Hernandez .40 .16
115 Tom Herr .20 .08
116 Dane Iorg .10 .04
117 Jim Kaat .20 .08
118 Tito Landrum .10 .04
119 Sixto Lezcano .10 .04
120 Mark Littell .10 .04
121 John Martin RC .10 .04
122 Silvio Martinez .10 .04
123 Ken Oberkfell .10 .04
124 Darrell Porter .20 .08
125 Mike Ramsey .10 .04
126 Orlando Sanchez .10 .04
127 Bob Shirley .10 .04
128 Lary Sorensen .10 .04
129 Bruce Sutter .20 .08
130 Bob Sykes .10 .04
131 Garry Templeton .10 .04
132 Gene Tenace .20 .08
133 Jerry Augustine .10 .04
134 Sal Bando .20 .08
135 Mark Brouhard .10 .04
136 Mike Caldwell .10 .04
137 Reggie Cleveland .10 .04
138 Cecil Cooper .20 .08
139 Jamie Easterly .10 .04
140 Marshall Edwards .10 .04
141 Rollie Fingers .20 .08
142 Jim Gantner .20 .08
143 Moose Haas .10 .04
144 Larry Hisle .10 .04
145 Roy Howell .10 .04
146 Rickey Keeton .10 .04
147 Randy Lerch .10 .04
148 Paul Molitor .40 .16
149 Don Money .10 .04
150 Charlie Moore .10 .04
151 Ben Oglivie .20 .08
152 Ted Simmons .20 .08
153 Jim Slaton .10 .04
154 Gorman Thomas .20 .08
155 Robin Yount 1.25 .50
156 Pete Vuckovich .10 .04
(Should precede Yount
in the team order)
157 Benny Ayala .10 .04
158 Mark Belanger .10 .04
159 Al Bumbry .10 .04
160 Terry Crowley .10 .04
161 Rich Dauer .10 .04
162 Doug DeCinces .20 .08
163 Rick Dempsey .20 .08
164 Jim Dwyer .10 .04
165 Mike Flanagan .20 .08
166 Dave Ford .10 .04
167 Dan Graham .10 .04
168 Wayne Krenchicki .10 .04
169 John Lowenstein .10 .04
170 Dennis Martinez .40 .16
171 Tippy Martinez .10 .04
172 Scott McGregor .10 .04
173 Jose Morales .10 .04
174 Eddie Murray .75 .30
175 Jim Palmer .20 .08
176 Cal Ripken RC 40.00 16.00
Fleer Ripken cards from 1982
through 1993 erroneously have 22
games played in 1981;not 23.
177 Gary Roenicke .10 .04
178 Lenn Sakata .10 .04
179 Ken Singleton .20 .08
180 Sammy Stewart .10 .04
181 Tim Stoddard .10 .04
182 Steve Stone .20 .08
183 Stan Bahnsen .10 .04
184 Ray Burris .10 .04
185 Gary Carter .40 .16
186 Warren Cromartie .10 .04
187 Andre Dawson .20 .08
188 Terry Francona .40 .16
189 Woodie Fryman .10 .04
190 Bill Gullickson .10 .04
191 Grant Jackson .10 .04
192 Wallace Johnson .10 .04
193 Charlie Lea .10 .04
194 Bill Lee .20 .08
195 Jerry Manuel .10 .04
196 Brad Mills .10 .04
197 John Milner .10 .04
198 Rowland Office .10 .04
199 David Palmer .10 .04
200 Larry Parrish .10 .04

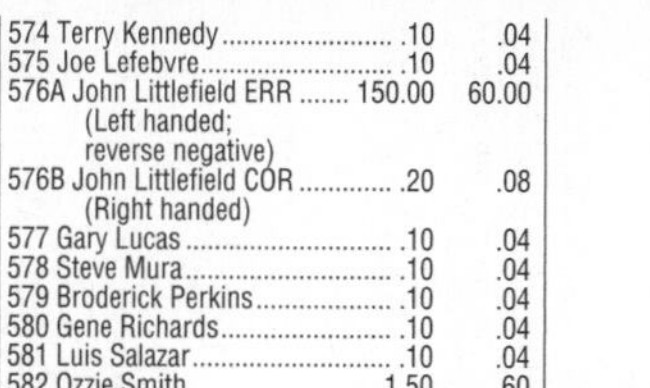

201 Mike Phillips .10 .04
202 Tim Raines .75 .30
203 Bobby Ramos .10 .04
204 Jeff Reardon .40 .16
205 Steve Rogers .10 .04
206 Scott Sanderson .10 .04
207 Rodney Scott UER .40 .16
(Photo actually
Tim Raines)
208 Elias Sosa .10 .04
209 Chris Speier .10 .04
210 Tim Wallach RC .40 .16
211 Jerry White .10 .04
212 Alan Ashby .10 .04
213 Cesar Cedeno .20 .08
214 Jose Cruz .20 .08
215 Kiko Garcia .10 .04
216 Phil Garner .20 .08
217 Danny Heep .10 .04
218 Art Howe .20 .08
219 Bob Knepper .10 .04
220 Frank LaCorte .10 .04
221 Joe Niekro .20 .08
222 Joe Pittman .10 .04
223 Terry Puhl .10 .04
224 Luis Pujols .10 .04
225 Craig Reynolds .10 .04
226 J.R. Richard .20 .08
227 Dave Roberts .10 .04
228 Vern Ruhle .10 .04
229 Nolan Ryan 4.00 1.60
230 Joe Sambito .10 .04
231 Tony Scott .10 .04
232 Dave Smith .10 .04
233 Harry Spilman .10 .04
234 Don Sutton .75 .30
235 Dickie Thon .10 .04
236 Denny Walling .10 .04
237 Gary Woods .10 .04
238 Luis Aguayo .10 .04
239 Ramon Aviles .10 .04
240 Bob Boone .20 .08
241 Larry Bowa .20 .08
242 Warren Brusstar .10 .04
243 Steve Carlton .20 .08
244 Larry Christenson .10 .04
245 Dick Davis .10 .04
246 Greg Gross .10 .04
247 Sparky Lyle .20 .08
248 Garry Maddox .10 .04
249 Gary Matthews .20 .08
250 Bake McBride .10 .04
251 Tug McGraw .20 .08
252 Keith Moreland .10 .04
253 Dickie Noles .10 .04
254 Mike Proly .10 .04
255 Ron Reed .10 .04
256 Pete Rose 2.50 1.00
257 Dick Ruthven .10 .04
258 Mike Schmidt 2.00 .80
259 Lonnie Smith .20 .08
260 Manny Trillo .10 .04
261 Del Unser .10 .04
262 George Vukovich .10 .04
263 Tom Brookens .10 .04
264 George Cappuzzello .10 .04
265 Marty Castillo .10 .04
266 Al Cowens .10 .04
267 Kirk Gibson .75 .30
268 Richie Hebner .20 .08
269 Ron Jackson .10 .04
270 Lynn Jones .10 .04
271 Steve Kemp .10 .04
272 Rick Leach .10 .04
273 Aurelio Lopez .10 .04
274 Jack Morris .20 .08
275 Kevin Saucier .10 .04
276 Lance Parrish .40 .16
277 Rick Peters .10 .04
278 Dan Petry .10 .04
279 Dave Rozema .10 .04
280 Stan Papi .10 .04
281 Dan Schatzeder .10 .04
282 Champ Summers .10 .04
283 Alan Trammell .40 .16
284 Lou Whitaker .20 .08
285 Milt Wilcox .10 .04
286 John Wockenfuss .10 .04
287 Gary Allenson .10 .04
288 Tom Burgmeier .10 .04
289 Bill Campbell .10 .04
290 Mark Clear .10 .04
291 Steve Crawford .10 .04
292 Dennis Eckersley .40 .16
293 Dwight Evans .40 .16
294 Rich Gedman .20 .08
295 Garry Hancock .10 .04
296 Glenn Hoffman .10 .04
297 Bruce Hurst .10 .04
298 Carney Lansford .20 .08
299 Rick Miller .10 .04
300 Reid Nichols .10 .04
301 Bob Ojeda RC .40 .16
302 Tony Perez .40 .16
303 Chuck Rainey .10 .04
304 Jerry Remy .10 .04
305 Jim Rice .20 .08
306 Joe Rudi .10 .04
307 Bob Stanley .10 .04
308 Dave Stapleton .10 .04
309 Frank Tanana .20 .08
310 Mike Torrez .10 .04
311 John Tudor .10 .04
312 Carl Yastrzemski 1.25 .50
313 Buddy Bell .20 .08
314 Steve Comer .10 .04
315 Danny Darwin .10 .04
316 John Ellis .10 .04
317 John Grubb .10 .04
318 Rick Honeycutt .10 .04
319 Charlie Hough .20 .08
320 Ferguson Jenkins .20 .08
321 John Henry Johnson .10 .04
322 Jim Kern .10 .04
323 Jon Matlack .10 .04
324 Doc Medich .10 .04
325 Mario Mendoza .10 .04
326 Al Oliver .20 .08
327 Pat Putnam .10 .04
328 Mickey Rivers .10 .04
329 Leon Roberts .10 .04
330 Billy Sample .10 .04
331 Bill Stein .10 .04
332 Jim Sundberg .10 .04
333 Mark Wagner .10 .04
334 Bump Wills .10 .04
335 Bill Almon .10 .04
336 Harold Baines .75 .30
337 Ross Baumgarten .10 .04
338 Tony Bernazard .10 .04
339 Britt Burns .10 .04
340 Richard Dotson .10 .04
341 Jim Essian .10 .04
342 Ed Farmer .10 .04
343 Carlton Fisk .40 .16
344 Kevin Hickey RC .10 .04
345 LaMarr Hoyt .10 .04
346 Lamar Johnson .10 .04
347 Jerry Koosman .20 .08
348 Rusty Kuntz .10 .04
349 Dennis Lamp .10 .04
350 Ron LeFlore .20 .08
351 Chet Lemon .10 .04
352 Greg Luzinski .20 .08
353 Bob Molinaro .10 .04
354 Jim Morrison .10 .04
355 Wayne Nordhagen .10 .04
356 Greg Pryor .10 .04
357 Mike Squires .10 .04
358 Steve Trout .10 .04
359 Alan Bannister .10 .04
360 Len Barker .10 .04
361 Bert Blyleven .40 .16
362 Joe Charboneau .20 .08
363 John Denny .10 .04
364 Bo Diaz .10 .04
365 Miguel Dilone .10 .04
366 Jerry Dybzinski .10 .04
367 Wayne Garland .10 .04
368 Mike Hargrove .20 .08
369 Toby Harrah .20 .08
370 Ron Hassey .20 .08
371 Von Hayes .20 .08
372 Pat Kelly .10 .04
373 Duane Kuiper .10 .04
374 Rick Manning .10 .04
375 Sid Monge .10 .04
376 Jorge Orta .10 .04
377 Dave Rosello .10 .04
378 Dan Spillner .10 .04
379 Mike Stanton .10 .04
380 Andre Thornton .10 .04
381 Tom Veryzer .10 .04
382 Rick Waits .10 .04
383 Doyle Alexander .10 .04
384 Vida Blue .20 .08
385 Fred Breining .10 .04
386 Enos Cabell .10 .04
387 Jack Clark .20 .08
388 Darrell Evans .20 .08
389 Tom Griffin .10 .04
390 Larry Herndon .10 .04
391 Al Holland .10 .04
392 Gary Lavelle .10 .04
393 Johnnie LeMaster .10 .04
394 Jerry Martin .10 .04
395 Milt May .10 .04
396 Greg Minton .10 .04
397 Joe Morgan .40 .16
398 Joe Pettini .10 .04
399 Allen Ripley .10 .04
400 Billy Smith .10 .04
401 Rennie Stennett .10 .04
402 Ed Whitson .10 .04
403 Jim Wohlford .10 .04
404 Willie Aikens .10 .04
405 George Brett 2.00 .80
406 Ken Brett .10 .04
407 Dave Chalk .10 .04
408 Rich Gale .10 .04
409 Cesar Geronimo .10 .04
410 Larry Gura .10 .04
411 Clint Hurdle .10 .04
412 Mike Jones .10 .04
413 Dennis Leonard .10 .04
414 Renie Martin .10 .04
415 Lee May .20 .08
416 Hal McRae .20 .08
417 Darryl Motley .10 .04
418 Rance Mulliniks .10 .04
419 Amos Otis .20 .08
420 Ken Phelps .10 .04
421 Jamie Quirk .10 .04
422 Dan Quisenberry .20 .08
423 Paul Splittorff .10 .04
424 U.L. Washington .10 .04
425 John Wathan .10 .04
426 Frank White .20 .08
427 Willie Wilson .20 .08
428 Brian Asselstine .10 .04
429 Bruce Benedict .10 .04
430 Tommy Boggs .10 .04
431 Larry Bradford .10 .04
432 Rick Camp .10 .04
433 Chris Chambliss .20 .08
434 Gene Garber .10 .04
435 Preston Hanna .10 .04
436 Bob Horner .20 .08
437 Glenn Hubbard .10 .04
438A All Hrabosky ERR 8.00 3.20
(Height 5'1"
All on reverse)
438B Al Hrabosky ERR .40 .16
(Height 5'1")
438C Al Hrabosky .20 .08
(Height 5'10")
439 Rufino Linares .10 .04
440 Rick Mahler .10 .04
441 Ed Miller .10 .04
442 John Montefusco .10 .04
443 Dale Murphy .75 .30
444 Phil Niekro .20 .08
445 Gaylord Perry .20 .08
446 Biff Pocoroba .10 .04
447 Rafael Ramirez .10 .04
448 Jerry Royster .10 .04
449 Claudell Washington .10 .04
450 Don Aase .10 .04
451 Don Baylor .40 .16
452 Juan Beniquez .10 .04
453 Rick Burleson .10 .04
454 Bert Campaneris .20 .08
455 Rod Carew .40 .16
456 Bob Clark .10 .04
457 Brian Downing .10 .04
458 Dan Ford .10 .04
459 Ken Forsch .10 .04
460A Dave Frost (5 mm .10 .04
space before ERA)
460B Dave Frost .10 .04
(1 mm space)
461 Bobby Grich .20 .08
462 Larry Harlow .10 .04
463 John Harris .10 .04
464 Andy Hassler .10 .04
465 Butch Hobson .10 .04
466 Jesse Jefferson .10 .04
467 Bruce Kison .10 .04
468 Fred Lynn .20 .08
469 Angel Moreno .10 .04
470 Ed Ott .10 .04
471 Fred Patek .10 .04
472 Steve Renko .10 .04
473 Mike Witt .20 .08
474 Geoff Zahn .10 .04
475 Gary Alexander .10 .04
476 Dale Berra .10 .04
477 Kurt Bevacqua .10 .04
478 Jim Bibby .10 .04
479 John Candelaria .10 .04
480 Victor Cruz .10 .04
481 Mike Easler .10 .04
482 Tim Foli .10 .04
483 Lee Lacy .10 .04
484 Vance Law .10 .04
485 Bill Madlock .20 .08
486 Willie Montanez .10 .04
487 Omar Moreno .10 .04
488 Steve Nicosia .10 .04
489 Dave Parker .20 .08
490 Tony Pena .20 .08
491 Pascual Perez .10 .04
492 Johnny Ray .20 .08
493 Rick Rhoden .10 .04
494 Bill Robinson .10 .04
495 Don Robinson .10 .04
496 Enrique Romo .10 .04
497 Rod Scurry .10 .04
498 Eddie Solomon .10 .04
499 Willie Stargell .40 .16
500 Kent Tekulve .20 .08
501 Jason Thompson .10 .04
502 Glenn Abbott .10 .04
503 Jim Anderson .10 .04
504 Floyd Bannister .10 .04
505 Bruce Bochte .10 .04
506 Jeff Burroughs .10 .04
507 Bryan Clark RC .10 .04
508 Ken Clay .10 .04
509 Julio Cruz .10 .04
510 Dick Drago .10 .04
511 Gary Gray .10 .04
512 Dan Meyer .10 .04
513 Jerry Narron .10 .04
514 Tom Paciorek .20 .08
515 Casey Parsons .10 .04
516 Lenny Randle .10 .04
517 Shane Rawley .10 .04
518 Joe Simpson .10 .04
519 Richie Zisk .10 .04
520 Neil Allen .10 .04
521 Bob Bailor .10 .04
522 Hubie Brooks .20 .08
523 Mike Cubbage .10 .04
524 Pete Falcone .10 .04
525 Doug Flynn .10 .04
526 Tom Hausman .10 .04
527 Ron Hodges .10 .04
528 Randy Jones .10 .04
529 Mike Jorgensen .10 .04
530 Dave Kingman .20 .08
531 Ed Lynch .10 .04
532 Mike G. Marshall .10 .04
533 Lee Mazzilli .10 .04
534 Dyar Miller .10 .04
535 Mike Scott .20 .08
536 Rusty Staub .20 .08
537 John Stearns .10 .04
538 Craig Swan .10 .04
539 Frank Taveras .10 .04
540 Alex Trevino .10 .04
541 Ellis Valentine .10 .04
542 Mookie Wilson .20 .08
543 Joel Youngblood .10 .04
544 Pat Zachry .10 .04
545 Glenn Adams .10 .04
546 Fernando Arroyo .10 .04
547 John Verhoeven .10 .04
548 Sal Butera .10 .04
549 John Castino .10 .04
550 Don Cooper .10 .04
551 Doug Corbett .10 .04
552 Dave Engle .10 .04
553 Roger Erickson .10 .04
554 Danny Goodwin .10 .04
555A Darrell Jackson .40 .16
(Black cap)
555B Darrell Jackson .20 .08
(Red cap with T)
555C Darrell Jackson 3.00 1.20
(Red cap, no emblem)
556 Pete Mackanin .10 .04
557 Jack O'Connor .10 .04
558 Hosken Powell .10 .04
559 Pete Redfern .10 .04
560 Roy Smalley .10 .04
561 Chuck Baker UER .10 .04
(Shortstop on front)
562 Gary Ward .10 .04
563 Rob Wilfong .10 .04
564 Al Williams .10 .04
565 Butch Wynegar .10 .04
566 Randy Bass RC .20 .08
567 Juan Bonilla RC .10 .04
568 Danny Boone .10 .04
569 John Curtis .10 .04
570 Juan Eichelberger .10 .04
571 Barry Evans .10 .04
572 Tim Flannery .10 .04
573 Ruppert Jones .10 .04
574 Terry Kennedy .10 .04
575 Joe Lefebvre .10 .04
576A John Littlefield ERR 150.00 60.00
(Left handed;
reverse negative)
576B John Littlefield COR .20 .08
(Right handed)
577 Gary Lucas .10 .04
578 Steve Mura .10 .04
579 Broderick Perkins .10 .04
580 Gene Richards .10 .04
581 Luis Salazar .10 .04
582 Ozzie Smith 1.50 .60
583 John Urrea .10 .04
584 Chris Welsh .10 .04
585 Rick Wise .10 .04
586 Doug Bird .10 .04
587 Tim Blackwell .10 .04
588 Bobby Bonds .20 .08
589 Bill Buckner .20 .08
590 Bill Caudill .10 .04
591 Hector Cruz .10 .04
592 Jody Davis .10 .04
593 Ivan DeJesus .10 .04
594 Steve Dillard .10 .04
595 Leon Durham .10 .04
596 Rawly Eastwick .10 .04
597 Steve Henderson .10 .04
598 Mike Krukow .10 .04
599 Mike Lum .10 .04
600 Randy Martz .10 .04
601 Jerry Morales .10 .04
602 Ken Reitz .10 .04
603 Lee Smith RC ERR 2.00 .80
(Cubs logo reversed)
603B Lee Smith RC COR 6.00 2.40
604 Dick Tidrow .10 .04
605 Jim Tracy .10 .04
606 Mike Tyson .10 .04
607 Ty Waller .10 .04
608 Danny Ainge 1.00 .40
609 Jorge Bell RC .75 .30
610 Mark Bomback .10 .04
611 Barry Bonnell .10 .04
612 Jim Clancy .10 .04
613 Damaso Garcia .10 .04
614 Jerry Garvin .10 .04
615 Alfredo Griffin .10 .04
616 Garth Iorg .10 .04
617 Luis Leal .10 .04
618 Ken Macha .10 .04
619 John Mayberry .10 .04
620 Joey McLaughlin .10 .04
621 Lloyd Moseby .10 .04
622 Dave Stieb .20 .08
623 Jackson Todd .10 .04
624 Willie Upshaw .10 .04
625 Otto Velez .10 .04
626 Ernie Whitt .10 .04
627 Alvis Woods .10 .04
628 All Star Game .20 .08
Cleveland, Ohio
629 Frank White .20 .08
Bucky Dent
630 Dan Driessen .20 .08
Dave Concepcion
George Foster
631 Bruce Sutter .10 .04
Top NL Relief Pitcher
632 Steve Carlton .20 .08
Carlton Fisk
633 Carl Yastrzemski .75 .30
3000th Game
634 Johnny Bench .75 .30
Tom Seaver
635 Fernando Valenzuela .20 .08
Gary Carter
636A Fernando Valenzuela: .75 .30
NL SO King "he" NL
636B Fernando Valenzuela: .40 .16
NL SO King "the" NL
637 Mike Schmidt .75 .30
Home Run King
638 Gary Carter .20 .08
Dave Parker
639 Perfect Game UER .20 .08
Len Barker
Bo Diaz
(Catcher actually
Ron Hassey)
640 Pete Rose .75 .30
Pete Rose Jr.
641 Lonnie Smith .75 .30
Mike Schmidt
Steve Carlton
642 Fred Lynn .20 .08
Dwight Evans
643 Rickey Henderson 1.25 .50
Most Hits and Runs
644 Rollie Fingers .20 .08
Most Saves AL
645 Tom Seaver .20 .08
Most 1981 Wins
646 Yankee Powerhouse .20 .08
Reggie Jackson
Dave Winfield
(Comma on back
after outfielder)
646B Yankee Powerhouse .20 .08
Reggie Jackson
Dave Winfield
(No comma)
647 CL: Yankees/Dodgers .10 .04
648 CL: A's/Reds .10 .04
649 CL: Cards/Brewers .10 .04
650 CL: Expos/Orioles .10 .04
651 CL: Astros/Phillies .10 .04
652 CL: Tigers/Red Sox .10 .04
653 CL: Rangers/White Sox .10 .04
654 CL: Giants/Indians .10 .04
655 CL: Royals/Braves .10 .04
656 CL: Angels/Pirates .10 .04
657 CL: Mariners/Mets .10 .04
658 CL: Padres/Twins .10 .04
659 CL: Blue Jays/Cubs .10 .04
660 Specials Checklist .10 .04

1982 Fleer Stamps

The stamps in this 242-piece set measure 1 13/16" by 2 1/2". The 1982 Fleer stamp set consists of different individual stamps issued in strips of 10 stamps each. The stamps were issued in packages with the Fleer team logo stickers. The backs are blank and an inexpensive album is available in which to place the stamps. A checklist is provided in the back of the album which lists 25 strips of 10 stamps. The checklist below lists the individual stamps plus the strip (with prefix G) to which the stamps are supposed to belong based on the album strip checklist. Complete strips have equal value to the sum of the individual stamps on the strip. Eight stamps have been doubly printed and are noted by two different strip numbers below. The numbering is essentially in team order.

Nm-Mt Ex-Mt
COMPLETE SET (242) 20.00 8.00
COMMON SHEET .75 .30
1 Fern. Valenzuela G20 .50 .20
2 Rick Monday G16 .05 .02
3 Ron Cey G9 .10 .04
4 Dusty Baker G20 .10 .04
5 Burt Hooton G10 .05 .02
6 Pedro Guerrero G23 .10 .04
7 Jerry Reuss G12 .05 .02
8 Bill Russell G7 .05 .02
9 Steve Garvey G21 .15 .06
10 Davey Lopes G19 .10 .04
11 Tom Seaver G7 1.00 .40
12 George Foster G17 .10 .04
13 Frank Pastore G12 .05 .02
14 Dave Collins G5 .05 .02
15 Dave Concepcion G21 .10 .04
16 Ken Griffey G6 .10 .04
17 Johnny Bench G20 1.00 .40
18 Ray Knight G16 .05 .02
19 Mario Soto G9 .05 .02
20 Ron Oester G19 .05 .02
21 Ken Oberkfell G21 .05 .02
22 Bob Forsch G4 .05 .02
23 Keith Hernandez G19 .10 .04
24 Dane Iorg G9 .05 .02
25 George Hendrick G2 .05 .02
26 Gene Tenace G24 .05 .02
27 Garry Templeton G12 .05 .02
28 Bruce Sutter G18 .10 .04
29 Darrell Porter G14 .05 .02
30 Tom Herr G3 .05 .02
31 Tim Raines G11 .50 .20
32 Chris Speier G13 .05 .02
33 Warren Cromartie G22 .05 .02
34 Larry Parrish G15 .05 .02
35 Andre Dawson G10 .75 .30
36 Steve Rogers G1/G25 .05 .02
37 Jeff Reardon G23 .15 .06
38 Rodney Scott G12 .05 .02
39 Gary Carter G14 .60 .24
40 Scott Sanderson G6 .05 .02
41 Cesar Cedeno G7 .05 .02
42 Nolan Ryan G10 6.00 2.40
43 Don Sutton G24 .25 .10
44 Terry Puhl G15 .05 .02
45 Joe Niekro G13 .10 .04
46 Tony Scott G16 .05 .02
47 Joe Sambito G1 .05 .02
48 Art Howe G9 .10 .04
49 Bob Knepper G18 .05 .02
50 Jose Cruz G22 .10 .04
51 Pete Rose G16 2.00 .80
52 Dick Ruthven G12 .05 .02
53 Mike Schmidt G14 2.00 .80
54 Steve Carlton G17 1.00 .40
55 Tug McGraw G4 .10 .04
56 Larry Bowa G4 .10 .04
57 Garry Maddox G18 .05 .02
58 Gary Matthews G4 .05 .02
59 Manny Trillo G15 .05 .02
60 Lonnie Smith G20 .05 .02
61 Vida Blue G11 .10 .04
62 Milt May G12 .05 .02
63 Joe Morgan G16 .50 .20
64 Enos Cabell G8 .05 .02
65 Jack Clark G18 .10 .04
66 Claud.Washington G19 .05 .02
67 Gaylord Perry G16 .50 .20
68 Phil Niekro G22 .50 .20
69 Bob Horner G7 .05 .02
70 Chris Chambliss G11 .05 .02
71 Dave Parker G15 .10 .04
72 Tony Pena G11 .05 .02
73 Kent Tekulve G23 .05 .02
74 Mike Easler G18 .05 .02
75 Tim Foli G13 .05 .02
76 Willie Stargell G21 .50 .20
77 Bill Madlock G5 .10 .04
78 Jim Bibby G14 .05 .02
79 Omar Moreno G17 .05 .02
80 Lee Lacy G2 .05 .02
81 Hubie Brooks G24 .05 .02
82 Rusty Staub G4 .10 .04
83 Ellis Valentine G13 .05 .02
84 Neil Allen G1 .05 .02
85 Dave Kingman G9 .15 .06
86 Mookie Wilson G3 .15 .06
87 Doug Flynn G11 .05 .02
88 Pat Zachry G8 .05 .02
89 John Stearns G6 .05 .02
90 Lee Mazzilli G2 .05 .02
91 Ken Reitz G23 .05 .02
92 Mike Krukow G11 .05 .02
93 Jerry Morales G10 .05 .02
94 Leon Durham G22 .05 .02
95 Ivan DeJesus G2 .05 .02
96 Bill Buckner G17 .10 .04
97 Jim Tracy G12 .05 .02
98 Steve Henderson G14 .05 .02

99 Dick Tidrow G14 .05 .02
100 Mike Tyson G5 .05 .02
101 Ozzie Smith G12 2.50 1.00
102 Ruppert Jones G24 .05 .02
103 Brod Perkins G10 .05 .02
104 Gene Richards G15 .05 .02
105 Terry Kennedy G22 .05 .02
106 Jim Bibby and .15 .06
Willie Stargell G4
107 Pete Rose and .75 .30
Larry Bowa G21
108 Fern.Valenzuela and .25 .10
Warren Spahn G1/G25
109 Pete Rose and .75 .30
Dave Concepcion G8
110 Reggie Jackson and 1.50 .60
Dave Winfield G3
111 Fernando Valenzuela .15 .06
and Tom Lasorda G4
112 Reggie Jackson G6 2.00 .80
113 Dave Winfield G3 1.50 .60
114 Lou Piniella G2 .10 .04
115 Tommy John G9 .10 .04
116 Rich Gossage G1/G25 .10 .04
117 Ron Davis G10 .05 .02
118 Rick Cerone G5 .05 .02
119 Graig Nettles G8 .10 .04
120 Ron Guidry G24 .10 .04
121 Willie Randolph G24 .10 .04
122 Dwayne Murphy G15 .05 .02
123 Rickey Henderson G16 2.50 1.00
124 Wayne Gross G6 .05 .02
125 Mike Norris G8 .05 .02
126 Rick Langford G20 .05 .02
127 Jim Spencer G17 .05 .02
128 Tony Armas G12 .05 .02
129 Matt Keough G7 .05 .02
130 Jeff Jones G19 .05 .02
131 Steve McCatty G3 .05 .02
132 Rollie Fingers G7 .30 .12
133 Jim Gantner G15 .05 .02
134 Gorman Thomas G6 .05 .02
135 Robin Yount G13 1.00 .40
136 Paul Molitor G22 1.50 .60
137 Ted Simmons G10 .10 .04
138 Ben Oglivie G23 .05 .02
139 Moose Haas G21 .05 .02
140 Cecil Cooper G24 .10 .04
141 Pete Vuckovich G10 .05 .02
142 Doug DeCinces G21 .05 .02
143 Jim Palmer G9 .50 .20
144 Steve Stone G16 .05 .02
145 Mike Flanagan G19 .05 .02
146 Rick Dempsey G9 .05 .02
147 Al Bumbry G14 .05 .02
148 Mark Belanger G8 .05 .02
149 Scott McGregor G23 .05 .02
150 Ken Singleton G10 .05 .02
151 Eddie Murray G5 2.50 1.00
152 Lance Parrish G20 .15 .06
153 Dave Rozema G15 .05 .02
154 Champ Summers G13 .05 .02
155 Alan Trammell G2 .50 .20
156 Lou Whitaker G1/G25 .25 .10
157 Milt Wilcox G5 .05 .02
158 Kevin Saucier G24 .05 .02
159 Jack Morris G14 .10 .04
160 Steve Kemp G7 .05 .02
161 Kirk Gibson G3 .25 .10
162 Carl Yastrzemski G3 .75 .30
163 Jim Rice G21 .15 .06
164 Carney Lansford G15 .10 .04
165 Dennis Eckersley G6 .50 .20
166 Mike Torrez G5 .05 .02
167 Dwight Evans G19 .10 .04
168 Glenn Hoffman G18 .05 .02
169 Bob Stanley G20 .05 .02
170 Tony Perez G16 .25 .10
171 Jerry Remy G13 .05 .02
172 Buddy Bell G5 .10 .04
173 Fergie Jenkins G17 .25 .10
174 Mickey Rivers G9 .05 .02
175 Bump Wills G2 .05 .02
176 Jon Matlack G20 .05 .02
177 Steve Comer G23 .05 .02
178 Al Oliver G1/G25 .10 .04
179 Bill Stein G3 .05 .02
180 Pat Putnam G14 .05 .02
181 Jim Sundberg G4 .05 .02
182 Ron LeFlore G4 .10 .04
183 Carlton Fisk G11 1.00 .40
184 Harold Baines G18 .25 .10
185 Bill Almon G2 .05 .02
186 Richard Dotson G9 .05 .02
187 Greg Luzinski G14 .10 .04
188 Mike Squires G13 .05 .02
189 Britt Burns G19 .05 .02
190 LaMarr Hoyt G6 .05 .02
191 Chet Lemon G22 .05 .02
192 Joe Charboneau G20 .05 .02
193 Toby Harrah G16 .05 .02
194 John Denny G22 .05 .02
195 Rick Manning G8 .05 .02
196 Miguel Dilone G15 .05 .02
197 Bo Diaz G13 .05 .02
198 Mike Hargrove G17 .10 .04
199 Bert Blyleven G11 .10 .04
200 Len Barker G7 .05 .02
201 Andre Thornton G18 .05 .02
202 George Brett G24 2.00 .80
203 U.L. Washington G25 .05 .02
204 Dan Quisenberry G17 .05 .02
205 Larry Gura G17 .05 .02
206 Willie Aikens G22 .05 .02
207 Willie Wilson G21 .05 .02
208 Dennis Leonard G8 .05 .02
209 Frank White G6 .10 .04
210 Hal McRae G23 .10 .04
211 Amos Otis G18 .05 .02
212 Don Aase G23 .05 .02
213 Butch Hobson G6 .05 .02
214 Fred Lynn G18 .10 .04
215 Brian Downing G10 .05 .02
216 Dan Ford G5 .05 .02
217 Rod Carew G5 .75 .30
218 Bobby Grich G19 .10 .04
219 Rick Burleson G11 .10 .04
220 Don Baylor G3 .10 .04
221 Ken Forsch G17 .05 .02
222 Bruce Bochte .05 .02
223 Richie Zisk .05 .02
224 Tom Paciorek .05 .02
225 Julio Cruz .05 .02
226 Jeff Burroughs .05 .02
227 Doug Corbett .05 .02
228 Roy Smalley .05 .02
229 Gary Ward .05 .02
230 John Castino .05 .02
231 Rob Wilfong .05 .02
232 Dave Stieb .10 .04
233 Otto Velez .05 .02
234 Damaso Garcia .05 .02
235 John Mayberry .05 .02
236 Alfredo Griffin .05 .02
237 Ted Williams 2.00 .80
Carl Yastrzemski
238 Rick Cerone .10 .04
Graig Nettles
239 Buddy Bell 1.50 .60
George Brett
240 Steve Carlton .25 .10
Jim Kaat
241 Steve Carlton .25 .10
Dave Parker
242 Ron Davis 4.00 1.60
Nolan Ryan
XX Stamp Album 2.00 .80

1983 Fleer Promo Sheet

This sheet, which measures approximately 7 1/2" by 10 1/2" featured information on the 1983 Fleer wax, cello and rack packs. The cards shown on the sheet are the same as their regular card from the set. Six different players are featured on this set.

Nm-Mt Ex-Mt
1 Rod Carew 3.00 1.20
Tom Paciorek
Jerry Dybzinski
Dan Driessen
Dusty Baker
John Butcher

1983 Fleer

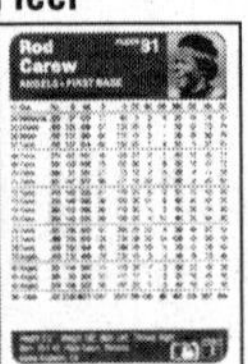

In 1983, for the third straight year, Fleer produced a baseball series of 660 standard-size cards. Of these, 1-628 are player cards, 629-646 are special cards, and 647-660 are checklist cards. The player cards are again ordered alphabetically within team and teams seeded in descending order based upon the previous season's standings. The front of each card has a colorful team logo at bottom left and the player's name and position at lower right. The reverses are done in shades of brown on white. Wax packs consisted of 15 cards plus logo stickers in a 38-pack box. Notable Rookie Cards include Wade Boggs, Tony Gwynn and Ryne Sandberg.

Nm-Mt Ex-Mt
COMPLETE SET (660) 60.00 24.00
1 Joaquin Andujar .10 .04
2 Doug Bair .10 .04
3 Steve Braun .10 .04
4 Glenn Brummer .10 .04
5 Bob Forsch .10 .04
6 David Green RC .10 .04
7 George Hendrick .10 .04
8 Keith Hernandez .40 .16
9 Tom Herr .20 .08
10 Dane Iorg .10 .04
11 Jim Kaat .20 .08
12 Jeff Lahti .10 .04
13 Tito Landrum .10 .04
14 Dave LaPoint .10 .04
15 Willie McGee RC 1.50 .60
16 Steve Mura .10 .04
17 Ken Oberkfell .10 .04
18 Darrell Porter .10 .04
19 Mike Ramsey .10 .04
20 Gene Roof .10 .04
21 Lonnie Smith .10 .04
22 Ozzie Smith 1.25 .50
23 John Stuper .10 .04
24 Bruce Sutter .20 .08
25 Gene Tenace .20 .08
26 Jerry Augustine .10 .04
27 Dwight Bernard .10 .04
28 Mark Brouhard .10 .04
29 Mike Caldwell .10 .04
30 Cecil Cooper .20 .08
31 Jamie Easterly .10 .04
32 Marshall Edwards .10 .04
33 Rollie Fingers .20 .08
34 Jim Gantner .10 .04
35 Moose Haas .10 .04
36 Roy Howell .10 .04
37 Pete Ladd .10 .04
38 Bob McClure .10 .04
39 Doc Medich .10 .04
40 Paul Molitor .40 .16
41 Don Money .10 .04
42 Charlie Moore .10 .04
43 Ben Oglivie .10 .04
44 Ed Romero .10 .04
45 Ted Simmons .20 .08
46 Jim Slaton .10 .04
47 Don Sutton .75 .30
48 Gorman Thomas .10 .04
49 Pete Vuckovich .10 .04
50 Ned Yost .10 .04
51 Robin Yount 1.25 .50
52 Benny Ayala .10 .04
53 Bob Bonner .10 .04
54 Al Bumbry .10 .04
55 Terry Crowley .10 .04
56 Storm Davis RC .10 .04
57 Rich Dauer .10 .04
58 Rick Dempsey UER .20 .08
(Posing batting lefty)
59 Jim Dwyer .10 .04
60 Mike Flanagan .20 .08
61 Dan Ford .10 .04
62 Glenn Gulliver .10 .04
63 John Lowenstein .10 .04
64 Dennis Martinez .20 .08
65 Tippy Martinez .10 .04
66 Scott McGregor .10 .04
67 Eddie Murray .75 .30
68 Joe Nolan .10 .04
69 Jim Palmer .20 .08
70 Cal Ripken 6.00 2.40
71 Gary Roenicke .10 .04
72 Lenn Sakata .10 .04
73 Ken Singleton .10 .04
74 Sammy Stewart .10 .04
75 Tim Stoddard .10 .04
76 Don Aase .10 .04
77 Don Baylor .40 .16
78 Juan Beniquez .10 .04
79 Bob Boone .20 .08
80 Rick Burleson .10 .04
81 Rod Carew .40 .16
82 Bobby Clark .10 .04
83 Doug Corbett .10 .04
84 John Curtis .10 .04
85 Doug DeCinces .20 .08
86 Brian Downing .10 .04
87 Joe Ferguson .10 .04
88 Tim Foli .10 .04
89 Ken Forsch .10 .04
90 Dave Goltz .10 .04
91 Bobby Grich .20 .08
92 Andy Hassler .10 .04
93 Reggie Jackson .40 .16
94 Ron Jackson .10 .04
95 Tommy John .40 .16
96 Bruce Kison .10 .04
97 Fred Lynn .20 .08
98 Ed Ott .10 .04
99 Steve Renko .10 .04
100 Luis Sanchez .10 .04
101 Rob Wilfong .10 .04
102 Mike Witt .10 .04
103 Geoff Zahn .10 .04
104 Willie Aikens .10 .04
105 Mike Armstrong .10 .04
106 Vida Blue .20 .08
107 Bud Black RC .20 .08
108 George Brett 2.00 .80
109 Bill Castro .10 .04
110 Onix Concepcion .10 .04
111 Dave Frost .10 .04
112 Cesar Geronimo .10 .04
113 Larry Gura .10 .04
114 Steve Hammond .10 .04
115 Don Hood .10 .04
116 Dennis Leonard .10 .04
117 Jerry Martin .10 .04
118 Lee May .20 .08
119 Hal McRae .20 .08
120 Amos Otis .20 .08
121 Greg Pryor .10 .04
122 Dan Quisenberry .20 .08
123 Don Slaught RC .40 .16
124 Paul Splittorff .10 .04
125 U.L. Washington .10 .04
126 John Wathan .10 .04
127 Frank White .20 .08
128 Willie Wilson .20 .08
129 Steve Bedrosian UER .20 .08
(Height 6'33")
130 Bruce Benedict .10 .04
131 Tommy Boggs .10 .04
132 Brett Butler .75 .30
133 Rick Camp .10 .04
134 Chris Chambliss .20 .08
135 Ken Dayley .10 .04
136 Gene Garber .10 .04
137 Terry Harper .10 .04
138 Bob Horner .10 .04
139 Glenn Hubbard .10 .04
140 Rufino Linares .10 .04
141 Rick Mahler .10 .04
142 Dale Murphy .75 .30
143 Phil Niekro .20 .08
144 Pascual Perez .10 .04
145 Biff Pocoroba .10 .04
146 Rafael Ramirez .10 .04
147 Jerry Royster .10 .04
148 Ken Smith .10 .04
149 Bob Walk .10 .04
150 Claudell Washington .10 .04
151 Bob Watson .20 .08
152 Larry Whisenton .10 .04
153 Porfirio Altamirano .10 .04
154 Marty Bystrom .10 .04
155 Steve Carlton .20 .08
156 Larry Christenson .10 .04
157 Ivan DeJesus .10 .04
158 John Denny .10 .04
159 Bob Dernier .10 .04
160 Bo Diaz .10 .04
161 Ed Farmer .10 .04
162 Greg Gross .10 .04
163 Mike Krukow .10 .04
164 Garry Maddox .10 .04
165 Gary Matthews .20 .08
166 Tug McGraw .20 .08
167 Bob Molinaro .10 .04
168 Sid Monge .10 .04
169 Ron Reed .10 .04
170 Bill Robinson .10 .04
171 Pete Rose 2.50 1.00
172 Dick Ruthven .10 .04
173 Mike Schmidt 2.00 .80
174 Manny Trillo .10 .04
175 Ozzie Virgil .10 .04
176 George Vukovich .10 .04
177 Gary Allenson .10 .04
178 Luis Aponte .10 .04
179 Wade Boggs RC 8.00 3.20
180 Tom Burgmeier .10 .04
181 Mark Clear .10 .04
182 Dennis Eckersley .40 .16
183 Dwight Evans .20 .08
184 Rich Gedman .10 .04
185 Glenn Hoffman .10 .04
186 Bruce Hurst .10 .04
187 Carney Lansford .20 .08
188 Rick Miller .10 .04
189 Reid Nichols .10 .04
190 Bob Ojeda .10 .04
191 Tony Perez .40 .16
192 Chuck Rainey .10 .04
193 Jerry Remy .10 .04
194 Jim Rice .20 .08
195 Bob Stanley .10 .04
196 Dave Stapleton .10 .04
197 Mike Torrez .10 .04
198 John Tudor .10 .04
199 Julio Valdez .10 .04
200 Carl Yastrzemski 1.25 .50
201 Dusty Baker .20 .08
202 Joe Beckwith .10 .04
203 Greg Brock .10 .04
204 Ron Cey .20 .08
205 Terry Forster .10 .04
206 Steve Garvey .20 .08
207 Pedro Guerrero .20 .08
208 Burt Hooton .10 .04
209 Steve Howe .10 .04
210 Ken Landreaux .10 .04
211 Mike Marshall .10 .04
212 Candy Maldonado RC .20 .08
213 Rick Monday .10 .04
214 Tom Niedenfuer .10 .04
215 Jorge Orta .10 .04
216 Jerry Reuss UER .20 .08
("Home:" omitted)
217 Ron Roenicke .10 .04
218 Vicente Romo .10 .04
219 Bill Russell .10 .04
220 Steve Sax .20 .08
221 Mike Scioscia .20 .08
222 Dave Stewart .20 .08
223 Derrel Thomas .10 .04
224 Fernando Valenzuela .40 .16
225 Bob Welch .20 .08
226 Ricky Wright .10 .04
227 Steve Yeager .10 .04
228 Bill Almon .10 .04
229 Harold Baines .75 .30
230 Salome Barojas .10 .04
231 Tony Bernazard .10 .04
232 Britt Burns .10 .04
233 Richard Dotson .10 .04
234 Ernesto Escarrega .10 .04
235 Carlton Fisk .40 .16
236 Jerry Hairston .10 .04
237 Kevin Hickey .10 .04
238 LaMarr Hoyt .20 .08
239 Steve Kemp .10 .04
240 Jim Kern .10 .04
241 Ron Kittle RC .40 .16
242 Jerry Koosman .20 .08
243 Dennis Lamp .10 .04
244 Rudy Law .10 .04
245 Vance Law .10 .04
246 Ron LeFlore .10 .04
247 Greg Luzinski .20 .08
248 Tom Paciorek .20 .08
249 Aurelio Rodriguez .20 .08
250 Mike Squires .10 .04
251 Steve Trout .10 .04
252 Jim Barr .10 .04
253 Dave Bergman .10 .04
254 Fred Breining .10 .04
255 Bob Brenly .10 .04
256 Jack Clark .20 .08
257 Chili Davis .75 .30
258 Darrell Evans .20 .08
259 Alan Fowlkes .10 .04
260 Rich Gale .10 .04
261 Atlee Hammaker .10 .04
262 Al Holland .10 .04
263 Duane Kuiper .10 .04
264 Bill Laskey .10 .04
265 Gary Lavelle .10 .04
266 Johnnie LeMaster .10 .04
267 Renie Martin .10 .04
268 Milt May .10 .04
269 Greg Minton .10 .04
270 Joe Morgan .40 .16
271 Tom O'Malley .10 .04
272 Reggie Smith .20 .08
273 Guy Sularz .10 .04
274 Champ Summers .10 .04
275 Max Venable .10 .04
276 Jim Wohlford .10 .04
277 Ray Burris .10 .04
278 Gary Carter .40 .16
279 Warren Cromartie .10 .04
280 Andre Dawson .20 .08
281 Terry Francona .20 .08
282 Doug Flynn .10 .04
283 Woodie Fryman .10 .04
284 Bill Gullickson .10 .04
285 Wallace Johnson .10 .04
286 Charlie Lea .10 .04
287 Randy Lerch .10 .04
288 Brad Mills .10 .04
289 Dan Norman .10 .04
290 Al Oliver .20 .08
291 David Palmer .10 .04
292 Tim Raines .75 .30
293 Jeff Reardon .20 .08
294 Steve Rogers .10 .04
295 Scott Sanderson .10 .04
296 Dan Schatzeder .10 .04
297 Bryn Smith .10 .04
298 Chris Speier .10 .04
299 Tim Wallach .20 .08
300 Jerry White .10 .04
301 Joel Youngblood .10 .04
302 Ross Baumgarten .10 .04
303 Dale Berra .10 .04
304 John Candelaria .10 .04
305 Dick Davis .10 .04
306 Mike Easler .10 .04
307 Richie Hebner .20 .08
308 Lee Lacy .10 .04
309 Bill Madlock .20 .08
310 Larry McWilliams .10 .04
311 John Milner .10 .04
312 Omar Moreno .10 .04
313 Jim Morrison .10 .04
314 Steve Nicosia .10 .04
315 Dave Parker .20 .08
316 Tony Pena .10 .04
317 Johnny Ray .10 .04
318 Rick Rhoden .10 .04
319 Don Robinson .10 .04
320 Enrique Romo .10 .04
321 Manny Sarmiento .10 .04
322 Rod Scurry .10 .04
323 Jimmy Smith .10 .04
324 Willie Stargell .40 .16
325 Jason Thompson .10 .04
326 Kent Tekulve .20 .08
327A Tom Brookens .10 .04
(Short .375" brown box
shaded in on card back)
327B Tom Brookens .10 .04
(Longer 1.25" brown box
shaded in on card back)
328 Enos Cabell .10 .04
329 Kirk Gibson .75 .30
330 Larry Herndon .10 .04
331 Mike Ivie .10 .04
332 Howard Johnson RC .75 .30
333 Lynn Jones .10 .04
334 Rick Leach .10 .04
335 Chet Lemon .10 .04
336 Jack Morris .20 .08
337 Lance Parrish .20 .08
338 Larry Pashnick .10 .04
339 Dan Petry .10 .04
340 Dave Rozema .10 .04
341 Dave Rucker .10 .04
342 Elias Sosa .10 .04
343 Dave Tobik .10 .04
344 Alan Trammell .40 .16
345 Jerry Turner .10 .04
346 Jerry Ujdur .10 .04
347 Pat Underwood .10 .04
348 Lou Whitaker .20 .08
349 Milt Wilcox .10 .04
350 Glenn Wilson .20 .08
351 John Wockenfuss .10 .04
352 Kurt Bevacqua .10 .04
353 Juan Bonilla .10 .04
354 Floyd Chiffer .10 .04
355 Luis DeLeon .10 .04
356 Dave Dravecky RC .75 .30
357 Dave Edwards .10 .04
358 Juan Eichelberger .10 .04
359 Tim Flannery .10 .04
360 Tony Gwynn RC 15.00 6.00
361 Ruppert Jones .10 .04
362 Terry Kennedy .10 .04
363 Joe Lefebvre .10 .04
364 Sixto Lezcano .10 .04
365 Tim Lollar .10 .04
366 Gary Lucas .10 .04
367 John Montefusco .10 .04
368 Broderick Perkins .10 .04
369 Joe Pittman .10 .04
370 Gene Richards .10 .04
371 Luis Salazar .10 .04
372 Eric Show .10 .04
373 Garry Templeton .10 .04
374 Chris Welsh .10 .04
375 Alan Wiggins .10 .04
376 Rick Cerone .10 .04
377 Dave Collins .10 .04
378 Roger Erickson .10 .04
379 George Frazier .10 .04
380 Oscar Gamble .10 .04
381 Rich Gossage .40 .16
382 Ken Griffey .20 .08
383 Ron Guidry .20 .08
384 Dave LaRoche .10 .04
385 Rudy May .10 .04
386 John Mayberry .10 .04
387 Lee Mazzilli .10 .04
388 Mike Morgan .10 .04
389 Jerry Mumphrey .10 .04
390 Bobby Murcer .20 .08
391 Graig Nettles .20 .08
392 Lou Piniella .20 .08
393 Willie Randolph .20 .08
394 Shane Rawley .10 .04
395 Dave Righetti .20 .08
396 Andre Robertson .10 .04
397 Roy Smalley .10 .04
398 Dave Winfield .20 .08
399 Butch Wynegar .10 .04
400 Chris Bando .10 .04
401 Alan Bannister .10 .04
402 Len Barker .10 .04
403 Tom Brennan .10 .04
404 Carmelo Castillo .10 .04
405 Miguel Dilone .10 .04
406 Jerry Dybzinski .10 .04
407 Mike Fischlin .10 .04
408 Ed Glynn UER .10 .04
(Photo actually
Bud Anderson)
409 Mike Hargrove .20 .08
410 Toby Harrah .10 .04
411 Ron Hassey .10 .04
412 Von Hayes .20 .08
413 Rick Manning .10 .04
414 Bake McBride .10 .04
415 Larry Milbourne .10 .04
416 Bill Nahorodny .10 .04
417 Jack Perconte .10 .04
418 Lary Sorensen .10 .04
419 Dan Spillner .10 .04
420 Rick Sutcliffe .20 .08
421 Andre Thornton .10 .04
422 Rick Waits .10 .04
423 Eddie Whitson .10 .04
424 Jesse Barfield .20 .08
425 Barry Bonnell .10 .04
426 Jim Clancy .10 .04
427 Damaso Garcia .10 .04
428 Jerry Garvin .10 .04
429 Alfredo Griffin .10 .04
430 Garth Iorg .10 .04
431 Roy Lee Jackson .10 .04
432 Luis Leal .10 .04
433 Buck Martinez .10 .04
434 Joey McLaughlin .10 .04
435 Lloyd Moseby .10 .04
436 Rance Mulliniks .10 .04
437 Dale Murray .10 .04
438 Wayne Nordhagen .10 .04
439 Geno Petralli .20 .08
440 Hosken Powell .10 .04

441 Dave Stieb .20 .08
442 Willie Upshaw .10 .04
443 Ernie Whitt .10 .04
444 Alvis Woods .10 .04
445 Alan Ashby .10 .04
446 Jose Cruz .20 .08
447 Kiko Garcia .10 .04
448 Phil Garner .20 .08
449 Danny Heep .10 .04
450 Art Howe .20 .08
451 Bob Knepper .10 .04
452 Alan Knicely .10 .04
453 Ray Knight .20 .08
454 Frank LaCorte .10 .04
455 Mike LaCoss .10 .04
456 Randy Moffitt .10 .04
457 Joe Niekro .20 .08
458 Terry Puhl .10 .04
459 Luis Pujols .10 .04
460 Craig Reynolds .10 .04
461 Bert Roberge .10 .04
462 Vern Ruhle .10 .04
463 Nolan Ryan 4.00 1.60
464 Joe Sambito .10 .04
465 Tony Scott .10 .04
466 Dave Smith .10 .04
467 Harry Spilman .10 .04
468 Dickie Thon .10 .04
469 Denny Walling .10 .04
470 Larry Andersen .10 .04
471 Floyd Bannister .10 .04
472 Jim Beattie .10 .04
473 Bruce Bochte .10 .04
474 Manny Castillo .10 .04
475 Bill Caudill .10 .04
476 Bryan Clark .10 .04
477 Al Cowens .10 .04
478 Julio Cruz .10 .04
479 Todd Cruz .10 .04
480 Gary Gray .10 .04
481 Dave Henderson .10 .04
482 Mike Moore RC .20 .08
483 Gaylord Perry .20 .08
484 Dave Revering .10 .04
485 Joe Simpson .10 .04
486 Mike Stanton .10 .04
487 Rick Sweet .10 .04
488 Ed VandeBerg .10 .04
489 Richie Zisk .10 .04
490 Doug Bird .10 .04
491 Larry Bowa .20 .08
492 Bill Buckner .20 .08
493 Bill Campbell .10 .04
494 Jody Davis .10 .04
495 Leon Durham .10 .04
496 Steve Henderson .10 .04
497 Willie Hernandez .20 .08
498 Ferguson Jenkins .20 .08
499 Jay Johnstone .20 .08
500 Junior Kennedy .10 .04
501 Randy Martz .10 .04
502 Jerry Morales .10 .04
503 Keith Moreland .10 .04
504 Dickie Noles .10 .04
505 Mike Proly .10 .04
506 Allen Ripley .10 .04
507 R.Sandberg RC UER 10.00 4.00
Should say High School
in Spokane, Washington
508 Lee Smith .75 .30
509 Pat Tabler .10 .04
510 Dick Tidrow .10 .04
511 Bump Wills .10 .04
512 Gary Woods .10 .04
513 Tony Armas .10 .04
514 Dave Beard .10 .04
515 Jeff Burroughs .10 .04
516 John D'Acquisto .10 .04
517 Wayne Gross .10 .04
518 Mike Heath .10 .04
519 R.Henderson UER 1.50 .60
Brock record listed
as 120 steals
520 Cliff Johnson .10 .04
521 Matt Keough .10 .04
522 Brian Kingman .10 .04
523 Rick Langford .10 .04
524 Dave Lopes .20 .08
525 Steve McCatty .10 .04
526 Dave McKay .10 .04
527 Dan Meyer .10 .04
528 Dwayne Murphy .10 .04
529 Jeff Newman .10 .04
530 Mike Norris .10 .04
531 Bob Owchinko .10 .04
532 Joe Rudi .10 .04
533 Jimmy Sexton .10 .04
534 Fred Stanley .10 .04
535 Tom Underwood .10 .04
536 Neil Allen .10 .04
537 Wally Backman .10 .04
538 Bob Bailor .10 .04
539 Hubie Brooks .20 .08
540 Carlos Diaz RC .10 .04
541 Pete Falcone .10 .04
542 George Foster .20 .08
543 Ron Gardenhire .10 .04
544 Brian Giles .10 .04
545 Ron Hodges .10 .04
546 Randy Jones .10 .04
547 Mike Jorgensen .10 .04
548 Dave Kingman .40 .16
549 Ed Lynch .10 .04
550 Jesse Orosco .10 .04
551 Rick Ownbey .10 .04
552 Charlie Puleo .10 .04
553 Gary Rajsich .10 .04
554 Mike Scott .20 .08
555 Rusty Staub .20 .08
556 John Stearns .10 .04
557 Craig Swan .10 .04
558 Ellis Valentine .10 .04
559 Tom Veryzer .10 .04
560 Mookie Wilson .20 .08
561 Pat Zachry .10 .04
562 Buddy Bell .20 .08
563 John Butcher .10 .04
564 Steve Comer .10 .04
565 Danny Darwin .10 .04
566 Bucky Dent .20 .08
567 John Grubb .10 .04
568 Rick Honeycutt .10 .04
569 Dave Hostetler .10 .04
570 Charlie Hough .20 .08
571 Lamar Johnson .10 .04
572 Jon Matlack .10 .04
573 Paul Mirabella .10 .04
574 Larry Parrish .10 .04
575 Mike Richardt .10 .04
576 Mickey Rivers .10 .04
577 Billy Sample .10 .04
578 Dave Schmidt .10 .04
579 Bill Stein .10 .04
580 Jim Sundberg .20 .08
581 Frank Tanana .20 .08
582 Mark Wagner .10 .04
583 George Wright RC .10 .04
584 Johnny Bench .75 .30
585 Bruce Berenyi .10 .04
586 Larry Biittner .10 .04
587 Cesar Cedeno .20 .08
588 Dave Concepcion .20 .08
589 Dan Driessen .10 .04
590 Greg Harris .10 .04
591 Ben Hayes .10 .04
592 Paul Householder .10 .04
593 Tom Hume .10 .04
594 Wayne Krenchicki .10 .04
595 Rafael Landestoy .10 .04
596 Charlie Leibrandt .10 .04
597 Eddie Milner .10 .04
598 Ron Oester .10 .04
599 Frank Pastore .10 .04
600 Joe Price .10 .04
601 Tom Seaver .40 .16
602 Bob Shirley .10 .04
603 Mario Soto .10 .04
604 Alex Trevino .10 .04
605 Mike Vail .10 .04
606 Duane Walker .10 .04
607 Tom Brunansky .20 .08
608 Bobby Castillo .10 .04
609 John Castino .10 .04
610 Ron Davis .10 .04
611 Lenny Faedo .10 .04
612 Terry Felton .10 .04
613 Gary Gaetti RC .75 .30
614 Mickey Hatcher .10 .04
615 Brad Havens .10 .04
616 Kent Hrbek .20 .08
617 Randy Johnson .10 .04
618 Tim Laudner .10 .04
619 Jeff Little .10 .04
620 Bobby Mitchell .10 .04
621 Jack O'Connor .10 .04
622 John Pacella .10 .04
623 Pete Redfern .10 .04
624 Jesus Vega .10 .04
625 Frank Viola RC .75 .30
626 Ron Washington .10 .04
627 Gary Ward .10 .04
628 Al Williams .10 .04
629 Carl Yastrzemski .75 .30
Dennis Eckersley
Mark Clear
630 Gaylord Perry .10 .04
Terry Bulling 5/6/82
631 Dave Concepcion .20 .08
Manny Trillo
632 Robin Yount .75 .30
Buddy Bell
633 Dave Winfield .10 .04
Kent Hrbek
634 Willie Stargell .75 .30
Pete Rose
635 Toby Harrah .20 .08
Andre Thornton
636 Ozzie Smith .75 .30
Lonnie Smith
637 Bo Diaz .20 .08
Gary Carter
638 Carlton Fisk .20 .08
Gary Carter
639 Rickey Henderson IA .75 .30
640 Ben Oglivie .40 .16
Reggie Jackson
641 Joel Youngblood .10 .04
August 4, 1982
642 Ron Hassey .20 .08
Len Barker
643 Black and Blue .20 .08
Vida Blue
644 Black and Blue .10 .04
Bud Black
645 Reggie Jackson Power .20 .08
646 Rickey Henderson Speed .75 .30
647 CL: Cards/Brewers .10 .04
648 CL: Orioles/Angels .10 .04
649 CL: Royals/Braves .10 .04
650 CL: Phillies/Red Sox .10 .04
651 CL: Dodgers/White Sox .10 .04
652 CL: Giants/Expos .10 .04
653 CL: Pirates/Tigers .10 .04
654 CL: Padres/Yankees .10 .04
655 CL: Indians/Blue Jays .10 .04
656 CL: Astros/Mariners .10 .04
657 CL: Cubs/A's .10 .04
658 CL: Mets/Rangers .10 .04
659 CL: Reds/Twins .10 .04
660 CL: Specials/Teams .10 .04

1983 Fleer Stamps

This 250-stamp set features color photos of players and team logos on stamps measuring approximately 1 1/4" by 1 13/16" each. The stamps were issued on four different sheets of 72 stamps each. There are 224 player stamps and 26 team logo stamps. The team logo stamps have double and triple prints. Baseball trivia quiz questions were also included with the stamps. The stamps are unnumbered and checklisted below in alphabetical order. Stamps were issued in three different colored Vend-A-Strip dispensors. Each row in a dispensor consisted of 18 stamps and 11 quizes.

Nm-Mt Ex-Mt
COMPLETE SET (250) 10.00 4.00
1 Willie Aikens .05 .02
2 Neil Allen .05 .02
3 Joaquin Andujar .05 .02
4 Alan Ashby .05 .02
5 Bob Bailor .05 .02
6 Harold Baines .15 .06
7 Dusty Baker .10 .04
8 Floyd Bannister .05 .02
9 Len Barker .05 .02
10 Don Baylor .10 .04
11 Dave Beard .05 .02
12 Jim Beattie .05 .02
13 Buddy Bell .10 .04
14 Johnny Bench .75 .30
15 Dale Berra .05 .02
16 Larry Biittner .05 .02
17 Vida Blue .10 .04
18 Bruce Bochte .05 .02
19 Wade Boggs 5.00 2.00
20 Bob Boone .10 .04
21 Larry Bowa .10 .04
22 George Brett 2.00 .80
23 Hubie Brooks .05 .02
24 Tom Brunansky .05 .02
25 Bill Buckner .10 .04
26 Al Bumbry .05 .02
27 Jeff Burroughs .05 .02
28 Enos Cabell .05 .02
29 Rod Carew .50 .20
30 Steve Carlton .40 .16
31 Gary Carter .40 .16
32 Bobby Castillo .05 .02
33 Bill Caudill .05 .02
34 Cesar Cedeno .10 .04
35 Rick Cerone .05 .02
36 Ron Cey .10 .04
37 Chris Chambliss .10 .04
38 Larry Christenson .05 .02
39 Jim Clancy .05 .02
40 Jack Clark .10 .04
41 Mark Clear .05 .02
42 Dave Concepcion .10 .04
43 Cecil Cooper .10 .04
44 Warren Cromartie .05 .02
45 Jose Cruz .10 .04
46 Danny Darwin .05 .02
47 Rich Dauer .05 .02
48 Ron Davis .05 .02
49 Andre Dawson .50 .20
50 Doug DeCinces .05 .02
51 Ivan DeJesus .05 .02
52 Luis DeLeon .05 .02
53 Bo Diaz .05 .02
54 Brian Downing .10 .04
55 Dan Driessen .05 .02
56 Leon Durham .05 .02
57 Mike Easler .05 .02
58 Dennis Eckersley .50 .20
59 Dwight Evans .15 .06
60 Rollie Fingers .40 .16
61 Carlton Fisk .50 .20
62 Mike Flanagan .05 .02
63 Bob Forsch .05 .02
64 Ken Forsch .05 .02
65 George Foster .10 .04
66 Gene Garber .10 .04
67 Damaso Garcia .05 .02
68 Phil Garner .05 .02
69 Steve Garvey .15 .06
70 Goose Gossage .15 .06
71 Ken Griffey .10 .04
72 John Grubb .05 .02
73 Ron Guidry .10 .04
74 Atlee Hammaker .05 .02
75 Mike Hargrove .10 .04
76 Toby Harrah .05 .02
77 Rickey Henderson 2.00 .80
78 Keith Hernandez .15 .06
79 Larry Herndon .05 .02
80 Tom Herr .05 .02
81 Al Holland .05 .02
82 Burt Hooton .05 .02
83 Bob Horner .05 .02
84 Art Howe .10 .04
85 Steve Howe .05 .02
86 LaMarr Hoyt .05 .02
87 Kent Hrbek .25 .10
88 Tom Hume .05 .02
89 Garth Iorg .05 .02
90 Reggie Jackson .75 .30
91 Ferguson Jenkins .30 .12
92 Tommy John .15 .06
93 Ruppert Jones .05 .02
94 Steve Kemp .05 .02
95 Bruce Kison .05 .02
96 Ray Knight .05 .02
97 Jerry Koosman .10 .04
98 Duane Kuiper .05 .02
99 Ken Landreaux .05 .02
100 Carney Lansford .05 .02
101 Bill Laskey .05 .02
102 Gary Lavelle .05 .02
103 Charlie Lea .05 .02
104 Ron LeFlore .05 .02
105 Dennis Leonard .05 .02
106 Sixto Lezcano .05 .02
107 Davey Lopes .10 .04
108 John Lowenstein .05 .02
109 Greg Luzinski .10 .04
110 Fred Lynn .15 .06
111 Garry Maddox .05 .02
112 Bill Madlock .10 .04
113 Rick Manning .05 .02
114 Dennis Martinez .10 .04
115 Tippy Martinez .05 .02
116 Randy Martz .05 .02
117 Jon Matlack .05 .02
118 Gary Matthews .10 .04
119 Milt May .05 .02
120 Lee Mazzilli .05 .02
121 Bob McClure .05 .02
122 Tug McGraw .10 .04
123 Scott McGregor .05 .02
124 Hal McRae .10 .04
125 Eddie Milner .05 .02
126 Greg Minton .05 .02
127 Paul Molitor .75 .30
128 Rick Monday .05 .02
129 John Montefusco .05 .02
130 Keith Moreland .05 .02
131 Joe Morgan .50 .20
132 Jerry Mumphrey .05 .02
133 Steve Mura .05 .02
134 Dale Murphy .40 .16
135 Dwayne Murphy .05 .02
136 Eddie Murray .50 .20
137 Graig Nettles .15 .06
138 Joe Niekro .10 .04
139 Phil Niekro .30 .12
140 Ken Oberkfell .05 .02
141 Ben Oglivie .05 .02
142 Al Oliver .15 .06
143 Amos Otis .10 .04
144 Tom Paciorek .05 .02
145 Jim Palmer .40 .16
146 Dave Parker .10 .04
147 Lance Parrish .15 .06
148 Larry Parrish .10 .04
149 Tony Pena .10 .04
150 Gaylord Perry .30 .12
151 Lou Piniella .10 .04
152 Darrell Porter .05 .02
153 Hosken Powell .05 .02
154 Dan Quisenberry .10 .04
155 Tim Raines .25 .10
156 Rafael Ramirez .05 .02
157 Willie Randolph .10 .04
158 Johnny Ray .05 .02
159 Jeff Reardon .10 .04
160 Ron Reed .05 .02
161 Jerry Reuss .10 .04
162 Rick Rhoden .05 .02
163 Jim Rice .10 .04
164 Mike Richardt .05 .02
165 Cal Ripken Jr. 4.00 1.60
166 Ron Roenicke .05 .02
167 Steve Rogers .05 .02
168 Pete Rose 1.00 .40
169 Jerry Royster .05 .02
170 Nolan Ryan 4.00 1.60
171 Manny Sarmiento .05 .02
172 Steve Sax .05 .02
173 Mike Schmidt 1.00 .40
174 Tom Seaver .50 .20
175 Eric Show .05 .02
176 Ted Simmons .15 .06
177 Ken Singleton .05 .02
178 Roy Smalley .05 .02
179 Lonnie Smith .05 .02
180 Ozzie Smith 2.00 .80
181 Reggie Smith .10 .04
182 Mario Soto .05 .02
183 Chris Speier .05 .02
184 Dan Spillner .05 .02
185 Bob Stanley .05 .02
186 Willie Stargell .30 .12
187 Rusty Staub .15 .06
188 Dave Stieb .10 .04
189 Jim Sundberg .05 .02
190 Rick Sutcliffe .05 .02
191 Bruce Sutter .10 .04
192 Don Sutton .30 .12
193 Craig Swan .05 .02
194 Kent Tekulve .05 .02
195 Gorman Thomas .05 .02
196 Jason Thompson .05 .02
197 Dickie Thon .05 .02
198 Andre Thornton .05 .02
199 Dick Tidrow .05 .02
200 Manny Trillo .05 .02
201 John Tudor .05 .02
202 Tom Underwood .05 .02
203 Willie Upshaw .05 .02
204 Ellis Valentine .05 .02
205 Fernando Valenzuela .30 .12
206 Ed VandeBerg .05 .02
207 Pete Vuckovich .05 .02
208 Gary Ward .05 .02
209 Claudell Washington .05 .02
210 U.L. Washington .05 .02
211 Bob Watson .10 .04
212 Lou Whitaker .25 .10
213 Frank White .05 .02
214 Milt Wilcox .05 .02
215 Al Williams .05 .02
216 Bump Wills .05 .02
217 Mookie Wilson .10 .04
218 Willie Wilson .05 .02
219 Dave Winfield .75 .30
220 John Wockenfuss .05 .02
221 Carl Yastrzemski .50 .20
222 Robin Yount .50 .20
223 Pat Zachry .05 .02
224 Richie Zisk .05 .02
225 Atlanta Braves TP .05 .02
226 Baltimore Orioles DP .05 .02
227 Boston Red Sox DP .05 .02
228 California Angels TP .05 .02
229 Chicago Cubs DP .05 .02
230 Chicago White Sox TP .05 .02
231 Cincinnati Reds TP .05 .02
232 Cleveland Indians TP .05 .02
233 Detroit Tigers DP .05 .02
234 Houston Astros DP .05 .02
235 Los Angeles Dodgers TP .05 .02
236 Kansas City Royals TP .05 .02
237 Milwaukee Brewers DP .05 .02
238 Minnesota Twins TP .05 .02
239 Montreal Expos TP .05 .02
240 New York Mets DP .05 .02
241 New York Yankees DP .05 .02
242 Oakland A's DP .05 .02
243 Philadelphia Phillies TP .05 .02
244 Pittsburgh Pirates TP .05 .02
245 St. Louis Cardinals DP .05 .02
246 San Diego Padres DP .05 .02
247 San Francisco Giants TP .05 .02
248 Seattle Mariners DP .05 .02
249 Texas Rangers DP .05 .02
250 Toronto Blue Jays DP .05 .02

1983 Fleer Stickers

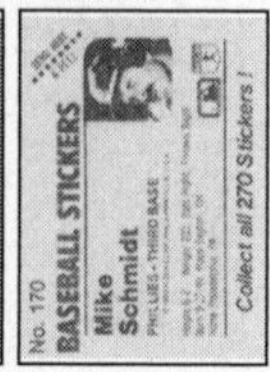

The stickers in this 270-sticker set measure approximately 1 13/16" by 2 1/2". The 1983 Fleer stickers set was issued in strips of ten stickers plus two team logos per strip. No album was issued for the stickers. The fronts contain player photos surrounded by a blue border with two red stars on the upper portion of a yellow frameline. While all of the players could be attained on 27 different strips, it was necessary to have 30 different strips to obtain all of the team logos. There are a few instances where the logo pictured on the front of the card relates to a different team checklisted on the back of the card. The backs of the logo stamps feature either a team checklist (CL) or poster offer (PO).

Nm-Mt Ex-Mt
COMPLETE SET 12.00 4.80
1 Bruce Sutter .10 .04
2 Willie McGee .30 .12
3 Darrell Porter .05 .02
4 Lonnie Smith .05 .02
5 Dane Iorg .05 .02
6 Keith Hernandez .10 .04
7 Joaquin Andujar .05 .02
8 Ken Oberkfell .05 .02
9 John Stuper .05 .02
10 Ozzie Smith 1.50 .60
11 Bob Forsch .05 .02
12 Jim Gantner .05 .02
13 Rollie Fingers .30 .12
14 Pete Vuckovich .05 .02
15 Ben Oglivie .05 .02
16 Don Sutton .30 .12
17 Bob McClure .05 .02
18 Robin Yount .40 .16
19 Paul Molitor .50 .20
20 Gorman Thomas .05 .02
21 Mike Caldwell .05 .02
22 Ted Simmons .10 .04
23 Cecil Cooper .10 .04
24 Steve Renko .05 .02
25 Tommy John .15 .06
26 Rod Carew .40 .16
27 Bruce Kison .05 .02
28 Ken Forsch .05 .02
29 Geoff Zahn .05 .02
30 Doug DeCinces .05 .02
31 Fred Lynn .10 .04
32 Reggie Jackson .75 .30
33 Don Baylor .10 .04
34 Bob Boone .10 .04
35 Brian Downing .05 .02
36 Rich Gossage .15 .06
37 Roy Smalley .05 .02
38 Graig Nettles .15 .06
39 Dave Winfield .50 .20
40 Lee Mazzilli .05 .02
41 Jerry Mumphrey .05 .02
42 Dave Collins .05 .02
43 Rick Cerone .05 .02
44 Willie Randolph .10 .04
45 Lou Piniella .10 .04
46 Ken Griffey .10 .04
47 Ron Guidry .10 .04
48 Jack Clark .05 .02
49 Reggie Smith .05 .02
50 Atlee Hammaker .05 .02
51 Fred Breining .05 .02
52 Gary Lavelle .05 .02
53 Chili Davis .25 .10
54 Greg Minton .05 .02
55 Joe Morgan .30 .12
56 Al Holland .05 .02
57 Bill Laskey .05 .02
58 Duane Kuiper .05 .02
59 Tom Burgmeier .05 .02
60 Carl Yastrzemski .50 .20
61 Mark Clear .05 .02
62 Mike Torrez .05 .02
63 Dennis Eckersley .30 .12
64 Wade Boggs 3.00 1.20
65 Bob Stanley .05 .02
66 Jim Rice .10 .04
67 Carney Lansford .05 .02
68 Jerry Remy .05 .02
69 Dwight Evans .15 .06
70 John Candelaria .05 .02
71 Bill Madlock .10 .04
72 Dave Parker .10 .04
73 Kent Tekulve .05 .02
74 Tony Pena .10 .04
75 Manny Sarmiento .05 .02
76 Johnny Ray .05 .02
77 Dale Berra .05 .02
78 Lee Lacy .05 .02
79 Jason Thompson .05 .02
80 Mike Easler .05 .02
81 Willie Stargell .30 .12
82 Rick Camp .05 .02
83 Bob Watson .10 .04
84 Bob Horner .05 .02
85 Rafael Ramirez .05 .02
86 Chris Chambliss .10 .04
87 Gene Garber .10 .04
88 Claudell Washington .05 .02
89 Steve Bedrosian .05 .02
90 Dale Murphy .50 .20
91 Phil Niekro .30 .12
92 Jerry Royster .05 .02
93 Bob Walk .05 .02
94 Frank White .05 .02
95 Dennis Leonard .05 .02
96 Vida Blue .10 .04
97 U.L. Washington .05 .02
98 George Brett 3.00 1.20

99 Amos Otis .05 .02
100 Dan Quisenberry .05 .02
101 Willie Aikens .05 .02
102 Hal McRae .05 .02
103 Larry Gura .05 .02
104 Willie Wilson .05 .02
105 Damaso Garcia .05 .02
106 Hosken Powell .05 .02
107 Joey McLaughlin .05 .02
108 Jim Clancy .05 .02
109 Barry Bonnell .05 .02
110 Garth Iorg .05 .02
111 Dave Stieb .10 .04
112 Fernando Valenzuela .15 .06
113 Steve Garvey .25 .10
114 Rick Monday .05 .02
115 Burt Hooten .05 .02
116 Bill Russell .05 .02
117 Pedro Guerrero .05 .02
118 Steve Sax .05 .02
119 Steve Howe .05 .02
120 Ken Landreaux .05 .02
121 Dusty Baker .10 .04
122 Ron Cey .10 .04
123 Jerry Reuss .10 .04
124 Bump Wills .05 .02
125 Keith Moreland .05 .02
126 Dick Tidrow .05 .02
127 Bill Campbell .05 .02
128 Larry Bowa .05 .02
129 Randy Martz .05 .02
130 Ferguson Jenkins .30 .12
131 Leon Durham .05 .02
132 Bill Buckner .10 .04
133 Ron Davis .05 .02
134 Jack O'Connor .05 .02
135 Kent Hrbek .10 .04
136 Gary Ward .05 .02
137 Al Williams .05 .02
138 Tom Brunansky .05 .02
139 Bobby Castillo .05 .02
140 Dusty Baker .15 .06
Dale Murphy
141 Nolan Ryan 2.50 1.00
Alan Ashby
142 Omar Moreno .05 .02
Lee Lacy
sic, Lacey
143 Al Oliver .50 .20
Pete Rose
144 Rickey Henderson .75 .30
145 Ray Knight .50 .20
Mike Schmidt
Pete Rose
146 Ben Oglivie .05 .02
Hal McRae
147 Ray Knight .05 .02
Tom Hume
148 Buddy Bell .25 .10
Carlton Fisk
149 Steve Kemp .05 .02
150 Rudy Law .05 .02
151 Ron LeFlore .05 .02
152 Jerry Koosman .10 .04
153 Carlton Fisk .50 .20
154 Salome Barojas .05 .02
155 Harold Baines .10 .04
156 Britt Burns .05 .02
157 Tom Paciorek .05 .02
158 Greg Luzinski .05 .02
159 LeMarr Hoyt .05 .02
160 George Wright .05 .02
161 Danny Darwin .05 .02
162 Lamar Johnson .05 .02
163 Charlie Hough .10 .04
164 Buddy Bell .10 .04
165 Jon Matlack .05 .02
166 Billy Sample .05 .02
167 Johnny Grubb .05 .02
168 Larry Parrish .10 .04
169 Ivan DeJesus .05 .02
170 Mike Schmidt 1.00 .40
171 Tug McGraw .05 .02
172 Ron Reed .05 .02
173 Garry Maddox .05 .02
174 Pete Rose 1.50 .60
175 Manny Trillo .05 .02
176 Steve Carlton .75 .30
177 Bo Diaz .05 .02
178 Gary Matthews .05 .02
179 Bill Caudill .05 .02
180 Ed VandeBerg .05 .02
181 Gaylord Perry .30 .12
182 Floyd Bannister .05 .02
183 Richie Zisk .05 .02
184 Al Cowens .05 .02
185 Bruce Bochte .05 .02
186 Jeff Burroughs .05 .02
187 Dave Beard .05 .02
188 Dave Lopes .05 .02
189 Dwayne Murphy .05 .02
190 Rick Langford .05 .02
191 Tom Underwood .05 .02
192 Rickey Henderson 2.00 .80
193 Mike Flanagan .05 .02
194 Scott McGregor .05 .02
195 Ken Singleton .05 .02
196 Rich Dauer .05 .02
197 John Lowenstein .05 .02
198 Cal Ripken 5.00 2.00
199 Dennis Martinez .10 .04
200 Jim Palmer .50 .20
201 Tippy Martinez .05 .02
202 Eddie Murray 1.00 .40
203 Al Bumbry .05 .02
204 Dickie Thon .05 .02
205 Phil Garner .05 .02
206 Jose Cruz .10 .04
207 Nolan Ryan 5.00 2.00
208 Ray Knight .05 .02
209 Terry Puhl .05 .02
210 Joe Niekro .05 .02
211 Art Howe .10 .04
212 Alan Ashby .05 .02
213 Tom Hume .05 .02
214 Johnny Bench .50 .20
215 Larry Biittner .05 .02
216 Mario Soto .05 .02
217 Dan Driessen .05 .02
218 Tom Seaver .50 .20
219 Dave Concepcion .10 .04
220 Wayne Krenchicki .05 .02
221 Cesar Cedeno .05 .02
222 Randy Jones .05 .02
223 Terry Kennedy .05 .02
224 Luis DeLeon .05 .02
225 Eric Show .05 .02
226 Tim Flannery .05 .02
227 Garry Templeton .05 .02
228 Tim Lollar .05 .02
229 Sixto Lezcano .05 .02
230 Bob Bailor .05 .02
231 Craig Swan .05 .02
232 Dave Kingman .10 .04
233 Mookie Wilson .10 .04
234 John Stearns .05 .02
235 Ellis Valentine .05 .02
236 Neil Allen .05 .02
237 Pat Zachry .05 .02
238 Rusty Staub .10 .04
239 George Foster .05 .02
240 Rick Sutcliffe .05 .02
241 Andre Thornton .05 .02
242 Mike Hargrove .10 .04
243 Dan Spillner .05 .02
244 Lary Sorensen .05 .02
245 Len Barker .05 .02
246 Rick Manning .05 .02
247 Toby Harrah .05 .02
248 Milt Wilcox .05 .02
249 Lou Whitaker .10 .04
250 Tom Brookens .05 .02
251 Chet Lemon .05 .02
252 Jack Morris .10 .04
253 Alan Trammell .25 .10
254 Johnny Wockenfuss .05 .02
255 Lance Parrish .15 .06
256 Larry Herndon .05 .02
257 Chris Speier .05 .02
258 Woodie Fryman .05 .02
259 Scott Sanderson .05 .02
260 Steve Rogers .05 .02
261 Warren Cromartie .05 .02
262 Gary Carter .40 .16
263 Bill Gullickson .05 .02
264 Andre Dawson .30 .12
265 Tim Raines .15 .06
266 Charlie Lea .05 .02
267 Jeff Reardon .10 .04
268 Al Oliver .10 .04
269 George Hendrick .05 .02
270 John Montefusco .05 .02
NNO Oakland A's CL .05 .02
NNO Montreal Expos CL .05 .02
NNO Boston Red Sox CL .05 .02
NNO California Angels PO .05 .02
NNO California Angels CL .05 .02
NNO Detroit Tigers CL .05 .02
NNO Los Angeles Dodgers CL .05 .02
NNO Kansas City Royals CL .05 .02
NNO St. Louis Cardinals PO .05 .02
NNO Baltimore Orioles CL .05 .02
NNO Montreal Expos PO .05 .02
NNO Pittsburgh Pirates PO .05 .02
NNO St. Louis Cardinals CL .05 .02
NNO San Diego Padres PO .05 .02
NNO Atlanta Braves PO .05 .02
NNO Texas Rangers CL .05 .02
NNO Kansas City Royals PO .05 .02
NNO New York Yankees CL .05 .02
NNO Toronto Blue Jays PO .05 .02
NNO Philadelphia Phillies PO .05 .02
NNO Chicago Cubs CL .05 .02
NNO Boston Red Sox PO .05 .02
NNO Pittsburgh Pirates CL .05 .02
NNO San Diego Padres CL .05 .02
NNO Cleveland Indians PO .05 .02
NNO Baltimore Orioles PO .05 .02
NNO New York Mets PO .05 .02
NNO Cincinnati Reds CL .05 .02
NNO Houston Astros PO .05 .02
NNO Milwaukee Brewers PO .05 .02
NNO Los Angeles Dodgers PO .05 .02
NNO Chicago White Sox PO .05 .02
NNO New York Yankees PO .05 .02
NNO Philadelphia Phillies CL .05 .02
NNO San Francisco Giants PO .05 .02
NNO Toronto Blue Jays CL .05 .02
NNO Minnesota Twins CL .05 .02
NNO Atlanta Braves CL .05 .02
NNO Cincinnati Reds PO .05 .02
NNO Detroit Tigers PO .05 .02
NNO New York Mets CL .05 .02
NNO Milwaukee Brewers CL .05 .02
NNO Cleveland Indians CL .05 .02
NNO Seattle Mariners CL .05 .02
NNO Seattle Mariners PO .05 .02
NNO Minnesota Twins PO .05 .02

1984 Fleer

The 1984 Fleer card 660-card standard-size set featured fronts with full-color team logos along with the player's name and position and the Fleer identification. Wax packs again consisted of 15 cards plus logo stickers. The set features many imaginative photos, several multi-player cards, and many more action shots than the 1983 card set. The backs are quite similar to the 1983 backs except that blue rather than brown ink is used. The player cards are alphabetized within team and the teams are ordered by their 1983 season finish and won-lost record. Specials (626-646) and checklist cards (647-660) make up the end of the set. The key Rookie Cards in this set are Don Mattingly, Darryl Strawberry and Andy Van Slyke.

Nm-Mt Ex-Mt
COMPLETE SET (660) 50.00 20.00
1 Mike Boddicker .15 .06
2 Al Bumbry .15 .06
3 Todd Cruz .15 .06
4 Rich Dauer .15 .06
5 Storm Davis .15 .06
6 Rick Dempsey .15 .06
7 Jim Dwyer .15 .06
8 Mike Flanagan .15 .06
9 Dan Ford .15 .06
10 John Lowenstein .15 .06
11 Dennis Martinez .40 .16
12 Tippy Martinez .15 .06
13 Scott McGregor .15 .06
14 Eddie Murray 1.50 .60
15 Joe Nolan .15 .06
16 Jim Palmer .40 .16
17 Cal Ripken 10.00 4.00
18 Gary Roenicke .15 .06
19 Lenn Sakata .15 .06
20 John Shelby .15 .06
21 Ken Singleton .15 .06
22 Sammy Stewart .15 .06
23 Tim Stoddard .15 .06
24 Marty Bystrom .15 .06
25 Steve Carlton .40 .16
26 Ivan DeJesus .15 .06
27 John Denny .15 .06
28 Bob Dernier .15 .06
29 Bo Diaz .15 .06
30 Kiko Garcia .15 .06
31 Greg Gross .15 .06
32 Kevin Gross RC .15 .06
33 Von Hayes .15 .06
34 Willie Hernandez .40 .16
35 Al Holland .15 .06
36 Charles Hudson .15 .06
37 Joe Lefebvre .15 .06
38 Sixto Lezcano .15 .06
39 Garry Maddox .15 .06
40 Gary Matthews .40 .16
41 Len Matuszek .15 .06
42 Tug McGraw .40 .16
43 Joe Morgan .75 .30
44 Tony Perez .75 .30
45 Ron Reed .15 .06
46 Pete Rose 5.00 2.00
47 Juan Samuel RC .75 .30
48 Mike Schmidt 4.00 1.60
49 Ozzie Virgil .15 .06
50 Juan Agosto .15 .06
51 Harold Baines 1.50 .60
52 Floyd Bannister .15 .06
53 Salome Barojas .15 .06
54 Britt Burns .15 .06
55 Julio Cruz .15 .06
56 Richard Dotson .15 .06
57 Jerry Dybzinski .15 .06
58 Carlton Fisk .75 .30
59 Scott Fletcher .15 .06
60 Jerry Hairston .15 .06
61 Kevin Hickey .15 .06
62 Marc Hill .15 .06
63 LaMarr Hoyt .15 .06
64 Ron Kittle .15 .06
65 Jerry Koosman .40 .16
66 Dennis Lamp .15 .06
67 Rudy Law .15 .06
68 Vance Law .15 .06
69 Greg Luzinski .40 .16
70 Tom Paciorek .40 .16
71 Mike Squires .15 .06
72 Dick Tidrow .15 .06
73 Greg Walker .40 .16
74 Glenn Abbott .15 .06
75 Howard Bailey .15 .06
76 Doug Bair .15 .06
77 Juan Berenguer .15 .06
78 Tom Brookens .40 .16
79 Enos Cabell .15 .06
80 Kirk Gibson 1.50 .60
81 John Grubb .15 .06
82 Larry Herndon .40 .16
83 Wayne Krenchicki .15 .06
84 Rick Leach .15 .06
85 Chet Lemon .15 .06
86 Aurelio Lopez .40 .16
87 Jack Morris .40 .16
88 Lance Parrish .75 .30
89 Dan Petry .40 .16
90 Dave Rozema .15 .06
91 Alan Trammell .75 .30
92 Lou Whitaker .40 .16
93 Milt Wilcox .15 .06
94 Glenn Wilson .40 .16
95 John Wockenfuss .15 .06
96 Dusty Baker .40 .16
97 Joe Beckwith .15 .06
98 Greg Brock .15 .06
99 Jack Fimple .15 .06
100 Pedro Guerrero .40 .16
101 Rick Honeycutt .15 .06
102 Burt Hooton .15 .06
103 Steve Howe .15 .06
104 Ken Landreaux .15 .06
105 Mike Marshall .15 .06
106 Rick Monday .15 .06
107 Jose Morales .15 .06
108 Tom Niedenfuer .15 .06
109 Alejandro Pena RC* .40 .16
110 Jerry Reuss UER .15 .06
("Home:" omitted)
111 Bill Russell .15 .06
112 Steve Sax .40 .16
113 Mike Scioscia .15 .06
114 Derrel Thomas .15 .06
115 Fernando Valenzuela .40 .16
116 Bob Welch .15 .06
117 Steve Yeager .15 .06
118 Pat Zachry .15 .06
119 Don Baylor .75 .30
120 Bert Campaneris .40 .16
121 Rick Cerone .15 .06
122 Ray Fontenot .15 .06
123 George Frazier .15 .06
124 Oscar Gamble .15 .06
125 Rich Gossage .75 .30
126 Ken Griffey .40 .16
127 Ron Guidry .40 .16
128 Jay Howell .15 .06
129 Steve Kemp .15 .06
130 Matt Keough .15 .06
131 Don Mattingly RC 20.00 8.00
132 John Montefusco .15 .06
133 Omar Moreno .15 .06
134 Dale Murray .15 .06
135 Graig Nettles .40 .16
136 Lou Piniella .40 .16
137 Willie Randolph .40 .16
138 Shane Rawley .15 .06
139 Dave Righetti .40 .16
140 Andre Robertson .15 .06
141 Bob Shirley .15 .06
142 Roy Smalley .15 .06
143 Dave Winfield .40 .16
144 Butch Wynegar .15 .06
145 Jim Acker .15 .06
146 Doyle Alexander .15 .06
147 Jesse Barfield .40 .16
148 Jorge Bell .40 .16
149 Barry Bonnell .15 .06
150 Jim Clancy .15 .06
151 Dave Collins .15 .06
152 Tony Fernandez RC 2.00 .80
153 Damaso Garcia .15 .06
154 Dave Geisel .15 .06
155 Jim Gott .15 .06
156 Alfredo Griffin .15 .06
157 Garth Iorg .15 .06
158 Roy Lee Jackson .15 .06
159 Cliff Johnson .15 .06
160 Luis Leal .15 .06
161 Buck Martinez .15 .06
162 Joey McLaughlin .15 .06
163 Randy Moffitt .15 .06
164 Lloyd Moseby .15 .06
165 Rance Mulliniks .15 .06
166 Jorge Orta .15 .06
167 Dave Stieb .15 .06
168 Willie Upshaw .15 .06
169 Ernie Whitt .15 .06
170 Len Barker .15 .06
171 Steve Bedrosian .15 .06
172 Bruce Benedict .15 .06
173 Brett Butler .75 .30
174 Rick Camp .15 .06
175 Chris Chambliss .40 .16
176 Ken Dayley .15 .06
177 Pete Falcone .15 .06
178 Terry Forster .15 .06
179 Gene Garber .15 .06
180 Terry Harper .15 .06
181 Bob Horner .15 .06
182 Glenn Hubbard .15 .06
183 Randy Johnson .15 .06
184 Craig McMurtry .15 .06
185 Donnie Moore .15 .06
186 Dale Murphy 1.50 .60
187 Phil Niekro .40 .16
188 Pascual Perez .15 .06
189 Biff Pocoroba .15 .06
190 Rafael Ramirez .15 .06
191 Jerry Royster .15 .06
192 Claudell Washington .15 .06
193 Bob Watson .40 .16
194 Jerry Augustine .15 .06
195 Mark Brouhard .15 .06
196 Mike Caldwell .15 .06
197 Tom Candiotti RC 1.50 .60
198 Cecil Cooper .40 .16
199 Rollie Fingers .40 .16
200 Jim Gantner .15 .06
201 Bob L. Gibson RC .15 .06
202 Moose Haas .15 .06
203 Roy Howell .15 .06
204 Pete Ladd .15 .06
205 Rick Manning .15 .06
206 Bob McClure .15 .06
207 Paul Molitor UER .75 .30
('83 stats should say
.270 BA and 608 AB)
208 Don Money .15 .06
209 Charlie Moore .15 .06
210 Ben Oglivie .15 .06
211 Chuck Porter .15 .06
212 Ed Romero .15 .06
213 Ted Simmons .40 .16
214 Jim Slaton .15 .06
215 Don Sutton 1.50 .60
216 Tom Tellmann .15 .06
217 Pete Vuckovich .15 .06
218 Ned Yost .15 .06
219 Robin Yount 2.50 1.00
220 Alan Ashby .15 .06
221 Kevin Bass .15 .06
222 Jose Cruz .40 .16
223 Bill Dawley .15 .06
224 Frank DiPino .15 .06
225 Bill Doran RC* .40 .16
226 Phil Garner .40 .16
227 Art Howe .40 .16
228 Bob Knepper .15 .06
229 Ray Knight .40 .16
230 Frank LaCorte .15 .06
231 Mike LaCoss .15 .06
232 Mike Madden .15 .06
233 Jerry Mumphrey .15 .06
234 Joe Niekro .40 .16
235 Terry Puhl .15 .06
236 Luis Pujols .15 .06
237 Craig Reynolds .15 .06
238 Vern Ruhle .15 .06
239 Nolan Ryan 8.00 3.20
240 Mike Scott .40 .16
241 Tony Scott .15 .06
242 Dave Smith .15 .06
243 Dickie Thon .15 .06
244 Denny Walling .15 .06
245 Dale Berra .15 .06
246 Jim Bibby .15 .06
247 John Candelaria .15 .06
248 Jose DeLeon RC .15 .06
249 Mike Easler .15 .06
250 Cecilio Guante .15 .06
251 Richie Hebner .15 .06
252 Lee Lacy .15 .06
253 Bill Madlock .40 .16
254 Milt May .15 .06
255 Lee Mazzilli .15 .06
256 Larry McWilliams .15 .06
257 Jim Morrison .15 .06
258 Dave Parker .40 .16
259 Tony Pena .15 .06
260 Johnny Ray .15 .06
261 Rick Rhoden .15 .06
262 Don Robinson .15 .06
263 Manny Sarmiento .15 .06
264 Rod Scurry .15 .06
265 Kent Tekulve .40 .16
266 Gene Tenace .40 .16
267 Jason Thompson .15 .06
268 Lee Tunnell .15 .06
269 Marvell Wynne .15 .06
270 Ray Burris .15 .06
271 Gary Carter .75 .30
272 Warren Cromartie .15 .06
273 Andre Dawson .40 .16
274 Doug Flynn .15 .06
275 Terry Francona .15 .06
276 Bill Gullickson .15 .06
277 Bob James .15 .06
278 Charlie Lea .15 .06
279 Bryan Little .15 .06
280 Al Oliver .40 .16
281 Tim Raines .75 .30
282 Bobby Ramos .15 .06
283 Jeff Reardon .40 .16
284 Steve Rogers .15 .06
285 Scott Sanderson .15 .06
286 Dan Schatzeder .15 .06
287 Bryn Smith .15 .06
288 Chris Speier .15 .06
289 Manny Trillo .15 .06
290 Mike Vail .15 .06
291 Tim Wallach .40 .16
292 Chris Welsh .15 .06
293 Jim Wohlford .15 .06
294 Kurt Bevacqua .15 .06
295 Juan Bonilla .15 .06
296 Bobby Brown .15 .06
297 Luis DeLeon .15 .06
298 Dave Dravecky .40 .16
299 Tim Flannery .15 .06
300 Steve Garvey .40 .16
301 Tony Gwynn 6.00 2.40
302 Andy Hawkins .15 .06
303 Ruppert Jones .15 .06
304 Terry Kennedy .15 .06
305 Tim Lollar .15 .06
306 Gary Lucas .15 .06
307 Kevin McReynolds RC .75 .30
308 Sid Monge .15 .06
309 Mario Ramirez .15 .06
310 Gene Richards .15 .06
311 Luis Salazar .15 .06
312 Eric Show .15 .06
313 Elias Sosa .15 .06
314 Garry Templeton .15 .06
315 Mark Thurmond .15 .06
316 Ed Whitson .15 .06
317 Alan Wiggins .15 .06
318 Neil Allen .15 .06
319 Joaquin Andujar .15 .06
320 Steve Braun .15 .06
321 Glenn Brummer .15 .06
322 Bob Forsch .15 .06
323 David Green .15 .06
324 George Hendrick .15 .06
325 Tom Herr .40 .16
326 Dane Iorg .15 .06
327 Jeff Lahti .15 .06
328 Dave LaPoint .15 .06
329 Willie McGee .75 .30
330 Ken Oberkfell .15 .06
331 Darrell Porter .15 .06
332 Jamie Quirk .15 .06
333 Mike Ramsey .15 .06
334 Floyd Rayford .15 .06
335 Lonnie Smith .15 .06
336 Ozzie Smith 2.50 1.00
337 John Stuper .15 .06
338 Bruce Sutter .40 .16
339 A.Van Slyke UER 1.50 .60
Batting and throwing
both wrong on card back
340 Dave Von Ohlen .15 .06
341 Willie Aikens .15 .06
342 Mike Armstrong .15 .06
343 Bud Black .15 .06
344 George Brett 4.00 1.60
345 Onix Concepcion .15 .06
346 Keith Creel .15 .06
347 Larry Gura .15 .06
348 Don Hood .15 .06
349 Dennis Leonard .15 .06
350 Hal McRae .40 .16
351 Amos Otis .40 .16
352 Gaylord Perry .40 .16
353 Greg Pryor .15 .06
354 Dan Quisenberry .15 .06
355 Steve Renko .15 .06
356 Leon Roberts .15 .06
357 Pat Sheridan .15 .06
358 Joe Simpson .15 .06
359 Don Slaught .40 .16
360 Paul Splittorff .15 .06
361 U.L. Washington .15 .06
362 John Wathan .15 .06
363 Frank White .40 .16
364 Willie Wilson .15 .06
365 Jim Barr .15 .06
366 Dave Bergman .15 .06
367 Fred Breining .15 .06
368 Bob Brenly .15 .06
369 Jack Clark .40 .16
370 Chili Davis .75 .30
371 Mark Davis .15 .06
372 Darrell Evans .40 .16
373 Atlee Hammaker .15 .06
374 Mike Krukow .15 .06
375 Duane Kuiper .15 .06
376 Bill Laskey .15 .06
377 Gary Lavelle .15 .06
378 Johnnie LeMaster .15 .06
379 Jeff Leonard .15 .06
380 Randy Lerch .15 .06
381 Renie Martin .15 .06
382 Andy McGaffigan .15 .06
383 Greg Minton .15 .06
384 Tom O'Malley .15 .06
385 Max Venable .15 .06
386 Brad Wellman .15 .06

387 Joel Youngblood .15 .06
388 Gary Allenson .15 .06
389 Luis Aponte .15 .06
390 Tony Armas .15 .06
391 Doug Bird .15 .06
392 Wade Boggs 4.00 1.60
393 Dennis Boyd .40 .16
394 Mike Brown UER P .15 .06
(shown with record of 31-104)
395 Mark Clear .15 .06
396 Dennis Eckersley .75 .30
397 Dwight Evans .40 .16
398 Rich Gedman .15 .06
399 Glenn Hoffman .15 .06
400 Bruce Hurst .15 .06
401 John Henry Johnson .15 .06
402 Ed Jurak .15 .06
403 Rick Miller .15 .06
404 Jeff Newman .15 .06
405 Reid Nichols .15 .06
406 Bob Ojeda .15 .06
407 Jerry Remy .15 .06
408 Jim Rice .40 .16
409 Bob Stanley .15 .06
410 Dave Stapleton .15 .06
411 John Tudor .15 .06
412 Carl Yastrzemski 1.50 .60
413 Buddy Bell .40 .16
414 Larry Biittner .15 .06
415 John Butcher .15 .06
416 Danny Darwin .15 .06
417 Bucky Dent .40 .16
418 Dave Hostetler .15 .06
419 Charlie Hough .40 .16
420 Bobby Johnson .15 .06
421 Odell Jones .15 .06
422 Jon Matlack .15 .06
423 Pete O'Brien RC* .40 .16
424 Larry Parrish .15 .06
425 Mickey Rivers .15 .06
426 Billy Sample .15 .06
427 Dave Schmidt .15 .06
428 Mike Smithson .15 .06
429 Bill Stein .15 .06
430 Dave Stewart .40 .16
431 Jim Sundberg .40 .16
432 Frank Tanana .40 .16
433 Dave Tobik .15 .06
434 Wayne Tolleson .15 .06
435 George Wright .15 .06
436 Bill Almon .15 .06
437 Keith Atherton .15 .06
438 Dave Beard .15 .06
439 Tom Burgmeier .15 .06
440 Jeff Burroughs .15 .06
441 Chris Codiroli .15 .06
442 Tim Conroy .15 .06
443 Mike Davis .15 .06
444 Wayne Gross .15 .06
445 Garry Hancock .15 .06
446 Mike Heath .15 .06
447 Rickey Henderson 2.50 1.00
448 Donnie Hill .15 .06
449 Bob Kearney .15 .06
450 Bill Krueger RC .15 .06
451 Rick Langford .15 .06
452 Carney Lansford .40 .16
453 Dave Lopes .40 .16
454 Steve McCatty .15 .06
455 Dan Meyer .15 .06
456 Dwayne Murphy .15 .06
457 Mike Norris .15 .06
458 Ricky Peters .15 .06
459 Tony Phillips RC 1.50 .60
460 Tom Underwood .15 .06
461 Mike Warren .15 .06
462 Johnny Bench 1.50 .60
463 Bruce Berenyi .15 .06
464 Dann Bilardello .15 .06
465 Cesar Cedeno .40 .16
466 Dave Concepcion .40 .16
467 Dan Driessen .15 .06
468 Nick Esasky .15 .06
469 Rich Gale .15 .06
470 Ben Hayes .15 .06
471 Paul Householder .15 .06
472 Tom Hume .15 .06
473 Alan Knicely .15 .06
474 Eddie Milner .15 .06
475 Ron Oester .15 .06
476 Kelly Paris .15 .06
477 Frank Pastore .15 .06
478 Ted Power .15 .06
479 Joe Price .15 .06
480 Charlie Puleo .15 .06
481 Gary Redus RC* .15 .06
482 Bill Scherrer .15 .06
483 Mario Soto .15 .06
484 Alex Trevino .15 .06
485 Duane Walker .15 .06
486 Larry Bowa .40 .16
487 Warren Brusstar .15 .06
488 Bill Buckner .40 .16
489 Bill Campbell .15 .06
490 Ron Cey .40 .16
491 Jody Davis .15 .06
492 Leon Durham .15 .06
493 Mel Hall .40 .16
494 Ferguson Jenkins .40 .16
495 Jay Johnstone .40 .16
496 Craig Lefferts RC .15 .06
497 Carmelo Martinez .15 .06
498 Jerry Morales .15 .06
499 Keith Moreland .15 .06
500 Dickie Noles .15 .06
501 Mike Proly .15 .06
502 Chuck Rainey .15 .06
503 Dick Ruthven .15 .06
504 Ryne Sandberg 6.00 2.40
505 Lee Smith 1.50 .60
506 Steve Trout .15 .06
507 Gary Woods .15 .06
508 Juan Beniquez .15 .06
509 Bob Boone .40 .16
510 Rick Burleson .15 .06
511 Rod Carew .75 .30
512 Bobby Clark .15 .06
513 John Curtis .15 .06
514 Doug DeCinces .15 .06
515 Brian Downing .15 .06
516 Tim Foli .15 .06
517 Ken Forsch .15 .06
518 Bobby Grich .40 .16
519 Andy Hassler .15 .06
520 Reggie Jackson .75 .30
521 Ron Jackson .15 .06
522 Tommy John .75 .30
523 Bruce Kison .15 .06
524 Steve Lubratich .15 .06
525 Fred Lynn .40 .16
526 Gary Pettis .15 .06
527 Luis Sanchez .15 .06
528 Daryl Sconiers .15 .06
529 Ellis Valentine .15 .06
530 Rob Wilfong .15 .06
531 Mike Witt .15 .06
532 Geoff Zahn .15 .06
533 Bud Anderson .15 .06
534 Chris Bando .15 .06
535 Alan Bannister .15 .06
536 Bert Blyleven .40 .16
537 Tom Brennan .15 .06
538 Jamie Easterly .15 .06
539 Juan Eichelberger .15 .06
540 Jim Essian .15 .06
541 Mike Fischlin .15 .06
542 Julio Franco .75 .30
543 Mike Hargrove .40 .16
544 Toby Harrah .40 .16
545 Ron Hassey .15 .06
546 Neal Heaton .15 .06
547 Bake McBride .15 .06
548 Broderick Perkins .15 .06
549 Lary Sorensen .15 .06
550 Dan Spillner .15 .06
551 Rick Sutcliffe .40 .16
552 Pat Tabler .15 .06
553 Gorman Thomas .15 .06
554 Andre Thornton .15 .06
555 George Vukovich .15 .06
556 Darrell Brown .15 .06
557 Tom Brunansky .40 .16
558 Randy Bush .15 .06
559 Bobby Castillo .15 .06
560 John Castino .15 .06
561 Ron Davis .15 .06
562 Dave Engle .15 .06
563 Lenny Faedo .15 .06
564 Pete Filson .15 .06
565 Gary Gaetti .75 .30
566 Mickey Hatcher .15 .06
567 Kent Hrbek .40 .16
568 Rusty Kuntz .15 .06
569 Tim Laudner .15 .06
570 Rick Lysander .15 .06
571 Bobby Mitchell .15 .06
572 Ken Schrom .15 .06
573 Ray Smith .15 .06
574 Tim Teufel RC .15 .06
575 Frank Viola .75 .30
576 Gary Ward .15 .06
577 Ron Washington .15 .06
578 Len Whitehouse .15 .06
579 Al Williams .15 .06
580 Bob Bailor .15 .06
581 Mark Bradley .15 .06
582 Hubie Brooks .15 .06
583 Carlos Diaz .15 .06
584 George Foster .40 .16
585 Brian Giles .15 .06
586 Danny Heep .15 .06
587 Keith Hernandez .75 .30
588 Ron Hodges .15 .06
589 Scott Holman .15 .06
590 Dave Kingman .75 .30
591 Ed Lynch .15 .06
592 Jose Oquendo RC .40 .16
593 Jesse Orosco .15 .06
594 Junior Ortiz .15 .06
595 Tom Seaver .75 .30
596 Doug Sisk .15 .06
597 Rusty Staub .40 .16
598 John Stearns .15 .06
599 Darryl Strawberry RC 3.00 1.20
600 Craig Swan .15 .06
601 Walt Terrell .15 .06
602 Mike Torrez .15 .06
603 Mookie Wilson .40 .16
604 Jamie Allen .15 .06
605 Jim Beattie .15 .06
606 Tony Bernazard .15 .06
607 Manny Castillo .15 .06
608 Bill Caudill .15 .06
609 Bryan Clark .15 .06
610 Al Cowens .15 .06
611 Dave Henderson .40 .16
612 Steve Henderson .15 .06
613 Orlando Mercado .15 .06
614 Mike Moore .15 .06
615 Ricky Nelson UER .15 .06
(Jamie Nelson's stats on back)
616 Spike Owen RC .40 .16
617 Pat Putnam .15 .06
618 Ron Roenicke .15 .06
619 Mike Stanton .15 .06
620 Bob Stoddard .15 .06
621 Rick Sweet .15 .06
622 Roy Thomas .15 .06
623 Ed VandeBerg .15 .06
624 Matt Young RC .15 .06
625 Richie Zisk .15 .06
626 Fred Lynn IA .40 .16
627 Manny Trillo IA .15 .06
628 Steve Garvey IA .15 .06
629 Rod Carew IA .40 .16
630 Wade Boggs IA 1.50 .60
631 Tim Raines IA .40 .16
632 Al Oliver IA .40 .16
633 Steve Sax IA .15 .06
634 Dickie Thon IA .15 .06
635 Dan Quisenberry .15 .06
Tippy Martinez
636 Joe Morgan 1.50 .60
Pete Rose
Tony Perez
637 Lance Parrish .75 .30
Bob Boone
638 George Brett 2.00 .80
Gaylord Perry
639 Dave Righetti .75 .30
Mike Warren
Bob Forsch
640 Johnny Bench 1.50 .60
Carl Yastrzemski
641 Gaylord Perry IA .15 .06
642 Steve Carlton IA .15 .06
643 Joe Altobelli MG .15 .06
Paul Owens MG
644 Rick Dempsey WS .40 .16
645 Mike Boddicker WS .15 .06
646 Scott McGregor WS .15 .06
647 CL: Orioles/Royals .15 .06
Joe Altobelli MG
648 CL: Phillies/Giants .15 .06
Paul Owens MG
649 CL: White Sox/Red Sox .75 .30
Tony LaRussa MG
650 CL: Tigers/Rangers .75 .30
Sparky Anderson MG
651 CL: Dodgers/A's .75 .30
Tommy Lasorda MG
652 CL: Yankees/Reds .75 .30
Billy Martin MG
653 CL: Blue Jays/Cubs .40 .16
Bobby Cox MG
654 CL: Braves/Angels .75 .30
Joe Torre MG
655 CL: Brewers/Indians .15 .06
Rene Lachemann MG
656 CL: Astros/Twins .15 .06
Bob Lillis MG
657 CL: Pirates/Mets .15 .06
Chuck Tanner MG
658 CL: Expos/Mariners .15 .06
Bill Virdon MG
659 CL: Padres/Specials .40 .16
Dick Williams MG
660 CL: Cardinals/Teams .75 .30
Whitey Herzog MG

1984 Fleer Update

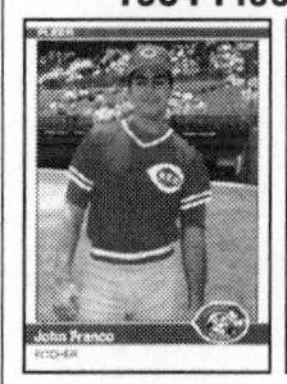
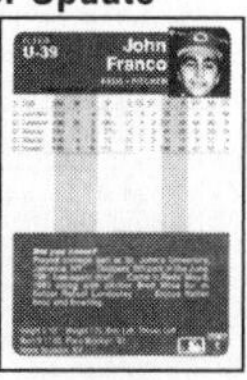

This set was Fleer's first update set and portrayed players with their proper team for the current year and rookies who were not in their regular issue. Like the Topps Traded sets of the time, the Fleer Update sets were distributed in factory set form through hobby dealers only. The set was quite popular with collectors, and, apparently, the print run was relatively short, as the set was quickly in short supply and exhibited a rapid and dramatic price increase in the mid to late 1980's. The cards are numbered on the back with a U prefix and placed in alphabetical order by player name. The key (extended) Rookie Cards in this set are Roger Clemens, John Franco, Dwight Gooden, Jimmy Key, Mark Langston, Kirby Puckett, and Bret Saberhagen. Collectors are urged to be careful if purchasing single cards of Clemens, Darling, Gooden, Puckett, Rose, or Saberhagen as these specific cards have been illegally reprinted. These fakes are blurry when compared to the real cards and have noticeably different printing dot patterns under 8X or greater magnification..

Nm-Mt Ex-Mt
COMP.FACT.SET (132) 300.00 120.00
1 Willie Aikens 1.00 .40
2 Luis Aponte 1.00 .40
3 Mark Bailey 1.00 .40
4 Bob Bailor 1.00 .40
5 Dusty Baker 1.50 .60
6 Steve Balboni 1.00 .40
7 Alan Bannister 1.00 .40
8 Marty Barrett 1.50 .60
9 Dave Beard 1.00 .40
10 Joe Beckwith 1.00 .40
11 Dave Bergman 1.00 .40
12 Tony Bernazard 1.00 .40
13 Bruce Bochte 1.00 .40
14 Barry Bonnell 1.00 .40
15 Phil Bradley 1.50 .60
16 Fred Breining 1.00 .40
17 Mike C. Brown 1.00 .40
18 Bill Buckner 1.50 .60
19 Ray Burris 1.00 .40
20 John Butcher 1.00 .40
21 Brett Butler 2.50 1.00
22 Enos Cabell 1.00 .40
23 Bill Campbell 1.00 .40
24 Bill Caudill 1.00 .40
25 Bobby Clark 1.00 .40
26 Bryan Clark 1.00 .40
27 Roger Clemens XRC 200.00 80.00
28 Jaime Cocanower 1.00 .40
29 Ron Darling XRC* 2.50 1.00
30 Alvin Davis XRC 1.50 .60
31 Bob Dernier 1.00 .40
32 Carlos Diaz 1.00 .40
33 Mike Easler 1.00 .40
34 Dennis Eckersley 2.50 1.00
35 Jim Essian 1.00 .40
36 Darrell Evans 1.50 .60
37 Mike Fitzgerald 1.00 .40
38 Tim Foli 1.00 .40
39 John Franco XRC 8.00 3.20
40 George Frazier 1.00 .40
41 Rich Gale 1.00 .40
42 Barbaro Garbey 1.00 .40
43 Dwight Gooden XRC 15.00 6.00
44 Rich Gossage 2.50 1.00
45 Wayne Gross 1.00 .40
46 Mark Gubicza XRC 1.50 .60
47 Jackie Gutierrez 1.00 .40
48 Toby Harrah 1.50 .60
49 Ron Hassey 1.00 .40
50 Richie Hebner 1.00 .40
51 Willie Hernandez 1.50 .60
52 Ed Hodge 1.00 .40
53 Ricky Horton 1.00 .40
54 Art Howe 1.50 .60
55 Dane Iorg 1.00 .40
56 Brook Jacoby 1.50 .60
57 Dion James XRC* 1.00 .40
58 Mike Jeffcoat 1.00 .40
59 Ruppert Jones 1.00 .40
60 Bob Kearney 1.00 .40
61 Jimmy Key XRC 2.50 1.00
62 Dave Kingman 2.50 1.00
63 Brad Komminsk 1.00 .40
64 Jerry Koosman 1.50 .60
65 Wayne Krenchicki 1.00 .40
66 Rusty Kuntz 1.00 .40
67 Frank LaCorte 1.00 .40
68 Dennis Lamp 1.00 .40
69 Tito Landrum 1.00 .40
70 Mark Langston XRC 4.00 1.60
71 Rick Leach 1.00 .40
72 Craig Lefferts 1.50 .60
73 Gary Lucas 1.00 .40
74 Jerry Martin 1.00 .40
75 Carmelo Martinez 1.00 .40
76 Mike Mason XRC 1.00 .40
77 Gary Matthews 1.50 .60
78 Andy McGaffigan 1.00 .40
79 Joey McLaughlin 1.00 .40
80 Joe Morgan 2.50 1.00
81 Darryl Motley 1.00 .40
82 Graig Nettles 1.50 .60
83 Phil Niekro 1.50 .60
84 Ken Oberkfell 1.00 .40
85 Al Oliver 1.50 .60
86 Jorge Orta 1.00 .40
87 Amos Otis 1.50 .60
88 Bob Owchinko 1.00 .40
89 Dave Parker 1.50 .60
90 Jack Perconte 1.00 .40
91 Tony Perez 2.50 1.00
92 Gerald Perry 1.50 .60
93 Kirby Puckett XRC 80.00 32.00
94 Shane Rawley 1.00 .40
95 Floyd Rayford 1.00 .40
96 Ron Reed 1.00 .40
97 R.J. Reynolds 1.00 .40
98 Gene Richards 1.00 .40
99 Jose Rijo XRC 4.00 1.60
100 Jeff D. Robinson 1.00 .40
101 Ron Romanick 1.00 .40
102 Pete Rose 12.00 4.80
103 Bret Saberhagen XRC 10.00 4.00
104 Scott Sanderson 1.00 .40
105 Dick Schofield XRC* 1.50 .60
106 Tom Seaver 2.50 1.00
107 Jim Slaton 1.00 .40
108 Mike Smithson 1.00 .40
109 Lary Sorensen 1.00 .40
110 Tim Stoddard 1.00 .40
111 Jeff Stone 1.00 .40
112 Champ Summers 1.00 .40
113 Jim Sundberg 1.50 .60
114 Rick Sutcliffe 1.50 .60
115 Craig Swan 1.00 .40
116 Derrel Thomas 1.00 .40
117 Gorman Thomas 1.00 .40
118 Alex Trevino 1.00 .40
119 Manny Trillo 1.00 .40
120 John Tudor 1.00 .40
121 Tom Underwood 1.00 .40
122 Mike Vail 1.00 .40
123 Tom Waddell 1.00 .40
124 Gary Ward 1.00 .40
125 Terry Whitfield 1.00 .40
126 Curtis Wilkerson 1.00 .40
127 Frank Williams 1.00 .40
128 Glenn Wilson 1.00 .40
129 John Wockenfuss 1.00 .40
130 Ned Yost 1.00 .40
131 Mike Young RC 1.00 .40
132 Checklist 1-132 1.00 .40

1984 Fleer Stickers

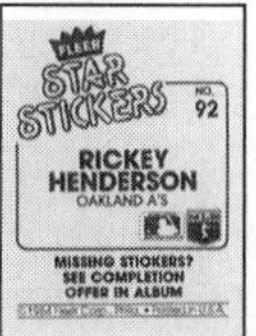

The stickers in this 126-sticker set measure approximately 1 15/16" by 2 1/2". The 1984 Fleer sticker set is a very attractive set with a beige border. Many players are featured more than once in the set due to the fact that the album issued to house the set contains league leader categories in which to place the stickers. The checklist below is ordered by categories, e.g., Game Winning RBI's (1-5), Batting Average (6-15), Home Runs (16-23), Hits (24-31), Slugging Percentage (32-39), Pinch Hits (40-43), Designated Hitter's Hits (44-47), On Base Percentage (48-55), Won/Lost Percentage (56-64), Earned Run Average (65-66), Saves (67-77), Strikeouts (78-87), Stolen Bases (88-95), Future Hall of Famers (96-103), Rookie Stars (104-113), World Series Batting (114-122) and Playoff Managers (123-126). These stickers were originally issued in packs of six for 25 cents plus a team logo.

Nm-Mt Ex-Mt
COMPLETE SET (126) 12.00 4.80
1 Dickie Thon .05 .02
2 Ken Landreaux .05 .02
3 Darrell Evans .15 .06
4 Harold Baines .15 .06
5 Dave Winfield .50 .20
6 Bill Madlock .05 .02
7 Lonnie Smith .05 .02
8 Jose Cruz .15 .06
9 George Hendrick .05 .02
10 Ray Knight .05 .02
11 Wade Boggs .60 .24
12 Rod Carew .50 .20
13 Lou Whitaker .25 .10
14 Alan Trammell .40 .16
15 Cal Ripken 2.00 .80
16 Mike Schmidt .75 .30
17 Dale Murphy .40 .16
18 Andre Dawson .40 .16
19 Pedro Guerrero .15 .06
20 Jim Rice .15 .06
21 Tony Armas .05 .02
22 Ron Kittle .05 .02
23 Eddie Murray .50 .20
24 Jose Cruz .15 .06
25 Andre Dawson .40 .16
26 Rafael Ramirez .05 .02
27 Al Oliver .15 .06
28 Wade Boggs .75 .30
29 Cal Ripken 2.00 .80
30 Lou Whitaker .15 .06
31 Cecil Cooper .15 .06
32 Dale Murphy .40 .16
33 Andre Dawson .40 .16
34 Pedro Guerrero .15 .06
35 Mike Schmidt .60 .24
36 George Brett 1.00 .40
37 Jim Rice .15 .06
38 Eddie Murray .40 .16
39 Carlton Fisk .40 .16
40 Rusty Staub .15 .06
41 Duane Walker .05 .02
42 Steve Braun .05 .02
43 Kurt Bevacqua .05 .02
44 Hal McRae .15 .06
45 Don Baylor .15 .06
46 Ken Singleton .05 .02
47 Greg Luzinski .15 .06
48 Mike Schmidt .40 .16
49 Keith Hernandez .15 .06
50 Dale Murphy .40 .16
51 Tim Raines .25 .10
52 Wade Boggs .75 .30
53 Rickey Henderson .75 .30
54 Rod Carew .50 .20
55 Ken Singleton .05 .02
56 John Denny .05 .02
57 John Candelaria .05 .02
58 Larry McWilliams .05 .02
59 Pascual Perez .05 .02
60 Jesse Orosco .15 .06
61 Moose Haas .05 .02
62 Richard Dotson .05 .02
63 Mike Flanagan .05 .02
64 Scott McGregor .05 .02
65 Atlee Hammaker .05 .02
66 Rick Honeycutt .05 .02
67 Lee Smith .40 .16
68 Al Holland .05 .02
69 Greg Minton .05 .02
70 Bruce Sutter .15 .06
71 Jeff Reardon .15 .06
72 Frank DiPino .05 .02
73 Dan Quisenberry .15 .06
74 Bob Stanley .05 .02
75 Ron Davis .05 .02
76 Bill Caudill .05 .02
77 Peter Ladd .05 .02
78 Steve Carlton .40 .16
79 Mario Soto .05 .02
80 Larry McWilliams .05 .02
81 Fernando Valenzuela .15 .06
82 Nolan Ryan 2.00 .80
83 Jack Morris .25 .10
84 Floyd Bannister .05 .02
85 Dave Stieb .05 .02
86 Dave Righetti .05 .02
87 Rick Sutcliffe .15 .06
88 Tim Raines .25 .10
89 Alan Wiggins .05 .02
90 Steve Sax .15 .06
91 Mookie Wilson .25 .10
92 Rickey Henderson .75 .30
93 Rudy Law .05 .02
94 Willie Wilson .15 .06
95 Julio Cruz .05 .02
96 Johnny Bench .50 .20
97 Carl Yastrzemski .50 .20
98 Gaylord Perry .40 .16
99 Pete Rose .75 .30
100 Joe Morgan .50 .20
101 Steve Carlton .50 .20
102 Jim Palmer .50 .20
103 Rod Carew .50 .20
104 Darryl Strawberry .60 .24
105 Craig McMurtry .05 .02
106 Mel Hall .05 .02
107 Lee Tunnell .05 .02
108 Bill Dawley .05 .02
109 Ron Kittle .05 .02
110 Mike Boddicker .05 .02
111 Julio Franco .25 .10
112 Daryl Sconiers .05 .02
113 Neal Heaton .05 .02
114 John Shelby .05 .02
115 Rick Dempsey .15 .06
116 John Lowenstein .05 .02
117 Jim Dwyer .05 .02
118 Bo Diaz .05 .02
119 Pete Rose .75 .30
120 Joe Morgan .50 .20
121 Gary Matthews .05 .02
122 Garry Maddox .05 .02
123 Paul Owens MG .05 .02
124 Tom Lasorda MG .25 .10
125 Joe Altobelli MG .05 .02
126 Tony LaRussa MG .15 .06

1985 Fleer

The 1985 Fleer set consists of 660 standard-size cards. Wax packs contained 15 cards plus logo stickers. Card fronts feature a full color photo, team logo along with the player's name and position. The borders enclosing the photo are color-coded to correspond to the player's team. The cards are ordered alphabetically within team. The teams are ordered based on their respective performance during the prior year. Subsets include Specials (626-643) and Major League Prospects (644-653). The black

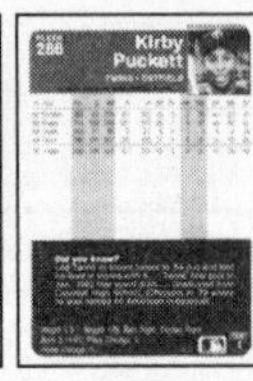

and white photo on the reverse is included for the third straight year. Rookie Cards include Roger Clemens, Eric Davis, Shawon Dunston, John Franco, Dwight Gooden, Orel Hershiser, Jimmy Key, Mark Langston, Terry Pendleton, Kirby Puckett and Bret Saberhagen

Nm-Mt Ex-Mt
COMPLETE SET (660) 80.00 32.00
1 Doug Bair .15 .06
2 Juan Berenguer .15 .06
3 Dave Bergman .15 .06
4 Tom Brookens .15 .06
5 Marty Castillo .15 .06
6 Darrell Evans .40 .16
7 Barbaro Garbey .15 .06
8 Kirk Gibson .40 .16
9 John Grubb .15 .06
10 Willie Hernandez .15 .06
11 Larry Herndon .15 .06
12 Howard Johnson .40 .16
13 Ruppert Jones .15 .06
14 Rusty Kuntz .15 .06
15 Chet Lemon .15 .06
16 Aurelio Lopez .15 .06
17 Sid Monge .15 .06
18 Jack Morris .40 .16
19 Lance Parrish .40 .16
20 Dan Petry .15 .06
21 Dave Rozema .15 .06
22 Bill Scherrer .15 .06
23 Alan Trammell .75 .30
24 Lou Whitaker .40 .16
25 Milt Wilcox .15 .06
26 Kurt Bevacqua .15 .06
27 Greg Booker .15 .06
28 Bobby Brown .15 .06
29 Luis DeLeon .15 .06
30 Dave Dravecky .40 .16
31 Tim Flannery .15 .06
32 Steve Garvey .40 .16
33 Rich Gossage .40 .16
34 Tony Gwynn 2.50 1.00
35 Greg Harris .15 .06
36 Andy Hawkins .15 .06
37 Terry Kennedy .15 .06
38 Craig Lefferts .15 .06
39 Tim Lollar .15 .06
40 Carmelo Martinez .15 .06
41 Kevin McReynolds .40 .16
42 Graig Nettles .40 .16
43 Luis Salazar .15 .06
44 Eric Show .15 .06
45 Garry Templeton .15 .06
46 Mark Thurmond .15 .06
47 Ed Whitson .15 .06
48 Alan Wiggins .15 .06
49 Rich Bordi .15 .06
50 Larry Bowa .40 .16
51 Warren Brusstar .15 .06
52 Ron Cey .40 .16
53 Henry Cotto RC .15 .06
54 Jody Davis .15 .06
55 Bob Dernier .15 .06
56 Leon Durham .15 .06
57 Dennis Eckersley .75 .30
58 George Frazier .15 .06
59 Richie Hebner .15 .06
60 Dave Lopes .40 .16
61 Gary Matthews .15 .06
62 Keith Moreland .15 .06
63 Rick Reuschel .15 .06
64 Dick Ruthven .15 .06
65 Ryne Sandberg 2.50 1.00
66 Scott Sanderson .15 .06
67 Lee Smith .75 .30
68 Tim Stoddard .15 .06
69 Rick Sutcliffe .40 .16
70 Steve Trout .15 .06
71 Gary Woods .15 .06
72 Wally Backman .15 .06
73 Bruce Berenyi .15 .06
74 Hubie Brooks UER .15 .06
(Kelvin Chapman's
stats on card back)
75 Kelvin Chapman .15 .06
76 Ron Darling .40 .16
77 Sid Fernandez .40 .16
78 Mike Fitzgerald .15 .06
79 George Foster .40 .16
80 Brent Gaff .15 .06
81 Ron Gardenhire .15 .06
82 Dwight Gooden RC 2.00 .80
83 Tom Gorman .15 .06
84 Danny Heep .15 .06
85 Keith Hernandez .75 .30
86 Ray Knight .15 .06
87 Ed Lynch .15 .06
88 Jose Oquendo .15 .06
89 Jesse Orosco .15 .06
90 Rafael Santana .15 .06
91 Doug Sisk .15 .06
92 Rusty Staub .40 .16
93 Darryl Strawberry 1.25 .50
94 Walt Terrell .15 .06
95 Mookie Wilson .40 .16
96 Jim Acker .15 .06
97 Willie Aikens .15 .06
98 Doyle Alexander .15 .06
99 Jesse Barfield .15 .06
100 George Bell .40 .16
101 Jim Clancy .15 .06
102 Dave Collins .15 .06
103 Tony Fernandez .40 .16
104 Damaso Garcia .15 .06
105 Jim Gott .15 .06
106 Alfredo Griffin .15 .06
107 Garth Iorg .15 .06
108 Roy Lee Jackson .15 .06
109 Cliff Johnson .15 .06
110 Jimmy Key RC 1.25 .50
111 Dennis Lamp .15 .06
112 Rick Leach .15 .06
113 Luis Leal .15 .06
114 Buck Martinez .15 .06
115 Lloyd Moseby .15 .06
116 Rance Mulliniks .15 .06
117 Dave Stieb .40 .16
118 Willie Upshaw .15 .06
119 Ernie Whitt .15 .06
120 Mike Armstrong .15 .06
121 Don Baylor .40 .16
122 Marty Bystrom .15 .06
123 Rick Cerone .15 .06
124 Joe Cowley .15 .06
125 Brian Dayett .15 .06
126 Tim Foli .15 .06
127 Ray Fontenot .15 .06
128 Ken Griffey .40 .16
129 Ron Guidry .40 .16
130 Toby Harrah .15 .06
131 Jay Howell .15 .06
132 Steve Kemp .15 .06
133 Don Mattingly 5.00 2.00
134 Bobby Meacham .15 .06
135 John Montefusco .15 .06
136 Omar Moreno .15 .06
137 Dale Murray .15 .06
138 Phil Niekro .40 .16
139 Mike Pagliarulo .15 .06
140 Willie Randolph .40 .16
141 Dennis Rasmussen .15 .06
142 Dave Righetti .40 .16
143 Jose Rijo RC .75 .30
144 Andre Robertson .15 .06
145 Bob Shirley .15 .06
146 Dave Winfield .40 .16
147 Butch Wynegar .15 .06
148 Gary Allenson .15 .06
149 Tony Armas .15 .06
150 Marty Barrett .15 .06
151 Wade Boggs 1.50 .60
152 Dennis Boyd .15 .06
153 Bill Buckner .40 .16
154 Mark Clear .15 .06
155 Roger Clemens RC 40.00 16.00
156 Steve Crawford .15 .06
157 Mike Easler .15 .06
158 Dwight Evans .40 .16
159 Rich Gedman .15 .06
160 Jackie Gutierrez .40 .16
(Wade Boggs
shown on deck)
161 Bruce Hurst .15 .06
162 John Henry Johnson .15 .06
163 Rick Miller .15 .06
164 Reid Nichols .15 .06
165 Al Nipper .15 .06
166 Bob Ojeda .15 .06
167 Jerry Remy .15 .06
168 Jim Rice .40 .16
169 Bob Stanley .15 .06
170 Mike Boddicker .15 .06
171 Al Bumbry .15 .06
172 Todd Cruz .15 .06
173 Rich Dauer .15 .06
174 Storm Davis .15 .06
175 Rick Dempsey .15 .06
176 Jim Dwyer .15 .06
177 Mike Flanagan .15 .06
178 Dan Ford .15 .06
179 Wayne Gross .15 .06
180 John Lowenstein .15 .06
181 Dennis Martinez .40 .16
182 Tippy Martinez .15 .06
183 Scott McGregor .15 .06
184 Eddie Murray 1.25 .50
185 Joe Nolan .15 .06
186 Floyd Rayford .15 .06
187 Cal Ripken 5.00 2.00
188 Gary Roenicke .15 .06
189 Lenn Sakata .15 .06
190 John Shelby .15 .06
191 Ken Singleton .15 .06
192 Sammy Stewart .15 .06
193 Bill Swaggerty .15 .06
194 Tom Underwood .15 .06
195 Mike Young .15 .06
196 Steve Balboni .15 .06
197 Joe Beckwith .15 .06
198 Bud Black .15 .06
199 George Brett 3.00 1.20
200 Onix Concepcion .15 .06
201 Mark Gubicza RC* .40 .16
202 Larry Gura .15 .06
203 Mark Huismann .15 .06
204 Dane Iorg .15 .06
205 Danny Jackson .15 .06
206 Charlie Leibrandt .15 .06
207 Hal McRae .40 .16
208 Darryl Motley .15 .06
209 Jorge Orta .15 .06
210 Greg Pryor .15 .06
211 Dan Quisenberry .40 .16
212 Bret Saberhagen RC 1.25 .50
213 Pat Sheridan .15 .06
214 Don Slaught .15 .06
215 U.L. Washington .15 .06
216 John Wathan .15 .06
217 Frank White .40 .16
218 Willie Wilson .15 .06
219 Neil Allen .15 .06
220 Joaquin Andujar .15 .06
221 Steve Braun .15 .06
222 Danny Cox .15 .06
223 Bob Forsch .15 .06
224 David Green .15 .06
225 George Hendrick .15 .06
226 Tom Herr .15 .06
227 Ricky Horton .15 .06
228 Art Howe .15 .06
229 Mike Jorgensen .15 .06
230 Kurt Kepshire .15 .06
231 Jeff Lahti .15 .06
232 Tito Landrum .15 .06
233 Dave LaPoint .15 .06
234 Willie McGee .40 .16
235 Tom Nieto .15 .06
236 Terry Pendleton RC 1.25 .50
237 Darrell Porter .15 .06
238 Dave Rucker .15 .06
239 Lonnie Smith .15 .06
240 Ozzie Smith 2.00 .80
241 Bruce Sutter .40 .16
242 Andy Van Slyke UER .40 .16
(Bats Right,
Throws Left)
243 Dave Von Ohlen .15 .06
244 Larry Andersen .15 .06
245 Bill Campbell .15 .06
246 Steve Carlton .40 .16
247 Tim Corcoran .15 .06
248 Ivan DeJesus .15 .06
249 John Denny .15 .06
250 Bo Diaz .15 .06
251 Greg Gross .15 .06
252 Kevin Gross .15 .06
253 Von Hayes .15 .06
254 Al Holland .15 .06
255 Charles Hudson .15 .06
256 Jerry Koosman .40 .16
257 Joe Lefebvre .15 .06
258 Sixto Lezcano .15 .06
259 Garry Maddox .15 .06
260 Len Matuszek .15 .06
261 Tug McGraw .40 .16
262 Al Oliver .40 .16
263 Shane Rawley .15 .06
264 Juan Samuel .15 .06
265 Mike Schmidt 3.00 1.20
266 Jeff Stone .15 .06
267 Ozzie Virgil .15 .06
268 Glenn Wilson .15 .06
269 John Wockenfuss .15 .06
270 Darrell Brown .15 .06
271 Tom Brunansky .40 .16
272 Randy Bush .15 .06
273 John Butcher .15 .06
274 Bobby Castillo .15 .06
275 Ron Davis .15 .06
276 Dave Engle .15 .06
277 Pete Filson .15 .06
278 Gary Gaetti .40 .16
279 Mickey Hatcher .15 .06
280 Ed Hodge .15 .06
281 Kent Hrbek .40 .16
282 Houston Jimenez .15 .06
283 Tim Laudner .15 .06
284 Rick Lysander .15 .06
285 Dave Meier .15 .06
286 Kirby Puckett RC 15.00 6.00
287 Pat Putnam .15 .06
288 Ken Schrom .15 .06
289 Mike Smithson .15 .06
290 Tim Teufel .15 .06
291 Frank Viola .40 .16
292 Ron Washington .15 .06
293 Don Aase .15 .06
294 Juan Beniquez .15 .06
295 Bob Boone .40 .16
296 Mike C. Brown .15 .06
297 Rod Carew .75 .30
298 Doug Corbett .15 .06
299 Doug DeCinces .15 .06
300 Brian Downing .15 .06
301 Ken Forsch .15 .06
302 Bobby Grich .40 .16
303 Reggie Jackson .75 .30
304 Tommy John .75 .30
305 Curt Kaufman .15 .06
306 Bruce Kison .15 .06
307 Fred Lynn .40 .16
308 Gary Pettis .15 .06
309 Ron Romanick .15 .06
310 Luis Sanchez .15 .06
311 Dick Schofield .15 .06
312 Daryl Sconiers .15 .06
313 Jim Slaton .15 .06
314 Derrel Thomas .15 .06
315 Rob Wilfong .15 .06
316 Mike Witt .15 .06
317 Geoff Zahn .15 .06
318 Len Barker .15 .06
319 Steve Bedrosian .15 .06
320 Bruce Benedict .15 .06
321 Rick Camp .15 .06
322 Chris Chambliss .40 .16
323 Jeff Dedmon .15 .06
324 Terry Forster .15 .06
325 Gene Garber .15 .06
326 Albert Hall .15 .06
327 Terry Harper .15 .06
328 Bob Horner .15 .06
329 Glenn Hubbard .15 .06
330 Randy Johnson .15 .06
331 Brad Komminsk .15 .06
332 Rick Mahler .15 .06
333 Craig McMurtry .15 .06
334 Donnie Moore .15 .06
335 Dale Murphy 1.25 .50
336 Ken Oberkfell .15 .06
337 Pascual Perez .15 .06
338 Gerald Perry .15 .06
339 Rafael Ramirez .15 .06
340 Jerry Royster .15 .06
341 Alex Trevino .15 .06
342 Claudell Washington .15 .06
343 Alan Ashby .15 .06
344 Mark Bailey .15 .06
345 Kevin Bass .15 .06
346 Enos Cabell .15 .06
347 Jose Cruz .40 .16
348 Bill Dawley .15 .06
349 Frank DiPino .15 .06
350 Bill Doran .15 .06
351 Phil Garner .40 .16
352 Bob Knepper .15 .06
353 Mike LaCoss .15 .06
354 Jerry Mumphrey .15 .06
355 Joe Niekro .15 .06
356 Terry Puhl .15 .06
357 Craig Reynolds .15 .06
358 Vern Ruhle .15 .06
359 Nolan Ryan 6.00 2.40
360 Joe Sambito .15 .06
361 Mike Scott .15 .06
362 Dave Smith .15 .06
363 Julio Solano .15 .06
364 Dickie Thon .15 .06
365 Denny Walling .15 .06
366 Dave Anderson .15 .06
367 Bob Bailor .15 .06
368 Greg Brock .15 .06
369 Carlos Diaz .15 .06
370 Pedro Guerrero .40 .16
371 Orel Hershiser RC 2.00 .80
372 Rick Honeycutt .15 .06
373 Burt Hooton .15 .06
374 Ken Howell .15 .06
375 Ken Landreaux .15 .06
376 Candy Maldonado .15 .06
377 Mike Marshall .15 .06
378 Tom Niedenfuer .15 .06
379 Alejandro Pena .15 .06
380 Jerry Reuss UER .15 .06
("Home:" omitted)
381 R.J. Reynolds .15 .06
382 German Rivera .15 .06
383 Bill Russell .15 .06
384 Steve Sax .15 .06
385 Mike Scioscia .15 .06
386 Franklin Stubbs .15 .06
387 Fernando Valenzuela .40 .16
388 Bob Welch .15 .06
389 Terry Whitfield .15 .06
390 Steve Yeager .15 .06
391 Pat Zachry .15 .06
392 Fred Breining .15 .06
393 Gary Carter .75 .30
394 Andre Dawson .40 .16
395 Miguel Dilone .15 .06
396 Dan Driessen .15 .06
397 Doug Flynn .15 .06
398 Terry Francona .15 .06
399 Bill Gullickson .15 .06
400 Bob James .15 .06
401 Charlie Lea .15 .06
402 Bryan Little .15 .06
403 Gary Lucas .15 .06
404 David Palmer .15 .06
405 Tim Raines .40 .16
406 Mike Ramsey .15 .06
407 Jeff Reardon .40 .16
408 Steve Rogers .15 .06
409 Dan Schatzeder .15 .06
410 Bryn Smith .15 .06
411 Mike Stenhouse .15 .06
412 Tim Wallach .40 .16
413 Jim Wohlford .15 .06
414 Bill Almon .15 .06
415 Keith Atherton .15 .06
416 Bruce Bochte .15 .06
417 Tom Burgmeier .15 .06
418 Ray Burris .15 .06
419 Bill Caudill .15 .06
420 Chris Codiroli .15 .06
421 Tim Conroy .15 .06
422 Mike Davis .15 .06
423 Jim Essian .15 .06
424 Mike Heath .15 .06
425 Rickey Henderson 1.50 .60
426 Donnie Hill .15 .06
427 Dave Kingman .40 .16
428 Bill Krueger .15 .06
429 Carney Lansford .40 .16
430 Steve McCatty .15 .06
431 Joe Morgan .75 .30
432 Dwayne Murphy .15 .06
433 Tony Phillips .15 .06
434 Lary Sorensen .15 .06
435 Mike Warren .15 .06
436 Curt Young .15 .06
437 Luis Aponte .15 .06
438 Chris Bando .15 .06
439 Tony Bernazard .15 .06
440 Bert Blyleven .40 .16
441 Brett Butler .40 .16
442 Ernie Camacho .15 .06
443 Joe Carter 1.25 .50
444 Carmelo Castillo .15 .06
445 Jamie Easterly .15 .06
446 Steve Farr RC .40 .16
447 Mike Fischlin .15 .06
448 Julio Franco .75 .30
449 Mel Hall .15 .06
450 Mike Hargrove .40 .16
451 Neal Heaton .15 .06
452 Brook Jacoby .15 .06
453 Mike Jeffcoat .15 .06
454 Don Schulze .15 .06
455 Roy Smith .15 .06
456 Pat Tabler .15 .06
457 Andre Thornton .15 .06
458 George Vukovich .15 .06
459 Tom Waddell .15 .06
460 Jerry Willard .15 .06
461 Dale Berra .15 .06
462 John Candelaria .15 .06
463 Jose DeLeon .15 .06
464 Doug Frobel .15 .06
465 Cecilio Guante .15 .06
466 Brian Harper .15 .06
467 Lee Lacy .15 .06
468 Bill Madlock .40 .16
469 Lee Mazzilli .15 .06
470 Larry McWilliams .15 .06
471 Jim Morrison .15 .06
472 Tony Pena .15 .06
473 Johnny Ray .15 .06
474 Rick Rhoden .15 .06
475 Don Robinson .15 .06
476 Rod Scurry .15 .06
477 Kent Tekulve .40 .16
478 Jason Thompson .15 .06
479 John Tudor .15 .06
480 Lee Tunnell .15 .06
481 Marvell Wynne .15 .06
482 Salome Barojas .15 .06
483 Dave Beard .15 .06
484 Jim Beattie .15 .06
485 Barry Bonnell .15 .06
486 Phil Bradley .40 .16
487 Al Cowens .15 .06
488 Alvin Davis RC* .40 .16
489 Dave Henderson .15 .06
490 Steve Henderson .15 .06
491 Bob Kearney .15 .06
492 Mark Langston RC .75 .30
493 Larry Milbourne .15 .06
494 Paul Mirabella .15 .06
495 Mike Moore .15 .06
496 Edwin Nunez .15 .06
497 Spike Owen .15 .06
498 Jack Perconte .15 .06
499 Ken Phelps .15 .06
500 Jim Presley .40 .16
501 Mike Stanton .15 .06
502 Bob Stoddard .15 .06
503 Gorman Thomas .15 .06
504 Ed VandeBerg .15 .06
505 Matt Young .15 .06
506 Juan Agosto .15 .06
507 Harold Baines .40 .16
508 Floyd Bannister .15 .06
509 Britt Burns .15 .06
510 Julio Cruz .15 .06
511 Richard Dotson .15 .06
512 Jerry Dybzinski .15 .06
513 Carlton Fisk .75 .30
514 Scott Fletcher .15 .06
515 Jerry Hairston .15 .06
516 Marc Hill .15 .06
517 LaMarr Hoyt .15 .06
518 Ron Kittle .15 .06
519 Rudy Law .15 .06
520 Vance Law .15 .06
521 Greg Luzinski .40 .16
522 Gene Nelson .15 .06
523 Tom Paciorek .40 .16
524 Ron Reed .15 .06
525 Bert Roberge .15 .06
526 Tom Seaver .75 .30
527 Roy Smalley .15 .06
528 Dan Spillner .15 .06
529 Mike Squires .15 .06
530 Greg Walker .15 .06
531 Cesar Cedeno .40 .16
532 Dave Concepcion .40 .16
533 Eric Davis RC 2.00 .80
534 Nick Esasky .15 .06
535 Tom Foley .15 .06
536 John Franco RC UER 1.25 .50
(Koufax misspelled
as Kofax on back)
537 Brad Gulden .15 .06
538 Tom Hume .15 .06
539 Wayne Krenchicki .15 .06
540 Andy McGaffigan .15 .06
541 Eddie Milner .15 .06
542 Ron Oester .15 .06
543 Bob Owchinko .15 .06
544 Dave Parker .40 .16
545 Frank Pastore .15 .06
546 Tony Perez .75 .30
547 Ted Power .15 .06
548 Joe Price .15 .06
549 Gary Redus .15 .06
550 Pete Rose 4.00 1.60
551 Jeff Russell .15 .06
552 Mario Soto .15 .06
553 Jay Tibbs .15 .06
554 Duane Walker .15 .06
555 Alan Bannister .15 .06
556 Buddy Bell .40 .16
557 Danny Darwin .15 .06
558 Charlie Hough .40 .16
559 Bobby Jones .15 .06
560 Odell Jones .15 .06
561 Jeff Kunkel .15 .06
562 Mike Mason RC .15 .06
563 Pete O'Brien .15 .06
564 Larry Parrish .15 .06
565 Mickey Rivers .15 .06
566 Billy Sample .15 .06
567 Dave Schmidt .15 .06
568 Donnie Scott .15 .06
569 Dave Stewart .40 .16
570 Frank Tanana .15 .06
571 Wayne Tolleson .15 .06
572 Gary Ward .15 .06
573 Curtis Wilkerson .15 .06
574 George Wright .15 .06
575 Ned Yost .15 .06
576 Mark Brouhard .15 .06
577 Mike Caldwell .15 .06
578 Bobby Clark .15 .06
579 Jaime Cocanower .15 .06
580 Cecil Cooper .40 .16
581 Rollie Fingers .40 .16
582 Jim Gantner .15 .06
583 Moose Haas .15 .06
584 Dion James .15 .06
585 Pete Ladd .15 .06
586 Rick Manning .15 .06
587 Bob McClure .15 .06
588 Paul Molitor .75 .30
589 Charlie Moore .15 .06
590 Ben Oglivie .15 .06
591 Chuck Porter .15 .06
592 Randy Ready RC* .15 .06
593 Ed Romero .15 .06
594 Bill Schroeder .15 .06
595 Ray Searage .15 .06
596 Ted Simmons .40 .16
597 Jim Sundberg .15 .06
598 Don Sutton 1.25 .50
599 Tom Tellmann .15 .06
600 Rick Waits .15 .06
601 Robin Yount 2.00 .80
602 Dusty Baker .40 .16
603 Bob Brenly .15 .06
604 Jack Clark .40 .16
605 Chili Davis .40 .16
606 Mark Davis .15 .06
607 Dan Gladden RC .40 .16
608 Atlee Hammaker .15 .06
609 Mike Krukow .15 .06
610 Duane Kuiper .15 .06
611 Bob Lacey .15 .06
612 Bill Laskey .15 .06
613 Gary Lavelle .15 .06
614 Johnnie LeMaster .15 .06
615 Jeff Leonard .15 .06
616 Randy Lerch .15 .06
617 Greg Minton .15 .06
618 Steve Nicosia .15 .06
619 Gene Richards .15 .06
620 Jeff D. Robinson .15 .06
621 Scot Thompson .15 .06
622 Manny Trillo .15 .06
623 Brad Wellman .15 .06
624 Frank Williams .15 .06
625 Joel Youngblood .15 .06

626 Cal Ripken IA 3.00 1.20
627 Mike Schmidt IA 1.25 .50
628 Sparky Anderson IA .40 .16
629 Dave Winfield .40 .16
Rickey Henderson
630 Mike Schmidt 2.00 .80
Ryne Sandberg
631 Darryl Strawberry 1.25 .50
Gary Carter
Steve Garvey
Ozzie Smith
632 Gary Carter .40 .16
Charlie Lea
633 Steve Garvey .40 .16
Rich Gossage
634 Dwight Gooden 1.25 .50
Juan Samuel
635 Willie Upshaw IA .15 .06
636 Lloyd Moseby IA .15 .06
637 HOLLAND: Al Holland .15 .06
638 TUNNELL .15 .06
Lee Tunnell
639 Reggie Jackson IA .75 .30
640 4000th Hit IA 1.25 .50
641 Cal Ripken Jr. 3.00 1.20
Cal Ripken Sr.
642 Cubs Division Champs .40 .16
643 Two Perfect Games .40 .16
and One No-Hitter:
Mike Witt
David Palmer
Jack Morris
644 Willie Lozado and .15 .06
Vic Mata
645 Kelly Gruber RC and .40 .16
Randy O'Neal
646 Jose Roman and .15 .06
Joel Skinner
647 Steve Kiefer RC and 1.25 .50
Danny Tartabull
648 Rob Dee RC and .40 .16
Alejandro Sanchez
649 Billy Hatcher RC and .75 .30
Shawon Dunston
650 Ron Robinson and .15 .06
Mike Bielecki
651 Zane Smith RC and .40 .16
Paul Zuvella
652 Joe Hesketh RC and .40 .16
Glenn Davis
653 John Russell and .15 .06
Steve Jeltz
654 CL: Tigers/Padres .15 .06
and Cubs/Mets
655 CL: Blue Jays/Yankees .15 .06
and Red Sox/Orioles
656 CL: Royals/Cardinals .15 .06
and Phillies/Twins
657 CL: Angels/Braves .15 .06
and Astros/Dodgers
658 CL: Expos/A's .15 .06
and Indians/Pirates
659 CL: Mariners/White Sox .15 .06
and Reds/Rangers
660 CL: Brewers/Giants .15 .06
and Special Cards

1985 Fleer Update

This 132-card standard-size update set was issued in factory set form exclusively through hobby dealers. Design is identical to the regular-issue 1985 Fleer cards except for the U prefixed card numbers on back. Cards are ordered alphabetically by the player's name. This set features the extended Rookie Cards of Vince Coleman, Darren Daulton, Ozzie Guillen and Mickey Tettleton.

Nm-Mt Ex-Mt
COMP.FACT.SET (132) 6.00 2.40
1 Don Aase .15 .06
2 Bill Almon .15 .06
3 Dusty Baker .40 .16
4 Dale Berra .15 .06
5 Karl Best .15 .06
6 Tim Birtsas .15 .06
7 Vida Blue .40 .16
8 Rich Bordi .15 .06
9 Daryl Boston XRC* .15 .06
10 Hubie Brooks .15 .06
11 Chris Brown .15 .06
12 Tom Browning XRC* .40 .16
13 Al Bumbry .15 .06
14 Tim Burke .15 .06
15 Ray Burris .15 .06
16 Jeff Burroughs .15 .06
17 Ivan Calderon XRC .15 .06
18 Jeff Calhoun .15 .06
19 Bill Campbell .15 .06
20 Don Carman .15 .06
21 Gary Carter .75 .30
22 Bobby Castillo .15 .06
23 Bill Caudill .15 .06
24 Rick Cerone .15 .06
25 Jack Clark .40 .16
26 Pat Clements .15 .06
27 Stu Cliburn .15 .06
28 Vince Coleman XRC 1.00 .40
29 Dave Collins .15 .06
30 Fritz Connally .15 .06
31 Henry Cotto .15 .06
32 Danny Darwin .15 .06
33 Darren Daulton XRC 2.00 .80
34 Jerry Davis .15 .06
35 Brian Dayett .15 .06
36 Ken Dixon .15 .06
37 Tommy Dunbar .15 .06
38 Mariano Duncan XRC 1.00 .40
39 Bob Fallon .15 .06
40 Brian Fisher XRC .15 .06
41 Mike Fitzgerald .15 .06
42 Ray Fontenot .15 .06
43 Greg Gagne XRC* .40 .16
44 Oscar Gamble .15 .06
45 Jim Gott .15 .06
46 David Green .15 .06
47 Alfredo Griffin .15 .06
48 Ozzie Guillen XRC .75 .30
49 Toby Harrah .15 .06
50 Ron Hassey .15 .06
51 Rickey Henderson 2.50 1.00
52 Steve Henderson .15 .06
53 George Hendrick .15 .06
54 Teddy Higuera XRC .40 .16
55 Al Holland .15 .06
56 Burt Hooton .15 .06
57 Jay Howell .15 .06
58 LaMarr Hoyt .15 .06
59 Tim Hulett XRC* .15 .06
60 Bob James .15 .06
61 Cliff Johnson .15 .06
62 Howard Johnson .40 .16
63 Ruppert Jones .15 .06
64 Steve Kemp .15 .06
65 Bruce Kison .15 .06
66 Mike LaCoss .15 .06
67 Lee Lacy .15 .06
68 Dave LaPoint .15 .06
69 Gary Lavelle .15 .06
70 Vance Law .15 .06
71 Manny Lee XRC .15 .06
72 Sixto Lezcano .15 .06
73 Tim Lollar .15 .06
74 Urbano Lugo .15 .06
75 Fred Lynn .40 .16
76 Steve Lyons .40 .16
77 Mickey Mahler .15 .06
78 Ron Mathis .15 .06
79 Len Matuszek .15 .06
80 O.McDowell XRC UER .40 .16
Part of bio
actually Roger's
81 R.McDowell XRC UER .40 .16
Part of bio
actually Oddibe's
82 Donnie Moore .15 .06
83 Ron Musselman .15 .06
84 Al Oliver .40 .16
85 Joe Orsulak XRC .40 .16
86 Dan Pasqua XRC* .40 .16
87 Chris Pittaro .15 .06
88 Rick Reuschel .15 .06
89 Earnie Riles .15 .06
90 Jerry Royster .15 .06
91 Dave Rozema .15 .06
92 Dave Rucker .15 .06
93 Vern Ruhle .15 .06
94 Mark Salas .15 .06
95 Luis Salazar .15 .06
96 Joe Sambito .15 .06
97 Billy Sample .15 .06
98 Alejandro Sanchez .15 .06
99 Calvin Schiraldi .15 .06
100 Rick Schu .15 .06
101 Larry Sheets .15 .06
102 Ron Shephard .15 .06
103 Nelson Simmons .15 .06
104 Don Slaught .15 .06
105 Roy Smalley .15 .06
106 Lonnie Smith .15 .06
107 Nate Snell .15 .06
108 Lary Sorensen .15 .06
109 Chris Speier .15 .06
110 Mike Stenhouse .15 .06
111 Tim Stoddard .15 .06
112 John Stuper .15 .06
113 Jim Sundberg .15 .06
114 Bruce Sutter .40 .16
115 Don Sutton 1.00 .40
116 Bruce Tanner .15 .06
117 Kent Tekulve .15 .06
118 Walt Terrell .15 .06
119 Mickey Tettleton XRC .75 .30
120 Rich Thompson .15 .06
121 Louis Thornton .15 .06
122 Alex Trevino .15 .06
123 John Tudor .15 .06
124 Jose Uribe .15 .06
125 Dave Valle XRC .15 .06
126 Dave Von Ohlen .15 .06
127 Curt Wardle .15 .06
128 U.L. Washington .15 .06
129 Ed Whitson .15 .06
130 Herm Winningham .15 .06
131 Rich Yett .15 .06
132 Checklist U1-U132 .15 .06

1985 Fleer Limited Edition

This 44-card set features standard size cards which were distributed in a colorful box as a complete set. The back of the box gives a complete checklist of the cards in the set. The cards are ordered alphabetically by the player's name. Backs of the cards are yellow and white whereas the fronts show a picture of the player inside a red banner-type border.

Nm-Mt Ex-Mt
COMP. FACT. SET (44) 8.00 3.20
1 Buddy Bell .05 .02
2 Bert Blyleven .10 .04
3 Wade Boggs .50 .20
4 George Brett 1.25 .50
5 Rod Carew .40 .16
6 Steve Carlton .40 .16
7 Alvin Davis .05 .02
8 Andre Dawson .25 .10
9 Steve Garvey .15 .06
10 Rich Gossage .10 .04
11 Tony Gwynn 1.50 .60
12 Keith Hernandez .10 .04
13 Kent Hrbek .10 .04
14 Reggie Jackson .50 .20
15 Dave Kingman .10 .04
16 Ron Kittle .05 .02
17 Mark Langston .05 .02
18 Jeff Leonard .05 .02
19 Bill Madlock .05 .02
20 Don Mattingly 1.25 .50
21 Jack Morris .10 .04
22 Dale Murphy .25 .10
23 Eddie Murray .50 .20
24 Tony Pena .10 .04
25 Dan Quisenberry .05 .02
26 Tim Raines .10 .04
27 Jim Rice .10 .04
28 Cal Ripken 2.50 1.00
29 Pete Rose .75 .30
30 Nolan Ryan 2.50 1.00
31 Ryne Sandberg 1.00 .40
32 Steve Sax .05 .02
33 Mike Schmidt .50 .20
34 Tom Seaver .40 .16
35 Ozzie Smith 1.00 .40
36 Mario Soto .05 .02
37 Dave Stieb .05 .02
38 Darryl Strawberry .10 .04
39 Rick Sutcliffe .05 .02
40 Alan Trammell .15 .06
41 Willie Upshaw .05 .02
42 Fernando Valenzuela .10 .04
43 Dave Winfield .30 .12
44 Robin Yount .50 .20

1985 Fleer Star Stickers

The stickers in this 126-sticker set measure approximately 1 15/16" by 2 1/2". The 1985 Fleer stickers set can be housed in a Fleer sticker album. Stickers are numbered on the fronts. A distinctive feature of the set is the inclusion of stop-action (designated SA in the checklist below) photos on cards 62 through 79. These photos are actually a series of six consecutive stickers which depict a player in action through the course of an activity; e.g., Eddie Murray's swing, Tom Seaver's wind-up and Mike Schmidt fielding. The backs of these stickers are blue and similar in design to past years.

Nm-Mt Ex-Mt
COMPLETE SET (126) 50.00 20.00
1 Pete Rose 3.00 1.20
2 Pete Rose 3.00 1.20
3 Pete Rose 3.00 1.20
4 Don Mattingly 8.00 3.20
5 Dave Winfield 1.25 .50
6 Wade Boggs 2.50 1.00
7 Buddy Bell .20 .08
8 Tony Gwynn 8.00 3.20
9 Lee Lacy .10 .04
10 Chili Davis .20 .08
11 Ryne Sandberg 4.00 1.60
12 Tony Armas .10 .04
13 Jim Rice .20 .08
14 Dave Kingman .20 .08
15 Alvin Davis .20 .08
16 Gary Carter 1.25 .50
17 Mike Schmidt 2.50 1.00
18 Dale Murphy .50 .20
19 Ron Cey .20 .08
20 Eddie Murray 1.50 .60
21 Harold Baines .20 .08
22 Kirk Gibson .20 .08
23 Jim Rice .20 .08
24 Gary Matthews .10 .04
25 Keith Hernandez .20 .08
26 Gary Carter 1.25 .50
27 George Hendrick .10 .04
28 Tony Armas .10 .04
29 Dave Kingman .20 .08
30 Dwayne Murphy .10 .04
31 Lance Parrish .20 .08
32 Andre Thornton .10 .04
33 Dale Murphy .50 .20
34 Mike Schmidt 2.50 1.00
35 Gary Carter 1.25 .50
36 Darryl Strawberry .20 .08
37 Don Mattingly 8.00 3.20
38 Larry Parrish .10 .04
39 George Bell .20 .08
40 Dwight Evans .20 .08
41 Cal Ripken 8.00 3.20
42 Tim Raines .20 .08
43 Johnny Ray .10 .04
44 Juan Samuel .10 .04
45 Ryne Sandberg 4.00 1.60
46 Mike Easler .10 .04
47 Andre Thornton .10 .04
48 Dave Kingman .20 .08
49 Don Baylor .20 .08
50 Rusty Staub .20 .08
51 Steve Braun .10 .04
52 Kevin Bass .10 .04
53 Greg Gross .10 .04
54 Rickey Henderson 5.00 2.00
55 Dave Collins .10 .04
56 Brett Butler .20 .08
57 Gary Pettis .10 .04
58 Tim Raines .20 .08
59 Juan Samuel .10 .04
60 Alan Wiggins .10 .04
61 Lonnie Smith .10 .04
62 Eddie Murray SA .75 .30
63 Eddie Murray SA .75 .30
64 Eddie Murray SA .75 .30
65 Eddie Murray SA .75 .30
66 Eddie Murray SA .75 .30
67 Eddie Murray SA .75 .30
68 Tom Seaver SA 1.00 .40
69 Tom Seaver SA 1.00 .40
70 Tom Seaver SA 1.00 .40
71 Tom Seaver SA 1.00 .40
72 Tom Seaver SA 1.00 .40
73 Tom Seaver SA 1.00 .40
74 Mike Schmidt SA 1.25 .50
75 Mike Schmidt SA 1.25 .50
76 Mike Schmidt SA 1.25 .50
77 Mike Schmidt SA 1.25 .50
78 Mike Schmidt SA 1.25 .50
79 Mike Schmidt SA 1.25 .50
80 Mike Boddicker .10 .04
81 Bert Blyleven .20 .08
82 Jack Morris .20 .08
83 Dan Petry .10 .04
84 Frank Viola .20 .08
85 Joaquin Andujar .10 .04
86 Mario Soto .10 .04
87 Dwight Gooden 2.50 1.00
88 Joe Niekro .10 .04
89 Rick Sutcliffe .10 .04
90 Mike Boddicker .10 .04
91 Dave Stieb .10 .04
92 Bert Blyleven .20 .08
93 Phil Niekro .60 .24
94 Alejandro Pena .10 .04
95 Dwight Gooden 2.50 1.00
96 Orel Hershiser 2.50 1.00
97 Rick Rhoden .10 .04
98 John Candelaria .10 .04
99 Dan Quisenberry .10 .04
100 Bill Caudill .10 .04
101 Willie Hernandez .10 .04
102 Dave Righetti .20 .08
103 Ron Davis .10 .04
104 Bruce Sutter .20 .08
105 Lee Smith .30 .12
106 Jesse Orosco .20 .08
107 Al Holland .10 .04
108 Goose Gossage .20 .08
109 Mark Langston .75 .30
110 Dave Stieb .20 .08
111 Mike Witt .10 .04
112 Bert Blyleven .20 .08
113 Dwight Gooden 2.50 1.00
114 Fernando Valenzuela .20 .08
115 Nolan Ryan 8.00 3.20
116 Mario Soto .10 .04
117 Ron Darling .20 .08
118 Dan Gladden .10 .04
119 Jeff Stone .10 .04
120 John Franco .75 .30
121 Barbaro Garbey .10 .04
122 Kirby Puckett 8.00 3.20
123 Roger Clemens 20.00 8.00
124 Bret Saberhagen .75 .30
125 Sparky Anderson MG .30 .12
126 Dick Williams MG .10 .04

1986 Fleer

The 1986 Fleer set consists of 660-card standard-size cards. Wax packs included 15 cards plus logo stickers. Card fronts feature dark blue borders (resulting in extremely condition sensitive cards commonly found with chipped edges), a team logo along with the player's name and position. The player cards are alphabetized within team and the teams are ordered by their 1985 season finish and won-lost record. Subsets include Specials (626-643) and Major League Prospects (644-653). The Dennis and Tippy Martinez cards were apparently switched in the set numbering, as their adjacent numbers (279 and 280) were reversed on the Orioles checklist card. The set includes the Rookie Cards of Rick Aguilera, Jose Canseco, Darren Daulton, Len Dykstra, Cecil Fielder, Andres Galarraga and Paul O'Neill.

Nm-Mt Ex-Mt
COMPLETE SET (660) 40.00 16.00
COMP.FACT.SET (660) 40.00 16.00
1 Steve Balboni .15 .06
2 Joe Beckwith .15 .06
3 Buddy Biancalana .15 .06
4 Bud Black .15 .06
5 George Brett 2.00 .80
6 Onix Concepcion .15 .06
7 Steve Farr .15 .06
8 Mark Gubicza .15 .06
9 Dane Iorg .15 .06
10 Danny Jackson .15 .06
11 Lynn Jones .15 .06
12 Mike Jones .15 .06
13 Charlie Leibrandt .15 .06
14 Hal McRae .25 .10
15 Omar Moreno .15 .06
16 Darryl Motley .15 .06
17 Jorge Orta .15 .06
18 Dan Quisenberry .15 .06
19 Bret Saberhagen .25 .10
20 Pat Sheridan .15 .06
21 Lonnie Smith .15 .06
22 Jim Sundberg .15 .06
23 John Wathan .15 .06
24 Frank White .25 .10
25 Willie Wilson .15 .06
26 Joaquin Andujar .15 .06
27 Steve Braun .15 .06
28 Bill Campbell .15 .06
29 Cesar Cedeno .25 .10
30 Jack Clark .25 .10
31 Vince Coleman RC* 1.00 .40
32 Danny Cox .15 .06
33 Ken Dayley .15 .06
34 Ivan DeJesus .15 .06
35 Bob Forsch .15 .06
36 Brian Harper .15 .06
37 Tom Herr .15 .06
38 Ricky Horton .15 .06
39 Kurt Kepshire .15 .06
40 Jeff Lahti .15 .06
41 Tito Landrum .15 .06
42 Willie McGee .25 .10
43 Tom Nieto .15 .06
44 Terry Pendleton .25 .10
45 Darrell Porter .25 .10
46 Ozzie Smith 1.25 .50
47 John Tudor .15 .06
48 Andy Van Slyke .25 .10
49 Todd Worrell RC .50 .20
50 Jim Acker .15 .06
51 Doyle Alexander .15 .06
52 Jesse Barfield .15 .06
53 George Bell .25 .10
54 Jeff Burroughs .15 .06
55 Bill Caudill .15 .06
56 Jim Clancy .15 .06
57 Tony Fernandez .15 .06
58 Tom Filer .15 .06
59 Damaso Garcia .15 .06
60 Tom Henke .25 .10
61 Garth Iorg .15 .06
62 Cliff Johnson .15 .06
63 Jimmy Key .75 .30
64 Dennis Lamp .15 .06
65 Gary Lavelle .15 .06
66 Buck Martinez .15 .06
67 Lloyd Moseby .15 .06
68 Rance Mulliniks .15 .06
69 Al Oliver .25 .10
70 Dave Stieb .15 .06
71 Louis Thornton .15 .06
72 Willie Upshaw .15 .06
73 Ernie Whitt .15 .06
74 Rick Aguilera RC .50 .20
75 Wally Backman .15 .06
76 Gary Carter .50 .20
77 Ron Darling .15 .06
78 Len Dykstra RC 1.50 .60
79 Sid Fernandez .25 .10
80 George Foster .25 .10
81 Dwight Gooden .75 .30
82 Tom Gorman .15 .06
83 Danny Heep .15 .06
84 Keith Hernandez .50 .20
85 Howard Johnson .25 .10
86 Ray Knight .25 .10
87 Terry Leach .15 .06
88 Ed Lynch .15 .06
89 Roger McDowell RC* .50 .20
90 Jesse Orosco .15 .06
91 Tom Paciorek .25 .10
92 Ronn Reynolds .15 .06
93 Rafael Santana .15 .06
94 Doug Sisk .15 .06
95 Rusty Staub .25 .10
96 Darryl Strawberry .50 .20
97 Mookie Wilson .25 .10
98 Neil Allen .15 .06
99 Don Baylor .50 .20
100 Dale Berra .15 .06
101 Rich Bordi .15 .06
102 Marty Bystrom .15 .06
103 Joe Cowley .15 .06
104 Brian Fisher RC .15 .06
105 Ken Griffey .25 .10
106 Ron Guidry .25 .10
107 Ron Hassey .15 .06
108 R.Henderson UER .75 .30
SB Record of 120, sic
109 Don Mattingly 2.50 1.00
110 Bobby Meacham .15 .06
111 John Montefusco .15 .06
112 Phil Niekro .25 .10
113 Mike Pagliarulo .15 .06
114 Dan Pasqua .15 .06
115 Willie Randolph .25 .10
116 Dave Righetti .15 .06
117 Andre Robertson .15 .06
118 Billy Sample .15 .06
119 Bob Shirley .15 .06
120 Ed Whitson .15 .06
121 Dave Winfield .25 .10
122 Butch Wynegar .15 .06
123 Dave Anderson .15 .06
124 Bob Bailor .15 .06
125 Greg Brock .15 .06
126 Enos Cabell .15 .06
127 Bobby Castillo .15 .06
128 Carlos Diaz .15 .06
129 Mariano Duncan RC* .50 .20
130 Pedro Guerrero .25 .10
131 Orel Hershiser .50 .20
132 Rick Honeycutt .15 .06
133 Ken Howell .15 .06
134 Ken Landreaux .15 .06
135 Bill Madlock .15 .06
136 Candy Maldonado .15 .06
137 Mike Marshall .15 .06
138 Len Matuszek .15 .06
139 Tom Niedenfuer .15 .06
140 Alejandro Pena .15 .06
141 Jerry Reuss .15 .06
142 Bill Russell .15 .06
143 Steve Sax .15 .06
144 Mike Scioscia .15 .06
145 Fernando Valenzuela .25 .10
146 Bob Welch .15 .06
147 Terry Whitfield .15 .06
148 Juan Beniquez .15 .06
149 Bob Boone .25 .10
150 John Candelaria .15 .06
151 Rod Carew .50 .20
152 Stu Cliburn .15 .06
153 Doug DeCinces .15 .06
154 Brian Downing .15 .06
155 Ken Forsch .15 .06
156 Craig Gerber .15 .06
157 Bobby Grich .25 .10
158 George Hendrick .15 .06
159 Al Holland .15 .06

160 Reggie Jackson .50 .20
161 Ruppert Jones .15 .06
162 Urbano Lugo .15 .06
163 Kirk McCaskill RC .15 .06
164 Donnie Moore .15 .06
165 Gary Pettis .15 .06
166 Ron Romanick .15 .06
167 Dick Schofield .15 .06
168 Daryl Sconiers .15 .06
169 Jim Slaton .15 .06
170 Don Sutton .75 .30
171 Mike Witt .15 .06
172 Buddy Bell .25 .10
173 Tom Browning .15 .06
174 Dave Concepcion .25 .10
175 Eric Davis .50 .20
176 Bo Diaz .15 .06
177 Nick Esasky .15 .06
178 John Franco .75 .30
179 Tom Hume .15 .06
180 Wayne Krenchicki .15 .06
181 Andy McGaffigan .15 .06
182 Eddie Milner .15 .06
183 Ron Oester .15 .06
184 Dave Parker .25 .10
185 Frank Pastore .15 .06
186 Tony Perez .50 .20
187 Ted Power .15 .06
188 Joe Price .15 .06
189 Gary Redus .15 .06
190 Ron Robinson .15 .06
191 Pete Rose 2.50 1.00
192 Mario Soto .15 .06
193 John Stuper .15 .06
194 Jay Tibbs .15 .06
195 Dave Van Gorder .15 .06
196 Max Venable .15 .06
197 Juan Agosto .15 .06
198 Harold Baines .50 .20
199 Floyd Bannister .15 .06
200 Britt Burns .15 .06
201 Julio Cruz .15 .06
202 Joel Davis .15 .06
203 Richard Dotson .15 .06
204 Carlton Fisk .50 .20
205 Scott Fletcher .15 .06
206 Ozzie Guillen RC* .50 .20
207 Jerry Hairston .15 .06
208 Tim Hulett .15 .06
209 Bob James .15 .06
210 Ron Kittle .15 .06
211 Rudy Law .15 .06
212 Bryan Little .15 .06
213 Gene Nelson .15 .06
214 Reid Nichols .15 .06
215 Luis Salazar .15 .06
216 Tom Seaver .50 .20
217 Dan Spillner .15 .06
218 Bruce Tanner .15 .06
219 Greg Walker .15 .06
220 Dave Wehrmeister .15 .06
221 Juan Berenguer .15 .06
222 Dave Bergman .15 .06
223 Tom Brookens .15 .06
224 Darrell Evans .25 .10
225 Barbaro Garbey .15 .06
226 Kirk Gibson .25 .10
227 John Grubb .15 .06
228 Willie Hernandez .15 .06
229 Larry Herndon .15 .06
230 Chet Lemon .15 .06
231 Aurelio Lopez .15 .06
232 Jack Morris .25 .10
233 Randy O'Neal .15 .06
234 Lance Parrish .25 .10
235 Dan Petry .15 .06
236 Alejandro Sanchez .15 .06
237 Bill Scherrer .15 .06
238 Nelson Simmons .15 .06
239 Frank Tanana .15 .06
240 Walt Terrell .15 .06
241 Alan Trammell .50 .20
242 Lou Whitaker .25 .10
243 Milt Wilcox .15 .06
244 Hubie Brooks .15 .06
245 Tim Burke .15 .06
246 Andre Dawson .25 .10
247 Mike Fitzgerald .15 .06
248 Terry Francona .15 .06
249 Bill Gullickson .15 .06
250 Joe Hesketh .15 .06
251 Bill Laskey .15 .06
252 Vance Law .15 .06
253 Charlie Lea .15 .06
254 Gary Lucas .15 .06
255 David Palmer .15 .06
256 Tim Raines .25 .10
257 Jeff Reardon .15 .06
258 Bert Roberge .15 .06
259 Dan Schatzeder .15 .06
260 Bryn Smith .15 .06
261 Randy St.Claire .15 .06
262 Scot Thompson .15 .06
263 Tim Wallach .15 .06
264 U.L. Washington .15 .06
265 Mitch Webster .15 .06
266 Herm Winningham .15 .06
267 Floyd Youmans .15 .06
268 Don Aase .15 .06
269 Mike Boddicker .15 .06
270 Rich Dauer .15 .06
271 Storm Davis .15 .06
272 Rick Dempsey .15 .06
273 Ken Dixon .15 .06
274 Jim Dwyer .15 .06
275 Mike Flanagan .15 .06
276 Wayne Gross .15 .06
277 Lee Lacy .15 .06
278 Fred Lynn .25 .10
279 Tippy Martinez .15 .06
280 Dennis Martinez .25 .10
281 Scott McGregor .15 .06
282 Eddie Murray .75 .30
283 Floyd Rayford .15 .06
284 Cal Ripken 3.00 1.20
285 Gary Roenicke .15 .06
286 Larry Sheets .15 .06
287 John Shelby .15 .06
288 Nate Snell .15 .06
289 Sammy Stewart .15 .06
290 Alan Wiggins .15 .06
291 Mike Young .15 .06
292 Alan Ashby .15 .06
293 Mark Bailey .15 .06
294 Kevin Bass .15 .06
295 Jeff Calhoun .15 .06
296 Jose Cruz .25 .10
297 Glenn Davis .25 .10
298 Bill Dawley .15 .06
299 Frank DiPino .15 .06
300 Bill Doran .15 .06
301 Phil Garner .25 .10
302 Jeff Heathcock .15 .06
303 Charlie Kerfeld .15 .06
304 Bob Knepper .15 .06
305 Ron Mathis .15 .06
306 Jerry Mumphrey .15 .06
307 Jim Pankovits .15 .06
308 Terry Puhl .15 .06
309 Craig Reynolds .15 .06
310 Nolan Ryan 4.00 1.60
311 Mike Scott .15 .06
312 Dave Smith .15 .06
313 Dickie Thon .15 .06
314 Denny Walling .15 .06
315 Kurt Bevacqua .15 .06
316 Al Bumbry .15 .06
317 Jerry Davis .15 .06
318 Luis DeLeon .15 .06
319 Dave Dravecky .25 .10
320 Tim Flannery .15 .06
321 Steve Garvey .25 .10
322 Rich Gossage .25 .10
323 Tony Gwynn 1.25 .50
324 Andy Hawkins .15 .06
325 LaMarr Hoyt .15 .06
326 Roy Lee Jackson .15 .06
327 Terry Kennedy .15 .06
328 Craig Lefferts .15 .06
329 Carmelo Martinez .15 .06
330 Lance McCullers .15 .06
331 Kevin McReynolds .15 .06
332 Greg Nettles .25 .10
333 Jerry Royster .15 .06
334 Eric Show .15 .06
335 Tim Stoddard .15 .06
336 Garry Templeton .15 .06
337 Mark Thurmond .15 .06
338 Ed Wojna .15 .06
339 Tony Armas .15 .06
340 Marty Barrett .15 .06
341 Wade Boggs .50 .20
342 Dennis Boyd .15 .06
343 Bill Buckner .25 .10
344 Mark Clear .15 .06
345 Roger Clemens 4.00 1.60
346 Steve Crawford .15 .06
347 Mike Easler .15 .06
348 Dwight Evans .25 .10
349 Rich Gedman .15 .06
350 Jackie Gutierrez .15 .06
351 Glenn Hoffman .15 .06
352 Bruce Hurst .15 .06
353 Bruce Kison .15 .06
354 Tim Lollar .15 .06
355 Steve Lyons .15 .06
356 Al Nipper .15 .06
357 Bob Ojeda .15 .06
358 Jim Rice .25 .10
359 Bob Stanley .15 .06
360 Mike Trujillo .15 .06
361 Thad Bosley .15 .06
362 Warren Brusstar .15 .06
363 Ron Cey .25 .10
364 Jody Davis .15 .06
365 Bob Dernier .15 .06
366 Shawon Dunston .25 .10
367 Leon Durham .15 .06
368 Dennis Eckersley .50 .20
369 Ray Fontenot .15 .06
370 George Frazier .15 .06
371 Billy Hatcher .15 .06
372 Dave Lopes .25 .10
373 Gary Matthews .15 .06
374 Ron Meridith .15 .06
375 Keith Moreland .15 .06
376 Reggie Patterson .15 .06
377 Dick Ruthven .15 .06
378 Ryne Sandberg 1.50 .60
379 Scott Sanderson .15 .06
380 Lee Smith .50 .20
381 Lary Sorensen .15 .06
382 Chris Speier .15 .06
383 Rick Sutcliffe .25 .10
384 Steve Trout .15 .06
385 Gary Woods .15 .06
386 Bert Blyleven .25 .10
387 Tom Brunansky .15 .06
388 Randy Bush .15 .06
389 John Butcher .15 .06
390 Ron Davis .15 .06
391 Dave Engle .15 .06
392 Frank Eufemia .15 .06
393 Pete Filson .15 .06
394 Gary Gaetti .25 .10
395 Greg Gagne .15 .06
396 Mickey Hatcher .15 .06
397 Kent Hrbek .25 .10
398 Tim Laudner .15 .06
399 Rick Lysander .15 .06
400 Dave Meier .15 .06
401 Kirby Puckett UER 2.00 .80
Card has him in NL,
should be AL
402 Mark Salas .15 .06
403 Ken Schrom .15 .06
404 Roy Smalley .15 .06
405 Mike Smithson .15 .06
406 Mike Stenhouse .15 .06
407 Tim Teufel .15 .06
408 Frank Viola .25 .10
409 Ron Washington .15 .06
410 Keith Atherton .15 .06
411 Dusty Baker .25 .10
412 Tim Birtsas .15 .06
413 Bruce Bochte .15 .06
414 Chris Codiroli .15 .06
415 Dave Collins .15 .06
416 Mike Davis .15 .06
417 Alfredo Griffin .15 .06
418 Mike Heath .15 .06
419 Steve Henderson .15 .06
420 Donnie Hill .15 .06
421 Jay Howell .15 .06
422 Tommy John .75 .30
423 Dave Kingman .25 .10
424 Bill Krueger .15 .06
425 Rick Langford .15 .06
426 Carney Lansford .25 .10
427 Steve McCatty .15 .06
428 Dwayne Murphy .15 .06
429 Steve Ontiveros RC .15 .06
430 Tony Phillips .15 .06
431 Jose Rijo .15 .06
432 Mickey Tettleton RC .50 .20
433 Luis Aguayo .15 .06
434 Larry Andersen .15 .06
435 Steve Carlton .25 .10
436 Don Carman .15 .06
437 Tim Corcoran .15 .06
438 Darren Daulton RC 1.50 .60
439 John Denny .15 .06
440 Tom Foley .15 .06
441 Greg Gross .15 .06
442 Kevin Gross .15 .06
443 Von Hayes .15 .06
444 Charles Hudson .15 .06
445 Garry Maddox .15 .06
446 Shane Rawley .15 .06
447 Dave Rucker .15 .06
448 John Russell .15 .06
449 Juan Samuel .15 .06
450 Mike Schmidt 2.00 .80
451 Rick Schu .15 .06
452 Dave Shipanoff .15 .06
453 Dave Stewart .25 .10
454 Jeff Stone .15 .06
455 Kent Tekulve .15 .06
456 Ozzie Virgil .15 .06
457 Glenn Wilson .15 .06
458 Jim Beattie .15 .06
459 Karl Best .15 .06
460 Barry Bonnell .15 .06
461 Phil Bradley .15 .06
462 Ivan Calderon RC* .50 .20
463 Al Cowens .15 .06
464 Alvin Davis .15 .06
465 Dave Henderson .15 .06
466 Bob Kearney .15 .06
467 Mark Langston .15 .06
468 Bob Long .15 .06
469 Mike Moore .15 .06
470 Edwin Nunez .15 .06
471 Spike Owen .15 .06
472 Jack Perconte .15 .06
473 Jim Presley .15 .06
474 Donnie Scott .15 .06
475 Bill Swift .15 .06
476 Danny Tartabull .25 .10
477 Gorman Thomas .15 .06
478 Roy Thomas .15 .06
479 Ed VandeBerg .15 .06
480 Frank Wills .15 .06
481 Matt Young .15 .06
482 Ray Burris .15 .06
483 Jaime Cocanower .15 .06
484 Cecil Cooper .25 .10
485 Danny Darwin .15 .06
486 Rollie Fingers .25 .10
487 Jim Gantner .15 .06
488 Bob L. Gibson .15 .06
489 Moose Haas .15 .06
490 Teddy Higuera RC* .50 .20
491 Paul Householder .15 .06
492 Pete Ladd .15 .06
493 Rick Manning .15 .06
494 Bob McClure .15 .06
495 Paul Molitor .50 .20
496 Charlie Moore .15 .06
497 Ben Oglivie .15 .06
498 Randy Ready .15 .06
499 Earnie Riles .15 .06
500 Ed Romero .15 .06
501 Bill Schroeder .15 .06
502 Ray Searage .15 .06
503 Ted Simmons .25 .10
504 Pete Vuckovich .15 .06
505 Rick Waits .15 .06
506 Robin Yount 1.25 .50
507 Len Barker .15 .06
508 Steve Bedrosian .15 .06
509 Bruce Benedict .15 .06
510 Rick Camp .15 .06
511 Rick Cerone .15 .06
512 Chris Chambliss .25 .10
513 Jeff Dedmon .15 .06
514 Terry Forster .15 .06
515 Gene Garber .15 .06
516 Terry Harper .15 .06
517 Bob Horner .15 .06
518 Glenn Hubbard .15 .06
519 Joe Johnson .15 .06
520 Brad Komminsk .15 .06
521 Rick Mahler .15 .06
522 Dale Murphy .75 .30
523 Ken Oberkfell .15 .06
524 Pascual Perez .15 .06
525 Gerald Perry .15 .06
526 Rafael Ramirez .15 .06
527 Steve Shields .15 .06
528 Zane Smith .15 .06
529 Bruce Sutter .25 .10
530 Milt Thompson RC .15 .06
531 Claudell Washington .15 .06
532 Paul Zuvella .15 .06
533 Vida Blue .25 .10
534 Bob Brenly .15 .06
535 Chris Brown .15 .06
536 Chili Davis .50 .20
537 Mark Davis .15 .06
538 Rob Deer .15 .06
539 Dan Driessen .15 .06
540 Scott Garrelts .15 .06
541 Dan Gladden .15 .06
542 Jim Gott .15 .06
543 David Green .15 .06
544 Atlee Hammaker .15 .06
545 Mike Jeffcoat .15 .06
546 Mike Krukow .15 .06
547 Dave LaPoint .15 .06
548 Jeff Leonard .15 .06
549 Greg Minton .15 .06
550 Alex Trevino .15 .06
551 Manny Trillo .15 .06
552 Jose Uribe .15 .06
553 Brad Wellman .15 .06
554 Frank Williams .15 .06
555 Joel Youngblood .15 .06
556 Alan Bannister .15 .06
557 Glenn Brummer .15 .06
558 Steve Buechele RC .50 .20
559 Jose Guzman RC .15 .06
560 Toby Harrah .15 .06
561 Greg Harris .15 .06
562 Dwayne Henry .15 .06
563 Burt Hooton .15 .06
564 Charlie Hough .25 .10
565 Mike Mason .15 .06
566 Oddibe McDowell .15 .06
567 Dickie Noles .15 .06
568 Pete O'Brien .15 .06
569 Larry Parrish .15 .06
570 Dave Rozema .15 .06
571 Dave Schmidt .15 .06
572 Don Slaught .15 .06
573 Wayne Tolleson .15 .06
574 Duane Walker .15 .06
575 Gary Ward .15 .06
576 Chris Welsh .15 .06
577 Curtis Wilkerson .15 .06
578 George Wright .15 .06
579 Chris Bando .15 .06
580 Tony Bernazard .15 .06
581 Brett Butler .25 .10
582 Ernie Camacho .15 .06
583 Joe Carter .75 .30
584 Carmen Castillo .15 .06
585 Jamie Easterly .15 .06
586 Julio Franco .25 .10
587 Mel Hall .15 .06
588 Mike Hargrove .25 .10
589 Neal Heaton .15 .06
590 Brook Jacoby .15 .06
591 Otis Nixon RC .50 .20
592 Jerry Reed .15 .06
593 Vern Ruhle .15 .06
594 Pat Tabler .15 .06
595 Rich Thompson .15 .06
596 Andre Thornton .15 .06
597 Dave Von Ohlen .15 .06
598 George Vukovich .15 .06
599 Tom Waddell .15 .06
600 Curt Wardle .15 .06
601 Jerry Willard .15 .06
602 Bill Almon .15 .06
603 Mike Bielecki .15 .06
604 Sid Bream .15 .06
605 Mike C. Brown .15 .06
606 Pat Clements .15 .06
607 Jose DeLeon .15 .06
608 Denny Gonzalez .15 .06
609 Cecilio Guante .15 .06
610 Steve Kemp .15 .06
611 Sammy Khalifa .15 .06
612 Lee Mazzilli .15 .06
613 Larry McWilliams .15 .06
614 Jim Morrison .15 .06
615 Joe Orsulak RC* .25 .10
616 Tony Pena .15 .06
617 Johnny Ray .15 .06
618 Rick Reuschel .15 .06
619 R.J. Reynolds .15 .06
620 Rick Rhoden .15 .06
621 Don Robinson .15 .06
622 Jason Thompson .15 .06
623 Lee Tunnell .15 .06
624 Jim Winn .15 .06
625 Marvell Wynne .15 .06
626 Dwight Gooden IA .50 .20
627 Don Mattingly IA 1.25 .50
628 Pete Rose 4192 .50 .20
629 Rod Carew 3000 Hits .25 .10
630 Tom Seaver .25 .10
Phil Niekro
631 Don Baylor Ouch .25 .10
632 Darryl Strawberry .25 .10
Tim Raines
633 Cal Ripken 1.50 .60
Alan Trammell
634 Wade Boggs 1.00 .40
George Brett
635 Bob Horner .50 .20
Dale Murphy
636 Willie McGee .25 .10
Vince Coleman
637 Vince Coleman IA .25 .10
638 Pete Rose .75 .30
Dwight Gooden
639 Wade Boggs 1.25 .50
Don Mattingly
640 Dale Murphy .50 .20
Steve Garvey
Dave Parker
641 Fernando Valenzuela .50 .20
Dwight Gooden
642 Jimmy Key .25 .10
Dave Stieb
643 Carlton Fisk .25 .10
Rich Gedman
644 Gene Walter RC and 5.00 2.00
Benito Santiago
645 Mike Woodard and .15 .06
Colin Ward
646 Kal Daniels RC and 4.00 1.60
Paul O'Neill
647 Andres Galarraga RC 3.00 1.20
Fred Toliver
648 Bob Kipper and .15 .06
Curt Ford
649 Jose Canseco RC and 8.00 3.20
Eric Plunk
650 Mark McLemore RC 1.00 .40
Gus Polidor
651 Rob Woodward and .15 .06
Mickey Brantley
652 Billy Joe Robidoux .15 .06
Mark Funderburk
653 Cecil Fielder RC and 1.50 .60
Cory Snyder
654 CL: Royals/Cardinals .15 .06
Blue Jays/Mets
655 CL: Yankees/Dodgers .15 .06
Angels/Reds UER
(168 Darly Sconiers)
656 CL: White Sox/Tigers .15 .06
Expos/Orioles
(279 Dennis,
280 Tippy)
657 CL: Astros/Padres .15 .06
Red Sox/Cubs
658 CL: Twins/A's .15 .06
Phillies/Mariners
659 CL: Brewers/Braves .15 .06
Giants/Rangers
660 CL: Indians/Pirates .15 .06
Special Cards

1986 Fleer All-Stars

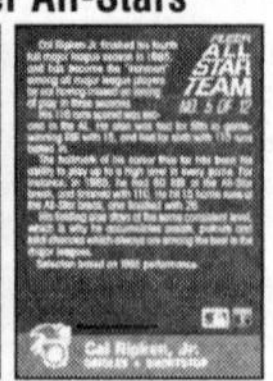

Randomly inserted in wax and cello packs, this 12-card standard-size set features top stars. The cards feature red backgrounds (American Leaguers) and blue backgrounds (National Leaguers). The 12 selections cover each position, left and right-handed starting pitchers, a reliever, and a designated hitter.

	Nm-Mt	Ex-Mt
COMPLETE SET (12)	25.00	10.00
1 Don Mattingly	8.00	3.20
2 Tom Herr	.50	.20
3 George Brett	6.00	2.40
4 Gary Carter	1.50	.60
5 Cal Ripken	10.00	4.00
6 Dave Parker	.75	.30
7 Rickey Henderson UER (Misspelled Ricky on card back)	2.50	1.00
8 Pedro Guerrero	.75	.30
9 Dan Quisenberry	.50	.20
10 Dwight Gooden	2.50	1.00
11 Gorman Thomas	.50	.20
12 John Tudor	.50	.20

1986 Fleer Future Hall of Famers

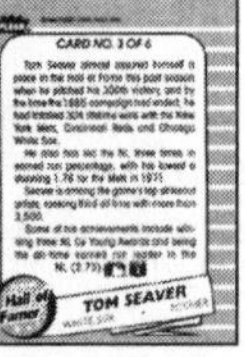

These six standard-size cards were issued one per Fleer three-packs. This set features players that Fleer predicts will be "Future Hall of Famers." The card backs describe career highlights, records, and honors won by the player.

	Nm-Mt	Ex-Mt
COMPLETE SET (6)	15.00	6.00
1 Pete Rose	6.00	2.40
2 Steve Carlton	.60	.24
3 Tom Seaver	1.25	.50
4 Rod Carew	1.25	.50
5 Nolan Ryan	10.00	4.00
6 Reggie Jackson	1.25	.50

1986 Fleer Wax Box Cards

The cards in this eight-card set measure the standard size and were found on the bottom of the Fleer regular issue wax pack and cello pack boxes as four-card panel. Cards have essentially the same design as the 1986 Fleer regular issue set. These eight cards (C1 to C8) are considered a separate set in their own right and are not typically included in a complete set of the regular issue 1986 Fleer cards. The value of the panel uncut is slightly greater, perhaps by 25 percent greater, than the value of the individual cards cut up carefully.

	Nm-Mt	Ex-Mt
COMPLETE SET (8)	6.00	2.40
C1 Royals Logo	.25	.10
C2 George Brett	3.00	1.20
C3 Ozzie Guillen	.75	.30
C4 Dale Murphy	.75	.30
C5 Cardinals Logo	.25	.10
C6 Tom Browning	.25	.10
C7 Gary Carter	1.00	.40
C8 Carlton Fisk	1.00	.40

1986 Fleer Update

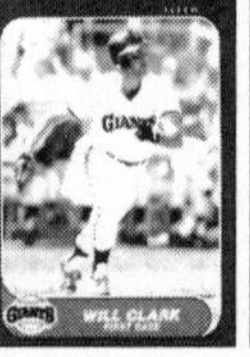

This 132-card standard-size set was distributed in factory set form through hobby dealers. In addition to the complete set of 132 cards, the box also contains 25 Team Logo Stickers.The card fronts look very similar to the 1986 Fleer regular issue. These cards are just as condition sensitive with most cards having chipped edges straight out of the box. The cards are numbered (with a U prefix) alphabetically according to player's last name. The extended

Rookie Cards in this set include Barry Bonds, Bobby Bonilla, Will Clark, Wally Joyner and John Kruk.

Nm-Mt Ex-Mt
COMP.FACT.SET (132) 50.00 20.00
1 Mike Aldrete .15 .06
2 Andy Allanson .15 .06
3 Neil Allen .15 .06
4 Joaquin Andujar .15 .06
5 Paul Assenmacher .15 .06
6 Scott Bailes .15 .06
7 Jay Baller .15 .06
8 Scott Bankhead .15 .06
9 Bill Bathe .15 .06
10 Don Baylor .25 .10
11 Billy Beane XRC 1.00 .40
12 Steve Bedrosian .15 .06
13 Juan Beniquez .15 .06
14 Barry Bonds XRC 40.00 16.00
15 Bobby Bonilla UER 1.00 .40
(Wrong birthday) XRC
16 Rich Bordi .15 .06
17 Bill Campbell .15 .06
18 Tom Candiotti .15 .06
19 John Cangelosi .15 .06
20 Jose Canseco UER 1.50 .60
(Headings on back
for a pitcher)
21 Chuck Cary .15 .06
22 Juan Castillo XRC .15 .06
23 Rick Cerone .15 .06
24 John Cerutti .15 .06
25 Will Clark XRC 2.00 .80
26 Mark Clear .15 .06
27 Darnell Coles .15 .06
28 Dave Collins .15 .06
29 Tim Conroy .15 .06
30 Ed Correa .15 .06
31 Joe Cowley .15 .06
32 Bill Dawley .15 .06
33 Rob Deer .25 .10
34 John Denny .15 .06
35 Jim Deshaies XRC .15 .06
36 Doug Drabek XRC 1.00 .40
37 Mike Easler .15 .06
38 Mark Eichhorn .15 .06
39 Dave Engle .15 .06
40 Mike Fischlin .15 .06
41 Scott Fletcher .15 .06
42 Terry Forster .15 .06
43 Terry Francona .15 .06
44 Andres Galarraga 1.25 .50
45 Lee Guetterman .15 .06
46 Bill Gullickson .15 .06
47 Jackie Gutierrez .15 .06
48 Moose Haas .15 .06
49 Billy Hatcher .15 .06
50 Mike Heath .15 .06
51 Guy Hoffman .15 .06
52 Tom Hume .15 .06
53 Pete Incaviglia XRC .50 .20
54 Dane Iorg .15 .06
55 Chris James XRC .15 .06
56 Stan Javier XRC* .50 .20
57 Tommy John 1.00 .40
58 Tracy Jones .15 .06
59 Wally Joyner XRC 1.00 .40
60 Wayne Krenchicki .15 .06
61 John Kruk XRC 1.50 .60
62 Mike LaCoss .15 .06
63 Pete Ladd .15 .06
64 Dave LaPoint .15 .06
65 Mike LaValliere XRC .50 .20
66 Rudy Law .15 .06
67 Dennis Leonard .15 .06
68 Steve Lombardozzi .15 .06
69 Aurelio Lopez .15 .06
70 Mickey Mahler .15 .06
71 Candy Maldonado .15 .06
72 Roger Mason XRC* .15 .06
73 Greg Mathews .15 .06
74 Andy McGaffigan .15 .06
75 Joel McKeon .15 .06
76 Kevin Mitchell XRC 1.00 .40
77 Bill Mooneyham .15 .06
78 Omar Moreno .15 .06
79 Jerry Mumphrey .15 .06
80 Al Newman .25 .10
81 Phil Niekro .25 .10
82 Randy Niemann .15 .06
83 Juan Nieves .15 .06
84 Bob Ojeda .15 .06
85 Rick Ownbey .15 .06
86 Tom Paciorek .25 .10
87 David Palmer .15 .06
88 Jeff Parrett XRC .15 .06
89 Pat Perry .15 .06
90 Dan Plesac .15 .06
91 Darrell Porter .25 .10
92 Luis Quinones .15 .06
93 Rey Quinones UER .15 .06
(Misspelled Quinonez)
94 Gary Redus .15 .06
95 Jeff Reed .15 .06
96 Bip Roberts XRC .50 .20
97 Billy Joe Robidoux .15 .06
98 Gary Roenicke .15 .06
99 Ron Roenicke .15 .06
100 Angel Salazar .15 .06
101 Joe Sambito .15 .06
102 Billy Sample .15 .06
103 Dave Schmidt .15 .06
104 Ken Schrom .15 .06
105 Ruben Sierra XRC 1.50 .60
106 Ted Simmons .25 .10
107 Sammy Stewart .15 .06
108 Kurt Stillwell .15 .06
109 Dale Sveum .15 .06
110 Tim Teufel .15 .06
111 Bob Tewksbury XRC .50 .20
112 Andres Thomas .15 .06
113 Jason Thompson .15 .06
114 Milt Thompson .25 .10
115 R. Thompson XRC .50 .20
116 Jay Tibbs .15 .06
117 Fred Toliver .15 .06
118 Wayne Tolleson .15 .06
119 Alex Trevino .15 .06
120 Manny Trillo .15 .06
121 Ed VandeBerg .15 .06
122 Ozzie Virgil .15 .06
123 Tony Walker .15 .06
124 Gene Walter .15 .06
125 Duane Ward XRC .50 .20
126 Jerry Willard .15 .06
127 Mitch Williams XRC .50 .20
128 Reggie Williams .15 .06
129 Bobby Witt XRC .50 .20
130 Marvell Wynne .15 .06
131 Steve Yeager .15 .06
132 Checklist 1-132 .15 .06

1986 Fleer League Leaders

This 44-card standard-size set is also sometimes referred to as the Walgreen's set. Although the set was distributed through Walgreen's, there is no mention on the cards or box of that fact. The cards are easily recognizable by the fact that they contain the phrase "Fleer League Leaders" at the top of the obverse. Both sides of the cards are designed with a blue stripe on white pattern. The checklist for the set is given on the outside of the red, white, blue, and gold box in which the set was packaged. A first year card of Jose Canseco highlights the set.

Nm-Mt Ex-Mt
COMP.FACT. SET (44) 6.00 2.40
1 Wade Boggs .50 .20
2 George Brett .75 .30
3 Jose Canseco 1.50 .60
4 Rod Carew .20 .08
5 Gary Carter .50 .20
6 Jack Clark .10 .04
7 Vince Coleman .10 .04
8 Jose Cruz .10 .04
9 Alvin Davis .05 .02
10 Mariano Duncan .05 .02
11 Leon Durham .05 .02
12 Carlton Fisk .40 .16
13 Julio Franco .10 .04
14 Scott Garrelts .05 .02
15 Steve Garvey .15 .06
16 Dwight Gooden .10 .04
17 Ozzie Guillen .15 .06
18 Willie Hernandez .05 .02
19 Bob Horner .05 .02
20 Kent Hrbek .10 .04
21 Charlie Leibrandt .05 .02
22 Don Mattingly .50 .20
23 Oddibe McDowell .05 .02
24 Willie McGee .10 .04
25 Keith Moreland .05 .02
26 Lloyd Moseby .05 .02
27 Dale Murphy .20 .08
28 Phil Niekro .40 .16
29 Joe Orsulak .05 .02
30 Dave Parker .10 .04
31 Lance Parrish .10 .04
32 Kirby Puckett .50 .20
33 Tim Raines .10 .04
34 Ernie Riles .05 .02
35 Cal Ripken 1.50 .60
36 Pete Rose .50 .20
37 Bret Saberhagen .10 .04
38 Juan Samuel .05 .02
39 Ryne Sandberg .50 .20
40 Tom Seaver .40 .16
41 Lee Smith .15 .06
42 Ozzie Smith .75 .30
43 Dave Stieb .05 .02
44 Robin Yount .30 .12

1986 Fleer Limited Edition

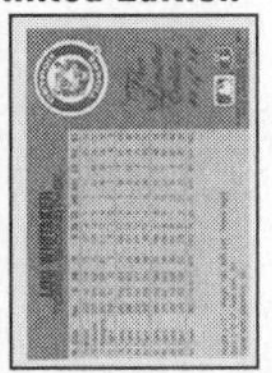

The 44-card boxed standard-size set was produced by Fleer for McCrory's. The cards have green and yellow borders. Card backs are printed in red and black on white card stock. The back of the original box gives a complete checklist of the players in the set. The set box also contains six logo stickers.

Nm-Mt Ex-Mt
COMP.FACT. SET (44) 6.00 2.40
1 Doyle Alexander .05 .02
2 Joaquin Andujar .05 .02
3 Harold Baines .15 .06
4 Wade Boggs .40 .16
5 Phil Bradley .05 .02
6 George Brett .50 .20
7 Hubie Brooks .05 .02
8 Chris Brown .05 .02
9 Tom Brunansky .05 .02
10 Gary Carter .40 .16
11 Vince Coleman .10 .04
12 Cecil Cooper .10 .04
13 Jose Cruz .10 .04
14 Mike Davis .05 .02
15 Carlton Fisk .40 .16
16 Julio Franco .10 .04
17 Damaso Garcia .05 .02
18 Rich Gedman .05 .02
19 Kirk Gibson .10 .04
20 Dwight Gooden .15 .06
21 Pedro Guerrero .05 .02
22 Tony Gwynn .75 .30
23 Rickey Henderson .75 .30
24 Orel Hershiser .15 .06
25 LaMarr Hoyt .05 .02
26 Reggie Jackson .50 .20
27 Don Mattingly .75 .30
28 Oddibe McDowell .05 .02
29 Willie McGee .10 .04
30 Paul Molitor .40 .16
31 Dale Murphy .20 .08
32 Eddie Murray .40 .16
33 Dave Parker .10 .04
34 Tony Pena .10 .04
35 Jeff Reardon .05 .02
36 Cal Ripken 1.50 .60
37 Pete Rose .50 .20
38 Bret Saberhagen .10 .04
39 Juan Samuel .05 .02
40 Ryne Sandberg .50 .20
41 Mike Schmidt .50 .20
42 Lee Smith .15 .06
43 Don Sutton .40 .16
44 Lou Whitaker .10 .04

1986 Fleer Mini

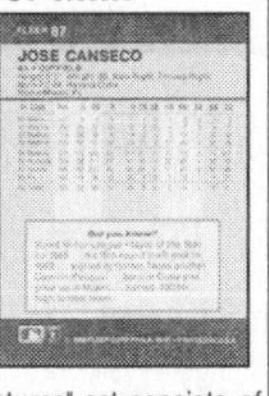

The Fleer "Classic Miniatures" set consists of 120 small cards with all new pictures of the players as compared to the 1986 Fleer regular issue. The cards are only 1 13/16" by 2 9/16", making them some of the smallest (in size) produced in the 1980's. Card backs provide career year-by-year statistics. The complete set was distributed in a red, white, and silver factory box along with 18 logo stickers. The card numbering is done in the same team order as the 1986 Fleer regular set. An early card of Jose Canseco is featured in this set.

Nm-Mt Ex-Mt
COMP.FACT SET (120) 8.00 3.20
1 George Brett .75 .30
2 Dan Quisenberry .05 .02
3 Bret Saberhagen .10 .04
4 Lonnie Smith .05 .02
5 Willie Wilson .05 .02
6 Jack Clark .10 .04
7 Vince Coleman .10 .04
8 Tom Herr .05 .02
9 Willie McGee .10 .04
10 Ozzie Smith .75 .30
11 John Tudor .05 .02
12 Jesse Barfield .05 .02
13 George Bell .10 .04
14 Tony Fernandez .10 .04
15 Damaso Garcia .05 .02
16 Dave Stieb .05 .02
17 Gary Carter .40 .16
18 Ron Darling .05 .02
19A Dwight Gooden .30 .12
(R on Mets logo)
19B Dwight Gooden .30 .12
(No R on Mets logo)
20 Keith Hernandez .10 .04
21 Darryl Strawberry .10 .04
22 Ron Guidry .10 .04
23 Rickey Henderson .60 .24
24 Don Mattingly .75 .30
25 Dave Righetti .05 .02
26 Dave Winfield .40 .16
27 Mariano Duncan .05 .02
28 Pedro Guerrero .10 .04
29 Bill Madlock .10 .04
30 Mike Marshall .05 .02
31 Fernando Valenzuela .15 .06
32 Reggie Jackson .50 .20
33 Gary Pettis .05 .02
34 Ron Romanick .05 .02
35 Don Sutton .30 .12
36 Mike Witt .05 .02
37 Buddy Bell .10 .04
38 Tom Browning .05 .02
39 Dave Parker .10 .04
40 Pete Rose .50 .20
41 Mario Soto .05 .02
42 Harold Baines .15 .06
43 Carlton Fisk .40 .16
44 Ozzie Guillen .15 .06
45 Ron Kittle .05 .02
46 Tom Seaver .40 .16
47 Kirk Gibson .10 .04
48 Jack Morris .15 .06
49 Lance Parrish .10 .04
50 Alan Trammell .15 .06
51 Lou Whitaker .10 .04
52 Hubie Brooks .05 .02
53 Andre Dawson .40 .16
54 Tim Raines .10 .04
55 Bryn Smith .05 .02
56 Tim Wallach .05 .02
57 Mike Boddicker .05 .02
58 Eddie Murray .40 .16
59 Cal Ripken 1.50 .60
60 John Shelby .05 .02
61 Mike Young .05 .02
62 Jose Cruz .10 .04
63 Glenn Davis .05 .02
64 Phil Garner .10 .04
65 Nolan Ryan 1.50 .60
66 Mike Scott .05 .02
67 Steve Garvey .10 .04
68 Rich Gossage .10 .04
69 Tony Gwynn 1.00 .40
70 Andy Hawkins .05 .02
71 Garry Templeton .05 .02
72 Wade Boggs .40 .16
73 Roger Clemens 1.00 .40
74 Dwight Evans .10 .04
75 Rich Gedman .05 .02
76 Jim Rice .10 .04
77 Shawon Dunston .05 .02
78 Leon Durham .05 .02
79 Keith Moreland .05 .02
80 Ryne Sandberg .50 .20
81 Rick Sutcliffe .05 .02
82 Bert Blyleven .10 .04
83 Tom Brunansky .05 .02
84 Kent Hrbek .10 .04
85 Kirby Puckett .50 .20
86 Bruce Bochte .05 .02
87 Jose Canseco .75 .30
88 Mike Davis .05 .02
89 Jay Howell .05 .02
90 Dwayne Murphy .05 .02
91 Steve Carlton .40 .16
92 Von Hayes .05 .02
93 Juan Samuel .05 .02
94 Mike Schmidt .40 .16
95 Glenn Wilson .05 .02
96 Phil Bradley .05 .02
97 Alvin Davis .05 .02
98 Jim Presley .05 .02
99 Danny Tartabull .05 .02
100 Cecil Cooper .10 .04
101 Paul Molitor .40 .16
102 Ernie Riles .05 .02
103 Robin Yount .40 .16
104 Bob Horner .05 .02
105 Dale Murphy .20 .08
106 Bruce Sutter .10 .04
107 Claudell Washington .05 .02
108 Chris Brown .05 .02
109 Chili Davis .10 .04
110 Scott Garrelts .05 .02
111 Oddibe McDowell .05 .02
112 Pete O'Brien .05 .02
113 Gary Ward .05 .02
114 Brett Butler .10 .04
115 Julio Franco .10 .04
116 Brook Jacoby .05 .02
117 Mike C. Brown .05 .02
118 Joe Orsulak .05 .02
119 Tony Pena .10 .04
120 R.J. Reynolds .05 .02

1986 Fleer Sluggers/Pitchers

Fleer produced this 44-card boxed standard-size set although it was primarily distributed by Kress, McCrory, Newberry, T.G.Y., and other similar stores. The set features 22 sluggers and 22 pitchers and is subtitled "Baseball's Best". The set was packaged in a red, white, blue, and yellow custom box along with six logo stickers. The set checklist is given on the back of the box. The card numbering is in alphabetical order by the player's name. The Will Clark and Bobby Witt cards were the first major league cards produced of those players. In addition, an early card of Jose Canseco is featured in this set.

Nm-Mt Ex-Mt
COMP.FACT SET (44) 6.00 2.40
1 Bert Blyleven .10 .04
2 Wade Boggs .40 .16
3 George Brett .75 .30
4 Tom Browning .05 .02
5 Jose Canseco 1.00 .40
6 Will Clark 1.00 .40
7 Roger Clemens .75 .30
8 Alvin Davis .05 .02
9 Julio Franco .10 .04
10 Kirk Gibson .10 .04
11 Dwight Gooden .10 .04
12 Rich Gossage .10 .04
13 Pedro Guerrero .05 .02
14 Ron Guidry .10 .04
15 Tony Gwynn .75 .30
16 Orel Hershiser .20 .08
17 Kent Hrbek .10 .04
18 Reggie Jackson .40 .16
19 Wally Joyner .40 .16
20 Charlie Leibrandt .05 .02
21 Don Mattingly .75 .30
22 Willie McGee .10 .04
23 Jack Morris .10 .04
24 Dale Murphy .20 .08
25 Eddie Murray .40 .16
26 Jeff Reardon .05 .02
27 Rick Reuschel .05 .02
28 Cal Ripken 1.50 .60
29 Pete Rose .50 .20
30 Nolan Ryan 1.50 .60
31 Bret Saberhagen .10 .04
32 Ryne Sandberg .50 .20
33 Mike Schmidt .50 .20
34 Tom Seaver .40 .16
35 Bryn Smith .05 .02
36 Mario Soto .05 .02
37 Dave Stieb .05 .02
38 Darryl Strawberry .10 .04
39 Rick Sutcliffe .05 .02
40 John Tudor .05 .02
41 Fernando Valenzuela .10 .04
42 Bobby Witt .10 .04
43 Mike Witt .05 .02
44 Robin Yount .40 .16

1986 Fleer Sluggers/Pitchers Box Cards

The cards in this six-card set each measure the standard size. Cards have essentially the same design as the 1986 Fleer Sluggers vs. Pitchers set of Baseball's Best. The cards were printed on the bottom of the counter display box which held 24 small boxed sets; hence theoretically these box cards are 1/24 as plentiful as the regular boxed set cards. These six cards, numbered M1 to M5 with one blank-back (unnumbered) card, are considered a separate set in their own right and are not typically included in a complete set of the 1986 Fleer Sluggers vs. Pitchers set of 44. The value of the panels uncut is slightly greater, perhaps by 25 percent greater, than the value of the individual cards cut up carefully.

Nm-Mt Ex-Mt
COMPLETE SET (6) 10.00 4.00
M1 Harold Baines 1.50 .60
M2 Steve Carlton 4.00 1.60
M3 Gary Carter 3.00 1.20
M4 Vince Coleman .75 .30
M5 Kirby Puckett 6.00 2.40
NNO Team Logo .50 .20
(Blank back)

1986 Fleer Sticker Cards

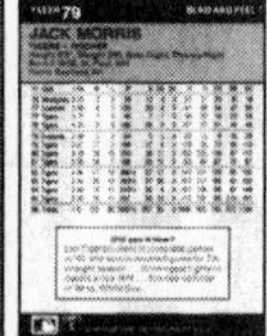

The standard-size stickers (made of card stock) 132-card set were distributed in wax packs and feature card photos on the front surrounded by a yellow border and a cranberry frame. The backs are printed in blue and black on white card stock. The backs contain year-by-year statistical information. They are numbered on the back in the upper left-hand corner. The card numbering is in alphabetical order by the player's name. A first year card of slugger Jose Canseco is featured in this set.

Nm-Mt Ex-Mt
COMPLETE SET (132) 15.00 6.00
1 Harold Baines .15 .06
2 Jesse Barfield .05 .02
3 Don Baylor .10 .04
4 Juan Beniquez .05 .02
5 Tim Birtsas .05 .02
6 Bert Blyleven .10 .04
7 Bruce Bochte .05 .02
8 Wade Boggs .50 .20
9 Dennis Boyd .05 .02
10 Phil Bradley .05 .02
11 George Brett 1.25 .50
12 Hubie Brooks .05 .02
13 Chris Brown .05 .02
14 Tom Browning .05 .02
15 Tom Brunansky .05 .02
16 Bill Buckner .10 .04
17 Britt Burns .05 .02
18 Brett Butler .10 .04
19 Jose Canseco 1.50 .60
20 Rod Carew .40 .16
21 Steve Carlton .40 .16
22 Don Carman .05 .02
23 Gary Carter .50 .20
24 Jack Clark .10 .04
25 Vince Coleman .10 .04
26 Cecil Cooper .10 .04
27 Jose Cruz .10 .04
28 Ron Darling .05 .02
29 Alvin Davis .05 .02
30 Jody Davis .05 .02
31 Mike Davis .05 .02
32 Andre Dawson .20 .08
33 Mariano Duncan .05 .02
34 Shawon Dunston .10 .04
35 Leon Durham .05 .02
36 Darrell Evans .10 .04
37 Tony Fernandez .10 .04
38 Carlton Fisk .40 .16
39 John Franco .20 .08
40 Julio Franco .10 .04
41 Damaso Garcia .05 .02
42 Scott Garrelts .05 .02
43 Steve Garvey .20 .08
44 Rich Gedman .05 .02
45 Kirk Gibson .10 .04
46 Dwight Gooden .15 .06
47 Pedro Guerrero .10 .04
48 Ron Guidry .10 .04
49 Ozzie Guillen .10 .04
50 Tony Gwynn 1.25 .50
51 Andy Hawkins .05 .02
52 Von Hayes .05 .02
53 Rickey Henderson 1.00 .40
54 Tom Henke .05 .02
55 Keith Hernandez .10 .04
56 Willie Hernandez .05 .02
57 Tommy Herr .05 .02
58 Orel Hershiser .15 .06
59 Teddy Higuera .05 .02
60 Bob Horner .05 .02
61 Charlie Hough .10 .04
62 Jay Howell .05 .02
63 LaMarr Hoyt .05 .02
64 Kent Hrbek .10 .04
65 Reggie Jackson .50 .20
66 Bob James .05 .02
67 Dave Kingman .10 .04
68 Ron Kittle .05 .02
69 Charlie Leibrandt .05 .02
70 Fred Lynn .10 .04
71 Mike Marshall .05 .02
72 Don Mattingly 1.25 .50
73 Oddibe McDowell .05 .02
74 Willie McGee .10 .04
75 Scott McGregor .05 .02
76 Paul Molitor .50 .20
77 Donnie Moore .05 .02
78 Keith Moreland .05 .02
79 Jack Morris .10 .04
80 Dale Murphy .20 .08
81 Eddie Murray .50 .20
82 Phil Niekro .40 .16
83 Joe Orsulak .05 .02

84 Dave Parker .10 .04
85 Lance Parrish .10 .04
86 Larry Parrish .05 .02
87 Tony Pena .10 .04
88 Gary Pettis .05 .02
89 Jim Presley .05 .02
90 Kirby Puckett 1.00 .40
91 Dan Quisenberry .05 .02
92 Tim Raines .10 .04
93 Johnny Ray .05 .02
94 Jeff Reardon .10 .04
95 Rick Reuschel .10 .04
96 Jim Rice .10 .04
97 Dave Righetti .05 .02
98 Earnie Riles .05 .02
99 Cal Ripken 2.50 1.00
100 Ron Romanick .05 .02
101 Pete Rose .75 .30
102 Nolan Ryan 2.50 1.00
103 Bret Saberhagen .10 .04
104 Mark Salas .05 .02
105 Juan Samuel .05 .02
106 Ryne Sandberg .75 .30
107 Mike Schmidt .50 .20
108 Mike Scott .05 .02
109 Tom Seaver .40 .16
110 Bryn Smith .05 .02
111 Dave Smith .10 .04
112 Lee Smith .15 .06
113 Ozzie Smith .75 .30
114 Mario Soto .05 .02
115 Dave Stieb .05 .02
116 Darryl Strawberry .10 .04
117 Bruce Sutter .10 .04
118 Garry Templeton .05 .02
119 Gorman Thomas .05 .02
120 Andre Thornton .05 .02
121 Alan Trammell .15 .06
122 John Tudor .05 .02
123 Fernando Valenzuela .20 .08
124 Frank Viola .10 .04
125 Gary Ward .05 .02
126 Lou Whitaker .10 .04
127 Frank White .10 .04
128 Glenn Wilson .05 .02
129 Willie Wilson .05 .02
130 Dave Winfield .40 .16
131 Robin Yount .40 .16
132 Dwight Gooden CL .20 .08
Dale Murphy

1986 Fleer Stickers Wax Box Cards

The bottoms of the Star Sticker wax boxes contained a set of four cards done in a similar format to the stickers; these cards (they are not stickers but truly cards) are numbered with the prefix S and are considered a separate set. Each individual card measures 2 1/2" by 3 1/2". The value of the panel uncut is slightly greater, perhaps by 25 percent greater, than the value of the individual cards cut up carefully.

Nm-Mt Ex-Mt
COMPLETE SET (4) 4.00 1.60
S1 Team Logo .25 .10
(Checklist back)
S2 Wade Boggs 2.00 .80
S3 Steve Garvey .75 .30
S4 Dave Winfield 1.50 .60

1987 Fleer

This set consists of 660 standard-size cards. Cards were primarily issued in 17-card wax packs, rack packs and hobby and retail factory sets. Card fronts feature a distinctive light blue and white blended border encasing a color photo. Cards are again organized numerically by teams with team ordering based on the previous seasons record. The last 36 cards in the set consist of Specials (625-643), Rookie Pairs (644-653), and checklists (654-660). The key Rookie Cards in this set are Barry Bonds, Bobby Bonilla, Will Clark, Chuck Finley, Bo Jackson, Wally Joyner, John Kruk, Barry Larkin and Devon White.

Nm-Mt Ex-Mt
COMPLETE SET (660) 80.00 32.00
COMP.FACT.SET (672) 80.00 32.00
1 Rick Aguilera .25 .10
2 Richard Anderson .15 .06
3 Wally Backman .15 .06
4 Gary Carter .40 .16
5 Ron Darling .15 .06
6 Len Dykstra .40 .16
7 Kevin Elster RC .50 .20
8 Sid Fernandez .15 .06
9 Dwight Gooden .40 .16
10 Ed Hearn .15 .06
11 Danny Heep .15 .06
12 Keith Hernandez .40 .16
13 Howard Johnson .15 .06
14 Ray Knight .15 .06
15 Lee Mazzilli .15 .06
16 Roger McDowell .15 .06
17 Kevin Mitchell RC * 1.25 .50
18 Randy Niemann .15 .06
19 Bob Ojeda .15 .06
20 Jesse Orosco .15 .06
21 Rafael Santana .15 .06
22 Doug Sisk .15 .06
23 Darryl Strawberry .40 .16
24 Tim Teufel .15 .06
25 Mookie Wilson .25 .10
26 Tony Armas .15 .06
27 Marty Barrett .15 .06
28 Don Baylor .25 .10
29 Wade Boggs .40 .16
30 Oil Can Boyd .15 .06
31 Bill Buckner .25 .10
32 Roger Clemens 1.50 .60
33 Steve Crawford .15 .06
34 Dwight Evans .25 .10
35 Rich Gedman .15 .06
36 Dave Henderson .15 .06
37 Bruce Hurst .15 .06
38 Tim Lollar .15 .06
39 Al Nipper .15 .06
40 Spike Owen .15 .06
41 Jim Rice .25 .10
42 Ed Romero .15 .06
43 Joe Sambito .15 .06
44 Calvin Schiraldi .15 .06
45 Tom Seaver UER .40 .16
Lifetime saves total 0, should be 1
46 Jeff Sellers .15 .06
47 Bob Stanley .15 .06
48 Sammy Stewart .15 .06
49 Larry Andersen .15 .06
50 Alan Ashby .15 .06
51 Kevin Bass .15 .06
52 Jeff Calhoun .15 .06
53 Jose Cruz .25 .10
54 Danny Darwin .15 .06
55 Glenn Davis .15 .06
56 Jim Deshaies RC * .25 .10
57 Bill Doran .15 .06
58 Phil Garner .15 .06
59 Billy Hatcher .15 .06
60 Charlie Kerfeld .15 .06
61 Bob Knepper .15 .06
62 Dave Lopes .25 .10
63 Aurelio Lopez .15 .06
64 Jim Pankovits .15 .06
65 Terry Puhl .15 .06
66 Craig Reynolds .15 .06
67 Nolan Ryan 3.00 1.20
68 Mike Scott .15 .06
69 Dave Smith .15 .06
70 Dickie Thon .15 .06
71 Tony Walker .15 .06
72 Denny Walling .15 .06
73 Bob Boone .25 .10
74 Rick Burleson .15 .06
75 John Candelaria .15 .06
76 Doug Corbett .15 .06
77 Doug DeCinces .15 .06
78 Brian Downing .15 .06
79 Chuck Finley RC 1.25 .50
80 Terry Forster .15 .06
81 Bob Grich .25 .10
82 George Hendrick .15 .06
83 Jack Howell .15 .06
84 Reggie Jackson .40 .16
85 Ruppert Jones .15 .06
86 Wally Joyner RC 1.25 .50
87 Gary Lucas .15 .06
88 Kirk McCaskill .15 .06
89 Donnie Moore .15 .06
90 Gary Pettis .15 .06
91 Vern Ruhle .15 .06
92 Dick Schofield .15 .06
93 Don Sutton .60 .24
94 Rob Wilfong .15 .06
95 Mike Witt .15 .06
96 Doug Drabek RC .50 .20
97 Mike Easler .15 .06
98 Mike Fischlin .15 .06
99 Brian Fisher .15 .06
100 Ron Guidry .25 .10
101 Rickey Henderson .60 .24
102 Tommy John .25 .10
103 Ron Kittle .15 .06
104 Don Mattingly 2.00 .80
105 Bobby Meacham .15 .06
106 Joe Niekro .15 .06
107 Mike Pagliarulo .15 .06
108 Dan Pasqua .15 .06
109 Willie Randolph .25 .10
110 Dennis Rasmussen .15 .06
111 Dave Righetti .15 .06
112 Gary Roenicke .15 .06
113 Rod Scurry .15 .06
114 Bob Shirley .15 .06
115 Joel Skinner .15 .06
116 Tim Stoddard .15 .06
117 Bob Tewksbury RC * .50 .20
118 Wayne Tolleson .15 .06
119 Claudell Washington .15 .06
120 Dave Winfield .25 .10
121 Steve Buechele .15 .06
122 Ed Correa .15 .06
123 Scott Fletcher .15 .06
124 Jose Guzman .15 .06
125 Toby Harrah .15 .06
126 Greg Harris .15 .06
127 Charlie Hough .25 .10
128 Pete Incaviglia RC * .50 .20
129 Mike Mason .15 .06
130 Oddibe McDowell .15 .06
131 Dale Mohorcic .15 .06
132 Pete O'Brien .15 .06
133 Tom Paciorek .25 .10
134 Larry Parrish .15 .06
135 Geno Petralli .15 .06
136 Darrell Porter .15 .06
137 Jeff Russell .15 .06
138 Ruben Sierra RC 1.25 .50
139 Don Slaught .15 .06
140 Gary Ward .15 .06
141 Curtis Wilkerson .15 .06
142 Mitch Williams RC * .50 .20
143 Bobby Witt RC UER .50 .20
(Tulsa misspelled as
Tusla; ERA should
be 6.43, not .643)
144 Dave Bergman .15 .06
145 Tom Brookens .15 .06
146 Bill Campbell .15 .06
147 Chuck Cary .15 .06
148 Darnell Coles .15 .06
149 Dave Collins .15 .06
150 Darrell Evans .25 .10
151 Kirk Gibson .25 .10
152 John Grubb .15 .06
153 Willie Hernandez .15 .06
154 Larry Herndon .15 .06
155 Eric King .15 .06
156 Chet Lemon .15 .06
157 Dwight Lowry .15 .06
158 Jack Morris .25 .10
159 Randy O'Neal .15 .06
160 Lance Parrish .25 .10
161 Dan Petry .15 .06
162 Pat Sheridan .15 .06
163 Jim Slaton .15 .06
164 Frank Tanana .15 .06
165 Walt Terrell .15 .06
166 Mark Thurmond .15 .06
167 Alan Trammell .40 .16
168 Lou Whitaker .25 .10
169 Luis Aguayo .15 .06
170 Steve Bedrosian .15 .06
171 Don Carman .15 .06
172 Darren Daulton .40 .16
173 Greg Gross .15 .06
174 Kevin Gross .15 .06
175 Von Hayes .15 .06
176 Charles Hudson .15 .06
177 Tom Hume .15 .06
178 Steve Jeltz .15 .06
179 Mike Maddux .15 .06
180 Shane Rawley .15 .06
181 Gary Redus .15 .06
182 Ron Roenicke .15 .06
183 Bruce Ruffin RC .25 .10
184 John Russell .15 .06
185 Juan Samuel .15 .06
186 Dan Schatzeder .15 .06
187 Mike Schmidt 1.50 .60
188 Rick Schu .15 .06
189 Jeff Stone .15 .06
190 Kent Tekulve .15 .06
191 Milt Thompson .15 .06
192 Glenn Wilson .15 .06
193 Buddy Bell .25 .10
194 Tom Browning .15 .06
195 Sal Butera .15 .06
196 Dave Concepcion .25 .10
197 Kal Daniels .15 .06
198 Eric Davis .40 .16
199 John Denny .15 .06
200 Bo Diaz .15 .06
201 Nick Esasky .15 .06
202 John Franco .25 .10
203 Bill Gullickson .15 .06
204 Barry Larkin RC 5.00 2.00
205 Eddie Milner .15 .06
206 Rob Murphy .15 .06
207 Ron Oester .15 .06
208 Dave Parker .25 .10
209 Tony Perez .40 .16
210 Ted Power .15 .06
211 Joe Price .15 .06
212 Ron Robinson .15 .06
213 Pete Rose 2.00 .80
214 Mario Soto .15 .06
215 Kurt Stillwell .15 .06
216 Max Venable .15 .06
217 Chris Welsh .15 .06
218 Carl Willis RC .25 .10
219 Jesse Barfield .15 .06
220 George Bell .15 .06
221 Bill Caudill .15 .06
222 John Cerutti .15 .06
223 Jim Clancy .15 .06
224 Mark Eichhorn .15 .06
225 Tony Fernandez .15 .06
226 Damaso Garcia .15 .06
227 Kelly Gruber ERR .15 .06
(Wrong birth year)
228 Tom Henke .15 .06
229 Garth Iorg .15 .06
230 Joe Johnson .15 .06
231 Cliff Johnson .15 .06
232 Jimmy Key .25 .10
233 Dennis Lamp .15 .06
234 Rick Leach .15 .06
235 Buck Martinez .15 .06
236 Lloyd Moseby .15 .06
237 Rance Mulliniks .15 .06
238 Dave Stieb .15 .06
239 Willie Upshaw .15 .06
240 Ernie Whitt .15 .06
241 Andy Allanson .15 .06
242 Scott Bailes .15 .06
243 Chris Bando .15 .06
244 Tony Bernazard .15 .06
245 John Butcher .15 .06
246 Brett Butler .25 .10
247 Ernie Camacho .15 .06
248 Tom Candiotti .15 .06
249 Joe Carter .60 .24
250 Carmen Castillo .15 .06
251 Julio Franco .25 .10
252 Mel Hall .15 .06
253 Brook Jacoby .15 .06
254 Phil Niekro .25 .10
255 Otis Nixon .15 .06
256 Dickie Noles .15 .06
257 Bryan Oelkers .15 .06
258 Ken Schrom .15 .06
259 Don Schulze .15 .06
260 Cory Snyder .15 .06
261 Pat Tabler .15 .06
262 Andre Thornton .15 .06
263 Rich Yett .15 .06
264 Mike Aldrete .15 .06
265 Juan Berenguer .15 .06
266 Vida Blue .25 .10
267 Bob Brenly .15 .06
268 Chris Brown .15 .06
269 Will Clark RC 3.00 1.20
270 Chili Davis .40 .16
271 Mark Davis .15 .06
272 Kelly Downs RC .25 .10
273 Scott Garrelts .15 .06
274 Dan Gladden .15 .06
275 Mike Krukow .15 .06
276 Randy Kutcher .15 .06
277 Mike LaCoss .15 .06
278 Jeff Leonard .15 .06
279 Candy Maldonado .15 .06
280 Roger Mason .15 .06
281 Bob Melvin .15 .06
282 Greg Minton .15 .06
283 Jeff D. Robinson .15 .06
284 Harry Spilman .15 .06
285 R.Thompson RC* .50 .20
286 Jose Uribe .15 .06
287 Frank Williams .15 .06
288 Joel Youngblood .15 .06
289 Jack Clark .25 .10
290 Vince Coleman .15 .06
291 Tim Conroy .15 .06
292 Danny Cox .15 .06
293 Ken Dayley .15 .06
294 Curt Ford .15 .06
295 Bob Forsch .15 .06
296 Tom Herr .15 .06
297 Ricky Horton .15 .06
298 Clint Hurdle .15 .06
299 Jeff Lahti .15 .06
300 Steve Lake .15 .06
301 Tito Landrum .15 .06
302 Mike LaValliere RC * .50 .20
303 Greg Mathews .15 .06
304 Willie McGee .25 .10
305 Jose Oquendo .15 .06
306 Terry Pendleton .25 .10
307 Pat Perry .15 .06
308 Ozzie Smith 1.00 .40
309 Ray Soff .15 .06
310 John Tudor .15 .06
311 Andy Van Slyke UER .25 .10
(Bats R, Throws L)
312 Todd Worrell .25 .10
313 Dann Bilardello .15 .06
314 Hubie Brooks .15 .06
315 Tim Burke .15 .06
316 Andre Dawson .25 .10
317 Mike Fitzgerald .15 .06
318 Tom Foley .15 .06
319 Andres Galarraga .40 .16
320 Joe Hesketh .15 .06
321 Wallace Johnson .15 .06
322 Wayne Krenchicki .15 .06
323 Vance Law .15 .06
324 Dennis Martinez .25 .10
325 Bob McClure .15 .06
326 Andy McGaffigan .15 .06
327 Al Newman .15 .06
328 Tim Raines .25 .10
329 Jeff Reardon .25 .10
330 Luis Rivera RC .25 .10
331 Bob Sebra .15 .06
332 Bryn Smith .15 .06
333 Jay Tibbs .15 .06
334 Tim Wallach .15 .06
335 Mitch Webster .15 .06
336 Jim Wohlford .15 .06
337 Floyd Youmans .15 .06
338 Chris Bosio RC .50 .20
339 Glenn Braggs RC .25 .10
340 Rick Cerone .15 .06
341 Mark Clear .15 .06
342 Bryan Clutterbuck .15 .06
343 Cecil Cooper .25 .10
344 Rob Deer .15 .06
345 Jim Gantner .15 .06
346 Ted Higuera .15 .06
347 John Henry Johnson .15 .06
348 Tim Leary .15 .06
349 Rick Manning .15 .06
350 Paul Molitor .40 .16
351 Charlie Moore .15 .06
352 Juan Nieves .15 .06
353 Ben Oglivie .15 .06
354 Dan Plesac .15 .06
355 Ernest Riles .15 .06
356 Billy Joe Robidoux .15 .06
357 Bill Schroeder .15 .06
358 Dale Sveum .15 .06
359 Gorman Thomas .15 .06
360 Bill Wegman .15 .06
361 Robin Yount 1.00 .40
362 Steve Balboni .15 .06
363 Scott Bankhead .15 .06
364 Buddy Biancalana .15 .06
365 Bud Black .15 .06
366 George Brett 1.50 .60
367 Steve Farr .15 .06
368 Mark Gubicza .15 .06
369 Bo Jackson RC 3.00 1.20
370 Danny Jackson .15 .06
371 Mike Kingery RC .25 .10
372 Rudy Law .15 .06
373 Charlie Leibrandt .15 .06
374 Dennis Leonard .15 .06
375 Hal McRae .25 .10
376 Jorge Orta .15 .06
377 Jamie Quirk .15 .06
378 Dan Quisenberry .15 .06
379 Bret Saberhagen .25 .10
380 Angel Salazar .15 .06
381 Lonnie Smith .15 .06
382 Jim Sundberg .15 .06
383 Frank White .25 .10
384 Willie Wilson .25 .10
385 Joaquin Andujar .15 .06
386 Doug Bair .15 .06
387 Dusty Baker .25 .10
388 Bruce Bochte .15 .06
389 Jose Canseco 1.50 .60
390 Chris Codiroli .15 .06
391 Mike Davis .15 .06
392 Alfredo Griffin .15 .06
393 Moose Haas .15 .06
394 Donnie Hill .15 .06
395 Jay Howell .15 .06
396 Dave Kingman .25 .10
397 Carney Lansford .25 .10
398 Dave Leiper .15 .06
399 Bill Mooneyham .15 .06
400 Dwayne Murphy .15 .06
401 Steve Ontiveros .15 .06
402 Tony Phillips .15 .06
403 Eric Plunk .15 .06
404 Jose Rijo .15 .06
405 Terry Steinbach RC .50 .20
406 Dave Stewart .25 .10
407 Mickey Tettleton .15 .06
408 Dave Von Ohlen .15 .06
409 Jerry Willard .15 .06
410 Curt Young .15 .06
411 Bruce Bochy .15 .06
412 Dave Dravecky .25 .10
413 Tim Flannery .15 .06
414 Steve Garvey .25 .10
415 Rich Gossage .25 .10
416 Tony Gwynn 1.00 .40
417 Andy Hawkins .15 .06
418 LaMarr Hoyt .15 .06
419 Terry Kennedy .15 .06
420 John Kruk RC 1.25 .50
421 Dave LaPoint .15 .06
422 Craig Lefferts .15 .06
423 Carmelo Martinez .15 .06
424 Lance McCullers .15 .06
425 Kevin McReynolds .15 .06
426 Graig Nettles .25 .10
427 Bip Roberts RC .50 .20
428 Jerry Royster .15 .06
429 Benito Santiago .40 .16
430 Eric Show .15 .06
431 Bob Stoddard .15 .06
432 Garry Templeton .15 .06
433 Gene Walter .15 .06
434 Ed Whitson .15 .06
435 Marvell Wynne .15 .06
436 Dave Anderson .15 .06
437 Greg Brock .15 .06
438 Enos Cabell .15 .06
439 Mariano Duncan .15 .06
440 Pedro Guerrero .15 .06
441 Orel Hershiser .25 .10
442 Rick Honeycutt .15 .06
443 Ken Howell .15 .06
444 Ken Landreaux .15 .06
445 Bill Madlock .25 .10
446 Mike Marshall .15 .06
447 Len Matuszek .15 .06
448 Tom Niedenfuer .15 .06
449 Alejandro Pena .15 .06
450 Dennis Powell .15 .06
451 Jerry Reuss .15 .06
452 Bill Russell .15 .06
453 Steve Sax .15 .06
454 Mike Scioscia .15 .06
455 Franklin Stubbs .15 .06
456 Alex Trevino .15 .06
457 Fernando Valenzuela .25 .10
458 Ed VandeBerg .15 .06
459 Bob Welch .15 .06
460 Reggie Williams .15 .06
461 Don Aase .15 .06
462 Juan Beniquez .15 .06
463 Mike Boddicker .15 .06
464 Juan Bonilla .15 .06
465 Rich Bordi .15 .06
466 Storm Davis .15 .06
467 Rick Dempsey .25 .10
468 Ken Dixon .15 .06
469 Jim Dwyer .15 .06
470 Mike Flanagan .15 .06
471 Jackie Gutierrez .15 .06
472 Brad Havens .15 .06
473 Lee Lacy .15 .06
474 Fred Lynn .25 .10
475 Scott McGregor .15 .06
476 Eddie Murray .60 .24
477 Tom O'Malley .15 .06
478 Cal Ripken Jr. 2.50 1.00
479 Larry Sheets .15 .06
480 John Shelby .15 .06
481 Nate Snell .15 .06
482 Jim Traber .15 .06
483 Mike Young .15 .06
484 Neil Allen .15 .06
485 Harold Baines .25 .10
486 Floyd Bannister .15 .06
487 Daryl Boston .15 .06
488 Ivan Calderon .15 .06
489 John Cangelosi .15 .06
490 Steve Carlton .25 .10
491 Joe Cowley .15 .06
492 Julio Cruz .15 .06
493 Bill Dawley .15 .06
494 Jose DeLeon .15 .06
495 Richard Dotson .15 .06
496 Carlton Fisk .40 .16
497 Ozzie Guillen .15 .06
498 Jerry Hairston .15 .06
499 Ron Hassey .15 .06
500 Tim Hulett .15 .06
501 Bob James .15 .06
502 Steve Lyons .15 .06
503 Joel McKeon .15 .06
504 Gene Nelson .15 .06
505 Dave Schmidt .15 .06
506 Ray Searage .15 .06
507 Bobby Thigpen RC .50 .20
508 Greg Walker .15 .06
509 Jim Acker .15 .06
510 Doyle Alexander .15 .06
511 Paul Assenmacher .40 .16
512 Bruce Benedict .15 .06
513 Chris Chambliss .25 .10
514 Jeff Dedmon .15 .06
515 Gene Garber .15 .06
516 Ken Griffey .25 .10
517 Terry Harper .15 .06
518 Bob Horner .15 .06
519 Glenn Hubbard .15 .06
520 Rick Mahler .15 .06
521 Omar Moreno .15 .06
522 Dale Murphy .60 .24
523 Ken Oberkfell .15 .06
524 Ed Olwine .15 .06
525 David Palmer .15 .06
526 Rafael Ramirez .15 .06
527 Billy Sample .15 .06
528 Ted Simmons .25 .10
529 Zane Smith .15 .06
530 Bruce Sutter .15 .06
531 Andres Thomas .15 .06
532 Ozzie Virgil .15 .06
533 Allan Anderson .15 .06
534 Keith Atherton .15 .06
535 Billy Beane .25 .10
536 Bert Blyleven .25 .10
537 Tom Brunansky .15 .06
538 Randy Bush .15 .06
539 George Frazier .15 .06
540 Gary Gaetti .25 .10
541 Greg Gagne .15 .06
542 Mickey Hatcher .15 .06
543 Neal Heaton .15 .06
544 Kent Hrbek .25 .10
545 Roy Lee Jackson .15 .06
546 Tim Laudner .15 .06

547 Steve Lombardozzi .15 .06
548 Mark Portugal RC * .25 .10
549 Kirby Puckett .60 .24
550 Jeff Reed .15 .06
551 Mark Salas .15 .06
552 Roy Smalley .15 .06
553 Mike Smithson .15 .06
554 Frank Viola .15 .06
555 Thad Bosley .15 .06
556 Ron Cey .25 .10
557 Jody Davis .15 .06
558 Ron Davis .15 .06
559 Bob Dernier .15 .06
560 Frank DiPino .15 .06
561 Shawon Dunston UER .15 .06
(Wrong birth year
listed on card back)
562 Leon Durham .15 .06
563 Dennis Eckersley .40 .16
564 Terry Francona .25 .10
565 Dave Gumpert .15 .06
566 Guy Hoffman .15 .06
567 Ed Lynch .15 .06
568 Gary Matthews .15 .06
569 Keith Moreland .15 .06
570 Jamie Moyer RC 2.00 .80
571 Jerry Mumphrey .15 .06
572 Ryne Sandberg 1.25 .50
573 Scott Sanderson .15 .06
574 Lee Smith .40 .16
575 Chris Speier .15 .06
576 Rick Sutcliffe .25 .10
577 Manny Trillo .15 .06
578 Steve Trout .15 .06
579 Karl Best .15 .06
580 Scott Bradley .15 .06
581 Phil Bradley .15 .06
582 Mickey Brantley .15 .06
583 Mike G. Brown P .15 .06
584 Alvin Davis .15 .06
585 Lee Guetterman .15 .06
586 Mark Huismann .15 .06
587 Bob Kearney .15 .06
588 Pete Ladd .15 .06
589 Mark Langston .15 .06
590 Mike Moore .15 .06
591 Mike Morgan .15 .06
592 John Moses .15 .06
593 Ken Phelps .15 .06
594 Jim Presley .15 .06
595 Rey Quinones UER .15 .06
(Quinonez on front)
596 Harold Reynolds .25 .10
597 Billy Swift .15 .06
598 Danny Tartabull .15 .06
599 Steve Yeager .15 .06
600 Matt Young .15 .06
601 Bill Almon .15 .06
602 Rafael Belliard RC .50 .20
603 Mike Bielecki .15 .06
604 Barry Bonds RC 60.00 24.00
605 Bobby Bonilla RC 1.25 .50
606 Sid Bream .15 .06
607 Mike C. Brown .15 .06
608 Pat Clements .15 .06
609 Mike Diaz .15 .06
610 Cecilio Guante .15 .06
611 Barry Jones .15 .06
612 Bob Kipper .15 .06
613 Larry McWilliams .15 .06
614 Jim Morrison .15 .06
615 Joe Orsulak .15 .06
616 Junior Ortiz .15 .06
617 Tony Pena .15 .06
618 Johnny Ray .15 .06
619 Rick Reuschel .15 .06
620 R.J. Reynolds .15 .06
621 Rick Rhoden .15 .06
622 Don Robinson .15 .06
623 Bob Walk .15 .06
624 Jim Winn .15 .06
625 Pete Incaviglia .60 .24
Jose Canseco
626 Don Sutton .25 .10
Phil Niekro
627 Dave Righetti .15 .06
Don Aase
628 Wally Joyner .60 .24
Jose Canseco
629 Gary Carter .40 .16
Sid Fernandez
Dwight Gooden
Keith Hernandez
Darryl Strawberry
630 Mike Scott .15 .06
Mike Krukow
631 Fernando Valenzuela .15 .06
John Franco
632 Bob Horner 4 Homers .15 .06
633 Jose Canseco .60 .24
Jim Rice
Kirby Puckett
634 Gary Carter .60 .24
Roger Clemens
635 Steve Carlton 4000K's .15 .06
636 Glenn Davis .60 .24
Eddie Murray
637 Wade Boggs .25 .10
Keith Hernandez
638 Don Mattingly 1.00 .40
Darryl Strawberry
639 Dave Parker .60 .24
Ryne Sandberg
640 Dwight Gooden .60 .24
Roger Clemens
641 Mike Witt .15 .06
Charlie Hough
642 Juan Samuel .25 .10
Tim Raines
643 Harold Baines .25 .10
Jesse Barfield
644 Dave Clark RC and .50 .20
Greg Swindell
645 Ron Karkovice RC .50 .20
Russ Morman
646 Devon White RC and 1.25 .50
Willie Fraser
647 Mike Stanley RC and .50 .20
Jerry Browne
648 Dave Magadan RC .50 .20
Phil Lombardi
649 Jose Gonzalez RC .25 .10
Ralph Bryant
650 Jimmy Jones RC and .25 .10
Randy Asadoor
651 Tracy Jones RC and .25 .10
Marvin Freeman
652 John Stefero and .50 .20
Kevin Seitzer RC
653 Rob Nelson and .25 .10
Steve Fireovid
654 CL: Mets/Red Sox .15 .06
Astros/Angels
655 CL: Yankees/Rangers .15 .06
Tigers/Phillies
656 CL: Reds/Blue Jays .15 .06
Indians/Giants
ERR (230/231 wrong)
657 CL: Cardinals/Expos .15 .06
Brewers/Royals
658 CL: A's/Padres .15 .06
Dodgers/Orioles
659 CL: White Sox/Braves .15 .06
Twins/Cubs
660 CL: Mariners/Pirates .15 .06
Special Cards
ER (580/581 wrong)

1987 Fleer Glossy

This set parallels the regular 1987 Fleer issue and signified a short-lived three year run of Glossy parallel cards likely produced in response to Topps' run of Tiffany parallel sets. The cards were issued in a special tin which also included a glossy version of the World Series set. These 672 standard-size are differentiated only by the gloss on the front. This set was produced in fairly large quantities, although still significantly less than regular issue cards. According to widely held beliefs in the hobby, somewhere between 75 and 100 thousand of these sets were produced.

Nm-Mt Ex-Mt
COMP.FACT.SET (672) 120.00 47.50
*STARS: .5X TO 1.2X BASIC CARDS
*ROOKIES: .5X TO 1.2X BASIC CARDS
FACTORY SET PRICE IS FOR SEALED SETS
OPENED SETS SELL FOR 50-60% OF SEALED

1987 Fleer All-Stars

This 12-card standard-size set was distributed as an insert in packs of the Fleer regular issue. The cards are designed with a color player photo superimposed on a gray or black background with yellow stars. The player's name, team, and position are printed in orange on black or gray at the bottom of the obverse. The card backs are done predominantly in gray, red, and black and are numbered on the back in the upper right hand corner.

Nm-Mt Ex-Mt
COMPLETE SET (12) 20.00 8.00
1 Don Mattingly 6.00 2.40
2 Gary Carter 1.25 .50
3 Tony Fernandez .50 .20
4 Steve Sax .50 .20
5 Kirby Puckett 2.00 .80
6 Mike Schmidt 5.00 2.00
7 Mike Easler .50 .20
8 Todd Worrell .75 .30
9 George Bell .50 .20
10 Fernando Valenzuela .75 .30
11 Roger Clemens 5.00 2.00
12 Tim Raines .75 .30

1987 Fleer Headliners

This six-card standard-size set was distributed one per rack pack as well as with three-pack wax pack rack packs. The obverse features the player photo against a beige background with irregular red stripes. The checklist below also lists each player's team affiliation. The set is sequenced in alphabetical order.

Nm-Mt Ex-Mt
COMPLETE SET (6) 6.00 2.40
1 Wade Boggs .60 .24
2 Jose Canseco 2.50 1.00
3 Dwight Gooden .60 .24
4 Rickey Henderson 1.00 .40
5 Keith Hernandez .60 .24
6 Jim Rice .40 .16

1987 Fleer Wax Box Cards

The cards in this 16-card set measure the standard, 2 1/2" by 3 1/2". Cards have essentially the same design as the 1987 Fleer regular issue set. The cards were printed on the bottoms of the regular issue wax pack boxes. These 16 cards (C1 to C16) are considered a separate set in their own right and are not typically included in a complete set of the regular issue 1987 Fleer cards. The value of the panel uncut is slightly greater, perhaps by 25 percent greater, than the value of the individual cards cut up carefully.

Nm-Mt Ex-Mt
COMPLETE SET (16) 10.00 4.00
C1 Mets Logo .10 .04
C2 Jesse Barfield .10 .04
C3 George Brett 3.00 1.20
C4 Dwight Gooden .50 .20
C5 Boston Logo .10 .04
C6 Keith Hernandez .25 .10
C7 Wally Joyner .75 .30
C8 Dale Murphy .75 .30
C9 Astros Logo .10 .04
C10 Dave Parker .25 .10
C11 Kirby Puckett 1.00 .40
C12 Dave Righetti .10 .04
C13 Angels Logo .10 .04
C14 Ryne Sandberg 2.00 .80
C15 Mike Schmidt 1.50 .60
C16 Robin Yount .75 .30

1987 Fleer World Series

This 12-card standard-size set of features highlights of the previous year's World Series between the Mets and the Red Sox. The sets were packaged as a complete set insert with the collated sets (of the 1987 Fleer regular issue) which were sold by Fleer directly to hobby card dealers; they were not available in the general retail candy store outlets.

Nm-Mt Ex-Mt
COMPLETE SET (12) 2.00 .80
1 Bruce Hurst .15 .06
2 Keith Hernandez and .25 .10
Wade Boggs
3 Roger Clemens HOR 1.50 .60
4 Gary Carter .40 .16
5 Ron Darling .15 .06
6 Marty Barrett .15 .06
7 Dwight Gooden .40 .16
8 Strategy at Work .25 .10
(Mets Conference)
9 Dwight Evans .25 .10
Congratulated by Rich Gedman
10 Dave Henderson .15 .06
11 Ray Knight .40 .16
Darryl Strawberry
12 Ray Knight .15 .06

1987 Fleer Update

This 132-card standard-size set was distributed exclusively in factory set form through hobby dealers. In addition to the complete set of 132 cards, the box also contained 25 Team Logo stickers. The cards look very similar to the 1987 Fleer regular issue except for the U-prefixed numbering on back. Cards are ordered alphabetically according to player's last name. The key extended Rookie Cards in this set are Ellis Burks, Greg Maddux, Fred McGriff and Matt Williams. In addition an early card of legendary slugger Mark McGwire highlights this set.

Nm-Mt Ex-Mt
COMP.FACT.SET (132) 15.00 6.00
1 Scott Bankhead .10 .04
2 Eric Bell .15 .06
3 Juan Beniquez .10 .04
4 Juan Berenguer .10 .04
5 Mike Birkbeck .15 .06
6 Randy Bockus .10 .04
7 Rod Booker .10 .04
8 Thad Bosley .10 .04
9 Greg Brock .10 .04
10 Bob Brower .10 .04
11 Chris Brown .10 .04
12 Jerry Browne .15 .06
13 Ralph Bryant .10 .04
14 DeWayne Buice .10 .04
15 Ellis Burks XRC .75 .30
16 Casey Candaele .10 .04
17 Steve Carlton .15 .06
18 Juan Castillo .15 .06
19 Chuck Crim .15 .06
20 Mark Davidson .10 .04
21 Mark Davis .10 .04
22 Storm Davis .10 .04
23 Bill Dawley .10 .04
24 Andre Dawson .15 .06
25 Brian Dayett .10 .04
26 Rick Dempsey .15 .06
27 Ken Dowell .10 .04
28 Dave Dravecky .15 .06
29 Mike Dunne .10 .04
30 Dennis Eckersley .25 .10
31 Cecil Fielder .25 .10
32 Brian Fisher .10 .04
33 Willie Fraser .15 .06
34 Ken Gerhart .10 .04
35 Jim Gott .10 .04
36 Dan Gladden .10 .04
37 Mike Greenwell XRC* .30 .12
38 Cecilio Guante .10 .04
39 Albert Hall .10 .04
40 Atlee Hammaker .10 .04
41 Mickey Hatcher .10 .04
42 Mike Heath .10 .04
43 Neal Heaton .10 .04
44 Mike Henneman XRC .30 .12
45 Guy Hoffman .10 .04
46 Charles Hudson .10 .04
47 Chuck Jackson .10 .04
48 Mike Jackson XRC .30 .12
49 Reggie Jackson .25 .10
50 Chris James .10 .04
51 Dion James .10 .04
52 Stan Javier .10 .04
53 Stan Jefferson .10 .04
54 Jimmy Jones .15 .06
55 Tracy Jones .10 .04
56 Terry Kennedy .10 .04
57 Mike Kingery .15 .06
58 Ray Knight .10 .04
59 Gene Larkin XRC .30 .12
60 Mike LaValliere .30 .12
61 Jack Lazorko .10 .04
62 Terry Leach .10 .04
63 Rick Leach .10 .04
64 Craig Lefferts .10 .04
65 Jim Lindeman .15 .06
66 Bill Long .10 .04
67 Mike Loynd XRC .10 .04
68 Greg Maddux XRC 5.00 2.00
69 Bill Madlock .15 .06
70 Dave Magadan .30 .12
71 Joe Magrane XRC .15 .06
72 Fred Manrique .10 .04
73 Mike Mason .10 .04
74 Lloyd McClendon XRC .30 .12
75 Fred McGriff 1.00 .40
76 Mark McGwire 5.00 2.00
77 Mark McLemore .15 .06
78 Kevin McReynolds .10 .04
79 Dave Meads .10 .04
80 Greg Minton .10 .04
81 John Mitchell XRC .15 .06
82 Kevin Mitchell .25 .10
83 John Morris .10 .04
84 Jeff Musselman .10 .04
85 Randy Myers XRC .75 .30
86 Gene Nelson .10 .04
87 Joe Niekro .10 .04
88 Tom Nieto .10 .04
89 Reid Nichols .10 .04
90 Matt Nokes XRC .30 .12
91 Dickie Noles .10 .04
92 Edwin Nunez .10 .04
93 Jose Nunez .10 .04
94 Paul O'Neill .40 .16
95 Jim Paciorek .10 .04
96 Lance Parrish .15 .06
97 Bill Pecota XRC .15 .06
98 Tony Pena .10 .04
99 Luis Polonia XRC .15 .06
100 Randy Ready .10 .04
101 Jeff Reardon .15 .06
102 Gary Redus .10 .04
103 Rick Rhoden .10 .04
104 Wally Ritchie .10 .04
105 Jeff M. Robinson UER .10 .04
(Wrong Jeff's
stats on back)
106 Mark Salas .10 .04
107 Dave Schmidt .10 .04
108 Kevin Seitzer UER .30 .12
(Wrong birth year)
109 John Shelby .10 .04
110 John Smiley XRC .30 .12
111 Lary Sorensen .10 .04
112 Chris Speier .10 .04
113 Randy St.Claire .10 .04
114 Jim Sundberg .10 .04
115 B.J. Surhoff XRC .75 .30
116 Greg Swindell .30 .12
117 Danny Tartabull .10 .04
118 Dorn Taylor .10 .04
119 Lee Tunnell .10 .04
120 Ed VandeBerg .10 .04
121 Andy Van Slyke .15 .06
122 Gary Ward .10 .04
123 Devon White .75 .30
124 Alan Wiggins .10 .04
125 Bill Wilkinson .10 .04
126 Jim Winn .10 .04
127 Frank Williams .10 .04
128 Ken Williams XRC .10 .04
129 Matt Williams XRC 1.50 .60
130 Herm Winningham .10 .04
131 Matt Young .10 .04
132 Checklist 1-132 .10 .04

1987 Fleer Update Glossy

This set parallels the regular Fleer Update issue. The cards were issued in a special tin. These 132 standard-size are differentiated only by the gloss on the front. This set was produced in fairly large quantities, although still significantly less than regular issue cards. Similar to the regular Glossy set -- it is believed that between 75 and 100 thousand of these sets were produced.

Nm-Mt Ex-Mt
COMP.FACT.SET (132) 15.00 6.00
*STARS: .4X TO 1X BASIC CARDS
*ROOKIES: .4X TO 1X BASIC CARDS

1987 Fleer Award Winners

This small set of 44 standard-size cards was produced for 7-Eleven stores by Fleer. The cards feature full color fronts and yellow, white, and black backs. The card fronts are distinguished by their yellow frame around the player's full-color photo. The box for the cards describes the set as the "1987 Limited Edition Baseball's Award Winners." The checklist for the set is given on the back of the set box. The card numbering is in alphabetical order by player's name.

Nm-Mt Ex-Mt
COMP.FACT SET (44) 5.00 2.00
1 Marty Barrett .05 .02
2 George Bell .05 .02
3 Bert Blyleven .10 .04
4 Bob Boone .10 .04
5 John Candelaria .05 .02
6 Jose Canseco .50 .20
7 Gary Carter .15 .06
8 Joe Carter .20 .08
9 Roger Clemens .75 .30
10 Cecil Cooper .10 .04
11 Eric Davis .15 .06
12 Tony Fernandez .10 .04
13 Scott Fletcher .05 .02
14 Bob Forsch .05 .02
15 Dwight Gooden .15 .06
16 Ron Guidry .10 .04
17 Ozzie Guillen .10 .04
18 Bill Gullickson .10 .04
19 Tony Gwynn .75 .30
20 Bob Knepper .05 .02
21 Ray Knight .05 .02
22 Mark Langston .05 .02
23 Candy Maldonado .05 .02
24 Don Mattingly .75 .30
25 Roger McDowell .05 .02
26 Dale Murphy .20 .08
27 Dave Parker .10 .04
28 Lance Parrish .10 .04
29 Gary Pettis .05 .02
30 Kirby Puckett .50 .20
31 Johnny Ray .05 .02
32 Dave Righetti .05 .02
33 Cal Ripken 1.50 .60
34 Bret Saberhagen .10 .04
35 Ryne Sandberg .50 .20
36 Mike Schmidt .50 .20
37 Mike Scott .10 .04
38 Ozzie Smith .75 .30
39 Robby Thompson .10 .04
40 Fernando Valenzuela .10 .04
41 Mitch Webster UER .05 .02
(Mike on front)
42 Frank White .10 .04
43 Mike Witt .05 .02
44 Todd Worrell .10 .04

1987 Fleer Baseball All-Stars

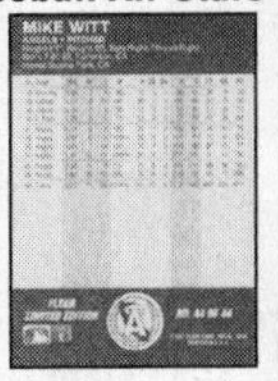

This small set of 44 standard-size cards was produced for Ben Franklin stores by Fleer. The cards feature full color fronts and red, white, and blue backs. The card fronts are easily distinguished by their white vertical stripes over a bright red background. The box for the cards proclaims "Limited Edition Baseball All-Stars" and is styled in the same manner and color scheme as the cards themselves. The checklist for the set is given on the back of the set box. The card numbering is in alphabetical order by player's name.

Nm-Mt Ex-Mt
COMP. FACT. SET (44) 6.00 2.40
1 Harold Baines .15 .06
2 Jesse Barfield .05 .02
3 Wade Boggs .50 .20
4 Dennis Boyd .05 .02
5 Scott Bradley .05 .02
6 Jose Canseco .50 .20
7 Gary Carter .40 .16
8 Joe Carter .20 .08
9 Mark Clear .05 .02
10 Roger Clemens .75 .30
11 Jose Cruz .10 .04
12 Chili Davis .15 .06
13 Jody Davis .05 .02
14 Rob Deer .05 .02
15 Brian Downing .05 .02
16 Sid Fernandez .05 .02
17 John Franco .10 .04
18 Andres Galarraga .40 .16
19 Dwight Gooden .15 .06
20 Tony Gwynn .75 .30
21 Charlie Hough .05 .02
22 Bruce Hurst .05 .02
23 Wally Joyner .20 .08
24 Carney Lansford .10 .04
25 Fred Lynn .10 .04
26 Don Mattingly .75 .30
27 Willie McGee .10 .04
28 Jack Morris .10 .04
29 Dale Murphy .20 .08
30 Bob Ojeda .05 .02
31 Tony Pena .10 .04
32 Kirby Puckett .50 .20
33 Dan Quisenberry .05 .02
34 Tim Raines .10 .04
35 Willie Randolph .10 .04
36 Cal Ripken 1.50 .60
37 Pete Rose .50 .20
38 Nolan Ryan 1.50 .60
39 Juan Samuel .05 .02
40 Mike Schmidt .50 .20
41 Ozzie Smith .75 .30
42 Andres Thomas .05 .02
43 Fernando Valenzuela .10 .04
44 Mike Witt .05 .02

1987 Fleer Exciting Stars

This small 44-card boxed standard-size set was produced by Fleer for distribution by the Cumberland Farm stores. The cards feature full color fronts. The set is titled "Baseball's Exciting Stars." Each individual boxed set includes the 44 cards and six logo stickers. The checklist for the set is found on the back panel of the box. The card numbering is in alphabetical order by player's name.

	Nm-Mt	Ex-Mt
COMP.FACT SET (44)	5.00	2.00
1 Don Aase	.05	.02
2 Rick Aguilera	.10	.04
3 Jesse Barfield	.05	.02
4 Wade Boggs	.40	.16
5 Oil Can Boyd	.05	.02
6 Sid Bream	.05	.02
7 Jose Canseco	.50	.20
8 Steve Carlton	.40	.16
9 Gary Carter	.40	.16
10 Will Clark	.75	.30
11 Roger Clemens	.75	.30
12 Danny Cox	.05	.02
13 Alvin Davis	.05	.02
14 Eric Davis	.15	.06
15 Rob Deer	.05	.02
16 Brian Downing	.05	.02
17 Gene Garber	.05	.02
18 Steve Garvey	.15	.06
19 Dwight Gooden	.15	.06
20 Mark Gubicza	.05	.02
21 Mel Hall	.05	.02
22 Terry Harper	.05	.02
23 Von Hayes	.05	.02
24 Rickey Henderson	.60	.24
25 Tom Henke	.05	.02
26 Willie Hernandez	.05	.02
27 Ted Higuera	.05	.02
28 Rick Honeycutt	.05	.02
29 Kent Hrbek	.10	.04
30 Wally Joyner	.20	.08
31 Charlie Kerfeld	.05	.02
32 Fred Lynn	.10	.04
33 Don Mattingly	.75	.30
34 Tim Raines	.10	.04
35 Dennis Rasmussen	.05	.02
36 Johnny Ray	.05	.02
37 Jim Rice	.10	.04
38 Pete Rose	.50	.20
39 Lee Smith	.15	.06
40 Cory Snyder	.05	.02
41 Darryl Strawberry	.10	.04
42 Kent Tekulve	.05	.02
43 Willie Wilson	.10	.04
44 Bobby Witt	.05	.02

1987 Fleer Game Winners

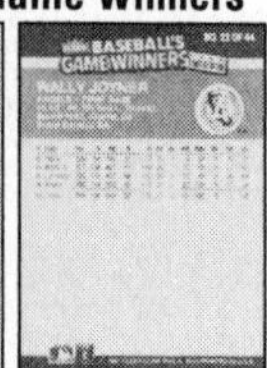

This small 44-card boxed standard-size set was produced by Fleer for distribution by several store chains, including Bi-Mart, Pay'n'Save, Mott's, M.E.Moses, and Winn's. The cards feature full color fronts. The set is titled "Baseball's Game Winners." Each individual boxed set includes the 44 cards and six logo stickers. The checklist for the set is found on the back panel of the box. The card numbering is in alphabetical order by player's name.

	Nm-Mt	Ex-Mt
COMP.FACT SET (44)	6.00	2.40
1 Harold Baines	.15	.06
2 Don Baylor	.10	.04
3 George Bell	.05	.02
4 Tony Bernazard	.05	.02
5 Wade Boggs	.50	.20
6 George Brett	.75	.30
7 Hubie Brooks	.05	.02
8 Jose Canseco	.75	.30
9 Gary Carter	.40	.16
10 Roger Clemens	.75	.30
11 Eric Davis	.10	.04
12 Glenn Davis	.05	.02
13 Shawon Dunston	.05	.02
14 Mark Eichhorn	.05	.02
15 Gary Gaetti	.10	.04
16 Steve Garvey	.15	.06
17 Kirk Gibson	.10	.04
18 Dwight Gooden	.15	.06
19 Von Hayes	.05	.02
20 Willie Hernandez	.05	.02
21 Ted Higuera	.05	.02
22 Wally Joyner	.20	.08
23 Bob Knepper	.05	.02
24 Mike Krukow	.05	.02
25 Jeff Leonard	.05	.02
26 Don Mattingly	.75	.30
27 Kirk McCaskill	.05	.02
28 Kevin McReynolds	.05	.02
29 Jim Morrison	.05	.02
30 Dale Murphy	.20	.08
31 Pete O'Brien	.05	.02
32 Bob Ojeda	.05	.02
33 Larry Parrish	.05	.02
34 Ken Phelps	.05	.02
35 Dennis Rasmussen	.05	.02
36 Ernest Riles	.05	.02
37 Cal Ripken	1.50	.60
38 Ron Robinson	.05	.02
39 Steve Sax	.05	.02
40 Mike Schmidt	.50	.20
41 John Tudor	.05	.02
42 Fernando Valenzuela	.10	.04
43 Mike Witt	.05	.02
44 Curt Young	.05	.02

1987 Fleer Hottest Stars

This 44-card boxed standard-size set was produced by Fleer for distribution by Revco stores all over the country. The cards feature full color fronts and red, white, and black backs. The card fronts are easily distinguished by their solid red outside borders and and white and blue inner borders framing the player's picture. The box for the cards proclaims "1987 Limited Edition Baseball's Hottest Stars" and is styled in the same manner and color scheme as the cards themselves. The checklist for the set is given on the back of the set box. The card numbering is in alphabetical order by player's name. An early card of Barry Bonds highlights this set.

	Nm-Mt	Ex-Mt
COMP.FACT.SET (44)	60.00	24.00
1 Joaquin Andujar	.10	.04
2 Harold Baines	.15	.06
3 Kevin Bass	.10	.04
4 Don Baylor	.15	.06
5 Barry Bonds	50.00	20.00
6 George Brett	1.00	.40
7 Tom Brunansky	.10	.04
8 Brett Butler	.15	.06
9 Jose Canseco	.75	.30
10 Roger Clemens	1.50	.60
11 Ron Darling	.10	.04
12 Eric Davis	.15	.06
13 Andre Dawson	.15	.06
14 Doug DeCinces	.10	.04
15 Leon Durham	.10	.04
16 Mark Eichhorn	.10	.04
17 Scott Garrelts	.10	.04
18 Dwight Gooden	.25	.10
19 Dave Henderson	.10	.04
20 Rickey Henderson	.40	.16
21 Keith Hernandez	.25	.10
22 Ted Higuera	.10	.04
23 Bob Horner	.15	.06
24 Pete Incaviglia	.15	.06
25 Wally Joyner	.40	.16
26 Mark Langston	.10	.04
27 Don Mattingly UER (Pirates logo on back)	1.25	.50
28 Dale Murphy	.40	.16
29 Kirk McCaskill	.10	.04
30 Willie McGee	.15	.06
31 Dave Righetti	.15	.06
32 Pete Rose	1.25	.50
33 Bruce Ruffin	.10	.04
34 Steve Sax	.10	.04
35 Mike Schmidt	1.00	.40
36 Larry Sheets	.10	.04
37 Eric Show	.10	.04
38 Dave Smith	.10	.04
39 Cory Snyder	.10	.04
40 Frank Tanana	.15	.06
41 Alan Trammell	.25	.10
42 Reggie Williams	.10	.04
43 Mookie Wilson	.15	.06
44 Todd Worrell	.15	.06

1987 Fleer League Leaders

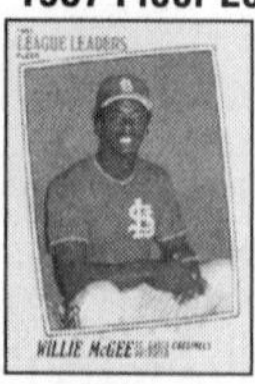

This small set of 44 standard-size cards was produced for Walgreens by Fleer. The cards feature full color fronts and red, white, and blue backs. The card fronts are easily distinguished by their light blue vertical stripes over a white background. The box for the cards proclaims a "Walgreens Exclusive" and is styled in the same manner and color scheme as the cards themselves. The checklist for the set is given on the back of the set box. The card numbering is in alphabetical order by player's name.

	Nm-Mt	Ex-Mt
COMP.FACT SET (44)	6.00	2.40
1 Jesse Barfield	.05	.02
2 Mike Boddicker	.05	.02
3 Wade Boggs	.50	.20
4 Phil Bradley	.05	.02
5 George Brett	.75	.30
6 Hubie Brooks	.05	.02
7 Chris Brown	.05	.02
8 Jose Canseco	.75	.30
9 Joe Carter	.20	.08
10 Roger Clemens	.75	.30
11 Vince Coleman	.05	.02
12 Joe Cowley	.05	.02
13 Kal Daniels	.05	.02
14 Glenn Davis	.05	.02
15 Jody Davis	.05	.02
16 Darrell Evans	.10	.04
17 Dwight Evans	.10	.04
18 John Franco	.10	.04
19 Julio Franco	.10	.04
20 Dwight Gooden	.15	.06
21 Rich Gossage	.10	.04
22 Tom Herr	.05	.02
23 Ted Higuera	.05	.02
24 Bob Horner	.05	.02
25 Pete Incaviglia	.10	.04
26 Wally Joyner	.20	.08
27 Dave Kingman	.10	.04
28 Don Mattingly	.75	.30
29 Willie McGee	.10	.04
30 Donnie Moore	.05	.02
31 Keith Moreland	.05	.02
32 Eddie Murray	.50	.20
33 Mike Pagliarulo	.05	.02
34 Larry Parrish	.05	.02
35 Tony Pena	.10	.04
36 Kirby Puckett	.50	.20
37 Pete Rose	.50	.20
38 Juan Samuel	.05	.02
39 Ryne Sandberg	.75	.30
40 Mike Schmidt	.50	.20
41 Darryl Strawberry	.10	.04
42 Greg Walker	.05	.02
43 Bob Welch	.05	.02
44 Todd Worrell	.05	.02

1987 Fleer Limited Edition

This 44-card boxed standard-size set was (mass) produced by Fleer for distribution by McCrory's and is sometimes referred to as the McCrory's set. The numerical checklist on the back of the box shows that the set is numbered alphabetically.

	Nm-Mt	Ex-Mt
COMP.FACT SET (44)	5.00	2.00
1 Floyd Bannister	.05	.02
2 Marty Barrett	.05	.02
3 Steve Bedrosian	.05	.02
4 George Bell	.05	.02
5 George Brett	.75	.30
6 Jose Canseco	.50	.20
7 Joe Carter	.20	.08
8 Will Clark	1.00	.40
9 Roger Clemens	.50	.20
10 Vince Coleman	.05	.02
11 Glenn Davis	.05	.02
12 Mike Davis	.05	.02
13 Len Dykstra	.15	.06
14 John Franco	.10	.04
15 Julio Franco	.10	.04
16 Steve Garvey	.15	.06
17 Kirk Gibson	.10	.04
18 Dwight Gooden	.15	.06
19 Tony Gwynn	.75	.30
20 Keith Hernandez	.10	.04
21 Teddy Higuera	.05	.02
22 Kent Hrbek	.10	.04
23 Wally Joyner	.20	.08
24 Mike Krukow	.05	.02
25 Mike Marshall	.05	.02
26 Don Mattingly	.75	.30
27 Oddibe McDowell	.05	.02
28 Jack Morris	.10	.04
29 Lloyd Moseby	.05	.02
30 Dale Murphy	.20	.08
31 Eddie Murray	.50	.20
32 Tony Pena	.10	.04
33 Jim Presley	.05	.02
34 Jeff Reardon	.10	.04
35 Jim Rice	.10	.04
36 Pete Rose	.50	.20
37 Mike Schmidt	.50	.20
38 Mike Scott	.05	.02
39 Lee Smith	.15	.06
40 Lonnie Smith	.05	.02
41 Gary Ward	.05	.02
42 Dave Winfield	.40	.16
43 Todd Worrell	.10	.04
44 Robin Yount	.40	.16

1987 Fleer Limited Box Cards

The cards in this six-card set each measure the standard size. Cards have essentially the same design as the 1987 Fleer Limited Edition cards which were distributed by McCrory's. The cards were printed on the bottom of the counter display box which held 24 small boxed sets; hence theoretically these box cards are 1/24 as plentiful as the regular boxed set cards. These six cards, numbered C1 to C6, are considered a separate set in their own right and are not typically included in a complete set of the 1987 Fleer Limited Edition set of 44. The value of the panels uncut is slightly greater, perhaps by 25 percent greater, than the value of the individual cards cut up carefully.

	Nm-Mt	Ex-Mt
COMPLETE SET (6)	2.00	.80
C1 Ron Darling	.25	.10
C2 Bill Buckner	.50	.20
C3 John Candelaria	.25	.10
C4 Jack Clark	.50	.20
C5 Bret Saberhagen	.50	.20
C6 Team Logo (Checklist back)	.25	.10

1987 Fleer Mini

The 1987 Fleer "Classic Miniatures" set consists of 120 small cards with all new pictures of the players as compared to the 1987 Fleer regular issue. The cards are only 1 13/16" by 2 9/16",

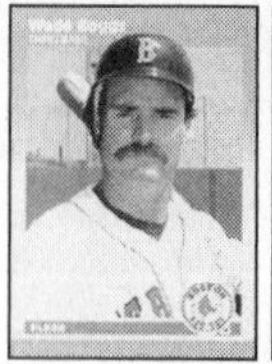

making them one of the smallest cards issued in the 1980's. Card backs provide career year-by-year statistics. The complete set was distributed in a blue, red, white, and silver factory box along with 18 logo stickers. The card numbering is by alphabetical order.

	Nm-Mt	Ex-Mt
COMP.FACT SET (120)	6.00	2.40
1 Don Aase	.05	.02
2 Joaquin Andujar	.05	.02
3 Harold Baines	.15	.06
4 Jesse Barfield	.05	.02
5 Kevin Bass	.05	.02
6 Don Baylor	.10	.04
7 George Bell	.05	.02
8 Tony Bernazard	.05	.02
9 Bert Blyleven	.10	.04
10 Wade Boggs	.40	.16
11 Phil Bradley	.05	.02
12 Sid Bream	.05	.02
13 George Brett	.75	.30
14 Hubie Brooks	.05	.02
15 Chris Brown	.05	.02
16 Tom Candiotti	.05	.02
17 Jose Canseco	.50	.20
18 Gary Carter	.15	.06
19 Joe Carter	.20	.08
20 Roger Clemens	.75	.30
21 Vince Coleman	.05	.02
22 Cecil Cooper	.10	.04
23 Ron Darling	.05	.02
24 Alvin Davis	.05	.02
25 Chili Davis	.15	.06
26 Eric Davis	.10	.04
27 Glenn Davis	.05	.02
28 Mike Davis	.05	.02
29 Doug DeCinces	.05	.02
30 Rob Deer	.05	.02
31 Jim Deshaies	.05	.02
32 Bo Diaz	.05	.02
33 Richard Dotson	.05	.02
34 Brian Downing	.05	.02
35 Shawon Dunston	.05	.02
36 Mark Eichhorn	.05	.02
37 Dwight Evans	.10	.04
38 Tony Fernandez	.10	.04
39 Julio Franco	.10	.04
40 Gary Gaetti	.10	.04
41 Andres Galarraga	.40	.16
42 Scott Garrelts	.05	.02
43 Steve Garvey	.15	.06
44 Kirk Gibson	.10	.04
45 Dwight Gooden	.15	.06
46 Ken Griffey	.10	.04
47 Mark Gubicza	.05	.02
48 Ozzie Guillen	.10	.04
49 Bill Gullickson	.05	.02
50 Tony Gwynn	.75	.30
51 Von Hayes	.05	.02
52 Rickey Henderson	.75	.30
53 Keith Hernandez	.10	.04
54 Willie Hernandez	.05	.02
55 Ted Higuera	.05	.02
56 Charlie Hough	.05	.02
57 Kent Hrbek	.10	.04
58 Pete Incaviglia	.10	.04
59 Wally Joyner	.30	.12
60 Bob Knepper	.05	.02
61 Mike Krukow	.05	.02
62 Mark Langston	.05	.02
63 Carney Lansford	.10	.04
64 Jim Lindeman	.05	.02
65 Bill Madlock	.10	.04
66 Don Mattingly	.75	.30
67 Kirk McCaskill	.05	.02
68 Lance McCullers	.05	.02
69 Keith Moreland	.05	.02
70 Jack Morris	.10	.04
71 Jim Morrison	.05	.02
72 Lloyd Moseby	.05	.02
73 Jerry Mumphrey	.05	.02
74 Dale Murphy	.20	.08
75 Eddie Murray	.50	.20
76 Pete O'Brien	.05	.02
77 Bob Ojeda	.05	.02
78 Jesse Orosco	.10	.04
79 Dan Pasqua	.05	.02
80 Dave Parker	.10	.04
81 Larry Parrish	.05	.02
82 Jim Presley	.05	.02
83 Kirby Puckett	.50	.20
84 Dan Quisenberry	.05	.02
85 Tim Raines	.10	.04
86 Dennis Rasmussen	.05	.02
87 Johnny Ray	.05	.02
88 Jeff Reardon	.10	.04
89 Jim Rice	.10	.04
90 Dave Righetti	.05	.02
91 Earnest Riles	.05	.02
92 Cal Ripken	1.50	.60
93 Ron Robinson	.05	.02
94 Juan Samuel	.05	.02
95 Ryne Sandberg	.60	.24
96 Steve Sax	.05	.02
97 Mike Schmidt	.40	.16
98 Ken Schrom	.05	.02
99 Mike Scott	.05	.02
100 Ruben Sierra	.40	.16
101 Lee Smith	.15	.06
102 Ozzie Smith	.75	.30
103 Cory Snyder	.05	.02
104 Kent Tekulve	.05	.02
105 Andres Thomas	.05	.02
106 Robby Thompson	.10	.04
107 Alan Trammell	.15	.06
108 John Tudor	.05	.02
109 Fernando Valenzuela	.10	.04
110 Greg Walker	.05	.02
111 Mitch Webster	.05	.02
112 Lou Whitaker	.10	.04
113 Frank White	.10	.04
114 Reggie Williams	.05	.02
115 Glenn Wilson	.05	.02
116 Willie Wilson	.10	.04
117 Dave Winfield	.50	.20
118 Mike Witt	.05	.02
119 Todd Worrell	.10	.04
120 Floyd Youmans	.05	.02

1987 Fleer Record Setters

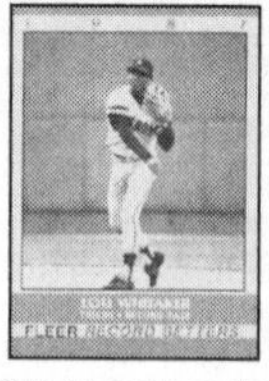
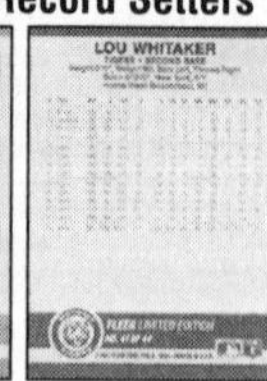

This 44-card boxed standard-size set was produced by Fleer for distribution by Eckerd's Drug Stores and is sometimes referred to as the Eckerd's set. Six team logo stickers are included in the box with the complete set. The numerical checklist on the back of the box shows that the set is numbered alphabetically.

	Nm-Mt	Ex-Mt
COMP.FACT SET (44)	5.00	2.00
1 George Brett	.50	.20
2 Chris Brown	.05	.02
3 Jose Canseco UER (3 of 444 on back)	.50	.20
4 Roger Clemens	.50	.20
5 Alvin Davis UER (5 of 441 on back, upside down one)	.05	.02
6 Shawon Dunston	.05	.02
7 Tony Fernandez	.10	.04
8 Carlton Fisk UER (8 of 44' on back)	.40	.16
9 Gary Gaetti UER (9 of 444 on back)	.10	.04
10 Gene Garber	.05	.02
11 Rich Gedman	.05	.02
12 Dwight Gooden	.15	.06
13 Ozzie Guillen	.10	.04
14 Bill Gullickson	.05	.02
15 Billy Hatcher	.05	.02
16 Orel Hershiser	.10	.04
17 Wally Joyner	.30	.12
18 Ray Knight	.05	.02
19 Craig Lefferts	.05	.02
20 Don Mattingly	.75	.30
21 Kevin Mitchell	.15	.06
22 Lloyd Moseby	.05	.02
23 Dale Murphy	.20	.08
24 Eddie Murray	.40	.16
25 Phil Niekro	.30	.12
26 Ben Oglivie	.05	.02
27 Jesse Orosco	.10	.04
28 Joe Orsulak	.05	.02
29 Larry Parrish	.05	.02
30 Tim Raines	.10	.04
31 Shane Rawley	.05	.02
32 Dave Righetti	.05	.02
33 Pete Rose	.50	.20
34 Steve Sax	.05	.02
35 Mike Schmidt	.50	.20
36 Mike Scott	.05	.02
37 Don Sutton	.30	.12
38 Alan Trammell	.15	.06
39 John Tudor	.05	.02
40 Gary Ward	.05	.02
41 Lou Whitaker	.10	.04
42 Willie Wilson	.10	.04
43 Todd Worrell	.10	.04
44 Floyd Youmans	.05	.02

1987 Fleer Sluggers/Pitchers

Fleer produced this 44-card boxed standard-size set although it was primarily distributed by McCrory, McLellan, Newberry, H.L.Green, T.G.Y., and other similar stores. The set features 28 sluggers and 16 pitchers and is subtitled "Baseball's Best". The set was packaged in a red, white, blue, and yellow custom box along with six logo stickers. The set checklist is given on the back of the box. The checklist on the back of the set box misspells McGwire as McGuire. The card numbering is in alphabetical order by player's name.

	Nm-Mt	Ex-Mt
COMP.FACT. SET (44)	10.00	4.00
1 Kevin Bass	.05	.02
2 Jesse Barfield	.05	.02
3 George Bell	.05	.02
4 Wade Boggs	.50	.20
5 Sid Bream	.05	.02
6 George Brett	.75	.30
7 Ivan Calderon	.05	.02
8 Jose Canseco	.50	.20
9 Jack Clark	.10	.04
10 Roger Clemens	1.00	.40
11 Eric Davis	.10	.04
12 Andre Dawson	.25	.10
13 Sid Fernandez	.05	.02
14 John Franco	.10	.04
15 Dwight Gooden	.15	.06
16 Pedro Guerrero	.05	.02
17 Tony Gwynn	.75	.30

18 Rickey Henderson .75 .30
19 Tom Henke .05 .02
20 Ted Higuera .05 .02
21 Pete Incaviglia .10 .04
22 Wally Joyner .30 .12
23 Jeff Leonard .05 .02
24 Joe Magrane .05 .02
25 Don Mattingly .75 .30
26 Mark McGwire 2.50 1.00
27 Jack Morris .10 .04
28 Dale Murphy .25 .10
29 Dave Parker .10 .04
30 Ken Phelps .05 .02
31 Kirby Puckett .50 .20
32 Tim Raines .10 .04
33 Jeff Reardon .10 .04
34 Dave Righetti .05 .02
35 Cal Ripken 2.00 .80
36 Bret Saberhagen .10 .04
37 Mike Schmidt .50 .20
38 Mike Scott .05 .02
39 Kevin Seitzer .25 .10
40 Darryl Strawberry .10 .04
41 Rick Sutcliffe .05 .02
42 Pat Tabler .05 .02
43 Fernando Valenzuela .10 .04
44 Mike Witt .05 .02

1987 Fleer Sluggers/Pitchers Box Cards

The cards in this six-card set each measure the standard size. Cards have essentially the same design as the 1987 Fleer Sluggers vs. Pitchers set of Baseball's Best. The cards were printed on the bottom of the counter display box which held 24 small boxed sets; hence theoretically these box cards are 1/24 as plentiful as the regular boxed set cards. These six cards, numbered M1 to M5 with one blank-back (unnumbered) card, are considered a separate set in their own right and are not typically included in a complete set of the 1987 Fleer Sluggers vs. Pitchers set of 44. The value of the panels uncut is slightly greater, perhaps by 25 percent greater, than the value of the individual cards cut up carefully.

Nm-Mt Ex-Mt
COMPLETE SET (6) 15.00 6.00
M1 Steve Bedrosian 1.00 .40
M2 Will Clark 10.00 4.00
M3 Vince Coleman 1.00 .40
M4 Bo Jackson 5.00 2.00
M5 Cory Snyder 1.00 .40
NNO Team Logo 1.00 .40
(Blank back)

1987 Fleer Sticker Cards

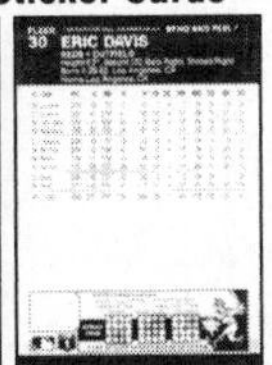

These Star Stickers were distributed as a separate issue by Fleer with five star stickers and a logo sticker in each wax pack. The 132-card (sticker) set features 2 1/2" by 3 1/2" full-color fronts and even statistics on the sticker back, which is an indication that the Fleer Company understands that these stickers are rarely used as stickers but more like traditional cards. The fronts are surrounded by a green border and the backs are printed in green and yellow on white card stock. The numbering is in alphabetical order by player's name.

Nm-Mt Ex-Mt
COMPLETE SET (132) 15.00 6.00
1 Don Aase .05 .02
2 Harold Baines .20 .08
3 Floyd Bannister .05 .02
4 Jesse Barfield .05 .02
5 Marty Barrett .05 .02
6 Kevin Bass .05 .02
7 Don Baylor .10 .04
8 Steve Bedrosian .05 .02
9 George Bell .05 .02
10 Bert Blyleven .10 .04
11 Mike Boddicker .05 .02
12 Wade Boggs .40 .16
13 Phil Bradley .05 .02
14 Sid Bream .05 .02
15 George Brett 1.25 .50
16 Hubie Brooks .05 .02
17 Tom Brunansky .05 .02
18 Tom Candiotti .05 .02
19 Jose Canseco .75 .30
20 Gary Carter .40 .16
21 Joe Carter .30 .12
22 Will Clark 1.25 .50
23 Mark Clear .05 .02
24 Roger Clemens 1.00 .40
25 Vince Coleman .05 .02
26 Jose Cruz .10 .04
27 Ron Darling .05 .02
28 Alvin Davis .05 .02
29 Chili Davis .20 .08
30 Eric Davis .20 .08
31 Glenn Davis .05 .02
32 Mike Davis .05 .02
33 Andre Dawson .30 .12
34 Doug DeCinces .05 .02
35 Brian Downing .05 .02
36 Shawon Dunston .05 .02
37 Mark Eichhorn .05 .02
38 Dwight Evans .10 .04
39 Tony Fernandez .10 .04
40 Bob Forsch .05 .02
41 John Franco .10 .04
42 Julio Franco .10 .04
43 Gary Gaetti .10 .04
44 Gene Garber .05 .02
45 Scott Garrelts .05 .02
46 Steve Garvey .20 .08
47 Kirk Gibson .10 .04
48 Dwight Gooden .20 .08
49 Ken Griffey .10 .04
50 Ozzie Guillen .10 .04
51 Bill Gullickson .05 .02
52 Tony Gwynn 1.25 .50
53 Mel Hall .05 .02
54 Greg A. Harris .05 .02
55 Von Hayes .05 .02
56 Rickey Henderson .75 .30
57 Tom Henke .05 .02
58 Keith Hernandez .10 .04
59 Willie Hernandez .05 .02
60 Ted Higuera .05 .02
61 Bob Horner .05 .02
62 Charlie Hough .05 .02
63 Jay Howell .05 .02
64 Kent Hrbek .10 .04
65 Bruce Hurst .05 .02
66 Pete Incaviglia .10 .04
67 Bob James .05 .02
68 Wally Joyner .40 .16
69 Mike Krukow .05 .02
70 Mark Langston .05 .02
71 Carney Lansford .10 .04
72 Fred Lynn .10 .04
73 Bill Madlock .10 .04
74 Don Mattingly 1.25 .50
75 Kirk McCaskill .05 .02
76 Lance McCullers .05 .02
77 Oddibe McDowell .05 .02
78 Paul Molitor .50 .20
79 Keith Moreland .05 .02
80 Jack Morris .10 .04
81 Jim Morrison .05 .02
82 Jerry Mumphrey .05 .02
83 Dale Murphy .30 .12
84 Eddie Murray .50 .20
85 Ben Oglivie .05 .02
86 Bob Ojeda .05 .02
87 Jesse Orosco .10 .04
88 Dave Parker .10 .04
89 Larry Parrish .05 .02
90 Tony Pena .10 .04
91 Jim Presley .05 .02
92 Kirby Puckett .50 .20
93 Dan Quisenberry .05 .02
94 Tim Raines .10 .04
95 Dennis Rasmussen .05 .02
96 Shane Rawley .05 .02
97 Johnny Ray .05 .02
98 Jeff Reardon .10 .04
99 Jim Rice .10 .04
100 Dave Righetti .05 .02
101 Cal Ripken 2.50 1.00
102 Pete Rose 1.00 .40
103 Nolan Ryan 2.50 1.00
104 Juan Samuel .05 .02
105 Ryne Sandberg 1.00 .40
106 Steve Sax .05 .02
107 Mike Schmidt .50 .20
108 Mike Scott .05 .02
109 Dave Smith .05 .02
110 Lee Smith .20 .08
111 Lonnie Smith .05 .02
112 Ozzie Smith 1.00 .40
113 Cory Snyder .05 .02
114 Darryl Strawberry .10 .04
115 Don Sutton .50 .20
116 Kent Tekulve .05 .02
117 Andres Thomas .05 .02
118 Alan Trammell .20 .08
119 John Tudor .05 .02
120 Fernando Valenzuela .10 .04
121 Bob Welch .10 .04
122 Lou Whitaker .10 .04
123 Frank White .10 .04
124 Reggie Williams .05 .02
125 Willie Wilson .10 .04
126 Dave Winfield .40 .16
127 Mike Witt .05 .02
128 Todd Worrell .10 .04
129 Curt Young .05 .02
130 Robin Yount .40 .16
131 Jose Canseco CL .75 .30
Don Mattingly
132 Bo Jackson CL .30 .12
Eric Davis

1987 Fleer Stickers Wax Box Cards

The bottoms of the Star Sticker wax boxes contained two different sets of four cards done in a similar format to the stickers; these cards (they are not stickers but truly cards) are numbered with the prefix S and are considered a separate set. The value of the panels uncut is slightly greater, perhaps by 25 percent greater, than the value of the individual cards cut up carefully. When cut properly, the individual cards measure standard size, 2 1/2" by 3 1/2".

Nm-Mt Ex-Mt
COMPLETE SET (8) 6.00 2.40
S1 Detroit Logo .10 .04
S2 Wade Boggs 1.50 .60
S3 Bert Blyleven .25 .10
S4 Jose Cruz .25 .10
S5 Glenn Davis .10 .04
S6 Phillies Logo .10 .04
S7 Bob Horner .10 .04
S8 Don Mattingly 4.00 1.60

1988 Fleer

This set consists of 660 standard-size cards. Cards were primarily issued in 15-card wax packs and hobby and retail factory sets. Each wax pack contained one of 26 different "Stadium Card" stickers. Card fronts feature a distinctive white background with red and blue diagonal stripes across the card. As in years past cards are organized numerically by teams and team order is based upon the previous season's record. Subsets include Specials (622-640), Rookie Pairs (641-653), and checklists (654-660). Rookie Cards in this set include Jay Bell, Ellis Burks, Ken Caminiti, Ron Gant, Tom Glavine, Mark Grace, Edgar Martinez, Jack McDowell and Matt Williams.

Nm-Mt Ex-Mt
COMPLETE SET (660) 15.00 6.00
COMP.RETAIL SET (660) 15.00 6.00
COMP.HOBBY SET (672) 15.00 6.00
1 Keith Atherton .10 .04
2 Don Baylor .15 .06
3 Juan Berenguer .10 .04
4 Bert Blyleven .15 .06
5 Tom Brunansky .10 .04
6 Randy Bush .10 .04
7 Steve Carlton .15 .06
8 Mark Davidson .10 .04
9 George Frazier .10 .04
10 Gary Gaetti .15 .06
11 Greg Gagne .10 .04
12 Dan Gladden .10 .04
13 Kent Hrbek .15 .06
14 Gene Larkin RC* .10 .04
15 Tim Laudner .10 .04
16 Steve Lombardozzi .10 .04
17 Al Newman .10 .04
18 Joe Niekro .10 .04
19 Kirby Puckett .30 .12
20 Jeff Reardon .15 .06
21A Dan Schatzeder ERR .15 .06
(Misspelled Schatzader on both sides of the card)
21B Dan Schatzeder COR .10 .04
22 Roy Smalley .10 .04
23 Mike Smithson .10 .04
24 Les Straker .10 .04
25 Frank Viola .10 .04
26 Jack Clark .15 .06
27 Vince Coleman .10 .04
28 Danny Cox .10 .04
29 Bill Dawley .10 .04
30 Ken Dayley .10 .04
31 Doug DeCinces .10 .04
32 Curt Ford .10 .04
33 Bob Forsch .10 .04
34 David Green .10 .04
35 Tom Herr .10 .04
36 Ricky Horton .10 .04
37 Lance Johnson RC .30 .12
38 Steve Lake .10 .04
39 Jim Lindeman .10 .04
40 Joe Magrane RC* .10 .04
41 Greg Mathews .10 .04
42 Willie McGee .15 .06
43 John Morris .10 .04
44 Jose Oquendo .10 .04
45 Tony Pena .10 .04
46 Terry Pendleton .15 .06
47 Ozzie Smith .50 .20
48 John Tudor .10 .04
49 Lee Tunnell .10 .04
50 Todd Worrell .15 .06
51 Doyle Alexander .10 .04
52 Dave Bergman .10 .04
53 Tom Brookens .10 .04
54 Darrell Evans .15 .06
55 Kirk Gibson .15 .06
56 Mike Heath .10 .04
57 Mike Henneman RC* .15 .06
58 Willie Hernandez .10 .04
59 Larry Herndon .10 .04
60 Eric King .10 .04
61 Chet Lemon .10 .04
62 Scott Lusader .10 .04
63 Bill Madlock .15 .06
64 Jack Morris .15 .06
65 Jim Morrison .10 .04
66 Matt Nokes RC* .10 .04
67 Dan Petry .10 .04
68A Jeff M. Robinson .20 .08
ERR, Stats for Jeff D. Robinson on card back
Born 12-13-60
68B Jeff M. Robinson .10 .04
COR, Born 12-14-61
69 Pat Sheridan .10 .04
70 Nate Snell .10 .04
71 Frank Tanana .10 .04
72 Walt Terrell .10 .04
73 Mark Thurmond .10 .04
74 Alan Trammell .20 .08
75 Lou Whitaker .15 .06
76 Mike Aldrete .10 .04
77 Bob Brenly .10 .04
78 Will Clark .30 .12
79 Chili Davis .20 .08
80 Kelly Downs .10 .04
81 Dave Dravecky .15 .06
82 Scott Garrelts .10 .04
83 Atlee Hammaker .10 .04
84 Dave Henderson .10 .04
85 Mike Krukow .10 .04
86 Mike LaCoss .10 .04
87 Craig Lefferts .10 .04
88 Jeff Leonard .10 .04
89 Candy Maldonado .10 .04
90 Eddie Milner .10 .04
91 Bob Melvin .10 .04
92 Kevin Mitchell .15 .06
93 Jon Perlman .10 .04
94 Rick Reuschel .10 .04
95 Don Robinson .10 .04
96 Chris Speier .10 .04
97 Harry Spilman .10 .04
98 Robby Thompson .10 .04
99 Jose Uribe .10 .04
100 Mark Wasinger .10 .04
101 Matt Williams RC 1.50 .60
102 Jesse Barfield .10 .04
103 George Bell .10 .04
104 Juan Beniquez .10 .04
105 John Cerutti .10 .04
106 Jim Clancy .10 .04
107 Rob Ducey .10 .04
108 Mark Eichhorn .10 .04
109 Tony Fernandez .10 .04
110 Cecil Fielder .20 .08
111 Kelly Gruber .10 .04
112 Tom Henke .10 .04
113A Garth Iorg ERR .20 .08
(Misspelled Iorq on card front)
113B Garth Iorg COR .10 .04
114 Jimmy Key .15 .06
115 Rick Leach .10 .04
116 Manny Lee .10 .04
117 Nelson Liriano .10 .04
118 Fred McGriff .30 .12
119 Lloyd Moseby .10 .04
120 Rance Mulliniks .10 .04
121 Jeff Musselman .10 .04
122 Jose Nunez .10 .04
123 Dave Stieb .10 .04
124 Willie Upshaw .10 .04
125 Duane Ward .10 .04
126 Ernie Whitt .10 .04
127 Rick Aguilera .15 .06
128 Wally Backman .10 .04
129 Mark Carreon RC .15 .06
130 Gary Carter .20 .08
131 David Cone .15 .06
132 Ron Darling .10 .04
133 Len Dykstra .15 .06
134 Sid Fernandez .10 .04
135 Dwight Gooden .20 .08
136 Keith Hernandez .20 .08
137 Gregg Jefferies RC .30 .12
138 Howard Johnson .10 .04
139 Terry Leach .10 .04
140 Barry Lyons .10 .04
141 Dave Magadan .10 .04
142 Roger McDowell .10 .04
143 Kevin McReynolds .10 .04
144 Keith A. Miller RC .10 .04
145 John Mitchell RC .10 .04
146 Randy Myers .20 .08
147 Bob Ojeda .10 .04
148 Jesse Orosco .10 .04
149 Rafael Santana .10 .04
150 Doug Sisk .10 .04
151 Darryl Strawberry .20 .08
152 Tim Teufel .10 .04
153 Gene Walter .10 .04
154 Mookie Wilson .15 .06
155 Jay Aldrich .10 .04
156 Chris Bosio .10 .04
157 Glenn Braggs .10 .04
158 Greg Brock .10 .04
159 Juan Castillo .10 .04
160 Mark Clear .10 .04
161 Cecil Cooper .15 .06
162 Chuck Crim .10 .04
163 Rob Deer .10 .04
164 Mike Felder .10 .04
165 Jim Gantner .10 .04
166 Ted Higuera .10 .04
167 Steve Kiefer .10 .04
168 Rick Manning .10 .04
169 Paul Molitor .20 .08
170 Juan Nieves .10 .04
171 Dan Plesac .10 .04
172 Earnest Riles .10 .04
173 Bill Schroeder .10 .04
174 Steve Stanicek .10 .04
175 B.J. Surhoff .15 .06
176 Dale Sveum .10 .04
177 Bill Wegman .10 .04
178 Robin Yount .50 .20
179 Hubie Brooks .10 .04
180 Tim Burke .10 .04
181 Casey Candaele .10 .04
182 Mike Fitzgerald .10 .04
183 Tom Foley .10 .04
184 Andres Galarraga .15 .06
185 Neal Heaton .10 .04
186 Wallace Johnson .10 .04
187 Vance Law .10 .04
188 Dennis Martinez .15 .06
189 Bob McClure .10 .04
190 Andy McGaffigan .10 .04
191 Reid Nichols .10 .04
192 Pascual Perez .10 .04
193 Tim Raines .15 .06
194 Jeff Reed .10 .04
195 Bob Sebra .10 .04
196 Bryn Smith .10 .04
197 Randy St.Claire .10 .04
198 Tim Wallach .10 .04
199 Mitch Webster .10 .04
200 Herm Winningham .10 .04
201 Floyd Youmans .10 .04
202 Brad Arnsberg .10 .04
203 Rick Cerone .10 .04
204 Pat Clements .10 .04
205 Henry Cotto .10 .04
206 Mike Easler .10 .04
207 Ron Guidry .15 .06
208 Bill Gullickson .10 .04
209 Rickey Henderson .30 .12
210 Charles Hudson .10 .04
211 Tommy John .15 .06
212 Roberto Kelly RC .30 .12
213 Ron Kittle .10 .04
214 Don Mattingly 1.00 .40
215 Bobby Meacham .10 .04
216 Mike Pagliarulo .10 .04
217 Dan Pasqua .10 .04
218 Willie Randolph .15 .06
219 Rick Rhoden .10 .04
220 Dave Righetti .10 .04
221 Jerry Royster .10 .04
222 Tim Stoddard .10 .04
223 Wayne Tolleson .10 .04
224 Gary Ward .10 .04
225 Claudell Washington .10 .04
226 Dave Winfield .15 .06
227 Buddy Bell .15 .06
228 Tom Browning .10 .04
229 Dave Concepcion .15 .06
230 Kal Daniels .10 .04
231 Eric Davis .15 .06
232 Bo Diaz .10 .04
233 Nick Esasky .10 .04
(Has a dollar sign before '87 SB totals)
234 John Franco .15 .06
235 Guy Hoffman .10 .04
236 Tom Hume .10 .04
237 Tracy Jones .10 .04
238 Bill Landrum .10 .04
239 Barry Larkin .30 .12
240 Terry McGriff .10 .04
241 Rob Murphy .10 .04
242 Ron Oester .10 .04
243 Dave Parker .15 .06
244 Pat Perry .10 .04
245 Ted Power .10 .04
246 Dennis Rasmussen .10 .04
247 Ron Robinson .10 .04
248 Kurt Stillwell .10 .04
249 Jeff Treadway RC .10 .04
250 Frank Williams .10 .04
251 Steve Balboni .10 .04
252 Bud Black .10 .04
253 Thad Bosley .10 .04
254 George Brett .75 .30
255 John Davis .10 .04
256 Steve Farr .10 .04
257 Gene Garber .10 .04
258 Jerry Don Gleaton .10 .04
259 Mark Gubicza .10 .04
260 Bo Jackson .30 .12
261 Danny Jackson .10 .04
262 Ross Jones .10 .04
263 Charlie Leibrandt .10 .04
264 Bill Pecota RC* .10 .04
265 Melido Perez RC .10 .04
266 Jamie Quirk .10 .04
267 Dan Quisenberry .10 .04
268 Bret Saberhagen .15 .06
269 Angel Salazar .10 .04
270 Kevin Seitzer UER .15 .06
(Wrong birth year)
271 Danny Tartabull .10 .04
272 Gary Thurman .10 .04
273 Frank White .15 .06
274 Willie Wilson .10 .04
275 Tony Bernazard .10 .04
276 Jose Canseco .30 .12
277 Mike Davis .10 .04
278 Storm Davis .10 .04
279 Dennis Eckersley .15 .06
280 Alfredo Griffin .10 .04
281 Rick Honeycutt .10 .04
282 Jay Howell .10 .04
283 Reggie Jackson .20 .08
284 Dennis Lamp .10 .04
285 Carney Lansford .15 .06
286 Mark McGwire 2.50 1.00
287 Dwayne Murphy .10 .04
288 Gene Nelson .10 .04
289 Steve Ontiveros .10 .04
290 Tony Phillips .10 .04
291 Eric Plunk .10 .04
292 Luis Polonia RC* .10 .04
293 Rick Rodriguez .10 .04
294 Terry Steinbach .15 .06
295 Dave Stewart .15 .06
296 Curt Young .10 .04
297 Luis Aguayo .10 .04
298 Steve Bedrosian .10 .04
299 Jeff Calhoun .10 .04
300 Don Carman .10 .04
301 Todd Frohwirth .10 .04
302 Greg Gross .10 .04
303 Kevin Gross .10 .04
304 Von Hayes .10 .04
305 Keith Hughes .10 .04
306 Mike Jackson RC* .15 .06
307 Chris James .10 .04
308 Steve Jeltz .10 .04
309 Mike Maddux .10 .04
310 Lance Parrish .10 .04
311 Shane Rawley .10 .04
312 Wally Ritchie .10 .04
313 Bruce Ruffin .10 .04
314 Juan Samuel .10 .04
315 Mike Schmidt .75 .30
316 Rick Schu .10 .04
317 Jeff Stone .10 .04
318 Kent Tekulve .10 .04
319 Milt Thompson .10 .04
320 Glenn Wilson .10 .04
321 Rafael Belliard .10 .04
322 Barry Bonds 3.00 1.20
323 Bobby Bonilla UER .15 .06
(Wrong birth year)
324 Sid Bream .10 .04
325 John Cangelosi .10 .04
326 Mike Diaz .10 .04
327 Doug Drabek .10 .04
328 Mike Dunne .10 .04
329 Brian Fisher .10 .04
330 Brett Gideon .10 .04
331 Terry Harper .10 .04
332 Bob Kipper .10 .04
333 Mike LaValliere .10 .04
334 Jose Lind RC .10 .04
335 Junior Ortiz .10 .04
336 Vicente Palacios .10 .04
337 Bob Patterson .10 .04
338 Al Pedrique .10 .04
339 R.J. Reynolds .10 .04
340 John Smiley RC* .15 .06
341 Andy Van Slyke UER .15 .06
(Wrong batting and throwing listed)
342 Bob Walk .10 .04
343 Marty Barrett .10 .04
344 Todd Benzinger RC* .10 .04
345 Wade Boggs .20 .08
346 Tom Bolton .10 .04
347 Oil Can Boyd .10 .04
348 Ellis Burks RC .75 .30
349 Roger Clemens .75 .30
350 Steve Crawford .10 .04
351 Dwight Evans .15 .06
352 Wes Gardner .10 .04
353 Rich Gedman .10 .04
354 Mike Greenwell .10 .04
355 Sam Horn RC .10 .04
356 Bruce Hurst .10 .04

357 John Marzano .10 .04
358 Al Nipper .10 .04
359 Spike Owen .10 .04
360 Jody Reed RC .15 .06
361 Jim Rice .15 .06
362 Ed Romero .10 .04
363 Kevin Romine .10 .04
364 Joe Sambito .10 .04
365 Calvin Schiraldi .10 .04
366 Jeff Sellers .10 .04
367 Bob Stanley .10 .04
368 Scott Bankhead .10 .04
369 Phil Bradley .10 .04
370 Scott Bradley .10 .04
371 Mickey Brantley .10 .04
372 Mike Campbell .10 .04
373 Alvin Davis .10 .04
374 Lee Guetterman .10 .04
375 Dave Hengel .10 .04
376 Mike Kingery .10 .04
377 Mark Langston .10 .04
378 Edgar Martinez RC 3.00 1.20
379 Mike Moore .10 .04
380 Mike Morgan .10 .04
381 John Moses .10 .04
382 Donell Nixon .10 .04
383 Edwin Nunez .10 .04
384 Ken Phelps .10 .04
385 Jim Presley .10 .04
386 Rey Quinones .10 .04
387 Jerry Reed .10 .04
388 Harold Reynolds .15 .06
389 Dave Valle .10 .04
390 Bill Wilkinson .10 .04
391 Harold Baines .15 .06
392 Floyd Bannister .10 .04
393 Daryl Boston .10 .04
394 Ivan Calderon .10 .04
395 Jose DeLeon .10 .04
396 Richard Dotson .10 .04
397 Carlton Fisk .20 .08
398 Ozzie Guillen .10 .04
399 Ron Hassey .10 .04
400 Donnie Hill .10 .04
401 Bob James .10 .04
402 Dave LaPoint .10 .04
403 Bill Lindsey .10 .04
404 Bill Long .10 .04
405 Steve Lyons .10 .04
406 Fred Manrique .10 .04
407 Jack McDowell RC .30 .12
408 Gary Redus .10 .04
409 Ray Searage .10 .04
410 Bobby Thigpen .10 .04
411 Greg Walker .10 .04
412 Ken Williams RC .10 .04
413 Jim Winn .10 .04
414 Jody Davis .10 .04
415 Andre Dawson .15 .06
416 Brian Dayett .10 .04
417 Bob Dernier .10 .04
418 Frank DiPino .10 .04
419 Shawon Dunston .10 .04
420 Leon Durham .10 .04
421 Les Lancaster .10 .04
422 Ed Lynch .10 .04
423 Greg Maddux 1.50 .60
424 Dave Martinez .10 .04
425A Keith Moreland ERR 1.50 .60
(Photo actually Jody Davis)
425B Keith Moreland COR .15 .06
(Bat on shoulder)
426 Jamie Moyer .30 .12
427 Jerry Mumphrey .10 .04
428 Paul Noce .10 .04
429 Rafael Palmeiro .60 .24
430 Wade Rowdon .10 .04
431 Ryne Sandberg .60 .24
432 Scott Sanderson .10 .04
433 Lee Smith .15 .06
434 Jim Sundberg .10 .04
435 Rick Sutcliffe .15 .06
436 Manny Trillo .10 .04
437 Juan Agosto .10 .04
438 Larry Andersen .10 .04
439 Alan Ashby .10 .04
440 Kevin Bass .10 .04
441 Ken Caminiti RC .75 .30
442 Rocky Childress .10 .04
443 Jose Cruz .10 .04
444 Danny Darwin .10 .04
445 Glenn Davis .10 .04
446 Jim Deshaies .10 .04
447 Bill Doran .10 .04
448 Ty Gainey .10 .04
449 Billy Hatcher .10 .04
450 Jeff Heathcock .10 .04
451 Bob Knepper .10 .04
452 Rob Mallicoat .10 .04
453 Dave Meads .10 .04
454 Craig Reynolds .10 .04
455 Nolan Ryan 1.50 .60
456 Mike Scott .10 .04
457 Dave Smith .10 .04
458 Denny Walling .10 .04
459 Robbie Wine .10 .04
460 Gerald Young .10 .04
461 Bob Brower .10 .04
462A Jerry Browne ERR 1.50 .60
(Photo actually Bob Brower, white player)
462B Jerry Browne COR .15 .06
(Black player)
463 Steve Buechele .10 .04
464 Edwin Correa .10 .04
465 Cecil Espy .10 .04
466 Scott Fletcher .10 .04
467 Jose Guzman .10 .04
468 Greg Harris .10 .04
469 Charlie Hough .15 .06
470 Pete Incaviglia .10 .04
471 Paul Kilgus .10 .04
472 Mike Loynd .10 .04
473 Oddibe McDowell .10 .04
474 Dale Mohorcic .10 .04
475 Pete O'Brien .10 .04
476 Larry Parrish .10 .04
477 Geno Petralli .10 .04
478 Jeff Russell .10 .04
479 Ruben Sierra .10 .04
480 Mike Stanley .15 .06
481 Curtis Wilkerson .10 .04
482 Mitch Williams .10 .04
483 Bobby Witt .10 .04
484 Tony Armas .10 .04
485 Bob Boone .15 .06
486 Bill Buckner .15 .06
487 DeWayne Buice .10 .04
488 Brian Downing .10 .04
489 Chuck Finley .20 .08
490 Willie Fraser UER .10 .04
(Wrong bio stats, for George Hendrick)
491 Jack Howell .10 .04
492 Ruppert Jones .10 .04
493 Wally Joyner .20 .08
494 Jack Lazorko .10 .04
495 Gary Lucas .10 .04
496 Kirk McCaskill .10 .04
497 Mark McLemore .10 .04
498 Darrell Miller .10 .04
499 Greg Minton .10 .04
500 Donnie Moore .10 .04
501 Gus Polidor .10 .04
502 Johnny Ray .10 .04
503 Mark Ryal .10 .04
504 Dick Schofield .10 .04
505 Don Sutton .30 .12
506 Devon White .15 .06
507 Mike Witt .10 .04
508 Dave Anderson .10 .04
509 Tim Belcher .15 .06
510 Ralph Bryant .10 .04
511 Tim Crews RC .10 .04
512 Mike Devereaux RC .15 .06
513 Mariano Duncan .10 .04
514 Pedro Guerrero .10 .04
515 Jeff Hamilton .10 .04
516 Mickey Hatcher .10 .04
517 Brad Havens .10 .04
518 Orel Hershiser .15 .06
519 Shawn Hillegas .10 .04
520 Ken Howell .10 .04
521 Tim Leary .10 .04
522 Mike Marshall .10 .04
523 Steve Sax .10 .04
524 Mike Scioscia .10 .04
525 Mike Sharperson .10 .04
526 John Shelby .10 .04
527 Franklin Stubbs .10 .04
528 Fernando Valenzuela .15 .06
529 Bob Welch .10 .04
530 Matt Young .10 .04
531 Jim Acker .10 .04
532 Paul Assenmacher .10 .04
533 Jeff Blauser RC .30 .12
534 Joe Boever .10 .04
535 Martin Clary .10 .04
536 Kevin Coffman .10 .04
537 Jeff Dedmon .10 .04
538 Ron Gant RC .75 .30
539 Tom Glavine RC 3.00 1.20
540 Ken Griffey .15 .06
541 Albert Hall .10 .04
542 Glenn Hubbard .10 .04
543 Dion James .10 .04
544 Dale Murphy .30 .12
545 Ken Oberkfell .10 .04
546 David Palmer .10 .04
547 Gerald Perry .10 .04
548 Charlie Puleo .10 .04
549 Ted Simmons .15 .06
550 Zane Smith .10 .04
551 Andres Thomas .10 .04
552 Ozzie Virgil .10 .04
553 Don Aase .10 .04
554 Jeff Ballard .10 .04
555 Eric Bell .10 .04
556 Mike Boddicker .10 .04
557 Ken Dixon .10 .04
558 Jim Dwyer .10 .04
559 Ken Gerhart .10 .04
560 Rene Gonzales RC .10 .04
561 Mike Griffin .10 .04
562 John Habyan UER .10 .04
(Misspelled Hayban on both sides of card)
563 Terry Kennedy .10 .04
564 Ray Knight .10 .04
565 Lee Lacy .10 .04
566 Fred Lynn .10 .04
567 Eddie Murray .30 .12
568 Tom Niedenfuer .10 .04
569 Bill Ripken RC* .10 .04
570 Cal Ripken 1.25 .50
571 Dave Schmidt .10 .04
572 Larry Sheets .10 .04
573 Pete Stanicek .10 .04
574 Mark Williamson .10 .04
575 Mike Young .10 .04
576 Shawn Abner .10 .04
577 Greg Booker .10 .04
578 Chris Brown .10 .04
579 Keith Comstock .10 .04
580 Joey Cora RC .30 .12
581 Mark Davis .10 .04
582 Tim Flannery .20 .08
(With surfboard)
583 Goose Gossage .20 .08
584 Mark Grant .10 .04
585 Tony Gwynn .50 .20
586 Andy Hawkins .10 .04
587 Stan Jefferson .10 .04
588 Jimmy Jones .10 .04
589 John Kruk .15 .06
590 Shane Mack .10 .04
591 Carmelo Martinez .10 .04
592 Lance McCullers UER .10 .04
(6'11" tall)
593 Eric Nolte .10 .04
594 Randy Ready .10 .04
595 Luis Salazar .10 .04
596 Benito Santiago .20 .08
597 Eric Show .10 .04
598 Garry Templeton .10 .04
599 Ed Whitson .10 .04
600 Scott Bailes .10 .04
601 Chris Bando .10 .04
602 Jay Bell RC .75 .30
603 Brett Butler .15 .06
604 Tom Candiotti .10 .04
605 Joe Carter .30 .12
606 Carmen Castillo .10 .04
607 Brian Dorsett .10 .04
608 John Farrell RC .10 .04
609 Julio Franco .10 .04
610 Mel Hall .10 .04
611 Tommy Hinzo .10 .04
612 Brook Jacoby .10 .04
613 Doug Jones RC .30 .12
614 Ken Schrom .10 .04
615 Cory Snyder .10 .04
616 Sammy Stewart .10 .04
617 Greg Swindell .10 .04
618 Pat Tabler .10 .04
619 Ed VandeBerg .10 .04
620 Eddie Williams RC .15 .06
621 Rich Yett .10 .04
622 Wally Joyner .15 .06
Cory Snyder
623 George Bell .10 .04
Pedro Guerrero
624 Mark McGwire 1.00 .40
Jose Canseco
625 Dave Righetti .10 .04
Dan Plesac
626 Bret Saberhagen .15 .06
Mike Witt
Jack Morris
627 John Franco .10 .04
Steve Bedrosian
628 Ozzie Smith .30 .12
Ryne Sandberg
629 Mark McGwire HL 1.25 .50
630 Mike Greenwell .30 .12
Ellis Burks
Todd Benzinger
631 Tony Gwynn .20 .08
Tim Raines
632 Mike Scott .15 .06
Orel Hershiser
633 Pat Tabler 1.25 .50
Mark McGwire
634 Tony Gwynn .20 .08
Vince Coleman
635 Tony Fernandez .50 .20
Cal Ripken
Alan Trammell
636 Mike Schmidt .30 .12
Gary Carter
637 Darryl Strawberry .15 .06
Eric Davis
638 Matt Nokes .20 .08
Kirby Puckett
639 Keith Hernandez .20 .08
Dale Murphy
640 Billy Ripken .75 .30
Cal Ripken
641 Mark Grace RC and 3.00 1.20
Darrin Jackson
642 Damon Berryhill RC .30 .12
Jeff Montgomery RC
643 Felix Fermin and .10 .04
Jesse Reid
644 Greg Myers RC and .10 .04
Greg Tabor
645 Joey Meyer and .10 .04
Jim Eppard
646 Adam Peterson .50 .20
Randy Velarde RC
647 Pete Smith and .15 .06
Chris Gwynn RC
648 Tom Newell and .10 .04
Greg Jelks
649 Mario Diaz RC .10 .04
Clay Parker
650 Jack Savage and .10 .04
Todd Simmons
651 John Burkett RC and .30 .12
Kirt Manwaring
652 Dave Otto RC and .40 .16
Walt Weiss
653 Jeff King RC and .15 .06
Randell Byers
654 CL: Twins/Cards .10 .04
Tigers/Giants UER
(90 Bob Melvin, 91 Eddie Milner)
655 CL: Blue Jays/Mets .10 .04
Brewers/Expos UER
(Mets listed before Blue Jays on card)
656 CL: Yankees/Reds .10 .04
Royals/A's
657 CL: Phillies/Pirates .10 .04
Red Sox/Mariners
658 CL: White Sox/Cubs .10 .04
Astros/Rangers
659 CL: Angels/Dodgers .10 .04
Braves/Orioles
660 CL: Padres/Indians .10 .04
Rookies/Specials

1988 Fleer Glossy

This 660 card set is a parallel to the regular Fleer issue. The cards are the same as the regular issue except for the glossy sheen on the front. The cards (along with the 12-card World Series insert set) were issued in a factory tin distributed exclusively through hobby dealers. Since many dealers had problems selling their 1987 sets, production was reduced for the 1988 issues. It is believed that between 40 and 60 thousand of these sets were produced.

Nm-Mt Ex-Mt
COMP.FACT.SET (672) 40.00 16.00
*STARS: .6X TO 1.5X BASIC CARDS
*ROOKIES: 1.5X TO 4X BASIC CARDS

1988 Fleer All-Stars

These 12 standard-size cards were inserted randomly in wax and cello packs of the 1988 Fleer set. The cards show the player silhouetted against a light green background with dark green stripes. The player's name, team, and position are printed in yellow at the bottom of the obverse. The card backs are done predominantly in green, white, and black. The players are the "best" at each position, three pitchers, eight position players, and a designated hitter.

Nm-Mt Ex-Mt
COMPLETE SET (12) 6.00 2.40
1 Matt Nokes .40 .16
2 Tom Henke .40 .16
3 Ted Higuera .40 .16
4 Roger Clemens 3.00 1.20
5 George Bell .40 .16
6 Andre Dawson .60 .24
7 Eric Davis .60 .24
8 Wade Boggs .75 .30
9 Alan Trammell .75 .30
10 Juan Samuel .40 .16
11 Jack Clark .60 .24
12 Paul Molitor .75 .30

1988 Fleer Headliners

This six-card standard-size set was distributed one per rack pack. The obverse features the player photo superimposed on a gray newsprint background. The cards are printed in red, black, and white on the back describing why that particular player made headlines the previous season. The set is sequenced in alphabetical order.

Nm-Mt Ex-Mt
COMPLETE SET (6) 6.00 2.40
1 Don Mattingly 1.25 .50
2 Mark McGwire 4.00 1.60
3 Jack Morris .20 .08
4 Darryl Strawberry .25 .10
5 Dwight Gooden .25 .10
6 Tim Raines .20 .08

1988 Fleer Wax Box Cards

The cards in this 16-card set measure the standard size. Cards have essentially the same design as the 1988 Fleer regular issue set. The cards were printed on the bottoms of the regular issue wax pack boxes. These 16 cards (C1 to C16) are considered a separate set in their own right and are not typically included in a complete set of the regular issue 1988 Fleer cards. The value of the panel uncut is slightly greater, perhaps by 25 percent greater, than the value of the individual cards cut up carefully.

Nm-Mt Ex-Mt
COMPLETE SET (16) 8.00 3.20
C1 Cardinals Logo .10 .04
C2 Dwight Evans .25 .10
C3 Andres Galarraga 1.00 .40
C4 Wally Joyner .25 .10
C5 Twins Logo .10 .04
C6 Dale Murphy 1.00 .40
C7 Kirby Puckett 1.25 .50
C8 Shane Rawley .10 .04
C9 Giants Logo .10 .04
C10 Ryne Sandberg 2.50 1.00
C11 Mike Schmidt 1.25 .50
C12 Kevin Seitzer .10 .04
C13 Tigers Logo .10 .04
C14 Dave Stewart .25 .10
C15 Tim Wallach .10 .04
C16 Todd Worrell .25 .10

1988 Fleer World Series

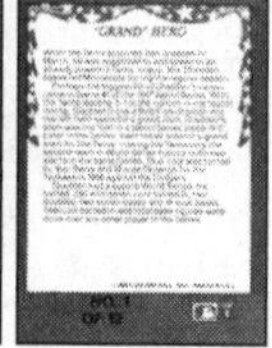

This 12-card standard-size set features highlights of the previous year's World Series between the Minnesota Twins and the St. Louis Cardinals. The sets were packaged as a complete set insert with the collated sets (of the 1988 Fleer regular issue) which were sold by Fleer directly to hobby card dealers; they were not available in the general retail candy store outlets. The set numbering is essentially in chronological order of the events from the immediate past World Series.

Nm-Mt Ex-Mt
COMPLETE SET (12) 2.00 .80
1 Dan Gladden .10 .04
2 Randy Bush .10 .04
3 John Tudor .10 .04
4 Ozzie Smith .50 .20
5 Todd Worrell .10 .04
Tony Pena
6 Vince Coleman .10 .04
7 Tom Herr .10 .04
Dan Driessen
8 Kirby Puckett .30 .12
9 Kent Hrbek .15 .06
10 Tom Herr .10 .04
11 Don Baylor .15 .06
12 Frank Viola .10 .04

1988 Fleer Update

This 132-card standard-size set was distributed exclusively in factory set form in a red, white and blue, cellophane-wrapped box through hobby dealers. In addition to the complete set of 132 cards, the box also contained 25 Team Logo stickers. The cards look very similar to the 1988 Fleer regular issue except for the U-prefixed numbering on back. Cards are ordered alphabetically by player's last name. This was the first Fleer Update set to adopt the Fleer "alphabetical within team" numbering system. The key extended Rookie Cards in this set are Roberto Alomar, Craig Biggio Al Leiter, John Smoltz and David Wells.

Nm-Mt Ex-Mt
COMP.FACT.SET (132) 8.00 3.20
1 Jose Bautista XRC .10 .04
2 Joe Orsulak .10 .04
3 Doug Sisk .10 .04
4 Craig Worthington .10 .04
5 Mike Boddicker .10 .04
6 Rick Cerone .10 .04
7 Larry Parrish .10 .04
8 Lee Smith .20 .08
9 Mike Smithson .10 .04
10 John Trautwein .10 .04
11 Sherman Corbett .10 .04
12 Chili Davis .30 .12
13 Jim Eppard .10 .04
14 Bryan Harvey XRC .20 .08
15 John Davis .10 .04
16 Dave Gallagher .10 .04
17 Ricky Horton .10 .04
18 Dan Pasqua .10 .04
19 Melido Perez .10 .04
20 Jose Segura .10 .04
21 Andy Allanson .10 .04
22 Jon Perlman .10 .04
23 Domingo Ramos .10 .04
24 Rick Rodriguez .10 .04
25 Willie Upshaw .10 .04
26 Paul Gibson .10 .04
27 Don Heinkel .10 .04
28 Ray Knight .10 .04
29 Gary Pettis .10 .04
30 Luis Salazar .10 .04
31 Mike Macfarlane XRC .10 .04
32 Jeff Montgomery .50 .20
33 Ted Power .10 .04
34 Israel Sanchez .10 .04
35 Kurt Stillwell .10 .04
36 Pat Tabler .10 .04
37 Don August .10 .04
38 Darryl Hamilton XRC .20 .08
39 Jeff Leonard .10 .04
40 Joey Meyer .10 .04
41 Allan Anderson .10 .04
42 Brian Harper .10 .04
43 Tom Herr .10 .04
44 Charlie Lea .10 .04
45 John Moses .10 .04
(Listed as Hohn on checklist card)
46 John Candelaria .10 .04
47 Jack Clark .20 .08
48 Richard Dotson .10 .04
49 Al Leiter XRC* .75 .30
50 Rafael Santana .10 .04
51 Don Slaught .10 .04
52 Todd Burns .10 .04
53 Dave Henderson .10 .04
54 Doug Jennings .10 .04
55 Dave Parker .20 .08
56 Walt Weiss .30 .12
57 Bob Welch .10 .04
58 Henry Cotto .10 .04
59 Mario Diaz UER .10 .04
(Listed as Marion on card front)
60 Mike Jackson .20 .08
61 Bill Swift .10 .04
62 Jose Cecena .10 .04
63 Ray Hayward .10 .04
64 Jim Steels UER .10 .04
(Listed as Jim Steele on card back)
65 Pat Borders XRC .20 .08
66 Sil Campusano .10 .04
67 Mike Flanagan .10 .04
68 Todd Stottlemyre XRC .50 .20
69 David Wells XRC 1.25 .50
70 Jose Alvarez XRC .10 .04
71 Paul Runge .10 .04
72 Cesar Jimenez .10 .04
(Card was intended for German Jiminez, it's his photo)
73 Pete Smith .10 .04
74 John Smoltz XRC 3.00 1.20
75 Damon Berryhill .10 .04
76 Goose Gossage .30 .12
77 Mark Grace 1.50 .60
78 Darrin Jackson .10 .04
79 Vance Law .10 .04
80 Jeff Pico .10 .04
81 Gary Varsho .10 .04
82 Tim Birtsas .10 .04
83 Rob Dibble XRC .75 .30
84 Danny Jackson .10 .04
85 Paul O'Neill .30 .12
86 Jose Rijo .10 .04

Card	Nm-Mt	Ex-Mt
87 Chris Sabo XRC	.20	.08
88 John Fishel	.10	.04
89 Craig Biggio XRC	2.00	.80
90 Terry Puhl	.10	.04
91 Rafael Ramirez	.10	.04
92 Louie Meadows	.10	.04
93 Kirk Gibson	.50	.20
94 Alfredo Griffin	.10	.04
95 Jay Howell	.10	.04
96 Jesse Orosco	.10	.04
97 Alejandro Pena	.10	.04
98 Tracy Woodson XRC*	.10	.04
99 John Dopson	.10	.04
100 Brian Holman XRC	.10	.04
101 Rex Hudler	.10	.04
102 Jeff Parrett	.10	.04
103 Nelson Santovenia	.10	.04
104 Kevin Elster	.10	.04
105 Jeff Innis	.10	.04
106 Mackey Sasser XRC*	.10	.04
107 Phil Bradley	.10	.04
108 Danny Clay	.10	.04
109 Greg A.Harris	.10	.04
110 Ricky Jordan XRC	.20	.08
111 David Palmer	.10	.04
112 Jim Gott	.10	.04
113 Tommy Gregg UER (Photo actually Randy Milligan)	.10	.04
114 Barry Jones	.10	.04
115 Randy Milligan XRC*	.10	.04
116 Luis Alicea XRC	.20	.08
117 Tom Brunansky	.10	.04
118 John Costello	.10	.04
119 Jose DeLeon	.10	.04
120 Bob Horner	.10	.04
121 Scott Terry	.10	.04
122 Roberto Alomar XRC	3.00	1.20
123 Dave Leiper	.10	.04
124 Keith Moreland	.10	.04
125 Mark Parent	.10	.04
126 Dennis Rasmussen	.10	.04
127 Randy Bockus	.10	.04
128 Brett Butler	.20	.08
129 Donell Nixon	.10	.04
130 Earnest Riles	.10	.04
131 Roger Samuels	.10	.04
132 Checklist U1-U132	.10	.04

1988 Fleer Update Glossy

This 132 card set is a parallel to the regular Fleer Update issue. Except for a glossy sheen on the front, the cards are identical to the regular Fleer issue. The cards were issued through hobby dealers in a special tin box. The cards are not as plentiful as the regular Fleer update set. Similar to the regular Glossy set, it is believed that between 40 and 60 thousand of these sets were produced.

	Nm-Mt	Ex-Mt
COMP.FACT.SET (132)	25.00	10.00

*STARS: 1X TO 2.5X BASIC CARDS ...
*ROOKIES: 1.25X TO 3X BASIC CARDS

1988 Fleer Award Winners

This small set of 44 standard-size cards was produced for 7-Eleven stores by Fleer. The cards feature full color fronts and red, white, and blue backs. The card fronts are distinguished by the red, white, and blue frame around the player's full-color photo. The box for the cards describes the set as the "1988 Limited Edition Baseball Award Winners." The checklist for the set is given on the back of the set box. The card numbering is in alphabetical order by player's name.

	Nm-Mt	Ex-Mt
COMP.FACT SET (44)	8.00	3.20
1 Steve Bedrosian	.05	.02
2 George Bell	.05	.02
3 Wade Boggs	.40	.16
4 Jose Canseco	.40	.16
5 Will Clark	.50	.20
6 Roger Clemens	.60	.24
7 Kal Daniels	.05	.02
8 Eric Davis	.10	.04
9 Andre Dawson	.30	.12
10 Mike Dunne	.05	.02
11 Dwight Evans	.10	.04
12 Carlton Fisk	.40	.16
13 Julio Franco	.05	.02
14 Dwight Gooden	.10	.04
15 Pedro Guerrero	.05	.02
16 Tony Gwynn	.75	.30
17 Orel Hershiser	.10	.04
18 Tom Henke	.05	.02
19 Ted Higuera	.05	.02
20 Charlie Hough	.10	.04
21 Wally Joyner	.10	.04
22 Jimmy Key	.10	.04
23 Don Mattingly	.75	.30
24 Mark McGwire	1.25	.50
25 Paul Molitor	.50	.20
26 Jack Morris	.10	.04
27 Dale Murphy	.30	.12
28 Terry Pendleton	.10	.04
29 Kirby Puckett	.40	.16
30 Tim Raines	.10	.04
31 Jeff Reardon	.10	.04
32 Harold Reynolds	.10	.04
33 Dave Righetti	.05	.02
34 Benito Santiago	.10	.04
35 Mike Schmidt	.50	.20
36 Mike Scott	.05	.02
37 Kevin Seitzer	.10	.04
38 Larry Sheets	.05	.02
39 Ozzie Smith	.75	.30
40 Darryl Strawberry	.10	.04
41 Rick Sutcliffe	.05	.02
42 Danny Tartabull	.05	.02
43 Alan Trammell	.20	.08
44 Tim Wallach	.05	.02

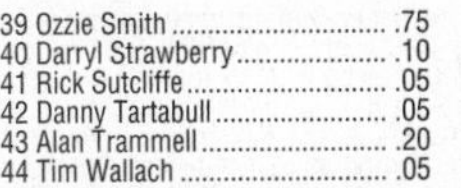

1988 Fleer Baseball All-Stars

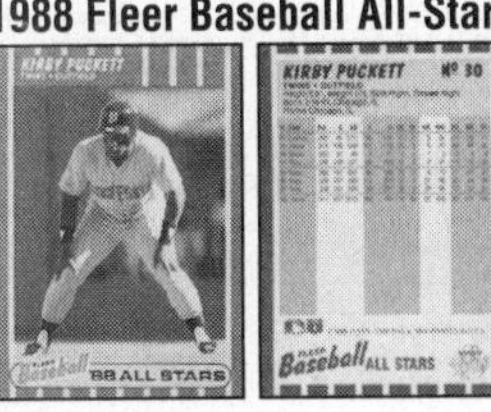

This small boxed set of 44 standard-size cards was produced exclusively for Ben Franklin Stores. The cards feature full color fronts and white and blue backs. The card fronts are distinguished by the yellow and blue striped background behind the player's full-color photo. The box for the cards describes the set as the "1988 Fleer Baseball All-Stars." The checklist for the set is given on the back of the set box. The card numbering is in alphabetical order by player's name.

	Nm-Mt	Ex-Mt
COMP.FACT SET (44)	6.00	2.40
1 George Bell	.05	.02
2 Wade Boggs	.40	.16
3 Bobby Bonilla	.10	.04
4 George Brett	.50	.20
5 Jose Canseco	.40	.16
6 Jack Clark	.10	.04
7 Will Clark	.50	.20
8 Roger Clemens	.75	.30
9 Eric Davis	.10	.04
10 Andre Dawson	.20	.08
11 Julio Franco	.05	.02
12 Dwight Gooden	.10	.04
13 Tony Gwynn	.75	.30
14 Orel Hershiser	.10	.04
15 Teddy Higuera	.05	.02
16 Charlie Hough	.10	.04
17 Kent Hrbek	.10	.04
18 Bruce Hurst	.05	.02
19 Wally Joyner	.10	.04
20 Mark Langston	.05	.02
21 Dave LaPoint	.05	.02
22 Candy Maldonado	.05	.02
23 Don Mattingly	.75	.30
24 Roger McDowell	.05	.02
25 Mark McGwire	1.25	.50
26 Jack Morris	.10	.04
27 Dale Murphy	.20	.08
28 Eddie Murray	.40	.16
29 Matt Nokes	.05	.02
30 Kirby Puckett	.40	.16
31 Tim Raines	.10	.04
32 Willie Randolph	.10	.04
33 Jeff Reardon	.10	.04
34 Nolan Ryan	1.50	.60
35 Juan Samuel	.05	.02
36 Mike Schmidt	.40	.16
37 Mike Scott	.05	.02
38 Kevin Seitzer	.10	.04
39 Ozzie Smith	.75	.30
40 Darryl Strawberry	.10	.04
41 Rick Sutcliffe	.05	.02
42 Alan Trammell	.15	.06
43 Tim Wallach	.05	.02
44 Dave Winfield	.40	.16

1988 Fleer Baseball MVP's

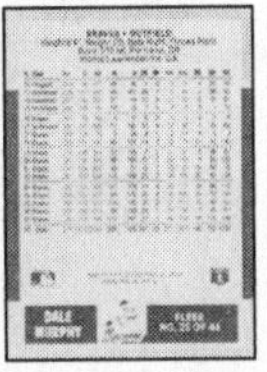

This small 44-card boxed standard-size set was produced by Fleer for distribution by the Toys'r'Us stores. The cards feature full color fronts. The set is titled "Baseball MVP." Each individual boxed set includes the 44 cards and six logo stickers. The checklist for the set is found on the back panel of the box. The card fronts have a vanilla-yellow and blue border. The box refers to Toys'r'Us but there is no mention of Toys'r'Us anywhere on the cards themselves. The card numbering is in alphabetical order by player's name.

	Nm-Mt	Ex-Mt
COMP.FACT SET (44)	8.00	3.20
1 George Bell	.05	.02
2 Wade Boggs	.40	.16
3 Jose Canseco	.40	.16
4 Ivan Calderon	.05	.02
5 Will Clark	.50	.20
6 Roger Clemens	.75	.30
7 Vince Coleman	.05	.02
8 Eric Davis	.10	.04
9 Andre Dawson	.20	.08
10 Dave Dravecky	.10	.04
11 Mike Dunne	.05	.02
12 Dwight Evans	.10	.04
13 Sid Fernandez	.05	.02
14 Tony Fernandez	.05	.02
15 Julio Franco	.10	.04
16 Dwight Gooden	.10	.04
17 Tony Gwynn	.75	.30
18 Ted Higuera	.05	.02
19 Charlie Hough	.10	.04
20 Wally Joyner	.15	.06
21 Mark Langston	.05	.02
22 Don Mattingly	.75	.30
23 Mark McGwire	1.25	.50
24 Jack Morris	.10	.04
25 Dale Murphy	.20	.08
26 Kirby Puckett	.30	.12
27 Tim Raines	.10	.04
28 Willie Randolph	.10	.04
29 Ryne Sandberg	.50	.20
30 Benito Santiago	.10	.04
31 Mike Schmidt	.50	.20
32 Mike Scott	.05	.02
33 Kevin Seitzer	.05	.02
34 Larry Sheets	.05	.02
35 Ozzie Smith	.75	.30
36 Dave Stewart	.10	.04
37 Darryl Strawberry	.10	.04
38 Rick Sutcliffe	.05	.02
39 Alan Trammell	.15	.06
40 Fernando Valenzuela	.10	.04
41 Frank Viola	.05	.02
42 Tim Wallach	.05	.02
43 Dave Winfield	.50	.20
44 Robin Yount	.40	.16

1988 Fleer Exciting Stars

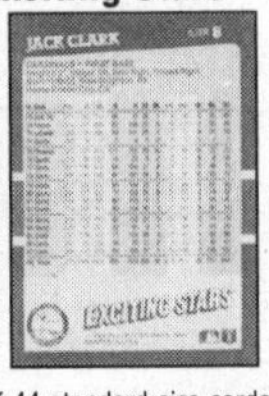

This small boxed set of 44 standard-size cards was produced exclusively for Cumberland Farm Stores. The cards feature full color fronts and red, white, and blue backs. The card fronts are distinguished by the framing of the player's full-color photo with a blue border with a red and white bar stripe across the middle. The box for the cards describes the set as the "1988 Fleer Baseball's Exciting Stars." The checklist for the set is given on the back of the set box. The card numbering is in alphabetical order by player's name.

	Nm-Mt	Ex-Mt
COMP.FACT SET (44)	5.00	2.00
1 Harold Baines	.15	.06
2 Kevin Bass	.05	.02
3 George Bell	.05	.02
4 Wade Boggs	.40	.16
5 Mickey Brantley	.05	.02
6 Sid Bream	.05	.02
7 Jose Canseco	.30	.12
8 Jack Clark	.10	.04
9 Will Clark	.50	.20
10 Roger Clemens	.75	.30
11 Vince Coleman	.05	.02
12 Eric Davis	.10	.04
13 Andre Dawson	.20	.08
14 Julio Franco	.10	.04
15 Dwight Gooden	.10	.04
16 Mike Greenwell	.05	.02
17 Tony Gwynn	.75	.30
18 Von Hayes	.05	.02
19 Tom Henke	.05	.02
20 Orel Hershiser	.10	.04
21 Teddy Higuera	.05	.02
22 Brook Jacoby	.05	.02
23 Wally Joyner	.15	.06
24 Jimmy Key	.10	.04
25 Don Mattingly	.75	.30
26 Mark McGwire	1.25	.50
27 Jack Morris	.10	.04
28 Dale Murphy	.20	.08
29 Matt Nokes	.05	.02
30 Kirby Puckett	.30	.12
31 Tim Raines	.10	.04
32 Ryne Sandberg	.50	.20
33 Benito Santiago	.10	.04
34 Mike Schmidt	.50	.20
35 Mike Scott	.05	.02
36 Kevin Seitzer	.10	.04
37 Larry Sheets	.05	.02
38 Ruben Sierra	.10	.04
39 Darryl Strawberry	.10	.04
40 Rick Sutcliffe	.05	.02
41 Danny Tartabull	.05	.02
42 Alan Trammell	.15	.06
43 Fernando Valenzuela	.10	.04
44 Devon White	.05	.02

1988 Fleer Hottest Stars

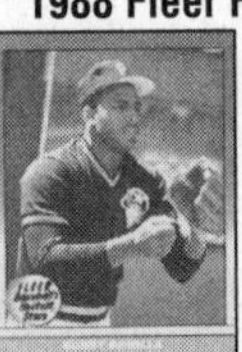

This 44-card boxed standard-size set was produced by Fleer for exclusive distribution by Revco Discount Drug stores all over the country. The cards feature full color fronts and red, white, and blue backs. The card fronts are easily distinguished by the flaming baseball in the lower right corner which says "Fleer Baseball's Hottest Stars." The player's picture is framed in red fading from orange down to yellow. The box for the cards proclaims "1988 Limited Edition Baseball's Hottest Stars" and is styled in blue, red, and yellow. The checklist for the set is given on the back of the set box. The box refers to Revco but there is no mention of Revco anywhere on the cards themselves. The card numbering is in alphabetical order by player's name.

	Nm-Mt	Ex-Mt
COMP.FACT SET (44)	5.00	2.00
1 George Bell	.05	.02
2 Wade Boggs	.40	.16
3 Bobby Bonilla	.10	.04
4 George Brett	.50	.20
5 Jose Canseco	.30	.12
6 Will Clark	.50	.20
7 Roger Clemens	.75	.30
8 Eric Davis	.10	.04
9 Andre Dawson	.20	.08
10 Tony Fernandez	.10	.04
11 Julio Franco	.10	.04
12 Gary Gaetti	.10	.04
13 Dwight Gooden	.10	.04
14 Mike Greenwell	.05	.02
15 Tony Gwynn	.75	.30
16 Rickey Henderson	.60	.24
17 Keith Hernandez	.10	.04
18 Tom Herr	.05	.02
19 Orel Hershiser	.10	.04
20 Ted Higuera	.05	.02
21 Wally Joyner	.10	.04
22 Jimmy Key	.10	.04
23 Mark Langston	.05	.02
24 Don Mattingly	.75	.30
25 Jack McDowell	.15	.06
26 Mark McGwire	1.25	.50
27 Kevin Mitchell	.10	.04
28 Jack Morris	.10	.04
29 Dale Murphy	.20	.08
30 Kirby Puckett	.30	.12
31 Tim Raines	.10	.04
32 Shane Rawley	.05	.02
33 Benito Santiago	.10	.04
34 Mike Schmidt	.50	.20
35 Mike Scott	.05	.02
36 Kevin Seitzer	.05	.02
37 Larry Sheets	.05	.02
38 Ruben Sierra	.10	.04
39 Dave Smith	.05	.02
40 Ozzie Smith	.75	.30
41 Darryl Strawberry	.10	.04
42 Rick Sutcliffe	.05	.02
43 Pat Tabler	.05	.02
44 Alan Trammell	.15	.06

1988 Fleer League Leaders

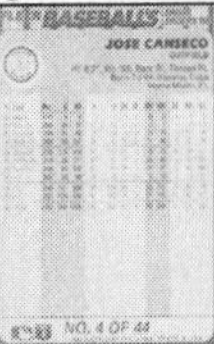

This small boxed set of 44 standard-size cards was produced exclusively for Walgreen Drug Stores. The cards feature full color fronts and pink, white, and blue backs. The card fronts are distinguished by the blue solid and striped background behind the player's full-color photo. The box for the cards describes the set as the "1988 Fleer Baseball's League Leaders." The checklist for the set is given on the back of the set box. The card numbering is in alphabetical order by player's name.

	Nm-Mt	Ex-Mt
COMP.FACT SET (44)	5.00	2.00
1 George Bell	.05	.02
2 Wade Boggs	.40	.16
3 Ivan Calderon	.05	.02
4 Jose Canseco	.40	.16
5 Will Clark	.50	.20
6 Roger Clemens	.75	.30
7 Vince Coleman	.05	.02
8 Eric Davis	.10	.04
9 Andre Dawson	.30	.12
10 Bill Doran	.05	.02
11 Dwight Evans	.10	.04
12 Julio Franco	.10	.04
13 Gary Gaetti	.10	.04
14 Andres Galarraga	.30	.12
15 Dwight Gooden	.10	.04
16 Tony Gwynn	.75	.30
17 Tom Henke	.05	.02
18 Keith Hernandez	.10	.04
19 Orel Hershiser	.10	.04
20 Ted Higuera	.05	.02
21 Kent Hrbek	.10	.04
22 Wally Joyner	.20	.08
23 Jimmy Key	.10	.04
24 Mark Langston	.05	.02
25 Don Mattingly	.75	.30
26 Mark McGwire	1.25	.50
27 Paul Molitor	.50	.20
28 Jack Morris	.10	.04
29 Dale Murphy	.30	.12
30 Kirby Puckett	.40	.16
31 Tim Raines	.10	.04
32 Rick Reuschel	.05	.02
33 Bret Saberhagen	.10	.04
34 Benito Santiago	.10	.04
35 Mike Schmidt	.50	.20
36 Mike Scott	.05	.02
37 Kevin Seitzer	.10	.04
38 Larry Sheets	.05	.02
39 Ruben Sierra	.10	.04
40 Darryl Strawberry	.10	.04
41 Rick Sutcliffe	.05	.02
42 Alan Trammell	.20	.08
43 Andy Van Slyke	.10	.04
44 Todd Worrell	.10	.04

1988 Fleer Mini

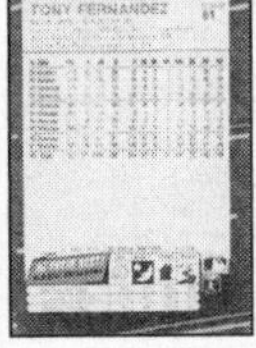

The 1988 Fleer "Classic Miniatures" set consists of 120 small cards with all new pictures of the players as compared to the 1988 Fleer regular issue. The cards are only 1 13/16" by 2 9/16", making them one of the smallest cards issued in the 1980's. Card backs provide career year-by-year statistics. The complete set was distributed in a green, red, white, and silver box along with 18 logo stickers. The card numbering is by alphabetical team order within league and alphabetically within each team. A rookie year card of Mark Grace highlights the set.

	Nm-Mt	Ex-Mt
COMP.FACT SET (120)	10.00	4.00
1 Eddie Murray	.50	.20
2 Dave Schmidt	.05	.02
3 Larry Sheets	.05	.02
4 Wade Boggs	.50	.20
5 Roger Clemens	.75	.30
6 Dwight Evans	.10	.04
7 Mike Greenwell	.05	.02
8 Sam Horn	.05	.02
9 Lee Smith	.10	.04
10 Brian Downing	.05	.02
11 Wally Joyner	.10	.04
12 Devon White	.05	.02
13 Mike Witt	.05	.02
14 Ivan Calderon	.05	.02
15 Ozzie Guillen	.10	.04
16 Jack McDowell	.15	.06
17 Kenny Williams	.15	.06
18 Joe Carter	.20	.08
19 Julio Franco	.10	.04
20 Pat Tabler	.05	.02
21 Doyle Alexander	.05	.02
22 Jack Morris	.10	.04
23 Matt Nokes	.05	.02
24 Walt Terrell	.05	.02
25 Alan Trammell	.15	.06
26 Bret Saberhagen	.10	.04
27 Kevin Seitzer	.10	.04
28 Danny Tartabull	.05	.02
29 Gary Thurman	.05	.02
30 Ted Higuera	.05	.02
31 Paul Molitor	.50	.20
32 Dan Plesac	.05	.02
33 Robin Yount	.30	.12
34 Gary Gaetti	.10	.04
35 Kent Hrbek	.10	.04
36 Kirby Puckett	.30	.12
37 Jeff Reardon	.10	.04
38 Frank Viola	.05	.02
39 Jack Clark	.10	.04
40 Rickey Henderson	.60	.24
41 Don Mattingly	.75	.30
42 Willie Randolph	.10	.04
43 Dave Righetti	.05	.02
44 Dave Winfield	.40	.16
45 Jose Canseco	.40	.16
46 Mark McGwire	1.25	.50
47 Dave Parker	.10	.04
48 Dave Stewart	.10	.04
49 Walt Weiss	.20	.08
50 Bob Welch	.05	.02
51 Mickey Brantley	.05	.02
52 Mark Langston	.05	.02
53 Harold Reynolds	.10	.04
54 Scott Fletcher	.05	.02
55 Charlie Hough	.10	.04
56 Pete Incaviglia	.05	.02
57 Larry Parrish	.05	.02
58 Ruben Sierra	.10	.04
59 George Bell	.05	.02
60 Mark Eichhorn	.05	.02
61 Tony Fernandez	.10	.04
62 Tom Henke	.10	.04
63 Jimmy Key	.10	.04
64 Dion James	.05	.02
65 Dale Murphy	.20	.08
66 Zane Smith	.05	.02
67 Andre Dawson	.20	.08
68 Mark Grace	1.50	.60
69 Jerry Mumphrey	.05	.02
70 Ryne Sandberg	.75	.30
71 Rick Sutcliffe	.05	.02
72 Kal Daniels	.05	.02
73 Eric Davis	.10	.04
74 John Franco	.10	.04
75 Ron Robinson	.05	.02
76 Jeff Treadway	.05	.02
77 Kevin Bass	.05	.02
78 Glenn Davis	.05	.02
79 Nolan Ryan	1.50	.60
80 Mike Scott	.05	.02
81 Dave Smith	.05	.02
82 Kirk Gibson	.10	.04
83 Pedro Guerrero	.05	.02
84 Orel Hershiser	.10	.04
85 Steve Sax	.05	.02
86 Fernando Valenzuela	.10	.04
87 Tim Burke	.05	.02
88 Andres Galarraga	.20	.08
89 Neal Heaton	.05	.02
90 Tim Raines	.10	.04
91 Tim Wallach	.05	.02
92 Dwight Gooden	.10	.04
93 Keith Hernandez	.10	.04
94 Gregg Jefferies	.15	.06
95 Howard Johnson	.05	.02
96 Roger McDowell	.05	.02
97 Darryl Strawberry	.10	.04
98 Steve Bedrosian	.05	.02
99 Von Hayes	.05	.02
100 Shane Rawley	.05	.02
101 Juan Samuel	.05	.02
102 Mike Schmidt	.30	.12
103 Bobby Bonilla	.10	.04
104 Mike Dunne	.05	.02
105 Andy Van Slyke	.10	.04
106 Vince Coleman	.05	.02
107 Bob Horner	.05	.02
108 Willie McGee	.10	.04
109 Ozzie Smith	.75	.30
110 John Tudor	.05	.02
111 Todd Worrell	.10	.04
112 Tony Gwynn	.75	.30
113 John Kruk	.10	.04
114 Lance McCullers	.05	.02
115 Benito Santiago	.10	.04

116 Will Clark .50 .20
117 Jeff Leonard .05 .02
118 Candy Maldonado .05 .02
119 Kirt Manwaring .05 .02
120 Don Robinson .05 .02

1988 Fleer Record Setters

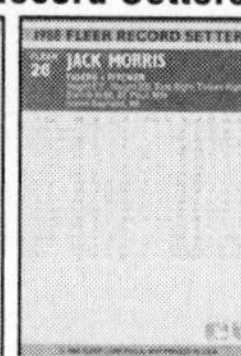

This small boxed set of 44 standard-size cards was produced exclusively for Eckerd's Drug Stores. The cards feature full color fronts and red, white, and blue backs. The card fronts are distinguished by the red and blue frame around the player's full-color photo. The box for the cards describes the set as the "1988 Baseball Record Setters." The checklist for the set is given on the back of the set box. The card numbering is in alphabetical order by player's name.

Nm-Mt Ex-Mt
COMP.FACT SET (44) 6.00 2.40
1 Jesse Barfield .05 .02
2 George Bell .05 .02
3 Wade Boggs .40 .16
4 Jose Canseco .30 .12
5 Jack Clark .10 .04
6 Will Clark .50 .20
7 Roger Clemens .75 .30
8 Alvin Davis .05 .02
9 Eric Davis .10 .04
10 Andre Dawson .20 .08
11 Mike Dunne .05 .02
12 John Franco .10 .04
13 Julio Franco .10 .04
14 Dwight Gooden .10 .04
15 Mark Gubicza .05 .02
(Listed as Gubiczo on box checklist)
16 Ozzie Guillen .10 .04
17 Tony Gwynn .75 .30
18 Orel Hershiser .10 .04
19 Teddy Higuera .05 .02
20 Howard Johnson UER .05 .02
(Missing '87 stats on card back)
21 Wally Joyner .15 .06
22 Jimmy Key .10 .04
23 Jeff Leonard .05 .02
24 Don Mattingly .75 .30
25 Mark McGwire 1.25 .50
26 Jack Morris .10 .04
27 Dale Murphy .20 .08
28 Larry Parrish .05 .02
29 Kirby Puckett .30 .12
30 Tim Raines .10 .04
31 Harold Reynolds .10 .04
32 Dave Righetti .05 .02
33 Cal Ripken 1.50 .60
34 Benito Santiago .10 .04
35 Mike Schmidt .50 .20
36 Mike Scott .05 .02
37 Kevin Seitzer .10 .04
38 Ozzie Smith .75 .30
39 Darryl Strawberry .10 .04
40 Rick Sutcliffe .05 .02
41 Alan Trammell .15 .06
42 Frank Viola .05 .02
43 Mitch Williams .05 .02
44 Todd Worrell .10 .04

1988 Fleer Sluggers/Pitchers

Fleer produced this 44-card boxed standard-size set although it was primarily distributed by McCrory, McLellan, J.J Newberry, H.L.Green, T.G.Y., and other similar stores. The set is subtitled "Baseball's Best". The set was packaged in a green custom box along with six logo stickers. The set checklist is given on the back of the box. The bottoms of the boxes which held the individual set boxes also contained a panel of six cards; these box bottom cards were numbered C1 through C6. The card numbering is in alphabetical order by player's name.

Nm-Mt Ex-Mt
COMP.FACT SET (44) 6.00 2.40
1 George Bell .05 .02
2 Wade Boggs .40 .16
3 Bobby Bonilla .10 .04
4 Tom Brunansky .05 .02
5 Ellis Burks .40 .16
6 Jose Canseco .30 .12
7 Joe Carter .20 .08
8 Will Clark .50 .20
9 Roger Clemens .75 .30
10 Eric Davis .10 .04
11 Glenn Davis .05 .02
12 Andre Dawson .20 .08
13 Dennis Eckersley .40 .16
14 Andres Galarraga .20 .08
15 Dwight Gooden .10 .04
16 Pedro Guerrero .05 .02
17 Tony Gwynn .75 .30
18 Orel Hershiser .10 .04
19 Ted Higuera .05 .02
20 Pete Incaviglia .05 .02
21 Danny Jackson .05 .02
22 Doug Jennings .05 .02
23 Mark Langston .05 .02
24 Dave LaPoint .05 .02
25 Mike LaValliere .05 .02
26 Don Mattingly .75 .30
27 Mark McGwire 1.25 .50
28 Dale Murphy .20 .08
29 Ken Phelps .05 .02
30 Kirby Puckett .30 .12
31 Johnny Ray .05 .02
32 Jeff Reardon .10 .04
33 Dave Righetti .05 .02
34 Cal Ripken UER 1.50 .60
(Misspelled Ripkin on card front)
35 Chris Sabo .10 .04
36 Mike Schmidt .50 .20
37 Mike Scott .05 .02
38 Kevin Seitzer .10 .04
39 Dave Stewart .10 .04
40 Darryl Strawberry .10 .04
41 Greg Swindell .05 .02
42 Frank Tanana .05 .02
43 Dave Winfield .50 .20
44 Todd Worrell .10 .04

1988 Fleer Sluggers/Pitchers Box Cards

The cards in this six-card set each measure the standard size. Cards have essentially the same design as the 1988 Fleer Sluggers vs. Pitchers set of Baseball's Best. The cards were printed on the bottom of the counter display box which held 24 small boxed sets; hence theoretically these box cards are 1/24 as plentiful as the regular boxed set cards. These six cards, numbered C1 to C6 are considered a separate set in their own right and are not typically included in a complete set of the 1988 Fleer Sluggers vs. Pitchers set of 44. The value of the panels uncut is slightly greater, perhaps by 25 percent greater, than the value of the individual cards cut up carefully.

Nm-Mt Ex-Mt
COMPLETE SET (6) 8.00 3.20
C1 Ron Darling 1.00 .40
C2 Rickey Henderson 3.00 1.20
C3 Carney Lansford 1.00 .40
C4 Rafael Palmeiro 3.00 1.20
C5 Frank Viola 1.00 .40
C6 Twins Logo 1.00 .40
(Checklist back)

1988 Fleer Sticker Cards

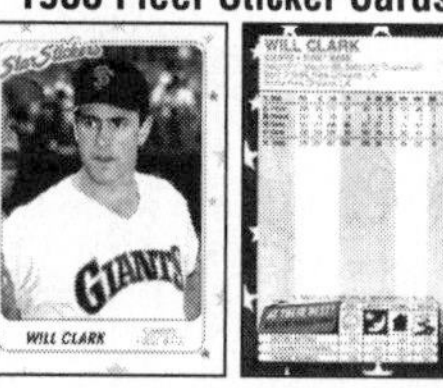

These Star Stickers were distributed as a separate issue by Fleer, with five star stickers and a logo sticker in each wax pack. The 132-card (sticker) set features 2 1/2" by 3 1/2" full-color fronts and even statistics on the sticker back, which is an indication that the Fleer Company understands that these stickers are rarely used as stickers but more like traditional cards. The fronts are surrounded by a silver-gray border and the backs are printed in red and black on white card stock. The set numbering is in alphabetical order within team and alphabetically by team within each league.

Nm-Mt Ex-Mt
COMPLETE SET (132) 12.00 4.80
1 Mike Boddicker .05 .02
2 Eddie Murray .50 .20
3 Cal Ripken 2.50 1.00
4 Larry Sheets .05 .02
5 Wade Boggs .50 .20
6 Ellis Burks 1.00 .40
7 Roger Clemens 1.25 .50
8 Dwight Evans .10 .04
9 Mike Greenwell .05 .02
10 Bruce Hurst .05 .02
11 Brian Downing .05 .02
12 Wally Joyner .10 .04
13 Mike Witt .05 .02
14 Ivan Calderon .05 .02
15 Jose DeLeon .05 .02
16 Ozzie Guillen .10 .04
17 Bobby Thigpen .05 .02
18 Joe Carter .20 .08
19 Julio Franco .10 .04
20 Brook Jacoby .05 .02
21 Cory Snyder .05 .02
22 Pat Tabler .05 .02
23 Doyle Alexander .05 .02
24 Kirk Gibson .10 .04
25 Mike Henneman .10 .04
26 Jack Morris .10 .04
27 Matt Nokes .05 .02
28 Walt Terrell .05 .02
29 Alan Trammell .15 .06
30 George Brett 1.25 .50
31 Charlie Leibrandt .05 .02
32 Bret Saberhagen .10 .04
33 Kevin Seitzer .05 .02
34 Danny Tartabull .05 .02
35 Frank White .10 .04
36 Rob Deer .05 .02
37 Ted Higuera .05 .02
38 Paul Molitor .50 .20
39 Dan Plesac .05 .02
40 Robin Yount .40 .16
41 Bert Blyleven .10 .04
42 Tom Brunansky .05 .02
43 Gary Gaetti .10 .04
44 Kent Hrbek .10 .04
45 Kirby Puckett .50 .20
46 Jeff Reardon .10 .04
47 Frank Viola .05 .02
48 Don Mattingly 1.25 .50
49 Mike Pagliarulo .05 .02
50 Willie Randolph .10 .04
51 Rick Rhoden .05 .02
52 Dave Righetti .05 .02
53 Dave Winfield .40 .16
54 Jose Canseco .40 .16
55 Carney Lansford .10 .04
56 Mark McGwire 2.00 .80
57 Dave Stewart .10 .04
58 Curt Young .05 .02
59 Alvin Davis .05 .02
60 Mark Langston .05 .02
61 Ken Phelps .05 .02
62 Harold Reynolds .10 .04
63 Scott Fletcher .05 .02
64 Charlie Hough .10 .04
65 Pete Incaviglia .05 .02
66 Oddibe McDowell .05 .02
67 Pete O'Brien .05 .02
68 Larry Parrish .05 .02
69 Ruben Sierra .10 .04
70 Jesse Barfield .05 .02
71 George Bell .05 .02
72 Tony Fernandez .10 .04
73 Tom Henke .05 .02
74 Jimmy Key .05 .02
75 Lloyd Moseby .05 .02
76 Dion James .05 .02
77 Dale Murphy .20 .08
78 Zane Smith .05 .02
79 Andre Dawson .20 .08
80 Ryne Sandberg 1.00 .40
81 Rick Sutcliffe .05 .02
82 Kal Daniels .05 .02
83 Eric Davis .10 .04
84 John Franco .10 .04
85 Kevin Bass .05 .02
86 Glenn Davis .05 .02
87 Bill Doran .05 .02
88 Nolan Ryan 2.50 1.00
89 Mike Scott .05 .02
90 Dave Smith .05 .02
91 Pedro Guerrero .05 .02
92 Orel Hershiser .10 .04
93 Steve Sax .05 .02
94 Fernando Valenzuela .10 .04
95 Tim Burke .05 .02
96 Andres Galarraga .20 .08
97 Tim Raines .10 .04
98 Tim Wallach .05 .02
99 Mitch Webster .05 .02
100 Ron Darling .05 .02
101 Sid Fernandez .05 .02
102 Dwight Gooden .10 .04
103 Keith Hernandez .10 .04
104 Howard Johnson .05 .02
105 Roger McDowell .05 .02
106 Darryl Strawberry .10 .04
107 Steve Bedrosian .05 .02
108 Von Hayes .05 .02
109 Shane Rawley .05 .02
110 Juan Samuel .05 .02
111 Mike Schmidt .50 .20
112 Milt Thompson .05 .02
113 Sid Bream .05 .02
114 Bobby Bonilla .05 .02
115 Mike Dunne .05 .02
116 Andy Van Slyke .10 .04
117 Vince Coleman .05 .02
118 Willie McGee .10 .04
119 Terry Pendleton .10 .04
120 Ozzie Smith 1.00 .40
121 John Tudor .05 .02
122 Todd Worrell .10 .04
123 Tony Gwynn 1.25 .50
124 John Kruk .10 .04
125 Benito Santiago .10 .04
126 Will Clark .50 .20
127 Dave Dravecky .10 .04
128 Jeff Leonard .05 .02
129 Candy Maldonado .05 .02
130 Rick Reuschel .05 .02
131 Don Robinson .05 .02
132 Checklist Card .05 .02

1988 Fleer Stickers Wax Box Cards

The bottoms of the Star Sticker wax boxes contained two different sets of four cards done in a similar format to the stickers; these cards (they are not stickers but truly cards) are numbered with the prefix S and are considered a separate set. The value of the panels uncut is slightly greater, perhaps by 25 percent greater, than the value of the individual cards cut up carefully.

Nm-Mt Ex-Mt
COMPLETE SET (8) 4.00 1.60
S1 Mark McGwire 5.00 2.00
Eric Davis
S2 Gary Carter 1.00 .40
S3 Kevin Mitchell .75 .30
S4 Ron Guidry .75 .30
S5 Rickey Henderson 2.00 .80
S6 Don Baylor .75 .30
S7 Giants Logo .50 .20
S8 Detroit Logo .50 .20

1988 Fleer Superstars

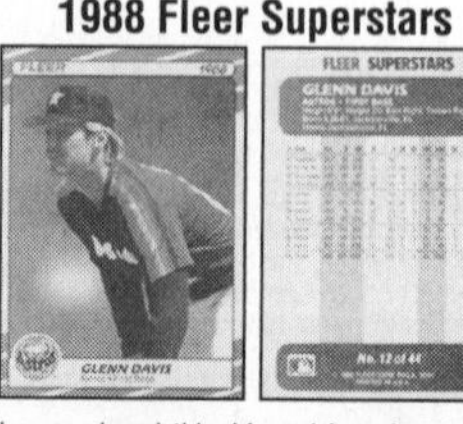

Fleer produced this 44-card boxed standard-size set although it was primarily distributed by McCrory, McLellan, J.J Newberry, H.L.Green, T.G.Y., and other similar stores. The set is subtitled "Fleer Superstars." The set was packaged in a red, white, blue, and yellow custom box along with six logo stickers. The set checklist is given on the back of the box. The bottoms of the boxes which held the individual set boxes also contained a panel of six cards; these box bottom cards were numbered C1 through C6. The card numbering is in alphabetical order by player's name.

Nm-Mt Ex-Mt
COMPLETE SET (44) 6.00 2.40
1 Steve Bedrosian .05 .02
2 George Bell .05 .02
3 Wade Boggs .40 .16
4 Barry Bonds 1.00 .40
5 Jose Canseco .30 .12
6 Joe Carter .20 .08
7 Jack Clark .10 .04
8 Will Clark .50 .20
9 Roger Clemens .75 .30
10 Alvin Davis .05 .02
11 Eric Davis .10 .04
12 Glenn Davis .05 .02
13 Andre Dawson .20 .08
14 Dwight Gooden .10 .04
15 Orel Hershiser .10 .04
16 Teddy Higuera .05 .02
17 Kent Hrbek .10 .04
18 Wally Joyner .10 .04
19 Jimmy Key .05 .02
20 John Kruk .10 .04
21 Jeff Leonard .05 .02
22 Don Mattingly .75 .30
23 Mark McGwire 1.25 .50
24 Kevin McReynolds .05 .02
25 Dale Murphy .20 .08
26 Matt Nokes .05 .02
27 Terry Pendleton .10 .04
28 Kirby Puckett .40 .16
29 Tim Raines .10 .04
30 Rick Rhoden .05 .02
31 Cal Ripken 1.50 .60
32 Benito Santiago .10 .04
33 Mike Schmidt .40 .16
34 Mike Scott .05 .02
35 Kevin Seitzer .10 .04
36 Ruben Sierra .10 .04
37 Cory Snyder .05 .02
38 Darryl Strawberry .10 .04
39 Rick Sutcliffe .05 .02
40 Danny Tartabull .05 .02
41 Alan Trammell .15 .06
42 Kenny Williams .10 .04
43 Mike Witt .05 .02
44 Robin Yount .40 .16

1988 Fleer Superstars Box Cards

The cards in this six-card set each measure the standard size. Cards have essentially the same design as the 1988 Fleer Superstars set. The cards were printed on the bottom of the counter display box which held 24 small boxed sets; hence theoretically these box cards are 1/24 as plentiful as the regular boxed set cards. These six cards, numbered C1 to C6 are considered a separate set in their own right and are not typically included in a complete set of the 1988 Fleer Superstars set of 44. The value of the panels uncut is slightly greater, perhaps by 25 percent greater, than the value of the individual cards cut up carefully.

Nm-Mt Ex-Mt
COMPLETE SET (6) 10.00 4.00
C1 Pete Incaviglia .50 .20
C2 Rickey Henderson 5.00 2.00
C3 Tony Fernandez .50 .20
C4 Shane Rawley .50 .20
C5 Ryne Sandberg 5.00 2.00
C6 Cardinals Logo .50 .20
(Checklist back)

1988 Fleer Team Leaders

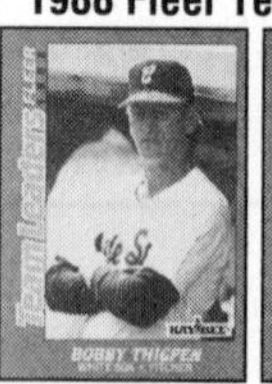

This 44-card boxed standard-size set was produced by Fleer for exclusive distribution by Kay Bee Toys and is sometimes referred to as the Fleer Kay Bee set. Six team logo stickers are included in the box with the complete set. The numerical checklist on the back of the box shows that the set is numbered alphabetically. The cards have a distinctive red border on the fronts. The Kay Bee logo is printed in the lower right corner of the obverse of each card.

Nm-Mt Ex-Mt
COMP.FACT SET (44) 8.00 3.20
1 George Bell .05 .02
2 Wade Boggs .50 .20
3 Jose Canseco .40 .16
4 Will Clark .60 .24
5 Roger Clemens .75 .30
6 Eric Davis .10 .04
7 Andre Dawson .30 .12
8 Julio Franco .10 .04
9 Andres Galarraga .30 .12
10 Dwight Gooden .10 .04
11 Tony Gwynn .75 .30
12 Tom Henke .05 .02
13 Orel Hershiser .10 .04
14 Kent Hrbek .10 .04
15 Ted Higuera .05 .02
16 Wally Joyner .20 .08
17 Jimmy Key .05 .02
18 Mark Langston .05 .02
19 Don Mattingly .75 .30
20 Willie McGee .10 .04
21 Mark McGwire 1.25 .50
22 Paul Molitor .50 .20
23 Jack Morris .10 .04
24 Dale Murphy .30 .12
25 Larry Parrish .05 .02
26 Kirby Puckett .40 .16
27 Tim Raines .10 .04
28 Jeff Reardon .10 .04
29 Dave Righetti .05 .02
30 Cal Ripken 1.50 .60
31 Don Robinson .05 .02
32 Bret Saberhagen .10 .04
33 Juan Samuel .05 .02
34 Mike Schmidt .50 .20
35 Mike Scott .05 .02
36 Kevin Seitzer .10 .04
37 Dave Smith .05 .02
38 Ozzie Smith .75 .30
39 Zane Smith .05 .02
40 Darryl Strawberry .10 .04
41 Rick Sutcliffe .05 .02
42 Bobby Thigpen .05 .02
43 Alan Trammell .20 .08
44 Andy Van Slyke .05 .02

1989 Fleer

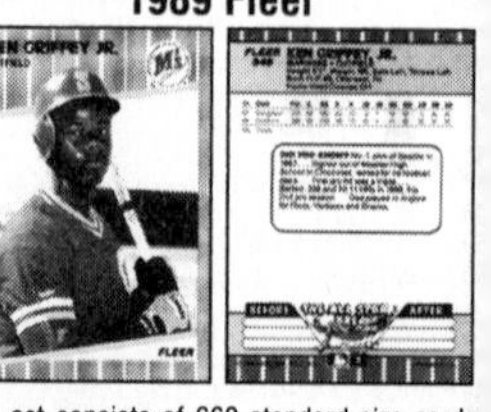

This set consists of 660 standard-size cards. Cards were primarily issued in 15-card wax packs, rack packs and hobby and retail factory sets. Card fronts feature a distinctive gray border background with white and yellow trim. Cards are again organized alphabetically within teams and teams ordered by previous season record. The last 33 cards in the set consist of Specials (628-639), Rookie Pairs (640-653), and checklists (654-660). Approximately half of the California Angels players have white rather than yellow halos. Certain Oakland A's player cards have red instead of green lines for front photo borders. Checklist cards are available either with or without positions listed for each player. Rookie Cards in this set include Craig Biggio, Ken Griffey Jr., Randy Johnson, Gary Sheffield, and John Smoltz. An interesting variation was discovered in late 1999 by Beckett Grading Services on the Randy Johnson RC (card number 381). It seems the most common version features a crudely-blacked out image of an outfield billboard. A scarcer version clearly reveals the words "Marlboro" on the billboard. A value for this variation is not provided due to scarcity. One of the hobby's most notorious errors and variations hails from this product. Card number 616, Billy Ripken, was originally published with a four-letter word imprinted on the bat. Needless to say, this caused quite a stir in 1989 and the card was quickly reprinted. Because of this, several different variations were printed with the final solution (and the most common version of this card) being a black box covering the bat knob. The first variation is still actively sought after in the hobby and the other versions are still sought after by collectors seeking a "master" set.

Nm-Mt Ex-Mt
COMPLETE SET (660) 15.00 6.00
COMP.FACT.SET (672) 15.00 6.00
1 Don Baylor .10 .04
2 Lance Blankenship RC .10 .04
3 Todd Burns UER .05 .02
(Wrong birthdate; before/after All-Star stats missing)
4 Greg Cadaret UER .05 .02
(All-Star Break stats show 3 losses, should be 2
5 Jose Canseco .25 .10
6 Storm Davis .05 .02
7 Dennis Eckersley .10 .04
8 Mike Gallego .05 .02
9 Ron Hassey .05 .02
10 Dave Henderson .05 .02
11 Rick Honeycutt .05 .02
12 Glenn Hubbard .05 .02
13 Stan Javier .05 .02
14 Doug Jennings .05 .02
15 Felix Jose RC .10 .04
16 Carney Lansford .10 .04
17 Mark McGwire 1.00 .40
18 Gene Nelson .05 .02
19 Dave Parker .10 .04
20 Eric Plunk .05 .02
21 Luis Polonia .05 .02
22 Terry Steinbach .10 .04
23 Dave Stewart .10 .04
24 Walt Weiss .05 .02
25 Bob Welch .05 .02
26 Curt Young .05 .02
27 Rick Aguilera .10 .04
28 Wally Backman .05 .02
29 Mark Carreon UER .05 .02
(After All-Star Break batting 7.14)
30 Gary Carter .15 .06
31 David Cone .10 .04
32 Ron Darling .05 .02
33 Len Dykstra .10 .04
34 Kevin Elster .05 .02
35 Sid Fernandez .05 .02
36 Dwight Gooden .15 .06
37 Keith Hernandez .15 .06
38 Gregg Jefferies .10 .04
39 Howard Johnson .05 .02
40 Terry Leach .05 .02
41 Dave Magadan UER .05 .02
(Bio says 15 doubles, should be 13)

2 Bob McClure .05 .02
3 Roger McDowell UER .05 .02
(Led Mets with 58, should be 62)
4 Kevin McReynolds .05 .02
5 Keith A. Miller .05 .02
6 Randy Myers .10 .04
7 Bob Ojeda .05 .02
8 Mackey Sasser .05 .02
9 Darryl Strawberry .15 .06
0 Tim Teufel .05 .02
1 Dave West RC .10 .04
2 Mookie Wilson .10 .04
3 Dave Anderson .05 .02
4 Tim Belcher .05 .02
5 Mike Davis .05 .02
6 Mike Devereaux .05 .02
7 Kirk Gibson .10 .04
8 Alfredo Griffin .05 .02
9 Chris Gwynn .05 .02
0 Jeff Hamilton .05 .02
1A Danny Heep ERR .25 .10
Lake Hills
1B Danny Heep COR .05 .02
San Antonio
2 Orel Hershiser .10 .04
3 Brian Holton .05 .02
4 Jay Howell .05 .02
5 Tim Leary .05 .02
6 Mike Marshall .05 .02
7 Ramon Martinez RC .25 .10
8 Jesse Orosco .05 .02
9 Alejandro Pena .05 .02
70 Steve Sax .05 .02
71 Mike Scioscia .05 .02
72 Mike Sharperson .05 .02
73 John Shelby .05 .02
74 Franklin Stubbs .05 .02
75 John Tudor .05 .02
76 Fernando Valenzuela .10 .04
77 Tracy Woodson .05 .02
78 Marty Barrett .05 .02
79 Todd Benzinger .05 .02
80 Mike Boddicker UER .05 .02
(Rochester in '76, should be '78)
81 Wade Boggs .15 .06
82 Oil Can Boyd .05 .02
83 Ellis Burks .15 .06
84 Rick Cerone .05 .02
85 Roger Clemens .50 .20
86 Steve Curry .05 .02
87 Dwight Evans .10 .04
88 Wes Gardner .05 .02
89 Rich Gedman .05 .02
90 Mike Greenwell .05 .02
91 Bruce Hurst .05 .02
92 Dennis Lamp .05 .02
93 Spike Owen .05 .02
94 Larry Parrish UER .05 .02
(Before All-Star Break batting 1.90)
95 Carlos Quintana RC .10 .04
96 Jody Reed .05 .02
97 Jim Rice .10 .04
98A Kevin Romine ERR .25 .10
(Photo actually Randy Kutcher batting)
98B Kevin Romine COR .05 .02
(Arms folded)
99 Lee Smith .10 .04
100 Mike Smithson .05 .02
101 Bob Stanley .05 .02
102 Allan Anderson .05 .02
103 Keith Atherton .05 .02
104 Juan Berenguer .05 .02
105 Bert Blyleven .10 .04
106 Eric Bullock UER .05 .02
Bats/Throws Right, should be Left
107 Randy Bush .05 .02
108 John Christensen .05 .02
109 Mark Davidson .05 .02
110 Gary Gaetti .10 .04
111 Greg Gagne .05 .02
112 Dan Gladden .05 .02
113 German Gonzalez .05 .02
114 Brian Harper .05 .02
115 Tom Herr .05 .02
116 Kent Hrbek .10 .04
117 Gene Larkin .05 .02
118 Tim Laudner .05 .02
119 Charlie Lea .05 .02
120 Steve Lombardozzi .05 .02
121A John Moses ERR .25 .10
Tempe
121B John Moses COR .05 .02
Phoenix
122 Al Newman .05 .02
123 Mark Portugal .05 .02
124 Kirby Puckett .25 .10
125 Jeff Reardon .10 .04
126 Fred Toliver .05 .02
127 Frank Viola .05 .02
128 Doyle Alexander .05 .02
129 Dave Bergman .05 .02
130A Tom Brookens ERR .75 .30
(Mike Heath back)
130B Tom Brookens COR .05 .02
131 Paul Gibson .05 .02
132A Mike Heath ERR .75 .30
(Tom Brookens back)
132B Mike Heath COR .05 .02
133 Don Heinkel .05 .02
134 Mike Henneman .05 .02
135 Guillermo Hernandez .05 .02
136 Eric King .05 .02
137 Chet Lemon .05 .02
138 Fred Lynn UER .05 .02
'74 and '75 stats missing
139 Jack Morris .10 .04
140 Matt Nokes .05 .02
141 Gary Pettis .05 .02
142 Ted Power .05 .02
143 Jeff M. Robinson .05 .02
144 Luis Salazar .05 .02
145 Steve Searcy .05 .02
146 Pat Sheridan .05 .02
147 Frank Tanana .05 .02
148 Alan Trammell .15 .06
149 Walt Terrell .05 .02
150 Jim Walewander .05 .02
151 Lou Whitaker .10 .04
152 Tim Birtsas .05 .02
153 Tom Browning .05 .02
154 Keith Brown .05 .02
155 Norm Charlton RC .25 .10
156 Dave Concepcion .10 .04
157 Kal Daniels .05 .02
158 Eric Davis .10 .04
159 Bo Diaz .05 .02
160 Rob Dibble RC .50 .20
161 Nick Esasky .10 .04
162 John Franco .10 .04
163 Danny Jackson .05 .02
164 Barry Larkin .25 .10
165 Rob Murphy .05 .02
166 Paul O'Neill .15 .06
167 Jeff Reed .05 .02
168 Jose Rijo .05 .02
169 Ron Robinson .05 .02
170 Chris Sabo RC .40 .16
171 Candy Sierra .05 .02
172 Van Snider .05 .02
173A Jeff Treadway 5.00 2.00
(Target registration mark above head on front in light blue)
173B Jeff Treadway .05 .02
(No target on front)
174 Frank Williams UER .05 .02
(After All-Star Break stats are jumbled)
175 Herm Winningham .05 .02
176 Jim Adduci .05 .02
177 Don August .05 .02
178 Mike Birkbeck .05 .02
179 Chris Bosio .05 .02
180 Glenn Braggs .05 .02
181 Greg Brock .05 .02
182 Mark Clear .05 .02
183 Chuck Crim .05 .02
184 Rob Deer .05 .02
185 Tom Filer .05 .02
186 Jim Gantner .05 .02
187 Darryl Hamilton RC .25 .10
188 Ted Higuera .05 .02
189 Odell Jones .05 .02
190 Jeffrey Leonard .05 .02
191 Joey Meyer .05 .02
192 Paul Mirabella .05 .02
193 Paul Molitor .15 .06
194 Charlie O'Brien .05 .02
195 Dan Plesac .05 .02
196 Gary Sheffield RC 1.50 .60
197 B.J. Surhoff .10 .04
198 Dale Sveum .05 .02
199 Bill Wegman .05 .02
200 Robin Yount .40 .16
201 Rafael Belliard .05 .02
202 Barry Bonds 1.25 .50
203 Bobby Bonilla .10 .04
204 Sid Bream .05 .02
205 Benny Distefano .05 .02
206 Doug Drabek .05 .02
207 Mike Dunne .05 .02
208 Felix Fermin .05 .02
209 Brian Fisher .05 .02
210 Jim Gott .05 .02
211 Bob Kipper .05 .02
212 Dave LaPoint .05 .02
213 Mike LaValliere .05 .02
214 Jose Lind .05 .02
215 Junior Ortiz .05 .02
216 Vicente Palacios .05 .02
217 Tom Prince .05 .02
218 Gary Redus .05 .02
219 R.J. Reynolds .05 .02
220 Jeff D. Robinson .05 .02
221 John Smiley .05 .02
222 Andy Van Slyke .10 .04
223 Bob Walk .05 .02
224 Glenn Wilson .05 .02
225 Jesse Barfield .05 .02
226 George Bell .05 .02
227 Pat Borders RC .25 .10
228 John Cerutti .05 .02
229 Jim Clancy .05 .02
230 Mark Eichhorn .05 .02
231 Tony Fernandez .05 .02
232 Cecil Fielder .10 .04
233 Mike Flanagan .05 .02
234 Kelly Gruber .05 .02
235 Tom Henke .05 .02
236 Jimmy Key .10 .04
237 Rick Leach .05 .02
238 Manny Lee UER .05 .02
(Bio says regular shortstop, sic, Tony Fernandez)
239 Nelson Liriano .05 .02
240 Fred McGriff .25 .10
241 Lloyd Moseby .05 .02
242 Rance Mulliniks .05 .02
243 Jeff Musselman .05 .02
244 Dave Stieb .05 .02
245 Todd Stottlemyre .15 .06
246 Duane Ward .05 .02
247 David Wells .10 .04
248 Ernie Whitt UER .05 .02
(HR total 21, should be 121)
249 Luis Aguayo .05 .02
250A Neil Allen ERR .75 .30
Sarasota, FL
250B Neil Allen COR .05 .02
Syosset, NY
251 John Candelaria .05 .02
252 Jack Clark .05 .02
253 Richard Dotson .05 .02
254 Rickey Henderson .25 .10
255 Tommy John .10 .04
256 Roberto Kelly .10 .04
257 Al Leiter .25 .10
258 Don Mattingly .60 .24
259 Dale Mohorcic .05 .02
260 Hal Morris RC .25 .10
261 Scott Nielsen .05 .02
262 Mike Pagliarulo UER .05 .02
(Wrong birthdate)
263 Hipolito Pena .05 .02
264 Ken Phelps .05 .02
265 Willie Randolph .10 .04
266 Rick Rhoden .05 .02
267 Dave Righetti .05 .02
268 Rafael Santana .05 .02
269 Steve Shields .05 .02
270 Joel Skinner .05 .02
271 Don Slaught .05 .02
272 Claudell Washington .05 .02
273 Gary Ward .05 .02
274 Dave Winfield .10 .04
275 Luis Aquino .05 .02
276 Floyd Bannister .05 .02
277 George Brett .60 .24
278 Bill Buckner .10 .04
279 Nick Capra .05 .02
280 Jose DeJesus .05 .02
281 Steve Farr .05 .02
282 Jerry Don Gleaton .05 .02
283 Mark Gubicza .05 .02
284 Tom Gordon RC UER .25 .10
(16.2 innings in '88, should be 15.2)
285 Bo Jackson .25 .10
286 Charlie Leibrandt .05 .02
287 Mike Macfarlane RC .25 .10
288 Jeff Montgomery .10 .04
289 Bill Pecota UER .05 .02
(Photo actually Brad Wellman)
290 Jamie Quirk .05 .02
291 Bret Saberhagen .10 .04
292 Kevin Seitzer .05 .02
293 Kurt Stillwell .05 .02
294 Pat Tabler .05 .02
295 Danny Tartabull .05 .02
296 Gary Thurman .05 .02
297 Frank White .10 .04
298 Willie Wilson .05 .02
299 Roberto Alomar .30 .12
300 S.Alomar Jr. RC UER .40 .16
Wrong birthdate, says 6/16/66, should say 6/18/66
301 Chris Brown .05 .02
302 Mike Brumley UER .05 .02
(133 hits in '88, should be 134)
303 Mark Davis .05 .02
304 Mark Grant .05 .02
305 Tony Gwynn .30 .12
306 Greg W. Harris RC .10 .04
307 Andy Hawkins .05 .02
308 Jimmy Jones .05 .02
309 John Kruk .10 .04
310 Dave Leiper .05 .02
311 Carmelo Martinez .05 .02
312 Lance McCullers .05 .02
313 Keith Moreland .05 .02
314 Dennis Rasmussen .05 .02
315 Randy Ready UER .05 .02
(1214 games in '88, should be 114)
316 Benito Santiago .10 .04
317 Eric Show .05 .02
318 Todd Simmons .05 .02
319 Garry Templeton .05 .02
320 Dickie Thon .05 .02
321 Ed Whitson .05 .02
322 Marvell Wynne .05 .02
323 Mike Aldrete .05 .02
324 Brett Butler .10 .04
325 Will Clark UER .25 .10
(Three consecutive 100 RBI seasons)
326 Kelly Downs UER .05 .02
('88 stats missing)
327 Dave Dravecky .10 .04
328 Scott Garrelts .05 .02
329 Atlee Hammaker .05 .02
330 Charlie Hayes RC .25 .10
331 Mike Krukow .05 .02
332 Craig Lefferts .05 .02
333 Candy Maldonado .05 .02
334 Kirt Manwaring UER .05 .02
(Bats Rights)
335 Bob Melvin .05 .02
336 Kevin Mitchell .10 .04
337 Donell Nixon .05 .02
338 Tony Perezchica .05 .02
339 Joe Price .05 .02
340 Rick Reuschel .05 .02
341 Earnest Riles .05 .02
342 Don Robinson .05 .02
343 Chris Speier .05 .02
344 Robby Thompson UER .05 .02
(West Plam Beach)
345 Jose Uribe .05 .02
346 Matt Williams .25 .10
347 Trevor Wilson RC .10 .04
348 Juan Agosto .05 .02
349 Larry Andersen .05 .02
350A Alan Ashby ERR 2.00 .80
(Throws Rig)
350B Alan Ashby COR .05 .02
351 Kevin Bass .05 .02
352 Buddy Bell .10 .04
353 Craig Biggio RC .75 .30
354 Danny Darwin .05 .02
355 Glenn Davis .05 .02
356 Jim Deshaies .05 .02
357 Bill Doran .05 .02
358 John Fishel .05 .02
359 Billy Hatcher .05 .02
360 Bob Knepper .05 .02
361 L.Meadows UER .05 .02
Bio says 10 EBH's and 6 SB's in '88, should be 3 and 4
362 Dave Meads .05 .02
363 Jim Pankovits .05 .02
364 Terry Puhl .05 .02
365 Rafael Ramirez .05 .02
366 Craig Reynolds .05 .02
367 Mike Scott .05 .02
(Card number listed as 368 on Astros CL)
368 Nolan Ryan 1.00 .40
(Card number listed as 367 on Astros CL)
369 Dave Smith .05 .02
370 Gerald Young .05 .02
371 Hubie Brooks .05 .02
372 Tim Burke .05 .02
373 John Dopson .05 .02
374 Mike R. Fitzgerald .05 .02
375 Tom Foley .05 .02
376 Andres Galarraga UER .10 .04
(Home: Caracus)
377 Neal Heaton .05 .02
378 Joe Hesketh .05 .02
379 Brian Holman RC .10 .04
380 Rex Hudler .05 .02
381 R.Johnson RC UER 3.00 1.20
Innings for '85 and '86 shown as 27 and 120, should be 27.1 and 119.2
381B R. Johnson Marlboro VAR
382 Wallace Johnson .05 .02
383 Tracy Jones .05 .02
384 Dave Martinez .05 .02
385 Dennis Martinez .10 .04
386 Andy McGaffigan .05 .02
387 Otis Nixon .05 .02
388 Johnny Paredes .05 .02
389 Jeff Parrett .05 .02
390 Pascual Perez .05 .02
391 Tim Raines .10 .04
392 Luis Rivera .05 .02
393 Nelson Santovenia .05 .02
394 Bryn Smith .05 .02
395 Tim Wallach .05 .02
396 Andy Allanson UER .05 .02
1214 hits in '88, should be 114
397 Rod Allen .05 .02
398 Scott Bailes .05 .02
399 Tom Candiotti .05 .02
400 Joe Carter .15 .06
401 Carmen Castillo UER .05 .02
(After All-Star Break batting 2.50)
402 Dave Clark UER .05 .02
(Card front shows position as Rookie; after All-Star Break batting 3.14)
403 John Farrell UER .05 .02
(Typo in runs allowed in '88)
404 Julio Franco .05 .02
405 Don Gordon .05 .02
406 Mel Hall .05 .02
407 Brad Havens .05 .02
408 Brook Jacoby .05 .02
409 Doug Jones .05 .02
410 Jeff Kaiser .05 .02
411 Luis Medina .05 .02
412 Cory Snyder .05 .02
413 Greg Swindell .05 .02
414 Ron Tingley UER .05 .02
(Hit HR in first ML at-bat, should be first AL at-bat)
415 Willie Upshaw .05 .02
416 Ron Washington .05 .02
417 Rich Yett .05 .02
418 Damon Berryhill .05 .02
419 Mike Bielecki .05 .02
420 Doug Dascenzo .05 .02
421 Jody Davis UER .05 .02
(Braves stats for '88 missing)
422 Andre Dawson .10 .04
423 Frank DiPino .05 .02
424 Shawon Dunston .05 .02
425 Rich Gossage .10 .04
426 Mark Grace UER .25 .10
(Minor League stats for '88 missing)
427 Mike Harkey RC .10 .04
428 Darrin Jackson .05 .02
429 Les Lancaster .05 .02
430 Vance Law .05 .02
431 Greg Maddux .50 .20
432 Jamie Moyer .10 .04
433 Al Nipper .05 .02
434 Rafael Palmeiro UER .25 .10
170 hits in '88, should be 178
435 Pat Perry .05 .02
436 Jeff Pico .05 .02
437 Ryne Sandberg .40 .16
438 Calvin Schiraldi .05 .02
439 Rick Sutcliffe .10 .04
440A Manny Trillo ERR 2.00 .80
(Throws Rig)
440B Manny Trillo COR .05 .02
441 Gary Varsho UER .05 .02
(Wrong birthdate; .303 should be .302; 11/28 should be 9/19)
442 Mitch Webster .05 .02
443 Luis Alicea RC .25 .10
444 Tom Brunansky .05 .02
445 Vince Coleman UER .05 .02
Third straight with 83 should be fourth straight with 81
446 John Costello UER .05 .02
(Home California, should be New York)
447 Danny Cox .05 .02
448 Ken Dayley .05 .02
449 Jose DeLeon .05 .02
450 Curt Ford .05 .02
451 Pedro Guerrero .05 .02
452 Bob Horner .05 .02
453 Tim Jones .05 .02
454 Steve Lake .05 .02
455 Joe Magrane UER .05 .02
(Des Moines, IO)
456 Greg Mathews .05 .02
457 Willie McGee .10 .04
458 Larry McWilliams .05 .02
459 Jose Oquendo .05 .02
460 Tony Pena .05 .02
461 Terry Pendleton .10 .04
462 Steve Peters UER .05 .02
(Lives in Harrah, not Harah)
463 Ozzie Smith .40 .16
464 Scott Terry .05 .02
465 Denny Walling .05 .02
466 Todd Worrell .05 .02
467 Tony Armas UER .05 .02
(Before All-Star Break batting 2.39)
468 Dante Bichette RC .40 .16
469 Bob Boone .10 .04
470 Terry Clark .05 .02
471 Stu Cliburn .05 .02
472 Mike Cook UER .05 .02
(TM near Angels logo missing from front)
473 Sherman Corbett .05 .02
474 Chili Davis .10 .04
475 Brian Downing .05 .02
476 Jim Eppard .05 .02
477 Chuck Finley .10 .04
478 Willie Fraser .05 .02
479 Bryan Harvey UER RC .25 .10
ML record shows 0-0, should be 7-5
480 Jack Howell .05 .02
481 Wally Joyner UER .10 .04
(Yorba Linda, GA)
482 Jack Lazorko .05 .02
483 Kirk McCaskill .05 .02
484 Mark McLemore .05 .02
485 Greg Minton .05 .02
486 Dan Petry .05 .02
487 Johnny Ray .05 .02
488 Dick Schofield .05 .02
489 Devon White .10 .04
490 Mike Witt .05 .02
491 Harold Baines .10 .04
492 Daryl Boston .05 .02
493 Ivan Calderon UER .05 .02
('80 stats shifted)
494 Mike Diaz .05 .02
495 Carlton Fisk .15 .06
496 Dave Gallagher .05 .02
497 Ozzie Guillen .05 .02
498 Shawn Hillegas .05 .02
499 Lance Johnson .10 .04
500 Barry Jones .05 .02
501 Bill Long .05 .02
502 Steve Lyons .05 .02
503 Fred Manrique .05 .02
504 Jack McDowell .10 .04
505 Donn Pall .05 .02
506 Kelly Paris .05 .02
507 Dan Pasqua .05 .02
508 Ken Patterson .05 .02
509 Melido Perez .05 .02
510 Jerry Reuss .05 .02
511 Mark Salas .05 .02
512 Bobby Thigpen UER .05 .02
('86 ERA 4.69, should be 4.68)
513 Mike Woodard .05 .02
514 Bob Brower .05 .02
515 Steve Buechele .05 .02
516 Jose Cecena .05 .02
517 Cecil Espy .05 .02
518 Scott Fletcher .05 .02
519 Cecilio Guante .05 .02
('87 Yankee stats are off-centered)
520 Jose Guzman .05 .02
521 Ray Hayward .05 .02
522 Charlie Hough .10 .04
523 Pete Incaviglia .05 .02
524 Mike Jeffcoat .05 .02
525 Paul Kilgus .05 .02
526 Chad Kreuter RC .25 .10
527 Jeff Kunkel .05 .02
528 Oddibe McDowell .05 .02
529 Pete O'Brien .05 .02
530 Geno Petralli .05 .02
531 Jeff Russell .05 .02
532 Ruben Sierra .05 .02
533 Mike Stanley .05 .02
534A Ed VandeBerg ERR 2.00 .80
(Throws Lef)
534B Ed VandeBerg COR .05 .02
535 Curtis Wilkerson ERR .05 .02
(Pitcher headings at bottom)
536 Mitch Williams .05 .02
537 Bobby Witt UER .05 .02
('85 ERA .643, should be 6.43)
538 Steve Balboni .05 .02
539 Scott Bankhead .05 .02
540 Scott Bradley .05 .02
541 Mickey Brantley .05 .02
542 Jay Buhner .10 .04
543 Mike Campbell .05 .02
544 Darnell Coles .05 .02
545 Henry Cotto .05 .02
546 Alvin Davis .05 .02
547 Mario Diaz .05 .02
548 Ken Griffey Jr. RC 8.00 3.20
549 Erik Hanson RC .25 .10
550 Mike Jackson UER .05 .02
(Lifetime ERA 3.345, should be 3.45)
551 Mark Langston .05 .02
552 Edgar Martinez .25 .10
553 Bill McGuire .05 .02
554 Mike Moore .05 .02
555 Jim Presley .05 .02
556 Rey Quinones .05 .02
557 Jerry Reed .05 .02
558 Harold Reynolds .10 .04
559 Mike Schooler .05 .02
560 Bill Swift .05 .02
561 Dave Valle .05 .02
562 Steve Bedrosian .05 .02
563 Phil Bradley .05 .02
564 Don Carman .05 .02
565 Bob Dernier .05 .02
566 Marvin Freeman .05 .02
567 Todd Frohwirth .05 .02
568 Greg Gross .05 .02
569 Kevin Gross .05 .02

570 Greg A. Harris .05 .02
571 Von Hayes .05 .02
572 Chris James .05 .02
573 Steve Jeltz .05 .02
574 Ron Jones UER .05 .02
(Led IL in '88 with
85, should be 75)
575 Ricky Jordan RC .25 .10
576 Mike Maddux .05 .02
577 David Palmer .05 .02
578 Lance Parrish .05 .02
579 Shane Rawley .05 .02
580 Bruce Ruffin .05 .02
581 Juan Samuel .05 .02
582 Mike Schmidt .50 .20
583 Kent Tekulve .05 .02
584 Milt Thompson UER .05 .02
(19 hits in '88,
should be 109)
585 Jose Alvarez RC .10 .04
586 Paul Assenmacher .05 .02
587 Bruce Benedict .05 .02
588 Jeff Blauser .10 .04
589 Terry Blocker .05 .02
590 Ron Gant .10 .04
591 Tom Glavine .25 .10
592 Tommy Gregg .05 .02
593 Albert Hall .05 .02
594 Dion James .05 .02
595 Rick Mahler .05 .02
596 Dale Murphy .25 .10
597 Gerald Perry .05 .02
598 Charlie Puleo .05 .02
599 Ted Simmons .10 .04
600 Pete Smith .05 .02
601 Zane Smith .05 .02
602 John Smoltz RC 1.00 .40
603 Bruce Sutter .05 .02
604 Andres Thomas .05 .02
605 Ozzie Virgil .05 .02
606 Brady Anderson RC .50 .20
607 Jeff Ballard .05 .02
608 Jose Bautista RC .10 .04
609 Ken Gerhart .05 .02
610 Terry Kennedy .05 .02
611 Eddie Murray .25 .10
612 Carl Nichols UER .05 .02
(Before All-Star Break
batting 1.88)
613 Tom Niedenfuer .05 .02
614 Joe Orsulak .05 .02
615 Oswald Peraza UER .05 .02
(Shown as Oswaldo)
616A Bill Ripken ERR 20.00 8.00
(Rick Face written
on knob of bat)
616B Bill Ripken 80.00 32.00
(Bat knob
whited out)
616C Bill Ripken 5.00 2.00
(Words on bat knob
scribbled out in White)
616D Bill Ripken 20.00 8.00
Words on Bat
scribbled out in Black
616E Bill Ripken DP .10 .04
(Black box covering
bat knob)
617 Cal Ripken .75 .30
618 Dave Schmidt .05 .02
619 Rick Schu .05 .02
620 Larry Sheets .05 .02
621 Doug Sisk .05 .02
622 Pete Stanicek .05 .02
623 Mickey Tettleton .05 .02
624 Jay Tibbs .05 .02
625 Jim Traber .05 .02
626 Mark Williamson .05 .02
627 Craig Worthington .05 .02
628 Jose Canseco 40/40 .10 .04
629 Tom Browning Perfect .05 .02
630 Roberto Alomar .25 .10
Sandy Alomar Jr. UER
(Names on card listed
in wrong order)
631 Will Clark .25 .10
Rafael Palmeiro UER
(Gallaraga, sic;
Clark 3 consecutive
100 RBI seasons;
third with 102 RBI's)
632 Darryl Strawberry .10 .04
Will Clark UER (Homeruns
should be two words)
633 Wade Boggs .10 .04
Carney Lansford UER
(Boggs hit .366 in
'86, should be '88)
634 Jose Canseco .50 .20
Terry Steinbach
Mark McGwire
635 Mark Davis .15 .06
Dwight Gooden
636 Danny Jackson .05 .02
David Cone UER
Hersheiser, sic
637 Chris Sabo .10 .04
Bobby Bonilla UER
Bobby Bonds, sic
638 Andres Galarraga UER .05 .02
(Misspelled Gallaraga
on card back)
Gerald Perry
639 Kirby Puckett .15 .06
Eric Davis
640 Steve Wilson and .05 .02
Cameron Drew
641 Kevin Brown and .25 .10
Kevin Reimer
642 Brad Pounders RC .10 .04
Jerald Clark
643 Mike Capel and .05 .02
Drew Hall
644 Joe Girardi RC and .40 .16
Rolando Roomes
645 Lenny Harris RC and .25 .10
Marty Brown
646 Luis DeLosSantos .05 .02
and Jim Campbell
647 Randy Kramer and .05 .02
Miguel Garcia
648 Torey Lovullo RC and .10 .04
Robert Palacios
649 Jim Corsi and .05 .02
Bob Milacki
650 Grady Hall and .05 .02
Mike Rochford
651 Terry Taylor RC .10 .04
Vance Lovelace
652 Ken Hill RC and .25 .10
Dennis Cook
653 Scott Service and .05 .02
Shane Turner
654 CL: Oakland/Mets .05 .02
Dodgers/Red Sox
(10 Henderson;
68 Jess Orosco)
655A CL: Twins/Tigers ERR .05 .02
Reds/Brewers
(179 Boslo and
Twins/Tigers positions
listed)
655B CL: Twins/Tigers COR .05 .02
Reds/Brewers
(179 Boslo but
Twins/Tigers positions
not listed)
656 CL: Pirates/Blue Jays .05 .02
Yankees/Royals
(225 Jess Barfield)
657 CL: Padres/Giants .05 .02
Astros/Expos
(367/368 wrong)
658 CL: Indians/Cubs .05 .02
Cardinals/Angels
(449 Deleon)
659 CL: White Sox/Rangers .05 .02
Mariners/Phillies
660 CL: Braves/Orioles .05 .02
Specials/Checklists
(632 hyphenated diff-
erently and 650 Hali;
595 Rich Mahler;
619 Rich Schu)

1989 Fleer Glossy

This 660 card set turned out to be the final parallel glossy issue for Fleer. These cards are identical to the regular Fleer cards except for the glossy sheen on the front. As many dealers did not order this product, this set is considerably scarcer than the regular 1989 Fleer set and the preceding years of Glossy parallels. Unlike the previous two seasons, the update set was not issued in Glossy form. It is estimated that Fleer made approximately 30,000 of these sets. The Ken Griffey Jr. card from this set is regarded as one of the most important early parallels in hobby history and is more often than not found with poor centering.

	Nm-Mt	Ex-Mt
COMP.FACT.SET (672)	120.00	47.50
*STARS: 3X TO 8X BASIC CARDS		
*ROOKIES: 4X TO 10X BASIC CARDS		

1989 Fleer All-Stars

This twelve-card standard-size subset was randomly inserted in Fleer wax and cello packs. The players selected are the 1989 Fleer Major League All-Star team. One player has been selected for each position along with a DH and three pitchers. The cards feature a distinctive green background on the card fronts. The set is sequenced in alphabetical order.

	Nm-Mt	Ex-Mt
COMPLETE SET (12)	5.00	2.00
1 Bobby Bonilla	.75	.30
2 Jose Canseco	2.00	.80
3 Will Clark	2.00	.80
4 Dennis Eckersley	.75	.30
5 Julio Franco	.40	.16
6 Mike Greenwell	.40	.16
7 Orel Hershiser	.75	.30
8 Paul Molitor	1.25	.50
9 Mike Scioscia	.40	.16
10 Darryl Strawberry	1.25	.50
11 Alan Trammell	1.25	.50
12 Frank Viola	.40	.16

1989 Fleer For The Record

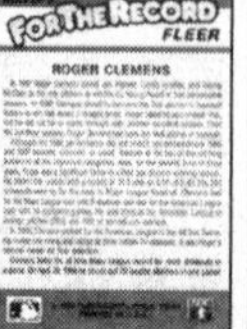

This six-card standard-size insert set was distributed one per rack pack. The set is subtitled "For The Record" and commemorates record-breaking events for those players from the previous season. The card backs are printed in red, black, and gray on white card stock. The set is sequenced in alphabetical order.

	Nm-Mt	Ex-Mt
COMPLETE SET (6)	8.00	3.20
1 Wade Boggs	1.00	.40
2 Roger Clemens	3.00	1.20
3 Andres Galarraga	.60	.24
4 Kirk Gibson	.60	.24
5 Greg Maddux	3.00	1.20
6 Don Mattingly UER (Won batting title '83, should say '84)	4.00	1.60

1989 Fleer Wax Box Cards

The cards in this 28-card set measure the standard 2 1/2" by 3 1/2". Cards have essentially the same design as the 1989 Fleer regular issue set. The cards were printed on the bottoms of the regular issue wax pack boxes. These 28 cards (C1 to C28) are considered a separate set in their own right and are not typically included in a complete set of the regular issue 1989 Fleer cards. The value of the panel uncut is slightly greater, perhaps by 25 percent greater, than the value of the individual cards cut up carefully. The wax box cards are further distinguished by the gray card stock used.

	Nm-Mt	Ex-Mt
COMPLETE SET (28)	10.00	4.00
C1 Mets Logo	.15	.06
C2 Wade Boggs	.75	.30
C3 George Brett	1.50	.60
C4 Jose Canseco UER ('88 strikeouts 121 and career strike-outs 49, should be 128 and 491)	1.50	.60
C5 A's Logo	.15	.06
C6 Will Clark	1.00	.40
C7 David Cone	.60	.24
C8 Andres Galarraga UER (Career average .289 should be .269)	.60	.24
C9 Dodgers Logo	.15	.06
C10 Kirk Gibson	.25	.10
C11 Mike Greenwell	.15	.06
C12 Tony Gwynn	2.50	1.00
C13 Tigers Logo	.15	.06
C14 Orel Hershiser	.25	.10
C15 Danny Jackson	.15	.06
C16 Wally Joyner	.25	.10
C17 Red Sox Logo	.15	.06
C18 Yankees Logo	.15	.06
C19 Fred McGriff UER (Career BA of .289 should be .269)	1.00	.40
C20 Kirby Puckett	2.00	.80
C21 Chris Sabo	.15	.06
C22 Kevin Seitzer	.15	.06
C23 Pirates Logo	.15	.06
C24 Astros Logo	.15	.06
C25 Darryl Strawberry	.25	.10
C26 Alan Trammell	.40	.16
C27 Andy Van Slyke	.15	.06
C28 Frank Viola	.15	.06

1989 Fleer World Series

This 12-card standard-size set features highlights of the previous year's World Series between the Dodgers and the Athletics. The sets were packaged as a complete set insert with the collated sets (of the 1989 Fleer regular issue) which were sold by Fleer directly to hobby card dealers; they were not available in the general retail candy store outlets. The Kirk Gibson card from this set highlights one of the most famous home runs in World Series history.

	Nm-Mt	Ex-Mt
COMPLETE SET (12)	2.00	.80
1 Mickey Hatcher	.05	.02
2 Tim Belcher	.05	.02
3 Jose Canseco	.25	.10
4 Mike Scioscia	.05	.02
5 Kirk Gibson	.10	.04
6 Orel Hershiser	.10	.04
7 Mike Marshall	.05	.02
8 Mark McGwire	1.00	.40
9 Steve Sax UER (actually 42 steals in '88)	.05	.02
10 Walt Weiss	.05	.02
11 Orel Hershiser	.10	.04
12 Dodger Blue World Champs	.10	.04

1989 Fleer Update

The 1989 Fleer Update set contains 132 standard-size cards. The cards were distributed exclusively in factory set form in grey and white, cellophane wrapped boxes through hobby dealers. The cards are identical in design to regular issue 1989 Fleer cards except for the U-prefixed numbering on back. The set numbering is in team order with players within teams ordered alphabetically. The set includes special cards for Nolan Ryan's 5,000th strikeout and Mike Schmidt's retirement. Rookie Cards include Kevin Appier, Joey (Albert) Belle, Deion Sanders, Greg Vaughn, Robin Ventura and Todd Zeile.

	Nm-Mt	Ex-Mt
COMP.FACT.SET (132)	5.00	2.00
1 Phil Bradley	.05	.02
2 Mike Devereaux	.05	.02
3 Steve Finley RC	.50	.20
4 Kevin Hickey	.05	.02
5 Brian Holton	.05	.02
6 Bob Milacki	.05	.02
7 Randy Milligan	.05	.02
8 John Dopson	.05	.02
9 Nick Esasky	.05	.02
10 Rob Murphy	.05	.02
11 Jim Abbott RC*	.50	.20
12 Bert Blyleven	.10	.04
13 Jeff Manto RC	.10	.04
14 Bob McClure	.05	.02
15 Lance Parrish	.05	.02
16 Lee Stevens RC	.25	.10
17 Claudell Washington	.05	.02
18 Mark Davis RC	.25	.10
19 Eric King	.05	.02
20 Ron Kittle	.05	.02
21 Matt Merullo	.05	.02
22 Steve Rosenberg	.05	.02
23 Robin Ventura RC	.75	.30
24 Keith Atherton	.05	.02
25 Joey Belle RC	1.50	.60
26 Jerry Browne	.05	.02
27 Felix Fermin	.05	.02
28 Brad Komminsk	.05	.02
29 Pete O'Brien	.05	.02
30 Mike Brumley	.05	.02
31 Tracy Jones	.05	.02
32 Mike Schwabe	.05	.02
33 Gary Ward	.05	.02
34 Frank Williams	.05	.02
35 Kevin Appier RC	.75	.30
36 Bob Boone	.10	.04
37 Luis DeLosSantos	.05	.02
38 Jim Eisenreich	.05	.02
39 Jaime Navarro RC	.10	.04
40 Bill Spiers RC	.25	.10
41 Greg Vaughn RC	.50	.20
42 Randy Veres	.05	.02
43 Wally Backman	.05	.02
44 Shane Rawley	.05	.02
45 Steve Balboni	.05	.02
46 Jesse Barfield	.05	.02
47 Alvaro Espinoza	.05	.02
48 Bob Geren RC	.05	.02
49 Mel Hall	.05	.02
50 Andy Hawkins	.05	.02
51 Hensley Meulens RC	.10	.04
52 Steve Sax	.05	.02
53 Deion Sanders RC	.75	.30
54 Rickey Henderson	.25	.10
55 Mike Moore	.05	.02
56 Tony Phillips	.05	.02
57 Greg Briley	.05	.02
58 Gene Harris RC	.10	.04
59 Randy Johnson	3.00	1.20
60 Jeffrey Leonard	.05	.02
61 Dennis Powell	.05	.02
62 Omar Vizquel RC	.50	.20
63 Kevin Brown	.25	.10
64 Julio Franco	.05	.02
65 Jamie Moyer	.10	.04
66 Rafael Palmeiro	.25	.10
67 Nolan Ryan	1.50	.60
68 Francisco Cabrera RC	.10	.04
69 Junior Felix RC	.10	.04
70 Al Leiter	.25	.10
71 Alex Sanchez	.05	.02
72 Geronimo Berroa	.05	.02
73 Derek Lilliquist RC	.10	.04
74 Lonnie Smith	.05	.02
75 Jeff Treadway	.05	.02
76 Paul Kilgus	.05	.02
77 Lloyd McClendon	.05	.02
78 Scott Sanderson	.05	.02
79 Dwight Smith RC	.25	.10
80 Jerome Walton	.25	.10
81 Mitch Williams	.05	.02
82 Steve Wilson	.05	.02
83 Todd Benzinger	.05	.02
84 Ken Griffey Sr.	.10	.04
85 Rick Mahler	.05	.02
86 Rolando Roomes	.05	.02
87 Scott Scudder RC	.10	.04
88 Jim Clancy	.05	.02
89 Rick Rhoden	.05	.02
90 Dan Schatzeder	.05	.02
91 Mike Morgan	.05	.02
92 Eddie Murray	.25	.10
93 Willie Randolph	.10	.04
94 Ray Searage	.05	.02
95 Mike Aldrete	.05	.02
96 Kevin Gross	.05	.02
97 Mark Langston	.05	.02
98 Spike Owen	.05	.02
99 Zane Smith	.05	.02
100 Don Aase	.05	.02
101 Barry Lyons	.05	.02
102 Juan Samuel	.05	.02
103 Wally Whitehurst RC	.10	.04
104 Dennis Cook	.05	.02
105 Len Dykstra	.10	.04
106 Charlie Hayes	.25	.10
107 Tommy Herr	.05	.02
108 Ken Howell	.05	.02
109 John Kruk	.10	.04
110 Roger McDowell	.05	.02
111 Terry Mulholland	.05	.02
112 Jeff Parrett	.05	.02
113 Neal Heaton	.05	.02
114 Jeff King	.05	.02
115 Randy Kramer	.05	.02
116 Bill Landrum	.05	.02
117 Cris Carpenter RC *	.10	.04
118 Frank DiPino	.05	.02
119 Ken Hill	.25	.10
120 Dan Quisenberry	.05	.02
121 Milt Thompson	.05	.02
122 Todd Zeile RC	.40	.16
123 Jack Clark	.05	.02
124 Bruce Hurst	.05	.02
125 Mark Parent	.05	.02
126 Bip Roberts	.10	.04
127 Jeff Brantley RC UER (Photo actually Joe Kmak)	.25	.10
128 Terry Kennedy	.05	.02
129 Mike LaCoss	.05	.02
130 Greg Litton	.05	.02
131 Mike Schmidt	.75	.30
132 Checklist 1-132	.05	.02

1989 Fleer Baseball All-Stars

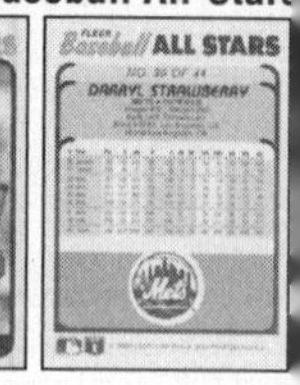

The 1989 Fleer Baseball All-Stars set contain 44 standard-size cards. The fronts ar yellowish beige with salmon pinstripes; th vertically oriented backs are red, white and pin and feature career stats. The card numbering o this set is ordered alphabetically by player' name. The cards were distributed through Be Franklin stores as a boxed set.

	Nm-Mt	Ex-Mt
COMP.FACT SET (44)	6.00	2.40
1 Doyle Alexander	.05	.02
2 George Bell	.05	.02
3 Wade Boggs	.40	.16
4 Bobby Bonilla	.10	.04
5 Jose Canseco	.40	.16
6 Will Clark	.75	.30
7 Roger Clemens	.75	.30
8 Vince Coleman	.05	.02
9 David Cone	.20	.08
10 Mark Davis	.05	.02
11 Andre Dawson	.20	.08
12 Dennis Eckersley	.40	.16
13 Andres Galarraga	.20	.08
14 Kirk Gibson	.10	.04
15 Dwight Gooden	.10	.04
16 Mike Greenwell	.05	.02
17 Mark Gubicza	.05	.02
18 Ozzie Guillen	.10	.04
19 Tony Gwynn	.75	.30
20 Rickey Henderson	.60	.24
21 Orel Hershiser	.10	.04
22 Danny Jackson	.05	.02
23 Doug Jones	.05	.02
24 Ricky Jordan	.05	.02
25 Bob Knepper	.05	.02
26 Barry Larkin	.50	.20
27 Vance Law	.05	.02
28 Don Mattingly	.75	.30
29 Mark McGwire	1.25	.50
30 Paul Molitor	.40	.16
31 Gerald Perry	.05	.02
32 Kirby Puckett	.40	.16
33 Johnny Ray	.05	.02
34 Harold Reynolds	.10	.04
35 Cal Ripken	1.50	.60
36 Don Robinson	.05	.02
37 Ruben Sierra	.10	.04
38 Dave Smith	.05	.02
39 Darryl Strawberry	.10	.04
40 Dave Stieb	.05	.02
41 Alan Trammell	.15	.06
42 Andy Van Slyke	.05	.02
43 Frank Viola	.05	.02
44 Dave Winfield	.40	.16

1989 Fleer Baseball MVP's

The 1989 Fleer Baseball MVP's set contains 44 standard-size cards. The fronts and backs are green and yellow. The horizontally oriented backs feature career stats. The card numbering of this set is ordered alphabetically by player's name. The cards were distributed through Toys 'R' Us stores as a boxed set.

	Nm-Mt	Ex-Mt
COMP.FACT SET (44)	8.00	3.20
1 Steve Bedrosian	.05	.02
2 George Bell	.05	.02
3 Wade Boggs	.40	.16
4 George Brett	.50	.20
5 Hubie Brooks	.05	.02
6 Jose Canseco	.30	.12
7 Will Clark	.50	.20
8 Roger Clemens	.50	.20
9 Eric Davis	.10	.04
10 Glenn Davis	.05	.02
11 Andre Dawson	.20	.08
12 Andres Galarraga	.20	.08
13 Kirk Gibson	.10	.04
14 Dwight Gooden	.10	.04
15 Mark Grace	.50	.20
16 Mike Greenwell	.05	.02
17 Tony Gwynn	.75	.30
18 Bryan Harvey	.05	.02
19 Orel Hershiser	.10	.04
20 Ted Higuera	.05	.02
21 Danny Jackson	.05	.02
22 Mike Jackson	.10	.04
23 Doug Jones	.05	.02
24 Greg Maddux	1.00	.40
25 Mike Marshall	.05	.02
26 Don Mattingly	.75	.30
27 Fred McGriff	.50	.20
28 Mark McGwire	1.25	.50
29 Kevin McReynolds	.05	.02
30 Jack Morris	.10	.04
31 Gerald Perry	.05	.02
32 Kirby Puckett	.40	.16

33 Chris Sabo .05 .02
34 Mike Scott .05 .02
35 Ruben Sierra .10 .04
36 Darryl Strawberry .10 .04
37 Danny Tartabull .05 .02
38 Bobby Thigpen .05 .02
39 Alan Trammell .15 .06
40 Andy Van Slyke .10 .04
41 Frank Viola .05 .02
42 Walt Weiss .05 .02
43 Dave Winfield .40 .16
44 Todd Worrell .10 .04

1989 Fleer Exciting Stars

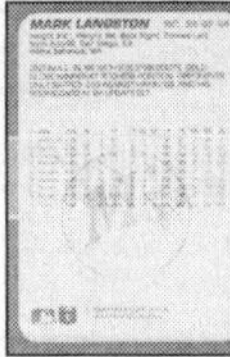

The 1989 Fleer Exciting Stars set contains 44 standard-size cards. The fronts have baby blue borders; the backs are pink and blue. The vertically oriented backs feature career stats. The card numbering of this set is ordered alphabetically by player's name. The cards were distributed as a boxed set.

Nm-Mt Ex-Mt
COMP.FACT SET (44) 6.00 2.40
1 Harold Baines .15 .06
2 Wade Boggs .40 .16
3 Jose Canseco .30 .12
4 Joe Carter .15 .06
5 Will Clark .50 .20
6 Roger Clemens .75 .30
7 Vince Coleman .05 .02
8 David Cone .20 .08
9 Eric Davis .10 .04
10 Glenn Davis .05 .02
11 Andre Dawson .20 .08
12 Dwight Evans .10 .04
13 Andres Galarraga .20 .08
14 Kirk Gibson .10 .04
15 Dwight Gooden .10 .04
16 Jim Gott .05 .02
17 Mark Grace .75 .30
18 Mike Greenwell .05 .02
19 Mark Gubicza .05 .02
20 Tony Gwynn .75 .30
21 Rickey Henderson .60 .24
22 Tom Henke .05 .02
23 Mike Henneman .05 .02
24 Orel Hershiser .10 .04
25 Danny Jackson .05 .02
26 Gregg Jefferies .05 .02
27 Ricky Jordan .05 .02
28 Wally Joyner .10 .04
29 Mark Langston .05 .02
30 Tim Leary .05 .02
31 Don Mattingly .75 .30
32 Mark McGwire 1.25 .50
33 Dale Murphy .20 .08
34 Kirby Puckett .40 .16
35 Chris Sabo .05 .02
36 Kevin Seitzer .05 .02
37 Ruben Sierra .10 .04
38 Ozzie Smith .75 .30
39 Dave Stewart .10 .04
40 Darryl Strawberry .10 .04
41 Alan Trammell .15 .06
42 Frank Viola .05 .02
43 Dave Winfield .40 .16
44 Robin Yount .40 .16

1989 Fleer Heroes of Baseball

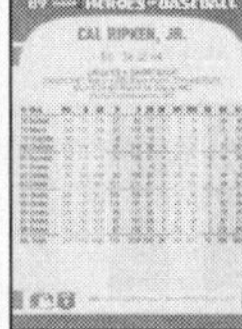

The 1989 Fleer Heroes of Baseball set contains 44 standard-size cards. The fronts and backs are red, white and blue. The vertically oriented backs feature career stats. The card numbering of this set is ordered alphabetically by player's name. The cards were distributed through Woolworth stores as a boxed set.

Nm-Mt Ex-Mt
COMP.FACT SET (44) 6.00 2.40
1 George Bell .05 .02
2 Wade Boggs .50 .20
3 Barry Bonds 1.00 .40
4 Tom Brunansky .05 .02
5 Jose Canseco .40 .16
6 Joe Carter .15 .06
7 Will Clark .50 .20
8 Roger Clemens 1.00 .40
9 David Cone .20 .08
10 Eric Davis .10 .04
11 Glenn Davis .05 .02
12 Andre Dawson .20 .08
13 Dennis Eckersley .40 .16
14 John Franco .10 .04
15 Gary Gaetti .10 .04
16 Andres Galarraga .20 .08
17 Kirk Gibson .10 .04
18 Dwight Gooden .10 .04
19 Mike Greenwell .05 .02
20 Tony Gwynn .75 .30
21 Bryan Harvey .05 .02
22 Orel Hershiser .10 .04
23 Ted Higuera .05 .02
24 Danny Jackson .05 .02
25 Ricky Jordan .05 .02
26 Don Mattingly .75 .30
27 Fred McGriff .40 .16
28 Mark McGwire 1.25 .50
29 Kevin McReynolds .05 .02
30 Gerald Perry .05 .02
31 Kirby Puckett .50 .20
32 Johnny Ray .05 .02
33 Harold Reynolds .10 .04
34 Cal Ripken 1.50 .60
35 Ryne Sandberg .50 .20
36 Kevin Seitzer .05 .02
37 Ruben Sierra .10 .04
38 Darryl Strawberry .10 .04
39 Bobby Thigpen .05 .02
40 Alan Trammell .15 .06
41 Andy Van Slyke .10 .04
42 Frank Viola .05 .02
43 Dave Winfield .40 .16
44 Robin Yount .50 .20

1989 Fleer League Leaders

The 1989 Fleer League Leaders set contains 44 standard-size cards. The fronts are red and yellow; the horizontally oriented backs are light blue and red, and feature career stats. The card numbering of this set is ordered alphabetically by player's name. The cards were distributed through Woolworth stores as a boxed set.

Nm-Mt Ex-Mt
COMP.FACT SET (44) 6.00 2.40
1 Allan Anderson .05 .02
2 Wade Boggs .40 .16
3 Jose Canseco .30 .12
4 Will Clark .50 .20
5 Roger Clemens .75 .30
6 Vince Coleman .05 .02
7 David Cone .20 .08
8 Kal Daniels .05 .02
9 Chili Davis .10 .04
10 Eric Davis .10 .04
11 Glenn Davis .05 .02
12 Andre Dawson .20 .08
13 John Franco .10 .04
14 Andres Galarraga .20 .08
15 Kirk Gibson .10 .04
16 Dwight Gooden .10 .04
17 Mark Grace .75 .30
18 Mike Greenwell .05 .02
19 Tony Gwynn .75 .30
20 Orel Hershiser .10 .04
21 Pete Incaviglia .05 .02
22 Danny Jackson .05 .02
23 Gregg Jefferies .05 .02
24 Joe Magrane .05 .02
25 Don Mattingly .75 .30
26 Fred McGriff .40 .16
27 Mark McGwire 1.25 .50
28 Dale Murphy .20 .08
29 Dan Plesac .05 .02
30 Kirby Puckett .50 .20
31 Harold Reynolds .10 .04
32 Cal Ripken 1.50 .60
33 Jeff M. Robinson .05 .02
34 Mike Scott .05 .02
35 Ozzie Smith .75 .30
36 Dave Stewart .10 .04
37 Darryl Strawberry .10 .04
38 Greg Swindell .05 .02
39 Bobby Thigpen .05 .02
40 Alan Trammell .15 .06
41 Andy Van Slyke .05 .02
42 Frank Viola .05 .02
43 Dave Winfield .40 .16
44 Robin Yount .50 .20

1989 Fleer Superstars

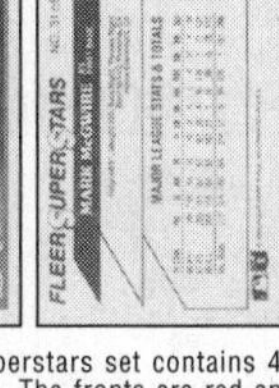

The 1989 Fleer Superstars set contains 44 standard-size cards. The fronts are red and beige; the horizontally oriented backs are yellow, and feature career stats. The card numbering of this set is ordered alphabetically by player's name. The cards were distributed as a boxed set. The back panel of the box contains the complete set checklist.

Nm-Mt Ex-Mt
COMP.FACT SET (44) 6.00 2.40
1 Roberto Alomar .75 .30
2 Harold Baines .10 .04
3 Tim Belcher .05 .02
4 Wade Boggs .40 .16
5 George Brett .75 .30
6 Jose Canseco .30 .12
7 Gary Carter .15 .06
8 Will Clark .50 .20
9 Roger Clemens .75 .30
10 Kal Daniels UER .05 .02
(Reverse negative photo on front)
11 Eric Davis .10 .04
12 Andre Dawson .20 .08
13 Tony Fernandez .10 .04
14 Scott Fletcher .05 .02
15 Andres Galarraga .20 .08
16 Kirk Gibson .10 .04
17 Dwight Gooden .10 .04
18 Jim Gott .05 .02
19 Mark Grace .75 .30
20 Mike Greenwell .05 .02
21 Tony Gwynn .75 .30
22 Rickey Henderson .60 .24
23 Orel Hershiser .10 .04
24 Ted Higuera .05 .02
25 Gregg Jefferies .05 .02
26 Wally Joyner .10 .04
27 Mark Langston .05 .02
28 Greg Maddux 1.50 .60
29 Don Mattingly .75 .30
30 Fred McGriff .40 .16
31 Mark McGwire 1.25 .50
32 Dan Plesac .05 .02
33 Kirby Puckett .40 .16
34 Jeff Reardon .10 .04
35 Chris Sabo .05 .02
36 Mike Schmidt .50 .20
37 Mike Scott .05 .02
38 Cory Snyder .05 .02
39 Darryl Strawberry .10 .04
40 Alan Trammell .15 .06
41 Frank Viola .05 .02
42 Walt Weiss .05 .02
43 Dave Winfield .50 .20
44 Todd Worrell UER .05 .02
(Statistical headings on back for hitter)

1990 Fleer

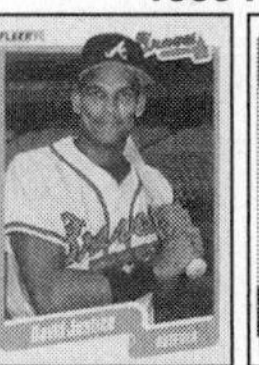

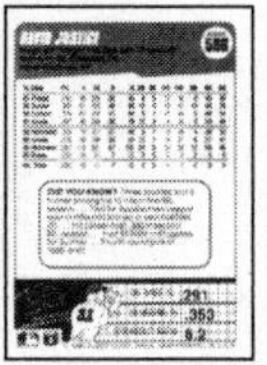

The 1990 Fleer set contains 660 standard-size cards. Cards were primarily issued in wax packs, rack packs and hobby and retail factory sets. Card fronts feature white outer borders with ribbon-like, colored inner borders. The set is again ordered numerically by teams based upon the previous season's record. Subsets include Decade Greats (621-630), Superstar Combinations (631-639), Rookie Prospects (640-653) and checklists (654-660). Rookie Cards of note include Moises Alou, Juan Gonzalez, David Justice, Sammy Sosa and Larry Walker.

Nm-Mt Ex-Mt
COMPLETE SET (660) 15.00 4.50
COMP.RETAIL SET (660) 8.00 2.40
COMP.HOBBY SET (672) 15.00 4.50
1 Lance Blankenship .05 .02
2 Todd Burns .05 .02
3 Jose Canseco .25 .07
4 Jim Corsi .05 .02
5 Storm Davis .05 .02
6 Dennis Eckersley .10 .03
7 Mike Gallego .05 .02
8 Ron Hassey .05 .02
9 Dave Henderson .05 .02
10 Rickey Henderson .25 .07
11 Rick Honeycutt .05 .02
12 Stan Javier .05 .02
13 Felix Jose .05 .02
14 Carney Lansford .10 .03
15 Mark McGwire UER .60 .18
(1989 runs listed as 4, should be 74)
16 Mike Moore .05 .02
17 Gene Nelson .05 .02
18 Dave Parker .10 .03
19 Tony Phillips .05 .02
20 Terry Steinbach .05 .02
21 Dave Stewart .10 .03
22 Walt Weiss .05 .02
23 Bob Welch .05 .02
24 Curt Young .05 .02
25 Paul Assenmacher .05 .02
26 Damon Berryhill .05 .02
27 Mike Bielecki .05 .02
28 Kevin Blankenship .05 .02
29 Andre Dawson .10 .03
30 Shawon Dunston .05 .02
31 Joe Girardi .15 .04
32 Mark Grace .15 .04
33 Mike Harkey .05 .02
34 Paul Kilgus .05 .02
35 Les Lancaster .05 .02
36 Vance Law .05 .02
37 Greg Maddux .40 .12
38 Lloyd McClendon .05 .02
39 Jeff Pico .05 .02
40 Ryne Sandberg .40 .12
41 Scott Sanderson .05 .02
42 Dwight Smith .05 .02
43 Rick Sutcliffe .10 .03
44 Jerome Walton .05 .02
45 Mitch Webster .05 .02
46 Curt Wilkerson .05 .02
47 Dean Wilkins .05 .02
48 Mitch Williams .05 .02
49 Steve Wilson .05 .02
50 Steve Bedrosian .05 .02
51 Mike Benjamin RC .10 .03
52 Jeff Brantley .05 .02
53 Brett Butler .10 .03
54 Will Clark UER .10 .03
(Did You Know says first in runs, should say tied for first)
55 Kelly Downs .05 .02
56 Scott Garrelts .05 .02
57 Atlee Hammaker .05 .02
58 Terry Kennedy .05 .02
59 Mike LaCoss .05 .02
60 Craig Lefferts .05 .02
61 Greg Litton .05 .02
62 Candy Maldonado .05 .02
63 Kirt Manwaring UER .05 .02
(No '88 Phoenix stats as noted in box)
64 Randy McCament .05 .02
65 Kevin Mitchell .05 .02
66 Donell Nixon .05 .02
67 Ken Oberkfell .05 .02
68 Rick Reuschel .05 .02
69 Ernest Riles .05 .02
70 Don Robinson .05 .02
71 Pat Sheridan .05 .02
72 Chris Speier .05 .02
73 Robby Thompson .05 .02
74 Jose Uribe .05 .02
75 Matt Williams .10 .03
76 George Bell .05 .02
77 Pat Borders .05 .02
78 John Cerutti .05 .02
79 Junior Felix .05 .02
80 Tony Fernandez .05 .02
81 Mike Flanagan .05 .02
82 Mauro Gozzo .05 .02
83 Kelly Gruber .05 .02
84 Tom Henke .05 .02
85 Jimmy Key .10 .03
86 Manny Lee .05 .02
87 Nelson Liriano UER .05 .02
(Should say "led the IL" instead of "led the TL")
88 Lee Mazzilli .05 .02
89 Fred McGriff .25 .07
90 Lloyd Moseby .05 .02
91 Rance Mulliniks .05 .02
92 Alex Sanchez .05 .02
93 Dave Stieb .10 .03
94 Todd Stottlemyre .10 .03
95 Duane Ward UER .05 .02
(Double line of '87 Syracuse stats)
96 David Wells .10 .03
97 Ernie Whitt .05 .02
98 Frank Wills .05 .02
99 Mookie Wilson .10 .03
100 Kevin Appier .25 .07
101 Luis Aquino .05 .02
102 Bob Boone .10 .03
103 George Brett .60 .18
104 Jose DeJesus .05 .02
105 Luis De Los Santos .05 .02
106 Jim Eisenreich .05 .02
107 Steve Farr .05 .02
108 Tom Gordon .10 .03
109 Mark Gubicza .05 .02
110 Bo Jackson .25 .07
111 Terry Leach .05 .02
112 Charlie Leibrandt .05 .02
113 Rick Luecken .05 .02
114 Mike Macfarlane .05 .02
115 Jeff Montgomery .10 .03
116 Bret Saberhagen .10 .03
117 Kevin Seitzer .05 .02
118 Kurt Stillwell .05 .02
119 Pat Tabler .05 .02
120 Danny Tartabull .05 .02
121 Gary Thurman .05 .02
122 Frank White .10 .03
123 Willie Wilson .05 .02
124 Matt Winters .05 .02
125 Jim Abbott .15 .04
126 Tony Armas .05 .02
127 Dante Bichette .25 .07
128 Bert Blyleven .10 .03
129 Chili Davis .10 .03
130 Brian Downing .05 .02
131 Mike Fetters RC .25 .07
132 Chuck Finley .10 .03
133 Willie Fraser .05 .02
134 Bryan Harvey .05 .02
135 Jack Howell .05 .02
136 Wally Joyner .10 .03
137 Jeff Manto .05 .02
138 Kirk McCaskill .05 .02
139 Bob McClure .05 .02
140 Greg Minton .05 .02
141 Lance Parrish .05 .02
142 Dan Petry .05 .02
143 Johnny Ray .05 .02
144 Dick Schofield .05 .02
145 Lee Stevens .10 .03
146 Claudell Washington .05 .02
147 Devon White .05 .02
148 Mike Witt .05 .02
149 Roberto Alomar .25 .07
150 Sandy Alomar Jr. .10 .03
151 Andy Benes .10 .03
152 Jack Clark .10 .03
153 Pat Clements .05 .02
154 Joey Cora .10 .03
155 Mark Davis .05 .02
156 Mark Grant .05 .02
157 Tony Gwynn .30 .09
158 Greg W. Harris .05 .02
159 Bruce Hurst .05 .02
160 Darrin Jackson .05 .02
161 Chris James .05 .02
162 Carmelo Martinez .05 .02
163 Mike Pagliarulo .05 .02
164 Mark Parent .05 .02
165 Dennis Rasmussen .05 .02
166 Bip Roberts .05 .02
167 Benito Santiago .10 .03
168 Calvin Schiraldi .05 .02
169 Eric Show .05 .02
170 Garry Templeton .05 .02
171 Ed Whitson .05 .02
172 Brady Anderson .10 .03
173 Jeff Ballard .10 .03
174 Phil Bradley .05 .02
175 Mike Devereaux .05 .02
176 Steve Finley .10 .03
177 Pete Harnisch .05 .02
178 Kevin Hickey .05 .02
179 Brian Holton .05 .02
180 Ben McDonald RC .25 .07
181 Bob Melvin .05 .02
182 Bob Milacki .05 .02
183 Randy Milligan UER .05 .02
(Double line of '87 stats)
184 Gregg Olson .10 .03
185 Joe Orsulak .05 .02
186 Bill Ripken .05 .02
187 Cal Ripken .75 .23
188 Dave Schmidt .05 .02
189 Larry Sheets .05 .02
190 Mickey Tettleton .05 .02
191 Mark Thurmond .05 .02
192 Jay Tibbs .05 .02
193 Jim Traber .05 .02
194 Mark Williamson .05 .02
195 Craig Worthington .05 .02
196 Don Aase .05 .02
197 Blaine Beatty .05 .02
198 Mark Carreon .05 .02
199 Gary Carter .15 .04
200 David Cone .10 .03
201 Ron Darling .05 .02
202 Kevin Elster .05 .02
203 Sid Fernandez .05 .02
204 Dwight Gooden .15 .04
205 Keith Hernandez .15 .04
206 Jeff Innis .05 .02
207 Gregg Jefferies .10 .03
208 Howard Johnson .05 .02
209 Barry Lyons UER .05 .02
(Double line of '87 stats)
210 Dave Magadan .05 .02
211 Kevin McReynolds .05 .02
212 Jeff Musselman .05 .02
213 Randy Myers .10 .03
214 Bob Ojeda .05 .02
215 Juan Samuel .05 .02
216 Mackey Sasser .05 .02
217 Darryl Strawberry .15 .04
218 Tim Teufel .05 .02
219 Frank Viola .05 .02
220 Juan Agosto .05 .02
221 Larry Andersen .05 .02
222 Eric Anthony RC .10 .03
223 Kevin Bass .05 .02
224 Craig Biggio .15 .04
225 Ken Caminiti .10 .03
226 Jim Clancy .05 .02
227 Danny Darwin .05 .02
228 Glenn Davis .05 .02
229 Jim Deshaies .05 .02
230 Bill Doran .05 .02
231 Bob Forsch .05 .02
232 Brian Meyer .05 .02
233 Terry Puhl .05 .02
234 Rafael Ramirez .05 .02
235 Rick Rhoden .05 .02
236 Dan Schatzeder .05 .02
237 Mike Scott .05 .02
238 Dave Smith .05 .02
239 Alex Trevino .05 .02
240 Glenn Wilson .05 .02
241 Gerald Young .05 .02
242 Tom Brunansky .05 .02
243 Cris Carpenter .05 .02
244 Alex Cole RC .10 .03
245 Vince Coleman .05 .02
246 John Costello .05 .02
247 Ken Dayley .05 .02
248 Jose DeLeon .05 .02
249 Frank DiPino .05 .02
250 Pedro Guerrero .05 .02
251 Ken Hill .10 .03
252 Joe Magrane .05 .02
253 Willie McGee UER .10 .03
(No decimal point before 353)
254 John Morris .05 .02
255 Jose Oquendo .05 .02
256 Tony Pena .05 .02
257 Terry Pendleton .10 .03
258 Ted Power .05 .02
259 Dan Quisenberry .05 .02
260 Ozzie Smith .40 .12
261 Scott Terry .05 .02
262 Milt Thompson .05 .02
263 Denny Walling .05 .02
264 Todd Worrell .05 .02
265 Todd Zeile .10 .03
266 Marty Barrett .05 .02
267 Mike Boddicker .05 .02
268 Wade Boggs .15 .04
269 Ellis Burks .15 .04
270 Rick Cerone .05 .02
271 Roger Clemens .50 .15
272 John Dopson .05 .02
273 Nick Esasky .05 .02
274 Dwight Evans .10 .03
275 Wes Gardner .05 .02
276 Rich Gedman .05 .02
277 Mike Greenwell .05 .02
278 Danny Heep .05 .02
279 Eric Hetzel .05 .02
280 Dennis Lamp .05 .02
281 Rob Murphy UER .05 .02
('89 stats say Reds, should say Red Sox)
282 Joe Price .05 .02
283 Carlos Quintana .05 .02
284 Jody Reed .05 .02
285 Luis Rivera .05 .02
286 Kevin Romine .05 .02
287 Lee Smith .10 .03
288 Mike Smithson .05 .02
289 Bob Stanley .05 .02
290 Harold Baines .10 .03
291 Kevin Brown .10 .03
292 Steve Buechele .05 .02
293 Scott Coolbaugh .05 .02
294 Jack Daugherty .05 .02
295 Cecil Espy .05 .02
296 Julio Franco .05 .02
297 Juan Gonzalez RC 1.50 .45
298 Cecilio Guante .05 .02
299 Drew Hall .05 .02
300 Charlie Hough .10 .03
301 Pete Incaviglia .05 .02
302 Mike Jeffcoat .05 .02
303 Chad Kreuter .05 .02
304 Jeff Kunkel .05 .02
305 Rick Leach .05 .02
306 Fred Manrique .05 .02
307 Jamie Moyer .10 .03

308 Rafael Palmeiro .15 .04
309 Geno Petralli .05 .02
310 Kevin Reimer .05 .02
311 Kenny Rogers .10 .03
312 Jeff Russell .05 .02
313 Nolan Ryan 1.00 .30
314 Ruben Sierra .05 .02
315 Bobby Witt .05 .02
316 Chris Bosio .05 .02
317 Glenn Braggs UER .05 .02
(Stats say 111 K's, but bio says 117 K's)
318 Greg Brock .05 .02
319 Chuck Crim .05 .02
320 Rob Deer .05 .02
321 Mike Felder .05 .02
322 Tom Filer .05 .02
323 Tony Fossas .05 .02
324 Jim Gantner .05 .02
325 Darryl Hamilton .05 .02
326 Teddy Higuera .05 .02
327 Mark Knudson .05 .02
328 Bill Krueger UER .05 .02
('86 stats missing)
329 Tim McIntosh RC .10 .03
330 Paul Molitor .15 .04
331 Jaime Navarro .05 .02
332 Charlie O'Brien .05 .02
333 Jeff Peterek .05 .02
334 Dan Plesac .05 .02
335 Jerry Reuss .05 .02
336 Gary Sheffield UER .25 .07
(Bio says played for 3 teams in '87, but stats say in '88)
337 Bill Spiers .05 .02
338 B.J. Surhoff .10 .03
339 Greg Vaughn .10 .03
340 Robin Yount .40 .12
341 Hubie Brooks .05 .02
342 Tim Burke .05 .02
343 Mike Fitzgerald .05 .02
344 Tom Foley .05 .02
345 Andres Galarraga .10 .03
346 Damaso Garcia .05 .02
347 Marquis Grissom RC .25 .07
348 Kevin Gross .05 .02
349 Joe Hesketh .05 .02
350 Jeff Huson RC .05 .02
351 Wallace Johnson .05 .02
352 Mark Langston .05 .02
353A Dave Martinez 2.00 .60
(Yellow on front)
353B Dave Martinez .05 .02
(Red on front)
354 Dennis Martinez UER .10 .03
('87 ERA is 616, should be 6.16)
355 Andy McGaffigan .05 .02
356 Otis Nixon .05 .02
357 Spike Owen .05 .02
358 Pascual Perez .05 .02
359 Tim Raines .10 .03
360 Nelson Santovenia .05 .02
361 Bryn Smith .05 .02
362 Zane Smith .05 .02
363 Larry Walker RC 1.00 .30
364 Tim Wallach .05 .02
365 Rick Aguilera .10 .03
366 Allan Anderson .05 .02
367 Wally Backman .05 .02
368 Doug Baker .05 .02
369 Juan Berenguer .05 .02
370 Randy Bush .05 .02
371 Carmelo Castillo .05 .02
372 Mike Dyer RC .05 .02
373 Gary Gaetti .10 .03
374 Greg Gagne .05 .02
375 Dan Gladden .05 .02
376 G.Gonzalez UER .05 .02
Bio says 31 saves in '88, but stats say 30
377 Brian Harper .05 .02
378 Kent Hrbek .10 .03
379 Gene Larkin .05 .02
380 Tim Laudner UER .05 .02
(No decimal point before '85 BA of 238)
381 John Moses .05 .02
382 Al Newman .05 .02
383 Kirby Puckett .25 .07
384 Shane Rawley .05 .02
385 Jeff Reardon .10 .03
386 Roy Smith .05 .02
387 Gary Wayne .05 .02
388 Dave West .05 .02
389 Tim Belcher .05 .02
390 Tim Crews UER .05 .02
(Stats say 163 IP for '83, but bio says 136)
391 Mike Davis .05 .02
392 Rick Dempsey .05 .02
393 Kirk Gibson .10 .03
394 Jose Gonzalez .05 .02
395 Alfredo Griffin .05 .02
396 Jeff Hamilton .05 .02
397 Lenny Harris .05 .02
398 Mickey Hatcher .05 .02
399 Orel Hershiser .10 .03
400 Jay Howell .05 .02
401 Mike Marshall .05 .02
402 Ramon Martinez .05 .02
403 Mike Morgan .05 .02
404 Eddie Murray .25 .07
405 Alejandro Pena .05 .02
406 Willie Randolph .10 .03
407 Mike Scioscia .05 .02
408 Ray Searage .05 .02
409 Fernando Valenzuela .10 .03
410 Jose Vizcaino RC .25 .07
411 John Wetteland .25 .07
412 Jack Armstrong .05 .02
413 Todd Benzinger UER .05 .02
(Bio says .323 at Pawtucket, but stats say .321)
414 Tim Birtsas .05 .02
415 Tom Browning .05 .02
416 Norm Charlton .05 .02
417 Eric Davis .10 .03
418 Rob Dibble .10 .03
419 John Franco .10 .03
420 Ken Griffey Sr. .10 .03
421 Chris Hammond RC .10 .03
(No 1989 used for "Did Not Play" stat, actually did play for Nashville in 1989)
422 Danny Jackson .05 .02
423 Barry Larkin .25 .07
424 Tim Leary .05 .02
425 Rick Mahler .05 .02
426 Joe Oliver .05 .02
427 Paul O'Neill .15 .04
428 Luis Quinones UER .05 .02
('86-'88 stats are omitted from card but included in totals)
429 Jeff Reed .05 .02
430 Jose Rijo .05 .02
431 Ron Robinson .05 .02
432 Rolando Roomes .05 .02
433 Chris Sabo .05 .02
434 Scott Scudder .05 .02
435 Herm Winningham .05 .02
436 Steve Balboni .05 .02
437 Jesse Barfield .05 .02
438 Mike Blowers RC .10 .03
439 Tom Brookens .05 .02
440 Greg Cadaret .05 .02
441 Alvaro Espinoza UER .05 .02
(Career games say 218, should be 219)
442 Bob Geren .05 .02
443 Lee Guetterman .05 .02
444 Mel Hall .05 .02
445 Andy Hawkins .05 .02
446 Roberto Kelly .05 .02
447 Don Mattingly .60 .18
448 Lance McCullers .05 .02
449 Hensley Meulens .05 .02
450 Dale Mohorcic .05 .02
451 Clay Parker .05 .02
452 Eric Plunk .05 .02
453 Dave Righetti .05 .02
454 Deion Sanders .25 .07
455 Steve Sax .05 .02
456 Don Slaught .05 .02
457 Walt Terrell .05 .02
458 Dave Winfield .10 .03
459 Jay Bell .10 .03
460 Rafael Belliard .05 .02
461 Barry Bonds .60 .18
462 Bobby Bonilla .10 .03
463 Sid Bream .05 .02
464 Benny Distefano .05 .02
465 Doug Drabek .05 .02
466 Jim Gott .05 .02
467 Billy Hatcher UER .05 .02
(.1 hits for Cubs in 1984)
468 Neal Heaton .05 .02
469 Jeff King .05 .02
470 Bob Kipper .05 .02
471 Randy Kramer .05 .02
472 Bill Landrum .05 .02
473 Mike LaValliere .05 .02
474 Jose Lind .05 .02
475 Junior Ortiz .05 .02
476 Gary Redus .05 .02
477 Rick Reed RC .25 .07
478 R.J. Reynolds .05 .02
479 Jeff D. Robinson .05 .02
480 John Smiley .05 .02
481 Andy Van Slyke .10 .03
482 Bob Walk .05 .02
483 Andy Allanson .05 .02
484 Scott Bailes .05 .02
485 Joey Belle UER .25 .07
(Has Jay Bell "Did You Know")
486 Bud Black .05 .02
487 Jerry Browne .05 .02
488 Tom Candiotti .05 .02
489 Joe Carter .10 .03
490 Dave Clark .05 .02
(No '84 stats)
491 John Farrell .05 .02
492 Felix Fermin .05 .02
493 Brook Jacoby .05 .02
494 Dion James .05 .02
495 Doug Jones .05 .02
496 Brad Komminsk .05 .02
497 Rod Nichols .05 .02
498 Pete O'Brien .05 .02
499 Steve Olin RC .10 .03
500 Jesse Orosco .05 .02
501 Joel Skinner .05 .02
502 Cory Snyder .05 .02
503 Greg Swindell .05 .02
504 Rich Yett .05 .02
505 Scott Bankhead .05 .02
506 Scott Bradley .05 .02
507 Greg Briley UER .05 .02
(28 SB's in bio, but 27 in stats)
508 Jay Buhner .10 .03
509 Darnell Coles .05 .02
510 Keith Comstock .05 .02
511 Henry Cotto .05 .02
512 Alvin Davis .05 .02
513 Ken Griffey Jr. .75 .23
514 Erik Hanson .05 .02
515 Gene Harris .05 .02
516 Brian Holman .05 .02
517 Mike Jackson .05 .02
518 Randy Johnson .40 .12
519 Jeffrey Leonard .05 .02
520 Edgar Martinez .15 .04
521 Dennis Powell .05 .02
522 Jim Presley .05 .02
523 Jerry Reed .05 .02
524 Harold Reynolds .10 .03
525 Mike Schooler .05 .02
526 Bill Swift .05 .02
527 Dave Valle .05 .02
528 Omar Vizquel .25 .07
529 Ivan Calderon .05 .02
530 Carlton Fisk UER .15 .04
(Bellow Falls, should be Bellows Falls)
531 Scott Fletcher .05 .02
532 Dave Gallagher .05 .02
533 Ozzie Guillen .05 .02
534 Greg Hibbard RC .10 .03
535 Shawn Hillegas .05 .02
536 Lance Johnson .05 .02
537 Eric King .05 .02
538 Ron Kittle .05 .02
539 Steve Lyons .05 .02
540 Carlos Martinez .05 .02
541 Tom McCarthy .05 .02
542 Matt Merullo .05 .02
(Had 5 ML runs scored entering '90, not 6)
543 Donn Pall UER .05 .02
(Stats say pro career began in '85, bio says '88)
544 Dan Pasqua .05 .02
545 Ken Patterson .05 .02
546 Melido Perez .05 .02
547 Steve Rosenberg .05 .02
548 Sammy Sosa RC 8.00 2.40
549 Bobby Thigpen .05 .02
550 Robin Ventura .25 .07
551 Greg Walker .05 .02
552 Don Carman .05 .02
553 Pat Combs .05 .02
(6 walks for Phillies in '89 in stats, brief bio says 4)
554 Dennis Cook .05 .02
555 Darren Daulton .10 .03
556 Len Dykstra .10 .03
557 Curt Ford .05 .02
558 Charlie Hayes .05 .02
559 Von Hayes .05 .02
560 Tommy Herr .05 .02
561 Ken Howell .05 .02
562 Steve Jeltz .05 .02
563 Ron Jones .05 .02
564 Ricky Jordan UER .05 .02
(Duplicate line of statistics on back)
565 John Kruk .10 .03
566 Steve Lake .05 .02
567 Roger McDowell .05 .02
568 Terry Mulholland UER .05 .02
(Did You Know refers to Dave Magadan)
569 Dwayne Murphy .05 .02
570 Jeff Parrett .05 .02
571 Randy Ready .05 .02
572 Bruce Ruffin .05 .02
573 Dickie Thon .05 .02
574 Jose Alvarez UER .05 .02
('78 and '79 stats are reversed)
575 Geronimo Berroa .05 .02
576 Jeff Blauser .05 .02
577 Joe Boever .05 .02
578 Marty Clary UER .05 .02
(No comma between city and state)
579 Jody Davis .05 .02
580 Mark Eichhorn .05 .02
581 Darrell Evans .10 .03
582 Ron Gant .10 .03
583 Tom Glavine .15 .04
584 Tommy Greene RC .10 .03
585 Tommy Gregg .05 .02
586 Dave Justice RC UER .50 .15
(Actually had 16 2B in Sumter in '86)
587 Mark Lemke .05 .02
588 Derek Lilliquist .05 .02
589 Oddibe McDowell .05 .02
590 Kent Mercker RC ERA .05 .02
(Bio says 2.75 ERA, stats say 2.68 ERA)
591 Dale Murphy .25 .07
592 Gerald Perry .05 .02
593 Lonnie Smith .05 .02
594 Pete Smith .05 .02
595 John Smoltz .25 .07
596 Mike Stanton RC UER .25 .07
(No comma between city and state)
597 Andres Thomas .05 .02
598 Jeff Treadway .05 .02
599 Doyle Alexander .05 .02
600 Dave Bergman .05 .02
601 Brian DuBois .05 .02
602 Paul Gibson .05 .02
603 Mike Heath .05 .02
604 Mike Henneman .05 .02
605 Guillermo Hernandez .05 .02
606 Shawn Holman .05 .02
607 Tracy Jones .05 .02
608 Chet Lemon .05 .02
609 Fred Lynn .05 .02
610 Jack Morris .10 .03
611 Matt Nokes .05 .02
612 Gary Pettis .05 .02
613 Kevin Ritz .05 .02
614 Jeff M. Robinson .05 .02
('88 stats are not in line)
615 Steve Searcy .05 .02
616 Frank Tanana .05 .02
617 Alan Trammell .15 .04
618 Gary Ward .05 .02
619 Lou Whitaker .10 .03
620 Frank Williams .05 .02
621A George Brett '80 2.00 .60
ERR (Had 10 .390 hitting seasons)
621B George Brett '80 .30 .09
COR
622 Fern.Valenzuela '81 .05 .02
623 Dale Murphy '82 .15 .04
624A Cal Ripken '83 ERR 5.00 1.50
(Misspelled Ripkin on card back)
624B Cal Ripken '83 COR .40 .12
625 Ryne Sandberg '84 .25 .07
626 Don Mattingly '85 .20 .06
627 Roger Clemens '86 .25 .07
628 George Bell '87 .05 .02
629 J.Canseco '88 UER .10 .03
Reggie won MVP in '83, should say '73
630A Will Clark '89 ERR 1.00 .30
(32 total bases on card back)
630B Will Clark '89 COR .25 .07
(321 total bases; technically still an error, listing only 24 runs)
631 Mark Davis .05 .02
Mitch Williams
632 Wade Boggs .10 .03
Mike Greenwell
633 Mark Gubicza .05 .02
Jeff Russell
634 Tony Fernandez .25 .07
Cal Ripken
635 Kirby Puckett .15 .04
Bo Jackson
636 Nolan Ryan .40 .12
Mike Scott
637 Will Clark .10 .03
Kevin Mitchell
638 Don Mattingly .30 .09
Mark McGwire
639 Howard Johnson .25 .07
Ryne Sandberg
640 Rudy Seanez RC .10 .03
Colin Charland
641 George Canale RC .25 .07
Kevin Maas UER
(Canale listed as INF on front, 1B on back)
642 Kelly Mann .25 .07
and Dave Hansen RC
643 Greg Smith .10 .03
and Stu Tate
644 Tom Drees .10 .03
and Dann Howitt
645 Mike Roesler RC .10 .03
and Derrick May
646 Scott Hemond .10 .03
and Mark Gardner RC
647 John Orton .10 .03
and Scott Leius RC
648 Rich Monteleone .10 .03
and Dana Williams
649 Mike Huff .10 .03
and Steve Frey
650 Chuck McElroy .50 .15
and Moises Alou RC
651 Bobby Rose .25 .07
and Mike Hartley
652 Matt Kinzer .10 .03
and Wayne Edwards
653 Delino DeShields RC .25 .07
and Jason Grimsley
654 CL: A's/Cubs .05 .02
Giants/Blue Jays
655 CL: Royals/Angels .05 .02
Padres/Orioles
656 CL: Mets/Astros .05 .02
Cards/Red Sox
657 CL: Rangers/Brewers .05 .02
Expos/Twins
658 CL: Dodgers/Reds .05 .02
Yankees/Pirates
659 CL: Indians/Mariners .05 .02
White Sox/Phillies
660A CL: Braves/Tigers .05 .02
Specials/Checklists
(Checklist-660 in smaller print on card front)
660B CL: Braves/Tigers .05 .02
Specials/Checklists
(Checklist-660 in normal print on card front)

1990 Fleer Canadian

The 1990 Fleer Canadian set contains 660 standard-size cards. The cards were distributed in wax packs exclusively in Canada. The Canadian set differs from the U.S. version only in that it shows copyright "FLEER LTD./LTEE PTD. IN CANADA" on the card backs. Although these Canadian cards were undoubtedly produced in much lesser quantities compared to the U.S. issue, the fact that the versions are so similar has kept the demand down over the years.

Nm-Mt Ex-Mt
COMPLETE SET (660) 60.00 18.00
*STARS: 2X to 5X BASIC CARDS
*ROOKIES: 2X to 4X BASIC CARDS

1990 Fleer All-Stars

The 1990 Fleer All-Star insert set includes 12 standard-size cards. The set was randomly inserted in 33-card cellos and wax packs. The set is sequenced in alphabetical order. The fronts are white with a light gray screen and bright red stripes. The player selection for the set is Fleer's opinion of the best Major Leaguer at each position.

Nm-Mt Ex-Mt
COMPLETE SET (12) 3.00 .90
1 Harold Baines .25 .07
2 Will Clark .25 .07
3 Mark Davis .15 .04
4 Howard Johnson UER .15 .04
(In middle of 5th line, the is misspelled th)
5 Joe Magrane .15 .04
6 Kevin Mitchell .15 .04
7 Kirby Puckett .60 .18
8 Cal Ripken 2.00 .60
9 Ryne Sandberg 1.00 .30
10 Mike Scott UER .15 .04
Astros spelled Asatros on back
11 Ruben Sierra .15 .04
12 Mickey Tettleton .15 .04

1990 Fleer League Standouts

This six-card standard-size insert set was distributed one per 45-card rack pack. The set is subtitled "Standouts" and commemorates outstanding events for those players from the previous season.

Nm-Mt Ex-Mt
COMPLETE SET (6) 6.00 1.80
1 Barry Larkin 2.00 .60
2 Don Mattingly 5.00 1.50
3 Darryl Strawberry 1.25 .35
4 Jose Canseco 2.00 .60
5 Wade Boggs 1.25 .35
6 Mark Grace UER 1.25 .35
(Chris Sabo misspelled as Cris)

1990 Fleer Soaring Stars

The 1990 Fleer Soaring Stars set was issued exclusively in jumbo cello packs. This 12-card, standard-size set features some of the most popular young players entering the 1990 season. The set gives the visual impression of rockets exploding in the air to honor these young players.

Nm-Mt Ex-Mt
COMPLETE SET (12) 15.00 4.50
1 Todd Zeile 1.00 .30
2 Mike Stanton .50 .15
3 Larry Walker 2.50 .75
4 Robin Ventura 2.00 .60
5 Scott Coolbaugh .50 .15
6 Ken Griffey Jr. 5.00 1.50
7 Tom Gordon 1.00 .30
8 Jerome Walton .50 .15
9 Junior Felix .50 .15
10 Jim Abbott 1.50 .45
11 Ricky Jordan .50 .15
12 Dwight Smith .50 .15

1990 Fleer Wax Box Cards

The 1990 Fleer wax box cards comprise seven different box bottoms with four cards each, for a total of 28 standard-size cards. The outer front borders are white; the inner, ribbon-like borders are different depending on the team. The vertically oriented backs are gray. The cards are numbered with a "C" prefix.

Nm-Mt Ex-Mt
COMPLETE SET (28) 12.00 3.60
C1 Giants Logo .10 .03
C2 Tim Belcher .10 .03
C3 Roger Clemens 2.50 .75
C4 Eric Davis .25 .07
C5 Glenn Davis .10 .03
C6 Cubs Logo .10 .03
C7 John Franco .25 .07
C8 Mike Greenwell .10 .03
C9 A's Logo .10 .03
C10 Ken Griffey Jr. 3.00 .90
C11 Pedro Guerrero .10 .03
C12 Tony Gwynn 2.50 .75
C13 Blue Jays Logo .10 .03
C14 Orel Hershiser .25 .07
C15 Bo Jackson .25 .07
C16 Howard Johnson .10 .03
C17 Mets Logo .10 .03
C18 Cardinals Logo .10 .03
C19 Don Mattingly 2.50 .75
C20 Mark McGwire 4.00 1.20
C21 Kevin Mitchell .10 .03
C22 Kirby Puckett 1.00 .30
C23 Royals Logo .10 .03
C24 Orioles Logo .10 .03
C25 Ruben Sierra .25 .07
C26 Dave Stewart .25 .07
C27 Jerome Walton .10 .03
C28 Robin Yount .75 .23

1990 Fleer World Series

This 12-card standard-size set was issued as an insert in with the Fleer factory sets, celebrating the 1989 World Series. This set marked the fourth year that Fleer issued a special World Series set in their factory (or vend) set. The design of these cards are different from the regular Fleer issue as the photo is framed by a white border with red and blue World Series cards and the player description in black.

Nm-Mt Ex-Mt
COMPLETE SET (12) 1.00 .30
1 Mike Moore .05 .02
2 Kevin Mitchell .05 .02
3 Terry Steinbach .05 .02
4 Will Clark .10 .03
5 Jose Canseco .25 .07
6 Walt Weiss .05 .02
7 Terry Steinbach .05 .02
8 Dave Stewart .10 .03
9 Dave Parker .10 .03
10 Dave Parker .10 .03
Jose Canseco
Will Clark
11 Rickey Henderson .25 .07
12 Oakland A's Celebrate .10 .03
Baseball's Best in 89

1990 Fleer Update

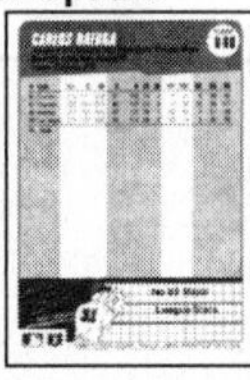

The 1990 Fleer Update set contains 132 standard-size cards. This set marked the seventh consecutive year Fleer issued an end of season Update set. The set was issued exclusively as a boxed set through hobby dealers. The set is checklisted alphabetically by team for each league and then alphabetically within each team. The fronts are styled the same as the 1990 Fleer regular issue set. The backs are numbered with the prefix "U" for Update. Rookie Cards in this set include Travis Fryman, Todd Hundley, John Olerud and Frank Thomas.

Nm-Mt Ex-Mt
COMP.FACT.SET (132) 4.00 1.20
1 Steve Avery .05 .02
2 Francisco Cabrera .05 .02
3 Nick Esasky .05 .02
4 Jim Kremers .05 .02
5 Greg Olson RC .10 .03
6 Jim Presley .05 .02
7 Shawn Boskie RC .10 .03
8 Joe Kraemer .05 .02
9 Luis Salazar .05 .02
10 Hector Villanueva .05 .02
11 Glenn Braggs .05 .02
12 Mariano Duncan .05 .02
13 Billy Hatcher .05 .02
14 Tim Layana .05 .02
15 Hal Morris .05 .02
16 Javier Ortiz .05 .02
17 Dave Rohde .05 .02
18 Eric Yelding .05 .02
19 Hubie Brooks .05 .02
20 Kal Daniels .05 .02
21 Dave Hansen .05 .02
22 Mike Hartley .05 .02
23 Stan Javier .05 .02
24 Jose Offerman RC .25 .07
25 Juan Samuel .05 .02
26 Dennis Boyd .05 .02
27 Delino DeShields .25 .07
28 Steve Frey .05 .02
29 Mark Gardner .05 .02
30 Chris Nabholz RC .10 .03
31 Bill Sampen .05 .02
32 Dave Schmidt .05 .02
33 Daryl Boston .05 .02
34 Chuck Carr RC .10 .03
35 John Franco .10 .03
36 Todd Hundley RC .25 .07
37 Julio Machado .05 .02
38 Alejandro Pena .05 .02
39 Darren Reed .05 .02
40 Kelvin Torve .05 .02
41 Darrel Akerfelds .05 .02
42 Jose DeJesus .05 .02
43 Dave Hollins RC UER .25 .07
(Misspelled Dane
on card back)
44 Carmelo Martinez .05 .02
45 Brad Moore .05 .02
46 Dale Murphy .25 .07
47 Wally Backman .05 .02
48 Stan Belinda RC .10 .03
49 Bob Patterson .05 .02
50 Ted Power .05 .02
51 Don Slaught .05 .02
52 Geronimo Pena RC .10 .03
53 Lee Smith .10 .03
54 John Tudor .05 .02
55 Joe Carter .10 .03
56 Thomas Howard .05 .02
57 Craig Lefferts .05 .02
58 Rafael Valdez .05 .02
59 Dave Anderson .05 .02
60 Kevin Bass .05 .02
61 John Burkett .05 .02
62 Gary Carter .15 .04
63 Rick Parker .05 .02
64 Trevor Wilson .05 .02
65 Chris Hoiles RC .25 .07
66 Tim Hulett .05 .02
67 Dave Johnson .05 .02
68 Curt Schilling 1.00 .30
69 David Segui RC .25 .07
70 Tom Brunansky .05 .02
71 Greg A. Harris .05 .02
72 Dana Kiecker .05 .02
73 Tim Naehring RC .10 .03
74 Tony Pena .05 .02
75 Jeff Reardon .10 .03
76 Jerry Reed .05 .02
77 Mark Eichhorn .05 .02
78 Mark Langston .05 .02
79 John Orton .05 .02
80 Luis Polonia .05 .02
81 Dave Winfield .10 .03
82 Cliff Young .05 .02
83 Wayne Edwards .05 .02
84 Alex Fernandez RC .25 .07
85 Craig Grebeck RC .10 .03
86 Scott Radinsky RC .10 .03
87 Frank Thomas RC 1.25 .35
88 Beau Allred RC .05 .02
89 Sandy Alomar Jr. .10 .03
90 Carlos Baerga RC .25 .07
91 Kevin Bearse .05 .02
92 Chris James .05 .02
93 Candy Maldonado .05 .02
94 Jeff Manto .05 .02
95 Cecil Fielder .10 .03
96 Travis Fryman RC .40 .12
97 Lloyd Moseby .05 .02
98 Edwin Nunez .05 .02
99 Tony Phillips .05 .02
100 Larry Sheets .05 .02
101 Mark Davis .05 .02
102 Storm Davis .05 .02
103 Gerald Perry .05 .02
104 Terry Shumpert .05 .02
105 Edgar Diaz .05 .02
106 Dave Parker .10 .03
107 Tim Drummond .05 .02
108 Junior Ortiz .05 .02
109 Park Pittman .05 .02
110 Kevin Tapani RC .25 .07
111 Oscar Azocar .05 .02
112 Jim Leyritz RC .25 .07
113 Kevin Maas .10 .03
114 Alan Mills RC .10 .03
115 Matt Nokes .05 .02
116 Pascual Perez .05 .02
117 Ozzie Canseco .05 .02
118 Scott Sanderson .05 .02
119 Tino Martinez .25 .07
120 Jeff Schaefer RC .05 .02
121 Matt Young .05 .02
122 Brian Bohanon RC .10 .03
123 Jeff Huson .05 .02
124 Ramon Manon .05 .02
125 Gary Mielke UER .05 .02
(Shown as Blue
Jay on front)
126 Willie Blair RC .10 .03
127 Glenallen Hill .05 .02
128 John Olerud RC UER .50 .15
(Listed as throwing
right, should be left)
129 Luis Sojo .05 .02
130 Mark Whiten RC .25 .07
131 Nolan Ryan 1.00 .30
132 Checklist U1-U132 .05 .02

1990 Fleer Award Winners

The 1990 Fleer Award Winners set was printed by Fleer for Hills stores (as well as for some 7/Eleven's) and released early in the summer of 1990. The original suggested retail price for the set at Hills was 2.49. The set features a player photo within a trophy design with the player's name, team and position at the base. This 44-card standard-size set is numbered in alphabetical order, although Will Clark erroneously precedes Jack Clark. Card number 10 is listed on the box checklist as being Ron Darling, but Darling is not in the set. Consequently the numbers on the box checklist between 10 and 37 are off by one. Darryl Strawberry (38) is not listed on the box, but is included in the set.

Nm-Mt Ex-Mt
COMP.FACT SET (44) 12.00 3.60
1 Jeff Ballard .05 .02
2 Tim Belcher .05 .02
3 Bert Blyleven .10 .03
4 Wade Boggs .40 .12
5 Bob Boone .10 .03
6 Jose Canseco .40 .12
7 Will Clark .50 .15
8 Jack Clark .10 .03
9 Vince Coleman .05 .02
10 Eric Davis .10 .03
11 Jose DeLeon .05 .02
12 Tony Fernandez .10 .03
13 Carlton Fisk .40 .12
14 Scott Garrelts .05 .02
15 Tom Gordon .15 .04
16 Ken Griffey Jr. 3.00 .90
17 Von Hayes .05 .02
18 Rickey Henderson .75 .23
19 Bo Jackson .60 .18
20 Howard Johnson .05 .02
21 Don Mattingly 1.00 .30
22 Fred McGriff .40 .12
23 Kevin Mitchell .05 .02
24 Gregg Olson .05 .02
25 Gary Pettis .05 .02
26 Kirby Puckett .50 .15
27 Harold Reynolds .10 .03
28 Jeff Russell .05 .02
29 Nolan Ryan 2.00 .60
30 Bret Saberhagen .10 .03
31 Ryne Sandberg .75 .23
32 Benito Santiago .10 .03
33 Mike Scott .05 .02
34 Ruben Sierra .10 .03
35 Lonnie Smith .05 .02
36 Ozzie Smith 1.00 .30
37 Dave Stewart .10 .03
38 Darryl Strawberry .10 .03
39 Greg Swindell .05 .02
40 Andy Van Slyke .05 .02
41 Tim Wallach .05 .02
42 Jerome Walton .05 .02
43 Mitch Williams .05 .02
44 Robin Yount .40 .12

1990 Fleer Baseball All-Stars

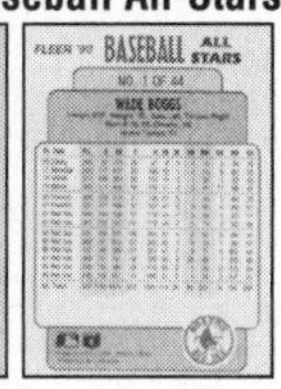

The 1990 Fleer Baseball All-Stars Set was produced by Fleer for the Ben Franklin chain and released early in the summer of 1990. This standard-size 44-card set features some of the best of today's players in alphabetical order. The design of the cards has vertical stripes on the front of the card. The set's custom box gives the set checklist on the back panel. The box also includes six peel-off team logo stickers each with a trivia quiz on back.

Nm-Mt Ex-Mt
COMP.FACT SET (44) 12.00 3.60
1 Wade Boggs .40 .12
2 Bobby Bonilla .05 .02
3 Tim Burke .05 .02
4 Jose Canseco .40 .12
5 Will Clark .50 .15
6 Eric Davis .10 .03
7 Glenn Davis .05 .02
8 Julio Franco .10 .03
9 Tony Fernandez .10 .03
10 Gary Gaetti .10 .03
11 Scott Garrelts .05 .02
12 Mark Grace .50 .15
13 Mike Greenwell .05 .02
14 Ken Griffey Jr. 3.00 .90
15 Mark Gubicza .05 .02
16 Pedro Guerrero .05 .02
17 Von Hayes .05 .02
18 Orel Hershiser .10 .03
19 Bruce Hurst .05 .02
20 Bo Jackson .50 .15
21 Howard Johnson .05 .02
22 Doug Jones .05 .02
23 Barry Larkin .50 .15
24 Don Mattingly 1.00 .30
25 Mark McGwire 1.50 .45
26 Kevin McReynolds .05 .02
27 Kevin Mitchell .05 .02
28 Dan Plesac .05 .02
29 Kirby Puckett .50 .15
30 Cal Ripken 2.00 .60
31 Bret Saberhagen .10 .03
32 Ryne Sandberg 1.00 .30
33 Steve Sax .05 .02
34 Ruben Sierra .10 .03
35 Ozzie Smith 1.00 .30
36 John Smoltz .15 .04
37 Darryl Strawberry .10 .03
38 Terry Steinbach .05 .02
39 Dave Stewart .10 .03
40 Bobby Thigpen .05 .02
41 Alan Trammell .15 .04
42 Devon White .05 .02
43 Mitch Williams .05 .02
44 Robin Yount .40 .12

1990 Fleer Baseball MVP's

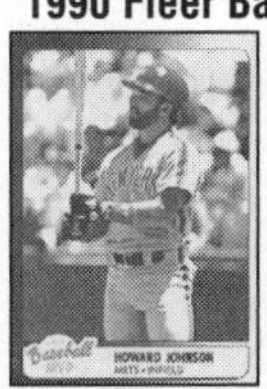
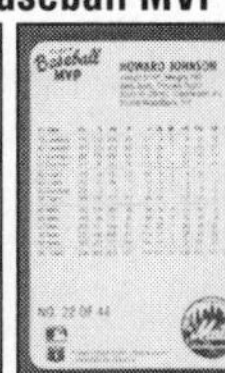

The 1990 Fleer Baseball MVP's were produced by Fleer exclusively for the Toys'R'Us chain and released early in the summer of 1990. This set has a multi-colored border, is standard size, and has 44 players arranged in alphabetical order. The set's custom box gives the set checklist on the back panel. The box also includes six peel-off team logo stickers.

Nm-Mt Ex-Mt
COMP.FACT SET (44) 12.00 3.60
1 George Bell .05 .02
2 Bert Blyleven .10 .03
3 Wade Boggs .40 .12
4 Bobby Bonilla .05 .02
5 George Brett 1.00 .30
6 Jose Canseco .40 .12
7 Will Clark .50 .15
8 Roger Clemens 1.00 .30
9 Eric Davis .10 .03
10 Glenn Davis .05 .02
11 Tony Fernandez .10 .03
12 Dwight Gooden .10 .03
13 Mike Greenwell .05 .02
14 Ken Griffey Jr. 2.50 .75
15 Pedro Guerrero .05 .02
16 Tony Gwynn 1.00 .30
17 Rickey Henderson .60 .18
18 Tom Herr .05 .02
19 Orel Hershiser .10 .03
20 Kent Hrbek .10 .03
21 Bo Jackson .50 .15
22 Howard Johnson .05 .02
23 Don Mattingly 1.00 .30
24 Fred McGriff .40 .12
25 Mark McGwire 1.50 .45
26 Kevin Mitchell .05 .02
27 Paul Molitor .40 .12
28 Dale Murphy .20 .06
29 Kirby Puckett .50 .15
30 Tim Raines .10 .03
31 Cal Ripken 2.00 .60
32 Bret Saberhagen .10 .03
33 Ryne Sandberg .75 .23
34 Ruben Sierra .10 .03
35 Dwight Smith .05 .02
36 Ozzie Smith 1.00 .30
37 Darryl Strawberry .10 .03
38 Dave Stewart .10 .03
39 Greg Swindell .05 .02
40 Bobby Thigpen .05 .02
41 Alan Trammell .15 .04
42 Jerome Walton .05 .02
43 Mitch Williams .05 .02
44 Robin Yount .40 .12

1990 Fleer League Leaders

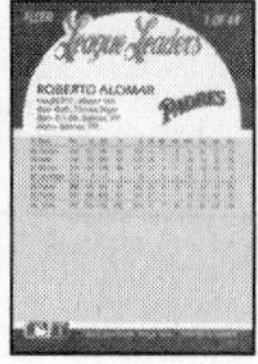

The 1990 Fleer League Leader set was issued by Fleer for Walgreen stores. This set design features solid blue borders with the players photo inset within the middle of the card. This 44-card, standard-size set is numbered in alphabetical order. The set's custom box gives the set checklist on the back panel. The box also includes six peel-off team logo stickers. The original suggested retail price for the set at Walgreen's was 2.49.

Nm-Mt Ex-Mt
COMP.FACT SET (44) 12.00 3.60
1 Roberto Alomar .75 .23
2 Tim Belcher .05 .02
3 George Bell .05 .02
4 Wade Boggs .40 .12
5 Jose Canseco .50 .15
6 Will Clark .50 .15
7 David Cone .20 .06
8 Eric Davis .10 .03
9 Glenn Davis .05 .02
10 Nick Esasky .05 .02
11 Dennis Eckersley .15 .04
12 Mark Grace .50 .15
13 Mike Greenwell .05 .02
14 Ken Griffey Jr. 3.00 .90
15 Mark Gubicza .05 .02
16 Pedro Guerrero .05 .02
17 Tony Gwynn 1.00 .30
18 Rickey Henderson .60 .18
19 Bo Jackson .50 .15
20 Doug Jones .05 .02
21 Ricky Jordan .05 .02
22 Barry Larkin .50 .15
23 Don Mattingly 1.00 .30
24 Fred McGriff .40 .12
25 Mark McGwire 1.50 .45
26 Kevin Mitchell .05 .02
27 Jack Morris .10 .03
28 Gregg Olson .05 .02
29 Dan Plesac .05 .02
30 Kirby Puckett .50 .15
31 Nolan Ryan 2.00 .60
32 Bret Saberhagen .10 .03
33 Ryne Sandberg 1.00 .30
34 Steve Sax .05 .02
35 Mike Scott .05 .02
36 Ruben Sierra .10 .03
37 Lonnie Smith .05 .02
38 Darryl Strawberry .10 .03
39 Bobby Thigpen .05 .02
40 Andy Van Slyke .10 .03
41 Tim Wallach .05 .02
42 Jerome Walton UER .05 .02
(Photo actually
Eric Yelding)
43 Devon White .05 .02
44 Robin Yount .40 .12

1991 Fleer

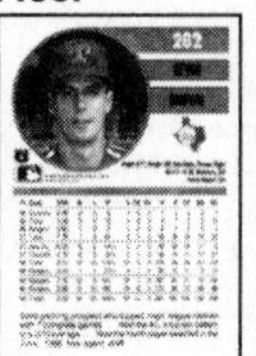

The 1991 Fleer set consists of 720 standard-size cards. Cards were primarily issued in wax packs, cello packs and factory sets. This set does not have what had been a Fleer tradition in prior years, the two-player Rookie Cards and there are less two-player special cards than in prior years. The design features bright yellow borders with the information in black indicating name, position, and team. The set is again ordered numerically by teams, followed by combination cards, rookie prospect pairs, and checklists. There are no notable Rookie Cards in this set. A number of the cards in the set can be found with photos cropped (very slightly) differently as Fleer used two separate printers in their attempt to maximize production.

Nm-Mt Ex-Mt
COMPLETE SET (720) 8.00 2.40
COMP.RETAIL SET (732) 10.00 3.00
COMP.HOBBY SET (732) 10.00 3.00
1 Troy Afenir .05 .02
2 Harold Baines .10 .03
3 Lance Blankenship .05 .02
4 Todd Burns .05 .02
5 Jose Canseco .25 .07
6 Dennis Eckersley .10 .03
7 Mike Gallego .05 .02
8 Ron Hassey .05 .02
9 Dave Henderson .05 .02
10 Rickey Henderson .25 .07
11 Rick Honeycutt .05 .02
12 Doug Jennings .05 .02
13 Joe Klink .05 .02
14 Carney Lansford .10 .03
15 Darren Lewis .05 .02
16 Willie McGee UER .10 .03
(Height 6'11")
17 Mark McGwire UER .60 .18
(183 extra base
hits in 1987)
18 Mike Moore .05 .02
19 Gene Nelson .05 .02
20 Dave Otto .05 .02
21 Jamie Quirk .05 .02
22 Willie Randolph .10 .03
23 Scott Sanderson .05 .02
24 Terry Steinbach .05 .02
25 Dave Stewart .10 .03
26 Walt Weiss .05 .02
27 Bob Welch .05 .02
28 Curt Young .05 .02
29 Wally Backman .05 .02
30 Stan Belinda UER .05 .02
(Born in Huntington,
should be State College)
31 Jay Bell .10 .03
32 Rafael Belliard .05 .02
33 Barry Bonds .60 .18
34 Bobby Bonilla .10 .03
35 Sid Bream .05 .02
36 Doug Drabek .05 .02
37 Carlos Garcia RC .05 .02
38 Neal Heaton .05 .02
39 Jeff King .05 .02
40 Bob Kipper .05 .02
41 Bill Landrum .05 .02
42 Mike LaValliere .05 .02
43 Jose Lind .05 .02
44 Carmelo Martinez .05 .02
45 Bob Patterson .05 .02
46 Ted Power .05 .02
47 Gary Redus .05 .02
48 R.J. Reynolds .05 .02
49 Don Slaught .05 .02
50 John Smiley .05 .02
51 Zane Smith .05 .02
52 Randy Tomlin RC .05 .02
53 Andy Van Slyke .10 .03
54 Bob Walk .05 .02
55 Jack Armstrong .05 .02
56 Todd Benzinger .05 .02
57 Glenn Braggs .05 .02
58 Keith Brown .05 .02
59 Tom Browning .05 .02
60 Norm Charlton .05 .02
61 Eric Davis .10 .03
62 Rob Dibble .10 .03
63 Bill Doran .05 .02
64 Mariano Duncan .05 .02
65 Chris Hammond .05 .02
66 Billy Hatcher .05 .02
67 Danny Jackson .05 .02
68 Barry Larkin .25 .07
69 Tim Layana .05 .02
(Black line over made
in first text line)
70 Terry Lee .05 .02
71 Rick Mahler .05 .02
72 Hal Morris .05 .02
73 Randy Myers .05 .02
74 Ron Oester .05 .02
75 Joe Oliver .05 .02
76 Paul O'Neill .15 .04
77 Luis Quinones .05 .02
78 Jeff Reed .05 .02
79 Jose Rijo .05 .02
80 Chris Sabo .05 .02
81 Scott Scudder .05 .02
82 Herm Winningham .05 .02
83 Larry Andersen .05 .02
84 Marty Barrett .05 .02
85 Mike Boddicker .05 .02
86 Wade Boggs .15 .04
87 Tom Bolton .05 .02
88 Tom Brunansky .05 .02
89 Ellis Burks .10 .03
90 Roger Clemens .50 .15
91 Scott Cooper .05 .02
92 John Dopson .05 .02
93 Dwight Evans .10 .03
94 Wes Gardner .05 .02
95 Jeff Gray .05 .02
96 Mike Greenwell .05 .02
97 Greg A. Harris .05 .02
98 Daryl Irvine .05 .02
99 Dana Kiecker .05 .02
100 Randy Kutcher .05 .02
101 Dennis Lamp .05 .02
102 Mike Marshall .05 .02
103 John Marzano .05 .02
104 Rob Murphy .05 .02
105 Tim Naehring .05 .02
106 Tony Pena .05 .02
107 Phil Plantier RC .05 .02
108 Carlos Quintana .05 .02
109 Jeff Reardon .10 .03
110 Jerry Reed .05 .02
111 Jody Reed .05 .02
112 Luis Rivera UER .05 .02
(Born 1/3/84)
113 Kevin Romine .05 .02
114 Phil Bradley .05 .02
115 Ivan Calderon .05 .02
116 Wayne Edwards .05 .02
117 Alex Fernandez .05 .02
118 Carlton Fisk .15 .04
119 Scott Fletcher .05 .02
120 Craig Grebeck .05 .02
121 Ozzie Guillen .05 .02
122 Greg Hibbard .05 .02
123 Lance Johnson UER .05 .02
(Born Cincinnati, should
be Lincoln Heights)
124 Barry Jones .05 .02

125 Ron Karkovice .05 .02
126 Eric King .05 .02
127 Steve Lyons .05 .02
128 Carlos Martinez .05 .02
129 Jack McDowell UER .05 .02
(Stanford misspelled as Standford on back)
130 Donn Pall .05 .02
(No dots over any i's in text)
131 Dan Pasqua .05 .02
132 Ken Patterson .05 .02
133 Melido Perez .05 .02
134 Adam Peterson .05 .02
135 Scott Radinsky .05 .02
136 Sammy Sosa .50 .15
137 Bobby Thigpen .05 .02
138 Frank Thomas .25 .07
139 Robin Ventura .10 .03
140 Daryl Boston .05 .02
141 Chuck Carr .05 .02
142 Mark Carreon .05 .02
143 David Cone .10 .03
144 Ron Darling .05 .02
145 Kevin Elster .05 .02
146 Sid Fernandez .05 .02
147 John Franco .10 .03
148 Dwight Gooden .15 .04
149 Tom Herr .05 .02
150 Todd Hundley .05 .02
151 Gregg Jefferies .05 .02
152 Howard Johnson .05 .02
153 Dave Magadan .05 .02
154 Kevin McReynolds .05 .02
155 Keith Miller UER .05 .02
(Text says Rochester in '87, stats say Tidewater, mixed up with other Keith Miller)
156 Bob Ojeda .05 .02
157 Tom O'Malley .05 .02
158 Alejandro Pena .05 .02
159 Darren Reed .05 .02
160 Mackey Sasser .05 .02
161 Darryl Strawberry .15 .04
162 Tim Teufel .05 .02
163 Kelvin Torve .05 .02
164 Julio Valera .05 .02
165 Frank Viola .10 .03
166 Wally Whitehurst .05 .02
167 Jim Acker .05 .02
168 Derek Bell .10 .03
169 George Bell .05 .02
170 Willie Blair .05 .02
171 Pat Borders .05 .02
172 John Cerutti .05 .02
173 Junior Felix .05 .02
174 Tony Fernandez .05 .02
175 Kelly Gruber UER .05 .02
(Born in Houston, should be Bellaire)
176 Tom Henke .05 .02
177 Glenallen Hill .05 .02
178 Jimmy Key .10 .03
179 Manny Lee .05 .02
180 Fred McGriff .15 .04
181 Rance Mulliniks .05 .02
182 Greg Myers .05 .02
183 John Olerud UER .10 .03
(Listed as throwing right, should be left)
184 Luis Sojo .05 .02
185 Dave Stieb .05 .02
186 Todd Stottlemyre .05 .02
187 Duane Ward .05 .02
188 David Wells .10 .03
189 Mark Whiten .05 .02
190 Ken Williams .05 .02
191 Frank Wills .05 .02
192 Mookie Wilson .10 .03
193 Don Aase .05 .02
194 Tim Belcher UER .05 .02
(Born Sparta, Ohio, should say Mt. Gilead)
195 Hubie Brooks .05 .02
196 Dennis Cook .05 .02
197 Tim Crews .05 .02
198 Kal Daniels .05 .02
199 Kirk Gibson .10 .03
200 Jim Gott .05 .02
201 Alfredo Griffin .05 .02
202 Chris Gwynn .05 .02
203 Dave Hansen .05 .02
204 Lenny Harris .05 .02
205 Mike Hartley .05 .02
206 Mickey Hatcher .05 .02
207 Carlos Hernandez .05 .02
208 Orel Hershiser .10 .03
209 Jay Howell UER .05 .02
(No 1982 Yankee stats)
210 Mike Huff .05 .02
211 Stan Javier .05 .02
212 Ramon Martinez .05 .02
213 Mike Morgan .05 .02
214 Eddie Murray .25 .07
215 Jim Neidlinger .05 .02
216 Jose Offerman .05 .02
217 Jim Poole .05 .02
218 Juan Samuel .05 .02
219 Mike Scioscia .05 .02
220 Ray Searage .05 .02
221 Mike Sharperson .05 .02
222 Fernando Valenzuela .10 .03
223 Jose Vizcaino .05 .02
224 Mike Aldrete .05 .02
225 Scott Anderson .05 .02
226 Dennis Boyd .05 .02
227 Tim Burke .05 .02
228 Delino DeShields .10 .03
229 Mike Fitzgerald .05 .02
230 Tom Foley .05 .02
231 Steve Frey .05 .02
232 Andres Galarraga .10 .03
233 Mark Gardner .05 .02
234 Marquis Grissom .05 .02
235 Kevin Gross .05 .02
(No date given for first Expos win)
236 Drew Hall .05 .02
237 Dave Martinez .05 .02
238 Dennis Martinez .10 .03
239 Dale Mohorcic .05 .02
240 Chris Nabholz .05 .02
241 Otis Nixon .05 .02
242 Junior Noboa .05 .02
243 Spike Owen .05 .02
244 Tim Raines .10 .03
245 Mel Rojas UER .05 .02
(Stats show 3.60 ERA, bio says 3.19 ERA)
246 Scott Ruskin .05 .02
247 Bill Sampen .05 .02
248 Nelson Santovenia .05 .02
249 Dave Schmidt .05 .02
250 Larry Walker .25 .07
251 Tim Wallach .05 .02
252 Dave Anderson .05 .02
253 Kevin Bass .05 .02
254 Steve Bedrosian .05 .02
255 Jeff Brantley .05 .02
256 John Burkett .05 .02
257 Brett Butler .10 .03
258 Gary Carter .15 .04
259 Will Clark .25 .07
260 Steve Decker RC .05 .02
261 Kelly Downs .05 .02
262 Scott Garrelts .05 .02
263 Terry Kennedy .05 .02
264 Mike LaCoss .05 .02
265 Mark Leonard .05 .02
266 Greg Litton .05 .02
267 Kevin Mitchell .05 .02
268 Randy O'Neal .05 .02
269 Rick Parker .05 .02
270 Rick Reuschel .05 .02
271 Ernest Riles .05 .02
272 Don Robinson .05 .02
273 Robby Thompson .05 .02
274 Mark Thurmond .05 .02
275 Jose Uribe .05 .02
276 Matt Williams .10 .03
277 Trevor Wilson .05 .02
278 Gerald Alexander .05 .02
279 Brad Arnsberg .05 .02
280 Kevin Belcher .05 .02
281 Joe Bitker .05 .02
282 Kevin Brown .10 .03
283 Steve Buechele .05 .02
284 Jack Daugherty .05 .02
285 Julio Franco .10 .03
286 Juan Gonzalez .25 .07
287 Bill Haselman .05 .02
288 Charlie Hough .10 .03
289 Jeff Huson .05 .02
290 Pete Incaviglia .05 .02
291 Mike Jeffcoat .05 .02
292 Jeff Kunkel .05 .02
293 Gary Mielke .05 .02
294 Jamie Moyer .10 .03
295 Rafael Palmeiro .15 .04
296 Geno Petralli .05 .02
297 Gary Pettis .05 .02
298 Kevin Reimer .05 .02
299 Kenny Rogers .10 .03
300 Jeff Russell .05 .02
301 John Russell .05 .02
302 Nolan Ryan 1.00 .30
303 Ruben Sierra .05 .02
304 Bobby Witt .05 .02
305 Jim Abbott UER .15 .04
(Text on back states he won Sullivan Award (outstanding amateur athlete) in 1989;should be '88)
306 Kent Anderson .05 .02
307 Dante Bichette .10 .03
308 Bert Blyleven .10 .03
309 Chili Davis .10 .03
310 Brian Downing .05 .02
311 Mark Eichhorn .05 .02
312 Mike Fetters .05 .02
313 Chuck Finley .10 .03
314 Willie Fraser .05 .02
315 Bryan Harvey .05 .02
316 Donnie Hill .05 .02
317 Wally Joyner .10 .03
318 Mark Langston .05 .02
319 Kirk McCaskill .05 .02
320 John Orton .05 .02
321 Lance Parrish .10 .03
322 Luis Polonia UER .05 .02
(1984 Madfison, should be Madison)
323 Johnny Ray .05 .02
324 Bobby Rose .05 .02
325 Dick Schofield .05 .02
326 Rick Schu .05 .02
327 Lee Stevens .05 .02
328 Devon White .05 .02
329 Dave Winfield .10 .03
330 Cliff Young .05 .02
331 Dave Bergman .05 .02
332 Phil Clark RC .05 .02
333 Darnell Coles .05 .02
334 Milt Cuyler .05 .02
335 Cecil Fielder .10 .03
336 Travis Fryman .10 .03
337 Paul Gibson .05 .02
338 Jerry Don Gleaton .05 .02
339 Mike Heath .05 .02
340 Mike Henneman .05 .02
341 Chet Lemon .05 .02
342 Lance McCullers .05 .02
343 Jack Morris .10 .03
344 Lloyd Moseby .05 .02
345 Edwin Nunez .05 .02
346 Clay Parker .05 .02
347 Dan Petry .05 .02
348 Tony Phillips .05 .02
349 Jeff M. Robinson .05 .02
350 Mark Salas .05 .02
351 Mike Schwabe .05 .02
352 Larry Sheets .05 .02
353 John Shelby .05 .02
354 Frank Tanana .05 .02
355 Alan Trammell .15 .04
356 Gary Ward .05 .02
357 Lou Whitaker .10 .03
358 Beau Allred .05 .02
359 Sandy Alomar Jr. .05 .02
360 Carlos Baerga .05 .02
361 Kevin Bearse .05 .02
362 Tom Brookens .05 .02
363 Jerry Browne UER .05 .02
(No dot over i in first text line)
364 Tom Candiotti .05 .02
365 Alex Cole .05 .02
366 John Farrell UER .05 .02
(Born in Neptune, should be Monmouth)
367 Felix Fermin .05 .02
368 Keith Hernandez .15 .04
369 Brook Jacoby .05 .02
370 Chris James .05 .02
371 Dion James .05 .02
372 Doug Jones .05 .02
373 Candy Maldonado .05 .02
374 Steve Olin .05 .02
375 Jesse Orosco .05 .02
376 Rudy Seanez .05 .02
377 Joel Skinner .05 .02
378 Cory Snyder .05 .02
379 Greg Swindell .05 .02
380 Sergio Valdez .05 .02
381 Mike Walker .05 .02
382 Colby Ward .05 .02
383 Turner Ward RC .10 .03
384 Mitch Webster .05 .02
385 Kevin Wickander .05 .02
386 Darrel Akerfelds .05 .02
387 Joe Boever .05 .02
388 Rod Booker .05 .02
389 Sil Campusano .05 .02
390 Don Carman .05 .02
391 Wes Chamberlain RC .05 .02
392 Pat Combs .05 .02
393 Darren Daulton .10 .03
394 Jose DeJesus .05 .02
395A Len Dykstra .10 .03
Name spelled Lenny on back
395B Len Dykstra .10 .03
Name spelled Len on back
396 Jason Grimsley .05 .02
397 Charlie Hayes .05 .02
398 Von Hayes .05 .02
399 David Hollins UER .05 .02
(Atl-bats, should say at-bats)
400 Ken Howell .05 .02
401 Ricky Jordan .05 .02
402 John Kruk .10 .03
403 Steve Lake .05 .02
404 Chuck Malone .05 .02
405 Roger McDowell UER .05 .02
(Says Phillies is saves, should say in)
406 Chuck McElroy .05 .02
407 Mickey Morandini .05 .02
408 Terry Mulholland .05 .02
409 Dale Murphy .25 .07
410A Randy Ready ERR .05 .02
(No Brewers stats listed for 1983)
410B Randy Ready COR .05 .02
411 Bruce Ruffin .05 .02
412 Dickie Thon .05 .02
413 Paul Assenmacher .05 .02
414 Damon Berryhill .05 .02
415 Mike Bielecki .05 .02
416 Shawn Boskie .05 .02
417 Dave Clark .05 .02
418 Doug Dascenzo .05 .02
419A Andre Dawson ERR .10 .03
(No stats for 1976)
419B Andre Dawson COR .10 .03
420 Shawon Dunston .05 .02
421 Joe Girardi .05 .02
422 Mark Grace .15 .04
423 Mike Harkey .05 .02
424 Les Lancaster .05 .02
425 Bill Long .05 .02
426 Greg Maddux .40 .12
427 Derrick May .05 .02
428 Jeff Pico .05 .02
429 Domingo Ramos .05 .02
430 Luis Salazar .05 .02
431 Ryne Sandberg .40 .12
432 Dwight Smith .05 .02
433 Greg Smith .05 .02
434 Rick Sutcliffe .10 .03
435 Gary Varsho .05 .02
436 Hector Villanueva .05 .02
437 Jerome Walton .05 .02
438 Curtis Wilkerson .05 .02
439 Mitch Williams .05 .02
440 Steve Wilson .05 .02
441 Marvell Wynne .05 .02
442 Scott Bankhead .05 .02
443 Scott Bradley .05 .02
444 Greg Briley .05 .02
445 Mike Brumley UER .05 .02
(Text 40 SB's in 1988, stats say 41)
446 Jay Buhner .10 .03
447 Dave Burba RC .10 .03
448 Henry Cotto .05 .02
449 Alvin Davis .05 .02
450 Ken Griffey Jr. .50 .15
(Bat around .300)
450A Ken Griffey Jr. 1.00 .30
(Bat .300)
451 Erik Hanson .05 .02
452 Gene Harris UER .05 .02
(63 career runs, should be 73)
453 Brian Holman .05 .02
454 Mike Jackson .05 .02
455 Randy Johnson .30 .09
456 Jeffrey Leonard .05 .02
457 Edgar Martinez .15 .04
458 Tino Martinez .15 .04
459 Pete O'Brien UER .05 .02
(1987 BA .266, should be .286)
460 Harold Reynolds .10 .03
461 Mike Schooler .05 .02
462 Bill Swift .05 .02
463 David Valle .05 .02
464 Omar Vizquel .10 .03
465 Matt Young .05 .02
466 Brady Anderson .10 .03
467 Jeff Ballard UER .05 .02
(Missing top of right parenthesis after Saberhagen in last text line)
468 Juan Bell .05 .02
469A Mike Devereaux .10 .03
(First line of text ends with six)
469B Mike Devereaux .10 .03
(First line of text ends with runs)
470 Steve Finley .10 .03
471 Dave Gallagher .05 .02
472 Leo Gomez .05 .02
473 Rene Gonzales .05 .02
474 Pete Harnisch .05 .02
475 Kevin Hickey .05 .02
476 Chris Hoiles .05 .02
477 Sam Horn .05 .02
478 Tim Hulett .05 .02
(Photo shows National Leaguer sliding into second base)
479 Dave Johnson .05 .02
480 Ron Kittle UER .05 .02
(Edmonton misspelled as Edmundton)
481 Ben McDonald .05 .02
482 Bob Melvin .05 .02
483 Bob Milacki .05 .02
484 Randy Milligan .05 .02
485 John Mitchell .05 .02
486 Gregg Olson .05 .02
487 Joe Orsulak .05 .02
488 Joe Price .05 .02
489 Bill Ripken .05 .02
490 Cal Ripken .75 .23
491 Curt Schilling .15 .04
492 David Segui .05 .02
493 Anthony Telford .05 .02
494 Mickey Tettleton .05 .02
495 Mark Williamson .05 .02
496 Craig Worthington .05 .02
497 Juan Agosto .05 .02
498 Eric Anthony .05 .02
499 Craig Biggio .15 .04
500 Ken Caminiti UER .10 .03
(Born 4/4, should be 4/21)
501 Casey Candaele .05 .02
502 Andujar Cedeno .05 .02
503 Danny Darwin .05 .02
504 Mark Davidson .05 .02
505 Glenn Davis .05 .02
506 Jim Deshaies .05 .02
507 Luis Gonzalez RC 1.25 .35
508 Bill Gullickson .05 .02
509 Xavier Hernandez .05 .02
510 Brian Meyer .05 .02
511 Ken Oberkfell .05 .02
512 Mark Portugal .05 .02
513 Rafael Ramirez .05 .02
514 Karl Rhodes .05 .02
515 Mike Scott .05 .02
516 Mike Simms .05 .02
517 Dave Smith .05 .02
518 Franklin Stubbs .05 .02
519 Glenn Wilson .05 .02
520 Eric Yelding UER .05 .02
(Text has 63 steals, stats have 64, which is correct)
521 Gerald Young .05 .02
522 Shawn Abner .05 .02
523 Roberto Alomar .25 .07
524 Andy Benes .05 .02
525 Joe Carter .10 .03
526 Jack Clark .10 .03
527 Joey Cora .05 .02
528 Paul Faries .05 .02
529 Tony Gwynn .30 .09
530 Atlee Hammaker .05 .02
531 Greg W. Harris .05 .02
532 Thomas Howard .05 .02
533 Bruce Hurst .05 .02
534 Craig Lefferts .05 .02
535 Derek Lilliquist .05 .02
536 Fred Lynn .05 .02
537 Mike Pagliarulo .05 .02
538 Mark Parent .05 .02
539 Dennis Rasmussen .05 .02
540 Bip Roberts .05 .02
541 Richard Rodriguez .05 .02
542 Benito Santiago .10 .03
543 Calvin Schiraldi .05 .02
544 Eric Show .05 .02
545 Phil Stephenson .05 .02
546 Garry Templeton UER .05 .02
(Born 3/24/57, should be 3/24/56)
547 Ed Whitson .05 .02
548 Eddie Williams .05 .02
549 Kevin Appier .10 .03
550 Luis Aquino .05 .02
551 Bob Boone .10 .03
552 George Brett .60 .18
553 Jeff Conine RC .50 .15
554 Steve Crawford .05 .02
555 Mark Davis .05 .02
556 Storm Davis .05 .02
557 Jim Eisenreich .05 .02
558 Steve Farr .05 .02
559 Tom Gordon .05 .02
560 Mark Gubicza .05 .02
561 Bo Jackson .25 .07
562 Mike Macfarlane .05 .02
563 Brian McRae RC .10 .03
564 Jeff Montgomery .05 .02
565 Bill Pecota .05 .02
566 Gerald Perry .05 .02
567 Bret Saberhagen .10 .03
568 Jeff Schulz .05 .02
569 Kevin Seitzer .05 .02
570 Terry Shumpert .05 .02
571 Kurt Stillwell .05 .02
572 Danny Tartabull .05 .02
573 Gary Thurman .05 .02
574 Frank White .10 .03
575 Willie Wilson .05 .02
576 Chris Bosio .05 .02
577 Greg Brock .05 .02
578 George Canale .05 .02
579 Chuck Crim .05 .02
580 Rob Deer .05 .02
581 Edgar Diaz .05 .02
582 Tom Edens .05 .02
583 Mike Felder .05 .02
584 Jim Gantner .05 .02
585 Darryl Hamilton .05 .02
586 Ted Higuera .05 .02
587 Mark Knudson .05 .02
588 Bill Krueger .05 .02
589 Tim McIntosh .05 .02
590 Paul Mirabella .05 .02
591 Paul Molitor .15 .04
592 Jaime Navarro .05 .02
593 Dave Parker .10 .03
594 Dan Plesac .05 .02
595 Ron Robinson .05 .02
596 Gary Sheffield .10 .03
597 Bill Spiers .05 .02
598 B.J. Surhoff .10 .03
599 Greg Vaughn .10 .03
600 Randy Veres .05 .02
601 Robin Yount .40 .12
602 Rick Aguilera .10 .03
603 Allan Anderson .05 .02
604 Juan Berenguer .05 .02
605 Randy Bush .05 .02
606 Carmelo Castillo .05 .02
607 Tim Drummond .05 .02
608 Scott Erickson .05 .02
609 Gary Gaetti .10 .03
610 Greg Gagne .05 .02
611 Dan Gladden .05 .02
612 Mark Guthrie .05 .02
613 Brian Harper .05 .02
614 Kent Hrbek .10 .03
615 Gene Larkin .05 .02
616 Terry Leach .05 .02
617 Nelson Liriano .05 .02
618 Shane Mack .05 .02
619 John Moses .05 .02
620 Pedro Munoz RC .05 .02
621 Al Newman .05 .02
622 Junior Ortiz .05 .02
623 Kirby Puckett .25 .07
624 Roy Smith .05 .02
625 Kevin Tapani .05 .02
626 Gary Wayne .05 .02
627 David West .05 .02
628 Cris Carpenter .05 .02
629 Vince Coleman .05 .02
630 Ken Dayley .05 .02
631A Jose DeLeon ERR .05 .02
(missing '79 Bradenton stats)
631B Jose DeLeon COR .05 .02
(with '79 Bradenton stats)
632 Frank DiPino .05 .02
633 Bernard Gilkey .05 .02
634A P.Guerrero ERR .10 .03
career SB shown as "$91"
634B Pedro Guerrero COR .10 .03
635 Ken Hill .05 .02
636 Felix Jose .05 .02
637 Ray Lankford .05 .02
638 Joe Magrane .05 .02
639 Tom Niedenfuer .05 .02
640 Jose Oquendo .05 .02
641 Tom Pagnozzi .05 .02
642 Terry Pendleton .10 .03
643 Mike Perez RC .10 .03
644 Bryn Smith .05 .02
645 Lee Smith .10 .03
646 Ozzie Smith .40 .12
647 Scott Terry .05 .02
648 Bob Tewksbury .05 .02
649 Milt Thompson .05 .02
650 John Tudor .05 .02
651 Denny Walling .05 .02
652 Craig Wilson .05 .02
653 Todd Worrell .05 .02
654 Todd Zeile .05 .02
655 Oscar Azocar .05 .02
656 Steve Balboni UER .05 .02
(Born 1/5/57, should be 1/16)
657 Jesse Barfield .05 .02
658 Greg Cadaret .05 .02
659 Chuck Cary .05 .02
660 Rick Cerone .05 .02
661 Dave Eiland .05 .02
662 Alvaro Espinoza .05 .02
663 Bob Geren .05 .02
664 Lee Guetterman .05 .02
665 Mel Hall .05 .02
666 Andy Hawkins .05 .02
667 Jimmy Jones .05 .02
668 Roberto Kelly .05 .02
669 Dave LaPoint UER .05 .02
(No '81 Brewers stats, totals also are wrong)
670 Tim Leary .05 .02
671 Jim Leyritz .05 .02
672 Kevin Maas .05 .02
673 Don Mattingly .60 .18
674 Matt Nokes .05 .02
675 Pascual Perez .05 .02
676 Eric Plunk .05 .02
677 Dave Righetti .10 .03
678 Jeff D. Robinson .05 .02
679 Steve Sax .05 .02
680 Mike Witt .05 .02
681 Steve Avery UER .05 .02
(Born in New Jersey, should say Michigan)
682 Mike Bell .05 .02
683 Jeff Blauser .05 .02
684 F.Cabrera UER .05 .02
Born 10/16, should say 10/10
685 Tony Castillo .05 .02
686 Marty Clary UER .05 .02
(Shown pitching righty, but bio has left)
687 Nick Esasky .05 .02
688 Ron Gant .10 .03
689 Tom Glavine .15 .04
690 Mark Grant .05 .02
691 Tommy Gregg .05 .02
692 Dwayne Henry .05 .02
693 Dave Justice .10 .03
694 Jimmy Kremers .05 .02

Card	Nm-Mt	Ex-Mt
695 Charlie Leibrandt	.05	.02
696 Mark Lemke	.05	.02
697 Oddibe McDowell	.05	.02
698 Greg Olson	.05	.02
699 Jeff Parrett	.05	.02
700 Jim Presley	.05	.02
701 Victor Rosario	.05	.02
702 Lonnie Smith	.05	.02
703 Pete Smith	.05	.02
704 John Smoltz	.15	.04
705 Mike Stanton	.05	.02
706 Andres Thomas	.05	.02
707 Jeff Treadway	.05	.02
708 Jim Vatcher	.05	.02
709 Ryne Sandberg	.25	.07
Cecil Fielder		
710 Barry Bonds	.75	.23
Ken Griffey Jr.		
711 Bobby Bonilla	.10	.03
Barry Larkin		
712 Bobby Thigpen	.05	.02
John Franco		
713 Andre Dawson	.25	.07
Ryne Sandberg UER		
(Ryno misspelled Rhino)		
714 CL:A's/Pirates	.05	.02
Reds/Red Sox		
715 CL:White Sox/Mets	.05	.02
Blue Jays/Dodgers		
716 CL:Expos/Giants	.05	.02
Rangers/Angels		
717 CL:Tigers/Indians	.05	.02
Phillies/Cubs		
718 CL:Mariners/Orioles	.05	.02
Astros/Padres		
719 CL:Royals/Brewers	.05	.02
Twins/Cardinals		
720 CL:Yankees/Braves	.05	.02
Superstars/Specials		

1991 Fleer All-Stars

or the sixth consecutive year Fleer issued an ll-Star insert set. This year the cards were nly available as random inserts in Fleer cello acks. This ten-card standard-size set is eminiscent of the 1971 Topps Greatest Moments set with two pictures on the (black-ordered) front as well as a photo on the back.

	Nm-Mt	Ex-Mt
OMPLETE SET (10)	15.00	4.50
Ryne Sandberg	3.00	.90
Barry Larkin	2.00	.60
Matt Williams	.75	.23
Cecil Fielder	.75	.23
Barry Bonds	5.00	1.50
Rickey Henderson	2.00	.60
Ken Griffey Jr.	4.00	1.20
Jose Canseco	2.00	.60
Benito Santiago	.75	.23
0 Roger Clemens	4.00	1.20

1991 Fleer Pro-Visions

his 12-card standard-size insert set features aintings by artist Terry Smith framed by istinctive black borders on each card front. he cards were randomly inserted in wax and ack packs. An additional four-card set was ssued only in 1991 Fleer factory sets. Those ards are numbered F1-F4. Unlike the 12 cards nserted in packs, these factory set cards eature white borders on front.

	Nm-Mt	Ex-Mt
OMPLETE REG.SET (12)	4.00	1.20
OMP.FACT.SET (4)	2.00	.60
Kirby Puckett UER	.75	.23
(.326 average,		
should be .328)		
Will Clark UER	.75	.23
(On tenth line, pennant		
misspelled pennent)		
Ruben Sierra UER	.15	.04
(No apostrophe		
in hasn't)		
Mark McGwire UER	2.00	.60
(Fisk won ROY in		
'72, not '82)		
Bo Jackson	.75	.23
(Bio says 6', others		
have him at 6'1")		
Jose Canseco UER	.75	.23
(Bio 6'3", 230,		
text has 6'4", 240)		
Dwight Gooden UER	.50	.15
(2.80 ERA in Lynchburg,		
should be 2.50)		
Mike Greenwell UER	.15	.04
(.328 BA and 87 RBI,		
should be .325 and 95)		
Roger Clemens	1.50	.45
0 Eric Davis	.30	.09
1 Don Mattingly	2.00	.60
2 Darryl Strawberry	.50	.15
1 Barry Bonds	2.00	.60
2 Rickey Henderson	.75	.23
F3 Ryne Sandberg	1.25	.35
F4 Dave Stewart	.30	.09

1991 Fleer Wax Box Cards

These cards were issued on the bottom of 1991 Fleer wax boxes. This set celebrated the spate of no-hitters in 1990 and were printed on three different boxes. These standard size cards, come four to a box, three about the no-hitters and one team logo card on each box. The cards are blank backed and are numbered on the front in a subtle way. They are ordered below as they are numbered, which is by chronological order of their no-hitters. Only the player cards are listed below since there was a different team logo card on each box.

	Nm-Mt	Ex-Mt
COMPLETE SET (9)	4.00	1.20
1 Mark Langston	.10	.03
and Mike Witt		
2 Randy Johnson	1.00	.30
3 Nolan Ryan	3.00	.90
4 Dave Stewart	.20	.06
5 Fernando Valenzuela	.20	.06
6 Andy Hawkins	.10	.03
7 Melido Perez	.10	.03
8 Terry Mulholland	.10	.03
9 Dave Stieb	.20	.06

1991 Fleer World Series

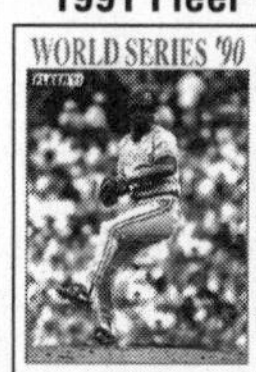

This eight-card set captures highlights from the 1990 World Series between the Cincinnati Reds and the Oakland Athletics. The set was only available as an insert with the 1991 Fleer factory sets. The standard-size cards have on the fronts color action photos, bordered in blue on a white card face. The words "World Series '90" appears in red and blue lettering above the pictures. The backs have a similar design, only with a summary of an aspect of the Series on a yellow background.

	Nm-Mt	Ex-Mt
COMPLETE SET (8)	.75	.23
1 Eric Davis	.10	.03
2 Billy Hatcher	.05	.02
3 Jose Canseco	.25	.07
4 Rickey Henderson	.25	.07
5 Chris Sabo	.05	.02
6 Dave Stewart	.10	.03
7 Jose Rijo	.05	.02
8 Reds Celebrate	.05	.02

1991 Fleer Update

The 1991 Fleer Update set contains 132 standard-size cards. The cards were distributed exclusively in factory set form through hobby dealers. Card design is identical to regular issue 1991 Fleer cards with the notable bright yellow borders except for the U-prefixed numbering on back. The cards are ordered alphabetically by team. The key Rookie Cards in this set are Jeff Bagwell and Ivan Rodriguez.

	Nm-Mt	Ex-Mt
COMP.FACT.SET (132)	5.00	1.50
1 Glenn Davis	.05	.02
2 Dwight Evans	.10	.03
3 Jose Mesa	.05	.02
4 Jack Clark	.10	.03
5 Danny Darwin	.05	.02
6 Steve Lyons	.05	.02
7 Mo Vaughn	.10	.03
8 Floyd Bannister	.05	.02
9 Gary Gaetti	.10	.03
10 Dave Parker	.10	.03
11 Joey Cora	.05	.02
12 Charlie Hough	.10	.03
13 Matt Merullo	.05	.02
14 Warren Newson	.05	.02
15 Tim Raines	.10	.03
16 Albert Belle	.10	.03
17 Glenallen Hill	.05	.02
18 Shawn Hillegas	.05	.02
19 Mark Lewis	.05	.02
20 Charles Nagy	.05	.02
21 Mark Whiten	.05	.02
22 John Cerutti	.05	.02
23 Rob Deer	.05	.02
24 Mickey Tettleton	.05	.02
25 Warren Cromartie	.05	.02
26 Kirk Gibson	.10	.03
27 David Howard	.05	.02
28 Brent Mayne	.05	.02
29 Dante Bichette	.10	.03
30 Mark Lee RC	.05	.02
31 Julio Machado	.05	.02
32 Edwin Nunez	.05	.02
33 Willie Randolph	.10	.03
34 Franklin Stubbs	.05	.02
35 Bill Wegman	.05	.02
36 Chili Davis	.10	.03
37 Chuck Knoblauch	.10	.03
38 Scott Leius	.05	.02
39 Jack Morris	.10	.03
40 Mike Pagliarulo	.05	.02
41 Lenny Webster	.05	.02
42 John Habyan	.05	.02
43 Steve Howe	.05	.02
44 Jeff Johnson	.05	.02
45 Scott Kamieniecki RC	.05	.02
46 Pat Kelly RC	.05	.02
47 Hensley Meulens	.05	.02
48 Wade Taylor	.05	.02
49 Bernie Williams	.25	.07
50 Kirk Dressendorfer RC	.05	.02
51 Ernest Riles	.05	.02
52 Rich DeLucia	.05	.02
53 Tracy Jones	.05	.02
54 Bill Krueger	.05	.02
55 Alonzo Powell	.05	.02
56 Jeff Schaefer	.05	.02
57 Russ Swan	.05	.02
58 John Barfield	.05	.02
59 Rich Gossage	.10	.03
60 Jose Guzman	.05	.02
61 Dean Palmer	.10	.03
62 Ivan Rodriguez RC	2.00	.60
63 Roberto Alomar	.25	.07
64 Tom Candiotti	.05	.02
65 Joe Carter	.10	.03
66 Ed Sprague	.05	.02
67 Pat Tabler	.05	.02
68 Mike Timlin RC	.10	.03
69 Devon White	.05	.02
70 Rafael Belliard	.05	.02
71 Juan Berenguer	.05	.02
72 Sid Bream	.05	.02
73 Marvin Freeman	.05	.02
74 Kent Mercker	.05	.02
75 Otis Nixon	.05	.02
76 Terry Pendleton	.10	.03
77 George Bell	.05	.02
78 Danny Jackson	.05	.02
79 Chuck McElroy	.05	.02
80 Gary Scott	.05	.02
81 Heathcliff Slocumb RC	.10	.03
82 Dave Smith	.05	.02
83 Rick Wilkins RC	.05	.02
84 Freddie Benavides	.05	.02
85 Ted Power	.05	.02
86 Mo Sanford	.05	.02
87 Jeff Bagwell RC	1.50	.45
88 Steve Finley	.10	.03
89 Pete Harnisch	.05	.02
90 Darryl Kile	.10	.03
91 Brett Butler	.10	.03
92 John Candelaria	.05	.02
93 Gary Carter	.15	.04
94 Kevin Gross	.05	.02
95 Bob Ojeda	.05	.02
96 Darryl Strawberry	.15	.04
97 Ivan Calderon	.05	.02
98 Ron Hassey	.05	.02
99 Gilberto Reyes	.05	.02
100 Hubie Brooks	.05	.02
101 Rick Cerone	.05	.02
102 Vince Coleman	.05	.02
103 Jeff Innis	.05	.02
104 Pete Schourek RC	.05	.02
105 Andy Ashby RC	.25	.07
106 Wally Backman	.05	.02
107 Darrin Fletcher	.05	.02
108 Tommy Greene	.05	.02
109 John Morris	.05	.02
110 Mitch Williams	.05	.02
111 Lloyd McClendon	.05	.02
112 Orlando Merced RC	.05	.02
113 Vicente Palacios	.05	.02
114 Gary Varsho	.05	.02
115 John Wehner	.05	.02
116 Rex Hudler	.05	.02
117 Tim Jones	.05	.02
118 Geronimo Pena	.05	.02
119 Gerald Perry	.05	.02
120 Larry Andersen	.05	.02
121 Jerald Clark	.05	.02
122 Scott Coolbaugh	.05	.02
123 Tony Fernandez	.05	.02
124 Darrin Jackson	.05	.02
125 Fred McGriff	.15	.04
126 Jose Mota RC	.05	.02
127 Tim Teufel	.05	.02
128 Bud Black	.05	.02
129 Mike Felder	.05	.02
130 Willie McGee	.10	.03
131 Dave Righetti	.10	.03
132 Checklist U1-U132	.05	.02

1992 Fleer

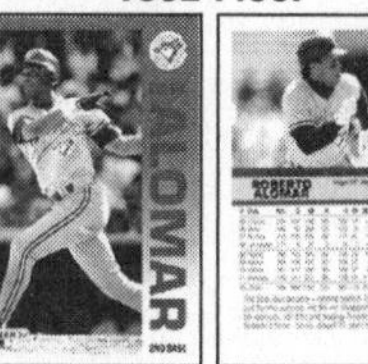
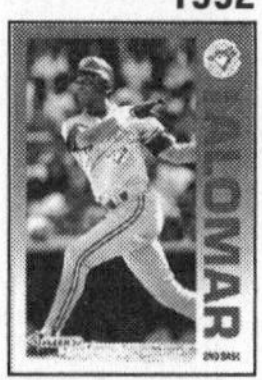

The 1992 Fleer set contains 720 standard-size cards issued in one comprehensive series. The cards were distributed in plastic wrapped packs, 35-card cello packs, 42-card rack packs and factory sets. The card fronts shade from metallic pale green to white as one moves down the face. The team logo and player's name appear to the right of the picture, running the length of the card. The cards are ordered alphabetically within and according to teams for each league with AL preceding NL. Topical subsets feature Major League Prospects (652-680), Record Setters (681-687), League Leaders (688-697), Super Star Specials (698-707) and Pro Visions (708-713). Rookie Cards include Scott Brosius and Vinny Castilla.

	Nm-Mt	Ex-Mt
COMPLETE SET (720)	10.00	3.00
COMP.HOBBY SET (732)	20.00	6.00
COMP.RETAIL SET (732)	20.00	6.00
1 Brady Anderson	.10	.03
2 Jose Bautista	.10	.03
3 Juan Bell	.10	.03
4 Glenn Davis	.10	.03
5 Mike Devereaux	.10	.03
6 Dwight Evans	.10	.03
7 Mike Flanagan	.10	.03
8 Leo Gomez	.10	.03
9 Chris Hoiles	.10	.03
10 Sam Horn	.10	.03
11 Tim Hulett	.10	.03
12 Dave Johnson	.10	.03
13 Chito Martinez	.10	.03
14 Ben McDonald	.10	.03
15 Bob Melvin	.10	.03
16 Luis Mercedes	.10	.03
17 Jose Mesa	.10	.03
18 Bob Milacki	.10	.03
19 Randy Milligan	.10	.03
20 Mike Mussina UER	.25	.07
(Card back refers		
to him as Jeff)		
21 Gregg Olson	.10	.03
22 Joe Orsulak	.10	.03
23 Jim Poole	.10	.03
24 Arthur Rhodes	.10	.03
25 Billy Ripken	.10	.03
26 Cal Ripken	.75	.23
27 David Segui	.10	.03
28 Roy Smith	.10	.03
29 Anthony Telford	.10	.03
30 Mark Williamson	.10	.03
31 Craig Worthington	.10	.03
32 Wade Boggs	.15	.04
33 Tom Bolton	.10	.03
34 Tom Brunansky	.10	.03
35 Ellis Burks	.10	.03
36 Jack Clark	.10	.03
37 Roger Clemens	.50	.15
38 Danny Darwin	.10	.03
39 Mike Greenwell	.10	.03
40 Joe Hesketh	.10	.03
41 Daryl Irvine	.10	.03
42 Dennis Lamp	.10	.03
43 Tony Pena	.10	.03
44 Phil Plantier	.10	.03
45 Carlos Quintana	.10	.03
46 Jeff Reardon	.10	.03
47 Jody Reed	.10	.03
48 Luis Rivera	.10	.03
49 Mo Vaughn	.10	.03
50 Jim Abbott	.15	.04
51 Kyle Abbott	.10	.03
52 Ruben Amaro	.10	.03
53 Scott Bailes	.10	.03
54 Chris Beasley	.10	.03
55 Mark Eichhorn	.10	.03
56 Mike Fetters	.10	.03
57 Chuck Finley	.10	.03
58 Gary Gaetti	.10	.03
59 Dave Gallagher	.10	.03
60 Donnie Hill	.10	.03
61 Bryan Harvey UER	.10	.03
(Lee Smith led the		
Majors with 47 saves)		
62 Wally Joyner	.10	.03
63 Mark Langston	.10	.03
64 Kirk McCaskill	.10	.03
65 John Orton	.10	.03
66 Lance Parrish	.10	.03
67 Luis Polonia	.10	.03
68 Bobby Rose	.10	.03
69 Dick Schofield	.10	.03
70 Luis Sojo	.10	.03
71 Lee Stevens	.10	.03
72 Dave Winfield	.10	.03
73 Cliff Young	.10	.03
74 Wilson Alvarez	.10	.03
75 Esteban Beltre	.10	.03
76 Joey Cora	.10	.03
77 Brian Drahman	.10	.03
78 Alex Fernandez	.10	.03
79 Carlton Fisk	.15	.04
80 Scott Fletcher	.10	.03
81 Craig Grebeck	.10	.03
82 Ozzie Guillen	.10	.03
83 Greg Hibbard	.10	.03
84 Charlie Hough	.10	.03
85 Mike Huff	.10	.03
86 Bo Jackson	.25	.07
87 Lance Johnson	.10	.03
88 Ron Karkovice	.10	.03
89 Jack McDowell	.10	.03
90 Matt Merullo	.10	.03
91 Warren Newson	.10	.03
92 Donn Pall UER	.10	.03
(Called Dunn on		
card back)		
93 Dan Pasqua	.10	.03
94 Ken Patterson	.10	.03
95 Melido Perez	.10	.03
96 Scott Radinsky	.10	.03
97 Tim Raines	.10	.03
98 Sammy Sosa	.40	.12
99 Bobby Thigpen	.10	.03
100 Frank Thomas	.25	.07
101 Robin Ventura	.10	.03
102 Mike Aldrete	.10	.03
103 Sandy Alomar Jr.	.10	.03
104 Carlos Baerga	.10	.03
105 Albert Belle	.10	.03
106 Willie Blair	.10	.03
107 Jerry Browne	.10	.03
108 Alex Cole	.10	.03
109 Felix Fermin	.10	.03
110 Glenallen Hill	.10	.03
111 Shawn Hillegas	.10	.03
112 Chris James	.10	.03
113 Reggie Jefferson	.10	.03
114 Doug Jones	.10	.03
115 Eric King	.10	.03
116 Mark Lewis	.10	.03
117 Carlos Martinez	.10	.03
118 Charles Nagy UER	.10	.03
(Throws right, but		
card says left)		
119 Rod Nichols	.10	.03
120 Steve Olin	.10	.03
121 Jesse Orosco	.10	.03
122 Rudy Seanez	.10	.03
123 Joel Skinner	.10	.03
124 Greg Swindell	.10	.03
125 Jim Thome	.25	.07
126 Mark Whiten	.10	.03
127 Scott Aldred	.10	.03
128 Andy Allanson	.10	.03
129 John Cerutti	.10	.03
130 Milt Cuyler	.10	.03
131 Mike Dalton	.10	.03
132 Rob Deer	.10	.03
133 Cecil Fielder	.10	.03
134 Travis Fryman	.10	.03
135 Dan Gakeler	.10	.03
136 Paul Gibson	.10	.03
137 Bill Gullickson	.10	.03
138 Mike Henneman	.10	.03
139 Pete Incaviglia	.10	.03
140 Mark Leiter	.10	.03
141 Scott Livingstone	.10	.03
142 Lloyd Moseby	.10	.03
143 Tony Phillips	.10	.03
144 Mark Salas	.10	.03
145 Frank Tanana	.10	.03
146 Walt Terrell	.10	.03
147 Mickey Tettleton	.10	.03
148 Alan Trammell	.15	.04
149 Lou Whitaker	.10	.03
150 Kevin Appier	.10	.03
151 Luis Aquino	.10	.03
152 Todd Benzinger	.10	.03
153 Mike Boddicker	.10	.03
154 George Brett	.60	.18
155 Storm Davis	.10	.03
156 Jim Eisenreich	.10	.03
157 Kirk Gibson	.10	.03
158 Tom Gordon	.10	.03
159 Mark Gubicza	.10	.03
160 David Howard	.10	.03
161 Mike Macfarlane	.10	.03
162 Brent Mayne	.10	.03
163 Brian McRae	.10	.03
164 Jeff Montgomery	.10	.03
165 Bill Pecota	.10	.03
166 Harvey Pulliam	.10	.03
167 Bret Saberhagen	.10	.03
168 Kevin Seitzer	.10	.03
169 Terry Shumpert	.10	.03
170 Kurt Stillwell	.10	.03
171 Danny Tartabull	.10	.03
172 Gary Thurman	.10	.03
173 Dante Bichette	.10	.03
174 Kevin D. Brown	.10	.03
175 Chuck Crim	.10	.03
176 Jim Gantner	.10	.03
177 Darryl Hamilton	.10	.03
178 Ted Higuera	.10	.03
179 Darren Holmes	.10	.03
180 Mark Lee	.10	.03
181 Julio Machado	.10	.03
182 Paul Molitor	.15	.04
183 Jaime Navarro	.10	.03
184 Edwin Nunez	.10	.03
185 Dan Plesac	.10	.03
186 Willie Randolph	.10	.03
187 Ron Robinson	.10	.03
188 Gary Sheffield	.10	.03
189 Bill Spiers	.10	.03
190 B.J. Surhoff	.10	.03
191 Dale Sveum	.10	.03
192 Greg Vaughn	.10	.03
193 Bill Wegman	.10	.03
194 Robin Yount	.40	.12
195 Rick Aguilera	.10	.03
196 Allan Anderson	.10	.03
197 Steve Bedrosian	.10	.03
198 Randy Bush	.10	.03
199 Larry Casian	.10	.03
200 Chili Davis	.10	.03
201 Scott Erickson	.10	.03
202 Greg Gagne	.10	.03
203 Dan Gladden	.10	.03
204 Brian Harper	.10	.03
205 Kent Hrbek	.10	.03
206 C.Knoblauch UER	.10	.03
Career hit total		
of 59 is wrong		
207 Gene Larkin	.10	.03
208 Terry Leach	.10	.03
209 Scott Leius	.10	.03
210 Shane Mack	.10	.03
211 Jack Morris	.10	.03
212 Pedro Munoz	.10	.03
213 Denny Neagle	.10	.03
214 Al Newman	.10	.03
215 Junior Ortiz	.10	.03
216 Mike Pagliarulo	.10	.03
217 Kirby Puckett	.25	.07
218 Paul Sorrento	.10	.03
219 Kevin Tapani	.10	.03
220 Lenny Webster	.10	.03
221 Jesse Barfield	.10	.03
222 Greg Cadaret	.10	.03
223 Dave Eiland	.10	.03
224 Alvaro Espinoza	.10	.03
225 Steve Farr	.10	.03
226 Bob Geren	.10	.03
227 Lee Guetterman	.10	.03
228 John Habyan	.10	.03
229 Mel Hall	.10	.03
230 Steve Howe	.10	.03
231 Mike Humphreys	.10	.03
232 Scott Kamieniecki	.10	.03
233 Pat Kelly	.10	.03
234 Roberto Kelly	.10	.03
235 Tim Leary	.10	.03
236 Kevin Maas	.10	.03
237 Don Mattingly	.60	.18
238 Hensley Meulens	.10	.03
239 Matt Nokes	.10	.03
240 Pascual Perez	.10	.03
241 Eric Plunk	.10	.03
242 John Ramos	.10	.03
243 Scott Sanderson	.10	.03
244 Steve Sax	.10	.03
245 Wade Taylor	.10	.03
246 Randy Velarde	.10	.03
247 Bernie Williams	.15	.04
248 Troy Afenir	.10	.03
249 Harold Baines	.10	.03
250 Lance Blankenship	.10	.03
251 Mike Bordick	.10	.03
252 Jose Canseco	.25	.07

253 Steve Chitren .10 .03
254 Ron Darling .10 .03
255 Dennis Eckersley .10 .03
256 Mike Gallego .10 .03
257 Dave Henderson .10 .03
258 R.Henderson UER .25 .07
Wearing 24 on front
and 22 on back
259 Rick Honeycutt .10 .03
260 Brook Jacoby .10 .03
261 Carney Lansford .10 .03
262 Mark McGwire .60 .18
263 Mike Moore .10 .03
264 Gene Nelson .10 .03
265 Jamie Quirk .10 .03
266 Joe Slusarski .10 .03
267 Terry Steinbach .10 .03
268 Dave Stewart .10 .03
269 Todd Van Poppel .10 .03
270 Walt Weiss .10 .03
271 Bob Welch .10 .03
272 Curt Young .10 .03
273 Scott Bradley .10 .03
274 Greg Briley .10 .03
275 Jay Buhner .10 .03
276 Henry Cotto .10 .03
277 Alvin Davis .10 .03
278 Rich DeLucia .10 .03
279 Ken Griffey Jr. .40 .12
280 Erik Hanson .10 .03
281 Brian Holman .10 .03
282 Mike Jackson .10 .03
283 Randy Johnson .25 .07
284 Tracy Jones .10 .03
285 Bill Krueger .10 .03
286 Edgar Martinez .15 .04
287 Tino Martinez .15 .04
288 Rob Murphy .10 .03
289 Pete O'Brien .10 .03
290 Alonzo Powell .10 .03
291 Harold Reynolds .10 .03
292 Mike Schooler .10 .03
293 Russ Swan .10 .03
294 Bill Swift .10 .03
295 Dave Valle .10 .03
296 Omar Vizquel .10 .03
297 Gerald Alexander .10 .03
298 Brad Arnsberg .10 .03
299 Kevin Brown .10 .03
300 Jack Daugherty .10 .03
301 Mario Diaz .10 .03
302 Brian Downing .10 .03
303 Julio Franco .10 .03
304 Juan Gonzalez .25 .07
305 Rich Gossage .10 .03
306 Jose Guzman .10 .03
307 Jose Hernandez RC .40 .12
308 Jeff Huson .10 .03
309 Mike Jeffcoat .10 .03
310 Terry Mathews .10 .03
311 Rafael Palmeiro .15 .04
312 Dean Palmer .10 .03
313 Geno Petralli .10 .03
314 Gary Pettis .10 .03
315 Kevin Reimer .10 .03
316 Ivan Rodriguez .25 .07
317 Kenny Rogers .10 .03
318 Wayne Rosenthal .10 .03
319 Jeff Russell .10 .03
320 Nolan Ryan 1.00 .30
321 Ruben Sierra .10 .03
322 Jim Acker .10 .03
323 Roberto Alomar .25 .07
324 Derek Bell .10 .03
325 Pat Borders .10 .03
326 Tom Candiotti .10 .03
327 Joe Carter .10 .03
328 Rob Ducey .10 .03
329 Kelly Gruber .10 .03
330 Juan Guzman .10 .03
331 Tom Henke .10 .03
332 Jimmy Key .10 .03
333 Manny Lee .10 .03
334 Al Leiter .10 .03
335 Bob MacDonald .10 .03
336 Candy Maldonado .10 .03
337 Rance Mulliniks .10 .03
338 Greg Myers .10 .03
339 John Olerud UER .10 .03
(1991 BA has .256,
but text says .258)
340 Ed Sprague .10 .03
341 Dave Stieb .10 .03
342 Todd Stottlemyre .10 .03
343 Mike Timlin .10 .03
344 Duane Ward .10 .03
345 David Wells .10 .03
346 Devon White .10 .03
347 Mookie Wilson .10 .03
348 Eddie Zosky .10 .03
349 Steve Avery .10 .03
350 Mike Bell .10 .03
351 Rafael Belliard .10 .03
352 Juan Berenguer .10 .03
353 Jeff Blauser .10 .03
354 Sid Bream .10 .03
355 Francisco Cabrera .10 .03
356 Marvin Freeman .10 .03
357 Ron Gant .10 .03
358 Tom Glavine .15 .04
359 Brian Hunter .10 .03
360 Dave Justice .10 .03
361 Charlie Leibrandt .10 .03
362 Mark Lemke .10 .03
363 Kent Mercker .10 .03
364 Keith Mitchell .10 .03
365 Greg Olson .10 .03
366 Terry Pendleton .10 .03
367 Armando Reynoso RC .25 .07
368 Deion Sanders .15 .04
369 Lonnie Smith .10 .03
370 Pete Smith .10 .03
371 John Smoltz .15 .04
372 Mike Stanton .10 .03
373 Jeff Treadway .10 .03
374 Mark Wohlers .10 .03
375 Paul Assenmacher .10 .03
376 George Bell .10 .03
377 Shawn Boskie .10 .03
378 Frank Castillo .10 .03
379 Andre Dawson .10 .03
380 Shawon Dunston .10 .03
381 Mark Grace .15 .04
382 Mike Harkey .10 .03
383 Danny Jackson .10 .03
384 Les Lancaster .10 .03
385 Ced Landrum .10 .03
386 Greg Maddux .40 .12
387 Derrick May .10 .03
388 Chuck McElroy .10 .03
389 Ryne Sandberg .40 .12
390 Heathcliff Slocumb .10 .03
391 Dave Smith .10 .03
392 Dwight Smith .10 .03
393 Rick Sutcliffe .10 .03
394 Hector Villanueva .10 .03
395 Chico Walker .10 .03
396 Jerome Walton .10 .03
397 Rick Wilkins .10 .03
398 Jack Armstrong .10 .03
399 Freddie Benavides .10 .03
400 Glenn Braggs .10 .03
401 Tom Browning .10 .03
402 Norm Charlton .10 .03
403 Eric Davis .10 .03
404 Rob Dibble .10 .03
405 Bill Doran .10 .03
406 Mariano Duncan .10 .03
407 Kip Gross .10 .03
408 Chris Hammond .10 .03
409 Billy Hatcher .10 .03
410 Chris Jones .10 .03
411 Barry Larkin .25 .07
412 Hal Morris .10 .03
413 Randy Myers .10 .03
414 Joe Oliver .10 .03
415 Paul O'Neill .15 .04
416 Ted Power .10 .03
417 Luis Quinones .10 .03
418 Jeff Reed .10 .03
419 Jose Rijo .10 .03
420 Chris Sabo .10 .03
421 Reggie Sanders .10 .03
422 Scott Scudder .10 .03
423 Glenn Sutko .10 .03
424 Eric Anthony .10 .03
425 Jeff Bagwell .25 .07
426 Craig Biggio .15 .04
427 Ken Caminiti .10 .03
428 Casey Candaele .10 .03
429 Mike Capel .10 .03
430 Andujar Cedeno .10 .03
431 Jim Corsi .10 .03
432 Mark Davidson .10 .03
433 Steve Finley .10 .03
434 Luis Gonzalez .15 .04
435 Pete Harnisch .10 .03
436 Dwayne Henry .10 .03
437 Xavier Hernandez .10 .03
438 Jimmy Jones .10 .03
439 Darryl Kile .10 .03
440 Rob Mallicoat .10 .03
441 Andy Mota .10 .03
442 Al Osuna .10 .03
443 Mark Portugal .10 .03
444 Scott Servais .10 .03
445 Mike Simms .10 .03
446 Gerald Young .10 .03
447 Tim Belcher .10 .03
448 Brett Butler .10 .03
449 John Candelaria .10 .03
450 Gary Carter .15 .04
451 Dennis Cook .10 .03
452 Tim Crews .10 .03
453 Kal Daniels .10 .03
454 Jim Gott .10 .03
455 Alfredo Griffin .10 .03
456 Kevin Gross .10 .03
457 Chris Gwynn .10 .03
458 Lenny Harris .10 .03
459 Orel Hershiser .10 .03
460 Jay Howell .10 .03
461 Stan Javier .10 .03
462 Eric Karros .10 .03
463 Ramon Martinez UER .10 .03
(Card says bats right,
should be left)
464 Roger McDowell UER .10 .03
(Wins add up to 54,
totals have 51)
465 Mike Morgan .10 .03
466 Eddie Murray .25 .07
467 Jose Offerman .10 .03
468 Bob Ojeda .10 .03
469 Juan Samuel .10 .03
470 Mike Scioscia .10 .03
471 Darryl Strawberry .15 .04
472 Bret Barberie .10 .03
473 Brian Barnes .10 .03
474 Eric Bullock .10 .03
475 Ivan Calderon .10 .03
476 Delino DeShields .10 .03
477 Jeff Fassero .10 .03
478 Mike Fitzgerald .10 .03
479 Steve Frey .10 .03
480 Andres Galarraga .10 .03
481 Mark Gardner .10 .03
482 Marquis Grissom .10 .03
483 Chris Haney .10 .03
484 Barry Jones .10 .03
485 Dave Martinez .10 .03
486 Dennis Martinez .10 .03
487 Chris Nabholz .10 .03
488 Spike Owen .10 .03
489 Gilberto Reyes .10 .03
490 Mel Rojas .10 .03
491 Scott Ruskin .10 .03
492 Bill Sampen .10 .03
493 Larry Walker .15 .04
494 Tim Wallach .10 .03
495 Daryl Boston .10 .03
496 Hubie Brooks .10 .03
497 Tim Burke .10 .03
498 Mark Carreon .10 .03
499 Tony Castillo .10 .03
500 Vince Coleman .10 .03
501 David Cone .10 .03
502 Kevin Elster .10 .03
503 Sid Fernandez .10 .03
504 John Franco .10 .03
505 Dwight Gooden .15 .04
506 Todd Hundley .10 .03
507 Jeff Innis .10 .03
508 Gregg Jefferies .10 .03
509 Howard Johnson .10 .03
510 Dave Magadan .10 .03
511 Terry McDaniel .10 .03
512 Kevin McReynolds .10 .03
513 Keith Miller .10 .03
514 Charlie O'Brien .10 .03
515 Mackey Sasser .10 .03
516 Pete Schourek .10 .03
517 Julio Valera .10 .03
518 Frank Viola .10 .03
519 Wally Whitehurst .10 .03
520 Anthony Young .10 .03
521 Andy Ashby .10 .03
522 Kim Batiste .10 .03
523 Joe Boever .10 .03
524 Wes Chamberlain .10 .03
525 Pat Combs .10 .03
526 Danny Cox .10 .03
527 Darren Daulton .10 .03
528 Jose DeJesus .10 .03
529 Len Dykstra .10 .03
530 Darrin Fletcher .10 .03
531 Tommy Greene .10 .03
532 Jason Grimsley .10 .03
533 Charlie Hayes .10 .03
534 Von Hayes .10 .03
535 Dave Hollins .10 .03
536 Ricky Jordan .10 .03
537 John Kruk .10 .03
538 Jim Lindeman .10 .03
539 Mickey Morandini .10 .03
540 Terry Mulholland .10 .03
541 Dale Murphy .25 .07
542 Randy Ready .10 .03
543 Wally Ritchie UER .10 .03
(Letters in data are
cut off on card)
544 Bruce Ruffin .10 .03
545 Steve Searcy .10 .03
546 Dickie Thon .10 .03
547 Mitch Williams .10 .03
548 Stan Belinda .10 .03
549 Jay Bell .10 .03
550 Barry Bonds .60 .18
551 Bobby Bonilla .10 .03
552 Steve Buechele .10 .03
553 Doug Drabek .10 .03
554 Neal Heaton .10 .03
555 Jeff King .10 .03
556 Bob Kipper .10 .03
557 Bill Landrum .10 .03
558 Mike LaValliere .10 .03
559 Jose Lind .10 .03
560 Lloyd McClendon .10 .03
561 Orlando Merced .10 .03
562 Bob Patterson .10 .03
563 Joe Redfield .10 .03
564 Gary Redus .10 .03
565 Rosario Rodriguez .10 .03
566 Don Slaught .10 .03
567 John Smiley .10 .03
568 Zane Smith .10 .03
569 Randy Tomlin .10 .03
570 Andy Van Slyke .10 .03
571 Gary Varsho .10 .03
572 Bob Walk .10 .03
573 John Wehner UER .10 .03
(Actually played for
Carolina in 1991,
not Cards)
574 Juan Agosto .10 .03
575 Cris Carpenter .10 .03
576 Jose DeLeon .10 .03
577 Rich Gedman .10 .03
578 Bernard Gilkey .10 .03
579 Pedro Guerrero .10 .03
580 Ken Hill .10 .03
581 Rex Hudler .10 .03
582 Felix Jose .10 .03
583 Ray Lankford .10 .03
584 Omar Olivares .10 .03
585 Jose Oquendo .10 .03
586 Tom Pagnozzi .10 .03
587 Geronimo Pena .10 .03
588 Mike Perez .10 .03
589 Gerald Perry .10 .03
590 Bryn Smith .10 .03
591 Lee Smith .10 .03
592 Ozzie Smith .40 .12
593 Scott Terry .10 .03
594 Bob Tewksbury .10 .03
595 Milt Thompson .10 .03
596 Todd Zeile .10 .03
597 Larry Andersen .10 .03
598 Oscar Azocar .10 .03
599 Andy Benes .10 .03
600 Ricky Bones .10 .03
601 Jerald Clark .10 .03
602 Pat Clements .10 .03
603 Paul Faries .10 .03
604 Tony Fernandez .10 .03
605 Tony Gwynn .30 .09
606 Greg W. Harris .10 .03
607 Thomas Howard .10 .03
608 Bruce Hurst .10 .03
609 Darrin Jackson .10 .03
610 Tom Lampkin .10 .03
611 Craig Lefferts .10 .03
612 Jim Lewis RC .10 .03
613 Mike Maddux .10 .03
614 Fred McGriff .15 .04
615 Jose Melendez .10 .03
616 Jose Mota .10 .03
617 Dennis Rasmussen .10 .03
618 Bip Roberts .10 .03
619 Rich Rodriguez .10 .03
620 Benito Santiago .10 .03
621 Craig Shipley .10 .03
622 Tim Teufel .10 .03
623 Kevin Ward .10 .03
624 Ed Whitson .10 .03
625 Dave Anderson .10 .03
626 Kevin Bass .10 .03
627 Rod Beck RC .25 .07
628 Bud Black .10 .03
629 Jeff Brantley .10 .03
630 John Burkett .10 .03
631 Will Clark .25 .07
632 Royce Clayton .10 .03
633 Steve Decker .10 .03
634 Kelly Downs .10 .03
635 Mike Felder .10 .03
636 Scott Garrelts .10 .03
637 Eric Gunderson .10 .03
638 Bryan Hickerson RC .10 .03
639 Darren Lewis .10 .03
640 Greg Litton .10 .03
641 Kirt Manwaring .10 .03
642 Paul McClellan .10 .03
643 Willie McGee .10 .03
644 Kevin Mitchell .10 .03
645 Francisco Oliveras .10 .03
646 Mike Remlinger .10 .03
647 Dave Righetti .10 .03
648 Robby Thompson .10 .03
649 Jose Uribe .10 .03
650 Matt Williams .10 .03
651 Trevor Wilson .10 .03
652 T.Goodwin MLP UER .10 .03
Timed in 3.5,
should be be timed
653 Terry Bross MLP .10 .03
654 M.Christopher MLP .10 .03
655 Kenny Lofton MLP .25 .07
656 Chris Cron MLP .10 .03
657 Willie Banks MLP .10 .03
658 Pat Rice MLP .10 .03
659A R.Maurer MLP ERR .75 .23
Name misspelled as
Mauer on card front
659B R.Maurer MLP COR .10 .03
660 Don Harris MLP .10 .03
661 Henry Rodriguez MLP .10 .03
662 Cliff Brantley MLP .10 .03
663 M.Linskey MLP UER .10 .03
220 pounds in data,
200 in text
664 Gary DiSarcina MLP .10 .03
665 Gil Heredia RC .25 .07
666 V.Castilla MLP RC .50 .15
667 Paul Abbott MLP .10 .03
668 M.Fariss MLP UER .10 .03
Called Paul on back
669 Jarvis Brown MLP .10 .03
670 Wayne Kirby MLP RC .10 .03
671 S.Brosius MLP RC .50 .15
672 Bob Hamelin MLP .10 .03
673 Joel Johnston MLP .10 .03
674 Tim Spehr MLP .10 .03
675A J.Gardner MLP ERR .75 .23
P on front,
should be SS
675B Jeff Gardner MLP COR .10 .03
676 Rico Rossy MLP .10 .03
677 R.Hernandez MLP RC .10 .03
678 Ted Wood MLP .10 .03
679 Cal Eldred MLP .10 .03
680 Sean Berry MLP .10 .03
681 Rickey Henderson RS .15 .04
682 Nolan Ryan RS .50 .15
683 Dennis Martinez RS .10 .03
684 Wilson Alvarez RS .10 .03
685 Joe Carter RS .10 .03
686 Dave Winfield RS .10 .03
687 David Cone RS .10 .03
688 Jose Canseco LL UER .10 .03
(Text on back has 42 stolen
bases in '88; should be 40)
689 Howard Johnson LL .10 .03
690 Julio Franco LL .10 .03
691 Terry Pendleton LL .10 .03
692 Cecil Fielder LL .10 .03
693 Scott Erickson LL .10 .03
694 Tom Glavine LL .10 .03
695 Dennis Martinez LL .10 .03
696 Bryan Harvey LL .10 .03
697 Lee Smith LL .10 .03
698 Roberto Alomar .10 .03
Sandy Alomar Jr.
699 Bobby Bonilla .10 .03
Will Clark
700 Mark Wohlers .10 .03
Kent Mercker
Alejandro Pena
701 Stacy Jones .15 .04
Bo Jackson
Gregg Olson
Frank Thomas
702 Paul Molitor .15 .04
Brett Butler
703 Cal Ripken .40 .12
Joe Carter
704 Barry Larkin .15 .04
Kirby Puckett
705 Mo Vaughn .10 .03
Cecil Fielder
706 Ramon Martinez .10 .03
Ozzie Guillen
707 Harold Baines .10 .03
Wade Boggs
708 Robin Yount PV .25 .07
709 K.Griffey Jr. PV UER .25 .07
Missing quotations on
back; BA has .322, but
was actually .327
710 Nolan Ryan PV .50 .15
711 Cal Ripken PV .40 .12
712 Frank Thomas PV .15 .04
713 Dave Justice PV .10 .03
714 Checklist 1-101 .10 .03
715 Checklist 102-194 .10 .03
716 Checklist 195-296 .10 .03
717 Checklist 297-397 .10 .03
718 Checklist 398-494 .10 .03
719 Checklist 495-596 .10 .03
720A CL 597-720 ERR .10 .03
659 Rob Mauer
720B CL 597-720 COR .10 .03
659 Rob Maurer

1992 Fleer All-Stars

Cards from this 24-card standard-size set were randomly inserted in plastic wrap packs. Selected members of the American and National League 1991 All-Star squads comprise this set.

	Nm-Mt	Ex-Mt
COMPLETE SET (24)	30.00	9.00
1 Felix Jose	.75	.23

2 Tony Gwynn	2.50	.75
3 Barry Bonds	5.00	1.50
4 Bobby Bonilla	.75	.23
5 Mike LaValliere	.75	.23
6 Tom Glavine	1.25	.35
7 Ramon Martinez	.75	.23
8 Lee Smith	.75	.23
9 Mickey Tettleton	.75	.23
10 Scott Erickson	.75	.23
11 Frank Thomas	2.00	.60
12 Danny Tartabull	.75	.23
13 Will Clark	2.00	.60
14 Ryne Sandberg	3.00	.90
15 Terry Pendleton	.75	.23
16 Barry Larkin	2.00	.60
17 Rafael Palmeiro	1.25	.35
18 Julio Franco	.75	.23
19 Robin Ventura	.75	.23
20 Cal Ripken UER (Candidte; total bases misspelled as based)	6.00	1.80
21 Joe Carter	.75	.23
22 Kirby Puckett	2.00	.60
23 Ken Griffey Jr.	3.00	.90
24 Jose Canseco	2.00	.60

1992 Fleer Clemens

Roger Clemens served as a spokesperson fo[r] Fleer during 1992 and was the exclusiv[e] subject of this 15-card standard-size set. Th[e] first 12-card Clemens "Career Highlight[s]" subseries was randomly inserted in 1992 Flee[r] packs. Two-thousand signed cards wer[e] randomly inserted in wax packs and could als[o] be won by entering a drawing. However, thes[e] cards are uncertifiable as they do not have an[y] distinguishable marks. Moreover, a three-car[d] Clemens subset (13-15) was available throug[h] a special mail-in offer. The glossy color photo[s] on the fronts are bordered in black an[d] accented with gold stripes and lettering on th[e] top of the card.

	Nm-Mt	Ex-Mt
COMPLETE SET (12)	12.00	3.60
COMMON CARD (1-12)	1.00	.30
COMMON MAIL (13-15)	1.00	.30
AU Roger Clemens AU Uncertified Signature	60.00	18.00
NNO Roger Clemens Paul Mullan Promo	6.00	1.80

1992 Fleer Lumber Company

The 1992 Fleer Lumber Company standard-siz[e] set features nine outstanding hitters in Majo[r] League Baseball. This set was only available a[s] a bonus in Fleer hobby factory sets.

	Nm-Mt	Ex-Mt
COMPLETE SET (9)	10.00	3.0[0]
L1 Cecil Fielder	.75	.2[3]
L2 Mickey Tettleton	.75	.2[3]
L3 Darryl Strawberry	1.25	.3[5]
L4 Ryne Sandberg	3.00	.9[0]
L5 Jose Canseco	2.00	.6[0]
L6 Matt Williams UER In 17th line, cycle is spelled cyle	.75	.2[3]
L7 Cal Ripken	6.00	1.8[0]
L8 Barry Bonds	5.00	1.5[0]
L9 Ron Gant	.75	.2[3]

1992 Fleer Rookie Sensations

Cards from the 20-card Fleer Rooki[e] Sensations set were randomly inserted in 199[2] Fleer 35-card cello packs. The cards wer[e] extremely popular upon release resulting [in] packs selling for levels far above suggeste[d] retail levels. The glossy color photos on th[e]

fronts have a white border on a royal blue card face. The words "Rookie Sensations" appear above the picture in gold foil lettering, while the player's name appears on a gold foil plaque beneath the picture. Through a mail-in offer for ten Fleer baseball card wrappers and 1.00 for postage and handling, Fleer offered an uncut 8 1/2" by 11" numbered promo sheet picturing ten of the 20-card set on each side in a reduced-size front-only format. The offer indicated an expiration date of July 31, 1992, or whenever the production quantity of 250,000 sheets was exhausted.

	Nm-Mt	Ex-Mt
COMPLETE SET (20)	50.00	15.00
1 Frank Thomas	5.00	1.50
2 Todd Van Poppel	1.50	.45
3 Orlando Merced	1.50	.45
4 Jeff Bagwell	5.00	1.50
5 Jeff Fassero	1.50	.45
6 Darren Lewis	1.50	.45
7 Milt Cuyler	1.50	.45
8 Mike Timlin	1.50	.45
9 Brian McRae	1.50	.45
10 Chuck Knoblauch	2.00	.60
11 Rich DeLucia	1.50	.45
12 Ivan Rodriguez	5.00	1.50
13 Juan Guzman	1.50	.45
14 Steve Chitren	1.50	.45
15 Mark Wohlers	1.50	.45
16 Wes Chamberlain	1.50	.45
17 Ray Lankford	1.50	.45
18 Chito Martinez	1.50	.45
19 Phil Plantier	1.50	.45
20 Scott Leius UER (Misspelled Lieus on card front)	1.50	.45

1992 Fleer Smoke 'n Heat

This 12-card standard-size set features outstanding major league pitchers, especially the premier fastball pitchers in both leagues. These cards were only available in Fleer's 1992 Christmas factory set.

	Nm-Mt	Ex-Mt
COMPLETE SET (12)	10.00	3.00
S1 Lee Smith	.75	.23
S2 Jack McDowell	.75	.23
S3 David Cone	.75	.23
S4 Roger Clemens	4.00	1.20
S5 Nolan Ryan	8.00	2.40
S6 Scott Erickson	.75	.23
S7 Tom Glavine	1.25	.35
S8 Dwight Gooden	1.25	.35
S9 Andy Benes	.75	.23
S10 Steve Avery	.75	.23
S11 Randy Johnson	2.00	.60
S12 Jim Abbott	1.25	.35

1992 Fleer Team Leaders

Cards from the 20-card Fleer Team Leaders set were randomly inserted in 1992 Fleer 42-card rack packs.

	Nm-Mt	Ex-Mt
COMPLETE SET (20)	40.00	12.00
1 Don Mattingly	10.00	3.00
2 Howard Johnson	1.50	.45
3 Chris Sabo UER (Where he it, should be Where he hit)	1.50	.45
4 Carlton Fisk	2.50	.75
5 Kirby Puckett	4.00	1.20
6 Cecil Fielder	1.50	.45
7 Tony Gwynn	5.00	1.50
8 Will Clark	4.00	1.20
9 Bobby Bonilla	1.50	.45
10 Len Dykstra	1.50	.45
11 Tom Glavine	2.50	.75
12 Rafael Palmeiro	2.50	.75
13 Wade Boggs	2.50	.75
14 Joe Carter	1.50	.45
15 Ken Griffey Jr.	6.00	1.80
16 Darryl Strawberry	2.50	.75
17 Cal Ripken	12.00	3.60
18 Danny Tartabull	1.50	.45
19 Jose Canseco	4.00	1.20
20 Andre Dawson	1.50	.45

1992 Fleer Update

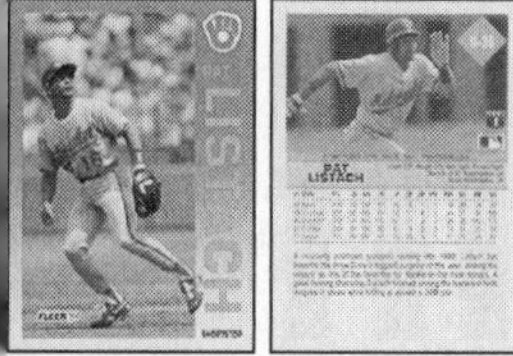

The 1992 Fleer Update set contains 132 standard-size cards. Cards were distributed exclusively in factory sets through hobby dealers. Factory sets included a four-card, black-bordered "92 Headliners" insert set for a total of 136 cards. Due to lackluster retail response for previous Fleer Update sets, wholesale orders for this product were low, resulting in a short print run. As word got out that the cards were in short supply, the secondary market prices soared not soon after release. The basic card design is identical to the regular issue 1992 Fleer cards except for the U-prefixed numbering on back. The cards are checklisted alphabetically within and according to teams for each league with AL preceding NL. Rookie Cards in this set include Jeff Kent and Mike Piazza. The Piazza card is widely recognized as one of the more desirable singles issued in the 1990's.

	Nm-Mt	Ex-Mt
COMP.FACT.SET (136)	100.00	30.00
COMPLETE SET (132)	100.00	30.00
1 Todd Frohwirth	.50	.15
2 Alan Mills	.50	.15
3 Rick Sutcliffe	1.00	.30
4 John Valentin RC	1.50	.45
5 Frank Viola	1.00	.30
6 Bob Zupcic RC	.50	.15
7 Mike Butcher	.50	.15
8 Chad Curtis RC	1.50	.45
9 Damion Easley RC	1.50	.45
10 Tim Salmon	2.50	.75
11 Julio Valera	.50	.15
12 George Bell	.50	.15
13 Roberto Hernandez	.50	.15
14 Shawn Jeter RC	.50	.15
15 Thomas Howard	.50	.15
16 Jesse Levis	.50	.15
17 Kenny Lofton	1.50	.45
18 Paul Sorrento	.50	.15
19 Rico Brogna	.50	.15
20 John Doherty RC	.50	.15
21 Dan Gladden	.50	.15
22 Buddy Groom RC	.50	.15
23 Shawn Hare RC	.50	.15
24 John Kiely	.50	.15
25 Kurt Knudsen	.50	.15
26 Gregg Jefferies	.50	.15
27 Wally Joyner	1.00	.30
28 Kevin Koslofski	.50	.15
29 Kevin McReynolds	.50	.15
30 Rusty Meacham	.50	.15
31 Keith Miller	.50	.15
32 Hipolito Pichardo RC	.50	.15
33 Jim Austin	.50	.15
34 Scott Fletcher	.50	.15
35 John Jaha RC	1.50	.45
36 Pat Listach RC	1.50	.45
37 Dave Nilsson	.50	.15
38 Kevin Seitzer	.50	.15
39 Tom Edens	.50	.15
40 Pat Mahomes RC	1.50	.45
41 John Smiley	.50	.15
42 Charlie Hayes	.50	.15
43 Sam Militello	.50	.15
44 Andy Stankiewicz	.50	.15
45 Danny Tartabull	.50	.15
46 Bob Wickman	.50	.15
47 Jerry Browne	.50	.15
48 Kevin Campbell	.50	.15
49 Vince Horsman	.50	.15
50 Troy Neel RC	.50	.15
51 Ruben Sierra	.50	.15
52 Bruce Walton	.50	.15
53 Willie Wilson	.50	.15
54 Bret Boone	2.50	.75
55 Dave Fleming	.50	.15
56 Kevin Mitchell	.50	.15
57 Jeff Nelson RC	2.50	.75
58 Shane Turner	.50	.15
59 Jose Canseco	2.50	.75
60 Jeff Frye RC	.50	.15
61 Danny Leon	.50	.15
62 Roger Pavlik RC	.50	.15
63 David Cone	1.00	.30
64 Pat Hentgen	.50	.15
65 Randy Knorr	.50	.15
66 Jack Morris	1.00	.30
67 Dave Winfield	1.00	.30
68 David Nied RC	.50	.15
69 Otis Nixon	.50	.15
70 Alejandro Pena	.50	.15
71 Jeff Reardon	1.00	.30
72 Alex Arias RC	.50	.15
73 Jim Bullinger	.50	.15
74 Mike Morgan	.50	.15
75 Rey Sanchez RC	1.50	.45
76 Bob Scanlan	.50	.15
77 Sammy Sosa	4.00	1.20
78 Scott Bankhead	.50	.15
79 Tim Belcher	.50	.15
80 Steve Foster	.50	.15
81 Willie Greene	.50	.15
82 Bip Roberts	.50	.15
83 Scott Ruskin	.50	.15
84 Greg Swindell	.50	.15
85 Juan Guerrero	.50	.15
86 Butch Henry	.50	.15
87 Doug Jones	.50	.15
88 Brian Williams RC	.50	.15
89 Tom Candiotti	.50	.15
90 Eric Davis	1.00	.30
91 Carlos Hernandez	.50	.15
92 Mike Piazza RC	60.00	18.00
93 Mike Sharperson	.50	.15
94 Eric Young RC	1.50	.45
95 Moises Alou	1.00	.30
96 Greg Colbrunn	.50	.15
97 Wil Cordero	.50	.15
98 Ken Hill	.50	.15
99 John Vander Wal RC	1.50	.45
100 John Wetteland	1.00	.30
101 Bobby Bonilla	1.00	.30
102 Eric Hillman RC	.50	.15
103 Pat Howell	.50	.15
104 Jeff Kent RC	10.00	3.00
105 Dick Schofield	.50	.15
106 Ryan Thompson RC	.50	.15
107 Chico Walker	.50	.15
108 Juan Bell	.50	.15
109 Mariano Duncan	.50	.15
110 Jeff Grotewold	.50	.15
111 Ben Rivera	.50	.15
112 Curt Schilling	1.50	.45
113 Victor Cole	.50	.15
114 Al Martin RC	1.50	.45
115 Roger Mason	.50	.15
116 Blas Minor	.50	.15
117 Tim Wakefield RC	4.00	1.20
118 Mark Clark RC	.50	.15
119 Rheal Cormier	.50	.15
120 Donovan Osborne	.50	.15
121 Todd Worrell	.50	.15
122 Jeremy Hernandez RC	.50	.15
123 Randy Myers	.50	.15
124 Frank Seminara RC	.50	.15
125 Gary Sheffield	1.00	.30
126 Dan Walters	.50	.15
127 Steve Hosey	.50	.15
128 Mike Jackson	.50	.15
129 Jim Pena	.50	.15
130 Cory Snyder	.50	.15
131 Bill Swift	.50	.15
132 Checklist U1-U132	.50	.15

1992 Fleer Update Headliners

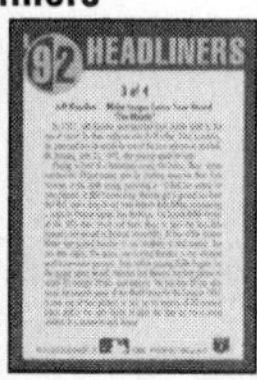

Each 1992 Fleer Update factory set included a four-card set of Headliner inserts. The cards are numbered separately and have a completely different design to the base cards. Each Headliner features UV coating and black borders. The set features a selection of stars that made headlines in the 1991 season. Cards are numbered on back X of 4.

	Nm-Mt	Ex-Mt
COMPLETE SET (4)	8.00	2.40
1 Ken Griffey Jr.	3.00	.90
2 Robin Yount	3.00	.90
3 Jeff Reardon	.75	.23
4 Cecil Fielder	.75	.23

1992 Fleer Citgo The Performer

This 24-card standard-size set was produced by Fleer for 7-Eleven. During April and May at any of the 1,600 participating 7-Eleven stores, customers who purchased eight gallons or more of mid-grade or premium Citgo-brand gasoline received a packet of five trading cards. During June or while supplies last, customers who wanted additional cards could receive three trading cards of their choice per eight gallon or more fill-up by sending in a self-addressed envelope with 1.00 to cover postage and handling. The front design has color action player photos, with a metallic blue-green border that fades to white as one moves down the card face. The card front prominently features "The Performer". The team logo, player's name, and his position appear in the wider right border. The top half of the backs have close-up photos, while the bottom half carry biography and complete career statistics.

	Nm-Mt	Ex-Mt
COMPLETE SET (24)	8.00	2.40
1 Nolan Ryan	1.25	.35
2 Frank Thomas	.40	.12
3 Ryne Sandberg	.50	.15
4 Ken Griffey Jr.	1.00	.30
5 Cal Ripken	1.25	.35
6 Roger Clemens	.75	.23
7 Cecil Fielder	.15	.04
8 Dave Justice	.30	.09
9 Wade Boggs	.40	.12
10 Tony Gwynn	.75	.23
11 Kirby Puckett	.40	.12
12 Darryl Strawberry	.15	.04
13 Jose Canseco	.30	.09
14 Barry Larkin	.30	.09
15 Terry Pendleton	.10	.03
16 Don Mattingly	.60	.18
17 Rickey Henderson	.60	.18
18 Ruben Sierra	.15	.04
19 Jeff Bagwell	.75	.23
20 Tom Glavine	.30	.09
21 Ramon Martinez	.15	.04
22 Will Clark	.30	.09
23 Barry Bonds	.60	.18
24 Roberto Alomar	.30	.09

1992 Fleer Gwynn Casa de Amparo

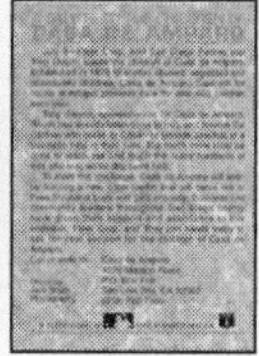

This one card set was produced by the Fleer Corporation for Casa de Amparo (Spanish for house of refuge) which provided care for over 600 children each year. Tony Gwynn served as a spokesperson for the house. The front features a color picture of Tony Gwynn hold Casa's Poster Child for 1992. The back displays information about Casa de Amparo.

	Nm-Mt	Ex-Mt
1 Tony Gwynn	5.00	1.50

1993 Fleer

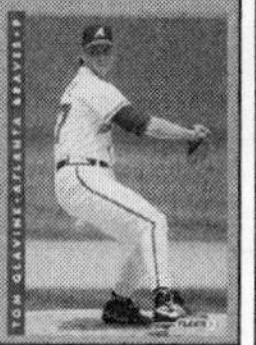

The 720-card 1993 Fleer baseball set contains two series of 360 standard-size cards. Cards were distributed in plastic wrapped packs, cello packs, jumbo packs and rack packs. For the first time in years, Fleer did not issue a factory set. In fact, Fleer discontinued issuing factory sets from 1993 through 1998. The cards are checklisted below alphabetically within and according to teams for each league with NL preceding AL. Topical subsets include League Leaders (344-348/704-708), Round Trippers (349-353/709-713), and Super Star Specials (354-357/714-717). Each series concludes with checklists (358-360/718-720). There are no key Rookie Cards in this set.

	Nm-Mt	Ex-Mt
COMPLETE SET (720)	40.00	12.00
COMP.SERIES 1 (360)	20.00	6.00
COMP.SERIES 2 (360)	20.00	6.00
1 Steve Avery	.10	.03
2 Sid Bream	.10	.03
3 Ron Gant	.20	.06
4 Tom Glavine	.30	.09
5 Brian Hunter	.10	.03
6 Ryan Klesko	.20	.06
7 Charlie Leibrandt	.10	.03
8 Kent Mercker	.10	.03
9 David Nied	.10	.03
10 Otis Nixon	.10	.03
11 Greg Olson	.10	.03
12 Terry Pendleton	.20	.06
13 Deion Sanders	.30	.09
14 John Smoltz	.30	.09
15 Mike Stanton	.10	.03
16 Mark Wohlers	.10	.03
17 Paul Assenmacher	.10	.03
18 Steve Buechele	.10	.03
19 Shawon Dunston	.10	.03
20 Mark Grace	.30	.09
21 Derrick May	.10	.03
22 Chuck McElroy	.10	.03
23 Mike Morgan	.10	.03
24 Rey Sanchez	.10	.03
25 Ryne Sandberg	.75	.23
26 Bob Scanlan	.10	.03
27 Sammy Sosa	.75	.23
28 Rick Wilkins	.10	.03
29 Bobby Ayala RC	.10	.03
30 Tim Belcher	.10	.03
31 Jeff Branson	.10	.03
32 Norm Charlton	.10	.03
33 Steve Foster	.10	.03
34 Willie Greene	.10	.03
35 Chris Hammond	.10	.03
36 Milt Hill	.10	.03
37 Hal Morris	.10	.03
38 Joe Oliver	.10	.03
39 Paul O'Neill	.30	.09
40 Tim Pugh RC	.10	.03
41 Jose Rijo	.10	.03
42 Bip Roberts	.10	.03
43 Chris Sabo	.10	.03
44 Reggie Sanders	.20	.06
45 Eric Anthony	.10	.03
46 Jeff Bagwell	.30	.09
47 Craig Biggio	.30	.09
48 Joe Boever	.10	.03
49 Casey Candaele	.10	.03
50 Steve Finley	.20	.06
51 Luis Gonzalez	.20	.06
52 Pete Harnisch	.10	.03
53 Xavier Hernandez	.10	.03
54 Doug Jones	.10	.03
55 Eddie Taubensee	.10	.03
56 Brian Williams	.10	.03
57 Pedro Astacio	.10	.03
58 Todd Benzinger	.10	.03
59 Brett Butler	.20	.06
60 Tom Candiotti	.10	.03
61 Lenny Harris	.10	.03
62 Carlos Hernandez	.10	.03
63 Orel Hershiser	.20	.06
64 Eric Karros	.20	.06
65 Ramon Martinez	.10	.03
66 Jose Offerman	.10	.03
67 Mike Scioscia	.10	.03
68 Mike Sharperson	.10	.03
69 Eric Young	.10	.03
70 Moises Alou	.20	.06
71 Ivan Calderon	.10	.03
72 Archi Cianfrocco	.10	.03
73 Wil Cordero	.10	.03
74 Delino DeShields	.10	.03
75 Mark Gardner	.10	.03
76 Ken Hill	.10	.03
77 Tim Laker RC	.10	.03
78 Chris Nabholz	.10	.03
79 Mel Rojas	.10	.03
80 John Vander Wal UER (Misspelled Vander Wall in letters on back)	.10	.03
81 Larry Walker	.30	.09
82 Tim Wallach	.10	.03
83 John Wetteland	.20	.06
84 Bobby Bonilla	.20	.06
85 Daryl Boston	.10	.03
86 Sid Fernandez	.10	.03
87 Eric Hillman	.10	.03
88 Todd Hundley	.10	.03
89 Howard Johnson	.10	.03
90 Jeff Kent	.50	.15
91 Eddie Murray	.50	.15
92 Bill Pecota	.10	.03
93 Bret Saberhagen	.20	.06
94 Dick Schofield	.10	.03
95 Pete Schourek	.10	.03
96 Anthony Young	.10	.03
97 Ruben Amaro	.10	.03
98 Juan Bell	.10	.03
99 Wes Chamberlain	.10	.03
100 Darren Daulton	.20	.06
101 Mariano Duncan	.10	.03
102 Mike Hartley	.10	.03
103 Ricky Jordan	.10	.03
104 John Kruk	.20	.06
105 Mickey Morandini	.10	.03
106 Terry Mulholland	.10	.03
107 Ben Rivera	.10	.03
108 Curt Schilling	.30	.09
109 Keith Shepherd RC	.10	.03
110 Stan Belinda	.10	.03
111 Jay Bell	.20	.06
112 Barry Bonds	1.25	.35
113 Jeff King	.10	.03
114 Mike LaValliere	.10	.03
115 Jose Lind	.10	.03
116 Roger Mason	.10	.03
117 Orlando Merced	.10	.03
118 Bob Patterson	.10	.03
119 Don Slaught	.10	.03
120 Zane Smith	.10	.03
121 Randy Tomlin	.10	.03
122 Andy Van Slyke	.20	.06
123 Tim Wakefield	.20	.06
124 Rheal Cormier	.10	.03
125 Bernard Gilkey	.10	.03
126 Felix Jose	.10	.03
127 Ray Lankford	.10	.03
128 Bob McClure	.10	.03
129 Donovan Osborne	.10	.03
130 Tom Pagnozzi	.10	.03
131 Geronimo Pena	.10	.03
132 Mike Perez	.10	.03
133 Lee Smith	.20	.06
134 Bob Tewksbury	.10	.03
135 Todd Worrell	.10	.03
136 Todd Zeile	.10	.03
137 Jerald Clark	.10	.03
138 Tony Gwynn	.60	.18
139 Greg W. Harris	.10	.03
140 Jeremy Hernandez	.10	.03
141 Darrin Jackson	.10	.03
142 Mike Maddux	.10	.03
143 Fred McGriff	.30	.09
144 Jose Melendez	.10	.03
145 Rich Rodriguez	.10	.03
146 Frank Seminara	.10	.03
147 Gary Sheffield	.20	.06
148 Kurt Stillwell	.10	.03
149 Dan Walters	.10	.03
150 Rod Beck	.10	.03
151 Bud Black	.10	.03
152 Jeff Brantley	.10	.03
153 John Burkett	.10	.03
154 Will Clark	.50	.15
155 Royce Clayton	.10	.03
156 Mike Jackson	.10	.03
157 Darren Lewis	.10	.03
158 Kirt Manwaring	.10	.03
159 Willie McGee	.20	.06
160 Cory Snyder	.10	.03
161 Bill Swift	.10	.03
162 Trevor Wilson	.10	.03
163 Brady Anderson	.20	.06
164 Glenn Davis	.10	.03
165 Mike Devereaux	.10	.03
166 Todd Frohwirth	.10	.03
167 Leo Gomez	.10	.03
168 Chris Hoiles	.10	.03
169 Ben McDonald	.10	.03
170 Randy Milligan	.10	.03
171 Alan Mills	.10	.03
172 Mike Mussina	.50	.15
173 Gregg Olson	.10	.03
174 Arthur Rhodes	.10	.03
175 David Segui	.10	.03
176 Ellis Burks	.20	.06
177 Roger Clemens	1.00	.30
178 Scott Cooper	.10	.03
179 Danny Darwin	.10	.03
180 Tony Fossas	.10	.03
181 Paul Quantrill	.10	.03
182 Jody Reed	.10	.03
183 John Valentin	.10	.03
184 Mo Vaughn	.20	.06
185 Frank Viola	.20	.06
186 Bob Zupcic	.10	.03
187 Jim Abbott	.30	.09
188 Gary DiSarcina	.10	.03
189 Damion Easley	.10	.03
190 Junior Felix	.10	.03
191 Chuck Finley	.20	.06
192 Joe Grahe	.10	.03
193 Bryan Harvey	.10	.03
194 Mark Langston	.10	.03
195 John Orton	.10	.03
196 Luis Polonia	.10	.03
197 Tim Salmon	.30	.09
198 Luis Sojo	.10	.03
199 Wilson Alvarez	.10	.03
200 George Bell	.10	.03
201 Alex Fernandez	.10	.03
202 Craig Grebeck	.10	.03
203 Ozzie Guillen	.10	.03
204 Lance Johnson	.10	.03
205 Ron Karkovice	.10	.03
206 Kirk McCaskill	.10	.03
207 Jack McDowell	.10	.03
208 Scott Radinsky	.10	.03
209 Tim Raines	.20	.06

210 Frank Thomas .50 .15
211 Robin Ventura .20 .06
212 Sandy Alomar Jr. .10 .03
213 Carlos Baerga .10 .03
214 Dennis Cook .10 .03
215 Thomas Howard .10 .03
216 Mark Lewis .10 .03
217 Derek Lilliquist .10 .03
218 Kenny Lofton .20 .06
219 Charles Nagy .10 .03
220 Steve Olin .10 .03
221 Paul Sorrento .10 .03
222 Jim Thome .50 .15
223 Mark Whiten .10 .03
224 Milt Cuyler .10 .03
225 Rob Deer .10 .03
226 John Doherty .10 .03
227 Cecil Fielder .20 .06
228 Travis Fryman .20 .06
229 Mike Henneman .10 .03
230 John Kiely UER .10 .03
(Card has batting stats of Pat Kelly)
231 Kurt Knudsen .10 .03
232 Scott Livingstone .10 .03
233 Tony Phillips .10 .03
234 Mickey Tettleton .10 .03
235 Kevin Appier .20 .06
236 George Brett 1.25 .35
237 Tom Gordon .10 .03
238 Gregg Jefferies .10 .03
239 Wally Joyner .20 .06
240 Kevin Koslofski .10 .03
241 Mike Macfarlane .10 .03
242 Brian McRae .10 .03
243 Rusty Meacham .10 .03
244 Keith Miller .10 .03
245 Jeff Montgomery .10 .03
246 Hipolito Pichardo .10 .03
247 Ricky Bones .10 .03
248 Cal Eldred .10 .03
249 Mike Fetters .10 .03
250 Darryl Hamilton .10 .03
251 Doug Henry .10 .03
252 John Jaha .10 .03
253 Pat Listach .10 .03
254 Paul Molitor .30 .09
255 Jaime Navarro .10 .03
256 Kevin Seitzer .10 .03
257 B.J. Surhoff .20 .06
258 Greg Vaughn .20 .06
259 Bill Wegman .10 .03
260 Robin Yount .75 .23
261 Rick Aguilera .10 .03
262 Chili Davis .20 .06
263 Scott Erickson .10 .03
264 Greg Gagne .10 .03
265 Mark Guthrie .10 .03
266 Brian Harper .10 .03
267 Kent Hrbek .20 .06
268 Terry Jorgensen .10 .03
269 Gene Larkin .10 .03
270 Scott Leius .10 .03
271 Pat Mahomes .10 .03
272 Pedro Munoz .10 .03
273 Kirby Puckett .50 .15
274 Kevin Tapani .10 .03
275 Carl Willis .10 .03
276 Steve Farr .10 .03
277 John Habyan .10 .03
278 Mel Hall .10 .03
279 Charlie Hayes .10 .03
280 Pat Kelly .10 .03
281 Don Mattingly 1.25 .35
282 Sam Militello .10 .03
283 Matt Nokes .10 .03
284 Melido Perez .10 .03
285 Andy Stankiewicz .10 .03
286 Danny Tartabull .10 .03
287 Randy Velarde .10 .03
288 Bob Wickman .10 .03
289 Bernie Williams .30 .09
290 Lance Blankenship .10 .03
291 Mike Bordick .10 .03
292 Jerry Browne .10 .03
293 Dennis Eckersley .20 .06
294 Rickey Henderson .50 .15
295 Vince Horsman .10 .03
296 Mark McGwire 1.25 .35
297 Jeff Parrett .10 .03
298 Ruben Sierra .10 .03
299 Terry Steinbach .10 .03
300 Walt Weiss .10 .03
301 Bob Welch .10 .03
302 Willie Wilson .10 .03
303 Bobby Witt .10 .03
304 Bret Boone .30 .09
305 Jay Buhner .20 .06
306 Dave Fleming .10 .03
307 Ken Griffey Jr. .75 .23
308 Erik Hanson .10 .03
309 Edgar Martinez .30 .09
310 Tino Martinez .30 .09
311 Jeff Nelson .10 .03
312 Dennis Powell .10 .03
313 Mike Schooler .10 .03
314 Russ Swan .10 .03
315 Dave Valle .10 .03
316 Omar Vizquel .20 .06
317 Kevin Brown .20 .06
318 Todd Burns .10 .03
319 Jose Canseco .50 .15
320 Julio Franco .20 .06
321 Jeff Frye .10 .03
322 Juan Gonzalez .50 .15
323 Jose Guzman .10 .03
324 Jeff Huson .10 .03
325 Dean Palmer .20 .06
326 Kevin Reimer .10 .03
327 Ivan Rodriguez .50 .15
328 Kenny Rogers .20 .06
329 Dan Smith .10 .03
330 Roberto Alomar .50 .15
331 Derek Bell .10 .03
332 Pat Borders .10 .03
333 Joe Carter .20 .06
334 Kelly Gruber .10 .03
335 Tom Henke .10 .03
336 Jimmy Key .20 .06
337 Manuel Lee .10 .03
338 Candy Maldonado .10 .03
339 John Olerud .20 .06
340 Todd Stottlemyre .10 .03
341 Duane Ward .10 .03
342 Devon White .10 .03
343 Dave Winfield .20 .06
344 Edgar Martinez LL .20 .06
345 Cecil Fielder LL .10 .03
346 Kenny Lofton LL .10 .03
347 Jack Morris LL .10 .03
348 Roger Clemens LL .50 .15
349 Fred McGriff RT .20 .06
350 Barry Bonds RT .60 .18
351 Gary Sheffield RT .10 .03
352 Darren Daulton RT .10 .03
353 Dave Hollins RT .10 .03
354 Pedro Martinez .50 .15
Ramon Martinez
355 Ivan Rodriguez .50 .15
Kirby Puckett
356 Ryne Sandberg .50 .15
Gary Sheffield
357 Roberto Alomar .20 .06
Chuck Knoblauch
Carlos Baerga
358 Checklist 1-120 .10 .03
359 Checklist 121-240 .10 .03
360 Checklist 241-360 .10 .03
361 Rafael Belliard .10 .03
362 Damon Berryhill .10 .03
363 Mike Bielecki .10 .03
364 Jeff Blauser .10 .03
365 Francisco Cabrera .10 .03
366 Marvin Freeman .10 .03
367 David Justice .20 .06
368 Mark Lemke .10 .03
369 Alejandro Pena .10 .03
370 Jeff Reardon .20 .06
371 Lonnie Smith .10 .03
372 Pete Smith .10 .03
373 Shawn Boskie .10 .03
374 Jim Bullinger .10 .03
375 Frank Castillo .10 .03
376 Doug Dascenzo .10 .03
377 Andre Dawson .20 .06
378 Mike Harkey .10 .03
379 Greg Hibbard .10 .03
380 Greg Maddux .75 .23
381 Ken Patterson .10 .03
382 Jeff D. Robinson .10 .03
383 Luis Salazar .10 .03
384 Dwight Smith .10 .03
385 Jose Vizcaino .10 .03
386 Scott Bankhead .10 .03
387 Tom Browning .10 .03
388 Darnell Coles .10 .03
389 Rob Dibble .20 .06
390 Bill Doran .10 .03
391 Dwayne Henry .10 .03
392 Cesar Hernandez .10 .03
393 Roberto Kelly .10 .03
394 Barry Larkin .50 .15
395 Dave Martinez .10 .03
396 Kevin Mitchell .10 .03
397 Jeff Reed .10 .03
398 Scott Ruskin .10 .03
399 Greg Swindell .10 .03
400 Dan Wilson .20 .06
401 Andy Ashby .10 .03
402 Freddie Benavides .10 .03
403 Dante Bichette .20 .06
404 Willie Blair .10 .03
405 Denis Boucher .10 .03
406 Vinny Castilla .20 .06
407 Braulio Castillo .10 .03
408 Alex Cole .10 .03
409 Andres Galarraga .20 .06
410 Joe Girardi .10 .03
411 Butch Henry .10 .03
412 Darren Holmes .10 .03
413 Calvin Jones .10 .03
414 Steve Reed RC .10 .03
415 Kevin Ritz .10 .03
416 Jim Tatum RC .10 .03
417 Jack Armstrong .10 .03
418 Bret Barberie .10 .03
419 Ryan Bowen .10 .03
420 Cris Carpenter .10 .03
421 Chuck Carr .10 .03
422 Scott Chiamparino .10 .03
423 Jeff Conine .20 .06
424 Jim Corsi .10 .03
425 Steve Decker .10 .03
426 Chris Donnels .10 .03
427 Monty Fariss .10 .03
428 Bob Natal .10 .03
429 Pat Rapp .10 .03
430 Dave Weathers .10 .03
431 Nigel Wilson .10 .03
432 Ken Caminiti .20 .06
433 Andujar Cedeno .10 .03
434 Tom Edens .10 .03
435 Juan Guerrero .10 .03
436 Pete Incaviglia .10 .03
437 Jimmy Jones .10 .03
438 Darryl Kile .20 .06
439 Rob Murphy .10 .03
440 Al Osuna .10 .03
441 Mark Portugal .10 .03
442 Scott Servais .10 .03
443 John Candelaria .10 .03
444 Tim Crews .10 .03
445 Eric Davis .20 .06
446 Tom Goodwin .10 .03
447 Jim Gott .10 .03
448 Kevin Gross .10 .03
449 Dave Hansen .10 .03
450 Jay Howell .10 .03
451 Roger McDowell .10 .03
452 Bob Ojeda .10 .03
453 Henry Rodriguez .10 .03
454 Darryl Strawberry .30 .09
455 Mitch Webster .10 .03
456 Steve Wilson .10 .03
457 Brian Barnes .10 .03
458 Sean Berry .10 .03
459 Jeff Fassero .10 .03
460 Darrin Fletcher .10 .03
461 Marquis Grissom .10 .03
462 Dennis Martinez .20 .06
463 Spike Owen .10 .03
464 Matt Stairs .10 .03
465 Sergio Valdez .10 .03
466 Kevin Bass .10 .03
467 Vince Coleman .10 .03
468 Mark Dewey .10 .03
469 Kevin Elster .10 .03
470 Tony Fernandez .10 .03
471 John Franco .20 .06
472 Dave Gallagher .10 .03
473 Paul Gibson .10 .03
474 Dwight Gooden .30 .09
475 Lee Guetterman .10 .03
476 Jeff Innis .10 .03
477 Dave Magadan .10 .03
478 Charlie O'Brien .10 .03
479 Willie Randolph .20 .06
480 Mackey Sasser .10 .03
481 Ryan Thompson .10 .03
482 Chico Walker .10 .03
483 Kyle Abbott .10 .03
484 Bob Ayrault .10 .03
485 Kim Batiste .10 .03
486 Cliff Brantley .10 .03
487 Jose DeLeon .10 .03
488 Len Dykstra .20 .06
489 Tommy Greene .10 .03
490 Jeff Grotewold .10 .03
491 Dave Hollins .10 .03
492 Danny Jackson .10 .03
493 Stan Javier .10 .03
494 Tom Marsh .10 .03
495 Greg Mathews .10 .03
496 Dale Murphy .50 .15
497 Todd Pratt RC .20 .06
498 Mitch Williams .10 .03
499 Danny Cox .10 .03
500 Doug Drabek .10 .03
501 Carlos Garcia .10 .03
502 Lloyd McClendon .10 .03
503 Denny Neagle .20 .06
504 Gary Redus .10 .03
505 Bob Walk .10 .03
506 John Wehner .10 .03
507 Luis Alicea .10 .03
508 Mark Clark .10 .03
509 Pedro Guerrero .20 .06
510 Rex Hudler .10 .03
511 Brian Jordan .20 .06
512 Omar Olivares .10 .03
513 Jose Oquendo .10 .03
514 Gerald Perry .10 .03
515 Bryn Smith .10 .03
516 Craig Wilson .10 .03
517 Tracy Woodson .10 .03
518 Larry Andersen .10 .03
519 Andy Benes .10 .03
520 Jim Deshaies .10 .03
521 Bruce Hurst .10 .03
522 Randy Myers .10 .03
523 Benito Santiago .20 .06
524 Tim Scott .10 .03
525 Tim Teufel .10 .03
526 Mike Benjamin .10 .03
527 Dave Burba .10 .03
528 Craig Colbert .10 .03
529 Mike Felder .10 .03
530 Bryan Hickerson .10 .03
531 Chris James .10 .03
532 Mark Leonard .10 .03
533 Greg Litton .10 .03
534 Francisco Oliveras .10 .03
535 John Patterson .10 .03
536 Jim Pena .10 .03
537 Dave Righetti .20 .06
538 Robby Thompson .10 .03
539 Jose Uribe .10 .03
540 Matt Williams .20 .06
541 Storm Davis .10 .03
542 Sam Horn .10 .03
543 Tim Hulett .10 .03
544 Craig Lefferts .10 .03
545 Chito Martinez .10 .03
546 Mark McLemore .10 .03
547 Luis Mercedes .10 .03
548 Bob Milacki .10 .03
549 Joe Orsulak .10 .03
550 Billy Ripken .10 .03
551 Cal Ripken Jr. 1.50 .45
552 Rick Sutcliffe .20 .06
553 Jeff Tackett .10 .03
554 Wade Boggs .30 .09
555 Tom Brunansky .10 .03
556 Jack Clark .20 .06
557 John Dopson .10 .03
558 Mike Gardiner .10 .03
559 Mike Greenwell .10 .03
560 Greg A. Harris .10 .03
561 Billy Hatcher .10 .03
562 Joe Hesketh .10 .03
563 Tony Pena .10 .03
564 Phil Plantier .10 .03
565 Luis Rivera .10 .03
566 Herm Winningham .10 .03
567 Matt Young .10 .03
568 Bert Blyleven .20 .06
569 Mike Butcher .10 .03
570 Chuck Crim .10 .03
571 Chad Curtis .10 .03
572 Tim Fortugno .10 .03
573 Steve Frey .10 .03
574 Gary Gaetti .20 .06
575 Scott Lewis .10 .03
576 Lee Stevens .10 .03
577 Ron Tingley .10 .03
578 Julio Valera .10 .03
579 Shawn Abner .10 .03
580 Joey Cora .10 .03
581 Chris Cron .10 .03
582 Carlton Fisk .30 .09
583 Roberto Hernandez .10 .03
584 Charlie Hough .20 .06
585 Terry Leach .10 .03
586 Donn Pall .10 .03
587 Dan Pasqua .10 .03
588 Steve Sax .10 .03
589 Bobby Thigpen .10 .03
590 Albert Belle .20 .06
591 Felix Fermin .10 .03
592 Glenallen Hill .10 .03
593 Brook Jacoby .10 .03
594 Reggie Jefferson .10 .03
595 Carlos Martinez .10 .03
596 Jose Mesa .10 .03
597 Rod Nichols .10 .03
598 Junior Ortiz .10 .03
599 Eric Plunk .10 .03
600 Ted Power .10 .03
601 Scott Scudder .10 .03
602 Kevin Wickander .10 .03
603 Skeeter Barnes .10 .03
604 Mark Carreon .10 .03
605 Dan Gladden .10 .03
606 Bill Gullickson .10 .03
607 Chad Kreuter .10 .03
608 Mark Leiter .10 .03
609 Mike Munoz .10 .03
610 Rich Rowland .10 .03
611 Frank Tanana .10 .03
612 Walt Terrell .10 .03
613 Alan Trammell .30 .09
614 Lou Whitaker .20 .06
615 Luis Aquino .10 .03
616 Mike Boddicker .10 .03
617 Jim Eisenreich .10 .03
618 Mark Gubicza .10 .03
619 David Howard .10 .03
620 Mike Magnante .10 .03
621 Brent Mayne .10 .03
622 Kevin McReynolds .10 .03
623 Ed Pierce RC .10 .03
624 Bill Sampen .10 .03
625 Steve Shifflett .10 .03
626 Gary Thurman .10 .03
627 Curt Wilkerson .10 .03
628 Chris Bosio .10 .03
629 Scott Fletcher .10 .03
630 Jim Gantner .10 .03
631 Dave Nilsson .10 .03
632 Jesse Orosco .10 .03
633 Dan Plesac .10 .03
634 Ron Robinson .10 .03
635 Bill Spiers .10 .03
636 Franklin Stubbs .10 .03
637 Willie Banks .10 .03
638 Randy Bush .10 .03
639 Chuck Knoblauch .20 .06
640 Shane Mack .10 .03
641 Mike Pagliarulo .10 .03
642 Jeff Reboulet .10 .03
643 John Smiley .10 .03
644 Mike Trombley .10 .03
645 Gary Wayne .10 .03
646 Lenny Webster .10 .03
647 Tim Burke .10 .03
648 Mike Gallego .10 .03
649 Dion James .10 .03
650 Jeff Johnson .10 .03
651 Scott Kamieniecki .10 .03
652 Kevin Maas .10 .03
653 Rich Monteleone .10 .03
654 Jerry Nielsen .10 .03
655 Scott Sanderson .10 .03
656 Mike Stanley .10 .03
657 Gerald Williams .10 .03
658 Curt Young .10 .03
659 Harold Baines .20 .06
660 Kevin Campbell .10 .03
661 Ron Darling .10 .03
662 Kelly Downs .10 .03
663 Eric Fox .10 .03
664 Dave Henderson .10 .03
665 Rick Honeycutt .10 .03
666 Mike Moore .10 .03
667 Jamie Quirk .10 .03
668 Jeff Russell .10 .03
669 Dave Stewart .20 .06
670 Greg Briley .10 .03
671 Dave Cochrane .10 .03
672 Henry Cotto .10 .03
673 Rich DeLucia .10 .03
674 Brian Fisher .10 .03
675 Mark Grant .10 .03
676 Randy Johnson .50 .15
677 Tim Leary .10 .03
678 Pete O'Brien .10 .03
679 Lance Parrish .20 .06
680 Harold Reynolds .20 .06
681 Shane Turner .10 .03
682 Jack Daugherty .10 .03
683 David Hulse RC .10 .03
684 Terry Mathews .10 .03
685 Al Newman .10 .03
686 Edwin Nunez .10 .03
687 Rafael Palmeiro .30 .09
688 Roger Pavlik .10 .03
689 Geno Petralli .10 .03
690 Nolan Ryan 2.00 .60
691 David Cone .20 .06
692 Alfredo Griffin .10 .03
693 Juan Guzman .10 .03
694 Pat Hentgen .10 .03
695 Randy Knorr .10 .03
696 Bob MacDonald .10 .03
697 Jack Morris .20 .06
698 Ed Sprague .10 .03
699 Dave Stieb .10 .03
700 Pat Tabler .10 .03
701 Mike Timlin .10 .03
702 David Wells .20 .06
703 Eddie Zosky .10 .03
704 Gary Sheffield LL .10 .03
705 Darren Daulton LL .10 .03
706 Marquis Grissom LL .10 .03
707 Greg Maddux LL .50 .15
708 Bill Swift LL .10 .03
709 Juan Gonzalez RT .30 .09
710 Mark McGwire RT .60 .18
711 Cecil Fielder RT .10 .03
712 Albert Belle RT .20 .06
713 Joe Carter RT .10 .03
714 Cecil Fielder SS .30 .09
Frank Thomas
715 Larry Walker SS .30 .09
Darren Daulton
716 Edgar Martinez SS .20 .06
Robin Ventura
717 Roger Clemens SS .50 .15
Dennis Eckersley
718 Checklist 361-480 .10 .03
719 Checklist 481-600 .10 .03
720 Checklist 601-720 .10 .03

1993 Fleer All-Stars

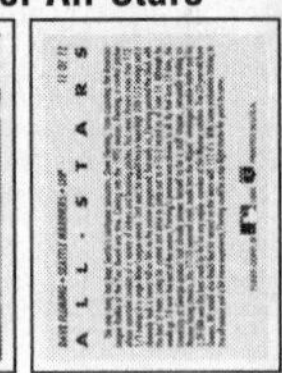

This 24-card standard-size set featuring members of the American and National league All-Star squads, was randomly inserted in wax packs. 12 American League players were seeded in series 1 packs and 12 National League players in series 2.

	Nm-Mt	Ex-Mt
COMPLETE SET (24)	40.00	12.00
COMPLETE SER.1 (12)	25.00	7.50
COMPLETE SER.2 (12)	15.00	4.50
AL1 Frank Thomas	3.00	.90
AL2 Roberto Alomar	3.00	.90
AL3 Edgar Martinez	2.00	.60
AL4 Pat Listach	.60	.18
AL5 Cecil Fielder	1.25	.35
AL6 Juan Gonzalez	3.00	.90
AL7 Ken Griffey Jr.	5.00	1.50
AL8 Joe Carter	1.25	.35
AL9 Kirby Puckett	3.00	.90
AL10 Brian Harper	.60	.18
AL11 Dave Fleming	.60	.18
AL12 Jack McDowell	.60	.18
NL1 Fred McGriff	2.00	.60
NL2 Delino DeShields	.60	.18
NL3 Gary Sheffield	1.25	.35
NL4 Barry Larkin	3.00	.90
NL5 Felix Jose	.60	.18
NL6 Larry Walker	2.00	.60
NL7 Barry Bonds	8.00	2.40
NL8 Andy Van Slyke	1.25	.35
NL9 Darren Daulton	1.25	.35
NL10 Greg Maddux	5.00	1.50
NL11 Tom Glavine	2.00	.60
NL12 Lee Smith	1.25	.35

1993 Fleer Glavine

As part of the Signature Series, this 12-card standard-size set spotlights Tom Glavine. An additional three cards (13-15) were available via a mail-in offer and are generally considered to be a separate set. The mail-in offer expired on September 30, 1993. Reportedly, a filmmaking problem during production resulted in eight variations in this 12-card insert set. Different backs appear on eight of the 12 cards. Cards 1-4 and 7-10 in wax packs feature card back text variations from those included in the rack and jumbo magazine packs. The text differences occur in the first few words of text on the card back. No corrections were made in Series I. The correct Glavine cards appeared in Series II wax, rack, and jumbo magazine packs. In addition, Tom Glavine signed cards for this set. Unlike some of the previous autograph cards from Fleer, these cards were certified as authentic by the manufacturer.

	Nm-Mt	Ex-Mt
COMPLETE SET (12)	4.00	1.20
COMMON CARD (1-12)	.50	.15
COMMON MAIL (13-15)	2.00	.60
AU Tom Glavine AU (Certified signature)	50.00	15.00

1993 Fleer Golden Moments

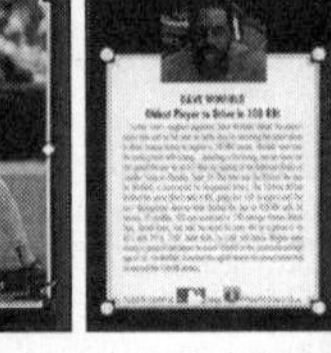

Cards from this six-card standard-size set featuring memorable moments from the previous season, were randomly inserted in 1993 Fleer wax packs, three each in series 1 and 2.

	Nm-Mt	Ex-Mt
COMPLETE SET (6)	12.00	3.60
COMPLETE SER.1 (3)	4.00	1.20
COMPLETE SER.2 (3)	8.00	2.40
A1 George Brett	6.00	1.80
A2 Mickey Morandini	.50	.15
A3 Dave Winfield	1.00	.30
B1 Dennis Eckersley	1.00	.30
B2 Bip Roberts	.50	.15
B3 Frank Thomas and Juan Gonzalez	2.50	.75

1993 Fleer Major League Prospects

Cards from this 36-card standard-size set featuring a selection of prospects, were randomly inserted in wax packs, 18 in each series. Early Cards of Pedro Martinez and Mike Piazza are featured within this set.

	Nm-Mt	Ex-Mt
COMPLETE SET (36)	30.00	9.00
COMPLETE SERIES 1 (18)	20.00	6.00
COMPLETE SERIES 2 (18)	10.00	3.00
A1 Melvin Nieves	.50	.15
A2 Sterling Hitchcock	.75	.23
A3 Tim Costo	.50	.15
A4 Manny Alexander	.50	.15
A5 Alan Embree	.50	.15
A6 Kevin Young	.75	.23
A7 J.T. Snow	2.00	.60
A8 Russ Springer	.50	.15
A9 Billy Ashley	.50	.15
A10 Kevin Rogers	.50	.15
A11 Steve Hosey	.50	.15
A12 Eric Wedge	.50	.15
A13 Mike Piazza	8.00	2.40
A14 Jesse Levis	.50	.15
A15 Rico Brogna	.50	.15
A16 Alex Arias	.50	.15
A17 Rod Brewer	.50	.15
A18 Troy Neel	.50	.15
B1 Scooter Tucker	.50	.15
B2 Kerry Woodson	.50	.15
B3 Greg Colbrunn	.50	.15
B4 Pedro Martinez	6.00	1.80
B5 Dave Silvestri	.50	.15
B6 Kent Bottenfield	.50	.15
B7 Rafael Bournigal	.50	.15
B8 J.T. Bruett	.50	.15
B9 Dave Mlicki	.50	.15
B10 Paul Wagner	.50	.15
B11 Mike Williams	.50	.15
B12 Henry Mercedes	.50	.15
B13 Scott Taylor	.50	.15
B14 Dennis Moeller	.50	.15
B15 Javy Lopez	1.25	.35
B16 Steve Cooke	.50	.15
B17 Pete Young	.50	.15
B18 Ken Ryan	.50	.15

1993 Fleer Pro-Visions

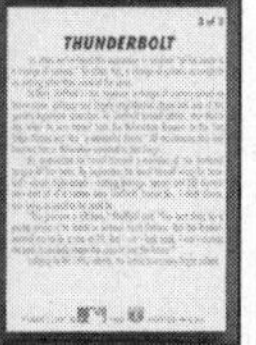

Cards from this six-card standard-size set, featuring a selection of superstars in fantasy paintings, were randomly inserted in poly packs, three each in series one and series two.

	Nm-Mt	Ex-Mt
COMPLETE SET (6)	5.00	1.50
COMPLETE SERIES 1 (3)	3.00	.90
COMPLETE SERIES 2 (3)	2.00	.60
A1 Roberto Alomar	3.00	.90
A2 Dennis Eckersley	1.25	.35
A3 Gary Sheffield	1.25	.35
B1 Andy Van Slyke	1.25	.35
B2 Tom Glavine	2.00	.60
B3 Cecil Fielder	1.25	.35

1993 Fleer Rookie Sensations

Cards from this 20-card standard-size set, featuring a selection of 1993's top rookies, were randomly inserted in cello packs, 10 in each series.

	Nm-Mt	Ex-Mt
COMPLETE SET (20)	20.00	6.00
COMPLETE SERIES 1 (10)	10.00	3.00
COMPLETE SERIES 2 (10)	10.00	3.00
RSA1 Kenny Lofton	2.00	.60
RSA2 Cal Eldred	1.00	.30
RSA3 Pat Listach	1.00	.30
RSA4 Roberto Hernandez	1.00	.30
RSA5 Dave Fleming	1.00	.30
RSA6 Eric Karros	2.00	.60
RSA7 Reggie Sanders	2.00	.60
RSA8 Derrick May	1.00	.30
RSA9 Mike Perez	1.00	.30
RSA10 Donovan Osborne	1.00	.30
RSB1 Moises Alou	2.00	.60
RSB2 Pedro Astacio	1.00	.30
RSB3 Jim Austin	1.00	.30
RSB4 Chad Curtis	1.00	.30
RSB5 Gary DiSarcina	1.00	.30
RSB6 Scott Livingstone	1.00	.30
RSB7 Sam Militello	1.00	.30
RSB8 Arthur Rhodes	1.00	.30
RSB9 Tim Wakefield	2.00	.60
RSB10 Bob Zupcic	1.00	.30

1993 Fleer Team Leaders

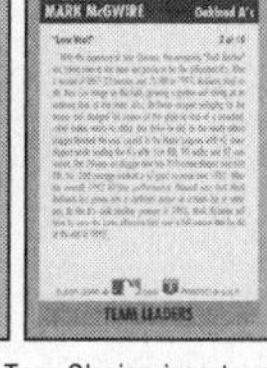

One Team Leader or Tom Glavine insert was seeded into each Fleer rack pack. Series 1 racks included 10 American League players, while series 2 racks included 10 National League players.

	Nm-Mt	Ex-Mt
COMPLETE SERIES 1 (10)	50.00	15.00
COMPLETE SERIES 2 (10)	20.00	6.00
AL1 Kirby Puckett	5.00	1.50
AL2 Mark McGwire	12.00	3.60
AL3 Pat Listach	1.00	.30
AL4 Roger Clemens	10.00	3.00
AL5 Frank Thomas	5.00	1.50
AL6 Carlos Baerga	1.00	.30
AL7 Brady Anderson	2.00	.60
AL8 Juan Gonzalez	5.00	1.50
AL9 Roberto Alomar	5.00	1.50
AL10 Ken Griffey Jr.	8.00	2.40
NL1 Will Clark	5.00	1.50
NL2 Terry Pendleton	2.00	.60
NL3 Ray Lankford	1.00	.30
NL4 Eric Karros	2.00	.60
NL5 Gary Sheffield	2.00	.60
NL6 Ryne Sandberg	8.00	2.40
NL7 Marquis Grissom	1.00	.30
NL8 John Kruk	2.00	.60
NL9 Jeff Bagwell	3.00	.90
NL10 Andy Van Slyke	2.00	.60

1993 Fleer Final Edition

This 300-card standard-size set was issued exclusively in factory set form (along with ten Diamond Tribute inserts) to update and feature rookies not in the regular 1993 Fleer set. The cards are identical in design to regular issue 1993 Fleer cards except for the F-prefixed numbering. Cards are ordered alphabetically within teams with NL preceding AL. The set closes with checklist cards (298-300). The only key Rookie Card in this set features Jim Edmonds.

	Nm-Mt	Ex-Mt
COMP.FACT.SET (310)	10.00	3.00
COMPLETE SET (300)	8.00	2.40
1 Steve Bedrosian	.10	.03
2 Jay Howell	.10	.03
3 Greg Maddux	.75	.23
4 Greg McMichael RC	.10	.03
5 Tony Tarasco RC	.10	.03
6 Jose Bautista	.10	.03
7 Jose Guzman	.10	.03
8 Greg Hibbard	.10	.03
9 Candy Maldonado	.10	.03
10 Randy Myers	.10	.03
11 Matt Walbeck RC	.10	.03
12 Turk Wendell	.10	.03
13 Willie Wilson	.10	.03
14 Greg Cadaret	.10	.03
15 Roberto Kelly	.10	.03
16 Randy Milligan	.10	.03
17 Kevin Mitchell	.10	.03
18 Jeff Reardon	.20	.06
19 John Roper	.10	.03
20 John Smiley	.10	.03
21 Andy Ashby	.10	.03
22 Dante Bichette	.20	.06
23 Willie Blair	.10	.03
24 Pedro Castellano	.10	.03
25 Vinny Castilla	.20	.06
26 Jerald Clark	.10	.03
27 Alex Cole	.10	.03
28 Scott Fredrickson RC	.10	.03
29 Jay Gainer RC	.10	.03
30 Andres Galarraga	.20	.06
31 Joe Girardi	.10	.03
32 Ryan Hawblitzel	.10	.03
33 Charlie Hayes	.10	.03
34 Darren Holmes	.10	.03
35 Chris Jones	.10	.03
36 David Nied	.10	.03
37 J.Owens RC	.10	.03
38 Lance Painter RC	.10	.03
39 Jeff Parrett	.10	.03
40 Steve Reed	.10	.03
41 Armando Reynoso	.10	.03
42 Bruce Ruffin	.10	.03
43 Danny Sheaffer RC	.10	.03
44 Keith Shepherd	.10	.03
45 Jim Tatum	.10	.03
46 Gary Wayne	.10	.03
47 Eric Young	.10	.03
48 Luis Aquino	.10	.03
49 Alex Arias	.10	.03
50 Jack Armstrong	.10	.03
51 Bret Barberie	.10	.03
52 Geronimo Berroa	.10	.03
53 Ryan Bowen	.10	.03
54 Greg Briley	.10	.03
55 Cris Carpenter	.10	.03
56 Chuck Carr	.10	.03
57 Jeff Conine	.20	.06
58 Jim Corsi	.10	.03
59 Orestes Destrade	.10	.03
60 Junior Felix	.10	.03
61 Chris Hammond	.10	.03
62 Bryan Harvey	.10	.03
63 Charlie Hough	.20	.06
64 Joe Klink	.10	.03
65 Richie Lewis RC UER (Refers to place of birth and residence as Illinois instead of Indiana)	.10	.03
66 Mitch Lyden RC	.10	.03
67 Bob Natal	.10	.03
68 Scott Pose RC	.10	.03
69 Rich Renteria	.10	.03
70 Benito Santiago	.20	.06
71 Gary Sheffield	.20	.06
72 Matt Turner RC	.10	.03
73 Walt Weiss	.10	.03
74 Darrell Whitmore RC	.10	.03
75 Nigel Wilson	.10	.03
76 Kevin Bass	.10	.03
77 Doug Drabek	.10	.03
78 Tom Edens	.10	.03
79 Chris James	.10	.03
80 Greg Swindell	.10	.03
81 Omar Daal RC	.50	.15
82 Raul Mondesi	.20	.06
83 Jody Reed	.10	.03
84 Cory Snyder	.10	.03
85 Rick Trlicek	.10	.03
86 Tim Wallach	.10	.03
87 Todd Worrell	.10	.03
88 Tavo Alvarez	.10	.03
89 Frank Bolick	.10	.03
90 Kent Bottenfield	.10	.03
91 Greg Colbrunn	.10	.03
92 Cliff Floyd	.30	.09
93 Lou Frazier RC	.10	.03
94 Mike Gardiner	.10	.03
95 Mike Lansing RC	.20	.06
96 Bill Risley	.10	.03
97 Jeff Shaw	.10	.03
98 Kevin Baez	.10	.03
99 Tim Bogar RC	.10	.03
100 Jeromy Burnitz	.20	.06
101 Mike Draper	.10	.03
102 Darrin Jackson	.10	.03
103 Mike Maddux	.10	.03
104 Joe Orsulak	.10	.03
105 Doug Saunders RC	.10	.03
106 Frank Tanana	.10	.03
107 Dave Telgheder RC	.10	.03
108 Larry Andersen	.10	.03
109 Jim Eisenreich	.10	.03
110 Pete Incaviglia	.10	.03
111 Danny Jackson	.10	.03
112 David West	.10	.03
113 Al Martin	.10	.03
114 Blas Minor	.10	.03
115 Dennis Moeller	.10	.03
116 William Pennyfeather	.10	.03
117 Rich Robertson RC	.10	.03
118 Ben Shelton	.10	.03
119 Lonnie Smith	.10	.03
120 Freddie Toliver	.10	.03
121 Paul Wagner	.10	.03
122 Kevin Young	.20	.06
123 Rene Arocha RC	.20	.06
124 Gregg Jefferies	.10	.03
125 Paul Kilgus	.10	.03
126 Les Lancaster	.10	.03
127 Joe Magrane	.10	.03
128 Rob Murphy	.10	.03
129 Erik Pappas	.10	.03
130 Stan Royer	.10	.03
131 Ozzie Smith	.75	.23
132 Tom Urbani RC	.10	.03
133 Mark Whiten	.10	.03
134 Derek Bell	.10	.03
135 Doug Brocail	.10	.03
136 Phil Clark	.10	.03
137 Mark Ettles RC	.10	.03
138 Jeff Gardner	.10	.03
139 Pat Gomez RC	.10	.03
140 Ricky Gutierrez	.10	.03
141 Gene Harris	.10	.03
142 Kevin Higgins	.10	.03
143 Trevor Hoffman	.20	.06
144 Phil Plantier	.10	.03
145 Kerry Taylor RC	.10	.03
146 Guillermo Velasquez	.10	.03
147 Wally Whitehurst	.10	.03
148 Tim Worrell RC	.10	.03
149 Todd Benzinger	.10	.03
150 Barry Bonds	1.25	.35
151 Greg Brummett RC	.10	.03
152 Mark Carreon	.10	.03
153 Dave Martinez	.10	.03
154 Jeff Reed	.10	.03
155 Kevin Rogers	.10	.03
156 Harold Baines	.20	.06
157 Damon Buford	.10	.03
158 Paul Carey RC	.10	.03
159 Jeffrey Hammonds	.10	.03
160 Jamie Moyer	.20	.06
161 Sherman Obando RC	.10	.03
162 John O'Donoghue RC	.10	.03
163 Brad Pennington	.10	.03
164 Jim Poole	.10	.03
165 Harold Reynolds	.20	.06
166 Fernando Valenzuela	.20	.06
167 Jack Voigt RC	.10	.03
168 Mark Williamson	.10	.03
169 Scott Bankhead	.10	.03
170 Greg Blosser	.10	.03
171 Jim Byrd RC	.10	.03
172 Ivan Calderon	.10	.03
173 Andre Dawson	.20	.06
174 Scott Fletcher	.10	.03
175 Jose Melendez	.10	.03
176 Carlos Quintana	.10	.03
177 Jeff Russell	.10	.03
178 Aaron Sele	.10	.03
179 Rod Correia RC	.10	.03
180 Chili Davis	.20	.06
181 Jim Edmonds RC	3.00	.90
182 Rene Gonzales	.10	.03
183 Hilly Hathaway RC	.10	.03
184 Torey Lovullo	.10	.03
185 Greg Myers	.10	.03
186 Gene Nelson	.10	.03
187 Troy Percival	.30	.09
188 Scott Sanderson	.10	.03
189 Darryl Scott RC	.10	.03
190 J.T. Snow RC	.50	.15
191 Russ Springer	.10	.03
192 Jason Bere	.10	.03
193 Rodney Bolton	.10	.03
194 Ellis Burks	.20	.06
195 Bo Jackson	.50	.15
196 Mike LaValliere	.10	.03
197 Scott Ruffcorn	.10	.03
198 Jeff Schwarz	.10	.03
199 Jerry DiPoto	.10	.03
200 Alvaro Espinoza	.10	.03
201 Wayne Kirby	.10	.03
202 Tom Kramer RC	.10	.03
203 Jesse Levis	.10	.03
204 Manny Ramirez	.50	.15
205 Jeff Treadway	.10	.03
206 Bill Wertz RC	.10	.03
207 Cliff Young	.10	.03
208 Matt Young	.10	.03
209 Kirk Gibson	.20	.06
210 Greg Gohr	.10	.03
211 Bill Krueger	.10	.03
212 Bob MacDonald	.10	.03
213 Mike Moore	.10	.03
214 David Wells	.20	.06
215 Billy Brewer	.10	.03
216 David Cone	.20	.06
217 Greg Gagne	.10	.03
218 Mark Gardner	.10	.03
219 Chris Haney	.10	.03
220 Phil Hiatt	.10	.03
221 Jose Lind	.10	.03
222 Juan Bell	.10	.03
223 Tom Brunansky	.10	.03
224 Mike Ignasiak	.10	.03
225 Joe Kmak	.10	.03
226 Tom Lampkin	.10	.03
227 Graeme Lloyd RC	.20	.06
228 Carlos Maldonado	.10	.03
229 Matt Mieske	.10	.03
230 Angel Miranda	.10	.03
231 Troy O'Leary RC	.50	.15
232 Kevin Reimer	.10	.03
233 Larry Casian	.10	.03
234 Jim Deshaies	.10	.03
235 Eddie Guardado RC	1.00	.30
236 Chip Hale	.10	.03
237 Mike Maksudian RC	.10	.03
238 David McCarty	.10	.03
239 Pat Meares RC	.20	.06
240 George Tsamis RC	.10	.03
241 Dave Winfield	.20	.06
242 Jim Abbott	.30	.09
243 Wade Boggs	.30	.09
244 Andy Cook RC	.10	.03
245 Russ Davis RC	.20	.06
246 Mike Humphreys	.10	.03
247 Jimmy Key	.20	.06
248 Jim Leyritz	.10	.03
249 Bobby Munoz	.10	.03
250 Paul O'Neill	.30	.09
251 Spike Owen	.10	.03
252 Dave Silvestri	.10	.03
253 Marcos Armas RC	.10	.03
254 Brent Gates	.10	.03
255 Rich Gossage	.20	.06
256 Scott Lydy RC	.10	.03
257 Henry Mercedes	.10	.03
258 Mike Mohler RC	.10	.03
259 Troy Neel	.10	.03
260 Edwin Nunez	.10	.03
261 Craig Paquette	.10	.03
262 Kevin Seitzer	.10	.03
263 Rich Amaral	.10	.03
264 Mike Blowers	.10	.03
265 Chris Bosio	.10	.03
266 Norm Charlton	.10	.03
267 Jim Converse RC	.10	.03
268 John Cummings RC	.10	.03
269 Mike Felder	.10	.03
270 Mike Hampton	.20	.06
271 Bill Haselman	.10	.03
272 Dwayne Henry	.10	.03
273 Greg Litton	.10	.03
274 Mackey Sasser	.10	.03
275 Lee Tinsley	.10	.03
276 David Wainhouse	.10	.03
277 Jeff Bronkey	.10	.03
278 Benji Gil	.10	.03
279 Tom Henke	.10	.03
280 Charlie Leibrandt	.10	.03
281 Robb Nen	.20	.06
282 Bill Ripken	.10	.03
283 Jon Shave RC	.10	.03
284 Doug Strange	.10	.03
285 Matt Whiteside RC	.10	.03
286 Scott Brow RC	.10	.03
287 Willie Canate RC	.10	.03
288 Tony Castillo	.10	.03
289 Domingo Cedeno RC	.10	.03
290 Darnell Coles	.10	.03
291 Danny Cox	.10	.03
292 Mark Eichhorn	.10	.03
293 Tony Fernandez	.10	.03
294 Al Leiter	.20	.06
295 Paul Molitor	.30	.09
296 Dave Stewart	.20	.06
297 Woody Williams RC	.75	.23
298 Checklist F1-F100	.10	.03
299 Checklist F101-F200	.10	.03
300 Checklist F201-F300	.10	.03

1993 Fleer Final Edition Diamond Tribute

Each Fleer Final Edition factory set contained a complete 10-card set of Diamond Tribute inserts. These cards are numbered separately and feature a totally different design from the base cards. Each card is numbered "X" of 10 on back.

	Nm-Mt	Ex-Mt
COMPLETE SET (10)	4.00	1.20
1 Wade Boggs	.50	.15
2 George Brett	2.00	.60
3 Andre Dawson	.30	.09
4 Carlton Fisk	.50	.15
5 Paul Molitor	.50	.15
6 Nolan Ryan	3.00	.90
7 Lee Smith	.30	.09
8 Ozzie Smith	1.25	.35
9 Dave Winfield	.30	.09
10 Robin Yount	1.25	.35

1993 Fleer Atlantic

This standard-size set of 25 cards features 24 high-profile players plus a checklist and was offered free in packs of five cards with a minimum purchase of eight gallons of Atlantic gasoline. The cards were available from June 14 to July 25, 1993, at participating Atlantic retailers in New York and Pennsylvania. The Atlantic Collector's Edition logo appears in the lower left. The cards are sequenced in alphabetical order. This set features one of the earliest cards picturing Barry Bonds as a member of the San Francisco Giants.

	Nm-Mt	Ex-Mt
COMPLETE SET (25)	8.00	2.40
1 Roberto Alomar	.40	.12
2 Barry Bonds	1.25	.35
3 Bobby Bonilla	.10	.03
4 Will Clark	.50	.15
5 Roger Clemens	1.25	.35
6 Darren Daulton	.20	.06
7 Dennis Eckersley	.30	.09
8 Cecil Fielder	.20	.06
9 Tom Glavine	.50	.15
10 Juan Gonzalez	.40	.12
11 Ken Griffey Jr.	1.50	.45
12 John Kruk	.20	.06
13 Greg Maddux	1.25	.35
14 Don Mattingly	1.25	.35
15 Fred McGriff	.30	.09
16 Mark McGwire	2.00	.60
17 Terry Pendleton	.10	.03
18 Kirby Puckett	.50	.15
19 Cal Ripken	2.50	.75
20 Nolan Ryan	2.50	.75
21 Ryne Sandberg	1.00	.30
22 Gary Sheffield	.50	.15
23 Frank Thomas	.50	.15
24 Andy Van Slyke	.10	.03
25 Checklist 1-25	.10	.03

1993 Fleer Fruit of the Loom

The 1993 Fleer Fruit of the Loom set consists of 66 cards measuring the standard size. Six-card packs were inserted in three-packs of Fruit of the Loom boys briefs. The cards have the same design as the regular issue 1993 Fleer. The only exception is the Fruit of the Loom logo which appears on the front. The cards are numbered on the back ordered alphabetically by player's name.

	Nm-Mt	Ex-Mt
COMPLETE SET (66)	60.00	18.00
1 Roberto Alomar	1.50	.45
2 Brady Anderson	.75	.23
3 Jeff Bagwell	3.00	.90
4 Albert Belle	.75	.23
5 Craig Biggio	1.00	.30
6 Barry Bonds	6.00	1.80
7 George Brett	6.00	1.80
8 Brett Butler	.75	.23
9 Jose Canseco	2.00	.60
10 Joe Carter	.75	.23
11 Will Clark	1.50	.45
12 Roger Clemens	6.00	1.80
13 Darren Daulton	.75	.23
14 Andre Dawson	1.50	.45
15 Delino DeShields	.50	.15
16 Rob Dibble	.75	.23
17 Doug Drabek	.50	.15
18 Dennis Eckersley	2.00	.60
19 Cecil Fielder	.75	.23
20 Travis Fryman	.75	.23
21 Tom Glavine	1.50	.45
22 Juan Gonzalez	2.50	.75
23 Dwight Gooden	.75	.23
24 Mark Grace	1.00	.30
25 Ken Griffey Jr.	6.00	1.80
26 Marquis Grissom	.75	.23
27 Juan Guzman	.50	.15
28 Tony Gwynn	6.00	1.80
29 Rickey Henderson	4.00	1.20
30 David Justice	1.50	.45
31 Eric Karros	1.00	.30
32 Chuck Knoblauch	1.50	.45

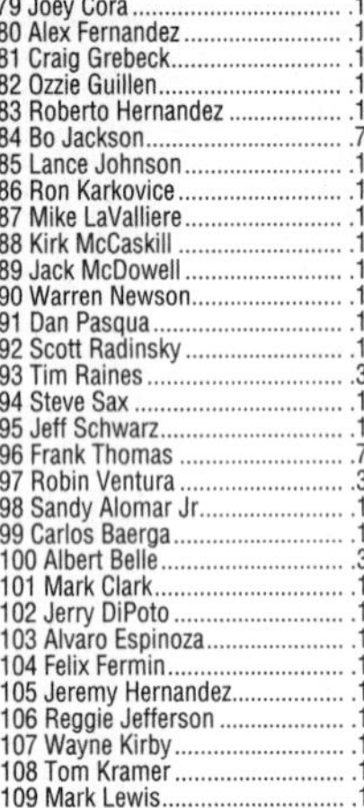
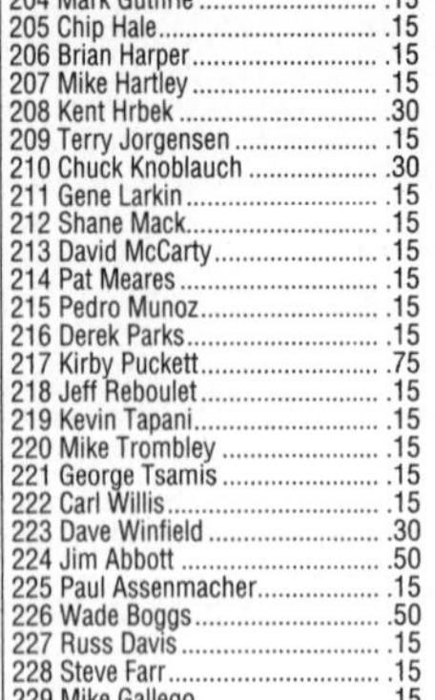
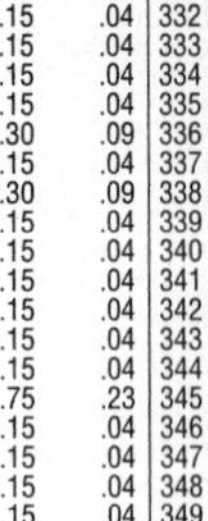
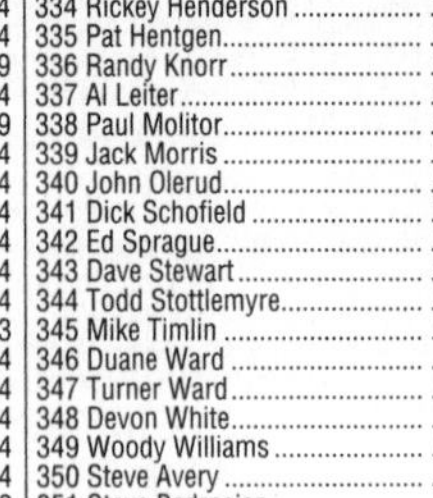
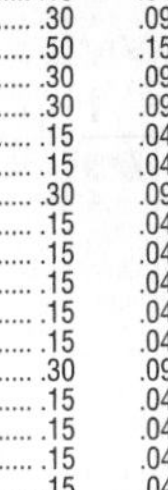
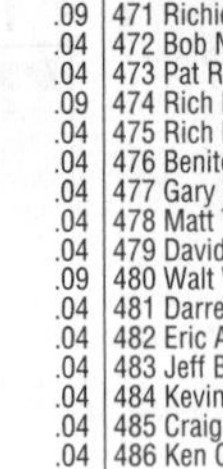
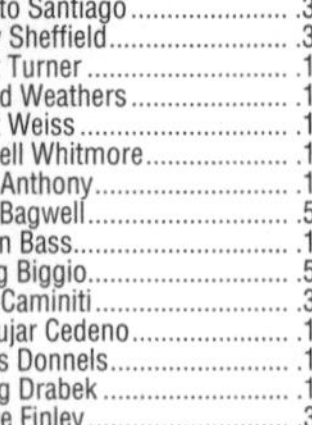

Card	Nm-Mt	Ex-Mt
33 John Kruk	.75	.23
34 Ray Lankford	.75	.23
35 Barry Larkin	1.50	.45
36 Pat Listach	.50	.15
37 Kenny Lofton	1.00	.30
38 Shane Mack	.50	.15
39 Greg Maddux	6.00	1.80
40 Dennis Martinez	.75	.23
41 Edgar Martinez	1.00	.30
42 Ramon Martinez	.50	.15
43 Don Mattingly	6.00	1.80
44 Jack McDowell	.50	.15
45 Fred McGriff	1.00	.30
46 Mark McGwire	10.00	3.00
47 Jeff Montgomery	.75	.23
48 Eddie Murray	1.50	.45
49 Charles Nagy	.50	.15
50 Tom Pagnozzi	.50	.15
51 Terry Pendleton	.50	.15
52 Kirby Puckett	3.00	.90
53 Jose Rijo	.50	.15
54 Cal Ripken	12.00	3.60
55 Nolan Ryan	12.00	3.60
56 Ryne Sandberg	4.00	1.20
57 Gary Sheffield	2.00	.60
58 Bill Swift	.50	.15
59 Danny Tartabull	.50	.15
60 Mickey Tettleton	.50	.15
61 Frank Thomas	2.00	.60
62 Andy Van Slyke	.50	.15
63 Robin Ventura	1.00	.30
64 Larry Walker	1.00	.30
65 Robin Yount	2.00	.60
66 Checklist 1-66	.50	.15

1994 Fleer

The 1994 Fleer baseball set consists of 720 standard-size cards. Cards were distributed in hobby, retail, and jumbo packs. The cards are numbered on the back, grouped alphabetically within teams, and checklisted below alphabetically according to teams for each league with AL preceding NL. The set closes with a Superstar Specials (706-713) subset. There are no key Rookie Cards in this set.

Card	Nm-Mt	Ex-Mt
COMPLETE SET (720)	40.00	12.00
1 Brady Anderson	.30	.09
2 Harold Baines	.30	.09
3 Mike Devereaux	.15	.04
4 Todd Frohwirth	.15	.04
5 Jeffrey Hammonds	.15	.04
6 Chris Hoiles	.15	.04
7 Tim Hulett	.15	.04
8 Ben McDonald	.15	.04
9 Mark McLemore	.15	.04
10 Alan Mills	.15	.04
11 Jamie Moyer	.30	.09
12 Mike Mussina	.75	.23
13 Gregg Olson	.15	.04
14 Mike Pagliarulo	.15	.04
15 Brad Pennington	.15	.04
16 Jim Poole	.15	.04
17 Harold Reynolds	.30	.09
18 Arthur Rhodes	.15	.04
19 Cal Ripken Jr.	2.50	.75
20 David Segui	.15	.04
21 Rick Sutcliffe	.30	.09
22 Fernando Valenzuela	.30	.09
23 Jack Voigt	.15	.04
24 Mark Williamson	.15	.04
25 Scott Bankhead	.15	.04
26 Roger Clemens	1.50	.45
27 Scott Cooper	.15	.04
28 Danny Darwin	.15	.04
29 Andre Dawson	.30	.09
30 Rob Deer	.15	.04
31 John Dopson	.15	.04
32 Scott Fletcher	.15	.04
33 Mike Greenwell	.15	.04
34 Greg A. Harris	.15	.04
35 Billy Hatcher	.15	.04
36 Bob Melvin	.15	.04
37 Tony Pena	.15	.04
38 Paul Quantrill	.15	.04
39 Carlos Quintana	.15	.04
40 Ernest Riles	.15	.04
41 Jeff Russell	.15	.04
42 Ken Ryan	.15	.04
43 Aaron Sele	.15	.04
44 John Valentin	.15	.04
45 Mo Vaughn	.30	.09
46 Frank Viola	.30	.09
47 Bob Zupcic	.15	.04
48 Mike Butcher	.15	.04
49 Rod Correia	.15	.04
50 Chad Curtis	.15	.04
51 Chili Davis	.30	.09
52 Gary DiSarcina	.15	.04
53 Damion Easley	.15	.04
54 Jim Edmonds	.50	.15
55 Chuck Finley	.30	.09
56 Steve Frey	.15	.04
57 Rene Gonzales	.15	.04
58 Joe Grahe	.15	.04
59 Hilly Hathaway	.15	.04
60 Stan Javier	.15	.04
61 Mark Langston	.15	.04
62 Phil Leftwich RC	.15	.04
63 Torey Lovullo	.15	.04
64 Joe Magrane	.15	.04
65 Greg Myers	.15	.04
66 Ken Patterson	.15	.04
67 Eduardo Perez	.15	.04
68 Luis Polonia	.15	.04
69 Tim Salmon	.50	.15
70 J.T. Snow	.30	.09
71 Ron Tingley	.15	.04
72 Julio Valera	.15	.04
73 Wilson Alvarez	.15	.04
74 Tim Belcher	.15	.04
75 George Bell	.15	.04
76 Jason Bere	.15	.04
77 Rod Bolton	.15	.04
78 Ellis Burks	.30	.09
79 Joey Cora	.15	.04
80 Alex Fernandez	.15	.04
81 Craig Grebeck	.15	.04
82 Ozzie Guillen	.15	.04
83 Roberto Hernandez	.15	.04
84 Bo Jackson	.75	.23
85 Lance Johnson	.15	.04
86 Ron Karkovice	.15	.04
87 Mike LaValliere	.15	.04
88 Kirk McCaskill	.15	.04
89 Jack McDowell	.15	.04
90 Warren Newson	.15	.04
91 Dan Pasqua	.15	.04
92 Scott Radinsky	.15	.04
93 Tim Raines	.30	.09
94 Steve Sax	.15	.04
95 Jeff Schwarz	.15	.04
96 Frank Thomas	.75	.23
97 Robin Ventura	.30	.09
98 Sandy Alomar Jr.	.15	.04
99 Carlos Baerga	.15	.04
100 Albert Belle	.30	.09
101 Mark Clark	.15	.04
102 Jerry DiPoto	.15	.04
103 Alvaro Espinoza	.15	.04
104 Felix Fermin	.15	.04
105 Jeremy Hernandez	.15	.04
106 Reggie Jefferson	.15	.04
107 Wayne Kirby	.15	.04
108 Tom Kramer	.15	.04
109 Mark Lewis	.15	.04
110 Derek Lilliquist	.15	.04
111 Kenny Lofton	.30	.09
112 Candy Maldonado	.15	.04
113 Jose Mesa	.15	.04
114 Jeff Mutis	.15	.04
115 Charles Nagy	.15	.04
116 Bob Ojeda	.15	.04
117 Junior Ortiz	.15	.04
118 Eric Plunk	.15	.04
119 Manny Ramirez	.50	.15
120 Paul Sorrento	.15	.04
121 Jim Thome	.75	.23
122 Jeff Treadway	.15	.04
123 Bill Wertz	.15	.04
124 Skeeter Barnes	.15	.04
125 Milt Cuyler	.15	.04
126 Eric Davis	.30	.09
127 John Doherty	.15	.04
128 Cecil Fielder	.30	.09
129 Travis Fryman	.30	.09
130 Kirk Gibson	.30	.09
131 Dan Gladden	.15	.04
132 Greg Gohr	.15	.04
133 Chris Gomez	.15	.04
134 Bill Gullickson	.15	.04
135 Mike Henneman	.15	.04
136 Kurt Knudsen	.15	.04
137 Chad Kreuter	.15	.04
138 Bill Krueger	.15	.04
139 Scott Livingstone	.15	.04
140 Bob MacDonald	.15	.04
141 Mike Moore	.15	.04
142 Tony Phillips	.15	.04
143 Mickey Tettleton	.15	.04
144 Alan Trammell	.50	.15
145 David Wells	.30	.09
146 Lou Whitaker	.30	.09
147 Kevin Appier	.30	.09
148 Stan Belinda	.15	.04
149 George Brett	2.00	.60
150 Billy Brewer	.15	.04
151 Hubie Brooks	.15	.04
152 David Cone	.30	.09
153 Gary Gaetti	.30	.09
154 Greg Gagne	.15	.04
155 Tom Gordon	.15	.04
156 Mark Gubicza	.15	.04
157 Chris Gwynn	.15	.04
158 John Habyan	.15	.04
159 Chris Haney	.15	.04
160 Phil Hiatt	.15	.04
161 Felix Jose	.15	.04
162 Wally Joyner	.30	.09
163 Jose Lind	.15	.04
164 Mike Macfarlane	.15	.04
165 Mike Magnante	.15	.04
166 Brent Mayne	.15	.04
167 Brian McRae	.15	.04
168 Kevin McReynolds	.15	.04
169 Keith Miller	.15	.04
170 Jeff Montgomery	.15	.04
171 Hipolito Pichardo	.15	.04
172 Rico Rossy	.15	.04
173 Juan Bell	.15	.04
174 Ricky Bones	.15	.04
175 Cal Eldred	.15	.04
176 Mike Fetters	.15	.04
177 Darryl Hamilton	.15	.04
178 Doug Henry	.15	.04
179 Mike Ignasiak	.15	.04
180 John Jaha	.15	.04
181 Pat Listach	.15	.04
182 Graeme Lloyd	.15	.04
183 Matt Mieske	.15	.04
184 Angel Miranda	.15	.04
185 Jaime Navarro	.15	.04
186 Dave Nilsson	.15	.04
187 Troy O'Leary	.15	.04
188 Jesse Orosco	.15	.04
189 Kevin Reimer	.15	.04
190 Kevin Seitzer	.15	.04
191 Bill Spiers	.15	.04
192 B.J. Surhoff	.30	.09
193 Dickie Thon	.15	.04
194 Jose Valentin	.15	.04
195 Greg Vaughn	.30	.09
196 Bill Wegman	.15	.04
197 Robin Yount	1.25	.35
198 Rick Aguilera	.15	.04
199 Willie Banks	.15	.04
200 Bernardo Brito	.15	.04
201 Larry Casian	.15	.04
202 Scott Erickson	.15	.04
203 Eddie Guardado	.30	.09
204 Mark Guthrie	.15	.04
205 Chip Hale	.15	.04
206 Brian Harper	.15	.04
207 Mike Hartley	.15	.04
208 Kent Hrbek	.30	.09
209 Terry Jorgensen	.15	.04
210 Chuck Knoblauch	.30	.09
211 Gene Larkin	.15	.04
212 Shane Mack	.15	.04
213 David McCarty	.15	.04
214 Pat Meares	.15	.04
215 Pedro Munoz	.15	.04
216 Derek Parks	.15	.04
217 Kirby Puckett	.75	.23
218 Jeff Reboulet	.15	.04
219 Kevin Tapani	.15	.04
220 Mike Trombley	.15	.04
221 George Tsamis	.15	.04
222 Carl Willis	.15	.04
223 Dave Winfield	.30	.09
224 Jim Abbott	.50	.15
225 Paul Assenmacher	.15	.04
226 Wade Boggs	.50	.15
227 Russ Davis	.15	.04
228 Steve Farr	.15	.04
229 Mike Gallego	.15	.04
230 Paul Gibson	.15	.04
231 Steve Howe	.15	.04
232 Dion James	.15	.04
233 Domingo Jean	.15	.04
234 Scott Kamieniecki	.15	.04
235 Pat Kelly	.15	.04
236 Jimmy Key	.30	.09
237 Jim Leyritz	.15	.04
238 Kevin Maas	.15	.04
239 Don Mattingly	2.00	.60
240 Rich Monteleone	.15	.04
241 Bobby Munoz	.15	.04
242 Matt Nokes	.15	.04
243 Paul O'Neill	.50	.15
244 Spike Owen	.15	.04
245 Melido Perez	.15	.04
246 Lee Smith	.30	.09
247 Mike Stanley	.15	.04
248 Danny Tartabull	.15	.04
249 Randy Velarde	.15	.04
250 Bob Wickman	.15	.04
251 Bernie Williams	.50	.15
252 Mike Aldrete	.15	.04
253 Marcos Armas	.15	.04
254 Lance Blankenship	.15	.04
255 Mike Bordick	.15	.04
256 Scott Brosius	.30	.09
257 Jerry Browne	.15	.04
258 Ron Darling	.15	.04
259 Kelly Downs	.15	.04
260 Dennis Eckersley	.30	.09
261 Brent Gates	.15	.04
262 Rich Gossage	.30	.09
263 Scott Hemond	.15	.04
264 Dave Henderson	.15	.04
265 Rick Honeycutt	.15	.04
266 Vince Horsman	.15	.04
267 Scott Lydy	.15	.04
268 Mark McGwire	2.00	.60
269 Mike Mohler	.15	.04
270 Troy Neel	.15	.04
271 Edwin Nunez	.15	.04
272 Craig Paquette	.15	.04
273 Ruben Sierra	.15	.04
274 Terry Steinbach	.15	.04
275 Todd Van Poppel	.15	.04
276 Bob Welch	.15	.04
277 Bobby Witt	.15	.04
278 Rich Amaral	.15	.04
279 Mike Blowers	.15	.04
280 Bret Boone UER (Name spelled Brett on front)	.30	.09
281 Chris Bosio	.15	.04
282 Jay Buhner	.30	.09
283 Norm Charlton	.15	.04
284 Mike Felder	.15	.04
285 Dave Fleming	.15	.04
286 Ken Griffey Jr.	1.25	.35
287 Erik Hanson	.15	.04
288 Bill Haselman	.15	.04
289 Brad Holman RC	.15	.04
290 Randy Johnson	.75	.23
291 Tim Leary	.15	.04
292 Greg Litton	.15	.04
293 Dave Magadan	.15	.04
294 Edgar Martinez	.50	.15
295 Tino Martinez	.50	.15
296 Jeff Nelson	.15	.04
297 Erik Plantenberg RC	.15	.04
298 Mackey Sasser	.15	.04
299 Brian Turang RC	.15	.04
300 Dave Valle	.15	.04
301 Omar Vizquel	.30	.09
302 Brian Bohanon	.15	.04
303 Kevin Brown	.30	.09
304 Jose Canseco UER (Back mentions 1991 as his 40/40 MVP season; should be '88)	.75	.23
305 Mario Diaz	.15	.04
306 Julio Franco	.30	.09
307 Juan Gonzalez	.75	.23
308 Tom Henke	.15	.04
309 David Hulse	.15	.04
310 Manuel Lee	.15	.04
311 Craig Lefferts	.15	.04
312 Charlie Leibrandt	.15	.04
313 Rafael Palmeiro	.50	.15
314 Dean Palmer	.30	.09
315 Roger Pavlik	.15	.04
316 Dan Peltier	.15	.04
317 Gene Petralli	.15	.04
318 Gary Redus	.15	.04
319 Ivan Rodriguez	.75	.23
320 Kenny Rogers	.30	.09
321 Nolan Ryan	3.00	.90
322 Doug Strange	.15	.04
323 Matt Whiteside	.15	.04
324 Roberto Alomar	.75	.23
325 Pat Borders	.15	.04
326 Joe Carter	.30	.09
327 Tony Castillo	.15	.04
328 Darnell Coles	.15	.04
329 Danny Cox	.15	.04
330 Mark Eichhorn	.15	.04
331 Tony Fernandez	.15	.04
332 Alfredo Griffin	.15	.04
333 Juan Guzman	.15	.04
334 Rickey Henderson	.75	.23
335 Pat Hentgen	.15	.04
336 Randy Knorr	.15	.04
337 Al Leiter	.30	.09
338 Paul Molitor	.50	.15
339 Jack Morris	.30	.09
340 John Olerud	.30	.09
341 Dick Schofield	.15	.04
342 Ed Sprague	.15	.04
343 Dave Stewart	.30	.09
344 Todd Stottlemyre	.15	.04
345 Mike Timlin	.15	.04
346 Duane Ward	.15	.04
347 Turner Ward	.15	.04
348 Devon White	.15	.04
349 Woody Williams	.30	.09
350 Steve Avery	.15	.04
351 Steve Bedrosian	.15	.04
352 Rafael Belliard	.15	.04
353 Damon Berryhill	.15	.04
354 Jeff Blauser	.15	.04
355 Sid Bream	.15	.04
356 Francisco Cabrera	.15	.04
357 Marvin Freeman	.15	.04
358 Ron Gant	.30	.09
359 Tom Glavine	.50	.15
360 Jay Howell	.15	.04
361 David Justice	.30	.09
362 Ryan Klesko	.30	.09
363 Mark Lemke	.15	.04
364 Javier Lopez	.30	.09
365 Greg Maddux	1.25	.35
366 Fred McGriff	.50	.15
367 Greg McMichael	.15	.04
368 Kent Mercker	.15	.04
369 Otis Nixon	.15	.04
370 Greg Olson	.15	.04
371 Bill Pecota	.15	.04
372 Terry Pendleton	.30	.09
373 Deion Sanders	.50	.15
374 Pete Smith	.15	.04
375 John Smoltz	.50	.15
376 Mike Stanton	.15	.04
377 Tony Tarasco	.15	.04
378 Mark Wohlers	.15	.04
379 Jose Bautista	.15	.04
380 Shawn Boskie	.15	.04
381 Steve Buechele	.15	.04
382 Frank Castillo	.15	.04
383 Mark Grace	.50	.15
384 Jose Guzman	.15	.04
385 Mike Harkey	.15	.04
386 Greg Hibbard	.15	.04
387 Glenallen Hill	.15	.04
388 Steve Lake	.15	.04
389 Derrick May	.15	.04
390 Chuck McElroy	.15	.04
391 Mike Morgan	.15	.04
392 Randy Myers	.15	.04
393 Dan Plesac	.15	.04
394 Kevin Roberson	.15	.04
395 Rey Sanchez	.15	.04
396 Ryne Sandberg	1.25	.35
397 Bob Scanlan	.15	.04
398 Dwight Smith	.15	.04
399 Sammy Sosa	1.25	.35
400 Jose Vizcaino	.15	.04
401 Rick Wilkins	.15	.04
402 Willie Wilson	.15	.04
403 Eric Yelding	.15	.04
404 Bobby Ayala	.15	.04
405 Jeff Branson	.15	.04
406 Tom Browning	.15	.04
407 Jacob Brumfield	.15	.04
408 Tim Costo	.15	.04
409 Rob Dibble	.30	.09
410 Willie Greene	.15	.04
411 Thomas Howard	.15	.04
412 Roberto Kelly	.15	.04
413 Bill Landrum	.15	.04
414 Barry Larkin	.75	.23
415 Larry Luebbers RC	.15	.04
416 Kevin Mitchell	.15	.04
417 Hal Morris	.15	.04
418 Joe Oliver	.15	.04
419 Tim Pugh	.15	.04
420 Jeff Reardon	.30	.09
421 Jose Rijo	.15	.04
422 Bip Roberts	.15	.04
423 John Roper	.15	.04
424 Johnny Ruffin	.15	.04
425 Chris Sabo	.15	.04
426 Juan Samuel	.15	.04
427 Reggie Sanders	.30	.09
428 Scott Service	.15	.04
429 John Smiley	.15	.04
430 Jerry Spradlin RC	.15	.04
431 Kevin Wickander	.15	.04
432 Freddie Benavides	.15	.04
433 Dante Bichette	.30	.09
434 Willie Blair	.15	.04
435 Daryl Boston	.15	.04
436 Kent Bottenfield	.15	.04
437 Vinny Castilla	.30	.09
438 Jerald Clark	.15	.04
439 Alex Cole	.15	.04
440 Andres Galarraga	.30	.09
441 Joe Girardi	.15	.04
442 Greg W. Harris	.15	.04
443 Charlie Hayes	.15	.04
444 Darren Holmes	.15	.04
445 Chris Jones	.15	.04
446 Roberto Mejia	.15	.04
447 David Nied	.15	.04
448 Jayhawk Owens	.15	.04
449 Jeff Parrett	.15	.04
450 Steve Reed	.15	.04
451 Armando Reynoso	.15	.04
452 Bruce Ruffin	.15	.04
453 Mo Sanford	.15	.04
454 Danny Sheaffer	.15	.04
455 Jim Tatum	.15	.04
456 Gary Wayne	.15	.04
457 Eric Young	.15	.04
458 Luis Aquino	.15	.04
459 Alex Arias	.15	.04
460 Jack Armstrong	.15	.04
461 Bret Barberie	.15	.04
462 Ryan Bowen	.15	.04
463 Chuck Carr	.15	.04
464 Jeff Conine	.30	.09
465 Henry Cotto	.15	.04
466 Orestes Destrade	.15	.04
467 Chris Hammond	.15	.04
468 Bryan Harvey	.15	.04
469 Charlie Hough	.30	.09
470 Joe Klink	.15	.04
471 Richie Lewis	.15	.04
472 Bob Natal	.15	.04
473 Pat Rapp	.15	.04
474 Rich Renteria	.15	.04
475 Rich Rodriguez	.15	.04
476 Benito Santiago	.30	.09
477 Gary Sheffield	.30	.09
478 Matt Turner	.15	.04
479 David Weathers	.15	.04
480 Walt Weiss	.15	.04
481 Darrell Whitmore	.15	.04
482 Eric Anthony	.15	.04
483 Jeff Bagwell	.50	.15
484 Kevin Bass	.15	.04
485 Craig Biggio	.50	.15
486 Ken Caminiti	.30	.09
487 Andujar Cedeno	.15	.04
488 Chris Donnels	.15	.04
489 Doug Drabek	.15	.04
490 Steve Finley	.30	.09
491 Luis Gonzalez	.30	.09
492 Pete Harnisch	.15	.04
493 Xavier Hernandez	.15	.04
494 Doug Jones	.15	.04
495 Todd Jones	.15	.04
496 Darryl Kile	.30	.09
497 Al Osuna	.15	.04
498 Mark Portugal	.15	.04
499 Scott Servais	.15	.04
500 Greg Swindell	.15	.04
501 Eddie Taubensee	.15	.04
502 Jose Uribe	.15	.04
503 Brian Williams	.15	.04
504 Billy Ashley	.15	.04
505 Pedro Astacio	.15	.04
506 Brett Butler	.30	.09
507 Tom Candiotti	.15	.04
508 Omar Daal	.15	.04
509 Jim Gott	.15	.04
510 Kevin Gross	.15	.04
511 Dave Hansen	.15	.04
512 Carlos Hernandez	.15	.04
513 Orel Hershiser	.30	.09
514 Eric Karros	.30	.09
515 Pedro Martinez	.75	.23
516 Ramon Martinez	.15	.04
517 Roger McDowell	.15	.04
518 Raul Mondesi	.30	.09
519 Jose Offerman	.15	.04
520 Mike Piazza	1.50	.45
521 Jody Reed	.15	.04
522 Henry Rodriguez	.15	.04
523 Mike Sharperson	.15	.04
524 Cory Snyder	.15	.04
525 Darryl Strawberry	.50	.15
526 Rick Trlicek	.15	.04
527 Tim Wallach	.15	.04
528 Mitch Webster	.15	.04
529 Steve Wilson	.15	.04
530 Todd Worrell	.15	.04
531 Moises Alou	.30	.09
532 Brian Barnes	.15	.04
533 Sean Berry	.15	.04
534 Greg Colbrunn	.15	.04
535 Delino DeShields	.15	.04
536 Jeff Fassero	.15	.04
537 Darrin Fletcher	.15	.04
538 Cliff Floyd	.30	.09
539 Lou Frazier	.15	.04
540 Marquis Grissom	.15	.04
541 Butch Henry	.15	.04
542 Ken Hill	.15	.04
543 Mike Lansing	.15	.04
544 Brian Looney RC	.15	.04
545 Dennis Martinez	.30	.09
546 Chris Nabholz	.15	.04
547 Randy Ready	.15	.04
548 Mel Rojas	.15	.04
549 Kirk Rueter	.30	.09
550 Tim Scott	.15	.04
551 Jeff Shaw	.15	.04
552 Tim Spehr	.15	.04
553 John Vander Wal	.15	.04
554 Larry Walker	.50	.15
555 John Wetteland	.30	.09
556 Rondell White	.30	.09
557 Tim Bogar	.15	.04
558 Bobby Bonilla	.30	.09
559 Jeromy Burnitz	.30	.09
560 Sid Fernandez	.15	.04
561 John Franco	.30	.09
562 Dave Gallagher	.15	.04
563 Dwight Gooden	.50	.1
564 Eric Hillman	.15	.0
565 Todd Hundley	.15	.0
566 Jeff Innis	.15	.0
567 Darrin Jackson	.15	.0
568 Howard Johnson	.15	.0
569 Bobby Jones	.15	.0
570 Jeff Kent	.30	.0
571 Mike Maddux	.15	.0
572 Jeff McKnight	.15	.0
573 Eddie Murray	.75	.2
574 Charlie O'Brien	.15	.0
575 Joe Orsulak	.15	.0
576 Bret Saberhagen	.30	.0
577 Pete Schourek	.15	.0
578 Dave Telgheder	.15	.0
579 Ryan Thompson	.15	.0
580 Anthony Young	.15	.0
581 Ruben Amaro	.15	.0
582 Larry Andersen	.15	.0
583 Kim Batiste	.15	.0
584 Wes Chamberlain	.15	.0
585 Darren Daulton	.30	.0
586 Mariano Duncan	.15	.0
587 Lenny Dykstra	.30	.0
588 Jim Eisenreich	.15	.0
589 Tommy Greene	.15	.0
590 Dave Hollins	.15	.0
591 Pete Incaviglia	.15	.0

592 Danny Jackson .15 .04
593 Ricky Jordan .15 .04
594 John Kruk .30 .09
595 Roger Mason .15 .04
596 Mickey Morandini .15 .04
597 Terry Mulholland .15 .04
598 Todd Pratt .15 .04
599 Ben Rivera .15 .04
600 Curt Schilling .50 .15
601 Kevin Stocker .15 .04
602 Milt Thompson .15 .04
603 David West .15 .04
604 Mitch Williams .15 .04
605 Jay Bell .30 .09
606 Dave Clark .15 .04
607 Steve Cooke .15 .04
608 Tom Foley .15 .04
609 Carlos Garcia .15 .04
610 Joel Johnston .15 .04
611 Jeff King .15 .04
612 Al Martin .15 .04
613 Lloyd McClendon .15 .04
614 Orlando Merced .15 .04
615 Blas Minor .15 .04
616 Denny Neagle .30 .09
617 Mark Petkovsek RC .15 .04
618 Tom Prince .15 .04
619 Don Slaught .15 .04
620 Zane Smith .15 .04
621 Randy Tomlin .15 .04
622 Andy Van Slyke .30 .09
623 Paul Wagner .15 .04
624 Tim Wakefield .30 .09
625 Bob Walk .15 .04
626 Kevin Young .15 .04
627 Luis Alicea .15 .04
628 Rene Arocha .15 .04
629 Rod Brewer .15 .04
630 Rheal Cormier .15 .04
631 Bernard Gilkey .15 .04
632 Lee Guetterman .15 .04
633 Gregg Jefferies .15 .04
634 Brian Jordan .30 .09
635 Les Lancaster .15 .04
636 Ray Lankford .15 .04
637 Rob Murphy .15 .04
638 Omar Olivares .15 .04
639 Jose Oquendo .15 .04
640 Donovan Osborne .15 .04
641 Tom Pagnozzi .15 .04
642 Erik Pappas .15 .04
643 Geronimo Pena .15 .04
644 Mike Perez .15 .04
645 Gerald Perry .15 .04
646 Ozzie Smith 1.25 .35
647 Bob Tewksbury .15 .04
648 Allen Watson .15 .04
649 Mark Whiten .15 .04
650 Tracy Woodson .15 .04
651 Todd Zeile .15 .04
652 Andy Ashby .15 .04
653 Brad Ausmus .15 .04
654 Billy Bean .15 .04
655 Derek Bell .15 .04
656 Andy Benes .15 .04
657 Doug Brocail .15 .04
658 Jarvis Brown .15 .04
659 Archi Cianfrocco .15 .04
660 Phil Clark .15 .04
661 Mark Davis .15 .04
662 Jeff Gardner .15 .04
663 Pat Gomez .15 .04
664 Ricky Gutierrez .15 .04
665 Tony Gwynn 1.00 .30
666 Gene Harris .15 .04
667 Kevin Higgins .15 .04
668 Trevor Hoffman .30 .09
669 Pedro Martinez RC .15 .04
670 Tim Mauser .15 .04
671 Melvin Nieves .15 .04
672 Phil Plantier .15 .04
673 Frank Seminara .15 .04
674 Craig Shipley .15 .04
675 Kerry Taylor .15 .04
676 Tim Teufel .15 .04
677 Guillermo Velasquez .15 .04
678 Wally Whitehurst .15 .04
679 Tim Worrell .15 .04
680 Rod Beck .15 .04
681 Mike Benjamin .15 .04
682 Todd Benzinger .15 .04
683 Bud Black .15 .04
684 Barry Bonds 2.00 .60
685 Jeff Brantley .15 .04
686 Dave Burba .15 .04
687 John Burkett .15 .04
688 Mark Carreon .15 .04
689 Will Clark .75 .23
690 Royce Clayton .15 .04
691 Bryan Hickerson .15 .04
692 Mike Jackson .15 .04
693 Darren Lewis .15 .04
694 Kirt Manwaring .15 .04
695 Dave Martinez .15 .04
696 Willie McGee .30 .09
697 John Patterson .15 .04
698 Jeff Reed .15 .04
699 Kevin Rogers .15 .04
700 Scott Sanderson .15 .04
701 Steve Scarsone .15 .04
702 Billy Swift .15 .04
703 Robby Thompson .15 .04
704 Matt Williams .30 .09
705 Trevor Wilson .15 .04
706 Fred McGriff .30 .09
Ron Gant
David Justice
707 John Olerud .30 .09
Paul Molitor
708 Mike Mussina .30 .09
Jack McDowell
709 Lou Whitaker .30 .09
Alan Trammell
710 Rafael Palmeiro .50 .15
Juan Gonzalez
711 Brett Butler .50 .15
Tony Gwynn
712 Kirby Puckett .50 .15
Chuck Knoblauch
713 Mike Piazza .75 .23
Eric Karros
714 Checklist 1 .15 .04
715 Checklist 2 .15 .04
716 Checklist 3 .15 .04
717 Checklist 4 .15 .04
718 Checklist 5 .15 .04
719 Checklist 6 .15 .04
720 Checklist 7 .15 .04
P69 Tim Salmon Promo 1.00 .30

1994 Fleer All-Rookies

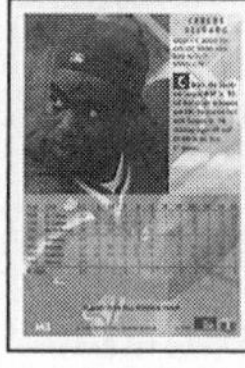

Collectors could redeem an All-Rookie Team Exchange card by mail for this nine-card set of top 1994 rookies at each position as chosen by Fleer. The expiration date to remeem this set was September 30, 1994. None of these players were in the basic 1994 Fleer set. The exchange card was randomly inserted into all 1994 Fleer packs.

	Nm-Mt	Ex-Mt
COMPLETE SET (9)	8.00	2.40
M1 Kurt Abbott	1.00	.30
M2 Rich Becker	.50	.15
M3 Carlos Delgado	1.50	.45
M4 Jorge Fabregas	.50	.15
M5 Bob Hamelin	.50	.15
M6 John Hudek	.50	.15
M7 Tim Hyers	.50	.15
M8 Luis Lopez	.50	.15
M9 James Mouton	.50	.15
NNO Exp. All-Rookie Exch.	.50	.15

1994 Fleer All-Stars

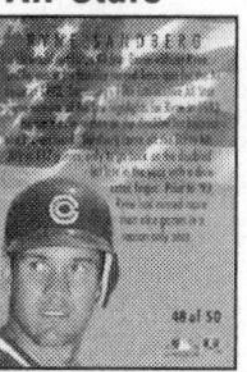

Fleer issued this 50-card standard-size set in 1994, to commemorate the All-Stars of the 1993 season. The cards were exclusively available in the Fleer wax packs at a rate of one in two. The set features 25 American League (1-25) and 25 National League (26-50) All-Stars. Each league's all-stars are sequenced in alphabetical order.

	Nm-Mt	Ex-Mt
COMPLETE SET (50)	25.00	7.50
1 Roberto Alomar	1.00	.30
2 Carlos Baerga	.20	.06
3 Albert Belle	.40	.12
4 Wade Boggs	.60	.18
5 Joe Carter	.40	.12
6 Scott Cooper	.20	.06
7 Cecil Fielder	.40	.12
8 Travis Fryman	.40	.12
9 Juan Gonzalez	1.00	.30
10 Ken Griffey Jr.	1.50	.45
11 Pat Hentgen	.20	.06
12 Randy Johnson	1.00	.30
13 Jimmy Key	.40	.12
14 Mark Langston	.20	.06
15 Jack McDowell	.20	.06
16 Paul Molitor	.60	.18
17 Jeff Montgomery	.20	.06
18 Mike Mussina	1.00	.30
19 John Olerud	.40	.12
20 Kirby Puckett	1.00	.30
21 Cal Ripken	3.00	.90
22 Ivan Rodriguez	1.00	.30
23 Frank Thomas	1.00	.30
24 Greg Vaughn	.40	.12
25 Duane Ward	.20	.06
26 Steve Avery	.20	.06
27 Rod Beck	.40	.12
28 Jay Bell	.40	.12
29 Andy Benes	.20	.06
30 Jeff Blauser	.20	.06
31 Barry Bonds	2.50	.75
32 Bobby Bonilla	.40	.12
33 John Burkett	.20	.06
34 Darren Daulton	.40	.12
35 Andres Galarraga	.40	.12
36 Tom Glavine	.60	.18
37 Mark Grace	.60	.18
38 Marquis Grissom	.20	.06
39 Tony Gwynn	1.25	.35
40 Bryan Harvey	.20	.06
41 Dave Hollins	.20	.06
42 David Justice	.40	.12
43 Darryl Kile	.40	.12
44 John Kruk	.40	.12
45 Barry Larkin	1.00	.30
46 Terry Mulholland	.20	.06
47 Mike Piazza	2.00	.60
48 Ryne Sandberg	1.50	.45
49 Gary Sheffield	.40	.12
50 John Smoltz	.60	.18

1994 Fleer Award Winners

Randomly inserted in foil packs at a rate of one in 37, this six-card standard-size set spotlights six outstanding players who received awards.

	Nm-Mt	Ex-Mt
COMPLETE SET (6)	8.00	2.40
1 Frank Thomas	1.25	.35
2 Barry Bonds	3.00	.90
3 Jack McDowell	.25	.07
4 Greg Maddux	2.00	.60
5 Tim Salmon	.75	.23
6 Mike Piazza	2.50	.75

1994 Fleer Golden Moments

These standard-size cards were issued one per blue retail jumbo pack. The fronts feature borderless color player action photos. A shrink-wrapped package containing a jumbo set was issued one per Fleer hobby case. Jumbos were later issued for retail purposes with a production number of 10,000. The standard-size cards are not individually numbered.

	Nm-Mt	Ex-Mt
COMPLETE SET (10)	30.00	9.00
1 Mark Whiten	.60	.18
2 Carlos Baerga	.60	.18
3 Dave Winfield	1.25	.35
4 Ken Griffey Jr.	5.00	1.50
5 Bo Jackson	3.00	.90
6 George Brett	8.00	2.40
7 Nolan Ryan	12.00	3.60
8 Fred McGriff	2.00	.60
9 Frank Thomas	3.00	.90
10 Chris Bosio Jim Abbott Darryl Kile	.60	.18

1994 Fleer Golden Moments Jumbo

These jumbo cards are parallel to the regular 1994 Fleer Golden Moments card. They were issued one set per hobby case. These cards were also later reissued for retail purposes. They are valued as a multiple of the regular Golden Moments cards

	Nm-Mt	Ex-Mt
COMPLETE SET (10)	35.00	10.50

*SINGLES: .4X TO 1X REGULAR GOLDEN MOMENTS

1994 Fleer League Leaders

Randomly inserted in all pack types at a rate of one in 17, this 28-card set features six statistical leaders each for the American (1-6) and the National (7-12) Leagues.

	Nm-Mt	Ex-Mt
COMPLETE SET (12)	5.00	1.50
1 John Olerud	.40	.12
2 Albert Belle	.40	.12
3 Rafael Palmeiro	.50	.15
4 Kenny Lofton	.40	.12
5 Jack McDowell	.25	.07
6 Kevin Appier	.40	.12
7 Andres Galarraga	.40	.12
8 Barry Bonds	1.50	.45
9 Lenny Dykstra	.40	.12
10 Chuck Carr	.25	.07
11 Tom Glavine UER No number on back of card	.50	.15
12 Greg Maddux	2.50	.75

1994 Fleer Lumber Company

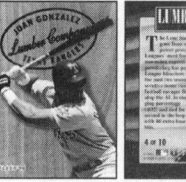

Randomly inserted in jumbo packs at a rate of one in five, this ten-card standard-size set features the best hitters in the game. The cards are numbered alphabetically.

	Nm-Mt	Ex-Mt
COMPLETE SET (10)	10.00	3.00
1 Albert Belle	.50	.15
2 Barry Bonds	3.00	.90
3 Ron Gant	.50	.15
4 Juan Gonzalez	1.25	.35
5 Ken Griffey Jr.	2.00	.60
6 David Justice	.50	.15
7 Fred McGriff	.75	.23
8 Rafael Palmeiro	.75	.23
9 Frank Thomas	1.25	.35
10 Matt Williams	.50	.15

1994 Fleer Major League Prospects

Randomly inserted in all pack types at a rate of one in six, this 35-card standard-size set showcases some of the outstanding young players in Major League Baseball. The cards are numbered on the back "X of 35" and are sequenced in alphabetical order.

	Nm-Mt	Ex-Mt
COMPLETE SET (35)	15.00	4.50
1 Kurt Abbott	.75	.23
2 Brian Anderson	.75	.23
3 Rich Aude	.25	.07
4 Cory Bailey	.25	.07
5 Danny Bautista	.25	.07
6 Marty Cordova	.25	.07
7 Tripp Cromer	.25	.07
8 Midre Cummings	.25	.07
9 Carlos Delgado	1.25	.35
10 Steve Dreyer	.25	.07
11 Steve Dunn	.25	.07
12 Jeff Granger	.25	.07
13 Tyrone Hill	.25	.07
14 Denny Hocking	.25	.07
15 John Hope	.25	.07
16 Butch Huskey	.25	.07
17 Miguel Jimenez	.25	.07
18 Chipper Jones	2.00	.60
19 Steve Karsay	.25	.07
20 Mike Kelly	.25	.07
21 Mike Lieberthal	.75	.23
22 Albie Lopez	.25	.07
23 Jeff McNeely	.25	.07
24 Danny Miceli	.25	.07
25 Nate Minchey	.25	.07
26 Marc Newfield	.25	.07
27 Darren Oliver	.75	.23
28 Luis Ortiz	.25	.07
29 Curtis Pride	.75	.23
30 Roger Salkeld	.25	.07
31 Scott Sanders	.25	.07
32 Dave Staton	.25	.07
33 Salomon Torres	.25	.07
34 Steve Trachsel	.25	.07
35 Chris Turner	.25	.07

1994 Fleer Pro-Visions

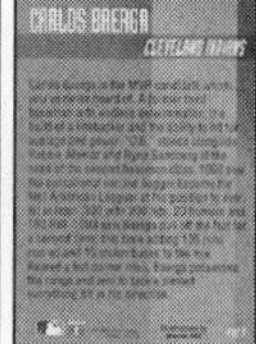

Randomly inserted in all pack types at a rate of one in 12, this nine-card standard-size set features on its fronts colorful artistic player caricatures with surrealistic backgrounds drawn by illustrator Wayne Still. When all nine cards are placed in order in a collector sheet, the backgrounds fit together to form a composite. The cards are numbered on the back "X of 9."

	Nm-Mt	Ex-Mt
COMPLETE SET (9)	4.00	1.20
1 Darren Daulton	.40	.12
2 John Olerud	.40	.12
3 Matt Williams	.40	.12
4 Carlos Baerga	.20	.06
5 Ozzie Smith	1.50	.45
6 Juan Gonzalez	1.00	.30
7 Jack McDowell	.20	.06
8 Mike Piazza	2.00	.60
9 Tony Gwynn	1.25	.35

1994 Fleer Rookie Sensations

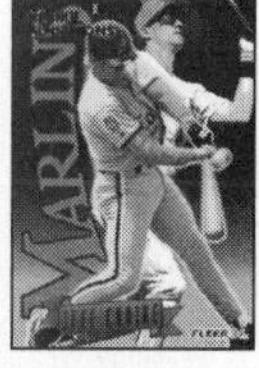

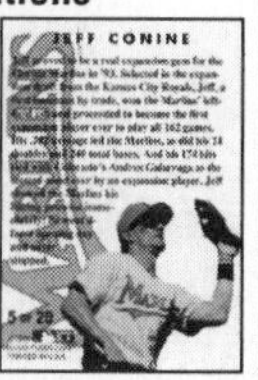

Randomly inserted in jumbo packs at a rate of one in four, this 20-card standard-size set features outstanding rookies. The fronts are "double exposed," with a player action cutout superimposed over a second photo. The cards are numbered on the back "X of 20" and are sequenced in alphabetical order.

	Nm-Mt	Ex-Mt
COMPLETE SET (20)	20.00	6.00
1 Rene Arocha	1.00	.30
2 Jason Bere	1.00	.30
3 Jeromy Burnitz	2.00	.60
4 Chuck Carr	1.00	.30
5 Jeff Conine	2.00	.60
6 Steve Cooke	1.00	.30
7 Cliff Floyd	2.00	.60
8 Jeffrey Hammonds	1.00	.30
9 Wayne Kirby	1.00	.30
10 Mike Lansing	1.00	.30
11 Al Martin	1.00	.30
12 Greg McMichael	1.00	.30
13 Troy Neel	1.00	.30
14 Mike Piazza	10.00	
15 Armando Reynoso	1.00	.30
16 Kirk Rueter	2.00	.60
17 Tim Salmon	3.00	.90
18 Aaron Sele	1.00	.30
19 J.T. Snow	2.00	.60
20 Kevin Stocker	1.00	.30

1994 Fleer Salmon

Spotlighting American League Rookie of the Year Tim Salmon, this 15-card standard size set was issued in two forms. Cards 1-12 were randomly inserted in packs (one in eight) and 13-15 were available through a mail-in offer. Ten wrappers and 1.50 were necessary to acquire the mail-ins. The mail-in expiration date was September 30, 1994. Salmon autographed more than 2,000 of his cards.

	Nm-Mt	Ex-Mt
COMPLETE SET (12)	15.00	4.50
COMMON CARD (1-12)	1.00	.30
COMMON MAIL (13-15)	1.00	.30
AU Tim Salmon AU (Certified autograph)	25.00	7.50

1994 Fleer Smoke 'n Heat

Randomly inserted in wax packs at a rate of one in 36, this 12-card standard-size set showcases the best pitchers in the game. The cards are numbered on the back "X of 12." and are sequenced in alphabetical order.

	Nm-Mt	Ex-Mt
COMPLETE SET (12)	60.00	18.00
1 Roger Clemens	10.00	3.00
2 David Cone	2.00	.60
3 Juan Guzman	1.00	.30
4 Pete Harnisch	1.00	.30
5 Randy Johnson	5.00	1.50
6 Mark Langston	1.00	.30
7 Greg Maddux	8.00	2.40
8 Mike Mussina	5.00	1.50
9 Jose Rijo	1.00	.30
10 Nolan Ryan	20.00	6.00
11 Curt Schilling	3.00	.90
12 John Smoltz	3.00	.90

1994 Fleer Team Leaders

Randomly inserted in all pack types, this 28-card standard-size set features Fleer's selected top player from each of the 28 major league teams. The card numbering is arranged alphabetically by city according to the American (1-14) and the National (15-28) Leagues.

	Nm-Mt	Ex-Mt
COMPLETE SET (28)	25.00	7.50
1 Cal Ripken	4.00	1.20
2 Mo Vaughn	.50	.15
3 Tim Salmon	.75	.23
4 Frank Thomas	1.25	.35
5 Carlos Baerga	.25	.07
6 Cecil Fielder	.50	.15
7 Brian McRae	.25	.07
8 Greg Vaughn	.50	.15
9 Kirby Puckett	1.25	.35
10 Don Mattingly	3.00	.90
11 Mark McGwire	3.00	.90
12 Ken Griffey Jr.	2.00	.60
13 Juan Gonzalez	1.25	.35
14 Paul Molitor	.75	.23
15 David Justice	.50	.15
16 Ryne Sandberg	2.00	.60
17 Barry Larkin	1.25	.35
18 Andres Galarraga	.50	.15
19 Gary Sheffield	.50	.15
20 Jeff Bagwell	.75	.23
21 Mike Piazza	2.50	.75
22 Marquis Grissom	.25	.07
23 Bobby Bonilla	.50	.15
24 Lenny Dykstra	.50	.15
25 Jay Bell	.50	.15
26 Gregg Jefferies	.25	.07
27 Tony Gwynn	1.50	.45
28 Will Clark	1.25	.35

1994 Fleer Update

This 200-card standard-size set highlights traded players in their new uniforms and promising young rookies. The Update set was exclusively distributed in factory set form through hobby dealers. A ten card Diamond Tribute set was included in each factory set for a total of 210 cards. The cards are numbered on the back, grouped alphabetically by team by league with AL preceding NL. Key Rookie Cards include Chan Ho Park and Alex Rodriguez.

Nm-Mt Ex-Mt
COMP.FACT.SET (210) 50.00 15.00
COMPLETE SET (200) 45.00 13.50
1 Mark Eichhorn .25 .07
2 Sid Fernandez .25 .07
3 Leo Gomez .25 .07
4 Mike Oquist .25 .07
5 Rafael Palmeiro .75 .23
6 Chris Sabo .25 .07
7 Dwight Smith .25 .07
8 Lee Smith .50 .15
9 Damon Berryhill .25 .07
10 Wes Chamberlain .25 .07
11 Gar Finnvold .25 .07
12 Chris Howard .25 .07
13 Tim Naehring .25 .07
14 Otis Nixon .25 .07
15 Brian Anderson RC .50 .15
16 Jorge Fabregas .25 .07
17 Rex Hudler .25 .07
18 Bo Jackson 1.25 .35
19 Mark Leiter .25 .07
20 Spike Owen .25 .07
21 Harold Reynolds .50 .15
22 Chris Turner .25 .07
23 Dennis Cook .25 .07
24 Jose DeLeon .25 .07
25 Julio Franco .50 .15
26 Joe Hall .25 .07
27 Darrin Jackson .25 .07
28 Dane Johnson .25 .07
29 Norberto Martin .25 .07
30 Scott Sanderson .25 .07
31 Jason Grimsley .25 .07
32 Dennis Martinez .50 .15
33 Jack Morris .50 .15
34 Eddie Murray 1.25 .35
35 Chad Ogea .25 .07
36 Tony Pena .25 .07
37 Paul Shuey .25 .07
38 Omar Vizquel .50 .15
39 Danny Bautista .25 .07
40 Tim Belcher .25 .07
41 Joe Boever .25 .07
42 Storm Davis .25 .07
43 Junior Felix .25 .07
44 Mike Gardiner .25 .07
45 Buddy Groom .25 .07
46 Juan Samuel .25 .07
47 Vince Coleman .25 .07
48 Bob Hamelin .25 .07
49 Dave Henderson .25 .07
50 Rusty Meacham .25 .07
51 Terry Shumpert .25 .07
52 Jeff Bronkey .25 .07
53 Alex Diaz .25 .07
54 Brian Harper .25 .07
55 Jose Mercedes .25 .07
56 Jody Reed .25 .07
57 Bob Scanlan .25 .07
58 Turner Ward .25 .07
59 Rich Becker .25 .07
60 Alex Cole .25 .07
61 Denny Hocking .25 .07
62 Scott Leius .25 .07
63 Pat Mahomes .25 .07
64 Carlos Pulido .25 .07
65 Dave Stevens .25 .07
66 Matt Walbeck .25 .07
67 Xavier Hernandez .25 .07
68 Sterling Hitchcock .25 .07
69 Terry Mulholland .25 .07
70 Luis Polonia .25 .07
71 Gerald Williams .25 .07
72 Mark Acre RC .25 .07
73 Geronimo Berroa .25 .07
74 Rickey Henderson 1.25 .35
75 Stan Javier .25 .07
76 Steve Karsay .25 .07
77 Carlos Reyes .25 .07
78 Bill Taylor RC .50 .15
79 Eric Anthony .25 .07
80 Bobby Ayala .25 .07
81 Tim Davis .25 .07
82 Felix Fermin .25 .07
83 Reggie Jefferson .25 .07
84 Keith Mitchell .25 .07
85 Bill Risley .25 .07
86 Alex Rodriguez RC 40.00 12.00
87 Roger Salkeld .25 .07
88 Dan Wilson .25 .07
89 Cris Carpenter .25 .07
90 Will Clark 1.25 .35
91 Jeff Frye .25 .07
92 Rick Helling .25 .07
93 Chris James .25 .07
94 Oddibe McDowell .25 .07
95 Billy Ripken .25 .07
96 Carlos Delgado .75 .23
97 Alex Gonzalez .25 .07
98 Shawn Green 1.25 .35
99 Darren Hall .25 .07
100 Mike Huff .25 .07
101 Mike Kelly .25 .07
102 Roberto Kelly .25 .07
103 Charlie O'Brien .25 .07
104 Jose Oliva .25 .07
105 Gregg Olson .25 .07
106 Willie Banks .25 .07
107 Jim Bullinger .25 .07
108 Chuck Crim .25 .07
109 Shawon Dunston .25 .07
110 Karl Rhodes .25 .07
111 Steve Trachsel .25 .07
112 Anthony Young .25 .07
113 Eddie Zambrano .25 .07
114 Bret Boone .50 .15
115 Jeff Brantley .25 .07
116 Hector Carrasco .25 .07
117 Tony Fernandez .25 .07
118 Tim Fortugno .25 .07
119 Erik Hanson .25 .07
120 Chuck McElroy .25 .07
121 Deion Sanders .75 .23
122 Ellis Burks .50 .15
123 Marvin Freeman .25 .07
124 Mike Harkey .25 .07
125 Howard Johnson .25 .07
126 Mike Kingery .25 .07
127 Nelson Liriano .25 .07
128 Marcus Moore .25 .07
129 Mike Munoz .25 .07
130 Kevin Ritz .25 .07
131 Walt Weiss .25 .07
132 Kurt Abbott RC .50 .15
133 Jerry Browne .25 .07
134 Greg Colbrunn .25 .07
135 Jeremy Hernandez .25 .07
136 Dave Magadan .25 .07
137 Kurt Miller .25 .07
138 Robb Nen .50 .15
139 Jesus Tavarez RC .25 .07
140 Sid Bream .25 .07
141 Tom Edens .25 .07
142 Tony Eusebio .25 .07
143 John Hudek RC .25 .07
144 Brian L. Hunter .25 .07
145 Orlando Miller .25 .07
146 James Mouton .25 .07
147 Shane Reynolds .25 .07
148 Rafael Bournigal .25 .07
149 Delino DeShields .25 .07
150 Garey Ingram RC .25 .07
151 Chan Ho Park RC 1.50 .45
152 Wil Cordero .25 .07
153 Pedro Martinez 1.25 .35
154 Randy Milligan .25 .07
155 Lenny Webster .25 .07
156 Rico Brogna .25 .07
157 Josias Manzanillo .25 .07
158 Kevin McReynolds .25 .07
159 Mike Remlinger .25 .07
160 David Segui .25 .07
161 Pete Smith .25 .07
162 Kelly Stinnett RC .50 .15
163 Jose Vizcaino .25 .07
164 Billy Hatcher .25 .07
165 Doug Jones .25 .07
166 Mike Lieberthal .50 .15
167 Tony Longmire .25 .07
168 Bobby Munoz .25 .07
169 Paul Quantrill .25 .07
170 Heathcliff Slocumb .25 .07
171 Fernando Valenzuela .50 .15
172 Mark Dewey .25 .07
173 Brian R. Hunter .25 .07
174 Jon Lieber .25 .07
175 Ravelo Manzanillo .25 .07
176 Dan Miceli .25 .07
177 Rick White .25 .07
178 Bryan Eversgerd .25 .07
179 John Habyan .25 .07
180 Terry McGriff .25 .07
181 Vicente Palacios .25 .07
182 Rich Rodriguez .25 .07
183 Rick Sutcliffe .50 .15
184 Donnie Elliott .25 .07
185 Joey Hamilton .25 .07
186 Tim Hyers RC .25 .07
187 Luis Lopez .25 .07
188 Ray McDavid .25 .07
189 Bip Roberts .25 .07
190 Scott Sanders .25 .07
191 Eddie Williams .25 .07
192 Steve Frey .25 .07
193 Pat Gomez .25 .07
194 Rich Monteleone .25 .07
195 Mark Portugal .25 .07
196 Darryl Strawberry .75 .23
197 Salomon Torres .25 .07
198 W.VanLandingham RC .25 .07
199 Checklist .25 .07
200 Checklist .25 .07

1994 Fleer Update Diamond Tribute

Each 1994 Fleer Update factory set contained a complete 10-card set of Diamond Tribute inserts. This was the third and final year that Fleer included an insert set in their factory boxed update sets. The 1994 Diamond Tribute inserts feature a player action shot cut out against a backdrop of clouds and baseballs. The selection once again focuses on the game's top veterans. Cards are numbered "X" of 10 on the back.

Nm-Mt Ex-Mt
COMPLETE SET (10) 2.00 .60
1 Barry Bonds 1.00 .30
2 Joe Carter .15 .04
3 Will Clark .40 .12
4 Roger Clemens .75 .23
5 Tony Gwynn .50 .15
6 Don Mattingly 1.00 .30
7 Fred McGriff .25 .07
8 Eddie Murray .40 .12
9 Kirby Puckett .40 .12
10 Cal Ripken 1.25 .35

1994 Fleer Sunoco

These 25 standard-size cards feature white-bordered color player action shots on their fronts. The cards are numbered on the back as "X of 25."

Nm-Mt Ex-Mt
COMPLETE SET (25) 6.00 1.80
1 Roberto Alomar .25 .07
2 Carlos Baerga .10 .03
3 Jeff Bagwell .50 .15
4 Jay Bell .10 .03
5 Barry Bonds 1.00 .30
6 Joe Carter .15 .04
7 Roger Clemens 1.00 .30
8 Darren Daulton .15 .04
9 Len Dykstra .15 .04
10 Cecil Fielder .15 .04
11 Tom Glavine .25 .07
12 Juan Gonzalez .40 .12
13 Ken Griffey Jr. 1.00 .30
14 David Justice .25 .07
15 John Kruk .15 .04
16 Greg Maddux 1.25 .35
17 Don Mattingly 1.00 .30
18 Jack McDowell .10 .03
19 John Olerud .15 .04
20 Mike Piazza 1.50 .45
21 Kirby Puckett .40 .12
22 Tim Salmon .25 .07
23 Frank Thomas .50 .15
24 Andy Van Slyke .10 .03
25 Checklist .10 .03

1995 Fleer

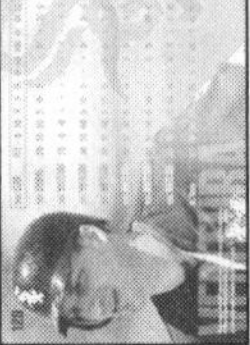

The 1995 Fleer set consists of 600 standard-size cards issued as one series. Each pack contained at least one insert card with some 'Hot Packs' containing nothing but insert cards. Full-bleed fronts have two player photos and, atypical of baseball cards fronts, biographical information such as height, weight, etc. The backgrounds are multi-colored. The backs are horizontal and contain year-by-year statistics along with a photo. There was a different design for each of baseball's six divisions. The checklist is arranged alphabetically by teams within each league with AL preceding NL. To preview the product prior to it's public release, Fleer printed up additional quantities of cards 26, 78, 155, 235, 285, 351, 509 and 514 and mailed them to dealers and hobby media.

Nm-Mt Ex-Mt
COMPLETE SET (600) 50.00 15.00
1 Brady Anderson .30 .09
2 Harold Baines .30 .09
3 Damon Buford .15 .04
4 Mike Devereaux .15 .04
5 Mark Eichhorn .15 .04
6 Sid Fernandez .15 .04
7 Leo Gomez .15 .04
8 Jeffrey Hammonds .15 .04
9 Chris Hoiles .15 .04
10 Rick Krivda .15 .04
11 Ben McDonald .15 .04
12 Mark McLemore .15 .04
13 Alan Mills .15 .04
14 Jamie Moyer .30 .09
15 Mike Mussina .75 .23
16 Mike Oquist .15 .04
17 Rafael Palmeiro .50 .15
18 Arthur Rhodes .15 .04
19 Cal Ripken Jr. 2.50 .75
20 Chris Sabo .15 .04
21 Lee Smith .30 .09
22 Jack Voigt .15 .04
23 Damon Berryhill .15 .04
24 Tom Brunansky .15 .04
25 Wes Chamberlain .15 .04
26 Roger Clemens 1.50 .45
27 Scott Cooper .15 .04
28 Andre Dawson .30 .09
29 Gar Finnvold .15 .04
30 Tony Fossas .15 .04
31 Mike Greenwell .15 .04
32 Joe Hesketh .15 .04
33 Chris Howard .15 .04
34 Chris Nabholz .15 .04
35 Tim Naehring .15 .04
36 Otis Nixon .15 .04
37 Carlos Rodriguez .15 .04
38 Rich Rowland .15 .04
39 Ken Ryan .15 .04
40 Aaron Sele .15 .04
41 John Valentin .15 .04
42 Mo Vaughn .30 .09
43 Frank Viola .30 .09
44 Danny Bautista .15 .04
45 Joe Boever .15 .04
46 Milt Cuyler .15 .04
47 Storm Davis .15 .04
48 John Doherty .15 .04
49 Junior Felix .15 .04
50 Cecil Fielder .30 .09
51 Travis Fryman .30 .09
52 Mike Gardiner .15 .04
53 Kirk Gibson .30 .09
54 Chris Gomez .15 .04
55 Buddy Groom .15 .04
56 Mike Henneman .15 .04
57 Chad Kreuter .15 .04
58 Mike Moore .15 .04
59 Tony Phillips .15 .04
60 Juan Samuel .15 .04
61 Mickey Tettleton .15 .04
62 Alan Trammell .50 .15
63 David Wells .30 .09
64 Lou Whitaker .30 .09
65 Jim Abbott .50 .15
66 Joe Ausanio .15 .04
67 Wade Boggs .50 .15
68 Mike Gallego .15 .04
69 Xavier Hernandez .15 .04
70 Sterling Hitchcock .15 .04
71 Steve Howe .15 .04
72 Scott Kamieniecki .15 .04
73 Pat Kelly .15 .04
74 Jimmy Key .30 .09
75 Jim Leyritz .15 .04
76 Don Mattingly UER 2.00 .60
Photo is a reversed negative
77 Terry Mulholland .15 .04
78 Paul O'Neill .50 .15
79 Melido Perez .15 .04
80 Luis Polonia .15 .04
81 Mike Stanley .15 .04
82 Danny Tartabull .15 .04
83 Randy Velarde .15 .04
84 Bob Wickman .15 .04
85 Bernie Williams .50 .15
86 Gerald Williams .15 .04
87 Roberto Alomar .75 .23
88 Pat Borders .15 .04
89 Joe Carter .30 .09
90 Tony Castillo .15 .04
91 Brad Cornett RC .15 .04
92 Carlos Delgado .30 .09
93 Alex Gonzalez .15 .04
94 Shawn Green .30 .09
95 Juan Guzman .15 .04
96 Darren Hall .15 .04
97 Pat Hentgen .15 .04
98 Mike Huff .15 .04
99 Randy Knorr .15 .04
100 Al Leiter .30 .09
101 Paul Molitor .50 .15
102 John Olerud .30 .09
103 Dick Schofield .15 .04
104 Ed Sprague .15 .04
105 Dave Stewart .30 .09
106 Todd Stottlemyre .15 .04
107 Devon White .30 .09
108 Woody Williams .15 .04
109 Wilson Alvarez .15 .04
110 Paul Assenmacher .15 .04
111 Jason Bere .15 .04
112 Dennis Cook .15 .04
113 Joey Cora .15 .04
114 Jose DeLeon .15 .04
115 Alex Fernandez .15 .04
116 Julio Franco .30 .09
117 Craig Grebeck .15 .04
118 Ozzie Guillen .15 .04
119 Roberto Hernandez .15 .04
120 Darrin Jackson .15 .04
121 Lance Johnson .15 .04
122 Ron Karkovice .15 .04
123 Mike LaValliere .15 .04
124 Norberto Martin .15 .04
125 Kirk McCaskill .15 .04
126 Jack McDowell .15 .04
127 Tim Raines .30 .09
128 Frank Thomas .75 .23
129 Robin Ventura .30 .09
130 Sandy Alomar Jr. .15 .04
131 Carlos Baerga .15 .04
132 Albert Belle .30 .09
133 Mark Clark .15 .04
134 Alvaro Espinoza .15 .04
135 Jason Grimsley .15 .04
136 Wayne Kirby .15 .04
137 Kenny Lofton .30 .09
138 Albie Lopez .15 .04
139 Dennis Martinez .30 .09
140 Jose Mesa .15 .04
141 Eddie Murray .75 .23
142 Charles Nagy .15 .04
143 Tony Pena .15 .04
144 Eric Plunk .15 .04
145 Manny Ramirez .30 .09
146 Jeff Russell .15 .04
147 Paul Shuey .15 .04
148 Paul Sorrento .15 .04
149 Jim Thome .75 .23
150 Omar Vizquel .30 .09
151 Dave Winfield .30 .09
152 Kevin Appier .30 .09
153 Billy Brewer .15 .04
154 Vince Coleman .15 .04
155 David Cone .30 .09
156 Gary Gaetti .30 .09
157 Greg Gagne .15 .04
158 Tom Gordon .15 .04
159 Mark Gubicza .15 .04
160 Bob Hamelin .15 .04
161 Dave Henderson .15 .04
162 Felix Jose .15 .04
163 Wally Joyner .30 .09
164 Jose Lind .15 .04
165 Mike Macfarlane .15 .04
166 Mike Magnante .15 .04
167 Brent Mayne .15 .04
168 Brian McRae .15 .04
169 Rusty Meacham .15 .04
170 Jeff Montgomery .15 .04
171 Hipolito Pichardo .15 .04
172 Terry Shumpert .15 .04
173 Michael Tucker .15 .04
174 Ricky Bones .15 .04
175 Jeff Cirillo .15 .04
176 Alex Diaz .15 .04
177 Cal Eldred .15 .04
178 Mike Fetters .15 .04
179 Darryl Hamilton .15 .04
180 Brian Harper .15 .04
181 John Jaha .15 .04
182 Pat Listach .15 .04
183 Graeme Lloyd .15 .04
184 Jose Mercedes .15 .04
185 Matt Mieske .15 .04
186 Dave Nilsson .15 .04
187 Jody Reed .15 .04
188 Bob Scanlan .15 .04
189 Kevin Seitzer .15 .04
190 Bill Spiers .15 .04
191 B.J. Surhoff .30 .09
192 Jose Valentin .15 .04
193 Greg Vaughn .30 .09
194 Turner Ward .15 .04
195 Bill Wegman .15 .04
196 Rick Aguilera .15 .04
197 Rich Becker .15 .04
198 Alex Cole .15 .04
199 Marty Cordova .15 .04
200 Steve Dunn .15 .04
201 Scott Erickson .15 .04
202 Mark Guthrie .15 .04
203 Chip Hale .15 .04
204 LaTroy Hawkins .15 .04
205 Denny Hocking .15 .04
206 Chuck Knoblauch .30 .09
207 Scott Leius .15 .04
208 Shane Mack .15 .04
209 Pat Mahomes .15 .04
210 Pat Meares .15 .04
211 Pedro Munoz .15 .04
212 Kirby Puckett .75 .23
213 Jeff Reboulet .15 .04
214 Dave Stevens .15 .04
215 Kevin Tapani .15 .04
216 Matt Walbeck .15 .04
217 Carl Willis .15 .04
218 Brian Anderson .15 .04
219 Chad Curtis .15 .04
220 Chili Davis .30 .09
221 Gary DiSarcina .15 .04
222 Damion Easley .15 .04
223 Jim Edmonds .30 .09
224 Chuck Finley .30 .09
225 Joe Grahe .15 .04
226 Rex Hudler .15 .04
227 Bo Jackson .75 .23
228 Mark Langston .15 .04
229 Phil Leftwich .15 .04
230 Mark Leiter .15 .04
231 Spike Owen .15 .04
232 Bob Patterson .15 .04
233 Troy Percival .30 .09
234 Eduardo Perez .15 .04
235 Tim Salmon .50 .15
236 J.T. Snow .30 .09
237 Chris Turner .15 .04
238 Mark Acre .15 .04
239 Geronimo Berroa .15 .04
240 Mike Bordick .15 .04
241 John Briscoe .15 .04
242 Scott Brosius .30 .09
243 Ron Darling .15 .04
244 Dennis Eckersley .30 .09
245 Brent Gates .15 .04
246 Rickey Henderson .75 .23
247 Stan Javier .15 .04
248 Steve Karsay .15 .04
249 Mark McGwire 2.00 .60
250 Troy Neel .15 .04
251 Steve Ontiveros .15 .04
252 Carlos Reyes .15 .04
253 Ruben Sierra .15 .04
254 Terry Steinbach .15 .04
255 Bill Taylor .15 .04
256 Todd Van Poppel .15 .04
257 Bobby Witt .15 .04
258 Rich Amaral .15 .04
259 Eric Anthony .15 .04
260 Bobby Ayala .15 .04
261 Mike Blowers .15 .04
262 Chris Bosio .15 .04
263 Jay Buhner .30 .09
264 John Cummings .15 .04
265 Tim Davis .15 .04
266 Felix Fermin .15 .04
267 Dave Fleming .15 .04
268 Goose Gossage .30 .09
269 Ken Griffey Jr. 1.25 .35
270 Reggie Jefferson .15 .04
271 Randy Johnson .75 .23
272 Edgar Martinez .50 .15
273 Tino Martinez .50 .15
274 Greg Pirkl .15 .04
275 Bill Risley .15 .04
276 Roger Salkeld .15 .04
277 Luis Sojo .15 .04
278 Mac Suzuki .15 .04
279 Dan Wilson .15 .04
280 Kevin Brown .30 .09
281 Jose Canseco .75 .23
282 Cris Carpenter .15 .04
283 Will Clark .75 .23
284 Jeff Frye .15 .04
285 Juan Gonzalez .75 .23
286 Rick Helling .15 .04
287 Tom Henke .15 .04
288 David Hulse .15 .04
289 Chris James .15 .04
290 Manuel Lee .15 .04
291 Oddibe McDowell .15 .04
292 Dean Palmer .30 .09
293 Roger Pavlik .15 .04
294 Bill Ripken .15 .04
295 Ivan Rodriguez .75 .23
296 Kenny Rogers .30 .09
297 Doug Strange .15 .04
298 Matt Whiteside .15 .04
299 Steve Avery .15 .04
300 Steve Bedrosian .15 .04
301 Rafael Belliard .15 .04
302 Jeff Blauser .15 .04
303 Dave Gallagher .15 .04
304 Tom Glavine .50 .15
305 David Justice .30 .09
306 Mike Kelly .15 .04

307 Roberto Kelly .15 .04
308 Ryan Klesko .30 .09
309 Mark Lemke .15 .04
310 Javier Lopez .30 .09
311 Greg Maddux 1.25 .35
312 Fred McGriff .50 .15
313 Greg McMichael .15 .04
314 Kent Mercker .15 .04
315 Charlie O'Brien .15 .04
316 Jose Oliva .15 .04
317 Terry Pendleton .30 .09
318 John Smoltz .50 .15
319 Mike Stanton .15 .04
320 Tony Tarasco .15 .04
321 Terrell Wade .15 .04
322 Mark Wohlers .15 .04
323 Kurt Abbott .15 .04
324 Luis Aquino .15 .04
325 Bret Barberie .15 .04
326 Ryan Bowen .15 .04
327 Jerry Browne .15 .04
328 Chuck Carr .15 .04
329 Matias Carrillo .15 .04
330 Greg Colbrunn .15 .04
331 Jeff Conine .30 .09
332 Mark Gardner .15 .04
333 Chris Hammond .15 .04
334 Bryan Harvey .15 .04
335 Richie Lewis .15 .04
336 Dave Magadan .15 .04
337 Terry Mathews .15 .04
338 Robb Nen .30 .09
339 Yorkis Perez .15 .04
340 Pat Rapp .15 .04
341 Benito Santiago .30 .09
342 Gary Sheffield .30 .09
343 Dave Weathers .15 .04
344 Moises Alou .30 .09
345 Sean Berry .15 .04
346 Wil Cordero .15 .04
347 Joey Eischen .15 .04
348 Jeff Fassero .15 .04
349 Darrin Fletcher .15 .04
350 Cliff Floyd .30 .09
351 Marquis Grissom .15 .04
352 Butch Henry .15 .04
353 Gil Heredia .15 .04
354 Ken Hill .15 .04
355 Mike Lansing .15 .04
356 Pedro Martinez .75 .23
357 Mel Rojas .15 .04
358 Kirk Rueter .15 .04
359 Tim Scott .15 .04
360 Jeff Shaw .15 .04
361 Larry Walker .50 .15
362 Lenny Webster .15 .04
363 John Wetteland .30 .09
364 Rondell White .30 .09
365 Bobby Bonilla .30 .09
366 Rico Brogna .15 .04
367 Jeromy Burnitz .30 .09
368 John Franco .30 .09
369 Dwight Gooden .50 .15
370 Todd Hundley .15 .04
371 Jason Jacome .15 .04
372 Bobby Jones .15 .04
373 Jeff Kent .30 .09
374 Jim Lindeman .15 .04
375 Josias Manzanillo .15 .04
376 Roger Mason .15 .04
377 Kevin McReynolds .15 .04
378 Joe Orsulak .15 .04
379 Bill Pulsipher .15 .04
380 Bret Saberhagen .30 .09
381 David Segui .15 .04
382 Pete Smith .15 .04
383 Kelly Stinnett .15 .04
384 Ryan Thompson .15 .04
385 Jose Vizcaino .15 .04
386 Toby Borland .15 .04
387 Ricky Bottalico .15 .04
388 Darren Daulton .30 .09
389 Mariano Duncan .15 .04
390 Lenny Dykstra .30 .09
391 Jim Eisenreich .15 .04
392 Tommy Greene .15 .04
393 Dave Hollins .15 .04
394 Pete Incaviglia .15 .04
395 Danny Jackson .15 .04
396 Doug Jones .15 .04
397 Ricky Jordan .15 .04
398 John Kruk .30 .09
399 Mike Lieberthal .30 .09
400 Tony Longmire .15 .04
401 Mickey Morandini .15 .04
402 Bobby Munoz .15 .04
403 Curt Schilling .50 .15
404 Heathcliff Slocumb .15 .04
405 Kevin Stocker .15 .04
406 Fernando Valenzuela .30 .09
407 David West .15 .04
408 Willie Banks .15 .04
409 Jose Bautista .15 .04
410 Steve Buechele .15 .04
411 Jim Bullinger .15 .04
412 Chuck Crim .15 .04
413 Shawon Dunston .15 .04
414 Kevin Foster .15 .04
415 Mark Grace .50 .15
416 Jose Hernandez .15 .04
417 Glenallen Hill .15 .04
418 Brooks Kieschnick .15 .04
419 Derrick May .15 .04
420 Randy Myers .15 .04
421 Dan Plesac .15 .04
422 Karl Rhodes .15 .04
423 Rey Sanchez .15 .04
424 Sammy Sosa 1.25 .35
425 Steve Trachsel .15 .04
426 Rick Wilkins .15 .04
427 Anthony Young .15 .04
428 Eddie Zambrano .15 .04
429 Bret Boone .30 .09
430 Jeff Branson .15 .04
431 Jeff Brantley .15 .04
432 Hector Carrasco .15 .04
433 Brian Dorsett .15 .04
434 Tony Fernandez .15 .04
435 Tim Fortugno .15 .04
436 Erik Hanson .15 .04
437 Thomas Howard .15 .04
438 Kevin Jarvis .15 .04
439 Barry Larkin .75 .23
440 Chuck McElroy .15 .04
441 Kevin Mitchell .15 .04
442 Hal Morris .15 .04
443 Jose Rijo .15 .04
444 John Roper .15 .04
445 Johnny Ruffin .15 .04
446 Deion Sanders .50 .15
447 Reggie Sanders .30 .09
448 Pete Schourek .15 .04
449 John Smiley .15 .04
450 Eddie Taubensee .15 .04
451 Jeff Bagwell .50 .15
452 Kevin Bass .15 .04
453 Craig Biggio .50 .15
454 Ken Caminiti .30 .09
455 Andujar Cedeno .15 .04
456 Doug Drabek .15 .04
457 Tony Eusebio .15 .04
458 Mike Felder .15 .04
459 Steve Finley .30 .09
460 Luis Gonzalez .30 .09
461 Mike Hampton .30 .09
462 Pete Harnisch .15 .04
463 John Hudek .15 .04
464 Todd Jones .15 .04
465 Darryl Kile .30 .09
466 James Mouton .15 .04
467 Shane Reynolds .15 .04
468 Scott Servais .15 .04
469 Greg Swindell .15 .04
470 Dave Veres RC .15 .04
471 Brian Williams .15 .04
472 Jay Bell .30 .09
473 Jacob Brumfield .15 .04
474 Dave Clark .15 .04
475 Steve Cooke .15 .04
476 Midre Cummings .15 .04
477 Mark Dewey .15 .04
478 Tom Foley .15 .04
479 Carlos Garcia .15 .04
480 Jeff King .15 .04
481 Jon Lieber .15 .04
482 Ravelo Manzanillo .15 .04
483 Al Martin .15 .04
484 Orlando Merced .15 .04
485 Danny Miceli .15 .04
486 Denny Neagle .30 .09
487 Lance Parrish .30 .09
488 Don Slaught .15 .04
489 Zane Smith .15 .04
490 Andy Van Slyke .30 .09
491 Paul Wagner .15 .04
492 Rick White .15 .04
493 Luis Alicea .15 .04
494 Rene Arocha .15 .04
495 Rheal Cormier .15 .04
496 Bryan Eversgerd .15 .04
497 Bernard Gilkey .15 .04
498 John Habyan .15 .04
499 Gregg Jefferies .15 .04
500 Brian Jordan .30 .09
501 Ray Lankford .15 .04
502 John Mabry .15 .04
503 Terry McGriff .15 .04
504 Tom Pagnozzi .15 .04
505 Vicente Palacios .15 .04
506 Geronimo Pena .15 .04
507 Gerald Perry .15 .04
508 Rich Rodriguez .15 .04
509 Ozzie Smith 1.25 .35
510 Bob Tewksbury .15 .04
511 Allen Watson .15 .04
512 Mark Whiten .15 .04
513 Todd Zeile .15 .04
514 Dante Bichette .30 .09
515 Willie Blair .15 .04
516 Ellis Burks .30 .09
517 Marvin Freeman .15 .04
518 Andres Galarraga .30 .09
519 Joe Girardi .15 .04
520 Greg W. Harris .15 .04
521 Charlie Hayes .15 .04
522 Mike Kingery .15 .04
523 Nelson Liriano .15 .04
524 Mike Munoz .15 .04
525 David Nied .15 .04
526 Steve Reed .15 .04
527 Kevin Ritz .15 .04
528 Bruce Ruffin .15 .04
529 John Vander Wal .15 .04
530 Walt Weiss .15 .04
531 Eric Young .15 .04
532 Billy Ashley .15 .04
533 Pedro Astacio .15 .04
534 Rafael Bournigal .15 .04
535 Brett Butler .30 .09
536 Tom Candiotti .15 .04
537 Omar Daal .15 .04
538 Delino DeShields .15 .04
539 Darren Dreifort .15 .04
540 Kevin Gross .15 .04
541 Orel Hershiser .30 .09
542 Garey Ingram .15 .04
543 Eric Karros .30 .09
544 Ramon Martinez .15 .04
545 Raul Mondesi .30 .09
546 Chan Ho Park .30 .09
547 Mike Piazza 1.25 .35
548 Henry Rodriguez .15 .04
549 Rudy Seanez .15 .04
550 Ismael Valdes .15 .04
551 Tim Wallach .15 .04
552 Todd Worrell .15 .04
553 Andy Ashby .15 .04
554 Brad Ausmus .15 .04
555 Derek Bell .15 .04
556 Andy Benes .15 .04
557 Phil Clark .15 .04
558 Donnie Elliott .15 .04
559 Ricky Gutierrez .15 .04
560 Tony Gwynn 1.00 .30
561 Joey Hamilton .15 .04
562 Trevor Hoffman .30 .09
563 Luis Lopez .15 .04
564 Pedro A. Martinez .15 .04
565 Tim Mauser .15 .04
566 Phil Plantier .15 .04
567 Bip Roberts .15 .04
568 Scott Sanders .15 .04
569 Craig Shipley .15 .04
570 Jeff Tabaka .15 .04
571 Eddie Williams .15 .04
572 Rod Beck .15 .04
573 Mike Benjamin .15 .04
574 Barry Bonds 2.00 .60
575 Dave Burba .15 .04
576 John Burkett .15 .04
577 Mark Carreon .15 .04
578 Royce Clayton .15 .04
579 Steve Frey .15 .04
580 Bryan Hickerson .15 .04
581 Mike Jackson .15 .04
582 Darren Lewis .15 .04
583 Kirt Manwaring .15 .04
584 Rich Monteleone .15 .04
585 John Patterson .15 .04
586 J.R. Phillips .15 .04
587 Mark Portugal .15 .04
588 Joe Rosselli .15 .04
589 Darryl Strawberry .50 .15
590 Bill Swift .15 .04
591 Robby Thompson .15 .04
592 W.VanLandingham .15 .04
593 Matt Williams .30 .09
594 Checklist .15 .04
595 Checklist .15 .04
596 Checklist .15 .04
597 Checklist .15 .04
598 Checklist .15 .04
599 Checklist .15 .04
600 Checklist .15 .04

1995 Fleer All-Fleer

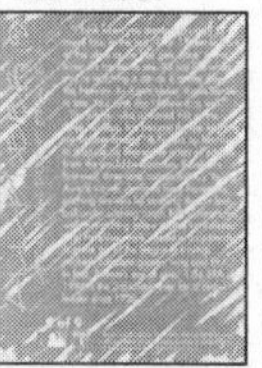

This nine-card standard-size set was available through a 1995 Fleer wrapper offer. Nine of the leading players for each position are featured in this set. The wrapper redemption offer expired on September 30, 1995. The fronts feature the player's photo covering most of the card with a small section on the right set off for the words "All Fleer 9" along with the player's name. The backs feature player information as to why they are among the best in the game.

	Nm-Mt	Ex-Mt
COMPLETE SET (9)	10.00	3.00
1 Mike Piazza	1.25	.35
2 Frank Thomas	.75	.23
3 Roberto Alomar	.75	.23
4 Cal Ripken	2.50	.75
5 Matt Williams	.30	.09
6 Barry Bonds	2.00	.60
7 Ken Griffey Jr.	1.25	.35
8 Tony Gwynn	1.00	.30
9 Greg Maddux	1.25	.35

1995 Fleer All-Rookies

This nine-card standard-size set was available through a Rookie Exchange redemption card randomly inserted in packs. The redemption deadline was 9/30/95. This set features players who made their major league debut in 1995. The fronts have an action photo with a grainy background. The player's name and team are in gold foil at the bottom. Horizontal backs have a player photo the left and minor league highlights to the right.

	Nm-Mt	Ex-Mt
COMPLETE SET (9)	3.00	.90
M1 Edgardo Alfonzo	.50	.15
M2 Jason Bates	.25	.07
M3 Brian Boehringer	.25	.07
M4 Darren Bragg	.25	.07
M5 Brad Clontz	.25	.07
M6 Jim Dougherty	.25	.07
M7 Todd Hollandsworth	.25	.07
M8 Rudy Pemberton	.25	.07
M9 Frank Rodriguez	.25	.07
NNO Exp. All-Rookie Exch.	.25	.07

1995 Fleer All-Stars

Randomly inserted in all pack types at a rate of one in three, this 25-card standard-size set showcases those that participated in the 1994 mid-season classic held in Pittsburgh. Horizontally designed, the fronts contain photos of American League stars with the back protraying the National League player from the same position. On each side, the 1994 All-Star Game logo appears in gold foil as does either the A.L. or N.L. logo in silver foil.

	Nm-Mt	Ex-Mt
COMPLETE SET (25)	10.00	3.00
1 Ivan Rodriguez Mike Piazza	1.50	.45
2 Frank Thomas Gregg Jefferies	1.00	.30
3 Robert Alomar Mariano Duncan	1.00	.30
4 Wade Boggs Matt Williams	.60	.18
5 Cal Ripken Jr. Ozzie Smith	3.00	.90
6 Joe Carter Barry Bonds	2.50	.75
7 Ken Griffey Jr. Tony Gwynn	1.50	.45
8 Kirby Puckett David Justice	1.00	.30
9 Jimmy Key Greg Maddux	1.50	.45
10 Chuck Knoblauch Wil Cordero	.40	.12
11 Scott Cooper Ken Caminiti	.40	.12
12 Will Clark Carlos Garcia	1.00	.30
13 Paul Molitor Jeff Bagwell	.60	.18
14 Travis Fryman Craig Biggio	.60	.18
15 Mickey Tettleton Fred McGriff	.60	.18
16 Kenny Lofton Moises Alou	.40	.12
17 Albert Belle Marquis Grissom	.40	.12
18 Paul O'Neill Dante Bichette	.60	.18
19 David Cone Ken Hill	.40	.12
20 Mike Mussina Doug Drabek	1.00	.30
21 Randy Johnson John Hudek	1.00	.30
22 Pat Hentgen Danny Jackson	.20	.06
23 Wilson Alvarez Rod Beck	.20	.06
24 Lee Smith Randy Myers	.40	.12
25 Jason Bere Doug Jones	.20	.06

1995 Fleer Award Winners

Randomly inserted in all pack types at a rate of one in 24, this six card standard-size set highlights the major award winners of 1994. Card fronts feature action photos that are full-bleed on the right border and have gold border on the left. Within the gold border are the player's name and Fleer Award Winner. The backs contain a photo with text that references 1994 accomplishments.

	Nm-Mt	Ex-Mt
COMPLETE SET (6)	5.00	1.50
1 Frank Thomas	1.25	.35
2 Jeff Bagwell	.75	.23
3 David Cone	.50	.15
4 Greg Maddux	2.00	.60
5 Bob Hamelin	.25	.07
6 Raul Mondesi	.50	.15

1995 Fleer League Leaders

Randomly inserted in all pack types at a rate of one in 12, this 10-card standard-size set features 1994 American and National League leaders in various categories. The horizontal cards have player photos on front and back. The back also has a brief write-up concerning the accomplishment.

	Nm-Mt	Ex-Mt
COMPLETE SET (10)	8.00	2.40
1 Paul O'Neill	.75	.23
2 Ken Griffey Jr.	2.00	.60
3 Kirby Puckett	1.25	.35
4 Jimmy Key	.50	.15
5 Randy Johnson	1.25	.35
6 Tony Gwynn	1.50	.45
7 Matt Williams	.50	.15
8 Jeff Bagwell	.75	.23
9 Greg Maddux Ken Hill	2.00	.60
10 Andy Benes	.25	.07

1995 Fleer Lumber Company

Randomly inserted in retail packs at a rate of one in 24, this standard-size set highlights 10 of the game's top sluggers. Full-bleed card fronts feature an action photo with the Lumber Company logo, which includes the player's name, toward the bottom of the photo. Card

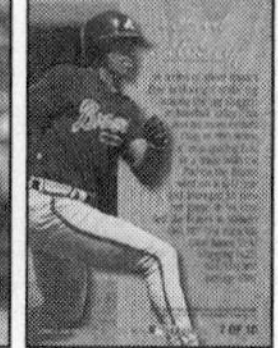

backs have a player photo and woodgrain background with a write-up that highlights individual achievements.

	Nm-Mt	Ex-Mt
COMPLETE SET (10)	30.00	9.00
1 Jeff Bagwell	2.50	.75
2 Albert Belle	1.50	.45
3 Barry Bonds	10.00	3.00
4 Jose Canseco	4.00	1.20
5 Joe Carter	1.50	.45
6 Ken Griffey Jr.	6.00	1.80
7 Fred McGriff	2.50	.75
8 Kevin Mitchell	.75	.23
9 Frank Thomas	4.00	1.20
10 Matt Williams	1.50	.45

1995 Fleer Major League Prospects

Randomly inserted in all pack types at a rate of one in six, this 10-card standard-size set spotlights major league hopefuls. Card fronts feature a player photo with the words "Major League Prospects" serving as part of the background. The player's name and team appear in silver foil at the bottom. The backs have a photo and a write-up on his minor league career.

	Nm-Mt	Ex-Mt
COMPLETE SET (10)	10.00	3.00
1 Garret Anderson	.50	.15
2 James Baldwin	.25	.07
3 Alan Benes	.25	.07
4 Armando Benitez	.50	.15
5 Ray Durham	.50	.15
6 Brian L. Hunter	.25	.07
7 Derek Jeter	4.00	1.20
8 Charles Johnson	.50	.15
9 Orlando Miller	.25	.07
10 Alex Rodriguez	4.00	1.20

1995 Fleer Pro-Visions

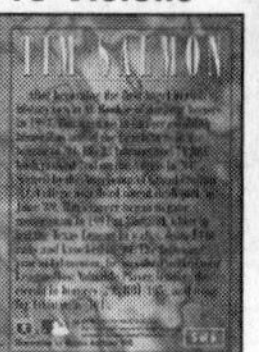

Randomly inserted in all pack types at a rate of one in nine, this six card standard-size set features top players illustrated by Wayne Anthony Still. The colorful artwork on front features the player in a surrealistic setting. The backs offer write-up on the player's previous season.

	Nm-Mt	Ex-Mt
COMPLETE SET (6)	3.00	.90
1 Mike Mussina	.75	.23
2 Raul Mondesi	.30	.09
3 Jeff Bagwell	.50	.15
4 Greg Maddux	1.25	.35
5 Tim Salmon	.50	.15
6 Manny Ramirez	.30	.09

1995 Fleer Rookie Sensations

Randomly inserted in 18-card packs, this 20-card standard-size set features top rookies from the 1994 season. The fronts have full-bleed color photos with the team and player's name in gold foil along the right edge. The backs also have full-bleed color photos along with player information.

	Nm-Mt	Ex-Mt
COMPLETE SET (20)	40.00	12.00
1 Kurt Abbott	2.00	.60
2 Rico Brogna	2.00	.60
3 Hector Carrasco	2.00	.60
4 Kevin Foster	2.00	.60
5 Chris Gomez	2.00	.60
6 Darren Hall	2.00	.60
7 Bob Hamelin	2.00	.60
8 Joey Hamilton	2.00	.60
9 John Hudek	2.00	.60

10 Ryan Klesko 4.00 1.20
11 Javier Lopez 4.00 1.20
12 Matt Mieske 2.00 .60
13 Raul Mondesi 4.00 1.20
14 Manny Ramirez 4.00 1.20
15 Shane Reynolds 2.00 .60
16 Bill Risley 2.00 .60
17 Johnny Ruffin 2.00 .60
18 Steve Trachsel 2.00 .60
19 W.VanLandingham 2.00 .60
20 Rondell White 4.00 1.20

1995 Fleer Team Leaders

Randomly inserted in 12-card hobby packs at a rate of one in 24, this 28-card standard-size set features top players from each team. Each team is represented with card the has the team's leading hitter on one side with the leading pitcher on the other side. The team logo, "Team Leaders" and the player's name are gold foil stamped on front and back.

Nm-Mt Ex-Mt
COMPLETE SET (28) 100.00 30.00
1 Cal Ripken Jr. 25.00 7.50
Mike Mussina
2 Mo Vaughn 15.00 4.50
Roger Clemens
3 Tim Salmon 5.00 1.50
Chuck Finley
4 Frank Thomas 8.00 2.40
Jack McDowell
5 Albert Belle 3.00 .90
Dennis Martinez
6 Cecil Fielder 3.00 .90
Mike Moore
7 Bob Hamelin 3.00 .90
David Cone
8 Greg Vaughn 3.00 .90
Ricky Bones
9 Kirby Puckett 8.00 2.40
Rick Aguilera
10 Don Mattingly 20.00 6.00
Jimmy Key
11 Ruben Sierra 3.00 .90
Dennis Eckersley
12 Ken Griffey Jr. 12.00 3.60
Randy Johnson
13 Jose Canseco 8.00 2.40
Kenny Rogers
14 Joe Carter 3.00 .90
Pat Hentgen
15 David Justice 12.00 3.60
Greg Maddux
16 Sammy Sosa 12.00 3.60
Steve Trachsel
17 Kevin Mitchell 1.50 .45
Jose Rijo
18 Dante Bichette 3.00 .90
Bruce Ruffin
19 Jeff Conine 3.00 .90
Robb Nen
20 Jeff Bagwell 5.00 1.50
Doug Drabek
21 Mike Piazza 12.00 3.60
Ramon Martinez
22 Moises Alou 3.00 .90
Ken Hill
23 Bobby Bonilla 3.00 .90
Bret Saberhagen
24 Darren Daulton 3.00 .90
Danny Jackson
25 Jay Bell 3.00 .90
Zane Smith
26 Gregg Jefferies 1.50 .45
Bob Tewksbury
27 Tony Gwynn 10.00 3.00
Andy Benes
28 Matt Williams 3.00 .90
Rod Beck

1995 Fleer Update

This 200-card standard-size set features many players who were either rookies in 1995 or played for new teams. These cards were issued in either 12-card packs with a suggested retail price of $1.49 or 18-card packs that had a suggested retail price of $2.29. Each Fleer Update pack included one card from several insert sets produced with this product. Hot packs featuring only these insert cards were included one every 72 packs. The full-bleed fronts have two player photos and, atypical of baseball card fronts, biographical information such as height, weight, etc. The backgrounds are multi-colored. The backs are horizontal, have yearly statistics, a photo, and are numbered with the prefix "U". The checklist is arranged alphabetically by team within each league's divisions. Key Rookie Cards in this set include Bobby Higginson and Hideo Nomo.

Nm-Mt Ex-Mt
COMPLETE SET (200) 15.00 4.50
1 Manny Alexander .10 .03
2 Bret Barberie .10 .03
3 Armando Benitez .20 .06
4 Kevin Brown .20 .06
5 Doug Jones .10 .03
6 Sherman Obando .10 .03
7 Andy Van Slyke .20 .06
8 Stan Belinda .10 .03
9 Jose Canseco .50 .15
10 Vaughn Eshelman .10 .03
11 Mike Macfarlane .10 .03
12 Troy O'Leary .10 .03
13 Steve Rodriguez .10 .03
14 Lee Tinsley .10 .03
15 Tim Vanegmond .10 .03
16 Mark Whiten .10 .03
17 Sean Bergman .10 .03
18 Chad Curtis .10 .03
19 John Flaherty .10 .03
20 Bob Higginson RC .50 .15
21 Felipe Lira .10 .03
22 Shannon Penn .10 .03
23 Todd Steverson .10 .03
24 Sean Whiteside .10 .03
25 Tony Fernandez .10 .03
26 Jack McDowell .10 .03
27 Andy Pettitte .30 .09
28 John Wetteland .20 .06
29 David Cone .20 .06
30 Mike Timlin .10 .03
31 Duane Ward .10 .03
32 Jim Abbott .30 .09
33 James Baldwin .10 .03
34 Mike Devereaux .10 .03
35 Ray Durham .20 .06
36 Tim Fortugno .10 .03
37 Scott Ruffcorn .10 .03
38 Chris Sabo .10 .03
39 Paul Assenmacher .10 .03
40 Bud Black .10 .03
41 Orel Hershiser .20 .06
42 Julian Tavarez .10 .03
43 Dave Winfield .20 .06
44 Pat Borders .10 .03
45 Melvin Bunch RC .10 .03
46 Tom Goodwin .10 .03
47 Jon Nunnally .10 .03
48 Joe Randa .10 .03
49 Dilson Torres RC .10 .03
50 Joe Vitiello .10 .03
51 David Hulse .10 .03
52 Scott Karl .10 .03
53 Mark Kiefer .10 .03
54 Derrick May .10 .03
55 Joe Oliver .10 .03
56 Al Reyes RC .10 .03
57 Steve Sparks RC .25 .07
58 Jerald Clark .10 .03
59 Eddie Guardado .20 .06
60 Kevin Maas .10 .03
61 David McCarty .10 .03
62 Brad Radke RC 1.00 .30
63 Scott Stahoviak .10 .03
64 Garret Anderson .20 .06
65 Shawn Boskie .10 .03
66 Mike James .10 .03
67 Tony Phillips .10 .03
68 Lee Smith .20 .06
69 Mitch Williams .10 .03
70 Jim Corsi .10 .03
71 Mark Harkey .10 .03
72 Dave Stewart .20 .06
73 Todd Stottlemyre .10 .03
74 Joey Cora .10 .03
75 Chad Kreuter .10 .03
76 Jeff Nelson .10 .03
77 Alex Rodriguez 1.25 .35
78 Ron Villone .10 .03
79 Bob Wells RC .25 .07
80 Jose Alberro RC .10 .03
81 Terry Burrows .10 .03
82 Kevin Gross .10 .03
83 Wilson Heredia .10 .03
84 Mark McLemore .10 .03
85 Otis Nixon .10 .03
86 Jeff Russell .10 .03
87 Mickey Tettleton .10 .03
88 Bob Tewksbury .10 .03
89 Pedro Borbon .10 .03
90 Marquis Grissom .10 .03
91 Chipper Jones .50 .15
92 Mike Mordecai .10 .03
93 Jason Schmidt .60 .18
94 John Burkett .10 .03
95 Andre Dawson .20 .06
96 Matt Dunbar RC .10 .03
97 Charles Johnson .20 .06
98 Terry Pendleton .20 .06
99 Rich Scheid .10 .03
100 Quilvio Veras .10 .03
101 Bobby Witt .10 .03
102 Eddie Zosky .10 .03
103 Shane Andrews .10 .03
104 Reid Cornelius .10 .03
105 Chad Fonville RC .10 .03
106 Mark Grudzielanek RC .40 .12
107 Roberto Kelly .10 .03
108 Carlos Perez RC .25 .07
109 Tony Tarasco .10 .03
110 Brett Butler .20 .06
111 Carl Everett .20 .06
112 Pete Harnisch .10 .03
113 Doug Henry .10 .03
114 Kevin Lomon RC .10 .03
115 Blas Minor .10 .03
116 Dave Mlicki .10 .03
117 Ricky Otero RC .10 .03
118 Norm Charlton .10 .03
119 Tyler Green .10 .03
120 Gene Harris .10 .03
121 Charlie Hayes .10 .03
122 Gregg Jefferies .10 .03
123 Michael Mimbs RC .10 .03
124 Paul Quantrill .10 .03
125 Frank Castillo .10 .03
126 Brian McRae .10 .03
127 Jaime Navarro .10 .03
128 Mike Perez .10 .03
129 Tanyon Sturtze .10 .03
130 Ozzie Timmons .10 .03
131 John Courtright .10 .03
132 Ron Gant .20 .06
133 Xavier Hernandez .10 .03
134 Brian Hunter .10 .03
135 Benito Santiago .20 .06
136 Pete Smith .10 .03
137 Scott Sullivan .10 .03
138 Derek Bell .10 .03
139 Doug Brocail .10 .03
140 Ricky Gutierrez .10 .03
141 Pedro A.Martinez .10 .03
142 Orlando Miller .10 .03
143 Phil Plantier .10 .03
144 Craig Shipley .10 .03
145 Rich Aude .10 .03
146 J.Christiansen RC .10 .03
147 Freddy Adrian Garcia RC .10 .03
148 Jim Gott .10 .03
149 Mark Johnson RC .25 .07
150 Esteban Loaiza .20 .06
151 Dan Plesac .10 .03
152 Gary Wilson RC .10 .03
153 Allen Battle .10 .03
154 Terry Bradshaw .10 .03
155 Scott Cooper .10 .03
156 Tripp Cromer .10 .03
157 John Frascatore RC .10 .03
158 John Habyan .10 .03
159 Tom Henke .10 .03
160 Ken Hill .10 .03
161 Danny Jackson .10 .03
162 Donovan Osborne .10 .03
163 Tom Urbani .10 .03
164 Roger Bailey .10 .03
165 Jorge Brito RC .10 .03
166 Vinny Castilla .20 .06
167 Darren Holmes .10 .03
168 Roberto Mejia .10 .03
169 Bill Swift .10 .03
170 Mark Thompson .10 .03
171 Larry Walker .30 .09
172 Greg Hansell .10 .03
173 Dave Hansen .10 .03
174 Carlos Hernandez .10 .03
175 Hideo Nomo RC 1.50 .45
176 Jose Offerman .10 .03
177 Antonio Osuna .10 .03
178 Reggie Williams .10 .03
179 Todd Williams .10 .03
180 Andres Berumen .10 .03
181 Ken Caminiti .20 .06
182 Andujar Cedeno .10 .03
183 Steve Finley .20 .06
184 Bryce Florie .10 .03
185 Dustin Hermanson .10 .03
186 Ray Holbert .10 .03
187 Melvin Nieves .10 .03
188 Roberto Petagine .10 .03
189 Jody Reed .10 .03
190 Fernando Valenzuela .20 .06
191 Brian Williams .10 .03
192 Mark Dewey .10 .03
193 Glenallen Hill .10 .03
194 Chris Hook RC .10 .03
195 Terry Mulholland .10 .03
196 Steve Scarsone .10 .03
197 Trevor Wilson .10 .03
198 Checklist .10 .03
199 Checklist .10 .03
200 Checklist .10 .03

1995 Fleer Update Diamond Tribute

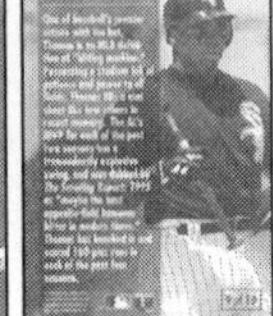

This 10-card standard-size set featuring some of baseball's leading stars were inserted at a stated rate of one in five packs. The cards are numbered in the lower right with an "X" of 10.

Nm-Mt Ex-Mt
COMPLETE SET (10) 8.00 2.40
1 Jeff Bagwell .50 .15
2 Albert Belle .30 .09
3 Barry Bonds 2.00 .60
4 David Cone .30 .09
5 Dennis Eckersley .30 .09
6 Ken Griffey Jr. 1.25 .35
7 Rickey Henderson .75 .23
8 Greg Maddux 1.25 .35
9 Frank Thomas .75 .23
10 Matt Williams .30 .09

1995 Fleer Update Headliners

Inserted one every three packs, this 20-card standard-size set features various major league stars. The cards are numbered in the lower left as "X" of 20.

Nm-Mt Ex-Mt
COMPLETE SET (20) 12.00 3.60
1 Jeff Bagwell .50 .15
2 Albert Belle .30 .09
3 Barry Bonds 2.00 .60
4 Jose Canseco .75 .23
5 Joe Carter .30 .09
6 Will Clark .75 .23
7 Roger Clemens 1.50 .45
8 Lenny Dykstra .30 .09
9 Cecil Fielder .30 .09
10 Juan Gonzalez .75 .23
11 Ken Griffey Jr. 1.25 .35
12 Kenny Lofton .30 .09
13 Greg Maddux 1.25 .35
14 Fred McGriff .50 .15
15 Mike Piazza 1.25 .35
16 Kirby Puckett .75 .23
17 Tim Salmon .50 .15
18 Frank Thomas .75 .23
19 Mo Vaughn .30 .09
20 Matt Williams .30 .09

1995 Fleer Update Rookie Update

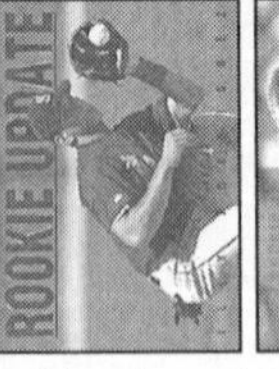
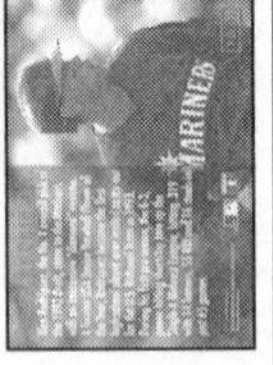

Inserted one in every four packs, this 10-card standard-size set features some of 1995's best rookies. The cards are numbered as "X of 10". Chipper Jones and Hideo Nomo are among the players included in this set.

Nm-Mt Ex-Mt
COMPLETE SET (10) 10.00 3.00
1 Shane Andrews .25 .07
2 Ray Durham .50 .15
3 Shawn Green .50 .15
4 Charles Johnson .50 .15
5 Chipper Jones 1.50 .45
6 Esteban Loaiza .50 .15
7 Hideo Nomo 2.00 .60
8 Jon Nunnally .25 .07
9 Alex Rodriguez 4.00 1.20
10 Julian Tavarez .25 .07

1995 Fleer Update Smooth Leather

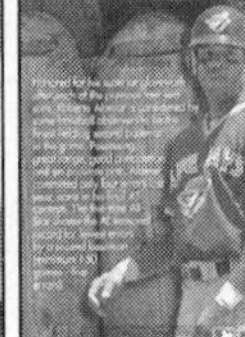

Inserted one every five jumbo packs, this 10-card standard-size set features many leading defensive wizards. The card fronts feature a player photo. Underneath the player photo, is his name along with the words "smooth leather" on the bottom. The right corner features a glove. All of this information as well as the "Fleer 95" logo is in gold print. All of this is on a card with a special leather-like coating. The back features a photo as well as fielding information. The cards are numbered in the lower left as "X of 10" and are sequenced in alphabetical order.

Nm-Mt Ex-Mt
COMPLETE SET (10) 25.00 7.50
1 Roberto Alomar 2.50 .75
2 Barry Bonds 6.00 1.80
3 Ken Griffey Jr. 4.00 1.20
4 Marquis Grissom .50 .15
5 Darren Lewis .50 .15
6 Kenny Lofton 1.00 .30
7 Don Mattingly 6.00 1.80
8 Cal Ripken 8.00 2.40
9 Ivan Rodriguez 2.50 .75
10 Matt Williams 1.00 .30

1995 Fleer Update Soaring Stars

This nine-card standard-size set was inserted one every 36 packs. The fronts feature the player's photo set against a prismatic background of baseballs. The player's name, the "Soaring Stars" logo as well as a star are all printed in gold foil at the bottom. The back has a player photo, his name as well as some career information. The cards are numbered in the upper right "X of 9" and are sequenced in alphabetical order.

Nm-Mt Ex-Mt
COMPLETE SET (9) 25.00 7.50
1 Moises Alou UER 2.50 .75
(says .399 BA in 1994)
2 Jason Bere 1.25 .35
3 Jeff Conine 2.50 .75
4 Cliff Floyd 2.50 .75
5 Pat Hentgen 1.25 .35
6 Kenny Lofton 2.50 .75
7 Raul Mondesi 2.50 .75
8 Mike Piazza 10.00 3.00
9 Tim Salmon 4.00 1.20

1996 Fleer

The 1996 Fleer baseball set consists of 600 standard-size cards issued in one series. Cards

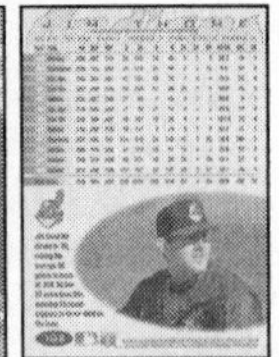

were issued in 11-card packs with a suggested retail price of $1.49. Borderless fronts are matte-finished and have full-color action shots with the player's name, team and position stamped in gold foil. Backs contain a biography and career stats on the top and a full-color head shot with a 1995 synopsis on the bottom. The matte finish on the cards was designed so collectors could have an easier surface for cards to be autographed. Fleer included in each pack a "Thanks a Million" scratch-off game card redeemable for instant-win prizes and a chance to bat for a million-dollar prize in a Major League park. Rookie Cards in this set include Matt Lawton and Mike Sweeney. A Cal Ripken promo was distributed to dealers and hobby media to preview the set.

Nm-Mt Ex-Mt
COMPLETE SET (600) 80.00 24.00
1 Manny Alexander .30 .09
2 Brady Anderson .30 .09
3 Harold Baines .30 .09
4 Armando Benitez .30 .09
5 Bobby Bonilla .30 .09
6 Kevin Brown .30 .09
7 Scott Erickson .30 .09
8 Curtis Goodwin .30 .09
9 Jeffrey Hammonds .30 .09
10 Jimmy Haynes .30 .09
11 Chris Hoiles .30 .09
12 Doug Jones .30 .09
13 Rick Krivda .30 .09
14 Jeff Manto .30 .09
15 Ben McDonald .30 .09
16 Jamie Moyer .30 .09
17 Mike Mussina .75 .23
18 Jesse Orosco .30 .09
19 Rafael Palmeiro .50 .15
20 Cal Ripken 2.50 .75
21 Rick Aguilera .30 .09
22 Luis Alicea .30 .09
23 Stan Belinda .30 .09
24 Jose Canseco .75 .23
25 Roger Clemens 1.50 .45
26 Vaughn Eshelman .30 .09
27 Mike Greenwell .30 .09
28 Erik Hanson .30 .09
29 Dwayne Hosey .30 .09
30 Mike Macfarlane UER .30 .09
31 Tim Naehring .30 .09
32 Troy O'Leary .30 .09
33 Aaron Sele .30 .09
34 Zane Smith .30 .09
35 Jeff Suppan .30 .09
36 Lee Tinsley .30 .09
37 John Valentin .30 .09
38 Mo Vaughn .30 .09
39 Tim Wakefield .30 .09
40 Jim Abbott .50 .15
41 Brian Anderson .30 .09
42 Garret Anderson .30 .09
43 Chili Davis .30 .09
44 Gary DiSarcina .30 .09
45 Damion Easley .30 .09
46 Jim Edmonds .30 .09
47 Chuck Finley .30 .09
48 Todd Greene .30 .09
49 Mike Harkey .30 .09
50 Mike James .30 .09
51 Mark Langston .30 .09
52 Greg Myers .30 .09
53 Orlando Palmeiro .30 .09
54 Bob Patterson .30 .09
55 Troy Percival .30 .09
56 Tony Phillips .30 .09
57 Tim Salmon .50 .15
58 Lee Smith .30 .09
59 J.T. Snow .30 .09
60 Randy Velarde .30 .09
61 Wilson Alvarez .30 .09
62 Luis Andujar .30 .09
63 Jason Bere .30 .09
64 Ray Durham .30 .09
65 Alex Fernandez .30 .09
66 Ozzie Guillen .30 .09
67 Roberto Hernandez .30 .09
68 Lance Johnson .30 .09
69 Matt Karchner .30 .09
70 Ron Karkovice .30 .09
71 Norberto Martin .30 .09
72 Dave Martinez .30 .09
73 Kirk McCaskill .30 .09
74 Lyle Mouton .30 .09
75 Tim Raines .30 .09
76 Mike Sirotka RC .50 .15
77 Frank Thomas .75 .23
78 Larry Thomas .30 .09
79 Robin Ventura .30 .09
80 Sandy Alomar Jr. .30 .09
81 Paul Assenmacher .30 .09
82 Carlos Baerga .30 .09
83 Albert Belle .30 .09
84 Mark Clark .30 .09
85 Alan Embree .30 .09
86 Alvaro Espinoza .30 .09
87 Orel Hershiser .30 .09
88 Ken Hill .30 .09
89 Kenny Lofton .30 .09
90 Dennis Martinez .30 .09
91 Jose Mesa .30 .09
92 Eddie Murray .75 .23
93 Charles Nagy .30 .09
94 Chad Ogea .30 .09
95 Tony Pena .30 .09
96 Herb Perry .30 .09
97 Eric Plunk .30 .09
98 Jim Poole .30 .09
99 Manny Ramirez .30 .09

100 Paul Sorrento .30 .09
101 Julian Tavarez .30 .09
102 Jim Thome .75 .23
103 Omar Vizquel .30 .09
104 Dave Winfield .30 .09
105 Danny Bautista .30 .09
106 Joe Boever .30 .09
107 Chad Curtis .30 .09
108 John Doherty .30 .09
109 Cecil Fielder .30 .09
110 John Flaherty .30 .09
111 Travis Fryman .30 .09
112 Chris Gomez .30 .09
113 Bob Higginson .30 .09
114 Mark Lewis .30 .09
115 Jose Lima .30 .09
116 Felipe Lira .30 .09
117 Brian Maxcy .30 .09
118 C.J. Nitkowski .30 .09
119 Phil Plantier .30 .09
120 Clint Sodowsky .30 .09
121 Alan Trammell .50 .15
122 Lou Whitaker .30 .09
123 Kevin Appier .30 .09
124 Johnny Damon .30 .09
125 Gary Gaetti .30 .09
126 Tom Goodwin .30 .09
127 Tom Gordon .30 .09
128 Mark Gubicza .30 .09
129 Bob Hamelin .30 .09
130 David Howard .30 .09
131 Jason Jacome .30 .09
132 Wally Joyner .30 .09
133 Keith Lockhart .30 .09
134 Brent Mayne .30 .09
135 Jeff Montgomery .30 .09
136 Jon Nunnally .30 .09
137 Juan Samuel .30 .09
138 Mike Sweeney RC 2.00 .60
139 Michael Tucker .30 .09
140 Joe Vitiello .30 .09
141 Ricky Bones .30 .09
142 Chuck Carr .30 .09
143 Jeff Cirillo .30 .09
144 Mike Fetters .30 .09
145 Darryl Hamilton .30 .09
146 David Hulse .30 .09
147 John Jaha .30 .09
148 Scott Karl .30 .09
149 Mark Kiefer .30 .09
150 Pat Listach .30 .09
151 Mark Loretta .30 .09
152 Mike Matheny .30 .09
153 Matt Mieske .30 .09
154 Dave Nilsson .30 .09
155 Joe Oliver .30 .09
156 Al Reyes .30 .09
157 Kevin Seitzer .30 .09
158 Steve Sparks .30 .09
159 B.J. Surhoff .30 .09
160 Jose Valentin .30 .09
161 Greg Vaughn .30 .09
162 Fernando Vina .30 .09
163 Rich Becker .30 .09
164 Ron Coomer .30 .09
165 Marty Cordova .30 .09
166 Chuck Knoblauch .30 .09
167 Matt Lawton RC .40 .12
168 Pat Meares .30 .09
169 Paul Molitor .50 .15
170 Pedro Munoz .30 .09
171 Jose Parra .30 .09
172 Kirby Puckett .75 .23
173 Brad Radke .30 .09
174 Jeff Reboulet .30 .09
175 Rich Robertson .30 .09
176 Frank Rodriguez .30 .09
177 Scott Stahoviak .30 .09
178 Dave Stevens .30 .09
179 Matt Walbeck .30 .09
180 Wade Boggs .50 .15
181 David Cone .30 .09
182 Tony Fernandez .30 .09
183 Joe Girardi .30 .09
184 Derek Jeter 2.00 .60
185 Scott Kamieniecki .30 .09
186 Pat Kelly .30 .09
187 Jim Leyritz .30 .09
188 Tino Martinez .50 .15
189 Don Mattingly 2.00 .60
190 Jack McDowell .30 .09
191 Jeff Nelson .30 .09
192 Paul O'Neill .50 .15
193 Melido Perez .30 .09
194 Andy Pettitte .50 .15
195 Mariano Rivera .50 .15
196 Ruben Sierra .30 .09
197 Mike Stanley .30 .09
198 Darryl Strawberry .50 .15
199 John Wetteland .30 .09
200 Bob Wickman .30 .09
201 Bernie Williams .50 .15
202 Mark Acre .30 .09
203 Geronimo Berroa .30 .09
204 Mike Bordick .30 .09
205 Scott Brosius .30 .09
206 Dennis Eckersley .30 .09
207 Brent Gates .30 .09
208 Jason Giambi .75 .23
209 Rickey Henderson .75 .23
210 Jose Herrera .30 .09
211 Stan Javier .30 .09
212 Doug Johns .30 .09
213 Mark McGwire 2.00 .60
214 Steve Ontiveros .30 .09
215 Craig Paquette .30 .09
216 Ariel Prieto .30 .09
217 Carlos Reyes .30 .09
218 Terry Steinbach .30 .09
219 Todd Stottlemyre .30 .09
220 Danny Tartabull .30 .09
221 Todd Van Poppel .30 .09
222 John Wasdin .30 .09
223 George Williams .30 .09
224 Steve Wojciechowski .30 .09
225 Rich Amaral .30 .09
226 Bobby Ayala .30 .09
227 Tim Belcher .30 .09
228 Andy Benes .30 .09
229 Chris Bosio .30 .09
230 Darren Bragg .30 .09
231 Jay Buhner .30 .09
232 Norm Charlton .30 .09
233 Vince Coleman .30 .09
234 Joey Cora .30 .09
235 Russ Davis .30 .09
236 Alex Diaz .30 .09
237 Felix Fermin .30 .09
238 Ken Griffey Jr. 1.25 .35
239 Sterling Hitchcock .30 .09
240 Randy Johnson .75 .23
241 Edgar Martinez .50 .15
242 Bill Risley .30 .09
243 Alex Rodriguez 1.50 .12
244 Luis Sojo .30 .09
245 Dan Wilson .30 .09
246 Bob Wolcott .30 .09
247 Will Clark .75 .23
248 Jeff Frye .30 .09
249 Benji Gil .30 .09
250 Juan Gonzalez .75 .23
251 Rusty Greer .30 .09
252 Kevin Gross .30 .09
253 Roger McDowell .30 .09
254 Mark McLemore .30 .09
255 Otis Nixon .30 .09
256 Luis Ortiz .30 .09
257 Mike Pagliarulo .30 .09
258 Dean Palmer .30 .09
259 Roger Pavlik .30 .09
260 Ivan Rodriguez .75 .23
261 Kenny Rogers .30 .09
262 Jeff Russell .30 .09
263 Mickey Tettleton .30 .09
264 Bob Tewksbury .30 .09
265 Dave Valle .30 .09
266 Matt Whiteside .30 .09
267 Roberto Alomar .75 .23
268 Joe Carter .30 .09
269 Tony Castillo .30 .09
270 Domingo Cedeno .30 .09
271 Tim Crabtree UER .30 .09
272 Carlos Delgado .30 .09
273 Alex Gonzalez .30 .09
274 Shawn Green .30 .09
275 Juan Guzman .30 .09
276 Pat Hentgen .30 .09
277 Al Leiter .30 .09
278 Sandy Martinez .30 .09
279 Paul Menhart .30 .09
280 John Olerud .30 .09
281 Paul Quantrill .30 .09
282 Ken Robinson .30 .09
283 Ed Sprague .30 .09
284 Mike Timlin .30 .09
285 Steve Avery .30 .09
286 Rafael Belliard .30 .09
287 Jeff Blauser .30 .09
288 Pedro Borbon .30 .09
289 Brad Clontz .30 .09
290 Mike Devereaux .30 .09
291 Tom Glavine .50 .15
292 Marquis Grissom .30 .09
293 Chipper Jones .75 .23
294 David Justice .30 .09
295 Mike Kelly .30 .09
296 Ryan Klesko .30 .09
297 Mark Lemke .30 .09
298 Javier Lopez .30 .09
299 Greg Maddux 1.25 .35
300 Fred McGriff .50 .15
301 Greg McMichael .30 .09
302 Kent Mercker .30 .09
303 Mike Mordecai .30 .09
304 Charlie O'Brien .30 .09
305 Eduardo Perez .30 .09
306 Luis Polonia .30 .09
307 Jason Schmidt .30 .09
308 John Smoltz .50 .15
309 Terrell Wade .30 .09
310 Mark Wohlers .30 .09
311 Scott Bullett .30 .09
312 Jim Bullinger .30 .09
313 Larry Casian .30 .09
314 Frank Castillo .30 .09
315 Shawon Dunston .30 .09
316 Kevin Foster .30 .09
317 Matt Franco .30 .09
318 Luis Gonzalez .30 .09
319 Mark Grace .50 .15
320 Jose Hernandez .30 .09
321 Mike Hubbard .30 .09
322 Brian McRae .30 .09
323 Randy Myers .30 .09
324 Jaime Navarro .30 .09
325 Mark Parent .30 .09
326 Mike Perez .30 .09
327 Rey Sanchez .30 .09
328 Ryne Sandberg 1.25 .35
329 Scott Servais .30 .09
330 Sammy Sosa 1.25 .35
331 Ozzie Timmons .30 .09
332 Steve Trachsel .30 .09
333 Todd Zeile .30 .09
334 Bret Boone .30 .09
335 Jeff Branson .30 .09
336 Jeff Brantley .30 .09
337 Dave Burba .30 .09
338 Hector Carrasco .30 .09
339 Mariano Duncan .30 .09
340 Ron Gant .30 .09
341 Lenny Harris .30 .09
342 Xavier Hernandez .30 .09
343 Thomas Howard .30 .09
344 Mike Jackson .30 .09
345 Barry Larkin .75 .23
346 Darren Lewis .30 .09
347 Hal Morris .30 .09
348 Eric Owens .30 .09
349 Mark Portugal .30 .09
350 Jose Rijo .30 .09
351 Reggie Sanders .30 .09
352 Benito Santiago .30 .09
353 Pete Schourek .30 .09
354 John Smiley .30 .09
355 Eddie Taubensee .30 .09
356 Jerome Walton .30 .09
357 David Wells .30 .09
358 Roger Bailey .30 .09
359 Jason Bates .30 .09
360 Dante Bichette .30 .09
361 Ellis Burks .30 .09
362 Vinny Castilla .30 .09
363 Andres Galarraga .30 .09
364 Darren Holmes .30 .09
365 Mike Kingery .30 .09
366 Curt Leskanic .30 .09
367 Quinton McCracken .30 .09
368 Mike Munoz .30 .09
369 David Nied .30 .09
370 Steve Reed .30 .09
371 Bryan Rekar .30 .09
372 Kevin Ritz .30 .09
373 Bruce Ruffin .30 .09
374 Bret Saberhagen .30 .09
375 Bill Swift .30 .09
376 John Vander Wal .30 .09
377 Larry Walker .50 .15
378 Walt Weiss .30 .09
379 Eric Young .30 .09
380 Kurt Abbott .30 .09
381 Alex Arias .30 .09
382 Jerry Browne .30 .09
383 John Burkett .30 .09
384 Greg Colbrunn .30 .09
385 Jeff Conine .30 .09
386 Andre Dawson .30 .09
387 Chris Hammond .30 .09
388 Charles Johnson .30 .09
389 Terry Mathews .30 .09
390 Robb Nen .30 .09
391 Joe Orsulak .30 .09
392 Terry Pendleton .30 .09
393 Pat Rapp .30 .09
394 Gary Sheffield .30 .09
395 Jesus Tavarez .30 .09
396 Marc Valdes .30 .09
397 Quilvio Veras .30 .09
398 Randy Veres .30 .09
399 Devon White .30 .09
400 Jeff Bagwell .50 .15
401 Derek Bell .30 .09
402 Craig Biggio .50 .15
403 John Cangelosi .30 .09
404 Jim Dougherty .30 .09
405 Doug Drabek .30 .09
406 Tony Eusebio .30 .09
407 Ricky Gutierrez .30 .09
408 Mike Hampton .30 .09
409 Dean Hartgraves .30 .09
410 John Hudek .30 .09
411 Brian L. Hunter .30 .09
412 Todd Jones .30 .09
413 Darryl Kile .30 .09
414 Dave Magadan .30 .09
415 Derrick May .30 .09
416 Orlando Miller .30 .09
417 James Mouton .30 .09
418 Shane Reynolds .30 .09
419 Greg Swindell .30 .09
420 Jeff Tabaka .30 .09
421 Dave Veres .30 .09
422 Billy Wagner .30 .09
423 Donne Wall .30 .09
424 Rick Wilkins .30 .09
425 Billy Ashley .30 .09
426 Mike Blowers .30 .09
427 Brett Butler .30 .09
428 Tom Candiotti .30 .09
429 Juan Castro .30 .09
430 John Cummings .30 .09
431 Delino DeShields .30 .09
432 Joey Eischen .30 .09
433 Chad Fonville .30 .09
434 Greg Gagne .30 .09
435 Dave Hansen .30 .09
436 Carlos Hernandez .30 .09
437 Todd Hollandsworth .30 .09
438 Eric Karros .30 .09
439 Roberto Kelly .30 .09
440 Ramon Martinez .30 .09
441 Raul Mondesi .30 .09
442 Hideo Nomo .75 .23
443 Antonio Osuna .30 .09
444 Chan Ho Park .30 .09
445 Mike Piazza 1.25 .35
446 Felix Rodriguez .30 .09
447 Kevin Tapani .30 .09
448 Ismael Valdes .30 .09
449 Todd Worrell .30 .09
450 Moises Alou .30 .09
451 Shane Andrews .30 .09
452 Yamil Benitez .30 .09
453 Sean Berry .30 .09
454 Wil Cordero .30 .09
455 Jeff Fassero .30 .09
456 Darrin Fletcher .30 .09
457 Cliff Floyd .30 .09
458 Mark Grudzielanek .30 .09
459 Gil Heredia .30 .09
460 Tim Laker .30 .09
461 Mike Lansing .30 .09
462 Pedro J.Martinez .75 .23
463 Carlos Perez .30 .09
464 Curtis Pride .30 .09
465 Mel Rojas .30 .09
466 Kirk Rueter .30 .09
467 F.P. Santangelo .30 .09
468 Tim Scott .30 .09
469 David Segui .30 .09
470 Tony Tarasco .30 .09
471 Rondell White .30 .09
472 Edgardo Alfonzo .30 .09
473 Tim Bogar .30 .09
474 Rico Brogna .30 .09
475 Damon Buford .30 .09
476 Paul Byrd .30 .09
477 Carl Everett .30 .09
478 John Franco .30 .09
479 Todd Hundley .30 .09
480 Butch Huskey .30 .09
481 Jason Isringhausen .30 .09
482 Bobby Jones .30 .09
483 Chris Jones .30 .09
484 Jeff Kent .30 .09
485 Dave Mlicki .30 .09
486 Robert Person .30 .09
487 Bill Pulsipher .30 .09
488 Kelly Stinnett .30 .09
489 Ryan Thompson .30 .09
490 Jose Vizcaino .30 .09
491 Howard Battle .30 .09
492 Toby Borland .30 .09
493 Ricky Bottalico .30 .09
494 Darren Daulton .30 .09
495 Lenny Dykstra .30 .09
496 Jim Eisenreich .30 .09
497 Sid Fernandez .30 .09
498 Tyler Green .30 .09
499 Charlie Hayes .30 .09
500 Gregg Jefferies .30 .09
501 Kevin Jordan .30 .09
502 Tony Longmire .30 .09
503 Tom Marsh .30 .09
504 Michael Mimbs .30 .09
505 Mickey Morandini .30 .09
506 Gene Schall .30 .09
507 Curt Schilling .50 .15
508 Heathcliff Slocumb .30 .09
509 Kevin Stocker .30 .09
510 Andy Van Slyke .30 .09
511 Lenny Webster .30 .09
512 Mark Whiten .30 .09
513 Mike Williams .30 .09
514 Jay Bell .30 .09
515 Jacob Brumfield .30 .09
516 Jason Christiansen .30 .09
517 Dave Clark .30 .09
518 Midre Cummings .30 .09
519 Angelo Encarnacion .30 .09
520 John Ericks .30 .09
521 Carlos Garcia .30 .09
522 Mark Johnson .30 .09
523 Jeff King .30 .09
524 Nelson Liriano .30 .09
525 Esteban Loaiza .30 .09
526 Al Martin .30 .09
527 Orlando Merced .30 .09
528 Dan Miceli .30 .09
529 Ramon Morel .30 .09
530 Denny Neagle .30 .09
531 Steve Parris .30 .09
532 Dan Plesac .30 .09
533 Don Slaught .30 .09
534 Paul Wagner .30 .09
535 John Wehner .30 .09
536 Kevin Young .30 .09
537 Allen Battle .30 .09
538 David Bell .30 .09
539 Alan Benes .30 .09
540 Scott Cooper .30 .09
541 Tripp Cromer .30 .09
542 Tony Fossas .30 .09
543 Bernard Gilkey .30 .09
544 Tom Henke .30 .09
545 Brian Jordan .30 .09
546 Ray Lankford .30 .09
547 John Mabry .30 .09
548 T.J. Mathews .30 .09
549 Mike Morgan .30 .09
550 Jose Oliva .30 .09
551 Jose Oquendo .30 .09
552 Donovan Osborne .30 .09
553 Tom Pagnozzi .30 .09
554 Mark Petkovsek .30 .09
555 Danny Sheaffer .30 .09
556 Ozzie Smith 1.25 .35
557 Mark Sweeney .30 .09
558 Allen Watson .30 .09
559 Andy Ashby .30 .09
560 Brad Ausmus .30 .09
561 Willie Blair .30 .09
562 Ken Caminiti .30 .09
563 Andujar Cedeno .30 .09
564 Glenn Dishman .30 .09
565 Steve Finley .30 .09
566 Bryce Florie .30 .09
567 Tony Gwynn 1.00 .30
568 Joey Hamilton .30 .09
569 Dustin Hermanson .30 .09
570 Trevor Hoffman .30 .09
571 Brian Johnson .30 .09
572 Marc Kroon .30 .09
573 Scott Livingstone .30 .09
574 Marc Newfield .30 .09
575 Melvin Nieves .30 .09
576 Jody Reed .30 .09
577 Bip Roberts .30 .09
578 Scott Sanders .30 .09
579 Fernando Valenzuela .30 .09
580 Eddie Williams .30 .09
581 Rod Beck .30 .09
582 Marvin Benard RC .30 .09
583 Barry Bonds 2.00 .60
584 Jamie Brewington RC .30 .09
585 Mark Carreon .30 .09
586 Royce Clayton .30 .09
587 Shawn Estes .30 .09
588 Glenallen Hill .30 .09
589 Mark Leiter .30 .09
590 Kirt Manwaring .30 .09
591 David McCarty .30 .09
592 Terry Mulholland .30 .09
593 John Patterson .30 .09
594 J.R. Phillips .30 .09
595 Deion Sanders .50 .15
596 Steve Scarsone .30 .09
597 Robby Thompson .30 .09
598 Sergio Valdez .30 .09
599 W.Van Landingham .30 .09
600 Matt Williams .30 .09
P20 Cal Ripken 3.00 .90
Promo

1996 Fleer Tiffany

The Tiffany Collection is a 600-card parallel set that has a special UV coating that replaces the matte finish of the regular cards and silver holographic foil that takes the place of gold foil for lettering. These cards were inserted in regular packs at one card per pack.

	Nm-Mt	Ex-Mt
*STARS: 2X TO 5X BASIC CARDS		
*ROOKIES: 4X TO 10X BASIC CARDS		

1996 Fleer Checklists

Checklist cards were seeded one per six regular packs and have glossy, borderless fronts with full-color shots of the Major League's best.

"Checklist" and the player's name are stamped in gold foil. Backs list the entire rundown of '96 Fleer cards printed in black type on a white background.

	Nm-Mt	Ex-Mt
COMPLETE SET (10)	4.00	1.20
1 Barry Bonds	1.00	.30
2 Ken Griffey Jr.	.60	.18
3 Chipper Jones	.40	.12
4 Greg Maddux	.60	.18
5 Mike Piazza	.60	.18
6 Manny Ramirez	.15	.04
7 Cal Ripken	1.25	.35
8 Frank Thomas	.40	.12
9 Mo Vaughn	.15	.04
10 Matt Williams	.15	.04

1996 Fleer Golden Memories

Randomly inserted at a rate of one in 10 regular packs, this 10-card standard-size set features important highlights of the 1995 season. Fronts have two action shots, one serving as a background, the other a full-color cutout. "Golden Memories" and player's name are printed vertically in white type. Backs contain a biography, player close-up and career statistics.

	Nm-Mt	Ex-Mt
COMPLETE SET (10)	8.00	2.40
1 Albert Belle	.40	.12
2 Barry Bonds Sammy Sosa	1.50	.45
3 Greg Maddux	1.50	.45
4 Edgar Martinez	.60	.18
5 Ramon Martinez	.40	.12
6 Mark McGwire	2.50	.75
7 Eddie Murray	1.00	.30
8 Cal Ripken	3.00	.90
9 Frank Thomas	1.00	.30
10 Alan Trammell Lou Whitaker	.60	.18

1996 Fleer Lumber Company

This retail-exclusive 12-card set was inserted one in every nine packs and features RBI and HR power hitters. The fronts display a color action player cut-out on a wood background with embossed printing. The backs carry a player photo and information about the player.

	Nm-Mt	Ex-Mt
COMPLETE SET (12)	25.00	7.50
1 Albert Belle	1.00	.30
2 Dante Bichette	1.00	.30
3 Barry Bonds	6.00	1.80
4 Ken Griffey Jr.	4.00	1.20
5 Mark McGwire	6.00	1.80
6 Mike Piazza	4.00	1.20
7 Manny Ramirez	1.00	.30
8 Tim Salmon	1.50	.45
9 Sammy Sosa	4.00	1.20
10 Frank Thomas	2.50	.75
11 Mo Vaughn	1.00	.30
12 Matt Williams	1.00	.30

1996 Fleer Postseason Glory

Randomly inserted in regular packs at a rate of one in five, this five-card standard-size set highlights great moments of the 1996 Divisional, League Championship and World Series games. Horizontal, white-bordered fronts feature a player in three full-color action cutouts with black strips on top and bottom. "Post-Season Glory" appears on top and the player's name is printed in silver hologram foil. White-bordered backs are split between a full-color player close-up and a description of his post-season play printed in white type on a black background.

Nm-Mt Ex-Mt
COMPLETE SET (5) 2.00 .60
1 Tom Glavine .25 .07
2 Ken Griffey Jr. .60 .18
3 Orel Hershiser .15 .04
4 Randy Johnson .40 .12
5 Jim Thome .40 .12

1996 Fleer Prospects

Randomly inserted at a rate of one in six regular packs, this ten-card standard-size set focuses on players moving up through the farm system. Borderless fronts have full-color head shots on one-color backgrounds. "Prospect" and the player's name are stamped in silver hologram foil. Backs feature a full-color action shot with a synopsis of talent printed in a green box.

Nm-Mt Ex-Mt
COMPLETE SET (10) 4.00 1.20
1 Yamil Benitez .50 .15
2 Roger Cedeno .50 .15
3 Tony Clark .50 .15
4 Micah Franklin .50 .15
5 Karim Garcia .50 .15
6 Todd Greene .50 .15
7 Alex Ochoa .50 .15
8 Ruben Rivera .50 .15
9 Chris Snopek .50 .15
10 Shannon Stewart 1.00 .30

1996 Fleer Road Warriors

Randomly inserted in regular packs at a rate of one in 13, this 10-card standard-size set focuses on players who thrive on the road. Fronts feature a full-color player cutout set against a winding rural highway background. "Road Warriors" is printed in reverse type with a hazy white border and the player's name is printed in white type underneath. Backs include the player's road stats, biography and a close-up shot.

Nm-Mt Ex-Mt
COMPLETE SET (10) 12.00 3.60
1 Derek Bell .50 .15
2 Tony Gwynn 1.50 .45
3 Greg Maddux 2.00 .60
4 Mark McGwire 3.00 .90
5 Mike Piazza 2.00 .60
6 Manny Ramirez .50 .15
7 Tim Salmon .75 .23
8 Frank Thomas 1.25 .35
9 Mo Vaughn .50 .15
10 Matt Williams .50 .15

1996 Fleer Rookie Sensations

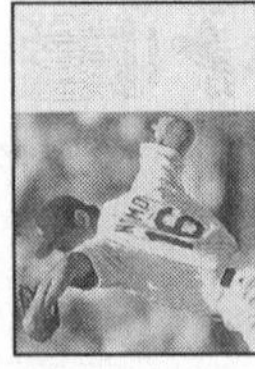

Randomly inserted at a rate of one in 11 regular packs, this 15-card standard-size set highlights 1995's best rookies. Borderless, horizontal fronts have a full-color action shot and a silver hologram strip containing the player's name and team logo. Horizontal backs have full-color head shots with a player profile all printed on a white background.

Nm-Mt Ex-Mt
COMPLETE SET (15) 15.00 4.50
1 Garret Anderson 1.25 .35
2 Marty Cordova 1.25 .35
3 Johnny Damon 1.25 .35
4 Ray Durham 1.25 .35
5 Carl Everett 1.25 .35
6 Shawn Green 1.25 .35
7 Brian L.Hunter 1.25 .35
8 Jason Isringhausen 1.25 .35
9 Charles Johnson 1.25 .35
10 Chipper Jones 3.00 .90
11 John Mabry 1.25 .35
12 Hideo Nomo 3.00 .90
13 Troy Percival 1.25 .35
14 Andy Pettitte 2.00 .60
15 Quilvio Veras 1.25 .35

1996 Fleer Smoke 'n Heat

Randomly inserted at a rate of one in nine regular packs, this 10-card standard-size set celebrates the pitchers with rifle arms and a high strikeout count. Fronts feature a full-color player cutout set against a red flame background. "Smoke 'n Heat" and the player's

name are printed in gold type. Backs feature the pitcher's 1995 numbers, a biography and career stats along with a full-color close-up.

Nm-Mt Ex-Mt
COMPLETE SET (10) 6.00 1.80
1 Kevin Appier .50 .15
2 Roger Clemens 2.50 .75
3 David Cone .50 .15
4 Chuck Finley .50 .15
5 Randy Johnson 1.25 .35
6 Greg Maddux 2.00 .60
7 Pedro Martinez 1.25 .35
8 Hideo Nomo 1.25 .35
9 John Smoltz .75 .23
10 Todd Stottlemyre .50 .15

1996 Fleer Team Leaders

This hobby-exclusive 28-card set was randomly inserted one in every nine packs and features statistical and inspirational leaders. The fronts display color action player cut-out on a foil background of the team name and logo. The backs carry a player portrait and player information.

Nm-Mt Ex-Mt
COMPLETE SET (28) 60.00 18.00
1 Cal Ripken 10.00 3.00
2 Mo Vaughn 1.25 .35
3 Jim Edmonds 1.25 .35
4 Frank Thomas 3.00 .90
5 Kenny Lofton 1.25 .35
6 Travis Fryman 1.25 .35
7 Gary Gaetti 1.25 .35
8 B.J. Surhoff 1.25 .35
9 Kirby Puckett 3.00 .90
10 Don Mattingly 8.00 2.40
11 Mark McGwire 8.00 2.40
12 Ken Griffey Jr. 5.00 1.50
13 Juan Gonzalez 3.00 .90
14 Joe Carter 1.25 .35
15 Greg Maddux 5.00 1.50
16 Sammy Sosa 5.00 1.50
17 Barry Larkin 3.00 .90
18 Dante Bichette 1.25 .35
19 Jeff Conine 1.25 .35
20 Jeff Bagwell 2.00 .60
21 Mike Piazza 5.00 1.50
22 Rondell White 1.25 .35
23 Rico Brogna 1.25 .35
24 Darren Daulton 1.25 .35
25 Jeff King 1.25 .35
26 Ray Lankford 1.25 .35
27 Tony Gwynn 4.00 1.20
28 Barry Bonds 8.00 2.40

1996 Fleer Tomorrow's Legends

Randomly inserted in regular packs at a rate of one in 13, this 10-card set focuses on young talent with bright futures. Multicolored fronts have four panels of art that serve as a background and a full-color player cutout. "Tomorrow's Legends" and player's name are printed in white type at the bottom. Backs include the player's '95 stats, biography and a full-color close-up shot.

Nm-Mt Ex-Mt
COMPLETE SET (10) 10.00 3.00
1 Garret Anderson .75 .23
2 Jim Edmonds .75 .23
3 Brian L.Hunter .75 .23
4 Jason Isringhausen .75 .23
5 Charles Johnson .75 .23
6 Chipper Jones 2.00 .60
7 Ryan Klesko .75 .23
8 Hideo Nomo 2.00 .60
9 Manny Ramirez .75 .23
10 Rondell White .75 .23

1996 Fleer Zone

This 12-card set was randomly inserted one in every 90 packs and features "unstoppable" hitters and "unhittable" pitchers. The fronts display a color action player cut-out printed on holographic foil. The backs carry a player portrait with information as to why they were selected for this set.

Nm-Mt Ex-Mt
COMPLETE SET (12) 100.00 30.00
1 Albert Belle 3.00 .90

2 Barry Bonds 20.00 6.00
3 Ken Griffey Jr. 12.00 3.60
4 Tony Gwynn 10.00 3.00
5 Randy Johnson 8.00 2.40
6 Kenny Lofton 3.00 .90
7 Greg Maddux 12.00 3.60
8 Edgar Martinez 5.00 1.50
9 Mike Piazza 12.00 3.60
10 Frank Thomas 8.00 2.40
11 Mo Vaughn 3.00 .90
12 Matt Williams 3.00 .90

1996 Fleer Update

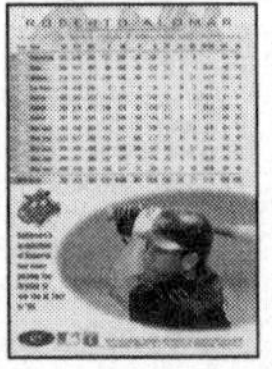

The 1996 Fleer Update set was issued in one series totalling 250 cards. The 11-card packs retailed for $1.49 each. The fronts feature color action player photos. The backs carry complete player stats and a "Did you know?" fact. The cards are grouped alphabetically within teams and checklisted below alphabetically according to teams for each league with AL preceding NL. The set contains the subset: Encore (U211-U245). Notable Rookie Cards include Tony Batista, Mike Cameron, Matt Mantei and Chris Singleton.

Nm-Mt Ex-Mt
COMPLETE SET (250) 30.00 9.00
U1 Roberto Alomar .75 .23
U2 Mike Devereaux .30 .09
U3 Scott McClain RC .30 .09
U4 Roger McDowell .30 .09
U5 Kent Mercker .30 .09
U6 Jimmy Myers RC .30 .09
U7 Randy Myers .30 .09
U8 B.J. Surhoff .30 .09
U9 Tony Tarasco .30 .09
U10 David Wells .30 .09
U11 Wil Cordero .30 .09
U12 Tom Gordon .30 .09
U13 Reggie Jefferson .30 .09
U14 Jose Malave .30 .09
U15 Kevin Mitchell .30 .09
U16 Jamie Moyer .30 .09
U17 Heathcliff Slocumb .30 .09
U18 Mike Stanley .30 .09
U19 George Arias .30 .09
U20 Jorge Fabregas .30 .09
U21 Don Slaught .30 .09
U22 Randy Velarde .30 .09
U23 Harold Baines .30 .09
U24 Mike Cameron RC 1.50 .45
U25 Darren Lewis .30 .09
U26 Tony Phillips .30 .09
U27 Bill Simas .30 .09
U28 Chris Snopek .30 .09
U29 Kevin Tapani .30 .09
U30 Danny Tartabull .30 .09
U31 Julio Franco .30 .09
U32 Jack McDowell .30 .09
U33 Kimera Bartee .30 .09
U34 Mark Lewis .30 .09
U35 Melvin Nieves .30 .09
U36 Mark Parent .30 .09
U37 Eddie Williams .30 .09
U38 Tim Belcher .30 .09
U39 Sal Fasano .30 .09
U40 Chris Haney .30 .09
U41 Mike Macfarlane .30 .09
U42 Jose Offerman .30 .09
U43 Joe Randa .30 .09
U44 Bip Roberts .30 .09
U45 Chuck Carr .30 .09
U46 Bobby Hughes .30 .09
U47 Graeme Lloyd .30 .09
U48 Ben McDonald .30 .09
U49 Kevin Wickander .30 .09
U50 Rick Aguilera .30 .09
U51 Mike Durant .30 .09
U52 Chip Hale .30 .09
U53 LaTroy Hawkins .30 .09
U54 Dave Hollins .30 .09
U55 Roberto Kelly .30 .09
U56 Paul Molitor .50 .15
U57 Dan Naulty .30 .09
U58 Mariano Duncan .30 .09
U59 Andy Fox .30 .09
U60 Joe Girardi .30 .09
U61 Dwight Gooden .50 .15
U62 Jimmy Key .30 .09
U63 Matt Luke .30 .09
U64 Tino Martinez .50 .15
U65 Jeff Nelson .30 .09
U66 Tim Raines .30 .09
U67 Ruben Rivera .30 .09
U68 Kenny Rogers .30 .09
U69 Gerald Williams .30 .09
U70 Tony Batista RC 1.25 .35
U71 Allen Battle .30 .09
U72 Jim Corsi .30 .09
U73 Steve Cox .30 .09
U74 Pedro Munoz .30 .09
U75 Phil Plantier .30 .09
U76 Scott Spiezio .30 .09
U77 Ernie Young .30 .09
U78 Russ Davis .30 .09
U79 Sterling Hitchcock .30 .09
U80 Edwin Hurtado .30 .09
U81 Raul Ibanez RC 1.00 .30
U82 Mike Jackson .30 .09
U83 Ricky Jordan .30 .09
U84 Paul Sorrento .30 .09
U85 Doug Strange .30 .09
U86 M.Brandenburg RC .30 .09
U87 Damon Buford .30 .09
U88 Kevin Elster .30 .09
U89 Darryl Hamilton .30 .09
U90 Ken Hill .30 .09
U91 Ed Vosberg .30 .09
U92 Craig Worthington .30 .09
U93 Tilson Brito RC .30 .09
U94 Giovanni Carrara RC .30 .09
U95 Felipe Crespo .30 .09
U96 Erik Hanson .30 .09
U97 Marty Janzen RC .30 .09
U98 Otis Nixon .30 .09
U99 Charlie O'Brien .30 .09
U100 Robert Perez .30 .09
U101 Paul Quantrill .30 .09
U102 Bill Risley .30 .09
U103 Juan Samuel .30 .09
U104 Jermaine Dye .30 .09
U105 W.Monds RC .30 .09
U106 Dwight Smith .30 .09
U107 Jerome Walton .30 .09
U108 Terry Adams .30 .09
U109 Leo Gomez .30 .09
U110 Robin Jennings .30 .09
U111 Doug Jones .30 .09
U112 Brooks Kieschnick .30 .09
U113 Dave Magadan .30 .09
U114 Jason Maxwell RC .30 .09
U115 Rodney Myers RC .30 .09
U116 Eric Anthony .30 .09
U117 Vince Coleman .30 .09
U118 Eric Davis .30 .09
U119 Steve Gibralter .30 .09
U120 Curtis Goodwin .30 .09
U121 Willie Greene .30 .09
U122 Mike Kelly .30 .09
U123 Marcus Moore .30 .09
U124 Chad Mottola .30 .09
U125 Chris Sabo .30 .09
U126 Roger Salkeld .30 .09
U127 Pedro Castellano .30 .09
U128 Trenidad Hubbard .30 .09
U129 Jayhawk Owens .30 .09
U130 Jeff Reed .30 .09
U131 Kevin Brown .30 .09
U132 Al Leiter .30 .09
U133 Matt Mantei RC .40 .12
U134 Dave Weathers .30 .09
U135 Devon White .30 .09
U136 Bob Abreu .30 .09
U137 Sean Berry .30 .09
U138 Doug Brocail .30 .09
U139 Richard Hidalgo .30 .09
U140 Alvin Morman .30 .09
U141 Mike Blowers .30 .09
U142 Roger Cedeno .30 .09
U143 Greg Gagne .30 .09
U144 Karim Garcia .30 .09
U145 Wilton Guerrero RC .40 .12
U146 Israel Alcantara RC .30 .09
U147 Omar Daal .30 .09
U148 Ryan McGuire .30 .09
U149 Sherman Obando .30 .09
U150 Jose Paniagua .30 .09
U151 Henry Rodriguez .30 .09
U152 Andy Stankiewicz .30 .09
U153 Dave Veres .30 .09
U154 Juan Acevedo .30 .09
U155 Mark Clark .30 .09
U156 Bernard Gilkey .30 .09
U157 Pete Harnisch .30 .09
U158 Lance Johnson .30 .09
U159 Brent Mayne .30 .09
U160 Rey Ordonez .30 .09
U161 Kevin Roberson .30 .09
U162 Paul Wilson .30 .09
U163 David Doster RC .30 .09
U164 Mike Grace RC .30 .09
U165 Rich Hunter RC .30 .09
U166 Pete Incaviglia .30 .09
U167 Mike Lieberthal .30 .09
U168 Terry Mulholland .30 .09
U169 Ken Ryan .30 .09
U170 Benito Santiago .30 .09
U171 Kevin Sefcik RC .30 .09
U172 Lee Tinsley .30 .09
U173 Todd Zeile .30 .09
U174 F.Cordova RC .40 .12
U175 Danny Darwin .30 .09
U176 Charlie Hayes .30 .09
U177 Jason Kendall .30 .09
U178 Mike Kingery .30 .09
U179 Jon Lieber .30 .09
U180 Zane Smith .30 .09
U181 Luis Alicea .30 .09
U182 Cory Bailey .30 .09
U183 Andy Benes .30 .09
U184 Pat Borders .30 .09
U185 Mike Busby RC .30 .09
U186 Royce Clayton .30 .09
U187 Dennis Eckersley .30 .09
U188 Gary Gaetti .30 .09
U189 Ron Gant .30 .09
U190 Aaron Holbert .30 .09
U191 Willie McGee .30 .09
U192 Miguel Mejia RC .30 .09
U193 Jeff Parrett .30 .09
U194 Todd Stottlemyre .30 .09
U195 Sean Bergman .30 .09
U196 Archi Cianfrocco .30 .09
U197 Rickey Henderson .75 .23
U198 Wally Joyner .30 .09
U199 Craig Shipley .30 .09
U200 Bob Tewksbury .30 .09
U201 Tim Worrell .30 .09
U202 Rich Aurilia RC 1.25 .35
U203 Doug Creek .30 .09
U204 Shawon Dunston .30 .09
U205 O.Fernandez RC .30 .09
U206 Mark Gardner .30 .09
U207 Stan Javier .30 .09
U208 Marcus Jensen .30 .09
U209 Chris Singleton RC .40 .12
U210 Allen Watson .30 .09
U211 Jeff Bagwell ENC .50 .15
U212 Derek Bell ENC .30 .09
U213 Albert Belle ENC .30 .09
U214 Wade Boggs ENC .50 .15
U215 Barry Bonds ENC 2.00 .60
U216 Jose Canseco ENC .75 .23
U217 Marty Cordova ENC .30 .09
U218 Jim Edmonds ENC .30 .09
U219 Cecil Fielder ENC .30 .09
U220 A.Galarraga ENC .30 .09
U221 Juan Gonzalez ENC .75 .23
U222 Mark Grace ENC .50 .15
U223 Ken Griffey Jr. ENC 1.25 .35
U224 Tony Gwynn ENC 1.00 .30
U225 J. Isringhausen ENC .30 .09
U226 Derek Jeter ENC 2.00 .60
U227 Randy Johnson ENC .75 .23
U228 Chipper Jones ENC .75 .23
U229 Ryan Klesko ENC .30 .09
U230 Barry Larkin ENC .75 .23
U231 Kenny Lofton ENC .30 .09
U232 Greg Maddux ENC 1.25 .35
U233 Raul Mondesi ENC .30 .09
U234 Hideo Nomo ENC .75 .23
U235 Mike Piazza ENC 1.25 .35
U236 Manny Ramirez ENC .30 .09
U237 Cal Ripken ENC 1.50 .45
U238 Tim Salmon ENC .50 .15
U239 Ryne Sandberg ENC 1.25 .35
U240 Reggie Sanders ENC .30 .09
U241 Gary Sheffield ENC .30 .09
U242 Sammy Sosa ENC 1.25 .35
U243 Frank Thomas ENC .75 .23
U244 Mo Vaughn ENC .30 .09
U245 Matt Williams ENC .30 .09
U246 Barry Bonds CL 1.00 .30
U247 Ken Griffey Jr. CL .75 .23
U248 Rey Ordonez CL .30 .09
U249 Ryne Sandberg CL .75 .23
U250 Frank Thomas CL .50 .15

1996 Fleer Update Tiffany

Inserted one per pack, these 250 cards parallel the basic Fleer Update cards. Unlike the basic cards, Tiffany inserts feature a layer of UV coating and a special logo on each card front.

Nm-Mt Ex-Mt
COMPLETE SET (250) 120.00 36.00
*STARS: 1.25X TO 3X BASIC CARDS .
*ROOKIES: 2X TO 5X BASIC CARDS ..

1996 Fleer Update Diamond Tribute

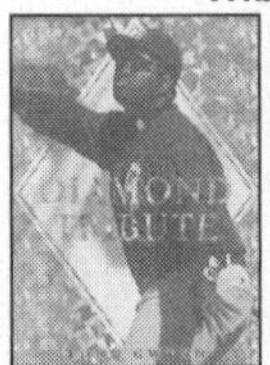

Randomly inserted in packs at a rate of one in 100, this 10-card set spotlights future Hall of Famers with holographic foils in a diamond design.

Nm-Mt Ex-Mt
COMPLETE SET (10) 150.00 45.00
1 Wade Boggs 6.00 1.80
2 Barry Bonds 25.00 7.50
3 Ken Griffey Jr. 15.00 4.50
4 Tony Gwynn 12.00 3.60
5 Rickey Henderson 10.00 3.00
6 Greg Maddux 15.00 4.50
7 Eddie Murray 10.00 3.00
8 Cal Ripken 30.00 9.00
9 Ozzie Smith 15.00 4.50
10 Frank Thomas 10.00 3.00

1996 Fleer Update Headliners

Randomly inserted exclusively in retail packs at a rate of one in 20, cards from this 20-card set feature raised textured printing. The fronts carry color action player photos with the word "headliner" running continuously across the background.

Nm-Mt Ex-Mt
COMPLETE SET (20) 40.00 12.00
1 Roberto Alomar 2.00 .60
2 Jeff Bagwell 1.25 .35
3 Albert Belle .75 .23
4 Barry Bonds 5.00 1.50
5 Cecil Fielder .75 .23
6 Juan Gonzalez 2.00 .60
7 Ken Griffey Jr. 3.00 .90
8 Tony Gwynn 2.50 .75
9 Randy Johnson 2.00 .60
10 Chipper Jones 2.00 .60
11 Ryan Klesko .75 .23
12 Kenny Lofton .75 .23
13 Greg Maddux 3.00 .90
14 Hideo Nomo 2.00 .60
15 Mike Piazza 3.00 .90
16 Manny Ramirez .75 .23
17 Cal Ripken 6.00 1.80
18 Tim Salmon 1.25 .35
19 Frank Thomas 2.00 .60
20 Matt Williams .75 .23

1996 Fleer Update New Horizons

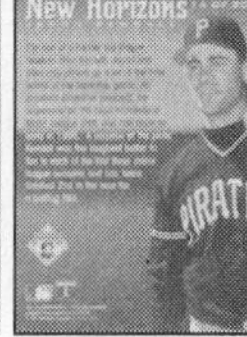

Randomly inserted in hobby packs only at a rate of one in five, this 20-card set features 1996 rookies and prospects. The fronts carry player action color photos printed on foil cards. The backs display a player portrait and information about the player.

	Nm-Mt	Ex-Mt
COMPLETE SET (20)	15.00	4.50
1 Bob Abreu	.50	.15
2 George Arias	.50	.15
3 Tony Batista	2.00	.60
4 Steve Cox	.50	.15
5 Jermaine Dye	.50	.15
6 Andy Fox	.50	.15
7 Mike Grace	.50	.15
8 Todd Greene	.50	.15
9 Wilton Guerrero	.50	.15
10 Richard Hidalgo	.50	.15
11 Raul Ibanez	2.00	.60
12 Robin Jennings	.50	.15
13 Marcus Jensen	.50	.15
14 Jason Kendall	.50	.15
15 Jason Maxwell	.50	.15
16 Ryan McGuire	.50	.15
17 Miguel Mejia	.50	.15
18 Wonderful Monds	.50	.15
19 Rey Ordonez	.50	.15
20 Paul Wilson	.50	.15

1996 Fleer Update Smooth Leather

Randomly inserted in packs at a rate of one in five, this 10-card set features defensive stars. The fronts display color player photos and gold foil printing. The backs carry a player portrait and information about why the player was selected for this set.

	Nm-Mt	Ex-Mt
COMPLETE SET (10)	10.00	3.00
1 Roberto Alomar	1.00	.30
2 Barry Bonds	2.50	.75
3 Will Clark	1.00	.30
4 Ken Griffey Jr.	1.50	.45
5 Kenny Lofton	.40	.12
6 Greg Maddux	1.50	.45
7 Raul Mondesi	.40	.12
8 Rey Ordonez	.40	.12
9 Cal Ripken	3.00	.90
10 Matt Williams	.40	.12

1996 Fleer Update Soaring Stars

Randomly inserted in packs at a rate of one in 11, this 10-card set features 10 of the hottest young players. The fronts carry color player cut-outs on a background of soaring baseballs in etched foil. The backs display another player photo on the same background with player information.

	Nm-Mt	Ex-Mt
COMPLETE SET (10)	25.00	7.50
1 Jeff Bagwell	1.25	.35
2 Barry Bonds	5.00	1.50
3 Juan Gonzalez	2.00	.60
4 Ken Griffey Jr.	3.00	.90
5 Chipper Jones	2.00	.60
6 Greg Maddux	3.00	.90
7 Mike Piazza	3.00	.90
8 Manny Ramirez	.75	.23
9 Frank Thomas	2.00	.60
10 Matt Williams	.75	.23

1997 Fleer

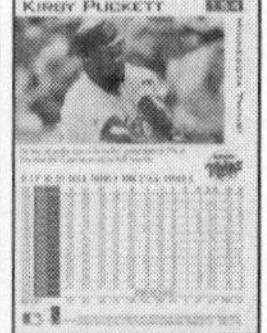

The 1997 Fleer set was issued in two series totaling 761 cards and distributed in 10-card packs with a suggested retail price of $1.49. The fronts feature color action player photos with a matte finish and gold foil printing. The backs carry another player photo with player information and career statistics. Cards 491-500 are a Checklist subset of Series one and feature black-and-white or sepia tone photos of big-name players. Series two contains the following subsets: Encore (696-720) which are redesigned cards of the big-name players from Series one, and Checklists (721-748). Cards 749 and 750 are expansion team logo cards with the insert checklists on the backs. Many dealers believe that cards numbered 751-761 were shortprinted. An Andruw Jones autographed Circa card numbered to 200 was also randomly inserted into packs. Rookie Cards in this set include Jose Cruz Jr., Brian Giles and Fernando Tatis.

	Nm-Mt	Ex-Mt
COMPLETE SET (761)	100.00	30.00
COMP. SERIES 1 (500)	60.00	18.00
COMP. SERIES 2 (261)	40.00	12.00
COMMON CARD (1-750)	.30	.09
COMMON CARD (751-761)	.50	.15
1 Roberto Alomar	.75	.23
2 Brady Anderson	.30	.09
3 Bobby Bonilla	.30	.09
4 Rocky Coppinger	.30	.09
5 Cesar Devarez	.30	.09
6 Scott Erickson	.30	.09
7 Jeffrey Hammonds	.30	.09
8 Chris Hoiles	.30	.09
9 Eddie Murray	.75	.23
10 Mike Mussina	.75	.23
11 Randy Myers	.30	.09
12 Rafael Palmeiro	.50	.15
13 Cal Ripken	2.50	.75
14 B.J. Surhoff	.30	.09
15 David Wells	.30	.09
16 Todd Zeile	.30	.09
17 Darren Bragg	.30	.09
18 Jose Canseco	.75	.23
19 Roger Clemens	1.50	.45
20 Wil Cordero	.30	.09
21 Jeff Frye	.30	.09
22 Nomar Garciaparra	1.25	.35
23 Tom Gordon	.30	.09
24 Mike Greenwell	.30	.09
25 Reggie Jefferson	.30	.09
26 Jose Malave	.30	.09
27 Tim Naehring	.30	.09
28 Troy O'Leary	.30	.09
29 Heathcliff Slocumb	.30	.09
30 Mike Stanley	.30	.09
31 John Valentin	.30	.09
32 Mo Vaughn	.30	.09
33 Tim Wakefield	.30	.09
34 Garret Anderson	.30	.09
35 George Arias	.30	.09
36 Shawn Boskie	.30	.09
37 Chili Davis	.30	.09
38 Jason Dickson	.30	.09
39 Gary DiSarcina	.30	.09
40 Jim Edmonds	.30	.09
41 Darin Erstad	.30	.09
42 Jorge Fabregas	.30	.09
43 Chuck Finley	.30	.09
44 Todd Greene	.30	.09
45 Mike Holtz	.30	.09
46 Rex Hudler	.30	.09
47 Mike James	.30	.09
48 Mark Langston	.30	.09
49 Troy Percival	.30	.09
50 Tim Salmon	.50	.15
51 Jeff Schmidt	.30	.09
52 J.T. Snow	.30	.09
53 Randy Velarde	.30	.09
54 Wilson Alvarez	.30	.09
55 Harold Baines	.30	.09
56 James Baldwin	.30	.09
57 Jason Bere	.30	.09
58 Mike Cameron	.30	.09
59 Ray Durham	.30	.09
60 Alex Fernandez	.30	.09
61 Ozzie Guillen	.30	.09
62 Roberto Hernandez	.30	.09
63 Ron Karkovice	.30	.09
64 Darren Lewis	.30	.09
65 Dave Martinez	.30	.09
66 Lyle Mouton	.30	.09
67 Greg Norton	.30	.09
68 Tony Phillips	.30	.09
69 Chris Snopek	.30	.09
70 Kevin Tapani	.30	.09
71 Danny Tartabull	.30	.09
72 Frank Thomas	.75	.23
73 Robin Ventura	.30	.09
74 Sandy Alomar Jr.	.30	.09
75 Albert Belle	.30	.09
76 Mark Carreon	.30	.09
77 Julio Franco	.30	.09
78 Brian Giles RC	1.50	.45
79 Orel Hershiser	.30	.09
80 Kenny Lofton	.30	.09
81 Dennis Martinez	.30	.09
82 Jack McDowell	.30	.09
83 Jose Mesa	.30	.09
84 Charles Nagy	.30	.09
85 Chad Ogea	.30	.09
86 Eric Plunk	.30	.09
87 Manny Ramirez	.30	.09
88 Kevin Seitzer	.30	.09
89 Julian Tavarez	.30	.09
90 Jim Thome	.75	.23
91 Jose Vizcaino	.30	.09
92 Omar Vizquel	.30	.09
93 Brad Ausmus	.30	.09
94 Kimera Bartee	.30	.09
95 Raul Casanova	.30	.09
96 Tony Clark	.30	.09
97 John Cummings	.30	.09
98 Travis Fryman	.30	.09
99 Bob Higginson	.30	.09
100 Mark Lewis	.30	.09
101 Felipe Lira	.30	.09
102 Phil Nevin	.30	.09
103 Melvin Nieves	.30	.09
104 Curtis Pride	.30	.09
105 A.J. Sager	.30	.09
106 Ruben Sierra	.30	.09
107 Justin Thompson	.30	.09
108 Alan Trammell	.50	.15
109 Kevin Appier	.30	.09
110 Tim Belcher	.30	.09
111 Jaime Bluma	.30	.09
112 Johnny Damon	.30	.09
113 Tom Goodwin	.30	.09
114 Chris Haney	.30	.09
115 Keith Lockhart	.30	.09
116 Mike Macfarlane	.30	.09
117 Jeff Montgomery	.30	.09
118 Jose Offerman	.30	.09
119 Craig Paquette	.30	.09
120 Joe Randa	.30	.09
121 Bip Roberts	.30	.09
122 Jose Rosado	.30	.09
123 Mike Sweeney	.30	.09
124 Michael Tucker	.30	.09
125 Jeromy Burnitz	.30	.09
126 Jeff Cirillo	.30	.09
127 Jeff D'Amico	.30	.09
128 Mike Fetters	.30	.09
129 John Jaha	.30	.09
130 Scott Karl	.30	.09
131 Jesse Levis	.30	.09
132 Mark Loretta	.30	.09
133 Mike Matheny	.30	.09
134 Ben McDonald	.30	.09
135 Matt Mieske	.30	.09
136 Marc Newfield	.30	.09
137 Dave Nilsson	.30	.09
138 Jose Valentin	.30	.09
139 Fernando Vina	.30	.09
140 Bob Wickman	.30	.09
141 Gerald Williams	.30	.09
142 Rick Aguilera	.30	.09
143 Rich Becker	.30	.09
144 Ron Coomer	.30	.09
145 Marty Cordova	.30	.09
146 Roberto Kelly	.30	.09
147 Chuck Knoblauch	.30	.09
148 Matt Lawton	.30	.09
149 Pat Meares	.30	.09
150 Travis Miller	.30	.09
151 Paul Molitor	.50	.15
152 Greg Myers	.30	.09
153 Dan Naulty	.30	.09
154 Kirby Puckett	.75	.23
155 Brad Radke	.30	.09
156 Frank Rodriguez	.30	.09
157 Scott Stahoviak	.30	.09
158 Dave Stevens	.30	.09
159 Matt Walbeck	.30	.09
160 Todd Walker	.30	.09
161 Wade Boggs	.50	.15
162 David Cone	.30	.09
163 Mariano Duncan	.30	.09
164 Cecil Fielder	.30	.09
165 Joe Girardi	.30	.09
166 Dwight Gooden	.50	.15
167 Charlie Hayes	.30	.09
168 Derek Jeter	2.00	.60
169 Jimmy Key	.30	.09
170 Jim Leyritz	.30	.09
171 Tino Martinez	.50	.15
172 Ramiro Mendoza RC	.40	.12
173 Jeff Nelson	.30	.09
174 Paul O'Neill	.50	.15
175 Andy Pettitte	.50	.15
176 Mariano Rivera	.50	.15
177 Ruben Rivera	.30	.09
178 Kenny Rogers	.30	.09
179 Darryl Strawberry	.50	.15
180 John Wetteland	.30	.09
181 Bernie Williams	.50	.15
182 Willie Adams	.30	.09
183 Tony Batista	.30	.09
184 Geronimo Berroa	.30	.09
185 Mike Bordick	.30	.09
186 Scott Brosius	.30	.09
187 Bobby Chouinard	.30	.09
188 Jim Corsi	.30	.09
189 Brent Gates	.30	.09
190 Jason Giambi	.75	.23
191 Jose Herrera	.30	.09
192 Damon Mashore	.30	.09
193 Mark McGwire	2.00	.60
194 Mike Mohler	.30	.09
195 Scott Spiezio	.30	.09
196 Terry Steinbach	.30	.09
197 Bill Taylor	.30	.09
198 John Wasdin	.30	.09
199 Steve Wojciechowski	.30	.09
200 Ernie Young	.30	.09
201 Rich Amaral	.30	.09
202 Jay Buhner	.30	.09
203 Norm Charlton	.30	.09
204 Joey Cora	.30	.09
205 Russ Davis	.30	.09
206 Ken Griffey Jr.	1.25	.35
207 Sterling Hitchcock	.30	.09
208 Brian Hunter	.30	.09
209 Raul Ibanez	.30	.09
210 Randy Johnson	.75	.23
211 Edgar Martinez	.50	.15
212 Jamie Moyer	.30	.09
213 Alex Rodriguez	1.25	.35
214 Paul Sorrento	.30	.09
215 Matt Wagner	.30	.09
216 Bob Wells	.30	.09
217 Dan Wilson	.30	.09
218 Damon Buford	.30	.09
219 Will Clark	.75	.23
220 Kevin Elster	.30	.09
221 Juan Gonzalez	.75	.23
222 Rusty Greer	.30	.09
223 Kevin Gross	.30	.09
224 Darryl Hamilton	.30	.09
225 Mike Henneman	.30	.09
226 Ken Hill	.30	.09
227 Mark McLemore	.30	.09
228 Darren Oliver	.30	.09
229 Dean Palmer	.30	.09
230 Roger Pavlik	.30	.09
231 Ivan Rodriguez	.75	.23
232 Mickey Tettleton	.30	.09
233 Bobby Witt	.30	.09
234 Jacob Brumfield	.30	.09
235 Joe Carter	.30	.09
236 Tim Crabtree	.30	.09
237 Carlos Delgado	.30	.09
238 Huck Flener	.30	.09
239 Alex Gonzalez	.30	.09
240 Shawn Green	.30	.09
241 Juan Guzman	.30	.09
242 Pat Hentgen	.30	.09
243 Marty Janzen	.30	.09
244 Sandy Martinez	.30	.09
245 Otis Nixon	.30	.09
246 Charlie O'Brien	.30	.09
247 John Olerud	.30	.09
248 Robert Perez	.30	.09
249 Ed Sprague	.30	.09
250 Mike Timlin	.30	.09
251 Steve Avery	.30	.09
252 Jeff Blauser	.30	.09
253 Brad Clontz	.30	.09
254 Jermaine Dye	.30	.09
255 Tom Glavine	.50	.15
256 Marquis Grissom	.30	.09
257 Andruw Jones	.30	.09
258 Chipper Jones	.75	.23
259 David Justice	.30	.09
260 Ryan Klesko	.30	.09
261 Mark Lemke	.30	.09
262 Javier Lopez	.30	.09
263 Greg Maddux	1.25	.35
264 Fred McGriff	.50	.15
265 Greg McMichael	.30	.09
266 Denny Neagle	.30	.09
267 Terry Pendleton	.30	.09
268 Eddie Perez	.30	.09
269 John Smoltz	.50	.15
270 Terrell Wade	.30	.09
271 Mark Wohlers	.30	.09
272 Terry Adams	.30	.09
273 Brant Brown	.30	.09
274 Leo Gomez	.30	.09
275 Luis Gonzalez	.30	.09
276 Mark Grace	.50	.15
277 Tyler Houston	.30	.09
278 Robin Jennings	.30	.09
279 Brooks Kieschnick	.30	.09
280 Brian McRae	.30	.09
281 Jaime Navarro	.30	.09
282 Ryne Sandberg	1.25	.35
283 Scott Servais	.30	.09
284 Sammy Sosa	1.25	.35
285 Dave Swartzbaugh	.30	.09
286 Amaury Telemaco	.30	.09
287 Steve Trachsel	.30	.09
288 Pedro Valdes	.30	.09
289 Turk Wendell	.30	.09
290 Bret Boone	.30	.09
291 Jeff Branson	.30	.09
292 Jeff Brantley	.30	.09
293 Eric Davis	.30	.09
294 Willie Greene	.30	.09
295 Thomas Howard	.30	.09
296 Barry Larkin	.75	.23
297 Kevin Mitchell	.30	.09
298 Hal Morris	.30	.09
299 Chad Mottola	.30	.09
300 Joe Oliver	.30	.09
301 Mark Portugal	.30	.09
302 Roger Salkeld	.30	.09
303 Reggie Sanders	.30	.09
304 Pete Schourek	.30	.09
305 John Smiley	.30	.09
306 Eddie Taubensee	.30	.09
307 Dante Bichette	.30	.09
308 Ellis Burks	.30	.09
309 Vinny Castilla	.30	.09
310 Andres Galarraga	.30	.09
311 Curt Leskanic	.30	.09
312 Quinton McCracken	.30	.09
313 Neifi Perez	.30	.09
314 Jeff Reed	.30	.09
315 Steve Reed	.30	.09
316 Armando Reynoso	.30	.09
317 Kevin Ritz	.30	.09
318 Bruce Ruffin	.30	.09
319 Larry Walker	.50	.15
320 Walt Weiss	.30	.09
321 Jamey Wright	.30	.09
322 Eric Young	.30	.09
323 Kurt Abbott	.30	.09
324 Alex Arias	.30	.09
325 Kevin Brown	.30	.09
326 Luis Castillo	.30	.09
327 Greg Colbrunn	.30	.09
328 Jeff Conine	.30	.09
329 Andre Dawson	.30	.09
330 Charles Johnson	.30	.09
331 Al Leiter	.30	.09
332 Ralph Milliard	.30	.09
333 Robb Nen	.30	.09
334 Pat Rapp	.30	.09
335 Edgar Renteria	.30	.09
336 Gary Sheffield	.30	.09
337 Devon White	.30	.09
338 Bob Abreu	.30	.09
339 Jeff Bagwell	.50	.15
340 Derek Bell	.30	.09
341 Sean Berry	.30	.09
342 Craig Biggio	.50	.15
343 Doug Drabek	.30	.09
344 Tony Eusebio	.30	.09
345 Ricky Gutierrez	.30	.09
346 Mike Hampton	.30	.09
347 Brian Hunter	.30	.09
348 Todd Jones	.30	.09
349 Darryl Kile	.30	.09
350 Derrick May	.30	.09
351 Orlando Miller	.30	.09
352 James Mouton	.30	.09
353 Shane Reynolds	.30	.09
354 Billy Wagner	.30	.09
355 Donne Wall	.30	.09
356 Mike Blowers	.30	.09
357 Brett Butler	.30	.09
358 Roger Cedeno	.30	.09
359 Chad Curtis	.30	.09
360 Delino DeShields	.30	.09
361 Greg Gagne	.30	.09
362 Karim Garcia	.30	.09
363 Wilton Guerrero	.30	.09
364 Todd Hollandsworth	.30	.09
365 Eric Karros	.30	.09
366 Ramon Martinez	.30	.09
367 Raul Mondesi	.30	.09
368 Hideo Nomo	.75	.23
369 Antonio Osuna	.30	.09
370 Chan Ho Park	.30	.09
371 Mike Piazza	1.25	.35
372 Ismael Valdes	.30	.09
373 Todd Worrell	.30	.09
374 Moises Alou	.30	.09
375 Shane Andrews	.30	.09
376 Yamil Benitez	.30	.09
377 Jeff Fassero	.30	.09
378 Darrin Fletcher	.30	.09
379 Cliff Floyd	.30	.09
380 Mark Grudzielanek	.30	.09
381 Mike Lansing	.30	.09
382 Barry Manuel	.30	.09
383 Pedro Martinez	.75	.23
384 Henry Rodriguez	.30	.09
385 Mel Rojas	.30	.09
386 F.P. Santangelo	.30	.09
387 David Segui	.30	.09
388 Ugueth Urbina	.30	.09
389 Rondell White	.30	.09
390 Edgardo Alfonzo	.30	.09
391 Carlos Baerga	.30	.09
392 Mark Clark	.30	.09
393 Alvaro Espinoza	.30	.09
394 John Franco	.30	.09
395 Bernard Gilkey	.30	.09
396 Pete Harnisch	.30	.09
397 Todd Hundley	.30	.09
398 Butch Huskey	.30	.09
399 Jason Isringhausen	.30	.09
400 Lance Johnson	.30	.09
401 Bobby Jones	.30	.09
402 Alex Ochoa	.30	.09
403 Rey Ordonez	.30	.09
404 Robert Person	.30	.09
405 Paul Wilson	.30	.09
406 Matt Beech	.30	.09
407 Ron Blazier	.30	.09
408 Ricky Bottalico	.30	.09
409 Lenny Dykstra	.30	.09
410 Jim Eisenreich	.30	.09
411 Bobby Estalella	.30	.09
412 Mike Grace	.30	.09
413 Gregg Jefferies	.30	.09
414 Mike Lieberthal	.30	.09
415 Wendell Magee	.30	.09
416 Mickey Morandini	.30	.09
417 Ricky Otero	.30	.09
418 Scott Rolen	.50	.15
419 Ken Ryan	.30	.09
420 Benito Santiago	.30	.09
421 Curt Schilling	.50	.15
422 Kevin Sefcik	.30	.09
423 Jermaine Allensworth	.30	.09
424 Trey Beamon	.30	.09
425 Jay Bell	.30	.09
426 Francisco Cordova	.30	.09
427 Carlos Garcia	.30	.09
428 Mark Johnson	.30	.09
429 Jason Kendall	.30	.09
430 Jeff King	.30	.09
431 Jon Lieber	.30	.09
432 Al Martin	.30	.09
433 Orlando Merced	.30	.09
434 Ramon Morel	.30	.09
435 Matt Ruebel	.30	.09
436 Jason Schmidt	.30	.09
437 Marc Wilkins	.30	.09
438 Alan Benes	.30	.09
439 Andy Benes	.30	.09
440 Royce Clayton	.30	.09
441 Dennis Eckersley	.30	.09
442 Gary Gaetti	.30	.09
443 Ron Gant	.30	.09
444 Aaron Holbert	.30	.09
445 Brian Jordan	.30	.09
446 Ray Lankford	.30	.09
447 John Mabry	.30	.09
448 T.J. Mathews	.30	.09
449 Willie McGee	.30	.09
450 Donovan Osborne	.30	.09
451 Tom Pagnozzi	.30	.09
452 Ozzie Smith	1.25	.35
453 Todd Stottlemyre	.30	.09
454 Mark Sweeney	.30	.09
455 Dmitri Young	.30	.09
456 Andy Ashby	.30	.09
457 Ken Caminiti	.30	.09
458 Archi Cianfrocco	.30	.09
459 Steve Finley	.30	.09
460 John Flaherty	.30	.09
461 Chris Gomez	.30	.09
462 Tony Gwynn	1.00	.30
463 Joey Hamilton	.30	.09
464 Rickey Henderson	.75	.23
465 Trevor Hoffman	.30	.09
466 Brian Johnson	.30	.09
467 Wally Joyner	.30	.09
468 Jody Reed	.30	.09
469 Scott Sanders	.30	.09
470 Bob Tewksbury	.30	.09
471 Fernando Valenzuela	.30	.09
472 Greg Vaughn	.30	.09
473 Tim Worrell	.30	.09
474 Rich Aurilia	.30	.09
475 Rod Beck	.30	.09
476 Marvin Benard	.30	.09
477 Barry Bonds	2.00	.60
478 Jay Canizaro	.30	.09
479 Shawon Dunston	.30	.09
480 Shawn Estes	.30	.09
481 Mark Gardner	.30	.09
482 Glenallen Hill	.30	.09
483 Stan Javier	.30	.09
484 Marcus Jensen	.30	.09
485 Bill Mueller RC	2.00	.60
486 Wm. VanLandingham	.30	.09
487 Allen Watson	.30	.09
488 Rick Wilkins	.30	.09
489 Matt Williams	.30	.09
490 Desi Wilson	.30	.09
491 Albert Belle CL	.30	.09
492 Ken Griffey Jr. CL	.75	.23
493 Andruw Jones CL	.30	.09

494 Chipper Jones CL .50 .15
495 Mark McGwire CL 1.00 .30
496 Paul Molitor CL .30 .09
497 Mike Piazza CL .75 .23
498 Cal Ripken CL 1.25 .35
499 Alex Rodriguez CL .75 .23
500 Frank Thomas CL .50 .15
501 Kenny Lofton .30 .09
502 Carlos Perez .30 .09
503 Tim Raines .30 .09
504 Danny Patterson .30 .09
505 Derrick May .30 .09
506 Dave Hollins .30 .09
507 Felipe Crespo .30 .09
508 Brian Banks .30 .09
509 Jeff Kent .30 .09
510 Bubba Trammell RC .40 .12
511 Robert Person .30 .09
512 David Arias-Ortiz RC 2.00 .60
513 Ryan Jones .30 .09
514 David Justice .30 .09
515 Will Cunnane .30 .09
516 Russ Johnson .30 .09
517 John Burkett .30 .09
518 Robinson Checo RC .30 .09
519 Ricardo Rincon RC .30 .09
520 Woody Williams .30 .09
521 Rick Helling .30 .09
522 Jorge Posada .50 .15
523 Kevin Orie .30 .09
524 Fernando Tatis RC .40 .12
525 Jermaine Dye .30 .09
526 Brian Hunter .30 .09
527 Greg McMichael .30 .09
528 Matt Wagner .30 .09
529 Richie Sexson .30 .09
530 Scott Ruffcorn .30 .09
531 Luis Gonzalez .30 .09
532 Mike Johnson RC .30 .09
533 Mark Petkovsek .30 .09
534 Doug Drabek .30 .09
535 Jose Canseco .75 .23
536 Bobby Bonilla .30 .09
537 J.T. Snow .30 .09
538 Shawon Dunston .30 .09
539 John Ericks .30 .09
540 Terry Steinbach .30 .09
541 Jay Bell .30 .09
542 Joe Borowski RC .30 .09
543 David Wells .30 .09
544 Justin Towle RC .30 .09
545 Mike Blowers .30 .09
546 Shannon Stewart .30 .09
547 Rudy Pemberton .30 .09
548 Bill Swift .30 .09
549 Osvaldo Fernandez .30 .09
550 Eddie Murray .75 .23
551 Don Wengert .30 .09
552 Brad Ausmus .30 .09
553 Carlos Garcia .30 .09
554 Jose Guillen .30 .09
555 Rheal Cormier .30 .09
556 Doug Brocail .30 .09
557 Rex Hudler .30 .09
558 Armando Benitez .30 .09
559 Eli Marrero .30 .09
560 Ricky Ledee RC .40 .12
561 Bartolo Colon .30 .09
562 Quilvio Veras .30 .09
563 Alex Fernandez .30 .09
564 Darren Dreifort .30 .09
565 Benji Gil .30 .09
566 Kent Mercker .30 .09
567 Glendon Rusch .30 .09
568 Ramon Tatis RC .30 .09
569 Roger Clemens 1.50 .45
570 Mark Lewis .30 .09
571 Emil Brown RC .30 .09
572 Jaime Navarro .30 .09
573 Sherman Obando .30 .09
574 John Wasdin .30 .09
575 Calvin Maduro .30 .09
576 Todd Jones .30 .09
577 Orlando Merced .30 .09
578 Cal Eldred .30 .09
579 Mark Gubicza .30 .09
580 Michael Tucker .30 .09
581 Tony Saunders RC .30 .09
582 Garvin Alston .30 .09
583 Joe Roa .30 .09
584 Brady Raggio RC .30 .09
585 Jimmy Key .30 .09
586 Marc Sagmoen RC .30 .09
587 Jim Bullinger .30 .09
588 Yorkis Perez .30 .09
589 Jose Cruz Jr. RC 1.25 .35
590 Mike Stanton .30 .09
591 Deivi Cruz RC .40 .12
592 Steve Karsay .30 .09
593 Mike Trombley .30 .09
594 Doug Glanville .30 .09
595 Scott Sanders .30 .09
596 Thomas Howard .30 .09
597 T.J. Staton RC .30 .09
598 Garrett Stephenson .30 .09
599 Rico Brogna .30 .09
600 Albert Belle .30 .09
601 Jose Vizcaino .30 .09
602 Chili Davis .30 .09
603 Shane Mack .30 .09
604 Jim Eisenreich .30 .09
605 Todd Zeile .30 .09
606 Brian Boehringer RC .30 .09
607 Paul Shuey .30 .09
608 Kevin Tapani .30 .09
609 John Wetteland .30 .09
610 Jim Leyritz .30 .09
611 Ray Montgomery RC .30 .09
612 Doug Bochtler .30 .09
613 Wady Almonte RC .30 .09
614 Danny Tartabull .30 .09
615 Orlando Miller .30 .09
616 Bobby Ayala .30 .09
617 Tony Graffanino .30 .09
618 Marc Valdes .30 .09
619 Ron Villone .30 .09
620 Derrek Lee .30 .09
621 Greg Colbrunn .30 .09
622 Felix Heredia RC .40 .12
623 Carl Everett .30 .09
624 Mark Thompson .30 .09
625 Jeff Granger .30 .09
626 Damian Jackson .30 .09
627 Mark Leiter .30 .09
628 Chris Holt .30 .09
629 Dario Veras RC .30 .09
630 Dave Burba .30 .09
631 Darryl Hamilton .30 .09
632 Mark Acre .30 .09
633 F.Hernandez RC .30 .09
634 Terry Mulholland .30 .09
635 Dustin Hermanson .30 .09
636 Delino DeShields .30 .09
637 Steve Avery .30 .09
638 Tony Womack RC .40 .12
639 Mark Whiten .30 .09
640 Marquis Grissom .30 .09
641 Xavier Hernandez .30 .09
642 Eric Davis .30 .09
643 Bob Tewksbury .30 .09
644 Dante Powell .30 .09
645 Carlos Castillo RC .30 .09
646 Chris Widger .30 .09
647 Moises Alou .30 .09
648 Pat Listach .30 .09
649 Edgar Ramos RC .30 .09
650 Deion Sanders .50 .15
651 John Olerud .30 .09
652 Todd Dunwoody .30 .09
653 Randall Simon RC .50 .15
654 Dan Carlson .30 .09
655 Matt Williams .30 .09
656 Jeff King .30 .09
657 Luis Alicea .30 .09
658 Brian Moehler RC .30 .09
659 Ariel Prieto .30 .09
660 Kevin Elster .30 .09
661 Mark Hutton .30 .09
662 Aaron Sele .30 .09
663 Graeme Lloyd .30 .09
664 John Burke .30 .09
665 Mel Rojas .30 .09
666 Sid Fernandez .30 .09
667 Pedro Astacio .30 .09
668 Jeff Abbott .30 .09
669 Darren Daulton .30 .09
670 Mike Bordick .30 .09
671 Sterling Hitchcock .30 .09
672 Damion Easley .30 .09
673 Armando Reynoso .30 .09
674 Pat Cline .30 .09
675 Orlando Cabrera RC .50 .15
676 Alan Embree .30 .09
677 Brian Bevil .30 .09
678 David Weathers .30 .09
679 Cliff Floyd .30 .09
680 Joe Randa .30 .09
681 Bill Haselman .30 .09
682 Jeff Fassero .30 .09
683 Matt Morris .30 .09
684 Mark Portugal .30 .09
685 Lee Smith .30 .09
686 Pokey Reese .30 .09
687 Benito Santiago .30 .09
688 Brian Johnson .30 .09
689 Brent Brede RC .30 .09
690 S.Hasegawa RC .75 .23
691 Julio Santana .30 .09
692 Steve Kline .30 .09
693 Julian Tavarez .30 .09
694 John Hudek .30 .09
695 Manny Alexander .30 .09
696 Roberto Alomar ENC .30 .09
697 Jeff Bagwell ENC .30 .09
698 Barry Bonds ENC .75 .23
699 Ken Caminiti ENC .30 .09
700 Juan Gonzalez ENC .30 .09
701 Ken Griffey Jr. ENC .75 .23
702 Tony Gwynn ENC .50 .15
703 Derek Jeter ENC 1.00 .30
704 Andruw Jones ENC .30 .09
705 Chipper Jones ENC .50 .15
706 Barry Larkin ENC .50 .15
707 Greg Maddux ENC .75 .23
708 Mark McGwire ENC 1.00 .30
709 Paul Molitor ENC .30 .09
710 Hideo Nomo ENC .30 .09
711 Andy Pettitte ENC .30 .09
712 Mike Piazza ENC .75 .23
713 Manny Ramirez ENC .30 .09
714 Cal Ripken ENC 1.25 .35
715 Alex Rodriguez ENC .75 .23
716 Ryne Sandberg ENC .75 .23
717 John Smoltz ENC .30 .09
718 Frank Thomas ENC .50 .15
719 Mo Vaughn ENC .30 .09
720 Bernie Williams ENC .30 .09
721 Tim Salmon CL .30 .09
722 Greg Maddux CL .75 .23
723 Cal Ripken CL 1.25 .35
724 Mo Vaughn CL .30 .09
725 Ryne Sandberg CL .75 .23
726 Frank Thomas CL .50 .15
727 Barry Larkin CL .30 .09
728 Manny Ramirez CL .30 .09
729 Andres Galarraga CL .30 .09
730 Tony Clark CL .30 .09
731 Gary Sheffield CL .30 .09
732 Jeff Bagwell CL .30 .09
733 Kevin Appier CL .30 .09
734 Mike Piazza CL .75 .23
735 Jeff Cirillo CL .30 .09
736 Paul Molitor CL .30 .09
737 Henry Rodriguez CL .30 .09
738 Todd Hundley CL .30 .09
739 Derek Jeter CL 1.00 .30
740 Mark McGwire CL 1.00 .30
741 Curt Schilling CL .30 .09
742 Jason Kendall CL .30 .09
743 Tony Gwynn CL .50 .15
744 Barry Bonds CL .75 .23
745 Ken Griffey Jr. CL .75 .23
746 Brian Jordan CL .30 .09
747 Juan Gonzalez CL .50 .15
748 Joe Carter CL .30 .09
749 Ariz. Diamondbacks CL Inserts .30 .09
750 Tampa Bay Devil Rays CL Inserts .30 .09
751 Hideki Irabu RC .75 .23
752 Jeremi Gonzalez RC .50 .15
753 Mario Valdez RC .50 .15
754 Aaron Boone .75 .23
755 Brett Tomko .50 .15
756 Jaret Wright RC .75 .23
757 Ryan McGuire .50 .15
758 Jason McDonald .50 .15
759 Adrian Brown RC .50 .15
760 Keith Foulke RC 2.00 .60
761 Bonus Checklist .50 .15
P489 M.Williams Promo 1.00 .30
NNO Andruw Jones 25.00 7.50
Circa AU/200

1997 Fleer Tiffany

Randomly inserted in series one and two packs at a rate of one in 20, this 751-card set is a parallel version of the regular set featuring a glossy holographic design, foil stamping, and UV coating.

Nm-Mt Ex-Mt
*STARS: 12.5X TO 30X BASIC CARDS
*ROOKIES: 6X TO 15X BASIC CARDS
*751-761: 4X TO 10X BASIC CARDS..

1997 Fleer Bleacher Blasters

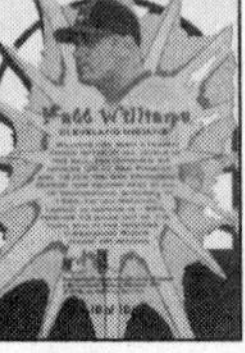

Randomly inserted in Fleer series two retail packs only at a rate of one in 36, this 10-card set features color action photos of power hitters who reach the bleachers with great frequency.

	Nm-Mt	Ex-Mt
COMPLETE SET (10)	80.00	24.00
1 Albert Belle	2.50	.75
2 Barry Bonds	15.00	4.50
3 Juan Gonzalez	6.00	1.80
4 Ken Griffey Jr.	10.00	3.00
5 Mark McGwire	15.00	4.50
6 Mike Piazza	10.00	3.00
7 Alex Rodriguez	10.00	3.00
8 Frank Thomas	6.00	1.80
9 Mo Vaughn	2.50	.75
10 Matt Williams	2.50	.75

1997 Fleer Decade of Excellence

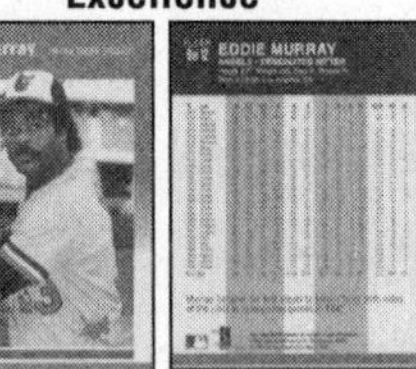

Randomly inserted in Fleer Series two hobby packs only at a rate of one in 36, this 12-card set spotlights players who started their major league careers no later than 1987. The set features photos of these players from the 1987 season in the 1987 Fleer Baseball card design.

	Nm-Mt	Ex-Mt
COMPLETE SET (12)	60.00	18.00
*RARE TRAD: 2X TO 5X BASIC DECADE		
RARE TRAD.STATED ODDS 1:360 HOBBY		
1 Wade Boggs	3.00	.90
2 Barry Bonds	12.00	3.60
3 Roger Clemens	10.00	3.00
4 Tony Gwynn	6.00	1.80
5 Rickey Henderson	5.00	1.50
6 Greg Maddux	8.00	2.40
7 Mark McGwire	12.00	3.60
8 Paul Molitor	3.00	.90
9 Eddie Murray	5.00	1.50
10 Cal Ripken	15.00	4.50
11 Ryne Sandberg	8.00	2.40
12 Matt Williams	2.00	.60

1997 Fleer Diamond Tribute

Randomly inserted in Fleer Series two packs at a rate of one in 288, this 12-card set features color action images of Baseball's top players on a dazzling foil background.

	Nm-Mt	Ex-Mt
1 Albert Belle	8.00	2.40
2 Barry Bonds	50.00	15.00
3 Juan Gonzalez	20.00	6.00
4 Ken Griffey Jr.	30.00	9.00
5 Tony Gwynn	25.00	7.50
6 Greg Maddux	30.00	9.00
7 Mark McGwire	50.00	15.00
8 Eddie Murray	20.00	6.00
9 Mike Piazza	30.00	9.00
10 Cal Ripken	60.00	18.00
11 Alex Rodriguez	30.00	9.00
12 Frank Thomas	20.00	6.00

1997 Fleer Golden Memories

Randomly inserted in first series packs at a rate of one in 16, this ten-card set commemorates

major achievements by individual players from the 1996 season. The fronts feature color player images on a background of the top portion of the sun and its rays. The backs carry player information.

	Nm-Mt	Ex-Mt
COMPLETE SET (10)	10.00	3.00
1 Barry Bonds	3.00	.90
2 Dwight Gooden	.75	.23
3 Todd Hundley	.50	.15
4 Mark McGwire	3.00	.90
5 Paul Molitor	.75	.23
6 Eddie Murray	1.25	.35
7 Hideo Nomo	1.25	.35
8 Mike Piazza	2.00	.60
9 Cal Ripken	4.00	1.20
10 Ozzie Smith	2.00	.60

1997 Fleer Goudey Greats

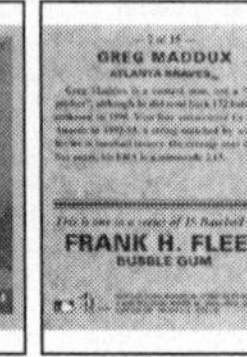

Randomly inserted in Fleer Series two packs at a rate of one in eight, this 15-card set features color player photos of today's stars on cards styled and sized to resemble the 1933 Goudey Baseball card set.

	Nm-Mt	Ex-Mt
COMPLETE SET (15)	15.00	4.50
*FOIL CARDS: 6X TO 15X BASIC GOUDEY		
FOIL SER.2 STATED ODDS 1:800		
1 Barry Bonds	3.00	.90
2 Ken Griffey Jr.	2.00	.60
3 Tony Gwynn	1.50	.45
4 Derek Jeter	3.00	.90
5 Chipper Jones	1.25	.35
6 Kenny Lofton	.50	.15
7 Greg Maddux	2.00	.60
8 Mark McGwire	3.00	.90
9 Eddie Murray	1.25	.35
10 Mike Piazza	2.00	.60
11 Cal Ripken	4.00	1.20
12 Alex Rodriguez	2.00	.60
13 Ryne Sandberg	2.00	.60
14 Frank Thomas	1.25	.35
15 Mo Vaughn	.50	.15

1997 Fleer Headliners

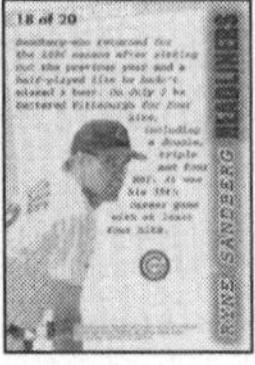

Randomly inserted in Fleer Series two packs at a rate of one in two, this 20-card set features color action photos of top players who make headlines for their teams. The backs carry player information.

	Nm-Mt	Ex-Mt
COMPLETE SET (20)	10.00	3.00
1 Jeff Bagwell	.30	.09
2 Albert Belle	.20	.06
3 Barry Bonds	1.25	.35
4 Ken Caminiti	.20	.06
5 Juan Gonzalez	.50	.15
6 Ken Griffey Jr.	.75	.23
7 Tony Gwynn	.60	.18
8 Derek Jeter	1.25	.35
9 Andruw Jones	.20	.06
10 Chipper Jones	.50	.15
11 Greg Maddux	.75	.23
12 Mark McGwire	1.25	.35
13 Paul Molitor	.30	.09
14 Eddie Murray	.50	.15
15 Mike Piazza	.75	.23
16 Cal Ripken	1.50	.45
17 Alex Rodriguez	.75	.23
18 Ryne Sandberg	.75	.23
19 John Smoltz	.30	.09
20 Frank Thomas	.50	.15

1997 Fleer Lumber Company

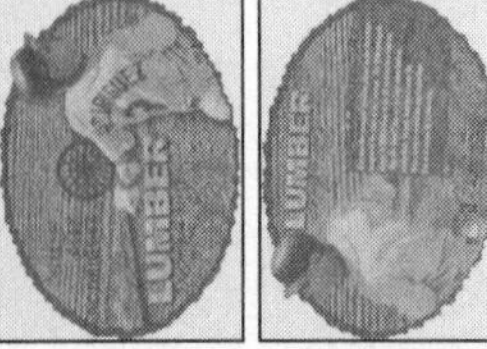

Randomly inserted exclusively in Fleer Series one retail packs, this 18-card set features a selection of the game's top sluggers. The innovative design displays pure die-cut circular borders, simulating the effect of a cut tree.

	Nm-Mt	Ex-Mt
COMPLETE SET (18)	120.00	36.00
1 Brady Anderson	3.00	.90
2 Jeff Bagwell	5.00	1.50
3 Albert Belle	3.00	.90
4 Barry Bonds	20.00	6.00
5 Jay Buhner	3.00	.90
6 Ellis Burks	3.00	.90
7 Andres Galarraga	3.00	.90
8 Juan Gonzalez	8.00	2.40
9 Ken Griffey Jr.	12.00	3.60
10 Todd Hundley	3.00	.90
11 Ryan Klesko	3.00	.90
12 Mark McGwire	20.00	6.00
13 Mike Piazza	12.00	3.60
14 Alex Rodriguez	12.00	3.60
15 Gary Sheffield	3.00	.90
16 Sammy Sosa	12.00	3.60
17 Frank Thomas	8.00	2.40
18 Mo Vaughn	3.00	.90

1997-98 Fleer Million Dollar Moments

Inserted one per pack into 1997 Fleer 2, 1997 Flair Showcase, 1998 Fleer 1 and 1998 Ultra 1; these 50 cards mix a selection of retired legends with today's stars, highlighting key moments in baseball history. The first 45 cards in the set are common to find. Cards 46-50 are extremely shortprinted with each card being tougher to find than the next as you work your way up to card number 50. Prior to the July 31st, 1998 deadline, collectors could mail in their 45-card sets (plus $5.99 for postage and handling) and receive a complete 50-card exchange set. The lucky collectors that managed to obtain one or more of the shortprinted cards could receive a shopping spree at card shops nationwide selected by Fleer. Each shortprinted card had to be mailed in along with a complete 45-card set to receive the following shopping allowances: number 46/$100, number 47/$250, number 48/$500, number 49/$1000. A grand prize of $1,000,000 cash (payable in increments of $50,000 annually over 20 years) was available for one collector that could obtain and redeem all five shortprint cards (numbers 46-50). This set was actually a part of a multi-sport promotion (baseball, basketball and football) for Fleer with each sport offering a separate $1,000,000 grand prize. In addition, 10,000 instant winner cards per sport (good for an assortment of material including shopping sprees, video games and various Fleer sets) were randomly seeded into packs. We are listing cards numbered from 46-50, however no prices are assigned for these cards.

	Nm-Mt	Ex-Mt
COMPLETE SET (45)	8.00	2.40
1 Checklist	.10	.03
2 Derek Jeter	.60	.18
3 Babe Ruth	1.50	.45
4 Barry Bonds	.60	.18
5 Brooks Robinson	.25	.07
6 Todd Hundley	.10	.03
7 Johnny Vander Meer	.10	.03
8 Cal Ripken	.75	.23
9 Bill Mazeroski	.15	.04
10 Chipper Jones	.25	.07
11 Frank Robinson	.15	.04
12 Roger Clemens	.50	.15
13 Bob Feller	.15	.04
14 Mike Piazza	.40	.12
15 Joe Nuxhall	.10	.03
16 Hideo Nomo	.25	.07
17 Jackie Robinson	.75	.23
18 Orel Hershiser	.10	.03
19 Bobby Thomson	.10	.03
20 Joe Carter	.10	.03
21 Al Kaline	.25	.07
22 Bernie Williams	.15	.04
23 Don Larsen	.15	.04
24 Rickey Henderson	.25	.07
25 Maury Wills	.10	.03
26 Andruw Jones	.10	.03
27 Bobby Richardson	.10	.03
28 Alex Rodriguez	.40	.12
29 Jim Bunning	.15	.04
30 Ken Caminiti	.10	.03
31 Bob Gibson	.15	.04
32 Frank Thomas	.25	.07
33 Mickey Lolich	.10	.03
34 John Smoltz	.15	.04
35 Ron Swoboda	.10	.03
36 Albert Belle	.10	.03
37 Chris Chambliss	.10	.03
38 Juan Gonzalez	.25	.07
39 Ron Blomberg	.10	.03
40 John Wetteland	.10	.03
41 Carlton Fisk	.25	.07
42 Mo Vaughn	.10	.03
43 Bucky Dent	.10	.03
44 Greg Maddux	.40	.12
45 Willie Stargell	.10	.03
46 Tony Gwynn SP		
47 Joel Youngblood SP		
48 Andy Pettitte SP		
49 Mookie Wilson SP		
50 Jeff Bagwell SP		

1997-98 Fleer Million Dollar Moments Redemption

This is the set received when a collector sent in his complete 45 card set along with the $5.99 for postage and handling. All 50 cards were sent in this exchange. The deadline for a collector sending in a card to acquire this redemption set was July 31, 1998. Unlike the pack insert, all 50 cards were produced in equal quantities.

	Nm-Mt	Ex-Mt
COMPLETE SET (45)	8.00	2.40
1 Checklist	.05	.02
2 Derek Jeter	1.50	.45
3 Babe Ruth	1.50	.45
4 Barry Bonds	.75	.23
5 Brooks Robinson	.25	.07
6 Todd Hundley	.10	.03
7 Johnny Vander Meer	.05	.02
8 Cal Ripken	1.00	.30
9 Bill Mazeroski	.20	.06
10 Chipper Jones	.60	.18
11 Frank Robinson	.25	.07
12 Roger Clemens	.75	.23
13 Bob Feller	.25	.07
14 Mike Piazza	.75	.23
15 Joe Nuxhall	.05	.02
16 Hideo Nomo	.40	.12
17 Jackie Robinson	1.00	.30
18 Orel Hershiser	.10	.03
19 Bobby Thomson	.05	.02
20 Joe Carter	.10	.03
21 Al Kaline	.25	.07
22 Bernie Williams	.20	.06
23 Don Larsen	.05	.02
24 Rickey Henderson	.30	.09
25 Maury Wills	.10	.03
26 Andruw Jones	.40	.12
27 Bobby Richardson	.05	.02
28 Alex Rodriguez	1.50	.45
29 Jim Bunning	.20	.06
30 Ken Caminiti	.15	.04
31 Bob Gibson	.20	.06
32 Frank Thomas	.50	.15
33 Mickey Lolich	.10	.03
34 John Smoltz	.10	.03
35 Ron Swoboda	.05	.02
36 Albert Belle	.10	.03
37 Chris Chambliss	.05	.02
38 Juan Gonzalez	.20	.06
39 Ron Blomberg	.05	.02
40 John Wetteland	.05	.02
41 Carlton Fisk	.40	.12
42 Mo Vaughn	.10	.03
43 Bucky Dent	.05	.02
44 Greg Maddux	.60	.18
45 Willie Stargell	.10	.03
46 Tony Gwynn	.50	.15
47 Joel Youngblood	.05	.02
48 Andy Pettitte	.15	.04
49 Mookie Wilson	.10	.03
50 Jeff Bagwell	.40	.12

1997 Fleer New Horizons

Randomly inserted in Fleer Series two packs at a rate of one in four, this 15-card set features borderless color action photos of Rookies and prospects. The backs carry player information.

	Nm-Mt	Ex-Mt
COMPLETE SET (15)	8.00	2.40
1 Bob Abreu	.50	.15
2 Jose Cruz Jr.	2.00	.60
3 Darin Erstad	.50	.15
4 Nomar Garciaparra	2.00	.60
5 Vladimir Guerrero	1.25	.35
6 Wilton Guerrero	.50	.15
7 Jose Guillen	.50	.15
8 Hideki Irabu	1.25	.35
9 Andruw Jones	.50	.15
10 Kevin Orie	.50	.15
11 Scott Rolen	.75	.23
12 Scott Spiezio	.50	.15
13 Bubba Trammell	.60	.18
14 Todd Walker	.50	.15
15 Dmitri Young	.50	.15

1997 Fleer Night and Day

Randomly inserted in Fleer Series one packs at a rate of one in 240, this ten-card set features color action photos of superstars who excel in day games, night games, or both and are printed on lenticular 3D cards. The backs carry player information.

	Nm-Mt	Ex-Mt
COMPLETE SET (10)	150.00	45.00
1 Barry Bonds	30.00	9.00
2 Ellis Burks	5.00	1.50
3 Juan Gonzalez	12.00	3.60
4 Ken Griffey Jr.	20.00	6.00
5 Mark McGwire	30.00	9.00
6 Mike Piazza	20.00	6.00
7 Manny Ramirez	5.00	1.50
8 Alex Rodriguez	20.00	6.00
9 John Smoltz	8.00	2.40
10 Frank Thomas	12.00	3.60

1997 Fleer Rookie Sensations

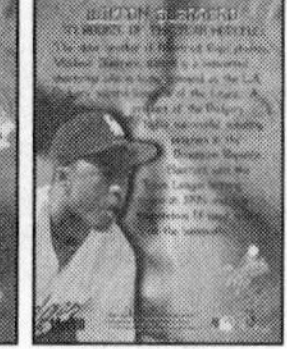

Randomly inserted in Fleer Series one packs at a rate of one in six, this 20-card set honors the top rookies from the 1996 season and the 1997 season rookies/prospects. The fronts freature color action player images on a multi-color swirling background. The backs carry a paragraph with information about the player.

	Nm-Mt	Ex-Mt
COMPLETE SET (20)	20.00	6.00
1 Jermaine Allensworth	.75	.23
2 James Baldwin	.75	.23
3 Alan Benes	.75	.23
4 Jermaine Dye	.75	.23
5 Darin Erstad	.75	.23
6 Todd Hollandsworth	.75	.23
7 Derek Jeter	5.00	1.50
8 Jason Kendall	.75	.23
9 Alex Ochoa	.75	.23
10 Rey Ordonez	.75	.23
11 Edgar Renteria	.75	.23
12 Bob Abreu	.75	.23
13 Nomar Garciaparra	3.00	.90
14 Wilton Guerrero	.75	.23
15 Andruw Jones	.75	.23
16 Wendell Magee	.75	.23
17 Neifi Perez	.75	.23
18 Scott Rolen	1.25	.35
19 Scott Spiezio	.75	.23
20 Todd Walker	.75	.23

1997 Fleer Soaring Stars

Randomly inserted in Fleer Series two packs at a rate of one in 12, this 12-card set features color action photos of players who enjoyed a meteoric rise to stardom and have all the skills to stay there. The player's image is set on a background of twinkling stars.

	Nm-Mt	Ex-Mt
COMPLETE SET (12)	30.00	9.00
*GLOWING: 4X TO 10X BASIC SOARING		
GLOWING: RANDOM INSERTS IN SER.2 PACKS		
LAST 20% OF PRINT RUN WAS GLOWING		
1 Albert Belle	.60	.18
2 Barry Bonds	4.00	1.20
3 Juan Gonzalez	1.50	.45
4 Ken Griffey Jr.	2.50	.75
5 Derek Jeter	4.00	1.20
6 Andruw Jones	.60	.18
7 Chipper Jones	1.50	.45
8 Greg Maddux	2.50	.75
9 Mark McGwire	4.00	1.20
10 Mike Piazza	2.50	.75
11 Alex Rodriguez	2.50	.75
12 Frank Thomas	1.50	.45

1997 Fleer Team Leaders

Randomly inserted in Fleer Series one packs at a rate of one in 20, this 28-card set honors statistical or inspirational leaders from each team on a die-cut card. The fronts feature color action player images with the player's face in the background. The backs carry a paragraph with information about the player.

	Nm-Mt	Ex-Mt
COMPLETE SET (28)	100.00	30.00
1 Cal Ripken	15.00	4.50
2 Mo Vaughn	2.00	.60
3 Jim Edmonds	2.00	.60
4 Frank Thomas	5.00	1.50
5 Albert Belle	2.00	.60
6 Bob Higginson	2.00	.60
7 Kevin Appier	2.00	.60
8 John Jaha	2.00	.60
9 Paul Molitor	3.00	.90
10 Andy Pettitte	3.00	.90
11 Mark McGwire	12.00	3.60
12 Ken Griffey Jr.	8.00	2.40
13 Juan Gonzalez	5.00	1.50
14 Pat Hentgen	2.00	.60
15 Chipper Jones	5.00	1.50
16 Mark Grace	3.00	.90
17 Barry Larkin	5.00	1.50
18 Ellis Burks	2.00	.60
19 Gary Sheffield	2.00	.60
20 Jeff Bagwell	3.00	.90
21 Mike Piazza	8.00	2.40
22 Henry Rodriguez	2.00	.60
23 Todd Hundley	2.00	.60
24 Curt Schilling	3.00	.90
25 Jeff King	2.00	.60
26 Brian Jordan	2.00	.60
27 Tony Gwynn	6.00	1.80
28 Barry Bonds	12.00	3.60

1997 Fleer Zone

Randomly inserted in Fleer Series one hobby packs only at a rate of one in 80, this 20-card set features color player images of some of the 1996 season's unstoppable hitters and unhittable pitchers on a holographic card. The backs carry another color photo with a paragraph about the player.

	Nm-Mt	Ex-Mt
COMPLETE SET (20)	200.00	60.00
1 Jeff Bagwell	6.00	1.80
2 Albert Belle	4.00	1.20
3 Barry Bonds	25.00	7.50
4 Ken Caminiti	4.00	1.20
5 Andres Galarraga	4.00	1.20
6 Juan Gonzalez	10.00	3.00
7 Ken Griffey Jr.	15.00	4.50
8 Tony Gwynn	12.00	3.60
9 Chipper Jones	10.00	3.00
10 Greg Maddux	15.00	4.50
11 Mark McGwire	25.00	7.50
12 Dean Palmer	4.00	1.20
13 Andy Pettitte	6.00	1.80
14 Mike Piazza	15.00	4.50
15 Alex Rodriguez	15.00	4.50
16 Gary Sheffield	4.00	1.20
17 John Smoltz	6.00	1.80
18 Frank Thomas	10.00	3.00
19 Jim Thome	10.00	3.00
20 Matt Williams	4.00	1.20

1997 Fleer Firestone

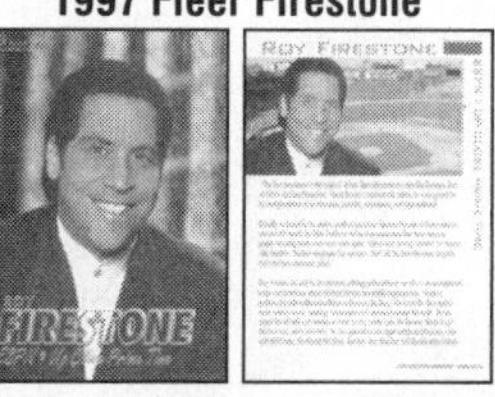

This one-card set features a color portrait with gold foil printing of Roy Firestone, the host of ESPN's "Up Close Prime Time." The back displays information about the interviewer.

	Nm-Mt	Ex-Mt
1 Roy Firestone	2.00	.60

1998 Fleer Diamond Skills Commemorative Sheet

This attractive eight-card unperforated sheet was distributed nationwide by hobby shops that participated in Fleer's Diamond Skills youth baseball program. Each shop that enrolled with Fleer in early April, 1998 received 25 sheets to give away to young baseball fans participating in the contest. From April 1st through June 30th, 1998, MLB and Fleer/SkyBox distributed more than 600,000 questionaire surveys. Each survey was then filled out and brought into an a local card shop, where the participating youth had to buy two packs of Fleer/SkyBox trading cards. In exchange for the two wrappers from those packs and the completed survey, the youth received one of these commemorative sheets.

	Nm-Mt	Ex-Mt
NNO Jim Edmonds Mike Piazza Scott Rolen Mark McGwire Jeff Bagwell Roger Clemens Cal Ripken Derek Jeter	5.00	1.50

1998 Fleer Mantle and Sons

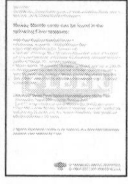

This special one-shot standard-sized card was distributed at Fleer's booth at the Sportsfest '98 show in Philadelphia as well as the National Convention in Chicago in the Summer of 1998. In conjunction with their licensing agreement with the Mantle family and accompanying 1998 Mantle promotions, Fleer brought Mantle's sons Danny and David to the aforementioned trade shows to sign this special card for collectors. The back of the card outlines Mickey Mantle's various card appearances in Fleer's 1998 products. Pricing is provided below for both signed and unsigned versions of this card.

	Nm-Mt	Ex-Mt
NNO Mickey Mantle w/sons AU. Danny Mantle David Mantle	10.00	3.00
NNO Mickey Mantle w/sons Danny Mantle David Mantle	3.00	.90

1998 Fleer Postcard Mantle Promo

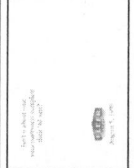

This one-card set features a color photo of Mickey Mantle as the A.L. Most Valuable Player in 1962 with a white border and measuring approximately 4 1/4" by 5 1/2". The white back has a date of August 5, 1998, and the words "Isn't it about time your customers complete their '63 set?" Only 3,500 of the cards were printed and are serially numbered.

	Nm-Mt	Ex-Mt
1 Mickey Mantle	5.00	1.50

1998 Fleer/SkyBox Player's Choice Sheet

This one-card set was given out at stadiums during the final weekend of the 1998 season and measures approximately 8 1/2" by 11". The card features color action player images of nominees for Outstanding Player, Pitcher and Rookie, Comeback Player of the Year, Man of the Year, and Player of the Year. One side displays the NL nominees and the other the AL ones. The players are checklisted below in alphabetical order.

	Nm-Mt	Ex-Mt
1 Moises Alou Rolando Arrojo Kevin Brown Jose Canseco Mike Caruso Roger Clemens Eric Davis Nomar Garciaparra Juan Gonzalez Ben Grieve Pete Harnisch Todd Helton Trevor Hoffman Brian Jordan Travis Lee Greg Maddux Pedro Martinez Mark McGwire Paul Molitor Alex Rodriguez Bret Saberhagen Sammy Sosa Greg Vaughn David Wells Kerry Wood	5.00	1.50

1999 Fleer Stan Musial NSCC Commemorative

This five-card over-sized (3 1/2" by 5") set was distributed to attendees of the 20th Annual National Sports Collectors Convention held in Atlanta in July, 1999. The cards were packaged in complete set form within a sealed clear plastic cello wrapper. An unnumbered Cover Card (bereft of any player images) displays the 20th National Convention logo on front and a checklist on back. This was the top card in each cello wrapped set. Card NC1 was a straight parallel of the basic issue 1999 Fleer Stan Musial card (number 6 within the basic Fleer set, but renumbered as NC1 for this set) and is the only standard-sized card in the set. Cards NC2-NC4 are quasi-reprints of selected cards from the 1999 Fleer Stan Musial Monumental Moments set - taking those standard sized cards and incorporating them into an over-sized card format with the famous Arch of St.Louis in the background.

	Nm-Mt	Ex-Mt
COMPLETE SET (5)	25.00	7.50
COMMON CARD (NC1-NC4)	5.00	1.50

1999 Fleer 23K McGwire

This card was issued by Fleer and commemorated the breaking of the single season homer record by Mark McGwire. The front has a relief photo of McGwire and a fascimile autograph. The back has information about the homer as well as the date listed on top. The card is also serial numbered on the back. However, it is possible that more of these cards were issued so any further information about this set is appreciated.

	Nm-Mt	Ex-Mt
1 Mark McGwire	10.00	3.00

1999 Fleer Diamond Skills Commemorative Sheet

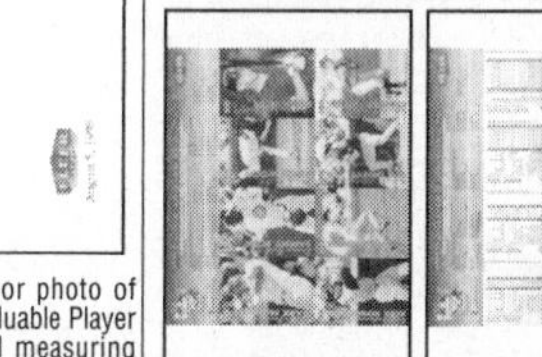

For the second year running, Fleer issued an attractive eight-card unperforated sheet. The sheet was distributed nationwide by hobby shops that participated in Fleer's Diamond Skills youth baseball program.

	Nm-Mt	Ex-Mt
NNO Mark McGwire Sammy Sosa Kerry Wood Derek Jeter Alex Rodriguez Nomar Garciaparra Ben Grieve Chipper Jones	5.00	1.50

1999 Fleer Spectra Star

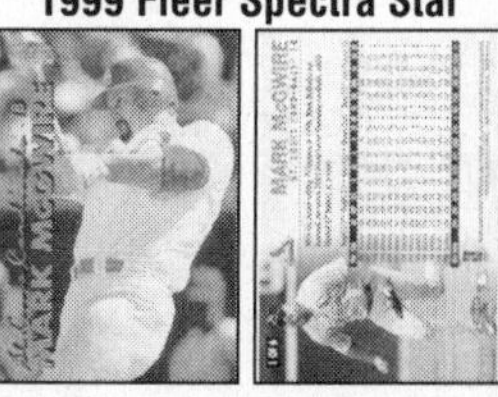

These six cards of baseball's leading superstars were issued by Fleer along with a kite. These cards are in the design of the 1999 Fleer set but are numbered "x" of 6. The kites were issued by Spectra Star.

	Nm-Mt	Ex-Mt
COMPLETE SET (6)	30.00	9.00
1 Mark McGwire	8.00	2.40
2 Ken Griffey Jr.	6.00	1.80
3 Derek Jeter	10.00	3.00
4 Greg Maddux	5.00	1.50
5 Mike Piazza	6.00	1.80
6 Sammy Sosa	5.00	1.50

1999 Fleer White Rose

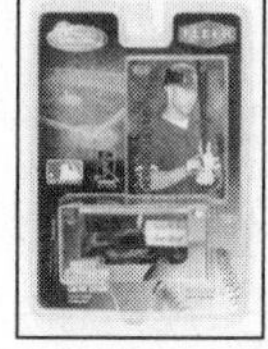

These 30 cards were issued along with a special truck in a combo package. The cards are sequenced thusly: Cards 1-14 are American League teams in alphabetical order; 15-26 are National League teams in alpha order, 27 and 28 are 1993 Expansion teams and 29 and 30 and 1998 Expansion team. The cards have the 1999 Fleer fronts and are specially numbered for this set. We are only pricing the cards here.

	Nm-Mt	Ex-Mt
COMPLETE SET (30)	80.00	24.00
1 Cal Ripken Jr.	10.00	3.00
2 Nomar Garciaparra	5.00	1.50
3 Tim Salmon	1.50	.45
4 Frank Thomas	3.00	.90
5 Jim Thome	2.50	.75
6 Tony Clark	1.00	.30
7 Johnny Damon	2.00	.60
8 Jeromy Burnitz	1.50	.45
9 Brad Radke	1.00	.30
10 Derek Jeter	10.00	3.00
11 Ben Grieve	1.50	.45
12 Ken Griffey Jr.	6.00	1.80
13 Ivan Rodriguez	3.00	.90
14 Carlos Delgado	2.50	.75
15 Greg Maddux	6.00	1.80
16 Sammy Sosa	5.00	1.50
17 Sean Casey	1.50	.45
18 Jeff Bagwell	3.00	.90

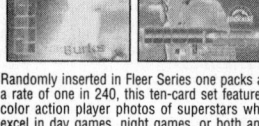

19 Raul Mondesi 1.00 .30
20 Vladimir Guerrero 4.00 1.20
21 Mike Piazza 6.00 1.80
22 Scott Rolen 2.50 .75
23 Jose Guillen 2.00 .60
24 Mark McGwire 8.00 2.40
25 Tony Gwynn 5.00 1.50
26 Barry Bonds 5.00 1.50
27 Larry Walker 1.50 .45
28 Livan Hernandez 1.00 .30
29 Matt Williams 1.50 .45
30 Wade Boggs 3.00 .90

2000 Fleer Club 3000

This set honors batters who have collected 3,000 hits and pitchers who have collected 3,000 strikeouts in their careers. The cards were seeded across all 2000 Fleer brands and each card in our checklist is marked with an abbreviation for the product it hails from. Pack odds are as follows - Fleer-distributed cards 1:36, Fleer Focus-distributed cards 1:36, Fleer Mystique-distributed cards 1:32, Fleer Showcase-distributed cards 1:24, and Ultra-distributed cards 1:24. These cards are unnumbered so we have sequenced them in alphabetical order by player initials.

Nm-Mt Ex-Mt
COMP.FLEER SET (3) 10.00 3.00
COMP.FOCUS SET (3) 10.00 3.00
COMP.MYSTIQUE SET (3) 12.00 3.60
COMP.SHOWCASE SET (2) 10.00 3.00
COMP.ULTRA SET (3) 10.00 3.00
BG Bob Gibson MYST 3.00 .90
CR Cal Ripken MYST 8.00 2.40
CY Carl Yastrzemski ULT 4.00 1.20
DW Dave Winfield MYST 3.00 .90
GB George Brett FLE 8.00 2.40
LB Lou Brock SHOW 3.00 .90
NR Nolan Ryan SHOW 6.00 1.80
PM Paul Molitor FOCUS 3.00 .90
RC Rod Carew FLE 3.00 .90
RY Robin Yount FLE 5.00 1.50
SC Steve Carlton FOCUS 3.00 .90
SM Stan Musial FOCUS 4.00 1.20
TG Tony Gwynn ULT 3.00 .90
WB Wade Boggs ULT 3.00 .90

2000 Fleer Club 3000 Memorabilia

Randomly inserted into all 2000 Fleer products, these cards feature game used memorabilia from legends of the game that have either collected 3,000 hits or struck out 3,000 batters during their career. The cards (and patterns of distribution) parallel the more common Club 3000 cards that lack the memorabilia elements. Each player has five different cards: A bat, a hat, a jersey, a combo of bat and jersey and a combo of bat, hat and jersey. Each card is sequentially numbered and detailed within our checklist. Please see the Fleer Club 3000 listing for specific information on which Fleer product each card was distributed in.

Nm-Mt Ex-Mt
BG1 Bob Gibson 25.00 7.50
Bat/265
BG2 Bob Gibson 60.00 18.00
Hat/55
BG3 Bob Gibson 15.00 4.50
Jersey/825
BG4 Bob Gibson 60.00 18.00
Bat-Jersey/100
BG5 Bob Gibson
Bat-Hat-Jsy/25
CR1 Cal Ripken 80.00 24.00
Bat/265
CR2 Cal Ripken 150.00 45.00
Hat/55
CR3 Cal Ripken 40.00 12.00
Jersey/825
CR4 Cal Ripken 150.00 45.00
Bat-Jersey/100
CR5 Cal Ripken
Bat-Hat-Jsy/25
CY1 Carl Yastrzemski 50.00 15.00
Bat/250
CY2 Carl Yastrzemski 100.00 30.00
Hat/100
CY3 Carl Yastrzemski 25.00 7.50
Jersey/440
CY4 Carl Yastrzemski 150.00 45.00
Bat/Jersey/100
CY5 Carl Yastrzemski
Bat/Hat/Jersey/25
DW1 Dave Winfield 15.00 4.50
Bat/270
DW2 Dave Winfield 50.00 15.00
Hat/55
DW3 Dave Winfield 10.00 3.00
Jersey/825
DW4 Dave Winfield 50.00 15.00
Bat-Jersey/100
DW5 Dave Winfield
Bat-Hat-Jsy/25
GB1 George Brett 40.00 12.00
Bat/240
GB2 George Brett 120.00 36.00
Hat/105
GB3 George Brett 25.00 7.50
Jersey/445
GB4 George Brett 120.00 36.00
Bat-Jersey/100
GB5 George Brett
Bat-Hat-Jersey/25
LB1 Lou Brock 25.00 7.50
Bat/270
LB2 Lou Brock 60.00 18.00
Hat/60
LB3 Lou Brock 15.00 4.50
Jersey/680
LB4 Lou Brock 60.00 18.00
Bat-Jersey/100
LB5 Lou Brock
Bat-Hat-Jsy/25
NR1 Nolan Ryan 80.00 24.00
Bat/265
NR2 Nolan Ryan 150.00 45.00
Hat/65
NR3 Nolan Ryan 40.00 12.00
Jersey/780
NR4 Nolan Ryan 150.00 45.00
Bat-Jersey/100
NR5 Nolan Ryan
Bat-Hat-Jsy/25
PM1 Paul Molitor 25.00 7.50
Bat/335
PM2 Paul Molitor 60.00 18.00
Hat/65
PM3 Paul Molitor 15.00 4.50
Jersey/975
PM4 Paul Molitor 60.00 18.00
Bat-Jersey/100
PM5 Paul Molitor
Bat-Hat-Jsy/25
RC1 Rod Carew 25.00 7.50
Bat/225
RC2 Rod Carew 60.00 18.00
Hat/105
RC3 Rod Carew 15.00 4.50
Jersey/395
RC4 Rod Carew 60.00 18.00
Bat-Jersey/100
RC5 Rod Carew
Bat-Hat-Jersey/25
RY1 Robin Yount 25.00 7.50
Bat/230
RY2 Robin Yount 80.00 24.00
Hat/105
RY3 Robin Yount 15.00 4.50
Jersey/445
RY4 Robin Yount 80.00 24.00
Bat-Jersey/100
RY5 Robin Yount
Bat-Hat-Jersey/25
SC1 Steve Carlton 15.00 4.50
Bat/325
SC2 Steve Carlton 50.00 15.00
Hat/65
SC3 Steve Carlton 10.00 3.00
Jersey/750
SC4 Steve Carlton 50.00 15.00
Bat-Jersey/100
SC5 Steve Carlton
Bat-Hat-Jsy/25
SM1 Stan Musial 60.00 18.00
Bat/325
SM2 Stan Musial 150.00 45.00
Hat/65
SM3 Stan Musial 40.00 12.00
Jersey/975
SM4 Stan Musial 150.00 45.00
Bat-Jersey/100
SM5 Stan Musial
Bat-Hat-Jsy/25
TG1 Tony Gwynn 50.00 15.00
Bat/260
TG2 Tony Gwynn 100.00 30.00
Hat/115
TG3 Tony Gwynn 30.00 9.00
Jersey/450
TG4 Tony Gwynn 100.00 30.00
Bat-Jersey/100
TG5 Tony Gwynn
Bat-Hat-Jersey/25
WB1 Wade Boggs 25.00 7.50
Bat/250
WB2 Wade Boggs 60.00 18.00
Hat/100
WB3 Wade Boggs 15.00 4.50
Jersey/440
WB4 Wade Boggs 60.00 18.00
Bat-Jersey/100
WB5 Wade Boggs
Bat-Hat-Jersey/25

2000 Fleer Japan Sheet

This sheet featured eight of the leading players in baseball. The cards feature the design of the Fleer 2000 set. These sheets were given away at the 2000 season-opening series between the Mets and Cubs in Japan.

Nm-Mt Ex-Mt
1 Sammy Sosa 5.00 1.50
Mike Piazza
Chipper Jones
Ivan Rodriguez
Cal Ripken Jr.
Pedro Martinez
Derek Jeter
Mo Vaughn

2000 Fleer Oreo

These two standard-size cards were issued by Fleer in conjunction with the "Oreo Stacking Contest 2000". These cards were given away to each youngster who attempted to pile Oreo cookies as high as they could. Both cards have special poses not in the regular Fleer sets. These cards are not numbered so we have placed them in alphabetical order.

Nm-Mt Ex-Mt
COMPLETE SET (2) 8.00 2.40
1 Ken Griffey Jr. 3.00 .90
2 Derek Jeter 5.00 1.50

2000 Fleer Twizzlers

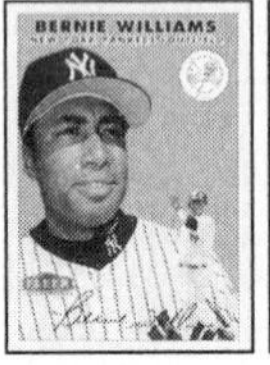

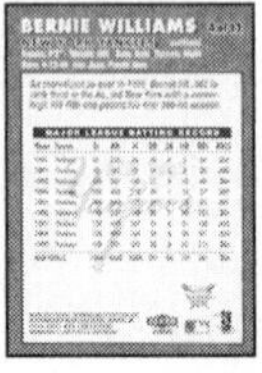

These 12 cards, designed in the style of 2000 Fleer, were inserted in packs ot Twizzlers. These cards are different from the regular Fleer cards as they are glossy on both sides and have a "team twizzler" logo on the back. The first six cards were issued to coincinde with the start of the 2000 season while the final six cards were issued approximately two months later.

Nm-Mt Ex-Mt
COMPLETE SET (12) 20.00 6.00
1 Mark McGwire 4.00 1.20
2 Cal Ripken Jr. 5.00 1.50
3 Chipper Jones 2.00 .60
4 Bernie Williams 1.00 .30
5 Alex Rodriguez 3.00 .90
6 Curt Schilling 1.00 .30
7 Ken Griffey Jr. 3.00 .90
8 Sammy Sosa 2.50 .75
9 Mike Piazza 3.00 .90
10 Pedro Martinez 1.25 .35
11 Kenny Lofton .75 .23
12 Larry Walker .50 .15

2001 Fleer Autographics

Randomly inserted into packs of Fleer Focus (1:72 w/memorabilia), Fleer Triple Crown (1:72 w/memorabilia cards), Ultra (1:48 w/memorabilia cards), 2002 Fleer Platinum Rack Packs (on average 1:6 racks contains an Autographics card) and 2002 Fleer Genuine (1:18 Hobby Direct box and 1:30 Hobby Distributor box), this insert set features authentic autographs from modern stars and prospects. The cards are designed horizontally with a full color player image at the side allowing plenty of room for the player's autograph. Card backs are unnumbered and feature Fleer's certificate of authenticity. Cards are checklisted alphabetically by player's last name and abbreviations indicating which brands each card was distributed in follows the player name. The brand legend is as follows: FC = Fleer Focus, TC = Fleer Triple Crown, UL = Ultra.

Nm-Mt Ex-Mt
FC SUFFIX ON FOCUS DISTRIBUTION
FS SUFFIX ON SHOWCASE DISTRIBUTION
FP'02 SUFFIX ON ULTRA DISTRIBUTION
GN SUFFIX ON GENUINE DISTRIBUTION
PM SUFFIX ON PREMIUM DISTRIBUTION
TC SUFFIX ON TRIPLE CROWN DISTRIBUTION
UL SUFFIX ON ULTRA DISTRIBUTION
1 Roberto Alomar 40.00 12.00
FC-FS-GN-PM-TC-UL
2 Jimmy Anderson TC-UL 10.00 3.00
3 Ryan Anderson TC 10.00 3.00
4 Rick Ankiel 10.00 3.00
FC-FS-GN-PM-TC
5 Albert Belle FC-FS-GN 15.00 4.50
6 Carlos Beltran FS-GN 15.00 4.50
7 Adrian Beltre 15.00 4.50
FC-FS-GN-PM-TC
8 Peter Bergeron 10.00 3.00
GN-PM-TC
9 Lance Berkman 15.00 4.50
FC-GN-TC-UL
10 Barry Bonds 120.00 36.00
FC-GN-TC-UL
11 Milton Bradley 15.00 4.50
FS-GN-TC
12 Ryan Bradley 10.00 3.00
GN'02
13 Dee Brown 10.00 3.00
FS-GN-PM-TC-FP'02
14 Roosevelt Brown 10.00 3.00
TC-UL
15 Jeromy Burnitz 15.00 4.50
FC-FS-GN-PM-UL
16 Pat Burrell 15.00 4.50
FC-FS-GN-PM-TC-UL
17 Alex Cabrera 10.00 3.00
UL
18 Sean Casey 15.00 4.50
FC-FS-GN-PM-TC
19 Eric Chavez 15.00 4.50
FC-GN-PM-TC-UL
20 Giuseppe Chiaramonte 10.00 3.00
TC
21 Joe Crede 10.00 3.00
FS-PM-TC-UL-FP'02
22 Jose Cruz Jr. 15.00 4.50
FS-GN-PM-TC
23 Johnny Damon 15.00 4.50
GN-PM-UL
24 Carlos Delgado 15.00 4.50
FC-GN-TC-UL
25 Ryan Dempster 10.00 3.00
FS-GN-TC-FP'02
26 J.D. Drew 15.00 4.50
FC-FS-GN-PM
27 Adam Dunn 25.00 7.50
FS-TC-UL-FP'02
28 Erubiel Durazo 10.00 3.00
FS-GN
29 Jermaine Dye 15.00 4.50
FC-FS-GN-PM
30 David Eckstein 10.00 3.00
FS-TC
31 Jim Edmonds 15.00 4.50
FC-GN-PM-TC-UL
32 Alex Escobar 10.00 3.00
FS-GN-PM
33 Seth Etherton 10.00 3.00
FS-GN
34 Adam Everett 10.00 3.00
FS-GN
35 Carlos Febles 10.00 3.00
FS-GN
36 Troy Glaus 25.00 7.50
FC-FS-GN-PM-TC
37 Chad Green 10.00 3.00
TC-UL
38 Ben Grieve 10.00 3.00
FC-FS-GN
39 Wilton Guerrero 10.00 3.00
GN'02
40 Tony Gwynn 60.00 18.00
FC-GN-PM-TC
41 Toby Hall 10.00 3.00
FS-GN
42 Todd Helton 25.00 7.50
FS-GN-PM-TC
43 Chad Hermansen 10.00 3.00
GN-PM-TC
44 Dustin Hermanson 10.00 3.00
PM-UL
45 Shea Hillenbrand 15.00 4.50
FS-GN-PM-TC
46 Aubrey Huff 15.00 4.50
FS-GN-PM-TC
47 Derek Jeter 120.00 36.00
GN-PM
48 D'Angelo Jimenez 10.00 3.00
FS
49 Randy Johnson 60.00 18.00
FC-GN-TC-UL
50 Chipper Jones 50.00 15.00
FC-GN-PMTC
51 Cesar King 10.00 3.00
GN
52 Paul Konerko 15.00 4.50
FS-GN-PM-FP'02
53 Corey Koskie 15.00 4.50
GN'02
54 Mike Lamb 10.00 3.00
FC-FS-GN-TC
55 Matt Lawton 10.00 3.00
FS-GN
56 Corey Lee 10.00 3.00
GN-TC-UL
57 Derrek Lee 15.00 4.50
FS-GN-PM-UL
58 Mike Lieberthal 15.00 4.50
FC-FS-GN-PM
59 Steve Lomasney 10.00 3.00
TC
60 Terrence Long 15.00 4.50
FC-GN-PM-TC-UL
61 Mike Lowell 15.00 4.50
FS-GN
62 Julio Lugo 10.00 3.00
FS-GN-PM-TC-UL
63 Greg Maddux 80.00 24.00
FC-GN
64 Jason Marquis 10.00 3.00
FS-GN-TC
65 Edgar Martinez 40.00 12.00
FC-FS-GN-UL
66 Justin Miller 10.00 3.00
GN-UL
67 Kevin Millwood 15.00 4.50
FC-FS-GN-PM
68 Eric Milton 10.00 3.00
FS-GN-PM
69 Bengie Molina 10.00 3.00
FS-GN-TC
70 Mike Mussina 40.00 12.00
FC-FS-GN-PM-TC
71 David Ortiz 15.00 4.50
GN'02
72 Russ Ortiz 15.00 4.50
FS-PM-UL
73 Pablo Ozuna 10.00 3.00
GN-PM-TC-UL
74 Corey Patterson 15.00 4.50
FC-FS-GN-PM-TC
75 Carl Pavano 15.00 4.50
PM
76 Jay Payton 10.00 3.00
FC-FS-GN-PM-TC
77 Wily Pena 10.00 3.00
TC
78 Josh Phelps 15.00 4.50
TC
79 Adam Piatt 10.00 3.00
FS-GN-TC-UL-FP'02
80 Juan Pierre 15.00 4.50
FC-FS-GN
81 Brad Radke 15.00 4.50
FC-FS-GN-PM-FP'02
82 Mark Redman 10.00 3.00
UL
83 Matt Riley 10.00 3.00
GN-TC
84 Cal Ripken 150.00 45.00
GN-PM
85 John Rocker 10.00 3.00
FS-GN
86 Alex Rodriguez 100.00 30.00
FS-GN-TC
87 Scott Rolen 25.00 7.50
FC-FS-GN-PM
88 Alex Sanchez 10.00 3.00
PM-TC
89 Fernando Seguignol 10.00 3.00
GN'02
90 Richie Sexson 15.00 4.50
FS-GN-PM-UL
91 Gary Sheffield 25.00 7.50
FC-FS-GN-PM-TC-UL
92 Alfonso Soriano 50.00 15.00
GN-PM-TC-UL
93 Dernell Stenson 15.00 4.50
GN-PM
94 Garrett Stephenson 10.00 3.00
PM
95 Shannon Stewart 15.00 4.50
FS-GN-PM-TC
96 Fernando Tatis 10.00 3.00
FC-GN-TC
97 Miguel Tejada 15.00 4.50
FS-FP'02
98 Jorge Toca 10.00 3.00
GN-PM
99 Robin Ventura 15.00 4.50
FC-FS-GN-PM
100 Jose Vidro 15.00 4.50
FS-GN-PM-TC-UL-FP'02
101 Billy Wagner 25.00 7.50
FS-PM
102 Kip Wells 10.00 3.00
FS-GN
103 Vernon Wells 15.00 4.50
GN-PM-UL
104 Rondell White 15.00 4.50
FS-GN
105 Bernie Williams 80.00 24.00
FP'02
106 Scott Williamson 10.00 3.00
GN
107 Preston Wilson 15.00 4.50
FS-GN-TC-UL
108 Kerry Wood 40.00 12.00
FC-FS-GN-PM-TC-FP'02
109 Jamey Wright 10.00 3.00
GN-UL
110 Julio Zuleta 10.00 3.00
FS-GN-PM-TC-UL

2001 Fleer Autographics Gold

Randomly inserted into a selection of Fleer products, this set is a complete parallel of the Autographics insert. These cards were produced with gold foil stamping on front and are individually serial numbered to 50. Corey Koskie was released exclusively in 2002 Fleer Platinum rack packs.

Nm-Mt Ex-Mt
*GOLD: 1X TO 2X BASIC AUTOS

2001 Fleer Autographics Silver

Randomly inserted into a selection of Fleer products, this set is a complete parallel of the Autographics insert. These cards were produced with silver foil stamping on front and are individually serial numbered to 250. Corey Koskie was distributed exclusively in 2002 Fleer Platinum rack packs.

Nm-Mt Ex-Mt
*SILVER: .75X TO 1.5X BASIC AUTOS

2001 Fleer Feel the Game

This insert set features game-used jersey cards of major league stars. The cards were distributed across several different Fleer products issued in 2001. Please note that the cards are listed below in alphabetical order for convience. Cards with "FC" listed after the players name were inserted into Fleer Focus packs (one Autographic or Feel Game in every 72 packs), "TC" listed after the players name were inserted into packs of Fleer Triple Crown (one Feel Game, Autographic or Crown of Gold in every 72 packs), while cards with "UL" after their name were inserted into Ultra packs (one Autographic or Feel Game in every 48 packs).

Nm-Mt Ex-Mt
*GOLD: 1.25X TO 2.5X BASIC FEEL GAME
1 Moises Alou FC-UL 10.00 3.00
2 Brady Anderson FC-UL 10.00 3.00
3 Adrian Beltre TC-UL 10.00 3.00
4 Dante Bichette FC-TC 10.00 3.00
5 Roger Cedeno TC 10.00 3.00
6 Ben Davis TC 10.00 3.00
7 Carlos Delgado TC-UL 10.00 3.00
8 J.D. Drew TC-UL 10.00 3.00
9 Jermaine Dye FC-UL 10.00 3.00
10 Jason Giambi TC-UL 15.00 4.50
11 Brian Giles FC-TC 10.00 3.00

12 Juan Gonzalez FC-TC 15.00 4.50
13 Rickey Henderson FC 15.00 4.50
14 Richard Hidalgo TC-UL 10.00 3.00
15 Chipper Jones TC-UL 15.00 4.50
16 Eric Karros TC-UL 10.00 3.00
17 Javy Lopez FC-TC 10.00 3.00
18 Tino Martinez FC-TC 15.00 4.50
19 Raul Mondesi TC-UL 10.00 3.00
20 Phil Nevin FC-TC 10.00 3.00
21 Chan Ho Park TC-UL 10.00 3.00
22 Ivan Rodriguez TC-UL 15.00 4.50
23 Matt Stairs FC-UL 10.00 3.00
24 Shannon Stewart FC-TC 10.00 3.00
25 Frank Thomas TC-UL 15.00 4.50
26 Jose Vidro FC-TC-UL 10.00 3.00
27 Matt Williams TC-UL 10.00 3.00
28 Preston Wilson TC-UL 10.00 3.00

2001 Fleer Ripken Cal to Greatness Jumbo

This one card set, features four different images of Ripken on front along with a large "8" on the right side. The top of the card features the words "8/10/81 -10-6/01" and "Cal to Greatness" on the top. The back of the card features various honors and records that Ripken owns. There is also a career batting line. On the bottom, the cards are serial numbered out of 2632, which was the number of games in Ripken's consecutive game hitting streak.

Nm-Mt Ex-Mt
NNO Cal Ripken 10.00 3.00

2001 Fleer Ripken Commemorative 50000

This set was issued by Fleer's and features highlights of the career of Cal Ripken Jr. Unlike the other set with a print run of 2632 sets, this set was issued to a print run of 50,000 sets and does not feature memorabilia cards. The set was issued in the following subsets: Career Highlights (1-12); The Streak (13-24); Final Season (25-35); Last Game (36-40) and Fleer Reprints (41-60).

Nm-Mt Ex-Mt
COMPLETE SET 10.00 3.00
COMMON CARD .50 .15

2002 Fleer

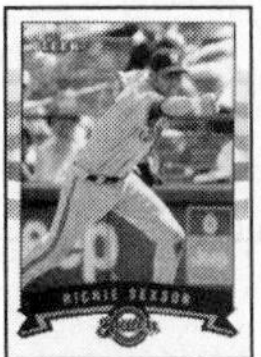
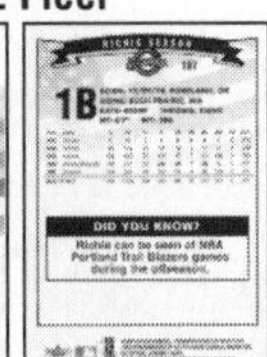

This 540 card set was issued in May, 2002. These cards were issued in 10 card packs which came packed 24 packs to a box and 10 boxes to a case and had an SRP of $2 per pack. Cards number 432 through 491 featured players who switched teams in the off season while cards 492 through 531 featured leading prospects and cards numbered 532 through 540 feature photos of important ballparks along with checklists on the back.

Nm-Mt Ex-Mt
COMPLETE SET (540) 100.00 30.00
COMMON CARD (1-540) .25 .07
COMMON CARD (492-531) .50 .15
1 Darin Erstad FP .25 .07
2 Randy Johnson FP .60 .18
3 Chipper Jones FP .60 .18
4 Jay Gibbons FP .25 .07
5 Nomar Garciaparra FP 1.00 .30
6 Sammy Sosa FP 1.00 .30
7 Frank Thomas FP .60 .18
8 Ken Griffey Jr. FP 1.00 .30
9 Jim Thome FP .60 .18
10 Todd Helton FP .40 .12
11 Jeff Weaver FP .25 .07
12 Cliff Floyd FP .25 .07
13 Jeff Bagwell FP .40 .12
14 Mike Sweeney FP .25 .07
15 Adrian Beltre FP .25 .07
16 Richie Sexson FP .25 .07
17 Brad Radke FP .25 .07
18 Vladimir Guerrero FP .60 .18
19 Mike Piazza FP 1.00 .30
20 Derek Jeter FP 1.25 .35
21 Eric Chavez FP .25 .07
22 Pat Burrell FP .25 .07
23 Brian Giles FP .25 .07
24 Trevor Hoffman FP .25 .07
25 Barry Bonds FP 1.00 .30
26 Ichiro Suzuki FP 1.00 .30
27 Albert Pujols FP 1.00 .30
28 Ben Grieve FP .25 .07
29 Alex Rodriguez FP 1.00 .30
30 Carlos Delgado FP .25 .07
31 Miguel Tejada .40 .12
32 Todd Hollandsworth .25 .07
33 Marlon Anderson .25 .07
34 Kerry Robinson .25 .07
35 Chris Richard .25 .07
36 Jamey Wright .25 .07
37 Ray Lankford .25 .07
38 Mike Bordick .40 .12
39 Danny Graves .25 .07
40 A.J. Pierzynski .40 .12
41 Shannon Stewart .40 .12
42 Tony Armas Jr. .25 .07
43 Brad Ausmus .25 .07
44 Alfonso Soriano .60 .18
45 Junior Spivey .25 .07
46 Brent Mayne .25 .07
47 Jim Thome 1.00 .30
48 Dan Wilson .25 .07
49 Geoff Jenkins .40 .12
50 Kris Benson .25 .07
51 Rafael Furcal .40 .12
52 Wiki Gonzalez .25 .07
53 Jeff Kent .40 .12
54 Curt Schilling .60 .18
55 Ken Harvey .25 .07
56 Roosevelt Brown .25 .07
57 David Segui .25 .07
58 Mario Valdez .25 .07
59 Adam Dunn .40 .12
60 Bob Howry .25 .07
61 Michael Barrett .25 .07
62 Garret Anderson .40 .12
63 Kelvim Escobar .25 .07
64 Ben Grieve .25 .07
65 Randy Johnson 1.00 .30
66 Jose Offerman .25 .07
67 Jason Kendall .40 .12
68 Joel Pineiro .40 .12
69 Alex Escobar .25 .07
70 Chris George .25 .07
71 Bobby Higginson .40 .12
72 Nomar Garciaparra 1.50 .45
73 Pat Burrell .40 .12
74 Lee Stevens .25 .07
75 Felipe Lopez .25 .07
76 Al Leiter .40 .12
77 Jim Edmonds .40 .12
78 Al Levine .25 .07
79 Raul Mondesi .40 .12
80 Jose Valentin .25 .07
81 Matt Clement .40 .12
82 Richard Hidalgo .40 .12
83 Jamie Moyer .40 .12
84 Brian Schneider .25 .07
85 John Franco .40 .12
86 Brian Buchanan .25 .07
87 Roy Oswalt .40 .12
88 Johnny Estrada .25 .07
89 Marcus Giles .40 .12
90 Carlos Valderrama .25 .07
91 Mark Mulder .40 .12
92 Mark Grace .60 .18
93 Andy Ashby .25 .07
94 Woody Williams .25 .07
95 Ben Petrick .25 .07
96 Roy Halladay .40 .12
97 Fred McGriff .60 .18
98 Shawn Green .40 .12
99 Todd Hundley .25 .07
100 Carlos Febles .25 .07
101 Jason Marquis .25 .07
102 Mike Redmond .25 .07
103 Shane Halter .25 .07
104 Trot Nixon .60 .18
105 Jeremy Giambi .25 .07
106 Carlos Delgado .40 .12
107 Richie Sexson .40 .12
108 Russ Ortiz .40 .12
109 David Ortiz .40 .12
110 Curtis Leskanic .25 .07
111 Jay Payton .25 .07
112 Travis Phelps .25 .07
113 J.T. Snow .40 .12
114 Edgar Renteria .40 .12
115 Freddy Garcia .40 .12
116 Cliff Floyd .40 .12
117 Charles Nagy .25 .07
118 Tony Batista .40 .12
119 Rafael Palmeiro .60 .18
120 Darren Dreifort .25 .07
121 Warren Morris .25 .07
122 Augie Ojeda .25 .07
123 Rusty Greer .40 .12
124 Esteban Yan .25 .07
125 Corey Patterson .40 .12
126 Matt Ginter .25 .07
127 Matt Lawton .25 .07
128 Miguel Batista .25 .07
129 Randy Winn .25 .07
130 Eric Milton .25 .07
131 Jack Wilson .25 .07
132 Sean Casey .40 .12
133 Mike Sweeney .40 .12
134 Jason Tyner .25 .07
135 Carlos Hernandez .25 .07
136 Shea Hillenbrand .40 .12
137 Shawn Wooten .25 .07
138 Peter Bergeron .25 .07
139 Travis Lee .25 .07
140 Craig Wilson .25 .07
141 Carlos Guillen .25 .07
142 Chipper Jones 1.00 .30
143 Gabe Kapler .25 .07
144 Raul Ibanez .25 .07
145 Eric Chavez .40 .12
146 D'Angelo Jimenez .25 .07
147 Chad Hermansen .25 .07
148 Joe Kennedy .25 .07
149 Mariano Rivera .60 .18
150 Jeff Bagwell .60 .18
151 Joe McEwing .25 .07
152 Ronnie Belliard .25 .07
153 Desi Relaford .25 .07
154 Vinny Castilla .40 .12
155 Tim Hudson .40 .12
156 Wilton Guerrero .25 .07
157 Raul Casanova .25 .07
158 Edgardo Alfonzo .40 .12
159 Derrek Lee .40 .12
160 Phil Nevin .40 .12
161 Roger Clemens 2.00 .60
162 Jason LaRue .25 .07
163 Brian Lawrence .25 .07
164 Adrian Beltre .40 .12
165 Troy Glaus .60 .18
166 Jeff Weaver .25 .07
167 B.J. Surhoff .40 .12
168 Eric Byrnes .25 .07
169 Mike Sirotka .25 .07
170 Bill Haselman .25 .07
171 Javier Vazquez .40 .12
172 Sidney Ponson .40 .12
173 Adam Everett .25 .07
174 Bubba Trammell .25 .07
175 Robb Nen .40 .12
176 Barry Larkin 1.00 .30
177 Tony Graffanino .25 .07
178 Rich Garces .25 .07
179 Juan Uribe .25 .07
180 Tom Glavine .60 .18
181 Eric Karros .40 .12
182 Michael Cuddyer .25 .07
183 Wade Miller .40 .12
184 Matt Williams .40 .12
185 Matt Morris .40 .12
186 Rickey Henderson 1.00 .30
187 Trevor Hoffman .40 .12
188 Wilson Betemit .25 .07
189 Steve Karsay .25 .07
190 Frank Catalanotto .25 .07
191 Jason Schmidt .40 .12
192 Roger Cedeno .25 .07
193 Magglio Ordonez .40 .12
194 Pat Hentgen .25 .07
195 Mike Lieberthal .40 .12
196 Andy Pettitte .60 .18
197 Jay Gibbons .40 .12
198 Rolando Arrojo .25 .07
199 Joe Mays .25 .07
200 Aubrey Huff .40 .12
201 Nelson Figueroa .25 .07
202 Paul Konerko .40 .12
203 Ken Griffey Jr. 1.50 .45
204 Brandon Duckworth .25 .07
205 Sammy Sosa 1.50 .45
206 Carl Everett .40 .12
207 Scott Rolen .60 .18
208 Orlando Hernandez .40 .12
209 Todd Helton .60 .18
210 Preston Wilson .40 .12
211 Gil Meche .40 .12
212 Bill Mueller .40 .12
213 Craig Biggio .60 .18
214 Dean Palmer .40 .12
215 Randy Wolf .40 .12
216 Jeff Suppan .25 .07
217 Jimmy Rollins .40 .12
218 Alexis Gomez .25 .07
219 Ellis Burks .40 .12
220 Ramon E. Martinez .25 .07
221 Ramiro Mendoza .25 .07
222 Einar Diaz .25 .07
223 Brent Abernathy .25 .07
224 Darin Erstad .40 .12
225 Reggie Taylor .25 .07
226 Jason Jennings .25 .07
227 Ray Durham .40 .12
228 John Parrish .25 .07
229 Kevin Young .25 .07
230 Xavier Nady .25 .07
231 Juan Cruz .25 .07
232 Greg Norton .25 .07
233 Barry Bonds 2.50 .75
234 Kip Wells .25 .07
235 Paul LoDuca .40 .12
236 Javy Lopez .40 .12
237 Luis Castillo .40 .12
238 Tom Gordon .25 .07
239 Mike Mordecai .25 .07
240 Damian Rolls .25 .07
241 Julio Lugo .25 .07
242 Ichiro Suzuki 1.50 .45
243 Tony Womack .25 .07
244 Matt Anderson .25 .07
245 Carlos Lee .40 .12
246 Alex Rodriguez 1.50 .45
247 Bernie Williams .60 .18
248 Scott Sullivan .25 .07
249 Mike Hampton .40 .12
250 Orlando Cabrera .25 .07
251 Benito Santiago .40 .12
252 Steve Finley .40 .12
253 Dave Williams .25 .07
254 Adam Kennedy .25 .07
255 Omar Vizquel .40 .12
256 Garrett Stephenson .25 .07
257 Fernando Tatis .25 .07
258 Mike Piazza 1.50 .45
259 Scott Spiezio .25 .07
260 Jacque Jones .40 .12
261 Russell Branyan .25 .07
262 Mark McLemore .25 .07
263 Mitch Meluskey .25 .07
264 Marlon Byrd .40 .12
265 Kyle Farnsworth .25 .07
266 Billy Sylvester .25 .07
267 C.C. Sabathia .40 .12
268 Mark Buehrle .40 .12
269 Geoff Blum .25 .07
270 Bret Prinz .25 .07
271 Placido Polanco .25 .07
272 John Olerud .40 .12
273 Pedro Martinez 1.00 .30
274 Doug Mientkiewicz .40 .12
275 Jason Bere .25 .07
276 Bud Smith .25 .07
277 Terrence Long .40 .12
278 Troy Percival .40 .12
279 Derek Jeter 2.50 .75
280 Eric Owens .25 .07
281 Jay Bell .40 .12
282 Mike Cameron .40 .12
283 Joe Randa .25 .07
284 Brian Roberts .40 .12
285 Ryan Klesko .40 .12
286 Ryan Dempster .25 .07
287 Cristian Guzman .40 .12
288 Tim Salmon .60 .18
289 Mark Johnson .25 .07
290 Brian Giles .40 .12
291 Jon Lieber .25 .07
292 Fernando Vina .40 .12
293 Mike Mussina 1.00 .30
294 Juan Pierre .40 .12
295 Carlos Beltran .40 .12
296 Vladimir Guerrero 1.00 .30
297 Orlando Merced .25 .07
298 Jose Hernandez .25 .07
299 Mike Lamb .25 .07
300 David Eckstein .25 .07
301 Mark Loretta .25 .07
302 Greg Vaughn .40 .12
303 Jose Vidro .40 .12
304 Jose Ortiz .25 .07
305 Mark Grudzielanek .25 .07
306 Rob Bell .25 .07
307 Elmer Dessens .25 .07
308 Tomas Perez .25 .07
309 Jerry Hairston Jr. .25 .07
310 Mike Stanton .25 .07
311 Todd Walker .40 .12
312 Jason Varitek .40 .12
313 Masato Yoshii .25 .07
314 Ben Sheets .40 .12
315 Roberto Hernandez .25 .07
316 Eli Marrero .25 .07
317 Josh Beckett .60 .18
318 Robert Fick .40 .12
319 Aramis Ramirez .40 .12
320 Bartolo Colon .40 .12
321 Kenny Kelly .25 .07
322 Luis Gonzalez .40 .12
323 John Smoltz .60 .18
324 Homer Bush .25 .07
325 Kevin Millwood .40 .12
326 Manny Ramirez .40 .12
327 Armando Benitez .40 .12
328 Luis Alicea .25 .07
329 Mark Kotsay .25 .07
330 Felix Rodriguez .25 .07
331 Eddie Taubensee .25 .07
332 John Burkett .25 .07
333 Ramon Ortiz .25 .07
334 Daryle Ward .25 .07
335 Jarrod Washburn .40 .12
336 Benji Gil .25 .07
337 Mike Lowell .40 .12
338 Larry Walker .60 .18
339 Andruw Jones .40 .12
340 Scott Elarton .25 .07
341 Tony McKnight .25 .07
342 Frank Thomas 1.00 .30
343 Kevin Brown .40 .12
344 Jermaine Dye .40 .12
345 Luis Rivas .25 .07
346 Jeff Conine .40 .12
347 Bobby Kielty .25 .07
348 Jeffrey Hammonds .25 .07
349 Keith Foulke .25 .07
350 Dave Martinez .25 .07
351 Adam Eaton .25 .07
352 Brandon Inge .25 .07
353 Tyler Houston .25 .07
354 Bobby Abreu .40 .12
355 Ivan Rodriguez 1.00 .30
356 Doug Glanville .25 .07
357 Jorge Julio .25 .07
358 Kerry Wood 1.00 .30
359 Eric Munson .25 .07
360 Joe Crede .25 .07
361 Denny Neagle .25 .07
362 Vance Wilson .25 .07
363 Neifi Perez .25 .07
364 Darryl Kile .40 .12
365 Jose Macias .25 .07
366 Michael Coleman .25 .07
367 Erubiel Durazo .25 .07
368 Darrin Fletcher .25 .07
369 Matt White .25 .07
370 Marvin Benard .25 .07
371 Brad Penny .25 .07
372 Chuck Finley .40 .12
373 Delino DeShields .25 .07
374 Adrian Brown .25 .07
375 Corey Koskie .40 .12
376 Kazuhiro Sasaki .40 .12
377 Brent Butler .25 .07
378 Paul Wilson .25 .07
379 Scott Williamson .25 .07
380 Mike Young .25 .07
381 Toby Hall .25 .07
382 Shane Reynolds .25 .07
383 Tom Goodwin .25 .07
384 Seth Etherton .25 .07
385 Billy Wagner .40 .12
386 Josh Phelps .25 .07
387 Kyle Lohse .25 .07
388 Jeremy Fikac .25 .07
389 Jorge Posada .60 .18
390 Bret Boone .40 .12
391 Angel Berroa .40 .12
392 Matt Mantei .25 .07
393 Alex Gonzalez .25 .07
394 Scott Strickland .25 .07
395 Charles Johnson .40 .12
396 Ramon Hernandez .25 .07
397 Damian Jackson .25 .07
398 Albert Pujols 2.00 .60
399 Gary Bennett .25 .07
400 Edgar Martinez .60 .18
401 Carl Pavano .25 .07
402 Chris Gomez .25 .07
403 Jaret Wright .25 .07
404 Lance Berkman .40 .12
405 Robert Person .25 .07
406 Brook Fordyce .25 .07
407 Adam Pettyjohn .25 .07
408 Chris Carpenter .25 .07
409 Rey Ordonez .25 .07
410 Eric Gagne .60 .18
411 Damion Easley .25 .07
412 A.J. Burnett .25 .07
413 Aaron Boone .40 .12
414 J.D. Drew .40 .12
415 Kelly Stinnett .25 .07
416 Mark Quinn .25 .07
417 Brad Radke .40 .12
418 Jose Cruz Jr. .40 .12
419 Greg Maddux 1.50 .45
420 Steve Cox .25 .07
421 Torii Hunter .40 .12
422 Sandy Alomar .25 .07
423 Barry Zito .60 .18
424 Bill Hall .25 .07
425 Marquis Grissom .25 .07
426 Rich Aurilia .40 .12
427 Royce Clayton .25 .07
428 Travis Fryman .40 .12
429 Pablo Ozuna .25 .07
430 David Dellucci .25 .07
431 Vernon Wells .40 .12
432 Gregg Zaun CP .25 .07
433 Alex Gonzalez CP .25 .07
434 Hideo Nomo CP 1.00 .30
435 Jeromy Burnitz CP .40 .12
436 Gary Sheffield CP .40 .12
437 Tino Martinez CP .60 .18
438 Tsuyoshi Shinjo CP .40 .12
439 Chan Ho Park CP .40 .12
440 Tony Clark CP .25 .07
441 Brad Fullmer CP .25 .07
442 Jason Giambi CP 1.00 .30
443 Billy Koch CP .25 .07
444 Mo Vaughn CP .40 .12
445 Alex Ochoa CP .25 .07
446 Darren Lewis CP .25 .07
447 John Rocker CP .25 .07
448 Scott Hatteberg CP .25 .07
449 Brady Anderson CP .40 .12
450 Chuck Knoblauch CP .40 .12
451 Pokey Reese CP .25 .07
452 Brian Jordan CP .40 .12
453 Albie Lopez CP .25 .07
454 David Bell CP .25 .07
455 Juan Gonzalez CP 1.00 .30
456 Terry Adams CP .25 .07
457 Kenny Lofton CP .40 .12
458 Shawn Estes CP .25 .07
459 Josh Fogg CP .25 .07
460 Dmitri Young CP .40 .12
461 Johnny Damon CP .40 .12
462 Chris Singleton CP .25 .07
463 Ricky Ledee CP .25 .07
464 Dustin Hermanson CP .25 .07
465 Aaron Sele CP .25 .07
466 Chris Stynes CP .25 .07
467 Matt Stairs CP .25 .07
468 Kevin Appier CP .40 .12
469 Omar Daal CP .25 .07
470 Moises Alou CP .40 .12
471 Juan Encarnacion CP .25 .07
472 Robin Ventura CP .40 .12
473 Eric Hinske CP .25 .07
474 Rondell White CP .40 .12
475 Carlos Pena CP .25 .07
476 Craig Paquette CP .25 .07
477 Marty Cordova CP .25 .07
478 Brett Tomko CP .25 .07
479 Reggie Sanders CP .40 .12
480 Roberto Alomar CP 1.00 .30
481 Jeff Cirillo CP .25 .07
482 Todd Zeile CP .40 .12
483 John Vander Wal CP .25 .07
484 Rick Helling CP .25 .07
485 Jeff D'Amico CP .25 .07
486 David Justice CP .40 .12
487 Jason Isringhausen CP .40 .12
488 Shigetoshi Hasegawa CP .40 .12
489 Eric Young CP .25 .07
490 David Wells CP .40 .12
491 Ruben Sierra CP .25 .07
492 Aaron Cook FF RC .75 .23
493 Takahito Nomura FF RC .75 .23
494 Austin Kearns FF .75 .23
495 Kazuhisa Ishii FF RC 4.00 1.20
496 Mark Teixeira FF 2.00 .60
497 Rene Reyes FF RC .75 .23
498 Tim Spooneybarger FF .50 .15
499 Ben Broussard FF .50 .15
500 Eric Cyr FF .50 .15
501 Anastacio Martinez FF RC .75 .23
502 Morgan Ensberg FF .75 .23
503 Steve Kent FF RC .75 .23
504 Franklin Nunez FF RC .75 .23
505 Adam Walker FF RC .75 .23
506 Anderson Machado FF RC .75 .23
507 Ryan Drese FF .50 .15
508 Luis Ugueto FF RC .75 .23
509 Jorge Nunez FF RC .75 .23
510 Colby Lewis FF .50 .15
511 Ron Calloway FF RC .75 .23
512 Hansel Izquierdo FF RC .75 .23
513 Jason Lane FF .50 .15
514 Rafael Soriano FF .75 .23
515 Jackson Melian FF .50 .15
516 Edwin Almonte FF RC .75 .23
517 Satoru Komiyama FF RC .75 .23
518 Corey Thurman FF RC .75 .23
519 Jorge De La Rosa FF RC .75 .23
520 Victor Martinez FF .75 .23
521 Dewon Brazelton FF .50 .15
522 Marlon Byrd FF .75 .23
523 Jae Seo FF .50 .15
524 Orlando Hudson FF .50 .15
525 Sean Burroughs FF .75 .23
526 Ryan Langerhans FF .50 .15
527 David Kelton FF .50 .15
528 So Taguchi FF RC 1.25 .35
529 Tyler Walker FF .50 .15
530 Hank Blalock FF 2.00 .60
531 Mark Prior FF 5.00 1.50
532 Yankee Stadium CL .40 .12
533 Fenway Park CL .40 .12
534 Wrigley Field CL .40 .12
535 Dodger Stadium CL .40 .12
536 Camden Yards CL .40 .12
537 PacBell Park CL .25 .07
538 Jacobs Field CL .25 .07
539 SAFECO Field CL .25 .07
540 Miller Field CL .25 .07
P279 Derek Jeter Promo

2002 Fleer Gold Backs

Randomly inserted in packs, this is a parallel to the 2002 Fleer set. These cards can be differentiated from the regular cards by either the "gold" stats or text used on the back of the cards. It was announced that 15 percent of the print run featured these gold backs.

Nm-Mt Ex-Mt
*GOLD BACK: .75X TO 2X BASIC
*GOLD BACK 492-531: .75X TO 2X BASIC

2002 Fleer Mini

Randomly inserted in retail packs, these cards parallel the 2002 Fleer set. They are printed to a smaller size than the regular set and also were printed to a stated print run of 50 serial numbered sets.

Nm-Mt Ex-Mt
*MINI: 10X TO 25X BASIC
*MINI 492-531: 5X TO 12X BASIC

2002 Fleer Tiffany

Randomly inserted in hobby packs, this is a parallel to the 2002 Fleer set and are printed to a stated print run of 200 serial numbered sets. These cards can be differentiated from the regular Fleer set by the glossy finish on the front.

Nm-Mt Ex-Mt
*TIFFANY: 4X TO 10X BASIC
*TIFFANY 492-531: 2X TO 5X BASIC

2002 Fleer Barry Bonds Career Highlights

Issued at overall odds of one in 12 hobby packs and one in 36 retail packs, these 10 cards feature highlights from Barry Bonds career. These cards were issued in different rates depending on which card number it was.

Nm-Mt Ex-Mt
COMPLETE SET (10) 40.00 12.00
COMMON CARD (1-3) 4.00 1.20
COMMON CARD (4-6) 5.00 1.50
COMMON CARD (7-9) 8.00 2.40
COMMON CARD (10) 5.00 1.50
1-3 ODDS 1:65 HOBBY, 1:225 RETAIL
4-6 ODDS 1:125 HOBBY, 1:400 RETAIL
7-9 ODDS 1:250 HOBBY, 1:500 RETAIL
10 ODDS 1:383 HOBBY, 1:800 RETAIL
OVERALL ODDS 1:12 HOBBY, 1:36 RETAIL

2002 Fleer Barry Bonds Career Highlights Autographs

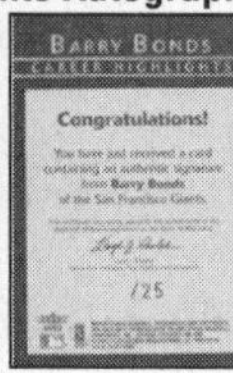

Randomly inserted in packs, these 10 cards not only parallel the Bonds Career Highlight set but also include an autograph from Barry Bonds on the card. Each card was issued to a stated print run of 25 serial numbered sets and due to market scarcity no pricing is provided.

Nm-Mt Ex-Mt
COMMON CARD (1-10) 200.00 60.00

2002 Fleer Classic Cuts Autographs

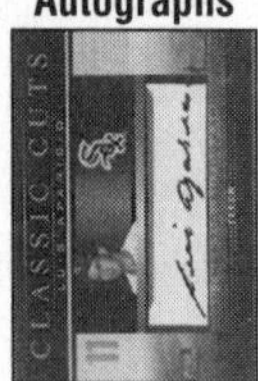

Inserted in packs at a stated rate of one in 432 hobby packs, these nine cards feature autographs from a retired legend. A few cards were issued to a smaller quantity and we have notated that information along with their stated print run next to their name in our checklist.

Nm-Mt Ex-Mt
BR-A Brooks Robinson SP/200 50.00 15.00
GP-A Gaylord Perry SP/225 20.00 6.00
HK-A Harmon Killebrew 50.00 15.00
JM-A Juan Marichal 15.00 4.50
LA-A Luis Aparicio 15.00 4.50
PR-A Phil Rizzuto SP/125 60.00 18.00
RC-A Ron Cey 15.00 4.50
RF-A Rollie Fingers SP/35
TL-A Tommy Lasorda SP/35

2002 Fleer Classic Cuts Game Used

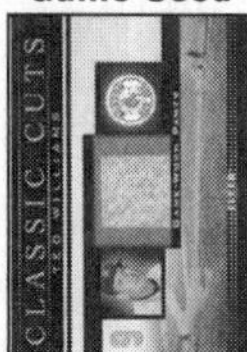

Inserted at stated odds of one in 24, these 94 cards feature retired players along with an authentic game-used memorabilia piece of that player. Some cards were issued in shorter quantites and we have provided the stated print run next to the player's name in our checklist.

Nm-Mt Ex-Mt
YBB Yogi Berra Bat/72
AD-J Andre Dawson Jsy 10.00 3.00
AT-B Alan Trammell Bat 15.00 4.50
BB-B Bobby Bonds Bat 10.00 3.00
BB-J Bobby Bonds Jsy 10.00 3.00
BD-B Bill Dickey Bat/200 25.00 7.50
BJ-J Bo Jackson Jsy 15.00 4.50
BM-B Billy Martin Bat/65
BR-B Brooks Robinson Bat/250 25.00 7.50
BT-B Bill Terry Bat/85
CF-B Carlton Fisk Bat 15.00 4.50
CF-J Carlton Fisk Jsy/150 25.00 7.50
CH-J Jim Hunter Jsy 15.00 4.50
CR-BG Cal Ripken Btg Glv/100 80.00 24.00
CR-FG Cal Ripken Fld Glv/60
CR-J Cal Ripken Jsy 50.00 15.00
CR-P Cal Ripken Pants/200 50.00 15.00
DE-B Dwight Evans Bat/250 15.00 4.50
DE-J Dwight Evans Jsy 10.00 3.00
DM-B Don Mattingly Bat/200 50.00 15.00
DM-J Don Mattingly Jsy 50.00 15.00
DM-P Don Mattingly Patch/50
DP-B Dave Parker Bat 10.00 3.00
DR-P Dave Righetti Patch
DW-B Dave Winfield Bat 10.00 3.00
DW-J Dave Winfield Jsy/231 15.00 4.50
DW-P Dave Winfield Pants 10.00 3.00
DW-P Dave Winfield Patch/25
DZ-J Don Zimmer Jsy/90
EM-B Eddie Mathews Bat/200 25.00 7.50
EM-B Eddie Murray Bat 15.00 4.50
EM-J Eddie Murray Jsy 15.00 4.50
EM-P Eddie Murray Patch/45
EW-J Earl Weaver Jsy 10.00 3.00
FL-B Fred Lynn Bat/25
GB-B George Brett Bat/250 40.00 12.00
GB-J George Brett Jsy/250 40.00 12.00
GH-B Gil Hodges Bat/200 25.00 7.50
GK-B George Kell Bat/150 25.00 7.50
HB-B Hank Bauer Bat 10.00 3.00
HG-B Hank Greenberg Bat/13
HW-B Hack Wilson Bat/8
HW-P Hoyt Wilhelm Pants/150 15.00 4.50
JB-B Johnny Bench Bat/100
JB-J Johnny Bench Jsy 15.00 4.50
JM-B Joe Morgan Bat/250 15.00 4.50
JP-J Jim Palmer Jsy/273 15.00 4.50
JR-B Jim Rice Bat/225 15.00 4.50
JR-J Jim Rice Jsy/90
JT-J Joe Torre Jsy/125 25.00 7.50
KG-B Kirk Gibson Bat 10.00 3.00
KP-B Kirby Puckett Bat/25
KP-J Kirby Puckett Jsy 15.00 4.50
LD-B Larry Doby Bat/250 15.00 4.50
LP-P Lou Piniella Pants 10.00 3.00
NF-B Nellie Fox Bat/200 25.00 7.50
NR-J Nolan Ryan Jsy 80.00 24.00
NR-P Nolan Ryan Pants/200 100.00 30.00
OC-B Orlando Cepeda Bat/45
OC-P Orlando Cepeda Pants 10.00 3.00
OS-J Ozzie Smith Jsy/250 25.00 7.50
PB-B Paul Blair Bat 10.00 3.00
PM-B Paul Molitor Bat/250 25.00 7.50
PM-P Paul Molitor Patch/110
PR-J Preacher Roe Jsy/19
PWR-J Pee Wee Reese Jsy/20
RC-B Roy Campanella Bat/7
RF-J Rollie Fingers Jsy 10.00 3.00
RJ-B Reggie Jackson Bat/50
RJ-P Reggie Jackson Pants 15.00 4.50
RK-B Ralph Kiner Bat/47
RM-P Roger Maris Pants/200 80.00 24.00
RS-B Ryne Sandberg Bat 30.00 9.00
RY-B Robin Yount Bat 15.00 4.50
SA-P Sparky Anderson Pants 10.00 3.00
SC-H Steve Carlton Hat/25
SC-P Steve Carlton Pants 10.00 3.00
SG-B Steve Garvey Bat 10.00 3.00
TJ-J Tommy John Jsy/55
TJ-P Tommy John Patch/15
TK-B Ted Kluszewski Bat/200 25.00 7.50
TK-P Ted Kluszewski Pants 15.00 4.50
TL-B Tony Lazzeri Bat/35
TM-P Thurman Munson Pants/10
TP-B Tony Perez Bat/250 15.00 4.50
TP-J Tony Perez Jsy 10.00 3.00
TW-B Ted Williams Bat 100.00 30.00
TW-P Ted Williams Pants 120.00 36.00
WB-B Wade Boggs Bat/99
WB-J Wade Boggs Jsy 15.00 4.50
WB-P Wade Boggs Patch/50
WM-J Willie McCovey Jsy/300 15.00 4.50
WR-P Willie Randolph Patch/18
WS-B Willie Stargell Bat/250 25.00 7.50

2002 Fleer Classic Cuts Game Used Autographs

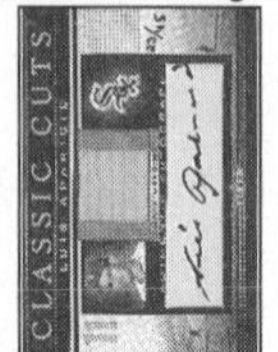

Randomly inserted in packs, these three cards feature not only a game-used piece from a retired player but also an authentic autograph. The stated print run for each player is listed next to their name in our checklist.

Nm-Mt Ex-Mt
BR-B Brooks Robinson Bat/45 100.00 30.00
LA-B Luis Aparicio Bat/45 40.00 12.00
RF-J Rollie Fingers Jsy/35

2002 Fleer Diamond Standouts

Randomly inserted in packs, these 10 cards have a stated print run of 1200 serial numbered sets. These cards feature players who most fans would consider the top 10 stars in Baseball.

Nm-Mt Ex-Mt
COMPLETE SET (10) 80.00 24.00

1 Mike Piazza 8.00 2.40
2 Derek Jeter 12.00 3.60
3 Ken Griffey Jr. 8.00 2.40
4 Barry Bonds 12.00 3.60
5 Sammy Sosa 8.00 2.40
6 Alex Rodriguez 8.00 2.40
7 Ichiro Suzuki 8.00 2.40
8 Greg Maddux 8.00 2.40
9 Jason Giambi 8.00 2.40
10 Nomar Garciaparra 8.00 2.40

2002 Fleer Golden Memories

Issued in packs at a stated rate of one in 24 packs, these 15 cards feature players who have earned many honors during their playing career.

Nm-Mt Ex-Mt
COMPLETE SET (15) 40.00 12.00
1 Frank Thomas 2.50 .75
2 Derek Jeter 6.00 1.80
3 Albert Pujols 5.00 1.50
4 Barry Bonds 6.00 1.80
5 Alex Rodriguez 4.00 1.20
6 Randy Johnson 2.50 .75
7 Jeff Bagwell 1.50 .45
8 Greg Maddux 4.00 1.20
9 Ivan Rodriguez 2.50 .75
10 Ichiro Suzuki 4.00 1.20
11 Mike Piazza 4.00 1.20
12 Pat Burrell 1.50 .45
13 Rickey Henderson 2.50 .75
14 Vladimir Guerrero 2.50 .75
15 Sammy Sosa 4.00 1.20

2002 Fleer Headliners

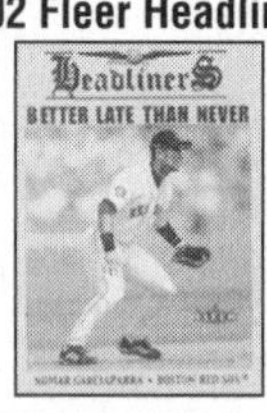

Issued at a stated rate of one in eight hobby packs and one in 12 retail packs, these 20 cards feature players who achieved noteworthy feats during the 2001 season.

Nm-Mt Ex-Mt
COMPLETE SET (20) 25.00 7.50
1 Randy Johnson 1.25 .35
2 Alex Rodriguez 2.00 .60
3 Todd Helton 1.00 .30
4 Pedro Martinez 1.25 .35
5 Ichiro Suzuki 2.00 .60
6 Vladimir Guerrero 1.25 .35
7 Derek Jeter 3.00 .90
8 Adam Dunn 1.00 .30
9 Luis Gonzalez 1.00 .30
10 Kazuhiro Sasaki 1.00 .30
11 Sammy Sosa 2.00 .60
12 Jason Giambi 1.25 .35
13 Ken Griffey Jr. 2.00 .60
14 Roger Clemens 2.50 .75
15 Brandon Duckworth 1.00 .30
16 Nomar Garciaparra 2.00 .60
17 Bud Smith 1.00 .30
18 Juan Gonzalez 1.25 .35
19 Chipper Jones 1.25 .35
20 Barry Bonds 3.00 .90

2002 Fleer Rookie Flashbacks

Issued at a stated rate of one in three retail packs, these 20 cards feature players who made their major league debut in 2001.

Nm-Mt Ex-Mt
COMPLETE SET (20) 25.00 7.50
1 Bret Prinz 1.00 .30
2 Albert Pujols 4.00 1.20
3 C.C. Sabathia 1.00 .30
4 Ichiro Suzuki 3.00 .90
5 Juan Cruz 1.00 .30
6 Jay Gibbons 1.00 .30
7 Bud Smith 1.00 .30
8 Johnny Estrada 1.00 .30
9 Roy Oswalt 1.00 .30
10 Tsuyoshi Shinjo 1.00 .30
11 Brandon Duckworth 1.00 .30
12 Jackson Melian 1.00 .30
13 Josh Beckett 1.25 .35
14 Morgan Ensberg 1.00 .30
15 Brian Lawrence 1.00 .30
16 Eric Hinske 1.00 .30
17 Juan Uribe 1.00 .30
18 Matt White 1.00 .30
19 Junior Spivey 1.00 .30
20 Wilson Betemit 1.00 .30

2002 Fleer Rookie Sensations

Randomly inserted in hobby packs and printed to a stated print run of 1500 serial numbered sets, these 20 cards feature players who made their major league debut in 2001.

Nm-Mt Ex-Mt
COMPLETE SET (20) 50.00 15.00
1 Bret Prinz 5.00 1.50
2 Albert Pujols 15.00 4.50
3 C.C. Sabathia 5.00 1.50
4 Ichiro Suzuki 12.00 3.60
5 Juan Cruz 5.00 1.50
6 Jay Gibbons 5.00 1.50
7 Bud Smith 5.00 1.50
8 Johnny Estrada 5.00 1.50
9 Roy Oswalt 5.00 1.50
10 Tsuyoshi Shinjo 5.00 1.50
11 Brandon Duckworth 5.00 1.50
12 Jackson Melian 5.00 1.50
13 Josh Beckett 5.00 1.50
14 Morgan Ensberg 5.00 1.50
15 Brian Lawrence 5.00 1.50
16 Eric Hinske 5.00 1.50
17 Juan Uribe 5.00 1.50
18 Matt White 5.00 1.50
19 Junior Spivey 5.00 1.50
20 Wilson Betemit 5.00 1.50

2002 Fleer Then and Now

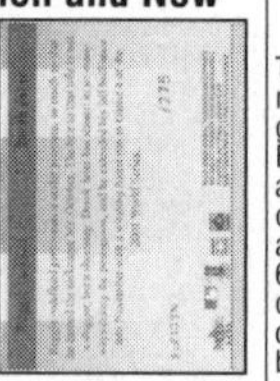

Randomly inserted in hobby packs, these 10 cards feature a player from the past who compares with one of today's stars. These cards are printed to a stated print run of 275 serial numbered sets.

Nm-Mt Ex-Mt
COMPLETE SET (10) 200.00 60.00
1 Eddie Mathews 15.00 4.50
Chipper Jones
2 Willie McCovey 30.00 9.00
Barry Bonds
3 Johnny Bench 20.00 6.00
Mika Piazza
4 Ernie Banks 20.00 6.00
Alex Rodriguez
5 Rickey Henderson 20.00 6.00
Ichiro Suzuki
6 Tom Seaver 25.00 7.50
Roger Clemens
7 Juan Marichal 15.00 4.50
Pedro Martinez
8 Reggie Jackson 30.00 9.00
Derek Jeter
9 Nolan Ryan 50.00 15.00
Kerry Wood
10 Joe Morgan 20.00 6.00
Ken Griffey Jr.

2002 Fleer Collection

This set, which combined a photo of a die cast car along with an Ultra card of the featured player was produced by Fleer and featured one player from each team. This set was issued by the Fleer Collectibles division of Fleer. We are pricing both the car and the card here.

MINT NRMT
COMPLETE SET 100.00 45.00
1 Troy Glaus 2.50 1.10
2 Luis Gonzalez 2.50 1.10
3 Chipper Jones 5.00 2.20
4 Cal Ripken Jr. 10.00 4.50
5 Nomar Garciaparra 5.00 2.20
6 Sammy Sosa 5.00 2.20
7 Frank Thomas 4.00 1.80
8 Ken Griffey Jr. 6.00 2.70
9 Jim Thome 2.50 1.10
10 Todd Helton 2.50 1.10
11 Tony Clark 1.00 .45
12 A.J. Burnett 1.00 .45
13 Jeff Bagwell 3.00 1.35
14 Mike Sweeney 2.50 1.10
15 Shawn Green 2.50 1.10
16 Ben Sheets 1.00 .45
17 Doug Mientkiewicz 1.00 .45
18 Vladimir Guerrero 4.00 1.80
19 Mike Piazza 5.00 2.20
20 Derek Jeter 10.00 4.50
21 Tim Hudson 2.50 1.10
22 Pat Burrell 1.50 .70
23 Jason Kendall 1.50 .70
24 Phil Nevin 1.50 .70
25 Barry Bonds 5.00 2.20
26 Ichiro Suzuki 10.00 4.50
27 Albert Pujols 6.00 2.70
28 Ben Grieve 1.00 .45
29 Alex Rodriguez 5.00 2.20
30 Carlos Delgado 3.00 1.35

2002 Fleer Bonds 4X MVP Jumbo

This one card jumbo set was made specificially for Shop at Home by Fleer. The card honors Barry Bonds as the only player ever to win 4 Most Valuable Player awards.

Nm-Mt Ex-Mt
NNO Barry Bonds 15.00 4.50

2002 Fleer Barry Bonds 600 Home Run Chasing History

This one card set, which measures 3 1/2" by 2 1/2" honors Barry Bonds 600th career homer. This card was issued to a stated print run of 600 serial numbered sets. This card has the bat piece used as part of the 600 on the left side of the card while the right side is used for both a portrait and action shot of Bonds along with an autograph. The back of the card gives congratulations for receiving this card as well as the individual serial numbering.

Nm-Mt Ex-Mt
1 Barry Bonds 100.00 30.00

2002 Fleer Barry Bonds 600 Home Run Jumbo

Nm-Mt Ex-Mt
BB-600 Barry Bonds 5.00 1.50

2002 Fleer Barry Bonds 600 Home Run Jumbo Game Used Autographed

This one card set, serial numbered to 600 and measuring 5 1/4" by 3 1/2", features a authentic game used bat piece and an autograph of Bonds. The left features a head shot was well as an action shot of Bonds. While the right side of the card features the bat piece as well as the autograph. The back has information about the 600th homer blast as well as serial numbering on the back. In addition, these cards come with certificates of authenticity which were issued by Goldin Sports Marketing.

Nm-Mt Ex-Mt
1 Barry Bonds 100.00 30.00

2002 Fleer Jeter Turn 2

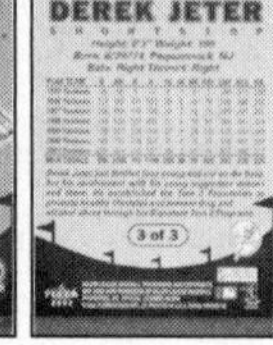

This three-card standard-size set feature Yankee superstar Derek Jeter and honors his work with his Turn 2 foundation. These three cards were originally distributed at a special banquet to raise money for the foundation. In addition, these cards were sent to every youngster who entered an essay contest at more than 100 after-school recreation centers in New York City.

Nm-Mt Ex-Mt
COMPLETE SET 5.00 1.50
COMMON CARD 2.00 .60

2003 Fleer 3D

This 72 "card" set was issued by Fleer late during the 2003 season and featured puzzle pieces which could be put together into a little statue of the player. The pieces came four "cards" and one statue to a package which had an $1.99 SRP. Please note that we are pricing the individual "cards" here. The set is broken up into 6 subsets: Sliding (1-12); Fielding (13-24); Diving Fielder (25-36); Left-Handed Batter (37-48); Right-Handed Batter (49-60); Pitching (61-72).

MINT NRMT
COMPLETE SET 20.00 9.00
1 Derek Jeter 2.50 1.10
2 Barry Bonds 1.25 .55
3 Ichiro Suzuki 2.00 .90
4 Jason Giambi .60 .25

5 Chipper Jones 1.25 .55
6 Alfonso Soriano .60 .25
7 Miguel Tejada .50 .23
8 Nomar Garciaparra 1.00 .45
9 Alex Rodriguez 1.25 .55
10 Ken Griffey Jr 1.25 .55
11 Sammy Sosa 1.25 .55
12 Albert Pujols 1.50 .70
13 Nomar Garciaparra H 1.00 .45
14 Nomar Garciaparra A 1.00 .45
15 Derek Jeter H 2.50 1.10
16 Derek Jeter A 2.50 1.10
17 Sammy Sosa 1.25 .55
18 Chipper Jones 1.25 .55
19 Alfonso Soriano H .60 .25
20 Alfonso Soriano A .60 .25
21 Alex Rodriguez H 1.25 .55
22 Alex Rodriguez A 1.25 .55
23 Miguel Tejada .50 .23
24 Albert Pujols 1.50 .70
25 Derek Jeter H 2.50 1.10
26 Derek Jeter A 2.50 1.10
27 Sammy Sosa H 1.25 .55
28 Sammy Sosa A 1.25 .55
29 Chipper Jones 1.25 .55
30 Alfonso Soriano H .60 .25
31 Alfonso Soriano A .60 .25
32 Miguel Tejada .50 .23
33 Nomar Garciaparra 1.25 .55
34 Alex Rodriguez 1.25 .55
35 Albert Pujols H 1.50 .70
36 Albert Pujols A 1.50 .70
37 Jason Giambi H .60 .25
38 Jason Giambi A .60 .25
39 Jason Giambi ALT .60 .25
40 Ken Griffey Jr H 1.25 .55
41 Ken Griffey Jr A 1.25 .55
42 Ken Griffey Jr ALT 1.25 .55
43 Barry Bonds H 1.25 .55
44 Barry Bonds A 1.25 .55
45 Barry Bonds ALT 1.25 .55
46 Ichiro Suzuki H 1.25 .55
47 Ichiro Suzuki A 1.25 .55
48 Ichiro Suzuki ALT 1.25 .55
49 Derek Jeter H 2.50 1.10
50 Derek Jeter A 2.50 1.10
51 Sammy Sosa H 1.25 .55
52 Sammy Sosa A 1.25 .55
53 Chipper Jones 1.25 .55
54 Alfonso Soriano H .60 .25
55 Alfonso Soriano A .60 .25
56 Miguel Tejada .50 .23
57 Nomar Garciaparra 1.25 .55
58 Alex Rodriguez 1.25 .55
59 Albert Pujols H 1.50 .70
60 Albert Pujols A 1.50 .70
61 Roger Clemens H 1.25 .55
62 Roger Clemens A 1.25 .55
63 Curt Schilling H .75 .35
64 Curt Schilling A .75 .35
65 Pedro Martinez H 1.25 .55
66 Pedro Martinez A 1.25 .55
67 Greg Maddux H 1.25 .55
68 Greg Maddux A 1.25 .55
69 Mark Prior H 1.25 .55
70 Mark Prior A 1.25 .55
71 Mariano Rivera H .50 .23
72 Mariano Rivera A .50 .23

2003 Fleer Barry Bonds 5 Time MVP

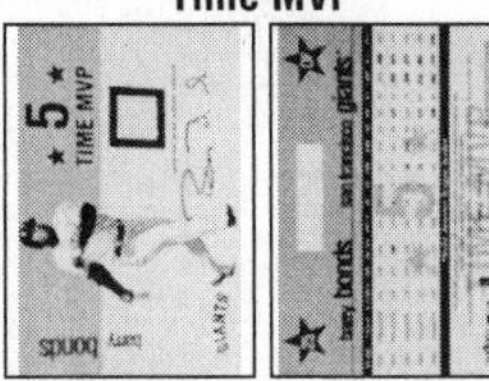

This one card set, features a bat chip and authentic autograph of Barry Bonds on the front and the card is serial numbered to 613 on the back.

Nm-Mt Ex-Mt

2003 Fleer Die Cast

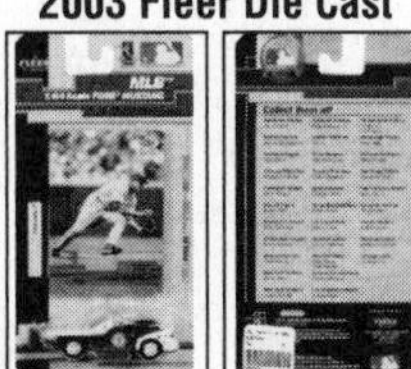

This 33 item set was issued as a combination card/die-cast card by Fleer. The car is set to a 1:64 scale while there is an also an Ultra card issued as part of the package. We are pricing the combination car/card here. Please note that these items are checklisted in alphabetical order.

Nm-Mt Ex-Mt
COMPLETE SET 100.00 30.00
1 Josh Beckett 5.00 1.50
2 Lance Berkman 3.00 .90
3 Barry Bonds 5.00 1.50
4 Pat Burrell 1.50 .45
5 Carlos Delgado 3.00 .90
6 Adam Dunn 2.50 .75
7 Robert Fick 1.00 .30
8 Jason Giambi 3.00 .90
9 Nomar Garciaparra 5.00 1.50
10 Jay Gibbons 1.50 .45
11 Brian Giles 2.50 .75
12 Troy Glaus 2.50 .75
13 Tom Glavine 2.50 .75
14 Shawn Green 3.00 .90
15 Ben Grieve 1.00 .30
16 Vladimir Guerrero 4.00 1.20

17 Todd Helton 5.00 1.50
18 Trevor Hoffman 1.50 .45
19 Torii Hunter 1.50 .45
20 Derek Jeter 10.00 3.00
21 Randy Johnson 5.00 1.50
22 Chipper Jones 5.00 1.50
23 Magglio Ordonez 2.50 .75
24 Mike Piazza 6.00 1.80
25 Albert Pujols 6.00 1.80
26 Alex Rodriguez 5.00 1.50
27 Richie Sexson 2.50 .75
28 Sammy Sosa 5.00 1.50
29 Ichiro Suzuki 8.00 2.40
30 Mike Sweeney 2.50 .75
31 Miguel Tejada 3.00 .90
32 Jim Thome 3.00 .90
33 Omar Vizquel 1.50 .45

2002 Fleer Authentix

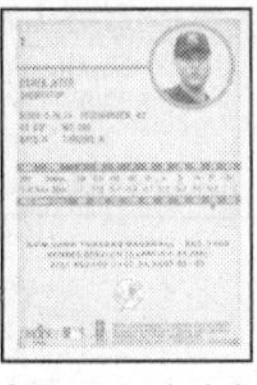

This 170-card base set features standard-size cards with a silhouetted action shot imposed over an old-school ticket design. These cards were issued in five card packs with an SRP of $3.99 with 24 packs in a box and 12 boxes in a case. Cards numbered 151 through 170 feature rookies and were randomly inserted into packs with a stated print run of 1850 serial numbered sets.

Nm-Mt Ex-Mt
COMP.SET w/o SP's (150) 40.00 12.00
COMMON CARD (1-135) .40 .12
COMMON CARD (136-150) .60 .18
COMMON CARD (151-170) 5.00 1.50
1 Derek Jeter 2.50 .75
2 Tim Hudson .40 .12
3 Robert Fick .40 .12
4 Javy Lopez .40 .12
5 Alfonso Soriano .60 .18
6 Ken Griffey Jr. 1.50 .45
7 Rafael Palmeiro .60 .18
8 Bernie Williams .60 .18
9 Adam Dunn .40 .12
10 Ivan Rodriguez 1.00 .30
11 Vladimir Guerrero 1.00 .30
12 Pedro Martinez 1.00 .30
13 Bret Boone .40 .12
14 Paul LoDuca .40 .12
15 Tony Batista .40 .12
16 Barry Bonds 2.50 .75
17 Craig Biggio .60 .18
18 Garret Anderson .40 .12
19 Mark Mulder .40 .12
20 Frank Thomas 1.00 .30
21 Alex Rodriguez 1.50 .45
22 Cristian Guzman .40 .12
23 Sammy Sosa 1.50 .45
24 Ichiro Suzuki 1.50 .45
25 Carlos Beltran .40 .12
26 Edgardo Alfonzo .40 .12
27 Josh Beckett .60 .18
28 Eric Chavez .40 .12
29 Roberto Alomar 1.00 .30
30 Raul Mondesi .40 .12
31 Mike Piazza 1.50 .45
32 Barry Larkin 1.00 .30
33 Ruben Sierra .40 .12
34 Tsuyoshi Shinjo .40 .12
35 Magglio Ordonez .40 .12
36 Ben Grieve .40 .12
37 Richie Sexson .40 .12
38 Manny Ramirez .40 .12
39 Jeff Kent .40 .12
40 Shawn Green .40 .12
41 Andruw Jones .40 .12
42 Aramis Ramirez .40 .12
43 Cliff Floyd .40 .12
44 Juan Pierre .40 .12
45 Jose Vidro .40 .12
46 Paul Konerko .40 .12
47 Greg Vaughn .40 .12
48 Geoff Jenkins .40 .12
49 Greg Maddux 1.50 .45
50 Ryan Klesko .40 .12
51 Corey Koskie .40 .12
52 Nomar Garciaparra 1.50 .45
53 Edgar Martinez .60 .18
54 Gary Sheffield .40 .12
55 Randy Johnson 1.00 .30
56 Bobby Abreu .40 .12
57 Mike Sweeney .40 .12
58 Chipper Jones 1.00 .30
59 Brian Giles .40 .12
60 Charles Johnson .40 .12
61 Ben Sheets .40 .12
62 Jason Giambi 1.00 .30
63 Todd Helton .60 .18
64 David Eckstein .40 .12
65 Troy Glaus .60 .18
66 Sean Casey .40 .12
67 Gabe Kapler .40 .12
68 Doug Mientkiewicz .40 .12
69 Curt Schilling .60 .18
70 Pat Burrell .40 .12
71 Albert Pujols 2.00 .60
72 Jermaine Dye .40 .12
73 Miguel Tejada .40 .12
74 Jim Thome 1.00 .30
75 Carlos Delgado .40 .12
76 Fred McGriff .60 .18
77 Mike Cameron .40 .12
78 Jeromy Burnitz .40 .12
79 Jay Gibbons .40 .12
80 Rich Aurilia .40 .12
81 Lance Berkman .40 .12
82 Brian Jordan .40 .12
83 Phil Nevin .40 .12
84 Moises Alou .40 .12

85 Reggie Sanders .40 .12
86 Scott Rolen .60 .18
87 Larry Walker .60 .18
88 Matt Williams .40 .12
89 Roger Clemens 2.00 .60
90 Juan Gonzalez 1.00 .30
91 Jose Cruz Jr. .40 .12
92 Tino Martinez .60 .18
93 Kerry Wood 1.00 .30
94 Freddy Garcia .40 .12
95 Jeff Bagwell .60 .18
96 Luis Gonzalez .40 .12
97 Jimmy Rollins .40 .12
98 Bobby Higginson .40 .12
99 Rondell White .40 .12
100 Jorge Posada .60 .18
101 Trot Nixon .60 .18
102 Jason Kendall .40 .12
103 Preston Wilson .40 .12
104 Corey Patterson .40 .12
105 Jose Valentin .40 .12
106 Carlos Lee .40 .12
107 Chris Richard .40 .12
108 Todd Walker .40 .12
109 Ellis Burks .40 .12
110 Brady Anderson .40 .12
111 Kazuhiro Sasaki .40 .12
112 Roy Oswalt .40 .12
113 Kevin Brown .40 .12
114 Jeff Weaver .40 .12
115 Todd Hollandsworth .40 .12
116 Joe Crede .40 .12
117 Tom Glavine .60 .18
118 Mike Lieberthal .40 .12
119 Tim Salmon .60 .18
120 Johnny Damon .40 .12
121 Brad Fullmer .40 .12
122 Mo Vaughn .40 .12
123 Torii Hunter .40 .12
124 Jamie Moyer .40 .12
125 Terrence Long .40 .12
126 Travis Lee .40 .12
127 Jacque Jones .40 .12
128 Lee Stevens .40 .12
129 Russ Ortiz .40 .12
130 Jeremy Giambi .40 .12
131 Mike Mussina 1.00 .30
132 Orlando Cabrera .40 .12
133 Barry Zito .60 .18
134 Robert Person .40 .12
135 Andy Pettitte .60 .18
136 Drew Henson FS .60 .18
137 Mark Teixeira FS 1.50 .45
138 David Espinosa FS .60 .18
139 Orlando Hudson FS .60 .18
140 Colby Lewis FS .60 .18
141 Bill Hall FS .60 .18
142 Michael Restovich FS .60 .18
143 Angel Berroa FS .60 .18
144 Dewon Brazelton FS .60 .18
145 Joe Thurston FS .60 .18
146 Mark Prior FS 3.00 .90
147 Dane Sardinha FS .60 .18
148 Marlon Byrd FS .60 .18
149 Jeff Deardorff FS .60 .18
150 Austin Kearns FS .60 .18
151 Anderson Machado TM RC 5.00 1.50
152 Kazuhisa Ishii TM RC 10.00 3.00
153 Eric Junge TM RC 5.00 1.50
154 Mark Corey TM RC 5.00 1.50
155 So Taguchi TM RC 8.00 2.40
156 Jorge Padilla TM RC 5.00 1.50
157 Steve Kent TM RC 5.00 1.50
158 Jaime Cerda TM RC 5.00 1.50
159 Hansel Izquierdo TM RC 5.00 1.50
160 Rene Reyes TM RC 5.00 1.50
161 Jorge Nunez TM RC 5.00 1.50
162 Corey Thurman TM RC 5.00 1.50
163 Jorge Sosa TM RC 5.00 1.50
164 Franklin Nunez TM RC 5.00 1.50
165 Adam Walker TM RC 5.00 1.50
166 Ryan Baerlocher TM RC 5.00 1.50
167 Ron Calloway TM RC 5.00 1.50
168 Miguel Asencio TM RC 5.00 1.50
169 Luis Ugueto TM RC 5.00 1.50
170 Felix Escalona TM RC 5.00 1.50

2002 Fleer Authentix Front Row

This 170-card set is a parallel to the base set. It features standard-size cards with a silhouetted action shot imposed over an old-school ticket design.

Nm-Mt Ex-Mt
*FRONT ROW 1-135: 4X TO 10X BASIC
*FRONT ROW 136-150: 4X TO 10X BASIC
*FRONT ROW 151-170: .75X TO 2X BASIC

2002 Fleer Authentix Second Row

This 170-card set is a parallel to the base set. It features standard-size cards with a silhouetted action shot imposed over an old-school ticket design. Cards were randomly seeded into packs and 250 serial-numbered sets were produced.

Nm-Mt Ex-Mt
*2ND ROW 1-135: 2.5X TO 6X BASIC
*2ND ROW 136-150: 2.5X TO 6X BASIC
*2ND ROW 151-170: .6X TO 1.5X BASIC

2002 Fleer Authentix Autograph AuthenTIX

This eight-card insert set presents special autographed cards of current and future stars. Cards were seeded into packs at a rate of 1:780 hobby and 1:2,200 retail. The standard-size cards feature embedded team replica tickets. This Ripped version comes with the tab "torn". Exchange cards were seeded into packs for Kazuhisa Ishii and David Espinosa with a redemption deadline of April 30th, 2003. Not all cards were printed to the same press run, we have notated these cards with an SP in our checklist and notated the stated press runs for these cards.

Nm-Mt Ex-Mt
AA-BR Brooks Robinson SP/145 40.00 12.00
AA-BS Ben Sheets SP/25
AA-DE David Espinosa 15.00 4.50
AA-DS Dane Sardinha 15.00 4.50
AA-KI Kazuhisa Ishii 40.00 12.00
AA-MP Mark Prior SP/145 100.00 30.00
AA-MT Mark Teixeira SP/25
AA-ST So Taguchi SP/150 25.00 7.50

2002 Fleer Authentix Ballpark Classics

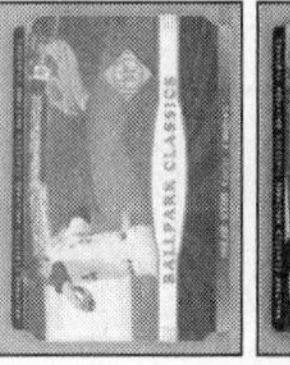

This 15-card insert set highlights fifteen Major League all-time greats. The standard-size cards have a brilliant design. Cards were seeded into packs at a rate of 1:22 hobby and 1:24 retail.

Nm-Mt Ex-Mt
COMPLETE SET (15) 80.00 24.00
1 Reggie Jackson 4.00 1.20
2 Don Mattingly 10.00 3.00
3 Duke Snider 4.00 1.20
4 Carlton Fisk 4.00 1.20
5 Cal Ripken 12.00 3.60
6 Willie McCovey 4.00 1.20
7 Robin Yount 6.00 1.80
8 Paul Molitor 4.00 1.20
9 George Brett 10.00 3.00
10 Ryne Sandberg 6.00 1.80
11 Nolan Ryan 10.00 3.00
12 Thurman Munson 6.00 1.80
13 Joe Morgan 4.00 1.20
14 Jim Rice 4.00 1.20
15 Babe Ruth 15.00 4.50

2002 Fleer Authentix Ballpark Classics Memorabilia

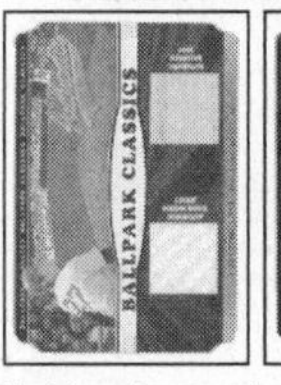

This 14-card insert set is a partial parallel to the Ballpark Classics insert. The standard-size cards feature not only a swatch of game-used memorabilia but also a piece of authentic stadium seat from either the Wrigley Field, Milwaukee County Stadium or Cleveland Stadium. Cards were seeded into hobby packs at a rate of 1:83 and retail packs at a rate of 1:440. A few cards were printed in smaller quantities and we have notated this inforrmation with an SP along with their stated print run in our checklist.

Nm-Mt Ex-Mt
CF Carlton Fisk Jsy 15.00 4.50
CR Cal Ripken Jsy 50.00 15.00
DM Don Mattingly Jsy 40.00 12.00
DS Duke Snider Bat SP/249 25.00 7.50
GB George Brett Jsy SP/482 40.00 12.00
JM Joe Morgan Bat 15.00 4.50
JR Jim Rice Jsy SP/487 15.00 4.50
NR Nolan Ryan Jsy 40.00 12.00
PM Paul Molitor Jsy 15.00 4.50
RJ Reggie Jackson Jsy SP/230 25.00 7.50
RS Ryne Sandberg Bat SP/82 100.00 30.00
RY Robin Yount Jsy SP/83 25.00 7.50
TM Thur Munson Cap SP/83 60.00 18.00
WM Willie McCovey Jsy SP/359 25.00 7.50

2002 Fleer Authentix Ballpark Classics Memorabilia Gold

This 15-card insert set is a parallel gold version to the Ballpark Classics Memorabilia insert. Babe Ruth, however, was featured only in this Gold set. Cards were randomly seeded into packs. Unlike the basic Memorabilia cards, each Gold parallel is serial-numbered to 100. The standard-size cards feature not only a swatch of game-used memorabilia but also a piece of authentic stadium seat from either the Wrigley Field, Milwaukee County Stadium or Cleveland Stadium.

Nm-Mt Ex-Mt
BR Babe Ruth Bat/Seat 200.00 60.00
CF Carlton Fisk Jsy/Seat 25.00 7.50
CR Cal Ripken Jsy/Seat 120.00 36.00
DM Don Mattingly Jsy/Seat 80.00 24.00
DS Duke Snider Bat/Seat 25.00 7.50
GB George Brett Jsy/Seat 60.00 18.00
JM Joe Morgan Bat/Seat 25.00 7.50
JR Jim Rice Jsy/Seat 25.00 7.50
NR Nolan Ryan Jsy/Seat 120.00 36.00
PM Paul Molitor Jsy/Seat 25.00 7.50
RJ Reggie Jackson Jsy/Seat 25.00 7.50
RS Ryne Sandberg Bat/Seat 100.00 30.00
RY Robin Yount Jsy/Seat 40.00 12.00
TM Thurman Munson Cap/Seat 50.00 15.00
WM Willie McCovey Jsy/Seat 25.00 7.50

2002 Fleer Authentix Bat AuthenTIX

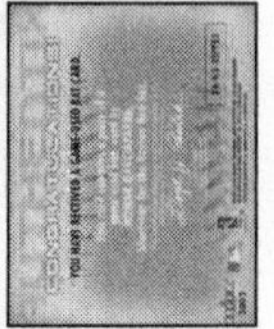

This 14-card insert set offers a piece of bat used by fourteen of MLB's biggest stars. Each standard-size card also features an embedded team replica ticket. This Ripped version comes with the tab "torn". Cards were randomly seeded into packs at a rate of 1:68 hobby. Many cards were issued to a different print run and we have notated that information in our checklist.

Nm-Mt Ex-Mt
BA-AJ Andruw Jones SP/171 15.00 4.50
BA-BB Barry Bonds SP/437 25.00 7.50
BA-BW Bernie Williams SP/44
BA-CJ Chipper Jones SP/37
BA-DH Drew Henson 10.00 3.00
BA-DJ Derek Jeter SP/197 50.00 15.00
BA-HN Hideo Nomo SP/41
BA-JG Juan Gonzalez SP/213 15.00 4.50
BA-JR Jimmy Rollins SP/409 15.00 4.50
BA-MR Manny Ramirez 10.00 3.00
BA-NG Nomar Garciaparra 25.00 7.50
BA-OH Orlando Hernandez 10.00 3.00
BA-PB Pat Burrell SP/468 15.00 4.50
BA-RD Ray Durham SP/52

2002 Fleer Authentix Jersey AuthenTIX

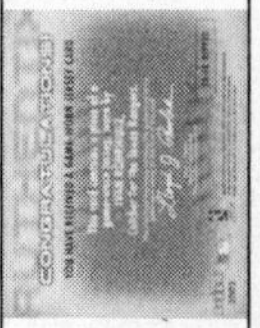

This 30-card insert set features standard-size game-worn jersey cards AND embedded team replica tickets! This "ripped" version comes with the tab "torn". Cards were seeded into hobby packs at a rate of 1:27 and retail packs at a rate of 1:43. Though the cards are not serial-numbered, representatives at Fleer revealed that the following players were produced in only half the quantity of others from this set: J.D. Drew, Jim Edmonds, Darin Erstad, Nomar Garciaparra, Luis Gonzalez, Andruw Jones, Manny Ramirez, Scott Rolen, Curt Schilling, Jim Thome and Bernie Williams.

Nm-Mt Ex-Mt
JA-AJ Andruw Jones SP 15.00 4.50
JA-AR Alex Rodriguez 15.00 4.50
JA-BB Barry Bonds 25.00 7.50
JA-BW Bernie Williams SP 20.00 6.00
JA-BZ Barry Zito 15.00 4.50
JA-CJ Chipper Jones 15.00 4.50
JA-DE Darin Erstad SP 15.00 4.50
JA-DJ Derek Jeter 30.00 9.00
JA-EC Eric Chavez 10.00 3.00
JA-FG Freddy Garcia 10.00 3.00
JA-FT Frank Thomas 15.00 4.50
JA-GM Greg Maddux 15.00 4.50
JA-IR Ivan Rodriguez 15.00 4.50
JA-JB Jeff Bagwell 15.00 4.50
JA-JD J.D. Drew SP 15.00 4.50
JA-JE Jim Edmonds SP 15.00 4.50
JA-JT Jim Thome SP 20.00 6.00
JA-LG Luis Gonzalez SP 15.00 4.50
JA-MO Magglio Ordonez 10.00 3.00
JA-MP Mike Piazza 15.00 4.50
JA-MR Manny Ramirez SP 15.00 4.50
JA-NG Nomar Garciaparra SP 25.00 7.50
JA-PL Paul LoDuca 10.00 3.00
JA-PM Pedro Martinez 15.00 4.50
JA-RA Roberto Alomar 15.00 4.50
JA-RJ Randy Johnson 15.00 4.50
JA-SG Shawn Green 10.00 3.00
JA-SR Scott Rolen SP 20.00 6.00
JA-TH Todd Helton 15.00 4.50
JACS Curt Schilling SP 20.00 6.00

2002 Fleer Authentix Jersey Autograph AuthenTIX

This 3-card insert set features standard-size game-worn jersey cards autographed by Derek Jeter, Chipper Jones and Greg Maddux. This Ripped version comes with the tab "torn". Cards were seeded into packs at a rate of 1:1387 hobby and 1:8,800 retail. Exchange cards were seeded into packs for Chipper Jones and Greg Maddux with a redemption deadline of April 30th, 2003. Though the cards are not serial-numbered, representatives at Fleer revealed that fifty copies of each card were produced.

Nm-Mt Ex-Mt
AJA-CJ Chipper Jones
AJA-DJ Derek Jeter 250.00 75.00
AJA-GM Greg Maddux

2002 Fleer Authentix Derek Jeter 1996 Autographics

This card, which was originally supposed to be issued in 2001 as part of the Derek Jeter legacy collection, was instead inserted into the 2002 Fleer Authentix set. This card had a stated print run of 100 serial numbered sets.

Nm-Mt Ex-Mt
NNO Derek Jeter 96/100 200.00 60.00

2002 Fleer Authentix Power Alley

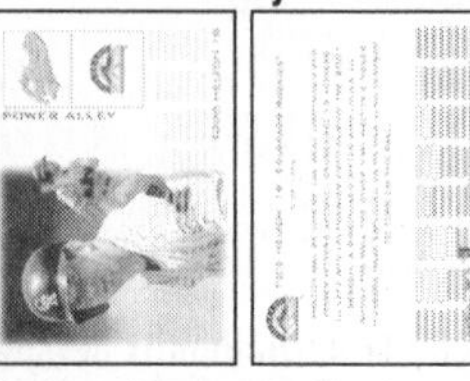

This 15-card insert set profiles the game's most hard-hitting sluggers. Cards were randomly seeded into packs ata a rate of 1:11.

Nm-Mt Ex-Mt
COMPLETE SET (15) 40.00 12.00
1 Sammy Sosa 4.00 1.20
2 Ken Griffey Jr. 4.00 1.20
3 Luis Gonzalez 2.00 .60
4 Alex Rodriguez 4.00 1.20
5 Shawn Green 2.00 .60
6 Barry Bonds 6.00 1.80
7 Todd Helton 2.00 .60
8 Jim Thome 2.50 .75
9 Troy Glaus 2.00 .60
10 Manny Ramirez 2.00 .60
11 Jeff Bagwell 2.00 .60
12 Jason Giambi 2.50 .75
13 Chipper Jones 2.50 .75
14 Mike Piazza 4.00 1.20
15 Albert Pujols 5.00 1.50

2003 Fleer Authentix

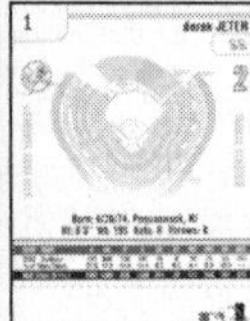

This 175 card set was distributed in two separate series. The primary Authentix product - containing the first 160 cards from the basic set - was issued in April, 2003. These cards were issued in five card packs with an $4 SRP. These packs were issued 24 to a box and 12 boxes to a case. Cards numbered 101 through 110 feature a Future Star subset. Cards numbered 111 through 125 featured a ticket to the majors subset and those cards were issued to a stated print run of 180 serial numbered sets. Cards numbered 126 through 160 feature Home Team extended cards. Those cards were issued in four ct home team packs where were issued one per home team box. In addition, one in 12 hobby boxes were issued as Home Team boxes. Cards 161-175 were randomly seeded within packs of Fleer Rookies and Greats of which was distributed in December, 2003. Each of these update cards was serial numbered to 1250 copies and continued the Ticket to the Majors prospect subset established in cards 111-125.

Nm-Mt Ex-Mt
COMP.LO SET w/o SP's (110) 25.00 7.50
COMMON CARD (1-100) .40 .12
COMMON CARD (101-110) .60 .18
COMMON (111-125/161-175) 4.00 1.20
COMMON CARD (126-132) 4.00 1.20
126-132 STATED PRINT RUN 1700 SETS
COMMON CARD (133-139/ 8.00 2.40
133-139 STATED PRINT RUN 210 SETS
COMMON CARD (140-153) 5.00 1.50
140-153 STATED PRINT RUN 560 SETS
COMMON CARD (154-160) 8.00 2.40
154-160 STATED PRINT RUN 280 SETS
1 Derek Jeter 2.50 .75
2 Tom Glavine .60 .18
3 Jason Jennings .40 .12
4 Craig Biggio .60 .18
5 Miguel Tejada .40 .12
6 Barry Bonds 2.50 .75
7 Juan Gonzalez 1.00 .30
8 Luis Gonzalez .40 .12
9 Johnny Damon .40 .12
10 Ellis Burks .40 .12
11 Frank Thomas 1.00 .30
12 Richie Sexson .40 .12
13 Roger Clemens 2.00 .60
14 Matt Morris .40 .12
15 Troy Glaus .60 .18
16 Tony Batista .40 .12
17 Magglio Ordonez .40 .12
18 Jose Vidro .40 .12
19 Barry Zito .60 .18
20 Chipper Jones 1.00 .30
21 Moises Alou .40 .12
22 Lance Berkman .40 .12
23 Jacque Jones .40 .12
24 Alfonso Soriano .60 .18
25 Sean Burroughs .40 .12
26 Scott Rolen .60 .18
27 Mark Grace .60 .18
28 Manny Ramirez .40 .12
29 Ken Griffey Jr. 1.50 .45
30 Josh Beckett .60 .18
31 Kazuhisa Ishii .40 .12
32 Pat Burrell .40 .12
33 Edgar Martinez .60 .18
34 Tim Salmon .60 .18
35 Raul Ibanez .40 .12
36 Vladimir Guerrero 1.00 .30
37 Jermaine Dye .40 .12
38 Rich Aurilia .40 .12
39 Rafael Palmeiro .60 .18
40 Kerry Wood 1.00 .30
41 Omar Vizquel .40 .12
42 Fred McGriff .60 .18
43 Ben Sheets .40 .12
44 Bernie Williams .60 .18
45 Brian Giles .40 .12
46 Jim Edmonds .40 .12
47 Garret Anderson .40 .12
48 Pedro Martinez 1.00 .30
49 Adam Dunn .40 .12
50 A.J. Burnett .40 .12
51 Eric Gagne .60 .18
52 Mo Vaughn .40 .12
53 Bobby Abreu .40 .12
54 Bret Boone .40 .12
55 Carlos Delgado .40 .12
56 Gary Sheffield .40 .12
57 Sammy Sosa 1.50 .45
58 Jim Thome 1.00 .30
59 Jeff Bagwell .60 .18
60 David Eckstein .40 .12
61 Jason Kendall .40 .12
62 Albert Pujols 2.00 .60
63 Curt Schilling .60 .18
64 Nomar Garciaparra 1.50 .45
65 Sean Casey .40 .12
66 Shawn Green .40 .12
67 Mike Piazza 1.50 .45
68 Ichiro Suzuki 1.50 .45
69 Eric Hinske .40 .12
70 Greg Maddux 1.50 .45
71 Larry Walker .60 .18
72 Roy Oswalt .40 .12
73 Alex Rodriguez 1.50 .45
74 Austin Kearns .40 .12
75 Cliff Floyd .40 .12
76 Kevin Brown .40 .12
77 Jason Giambi 1.00 .30
78 Jorge Julio .40 .12
79 Carlos Lee .40 .12
80 Mike Sweeney .40 .12
81 Edgardo Alfonzo .40 .12
82 Eric Chavez .40 .12
83 Andruw Jones .40 .12
84 Mark Prior 2.00 .60
85 Todd Helton .60 .18
86 Torii Hunter .40 .12
87 Ryan Klesko .40 .12
88 Aubrey Huff .40 .12
89 Randy Johnson 1.00 .30
90 Barry Larkin 1.00 .30
91 Mike Lowell .40 .12
92 Jimmy Rollins .40 .12
93 Darin Erstad .40 .12
94 Jay Gibbons .40 .12
95 Paul Konerko .40 .12
96 Bobby Higginson .40 .12
97 Carlos Beltran .40 .12
98 Bartolo Colon .40 .12
99 Jeff Kent .40 .12
100 Ivan Rodriguez 1.00 .30
101 Joe Borchard FS .60 .18
102 Mark Teixeira FS 1.00 .30
103 Francisco Rodriguez FS .60 .18
104 Chris Snelling FS .60 .18
105 Hee Seop Choi FS .60 .18
106 Hank Blalock FS 1.00 .30
107 Marlon Byrd FS .60 .18
108 Michael Restovich FS .60 .18
109 Victor Martinez FS .60 .18
110 Lyle Overbay FS .60 .18
111 Brian Stokes TM RC 4.00 1.20
112 Josh Hall TM RC 5.00 1.50
113 Chris Waters TM RC 4.00 1.20
114 Lew Ford TM RC 5.00 1.50
115 Ian Ferguson TM RC 4.00 1.20
116 Josh Willingham TM RC 6.00 1.80
117 Josh Stewart TM RC 4.00 1.20
118 Pete LaForest TM RC 5.00 1.50
119 Jose Contreras TM RC 8.00 2.40
120 Terrmel Sledge TM RC 5.00 1.50
121 Guillermo Quiroz TM RC 6.00 1.80
122 Alejandro Machado TM RC 4.00 1.20
123 Nook Logan TM RC 4.00 1.20
124 Rontrez Johnson TM RC 4.00 1.20
125 Hideki Matsui TM RC 15.00 4.50
126 Phil Rizzuto HT 5.00 1.50
127 Robin Ventura HT 4.00 1.20
128 Andy Pettitte HT 5.00 1.50
129 Mike Mussina HT 5.00 1.50
130 Mariano Rivera HT 5.00 1.50
131 Jeff Weaver HT 4.00 1.20
132 David Wells HT 4.00 1.20
133 Tommy Lasorda HT 8.00 2.40
134 Pee Wee Reese HT 10.00 3.00
135 Hideo Nomo HT 15.00 4.50
136 Adrian Beltre HT 8.00 2.40
137 Chin-Feng Chen HT 8.00 2.40
138 Odalis Perez HT 8.00 2.40
139 Dave Roberts HT 8.00 2.40
140 Bobby Doerr HT 5.00 1.50
141 Jason Varitek HT 5.00 1.50
142 Trot Nixon HT 8.00 2.40
143 Tim Wakefield HT 5.00 1.50
144 John Burkett HT 5.00 1.50
145 Jeremy Giambi HT 5.00 1.50
146 Casey Fossum HT 5.00 1.50
147 Phil Niekro HT 5.00 1.50
148 Warren Spahn HT 8.00 2.40
149 Rafael Furcal HT 5.00 1.50
150 Vinny Castilla HT 5.00 1.50
151 Javy Lopez HT 5.00 1.50
152 Jason Marquis HT 5.00 1.50
153 Mike Hampton HT 5.00 1.50
154 Gaylord Perry HT 8.00 2.40
155 Ruben Sierra HT 8.00 2.40
156 Mike Cameron HT 8.00 2.40
157 Freddy Garcia HT 8.00 2.40
158 Joel Pineiro HT 8.00 2.40
159 Jamie Moyer HT 8.00 2.40
160 Carlos Guillen HT 8.00 2.40
161 Chien-Ming Wang TM RC 6.00 1.80
162 Rickie Weeks TM RC 12.00 3.60
163 Brandon Webb TM RC 8.00 2.40
164 Craig Brazell TM RC 5.00 1.50
165 Michael Hessman TM RC 4.00 1.20
166 Ryan Wagner TM RC 5.00 1.50
167 Matt Kata TM RC 5.00 1.50
168 Edwin Jackson TM RC 10.00 3.00
169 Mike Ryan TM RC 5.00 1.50
170 Delmon Young TM RC 15.00 4.50
171 Bo Hart TM RC 6.00 1.80
172 Jeff Duncan TM RC 5.00 1.50
173 Robby Hammock TM RC 5.00 1.50
174 Jeremy Bonderman TM RC 5.00 1.50
175 Clint Barmes TM RC 5.00 1.50

2003 Fleer Authentix Balcony

Randomly inserted in packs, this is a parallel of the first 125 cards in the Fleer Authentix set. These cards were issued to a stated print run of 250 serial numbered sets.

Nm-Mt Ex-Mt
*BALCONY 1-100: 2X TO 5X BASIC
*BALCONY 101-110: 2X TO 5X BASIC
*BALCONY 111-125: .5X TO 1.2X BASIC

2003 Fleer Authentix Club Box

Randomly inserted into packs, this set parallels the first 125 cards of the Fleer Authentix set. These cards were issued to a stated print run of 100 serial numbered sets.

Nm-Mt Ex-Mt
*CLUB BOX 1-100: 4X TO 10X BASIC
*CLUB BOX 101-110: 4X TO 10X BASIC
*CLUB BOX 111-125: .6X TO 1.5X BASIC

2003 Fleer Authentix Autograph Front Row

Randomly inserted into packs, these cards feature authentic autographs of the two featured players. These cards were issued to a stated print run of 50 serial numbered sets.

Nm-Mt Ex-Mt
BB Barry Bonds
DJ Derek Jeter

2003 Fleer Authentix Autograph Second Row

Randomly inserted in packs, this card features Yankee superstar Derek Jeter. This card was issued to a stated print run of 150 serial numbered sets.

Nm-Mt Ex-Mt
DJ Derek Jeter 150.00 45.00

2003 Fleer Authentix Autograph Third Row

Randomly inserted into packs, these two cards feature authentic autographs. Each of these cards was issued to a stated print run of 250 serial numbered sets.

Nm-Mt Ex-Mt
BB Barry Bonds 175.00 52.50
DJ Derek Jeter 120.00 36.00

2003 Fleer Authentix Ballpark Classics

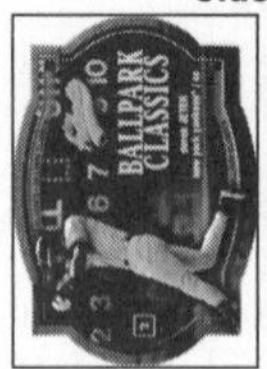

Issued at a stated rate of one in 12 hobby packs and one in 18 retail packs, these 10 cards feature some of the leading players in baseball.

Nm-Mt Ex-Mt
COMPLETE SET (10) 25.00 7.50
1 Derek Jeter 6.00 1.80
2 Randy Johnson 2.00 .60
3 Nomar Garciaparra 4.00 1.20
4 Barry Bonds 6.00 1.80
5 Alfonso Soriano 2.00 .60
6 Alex Rodriguez 4.00 1.20
7 Jim Thome 2.00 .60
8 Chipper Jones 2.00 .60
9 Mike Piazza 4.00 1.20
10 Ichiro Suzuki 4.00 1.20

2003 Fleer Authentix Game Bat

Inserted at a stated rate of one in 78 hobby packs and one in 202 retail packs, these nine cards feature a game-use bat piece. The Jason Giambi card was issued in shorter quantities and we have notated that card as an SP in our checklist.

Nm-Mt Ex-Mt
*UNRIPPED: .75X TO 2X BASIC GAME BAT

UNRIPPED RANDOM INSERTS IN PACKS
UNRIPPED PRINT RUN 50 SERIAL #'d SETS
AD Adam Dunn 8.00 2.40
CJ Chipper Jones 10.00 3.00
DJ Derek Jeter 25.00 7.50
JG Jason Giambi SP 12.00 3.60
JT Jim Thome 10.00 3.00
MR Manny Ramirez 8.00 2.40
NG Nomar Garciaparra 15.00 4.50
SS Sammy Sosa 15.00 4.50
VG Vladimir Guerrero 10.00 3.00

2003 Fleer Authentix Game Jersey

Issued at a stated rate of one in 10 hobby packs and one in 41 retail packs, these 24 cards feature game-used jersey pieces. The Derek Jeter and Randy Johnson cards were issued in shorter quantity and we have notated those cards with an SP in our checklist.

Nm-Mt Ex-Mt
*UNRIPPED: .75X TO 2X BASIC GAME JSY
UNRIPPED RANDOM INSERTS IN PACKS
UNRIPPED PRINT RUN 50 SERIAL #'d SETS
AD Adam Dunn 8.00 2.40
AR Alex Rodriguez 15.00 4.50
AS Alfonso Soriano 10.00 3.00
CD Carlos Delgado 8.00 2.40
CJ Chipper Jones 10.00 3.00
DJ Derek Jeter SP 30.00 9.00
EH Eric Hinske 8.00 2.40
GM Greg Maddux 10.00 3.00
JB Jeff Bagwell 10.00 3.00
JB2 Josh Beckett 10.00 3.00
KW Kerry Wood 10.00 3.00
LB Lance Berkman 8.00 2.40
MB Mark Buehrle 8.00 2.40
MP Mike Piazza 10.00 3.00
MR Manny Ramirez 8.00 2.40
MT Miguel Tejada 8.00 2.40
NG Nomar Garciaparra 15.00 4.50
PB Pat Burrell 8.00 2.40
RC Roger Clemens 15.00 4.50
RJ Randy Johnson SP 10.00 3.00
SB Sean Burroughs 8.00 2.40
SS Sammy Sosa 15.00 4.50
TH Torii Hunter 8.00 2.40
VG Vladimir Guerrero 10.00 3.00

2003 Fleer Authentix Game Jersey All-Star

Randomly inserted in packs, these cards feature special "all-star" versions of the game jersey set. These cards are issued to varying print runs and we have notated that information next to the player's name in our checklist. Please note that for cards with a print run of 25 or fewer copies, no pricing is provided due to market scarcity.

Nm-Mt Ex-Mt
AD Adam Dunn/91 15.00 4.50
AR Alex Rodriguez/111 40.00 12.00
AS Alfonso Soriano/21
CJ Chipper Jones/14
DJ Derek Jeter/81 60.00 18.00
LB Lance Berkman/103 15.00 4.50
MB Mark Buehrle/88 15.00 4.50
MP Mike Piazza/109 30.00 9.00
MR Manny Ramirez/78 15.00 4.50
MT Miguel Tejada/52 30.00 9.00
NG Nomar Garciaparra/53 60.00 18.00
SS Sammy Sosa/8
TH Torii Hunter/64 30.00 9.00
VG Vladimir Guerrero/66 40.00 12.00

2003 Fleer Authentix Game Jersey Autograph Front Row

Randomly inserted into packs, these cards feature not only a game-used jersey swatch but also an authentic autograph of the featured player. These cards were issued to a stated print run of 100 serial numbered sets.

Nm-Mt Ex-Mt
DJ Derek Jeter 150.00 45.00
NR Nolan Ryan 150.00 45.00

2003 Fleer Authentix Game Jersey Autograph Second Row

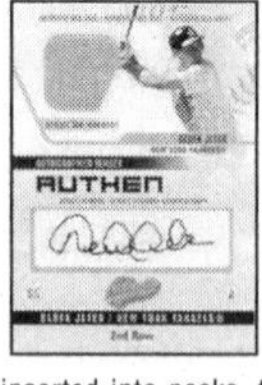

Randomly inserted into packs, these cards feature not only a game-used jersey swatch but also an authentic autograph of the featured player. These cards were issued to a stated print run of 200 serial numbered sets.

Nm-Mt Ex-Mt
DJ Derek Jeter 150.00 45.00
NR Nolan Ryan 150.00 45.00

2003 Fleer Authentix Game Jersey Autograph Third Row

Randomly inserted into packs, this card features not only a game-used jersey swatch but also an authentic autograph of the featured player. This card was issued to a stated print run of 300 serial numbered sets.

Nm-Mt Ex-Mt
DJ Derek Jeter 120.00 36.00

2003 Fleer Authentix Game Jersey Game of the Week

Inserted at a stated rate of one in 240 hobby packs and one in 420 retail packs, these 10 cards feature two players. These cards were issued in either group A or group B and the cards in the Group A are twice as scarce as the Group B cards. We have notated next to the card which group these cards belonged to.

Nm-Mt Ex-Mt
*UNRIPPED: 1X TO 2.5X BASIC GAME A
*UNRIPPED: .75X TO 2X BASIC GAME B
UNRIPPED RANDOM INSERTS IN PACKS
UNRIPPED PRINT RUN 50 SERIAL #'d SETS
AD-LB Adam Dunn 15.00 4.50
Lance Berkman A
AR-MT Alex Rodriguez 30.00 9.00
Miguel Tejada A
AS-SS Alfonso Soriano 30.00 9.00
Sammy Sosa A
CJ-PB Chipper Jones 25.00 7.50
Pat Burrell B
DJ-MT Derek Jeter 40.00 12.00
Miguel Tejada A
DJ-NG Derek Jeter 60.00 18.00
Nomar Garciaparra A
EH-TH Eric Hinske 15.00 4.50
Torii Hunter A
GM-RJ Greg Maddux 30.00 9.00
Randy Johnson B
MP-SS Mike Piazza 40.00 12.00
Sammy Sosa A
TH-AS Torii Hunter 15.00 4.50
Alfonso Soriano A

2003 Fleer Authentix Hometown Heroes Memorabilia

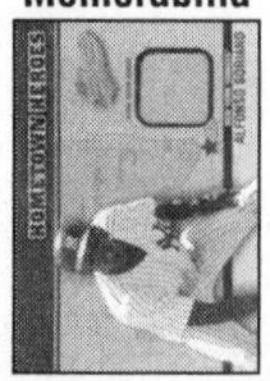

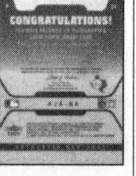

Inserted at a stated rate of one per home town hero packs, these 20 cards feature a game-used piece from players from the most popular franchises in the game. A few cards were announced to have a stated print run of 300 or fewer cards and we have notated that information next to the player's name in our checklist.

Nm-Mt Ex-Mt
I Ichiro Suzuki Base SP/100 40.00 12.00
AJ Andruw Jones Jsy SP/150
AS Alfonso Soriano Jsy 15.00 4.50
BB Bret Boone Jsy SP/200 15.00 4.50
CC Chin-Feng Chen Jsy SP/150 50.00 15.00
CJ Chipper Jones Jsy
DJ Derek Jeter Jsy 40.00 12.00
EM Edgar Martinez Jsy SP/200 25.00 7.50
FG Freddy Garcia Jsy SP/200
GM Greg Maddux Jsy
GS Gary Sheffield Jsy SP/100 15.00 4.50
JD Johnny Damon Jsy SP/100
JG Jason Giambi Bat SP/300 25.00 7.50
KB Kevin Brown Jsy SP/150 15.00 4.50
KI Kazuhisa Ishii Jsy SP/100 15.00 4.50
MR Manny Ramirez Jsy 10.00 3.00
NG Nomar Garciaparra Jsy 40.00 12.00
PM Pedro Martinez Jsy SP/100 25.00 7.50
RC Roger Clemens Jsy 25.00 7.50
SG Shawn Green Jsy SP/100 15.00 4.50

2003 Fleer Authentix Ticket Studs

Issued at a stated rate of one in six packs, these 15 cards feature cards which look like tickets and feature some of the leading superstars in baseball.

Nm-Mt Ex-Mt
COMPLETE SET (15) 25.00 7.50
1 Curt Schilling 2.00 .60
2 Greg Maddux 4.00 1.20
3 Torii Hunter 2.00 .60
4 Mike Piazza 4.00 1.20
5 Pedro Martinez 2.00 .60
6 Nomar Garciaparra 4.00 1.20
7 Derek Jeter 6.00 1.80
8 Alex Rodriguez 4.00 1.20
9 Alfonso Soriano 2.00 .60
10 Pat Burrell 2.00 .60
11 Barry Bonds 6.00 1.80
12 Jason Giambi 2.00 .60
13 Sammy Sosa 4.00 1.20
14 Vladimir Guerrero 2.00 .60
15 Ichiro Suzuki 4.00 1.20

2004 Fleer Authentix

This 140-card set was released in March, 2004. The set was issued in both hobby and retail format. The hobby version was issued in five-card packs with an $4 SRP which came 24 packs to a box and six boxes to a case. The retail packs were also issued in five-card packs with an $2 SRP and those packs came 24 packs to a box and six boxes to a case. In the hobby version it is important to note that one of every six boxes in an sealed case is an "Yankee" home team box. The Yankee cards are cards numbered 131 through 140 and were issued four per yankees home team pack. Those cards were issued to a stated print run of approximately 800 sets. In addition cards 101 through 130 feature leading prospect which were issued at a stated rate of one in 11 hobby packs and one in 34 retail packs. Each of those cards were issued to a stated print run of 999 serial numbered sets.

Nm-Mt Ex-Mt
COMP.SET w/o SP's (100) 25.00 7.50
COMMON CARD (1-100) .40 .12
COMMON CARD (101-130) 5.00 1.50
COMMON CARD (131-140) 8.00 2.40
1 Albert Pujols 2.00 .60
2 Derek Jeter 2.50 .75
3 Jody Gerut .40 .12
4 Mark Teixeira .40 .12
5 Tom Glavine .60 .18
6 Kerry Wood 1.00 .30
7 Ichiro Suzuki 1.50 .45
8 Jose Vidro .40 .12
9 Mark Prior 2.00 .60
10 Jim Edmonds .40 .12
11 Richie Sexson .40 .12
12 Jay Gibbons .40 .12
13 Jason Kendall .40 .12
14 Lance Berkman .40 .12
15 Andruw Jones .40 .12
16 Jim Thome 1.00 .30
17 Josh Beckett .60 .18
18 Troy Glaus .60 .18
19 Jason Giambi 1.00 .30
20 Sammy Sosa 1.50 .45
21 Bret Boone .40 .12
22 Eric Gagne .60 .18
23 Nomar Garciaparra 1.50 .45
24 Geoff Jenkins .40 .12
25 Ivan Rodriguez 1.00 .30
26 Preston Wilson .40 .12
27 Alex Rodriguez 1.50 .45
28 Jorge Posada .60 .18
29 Ken Griffey Jr. 1.50 .45
30 Rocco Baldelli 1.00 .30
31 Shannon Stewart .40 .12
32 Frank Thomas 1.00 .30
33 Edgar Renteria .40 .12
34 Torii Hunter .40 .12
35 Corey Patterson .40 .12
36 Edgar Martinez .60 .18
37 Jeff Bagwell .60 .18
38 Greg Maddux 1.50 .45
39 Mike Lieberthal .40 .12
40 Craig Biggio .60 .18
41 Randy Johnson 1.00 .30
42 Marlon Byrd .40 .12
43 Jay Payton .40 .12
44 Carlos Delgado .40 .12
45 Scott Podsednik 1.00 .30
46 Pedro Martinez 1.00 .30
47 Carlos Beltran .40 .12
48 Mike Sweeney .40 .12
49 Gary Sheffield .40 .12
50 Pat Burrell .40 .12
51 Shawn Green .40 .12
52 Tony Batista .40 .12
53 Brian Giles .40 .12
54 Roy Oswalt .40 .12
55 Brandon Webb .40 .12
56 Miguel Tejada .40 .12
57 Miguel Cabrera 1.00 .30
58 Luis Gonzalez .40 .12
59 Billy Wagner .40 .12
60 Craig Monroe .40 .12
61 Vernon Wells .40 .12
62 Bernie Williams .60 .18
63 Austin Kearns .40 .12
64 Aubrey Huff .40 .12
65 Mike Piazza 1.50 .45
66 Magglio Ordonez .40 .12
67 Bo Hart .40 .12
68 Hideo Nomo 1.00 .30
69 Curt Schilling .60 .18
70 Barry Zito .60 .18
71 Todd Helton .60 .18
72 Roy Halladay .40 .12
73 Alfonso Soriano .60 .18
74 Roberto Alomar 1.00 .30
75 Scott Rolen .60 .18
76 Manny Ramirez .40 .12
77 Sean Burroughs .40 .12
78 Angel Berroa .40 .12
79 Javy Lopez .40 .12
80 Reggie Sanders .40 .12
81 Juan Pierre .40 .12
82 Chipper Jones 1.00 .30
83 Bobby Abreu .40 .12
84 Dontrelle Willis .40 .12
85 Tim Salmon .60 .18
86 Eric Chavez .40 .12
87 Adam Dunn .40 .12
88 Rafael Palmeiro .60 .18
89 Hideki Matsui 1.50 .45
90 Esteban Loaiza .40 .12
91 Darin Erstad .40 .12
92 Vladimir Guerrero 1.00 .30
93 David Ortiz .40 .12
94 Jason Schmidt .40 .12
95 Dmitri Young .40 .12
96 Garret Anderson .40 .12
97 Mark Mulder .40 .12
98 Omar Vizquel .40 .12
99 Hank Blalock .40 .12
100 Jose Reyes .60 .18
101 Rickie Weeks TM 8.00 2.40
102 Chad Gaudin TM 5.00 1.50
103 Ryan Wagner TM 5.00 1.50
104 Koyie Hill TM 5.00 1.50
105 Rich Harden TM 5.00 1.50
106 Edwin Jackson TM 8.00 2.40
107 Khalil Greene TM 5.00 1.50
108 Chien-Ming Wang TM 5.00 1.50
109 Matt Kata TM 5.00 1.50
110 Chin-Hui Tsao TM 5.00 1.50
111 Dan Haren TM 5.00 1.50
112 Delmon Young TM 8.00 2.40
113 Mike Hessman TM 5.00 1.50
114 Bobby Crosby TM 8.00 2.40
115 Cory Sullivan TM RC 5.00 1.50
116 Brandon Watson TM 5.00 1.50
117 Aaron Miles TM 5.00 1.50
118 Jonny Gomes TM 5.00 1.50
119 Graham Koonce TM 8.00 2.40
120 Shawn Hill TM RC 5.00 1.50
121 Garrett Atkins TM 5.00 1.50
122 John Gall TM RC 5.00 1.50
123 Chad Bentz TM RC 5.00 1.50
124 Alfredo Simon TM RC 5.00 1.50
125 Josh Labandeira TM RC 5.00 1.50
126 Ryan Howard TM 5.00 1.50
127 Jason Bartlett TM RC 15.00 4.50
128 Dallas McPherson TM 5.00 1.50
129 Greg Dobbs TM RC 5.00 1.50
130 Jerry Gil TM RC 5.00 1.50
131 Aaron Boone EXT 8.00 2.40
132 Javier Vazquez EXT 8.00 2.40
133 Mariano Rivera EXT 10.00 3.00
134 Kevin Brown EXT 8.00 2.40
135 Mike Mussina EXT 10.00 3.00
136 Ruben Sierra EXT 8.00 2.40
137 Enrique Wilson EXT 8.00 2.40
138 Erick Almonte EXT 8.00 2.40
139 Jose Contreras EXT 8.00 2.40
140 Drew Henson EXT 8.00 2.40

2004 Fleer Authentix Balcony

Nm-Mt Ex-Mt
*BALCONY 1-100: 4X TO 10X BASIC..
*BALCONY 101-130: .6X TO 1.5X BASIC
*BALCONY 101-130: .6X TO 1.5X BASIC RC
OVERALL PARALLEL ODDS 1:6 H, 1:48 R
STATED PRINT RUN 100 SERIAL #'d SETS

2004 Fleer Authentix Club Box

Nm-Mt Ex-Mt
OVERALL PARALLEL ODDS 1:6 H, 1:48 R
STATED PRINT RUN 25 SERIAL #'d SETS
NO PRICING DUE TO SCARCITY

2004 Fleer Authentix Standing Room Only

Nm-Mt Ex-Mt
OVERALL PARALLEL ODDS 1:6 H, 1:48 R
STATED PRINT RUN 5 SERIAL #'d SETS
NO PRICING DUE TO SCARCITY

2004 Fleer Authentix Ticket to the Majors Autograph Boosters

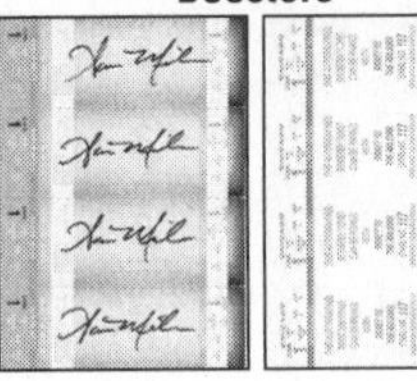

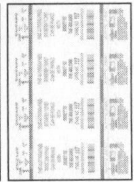

This very innovative idea was included in Authentix packs at stated rates of one in 200 hobby and one in 1560 retail packs. Each of these "non-torn" cards have four autographs on a "ticket" which the lucky collector who pulled these cards could then replace the regular card with an autograph instead of the standard ticket. A few players did not return their tickets in time for inclusion in the product and those cards could be redeemed immediately when the player's returned their tickets. In addition, there is no expiration date on those exchange cards.

Nm-Mt Ex-Mt
STATED ODDS 1:200 HOBBY, 1:1560 RETAIL
STATED PRINT RUN 50 SERIAL #'d SETS
LISTED PRICES ARE FOR NON-TORN CARDS
101 Rickie Weeks 100.00 30.00
103 Ryan Wagner 40.00 12.00
105 Rich Harden 60.00 18.00
106 Edwin Jackson 60.00 18.00
107 Khalil Greene 40.00 12.00
112 Delmon Young 100.00 30.00
114 Bobby Crosby EXCH 60.00 18.00
115 Cory Sullivan 25.00 7.50
117 Aaron Miles 40.00 12.00
118 Jonny Gomes 25.00 7.50
119 Graham Koonce 60.00 18.00
121 Garrett Atkins 25.00 7.50
122 John Gall 25.00 7.50
123 Chad Bentz 25.00 7.50
124 Alfredo Simon EXCH 25.00 7.50
125 John Labandeira 25.00 7.50
126 Ryan Howard 25.00 7.50
127 Jason Bartlett 50.00 15.00
128 Dallas McPherson 40.00 12.00
130 Jerry Gil EXCH 25.00 7.50

2004 Fleer Authentix Autograph All-Star

Nm-Mt Ex-Mt
STATED PRINT RUN 75 SERIAL #'d SETS
CHAMPIONSHIP PRINT RUN 25 #'d SETS
NO CHAMP.PRICING DUE TO SCARCITY
RANDOM INSERTS IN PACKS
EXCHANGE DEADLINE INDEFINITE
AB Angel Berroa EXCH 25.00 7.50
AP Albert Pujols 150.00 45.00
EG Eric Gagne 40.00 12.00
JP Juan Pierre 25.00 7.50
MB Marlon Byrd 15.00 4.50
MC Miguel Cabrera EXCH 40.00 12.00
RB Rocco Baldelli 40.00 12.00
RH Roy Halladay 25.00 7.50
TN Trot Nixon 40.00 12.00
VW Vernon Wells 25.00 7.50

2004 Fleer Authentix Ballpark Classics

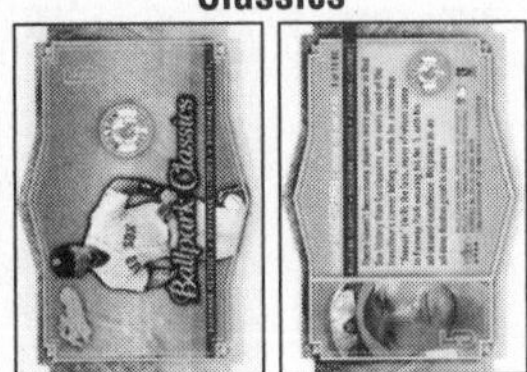

Nm-Mt Ex-Mt
STATED ODDS 1:12 HOBBY, 1:18 RETAIL
1 Nomar Garciaparra 5.00 1.50
2 Alfonso Soriano 3.00 .90
3 Chipper Jones 3.00 .90
4 Albert Pujols 6.00 1.80
5 Jason Giambi 3.00 .90
6 Mark Prior 6.00 1.80
7 Sammy Sosa 5.00 1.50
8 Derek Jeter 8.00 2.40
9 Greg Maddux 5.00 1.50
10 Alex Rodriguez 5.00 1.50

2004 Fleer Authentix Ballpark Classics Jersey

Nm-Mt Ex-Mt
STATED ODDS 1:37 HOBBY, 1:240 RETAIL
AP Albert Pujols 15.00 4.50
AR Alex Rodriguez 10.00 3.00
AS Alfonso Soriano 10.00 3.00
CJ Chipper Jones 10.00 3.00
DJ Derek Jeter 20.00 6.00
GM Greg Maddux 10.00 3.00
JG Jason Giambi 10.00 3.00
MP Mark Prior 15.00 4.50
NG Nomar Garciaparra 15.00 4.50
SS Sammy Sosa 15.00 4.50

2004 Fleer Authentix Game Jersey

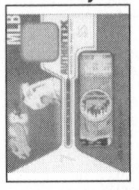

Nm-Mt Ex-Mt
STATED ODDS 1:16 HOBBY, 1:71 RETAIL
*UNRIPPED: .6X TO 1.5X BASIC
UNRIPPED RANDOM INSERTS IN PACKS
UNRIPPED PRINT RUN 50 SERIAL #'d SETS
*GOLD p/r 51-89: .6X TO 1.5X BASIC.
*GOLD p/r 38-44: .75X TO 2X BASIC..
GOLD RANDOM INSERTS IN PACKS ..
GOLD PRINT B/WN 25-89 COPIES PER
NO GOLD PRICING ON QTY OF 25 OR LESS
GOLD UNRIPPED RANDOM IN HOBBY ONLY
GOLD UNRIPPED PRINT 1 SERIAL #'d SET
NO GOLD UNRIPPED PRICING AVAILABLE
AK Austin Kearns 8.00 2.40
AP Albert Pujols 15.00 4.50
AR Alex Rodriguez 10.00 3.00
AS Alfonso Soriano 10.00 3.00
BZ Barry Zito 10.00 3.00
CJ Chipper Jones 10.00 3.00
DJ Derek Jeter 20.00 6.00
DW Dontrelle Willis 8.00 2.40
GM Greg Maddux 10.00 3.00
HC Hee Seop Choi 8.00 2.40
IR Ivan Rodriguez 10.00 3.00
JB Josh Beckett 10.00 3.00
JB2 Jeff Bagwell 10.00 3.00
JG Jason Giambi 10.00 3.00
JP Juan Pierre 8.00 2.40
JR Jose Reyes 10.00 3.00
JT Jim Thome 10.00 3.00
KW Kerry Wood 10.00 3.00
MC Miguel Cabrera 10.00 3.00
MP Mark Prior 15.00 4.50
MT Mark Teixeira 8.00 2.40
NG Nomar Garciaparra 15.00 4.50
RJ Randy Johnson 10.00 3.00
SS Sammy Sosa 15.00 4.50
TH Torii Hunter 8.00 2.40

2004 Fleer Authentix Game Jersey Autograph Regular Season

Nm-Mt Ex-Mt
STATED PRINT RUN 100 SERIAL #'d SETS
*ALL-STAR: .5X TO 1.2X BASIC
ALL-STAR PRINT RUN 50 SERIAL #'d SETS
CHAMPIONSHIP PRINT 10 SERIAL #'d SETS
NO CHAMP.PRICING DUE TO SCARCITY
RANDOM INSERTS IN PACKS
EXCHANGE DEADLINE INDEFINITE
AB Angel Berroa EXCH 25.00 7.50
AP Albert Pujols 150.00 45.00
EG Eric Gagne 40.00 12.00
JP Juan Pierre 25.00 7.50
MB Marlon Byrd 15.00 4.50
MC Miguel Cabrera EXCH 40.00 12.00
RB Rocco Baldelli 40.00 12.00
RH Roy Halladay 25.00 7.50
TN Trot Nixon 40.00 12.00
VW Vernon Wells 25.00 7.50

2004 Fleer Authentix Game Jersey Dual

Nm-Mt Ex-Mt
STATED ODDS 1:120 HOBBY, 1:420 RETAIL
*UNRIPPED: .6X TO 1.5X BASIC
UNRIPPED RANDOM INSERTS IN PACKS
UNRIPPED PRINT RUN 50 SERIAL #'d SETS
ARDJ Alex Rodriguez 50.00 15.00
Derek Jeter
CJAP Chipper Jones 20.00 6.00
Albert Pujols
DWKW Dontrelle Willis 15.00 4.50
Kerry Wood
JBAK Jeff Bagwell 15.00 4.50
Austin Kearns
JBMP Josh Beckett 25.00 7.50
Mark Prior
JGBZ Jason Giambi 15.00 4.50
Barry Zito
JRJP Jose Reyes 15.00 4.50
Juan Pierre
JTIR Jim Thome 15.00 4.50
Ivan Rodriguez
MCMT Miguel Cabrera 15.00 4.50
Mark Teixeira
NGAS Nomar Garciaparra 15.00 4.50
Alfonso Soriano

2004 Fleer Authentix Ticket for Four

Nm-Mt Ex-Mt
RANDOM INSERTS IN PACKS
STATED PRINT RUN 100 SERIAL #'d SETS
GJBH Jason Giambi 25.00 7.50
Randy Johnson
Jeff Bagwell
Torii Hunter
GRJR Nomar Garciaparra 60.00 18.00
Alex Rodriguez
Derek Jeter
Jose Reyes
GSJP Nomar Garciaparra 40.00 12.00
Alfonso Soriano
Chipper Jones
Albert Pujols
GTTB Jason Giambi 25.00 7.50
Jim Thome
Mark Teixeira
Jeff Bagwell
JPSH Chipper Jones 40.00 12.00
Albert Pujols
Sammy Sosa
Torii Hunter
MJWZ Greg Maddux 30.00 9.00
Randy Johnson
Kerry Wood
Barry Zito
PMKR Mark Prior 40.00 12.00
Greg Maddux
Austin Kearns
Ivan Rodriguez
RCCP Ivan Rodriguez 25.00 7.50
Miguel Cabrera
Hee Seop Choi
Juan Pierre
SJRT Sammy Sosa 50.00 15.00
Derek Jeter
Alex Rodriguez
Jim Thome
WBPW Dontrelle Willis 40.00 12.00
Josh Beckett
Mark Prior
Kerry Wood

2004 Fleer Authentix Ticket Studs

Nm-Mt Ex-Mt
STATED ODDS 1:6 HOBBY, 1:8 RETAIL
1 Nomar Garciaparra 4.00 1.20
2 Josh Beckett 2.50 .75
3 Derek Jeter 6.00 1.80
4 Mark Prior 5.00 1.50
5 Albert Pujols 5.00 1.50
6 Alfonso Soriano 2.50 .75
7 Jim Thome 2.50 .75
8 Ichiro Suzuki 4.00 1.20
9 Hideki Matsui 4.00 1.20
10 Dontrelle Willis 1.50 .45
11 Mike Schmidt 6.00 1.80
12 Nolan Ryan 8.00 2.40
13 Reggie Jackson 3.00 .90
14 Tom Seaver 3.00 .90
15 Brooks Robinson 3.00 .90

2004 Fleer Authentix Yankees Game Used Unripped

Nm-Mt Ex-Mt
ONE GU YANKS CARD PER YANKS HT PACK
*UNRIPPED 50: X TO X BASIC
UNRIPPED 50 RANDOM IN YANKS HOME TM
UNRIPPED 50 PRINT 50 SERIAL #'d SETS
DJ Derek Jeter Jsy 20.00 6.00
DM Don Mattingly Jsy 25.00 7.50

PR Phil Rizzuto Pants 15.00 4.50
RJ Reggie Jackson Jsy 15.00 4.50

2004 Fleer Authentix Yankees Game Used Dual Unripped

Nm-Mt Ex-Mt
ONE GU YANKS CARD PER YANKS HT PACK
STATED PRINT RUN 25 SERIAL #'d SETS
NO PRICING DUE TO SCARCITY
DMRJ Don Mattingly Jsy
Reggie Jackson Jsy
PRDJ Phil Rizzuto Pants
Derek Jeter Jsy

2001 Fleer Authority

This product was released in late December 2001, and featured a 150-card base set that was broken into tiers as follows: 100 Base Veterans, and 50 Prospects (serial numbered to 2001). Each pack contained five cards.

Nm-Mt Ex-Mt
COMP.SET w/o SP's (100) 25.00 7.50
COMMON CARD (1-100) .40 .12
COMMON (101-150) 5.00 1.50
1 Mark Grace .60 .18
2 Paul Konerko .40 .12
3 Sean Casey .40 .12
4 Jim Thome 1.00 .30
5 Todd Helton .60 .18
6 Tony Clark .40 .12
7 Jeff Bagwell .60 .18
8 Mike Sweeney .40 .12
9 Eric Karros .40 .12
10 Richie Sexson .40 .12
11 Doug Mientkiewicz .40 .12
12 Ryan Klesko .40 .12
13 John Olerud .40 .12
14 Mark McGwire 2.50 .75
15 Fred McGriff .60 .18
16 Rafael Palmeiro .60 .18
17 Carlos Delgado .40 .12
18 Roberto Alomar 1.00 .30
19 Craig Biggio .60 .18
20 Jose Vidro .40 .12
21 Edgardo Alfonzo .40 .12
22 Jeff Kent .40 .12
23 Bret Boone .40 .12
24 Rafael Furcal .40 .12
25 Nomar Garciaparra 1.50 .45
26 Barry Larkin 1.00 .30
27 Cristian Guzman .40 .12
28 Derek Jeter 2.50 .75
29 Miguel Tejada .40 .12
30 Jimmy Rollins .40 .12
31 Rich Aurilia .40 .12
32 Alex Rodriguez 1.50 .45
33 Cal Ripken 3.00 .90
34 Troy Glaus .60 .18
35 Matt Williams .40 .12
36 Chipper Jones 1.00 .30
37 Jeff Cirillo .40 .12
38 Robin Ventura .40 .12
39 Eric Chavez .40 .12
40 Scott Rolen .60 .18
41 Phil Nevin .40 .12
42 Mike Piazza 1.50 .45
43 Jorge Posada .60 .18
44 Jason Kendall .40 .12
45 Ivan Rodriguez 1.00 .30
46 Frank Thomas 1.00 .30
47 Edgar Martinez .60 .18
48 Darin Erstad .40 .12
49 Tim Salmon .60 .18
50 Luis Gonzalez .40 .12
51 Andruw Jones .40 .12
52 Carl Everett .40 .12
53 Manny Ramirez .40 .12
54 Sammy Sosa 1.50 .45
55 Rondell White .40 .12
56 Magglio Ordonez .40 .12
57 Ken Griffey Jr. 1.50 .45
58 Juan Gonzalez 1.00 .30
59 Larry Walker .60 .18
60 Bobby Higginson .40 .12
61 Cliff Floyd .40 .12
62 Preston Wilson .40 .12
63 Moises Alou .40 .12
64 Lance Berkman .40 .12
65 Richard Hidalgo .40 .12
66 Jermaine Dye .40 .12
67 Mark Quinn .40 .12
68 Shawn Green .40 .12
69 Gary Sheffield .40 .12
70 Jeromy Burnitz .40 .12
71 Geoff Jenkins .40 .12
72 Vladimir Guerrero 1.00 .30
73 Bernie Williams .60 .18
74 Johnny Damon .40 .12
75 Jason Giambi 1.00 .30
76 Bobby Abreu .40 .12
77 Pat Burrell .40 .12
78 Brian Giles .40 .12
79 Tony Gwynn 1.25 .35
80 Barry Bonds 2.50 .75
81 J.D. Drew .40 .12
82 Jim Edmonds .40 .12
83 Greg Vaughn .40 .12
84 Raul Mondesi .40 .12
85 Shannon Stewart .40 .12
86 Randy Johnson 1.00 .30
87 Curt Schilling .60 .18
88 Tom Glavine .60 .18
89 Greg Maddux 1.50 .45
90 Pedro Martinez 1.00 .30
91 Kerry Wood 1.00 .30
92 David Wells .40 .12
93 Bartolo Colon .40 .12
94 Mike Hampton .40 .12
95 Kevin Brown .40 .12
96 Al Leiter .40 .12
97 Roger Clemens 2.00 .60
98 Mike Mussina 1.00 .30
99 Tim Hudson .40 .12
100 Kazuhiro Sasaki .40 .12
101 Ichiro Suzuki RC 40.00 12.00
102 Albert Pujols RC 50.00 15.00
103 Drew Henson RC 8.00 2.40
104 Adam Pettyjohn RC 5.00 1.50
105 Adrian Hernandez RC 5.00 1.50
106 Andy Morales RC 5.00 1.50
107 Tsuyoshi Shinjo RC 8.00 2.40
108 Juan Uribe RC 5.00 1.50
109 Jack Wilson RC 5.00 1.50
110 Jason Smith RC 5.00 1.50
111 Junior Spivey RC 6.00 1.80
112 Wilson Betemit RC 5.00 1.50
113 Elpidio Guzman RC 5.00 1.50
114 Esix Snead RC 5.00 1.50
115 Winston Abreu RC 5.00 1.50
116 Jeremy Owens RC 5.00 1.50
117 Jay Gibbons RC 8.00 2.40
118 Luis Lopez 5.00 1.50
119 Ryan Freel RC 5.00 1.50
120 Rafael Soriano RC 8.00 2.40
121 Johnny Estrada RC 6.00 1.80
122 Bud Smith RC 5.00 1.50
123 Jackson Melian RC 5.00 1.50
124 Matt White RC 5.00 1.50
125 Travis Hafner RC 8.00 2.40
126 Morgan Ensberg RC 8.00 2.40
127 Endy Chavez RC 5.00 1.50
128 Brett Prinz RC 5.00 1.50
129 Juan Diaz RC 5.00 1.50
130 Erick Almonte RC 5.00 1.50
131 Rob Mackowiak RC 5.00 1.50
132 Carlos Valderrama RC 5.00 1.50
133 Wilkin Ruan RC 5.00 1.50
134 Angel Berroa RC 10.00 3.00
135 Henry Mateo RC 5.00 1.50
136 Bill Ortega RC 5.00 1.50
137 Billy Sylvester RC 5.00 1.50
138 Andres Torres RC 5.00 1.50
139 Nate Frese RC 5.00 1.50
140 Casey Fossum RC 5.00 1.50
141 Ricardo Rodriguez RC 5.00 1.50
142 Brian Roberts RC 5.00 1.50
143 Carlos Garcia RC 5.00 1.50
144 Brian Lawrence RC 5.00 1.50
145 Cory Aldridge RC 5.00 1.50
146 Mark Teixeira RC 25.00 7.50
147 Juan Cruz RC 5.00 1.50
148 B. Duckworth RC 5.00 1.50
149 Dewon Brazelton RC 6.00 1.80
150 Mark Prior RC 50.00 15.00
MM4 Derek Jeter 15.00 4.50
MM/2000
MM4AU Derek Jeter 150.00 45.00
MM AU/100
NNO Derek Jeter 150.00 45.00
93 AU/500

2001 Fleer Authority Prominence 125/75

This 150-card insert is actually a parallel of the 2001 Fleer Authority base set. The set is broken into tiers as follows: 100 Base Veterans (numbered to 125), and 50 Prospects (numbered to 75).

Nm-Mt Ex-Mt
COMMON CARD (101-100) 4.00 1.20
*STARS 1-100: 5X TO 12X BASIC
COMMON CARD (101-150) 8.00 2.40
*ROOKIES 101-150: 1.25X TO 3X BASIC

2001 Fleer Authority Diamond Cuts Memorabilia

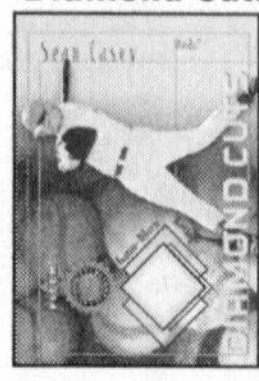

This 111-card insert set features various swatches of game-used memorabilia including shoes, hats, bats and jerseys. Overall odds on these cards were 1:10 packs. Please note that Manny Ramirez had 100 red Batting Glove cards and 100 blue Batting Glove cards. Print runs listed below.

Nm-Mt Ex-Mt
1 Rick Ankiel Shoes/400 15.00 4.50
2 Jeff Bagwell Jsy/1000 15.00 4.50
3 Adrian Beltre Hat/240 15.00 4.50
4 Craig Biggio Bat/800 15.00 4.50
5 Barry Bonds Hat/240 50.00 15.00
6 Barry Bonds Jsy/1000 25.00 7.50
7 Barry Bonds Pants/800 25.00 7.50
8 Barry Bonds Shoes/400 40.00 12.00
9 B.Bonds Wristband/100 80.00 24.00
10 Kevin Brown Hat/240 15.00 4.50
11 Kevin Brown Pants/800 10.00 3.00
12 Eric Byrnes Bat/800 10.00 3.00
13 Sean Casey Jsy/1000 10.00 3.00
14 Eric Chavez Hat/240 15.00 4.50
15 Bartolo Colon Hat/240 15.00 4.50
16 Erubiel Durazo Bat/800 10.00 3.00
17 Ray Durham Bat/800 10.00 3.00
18 Jim Edmonds Hat/240 15.00 4.50
19 J.Edmonds Shoes/400 15.00 4.50
20 Darin Erstad Hat/240 15.00 4.50
21 Carlos Febles Bat/800 10.00 3.00
22 Carlos Febles Shoes/400 15.00 4.50
23 Rafael Furcal Hat/240 15.00 4.50
24 Brian Giles Pants/800 10.00 3.00
25 Juan Gonzalez Btg Glv/100 30.00 9.00
26 Juan Gonzalez Hat/240 25.00 7.50
27 Luis Gonzalez Hat/240 15.00 4.50
28 Shawn Green Bat/800 10.00 3.00
29 S.Green Btg Glv/100 20.00 6.00
30 V.Guerrero Bat/800 15.00 4.50
31 Tony Gwynn Bat/975 15.00 4.50
32 J.Hairston Jr. Hat/240 15.00 4.50
33 Mike Hampton Hat/240 15.00 4.50
34 M.Hampton Shoes/400 15.00 4.50
35 Jason Hart Bat/800 10.00 3.00
36 Todd Helton Jsy/1000 15.00 4.50
37 Todd Helton Pants/800 15.00 4.50
38 O.Hernandez Bat/800 10.00 3.00
39 R.Hidalgo Bat/800 10.00 3.00
40 R.Hidalgo Btg Glv/200 15.00 4.50
41 Derek Jeter Bat/800 40.00 12.00
42 D.Jeter Btg Glv/150 80.00 24.00
43 Derek Jeter Jsy/1000 40.00 12.00
44 Derek Jeter Pants/800 40.00 12.00
45 Derek Jeter Shoes/400 60.00 18.00
46 R.Johnson Hat/240 25.00 7.50
47 Chipper Jones Bat/800 15.00 4.50
48 C. Jones Jsy/1000 15.00 4.50
49 Andruw Jones Bat/800 10.00 3.00
50 Andruw Jones Hat/240 15.00 4.50
51 Jason Kendall Hat/240 15.00 4.50
52 Jason Kendall Base/250 15.00 4.50
53 Barry Larkin Base/250 25.00 7.50
54 Barry Larkin Jsy/1000 15.00 4.50
55 Matt Lawton Hat/240 15.00 4.50
56 M.Lieberthal Btg Glv/100 20.00 6.00
57 Mike Lieberthal Wristband/25
58 Kenny Lofton Bat/800 10.00 3.00
59 E.Martinez Btg Glv/200 25.00 7.50
60 P.Martinez Shoes/400 20.00 6.00
61 Raul Mondesi Bat/800 10.00 3.00
62 R.Mondesi Btg Glv/100 20.00 6.00
63 Hideo Nomo Bat/800 25.00 7.50
64 Hideo Nomo Hat/240 60.00 18.00
65 Magglio Ordonez Base/250 15.00 4.50
66 M.Ordonez Btg Glv/200 15.00 4.50
67 M.Ordonez Hat/240 15.00 4.50
68 David Ortiz Base/250 15.00 4.50
69 David Ortiz Bat/800 10.00 3.00
70 R.Palmeiro Bat/800 15.00 4.50
71 R.Palmeiro Hat/240 25.00 7.50
72 R.Palmeiro Jsy/1000 25.00 7.50
73 Chan Ho Park Hat/240 15.00 4.50
74 Mike Piazza Bat/800 25.00 7.50
75 Mike Piazza Jsy/1000 25.00 7.50
76 Mike Piazza Shoes/400 40.00 12.00
77 Albert Pujols Pants/800 50.00 15.00
78 M.Ramirez Bat/800 10.00 3.00
79 M.Ramirez Btg Glv/200 15.00 4.50
80 M.Ramirez Hat/240 15.00 4.50
81 M.Ramirez Jsy/1000 15.00 4.50
82 Cal Ripken Btg Glv/100 100.00 30.00
83 Cal Ripken Pants/800 40.00 12.00
84 Ivan Rodriguez Base/250 25.00 7.50
85 I.Rodriguez Btg Glv/100 30.00 9.00
86 Ivan Rodriguez Hat/240 25.00 7.50
87 I.Rodriguez Pants/800 15.00 4.50
88 I.Rodriguez Shoes/400 20.00 6.00
89 Ivan Rodriguez Wristband/50
90 Scott Rolen Base/250 25.00 7.50
91 Scott Rolen Hat/240 25.00 7.50
92 J.Sandberg Bat/800 10.00 3.00
93 D.Sanders Jsy/1000 15.00 4.50
94 Tsuy Shinjo Bat/800 15.00 4.50
95 T.Shinjo Wristband/150 25.00 7.50
96 J.T. Snow Bat/800 10.00 3.00
97 J.T. Snow Jsy/1000 10.00 3.00
98 A.Soriano Hat/240 25.00 7.50
99 Ichiro Suzuki Bat/350 80.00 24.00
100 Ichiro Suzuki Hat/240 100.00 30.00
101 M.Sweeney Hat/240 15.00 4.50
102 Mike Sweeney Wristband/25
103 M.Tejada Hat/240 15.00 4.50
104 Frank Thomas Base/250 25.00 7.50
105 F.Thomas Bat/800 15.00 4.50
106 F.Thomas Hat/240 25.00 7.50
107 Jim Thome Bat/800 15.00 4.50
108 Jim Thome Wristband/50
109 Larry Walker Bat/800 15.00 4.50
110 L.Walker Jsy/1000 15.00 4.50
111 B.Williams Bat/800 15.00 4.50

2001 Fleer Authority Figures

This 20-card insert pairs veteran players with comparable prospects. Each card is serial numbered to 1750.

Nm-Mt Ex-Mt
COMPLETE SET (20) 150.00 45.00
1 Mark McGwire 20.00 6.00
Albert Pujols
2 Kazuhiro Sasaki 15.00 4.50
Ichiro Suzuki
3 Derek Jeter 12.00 3.60
Drew Henson
4 Ken Griffey Jr. 10.00 3.00
Jackson Melian
5 Chipper Jones 6.00 1.80
Wilson Betemit
6 Jeff Bagwell 5.00 1.50
Morgan Ensberg
7 Cal Ripken 30.00 9.00
Jay Gibbons
8 Mike Piazza 8.00 2.40
Tsuyoshi Shinjo
9 Luis Gonzalez 3.00 .90
Junior Spivey
10 Barry Bonds 15.00 4.50
Carlos Valderrama
11 Todd Helton 3.00 .90
Juan Uribe
12 Roger Clemens 12.00 3.60
Adrian Hernandez
13 Alex Rodriguez 8.00 2.40
Travis Hafner
14 Scott Rolen 4.00 1.20
Johnny Estrada
15 Brian Giles 3.00 .90
Rob Mackowiak
16 Randy Johnson 6.00 1.80
Bret Prinz
17 Carlos Delgado 3.00 .90
Luis Lopez
18 Manny Ramirez 3.00 .90
Juan Diaz
19 Mike Sweeney 3.00 .90
Endy Chavez
20 Sammy Sosa 10.00 3.00
Jaisen Randolph

2001 Fleer Authority Seal of Approval

This 15-card insert features seasoned veterans that have received the "Seal of Approval" from fans across America. These cards were inserted into packs at a rate of 1:20.

Nm-Mt Ex-Mt
COMPLETE SET (15) 120.00 36.00
1 Derek Jeter 12.00 3.60
2 Alex Rodriguez 8.00 2.40
3 Nomar Garciaparra 8.00 2.40
4 Cal Ripken 15.00 4.50
5 Mike Piazza 8.00 2.40
6 Mark McGwire 12.00 3.60
7 Tony Gwynn 6.00 1.80
8 Barry Bonds 12.00 3.60
9 Greg Maddux 8.00 2.40
10 Chipper Jones 5.00 1.50
11 Roger Clemens 10.00 3.00
12 Ken Griffey Jr. 8.00 2.40
13 Vladimir Guerrero 5.00 1.50
14 Sammy Sosa 8.00 2.40
15 Todd Helton 5.00 1.50

2003 Fleer Avant

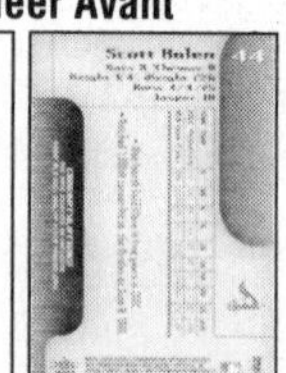

This 90 card set was released in September, 2003. This set was issued in 10 card packs with a $6.99 SRP which came 18 to a box and 6 boxes to a case. The first 65 cards of the set featured active veteran players while cards 66 through 75 featured retired players and those cards were printed to a stated print run 799 serial numbered sets. Cards numbered 76 through 90 featured rookies and prospects and those cards were issued to a stated print run of 699 serial numbered sets.

MINT NRMT
COMP.SET w/o SP's (65) 50.00 22.00
COMMON CARD (1-65) 1.00 .45
COMMON CARD (76-90) 5.00 2.20
1 Adam Dunn 1.00 .45
2 Barry Zito 1.50 .70
3 Preston Wilson 1.00 .45
4 Barry Bonds 6.00 2.70
5 Hank Blalock 1.50 .70
6 Omar Vizquel 1.50 .70
7 Brian Giles 1.00 .45
8 Kerry Wood 2.50 1.10
9 Miguel Tejada 1.00 .45
10 Magglio Ordonez 1.00 .45
11 Randy Johnson 2.50 1.10
12 Jeff Bagwell 1.50 .70
13 Pat Burrell 1.00 .45
14 Jason Giambi 2.50 1.10
15 Mark Prior 5.00 2.20
16 Roger Clemens 5.00 2.20
17 Sammy Sosa 4.00 1.80
18 Jay Gibbons 1.00 .45
19 Torii Hunter 1.00 .45
20 Ichiro Suzuki 4.00 1.80
21 Derek Jeter 6.00 2.70
22 Tom Glavine 1.50 .70
23 Alfonso Soriano 1.50 .70
24 Manny Ramirez 1.00 .45
25 Frank Thomas 2.50 1.10
26 Carlos Pena 1.00 .45
27 Alex Rodriguez 4.00 1.80
28 Edgar Martinez 1.50 .70
29 Larry Walker 1.50 .70
30 Rafael Palmeiro 1.50 .70
31 Mike Piazza 4.00 1.80
32 Nomar Garciaparra 4.00 1.80
33 Lance Berkman 1.00 .45
34 Vladimir Guerrero 2.50 1.10
35 Troy Glaus 1.50 .70
36 Ivan Rodriguez 2.50 1.10
37 Mark Mulder 1.00 .45
38 Curt Schilling 1.50 .70
39 Mike Sweeney 1.00 .45
40 Albert Pujols 5.00 2.20
41 Tim Hudson 1.00 .45
42 Greg Maddux 4.00 1.80
43 Shawn Green 1.50 .70
44 Scott Rolen 1.50 .70
45 Gary Sheffield 1.00 .45
46 Richie Sexson 1.00 .45
47 Aubrey Huff 1.00 .45
48 Luis Gonzalez 1.00 .45
49 Todd Helton 1.50 .70
50 Xavier Nady 1.00 .45
51 Juan Gonzalez 2.50 1.10
52 Pedro Martinez 2.50 1.10
53 Garret Anderson 1.00 .45
54 Craig Biggio 1.50 .70
55 Bret Boone 1.00 .45
56 Ken Griffey Jr. 4.00 1.80
57 Kevin Millwood 1.00 .45
58 Carlos Delgado 1.00 .45
59 Chipper Jones 2.50 1.10
60 Hideo Nomo 2.50 1.10
61 Jim Edmonds 1.50 .70
62 Austin Kearns 1.00 .45
63 Jim Thome 2.50 1.10
64 Vernon Wells 1.00 .45
65 Mike Lowell 1.00 .45
66 Whitey Ford RET 8.00 3.60
67 Bob Gibson RET 8.00 3.60
68 Reggie Jackson RET 8.00 3.60
69 Willie McCovey RET 8.00 3.60
70 Phil Rizzuto RET 8.00 3.60
71 Al Kaline RET 8.00 3.60
72 Brooks Robinson RET 8.00 3.60
73 Nolan Ryan RET 12.00 5.50
74 Mike Schmidt RET 10.00 4.50
75 Tom Seaver RET 8.00 3.60
76 Hideki Matsui ROO RC 20.00 9.00
77 Rocco Baldelli ROO 15.00 6.75
78 Jose Contreras ROO RC 10.00 4.50
79 Hee Seop Choi ROO 5.00 2.20
80 Jeremy Bonderman ROO RC 8.00 3.60
81 Bo Hart ROO RC 10.00 4.50
82 Brandon Webb ROO RC 12.00 5.50
83 Ron Calloway ROO 5.00 2.20
84 Jesse Foppert ROO 5.00 2.20
85 Kyle Snyder ROO 5.00 2.20
86 Mark Teixeira ROO 8.00 3.60
87 Jose Reyes ROO 8.00 3.60
88 Dontrelle Willis ROO 8.00 3.60
89 Reed Johnson ROO 5.00 2.20
90 Rickie Weeks ROO RC 20.00 9.00
P39 Derek Jeter Promo 2.00 .90

2003 Fleer Avant Black and White

MINT NRMT
*B/W 1-65: 1.25X TO 3X BASIC
*B/W 66-75: .6X TO 1.5X BASIC
*B/W 76-90: .6X TO 1.5X BASIC
*B/W 76-90: .6X TO 1.5X BASIC RC'S
RANDOM INSERTS IN PACKS
STATED PRINT RUN 199 SERIAL #'d SETS

2003 Fleer Avant Autograph Blue

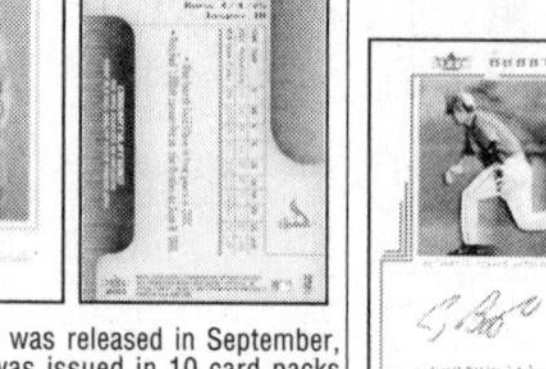
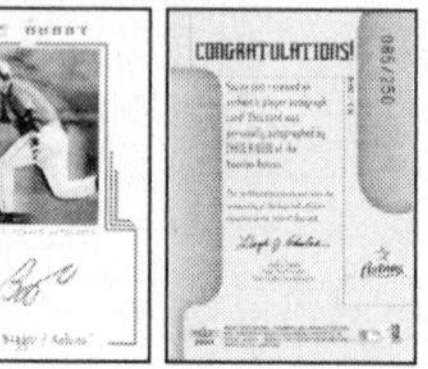

Randomly inserted into packs, these cards feature authentic autographs from the featured player with the card having blue ink surrounding the autograph. Please note that although most cards were issued to a stated print run of 300 sets a few were issued in smaller quantites and that information in noted next to the players name in our checklist.

MINT NRMT
AH Aubrey Huff/300 15.00 6.75
AK Al Kaline/200 30.00 13.50
BG Bob Gibson/250 30.00 13.50
BH Bo Hart/300 25.00 11.00
BR Brooks Robinson/300 30.00 13.50
BW Brandon Webb/300 40.00 18.00
CB Craig Biggio/250 25.00 11.00
DW Dontrelle Willis/300 25.00 11.00
EM Edgar Martinez/246 25.00 11.00
HB Hank Blalock/300 25.00 11.00
JR Jose Reyes/300 25.00 11.00
RB Rocco Baldelli/250 50.00 22.00
VW Vernon Wells/250 15.00 6.75

2003 Fleer Avant Autograph Copper

All the players in this set signed 150 copies except for Manny Ramirez, who signed 100 cards in copper ink.

MINT NRMT
*ACTIVE: .5X TO 1.2X BLUE AUTOS
*ROOKIES: .5X TO 1.2X BLUE AUTOS
*RETIRED: .5X TO 1.2X BLUE AUTOS
RANDOM INSERTS IN PACKS
PRINT RUNS B/WN 100-150 COPIES PER
BZ Barry Zito/150 30.00 13.50
CP Carlos Pena/150 20.00 9.00
ML Mike Lowell/150 20.00 9.00
MR Manny Ramirez/100 50.00 22.00
MT Miguel Tejada/150 20.00 9.00

2003 Fleer Avant Autograph Gold

MINT NRMT
RANDOM INSERTS IN PACKS
STATED PRINT RUN 25 SERIAL #'d SETS
NO PRICING DUE TO SCARCITY

2003 Fleer Avant Autograph Silver

MINT NRMT
*SILVER: .5X TO 1.2X COPPER AUTO
RANDOM INSERTS IN PACKS
STATED PRINT RUN 75 SERIAL #'d SETS
DJ Derek Jeter 120.00 55.00

2003 Fleer Avant Material

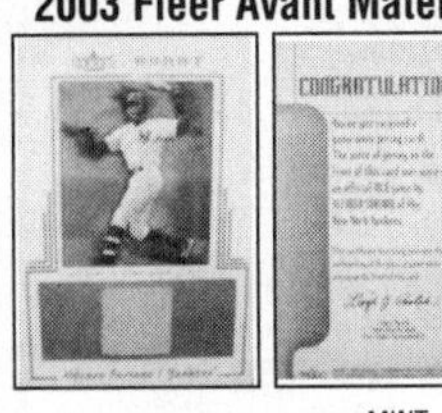

MINT NRMT
RANDOM INSERTS IN PACKS
STATED PRINT RUN 50 SERIAL #'d SETS
AR Alex Rodriguez Jsy 25.00 11.00
AS Alfonso Soriano Jsy 20.00 9.00
BB Barry Bonds Base
BZ Barry Zito Jsy
CJ Chipper Jones Jsy 20.00 9.00
DJ Derek Jeter Jsy
GM Greg Maddux Jsy 20.00 9.00
JG Jason Giambi Jsy 20.00 9.00
JT Jim Thome Jsy 20.00 9.00
MT Miguel Tejada Jsy 15.00 6.75
NG Nomar Garciaparra Jsy 25.00 11.00
RB Rocco Baldelli Jsy
RJ Randy Johnson Jsy 20.00 9.00
SS Sammy Sosa Jsy 25.00 11.00
VG Vladimir Guerrero Jsy 20.00 9.00

2003 Fleer Avant Candid Collection

MINT NRMT
RANDOM INSERTS IN PACKS
STATED PRINT RUN 500 SERIAL #'d SETS
1 Derek Jeter 12.00 5.50
2 Mike Piazza 8.00 3.60
3 Albert Pujols 10.00 4.50
4 Randy Johnson 8.00 3.60
5 Alex Rodriguez 8.00 3.60
6 Vladimir Guerrero 8.00 3.60
7 Troy Glaus 8.00 3.60
8 Ichiro Suzuki 8.00 3.60
9 Barry Zito 8.00 3.60
10 Jim Thome 8.00 3.60
11 Sammy Sosa 8.00 3.60
12 Greg Maddux 8.00 3.60
13 Barry Bonds 12.00 5.50
14 Jason Giambi 8.00 3.60
15 Nomar Garciaparra 8.00 3.60

2003 Fleer Avant Candid Collection Game Jersey

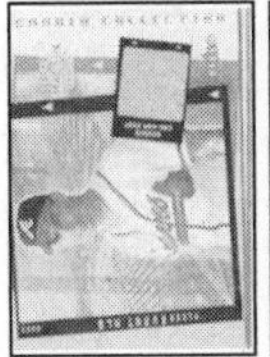
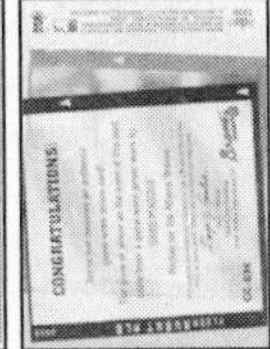

MINT NRMT
RANDOM INSERTS IN PACKS
STATED PRINT RUN 150 SERIAL #'d SETS
AR Alex Rodriguez 20.00 9.00
BZ Barry Zito 15.00 6.75
DJ Derek Jeter 30.00 13.50
GM Greg Maddux 15.00 6.75
JG Jason Giambi 15.00 6.75
JT Jim Thome 15.00 6.75
MP Mike Piazza 15.00 6.75
NG Nomar Garciaparra 20.00 9.00
RJ Randy Johnson 15.00 6.75
SS Sammy Sosa 20.00 9.00

2003 Fleer Avant Hall of Frame

MINT NRMT
RANDOM INSERTS IN PACKS
STATED PRINT RUN 299 SERIAL #'d SETS
1 Richie Ashburn 10.00 4.50
2 Rod Carew 10.00 4.50
3 Whitey Ford 10.00 4.50
4 Bob Gibson 10.00 4.50
5 Reggie Jackson 10.00 4.50
6 Harmon Killebrew 10.00 4.50
7 Willie McCovey 10.00 4.50
8 Phil Rizzuto 10.00 4.50
9 Al Kaline 10.00 4.50
10 Brooks Robinson 10.00 4.50
11 Nolan Ryan 20.00 9.00
12 Mike Schmidt 15.00 6.75
13 Tom Seaver 10.00 4.50
14 Warren Spahn 10.00 4.50

2003 Fleer Avant Hall of Frame Game Used

MINT NRMT
RANDOM INSERTS IN PACKS
STATED PRINT RUN 99 SERIAL #'d SETS
AK Al Kaline Jsy 30.00 13.50
MS Mike Schmidt Bat 40.00 18.00
NR Nolan Ryan Patch 80.00 36.00
RJ Reggie Jackson Pants 25.00 11.00
WM Willie McCovey Jsy 25.00 11.00

2003 Fleer Avant On Display

MINT NRMT
RANDOM INSERTS IN PACKS
STATED PRINT RUN 399 SERIAL #'d SETS
1 Derek Jeter 15.00 6.75
2 Barry Bonds 15.00 6.75
3 Rocco Baldelli 20.00 9.00
4 Alex Rodriguez 10.00 4.50
5 Alfonso Soriano 10.00 4.50
6 Sammy Sosa 10.00 4.50
7 Nomar Garciaparra 10.00 4.50
8 Hideki Matsui 20.00 9.00
9 Miguel Tejada 8.00 3.60
10 Chipper Jones 10.00 4.50

2003 Fleer Avant On Display Game Used

MINT NRMT
RANDOM INSERTS IN PACKS
STATED PRINT RUN 250 SERIAL #'d SETS
AR Alex Rodriguez Jsy 15.00 6.75
AS Alfonso Soriano Jsy 10.00 4.50
BB Barry Bonds Base 15.00 6.75
CJ Chipper Jones Jsy 10.00 4.50
DJ Derek Jeter Jsy 25.00 11.00
HM Hideki Matsui Base 40.00 18.00
MT Miguel Tejada Jsy 8.00 3.60
NG Nomar Garciaparra Jsy 20.00 9.00
RB Rocco Baldelli Jsy 25.00 11.00
SS Sammy Sosa Jsy 20.00 9.00

2002 Fleer Box Score

Fleer released this innovative 310 card set in July, 2002. The set was released in boxes which contained 18 seven-card packs as well as a box featuring a full subset of one of the speciality subsets issued. Cards 1-125 feature active veteran players while cards 126-150 feature rookies and prospects. Cards numbered 126 through 150 were issued to a stated print run of 2499 sets. Cards numbered 151-190, which were issued in their own special box featured rising stars. Cards numbered 191-230 featured players born outside the USA, cards 231-270 featured players who have participated in All-Star games and cards 271-310 feature players enshrined in Cooperstown. Each of the cards numbered from 151-310 were printed to a stated print run of 2,950 sets.

Nm-Mt Ex-Mt
COMP.SET w/o SP's (125) 25.00 7.50
COMMON CARD (1-125) .40 .12
COMMON CARD (126-150) 5.00 1.50
COMP.RISING STAR SET (40) 25.00 7.50
COMMON CARD (151-190) 2.00 .60
COMP.INT'L SET (40) 25.00 7.50
COMMON CARD (191-230) 2.00 .60
COMP.ALL-STAR SET (40) 25.00 7.50
COMMON CARD (231-270) 2.00 .60
COMP.COOPERSTOWN SET (40) 40.00 12.00
COMMON CARD (271-310) 2.00 .60
1 Derek Jeter 2.50 .75
2 Kevin Brown .40 .12
3 Nomar Garciaparra 1.50 .45
4 Mark Buehrle .40 .12
5 Mike Piazza 1.50 .45
6 David Justice .40 .12
7 Tino Martinez .60 .18
8 Paul Konerko .40 .12
9 Larry Walker .60 .18
10 Ben Sheets .40 .12
11 Mike Cameron .40 .12
12 David Wells .40 .12
13 Barry Zito .60 .18
14 Pat Burrell .40 .12
15 Mike Mussina 1.00 .30
16 Bud Smith .40 .12
17 Brian Jordan .40 .12
18 Chris Singleton .40 .12
19 Daryle Ward .40 .12
20 Russ Ortiz .40 .12
21 Jason Kendall .40 .12
22 Kerry Wood 1.00 .30
23 Jeff Weaver .40 .12
24 Tony Armas Jr. .40 .12
25 Toby Hall .40 .12
26 Brian Giles .40 .12
27 Juan Pierre .40 .12
28 Ken Griffey Jr. 1.50 .45
29 Mike Sweeney .40 .12
30 John Smoltz .60 .18
31 Sean Casey .40 .12
32 Jeremy Giambi .40 .12
33 Mike Lieberthal .40 .12
34 Rich Aurilia .40 .12
35 Matt Lawton .40 .12
36 Dmitri Young .40 .12
37 Wade Miller .40 .12
38 Jason Giambi 1.00 .30
39 Jeff Cirillo .40 .12
40 Mark Grace .60 .18
41 Frank Thomas 1.00 .30
42 Preston Wilson .40 .12
43 Brad Radke .40 .12
44 Greg Maddux 1.50 .45
45 Adam Dunn .40 .12
46 Roy Oswalt .40 .12
47 Troy Glaus .60 .18
48 Edgar Martinez .60 .18
49 Billy Koch .40 .12
50 Chipper Jones 1.00 .30
51 Lance Berkman .40 .12
52 Shannon Stewart .40 .12
53 Eddie Guardado .40 .12
54 C.C. Sabathia .40 .12
55 Craig Biggio .60 .18
56 Roger Clemens 2.00 .60
57 Jimmy Rollins .40 .12
58 Carlos Delgado .40 .12
59 Tony Clark .40 .12
60 Mike Hampton .40 .12
61 Jeromy Burnitz .40 .12
62 Jorge Posada .60 .18
63 Todd Helton .60 .18
64 Richie Sexson .40 .12
65 Ryan Klesko .40 .12
66 Cliff Floyd .40 .12
67 Eric Milton .40 .12
68 Scott Rolen .60 .18
69 Steve Finley .40 .12
70 Ray Durham .40 .12
71 Jeff Bagwell .60 .18
72 Geoff Jenkins .40 .12
73 Jamie Moyer .40 .12
74 David Eckstein .40 .12
75 Johnny Damon .40 .12
76 Pokey Reese .40 .12
77 Mo Vaughn .40 .12
78 Trevor Hoffman .40 .12
79 Albert Pujols 2.00 .60
80 Ben Grieve .40 .12
81 Matt Morris .40 .12
82 Aubrey Huff .40 .12
83 Darin Erstad .40 .12
84 Garret Anderson .40 .12
85 Jacque Jones .40 .12
86 Matt Anderson .40 .12
87 Jose Vidro .40 .12
88 Carlos Lee .40 .12
89 Jeff Suppan .40 .12
90 Al Leiter .40 .12
91 Jeff Kent .40 .12
92 Randy Johnson 1.00 .30
93 Moises Alou .40 .12
94 Bobby Higginson .40 .12
95 Phil Nevin .40 .12
96 Alex Rodriguez 1.50 .45
97 Luis Gonzalez .40 .12
98 A.J. Burnett .40 .12
99 Torii Hunter .40 .12
100 Ivan Rodriguez 1.00 .30
101 Pedro Martinez 1.00 .30
102 Brady Anderson .40 .12
103 Paul LoDuca .40 .12
104 Eric Chavez .40 .12
105 Tim Salmon .60 .18
106 Javier Vazquez .40 .12
107 Bret Boone .40 .12
108 Greg Vaughn .40 .12
109 J.D. Drew .40 .12
110 Jay Gibbons .40 .12
111 Jim Thome 1.00 .30
112 Shawn Green .40 .12
113 Tim Hudson .40 .12
114 John Olerud .40 .12
115 Raul Mondesi .40 .12
116 Curt Schilling .60 .18
117 Corey Patterson .40 .12
118 Robert Fick .40 .12
119 Corey Koskie .40 .12
120 Juan Gonzalez 1.00 .30
121 Jerry Hairston Jr. .40 .12
122 Gary Sheffield .40 .12
123 Mark Mulder .40 .12
124 Barry Bonds 2.50 .75
125 Jim Edmonds .40 .12
126 Franklyn German RP RC 5.00 1.50
127 Rodrigo Rosario RP RC 5.00 1.50
128 Ryan Ludwick RP 5.00 1.50
129 Jorge De La Rosa RP RC 5.00 1.50
130 Jason Lane RP 5.00 1.50
131 Brian Mallette RP RC 5.00 1.50
132 Chris Baker RP RC 5.00 1.50
133 Kyle Kane RP RC 5.00 1.50
134 Doug Devore RP RC 5.00 1.50
135 Raul Chavez RP RC 5.00 1.50
136 Miguel Asencio RP RC 5.00 1.50
137 Luis C.Garcia RP RC 5.00 1.50
138 Nick Johnson RP 5.00 1.50
139 Mike Crudale RP RC 5.00 1.50
140 P.J. Bevis RP RC 5.00 1.50
141 Josh Hancock RP RC 5.00 1.50
142 Jeremy Lambert RP RC 5.00 1.50
143 Ben Broussard RP 5.00 1.50
144 John Ennis RP RC 5.00 1.50
145 Wilson Valdez RP RC 5.00 1.50
146 Eric Good RP RC 5.00 1.50
147 Elio Serrano RP RC 5.00 1.50
148 Jaime Cerda RP RC 5.00 1.50
149 Hank Blalock RP 8.00 2.40
150 Brandon Duckworth RP 5.00 1.50
151 Drew Henson RS 2.00 .60
152 Kazuhisa Ishii RS RC 5.00 1.50
153 Earl Snyder RS RC 2.00 .60
154 J.M. Gold RS 2.00 .60
155 Satoru Komiyama RS RC 2.00 .60
156 Marlon Byrd RS 2.00 .60
157 So Taguchi RS RC 3.00 .90
158 Eric Hinske RS 2.00 .60
159 Mark Prior RS 10.00 3.00
160 Jorge Padilla RS RC 2.00 .60
161 Rene Reyes RS RC 2.00 .60
162 Jorge Nunez RS RC 2.00 .60
163 Nelson Castro RS RC 2.00 .60
164 Anderson Machado RS RC 2.00 .60
165 Mark Teixeira RS 3.00 .90
166 Orlando Hudson RS 2.00 .60
167 Edwin Almonte RS RC 2.00 .60
168 Luis Ugueto RS RC 2.00 .60
169 Felix Escalona RS RC 2.00 .60
170 Ron Calloway RS RC 2.00 .60
171 Kevin Mench RS 2.00 .60
172 Takahito Nomura RS RC 2.00 .60
173 Sean Burroughs RS 2.00 .60
174 Steve Kent RS RC 2.00 .60
175 Jorge Sosa RS RC 2.00 .60
176 Mike Moriarty RS RC 2.00 .60
177 Carlos Pena RS 2.00 .60
178 Anastacio Martinez RS RC 2.00 .60
179 Reed Johnson RS RC 3.00 .90
180 Juan Brito RS RC 2.00 .60
181 Wilson Betemit RS 2.00 .60
182 Mike Rivera RS 2.00 .60
183 David Espinosa RS 2.00 .60
184 Todd Donovan RS RC 2.00 .60
185 Morgan Ensberg RS 2.00 .60
186 Dewon Brazelton RS 2.00 .60
187 Ben Howard RS RC 2.00 .60
188 Austin Kearns RS 2.00 .60
189 Josh Beckett RS 3.00 .90
190 Brandon Backe RS RC 2.00 .60
191 Ichiro Suzuki IRT 6.00 1.80
192 Tsuyoshi Shinjo IRT 2.00 .60
193 Hideo Nomo IRT 4.00 1.20
194 Kazuhiro Sasaki IRT 2.00 .60
195 Edgardo Alfonzo IRT 2.00 .60
196 Chan Ho Park IRT 2.00 .60
197 Carlos Hernandez IRT 2.00 .60
198 Byung-Hyun Kim IRT 2.00 .60
199 Omar Vizquel IRT 2.00 .60
200 Freddy Garcia IRT 2.00 .60
201 Richard Hidalgo IRT 2.00 .60
202 Maggio Ordonez IRT 2.00 .60
203 Bob Abreu IRT 2.00 .60
204 Roger Cedeno IRT 2.00 .60
205 Andruw Jones IRT 2.00 .60
206 Mariano Rivera IRT 2.50 .75
207 Jose Macias IRT 2.00 .60
208 Orlando Hernandez IRT 2.00 .60
209 Rafael Palmeiro IRT 2.50 .75
210 Danys Baez IRT 2.00 .60
211 Bernie Williams IRT 2.50 .75
212 Carlos Beltran IRT 2.00 .60
213 Roberto Alomar IRT 4.00 1.20
214 Jose Cruz Jr. IRT 2.00 .60
215 Ryan Dempster IRT 2.00 .60
216 Erubiel Durazo IRT 2.00 .60
217 Carlos Pena IRT 2.00 .60
218 Sammy Sosa IRT 6.00 1.80
219 Adrian Beltre IRT 2.00 .60
220 Aramis Ramirez IRT 2.00 .60
221 Alfonso Soriano IRT 2.50 .75
222 Vladimir Guerrero IRT 4.00 1.20
223 Juan Uribe IRT 2.00 .60
224 Cristian Guzman IRT 2.00 .60
225 Manny Ramirez IRT 2.00 .60
226 Juan Cruz IRT 2.00 .60
227 Ramon Ortiz IRT 2.00 .60
228 Juan Encarnacion IRT 2.00 .60
229 Bartolo Colon IRT 2.00 .60
230 Miguel Tejada IRT 2.00 .60
231 Cal Ripken AS 12.00 3.60
232 Derek Jeter AS 10.00 3.00
233 Pedro Martinez AS 4.00 1.20
234 Roberto Alomar AS 4.00 1.20
235 Sandy Alomar Jr. AS 2.00 .60
236 Mike Piazza AS 6.00 1.80
237 Jeff Conine AS 2.00 .60
238 Fred McGriff AS 2.50 .75
239 Kirby Puckett AS 4.00 1.20
240 Ken Griffey Jr. AS 6.00 1.80
241 Roger Clemens AS 8.00 2.40
242 Joe Morgan AS 2.00 .60
243 Willie McCovey AS 2.00 .60
244 Brooks Robinson AS 4.00 1.20
245 Juan Marichal AS 2.00 .60
246 Todd Helton AS 2.50 .75
247 Alex Rodriguez AS 6.00 1.80
248 Barry Bonds AS 10.00 3.00
249 Nomar Garciaparra AS 6.00 1.80
250 Jeff Bagwell AS 2.50 .75
251 Kenny Lofton AS 2.00 .60
252 Barry Larkin AS 4.00 1.20
253 Tom Glavine AS 2.50 .75
254 Magglio Ordonez AS 2.00 .60
255 Randy Johnson AS 4.00 1.20
256 Chipper Jones AS 4.00 1.20
257 Kevin Brown AS 2.00 .60
258 Rickey Henderson AS 4.00 1.20
259 Greg Maddux AS 6.00 1.80
260 Jim Thome AS 4.00 1.20
261 Rafael Palmeiro AS 2.50 .75
262 Frank Thomas AS 4.00 1.20
263 Manny Ramirez AS 2.00 .60
264 Travis Fryman AS 2.00 .60
265 Gary Sheffield AS 2.00 .60
266 Bernie Williams AS 2.50 .75
267 Matt Williams AS 2.00 .60
268 Ivan Rodriguez AS 4.00 1.20
269 Mike Mussina AS 4.00 1.20
270 Larry Walker AS 2.50 .75
271 Jim Palmer CT 2.00 .60
272 Cal Ripken CT 15.00 4.50
273 Brooks Robinson CT 5.00 1.50
274 Bobby Doerr CT 2.00 .60
275 Ernie Banks CT 5.00 1.50
276 Fergie Jenkins CT 2.00 .60
277 Luis Aparicio CT 2.00 .60
278 Hoyt Wilhelm CT 2.00 .60
279 Tom Seaver CT 3.00 .90
280 Joe Morgan CT 2.00 .60
281 Lou Boudreau CT 2.00 .60
282 Larry Doby CT 2.00 .60
283 Jim Bunning CT 2.00 .60
284 George Kell CT 2.00 .60
285 Pee Wee Reese CT 3.00 .90
286 Eddie Mathews CT 5.00 1.50
287 Robin Yount CT 8.00 2.40
288 Rod Carew CT 3.00 .90
289 Monte Irvin CT 2.00 .60
290 Yogi Berra CT 5.00 1.50
291 Whitey Ford CT 3.00 .90
292 Reggie Jackson CT 3.00 .90
293 Rollie Fingers CT 2.00 .60
294 Catfish Hunter CT 3.00 .90
295 Richie Ashburn CT 3.00 .90
296 Willie Stargell CT 3.00 .90
297 Ralph Kiner CT 3.00 .90
298 Orlando Cepeda CT 2.00 .60
299 Juan Marichal CT 2.00 .60
300 Gaylord Perry CT 2.00 .60
301 Willie McCovey CT 2.00 .60
302 Red Schoendienst CT 2.00 .60
303 Nolan Ryan CT 12.00 3.60
304 Bob Gibson CT 3.00 .90
305 Al Kaline CT 5.00 1.50
306 Harmon Killebrew CT 5.00 1.50
307 Stan Musial CT 8.00 2.40
308 Phil Rizzuto CT 3.00 .90
309 Mike Schmidt CT 12.00 3.60
310 Enos Slaughter CT 2.00 .60
P124 Barry Bonds Promo 2.00 .60

2002 Fleer Box Score Classic Miniatures

Issued as a special box within the Box Score unopened boxes, this is a 40-card partial parallel to the Box Score set. These cards are smaller than the regular cards are have a stated print run of 2950 serial numbered sets.

Nm-Mt Ex-Mt
1 Derek Jeter 10.00 3.00
3 Nomar Garciaparra 6.00 1.80
5 Mike Piazza 6.00 1.80
9 Larry Walker 2.50 .75
11 Mike Cameron 1.50 .45
14 Pat Burrell 1.50 .45
26 Brian Giles 1.50 .45
28 Ken Griffey Jr. 6.00 1.80
29 Mike Sweeney 1.50 .45
38 Jason Giambi 4.00 1.20
41 Frank Thomas 4.00 1.20
44 Greg Maddux 6.00 1.80
45 Adam Dunn 1.50 .45
46 Roy Oswalt 1.50 .45
47 Troy Glaus 2.50 .75
50 Chipper Jones 4.00 1.20
51 Lance Berkman 1.50 .45
56 Roger Clemens 8.00 2.40
57 Jimmy Rollins 1.50 .45
58 Carlos Delgado 1.50 .45
63 Todd Helton 2.50 .75
64 Richie Sexson 1.50 .45
66 Cliff Floyd 1.50 .45
71 Jeff Bagwell 2.50 .75
79 Albert Pujols 8.00 2.40
92 Randy Johnson 4.00 1.20
95 Phil Nevin 1.50 .45
96 Alex Rodriguez 6.00 1.80
97 Luis Gonzalez 1.50 .45
99 Torii Hunter 1.50 .45
100 Ivan Rodriguez 4.00 1.20
101 Pedro Martinez 4.00 1.20
104 Eric Chavez 1.50 .45
107 Bret Boone 1.50 .45
109 J.D. Drew 1.50 .45
111 Jim Thome 4.00 1.20
112 Shawn Green 1.50 .45
113 Tim Hudson 1.50 .45
116 Curt Schilling 2.50 .75
124 Barry Bonds 10.00 3.00

2002 Fleer Box Score Classic Miniatures First Edition

Randomly issued in Classic Miniature mini-boxes, this is a parallel to the Mini parallel set. Each of these cards were issued to a stated print run of 100 serial numbered sets.

Nm-Mt Ex-Mt
*CLASSIC MINIS 1ST ED: 4X TO 10X BASIC

2002 Fleer Box Score Classic Miniatures Game Used

This 10-card set was inserted at a stated rate of one per classic mini box. Each card features a piece of game-used memorabilia as well as the card.

Nm-Mt Ex-Mt
1 Derek Jeter Bat 25.00 7.50
2 Mike Piazza Jsy 15.00 4.50
3 Adam Dunn Jsy 15.00 4.50

4 Chipper Jones Bat 20.00 6.00
5 Roger Clemens Jsy 20.00 6.00
6 Alex Rodriguez Jsy 15.00 4.50
7 Pedro Martinez Jsy 20.00 6.00
8 Jim Thome Bat 20.00 6.00
9 Curt Schilling Jsy 15.00 4.50
10 Barry Bonds Bat 25.00 7.50

2002 Fleer Box Score First Edition

Randomly inserted in Box Score, this is a parallel to the basic set. Each of these cards have a stated print run of 100 serial numbered sets.

Nm-Mt Ex-Mt
*1ST ED. 1-125: 4X TO 10X BASIC CARDS
*1ST ED. 126-150: .5X TO 1.2X BASIC
*1ST ED. 151-190: 1X TO 2.5X BASIC
*1ST ED. 191-230: 1X TO 2.5X BASIC
*1ST ED. 231-270: 1X TO 2.5X BASIC
*1ST ED. 271-310: 1X TO 2.5X BASIC
151-190 ONE SUBSET PER RS 1ST ED. BOX
191-230 ONE SUBSET PER IRT 1ST ED. BOX
231-270 ONE SUBSET PER AS 1ST ED. BOX
271-310 ONE SUBSET PER CT 1ST ED. BOX
STATED PRINT RUN 100 SERIAL #'d SETS

2002 Fleer Box Score All-Star Lineup Game Used

This 10-card set was inserted at a stated rate of one per All-Star box. Each card features two pieces of game-used memorabilia as well as the card. Please note that the Jeter/Garciaparra/Rodriguez card has either Alex Rodriguez bat or Alex Rodriguez jersey swatches on it. There is no price differential for either version of this card.

Nm-Mt Ex-Mt
1 Derek Jeter Bat 60.00 18.00
Nomar Garciaparra Bat
Alex Rodriguez Jsy
1A Derek Jeter Bat 60.00 18.00
Nomar Garciaparra Bat
Alex Rodriguez Bat
2 Joe Morgan Bat 25.00 7.50
Willie McCovey Jsy
Brooks Robinson Bat
3 Ivan Rodriguez Jsy 25.00 7.50
Rafael Palmeiro Bat
Alex Rodriguez Jsy
4 Bernie Williams Jsy 50.00 15.00
Derek Jeter Bat
Mike Mussina Jsy
5 Barry Bonds Bat 50.00 15.00
Cal Ripken Jsy
Frank Thomas Jsy
6 Cal Ripken Jsy 80.00 24.00
Derek Jeter Bat
Pedro Martinez Jsy
Roberto Alomar Bat
7 Mike Piazza Jsy 60.00 18.00
Barry Bonds Bat
Ken Griffey Jr. Base
Jeff Bagwell Bat
8 Roger Clemens Jsy 80.00 24.00
Greg Maddux Jsy
Randy Johnson Jsy
Pedro Martinez Jsy
9 Todd Helton Jsy 40.00 12.00
Roberto Alomar Bat
Alex Rodriguez Jsy
Chipper Jones Jsy
10 Ken Griffey Jr Base 50.00 15.00
Barry Bonds Bat
Manny Ramirez Jsy
Larry Walker Jsy

2002 Fleer Box Score Amazing Greats

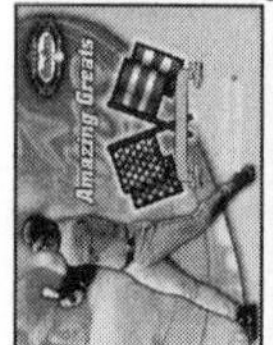

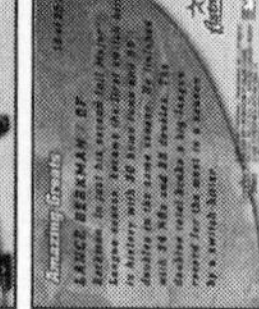

Inserted in packs at stated odds of one in five, these 20 cards feature some of the leading players in baseball.

Nm-Mt Ex-Mt
COMPLETE SET (20) 40.00 12.00
1 Derek Jeter 6.00 1.80
2 Barry Bonds 6.00 1.80
3 Mike Piazza 4.00 1.20
4 Ivan Rodriguez 2.50 .75
5 Todd Helton 1.50 .45
6 Nomar Garciaparra 4.00 1.20
7 Jim Thome 2.50 .75
8 Bernie Williams 1.50 .45
9 Kazuhiro Sasaki 1.50 .45
10 Torii Hunter 1.50 .45
11 Bret Boone 1.50 .45
12 Tim Hudson 1.50 .45
13 Randy Johnson 2.50 .75
14 Rafael Palmeiro 1.50 .45
15 Scott Rolen 1.50 .45
16 Carlos Delgado 1.50 .45
17 Chipper Jones 2.50 .75
18 Lance Berkman 1.50 .45
19 Frank Thomas 2.50 .75
20 Greg Maddux 4.00 1.20

2002 Fleer Box Score Amazing Greats Single Swatch

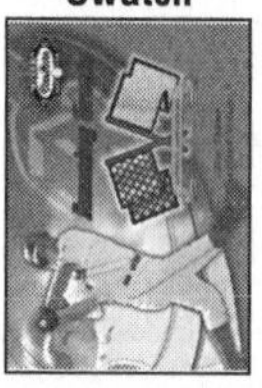

Inserted in packs at stated odds of one in 13, these cards are a partial parallel to the Amazing Greats insert set and feature a game-worn uniform swatch of the featured player.

Nm-Mt Ex-Mt
1 Lance Berkman 10.00 3.00
2 Barry Bonds 25.00 7.50
3 Bret Boone 10.00 3.00
4 Carlos Delgado 10.00 3.00
5 Nomar Garciaparra 20.00 6.00
6 Torii Hunter 10.00 3.00
7 Derek Jeter 25.00 7.50
8 Greg Maddux 15.00 4.50
9 Rafael Palmeiro 15.00 4.50
10 Mike Piazza 15.00 4.50
11 Ivan Rodriguez 15.00 4.50
12 Scott Rolen 15.00 4.50
13 Kazuhiro Sasaki 10.00 3.00
14 Frank Thomas 15.00 4.50
15 Jim Thome Bat 15.00 4.50
16 Bernie Williams 15.00 4.50

2002 Fleer Box Score Amazing Greats Dual Swatch

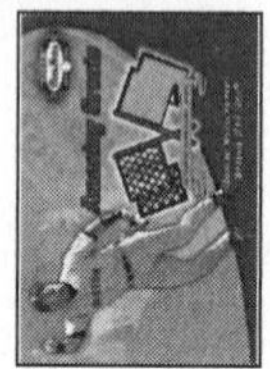

Inserted in packs at stated odds of one in 90, these cards are a partial parallel to the Amazing Greats insert set and feature two game-worn uniform swatches of the featured player.

Nm-Mt Ex-Mt
1 Lance Berkman 15.00 4.50
2 Barry Bonds 40.00 12.00
3 Bret Boone 15.00 4.50
4 Carlos Delgado 15.00 4.50
5 Nomar Garciaparra 30.00 9.00
6 Torii Hunter 15.00 4.50
7 Derek Jeter 40.00 12.00
8 Greg Maddux 25.00 7.50
9 Rafael Palmeiro 25.00 7.50
10 Mike Piazza 25.00 7.50
11 Ivan Rodriguez 25.00 7.50
12 Scott Rolen 25.00 7.50
13 Kazuhiro Sasaki 15.00 4.50
14 Frank Thomas 25.00 7.50
15 Bernie Williams 25.00 7.50

2002 Fleer Box Score Amazing Greats Patch

Randomly Inserted in packs, these cards are a partial parallel to the Amazing Greats insert set and feature a game-worn patch swatch of the featured player.

Nm-Mt Ex-Mt
1 Lance Berkman 25.00 7.50
2 Barry Bonds 60.00 18.00
3 Bret Boone 25.00 7.50
4 Carlos Delgado 25.00 7.50
5 Nomar Garciaparra 50.00 15.00
6 Torii Hunter 25.00 7.50
7 Derek Jeter 60.00 18.00
8 Greg Maddux 40.00 12.00
9 Rafael Palmeiro 40.00 12.00
10 Mike Piazza 40.00 12.00
11 Ivan Rodriguez 40.00 12.00
12 Scott Rolen 40.00 12.00
13 Kazuhiro Sasaki 25.00 7.50
14 Frank Thomas 40.00 12.00
15 Bernie Williams 40.00 12.00

2002 Fleer Box Score Bat Rack Quads

Randomly inserted in packs, these 13 cards feature bat pieces from each of the four player featured on the card. Each card has a stated print run of 150 serial numbered cards.

Nm-Mt Ex-Mt
1 Torii Hunter 40.00 12.00
Cristian Guzman
Frank Thomas
Magglio Ordonez
2 Alex Rodriguez 60.00 18.00
Ivan Rodriguez
Eric Chavez
Miguel Tejada
3 Derek Jeter 120.00 36.00
Alfonso Soriano
Mike Piazza
Roberto Alomar
4 Barry Bonds 120.00 36.00
Lance Berkman
Alex Rodriguez
Nomar Garciaparra
5 Ivan Rodriguez 120.00 36.00
Mike Piazza
Chipper Jones
Barry Bonds
6 Alex Rodriguez 120.00 36.00
Nomar Garciaparra
Derek Jeter
Miguel Tejada
7 Roberto Alomar 40.00 12.00
Mo Vaughn
Jeff Bagwell
Craig Biggio
8 Rafael Palmeiro 40.00 12.00
Carlos Delgado
Jim Thome
Frank Thomas
9 Magglio Ordonez 40.00 12.00
Bernie Williams
Juan Gonzalez
Manny Ramirez
10 Chipper Jones 40.00 12.00
Adam Dunn
Jeff Bagwell
Mo Vaughn
11 Alex Rodriguez 60.00 18.00
Rafael Palmeiro
Bernie Williams
Alfonso Soriano
12 Carlos Pena 40.00 12.00
Eric Chavez
Carlos Delgado
Juan Gonzalez
13 Adam Dunn 40.00 12.00
Lance Berkman
Jim Thome
Manny Ramirez

2002 Fleer Box Score Bat Rack Trios

Randomly inserted in packs, these 10 cards feature bat pieces from each of the four player featured on the card. Each card has a stated print run of 300 serial numbered cards.

Nm-Mt Ex-Mt
1 Derek Jeter 80.00 24.00
Alfonso Soriano
Bernie Williams
2 Mike Piazza 40.00 12.00
Roberto Alomar
Mo Vaughn
3 Jeff Bagwell 40.00 12.00
Lance Berkman
Craig Biggio
4 Eric Chavez 25.00 7.50
Miguel Tejada
Carlos Pena
5 Alex Rodriguez 50.00 15.00
Ivan Rodriguez
Rafael Palmeiro
6 Chipper Jones 25.00 7.50
Gary Sheffield
Andruw Jones
7 Carlos Delgado 25.00 7.50
Jim Thome
Frank Thomas
8 Derek Jeter 80.00 24.00
Nomar Garciaparra
Alex Rodriguez
9 Barry Bonds 50.00 15.00
Adam Dunn
Chipper Jones
10 Magglio Ordonez 25.00 7.50
Juan Gonzalez
Manny Ramirez

2002 Fleer Box Score Debuts

Randomly inserted in packs, these 15 innovative cards feature players who debuted in the majors in 2002. These cards are unique as

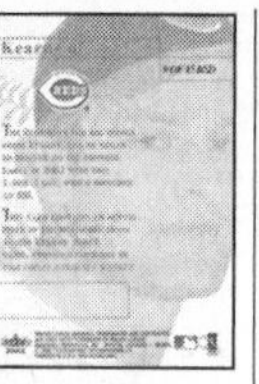

the actual "box score" from their debut game as printed in what was then called "U.S.A. Today Baseball Weekly" was included on each card. Each of these cards have a stated print run of 2,002 sets.

Nm-Mt Ex-Mt
COMPLETE SET (15) 100.00 30.00
1 Hank Blalock 10.00 3.00
2 Eric Hinske 5.00 1.50
3 Kazuhisa Ishii 15.00 4.50
4 Sean Burroughs 5.00 1.50
5 Andres Torres 5.00 1.50
6 Satoru Komiyama 5.00 1.50
7 Mark Prior 20.00 6.00
8 Kevin Mench 5.00 1.50
9 Austin Kearns 5.00 1.50
10 Earl Snyder 5.00 1.50
11 Jon Rauch 5.00 1.50
12 Jason Lane 5.00 1.50
13 Ben Howard 5.00 1.50
14 Bobby Hill 5.00 1.50
15 Dennis Tankersley 5.00 1.50

2002 Fleer Box Score Hall of Fame Material

This 10-card set was inserted at a stated rate of one per Cooperstown box. Each card features a piece of game-used memorabilia on the card.

Nm-Mt Ex-Mt
1 Jim Palmer Jsy 15.00 4.50
2 Cal Ripken Jsy 40.00 12.00
3 Brooks Robinson Bat 15.00 4.50
4 Joe Morgan Bat 15.00 4.50
5 Eddie Mathews Bat 15.00 4.50
6 Robin Yount Jsy 15.00 4.50
7 Reggie Jackson Jsy 15.00 4.50
8 Catfish Hunter Jsy 15.00 4.50
9 Willie McCovey Jsy 15.00 4.50
10 Nolan Ryan Jsy 50.00 15.00

2002 Fleer Box Score Press Clippings

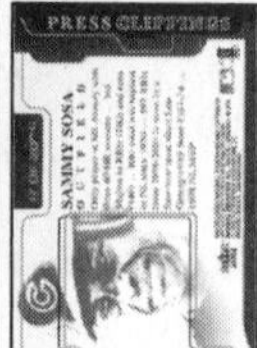

Inserted in packs at stated odds of one in 90, these 20 cards feature players who gather a great deal of press coverage.

Nm-Mt Ex-Mt
COMPLETE SET (20) 200.00 60.00
1 Mark Mulder 8.00 2.40
2 Curt Schilling 8.00 2.40
3 Alfonso Soriano 8.00 2.40
4 Jeff Bagwell 8.00 2.40
5 J.D. Drew 8.00 2.40
6 Pedro Martinez 10.00 3.00
7 Bob Abreu 8.00 2.40
8 Alex Rodriguez 15.00 4.50
9 Mike Sweeney 8.00 2.40
10 Carlos Pena 8.00 2.40
11 Josh Beckett 8.00 2.40
12 Roger Clemens 20.00 6.00
13 Manny Ramirez 8.00 2.40
14 Adam Dunn 8.00 2.40
15 Kazuhisa Ishii 12.00 3.60
16 Ken Griffey Jr. 15.00 4.50
17 Sammy Sosa 15.00 4.50
18 Ichiro Suzuki 15.00 4.50
19 Albert Pujols 20.00 6.00
20 Troy Glaus 8.00 2.40

2002 Fleer Box Score Press Clippings Game Used

Inserted in packs at stated odds of one in 13, these 20 cards are a partial parallel to the Press Clippings insert set.

Nm-Mt Ex-Mt
1 Bob Abreu Jsy 10.00 3.00
2 Jeff Bagwell Jsy 15.00 4.50
3 Josh Beckett Jsy 15.00 4.50
5 Roger Clemens Jsy SP/40
5 J.D. Drew Jsy 10.00 3.00
6 Adam Dunn Jsy 10.00 3.00
7 Troy Glaus Base 15.00 4.50
8 Ken Griffey Jr. Base 15.00 4.50
9 Kazuhisa Ishii Jsy SP/350 15.00 4.50
10 Pedro Martinez Jsy 20.00 6.00
11 Mark Mulder Jsy 10.00 3.00
12 Carlos Pena Jsy 10.00 3.00
13 Albert Pujols Base 15.00 4.50
14 Manny Ramirez Jsy 10.00 3.00
15 Alex Rodriguez Jsy 15.00 4.50
16 Curt Schilling Jsy 15.00 4.50
17 Alfonso Soriano Bat 15.00 4.50
18 Sammy Sosa Base 15.00 4.50
19 Ichiro Suzuki Base 25.00 7.50
20 Mike Sweeney Jsy 10.00 3.00

2002 Fleer Box Score Wave of the Future Game Used

This 10-card set was inserted at a stated rate of one per Rising Star mini box. Each card features a piece of game-used memorabilia on the card. A few cards in this set were produced in shorter quantities and we have notated the stated print run next to their name.

Nm-Mt Ex-Mt
1 Drew Henson Bat 8.00 2.40
2 Kazuhisa Ishii Bat 10.00 3.00
3 Marlon Byrd Pants 8.00 2.40
4 So Taguchi Bat 10.00 3.00
5 Jorge Padilla Pants SP/75 15.00 4.50
6 Rene Reyes Pants 8.00 2.40
7 Mark Teixeira Pants SP/100 20.00 6.00
8 Carlos Pena Bat 8.00 2.40
9 Austin Kearns Pants 8.00 2.40
10 Josh Beckett Jsy SP/50 25.00 7.50

2002 Fleer Box Score World Piece Game Used

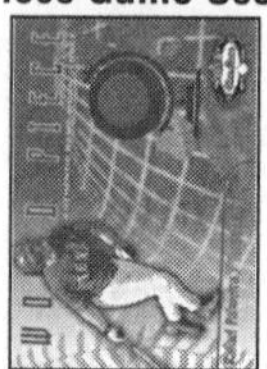

This 10-card set was inserted at a stated rate of one per International mini box. Each card features a piece of game-used memorabilia on the card.

Nm-Mt Ex-Mt
1 Ichiro Suzuki Base 25.00 7.50
2 Tsuyoshi Shinjo Bat 10.00 3.00
3 Hideo Nomo Jsy 30.00 9.00
4 Kazuhiro Sasaki Jsy 10.00 3.00
5 Chan Ho Park Jsy 10.00 3.00
6 Magglio Ordonez Jsy 10.00 3.00
7 Andruw Jones Jsy 10.00 3.00
8 Rafael Palmeiro Jsy 15.00 4.50
9 Bernie Williams Jsy 15.00 4.50
10 Roberto Alomar Bat 15.00 4.50

2003 Fleer Box Score

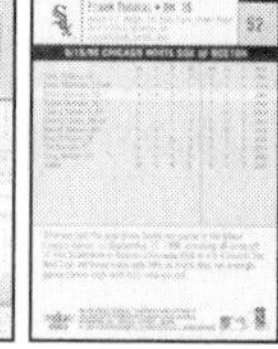

This 245 card set was released in July, 2003. The first 100 cards feature veteran players. Cards numbered 101 through 110 feature players who made their major league debut in 2003 and the USA Today Box Score of their debut game is embedded into the card. Those cards were issued to a stated print run of 599 serial numbered sets. Cards numbered 111 through 125 feature 2003 rookies and those cards were issued at a stated rate of one in six. Cards numbered 126 through 155 comprise a rising star subset which were issued one per rising star box. Cards numbered 156 through 185 feature All-Stars and those cards were all issued as a complete run in the All-Star box. Cards numbered 186-215 feature leading players born overseas and those cards were issued as a complete run in International boxes. And then cards numbered 216 through 245 feature a mix of current and retired New York Yankees and those cards were issued in a special Bronx Bomber box. All cards numbered between 126 and 245 were issued to a stated print run of 2400 sets. Card number 224 was not issued in this set.

Nm-Mt Ex-Mt
COMP.SET w/o SP's (100) 25.00 7.50
COMMON CARD (1-100) .40 .12
COMMON CARD (101-110) 5.00 1.50
COMMON CARD (111-125) 3.00 .90
COMP.RS SET (30) 25.00 7.50
COMMON CARD (126-155) 2.00 .60

COMP.AS SET (30) 25.00 7.50
COMMON CARD (156-185) 2.00 .60
COMP.IRT SET (30) 25.00 7.50
COMMON CARD (186-215) 2.00 .60
COMP.BRX SET (29) 40.00 12.00
COMMON CARD (216-245) 2.00 .60
1 Troy Glaus .60 .18
2 Derek Jeter 2.50 .75
3 Alex Rodriguez 1.50 .45
4 Barry Zito .60 .18
5 Darin Erstad .40 .12
6 Tim Hudson .40 .12
7 Josh Beckett .60 .18
8 Adam Dunn .40 .12
9 Tim Salmon .40 .12
10 Ivan Rodriguez 1.00 .30
11 Mark Buehrle .40 .12
12 Sammy Sosa 1.50 .45
13 Vicente Padilla .40 .12
14 Randy Johnson 1.00 .30
15 Lance Berkman .40 .12
16 Jim Thome 1.00 .30
17 Luis Gonzalez .40 .12
18 Craig Biggio .60 .18
19 Cliff Floyd .40 .12
20 Pat Burrell .40 .12
21 Matt Morris .40 .12
22 Torii Hunter .40 .12
23 Curt Schilling .60 .18
24 Paul Konerko .40 .12
25 Jeff Bagwell .60 .18
26 Mike Piazza 1.50 .45
27 A.J. Burnett .40 .12
28 Jimmy Rollins .40 .12
29 Greg Maddux 1.50 .45
30 Jeff Kent .40 .12
31 Bobby Abreu .40 .12
32 Chipper Jones 1.00 .30
33 Mike Sweeney .40 .12
34 Jason Kendall .40 .12
35 Gary Sheffield .40 .12
36 Carlos Beltran .40 .12
37 Brian Giles .40 .12
38 Jim Edmonds .40 .12
39 Roger Clemens 2.00 .60
40 Andruw Jones .40 .12
41 Paul Lo Duca .40 .12
42 Ryan Klesko .40 .12
43 Jay Gibbons .40 .12
44 Shawn Green .40 .12
45 Sean Burroughs .40 .12
46 Magglio Ordonez .40 .12
47 Tony Batista .40 .12
48 J.D. Drew .40 .12
49 Hideo Nomo 1.00 .30
50 Edgardo Alfonzo .40 .12
51 Nomar Garciaparra 1.50 .45
52 Frank Thomas 1.00 .30
53 Kazuhisa Ishii .40 .12
54 Rich Aurilia .40 .12
55 Shea Hillenbrand .40 .12
56 Tom Glavine .60 .18
57 Richie Sexson .40 .12
58 Mo Vaughn .40 .12
59 Barry Bonds 2.50 .75
60 Carlos Delgado .40 .12
61 Pedro Martinez 1.00 .30
62 Jacque Jones .40 .12
63 Edgar Martinez .60 .18
64 Manny Ramirez .40 .12
65 Bret Boone .40 .12
66 Kerry Wood 1.00 .30
67 Roy Oswalt .40 .12
68 Cristian Guzman .40 .12
69 Moises Alou .40 .12
70 Bartolo Colon .40 .12
71 Ichiro Suzuki 1.50 .45
72 Jose Vidro .40 .12
73 Scott Rolen .60 .18
74 Mark Prior 2.00 .60
75 Vladimir Guerrero 1.00 .30
76 Albert Pujols 1.50 .45
77 Aubrey Huff .40 .12
78 Ken Griffey Jr. 1.50 .45
79 Roberto Alomar 1.00 .30
80 Ben Grieve .40 .12
81 Miguel Tejada .40 .12
82 Austin Kearns .40 .12
83 Jason Giambi 1.00 .30
84 John Olerud .40 .12
85 Omar Vizquel .40 .12
86 Juan Gonzalez 1.00 .30
87 Larry Walker .60 .18
88 Jorge Posada .60 .18
89 Rafael Palmeiro .60 .18
90 Todd Helton .60 .18
91 Bernie Williams .60 .18
92 Garret Anderson .40 .12
93 Eric Hinske .40 .12
94 Mike Lowell .40 .12
95 Jason Jennings .40 .12
96 Eric Chavez .40 .12
97 Alfonso Soriano .60 .18
98 David Eckstein .40 .12
99 Bobby Higginson .40 .12
100 Roy Halladay .40 .12
101 Robby Hammock BSD RC 8.00 2.40
102 Hideki Matsui BSD RC 20.00 6.00
103 Chase Utley BSD 5.00 1.50
104 Oscar Villarreal BSD RC 5.00 1.50
105 Jose Contreras BSD RC 10.00 3.00
106 Rocco Baldelli BSD 15.00 4.50
107 Jesse Foppert BSD 5.00 1.50
108 Jer. Bonderman BSD RC 8.00 2.40
109 Shane Victorino BSD RC 5.00 1.50
110 Ron Calloway BSD 5.00 1.50
111 Brandon Webb ROO RC 10.00 3.00
112 Guillermo Quiroz ROO RC 5.00 1.50
113 Clint Barmes ROO RC 5.00 1.50
114 Pete LaForest ROO RC 5.00 1.50
115 Craig Brazell ROO RC 5.00 1.50
116 Todd Wellemeyer ROO RC 5.00 1.50
117 Bernie Castro ROO RC 3.00 .90
118 Al. Machado ROO RC 3.00 .90
119 Terrmel Sledge ROO RC 5.00 1.50
120 Ian Ferguson ROO RC 3.00 .90
121 Lew Ford ROO RC 5.00 1.50
122 Nook Logan ROO RC 3.00 .90
123 Mike Nicolas ROO RC 3.00 .90
124 Jeff Duncan ROO RC 5.00 1.50
125 Tim Olson ROO RC 5.00 1.50
126 Michael Hessman RS RC 2.00 .60
127 Francisco Rosario RS RC 2.00 .60
128 Felix Sanchez RS RC 2.00 .60
129 Andrew Brown RS RC 2.00 .60
130 Matt Bruback RS RC 2.00 .60
131 Diegomar Markwell RS RC 2.00 .60
132 Josh Willingham RS RC 4.00 1.20
133 Wes Obermueller RS 2.00 .60
134 Phil Seibel RS RC 2.00 .60
135 Arnie Munoz RS RC 2.00 .60
136 Matt Kata RS RC 3.00 .90
137 Joe Valentine RS RC 2.00 .60
138 Ricardo Rodriguez RS 2.00 .60
139 Lyle Overbay RS 2.00 .60
140 Brian Stokes RS RC 2.00 .60
141 Josh Hall RS RC 3.00 .90
142 Kevin Hooper RS 2.00 .60
143 Chien-Ming Wang RS RC 6.00 1.80
144 Prentice Redman RS RC 2.00 .60
145 Chris Waters RS RC 2.00 .60
146 Jon Leicester RS RC 2.00 .60
147 Daniel Cabrera RS RC 2.00 .60
148 Alfredo Gonzalez RS RC 2.00 .60
149 Doug Waechter RS RC 3.00 .90
150 Brandon Larson RS 2.00 .60
151 Beau Kemp RS RC 2.00 .60
152 Cory Stewart RS RC 2.00 .60
153 Francisco Rodriguez RS 2.00 .60
154 Hee Seop Choi RS 2.00 .60
155 Mike Neu RS RC 2.00 .60
156 Derek Jeter AS 10.00 3.00
157 Alex Rodriguez AS 6.00 1.80
158 Nomar Garciaparra AS 6.00 1.80
159 Barry Bonds AS 10.00 3.00
160 Sammy Sosa AS 6.00 1.80
161 Vladimir Guerrero AS 4.00 1.20
162 Roger Clemens AS 8.00 2.40
163 Randy Johnson AS 4.00 1.20
164 Greg Maddux AS 6.00 1.80
165 Ken Griffey Jr. AS 6.00 1.80
166 Mike Piazza AS 6.00 1.80
167 Ichiro Suzuki AS 6.00 1.80
168 Barry Larkin AS 4.00 1.20
169 Lance Berkman AS 2.00 .60
170 Jim Thome AS 4.00 1.20
171 Jason Giambi AS 4.00 1.20
172 Gary Sheffield AS 2.00 .60
173 Ivan Rodriguez AS 4.00 1.20
174 Miguel Tejada AS 2.00 .60
175 Manny Ramirez AS 2.00 .60
176 Mike Sweeney AS 2.00 .60
177 Larry Walker AS 2.50 .75
178 Jeff Bagwell AS 2.50 .75
179 Chipper Jones AS 4.00 1.20
180 Craig Biggio AS 2.50 .75
181 Curt Schilling AS 2.50 .75
182 Pedro Martinez AS 4.00 1.20
183 Roberto Alomar AS 4.00 1.20
184 Bernie Williams AS 2.50 .75
185 Magglio Ordonez AS 2.00 .60
186 Jose Contreras IRT 6.00 1.80
187 Rafael Palmeiro IRT 2.50 .75
188 Andruw Jones IRT 2.00 .60
189 Bartolo Colon IRT 2.00 .60
190 Vladimir Guerrero IRT 4.00 1.20
191 Pedro Martinez IRT 4.00 1.20
192 Albert Pujols IRT 6.00 1.80
193 Manny Ramirez IRT 2.00 .60
194 Felix Rodriguez IRT 2.00 .60
195 Alfonso Soriano IRT 2.50 .75
196 Sammy Sosa IRT 6.00 1.80
197 Miguel Tejada IRT 2.00 .60
198 Kazuhisa Ishii IRT 2.00 .60
199 Hideki Matsui IRT 15.00 4.50
200 Hideo Nomo IRT 4.00 1.20
201 Tomo Ohka IRT 2.00 .60
202 Kazuhiro Sasaki IRT 2.00 .60
203 Tsuyoshi Shinjo IRT 2.00 .60
204 Ichiro Suzuki IRT 6.00 1.80
205 Vicente Padilla IRT 2.00 .60
206 Carlos Beltran IRT 2.00 .60
207 Jose Cruz Jr. IRT 2.00 .60
208 Carlos Delgado IRT 2.00 .60
209 Juan Gonzalez IRT 4.00 1.20
210 Jorge Posada IRT 2.50 .75
211 Ivan Rodriguez IRT 4.00 1.20
212 Hee Seop Choi IRT 2.00 .60
213 Bobby Abreu IRT 2.00 .60
214 Magglio Ordonez IRT 2.00 .60
215 Francisco Rodriguez IRT 2.00 .60
216 Juan Acevedo BRX 2.00 .60
217 Erick Almonte BRX 2.00 .60
218 Yogi Berra BRX 4.00 1.20
219 Brandon Claussen BRX 2.00 .60
220 Roger Clemens BRX 8.00 2.40
221 Jose Contreras BRX 6.00 1.80
222 Whitey Ford BRX 2.50 .75
223 Jason Giambi BRX 4.00 1.20
224 Does Not Exist
225 Michel Hernandez BRX RC 2.00 .60
226 Sterling Hitchcock BRX 2.00 .60
227 Catfish Hunter BRX 2.50 .75
228 Reggie Jackson BRX 2.50 .75
229 Derek Jeter BRX 10.00 3.00
230 Nick Johnson BRX 2.00 .60
231 Hideki Matsui BRX 15.00 4.50
232 Raul Mondesi BRX 2.00 .60
233 Mike Mussina BRX 4.00 1.20
234 Andy Pettitte BRX 2.50 .75
235 Jorge Posada BRX 2.50 .75
236 Mariano Rivera BRX 2.50 .75
237 Phil Rizzuto BRX 2.50 .75
238 Enos Slaughter BRX 2.00 .60
239 Alfonso Soriano BRX 2.50 .75
240 Robin Ventura BRX 2.00 .60
241 Chien-Ming Wang BRX RC 6.00 1.80
242 Jeff Weaver BRX 2.00 .60
243 David Wells BRX 2.00 .60
244 Bernie Williams BRX 2.50 .75
245 Todd Zeile BRX 2.00 .60

2003 Fleer Box Score Classic Miniatures

Nm-Mt Ex-Mt
COMPLETE SET (30) 25.00 7.50
*CLASSIC MINIS: 1.5X TO 4X BASIC..
ONE SET PER CLASSIC MINI BOX
STATED PRINT RUN 2400 SETS

2003 Fleer Box Score Classic Miniatures Game Jersey

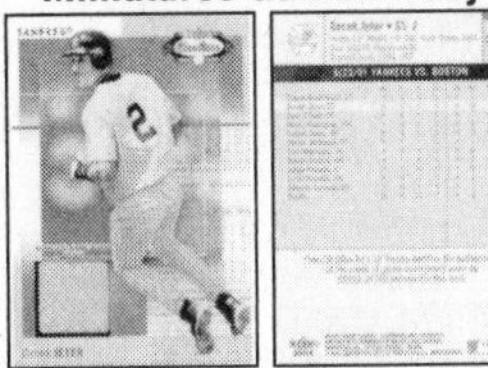

Nm-Mt Ex-Mt
ONE PER CLASSIC MINI BOX
SP PRINT RUNS PROVIDED BY FLEER
SP'S ARE NOT SERIAL-NUMBERED
AK Austin Kearns 8.00 2.40
DJ Derek Jeter 25.00 7.50
GM Greg Maddux 10.00 3.00
HN Hideo Nomo 15.00 4.50
JG Jason Giambi 10.00 3.00
JT Jim Thome SP/150 10.00 3.00
MP Mark Prior SP/150 15.00 4.50
MT Miguel Tejada 8.00 2.40
NG Nomar Garciaparra 15.00 4.50
VG Vladimir Guerrero SP/250 10.00 3.00

2003 Fleer Box Score First Edition

Nm-Mt Ex-Mt
*1ST ED. 1-100: 4X TO 10X BASIC
*1ST ED. 101-110: .4X TO 1X BASIC..
*1ST ED. 111-125: 1X TO 2.5X BASIC
*1ST ED. 126-155: 1X TO 2.5X BASIC
*1ST ED. 156-185: 1X TO 2.5X BASIC
*1ST ED. 186-215: 1X TO 2.5X BASIC
*1ST ED. 216-245: 1X TO 2.5X BASIC
1-125 RANDOM INSERTS IN PACKS
126-155 ONE SUBSET PER RS 1ST ED. BOX
156-185 ONE SUBSET PER AS 1ST ED. BOX
186-215 ONE SUBSET PER IRT 1ST ED. BOX
216-245 ONE SUBSET PER BRX 1ST ED. BOX
1-125 PRINT RUN 150 SERIAL #'d SETS
126-245 PRINT RUN 100 SERIAL #'d SETS
CARD 224 DOES NOT EXIST
102 Hideki Matsui BSD 40.00 12.00
143 Chien-Ming Wang RS 15.00 4.50
231 Hideki Matsui BRX 40.00 12.00
241 Chien-Ming Wang BRX 15.00 4.50

2003 Fleer Box Score All-Star Line Up Autographs

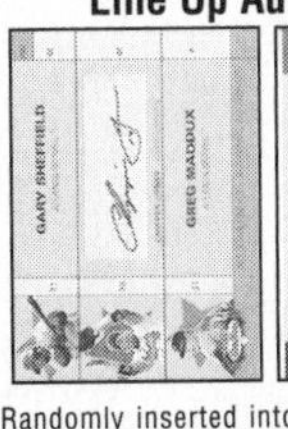
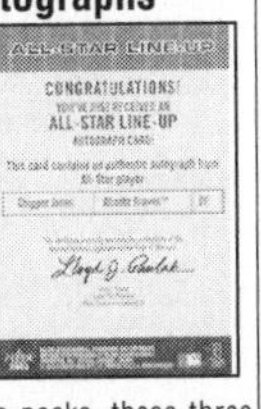

Randomly inserted into packs, these three cards feature authentic autographs from one of the players on the card. Please note that we have put the stated print run next to the player's name in our checklist.

Nm-Mt Ex-Mt
CJ Chipper Jones AU/170 50.00 15.00
Gary Sheffield
Greg Maddux
JT Jim Thome AU/260 40.00 12.00
Roberto Alomar
Alex Rodriguez
Nomar Garciaparra
RJ Randy Johnson AU/270 80.00 24.00
Roger Clemens
Greg Maddux

2003 Fleer Box Score All-Star Line Up Autographs Gold

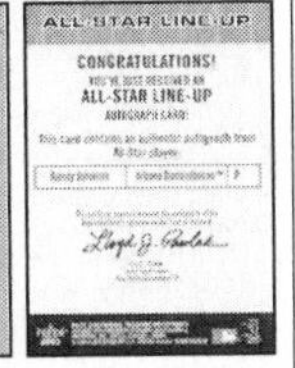

Nm-Mt Ex-Mt
RANDOM INSERTS IN PACKS
STATED PRINT RUN 50 SERIAL #'d SETS
CJ Chipper Jones AU
Gary Sheffield
Greg Maddux
JT Jim Thome
Roberto Alomar
Alex Rodriguez
Nomar Garciaparra
RJ Randy Johnson
Roger Clemens
Greg Maddux

2003 Fleer Box Score All-Star Lineup Game Used

Issued at a stated rate of one per All-Stars box, these 10 cards feature anywhere from two to four memorabilia pieces on them. A couple of the cards were produced in shorter supply and those cards we have notated with an SP in our checklist. In addition, the two cards featuring Barry Bonds have no game-used memorabilia of Bonds on the card.

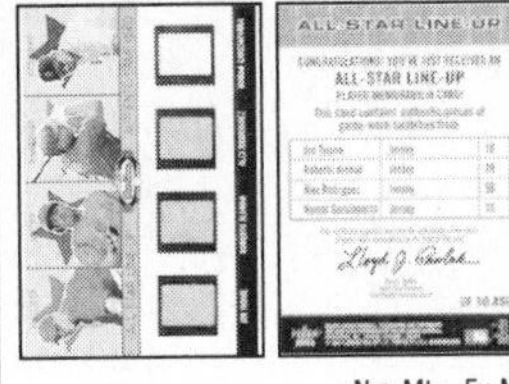

Nm-Mt Ex-Mt
1 Derek Jeter Jsy 50.00 15.00
Alex Rodriguez Jsy
Nomar Garciaparra Jsy
2 Barry Bonds 20.00 6.00
Sammy Sosa Jsy
Vladimir Guerrero Jsy SP/200
3 Roger Clemens Jsy 40.00 12.00
Randy Johnson Jsy
Greg Maddux Jsy
4 Jason Giambi Jsy 60.00 18.00
Alfonso Soriano Jsy
Derek Jeter Jsy SP/50
5 Craig Biggio Jsy 25.00 7.50
Jeff Bagwell Jsy
Lance Berkman Jsy SP/150
6 Chipper Jones Jsy 40.00 12.00
Gary Sheffield Jsy
Greg Maddux Jsy
7 Ivan Rodriguez Jsy 50.00 15.00
Mike Piazza Jsy
Randy Johnson Jsy
Roger Clemens Jsy
8 Barry Bonds 25.00 7.50
Ken Griffey Jr. Base
Manny Ramirez Base
Ichiro Suzuki Base SP/175
9 Roberto Alomar Jsy 50.00 15.00
Mike Piazza Jsy
Alfonso Soriano Jsy
Jason Giambi Jsy
10 Jim Thome Jsy 50.00 15.00
Roberto Alomar Jsy
Alex Rodriguez Jsy
Nomar Garciaparra Jsy SP/100

2003 Fleer Box Score Bat Rack Quads

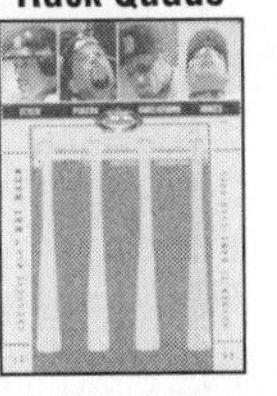

Randomly inserted in packs, these seven cards feature four game-used bat pieces on each card. Each of these cards were issued to a stated print run of 50 serial numbered sets.

Nm-Mt Ex-Mt
1 Derek Jeter 60.00 18.00
Torii Hunter
Troy Glaus
Miguel Tejada
2 Derek Jeter 100.00 30.00
Mike Piazza
Nomar Garciaparra
Chipper Jones
3 Vladimir Guerrero 50.00 15.00
Lance Berkman
Sammy Sosa
Scott Rolen
4 Jason Giambi 50.00 15.00
Alfonso Soriano
Alex Rodriguez
Troy Glaus
5 Alex Rodriguez 50.00 15.00
Jim Thome
Sammy Sosa
Scott Rolen
6 Jason Giambi 50.00 15.00
Jim Thome
Mike Piazza
Chipper Jones
7 Nomar Garciaparra
Miguel Tejada
Vladimir Guerrero
Alfonso Soriano

2003 Fleer Box Score Bat Rack Trios

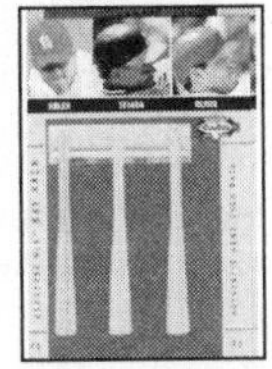

Randomly inserted into packs, these 10 cards feature three game-used bat pieces on them. Each of these cards were issued to a stated print run of 250 serial numbered sets.

Nm-Mt Ex-Mt
1 Derek Jeter 50.00 15.00
Alfonso Soriano
Jason Giambi
2 Scott Rolen 20.00 6.00
Miguel Tejada
Troy Glaus
3 Jim Thome 25.00 7.50
Chipper Jones
Mike Piazza
4 Troy Glaus 40.00 12.00
Nomar Garciaparra
Alfonso Soriano
5 Lance Berkman 25.00 7.50
Vladimir Guerrero
Sammy Sosa
6 Chipper Jones 20.00 6.00
Lance Berkman
Vladimir Guerrero
7 Torii Hunter 25.00 7.50
Jason Giambi
Nomar Garciaparra
8 Derek Jeter 40.00 12.00
Miguel Tejada
Alex Rodriguez
9 Scott Rolen 40.00 12.00
Sammy Sosa
Alex Rodriguez
10 Torii Hunter 25.00 7.50
Jim Thome
Mike Piazza

2003 Fleer Box Score Bronx Bombers Game Jersey

Inserted at a stated rate of one per Bronx Bombers box, these nine cards feature game-used jersey swatches of current New York Yankees. Please note that card number two was never issued and Nick Johnson was produced to a shorter quantity then the other cards in this set.

Nm-Mt Ex-Mt
1 Roger Clemens 20.00 6.00
3 Jason Giambi 15.00 4.50
4 Derek Jeter 30.00 9.00
5 Alfonso Soriano 15.00 4.50
6 Bernie Williams 15.00 4.50
7 Nick Johnson SP/150 10.00 3.00
8 Jorge Posada 15.00 4.50
9 Mike Mussina 20.00 6.00
10 Robin Ventura 10.00 3.00

2003 Fleer Box Score Jersey Rack Trios

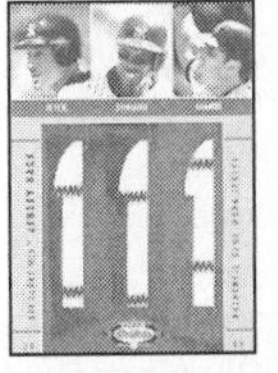

Randomly inserted in packs, these 10 cards feature three game-used bat pieces on them. Eachof these cards were issued to a stated print run of 350 serial numbered sets.

Nm-Mt Ex-Mt
1 Derek Jeter 50.00 15.00
Alfonso Soriano
Jason Giambi
2 Curt Schilling 25.00 7.50
Randy Johnson
Greg Maddux
3 Roger Clemens 25.00 7.50
Pedro Martinez
Barry Zito
4 Alex Rodriguez 40.00 12.00
Vladimir Guerrero
Sammy Sosa
5 Derek Jeter 50.00 15.00
Nomar Garciaparra
Alex Rodriguez
6 Lance Berkman 25.00 7.50
Sammy Sosa
Torii Hunter
7 Vladimir Guerrero 25.00 7.50
Jim Thome
Alex Rodriguez
8 Derek Jeter 40.00 12.00
Miguel Tejada
Nomar Garciaparra
9 Alfonso Soriano 20.00 6.00
Eric Chavez
Jim Thome
10 Miguel Tejada 20.00 6.00
Eric Chavez
Barry Zito

2003 Fleer Box Score Jersey Rack Quads

Randomly inserted into packs, these eight cards feature four game-used jersey swatches. These cards were issued to a stated print run of 150 serial numbered sets.

Nm-Mt Ex-Mt
1 Derek Jeter 60.00 18.00
Alex Rodriguez
Nomar Garciaparra
Miguel Tejada

Card	Nm-Mt	Ex-Mt
2 Roger Clemens	100.00	30.00
Jason Giambi		
Alfonso Soriano		
Derek Jeter		
3 Randy Johnson	80.00	24.00
Greg Maddux		
Roger Clemens		
Pedro Martinez		
4 Curt Schilling	40.00	12.00
Vladimir Guerrero		
Randy Johnson		
Alex Rodriguez		
5 Jason Giambi	40.00	12.00
Jim Thome		
Sammy Sosa		
Vladimir Guerrero		
6 Eric Chavez	50.00	15.00
Alfonso Soriano		
Jim Thome		
Sammy Sosa		
7 Barry Zito	40.00	12.00
Greg Maddux		
Pedro Martinez		
Curt Schilling		
8 Nomar Garciaparra	40.00	12.00
Miguel Tejada		
Barry Zito		
Eric Chavez		

2003 Fleer Box Score Press Clippings

	Nm-Mt	Ex-Mt
STATED ODDS 1:18		
1 Derek Jeter	8.00	2.40
2 Nomar Garciaparra	5.00	1.50
3 Miguel Tejada	3.00	.90
4 Barry Bonds	8.00	2.40
5 Alex Rodriguez	5.00	1.50
6 Sammy Sosa	5.00	1.50
7 Lance Berkman	3.00	.90
8 Torii Hunter	3.00	.90
9 Troy Glaus	3.00	.90
10 Eric Chavez	3.00	.90
11 Tim Hudson	3.00	.90
12 Randy Johnson	3.00	.90
13 Mike Piazza	5.00	1.50
14 Roberto Alomar	3.00	.90
15 Jim Thome	3.00	.90
16 Alfonso Soriano	3.00	.90
17 Roger Clemens	6.00	1.80
18 Pedro Martinez	3.00	.90
19 Mark Prior	6.00	1.80
20 Curt Schilling	3.00	.90

2003 Fleer Box Score Press Clippings Dual

	Nm-Mt	Ex-Mt
RANDOM INSERTS IN PACKS		
STATED PRINT RUN 250 SERIAL #'d SETS		
1 Derek Jeter	15.00	4.50
Nomar Garciaparra		
2 Miguel Tejada	10.00	3.00
Barry Bonds		
3 Alex Rodriguez	10.00	3.00
Sammy Sosa		
4 Lance Berkman	8.00	2.40
Torii Hunter		
5 Troy Glaus	8.00	2.40
Eric Chavez		
6 Tim Hudson	8.00	2.40
Randy Johnson		
7 Mike Piazza	10.00	3.00
Roberto Alomar		
8 Jim Thome	8.00	2.40
Alfonso Soriano		
9 Roger Clemens	8.00	2.40
Pedro Martinez		
10 Mark Prior	10.00	3.00
Curt Schilling		

2003 Fleer Box Score Press Clippings Dual Patch

	Nm-Mt	Ex-Mt
RANDOM INSERTS IN PACKS		
PRINT RUNS B/WN 100-150 COPIES PER		
1 Derek Jeter	100.00	30.00
Nomar Garciaparra/100		
2 Miguel Tejada	25.00	7.50
Troy Glaus/150		
3 Alex Rodriguez	60.00	18.00
Sammy Sosa/150		
4 Lance Berkman	25.00	7.50
Torii Hunter/150		
5 Troy Glaus	25.00	7.50
Eric Chavez/150		
6 Tim Hudson	25.00	7.50
Randy Johnson/150		
7 Mike Piazza	50.00	15.00
Roberto Alomar/150		
8 Jim Thome	25.00	7.50
Alfonso Soriano/100		
9 Roger Clemens	50.00	15.00
Pedro Martinez/100		
10 Mark Prior	50.00	15.00
Curt Schilling/150		
11 Kerry Wood	25.00	7.50
Kris Benson/150		
12 Rafael Palmeiro	25.00	7.50
Jeff Bagwell/150		
13 Andruw Jones	25.00	7.50
Gary Sheffield/150		
14 Manny Ramirez	25.00	7.50
Carlos Beltran/150		
15 Todd Helton	25.00	7.50
Erubiel Durazo/150		

2003 Fleer Box Score Press Clippings Game Jersey

	Nm-Mt	Ex-Mt
STATED ODDS 1:12		
SP PRINT RUNS PROVIDED BY FLEER		
SP'S ARE NOT SERIAL-NUMBERED		
AJ Andruw Jones	5.00	1.50
AR Alex Rodriguez	10.00	3.00
AS Alfonso Soriano	8.00	2.40
CB Carlos Beltran SP/250	5.00	1.50
CS Curt Schilling	8.00	2.40
DJ Derek Jeter	20.00	6.00
EC Eric Chavez	5.00	1.50
ED Erubiel Durazo SP/250	5.00	1.50
GS Gary Sheffield SP/250	5.00	1.50
JB Jeff Bagwell	8.00	2.40
JT Jim Thome	8.00	2.40
KB Kris Benson SP/250	5.00	1.50
KW Kerry Wood SP/250	8.00	2.40
LB Lance Berkman SP/250	5.00	1.50
MP1 Mike Piazza	10.00	3.00
MP2 Mark Prior	15.00	4.50
MR Manny Ramirez SP/250	5.00	1.50
MT Miguel Tejada	5.00	1.50
NG Nomar Garciaparra	15.00	4.50
PM Pedro Martinez	8.00	2.40
RA Roberto Alomar	8.00	2.40
RC Roger Clemens	15.00	4.50
RJ Randy Johnson	8.00	2.40
RP Rafael Palmeiro	8.00	2.40
SS Sammy Sosa	15.00	4.50
TG Troy Glaus	8.00	2.40
TH1 Todd Helton SP/250	8.00	2.40
TH2 Tim Hudson	5.00	1.50
TH3 Torii Hunter	5.00	1.50

2003 Fleer Box Score Wave of the Future Game Used

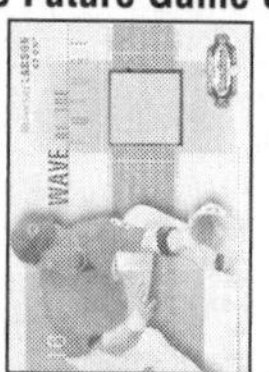

Issued at a stated rate of one per rising star box, these 10 cards feature not only a promising youngster but also a game-used memorabilia piece of that player. The Francisco Rodriguez card was issued to a stated print run of 125 cards.

	Nm-Mt	Ex-Mt
1 Lyle Overbay Bat	8.00	2.40
2 Brandon Larson Bat	8.00	2.40
3 Ricardo Rodriguez Jsy	8.00	2.40
4 Hee Seop Choi Jsy	8.00	2.40
5 Fran Rodriguez Jsy SP/125	10.00	3.00
6 Ron Calloway Jsy	8.00	2.40
7 Jeremy Bonderman Bat	10.00	3.00
8 Chase Utley Jsy	8.00	2.40

2003 Fleer Box Score World Piece Game Jersey

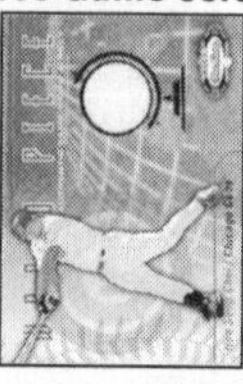

Inserted one per International Box, these 10 cards feature game-used jersey swatches of players born outside the USA. A few of these cards were issued to a smaller quantity and we have noted the announced print run next to the player's name in our checklist.

	Nm-Mt	Ex-Mt
1 Francisco Rodriguez SP/100	8.00	2.40
2 Vladimir Guerrero SP/200	10.00	3.00
3 Pedro Martinez	10.00	3.00
4 Sammy Sosa	15.00	4.50
5 Miguel Tejada	8.00	2.40
6 Hideo Nomo	10.00	3.00
7 Kazuhiro Sasaki	8.00	2.40
8 Jose Cruz Jr. SP/100	8.00	2.40
9 Ivan Rodriguez	10.00	3.00
10 Hee Seop Choi	8.00	2.40

1999 Fleer Brilliants

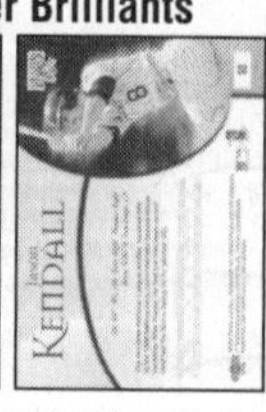

The 1999 Fleer Brilliants set was issued in June 1999 in one series for a total of 175 cards. The set was distributed in five-card packs with an original SRP of $4.99. The fronts feature color action player images on a black-and-white, high-contrast, super-bright mirror background printed on 24-point styrene card stock and laminated with radial-etched mirror foil. The set contains the Rookie subset (126-175) with an insertion rate in packs of 1:2. A promotional sample card featuring J.D. Drew was distributed to dealer accounts and hobby media a few months prior to the product's national release. This card can be easily identified by the "PROMOTIONAL SAMPLE" text running diagonally across the front and back. Notable Rookie Cards include Pat Burrell and Freddy Garcia.

	Nm-Mt	Ex-Mt
COMPLETE SET (175)	100.00	30.00
COMP.SET w/o SP's (125)	50.00	15.00
COMMON CARD (1-125)	.50	.15
COMMON (126-175)	.75	.23
1 Mark McGwire	3.00	.90
2 Derek Jeter	3.00	.90
3 Nomar Garciaparra	2.00	.60
4 Travis Lee	.50	.15
5 Jeff Bagwell	.75	.23
6 Andres Galarraga	.50	.15
7 Pedro Martinez	1.25	.35
8 Cal Ripken	4.00	1.20
9 Vladimir Guerrero	1.25	.35
10 Chipper Jones	1.25	.35
11 Rusty Greer	.50	.15
12 Omar Vizquel	.50	.15
13 Quinton McCracken	.50	.15
14 Jaret Wright	.50	.15
15 Mike Mussina	1.25	.35
16 Jason Giambi	1.25	.35
17 Tony Clark	.50	.15
18 Troy O'Leary	.50	.15
19 Troy Percival	.50	.15
20 Kerry Wood	1.25	.35
21 Vinny Castilla	.50	.15
22 Chris Carpenter	.50	.15
23 Richie Sexson	.50	.15
24 Ken Griffey Jr.	2.00	.60
25 Barry Bonds	3.00	.90
26 Carlos Delgado	.50	.15
27 Frank Thomas	1.25	.35
28 Manny Ramirez	.50	.15
29 Shawn Green	.50	.15
30 Mike Piazza	2.00	.60
31 Tino Martinez	.75	.23
32 Dante Bichette	.50	.15
33 Scott Rolen	.75	.23
34 Gabe Alvarez	.50	.15
35 Raul Mondesi	.50	.15
36 Damion Easley	.50	.15
37 Jeff Kent	.50	.15
38 Al Leiter	.50	.15
39 Alex Rodriguez	2.00	.60
40 Jeff King	.50	.15
41 Mark Grace	.75	.23
42 Larry Walker	.75	.23
43 Moises Alou	.50	.15
44 Juan Gonzalez	1.25	.35
45 Rolando Arrojo	.50	.15
46 Tom Glavine	.75	.23
47 Johnny Damon	.50	.15
48 Livan Hernandez	.50	.15
49 Craig Biggio	.75	.23
50 Dmitri Young	.50	.15
51 Chan Ho Park	.50	.15
52 Todd Walker	.50	.15
53 Derrek Lee	.50	.15
54 Todd Helton	.75	.23
55 Ray Lankford	.50	.15
56 Jim Thome	1.25	.35
57 Matt Lawton	.50	.15
58 Matt Anderson	.50	.15
59 Jose Offerman	.50	.15
60 Eric Karros	.50	.15
61 Orlando Hernandez	.50	.15
62 Ben Grieve	.50	.15
63 Bobby Abreu	.50	.15
64 Kevin Young	.50	.15
65 John Olerud	.50	.15
66 Sammy Sosa	2.00	.60
67 Andy Ashby	.50	.15
68 Juan Encarnacion	.50	.15
69 Shane Reynolds	.50	.15
70 Bernie Williams	.75	.23
71 Mike Cameron	.50	.15
72 Troy Glaus	.75	.23
73 Gary Sheffield	.50	.15
74 Jeromy Burnitz	.50	.15
75 Mike Caruso	.50	.15
76 Chuck Knoblauch	.50	.15
77 Kenny Rogers	.50	.15
78 David Cone	.50	.15
79 Tony Gwynn	1.50	.45
80 Jay Buhner	.50	.15
81 Paul O'Neill	.75	.23
82 Charles Nagy	.50	.15
83 Javy Lopez	.50	.15
84 Scott Erickson	.50	.15
85 Trevor Hoffman	.50	.15
86 Andruw Jones	.50	.15
87 Ray Durham	.50	.15
88 Jorge Posada	.75	.23
89 Edgar Martinez	.75	.23
90 Tim Salmon	.75	.23
91 Bobby Higginson	.50	.15
92 Adrian Beltre	.50	.15
93 Jason Kendall	.50	.15
94 Henry Rodriguez	.50	.15
95 Greg Maddux	2.00	.60
96 David Justice	.50	.15
97 Ivan Rodriguez	1.25	.35
98 Curt Schilling	.75	.23
99 Matt Williams	.50	.15
100 Darin Erstad	.50	.15
101 Rafael Palmeiro	.75	.23
102 David Wells	.50	.15
103 Barry Larkin	1.25	.35
104 Robin Ventura	.50	.15
105 Edgar Renteria	.50	.15
106 Andy Pettitte	.75	.23
107 Albert Belle	.50	.15
108 Steve Finley	.50	.15
109 Fernando Vina	.50	.15
110 Rondell White	.50	.15
111 Kevin Brown	.75	.23
112 Jose Canseco	1.25	.35
113 Roger Clemens	2.50	.75
114 Todd Hundley	.50	.15
115 Will Clark	1.25	.35
116 Jim Edmonds	.50	.15
117 Randy Johnson	1.25	.35
118 Denny Neagle	.50	.15
119 Brian Jordan	.50	.15
120 Dean Palmer	.50	.15
121 Roberto Alomar	1.25	.35
122 Ken Caminiti	.50	.15
123 Brian Giles	.50	.15
124 Todd Stottlemyre	.50	.15
125 Mo Vaughn	.50	.15
126 J.D. Drew	.75	.23
127 Ryan Minor	.75	.23
128 Gabe Kapler	.75	.23
129 Jeremy Giambi	.75	.23
130 Eric Chavez	.75	.23
131 Ben Davis	.75	.23
132 Rob Fick	.75	.23
133 George Lombard	.75	.23
134 Calvin Pickering	.75	.23
135 Preston Wilson	.75	.23
136 Corey Koskie	.75	.23
137 Russell Branyan	.75	.23
138 Bruce Chen	.75	.23
139 Matt Clement	.75	.23
140 Pat Burrell RC	4.00	1.20
141 Freddy Garcia RC	1.25	.35
142 Brian Simmons	.75	.23
143 Carlos Febles	.75	.23
144 Carlos Guillen	.75	.23
145 Fernando Seguignol	.75	.23
146 Carlos Beltran	.75	.23
147 Edgard Clemente	.75	.23
148 Mitch Meluskey	.75	.23
149 Ryan Bradley	.75	.23
150 Marlon Anderson	.75	.23
151 A.J. Burnett RC	1.25	.35
152 Scott Hunter RC	.75	.23
153 Mark Johnson	.75	.23
154 Angel Pena	.75	.23
155 Roy Halladay	.75	.23
156 Chad Allen RC	.75	.23
157 Trot Nixon	.75	.23
158 Ricky Ledee	.75	.23
159 Gary Bennett RC	.75	.23
160 Micah Bowie RC	.75	.23
161 D.Mientkiewicz RC	1.50	.45
162 Danny Klassen	.75	.23
163 Willis Otanez	.75	.23
164 Jin Ho Cho	.75	.23
165 Mike Lowell	.75	.23
166 Armando Rios	.75	.23
167 Warren Morris	.75	.23
168 Michael Barrett	.75	.23
169 Alex Gonzalez	.75	.23
170 Masao Kida RC	.75	.23
171 Peter Tucci	.75	.23
172 Luis Saturria RC	.75	.23
173 Kris Benson	.75	.23
174 Mario Encarnacion RC	.75	.23
175 Roosevelt Brown RC	.75	.23
NNO J.D. Drew Sample	1.00	.30

1999 Fleer Brilliants 24-Karat Gold

Randomly inserted in packs, this 175-card set is parallel to the base set with a gold background, rainbow-holographic reflective mirror foil, and a 24-kt. gold logo. Each card is serial numbered to 24 on the back.

	Nm-Mt	Ex-Mt
*STARS 1-125: 20X TO 50X BASIC		
*ROOKIES: 126-175: 12.5X TO 25X BASIC		

1999 Fleer Brilliants Blue

Randomly inserted into packs, this 175-card set is parallel to the base set. It is distinguished by its blue background and a "B" prefix on the card number. Cards 1-125 have an insertion rate of 1:3 packs, and Cards 126-175 have a 1:6 packs insertion rate.

	Nm-Mt	Ex-Mt
*STARS 1-125: 1.25X TO 3X BASIC CARDS		
*ROOKIES: 126-175: .5X TO 1.25X BASIC		

1999 Fleer Brilliants Gold

Randomly inserted into packs, this 175-card set is parallel to the base set with gold backgrounds, super-bright mirror foil, and a "G" prefix on the card number. Each card is serial numbered to 99 on the back.

	Nm-Mt	Ex-Mt
*STARS 1-125: 10X TO 25X BASIC		
*ROOKIES 126-175: 5X TO 12X BASIC		

1999 Fleer Brilliants Illuminators

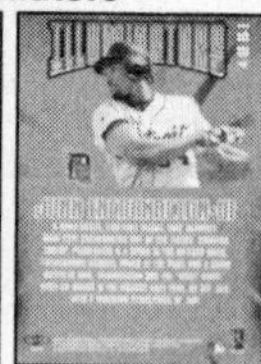

Randomly inserted into packs at the rate of one in 10, this 15-card set features color photos of top young stars printed on team color-coded, super-bright mirror-foil cards.

	Nm-Mt	Ex-Mt
COMPLETE SET (15)	25.00	7.50
1 Kerry Wood	4.00	1.20
2 Ben Grieve	1.50	.45
3 J.D. Drew	2.50	.75
4 Juan Encarnacion	1.50	.45
5 Travis Lee	1.50	.45
6 Todd Helton	2.50	.75
7 Troy Glaus	2.50	.75
8 Ricky Ledee	2.50	.75
9 Eric Chavez	2.50	.75
10 Ben Davis	2.50	.75
11 George Lombard	2.50	.75
12 Jeremy Giambi	2.50	.75
13 Richie Sexson	1.50	.45
14 Corey Koskie	2.50	.75
15 Russell Branyan	2.50	.75

1999 Fleer Brilliants Shining Stars

Randomly inserted into packs at the rate of one in 20, this 15-card set features color action cut-outs of top players silhouetted on a background of stars and printed on styrene cards with two-sided mirrored foil.

	Nm-Mt	Ex-Mt
COMPLETE SET (15)	120.00	36.00
*PULSAR: 2X TO 5X BASIC SHINING STAR		
PULSAR STATED ODDS 1:400		
1 Ken Griffey Jr.	8.00	2.40
2 Mark McGwire	12.00	3.60
3 Sammy Sosa	8.00	2.40
4 Derek Jeter	12.00	3.60
5 Nomar Garciaparra	8.00	2.40
6 Alex Rodriguez	8.00	2.40
7 Mike Piazza	8.00	2.40
8 Juan Gonzalez	5.00	1.50
9 Chipper Jones	5.00	1.50
10 Cal Ripken	15.00	4.50
11 Frank Thomas	5.00	1.50
12 Greg Maddux	8.00	2.40
13 Roger Clemens	10.00	3.00
14 Vladimir Guerrero	5.00	1.50
15 Manny Ramirez	2.00	.60

2003 Fleer Double Header

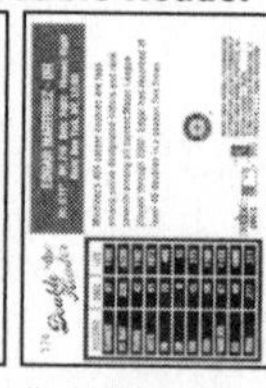

This set, which in actuality is 240 cards, was released in January, 2003. Although the card numbers actually go up to 300, the final 120 cards were actually issued as "flip cards" which featured two players on each card. These cards were issued in eight card packs which came 20 packs to a box and 20 boxes to a case with an SRP of $3. Cards numbered 181 through 236 feature two teammates. Cards numbered 237 through 252 feature players who have something in common. Cards numbered 253 through 270 feature All-Star game starters. Cards numbered 271 through 300 feature 15 pairs of prospect from the same organization. A promotional card of Derek Jeter was issued in advance of this set to show what these cards would look like. That card is priced at the end of our checklist

	Nm-Mt	Ex-Mt
COMPLETE SET (240)	80.00	24.00
COMMON CARD (1-180)	.40	.12
COMMON CARD (181-270)	.50	.15
COMMON CARD (271-300)	1.00	.30
1 Ramon Vazquez	.40	.12
2 Derek Jeter	2.50	.75
3 Orlando Hudson	.40	.12
4 Miguel Tejada	.40	.12
5 Steve Finley	.40	.12
6 Brad Wilkerson	.40	.12
7 Craig Biggio	.60	.18
8 Marlon Anderson	.40	.12
9 Phil Nevin	.40	.12
10 Hideo Nomo	1.00	.30
11 Barry Larkin	1.00	.30
12 Alfonso Soriano	.60	.18
13 Rodrigo Lopez	.40	.12
14 Paul Konerko	.40	.12
15 Carlos Beltran	.40	.12

16 Garret Anderson .40 .12
17 Kazuhisa Ishii .40 .12
18 Eddie Guardado .40 .12
19 Juan Gonzalez 1.00 .30
20 Mark Mulder .40 .12
21 Sammy Sosa 1.50 .45
22 Kazuhiro Sasaki .40 .12
23 Jose Cruz Jr. .40 .12
24 Tomo Ohka .40 .12
25 Barry Bonds 2.50 .75
26 Carlos Delgado .40 .12
27 Scott Rolen .60 .18
28 Steve Cox .40 .12
29 Mike Sweeney .40 .12
30 Ryan Klesko .40 .12
31 Greg Maddux 1.50 .45
32 Derek Lowe .40 .12
33 David Wells .40 .12
34 Kerry Wood 1.00 .30
35 Randall Simon .40 .12
36 Ben Howard .40 .12
37 Jeff Suppan .40 .12
38 Curt Schilling .60 .18
39 Eric Gagne .60 .18
40 Raul Mondesi .40 .12
41 Jeffrey Hammonds .40 .12
42 Mo Vaughn .40 .12
43 Sidney Ponson .40 .12
44 Adam Dunn .40 .12
45 Pedro Martinez 1.00 .30
46 Jason Simontacchi .40 .12
47 Tom Glavine .60 .18
48 Torii Hunter .40 .12
49 Gabe Kapler .40 .12
50 Andy Van Hekken .40 .12
51 Ichiro Suzuki 1.50 .45
52 Andruw Jones .40 .12
53 Bobby Abreu .40 .12
54 Junior Spivey .40 .12
55 Ray Durham .40 .12
56 Mark Buehrle .40 .12
57 Drew Henson .40 .12
58 Brandon Duckworth .40 .12
59 Rob Mackowiak .40 .12
60 Josh Beckett .60 .18
61 Chan Ho Park .40 .12
62 John Smoltz .60 .18
63 Jimmy Rollins .40 .12
64 Orlando Cabrera .40 .12
65 Johnny Damon .40 .12
66 Austin Kearns .40 .12
67 Tsuyoshi Shinjo .40 .12
68 Tim Hudson .40 .12
69 Coco Crisp .40 .12
70 Darin Erstad .40 .12
71 Jacque Jones .40 .12
72 Vicente Padilla .40 .12
73 Hee Seop Choi .40 .12
74 Shea Hillenbrand .40 .12
75 Edgardo Alfonzo .40 .12
76 Pat Burrell .40 .12
77 Ben Sheets .40 .12
78 Ivan Rodriguez 1.00 .30
79 Josh Phelps .40 .12
80 Adam Kennedy .40 .12
81 Eric Chavez .40 .12
82 Bobby Higginson .40 .12
83 Nomar Garciaparra 1.50 .45
84 J.D. Drew .40 .12
85 Carl Crawford .40 .12
86 Matt Morris .40 .12
87 Chipper Jones 1.00 .30
88 Luis Gonzalez .40 .12
89 Richie Sexson .40 .12
90 Eric Milton .40 .12
91 Andres Galarraga .40 .12
92 Paul Lo Duca .40 .12
93 Mark Grace .60 .18
94 Ben Grieve .40 .12
95 Mike Lowell .40 .12
96 Roberto Alomar 1.00 .30
97 Wade Miller .40 .12
98 Sean Casey .40 .12
99 Roger Clemens 2.00 .60
100 Matt Williams .40 .12
101 Brian Giles .40 .12
102 Jim Thome 1.00 .30
103 Troy Glaus .60 .18
104 Joe Borchard .40 .12
105 Vladimir Guerrero 1.00 .30
106 Kevin Mench .40 .12
107 Omar Vizquel .40 .12
108 Magglio Ordonez .40 .12
109 Ken Griffey Jr. 1.50 .45
110 Mike Piazza 1.50 .45
111 Mark Teixeira .60 .18
112 Jason Jennings .40 .12
113 Ellis Burks .40 .12
114 Jason Varitek .40 .12
115 Larry Walker .60 .18
116 Frank Thomas 1.00 .30
117 Ramon Ortiz .40 .12
118 Mark Quinn .40 .12
119 Preston Wilson .40 .12
120 Carlos Lee .40 .12
121 Brian Lawrence .40 .12
122 Tim Salmon .60 .18
123 Shawn Green .40 .12
124 Randy Johnson 1.00 .30
125 Jeff Bagwell .60 .18
126 C.C. Sabathia .40 .12
127 Bernie Williams .60 .18
128 Roy Oswalt .40 .12
129 Albert Pujols 2.00 .60
130 Reggie Sanders .40 .12
131 Jeff Conine .40 .12
132 John Olerud .40 .12
133 Lance Berkman .40 .12
134 Geoff Jenkins .40 .12
135 Jim Edmonds .40 .12
136 Todd Helton .60 .18
137 Jason Kendall .40 .12
138 Robin Ventura .40 .12
139 Randy Winn .40 .12
140 Carl Everett .40 .12
141 Jose Vidro .40 .12
142 Pokey Reese .40 .12
143 Edgar Renteria .40 .12
144 Alex Rodriguez 1.50 .45
145 Doug Mientkiewicz .40 .12
146 Aramis Ramirez .40 .12
147 Bobby Hill .40 .12
148 Jorge Posada .60 .18
149 Sean Burroughs .40 .12
150 Jeff Kent .40 .12
151 Tino Martinez .40 .12
152 Mark Prior 1.50 .45
153 Brad Radke .40 .12
154 Al Leiter .40 .12
155 Eric Karros .40 .12
156 Manny Ramirez .40 .12
157 Jason Lane .40 .12
158 Mike Lieberthal .40 .12
159 Shannon Stewart .40 .12
160 Robert Fick .40 .12
161 Derrek Lee .40 .12
162 Jason Giambi 1.00 .30
163 Rafael Palmeiro .60 .18
164 Jay Payton .40 .12
165 Adrian Beltre .40 .12
166 Marlon Byrd .40 .12
167 Bret Boone .40 .12
168 Roy Halladay .40 .12
169 Freddy Garcia .40 .12
170 Rich Aurilia .40 .12
171 Jared Sandberg .40 .12
172 Paul Byrd .40 .12
173 Gary Sheffield .40 .12
174 Edgar Martinez .60 .18
175 Eric Hinske .40 .12
176 Milton Bradley .40 .12
177 David Eckstein .40 .12
178 Jay Gibbons .40 .12
179 Corey Patterson .40 .12
180 Barry Zito .60 .18
181-82 Darin Erstad .75 .23
Troy Glaus
183-84 Curt Schilling 1.25 .35
Randy Johnson
185-86 Andruw Jones 1.25 .35
Chipper Jones
187-88 Tony Batista .50 .15
Jay Gibbons
189-90 Pedro Martinez 2.00 .60
Nomar Garciaparra
191-92 Sammy Sosa 2.00 .60
Kerry Wood
193-94 Paul Konerko .75 .23
Joe Borchard
195-96 Austin Kearns .75 .23
Adam Dunn
197-98 Omar Vizquel 1.25 .35
Jim Thome
199-00 Larry Walker .75 .23
Todd Helton
201-02 Josh Beckett 1.25 .35
Luis Castillo
203-04 Craig Biggio .75 .23
Jeff Bagwell
205-06 Paul Byrd .50 .15
Mike Sweeney
207-08 Adrian Beltre .75 .23
Shawn Green
209-10 Jose Hernandez .50 .15
Richie Sexson
211-12 Jacque Jones .75 .23
Torii Hunter
213-14 Vladimir Guerrero 1.25 .35
Jose Vidro
215-16 Edgardo Alfonzo 2.00 .60
Mike Piazza
217-18 Roger Clemens 2.50 .75
Derek Jeter
219-20 Eric Chavez .75 .23
Miguel Tejada
221-22 Marlon Byrd .75 .23
Pat Burrell
223-24 Jason Kendall .50 .15
Brian Giles
225-26 Phil Nevin .75 .23
Sean Burroughs
227-28 Jeff Kent 2.50 .75
Barry Bonds
229-30 Kazuhiro Sasaki 2.00 .60
Ichiro Suzuki
231-32 Albert Pujols 2.00 .60
J.D. Drew
233-34 Juan Gonzalez 2.00 .60
Ivan Rodriguez
235-36 Eric Hinske .50 .15
Orlando Hudson
237-38 Lance Berkman 1.25 .35
Chipper Jones
239-40 Alex Rodriguez 2.50 .75
Derek Jeter
241-42 Ichiro Suzuki 2.00 .60
Hideo Nomo
243-44 Manny Ramirez .75 .23
Bernie Williams
245-46 Tom Glavine 2.00 .60
Roger Clemens
247-48 Ken Griffey Jr. 2.00 .60
Barry Larkin
249-50 Mark Teixeira 3.00 .90
Mark Prior
251-52 Albert Pujols 2.00 .60
Drew Henson
253-54 Jason Giambi 2.00 .60
Todd Helton AS
255-56 Jose Vidro .75 .23
Alfonso Soriano AS
257-58 Shea Hillenbrand .75 .23
Scott Rolen AS
259-60 Jimmy Rollins 2.00 .60
Alex Rodriguez AS
261-62 Torii Hunter 1.25 .35
Vladimir Guerrero AS
263-64 Ichiro Suzuki AS 2.00 .60
Sammy Sosa AS
265-66 Barry Bonds 2.50 .75
Manny Ramirez AS
267-68 Mike Piazza 2.00 .60
Jorge Posada AS
269-70 Robin Yount 3.00 .90
Ozzie Smith AS
271-72 Josh Hancock 1.00 .30
Freddy Sanchez OD
273-74 Ryan Bukvich 1.00 .30
Shawn Sedlacek OD
275-76 Doug Devore 1.00 .30
Rene Reyes OD
277-78 Hank Blalock 1.50 .45
Travis Hafner OD
279-80 Eric Junge 1.00 .30
Brett Myers OD
281-82 Brad Lidge 1.00 .30
Jeriome Robertson OD
283-84 Miguel Asencio 1.00 .30
Runelvys Hernandez OD
285-86 Fernando Rodney 1.00 .30
Barry Wesson OD
287-88 Victor Alvarez 1.00 .30
David Ross OD
289-90 Tony Torcato 1.00 .30
Chris Snelling OD
291-92 Kirk Saarloos 1.00 .30
Morgan Ensberg OD
293-94 Josh Bard 1.00 .30
Wil Nieves OD
295-96 Jung Bong 1.00 .30
Trey Hodges OD
297-98 Kevin Cash 1.00 .30
Reed Johnson OD
299-00 Chone Figgins 1.00 .30
John Lackey OD
P2 Derek Jeter Promo 3.00 .90

2003 Fleer Double Header Flip Card Game Used

Inserted at a stated rate of one in 20, these cards feature game-used memorabilia of the featured player. A few cards were issued in shorter supply and we have provided that print run information in our checklist next to the player's name.

Nm-Mt Ex-Mt
*GOLD: .75X TO 2X BASIC GAME USED
*GOLD: .6X TO 1.5X BASIC GAME USED SP
GOLD RANDOM INSERTS IN PACKS..
GOLD PRINT RUN 100 SERIAL #'d SETS
1 Roberto Alomar Bat SP/200 15.00 4.50
2 Jeff Bagwell Jsy 10.00 3.00
3 Adrian Beltre Jsy 8.00 2.40
4 Barry Bonds Bat SP/200 25.00 7.50
5 Roger Clemens Jsy SP/200 20.00 6.00
6 J.D. Drew Jsy 8.00 2.40
7 Adam Dunn Jsy SP/200 10.00 3.00
8 N.Garciaparra Jsy SP/200 20.00 6.00
9 Mark Grace Jsy 10.00 3.00
10 Todd Helton Jsy SP/200 15.00 4.50
11 Derek Jeter Jsy SP/200 25.00 7.50
12 Randy Johnson Jsy SP/200 15.00 4.50
13 Chipper Jones Jsy 10.00 3.00
14 Eric Karros Jsy 8.00 2.40
15 Barry Larkin Jsy SP/200 15.00 4.50
16 Greg Maddux Jsy SP/200 15.00 4.50
17 Hideo Nomo Jsy SP/200 15.00 4.50
18 Kazuhisa Ishii Jsy 8.00 2.40
19 Mike Piazza Jsy SP/200 15.00 4.50
20 Jorge Posada Jsy SP/200 15.00 4.50
21 Mark Prior Jsy SP/200 20.00 6.00
22 Alex Rodriguez Jsy 15.00 4.50
23 Kazuhiro Sasaki Jsy SP/200 10.00 3.00
24 Curt Schilling Jsy SP/200 15.00 4.50
25 Alfonso Soriano Jsy 10.00 3.00
26 Miguel Tejada Jsy 8.00 2.40
27 Jim Thome Jsy SP/200 15.00 4.50
28 Robin Ventura Jsy 8.00 2.40
29 Bernie Williams Jsy SP/200 15.00 4.50
30 Kerry Wood Jsy SP/200 15.00 4.50

2003 Fleer Double Header Keystone Combinations

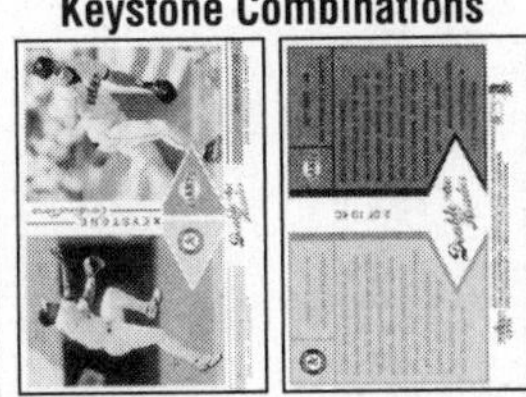

Inserted at a stated rate of one in 10, these 10 cards feature a pair of middle infielders.

Nm-Mt Ex-Mt
1 Derek Jeter 6.00 1.80
Bret Boone
2 Miguel Tejada 2.00 .60
Jeff Kent
3 Nomar Garciaparra 4.00 1.20
Ray Durham
4 Omar Vizquel 2.50 .75
Roberto Alomar
5 Pee Wee Reese 2.00 .60
Joe Morgan
6 Alex Rodriguez 4.00 1.20
Craig Biggio
7 Orlando Hudson 2.00 .60
Jose Vidro
8 Phil Rizzuto 2.00 .60
Alfonso Soriano
9 Alex Rodriguez 4.00 1.20
Miguel Tejada
10 Nomar Garciaparra 5.00 1.50
Derek Jeter

2003 Fleer Double Header Keystone Combinations Memorabilia

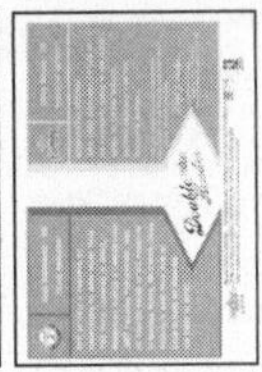
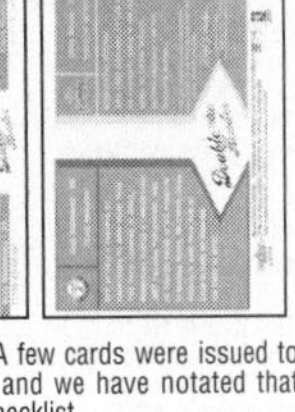

Inserted at a stated rate of one in 40, these 14 cards features two players but only one memorabilia piece. A few cards were issued to a shorter print run and we have notated that information in our checklist.

Nm-Mt Ex-Mt
1 Roberto Alomar Jsy 10.00 3.00
Omar Vizquel
2 Craig Biggio Jsy 10.00 3.00
Alex Rodriguez
3 Bret Boone Jsy 8.00 2.40
Derek Jeter
4 Nomar Garciaparra Jsy 20.00 6.00
Ray Durham SP/175
5 Nomar Garciaparra Jsy 20.00 6.00
Derek Jeter SP/175
6 Derek Jeter Jsy 25.00 7.50
Bret Boone SP/175
7 Derek Jeter Jsy 25.00 7.50
Nomar Garciaparra SP/175
8 Jeff Kent Jsy 8.00 2.40
Miguel Tejada
9 Alex Rodriguez Jsy 15.00 4.50
Craig Biggio SP/200
10 Alex Rodriguez Bat 15.00 4.50
Miguel Tejada
11 Alfonso Soriano Jsy 15.00 4.50
Phil Rizzuto SP/75
12 Miguel Tejada Jsy 8.00 2.40
Jeff Kent
13 Miguel Tejada Jsy 8.00 2.40
Alex Rodriguez
14 Jose Vidro Jsy 8.00 2.40
Orlando Hudson

2003 Fleer Double Header Let's Play Too

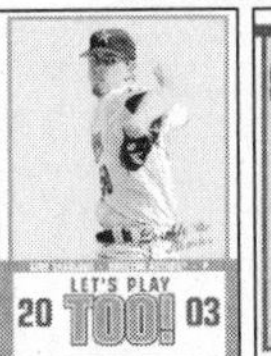

Inserted at a stated rate of one in five, this 15 card set featured leading prospects entering the 2003 season.

Nm-Mt Ex-Mt
COMPLETE SET (15) 15.00 4.50
1 Chris Snelling 2.00 .60
2 Kevin Mench 2.00 .60
3 Brett Myers 2.00 .60
4 Julius Matos 2.00 .60
5 Drew Henson 2.00 .60
6 Joe Borchard 2.00 .60
7 Felix Escalona 2.00 .60
8 Kirk Saarloos 2.00 .60
9 Ben Howard 2.00 .60
10 Hee Seop Choi 2.00 .60
11 Rene Reyes 2.00 .60
12 Josh Bard 2.00 .60
13 Marlon Byrd 2.00 .60
14 Coco Crisp 2.00 .60
15 Reed Johnson 2.00 .60

2003 Fleer Double Header Matinee Idols

Inserted at a stated rate of one in 20, this 15 card set featured leading Hall of Famers from the post World War 2 era.

Nm-Mt Ex-Mt
1 Yogi Berra 5.00 1.50
2 Richie Ashburn 5.00 1.50
3 Whitey Ford 5.00 1.50
4 Eddie Mathews 5.00 1.50
5 Jim Palmer 5.00 1.50
6 Al Kaline 5.00 1.50
7 Brooks Robinson 5.00 1.50
8 Willie McCovey 5.00 1.50
9 Billy Williams 5.00 1.50
10 Willie Stargell 5.00 1.50
11 Nolan Ryan 12.00 3.60
12 Rod Carew 5.00 1.50
13 Reggie Jackson 5.00 1.50
14 Tom Seaver 5.00 1.50
15 Mike Schmidt 10.00 3.00

2003 Fleer Double Header Twin Bill

Inserted at a stated rate of one in 10, these 20 two player cards feature only elite players.

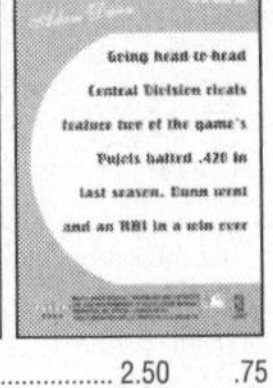

Nm-Mt Ex-Mt
1A Barry Bonds 6.00 1.80
1B Lance Berkman 2.00 .60
2A Derek Jeter 6.00 1.80
2B Alex Rodriguez 4.00 1.20
3A Roger Clemens 5.00 1.50
3B Pedro Martinez 2.50 .75
4A Roberto Alomar 2.50 .75
4B Chipper Jones 2.50 .75
5A Barry Zito 2.00 .60
5B Ichiro Suzuki 4.00 1.20
6A Sammy Sosa 4.00 1.20
6B Ken Griffey Jr. 4.00 1.20
7A Bernie Williams 2.00 .60
7B Manny Ramirez 2.00 .60
8A Nomar Garciaparra 4.00 1.20
8B Derek Jeter 6.00 1.80
9A Randy Johnson 2.50 .75
9B Greg Maddux 4.00 1.20
10A Albert Pujols 5.00 1.50
10B Adam Dunn 2.00 .60

2003 Fleer Double Header Twin Bill Dual Swatch

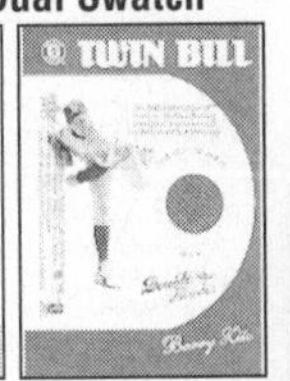

Randomly inserted into packs, these seven cards feature two pieces of authentic game-used jersey swatches on each card.

Nm-Mt Ex-Mt
BB-AD Barry Bonds
Adam Dunn
DJ-AR Derek Jeter
Alex Rodriguez
MR-PM Manny Ramirez
Pedro Martinez
NG-DJ Nomar Garciaparra
Derek Jeter
RA-MR Roberto Alomar
Manny Ramirez
RC-BW Roger Clemens
Bernie Williams
RJ-BZ Randy Johnson
Barry Zito

2003 Fleer Double Header Twin Bill Single Swatch

Inserted at a stated rate of one in 200, these 12 cards feature authentic jersey swatches on the card. The print run information for these cards (except for Roberto Alomar) is given next to the player's name.

Nm-Mt Ex-Mt
1 Roberto Alomar 15.00 4.50
2 Barry Bonds SP/100 30.00 9.00
3 Roger Clemens SP/100 25.00 7.50
4 Adam Dunn SP/100 20.00 6.00
5 Nomar Garciaparra SP/100 25.00 7.50
6 Derek Jeter SP/100 40.00 12.00
7 Randy Johnson SP/100 20.00 6.00
8 Pedro Martinez SP/100 20.00 6.00
9 Manny Ramirez SP/75
10 Alex Rodriguez SP/100 25.00 7.50
11 Bernie Williams SP/100 20.00 6.00
12 Barry Zito SP/100 20.00 6.00

1994 Fleer Extra Bases

Measuring 2 1/2" by 4 3/4", this 400 card set was issued by Fleer. Each pack contained at least one insert card. Full-bleed fronts contain a large color photo with the player's name and Extra Bases logo at the bottom. The backs are also full-bleed with a large player photo and statistics. The checklist was arranged alphabetically by team and league starting with the American League. Within each team, the player listings are alphabetical. Rookie Cards include Ray Durham and Chan Ho Park.

Nm-Mt Ex-Mt
COMPLETE SET (400) 40.00 12.00
1 Brady Anderson .30 .09
2 Harold Baines .30 .09
3 Mike Devereaux .15 .04
4 Sid Fernandez .15 .04
5 Jeffrey Hammonds .15 .04
6 Chris Hoiles .15 .04

7 Ben McDonald .15 .04
8 Mark McLemore .15 .04
9 Mike Mussina .75 .23
10 Mike Oquist .15 .04
11 Rafael Palmeiro .50 .15
12 Cal Ripken Jr. 2.50 .75
13 Chris Sabo .15 .04
14 Lee Smith .30 .09
15 Wes Chamberlain .15 .04
16 Roger Clemens 1.50 .45
17 Scott Cooper .15 .04
18 Danny Darwin .15 .04
19 Andre Dawson .30 .09
20 Mike Greenwell .15 .04
21 Tim Naehring .15 .04
22 Otis Nixon .15 .04
23 Jeff Russell .15 .04
24 Ken Ryan .15 .04
25 Aaron Sele .15 .04
26 John Valentin .15 .04
27 Mo Vaughn .30 .09
28 Frank Viola .30 .09
29 Brian Anderson RC .30 .09
30 Chad Curtis .15 .04
31 Chili Davis .30 .09
32 Gary DiSarcina .15 .04
33 Damion Easley .15 .04
34 Jim Edmonds .50 .15
35 Chuck Finley .30 .09
36 Bo Jackson .75 .23
37 Mark Langston .15 .04
38 Harold Reynolds .30 .09
39 Tim Salmon .50 .15
40 Wilson Alvarez .15 .04
41 James Baldwin .15 .04
42 Jason Bere .15 .04
43 Joey Cora .15 .04
44 Ray Durham RC 1.00 .30
45 Alex Fernandez .15 .04
46 Julio Franco .30 .09
47 Ozzie Guillen .15 .04
48 Darrin Jackson .15 .04
49 Lance Johnson .15 .04
50 Ron Karkovice .15 .04
51 Jack McDowell .15 .04
52 Tim Raines .30 .09
53 Frank Thomas .75 .23
54 Robin Ventura .30 .09
55 Sandy Alomar Jr. .15 .04
56 Carlos Baerga .15 .04
57 Albert Belle .30 .09
58 Mark Clark .15 .04
59 Wayne Kirby .15 .04
60 Kenny Lofton .30 .09
61 Dennis Martinez .30 .09
62 Jose Mesa .15 .04
63 Jack Morris .30 .09
64 Eddie Murray .75 .23
65 Charles Nagy .15 .04
66 Manny Ramirez .50 .15
67 Paul Shuey .15 .04
68 Paul Sorrento .15 .04
69 Jim Thome .75 .23
70 Omar Vizquel .30 .09
71 Eric Davis .30 .09
72 John Doherty .15 .04
73 Cecil Fielder .30 .09
74 Travis Fryman .30 .09
75 Kirk Gibson .30 .09
76 Gene Harris .15 .04
77 Mike Henneman .15 .04
78 Mike Moore .15 .04
79 Tony Phillips .15 .04
80 Mickey Tettleton .15 .04
81 Alan Trammell .50 .15
82 Lou Whitaker .30 .09
83 Kevin Appier .30 .09
84 Vince Coleman .15 .04
85 David Cone .30 .09
86 Gary Gaetti .30 .09
87 Greg Gagne .15 .04
88 Tom Gordon .15 .04
89 Jeff Granger .15 .04
90 Bob Hamelin .15 .04
91 Dave Henderson .15 .04
92 Felix Jose .15 .04
93 Wally Joyner .30 .09
94 Jose Lind .15 .04
95 Mike Macfarlane .15 .04
96 Brian McRae .15 .04
97 Jeff Montgomery .15 .04
98 Ricky Bones .15 .04
99 Jeff Bronkey .15 .04
100 Alex Diaz RC .15 .04
101 Cal Eldred .15 .04
102 Darryl Hamilton .15 .04
103 Brian Harper .15 .04
104 John Jaha .15 .04
105 Pat Listach .15 .04
106 Dave Nilsson .15 .04
107 Jody Reed .15 .04
108 Kevin Seitzer .15 .04
109 Greg Vaughn .30 .09
110 Turner Ward .15 .04
111 Wes Weger RC .15 .04
112 Bill Wegman .15 .04
113 Rick Aguilera .30 .09
114 Rich Becker .15 .04
115 Alex Cole .15 .04
116 Scott Erickson .15 .04
117 Kent Hrbek .30 .09
118 Chuck Knoblauch .30 .09
119 Scott Leius .15 .04
120 Shane Mack .15 .04
121 Pat Mahomes .15 .04
122 Pat Meares .15 .04
123 Kirby Puckett .75 .23
124 Kevin Tapani .15 .04
125 Matt Walbeck .15 .04
126 Dave Winfield .30 .09
127 Jim Abbott .50 .15
128 Wade Boggs .50 .15
129 Mike Gallego .15 .04
130 Xavier Hernandez .15 .04
131 Pat Kelly .15 .04
132 Jimmy Key .30 .09
133 Don Mattingly 2.00 .60
134 Terry Mulholland .15 .04
135 Matt Nokes .15 .04
136 Paul O'Neill .50 .15
137 Melido Perez .15 .04
138 Luis Polonia .15 .04
139 Mike Stanley .15 .04
140 Danny Tartabull .15 .04
141 Randy Velarde .15 .04
142 Bernie Williams .50 .15
143 Mark Acre RC .15 .04
144 Geronimo Berroa .15 .04
145 Mike Bordick .30 .09
146 Scott Brosius .30 .09
147 Ron Darling .15 .04
148 Dennis Eckersley .30 .09
149 Brent Gates .15 .04
150 Rickey Henderson .75 .23
151 Stan Javier .15 .04
152 Steve Karsay .15 .04
153 Mark McGwire 2.00 .60
154 Troy Neel .15 .04
155 Ruben Sierra .15 .04
156 Terry Steinbach .15 .04
157 Bill Taylor RC .30 .09
158 Rich Amaral .15 .04
159 Eric Anthony .15 .04
160 Bobby Ayala .15 .04
161 Chris Bosio .15 .04
162 Jay Buhner .30 .09
163 Tim Davis .15 .04
164 Felix Fermin .15 .04
165 Dave Fleming .15 .04
166 Ken Griffey Jr. 1.25 .35
167 Reggie Jefferson .15 .04
168 Randy Johnson .75 .23
169 Edgar Martinez .50 .15
170 Tino Martinez .50 .15
171 Bill Risley .15 .04
172 Roger Salkeld .15 .04
173 Mac Suzuki RC .75 .23
174 Dan Wilson .15 .04
175 Kevin Brown .30 .09
176 Jose Canseco .75 .23
177 Will Clark .75 .23
178 Juan Gonzalez .75 .23
179 Rick Helling .15 .04
180 Tom Henke .15 .04
181 Chris James .15 .04
182 Manuel Lee .15 .04
183 Dean Palmer .30 .09
184 Ivan Rodriguez .75 .23
185 Kenny Rogers .30 .09
186 Roberto Alomar .75 .23
187 Pat Borders .15 .04
188 Joe Carter .30 .09
189 Carlos Delgado .50 .15
190 Juan Guzman .15 .04
191 Pat Hentgen .15 .04
192 Paul Molitor .50 .15
193 John Olerud .30 .09
194 Ed Sprague .15 .04
195 Dave Stewart .30 .09
196 Todd Stottlemyre .15 .04
197 Duane Ward .15 .04
198 Devon White .15 .04
199 Steve Avery .15 .04
200 Jeff Blauser .15 .04
201 Tom Glavine .50 .15
202 David Justice .30 .09
203 Mike Kelly .15 .04
204 Roberto Kelly .15 .04
205 Ryan Klesko .30 .09
206 Mark Lemke .15 .04
207 Javier Lopez .30 .09
208 Greg Maddux 1.25 .35
209 Fred McGriff .50 .15
210 Greg McMichael .15 .04
211 Kent Mercker .15 .04
212 Terry Pendleton .30 .09
213 John Smoltz .50 .15
214 Tony Tarasco .15 .04
215 Willie Banks .15 .04
216 Steve Buechele .15 .04
217 Shawon Dunston .15 .04
218 Mark Grace .50 .15
219 Brooks Kieschnick RC .30 .09
220 Derrick May .15 .04
221 Randy Myers .30 .09
222 Karl Rhodes .15 .04
223 Rey Sanchez .15 .04
224 Sammy Sosa 1.25 .35
225 Steve Trachsel .15 .04
226 Rick Wilkins .15 .04
227 Bret Boone .30 .09
228 Jeff Brantley .15 .04
229 Tom Browning .15 .04
230 Hector Carrasco .15 .04
231 Rob Dibble .30 .09
232 Erik Hanson .15 .04
233 Barry Larkin .75 .23
234 Kevin Mitchell .15 .04
235 Hal Morris .15 .04
236 Joe Oliver .15 .04
237 Jose Rijo .15 .04
238 Johnny Ruffin .15 .04
239 Deion Sanders .50 .15
240 Reggie Sanders .30 .09
241 John Smiley .15 .04
242 Dante Bichette .30 .09
243 Ellis Burks .30 .09
244 Andres Galarraga .30 .09
245 Joe Girardi .15 .04
246 Greg W.Harris .15 .04
247 Charlie Hayes .15 .04
248 Howard Johnson .15 .04
249 Roberto Mejia .15 .04
250 Marcus Moore .15 .04
251 David Nied .15 .04
252 Armando Reynoso .15 .04
253 Bruce Ruffin .15 .04
254 Mark Thompson .15 .04
255 Walt Weiss .15 .04
256 Kurt Abbott RC .30 .09
257 Bret Barberie .15 .04
258 Chuck Carr .15 .04
259 Jeff Conine .30 .09
260 Chris Hammond .15 .04
261 Bryan Harvey .15 .04
262 Jeremy Hernandez .15 .04
263 Charlie Hough .30 .09
264 Dave Magadan .15 .04
265 Benito Santiago .30 .09
266 Gary Sheffield .30 .09
267 David Weathers .15 .04
268 Jeff Bagwell .50 .15
269 Craig Biggio .50 .15
270 Ken Caminiti .30 .09
271 Andujar Cedeno .15 .04
272 Doug Drabek .15 .04
273 Steve Finley .30 .09
274 Luis Gonzalez .30 .09
275 Pete Harnisch .15 .04
276 John Hudek RC .15 .04
277 Darryl Kile .30 .09
278 Orlando Miller .15 .04
279 James Mouton .15 .04
280 Shane Reynolds .15 .04
281 Scott Servais .15 .04
282 Greg Swindell .15 .04
283 Pedro Astacio .15 .04
284 Brett Butler .30 .09
285 Tom Candiotti .15 .04
286 Delino DeShields .15 .04
287 Kevin Gross .15 .04
288 Orel Hershiser .30 .09
289 Eric Karros .30 .09
290 Ramon Martinez .15 .04
291 Raul Mondesi .30 .09
292 Jose Offerman .15 .04
293 Chan Ho Park RC 1.00 .30
294 Mike Piazza 1.25 .35
295 Henry Rodriguez .15 .04
296 Cory Snyder .15 .04
297 Tim Wallach .15 .04
298 Todd Worrell .15 .04
299 Moises Alou .30 .09
300 Sean Berry .15 .04
301 Wil Cordero .15 .04
302 Joey Eischen .15 .04
303 Jeff Fassero .15 .04
304 Darrin Fletcher .15 .04
305 Cliff Floyd .30 .09
306 Marquis Grissom .15 .04
307 Ken Hill .15 .04
308 Mike Lansing .15 .04
309 Pedro J.Martinez .75 .23
310 Mel Rojas .15 .04
311 Kirk Rueter .30 .09
312 Larry Walker .50 .15
313 John Wetteland .30 .09
314 Rondell White .30 .09
315 Bobby Bonilla .30 .09
316 John Franco .30 .09
317 Dwight Gooden .50 .15
318 Todd Hundley .15 .04
319 Bobby Jones .15 .04
320 Jeff Kent .30 .09
321 Kevin McReynolds .15 .04
322 Bill Pulsipher .15 .04
323 Bret Saberhagen .30 .09
324 David Segui .15 .04
325 Pete Smith .15 .04
326 Kelly Stinnett RC .15 .04
327 Ryan Thompson .15 .04
328 Jose Vizcaino .15 .04
329 Ricky Bottalico RC .30 .09
330 Darren Daulton .30 .09
331 Mariano Duncan .15 .04
332 Lenny Dykstra .30 .09
333 Tommy Greene .15 .04
334 Billy Hatcher .15 .04
335 Dave Hollins .15 .04
336 Pete Incaviglia .15 .04
337 Danny Jackson .15 .04
338 Doug Jones .15 .04
339 Ricky Jordan .15 .04
340 John Kruk .30 .09
341 Curt Schilling .50 .15
342 Kevin Stocker .15 .04
343 Jay Bell .30 .09
344 Steve Cooke .15 .04
345 Carlos Garcia .15 .04
346 Brian Hunter .15 .04
347 Jeff King .15 .04
348 Al Martin .15 .04
349 Orlando Merced .15 .04
350 Denny Neagle .15 .04
351 Don Slaught .15 .04
352 Andy Van Slyke .30 .09
353 Paul Wagner .15 .04
354 Rick White RC .15 .04
355 Luis Alicea .15 .04
356 Rene Arocha .15 .04
357 Rheal Cormier .15 .04
358 Bernard Gilkey .15 .04
359 Gregg Jefferies .15 .04
360 Ray Lankford .15 .04
361 Tom Pagnozzi .15 .04
362 Mike Perez .15 .04
363 Ozzie Smith 1.25 .35
364 Bob Tewksbury .15 .04
365 Mark Whiten .15 .04
366 Todd Zeile .30 .09
367 Andy Ashby .15 .04
368 Brad Ausmus .15 .04
369 Derek Bell .15 .04
370 Andy Benes .15 .04
371 Archi Cianfrocco .15 .04
372 Tony Gwynn 1.00 .30
373 Trevor Hoffman .30 .09
374 Tim Hyers RC .15 .04
375 Pedro Martinez RC .15 .04
376 Phil Plantier .15 .04
377 Bip Roberts .15 .04
378 Scott Sanders .15 .04
379 Dave Staton .15 .04
380 Wally Whitehurst .15 .04
381 Rod Beck .15 .04
382 Todd Benzinger .15 .04
383 Barry Bonds 2.00 .60
384 John Burkett .15 .04
385 Royce Clayton .15 .04
386 Bryan Hickerson .15 .04
387 Mike Jackson .15 .04
388 Darren Lewis .15 .04
389 Kirt Manwaring .15 .04
390 Willie McGee .30 .09
391 Mark Portugal .15 .04
392 Bill Swift .15 .04
393 Robby Thompson .15 .04
394 Salomon Torres .15 .04
395 Matt Williams .30 .09
396 Checklist .15 .04
397 Checklist .15 .04
398 Checklist .15 .04
399 Checklist .15 .04
400 Checklist .15 .04
P1 Paul Molitor Promo 2.00 .60

1994 Fleer Extra Bases Game Breakers

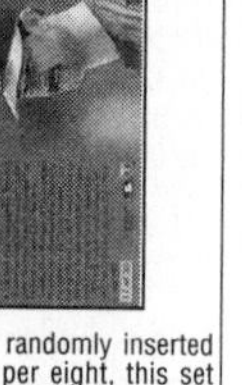

Consisting of 30 cards and randomly inserted in packs at a rate of three per eight, this set features top run producers from around the major leagues. The cards measure 2 1/2" by 4 11/16" and are horizontally designed. There are two photos on the front that bleed into one another. The back has a photo and career highlights.

Nm-Mt Ex-Mt
COMPLETE SET (30) 20.00 6.00
1 Jeff Bagwell 1.00 .30
2 Rod Beck .50 .15
3 Albert Belle .75 .23
4 Barry Bonds 4.00 1.20
5 Jose Canseco 1.50 .45
6 Joe Carter .75 .23
7 Roger Clemens 3.00 .90
8 Darren Daulton .75 .23
9 Lenny Dykstra .75 .23
10 Cecil Fielder .75 .23
11 Tom Glavine 1.00 .30
12 Juan Gonzalez 1.50 .45
13 Mark Grace 1.00 .30
14 Ken Griffey Jr. 2.50 .75
15 David Justice .75 .23
16 Greg Maddux 2.50 .75
17 Don Mattingly 4.00 1.20
18 Ben McDonald .50 .15
19 Fred McGriff 1.00 .30
20 Paul Molitor 1.00 .30
21 John Olerud .75 .23
22 Mike Piazza 2.50 .75
23 Kirby Puckett 1.50 .45
24 Cal Ripken Jr. 5.00 1.50
25 Tim Salmon 1.00 .30
26 Gary Sheffield .75 .23
27 Frank Thomas 1.50 .45
28 Mo Vaughn .75 .23
29 Matt Williams .75 .23
30 Dave Winfield .75 .23

1994 Fleer Extra Bases Major League Hopefuls

Randomly inserted in packs at a rate of one in eight, this 10-card set features top minor league performers. Cards measure 2 1/2" by 4 11/16". Computer generated fronts contain multiple player photos. The backs have a player photo and a write-up about the player's minor league exploits.

Nm-Mt Ex-Mt
COMPLETE SET (10) 6.00 1.80
1 James Baldwin .50 .15
2 Ricky Bottalico .75 .23
3 Ray Durham 2.00 .60
4 Joey Eischen .50 .15
5 Brooks Kieschnick .75 .23
6 Orlando Miller .50 .15
7 Bill Pulsipher .50 .15
8 Mac Suzuki 1.50 .45
9 Mark Thompson .50 .15
10 Wes Weger .50 .15

1994 Fleer Extra Bases Pitchers Duel

This 10-card set measures 2 1/2" by 4 3/4". These cards were available through a wrapper offer which was good through March 31, 1995. Each card features two leading pitchers.

Nm-Mt Ex-Mt
COMPLETE SET (10) 12.00 3.60
1 Roger Clemens 3.00 .90
Jack McDowell
2 Ben McDonald 1.00 .30
Randy Johnson
3 David Cone .75 .23
Jimmy Key
4 Mike Mussina 1.50 .45
Aaron Sele
5 Chuck Finley .75 .23
Wilson Alvarez
6 Curt Schilling 1.00 .30
Steve Avery
7 Greg Maddux 2.50 .75
Jose Rijo
8 Bob Tewksbury .75 .23
Bret Saberhagen
9 Tom Glavine 1.00 .30
Bill Swift
10 Doug Drabek .75 .23
Orel Hershiser

1994 Fleer Extra Bases Rookie Standouts

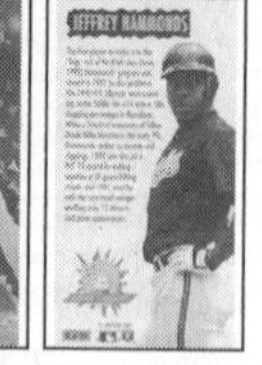

Randomly inserted in packs at a rate of one in four, this 20-card set features those that had potential for being top rookies in 1994. The cards measure 2 1/2" by 4 11/16". Card fronts have an action photo of the player. The background is somewhat blurred and a jagged outline appears around the player as if to allow him to stand out from the rest of the card. The backs have a player photo and text on a white background.

Nm-Mt Ex-Mt
COMPLETE SET (20) 12.00 3.60
1 Kurt Abbott .75 .23
2 Brian Anderson .75 .23
3 Hector Carrasco .50 .15
4 Tim Davis .50 .15
5 Carlos Delgado 1.00 .30
6 Cliff Floyd .75 .23
7 Bob Hamelin .50 .15
8 Jeffrey Hammonds .50 .15
9 Rick Helling .50 .15
10 Steve Karsay .50 .15
11 Ryan Klesko .75 .23
12 Javier Lopez .75 .23
13 Raul Mondesi .75 .23
14 James Mouton .50 .15
15 Chan Ho Park 2.00 .60
16 Manny Ramirez 1.00 .30
17 Tony Tarasco .50 .15
18 Steve Trachsel .50 .15
19 Rick White .50 .15
20 Rondell White .75 .23

1994 Fleer Extra Bases Second Year Stars

Randomly inserted in packs at a rate of one in four, Second Year Stars takes a look at 20 top second year players and reflects on their rookie campaigns of 1993. The cards measure 2 1/2" by 4 11/16". Card fronts feature multiple photos including a large full bleed photo of the player and four smaller photos that give the appearance of being captured on film. These smaller photos run the length of the card and are on the left.

Nm-Mt Ex-Mt
COMPLETE SET (20) 10.00 3.00
1 Bobby Ayala .50 .15
2 Jason Bere .50 .15
3 Chuck Carr .50 .15
4 Jeff Conine .75 .23
5 Steve Cooke .50 .15
6 Wil Cordero .50 .15
7 Carlos Garcia .50 .15
8 Brent Gates .50 .15
9 Trevor Hoffman .75 .23
10 Wayne Kirby .50 .15
11 Al Martin .50 .15
12 Pedro Martinez 1.50 .45
13 Greg McMichael .50 .15
14 Troy Neel .50 .15
15 David Nied .50 .15
16 Mike Piazza 2.50 .75
17 Kirk Rueter .75 .23
18 Tim Salmon 1.00 .30
19 Aaron Sele .50 .15
20 Kevin Stocker .50 .15

2002 Fleer Fall Classics

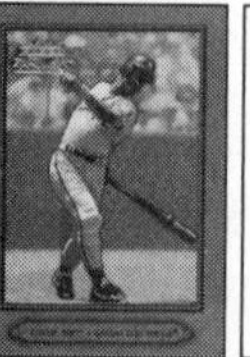

This 120 card set was released in late August, 2002. This set was issued in five card packs which came 24 packs to a box and six boxes to a case with an SRP of $6 per pack. Twenty players in this set participated in the World Series with at least two different teams and one of the varieties is printed in significantly lesser quantities than the more common version. We have notated for those players both the teams mentioned and also noted which version is the short printed version. The final ten cards of the set are mulit-player cards with something in common.

	Nm-Mt	Ex-Mt
COMPLETE SET (100)	30.00	9.00
COMMON CARD (1-100)	.50	.15
COMMON SP	5.00	1.50
1 Rabbit Maranville	.50	.15
2 Tris Speaker	.75	.23
3 Harmon Killebrew	1.25	.35
4 Lou Gehrig	2.50	.75
5 Lou Boudreau	.50	.15
6 Al Kaline	1.25	.35
7A Paul Molitor Blue Jays	.75	.23
7B Paul Molitor Brewers SP	8.00	2.40
8 Cal Ripken	4.00	1.20
9 Yogi Berra	1.25	.35
10 Phil Rizzuto	.75	.23
11A Luis Aparicio W.Sox	.50	.15
11B Luis Aparicio O's SP	5.00	1.50
12 Stan Musial	2.00	.60
13 Mel Ott	1.25	.35
14 Larry Doby	.50	.15
15 Ozzie Smith	2.00	.60
16A Babe Ruth Yankees	5.00	1.50
16B Babe Ruth Red Sox SP	15.00	4.50
17A Red Schoendienst Braves	.50	.15
17B R.Schoendienst Cards SP	5.00	1.50
18 Rollie Fingers	.50	.15
19 Thurman Munson	2.00	.60
20 Lou Brock	.75	.23
21A Paul O'Neill Yankees	.75	.23
21B Paul O'Neill Reds SP	8.00	2.40
22 Jim Palmer	.50	.15
23 Kirby Puckett	1.25	.35
24A Tony Perez Reds	.50	.15
24B Tony Perez Phils SP	5.00	1.50
25 Don Larsen	.50	.15
26A Steve Garvey Dodgers	.50	.15
26B Steve Garvey Padres SP	5.00	1.50
27A Jim Hunter A's	.75	.23
27B Jim Hunter Yankees SP	8.00	2.40
28 Juan Marichal	.50	.15
29 Pee Wee Reese	.75	.23
30 Orlando Cepeda	.50	.15
31 Goose Gossage	.50	.15
32 Ray Knight	.50	.15
33 Eddie Murray	1.25	.35
34 Nolan Ryan	3.00	.90
35 Alan Trammell	.75	.23
36 Grover Alexander	1.25	.35
37 Joe Carter	.50	.15
38 Rogers Hornsby	1.25	.35
39 Jimmie Foxx	1.25	.35
40 Mike Schmidt	2.50	.75
41 Eddie Mathews	1.25	.35
42 Jackie Robinson	1.50	.45
43A Eddie Collins A's	.50	.15
43B Ed. Collins White Sox SP	5.00	1.50
44 Willie McCovey	.50	.15
45 Bob Gibson	.75	.23
46A Keith Hernandez Mets	.75	.23
46B Keith Hernandez Cards SP	8.00	2.40
47 Brooks Robinson	1.25	.35
48 Mordecai Brown	.50	.15
49 Gary Carter	.75	.23
50A Kirk Gibson Dodgers	.50	.15
50B Kirk Gibson Tigers SP	5.00	1.50
51 Johnny Mize	.50	.15
52 Johnny Podres	.50	.15
53 Darrell Porter	.50	.15
54 Willie Stargell	.75	.23
55A Lenny Dykstra Mets	.50	.15
55B Lenny Dykstra Phillies SP	5.00	1.50
56 Christy Mathewson	1.25	.35
57 Walter Johnson	1.25	.35
58 Whitey Ford	.75	.23
59 Lefty Grove	.75	.23
60 Duke Snider	.75	.23
61 Cy Young	1.25	.35
62A Dave Winfield Blue Jays	.50	.15
62B Dave Winfield Yankees SP	5.00	1.50
63 Robin Yount	2.00	.60
64 Fred Lynn	.50	.15
65 Ty Cobb	2.00	.60
66 Joe Morgan	.50	.15
67 Bill Mazeroski	.50	.15
68 Frank Baker	.50	.15
69 Chief Bender	.50	.15
70 Carlton Fisk	.75	.23
71 Jerry Coleman	.50	.15
72 Frankie Frisch	.50	.15
73A Wade Boggs Red Sox	.75	.23
73B Wade Boggs Yankees SP	8.00	2.40
74 Johnny Bench	1.25	.35
75A Roger Maris Yankees	2.00	.60
75B Roger Maris Cards SP	10.00	3.00
76 Dom DiMaggio	.50	.15
77 George Brett	3.00	.90
78A Dave Parker Pirates	.50	.15
78B Dave Parker A's SP	5.00	1.50
79 Hank Greenberg	1.25	.35
80 Pepper Martin	.75	.23
81A Graig Nettles Yankees	.50	.15
81B Graig Nettles Padres SP	5.00	1.50
82 Dennis Eckersley	.50	.15
83 Donn Clendenon	.50	.15
84 Tom Seaver	.75	.23
85 Honus Wagner	2.00	.60
86A Reggie Jackson Yankees	.75	.23
86B Reggie Jackson A's SP	8.00	2.40
87A Goose Goslin Senators	.50	.15
87B Goose Goslin Tigers SP	5.00	1.50
88 Tony Kubek	.75	.23
89 Roy Campanella	1.25	.35
90A Steve Carlton Phillies	.50	.15
90B Steve Carlton Cards SP	5.00	1.50
91 Lou Gehrig / Mel Ott	1.50	.45
92 Eddie Collins / Joe Morgan	.50	.15
93 George Brett / Mike Schmidt	2.50	.75
94 Cal Ripken / Ozzie Smith	2.50	.75
95 Thurman Munson / Johnny Bench	1.25	.35
96 Willie Stargell / Stan Musial / Pepper Martin	1.25	.35
97 Babe Ruth / Kirby Puckett / Reggie Jackson	2.50	.75
98 Cy Young / Bob Gibson	.75	.23
99 Whitey Ford / Steve Carlton	.75	.23
100 Paul Molitor / Lou Brock	.75	.23

2002 Fleer Fall Classics Championship Gold

Randomly inserted in packs, this is a full parallel to the Fall Classics Set. Each card, whether or not it was short printed in the base set, has a stated print run of 50 serial numbered sets.

Nm-Mt Ex-Mt

*GOLD POST-WAR: 8X TO 20X BASIC
*GOLD PRE-WAR: 5X TO 12X BASIC .
*GOLD POST-WAR: .75X TO 2X BASIC SP's
*GOLD PRE-WAR: .5X TO 1.2X BASIC SP's

2002 Fleer Fall Classics HOF Plaque

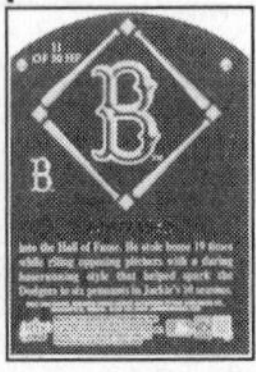

Randomly inserted in packs, these 30 cards feature hall of famers on cards designed similarly to those plaques a fan would see at the Hall of Fame in Cooperstown. Each card has a stated print run based on the year of their induction into the Hall of Fame.

	Nm-Mt	Ex-Mt
COMPLETE SET (30)	120.00	36.00
1 Babe Ruth/1936	15.00	4.50
2 Christy Mathewson/1936	5.00	1.50
3 Honus Wagner/1936	8.00	2.40
4 Ty Cobb/1936	8.00	2.40
5 Walter Johnson/1936	5.00	1.50
6 Cy Young/1937	5.00	1.50
7 Tris Speaker/1937	3.00	.90
8 Eddie Collins/1939	3.00	.90
9 Lou Gehrig/1939	10.00	3.00
10 Jimmie Foxx/1951	5.00	1.50
11 Jackie Robinson/1962	6.00	1.80
12 Stan Musial/1969	8.00	2.40
13 Yogi Berra/1972	5.00	1.50
14 Duke Snider/1980	3.00	.90
15 Juan Marichal/1983	3.00	.90
16 Luis Aparicio/1984	3.00	.90
17 Pee Wee Reese/1984	3.00	.90
18 Willie McCovey/1986	3.00	.90
19 Willie Stargell/1988	3.00	.90
20 Johnny Bench/1989	5.00	1.50
21 Joe Morgan/1990	3.00	.90
22 Jim Palmer/1990	3.00	.90
23 Tom Seaver/1992	3.00	.90
24 Reggie Jackson/1993	3.00	.90
25 Steve Carlton/1994	3.00	.90
26 George Brett/1999	12.00	3.60
27 Nolan Ryan/1999	12.00	3.60
28 Robin Yount/1999	8.00	2.40
29 Kirby Puckett/2001	5.00	1.50
30 Ozzie Smith/2002	8.00	2.40

2002 Fleer Fall Classics MVP Collection Game Used

Inserted into packs at a stated rate of one in 100 hobby and one in 240 retail, these 11 cards feature memorabilia pieces from players who won the World Series MVP award. Many of these cards have stated print runs of 250 or fewer cards and we have notated that information next to their name in our checklist.

	Nm-Mt	Ex-Mt
AT Alan Trammell Jsy	15.00	4.50
BR B.Robinson Bat SP/250	25.00	7.50
DC Donn Clendenon Pants	10.00	3.00
DP Darrell Porter Bat SP/250	10.00	3.00
JB Johnny Bench Jsy SP/200	25.00	7.50
PM Paul Molitor Bat SP/250	15.00	4.50
RF Rollie Fingers Jsy SP/200	10.00	3.00
RJNY Reggie Jackson Yanks Jsy	15.00	4.50
RJOK R.Jackson A's Jsy SP/50	30.00	9.00
RK Ray Knight Bat	10.00	3.00
WS Willie Stargell Jsy SP/200	15.00	4.50

2002 Fleer Fall Classics MVP Collection Game Used Patch

These five cards form a partial parallel of the MVP Collection insert set. These cards are all printed to a stated print run which matches the last two digits of the year these players won the World Series MVP award.

	Nm-Mt	Ex-Mt
AT Alan Trammell Jsy /84	50.00	15.00
BR Brooks Robinson Bat/70	60.00	18.00
JB Johnny Bench Jsy/76	60.00	18.00
RF Rollie Fingers Jsy/74	25.00	7.50
RJNY R.Jackson Yanks Jsy/77	50.00	15.00

2002 Fleer Fall Classics October Legends Game Used

Issued in hobby pack at stated odds of one in 48 hobby and one in 200 retail, these 26 cards feature memorabilia from various World Series heroes. Many of these cards have stated print runs of 225 or fewer and we have notated that information next to their name in our checklist.

	Nm-Mt	Ex-Mt
CR Cal Ripken Jsy SP/50		
DE Dennis Eckersley Jsy	10.00	3.00
DP Dave Parker Bat SP/50	20.00	6.00
DP Darrell Porter Bat SP/150	10.00	3.00
DS Duke Snider Pants SP/200	20.00	6.00
EM Eddie Murray Jsy	15.00	4.50
FF Frankie Frisch Pants SP/25		
GB George Brett Jsy	25.00	7.50
GC Gary Carter Jsy SP/200	20.00	6.00
JM Joe Morgan Bat	10.00	3.00
JMA Juan Marichal Jsy	10.00	3.00
KH Keith Hernandez Bat SP/100	25.00	7.50
KHJ K.Hernandez Jsy SP/150	25.00	7.50
LD Lenny Dykstra Bat SP/200	15.00	4.50
PM Pepper Martin Bat	25.00	7.50
PM Paul Molitor Bat SP/150	25.00	7.50
PO Paul O'Neill Jsy	15.00	4.50
PWR Pee Wee Reese Pants SP/200	20.00	6.00
RF Rollie Fingers Jsy	10.00	3.00
RM Roger Maris Jsy	80.00	24.00
RS R.Schoendienst Pants SP/210	15.00	4.50
RY Robin Yount Bat	15.00	4.50
TP Tony Perez Jsy	10.00	3.00
WB Wade Boggs Jsy	15.00	4.50
WM Willie McCovey Jsy SP/150	15.00	4.50
WS Willie Stargell Jsy SP/225	20.00	6.00

2002 Fleer Fall Classics October Legends Game Used Gold

Randomly inserted in packs, this is a parallel to the October Legends insert set. These cards were issued to a stated print run of 100 serial numbered sets.

Nm-Mt Ex-Mt

*GOLD: .6X TO 1.5X BASIC OCT.LGD.
*GOLD: .5X TO 1.2X BASIC OCT.LGD SP
*GOLD: .4X TO 1X BASIC OCT.LGD SP/50

2002 Fleer Fall Classics October Legends Game Used Dual

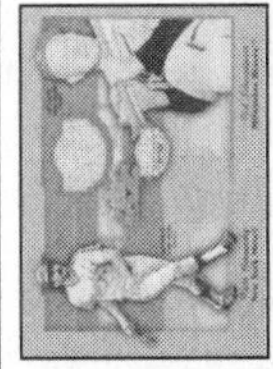

Inserted in packs at stated odds of one in 60 hobby and one in 244 retail, these 15 cards feature two players as well as game-used swatches of memorabilia from each player. A few cards were printed to a shorter quantity and we have notated that information along with the stated print run information next to their name in our checklist.

	Nm-Mt	Ex-Mt
1 Cal Ripken Jsy / Eddie Murray Jsy SP/100	60.00	18.00
2 Cal Ripken Bat / Eddie Murray Jsy SP/200	50.00	15.00
3 Duke Snider Pants / Pee Wee Reese Pants SP/200	40.00	12.00
4 George Brett Jsy / Darrell Porter Bat SP/150	50.00	15.00
5 Gary Carter Jsy / Keith Hernandez Bat	20.00	6.00
6 Juan Marichal Jsy / Willie McCovey Jsy	20.00	6.00
7 Joe Morgan Bat / Tony Perez Jsy	20.00	6.00
8 Keith Hernandez Jsy / Red Schoendienst Pants	20.00	6.00
9 Lenny Dykstra Bat / Gary Carter Jsy	20.00	6.00
10 Pepper Martin Bat / Frankie Frisch Pants	25.00	7.50
11 Rollie Fingers Jsy / Dennis Eckersley Jsy	20.00	6.00
12 Roger Maris Jsy / Paul O'Neill Jsy SP/200	60.00	18.00
13 Robin Yount Bat / Paul Molitor Bat SP/150	50.00	15.00
14 Wade Boggs Jsy / Keith Hernandez Jsy	20.00	6.00
15 Willie Stargell Jsy / Dave Parker Bat	20.00	6.00

2002 Fleer Fall Classics Pennant Chase Game Used

Inserted at stated odds of one in 48 hobby and one in 200 retail, these seven cards feature memorabilia items from players who participated in many pennant races. Every player in this set was a major cog for either the Boston Red Sox or the New York Yankees. The Yogi Berra card was printed in shorter supply and we have notated that stated print run information next to his name in our checklist.

	Nm-Mt	Ex-Mt
CF Carlton Fisk Bat	15.00	4.50
DW Dave Winfield Bat	15.00	4.50
FL Fred Lynn Bat	15.00	4.50
RJ Reggie Jackson Jsy	15.00	4.50
TM Thurman Munson Bat	40.00	12.00
WB Wade Boggs Jsy	15.00	4.50
YB Yogi Berra Pants SP/150	25.00	7.50

2002 Fleer Fall Classics Pennant Chase Game Used Dual

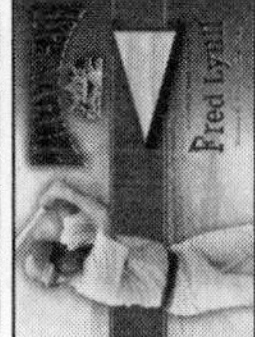

Randomly inserted in packs, these three cards feature two players and a game-used piece from each player on the card. These cards have a stated print run of 50 serial numbered sets.

	Nm-Mt	Ex-Mt
CFRJ Carlton Fisk Bat / Reggie Jackson Jsy	50.00	15.00
FLTM Fred Lynn Bat / Thurman Munson Bat	80.00	24.00
WBDW Wade Boggs Jsy / Dave Winfield Bat	50.00	15.00

2002 Fleer Fall Classics Rival Factions

Randomly inserted in packs, these 43 cards feature two players on each card. This set was issued in three tiers with cards numbered 1 through 24 having a stated print of 1000 serial numbered set, cards 25-34 had a stated print run of 500 serial numbered sets and cards numbered 35-43 had a stated print run of 50 serial numbered sets.

	Nm-Mt	Ex-Mt
1 Carlton Fisk / Thurman Munson	10.00	3.00
2 Frank Baker / Babe Ruth	20.00	6.00
3 Jimmie Foxx / Lou Gehrig	10.00	3.00
4 Steve Carlton / Nolan Ryan	15.00	4.50
5 Mordecai Brown / Honus Wagner	10.00	3.00
6 Frankie Frisch / Duke Snider	4.00	1.20
7 Ozzie Smith / Alan Trammell	10.00	3.00
8 Larry Doby / Jackie Robinson	8.00	2.40
9 Steve Garvey / Tony Perez	4.00	1.20
10 Johnny Bench / Willie Stargell	6.00	1.80
11 Ty Cobb / Eddie Collins	10.00	3.00
12 Reggie Jackson / Brooks Robinson	6.00	1.80
13 Yogi Berra / Roy Campanella	6.00	1.80
14 Orlando Cepeda / Willie McCovey	4.00	1.20
15 Al Kaline / Jim Palmer	6.00	1.80
16 George Brett / Kirby Puckett	12.00	3.60
17 Bob Gibson / Tom Seaver	4.00	1.20
18 Cal Ripken / Robin Yount	20.00	6.00
19 Johnny Mize / Mel Ott	6.00	1.80
20 Stan Musial / Pee Wee Reese	10.00	3.00
21 Hank Greenberg / Lefty Grove	6.00	1.80
22 Dave Parker / Mike Schmidt	12.00	3.60
23 Bill Mazeroski / Joe Morgan	4.00	1.20
24 Johnny Bench / Carlton Fisk	6.00	1.80
25 George Brett / Mike Schmidt	20.00	6.00
26 Pee Wee Reese / Phil Rizzuto	5.00	1.50
27 Cal Ripken / Alan Trammell	25.00	7.50
28 Catfish Hunter / Tom Seaver	5.00	1.50
29 Ty Cobb / Honus Wagner	12.00	3.60
30 Steve Carlton / Lefty Grove	5.00	1.50
31 Ozzie Smith / Robin Yount	12.00	3.60
32 Frankie Frisch / Joe Morgan	5.00	1.50
33 Hank Greenberg / Jackie Robinson	10.00	3.00
34 Jimmie Foxx / Pepper Martin	8.00	2.40
35 Lou Gehrig / Cal Ripken	150.00	45.00
36 Ozzie Smith / Honus Wagner	50.00	15.00
37 Reggie Jackson / Dave Winfield	25.00	7.50
38 Ty Cobb / Rogers Hornsby	40.00	12.00
39 Babe Ruth / Roger Maris	80.00	24.00
40 Yogi Berra / Thurman Munson	40.00	12.00
41 Nolan Ryan / Tom Seaver	60.00	18.00
42 Joe Morgan / Jackie Robinson	30.00	9.00
43 Jimmie Foxx / Mel Ott	25.00	7.50

2002 Fleer Fall Classics Rival Factions Game Used

Inserted in packs at state odds of one in 32 hobby and one 121 retail, these 63 cards feature two players on the card but only one memorabilia piece. We have put the player with the memorabilia piece first in our checklist along with what type of piece it is. In addition, many cards were printed to shorter supply and we have notated that stated print run information next to the card in our checklist.

	Nm-Mt	Ex-Mt
1 Frank Baker Bat / Babe Ruth	50.00	15.00
2 Johnny Bench Jsy / Carlton Fisk/75	30.00	9.00
3 Johnny Bench Jsy / Willie Stargell/55	30.00	9.00
4 Yogi Berra Pants / Roy Campanella/225	20.00	6.00
5 Yogi Berra Pants / Thurman Munson	20.00	6.00
6 George Brett Jsy / Kirby Puckett/200	40.00	12.00
7 George Brett Jsy / Mike Schmidt	40.00	12.00
8 Steve Carlton Pants / Lefty Grove	15.00	4.50
9 Steve Carlton Pants / Nolan Ryan/225	20.00	6.00
10 Orlando Cepeda Bat / Willie McCovey	15.00	4.50
11 Larry Doby Bat / Jackie Robinson	15.00	4.50
12 Carlton Fisk Jsy / Johnny Bench/200	20.00	6.00
13 Carlton Fisk Jsy / Thurman Munson/200	20.00	6.00
14 Jimmie Foxx Bat / Lou Gehrig/100	50.00	15.00
15 Jimmie Foxx Bat / Pepper Martin/50	60.00	18.00
16 Jimmie Foxx Bat / Mel Ott/100	50.00	15.00
17 Frankie Frisch Pants / Joe Morgan/75	30.00	9.00
18 Frankie Frisch Pants / Duke Snider/200	25.00	7.50
19 Steve Garvey Jsy / Tony Perez	15.00	4.50
20 Hank Greenberg Bat / Lefty Grove/45	60.00	18.00
21 Hank Greenberg Bat / Jackie Robinson/75	50.00	15.00
22 Jim Hunter Jsy / Tom Seaver	20.00	6.00
23 Reggie Jackson Jsy / Brooks Robinson/50	30.00	9.00
24 Reggie Jackson Jsy / Dave Winfield/100	25.00	7.50
25 Roger Maris Jsy / Babe Ruth	80.00	24.00
26 Pepper Martin Bat / Jimmie Foxx/50	30.00	9.00
27 Willie McCovey Jsy / Orlando Cepeda/200	20.00	6.00
28 Johnny Mize Bat / Mel Ott/95	15.00	4.50

29 Joe Morgan Pants 20.00 6.00
Frankie Frisch
30 Joe Morgan Pants 20.00 6.00
Jackie Robinson/275
31 Joe Morgan Pants 20.00 6.00
Bill Mazeroski/200
32 Thurman Munson Jsy 50.00 15.00
Yogi Berra/50
33 Thurman Munson Jsy
Carlton Fisk/25
34 Jim Palmer Pants 15.00 4.50
Al Kaline
35 Dave Parker Bat 15.00 4.50
Mike Schmidt/100
36 Tony Perez Jsy 20.00 6.00
Steve Garvey/250
37 Kirby Puckett Bat 20.00 6.00
George Brett/250
38 Pee Wee Reese Pants 20.00 6.00
Stan Musial
39 Pee Wee Reese Pants 20.00 6.00
Phil Rizzuto/250
40 Cal Ripken Jsy 40.00 12.00
Lou Gehrig
41 Cal Ripken Jsy 40.00 12.00
Alan Trammell/225
42 Cal Ripken Jsy 40.00 12.00
Robin Yount/200
43 Brooks Robinson Bat 20.00 6.00
Reggie Jackson
44 Jackie Robinson Bat 60.00 18.00
Larry Doby/50
45 Jackie Robinson Pants 50.00 15.00
Hank Greenberg/75
46 Jackie Robinson Pants 50.00 15.00
Joe Morgan/75
47 Babe Ruth Bat
Frank Baker/25
48 Babe Ruth Bat
Roger Maris/25
49 Nolan Ryan Jsy 50.00 15.00
Steve Carlton/200
50 Nolan Ryan Jsy 50.00 15.00
Tom Seaver/200
51 Tom Seaver Pants 20.00 6.00
Bob Gibson
52 Tom Seaver Pants 20.00 6.00
Jim Hunter/225
53 Tom Seaver Pants 20.00 6.00
Nolan Ryan/150
54 Ozzie Smith Jsy 25.00 7.50
Alan Trammell/100
55 Ozzie Smith Jsy 20.00 6.00
Honus Wagner
56 Ozzie Smith Jsy 20.00 6.00
Robin Yount/175
57 Duke Snider Pants 20.00 6.00
Frankie Frisch/200
58 Willie Stargell Jsy 20.00 6.00
Johnny Bench/200
59 Alan Trammell Jsy 20.00 6.00
Ozzie Smith/250
60 Alan Trammell Jsy 20.00 6.00
Cal Ripken
61 Dave Winfield Jsy 15.00 4.50
Reggie Jackson/100
62 Robin Yount Jsy 25.00 7.50
Ozzie Smith/250
63 Robin Yount Jsy 25.00 7.50
Cal Ripken/200

2002 Fleer Fall Classics Rival Factions Game Used Dual

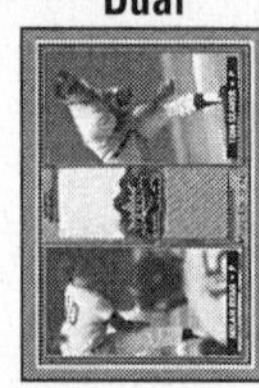

Inserted in packs at stated odds of one in 60 hobby and one in 244 retail, these 24 cards feature two players along with a game-used memorabilia piece for each player. A few cards were issued to a shorter print run and we have notated that information next to the card in our checklist.

Nm-Mt Ex-Mt
1 Babe Ruth Bat
Roger Maris Jsy SP/25
2 Carlton Fisk Jsy 40.00 12.00
Thurman Munson Jsy
3 Catfish Hunter Jsy 25.00 7.50
Tom Seaver Pants
4 Cal Ripken Jsy 50.00 15.00
Alan Trammell Jsy
5 Cal Ripken Jsy 60.00 18.00
Robin Yount Jsy
6 Frank Baker Bat
Babe Ruth Bat SP/25
7 Frankie Frisch Pants 25.00 7.50
Duke Snider Pants
8 Frankie Frisch Pants 25.00 7.50
Joe Morgan Pants
9 George Brett Jsy 50.00 15.00
Kirby Puckett Bat
10 Hank Greenberg Bat 150.00 45.00
Jackie Robinson Pants SP/50
11 Johnny Bench Jsy 30.00 9.00
Carlton Fisk Jsy
12 Johnny Bench Jsy 30.00 9.00
Willie Stargell Jsy
13 Jimmie Foxx Bat 60.00 18.00
Pepper Martin Bat SP/200
14 Joe Morgan Pants 80.00 24.00
Jackie Robinson Pants SP/50
15 Larry Doby Bat 80.00 24.00
Jackie Robinson Pants SP/75
16 Nolan Ryan Jsy 80.00 24.00
Tom Seaver Pants
17 Orlando Cepeda Bat 25.00 7.50
Willie McCovey Jsy SP/200
18 Ozzie Smith Jsy 30.00 9.00
Alan Trammell Jsy
19 Ozzie Smith Jsy 30.00 9.00
Robin Yount Jsy
20 Reggie Jackson Jsy 30.00 9.00
Brooks Robinson Bat
21 Reggie Jackson Jsy 25.00 7.50
Dave Winfield Jsy SP/150
22 Steve Carlton Pants 80.00 24.00
Nolan Ryan Jsy
23 Steve Garvey Jsy 20.00 6.00
Tony Perez Jsy
24 Yogi Berra Pants 80.00 24.00
Thurman Munson Jsy

2002 Fleer Fall Classics Rival Factions Game Used Dual Patch

Randomly inserted in packs, these 10 cards feature two players along with a jersey patch for each player on the card. These cards were printed to a stated print run of 50 serial numbered sets.

Nm-Mt Ex-Mt
CFTM Carlton Fisk 100.00 30.00
Thurman Munson
CRAT Cal Ripken 150.00 45.00
Alan Trammell
CRRY Cal Ripken 150.00 45.00
Robin Yount
JBCF Johnny Bench 80.00 24.00
Carlton Fisk
JBWS Johnny Bench 80.00 24.00
Willie Stargell
OSAT Ozzie Smith 80.00 24.00
Alan Trammell
OSRY Ozzie Smith 80.00 24.00
Robin Yount
RJDW Reggie Jackson 50.00 15.00
Dave Winfield
SCNR Steve Carlton 150.00 45.00
Nolan Ryan
SGTP Steve Garvey 50.00 15.00
Tony Perez

2002 Fleer Fall Classics Rival Factions Game Used Quad

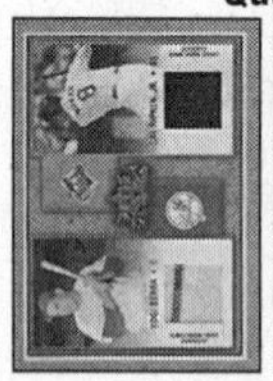

Randomly inserted in packs, these 10 cards feature four players on the card along with a game-worn memorabilia piece for each of the four players on the card. Each card has a stated print run of 25 serial numbered set and therefore no pricing is available due to market scarcity.

Nm-Mt Ex-Mt
1 Babe Ruth Bat
Roger Maris Jsy
Yogi Berra Bat
Thurman Munson Jsy
2 Hank Greenberg Bat
Frank Baker Bat
Jimmie Foxx Bat
Johnny Mize Bat
3 Johnny Bench Jsy
Joe Morgan Pants
Tom Seaver Pants
Tony Perez Jsy
4 Pee Wee Reese Pants
Duke Snider Pants
Yogi Berra Pants
Johnny Mize Bat
5 Nolan Ryan Jsy
Tom Seaver Pants
Brooks Robinson Bat
Jim Palmer Pants
6 Ozzie Smith Jsy
Alan Trammell Jsy
Cal Ripken Jsy
Robin Yount Jsy
7 Reggie Jackson Jsy
Catfish Hunter Jsy
Johnny Bench Jsy
Tony Perez Jsy
8 Steve Carlton Pants
Nolan Ryan Jsy
Tom Seaver Pants
Jim Palmer Pants
9 Yogi Berra Pants
Cal Ripken Jsy
Joe Morgan Pants
Willie Stargell Jsy
10 Yogi Berra Pants
Thurman Munson Jsy
Johnny Bench Jsy
Carlton Fisk Jsy

2002 Fleer Fall Classics Series of Champions

Inserted at stated odds of one in six, this 19 card insert set features players who had

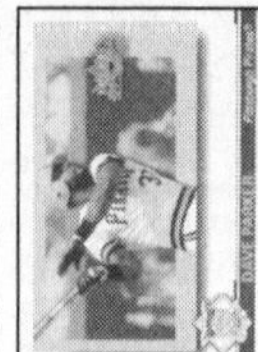

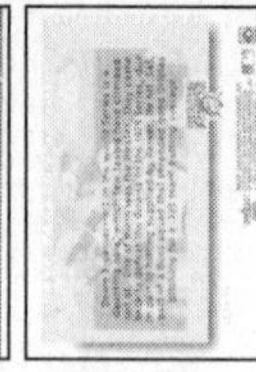

important impacts on a World Series.

Nm-Mt Ex-Mt
COMPLETE SET (19) 40.00 12.00
1 Yogi Berra 3.00 .90
2 Wade Boggs 2.00 .60
3 Dave Parker 2.00 .60
4 Joe Carter 2.00 .60
5 Kirk Gibson 2.00 .60
6 Reggie Jackson 2.00 .60
7 Tony Kubek 2.00 .60
8 Don Larsen 2.00 .60
9 Bill Mazeroski 2.00 .60
10 Eddie Murray 3.00 .90
11 Graig Nettles 2.00 .60
12 Tony Perez 2.00 .60
13 Phil Rizzuto 2.00 .60
14 Mike Schmidt 6.00 1.80
15 Red Schoendienst 2.00 .60
16 Duke Snider 2.00 .60
17 Ty Cobb 5.00 1.50
18 Lou Gehrig 6.00 1.80
19 Babe Ruth 10.00 3.00

2002 Fleer Fall Classics Series of Champions Game Used

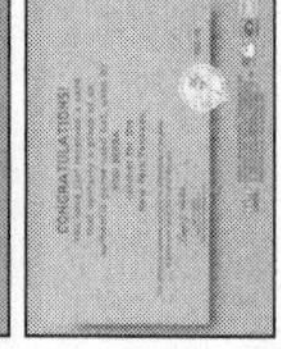

Inserted in hobby packs at stated odds of one in 36 and retail packs at odds of one in 135, these 13 cards form a partial parallel to the Series of Champions insert set. The Babe Ruth card was issued to a stated print run of 25 sets and is therefore not priced due to market scarcity.

Nm-Mt Ex-Mt
BR Babe Ruth Bat SP/25
DP Dave Parker Bat 10.00 3.00
DS Duke Snider Bat 15.00 4.50
EM Eddie Murray Bat 15.00 4.50
GN Graig Nettles Bat 10.00 3.00
JC Joe Carter Bat 10.00 3.00
KG Kirk Gibson Bat 10.00 3.00
RJ Reggie Jackson Bat 15.00 4.50
RS Red Schoendienst Pants 10.00 3.00
TK Tony Kubek Bat 15.00 4.50
TP Tony Perez Bat 10.00 3.00
WB Wade Boggs Jsy 15.00 4.50
YB Yogi Berra Bat 15.00 4.50

2002 Fleer Fall Classics Series of Champions Game Used Gold

Randomly inserted in packs, this is a parallel of the Series of Champions insert set. These cards can be identified by their stated print run of 100 serial numbered sets.

Nm-Mt Ex-Mt
*GOLD: .6X TO 1.5X BASIC CHAMPIONS
BR Babe Ruth Bat 200.00 60.00

2002 Fleer Fall Classics Series of Champions Bat Knob

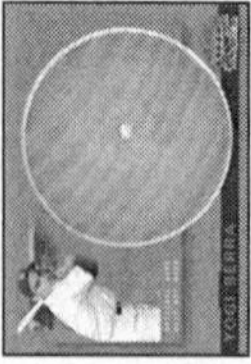

Randomly inserted in packs, these 10 cards form a partial parallel to the Series of Champions insert set. Each card features a piece of the bat knob and was issued to a stated print run of 10 serial numbered sets. Due to market scarcity, no pricing is provided.

Nm-Mt Ex-Mt
DP Dave Parker
DS Duke Snider
EM Eddie Murray
GN Graig Nettles
JC Joe Carter
KG Kirk Gibson
RJ Reggie Jackson
TK Tony Kubek
TP Tony Perez
YB Yogi Berra

2003 Fleer Fall Classics

This 106 card set was released in August, 2003. This set was issued in five card packs with a $5 SRP which were 24 packs to a box and 12 boxes to a case. Please note that 19 players in the set, who participated with 2 different teams in the World Series have

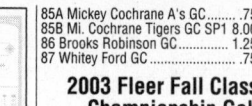

variations in which one of the two cards are significantly harder. Please note that there are also 2 different SP types and we have notated that information in our checklist. Cards numbered 64 to 70 are from the Dynasty Foundation subset while cards numbered 71 through 87 are from the Gallery of Champions subset.

MINT NRMT
COMP. SET w/o SP's (87) 25.00 11.00
COMMON CARD (1-87) .50 .23
COMMON SP1 5.00 2.20
SP1 STATED ODDS 1:18 H, 1:36 R
COMMON SP2 5.00 2.20
SP2 STATED ODDS 1:1 LGD STAR
1 Rod Carew .75 .35
2 Bobby Doerr .50 .23
3A Eddie Mathews Braves 1.25 .55
3B Eddie Mathews Tigers SP2 10.00 4.50
4 Tom Seaver .75 .35
5 Lou Brock .75 .35
6A Nolan Ryan Mets 3.00 1.35
6B Nolan Ryan Astros SP2 12.00 5.50
7 Pee Wee Reese .75 .35
8 Robin Yount 2.00 .90
9 Bob Feller .75 .35
10 Harmon Killebrew 1.25 .55
11 Hal Newhouser .50 .23
12 Al Kaline 1.25 .55
13 Hoyt Wilhelm .50 .23
14 Early Wynn .50 .23
15A Yogi Berra Yanks 1.25 .55
15B Yogi Berra Mets SP2 10.00 4.50
16 Billy Williams .50 .23
17 Rollie Fingers .50 .23
18A Sparky Anderson Tigers .50 .23
18B Sp. Anderson Reds SP1 5.00 2.20
19 Lou Boudreau .50 .23
20 Warren Spahn .75 .35
21 Enos Slaughter .50 .23
22 Luis Aparicio .50 .23
23 Phil Rizzuto .75 .35
24 Willie McCovey .50 .23
25 Joe Morgan .50 .23
26 Alan Trammell .50 .23
27 Eddie Plank .50 .23
28 Lefty Grove .75 .35
29 Walter Johnson 1.25 .55
30 Roy Campanella 1.25 .55
31 Carlton Fisk .75 .35
32 Bill Dickey .75 .35
33A Rogers Hornsby Cards 1.25 .55
33B Rogers Hornsby Cubs SP1 10.00 4.50
34 Wade Boggs .75 .35
35 Chick Stahl .50 .23
36A Don Drysdale Brooklyn 1.25 .55
36B Don Drysdale LA SP1 10.00 4.50
37 Jose Canseco 1.25 .55
38A Roger Maris Cards 2.00 .90
38B Roger Maris Yanks SP2 10.00 4.50
39 Cal Ripken 4.00 1.80
40A Kiki Cuyler Pirates .50 .23
40B Kiki Cuyler Cubs SP1 5.00 2.20
41 Hank Greenberg 1.25 .55
42 Bud Harrelson .50 .23
43A Eddie Murray O's 1.25 .55
43B Eddie Murray Indians SP2 10.00 4.50
44 Jimmy Sebring .50 .23
45 Ozzie Smith 2.00 .90
46A Darryl Strawberry Mets .75 .35
46B D. Strawberry Yanks SP2 8.00 3.60
47 Dave Parker .50 .23
48A Gil Hodges Dodgers .75 .35
48B Gil Hodges Mets SP2 8.00 3.60
49 Joe Carter .50 .23
50A Leo Durocher Cards .50 .23
50B Leo Durocher Giants SP1 5.00 2.20
51 Christy Mathewson 1.25 .55
52 Elston Howard .50 .23
53 Hughie Jennings .50 .23
54 Nellie Fox .75 .35
55 Carl Yastrzemski 2.00 .90
56A Frank Robinson O's .50 .23
56B Frank Robinson Reds SP2 5.00 2.20
57 Dennis Eckersley .50 .23
58A Grover Alexander Phils .75 .35
58B G.C. Alexander Cards SP1 8.00 3.60
59 Carl Hubbell .75 .35
60 Dave Winfield .50 .23
61 Honus Wagner 2.00 .90
62A Duke Snider Brooklyn .75 .35
62B Duke Snider LA SP2 8.00 3.60
63A Frankie Frisch Giants .50 .23
63B Frankie Frisch Cards SP1 5.00 2.20
64 Dizzy Dean DF .75 .35
65 Bob Gibson DF .75 .35
66 Johnny Bench DF 1.25 .55
67 Ty Cobb DF 2.00 .90
68 Lou Gehrig DF 2.50 1.10
69 Catfish Hunter DF .75 .35
70 Willie Stargell DF .75 .35
71A Reggie Jackson A's GC .75 .35
71B Reg. Jackson Yanks GC SP2 8.00 3.60
72 George Brett GC 3.00 1.35
73A Babe Ruth Sox GC 4.00 1.80
73B Babe Ruth Yanks GC SP1 15.00 6.75
74 Cy Young GC 1.25 .55
75 Jim Palmer GC .50 .23
76 Mickey Lolich GC .50 .23
77 Stan Musial GC 2.00 .90
78 Steve Carlton GC .50 .23
79 Roberto Clemente GC 3.00 1.35
80 John McGraw GC .75 .35
81 Paul Molitor GC .75 .35
82 Red Ruffing GC .50 .23
83 Connie Mack GC .50 .23
84 Mike Schmidt GC 2.50 1.10

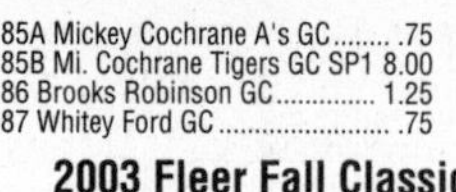

85A Mickey Cochrane A's GC .75 .35
85B Mi. Cochrane Tigers GC SP1 8.00 3.60
86 Brooks Robinson GC 1.25 .55
87 Whitey Ford GC .75 .35

2003 Fleer Fall Classics Championship Gold

MINT NRMT
*GOLD POST-WAR: 8X TO 20X BASIC
*GOLD PRE-WAR: 5X TO 12X BASIC
*GOLD POST-WAR: .75X TO 2X BASIC SP1
*GOLD PRE-WAR: .5X TO 1.2X BASIC SP1
*GOLD POST-WAR: .75X TO 2X BASIC SP2
RANDOM INSERTS IN PACKS
STATED PRINT RUN 50 SERIAL #'d SETS

2003 Fleer Fall Classics All-American Autographs

Randomly inserted into packs, these 14 cards feature autographs from players who participated in the World Series. Since there are varying print runs, we have notated the stated print run next to the player's name in our checklist.

MINT NRMT
AK Al Kaline/325 25.00 11.00
AT Alan Trammell/150 15.00 6.75
BF Bob Feller/300 20.00 9.00
BM Bill Mazeroski/75 20.00 9.00
BR Brooks Robinson/325 25.00 11.00
BS Moose Skowron/150 15.00 6.75
CF Carlton Fisk/75 30.00 13.50
FL Fred Lynn/275 15.00 6.75
HK Harmon Killebrew/150 40.00 18.00
LA Luis Aparicio/150 15.00 6.75
PR Preacher Roe/450 15.00 6.75
RB Rick Burleson/250 10.00 4.50
VB Vida Blue/450 10.00 4.50
WS Warren Spahn/75 40.00 18.00

2003 Fleer Fall Classics All-American Autographs 100

MINT NRMT
RANDOM INSERTS IN PACKS
STATED PRINT RUN 100 SERIAL #'d SETS
AK Al Kaline 40.00 18.00
AT Alan Trammell 20.00 9.00
BF Bob Feller 30.00 13.50
BM Bill Mazeroski 20.00 9.00
BR Brooks Robinson 40.00 18.00
BS Moose Skowron 20.00 9.00
CF Carlton Fisk 30.00 13.50
DS Duke Snider 30.00 13.50
FL Fred Lynn 20.00 9.00
HK Harmon Killebrew 50.00 22.00
JP Jim Palmer 20.00 9.00
LA Luis Aparicio 20.00 9.00
PR Preacher Roe 20.00 9.00
RB Rick Burleson 15.00 6.75
SC Steve Carlton 30.00 13.50
VB Vida Blue 15.00 6.75
WS Warren Spahn 40.00 18.00

2003 Fleer Fall Classics All-American Autographs 50

MINT NRMT
*AUTO 50: .5X TO 1.2X AUTO 100
RANDOM INSERTS IN PACKS
STATED PRINT RUN 50 SERIAL #'d SETS
MS Mike Schmidt 80.00 36.00
OS Ozzie Smith 80.00 36.00

2003 Fleer Fall Classics All-American Game Used

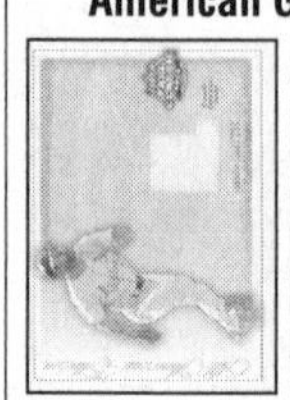

MINT NRMT
RANDOM INSERTS IN PACKS
STATED PRINT RUN 100 SERIAL #'d SETS
AK Al Kaline Bat 25.00 11.00
AT Alan Trammell Jsy 15.00 6.75
BM Bill Mazeroski Bat 15.00 6.75
BR Brooks Robinson Bat 25.00 11.00
CR Cal Ripken Jsy 80.00 36.00
DS Duke Snider Pants 25.00 11.00
EMA Eddie Mathews Bat 25.00 11.00
EMU Eddie Murray Jsy 25.00 11.00
FR Frank Robinson Bat 15.00 6.75
GH Gil Hodges Bat
LA Luis Aparicio Jsy 15.00 6.75
NR Nolan Ryan Jsy
OS Ozzie Smith Jsy 40.00 18.00
RJ Reggie Jackson Jsy 25.00 11.00
SM Stan Musial Jsy 50.00 22.00
TS Tom Seaver Jsy 25.00 11.00
WB Wade Boggs Patch 25.00 11.00
YB Yogi Berra Pants 25.00 11.00

2003 Fleer Fall Classics All-American Game Used Autographs

MINT NRMT

RANDOM INSERTS IN PACKS ....
STATED PRINT RUN 25 SERIAL #'d SETS
NO PRICING DUE TO SCARCITY ....

AK Al Kaline Bat
AT Alan Trammell Patch
BM Bill Mazeroski Bat
BR Brooks Robinson Bat
BS Moose Skowron Bat
CF Carlton Fisk Jsy
DS Duke Snider Pants
FL Fred Lynn Patch
GB George Brett Jsy
HK Harmon Killebrew Bat
JB Johnny Bench Patch
LA Luis Aparicio Jsy
MS Mike Schmidt Jsy
NR Nolan Ryan Jsy
OS Ozzie Smith Patch
SC Steve Carlton Jsy
SM Stan Musial Bat

2003 Fleer Fall Classics Legendary Collection Memorabilia

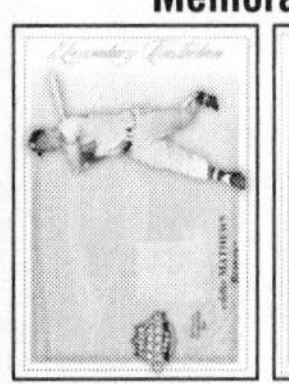

STATED ODDS 1:1 LGD STAR ....
SP INFO PROVIDED BY FLEER ....

	MINT	NRMT
DSO Duke Snider Pants	10.00	4.50
DSY Darryl Strawberry Bat	10.00	4.50
EM Eddie Mathews Bat SP	20.00	9.00
EMY Eddie Murray Bat	10.00	4.50
FR Frank Robinson Bat	10.00	4.50
GH Gil Hodges Jsy SP	15.00	6.75
NR Nolan Ryan Jsy	40.00	18.00
RJ Reggie Jackson Jsy	10.00	4.50
RM Roger Maris Pants SP	50.00	22.00
YB Yogi Berra Pants	10.00	4.50

2003 Fleer Fall Classics Pennant Aggression

RANDOM INSERTS IN PACKS ....
PRINT RUNS B/WN 1908-1985 COPIES PER

	MINT	NRMT
1 Ty Cobb/1908	8.00	3.60
2 Honus Wagner/1909	8.00	3.60
3 Walter Johnson/1924	5.00	2.20
4 Jimmie Foxx/1930	5.00	2.20
5 Frankie Frisch/1931	3.00	1.35
6 Pee Wee Reese/1947	5.00	2.20
7 Yogi Berra/1951	5.00	2.20
8 Roy Campanella/1953	5.00	2.20
9 Whitey Ford/1961	5.00	2.20
10 Frank Robinson/1966	3.00	1.35
11 Carl Yastrzemski/1967	8.00	3.60
12 Brooks Robinson/1970	5.00	2.20
13 Johnny Bench/1972	5.00	2.20
14 Reggie Jackson/1973	5.00	2.20
15 Catfish Hunter/1974	5.00	2.20
16 Joe Morgan/1975	3.00	1.35
17 Thurman Munson/1976	6.00	2.70
18 Willie Stargell/1979	5.00	2.20
19 Mike Schmidt/1980	10.00	4.50
20 George Brett/1985	12.00	5.50

2003 Fleer Fall Classics Pennant Aggression Game Used

MINT NRMT

STATED PRINT RUN 100 SERIAL #'d SETS
*PATCH: 1X TO 2X BASIC...................
PATCH PRINT RUN 50 SERIAL #'d SETS
RANDOM INSERTS IN PACKS ....

	MINT	NRMT
BR Brooks Robinson Bat	25.00	11.00
CH Catfish Hunter Jsy	25.00	11.00
CM Joe Morgan Jsy	15.00	6.75
CY Carl Yastrzemski Jsy	40.00	18.00
FR Frank Robinson Jsy	15.00	6.75
GB George Brett Jsy	80.00	36.00
JB Johnny Bench Jsy	25.00	11.00
MS Mike Schmidt Jsy	40.00	18.00
RJ Reggie Jackson Jsy	25.00	11.00
TM Thurman Munson Jsy	40.00	18.00
WS Willie Stargell Jsy	25.00	11.00
YB Yogi Berra Jsy	25.00	11.00

2003 Fleer Fall Classics Postseason Glory

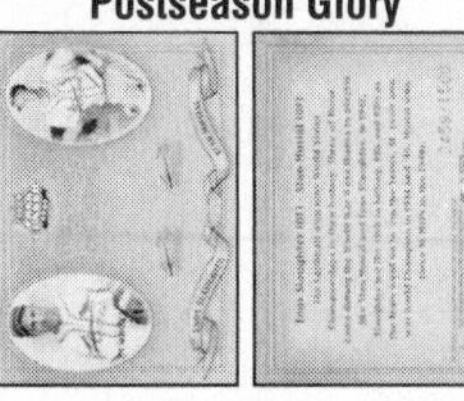

Randomly inserted into packs, these 30 cards link a few of the greats that have made pennant races and World Series so memorable over the years. Please note that there is a sliding scale for the print runs for these cards and cards 1-15 are serial numbered to 1500 while cards 16 through 25 are numbered to 750 and cards numbered 26 to 30 are serial numbered to 100. Card number 17 was never issued for this set.

	MINT	NRMT
1 Carlton Fisk Carl Yastrzemski	8.00	3.60
2 Enos Slaughter Stan Musial	8.00	3.60
3 Reggie Jackson Thurman Munson	6.00	2.70
4 Eddie Plank Christy Mathewson	5.00	2.20
5 Cy Young Jimmy Sebring	5.00	2.20
6 Yogi Berra Whitey Ford	5.00	2.20
7 Mickey Lolich Alan Trammell	5.00	2.20
8 Eddie Mathews Red Schoendienst	5.00	2.20
9 Roy Campanella Pee Wee Reese	5.00	2.20
10 Joe Carter Bill Mazeroski	3.00	1.35
11 Brooks Robinson Frank Robinson	5.00	2.20
12 Tom Seaver Gil Hodges	5.00	2.20
13 Robin Yount Paul Molitor	8.00	3.60
14 Dave Parker Willie Stargell	5.00	2.20
15 Cal Ripken Jim Palmer	15.00	6.75
16 Babe Ruth Whitey Ford	15.00	6.75
18 Lou Brock Bob Gibson	6.00	2.70
19 Mike Schmidt Brooks Robinson	12.00	5.50
20 Johnny Bench Thurman Munson	8.00	3.60
21 Nolan Ryan Walter Johnson	12.00	5.50
22 Don Drysdale Duke Snider	6.00	2.70
23 Joe Carter Paul Molitor	6.00	2.70
24 Hughie Jennings Ty Cobb	10.00	4.50
25 Cal Ripken Eddie Murray	20.00	9.00
26 Mike Schmidt Steve Carlton	25.00	11.00
27 Roberto Clemente Willie Stargell	50.00	22.00
28 Jim Palmer Nolan Ryan	40.00	18.00
29 Joe Morgan Johnny Bench	15.00	6.75
30 Lou Gehrig Babe Ruth	50.00	22.00

2003 Fleer Fall Classics Postseason Glory Dual Patch

MINT NRMT

*PATCH: 1X TO 2X BASIC DUAL JSY .
RANDOM INSERTS IN PACKS ....
STATED PRINT RUN 50 SERIAL #'d SETS

	MINT	NRMT
LBBG Lou Brock Bob Gibson	60.00	27.00

2003 Fleer Fall Classics Postseason Glory Dual Swatch

MINT NRMT

RANDOM INSERTS IN PACKS ....

STATED PRINT RUN 100 SERIAL #'d SETS

	MINT	NRMT
BRFR Brooks Robinson Bat Frank Robinson Bat	40.00	18.00
CFCY Carlton Fisk Jsy Carl Yastrzemski Jsy	60.00	27.00
CREM Cal Ripken Jsy Eddie Murray Jsy	100.00	45.00
DDDS Don Drysdale Jsy Duke Snider Pants	40.00	18.00
JMJB Joe Morgan Jsy Johnny Bench Jsy	40.00	18.00
JPNR Jim Palmer Jsy Nolan Ryan Jsy	60.00	27.00
MSSC Mike Schmidt Jsy Steve Carlton Jsy	40.00	18.00
RJTM Reggie Jackson Jsy Thurman Munson Pants	80.00	36.00
RYPM Robin Yount Jsy Paul Molitor Jsy	40.00	18.00
YBWF Yogi Berra Pants Whitey Ford Jsy	40.00	18.00

2003 Fleer Fall Classics Postseason Glory Quad Patch

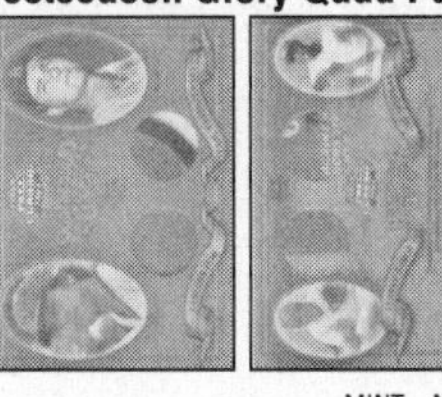

MINT NRMT

RANDOM INSERTS IN PACKS ....
STATED PRINT RUN 1 SERIAL #'d SET
NO PRICING DUE TO SCARCITY ....

2003 Fleer Fall Classics Postseason Glory Quad Swatch

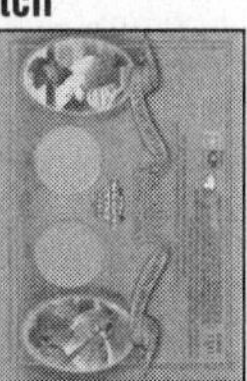

MINT NRMT

RANDOM INSERTS IN PACKS ....
STATED PRINT RUN 25 SERIAL #'d SETS
NO PRICING DUE TO SCARCITY ....

BFJM Yogi Berra Pants
Whitey Ford Jsy
Reggie Jackson Jsy
Thurman Munson Pants
FGPR Whitey Ford Jsy
Bob Gibson Jsy
Jim Palmer Jsy
Nolan Ryan Jsy
FYMB Carlton Fisk Jsy
Carl Yastrzemski Jsy
Joe Morgan Jsy
Johnny Bench Jsy
JRMR Reggie Jackson Bat
Babe Ruth Bat
Eddie Mathews Bat
Frank Robinson Bat
JSBR Reggie Jackson Jsy
Willie Stargell Bat
Johnny Bench Jsy
Brooks Robinson Bat
MYMR Robin Yount Jsy
Paul Molitor Jsy
Cal Ripken Jsy
Eddie Murray Jsy
RMSS Cal Ripken Jsy
Joe Morgan Jsy
Mike Schmidt Jsy
Willie Stargell Bat
RRPR Brooks Robinson Bat
Frank Robinson Bat
Cal Ripken Jsy
Jim Palmer Jsy

2003 Fleer Fall Classics Postseason Glory Single Patch

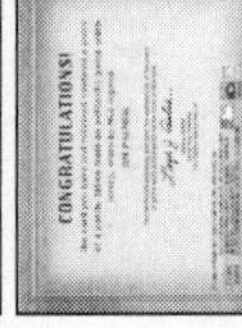

MINT NRMT

RANDOM INSERTS IN PACKS ....
STATED PRINT RUN 75 SERIAL #'d SETS

	MINT	NRMT
BG Bob Gibson-Brock	40.00	18.00
CF Carlton Fisk-Yaz	40.00	18.00
CR Cal Ripken-Murray	100.00	45.00
CY Carl Yastrzemski-Fisk	80.00	36.00
EM Eddie Murray-Ripken	40.00	18.00
JB Johnny Bench-Morgan	40.00	18.00
JM Joe Morgan-Bench	25.00	11.00
JP Jim Palmer-Ryan	25.00	11.00
LB Lou Brock-Gibson	40.00	18.00
MS Mike Schmidt-Carlton	60.00	27.00
NR Nolan Ryan-Palmer	100.00	45.00
PM Paul Molitor-Yount	40.00	18.00
RY Robin Yount-Molitor	60.00	27.00
SC Steve Carlton-Schmidt	25.00	11.00

2003 Fleer Fall Classics Postseason Glory Single Swatch

MINT NRMT

RANDOM INSERTS IN PACKS ....
STATED PRINT RUN 150 SERIAL #'d SETS

	MINT	NRMT
BG Bob Gibson Jsy-Brock	15.00	6.75
BRO Brooks Robinson Bat-F.Rob	15.00	6.75
BRU Babe Ruth Bat-Gehrig	150.00	70.00
CF Carlton Fisk Jsy-Yaz	15.00	6.75
CR Cal Ripken Jsy-Murray	50.00	22.00
CY Carl Yastrzemski Jsy-Fisk	40.00	18.00
DD Don Drysdale Jsy-Snider	15.00	6.75
DP Dave Parker Bat-Stargell	10.00	4.50
DS Duke Snider Pants-Drysdale	15.00	6.75
EM Eddie Murray Jsy-Ripken	25.00	11.00
FR Frank Robinson Bat-Brooks	10.00	4.50
JB Johnny Bench Jsy-Morgan	15.00	6.75
JC Joe Carter Bat-Molitor	10.00	4.50
JM Joe Morgan Jsy-Bench	10.00	4.50
JP Jim Palmer Jsy-Ryan	15.00	6.75
LB Lou Brock Jsy-Gibson	15.00	6.75
MS Mike Schmidt Jsy-Carlton	30.00	13.50
NR Nolan Ryan Jsy-Palmer	50.00	22.00
PMC Paul Molitor Jsy-Carter	15.00	6.75
PMY Paul Molitor Jsy-Yount	25.00	11.00
RJ Reggie Jackson Jsy-Munson	15.00	6.75
RY Robin Yount Jsy-Molitor	25.00	11.00
SC Steve Carlton Jsy-Schmidt	10.00	4.50
TMO T.Munson Pants-Reggie	25.00	11.00
WF Whitey Ford Jsy-Berra	15.00	6.75
WS Willie Stargell Bat-Parker	15.00	6.75
YB Yogi Berra Pants-Ford	15.00	6.75

2003 Fleer Fall Classics Series Contenders Bat

A few cards in this set were produced in smaller quantities and we have notated that information with an SP next to the player's name in our checklist.

STATED ODDS 1:111 RETAIL ....
KNOBS PRINT RUN B/WN 9-10 COPIES PER
NO KNOBS PRICING DUE TO SCARCITY

	MINT	NRMT
AK Al Kaline	25.00	11.00
BD Bill Dickey	15.00	6.75
CF Carlton Fisk	15.00	6.75
DM Don Mattingly	40.00	18.00
DS Darryl Strawberry	15.00	6.75
HK Harmon Killebrew	25.00	11.00
JC Jose Canseco	25.00	11.00
PR Phil Rizzuto SP	15.00	6.75
WM Willie McCovey SP	15.00	6.75

2003 Fleer Fall Classics Series Contenders Bat Knobs

MINT NRMT

RANDOM INSERTS IN PACKS ....
PRINT RUNS B/WN 9-10 COPIES PER
NO PRICING DUE TO SCARCITY ....

2003 Fleer Fall Classics Yankees Penstripes Autographs Anniversary

Randomly inserted into packs, these five cards feature authentic autographs from players who participated with the Yankees in the World Series. Each of the cards were issued to a stated print run of 100 serial numbered sets.

MINT NRMT

WS PRINT RUN 26 SERIAL #'d SETS .
NO WS PRICING DUE TO SCARCITY ..
RANDOM INSERTS IN PACKS ....

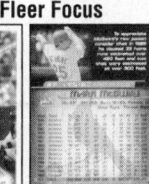

	MINT	NRMT
BS Moose Skowron	25.00	11.00
DM Don Mattingly	120.00	55.00
DW Dave Winfield	40.00	18.00
RJ Reggie Jackson	40.00	18.00
WB Wade Boggs	40.00	18.00

2000 Fleer Focus

The 2000 Fleer Focus product was released in April, 2000 as a 250-card set. The set features 225-player cards (cards 1-225), and 25-prospect cards (cards 226-250). Cards numbered 226 through 250 were issued in two separate varieties. The first 999 of each of these cards feature a portrait shot on the front of the featured prospect. The next 3,000 cards issued have an action shot on the front of the featured prospect. Due to how this set was issued, collectors can consider the set complete minus short prints at 225 cards; complete with the more common pose of the prospect player at 250 cards; or complete as a master set with all 275 cards.

	Nm-Mt	Ex-Mt
COMP.MASTER SET (275)	500.00	150.00
COMP.SET w/2999's (250)	150.00	45.00
COMP.SET w/o SP's (225)	25.00	7.50
COMMON CARD (1-225)	.30	.09
COMMON (226-250)	5.00	1.50
COMMON (226P-250P)	10.00	3.00
1 Nomar Garciaparra	1.25	.35
2 Adrian Beltre	.30	.09
3 Miguel Tejada	.30	.09
4 Joe Randa	.30	.09
5 Larry Walker	.50	.15
6 Jeff Weaver	.30	.09
7 Jay Bell	.30	.09
8 Ivan Rodriguez	.75	.23
9 Edgar Martinez	.50	.15
10 Desi Relaford	.30	.09
11 Derek Jeter	2.00	.60
12 Delino DeShields	.30	.09
13 Craig Biggio	.50	.15
14 Chuck Knoblauch	.30	.09
15 Chuck Finley	.30	.09
16 Brett Tomko	.30	.09
17 Bobby Higginson	.30	.09
18 Pedro Martinez	.75	.23
19 Troy O'Leary	.30	.09
20 Rickey Henderson	.75	.23
21 Robb Nen	.30	.09
22 Rolando Arrojo	.30	.09
23 Rondell White	.30	.09
24 Royce Clayton	.30	.09
25 Rusty Greer	.30	.09
26 Stan Spencer	.30	.09
27 Steve Finley	.30	.09
28 Tom Goodwin	.30	.09
29 Troy Percival	.30	.09
30 Wilton Guerrero	.30	.09
31 Roberto Alomar	.75	.23
32 Mike Hampton	.30	.09
33 Michael Barrett	.30	.09
34 Curt Schilling	.50	.15
35 Bill Mueller	.30	.09
36 Bernie Williams	.50	.15
37 John Smoltz	.50	.15
38 B.J. Surhoff	.30	.09
39 Pete Harnisch	.30	.09
40 Juan Encarnacion	.30	.09
41 Derrek Lee	.30	.09
42 Jeff Shaw	.30	.09
43 David Cone	.30	.09
44 Jason Christiansen	.30	.09
45 Jeff Kent	.30	.09
46 Randy Johnson	.75	.23
47 Todd Walker	.30	.09
48 Jose Lima	.30	.09
49 Jason Giambi	.75	.23
50 Ken Griffey Jr. Reds	1.25	.35
51 Bartolo Colon	.30	.09
52 Mike Lieberthal	.30	.09
53 Shane Reynolds	.30	.09
54 Travis Lee	.30	.09
55 Travis Fryman	.30	.09
56 John Valentin	.30	.09
57 Joey Hamilton	.30	.09
58 Jay Buhner	.30	.09
59 Brad Radke	.30	.09
60 A.J. Burnett	.30	.09
61 Roy Halladay	.30	.09
62 Raul Mondesi	.30	.09
63 Matt Mantei	.30	.09
64 Mark Grace	.50	.15
65 David Justice	.30	.09
66 Billy Wagner	.30	.09
67 Eric Milton	.30	.09
68 Eric Chavez	.30	.09
69 Doug Glanville	.30	.09
70 Ray Durham	.30	.09
71 Mike Sirotka	.30	.09
72 Greg Vaughn	.30	.09
73 Brian Jordan	.30	.09
74 Alex Gonzalez	.30	.09

75 Alex Rodriguez 1.25 .35
76 David Nilsson .30 .09
77 Robin Ventura .50 .15
78 Kevin Young .30 .09
79 Wilson Alvarez .30 .09
80 Matt Williams .30 .09
81 Ismael Valdes .30 .09
82 Kenny Lofton .30 .09
83 Carlos Beltran .30 .09
84 Doug Mientkiewicz .30 .09
85 Wally Joyner .30 .09
86 J.D. Drew .30 .09
87 Carlos Delgado .30 .09
88 Tony Womack .30 .09
89 Eric Young .30 .09
90 Manny Ramirez .30 .09
91 Johnny Damon .30 .09
92 Torii Hunter .30 .09
93 Kenny Rogers .30 .09
94 Trevor Hoffman .30 .09
95 John Wetteland .30 .09
96 Ray Lankford .30 .09
97 Tom Glavine .50 .15
98 Carlos Lee .30 .09
99 Richie Sexson .30 .09
100 Carlos Febles .30 .09
101 Chad Allen .30 .09
102 Sterling Hitchcock .30 .09
103 Joe McEwing .30 .09
104 Justin Thompson .30 .09
105 Jim Edmonds .30 .09
106 Kerry Wood .75 .23
107 Jim Thome .75 .23
108 Jeremy Giambi .30 .09
109 Mike Piazza 1.25 .35
110 Darryl Kile .30 .09
111 Darin Erstad .30 .09
112 Kyle Farnsworth .30 .09
113 Omar Vizquel .30 .09
114 Orber Moreno .30 .09
115 Al Leiter .30 .09
116 John Olerud .30 .09
117 Aaron Sele .30 .09
118 Chipper Jones .75 .23
119 Paul Konerko .30 .09
120 Chris Singleton .30 .09
121 Fernando Vina .30 .09
122 Andy Ashby .30 .09
123 Eli Marrero .30 .09
124 Edgar Renteria .30 .09
125 Roberto Hernandez .30 .09
126 Andruw Jones .30 .09
127 Magglio Ordonez .30 .09
128 Bob Wickman .30 .09
129 Tony Gwynn 1.00 .30
130 Mark McGwire 2.00 .60
131 Albert Belle .30 .09
132 Pokey Reese .30 .09
133 Tony Clark .30 .09
134 Jeff Bagwell .50 .15
135 Mark Grudzielanek .30 .09
136 Dustin Hermanson .30 .09
137 Reggie Sanders .30 .09
138 Ryan Rupe .30 .09
139 Kevin Millwood .30 .09
140 Bret Saberhagen .30 .09
141 Juan Guzman .30 .09
142 Alex Gonzalez .30 .09
143 Gary Sheffield .30 .09
144 Roger Clemens 1.50 .45
145 Ben Grieve .30 .09
146 Bobby Abreu .30 .09
147 Brian Giles .30 .09
148 Quinton McCracken .30 .09
149 Freddy Garcia .30 .09
150 Erubiel Durazo .30 .09
151 Sidney Ponson .30 .09
152 Scott Williamson .30 .09
153 Ken Caminiti .30 .09
154 Vladimir Guerrero .75 .23
155 Andy Pettitte .50 .15
156 Edwards Guzman .30 .09
157 Shannon Stewart .30 .09
158 Greg Maddux 1.25 .35
159 Mike Stanley .30 .09
160 Sean Casey .30 .09
161 Cliff Floyd .30 .09
162 Devon White .30 .09
163 Scott Brosius .30 .09
164 Marlon Anderson .30 .09
165 Jason Kendall .30 .09
166 Ryan Klesko .30 .09
167 Sammy Sosa 1.25 .35
168 Frank Thomas .75 .23
169 Geoff Jenkins .30 .09
170 Jason Schmidt .30 .09
171 Dan Wilson .30 .09
172 Jose Canseco .75 .23
173 Troy Glaus .50 .15
174 Mariano Rivera .50 .15
175 Scott Rolen .50 .15
176 J.T. Snow .30 .09
177 Rafael Palmeiro .50 .15
178 A.J. Hinch .30 .09
179 Jose Offerman .30 .09
180 Jeff Cirillo .30 .09
181 Dean Palmer .30 .09
182 Jose Rosado .30 .09
183 Armando Benitez .30 .09
184 Brady Anderson .30 .09
185 Cal Ripken 2.50 .75
186 Barry Larkin .75 .23
187 Damion Easley .30 .09
188 Moises Alou .30 .09
189 Todd Hundley .30 .09
190 Tim Hudson .50 .15
191 Livan Hernandez .30 .09
192 Fred McGriff .50 .15
193 Orlando Hernandez .30 .09
194 Tim Salmon .50 .15
195 Mike Mussina .75 .23
196 Todd Helton .50 .15
197 Juan Gonzalez .75 .23
198 Kevin Brown .50 .15
199 Ugueth Urbina .30 .09
200 Matt Stairs .30 .09
201 Shawn Estes .30 .09
202 Gabe Kapler .30 .09
203 Javy Lopez .30 .09
204 Henry Rodriguez .30 .09
205 Dante Bichette .30 .09
206 Jeromy Burnitz .30 .09
207 Todd Zeile .30 .09
208 Rico Brogna .30 .09
209 Warren Morris .30 .09
210 David Segui .30 .09
211 Vinny Castilla .30 .09
212 Mo Vaughn .30 .09
213 Charles Johnson .30 .09
214 Neifi Perez .30 .09
215 Shawn Green .30 .09
216 Carl Pavano .30 .09
217 Tino Martinez .50 .15
218 Barry Bonds 2.00 .60
219 David Wells .30 .09
220 Paul O'Neill .50 .15
221 Masato Yoshii .30 .09
222 Kris Benson .30 .09
223 Fernando Tatis .30 .09
224 Lee Stevens .30 .09
225 Jose Cruz Jr. .30 .09
226 Rick Ankiel 5.00 1.50
226P Rick Ankiel PORT 10.00 3.00
227 Matt Riley 5.00 1.50
227P Matt Riley PORT 10.00 3.00
228 Norm Hutchins 5.00 1.50
228P N.Hutchins PORT 10.00 3.00
229 Ruben Mateo 5.00 1.50
229P Ruben Mateo PORT 10.00 3.00
230 Ben Petrick 5.00 1.50
230P Ben Petrick PORT 10.00 3.00
231 Mario Encarnacion 5.00 1.50
231P M.Encarnacion PORT 10.00 3.00
232 Nick Johnson 5.00 1.50
232P Nick Johnson PORT 10.00 3.00
233 Adam Piatt 5.00 1.50
233P Adam Piatt PORT 10.00 3.00
234 Mike Darr 5.00 1.50
234P Mike Darr PORT 10.00 3.00
235 Chad Hermansen 5.00 1.50
235P C.Hermansen PORT 10.00 3.00
236 Wily Pena 5.00 1.50
236P Wily Pena PORT 10.00 3.00
237 Octavio Dotel 5.00 1.50
237P Octavio Dotel PORT 10.00 3.00
238 Vernon Wells 5.00 1.50
238P Vernon Wells PORT 10.00 3.00
239 Daryle Ward 5.00 1.50
239P Daryle Ward PORT 10.00 3.00
240 Adam Kennedy 5.00 1.50
240P A.Kennedy PORT 10.00 3.00
241 Angel Pena 5.00 1.50
241P Angel Pena PORT 10.00 3.00
242 Lance Berkman 5.00 1.50
242P L.Berkman PORT 10.00 3.00
243 Gabe Molina 5.00 1.50
243P Gabe Molina PORT 10.00 3.00
244 Steve Lomasney 5.00 1.50
244P S.Lomasney PORT 10.00 3.00
245 Jacob Cruz 5.00 1.50
245P Jacob Cruz PORT 10.00 3.00
246 Mark Quinn 5.00 1.50
246P Mark Quinn PORT 10.00 3.00
247 Eric Munson 5.00 1.50
247P Eric Munson PORT 10.00 3.00
248 Alfonso Soriano 8.00 2.40
248P A.Soriano PORT 12.00 3.60
249 Kip Wells 5.00 1.50
249P Kip Wells PORT 10.00 3.00
250 Josh Beckett 5.00 1.50
250P Josh Beckett PORT 15.00 4.50

2000 Fleer Focus Masterpiece Errors

Randomly inserted into packs, this set features error cards of 25 of the Masterpiece edition parallels. The cards look just like the Masterpiece parallels, however, these cards lack the "One of One" stamp on the back of the card.

Nm-Mt Ex-Mt
50 Ken Griffey Jr. Reds 15.00 4.50
202 Gabe Kapler 4.00 1.20
203 Javy Lopez 4.00 1.20
204 Henry Rodriguez 4.00 1.20
205 Dante Bichette 4.00 1.20
206 Jeromy Burnitz 4.00 1.20
207 Todd Zeile 4.00 1.20
208 Rico Brogna 4.00 1.20
209 Warren Morris 4.00 1.20
210 David Segui 4.00 1.20
211 Vinny Castilla 4.00 1.20
212 Mo Vaughn 4.00 1.20
213 Charles Johnson 4.00 1.20
214 Neifi Perez 4.00 1.20
215 Shawn Green 4.00 1.20
216 Carl Pavano 4.00 1.20
217 Tino Martinez 6.00 1.80
218 Barry Bonds 25.00 7.50
219 David Wells 4.00 1.20
220 Paul O'Neill 6.00 1.80
221 Masato Yoshii 4.00 1.20
222 Kris Benson 4.00 1.20
223 Fernando Tatis 4.00 1.20
224 Lee Stevens 4.00 1.20
225 Jose Cruz Jr. 4.00 1.20

2000 Fleer Focus Masterpiece Mania

Randomly inserted into packs, this 250-card set is a complete parallel of the Fleer Focus base set. There were only 300 serial numbered sets of this insert produced.

Nm-Mt Ex-Mt
*STARS 1-225: 6X TO 15X BASIC CARDS
*ROOKIES 226-250: .5X TO 1.2X BASIC

2000 Fleer Focus Feel the Game

Randomly inserted into packs at one in 288, this 10-card insert set features game-used jersey patches of some of the best players in major league baseball.

Nm-Mt Ex-Mt
1 Cal Ripken 50.00 15.00
2 Randy Johnson 15.00 4.50
3 Alex Rodriguez 25.00 7.50
4 Scott Rolen 15.00 4.50

5 Javy Lopez 10.00 3.00
6 Vladimir Guerrero 15.00 4.50
7 Tom Glavine 15.00 4.50
8 Tim Salmon 15.00 4.50
9 Adrian Beltre 10.00 3.00
10 Miguel Tejada 10.00 3.00

2000 Fleer Focus Focal Points

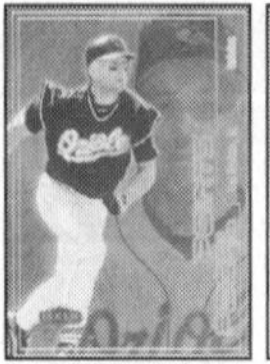

Randomly inserted into packs at one in six, this set features 15 players that play the game with style and grace. Card backs carry a "F" prefix.

Nm-Mt Ex-Mt
COMPLETE SET (15) 25.00 7.50
*STRIKING: 8X TO 20X BASIC FOCAL
STRIKING RANDOM IN HOBBY PACKS
STRIKING PRINT RUN 50 SERIAL #'d SETS
F1 Mark McGwire 3.00 .90
F2 Tony Gwynn 1.50 .45
F3 Nomar Garciaparra 2.00 .60
F4 Juan Gonzalez 1.25 .35
F5 Jeff Bagwell .75 .23
F6 Chipper Jones 1.25 .35
F7 Cal Ripken 4.00 1.20
F8 Alex Rodriguez 2.00 .60
F9 Scott Rolen .75 .23
F10 Vladimir Guerrero 1.25 .35
F11 Mike Piazza 2.00 .60
F12 Frank Thomas 1.25 .35
F13 Ken Griffey Jr. 2.00 .60
F14 Sammy Sosa 2.00 .60
F15 Derek Jeter 3.00 .90

2000 Fleer Focus Fresh Ink

Randomly inserted into packs at one in 96, this 48-card set features certified autographs of players such as J.D. Drew, Tony Gwynn, and Shawn Green. Exchange cards for Troy Glaus and Mike Lieberthal had an exchange deadline of 5/31/01. The Tony Gwynn and Derek Jeter cards were not on original checklists and were late additions seeded into packs just prior to shipping. According to Fleer, Jeter signed only 100 cards (though they are not serial numbered). The cards are unnumbered and checklisted in alphabetical order by player's last name.

Nm-Mt Ex-Mt
1 Chad Allen 10.00 3.00
2 Michael Barrett 10.00 3.00
3 Josh Beckett 40.00 12.00
4 Rob Bell 10.00 3.00
5 Adrian Beltre 15.00 4.50
6 Milton Bradley 15.00 4.50
7 Rico Brogna 10.00 3.00
8 Mike Cameron 15.00 4.50
9 Eric Chavez 15.00 4.50
10 Bruce Chen 10.00 3.00
11 Johnny Damon 15.00 4.50
12 Ben Davis 10.00 3.00
13 J.D. Drew 15.00 4.50
14 Erubiel Durazo 15.00 4.50
15 Jeremy Giambi 10.00 3.00
16 Jason Giambi 40.00 12.00
17 Doug Glanville 10.00 3.00
18 Troy Glaus 25.00 7.50
19 Shawn Green 15.00 4.50
20 Tony Gwynn 60.00 18.00
21 Mike Hampton 15.00 4.50
22 Tim Hudson 25.00 7.50
23 John Jaha 10.00 3.00
24 Derek Jeter 150.00 45.00
25 D'Angelo Jimenez 10.00 3.00
26 Nick Johnson 15.00 4.50
27 Randy Johnson SP 100.00 30.00
28 Andruw Jones 25.00 7.50
29 Jason Kendall 15.00 4.50
30 Adam Kennedy 15.00 4.50
31 Mike Lieberthal 15.00 4.50
32 Edgar Martinez 40.00 12.00
33 Aaron McNeal 15.00 4.50
34 Kevin Millwood 15.00 4.50
35 Mike Mussina 40.00 12.00
36 Magglio Ordonez 15.00 4.50
37 Eric Owens 10.00 3.00
38 Rafael Palmeiro 40.00 12.00
39 Wily Pena 10.00 3.00
40 Adam Piatt 10.00 3.00
41 Cal Ripken 120.00 36.00
42 Alex Rodriguez 100.00 30.00
43 Tim Salmon 25.00 7.50
44 Chris Singleton 10.00 3.00
45 Mike Sweeney 15.00 4.50
46 Jose Vidro 15.00 4.50
47 Rondell White 15.00 4.50
48 Jaret Wright 10.00 3.00

2000 Fleer Focus Future Vision

Randomly inserted into packs at one in nine, this 15-card insert set features the year's top rookies with an innovative twist. Card backs carry a "FV" prefix.

Nm-Mt Ex-Mt
COMPLETE SET (15) 15.00 4.50
FV1 Rick Ankiel 1.00 .30
FV2 Matt Riley 1.00 .30
FV3 Ruben Mateo 1.00 .30
FV4 Ben Petrick 1.00 .30
FV5 Mario Encarnacion 1.00 .30
FV6 Octavio Dotel 1.00 .30
FV7 Vernon Wells 1.00 .30
FV8 Adam Kennedy 1.00 .30
FV9 Lance Berkman 1.00 .30
FV10 Chad Hermansen 1.00 .30
FV11 Mark Quinn 1.00 .30
FV12 Eric Munson 1.00 .30
FV13 Alfonso Soriano 2.00 .60
FV14 Kip Wells 1.00 .30
FV15 Josh Beckett 2.50 .75

2000 Fleer Focus Pocus

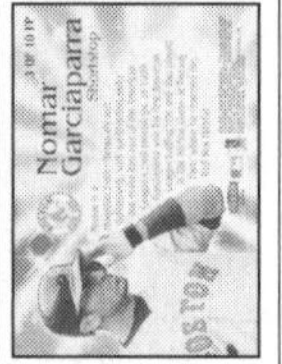

Randomly inserted into packs at one in 14, this set features 10 stars that display wizardry on the diamond. Card backs carry a "FP" prefix.

Nm-Mt Ex-Mt
COMPLETE SET (10) 50.00 15.00
FP1 Cal Ripken 8.00 2.40
FP2 Tony Gwynn 3.00 .90
FP3 Nomar Garciaparra 4.00 1.20
FP4 Juan Gonzalez 2.50 .75
FP5 Mike Piazza 4.00 1.20
FP6 Mark McGwire 6.00 1.80
FP7 Chipper Jones 2.50 .75
FP8 Ken Griffey Jr. 4.00 1.20
FP9 Derek Jeter 6.00 1.80
FP10 Alex Rodriguez 4.00 1.20

2001 Fleer Focus

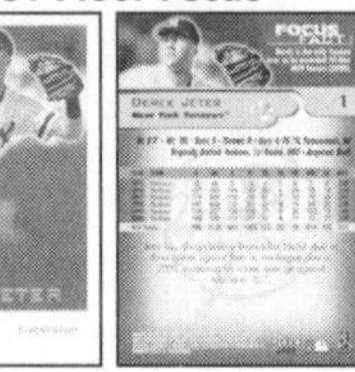

The 2001 Fleer Focus product was released in late January, 2001. Each pack contained 10 cards, and carried a suggested retail price of $2.99. The 240-card base set is broken into tiers as follows: Base Veterans (1-200), and Prospects (201-240 - individually serial numbered by position). Breakdowns for the prospect cards are as follows: First Baseman (201-207) - 2,499 of each, Third Baseman (208-211) - 2,999 of each, Catcher (212) - 3,499 of each, Outfielders (213-224) - 1,999 of each, Pitchers (225-235) - 4,999 of each and Second Baseman/Shortstops (236-240) - 3,999 of each. Though not confirmed by the manufacturer, reports from dealers indicate that on average each 24-pack box of Focus contained three Prospect cards. An additional ten cards (241-250) featuring a selection of top prosects was distributed in late December, 2001 within Fleer Platinum RC packs. Each of these cards is serial numbered to 999 copies.

Nm-Mt Ex-Mt
COMP.SET w/o SP's (200) 25.00 7.50
COMMON CARD (1-200) .30 .09
COMMON (201-240) 5.00 1.50
COMMON (241-250) 10.00 3.00
1 Derek Jeter 2.00 .60
2 Manny Ramirez .30 .09
3 Ken Griffey Jr. 1.25 .35
4 Ken Caminiti .30 .09
5 Joe Randa .30 .09
6 Jason Kendall .30 .09
7 Ron Coomer .30 .09
8 Rondell White .30 .09
9 Tino Martinez .50 .15
10 Nomar Garciaparra 1.25 .35
11 Tony Batista .30 .09
12 Todd Stottlemyre .30 .09
13 Ryan Klesko .30 .09
14 Darin Erstad .30 .09
15 Todd Walker .30 .09
16 Al Leiter .30 .09
17 Carl Everett .30 .09
18 Bobby Abreu .30 .09
19 Raul Mondesi .30 .09
20 Vladimir Guerrero .75 .23
21 Mike Bordick .30 .09
22 Aaron Sele .30 .09
23 Ray Lankford .30 .09
24 Roger Clemens 1.50 .45
25 Kevin Young .30 .09
26 Brad Radke .30 .09
27 Todd Hundley .30 .09
28 Ellis Burks .30 .09
29 Lee Stevens .30 .09
30 Eric Karros .30 .09
31 Darren Dreifort .30 .09
32 Ivan Rodriguez .75 .23
33 Pedro Martinez .75 .23
34 Travis Fryman .30 .09
35 Garret Anderson .30 .09
36 Rafael Palmeiro .50 .15
37 Jason Giambi .75 .23
38 Jeromy Burnitz .30 .09
39 Robin Ventura .30 .09
40 Derek Bell .30 .09
41 Carlos Guillen .30 .09
42 Albert Belle .30 .09
43 Henry Rodriguez .30 .09
44 Brian Jordan .30 .09
45 Mike Sweeney .30 .09
46 Ruben Rivera .30 .09
47 Greg Maddux 1.25 .35
48 Corey Koskie .30 .09
49 Sandy Alomar Jr. .30 .09
50 Mike Mussina .75 .23
51 Tom Glavine .50 .15
52 Aaron Boone .30 .09
53 Frank Thomas .75 .23
54 Kenny Lofton .30 .09
55 Danny Graves .30 .09
56 Jose Valentin .30 .09
57 Travis Lee .30 .09
58 Jim Edmonds .30 .09
59 Jim Thome .75 .23
60 Steve Finley .30 .09
61 Shawn Green .30 .09
62 Lance Berkman .30 .09
63 Mark Quinn .30 .09
64 Randy Johnson .75 .23
65 Dmitri Young .30 .09
66 Andy Pettitte .50 .15
67 Paul O'Neill .50 .15
68 Gil Heredia .30 .09
69 Russell Branyan .30 .09
70 Alex Rodriguez 1.25 .35
71 Geoff Jenkins .30 .09
72 Eric Chavez .30 .09
73 Cal Ripken 2.50 .75
74 Mark Kotsay .30 .09
75 Jeff D'Amico .30 .09
76 Tony Womack .30 .09
77 Eric Milton .30 .09
78 Joe Girardi .30 .09
79 Peter Bergeron .30 .09
80 Miguel Tejada .30 .09
81 Luis Gonzalez .30 .09
82 Doug Glanville .30 .09
83 Gerald Williams .30 .09
84 Troy O'Leary .30 .09
85 Brian Giles .30 .09
86 Miguel Cairo .30 .09
87 Magglio Ordonez .30 .09
88 Rick Helling .30 .09
89 Bruce Chen .30 .09
90 Jason Varitek .30 .09
91 Mike Lieberthal .30 .09
92 Shawn Estes .30 .09
93 Rick Ankiel .30 .09
94 Tim Salmon .50 .15
95 Jacque Jones .30 .09
96 Johnny Damon .30 .09
97 Larry Walker .50 .15
98 Ruben Mateo .30 .09
99 Brad Fullmer .30 .09
100 Edgardo Alfonzo .30 .09
101 Mark Mulder .30 .09
102 Tony Gwynn 1.00 .30
103 Mike Cameron .30 .09
104 Richie Sexson .30 .09
105 Barry Larkin .75 .23
106 Mike Piazza 1.25 .35
107 Eric Young .30 .09
108 Edgar Renteria .30 .09
109 Todd Zeile .30 .09
110 Luis Castillo .30 .09
111 Sammy Sosa 1.25 .35
112 David Justice .30 .09
113 Delino DeShields .30 .09
114 Mariano Rivera .50 .15
115 Edgar Martinez .50 .15
116 Ray Durham .30 .09
117 Brady Anderson .30 .09
118 Eric Owens .30 .09
119 Alex Gonzalez .30 .09
120 Jay Buhner .30 .09
121 Greg Vaughn .30 .09
122 Mike Lowell .30 .09
123 Marquis Grissom .30 .09
124 Matt Williams .30 .09
125 Dean Palmer .30 .09
126 Troy Glaus .50 .15
127 Bret Boone .30 .09
128 David Ortiz .30 .09
129 Glenallen Hill .30 .09
130 Chipper Jones .75 .23
131 Tony Clark .30 .09
132 Terrence Long .30 .09
133 Chuck Finley .30 .09
134 Jeff Bagwell .50 .15
135 J.T. Snow .30 .09
136 Andruw Jones .30 .09
137 Carlos Delgado .30 .09
138 Mo Vaughn .30 .09
139 Derrek Lee .30 .09
140 Bobby Estalella .30 .09
141 Kerry Wood .75 .23
142 Jose Vidro .30 .09
143 Ben Grieve .30 .09
144 Barry Bonds 2.00 .60
145 Javy Lopez .30 .09
146 Adam Kennedy .30 .09
147 Jeff Cirillo .30 .09

148 Cliff Floyd .30 .09
149 Carl Pavano .30 .09
150 Bobby Higginson .30 .09
151 Kevin Brown .30 .09
152 Fernando Tatis .30 .09
153 Matt Lawton .30 .09
154 Damion Easley .30 .09
155 Curt Schilling .50 .15
156 Mark McGwire 2.00 .60
157 Mark Grace .50 .15
158 Adrian Beltre .30 .09
159 Jorge Posada .50 .15
160 Richard Hidalgo .30 .09
161 Vinny Castilla .30 .09
162 Bernie Williams .50 .15
163 John Olerud .30 .09
164 Todd Helton .50 .15
165 Craig Biggio .50 .15
166 David Wells .30 .09
167 Phil Nevin .30 .09
168 Andres Galarraga .30 .09
169 Moises Alou .30 .09
170 Denny Neagle .30 .09
171 Jeffrey Hammonds .30 .09
172 Sean Casey .30 .09
173 Gary Sheffield .30 .09
174 Carlos Lee .30 .09
175 Juan Encarnacion .30 .09
176 Roberto Alomar .75 .23
177 Kenny Rogers .30 .09
178 Charles Johnson .30 .09
179 Shannon Stewart .30 .09
180 B.J. Surhoff .30 .09
181 Paul Konerko .30 .09
182 Jermaine Dye .30 .09
183 Scott Rolen .50 .15
184 Fred McGriff .50 .15
185 Juan Gonzalez .75 .23
186 Carlos Beltran .30 .09
187 Jay Payton .30 .09
188 Chad Hermansen .30 .09
189 Pat Burrell .30 .09
190 Omar Vizquel .30 .09
191 Trot Nixon .50 .15
192 Mike Hampton .30 .09
193 Kris Benson .30 .09
194 Gabe Kapler .30 .09
195 Rickey Henderson .75 .23
196 J.D. Drew .30 .09
197 Pokey Reese .30 .09
198 Jeff Kent .30 .09
199 Jose Cruz Jr. .30 .09
200 Preston Wilson .30 .09
201 Eric Munson/2499 5.00 1.50
202 Alex Cabrera/2499 5.00 1.50
203 Nate Rolison/2499 5.00 1.50
204 Julio Zuleta/2499 5.00 1.50
205 Chris Richard/2499 5.00 1.50
206 Dernell Stenson/2499 5.00 1.50
207 Aaron McNeal/2499 5.00 1.50
208 Aubrey Huff/2999 5.00 1.50
209 Mike Lamb/2999 5.00 1.50
210 Xavier Nady/2999 5.00 1.50
211 Joe Crede/2999 5.00 1.50
212 Ben Petrick/3499 5.00 1.50
213 M.Burkhart/1999 5.00 1.50
214 Jason Tyner/1999 5.00 1.50
215 Juan Pierre/1999 5.00 1.50
216 Adam Dunn/1999 5.00 1.50
217 Adam Piatt/1999 5.00 1.50
218 Eric Byrnes/1999 5.00 1.50
219 Corey Patterson/1999 5.00 1.50
220 Kenny Kelly/1999 5.00 1.50
221 Tike Redman/1999 5.00 1.50
222 Luis Matos/1999 5.00 1.50
223 Timo Perez/1999 5.00 1.50
224 Vernon Wells/1999 5.00 1.50
225 Barry Zito/4999 8.00 2.40
226 Adam Bernero/4999 5.00 1.50
227 Kazuhiro Sasaki/4999 5.00 1.50
228 O.Mairena/4999 5.00 1.50
229 Mark Buehrle/4999 5.00 1.50
230 Ryan Dempster/4999 5.00 1.50
231 Tim Hudson/4999 5.00 1.50
232 Scott Downs/4999 5.00 1.50
233 A.J. Burnett/4999 5.00 1.50
234 Adam Eaton/4999 5.00 1.50
235 P.Crawford/4999 5.00 1.50
236 Jace Brewer/3999 5.00 1.50
237 Jose Ortiz/3999 5.00 1.50
238 Rafael Furcal/3999 5.00 1.50
239 Julio Lugo/3999 5.00 1.50
240 T. De la Rosa/3999 5.00 1.50
241 T. Shinjo/999 RC 12.00 3.60
242 W. Betemit/999 RC 10.00 3.00
243 J. Owens/999 RC 10.00 3.00
244 Drew Henson/999 RC 12.00 3.60
245 Albert Pujols/999 RC 50.00 15.00
246 Travis Hafner/999 RC 10.00 3.00
247 Ichiro Suzuki/999 RC 40.00 12.00
248 E. Guzman/999 RC 10.00 3.00
249 Matt White/999 RC 10.00 3.00
250 Junior Spivey/999 RC 10.00 3.00

2001 Fleer Focus Green

Randomly inserted into packs, this 240-card set is a complete parallel of the 2001 Fleer Focus base set. Each card is individually serial numbered to either the player's batting average or ERA. Please note that these cards were produced with green foil lettering on the card fronts, and are serial numbered on the back of each card.

Nm-Mt Ex-Mt
*1-200 PRINT RUN b/wn 401-600: 3X TO 8X
*1-200 PRINT RUN b/wn 250-400: 4X TO 10X
*1-200 PRINT RUN b/wn 201-250: 5X TO 12X
*1-200 PRINT RUN b/wn 151-200: 6X TO 15X

2001 Fleer Focus Bat Company

Randomly inserted into packs at one in 24, this 10-card insert features players that crank out hits on a consistent basis. Card backs carry a "BC" prefix.

Nm-Mt Ex-Mt
COMPLETE SET (10) 80.00 24.00
*VIP: 3X TO 6X BASIC BAT CO.

VIP RANDOM INSERTS IN PACKS
VIP PRINT RUN 50 SERIAL #'d SETS
BC1 Barry Bonds 12.00 3.60
BC2 Mark McGwire 12.00 3.60
BC3 Sammy Sosa 8.00 2.40
BC4 Ken Griffey Jr. 8.00 2.40
BC5 Mike Piazza 8.00 2.40
BC6 Derek Jeter 12.00 3.60
BC7 Gary Sheffield 4.00 1.20
BC8 Frank Thomas 5.00 1.50
BC9 Chipper Jones 5.00 1.50
BC10 Alex Rodriguez 8.00 2.40

2001 Fleer Focus Big Innings

Randomly inserted into packs at one in six, this 25-card insert features players that are at the beginning of their promising careers. Card backs carry a "BI" prefix.

Nm-Mt Ex-Mt
COMPLETE SET (25) 40.00 12.00
*VIP: 6X TO 12X BASIC BIG.INN.
VIP RANDOM INSERTS IN PACKS
VIP PRINT RUN 50 SERIAL #'d SETS
BI1 Rick Ankiel 1.50 .45
BI2 Andruw Jones 1.50 .45
BI3 Brian Giles 1.50 .45
BI4 Derek Jeter 6.00 1.80
BI5 Rafael Furcal 1.50 .45
BI6 Richie Sexson 1.50 .45
BI7 Jay Payton 1.50 .45
BI8 Carlos Delgado 1.50 .45
BI9 Jermaine Dye 1.50 .45
BI10 Darin Erstad 1.50 .45
BI11 Pat Burrell 1.50 .45
BI12 Richard Hidalgo 1.50 .45
BI13 Adrian Beltre 1.50 .45
BI14 Todd Helton 1.50 .45
BI15 Vladimir Guerrero 2.50 .75
BI16 Nomar Garciaparra 4.00 1.20
BI17 Gabe Kapler 1.50 .45
BI18 Carlos Lee 1.50 .45
BI19 J.D. Drew 1.50 .45
BI20 Troy Glaus 1.50 .45
BI21 Scott Rolen 1.50 .45
BI22 Alex Rodriguez 4.00 1.20
BI23 Magglio Ordonez 1.50 .45
BI24 Miguel Tejada 1.50 .45
BI25 Ruben Mateo 1.50 .45

2001 Fleer Focus Diamond Vision

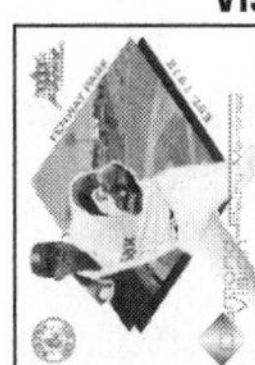

Randomly inserted into packs at one in 12, this 15-card insert features players that keep the ballparks packed on a nightly basis. Card backs carry a "DV" prefix.

Nm-Mt Ex-Mt
COMPLETE SET (15) 60.00 18.00
*VIP: 6X TO 12X BASIC DIAM.VIS.
VIP RANDOM INSERTS IN PACKS
VIP PRINT RUN 50 SERIAL #'d SETS
DV1 Derek Jeter 6.00 1.80
DV2 Nomar Garciaparra 4.00 1.20
DV3 Cal Ripken 8.00 2.40
DV4 Jeff Bagwell 2.00 .60
DV5 Mark McGwire 6.00 1.80
DV6 Ken Griffey Jr. 4.00 1.20
DV7 Pedro Martinez 2.50 .75
DV8 Carlos Delgado 2.00 .60
DV9 Chipper Jones 2.50 .75
DV10 Barry Bonds 6.00 1.80
DV11 Mike Piazza 4.00 1.20
DV12 Sammy Sosa 4.00 1.20
DV13 Alex Rodriguez 4.00 1.20
DV14 Frank Thomas 2.50 .75
DV15 Randy Johnson 2.50 .75

2001 Fleer Focus ROY Collection

Randomly inserted into packs at one in 24, this 25-card insert features players that have won the Rookie of the Year award. Card backs carry a "ROY" prefix. Please note that card number ROY23 (originally intended for 1981 Rookie of the Year Fernando Valenzuela) was switched at the last minute to 1998 Rookie of the Year Kerry Wood.

Nm-Mt Ex-Mt
COMPLETE SET (25) 200.00 60.00
ROY1 Luis Aparicio 4.00 1.20

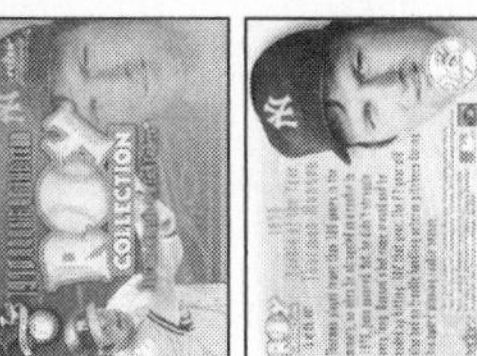

ROY2 Johnny Bench 8.00 2.40
ROY3 Joe Black 4.00 1.20
ROY4 Rod Carew 5.00 1.50
ROY5 Orlando Cepeda 4.00 1.20
ROY6 Carlton Fisk 5.00 1.50
ROY7 Ben Grieve 4.00 1.20
ROY8 Frank Howard 4.00 1.20
ROY9 Derek Jeter 15.00 4.50
ROY10 Fred Lynn 4.00 1.20
ROY11 Willie Mays 15.00 4.50
ROY12 Willie McCovey 4.00 1.20
ROY13 Mark McGwire 15.00 4.50
ROY14 Raul Mondesi 4.00 1.20
ROY15 Thurman Munson 10.00 3.00
ROY16 Eddie Murray 8.00 2.40
ROY17 Mike Piazza 10.00 3.00
ROY18 Cal Ripken 20.00 6.00
ROY19 Frank Robinson 5.00 1.50
ROY20 Jackie Robinson 10.00 3.00
ROY21 Scott Rolen 5.00 1.50
ROY22 Tom Seaver 5.00 1.50
ROY23 Kerry Wood 8.00 2.40
ROY24 David Justice 4.00 1.20
ROY25 Billy Williams 4.00 1.20

2001 Fleer Focus ROY Collection Memorabilia

Randomly inserted into packs at one in 288, this 21-card insert is a partial parallel of the ROY Collection insert. This parallel features swatches of game-used memorabilia from players that have won the Rookie of the Year award. Card backs carry a "ROY" prefix. Please note that card number ROY21 (intended for 1981 Rookie of the Year Fernando Valenzuela) does not exist.

Nm-Mt Ex-Mt
ROY1 Luis Aparicio Bat 15.00 4.50
ROY2 Johnny Bench Jsy 25.00 7.50
ROY3 Orlando Cepeda Bat 15.00 4.50
ROY4 Carlton Fisk Jsy 25.00 7.50
ROY5 Ben Grieve Jsy 15.00 4.50
ROY6 Frank Howard Bat 15.00 4.50
ROY7 Derek Jeter Jsy 80.00 24.00
ROY8 Fred Lynn Bat 15.00 4.50
ROY9 Willie Mays Jsy 80.00 24.00
ROY10 W. McCovey Bat 15.00 4.50
ROY11 Mark McGwire Ball 100.00 30.00
ROY12 Raul Mondesi Bat 15.00 4.50
ROY13 T. Munson Bat 50.00 15.00
ROY14 Eddie Murray Jsy 25.00 7.50
ROY15 Mike Piazza Base 25.00 7.50
ROY16 Cal Ripken Jsy 80.00 24.00
ROY17 F. Robinson Bat 25.00 7.50
ROY18 J. Robinson Pants 120.00 36.00
ROY19 Scott Rolen Bat 25.00 7.50
ROY20 Tom Seaver Jsy 25.00 7.50
ROY22 David Justice Jsy 15.00 4.50

2001 Fleer Focus ROY Collection Memorabilia Autograph

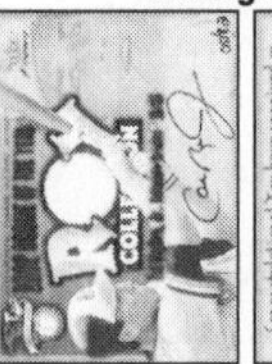

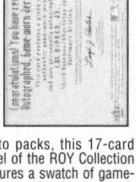

Randomly inserted into packs, this 17-card insert is a partial parallel of the ROY Collection insert. This parallel features a swatch of game-used memorabilia and an authentic autograph of players that have won the Rookie of the Year award. Please note that these cards are serial numbered to the year in which each player won the ROY award (i.e. 1972=72). Card backs carry a "ROYSM" prefix. Please note that the Willie Mays, Carlton Fisk and Luis Aparicio cards packed out as exchange cards with a redemption deadline of February 1st, 2002. Also, card ROYSM17 (originally intended for Fernando Valenzuela) does not exist, thus the set is complete at 17 cards despite being numbered to 18.

Nm-Mt Ex-Mt
1 Luis Aparicio Bat/56 50.00 15.00
2 Johnny Bench Jsy/68 150.00 45.00
3 Orlando Cepeda Bat/58 50.00 15.00
4 Carlton Fisk Jsy/72 80.00 24.00
5 Ben Grieve Jsy/98 50.00 15.00
6 Frank Howard Bat/60 50.00 15.00
7 Derek Jeter Jsy/96 300.00 90.00
8 Fred Lynn Bat/75 50.00 15.00
9 Willie Mays Jsy/51 300.00 90.00
10 Willie McCovey Bat/59 80.00 24.00
11 Raul Mondesi Bat/94 50.00 15.00
12 Eddie Murray Jsy/77 100.00 30.00
13 Cal Ripken Jsy/82 400.00 120.00
14 Frank Robinson Bat/57 100.00 30.00
15 Scott Rolen Bat/97 80.00 24.00
16 Tom Seaver Jsy/67 150.00 45.00
18 David Justice Jsy/90 50.00 15.00

2002 Fleer Focus JE

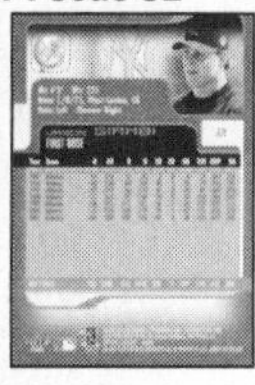

This 260 card standard-size set was issued in June, 2002. The product was issued in 10 card packs which were packaged 24 packs to a box and 16 boxes to a case with an SRP of $3 per pack. Cards numbered 225 through 260 feature rookies and prospects and were issued at a stated rate of one in four hobby packs and one in eight retail packs.

Nm-Mt Ex-Mt
COMPLETE SET (260) 100.00 30.00
COMP.SET w/o SP's (225) 25.00 7.50
COMMON CARD (1-225) .30 .09
COMMON CARD (226-260) 2.00 .60
1 Mike Piazza 1.25 .35
2 Jason Giambi .75 .23
3 Jim Thome .75 .23
4 John Olerud .30 .09
5 J.D. Drew .30 .09
6 Richard Hidalgo .30 .09
7 Rusty Greer .30 .09
8 Tony Batista .30 .09
9 Omar Vizquel .30 .09
10 Randy Johnson .75 .23
11 Cristian Guzman .30 .09
12 Mark Grace .50 .15
13 Jeff Cirillo .30 .09
14 Mike Cameron .30 .09
15 Jeromy Burnitz .30 .09
16 Pokey Reese .30 .09
17 Richie Sexson .30 .09
18 Joe Randa .30 .09
19 Aramis Ramirez .30 .09
20 Pedro Martinez .75 .23
21 Todd Hollandsworth .30 .09
22 Rondell White .30 .09
23 Tsuyoshi Shinjo .30 .09
24 Melvin Mora .30 .09
25 Tim Hudson .30 .09
26 Darrin Fletcher .30 .09
27 Bill Mueller .30 .09
28 Jeff Weaver .30 .09
29 Tony Clark .30 .09
30 Tom Glavine .50 .15
31 Jarrod Washburn .30 .09
32 Greg Vaughn .30 .09
33 Lee Stevens .30 .09
34 Charles Johnson .30 .09
35 Lance Berkman .30 .09
36 Bud Smith .30 .09
37 Keith Foulke .30 .09
38 Ben Davis .30 .09
39 Daryle Ward .30 .09
40 Bernie Williams .50 .15
41 Dean Palmer .30 .09
42 Mark Mulder .30 .09
43 Jason LaRue .30 .09
44 Jay Gibbons .30 .09
45 Brandon Duckworth .30 .09
46 Carlos Delgado .30 .09
47 Barry Zito .50 .15
48 Matt Morris .30 .09
49 J.T. Snow .30 .09
50 Albert Pujols 1.50 .45
51 Brad Fullmer .30 .09
52 Damion Easley .30 .09
53 Pat Burrell .30 .09
54 Kevin Brown .30 .09
55 Todd Walker .30 .09
56 Rich Garces .30 .09
57 Carlos Pena .30 .09
58 Paul LoDuca .30 .09
59 Mike Lieberthal .30 .09
60 Barry Larkin .75 .23
61 Jon Lieber .30 .09
62 Jose Cruz Jr. .30 .09
63 Mo Vaughn .30 .09
64 Ivan Rodriguez .75 .23
65 Jorge Posada .50 .15
66 Magglio Ordonez .30 .09
67 Juan Encarnacion .30 .09
68 Shawn Estes .30 .09
69 Kevin Appier .30 .09
70 Jeff Bagwell .50 .15
71 Tim Wakefield .30 .09
72 Shannon Stewart .30 .09
73 Scott Rolen .50 .15
74 Bobby Higginson .30 .09
75 Jim Edmonds .30 .09
76 Adam Dunn .30 .09
77 Eric Chavez .30 .09
78 Adrian Beltre .30 .09
79 Jason Varitek .30 .09
80 Barry Bonds 2.00 .60
81 Edgar Renteria .30 .09
82 Raul Mondesi .30 .09
83 Eric Karros .30 .09
84 Ken Griffey Jr. 1.25 .35
85 Jermaine Dye .30 .09
86 Carlos Beltran .30 .09
87 Mark Quinn .30 .09
88 Terrence Long .30 .09
89 Shawn Green .30 .09
90 Nomar Garciaparra 1.25 .35
91 Sean Casey .30 .09
92 Homer Bush .30 .09
93 Bob Abreu .30 .09
94 Jamey Wright .30 .09
95 Tony Womack .30 .09
96 Larry Walker .50 .15
97 Doug Mientkiewicz .30 .09
98 Jimmy Rollins .30 .09
99 Brady Anderson .30 .09
100 Derek Jeter 2.00 .60
101 Kevin Young .30 .09
102 Juan Pierre .30 .09
103 Edgar Martinez .50 .15
104 Corey Koskie .30 .09
105 Jeffrey Hammonds .30 .09
106 Luis Gonzalez .30 .09
107 Travis Fryman .30 .09
108 Kerry Wood .75 .23
109 Rafael Palmeiro .50 .15
110 Ichiro Suzuki 1.25 .35
111 Russ Ortiz .30 .09
112 Jeff Kent .30 .09
113 Scott Erickson .30 .09
114 Bruce Chen .30 .09
115 Craig Biggio .50 .15
116 Robin Ventura .30 .09
117 Alex Rodriguez 1.25 .35
118 Roy Oswalt .30 .09
119 Fred McGriff .50 .15
120 Juan Gonzalez .75 .23
121 David Justice .30 .09
122 Pat Hentgen .30 .09
123 Hideo Nomo .75 .23
124 Ramon Ortiz .30 .09
125 David Ortiz .30 .09
126 Phil Nevin .30 .09
127 Ryan Dempster .30 .09
128 Toby Hall .30 .09
129 Vladimir Guerrero .75 .23
130 Chipper Jones .75 .23
131 Russell Branyan .30 .09
132 Jose Vidro .30 .09
133 Bubba Trammell .30 .09
134 Tino Martinez .50 .15
135 Greg Maddux 1.25 .35
136 Derrek Lee .30 .09
137 Troy Glaus .50 .15
138 Joe Crede .30 .09
139 Steve Cox .30 .09
140 Sammy Sosa 1.25 .35
141 Corey Patterson .30 .09
142 Vernon Wells .30 .09
143 Matt Lawton .30 .09
144 Gabe Kapler .30 .09
145 Johnny Damon .30 .09
146 Marty Cordova .30 .09
147 Moises Alou .30 .09
148 Fernando Tatis .30 .09
149 Tanyon Sturtze .30 .09
150 Roger Clemens 1.50 .45
151 Paul Konerko .30 .09
152 Chan Ho Park .30 .09
153 Marcus Giles .30 .09
154 David Eckstein .30 .09
155 Mike Lowell .30 .09
156 Preston Wilson .30 .09
157 John Vander Wal .30 .09
158 Tim Salmon .50 .15
159 Andy Pettitte .50 .15
160 Mike Mussina .75 .23
161 Doug Davis .30 .09
162 Peter Bergeron .30 .09
163 Rich Aurilia .30 .09
164 Eric Milton .30 .09
165 Geoff Jenkins .30 .09
166 Todd Helton .50 .15
167 Bret Boone .30 .09
168 Kris Benson .30 .09
169 Brian Anderson .30 .09
170 Roberto Alomar .75 .23
171 Javier Vazquez .30 .09
172 Scott Schoeneweis .30 .09
173 Ryan Klesko .30 .09
174 Jacque Jones .30 .09
175 Andruw Jones .30 .09
176 Aubrey Huff .30 .09
177 Mark Buehrle .30 .09
178 Josh Beckett .50 .15
179 Ben Sheets .30 .09
180 Curt Schilling .50 .15
181 C.C. Sabathia .30 .09
182 Denny Neagle .30 .09
183 Jamie Moyer .30 .09
184 Jason Kendall .30 .09
185 Dee Brown .30 .09
186 Frank Thomas .75 .23
187 Damian Rolls .30 .09
188 Carlos Lee .30 .09
189 Kevin Jarvis .30 .09
190 Manny Ramirez .30 .09
191 Cliff Floyd .30 .09
192 Freddy Garcia .30 .09
193 Orlando Cabrera .30 .09
194 Mike Sweeney .30 .09
195 Gary Sheffield .30 .09
196 Rafael Furcal .30 .09
197 Esteban Loaiza .30 .09
198 Mike Hampton .30 .09
199 Brian Giles .30 .09
200 Darin Erstad .30 .09
201 David Wells .30 .09
202 Kenny Lofton .30 .09
203 Aaron Sele .30 .09
204 Jason Schmidt .30 .09
205 Javy Lopez .30 .09
206 Dmitri Young .30 .09
207 Darryl Kile .30 .09
208 Matt Williams .30 .09
209 Joe Kennedy .30 .09
210 Chuck Knoblauch .30 .09
211 Brian Jordan .30 .09
212 Robert Person .30 .09
213 Alex Ochoa .30 .09
214 Steve Finley .30 .09
215 Ben Petrick .30 .09
216 Al Leiter .30 .09
217 Mark Kotsay .30 .09
218 Miguel Tejada .30 .09
219 David Segui .30 .09
220 A.J. Burnett .30 .09
221 Marlon Anderson .30 .09
222 Wiki Gonzalez .30 .09
223 Jeff Suppan .30 .09
224 Dave Roberts .30 .09
225 Jose Hernandez .30 .09

226 Angel Berroa ROO	2.00	.60
227 Sean Burroughs ROO	2.00	.60
228 Luis Martinez ROO RC	2.00	.60
229 Adrian Burnside ROO RC	2.00	.60
230 John Ennis ROO RC	2.00	.60
231 An. Martinez ROO RC	2.00	.60
232 Hank Blalock ROO	3.00	.90
233 Eric Hinske ROO	2.00	.60
234 Chris Booker ROO RC	2.00	.60
235 Colin Young ROO RC	2.00	.60
236 Mark Corey ROO RC	2.00	.60
237 Satoru Komiyama ROO RC	2.00	.60
238 So Taguchi ROO RC	3.00	.90
239 Elio Serrano ROO RC	2.00	.60
240 Reed Johnson ROO RC	3.00	.90
241 Jeremy Lambert ROO RC	2.00	.60
242 Chris Baker ROO RC	2.00	.60
243 Orlando Hudson ROO	2.00	.60
244 Travis Hughes ROO RC	2.00	.60
245 Kevin Frederick ROO RC	2.00	.60
246 Rodrigo Rosario ROO RC	2.00	.60
247 Jeremy Ward ROO RC	2.00	.60
248 Kazuhisa Ishii ROO RC	5.00	1.50
249 Austin Kearns ROO	2.00	.60
250 Kyle Kane ROO RC	2.00	.60
251 Cam Esslinger ROO RC	2.00	.60
252 Jeff Austin ROO RC	2.00	.60
253 Brian Mallette ROO RC	2.00	.60
254 Mark Prior ROO	10.00	3.00
255 Mark Teixeira ROO	3.00	.90
256 Carlos Valderrama ROO	2.00	.60
257 Jason Hart ROO	2.00	.60
258 Takahito Nomura ROO RC	2.00	.60
259 Matt Thornton ROO RC	2.00	.60
260 Marlon Byrd ROO	2.00	.60

2002 Fleer Focus JE Century Parallel

Randomly inserted into packs, this is a parallel to the basic set. Each card is serial numbered to the players's uniform number plus 100. Since each player has a different amount of cards printed we have put that information next to the player's name.

	Nm-Mt	Ex-Mt
*CENTURY 1-225: 6X TO 15X BASIC..		
*CENTURY 226-260: 1X TO 2.5X BASIC		
RANDOM INSERTS IN HOBBY PACKS		
PRINT RUNS RANGE FROM 101-199 OF EACH		
SEE BECKETT.COM FOR ALL PRINT RUNS		

2002 Fleer Focus JE Jersey Parallel

Randomly inserted into packs, this is a parallel to the basic set. Each card is serial numbered to the players's uniform number. Since each player has a different amount of cards printed we have put that information next to the player's name. Players with a print run of 25 or less are not priced due to market scarcity.

	Nm-Mt	Ex-Mt
*1-225 PRINT RUN b/wn 26-35 20X TO 50X		
*1-225 PRINT RUN b/wn 36-50 15X TO 40X		
*1-225 PRINT RUN b/wn 51-65 12.5X TO 30X		
*1-225 PRINT RUN b/wn 66-80 10X TO 25X		
COMMON (226-260) p/r 81-99	6.00	1.80
UNLISTED 226-260 p/r 81-99	15.00	4.50
COMMON (226-260) p/r 66-80	8.00	2.40
UNLISTED 226-260 p/r 66-80	20.00	6.00
COMMON (226-260) p/r 51-65	10.00	3.00
SEMIS 226-260 p/r 51-65	15.00	4.50
COMMON (226-260) p/r 36-50	12.00	3.60
UNLISTED 226-260 p/r 26-35	40.00	12.00
RANDOM INSERTS IN HOBBY PACKS		
PRINT RUNS BASED ON UNIFORM NUMBER		
SEE BECKETT.COM FOR PRINT RUNS		
NO PRICING ON QUANTITIES OF 25 OR LESS		

2002 Fleer Focus JE Blue Chips

Inserted at stated odds of one in six hobby and one in 12 retail, this 15 card set honors some of the best young talent in baseball.

	Nm-Mt	Ex-Mt
COMPLETE SET (15)	15.00	4.50
1 Albert Pujols	5.00	1.50
2 Sean Burroughs	1.00	.30
3 Vernon Wells	1.00	.30
4 Adam Dunn	1.00	.30
5 Pat Burrell	1.00	.30
6 Juan Pierre	1.00	.30
7 Russell Branyan	1.00	.30
8 Carlos Pena	1.00	.30
9 Toby Hall	1.00	.30
10 Hank Blalock	2.50	.75
11 Alfonso Soriano	1.50	.45
12 Jimmy Rollins	1.00	.30
13 Jose Ortiz	1.00	.30
14 Eric Hinske	1.00	.30
15 Nick Johnson	1.00	.30

2002 Fleer Focus JE Blue Chips Game Used

Inserted at stated odds of one in 96 hobby and one in 180 retail, these two cards feature game-used memorabilia of two of the young stars in the Blue Chips insert set.

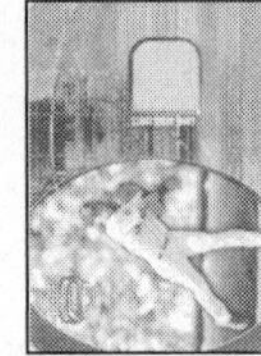

	Nm-Mt	Ex-Mt
1 Russell Branyan Pants	10.00	3.00
2 Nick Johnson Jsy	10.00	3.00

2002 Fleer Focus JE Blue Chips Game Used Patch

Randomly inserted into packs, this card featured a game-used patch of the featured player from the Blue Chips set. This card has a stated print run of 100 serial numbered sets.

	Nm-Mt	Ex-Mt
1 Nick Johnson	25.00	7.50

2002 Fleer Focus JE Intl Diamond Co.

Inserted into packs at a stated rate of one in eight hobby and one in 12 retail, this 25 card set features 25 players born outside the continental United States.

	Nm-Mt	Ex-Mt
COMPLETE SET (25)	40.00	12.00
1 Bobby Abreu	2.00	.60
2 Adrian Beltre	2.00	.60
3 Jorge Posada	2.00	.60
4 Vladimir Guerrero	3.00	.90
5 Rafael Palmeiro	2.00	.60
6 Sammy Sosa	5.00	1.50
7 Larry Walker	2.00	.60
8 Manny Ramirez	2.00	.60
9 Ichiro Suzuki	5.00	1.50
10 Jose Cruz Jr.	2.00	.60
11 Juan Gonzalez	3.00	.90
12 Bernie Williams	2.00	.60
13 Ivan Rodriguez	3.00	.90
14 Moises Alou	2.00	.60
15 Cristian Guzman	2.00	.60
16 Andruw Jones	2.00	.60
17 Aramis Ramirez	2.00	.60
18 Raul Mondesi	2.00	.60
19 Edgar Martinez	2.00	.60
20 Magglio Ordonez	2.00	.60
21 Roberto Alomar	3.00	.90
22 Chan Ho Park	2.00	.60
23 Kazuhiro Sasaki	2.00	.60
24 Tsuyoshi Shinjo	2.00	.60
25 Hideo Nomo	3.00	.90

2002 Fleer Focus JE Intl Diamond Co. Game Used

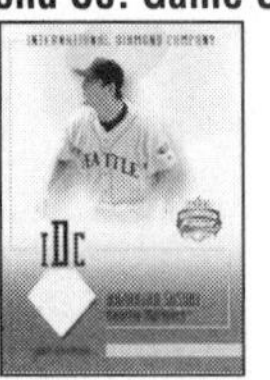

Inserted at stated odds of one in 144 hobby and one in 180 retail, these ten cards feature game-used memorabilia of ten of the players featured in in the International Diamond Company insert set.

	Nm-Mt	Ex-Mt
1 Andruw Jones Jsy	10.00	3.00
2 Edgar Martinez Jsy	15.00	4.50
3 Raul Mondesi Jsy	10.00	3.00
4 Hideo Nomo Jsy	40.00	12.00
5 Rafael Palmeiro Jsy	15.00	4.50
6 Chan Ho Park Jsy	10.00	3.00
7 Aramis Ramirez Pants	10.00	3.00
8 Manny Ramirez Jsy	10.00	3.00
9 Ivan Rodriguez Jsy	15.00	4.50
10 Kazuhiro Sasaki Jsy SP/307	10.00	3.00

2002 Fleer Focus JE Intl Diamond Co. Game Used Patch

Randomly inserted into packs, these six cards feature game-used patches of the featured player from the International Diamond Company insert set. These cards have a stated print run of 100 serial numbered sets.

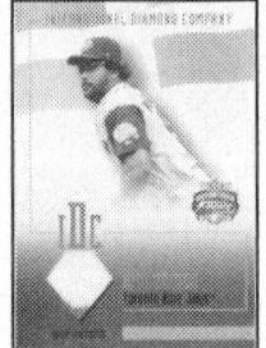

	Nm-Mt	Ex-Mt
1 Edgar Martinez	30.00	9.00
2 Raul Mondesi	25.00	7.50
3 Hideo Nomo	150.00	45.00
4 Chan Ho Park	25.00	7.50
5 Manny Ramirez	25.00	7.50
6 Ivan Rodriguez	40.00	12.00

2002 Fleer Focus JE K Corps

Inserted in packs at a stated rate of one in 12, these 15 cards feature some of the top pitchers in baseball.

	Nm-Mt	Ex-Mt
COMPLETE SET (15)	25.00	7.50
1 Roger Clemens	5.00	1.50
2 Randy Johnson	2.50	.75
3 Tom Glavine	1.50	.45
4 Josh Beckett	1.50	.45
5 Matt Morris	1.50	.45
6 Curt Schilling	1.50	.45
7 Greg Maddux	4.00	1.20
8 Tim Hudson	1.50	.45
9 Roy Oswalt	1.50	.45
10 Kerry Wood	2.50	.75
11 Barry Zito	1.50	.45
12 Kevin Brown	1.50	.45
13 Ryan Dempster	1.50	.45
14 Ben Sheets	1.50	.45
15 Pedro Martinez	2.50	.75

2002 Fleer Focus JE K Corps Game Used

Inserted at stated odds of one in 96 hobby and one in 180 retail, these six cards feature game-used memorabilia of ten of the players featured in in the K Corps insert set. A couple of the player were printed in shorter supply and we have printed the stated print run next to the player's name in our checklist.

	Nm-Mt	Ex-Mt
1 Kevin Brown Jsy	10.00	3.00
2 Randy Johnson Jsy SP/316	15.00	4.50
3 Greg Maddux Jsy	15.00	4.50
4 Pedro Martinez Jsy	15.00	4.50
5 Curt Schilling Jsy	15.00	4.50
6 Barry Zito Jsy SP/220	15.00	4.50

2002 Fleer Focus JE K Corps Game Used Patch

Randomly inserted into packs, these three cards feature game-used patches of the featured player from the K Corps insert set. These cards have a stated print run of 100 serial numbered sets.

	Nm-Mt	Ex-Mt
1 Kevin Brown	25.00	7.50
2 Pedro Martinez	40.00	12.00
3 Curt Schilling	30.00	9.00

2002 Fleer Focus JE Kings of Swing

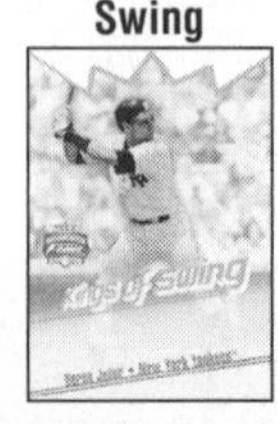

Inserted at stated odds of one in 48, this 20 card insert set featues some of baseball's heaviest hitters.

	Nm-Mt	Ex-Mt
COMPLETE SET (20)	150.00	45.00
1 Barry Bonds	15.00	4.50
2 Mike Piazza	10.00	3.00
3 Albert Pujols	12.00	3.60
4 Todd Helton	5.00	1.50
5 Ken Griffey Jr.	10.00	3.00
6 Alex Rodriguez	10.00	3.00
7 Sammy Sosa	10.00	3.00
8 Troy Glaus	5.00	1.50
9 Derek Jeter	15.00	4.50
10 Ichiro Suzuki	10.00	3.00
11 Manny Ramirez	5.00	1.50
12 Roberto Alomar	6.00	1.80
13 Juan Gonzalez	6.00	1.80
14 Shawn Green	5.00	1.50
15 Vladimir Guerrero	6.00	1.80
16 Nomar Garciaparra	10.00	3.00
17 Adam Dunn	5.00	1.50
18 Jason Giambi	6.00	1.80
19 Edgar Martinez	5.00	1.50
20 Chipper Jones	6.00	1.80

2002 Fleer Focus JE Kings of Swing Game Used

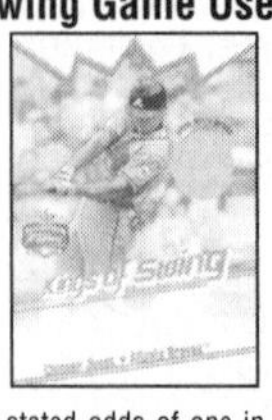

Inserted at stated odds of one in 108 hobby and one in 180 retail, these six cards feature game-used memorabilia of ten of the players featured in in the Kings of Swing insert set.

	Nm-Mt	Ex-Mt
1 Shawn Green Jsy	15.00	4.50
2 Todd Helton Jsy	15.00	4.50
3 Derek Jeter Jsy SP/348	40.00	12.00
4 Chipper Jones Jsy	15.00	4.50
5 Edgar Martinez Jsy	15.00	4.50
6 Mike Piazza Jsy	15.00	4.50
7 Manny Ramirez Jsy	15.00	4.50
8 Alex Rodriguez Jsy	15.00	4.50

2002 Fleer Focus JE Kings of Swing Game Used Patch

Randomly inserted into packs, these five cards feature game-used patches of the featured player from the Kings of Swing insert set. These cards have a stated print run of 100 serial numbered sets.

	Nm-Mt	Ex-Mt
1 Shawn Green	30.00	9.00
2 Todd Helton	30.00	9.00
3 Edgar Martinez	30.00	9.00
4 Mike Piazza	50.00	15.00
5 Manny Ramirez	30.00	9.00

2002 Fleer Focus JE Larger than Life

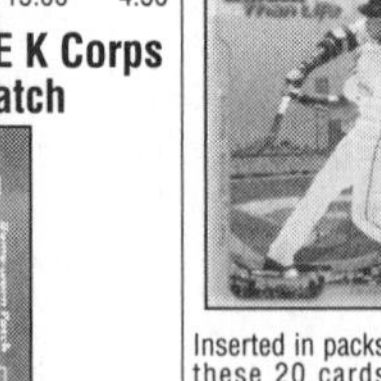

Inserted in packs at a stated rate of one in 240, these 20 cards feature players who have achieved spectacular feats on the field.

	Nm-Mt	Ex-Mt
1 Jason Giambi	15.00	4.50
2 Carlos Delgado	10.00	3.00
3 Alex Rodriguez	25.00	7.50
4 Preston Wilson	10.00	3.00
5 Frank Thomas	15.00	4.50
6 Nomar Garciaparra	25.00	7.50
7 Jim Edmonds	10.00	3.00
8 Jim Thome	15.00	4.50
9 Barry Bonds	40.00	12.00
10 Mo Vaughn	10.00	3.00
11 Ichiro Suzuki	25.00	7.50
12 Ivan Rodriguez	15.00	4.50
13 Gary Sheffield	10.00	3.00
14 Derek Jeter	40.00	12.00
15 Jeff Bagwell	15.00	4.50
16 Mike Piazza	25.00	7.50
17 J.D. Drew	10.00	3.00
18 Sammy Sosa	25.00	7.50
19 Albert Pujols	30.00	9.00
20 Luis Gonzalez	10.00	3.00

2002 Fleer Focus JE Larger than Life Game Used

Inserted at stated odds of one in 144 hobby and one in 180 retail, these ten cards feature game-used memorabilia of ten of the players featured in in the Larger than Life insert set. The Jeff Bagwell card was produced to a stated

print run of 20 cards and therefore is not priced due to market scarcity.

	Nm-Mt	Ex-Mt
1 Jeff Bagwell Jsy SP/20		
2 Jim Edmonds Jsy	10.00	3.00
3 Luis Gonzalez Jsy	10.00	3.00
4 Derek Jeter Jsy	30.00	9.00
5 Mike Piazza Jsy	20.00	6.00
6 Alex Rodriguez Jsy	20.00	6.00
7 Ivan Rodriguez Jsy	15.00	4.50
8 Frank Thomas Jsy	15.00	4.50
9 Mo Vaughn Jsy	10.00	3.00
10 Preston Wilson Jsy	10.00	3.00

2002 Fleer Focus JE Larger than Life Game Used Patch

Randomly inserted into packs, these six cards feature game-used patches of the featured player from the Larger than Life insert set. These cards have a stated print run of 100 serial numbered sets.

	Nm-Mt	Ex-Mt
1 Jim Edmonds	25.00	7.50
2 Luis Gonzalez	25.00	7.50
3 Mike Piazza	50.00	15.00
4 Ivan Rodriguez	40.00	12.00
5 Frank Thomas	40.00	12.00
6 Preston Wilson	25.00	7.50

2002 Fleer Focus JE Materialistic Away

Inserted in packs at a stated rate of one in 24, these 15 cards are printed on a jersey-like material and feature the game's best players on a simulation away jersey.

	Nm-Mt	Ex-Mt
COMPLETE SET (15)	120.00	36.00
1 Derek Jeter	15.00	4.50
2 Alex Rodriguez	10.00	3.00
3 Mike Piazza	10.00	3.00
4 Ivan Rodriguez	6.00	1.80
5 Chipper Jones	6.00	1.80
6 Todd Helton	4.00	1.20
7 Nomar Garciaparra	10.00	3.00
8 Barry Bonds	15.00	4.50
9 Ichiro Suzuki	10.00	3.00
10 Ken Griffey Jr.	10.00	3.00
11 Jason Giambi	6.00	1.80
12 Sammy Sosa	10.00	3.00
13 Albert Pujols	12.00	3.60
14 Pedro Martinez	6.00	1.80
15 Vladimir Guerrero	6.00	1.80

2002 Fleer Focus JE Materialistic Home

Randomly inserted in packs, these 15 cards are printed on a jersey-like material and feature the game's best players on a simulation home jersey. Each card is printed to a stated print run of 50 serial numbered sets.

	Nm-Mt	Ex-Mt
*HOME: 1.5X TO 4X BASIC AWAY		

2002 Fleer Focus JE Materialistic Jumbos Away

Inserted one per hobby box, these 15 cards are oversized versions of the Materialistic Away insert set.

	Nm-Mt	Ex-Mt
*JUMBO AWAY: .5X TO 1.2X BASIC AWAY		

2003 Fleer Focus JE

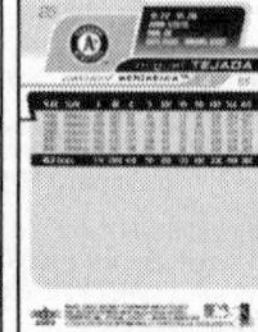

This 180 card set was released in May, 2003. The set was issued in seven card packs with an SRP of $3 which were issued 24 packs to a box and 16 boxes to a case. Cards number 161 through 180, which were issued at a stated rate of one in four featured leading prospects.

	Nm-Mt	Ex-Mt
COMPLETE SET (180)	50.00	15.00
COMP.SET w/o SP's (160)	20.00	6.00
COMMON CARD (1-160)	.30	.09
COMMON CARD (161-180)	2.00	.60
1 Derek Jeter	2.00	.60
2 Preston Wilson	.30	.09
3 Trevor Hoffman	.30	.09
4 Moises Alou	.30	.09
5 Roberto Alomar	.75	.23
6 Tim Salmon	.50	.15
7 Mike Lowell	.30	.09
8 Barry Bonds	2.00	.60
9 Fred McGriff	.50	.15
10 Mo Vaughn	.30	.09
11 Junior Spivey	.30	.09
12 Roy Oswalt	.30	.09
13 Ichiro Suzuki	1.25	.35
14 Magglio Ordonez	.30	.09
15 Adam Kennedy	.30	.09
16 Randy Johnson	.75	.23
17 Carlos Beltran	.30	.09
18 John Olerud	.30	.09
19 Joe Borchard	.30	.09
20 Alfonso Soriano	.50	.15
21 Curt Schilling	.50	.15
22 Mike Sweeney	.30	.09
23 Tino Martinez	.50	.15
24 Barry Larkin	.75	.23
25 Miguel Tejada	.30	.09
26 Chipper Jones	.75	.23
27 Kevin Brown	.30	.09
28 J.D. Drew	.30	.09
29 Sean Casey	.30	.09
30 Bernie Williams	.50	.15
31 Troy Percival	.30	.09
32 Jeff Bagwell	.50	.15
33 Kenny Lofton	.30	.09
34 Kerry Wood	.75	.23
35 Armando Benitez	.30	.09
36 David Eckstein	.30	.09
37 Wade Miller	.30	.09
38 Edgar Martinez	.50	.15
39 Mark Prior	1.50	.45
40 Mike Piazza	1.25	.35
41 Shea Hillenbrand	.30	.09
42 Bartolo Colon	.30	.09
43 Darin Erstad	.30	.09
44 A.J. Burnett	.30	.09
45 Jeff Kent	.30	.09
46 Corey Patterson	.30	.09
47 Ty Wigginton	.30	.09
48 Troy Glaus	.50	.15
49 Josh Beckett	.50	.15
50 Brian Lawrence	.30	.09
51 Frank Thomas	.75	.23
52 Jason Giambi	.75	.23
53 Luis Gonzalez	.30	.09
54 Raul Ibanez	.30	.09
55 Kazuhiro Sasaki	.30	.09
56 Mark Buehrle	.30	.09
57 Roger Clemens	1.50	.45
58 Matt Williams	.30	.09
59 Joe Randa	.30	.09
60 Jamie Moyer	.30	.09
61 Paul Konerko	.30	.09
62 Mike Mussina	.75	.23
63 Javy Lopez	.30	.09
64 Brian Jordan	.30	.09
65 Scott Rolen	.50	.15
66 Aaron Boone	.30	.09
67 Eric Chavez	.30	.09
68 Mark Grace	.50	.15
69 Shawn Green	.30	.09
70 Albert Pujols	1.50	.45
71 Sammy Sosa	1.25	.35
72 Edgardo Alfonzo	.30	.09
73 Garret Anderson	.30	.09
74 Lance Berkman	.30	.09
75 Bret Boone	.30	.09
76 Joe Crede	.30	.09
77 Al Leiter	.30	.09
78 Jarrod Washburn	.30	.09
79 Craig Biggio	.50	.15
80 Rich Aurilia	.30	.09
81 Adam Dunn	.30	.09
82 Jermaine Dye	.30	.09
83 Tom Glavine	.50	.15
84 Eric Gagne	.50	.15
85 Jared Sandberg	.30	.09
86 Jim Thome	.75	.23
87 Barry Zito	.50	.15
88 Gary Sheffield	.30	.09
89 Paul Lo Duca	.30	.09
90 Matt Morris	.30	.09
91 Juan Pierre	.30	.09
92 Randy Wolf	.30	.09
93 Jay Gibbons	.30	.09
94 Brad Radke	.30	.09
95 Carlos Delgado	.30	.09
96 Carlos Pena	.30	.09
97 Brian Giles	.30	.09
98 Rodrigo Lopez	.30	.09
99 Jacque Jones	.30	.09
100 Juan Gonzalez	.75	.23
101 Randall Simon	.30	.09
102 Mike Williams	.30	.09
103 Derek Lowe	.30	.09
104 Brad Wilkerson	.30	.09
105 Eric Hinske	.30	.09
106 Luis Castillo	.30	.09
107 Phil Nevin	.30	.09
108 Manny Ramirez	.30	.09
109 Vladimir Guerrero	.75	.23
110 Roy Halladay	.30	.09
111 Ellis Burks	.30	.09
112 Bobby Abreu	.30	.09
113 Tony Batista	.30	.09
114 Richie Sexson	.30	.09
115 Rafael Palmeiro	.50	.15
116 Todd Helton	.50	.15
117 Pat Burrell	.30	.09
118 John Smoltz	.50	.15
119 Ben Sheets	.30	.09
120 Aubrey Huff	.30	.09
121 Andruw Jones	.30	.09
122 Kazuhisa Ishii	.30	.09
123 Jim Edmonds	.30	.09
124 Austin Kearns	.30	.09
125 Mark Mulder	.30	.09
126 Greg Maddux	1.25	.35
127 Jose Hernandez	.30	.09
128 Ben Grieve	.30	.09
129 Ken Griffey Jr.	1.25	.35
130 Tim Hudson	.30	.09
131 Jorge Julio	.30	.09
132 Torii Hunter	.30	.09
133 Ivan Rodriguez	.75	.23
134 Jason Jennings	.30	.09
135 Jason Kendall	.30	.09
136 Nomar Garciaparra	1.25	.35
137 Michael Cuddyer	.30	.09
138 Shannon Stewart	.30	.09
139 Larry Walker	.50	.15
140 Aramis Ramirez	.30	.09
141 Johnny Damon	.30	.09
142 Orlando Cabrera	.30	.09
143 Vernon Wells	.30	.09
144 Bobby Higginson	.30	.09
145 Sean Burroughs	.30	.09
146 Pedro Martinez	.75	.23
147 Jose Vidro	.30	.09
148 Orlando Hudson	.30	.09
149 Robert Fick	.30	.09
150 Ryan Klesko	.30	.09
151 Kevin Millwood	.30	.09
152 Alex Sanchez	.30	.09
153 Randy Winn	.30	.09
154 Omar Vizquel	.30	.09
155 Mike Lieberthal	.30	.09
156 Marty Cordova	.30	.09
157 Cristian Guzman	.30	.09
158 Alex Rodriguez	1.25	.35
159 C.C. Sabathia	.30	.09
160 Jimmy Rollins	.30	.09
161 Josh Willingham HP RC	4.00	1.20
162 Lance Niekro HP	2.00	.60
163 Nook Logan HP RC	2.00	.60
164 Chase Utley HP	2.00	.60
165 Pete LaForest HP RC	3.00	.90
166 Victor Martinez HP	2.00	.60
167 Adam LaRoche HP	3.00	.90
168 Ian Ferguson HP RC	2.00	.60
169 Mark Teixeira HP	3.00	.90
170 Chris Waters HP RC	2.00	.60
171 Hideki Matsui HP RC	8.00	2.40
172 Alejandro Machado HP RC	2.00	.60
173 Francisco Rosario HP RC	2.00	.60
174 Terrmel Sledge HP RC	3.00	.90
175 Guillermo Quiroz HP RC	3.00	.90
176 Lew Ford HP RC	3.00	.90
177 Hank Blalock HP	3.00	.90
178 Lyle Overbay HP	2.00	.60
179 Matt Bruback HP RC	2.00	.60
180 Jose Contreras HP RC	4.00	1.20

2003 Fleer Focus JE Century Parallel

Randomly inserted into packs, this is a parallel to the basic Focus JE set. These cards were issued to a stated print run of the player's uniform number plus 100. Please note that we have put the stated print run next to the player's name in our checklist.

Nm-Mt Ex-Mt

*CENTURY 1-160: 6X TO 15X BASIC..
*CENTURY 161-180: 1X TO 2.5X BASIC
RANDOM INSERTS IN PACKS
PRINT RUNS BASED ON JSY NUMBER +100

2003 Fleer Focus JE Franchise Focus

Inserted at a stated rate of one in four, this 20-card set features players who are among the keys to their franchise.

	Nm-Mt	Ex-Mt
COMPLETE SET (20)	15.00	4.50
1 Troy Glaus	1.00	.30
2 Randy Johnson	1.25	.35
3 Chipper Jones	1.25	.35
4 Nomar Garciaparra	2.00	.60
5 Sammy Sosa	2.00	.60
6 Ken Griffey Jr.	2.00	.60
7 Jeff Bagwell	1.00	.30
8 Mike Sweeney	1.00	.30
9 Shawn Green	1.00	.30
10 Torii Hunter	1.00	.30
11 Vladimir Guerrero	1.25	.35
12 Mike Piazza	2.00	.60
13 Jason Giambi	1.25	.35
14 Barry Zito	1.00	.30
15 Pat Burrell	1.00	.30
16 Barry Bonds	3.00	.90
17 Ichiro Suzuki	2.00	.60
18 Albert Pujols	2.50	.75
19 Alex Rodriguez	2.00	.60
20 Carlos Delgado	1.00	.30

2003 Fleer Focus JE Home and Aways Game Jersey

Inserted at a stated rate of one in 288, this nine card set features a home jersey swatch on one side and a visiting jersey swatch on the other side of the card.

	Nm-Mt	Ex-Mt
AR Alex Rodriguez	30.00	9.00
AS Alfonso Soriano	15.00	4.50
CJ Chipper Jones	15.00	4.50
DJ Derek Jeter	50.00	15.00
GM Greg Maddux	20.00	6.00
JD J.D. Drew	15.00	4.50
LB Lance Berkman	15.00	4.50
NG Nomar Garciaparra	30.00	9.00
RO Roy Oswalt	15.00	4.50

2003 Fleer Focus JE Materialistic Action Away

Inserted in packs at a stated rate of one in 192, this 15-card set features leading players as well as a swatch of their visiting uniform.

Nm-Mt Ex-Mt

*HOME: .75X TO 2X BASIC AWAY......
HOME RANDOM INSERTS IN PACKS .
HOME PRINT RUN 50 SERIAL #'d SETS

	Nm-Mt	Ex-Mt
I Ichiro Suzuki	15.00	4.50
AD Adam Dunn	15.00	4.50
AP Albert Pujols	15.00	4.50
AR Alex Rodriguez	15.00	4.50
AS Alfonso Soriano	15.00	4.50
CJ Chipper Jones	15.00	4.50
DJ Derek Jeter	25.00	7.50
GM Greg Maddux	15.00	4.50
JG Jason Giambi	15.00	4.50
KG Ken Griffey Jr.	15.00	4.50
MP Mike Piazza	15.00	4.50
NG Nomar Garciaparra	15.00	4.50
PB Pat Burrell	15.00	4.50
RC Roger Clemens	20.00	6.00
SS Sammy Sosa	15.00	4.50

2003 Fleer Focus JE Materialistic Oversized

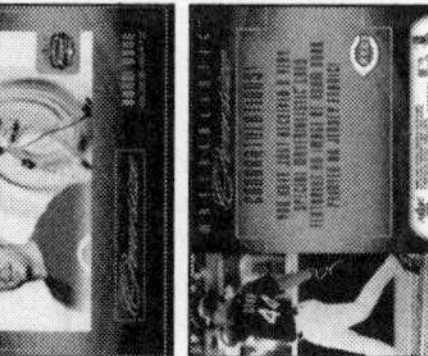

Issued as a box topper, these "oversized" cards featured not only a larger card but also a larger jersey swatch piece. These cards were issued in special wrappers which differentiated these cards from the regular packs.

	Nm-Mt	Ex-Mt
I Ichiro Suzuki	8.00	2.40
AD Adam Dunn	5.00	1.50
AP Albert Pujols	10.00	3.00
AR Alex Rodriguez	8.00	2.40
AS Alfonso Soriano	5.00	1.50
CJ Chipper Jones	5.00	1.50
DJ Derek Jeter	12.00	3.60
GM Greg Maddux	8.00	2.40
JG Jason Giambi	5.00	1.50
KG Ken Griffey Jr.	8.00	2.40
MP Mike Piazza	8.00	2.40
NG Nomar Garciaparra	8.00	2.40
PB Pat Burrell	5.00	1.50
RC Roger Clemens	10.00	3.00
RJ Reggie Jackson	5.00	1.50
SS Sammy Sosa	8.00	2.40

2003 Fleer Focus JE Materialistic Oversized Autographs

Randomly inserted in jumbo packs, these three cards feature not only the oversize cards but also authentic autographs of the featured player. The stated print runs for these players appears next to their name in our checklist.

	Nm-Mt	Ex-Mt
CJ Chipper Jones/80	100.00	30.00
DJ Derek Jeter/360	150.00	45.00
RJ Reggie Jackson/360	60.00	18.00

2003 Fleer Focus JE Materialistic Plus Game Jersey

Randomly inserted in packs, these nine cards feature leading players along with a game-used jersey swatch of the featured player. These

cards were issued to a stated print run of 250 serial numbered sets.

	Nm-Mt	Ex-Mt
AD Adam Dunn	10.00	3.00
AR Alex Rodriguez	20.00	6.00
AS Alfonso Soriano	15.00	4.50
CJ Chipper Jones	15.00	4.50
DJ Derek Jeter	30.00	9.00
GM Greg Maddux	25.00	7.50
MP Mike Piazza	25.00	7.50
NG Nomar Garciaparra	25.00	7.50
RC Roger Clemens	25.00	7.50

2003 Fleer Focus JE Materialistic Portrait Away

Issued at a stated rate of one in 576, this 15 card set features portraits of leading players in their away uniforms.

Nm-Mt Ex-Mt

HOME RANDOM INSERTS IN PACKS .
HOME PRINT RUN 1 SERIAL #'d SET .
NO HOME PRICING DUE TO SCARCITY

	Nm-Mt	Ex-Mt
I Ichiro Suzuki	25.00	7.50
AD Adam Dunn	20.00	6.00
AP Albert Pujols	30.00	9.00
AR Alex Rodriguez	25.00	7.50
AS Alfonso Soriano	20.00	6.00
CJ Chipper Jones	20.00	6.00
DJ Derek Jeter	40.00	12.00
GM Greg Maddux	25.00	7.50
JG Jason Giambi	20.00	6.00
KG Ken Griffey Jr.	25.00	7.50
MP Mike Piazza	25.00	7.50
NG Nomar Garciaparra	25.00	7.50
PB Pat Burrell	20.00	6.00
RC Roger Clemens	30.00	9.00
SS Sammy Sosa	25.00	7.50

2003 Fleer Focus JE MLB Shirtified

Inserted at a stated rate of one in 24, this 15-card set features leading players along with various jersey designs.

	Nm-Mt	Ex-Mt
1 Manny Ramirez	2.50	.75
2 Jarrod Washburn	2.50	.75
3 Greg Maddux	6.00	1.80
4 Austin Kearns	2.50	.75
5 Jim Thome	4.00	1.20
6 Kazuhisa Ishii	2.50	.75
7 Mike Piazza	6.00	1.80
8 Alfonso Soriano	2.50	.75
9 Pat Burrell	2.50	.75
10 Derek Jeter	10.00	3.00
11 Miguel Tejada	2.50	.75
12 Roger Clemens	8.00	2.40
13 Alex Rodriguez	6.00	1.80
14 Roy Oswalt	2.50	.75
15 Richie Sexson	2.50	.75

2003 Fleer Focus JE MLB Shirtified Game Jersey

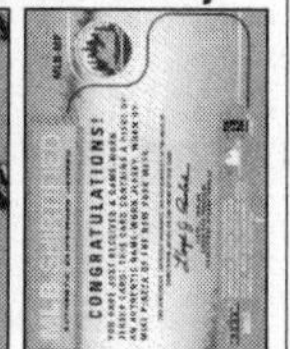

Issued at a stated rate of one in 35, this is a partial parallel to the MLB Shirtified set. These cards feature a game worn jersey swatch on them.

	Nm-Mt	Ex-Mt
AR Alex Rodriguez	15.00	4.50
AS Alfonso Soriano	10.00	3.00
DJ Derek Jeter	25.00	7.50
GM Greg Maddux	10.00	3.00
MP Mike Piazza	10.00	3.00
MR Manny Ramirez	8.00	2.40
MT Miguel Tejada	8.00	2.40
RC Roger Clemens	15.00	4.50
RO Roy Oswalt	8.00	2.40
RS Richie Sexson	8.00	2.40

2003 Fleer Focus JE MLB Shirtified Patch

Randomly inserted into packs, this is a parallel to the MLB Shirtified Game Jersey set. These cards feature authentic patches and this set was issued to a stated print run of 200 serial numbered sets.

Nm-Mt Ex-Mt

*PREMIUM LOGOS: 2X HI COLUMN ..
*4 OR MORE COLORS: 1.5X HI COLUMN

	Nm-Mt	Ex-Mt
AR Alex Rodriguez	40.00	12.00
AS Alfonso Soriano	25.00	7.50
DJ Derek Jeter	60.00	18.00
GM Greg Maddux	40.00	12.00
MP Mike Piazza	40.00	12.00
MR Manny Ramirez	20.00	6.00
MT Miguel Tejada	20.00	6.00
RC Roger Clemens	40.00	12.00
RO Roy Oswalt	20.00	6.00
RS Richie Sexson	20.00	6.00

2003 Fleer Focus JE Team Colors

Inserted at a stated rate of one in 12, this 20 card set feature both an action and a portrait shot of the featured player.

	Nm-Mt	Ex-Mt
1 Alex Rodriguez	4.00	1.20
2 Mark Prior	5.00	1.50
3 Derek Jeter	6.00	1.80
4 Curt Schilling	1.50	.45
5 Pat Burrell	1.50	.45
6 Josh Beckett	1.50	.45
7 Sean Burroughs	1.50	.45
8 Troy Glaus	1.50	.45
9 Torii Hunter	1.50	.45
10 Jeff Bagwell	2.50	.75
11 Pedro Martinez	2.50	.75
12 Mike Piazza	4.00	1.20
13 Lance Berkman	1.50	.45
14 Nomar Garciaparra	4.00	1.20
15 Chipper Jones	2.50	.75
16 Eric Chavez	1.50	.45
17 Barry Zito	1.50	.45
18 Barry Bonds	6.00	1.80
19 Adam Dunn	1.50	.45
20 Randy Johnson	2.50	.75

2003 Fleer Focus JE Team Colors Game Jersey

Inserted at a stated rate of one in 28, this is a partial parallel to the Team Colors set. These cards feature a game-used jersey swatch on them.

	Nm-Mt	Ex-Mt
AD Adam Dunn	8.00	2.40
CJ Chipper Jones	10.00	3.00
CS Curt Schilling	10.00	3.00
DJ Derek Jeter	25.00	7.50
EC Eric Chavez	8.00	2.40
JBA Jeff Bagwell	10.00	3.00
JBE Josh Beckett	10.00	3.00
LB Lance Berkman	8.00	2.40
NG Nomar Garciaparra	15.00	4.50
PM Pedro Martinez	10.00	3.00
RJ Randy Johnson	10.00	3.00
TG Troy Glaus	10.00	3.00

2003 Fleer Focus JE Team Colors Game Jersey Multi Color

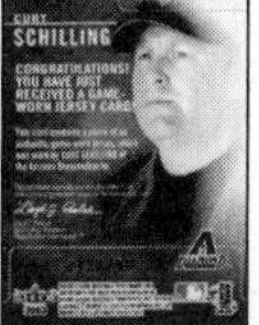

Randomly inserted in packs, this is a partial parallel to the Team Colors set. These cards feature multi-color pieces of the game-used jersery of the featured player. These cards were issued to a stated print run of 250 serial numbered sets.

	Nm-Mt	Ex-Mt
*4 OR MORE COLORS: 1.5X HI COLUMN		
AD Adam Dunn	20.00	6.00
AR Alex Rodriguez	40.00	12.00
CJ Chipper Jones	25.00	7.50
CS Curt Schilling	25.00	7.50
DJ Derek Jeter	50.00	15.00
EC Eric Chavez	20.00	6.00
JBA Jeff Bagwell	25.00	7.50
JBE Josh Beckett	25.00	7.50
LB Lance Berkman	20.00	6.00
MP Mike Piazza	40.00	12.00
NG Nomar Garciaparra	40.00	12.00
PM Pedro Martinez	25.00	7.50
RJ Randy Johnson	25.00	7.50
TG Troy Glaus	25.00	7.50

2001 Fleer Futures

The 2001 Fleer Futures product was released in late March, 2001 and features a 220-card base set that was broken into tiers as follows: Base Veterans (1-180), and Bright Futures Prospects (181-220). Each pack contained eight cards and carried a suggested retail price of $2.99. Please note that a three-card group of regular cards were inserted as a boxtopper on top of Futures Boxes so collectors could see what the cards looked like. An additional ten cards (221-230) featuring a selection of top prosects was distributed in late December, 2001 within Fleer Platinum RC packs. Each of these cards is serial numbered to 2499 copies.

	Nm-Mt	Ex-Mt
COMPLETE SET (220)	25.00	7.50
COMMON CARD (1-220)	.30	.09
COMMON (221-230)	5.00	1.50
1 Darin Erstad	.30	.09
2 Manny Ramirez	.30	.09
3 Darryl Kile	.30	.09
4 Troy O'Leary	.30	.09
5 Mark Quinn	.30	.09
6 Brian Giles	.30	.09
7 Randy Johnson	.75	.23
8 Todd Walker	.30	.09
9 Mike Piazza	1.25	.35
10 Fred McGriff	.50	.15
11 Sammy Sosa	1.25	.35
12 Chan Ho Park	.30	.09
13 John Rocker	.30	.09
14 Luis Castillo	.30	.09
15 Eric Chavez	.30	.09
16 Carlos Delgado	.30	.09
17 Sean Casey	.30	.09
18 Corey Koskie	.30	.09
19 John Olerud	.30	.09
20 Nomar Garciaparra	1.25	.35
21 Craig Biggio	.50	.15
22 Pat Burrell	.30	.09
23 Ben Molina	.30	.09
24 Jim Thome	.75	.23
25 Rey Ordonez	.30	.09
26 Fernando Tatis	.30	.09
27 Eric Young	.30	.09
28 Eric Karros	.30	.09
29 Adam Eaton	.30	.09
30 Brian Jordan	.30	.09
31 Jorge Posada	.50	.15
32 Gabe Kapler	.30	.09
33 Keith Foulke	.30	.09
34 Ron Coomer	.30	.09
35 Chipper Jones	.75	.23
36 Miguel Tejada	.30	.09
37 David Wells	.30	.09
38 Carlos Lee	.30	.09
39 Barry Bonds	2.00	.60
40 Derrek Lee	.30	.09
41 Tim Hudson	.30	.09
42 Billy Koch	.30	.09
43 Dmitri Young	.30	.09
44 Vladimir Guerrero	.75	.23
45 Rickey Henderson	.75	.23
46 Jeff Bagwell	.50	.15
47 Robert Person	.30	.09
48 Brady Anderson	.30	.09
49 Lance Berkman	.30	.09
50 Mike Lieberthal	.30	.09
51 Adam Kennedy	.30	.09
52 Russell Branyan	.30	.09
53 Robin Ventura	.30	.09
54 Mark McGwire	2.00	.60
55 Tony Gwynn	1.00	.30
56 Matt Williams	.30	.09
57 Jeff Cirillo	.30	.09
58 Roger Clemens	1.50	.45
59 Ivan Rodriguez	.75	.23
60 Brad Radke	.30	.09
61 Kazuhiro Sasaki	.30	.09
62 Cal Ripken	2.50	.75
63 Ken Caminiti	.30	.09
64 Bob Abreu	.30	.09
65 Troy Glaus	.50	.15
66 Sandy Alomar Jr.	.30	.09
67 Jose Vidro	.30	.09
68 Pedro Martinez	.75	.23
69 Kevin Young	.30	.09
70 Jay Bell	.30	.09
71 Larry Walker	.50	.15
72 Derek Jeter	2.00	.60
73 Miguel Cairo	.30	.09
74 Magglio Ordonez	.30	.09
75 Jeromy Burnitz	.30	.09
76 J.T. Snow	.30	.09
77 Andres Galarraga	.30	.09
78 Ryan Dempster	.30	.09
79 Ken Griffey Jr.	1.25	.35
80 Aaron Sele	.30	.09
81 Tom Glavine	.50	.15
82 Hideo Nomo	.75	.23
83 Orlando Hernandez	.30	.09
84 Tony Batista	.30	.09
85 Aaron Boone	.30	.09
86 Jacque Jones	.30	.09
87 Delino DeShields	.30	.09
88 Garret Anderson	.30	.09
89 Fernando Seguignol	.30	.09
90 Jim Edmonds	.30	.09
91 Frank Thomas	.75	.23
92 Adrian Beltre	.30	.09
93 Ellis Burks	.30	.09
94 Andruw Jones	.30	.09
95 Tony Clark	.30	.09
96 Danny Graves	.30	.09
97 Alex Rodriguez	1.25	.35
98 Mike Mussina	.75	.23
99 Scott Elarton	.30	.09
100 Jason Giambi	.75	.23
101 Jay Payton	.30	.09
102 Gerald Williams	.30	.09
103 Kerry Wood	.75	.23
104 Shawn Green	.30	.09
105 Greg Maddux	1.25	.35
106 Juan Encarnacion	.30	.09
107 Bernie Williams	.50	.15
108 Mike Lamb	.30	.09
109 Charles Johnson	.30	.09
110 Richie Sexson	.30	.09
111 Jeff Kent	.30	.09
112 Albert Belle	.30	.09
113 Cliff Floyd	.30	.09
114 Ben Grieve	.30	.09
115 Tim Salmon	.50	.15
116 Carl Pavano	.30	.09
117 Rick Ankiel	.30	.09
118 Dante Bichette	.30	.09
119 Johnny Damon	.30	.09
120 Brian Anderson	.30	.09
121 Roberto Alomar	.75	.23
122 Mike Hampton	.30	.09
123 Greg Vaughn	.30	.09
124 Carl Everett	.30	.09
125 Moises Alou	.30	.09
126 Jason Kendall	.30	.09
127 Omar Vizquel	.30	.09
128 Mark Grace	.50	.15
129 Kevin Brown	.30	.09
130 Phil Nevin	.30	.09
131 Kevin Millwood	.30	.09
132 Bobby Higginson	.30	.09
133 Ruben Mateo	.30	.09
134 Luis Gonzalez	.30	.09
135 Dean Palmer	.30	.09
136 Mariano Rivera	.50	.15
137 Rick Helling	.30	.09
138 Paul Konerko	.30	.09
139 Marquis Grissom	.30	.09
140 Robb Nen	.30	.09
141 Javy Lopez	.30	.09
142 Preston Wilson	.30	.09
143 Terrence Long	.30	.09
144 Shannon Stewart	.30	.09
145 Barry Larkin	.75	.23
146 Cristian Guzman	.30	.09
147 Jay Buhner	.30	.09
148 Jermaine Dye	.30	.09
149 Kris Benson	.30	.09
150 Curt Schilling	.50	.15
151 Todd Helton	.50	.15
152 Paul O'Neill	.50	.15
153 Rafael Palmeiro	.50	.15
154 Ray Durham	.30	.09
155 Geoff Jenkins	.30	.09
156 Livan Hernandez	.30	.09
157 Rafael Furcal	.30	.09
158 Juan Gonzalez	.75	.23
159 Tino Martinez	.50	.15
160 Raul Mondesi	.30	.09
161 Matt Lawton	.30	.09
162 Edgar Martinez	.50	.15
163 Richard Hidalgo	.30	.09
164 Scott Rolen	.50	.15
165 Chuck Finley	.30	.09
166 Edgardo Alfonzo	.30	.09
167 J.D. Drew	.30	.09
168 Trot Nixon	.50	.15
169 Carlos Beltran	.30	.09
170 Ryan Klesko	.30	.09
171 Mo Vaughn	.30	.09
172 Kenny Lofton	.30	.09
173 Al Leiter	.30	.09
174 Rondell White	.30	.09
175 Mike Sweeney	.30	.09
176 Trevor Hoffman	.30	.09
177 Steve Finley	.30	.09
178 Jeffrey Hammonds	.30	.09
179 David Justice	.30	.09
180 Gary Sheffield	.30	.09
181 Eric Munson BF	.30	.09
182 Luis Matos BF	.30	.09
183 Alex Cabrera BF	.30	.09
184 Randy Keisler BF	.30	.09
185 Nate Rolison BF	.30	.09
186 Jason Hart BF	.30	.09
187 Timo Perez BF	.30	.09
188 Adam Bernero BF	.30	.09
189 Barry Zito BF	.75	.23
190 Ryan Kohlmeier BF	.30	.09
191 Joey Nation BF	.30	.09
192 Oswaldo Mairena BF	.30	.09
193 Aubrey Huff BF	.30	.09
194 Mark Buehrle BF	.30	.09
195 Jace Brewer BF	.30	.09
196 Julio Zuleta BF	.30	.09
197 Xavier Nady BF	.30	.09
198 Vernon Wells BF	.30	.09
199 Joe Crede BF	.30	.09
200 Scott Downs BF	.30	.09
201 Ben Petrick BF	.30	.09
202 A.J. Burnett BF	.30	.09
203 Esix Snead BF RC	.30	.09
204 Dernell Stenson BF	.30	.09
205 Jose Ortiz BF	.30	.09
206 Paxton Crawford BF	.30	.09
207 Jason Tyner BF	.30	.09
208 Jimmy Rollins BF	.30	.09
209 Juan Pierre BF	.30	.09
210 Keith Ginter BF	.30	.09
211 Adam Dunn BF	.30	.09
212 Larry Barnes BF	.30	.09
213 Adam Piatt BF	.30	.09
214 Rodney Lindsey BF	.30	.09
215 Eric Byrnes BF	.30	.09
216 Julio Lugo BF	.30	.09
217 Corey Patterson BF	.30	.09
218 Reggie Taylor BF	.30	.09
219 Kenny Kelly BF	.30	.09
220 Tike Redman BF	.30	.09
221 D.Henson/2499 RC	6.00	1.80
222 J.Estrada/2499 RC	5.00	1.50
223 E.Guzman/2499 RC	5.00	1.50
224 Albert Pujols/2499 RC	40.00	12.00
225 W.Betemit/2499 RC	5.00	1.50
226 M.Teixeira/2499 RC	15.00	4.50
227 T.Shinjo/2499 RC	6.00	1.80
228 Matt White/2499 RC	5.00	1.50
229 A.Hernandez/2499 RC	5.00	1.50
230 I.Suzuki/2499 RC	25.00	7.50

2001 Fleer Futures Black Gold

Randomly inserted into packs, this 220-card set is a complete parallel of the 2001 Fleer Futures base set. Each card in this set features a black foil background, and is individually serial numbered to 499.

	Nm-Mt	Ex-Mt
*STARS 1-180: 3X TO 8X BASE HI		
*BF 181-220: 3X TO 8X BASE HI		
*BF RC'S 181-220: 3X TO 8X BASE HI		

2001 Fleer Futures September Call-Ups Memorabilia

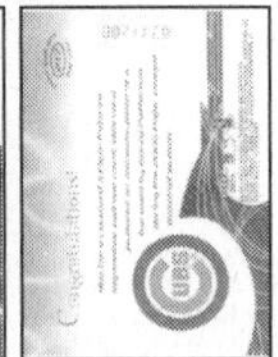

Randomly inserted into packs, this 15-card insert is a partial parallel of the Bright Future cards found in the 2001 Fleer Futures base set. This set features cards of young prospects with a swatch of game-used memorabilia that includes Caps, Bats, Gloves, and Cleats. Please note that there were only 200 of each card produced.

	Nm-Mt	Ex-Mt
184 R. Keisler Cap/Cleat	8.00	2.40
185 Nate Rolison Bat	8.00	2.40
187 Timo Perez Bat	8.00	2.40
191 Joey Nation Glove	8.00	2.40
192 O. Mairena Glove	8.00	2.40
195 Jace Brewer Bat	8.00	2.40
197 Xavier Nady Glove	8.00	2.40
199 Joe Crede Bat	8.00	2.40
205 Jose Ortiz Bat	8.00	2.40
208 Jimmy Rollins Glove	8.00	2.40
210 Keith Ginter Bat	8.00	2.40
214 Rodney Lindsey Bat	8.00	2.40
217 Corey Patterson Bat	8.00	2.40
218 Reggie Taylor Bat	8.00	2.40
219 Kenny Kelly Bat	8.00	2.40

2001 Fleer Futures Bases Loaded

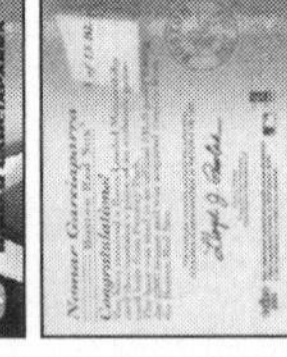

Randomly inserted into hobby packs at one in 134, this 15-card insert features a piece of game-used base from the player's home stadium. Card backs carry a "BL" prefix.

	Nm-Mt	Ex-Mt
BL1 Ken Griffey Jr.	15.00	4.50
BL2 Mark McGwire	40.00	12.00
BL3 Carlos Delgado	8.00	2.40
BL4 Chipper Jones	10.00	3.00
BL5 Nomar Garciaparra	15.00	4.50
BL6 Cal Ripken	25.00	7.50
BL7 Sammy Sosa	15.00	4.50
BL8 Jeff Bagwell	10.00	3.00
BL9 Vladimir Guerrero	10.00	3.00
BL10 Tony Gwynn	10.00	3.00
BL11 Frank Thomas	10.00	3.00
BL12 Mike Piazza	10.00	3.00
BL13 Jason Giambi	10.00	3.00
BL14 Troy Glaus	10.00	3.00
BL15 Pat Burrell	8.00	2.40

2001 Fleer Futures Bats to the Future

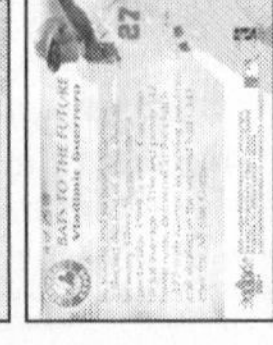

Randomly inserted into packs at one in 28, this 25-card insert features the top Silver Slugger winners in baseball history. Card backs carry a "BF" prefix.

	Nm-Mt	Ex-Mt
COMPLETE SET (25)	200.00	60.00
BF1 Mike Schmidt	15.00	4.50
BF2 Carlton Fisk	5.00	1.50
BF3 Paul Molitor	5.00	1.50
BF4 Vladimir Guerrero	6.00	1.80
BF5 Dave Parker	5.00	1.50
BF6 Chipper Jones	6.00	1.80
BF7 Carlos Delgado	5.00	1.50
BF8 Tony Gwynn	8.00	2.40
BF9 Reggie Jackson	5.00	1.50
BF10 Eddie Murray	6.00	1.80
BF11 Robin Yount	10.00	3.00
BF12 Alan Trammell	5.00	1.50
BF13 Frank Thomas	6.00	1.80
BF14 Cal Ripken	20.00	6.00
BF15 Don Mattingly	25.00	7.50
BF16 Jim Rice	5.00	1.50
BF17 Juan Gonzalez	6.00	1.80
BF18 Todd Helton	5.00	1.50
BF19 George Brett	15.00	4.50
BF20 Barry Bonds	15.00	4.50
BF21 Kirk Gibson	5.00	1.50
BF22 Matt Williams	5.00	1.50
BF23 Dave Winfield	5.00	1.50
BF24 Ryne Sandberg	15.00	4.50
BF25 Ivan Rodriguez	6.00	1.80

2001 Fleer Futures Bats to the Future Game Bat

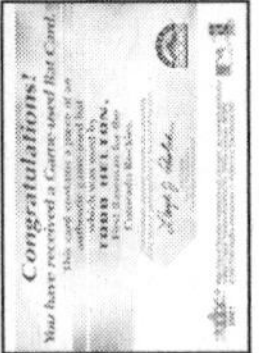

Randomly inserted into packs at one in 114, this 25-card insert features pieces of actual game-used lumber. Cards are listed below in alphabetical order for convenience.

	Nm-Mt	Ex-Mt
1 Barry Bonds	30.00	9.00
2 George Brett	40.00	12.00
3 Carlos Delgado	10.00	3.00
4 Carlton Fisk	25.00	7.50
5 Kirk Gibson	15.00	4.50
6 Juan Gonzalez	15.00	4.50
7 Vladimir Guerrero	15.00	4.50
8 Tony Gwynn	15.00	4.50
9 Todd Helton	15.00	4.50
10 Reggie Jackson	25.00	7.50
11 Chipper Jones	15.00	4.50
12 Don Mattingly	40.00	12.00
13 Paul Molitor	25.00	7.50
14 Eddie Murray	25.00	7.50
15 Dave Parker	15.00	4.50
16 Jim Rice	15.00	4.50
17 Cal Ripken	50.00	15.00
18 Ivan Rodriguez	15.00	4.50
19 Ryne Sandberg	40.00	12.00
20 Mike Schmidt	40.00	12.00
21 Frank Thomas	15.00	4.50
22 Alan Trammell	25.00	7.50
23 Matt Williams	10.00	3.00
24 Dave Winfield	15.00	4.50
25 Robin Yount	25.00	7.50

2001 Fleer Futures Bats to the Future Game Bat Autograph

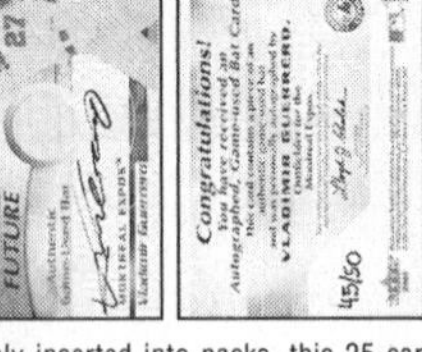

Randomly inserted into packs, this 25-card insert features both an autograph and a piece of actual game-used lumber. Cards are listed below in alphabetical order for convenience. Please note that there were only 50 of each card produced. Also note that Jim Rice and Eddie Murray packed out as exchange cards with a redemption deadline of March 1st, 2002.

	Nm-Mt	Ex-Mt
1 Barry Bonds	250.00	75.00
2 George Brett	200.00	60.00
3 Carlos Delgado	50.00	15.00
4 Carlton Fisk	80.00	24.00
5 Kirk Gibson	50.00	15.00
6 Juan Gonzalez	100.00	30.00
7 Vladimir Guerrero	100.00	30.00
8 Tony Gwynn	120.00	36.00
9 Todd Helton	80.00	24.00
10 Reggie Jackson	120.00	36.00
11 Chipper Jones	100.00	30.00
12 Don Mattingly	200.00	60.00
13 Paul Molitor	80.00	24.00
14 Eddie Murray	120.00	36.00
15 Dave Parker	50.00	15.00
16 Jim Rice	50.00	15.00
17 Cal Ripken	250.00	75.00
18 Ivan Rodriguez	100.00	30.00
19 Ryne Sandberg	200.00	60.00
20 Mike Schmidt	150.00	45.00
21 Frank Thomas	100.00	30.00
22 Alan Trammell	80.00	24.00
23 Matt Williams	50.00	15.00
24 Dave Winfield	80.00	24.00
25 Robin Yount	120.00	36.00

2001 Fleer Futures Characteristics

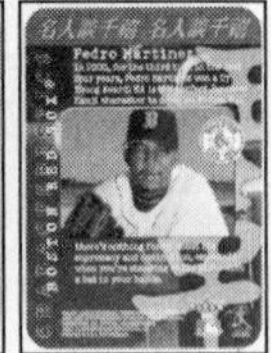

Randomly inserted into packs at one in nine, this 15-card insert pairs up players with the Japanese "Kanji" characters that describe their skills. Card backs carry a "C" prefix.

	Nm-Mt	Ex-Mt
COMPLETE SET (15)	40.00	12.00
C1 Derek Jeter	5.00	1.50
C2 Mark McGwire	5.00	1.50
C3 Nomar Garciaparra	3.00	.90
C4 Sammy Sosa	3.00	.90
C5 Pedro Martinez	2.00	.60
C6 Chipper Jones	2.00	.60
C7 Cal Ripken	6.00	1.80
C8 Todd Helton	1.50	.45
C9 Jim Edmonds	1.50	.45
C10 Ken Griffey Jr.	3.00	.90
C11 Alex Rodriguez	3.00	.90
C12 Mike Piazza	3.00	.90
C13 Vladimir Guerrero	2.00	.60
C14 Frank Thomas	2.00	.60
C15 Carlos Delgado	1.50	.45

2001 Fleer Futures Hot Commodities

Randomly inserted into packs at one in 14, this 10-card insert set features players that every ballclub wishes they had on their team. Card backs carry a "HC" prefix.

	Nm-Mt	Ex-Mt
COMPLETE SET (10)	40.00	12.00
HC1 Mark McGwire	5.00	1.50
HC2 Ken Griffey Jr.	3.00	.90
HC3 Derek Jeter	5.00	1.50
HC4 Cal Ripken	6.00	1.80
HC5 Chipper Jones	2.00	.60
HC6 Barry Bonds	5.00	1.50
HC7 Mike Piazza	3.00	.90
HC8 Sammy Sosa	3.00	.90
HC9 Alex Rodriguez	3.00	.90
HC10 Frank Thomas	2.00	.60

2001 Fleer Game Time

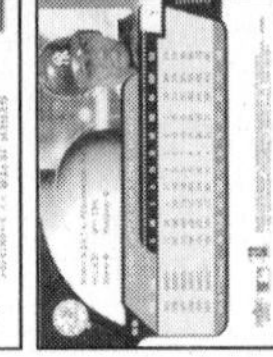

The 2001 Fleer Game Time product was released in June, 2001 and featured a 121-card base set that was broken into tiers as follows: Base Veterans (1-90), and Next Game Rookies (91-121) serial numbered to 2000. Each pack contained five cards and carried a suggested retail price of $3.99.

	Nm-Mt	Ex-Mt
COMP.SET w/o SP's (90)	25.00	7.50
COMMON CARD (1-90)	.40	.12
COMMON NG (91-121)	4.00	1.20
1 Derek Jeter	2.50	.75
2 Nomar Garciaparra	1.50	.45
3 Alex Rodriguez	1.50	.45
4 Jason Kendall	.40	.12
5 Barry Bonds	2.50	.75
6 David Wells	.40	.12
7 Craig Biggio	.60	.18
8 Adrian Beltre	.40	.12
9 Pat Burrell	.40	.12
10 Rafael Palmeiro	.60	.18
11 Jim Thome	1.00	.30
12 Mike Lowell	.40	.12
13 Trevor Hoffman	.40	.12
14 Pokey Reese	.40	.12
15 Juan Encarnacion	.40	.12
16 Shawn Green	.40	.12
17 Kerry Wood	1.00	.30
18 Richard Hidalgo	.40	.12
19 Scott Rolen	.60	.18
20 Jeff Kent	.40	.12
21 Alex Gonzalez	.40	.12
22 Matt Williams	.40	.12
23 Mike Sweeney	.40	.12
24 Edgar Martinez	.60	.18
25 Sammy Sosa	1.50	.45
26 Bobby Higginson	.40	.12
27 Kevin Brown	.40	.12
28 Mike Lieberthal	.40	.12
29 Pedro Martinez	1.00	.30
30 Jeff Weaver	.40	.12
31 Greg Maddux	1.50	.45
32 Mike Hampton	.40	.12
33 Vladimir Guerrero	1.00	.30
34 Greg Vaughn	.40	.12
35 Manny Ramirez	.40	.12

36 Carlos Beltran	.40	.12
37 Eric Chavez	.40	.12
38 Troy Glaus	.60	.18
39 Todd Helton	.60	.18
40 Gary Sheffield	.40	.12
41 Brady Anderson	.40	.12
42 Juan Gonzalez	1.00	.30
43 Tim Hudson	.40	.12
44 Kenny Lofton	.40	.12
45 Al Leiter	.40	.12
46 Eric Owens	.40	.12
47 Roberto Alomar	1.00	.30
48 Preston Wilson	.40	.12
49 Tony Gwynn	1.25	.35
50 Cal Ripken	3.00	.90
51 Ben Petrick	.40	.12
52 Jason Giambi	1.00	.30
53 Ben Grieve	.40	.12
54 Albert Belle	.40	.12
55 Jose Vidro	.40	.12
56 Barry Zito	1.00	.30
57 Ivan Rodriguez	1.00	.30
58 Jeff Bagwell	.60	.18
59 Geoff Jenkins	.40	.12
60 Roger Clemens	2.00	.60
61 John Olerud	.40	.12
62 Randy Johnson	1.00	.30
63 Matt Lawton	.40	.12
64 Mark McGwire	2.50	.75
65 Brad Radke	.40	.12
66 Frank Thomas	1.00	.30
67 Edgardo Alfonzo	.40	.12
68 Brian Giles	.40	.12
69 J.T. Snow	.40	.12
70 Carlos Delgado	.40	.12
71 Chipper Jones	1.00	.30
72 Mark Quinn	.40	.12
73 Mike Mussina	1.00	.30
74 Rick Ankiel	.40	.12
75 Rafael Furcal	.40	.12
76 Jim Edmonds	.40	.12
77 Vinny Castilla	.40	.12
78 Sean Casey	.40	.12
79 Derrek Lee	.40	.12
80 Mike Piazza	1.50	.45
81 Warren Morris	.40	.12
82 Tim Salmon	.60	.18
83 Jeromy Burnitz	.40	.12
84 Freddy Garcia	.40	.12
85 Ken Griffey Jr.	1.50	.45
86 Andruw Jones	.40	.12
87 Darryl Kile	.40	.12
88 Magglio Ordonez	.40	.12
89 Bernie Williams	.60	.18
90 Timo Perez	.40	.12
91 Ichiro Suzuki NG RC	25.00	7.50
92 Larry Barnes	4.00	1.20
Darin Erstad		
93 J. Randolph NG RC	4.00	1.20
94 Paul Phillips NG RC	4.00	1.20
95 Esix Snead NG RC	4.00	1.20
96 Matt White NG RC	4.00	1.20
97 Ryan Freel NG RC	4.00	1.20
98 Winston Abreu NG RC	4.00	1.20
99 Junior Spivey NG RC	5.00	1.50
100 Randy Keisler	8.00	2.40
Roger Clemens		
101 Mike Piazza	6.00	1.80
Brian Cole		
102 Aubrey Huff	5.00	1.50
Chipper Jones		
103 Corey Patterson	5.00	1.50
Sammy Sosa		
104 Sun Woo Kim	5.00	1.50
Pedro Martinez		
105 Drew Henson NG RC	6.00	1.80
106 C. Vargas NG RC	4.00	1.20
107 Rafael Furcal	4.00	1.20
Cesar Izturis		
108 Paxton Crawford	5.00	1.50
Pedro Martinez		
109 A. Hernandez NG RC	4.00	1.20
110 Jace Brewer	10.00	3.00
Derek Jeter		
111 Andy Morales NG RC	4.00	1.20
112 W. Betemit NG RC	4.00	1.20
113 Juan Diaz NG RC	4.00	1.20
114 Erick Almonte NG RC	4.00	1.20
115 Nick Punto NG RC	4.00	1.20
116 T. Shinjo NG RC	6.00	1.80
117 Jay Gibbons NG RC	6.00	1.80
118 Andres Torres NG RC	4.00	1.20
119 Alexis Gomez NG RC	4.00	1.20
120 Wilkin Ruan NG RC	4.00	1.20
121 Albert Pujols NG RC	40.00	12.00
MM2 Derek Jeter/1996	12.00	3.60
MM2 Derek Jeter AU/96	120.00	36.00

2001 Fleer Game Time Next Game Extra

Randomly inserted into packs, this 31-card insert is actually a parallel of the Next game Rookies from the Fleer Game Time base set. Each card was produced with the words "Next Game Extra" on the card fronts. Please note that each card is serial numbered to 200 on the card back.

	Nm-Mt	Ex-Mt
COMMON CARD (91-121)	15.00	4.50
*EXTRA: .75X TO 2X BASIC CARDS ...		

2001 Fleer Game Time Famers Lumber

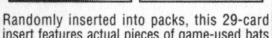

Randomly inserted into packs, this 29-card insert features actual pieces of game-used bats from Hall of Famers like Carlton Fisk and Roberto Clemente. Please note that each card is serial numbered to 100.

	Nm-Mt	Ex-Mt
1 Luis Aparicio	15.00	4.50
2 Hank Bauer	15.00	4.50
3 Paul Blair	15.00	4.50
4 Bobby Bonds	15.00	4.50
5 Orlando Cepeda	15.00	4.50
6 Roberto Clemente	150.00	45.00
7 Rocky Colavito	25.00	7.50
8 Bucky Dent	15.00	4.50
9 Bill Dickey	25.00	7.50
10 Larry Doby	15.00	4.50
11 Carlton Fisk	25.00	7.50
12 Hank Greenberg	80.00	24.00
13 Elston Howard	25.00	7.50
14 Frank Howard	15.00	4.50
15 Reggie Jackson	25.00	7.50
16 Harmon Killebrew	25.00	7.50
17 Tony Lazzeri	15.00	4.50
18 Roger Maris	80.00	24.00
19 Johnny Mize	15.00	4.50
20 Thurman Munson	50.00	15.00
21 Tony Perez	15.00	4.50
22 Jim Rice	15.00	4.50
23 Phil Rizzuto	25.00	7.50
24 Bill Skowron	25.00	7.50
25 Enos Slaughter	15.00	4.50
26 Duke Snider	25.00	7.50
27 Willie Stargell	25.00	7.50
28 Bill Terry	25.00	7.50
29 Ted Williams	150.00	45.00

2001 Fleer Game Time Let's Play Two

Randomly inserted into packs at one in 24, this 15-card insert set features cards of players that play the same position. Card backs carry a "LT" prefix.

	Nm-Mt	Ex-Mt
COMPLETE SET (15)	120.00	36.00
LT1 Nomar Garciaparra	10.00	3.00
Derek Jeter		
LT2 Mark McGwire	12.00	3.60
Sammy Sosa		
LT3 Pedro Martinez	5.00	1.50
Randy Johnson		
LT4 Vladimir Guerrero	5.00	1.50
Carlos Delgado		
LT5 Mike Piazza	12.00	3.60
Roger Clemens		
LT6 Alex Rodriguez	8.00	2.40
Miguel Tejada		
LT7 Chipper Jones	5.00	1.50
Troy Glaus		
LT8 Alex Rodriguez	12.00	3.60
Derek Jeter		
LT9 Cal Ripken	15.00	4.50
Derek Jeter		
LT10 Jason Giambi	12.00	3.60
Mark McGwire		
LT11 Jeff Bagwell	5.00	1.50
Craig Biggio		
LT12 Tom Glavine	8.00	2.40
Greg Maddux		
LT13 Ken Griffey Jr.	12.00	3.60
Barry Bonds		
LT14 Manny Ramirez	5.00	1.50
Pedro Martinez		
LT15 Ivan Rodriguez	8.00	2.40
Alex Rodriguez		

2001 Fleer Game Time Lumber

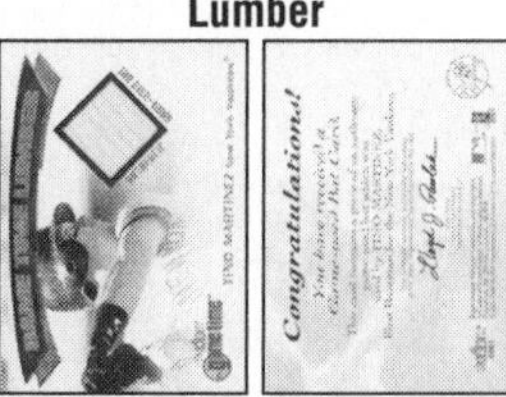

Randomly inserted into packs at one in 40, this 28-card insert features actual pieces of game-used bat from players like Barry Bonds and Nomar Garciaparra.

	Nm-Mt	Ex-Mt
1 Roberto Alomar	15.00	4.50
2 Rick Ankiel	10.00	3.00
3 Adrian Beltre	10.00	3.00
4 Barry Bonds	30.00	9.00
5 Kevin Brown	10.00	3.00
6 Ken Caminiti	10.00	3.00
7 Eric Chavez	10.00	3.00
8 Carlos Delgado	10.00	3.00
9 J.D. Drew	10.00	3.00
10 Erubiel Durazo	10.00	3.00
11 Carl Everett	10.00	3.00
12 Rafael Furcal	10.00	3.00
13 Nomar Garciaparra	20.00	6.00
14 Brian Giles	10.00	3.00
15 Juan Gonzalez	15.00	4.50
16 Todd Helton	15.00	4.50
17 Randy Johnson	15.00	4.50
18 Chipper Jones	15.00	4.50
19 Pedro Martinez	15.00	4.50
20 Tino Martinez	15.00	4.50
21 Cal Ripken SP/275	50.00	15.00
22 Ivan Rodriguez	15.00	4.50
23 Frank Thomas	15.00	4.50
24 Jim Thome	15.00	4.50
25 Bernie Williams	15.00	4.50

2001 Fleer Game Time New Order

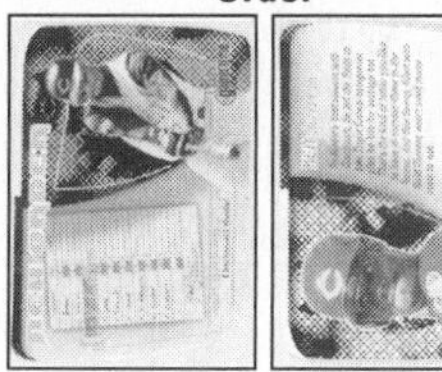

Randomly inserted into packs at one in 12, this 15-card insert set features players that are the future foundations of their ballclubs. Card backs carry a "NO" prefix.

	Nm-Mt	Ex-Mt
COMPLETE SET (15)	40.00	12.00
NO1 Derek Jeter	6.00	1.80
NO2 Nomar Garciaparra	4.00	1.20
NO3 Alex Rodriguez	4.00	1.20
NO4 Mark McGwire	6.00	1.80
NO5 Sammy Sosa	4.00	1.20
NO6 Carlos Delgado	1.50	.45
NO7 Troy Glaus	1.50	.45
NO8 Jason Giambi	2.50	.75
NO9 Mike Piazza	4.00	1.20
NO10 Todd Helton	1.50	.45
NO11 Vladimir Guerrero	2.50	.75
NO12 Manny Ramirez	1.50	.45
NO13 Frank Thomas	2.50	.75
NO14 Ken Griffey Jr.	4.00	1.20
NO15 Chipper Jones	2.50	.75

2001 Fleer Game Time Sticktoitness

Randomly inserted into packs at one in 8, this 20-card insert set features players that stick to the game plan. Card backs carry a "S" prefix.

	Nm-Mt	Ex-Mt
COMPLETE SET (20)	50.00	15.00
S1 Derek Jeter	6.00	1.80
S2 Nomar Garciaparra	4.00	1.20
S3 Alex Rodriguez	4.00	1.20
S4 Jeff Bagwell	1.50	.45
S5 Bernie Williams	1.50	.45
S6 Eric Chavez	1.50	.45
S7 Richard Hidalgo	1.50	.45
S8 Ichiro Suzuki	15.00	4.50
S9 Troy Glaus	1.50	.45
S10 Magglio Ordonez	1.50	.45
S11 Corey Patterson	1.50	.45
S12 Todd Helton	1.50	.45
S13 Jim Edmonds	1.50	.45
S14 Rafael Furcal	1.50	.45
S15 Mo Vaughn	1.50	.45
S16 Pat Burrell	1.50	.45
S17 Adrian Beltre	1.50	.45
S18 Andruw Jones	1.50	.45
S19 Manny Ramirez	1.50	.45
S20 Sean Casey	1.50	.45

2001 Fleer Game Time Uniformity

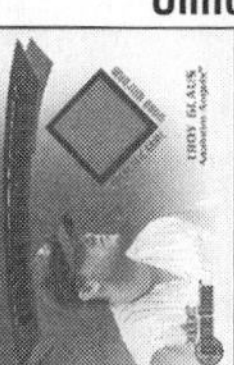
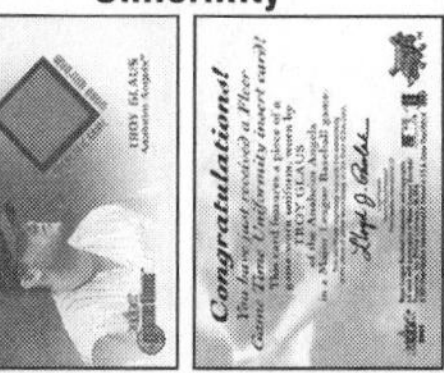

Randomly inserted into packs at one in 25, this 23-card insert set features swatches of actual game-used jerseys. The cards have been listed below in alphabetical order for convenience.

	Nm-Mt	Ex-Mt
1 Barry Bonds	25.00	7.50
2 Kevin Brown	10.00	3.00
3 Jay Buhner	10.00	3.00
4 Jeromy Burnitz	10.00	3.00
5 Andres Galarraga	10.00	3.00
6 Troy Glaus	15.00	4.50
7 Vladimir Guerrero	15.00	4.50
8 Carlos Guillen	10.00	3.00
9 Tony Gwynn	15.00	4.50
10 Brian Jordan	10.00	3.00
11 Greg Maddux	15.00	4.50
12 Fred McGriff	15.00	4.50
13 John Olerud	10.00	3.00
14 Magglio Ordonez	10.00	3.00
15 Ben Petrick	10.00	3.00
16 Brad Radke	10.00	3.00
17 Ivan Rodriguez	15.00	4.50
18 Fernando Seguignol	10.00	3.00
19 Gary Sheffield	10.00	3.00
20 Robin Ventura	10.00	3.00
21 Larry Walker	15.00	4.50
22 Rondell White	10.00	3.00
23 Matt Williams	10.00	3.00

2000 Fleer Gamers

The 2000 Fleer Gamers product was released in May,2000 as a 120-card set that featured 90

player cards, 20 Next Gamers cards (1:3), and 10 Fame Game cards (1:8). Each pack contained 5-cards and carried a suggested retail price of $2.99. An Alex Rodriguez Sample card was distributed to dealers and hobby media several weeks prior to the produt's release date.

	Nm-Mt	Ex-Mt
COMPLETE SET (120)	80.00	24.00
COMP.SET w/o SP's (90)	25.00	7.50
COMMON CARD (1-90)	.30	.09
COMMON NG (91-110)	2.00	.60
COMMON FG (111-120)	3.00	.90
1 Cal Ripken	2.50	.75
2 Derek Jeter	2.00	.60
3 Alex Rodriguez	1.25	.35
4 Alex Gonzalez	.30	.09
5 Nomar Garciaparra	1.25	.35
6 Brian Giles	.30	.09
7 Chris Singleton	.30	.09
8 Kevin Brown	.50	.15
9 J.D. Drew	.30	.09
10 Raul Mondesi	.30	.09
11 Sammy Sosa	1.25	.35
12 Carlos Beltran	.30	.09
13 Eric Chavez	.30	.09
14 Gabe Kapler	.30	.09
15 Tim Salmon	.50	.15
16 Manny Ramirez	.30	.09
17 Orlando Hernandez	.30	.09
18 Jeff Kent	.30	.09
19 Juan Gonzalez	.75	.23
20 Moises Alou	.30	.09
21 Jason Giambi	.75	.23
22 Ivan Rodriguez	.75	.23
23 Geoff Jenkins	.30	.09
24 Ken Griffey Jr.	1.25	.35
25 Mark McGwire	2.00	.60
26 Jose Canseco	.75	.23
27 Roberto Alomar	.75	.23
28 Craig Biggio	.50	.15
29 Scott Rolen	.50	.15
30 Vinny Castilla	.30	.09
31 Greg Maddux	1.25	.35
32 Pedro Martinez	.75	.23
33 Mike Piazza	1.25	.35
34 Albert Belle	.30	.09
35 Frank Thomas	.75	.23
36 Bobby Abreu	.30	.09
37 Edgar Martinez	.50	.15
38 Pokey Reese	.30	.09
39 Preston Wilson	.30	.09
40 Mike Lieberthal	.30	.09
41 Andruw Jones	.30	.09
42 Damion Easley	.30	.09
43 Mike Cameron	.30	.09
44 Todd Walker	.30	.09
45 Jason Kendall	.30	.09
46 Sean Casey	.30	.09
47 Corey Koskie	.30	.09
48 Warren Morris	.30	.09
49 Andres Galarraga	.30	.09
50 Dean Palmer	.30	.09
51 Jose Vidro	.30	.09
52 Brian Jordan	.30	.09
53 Tony Clark	.30	.09
54 Vladimir Guerrero	.75	.23
55 Mo Vaughn	.30	.09
56 Richie Sexson	.30	.09
57 Tino Martinez	.50	.15
58 Eric Owens	.30	.09
59 Matt Williams	.30	.09
60 Omar Vizquel	.30	.09
61 Rickey Henderson	.75	.23
62 J.T. Snow	.30	.09
63 Mark Grace	.50	.15
64 Carlos Febles	.30	.09
65 Paul O'Neill	.50	.15
66 Randy Johnson	.75	.23
67 Kenny Lofton	.30	.09
68 Roger Cedeno	.30	.09
69 Shawn Green	.30	.09
70 Chipper Jones	.75	.23
71 Jeff Cirillo	.30	.09
72 Robin Ventura	.50	.15
73 Paul Konerko	.30	.09
74 Jeromy Burnitz	.30	.09
75 Ben Grieve	.30	.09
76 Troy Glaus	.50	.15
77 Jim Thome	.75	.23
78 Bernie Williams	.50	.15
79 Barry Bonds	2.00	.60
80 Ray Durham	.30	.09
81 Adrian Beltre	.30	.09
82 Ray Lankford	.30	.09
83 Carlos Delgado	.30	.09
84 Erubiel Durazo	.30	.09
85 Larry Walker	.50	.15
86 Edgardo Alfonzo	.30	.09
87 Rafael Palmeiro	.50	.15
88 Magglio Ordonez	.30	.09
89 Jeff Bagwell	.50	.15
90 Tony Gwynn	1.00	.30
91 Norm Hutchins NG	2.00	.60
92 D.Turnbow NG RC	2.00	.60
93 Matt Riley NG	2.00	.60
94 David Eckstein NG	2.00	.60
95 Dernell Stenson NG	2.00	.60
96 Joe Crede NG	2.00	.60
97 Ben Petrick NG	2.00	.60
98 Eric Munson NG	2.00	.60
99 Pablo Ozuna NG	2.00	.60
100 Josh Beckett NG	5.00	1.50
101 Aaron McNeal NG RC	2.00	.60
102 Milton Bradley NG	2.00	.60
103 Alex Escobar NG	2.00	.60
104 Alfonso Soriano NG	4.00	1.20
105 Wily Pena NG	2.00	.60
106 Nick Johnson NG	2.00	.60
107 Adam Piatt NG	2.00	.60
108 Pat Burrell NG	2.50	.75
109 Rick Ankiel NG	2.00	.60
110 Vernon Wells NG	2.00	.60
111 Alex Rodriguez FG	4.00	1.20
112 Cal Ripken FG	8.00	2.40
113 Mark McGwire FG	6.00	1.80
114 Ken Griffey Jr. FG	4.00	1.20
115 Mike Piazza FG	4.00	1.20
116 Nomar Garciaparra FG	4.00	1.20
117 Derek Jeter FG	6.00	1.80
118 Chipper Jones FG	3.00	.90
119 Sammy Sosa FG	4.00	1.20
120 Tony Gwynn FG	3.00	.90
S3 Alex Rodriguez Sample	2.00	.60

2000 Fleer Gamers Extra

Randomly inserted into packs, this 120-card insert parallels the Gamers base set. Please note that cards (1-90) were inserted into packs at a rate of one per 24, cards (91-110) were inserted at one in 36, and cards (111-120) were inserted at one in 36. Cards feature a gold foil background rather than the silver foil featured in the base set.

	Nm-Mt	Ex-Mt
*EXTRA 1-90: 6X TO 15X BASIC 1-90		
*EXTRA 91-110: .5X TO 1.2X BASIC 91-110		
*EXTRA 111-120: .6X TO 1.5X BASIC 111-120		

2000 Fleer Gamers Cal to Greatness

Randomly inserted into packs, this 15-card set pays tribute to Cal Ripken. Cards (1-5) in the set were seeded into packs at one in nine, cards (6-10) were seeded at one in 25, and cards (11-15) were seeded at one in 144. Card backs carry a "CTA" prefix.

	Nm-Mt	Ex-Mt
COMPLETE SET (15)	100.00	30.00
COMMON (CTA1-CTA5)	5.00	1.50
COMMON (CTA6-CTA10)	10.00	3.00
COMMON (CTA11-CTA15)	25.00	7.50

2000 Fleer Gamers Change the Game

Randomly inserted into packs at one in 24, this 15-card insert set features players that have changed the way baseball has been played in the past. Card backs carry a "CG" prefix.

	Nm-Mt	Ex-Mt
COMPLETE SET (15)	100.00	30.00
CG1 Alex Rodriguez	8.00	2.40
CG2 Cal Ripken	15.00	4.50
CG3 Chipper Jones	5.00	1.50
CG4 Derek Jeter	12.00	3.60
CG5 Ken Griffey Jr.	8.00	2.40
CG6 Mark McGwire	12.00	3.60
CG7 Mike Piazza	8.00	2.40
CG8 Nomar Garciaparra	8.00	2.40
CG9 Sammy Sosa	8.00	2.40
CG10 Tony Gwynn	6.00	1.80
CG11 Ivan Rodriguez	5.00	1.50
CG12 Pedro Martinez	5.00	1.50
CG13 Juan Gonzalez	5.00	1.50
CG14 Vladimir Guerrero	5.00	1.50
CG15 Manny Ramirez	2.00	.60

2000 Fleer Gamers Determined

Randomly inserted into packs at one in 12, this 15-card insert set features players that are determined to win. Card backs carry a "D" prefix.

	Nm-Mt	Ex-Mt
COMPLETE SET (15)	60.00	18.00
D1 Nomar Garciaparra	4.00	1.20
D2 Chipper Jones	2.50	.75
D3 Derek Jeter	6.00	1.80
D4 Mike Piazza	4.00	1.20
D5 Jeff Bagwell	1.50	.45
D6 Mark McGwire	6.00	1.80
D7 Greg Maddux	4.00	1.20
D8 Sammy Sosa	4.00	1.20
D9 Ken Griffey Jr.	4.00	1.20
D10 Alex Rodriguez	4.00	1.20

D11 Tony Gwynn	3.00	.90
D12 Cal Ripken	8.00	2.40
D13 Barry Bonds	6.00	1.80
D14 Juan Gonzalez	2.50	.75
D15 Sean Casey	1.00	.30

2000 Fleer Gamers Lumber

Randomly inserted into packs at one in 36, this 48-card insert features chips from actual player used bats. This set represents one of the earliest attempts by a major manufacturer to seed game-used bat cards at a one per box ratio.

	Nm-Mt	Ex-Mt
1 Edgardo Alfonzo	10.00	3.00
2 Roberto Alomar	15.00	4.50
3 Moises Alou	10.00	3.00
4 Carlos Beltran	10.00	3.00
5 Adrian Beltre	10.00	3.00
6 Wade Boggs	15.00	4.50
7 Barry Bonds	40.00	12.00
8 Jeromy Burnitz	10.00	3.00
9 Mike Cameron	10.00	3.00
10 Sean Casey	10.00	3.00
11 Roger Cedeno	10.00	3.00
12 Eric Chavez	10.00	3.00
13 Tony Clark	10.00	3.00
14 Carlos Delgado	10.00	3.00
15 J.D. Drew	10.00	3.00
16 Erubiel Durazo	10.00	3.00
17 Ray Durham	10.00	3.00
18 Damion Easley	10.00	3.00
19 Carlos Febles	10.00	3.00
20 Jason Giambi	15.00	4.50
21 Shawn Green	10.00	3.00
22 Vladimir Guerrero	15.00	4.50
23 Norm Hutchins	10.00	3.00
24 Derek Jeter	40.00	12.00
25 Chipper Jones	15.00	4.50
26 Gabe Kapler	10.00	3.00
27 Jason Kendall	10.00	3.00
28 Paul Konerko	10.00	3.00
29 Ray Lankford	10.00	3.00
30 Mike Lieberthal	10.00	3.00
31 Edgar Martinez	15.00	4.50
32 Raul Mondesi	10.00	3.00
33 Warren Morris	10.00	3.00
34 Magglio Ordonez	10.00	3.00
35 Rafael Palmeiro	15.00	4.50
36 Pokey Reese	10.00	3.00
37 Cal Ripken	40.00	12.00
38 Alex Rodriguez	25.00	7.50
39 Ivan Rodriguez	15.00	4.50
40 Scott Rolen	15.00	4.50
41 Chris Singleton	10.00	3.00
42 Alfonso Soriano	15.00	4.50
43 Frank Thomas	15.00	4.50
44 Jim Thome	15.00	4.50
45 Robin Ventura	10.00	3.00
46 Jose Vidro	10.00	3.00
47 Bernie Williams	15.00	4.50
48 Matt Williams	10.00	3.00

2000 Fleer Gamers Signed Lumber

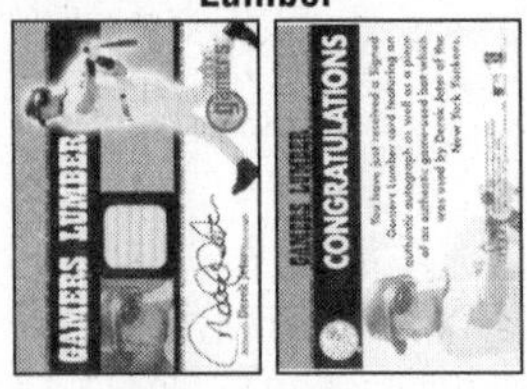

Randomly inserted into packs at one in 287, this 12-card autographed insert set features chips from actual player used bats and parallels the more common lumber inserts. Cards are not numbered, and are listed below in alphabetical order. Sean Casey, Shawn Green and Alex Rodriguez were exchange cards and collectors had to mail in those cards by May 1, 2001.

	Nm-Mt	Ex-Mt
1 Roberto Alomar	50.00	15.00
2 Sean Casey	30.00	9.00
3 Eric Chavez	30.00	9.00
4 Tony Clark	25.00	7.50
5 Erubiel Durazo	30.00	9.00
6 Shawn Green	30.00	9.00
7 Derek Jeter	150.00	45.00
8 Paul Konerko	30.00	9.00
9 Rafael Palmeiro	50.00	15.00
10 Alex Rodriguez	120.00	36.00
11 Alfonso Soriano	60.00	18.00
12 Robin Ventura	30.00	9.00

2001 Fleer Genuine

The 2001 Fleer Genuine product was released in May, 2001 and featured a 130-card base set that was broken into tiers as follows: Base Veterans (1-100), and Rookies (100-130) featuring game-used materials and are serial numbered to 1500. Each pack contained five cards and carried a suggested retail price of $4.99. 500 exchange cards were seeded into packs for a Derek Jeter signed uncut sheet.

	Nm-Mt	Ex-Mt
COMP.SET w/o SP's (90)	25.00	7.50
COMMON CARD (1-100)	.50	.15
COMMON (101-130)	5.00	1.50
1 Derek Jeter	3.00	.90
2 Nomar Garciaparra	2.00	.60
3 Alex Rodriguez	2.00	.60
4 Frank Thomas	1.25	.35
5 Travis Fryman	.50	.15
6 Gary Sheffield	.50	.15
7 Jason Giambi	1.25	.35
8 Trevor Hoffman	.50	.15
9 Todd Helton	.75	.23
10 Ivan Rodriguez	1.25	.35
11 Roberto Alomar	1.25	.35
12 Barrry Zito	1.25	.35
13 Kevin Brown	.50	.15
14 Shawn Green	.50	.15
15 Kenny Lofton	.50	.15
16 Jeff Weaver	.50	.15
17 Geoff Jenkins	.50	.15
18 Carlos Delgado	.50	.15
19 Mark Grace	.75	.23
20 Ken Griffey Jr.	2.00	.60
21 David Justice	.50	.15
22 Brian Giles	.50	.15
23 Scott Williamson	.50	.15
24 Richie Sexson	.50	.15
25 John Olerud	.50	.15
26 Sammy Sosa	2.00	.60
27 Bobby Higginson	.50	.15
28 Matt Lawton	.50	.15
29 Vinny Castilla	.50	.15
30 Alex Gonzalez	.50	.15
31 Manny Ramirez	.50	.15
32 Brad Radke	.50	.15
33 Cal Ripken	4.00	1.20
34 Richard Hidalgo	.50	.15
35 Al Leiter	.50	.15
36 Freddy Garcia	.50	.15
37 Juan Encarnacion	.50	.15
38 Corey Koskie	.50	.15
39 Greg Vaughn	.50	.15
40 Rafael Palmeiro	.75	.23
41 Vladimir Guerrero	1.25	.35
42 Troy Glaus	.75	.23
43 Mike Hampton	.50	.15
44 Jose Vidro	.50	.15
45 Ryan Rupe	.50	.15
46 Troy O'Leary	.50	.15
47 Ben Petrick	.50	.15
48 Mike Lieberthal	.50	.15
49 Mike Sweeney	.50	.15
50 Scott Rolen	.75	.23
51 Albert Belle	.75	.23
52 Mark Quinn	.50	.15
53 Mike Piazza	2.00	.60
54 Mark McGwire	3.00	.90
55 Brady Anderson	.50	.15
56 Carlos Beltran	.50	.15
57 Michael Barrett	.50	.15
58 Jason Kendall	.50	.15
59 Jim Edmonds	.50	.15
60 Matt Williams	.50	.15
61 Pokey Reese	.50	.15
62 Bernie Williams	.75	.23
63 Barry Bonds	3.00	.90
64 David Wells	.50	.15
65 Chipper Jones	1.25	.35
66 Jim Parque	.50	.15
67 Derrek Lee	.50	.15
68 Darin Erstad	.50	.15
69 Edgar Martinez	.75	.23
70 Kerry Wood	1.25	.35
71 Omar Vizquel	.50	.15
72 Jeromy Burnitz	.50	.15
73 Warren Morris	.50	.15
74 Rick Ankiel	.50	.15
75 Andruw Jones	.50	.15
76 Paul Konerko	.50	.15
77 Mike Lowell	.50	.15
78 Roger Clemens	2.50	.75
79 Tim Hudson	.50	.15
80 Rafael Furcal	.50	.15
81 Craig Biggio	.75	.23
82 Edgardo Alfonzo	.50	.15
83 Pat Burrell	.50	.15
84 Adrian Beltre	.50	.15
85 Tony Gwynn	1.50	.45
86 J.T. Snow	.50	.15
87 Randy Johnson	1.25	.35
88 Sean Casey	.50	.15
89 Preston Wilson	.50	.15
90 Mike Mussina	1.25	.35
91 Eric Chavez	.50	.15
92 Tim Salmon	.75	.23
93 Pedro Martinez	1.25	.35
94 Darryl Kile	.50	.15
95 Greg Maddux	2.00	.60
96 Magglio Ordonez	.50	.15
97 Jeff Bagwell	.75	.23
98 Timo Perez	.50	.15
99 Jeff Kent	.50	.15
100 Eric Owens	.50	.15
101 Ichiro Suzuki GU RC	40.00	12.00
102 E. Guzman GU RC	5.00	1.50
103 T. Shinjo GU RC	8.00	2.40
104 Travis Hafner GU RC	8.00	2.40
105 Larry Barnes GU	5.00	1.50
106 J. Randolph GU RC	5.00	1.50
107 Paul Phillips GU RC	5.00	1.50
108 Erick Almonte GU RC	5.00	1.50
109 Nick Punto GU RC	5.00	1.50
110 Jack Wilson GU RC	5.00	1.50
111 Jeremy Owens GU RC	5.00	1.50
112 Esix Snead GU RC	5.00	1.50
113 Jay Gibbons GU RC	8.00	2.40
114 A. Hernandez GU RC	5.00	1.50
115 Matt White GU RC	5.00	1.50
116 Ryan Freel GU RC	5.00	1.50
117 Martin Vargas GU RC	5.00	1.50
118 Winston Abreu GU RC	5.00	1.50
119 Junior Spivey GU RC	6.00	1.80
120 Paxton Crawford GU	5.00	1.50
121 Randy Keisler GU	5.00	1.50
122 Juan Diaz GU RC	5.00	1.50
123 Aaron Rowand GU	5.00	1.50
124 Toby Hall GU	5.00	1.50
125 Brian Cole GU	5.00	1.50
126 Aubrey Huff GU	5.00	1.50
127 Corey Patterson GU	5.00	1.50
128 Sun Woo Kim GU	5.00	1.50
129 Jace Brewer GU	5.00	1.50
130 Cesar Izturis GU	5.00	1.50
NNO Derek Jeter	120.00	36.00
AU Sheet/500 EXCH		

2001 Fleer Genuine At Large

Randomly inserted into packs at one in 23, this 15-card insert features major league talents "at large". Card backs carry an "ALG" prefix.

	Nm-Mt	Ex-Mt
COMPLETE SET (15)	120.00	36.00
ALG1 Derek Jeter	12.00	3.60
ALG2 Nomar Garciaparra	8.00	2.40
ALG3 Mark McGwire	12.00	3.60
ALG4 Pedro Martinez	5.00	1.50
ALG5 Tony Gwynn	6.00	1.80
ALG6 Roger Clemens	10.00	3.00
ALG7 Ivan Rodriguez	5.00	1.50
ALG8 Sammy Sosa	8.00	2.40
ALG9 Magglio Ordonez	3.00	.90
ALG10 Jason Giambi	5.00	1.50
ALG11 Carlos Delgado	3.00	.90
ALG12 Chipper Jones	5.00	1.50
ALG13 Mike Piazza	8.00	2.40
ALG14 Cal Ripken	15.00	4.50
ALG15 Ken Griffey Jr.	8.00	2.40

2001 Fleer Genuine Coverage Plus

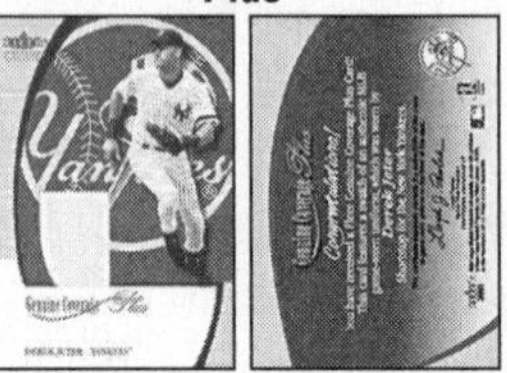

Randomly inserted into hobby packs, this 10-card insert features jersey swatches from players like Derek Jeter and Cal Ripken. Cards are listed below in alphabetical order for convenience. Please note that there were only 150 serial numbered sets produced.

	Nm-Mt	Ex-Mt
1 Barry Bonds	50.00	15.00
2 Darin Erstad	15.00	4.50
3 Troy Glaus	20.00	6.00
4 Tony Gwynn	25.00	7.50
5 Derek Jeter	50.00	15.00
6 Randy Johnson	20.00	6.00
7 Andruw Jones	15.00	4.50
8 Chipper Jones	20.00	6.00
9 Cal Ripken	50.00	15.00
10 Frank Thomas	20.00	6.00

2001 Fleer Genuine Final Cut

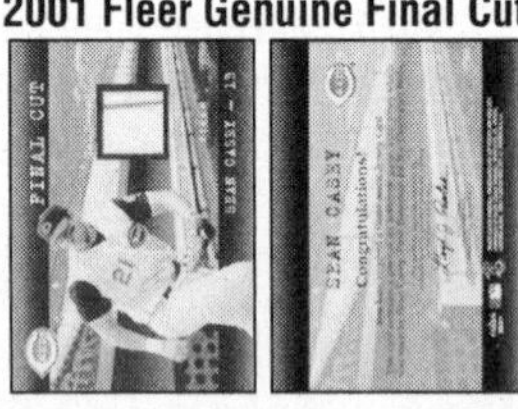

Randomly inserted into packs at one in 30, this 28-card insert features jersey swatches from players like Derek Jeter and Cal Ripken. Cards are listed below in alphabetical order for convenience. Representatives at Fleer announced specific print runs on several short-printed cards within this set, though the cards lack actual serial-numbering. Don Larsen, Ron Guidry and Reggie Jackson were not intended for public release. It's rumored that Willie Randolph and Dave Righetti were also not intended for public release. The Guidry, Larsen, Randolph and Righetti cards are extremely scarce (estimated only a few copies of each exist) as Fleer attempted to pull all of the copies they could find from production prior to shipping.

	Nm-Mt	Ex-Mt
*MULTI-COLOR PATCH: .75X TO 2X BASIC		
1 Wade Boggs	15.00	4.50
2 Barry Bonds SP/330	50.00	15.00
3 George Brett	25.00	7.50
4 Sean Casey	10.00	3.00
5 J.D. Drew SP/75	25.00	7.50
6 Bob Gibson SP/200	40.00	12.00
7 Troy Glaus	15.00	4.50
8 Ron Guidry SP		
9 Tony Gwynn	15.00	4.50
10 Reggie Jackson SP		
11 Andruw Jones SP/135	25.00	7.50
12 Chipper Jones	15.00	4.50
13 Don Larsen SP		
14 Greg Maddux	15.00	4.50
15 Edgar Martinez SP/130 UER	40.00	12.00
Card says it is part of a batting glove but the pieces are game worn jersey swatches		
16 Willie Randolph SP		
17 Pokey Reese	10.00	3.00
18 Dave Righetti SP		
19 Cal Ripken	40.00	12.00
20 Ivan Rodriguez SP/120	40.00	12.00
21 Scott Rolen	15.00	4.50
22 Tim Salmon	15.00	4.50
23 Miguel Tejada SP/170	25.00	7.50
24 Frank Thomas	15.00	4.50
25 Robin Ventura	10.00	3.00
26 Larry Walker	15.00	4.50
27 Matt Williams	10.00	3.00
28 Robin Yount	15.00	4.50

2001 Fleer Genuine High Interest

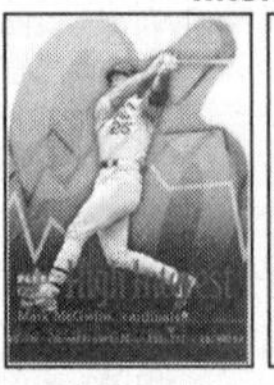

Randomly inserted into packs at one in 23, this 15-card insert features players that have earned the respect of the fans year in year out. Cards backs carry a "HI" prefix.

	Nm-Mt	Ex-Mt
COMPLETE SET (15)	100.00	30.00
HI1 Derek Jeter	12.00	3.60
HI2 Nomar Garciaparra	8.00	2.40
HI3 Greg Maddux	8.00	2.40
HI4 Todd Helton	3.00	.90
HI5 Sammy Sosa	8.00	2.40
HI6 Jeff Bagwell	3.00	.90
HI7 Jason Giambi	5.00	1.50
HI8 Frank Thomas	5.00	1.50
HI9 Andruw Jones	3.00	.90
HI10 Jim Edmonds	3.00	.90
HI11 Bernie Williams	3.00	.90
HI12 Randy Johnson	5.00	1.50
HI13 Ken Griffey Jr.	8.00	2.40
HI14 Pedro Martinez	5.00	1.50
HI15 Mark McGwire	12.00	3.60

2001 Fleer Genuine Material Issue

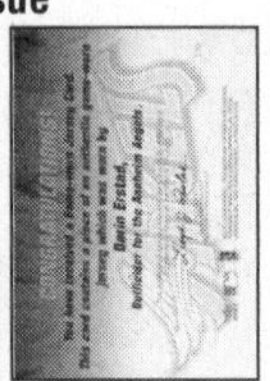

Randomly inserted into hobby packs at one in 30, this 19-card insert features game-used jersey swatches from players like Tony Gwynn and Pedro Martinez. Cards have been listed in alphabetical order for convenience. Representatives at Fleer announced that Pedro Martinez and Curt Schilling were both shortprints. Though the cards lack actual serial-numbering, it was announced that 60 copies of the Martinez card and 120 copies of the Schilling card were produced.

	Nm-Mt	Ex-Mt
*MULTI-COLOR PATCH: 1X TO 2.5X BASIC		
1 Steve Carlton SP *	25.00	7.50
2 J.D. Drew	10.00	3.00
3 Darin Erstad	10.00	3.00
4 Troy Glaus	15.00	4.50
5 Tom Glavine	15.00	4.50
6 Tony Gwynn	15.00	4.50
7 Randy Johnson	15.00	4.50
8 Chipper Jones	15.00	4.50
9 Greg Maddux	15.00	4.50
10 Edgar Martinez SP *	30.00	9.00
11 Pedro Martinez SP/60	50.00	15.00
12 Kevin Millwood	10.00	3.00
13 Paul Molitor SP *	30.00	9.00
14 Cal Ripken	40.00	12.00
15 Scott Rolen	15.00	4.50
16 Nolan Ryan	50.00	15.00
17 Curt Schilling SP/120	30.00	9.00
18 Frank Thomas	15.00	4.50
19 Robin Ventura	10.00	3.00

2001 Fleer Genuine Names Of The Game

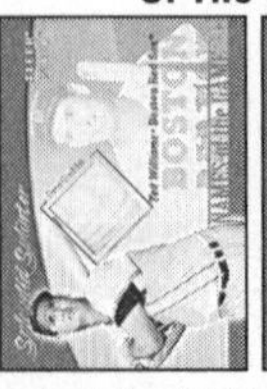

Randomly inserted into packs, this 34-card insert features swatches of game-used memorabilia (either bat or jersey). Cards have been listed below in alphabetical order for convenience. Please note that there were only 50 serial numbered sets produced.

	Nm-Mt	Ex-Mt
1 Yogi Berra Bat	40.00	12.00
2 Orlando Cepeda Bat	25.00	7.50
3 Rocky Colavito Bat	40.00	12.00
4 Andre Dawson Jsy	25.00	7.50
5 Bucky Dent Bat	25.00	7.50
6 Rollie Fingers Jsy	25.00	7.50
7 Carlton Fisk Bat	40.00	12.00
8 Whitey Ford Jsy	40.00	12.00
9 Jimmie Foxx Bat	120.00	36.00
10 Hank Greenberg Bat	100.00	30.00
11 Catfish Hunter Jsy	40.00	12.00
12 Reggie Jackson Jsy	40.00	12.00
13 Randy Johnson Jsy	40.00	12.00
14 Chipper Jones Bat	40.00	12.00
15 Harmon Killebrew Bat	40.00	12.00
16 Tony Lazzeri Bat	25.00	7.50
17 Don Mattingly Bat	100.00	30.00
18 Willie McCovey Bat	25.00	7.50
19 Johnny Mize Bat	25.00	7.50
20 Pee Wee Reese Jsy	40.00	12.00
21 Cal Ripken Bat	100.00	30.00
22 Phil Rizzuto Bat	40.00	12.00
23 Ivan Rodriguez Bat	40.00	12.00
24 Preacher Roe Jsy	40.00	12.00
25 Babe Ruth Bat	300.00	90.00
26 Nolan Ryan Jsy	100.00	30.00
27 Tom Seaver Jsy	40.00	12.00
28 Bill Skowron Bat	40.00	12.00
29 Enos Slaughter Bat	25.00	7.50
30 Duke Snider Bat	40.00	12.00
31 Willie Stargell Bat	40.00	12.00
32 Bill Terry Bat	40.00	12.00
33 Ted Williams Bat	150.00	45.00
34 Hack Wilson Bat	120.00	36.00

2001 Fleer Genuine Names Of The Game Autographs

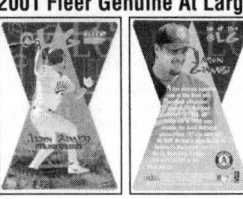

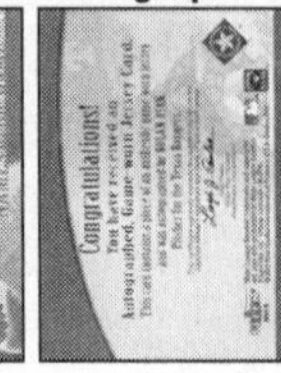

Randomly inserted into packs, this 22-card insert features swatches of game-used memorabilia (either bat or jersey) and an authentic autograph from the depicted player. Cards have been listed below in alphabetical order for convenience. Please note that there were only 100 serial numbered sets produced.

	Nm-Mt	Ex-Mt
1 Yogi Berra Bat	100.00	30.00
2 Orlando Cepeda Bat	40.00	12.00
3 Rocky Colavito Bat	100.00	30.00
4 Andre Dawson Jsy	40.00	12.00
5 Bucky Dent Bat	40.00	12.00
6 Rollie Fingers Jsy	40.00	12.00
7 Carlton Fisk Bat	60.00	18.00
8 Whitey Ford Jsy	60.00	18.00
9 Reggie Jackson Jsy	100.00	30.00
10 Randy Johnson Jsy	100.00	30.00
11 Chipper Jones Bat	100.00	30.00
12 Harmon Killebrew Bat	100.00	30.00
13 Don Mattingly Bat	150.00	45.00
14 Willie McCovey Bat	60.00	18.00
15 Cal Ripken Bat	250.00	75.00
16 Ivan Rodriguez Bat	100.00	30.00
17 Preacher Roe Jsy	60.00	18.00
18 Nolan Ryan Jsy	200.00	60.00
19 Tom Seaver Jsy	60.00	18.00
20 Bill Skowron Bat	60.00	18.00
21 Enos Slaughter Bat	60.00	18.00
22 Duke Snider Bat	60.00	18.00

2001 Fleer Genuine Pennant Aggression

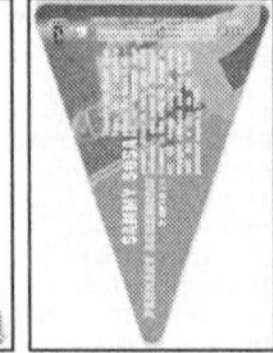

Randomly inserted into packs at one in 23, this 10-card insert features players that play very aggressively down the stretch for the pennant. Card backs carry a "PA" prefix.

	Nm-Mt	Ex-Mt
COMPLETE SET (10)	60.00	18.00
PA1 Derek Jeter	10.00	3.00
PA2 Alex Rodriguez	6.00	1.80
PA3 Nomar Garciaparra	6.00	1.80
PA4 Mark McGwire	10.00	3.00
PA5 Ken Griffey Jr.	6.00	1.80
PA6 Mike Piazza	6.00	1.80
PA7 Sammy Sosa	6.00	1.80
PA8 Barry Bonds	10.00	3.00
PA9 Chipper Jones	4.00	1.20
PA10 Pedro Martinez	4.00	1.20

2001 Fleer Genuine Tip Of The Cap

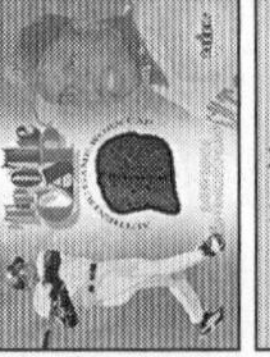

Randomly inserted into hobby packs, this 13-card insert features swatches of game-used hat. Cards have been listed below in alphabetical order for convenience. Please note that there were only 150 serial numbered sets produced.

	Nm-Mt	Ex-Mt
1 Roberto Alomar	25.00	7.50
2 Barry Bonds	60.00	18.00
3 Eric Chavez	15.00	4.50
4 Troy Glaus	25.00	7.50
5 Shawn Green	15.00	4.50
6 Vladimir Guerrero	25.00	7.50
7 Randy Johnson	25.00	7.50
8 Andruw Jones	15.00	4.50
9 Javy Lopez	15.00	4.50
10 Pedro Martinez	25.00	7.50
11 Rafael Palmeiro	25.00	7.50
12 Ivan Rodriguez	25.00	7.50
13 Miguel Tejada	15.00	4.50

2002 Fleer Genuine

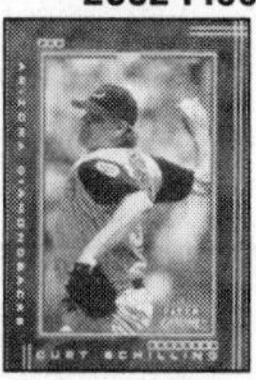
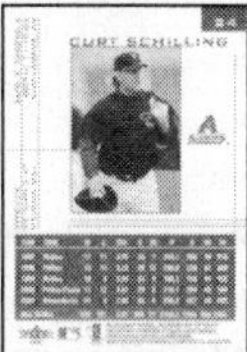

This 140 card was released in May, 2002. These cards were issued in five card packs with an SRP of $4.99 per pack and they were issued 24 packs to a box and six boxes per case. The first 100 card feature veteran players and the final forty player feature prospect cards. Cards number 101 through 140 have a stated print run of 2002 serial numbered sets.

	Nm-Mt	Ex-Mt
COMP.SET w/o SP's (100)	25.00	7.50
COMMON CARD (1-100)	.50	.15
COMMON CARD (101-140)	5.00	1.50
1 Alex Rodriguez	2.00	.60
2 Manny Ramirez	.50	.15
3 Jim Thome	1.25	.35
4 Eric Milton	.50	.15
5 Todd Helton	.75	.23
6 Mike Mussina	1.25	.35
7 Ichiro Suzuki	2.00	.60
8 Randy Johnson	1.25	.35
9 Mark Mulder	.50	.15
10 Johnny Damon	.50	.15
11 Sean Casey	.50	.15
12 Albert Pujols	2.50	.75
13 Mark Grace	.75	.23
14 Moises Alou	.50	.15
15 Raul Mondesi	.50	.15
16 Cliff Floyd	.50	.15
17 Vladimir Guerrero	1.25	.35
18 Pat Burrell	.50	.15
19 Ryan Klesko	.50	.15
20 Mike Hampton	.50	.15
21 Shawn Green	.50	.15
22 Rich Aurilia	.50	.15
23 Matt Morris	.50	.15
24 Curt Schilling	.75	.23
25 Kevin Brown	.50	.15
26 Adrian Beltre	.50	.15
27 Joe Mays	.50	.15
28 Luis Gonzalez	.50	.15
29 Barry Larkin	1.25	.35
30 A.J. Burnett	.50	.15
31 Eric Munson	.50	.15
32 Juan Gonzalez	1.25	.35
33 Lance Berkman	.50	.15
34 Fred McGriff	.75	.23
35 Paul Konerko	.50	.15
36 Pedro Martinez	1.25	.35
37 Adam Dunn	.50	.15
38 Jeromy Burnitz	.50	.15
39 Mike Sweeney	.50	.15
40 Bret Boone	.50	.15
41 Ken Griffey Jr.	2.00	.60
42 Eric Chavez	.50	.15
43 Mark Quinn	.50	.15
44 Roberto Alomar	1.25	.35
45 Bobby Abreu	.50	.15
46 Bartolo Colon	.50	.15
47 Jimmy Rollins	.50	.15
48 Chipper Jones	1.25	.35
49 Ben Sheets	.50	.15
50 Freddy Garcia	.50	.15
51 Sammy Sosa	2.00	.60
52 Rafael Palmeiro	.75	.23
53 Preston Wilson	.50	.15
54 Troy Glaus	.75	.23
55 Josh Beckett	.75	.23
56 C.C. Sabathia	.50	.15
57 Magglio Ordonez	.50	.15
58 Brian Giles	.50	.15
59 Darin Erstad	.50	.15
60 Gary Sheffield	.50	.15
61 Paul LoDuca	.50	.15
62 Derek Jeter	3.00	.90
63 Greg Maddux	2.00	.60
64 Kerry Wood	1.25	.35
65 Toby Hall	.50	.15
66 Barry Bonds	3.00	.90
67 Jeff Bagwell	.75	.23
68 Jason Kendall	.50	.15
69 Richard Hidalgo	.50	.15
70 J.D. Drew	.50	.15
71 Tom Glavine	.75	.23
72 Javier Vazquez	.50	.15
73 Doug Mientkiewicz	.50	.15
74 Jason Giambi	1.25	.35
75 Carlos Delgado	.50	.15
76 Aramis Ramirez	.50	.15
77 Torii Hunter	.50	.15
78 Ivan Rodriguez	1.25	.35
79 Charles Johnson	.50	.15
80 Jeff Kent	.50	.15
81 Jacque Jones	.50	.15
82 Larry Walker	.75	.23
83 Cristian Guzman	.50	.15
84 Jermaine Dye	.50	.15
85 Roger Clemens	2.50	.75
86 Mike Piazza	2.00	.60
87 Craig Biggio	.75	.23
88 Phil Nevin	.50	.15
89 Jeff Cirillo	.50	.15
90 Barry Zito	.75	.23
91 Ryan Dempster	.50	.15
92 Mark Buehrle	.50	.15
93 Nomar Garciaparra	2.00	.60
94 Frank Thomas	1.25	.35
95 Jim Edmonds	.50	.15
96 Geoff Jenkins	.50	.15
97 Scott Rolen	.75	.23
98 Tim Hudson	.50	.15
99 Shannon Stewart	.50	.15
100 Richie Sexson	.50	.15
101 Orlando Hudson UP	5.00	1.50
102 Doug Devore UP RC	5.00	1.50
103 Rene Reyes UP RC	5.00	1.50
104 Steve Bechler UP RC	5.00	1.50
105 Jorge Nunez UP RC	5.00	1.50
106 Mitch Wylie UP RC	5.00	1.50
107 Jaime Cerda UP RC	5.00	1.50
108 Brandon Puffer UP RC	5.00	1.50
109 Tyler Yates UP RC	8.00	2.40
110 Bill Hall UP	5.00	1.50
111 Pete Zamora UP RC	5.00	1.50
112 Jeff Deardorff UP	5.00	1.50
113 J.J. Putz UP RC	5.00	1.50
114 Scotty Layfield UP RC	5.00	1.50
115 Brandon Backe UP RC	5.00	1.50
116 Andy Pratt UP RC	5.00	1.50
117 Mark Prior UP	15.00	4.50
118 Franklyn German UP RC	5.00	1.50
119 Todd Donovan UP RC	5.00	1.50
120 Franklin Nunez UP RC	5.00	1.50
121 Adam Walker UP RC	5.00	1.50
122 Ron Calloway UP RC	5.00	1.50
123 Tim Kalita UP RC	5.00	1.50
124 Kazuhisa Ishii UP RC	10.00	3.00
125 Mark Teixeira UP	8.00	2.40
126 Nate Field UP RC	5.00	1.50
127 Nelson Castro UP RC	5.00	1.50
128 So Taguchi UP RC	8.00	2.40
129 Marlon Byrd UP	5.00	1.50
130 Drew Henson UP	5.00	1.50
131 Kenny Kelly UP	5.00	1.50
132 John Ennis UP RC	5.00	1.50
133 Anastacio Martinez UP RC	5.00	1.50
134 Matt Guerrier UP	5.00	1.50
135 Tom Wilson UP RC	5.00	1.50
136 Ben Howard UP RC	5.00	1.50
137 Chris Baker UP RC	5.00	1.50
138 Kevin Frederick UP RC	5.00	1.50
139 Wilson Valdez UP RC	5.00	1.50
140 Austin Kearns UP	5.00	1.50

2002 Fleer Genuine Bats Incredible

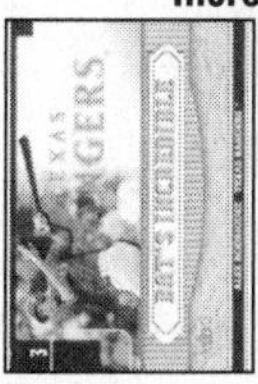

Inserted in packs at a stated rate of one in 10 hobby and one in 20 retail, these 25 cards feature some of the leading hitters in baseball.

	Nm-Mt	Ex-Mt
COMPLETE SET (25)	100.00	30.00
BI1 Todd Helton	2.50	.75
BI2 Chipper Jones	4.00	1.20
BI3 Luis Gonzalez	2.50	.75
BI4 Barry Bonds	10.00	3.00
BI5 Jason Giambi	4.00	1.20
BI6 Alex Rodriguez	6.00	1.80
BI7 Manny Ramirez	2.50	.75
BI8 Jeff Bagwell	2.50	.75
BI9 Shawn Green	2.50	.75
BI10 Albert Pujols	8.00	2.40
BI11 Paul LoDuca	2.50	.75
BI12 Mike Piazza	6.00	1.80
BI13 Derek Jeter	10.00	3.00
BI14 Edgar Martinez	2.50	.75
BI15 Juan Gonzalez	4.00	1.20
BI16 Magglio Ordonez	2.50	.75
BI17 Jermaine Dye	2.50	.75
BI18 Larry Walker	2.50	.75
BI19 Phil Nevin	2.50	.75
BI20 Ivan Rodriguez	4.00	1.20
BI21 Ichiro Suzuki	6.00	1.80
BI22 J.D. Drew	2.50	.75
BI23 Vladimir Guerrero	4.00	1.20
BI24 Sammy Sosa	6.00	1.80
BI25 Ken Griffey Jr.	6.00	1.80

2002 Fleer Genuine Bats Incredible Game Used

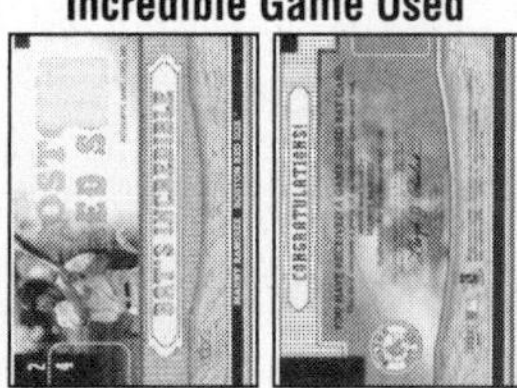

Inserted at a stated rate of one in 18 hobby and one in 90 retail packs, these 12 cards partially parallel the Bats Incredible insert set. These cards have a bat chip on them in addition to the player's photo.

	Nm-Mt	Ex-Mt
1 Todd Helton	10.00	3.00
2 Chipper Jones	15.00	4.50
3 J.D. Drew	10.00	3.00
4 Alex Rodriguez	15.00	4.50
5 Manny Ramirez	10.00	3.00
6 Shawn Green	10.00	3.00
7 Derek Jeter	25.00	7.50
8 Edgar Martinez	10.00	3.00
9 Juan Gonzalez	10.00	3.00
10 Jermaine Dye	8.00	2.40
11 Phil Nevin	8.00	2.40
12 Ivan Rodriguez	10.00	3.00

2002 Fleer Genuine Ink

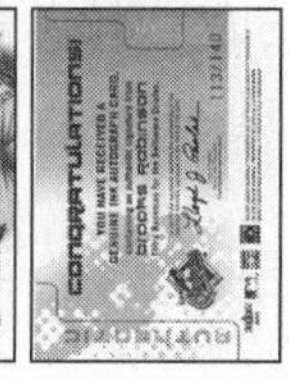

Randomly inserted in packs, these cards feature authentic autographs of the players featued. These cards all have diferent print runs and we have listed the stated print run next to the player's name. Paul Molitor did not sign his cards in time for inclusion in packs and those cards could be redeemed until June 1, 2003.

	Nm-Mt	Ex-Mt
1 Barry Bonds/150	175.00	52.50
2 Ron Cey/975	15.00	4.50
3 Derek Jeter/150	150.00	45.00
4 Al Kaline/300	80.00	24.00
5 Don Mattingly/50	120.00	36.00
6 Paul Molitor/365	50.00	15.00
7 Dale Murphy/700	50.00	15.00
8 Phil Rizzuto/700	30.00	9.00
9 Brooks Robinson/140	80.00	24.00
10 Maury Wills/975	15.00	4.50

2002 Fleer Genuine Leaders

Inserted into packs at a stated rate of one in six hobby and one in eight retail, these 15 cards honor some of the leading players in the game.

	Nm-Mt	Ex-Mt
COMPLETE SET (15)	40.00	12.00
1 Sammy Sosa	4.00	1.20
2 Todd Helton	1.50	.45
3 Alex Rodriguez	4.00	1.20
4 Roger Clemens	5.00	1.50
5 Barry Bonds	6.00	1.80
6 Randy Johnson	2.50	.75
7 Albert Pujols	5.00	1.50
8 Curt Schilling	1.50	.45
9 Bernie Williams	1.50	.45
10 Ken Griffey Jr.	4.00	1.20
11 Pedro Martinez	2.50	.75
12 Juan Gonzalez	2.50	.75
13 Hideo Nomo	2.50	.75
14 Bret Boone	1.50	.45
15 Ichiro Suzuki	4.00	1.20

2002 Fleer Genuine Leaders Game Jersey

Inserted into packs at stated odds of one in 11 hobby and one in 566 retail, these nine cards partially parallel the Leaders insert set. These cards feature a game jersey swatch on them in addition to the player's photo.

	Nm-Mt	Ex-Mt
1 Todd Helton	15.00	4.50
2 Alex Rodriguez	15.00	4.50
3 Roger Clemens	20.00	6.00
4 Barry Bonds	25.00	7.50
5 Randy Johnson	15.00	4.50
6 Bernie Williams	15.00	4.50
7 Curt Schilling	15.00	4.50
8 Hideo Nomo	20.00	6.00
9 Pedro Martinez	15.00	4.50

2002 Fleer Genuine Names of the Game

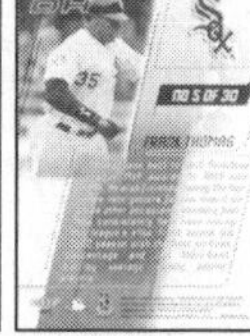

Issued in packs at stated odds of one in 10 hobby and one in 20 retail, these 30 cards feature a good mix of the leading players in baseball.

	Nm-Mt	Ex-Mt
COMPLETE SET (30)	120.00	36.00
1 Mike Piazza	8.00	2.40
2 Chipper Jones	5.00	1.50
3 Jim Edmonds	3.00	.90
4 Barry Larkin	5.00	1.50
5 Frank Thomas	5.00	1.50
6 Manny Ramirez	3.00	.90
7 Carlos Delgado	3.00	.90
8 Brian Giles	3.00	.90
9 Kerry Wood	5.00	1.50
10 Derek Jeter	12.00	3.60
11 Adam Dunn	3.00	.90
12 Gary Sheffield	3.00	.90
13 Luis Gonzalez	3.00	.90
14 Mark Mulder	3.00	.90
15 Roberto Alomar	5.00	1.50
16 Scott Rolen	3.00	.90
17 Tom Glavine	3.00	.90
18 Bobby Abreu	3.00	.90
19 Nomar Garciaparra	8.00	2.40
20 Darin Erstad	3.00	.90
21 Cliff Floyd	3.00	.90
22 Tim Hudson	3.00	.90
23 Jim Thome	5.00	1.50
24 Nolan Ryan	12.00	3.60
25 Reggie Jackson	3.00	.90
26 Rafael Palmeiro	3.00	.90
27 Ken Griffey Jr.	8.00	2.40
28 Sammy Sosa	8.00	2.40
29 Vladimir Guerrero	5.00	1.50
30 Ichiro Suzuki	8.00	2.40

2002 Fleer Genuine Names of the Game Memorabilia

Inserted in packs at stated odds of one in 24 hobby and one in 100 retail, these 19 cards are a partial parallel of the Names of the Game memorabilia set. These cards feature a memorabilia item to go with the player's photo. The Nomar Garciaparra card was issued in shorter supply and we have notated that information along with the stated print run for that card.

	Nm-Mt	Ex-Mt
1 Roberto Alomar	15.00	4.50
2 Carlos Delgado	10.00	3.00
3 Jim Edmonds	10.00	3.00
4 Darin Erstad	10.00	3.00
5 Cliff Floyd	10.00	3.00
6 Nomar Garciaparra SP/90		
7 Brian Giles	10.00	3.00
8 Luis Gonzalez	10.00	3.00
9 Tim Hudson	10.00	3.00
10 Derek Jeter	30.00	9.00
11 Chipper Jones	15.00	4.50
12 Barry Larkin	15.00	4.50
13 Mark Mulder	10.00	3.00
14 Rafael Palmeiro	15.00	4.50
15 Mike Piazza	15.00	4.50
16 Manny Ramirez	10.00	3.00
17 Scott Rolen	15.00	4.50
18 Nolan Ryan	40.00	12.00
19 Jim Thome	15.00	4.50

2002 Fleer Genuine Programs

Inserted one per hobby distributor box, these feature a mix of All-Star game and World Series programs from the past 20 years.

	Nm-Mt	Ex-Mt
1 1987 All-Star Game		
2 1988 All-Star Game		
3 1990 All-Star Game		
4 1991 All-Star Game		
5 1992 All-Star Game		
6 1993 All-Star Game		
7 1994 All-Star Game		
8 1995 All-Star Game		
9 1996 All-Star Game		
10 1997 All-Star Game		
11 1998 All-Star Game		
12 1999 All-Star Game		
13 2001 All-Star Game/P.Martinez		
14 2001 All-Star Game/K.Griffey Jr.		
15 2001 All-Star Game/M.Piazza		
16 2001 All-Star Game/D.Jeter		
17 1984 World Series		
18 1987 World Series		
19 1989 World Series		
20 1990 World Series		
21 1991 World Series		
22 1992 World Series		
23 1993 World Series		
24 1995 World Series		
25 1996 World Series		
26 1997 World Series		
27 1998 World Series		
28 1999 World Series		
29 2001 World Series		

2002 Fleer Genuine Tip of the Cap

Inserted in packs at stated odds of one in six hobby and one in eight retail, this 25 cards feature a nice mix of active and retired players.

	Nm-Mt	Ex-Mt
COMPLETE SET (25)	60.00	18.00
1 Alex Rodriguez	5.00	1.50
2 Derek Jeter	8.00	2.40
3 Kazuhiro Sasaki	2.00	.60
4 Barry Bonds	8.00	2.40
5 J.D. Drew	2.00	.60
6 Tsuyoshi Shinjo	2.00	.60
7 Alfonso Soriano	2.00	.60
8 Albert Pujols	6.00	1.80
9 Tom Seaver	2.00	.60
10 Drew Henson	2.00	.60
11 Dave Winfield	2.00	.60
12 Carlos Delgado	2.00	.60
13 Lou Boudreau	2.00	.60
14 Shawn Green	2.00	.60
15 Roger Clemens	6.00	1.80
16 Randy Johnson	3.00	.90
17 Sammy Sosa	5.00	1.50
18 Rafael Palmeiro	2.00	.60
19 Ken Griffey Jr.	5.00	1.50
20 Ichiro Suzuki	5.00	1.50
21 Eric Chavez	2.00	.60
22 Andruw Jones	2.00	.60
23 Miguel Tejada	2.00	.60
24 Pedro Martinez	3.00	.90
25 Tim Salmon	2.00	.60

2002 Fleer Genuine Tip of the Cap Game Used

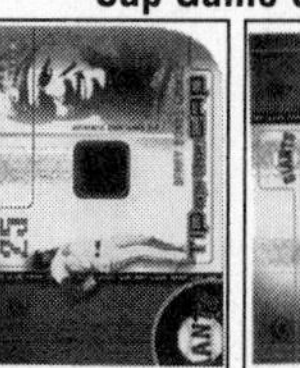

Randomly inserted into packs, these 26 cards feature pieces of memorabilia worn by the featured player. These cards all have different stated print runs and we have listed that information next to their names in our checklist.

	Nm-Mt	Ex-Mt
1 Adrian Beltre/6		
2 Barry Bonds/32		
3 Lou Boudreau/303	25.00	7.50
4 Kevin Brown/6		
5 Eric Chavez/14		
6 Bartolo Colon/16		
7 Carlos Delgado/219	20.00	6.00
8 J.D. Drew/8		
9 Jim Edmonds/8		
10 Darin Erstad/22		
11 Rafael Furcal/12		
12 Juan Gonzalez/6		
13 Luis Gonzalez/12		
14 Shawn Green/4		
15 Drew Henson/361	20.00	6.00
16 Randy Johnson/74		
17 Andruw Jones/19		
18 Jason Kendall/41		
19 Pedro Martinez/2		
20 Rafael Palmeiro/300	25.00	7.50
21 Alex Rodriguez/670	25.00	7.50
22 Tim Salmon/6		
23 Tom Seaver/224	25.00	7.50
24 Alfonso Soriano/4		
25 Miguel Tejada/225	20.00	6.00
26 Dave Winfield/363	20.00	6.00

2002 Fleer Genuine Touch Em All

Inserted into packs at stated odds of one in 10 hobby and one in 20 retail, these 25 cards feature the leading sluggers in the game.

	Nm-Mt	Ex-Mt
COMPLETE SET (25)	100.00	30.00
1 Derek Jeter	10.00	3.00
2 Sammy Sosa	6.00	1.80
3 Albert Pujols	8.00	2.40
4 Vladimir Guerrero	4.00	1.20
5 Ken Griffey Jr.	6.00	1.80
6 Nomar Garciaparra	6.00	1.80
7 Luis Gonzalez	2.50	.75
8 Barry Bonds	10.00	3.00
9 Manny Ramirez	2.50	.75
10 Jason Giambi	4.00	1.20
11 Chipper Jones	4.00	1.20
12 Ichiro Suzuki	6.00	1.80
13 Alex Rodriguez	6.00	1.80
14 Juan Gonzalez	4.00	1.20
15 Todd Helton	2.50	.75
16 Roberto Alomar	4.00	1.20
17 Jeff Bagwell	2.50	.75
18 Mike Piazza	6.00	1.80
19 Gary Sheffield	2.50	.75
20 Ivan Rodriguez	4.00	1.20
21 Frank Thomas	4.00	1.20
22 Bobby Abreu	2.50	.75
23 J.D. Drew	2.50	.75
24 Scott Rolen	2.50	.75
25 Darin Erstad	2.50	.75

2002 Fleer Genuine Touch Em All Game Base

Randomly inserted into packs, these 25 cards parallel the Touch Em All insert set. These

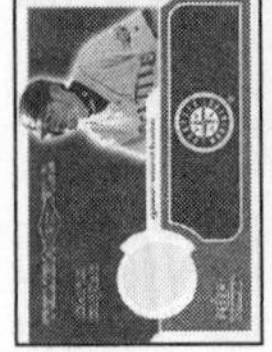

cards feature a piece of a game base used by the player in a game. These cards were issued to a stated print run of 350 serial numbered sets.

	Nm-Mt	Ex-Mt
1 Derek Jeter	25.00	7.50
2 Sammy Sosa	15.00	4.50
3 Albert Pujols	20.00	6.00
4 Vladimir Guerrero	15.00	4.50
5 Ken Griffey Jr.	15.00	4.50
6 Nomar Garciaparra	15.00	4.50
7 Luis Gonzalez	10.00	3.00
8 Barry Bonds	25.00	7.50
9 Manny Ramirez	10.00	3.00
10 Jason Giambi	15.00	4.50
11 Chipper Jones	15.00	4.50
12 Ichiro Suzuki	25.00	7.50
13 Alex Rodriguez	15.00	4.50
14 Juan Gonzalez	15.00	4.50
15 Todd Helton	15.00	4.50
16 Roberto Alomar	15.00	4.50
17 Jeff Bagwell	15.00	4.50
18 Mike Piazza	15.00	4.50
19 Gary Sheffield	10.00	3.00
20 Ivan Rodriguez	15.00	4.50
21 Frank Thomas	15.00	4.50
22 Bobby Abreu	10.00	3.00
23 J.D. Drew	10.00	3.00
24 Scott Rolen	15.00	4.50
25 Darin Erstad	10.00	3.00

2003 Fleer Genuine

This 145-card set was distributed in two separate series. The primary Genuine product - of which contained the first 130 cards from the basic set - was released in July, 2003. This set was issued in five card packs with an $5 SRP which came 24 packs to a box and 12 boxes to a case. Cards numbered 1 through 100 feature veterans while cards numbered 101 through 130 feature a mix of rookies and prospects and those cards were issued to a stated print run of 799 serial numbered sets. Cards 131-145 were randomly seeded within packs of Fleer Rookies and Greats of which was distributed in December, 2003. These fifteen update cards continued the Genuine Upside prospect subset established with cards 101-130 from the primary "low series" set. Each update card was serial numbered to 1000 copies.

	MINT	NRMT
COMP.LO SET w/o SP's (100)	25.00	11.00
COMMON CARD (1-100)	.50	.23
COMMON CARD (101-145)	5.00	2.20
1 Derek Jeter	3.00	1.35
2 Mo Vaughn	.50	.23
3 Adam Dunn	.50	.23
4 Aubrey Huff	.50	.23
5 Jacque Jones	.50	.23
6 Kerry Wood	1.25	.55
7 Barry Bonds	3.00	1.35
8 Kevin Brown	.50	.23
9 Sammy Sosa	2.00	.90
10 Ray Durham	.50	.23
11 Carlos Beltran	.50	.23
12 Tony Batista	.50	.23
13 Bobby Abreu	.50	.23
14 Craig Biggio	.75	.35
15 Gary Sheffield	.50	.23
16 Jermaine Dye	.50	.23
17 Carlos Pena	.50	.23
18 Tim Salmon	.75	.35
19 Mike Piazza	2.00	.90
20 Moises Alou	.50	.23
21 Edgardo Alfonzo	.50	.23
22 Mike Sweeney	.50	.23
23 Jay Gibbons	.50	.23
24 Kevin Millwood	.50	.23
25 A.J. Burnett	.50	.23
26 Austin Kearns	.50	.23
27 Rafael Palmeiro	.75	.35
28 Vladimir Guerrero	1.25	.55
29 Paul Konerko	.50	.23
30 Scott Rolen	.75	.35
31 Fred McGriff	.75	.35
32 Frank Thomas	1.25	.55
33 John Olerud	.50	.23
34 Eric Gagne	.75	.35
35 Nomar Garciaparra	2.00	.90
36 Ryan Klesko	.50	.23
37 Lance Berkman	.50	.23
38 Andruw Jones	.50	.23
39 Pat Burrell	.50	.23
40 Juan Encarnacion	.50	.23
41 Curt Schilling	.75	.35
42 Jason Giambi	1.25	.55
43 Barry Larkin	1.25	.55
44 Alex Rodriguez	2.00	.90
45 Kazuhisa Ishii	.50	.23
46 Pedro Martinez	1.25	.55
47 Sean Burroughs	.50	.23
48 Roy Oswalt	.50	.23
49 Chipper Jones	1.25	.55
50 Barry Zito	.75	.35
51 Jeff Kent	.50	.23
52 Rodrigo Lopez	.50	.23
53 Jim Thome	1.25	.55
54 Ivan Rodriguez	1.25	.55
55 Luis Gonzalez	.50	.23
56 Alfonso Soriano	.75	.35
57 Josh Beckett	.75	.35
58 Junior Spivey	.50	.23
59 Bernie Williams	.75	.35
60 Omar Vizquel	.50	.23
61 Eric Hinske	.50	.23
62 Jose Vidro	.50	.23
63 Bartolo Colon	.50	.23
64 Jim Edmonds	.50	.23
65 Ben Sheets	.50	.23
66 Mark Prior	2.50	1.10
67 Edgar Martinez	.75	.35
68 Raul Ibanez	.50	.23
69 Darin Erstad	.50	.23
70 Roger Clemens	2.50	1.10
71 C.C. Sabathia	.50	.23
72 Carlos Delgado	.50	.23
73 Tom Glavine	.75	.35
74 Magglio Ordonez	.50	.23
75 Ichiro Suzuki	2.00	.90
76 Johnny Damon	.50	.23
77 Brian Giles	.50	.23
78 Jeff Bagwell	.75	.35
79 Greg Maddux	2.00	.90
80 Eric Chavez	.50	.23
81 Larry Walker	.75	.35
82 Randy Johnson	1.25	.55
83 Miguel Tejada	.50	.23
84 Todd Helton	.75	.35
85 Jarrod Washburn	.50	.23
86 Troy Glaus	.75	.35
87 Ken Griffey Jr.	2.00	.90
88 Albert Pujols	2.50	1.10
89 Torii Hunter	.50	.23
90 Joe Crede	.50	.23
91 Matt Morris	.50	.23
92 Shawn Green	.50	.23
93 Manny Ramirez	.50	.23
94 Jason Kendall	.50	.23
95 Preston Wilson	.50	.23
96 Garret Anderson	.50	.23
97 Cliff Floyd	.50	.23
98 Sean Casey	.50	.23
99 Juan Gonzalez	1.25	.55
100 Richie Sexson	.50	.23
101 Joe Borchard GU	5.00	2.20
102 Josh Stewart GU RC	5.00	2.20
103 Francisco Rodriguez GU	5.00	2.20
104 Jeremy Bonderman GU RC	8.00	3.60
105 Walter Young GU	5.00	2.20
106 Brandon Webb GU RC	10.00	4.50
107 Lyle Overbay GU	5.00	2.20
108 Jose Contreras GU RC	8.00	3.60
109 Victor Martinez GU	5.00	2.20
110 Hideki Matsui GU RC	15.00	6.75
111 Brian Stokes GU RC	5.00	2.20
112 Daniel Cabrera GU RC	5.00	2.20
113 Josh Willingham GU RC	8.00	3.60
114 Mark Teixeira GU	8.00	3.60
115 Pete LaForest GU RC	8.00	3.60
116 Chris Waters GU RC	5.00	2.20
117 Chien-Ming Wang GU RC	8.00	3.60
118 Ian Ferguson GU RC	5.00	2.20
119 Rocco Baldelli GU	10.00	4.50
120 Termel Sledge GU RC	8.00	3.60
121 Hank Blalock GU	8.00	3.60
122 Alejandro Machado GU RC	5.00	2.20
123 Hee Seop Choi GU	5.00	2.20
124 Guillermo Quiroz GU RC	8.00	3.60
125 Chase Utley GU	5.00	2.20
126 Nook Logan GU RC	5.00	2.20
127 Josh Hall GU RC	8.00	3.60
128 Ryan Church GU	5.00	2.20
129 Lew Ford GU RC	8.00	3.60
130 Francisco Rosario GU RC	5.00	2.20
131 Dan Haren GU RC	8.00	3.60
132 Rickie Weeks GU RC	15.00	6.75
133 Prentice Redman GU RC	5.00	2.20
134 Craig Brazell GU RC	8.00	3.60
135 Jon Leicester GU RC	5.00	2.20
136 Ryan Wagner GU RC	8.00	3.60
137 Matt Kata GU RC	8.00	3.60
138 Edwin Jackson GU RC	12.00	5.50
139 Mike Ryan GU RC	8.00	3.60
140 Delmon Young GU RC	15.00	6.75
141 Bo Hart GU RC	8.00	3.60
142 Jeff Duncan GU RC	8.00	3.60
143 Robby Hammock GU RC	8.00	3.60
144 Michael Hessman GU RC	5.00	2.20
145 Clint Barmes GU RC	8.00	3.60

2003 Fleer Genuine Reflection Ascending

	MINT	NRMT
*1-100 PRINT RUN b/wn 26-35: 10X TO 25X		
*1-100 PRINT RUN b/wn 36-50: 8X TO 20X		
*1-100 PRINT RUN b/wn 51-65: 6X TO 15X		
*1-100 PRINT RUN b/wn 66-80: 5X TO 12X		
*1-100 PRINT RUN b/wn 81-100: 4X TO 10X		
*101-130 P/R b/wn 101-130: .6X TO 1.5X		
*101-130 P/R b/wn 101-130: .6X TO 1.5X RC		
RANDOM INSERTS IN PACKS		
PRINT RUNS B/WN 1-130 COPIES PER CARD		
1-25 NOT PRICED DUE TO SCARCITY		

2003 Fleer Genuine Reflection Descending

	MINT	NRMT
*1-100 PRINT RUN b/wn 130-101: 3X TO 8X		
*1-100 PRINT RUN b/wn 100-81: 4X TO 10X		
*1-100 PRINT RUN b/wn 80-66: 5X TO 12X		
*1-100 PRINT RUN b/wn 65-51: 6X TO 15X		
*1-100 PRINT RUN b/wn 50-36: 8X TO 20X		
*1-100 PRINT RUN b/wn 35-31: 10X TO 25X		
RANDOM INSERTS IN PACKS		
PRINT RUNS B/WN 1-130 COPIES PER CARD		
101-105 RC'S NOT PRICED DUE TO SCARCITY		
106-130 NOT PRICED DUE TO SCARCITY		

2003 Fleer Genuine Article Insider Game Jersey

Inserted into packs at a stated rate of one in 24, these 25 cards feature game-used swatches

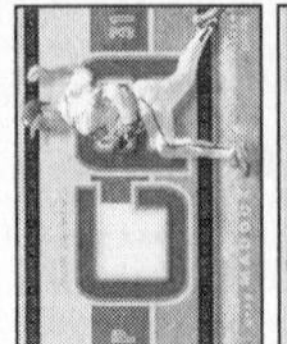

from some major league stars. Several of the cards in this set were produced in smaller quantities and we have noted the announced print run next to the player's name in our checklist.

	MINT	NRMT
AD Adam Dunn	8.00	3.60
AJ Andruw Jones SP/200	8.00	3.60
AR Alex Rodriguez SP/50		
AS Alfonso Soriano SP/300	10.00	4.50
CJ Chipper Jones	10.00	4.50
CS Curt Schilling	10.00	4.50
DJ Derek Jeter SP/450	25.00	11.00
DM Don Mattingly Pants	25.00	11.00
JB Jeff Bagwell	10.00	4.50
JG Jason Giambi SP/50		
LB Lance Berkman	8.00	3.60
MO Magglio Ordonez	8.00	3.60
MP Mike Piazza SP/100	20.00	9.00
MS Greg Maddux	10.00	4.50
MT Miguel Tejada SP/100	15.00	6.75
NG Nomar Garciaparra	15.00	6.75
PG Pat Burrell	8.00	3.60
PM Pedro Martinez	10.00	4.50
RJ Randy Johnson	10.00	4.50
SG Shawn Green	8.00	3.60
SS Sammy Sosa SP/300	15.00	6.75
TG Troy Glaus	10.00	4.50
TH Torii Hunter	8.00	3.60
TH2 Todd Helton	10.00	4.50
VG Vladimir Guerrero SP/100	20.00	9.00

2003 Fleer Genuine Article Insider Game Jersey Tag

Randomly inserted into packs, these 19 cards feature pieces of the "tags" used on uniforms. Each of these cards were issued to a stated print run of 10 serial numbered sets and no pricing is available due to market scarcity.

	MINT	NRMT
AJ Andruw Jones		
AR Alex Rodriguez		
AS Alfonso Soriano		
CJ Chipper Jones		
CS Curt Schilling		
JB Jeff Bagwell		
LB Lance Berkman		
MP Mike Piazza		
MT Miguel Tejada		
NG Nomar Garciaparra		
PB Pat Burrell		
PM Pedro Martinez		
RJ Randy Johnson		
SG Shawn Green		
SS Sammy Sosa		
TG Troy Glaus		
THe Todd Helton		
THu Torii Hunter		
VG Vladimir Guerrero		

2003 Fleer Genuine Article Insider Game Jersey Autographs

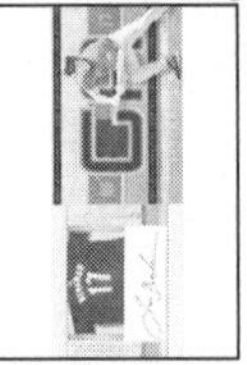

Randomly inserted into packs, these two cards parallel the Insider Game Jersey insert set but also have an autograph of the featured player.

	MINT	NRMT
RANDOM INSERTS IN PACKS		
PRINTS B/WN 165-170 COPIES PER CARD		
GA-DM Don Mattingly Pants	100.00	45.00
GA-LB Lance Berkman	25.00	11.00

2003 Fleer Genuine Article Insider Game Jersey Autographs VIP Blue

	MINT	NRMT
RANDOM INSERTS IN PACKS		
STATED PRINT RUN 50 SERIAL #'d SETS		
GA-DM Don Mattingly Pants	200.00	90.00
GA-LB Lance Berkman	50.00	22.00

2003 Fleer Genuine Article Insider Game Jersey Autographs VIP Red

	MINT	NRMT
RANDOM INSERTS IN PACKS		
STATED PRINT RUN 100 SERIAL #'d SETS		
GA-DJ Derek Jeter	150.00	70.00
GA-DM Don Mattingly Pants	150.00	70.00
GA-LB Lance Berkman	40.00	18.00

2003 Fleer Genuine Longball Threats

	MINT	NRMT
COMPLETE SET (15)	25.00	11.00
STATED ODDS 1:8		
1 Derek Jeter	6.00	2.70

	MINT	NRMT
Nomar Garciaparra		
2 Jim Thome	2.50	1.10
Pat Burrell		
3 Alex Rodriguez	4.00	1.80
Rafael Palmeiro		
4 Alfonso Soriano	8.00	3.60
Hideki Matsui		
5 Torii Hunter	2.50	1.10
Vladimir Guerrero		
6 Mike Sweeney	1.50	.70
Phil Nevin		
7 Mike Piazza	4.00	1.80
Sammy Sosa		
8 Shawn Green	2.50	1.10
Jason Giambi		
9 Magglio Ordonez	1.50	.70
Andruw Jones		
10 Eric Chavez	1.50	.70
Carlos Delgado		
11 Manny Ramirez	1.50	.70
Jeff Bagwell		
12 Scott Rolen	1.50	.70
Troy Glaus		
13 Barry Bonds	6.00	2.70
Miguel Tejada		
14 Albert Pujols	5.00	2.20
Lance Berkman		
15 Chipper Jones	2.50	1.10
Todd Helton		

2003 Fleer Genuine Longball Threats Dual Patch

	MINT	NRMT
RANDOM INSERTS IN PACKS		
PRINT RUNS B/WN 36-100 COPIES PER CARD		
1 Derek Jeter	100.00	45.00
Nomar Garciaparra		
2 Jim Thome	25.00	11.00
Pat Burrell		
3 Alex Rodriguez	50.00	22.00
Rafael Palmeiro		
5 Torii Hunter	40.00	18.00
Vladimir Guerrero		
6 Mike Sweeney	40.00	18.00
Phil Nevin		
7 Mike Piazza	60.00	27.00
Sammy Sosa		
8 Shawn Green	25.00	11.00
Jason Giambi		
9 Magglio Ordonez	15.00	6.75
Andruw Jones		
11 Manny Ramirez	40.00	18.00
Jeff Bagwell		
12 Scott Rolen	40.00	18.00
Troy Glaus		
15 Chipper Jones	40.00	18.00
Todd Helton		

2003 Fleer Genuine Longball Threats Dual Swatch

	MINT	NRMT
STATED ODDS 1:72		
1 Derek Jeter	40.00	18.00
Nomar Garciaparra		
2 Jim Thome	15.00	6.75
Pat Burrell		
3 Alex Rodriguez	25.00	11.00
Rafael Palmeiro		
5 Torii Hunter	15.00	6.75
Vladimir Guerrero		
6 Mike Sweeney	10.00	4.50
Phil Nevin		
7 Mike Piazza	25.00	11.00
Sammy Sosa		
8 Shawn Green	15.00	6.75
Jason Giambi		
9 Magglio Ordonez	10.00	4.50
Andruw Jones		
11 Manny Ramirez	10.00	4.50
Jeff Bagwell		
12 Scott Rolen	15.00	6.75
Troy Glaus		
15 Chipper Jones	15.00	6.75
Todd Helton		

2003 Fleer Genuine Longball Threats Single Swatch

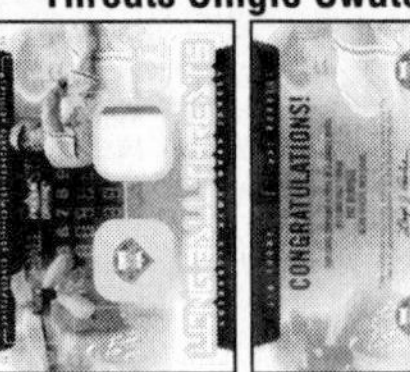

	MINT	NRMT
STATED ODDS 1:13		
SP PRINT RUNS PROVIDED BY FLEER		
SP'S ARE NOT SERIAL-NUMBERED		
1A Derek Jeter Jsy	25.00	11.00
Nomar Garciaparra SP/300		
1B Nomar Garciaparra Jsy	15.00	6.75
Derek Jeter		
2A Jim Thome Jsy	10.00	4.50
Pat Burrell		
2B Pat Burrell Jsy	8.00	3.60
Jim Thome		
3B Rafael Palmeiro Jsy	10.00	4.50
Alex Rodriguez		
4A Alfonso Soriano Jsy	25.00	11.00
Hideki Matsui SP/250		
5A Torii Hunter Jsy	8.00	3.60
Vladimir Guerrero		
5B Vladimir Guerrero Jsy	10.00	4.50
Torii Hunter		
6A Mike Sweeney Jsy	8.00	3.60
Phil Nevin		
6B Phil Nevin Jsy	8.00	3.60
Mike Sweeney SP/300		
7A Mike Piazza Jsy	15.00	6.75
Sammy Sosa		
7B Sammy Sosa Jsy	25.00	11.00
Mike Piazza SP/100		
8A Shawn Green Jsy	8.00	3.60
Jason Giambi		
8B Jason Giambi Jsy		
Shawn Green SP/50		
9A Magglio Ordonez Jsy	8.00	3.60
Andruw Jones		
9B Andruw Jones Jsy	8.00	3.60
Magglio Ordonez SP/200		
10B Carlos Delgado Jsy	8.00	3.60
Eric Chavez		
11A Manny Ramirez Jsy	8.00	3.60
Jeff Bagwell		
11B Jeff Bagwell Jsy	10.00	4.50
Manny Ramirez SP/450		
12A Scott Rolen Jsy	10.00	4.50
Troy Glaus		
12B Troy Glaus Jsy	10.00	4.50
Scott Rolen		
13B Miguel Tejada Jsy	8.00	3.60
Barry Bonds		
14B Lance Berkman Jsy	8.00	3.60
Albert Pujols		
15A Chipper Jones Jsy	10.00	4.50
Todd Helton		
15B Todd Helton Jsy	10.00	4.50
Chipper Jones		

2003 Fleer Genuine Tools of the Game

	MINT	NRMT
STATED ODDS 1:20		
1 Adam Dunn	3.00	1.35
2 Chipper Jones	5.00	2.20
3 Torii Hunter	3.00	1.35
4 Mike Piazza	8.00	3.60
5 Hideki Matsui	10.00	4.50
6 Nomar Garciaparra	8.00	3.60
7 Derek Jeter	12.00	5.50
8 Alex Rodriguez	8.00	3.60
9 Alfonso Soriano	3.00	1.35
10 Pat Burrell	3.00	1.35
11 Barry Bonds	12.00	5.50
12 Jason Giambi	5.00	2.20
13 Sammy Sosa	8.00	3.60
14 Vladimir Guerrero	5.00	2.20
15 Ichiro Suzuki	8.00	3.60

2003 Fleer Genuine Tools of the Game Bat

	MINT	NRMT
STATED ODDS 1:42		
1 Adam Dunn	8.00	3.60
4 Mike Piazza	15.00	6.75
7 Derek Jeter	20.00	9.00
8 Alex Rodriguez	15.00	6.75
9 Alfonso Soriano	10.00	4.50
12 Jason Giambi	10.00	4.50
13 Sammy Sosa	15.00	6.75
14 Vladimir Guerrero	10.00	4.50

2003 Fleer Genuine Tools of the Game Bat-Jersey

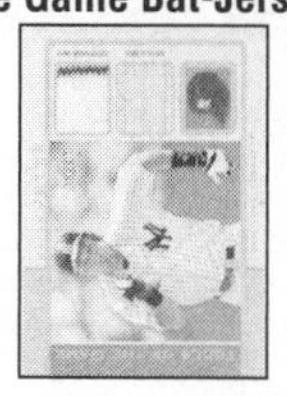

MINT NRMT
RANDOM INSERTS IN PACKS
STATED PRINT RUN 250 SERIAL #'d SETS
1 Adam Dunn 15.00 6.75
4 Mike Piazza 30.00 13.50
7 Derek Jeter 40.00 18.00
8 Alex Rodriguez
9 Alfonso Soriano 20.00 9.00
12 Jason Giambi 20.00 9.00
13 Sammy Sosa 30.00 13.50
14 Vladimir Guerrero 20.00 9.00

2003 Fleer Genuine Tools of the Game Bat-Jersey-Cap

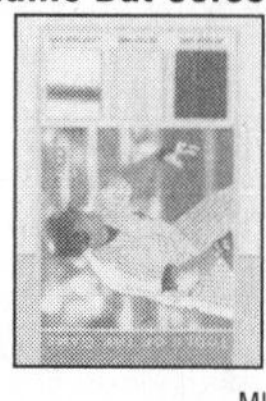

MINT NRMT
RANDOM INSERTS IN PACKS
STATED PRINT RUN 100 SERIAL #'d SETS
1 Adam Dunn 25.00 11.00
4 Mike Piazza 60.00 27.00
7 Derek Jeter 100.00 45.00
8 Alex Rodriguez 60.00 27.00
9 Alfonso Soriano 40.00 18.00
12 Jason Giambi 40.00 18.00
13 Sammy Sosa 60.00 27.00
14 Vladimir Guerrero 40.00 18.00

2000 Fleer Greats of the Game

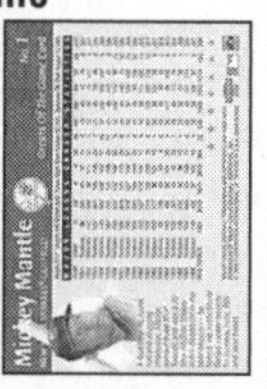

The 2000 Fleer Greats of the Game set was released in late March, 2000 as a 107-card set that features some of the greatest players to ever play the game. There was only one series offered. Each pack contained six cards and carried a suggested retail price of 4.99. A promotional sample card featuring Nolan Ryan was distributed to dealers and hobby media several weeks before the product went live. Card fronts featured an attractive burgundy frame with (in most cases) a full color player image. Fueled by a great selection of autographs, the popular Yankee Clippings game-used jersey inserts and the aforementioned superior design of the base set, the product turned out to be one of the most popular releases of the 2000 calendar.

Nm-Mt Ex-Mt
COMPLETE SET (107) 40.00 12.00
1 Mickey Mantle 10.00 3.00
2 Gil Hodges 1.50 .45
3 Monte Irvin 1.00 .30
4 Satchel Paige 1.50 .45
5 Roy Campanella 1.50 .45
6 Richie Ashburn 1.00 .30
7 Roger Maris 2.50 .75
8 Ozzie Smith 2.50 .75
9 Reggie Jackson 1.00 .30
10 Eddie Mathews 1.50 .45
11 Dave Righetti .60 .18
12 Dave Winfield .60 .18
13 Lou Whitaker .60 .18
14 Phil Garner .60 .18
15 Ron Cey .60 .18
16 Brooks Robinson 1.50 .45
17 Bruce Sutter .60 .18
18 Dave Parker .60 .18
19 Johnny Bench 1.50 .45
20 Fernando Valenzuela .60 .18
21 George Brett 4.00 1.20
22 Paul Molitor 1.00 .30
23 Hoyt Wilhelm .60 .18
24 Luis Aparicio .60 .18
25 Frank White .60 .18
26 Herb Score .60 .18
27 Kirk Gibson .60 .18
28 Mike Schmidt 3.00 .90
29 Don Baylor .60 .18
30 Joe Pepitone .60 .18
31 Hal McRae .60 .18
32 Lee Smith .60 .18
33 Nolan Ryan 4.00 1.20
34 Bill Mazeroski 1.00 .30
35 Bobby Doerr 1.00 .30
36 Duke Snider 1.00 .30
37 Dick Groat .60 .18
38 Larry Doby .60 .18
39 Kirby Puckett 1.50 .45
40 Steve Carlton .60 .18
41 Dennis Eckersley .60 .18
42 Jim Bunning 1.00 .30
43 Ron Guidry .60 .18
44 Alan Trammell 1.00 .30
45 Bob Feller 1.00 .30
46 Dave Concepcion .60 .18
47 Dwight Evans .60 .18
48 Enos Slaughter .60 .18
49 Tom Seaver 1.00 .30
50 Tony Oliva .60 .18
51 Mel Stottlemyre .60 .18
52 Tommy John .60 .18
53 Willie McCovey .60 .18
54 Red Schoendienst .60 .18
55 Gorman Thomas .60 .18
56 Ralph Kiner .60 .18
57 Robin Yount 2.50 .75
58 Andre Dawson .60 .18
59 Al Kaline 1.50 .45
60 Dom DiMaggio 1.00 .30
61 Juan Marichal .60 .18
62 Jack Morris .60 .18
63 Warren Spahn 1.00 .30
64 Preacher Roe .60 .18
65 Darrell Evans .60 .18
66 Jim Bouton .60 .18
67 Rocky Colavito 1.00 .30
68 Bob Gibson 1.00 .30
69 Whitey Ford 1.00 .30
70 Moose Skowron .60 .18
71 Boog Powell .60 .18
72 Al Lopez 1.00 .30
73 Lou Brock 1.00 .30
74 Mickey Lolich .60 .18
75 Rod Carew 1.00 .30
76 Bob Lemon 1.00 .30
77 Frank Howard .60 .18
78 Phil Rizzuto 1.50 .45
79 Carl Yastrzemski 2.50 .75
80 Rico Carty .60 .18
81 Jim Kaat .60 .18
82 Bert Blyleven .60 .18
83 George Kell 1.00 .30
84 Jim Palmer .60 .18
85 Maury Wills .60 .18
86 Jim Rice .60 .18
87 Joe Carter .60 .18
88 Clete Boyer .60 .18
89 Yogi Berra 1.50 .45
90 Cecil Cooper .60 .18
91 Davey Johnson .60 .18
92 Lou Boudreau 1.00 .30
93 Orlando Cepeda .60 .18
94 Tommy Henrich .60 .18
95 Hank Bauer .60 .18
96 Don Larsen .60 .18
97 Vida Blue .60 .18
98 Ben Oglivie .60 .18
99 Don Mattingly 4.00 1.20
100 Dale Murphy 1.50 .45
101 Ferguson Jenkins .60 .18
102 Bobby Bonds .60 .18
103 Dick Allen .60 .18
104 Stan Musial 2.50 .75
105 Gaylord Perry .60 .18
106 Willie Randolph .60 .18
107 Willie Stargell 1.00 .30
P33 Nolan Ryan Promo 1.50 .45

2000 Fleer Greats of the Game Autographs

Randomly inserted in packs at one in six, this 90-card insert features autographed cards of some of the greatest players in major league history. The card design closely parallels the attractive basic issue cards, except of course for the player's singature. Representatives at Fleer eventually released cryptic details on a few cards confirming widespread belief on suspected shortprints within the set. It's known that the scarcest cards are Johnny Bench and Mike Schmidt. Several other cards from this set experienced amazing surges iin value throughout the course of the year 2000 as collectors scrambled to complete their sets in the midst of heavy demand and rumours of additional short prints. Also, Herb Score mistakenly signed several of his basic autographs with an "ROY 55" notation. Score was supposed so sign only 55 purple-bordered Memorable Moments variations. Finally, a Derek Jeter card was released in early 2004. It's believed that the card was only made available as a redemption to collectors for autograph exchange cards of other players that they could not fulfill. Please note that these cards are unnumbered and we have sequenced them in alphabetical order.

Nm-Mt Ex-Mt
1 Luis Aparicio 15.00 4.50
2 Hank Bauer 15.00 4.50
3 Don Baylor 15.00 4.50
4 Johnny Bench SP 200.00 60.00
5 Yogi Berra SP 175.00 52.50
6 Vida Blue 15.00 4.50
7 Bert Blyleven 15.00 4.50
8 Bobby Bonds 25.00 7.50
9 Lou Boudreau 120.00 36.00
10 Jim Bouton 25.00 7.50
11 Clete Boyer 15.00 4.50
12 George Brett SP 200.00 60.00
13 Lou Brock 25.00 7.50
14 Jim Bunning 25.00 7.50
15 Rod Carew 40.00 12.00
16 Steve Carlton 25.00 7.50
17 Joe Carter SP 120.00 36.00
18 Orlando Cepeda 15.00 4.50
19 Ron Cey 10.00 3.00
20 Rocky Colavito 50.00 15.00
21 Dave Concepcion 15.00 4.50
21A Dave Concepcion 15.00 4.50
Signed in Red Ink
22 Cecil Cooper 10.00 3.00
23 Andre Dawson 10.00 3.00
24 Dom DiMaggio 120.00 36.00
25 Bobby Doerr 15.00 4.50
26 Darrell Evans 10.00 3.00
27 Bob Feller 25.00 7.50
28 Whitey Ford SP 150.00 45.00
29 Phil Garner 10.00 3.00
30 Bob Gibson 25.00 7.50
31 Kirk Gibson 25.00 7.50
32 Dick Groat 15.00 4.50
33 Ron Guidry 15.00 4.50
34 Tommy Henrich SP 150.00 45.00
35 Frank Howard 15.00 4.50
36 Reggie Jackson SP 150.00 45.00
37 Ferguson Jenkins 15.00 4.50
38 Derek Jeter EXCH
39 Tommy John 15.00 4.50
40 Davey Johnson 10.00 3.00
41 Jim Kaat 15.00 4.50
42 Al Kaline 40.00 12.00
43 George Kell 15.00 4.50
44 Ralph Kiner 25.00 7.50
45 Don Larsen 25.00 7.50
46 Mickey Lolich 15.00 4.50
47 Juan Marichal 60.00 18.00
48 Eddie Mathews 100.00 30.00
49 Don Mattingly SP 300.00 90.00
50 Bill Mazeroski 25.00 7.50
51 Willie McCovey SP 120.00 36.00
52 Hal McRae 10.00 3.00
53 Paul Molitor 40.00 12.00
54 Jack Morris 15.00 4.50
55 Dale Murphy 40.00 12.00
56 Stan Musial SP 100.00 30.00
57 Ben Oglivie 10.00 3.00
58 Tony Oliva 15.00 4.50
59 Jim Palmer SP 100.00 30.00
60 Dave Parker 15.00 4.50
61 Joe Pepitone 15.00 4.50
62 Gaylord Perry 15.00 4.50
63 Boog Powell 15.00 4.50
64 Kirby Puckett SP 175.00 52.50
65 Willie Randolph 15.00 4.50
66 Jim Rice 25.00 7.50
67 Dave Righetti 15.00 4.50
68 Phil Rizzuto SP 175.00 52.50
69 Brooks Robinson 40.00 12.00
70 Preacher Roe 15.00 4.50
71 Nolan Ryan 150.00 45.00
72 Mike Schmidt SP 250.00 75.00
73 Red Schoendienst 25.00 7.50
74 Herb Score 15.00 4.50
Card has no ROY 55 on signature
75 Herb Score 40.00 12.00
ROY 55 in signature
76 Tom Seaver 100.00 30.00
77 Moose Skowron 15.00 4.50
78 Enos Slaughter 25.00 7.50
79 Lee Smith 15.00 4.50
80 Ozzie Smith SP 200.00 60.00
81 Duke Snider SP 175.00 52.50
82 Warren Spahn SP 120.00 36.00
83 Willie Stargell 50.00 15.00
84 Bruce Sutter 15.00 4.50
85 Gorman Thomas 10.00 3.00
86 Alan Trammell 25.00 7.50
87 Frank White 15.00 4.50
88 Hoyt Wilhelm 25.00 7.50
89 Maury Wills 15.00 4.50
90 Carl Yastrzemski 60.00 18.00
91 Robin Yount SP 150.00 45.00

2000 Fleer Greats of the Game Autographs Memorable Moments

Randomly inserted in packs, this insert features autographs of Ron Guidry, Nolan Ryan, Herb Score and Tom Seaver. Each card is autographed and contains a notion by the player related to a career achievement. Each card is serial-numbered to the year of that achievement. The fronts of these cards are purple-bordered instead of burgandy-bordered. Please note that Herb Score signed some of his regular burgandy-bordered autograph cards with the "HOF 55" notation. Please refer to the basic autograph set for price listings on that card.

Nm-Mt Ex-Mt
1 Ron Guidry/CY 78 120.00 36.00
2 Nolan Ryan/HOF 99 400.00 120.00
3 Herb Score/ROY 55 100.00 30.00
4 Tom Seaver/CY 69 250.00 75.00

2000 Fleer Greats of the Game Retrospection

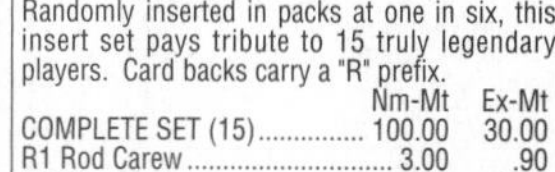

Randomly inserted in packs at one in six, this insert set pays tribute to 15 truly legendary players. Card backs carry a "R" prefix.

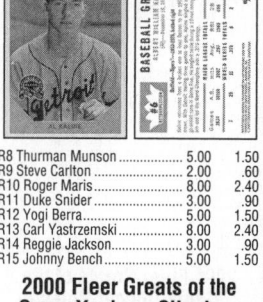

Nm-Mt Ex-Mt
COMPLETE SET (15) 100.00 30.00
R1 Rod Carew 3.00 .90
R2 Stan Musial 8.00 2.40
R3 Nolan Ryan 12.00 3.60
R4 Tom Seaver 3.00 .90
R5 Brooks Robinson 5.00 1.50
R6 Al Kaline 5.00 1.50
R7 Mike Schmidt 10.00 3.00
R8 Thurman Munson 5.00 1.50
R9 Steve Carlton 2.00 .60
R10 Roger Maris 8.00 2.40
R11 Duke Snider 3.00 .90
R12 Yogi Berra 5.00 1.50
R13 Carl Yastrzemski 8.00 2.40
R14 Reggie Jackson 3.00 .90
R15 Johnny Bench 5.00 1.50

2000 Fleer Greats of the Game Yankees Clippings

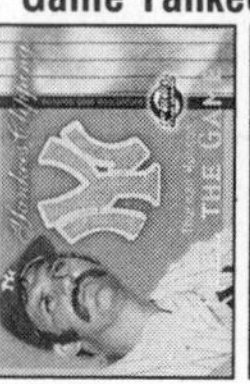
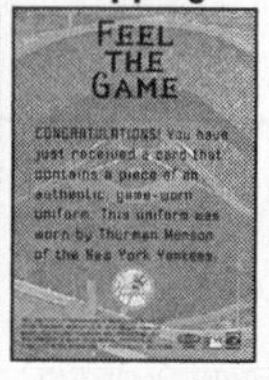

Randomly inserted in packs at one in 48, this insert set features 15 cards that contain pieces of game-used jerseys of legendary New York Yankee players. Card backs carry a "YC" prefix. This set represents one of the earliest attempts by manufacturers to incorporate a theme into a memorabilia-based insert.

Nm-Mt Ex-Mt
YC1 Mickey Mantle 300.00 90.00
YC2 Ron Guidry 40.00 12.00
YC3 Don Larsen 40.00 12.00
YC4 Elston Howard 40.00 12.00
YC5 Mel Stottlemyre 25.00 7.50
YC6 Don Mattingly 100.00 30.00
YC7 Reggie Jackson 60.00 18.00
YC8 Tommy John 25.00 7.50
YC9 Dave Winfield 25.00 7.50
YC10 Willie Randolph 25.00 7.50
Uniform is home pinstripes
YC10A Willie Randolph 25.00 7.50
Grey Uniform
YC11 Tommy Henrich 25.00 7.50
YC12 Billy Martin 60.00 18.00
YC13 Dave Righetti 25.00 7.50
YC14 Joe Pepitone 25.00 7.50
YC15 Thurman Munson 80.00 24.00

2001 Fleer Greats of the Game Promo Sheets

These six promo sheets were inserted into Sports Cards Magazine starting in February, 2001. Each uncut sheet features six Greats of the Game trading cards. Please note that Fleer released these one month at a time.

Nm-Mt Ex-Mt
COMPLETE SET (6) 18.00 5.50
1 Rick Ankiel 3.00 .90
Jeff Bagwell
Barry Bonds
Pat Burrell
Roger Clemens
Carlos Delgado
2 J.D. Drew 3.00 .90
Jim Edmonds
Darin Erstad
Andres Galarraga
Nomar Garciaparra
Jason Giambi
3 Troy Glaus 3.00 .90
Roberto Alomar
Ken Griffey Jr.
Vladimir Guerrero
Tony Gwynn
Todd Helton
4 Derek Jeter 3.00 .90
Randy Johnson
Chipper Jones
Andruw Jones
Greg Maddux
Pedro Martinez
5 Mark McGwire 3.00 .90
Magglio Ordonez
Mike Piazza
Manny Ramirez
Cal Ripken
Alex Rodriguez
6 Ivan Rodriguez 3.00 .90
Jeff Kent
Gary Sheffield
Sammy Sosa
Frank Thomas
Bernie Williams

2001 Fleer Greats of the Game

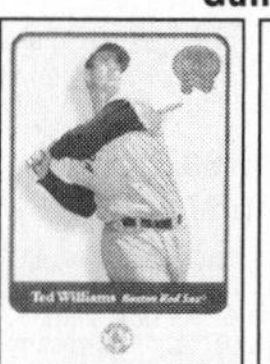

The 2001 Fleer Greats of the Game product was released in March, 2001 and features a 137-card base set that includes many players that are in the Major League Hall of Fame. Each pack contains five cards and carried a suggested retail price of $4.99.

Nm-Mt Ex-Mt
COMPLETE SET (137) 50.00 15.00
1 Roberto Clemente 6.00 1.80
2 George Anderson 1.00 .30
3 Babe Ruth 8.00 2.40
4 Paul Molitor 1.50 .45
5 Don Larsen 1.00 .30
6 Cy Young 2.50 .75
7 Billy Martin 1.50 .45
8 Lou Brock 1.50 .45
9 Fred Lynn 1.00 .30
10 Johnny VanderMeer 1.00 .30
11 Harmon Killebrew 2.50 .75
12 Dave Winfield 1.00 .30
13 Orlando Cepeda 1.00 .30
14 Johnny Mize 1.50 .45
15 Walter Johnson 2.50 .75
16 Roy Campanella 2.50 .75
17 Monte Irvin 1.50 .45
18 Mookie Wilson 1.00 .30
19 Elston Howard 1.50 .45
20 Walter Alston 1.00 .30
21 Rollie Fingers 1.00 .30
22 Brooks Robinson 2.50 .75
23 Hank Greenberg 2.50 .75
24 Maury Wills 1.00 .30
25 Rich Gossage 1.00 .30
26 Leon Day 1.00 .30
27 Jimmie Foxx 2.50 .75
28 Alan Trammell 1.50 .45
29 Dennis Martinez 1.00 .30
30 Don Drysdale 2.50 .75
31 Bob Feller 1.50 .45
32 Jackie Robinson 3.00 .90
33 Whitey Ford 1.50 .45
34 Enos Slaughter 1.00 .30
35 Rod Carew 1.50 .45
36 Eddie Mathews 2.50 .75
37 Ron Cey 1.00 .30
38 Thurman Munson 3.00 .90
39 Henry Kimbro 1.00 .30
40 Ty Cobb 4.00 1.20
41 Rocky Colavito 2.50 .75
42 Satchel Paige 2.50 .75
43 Andre Dawson 1.00 .30
44 Phil Rizzuto 2.50 .75
45 Roger Maris 4.00 1.20
46 Bobby Bonds 1.00 .30
47 Joe Carter 1.00 .30
48 Christy Mathewson 2.50 .75
49 Tony Lazzeri 1.00 .30
50 Gil Hodges 2.50 .75
51 Ray Dandridge 1.00 .30
52 Gaylord Perry 1.00 .30
53 Ernie Banks 2.50 .75
54 Lou Gehrig 5.00 1.50
55 George Kell 1.50 .45
56 Wes Parker 1.00 .30
57 Sam Jethroe 1.00 .30
58 Joe Morgan 1.00 .30
59 Steve Garvey 1.00 .30
60 Joe Torre 1.00 .30
61 Roger Craig 1.00 .30
62 Warren Spahn 1.50 .45
63 Willie McCovey 1.00 .30
64 Cool Papa Bell 1.00 .30
65 Frank Robinson 1.50 .45
66 Richie Allen 1.00 .30
67 Bucky Dent 1.00 .30
68 George Foster 1.00 .30
69 Hoyt Wilhelm 1.00 .30
70 Phil Niekro 1.00 .30
71 Buck Leonard 1.00 .30
72 Preacher Roe 1.00 .30
73 Yogi Berra 2.50 .75
74 Joe Black 1.00 .30
75 Nolan Ryan 6.00 1.80
76 Pop Lloyd 1.00 .30
77 Lester Lockett 1.00 .30
78 Paul Blair 1.00 .30
79 Ryne Sandberg 4.00 1.20
80 Bill Perkins 1.00 .30
81 Frank Howard 1.00 .30
82 Hack Wilson 1.50 .45
83 Robin Yount 4.00 1.20
84 Harry Heilmann 1.00 .30
85 Mike Schmidt 5.00 1.50
86 Vida Blue 1.00 .30
87 George Brett 6.00 1.80
88 Juan Marichal 1.00 .30
89 Tom Seaver 1.50 .45
90 Bill Skowron 1.00 .30
91 Don Mattingly 6.00 1.80
92 Jim Bunning 1.50 .45
93 Eddie Murray 2.50 .75
94 Tommy Lasorda 1.00 .30
95 Pee Wee Reese 2.50 .75
96 Bill Dickey 1.50 .45
97 Ozzie Smith 4.00 1.20
98 Dale Murphy 2.50 .75
99 Artie Wilson 1.00 .30
100 Bill Terry 1.00 .30
101 Jim Hunter 1.50 .45
102 Don Sutton 1.00 .30
103 Luis Aparicio 1.00 .30
104 Reggie Jackson 1.50 .45
105 Ted Radcliffe 1.00 .30
106 Carl Erskine 1.00 .30
107 Johnny Bench 2.50 .75
108 Carl Furillo 1.00 .30
109 Stan Musial 4.00 1.20
110 Carlton Fisk 1.50 .45
111 Rube Foster 1.00 .30
112 Tony Oliva 1.00 .30
113 Hank Bauer 1.00 .30
114 Jim Rice 1.00 .30
115 Willie Mays 5.00 1.50
116 Ralph Kiner 1.00 .30
117 Al Kaline 2.50 .75
118 Billy Williams 1.00 .30
119 Buck O'Neil 1.00 .30
120 Tony Perez 1.00 .30
121 Dave Parker 1.00 .30
122 Kirk Gibson 1.00 .30
123 Lou Piniella 1.00 .30
124 Ted Williams 6.00 1.80
125 Steve Carlton 1.00 .30

126 Dizzy Dean 2.50 .75
127 Willie Stargell 1.50 .45
128 Joe Niekro 1.00 .30
129 Lloyd Waner 1.50 .45
130 Wade Boggs 1.50 .45
131 Wilmer Fields 1.00 .30
132 Bill Mazeroski 1.50 .45
133 Duke Snider 1.50 .45
134 Joe Williams 1.00 .30
135 Bob Gibson 1.50 .45
136 Jim Palmer 1.00 .30
137 Oscar Charleston 1.00 .30

2001 Fleer Greats of the Game Autographs

Randomly inserted into packs at one in eight Hobby, and one in 20 Retail, this 93-card insert set features authentic autographs from legendary players such as Nolan Ryan, Mike Schmidt, and recently inducted Hall of Famer Dave Winfield. Please note, the following players packed out as exchange cards with a redemption deadline of March 1st, 2002: Luis Aparicio, Sam Jethroe, Tommy Lasorda, Juan Marichal, Willie Mays, Phil Rizzuto and Willie Stargell. In addition, the following players had about 50 percent actual signed cards and 50 percent exchange cards seeded into packs: Jim Bunning, Ron Cey, Rollie Fingers, Carlton Fisk, Harmon Killebrew, Gaylord Perry and Brooks Robinson. Also, representatives at Fleer announced specific print runs for several short-printed cards within this set. Though the cards lack actual serial-numbering, the announced quantities for these SP's have been added to our checklist. Willie Stargell passed on before he could sign his card and Fleer used various redemption cards to send to those collectors who had pulled one of those cards from packs.

Nm-Mt Ex-Mt
1 Richie Allen 15.00 4.50
2 Sparky Anderson 15.00 4.50
3 Luis Aparicio 15.00 4.50
4 Ernie Banks SP/250 120.00 36.00
5 Hank Bauer 15.00 4.50
6 Johnny Bench SP/400 120.00 36.00
7 Yogi Berra SP/500 80.00 24.00
8 Joe Black 15.00 4.50
9 Paul Blair 15.00 4.50
9A Paul Blair 15.00 4.50
Double-Signed
10 Vida Blue 15.00 4.50
11 Wade Boggs 50.00 15.00
12 Bobby Bonds 25.00 7.50
13 George Brett SP/247 200.00 60.00
14 Lou Brock SP/500 50.00 15.00
15 Jim Bunning 25.00 7.50
16 Rod Carew 25.00 7.50
17 Steve Carlton 30.00 9.00
18 Joe Carter 15.00 4.50
19 Orlando Cepeda 15.00 4.50
20 Ron Cey 15.00 4.50
21 Rocky Colavito 25.00 7.50
22 Roger Craig 15.00 4.50
23 Andre Dawson 15.00 4.50
24 Bucky Dent 15.00 4.50
25 Carl Erskine 15.00 4.50
26 Bob Feller 25.00 7.50
27 Wilmer Fields 15.00 4.50
28 Rollie Fingers 15.00 4.50
29 Carlton Fisk 50.00 15.00
30 Whitey Ford 40.00 12.00
31 George Foster 15.00 4.50
32 Steve Garvey SP/400 50.00 15.00
33 Bob Gibson 30.00 9.00
34 Kirk Gibson 15.00 4.50
35 Rich Gossage 15.00 4.50
36 Frank Howard 15.00 4.50
37 Monte Irvin 25.00 7.50
38 Reg. Jackson SP/400 80.00 24.00
39 Sam Jethroe 15.00 4.50
40 Al Kaline 40.00 12.00
41 George Kell 25.00 7.50
42 H. Killebrew EXCH* 30.00 9.00
43 Ralph Kiner 25.00 7.50
44 Don Larsen 25.00 7.50
45 Tommy Lasorda SP/400 50.00 15.00
46 Lester Lockett 15.00 4.50
47 Fred Lynn 15.00 4.50
48 Juan Marichal 15.00 4.50
49 Dennis Martinez 15.00 4.50
50 Don Mattingly 100.00 30.00
51 Willie Mays SP/100 500.00 150.00
52 Bill Mazeroski UER 25.00 7.50
Baltimore Elite Giants logo on card back
53 Willie McCovey 25.00 7.50
54 Paul Molitor 25.00 7.50
55 Joe Morgan 15.00 4.50
56 Dale Murphy 40.00 12.00
57 Eddie Murray SP/140 300.00 90.00
58 Stan Musial SP/525 100.00 30.00
59 Joe Niekro 15.00 4.50
60 Phil Niekro 15.00 4.50
61 Tony Oliva 15.00 4.50
62 Buck O'Neil 25.00 7.50
63 Jim Palmer SP/600 25.00 7.50
64 Dave Parker 15.00 4.50
65 Tony Perez 25.00 7.50
66 Gaylord Perry 15.00 4.50
67 Lou Piniella 15.00 4.50
68 Ted Radcliffe 15.00 4.50
69 Jim Rice 25.00 7.50
70 Phil Rizzuto 100.00 30.00
EXCH SP/425
71 Brooks Robinson 30.00 9.00
72 Frank Robinson 30.00 9.00
73 Preacher Roe 15.00 4.50
74 Nolan Ryan SP/650 120.00 36.00
75 Ryne Sandberg 60.00 18.00
76 Mike Schmidt SP/213 250.00 75.00
77 Tom Seaver 50.00 15.00
78 Bill Skowron 15.00 4.50
79 Enos Slaughter 25.00 7.50
80 Ozzie Smith 60.00 18.00
81 Duke Snider SP/600 80.00 24.00
82 Warren Spahn 40.00 12.00
83 Willie Stargell NO AU 25.00 7.50
84 Don Sutton 15.00 4.50
85 Joe Torre SP/500 60.00 18.00
86 Alan Trammell 25.00 7.50
87 Hoyt Wilhelm 15.00 4.50
88 Billy Williams 15.00 4.50
89 Maury Wills 15.00 4.50
90 Artie Wilson 15.00 4.50
91 Mookie Wilson 15.00 4.50
92 Dave Winfield SP/370 80.00 24.00
93 Robin Yount SP/400 100.00 30.00

2001 Fleer Greats of the Game Dodger Blues

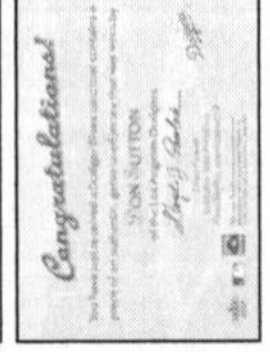

Randomly inserted into packs at one in 36 Hobby, this 15-card insert set features swatches from actual game-used Jerseys, Uniforms, and Bats from legendary Dodger players. The cards have been listed below in alphabetical order for convenience. Please note, according to representatives at Fleer less than 200 of each SP was produced.

Nm-Mt Ex-Mt
1 Walter Alston Jsy 15.00 4.50
2 Walter Alston Uniform 15.00 4.50
3 Roy Campanella Bat SP 120.00 36.00
4 Roger Craig Jsy 15.00 4.50
5 Don Drysdale Jsy 25.00 7.50
6 Carl Furillo Jsy 15.00 4.50
7 Steve Garvey Jsy 15.00 4.50
8 Gil Hodges Uniform 25.00 7.50
9 Wes Parker Bat 15.00 4.50
10 Wes Parker Jsy 15.00 4.50
11 Pee Wee Reese Jsy 25.00 7.50
12 Jackie Robinson 200.00 60.00
Uniform SP
13 Preacher Roe Jsy 25.00 7.50
14 Duke Snider Bat SP 120.00 36.00
15 Don Sutton Jsy 15.00 4.50

2001 Fleer Greats of the Game Feel the Game Classics

Randomly inserted into packs at one in 72 Hobby, and one in 400 Retail, this 24-card insert features swatches of actual game-used Bats or Jerseys from legendary players like Babe Ruth and Roger Maris. Please note that the cards are listed below in alphabetical order. Though the cards lack actual serial-numbering, specific print runs for several short-printed cards was publicly announced by representativces at Fleer. These figures are detailed in our checklist.

Nm-Mt Ex-Mt
1 L. Aparicio Bat SP/200 25.00 7.50
2 George Brett Jsy SP/300 50.00 15.00
3 Lou Brock Jsy 15.00 4.50
4 O. Cepeda Bat SP/300 25.00 7.50
5 Whitey Ford Jsy 15.00 4.50
6 Hank Greenberg Bat SP/300 80.00 24.00
7 Elston Howard Bat SP/300 25.00 7.50
8 Jim Hunter Jsy 15.00 4.50
9 Harmon Killebrew Bat 15.00 4.50
10 Roger Maris Bat 80.00 24.00
11 Eddie Mathews Bat 15.00 4.50
12 Willie McCovey 25.00 7.50
Bat SP/200
13 Johnny Mize Bat 15.00 4.50
14 Paul Molitor Jsy 15.00 4.50
15 Jim Palmer Jsy 10.00 3.00
16 Tony Perez Bat 10.00 3.00
17 B.Robinson Bat SP/144 25.00 7.50
18 Babe Ruth Bat SP/250 250.00 75.00
19 Mike Schmidt Jsy 40.00 12.00
20 Tom Seaver Jsy 15.00 4.50
21 Enos Slaughter 25.00 7.50
Bat SP/200
22 Willie Stargell Jsy 15.00 4.50
23 Hack Wilson Bat 80.00 24.00
24 Harry Heilmann Bat 10.00 3.00

2001 Fleer Greats of the Game Retrospection

Randomly inserted into hobby and retail packs at one in six, this 10-card insert set takes a look at the careers of some of the best players to have ever played the game. Card backs carry a "RC" prefix.

Nm-Mt Ex-Mt
COMPLETE SET (10) 30.00 9.00
RC1 Babe Ruth 15.00 4.50

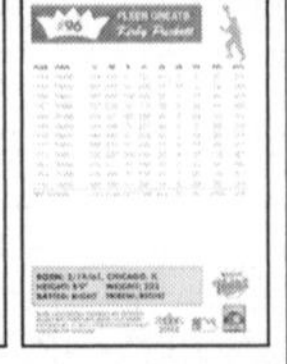

RC2 Stan Musial 6.00 1.80
RC3 Jimmie Foxx 5.00 1.50
RC4 Roberto Clemente 10.00 3.00
RC5 Ted Williams 12.00 3.60
RC6 Mike Schmidt 8.00 2.40
RC7 Cy Young 5.00 1.50
RC8 Satchel Paige 5.00 1.50
RC9 Hank Greenberg 5.00 1.50
RC10 Jim Bunning 3.00 .90

2002 Fleer Greats of the Game

This product was released in mid-December 2001, and featured a 100-card base set of Hall of Famers like Cy Young and Ted Williams. Each pack contained five-cards and carried a suggested retail price of $4.99.

Nm-Mt Ex-Mt
COMPLETE SET (100) 50.00 15.00
1 Cal Ripken 8.00 2.40
2 Paul Molitor 1.50 .45
3 Roberto Clemente 5.00 1.50
4 Cy Young 2.50 .75
5 Tris Speaker 2.50 .75
6 Lou Brock 1.50 .45
7 Fred Lynn 1.00 .30
8 Harmon Killebrew 2.50 .75
9 Ted Williams 6.00 1.80
10 Dave Winfield 1.00 .30
11 Orlando Cepeda 1.00 .30
12 Johnny Mize 1.50 .45
13 Walter Johnson 2.50 .75
14 Roy Campanella 2.50 .75
15 George Sisler 1.00 .30
16 Bo Jackson 2.50 .75
17 Rollie Fingers 1.00 .30
18 Brooks Robinson 2.50 .75
19 Billy Williams 1.00 .30
20 Maury Wills 1.00 .30
21 Jimmie Foxx 2.50 .75
22 Alan Trammell 1.50 .45
23 Rogers Hornsby 2.50 .75
24 Don Drysdale 2.50 .75
25 Bob Feller 1.50 .45
26 Jackie Robinson 3.00 .90
27 Whitey Ford 1.50 .45
28 Enos Slaughter 1.00 .30
29 Rod Carew 1.50 .45
30 Eddie Mathews 2.50 .75
31 Ron Cey 1.00 .30
32 Thurman Munson 3.00 .90
33 Ty Cobb 4.00 1.20
34 Rocky Colavito 2.50 .75
35 Satchel Paige 2.50 .75
36 Andre Dawson 1.00 .30
37 Phil Rizzuto 2.50 .75
38 Roger Maris 4.00 1.20
39 Earl Weaver 1.00 .30
40 Joe Carter 1.00 .30
41 Christy Mathewson 2.50 .75
42 Tony Lazzeri 1.00 .30
43 Gil Hodges 2.50 .75
44 Gaylord Perry 1.00 .30
45 Steve Carlton 1.00 .30
46 George Kell 1.50 .45
47 Mickey Cochrane 1.50 .45
48 Joe Morgan 1.00 .30
49 Steve Garvey 1.00 .30
50 Bob Gibson 1.50 .45
51 Lefty Grove 1.50 .45
52 Warren Spahn 1.50 .45
53 Willie McCovey 1.00 .30
54 Frank Robinson 1.50 .45
55 Rich Gossage 1.00 .30
56 Hank Bauer 1.00 .30
57 Hoyt Wilhelm 1.00 .30
58 Mel Ott 2.50 .75
59 Preacher Roe 1.00 .30
60 Yogi Berra 2.50 .75
61 Nolan Ryan 6.00 1.80
62 Dizzy Dean 2.50 .75
63 Ryne Sandberg 4.00 1.20
64 Frank Howard 1.00 .30
65 Hack Wilson 1.50 .45
66 Robin Yount 4.00 1.20
67 Al Kaline 2.50 .75
68 Mike Schmidt 5.00 1.50
69 Vida Blue 1.00 .30
70 George Brett 6.00 1.80
71 Sparky Anderson 1.00 .30
72 Tom Seaver 1.50 .45
73 Bill Skowron 1.00 .30
74 Don Mattingly 6.00 1.80
75 Carl Yastrzemski 4.00 1.20
76 Eddie Murray 2.50 .75
77 Jim Palmer 1.00 .30
78 Bill Dickey 1.50 .45
79 Ozzie Smith 4.00 1.20
80 Dale Murphy 2.50 .75
81 Nap Lajoie 2.50 .75
82 Jim Hunter 1.50 .45
83 Duke Snider 1.50 .45
84 Luis Aparicio 1.00 .30
85 Reggie Jackson 1.50 .45
86 Honus Wagner 3.00 .90
87 Johnny Bench 2.50 .75
88 Stan Musial 4.00 1.20
89 Carlton Fisk 1.50 .45
90 Tony Oliva 1.00 .30
91 Wade Boggs 1.50 .45
92 Jim Rice 1.00 .30
93 Bill Mazeroski 1.50 .45
94 Ralph Kiner 1.00 .30
95 Tony Perez 1.00 .30
96 Kirby Puckett 2.50 .75
97 Bobby Bonds 1.00 .30
98 Bill Terry 1.00 .30
99 Juan Marichal 1.00 .30
100 Hank Greenberg 2.50 .75

2002 Fleer Greats of the Game Autographs

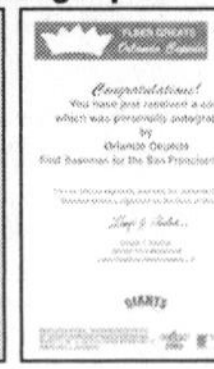

Randomly inserted into packs at one in 24, this insert set features authentic autographs from legendary players such as Nolan Ryan, Bob Gibson, and recently inducted Hall of Famer Ozzie Smith. Please note that a few of the players were short-printed and are listed below with an "SP" after their name. A number of exchange cards with a redemption deadline of 12/01/02 were seeded into packs. The following players were available via redemption: Al Kaline, Alan Trammell, Bobby Bonds, Bob Feller, Carlton Fisk, Rocky Colavito, Cal Ripken, Dave Winfield, Eddie Murray, Enos Slaughter, Harmon Killebrew, Juan Marichal, Kirby Puckett, Luis Aparicio, Lou Brock, Mike Schmidt, Dale Murphy, Maury Wills, Nolan Ryan, Ozzie Smith, Phil Rizzuto, Rod Carew, Rollie Fingers, Rich Gossage, Ralph Kiner, Robin Yount, Steve Garvey, Whitey Ford, Willie McCovey and Yogi Berra.

Nm-Mt Ex-Mt
AD Andre Dawson 15.00 4.50
AK Al Kaline 40.00 12.00
AT Alan Trammell 25.00 7.50
BB Bobby Bonds 25.00 7.50
BF Bob Feller 25.00 7.50
BG Bob Gibson SP/200 30.00 9.00
BM Bill Mazeroski SP/200 30.00 9.00
BR Brooks Robinson 30.00 9.00
BS Bill Skowron 15.00 4.50
BW Billy Williams 15.00 4.50
CE Ron Cey 10.00 3.00
CF C.Fisk SP/100 EXCH 80.00 24.00
CO Rocky Colavito 40.00 12.00
CR C.Ripken SP/100 EXCH 200.00 60.00
CY C.Yastrzemski SP/200 80.00 24.00
DM Don Mattingly SP/300 80.00 24.00
DP Dave Parker 15.00 4.50
DS Duke Snider 25.00 7.50
DW D.Winfield SP/250 EXCH 30.00 9.00
EM E.Murray SP/250 EXCH 80.00 24.00
ES Enos Slaughter 25.00 7.50
FH Frank Howard 15.00 4.50
FL Fred Lynn 15.00 4.50
FR F.Robinson SP/250 30.00 9.00
GB George Brett SP/150 150.00 45.00
GK George Kell 25.00 7.50
GP Gaylord Perry 15.00 4.50
HB Hank Bauer 15.00 4.50
HK H.Killebrew EXCH 30.00 9.00
HW Hoyt Wilhelm 15.00 4.50
JB Johnny Bench 60.00 18.00
JC Joe Carter 15.00 4.50
JM Juan Marichal 15.00 4.50
JM Joe Morgan 15.00 4.50
JP Jim Palmer 25.00 7.50
JR Jim Rice 15.00 4.50
KP K.Puckett SP/250 EXCH 80.00 24.00
LA Luis Aparicio 15.00 4.50
LB L.Brock SP/250 EXCH 30.00 9.00
MS M.Schmidt SP/150 EXCH 120.00 36.00
MU Dale Murphy 40.00 12.00
MW Maury Wills 15.00 4.50
NR N.Ryan SP/150 EXCH 120.00 36.00
OC Orlando Cepeda 15.00 4.50
OS Ozzie Smith SP/300 80.00 24.00
PB Paul Blair 10.00 3.00
PM Paul Molitor 25.00 7.50
PR P.Rizzuto SP/300 EXCH 60.00 18.00
PR Preacher Roe 15.00 4.50
RC R.Carew SP/250 EXCH 50.00 15.00
RF Rollie Fingers 15.00 4.50
RG Rich Gossage 15.00 4.50
RJ R.Jackson SP/150 80.00 24.00
RK R.Kiner SP/250 EXCH 25.00 7.50
RS R.Sandberg SP/200 80.00 24.00
RY R.Yount SP/250 EXCH 80.00 24.00
SA Sparky Anderson 15.00 4.50
SC Steve Carlton 30.00 9.00
SG Steve Garvey 15.00 4.50
SM Stan Musial SP/200 80.00 24.00
TO Tony Oliva 15.00 4.50
TP Tony Perez 15.00 4.50
TS Tom Seaver SP/150 60.00 18.00
VB Vida Blue 15.00 4.50
WB Wade Boggs 25.00 7.50
WF Whitey Ford 40.00 12.00
WM Willie McCovey 25.00 7.50
WS Warren Spahn 40.00 12.00
YB Yogi Berra 50.00 15.00

2002 Fleer Greats of the Game Dueling Duos

This 29-card insert pairs contemporaries that competed against each other in their respective eras. These cards were inserted into packs at one in six.

Nm-Mt Ex-Mt
1 Johnny Bench 4.00 1.20
Carlton Fisk
2 Roy Campanella 5.00 1.50
Yogi Berra
3 Stan Musial 8.00 2.40
Ted Williams
4 Carl Yastrzemski 5.00 1.50
Reggie Jackson
5 Babe Ruth 10.00 3.00
Jimmie Foxx
6 Kirby Puckett 8.00 2.40
Don Mattingly
7 Steve Carlton 8.00 2.40
Nolan Ryan
8 Wade Boggs 10.00 3.00
Don Mattingly
9 Brooks Robinson 5.00 1.50
Roger Maris
10 Paul Molitor 10.00 3.00
Don Mattingly
11 Sparky Anderson 3.00 .90
Earl Weaver
12 Bob Gibson 3.00 .90
Duke Snider
13 Yogi Berra 5.00 1.50
Gil Hodges
14 Joe Morgan 6.00 1.80
Ryne Sandberg
15 Tony Perez 5.00 1.50
Carl Yastrzemski
16 Jimmie Foxx 4.00 1.20
Bill Dickey
17 Ralph Kiner 3.00 .90
Duke Snider
18 Nellie Fox 3.00 .90
Rocky Colavito
19 Willie McCovey 4.00 1.20
Johnny Bench
20 Duke Snider 3.00 .90
Eddie Mathews
21 Reggie Jackson 3.00 .90
Jim Rice
22 Eddie Murray 4.00 1.20
Jim Rice
23 Paul Molitor 3.00 .90
Dave Winfield
24 Robin Yount 5.00 1.50
Dave Winfield
25 Enos Slaughter 3.00 .90
Ted Kluszewski
26 Wade Boggs 10.00 3.00
George Brett
27 George Brett 10.00 3.00
Mike Schmidt
28 George Brett 10.00 3.00
Eddie Murray
29 George Brett 12.00 3.60
Cal Ripken

2002 Fleer Greats of the Game Dueling Duos Autographs

This six-card insert set is a partial parallel of the 2002 Fleer Greats of the Game Dueling Duos insert, and features dual autographs from greats like Bench/Fisk. Each card is individually serial numbered to 25. Due to market scarcity, no pricing is provided. The following cards were distributed in packs as exchange cards with a redemption deadline of 12/01/02: Bench/Fisk, Boggs/Mattingly, Brett/Schmidt and Puckett/Mattingly.

Nm-Mt Ex-Mt
1 Johnny Bench
Carlton Fisk
2 Wade Boggs
Don Mattingly
3 George Brett
Mike Schmidt
4 Kirby Puckett
Don Mattingly
5 Duke Snider
Bob Gibson
6 Carl Yastrzemski
Reggie Jackson

2002 Fleer Greats of the Game Dueling Duos Game Used Single

This 54-card insert features a single swatch of game-used jersey, and was inserted into packs at 1:24. Please note that a few of the players were short-printed and are notated as such in our checklist.

Nm-Mt Ex-Mt
BD1 Jimmie Foxx 20.00 6.00
Bill Dickey Bat
BG1 Bob Gibson Jsy 20.00 6.00
Duke Snider SP/200
BR1 Brooks Robinson Bat 25.00 7.50
Roger Maris

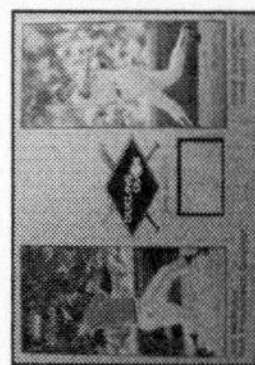

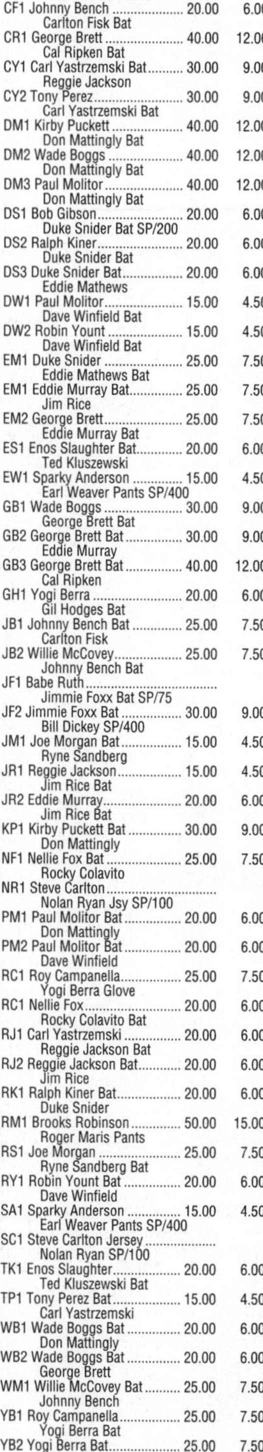

Card	Nm-Mt	Ex-Mt
BR1 Babe Ruth Bat		
Jimmie Foxx SP/75		
CF1 Johnny Bench	20.00	6.00
Carlton Fisk Bat		
CR1 George Brett	40.00	12.00
Cal Ripken Bat		
CY1 Carl Yastrzemski Bat	30.00	9.00
Reggie Jackson		
CY2 Tony Perez	30.00	9.00
Carl Yastrzemski Bat		
DM1 Kirby Puckett	40.00	12.00
Don Mattingly Bat		
DM2 Wade Boggs	40.00	12.00
Don Mattingly Bat		
DM3 Paul Molitor	40.00	12.00
Don Mattingly Bat		
DS1 Bob Gibson	20.00	6.00
Duke Snider Bat SP/200		
DS2 Ralph Kiner	20.00	6.00
Duke Snider Bat		
DS3 Duke Snider Bat	20.00	6.00
Eddie Mathews		
DW1 Paul Molitor	15.00	4.50
Dave Winfield Bat		
DW2 Robin Yount	15.00	4.50
Dave Winfield Bat		
EM1 Duke Snider	25.00	7.50
Eddie Mathews Bat		
EM1 Eddie Murray Bat	25.00	7.50
Jim Rice		
EM2 George Brett	25.00	7.50
Eddie Murray Bat		
ES1 Enos Slaughter Bat	20.00	6.00
Ted Kluszewski		
EW1 Sparky Anderson	15.00	4.50
Earl Weaver Pants SP/400		
GB1 Wade Boggs	30.00	9.00
George Brett Bat		
GB2 George Brett Bat	30.00	9.00
Eddie Murray		
GB3 George Brett Bat	40.00	12.00
Cal Ripken		
GH1 Yogi Berra	20.00	6.00
Gil Hodges Bat		
JB1 Johnny Bench Bat	25.00	7.50
Carlton Fisk		
JB2 Willie McCovey	25.00	7.50
Johnny Bench Bat		
JF1 Babe Ruth		
Jimmie Foxx Bat SP/75		
JF2 Jimmie Foxx Bat	30.00	9.00
Bill Dickey SP/400		
JM1 Joe Morgan Bat	15.00	4.50
Ryne Sandberg		
JR1 Reggie Jackson	15.00	4.50
Jim Rice Bat		
JR2 Eddie Murray	20.00	6.00
Jim Rice Bat		
KP1 Kirby Puckett Bat	30.00	9.00
Don Mattingly		
NF1 Nellie Fox Bat	25.00	7.50
Rocky Colavito		
NR1 Steve Carlton		
Nolan Ryan Jsy SP/100		
PM1 Paul Molitor Bat	20.00	6.00
Don Mattingly		
PM2 Paul Molitor Bat	20.00	6.00
Dave Winfield		
RC1 Roy Campanella	25.00	7.50
Yogi Berra Glove		
RC1 Nellie Fox	20.00	6.00
Rocky Colavito Bat		
RJ1 Carl Yastrzemski	20.00	6.00
Reggie Jackson Bat		
RJ2 Reggie Jackson Bat	20.00	6.00
Jim Rice		
RK1 Ralph Kiner Bat	20.00	6.00
Duke Snider		
RM1 Brooks Robinson	50.00	15.00
Roger Maris Pants		
RS1 Joe Morgan	25.00	7.50
Ryne Sandberg Bat		
RY1 Robin Yount Bat	20.00	6.00
Dave Winfield		
SA1 Sparky Anderson	15.00	4.50
Earl Weaver Pants SP/400		
SC1 Steve Carlton Jersey		
Nolan Ryan SP/100		
TK1 Enos Slaughter	20.00	6.00
Ted Kluszewski Bat		
TP1 Tony Perez Bat	15.00	4.50
Carl Yastrzemski		
WB1 Wade Boggs Bat	20.00	6.00
Don Mattingly		
WB2 Wade Boggs Bat	20.00	6.00
George Brett		
WM1 Willie McCovey Bat	25.00	7.50
Johnny Bench		
YB1 Roy Campanella	25.00	7.50
Yogi Berra Bat		
YB2 Yogi Berra Bat	25.00	7.50
Gil Hodges		

2002 Fleer Greats of the Game Dueling Duos Game Used Double

This 27-card insert is a partial parallel of the 2002 Fleer Greats of the Game Dueling Duos insert. Each card features dual jersey swatches from greats like Boggs/Brett, and is individually serial numbered to 25. Due to market scarcity, no pricing is provided.

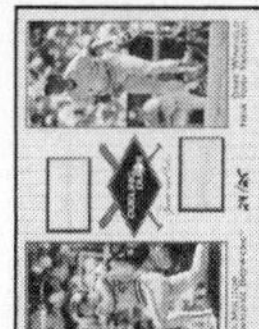

Card	Nm-Mt	Ex-Mt
1 Sparky Anderson		
Earl Weaver		
2 Johnny Bench		
Carlton Fisk		
3 Yogi Berra		
Gil Hodges		
4 Wade Boggs		
George Brett		
5 Wade Boggs		
Don Mattingly		
6 George Brett		
Eddie Murray		
7 George Brett		
Cal Ripken		
8 Roy Campanella		
Yogi Berra		
9 Steve Carlton		
Nolan Ryan		
10 Nellie Fox		
Rocky Colavito		
11 Jimmie Foxx		
Bill Dickey		
12 Bob Gibson		
Duke Snider		
13 Reggie Jackson		
Jim Rice		
14 Ralph Kiner		
Duke Snider		
15 Willie McCovey		
Johnny Bench		
16 Paul Molitor		
Don Mattingly		
17 Paul Molitor		
Dave Winfield		
18 Joe Morgan		
Ryne Sandberg		
19 Eddie Murray		
Jim Rice		
20 Tony Perez		
Carl Yastrzemski		
21 Kirby Puckett		
Don Mattingly		
22 Brooks Robinson		
Roger Maris		
23 Babe Ruth		
Jimmie Foxx		
24 Enos Slaughter		
Ted Kluszewski		
25 Duke Snider		
Eddie Mathews		
26 Carl Yastrzemski		
Reggie Jackson		
27 Robin Yount		
Dave Winfield		

2002 Fleer Greats of the Game Through the Years Level 1

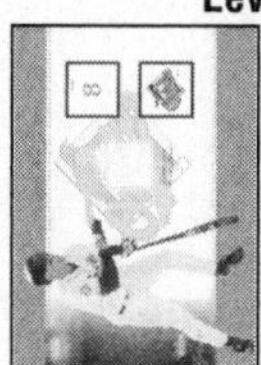

This 31-card insert features swatches of authentic game-used jersey on a silver-foil based card. These cards were inserted into packs at a rate of 1:24.

Card	Nm-Mt	Ex-Mt
1 Johnny Bench Pants	20.00	6.00
2 Vida Blue	15.00	4.50
3 Wade Boggs	15.00	4.50
4 George Brett	25.00	7.50
5 Carlton Fisk Hitting	15.00	4.50
6 Carlton Fisk Fielding	15.00	4.50
7 Bo Jackson Royals	20.00	6.00
8 Bo Jackson White Sox	20.00	6.00
9 Reggie Jackson A's	15.00	4.50
10 Reggie Jackson Angels	15.00	4.50
11 Ted Kluszewski	15.00	4.50
12 Don Mattingly	25.00	7.50
13 Willie McCovey	15.00	4.50
14 Paul Molitor Blue Jays	15.00	4.50
15 Paul Molitor Brewers	15.00	4.50
16 Eddie Murray	20.00	6.00
17 Jim Palmer	15.00	4.50
18 Tony Perez	15.00	4.50
19 J.Rice Red Sox Home	15.00	4.50
20 Jim Rice Red Sox Road	15.00	4.50
21 C.Ripken Orioles Hitting	40.00	12.00
22 Cal Ripken Orioles Fielding	40.00	12.00
23 Brooks Robinson Bat	20.00	6.00
24 Frank Robinson	15.00	4.50
25 J.Robinson Pants SP/200	80.00	24.00
26 Nolan Ryan	40.00	12.00
27 Hoyt Wilhelm	15.00	4.50
28 Ted Williams SP/350	100.00	30.00
29 Dave Winfield	15.00	4.50
30 Carl Yastrzemski	25.00	7.50
31 Robin Yount	20.00	6.00

2002 Fleer Greats of the Game Through the Years Level 1 Patch

This 27-card insert features swatches of authentic jersey patch on a gold-foil based card. Each card is also individually serial numbered to 100.

Card	Nm-Mt	Ex-Mt
1 Johnny Bench	50.00	15.00
2 Wade Boggs	40.00	12.00
3 George Brett	100.00	30.00
4 Carlton Fisk Hitting	40.00	12.00
5 Carlton Fisk Fielding	40.00	12.00
6 Bo Jackson Royals	50.00	15.00
7 Bo Jackson White Sox	50.00	15.00
8 Reggie Jackson A's	40.00	12.00
9 Reggie Jackson Angels	40.00	12.00
10 Ted Kluszewski	40.00	12.00
11 Don Mattingly	100.00	30.00
12 Willie McCovey	40.00	12.00
13 Paul Molitor Blue Jays	40.00	12.00
14 Paul Molitor Brewers	40.00	12.00
15 Eddie Murray	50.00	15.00
16 Jim Palmer	40.00	12.00
17 Tony Perez	40.00	12.00
18 Jim Rice Red Sox	40.00	12.00
19 Jim Rice Red Sox	40.00	12.00
20 Cal Ripken Hitting	120.00	36.00
21 Cal Ripken Fielding	120.00	36.00
22 Frank Robinson	40.00	12.00
23 Nolan Ryan	100.00	30.00
24 Ted Williams	150.00	45.00
25 Dave Winfield	40.00	12.00
26 Carl Yastrzemski	80.00	24.00
27 Robin Yount	60.00	18.00

2002 Fleer Greats of the Game Through the Years Level 2

This 22-card insert features swatches of authentic game-used jersey on a silver-foil based card. These cards were individually serial numbered to 100.

Card	Nm-Mt	Ex-Mt
1 Johnny Bench	50.00	15.00
2 Wade Boggs	40.00	12.00
3 George Brett	100.00	30.00
4 Carlton Fisk White Sox	40.00	12.00
5 Bo Jackson Royals	50.00	15.00
6 Bo Jackson White Sox	50.00	15.00
7 Reggie Jackson A's	40.00	12.00
8 Ted Kluszewski	40.00	12.00
9 Don Mattingly	100.00	30.00
10 Willie McCovey	40.00	12.00
11 Paul Molitor Brewers	40.00	12.00
12 Eddie Murray	50.00	15.00
13 Jim Palmer	40.00	12.00
14 Jim Rice Home	40.00	12.00
15 Jim Rice Road	40.00	12.00
16 Cal Ripken Hitting	120.00	36.00
17 Cal Ripken Fielding	120.00	36.00
18 Nolan Ryan	100.00	30.00
19 Ted Williams	150.00	45.00
20 Dave Winfield	40.00	12.00
21 Carl Yastrzemski	80.00	24.00
22 Robin Yount	60.00	18.00

2002 Fleer Greats of the Game Through the Years Level 3

This 19-card insert features swatches of authentic game-used jersey on a silver-foil based card. These cards were individually serial numbered to 25. Due to market scarcity, no pricing is provided for these cards.

Card	Nm-Mt	Ex-Mt
1 Johnny Bench		
2 Wade Boggs		
3 George Brett		
4 Carlton Fisk White Sox		
5 Reggie Jackson A's		
6 Ted Kluszewski		
7 Don Mattingly		
8 Willie McCovey		
9 Paul Molitor Brewers		
10 Eddie Murray		
11 Jim Rice Home		
12 Jim Rice Road		
13 Cal Ripken Hitting		
14 Cal Ripken Batting		
15 Nolan Ryan		
16 Ted Williams		
17 Dave Winfield		
18 Carl Yastrzemski		
19 Robin Yount		

2003 Fleer Hardball

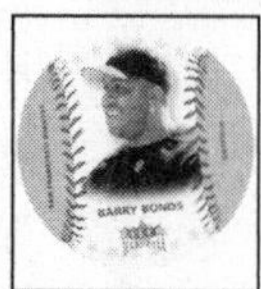

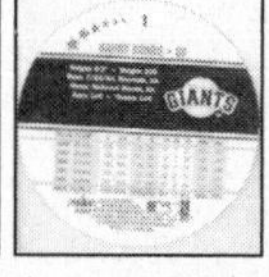

This innovative 280 card set was released in March, 2003. These cards, which are more accurately described as discs, are designed in the style of the discs which were popular in the 1980's. These cards were issued in seven card hobby packs with an SRP of $4 per pack. These packs were issued 24 packs to a box and 12 boxes to a case. In addition, these cards were also issued in seven card retail packs. Those cards had an SRP of $ 3 per pack as there was not as much in them as in the hobby packs. The following subsets were issued in shorter quantity in packs. Cards numbered 241 through 265 featued All-Around stars and cards numbered 266 through 280 feature rookies on deck. These cards were issued at stated rates of one in two hobby packs, one in four retail packs and one in five blaster packs.

Card	Nm-Mt	Ex-Mt
COMPLETE SET (280)	150.00	45.00
COMP.SET w/o SP's (240)	80.00	24.00
COMMON CARD (1-240)	.40	.12
COMMON CARD (241-265)	1.50	.45
COMMON CARD (266-280)	1.50	.45
1 Barry Bonds	2.50	.75
2 Derek Jeter	2.50	.75
3 Jason Varitek	.40	.12
4 Magglio Ordonez	.40	.12
5 Ryan Dempster	.40	.12
6 Adam Everett	.40	.12
7 Paul LoDuca	.40	.12
8 Brad Wilkerson	.40	.12
9 Al Leiter	.40	.12
10 Jermaine Dye	.40	.12
11 Rob Mackowiak	.40	.12
12 J.T. Snow	.40	.12
13 Juan Gonzalez	1.00	.30
14 Eric Hinske	.40	.12
15 Greg Maddux	1.50	.45
16 Moises Alou	.40	.12
17 Carlos Lee	.40	.12
18 Richard Hidalgo	.40	.12
19 Jorge Posada	.60	.18
20 Mike Lieberthal	.40	.12
21 Jeff Cirillo	.40	.12
22 Corey Patterson	.40	.12
23 C.C. Sabathia	.40	.12
24 Brian Giles	.40	.12
25 Edgar Martinez	.60	.18
26 Trot Nixon	.60	.18
27 Kerry Wood	1.00	.30
28 Austin Kearns	.40	.12
29 Lance Berkman	.40	.12
30 Hideo Nomo	1.00	.30
31 Brad Radke	.40	.12
32 John Valentin	.40	.12
33 Tim Hudson	.40	.12
34 Aramis Ramirez	.40	.12
35 Kevin Mench	.40	.12
36 Kevin Appier	.40	.12
37 Chris Richard	.40	.12
38 Ruben Mateo	.40	.12
39 Juan Pierre	.40	.12
40 Nick Neugebauer	.40	.12
41 Mike Mussina	1.00	.30
42 Rich Aurilia	.40	.12
43 Albert Pujols	2.00	.60
44 Carlos Delgado	.40	.12
45 Junior Spivey	.40	.12
46 Marcus Giles	.40	.12
47 Johnny Damon	.40	.12
48 Mark Prior	2.00	.60
49 Omar Vizquel	.40	.12
50 Craig Biggio	.60	.18
51 Chuck Knoblauch	.40	.12
52 Eric Milton	.40	.12
53 Jeromy Burnitz	.40	.12
54 Jim Thome	1.00	.30
55 Steve Finley	.40	.12
56 Kevin Millwood	.40	.12
57 Alex Gonzalez	.40	.12
58 Ben Broussard	.40	.12
59 Derrek Lee	.40	.12
60 Joe Randa	.40	.12
61 Doug Mientkiewicz	.40	.12
62 Jason Phillips	.40	.12
63 Brett Myers	.40	.12
64 Josh Fogg	.40	.12
65 Reggie Sanders	.40	.12
66 Chipper Jones	1.00	.30
67 Roosevelt Brown	.40	.12
68 Matt Lawton	.40	.12
69 Charles Johnson	.40	.12
70 Mark Quinn	.40	.12
71 Jacque Jones	.40	.12
72 Armando Benitez	.40	.12
73 Bobby Abreu	.40	.12
74 Jason Kendall	.40	.12
75 Jeff Kent	.40	.12
76 Mark Teixeira	.60	.18
77 Garret Anderson	.40	.12
78 Jerry Hairston Jr.	.40	.12
79 Tony Graffanino	.40	.12
80 Josh Beckett	.60	.18
81 Eric Gagne	.60	.18
82 Fernando Tatis	.40	.12
83 Brett Tomko	.40	.12
84 Fernando Vina	.40	.12
85 Rafael Palmeiro	.60	.18
86 Luis Gonzalez	.40	.12
87 Javy Lopez	.40	.12
88 Shea Hillenbrand	.40	.12
89 Hee Seop Choi	.40	.12
90 Preston Wilson	.40	.12
91 Neifi Perez	.40	.12
92 Ray Lankford	.40	.12
93 Tsuyoshi Shinjo	.40	.12
94 Ben Grieve	.40	.12
95 Jarrod Washburn	.40	.12
96 Gary Sheffield	.40	.12
97 Derek Lowe	.40	.12
98 Tony Womack	.40	.12
99 Milton Bradley	.40	.12
100 Brad Penny	.40	.12
101 Mike Sweeney	.40	.12
102 A.J. Pierzynski	.40	.12
103 Edgardo Alfonzo	.40	.12
104 Marlon Byrd	.40	.12
105 Sean Burroughs	.40	.12
106 Kazuhiro Sasaki	.40	.12
107 Damian Rolls	.40	.12
108 Troy Glaus	.60	.18
109 Rafael Furcal	.40	.12
110 Nomar Garciaparra	1.50	.45
111 Josh Bard	.40	.12
112 Alex Gonzalez	.40	.12
113 Cristian Guzman	.40	.12
114 Roger Cedeno	.40	.12
115 Freddy Garcia	.40	.12
116 Travis Phelps	.40	.12
117 Juan Cruz	.40	.12
118 Frank Thomas	1.00	.30
119 Jaret Wright	.40	.12
120 Carlos Beltran	.40	.12
121 Ronnie Belliard	.40	.12
122 Roger Clemens	2.00	.60
123 Vicente Padilla	.40	.12
124 Joel Pineiro	.40	.12
125 Jared Sandberg	.40	.12
126 Tom Glavine	.60	.18
127 Matt Clement	.40	.12
128 Aaron Rowand	.40	.12
129 Alex Escobar	.40	.12
130 Randy Wolf	.40	.12
131 Ichiro Suzuki	1.50	.45
132 Toby Hall	.40	.12
133 Scott Spiezio	.40	.12
134 Bobby Higginson	.40	.12
135 A.J. Burnett	.40	.12
136 Cesar Izturis	.40	.12
137 Roberto Alomar	1.00	.30
138 Trevor Hoffman	.40	.12
139 Edgar Renteria	.40	.12
140 Rusty Greer	.40	.12
141 David Eckstein	.40	.12
142 Pedro Martinez	1.00	.30
143 Joe Crede	.40	.12
144 Robert Fick	.40	.12
145 Mike Lowell	.40	.12
146 Brian Jordan	.40	.12
147 Mark Mulder	.40	.12
148 Scott Rolen	.60	.18
149 Eddie Guardado	.40	.12
150 Adam Kennedy	.40	.12
151 Ken Griffey Jr.	1.50	.45
152 Larry Walker	.60	.18
153 Carlos Pena	.40	.12
154 Geoff Jenkins	.40	.12
155 Bartolo Colon	.40	.12
156 Mariano Rivera	.60	.18
157 Robb Nen	.40	.12
158 Bret Boone	.40	.12
159 Shannon Stewart	.40	.12
160 Chris Singleton	.40	.12
161 Todd Walker	.40	.12
162 Jay Payton	.40	.12
163 Zach Day	.40	.12
164 Bernie Williams	.60	.18
165 Bubba Trammell	.40	.12
166 Matt Morris	.40	.12
167 Jose Cruz Jr.	.40	.12
168 Mark Grace	.60	.18
169 Andruw Jones	.40	.12
170 Cliff Floyd	.40	.12
171 Antonio Alfonseca	.40	.12
172 Jeff Bagwell	.60	.18
173 Shawn Green	.40	.12
174 Joe Mays	.40	.12
175 Mike Piazza	1.50	.45
176 Adam Piatt	.40	.12
177 Pokey Reese	.40	.12
178 Carl Everett	.40	.12
179 Tim Salmon	.60	.18
180 Rodrigo Lopez	.40	.12
181 Brandon Inge	.40	.12
182 Kazuhisa Ishii	.40	.12
183 Jose Vidro	.40	.12
184 Barry Zito	.60	.18
185 Phil Nevin	.40	.12
186 J.D. Drew	.40	.12
187 Vernon Wells	.40	.12
188 Darin Erstad	.40	.12
189 Barry Larkin	1.00	.30
190 Jason Jennings	.40	.12
191 Luis Castillo	.40	.12
192 Adrian Beltre	.40	.12
193 Tony Armas	.40	.12
194 Terrence Long	.40	.12
195 Mark Kotsay	.40	.12
196 Tino Martinez	.60	.18
197 Jayson Werth	.40	.12
198 Eric Chavez	.40	.12
199 Matt Williams	.40	.12
200 Jon Lieber	.40	.12
201 Eddie Taubensee	.40	.12
202 Shane Reynolds	.40	.12
203 Alex Sanchez	.40	.12
204 Jason Giambi	1.00	.30
205 Jimmy Rollins	.40	.12
206 Jamie Moyer	.40	.12
207 Francisco Rodriguez	.40	.12
208 Marty Cordova	.40	.12
209 Aaron Boone	.40	.12
210 Mike Hampton	.40	.12
211 Mark Redman	.40	.12
212 Richie Sexson	.40	.12
213 Andy Pettitte	.60	.18
214 Livan Hernandez	.40	.12
215 Jason Isringhausen	.40	.12
216 Curt Schilling	.60	.18
217 Manny Ramirez	.40	.12
218 Jose Valentin	.40	.12
219 Brent Butler	.40	.12
220 Billy Wagner	.40	.12
221 Ben Sheets	.40	.12
222 Jeff Weaver	.40	.12
223 Brent Abernathy	.40	.12
224 Jay Gibbons	.40	.12
225 Sean Casey	.40	.12
226 Greg Norton	.40	.12
227 Andy Van Hekken	.40	.12
228 Kevin Brown	.40	.12
229 Orlando Cabrera	.40	.12
230 Scott Hatteberg	.40	.12
231 Ryan Klesko	.40	.12
232 Roy Halladay	.40	.12
233 Randy Johnson	1.00	.30
234 Mark Buehrle	.40	.12
235 Todd Helton	.60	.18
236 Jeffrey Hammonds	.40	.12
237 Sidney Ponson	.40	.12
238 Kip Wells	.40	.12
239 John Olerud	.40	.12
240 Aubrey Huff	.40	.12
241 Derek Jeter AAS	4.00	1.20
242 Barry Bonds AAS	4.00	1.20
243 Ichiro Suzuki AAS	2.50	.75
244 Troy Glaus AAS	1.50	.45
245 Alex Rodriguez AAS	2.50	.75
246 Sammy Sosa AAS	2.50	.75
247 Lance Berkman AAS	1.50	.45

248 Jason Giambi AAS 2.00 .60
249 Nomar Garciaparra AAS 2.50 .75
250 Miguel Tejada AAS 1.50 .45
251 Albert Pujols AAS 3.00 .90
252 Mike Piazza AAS 2.50 .75
253 Vladimir Guerrero AAS 2.00 .60
254 Shawn Green AAS 1.50 .45
255 Todd Helton AAS 1.50 .45
256 Ken Griffey Jr. AAS 2.50 .75
257 Torii Hunter AAS 1.50 .45
258 Chipper Jones AAS 2.00 .60
259 Alfonso Soriano AAS 1.50 .45
260 Luis Gonzalez AAS 1.50 .45
261 Pedro Martinez AAS 2.00 .60
262 Tim Hudson AAS 1.50 .45
263 Roger Clemens AAS 3.00 .90
264 Greg Maddux AAS 2.50 .75
265 Randy Johnson AAS 2.00 .60
266 Vinny Chulk OD 1.50 .45
267 Jose Castillo OD 1.50 .45
268 Craig Brazell OD RC 2.00 .60
269 Felix Sanchez OD RC 1.50 .45
270 John Webb OD 1.50 .45
271 Josh Hall OD RC 2.00 .60
272 Alexis Rios OD 5.00 1.50
273 Phil Seibel OD RC 1.50 .45
274 Prentice Redman OD RC 1.50 .45
275 Walter Young OD 1.50 .45
276 Nic Jackson OD 1.50 .45
277 Adam Morrissey OD 1.50 .45
278 Bobby Jenks OD 1.50 .45
279 Rodrigo Rosario OD 1.50 .45
280 Chin-Feng Chen OD 1.50 .45

2003 Fleer Hardball Gold

Inserted in packs at a stated rate of one in four hobby, one in six retail and one in 10 blaster; this is a parallel of the Fleer Hardball set. These cards can be identified as they feature gold foil.

Nm-Mt Ex-Mt
*GOLD 1-240: 1.5X TO 4X BASIC
*GOLD 241-265: 1X TO 2.5X BASIC
*GOLD 266-280: .75X TO 2X BASIC

2003 Fleer Hardball Platinum

Randomly inserted in hobby packs, this is a parallel to the Fleer Hardball set. These cards were issued to a stated print run of 50 serial numbered sets.

Nm-Mt Ex-Mt
*PLATINUM 1-240: 8X TO 20X BASIC
*PLATINUM 241-265: 5X TO 12X BASIC
*PLATINUM 266-280: 2X TO 5X BASIC

2003 Fleer Hardball Discs

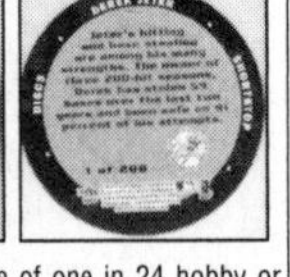

Issued at a stated rate of one in 24 hobby or retail and one in 50 blaster packs, these 20 cards truly are called discs and feature the leading players in football.

Nm-Mt Ex-Mt
1 Derek Jeter 10.00 3.00
2 Barry Bonds 10.00 3.00
3 Ichiro Suzuki 6.00 1.80
4 Sammy Sosa 6.00 1.80
5 Nomar Garciaparra 6.00 1.80
6 Lance Berkman 3.00 .90
7 Jason Giambi 4.00 1.20
8 Mike Piazza 6.00 1.80
9 Shawn Green 3.00 .90
10 Barry Zito 3.00 .90
11 Albert Pujols 8.00 2.40
12 Alex Rodriguez 6.00 1.80
13 Tim Salmon 3.00 .90
14 Eric Chavez 3.00 .90
15 Ken Griffey Jr. 6.00 1.80
16 Alfonso Soriano 3.00 .90
17 Vladimir Guerrero 4.00 1.20
18 Francisco Rodriguez 3.00 .90
19 Miguel Tejada 3.00 .90
20 Randy Johnson 4.00 1.20

2003 Fleer Hardball On the Ball

Issued at a stated rate of one in 12 hobby, one in 18 retail and one in 20 blaster, these 15 cards feature leading players against a baseball type background.

Nm-Mt Ex-Mt
1 Derek Jeter 6.00 1.80
2 Barry Bonds 6.00 1.80
3 Nomar Garciaparra 4.00 1.20
4 Alfonso Soriano 2.00 .60
5 Mike Piazza 4.00 1.20
6 Alex Rodriguez 4.00 1.20
7 Chipper Jones 2.50 .75
8 Randy Johnson 2.50 .75
9 Pedro Martinez 2.50 .75
10 Albert Pujols 5.00 1.50
11 Vladimir Guerrero 2.50 .75
12 Sammy Sosa 4.00 1.20
13 Ichiro Suzuki 4.00 1.20
14 Troy Glaus 2.00 .60
15 Jason Giambi 2.50 .75

2003 Fleer Hardball On the Ball Game Used

Inserted in packs at a stated rate of one in 18 hobby, one in 30 retail and one in 10 blaster

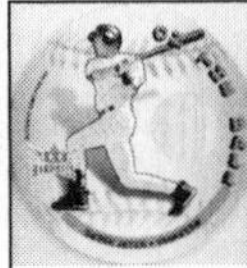

packs, these 10 cards parallel the On the Ball insert set by featuring an authentic game-used memorabilia piece.

Nm-Mt Ex-Mt
1 Barry Bonds Jsy 20.00 6.00
2 Nomar Garciaparra Jsy 15.00 4.50
3 Troy Glaus Jsy 10.00 3.00
4 Derek Jeter Bat 20.00 6.00
5 Randy Johnson Jsy 10.00 3.00
6 Chipper Jones Bat 10.00 3.00
7 Pedro Martinez Jsy 10.00 3.00
8 Mike Piazza Jsy 15.00 4.50
9 Alex Rodriguez Jsy 15.00 4.50
10 Alfonso Soriano Jsy 10.00 3.00

2003 Fleer Hardball Round Numbers

Randomly inserted in packs, these cards feature retired players along with their uniform name designed on the front. These cards were issued to a stated print run of 1000 serial numbered sets.

Nm-Mt Ex-Mt
1 Nolan Ryan 12.00 3.60
2 Al Kaline 8.00 2.40
3 Mike Schmidt 10.00 3.00
4 Yogi Berra 8.00 2.40
5 Brooks Robinson 8.00 2.40
6 Tom Seaver 8.00 2.40
7 Willie McCovey 8.00 2.40
8 Harmon Killebrew 8.00 2.40
9 Richie Ashburn 8.00 2.40
10 Lou Brock 8.00 2.40
11 Jim Palmer 8.00 2.40
12 Willie Stargell 8.00 2.40
13 Whitey Ford 8.00 2.40
14 Robin Yount 12.00 3.60

2003 Fleer Hardball Round Numbers Game Used

Inserted at a stated rate of one in 288 hobby packs and one in 566 retail packs, these four cards partially parallel the round numbers insert set. The cards with asterisks next to their name in our data base are perceived to have been issued in larger supply.

Nm-Mt Ex-Mt
1 Al Kaline Jsy * 25.00 7.50
2 Mike Schmidt Jsy * 25.00 7.50
3 Harmon Killebrew Bat 50.00 15.00
4 Lou Brock Jsy 30.00 9.00

2003 Fleer Hardball Round Trippers

Issued at a stated rate of one in eight hobby packs, one in 12 retail packs and one in 20 blaster packs, these cards show players set against a basepath background.

Nm-Mt Ex-Mt
1 Alfonso Soriano 2.00 .60
2 Alex Rodriguez 4.00 1.20
3 Lance Berkman 2.00 .60
4 Shawn Green 2.00 .60
5 Pat Burrell 2.00 .60
6 Andruw Jones 2.00 .60
7 Garret Anderson 2.00 .60
8 Miguel Tejada 2.00 .60
9 Mike Piazza 4.00 1.20
10 Eric Chavez 2.00 .60
11 Rafael Palmeiro 2.00 .60
12 Chipper Jones 2.50 .75
13 Manny Ramirez 2.00 .60
14 Jeff Bagwell 2.00 .60
15 Torii Hunter 2.00 .60
16 Nomar Garciaparra 4.00 1.20
17 Sammy Sosa 4.00 1.20
18 Vladimir Guerrero 2.50 .75
19 Troy Glaus 2.00 .60
20 Jason Giambi 2.50 .75

2003 Fleer Hardball Round Trippers Rounding First

Randomly inserted into hobby packs, these cards feature not only the featured player but a game-used memorabilia piece from their career. Since each card was issued to a

different print run, we have notated that information next to their name in our checklist.

Nm-Mt Ex-Mt
1 Garret Anderson Bat/40
2 Jeff Bagwell Bat/344 10.00 3.00
3 Lance Berkman Jsy/529 8.00 2.40
4 Pat Burrell Bat/502 8.00 2.40
5 Eric Chavez Jsy/572 8.00 2.40
6 Nomar Garciaparra Bat/529 15.00 4.50
7 Shawn Green Bat/249 8.00 2.40
8 Andruw Jones Jsy/569 8.00 2.40
9 Chipper Jones Jsy/570 10.00 3.00
10 Rafael Palmeiro Jsy/515 10.00 3.00
11 Mike Piazza Bat/289 25.00 7.50
12 Manny Ramirez Jsy/530 8.00 2.40
13 Alex Rodriguez Jsy/536 20.00 6.00
14 Alfonso Soriano Jsy/228 10.00 3.00
15 Miguel Tejada Jsy/524 8.00 2.40

2003 Fleer Hardball Signatures

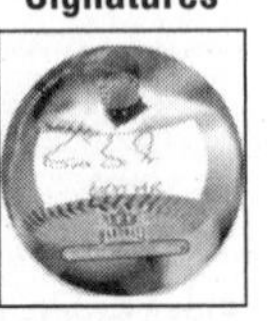

Randomly inserted into packs, these two cards feature authentic signatures of either Barry Bonds or Derek Jeter. We have printed the provided print run information next to the player's name in our checklist.

Nm-Mt Ex-Mt
1 Barry Bonds/255 175.00 52.50
2 Barry Bonds HR 600/100 300.00 90.00
3 Barry Bonds #25/25
4 Derek Jeter/500 100.00 30.00

2002 Fleer Hot Prospects

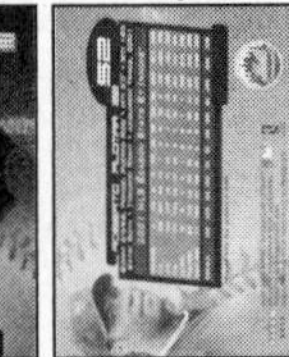

This 125 standard-size set was released in August, 2002. It was issued in five card packs with an $3 SRP which were issued 15 packs to a box and 6 boxes to a case. Cards numbered 81-105 feature not only a rookie/prospect card but also has a game-used memorabilia piece attached to the card while cards numbered 106 through 125 just features rookies. Cards 81-105 have a stated print run of 1000 serial numbered sets and cards 106-125 have a stated print run of 1500 sets.

Nm-Mt Ex-Mt
COMP.SET w/o SP's (80) 30.00 9.00
COMMON CARD (1-80) .50 .15
COMMON CARD (81-105) 10.00 3.00
COMMON CARD (106-125) 5.00 1.50
1 Derek Jeter 3.00 .90
2 Garret Anderson .50 .15
3 Scott Rolen .75 .23
4 Bret Boone .50 .15
5 Lance Berkman .50 .15
6 Andruw Jones .50 .15
7 Ivan Rodriguez 1.25 .35
8 Bernie Williams .75 .23
9 Cristian Guzman .50 .15
10 Mo Vaughn .50 .15
11 Troy Glaus .75 .23
12 Tim Salmon .75 .23
13 Jason Giambi 1.25 .35
14 Cliff Floyd .50 .15
15 Tim Hudson .50 .15
16 Curt Schilling .75 .23
17 Sammy Sosa 2.00 .60
18 Alex Rodriguez 2.00 .60
19 Chuck Knoblauch .50 .15
20 Jason Kendall .50 .15
21 Ben Sheets .50 .15
22 Nomar Garciaparra 2.00 .60
23 Ryan Klesko .50 .15
24 Greg Vaughn .50 .15
25 Rafael Palmeiro .75 .23
26 Miguel Tejada .50 .15
27 Shea Hillenbrand .50 .15
28 Jim Thome 1.25 .35
29 Randy Johnson 1.25 .35
30 Barry Larkin 1.25 .35
31 Paul LoDuca .50 .15
32 Pedro Martinez 1.25 .35
33 Luis Gonzalez .50 .15
34 Carlos Delgado .50 .15
35 Richie Sexson .50 .15
36 Albert Pujols 2.50 .75
37 Bobby Abreu .50 .15
38 Gary Sheffield .50 .15
39 Magglio Ordonez .50 .15
40 Eric Chavez .50 .15
41 Jeff Bagwell .75 .23
42 Doug Mientkiewicz .50 .15
43 Moises Alou .50 .15
44 Todd Helton .75 .23
45 Ichiro Suzuki 2.00 .60
46 Jose Cruz Jr. .50 .15
47 Freddy Garcia .50 .15
48 Tino Martinez .75 .23
49 Roger Clemens 2.50 .75
50 Greg Maddux 2.00 .60
51 Mike Piazza 2.00 .60
52 Roberto Alomar 1.25 .35
53 Adam Dunn .50 .15
54 Kerry Wood 1.25 .35
55 Edgar Martinez .75 .23
56 Ken Griffey Jr. 2.00 .60
57 Juan Gonzalez 1.25 .35
58 Pat Burrell .50 .15
59 Corey Koskie .50 .15
60 Jose Vidro .50 .15
61 Ben Grieve .50 .15
62 Barry Bonds 3.00 .90
63 Raul Mondesi .50 .15
64 Jimmy Rollins .50 .15
65 Mike Sweeney .50 .15
66 Josh Beckett .75 .23
67 Chipper Jones 1.25 .35
68 Jeff Kent .50 .15
69 Tony Batista .50 .15
70 Phil Nevin .50 .15
71 Brian Jordan .50 .15
72 Rich Aurilia .50 .15
73 Brian Giles .50 .15
74 Frank Thomas 1.25 .35
75 Larry Walker .75 .23
76 Shawn Green .50 .15
77 Manny Ramirez .50 .15
78 Craig Biggio .75 .23
79 Vladimir Guerrero 1.25 .35
80 Jeromy Burnitz .50 .15
81 Mark Teixeira FS Pants 15.00 4.50
82 Corey Thurman FS Pants RC 10.00 3.00
83 Mark Prior FS Bat 25.00 7.50
84 Marlon Byrd FS Pants 10.00 3.00
85 Austin Kearns FS Pants 10.00 3.00
86 Satoru Komiyama FS Jsy RC 10.00 3.00
87 So Taguchi FS Bat RC 12.00 3.60
88 Jorge Padilla FS Pants RC 10.00 3.00
89 Rene Reyes FS Pants RC 10.00 3.00
90 Jorge Nunez FS Pants RC 10.00 3.00
91 Ron Calloway FS Pants RC 10.00 3.00
92 Kazuhisa Ishii FS Jsy RC 15.00 4.50
93 Dewon Brazelton FS Pants 10.00 3.00
94 Angel Berroa FS Pants 10.00 3.00
95 Felix Escalona FS Pants RC 10.00 3.00
96 Sean Burroughs FS Bat 10.00 3.00
97 Br. Duckworth FS Pants 10.00 3.00
98 Hank Blalock FS Pants 15.00 4.50
99 Eric Hinske FS Pants 10.00 3.00
100 Carlos Pena FS Jsy 10.00 3.00
101 Morgan Ensberg FS Pants 10.00 3.00
102 Ryan Ludwick FS Pants 10.00 3.00
103 C. Snelling FS Pants RC 12.00 3.60
104 Jason Lane FS Pants 10.00 3.00
105 Drew Henson FS Bat 10.00 3.00
106 Bobby Kielty HP 5.00 1.50
107 Earl Snyder HP RC 5.00 1.50
108 Nate Field HP RC 5.00 1.50
109 Juan Diaz HP 5.00 1.50
110 Ryan Anderson HP 5.00 1.50
111 Esteban German HP 5.00 1.50
112 Takahito Nomura HP RC 5.00 1.50
113 David Kelton HP 5.00 1.50
114 Steve Kent HP RC 5.00 1.50
115 Colby Lewis HP 5.00 1.50
116 Jason Simontacchi HP RC 5.00 1.50
117 Rodrigo Rosario HP RC 5.00 1.50
118 Ben Howard HP RC 5.00 1.50
119 Hansel Izquierdo HP RC 5.00 1.50
120 John Ennis HP RC 5.00 1.50
121 Anderson Machado HP RC 5.00 1.50
122 Luis Ugueto HP RC 5.00 1.50
123 Anastacio Martinez HP RC 5.00 1.50
124 Reed Johnson HP RC 8.00 2.40
125 Juan Cruz HP 5.00 1.50

2002 Fleer Hot Prospects Future Swatch Autographs

Randomly inserted into packs, these four cards feature autographs of the noted rookie player. Each card has a stated print run of 100 serial numbered sets. All four of these cards were issued as redemptions within packs - each with an exchange deadline of July 31, 2003.

Nm-Mt Ex-Mt
83 Mark Prior FS Bat EXCH 120.00 36.00
87 So Taguchi FS Bat EXCH 25.00 7.50
89 Rene Reyes FS Pants EXCH 15.00 4.50
105 Drew Henson FS Bat 25.00 7.50

2002 Fleer Hot Prospects Co-Stars

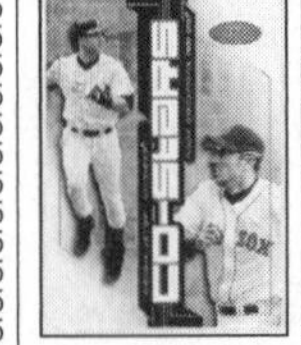
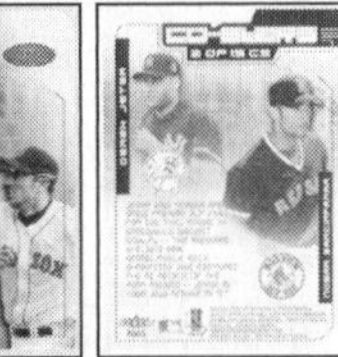

Inserted in hobby packs at a stated rate of one in six, these 15 cards feature two players with something in common who are either stars or upcoming prospects.

Nm-Mt Ex-Mt
COMPLETE SET (15) 50.00 15.00
1 Barry Bonds 8.00 2.40
Alex Rodriguez
2 Derek Jeter 6.00 1.80
Nomar Garciaparra
3 Andruw Jones 3.00 .90
Chipper Jones
4 Juan Gonzalez 3.00 .90
Jim Thome
5 Pedro Martinez 3.00 .90
Randy Johnson
6 Adam Dunn 2.00 .60
Pat Burrell
7 Frank Thomas 3.00 .90
Manny Ramirez
8 Jeff Bagwell 2.00 .60
Lance Berkman
9 So Taguchi 8.00 2.40
Kazuhisa Ishii
10 Jimmy Rollins 2.00 .60
Miguel Tejada
11 Morgan Ensberg 2.00 .60
Carlos Pena
12 Adam Dunn 2.00 .60
Austin Kearns
13 Vladimir Guerrero 3.00 .90
Scott Rolen
14 Drew Henson 2.00 .60
Xavier Nady
15 Mike Piazza 5.00 1.50
Ivan Rodriguez

2002 Fleer Hot Prospects Inside Barry Bonds Memorabilia

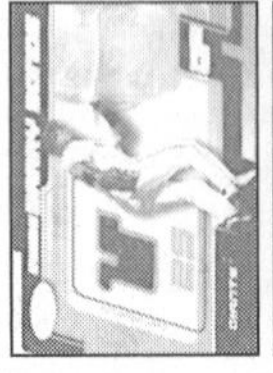

Randomly inserted into packs, these eight cards feature different Barry Bonds memorabilia. Since each card has a different stated print run, we have put that information next to the player's name in our checklist along with the specific item cut up for use on the card.

Nm-Mt Ex-Mt
1 B.Bonds Home Pants/1000 25.00 7.50
2 B.Bonds Away Pants/900 25.00 7.50
3 B.Bonds Away Jsy/800 25.00 7.50
4 B.Bonds Bat/700 25.00 7.50
5 B.Bonds Base/600 20.00 6.00
6 B.Bonds Cleats/500 30.00 9.00
7 B.Bonds Btg Glv/400 30.00 9.00
8 B.Bonds Cap/300 40.00 12.00

2002 Fleer Hot Prospects Jerseygraphs

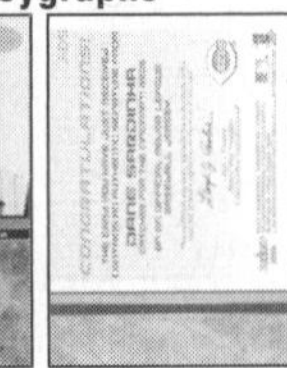

Inserted in hobby packs at stated odds of one in 186, these nine cards feature the player's signature on actual MLB jersey material. A few players were produced in shorter quantities and we have put that stated information next to their name in our checklist.

Nm-Mt Ex-Mt
J-AB Adrian Beltre SP/169 25.00 7.50
J-BB Barry Bonds SP/65
J-CJ Chipper Jones SP/100 100.00 30.00
J-DE David Espinosa 15.00 4.50
J-DH Drew Henson 40.00 12.00
J-DJ Derek Jeter SP/108 200.00 60.00
J-DS Dane Sardinha 15.00 4.50
J-GM Kazuhisa Ishii SP/40
J-ST So Taguchi SP/100 50.00 15.00

2002 Fleer Hot Prospects MLB Hot Materials

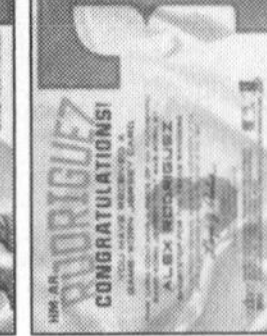

Inserted at a stated rate of one in nine, these 44 cards feature material worn and used by a variety of stars and rookies. A few players were printed in shorter quantities and we have provided the stated print run information next to their name in our checklist.

Nm-Mt Ex-Mt
AD2 Adam Dunn Jsy 10.00 3.00
AR Alex Rodriguez Jsy 15.00 4.50
BB Bret Boone Bat 10.00 3.00
BB2 Barry Bonds Pants 25.00 7.50
BD Brandon Duckworth Pants 10.00 3.00
BG Brian Giles Pants 10.00 3.00
BW Bernie Williams Jsy 15.00 4.50
CD Carlos Delgado Jsy 10.00 3.00
CG Cristian Guzman Bat SP/261 15.00 4.50
CP Carlos Pena Jsy SP/120 15.00 4.50
CP2 Corey Patterson Jsy 10.00 3.00

CS Curt Schilling Jsy 15.00 4.50
FG Freddy Garcia Jsy 10.00 3.00
FT Frank Thomas Jsy 15.00 4.50
GK Gabe Kapler Jsy 10.00 3.00
GM Greg Maddux Jsy 15.00 4.50
GS Gary Sheffield Bat 10.00 3.00
IR Ivan Rodriguez Jsy 15.00 4.50
JB Josh Beckett Jsy 15.00 4.50
JB2 Jeff Bagwell Jsy SP/108 20.00 6.00
JG Juan Gonzalez Jsy 15.00 4.50
JT Jim Thome Bat 15.00 4.50
JU Juan Uribe Bat 10.00 3.00
KI Kazuhisa Ishii Jsy SP/70
LB Lance Berkman Jsy 10.00 3.00
MM Mark Mulder Jsy 10.00 3.00
MO Moises Alou Bat 10.00 3.00
MO Magglio Ordonez Jsy 10.00 3.00
MP Mike Piazza Jsy 15.00 4.50
MS Mike Sweeney Jsy 10.00 3.00
NJ Nick Johnson Jsy 10.00 3.00
PL Paul LoDuca Jsy 10.00 3.00
PM Pedro Martinez Jsy 15.00 4.50
RF Rafael Furcal Jsy 10.00 3.00
RO Roy Oswalt Jsy 10.00 3.00
RP Rafael Palmeiro Jsy 15.00 4.50
SB Sean Burroughs Bat SP/350 15.00 4.50
SG Shawn Green Jsy 10.00 3.00
ST So Taguchi Bat 10.00 3.00
TA Tony Armas Jr. Jsy 10.00 3.00
TH Todd Helton Jsy 15.00 4.50
TH Torii Hunter Bat 10.00 3.00
TM Tino Martinez Bat 15.00 4.50
VW Vernon Wells Bat 10.00 3.00

2002 Fleer Hot Prospects MLB Hot Tandems

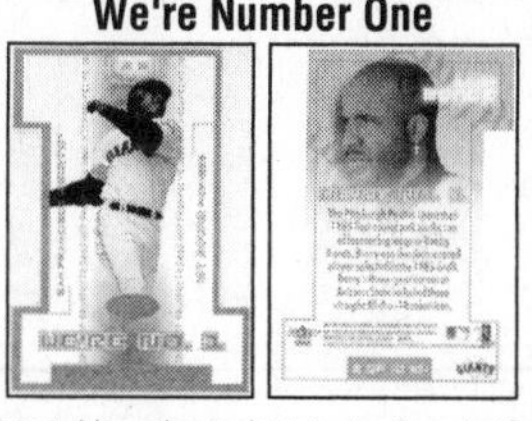

Randomly inserted in packs, these 45 cards feature dual memorabilia cards of two players who have something in common.

	Nm-Mt	Ex-Mt
ADCP Adam Dunn Jsy / Corey Patterson Jsy	15.00	4.50
ADLB Adam Dunn Jsy / Lance Berkman Jsy	15.00	4.50
ARIR Alex Rodriguez Jsy / Ivan Rodriguez Jsy	40.00	12.00
BBDJ Barry Bonds Pants / Derek Jeter Jsy	80.00	24.00
BBFG Bret Boone Bat / Freddy Garcia Jsy	15.00	4.50
BBKI Barry Bonds Pants / Kazuhisa Ishii Jsy	40.00	12.00
BBTH Bret Boone Bat / Torii Hunter Bat	30.00	9.00
BDJB Brandon Duckworth Pants / Josh Beckett Jsy	20.00	6.00
BDRO Brandon Duckworth Pants / Roy Oswalt Jsy	15.00	4.50
BWJP Bernie Williams Jsy / Jorge Posada Bat	20.00	6.00
BWNJ Bernie Williams Jsy / Nick Johnson Jsy	20.00	6.00
CDVW Carlos Delgado Jsy / Vernon Wells Bat	15.00	4.50
CGTH Cristian Guzman Bat / Torii Hunter Bat	15.00	4.50
CPCP Carlos Pena Jsy / Corey Patterson Jsy	15.00	4.50
CPNJ Carlos Pena Jsy / Nick Johnson Jsy	15.00	4.50
CSGM Curt Schilling Jsy / Greg Maddux Jsy	30.00	9.00
CSPM Curt Schilling Jsy / Pedro Martinez Jsy	25.00	7.50
FTMO Frank Thomas Jsy / Magglio Ordonez Jsy	25.00	7.50
GKJG Gabe Kapler Jsy / Juan Gonzalez Jsy	25.00	7.50
GKRP Gabe Kapler Jsy / Rafael Palmeiro Jsy	20.00	6.00
GMPM Greg Maddux Jsy / Pedro Martinez Jsy	30.00	9.00
GSRF Gary Sheffield Bat / Rafael Furcal Jsy	15.00	4.50
HBAK Hank Blalock Pants / Austin Kearns Pants	15.00	4.50
HBMT Hank Blalock Pants / Mark Teixeira Pants	25.00	7.50
JBLB Jeff Bagwell Jsy / Lance Berkman Jsy	20.00	6.00
JBMP Jeff Bagwell Jsy / Mike Piazza Jsy	30.00	9.00
JBRO Josh Beckett Jsy / Roy Oswalt Jsy	20.00	6.00
JGRP Juan Gonzalez Jsy / Rafael Palmeiro Jsy	25.00	7.50
JPMP Jorge Posada Bat / Mike Piazza Jsy	30.00	9.00
JTSG Jim Thome Bat / Shawn Green Jsy	25.00	7.50
JUCG Juan Uribe Bat / Cristian Guzman Bat	15.00	4.50
JUMT Juan Uribe Bat / Miguel Tejada Jsy	15.00	4.50
KIDJ Kazuhisa Ishii Jsy / Derek Jeter Jsy	40.00	12.00
KIMP Kazuhisa Ishii Jsy / Mark Prior Bat	30.00	9.00
KISK Kazuhisa Ishii Jsy / Satoru Komiyama Jsy	25.00	7.50
KIST Kazuhisa Ishii Jsy / So Taguchi Bat	25.00	7.50
MAMO Moises Alou Bat / Magglio Ordonez Jsy	15.00	4.50
MBAK Marlon Byrd Pants / Austin Kearns Pants	15.00	4.50
MBJP Marlon Byrd Pants / Jorge Padilla Pants	15.00	4.50
MMMT Mark Mulder Jsy / Miguel Tejada Jsy	15.00	4.50
MSTH Mike Sweeney Jsy / Todd Helton Jsy	20.00	6.00
PLSG Paul LoDuca Jsy / Shawn Green Jsy	15.00	4.50
SBDH Sean Burroughs Bat / Drew Henson Bat	15.00	4.50
TAFG Tony Armas Jr. Jsy / Freddy Garcia Jsy	15.00	4.50
TMTH Tino Martinez Bat / Todd Helton Jsy	20.00	6.00

2002 Fleer Hot Prospects We're Number One

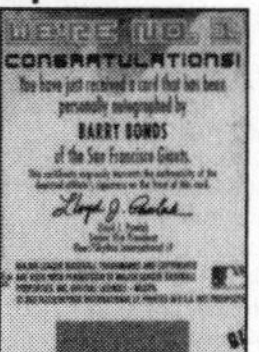

Inserted in packs at a stated rate of one in 15, these 10 cards feature players who had been drafted in the first round of the amateur draft.

	Nm-Mt	Ex-Mt
COMPLETE SET (10)	50.00	15.00
AR Alex Rodriguez	8.00	2.40
BB Barry Bonds	12.00	3.60
CJ Chipper Jones	4.00	1.20
DJ Derek Jeter	12.00	3.60
JD J.D. Drew	2.50	.75
KG Ken Griffey Jr.	8.00	2.40
MR Manny Ramirez	2.50	.75
NG Nomar Garciaparra	8.00	2.40
RC Roger Clemens	10.00	3.00
TH Todd Helton	2.50	.75

2002 Fleer Hot Prospects We're Number One Autographs

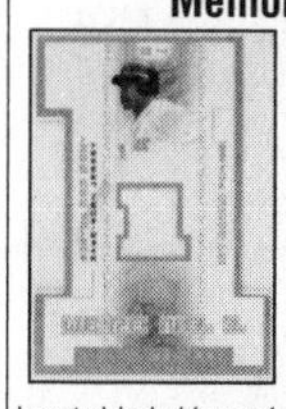

These two cards form a partial parallel to the We're Number One insert set. The two player, Bonds and Jeter each signed the number of cards numbered to the last two digits of their draft year.

	Nm-Mt	Ex-Mt
BB Barry Bonds/85	250.00	75.00
DJ Derek Jeter/92		

2002 Fleer Hot Prospects We're Number One Memorabilia

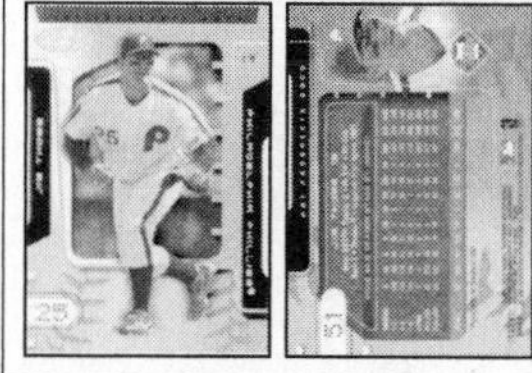

Inserted in hobby packs at stated odds, these nine cards form a partial parallel to the We're Number One insert set. With the exception of Ken Griffey Jr, each player has a game-used jersery swatch attached to it. Griffey's memorabilia piece comes from a game-used base.

	Nm-Mt	Ex-Mt
AR Alex Rodriguez Jsy	15.00	4.50
BB Barry Bonds Jsy	25.00	7.50
CJ Chipper Jones Jsy	15.00	4.50
DJ Derek Jeter Jsy	25.00	7.50
JD J.D. Drew Jsy	15.00	4.50
KG Ken Griffey Jr. Base SP	20.00	6.00
MR Manny Ramirez Jsy	15.00	4.50
NG Nomar Garciaparra Jsy	20.00	6.00
TH Todd Helton Jsy	15.00	4.50

2003 Fleer Hot Prospects

This 127-card set was distributed in two separate releases. The primary Hot Prospects product - containing the first 119 cards from the basic set - was released in August, 2003. This set was issued in five card packs with a $12 SRP which came 15 packs to a box and 12 boxes to a case. Cards numbered 1 through 80 feature veterans. Cards 81-119 feature a selection of prospects and rookies with many cards including a certified autograph or game used element (and in some cases both). One card from this run was guaranteed within each sealed box. In addition, all of these prospect cards are serial numbered to quantities ranging between 400-1250 copies per. Please note that cards 88, 96, 106 and 108 were never produced. Cards 120-127 were randomly seeded within packs of Fleer Rookies and Greats of which was distributed in December, 2003. These eight update cards (featuring a selection of top prospects) were all serial numbered to a mere 250 copies per and all included a game used element.

	MINT	NRMT
COMP.LO SET w/o SP's (80)	30.00	13.50
COMMON CARD (1-80)	.50	.23
FS BAT/JSY PRINT RUN 1250 #'d SETS		
CUT AU PRINT RUN 500 SERIAL #'d SETS		
GG AU PRINT RUN 400 SERIAL #'d SETS		
COMMON CARD (120-127)	10.00	4.50
1 Derek Jeter	3.00	1.35
2 Ryan Klesko	.50	.23
3 Troy Glaus	.75	.35
4 Jeff Kent	.50	.23
5 Frank Thomas	1.25	.55
6 Gary Sheffield	.50	.23
7 Jim Edmonds	.50	.23
8 Pat Burrell	.50	.23
9 Jacque Jones	.50	.23
10 Jason Jennings	.50	.23
11 Pedro Martinez	1.25	.55
12 Rafael Palmeiro	.75	.35
13 Jason Kendall	.50	.23
14 Tom Glavine	.75	.35
15 Josh Beckett	.75	.35
16 Luis Gonzalez	.50	.23
17 Edgar Martinez	.75	.35
18 Miguel Tejada	.50	.23
19 Fred McGriff	.75	.35
20 Adam Dunn	.50	.23
21 Lance Berkman	.50	.23
22 Magglio Ordonez	.50	.23
23 Darin Erstad	.50	.23
24 Rich Aurilia	.50	.23
25 Mike Piazza	2.00	.90
26 Shawn Green	.50	.23
27 Larry Walker	.75	.35
28 Manny Ramirez	.50	.23
29 Juan Gonzalez	1.25	.55
30 Eric Chavez	.50	.23
31 Torii Hunter	.50	.23
32 A.J. Burnett	.50	.23
33 Sammy Sosa	2.00	.90
34 Eric Hinske	.50	.23
35 Brian Giles	.50	.23
36 Mike Sweeney	.50	.23
37 Sean Casey	.50	.23
38 Chipper Jones	1.25	.55
39 Scott Rolen	.75	.35
40 Jason Giambi	1.25	.55
41 Mo Vaughn	.50	.23
42 Roy Oswalt	.50	.23
43 Paul Konerko	.50	.23
44 Tim Salmon	.75	.35
45 Edgardo Alfonzo	.50	.23
46 Jermaine Dye	.50	.23
47 Ben Sheets	.50	.23
48 Todd Helton	.75	.35
49 Greg Maddux	2.00	.90
50 Albert Pujols	2.50	1.10
51 Jim Thome	1.25	.55
52 Vladimir Guerrero	1.25	.55
53 Ivan Rodriguez	1.25	.55
54 Nomar Garciaparra	2.00	.90
55 Alex Rodriguez	2.00	.90
56 Alfonso Soriano	.75	.35
57 Kazuhisa Ishii	.50	.23
58 Austin Kearns	.50	.23
59 Curt Schilling	.75	.35
60 Bret Boone	.50	.23
61 Mark Prior	2.50	1.10
62 Garret Anderson	.50	.23
63 Barry Bonds	3.00	1.35
64 Roger Clemens	2.50	1.10
65 Jeff Bagwell	.75	.35
66 Omar Vizquel	.50	.23
67 Jay Gibbons	.50	.23
68 Aubrey Huff	.50	.23
69 Bobby Abreu	.50	.23
70 Richie Sexson	.50	.23
71 Bobby Higginson	.50	.23
72 Kerry Wood	1.25	.55
73 Carlos Delgado	.50	.23
74 Sean Burroughs	.50	.23
75 Jose Vidro	.50	.23
76 Ken Griffey Jr.	2.00	.90
77 Randy Johnson	1.25	.55
78 Ichiro Suzuki	2.00	.90
79 Barry Zito	.75	.35
80 Carlos Beltran	.50	.23
81 Joe Borchard FS Jsy	8.00	3.60
82 Mark Teixeira FS Bat	10.00	4.50
83 Brandon Webb FS Jsy RC	15.00	6.75
84 S.Victorino Pants AU RC	15.00	6.75
85 Hee Seop Choi FS Jsy	8.00	3.60
86 Hank Blalock FS Bat	10.00	4.50
87 Brett Myers FS Jsy	8.00	3.60
88 Does Not Exist		
89 Jesse Foppert FS Jsy	8.00	3.60
90 Lyle Overbay FS Jsy	8.00	3.60
91 Brian Stokes Pants AU RC	15.00	6.75
92 Josh Hall Bat AU RC	25.00	11.00
93 Chris Waters Pants AU RC	15.00	6.75
94 Lew Ford Pants AU RC	25.00	11.00
95 Ian Ferguson AU RC	10.00	4.50
96 Does Not Exist		
97 Josh Stewart AU RC	10.00	4.50
98 Pete LaForest AU RC	15.00	6.75
99 Jose Contreras Jsy AU/300 RC	50.00	22.00
100 Termel Sledge AU RC	15.00	6.75
101 Guillermo Quiroz AU RC	20.00	9.00
102 Alejandro Machado AU RC	10.00	4.50
103 Nook Logan Pants AU RC	15.00	6.75
104 R.Hammock Pants AU RC	25.00	11.00
105 Hideki Matsui FS Base RC	20.00	9.00
106 Does Not Exist		
107 Rocco Baldelli FS Jsy	15.00	6.75
108 Does Not Exist		
109 T.Wellemeyer Pants AU RC	25.00	11.00
110 Mi. Hessman Pants AU RC	15.00	6.75
111 J.Bonderman Pants AU RC	25.00	11.00
112 Craig Brazell Pants AU RC	25.00	11.00
113 Franc Rosario Pants AU RC	15.00	6.75
114 Jeff Duncan Pants AU RC	25.00	11.00
115 Dan. Cabrera Pants AU RC	15.00	6.75
116 Dontrelle Willis Pants AU	40.00	18.00
117 Cory Stewart AU RC	10.00	4.50
118 Tim Olson Pants AU RC	25.00	11.00
119 C.Wang Pants AU/500 RC	40.00	18.00
120 Josh Willingham Pants RC	10.00	4.50
121 Rickie Weeks Bat RC	25.00	11.00
122 Prentice Redman Pants RC	10.00	4.50
123 Mike Ryan Pants RC	15.00	6.75
124 Oscar Villarreal Pants RC	10.00	4.50
125 Ryan Wagner Pants RC	15.00	6.75
126 Bo Hart Pants RC	15.00	6.75
127 Edwin Jackson Pants RC	20.00	9.00

2003 Fleer Hot Prospects Class Of

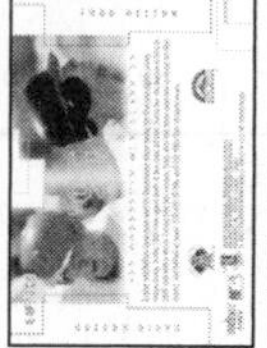

	MINT	NRMT
COMPLETE SET (10)	30.00	13.50
STATED ODDS 1:15		
1 Barry Zito / Josh Beckett	2.50	1.10
2 Pat Burrell / J.D. Drew	2.50	1.10
3 Mark Prior / Mark Teixeira	8.00	3.60
4 Austin Kearns / Sean Burroughs	2.50	1.10
5 Troy Glaus / Lance Berkman	2.50	1.10
6 Darin Erstad / Todd Helton	2.50	1.10
7 Manny Ramirez / Shawn Green	2.50	1.10
8 Matt Morris / Kerry Wood	4.00	1.80
9 Nomar Garciaparra / Paul Konerko	6.00	2.70
10 Alex Rodriguez / Torii Hunter	6.00	2.70

2003 Fleer Hot Prospects Class Of Game Used

	MINT	NRMT
RANDOM INSERTS IN PACKS		
STATED PRINT RUN 375 SERIAL #'d SETS		
AKSB Austin Kearns Jsy / Sean Burroughs Jsy	10.00	4.50
ARTH Alex Rodriguez Jsy / Torii Hunter Jsy	20.00	9.00
BZJB Barry Zito Jsy / Josh Beckett Jsy	15.00	6.75
DETH Darin Erstad Jsy / Todd Helton Jsy	15.00	6.75
MMKW Matt Morris Jsy / Kerry Wood Jsy	15.00	6.75
MPMT Mark Prior Jsy / Mark Teixeira Bat	30.00	13.50
MRSG Manny Ramirez Jsy / Shawn Green Jsy	10.00	4.50
NGPK Nomar Garciaparra Jsy / Paul Konerko Jsy	20.00	9.00
PBJD Pat Burrell Jsy / J.D. Drew Jsy	10.00	4.50
TGLB Troy Glaus Jsy / Lance Berkman Jsy	15.00	6.75

2003 Fleer Hot Prospects Cream of the Crop

	MINT	NRMT
COMPLETE SET (15)	50.00	22.00
STATED ODDS 1:5		
1 Barry Bonds	6.00	2.70
2 Derek Jeter	6.00	2.70
3 Ichiro Suzuki	4.00	1.80
4 Nomar Garciaparra	4.00	1.80
5 Roger Clemens	5.00	2.20
6 Alex Rodriguez	4.00	1.80
7 Greg Maddux	4.00	1.80
8 Mike Piazza	4.00	1.80
9 Sammy Sosa	4.00	1.80
10 Jason Giambi	2.50	1.10
11 Hideki Matsui	10.00	4.50
12 Albert Pujols	5.00	2.20
13 Vladimir Guerrero	2.50	1.10
14 Jim Thome	2.50	1.10
15 Pedro Martinez	2.50	1.10

2003 Fleer Hot Prospects MLB Hot Materials

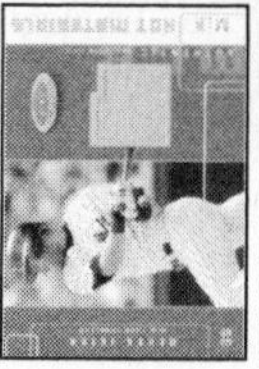

	MINT	NRMT
STATED PRINT RUN 499 SERIAL #'d SETS		
*RED HOT: .75X TO 2X BASIC		
RED HOT PRINT RUN 50 SERIAL #'d SETS		
RANDOM INSERTS IN PACKS		
AD Adam Dunn Jsy	8.00	3.60
AR Alex Rodriguez Jsy	15.00	6.75
AS Alfonso Soriano Jsy	10.00	4.50
BA Tom Glavine Jsy	10.00	4.50
CD Carlos Delgado Jsy	8.00	3.60
CJ Chipper Jones Jsy	10.00	4.50
DJ Derek Jeter Jsy	25.00	11.00
GM Greg Maddux Jsy	10.00	4.50
HC Hee Seop Choi Jsy	8.00	3.60
JB Josh Beckett Jsy	10.00	4.50
JG Jason Giambi Jsy	10.00	4.50
JT Jim Thome Jsy	10.00	4.50
LB Lance Berkman Bat	8.00	3.60
LO Lyle Overbay Jsy	8.00	3.60
MPI Mike Piazza Jsy	10.00	4.50
MPR Mark Prior Jsy	15.00	6.75
MR Manny Ramirez Jsy	8.00	3.60
MS Mike Sweeney Jsy	8.00	3.60
MTJ Miguel Tejada Jsy	8.00	3.60
MTX Mark Teixeira Bat	10.00	4.50
NG Nomar Garciaparra Jsy	15.00	6.75
PB Pat Burrell Jsy	8.00	3.60
RJ Randy Johnson Jsy	10.00	4.50
RP Rafael Palmeiro Jsy	10.00	4.50
SG Shawn Green Jsy	8.00	3.60
SS Sammy Sosa Jsy	15.00	6.75
TG Troy Glaus Jsy	10.00	4.50
THE Todd Helton Jsy	10.00	4.50
THU Torii Hunter Jsy	8.00	3.60
VG Vladimir Guerrero Jsy	10.00	4.50

2003 Fleer Hot Prospects MLB Hot Tandems

	MINT	NRMT
STATED PRINT RUN 100 SERIAL #'d SETS		
RED HOT PRINT RUN 10 SERIAL #'d SETS		
NO RED HOT PRICING DUE TO SCARCITY		
RANDOM INSERTS IN PACKS		
ARMT Alex Rodriguez Jsy / Miguel Tejada Jsy	25.00	11.00
CJDJ Chipper Jones Jsy / Derek Jeter Jsy	40.00	18.00
DJMT Derek Jeter Jsy / Miguel Tejada Jsy	40.00	18.00
DJNG Derek Jeter Jsy / Nomar Garciaparra Jsy	40.00	18.00
HCLO Hee Seop Choi Jsy / Lyle Overbay Jsy	15.00	6.75
JBGM Josh Beckett Jsy / Greg Maddux Jsy	20.00	9.00
JGTG Jason Giambi Jsy / Troy Glaus Jsy	15.00	6.75
JTJG Jim Thome Jsy / Jason Giambi Jsy	15.00	6.75
LBAD Lance Berkman Bat / Adam Dunn Jsy	15.00	6.75
LORJ Lyle Overbay Jsy / Randy Johnson Jsy	15.00	6.75
MPCJ Mike Piazza Jsy / Chipper Jones Jsy	20.00	9.00
MPDJ Mike Piazza Jsy / Derek Jeter Jsy	40.00	18.00
MPJB Mark Prior Jsy / Josh Beckett Jsy	25.00	11.00
MPSS Mark Prior Jsy / Sammy Sosa Jsy	25.00	11.00
MTAR Mark Teixeira Bat / Alex Rodriguez Jsy	25.00	11.00
NGMT Nomar Garciaparra Jsy / Miguel Tejada Jsy	25.00	11.00
PBJT Pat Burrell Jsy / Jim Thome Jsy	15.00	6.75
RJGM Randy Johnson Jsy / Greg Maddux Jsy	20.00	9.00
RPAD Rafael Palmeiro Jsy / Adam Dunn Jsy	15.00	6.75
RPMT Rafael Palmeiro Jsy / Mark Teixeira Bat	15.00	6.75
SSPB Sammy Sosa Jsy / Pat Burrell Jsy	25.00	11.00
TGSG Troy Glaus Jsy / Shawn Green Jsy	15.00	6.75
THAD Torii Hunter Jsy / Lance Berkman Bat	15.00	6.75
THVG Torii Hunter Jsy / Vladimir Guerrero Jsy	15.00	6.75
VGSG Vladimir Guerrero Jsy / Shawn Green Jsy	15.00	6.75

2003 Fleer Hot Prospects MLB Hot Triple Patch

	MINT	NRMT
RANDOM INSERTS IN PACKS		
STATED PRINT RUN 50 SERIAL #'d SETS		
BGJ Lance Berkman / Troy Glaus / Chipper Jones	50.00	22.00
BTB Pat Burrell / Jim Thome / Lance Berkman	50.00	22.00
DJB Adam Dunn / Randy Johnson / Josh Beckett	50.00	22.00
GGJ Vladimir Guerrero / Troy Glaus / Chipper Jones	50.00	22.00
GRT Jason Giambi / Alex Rodriguez / Miguel Tejada	60.00	27.00
GSP Nomar Garciaparra / Sammy Sosa / Mike Piazza	100.00	45.00
GTD Jason Giambi / Miguel Tejada / Adam Dunn	50.00	22.00
HSG Torii Hunter / Sammy Sosa / Vladimir Guerrero		
JGR Derek Jeter / Nomar Garciaparra / Alex Rodriguez	150.00	70.00
JHP Derek Jeter / Torii Hunter / Mark Prior	120.00	55.00
JSG Randy Johnson / Alfonso Soriano / Shawn Green	50.00	22.00
PBM Mark Prior / Josh Beckett / Greg Maddux	120.00	55.00
PBT Mike Piazza / Pat Burrell / Jim Thome	60.00	27.00
PCT Rafael Palmeiro / Hee Seop Choi / Mark Teixeira	50.00	22.00
SMG Alfonso Soriano / Greg Maddux / Shawn Green	80.00	36.00

2003 Fleer Hot Prospects PlayerGraphs

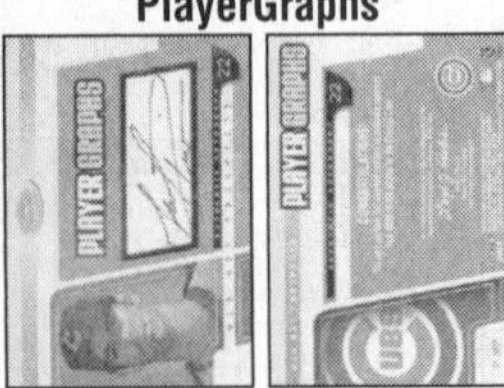

Randomly inserted in packs, these 11 cards feature authentic autographs from the featured player. Each of these cards were issued to a stated print run of 400 serial numbered sets.

	MINT	NRMT
*RED HOT: .6X TO 1.5X BASIC		
RED HOT PRINT RUN 100 SERIAL #'d SETS		
RANDOM INSERTS IN PACKS		
AH Aubrey Huff	15.00	6.75
BM Brett Myers	15.00	6.75
CZ Carlos Zambrano	25.00	11.00
FR Francisco Rodriguez	15.00	6.75
HB Hank Blalock	25.00	11.00
JR Jose Reyes	25.00	11.00
MP Mark Prior	60.00	27.00
MT Mark Teixiera	25.00	11.00
RO Roy Oswalt	15.00	6.75
VW Vernon Wells	15.00	6.75
XN Xavier Nady	15.00	6.75

2001 Fleer Legacy

The 2001 Fleer Legacy product was released in mid-July, 2001 and featured a 105-card base set that was broken into tiers as follows: Base Veterans (1-90) and Prospects (91-105) that are individually serial numbered to 799. Please note that the first 300 serial-numbered cards of Albert Pujols packed out as exchange cards for a copy actually signed by Pujols. Card number 98 does not exist. Each box contained 15 packs with five cards per pack.

	Nm-Mt	Ex-Mt
COMP.SET w/o SP's (90)	40.00	12.00
COMMON CARD (1-90)	1.00	.30
COMMON AUTO (91-100)	15.00	4.50
COMMON CARD (101-105)	10.00	3.00
1 Pedro Martinez	2.50	.75
2 Andruw Jones	1.00	.30
3 Mike Hampton	1.00	.30
4 Gary Sheffield	1.00	.30
5 Barry Zito	2.50	.75
6 J.D. Drew	1.00	.30
7 Charles Johnson	1.00	.30
8 David Wells	1.00	.30
9 Kazuhiro Sasaki	1.00	.30
10 Vladimir Guerrero	2.50	.75
11 Pat Burrell	1.00	.30
12 Ruben Mateo	1.00	.30
13 Greg Maddux	4.00	1.20
14 Sean Casey	1.00	.30
15 Craig Biggio	1.50	.45
16 Bernie Williams	1.50	.45
17 Jeff Kent	1.00	.30
18 Nomar Garciaparra	4.00	1.20
19 Cal Ripken	8.00	2.40
20 Larry Walker	1.50	.45
21 Adrian Beltre	1.00	.30
22 Johnny Damon	1.00	.30
23 Rick Ankiel	1.00	.30
24 Matt Williams	1.00	.30
25 Magglio Ordonez	1.00	.30
26 Richard Hidalgo	1.00	.30
27 Robin Ventura	1.00	.30
28 Jason Kendall	1.00	.30
29 Tony Batista	1.00	.30
30 Chipper Jones	2.50	.75
31 Jim Thome	2.50	.75
32 Kevin Brown	1.00	.30
33 Mike Mussina	2.50	.75
34 Mark McGwire	6.00	1.80
35 Darin Erstad	1.00	.30
36 Manny Ramirez	1.00	.30
37 Bobby Higginson	1.00	.30
38 Richie Sexson	1.00	.30
39 Jason Giambi	2.50	.75
40 Alex Rodriguez	4.00	1.20
41 Mark Grace	1.50	.45
42 Ken Griffey Jr.	4.00	1.20
43 Moises Alou	1.00	.30
44 Edgardo Alfonzo	1.00	.30
45 Phil Nevin	1.00	.30
46 Rafael Palmeiro	1.50	.45
47 Javy Lopez	1.00	.30
48 Juan Gonzalez	2.50	.75
49 Jermaine Dye	1.00	.30
50 Roger Clemens	5.00	1.50
51 Barry Bonds	6.00	1.80
52 Carl Everett	1.00	.30
53 Ben Sheets	1.00	.30
54 Juan Encarnacion	1.00	.30
55 Jeromy Burnitz	1.00	.30
56 Miguel Tejada	1.00	.30
57 Ben Grieve	1.00	.30
58 Randy Johnson	2.50	.75
59 Frank Thomas	2.50	.75
60 Preston Wilson	1.00	.30
61 Mike Piazza	4.00	1.20
62 Brian Giles	1.00	.30
63 Carlos Delgado	1.00	.30
64 Tom Glavine	1.50	.45
65 Roberto Alomar	2.50	.75
66 Mike Sweeney	1.00	.30
67 Orlando Hernandez	1.00	.30
68 Edgar Martinez	1.50	.45
69 Tim Salmon	1.50	.45
70 Kerry Wood	2.50	.75
71 Jack Wilson RC	1.00	.30
72 Matt Lawton	1.00	.30
73 Scott Rolen	1.50	.45
74 Ivan Rodriguez	2.50	.75
75 Steve Finley	1.00	.30
76 Barry Larkin	2.50	.75
77 Jeff Bagwell	1.50	.45
78 Derek Jeter	6.00	1.80
79 Tony Gwynn	3.00	.90
80 Raul Mondesi	1.00	.30
81 Rafael Furcal	1.00	.30
82 Todd Helton	1.50	.45
83 Shawn Green	1.00	.30
84 Tim Hudson	1.00	.30
85 Jim Edmonds	1.00	.30
86 Troy Glaus	1.50	.45
87 Sammy Sosa	4.00	1.20
88 Cliff Floyd	1.00	.30
89 Jose Vidro	1.00	.30
90 Bob Abreu	1.00	.30
91 Drew Henson AU RC	50.00	15.00
92 Andy Morales AU RC	15.00	4.50
93 Wilson Betemit AU RC	15.00	4.50
94 Elpidio Guzman AU RC	15.00	4.50
95 Esix Snead AU RC	15.00	4.50
96 Winston Abreu AU RC	15.00	4.50
97 Jeremy Owens AU RC	15.00	4.50
98 Does Not Exist		
99 Junior Spivey AU RC	25.00	7.50
100 J. Randolph AU RC	15.00	4.50
101 Ichiro Suzuki RC	60.00	18.00
102 Albert Pujols RC/499	80.00	24.00
102AU Albert Pujols AU/300	300.00	90.00
103 Tsuyoshi Shinjo RC	15.00	4.50
104 Jay Gibbons RC	15.00	4.50
105 Juan Uribe RC	10.00	3.00

2001 Fleer Legacy Ultimate

Randomly inserted into packs, this 105-card set is actually a complete parallel of the 2001 Fleer Legacy base set. These cards have a gold backdrop, and are serial numbered to 250.

	Nm-Mt	Ex-Mt
*STARS 1-90: 2.5X TO 6X BASIC CARDS		
*ROOKIES 91-100: .2X TO .5X BASIC CARDS		
*ROOKIES 101-105: .4X TO 1X BASIC CARDS		

2001 Fleer Legacy Hit Kings

Randomly inserted into packs at one in 13, this 29-card insert features actual chips from game-used bats from the major leagues top hitters Cards have been listed in alphabetical order for convenience.

	Nm-Mt	Ex-Mt
1 Rick Ankiel	10.00	3.00
2 Tony Batista	10.00	3.00
3 Carlos Beltran	10.00	3.00
4 Adrian Beltre	10.00	3.00
5 Barry Bonds	30.00	9.00
6 George Brett	25.00	7.50
7 Jose Canseco	15.00	4.50
8 Roger Cedeno	10.00	3.00
9 Johnny Damon	10.00	3.00
10 Erubiel Durazo	10.00	3.00
11 Juan Encarnacion	10.00	3.00
12 Troy Glaus	15.00	4.50
13 Shawn Green	10.00	3.00
14 Vladimir Guerrero	15.00	4.50
15 Reggie Jackson	15.00	4.50
16 Andruw Jones	10.00	3.00
17 Jason Kendall	10.00	3.00
18 Ralph Kiner	15.00	4.50
19 Billy Martin	15.00	4.50
20 Ruben Mateo	10.00	3.00
21 Stan Musial	25.00	7.50
22 Troy O'Leary	10.00	3.00
23 Magglio Ordonez	10.00	3.00
24 Corey Patterson	10.00	3.00
25 Juan Pierre	10.00	3.00
26 Ivan Rodriguez	15.00	4.50
27 Tim Salmon	15.00	4.50
28 Jim Thome	15.00	4.50
29 Jose Vidro	10.00	3.00

2001 Fleer Legacy Hit Kings Short Prints

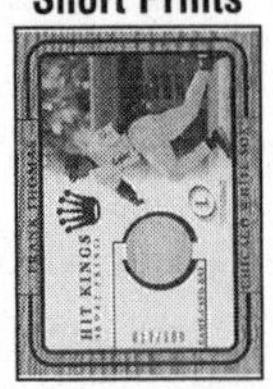

Randomly inserted into packs, this 10-card insert features actual chips from game-used bats from the major leagues top hitters Cards have been listed in alphabetical order for convenience. Please note that there were only 100 serial numbered sets produced. These cards also have a special red-foil stamping on the card fronts.

	Nm-Mt	Ex-Mt
1 Johnny Bench	40.00	12.00
2 Wade Boggs	40.00	12.00
3 Roger Clemens	80.00	24.00
4 Steve Garvey	25.00	7.50
5 Tony Gwynn	50.00	15.00
6 Eddie Mathews	40.00	12.00
7 Joe Morgan	25.00	7.50
8 Scott Rolen	40.00	12.00
9 Frank Thomas	40.00	12.00
10 Robin Yount	40.00	12.00

2001 Fleer Legacy Hot Gloves

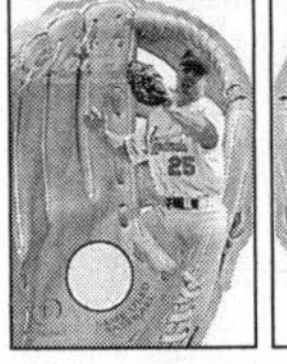

Randomly inserted into packs at one in 180, this 15-card insert featured actual swatches of game-used gloves. Unfortunately, redemption cards had to be placed into packs for all fifteen cards. The exchange deadline was 07/01/02. Prices below refer to actual memorabilia cards. The redemption cards are valued at 25 percent of isted values.

	Nm-Mt	Ex-Mt
*REDEMPTION CARDS: .25X VALUE..		
1 Andruw Jones	25.00	7.50
2 Mike Mussina	40.00	12.00
3 Roberto Alomar	40.00	12.00
4 Tony Gwynn	50.00	15.00
5 Bernie Williams	40.00	12.00
6 Ivan Rodriguez	40.00	12.00
7 Ken Griffey Jr.	80.00	24.00
8 Robin Ventura	25.00	7.50
9 Cal Ripken	100.00	30.00
10 Jeff Bagwell	40.00	12.00
11 Mark McGwire	150.00	45.00
12 Rafael Palmeiro	40.00	12.00
13 Scott Rolen	40.00	12.00
14 Barry Bonds	100.00	30.00
15 Greg Maddux	60.00	18.00

2001 Fleer Legacy MLB Autograph Fitted Caps

Inserted at one per box (chiptopper), this collection features actual autographed hats from both modern-day and classic players. Hats have been listed in alphabetical order for convenience. Specific quantities for caps in short supply were announced by Fleer shortly after the product went live. Those figures are detailed within our checklist. According to Fleer, no more than 500 of each cap was signed. Exchange cards, with a redemption deadline of July 1st, 2002, were seeded into packs for the following players: Pat Burrell, Darin Erstad, Nomar Garciaparra, Paul Molitor, Jim Thome and Robin Yount.

	Nm-Mt	Ex-Mt
1 Edgardo Alfonzo	40.00	12.00
2 Roberto Alomar	80.00	24.00
3 Ernie Banks SP/100	150.00	45.00
4 Adrian Beltre	40.00	12.00
5 Johnny Bench SP/100	150.00	45.00
6 Lance Berkman	40.00	12.00
7 Yogi Berra SP/200	150.00	45.00
8 Craig Biggio	50.00	15.00
9 Barry Bonds	400.00	120.00
10 Jeromy Burnitz	40.00	12.00
11 Pat Burrell	40.00	12.00
12 Steve Carlton	50.00	15.00
13 Sean Casey	40.00	12.00
14 Orlando Cepeda	40.00	12.00
15 Eric Chavez	40.00	12.00
16 Tony Clark	40.00	12.00
17 Roger Clemens SP/100	300.00	90.00
18 Johnny Damon	40.00	12.00
19 Dom DiMaggio SP/200	100.00	30.00
20 J.D. Drew	40.00	12.00
21 Jermaine Dye	40.00	12.00
22 Darin Erstad	40.00	12.00
23 Carlton Fisk SP/150	120.00	36.00
24 Rafael Furcal	40.00	12.00
25 Nomar Garciaparra SP/150	200.00	60.00
26 Jason Giambi	80.00	24.00
27 Troy Glaus	50.00	15.00
28 Tom Glavine	80.00	24.00
29 Juan Gonzalez	80.00	24.00
30 Luis Gonzalez	40.00	12.00
31 Tony Gwynn	120.00	36.00
32 Drew Henson	50.00	15.00
33 Derek Jeter	300.00	90.00
34 Andruw Jones	50.00	15.00
35 David Justice	40.00	12.00
36 Paul Konerko	40.00	12.00
37 Don Mattingly	200.00	60.00
38 Willie McCovey	50.00	15.00
39 Paul Molitor	60.00	18.00
40 Stan Musial SP/200	200.00	60.00
41 Mike Mussina	80.00	24.00
42 Jim Palmer	40.00	12.00
43 Corey Patterson	40.00	12.00
44 Kirby Puckett SP/200	100.00	30.00
45 Cal Ripken SP/200	300.00	90.00
46 Brooks Robinson	80.00	24.00
47 Ivan Rodriguez	80.00	24.00
48 Scott Rolen	50.00	15.00
49 Nolan Ryan SP/150		
50 Mike Schmidt SP/150	150.00	45.00
51 Tom Seaver SP/100	150.00	45.00
52 Ben Sheets	40.00	12.00
53 Ozzie Smith	120.00	36.00
54 Duke Snider	50.00	15.00
55 Miguel Tejada	40.00	12.00
56 Jim Thome	80.00	24.00
57 Matt Williams	40.00	12.00
58 Dave Winfield SP/150	100.00	30.00
59 C.Yastrzemski SP/150	150.00	45.00
60 Robin Yount	120.00	36.00
61 Barry Zito	80.00	24.00

2001 Fleer Legacy MLB Game Issue Base

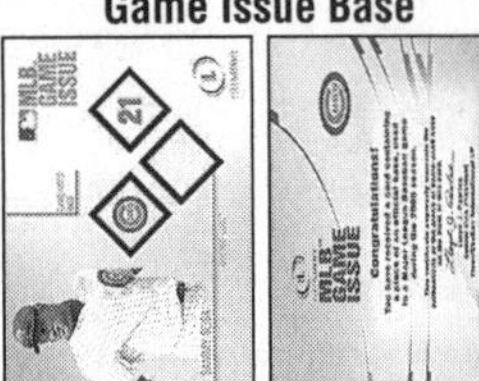

Randomly inserted into packs at one in 52, this 15-card insert features actual swatches from game-used bases from top major league talents. Cards have been listed in alphabetical order for convenience.

	Nm-Mt	Ex-Mt
1 Barry Bonds	30.00	9.00
2 Pat Burrell	10.00	3.00
3 Troy Glaus	10.00	3.00
4 Ken Griffey Jr.	15.00	4.50
5 Tony Gwynn	15.00	4.50
6 Todd Helton	10.00	3.00
7 Derek Jeter	30.00	9.00
8 Chipper Jones	10.00	3.00
9 Mark McGwire	50.00	15.00
10 Mike Piazza	20.00	6.00
11 Cal Ripken	40.00	12.00
12 Alex Rodriguez	25.00	7.50
13 Scott Rolen	10.00	3.00
14 Sammy Sosa	15.00	4.50
15 Frank Thomas	10.00	3.00

2001 Fleer Legacy MLB Game Issue Base-Ball

Randomly inserted into packs, this 15-card insert features actual swatches from both game-used bases and baseballs from top major league talents. Cards have been listed in alphabetical order for convenience. Please note that there were only 100 serial numbered sets produced.

	Nm-Mt	Ex-Mt
1 Barry Bonds	80.00	24.00
2 Pat Burrell	25.00	7.50
3 Troy Glaus	25.00	7.50
4 Ken Griffey Jr.	50.00	15.00
5 Tony Gwynn	50.00	15.00
6 Todd Helton	25.00	7.50
7 Derek Jeter	80.00	24.00
8 Chipper Jones	40.00	12.00
9 Mark McGwire	150.00	45.00
10 Mike Piazza	80.00	24.00
11 Cal Ripken	100.00	30.00
12 Scott Rolen	25.00	7.50
13 Alex Rodriguez	80.00	24.00
14 Sammy Sosa	60.00	18.00
15 Frank Thomas	40.00	12.00

2001 Fleer Legacy MLB Game Issue Base-Ball-Jersey

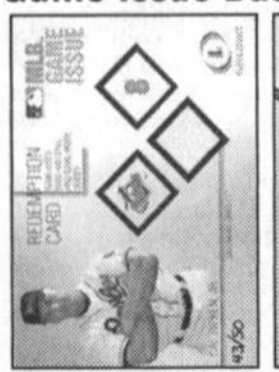

Randomly inserted into packs, this 10-card insert features actual swatches from game-used bases, baseballs, and jerseys from top major league talents. Cards have been listed in alphabetical order for convenience. Please note that there were only 50 serial numbered sets produced. Exchange cards, with a redemption deadline of July 1st, 2002, were seeded into packs for the following players: Barry Bonds, Pat Burrell, Tony Gwynn, Cal Ripken and Scott Rolen.

	Nm-Mt	Ex-Mt
1 Barry Bonds	150.00	45.00
2 Pat Burrell	50.00	15.00
3 Troy Glaus	50.00	15.00
4 Tony Gwynn	100.00	30.00
5 Todd Helton	50.00	15.00
6 Derek Jeter	150.00	45.00
7 Chipper Jones	80.00	24.00
8 Cal Ripken	200.00	60.00
9 Scott Rolen	50.00	15.00
10 Frank Thomas	80.00	24.00

2001 Fleer Legacy Tailor Made

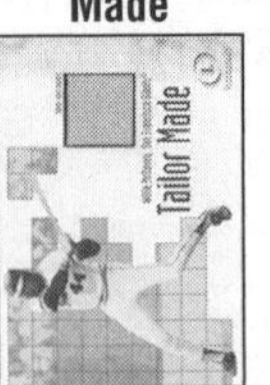

Randomly inserted into packs at one in 15, this 23-card insert features actual swatches of game-used jersey from top major league talents like Barry Bonds and Reggie Jackson. Cards have been listed in alphabetical order for convenience.

	Nm-Mt	Ex-Mt
*MULTI-COLOR PATCH: .75X TO 2X BASIC		
1 Edgardo Alfonzo	10.00	3.00
2 Rick Ankiel	10.00	3.00
3 Barry Bonds	30.00	9.00
4 Kevin Brown	10.00	3.00
5 Orlando Cepeda	10.00	3.00
6 Carlos Delgado	10.00	3.00
7 J.D. Drew	10.00	3.00
8 Shawn Green	10.00	3.00
9 Todd Helton	15.00	4.50
10 Reggie Jackson	15.00	4.50
11 Jason Kendall	10.00	3.00
12 Greg Maddux	15.00	4.50
13 Don Mattingly	50.00	15.00
14 Willie McCovey	10.00	3.00
15 Rafael Palmeiro	15.00	4.50
16 Lou Piniella	10.00	3.00
17 Manny Ramirez	10.00	3.00
18 Cal Ripken	50.00	15.00
19 Ivan Rodriguez	15.00	4.50
20 Nolan Ryan	50.00	15.00
21 Curt Schilling	15.00	4.50
22 Rondell White	10.00	3.00
23 Dave Winfield	10.00	3.00

2002 Fleer Maximum

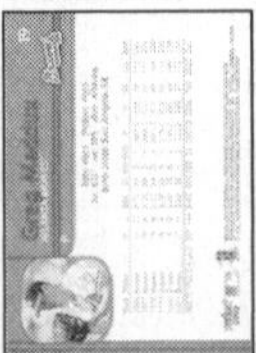

This 270 card set was released in February, 2002. These cards were issued in 15 card packs which were packaged 16 packs to a box and 12 boxes to a case. The set has 200 base cards, 50 rookies and prospects (201-250) and 20 Impact cards (251-270). Cards numbered

201-250 were randomly inserted in packs are all serial numbered to 500. Cards numbered 251-270 were inserted one per hobby pack.

	Nm-Mt	Ex-Mt
COMP.SET w/o SP's (200)	40.00	12.00
COMP.IMPACT SET (20)	25.00	7.50
COMMON CARD (1-200)	.40	.12
COMMON CARD (201-250)	10.00	3.00
COMMON CARD (251-270)	.75	.23
1 Barry Bonds	2.50	.75
2 Alex Rodriguez	1.50	.45
3 Jim Edmonds	.40	.12
4 Manny Ramirez	.40	.12
5 Jeff Bagwell	.60	.18
6 Kazuhiro Sasaki	.40	.12
7 Jason Giambi	1.00	.30
8 J.D. Drew	.40	.12
9 Barry Larkin	1.00	.30
10 Chipper Jones	1.00	.30
11 Rafael Palmeiro	.60	.18
12 Roberto Alomar	1.00	.30
13 Randy Johnson	1.00	.30
14 Juan Gonzalez	1.00	.30
15 Gary Sheffield	.40	.12
16 Larry Walker	.60	.18
17 Todd Helton	.60	.18
18 Ivan Rodriguez	1.00	.30
19 Greg Maddux	1.50	.45
20 Mike Piazza	1.50	.45
21 Tsuyoshi Shinjo	.40	.12
22 Luis Gonzalez	.40	.12
23 Pedro Martinez	1.00	.30
24 Albert Pujols	2.00	.60
25 Jose Canseco	1.00	.30
26 Edgar Martinez	.60	.18
27 Moises Alou	.40	.12
28 Vladimir Guerrero	1.00	.30
29 Shawn Green	.40	.12
30 Miguel Tejada	.40	.12
31 Bernie Williams	.60	.18
32 Frank Thomas	1.00	.30
33 Jim Thome	1.00	.30
34 Derek Jeter	2.50	.75
35 Julio Lugo	.40	.12
36 Mo Vaughn	.40	.12
37 Steve Cox	.40	.12
38 Brad Radke	.40	.12
39 Brian Jordan	.40	.12
40 Garret Anderson	.40	.12
41 Ichiro Suzuki	1.50	.45
42 Mike Lieberthal	.40	.12
43 Preston Wilson	.40	.12
44 Bud Smith	.40	.12
45 Curt Schilling	.60	.18
46 Eric Chavez	.40	.12
47 Javier Vazquez	.40	.12
48 Jose Ortiz	.40	.12
49 Mike Sweeney	.40	.12
50 Travis Fryman	.40	.12
51 Brady Anderson	.40	.12
52 Chan Ho Park	.40	.12
53 C.C. Sabathia	.40	.12
54 Jack Wilson	.40	.12
55 Joe Crede	.40	.12
56 Mike Mussina	1.00	.30
57 Sean Casey	.40	.12
58 Bobby Abreu	.40	.12
59 Joe Randa	.40	.12
60 Jose Vidro	.40	.12
61 Juan Uribe	.40	.12
62 Mark Grace	.60	.18
63 Matt Morris	.40	.12
64 Omar Vizquel	.40	.12
65 Darryl Kile	.40	.12
66 Dee Brown	.40	.12
67 Fernando Tatis	.40	.12
68 Jeff Cirillo	.40	.12
69 Johnny Damon	.40	.12
70 Milton Bradley	.40	.12
71 Reggie Sanders	.40	.12
72 Al Leiter	.40	.12
73 Andres Galarraga	.40	.12
74 Ellis Burks	.40	.12
75 Jermaine Dye	.40	.12
76 Juan Pierre	.40	.12
77 Junior Spivey	.40	.12
78 Mark Quinn	.40	.12
79 Ben Sheets	.40	.12
80 Brad Fullmer	.40	.12
81 Bubba Trammell	.40	.12
82 Dante Bichette	.40	.12
83 Ken Griffey Jr.	1.50	.45
84 Paul O'Neill	.60	.18
85 Robert Fick	.40	.12
86 Bret Boone	.40	.12
87 Raul Mondesi	.40	.12
88 Josh Beckett	.60	.18
89 Geoff Jenkins	.40	.12
90 Ramon Ortiz	.40	.12
91 Robin Ventura	.40	.12
92 Tom Glavine	.60	.18
93 Jimmy Rollins	.40	.12
94 Jamie Moyer	.40	.12
95 Magglio Ordonez	.40	.12
96 Mike Lowell	.40	.12
97 Ryan Dempster	.40	.12
98 Scott Schoeneweis	.40	.12
99 Todd Zeile	.40	.12
100 A.J. Burnett	.40	.12
101 Aaron Sele	.40	.12
102 Cal Ripken	3.00	.90
103 Carlos Beltran	.40	.12
104 David Eckstein	.40	.12
105 Jason Marquis	.40	.12
106 Matt Lawton	.40	.12
107 Ben Grieve	.40	.12
108 Brian Giles	.40	.12
109 Josh Towers	.40	.12
110 Lance Berkman	.40	.12
111 Sammy Sosa	1.50	.45
112 Torii Hunter	.40	.12
113 Aubrey Huff	.40	.12
114 Craig Biggio	.60	.18
115 Doug Mientkiewicz	.40	.12
116 Fred McGriff	.60	.18
117 Jason Johnson	.40	.12
118 Pat Burrell	.40	.12
119 Aaron Boone	.40	.12
120 Carlos Delgado	.40	.12
121 Nomar Garciaparra	1.50	.45
122 Richie Sexson	.40	.12
123 Russ Ortiz	.40	.12
124 Tim Hudson	.40	.12
125 Tony Clark	.40	.12
126 Jeromy Burnitz	.40	.12
127 Jose Cruz	.40	.12
128 Juan Encarnacion	.40	.12
129 Mark Mulder	.40	.12
130 Mike Hampton	.40	.12
131 Rich Aurilia	.40	.12
132 Trot Nixon	.60	.18
133 Greg Vaughn	.40	.12
134 Jacque Jones	.40	.12
135 Jason Kendall	.40	.12
136 Jay Gibbons	.40	.12
137 Mark Buehrle	.40	.12
138 Richard Hidalgo	.40	.12
139 Rondell White	.40	.12
140 Cristian Guzman	.40	.12
141 Andy Pettitte	.60	.18
142 Chris Richard	.40	.12
143 Paul LoDuca	.40	.12
144 Phil Nevin	.40	.12
145 Ray Durham	.40	.12
146 Todd Walker	.40	.12
147 Bartolo Colon	.40	.12
148 Ben Petrick	.40	.12
149 Freddy Garcia	.40	.12
150 Jon Lieber	.40	.12
151 Jose Hernandez	.40	.12
152 Matt Williams	.40	.12
153 Shannon Stewart	.40	.12
154 Adrian Beltre	.40	.12
155 Carlos Lee	.40	.12
156 Frank Catalanotto	.40	.12
157 Jorge Posada	.60	.18
158 Pokey Reese	.40	.12
159 Ryan Klesko	.40	.12
160 Ugueth Urbina	.40	.12
161 Adam Dunn	.40	.12
162 Alfonso Soriano	.60	.18
163 Ben Davis	.40	.12
164 Paul Konerko	.40	.12
165 Eric Karros	.40	.12
166 Jeff Weaver	.40	.12
167 Ruben Sierra	.40	.12
168 Bobby Higginson	.40	.12
169 Eric Milton	.40	.12
170 Kerry Wood	1.00	.30
171 Roy Oswalt	.40	.12
172 Scott Rolen	.60	.18
173 Tim Salmon	.40	.12
174 Aramis Ramirez	.40	.12
175 Jason Tyner	.40	.12
176 Juan Cruz	.40	.12
177 Keith Foulke	.40	.12
178 Kevin Brown	.40	.12
179 Roger Clemens	2.00	.60
180 Tony Batista	.40	.12
181 Andruw Jones	.40	.12
182 Cliff Floyd	.40	.12
183 Darin Erstad	.40	.12
184 Joe Mays	.40	.12
185 Mike Cameron	.40	.12
186 Robert Person	.40	.12
187 Jeff Kent	.40	.12
188 Gabe Kapler	.40	.12
189 Jason Jennings	.40	.12
190 Jason Varitek	.40	.12
191 Barry Zito	.60	.18
192 Rickey Henderson	1.00	.30
193 Tino Martinez	.60	.18
194 Brandon Duckworth	.40	.12
195 Corey Koskie	.40	.12
196 Derrek Lee	.40	.12
197 Javy Lopez	.40	.12
198 John Olerud	.40	.12
199 Terrence Long	.40	.12
200 Troy Glaus	.60	.18
201 Scott MacRae RHW	10.00	3.00
202 Scott Chiasson RHW	10.00	3.00
203 Bart Miadich RHW	10.00	3.00
204 Brian Bowles RHW	10.00	3.00
205 David Williams RHW	10.00	3.00
206 Victor Zambrano RHW	10.00	3.00
207 Joe Beimel RHW	10.00	3.00
208 Scott Stewart RHW	10.00	3.00
209 Bob File RHW	10.00	3.00
210 Ryan Jensen RHW	10.00	3.00
211 Jason Karnuth RHW	10.00	3.00
212 Brandon Knight RHW	10.00	3.00
213 Andy Shibilo RHW RC	10.00	3.00
214 Chad Ricketts RHW RC	10.00	3.00
215 Mark Prior RHW	25.00	7.50
216 Chad Paronto RHW	10.00	3.00
217 Corky Miller RHW	10.00	3.00
218 Luis Pineda RHW	10.00	3.00
219 Ramon Vazquez RHW	10.00	3.00
220 Tony Cogan RHW	10.00	3.00
221 Roy Smith RHW	10.00	3.00
222 Mark Lukasiewicz RHW	10.00	3.00
223 Mike Rivera RHW	10.00	3.00
224 Brad Voyles RHW	10.00	3.00
225 Jamie Burke RHW RC	10.00	3.00
226 Justin Duchscherer RTC	10.00	3.00
227 Eric Cyr RTC	10.00	3.00
228 Mark Lukasiewicz RTC	10.00	3.00
229 Marlon Byrd RTC	10.00	3.00
230 Chris Piersoll RTC RC	10.00	3.00
231 Ramon Vazquez RTC	10.00	3.00
232 Tony Cogan RTC	10.00	3.00
233 Roy Smith RTC	10.00	3.00
234 Franklin Nunez RTC RC	10.00	3.00
235 Corky Miller RTC	10.00	3.00
236 Jorge Nunez RTC RC	10.00	3.00
237 Joe Beimel RTC	10.00	3.00
238 Eric Knott RTC	10.00	3.00
239 Victor Zambrano RTC	10.00	3.00
240 Jason Karnuth RTC	10.00	3.00
241 Jason Middlebrook RTC	10.00	3.00
242 Scott Stewart RTC	10.00	3.00
243 Tim Spooneybarger RTC	10.00	3.00
244 David Williams RTC	10.00	3.00
245 Bart Miadich RTC	10.00	3.00
246 Mike Koplove RTC	10.00	3.00
247 Ryan Jensen RTC	10.00	3.00
248 Jeremy Fikac RTC	10.00	3.00
249 Bob File RTC	10.00	3.00
250 Craig Monroe RTC	10.00	3.00
251 Albert Pujols MI	3.00	.90
252 Ichiro Suzuki MI	2.50	.75
253 Nomar Garciaparra MI	2.50	.75
254 Barry Bonds MI	4.00	1.20
255 Jason Giambi MI	1.50	.45
256 Derek Jeter MI	4.00	1.20
257 Roberto Alomar MI	1.50	.45
258 Roger Clemens MI	3.00	.90
259 Mike Piazza MI	2.50	.75
260 Vladimir Guerrero MI	1.50	.45
261 Todd Helton MI	1.00	.30
262 Shawn Green MI	.75	.23
263 Chipper Jones MI	1.50	.45
264 Pedro Martinez MI	1.50	.45
265 Pat Burrell MI	.75	.23
266 Sammy Sosa MI	2.50	.75
267 Ken Griffey Jr. MI	2.50	.75
268 Cal Ripken MI	5.00	1.50
269 Kerry Wood MI	1.50	.45
270 Alex Rodriguez MI	2.50	.75
NNO Derek Jeter Promo	3.00	.90

2002 Fleer Maximum To the Max

Randomly inserted into hobby packs, this set parallels the Fleer Maximum set. These cards all have different print runs which we have noted in our checklist.

Nm-Mt Ex-Mt
* 1-200 PRINT RUN b/wn 201-417 4X TO 10X
* 1-200 PRINT RUN b/wn 151-200 5X TO 12X
* 1-200 PRINT RUN b/wn 121-150 6X TO 15X
* 1-200 PRINT RUN b/wn 81-120 8X TO 20X
* 1-200 PRINT RUN b/wn 66-80 10X TO 25X
* 1-200 PRINT RUN b/wn 51-65 12.5X TO 30X
* 1-200 PRINT RUN b/wn 36-50 15X TO 40X
* 1-200 PRINT RUN b/wn 26-35 20X TO 50X
* 1-200 PRINT RUN b/wn 21-25 25X TO 60X
1-200 PRINT RUN b/wn 24-417 OF EACH
* ROOKIES 151-200: .4X TO 1X BASIC
151-200 PRINT RUN 100 SERIAL #'d SETS
*IMPACT 251-270: 2.5X TO 6X BASIC
251-270 PRINT RUN b/wn 233-372 OF EACH
RANDOM INSERTS IN HOBBY PACKS
SEE BECKETT.COM FOR EXACT PRINT RUNS

2002 Fleer Maximum Americas Game

Inserted into retail packs at stated odds of one in 10, these 25 cards feature some of the fan favorites.

	Nm-Mt	Ex-Mt
COMPLETE SET (25)	60.00	18.00
1 Pedro Martinez	3.00	.90
2 Miguel Tejada	1.25	.35
3 Randy Johnson	3.00	.90
4 Barry Bonds	8.00	2.40
5 Rafael Palmeiro	2.00	.60
6 Mike Piazza	5.00	1.50
7 Greg Maddux	5.00	1.50
8 Jeff Bagwell	2.00	.60
9 Edgar Martinez	2.00	.60
10 Albert Pujols	6.00	1.80
11 Todd Helton	2.00	.60
12 Chipper Jones	3.00	.90
13 Luis Gonzalez	1.25	.35
14 Jason Giambi	3.00	.90
15 Kazuhiro Sasaki	1.25	.35
16 Dave Winfield	1.25	.35
17 Reggie Jackson	2.00	.60
18 Tom Glavine	2.00	.60
19 Carlos Delgado	1.25	.35
20 Bobby Abreu	1.25	.35
21 Larry Walker	2.00	.60
22 J.D. Drew	1.25	.35
23 Alex Rodriguez	5.00	1.50
24 Frank Thomas	3.00	.90
25 C.C. Sabathia	1.25	.35

2002 Fleer Maximum Americas Game Jersey

These cards were Inserted into hobby packs at stated odds of one in 24 and retail packs at stated odds of one in 72. This is a partial parallel of the America's game insert set and features a star-shaped swatch of a game-used jersey on every card. Cards with asterisks next to them are perceived to be produced in shorter quantity.

Nm-Mt Ex-Mt
*GOLD: .75X TO 2X BASIC AMERICA JERSEY
GOLD RANDOM INSERTS IN PACKS..
GOLD PRINT RUN 100 SERIAL #'d SETS

	Nm-Mt	Ex-Mt
1 Jeff Bagwell	15.00	4.50
2 Craig Biggio *	15.00	4.50
3 Barry Bonds Pants	25.00	7.50
4 Carlos Delgado	10.00	3.00
5 J.D. Drew	10.00	3.00
6 Jason Giambi *	15.00	4.50
7 Tom Glavine *	15.00	4.50
8 Luis Gonzalez	10.00	3.00
9 Todd Helton	15.00	4.50
10 Reggie Jackson Pants*	15.00	4.50
11 Randy Johnson	15.00	4.50
12 Chipper Jones	15.00	4.50
13 Greg Maddux	15.00	4.50
14 Edgar Martinez	15.00	4.50
15 Pedro Martinez *	15.00	4.50
16 Rafael Palmeiro	15.00	4.50
17 Chan Ho Park	10.00	3.00
18 Mike Piazza	15.00	4.50
19 Albert Pujols	25.00	7.50
20 Kazuhiro Sasaki	10.00	3.00
21 Miguel Tejada *	10.00	3.00
22 Frank Thomas	15.00	4.50
23 Larry Walker	15.00	4.50
24 Dave Winfield *	10.00	3.00

2002 Fleer Maximum Americas Game Four Score

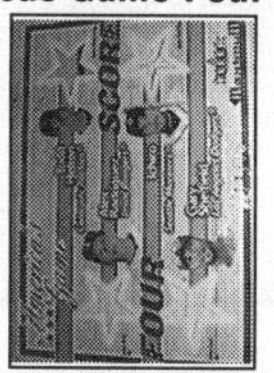

Randomly inserted into packs, these two cards feature four players on the card along with a memorabilia piece related to that player. These cards have a stated print run of 15 copies and due to market scarcity, no pricing is provided.

Nm-Mt Ex-Mt
FS1 Mike Piazza Pants
Derek Jeter Jsy
Ichiro Suzuki Base
Albert Pujols Jsy
FS2 Todd Helton Jsy
Alex Rodriguez Bat
Ichiro Suzuki Base
Gary Sheffield Bat

2002 Fleer Maximum Americas Game Stars and Stripes

Randomly inserted into packs, these nine cards feature both a jersey swatch as well as a bat chip on the card. These cards are serial numbered to 25 and no pricing is provided due to market scarcity.

Nm-Mt Ex-Mt
SS1 Mike Piazza
SS2 Chipper Jones
SS3 Barry Bonds
SS4 Luis Gonzalez
SS5 Ivan Rodriguez
SS6 Jason Giambi
SS7 Randy Johnson
SS8 Edgar Martinez
SS9 Todd Helton

2002 Fleer Maximum Coverage

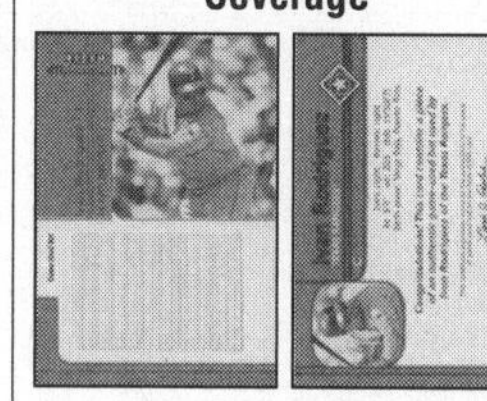

Randomly inserted into packs these cards provide a large swatch of a game-used jersey or bat from the featured player. These cards have a stated print run of 100 copies. An exchange card with a deadline of March 1st, 2003 was seeded into packs for the Barry Bonds bat card.

	Nm-Mt	Ex-Mt
1 Roberto Alomar Bat	40.00	12.00
2 Jeff Bagwell Jsy	25.00	7.50
3 Barry Bonds Bat	80.00	24.00
4 Jose Canseco Bat	40.00	12.00
5 J.D. Drew Bat		
6 Jim Edmonds Bat	25.00	7.50
7 Jason Giambi Bat	40.00	12.00
8 Juan Gonzalez Bat		
9 Luis Gonzalez Jsy	25.00	7.50
10 Todd Helton Jsy	25.00	7.50
11 Randy Johnson Jsy	40.00	12.00
12 Chipper Jones Bat	40.00	12.00
13 Greg Maddux Jsy	50.00	15.00
14 Pedro Martinez Jsy	40.00	12.00
15 Rafael Palmeiro Pants		
16 Albert Pujols Jsy	80.00	24.00
17 Manny Ramirez Bat	25.00	7.50
18 Alex Rodriguez Bat		
19 Ivan Rodriguez Bat	40.00	12.00
20 Kazuhiro Sasaki Jsy		
21 Gary Sheffield Bat	25.00	7.50
22 Tsuyoshi Shinjo Bat	25.00	7.50

2002 Fleer Maximum Coverage Autographs

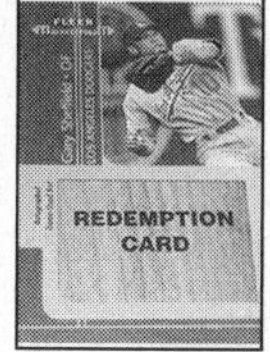

Exchange cards witrh a redemption deadline of March 1st, 2003 were andomly inserted into packs for upgraded parallels (whereby the player's signed the cards) of the Coverage insert set. Thes actual cards mailed out to collectors from Fleer are autographed and have varying stated print runs which we have noted in our checklist.

Nm-Mt Ex-Mt
1 Barry Bonds Pants/50
2 J.D. Drew Bat/100
3 Jim Edmonds Bat/100
4 Drew Henson Bat/100
5 Chipper Jones Bat/50
6 Albert Pujols Jsy/100
7 Gary Sheffield Bat/100

2002 Fleer Maximum Derek Jeter Legacy Collection

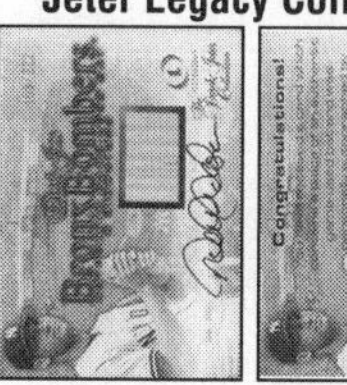

These four card feature Derek Jeter memorabilia items. The memorabilia cards were inserted at stated odds of one in 236 while the auto cards were randomly inserted into packs.

	Nm-Mt	Ex-Mt
1 D.Jeter Bronx Bat	50.00	15.00
2 D.Jeter Bronx Bat AU/222	200.00	60.00
3 D.Jeter Columbus Jsy	50.00	15.00
4 D.Jeter Columbus Jsy AU	250.00	75.00

2002 Fleer Maximum Power

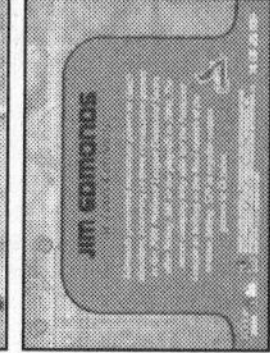

Inserted into retail packs at stated odds of one in 20, these 25 cards feature heavy hitters who produce for their teams.

	Nm-Mt	Ex-Mt
COMPLETE SET (25)	100.00	30.00
1 Luis Gonzalez	2.00	.60
2 Jimmy Rollins	2.00	.60
3 Larry Walker	3.00	.90
4 Frank Thomas	5.00	1.50
5 Manny Ramirez	2.00	.60
6 Barry Bonds	12.00	3.60
7 Jim Thome	5.00	1.50
8 Tsuyoshi Shinjo	2.00	.60
9 Bernie Williams	3.00	.90
10 Chipper Jones	5.00	1.50
11 Shawn Green	2.00	.60
12 Drew Henson	2.00	.60
13 Juan Gonzalez	5.00	1.50
14 Jim Edmonds	2.00	.60
15 Moises Alou	2.00	.60
16 Roberto Alomar	5.00	1.50
17 Jose Canseco	5.00	1.50
18 Ivan Rodriguez	5.00	1.50
19 Barry Larkin	5.00	1.50
20 Mike Piazza	8.00	2.40
21 Gary Sheffield	2.00	.60
22 J.D. Drew	2.00	.60
23 Alex Rodriguez	8.00	2.40
24 Jason Giambi	5.00	1.50
25 Todd Helton	3.00	.90

2002 Fleer Maximum Power Bat

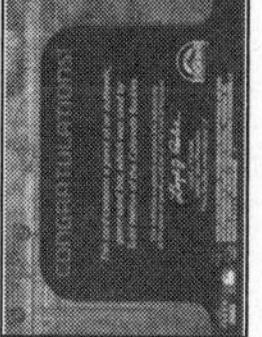

Inserted into packs at stated odds of one in 24 hobby and one in 72 retail, these 23 cards feature bat chips of these leading hitters. A few players were produced in lesser quantites and we have notated those quantities in our checklist. In addition, a few players had their distribution evenly split between retail and hobby packs and those players are noted in our checklist with asterisks.

Nm-Mt Ex-Mt
GOLD RANDOM INSERTS IN PACKS ..
GOLD PRINT RUN 25 SERIAL #'d SETS
GOLD NO PRICING DUE TO SCARCITY
1 Roberto Alomar 15.00 4.50
2 Moises Alou SP/150
3 Barry Bonds * 25.00 7.50
4 Jose Canseco 15.00 4.50
5 J.D. Drew SP/200 10.00 3.00
6 Jim Edmonds 10.00 3.00
7 Jason Giambi 15.00 4.50
8 Juan Gonzalez 15.00 4.50
9 Luis Gonzalez 10.00 3.00
10 Shawn Green 10.00 3.00
11 Todd Helton 15.00 4.50
12 Chipper Jones * 15.00 4.50
13 Barry Larkin SP/50
14 Mike Piazza * 15.00 4.50
15 Manny Ramirez 10.00 3.00
16 Alex Rodriguez * 15.00 4.50
17 Ivan Rodriguez 15.00 4.50
18 Gary Sheffield 10.00 3.00
19 Tsuyoshi Shinjo 10.00 3.00
20 Frank Thomas 15.00 4.50
21 Jim Thome 15.00 4.50
22 Larry Walker 15.00 4.50
23 Bernie Williams SP/175

1999 Fleer Mystique

This 160-card set features color action player photos with a palette name box and shadowed "Mystique" in the background. The cards were issued in four-card packs with an SRP of $4.99 per pack. The backs carry player statistics. The set included the following two subsets: Rookies (101-150) serially numbered to 2,999, and Stars (151-160) serially numbered to 2,500. The cards with "SP" following the player's name in our checklist were distributed only as peel offs. Peel off cards were seeded at a rate of one per pack. Collectors had to peel off the sparkling foil coating off the front and back of the card to reveal what it was (hence the name "Mystique"). Peel off cards were either short printed super stars from the basic set (1-100), a serial numbered Prospect or Star card (101-160) or an insert card. A promo card featuring J.D. Drew was distributed to dealers and hobby media several weeks prior to the product's release. This Drew card is easily identified by the text "PROMOTIONAL SAMPLE" running diagonally across the front and back of the card. This set contains Pat Burrell's "Best" Rookie Card. The Phillies player had 25 Rookie Cards issued in 1999 and the Fleer Mystique was the only one that was serial numbered. That, in large part, boosted this card to the top of many collectors wantlists after the product's release.

Nm-Mt Ex-Mt
COMPLETE SET (160) 250.00 75.00
COMP.SHORT SET (100) 40.00 12.00
COMMON CARD (1-100) .40 .12
COMMON SP (1-100) 1.00 .30
COMMON (101-150) 5.00 1.50
COMMON (151-160) 5.00 1.50
1 Ken Griffey Jr. SP 2.50 .75
2 Livan Hernandez .40 .12
3 Jeff Kent .40 .12
4 Brian Jordan .40 .12
5 Kevin Young .40 .12
6 Vinny Castilla .40 .12
7 Orlando Hernandez SP 1.00 .30
8 Bobby Abreu .40 .12
9 Vladimir Guerrero SP 1.50 .45
10 Chuck Knoblauch .40 .12
11 Nomar Garciaparra SP 2.50 .75
12 Jeff Bagwell .60 .18
13 Todd Walker .40 .12
14 Johnny Damon .40 .12
15 Mike Caruso .40 .12
16 Cliff Floyd .40 .12
17 Andy Pettitte .60 .18
18 Cal Ripken SP 5.00 1.50
19 Brian Giles .40 .12
20 Robin Ventura .40 .12
21 Alex Gonzalez .40 .12
22 Randy Johnson 1.00 .30
23 Raul Mondesi .40 .12
24 Ken Caminiti .40 .12
25 Tom Glavine .60 .18
26 Derek Jeter SP 4.00 1.20
27 Carlos Delgado .40 .12
28 Adrian Beltre .40 .12
29 Tino Martinez .60 .18
30 Todd Helton .60 .18
31 Juan Gonzalez SP 1.50 .45
32 Henry Rodriguez .40 .12
33 Jim Thome 1.00 .30
34 Paul O'Neill .60 .18
35 Scott Rolen SP 1.00 .30
36 Rafael Palmeiro .60 .18
37 Will Clark 1.00 .30
38 Todd Hundley .40 .12
39 Andruw Jones SP 1.00 .30
40 Rolando Arrojo .40 .12
41 Barry Larkin 1.00 .30
42 Tim Salmon .60 .18
43 Rondell White .40 .12
44 Curt Schilling .60 .18
45 Chipper Jones SP 1.50 .45
46 Jeromy Burnitz .40 .12
47 Mo Vaughn .40 .12
48 Tony Clark .40 .12
49 Fernando Tatis .40 .12
50 Dmitri Young .40 .12
51 Wade Boggs .60 .18
52 Rickey Henderson 1.00 .30
53 Manny Ramirez SP 1.00 .30
54 Edgar Martinez .60 .18
55 Jason Giambi 1.00 .30
56 Jason Kendall .40 .12
57 Eric Karros .40 .12
58 Jose Canseco SP 1.50 .45
59 Shawn Green .40 .12
60 Ellis Burks .40 .12
61 Derek Bell .40 .12
62 Shannon Stewart .40 .12
63 Roger Clemens SP 3.00 .90
64 Sean Casey SP 1.00 .30
65 Jose Offerman .40 .12
66 Sammy Sosa SP 2.50 .75
67 Frank Thomas SP 1.50 .45
68 Tony Gwynn SP 1.50 .45
69 Roberto Alomar 1.00 .30
70 Mark McGwire SP 4.00 1.20
71 Troy Glaus .60 .18
72 Ray Durham .40 .12
73 Jeff Cirillo .40 .12
74 Alex Rodriguez SP 2.50 .75
75 Jose Cruz Jr. .40 .12
76 Juan Encarnacion .40 .12
77 Mark Grace .60 .18
78 Barry Bonds SP 4.00 1.20
79 Ivan Rodriguez SP 1.50 .45
80 Greg Vaughn .40 .12
81 Greg Maddux SP 2.50 .75
82 Albert Belle .40 .12
83 John Olerud .40 .12
84 Kenny Lofton .40 .12
85 Bernie Williams .60 .18
86 Matt Williams .40 .12
87 Ray Lankford .40 .12
88 Darin Erstad .40 .12
89 Ben Grieve .40 .12
90 Craig Biggio .60 .18
91 Dean Palmer .40 .12
92 Reggie Sanders .40 .12
93 Dante Bichette .40 .12
94 Pedro Martinez SP 1.50 .45
95 Larry Walker .60 .18
96 David Wells .40 .12
97 Travis Lee SP 1.00 .30
98 Mike Piazza SP 2.50 .75
99 Mike Mussina 1.00 .30
100 Kevin Brown .60 .18
101 Ruben Mateo PROS 5.00 1.50
102 Rob. Ramirez RC 5.00 1.50
103 Glen Barker PROS RC 5.00 1.50
104 C. Bellinger PROS RC 5.00 1.50
105 Carlos Guillen PROS 5.00 1.50
106 S.Schoeneweis PROS 5.00 1.50
107 C.Gubanich PROS RC 5.00 1.50
108 S.Williamson PROS 5.00 1.50
109 E.Guzman PROS RC 5.00 1.50
110 A.J. Burnett PROS RC 10.00 3.00
111 Jeremy Giambi PROS 5.00 1.50
112 Trot Nixon PROS 8.00 2.40
113 J.D. Drew PROS 5.00 1.50
114 Roy Halladay PROS 5.00 1.50
115 J.Macias PROS RC 5.00 1.50
116 Corey Koskie PROS 5.00 1.50
117 Ryan Rupe PROS RC 5.00 1.50
118 S.Hunter PROS RC 5.00 1.50
119 Rob Fick PROS 5.00 1.50
120 M.Christensen PROS 5.00 1.50
121 Carlos Febles PROS 5.00 1.50
122 Gabe Kapler PROS 5.00 1.50
123 Jeff Liefer PROS 5.00 1.50
124 Warren Morris PROS 5.00 1.50
125 Chris Pritchett PROS 5.00 1.50
126 Torii Hunter PROS 5.00 1.50
127 Armando Rios PROS 5.00 1.50
128 Ricky Ledee PROS 5.00 1.50
129 K.Dransfeldt RC 5.00 1.50
130 J.Zimmerman RC 5.00 1.50
131 Eric Chavez PROS 5.00 1.50
132 F.Garcia PROS RC 10.00 3.00
133 Jose Jimenez PROS 5.00 1.50
134 Pat Burrell PROS RC 50.00 15.00
135 J.McEwing PROS RC 5.00 1.50
136 Kris Benson PROS 5.00 1.50
137 Joe Mays PROS RC 8.00 2.40
138 R.Roque PROS RC 5.00 1.50
139 C.Guzman PROS 5.00 1.50
140 Michael Barrett PROS 5.00 1.50
141 D.Mientkiewicz RC 12.00 3.60
142 Jeff Weaver PROS RC 8.00 2.40
143 Mike Lowell PROS 5.00 1.50
144 J.Phillips PROS RC 5.00 1.50
145 M.Anderson PROS 5.00 1.50
146 B.Hinchliffe PROS RC 5.00 1.50
147 Matt Clement PROS 5.00 1.50
148 Terrence Long PROS 5.00 1.50
149 Carlos Beltran PROS 5.00 1.50
150 Preston Wilson PROS 5.00 1.50
151 Ken Griffey Jr. STAR 8.00 2.40
152 Mark McGwire STAR 12.00 3.60
153 Sammy Sosa STAR 8.00 2.40
154 Mike Piazza STAR 8.00 2.40
155 Alex Rodriguez STAR 8.00 2.40
156 N.Garciaparra STAR 8.00 2.40
157 Cal Ripken STAR 15.00 4.50
158 Greg Maddux STAR 8.00 2.40
159 Derek Jeter STAR 12.00 3.60
160 Juan Gonzalez STAR 5.00 1.50
P113 J.D. Drew Promo 1.00 .30

1999 Fleer Mystique Gold

Randomly inserted into packs at the rate of one in eight, this 100-card set is a partial parallel gold version of the base set (cards 1-100).

Nm-Mt Ex-Mt
*GOLD: 1.5X TO 4X BASIC CARDS
*GOLD: 1X TO 2.5X BASIC SP's

1999 Fleer Mystique Destiny

Randomly inserted into packs, this ten-card set features color photos of top young players printed on silver holofoil cards and sequentially numbered to 999.

Nm-Mt Ex-Mt
COMPLETE SET (10) 120.00 36.00
1 Tony Gwynn 12.00 3.60
2 Juan Gonzalez 12.00 3.60
3 Scott Rolen 8.00 2.40

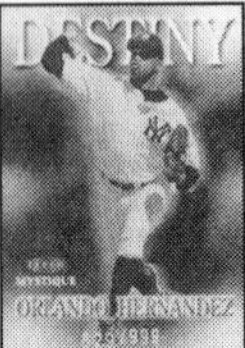
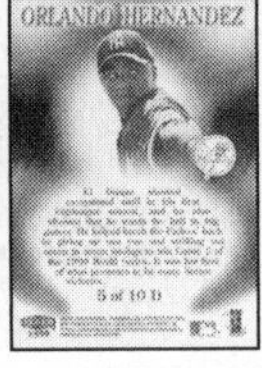

4 Nomar Garciaparra 20.00 6.00
5 Orlando Hernandez 8.00 2.40
6 Andruw Jones 8.00 2.40
7 Vladimir Guerrero 12.00 3.60
8 Darin Erstad 3.00 .90
9 Manny Ramirez 8.00 2.40
10 Roger Clemens 25.00 7.50

1999 Fleer Mystique Established

Randomly inserted into packs, this 10-card set features color action photos of veteran stars printed on plastic, highlighted with silver and red holofoil, and covered with opaque blue film. The cards are sequentially numbered on the back to 100.

Nm-Mt Ex-Mt
COMPLETE SET (10) 500.00 150.00
1 Ken Griffey Jr. 40.00 12.00
2 Derek Jeter 60.00 18.00
3 Chipper Jones 25.00 7.50
4 Greg Maddux 40.00 12.00
5 Mark McGwire 60.00 18.00
6 Mike Piazza 40.00 12.00
7 Cal Ripken 80.00 24.00
8 Alex Rodriguez 40.00 12.00
9 Sammy Sosa 40.00 12.00
10 Frank Thomas 25.00 7.50

1999 Fleer Mystique Feel the Game

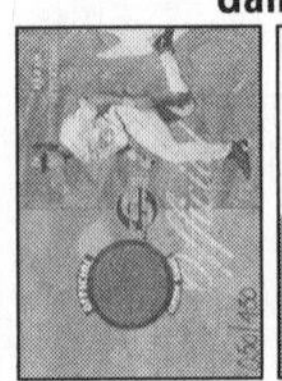

Randomly inserted into packs, this seven-card set features pieces of actual game-used equipment by top players. Each card is serial numbered by hand on the front. The print run for each card is listed after the player's name in the checklist below.

Nm-Mt Ex-Mt
1 Adrian Beltre 15.00 4.50
Shoe/430
2 J.D.Drew 15.00 4.50
Jersey/450
3 Juan Gonzalez 25.00 7.50
Batting Glove/415
4 Tony Gwynn 25.00 7.50
Jersey/435
5 Kevin Millwood 15.00 4.50
Jersey/435
6 Alex Rodriguez 40.00 12.00
Batting Glove/345
7 Frank Thomas 25.00 7.50
Jersey/450

1999 Fleer Mystique Fresh Ink

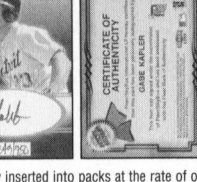

Randomly inserted into packs at the rate of one in 48, this 26-card set features autographed color action photos of top rookies and veterans. Each autograph is authenticated with the Fleer Seal of Authenticity and a certificate printed on the back of each card. The cards are unnumbered and checklisted in alphabetical order. The print run follows the player's name in our checklist.

Nm-Mt Ex-Mt
1 Roberto Alomar/500 40.00 12.00
2 Michael Barrett/1000 10.00 3.00
3 Kris Benson/500 10.00 3.00
4 Micah Bowie/1000 10.00 3.00
5 A.J. Burnett/1000 15.00 4.50
6 Pat Burrell/500 40.00 12.00
7 Ken Caminiti/250 20.00 6.00
8 Jose Canseco/250 50.00 15.00
9 Sean Casey/1000 15.00 4.50
10 Edgard Clemente/1000 10.00 3.00
11 Bartolo Colon/500 15.00 4.50
12 J.D. Drew/400 15.00 4.50
13 Juan Encarnacion/1000 10.00 3.00
14 Troy Glaus/400 25.00 7.50
15 Juan Gonzalez/250 80.00 24.00
16 Shawn Green/250 30.00 9.00
17 Tony Gwynn/250 50.00 15.00
18 Chipper Jones/500 50.00 15.00
19 Gabe Kapler/750 10.00 3.00
20 Barry Larkin/250 50.00 15.00
21 Doug Mientkiewicz/500 15.00 4.50
22 Alex Rodriguez/200 120.00 36.00
23 Scott Rolen/140 50.00 15.00
24 Fernando Tatis/750 10.00 3.00
25 Robin Ventura/500 15.00 4.50
26 Todd Walker/1000 15.00 4.50

1999 Fleer Mystique Prophetic

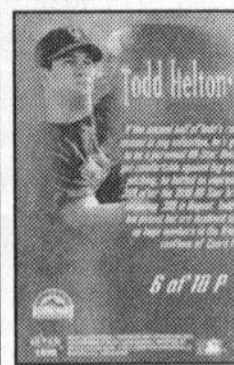

Randomly inserted into packs, this 10-card set features color photos of top rookies and other young players printed with silver/blue holofoil highlights, gold foil stamping, and covered with opaque blue film. The cards are serially numbered on back to 1999. An early numbered card of Pat Burrell is in this set.

Nm-Mt Ex-Mt
COMPLETE SET (10) 50.00 15.00
1 Eric Chavez 3.00 .90
2 J.D. Drew 3.00 .90
3 A.J. Burnett 5.00 1.50
4 Ben Grieve 3.00 .90
5 Gabe Kapler 3.00 .90
6 Todd Helton 3.00 .90
7 Troy Glaus 3.00 .90
8 Travis Lee 3.00 .90
9 Pat Burrell 12.00 3.60
10 Kerry Wood 5.00 1.50

2000 Fleer Mystique

The 2000 Fleer Mystique product was released in August,2000 as a 175-card set that featured 125 veteran players (1-125) and 50 prospect cards (126-175) that were individually serial numbered to 2000. Each pack contained five cards and carried a suggested retail price of $4.99. Notable Rookie Cards include Kasahiro Sasaki. Please note that two Dave Winfield exchange cards were inserted into the product (a signed helmet exchange card numbered to 40, and a signed baseball exchange card numbered to 20. The exchange deadline for both cards was July 7th, 2001. Also note that a Cal Ripken promo card was sent to hobby dealers and members of the media to promote the release of the 2000 Fleer Mystique baseball product. This card is identical to card number 54 from the 2000 Fleer Mystique base set, except for the fact that this card has "Promotional Sample" stamped across the back of the card.

Nm-Mt Ex-Mt
COMP.SET w/o SP's (125) 40.00 12.00
COMMON CARD (1-125) .50 .15
COMMON (126-175) 5.00 1.50
1 Derek Jeter 3.00 .90
2 David Justice .50 .15
3 Kevin Brown .75 .23
4 Jason Giambi 1.25 .35
5 Jose Canseco 1.25 .35
6 Mark Grace .75 .23
7 Hideo Nomo 1.25 .35
8 Edgardo Alfonzo .50 .15
9 Barry Bonds 3.00 .90
10 Pedro Martinez 1.25 .35
11 Juan Gonzalez 1.25 .35
12 Vladimir Guerrero 1.25 .35
13 Chuck Finley .50 .15
14 Brian Jordan .50 .15
15 Richie Sexson .50 .15
16 Chan Ho Park .50 .15
17 Tim Hudson .75 .23
18 Fred McGriff .75 .23
19 Darin Erstad .50 .15
20 Chris Singleton .50 .15
21 Jeff Bagwell .75 .23
22 David Cone .50 .15
23 Edgar Martinez .75 .23
24 Greg Maddux 2.00 .60
25 Jim Thome 1.25 .35
26 Eric Karros .50 .15
27 Bob Abreu .50 .15
28 Greg Vaughn .50 .15
29 Kevin Millwood .50 .15
30 Omar Vizquel .50 .15
31 Marquis Grissom .50 .15
32 Mike Lieberthal .50 .15
33 Gabe Kapler .50 .15
34 Brady Anderson .50 .15
35 Jeff Cirillo .50 .15
36 Geoff Jenkins .50 .15
37 Scott Rolen .75 .23
38 Rafael Palmeiro .75 .23
39 Randy Johnson 1.25 .35
40 Barry Larkin 1.25 .35
41 Johnny Damon .50 .15
42 Andy Pettitte .75 .23
43 Mark McGwire 3.00 .90
44 Albert Belle .50 .15
45 Derrick Gibson .50 .15
46 Corey Koskie .50 .15
47 Curt Schilling .75 .23
48 Ivan Rodriguez 1.25 .35
49 Mike Mussina 1.25 .35
50 Todd Helton .75 .23
51 Matt Lawton .50 .15
52 Jason Kendall .50 .15
53 Kenny Rogers .50 .15
54 Cal Ripken 4.00 1.20
55 Larry Walker .75 .23
56 Eric Milton .50 .15
57 Warren Morris .50 .15
58 Carlos Delgado .50 .15
59 Kerry Wood 1.25 .35
60 Cliff Floyd .50 .15
61 Mike Piazza 2.00 .60
62 Jeff Kent .50 .15
63 Sammy Sosa 2.00 .60
64 Alex Fernandez .50 .15
65 Mike Hampton .50 .15
66 Livan Hernandez .50 .15
67 Matt Williams .50 .15
68 Roberto Alomar 1.25 .35
69 Jermaine Dye .50 .15
70 Bernie Williams .75 .23
71 Edgar Martinez .75 .23
72 Tom Glavine .75 .23
73 Bartolo Colon .50 .15
74 Jason Varitek .50 .15
75 Eric Chavez .50 .15
76 Fernando Tatis .50 .15
77 Adrian Beltre .50 .15
78 Paul Konerko .50 .15
79 Mike Lowell .50 .15
80 Robin Ventura .50 .15
81 Russ Ortiz .50 .15
82 Troy Glaus .75 .23
83 Frank Thomas 1.25 .35
84 Craig Biggio .75 .23
85 Orlando Hernandez .50 .15
86 John Olerud .50 .15
87 Chipper Jones 1.25 .35
88 Manny Ramirez .50 .15
89 Shawn Green .50 .15
90 Ben Grieve .50 .15
91 Vinny Castilla .50 .15
92 Tim Salmon .75 .23
93 Dante Bichette .50 .15
94 Ken Caminiti .50 .15
95 Andruw Jones .50 .15
96 Alex Rodriguez 2.00 .60
97 Erubiel Durazo .50 .15
98 Sean Casey .50 .15
99 Carlos Beltran .50 .15
100 Paul O'Neill .75 .23
101 Ray Lankford .50 .15
102 Troy O'Leary .50 .15
103 Bobby Higginson .50 .15
104 Rondell White .50 .15
105 Tony Gwynn 1.50 .45
106 Jim Edmonds .50 .15
107 Magglio Ordonez .50 .15
108 Preston Wilson .50 .15
109 Roger Clemens 2.50 .75
110 Ken Griffey Jr. 2.50 .75
111 Nomar Garciaparra 2.00 .60
112 Juan Encarnacion .50 .15
113 Michael Barrett .50 .15
114 Matt Clement .50 .15
115 David Wells .50 .15
116 Mo Vaughn .50 .15
117 Mike Cameron .50 .15
118 Jose Lima .50 .15
119 Tino Martinez .75 .23
120 J.D. Drew .50 .15
121 Carl Everett .50 .15
122 Tony Clark .50 .15
123 Brad Radke .50 .15
124 Kevin Young .50 .15
125 Raul Mondesi .50 .15
126 Cole Liniak PROS 5.00 1.50
127 A.Soriano PROS 8.00 2.40
128 Lance Berkman PROS 5.00 1.50
129 D.Young PROS RC 5.00 1.50
130 F.Cordero PROS 5.00 1.50
131 Robert Fick PROS 5.00 1.50
132 Matt LeCroy PROS 5.00 1.50
133 Adam Piatt PROS 5.00 1.50
134 D.Turnbow PROS RC 5.00 1.50
135 Mark Quinn PROS 5.00 1.50
136 Kip Wells PROS 5.00 1.50
137 Rob Bell PROS 5.00 1.50
138 Brad Penny PROS 5.00 1.50
139 Pat Burrell PROS 8.00 2.40
140 Danys Baez PROS RC 8.00 2.40
141 C.Hermansen PROS 5.00 1.50
142 S.Lomasney PROS 5.00 1.50
143 Peter Bergeron PROS 5.00 1.50
144 J.Anderson PROS 5.00 1.50
145 Mike Darr PROS 5.00 1.50
146 Jacob Cruz PROS 5.00 1.50
147 K.Sasaki PROS RC 10.00 3.00
148 Ben Petrick PROS 5.00 1.50
149 Rick Ankiel PROS 5.00 1.50
150 A.McNeal PROS RC 5.00 1.50
151 Octavio Dotel PROS 5.00 1.50
152 Juan Pena PROS 5.00 1.50
153 Nick Johnson PROS 5.00 1.50
154 Wilton Veras PROS 5.00 1.50
155 Wily Pena PROS 5.00 1.50
156 Mark Mulder PROS 8.00 2.40
157 Daryle Ward PROS 5.00 1.50
158 C.Durbin PROS RC 5.00 1.50
159 Angel Pena PROS 5.00 1.50
160 DeWayne Wise PROS 5.00 1.50
161 Tarrik Brock PROS 5.00 1.50
162 Marcus Jensen PROS 5.00 1.50
163 Kevin Barker PROS 5.00 1.50
164 B.J. Ryan PROS 5.00 1.50
165 Cesar King PROS 5.00 1.50
166 Geoff Blum PROS 5.00 1.50
167 Ruben Mateo PROS 5.00 1.50
168 Ramon Ortiz PROS 5.00 1.50
169 Eric Munson PROS 5.00 1.50
170 Josh Beckett PROS 10.00 3.00
171 Rafael Furcal PROS 5.00 1.50

172 Matt Riley PROS 5.00 1.50
173 J.Santana PROS RC 20.00 6.00
174 Mark Johnson PROS 5.00 1.50
175 Adam Kennedy PROS 5.00 1.50
P54 Cal Ripken PROMO 2.50 .75
DW1 D.Winfield Ball/20
DW2 Dave Winfield 100.00 30.00
Helmet/40

2000 Fleer Mystique Gold

Randomly inserted into packs at one in 20, this 175-card set is a complete parallel of the 2000 Fleer Mystique base set. Each card in the set features gold foil instead of the silver foil found on the base set.

Nm-Mt Ex-Mt
*STARS 1-125: 5X TO 12X BASIC CARDS
*PROSPECTS 126-175: .5X TO 1.2X BASIC

2000 Fleer Mystique Diamond Dominators

Randomly inserted into packs at one in five, this 10-card set features players that dominate their opponents on the field. Card backs carry a "DD" prefix.

Nm-Mt Ex-Mt
COMPLETE SET (10) 20.00 6.00
DD1 Manny Ramirez .40 .12
DD2 Pedro Martinez 1.00 .30
DD3 Sean Casey .40 .12
DD4 Vladimir Guerrero 1.00 .30
DD5 Sammy Sosa 1.50 .45
DD6 Nomar Garciaparra 1.50 .45
DD7 Mark McGwire 2.50 .75
DD8 Ken Griffey Jr. 2.00 .60
DD9 Derek Jeter 2.50 .75
DD10 Alex Rodriguez 1.50 .45

2000 Fleer Mystique Feel the Game

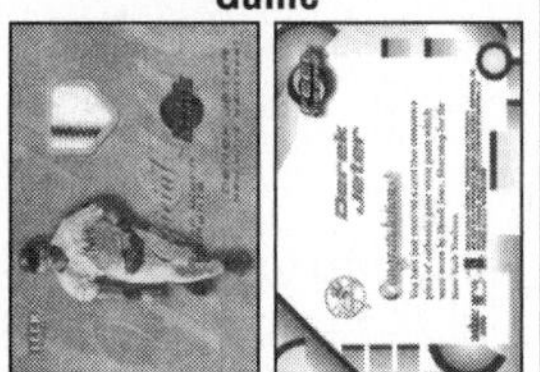

Randomly inserted into packs at one in 120, this 14-card set features game-worn jersey cards and game-used bat cards of some of the best players in major league baseball. The cards are unnumbered and listed below in alphabetical order by each player's last name in our checklist.

Nm-Mt Ex-Mt
1 Michael Barrett Bat 8.00 2.40
2 Carlos Beltran Bat 10.00 3.00
3 Barry Bonds Bat 40.00 12.00
4 Pat Burrell Bat 15.00 4.50
5 Shawn Green Bat 10.00 3.00
6 Vladimir Guerrero Bat 15.00 4.50
7 Tony Gwynn Jsy 15.00 4.50
8 Derek Jeter Pants 40.00 12.00
9 Chipper Jones Jsy 15.00 4.50
10 Rafael Palmeiro Bat 15.00 4.50
11 Cal Ripken Jsy 40.00 12.00
12 Alex Rodriguez Bat 25.00 7.50
13 Alex Rodriguez Jsy 25.00 7.50
14 Frank Thomas Bat 15.00 4.50

2000 Fleer Mystique Fresh Ink

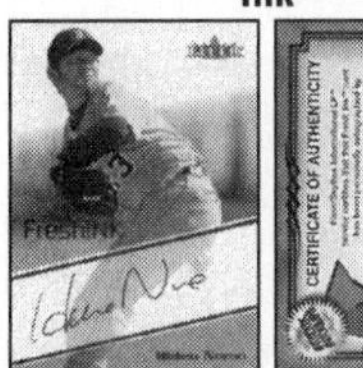
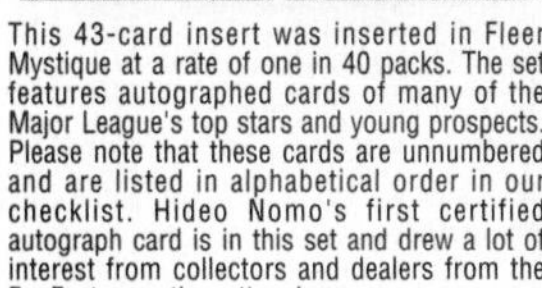

This 43-card insert was inserted in Fleer Mystique at a rate of one in 40 packs. The set features autographed cards of many of the Major League's top stars and young prospects. Please note that these cards are unnumbered and are listed in alphabetical order in our checklist. Hideo Nomo's first certified autograph card is in this set and drew a lot of interest from collectors and dealers from the Far East upon the set's release.

Nm-Mt Ex-Mt
1 Chad Allen 10.00 3.00
2 Glen Barker 10.00 3.00
3 Michael Barrett 10.00 3.00
4 Josh Beckett 40.00 12.00
5 Lance Berkman SP 40.00 12.00
6 Kent Bottenfield 10.00 3.00
7 Milton Bradley 15.00 4.50
8 Orlando Cabrera 10.00 3.00
9 Sean Casey 15.00 4.50
10 Roger Cedeno 10.00 3.00
11 Will Clark 40.00 12.00
12 Russ Davis 10.00 3.00
13 Carlos Delgado 15.00 4.50
14 Einar Diaz 10.00 3.00
15 J.D. Drew 15.00 4.50
16 Damion Easley 10.00 3.00
17 Carlos Febles 10.00 3.00
18 Doug Glanville 10.00 3.00
19 Alex Gonzalez 10.00 3.00
20 Tony Gwynn 50.00 15.00
21 Mike Hampton 15.00 4.50
22 Bobby Howry 10.00 3.00
23 John Jaha 10.00 3.00
24 Nick Johnson 15.00 4.50
25 Andruw Jones 25.00 7.50
26 Adam Kennedy 15.00 4.50
27 Mike Lieberthal 15.00 4.50
28 Jose Macias 10.00 3.00
29 Raul Mondesi 15.00 4.50
30 Heath Murray 10.00 3.00
31 Mike Mussina 40.00 12.00
32 Hideo Nomo 500.00 150.00
33 Magglio Ordonez 15.00 4.50
34 Eric Owens 10.00 3.00
35 Adam Piatt 10.00 3.00
36 Cal Ripken 120.00 36.00
37 Tim Salmon 25.00 7.50
38 Chris Singleton 10.00 3.00
39 J.T. Snow 15.00 4.50
40 Mike Sweeney 15.00 4.50
41 Wilton Veras 10.00 3.00
42 Jose Vidro 15.00 4.50
43 Rondell White 15.00 4.50
44 Jaret Wright 10.00 3.00

2000 Fleer Mystique High Praise

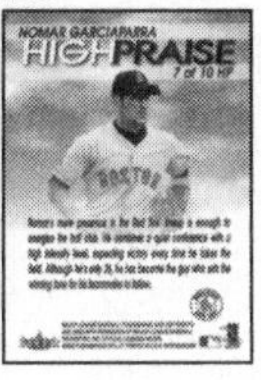

Randomly inserted into packs at one in 20, this 10-card set features players that are praised when they take the field. Card backs carry a "HP" prefix.

Nm-Mt Ex-Mt
COMPLETE SET (10) 60.00 18.00
HP1 Mark McGwire 6.00 1.80
HP2 Ken Griffey Jr. 5.00 1.50
HP3 Alex Rodriguez 4.00 1.20
HP4 Derek Jeter 6.00 1.80
HP5 Sammy Sosa 4.00 1.20
HP6 Mike Piazza 4.00 1.20
HP7 Nomar Garciaparra 4.00 1.20
HP8 Cal Ripken 8.00 2.40
HP9 Tony Gwynn 3.00 .90
HP10 Shawn Green 1.00 .30

2000 Fleer Mystique Rookie I.P.O.

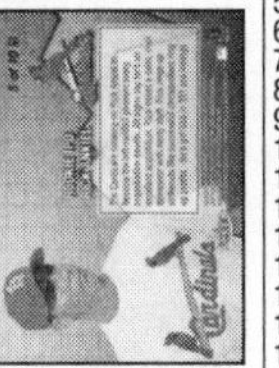

Randomly inserted into packs at one in 10, this 10-card set features top prospects/rookies of the 2000 season. Card backs carry a "RI" prefix.

Nm-Mt Ex-Mt
COMPLETE SET (10) 15.00 4.50
RI1 Josh Beckett 2.50 .75
RI2 Eric Munson 1.00 .30
RI3 Pat Burrell 1.25 .35
RI4 Alfonso Soriano 2.00 .60
RI5 Rick Ankiel 1.00 .30
RI6 Ruben Mateo 1.00 .30
RI7 Mark Quinn 1.00 .30
RI8 Kip Wells 1.00 .30
RI9 Ben Petrick 1.00 .30
RI10 Nick Johnson 1.00 .30

2000 Fleer Mystique Seismic Activity

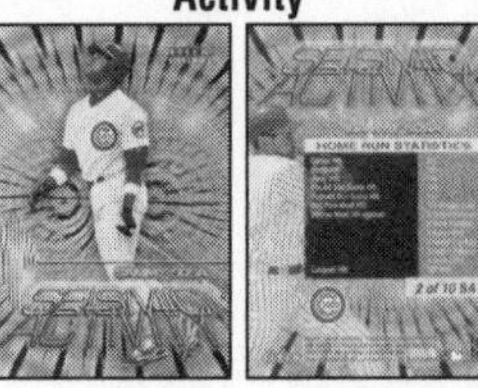

Randomly inserted into packs at one in 40, this 10-card set features players that register seismic activity everytime they swing the bat. Card backs carry a "SA" prefix.

Nm-Mt Ex-Mt
COMPLETE SET (10) 80.00 24.00
*RICHTER 100: 1.5X TO 4X BASIC SEISMIC
RICHTER 100 RANDOM INSERTS IN PACKS
RICHTER 100 PRINT RUN 100 SERIAL #'d SETS
SA1 Ken Griffey Jr. 10.00 3.00
SA2 Sammy Sosa 8.00 2.40
SA3 Derek Jeter 12.00 3.60
SA4 Mark McGwire 12.00 3.60
SA5 Manny Ramirez 2.00 .60
SA6 Mike Piazza 8.00 2.40
SA7 Vladimir Guerrero 5.00 1.50
SA8 Chipper Jones 5.00 1.50
SA9 Alex Rodriguez 8.00 2.40
SA10 Jeff Bagwell 3.00 .90

2000 Fleer Mystique Supernaturals

Randomly inserted into packs at one in 16, this 10-card set features players that seem to have supernatural skills on the playing field. Card backs carry a "S" prefix.

Nm-Mt Ex-Mt
COMPLETE SET (10) 20.00 6.00
S1 Alex Rodriguez 2.00 .60
S2 Chipper Jones 1.25 .35
S3 Derek Jeter 3.00 .90
S4 Ivan Rodriguez 1.25 .35
S5 Ken Griffey Jr. 2.50 .75
S6 Mark McGwire 3.00 .90
S7 Mike Piazza 2.00 .60
S8 Nomar Garciaparra 2.00 .60
S9 Sammy Sosa 2.00 .60
S10 Vladimir Guerrero 1.25 .35

2003 Fleer Mystique

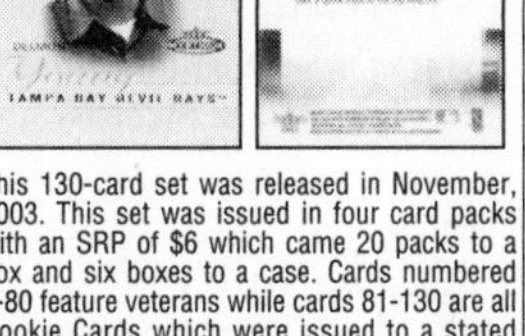

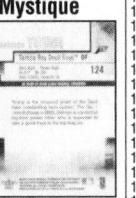

This 130-card set was released in November, 2003. This set was issued in four card packs with an SRP of $6 which came 20 packs to a box and six boxes to a case. Cards numbered 1-80 feature veterans while cards 81-130 are all Rookie Cards which were issued to a stated print run of 699 serial numbered sets. Those last 50 cards were inserted into packs at a stated rate of one in five.

MINT NRMT
COMP.SET w/o SP's (80) 40.00 18.00
COMMON CARD (1-80) .50 .23
COMMON CARD (81-130) 5.00 2.20
1 Alex Rodriguez 2.00 .90
2 Derek Jeter 3.00 1.35
3 Jose Vidro .50 .23
4 Miguel Tejada .50 .23
5 Albert Pujols 2.50 1.10
6 Rocco Baldelli 2.00 .90
7 Jose Reyes .75 .35
8 Hideo Nomo 1.25 .55
9 Hank Blalock .75 .35
10 Chipper Jones 1.25 .55
11 Barry Larkin 1.25 .55
12 Alfonso Soriano .75 .35
13 Aramis Ramirez .50 .23
14 Darin Erstad .50 .23
15 Jim Edmonds .50 .23
16 Garret Anderson .50 .23
17 Todd Helton .75 .35
18 Jason Kendall .50 .23
19 Aubrey Huff .50 .23
20 Troy Glaus .75 .35
21 Sammy Sosa 2.00 .90
22 Roger Clemens 2.50 1.10
23 Mark Teixeira .75 .35
24 Barry Bonds 3.00 1.35
25 Jim Thome 1.25 .55
26 Carlos Delgado .50 .23
27 Vladimir Guerrero 1.25 .55
28 Austin Kearns .50 .23
29 Pat Burrell .50 .23
30 Ken Griffey Jr. 2.00 .90
31 Greg Maddux 2.00 .90
32 Corey Patterson .50 .23
33 Larry Walker .75 .35
34 Kerry Wood 1.25 .55
35 Frank Thomas 1.25 .55
36 Dontrelle Willis 1.25 .55
37 Randy Johnson 1.25 .55
38 Curt Schilling .75 .35
39 Jay Gibbons .50 .23
40 Dmitri Young .50 .23
41 Edgar Martinez .75 .35
42 Kevin Brown .50 .23
43 Scott Rolen .75 .35
44 Adam Dunn .50 .23
45 Pedro Martinez 1.25 .55
46 Corey Koskie .50 .23
47 Tom Glavine .75 .35
48 Torii Hunter .50 .23
49 Shawn Green .50 .23
50 Nomar Garciaparra 2.00 .90
51 Bernie Williams .75 .35
52 Milton Bradley .50 .23
53 Jason Giambi 1.25 .55
54 Mike Lieberthal .50 .23
55 Jeff Bagwell .75 .35
56 Carlos Pena .50 .23
57 Lance Berkman .50 .23
58 Jose Cruz Jr. .50 .23
59 Josh Beckett .75 .35
60 Mark Mulder .50 .23
61 Mike Piazza 2.00 .90
62 Mark Prior 2.50 1.10
63 Sean Burroughs .50 .23
64 Angel Berroa .50 .23
65 Geoff Jenkins .50 .23
66 Magglio Ordonez .50 .23
67 Craig Biggio .75 .35
68 Roberto Alomar 1.25 .55
69 Hee Seop Choi .50 .23
70 J.D. Drew .50 .23
71 Richie Sexson .50 .23
72 Brian Giles .50 .23
73 Gary Sheffield .50 .23
74 Manny Ramirez .50 .23
75 Barry Zito .75 .35
76 Andruw Jones .50 .23
77 Ivan Rodriguez 1.25 .55
78 Ichiro Suzuki 2.00 .90
79 Mike Sweeney .50 .23
80 Vernon Wells .50 .23
81 Craig Brazell RU RC 8.00 3.60
82 Wilfredo Ledezma RU RC 5.00 2.20
83 Josh Willingham RU RC 10.00 4.50
84 Chien-Ming Wang RU RC 10.00 4.50
85 Mike Ryan RU RC 8.00 3.60
86 Mike Gallo RU RC 5.00 2.20
87 Rickie Weeks RU RC 20.00 9.00
88 Brian Stokes RU RC 5.00 2.20
89 Humberto Quintero RU RC 5.00 2.20
90 Ramon Nivar RU RC 8.00 3.60
91 Jeremy Griffiths RU RC 8.00 3.60
92 Terrmel Sledge RU RC 8.00 3.60
93 Brandon Webb RU RC 12.00 5.50
94 David DeJesus RU RC 8.00 3.60
95 Doug Waechter RU RC 8.00 3.60
96 Jeremy Bonderman RU RC 8.00 3.60
97 Felix Sanchez RU RC 5.00 2.20
98 Colin Porter RU RC 5.00 2.20
99 Francisco Cruceta RU RC 5.00 2.20
100 Hideki Matsui RU RC 20.00 9.00
101 Chris Waters RU RC 5.00 2.20
102 Dan Haren RU RC 8.00 3.60
103 Lew Ford RU RC 8.00 3.60
104 Oscar Villarreal RU RC 5.00 2.20
105 Ryan Wagner RU RC 10.00 4.50
106 Prentice Redman RU RC 5.00 2.20
107 Josh Stewart RU RC 5.00 2.20
108 Carlos Mendez RU RC 5.00 2.20
109 Michael Hessman RU RC 5.00 2.20
110 Josh Hall RU RC 8.00 3.60
111 Daniel Garcia RU RC 5.00 2.20
112 Matt Kata RU RC 8.00 3.60
113 Michel Hernandez RU RC 5.00 2.20
114 Sergio Mitre RU RC 8.00 3.60
115 Pete LaForest RU RC 8.00 3.60
116 Edwin Jackson RU RC 15.00 6.75
117 Matt Diaz RU RC 8.00 3.60
118 Greg Aquino RU RC 5.00 2.20
119 Jose Contreras RU RC 10.00 4.50
120 Jeff Duncan RU RC 8.00 3.60
121 Richard Fischer RU RC 5.00 2.20
122 Todd Wellemeyer RU RC 8.00 3.60
123 Robby Hammock RU RC 8.00 3.60
124 Delmon Young RU RC 25.00 11.00
125 Clint Barmes RU RC 8.00 3.60
126 Phil Seibel RU RC 5.00 2.20
127 Bo Hart RU RC 10.00 4.50
128 Jon Leicester RU RC 5.00 2.20
129 Chad Gaudin RU RC 5.00 2.20
130 Guillermo Quiroz RU RC 10.00 4.50

2003 Fleer Mystique Blue Die Cuts

MINT NRMT
*BLUE DIE CUTS: .6X TO 1.5X BASIC.
TWO PER MYSTERY PACK
STATED PRINT RUN 200 SERIAL #'d SETS

2003 Fleer Mystique Gold

MINT NRMT
*GOLD: 4X TO 10X BASIC
STATED ODDS 1:18
1-80 PRINT RUN 75 SERIAL #'d SETS
81-130 PRINT RUN 25 SERIAL #'d SETS
81-130 NO PRICING DUE TO SCARCITY

2003 Fleer Mystique Awe Pairs

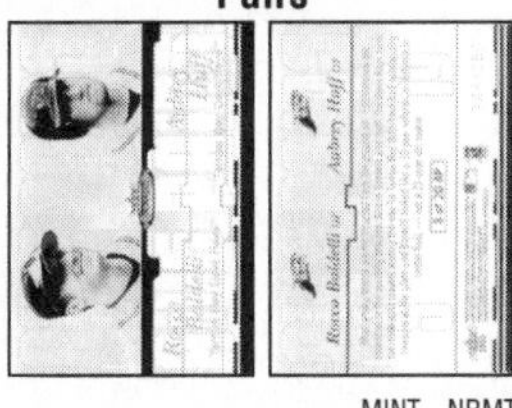

MINT NRMT
OVERALL #'d INSERT ODDS 1:10
STATED PRINT RUN 250 SERIAL #'d SETS
*GOLD: .75X TO 2X BASIC AWE
OVERALL #'d INSERT PARALLEL ODDS 1:30
GOLD PRINT RUNS B/WN 63-101 COPIES PER
1 Nomar Garciaparra 8.00 3.60
Pedro Martinez
2 Derek Jeter 12.00 5.50
Alfonso Soriano
3 Rocco Baldelli 8.00 3.60
Aubrey Huff
4 Carlos Delgado 5.00 2.20
Vernon Wells
5 Troy Glaus 5.00 2.20
Garret Anderson
6 Ichiro Suzuki 8.00 3.60
Bret Boone
7 Alex Rodriguez 8.00 3.60
Hank Blalock
8 Chipper Jones 5.00 2.20
Andruw Jones
9 Dontrelle Willis 5.00 2.20
Mike Lowell
10 Vladimir Guerrero 5.00 2.20
Orlando Cabrera
11 Tom Glavine 8.00 3.60
Mike Piazza
12 Jim Thome 5.00 2.20
Mike Lieberthal
13 Sammy Sosa 8.00 3.60
Corey Patterson
14 Jeff Bagwell 5.00 2.20
Lance Berkman
15 Geoff Jenkins 5.00 2.20
Richie Sexson
16 Albert Pujols 10.00 4.50
Jim Edmonds
17 Todd Helton 5.00 2.20
Larry Walker
18 Paul Lo Duca 5.00 2.20
Shawn Green
19 Ryan Klesko 5.00 2.20
Sean Burroughs
20 Barry Bonds 12.00 5.50
Rich Aurilia

2003 Fleer Mystique Awe Pairs Memorabilia

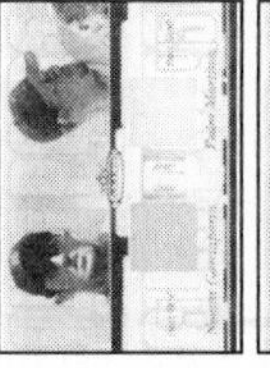

MINT NRMT
OVERALL #'d GU INSERT ODDS 1:20.
STATED PRINT RUN 100 SERIAL #'d SETS
OVERALL #'d GU PARALLEL ODDS 1:350
GOLD PRINT RUN 10 SERIAL #'d SETS
NO GOLD PRICING DUE TO SCARCITY
APJE Albert Pujols Jsy 25.00 11.00
Jim Edmonds Jsy
ARHB Alex Rodriguez Jsy 20.00 9.00
Hank Blalock Bat
CDVW Carlos Delgado Jsy 10.00 4.50
Vernon Wells Bat
CJAJ Chipper Jones Jsy 15.00 6.75
Andruw Jones Jsy
DJAS Derek Jeter Jsy 30.00 13.50
Alfonso Soriano Jsy
DWML Dontrelle Willis Jsy 15.00 6.75
Mike Lowell Bat
GJRS Geoff Jenkins Bat 10.00 4.50
Richie Sexson Bat
JBLB Jeff Bagwell Jsy 15.00 6.75
Lance Berkman Jsy
JTML Jim Thome Jsy 15.00 6.75
Mike Lieberthal Bat
NGPM Nomar Garciaparra Jsy 20.00 9.00
Pedro Martinez Jsy
PLDSG Paul Lo Duca Jsy 10.00 4.50
Shawn Green Jsy
RBAH Rocco Baldelli Jsy 25.00 11.00
Aubrey Huff Bat
RKSB Ryan Klesko Bat 10.00 4.50
Sean Burroughs Jsy
SSCP Sammy Sosa Jsy 20.00 9.00
Corey Patterson Jsy
TGGA Troy Glaus Jsy 15.00 6.75
Garret Anderson Bat
TGMP Tom Glavine Jsy 15.00 6.75
Mike Piazza Jsy
THLW Todd Helton Jsy 15.00 6.75
Larry Walker Jsy
VGOC Vladimir Guerrero Jsy 15.00 6.75
Orlando Cabrera Bat

2003 Fleer Mystique Diamond Dominators

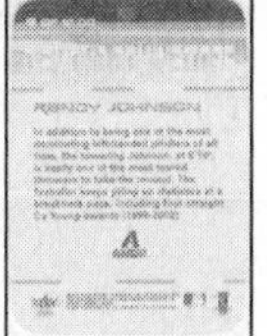

MINT NRMT
OVERALL #'d INSERT ODDS 1:10
STATED PRINT RUN 100 SERIAL #'d SETS
*GOLD p/r 51-75: .6X TO 1.5X BASIC.
*GOLD p/r 44-45: .75X TO 2X BASIC..
*GOLD p/r 31: 1.25X TO 3X BASIC
OVERALL #'d INSERT PARALLEL ODDS 1:30
GOLD PRINT RUNS B/WN 3-75 COPIES PER
NO GOLD PRICING ON QTY OF 25 OR LESS
1 Mike Piazza 12.00 5.50
2 Greg Maddux 12.00 5.50
3 Alfonso Soriano 8.00 3.60
4 Barry Zito 8.00 3.60
5 Alex Rodriguez 12.00 5.50
6 Roger Clemens 15.00 6.75
7 Sammy Sosa 12.00 5.50
8 Adam Dunn 8.00 3.60
9 Randy Johnson 8.00 3.60
10 Pedro Martinez 8.00 3.60

2003 Fleer Mystique Diamond Dominators Memorabilia

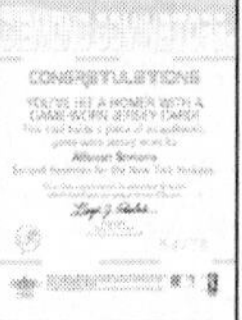

MINT NRMT
OVERALL #'d GU INSERT ODDS 1:20.
STATED PRINT RUN 75 SERIAL #'d SETS

OVERALL #'d GU PARALLEL ODDS 1:350
GOLD PRINT RUN 10 SERIAL #'d SETS
NO GOLD PRICING DUE TO SCARCITY
AD Adam Dunn Bat 12.00 5.50
AR Alex Rodriguez Jsy 20.00 9.00
AS Alfonso Soriano Jsy 15.00 6.75
BZ Barry Zito Jsy 15.00 6.75
GM Greg Maddux Jsy 20.00 9.00
MP Mike Piazza Jsy 20.00 9.00
PM Pedro Martinez Jsy 15.00 6.75
RC Roger Clemens Jsy 25.00 11.00
RJ Randy Johnson Jsy 15.00 6.75
SS Sammy Sosa Jsy 25.00 11.00

2003 Fleer Mystique Ink Appeal

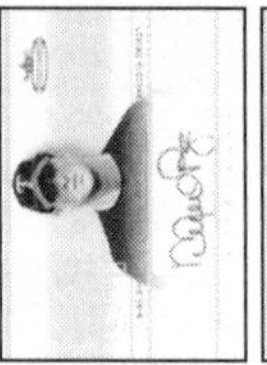
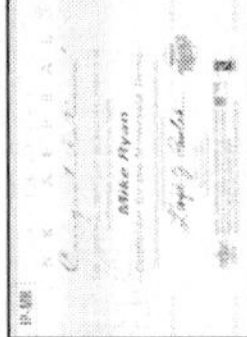

MINT NRMT
OVERALL INK APPEAL ODDS 1:150
STATED PRINT RUN 50 SERIAL #'d SETS
AH Aubrey Huff 25.00 11.00
BH Bo Hart 40.00 18.00
CP Corey Patterson 25.00 11.00
DW Dontrelle Willis
HB Hank Blalock 40.00 18.00
JR Jose Reyes 50.00 22.00
JW Josh Willingham 30.00 13.50
MR Mike Ryan 25.00 11.00
RB Rocco Baldelli 80.00 36.00
RW Rickie Weeks
TH Torii Hunter 25.00 11.00

2003 Fleer Mystique Ink Appeal Gold

MINT NRMT
OVERALL INK APPEAL ODDS 1:150
PRINT RUNS B/WN 2-70 COPIES PER
NO PRICING ON QTY OF 25 OR LESS.
AH Aubrey Huff/19
BH Bo Hart/31
CP Corey Patterson/20
DW Dontrelle Willis/35
HB Hank Blalock/9
JR Jose Reyes/7
JW Josh Willingham/70 30.00 13.50
MR Mike Ryan/54 25.00 11.00
RB Rocco Baldelli/5
RW Rickie Weeks/2
TH Torii Hunter/48 25.00 11.00

2003 Fleer Mystique Ink Appeal Dual

MINT NRMT
OVERALL INK APPEAL ODDS 1:150
STATED PRINT RUN 20 SERIAL #'d SETS
NO PRICING DUE TO SCARCITY
AHRB Aubrey Huff
Rocco Baldelli
BWDW Brandon Webb
Dontrelle Willis
CPWL Carlos Pena
Wilfredo Ledezma
JWML Josh Willingham
Mike Lowell
SRBH Scott Rolen
Bo Hart
THMR Torii Hunter
Mike Ryan

2003 Fleer Mystique Ink Appeal Dual Gold

MINT NRMT
OVERALL INK APPEAL ODDS 1:150
STATED PRINT RUN 5 SERIAL #'d SETS
NO PRICING DUE TO SCARCITY

2003 Fleer Mystique Rare Finds

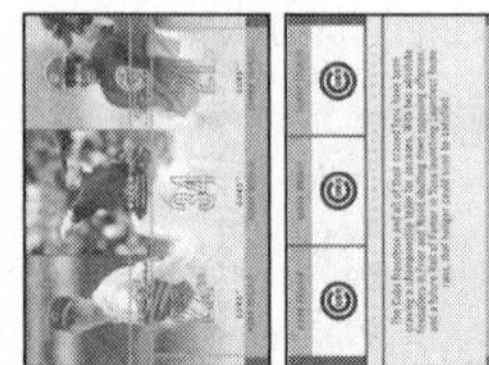

MINT NRMT
OVERALL #'d INSERT ODDS 1:10
STATED PRINT RUN 250 SERIAL #'d SETS
1 Jason Giambi 12.00 5.50
Roger Clemens
Derek Jeter
2 Randy Johnson 10.00 4.50
Curt Schilling
Brandon Webb
3 Nomar Garciaparra 8.00 3.60
Pedro Martinez
Manny Ramirez
4 Mark Prior 10.00 4.50
Kerry Wood
Sammy Sosa
5 Jeff Bagwell 5.00 2.20
Craig Biggio
Lance Berkman
6 Austin Kearns 5.00 2.20
Adam Dunn
Barry Larkin
7 Jim Edmonds 5.00 2.20
Scott Rolen
J.D. Drew
8 Chipper Jones 8.00 3.60
Andruw Jones
Greg Maddux
9 Barry Zito 5.00 2.20
Miguel Tejada
Mark Mulder
10 Alex Rodriguez 8.00 3.60
Mark Teixeira
Rafael Palmeiro

2003 Fleer Mystique Rare Finds Single Swatch

MINT NRMT
OVERALL RF SWATCH ODDS 1:1 MYSTERY
STATED PRINT RUN 150 SERIAL #'d SETS
GOLD RANDOM IN MYSTERY PACKS
GOLD PRINT RUN 15 SERIAL #'d SETS
NO GOLD PRICING DUE TO SCARCITY
AK Austin Kearns Jsy 8.00 3.60
Adam Dunn
Barry Larkin
AR Alex Rodriguez Jsy 15.00 6.75
Mark Teixeira
Rafael Palmeiro
BL Barry Larkin Jsy 10.00 4.50
Austin Kearns
Adam Dunn
BW Brandon Webb Jsy 15.00 6.75
Randy Johnson
Curt Schilling
CJ Chipper Jones Jsy 10.00 4.50
Andruw Jones
Greg Maddux
DJ Derek Jeter Jsy 20.00 9.00
Jason Giambi
Roger Clemens
GM Greg Maddux Jsy 10.00 4.50
Chipper Jones
Andruw Jones
JB Jeff Bagwell Jsy 10.00 4.50
Craig Biggio
Lance Berkman
JD J.D. Drew Jsy 8.00 3.60
Jim Edmonds
Scott Rolen
JG Jason Giambi Jsy 10.00 4.50
Roger Clemens
Derek Jeter
MM Mark Mulder Jsy 8.00 3.60
Barry Zito
Miguel Tejada
MP Mark Prior Jsy 15.00 6.75
Kerry Wood
Sammy Sosa
MTJ Miguel Tejada Jsy 8.00 3.60
Barry Zito
Mark Mulder
MTX Mark Teixeira Jsy 10.00 4.50
Alex Rodriguez
Rafael Palmeiro
NG Nomar Garciaparra Jsy 15.00 6.75
Pedro Martinez
Manny Ramirez
PM Nomar Garciaparra 10.00 4.50
Pedro Martinez Jsy
Manny Ramirez
RC Roger Clemens Jsy 15.00 6.75
Jason Giambi
Derek Jeter
RJ Randy Johnson Jsy 10.00 4.50
Curt Schilling
Brandon Webb
SR Scott Rolen Jsy 10.00 4.50
Jim Edmonds
J.D. Drew
SS Sammy Sosa Jsy 15.00 6.75
Mark Prior
Kerry Wood

2003 Fleer Mystique Rare Finds Double Swatch

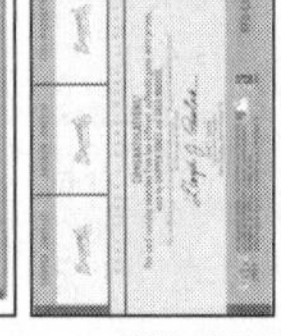

MINT NRMT
OVERALL RF SWATCH ODDS 1:1 MYSTERY
STATED PRINT RUN 75 SERIAL #'d SETS
GOLD RANDOM IN MYSTERY PACKS
GOLD PRINT RUN 10 SERIAL #'d SETS
NO GOLD PRICING DUE TO SCARCITY
AJGM Andruw Jones Jsy 15.00 6.75
Greg Maddux Jsy
Chipper Jones
AKAD Austin Kearns Jsy 10.00 4.50
Adam Dunn Jsy
Barry Larkin
ARMT Alex Rodriguez Jsy 25.00 11.00
Mark Teixeira Jsy
Rafael Palmeiro
BZMT Barry Zito Jsy 15.00 6.75
Miguel Tejada Jsy
Mark Mulder
CJGM Chipper Jones Jsy 25.00 11.00
Greg Maddux Jsy
Andruw Jones
JBCB Jeff Bagwell Jsy 15.00 6.75
Craig Biggio Jsy
Lance Berkman
JESR Jim Edmonds Jsy 15.00 6.75
Scott Rolen Jsy
J.D. Drew
JGDJ Jason Giambi Jsy 30.00 13.50
Derek Jeter Jsy
Roger Clemens
MPKW Mark Prior Jsy 30.00 13.50
Kerry Wood Jsy
Sammy Sosa
MPSS Mark Prior Jsy 40.00 18.00
Sammy Sosa Jsy
Kerry Wood
NGMR Nomar Garciaparra Jsy 30.00 13.50
Manny Ramirez Jsy
Pedro Martinez
PMMR Pedro Martinez Jsy 15.00 6.75
Manny Ramirez Jsy
Nomar Garciaparra
RCDJ Roger Clemens Jsy 50.00 22.00
Derek Jeter Jsy
Jason Giambi
RJBW Randy Johnson Jsy 25.00 11.00
Brandon Webb Jsy
Curt Schilling
RJCS Randy Johnson Jsy 15.00 6.75
Curt Schilling Jsy
Brandon Webb

2003 Fleer Mystique Rare Finds Triple Swatch

MINT NRMT
OVERALL RF SWATCH ODDS 1:1 MYSTERY
STATED PRINT RUN 50 SERIAL #'d SETS
GOLD RANDOM IN MYSTERY PACKS
GOLD PRINT RUN 5 SERIAL #'d SETS
NO GOLD PRICING DUE TO SCARCITY
AAB Austin Kearns Jsy 25.00 11.00
Adam Dunn Jsy
Barry Larkin Jsy
AMR Alex Rodriguez Jsy 40.00 18.00
Mark Teixeira Jsy
Rafael Palmeiro Bat
BMM Barry Zito Jsy 25.00 11.00
Miguel Tejada Jsy
Mark Mulder Jsy
CAG Chipper Jones Jsy 60.00 27.00
Andruw Jones Jsy
Greg Maddux Jsy
JCL Jeff Bagwell Jsy 25.00 11.00
Craig Biggio Jsy
Lance Berkman Jsy
JRD Jason Giambi Jsy 100.00 45.00
Roger Clemens Jsy
Derek Jeter Jsy
JSJ Jim Edmonds Jsy 40.00 18.00
Scott Rolen Jsy
J.D. Drew Jsy
MKS Mark Prior Jsy 80.00 36.00
Kerry Wood Jsy
Sammy Sosa Jsy
NPM Nomar Garciaparra Jsy 80.00 36.00
Pedro Martinez Jsy
Manny Ramirez Jsy
RCB Randy Johnson Jsy 40.00 18.00
Curt Schilling Jsy
Brandon Webb Jsy

2003 Fleer Mystique Rare Finds Autograph

MINT NRMT
OVERALL RF AUTO ODDS 1:650 MYSTERY
STATED PRINT RUN 15 SERIAL #'d SETS
NO PRICING DUE TO SCARCITY
AK Austin Kearns
BW Brandon Webb
CJ Chipper Jones
MT Miguel Tejada
SR Scott Rolen

2003 Fleer Mystique Rare Finds Autograph Jersey

MINT NRMT
RANDOM INSERTS IN MYSTERY PACKS

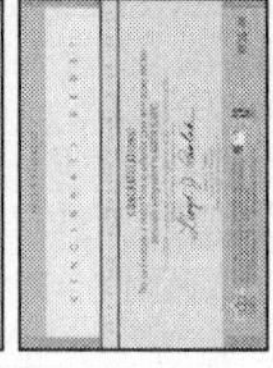

STATED PRINT RUN 5 SERIAL #'d SETS
NO PRICING DUE TO SCARCITY

2003 Fleer Mystique Secret Weapons

MINT NRMT
OVERALL #'d INSERT ODDS 1:10
STATED PRINT RUN 250 SERIAL #'d SETS
*GOLD p/r 224-307: .4X TO 1X BASIC SW
*GOLD p/r 100: .6X TO 1.5X BASIC SW
OVERALL #'d INSERT PARALLEL ODDS 1:30
GOLD PRINT RUNS B/WN 100-307 COPIES PER
1 Hank Blalock 5.00 2.20
2 Dontrelle Willis 5.00 2.20
3 Jose Reyes 5.00 2.20
4 Bo Hart 10.00 4.50
5 Corey Patterson 5.00 2.20
6 Hideki Matsui 20.00 9.00
7 Mark Teixeira 5.00 2.20
8 Brandon Webb 12.00 5.50
9 Rocco Baldelli 12.00 5.50
10 Mark Prior 10.00 4.50

2003 Fleer Mystique Shining Stars

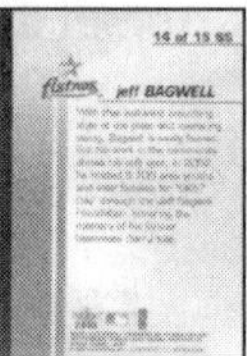

MINT NRMT
OVERALL #'d INSERT ODDS 1:10
STATED PRINT RUN 300 SERIAL #'d SETS
*GOLD p/r 419-658: .3X TO .8X BASIC SS
*GOLD p/r 269-381: .4X TO 1X BASIC SS
*GOLD p/r 173-234: .5X TO 1.2X BASIC SS
*GOLD p/r 114-127: .6X TO 1.5X BASIC SS
*GOLD p/r 96: .75X TO 2X BASIC SS
*GOLD p/r 28-29: 2X TO 5X BASIC SS
OVERALL #'d INSERT PARALLEL ODDS 1:30
GOLD PRINT RUNS B/WN 28-658 COPIES PER
1 Derek Jeter 12.00 5.50
2 Barry Bonds 12.00 5.50
3 Nomar Garciaparra 8.00 3.60
4 Austin Kearns 5.00 2.20
5 Vladimir Guerrero 5.00 2.20
6 Jim Thome 5.00 2.20
7 Ichiro Suzuki 8.00 3.60
8 Jason Giambi 5.00 2.20
9 Albert Pujols 10.00 4.50
10 Ken Griffey Jr. 8.00 3.60
11 Chipper Jones 5.00 2.20
12 Scott Rolen 5.00 2.20
13 Manny Ramirez 5.00 2.20
14 Jeff Bagwell 5.00 2.20
15 Torii Hunter 5.00 2.20

2003 Fleer Mystique Shining Stars Jersey

MINT NRMT
STATED PRINT RUN 100 SERIAL #'d SETS
*PATCH: .75X TO 2X BASIC SS JSY
PATCH PRINT RUN 50 SERIAL #'d SETS
OVERALL #'d GU INSERT ODDS 1:20
AJ Andruw Jones 10.00 4.50
AK Austin Kearns 10.00 4.50
AP Albert Pujols 20.00 9.00
CD Carlos Delgado 10.00 4.50
CJ Chipper Jones 12.00 5.50
DJ Derek Jeter 25.00 11.00
JB Jeff Bagwell 12.00 5.50
JG Jason Giambi 12.00 5.50
JT Jim Thome 12.00 5.50
MR Manny Ramirez 10.00 4.50
NG Nomar Garciaparra 20.00 9.00
SR Scott Rolen 12.00 5.50
THE Todd Helton 12.00 5.50
THU Torii Hunter 10.00 4.50
VG Vladimir Guerrero 12.00 5.50

2003 Fleer Patchworks

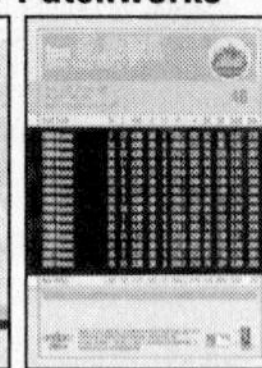

This 115 card set was released in May, 2003. This set was issued in five-card packs which were issued in five card packs with a $4.99 SRP which came 24 packs to a box and 12 boxes to a case. The set consists of 90 veterans (1-90) and 25 rookies and leading prospects (91-115). The final 25 cards were randomly inserted in packs and issued to a stated print run of 1500 serial numbered sets.

Nm-Mt Ex-Mt
COMP.SET w/o SP's (90) 15.00 4.50
COMMON CARD (1-90) .40 .12
COMMON CARD (91-115) 4.00 1.20
1 Luis Castillo .40 .12
2 Derek Jeter 2.50 .75
3 Vladimir Guerrero 1.00 .30
4 Bobby Higginson .40 .12
5 Pat Burrell .40 .12
6 Ivan Rodriguez 1.00 .30
7 Craig Biggio .60 .18
8 Troy Glaus .60 .18
9 Barry Bonds 2.50 .75
10 Hideo Nomo 1.00 .30
11 Barry Larkin 1.00 .30
12 Roberto Alomar 1.00 .30
13 Rodrigo Lopez .40 .12
14 Eric Chavez .40 .12
15 Shawn Green .40 .12
16 Joe Randa .40 .12
17 Mark Grace .60 .18
18 Jason Kendall .40 .12
19 Hee Seop Choi .40 .12
20 Luis Gonzalez .40 .12
21 Sammy Sosa 1.50 .45
22 Larry Walker .60 .18
23 Phil Nevin .40 .12
24 Manny Ramirez .40 .12
25 Jim Thome 1.00 .30
26 Randy Johnson 1.00 .30
27 Jose Vidro .40 .12
28 Austin Kearns .40 .12
29 Mike Sweeney .40 .12
30 Maggio Ordonez .40 .12
31 Mike Piazza 1.50 .45
32 Eric Hinske .40 .12
33 Alex Rodriguez 1.50 .45
34 Kerry Wood 1.00 .30
35 Matt Morris .40 .12
36 Lance Berkman .40 .12
37 Michael Cuddyer .40 .12
38 Curt Schilling .60 .18
39 Sean Burroughs .40 .12
40 Ken Griffey Jr. 1.50 .45
41 Edgardo Alfonzo .40 .12
42 Carlos Pena .40 .12
43 Adam Dunn .40 .12
44 Pedro Martinez 1.00 .30
45 Miguel Tejada .40 .12
46 Tom Glavine .60 .18
47 Torii Hunter .40 .12
48 Jason Giambi 1.00 .30
49 Tony Batista .40 .12
50 Ben Grieve .40 .12
51 Ichiro Suzuki 1.50 .45
52 Bobby Abreu .40 .12
53 Todd Helton .60 .18
54 Kazuhiro Sasaki .40 .12
55 Nomar Garciaparra 1.50 .45
56 Francisco Rodriguez .40 .12
57 Ellis Burks .40 .12
58 Frank Thomas 1.00 .30
59 Greg Maddux 1.50 .45
60 Josh Beckett .60 .18
61 Brad Wilkerson .40 .12
62 Joe Borchard .40 .12
63 Carlos Delgado .40 .12
64 Alfonso Soriano .60 .18
65 Chipper Jones 1.00 .30
66 J.D. Drew .40 .12
67 Mark Prior 2.00 .60
68 Rafael Palmeiro .60 .18
69 Jeff Kent .40 .12
70 Adrian Beltre .40 .12
71 Marlon Byrd .40 .12
72 Orlando Hudson .40 .12
73 Junior Spivey .40 .12
74 Jeff Bagwell .60 .18
75 Barry Zito .60 .18
76 Roger Clemens 2.00 .60
77 Aubrey Huff .40 .12
78 Geoff Jenkins .40 .12
79 Andruw Jones .40 .12
80 Scott Rolen .60 .18
81 Omar Vizquel .40 .12
82 Darin Erstad .40 .12
83 Bernie Williams .60 .18
84 Freddy Garcia .40 .12
85 Richie Sexson .40 .12
86 Josh Phelps .40 .12
87 Albert Pujols 2.00 .60
88 Aramis Ramirez .40 .12
89 Shea Hillenbrand .40 .12
90 Cristian Guzman .40 .12
91 Adam LaRoche RR 5.00 1.50
92 David Pember RR RC 4.00 1.20
93 Terrmel Sledge RR RC 5.00 1.50
94 Hideki Matsui RR RC 15.00 4.50
95 Nook Logan RR RC 4.00 1.20
96 Jose Contreras RR RC 8.00 2.40
97 Pete LaForest RR RC 5.00 1.50
98 Rich Fischer RR RC 4.00 1.20
99 Francisco Rosario RR RC 4.00 1.20
100 Josh Willingham RR RC 6.00 1.80
101 Alejandro Machado RR RC 4.00 1.20
102 Lew Ford RR RC 5.00 1.50
103 Joe Valentine RR RC 4.00 1.20

104 Guillermo Quiroz RR RC 8.00 2.40
105 Chien-Ming Wang RR RC 8.00 2.40
106 Jhonny Peralta RR RC 4.00 1.20
107 Shane Victorino RR RC 4.00 1.20
108 Prentice Redman RR RC 4.00 1.20
109 Matt Bruback RR RC 4.00 1.20
110 Lance Niekro RR 4.00 1.20
111 Travis Hughes RR 4.00 1.20
112 Nic Jackson RR 4.00 1.20
113 Hector Luna RR RC 4.00 1.20
114 Cliff Lee RR 4.00 1.20
115 Tim Olson RR RC 5.00 1.50

2003 Fleer Patchworks Star Ruby

Nm-Mt Ex-Mt
*RUBY 1-90: 4X TO 10X BASIC
*RUBY 91-115: .6X TO 1.5X BASIC
RANDOM INSERTS IN PACKS
STATED PRINT RUN 100 SERIAL #'d SETS

2003 Fleer Patchworks Diamond Ink

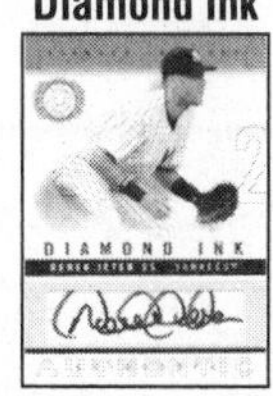

Randomly inserted into packs, these six cards feature authentic signed autographs from four different players. Derek Jeter signed his cards in a mix of Black, blue and red ink. We have printed the stated print run next to the player's name in our checklist.

Nm-Mt Ex-Mt
DJ1 Derek Jeter Black/210 150.00 45.00
DJ2 Derek Jeter Blue/101 150.00 45.00
DJ3 Derek Jeter Red/50 200.00 60.00
MP Mark Prior/88 120.00 36.00
MS Mike Schmidt/194 80.00 24.00
TG Troy Glaus/351 25.00 7.50

2003 Fleer Patchworks Game-Worn Patch Level 1 Single

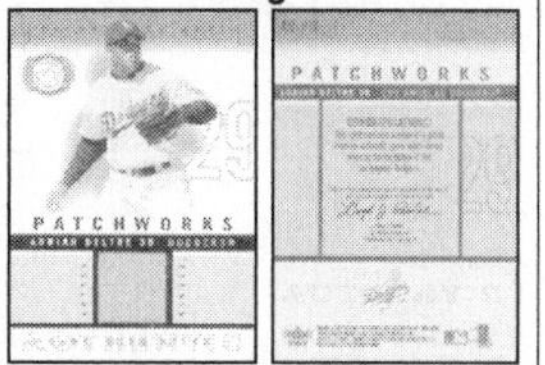

Randomly inserted into packs, these 17 cards feature a single color patch swatch. Please note that the second level cards feature dual-colored swatches and level 3 features multi-colored swatches. The level 1 patches were issued to a stated print run of 250 serial numbered sets.

Nm-Mt Ex-Mt
AB Adrian Beltre 10.00 3.00
AJ Andruw Jones 10.00 3.00
AR Alex Rodriguez
BA Bob Abreu 10.00 3.00
BW Bernie Williams 15.00 4.50
CD Carlos Delgado
EC Eric Chavez 10.00 3.00
FT Frank Thomas 15.00 4.50
GM Greg Maddux 15.00 4.50
JB Josh Beckett 15.00 4.50
KS Kazuhiro Sasaki 10.00 3.00
KW Kerry Wood 15.00 4.50
LB Lance Berkman 10.00 3.00
MG Mark Grace 15.00 4.50
RA Roberto Alomar 15.00 4.50
RO Roy Oswalt 10.00 3.00
VG Vladimir Guerrero 15.00 4.50

2003 Fleer Patchworks Game-Worn Patch Level 2 Dual

Nm-Mt Ex-Mt
RANDOM INSERTS IN PACKS
STATED PRINT RUN 100 SERIAL #'d SETS
AB Adrian Beltre 25.00 7.50
AJ Andruw Jones 25.00 7.50
AR Alex Rodriguez 50.00 15.00
BA Bob Abreu 25.00 7.50
BW Bernie Williams 30.00 9.00
CD Carlos Delgado 25.00 7.50
CS Curt Schilling 30.00 9.00
EC Eric Chavez 25.00 7.50
FT Frank Thomas 30.00 9.00
GM Greg Maddux 40.00 12.00
JB Josh Beckett 30.00 9.00
KS Kazuhiro Sasaki 25.00 7.50
KW Kerry Wood 30.00 9.00
LB Lance Berkman 25.00 7.50
MG Mark Grace 30.00 9.00
RA Roberto Alomar 30.00 9.00
RO Roy Oswalt 25.00 7.50
VG Vladimir Guerrero 30.00 9.00

2003 Fleer Patchworks Game-Worn Patch Level 3 Multi

Nm-Mt Ex-Mt
RANDOM INSERTS IN PACKS
STATED PRINT RUN 50 SERIAL #'d SETS
AB Adrian Beltre 30.00 9.00
AJ Andruw Jones 30.00 9.00
AR Alex Rodriguez 60.00 18.00
BA Bob Abreu 30.00 9.00
BW Bernie Williams 40.00 12.00
CD Carlos Delgado 30.00 9.00
CS Curt Schilling 40.00 12.00
EC Eric Chavez 30.00 9.00
FT Frank Thomas 40.00 12.00
GM Greg Maddux 50.00 15.00
JB Josh Beckett 40.00 12.00
KS Kazuhiro Sasaki 30.00 9.00
KW Kerry Wood 40.00 12.00
LB Lance Berkman 30.00 9.00
MG Mark Grace 40.00 12.00
RA Roberto Alomar 40.00 12.00
RO Roy Oswalt 30.00 9.00
VG Vladimir Guerrero 40.00 12.00

2003 Fleer Patchworks Licensed Apparel Jersey

Nm-Mt Ex-Mt
STATED PRINT RUN 500 SERIAL #'d SETS
*ONE-COLOR PATCH: .75X TO 2X BASIC APP
*MULTI-COLOR PATCH: 1.25 TO 3X BASIC APP
PATCH PRINT RUN 300 SERIAL #'d SETS
RANDOM INSERTS IN PACKS
AD Adam Dunn 8.00 2.40
CB Carlos Beltran 8.00 2.40
CJ Chipper Jones 10.00 3.00
DE Darin Erstad 8.00 2.40
DJ Derek Jeter 25.00 7.50
JD J.D. Drew 8.00 2.40
JR Jimmy Rollins 8.00 2.40
KB Kevin Brown 8.00 2.40
MM Mike Mussina 15.00 4.50
MO Maggio Ordonez 8.00 2.40
MP Mike Piazza 15.00 4.50
PK Paul Konerko 8.00 2.40
SG Shawn Green 8.00 2.40
SS Shannon Stewart 8.00 2.40
TH Todd Helton 10.00 3.00

2003 Fleer Patchworks Licensed Apparel Patch

Nm-Mt Ex-Mt
RANDOM INSERTS IN PACKS
STATED PRINT RUN 300 SERIAL #'d SETS

2003 Fleer Patchworks National Pastime

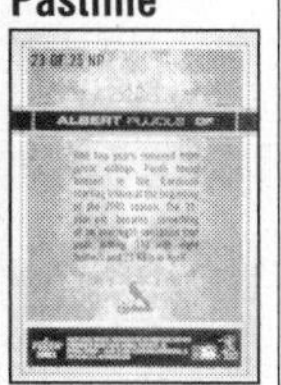

Nm-Mt Ex-Mt
STATED ODDS 1:12
1 Barry Bonds 6.00 1.80
2 Kazuhiro Sasaki 2.00 .60
3 Mike Piazza 4.00 1.20
4 Barry Zito 2.00 .60
5 Sammy Sosa 4.00 1.20
6 Pedro Martinez 2.50 .75
7 Craig Biggio 2.00 .60
8 Rafael Palmeiro 2.00 .60
9 Greg Maddux 4.00 1.20
10 Manny Ramirez 2.00 .60
11 Adam Dunn 2.00 .60
12 Omar Vizquel 2.00 .60
13 Hideo Nomo 2.50 .75
14 Alex Rodriguez 4.00 1.20
15 Pat Burrell 2.00 .60
16 Nomar Garciaparra 4.00 1.20
17 Randy Johnson 2.50 .75
18 Juan Gonzalez 2.50 .75
19 Chipper Jones 2.50 .75
20 Frank Thomas 2.50 .75
21 Vladimir Guerrero 2.50 .75
22 Troy Glaus 2.00 .60
23 Albert Pujols 5.00 1.50
24 Ichiro Suzuki 4.00 1.20
25 Ken Griffey Jr. 4.00 1.20

2003 Fleer Patchworks National Patchtime Commemorative

Randomly inserted into packs, these cards feature a commemorative patch piece from the featured uniform. These cards were issued to a stated print run of 25 serial numbered sets and no pricing is available due to market scarcity.

Nm-Mt Ex-Mt
AR Alex Rodriguez
BZ Barry Zito
CB Craig Biggio
FT Frank Thomas
GM Greg Maddux
MP Mike Piazza
PM Pedro Martinez
RP Rafael Palmeiro
SS Sammy Sosa
TG Troy Glaus
VG Vladimir Guerrero

2003 Fleer Patchworks National Patchtime Nameplate

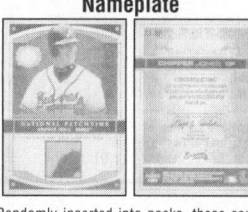

Randomly inserted into packs, these cards feature pieces from the player's uniform name. These cards were issued to a stated print run of 50 serial numbered sets.

Nm-Mt Ex-Mt
AR Alex Rodriguez 50.00 15.00
BZ Barry Zito 40.00 12.00
CB Craig Biggio 40.00 12.00
CJ Chipper Jones 40.00 12.00
FT Frank Thomas 40.00 12.00
GM Greg Maddux 40.00 12.00
HN Hideo Nomo 80.00 24.00
MP Mike Piazza 40.00 12.00
NG Nomar Garciaparra 60.00 18.00
PB Pat Burrell 30.00 9.00
RJ Randy Johnson 40.00 12.00
RP Rafael Palmeiro 40.00 12.00
SS Sammy Sosa 60.00 18.00
TG Troy Glaus 40.00 12.00
VG Vladimir Guerrero 40.00 12.00

2003 Fleer Patchworks National Patchtime Number

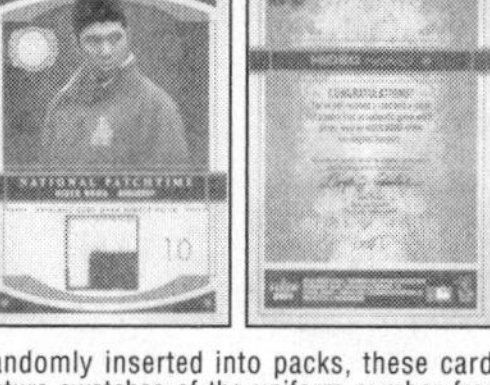

Randomly inserted into packs, these cards feature swatches of the uniform number from the game-used jersey cut up for this insert set. These cards were issued to a stated print run of 75 serial numbered sets.

Nm-Mt Ex-Mt
AR Alex Rodriguez 40.00 12.00
BZ Barry Zito 30.00 9.00
CB Craig Biggio 30.00 9.00
CJ Chipper Jones 30.00 9.00
FT Frank Thomas 30.00 9.00
GM Greg Maddux 30.00 9.00
HN Hideo Nomo 60.00 18.00
MP Mike Piazza 30.00 9.00
MR Manny Ramirez 25.00 7.50
NG Nomar Garciaparra 50.00 15.00
PB Pat Burrell 25.00 7.50
PM Pedro Martinez 30.00 9.00
RJ Randy Johnson 30.00 9.00
RP Rafael Palmeiro 30.00 9.00
SS Sammy Sosa 40.00 12.00
VG Vladimir Guerrero 30.00 9.00

2003 Fleer Patchworks National Patchtime Team Name

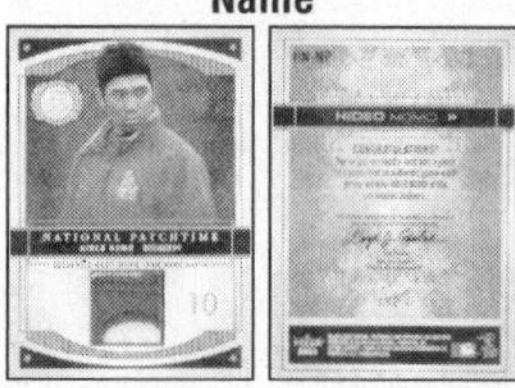

Randomly inserted into packs, these cards feature a swatch of the team name from the uniform used to create this game-used set. These cards were issued to a stated print run of 100 serial numbered sets.

Nm-Mt Ex-Mt
AR Alex Rodriguez 40.00 12.00
BZ Barry Zito 30.00 9.00
CJ Chipper Jones 30.00 9.00
FT Frank Thomas 30.00 9.00
GM Greg Maddux 40.00 12.00
HN Hideo Nomo 60.00 18.00
MP Mike Piazza 40.00 12.00
NG Nomar Garciaparra 50.00 15.00
OV Omar Vizquel 25.00 7.50
PB Pat Burrell 25.00 7.50
RJ Randy Johnson 30.00 9.00
RP Rafael Palmeiro 30.00 9.00
SS Sammy Sosa 40.00 12.00
TG Troy Glaus 30.00 9.00
VG Vladimir Guerrero 30.00 9.00

2003 Fleer Patchworks National Patchtime Trim

Randomly inserted into packs, these cards feature pieces cut from the uniform "trim". These cards were issued to a stated print run of 200 serial numbered sets.

Nm-Mt Ex-Mt
AR Alex Rodriguez 30.00 9.00
CJ Chipper Jones 25.00 7.50
FT Frank Thomas 25.00 7.50
GM Greg Maddux 30.00 9.00
HN Hideo Nomo 50.00 15.00
MP Mike Piazza 30.00 9.00
MR Manny Ramirez 15.00 4.50
NG Nomar Garciaparra 40.00 12.00
PM Pedro Martinez 25.00 7.50
RP Rafael Palmeiro 25.00 7.50
VG Vladimir Guerrero 25.00 7.50

2003 Fleer Patchworks Numbers Game

Nm-Mt Ex-Mt
STATED ODDS 1:24
1 Ichiro Suzuki 5.00 1.50
2 Derek Jeter 8.00 2.40
3 Alex Rodriguez 5.00 1.50
4 Miguel Tejada 3.00 .90
5 Nomar Garciaparra 5.00 1.50
6 Jason Giambi 3.00 .90
7 J.D. Drew 3.00 .90
8 Barry Bonds 8.00 2.40
9 Alfonso Soriano 3.00 .90
10 Jeff Bagwell 3.00 .90
11 Barry Larkin 3.00 .90
12 Roberto Alomar 3.00 .90
13 Larry Walker 3.00 .90
14 Roger Clemens 6.00 1.80
15 Ken Griffey Jr. 5.00 1.50

2003 Fleer Patchworks Numbers Game Jersey

Nm-Mt Ex-Mt
STATED ODDS 1:33
AR Alex Rodriguez 10.00 3.00
AS Alfonso Soriano 8.00 2.40
BL Barry Larkin 8.00 2.40
DJ Derek Jeter 12.00 3.60
JB Jeff Bagwell 8.00 2.40
JG Jason Giambi 8.00 2.40
LW Larry Walker 8.00 2.40
MT Miguel Tejada 8.00 2.40
RA Roberto Alomar 8.00 2.40
RC Roger Clemens 15.00 4.50

2003 Fleer Patchworks Numbers Game Patch

Nm-Mt Ex-Mt
RANDOM INSERTS IN PACKS
STATED PRINT RUN 300 SERIAL #'d SETS
AR Alex Rodriguez 40.00 12.00
AS Alfonso Soriano 25.00 7.50
BL Barry Larkin 25.00 7.50
DJ Derek Jeter 50.00 15.00
JB Jeff Bagwell 25.00 7.50
JG Jason Giambi 25.00 7.50
LW Larry Walker 25.00 7.50
MT Miguel Tejada 15.00 4.50
RA Roberto Alomar 25.00 7.50
RC Roger Clemens 40.00 12.00

2003 Fleer Patchworks Past Present Future

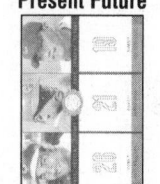

Nm-Mt Ex-Mt
STATED ODDS 1:72
1 Eddie Mathews 10.00 3.00
Rafael Palmeiro
Alex Rodriguez
2 Phil Rizzuto 12.00 3.60
Derek Jeter
Alfonso Soriano
3 Reggie Jackson 10.00 3.00
Barry Bonds
Sammy Sosa
4 Billy Williams 10.00 3.00
Sammy Sosa
Hee Seop Choi
5 Joe Morgan 10.00 3.00
Roberto Alomar
Alfonso Soriano
6 Yogi Berra 10.00 3.00
Mike Piazza
Josh Phelps
7 Nolan Ryan 12.00 3.60
Roger Clemens
Kerry Wood
8 Mike Schmidt 10.00 3.00
Scott Rolen
Eric Hinske
9 Barry Bonds 10.00 3.00
Alex Rodriguez
Alfonso Soriano
10 Yogi Berra 15.00 4.50
Derek Jeter
Hideki Matsui

2003 Fleer Patchworks Patch Present Future Single

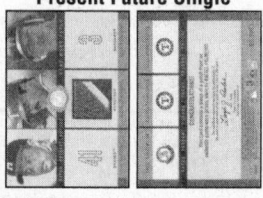

Randomly inserted into packs, these cards features three players on the card with one of the players having a game-worn swatch embedded on the card. These cards were issued to a stated print run of 200 serial numbered sets.

Nm-Mt Ex-Mt
AR1 Eddie Mathews 40.00 12.00
Rafael Palmeiro
Alex Rodriguez Patch
AR2 Barry Bonds
Alex Rodriguez Patch
Alfonso Soriano
AS1 Phil Rizzuto 25.00 7.50
Derek Jeter
Alfonso Soriano Patch
AS2 Joe Morgan 25.00 7.50
Roberto Alomar
Alfonso Soriano Patch
AS3 Barry Bonds 25.00 7.50
Alex Rodriguez
Alfonso Soriano Patch
BB Reggie Jackson 50.00 15.00
Barry Bonds Patch
Sammy Sosa
DJ1 Phil Rizzuto 60.00 18.00
Derek Jeter Patch
Alfonso Soriano
DJ2 Yogi Berra 60.00 18.00
Derek Jeter Patch
Hideki Matsui
EH Mike Schmidt 15.00 4.50
Scott Rolen
Eric Hinske Patch
KW Nolan Ryan 40.00 12.00
Roger Clemens
Kerry Wood Patch
MP Yogi Berra 40.00 12.00
Mike Piazza Patch
Josh Phelps
RA Joe Morgan 40.00 12.00
Roberto Alomar Patch
Alfonso Soriano
RC Nolan Ryan 60.00 18.00
Roger Clemens Patch
Kerry Wood
RP Eddie Mathews 25.00 7.50
Rafael Palmeiro Patch
Alex Rodriguez
SR Mike Schmidt
Scott Rolen Patch
Eric Hinske
SS1 Reggie Jackson 25.00 7.50
Barry Bonds
Sammy Sosa Patch
SS2 Billy Williams 40.00 12.00
Sammy Sosa Patch
Hee Seop Choi

2003 Fleer Patchworks Patch Present Future Dual

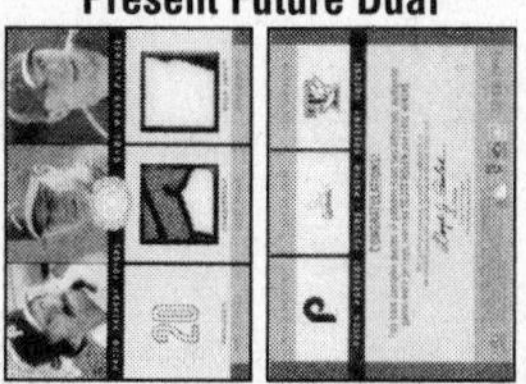

Randomly inserted into packs, this partial parallel to the Patch Present Future Set features three players on the card with the two active players having a patch piece embedded on the card. These cards were issued to a stated print run of 100 serial numbered sets.

Nm-Mt Ex-Mt
ARAS Barry Bonds 80.00 24.00
Alex Rodriguez Patch
Alfonso Soriano Patch
DJAS Phil Rizzuto 100.00 30.00
Derek Jeter Patch
Alfonso Soriano Patch
RAAS Joe Morgan 60.00 18.00
Roberto Alomar Patch
Alfonso Soriano Patch
RCKW Nolan Ryan 80.00 24.00
Roger Clemens Patch
Kerry Wood Patch
RPAR Eddie Mathews 80.00 24.00
Rafael Palmeiro Patch

Alex Rodriguez Patch
SREH Mike Schmidt 60.00 18.00
Scott Rolen Patch
Eric Hinske Patch

2001 Fleer Platinum

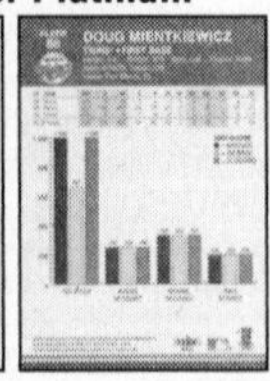

This 601-card set was distributed in two separate series. Series 1 was released in late May, 2001 with cards distributed in 10-card hobby packs with a suggested retail price of $2.99 and a 25-card jumbo pack for $9.99. Series 2 (entitled Platinum RC edition) was released in late December, 2001. The set features player photos printed in the original 1981 Fleer design. The first series contains 250 regular cards plus 31 dual short printed cards (251-280/301) and 20 All-Star cards (281-300) both with an insertion rate of 1:6 in the hobby packs and 1:2 in the jumbo packs. The second series set contains 300 cards composed of basic (302-401), Chart Toppers (402-431), Team Leaders (432-461), Franchise Futures (462-481), Postseason Glory (482-501) and Rookies (502-601), seeded at a rate of 1:3 packs). Notable Rookie Cards include Ichiro, Albert Pujols and Mark Tiexeira. According to representatives at Fleer, card 529 (Mark Prior RC) and card 402 (Freddy Garcia CT) were mistakenly switched with each other on the printing forms - thereby making card 402 a short-print (available at the same ratio as cards 502-601) and card 529 a basic card (available at the same rate as cards 302-501).

Nm-Mt Ex-Mt
COMP. SERIES 1 (301) 200.00 60.00
COMP. SERIES 2 (300) 200.00 60.00
COMP.SER.1 w/o SP's (250) 40.00 12.00
COMP.SER.2 w/o SP's (200) 40.00 12.00
COMMON (1-250/302-501) .30 .09
COMMON (251-280) 2.00 .60
COMMON AS (281-300) 2.00 .60
COMMON (502-601) 2.00 .60
1 Bobby Abreu .30 .09
2 Brad Radke .30 .09
3 Bill Mueller .30 .09
4 Adam Eaton .30 .09
5 Antonio Alfonseca .30 .09
6 Manny Ramirez .30 .09
7 Adam Kennedy .30 .09
8 Jose Valentin .30 .09
9 Jaret Wright .30 .09
10 Aramis Ramirez .30 .09
11 Jeff Kent .30 .09
12 Juan Encarnacion .30 .09
13 Sandy Alomar Jr. .30 .09
14 Joe Randa .30 .09
15 Darryl Kile .30 .09
16 Darren Dreifort .30 .09
17 Matt Kinney .30 .09
18 Pokey Reese .30 .09
19 Ryan Klesko .30 .09
20 Shawn Estes .30 .09
21 Moises Alou .30 .09
22 Edgar Renteria .30 .09
23 Chuck Knoblauch .30 .09
24 Carl Everett .30 .09
25 Garret Anderson .30 .09
26 Shane Reynolds .30 .09
27 Billy Koch .30 .09
28 Carlos Febles .30 .09
29 Brian Anderson .30 .09
30 Armando Rios .30 .09
31 Ryan Kohlmeier .30 .09
32 Steve Finley .30 .09
33 Brady Anderson .30 .09
34 Cal Ripken 2.50 .75
35 Paul Konerko .30 .09
36 Chuck Finley .30 .09
37 Rick Ankiel .30 .09
38 Mariano Rivera .50 .15
39 Corey Koskie .30 .09
40 Cliff Floyd .30 .09
41 Kevin Appier .30 .09
42 Henry Rodriguez .30 .09
43 Mark Kotsay .30 .09
44 Brook Fordyce .30 .09
45 Brad Ausmus .30 .09
46 Alfonso Soriano .50 .15
47 Ray Lankford .30 .09
48 Keith Foulke .30 .09
49 Rich Aurilia .30 .09
50 Alex Rodriguez 1.50 .45
51 Eric Byrnes .30 .09
52 Travis Fryman .30 .09
53 Jeff Bagwell .50 .15
54 Scott Rolen .50 .15
55 Matt Lawton .30 .09
56 Brad Fullmer .30 .09
57 Tony Batista .30 .09
58 Nate Rolison .30 .09
59 Carlos Lee .30 .09
60 Rafael Furcal .30 .09
61 Jay Bell .30 .09
62 Jimmy Rollins .30 .09
63 Derrek Lee .30 .09
64 Andres Galarraga .30 .09
65 Derek Bell .30 .09
66 Tim Salmon .50 .15
67 Travis Lee .30 .09
68 Kevin Millwood .30 .09
69 Albert Belle .30 .09
70 Kazuhiro Sasaki .30 .09
71 Al Leiter .30 .09
72 Britt Reames .30 .09
73 Carlos Beltran .30 .09
74 Curt Schilling .50 .15
75 Curtis Leskanic .30 .09
76 Jeremy Giambi .30 .09
77 Adrian Beltre .30 .09
78 David Segui .30 .09
79 Mike Lieberthal .30 .09
80 Brian Giles .30 .09
81 Marvin Benard .30 .09
82 Aaron Sele .30 .09
83 Kenny Lofton .30 .09
84 Doug Glanville .30 .09
85 Kris Benson .30 .09
86 Richie Sexson .30 .09
87 Javy Lopez .30 .09
88 Doug Mientkiewicz .30 .09
89 Peter Bergeron .30 .09
90 Gary Sheffield .30 .09
91 Derek Lowe .30 .09
92 Tom Glavine .50 .15
93 Lance Berkman .30 .09
94 Chris Singleton .30 .09
95 Mike Lowell .30 .09
96 Luis Gonzalez .30 .09
97 Dante Bichette .30 .09
98 Mike Sirotka .30 .09
99 Julio Lugo .30 .09
100 Juan Gonzalez .75 .23
101 Craig Biggio .50 .15
102 Armando Benitez .30 .09
103 Greg Maddux 1.25 .35
104 Mark Grace .50 .15
105 John Smoltz .50 .15
106 J.T. Snow .30 .09
107 Al Martin .30 .09
108 Danny Graves .30 .09
109 Barry Bonds 2.00 .60
110 Lee Stevens .30 .09
111 Pedro Martinez .75 .23
112 Shawn Green .30 .09
113 Bret Boone .30 .09
114 Matt Stairs .30 .09
115 Tino Martinez .50 .15
116 Rusty Greer .30 .09
117 Mike Bordick .30 .09
118 Garrett Stephenson .30 .09
119 Edgar Martinez .50 .15
120 Ben Grieve .30 .09
121 Milton Bradley .30 .09
122 Aaron Boone .30 .09
123 Ruben Mateo .30 .09
124 Ken Griffey Jr. 1.25 .35
125 Russell Branyan .30 .09
126 Shannon Stewart .30 .09
127 Fred McGriff .50 .15
128 Ben Petrick .30 .09
129 Kevin Brown .30 .09
130 B.J. Surhoff .30 .09
131 Mark McGwire 2.00 .60
132 Carlos Guillen .30 .09
133 Adrian Brown .30 .09
134 Mike Sweeney .30 .09
135 Eric Milton .30 .09
136 Cristian Guzman .30 .09
137 Ellis Burks .30 .09
138 Fernando Tatis .30 .09
139 Bengie Molina .30 .09
140 Tony Gwynn 1.00 .30
141 Jeromy Burnitz .30 .09
142 Miguel Tejada .30 .09
143 Raul Mondesi .30 .09
144 Jeffrey Hammonds .30 .09
145 Pat Burrell .30 .09
146 Frank Thomas .75 .23
147 Eric Munson .30 .09
148 Mike Hampton .30 .09
149 Mike Cameron .30 .09
150 Jim Thome .75 .23
151 Mike Mussina .75 .23
152 Rick Helling .30 .09
153 Ken Caminiti .30 .09
154 John VanderWal .30 .09
155 Denny Neagle .30 .09
156 Robb Nen .30 .09
157 Jose Canseco .75 .23
158 Mo Vaughn .30 .09
159 Phil Nevin .30 .09
160 Pat Hentgen .30 .09
161 Sean Casey .30 .09
162 Greg Vaughn .30 .09
163 Trot Nixon .50 .15
164 Roberto Hernandez .30 .09
165 Vinny Castilla .30 .09
166 Robin Ventura .30 .09
167 Alex Ochoa .30 .09
168 Orlando Hernandez .30 .09
169 Luis Castillo .30 .09
170 Quilvio Veras .30 .09
171 Troy O'Leary .30 .09
172 Livan Hernandez .30 .09
173 Roger Cedeno .30 .09
174 Jose Vidro .30 .09
175 John Olerud .30 .09
176 Richard Hidalgo .30 .09
177 Eric Chavez .30 .09
178 Fernando Vina .30 .09
179 Chris Stynes .30 .09
180 Bobby Higginson .30 .09
181 Bruce Chen .30 .09
182 Omar Vizquel .30 .09
183 Rey Ordonez .30 .09
184 Trevor Hoffman .30 .09
185 Jeff Cirillo .30 .09
186 Billy Wagner .30 .09
187 David Ortiz .30 .09
188 Tim Hudson .30 .09
189 Tony Clark .30 .09
190 Larry Walker .50 .15
191 Eric Owens .30 .09
192 Aubrey Huff .30 .09
193 Royce Clayton .30 .09
194 Todd Walker .30 .09
195 Rafael Palmeiro .50 .15
196 Todd Hundley .30 .09
197 Roger Clemens 1.50 .45
198 Jeff Weaver .30 .09
199 Dean Palmer .30 .09
200 Geoff Jenkins .30 .09
201 Matt Clement .30 .09
202 David Wells .30 .09
203 Chan Ho Park .30 .09
204 Hideo Nomo .75 .23
205 Bartolo Colon .30 .09
206 John Wetteland .30 .09
207 Corey Patterson .30 .09
208 Freddy Garcia .30 .09
209 David Cone .30 .09
210 Rondell White .30 .09
211 Carl Pavano .30 .09
212 Charles Johnson .30 .09
213 Ron Coomer .30 .09
214 Matt Williams .30 .09
215 Jay Payton .30 .09
216 Nick Johnson .30 .09
217 Deivi Cruz .30 .09
218 Scott Elarton .30 .09
219 Neifi Perez .30 .09
220 Jason Isringhausen .30 .09
221 Jose Cruz Jr. .30 .09
222 Gerald Williams .30 .09
223 Timo Perez .30 .09
224 Damion Easley .30 .09
225 Jeff D'Amico .30 .09
226 Preston Wilson .30 .09
227 Robert Person .30 .09
228 Jacque Jones .30 .09
229 Johnny Damon .30 .09
230 Tony Womack .30 .09
231 Adam Piatt .30 .09
232 Brian Jordan .30 .09
233 Ben Davis .30 .09
234 Kerry Wood .75 .23
235 Mike Piazza 1.25 .35
236 David Justice .30 .09
237 Dave Veres .30 .09
238 Eric Young .30 .09
239 Juan Pierre .30 .09
240 Gabe Kapler .30 .09
241 Ryan Dempster .30 .09
242 Dmitri Young .30 .09
243 Jorge Posada .50 .15
244 Eric Karros .30 .09
245 J.D. Drew .30 .09
246 Todd Zeile .30 .09
247 Mark Quinn .30 .09
248 Kenny Kelly UER .30 .09
Listed as a Mariner on the front
249 Jermaine Dye .30 .09
250 Barry Zito .75 .23
251 Jason Hart 2.00 .60
Larry Barnes
252 Ichiro Suzuki RC 25.00 7.50
Elpidio Guzman RC
253 Tsuyoshi Shinjo RC 5.00 1.50
Brian Cole
254 John Barnes 2.00 .60
Adrian Hernandez RC
255 Jason Tyner 2.00 .60
Jace Brewer
256 Brian Buchanan 2.00 .60
Luis Rivas
257 Brent Abernathy 2.00 .60
Jose Ortiz
258 Marcus Giles 2.00 .60
Keith Ginter
259 Tike Redman 2.00 .60
Jaisen Randolph RC
260 Dane Sardinha 2.00 .60
David Espinosa
261 Josh Beckett 3.00 .90
Craig House
262 Jack Cust 2.00 .60
Hiram Bocachica
263 Alex Escobar 2.00 .60
Esix Snead RC
264 Chris Richard 2.00 .60
Vernon Wells
265 Pedro Feliz 2.00 .60
Xavier Nady
266 Brandon Inge 2.00 .60
Joe Crede
267 Ben Sheets 3.00 .90
Roy Oswalt
268 Drew Henson RC 6.00 1.80
Andy Morales RC
269 C.C. Sabathia 2.00 .60
Justin Miller
270 David Eckstein 2.00 .60
Jason Grabowski
271 Dee Brown 2.00 .60
Chris Wakeland
272 Junior Spivey RC 4.00 1.20
Alex Cintron
273 Elvis Pena 2.00 .60
Juan Uribe RC
274 Carlos Pena 2.00 .60
Jason Romano
275 Winston Abreu 2.00 .60
Wilson Betemit
276 Jose Mieses RC 2.00 .60
Nick Neugebauer
277 Shea Hillenbrand 2.00 .60
Dernell Stenson
278 Jared Sandberg 2.00 .60
Toby Hall
279 Jay Gibbons RC 5.00 1.50
Ivanon Coffie
280 Pablo Ozuna 2.00 .60
Santiago Perez
281 N.Garciaparra AS 8.00 2.40
282 Derek Jeter AS 12.00 3.60
283 Jason Giambi AS 5.00 1.50
284 Magglio Ordonez AS 2.00 .60
285 Ivan Rodriguez AS 5.00 1.50
286 Troy Glaus AS 3.00 .90
287 Carlos Delgado AS 2.00 .60
288 Darin Erstad AS 2.00 .60
289 Bernie Williams AS 3.00 .90
290 Roberto Alomar AS 5.00 1.50
291 Barry Larkin AS 5.00 1.50
292 Chipper Jones AS 5.00 1.50
293 Vladimir Guerrero AS 5.00 1.50
294 Sammy Sosa AS 8.00 2.40
295 Todd Helton AS 3.00 .90
296 Randy Johnson AS 5.00 1.50
297 Jason Kendall AS 2.00 .60
298 Jim Edmonds AS 2.00 .60
299 Andruw Jones AS 2.00 .60
300 Edgardo Alfonzo AS 2.00 .60
301 Albert Pujols RC 60.00 18.00
Donaldo Mendez RC/1500
302 Shawn Wooten .30 .09
303 Todd Walker .30 .09
304 Brian Buchanan .30 .09
305 Jim Edmonds .30 .09
306 Jarrod Washburn .30 .09
307 Jose Rijo .30 .09
308 Tim Raines .30 .09
309 Matt Morris .30 .09
310 Troy Glaus .50 .15
311 Barry Larkin .75 .23
312 Javier Vazquez .30 .09
313 Placido Polanco .30 .09
314 Darin Erstad .30 .09
315 Marty Cordova .30 .09
316 Vladimir Guerrero .75 .23
317 Kerry Robinson .30 .09
318 Byung-Hyun Kim .30 .09
319 C.C. Sabathia .30 .09
320 Edgardo Alfonzo .30 .09
321 Jason Tyner .30 .09
322 Reggie Sanders .30 .09
323 Roberto Alomar .75 .23
324 Matt Lawton .30 .09
325 Brent Abernathy .30 .09
326 Randy Johnson .75 .23
327 Todd Helton .50 .15
328 Andy Pettitte .50 .15
329 Josh Beckett .50 .15
330 Mark DeRosa .30 .09
331 Jose Ortiz .30 .09
332 Derek Jeter 2.00 .60
333 Toby Hall .30 .09
334 Wes Helms .30 .09
335 Jose Macias .30 .09
336 Bernie Williams .50 .15
337 Ivan Rodriguez .75 .23
338 Chipper Jones .75 .23
339 Brandon Inge .30 .09
340 Jason Giambi .75 .23
341 Frank Catalanotto .30 .09
342 Andruw Jones .30 .09
343 Carlos Hernandez .30 .09
344 Jermaine Dye .30 .09
345 Mike Lamb .30 .09
346 Ken Caminiti .30 .09
347 A.J. Burnett .30 .09
348 Terrence Long .30 .09
349 Ruben Sierra .30 .09
350 Marcus Giles UER .30 .09
Listed as a pitcher on the back
351 Wade Miller .30 .09
352 Mark Mulder .30 .09
353 Carlos Delgado .30 .09
354 Chris Richard .30 .09
355 Dayle Ward .30 .09
356 Brad Penny .30 .09
357 Vernon Wells .30 .09
358 Jason Johnson .30 .09
359 Tim Redding .30 .09
360 Marlon Anderson .30 .09
361 Carlos Pena .30 .09
362 Nomar Garciaparra 1.25 .35
363 Roy Oswalt .50 .15
364 Todd Ritchie .30 .09
365 Jose Mesa .30 .09
366 Shea Hillenbrand .30 .09
367 Dee Brown .30 .09
368 Jason Kendall .30 .09
369 Vinny Castilla .30 .09
370 Fred McGriff .50 .15
371 Neifi Perez .30 .09
372 Xavier Nady .30 .09
373 Abraham Nunez .30 .09
374 Jon Lieber .30 .09
375 Paul LoDuca .30 .09
376 Bubba Trammell .30 .09
377 Brady Clark .30 .09
378 Joel Pineiro .75 .23
379 Mark Grudzielanek .30 .09
380 D'Angelo Jimenez .30 .09
381 Junior Herndon .30 .09
382 Magglio Ordonez .30 .09
383 Ben Sheets .30 .09
384 John Vander Wal .30 .09
385 Pedro Astacio .30 .09
386 Jose Canseco .75 .23
387 Jose Hernandez .30 .09
388 Eric Davis .30 .09
389 Sammy Sosa 1.25 .35
390 Mark Buehrle .30 .09
391 Mark Loretta .30 .09
392 Andres Galarraga .30 .09
393 Scott Spiezio .30 .09
394 Joe Crede .30 .09
395 Luis Rivas .30 .09
396 David Bell .30 .09
397 Einar Diaz .30 .09
398 Adam Dunn .30 .09
399 A.J. Pierzynski .30 .09
400 Jamie Moyer .30 .09
401 Nick Johnson .30 .09
402 Freddy Garcia CT SP 10.00 3.00
403 Hideo Nomo CT .30 .09
404 Mark Mulder CT .30 .09
405 Steve Sparks CT .30 .09
406 Mariano Rivera CT .30 .09
407 Mark Buerhle .50 .15
Mike Mussina CT
408 Randy Johnson CT .50 .15
409 Randy Johnson CT .50 .15
410 Curt Schilling .30 .09
Matt Morris CT
411 Greg Maddux CT .75 .23
412 Robb Nen CT .30 .09
413 Randy Johnson CT .50 .15
414 Barry Bonds CT .75 .23
415 Jason Giambi CT .30 .09
416 Ichiro Suzuki CT 5.00 1.50
417 Ichiro Suzuki CT 5.00 1.50
418 Alex Rodriguez CT .75 .23
419 Bret Boone CT .30 .09
420 Ichiro Suzuki CT 5.00 1.50
421 Alex Rodriguez CT .75 .23
422 Jason Giambi CT .30 .09
423 Alex Rodriguez CT .75 .23
424 Larry Walker CT .30 .09
425 Rich Aurilia CT .30 .09
426 Barry Bonds CT .75 .23
427 Sammy Sosa CT .75 .23
428 Jimmy Rollins .30 .09
Juan Pierre CT
429 Sammy Sosa CT .75 .23
430 Lance Berkman CT .30 .09
431 Sammy Sosa CT .75 .23
432 Carlos Delgado TL .30 .09
433 Alex Rodriguez TL .75 .23
434 Greg Vaughn TL .30 .09
435 Albert Pujols TL 15.00 4.50
436 Ichiro Suzuki TL 5.00 1.50
437 Barry Bonds TL .75 .23
438 Phil Nevin TL .30 .09
439 Brian Giles TL .30 .09
440 Bobby Abreu TL .30 .09
441 Jason Giambi TL .30 .09
442 Derek Jeter TL 1.00 .30
443 Mike Piazza TL .75 .23
444 Vladimir Guerrero TL .50 .15
445 Corey Koskie TL .30 .09
446 Richie Sexson TL .30 .09
447 Shawn Green TL .30 .09
448 Mike Sweeney TL .30 .09
449 Jeff Bagwell TL .30 .09
450 Cliff Floyd TL .30 .09
451 Roger Cedeno TL .30 .09
452 Todd Helton TL .30 .09
453 Juan Gonzalez TL .50 .15
454 Sean Casey TL .30 .09
455 Magglio Ordonez TL .30 .09
456 Sammy Sosa TL .75 .23
457 Manny Ramirez TL .30 .09
458 Jeff Conine TL .30 .09
459 Chipper Jones TL .50 .15
460 Luis Gonzalez TL .30 .09
461 Troy Glaus TL .30 .09
462 Ivan Rodriguez .50 .15
Jason Romano FF
463 Luis Gonzalez .30 .09
Jack Cust FF
464 Jim Thome .30 .09
C.C. Sabathia FF
465 Jason Giambi .30 .09
Jason Hart FF
466 Jeff Bagwell .50 .15
Roy Oswalt FF
467 Sammy Sosa .75 .23
Corey Patterson FF
468 Mike Piazza .75 .23
Alex Escobar FF
469 Ken Griffey Jr. .75 .23
Adam Dunn FF
470 Roger Clemens .75 .23
Nick Johnson FF
471 Cliff Floyd .30 .09
Josh Beckett FF
472 Cal Ripken Jr. 1.25 .35
Jerry Hairston Jr. FF
473 Phil Nevin .30 .09
Xavier Nady FF
474 Scott Rolen .30 .09
Jimmy Rollins FF
475 Barry Larkin .50 .15
David Espinosa FF
476 Larry Walker .50 .15
Jose Ortiz FF
477 Chipper Jones .50 .15
Marcus Giles FF
478 Craig Biggio .30 .09
Keith Ginter FF
479 Magglio Ordonez .30 .09
Aaron Rowand FF
480 Alex Rodriguez .75 .23
Carlos Pena FF
481 Derek Jeter 1.00 .30
Alfonso Soriano FF
482 Erubiel Durazo PG .30 .09
483 Bernie Williams PG .30 .09
484 Team Photo PG .30 .09
485 Team Photo PG .30 .09
486 Andy Pettitte PG .30 .09
487 Curt Schilling PG .30 .09
488 Randy Johnson PG .50 .15
489 Rudolph Guiliani PG .75 .23
Mayor of New York City
490 George W. Bush PG 2.50 .75
President of United States
491 Roger Clemens PG .75 .23
492 Mariano Rivera PG .50 .15
493 Tino Martinez PG .30 .09
494 Derek Jeter PG 1.00 .30
495 Scott Brosius PG .30 .09
496 Alfonso Soriano PG .30 .09
497 Matt Williams PG .30 .09
498 Tony Womack PG .30 .09
499 Luis Gonzalez PG .30 .09
500 Arizona Diamondbacks PG .75 .23
501 Randy Johnson .50 .15
Curt Schilling
Co-MVP's PG
502 Josh Fogg RC 2.00 .60
503 Elpidio Guzman RC 2.00 .60
504 Corky Miller RC 2.00 .60
505 Cesar Crespo RC 2.00 .60
506 Carlos Garcia RC 2.00 .60
507 Carlos Valderrama RC 2.00 .60
508 Joe Kennedy RC 2.00 .60
509 Henry Mateo RC 2.00 .60
510 B. Duckworth RC 2.00 .60
511 Ichiro Suzuki 15.00 4.50
512 Zach Day RC 3.00 .90
513 Ryan Freel RC 2.00 .60
514 Brian Lawrence RC 2.00 .60
515 Alexis Gomez RC 2.00 .60
516 Will Ohman RC 2.00 .60
517 Juan Diaz RC 2.00 .60
518 Juan Moreno RC 2.00 .60
519 Rob Mackowiak RC 2.00 .60
520 Horacio Ramirez RC 3.00 .90
521 Albert Pujols 40.00 12.00
522 Tsuyoshi Shinjo 4.00 1.20
523 Ryan Drese RC 2.00 .60
524 Angel Berroa RC 5.00 1.50
525 Josh Towers RC 2.00 .60
526 Junior Spivey 3.00 .90
527 Greg Miller RC 2.00 .60
528 Esix Snead 2.00 .60
529 Mark Prior DP RC 30.00 9.00
530 Drew Henson 4.00 1.20
531 Brian Reith RC 2.00 .60
532 Andres Torres RC 2.00 .60
533 Casey Fossum RC 2.00 .60
534 Wilmy Caceres RC 2.00 .60
535 Matt White RC 2.00 .60
536 Wilkin Ruan RC 2.00 .60
537 Rick Bauer RC 2.00 .60
538 Morgan Ensberg RC 4.00 1.20
539 Geronimo Gil RC 2.00 .60

540 Dewon Brazelton RC 3.00 .90
541 Johnny Estrada RC 3.00 .90
542 Claudio Vargas RC 2.00 .60
543 Donaldo Mendez 2.00 .60
544 Kyle Lohse RC 3.00 .90
545 Nate Frese RC 2.00 .60
546 Christian Parker RC 2.00 .60
547 Blaine Neal RC 2.00 .60
548 Travis Hafner RC 5.00 1.50
549 Billy Sylvester RC 2.00 .60
550 Adam Pettyjohn RC 2.00 .60
551 Bill Ortega RC 2.00 .60
552 Jose Acevedo RC 2.00 .60
553 Steve Green RC 2.00 .60
554 Jay Gibbons 4.00 1.20
555 Bert Snow RC 2.00 .60
556 Erick Almonte RC 2.00 .60
557 Jeremy Owens RC 2.00 .60
558 Sean Douglass RC 2.00 .60
559 Jason Smith RC 2.00 .60
560 Ricardo Rodriguez RC 2.00 .60
561 Mark Teixeira RC 12.00 3.60
562 Tyler Walker RC 2.00 .60
563 Juan Uribe 2.00 .60
564 Bud Smith RC 2.00 .60
565 Angel Santos RC 2.00 .60
566 Brandon Lyon RC 2.00 .60
567 Eric Hinske RC UER 3.00 .90
Front says he is a pitcher
568 Nick Punto RC 2.00 .60
569 Winston Abreu 2.00 .60
570 Jason Phillips RC 25.00 7.50
571 Rafael Soriano RC 5.00 1.50
572 Wilson Betemit 2.00 .60
573 Endy Chavez RC 2.00 .60
574 Juan Cruz RC 2.00 .60
575 Cory Aldridge RC 2.00 .60
576 Adrian Hernandez 2.00 .60
577 Brandon Larson RC 2.00 .60
578 Bret Prinz RC 2.00 .60
579 Jackson Melian RC 2.00 .60
580 Dave Maurer RC 2.00 .60
581 Jason Michaels RC 2.00 .60
582 Travis Phelps RC 2.00 .60
583 Cody Ransom RC 2.00 .60
584 Benito Baez RC 2.00 .60
585 Brian Roberts RC 2.00 .60
586 Nate Teut RC 2.00 .60
587 Jack Wilson RC 2.00 .60
588 Willie Harris RC 2.00 .60
589 Martin Vargas RC 2.00 .60
590 Steve Torrealba RC 2.00 .60
591 Stubby Clapp RC 2.00 .60
592 Dan Wright 2.00 .60
593 Mike Rivera RC 2.00 .60
594 Luis Pineda RC 2.00 .60
595 Lance Davis RC 2.00 .60
596 Ramon Vazquez RC 2.00 .60
597 Dustan Mohr RC 2.00 .60
598 Troy Mattes RC 2.00 .60
599 Grant Balfour RC 2.00 .60
600 Jared Fernandez RC 2.00 .60
601 Jorge Julio RC 2.00 .60

2001 Fleer Platinum Parallel

Randomly inserted in hobby packs, this 600-card set is a parallel version of the base set. Cards 1-250 and 302-501 are sequentially numbered to 201 and cards 251-300 and 502-601 to 21. Card number 300 was never produced as a Parallel.

Nm-Mt Ex-Mt
*STARS 1-250/302-501: 2.5X TO 6X BASIC
*SUBSET RC'S 402-501: 2X TO 5X BASIC

2001 Fleer Platinum 20th Anniversary Reprints

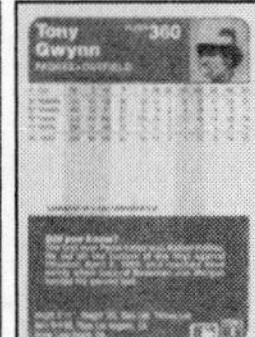

Randomly inserted in hobby packs at the rate of one in eight and in jumbo packs at the rate of one in four, this 18-card set features reprints of Fleer's best rookie cards from the past 20 years of cards.

Nm-Mt Ex-Mt
COMPLETE SET (18) 60.00 18.00
1 Cal Ripken 82F 12.00 3.60
2 Wade Boggs 83F 2.50 .75
3 Ryne Sandberg 83F 6.00 1.80
4 Tony Gwynn 83F 5.00 1.50
5 Don Mattingly 84F 10.00 3.00
6 Roger Clemens 85F 8.00 2.40
7 Kirby Puckett 85F 4.00 1.20
8 Jose Canseco 86LL 4.00 1.20
9 Barry Bonds 87F 10.00 3.00
10 Ken Griffey Jr. 89F 6.00 1.80
11 Sammy Sosa 90F 6.00 1.80
12 Ivan Rodriguez 91UU 4.00 1.20
13 Jeff Bagwell 91UU 2.50 .75
14 J.D. Drew 98UPD 2.50 .75
15 Troy Glaus 98UPD 2.50 .75
16 Rick Ankiel 99UPD 2.50 .75
17 Xavier Nady 00GL 2.50 .75
18 Jose Ortiz 00GL 2.50 .75

2001 Fleer Platinum Classic Combinations

Randomly inserted in packs, this 40-card set features dual player cards which pair some of the greatest players in the game. Cards 1-10 are serially numbered to 250, 11-20 to 500, 21-30 to 1,000, and 31-40 to 2,000.

Nm-Mt Ex-Mt
COMPLETE SET (40) 800.00 240.00
COMMON (CC1-CC10) 20.00 6.00
COMMON (CC11-CC20) 15.00 4.50
COMMON (CC21-CC30) 8.00 2.40

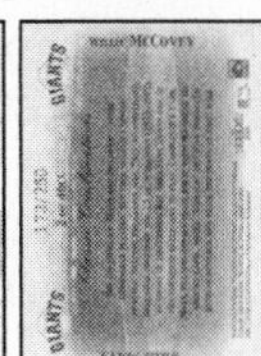

COMMON (CC31-CC40) 5.00 1.50
CC1 Derek Jeter 20.00 6.00
Alex Rodriguez
CC2 Willie Mays 25.00 7.50
Willie McCovey
CC3 Lou Gehrig 40.00 12.00
Babe Ruth
CC4 Mark McGwire 30.00 9.00
Ken Griffey Jr.
CC5 Johnny Bench 20.00 6.00
Roy Campanella
CC6 Ted Williams 30.00 9.00
Nomar Garciaparra
CC7 Yogi Berra 20.00 6.00
Mike Piazza
CC8 Ernie Banks 20.00 6.00
Sammy Sosa
CC9 Nolan Ryan 30.00 9.00
Randy Johnson
CC10 Roberto Clemente 30.00 9.00
Vladimir Guerrero
CC11 Stan Musial 30.00 9.00
Lou Gehrig
CC12 Bill Mazeroski 25.00 7.50
Roberto Clemente
CC13 Ernie Banks 15.00 4.50
Alex Rodriguez
CC14 Phil Rizzuto 25.00 7.50
Derek Jeter
CC15 Mike Piazza 15.00 4.50
Johnny Bench
CC16 Mark McGwire 25.00 7.50
Sammy Sosa
CC17 Ted Williams 25.00 7.50
Tony Gwynn
CC18 Eddie Mathews 20.00 6.00
Mike Schmidt
CC19 Barry Bonds 25.00 7.50
Willie Mays
CC20 Nolan Ryan 30.00 9.00
Pedro Martinez
CC21 Barry Bonds 20.00 6.00
Ken Griffey Jr.
CC22 Willie McCovey 5.00 1.50
Reggie Jackson
CC23 Roberto Clemente 20.00 6.00
Sammy Sosa
CC24 Willie Mays 15.00 4.50
Ernie Banks
CC25 Eddie Mathews 8.00 2.40
Chipper Jones
CC26 Mike Schmidt 15.00 4.50
Brooks Robinson
CC27 Stan Musial 20.00 6.00
Mark McGwire
CC28 Ted Williams 20.00 6.00
Roger Maris
CC29 Yogi Berra 5.00 1.50
Roy Campanella
CC30 Johnny Bench 8.00 2.40
Tony Perez
CC31 Bill Mazeroski 5.00 1.50
Joe Carter
CC32 Mike Piazza 8.00 2.40
Roy Campanella
CC33 Ernie Banks 5.00 1.50
Craig Biggio
CC34 Frank Robinson 5.00 1.50
Brooks Robinson
CC35 Mike Schmidt 10.00 3.00
Scott Rolen
CC36 Roger Maris 12.00 3.60
Mark McGwire
CC37 Stan Musial 8.00 2.40
Tony Gwynn
CC38 Ted Williams 12.00 3.60
Bill Terry
CC39 Derek Jeter 12.00 3.60
Reggie Jackson
CC40 Yogi Berra 5.00 1.50
Bill Dickey

2001 Fleer Platinum Classic Combinations Memorabilia

Randomly inserted in packs, this 11-card set features dual player cards which pair some of the greatest players in the game and contain pieces of game-used bats. Only 25 serially numbered sets were produced.

Nm-Mt Ex-Mt
1 Yogi Berra
Bill Dickey
2 Yogi Berra
Roy Campanella
3 Roberto Clemente Bat
Vladimir Guerrero Bat
4 Eddie Mathews
Chipper Jones
5 Willie McCovey
Reggie Jackson
6 Phil Rizzuto
Derek Jeter
7 Frank Robinson
Brooks Robinson
8 Mike Schmidt
Brooks Robinson
9 Mike Schmidt
Scott Rolen
10 Ted Williams
Bill Terry
11 Ted Williams
Tony Gwynn

2001 Fleer Platinum Classic Combinations Retail

Randomly inserted into retail packs at the rate of one in 20, this 40-card set is a parallel version of the regular insert set.

Nm-Mt Ex-Mt
COMPLETE SET (40) 300.00 90.00
CC1 Derek Jeter 12.00 3.60
Alex Rodriguez
CC2 Willie Mays 10.00 3.00
Willie McCovey
CC3 Lou Gehrig 15.00 4.50
Babe Ruth
CC4 Mark McGwire 12.00 3.60
Ken Griffey Jr.
CC5 Johnny Bench
Roy Campanella
CC6 Ted Williams 12.00 3.60
Nomar Garciaparra
CC7 Yogi Berra 8.00 2.40
Mike Piazza
CC8 Ernie Banks 8.00 2.40
Sammy Sosa
CC9 Nolan Ryan 12.00 3.60
Randy Johnson
CC10 Roberto Clemente 12.00 3.60
Vladimir Guerrero
CC11 Stan Musial 10.00 3.00
Lou Gehrig
CC12 Bill Mazeroski 12.00 3.60
Roberto Clemente
CC13 Ernie Banks 8.00 2.40
Alex Rodriguez
CC14 Phil Rizzuto 12.00 3.60
Derek Jeter
CC15 Mike Piazza 8.00 2.40
Johnny Bench
CC16 Mark McGwire 12.00 3.60
Sammy Sosa
CC17 Ted Williams 12.00 3.60
Tony Gwynn
CC18 Eddie Mathews 10.00 3.00
Mike Schmidt
CC19 Barry Bonds 12.00 3.60
Willie Mays
CC20 Nolan Ryan 12.00 3.60
Pedro Martinez
CC21 Barry Bonds 12.00 3.60
Ken Griffey Jr.
CC22 Willie McCovey 4.00 1.20
Reggie Jackson
CC23 Roberto Clemente 12.00 3.60
Sammy Sosa
CC24 Willie Mays 8.00 2.40
Ernie Banks
CC25 Eddie Mathews 5.00 1.50
Chipper Jones
CC26 Mike Schmidt 10.00 3.00
Brooks Robinson
CC27 Stan Musial 12.00 3.60
Mark McGwire
CC28 Ted Williams 12.00 3.60
Roger Maris
CC29 Yogi Berra 5.00 1.50
Roy Campanella
CC30 Johnny Bench 5.00 1.50
Tony Perez
CC31 Bill Mazeroski 4.00 1.20
Joe Carter
CC32 Mike Piazza 8.00 2.40
Roy Campanella
CC33 Ernie Banks 5.00 1.50
Craig Biggio
CC34 Frank Robinson 5.00 1.50
Brooks Robinson
CC35 Mike Schmidt 10.00 3.00
Scott Rolen
CC36 Roger Maris 12.00 3.60
Mark McGwire
CC37 Stan Musial 8.00 2.40
Tony Gwynn
CC38 Ted Williams 12.00 3.60
Bill Terry
CC39 Derek Jeter 12.00 3.60
Reggie Jackson
CC40 Yogi Berra 5.00 1.50
Bill Dickey

2001 Fleer Platinum Grandstand Greats

Randomly inserted in hobby packs at the rate of one in 12 and in jumbo packs at the rate of one in six, this 20-card set features color photos of the crowd-pleasers of the League.

Nm-Mt Ex-Mt
COMPLETE SET (20) 80.00 24.00
GG1 Chipper Jones 3.00 .90
GG2 Alex Rodriguez 5.00 1.50
GG3 Jeff Bagwell 2.00 .60
GG4 Troy Glaus 2.00 .60
GG5 Manny Ramirez 2.00 .60
GG6 Derek Jeter 8.00 2.40
GG7 Tony Gwynn 4.00 1.20
GG8 Greg Maddux 5.00 1.50
GG9 Nomar Garciaparra 5.00 1.50
GG10 Sammy Sosa 5.00 1.50
GG11 Mike Piazza 5.00 1.50
GG12 Barry Bonds 8.00 2.40
GG13 Mark McGwire 8.00 2.40
GG14 Vladimir Guerrero 3.00 .90
GG15 Ivan Rodriguez 3.00 .90
GG16 Ken Griffey Jr. 5.00 1.50
GG17 Todd Helton 2.00 .60
GG18 Cal Ripken 10.00 3.00
GG19 Pedro Martinez 3.00 .90
GG20 Frank Thomas 3.00 .90

2001 Fleer Platinum Lumberjacks

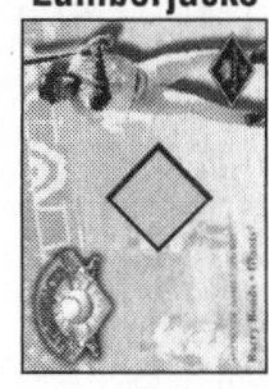

This 27-card insert set features game-used bat chips from greats like Derek Jeter and Ivan Rodriguez. These cards were inserted at a stated rate of one per rack pack

Nm-Mt Ex-Mt
1 Roberto Alomar 15.00 4.50
2 Moises Alou 10.00 3.00
3 Adrian Beltre 10.00 3.00
4 Lance Berkman 10.00 3.00
5 Barry Bonds 25.00 7.50
6 Bret Boone 10.00 3.00
7 J.D. Drew
8 Adam Dunn 10.00 3.00
9 Darin Erstad 10.00 3.00
10 Cliff Floyd 10.00 3.00
11 Brian Giles 10.00 3.00
12 Luis Gonzalez 10.00 3.00
13 Vladimir Guerrero 15.00 4.50
14 Cristian Guzman 10.00 3.00
15 Tony Gwynn 15.00 4.50
16 Todd Helton 15.00 4.50
17 Drew Henson 15.00 4.50
18 Derek Jeter 25.00 7.50
19 Chipper Jones 15.00 4.50
20 Mike Piazza 15.00 4.50
21 Albert Pujols 40.00 12.00
22 Manny Ramirez 10.00 3.00
23 Cal Ripken
24 Ivan Rodriguez 15.00 4.50
25 Gary Sheffield 10.00 3.00
26 Mike Sweeney 10.00 3.00
27 Larry Walker 15.00 4.50

2001 Fleer Platinum Lumberjacks Autographs

This eight-card set is a partial parallel to the 2001 Fleer Platinum Lumberjacks insert. Each card is autographed and individually serial numbered to 100. Not all the cards were signed in time for inclusion in packs and those exchange cards could be redeemed until November 30, 2002. The following players were seeded into packs as exchange cards: Barry Bonds, Derek Jeter, Albert Pujols and Cal Ripken.

Nm-Mt Ex-Mt
6 Barry Bonds 300.00 90.00
7 J.D. Drew
8 Adam Dunn 100.00 30.00
12 Luis Gonzalez 80.00 24.00
18 Derek Jeter 200.00 60.00
21 Albert Pujols 250.00 75.00
23 Cal Ripken 200.00 60.00
26 Mike Sweeney

2001 Fleer Platinum Nameplates

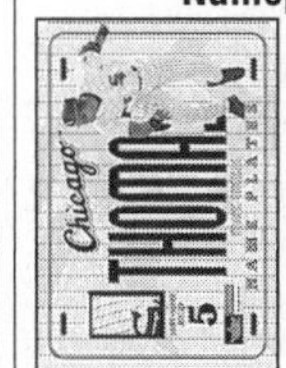

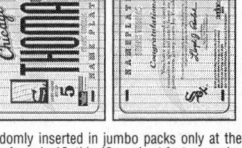

Randomly inserted in jumbo packs only at the rate of one in 12, this 42-card set features color images of top players on a license plate design background and pieces of actual name plates from players' uniforms embedded in the cards.

Nm-Mt Ex-Mt
1 Carlos Beltran/90 25.00 7.50
2 Adrian Beltre/55* 25.00 7.50
3 Sean Casey/21
4 J.D. Drew/170 25.00 7.50
5 Darin Erstad/39 25.00 7.50
6 Troy Glaus/85 40.00 12.00
7 Tom Glavine/125 40.00 12.00
8 Vladimir Guerrero/80 40.00 12.00
9 Vladimir Guerrero/90 40.00 12.00
10 Tony Gwynn/35 120.00 36.00
11 Tony Gwynn/65 60.00 18.00
12 Tony Gwynn/70 60.00 18.00
13 Jeffrey Hammonds/135 25.00 7.50
14 Randy Johnson/99 40.00 12.00
15 Chipper Jones/95 40.00 12.00
16 Javy Lopez/49* 25.00 7.50
17 Greg Maddux/180 80.00 24.00
18 Edgar Martinez/87 40.00 12.00
19 Pedro Martinez/120 40.00 12.00
20 Kevin Millwood/130 25.00 7.50
21 Stan Musial/30 200.00 60.00
22 Mike Mussina/91 40.00 12.00
23 Manny Ramirez/75 25.00 7.50
24 Manny Ramirez/105 25.00 7.50
25 Cal Ripken/19
26 Cal Ripken/21
27 Cal Ripken/23
28 Cal Ripken/110 150.00 45.00
29 Ivan Rodriguez/177 40.00 12.00
30 Scott Rolen/65 40.00 12.00
31 Scott Rolen/125 40.00 12.00
32 Nolan Ryan/40 200.00 60.00
33 Nolan Ryan/55 200.00 60.00
34 Curt Schilling/110* 40.00 12.00
35 Frank Thomas/35 50.00 15.00
36 Frank Thomas/75 40.00 12.00
37 Frank Thomas/80 40.00 12.00
38 Robin Ventura/99 25.00 7.50
39 Larry Walker/79 40.00 12.00
40 Larry Walker/85 40.00 12.00
41 Matt Williams/175 25.00 7.50
42 Dave Winfield/80 25.00 7.50

2001 Fleer Platinum National Patch Time

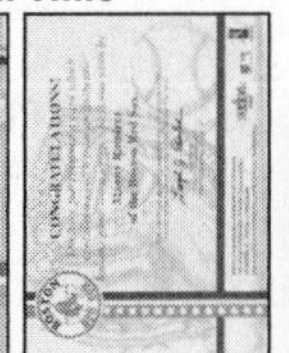

Randomly inserted in first and second series hobby packs at the rate of one in 24 and first and second series retail packs at the rate of one in 36, this set features color images of superstars of baseball with authentic game-worn jersey and pants swatches embedded in the cards. Jersey cards featureing the following players: Mo Vaughn, Kazuhiro Sasaki, Aaron Sele, Todd Walker, Jorge Posada, Vida Blue, Jim Palmer, Jim Rice, Mike Mussina, and Carl Yastrzemski were produced. However, due to MLB regulations these cards were pulled at the last minute from series one packs. Vaughn and Sasaki were eventually seeded into second series packs and a lone Mike Mussina copy was verified as coming from a second series pack, but no Mussina's or Yastrzemski's were intended for release.

Nm-Mt Ex-Mt
1 Edgardo Alfonzo S1 10.00 3.00
2 B.Anderson Pants S1 10.00 3.00
3 Jeff Bagwell S2 15.00 4.50
4 Adrian Beltre S2 10.00 3.00
5 Wade Boggs S1 15.00 4.50
6 Barry Bonds S2 25.00 7.50
7 George Brett S1 40.00 12.00
8 Eric Chavez S2 10.00 3.00
9 Jeff Cirillo S1 10.00 3.00
10 R.Clemens Gray S1 25.00 7.50
11 R.Clemens White S2 25.00 7.50
12 Pedro Martinez S1 15.00 4.50
12 J.D. Drew S2 10.00 3.00
13 Darin Erstad S2 10.00 3.00
14 Carl Everett S1 10.00 3.00
15 Rollie Fingers Pants S1 10.00 3.00
16 Freddy Garcia White S1 10.00 3.00
17 Freddy Garcia White S2 10.00 3.00
18 Jason Giambi SP S2 15.00 4.50
19 Juan Gonzalez SP S2 15.00 4.50
20 Mark Grace S2 15.00 4.50
21 Shawn Green S2 10.00 3.00
22 Ben Grieve S2 10.00 3.00
23 Vladimir Guerrero S2 15.00 4.50
24 Tony Gwynn White S1 15.00 4.50
25 Tony Gwynn White S2 15.00 4.50
26 Todd Helton S2 15.00 4.50
27 Randy Johnson S2 15.00 4.50
28 Chipper Jones S2 15.00 4.50
29 David Justice S2 10.00 3.00
30 Jason Kendall S1 10.00 3.00
31 Jeff Kent S2 10.00 3.00
32 Paul LoDuca S2 10.00 3.00
33 Greg Maddux White S1 15.00 4.50
34 G.Maddux Gray-White S2 15.00 4.50
36 Fred McGriff S1 15.00 4.50
37 Eddie Murray S1 15.00 4.50
38 Mike Mussina S2 SP
39 John Olerud S2 10.00 3.00
40 M.Ordonez Gray S1 10.00 3.00
41 M.Ordonez Gray SP S2 10.00 3.00
42 Adam Piatt S1 10.00 3.00
43 Jorge Posada S2 15.00 4.50
44 Manny Ramirez S1 10.00 3.00
45 Cal Ripken Black S1 50.00 15.00
46 C.Ripken Gray-White S2 50.00 15.00
47 Mariano Rivera S2 15.00 4.50
48 Ivan Rodriguez Blue S1 15.00 4.50
49 I.Rodriguez Blue-WhiteS2 15.00 4.50
50 Scott Rolen S2 15.00 4.50
51 Nolan Ryan S1 40.00 12.00
52 Kazuhiro Sasaki S2 10.00 3.00
53 Mike Schmidt S1 25.00 7.50
54 Tom Seaver S1 15.00 4.50
55 Aaron Sele S2 10.00 3.00
56 Gary Sheffield S2 10.00 3.00
57 Ozzie Smith S1 15.00 4.50
58 John Smoltz S2 15.00 4.50
59 Frank Thomas S2 15.00 4.50
60 Mo Vaughn S2 10.00 3.00
61 Robin Ventura S2 10.00 3.00
62 Rondell White S1 10.00 3.00
63 Bernie Williams S2 15.00 4.50
64 Dave Winfield S1 10.00 3.00

2001 Fleer Platinum Prime Numbers

This 15-card insert set was issued in jumbo packs at 1:12, and features game-used jersey swatches from veteran players like Cal Ripken and Chipper Jones.

	Nm-Mt	Ex-Mt
1 Jeff Bagwell	25.00	7.50
2 Cal Ripken	100.00	30.00
3 Barry Bonds	80.00	24.00
4 Todd Helton		
5 Derek Jeter	80.00	24.00
6 Tony Gwynn	40.00	12.00
7 Kazuhiro Sasaki	15.00	4.50
8 Chan Ho Park	15.00	4.50
9 Sean Casey		
10 Chipper Jones	25.00	7.50
11 Pedro Martinez	25.00	7.50
12 Mike Piazza	50.00	15.00
13 Carlos Delgado	15.00	4.50
14 Craig Biggio		
15 Roger Clemens	60.00	18.00

2001 Fleer Platinum Rack Pack Autographs

Randomly inserted in rack packs only, this 21-card set features actual autographed player cards and autographics cards from the last 20 years. These cards were almost all originally inserted in Fleer packs and were bought back for signing for this product.

	Nm-Mt	Ex-Mt
1 H.Aaron 1997 SI/90	120.00	36.00
2 L.Brock 1998 SITN/15		
3 Roger Clemens 1998 SITN/125	100.00	30.00
4 Jose Cruz Jr. 1997 No Brand	5.00	1.50
5 J.Drew 1999 SI One's/10*		
6 S.Garvey 1987 Fleer/15*		
7 Bob Gibson 1998 SITN/300	30.00	9.00
8 B.Grieve No Brand/100*	5.00	1.50
9 T.Gwynn 1998 SITN/125	60.00	18.00
10 Wes Helms 1997 No Brand	5.00	1.50
11 Harmon Killebrew 1998 SITN/300	40.00	12.00
12 Paul Konerko No Brand/135*	15.00	4.50
13 W.Mays 1997 SI/115	150.00	45.00
14 Willie Mays 1998 SITN/120	150.00	45.00
15 K.Puckett 1997 SI/105	80.00	24.00
16 C.Ripken 1997 SI/5		
17 Brooks Robinson 1998 SITN/40	120.00	36.00
18 Frank Robinson 1997 SI/115	30.00	9.00
19 Scott Rolen 1998 SITN/150	30.00	9.00
20 Alex Rodriguez 1997 SI/94	150.00	45.00
21 Alex Rodriguez 1998 Promo/150	100.00	30.00

2001 Fleer Platinum Tickets Autographs

Randomly inserted in hobby boxes, this nine-card set is a partial parallel version of the regular insert set and is distinguished by the autographs on the tickets.

	Nm-Mt	Ex-Mt
1 George Brett 3000th Hit 9/30/92		
2 Rod Carew 3000th Hit 8/4/85		
3 Steve Carlton 300th Win 9/23/83	30.00	9.00
4 Bob Gibson 1968 WS		
5 Stan Musial Last Game 9/29/63		
6 Cal Ripken 1991 AS MVP		
7 Cal Ripken 400th HR		
8 Mike Schmidt 500th HR 4/18/87		
9 Mike Schmidt Opening Day		

2001 Fleer Platinum Winning Combinations

This 40-card insert was issued in Series two hobby packs. The set pairs players that have similar abilities. Each card is serial numbered to either 2000, 1000, 500, or 250.

	Nm-Mt	Ex-Mt
1 Derek Jeter / Ozzie Smith/2000	12.00	3.60
2 Barry Bonds / Mark McGwire/500	25.00	7.50
3 Ichiro Suzuki / Albert Pujols/250	60.00	18.00
4 Ted Williams / Manny Ramirez/1000	20.00	6.00
5 Tony Gwynn / Cal Ripken/250	40.00	12.00
6 Mike Piazza / Derek Jeter/500	25.00	7.50
7 Dave Winfield / Tony Gwynn/2000	6.00	1.80
8 Hideo Nomo / Ichiro Suzuki/2000	20.00	6.00
9 Cal Ripken / Ozzie Smith/1000	25.00	7.50
10 Mark McGwire / Albert Pujols/2000	15.00	4.50
11 Jeff Bagwell / Craig Biggio/1000	8.00	2.40
12 Bobby Bonds / Barry Bonds/250	30.00	9.00
13 Ted Williams / Stan Musial/250	30.00	9.00
14 Babe Ruth / Reggie Jackson/500	30.00	9.00
15 Kazuhiro Sasaki / Ichiro Suzuki/500	40.00	12.00
16 Nolan Ryan / Roger Clemens/500	25.00	7.50
17 Roger Clemens / Derek Jeter/250	30.00	9.00
18 Mike Piazza / Ivan Rodriguez/1000	12.00	3.60
19 Vladimir Guerrero / Sammy Sosa/2000	8.00	2.40
20 Barry Bonds / Sammy Sosa/250	30.00	9.00
21 Roger Clemens / Greg Maddux/1000	15.00	4.50
22 Juan Gonzalez / Manny Ramirez/2000	5.00	1.50
23 Todd Helton / Jason Giambi/2000	5.00	1.50
24 Jeff Bagwell / Lance Berkman/2000	5.00	1.50
25 Mike Sweeney / George Brett/1000	15.00	4.50
26 Luis Gonzalez / Babe Ruth/2000	15.00	4.50
27 Bill Skowron / Don Mattingly/250	40.00	12.00
28 Yogi Berra / Cal Ripken/2000	15.00	4.50
29 Pedro Martinez / Nomar Garciaparra/500	15.00	4.50
30 Ted Kluszewski / Frank Robinson/1000	8.00	2.40
31 Curt Schilling / Randy Johnson/1000	8.00	2.40
32 Ken Griffey Jr. / Cal Ripken/500	30.00	9.00
33 Mike Piazza / Johnny Bench/1000	12.00	3.60
34 Stan Musial / Albert Pujols	40.00	12.00
35 Jackie Robinson / Nellie Fox	12.00	3.60
36 Lefty Grove / Steve Carlton/250	15.00	4.50
37 Ty Cobb / Tony Gwynn/250	20.00	6.00
38 Albert Pujols / Frank Robinson/1000	25.00	7.50
39 Ryne Sandberg / Sammy Sosa/500	25.00	7.50
40 Cal Ripken / Lou Gehrig/250	40.00	12.00

2001 Fleer Platinum Winning Combinations Blue

This 40-card insert is a complete parallel of the 2001 Fleer Platinum Winning Combinations insert. Each blue bordered card can be found in jumbo packs at a rate of 1:12, rack packs at 1:6, and retail packs at 1:20.

	Nm-Mt	Ex-Mt
COMPLETE SET (40)	300.00	90.00
1 Derek Jeter / Ozzie Smith	12.00	3.60
2 Barry Bonds / Mark McGwire	12.00	3.60
3 Ichiro Suzuki / Albert Pujols	25.00	7.50
4 Ted Williams / Manny Ramirez	12.00	3.60
5 Tony Gwynn / Cal Ripken	15.00	4.50
6 Mike Piazza / Derek Jeter	12.00	3.60
7 Dave Winfield / Tony Gwynn	6.00	1.80
8 Hideo Nomo / Ichiro Suzuki	20.00	6.00
9 Cal Ripken / Ozzie Smith	15.00	4.50
10 Mark McGwire / Albert Pujols	20.00	6.00
11 Jeff Bagwell / Craig Biggio	5.00	1.50
12 Bobby Bonds / Barry Bonds	12.00	3.60
13 Ted Williams / Stan Musial	12.00	3.60
14 Babe Ruth / Reggie Jackson	15.00	4.50
15 Kazuhiro Sasaki / Ichiro Suzuki	15.00	4.50
16 Nolan Ryan / Roger Clemens	12.00	3.60
17 Roger Clemens / Derek Jeter	12.00	3.60
18 Mike Piazza / Ivan Rodriguez	8.00	2.40
19 Vladimir Guerrero / Sammy Sosa	8.00	2.40
20 Barry Bonds / Sammy Sosa	12.00	3.60
21 Roger Clemens / Greg Maddux	10.00	3.00
22 Juan Gonzalez / Manny Ramirez	5.00	1.50
23 Todd Helton / Jason Giambi	5.00	1.50
24 Jeff Bagwell / Lance Berkman	5.00	1.50
25 Mike Sweeney / George Brett	12.00	3.60
26 Luis Gonzalez / Babe Ruth	15.00	4.50
27 Bill Skowron / Don Mattingly	12.00	3.60
28 Yogi Berra / Cal Ripken	15.00	4.50
29 Pedro Martinez / Nomar Garciaparra	8.00	2.40
30 Ted Kluszewski / Frank Robinson	5.00	1.50
31 Curt Schilling / Randy Johnson	5.00	1.50
32 Ken Griffey Jr. / Cal Ripken	15.00	4.50
33 Mike Piazza / Johnny Bench	8.00	2.40
34 Stan Musial / Albert Pujols	15.00	4.50
35 Jackie Robinson / Nellie Fox	6.00	1.80
36 Lefty Grove / Steve Carlton	5.00	1.50
37 Ty Cobb / Tony Gwynn	8.00	2.40
38 Albert Pujols / Frank Robinson	15.00	4.50
39 Ryne Sandberg / Sammy Sosa	8.00	2.40
40 Cal Ripken / Lou Gehrig	15.00	4.50

2001 Fleer Platinum Winning Combinations Memorabilia

This 25-card set is a partial parallel of the 2001 Fleer Platinum Winning Combinations insert, each card features game-used memorabilia. These cards were inserted into Series two hobby/jumbo packs, and are individually serial numbered to 25. Due to market scarcity, no pricing is provided.

	Nm-Mt	Ex-Mt
1 Derek Jeter / Ozzie Smith		
3 Ichiro Suzuki / Albert Pujols		
4 Ted Williams / Manny Ramirez		
5 Tony Gwynn / Cal Ripken		
6 Mike Piazza / Derek Jeter		
7 Dave Winfield / Tony Gwynn		
8 Hideo Nomo / Ichiro Suzuki		
9 Cal Ripken / Ozzie Smith		
11 Jeff Bagwell / Craig Biggio		
12 Bobby Bonds / Barry Bonds		
14 Babe Ruth / Reggie Jackson		
15 Kazuhiro Sasaki / Ichiro Suzuki		
16 Nolan Ryan / Roger Clemens		
17 Roger Clemens / Derek Jeter		
18 Mike Piazza / Ivan Rodriguez		
21 Roger Clemens / Greg Maddux		
22 Juan Gonzalez / Manny Ramirez		
24 Jeff Bagwell / Lance Berkman		
25 Mike Sweeney / George Brett		
26 Luis Gonzalez / Babe Ruth		
27 Bill Skowron / Don Mattingly		
30 Ted Kluszewski / Frank Robinson		
33 Mike Piazza / Johnny Bench		
35 Jackie Robinson / Nellie Fox		
38 Albert Pujols / Frank Robinson		

2002 Fleer Platinum

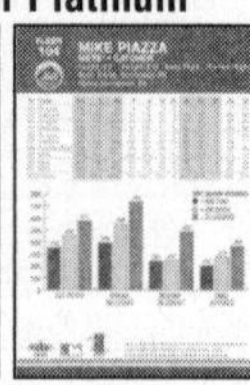

This 301 card set was issued in early Spring, 2002. These cards were issued in three different ways: 10 card hobby and retail packs. These packs were issued 24 packs to a box and six boxes to a case and had an SRP of $3. This product was also issued in 25 card jumbo packs which were packaged 12 to a box and eight boxes to a case. These cards had an SRP of $6. In addition, these cards were also issued in 45-card rack packs which were issued six packs to a box and two boxes to a case. These packs had an SRP of $10 per pack. The first 250 cards were basic cards while cards 251 through 260 are a Decade of Dominance subset, cards 261-270 feature the 10 players considered among the best young prospect and then 271-300 feature dual players prospects. Cards numbered 301 and 302 feature Japanese imports for 2002, So Taguchi and Kazuhisa Ishii. Card number 280 was not issued upon release of this set but was scheduled for release later in the 2002 season. At season's end, it was decided by the manufacturer to NOT release this card. A few copies of this card (with a large square box cut out from Satoru Komiyama's image) erroneously made their way into packs. Due to scarcity, a value has not been established. In addition, 73 redemption cards were seeded into packs whereby the holder of the card could exchange it for an actual vintage 1986 Fleer Update Bonds XRC signed and certified by Barry himself and hand-numbered "X/73". The deadline to send this card in was April 30th, 2003.

	Nm-Mt	Ex-Mt
COMPLETE SET (301)	200.00	60.00
COMP.SET w/o SP's (250)	25.00	7.50
COMMON CARD (1-250)	.30	.09
COMMON CARD (251-260)	3.00	.90
COMMON CARD (261-270)	3.00	.90
COMMON CARD (271-302)	3.00	.90
1 Garret Anderson	.30	.09
2 Randy Johnson	.75	.23
3 Chipper Jones	.75	.23
4 David Cone	.30	.09
5 Corey Patterson	.30	.09
6 Carlos Lee	.30	.09
7 Barry Larkin	.75	.23
8 Jim Thome	.75	.23
9 Larry Walker	.50	.15
10 Randall Simon	.30	.09
11 Charles Johnson	.30	.09
12 Richard Hidalgo	.30	.09
13 Mark Quinn	.30	.09
14 Paul LoDuca	.30	.09
15 Cristian Guzman	.30	.09
16 Orlando Cabrera	.30	.09
17 Al Leiter	.30	.09
18 Nick Johnson	.30	.09
19 Eric Chavez	.30	.09
20 Miguel Tejada	.30	.09
21 Mike Lieberthal	.30	.09
22 Rob Mackowiak	.30	.09
23 Ryan Klesko	.30	.09
24 Jeff Kent	.30	.09
25 Edgar Martinez	.50	.15
26 Steve Kline	.30	.09
27 Toby Hall	.30	.09
28 Rusty Greer	.30	.09
29 Jose Cruz Jr.	.30	.09
30 Darin Erstad	.30	.09
31 Reggie Sanders	.30	.09
32 Javy Lopez	.30	.09
33 Carl Everett	.30	.09
34 Sammy Sosa	1.25	.35
35 Magglio Ordonez	.30	.09
36 Todd Walker	.30	.09
37 Omar Vizquel	.30	.09
38 Matt Anderson	.30	.09
39 Jeff Weaver	.30	.09
40 Derrek Lee	.30	.09
41 Julio Lugo	.30	.09
42 Joe Randa	.30	.09
43 Chan Ho Park	.30	.09
44 Torii Hunter	.30	.09
45 Vladimir Guerrero	.75	.23
46 Rey Ordonez	.30	.09
47 Tino Martinez	.50	.15
48 Johnny Damon	.30	.09
49 Barry Zito	.50	.15
50 Robert Person	.30	.09
51 Aramis Ramirez	.30	.09
52 Mark Kotsay	.30	.09
53 Jason Schmidt	.30	.09
54 Jamie Moyer	.30	.09
55 David Justice	.30	.09
56 Aubrey Huff	.30	.09
57 Rick Helling	.30	.09
58 Carlos Delgado	.30	.09
59 Troy Glaus	.50	.15
60 Curt Schilling	.50	.15
61 Greg Maddux	1.25	.35
62 Nomar Garciaparra	1.25	.35
63 Kerry Wood	.75	.23
64 Frank Thomas	.75	.23
65 Dmitri Young	.30	.09
66 Alex Ochoa	.30	.09
67 Jose Macias	.30	.09
68 Antonio Alfonseca	.30	.09
69 Mike Lowell	.30	.09
70 Wade Miller	.30	.09
71 Mike Sweeney	.30	.09
72 Gary Sheffield	.30	.09
73 Corey Koskie	.30	.09
74 Lee Stevens	.30	.09
75 Jay Payton	.30	.09
76 Mike Mussina	.75	.23
77 Jermaine Dye	.30	.09
78 Bobby Abreu	.30	.09
79 Scott Rolen	.50	.15
80 Todd Ritchie	.30	.09
81 D'Angelo Jimenez	.30	.09
82 Robb Nen	.30	.09
83 John Olerud	.30	.09
84 Matt Morris	.30	.09
85 Joe Kennedy	.30	.09
86 Gabe Kapler	.30	.09
87 Chris Carpenter	.30	.09
88 David Eckstein	.30	.09
89 Matt Williams	.30	.09
90 John Smoltz	.50	.15
91 Pedro Martinez	.75	.23
92 Eric Young	.30	.09
93 Jose Valentin	.30	.09
94 Erubiel Durazo	.30	.09
95 Jeff Cirillo	.30	.09
96 Brandon Inge	.30	.09
97 Josh Beckett	.50	.15
98 Preston Wilson	.30	.09
99 Damian Jackson	.30	.09
100 Adrian Beltre	.30	.09
101 Jeromy Burnitz	.30	.09
102 Joe Mays	.30	.09
103 Michael Barrett	.30	.09
104 Mike Piazza	1.25	.35
105 Brady Anderson	.30	.09
106 Jason Giambi Yankees	.75	.23
107 Marlon Anderson	.30	.09
108 Jimmy Rollins	.30	.09
109 Jack Wilson	.30	.09
110 Brian Lawrence	.30	.09
111 Russ Ortiz	.30	.09
112 Kazuhiro Sasaki	.30	.09
113 Placido Polanco	.30	.09
114 Damian Rolls	.30	.09
115 Rafael Palmeiro	.50	.15
116 Brad Fullmer	.30	.09
117 Tim Salmon	.50	.15
118 Tony Womack	.30	.09
119 Tony Batista	.30	.09
120 Trot Nixon	.50	.15
121 Mark Buehrle	.30	.09
122 Derek Jeter	2.00	.60
123 Ellis Burks	.30	.09
124 Mike Hampton	.30	.09
125 Roger Cedeno	.30	.09
126 A.J. Burnett	.30	.09
127 Moises Alou	.30	.09
128 Billy Wagner	.30	.09
129 Kevin Brown	.30	.09
130 Jose Hernandez	.30	.09
131 Doug Mientkiewicz	.30	.09
132 Javier Vazquez	.30	.09
133 Tsuyoshi Shinjo	.30	.09
134 Andy Pettitte	.50	.15
135 Tim Hudson	.30	.09
136 Pat Burrell	.30	.09
137 Brian Giles	.30	.09
138 Kevin Young	.30	.09
139 Xavier Nady	.30	.09
140 J.T. Snow	.30	.09
141 Aaron Sele	.30	.09
142 Albert Pujols	1.50	.45
143 Jason Tyner	.30	.09
144 Ivan Rodriguez	.75	.23
145 Raul Mondesi	.30	.09
146 Matt Lawton	.30	.09
147 Rafael Furcal	.30	.09
148 Jeff Conine	.30	.09
149 Hideo Nomo	.75	.23
150 Jose Canseco	.75	.23
151 Aaron Boone	.30	.09
152 Bartolo Colon	.30	.09
153 Todd Helton	.50	.15
154 Tony Clark	.30	.09
155 Pablo Ozuna	.30	.09
156 Jeff Bagwell	.50	.15
157 Carlos Beltran	.30	.09
158 Shawn Green	.30	.09
159 Geoff Jenkins	.30	.09
160 Eric Milton	.30	.09
161 Jose Vidro	.30	.09
162 Robin Ventura	.30	.09
163 Jorge Posada	.50	.15
164 Terrence Long	.30	.09
165 Brandon Duckworth	.30	.09
166 Chad Hermansen	.30	.09
167 Ben Davis	.30	.09
168 Phil Nevin	.30	.09
169 Bret Boone	.30	.09
170 J.D. Drew	.30	.09
171 Edgar Renteria	.30	.09
172 Randy Winn	.30	.09
173 Alex Rodriguez	1.25	.35
174 Shannon Stewart	.30	.09
175 Steve Finley	.30	.09
176 Marcus Giles	.30	.09
177 Jay Gibbons	.30	.09
178 Manny Ramirez	.30	.09
179 Ray Durham	.30	.09
180 Sean Casey	.30	.09
181 Travis Fryman	.30	.09
182 Denny Neagle	.30	.09
183 Deivi Cruz	.30	.09
184 Luis Castillo	.30	.09
185 Lance Berkman	.30	.09
186 Dee Brown	.30	.09
187 Jeff Shaw	.30	.09
188 Mark Loretta	.30	.09
189 David Ortiz	.30	.09
190 Edgardo Alfonzo	.30	.09
191 Roger Clemens	1.50	.45
192 Mariano Rivera	.50	.15
193 Jeremy Giambi	.30	.09
194 Johnny Estrada	.30	.09
195 Craig Wilson	.30	.09
196 Adam Eaton	.30	.09
197 Rich Aurilia	.30	.09

198 Mike Cameron .30 .09
199 Jim Edmonds .30 .09
200 Fernando Vina .30 .09
201 Greg Vaughn .30 .09
202 Mike Young .30 .09
203 Vernon Wells .30 .09
204 Luis Gonzalez .30 .09
205 Tom Glavine .50 .15
206 Chris Richard .30 .09
207 Jon Lieber .30 .09
208 Keith Foulke .30 .09
209 Rondell White .30 .09
210 Bernie Williams .50 .15
211 Juan Pierre .30 .09
212 Juan Encarnacion .30 .09
213 Ryan Dempster .30 .09
214 Tim Redding .30 .09
215 Jeff Suppan .30 .09
216 Mark Grudzielanek .30 .09
217 Richie Sexson .30 .09
218 Brad Radke .30 .09
219 Armando Benitez .30 .09
220 Orlando Hernandez .30 .09
221 Alfonso Soriano .50 .15
222 Mark Mulder .30 .09
223 Travis Lee .30 .09
224 Jason Kendall .30 .09
225 Trevor Hoffman .30 .09
226 Barry Bonds 2.00 .60
227 Freddy Garcia .30 .09
228 Darryl Kile .30 .09
229 Ben Grieve .30 .09
230 Frank Catalanotto .30 .09
231 Ruben Sierra .30 .09
232 Homer Bush .30 .09
233 Mark Grace .50 .15
234 Andruw Jones .30 .09
235 Brian Roberts .30 .09
236 Fred McGriff .50 .15
237 Paul Konerko .30 .09
238 Ken Griffey Jr. 1.25 .35
239 John Burkett .30 .09
240 Juan Uribe .30 .09
241 Bobby Higginson .30 .09
242 Cliff Floyd .30 .09
243 Craig Biggio .50 .15
244 Neifi Perez .30 .09
245 Eric Karros .30 .09
246 Ben Sheets .30 .09
247 Tony Armas Jr. .30 .09
248 Mo Vaughn .30 .09
249 David Wells .30 .09
250 Juan Gonzalez .75 .23
251 Barry Bonds DD 8.00 2.40
252 Sammy Sosa DD 5.00 1.50
253 Ken Griffey Jr. DD 5.00 1.50
254 Roger Clemens DD 6.00 1.80
255 Greg Maddux DD 5.00 1.50
256 Chipper Jones DD 3.00 .90
257 Alex Rodriguez 6.00 1.80
Derek Jeter
Nomar Garciaparra DD
258 Roberto Alomar DD 3.00 .90
259 Jeff Bagwell DD 3.00 .90
260 Mike Piazza DD 5.00 1.50
261 Mark Teixeira BB 4.00 1.20
262 Mark Prior BB 6.00 1.80
263 Alex Escobar BB 3.00 .90
264 C.C. Sabathia BB 3.00 .90
265 Drew Henson BB 3.00 .90
266 Wilson Betemit BB 3.00 .90
267 Roy Oswalt BB 3.00 .90
268 Adam Dunn BB 3.00 .90
269 Bud Smith BB 3.00 .90
270 Dewon Brazelton BB 3.00 .90
271 Brandon Backe RC 3.00 .90
Jason Standridge
272 Wilfredo Rodriguez 3.00 .90
Carlos Hernandez
273 Geronimo Gil 3.00 .90
Luis Rivera
274 Carlos Pena 3.00 .90
Jovanny Cedeno
275 Austin Kearns 3.00 .90
Ben Broussard
276 Jorge De La RosaRC 3.00 .90
Kenny Kelly
277 Ryan Drese 3.00 .90
Victor Martinez
278 Joel Pinero 3.00 .90
Nate Cornejo
279 David Kelton 3.00 .90
Carlos Zambrano
280 Bill Ortega
Satoru Komiyama ERR
Not intended for public release
Card features large cut out square over Komiyama image
281 Donnie Bridges 3.00 .90
Wilkin Ruan
282 Wily Mo Pena 4.00 1.20
Brandon Claussen
283 Jason Jennings 3.00 .90
Rene Reyes RC
284 Steve Green 3.00 .90
Alfredo Amezaga
285 Eric Hinske 3.00 .90
Felipe Lopez
286 Anderson Machado RC 3.00 .90
Brad Baisley
287 Carlos Garcia 3.00 .90
Sean Douglass
288 Pat Strange 3.00 .90
Jae Weong Seo
289 Marcus Thames 3.00 .90
Alex Graman
290 Matt Childers RC 3.00 .90
Hansel Izquierdo RC
291 Ron Calloway RC 3.00 .90
Adam Walker RC
292 J.R. House 3.00 .90
J.J. Davis
293 Ryan Anderson 3.00 .90
Rafael Soriano
294 Mike Bynum 3.00 .90
Dennis Tankersley
295 Kurt Ainsworth 3.00 .90
Carlos Valderrama
296 Billy Hall 3.00 .90
Cristian Guerrero
297 Miguel Olivo 3.00 .90
Danny Wright
298 Marlon Byrd 3.00 .90
Jorge Padilla RC
299 Juan Cruz 3.00 .90
Ben Christensen
300 Adam Johnson 3.00 .90
Michael Restovich
301 So Taguchi SP RC 3.00 .90
302 Kazuhisa Ishii SP RC 4.00 1.20
NNO Barry Bonds 1986 AU/73 500.00 150.00

2002 Fleer Platinum Parallel

Randomly inserted into packs, this is a parallel set version of the 2002 Fleer Platinum set. These cards have a stated print run of 202 cards for cards numbered 1 through 250 and 22 for cards numbered 251-302. Please note that no pricing is provided for cards numbered 251-302 due to market scarcity.

Nm-Mt Ex-Mt
*PARALLEL 1-250: 2.5X TO 6X BASIC

2002 Fleer Platinum Clubhouse Memorabilia

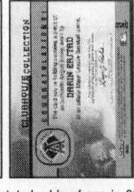

Inserted into packs at stated odds of one in 32 hobby and one in 44 retail packs, these 39 cards feature game-used memorabilia pieces. Fleer has stated the print runs for each of these cards and we have notated that information in our checklist.

Nm-Mt Ex-Mt
1 Edgardo Alfonzo Jsy/1000 10.00 3.00
2 Rick Ankiel Jsy/500 10.00 3.00
3 Adrian Beltre Jsy/875 10.00 3.00
4 Craig Biggio Bat/600 15.00 4.50
5 Barry Bonds Jsy/1000 30.00 9.00
6 Sean Casey Jsy/800 10.00 3.00
7 Eric Chavez Jsy/1000 10.00 3.00
8 Roger Clemens Jsy/1000 25.00 7.50
9 Johnny Damon Bat/700 10.00 3.00
10 Carlos Delgado Jsy/750 10.00 3.00
11 J.D. Drew Jsy/1000 10.00 3.00
12 Darin Erstad Jsy/850 10.00 3.00
13 N.Garciaparra Jsy/750 20.00 6.00
14 Juan Gonzalez Bat/1000 15.00 4.50
15 Todd Helton Jsy/925 15.00 4.50
16 Tim Hudson Jsy/825 10.00 3.00
17 D.Jeter Pants/1000 30.00 9.00
18 Randy Johnson Jsy/1000 15.00 4.50
19 A.Jones Jsy/1000 10.00 3.00
20 Jason Kendall Jsy/1000 10.00 3.00
21 Paul LoDuca Jsy/1000 10.00 3.00
22 Greg Maddux Jsy/875 15.00 4.50
23 Pedro Martinez Jsy/775 15.00 4.50
24 Raul Mondesi Bat/575 10.00 3.00
25 M.Ordonez Jsy/575 10.00 3.00
26 Mike Piazza Jsy/950 15.00 4.50
27 Mike Piazza Pants/1000 15.00 4.50
28 M.Ramirez Jsy/1000 10.00 3.00
29 Mariano Rivera Jsy/725 15.00 4.50
30 Alex Rodriguez Jsy/850 20.00 6.00
31 I.Rodriguez Jsy/1000 15.00 4.50
32 Scott Rolen Jsy/120 15.00 4.50
33 K.Sasaki Jsy/1000 10.00 3.00
34 Curt Schilling Jsy/1000 15.00 4.50
35 Gary Sheffield Bat/775 10.00 3.00
36 Gary Sheffield Jsy/800 10.00 3.00
37 Frank Thomas Jsy/850 15.00 4.50
38 Jim Thome Bat/750 15.00 4.50
39 Omar Vizquel Jsy/1000 10.00 3.00

2002 Fleer Platinum Clubhouse Memorabilia Combos

Inserted at a stated rate of one in 96 hobby packs and one in 192 retail packs, these 39 cards parallel the Clubhouse Memorabilia set. These cards can be differentiated by their having two distinct pieces of game-used memorabilia attached to the front. Since these cards have distinct press runs, we have notated that information in our checklist.

Nm-Mt Ex-Mt
1 Edgardo Alfonzo Ball-Jsy/125 15.00 4.50
2 Rick Ankiel Bat-Jsy/200 15.00 4.50
3 Adrian Beltre Ball-Jsy/125 15.00 4.50
4 Craig Biggio Jsy-Bat/50
5 Barry Bonds Glove-Jsy/275 50.00 15.00
6 Sean Casey Ball-Jsy/125 15.00 4.50
7 Eric Chavez Base-Jsy/325 15.00 4.50
8 Roger Clemens Base-Jsy/325 40.00 12.00
9 Johnny Damon Base-Bat/175 15.00 4.50
10 Carlos Delgado Base-Jsy/325 15.00 4.50
11 J.D. Drew Ball-Jsy/125 15.00 4.50
12 Darin Erstad Bat-Jsy/125 15.00 4.50
13 N.Garciaparra Bat-Jsy/275 40.00 12.00
14 Juan Gonzalez Jsy-Bat/75 25.00 7.50
15 Todd Helton Jsy-Bat/35
16 Tim Hudson Bat-Jsy/200 15.00 4.50
17 D.Jeter Btg Glv-Pants/200 50.00 15.00
18 Randy Johnson Bat-Jsy/125 25.00 7.50
19 And Jones Btg Glv-Jsy/100 15.00 4.50
20 Jason Kendall Bat-Jsy/50
21 Paul LoDuca Ball-Jsy/125 15.00 4.50
22 Greg Maddux Ball-Jsy/275 25.00 7.50
23 Pedro Martinez Base-Jsy/300 25.00 7.50
24 Raul Mondesi Bat-Btg Glv/75
25 M.Ordonez Bat-Jsy/325 15.00 4.50
26 Mike Piazza Ball-Jsy/125 40.00 12.00
27 Mike Piazza Ball-Pants/125 40.00 12.00
28 M.Ramirez Base-Jsy/350 15.00 4.50
29 Mariano Rivera Base-Jsy/175 25.00 7.50
30 Alex Rodriguez Base-Jsy/300 30.00 9.00
31 I.Rodriguez Btg Glv-Glv/100 25.00 7.50
32 Scott Rolen Ball-Jsy/125 25.00 7.50
33 K.Sasaki Base-Jsy/350 15.00 4.50
34 Curt Schilling Ball-Jsy/125 25.00 7.50
35 Gary Sheffield Ball-Bat/125 15.00 4.50
36 Gary Sheffield Ball-Jsy/125 15.00 4.50
37 Frank Thomas Base-Jsy/275 25.00 7.50
38 Jim Thome Base-Bat/275 25.00 7.50
39 Omar Vizquel Base-Jsy/300 15.00 4.50

2002 Fleer Platinum Cornerstones

These cards were distributed in jumbo packs (1:12), rack packs (1:6) and retail packs (1:20). Each card features two prominent active and retired ballplayers paired up in a horizontal design with an image of a base floating in front of them. The cards are identical in design to the hobby-only Cornerstones Numbered except these cards lack serial-numbering, feature the word "Cornerstones" in brown lettering on front (the hobby-only versions are serial-numbered on back and feature white lettering for the "Cornerstones" moniker on front and oddly enough are entirely devoid of any checklist card number on back. The cards have been checklisted in our database using the same order as the hobby Cornerstones set.

Nm-Mt Ex-Mt
COMPLETE SET (40) 200.00 60.00
1 Bill Terry 3.00 .90
Johnny Mize
2 Cal Ripken 15.00 4.50
Eddie Murray
3 Eddie Mathews 5.00 1.50
Chipper Jones
4 Albert Pujols 10.00 3.00
George Sisler
5 Sean Casey 3.00 .90
Tony Perez
6 Jimmie Foxx 5.00 1.50
Scott Rolen
7 Wade Boggs 12.00 3.60
George Brett
8 Rod Carew 3.00 .90
Troy Glaus
9 Jeff Bagwell 3.00 .90
Rafael Palmeiro
10 Willie Stargell 3.00 .90
Pie Traynor
11 Cal Ripken 15.00 4.50
Brooks Robinson
12 Tony Perez 3.00 .90
Ted Kluszewski
13 Jason Giambi 10.00 3.00
Don Mattingly
14 Hank Greenberg 5.00 1.50
Jimmie Foxx
15 Ernie Banks 5.00 1.50
Willie McCovey
16 Jim Thome 5.00 1.50
Travis Fryman
17 Ted Kluszewski 3.00 .90
Sean Casey
18 Gil Hodges 5.00 1.50
Johnny Mize
19 Brooks Robinson 5.00 1.50
Boog Powell
20 Bill Terry 3.00 .90
George Sisler
21 Wade Boggs 12.00 3.60
Don Mattingly
22 Jason Giambi Yankees 5.00 1.50
Carlos Delgado
23 Willie Stargell 3.00 .90
Bill Madlock
24 Mark Grace 3.00 .90
Matt Williams
25 Paul Molitor 12.00 3.60
George Brett
26 Carlos Delgado 3.00 .90
Mo Vaughn
27 Bill Terry 3.00 .90
Willie McCovey
28 Mike Sweeney 12.00 3.60
George Brett
29 Eddie Mathews 5.00 1.50
Ernie Banks
30 Eric Karros 5.00 1.50
Gil Hodges
31 Paul Molitor 12.00 3.60
Don Mattingly
32 Brooks Robinson 5.00 1.50
Rod Carew
33 Chipper Jones 10.00 3.00
Albert Pujols
34 Harry Heilmann 5.00 1.50
Hank Greenberg
35 Frank Thomas 5.00 1.50
Carlos Delgado
36 Jeff Bagwell 3.00 .90
Todd Helton
37 Rafael Palmeiro 3.00 .90
Fred McGriff
38 Cal Ripken 15.00 4.50
Wade Boggs
39 Orlando Cepeda 3.00 .90
Willie McCovey
40 John Olerud 3.00 .90
Mark Grace

2002 Fleer Platinum Cornerstones Memorabilia

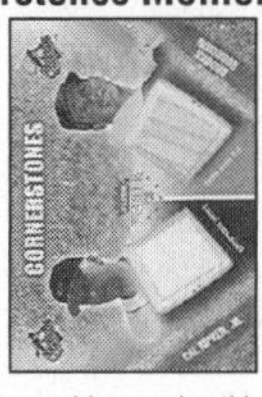

Randomly inserted into packs, this 22-card set is a partial parallel of the Cornerstones insert set. These cards have two pieces of memorabilia and all have stated print runs of 25 serial numbered sets. Due to market scarcity, no pricing is provided for this set.

Nm-Mt Ex-Mt
1 Bill Terry Bat
Johnny Mize Bat
2 Cal Ripken Jsy
Eddie Murray Jsy
3 Eddie Mathews Bat
Chipper Jones Jsy
5 Sean Casey Jsy
Tony Perez Bat
6 Jimmie Foxx Bat
Scott Rolen Jsy
7 Wade Boggs Jsy
George Brett Jsy
9 Jeff Bagwell Bat
Rafael Palmeiro Jsy
11 Cal Ripken Jsy
Brooks Robinson Bat
12 Tony Perez Bat
Ted Kluszewski Jsy
14 Hank Greenberg Bat
Jimmie Foxx Bat
16 Jim Thome Bat
Travis Fryman Bat
17 Ted Kluszewski Jsy
Sean Casey Jsy
21 Wade Boggs Jsy
Don Mattingly Jsy
25 Paul Molitor Jsy
George Brett Jsy
27 Bill Terry Bat
Willie McCovey Jsy
28 Mike Sweeney Bat
George Brett Jsy
31 Paul Molitor Jsy
Don Mattingly Jsy
35 Frank Thomas Jsy
Carlos Delgado Jsy
36 Jeff Bagwell Bat
Todd Helton Jsy
38 Cal Ripken Jsy
Wade Boggs Jsy
39 Orlando Cepeda Jsy
Willie McCovey Jsy
40 John Olerud Jsy
Mark Grace Jsy

2002 Fleer Platinum Cornerstones Numbered

Randomly inserted into hobby packs, these 40 cards have different print runs depending on which group of cards they belong to. Cards numbered 1-10 were printed to a stated print run of 250 serial numbered sets while cards numbered 11-20 have a stated print run of 500 sets. Cards numbered 21-30 have a stated print run of 1000 sets and cards numbered 31-40 have a stated print run of 2000 sets. Other than Harry Heilmann, most of the players played a significant part of their career at either first or third base.

Nm-Mt Ex-Mt
COMMON CARD (1-10) 15.00 4.50
COMMON CARD (11-20) 10.00 3.00
COMMON CARD (21-30) 8.00 2.40
COMMON CARD (31-40) 5.00 1.50
1 Bill Terry 15.00 4.50
Johnny Mize
2 Cal Ripken 40.00 12.00
Eddie Murray
3 Eddie Mathews 15.00 4.50
Chipper Jones
4 Albert Pujols 25.00 7.50
George Sisler
5 Sean Casey 15.00 4.50
Tony Perez
6 Jimmie Foxx 15.00 4.50
Scott Rolen
7 Wade Boggs 30.00 9.00
George Brett
8 Rod Carew 15.00 4.50
Troy Glaus
9 Jeff Bagwell 15.00 4.50
Rafael Palmeiro
10 Willie Stargell 15.00 4.50
Pie Traynor
11 Cal Ripken 30.00 9.00
Brooks Robinson
12 Tony Perez 10.00 3.00
Ted Kluszewski
13 Jason Giambi 30.00 9.00
Don Mattingly
14 Hank Greenberg 10.00 3.00
Jimmie Foxx
15 Ernie Banks 10.00 3.00
Willie McCovey
16 Jim Thome 10.00 3.00
Travis Fryman
17 Ted Kluszewski 10.00 3.00
Sean Casey
18 Gil Hodges 10.00 3.00
Johnny Mize
19 Brooks Robinson 10.00 3.00
Boog Powell
20 Bill Terry 10.00 3.00
George Sisler
21 Wade Boggs 20.00 6.00
Don Mattingly
22 Jason Giambi Yankees 8.00 2.40
Carlos Delgado
23 Willie Stargell 8.00 2.40
Bill Madlock
24 Mark Grace 8.00 2.40
Matt Williams
25 Paul Molitor 15.00 4.50
George Brett
26 Carlos Delgado 8.00 2.40
Mo Vaughn
27 Bill Terry 8.00 2.40
Willie McCovey
28 Mike Sweeney 15.00 4.50
George Brett
29 Eddie Mathews 8.00 2.40
Ernie Banks
30 Eric Karros 8.00 2.40
Gil Hodges
31 Paul Molitor 12.00 3.60
Don Mattingly
32 Brooks Robinson 5.00 1.50
Rod Carew
33 Chipper Jones 10.00 3.00
Albert Pujols
34 Harry Heilmann 5.00 1.50
Hank Greenberg
35 Frank Thomas 5.00 1.50
Carlos Delgado
36 Jeff Bagwell 5.00 1.50
Todd Helton
37 Rafael Palmeiro 5.00 1.50
Fred McGriff
38 Cal Ripken 15.00 4.50
Wade Boggs
39 Orlando Cepeda 5.00 1.50
Willie McCovey
40 John Olerud 5.00 1.50
Mark Grace

2002 Fleer Platinum Fence Busters

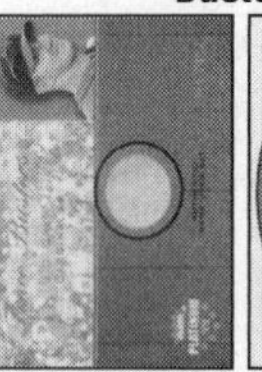

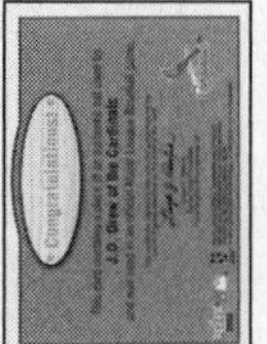

Randomly inserted into rack packs, these 22 cards feature some of the leading hitters in the game. We have provided the stated print runs for these cards in our checklist. The Jeff Bagwell card was not ready when Fleer went to press with this set and that card could be redeemed until April 30th, 2003.

Nm-Mt Ex-Mt
1 Roberto Alomar/800 15.00 4.50
2 Moises Alou/800 10.00 3.00
3 Jeff Bagwell/400 15.00 4.50
4 Barry Bonds/700 30.00 9.00
5 J.D. Drew/800 10.00 3.00
6 Jim Edmonds/500 10.00 3.00
7 Brian Giles/700 10.00 3.00
8 Luis Gonzalez/625 10.00 3.00
9 Shawn Green/800 10.00 3.00
10 Todd Helton/675 15.00 4.50
11 Derek Jeter/400 30.00 9.00
12 Andruw Jones/800 10.00 3.00
13 Chipper Jones/800 15.00 4.50
14 Tino Martinez/800 15.00 4.50
15 Rafael Palmeiro/800 15.00 4.50
16 Mike Piazza/800 15.00 4.50
17 Manny Ramirez/800 10.00 3.00
18 Alex Rodriguez/675 20.00 6.00
19 Miguel Tejada/700 10.00 3.00
20 Frank Thomas/800 15.00 4.50
21 Jim Thome/800 15.00 4.50
22 Larry Walker/750 15.00 4.50

2002 Fleer Platinum Fence Busters Autographs

Randomly inserted into rack packs, these four cards feature signed copies of the Fence Busters insert set. These cards were all serial numbered to the selected player's 2001 home run total. All of these cards were issued as exchange cards and could be redeemed until April 30th, 2003.

Nm-Mt Ex-Mt
1 Jeff Bagwell/39
2 Barry Bonds/73 300.00 90.00
3 Derek Jeter/21
4 Miguel Tejada/31

2002 Fleer Platinum National Patch Time

Inserted at stated odds at one in 12 jumbo packs, these 19 cards feature the selected player as well as game-worn jersey patch swatch of the featured player. The stated print

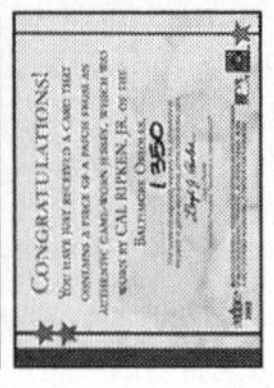

runs for the players are listed next to their name in our checklist.

	Nm-Mt	Ex-Mt
1 Barry Bonds/75	120.00	36.00
2 Pat Burrell/285	40.00	12.00
3 Jose Canseco/150	60.00	18.00
4 Carlos Delgado/70	50.00	15.00
5 J.D. Drew/210	40.00	12.00
6 Adam Dunn/75	50.00	15.00
7 Darin Erstad/315	40.00	12.00
8 Juan Gonzalez/50	80.00	24.00
9 Todd Helton/110	50.00	15.00
10 Derek Jeter/65	120.00	36.00
11 Greg Maddux/775	40.00	12.00
12 Pedro Martinez/45	80.00	24.00
13 Magglio Ordonez/85	50.00	15.00
14 Manny Ramirez/100	50.00	15.00
15 Cal Ripken/350	100.00	30.00
16 Alex Rodriguez/325	60.00	18.00
17 Ivan Rodriguez/225	50.00	15.00
18 Kazuhiro Sasaki/310	40.00	12.00
19 Miguel Tejada/55	50.00	15.00

2002 Fleer Platinum Wheelhouse

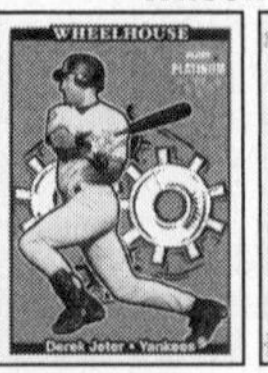
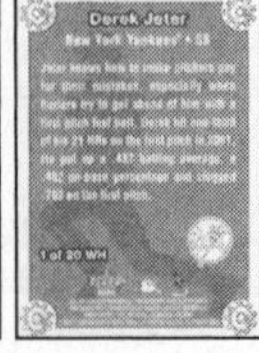

Inserted at stated odds of one in 12 hobby and one in 20 retail, these 20 cards feature some of the leading hitters in baseball.

	Nm-Mt	Ex-Mt
COMPLETE SET (20)	80.00	24.00
1 Derek Jeter	8.00	2.40
2 Barry Bonds	8.00	2.40
3 Luis Gonzalez	3.00	.90
4 Jason Giambi	3.00	.90
5 Ivan Rodriguez	3.00	.90
6 Mike Piazza	5.00	1.50
7 Troy Glaus	3.00	.90
8 Nomar Garciaparra	5.00	1.50
9 Juan Gonzalez	3.00	.90
10 Sammy Sosa	5.00	1.50
11 Albert Pujols	6.00	1.80
12 Ken Griffey Jr.	5.00	1.50
13 Scott Rolen	3.00	.90
14 Jeff Bagwell	3.00	.90
15 Ichiro Suzuki	5.00	1.50
16 Todd Helton	3.00	.90
17 Chipper Jones	3.00	.90
18 Alex Rodriguez	5.00	1.50
19 Vladimir Guerrero	3.00	.90
20 Manny Ramirez	3.00	.90

2003 Fleer Platinum

This 250 card set was release in February, 2003. These cards were issued in a variety of manners. Each box contained 14 wax packs as well as 4 jumbo packs and one rack pack. The wax packs had an SRP of $3, while the jumbos had an SRP of $5 amd the rack packs had an SRP of $10. There are several subsets in the product. Cards numbered 201 through 220 feature Unsung Heroes. Cards numbered 221 through 250 are prospects but those cards were issued in different ratios throughout the set.

	Nm-Mt	Ex-Mt
COMP.SET w/o SP's (220)	25.00	7.50
COMMON CARD (1-220)	.30	.09
COMMON CARD (221-235)	2.00	.60
221-235 ODDS 1:4 WAX, 1:2 JUMBO, 1:1 RACK		
COMMON CARD (236-240)	2.00	.60
236-240 ODDS 1:12 WAX		
COMMON CARD (241-245)	3.00	.90
241-245 ODDS 1:6 JUMBO		
COMMON CARD (246-250)	3.00	.90
246-250 ODDS 1:2 RACK		
1 Barry Bonds	2.00	.60
2 Sean Casey	.30	.09
3 Todd Walker	.30	.09
4 Tony Batista	.30	.09
5 Todd Zeile	.30	.09
6 Ruben Sierra	.30	.09
7 Jose Cruz Jr.	.30	.09
8 Ben Grieve	.30	.09
9 Rob Mackowiak	.30	.09
10 Gary Sheffield	.30	.09
11 Armando Benitez	.30	.09
12 Tim Hudson	.30	.09
13 Eric Milton	.30	.09
14 Andy Pettitte	.50	.15
15 Jeff Bagwell	.50	.15
16 Jeff Kent	.30	.09
17 Joe Randa	.30	.09
18 Benito Santiago	.30	.09
19 Russell Branyan	.30	.09
20 Cliff Floyd	.30	.09
21 Chris Richard	.30	.09
22 Randy Winn	.30	.09
23 Freddy Garcia	.30	.09
24 Derek Lowe	.30	.09
25 Ben Sheets	.30	.09
26 Fred McGriff	.50	.15
27 Bret Boone	.30	.09
28 Jose Hernandez	.30	.09
29 Phil Nevin	.30	.09
30 Mike Piazza	1.25	.35
31 Bobby Abreu	.30	.09
32 Darin Erstad	.30	.09
33 Andruw Jones	.30	.09
34 Brad Wilkerson	.30	.09
35 Brian Lawrence	.30	.09
36 Vladimir Nunez	.30	.09
37 Kazuhiro Sasaki	.30	.09
38 Carlos Delgado	.30	.09
39 Steve Cox	.30	.09
40 Adrian Beltre	.30	.09
41 Josh Bard	.30	.09
42 Randall Simon	.30	.09
43 Johnny Damon	.30	.09
44 Ken Griffey Jr.	1.25	.35
45 Sammy Sosa	1.25	.35
46 Kevin Brown	.30	.09
47 Kazuhisa Ishii	.30	.09
48 Matt Morris	.30	.09
49 Mark Prior	1.50	.45
50 Kip Wells	.30	.09
51 Hee Seop Choi	.30	.09
52 Craig Biggio	.50	.15
53 Derek Jeter	2.00	.60
54 Albert Pujols	1.50	.45
55 Joe Borchard	.30	.09
56 Robert Fick	.30	.09
57 Jacque Jones	.30	.09
58 Juan Pierre	.30	.09
59 Bernie Williams	.50	.15
60 Elmer Dessens	.30	.09
61 Al Leiter	.30	.09
62 Curt Schilling	.50	.15
63 Carlos Pena	.30	.09
64 Tino Martinez	.50	.15
65 Fernando Vina	.30	.09
66 Aaron Boone	.30	.09
67 Michael Barrett	.30	.09
68 Frank Thomas	.75	.23
69 J.D. Drew	.30	.09
70 Vladimir Guerrero	.75	.23
71 Shannon Stewart	.30	.09
72 Mark Buehrle	.30	.09
73 Jamie Moyer	.30	.09
74 Brad Radke	.30	.09
75 Mike Williams	.30	.09
76 Ryan Klesko	.30	.09
77 Roberto Alomar	.75	.23
78 Edgardo Alfonzo	.30	.09
79 Matt Williams	.30	.09
80 Edgar Martinez	.50	.15
81 Shawn Green	.30	.09
82 Kenny Lofton	.30	.09
83 Josh Beckett	.50	.15
84 Trevor Hoffman	.30	.09
85 Kevin Millwood	.30	.09
86 Odalis Perez	.30	.09
87 Jarrod Washburn	.30	.09
88 Jason Giambi	.75	.23
89 Eric Young	.30	.09
90 Barry Larkin	.75	.23
91 Aramis Ramirez	.30	.09
92 Ivan Rodriguez	.75	.23
93 Steve Finley	.30	.09
94 Brian Jordan	.30	.09
95 Manny Ramirez	.30	.09
96 Preston Wilson	.30	.09
97 Rodrigo Lopez	.30	.09
98 Ramon Ortiz	.30	.09
99 Jim Thome	.75	.23
100 Luis Castillo	.30	.09
101 Alex Rodriguez	1.25	.35
102 Jared Sandberg	.30	.09
103 Ellis Burks	.30	.09
104 Pat Burrell	.30	.09
105 Brian Giles	.30	.09
106 Mark Kotsay	.30	.09
107 Dave Roberts	.30	.09
108 Roy Halladay	.30	.09
109 Chan Ho Park	.30	.09
110 Erubiel Durazo	.30	.09
111 Bobby Hill	.30	.09
112 Cristian Guzman	.30	.09
113 Troy Glaus	.50	.15
114 Lance Berkman	.30	.09
115 Juan Encarnacion	.30	.09
116 Chipper Jones	.75	.23
117 Corey Patterson	.30	.09
118 Vernon Wells	.30	.09
119 Matt Clement	.30	.09
120 Billy Koch	.30	.09
121 Hideo Nomo	.75	.23
122 Derrek Lee	.30	.09
123 Todd Helton	.50	.15
124 Sean Burroughs	.30	.09
125 Jason Kendall	.30	.09
126 Dmitri Young	.30	.09
127 Adam Dunn	.30	.09
128 Bobby Higginson	.30	.09
129 Raul Mondesi	.30	.09
130 Bubba Trammell	.30	.09
131 A.J. Burnett	.30	.09
132 Randy Johnson	.75	.23
133 Mark Mulder	.30	.09
134 Mariano Rivera	.50	.15
135 Kerry Wood	.75	.23
136 Mo Vaughn	.30	.09
137 Jimmy Rollins	.30	.09
138 Jose Valentin	.30	.09
139 Brad Fullmer	.30	.09
140 Mike Cameron	.30	.09
141 Luis Gonzalez	.30	.09
142 Kevin Appier	.30	.09
143 Mike Hampton	.30	.09
144 Pedro Martinez	.75	.23
145 Javier Vazquez	.30	.09
146 Doug Mientkiewicz	.30	.09
147 Adam Kennedy	.30	.09
148 Rafael Furcal	.30	.09
149 Eric Chavez	.30	.09
150 Mike Lieberthal	.30	.09
151 Moises Alou	.30	.09
152 Jermaine Dye	.30	.09
153 Torii Hunter	.30	.09
154 Trot Nixon	.50	.15
155 Larry Walker	.50	.15
156 Jorge Julio	.30	.09
157 Mike Mussina	.75	.23
158 Kirk Rueter	.30	.09
159 Rafael Palmeiro	.50	.15
160 Pokey Reese	.30	.09
161 Miguel Tejada	.30	.09
162 Robin Ventura	.30	.09
163 Raul Ibanez	.30	.09
164 Roger Cedeno	.30	.09
165 Juan Gonzalez	.75	.23
166 Carlos Lee	.30	.09
167 Tim Salmon	.50	.15
168 Orlando Hernandez	.30	.09
169 Wade Miller	.30	.09
170 Troy Percival	.30	.09
171 Billy Wagner	.30	.09
172 Jeff Conine	.30	.09
173 Junior Spivey	.30	.09
174 Edgar Renteria	.30	.09
175 Scott Rolen	.50	.15
176 Jason Varitek	.30	.09
177 Ben Broussard	.30	.09
178 Jeremy Giambi	.30	.09
179 Gabe Kapler	.30	.09
180 Armando Rios	.30	.09
181 Ichiro Suzuki	1.25	.35
182 Tom Glavine	.50	.15
183 Greg Maddux	1.25	.35
184 Roy Oswalt	.30	.09
185 John Smoltz	.50	.15
186 Eric Karros	.30	.09
187 Alfonso Soriano	.50	.15
188 Nomar Garciaparra	1.25	.35
189 Joe Crede	.30	.09
190 Javy Lopez	.30	.09
191 Carlos Beltran	.30	.09
192 Jim Edmonds	.30	.09
193 Geoff Jenkins	.30	.09
194 Magglio Ordonez	.30	.09
195 Daryle Ward	.30	.09
196 Roger Clemens	1.50	.45
197 Byung-Hyun Kim	.30	.09
198 Robb Nen	.30	.09
199 C.C. Sabathia	.30	.09
200 Barry Zito	.50	.15
201 Mark Grace UH	.30	.09
202 Paul Konerko UH	.30	.09
203 Mike Sweeney UH	.30	.09
204 John Olerud UH	.30	.09
205 Jose Vidro UH	.30	.09
206 Ray Durham UH	.30	.09
207 Omar Vizquel UH	.30	.09
208 Shea Hillenbrand UH	.30	.09
209 Mike Lowell UH	.30	.09
210 Aubrey Huff UH	.30	.09
211 Eric Hinske UH	.30	.09
212 Paul Lo Duca UH	.30	.09
213 Jay Gibbons UH	.30	.09
214 Austin Kearns UH	.30	.09
215 Richie Sexson UH	.30	.09
216 Garret Anderson UH	.30	.09
217 Eric Gagne UH	.30	.09
218 Jason Jennings UH	.30	.09
219 Damian Moss UH	.30	.09
220 David Eckstein UH	.30	.09
221 Mark Teixeira PROS	3.00	.90
222 Bill Hall PROS	2.00	.60
223 Bobby Jenks PROS	2.00	.60
224 Adam Morrissey PROS	2.00	.60
225 Rodrigo Rosario PROS	2.00	.60
226 Brett Myers PROS	2.00	.60
227 Tony Alvarez PROS	2.00	.60
228 Willie Bloomquist PROS	2.00	.60
229 Ben Howard PROS	2.00	.60
230 Nic Jackson PROS	2.00	.60
231 Carl Crawford PROS	2.00	.60
232 Omar Infante PROS	2.00	.60
233 Francisco Rodriguez PROS	2.00	.60
234 Andy Van Hekken PROS	2.00	.60
235 Kirk Saarloos PROS	2.00	.60
236 Dusty Wathan PROS RC	2.00	.60
237 Jamey Carroll PROS	2.00	.60
238 Jason Phillips PROS	2.00	.60
239 Jose Castillo PROS	2.00	.60
240 Arnaldo Munoz PROS RC	2.00	.60
241 Orlando Hudson PROS	3.00	.90
242 Drew Henson PROS	3.00	.90
243 Jason Lane PROS	3.00	.90
244 Vinny Chulk PROS	3.00	.90
245 Prentice Redman PROS RC	3.00	.90
246 Marlon Byrd PROS	3.00	.90
247 Chin-Feng Chen PROS	3.00	.90
248 Craig Brazell PROS RC	5.00	1.50
249 John Webb PROS	3.00	.90
250 Adam LaRoche PROS	5.00	1.50

2003 Fleer Platinum Finish

Randomly inserted in packs, this is a parallel to the Fleer Platinum set. These cards with a "finished" type front were issued to a stated print run of 100 serial numbered sets.

	Nm-Mt	Ex-Mt
*FINISH 1-220: 3X TO 8X BASIC		
*FINISH 221-235: 1X TO 2.5X BASIC		
*FINISH 236-240: 1X TO 2.5X BASIC		
*FINISH 241-245: .6X TO 1.5X BASIC		
*FINISH 2446-250: .6X TO 1.5X BASIC		

2003 Fleer Platinum Barry Bonds Chasing History Game Used

Randomly inserted in packs, these five cards feature game used swatches from both Barry Bonds and various retired players whose records he was chasing. The cards with two game-worn swatches were issued to a stated print run of 250 serial numbered sets while the five player card was issued to a stated print run of 25 serial numbered sets.

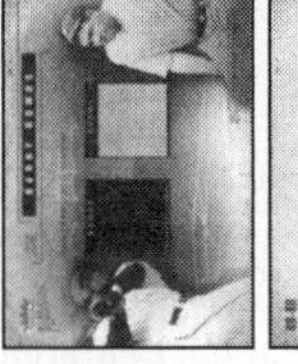
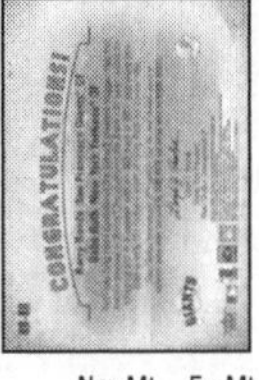

	Nm-Mt	Ex-Mt
BB Barry Bonds / Bobby Bonds	40.00	12.00
BR Barry Bonds / Babe Ruth	250.00	75.00
RM Barry Bonds / Roger Maris	80.00	24.00
WM Barry Bonds / Willie McCovey	40.00	12.00
CH Barry Bonds / Bobby Bonds / Roger Maris / Willie McCovey / Babe Ruth		

2003 Fleer Platinum Guts and Glory

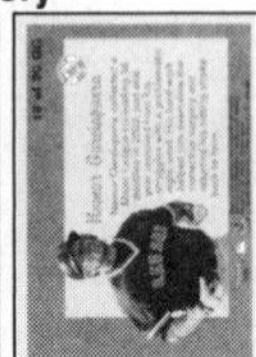

Inserted at a stated rate of one in four wax packs, one in two jumbo and one per rack pack, this 20 card set features some of the leading players in baseball.

	Nm-Mt	Ex-Mt
COMPLETE SET (20)	25.00	7.50
1 Jason Giambi	1.25	.35
2 Alfonso Soriano	1.00	.30
3 Scott Rolen	1.00	.30
4 Ivan Rodriguez	1.25	.35
5 Barry Bonds	3.00	.90
6 Jim Edmonds	1.00	.30
7 Darin Erstad	1.00	.30
8 Brian Giles	1.00	.30
9 Luis Gonzalez	1.00	.30
10 Adam Dunn	1.00	.30
11 Torii Hunter	1.00	.30
12 Andruw Jones	1.00	.30
13 Sammy Sosa	2.00	.60
14 Ichiro Suzuki	2.00	.60
15 Miguel Tejada	1.00	.30
16 Roger Clemens	2.50	.75
17 Curt Schilling	1.00	.30
18 Nomar Garciaparra	2.00	.60
19 Derek Jeter	3.00	.90
20 Alex Rodriguez	2.00	.60

2003 Fleer Platinum Heart of the Order

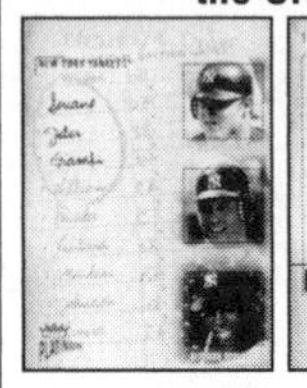
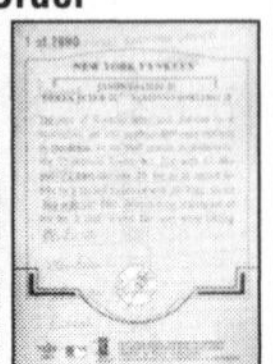

Inserted in packs at a rate of one in 12 wax, one in six jumbo and one in three rack, these cards feature three players who are the key offensive weapons for their teams.

	Nm-Mt	Ex-Mt
1 Jason Giambi / Derek Jeter / Alfonso Soriano	4.00	1.20
2 Todd Helton / Preston Wilson / Larry Walker	2.00	.60
3 Rafael Palmeiro / Alex Rodriguez / Ivan Rodriguez	3.00	.90
4 Adam Dunn / Ken Griffey Jr. / Austin Kearns	3.00	.90
5 Jeff Bagwell / Craig Biggio / Lance Berkman	2.00	.60
6 Eric Chavez / Miguel Tejada / Jermaine Dye	2.00	.60
7 Troy Glaus / Garrett Anderson / Darin Erstad	2.00	.60
8 Mike Piazza / Mo Vaughn / Roberto Alomar	3.00	.90
9 Torii Hunter / Jacque Jones / Corey Koskie	2.00	.60
10 Barry Bonds / Jeff Kent / Rich Aurilia	5.00	1.50
11 Pat Burrell / Bobby Abreu / Jimmy Rollins	2.00	.60
12 Shawn Green / Adrian Beltre / Paul Lo Duca	2.00	.60
13 Vladimir Guerrero / Brad Wilkerson / Jose Vidro	2.00	.60
14 Chipper Jones / Andruw Jones / Gary Sheffield	2.00	.60
15 Ichiro Suzuki / Bret Boone / Edgar Martinez	3.00	.90
16 Albert Pujols / Scott Rolen / J.D. Drew	4.00	1.20
17 Sammy Sosa / Fred McGriff / Moises Alou	3.00	.90
18 Nomar Garciaparra / Shea Hillenbrand / Manny Ramirez	3.00	.90
19 Frank Thomas / Magglio Ordonez / Paul Konerko	2.00	.60
20 Jason Kendall / Brian Giles / Amaris Ramirez	2.00	.60

2003 Fleer Platinum Heart of the Order Game Used

Inserted at a stated rate of one in two rack packs, this is a partial parallel to the Heart of the Order set. These cards feature a game-used memorabilia piece form one of the players on the card along with photos of the other two players. Each of these cards was issued to a stated print run of 400 serial numbered sets.

	Nm-Mt	Ex-Mt
AB Adrian Beltre Jsy / Shawn Green / Paul Lo Duca	8.00	2.40
AK Austin Kearns Pants / Adam Dunn / Ken Griffey Jr.	8.00	2.40
AS Alfonso Soriano Bat / Jason Giambi / Derek Jeter	10.00	3.00
BB Bret Boone Jsy / Edgar Martinez / Ichiro Suzuki	8.00	2.40
BG Brian Giles Bat / Jason Kendall / Aramis Ramirez	8.00	2.40
CJ Chipper Jones Jsy / Andruw Jones / Gary Sheffield	15.00	4.50
DE Darin Erstad Jsy / Garret Anderson / Troy Glaus	8.00	2.40
FT Frank Thomas Jsy / Paul Konerko / Magglio Ordonez	15.00	4.50
JD J.D. Drew Jsy / Albert Pujols / Scott Rolen	8.00	2.40
JK Jeff Kent Jsy / Rich Aurilia / Barry Bonds	8.00	2.40
JR Jimmy Rollins Jsy / Bob Abreu / Pat Burrell	8.00	2.40
JV Jose Vidro Jsy / Vladimir Guerrero / Brad Wilkerson	8.00	2.40
LB Lance Berkman Bat / Jeff Bagwell / Craig Biggio	8.00	2.40
MP Mike Piazza Jsy / Roberto Alomar / Mo Vaughn	15.00	4.50
MR Manny Ramirez Jsy / Nomar Garciaparra / Shea Hillenbrand	8.00	2.40
RP Rafael Palmeiro Jsy / Alex Rodriguez / Ivan Rodriguez	10.00	3.00
SS Sammy Sosa Jsy / Moises Alou / Fred McGriff	15.00	4.50
TH Todd Helton Jsy / Larry Walker / Preston Wilson	10.00	3.00

2003 Fleer Platinum MLB Scouting Report

Randomly inserted in packs, this 32 card set features information about the noted player. Each card has some scouting type information to go with some hitting charts. These cards were issued to a stated print run of 400 serial numbered sets.

	Nm-Mt	Ex-Mt
1 Jason Giambi	4.00	1.20
2 Paul Konerko	4.00	1.20
3 Jim Thome	4.00	1.20
4 Alfonso Soriano	4.00	1.20
5 Troy Glaus	4.00	1.20
6 Eric Hinske	4.00	1.20
7 Paul Lo Duca	4.00	1.20

8 Mike Piazza 6.00 1.80
9 Marlon Byrd 4.00 1.20
10 Garret Anderson 4.00 1.20
11 Barry Bonds 10.00 3.00
12 Pat Burrell 4.00 1.20
13 Joe Crede 4.00 1.20
14 J.D. Drew 4.00 1.20
15 Ken Griffey Jr. 6.00 1.80
16 Vladimir Guerrero 4.00 1.20
17 Torii Hunter 4.00 1.20
18 Chipper Jones 4.00 1.20
19 Austin Kearns 4.00 1.20
20 Albert Pujols 8.00 2.40
21 Manny Ramirez 4.00 1.20
22 Gary Sheffield 4.00 1.20
23 Sammy Sosa 6.00 1.80
24 Ichiro Suzuki 6.00 1.80
25 Bernie Williams 4.00 1.20
26 Randy Johnson 4.00 1.20
27 Greg Maddux 6.00 1.80
28 Hideo Nomo 4.00 1.20
29 Nomar Garciaparra 6.00 1.80
30 Derek Jeter 10.00 3.00
31 Alex Rodriguez 6.00 1.80
32 Miguel Tejada 4.00 1.20

2003 Fleer Platinum MLB Scouting Report Game Used

Randomly inserted in wax packs, this is a partial parallel to the Scouting Report insert set. These cards feature a game used piece to go with the scouting report information. These cards were issued to a stated print run of 250 serial numbered sets.

Nm-Mt Ex-Mt
3 Jim Thome Jsy 15.00 4.50
4 Alfonso Soriano Bat 15.00 4.50
8 Mike Piazza Jsy 15.00 4.50
11 Barry Bonds Jsy 25.00 7.50
14 J.D. Drew Jsy 10.00 3.00
18 Chipper Jones Jsy 15.00 4.50
19 Austin Kearns Pants 10.00 3.00
21 Manny Ramirez Jsy 10.00 3.00
23 Sammy Sosa Jsy 20.00 6.00
26 Randy Johnson Jsy 15.00 4.50
27 Greg Maddux Jsy 15.00 4.50
28 Hideo Nomo Jsy 30.00 9.00
30 Derek Jeter Jsy 25.00 7.50

2003 Fleer Platinum Nameplates

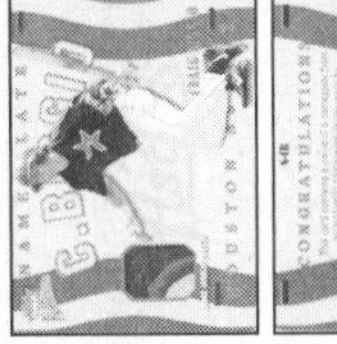

Inserted at a stated rate of one in eight jumbo packs, these 41 cards feature different amounts of the featured players. We have notated the print runs for the players in our checklist.

Nm-Mt Ex-Mt
AD Adam Dunn/117 25.00 7.50
AJ Andruw Jones/170 25.00 7.50
AR Alex Rodriguez/248 50.00 15.00
BB Barry Bonds/251 60.00 18.00
BL Barry Larkin/97 50.00 15.00
BZ Barry Zito/248 25.00 7.50
CB Craig Biggio/152 25.00 7.50
CC Chin-Feng Chen/110 120.00 36.00
CJ Chipper Jones/251 30.00 9.00
CK Corey Koskie/130 25.00 7.50
EH Eric Hinske/173 25.00 7.50
EM Edgar Martinez/176 25.00 7.50
FT Frank Thomas/58 50.00 15.00
FT Frank Thomas/93 50.00 15.00
GM Greg Maddux/248 40.00 12.00
HN Hideo Nomo/150
IR Ivan Rodriguez/189 40.00 12.00
JB Jeff Bagwell/121 40.00 12.00
JD Johnny Damon/35 50.00 15.00
JO John Olerud/180 25.00 7.50
JR Jimmy Rollins/74 25.00 7.50
JT Jim Thome/158 40.00 12.00
KI Kazuhisa Ishii/35 50.00 15.00
KS Kazuhiro Sasaki/82 25.00 7.50
KW Kerry Wood/49 80.00 24.00
LB Lance Berkman/176 25.00 7.50
LW Larry Walker/161 25.00 7.50
MP Mike Piazza/200 40.00 12.00
MP2 Mark Prior/123 50.00 15.00
MR Manny Ramirez/94 25.00 7.50
MS Mike Sweeney/175 25.00 7.50
MT Miguel Tejada/225 25.00 7.50
NG Nomar Garciaparra/258 40.00 12.00
PB Pat Burrell/176 25.00 7.50
PM Pedro Martinez/244 30.00 9.00
PN Phil Nevin/134
RC Roger Clemens/141 60.00 18.00
RJ Randy Johnson/142
RO Roy Oswalt/155 25.00 7.50
RP Rafael Palmeiro/245 25.00 7.50
RS Richie Sexson/160 25.00 7.50
VG Vladimir Guerrero/102 50.00 15.00

2003 Fleer Platinum Portraits

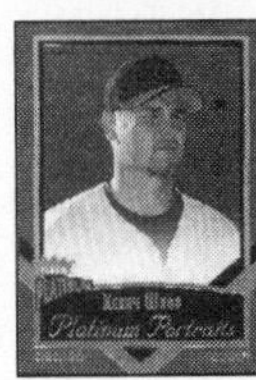

Inserted at a stated rate of one in 20 wax packs, one in 10 jumbo packs and one in five rack packs, these 20 cards feature painting like cards of the featured player.

Nm-Mt Ex-Mt
1 Josh Beckett 3.00 .90
2 Roberto Alomar 3.00 .90
3 Alfonso Soriano 3.00 .90
4 Mike Piazza 5.00 1.50
5 Ivan Rodriguez 3.00 .90
6 Edgar Martinez 3.00 .90
7 Barry Bonds 8.00 2.40
8 Adam Dunn 3.00 .90
9 Juan Gonzalez 3.00 .90
10 Chipper Jones 3.00 .90
11 Albert Pujols 6.00 1.80
12 Magglio Ordonez 3.00 .90
13 Shea Hillenbrand 3.00 .90
14 Larry Walker 3.00 .90
15 Pedro Martinez 3.00 .90
16 Kerry Wood 3.00 .90
17 Barry Zito 3.00 .90
18 Nomar Garciaparra 5.00 1.50
19 Derek Jeter 8.00 2.40
20 Alex Rodriguez 5.00 1.50

2003 Fleer Platinum Portraits Game Jersey

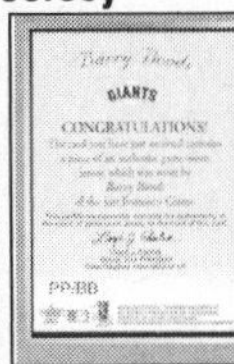

Inserted at a stated rate of one in 86 wax packs, this is a partial parallel to the Portraits insert set. These cards feature a game-worn jersey swatch on the front. The Derek Jeter card was issued in smaller quantity and we have notated that information in our data base.

Nm-Mt Ex-Mt
1 Josh Beckett 10.00 3.00
4 Mike Piazza 15.00 4.50
5 Ivan Rodriguez 10.00 3.00
7 Barry Bonds 20.00 6.00
8 Adam Dunn 8.00 2.40
10 Chipper Jones 10.00 3.00
15 Pedro Martinez 10.00 3.00
16 Kerry Wood 10.00 3.00
17 Barry Zito 10.00 3.00
18 Nomar Garciaparra 15.00 4.50
19 Derek Jeter SP/150 30.00 9.00

2003 Fleer Platinum Portraits Game Patch

Inserted at a stated rate of one in 86 wax packs, this is a partial parallel to the Portraits insert set. These cards feature a game-worn jersey swatch on the front. These cards were issued to a stated print run of 100 serial numbered sets.

Nm-Mt Ex-Mt
4 Mike Piazza 60.00 18.00
5 Ivan Rodriguez 40.00 12.00
7 Barry Bonds 60.00 18.00
8 Adam Dunn 40.00 12.00
10 Chipper Jones 40.00 12.00
15 Pedro Martinez 40.00 12.00
16 Kerry Wood 40.00 12.00
17 Barry Zito 40.00 12.00
18 Nomar Garciaparra 60.00 18.00
19 Derek Jeter

2004 Fleer Platinum

This 200-card set was released in February, 2004. The set was issued in seven-card packs with an $3 SRP which came 18 packs to a box and 16 boxes to a case. In addition, every hobby box had four jumbo packs included. Those jumbo packs had 20 cards in them. Plus rack packs were issued; those packs had 30 cards in each pack. Cards numbered 1-135 are major league veterans while cards numbered 136-143 were issued at a stated rate of one in three wax and one in 12 retail packs. Cards numbered 144-151 were issued at a stated rate of one per jumbo while cards 152 through 157 were issued exclusively in rack packs at a rate of one per and according to Fleer the stated print run of those cards was approximately 1000 cards. The set closes with the following subsets: UH (cards numbered 158 through 182 while cards numbered 183 through 200 feature multi-player prospect cards.

Nm-Mt Ex-Mt
COMP.SET w/o SP's (178) 25.00 7.50
COMMON (1-135/158-182) .30 .09
COMMON CARD (183-200) 1.00 .30
183-200 ARE NOT SHORT-PRINTS
COMMON CARD (136-143) 1.50 .45
136-143 ODDS 1:3 WAX, 1:12 RETAIL
COMMON CARD (144-151) 2.50 .75
144-151 ODDS ONE PER JUMBO
COMMON CARD (152-157) 8.00 2.40
152-157 ODDS ONE PER RACK PACK
152-157 STATED PRINT RUN APPX.1000 SETS
152-157 PRINT RUN PROVIDED BY FLEER
152-157 ARE NOT SERIAL-NUMBERED
1 Luis Castillo .30 .09
2 Preston Wilson .30 .09
3 Johan Santana .30 .09
4 Fred McGriff .50 .15
5 Albert Pujols 1.50 .45
6 Reggie Sanders .30 .09
7 Ivan Rodriguez .75 .23
8 Roy Halladay .30 .09
9 Brian Giles .30 .09
10 Bernie Williams .50 .15
11 Barry Larkin .75 .23
12 Marlon Anderson .30 .09
13 Ramon Ortiz .30 .09
14 Luis Matos .30 .09
15 Esteban Loaiza .30 .09
16 Orlando Cabrera .30 .09
17 Jamie Moyer .30 .09
18 Tino Martinez .50 .15
19 Josh Beckett .50 .15
20 Derek Jeter 2.00 .60
21 Derek Lowe .30 .09
22 Jack Wilson .30 .09
23 Bret Boone .30 .09
24 Matt Morris .30 .09
25 Javier Vazquez .30 .09
26 Joe Crede .30 .09
27 Jose Vidro .30 .09
28 Mike Piazza 1.25 .35
29 Curt Schilling .50 .15
30 Alex Rodriguez 1.25 .35
31 John Olerud .30 .09
32 Dontrelle Willis .30 .09
33 Larry Walker .50 .15
34 Joe Randa .30 .09
35 Paul Lo Duca .30 .09
36 Marlon Byrd .30 .09
37 Bo Hart .30 .09
38 Rafael Palmeiro .50 .15
39 Garret Anderson .30 .09
40 Tom Glavine .50 .15
41 Ichiro Suzuki 1.25 .35
42 Derek Lee .30 .09
43 Lance Berkman .30 .09
44 Nomar Garciaparra 1.25 .35
45 Mike Sweeney .30 .09
46 A.J. Burnett .30 .09
47 Sean Casey .30 .09
48 Eric Gagne .50 .15
49 Joel Pineiro .30 .09
50 Russ Ortiz .30 .09
51 Placido Polanco .30 .09
52 Sammy Sosa 1.25 .35
53 Mark Teixeira .30 .09
54 Randy Wolf .30 .09
55 Vladimir Guerrero .75 .23
56 Tim Hudson .30 .09
57 Lew Ford .30 .09
58 Carlos Delgado .30 .09
59 Darin Erstad .30 .09
60 Mike Lieberthal .30 .09
61 Craig Biggio .50 .15
62 Ryan Klesko .30 .09
63 C.C. Sabathia .30 .09
64 Carlos Lee .30 .09
65 Al Leiter .30 .09
66 Brandon Webb .30 .09
67 Jacque Jones .30 .09
68 Kerry Wood .75 .23
69 Omar Vizquel .30 .09
70 Jeremy Bonderman .30 .09
71 Kevin Brown .30 .09
72 Richie Sexson .30 .09
73 Zach Day .30 .09
74 Mike Mussina .75 .23
75 Sidney Ponson .30 .09
76 Andruw Jones .30 .09
77 Woody Williams .30 .09
78 Kazuhiro Sasaki .30 .09
79 Matt Clement .30 .09
80 Shea Hillenbrand .30 .09
81 Bartolo Colon .30 .09
82 Ken Griffey Jr. 1.25 .35
83 Todd Helton .50 .15
84 Dmitri Young .30 .09
85 Richard Hidalgo .30 .09
86 Carlos Beltran .30 .09
87 Brad Wilkerson .30 .09
88 Andy Pettitte .50 .15
89 Miguel Tejada .30 .09
90 Edgar Martinez .50 .15
91 Vernon Wells .30 .09
92 Magglio Ordonez .30 .09
93 Tony Batista .30 .09
94 Jose Reyes .50 .15
95 Matt Stairs .30 .09
96 Manny Ramirez .30 .09
97 Carlos Pena .30 .09
98 A.J. Pierzynski .30 .09
99 Jim Thome .75 .23
100 Aubrey Huff .30 .09
101 Roberto Alomar .75 .23
102 Luis Gonzalez .30 .09
103 Chipper Jones .75 .23
104 Jay Gibbons .30 .09
105 Adam Dunn .30 .09
106 Jay Payton .30 .09
107 Scott Podsednik .75 .23
108 Roy Oswalt .30 .09
109 Milton Bradley .30 .09
110 Shawn Green .30 .09
111 Ryan Wagner .30 .09
112 Eric Chavez .30 .09
113 Pat Burrell .30 .09
114 Frank Thomas .75 .23
115 Jason Kendall .30 .09
116 Jake Peavy .30 .09
117 Mike Cameron .30 .09
118 Jim Edmonds .30 .09
119 Hank Blalock .30 .09
120 Troy Glaus .50 .15
121 Jeff Kent .30 .09
122 Jason Schmidt .30 .09
123 Corey Patterson .30 .09
124 Austin Kearns .30 .09
125 Edwin Jackson .30 .09
126 Alfonso Soriano .50 .15
127 Bobby Abreu .30 .09
128 Scott Rolen .50 .15
129 Jeff Bagwell .50 .15
130 Shannon Stewart .30 .09
131 Rich Aurilia .30 .09
132 Ty Wigginton .30 .09
133 Randy Johnson .75 .23
134 Rocco Baldelli .75 .23
135 Hideo Nomo .75 .23
136 Greg Maddux WE 3.00 .90
137 Johnny Damon WE 1.50 .45
138 Mark Prior WE 4.00 1.20
139 Corey Koskie WE 1.50 .45
140 Miguel Cabrera WE 2.00 .60
141 Hideki Matsui WE 3.00 .90
142 Jose Cruz Jr. WE 1.50 .45
143 Barry Zito WE 1.50 .45
144 Javy Lopez JE 2.50 .75
145 Jason Varitek JE 2.50 .75
146 Moises Alou JE 2.50 .75
147 Torii Hunter JE 2.50 .75
148 Juan Encarnacion JE 2.50 .75
149 Jorge Posada JE 2.50 .75
150 Marquis Grissom JE 2.50 .75
151 Rich Harden JE 2.50 .75
152 Gary Sheffield RE 8.00 2.40
153 Pedro Martinez RE 10.00 3.00
154 Brad Radke RE 8.00 2.40
155 Mike Lowell RE 8.00 2.40
156 Jason Giambi RE 10.00 3.00
157 Mark Mulder RE 8.00 2.40
158 Ben Weber UH .30 .09
159 Mark DeRosa UH .30 .09
160 Melvin Mora UH .30 .09
161 Bill Mueller UH .30 .09
162 Jon Garland UH .30 .09
163 Jody Gerut UH .30 .09
164 Javier Lopez UH .30 .09
165 Craig Monroe UH .30 .09
166 Juan Pierre UH .30 .09
167 Morgan Ensberg UH .30 .09
168 Angel Berroa UH .30 .09
169 Geoff Jenkins UH .30 .09
170 Matt LeCroy UH .30 .09
171 Livan Hernandez UH .30 .09
172 Jason Phillips UH .30 .09
173 Mariano Rivera UH .50 .15
174 Erubiel Durazo UH .30 .09
175 Jason Michaels UH .30 .09
176 Kip Wells UH .30 .09
177 Ray Durham UH .30 .09
178 Randy Winn UH .30 .09
179 Edgar Renteria UH .30 .09
180 Carl Crawford UH .30 .09
181 Laynce Nix UH .30 .09
182 Greg Myers UH .30 .09
183 Delmon Young 3.00 .90
Chad Gaudin
184 Humberto Quintero 1.00 .30
Bernie Castro
185 Craig Brazell 1.00 .30
Danny Garcia
186 Ryan Wing 1.00 .30
Francisco Cruceta
187 William Bergolla RC 1.50 .45
Josh Hall
188 Clint Barmes 1.50 .45
Garrett Atkins
189 Chris Bootcheck 1.00 .30
Richard Fischer
190 Edgar Gonzalez 1.50 .45
Matt Kata
191 Andrew Brown 1.00 .30
Koyie Hill
192 John Gall RC 1.50 .45
Dan Haren
193 Chad Bentz RC 1.50 .45
Luis Ayala
194 Hector Gimenez RC 1.50 .45
Eric Bruntlett
195 Boof Bonser 1.00 .30
Rob Bowen
196 Chris Snelling 1.50 .45
Rett Johnson
197 Rickie Weeks 3.00 .90
Adam Morrissey
198 Noah Lowry 1.50 .45
Todd Linden
199 Chris Waters 1.00 .30
Brett Evert
200 Jorge De Paula 1.50 .45
Chien-Ming Wang

2004 Fleer Platinum Finish

Nm-Mt Ex-Mt
*FINISH 1-135/158-182: 3X TO 8X BASIC
*FINISH 183-200: 1X TO 2.5X BASIC
*FINISH 136-143: 1.25X TO 3X BASIC
*FINISH 144-151: .75X TO 2X BASIC
*FINISH 152-157: .25X TO .6X BASIC
STATED ODDS 1:15 WAX
STATED PRINT RUN 100 SERIAL #'d SETS

2004 Fleer Platinum Big Signs

Nm-Mt Ex-Mt
ODDS 1:9 WAX, 1:2 JUMBO, 1:8 RETAIL
1 Albert Pujols 3.00 .90
2 Derek Jeter 4.00 1.20

3 Mike Piazza 2.50 .75
4 Jason Giambi 1.50 .45
5 Ichiro Suzuki 2.50 .75
6 Nomar Garciaparra 2.50 .75
7 Mark Prior 3.00 .90
8 Randy Johnson 1.50 .45
9 Greg Maddux 2.50 .75
10 Sammy Sosa 2.50 .75
11 Ken Griffey Jr. 2.50 .75
12 Dontrelle Willis 1.50 .45
13 Alex Rodriguez 2.50 .75
14 Chipper Jones 1.50 .45
15 Hank Blalock 1.50 .45

2004 Fleer Platinum Big Signs Autographs

Albert Pujols and Chipper Jones did not return their cards in time for pack out. Please note there is no expiration date to return these cards by.

Nm-Mt Ex-Mt
RANDOM INSERTS IN WAX PACKS
STATED PRINT RUN 100 SERIAL #'d SETS
EXCHANGE DEADLINE INDEFINITE
AP Albert Pujols EXCH 200.00 60.00
CJ Chipper Jones EXCH 50.00 15.00
DW Dontrelle Willis 25.00 7.50
HB Hank Blalock 25.00 7.50

2004 Fleer Platinum Classic Combinations

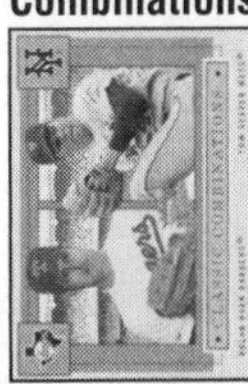

Nm-Mt Ex-Mt
STATED ODDS 1:108 WAX, 1:270 RETAIL
1 Ivan Rodriguez 12.00 3.60
Mike Piazza
2 Alex Rodriguez 12.00 3.60
Sammy Sosa
3 Dontrelle Willis 8.00 2.40
Angel Berroa
4 Nomar Garciaparra 20.00 6.00
Derek Jeter
5 Ichiro Suzuki 12.00 3.60
Hideo Nomo
6 Josh Beckett 8.00 2.40
Kerry Wood
7 Albert Pujols 15.00 4.50
Carlos Delgado
8 Alfonso Soriano 8.00 2.40
Joe Morgan
9 Jason Giambi 8.00 2.40
Reggie Jackson
10 Nolan Ryan 25.00 7.50
Tom Seaver

2004 Fleer Platinum Clubhouse Memorabilia

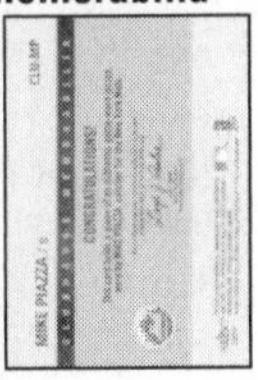

Nm-Mt Ex-Mt
STATED ODDS 1:24 WAX, 1:96 RETAIL
SP INFO PROVIDED BY FLEER
*DUAL: 1X TO 2.5X BASIC
*DUAL: .75X TO 2X BASIC SP
DUAL RANDOM IN WAX AND RETAIL
DUAL PRINT RUN 50 SERIAL #'d SETS
DUAL FEATURE TWO JSY SWATCHES
AK Austin Kearns 8.00 2.40
AP Albert Pujols SP 20.00 6.00
AR Alex Rodriguez 10.00 3.00
AS Alfonso Soriano SP 10.00 3.00
CJ Chipper Jones SP 10.00 3.00
DJ Derek Jeter 20.00 6.00
DW Dontrelle Willis 8.00 2.40
GM Greg Maddux 10.00 3.00
HB Hank Blalock 8.00 2.40
HN Hideo Nomo 15.00 4.50
JB Josh Beckett 10.00 3.00
JG Jason Giambi 10.00 3.00

JT Jim Thome 10.00 3.00
MPI Mike Piazza 10.00 3.00
MPR Mark Prior SP 20.00 6.00
MT Miguel Tejada 8.00 2.40
NG Nomar Garciaparra 10.00 3.00
RB Rocco Baldelli 10.00 3.00
RS Richie Sexson 8.00 2.40
SS Sammy Sosa 15.00 4.50
THE Todd Helton 10.00 3.00
THU Torii Hunter 8.00 2.40
VG Vladimir Guerrero 10.00 3.00

2004 Fleer Platinum Inscribed

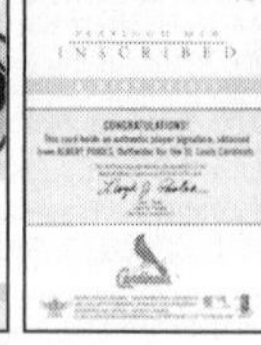

Nm-Mt Ex-Mt
ONE PER RACK PACK
PRINT RUNS B/WN 20-315 COPIES PER
EXCH PRINT RUNS PROVIDED BY FLEER
EXCHANGE DEADLINE INDEFINITE
NO PRICING ON QTY OF 25 OR LESS.
1-CS Randy Johnson/150 EXCH
2-AS Adam LaRoche/200 EXCH 25.00 7.50
AB Angel Berroa/210 15.00 4.50
AP Albert Pujols/100 175.00 52.50
BL Barry Larkin/75 EXCH 50.00 15.00
BWA Billy Wagner/300 EXCH 25.00 7.50
BWE Brandon Webb/150 25.00 7.50
CBE Chad Bentz/310 10.00 3.00
CBO Chris Bootcheck/210 10.00 3.00
CSN Chris Snelling/310 10.00 3.00
DH Dan Haren/200 15.00 4.50
DM Dallas McPherson/160 15.00 4.50
DW Dontrelle Willis/25
DY Delmon Young/210 40.00 12.00
EG Eric Gagne/130 40.00 12.00
EJ Edwin Jackson/200 25.00 7.50
JR1 Jose Reyes/20
JR2 Jose Reyes/150 EXCH
JV Javier Vazquez/160 50.00 15.00
KG Khalil Greene/310 25.00 7.50
KH Koyie Hill/300 10.00 3.00
LN Laynce Nix/200 25.00 7.50
MB Marlon Byrd/255 10.00 3.00
MC Miguel Cabrera/200 EXCH 25.00 7.50
MK Matt Kata/315 15.00 4.50
RB Rocco Baldelli/100 40.00 12.00
RHA Rich Harden/200
RHO Ryan Howard/160 10.00 3.00
RWA Ryan Wagner/275 EXCH 15.00 4.50
RWE Rickie Weeks/200
SP Scott Podsednik/180 50.00 15.00
SR Scott Rolen/55
VW Vernon Wells/200 15.00 4.50

2004 Fleer Platinum MLB Scouting Report

Nm-Mt Ex-Mt
ODDS 1:45 WAX, 1:96 JUMBO, 1:190 RETAIL
STATED PRINT RUN 400 SERIAL #'d SETS
1 Josh Beckett 4.00 1.20
2 Todd Helton 4.00 1.20
3 Rocco Baldelli 4.00 1.20
4 Pedro Martinez 4.00 1.20
5 Jeff Bagwell 4.00 1.20
6 Mark Prior 8.00 2.40
7 Ichiro Suzuki 6.00 1.80
8 Barry Zito 4.00 1.20
9 Manny Ramirez 4.00 1.20
10 Miguel Cabrera 4.00 1.20
11 Richie Sexson 4.00 1.20
12 Hideki Matsui 6.00 1.80
13 Magglio Ordonez 4.00 1.20
14 Brandon Webb 4.00 1.20
15 Kerry Wood 4.00 1.20

2004 Fleer Platinum MLB Scouting Report Game Jersey

Nm-Mt Ex-Mt
RANDOM IN WAX AND RETAIL PACKS
STATED PRINT RUN 250 SERIAL #'d SETS
BW Brandon Webb 10.00 3.00
JB Josh Beckett 15.00 4.50
JBAG Jeff Bagwell 15.00 4.50
KW Kerry Wood 15.00 4.50
MP Mark Prior 20.00 6.00
MR Manny Ramirez 10.00 3.00
PM Pedro Martinez 15.00 4.50
RB Rocco Baldelli 15.00 4.50
TH Todd Helton 15.00 4.50

2004 Fleer Platinum Nameplates Player

Nm-Mt Ex-Mt
OVERALL NAMEPLATES ODDS 1:4 JUMBO
PRINT RUNS B/WN 25-320 COPIES PER
NO PRICING ON QTY OF 25 OR LESS.
AK Austin Kearns/310 15.00 4.50
AP Albert Pujols/190 40.00 12.00
AR Alex Rodriguez/225 25.00 7.50
BZ Barry Zito/170 20.00 6.00
CJ Chipper Jones/150 25.00 7.50
CS Curt Schilling/260 20.00 6.00
GS Gary Sheffield/115 20.00 6.00
HB Hank Blalock/200 15.00 4.50
HN Hideo Nomo/85 50.00 15.00
HSC Hee Seop Choi/70 20.00 6.00
JB Josh Beckett/255 20.00 6.00
JP Juan Pierre/50 25.00 7.50
JR Jose Reyes/310 20.00 6.00
KB Kevin Brown/80 15.00 4.50
KW Kerry Wood/290 20.00 6.00
LC Luis Castillo/75 15.00 4.50
MB Marlon Byrd/75 15.00 4.50
MC Miguel Cabrera/75 25.00 7.50
MR Manny Ramirez/210 15.00 4.50
MT Mark Teixeira/250 15.00 4.50
NG Nomar Garciaparra/320 25.00 7.50
RJ Randy Johnson/200 20.00 6.00
RS Richie Sexson/165 15.00 4.50
SS Sammy Sosa/260 25.00 7.50
TG Tom Glavine/25

2004 Fleer Platinum Nameplates Team

Nm-Mt Ex-Mt
OVERALL NAMEPLATES ODDS 1:4 JUMBO
PRINT RUNS B/WN 105-515 COPIES PER
AK Austin Kearns/515 10.00 3.00
AP Albert Pujols/470 30.00 9.00
AR Alex Rodriguez/510 20.00 6.00
BZ Barry Zito/515 15.00 4.50
CJ Chipper Jones/420 15.00 4.50
CS Curt Schilling/250 20.00 6.00
GS Gary Sheffield/500 10.00 3.00
HB Hank Blalock/515 10.00 3.00
HN Hideo Nomo/390 20.00 6.00
HSC Hee Seop Choi/220 15.00 4.50
JB Josh Beckett/390 15.00 4.50
JP Juan Pierre/110 20.00 6.00
JR Jose Reyes/510 15.00 4.50
KB Kevin Brown/220 10.00 3.00
KW Kerry Wood/510 10.00 3.00
LC Luis Castillo/225 10.00 3.00
MB Marlon Byrd/470 10.00 3.00
MC Miguel Cabrera/105 25.00 7.50
MR Manny Ramirez/480 10.00 3.00
MT Mark Teixeira/505 10.00 3.00
NG Nomar Garciaparra/250 25.00 7.50
RJ Randy Johnson/290 20.00 6.00
RS Richie Sexson/420 10.00 3.00
SS Sammy Sosa/490 25.00 7.50

2004 Fleer Platinum Portraits

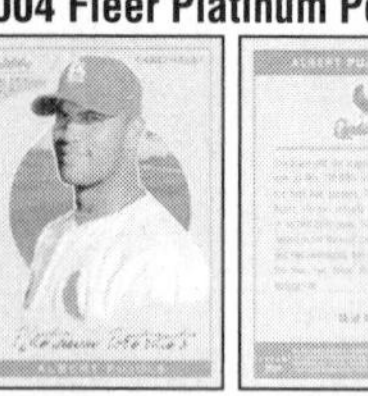

Nm-Mt Ex-Mt
ODDS 1:18 WAX, 1:4 JUMBO, 1:24 RETAIL
1 Jason Giambi 3.00 .90
2 Nomar Garciaparra 5.00 1.50
3 Vladimir Guerrero 3.00 .90
4 Mark Prior 6.00 1.80
5 Jim Thome 3.00 .90
6 Derek Jeter 8.00 2.40
7 Sammy Sosa 5.00 1.50
8 Alex Rodriguez 5.00 1.50
9 Greg Maddux 5.00 1.50
10 Albert Pujols 6.00 1.80

2004 Fleer Platinum Portraits Game Jersey

Nm-Mt Ex-Mt
STATED ODDS 1:48 WAX, 1:120 RETAIL
SP INFO PROVIDED BY FLEER
*PATCH: .75X TO 2X BASIC
*PATCH: .6X TO 1.5X BASIC SP
PATCH RANDOM IN WAX AND RETAIL
PATCH PRINT RUN 100 SERIAL #'d SETS
AP Albert Pujols 15.00 4.50
AR Alex Rodriguez 10.00 3.00
DJ Derek Jeter 20.00 6.00

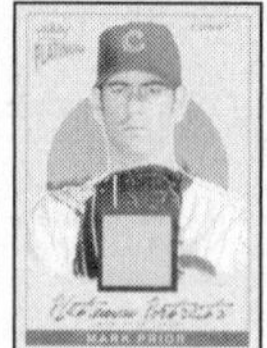
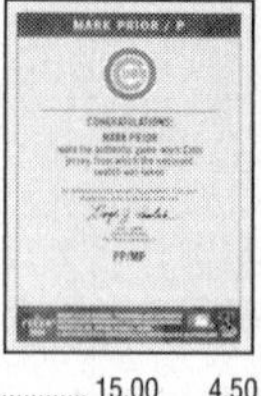

GM Greg Maddux SP 15.00 4.50
JG Jason Giambi 10.00 3.00
JT Jim Thome 10.00 3.00
MP Mark Prior SP 20.00 6.00
NG Nomar Garciaparra 10.00 3.00
SS Sammy Sosa 10.00 3.00
VG Vladimir Guerrero 10.00 3.00

2001 Fleer Premium

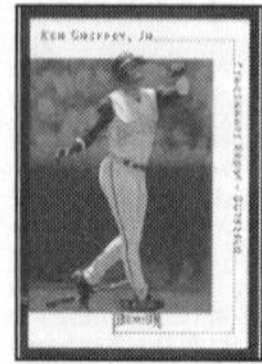

The 2001 Fleer Premium product was released in early April, 2001 and features a 235-card base set that was broken into tiers as follows: Base Veterans (1-200), and Prospects (201-235) which were individually serial numbered to 1999. Please note that cards 231-235 all packed out as exchange cards and needed to have been exchanged to Fleer by 5/01/02. Each pack contained eight cards and carried a suggested retail price of $3.99.

Nm-Mt Ex-Mt
COMP.SET w/o SP's (200) 30.00 9.00
COMMON CARD (1-200) .40 .12
COMMON (201-230) 8.00 2.40
COMMON (231-235) 8.00 2.40
1 Cal Ripken 3.00 .90
2 Derek Jeter 2.50 .75
3 Edgardo Alfonzo .40 .12
4 Luis Castillo .40 .12
5 Mike Lieberthal .40 .12
6 Kazuhiro Sasaki .40 .12
7 Jeff Kent .40 .12
8 Eric Karros .40 .12
9 Tom Glavine .60 .18
10 Jeromy Burnitz .40 .12
11 Travis Fryman .40 .12
12 Ron Coomer .40 .12
13 Jeff D'Amico .40 .12
14 Carlos Febles .40 .12
15 Kevin Brown .40 .12
16 Deivi Cruz .40 .12
17 Tino Martinez .60 .18
18 Bobby Abreu .40 .12
19 Roger Clemens 2.00 .60
20 Jeffrey Hammonds .40 .12
21 Peter Bergeron .40 .12
22 Ray Lankford .40 .12
23 Scott Rolen .60 .18
24 Jermaine Dye .40 .12
25 Rusty Greer .40 .12
26 Frank Thomas 1.00 .30
27 Jeff Bagwell .60 .18
28 Cliff Floyd .40 .12
29 Chris Singleton .40 .12
30 Steve Finley .40 .12
31 Orlando Hernandez .40 .12
32 Tom Goodwin .40 .12
33 Larry Walker .60 .18
34 Mike Sweeney .40 .12
35 Tim Hudson .40 .12
36 Kerry Wood 1.00 .30
37 Mike Lowell .40 .12
38 Andruw Jones .75 .23
39 Alex Gonzalez .40 .12
40 Juan Gonzalez .75 .23
41 J.D. Drew .40 .12
42 Mark McLemore .40 .12
43 Royce Clayton .40 .12
44 Paul O'Neill .60 .18
45 Carlos Beltran .40 .12
46 Phil Nevin .40 .12
47 Rondell White .40 .12
48 Gerald Williams .40 .12
49 Geoff Jenkins .40 .12
50 Marvin Benard .40 .12
51 Alex Rodriguez 1.50 .45
52 Moises Alou .40 .12
53 Mike Lansing .40 .12
54 Omar Vizquel .40 .12
55 Eric Chavez .40 .12
56 Mark Quinn .40 .12
57 Mike Lamb .40 .12
58 Rick Ankiel .40 .12
59 Lance Berkman .40 .12
60 Jeff Conine .40 .12
61 B.J. Surhoff .40 .12
62 Todd Helton .60 .18
63 J.T. Snow .40 .12
64 John VanderWal .40 .12
65 Johnny Damon .40 .12
66 Bobby Higginson .40 .12
67 Carlos Delgado .75 .23
68 Shawn Green .40 .12
69 Mike Redmond .40 .12
70 Mike Piazza 1.50 .45
71 Adrian Beltre .40 .12
72 Juan Encarnacion .40 .12
73 Chipper Jones 1.00 .30
74 Garret Anderson .40 .12
75 Paul Konerko .40 .12
76 Barry Larkin 1.00 .30
77 Tony Gwynn 1.25 .35
78 Rafael Palmeiro .60 .18
79 Randy Johnson 1.00 .30
80 Mark Grace .75 .23
81 Javy Lopez .40 .12
82 Gabe Kapler .40 .12
83 Henry Rodriguez .40 .12
84 Raul Mondesi .40 .12
85 Adam Piatt .40 .12
86 Marquis Grissom .40 .12
87 Charles Johnson .40 .12
88 Sean Casey .40 .12
89 Manny Ramirez .40 .12
90 Curt Schilling .60 .18
91 Fernando Tatis .40 .12
92 Derek Bell .40 .12
93 Tony Clark .40 .12
94 Homer Bush .40 .12
95 Nomar Garciaparra 1.50 .45
96 Vinny Castilla .40 .12
97 Ben Davis .40 .12
98 Carl Everett .40 .12
99 Damion Easley .40 .12
100 Craig Biggio .60 .18
101 Todd Hollandsworth .40 .12
102 Jay Payton .40 .12
103 Gary Sheffield .40 .12
104 Sandy Alomar Jr. .40 .12
105 Doug Glanville .40 .12
106 Barry Bonds 2.50 .75
107 Tim Salmon .60 .18
108 Terrence Long .40 .12
109 Jorge Posada .60 .18
110 Jose Offerman .40 .12
111 Edgar Martinez .60 .18
112 Jeremy Giambi .40 .12
113 Dean Palmer .40 .12
114 Roberto Alomar .75 .23
115 Aaron Boone .40 .12
116 Adam Kennedy .40 .12
117 Joe Randa .40 .12
118 Jose Vidro .40 .12
119 Tony Batista .40 .12
120 Kevin Young .40 .12
121 Preston Wilson .40 .12
122 Jason Kendall .40 .12
123 Mark Kotsay .40 .12
124 Timo Perez .40 .12
125 Eric Young .40 .12
126 Greg Maddux 1.50 .45
127 Richard Hidalgo .40 .12
128 Brian Giles .40 .12
129 Fred McGriff .60 .18
130 Troy Glaus .60 .18
131 Todd Walker .40 .12
132 Brady Anderson .40 .12
133 Jim Edmonds .40 .12
134 Ben Grieve .40 .12
135 Greg Vaughn .40 .12
136 Robin Ventura .40 .12
137 Sammy Sosa 1.50 .45
138 Rich Aurilia .40 .12
139 Jose Valentin .40 .12
140 Trot Nixon .60 .18
141 Troy Percival .40 .12
142 Bernie Williams .60 .18
143 Warren Morris .40 .12
144 Jacque Jones .40 .12
145 Danny Bautista .40 .12
146 A.J. Pierzynski .40 .12
147 Mark McGwire 2.50 .75
148 Rafael Furcal .40 .12
149 Ray Durham .40 .12
150 Mike Mussina .75 .23
151 Jay Bell .40 .12
152 David Wells .40 .12
153 Ken Caminiti .40 .12
154 Jim Thome 1.00 .30
155 Ivan Rodriguez 1.00 .30
156 Milton Bradley .40 .12
157 Ken Griffey Jr. 1.50 .45
158 Al Leiter .40 .12
159 Corey Koskie .40 .12
160 Shannon Stewart .40 .12
161 Mo Vaughn .40 .12
162 Pedro Martinez 1.00 .30
163 Todd Hundley .40 .12
164 Darin Erstad .75 .23
165 Ruben Rivera .40 .12
166 Richie Sexson .40 .12
167 Andres Galarraga .40 .12
168 Darryl Kile .40 .12
169 Jose Cruz Jr. .40 .12
170 David Justice .40 .12
171 Vladimir Guerrero 1.00 .30
172 Jeff Cirillo .40 .12
173 John Olerud .40 .12
174 Devon White .40 .12
175 Ron Belliard .40 .12
176 Pokey Reese .40 .12
177 Mike Hampton .40 .12
178 David Ortiz .40 .12
179 Magglio Ordonez .40 .12
180 Ruben Mateo .40 .12
181 Carlos Lee .40 .12
182 Matt Williams .40 .12
183 Miguel Tejada .40 .12
184 Scott Elarton .40 .12
185 Bret Boone .40 .12
186 Pat Burrell .40 .12
187 Brad Radke .40 .12
188 Brian Jordan .40 .12
189 Matt Lawton .40 .12
190 Al Martin .40 .12
191 Albert Belle .40 .12
192 Tony Womack .40 .12
193 Roger Cedeno .40 .12
194 Travis Lee .40 .12
195 Dmitri Young .40 .12
196 Jay Buhner .40 .12
197 Jason Giambi .75 .23
198 Jason Tyner .40 .12
199 Ben Petrick .40 .12
200 Jose Canseco .75 .23
201 Nick Johnson 8.00 2.40
202 Jace Brewer 8.00 2.40
203 Ryan Freel RC 8.00 2.40
204 Jaisen Randolph RC 8.00 2.40
205 Marcus Giles 8.00 2.40
206 Claudio Vargas RC 8.00 2.40
207 Brian Cole 8.00 2.40
208 Scott Hodges 8.00 2.40
209 Winston Abreu RC 8.00 2.40
210 Shea Hillenbrand 8.00 2.40
211 Larry Barnes 8.00 2.40
212 Paul Phillips RC 8.00 2.40
213 Pedro Santana RC 8.00 2.40
214 Ivanon Coffie 8.00 2.40
215 Junior Spivey RC 10.00 3.00
216 Donzell McDonald 8.00 2.40
217 Vernon Wells 8.00 2.40
218 Corey Patterson 8.00 2.40
219 Sang-Hoon Lee 8.00 2.40
220 Jack Cust 8.00 2.40
221 Jason Romano 8.00 2.40
222 Jack Wilson RC 8.00 2.40
223 Adam Everett 8.00 2.40
224 Esix Snead RC 8.00 2.40
225 Jason Hart 8.00 2.40
226 Joe Lawrence 8.00 2.40
227 Brandon Inge 8.00 2.40
228 Alex Escobar 8.00 2.40
229 Abraham Nunez 8.00 2.40
230 Jared Sandberg 8.00 2.40
231 Ichiro Suzuki RC 40.00 12.00
232 Tsuyoshi Shinjo RC 12.00 3.60
233 Albert Pujols RC 60.00 18.00
234 Wilson Betemit RC 8.00 2.40
235 Drew Henson RC 20.00 6.00
MM1 D.Jeter MM/1995 12.00 3.60
NNO D.Jeter MM AU/95 EX 120.00 36.00

2001 Fleer Premium Star Ruby

Randomly inserted into packs, this set is a parallel of the first 230 cards of the 2001 Fleer Premium base set. Each card was produced with ruby-red foil stamping and are individually serial numbered to 125.

Nm-Mt Ex-Mt
*RUBY 1-200: 5X TO 12X BASE HI
*RUBY 201-230: .3X TO .8X BASE HI

2001 Fleer Premium A Time for Heroes

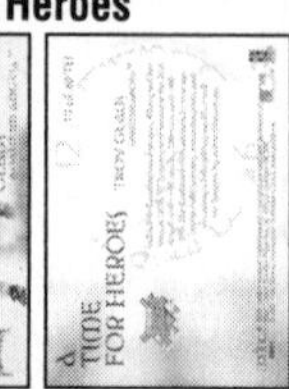

Randomly inserted into packs at one in 20, this 20-card insert set pays homage to the heroes who have emerged in the modern game Card backs carry an "ATFH" prefix.

Nm-Mt Ex-Mt
COMPLETE SET (20) 80.00 24.00
ATFH1 Darin Erstad 2.00 .60
ATFH2 Alex Rodriguez 6.00 1.80
ATFH3 Shawn Green 2.00 .60
ATFH4 Jeff Bagwell 2.50 .75
ATFH5 Sammy Sosa 6.00 1.80
ATFH6 Derek Jeter 10.00 3.00
ATFH7 Nomar Garciaparra 6.00 1.80
ATFH8 Carlos Delgado 2.00 .60
ATFH9 Pat Burrell 2.00 .60
ATFH10 Tony Gwynn 5.00 1.50
ATFH11 Chipper Jones 4.00 1.20
ATFH12 Jason Giambi 4.00 1.20
ATFH13 Magglio Ordonez 2.00 .60
ATFH14 Troy Glaus 2.50 .75
ATFH15 Ivan Rodriguez 4.00 1.20
ATFH16 Andruw Jones 2.00 .60
ATFH17 Vladimir Guerrero 4.00 1.20
ATFH18 Ken Griffey Jr. 6.00 1.80
ATFH19 J.D. Drew 2.00 .60
ATFH20 Todd Helton 2.50 .75

2001 Fleer Premium Brother Wood

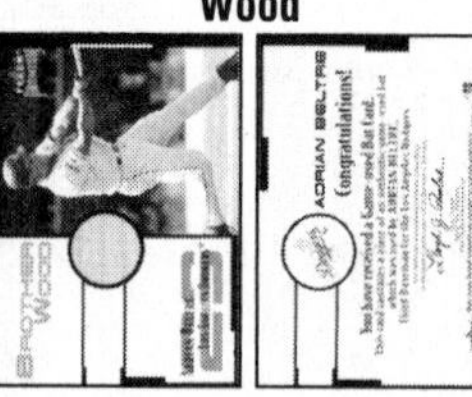

Randomly inserted into packs at one in 108, this 9-card insert set features actual pieces of game-used bats. Card backs carry a "BW" prefix.

Nm-Mt Ex-Mt
BW1 Vladimir Guerrero 15.00 4.50
BW2 Andruw Jones 10.00 3.00
BW3 Corey Patterson 10.00 3.00
BW4 Magglio Ordonez 10.00 3.00
BW5 Jason Giambi 15.00 4.50
BW6 Rafael Palmeiro 15.00 4.50
BW7 Eric Chavez 10.00 3.00
BW8 Pat Burrell 10.00 3.00
BW9 Adrian Beltre 10.00 3.00

2001 Fleer Premium Decades of Excellence

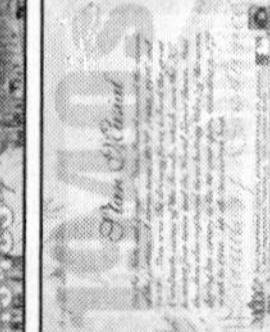

Randomly inserted into packs at one in 12, this 50-card insert spans 80 years of baseball, and pays homage to the best players from each decade. Card backs carry a "DE" prefix. The Willie Mays card was not supposed to exist but several copies have been found in packs and is tagged an SP without pricing in our checklist.

	Nm-Mt	Ex-Mt
COMPLETE SET (50)	350.00	105.00
DE1 Lou Gehrig Babe Ruth	20.00	6.00
DE2 Lloyd Waner	3.00	.90
DE3 Jimmie Foxx	5.00	1.50
DE4 Hank Greenberg	5.00	1.50
DE5 Ted Williams UER	15.00	4.50
DE6 Johnny Mize	3.00	.90
DE7 Enos Slaughter	3.00	.90
DE8 Jackie Robinson	6.00	1.80
DE9 Stan Musial	8.00	2.40
DE10 Duke Snider	3.00	.90
DE11 Eddie Mathews	5.00	1.50
DE12 Roy Campanella	5.00	1.50
DE13 Yogi Berra	5.00	1.50
DE14 Pee Wee Reese	5.00	1.50
DE15 Phil Rizzuto	5.00	1.50
DE16 Al Kaline	5.00	1.50
DE17 Willie Mays SP		
DE18 Frank Howard	3.00	.90
DE19 Roberto Clemente	15.00	4.50
DE20 Bob Gibson	3.00	.90
DE21 Roger Maris	8.00	2.40
DE22 Don Drysdale	5.00	1.50
DE23 Maury Wills	3.00	.90
DE24 Tom Seaver	3.00	.90
DE25 Reggie Jackson	3.00	.90
DE26 Johnny Bench	5.00	1.50
DE27 Carlton Fisk	3.00	.90
DE28 Rod Carew	3.00	.90
DE29 Steve Carlton	3.00	.90
DE30 Mike Schmidt	12.00	3.60
DE31 Nolan Ryan	15.00	4.50
DE32 Rickey Henderson	5.00	1.50
DE33 Roger Clemens	10.00	3.00
DE34 Don Mattingly	15.00	4.50
DE35 George Brett	12.00	3.60
DE36 Greg Maddux	8.00	2.40
DE37 Cal Ripken	15.00	4.50
DE38 Chipper Jones	5.00	1.50
DE39 Barry Bonds	12.00	3.60
DE40 Ivan Rodriguez	5.00	1.50
DE41 Mark McGwire Sammy Sosa	15.00	4.50
DE42 Ken Griffey Jr.	8.00	2.40
DE43 Tony Gwynn	6.00	1.80
DE44 Vladimir Guerrero	5.00	1.50
DE45 Shawn Green	3.00	.90
DE46 Alex Rodriguez Derek Jeter Nomar Garciaparra	12.00	3.60
DE47 Pat Burrell	3.00	.90
DE48 Rick Ankiel	3.00	.90
DE49 Eric Chavez	3.00	.90
DE50 Troy Glaus	3.00	.90

2001 Fleer Premium Decades of Excellence Autograph

Randomly inserted into hobby packs, this 20-card insert set is a partial parallel of the 2001 Fleer Premium Decades of Excellence insert set. The set features authentic autographs from the player depicted on each card. Please note that each card is serial numbered to the year in which the player made his major league debut.

	Nm-Mt	Ex-Mt
1 Rick Ankiel/99	40.00	12.00
2 Johnny Bench/67	100.00	30.00
3 Barry Bonds/86	250.00	75.00
4 George Brett/73	150.00	45.00
5 Rod Carew/67	60.00	18.00
6 Steve Carlton/65	60.00	18.00
7 Eric Chavez/98	40.00	12.00
8 Carlton Fisk/69	60.00	18.00
9 Bob Gibson/59	60.00	18.00
10 Tony Gwynn/82	100.00	30.00
11 Reggie Jackson/67	100.00	30.00
12 Chipper Jones/93	100.00	30.00
13 Al Kaline/53	120.00	36.00
14 Don Mattingly/82	150.00	45.00
15 Cal Ripken/81	200.00	60.00
16 Nolan Ryan/66	150.00	45.00
17 Mike Schmidt/72	150.00	45.00
18 Tom Seaver/67	60.00	18.00
19 Enos Slaughter/38	60.00	18.00
20 Maury Wills/59	40.00	12.00

2001 Fleer Premium Decades of Excellence Memorabilia

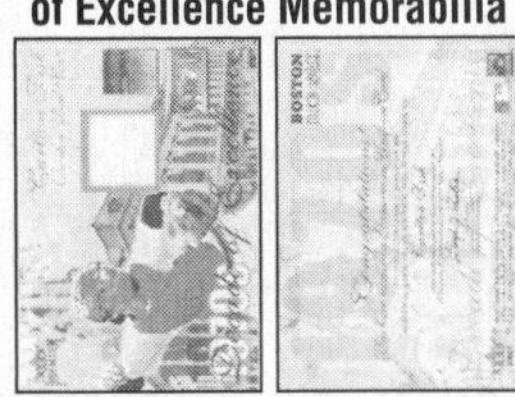

Randomly inserted into hobby packs at one in 217, this 21-card insert is a partial parallel of the 2001 Fleer Premium Decades of Excellence insert. Each of these cards features either a swatch of game-used jersey or a sliver of game-used bat. Please note that the Carlton Fisk and Roger Maris cards feature swatches of game-used uniform. The cards have been listed below in alphabetical order for convenience. Though the cards lack actual serial-numbering, representatives at Fleer publicly announced specific print runs on several short-printed cards within this set. That information is detailed within our checklist.

	Nm-Mt	Ex-Mt
1 Rick Ankiel Jsy	15.00	4.50
2 Barry Bonds Jsy		
3 Pat Burrell Jsy	15.00	4.50
4 Roy Campanella Bat SP/50	80.00	24.00
5 Eric Chavez Bat	15.00	4.50
6 Roberto Clemente Bat SP/50	150.00	45.00
7 Carlton Fisk Uniform	25.00	7.50
8 Jimmie Foxx Bat SP/50	100.00	30.00
9 Shawn Green Bat	15.00	4.50
10 Tony Gwynn Jsy	30.00	9.00
11 Reggie Jackson Jsy	25.00	7.50
12 Greg Maddux Jsy	40.00	12.00
13 Roger Maris Uniform		
14 Pee Wee Reese Jsy	25.00	7.50
15 Cal Ripken Jsy SP/50		
16 Ivan Rodriguez Bat	25.00	7.50
17 Nolan Ryan Jsy		
18 Mike Schmidt Jsy		
19 Tom Seaver Jsy		
20 Duke Snider Bat	25.00	7.50
21 Ted Williams Jsy SP/50	150.00	45.00

2001 Fleer Premium Diamond Dominators

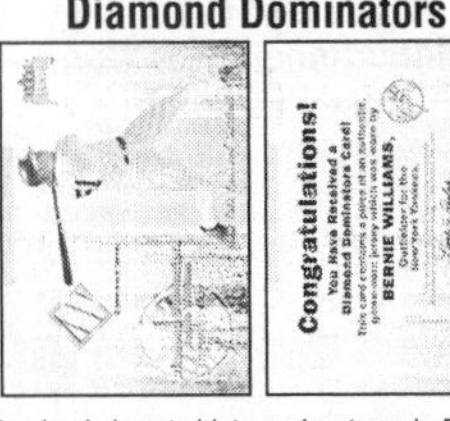

Randomly inserted into packs at one in 51, this 14-card insert features swatches of game-used jerseys of the players depicted below. Card backs carry a "DD" prefix.

	Nm-Mt	Ex-Mt
DD1 Troy Glaus	15.00	4.50
DD2 Darin Erstad	10.00	3.00
DD3 J.D. Drew	10.00	3.00
DD4 Barry Bonds	40.00	12.00
DD5 Roger Clemens	30.00	9.00
DD6 Vladimir Guerrero	15.00	4.50
DD7 Tony Gwynn	20.00	6.00
DD8 Greg Maddux	25.00	7.50
DD9 Cal Ripken	50.00	15.00
DD10 Ivan Rodriguez	15.00	4.50
DD11 Frank Thomas	15.00	4.50
DD12 Bernie Williams	15.00	4.50
DD13 Jeromy Burnitz	10.00	3.00
DD14 Juan Gonzalez	15.00	4.50

2001 Fleer Premium Diamond Patches

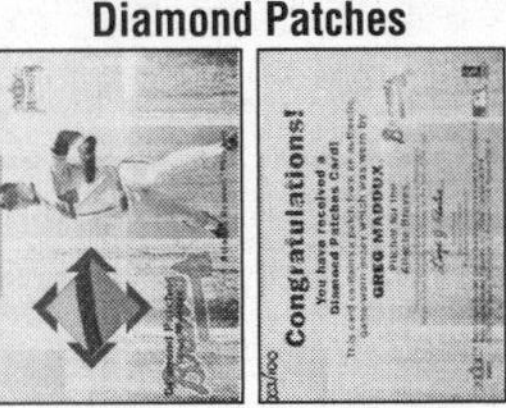

Randomly inserted into packs, this 14-card insert features swatches of jersey patches of the players depicted below. Card backs carry a "DD" prefix. Please note that there were only 100 of each card produced.

	Nm-Mt	Ex-Mt
DD1 Troy Glaus	80.00	24.00
DD2 Darin Erstad	50.00	15.00
DD3 J.D. Drew	50.00	15.00
DD4 Barry Bonds	120.00	36.00
DD5 Roger Clemens	100.00	30.00
DD6 Vladimir Guerrero	80.00	24.00
DD7 Tony Gwynn	80.00	24.00
DD8 Greg Maddux	80.00	24.00
DD9 Cal Ripken	120.00	36.00
DD10 Ivan Rodriguez	80.00	24.00
DD11 Frank Thomas	80.00	24.00
DD12 Bernie Williams	80.00	24.00
DD13 Jeromy Burnitz	50.00	15.00
DD14 Juan Gonzalez	80.00	24.00

2001 Fleer Premium Grip It and Rip It

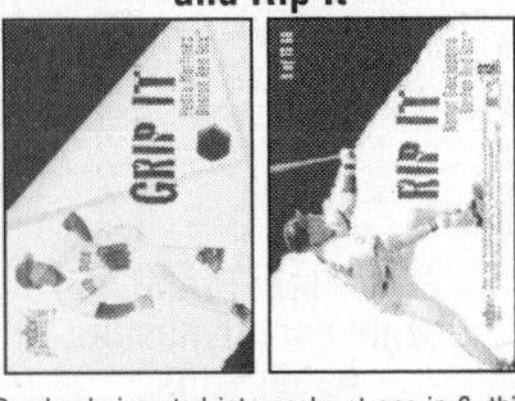

Randomly inserted into packs at one in 6, this 15-card insert pairs up teammates that get the job done with their ability to catch and hit. Card backs carry a "GRP" prefix.

	Nm-Mt	Ex-Mt
COMPLETE SET (15)	30.00	9.00
GRP1 Roger Clemens Derek Jeter	3.00	.90
GRP2 Scott Rolen Pat Burrell	1.00	.30
GRP3 Greg Maddux Andruw Jones	2.00	.60
GRP4 Shannon Stewart Carlos Delgado	1.00	.30
GRP5 Shawn Estes Barry Bonds	3.00	.90
GRP6 Cal Eldred Frank Thomas	1.25	.35
GRP7 Mark McGwire Jim Edmonds	3.00	.90
GRP8 Jose Vidro Vladimir Guerrero	1.25	.35
GRP9 Pedro Martinez Nomar Garciaparra	2.00	.60
GRP10 Tom Glavine Chipper Jones	1.25	.35
GRP11 Ken Griffey Jr. Sean Casey	2.00	.60
GRP12 Jeff Bagwell Moises Alou	1.00	.30
GRP13 Troy Glaus Darin Erstad	1.00	.30
GRP14 Mike Piazza Robin Ventura	2.00	.60
GRP15 Eric Chavez Jason Giambi	1.25	.35

2001 Fleer Premium Grip It and Rip It Plus

Randomly inserted into hobby packs, this 15-card set is a complete parallel of the 2001 Fleer Premium Grip It and Rip It insert. Each of these cards feature either a swatch of game-used base and bat, or a swatch of game-used ball and bat. Please note that each Base/Bat card is serial numbered to 200, while each Ball/Bat card is serial numbered to 100.

	Nm-Mt	Ex-Mt
GRP1 Roger Clemens Ball Derek Jeter Bat	120.00	36.00
GRP2 Scott Rolen Base Pat Burrell Bat/200	25.00	7.50
GRP3 Greg Maddux Ball Andruw Jones Bat/100	80.00	24.00
GRP4 Shan. Stewart Base Carlos Delgado Bat	15.00	4.50
GRP5 Shawn Estes Barry Bonds	100.00	30.00
GRP6 Cal Eldred Frank Thomas	25.00	7.50
GRP7 Mark McGwire Ball Jim Edmonds Bat/100	150.00	45.00
GRP8 Jose Vidro Base Vladimir Guerrero Bat/200	25.00	7.50
GRP9 Pedro Martinez Nomar Garciaparra	80.00	24.00
GRP10 Tom Glavine Chipper Jones	25.00	7.50
GRP11 K. Griffey Jr. Base Sean Casey Bat/200	40.00	12.00
GRP12 Jeff Bagwell Base Moises Alou Bat/200	25.00	7.50
GRP13 Troy Glaus Base Darin Erstad Bat/200	25.00	7.50
GRP14 Mike Piazza Ball Robin Ventura Bat	80.00	24.00
GRP15 Eric Chavez Base Jason Giambi Bat/200	25.00	7.50

2001 Fleer Premium Heroes Game Jersey

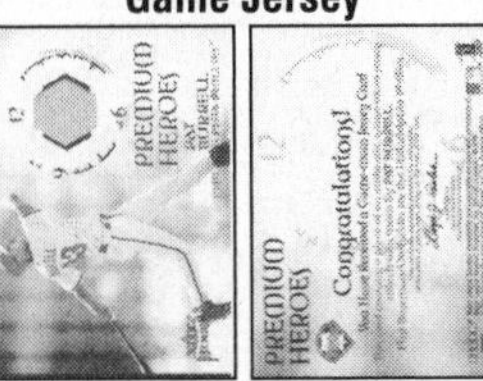

Randomly inserted into hobby packs at one in 101, this 10-card insert is a partial parallel of the 2001 Fleer Premium A Time For Heroes insert. Each of these cards features a swatch of game-used jersey. The cards are listed below in alphabetical order for convenience.

	Nm-Mt	Ex-Mt
1 Pat Burrell	10.00	3.00
2 J.D. Drew	10.00	3.00
3 Jason Giambi	15.00	4.50
4 Troy Glaus	15.00	4.50
5 Shawn Green	10.00	3.00
6 Todd Helton	15.00	4.50
7 Derek Jeter	50.00	15.00
8 Andruw Jones	10.00	3.00
9 Chipper Jones	15.00	4.50
10 Ivan Rodriguez	15.00	4.50

2001 Fleer Premium Home Field Advantage

Randomly inserted into packs at one in 72 Hobby, and 1:144 Retail this 15-card insert features players with their home field in the background. Card backs carry a "HFA" prefix.

	Nm-Mt	Ex-Mt
COMPLETE SET (15)	200.00	60.00
HFA1 Mike Piazza	12.00	3.60
HFA2 Derek Jeter	20.00	6.00
HFA3 Ken Griffey Jr.	12.00	3.60
HFA4 Carlos Delgado	6.00	1.80
HFA5 Chipper Jones	8.00	2.40
HFA6 Alex Rodriguez	12.00	3.60
HFA7 Sammy Sosa	12.00	3.60
HFA8 Scott Rolen	6.00	1.80
HFA9 Nomar Garciaparra	12.00	3.60
HFA10 Todd Helton	6.00	1.80
HFA11 Vladimir Guerrero	8.00	2.40
HFA12 Jeff Bagwell	6.00	1.80
HFA13 Barry Bonds	20.00	6.00
HFA14 Cal Ripken	25.00	7.50
HFA15 Mark McGwire	20.00	6.00

2001 Fleer Premium Home Field Advantage Game Wall

Randomly inserted into packs, this 15-card insert is a complete parallel of the 2001 Fleer Premium Home Field Advantage insert. Each of these cards feature a swatch of actual game-used wall. Card backs carry a "HFA" prefix.

	Nm-Mt	Ex-Mt
HFA1 Mike Piazza	40.00	12.00
HFA2 Derek Jeter	60.00	18.00
HFA3 Ken Griffey Jr.	40.00	12.00
HFA4 Carlos Delgado	15.00	4.50
HFA5 Chipper Jones	25.00	7.50
HFA6 Alex Rodriguez	40.00	12.00
HFA7 Sammy Sosa	40.00	12.00
HFA8 Scott Rolen	25.00	7.50
HFA9 Nomar Garciaparra	40.00	12.00
HFA10 Todd Helton	25.00	7.50
HFA11 Vladimir Guerrero	25.00	7.50
HFA12 Jeff Bagwell	25.00	7.50
HFA13 Barry Bonds	60.00	18.00
HFA14 Cal Ripken	80.00	24.00
HFA15 Mark McGwire	80.00	24.00

2001 Fleer Premium Performers Game Base

Randomly inserted into hobby packs, this 15-card insert set is a complete parallel of the 2001 Fleer Premium Solid Performers insert. Each of these cards feature a swatch of game-used base. Card backs carry a "SP" prefix. Also note that there were only 150 of each card produced.

	Nm-Mt	Ex-Mt
SP1 Mark McGwire	80.00	24.00
SP2 Alex Rodriguez	40.00	12.00
SP3 Nomar Garciaparra	30.00	9.00
SP4 Derek Jeter	50.00	15.00
SP5 Vladimir Guerrero	20.00	6.00
SP6 Todd Helton	20.00	6.00
SP7 Chipper Jones	20.00	6.00
SP8 Mike Piazza	30.00	9.00
SP9 Ivan Rodriguez	20.00	6.00
SP10 Tony Gwynn	30.00	9.00
SP11 Cal Ripken	60.00	18.00
SP12 Barry Bonds	50.00	15.00
SP13 Jeff Bagwell	20.00	6.00
SP14 Ken Griffey Jr.	30.00	9.00
SP15 Sammy Sosa	30.00	9.00

2001 Fleer Premium Solid Performers

Randomly inserted into packs at one in 20, this 15-card insert features players that ballclubs build their franchise around. Card backs carry a "SP" prefix.

	Nm-Mt	Ex-Mt
COMPLETE SET (15)	80.00	24.00
SP1 Mark McGwire	8.00	2.40
SP2 Alex Rodriguez	5.00	1.50
SP3 Nomar Garciaparra	5.00	1.50
SP4 Derek Jeter	8.00	2.40
SP5 Vladimir Guerrero	3.00	.90
SP6 Todd Helton	3.00	.90
SP7 Chipper Jones	3.00	.90
SP8 Mike Piazza	5.00	1.50
SP9 Ivan Rodriguez	3.00	.90
SP10 Tony Gwynn	4.00	1.20
SP11 Cal Ripken	10.00	3.00
SP12 Barry Bonds	8.00	2.40
SP13 Jeff Bagwell	3.00	.90
SP14 Ken Griffey Jr.	5.00	1.50
SP15 Sammy Sosa	5.00	1.50

2002 Fleer Premium

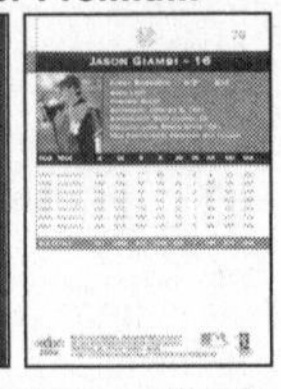

This 240 card set was released in early spring, 2002. This set was issued in 10 card packs which were issued 24 packs to a box. Cards numbered from 201 through 240 featured leading prospects entering the 2002 season and were seeded at stated odds of one in two packs. In late May, Fleer announced their "Player to be Named" program, whereby collectors could send in 10 copies of any of the short-printed prospect cards (201-240) and in turn receive ten new prospect cards (241-250) each serial numbered to 2002. The "Player to be Named" cards were actually released in October, 2002.

	Nm-Mt	Ex-Mt
COMP.MASTER SET (250)	120.00	36.00
COMPLETE SET (240)	80.00	24.00
COMP.SET w/o SP'S (200)	30.00	9.00
COMP.UPDATE SET (10)	40.00	12.00
COMMON CARD (1-200)	.40	.12
COMMON CARD (201-240)	2.00	.60
COMMON CARD (241-250)	4.00	1.20
1 Garret Anderson	.40	.12
2 Derek Jeter	2.50	.75
3 Ken Griffey Jr.	1.50	.45
4 Luis Castillo	.40	.12
5 Richie Sexson	.40	.12
6 Mike Mussina	1.00	.30
7 Rickey Henderson	1.00	.30
8 Bud Smith	.40	.12
9 David Eckstein	.40	.12
10 Nomar Garciaparra	1.50	.45
11 Barry Larkin	1.00	.30
12 Cliff Floyd	.40	.12
13 Ben Sheets	.40	.12
14 Jorge Posada	.60	.18
15 Phil Nevin	.40	.12
16 Fernando Vina	.40	.12
17 Darin Erstad	.40	.12
18 Shea Hillenbrand	.40	.12
19 Todd Walker	.40	.12
20 Charles Johnson	.40	.12
21 Cristian Guzman	.40	.12
22 Mariano Rivera	.60	.18
23 Bubba Trammell	.40	.12
24 Brent Abernathy	.40	.12
25 Troy Glaus	.60	.18
26 Pedro Martinez	1.00	.30
27 Dmitri Young	.40	.12
28 Derrek Lee	.40	.12
29 Torii Hunter	.40	.12
30 Alfonso Soriano	.60	.18
31 Rich Aurilia	.40	.12
32 Ben Grieve	.40	.12
33 Tim Salmon	.60	.18
34 Trot Nixon	.60	.18
35 Roberto Alomar	1.00	.30
36 Mike Lowell	.40	.12
37 Jacque Jones	.40	.12
38 Bernie Williams	.60	.18
39 Barry Bonds	2.50	.75
40 Toby Hall	.40	.12
41 Mo Vaughn	.40	.12
42 Hideo Nomo	1.00	.30
43 Travis Fryman	.40	.12
44 Preston Wilson	.40	.12
45 Corey Koskie	.40	.12
46 Eric Chavez	.40	.12
47 Andres Galarraga	.40	.12
48 Greg Vaughn	.40	.12
49 Shawn Wooten	.40	.12
50 Manny Ramirez	.40	.12
51 Juan Gonzalez	1.00	.30
52 Moises Alou	.40	.12
53 Joe Mays	.40	.12
54 Johnny Damon	.40	.12
55 Jeff Kent	.40	.12
56 Frank Catalanotto	.40	.12
57 Steve Finley	.40	.12
58 Jason Varitek	.40	.12
59 Kenny Lofton	.40	.12
60 Jeff Bagwell	.60	.18
61 Doug Mientkiewicz	.40	.12
62 Jermaine Dye	.40	.12
63 John Vander Wal	.40	.12
64 Gabe Kapler	.40	.12
65 Luis Gonzalez	.40	.12
66 Jon Lieber	.40	.12
67 C.C. Sabathia	.40	.12
68 Lance Berkman	.40	.12
69 Eric Milton	.40	.12
70 Jason Giambi Yankees	1.00	.30
71 Ichiro Suzuki	1.50	.45
72 Rafael Palmeiro	.60	.18
73 Mark Grace	.60	.18
74 Fred McGriff	.60	.18
75 Jim Thome	1.00	.30
76 Craig Biggio	.60	.18
77 A.J. Pierzynski	.40	.12
78 Ramon Hernandez	.40	.12
79 Paul Abbott	.40	.12
80 Alex Rodriguez	1.50	.45
81 Randy Johnson	1.00	.30
82 Corey Patterson	.40	.12
83 Omar Vizquel	.40	.12
84 Richard Hidalgo	.40	.12

85 Luis Rivas .40 .12
86 Tim Hudson .40 .12
87 Bret Boone .40 .12
88 Ivan Rodriguez 1.00 .30
89 Junior Spivey .40 .12
90 Sammy Sosa 1.50 .45
91 Jeff Cirillo .40 .12
92 Roy Oswalt .40 .12
93 Orlando Cabrera .40 .12
94 Terrence Long .40 .12
95 Mike Cameron .40 .12
96 Homer Bush .40 .12
97 Reggie Sanders .40 .12
98 Rondell White .40 .12
99 Mike Hampton .40 .12
100 Carlos Beltran .40 .12
101 Vladimir Guerrero 1.00 .30
102 Miguel Tejada .40 .12
103 Freddy Garcia .40 .12
104 Jose Cruz Jr. .40 .12
105 Curt Schilling .60 .18
106 Kerry Wood 1.00 .30
107 Todd Helton .60 .18
108 Neifi Perez .40 .12
109 Javier Vazquez .40 .12
110 Barry Zito .60 .18
111 Edgar Martinez .60 .18
112 Carlos Delgado .40 .12
113 Matt Williams .40 .12
114 Eric Young .40 .12
115 Alex Ochoa .40 .12
116 Mark Quinn .40 .12
117 Jose Vidro .40 .12
118 Bobby Abreu .40 .12
119 David Bell .40 .12
120 Brad Fullmer .40 .12
121 Rafael Furcal .40 .12
122 Ray Durham .40 .12
123 Jose Ortiz .40 .12
124 Joe Randa .40 .12
125 Edgardo Alfonzo .40 .12
126 Marlon Anderson .40 .12
127 Jamie Moyer .40 .12
128 Alex Gonzalez .40 .12
129 Marcus Giles .40 .12
130 Keith Foulke .40 .12
131 Juan Pierre .40 .12
132 Mike Sweeney .40 .12
133 Matt Lawton .40 .12
134 Pat Burrell .40 .12
135 John Olerud .40 .12
136 Raul Mondesi .40 .12
137 Tom Glavine .60 .18
138 Paul Konerko .40 .12
139 Larry Walker .60 .18
140 Adrian Beltre .40 .12
141 Al Leiter .40 .12
142 Mike Lieberthal .40 .12
143 Kazuhiro Sasaki .40 .12
144 Shannon Stewart .40 .12
145 Andruw Jones .40 .12
146 Carlos Lee .40 .12
147 Roger Cedeno .40 .12
148 Kevin Brown .40 .12
149 Jay Payton .40 .12
150 Scott Rolen .60 .18
151 J.D. Drew .40 .12
152 Chipper Jones 1.00 .30
153 Magglio Ordonez .40 .12
154 Tony Clark .40 .12
155 Shawn Green .40 .12
156 Mike Piazza 1.50 .45
157 Jimmy Rollins .40 .12
158 Jim Edmonds .40 .12
159 Javy Lopez .40 .12
160 Chris Singleton .40 .12
161 Juan Encarnacion .40 .12
162 Eric Karros .40 .12
163 Tsuyoshi Shinjo .40 .12
164 Brian Giles .40 .12
165 Darryl Kile .40 .12
166 Greg Maddux 1.50 .45
167 Frank Thomas 1.00 .30
168 Shane Halter .40 .12
169 Paul LoDuca .40 .12
170 Robin Ventura .40 .12
171 Jason Kendall .40 .12
172 Jason Hart .40 .12
173 Brady Anderson .40 .12
174 Jose Valentin .40 .12
175 Bobby Higginson .40 .12
176 Gary Sheffield .40 .12
177 Roger Clemens 2.00 .60
178 Aramis Ramirez .40 .12
179 Matt Morris .40 .12
180 Jeff Conine .40 .12
181 Aaron Boone .40 .12
182 Jose Macias .40 .12
183 Jeromy Burnitz .40 .12
184 Carl Everett .40 .12
185 Trevor Hoffman .40 .12
186 Placido Polanco .40 .12
187 Jay Gibbons .40 .12
188 Sean Casey .40 .12
189 Josh Beckett .60 .18
190 Jeffrey Hammonds .40 .12
191 Chuck Knoblauch .40 .12
192 Ryan Klesko .40 .12
193 Albert Pujols 2.00 .60
194 Chris Richard .40 .12
195 Adam Dunn .40 .12
196 A.J. Burnett .40 .12
197 Geoff Jenkins .40 .12
198 Tino Martinez .60 .18
199 Ray Lankford .40 .12
200 Edgar Renteria .40 .12
201 Eric Cyr PROS 2.00 .60
202 Travis Phelps PROS 2.00 .60
203 Rick Bauer PROS 2.00 .60
204 Mark Prior PROS 10.00 3.00
205 Wilson Betemit PROS 2.00 .60
206 Dewon Brazelton PROS 2.00 .60
207 Cody Ransom PROS 2.00 .60
208 Donnie Bridges PROS 2.00 .60
209 Justin Duchscherer PROS 2.00 .60
210 Nate Cornejo PROS 2.00 .60
211 Jason Romano PROS 2.00 .60
212 Juan Cruz PROS 2.00 .60
213 Pedro Santana PROS 2.00 .60
214 Ryan Drese PROS 2.00 .60
215 Bert Snow PROS 2.00 .60
216 Nate Frese PROS 2.00 .60
217 Rafael Soriano PROS 2.00 .60
218 Franklin Nunez PROS RC 2.00 .60
219 Tim Spooneybarger PROS 2.00 .60
220 Willie Harris PROS 2.00 .60
221 Billy Sylvester PROS 2.00 .60
222 Carlos Hernandez PROS 2.00 .60
223 Mark Teixeira PROS 4.00 1.20
224 Adrian Hernandez PROS 2.00 .60
225 Andres Torres PROS 2.00 .60
226 Marlon Byrd PROS 2.00 .60
227 Juan Rivera PROS 2.00 .60
228 Adam Johnson PROS 2.00 .60
229 Justin Kaye PROS 2.00 .60
230 Kyle Kessel PROS 2.00 .60
231 Horacio Ramirez PROS 2.00 .60
232 Brandon Larson PROS 2.00 .60
233 Luis Lopez PROS 2.00 .60
234 Rob Mackowiak PROS 2.00 .60
235 Henry Mateo PROS 2.00 .60
236 Corky Miller PROS 2.00 .60
237 Greg Miller PROS 2.00 .60
238 Dustan Mohr PROS 2.00 .60
239 Bill Ortega PROS 2.00 .60
240 Billy Hall PROS 2.00 .60
241 Kazuhisa Ishii UPD RC 8.00 2.40
242 So Taguchi UPD RC 5.00 1.50
243 Takahito Nomura UPD RC 4.00 1.20
244 Satoru Komiyama UPD RC 4.00 1.20
245 Jorge Padilla UPD RC 4.00 1.20
246 Anastacio Martinez UPD RC 4.00 1.20
247 Rodrigo Rosario UPD RC 4.00 1.20
248 Ben Howard UPD RC 4.00 1.20
249 Reed Johnson UPD RC 5.00 1.50
250 Mike Crudale UPD RC 4.00 1.20
P2 Derek Jeter Promo 2.50 .75

2002 Fleer Premium Star Ruby

Randomly inserted into packs, this is a parallel of the 2002 Fleer Premium set. These cards were serial numbered to a stated print run of 125 sets. Cards 241-250 were available exclusively through the "Player to be Named" mail exchange program. The first 50 collectors that sent in cards for the "Player to be Named" program (of which was announced in May, 2002) received the Star Ruby parallel versions along with the basic update cards.

Nm-Mt Ex-Mt
*STARS 1-200: 5X TO 12X BASIC ......
*PROSPECTS 201-240: 1X TO 2.5X BASIC

2002 Fleer Premium Diamond Stars

Issued at stated odds of one in 72, these 20 cards feature some of the leading players in baseball as the 2002 season began.

Nm-Mt Ex-Mt
COMPLETE SET (20) 200.00 60.00
1 Pedro Martinez 8.00 2.40
2 Derek Jeter 20.00 6.00
3 Sammy Sosa 12.00 3.60
4 Ken Griffey Jr. 12.00 3.60
5 Chipper Jones 8.00 2.40
6 Roger Clemens 15.00 4.50
7 Ichiro Suzuki 12.00 3.60
8 Jeff Bagwell 5.00 1.50
9 Luis Gonzalez 5.00 1.50
10 Manny Ramirez 5.00 1.50
11 Alex Rodriguez 12.00 3.60
12 Kazuhiro Sasaki 5.00 1.50
13 Mike Piazza 12.00 3.60
14 Vladimir Guerrero 8.00 2.40
15 Randy Johnson 8.00 2.40
16 Ivan Rodriguez 8.00 2.40
17 Nomar Garciaparra 12.00 3.60
18 Barry Bonds 20.00 6.00
19 Todd Helton 5.00 1.50
20 Greg Maddux 12.00 3.60

2002 Fleer Premium Diamond Stars Autograph

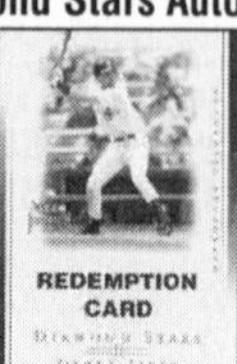

Randomly inserted in packs, and with a stated (though not serial numbered) print run of 100 copies, this card features an autograph of Derek Jeter. As Jeter did not sign these cards in time for insertion into the product, the exchange cards seeded into packs could be redeemed until April 1, 2003.

Nm-Mt Ex-Mt
1 Derek Jeter 150.00 45.00

2002 Fleer Premium Diamond Stars Game Used

Issued at stated odds of one in 105, these 12 cards feature players from the Diamond Stars insert set along with a game-used memorabilia piece featuring that player.

Nm-Mt Ex-Mt
1 Barry Bonds Jsy 25.00 7.50

2 Manny Ramirez Jsy 15.00 4.50
3 Ivan Rodriguez Jsy 15.00 4.50
4 Kazuhiro Sasaki Jsy 15.00 4.50
5 Roger Clemens Jsy 25.00 7.50
6 Alex Rodriguez Jsy 20.00 6.00
7 Derek Jeter Bat 40.00 12.00
8 Chipper Jones Jsy 15.00 4.50
9 Todd Helton Pants 15.00 4.50
10 Luis Gonzalez Jsy 15.00 4.50
11 Mike Piazza Jsy 15.00 4.50
12 N.Garciaparra Bat SP/150 40.00 12.00

2002 Fleer Premium Diamond Stars Game Used Premium

Randomly inserted into packs and with a stated print run of 75 serial numbered cards, these 10 cards feature players from the diamond star insert set along with a game-used patch piece.

Nm-Mt Ex-Mt
1 Barry Bonds 100.00 30.00
2 Roger Clemens 100.00 30.00
3 Todd Helton 50.00 15.00
4 Chipper Jones 50.00 15.00
5 Manny Ramirez 40.00 12.00
6 Alex Rodriguez 80.00 24.00
7 Ivan Rodriguez 50.00 15.00
8 Luis Gonzalez 40.00 12.00
9 Mike Piazza 50.00 15.00
10 Kazuhiro Sasaki 40.00 12.00

2002 Fleer Premium Diamond Stars Dual Game Used

Randomly inserted into packs and with a stated print run of 100 serial numbered sets, these seven cards feature two game-used swatches of featured players from this set.

Nm-Mt Ex-Mt
1 Barry Bonds Jsy-Pants 100.00 30.00
2 Todd Helton Jsy-Bat 50.00 15.00
3 Derek Jeter Jsy-Bat 100.00 30.00
4 Chipper Jones Jsy-Bat 50.00 15.00
5 Mike Piazza Bat-Jsy 50.00 15.00
6 Manny Ramirez Jsy-Jsy 40.00 12.00
7 Alex Rodriguez Jsy-Hat 60.00 18.00

2002 Fleer Premium Diamond Stars Dual Game Used Premium

Randomly inserted into packs and with a stated print run of 25 serial numbered sets, these five cards feature three game-used swatches of featured players from this set. Due to market scarcity, no pricing is provided for these cards.

Nm-Mt Ex-Mt
1 Barry Bonds Patch-Btg Glv
2 Chipper Jones Btg Glv-Patch
3 Manny Ramirez Patch-Patch
4 Mike Piazza Patch-Bat
5 Alex Rodriguez Patch-Btg Glv

2002 Fleer Premium International Pride

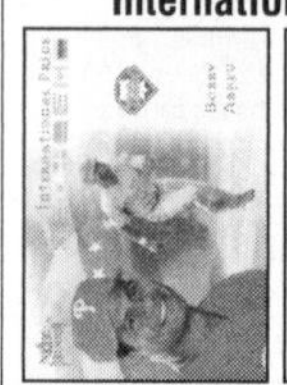

Issued at stated odds of one in six, these 15 cards feature leading players born outside the continental United States.

Nm-Mt Ex-Mt
COMPLETE SET (15) 25.00 7.50
1 Larry Walker 2.00 .60
2 Albert Pujols 4.00 1.20
3 Juan Gonzalez 2.00 .60
4 Ichiro Suzuki 3.00 .90
5 Rafael Palmeiro 2.00 .60
6 Carlos Delgado 2.00 .60
7 Kazuhiro Sasaki 2.00 .60
8 Vladimir Guerrero 2.00 .60
9 Bobby Abreu 2.00 .60
10 Ivan Rodriguez 2.00 .60
11 Tsuyoshi Shinjo 2.00 .60
12 Pedro Martinez 2.00 .60
13 Andruw Jones 2.00 .60
14 Sammy Sosa 3.00 .90
15 Chan Ho Park 2.00 .60

2002 Fleer Premium International Pride Game Used

Issued at stated odds of one in 90, these 10 cards feature players from the International Pride insert set along with a game-used memorabilia piece.

Nm-Mt Ex-Mt
1 Carlos Delgado Jsy 15.00 4.50
2 Juan Gonzalez Jsy 15.00 4.50
3 Andruw Jones Bat 15.00 4.50
4 Pedro Martinez Jsy 15.00 4.50
5 Rafael Palmeiro Jsy 15.00 4.50
6 Chan Ho Park Jsy 15.00 4.50
7 Albert Pujols Jsy 25.00 7.50
8 Ivan Rodriguez Bat 15.00 4.50
9 Kazuhiro Sasaki Jsy 15.00 4.50
10 Tsuyoshi Shinjo Jsy 15.00 4.50

2002 Fleer Premium International Pride Game Used Premium

Randomly inserted into packs and with a stated print run of 75 serial numbered sets, these 10 cards feature players from the International Pride insert set along with a game-used jersey patch of said player.

Nm-Mt Ex-Mt
1 Carlos Delgado 40.00 12.00
2 Juan Gonzalez 50.00 15.00
3 Andruw Jones 40.00 12.00
4 Pedro Martinez 50.00 15.00
5 Chan Ho Park 40.00 12.00
6 Ivan Rodriguez 50.00 15.00
7 Tsuyoshi Shinjo 40.00 12.00
8 Rafael Palmeiro 50.00 15.00
9 Albert Pujols 100.00 30.00
10 Kazuhiro Sasaki 40.00 12.00

2002 Fleer Premium Legendary Dynasties

Inserted at stated odds of one in 18, these 36 cards feature players from some of the greatest past and present teams in major league history.

Nm-Mt Ex-Mt
COMPLETE SET (36) 250.00 75.00
*GOLD: .6X TO 1.5X BASIC DYNASTY
GOLD RANDOM INSERT IN PACKS ....
GOLD PRINT RUN 300 SERIAL #'d SETS
1 Honus Wagner 10.00 3.00
2 Christy Mathewson 10.00 3.00
3 Lou Gehrig 12.00 3.60
4 Babe Ruth 20.00 6.00
5 Jimmie Foxx 10.00 3.00
6 Lefty Grove 8.00 2.40
7 Al Simmons 5.00 1.50
8 Bill Dickey 8.00 2.40
9 Stan Musial 10.00 3.00
10 Enos Slaughter 5.00 1.50
11 Johnny Mize 5.00 1.50
12 Yogi Berra 10.00 3.00
13 Whitey Ford 8.00 2.40
14 Jackie Robinson 8.00 2.40
15 Duke Snider 8.00 2.40
16 Roger Maris 10.00 3.00
17 Jim Palmer 5.00 1.50
18 Don Drysdale 10.00 3.00
19 Brooks Robinson 10.00 3.00
20 Rollie Fingers 5.00 1.50
21 Reggie Jackson 8.00 2.40
22 Joe Morgan 5.00 1.50
23 Johnny Bench 10.00 3.00
24 Thurman Munson 10.00 3.00
25 Jose Canseco 5.00 1.50
26 Tom Glavine 5.00 1.50
27 Chipper Jones 5.00 1.50
28 Greg Maddux 8.00 2.40
29 Roberto Alomar 5.00 1.50
30 David Cone 5.00 1.50
31 Jim Thome 5.00 1.50
32 Manny Ramirez 5.00 1.50
33 Roger Clemens 10.00 3.00
34 Derek Jeter 12.00 3.60
35 Bernie Williams 5.00 1.50
36 Alfonso Soriano 5.00 1.50

2002 Fleer Premium Legendary Dynasties Autographs

Randomly inserted into packs, these nine cards feature autographs of selected players from the legendary dynasty set. These cards are all serial numbered to a year in which the player's team won the World Series - except for Brooks Robinson's card of which honors his 1964 MVP campaign. Since all cards have different print runs, we have notated that information in our checklist. In addition, all cards were issued

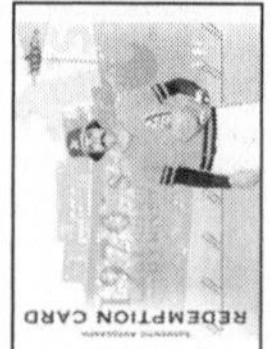

as exchange cards and these cards could be redeemed until April 1, 2003.

Nm-Mt Ex-Mt
1 Johnny Bench/76
2 Yogi Berra/51
3 Rollie Fingers/74
4 Tom Glavine/95
5 Reggie Jackson/73
6 Derek Jeter/96 150.00 45.00
7 Greg Maddux/95
8 Jim Palmer/70
9 Brooks Robinson/64

2002 Fleer Premium Legendary Dynasties Game Used

Issued at stated odds of one in 120, these 22 cards feature a game-worn memorabilia piece from 22 of the players featured in the Legendary Dynasty insert set. A few cards were issued in shorter supply, we have notated those cards with a SP in our checklist and their print run as well.

Nm-Mt Ex-Mt
1 Roberto Alomar Jsy 20.00 6.00
2 Johnny Bench Jsy 20.00 6.00
3 Yogi Berra Bat SP/75
4 Roger Clemens Jsy 30.00 9.00
5 Bill Dickey Bat SP/200 25.00 7.50
6 Rollie Fingers Jsy 15.00 4.50
7 Whitey Ford Jsy SP/25
8 Reggie Jackson Bat SP/250 40.00 12.00
9 Derek Jeter Bat 40.00 12.00
10 Chipper Jones Jsy 20.00 6.00
11 Roger Maris Bat SP/225 60.00 18.00
12 Johnny Mize Bat SP/225 25.00 7.50
13 Joe Morgan Bat 15.00 4.50
14 T.Munson Bat SP/250 50.00 15.00
15 Jim Palmer Jsy 15.00 4.50
16 Manny Ramirez Jsy 15.00 4.50
17 Brooks Robinson Bat SP/200 40.00 12.00
18 J.Robinson Pants SP/150 80.00 24.00
19 Babe Ruth Bat SP/60 200.00 60.00
20 Duke Snider Bat SP/250 40.00 12.00
21 Alfonso Soriano Jsy 20.00 6.00
22 Bernie Williams Jsy 20.00 6.00

2002 Fleer Premium Legendary Dynasties Game Used Premium

Randomly inserted into packs, these 12 cards feature players from the set along with a game-worn jersey patch swatch. These cards are all serial numbered to the highest win total any of their teams accomplished and we have notated that information in our checklist.

Nm-Mt Ex-Mt
1 Rollie Fingers/93 25.00 7.50
2 Roger Clemens/114 80.00 24.00
3 Roger Maris/109 100.00 30.00
4 Roberto Alomar/96 50.00 15.00
5 Reggie Jackson/93 40.00 12.00
6 Manny Ramirez/99 25.00 7.50
7 Johnny Bench/108 50.00 15.00
8 Jim Palmer/109 25.00 7.50
9 Derek Jeter/114 120.00 36.00
10 Alfonso Soriano/99 40.00 12.00
11 Chipper Jones/106 50.00 15.00
12 Bernie Williams/114 40.00 12.00

2002 Fleer Premium On Base!

Randomly inserted in packs, these 30 cards feature some of the leading offensive forces in baseball. These cards are all printed to stated print run of the player's 2002 on-base percentage. We have notated those print runs in our checklist.

Nm-Mt Ex-Mt
COMPLETE SET (30) 250.00 75.00
1 Frank Thomas/316 8.00 2.40
2 Ivan Rodriguez/347 8.00 2.40
3 Nomar Garciaparra/352 12.00 3.60
4 Ken Griffey Jr./365 12.00 3.60
5 Juan Gonzalez/370 8.00 2.40
6 Shawn Green/372 5.00 1.50
7 Vladimir Guerrero/377 8.00 2.40
8 Derek Jeter/377 20.00 6.00

9 Scott Rolen/378 5.00 1.50
10 Ichiro Suzuki/381 15.00 4.50
11 Mike Piazza/384 12.00 3.60
12 Bernie Williams/395 5.00 1.50
13 Moises Alou/396 5.00 1.50
14 Jeff Bagwell/397 5.00 1.50
15 Alex Rodriguez/399 12.00 3.60
16 Albert Pujols/403 15.00 4.50
17 Manny Ramirez/405 5.00 1.50
18 Carlos Delgado/408 5.00 1.50
19 Jim Edmonds/410 5.00 1.50
20 Roberto Alomar/415 8.00 2.40
21 Jim Thome/416 8.00 2.40
22 Gary Sheffield/417 5.00 1.50
23 Chipper Jones/427 8.00 2.40
24 Luis Gonzalez/429 5.00 1.50
25 Lance Berkman/430 5.00 1.50
26 Todd Helton/432 5.00 1.50
27 Sammy Sosa/437 12.00 3.60
28 Larry Walker/449 5.00 1.50
29 Jason Giambi/477 8.00 2.40
30 Barry Bonds/515 20.00 6.00

2002 Fleer Premium On Base! Game Used

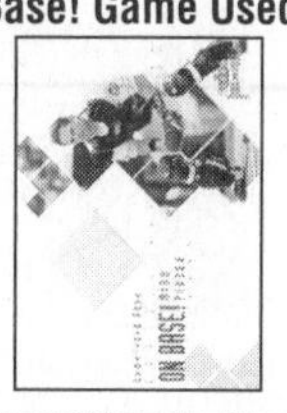

Randomly inserted into packs, this set parallels the On Base! Insert set and was issued in a quantity of 100 serial numbered sets. These cards all feature a game-used piece of the featured player.

Nm-Mt Ex-Mt
1 Luis Gonzalez 10.00 3.00
2 Chipper Jones 15.00 4.50
3 Gary Sheffield 10.00 3.00
4 Nomar Garciaparra 25.00 7.50
5 Manny Ramirez 10.00 3.00
6 Moises Alou 10.00 3.00
7 Sammy Sosa 25.00 7.50
8 Frank Thomas 15.00 4.50
9 Ken Griffey Jr. 25.00 7.50
10 Jim Thome 15.00 4.50
11 Todd Helton 15.00 4.50
12 Larry Walker 15.00 4.50
13 Jeff Bagwell 15.00 4.50
14 Lance Berkman 10.00 3.00
15 Shawn Green 10.00 3.00
16 Vladimir Guerrero 15.00 4.50
17 Roberto Alomar 15.00 4.50
18 Mike Piazza 25.00 7.50
19 Jason Giambi 15.00 4.50
20 Derek Jeter 40.00 12.00
21 Bernie Williams 15.00 4.50
22 Scott Rolen 15.00 4.50
23 Barry Bonds 40.00 12.00
24 Ichiro Suzuki 40.00 12.00
25 Jim Edmonds 10.00 3.00
26 Albert Pujols 30.00 9.00
27 Juan Gonzalez 15.00 4.50
28 Alex Rodriguez 30.00 9.00
29 Ivan Rodriguez 15.00 4.50
30 Carlos Delgado 10.00 3.00

2001 Fleer Red Sox 100th

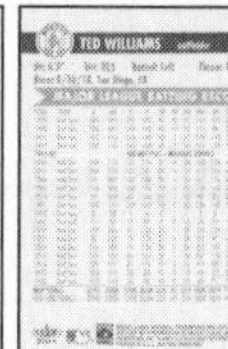

The 2001 Fleer Red Sox product released in late June, 2001 and featured a 100-card base set. The set was broken into three subsets: Red Sox Players (1-77), Beantown's Best (78-92), and Fenway Park cards (93-100). Each pack contained five cards, and carried a suggested retail price of $2.99. A Field the Game exchange card was randomly seeded into packs. Each of these cards was serial numbered of 7,150. Collectors received a special card that included an actual piece of Fenway Park. The deadline to exchange these cards was August 1st, 2002.

Nm-Mt Ex-Mt
COMPLETE SET (100) 25.00 7.50
1 Carl Yastrzemski 3.00 .90
2 Mel Parnell .50 .15
3 Birdie Tebbetts .50 .15
4 Tex Hughson .50 .15
5 Nomar Garciaparra 3.00 .90
6 Fred Lynn .75 .23
7 John Valentin .50 .15
8 Rico Petrocelli .50 .15
9 Ted Williams 5.00 1.50
10 Roger Clemens 4.00 1.20
11 Luis Aparicio .75 .23
12 Cy Young 2.00 .60
13 Carlton Fisk 1.25 .35
14 Pedro Martinez 2.00 .60
15 Joe Dobson .50 .15
16 Babe Ruth 6.00 1.80
17 Doc Cramer .50 .15
18 Pete Runnels .50 .15
19 Tony Conigliaro 1.25 .35
20 Bill Monbouquette .50 .15
21 Boo Ferriss .50 .15
22 Harry Hooper 1.25 .35
23 Tony Armas .50 .15
24 Joe Cronin .75 .23
25 Rick Ferrell .75 .23
26 Wade Boggs 1.25 .35
27 Don Baylor .75 .23
28 Jeff Reardon .75 .23
29 Joe Wood 1.25 .35
30 Mo Vaughn .75 .23
31 Walt Dropo .50 .15
32 Vern Stephens .50 .15
33 Bernie Carbo .50 .15
34 George Scott .50 .15
35 Lefty Grove 2.00 .60
36 Dom DiMaggio 2.00 .60
37 Dennis Eckersley .75 .23
38 Johnny Pesky .75 .23
39 Jim Lonborg .50 .15
40 Jimmy Piersall .75 .23
41 Tris Speaker 2.00 .60
42 Frank Malzone .50 .15
43 Bobby Doerr 1.25 .35
44 Jimmie Foxx 2.00 .60
45 Tony Pena .50 .15
46 Billy Goodman .50 .15
47 Jim Rice .75 .23
48 Reggie Smith .75 .23
49 Bill Buckner .75 .23
50 Earl Wilson .50 .15
51 Rick Burleson .50 .15
52 George Kell 1.25 .35
53 Dick Radatz .50 .15
54 Dwight Evans .75 .23
55 Luis Tiant .75 .23
56 Elijah Green .50 .15
57 Gene Conley .50 .15
58 Jackie Jensen .75 .23
59 Mike Fornieles .50 .15
60 Dutch Leonard .50 .15
61 Jake Stahl .50 .15
62 Don Schwall .50 .15
63 Jimmy Collins .75 .23
64 Herb Pennock 1.25 .35
65 Red Ruffing 1.25 .35
66 Carney Lansford .75 .23
67 Dick Stuart .50 .15
68 Dave Morehead .50 .15
69 Harry Agganis .75 .23
70 Lou Boudreau MGR 1.25 .35
71 Joe Morgan MGR .50 .15
72 Don Zimmer MGR .75 .23
73 Tom Yawkey OWN .75 .23
74 Jean Yawkey OWN .50 .15
75 Boston Red Sox .75 .23
Origin of the Red Sox
76 Boston Red Sox .75 .23
The First Season - 1901
77 Boston Red Sox .75 .23
World Series Triumphs
78 Carl Yastrzemski BB 2.00 .60
79 Carlton Fisk BB .75 .23
80 Dom DiMaggio BB .75 .23
81 Wade Boggs BB .75 .23
82 Nomar Garciaparra BB 2.00 .60
83 Pedro Martinez BB 1.25 .35
84 Ted Williams BB 2.50 .75
85 Jim Rice BB .50 .15
86 Fred Lynn BB .50 .15
87 Mo Vaughn BB .50 .15
88 Bobby Doerr BB UER .75 .23
Card Pictures Lou Boudreau
89 Bernie Carbo BB .50 .15
90 Dennis Eckersley BB .75 .23
91 Jimmy Piersall BB .50 .15
92 Luis Tiant BB .50 .15
93 Fenway Park .50 .15
Jimmy Fund signage
94 Fenway Park .50 .15
Green Monster w/Ads
95 Fenway Park .50 .15
Green Monster w/All-Star logo
96 Fenway Park .50 .15
Ladder shot on Green Monster
97 Fenway Park .50 .15
Manual scoreboard
98 Fenway Park .50 .15
Panoramic of Fenway Park
99 Fenway Park .50 .15
Lansdowne Street
100 Fenway Park .50 .15
1999 All-Star Game
NNO Field the Game/7150 EXCH 40.00 12.00

2001 Fleer Red Sox 100th BoSox Sigs

Randomly inserted into packs at one in 96, this 16-card insert set features authentic autographs from Red Sox greats like Roger Clemens and Nomar Garciaparra. Please note that Boggs, Clemens, Fisk, Garciaparra, Rice, Yastrzemski all packed out as exchange cards with a redemption deadline of 07/31/02.

Nm-Mt Ex-Mt
1 Wade Boggs 100.00 30.00
2 Bill Buckner 25.00 7.50
3 Bernie Carbo 25.00 7.50
4 Roger Clemens 300.00 90.00
SP/100 EXCH
5 Dom DiMaggio 100.00 30.00
6 Bobby Doerr 40.00 12.00
7 Dennis Eckersley 80.00 24.00
8 Dwight Evans 100.00 30.00
9 Carlton Fisk 120.00 36.00
10 N.Garciaparra EXCH 250.00 75.00
11 Jim Lonborg 25.00 7.50
12 Fred Lynn 80.00 24.00
13 Rico Petrocelli 25.00 7.50
14 Jim Rice 80.00 24.00
15 Luis Tiant 25.00 7.50
16 C.Yastrzemski SP/200 200.00 60.00

2001 Fleer Red Sox 100th MLB Autographed Fitted Caps

Inserted one per deluxe box, these signed caps feature some of the Boston Red Sox leading players of the past. An exchange card with a redemption deadline of 07/31/02 was seeded into packs for Nomar Garciaparra's cap.

Nm-Mt Ex-Mt
1 Wade Boggs
2 Bill Buckner 30.00 9.00
3 Bernie Carbo 30.00 9.00
4 Roger Clemens
5 Bobby Doerr 40.00 12.00
6 Dennis Eckersley 60.00 18.00
7 Dwight Evans 30.00 9.00
8 Nomar Garciaparra
9 Jim Lonborg 30.00 9.00
10 Johnny Pesky 30.00 9.00
11 Rico Petrocelli 30.00 9.00
12 Jim Rice 40.00 12.00
13 Luis Tiant 30.00 9.00

2001 Fleer Red Sox 100th Splendid Splinters

Randomly inserted into packs at one in 10, this 15-card insert features some of the best hitters in Red Sox history. Card backs carry a "SS" prefix.

Nm-Mt Ex-Mt
COMPLETE SET (15) 30.00 9.00
SS1 Babe Ruth 8.00 2.40
SS2 Dom DiMaggio 2.50 .75
SS3 Carlton Fisk 1.50 .45
SS4 Carl Yastrzemski 4.00 1.20
SS5 Nomar Garciaparra 5.00 1.50
SS6 Wade Boggs 1.50 .45
SS7 Ted Williams 8.00 2.40
SS8 Jim Rice 1.00 .30
SS9 Mo Vaughn 1.00 .30
SS10 Tris Speaker 2.50 .75
SS11 Dwight Evans 1.00 .30
SS12 Jimmie Foxx 3.00 .90
SS13 Bobby Doerr 1.50 .45
SS14 Fred Lynn 1.00 .30
SS15 Johnny Pesky 1.00 .30

2001 Fleer Red Sox 100th Splendid Splinters Game Bat

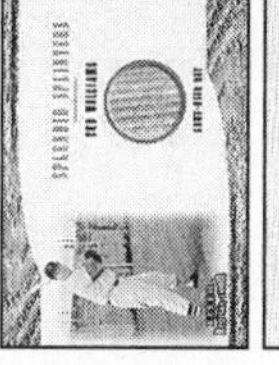

Randomly inserted into packs at one in 96, this eight-card insert set features game-used bat chips from Red Sox greats like Babe Ruth and Nomar Garciaparra. Card backs carry a "SS" prefix. Though they lack actual serial-numbering, the Jimmie Foxx, Babe Ruth and Ted Williams cards were announced by Fleer to be short-prints with 100 copies of each card produced.

Nm-Mt Ex-Mt
1 Wade Boggs 50.00 15.00
2 Dwight Evans 30.00 9.00
3 Jimmie Foxx SP/100 200.00 60.00
4 Nomar Garciaparra 60.00 18.00
5 Jim Rice 30.00 9.00
6 Babe Ruth SP/100 350.00 105.00
7 Ted Williams SP/100 300.00 90.00
8 Carl Yastrzemski 60.00 18.00

2001 Fleer Red Sox 100th Threads

Randomly inserted into packs at one in 96, this nine card insert set features game-used jersey swatches from Red Sox greats like Wade Boggs and Ted Williams. Though they lack actual serial-numbering, the cards of Carlton Fisk, Pedro Martinez and Ted Williams were announced by Fleer to be short-prints with 100 copies of each card produced.

Nm-Mt Ex-Mt
1 Wade Boggs 50.00 15.00
2 Roger Clemens 60.00 18.00
3 Dwight Evans 30.00 9.00
4 Carlton Fisk SP/100 60.00 18.00
5 Pedro Martinez SP/100 60.00 18.00
6 Jim Rice 50.00 15.00
7 Ted Williams SP/100 200.00 60.00
8 Carl Yastrzemski 60.00 18.00
9 Don Zimmer 30.00 9.00

2001 Fleer Red Sox 100th Yawkey's Heroes

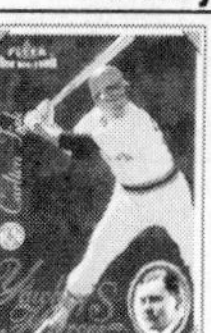

Randomly inserted into packs at one in four, this 20-card insert set features Red Sox greats like Babe Ruth, Ted Williams, and Nomar Garciaparra. Card backs carry a "YH" prefix.

Nm-Mt Ex-Mt
COMPLETE SET (20) 15.00 4.50
YH1 Bobby Doerr 1.25 .35
YH2 Dom DiMaggio 2.00 .60
YH3 Jim Rice .75 .23
YH4 Wade Boggs 1.25 .35
YH5 Carlton Fisk 1.25 .35
YH6 Nomar Garciaparra 3.00 .90
YH7 Dennis Eckersley .75 .23
YH8 Carl Yastrzemski 3.00 .90
YH9 Ted Williams 5.00 1.50
YH10 Tony Conigliaro 1.25 .35
YH11 Tony Armas .75 .23
YH12 Joe Cronin 2.00 .60
YH13 Mo Vaughn .75 .23
YH14 Johnny Pesky .75 .23
YH15 Jim Lonborg .75 .23
YH16 Luis Tiant .75 .23
YH17 Tony Pena .75 .23
YH18 Dwight Evans .75 .23
YH19 Fred Lynn .75 .23
YH20 Jimmy Piersall .75 .23

2003 Fleer Rookies and Greats

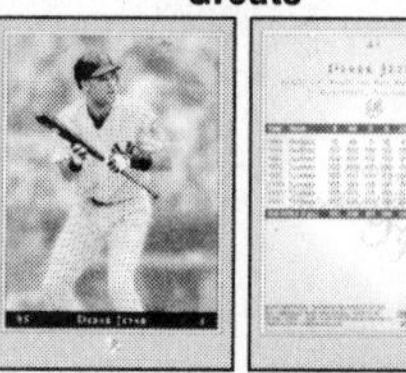

This 75-card standard-size set was released in December, 2003. The set was issued in five-card packs with an $6 SRP which came 20 packs to a box and six boxes to a case. Cards numbered 1-60 feature active stars while cards 61-75 feature a select group of retired greats. In additon, update cards for the following products: Flair, Fleer Authentix, Fleer Genuine, Fleer Hot Prospects, Fleer Showcase and Ultra were also inserted into these packs.

MINT NRMT
COMPLETE SET (75) 25.00 11.00
1 Troy Glaus .60 .25
2 Gary Sheffield .40 .18
3 Sammy Sosa 1.50 .70
4 Mark Prior 2.00 .90
5 Dontrelle Willis 1.00 .45
6 Shawn Green .40 .18
7 Vladimir Guerrero 1.00 .45
8 Jose Reyes .60 .25
9 Miguel Tejada .40 .18
10 Bret Boone .40 .18
11 Rocco Baldelli 1.50 .70
12 Rafael Palmeiro .60 .25
13 Ichiro Suzuki 1.50 .70
14 Carlos Delgado .40 .18
15 Garret Anderson .40 .18
16 Richie Sexson .40 .18
17 Roger Clemens 2.00 .90
18 Barry Zito .60 .25
19 Jim Thome 1.00 .45
20 Alex Rodriguez 1.50 .70
21 Randy Johnson 1.00 .45
22 Chipper Jones 1.00 .45
23 Kerry Wood 1.00 .45
24 Ken Griffey Jr. 1.50 .70
25 Ivan Rodriguez 1.00 .45
26 Jeff Kent .40 .18
27 Todd Helton .60 .25
28 Jeff Bagwell .60 .25
29 Hideo Nomo 1.00 .45
30 Torii Hunter .40 .18
31 Brian Giles .40 .18
32 Albert Pujols 2.00 .90
33 Vernon Wells .40 .18
34 Nomar Garciaparra 1.50 .70
35 Magglio Ordonez .40 .18
36 C.C. Sabathia .40 .18
37 Preston Wilson .40 .18
38 Mike Sweeney .40 .18
39 Jose Vidro .40 .18
40 Jason Giambi 1.00 .45
41 Derek Jeter 2.50 1.10
42 Mike Piazza 1.50 .70
43 Rich Harden .60 .25
44 Jason Kendall .40 .18
45 Barry Bonds 2.50 1.10
46 Barry Larkin 1.00 .45
47 Dmitri Young .40 .18
48 Craig Biggio .60 .25
49 Angel Berroa .40 .18
50 Alfonso Soriano .60 .25
51 Kevin Millwood .40 .18
52 Edgar Martinez .60 .25
53 Jim Edmonds .40 .18
54 Curt Schilling .60 .25
55 Jay Gibbons .40 .18
56 Pedro Martinez 1.00 .45
57 Greg Maddux 1.50 .70
58 Manny Ramirez .40 .18
59 Frank Thomas 1.00 .45
60 Adam Dunn .40 .18
61 Babe Ruth GR 4.00 1.80
62 Bob Gibson GR 1.50 .70
63 Willie Stargell GR 1.50 .70
64 Mike Schmidt GR 3.00 1.35
65 Nolan Ryan GR 4.00 1.80
66 Tom Seaver GR 1.50 .70
67 Brooks Robinson GR 1.50 .70
68 Willie McCovey GR 1.50 .70
69 Harmon Killebrew GR 1.50 .70
70 Al Kaline GR 1.50 .70
71 Reggie Jackson GR 1.50 .70
72 Eddie Mathews GR 1.50 .70
73 Ralph Kiner GR 1.00 .45
74 Cal Ripken GR 5.00 2.20
75 Phil Rizzuto GR 1.50 .70

2003 Fleer Rookies and Greats Blue

MINT NRMT
*BLUE 1-60: 2X TO 5X BASIC
*BLUE 61-75: 1.25X TO 3X BASIC
STATED ODDS 1:10
STATED PRINT RUN 250 SERIAL #'d SETS

2003 Fleer Rookies and Greats Boyhood Idols Game Used

MINT NRMT
OVERALL AU-GU ODDS 1:7
STATED PRINT RUN 615 SERIAL #'d SETS
BD Bucky Dent Jsy 10.00 4.50
BR Brooks Robinson Jsy 15.00 6.75
CF Carlton Fisk Jsy 15.00 6.75
CR Cal Ripken Jsy 30.00 13.50
DM Don Mattingly Jsy 25.00 11.00
FH Frank Howard Bat 10.00 4.50
HK Harmon Killebrew Pants 15.00 6.75
JC Joe Carter Bat 10.00 4.50
JM Joe Morgan Jsy 10.00 4.50
JP Jim Palmer Jsy 10.00 4.50
MS Mike Schmidt Jsy 20.00 9.00
MS2 Moose Skowron Pants 10.00 4.50
NR Nolan Ryan Jsy 25.00 11.00
RY Robin Yount Jsy 15.00 6.75

2003 Fleer Rookies and Greats Boyhood Idols Game Used Autograph

MINT NRMT
OVERALL AU-GU ODDS 1:7
PRINT RUNS B/WN 40-50 COPIES PER
BD Bucky Dent Jsy/50 30.00 13.50
BR Brooks Robinson Jsy/50 60.00 27.00
CF Carlton Fisk Jsy/50 50.00 22.00
FH Frank Howard Bat/50 30.00 13.50
HK Harmon Killebrew Pants/40 60.00 27.00
JC Joe Carter Bat/50 30.00 13.50
JP Jim Palmer Jsy/50 30.00 13.50
MS2 Moose Skowron Pants/50 30.00 13.50

2003 Fleer Rookies and Greats Dynamic Debuts

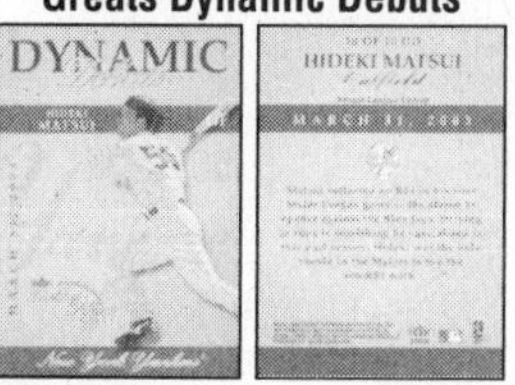

MINT NRMT
STATED ODDS 1:10
1 Rickie Weeks 8.00 3.60
2 Brandon Webb 5.00 2.20
3 Jose Reyes 3.00 1.35
4 Bo Hart 4.00 1.80
5 Dontrelle Willis 3.00 1.35
6 Rich Harden 3.00 1.35
7 Ryan Wagner 3.00 1.35
8 Rocco Baldelli 5.00 2.20
9 Mark Teixeira 3.00 1.35
10 Hideki Matsui 8.00 3.60

2003 Fleer Rookies and Greats Dynamic Debuts Autograph

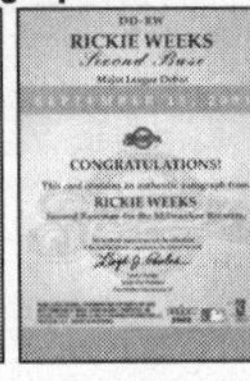

OVERALL AU-GU ODDS 1:7
STATED PRINT RUN 100 SERIAL #'d SETS

	MINT	NRMT
BH Bo Hart	40.00	18.00
DW Dontrelle Willis	30.00	13.50
JR Jose Reyes	30.00	13.50
RW Rickie Weeks	50.00	22.00
RW2 Ryan Wagner	30.00	13.50

2003 Fleer Rookies and Greats Looming Large

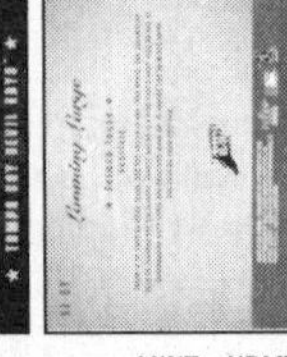

STATED PRINT RUN 500 SERIAL #'d SETS
RARE PRINT RUN 15 SERIAL #'d SETS
NO RARE PRICING DUE TO SCARCITY
*UNCOMMON: .75X TO 2X BASIC
UNCOMMON PRINT RUN 150 SERIAL #'d SETS
RANDOM INSERTS IN PACKS

	MINT	NRMT
BH Bo Hart	5.00	2.20
BW Brandon Webb	6.00	2.70
CB Clint Barmes	4.00	1.80
CW Chien-Ming Wang	5.00	2.20
DY Delmon Young	10.00	4.50
EJ Edwin Jackson	8.00	3.60
HM Hideki Matsui	10.00	4.50
JB Jeremy Bonderman	4.00	1.80
JC Jose Contreras	5.00	2.20
JD Jeff Duncan	4.00	1.80
MH Michael Hessman	4.00	1.80
MK Matt Kata	4.00	1.80
RH Robby Hammock	4.00	1.80
RW Rickie Weeks	10.00	4.50
RW2 Ryan Wagner	4.00	1.80

2003 Fleer Rookies and Greats Naturals

STATED ODDS 1:5
*UNCOMMON: 1.5X TO 4X BASIC
UNCOMMON RANDOM INSERTS IN PACKS
UNCOMMON PRINT RUN 75 SERIAL #'d SETS

	MINT	NRMT
TN1 Cal Ripken	10.00	4.50
TN2 Mike Schmidt	6.00	2.70
TN3 Derek Jeter	6.00	2.70
TN4 Joe Carter	2.00	.90
TN5 Nomar Garciaparra	4.00	1.80
TN6 Frank Howard	2.00	.90
TN7 Al Kaline	3.00	1.35
TN8 Albert Pujols	5.00	2.20
TN9 Nolan Ryan	8.00	3.60
TN10 Duke Snider	3.00	1.35
TN11 Alex Rodriguez	4.00	1.80
TN12 Brooks Robinson	3.00	1.35
TN13 Roger Clemens	5.00	2.20
TN14 Sammy Sosa	4.00	1.80
TN15 Jim Palmer	2.00	.90
TN16 Alfonso Soriano	2.50	1.10
TN17 Don Mattingly	8.00	3.60
TN18 Harmon Killebrew	3.00	1.35
TN19 Bob Feller	3.00	1.35
TN20 Reggie Jackson	3.00	1.35
TN21 Ichiro Suzuki	4.00	1.80
TN22 Barry Bonds	6.00	2.70
TN23 Hideki Matsui	8.00	3.60
TN24 Willie Stargell	3.00	1.35
TN25 Pee Wee Reese	3.00	1.35

2003 Fleer Rookies and Greats Naturals Autograph

OVERALL AU-GU ODDS 1:7
STATED PRINT RUN 50 SERIAL #'d SETS

	MINT	NRMT
AK Al Kaline	50.00	22.00
BF Bob Feller	40.00	18.00
BR Brooks Robinson	50.00	22.00
CR Cal Ripken	150.00	70.00
DS Duke Snider	40.00	18.00
FH Frank Howard	40.00	18.00
HK Harmon Killebrew	50.00	22.00
JC Joe Carter	25.00	11.00
JP Jim Palmer	25.00	11.00
NR Nolan Ryan	120.00	55.00

2003 Fleer Rookies and Greats Naturals Game Used

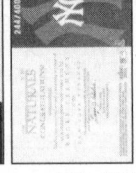

PRINT RUNS B/WN 250-400 COPIES PER
PATCH PRINT RUN 25 SERIAL #'d SETS
NO PATCH PRICING DUE TO SCARCITY
OVERALL AU-GU ODDS 1:7

	MINT	NRMT
AK Al Kaline Bat/250	15.00	6.75
AP Albert Pujols Jsy/250	20.00	9.00
AR Alex Rodriguez Jsy/250	10.00	4.50
AS Alfonso Soriano Jsy/250	10.00	4.50
BR Brooks Robinson Jsy/400	15.00	6.75
CR Cal Ripken Jsy/250	30.00	13.50
DJ Derek Jeter Jsy/250	25.00	11.00
DM Don Mattingly Jsy/250	25.00	11.00
DS Duke Snider Jsy/250	15.00	6.75
FH Frank Howard Bat/400	10.00	4.50
HK Harmon Killebrew Pants/400	15.00	6.75
JC Joe Carter Bat/250	10.00	4.50
JP Jim Palmer Jsy/250	10.00	4.50
MS Mike Schmidt Jsy/250	20.00	9.00
NG Nomar Garciaparra Jsy/250.	15.00	6.75
NR Nolan Ryan Jsy/400	25.00	11.00
RC Roger Clemens Jsy/400	15.00	6.75
RJ Reggie Jackson Jsy/400	15.00	6.75
SS Sammy Sosa Jsy/250	15.00	6.75

2003 Fleer Rookies and Greats Naturals Game Used Autograph

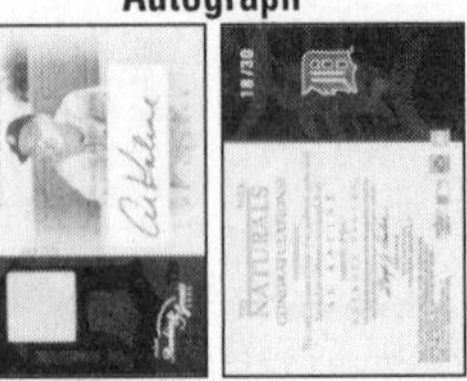

OVERALL AU-GU ODDS 1:7
STATED PRINT RUN 30 SERIAL #'d SETS
AU PATCH PRINT RUN 5 SERIAL #'d SETS
NO AU PATCH PRICING DUE TO SCARCITY

	MINT	NRMT
AK Al Kaline Bat	80.00	36.00
BR Brooks Robinson Jsy	80.00	36.00
CR Cal Ripken Jsy	200.00	90.00
DS Duke Snider Jsy	60.00	27.00
FH Frank Howard Bat	40.00	18.00
HK Harmon Killebrew Pants	80.00	36.00
JC Joe Carter Bat	40.00	18.00
JP Jim Palmer Jsy	40.00	18.00
NR Nolan Ryan Jsy	150.00	70.00

2003 Fleer Rookies and Greats Through the Years Game Used

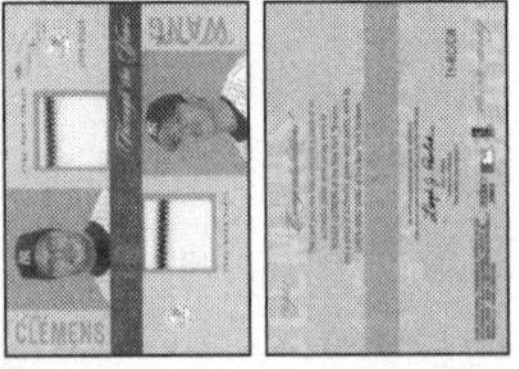

STATED PRINT RUN 360 SERIAL #'d SETS
PATCH PRINT RUN 25 SERIAL #'d SETS
NO PATCH PRICING DUE TO SCARCITY
OVERALL AU-GU ODDS 1:7
ALL ARE DUAL JSY UNLESS NOTED

	MINT	NRMT
ARMT Alex Rodriguez Jsy Mark Teixeira Jsy	15.00	6.75
BHLB Bo Hart Pants Lou Brock Jsy	20.00	9.00
BLJM Barry Larkin Jsy Joe Morgan Jsy	15.00	6.75
DJPR Derek Jeter Jsy Phil Rizzuto Pants	40.00	18.00
EMCJ Eddie Mathews Pants Chipper Jones Jsy	20.00	9.00
HKTH Harmon Killebrew Pants.. Torii Hunter Jsy	20.00	9.00
JCMM Jose Contreras Jsy Mike Mussina Jsy	15.00	6.75
JGRJ Jason Giambi Jsy Reggie Jackson Jsy	15.00	6.75
JTMS Jim Thome Jsy Mike Schmidt Jsy	30.00	13.50
MHCJ Michael Hessman Pants . Chipper Jones Jsy	15.00	6.75
MPJR Mike Piazza Jsy Jose Reyes Jsy	15.00	6.75
NGBD Nomar Garciaparra Jsy Bobby Doerr Bat	25.00	11.00
NRHB Nolan Ryan Jsy Hank Blalock Jsy	40.00	18.00
PRJR Phil Rizzuto Pants Jose Reyes Jsy	20.00	9.00
RCCW Roger Clemens Jsy Chien-Ming Wang Pants	30.00	13.50
RJBW Randy Johnson Jsy Brandon Webb Jsy	15.00	6.75
RYSP Robin Yount Jsy Scott Podsednik Bat	25.00	11.00
SCKM Steve Carlton Jsy Kevin Millwood Jsy	10.00	4.50
SSMP Sammy Sosa Jsy Mark Prior Jsy	30.00	13.50
WMBB Willie McCovey Pants Barry Bonds Base	25.00	11.00

2000 Fleer Showcase

The 2000 Fleer Showcase product was released in October, 2000. The product featured a 140-card base set that was broken into tiers as follows: 100 Base Veterans (1-100). 40 Prospects (101-140). Please note that cards 101-115 were serial numbered to 1000, and cards 116-140 were serial numbered to 2000. Each pack contained five cards and carried a suggested retail price of $3.99.

	Nm-Mt	Ex-Mt
COMPLETE SET (140)	600.00	180.00
COMP.SET w/o SP's (100)	30.00	9.00
COMMON CARD (1-100)	.50	.15
COMMON (101-115)	10.00	3.00
COMMON (116-140)	8.00	2.40
1 Alex Rodriguez	2.00	.60
2 Derek Jeter	3.00	.90
3 Jeromy Burnitz	.50	.15
4 John Olerud	.50	.15
5 Paul Konerko	.50	.15
6 Johnny Damon	.50	.15
7 Curt Schilling	.75	.23
8 Barry Larkin	1.25	.35
9 Adrian Beltre	.50	.15
10 Scott Rolen	.75	.23
11 Carlos Delgado	.50	.15
12 Pedro Martinez	1.25	.35
13 Todd Helton	.75	.23
14 Jacque Jones	.50	.15
15 Jeff Kent	.50	.15
16 Darin Erstad	.50	.15
17 Juan Encarnacion	.50	.15
18 Roger Clemens	2.50	.75
19 Tony Gwynn	1.50	.45
20 Nomar Garciaparra	2.00	.60
21 Roberto Alomar	1.25	.35
22 Matt Lawton	.50	.15
23 Rich Aurilia	.50	.15
24 Charles Johnson	.50	.15
25 Jim Thome	1.25	.35
26 Eric Milton	.50	.15
27 Barry Bonds	3.00	.90
28 Albert Belle	.50	.15
29 Travis Fryman	.50	.15
30 Ken Griffey Jr.	2.00	.60
31 Phil Nevin	.50	.15
32 Chipper Jones	1.25	.35
33 Craig Biggio	.75	.23
34 Mike Hampton	.50	.15
35 Fred McGriff	.75	.23
36 Cal Ripken	4.00	1.20
37 Manny Ramirez	.50	.15
38 Jose Vidro	.50	.15
39 Trevor Hoffman	.50	.15
40 Tom Glavine	.75	.23
41 Frank Thomas	1.25	.35
42 Chris Widger	.50	.15
43 J.D. Drew	.50	.15
44 Andres Galarraga	.50	.15
45 Pokey Reese	.50	.15
46 Mike Piazza	2.00	.60
47 Kevin Young	.50	.15
48 Sean Casey	.50	.15
49 Carlos Beltran	.50	.15
50 Jason Kendall	.50	.15
51 Vladimir Guerrero	1.25	.35
52 Jermaine Dye	.50	.15
53 Brian Giles	.50	.15
54 Andruw Jones	.50	.15
55 Richard Hidalgo	.50	.15
56 Robin Ventura	.50	.15
57 Ivan Rodriguez	1.25	.35
58 Greg Maddux	2.00	.60
59 Billy Wagner	.50	.15
60 Ruben Mateo	.50	.15
61 Troy Glaus	.75	.23
62 Dean Palmer	.50	.15
63 Eric Chavez	.50	.15
64 Edgar Martinez	.75	.23
65 Randy Johnson	1.25	.35
66 Preston Wilson	.50	.15
67 Orlando Hernandez	.50	.15
68 Jim Edmonds	.50	.15
69 Carl Everett	.50	.15
70 Larry Walker	.75	.23
71 Ron Belliard	.50	.15
72 Sammy Sosa	2.00	.60
73 Matt Williams	.50	.15
74 Cliff Floyd	.50	.15
75 Bernie Williams	.75	.23
76 Fernando Tatis	.50	.15
77 Steve Finley	.50	.15
78 Jeff Bagwell	.75	.23
79 Edgardo Alfonzo	.50	.15
80 Jose Canseco	1.25	.35
81 Magglio Ordonez	.50	.15
82 Shawn Green	.50	.15
83 Bobby Abreu	.50	.15
84 Tony Batista	.50	.15
85 Mo Vaughn	.50	.15
86 Juan Gonzalez	1.25	.35
87 Paul O'Neill	.75	.23
88 Mark McGwire	3.00	.90
89 Mark Grace	.75	.23
90 Kevin Brown	.50	.15
91 Ben Grieve	.50	.15
92 Shannon Stewart	.50	.15
93 Erubiel Durazo	.50	.15
94 Antonio Alfonseca	.50	.15
95 Jeff Cirillo	.50	.15
96 Greg Vaughn	.50	.15
97 Kerry Wood	1.25	.35
98 Geoff Jenkins	.50	.15
99 Jason Giambi	1.25	.35
100 Rafael Palmeiro	.75	.23
101 Rafael Furcal PROS	10.00	3.00
102 Pablo Ozuna PROS	10.00	3.00
103 Brad Penny PROS	10.00	3.00
104 Mark Mulder PROS	12.00	3.60
105 Adam Piatt PROS	10.00	3.00
106 Mike Lamb PROS RC	10.00	3.00
107 K.Sasaki PROS RC	15.00	4.50
108 A.McNeal PROS RC	10.00	3.00
109 Pat Burrell PROS	12.00	3.60
110 Rick Ankiel PROS	10.00	3.00
111 Eric Munson PROS	10.00	3.00
112 Josh Beckett PROS	15.00	4.50
113 Adam Kennedy PROS	10.00	3.00
114 Alex Escobar PROS	10.00	3.00
115 C.Hermansen PROS	10.00	3.00
116 Kip Wells PROS	8.00	2.40
117 Matt LeCroy PROS	8.00	2.40
118 Julio Ramirez PROS	8.00	2.40
119 Ben Petrick PROS	8.00	2.40
120 Nick Johnson PROS	8.00	2.40
121 G.Dawkins PROS	8.00	2.40
122 Julio Zuleta PROS RC	8.00	2.40
123 A.Soriano PROS	10.00	3.00
124 K.McDonald RC	8.00	2.40
125 Kory DeHaan PROS	8.00	2.40
126 Vernon Wells PROS	8.00	2.40
127 D.Stenson PROS	8.00	2.40
128 David Eckstein PROS	8.00	2.40
129 Robert Fick PROS	8.00	2.40
130 Cole Liniak PROS	8.00	2.40
131 Mark Quinn PROS	8.00	2.40
132 Eric Gagne PROS	10.00	3.00
133 Wily Mo Pena PROS	8.00	2.40
134 A.Thompson RC	8.00	2.40
135 Steve Sisco PROS RC	8.00	2.40
136 P.Rigdon PROS RC	8.00	2.40
137 Rob Bell PROS	8.00	2.40
138 Carlos Guillen PROS	8.00	2.40
139 Jimmy Rollins PROS	8.00	2.40
140 Jason Conti PROS	8.00	2.40

2000 Fleer Showcase Legacy Collection

Randomly inserted into packs, this 140-card set is a complete parallel of the 2000 Fleer Showcase base set. Each card in the set is individually serial numbered to 20.

Nm-Mt Ex-Mt
*STARS 1-100: 25X TO 60X BASIC

2000 Fleer Showcase Prospect Showcase First

Randomly inserted into packs, this 40-card set features MLB's top prospects. Each card is individually serial numbered to 500.

Nm-Mt Ex-Mt
*PROSPECT 1-15: .4X TO 1X BASIC...
*PROSPECT RC 1-15: .5X TO 1.2X BASIC
*PROSPECT 16-40: .6X TO 1.5X BASIC
*PROSPECT RC 16-40: .75X TO 2X BASIC

2000 Fleer Showcase Consummate Prose

Randomly inserted into packs at one in six, this 15-card die-cut set features players that perform at a higher level. Card backs carry a "CP" prefix.

	Nm-Mt	Ex-Mt
COMPLETE SET (15)	30.00	9.00
CP1 Jeff Bagwell	1.00	.30
CP2 Alex Rodriguez	2.50	.75
CP3 Chipper Jones	1.50	.45
CP4 Derek Jeter	4.00	1.20
CP5 Manny Ramirez	.60	.18
CP6 Tony Gwynn	2.00	.60
CP7 Sammy Sosa	2.50	.75
CP8 Ivan Rodriguez	1.50	.45
CP9 Greg Maddux	2.50	.75
CP10 Ken Griffey Jr.	2.50	.75
CP11 Rick Ankiel	1.50	.45
CP12 Cal Ripken	5.00	1.50
CP13 Pedro Martinez	1.50	.45
CP14 Mike Piazza	2.50	.75
CP15 Mark McGwire	4.00	1.20

2000 Fleer Showcase Feel the Game

Randomly inserted into packs at one in 72, this 10-card insert features game-used jersey cards of some of the biggest names in MLB. Card backs carry a "FG" prefix.

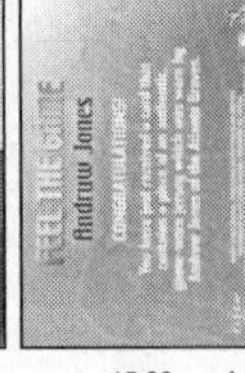

	Nm-Mt	Ex-Mt
FG1 Barry Bonds	40.00	12.00
FG2 Gookie Dawkins	8.00	2.40
FG3 Darin Erstad	10.00	3.00
FG4 Troy Glaus	15.00	4.50
FG5 Scott Rolen	15.00	4.50
FG6 Alex Rodriguez	25.00	7.50
FG7 Andruw Jones	10.00	3.00
FG8 Robin Ventura	10.00	3.00
FG9 Sean Casey	10.00	3.00
FG10 Cal Ripken	50.00	15.00

2000 Fleer Showcase Final Answer

Randomly inserted into packs at one in 10, this 10-card set features hitters that get the job done in clutch situations. Card backs carry a "FA" prefix.

	Nm-Mt	Ex-Mt
COMPLETE SET (10)	40.00	12.00
FA1 Alex Rodriguez	4.00	1.20
FA2 Vladimir Guerrero	2.50	.75
FA3 Cal Ripken	8.00	2.40
FA4 Sammy Sosa	4.00	1.20
FA5 Barry Bonds	6.00	1.80
FA6 Derek Jeter	6.00	1.80
FA7 Ken Griffey Jr.	4.00	1.20
FA8 Mike Piazza	4.00	1.20
FA9 Nomar Garciaparra	4.00	1.20
FA10 Mark McGwire	6.00	1.80

2000 Fleer Showcase Fresh Ink

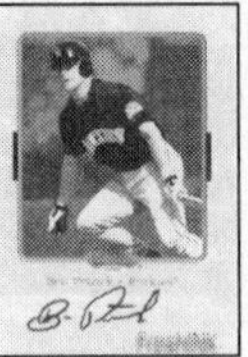

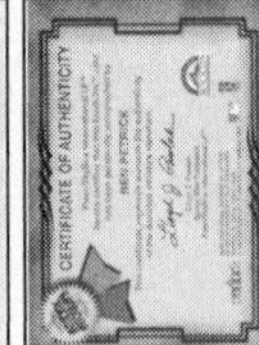

Randomly inserted into packs at one in 24, this 38-card insert set features autographs of many of MLB's top stars and prospects. Please note that Josh Beckett and Brad Penny packed out as exchange cards and must be submited to Fleer by 07/01/01. These cards are not numbered and we have sequenced them in alphabetical order in our checklist.

	Nm-Mt	Ex-Mt
1 Rick Ankiel	10.00	3.00
2 Josh Beckett	40.00	12.00
3 Barry Bonds	175.00	52.50
4 A.J. Burnett	15.00	4.50
5 Pat Burrell	25.00	7.50
6 Ken Caminiti	15.00	4.50
7 Sean Casey	15.00	4.50
8 Jose Cruz Jr.	15.00	4.50
9 Gookie Dawkins	10.00	3.00
10 Erubiel Durazo	15.00	4.50
11 Juan Encarnacion	10.00	3.00
12 Darin Erstad	15.00	4.50
13 Rafael Furcal	15.00	4.50
14 Nomar Garciaparra	120.00	36.00
15 Jason Giambi	40.00	12.00
16 Jeremy Giambi	10.00	3.00
17 Brian Giles	15.00	4.50
18 Troy Glaus	25.00	7.50
19 Vladimir Guerrero	40.00	12.00
20 Chad Hermansen	10.00	3.00
21 Randy Johnson	80.00	24.00
22 Andruw Jones	25.00	7.50
23 Jason Kendall	15.00	4.50
24 Paul Konerko	15.00	4.50
25 Mike Lowell	15.00	4.50
26 Aaron McNeal	15.00	4.50
27 Warren Morris	10.00	3.00
28 Paul O'Neill	25.00	7.50
29 Magglio Ordonez	15.00	4.50
30 Pablo Ozuna	10.00	3.00
31 Brad Penny	15.00	4.50
32 Ben Petrick	10.00	3.00
33 Pokey Reese	10.00	3.00
34 Cal Ripken	150.00	45.00
35 Alex Rodriguez	100.00	30.00
36 Scott Rolen	25.00	7.50
37 Jose Vidro	15.00	4.50
38 Kip Wells	10.00	3.00

2000 Fleer Showcase License to Skill

Randomly inserted into packs at one in 20, this 10-card set features highly skilled players. Card backs carry a "LS" prefix.

	Nm-Mt	Ex-Mt
COMPLETE SET (10)	80.00	24.00
LS1 Vladimir Guerrero	5.00	1.50
LS2 Pedro Martinez	5.00	1.50
LS3 Nomar Garciaparra	8.00	2.40
LS4 Ivan Rodriguez	5.00	1.50
LS5 Mark McGwire	12.00	3.60

LS6 Derek Jeter 12.00 3.60
LS7 Ken Griffey Jr. 8.00 2.40
LS8 Randy Johnson 5.00 1.50
LS9 Sammy Sosa 8.00 2.40
LS10 Alex Rodriguez 8.00 2.40

2000 Fleer Showcase Long Gone

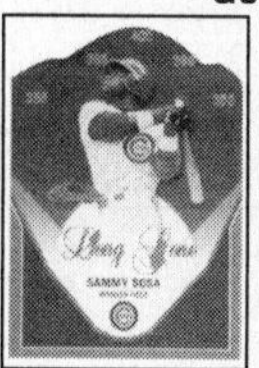
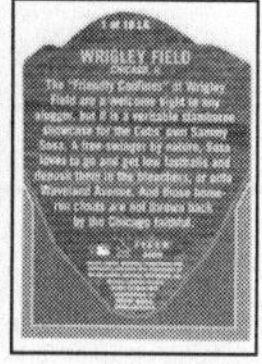

Randomly inserted into packs at one in 20, this 10-card set features hitters that are known for hitting the longball. Card backs carry a "LG" prefix.

Nm-Mt Ex-Mt
COMPLETE SET (10) 25.00 7.50
LG1 Sammy Sosa 3.00 .90
LG2 Derek Jeter 5.00 1.50
LG3 Nomar Garciaparra 3.00 .90
LG4 Juan Gonzalez 2.00 .60
LG5 Vladimir Guerrero 2.00 .60
LG6 Barry Bonds 5.00 1.50
LG7 Jeff Bagwell 1.25 .35
LG8 Alex Rodriguez 3.00 .90
LG9 Ken Griffey Jr. 3.00 .90
LG10 Mark McGwire 5.00 1.50

2000 Fleer Showcase Noise of Summer

Randomly inserted into packs at one in 10, this 10-card set features players that make plenty of noise during the season. Card backs carry a "NS" prefix.

Nm-Mt Ex-Mt
COMPLETE SET (10) 40.00 12.00
NS1 Chipper Jones 2.50 .75
NS2 Jeff Bagwell 1.50 .45
NS3 Manny Ramirez 1.00 .30
NS4 Mark McGwire 6.00 1.80
NS5 Ken Griffey Jr. 4.00 1.20
NS6 Mike Piazza 4.00 1.20
NS7 Pedro Martinez 2.50 .75
NS8 Alex Rodriguez 4.00 1.20
NS9 Derek Jeter 6.00 1.80
NS10 Randy Johnson 2.50 .75

2000 Fleer Showcase Sweet Sigs

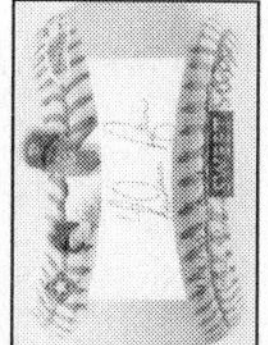
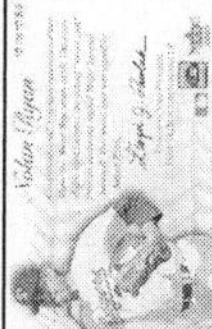

Randomly inserted into packs at one in 250, this 10-card set features autographs of MLB players like Alex Rodriguez and Nolan Ryan. Card backs carry a "SS" prefix. A month after the product went live, representatives at Fleer publicly released print run information on three short-printed cards (Clemens, Garciaparra and A.Rodriguez). Exact amounts are provided in our checklist.

Nm-Mt Ex-Mt
SS1 N.Garciaparra SP/53 250.00 75.00
SS2 Alex Rodriguez SP/67 250.00 75.00
SS3 Tony Gwynn 50.00 15.00
SS4 Roger Clemens SP/79 200.00 60.00
SS5 Scott Rolen 50.00 15.00
SS6 Greg Maddux 100.00 30.00
SS7 Jose Cruz Jr. 25.00 7.50
SS8 Tony Womack 15.00 4.50
SS9 Jay Buhner 25.00 7.50
SS10 Nolan Ryan 150.00 45.00

2001 Fleer Showcase

This 160-card set was distributed in five-card packs with a suggested retial price of $4.99. The set features color player images on Satin technology and contains the following subsets: Avant (101-115), Rookie Avant (116-125), and Rookie Showcase (126-160) with the first 20 sequentially numbered to 1,500 and the next 15 to 2,000)

Nm-Mt Ex-Mt
COMP.SET w/o SP's (100) 30.00 9.00
COMMON CARD (1-100) .50 .15
COMMON (101-115) 5.00 1.50
COMMON (116-125) 15.00 4.50
COMMON (126 -160) 8.00 2.40
1 Tony Gwynn 1.50 .45
2 Barry Larkin 1.25 .35
3 Chan Ho Park .50 .15
4 Darin Erstad .50 .15
5 Rafael Furcal .50 .15
6 Roger Cedeno .50 .15
7 Timo Perez .50 .15
8 Rick Ankiel .50 .15
9 Pokey Reese .50 .15
10 Jeromy Burnitz .50 .15
11 Phil Nevin .50 .15
12 Matt Williams .50 .15
13 Mike Hampton .50 .15
14 Fernando Tatis .50 .15
15 Kazuhiro Sasaki .50 .15
16 Jim Thome 1.25 .35
17 Geoff Jenkins .50 .15
18 Jeff Kent .50 .15
19 Tom Glavine .75 .23
20 Dean Palmer .50 .15
21 Todd Zeile .50 .15
22 Edgar Renteria .50 .15
23 Andruw Jones .50 .15
24 Juan Encarnacion .50 .15
25 Robin Ventura .50 .15
26 J.D. Drew .50 .15
27 Ray Durham .50 .15
28 Richard Hidalgo .50 .15
29 Eric Chavez .50 .15
30 Rafael Palmeiro .75 .23
31 Steve Finley .50 .15
32 Jeff Weaver .50 .15
33 Al Leiter .50 .15
34 Jim Edmonds .50 .15
35 Garret Anderson .50 .15
36 Larry Walker .75 .23
37 Jose Vidro .50 .15
38 Mike Cameron .50 .15
39 Brady Anderson .50 .15
40 Mike Lowell .50 .15
41 Bernie Williams .75 .23
42 Gary Sheffield .50 .15
43 John Smoltz .75 .23
44 Mike Mussina 1.25 .35
45 Greg Vaughn .50 .15
46 Juan Gonzalez 1.25 .35
47 Matt Lawton .50 .15
48 Robb Nen .50 .15
49 Brad Radke .50 .15
50 Edgar Martinez .75 .23
51 Mike Bordick .50 .15
52 Shawn Green .50 .15
53 Carl Everett .50 .15
54 Adrian Beltre .50 .15
55 Kerry Wood 1.25 .35
56 Kevin Brown .50 .15
57 Brian Giles .50 .15
58 Greg Maddux 2.00 .60
59 Preston Wilson .50 .15
60 Orlando Hernandez .50 .15
61 Ben Grieve .50 .15
62 Jermaine Dye .50 .15
63 Travis Lee .50 .15
64 Jose Cruz Jr. .50 .15
65 Rondell White .50 .15
66 Carlos Beltran .50 .15
67 Scott Rolen .75 .23
68 Brad Fullmer .50 .15
69 David Wells .50 .15
70 Mike Sweeney .50 .15
71 Barry Zito 1.25 .35
72 Tony Batista .50 .15
73 Curt Schilling .75 .23
74 Jeff Cirillo .50 .15
75 Edgardo Alfonzo .50 .15
76 John Olerud .50 .15
77 Carlos Lee .50 .15
78 Moises Alou .50 .15
79 Tim Hudson .50 .15
80 Andres Galarraga .50 .15
81 Roberto Alomar 1.25 .35
82 Richie Sexson .50 .15
83 Trevor Hoffman .50 .15
84 Omar Vizquel .50 .15
85 Jacque Jones .50 .15
86 J.T. Snow .50 .15
87 Sean Casey .50 .15
88 Craig Biggio .75 .23
89 Mariano Rivera .75 .23
90 Rusty Greer .50 .15
91 Barry Bonds 3.00 .90
92 Pedro Martinez 1.25 .35
93 Cal Ripken 4.00 1.20
94 Pat Burrell .50 .15
95 Chipper Jones 1.25 .35
96 Magglio Ordonez .50 .15
97 Jeff Bagwell .75 .23
98 Randy Johnson 1.25 .35
99 Frank Thomas 1.25 .35
100 Jason Kendall .50 .15
101 N.Garciaparra AC 12.00 3.60
102 Mark McGwire AC 20.00 6.00
103 Troy Glaus AC 5.00 1.50
104 Ivan Rodriguez AC 8.00 2.40
105 Manny Ramirez AC 5.00 1.50
106 Derek Jeter AC 20.00 6.00
107 Alex Rodriguez AC 12.00 3.60
108 Ken Griffey Jr. AC 12.00 3.60
109 Todd Helton AC 5.00 1.50
110 Sammy Sosa AC 12.00 3.60
111 Vladimir Guerrero AC 8.00 2.40
112 Mike Piazza AC 12.00 3.60
113 Roger Clemens AC 15.00 4.50
114 Jason Giambi AC 8.00 2.40
115 Carlos Delgado AC 5.00 1.50
116 Ichiro Suzuki AC RC 80.00 24.00
117 M.Ensberg AC RC 25.00 7.50
118 C. Valderrama AC RC 15.00 4.50
119 Erick Almonte AC RC 15.00 4.50
120 T.Shinjo AC RC 25.00 7.50
121 Albert Pujols AC RC 100.00 30.00
122 Wilson Betemit AC RC 15.00 4.50
123 A.Hernandez AC RC 15.00 4.50
124 J.Melian AC RC 15.00 4.50
125 Drew Henson AC RC 25.00 7.50
126 Paul Phillips RS RC 8.00 2.40
127 Esix Snead RS RC 8.00 2.40
128 Ryan Freel RS RC 8.00 2.40
129 Junior Spivey RS RC 10.00 3.00
130 E.Guzman RS RC 8.00 2.40
131 Juan Diaz RS RC 8.00 2.40
132 Andres Torres RS RC 8.00 2.40
133 Jay Gibbons RS RC 12.00 3.60
134 Bill Ortega RS RC 8.00 2.40
135 Alexis Gomez RS RC 8.00 2.40
136 Wilkin Ruan RS RC 8.00 2.40
137 Henry Mateo RS RC 8.00 2.40
138 Juan Uribe RS RC 8.00 2.40
139 J.Estrada RS RC 10.00 3.00
140 J.Randolph RS RC 8.00 2.40
141 Eric Hinske RS RC 10.00 3.00
142 Jack Wilson RS RC 8.00 2.40
143 Cody Ransom RS RC 8.00 2.40
144 Nate Frese RS RC 8.00 2.40
145 John Grabow RS RC 8.00 2.40
146 C.Parker RS RC 8.00 2.40
147 B.Lawrence RS RC 8.00 2.40
148 B. Duckworth RS RC 8.00 2.40
149 Winston Abreu RS RC 8.00 2.40
150 H.Ramirez RS RC 10.00 3.00
151 Nick Maness RS RC 8.00 2.40
152 Blaine Neal RS RC 8.00 2.40
153 Billy Sylvester RS RC 8.00 2.40
154 David Elder RS RC 8.00 2.40
155 Bert Snow RS RC 8.00 2.40
156 Claudio Vargas RS RC 8.00 2.40
157 Martin Vargas RS RC 8.00 2.40
158 Grant Balfour RS RC 8.00 2.40
159 Randy Keisler RS 8.00 2.40
160 Zach Day RS RC 10.00 3.00
P1 Tony Gwynn Promo 2.00 .60
MM5 D.Jeter MM/2000 12.00 3.60
NNO D.Jeter MM AU/100 120.00 36.00

2001 Fleer Showcase Legacy

Randomly inserted in hobby packs only, this 160-card set is a parallel version of the base set. Only 50 serially numbered sets were produced.

Nm-Mt Ex-Mt
*STARS 1-100: 8X TO 20X BASIC 1-100
*AVANT 101-115: 1.25X TO 3X BASIC 101-115
*AVANT 116-125: .75X TO 2X BASIC 116-125
*RS 126-145: 1.25X TO 3X BASIC 126-145
*RS 146-160: 1.5X TO 4X BASIC 146-160

2001 Fleer Showcase Awards Showcase

Randomly inserted in retail packs only at the rate of one in 20, this 20-card set features color photos of some of the big award winners from the 2000 season.

Nm-Mt Ex-Mt
COMPLETE SET (20) 60.00 18.00
AS1 Derek Jeter 8.00 2.40
AS2 Derek Jeter 8.00 2.40
AS3 Jason Giambi 3.00 .90
AS4 Jeff Kent 1.25 .35
AS5 Pedro Martinez 3.00 .90
AS6 Randy Johnson 3.00 .90
AS7 Kazuhiro Sasaki 1.25 .35
AS8 Rafael Furcal 1.25 .35
AS9 Carlos Delgado 1.25 .35
AS10 Todd Helton 2.00 .60
AS11 Ivan Rodriguez 3.00 .90
AS12 Darin Erstad 1.25 .35
AS13 Bernie Williams 2.00 .60
AS14 Greg Maddux 5.00 1.50
AS15 Jim Edmonds 1.25 .35
AS16 Andruw Jones 1.25 .35
AS17 Nomar Garciaparra 5.00 1.50
AS18 Todd Helton 2.00 .60
AS19 Troy Glaus 2.00 .60
AS20 Sammy Sosa 5.00 1.50

2001 Fleer Showcase Awards Showcase Memorabilia

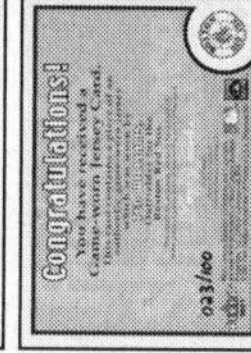

Randomly inserted in hobby packs only, this 34-card set features color photos of players who were Cy Young and MVP winners with pieces of memorabilia embedded in the cards. Only 100 serially numbered sets were produced.

Nm-Mt Ex-Mt
1 Johnny Bench Jsy 25.00 7.50
2 Yogi Berra Bat 25.00 7.50
3 George Brett Jsy 40.00 12.00
4 Lou Brock Bat 25.00 7.50
5 Roy Campanella Bat 40.00 12.00
6 Steve Carlton Jsy 15.00 4.50
7 Roger Clemens Jsy 50.00 15.00
9 Andre Dawson Jsy 15.00 4.50
10 Whitey Ford Jsy 25.00 7.50
12 Jimmie Foxx Bat 60.00 18.00
14 Kirk Gibson Bat 15.00 4.50
15 Tom Glavine Jsy 25.00 7.50
16 Juan Gonzalez Bat 25.00 7.50
17 Elston Howard Bat 25.00 7.50
18 Jim Hunter Jsy 25.00 7.50
19 Reggie Jackson Bat 25.00 7.50
20 Randy Johnson Jsy 25.00 7.50
21 Chipper Jones Bat 25.00 7.50
22 Harmon Killebrew Bat 25.00 7.50
23 Fred Lynn Bat 15.00 4.50
24 Greg Maddux Jsy 25.00 7.50
25 Don Mattingly Bat 80.00 24.00
27 Willie McCovey Jsy 15.00 4.50
28 Jim Palmer Jsy 15.00 4.50
29 Jim Rice Bat 15.00 4.50
30 Brooks Robinson Bat 25.00 7.50
31 Frank Robinson Bat 25.00 7.50
32 Jackie Robinson Pants 80.00 24.00
33 Ivan Rodriguez Jsy 25.00 7.50
34 Mike Schmidt Jsy 40.00 12.00
35 Tom Seaver Jsy 25.00 7.50
36 Willie Stargell Jsy 25.00 7.50
37 Ted Williams Jsy 150.00 45.00
38 Robin Yount Jsy 25.00 7.50

2001 Fleer Showcase Sticks

Randomly inserted into hobby packs at the rate of one in 24, this 36-card set color player photos with pieces of game-used bats embedded in the cards.

Nm-Mt Ex-Mt
1 Roberto Alomar 15.00 4.50
2 Rick Ankiel 10.00 3.00
3 Adrian Beltre 10.00 3.00
4 Barry Bonds 30.00 9.00
5 Pat Burrell 10.00 3.00
6 Roger Cedeno 10.00 3.00
7 Tony Clark 10.00 3.00
8 Roger Clemens 25.00 7.50
9 Carlos Delgado 10.00 3.00
10 J.D. Drew 10.00 3.00
11 Steve Finley 10.00 3.00
12 Rafael Furcal 10.00 3.00
13 Alex Gonzalez 10.00 3.00
14 Juan Gonzalez 15.00 4.50
15 Shawn Green 10.00 3.00
16 Vladimir Guerrero 15.00 4.50
17 Richard Hidalgo 10.00 3.00
18 Reggie Jackson 15.00 4.50
19 Randy Johnson 15.00 4.50
20 Andruw Jones 10.00 3.00
21 Chipper Jones 15.00 4.50
22 Al Kaline 15.00 4.50
23 George Kell 15.00 4.50
24 Jason Kendall 10.00 3.00
25 Magglio Ordonez 10.00 3.00
26 Adam Piatt 10.00 3.00
27 Jorge Posada 15.00 4.50
28 Ivan Rodriguez 15.00 4.50
29 Scott Rolen 15.00 4.50
30 Tsuyoshi Shinjo 15.00 4.50
31 Shannon Stewart 10.00 3.00
32 Ichiro Suzuki 60.00 18.00
33 Frank Thomas 15.00 4.50
34 Jim Thome 15.00 4.50
35 Jose Vidro 10.00 3.00
36 Preston Wilson 10.00 3.00

2001 Fleer Showcase Sweet Sigs Leather

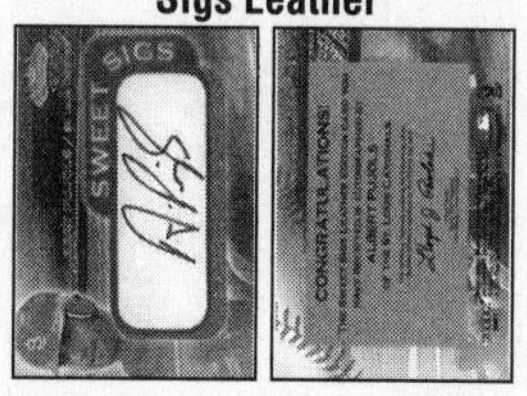

Randomly inserted in hobby packs at the rate of one in 24, this 23 card set features color player head shots with their autograph printed on a piece of simulated baseball leather. The following players cards were seeded into packs as exchange cards with a redemption deadline of 11/01/02: Bob Abreu, Wilson Betemit, Russell Branyan, Pat Burrell, Sean Casey, Eric Chavez, Rafael Furcal, Nomar Garciaparra, Juan Gonzalez, Elpidio Guzman, Brandon Inge, Willie Mays, Jackson Melian, Xavier Nady, Jose Ortiz, Ben Sheets and Mike Sweeney.

Nm-Mt Ex-Mt
1 Bob Abreu SP/100 40.00 12.00
2 Wilson Betemit 15.00 4.50
3 Russell Branyan 15.00 4.50
4 Pat Burrell SP/75 40.00 12.00
5 Sean Casey SP/75 40.00 12.00
6 E.Chavez SP/100 EXCH 40.00 12.00
7 Rafael Furcal EXCH 15.00 4.50
8 Nomar Garciaparra 200.00 60.00
SP/55 EXCH
9 Brian Giles SP/75 40.00 12.00
10 Juan Gonzalez 80.00 24.00
SP/75 EXCH
11 Elpidio Guzman 15.00 4.50
12 Drew Henson SP/75 40.00 12.00
13 Brandon Inge 15.00 4.50
14 Derek Jeter SP/75 250.00 75.00
15 Andruw Jones SP/85 50.00 15.00
16 W.Mays SP/60 EXCH 200.00 60.00
17 Jackson Melian 15.00 4.50
18 Xavier Nady 15.00 4.50
19 Jose Ortiz 15.00 4.50
20 Albert Pujols SP/75 300.00 90.00
21 Ben Sheets 15.00 4.50
22 Mike Sweeney 15.00 4.50
23 Miguel Tejada SP/75 40.00 12.00

2001 Fleer Showcase Sweet Sigs Lumber

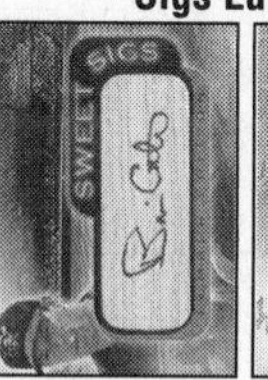

Randomly inserted in hobby packs at the rate of one in 24, this 23-card set features color player photos with their autograph printed on a piece of ash designed to look like a bat. The following players cards were seeded into packs as exchange cards with a redemption deadline of 11/01/02: Bob Abreu, Wilson Betemit, Russell Branyan, Sean Casey, Eric Chavez, Rafael Furcal, Nomar Garciaparra, Juan Gonzalez, Elpidio Guzman, Brandon Inge, Jackson Melian, Xavier Nady, Jose Ortiz, Ben Sheets and Mike Sweeney.

Nm-Mt Ex-Mt
1 Bob Abreu 15.00 4.50
2 Wilson Betemit 15.00 4.50
3 Russell Branyan 15.00 4.50
4 Pat Burrell SP/300 25.00 7.50
5 Sean Casey SP/300 25.00 7.50
6 Eric Chavez 15.00 4.50
7 Rafael Furcal 15.00 4.50
8 Nomar Garciaparra 150.00 45.00
SP/155 EXCH
9 Brian Giles SP/155 25.00 7.50
10 Juan Gonzalez 50.00 15.00
SP/300 EXCH
11 Elpidio Guzman 15.00 4.50
12 Drew Henson SP/145 30.00 9.00
13 Brandon Inge 15.00 4.50
14 Derek Jeter SP/300 150.00 45.00
15 Andruw Jones SP/300 30.00 9.00
16 Willie Mays SP/155
17 Jackson Melian 15.00 4.50
18 Xavier Nady 15.00 4.50
19 Jose Ortiz 15.00 4.50
20 Albert Pujols SP/150 200.00 60.00
21 Ben Sheets 15.00 4.50
22 Mike Sweeney 15.00 4.50
23 Miguel Tejada SP/300 25.00 7.50

2001 Fleer Showcase Sweet Sigs Wall

Randomly inserted in hobby packs at the rate of one in 24, this 23-card set features color player photos with their autograph printed on an actual piece of game-used outfield wall. The following players cards were seeded into packs as exchange cards with a redemption deadline of 11/01/02: Bob Abreu, Wilson Betemit, Russell Branyan, Pat Burrell, Eric Chavez, Rafael Furcal, Nomar Garciaparra, Juan Gonzalez, Elpidio Guzman, Brandon Inge, Willie Mays, Jackson Melian, Xavier Nady, Jose Ortiz and Ben Sheets.

Nm-Mt Ex-Mt
1 Bob Abreu 15.00 4.50
2 Wilson Betemit 15.00 4.50
3 Russell Branyan 15.00 4.50
4 Pat Burrell SP/93 30.00 9.00
5 Sean Casey SP/98 30.00 9.00
6 Eric Chavez 15.00 4.50
7 Rafael Furcal 15.00 4.50
8 Nomar Garciaparra 200.00 60.00
SP/80 EXCH
9 Brian Giles SP/100 30.00 9.00
10 Juan Gonzalez 100.00 30.00
SP/30 EXCH
11 Elpidio Guzman 15.00 4.50
12 Drew Henson SP/100 40.00 12.00
13 Brandon Inge 15.00 4.50
14 Derek Jeter SP/90 200.00 60.00
15 Andruw Jones SP/200 40.00 12.00
16 W.Mays SP/85 EXCH 150.00 45.00
17 Jackson Melian 15.00 4.50
18 Xavier Nady 15.00 4.50
19 Jose Ortiz 15.00 4.50
20 Albert Pujols SP/80 300.00 90.00
21 Ben Sheets 15.00 4.50
22 Mike Sweeney
23 Miguel Tejada SP/120 30.00 9.00

2002 Fleer Showcase

This 166 card standard-size set was released in June, 2002. It was issued in five card packs

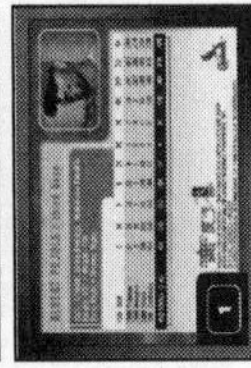

which came 24 packs to a box and four boxes to a case. Each pack had an SRP of $5. Cards numbered 1-125 featured standard cards of veterans while cards 126-135 featured special veteran "avant" cards (seeded at a rate of 1:12 packs) and cards numbered 136-166 feature rookies/prospects (randomly seeded into packs at an undisclosed rate). Those rookie/prospect cards were issued in the following way: cards 136-141 have a stated print run of 500 serial numbered sets, cards numbered 142-156 have a stated print run of 1000 serial numbered sets and cards numbered 157-166 have a stated print run of 1500 serial numbered sets.

	Nm-Mt	Ex-Mt
COMP.SET w/o SP's (125)	30.00	9.00
COMMON CARD (1-125)	.50	.15
COMMON CARD (126-135)	8.00	2.40
COMMON CARD (136-141)	10.00	3.00
COMMON CARD (142-166)	8.00	2.40
1 Albert Pujols	2.50	.75
2 Pedro Martinez	1.25	.35
3 Frank Thomas	1.25	.35
4 Gary Sheffield	.50	.15
5 Roberto Alomar	1.25	.35
6 Luis Gonzalez	.50	.15
7 Bobby Abreu	.50	.15
8 Carlos Lee	.50	.15
9 Preston Wilson	.50	.15
10 Todd Helton	.75	.23
11 Juan Gonzalez	1.25	.35
12 Chuck Knoblauch	.50	.15
13 Jason Kendall	.50	.15
14 Aaron Sele	.50	.15
15 Greg Vaughn	.50	.15
16 Fred McGriff	.75	.23
17 Doug Mientkiewicz	.50	.15
18 Richard Hidalgo	.50	.15
19 Alfonso Soriano	.75	.23
20 Matt Williams	.50	.15
21 Bobby Higginson	.50	.15
22 Mo Vaughn	.50	.15
23 Andruw Jones	.50	.15
24 Omar Vizquel	.50	.15
25 Bret Boone	.50	.15
26 Bernie Williams	.75	.23
27 Rafael Furcal	.50	.15
28 Jeff Bagwell	.75	.23
29 Marty Cordova	.50	.15
30 Lance Berkman	.50	.15
31 Vernon Wells	.50	.15
32 Garret Anderson	.50	.15
33 Larry Bigbie	.50	.15
34 Steve Finley	.50	.15
35 Barry Bonds	3.00	.90
36 Eric Chavez	.50	.15
37 Tony Clark	.50	.15
38 Roger Clemens	2.50	.75
39 Adam Dunn	.50	.15
40 Roger Cedeno	.50	.15
41 Carlos Delgado	.50	.15
42 Jermaine Dye	.50	.15
43 Brian Jordan	.50	.15
44 Darin Erstad	.50	.15
45 Paul LoDuca	.50	.15
46 Jim Edmonds	.50	.15
47 Tom Glavine	.75	.23
48 Cliff Floyd	.50	.15
49 Jon Lieber	.50	.15
50 Adrian Beltre	.50	.15
51 Joel Pineiro	.50	.15
52 Jim Thome	1.25	.35
53 Jimmy Rollins	.50	.15
54 Pat Burrell	.50	.15
55 Jeromy Burnitz	.50	.15
56 Larry Walker	.75	.23
57 Damon Minor	.50	.15
58 John Olerud	.50	.15
59 Carlos Beltran	.50	.15
60 Vladimir Guerrero	1.25	.35
61 David Justice	.50	.15
62 Phil Nevin	.50	.15
63 Tino Martinez	.75	.23
64 Curt Schilling	.75	.23
65 Corey Patterson	.50	.15
66 Aubrey Huff	.50	.15
67 Mark Grace	.75	.23
68 Rafael Palmeiro	.75	.23
69 Jorge Posada	.75	.23
70 Craig Biggio	.75	.23
71 Manny Ramirez	.50	.15
72 Mark Quinn	.50	.15
73 Raul Mondesi	.50	.15
74 Shawn Green	.50	.15
75 Brian Giles	.50	.15
76 Paul Konerko	.50	.15
77 Troy Glaus	.75	.23
78 Mike Mussina	1.25	.35
79 Greg Maddux	2.00	.60
80 Edgar Martinez	.75	.23
81 Jose Vidro	.50	.15
82 Scott Rolen	.75	.23
83 Ben Grieve	.50	.15
84 Jeff Kent	.50	.15
85 Magglio Ordonez	.50	.15
86 Freddy Garcia	.50	.15
87 Ivan Rodriguez	1.25	.35
88 Pokey Reese	.50	.15
89 Shannon Stewart	.50	.15
90 Randy Johnson	1.25	.35
91 Cristian Guzman	.50	.15
92 Tsuyoshi Shinjo	.50	.15
93 Steve Cox	.50	.15
94 Mike Sweeney	.50	.15
95 Robert Fick	.50	.15
96 Sean Casey	.50	.15
97 Tim Hudson	.50	.15
98 Bud Smith	.50	.15
99 Corey Koskie	.50	.15
100 Richie Sexson	.50	.15
101 Aramis Ramirez	.50	.15
102 Barry Larkin	1.25	.35
103 Rich Aurilia	.50	.15
104 Charles Johnson	.50	.15
105 Ryan Klesko	.50	.15
106 Ben Sheets	.50	.15
107 J.D. Drew	.50	.15
108 Jay Gibbons	.50	.15
109 Kerry Wood	1.25	.35
110 C.C. Sabathia	.50	.15
111 Eric Munson	.50	.15
112 Josh Beckett	.75	.23
113 Javier Vazquez	.50	.15
114 Barry Zito	.75	.23
115 Kazuhiro Sasaki	.50	.15
116 Bubba Trammell	.50	.15
117 Russell Branyan	.50	.15
118 Todd Walker	.50	.15
119 Mike Hampton	.50	.15
120 Jeff Weaver	.50	.15
121 Geoff Jenkins	.50	.15
122 Edgardo Alfonzo	.50	.15
123 Mike Lieberthal	.50	.15
124 Mike Lowell	.50	.15
125 Kevin Brown	.50	.15
126 Derek Jeter AC	20.00	6.00
127 Ichiro Suzuki AC	12.00	3.60
128 Nomar Garciaparra AC	12.00	3.60
129 Ken Griffey Jr. AC	12.00	3.60
130 Jason Giambi AC	8.00	2.40
131 Alex Rodriguez AC	12.00	3.60
132 Chipper Jones AC	8.00	2.40
133 Mike Piazza AC	12.00	3.60
134 Sammy Sosa AC	12.00	3.60
135 Hideo Nomo AC	8.00	2.40
136 Kazuhisa Ishii AC RC	15.00	4.50
137 Satoru Komiyama AC RC	10.00	3.00
138 So Taguchi AC RC	15.00	4.50
139 Jorge Padilla AC RC	10.00	3.00
140 Rene Reyes AC RC	10.00	3.00
141 Jorge Nunez AC RC	10.00	3.00
142 Nelson Castro RS	8.00	2.40
143 Anderson Machado RS RC	8.00	2.40
144 Edwin Almonte RS RC	8.00	2.40
145 Luis Ugueto RS RC	8.00	2.40
146 Felix Escalona RS RC	8.00	2.40
147 Ron Calloway RS RC	8.00	2.40
148 Hansel Izquierdo RS RC	8.00	2.40
149 Mark Teixeira RS	10.00	3.00
150 Orlando Hudson RS	8.00	2.40
151 Aaron Cook RS RC	8.00	2.40
152 Aaron Taylor RS RC	8.00	2.40
153 Takahito Nomura RS RC	8.00	2.40
154 Matt Thornton RS RC	8.00	2.40
155 Mark Prior RS	15.00	4.50
156 Reed Johnson RS RC	10.00	3.00
157 Doug DeVore RS RC	8.00	2.40
158 Ben Howard RS RC	8.00	2.40
159 Francis Beltran RS RC	8.00	2.40
160 Brian Mallette RS RC	8.00	2.40
161 Sean Burroughs RS	8.00	2.40
162 Michael Restovich RS	8.00	2.40
163 Austin Kearns RS	8.00	2.40
164 Marlon Byrd RS	8.00	2.40
165 Hank Blalock RS	10.00	3.00
166 Mike Rivera RS	8.00	2.40

2002 Fleer Showcase Legacy

Issued at a stated rate of one per hobby box, this is a complete parallel of the Fleer Showcase set. Each of these cards have a stated print run of 175 serial numbered sets.

Nm-Mt Ex-Mt

*LEGACY 1-125: ,,2.5X TO ,,6X BASIC
*LEGACY 126-135: ,,.5X TO ,,1.2X BASIC
*LEGACY 136-141: ,,.4X TO ,,1X BASIC
*LEGACY 142-166: ,,.5X TO ,,1.2X BASIC

2002 Fleer Showcase Baseball's Best

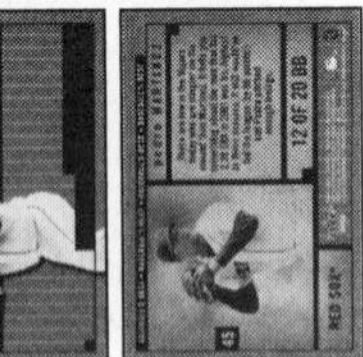

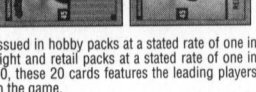

Issued in hobby packs at a stated rate of one in eight and retail packs at a stated rate of one in 10, these 20 cards features the leading players in the game.

	Nm-Mt	Ex-Mt
COMPLETE SET (20)	60.00	18.00
1 Derek Jeter	8.00	2.40
2 Barry Bonds	8.00	2.40
3 Mike Piazza	5.00	1.50
4 Alex Rodriguez	5.00	1.50
5 Pat Burrell	2.00	.60
6 Rafael Palmeiro	2.00	.60
7 Nomar Garciaparra	5.00	1.50
8 Todd Helton	2.00	.60
9 Roger Clemens	6.00	1.80
10 Shawn Green	2.00	.60
11 Chipper Jones	3.00	.90
12 Pedro Martinez	3.00	.90
13 Luis Gonzalez	2.00	.60
14 Randy Johnson	3.00	.90
15 Ichiro Suzuki	5.00	1.50
16 Ken Griffey Jr.	5.00	1.50
17 Vladimir Guerrero	3.00	.90
18 Sammy Sosa	5.00	1.50
19 Jason Giambi	3.00	.90
20 Albert Pujols	6.00	1.80

2002 Fleer Showcase Baseball's Best Memorabilia

Inserted in packs at stated odds of one in 12 hobby and one in 36 retail, these 19 cards are a partial parallel of the Baseball's Best insert set.

Each of these cards have a memorabilia piece attached to them.

	Nm-Mt	Ex-Mt
*MULTI-COLOR PATCH: 1X TO 2.5X BASIC		
1 Derek Jeter Jsy	20.00	6.00
2 Barry Bonds Jsy	20.00	6.00
3 Mike Piazza Jsy	10.00	3.00
4 Alex Rodriguez Bat	15.00	4.50
6 Rafael Palmeiro Jsy	10.00	3.00
7 Nomar Garciaparra Jsy	15.00	4.50
8 Todd Helton Bat SP/350	10.00	3.00
9 Roger Clemens Jsy	15.00	4.50
10 Shawn Green Jsy	8.00	2.40
11 Chipper Jones Jsy	10.00	3.00
12 Pedro Martinez Jsy	10.00	3.00
13 Luis Gonzalez Jsy	8.00	2.40
14 Randy Johnson Jsy	10.00	3.00
15 Ichiro Suzuki Base	20.00	6.00
16 Ken Griffey Jr. Base	15.00	4.50
17 Vladimir Guerrero Base	8.00	2.40
18 Sammy Sosa Base	15.00	4.50
19 Jason Giambi Base	10.00	3.00
20 Albert Pujols Base	15.00	4.50

2002 Fleer Showcase Baseball's Best Memorabilia Gold

Randomly inserted in packs, these 19 cards are a parallel of the Baseball's Best Memorabilia insert set. Each of these cards have a stated print run of 100 serial numbered sets.

Nm-Mt Ex-Mt

*GOLD: 1X TO 2.5X BASIC MEMORABILIA

2002 Fleer Showcase Baseball's Best Memorabilia Autographs Gold

Randomly inserted in packs, these two cards are a parallel of the Baseball's Best Memorabilia insert set. Each of these cards have a stated print run of 100 serial numbered sets. Each of these cards feature not only the memorabilia swatch but also the player's autograph.

	Nm-Mt	Ex-Mt
1 Derek Jeter Jsy	200.00	60.00
2 Barry Bonds Jsy	200.00	60.00

2002 Fleer Showcase Baseball's Best Memorabilia Autographs Silver

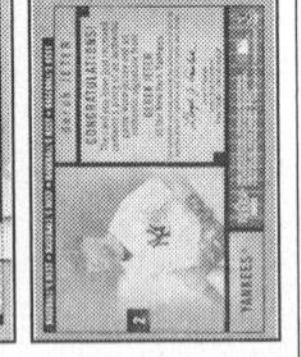

Randomly inserted in packs, these two cards are a parallel of the Baseball's Best Memorabilia insert set. Each of these cards have a stated print run of 400 serial numbered sets. Each of these cards feature not only the memorabilia swatch but also the player's autograph.

	Nm-Mt	Ex-Mt
1 Derek Jeter Jsy	150.00	45.00
2 Barry Bonds Jsy	175.00	52.50

2002 Fleer Showcase Derek Jeter Legacy Collection

Randomly inserted in packs, these 22 cards trace the entire career of Yankee superstar Derek Jeter who helped lead the Yankees to five pennants and four world championships in the first six years of his career.

	Nm-Mt	Ex-Mt
COMPLETE SET (22)	100.00	30.00
COMMON CARD (1-22)	8.00	2.40

2002 Fleer Showcase Derek Jeter Legacy Collection Memorabilia

Randomly inserted in packs, these four cards feature various memorabilia which were part of Derek Jeter's career. Each card was printed to a different stated print run and we have notated that information in our checklist.

	Nm-Mt	Ex-Mt
1 D.Jeter YC Jsy/300	150.00	45.00
2 Derek Jeter Combo Jsy/175	150.00	45.00
Features white NY Yankees swatch and Blue Columbus Bombers swatch		
3 D.Jeter WS Ball/50	200.00	60.00
4 D.Jeter Fldg Glv/425	100.00	30.00

2002 Fleer Showcase Sweet Sigs Leather

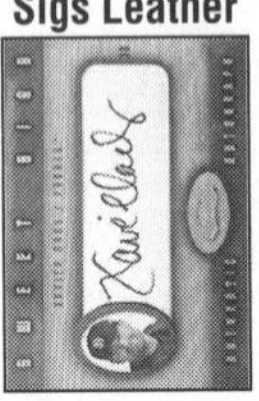

Randomly inserted in packs, these 13 cards feature player signatures on actual non game-used leather. Since each player signed a different amount of cards we have put that stated information next to their name in our checklist. A few players signed less than 38 cards and those cards are not priced due to market scarcity.

	Nm-Mt	Ex-Mt
1 Bobby Abreu/10		
2 Russell Branyan/90	15.00	4.50
3 Pat Burrell/35		
4 Sean Casey/35		
5 Eric Chavez/20		
6 Rafael Furcal/92	25.00	7.50
7 Nomar Garciaparra/5		
8 Brandon Inge/122	12.00	3.60
9 Jackson Melian/37		
10 Xavier Nady/301	15.00	4.50
11 Jose Ortiz/50	20.00	6.00
12 Ben Sheets/60	30.00	9.00
13 Mike Sweeney/103	20.00	6.00

2002 Fleer Showcase Sweet Sigs Lumber

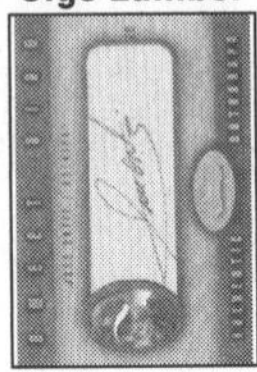

Randomly inserted in packs, these 13 cards feature player signatures on actual non game-used wood. Since each player signed a different amount of cards we have put that stated information next to their name in our checklist.

	Nm-Mt	Ex-Mt
1 Bobby Abreu/231	15.00	4.50
2 Russell Branyan/425	10.00	3.00
3 Pat Burrell/115	20.00	6.00
4 Sean Casey/64	30.00	9.00
5 Eric Chavez/256	15.00	4.50
6 Rafael Furcal/530	15.00	4.50
7 Nomar Garciaparra/25		
8 Brandon Inge/528	10.00	3.00
9 Jackson Melian/636	10.00	3.00
10 Xavier Nady/589	10.00	3.00
11 Jose Ortiz/515	10.00	3.00
12 Ben Sheets/458	15.00	4.50
13 Mike Sweeney/495	15.00	4.50

2002 Fleer Showcase Sweet Sigs Wall

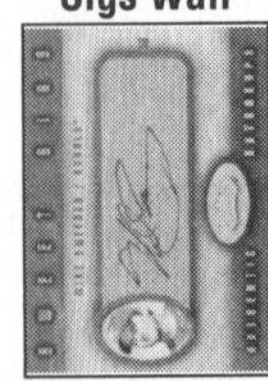

Randomly inserted in packs, these 13 cards feature player signatures on actual non game-used wall pieces. Since each player signed a different amount of cards we have put that stated information next to their name in our checklist. Cards with a print run of 35 or fewer are not priced due to market scarcity.

	Nm-Mt	Ex-Mt
1 Bobby Abreu/70	30.00	9.00
2 Russell Branyan/200	10.00	3.00
3 Pat Burrell/35		
4 Sean Casey/35		
5 Eric Chavez/108	20.00	6.00
6 Rafael Furcal/207	15.00	4.50
7 Nomar Garciaparra/25		
8 Brandon Inge/187	12.00	3.60
9 Jackson Melian/146	12.00	3.60
10 Xavier Nady/286	10.00	3.00
11 Jose Ortiz/116	12.00	3.60
12 Ben Sheets/150	20.00	6.00
13 Mike Sweeney/371	15.00	4.50

2003 Fleer Showcase

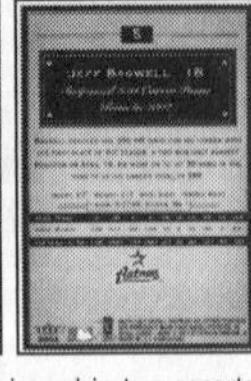

This 145-card set was issued in two separtate series. The primary Showcase product was released in March, 2003. Cards 1-95 are active ballplayers and 96- 105 feature retired players. Cards 106 through 135 are a subset entitled Showcasing Talent of which features a selection of top prospects. Three pack types were produced for this product (Jersey, Leather and Lumber) eight of each were placed into the 24-ct sealed boxes. Each pack type contained a selection of commonly available cards plus other inserts and subsets of which were exclusive to the theme. Cards 136-145 were randomly seeded within Fleer Rookies and Greats packs of which was distributed in December, 2003. Each of these 10 update cards features a top prospect and is serial numbered to 750 copies.

	Nm-Mt	Ex-Mt
COMP.LO SET w/o SP's (105)	25.00	7.50
COMMON CARD (1-95)	.50	.15
COMMON CARD (96-105)	1.00	.30
COMMON CARD (106-135)	3.00	.90
106-135 ODDS 1:3 HOBBY, 1:12 RETAIL		
106-115 DIST IN JERSEY AND RETAIL PACKS		
116-125 DIST IN LEATHER AND RETAIL PACKS		
126-135 DIST IN LUMBER AND RETAIL PACKS		
COMMON CARD (136-145)	5.00	1.50
1 David Eckstein	.50	.15
2 Curt Schilling	.75	.23
3 Jay Gibbons	.50	.15
4 Kerry Wood	1.25	.35
5 Jeff Bagwell	.75	.23
6 Hideo Nomo	1.25	.35
7 Tim Hudson	.50	.15
8 J.D. Drew	.50	.15
9 Josh Phelps	.50	.15
10 Bartolo Colon	.50	.15
11 Bobby Abreu	.50	.15
12 Matt Morris	.50	.15
13 Kazuhiro Sasaki	.50	.15
14 Sean Burroughs	.50	.15
15 Vicente Padilla	.50	.15
16 Jorge Posada	.75	.23
17 Torii Hunter	.50	.15
18 Richie Sexson	.50	.15
19 Lance Berkman	.50	.15
20 Todd Helton	.75	.23
21 Paul Konerko	.50	.15
22 Pedro Martinez	1.25	.35
23 Rodrigo Lopez	.50	.15
24 Gary Sheffield	.50	.15
25 Darin Erstad	.50	.15
26 Nomar Garciaparra	2.00	.60
27 Adam Dunn	.50	.15
28 Jason Giambi	1.25	.35
29 Miguel Tejada	.50	.15
30 Chipper Jones	1.25	.35
31 Alex Rodriguez	2.00	.60
32 Barry Bonds	3.00	.90
33 Roger Clemens	2.50	.75
34 Sammy Sosa	2.00	.60
35 Randy Johnson	1.25	.35
36 Tim Salmon	.75	.23
37 Shea Hillenbrand	.50	.15
38 Larry Walker	.75	.23
39 A.J. Burnett	.50	.15
40 Shawn Green	.50	.15
41 Cristian Guzman	.50	.15
42 Bernie Williams	.75	.23
43 Mark Mulder	.50	.15
44 Brian Giles	.50	.15
45 Bret Boone	.50	.15
46 Juan Gonzalez	1.25	.35
47 Roy Halladay	.50	.15
48 Wade Miller	.50	.15
49 Jeff Kent	.50	.15
50 Carlos Delgado	.50	.15
51 Mike Lowell	.50	.15
52 Jim Edmonds	.50	.15
53 Ivan Rodriguez	1.25	.35
54 Aubrey Huff	.50	.15
55 Ryan Klesko	.50	.15
56 Paul Lo Duca	.50	.15
57 Roy Oswalt	.50	.15
58 Omar Vizquel	.50	.15
59 Manny Ramirez	.50	.15
60 Andruw Jones	.50	.15
61 Troy Glaus	.75	.23
62 Ichiro Suzuki	2.00	.60
63 Albert Pujols	2.50	.75
64 Derek Jeter	3.00	.90
65 Mark Prior	2.50	.75
66 Ken Griffey Jr.	2.00	.60
67 Vladimir Guerrero	1.25	.35
68 Mike Piazza	2.00	.60
69 Alfonso Soriano	.75	.23
70 Greg Maddux	2.00	.60
71 Adam Kennedy	.50	.15
72 Junior Spivey	.50	.15
73 Tom Glavine	.75	.23
74 Derek Lowe	.50	.15

75 Magglio Ordonez .50 .15
76 Jim Thome 1.25 .35
77 Robert Fick .50 .15
78 Josh Beckett .75 .23
79 Mike Sweeney .50 .15
80 Kazuhisa Ishii .50 .15
81 Roberto Alomar 1.25 .35
82 Barry Zito .75 .23
83 Pat Burrell .50 .15
84 Scott Rolen .75 .23
85 John Olerud .50 .15
86 Eric Hinske .50 .15
87 Rafael Palmeiro .75 .23
88 Edgar Martinez .75 .23
89 Eric Chavez .50 .15
90 Jose Vidro .50 .15
91 Craig Biggio .75 .23
92 Rich Aurilia .50 .15
93 Austin Kearns .50 .15
94 Luis Gonzalez .50 .15
95 Garret Anderson .50 .15
96 Yogi Berra 2.00 .60
97 Al Kaline 2.00 .60
98 Robin Yount 3.00 .90
99 Reggie Jackson 1.50 .45
100 Harmon Killebrew 2.00 .60
101 Eddie Mathews 2.00 .60
102 Willie McCovey 1.00 .30
103 Nolan Ryan 4.00 1.20
104 Mike Schmidt 2.50 .75
105 Tom Seaver 1.50 .45
106 Francisco Rodriguez ST 3.00 .90
107 Carl Crawford ST 3.00 .90
108 Ben Howard ST 3.00 .90
109 Hank Blalock ST 5.00 1.50
110 Hee Seop Choi ST 3.00 .90
111 Kirk Saarloos ST 3.00 .90
112 Lew Ford ST RC 5.00 1.50
113 Andy Van Hekken ST 3.00 .90
114 Drew Henson ST 3.00 .90
115 Marlon Byrd ST 3.00 .90
116 Jayson Werth ST 3.00 .90
117 Willie Bloomquist ST 3.00 .90
118 Joe Borchard ST 3.00 .90
119 Mark Teixeira ST 5.00 1.50
120 Bobby Hill ST 3.00 .90
121 Jason Lane ST 3.00 .90
122 Omar Infante ST 3.00 .90
123 Victor Martinez ST 3.00 .90
124 Jorge Padilla ST 3.00 .90
125 John Lackey ST 3.00 .90
126 Anderson Machado ST 3.00 .90
127 Rodrigo Rosario ST 3.00 .90
128 Freddy Sanchez ST 3.00 .90
129 Tony Alvarez ST 3.00 .90
130 Matt Thornton ST 3.00 .90
131 Joe Thurston ST 3.00 .90
132 Brett Myers ST 3.00 .90
133 Nook Logan ST RC 3.00 .90
134 Chris Snelling ST 3.00 .90
135 Terrmel Sledge ST RC 5.00 1.50
136 Chien-Ming Wang ST RC 8.00 2.40
137 Rickie Weeks ST RC 15.00 4.50
138 Brandon Webb ST RC 10.00 3.00
139 Hideki Matsui ST RC 15.00 4.50
140 Michael Hessman ST RC 5.00 1.50
141 Ryan Wagner ST RC 8.00 2.40
142 Bo Hart ST RC 8.00 2.40
143 Edwin Jackson ST RC 12.00 3.60
144 Jose Contreras ST RC 8.00 2.40
145 Delmon Young ST RC 15.00 4.50

2003 Fleer Showcase Legacy

This 135 card set was distributed exclusively in three separate forms of hobby packs. Cards 1-35 and 126-135 were available exclusively in hobby Lumber packs (signified by an orange-bar wrapper), 36-70 and 116-125 in hobby Leather packs (signified by brown-bar wrapper) and 71-105 and 106-115 in hobby Jersey packs (signified by a gray-bar wrapper). Only 150 serial numbered sets were produced. Each card 's serial numbered on back in gold foil.

Nm-Mt Ex-Mt
*LEGACY 1-95: 2.5X TO 6X BASIC
*LEGACY 96-105: 3X TO 8X BASIC
*LEGACY 106-135: .6X TO 1.5X BASIC

2003 Fleer Showcase Baseball's Best

Issued at a stated rate of one in eight leather packs and one in 24 retail packs, this 15-card insert set features the best players in basbeball.

Nm-Mt Ex-Mt
1 Curt Schilling 3.00 .90
2 Barry Zito 3.00 .90
3 Torii Hunter 3.00 .90
4 Pedro Martinez 3.00 .90
5 Bernie Williams 3.00 .90
6 Magglio Ordonez 3.00 .90
7 Alfonso Soriano 3.00 .90
8 Hideo Nomo 3.00 .90
9 Jason Giambi 3.00 .90
10 Sammy Sosa 5.00 1.50
11 Vladimir Guerrero 3.00 .90
12 Ken Griffey Jr. 5.00 1.50
13 Troy Glaus 3.00 .90
14 Ichiro Suzuki 5.00 1.50
15 Albert Pujols 6.00 1.80

2003 Fleer Showcase Baseball's Best Game Jersey

These cards parallel the Baseball's Best insert set. Although the wrappper stated odds list these cards as 1:27 Leather hobby packs - our

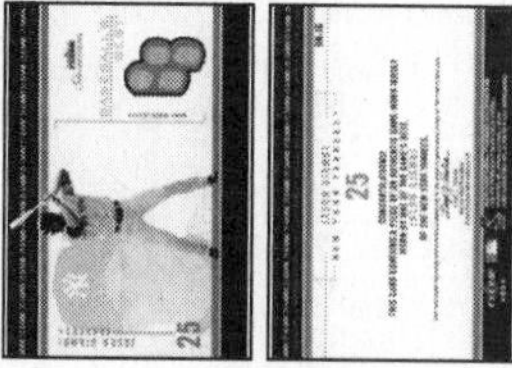

analysis of the case breakdown, coupled with reports from dealers in the field indicates the cards were actually seeded at a rate of 1:9 Leather hobby packs.

Nm-Mt Ex-Mt
1B Curt Schilling 10.00 3.00
2 Barry Zito 10.00 3.00
3 Torii Hunter 8.00 2.40
4 Pedro Martinez 10.00 3.00
5 Bernie Williams 10.00 3.00
6 Magglio Ordonez 8.00 2.40
7 Alfonso Soriano 10.00 3.00
8 Hideo Nomo Sox 10.00 3.00
9 Jason Giambi 10.00 3.00
10 Sammy Sosa 15.00 4.50

2003 Fleer Showcase Hot Gloves

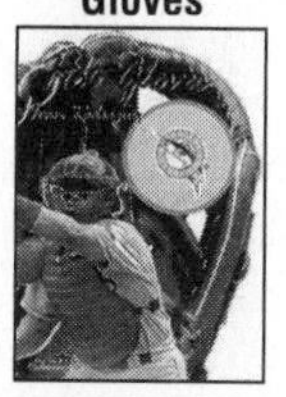

Inserted at a stated rate of one in 144 leather and one in 288 retail packs these 10 cards features some of the leading defensive players in baseball.

Nm-Mt Ex-Mt
1 Greg Maddux 25.00 7.50
2 Ivan Rodriguez 15.00 4.50
3 Derek Jeter 40.00 12.00
4 Mike Piazza 25.00 7.50
5 Nomar Garciaparra 25.00 7.50
6 Andruw Jones 15.00 4.50
7 Scott Rolen 15.00 4.50
8 Barry Bonds 40.00 12.00
9 Roger Clemens 30.00 9.00
10 Alex Rodriguez 25.00 7.50

2003 Fleer Showcase Hot Gloves Game Jersey

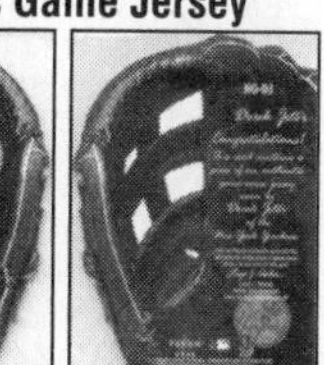

Randomly inserted in lumber packs, this is a parallel to the Hot Gloves insert set. These cards have a game-worn jersey card as well as the player's photo pictured.

Nm-Mt Ex-Mt
1 Greg Maddux 20.00 6.00
2 Ivan Rodriguez 15.00 4.50
3 Derek Jeter 30.00 9.00
4 Mike Piazza 20.00 6.00
5 Nomar Garciaparra 20.00 6.00
6 Andruw Jones 15.00 4.50
7 Scott Rolen 15.00 4.50
8 Barry Bonds 30.00 9.00
9 Roger Clemens 25.00 7.50
10 Alex Rodriguez 20.00 6.00

2003 Fleer Showcase Sweet Sigs

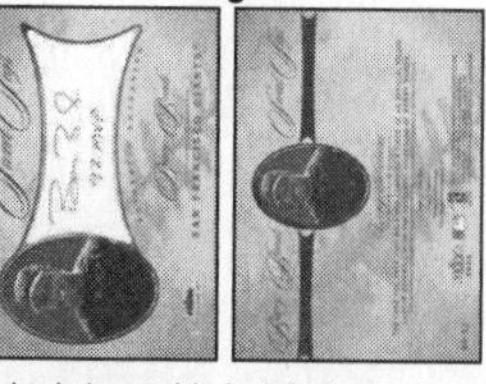

Randomly inserted in both leather and retail packs, these cards feature authentic signatures of either Barry Bonds or Derek Jeter. As these cards are issued to various print runs, we have notated that information in our checklist.

Nm-Mt Ex-Mt
BB1 Barry Bonds 90 MVP/150 175.00 52.50
BB2 Barry Bonds 92 MVP/100 175.00 52.50
BB3 Barry Bonds 93 MVP/75 200.00 60.00
BB4 Barry Bonds 01 MVP/50 250.00 75.00
BB5 Barry Bonds 02 MVP/25
BB6 Barry Bonds 5X MVP/5
DJ2 Derek Jeter Blue Ink/250 150.00 45.00
DJ3 Derek Jeter Red Ink/50 250.00 75.00

2003 Fleer Showcase Sweet Stitches

Issued at a stated rate of one in eight jersey packs and one in 24 retail packs, these 10 cards feature information about what various stars do in their off-field activities.

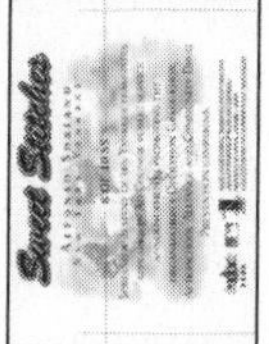

Nm-Mt Ex-Mt
1 Derek Jeter 8.00 2.40
2 Randy Johnson 3.00 .90
3 Jeff Bagwell 3.00 .90
4 Nomar Garciaparra 5.00 1.50
5 Roger Clemens 6.00 1.80
6 Todd Helton 3.00 .90
7 Barry Bonds 8.00 2.40
8 Alfonso Soriano 3.00 .90
9 Miguel Tejada 3.00 .90
10 Mark Prior 6.00 1.80

2003 Fleer Showcase Sweet Stitches Game Jersey

Randomly inserted in jersey packs, this is a parallel to the Sweet Stitches insert set. These cards feature game-used jersey pieces and were issued to assorted print runs and we have notated that information next to the player's name in our checklist.

Nm-Mt Ex-Mt
1 Derek Jeter/599 25.00 7.50
2 Randy Johnson/899 10.00 3.00
3 Jeff Bagwell/899 10.00 3.00
4 Nomar Garciaparra/899 15.00 4.50
5 Roger Clemens/599 20.00 6.00
6 Todd Helton/899 10.00 3.00
7 Barry Bonds/899 20.00 6.00
8 Alfonso Soriano/599 10.00 3.00
9 Miguel Tejada/899 8.00 2.40
10 Mark Prior/899 15.00 4.50
11 Sammy Sosa/899 15.00 4.50
12 J.D. Drew/899 8.00 2.40
13 Alex Rodriguez/899 15.00 4.50
14 Mike Piazza/899 15.00 4.50

2003 Fleer Showcase Sweet Stitches Patch

Randomly inserted in jersey packs, this is a parallel to the sweet stitches insert set. These cards feature game-used jersey patch pieces and were issued to assorted print runs and we have notated that information next to the player's name in our checklist.

Nm-Mt Ex-Mt
1 Derek Jeter/50
2 Randy Johnson/150 40.00 12.00
3 Jeff Bagwell/150 40.00 12.00
4 Nomar Garciaparra/150 60.00 18.00
5 Roger Clemens/50
6 Todd Helton/75 50.00 15.00
7 Barry Bonds/150 80.00 24.00
8 Alfonso Soriano/50 40.00 12.00
9 Miguel Tejada/150 25.00 7.50
10 Mark Prior/150 60.00 18.00
11 Sammy Sosa/150 60.00 18.00
12 J.D. Drew/150 25.00 7.50
13 Alex Rodriguez/150 60.00 18.00
14 Mike Piazza/150 60.00 18.00

2003 Fleer Showcase Thunder Sticks

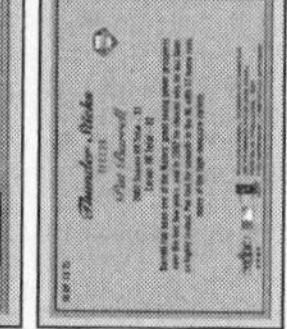

Inserted in packs at a stated rate of one in eight lumber and one in 24 retail, these 10 cards feature some of the leading power hitters in baseball.

Nm-Mt Ex-Mt
1 Adam Dunn 3.00 .90
2 Alex Rodriguez 5.00 1.50
3 Barry Bonds 8.00 2.40
4 Jim Thome 3.00 .90
5 Chipper Jones 3.00 .90
6 Manny Ramirez 3.00 .90
7 Carlos Delgado 3.00 .90
8 Mike Piazza 5.00 1.50
9 Shawn Green 3.00 .90
10 Pat Burrell 3.00 .90

2003 Fleer Showcase Thunder Sticks Game Bat

Randomly inserted in lumber packs, these cards parallel the Thunder Sticks insert set. These cards feature a game bat piece and were issued to a varying amount of cards. We have notated the print run information next to the player's name in our checklist.

Nm-Mt Ex-Mt
*GOLD: 1X TO 2.5X BASIC CARDS
GOLD PRINT RUN 99 SERIAL #'d SETS
1 Adam Dunn/799 8.00 2.40
2 Alex Rodriguez/799 15.00 4.50
3 Barry Bonds/899 20.00 6.00
4 Jim Thome/799 10.00 3.00
5 Chipper Jones/799 10.00 3.00
6 Manny Ramirez/799 8.00 2.40
7 Troy Glaus/799 10.00 3.00
8 Vladimir Guerrero/799 10.00 3.00
9 Shawn Green/799 8.00 2.40
10 Pat Burrell/799 8.00 2.40

2004 Fleer Showcase

Nm-Mt Ex-Mt
COMP.SET w/o SP's (100) 25.00 7.50
COMMON CARD (1-100) .50 .15
COMMON CARD (101-130) 4.00 1.20
101-130 ODDS 1:6 HOBBY, 1:12 RETAIL
1 Corey Patterson .50 .15
2 Ken Griffey Jr. 2.00 .60
3 Preston Wilson .50 .15
4 Juan Pierre .50 .15
5 Jose Reyes .75 .23
6 Jason Schmidt .50 .15
7 Rocco Baldelli 1.25 .35
8 Carlos Delgado .50 .15
9 Hideki Matsui 2.00 .60
10 Nomar Garciaparra 2.00 .60
11 Brian Giles .50 .15
12 Darin Erstad .50 .15
13 Larry Walker .75 .23
14 Bernie Williams .75 .23
15 Laynce Nix .50 .15
16 Manny Ramirez .50 .15
17 Magglio Ordonez .50 .15
18 Khalil Greene .50 .15
19 Jim Edmonds .50 .15
20 Troy Glaus .75 .23
21 Curt Schilling .75 .23
22 Chipper Jones 1.25 .35
23 Sammy Sosa 2.00 .60
24 Frank Thomas 1.25 .35
25 Todd Helton .75 .23
26 Craig Biggio .75 .23
27 Shannon Stewart .50 .15
28 Mark Mulder .50 .15
29 Mike Lieberthal .50 .15
30 Reggie Sanders .50 .15
31 Edgar Martinez .75 .23
32 Bo Hart .50 .15
33 Mark Teixeira .50 .15
34 Jay Gibbons .50 .15
35 Roberto Alomar 1.25 .35
36 Kip Wells .50 .15
37 J.D. Drew .50 .15
38 Jason Varitek .50 .15
39 Craig Monroe .50 .15
40 Roy Oswalt .50 .15
41 Edgardo Alfonzo .50 .15
42 Roy Halladay .50 .15
43 Gary Sheffield .50 .15
44 Lance Berkman .50 .15
45 Torii Hunter .50 .15
46 Vladimir Guerrero 1.25 .35
47 Marlon Byrd .50 .15
48 Austin Kearns .50 .15
49 Angel Berroa .50 .15
50 Geoff Jenkins .50 .15
51 Aubrey Huff .50 .15
52 Dontrelle Willis .50 .15
53 Tony Batista .50 .15
54 Shawn Green .50 .15
55 Jason Kendall .50 .15
56 Garret Anderson .50 .15
57 Andruw Jones .50 .15
58 Dmitri Young .50 .15
59 Richie Sexson .50 .15
60 Jorge Posada .75 .23
61 Bobby Abreu .50 .15
62 Vernon Wells .50 .15
63 Javy Lopez .50 .15
64 Josh Beckett .75 .23
65 Eric Chavez .50 .15
66 Tim Salmon .75 .23
67 Brandon Webb .50 .15
68 Pedro Martinez 1.25 .35
69 Kerry Wood 1.25 .35
70 Jose Vidro .50 .15
71 Alfonso Soriano .75 .23
72 Barry Zito .75 .23
73 Sean Burroughs .50 .15
74 Jamie Moyer .50 .15
75 Luis Gonzalez .50 .15
76 Adam Dunn .50 .15
77 Mike Piazza 2.00 .60
78 Pat Burrell .50 .15
79 Scott Rolen .75 .23
80 Milton Bradley .50 .15
81 Mike Sweeney .50 .15
82 Hank Blalock .50 .15
83 Esteban Loaiza .50 .15
84 Hideo Nomo 1.25 .35
85 Derek Jeter 3.00 .90
86 Albert Pujols 2.50 .75
87 Greg Maddux 2.00 .60
88 Mark Prior 2.50 .75
89 Mike Lowell .50 .15
90 Jeff Bagwell .75 .23
91 Scott Podsednik 1.25 .35
92 Tom Glavine .75 .23
93 Jason Giambi 1.25 .35
94 Jim Thome 1.25 .35
95 Ichiro Suzuki 2.00 .60
96 Randy Johnson 1.25 .35
97 Omar Vizquel .50 .15
98 Ivan Rodriguez 1.25 .35
99 Miguel Tejada .50 .15
100 Alex Rodriguez 2.00 .60
101 Rickie Weeks ST 5.00 1.50
102 Chad Gaudin ST 4.00 1.20
103 Rich Harden ST 4.00 1.20
104 Edwin Jackson ST 5.00 1.50
105 Chien-Ming Wang ST 4.00 1.20
106 Matt Kata ST 4.00 1.20
107 Delmon Young ST 5.00 1.50
108 Ryan Wagner ST 4.00 1.20
109 Jeff Duncan ST 4.00 1.20
110 Prentice Redman ST 4.00 1.20
111 Clint Barmes ST 4.00 1.20
112 Jeremy Guthrie ST 4.00 1.20
113 Brian Stokes ST 4.00 1.20
114 David DeJesus ST 4.00 1.20
115 Felix Sanchez ST 4.00 1.20
116 Josh Stewart ST 4.00 1.20
117 Daniel Garcia ST 4.00 1.20
118 Jon Leicester ST 4.00 1.20
119 Francisco Cruceta ST 4.00 1.20
120 Oscar Villarreal ST 4.00 1.20
121 Michael Hessman ST 4.00 1.20
122 Michel Hernandez ST 4.00 1.20
123 Richard Fischer ST 4.00 1.20
124 Robby Hammock ST 4.00 1.20
125 Guillermo Quiroz ST 4.00 1.20
126 Craig Brazell ST 4.00 1.20
127 Wilfredo Ledezma ST 4.00 1.20
128 Josh Willingham ST 4.00 1.20
129 Ramon Nivar ST 4.00 1.20
130 Matt Diaz ST 4.00 1.20

2004 Fleer Showcase Legacy

Nm-Mt Ex-Mt
*LEGACY 1-100: 6X TO 15X BASIC
*LEGACY 101-130: 1.5X TO 4X BASIC
OVERALL PARALLEL ODDS 1:24
STATED PRINT RUN 99 SERIAL #'d SETS

2004 Fleer Showcase Masterpiece

Nm-Mt Ex-Mt
OVERALL PARALLEL ODDS 1:24
STATED PRINT RUN 1 SERIAL #'d SET
NO PRICING DUE TO SCARCITY

2004 Fleer Showcase Baseballs Best

Nm-Mt Ex-Mt
STATED ODDS 1:24 HOBBY, 1:12 RETAIL
1 Derek Jeter 8.00 2.40
2 Mark Prior 6.00 1.80
3 Mike Piazza 5.00 1.50
4 Jeff Bagwell 3.00 .90
5 Kerry Wood 3.00 .90
6 Ivan Rodriguez 3.00 .90
7 Albert Pujols 6.00 1.80
8 Jim Thome 3.00 .90
9 Sammy Sosa 5.00 1.50
10 Vladimir Guerrero 3.00 .90
11 Eric Gagne 3.00 .90
12 Randy Johnson 3.00 .90
13 Todd Helton 3.00 .90
14 Chipper Jones 3.00 .90
15 Alex Rodriguez 5.00 1.50

2004 Fleer Showcase Baseballs Best Game Used

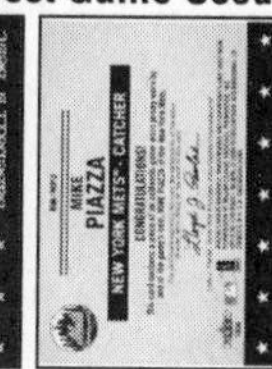

Nm-Mt Ex-Mt
STATED ODDS 1:72 HOBBY, 1:48 RETAIL
*PATCH: 1.5X TO 4X BASIC
PATCH RANDOM INSERTS IN PACKS
PATCH PRINT RUN 50 SERIAL #'d SETS
*GOLD: .5X TO 1.2X BASIC
GOLD RANDOM INSERTS IN PACKS
GOLD PRINT RUN 150 SERIAL #'d SETS
*REWARD: 1X TO 2.5X BASIC
REWARD ISSUED ONLY IN DEALER PACKS
REWARD PRINTS B/WN 29-44 COPIES PER
AP Albert Pujols Jsy 15.00 4.50
AR Alex Rodriguez Jsy 10.00 3.00
CJ Chipper Jones Jsy 10.00 3.00
DJ Derek Jeter Bat 20.00 6.00
EG Eric Gagne Jsy 10.00 3.00
IR Ivan Rodriguez Jsy 10.00 3.00
JB Jeff Bagwell Jsy 10.00 3.00
JT Jim Thome Jsy 10.00 3.00
KW Kerry Wood Jsy 10.00 3.00
MPI Mike Piazza Jsy 10.00 3.00
MPR Mark Prior Jsy 15.00 4.50
RJ Randy Johnson Jsy 10.00 3.00
SS Sammy Sosa Jsy 10.00 3.00
TH Todd Helton Jsy 10.00 3.00
VG Vladimir Guerrero Jsy 10.00 3.00

2004 Fleer Showcase Grace

Nm-Mt Ex-Mt
STATED ODDS 1:12 HOBBY/RETAIL
1 Kerry Wood 3.00 .90

2 Derek Jeter 8.00 2.40
3 Nomar Garciaparra 5.00 1.50
4 Mike Piazza 5.00 1.50
5 Mark Prior 6.00 1.80
6 Jose Reyes 3.00 .90
7 Dontrelle Willis 3.00 .90
8 Pedro Martinez 3.00 .90
9 Tim Hudson 3.00 .90
10 Troy Glaus 3.00 .90
11 Hank Blalock 3.00 .90
12 Albert Pujols 6.00 1.80
13 Juan Pierre 3.00 .90
14 Angel Berroa 3.00 .90
15 Rocco Baldelli 3.00 .90
16 Carlos Delgado 3.00 .90
17 Manny Ramirez 3.00 .90
18 Alex Rodriguez 5.00 1.50
19 Andruw Jones 3.00 .90
20 Luis Gonzalez 3.00 .90

2004 Fleer Showcase Grace Game Used

Nm-Mt Ex-Mt
STATED ODDS 1:48 HOBBY/RETAIL
*PATCH: 1.5X TO 4X BASIC
PATCH RANDOM INSERTS IN PACKS
PATCH PRINT RUN 50 SERIAL #'d SETS
*GOLD: .5X TO 1.2X BASIC
GOLD RANDOM INSERTS IN PACKS
GOLD PRINT RUN 150 SERIAL #'d SETS
*REWARD p/r 44-55: 1X TO 2.5X BASIC
REWARD ISSUED ONLY IN DEALER PACKS
REWARD PRINTS B/WN 23-55 COPIES PER
NO REWARD PRICING ON QTY OF 23
AP Albert Pujols Jsy 15.00 4.50
AR Alex Rodriguez Jsy 10.00 3.00
DJ Derek Jeter Bat 20.00 6.00
DW Dontrelle Willis Jsy 8.00 2.40
MPI Mike Piazza Jsy 10.00 3.00
MPR Mark Prior Jsy 15.00 4.50
MR Manny Ramirez Jsy 8.00 2.40
NG Nomar Garciaparra Jsy 10.00 3.00
PM Pedro Martinez Jsy 10.00 3.00
RB Rocco Baldelli Jsy 10.00 3.00

2004 Fleer Showcase Hot Gloves

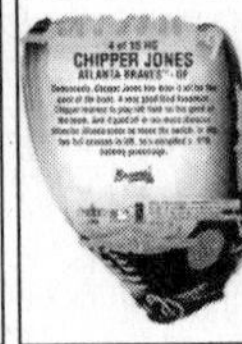

Nm-Mt Ex-Mt
STATED ODDS 1:288 HOBBY, 1:576 RETAIL
NO MORE THAN 120 SETS PRODUCED
PRINT RUN INFO PROVIDED BY FLEER
CARDS ARE NOT SERIAL-NUMBERED
1 Derek Jeter 50.00 15.00
2 Nomar Garciaparra 30.00 9.00
3 Alex Rodriguez 30.00 9.00
4 Chipper Jones 25.00 7.50
5 Torii Hunter 25.00 7.50
6 Ichiro Suzuki 40.00 12.00
7 Mark Prior 40.00 12.00
8 Vladimir Guerrero 25.00 7.50
9 Albert Pujols 40.00 12.00
10 Ivan Rodriguez 25.00 7.50
11 Hideki Matsui 60.00 18.00
12 Sammy Sosa 40.00 12.00
13 Jim Thome 25.00 7.50
14 Rocco Baldelli 25.00 7.50
15 Jeff Bagwell 25.00 7.50

2004 Fleer Showcase Hot Gloves Game Used

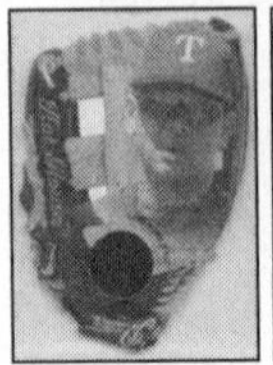
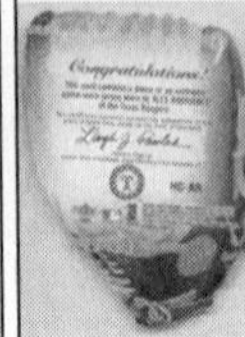

Nm-Mt Ex-Mt
RANDOM INSERTS IN PACKS
STATED PRINT RUN 50 SERIAL #'d SETS
AP Albert Pujols Jsy 60.00 18.00
AR Alex Rodriguez Jsy 50.00 15.00
CJ Chipper Jones Jsy 30.00 9.00
DJ Derek Jeter Jsy 80.00 24.00
HM Hideki Matsui Base 100.00 30.00
IR Ivan Rodriguez Jsy 30.00 9.00
IS Ichiro Suzuki Base 120.00 36.00
JB Jeff Bagwell Jsy 30.00 9.00
JT Jim Thome Jsy 30.00 9.00
MP Mark Prior Jsy 60.00 18.00
NG Nomar Garciaparra Jsy 50.00 15.00
RB Rocco Baldelli Jsy 30.00 9.00
SS Sammy Sosa Jsy 50.00 15.00
TH Torii Hunter Jsy 30.00 9.00
VG Vladimir Guerrero Jsy 30.00 9.00

2004 Fleer Showcase Pujols Legacy Collection

Nm-Mt Ex-Mt
COMMON CARD (1-10) 8.00 2.40
STATED ODDS 1:24
STATED PRINT RUN 1000 SERIAL #'d SETS

2004 Fleer Showcase Pujols Legacy Collection Autograph

Nm-Mt Ex-Mt
OVERALL AUTOGRAPH ODDS 1:24
PRINT RUNS B/WN 1-10 COPIES PER
NO PRICING DUE TO SCARCITY
1 Albert Pujols Draft 99/1
2 Albert Pujols 01 ROY/2
3 Albert Pujols 01 Slugger/3
4 Albert Pujols 4 Pos/4
5 Albert Pujols NL Records/5
6 Albert Pujols 2X AS/6
7 Albert Pujols HR Record/7
8 Albert Pujols 300-100-100/8
9 Albert Pujols 03 Btg Champ/9
10 Albert Pujols 03 POY/10

2004 Fleer Showcase Pujols Legacy Collection Game Jersey

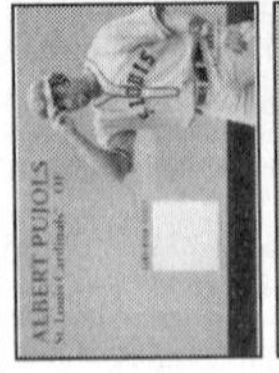
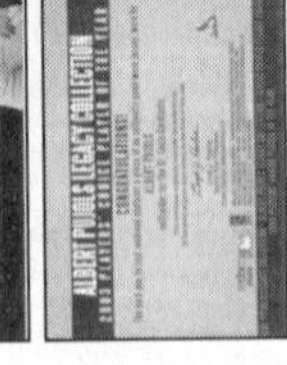

Nm-Mt Ex-Mt
RANDOM INSERTS IN PACKS
PRINT RUNS B/WN 10-100 COPIES PER
NO PRICING ON QTY OF 40 OR LESS.
1 Albert Pujols Draft 99/10
2 Albert Pujols 01 ROY/20
3 Albert Pujols 01 Slugger/30
4 Albert Pujols 4 Pos/40
5 Albert Pujols NL Records/50 30.00 9.00
6 Albert Pujols 2X AS/60 30.00 9.00
7 Albert Pujols HR Record/70 25.00 7.50
8 Albert Pujols 300-100-100/80 25.00 7.50
9 Albert Pujols 03 Btg Champ/90 25.00 7.50
10 Albert Pujols 03 POY/100 25.00 7.50

2004 Fleer Showcase Sweet Sigs

Nm-Mt Ex-Mt
OVERALL AUTOGRAPH ODDS 1:24
PRINT RUNS B/WN 26-1000 COPIES PER
EXCH.PRINT RUNS PROVIDED BY FLEER
EXCHANGE DEADLINE INDEFINITE
AK Austin Kearns/224 15.00 4.50
AP1 Albert Pujols/150 EXCH 200.00 60.00
AP2 A.Pujols NNO/300 EXCH 150.00 45.00
BH Bo Hart/667 25.00 7.50
BW Brandon Webb/1000 15.00 4.50
BZ Barry Zito/248 40.00 12.00
CPA Corey Patterson/176 20.00 6.00
CPE Carlos Pena/48 20.00 6.00
CW Chien Mien-Wang/35 60.00 18.00
DW Dontrelle Willis/26 60.00 18.00
DY Delmon Young/1000 EXCH 40.00 12.00
HB Hank Blalock/824 25.00 7.50
JG John Gall/900 EXCH 10.00 3.00
JR Jose Reyes/115 30.00 9.00
JW Josh Willingham/180 20.00 6.00
ML Mike Lowell/44 25.00 7.50
MR Michael Ryan/288 10.00 3.00
MT Miguel Tejada/52 25.00 7.50
RWA Ryan Wagner/700 EXCH 15.00 4.50
RWE Rickie Weeks/416 40.00 12.00
SR Scott Rolen/200 40.00 12.00
TB Taylor Buchholz/900 EXCH 10.00 3.00
TH Torii Hunter/294 15.00 4.50
WL Wilfredo Ledezma/376 10.00 3.00

2004 Fleer Showcase Sweet Sigs Game Jersey

Nm-Mt Ex-Mt
OVERALL AUTOGRAPH ODDS 1:24
STATED PRINT RUN 5 SERIAL #'d CARDS
NO PRICING DUE TO SCARCITY
AP Albert Pujols/5

2003 Fleer Splendid Splinters

This 150-card set was issued in April, 2003. These cards were issued in five card packs with an $5 SRP which came 24 packs to a box and 12 boxes to a case. Cards number 1 through 90 feature veterans while cards number 91 through 110 feature "simulated wood" cards of veterans. Cards numbered 111 through 140 feature leading prospects while cards numbered 141 through 150 feature prospects with simulated wood. Please note, that an autograph baseball of Ted Williams (authenticated by Green Diamonds) was a special bonus for distributors ordering this product. The ball, however, has no special notation from Fleer and is just priced as an Ted Williams signed ball.

Nm-Mt Ex-Mt
COMP.SET w/o SP's (90) 15.00 4.50
COMMON CARD (1-90) .30 .09
COMMON CARD (91-110) 8.00 2.40
COMMON CARD (111-140) 3.00 .90
COMMON CARD (141-150) 5.00 1.50
1 David Eckstein .30 .09
2 Barry Larkin .75 .23
3 Edgardo Alfonzo .30 .09
4 Darin Erstad .30 .09
5 Ellis Burks .30 .09
6 Omar Vizquel .30 .09
7 Bartolo Colon .30 .09
8 Roberto Alomar .75 .23
9 Garret Anderson .30 .09
10 Al Leiter .30 .09
11 Tim Salmon .50 .15
12 Larry Walker .50 .15
13 Jorge Posada .50 .15
14 Curt Schilling .50 .15
15 Jason Jennings .30 .09
16 Jason Giambi .75 .23
17 Robert Fick .30 .09
18 Kazuhiro Sasaki .30 .09
19 Bernie Williams .50 .15
20 Junior Spivey .30 .09
21 Mike Lowell .30 .09
22 Luis Gonzalez .30 .09
23 Josh Beckett .50 .15
24 John Smoltz .50 .15
25 Mike Mussina .75 .23
26 Gary Sheffield .30 .09
27 Tom Glavine .50 .15
28 Tim Hudson .30 .09
29 Austin Kearns .30 .09
30 Andruw Jones .30 .09
31 Roger Clemens 1.50 .45
32 Mark Mulder .30 .09
33 Jay Gibbons .30 .09
34 Jeff Kent .30 .09
35 Barry Zito .50 .15
36 Rodrigo Lopez .30 .09
37 Jeff Bagwell .50 .15
38 Eric Chavez .30 .09
39 Pedro Martinez .75 .23
40 Lance Berkman .30 .09
41 Bobby Abreu .30 .09
42 Wade Miller .30 .09
43 Bret Boone .30 .09
44 Vicente Padilla .30 .09
45 Shea Hillenbrand .30 .09
46 Roy Oswalt .30 .09
47 Pat Burrell .30 .09
48 Manny Ramirez .30 .09
49 Craig Biggio .50 .15
50 Randy Wolf .30 .09
51 Kerry Wood .75 .23
52 Mike Sweeney .30 .09
53 Brian Giles .30 .09
54 Kazuhisa Ishii .30 .09
55 Jason Kendall .30 .09
56 Hideo Nomo .75 .23
57 Josh Phelps .30 .09
58 Sean Burroughs .30 .09
59 Paul Konerko .30 .09
60 Shawn Green .30 .09
61 Ryan Klesko .30 .09
62 Magglio Ordonez .30 .09
63 Paul Lo Duca .30 .09
64 Edgar Martinez .50 .15
65 J.D. Drew .30 .09
66 Phil Nevin .30 .09
67 Jim Edmonds .30 .09
68 Matt Morris .30 .09
69 Aubrey Huff .30 .09
70 Adam Dunn .30 .09
71 John Olerud .30 .09
72 Juan Gonzalez .75 .23
73 Scott Rolen .50 .15
74 Rafael Palmeiro .50 .15
75 Roy Halladay .30 .09
76 Kevin Brown .30 .09
77 Ivan Rodriguez .75 .23
78 Eric Hinske .30 .09
79 Frank Thomas .75 .23
80 Carlos Delgado .30 .09
81 Bobby Higginson .30 .09
82 Trevor Hoffman .30 .09
83 Cliff Floyd .30 .09
84 Derek Lowe .30 .09
85 Richie Sexson .30 .09
86 Rich Aurilia .30 .09
87 Sean Casey .30 .09
88 Cristian Guzman .30 .09
89 Randy Winn .30 .09
90 Jose Vidro .30 .09
91 Mark Prior Wood 15.00 4.50
92 Derek Jeter Wood 20.00 6.00
93 Alex Rodriguez Wood 15.00 4.50
94 Greg Maddux Wood 15.00 4.50
95 Troy Glaus Wood 10.00 3.00
96 Vladimir Guerrero Wood 10.00 3.00
97 Todd Helton Wood 10.00 3.00
98 Albert Pujols Wood 15.00 4.50
99 Torii Hunter Wood 8.00 2.40
100 Mike Piazza Wood 15.00 4.50
101 Ichiro Suzuki Wood 15.00 4.50
102 Sammy Sosa Wood 15.00 4.50
103 Ken Griffey Jr. Wood 15.00 4.50
104 Nomar Garciaparra Wood 15.00 4.50
105 Barry Bonds Wood 20.00 6.00
106 Chipper Jones Wood 10.00 3.00
107 Jim Thome Wood 10.00 3.00
108 Miguel Tejada Wood 8.00 2.40
109 Randy Johnson Wood 10.00 3.00
110 Alfonso Soriano Wood 10.00 3.00
111 Guillermo Quiroz BB RC 6.00 1.80
112 Josh Willingham BB RC 6.00 1.80
113 Alejandro Machado BB RC 3.00 .90
114 Chris Waters BB RC 3.00 .90
115 Adam LaRoche BB 5.00 1.50
116 Prentice Redman BB RC 3.00 .90
117 Jhonny Peralta BB RC 3.00 .90
118 Francisco Rosario BB RC 3.00 .90
119 Shane Victorino BB RC 3.00 .90
120 Chien-Ming Wang BB RC 8.00 2.40
121 Matt Bruback BB RC 3.00 .90
122 Rontrez Johnson BB RC 3.00 .90
123 Josh Hall BB RC 5.00 1.50
124 Matt Kata BB RC 5.00 1.50
125 Hector Luna BB RC 3.00 .90
126 Josh Stewart BB RC 3.00 .90
127 Craig Brazell BB RC 5.00 1.50
128 Tim Olson BB RC 5.00 1.50
129 Michel Hernandez BB RC 3.00 .90
130 Michael Hessman BB RC 3.00 .90
131 Clint Barmes BB RC 5.00 1.50
132 Justin Morneau BB 3.00 .90
133 Chris Snelling BB 3.00 .90
134 Bobby Jenks BB 3.00 .90
135 Tim Hummell BB 3.00 .90
136 Adam Morrissey BB 3.00 .90
137 Carl Crawford BB 3.00 .90
138 Garrett Atkins BB 3.00 .90
139 Jung Bong BB 3.00 .90
140 Ken Harvey BB 3.00 .90
141 Chin-Feng Chen Wood 10.00 3.00
142 Hee Seop Choi Wood 5.00 1.50
143 Lance Niekro Wood 5.00 1.50
144 Mark Teixeira Wood 8.00 2.40
145 Nook Logan Wood RC 5.00 1.50
146 Terrmel Sledge Wood RC 8.00 2.40
147 Lew Ford Wood RC 8.00 2.40
148 Ian Ferguson Wood RC 5.00 1.50
149 Hid Matsui Wood/499 RC 20.00 6.00
150 Jose Contreras Wood RC 10.00 3.00

2003 Fleer Splendid Splinters Bat Chips

Randomly inserted into packs, this 19-card set is a partial parallel to the base set. These cards feature game-used bat chips of the featured player.

Nm-Mt Ex-Mt
16 Jason Giambi 10.00 3.00
19 Bernie Williams 10.00 3.00
26 Gary Sheffield 8.00 2.40
37 Jeff Bagwell 10.00 3.00
48 Manny Ramirez 8.00 2.40
61 Ryan Klesko 8.00 2.40
70 Adam Dunn 8.00 2.40
87 Sean Casey 8.00 2.40
92 Derek Jeter 25.00 7.50
93 Alex Rodriguez 15.00 4.50
95 Troy Glaus 10.00 3.00
96 Vladimir Guerrero 10.00 3.00
100 Mike Piazza 15.00 4.50
102 Sammy Sosa 15.00 4.50
104 Nomar Garciaparra 15.00 4.50
105 Barry Bonds 25.00 7.50
107 Jim Thome 10.00 3.00
108 Miguel Tejada 8.00 2.40
110 Alfonso Soriano 10.00 3.00

2003 Fleer Splendid Splinters Family Tree

Inserted at a stated rate of one in 12, these 10 cards feature two related major league players.

Nm-Mt Ex-Mt
COMPLETE SET (10) 25.00 7.50
1 Lance Niekro 2.00 .60
Phil Niekro
2 Bob Boone 2.00 .60
Bret Boone
3 Sandy Alomar Jr. 2.50 .75
Roberto Alomar
4 Ken Griffey Sr. 4.00 1.20
Ken Griffey Jr.
5 Jason Giambi 2.50 .75
Jeremy Giambi
6 Bobby Bonds 6.00 1.80
Barry Bonds
7 Tony Perez 2.00 .60
Eduardo Perez
8 Brian Giles 2.00 .60
Marcus Giles
9 Felipe Alou MG 2.00 .60
Moises Alou
10 Pedro Martinez 2.50 .75
Ramon Martinez

2003 Fleer Splendid Splinters Home Run Club

Inserted at a stated rate of one in 72, this 12-card set features some of the leading home run hitters.

Nm-Mt Ex-Mt
1 Barry Bonds 15.00 4.50
2 Jason Giambi 8.00 2.40
3 Sammy Sosa 10.00 3.00
4 Jim Thome 8.00 2.40
5 Lance Berkman 8.00 2.40
6 Alfonso Soriano 8.00 2.40
7 Vladimir Guerrero 8.00 2.40
8 Shawn Green 8.00 2.40
9 Troy Glaus 8.00 2.40
10 Pat Burrell 8.00 2.40
11 Alex Rodriguez 10.00 3.00
12 Mike Piazza 10.00 3.00

2003 Fleer Splendid Splinters Home Run Club Autographs

Randomly inserted in packs, this seven-card set features autographs from some leading players. As the player's signed in different ink, we have notated which color ink the player signed the card in as well as the stated print run for each card.

Nm-Mt Ex-Mt
BB1 Barry Bonds Black Ink/150 175.00 52.50
CR1 Cal Ripken Black Ink/300 120.00 36.00
CR2 Cal Ripken Blue Ink/150 150.00 45.00
CR3 Cal Ripken Red Ink/50 250.00 75.00
DJ1 Derek Jeter Black Ink/400 100.00 30.00
DJ2 Derek Jeter Blue Ink/250 120.00 36.00
DJ3 Derek Jeter Red Ink/50 150.00 45.00

2003 Fleer Splendid Splinters Home Run Club Memorabilia

Randomly inserted in packs, these cards feature not only leading home run hitters but also a game-used memorabilia piece attached to the card. Each of these cards were issued to a stated print run of 599 serial numbered sets.

Nm-Mt Ex-Mt
1 Barry Bonds Jsy 25.00 7.50
2 Jason Giambi Bat 10.00 3.00
3 Sammy Sosa Jsy 15.00 4.50
4 Jim Thome Bat 10.00 3.00
5 Lance Berkman Bat 8.00 2.40
6 Alfonso Soriano Jsy 10.00 3.00
7 Vladimir Guerrero Jsy 10.00 3.00
8 Shawn Green Jsy 8.00 2.40
9 Troy Glaus Bat 10.00 3.00
10 Pat Burrell Bat 8.00 2.40
11 Alex Rodriguez Jsy 15.00 4.50
12 Mike Piazza Jsy 15.00 4.50
13 Todd Helton Jsy 10.00 3.00
14 Rafael Palmeiro Jsy 10.00 3.00

2003 Fleer Splendid Splinters Knothole Gang

Issued at a stated rate of one in 24, this 15 card set features a look at players as if they were being looked through a knothole. Knotholes were popular ways for fans (primarily kids) to look into a ballfield for either free or a nominal cost before the expansion era.

Nm-Mt Ex-Mt
1 Derek Jeter 8.00 2.40
2 Barry Bonds 8.00 2.40
3 Sammy Sosa 5.00 1.50
4 Jason Giambi 3.00 .90
5 Alfonso Soriano 2.50 .75
6 Roger Clemens 6.00 1.80
7 Miguel Tejada 2.50 .75
8 Greg Maddux 5.00 1.50
9 Randy Johnson 3.00 .90
10 Chipper Jones 3.00 .90
11 Nomar Garciaparra 5.00 1.50
12 Alex Rodriguez 5.00 1.50
13 Ichiro Suzuki 5.00 1.50
14 Vladimir Guerrero 3.00 .90
15 Albert Pujols 6.00 1.80

2003 Fleer Splendid Splinters Knothole Gang Game Jersey

Issued at a stated rate of one in 40, this is a parallel to the Knothole Gang set. These cards feature game-used jersey swatches as well as the player's photo.

Nm-Mt Ex-Mt
AR Alex Rodriguez 15.00 4.50
AS Alfonso Soriano 10.00 3.00
BB Barry Bonds 20.00 6.00

CJ Chipper Jones 10.00 3.00
DJ Derek Jeter 20.00 6.00
GM Greg Maddux 10.00 3.00
LB Lance Berkman 8.00 2.40
MO Magglio Ordonez 8.00 2.40
MT Miguel Tejada 8.00 2.40
NG Nomar Garciaparra 15.00 4.50
RC Roger Clemens 15.00 4.50
RJ Randy Johnson 10.00 3.00
SS Sammy Sosa 15.00 4.50
TH Torii Hunter 8.00 2.40
VG Vladimir Guerrero 10.00 3.00

2003 Fleer Splendid Splinters Knothole Gang Patch

Randomly inserted in packs, this is a partial parallel to the Knothole Gang set. These cards feature game-used patch pieces and was issued to a stated print run of 99 serial numbered sets.

Nm-Mt Ex-Mt
AR Alex Rodriguez 50.00 15.00
AS Alfonso Soriano 40.00 12.00
BB Barry Bonds 80.00 24.00
CJ Chipper Jones 30.00 9.00
DJ Derek Jeter 80.00 24.00
GM Greg Maddux 50.00 15.00
MT Miguel Tejada 25.00 7.50
NG Nomar Garciaparra 50.00 15.00
RC Roger Clemens 40.00 12.00
RJ Randy Johnson 40.00 12.00
SS Sammy Sosa 40.00 12.00
VG Vladimir Guerrero 25.00 7.50

2003 Fleer Splendid Splinters Knothole Gang Triple Jersey

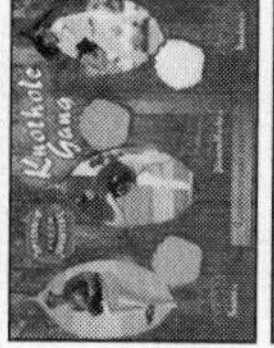

Randomly inserted in packs, these five cards feature not only three players but also game-used jersey swatches for each of the players on the card. These cards were issued to a stated print run of 29 serial numbered sets.

Nm-Mt Ex-Mt
BBCJMT Barry Bonds
Chipper Jones
Miguel Tejada
BBSSVG Barry Bonds
Sammy Sosa
Vladimir Guerrero
DJNGAR Derek Jeter
Nomar Garciaparra
Alex Rodriguez
DJRCAS Derek Jeter
Roger Clemens
Alfonso Soriano
GMRJRC Greg Maddux
Randy Johnson
Roger Clemens

2003 Fleer Splendid Splinters Wood

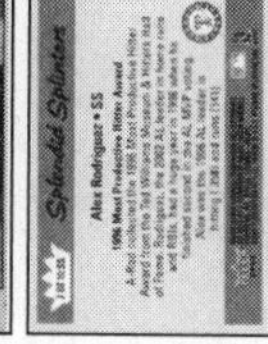

Inserted at a stated rate of one in 24, this 10 card set feature active hitters who have received an award from the Ted Williams Museum.

Nm-Mt Ex-Mt
COMPLETE SET (10) 50.00 15.00
1 Derek Jeter 12.00 3.60
2 Barry Bonds 12.00 3.60
3 Scott Rolen 5.00 1.50
4 Nomar Garciaparra 8.00 2.40
5 Sammy Sosa 8.00 2.40
6 Alfonso Soriano 5.00 1.50
7 Alex Rodriguez 8.00 2.40
8 Mike Piazza 8.00 2.40
9 Manny Ramirez 5.00 1.50
10 Jeff Bagwell 5.00 1.50

2003 Fleer Splendid Splinters Wood Game Bat

Randomly inserted in packs, this is a partial parallel to the Wood insert set. Each of these cards feature a game-used bat chip and were issued to a stated print run of 349 serial numbered sets.

Nm-Mt Ex-Mt
AR Alex Rodriguez 15.00 4.50
AS Alfonso Soriano 10.00 3.00
BB Barry Bonds 25.00 7.50

DJ Derek Jeter 25.00 7.50
JB Jeff Bagwell 10.00 3.00
MP Mike Piazza 15.00 4.50
MR Manny Ramirez 8.00 2.40
NG Nomar Garciaparra 15.00 4.50
SS Sammy Sosa 15.00 4.50

2003 Fleer Splendid Splinters Wood Game Bat Dual

Randomly inserted into packds, these four cards feature two leading hitters as well as game-used bat chips from the featured players. Each of these cards were issued to a stated print run of 99 serial numbered sets.

Nm-Mt Ex-Mt
ARNG Alex Rodriguez 60.00 18.00
Nomar Garciaparra
BBSS Barry Bonds 80.00 24.00
Sammy Sosa
DJAS Derek Jeter 80.00 24.00
Alfonso Soriano
MPJB Mike Piazza 40.00 12.00
Jeff Bagwell

1998 Fleer Tradition

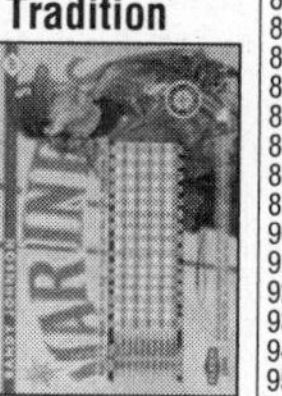

The 600-card 1998 Fleer set was issued in two series. Series one consists of 350 cards and Series two consists of 250 cards. The packs for either series consisted of 12 cards and had a SRP of $1.49. Card fronts feature borderless color action player photos with UV-coating and foil stamping. The backs display player information and career statistics. The set contains the following topical subsets: Smoke 'N Heat (301-310), Golden Memories (311-320), Tale of the Tape (321-340) and Unforgettable Moments (576-600). The Golden Memories (1:6 packs), Tale of the Tape (1:4 packs) and Unforgettable Moments (1:4 packs) cards are shortprinted. An Alex Rodriguez Promo card was distributed to dealers along with their 1998 Fleer series one order forms. The card can be readily distinguished by the "Promotional Sample" text running diagonally across both the front and back of the card. 50 Fleer Flashback Exchange cards were hand-numbered and randomly inserted into packs. Each of these cards could be exchanged for a framed, uncut press sheet from one of Fleer's baseball sets dating anywhere from 1981 to 1993.

Nm-Mt Ex-Mt
COMPLETE SET (600) 150.00 45.00
COMP. SERIES 1 (350) 90.00 27.00
COMP. SERIES 2 (250) 60.00 18.00
COMMON CARD (1-600) .30 .09
COMMON GM (311-320) .50 .15
COMMON TT (321-340) .60 .18
COMMON UM (576-600) .75 .23
1 Ken Griffey Jr. 1.25 .35
2 Derek Jeter 2.00 .60
3 Gerald Williams .30 .09
4 Carlos Delgado .30 .09
5 Nomar Garciaparra 1.25 .35
6 Gary Sheffield .30 .09
7 Jeff King .30 .09
8 Cal Ripken 2.50 .75
9 Matt Williams .30 .09
10 Chipper Jones .75 .23
11 Chuck Knoblauch .30 .09
12 Mark Grudzielanek .30 .09
13 Edgardo Alfonzo .30 .09
14 Andres Galarraga .30 .09
15 Tim Salmon .50 .15
16 Reggie Sanders .30 .09
17 Tony Clark .30 .09
18 Jason Kendall .30 .09
19 Juan Gonzalez .75 .23
20 Ben Grieve .30 .09
21 Roger Clemens 1.50 .45
22 Raul Mondesi .30 .09
23 Robin Ventura .30 .09
24 Derrek Lee .30 .09
25 Mark McGwire 2.00 .60
26 Luis Gonzalez .30 .09
27 Kevin Brown .50 .15
28 Kirk Rueter .30 .09
29 Bobby Estalella .30 .09
30 Shawn Green .30 .09
31 Greg Maddux 1.25 .35
32 Jorge Velandia .30 .09
33 Larry Walker .50 .15
34 Joey Cora .30 .09
35 Frank Thomas .75 .23
36 Curtis King RC .30 .09
37 Aaron Boone .30 .09
38 Curt Schilling .50 .15
39 Bruce Aven .30 .09
40 Ben McDonald .30 .09
41 Andy Ashby .30 .09
42 Jason McDonald .30 .09
43 Eric Davis .30 .09
44 Mark Grace .50 .15
45 Pedro Martinez .75 .23
46 Lou Collier .30 .09
47 Chan Ho Park .30 .09
48 Shane Halter .30 .09
49 Brian Hunter .30 .09
50 Jeff Bagwell .50 .15
51 Bernie Williams .50 .15
52 J.T. Snow .30 .09
53 Todd Greene .30 .09
54 Shannon Stewart .30 .09
55 Darren Bragg .30 .09
56 Fernando Tatis .30 .09
57 Darryl Kile .30 .09
58 Chris Stynes .30 .09
59 Javier Valentin .30 .09
60 Brian McRae .30 .09
61 Tom Evans .30 .09
62 Randall Simon .30 .09
63 Darrin Fletcher .30 .09
64 Jaret Wright .30 .09
65 Luis Ordaz .30 .09
66 Jose Canseco .75 .23
67 Edgar Renteria .30 .09
68 Jay Buhner .30 .09
69 Paul Konerko .30 .09
70 Adrian Brown .30 .09
71 Chris Carpenter .30 .09
72 Mike Lieberthal .30 .09
73 Dean Palmer .30 .09
74 Jorge Fabregas .30 .09
75 Stan Javier .30 .09
76 Damion Easley .30 .09
77 David Cone .30 .09
78 Aaron Sele .30 .09
79 Antonio Alfonseca .30 .09
80 Bobby Jones .30 .09
81 David Justice .30 .09
82 Jeffrey Hammonds .30 .09
83 Doug Glanville .30 .09
84 Jason Dickson .30 .09
85 Brad Radke .30 .09
86 David Segui .30 .09
87 Greg Vaughn .30 .09
88 Mike Cather RC .30 .09
89 Alex Fernandez .30 .09
90 Billy Taylor .30 .09
91 Jason Schmidt .30 .09
92 Mike DeJean RC .30 .09
93 Domingo Cedeno .30 .09
94 Jeff Cirillo .30 .09
95 Manny Aybar RC .30 .09
96 Jaime Navarro .30 .09
97 Dennis Reyes .30 .09
98 Barry Larkin .75 .23
99 Troy O'Leary .30 .09
100 Alex Rodriguez 1.25 .35
101 Pat Hentgen .30 .09
102 Bubba Trammell .30 .09
103 Glendon Rusch .30 .09
104 Kenny Lofton .30 .09
105 Craig Biggio .50 .15
106 Kelvim Escobar .30 .09
107 Mark Kotsay .30 .09
108 Rondell White .30 .09
109 Darren Oliver .30 .09
110 Jim Thome .75 .23
111 Rich Becker .30 .09
112 Chad Curtis .30 .09
113 Dave Hollins .30 .09
114 Bill Mueller .30 .09
115 Antone Williamson .30 .09
116 Tony Womack .30 .09
117 Randy Myers .30 .09
118 Rico Brogna .30 .09
119 Pat Watkins .30 .09
120 Eli Marrero .30 .09
121 Jay Bell .30 .09
122 Kevin Tapani .30 .09
123 Todd Erdos RC .30 .09
124 Neifi Perez .30 .09
125 Todd Hundley .30 .09
126 Jeff Abbott .30 .09
127 Todd Zeile .30 .09
128 Travis Fryman .30 .09
129 Sandy Alomar Jr. .30 .09
130 Fred McGriff .50 .15
131 Richard Hidalgo .30 .09
132 Scott Spiezio .30 .09
133 John Valentin .30 .09
134 Quilvio Veras .30 .09
135 Mike Lansing .30 .09
136 Paul Molitor .50 .15
137 Randy Johnson .75 .23
138 Harold Baines .30 .09
139 Doug Jones .30 .09
140 Abraham Nunez .30 .09
141 Alan Benes .30 .09
142 Matt Perisho .30 .09
143 Chris Clemons .30 .09
144 Andy Pettitte .50 .15
145 Jason Giambi .75 .23
146 Moises Alou .30 .09
147 Chad Fox RC .30 .09
148 Felix Martinez .30 .09
149 Carlos Mendoza RC .30 .09
150 Scott Rolen .50 .15
151 Jose Cabrera RC .30 .09
152 Justin Thompson .30 .09
153 Ellis Burks .30 .09
154 Pokey Reese .30 .09
155 Bartolo Colon .30 .09
156 Ray Durham .30 .09
157 Ugueth Urbina .30 .09
158 Tom Goodwin .30 .09
159 Dave Dellucci RC .30 .09
160 Rod Beck .30 .09
161 Ramon Martinez .30 .09
162 Joe Carter .30 .09
163 Kevin Orie .30 .09
164 Trevor Hoffman .30 .09
165 Emil Brown .30 .09
166 Robb Nen .30 .09
167 Paul O'Neill .50 .15
168 Ryan Long .30 .09
169 Ray Lankford .30 .09
170 Ivan Rodriguez .75 .23
171 Rick Aguilera .30 .09
172 Deivi Cruz .30 .09
173 Ricky Bottalico .30 .09
174 Garret Anderson .30 .09
175 Jose Vizcaino .30 .09
176 Omar Vizquel .30 .09
177 Jeff Blauser .30 .09
178 Orlando Cabrera .30 .09
179 Russ Johnson .30 .09
180 Matt Stairs .30 .09
181 Will Cunnane .30 .09
182 Adam Riggs .30 .09
183 Matt Morris .30 .09
184 Mario Valdez .30 .09
185 Larry Sutton .30 .09
186 Marc Pisciotta RC .30 .09
187 Dan Wilson .30 .09
188 John Franco .30 .09
189 Darren Daulton .30 .09
190 Todd Helton .50 .15
191 Brady Anderson .30 .09
192 Ricardo Rincon .30 .09
193 Kevin Stocker .30 .09
194 Jose Valentin .30 .09
195 Ed Sprague .30 .09
196 Ryan McGuire .30 .09
197 Scott Eyre .30 .09
198 Steve Finley .30 .09
199 T.J. Mathews .30 .09
200 Mike Piazza 1.25 .35
201 Mark Wohlers .30 .09
202 Brian Giles .30 .09
203 Eduardo Perez .30 .09
204 Shigetoshi Hasegawa .30 .09
205 Mariano Rivera .50 .15
206 Jose Rosado .30 .09
207 Michael Coleman .30 .09
208 James Baldwin .30 .09
209 Russ Davis .30 .09
210 Billy Wagner .30 .09
211 Sammy Sosa 1.25 .35
212 Frank Catalanotto RC .50 .15
213 Delino DeShields .30 .09
214 John Olerud .30 .09
215 Heath Murray .30 .09
216 Jose Vidro .30 .09
217 Jim Edmonds .30 .09
218 Shawon Dunston .30 .09
219 Homer Bush .30 .09
220 Midre Cummings .30 .09
221 Tony Saunders .30 .09
222 Jeromy Burnitz .30 .09
223 Enrique Wilson .30 .09
224 Chili Davis .30 .09
225 Jerry DiPoto .30 .09
226 Dante Powell .30 .09
227 Javier Lopez .30 .09
228 Kevin Polcovich .30 .09
229 Deion Sanders .50 .15
230 Jimmy Key .30 .09
231 Rusty Greer .30 .09
232 Reggie Jefferson .30 .09
233 Ron Coomer .30 .09
234 Bobby Higginson .30 .09
235 Magglio Ordonez RC 2.00 .60
236 Miguel Tejada .50 .15
237 Rick Gorecki .30 .09
238 Charles Johnson .30 .09
239 Lance Johnson .30 .09
240 Derek Bell .30 .09
241 Will Clark .75 .23
242 Brady Raggio .30 .09
243 Orel Hershiser .30 .09
244 Vladimir Guerrero .75 .23
245 John LeRoy .30 .09
246 Shawn Estes .30 .09
247 Brett Tomko .30 .09
248 Dave Nilsson .30 .09
249 Edgar Martinez .50 .15
250 Tony Gwynn 1.00 .30
251 Mark Bellhorn .30 .09
252 Jed Hansen .30 .09
253 Butch Huskey .30 .09
254 Eric Young .30 .09
255 Vinny Castilla .30 .09
256 Hideki Irabu .30 .09
257 Mike Cameron .30 .09
258 Juan Encarnacion .30 .09
259 Brian Rose .30 .09
260 Brad Ausmus .30 .09
261 Dan Serafini .30 .09
262 Willie Greene .30 .09
263 Troy Percival .30 .09
264 Jeff Wallace .30 .09
265 Richie Sexson .30 .09
266 Rafael Palmeiro .50 .15
267 Brad Fullmer .30 .09
268 Jeremi Gonzalez .30 .09
269 Rob Stanifer RC .30 .09
270 Mickey Morandini .30 .09
271 Andruw Jones .30 .09
272 Royce Clayton .30 .09
273 T.Kashiwada RC .30 .09
274 Steve Woodard .30 .09
275 Jose Cruz Jr. .30 .09
276 Keith Foulke .30 .09
277 Brad Rigby .30 .09
278 Tino Martinez .50 .15
279 Todd Jones .30 .09
280 John Wetteland .30 .09
281 Alex Gonzalez .30 .09
282 Ken Cloude .30 .09
283 Jose Guillen .30 .09
284 Danny Clyburn .30 .09
285 David Ortiz .30 .09
286 John Thomson .30 .09
287 Kevin Appier .30 .09
288 Ismael Valdes .30 .09
289 Gary DiSarcina .30 .09
290 Todd Dunwoody .30 .09
291 Wally Joyner .30 .09
292 Charles Nagy .30 .09
293 Jeff Shaw .30 .09
294 Kevin Millwood RC 1.25 .35
295 Rigo Beltran RC .30 .09
296 Jeff Frye .30 .09
297 Oscar Henriquez .30 .09
298 Mike Thurman .30 .09
299 Garrett Stephenson .30 .09
300 Barry Bonds 2.00 .60
301 Roger Clemens SH .75 .23
302 David Cone SH .30 .09
303 Hideki Irabu SH .30 .09
304 Randy Johnson SH .50 .15
305 Greg Maddux SH .75 .23
306 Pedro Martinez SH .50 .15
307 Mike Mussina SH .50 .15
308 Andy Pettitte SH .30 .09
309 Curt Schilling SH .30 .09
310 John Smoltz SH .30 .09
311 Roger Clemens GM 2.50 .75
312 Jose Cruz JR. GM .50 .15
313 N.Garciaparra GM 2.00 .60
314 Ken Griffey Jr. GM 2.00 .60
315 Tony Gwynn GM 1.50 .45
316 Hideki Irabu GM .50 .15
317 Randy Johnson GM 1.25 .35
318 Mark McGwire GM 3.00 .90
319 Curt Schilling GM .75 .23
320 Larry Walker GM .75 .23
321 Jeff Bagwell TT 1.00 .30
322 Albert Belle TT .60 .18
323 Barry Bonds TT 4.00 1.20
324 Jay Buhner TT .60 .18
325 Tony Clark TT .60 .18
326 Jose Cruz Jr. TT .60 .18
327 Andres Galarraga TT .60 .18
328 Juan Gonzalez TT 1.50 .45
329 Ken Griffey Jr. TT 2.50 .75
330 Andruw Jones TT .60 .18
331 Tino Martinez TT 1.00 .30
332 Mark McGwire TT 4.00 1.20
333 Rafael Palmeiro TT 1.00 .30
334 Mike Piazza TT 2.50 .75
335 Manny Ramirez TT .60 .18
336 Alex Rodriguez TT 2.50 .75
337 Frank Thomas TT 1.50 .45
338 Jim Thome TT 1.50 .45
339 Mo Vaughn TT .60 .18
340 Larry Walker TT 1.00 .30
341 Jose Cruz Jr. CL .30 .09
342 Ken Griffey Jr. CL .75 .23
343 Derek Jeter CL 1.00 .30
344 Andruw Jones CL .30 .09
345 Chipper Jones CL .50 .15
346 Greg Maddux CL .75 .23
347 Mike Piazza CL .75 .23
348 Cal Ripken CL 1.25 .35
349 Alex Rodriguez CL .75 .23
350 Frank Thomas CL .50 .15
351 Mo Vaughn .30 .09
352 Andres Galarraga .30 .09
353 Roberto Alomar .75 .23
354 Darin Erstad .30 .09
355 Albert Belle .30 .09
356 Matt Williams .30 .09
357 Darryl Kile .30 .09
358 Kenny Lofton .30 .09
359 Orel Hershiser .30 .09
360 Bob Abreu .30 .09
361 Chris Widger .30 .09
362 Glenallen Hill .30 .09
363 Chili Davis .30 .09
364 Kevin Brown .50 .15
365 Marquis Grissom .30 .09
366 Livan Hernandez .30 .09
367 Moises Alou .30 .09
368 Matt Lawton .30 .09
369 Rey Ordonez .30 .09
370 Kenny Rogers .30 .09
371 Lee Stevens .30 .09
372 Wade Boggs .50 .15
373 Luis Gonzalez .30 .09
374 Jeff Conine .30 .09
375 Esteban Loaiza .30 .09
376 Jose Canseco .75 .23
377 Henry Rodriguez .30 .09
378 Dave Burba .30 .09
379 Todd Hollandsworth .30 .09
380 Ron Gant .30 .09
381 Pedro Martinez .75 .23
382 Ryan Klesko .30 .09
383 Derrek Lee .30 .09
384 Doug Glanville .30 .09
385 David Wells .30 .09
386 Ken Caminiti .30 .09
387 Damon Hollins .30 .09
388 Manny Ramirez .30 .09
389 Mike Mussina .75 .23
390 Jay Bell .30 .09
391 Mike Piazza 1.25 .35
392 Mike Lansing .30 .09
393 Mike Hampton .30 .09
394 Geoff Jenkins .30 .09
395 Jimmy Haynes .30 .09
396 Scott Servais .30 .09
397 Kent Mercker .30 .09
398 Jeff Kent .30 .09
399 Kevin Elster .30 .09
400 Masato Yoshii RC .50 .15
401 Jose Vizcaino .30 .09
402 Javier Martinez RC .30 .09
403 David Segui .30 .09
404 Tony Saunders .30 .09
405 Karim Garcia .30 .09
406 Armando Benitez .30 .09
407 Joe Randa .30 .09
408 Vic Darensbourg .30 .09
409 Sean Casey .30 .09
410 Eric Milton .30 .09
411 Trey Moore .30 .09
412 Mike Stanley .30 .09
413 Tom Gordon .30 .09
414 Hal Morris .30 .09
415 Braden Looper .30 .09
416 Mike Kelly .30 .09
417 John Smoltz .50 .15
418 Roger Cedeno .30 .09
419 Al Leiter .30 .09
420 Chuck Knoblauch .30 .09
421 Felix Rodriguez .30 .09

422 Bip Roberts .30 .09
423 Ken Hill .30 .09
424 Jermaine Allensworth .30 .09
425 Esteban Yan RC .30 .09
426 Scott Karl .30 .09
427 Sean Berry .30 .09
428 Rafael Medina .30 .09
429 Javier Vazquez .30 .09
430 Rickey Henderson .75 .23
431 Adam Butler .30 .09
432 Todd Stottlemyre .30 .09
433 Yamil Benitez .30 .09
434 Sterling Hitchcock .30 .09
435 Paul Sorrento .30 .09
436 Bobby Ayala .30 .09
437 Tim Raines .30 .09
438 Chris Hoiles .30 .09
439 Rod Beck .30 .09
440 Donnie Sadler .30 .09
441 Charles Johnson .30 .09
442 Russ Ortiz .30 .09
443 Pedro Astacio .30 .09
444 Wilson Alvarez .30 .09
445 Mike Blowers .30 .09
446 Todd Zeile .30 .09
447 Mel Rojas .30 .09
448 F.P. Santangelo .30 .09
449 Dmitri Young .30 .09
450 Brian Anderson .30 .09
451 Cecil Fielder .30 .09
452 Roberto Hernandez .30 .09
453 Todd Walker .30 .09
454 Tyler Green .30 .09
455 Jorge Posada .50 .15
456 Geronimo Berroa .30 .09
457 Jose Silva .30 .09
458 Bobby Bonilla .30 .09
459 Walt Weiss .30 .09
460 Darren Dreifort .30 .09
461 B.J. Surhoff .30 .09
462 Quinton McCracken .30 .09
463 Derek Lowe .30 .09
464 Jorge Fabregas .30 .09
465 Joey Hamilton .30 .09
466 Brian Jordan .30 .09
467 Allen Watson .30 .09
468 John Jaha .30 .09
469 Heathcliff Slocumb .30 .09
470 Gregg Jefferies .30 .09
471 Scott Brosius .30 .09
472 Chad Ogea .30 .09
473 A.J. Hinch .30 .09
474 Bobby Smith .30 .09
475 Brian Moehler .30 .09
476 DaRond Stovall .30 .09
477 Kevin Young .30 .09
478 Jeff Suppan .30 .09
479 Marty Cordova .30 .09
480 John Halama RC .30 .09
481 Bubba Trammell .30 .09
482 Mike Caruso .30 .09
483 Eric Karros .30 .09
484 Jamey Wright .30 .09
485 Mike Sweeney .30 .09
486 Aaron Sele .30 .09
487 Cliff Floyd .30 .09
488 Jeff Brantley .30 .09
489 Jim Leyritz .30 .09
490 Denny Neagle .30 .09
491 Travis Fryman .30 .09
492 Carlos Baerga .30 .09
493 Eddie Taubensee .30 .09
494 Darryl Strawberry .50 .15
495 Brian Johnson .30 .09
496 Randy Myers .30 .09
497 Jeff Blauser .30 .09
498 Jason Wood .30 .09
499 Rolando Arrojo RC .30 .09
500 Johnny Damon .30 .09
501 Jose Mercedes .30 .09
502 Tony Batista .30 .09
503 Mike Piazza Mets 1.25 .35
504 Hideo Nomo .75 .23
505 Chris Gomez .30 .09
506 Jesus Sanchez RC .30 .09
507 Al Martin .30 .09
508 Brian Edmondson .30 .09
509 Joe Girardi .30 .09
510 Shayne Bennett .30 .09
511 Joe Carter .30 .09
512 Dave Mlicki .30 .09
513 Rich Butler RC .30 .09
514 Dennis Eckersley .30 .09
515 Travis Lee .30 .09
516 John Mabry .30 .09
517 Jose Mesa .30 .09
518 Phil Nevin .30 .09
519 Raul Casanova .30 .09
520 Mike Fetters .30 .09
521 Gary Sheffield .30 .09
522 Terry Steinbach .30 .09
523 Steve Trachsel .30 .09
524 Josh Booty .30 .09
525 Darryl Hamilton .30 .09
526 Mark McLemore .30 .09
527 Kevin Stocker .30 .09
528 Bret Boone .30 .09
529 Shane Andrews .30 .09
530 Robb Nen .30 .09
531 Carl Everett .30 .09
532 LaTroy Hawkins .30 .09
533 Fernando Vina .30 .09
534 Michael Tucker .30 .09
535 Mark Langston .30 .09
536 Mickey Mantle 5.00 1.50
537 Bernard Gilkey .30 .09
538 Francisco Cordova .30 .09
539 Mike Bordick .30 .09
540 Fred McGriff .50 .15
541 Cliff Politte .30 .09
542 Jason Varitek .30 .09
543 Shawon Dunston .30 .09
544 Brian Meadows .30 .09
545 Pat Meares .30 .09
546 Carlos Perez .30 .09
547 Desi Relaford .30 .09
548 Antonio Osuna .30 .09
549 Devon White .30 .09
550 Sean Runyan .30 .09
551 Mickey Morandini .30 .09
552 Dave Martinez .30 .09
553 Jeff Fassero .30 .09
554 Ryan Jackson RC .30 .09
555 Stan Javier .30 .09
556 Jaime Navarro .30 .09
557 Jose Offerman .30 .09
558 Mike Lowell RC 1.50 .45
559 Darrin Fletcher .30 .09
560 Mark Lewis .30 .09
561 Dante Bichette .30 .09
562 Chuck Finley .30 .09
563 Kerry Wood .75 .23
564 Andy Benes .30 .09
565 Freddy Garcia .30 .09
566 Tom Glavine .50 .15
567 Jon Nunnally .30 .09
568 Miguel Cairo .30 .09
569 Shane Reynolds .30 .09
570 Roberto Kelly .30 .09
571 Jose Cruz Jr. CL .30 .09
572 Ken Griffey Jr. CL .75 .23
573 Mark McGwire CL 1.00 .30
574 Cal Ripken CL 1.25 .35
575 Frank Thomas CL .50 .15
576 Jeff Bagwell UM 1.25 .35
577 Barry Bonds UM 5.00 1.50
578 Tony Clark UM .75 .23
579 Roger Clemens UM 4.00 1.20
580 Jose Cruz Jr. UM .75 .23
581 N.Garciaparra UM 3.00 .90
582 Juan Gonzalez UM 2.00 .60
583 Ben Grieve UM .75 .23
584 Ken Griffey Jr. UM 3.00 .90
585 Tony Gwynn UM 2.50 .75
586 Derek Jeter UM 5.00 1.50
587 Randy Johnson UM 2.00 .60
588 Chipper Jones UM 2.00 .60
589 Greg Maddux UM 3.00 .90
590 Mark McGwire UM 5.00 1.50
591 Paul Molitor UM 1.25 .35
592 Andy Pettitte UM 1.25 .35
593 Cal Ripken UM 6.00 1.80
594 Alex Rodriguez UM 3.00 .90
595 Scott Rolen UM 1.25 .35
596 Curt Schilling UM 1.25 .35
597 Frank Thomas UM 2.00 .60
598 Jim Thome UM 2.00 .60
599 Larry Walker UM 1.25 .35
600 Bernie Williams UM 1.25 .35
P100 A.Rodriguez Promo 1.50 .45

1998 Fleer Tradition Vintage '63

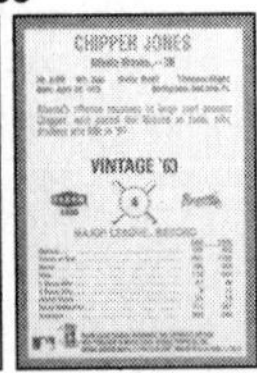

Randomly inserted one in every first and second series hobby pack, this 128-card set commemorates the 35th anniversary of the Fleer set and features color photos of top players printed in the 1963 Fleer Baseball card design.

Nm-Mt Ex-Mt
1 Jason Dickson .40 .12
2 Tim Salmon .60 .18
3 Andruw Jones .40 .12
4 Chipper Jones 1.00 .30
5 Kenny Lofton .40 .12
6 Greg Maddux 1.50 .45
7 Rafael Palmeiro .60 .18
8 Cal Ripken 3.00 .90
9 Nomar Garciaparra 1.50 .45
10 Mark Grace .60 .18
11 Sammy Sosa 1.50 .45
12 Frank Thomas 1.00 .30
13 Deion Sanders .60 .18
14 Sandy Alomar Jr. .40 .12
15 David Justice .40 .12
16 Jim Thome 1.00 .30
17 Matt Williams .40 .12
18 Jaret Wright .40 .12
19 Vinny Castilla .40 .12
20 Andres Galarraga .40 .12
21 Todd Helton .60 .18
22 Larry Walker .60 .18
23 Tony Clark .40 .12
24 Moises Alou .40 .12
25 Kevin Brown .60 .18
26 Charles Johnson .40 .12
27 Edgar Renteria .40 .12
28 Gary Sheffield .40 .12
29 Jeff Bagwell .60 .18
30 Craig Biggio .60 .18
31 Raul Mondesi .40 .12
32 Mike Piazza 1.50 .45
33 Chuck Knoblauch .40 .12
34 Paul Molitor .60 .18
35 Vladimir Guerrero 1.00 .30
36 Pedro Martinez 1.00 .30
37 Todd Hundley .40 .12
38 Derek Jeter 2.50 .75
39 Tino Martinez .60 .18
40 Paul O'Neill .60 .18
41 Andy Pettitte .60 .18
42 Mariano Rivera .60 .18
43 Bernie Williams .60 .18
44 Ben Grieve .40 .12
45 Scott Rolen .60 .18
46 Curt Schilling .60 .18
47 Jason Kendall .40 .12
48 Tony Womack .40 .12
49 Ray Lankford .40 .12
50 Mark McGwire 2.50 .75
51 Matt Morris .40 .12
52 Tony Gwynn 1.25 .35
53 Barry Bonds 2.50 .75
54 Jay Buhner .40 .12
55 Ken Griffey Jr. 1.50 .45
56 Randy Johnson 1.00 .30
57 Edgar Martinez .60 .18
58 Alex Rodriguez 1.50 .45
59 Juan Gonzalez 1.00 .30
60 Rusty Greer .40 .12
61 Ivan Rodriguez 1.00 .30
62 Roger Clemens 2.00 .60
63 Jose Cruz Jr. .40 .12
64 Darin Erstad .40 .12
65 Jay Bell .40 .12
66 Andy Benes .40 .12
67 Mickey Mantle 6.00 1.80
68 Karim Garcia .40 .12
69 Travis Lee .40 .12
70 Matt Williams .40 .12
71 Andres Galarraga .40 .12
72 Tom Glavine .60 .18
73 Ryan Klesko .40 .12
74 Denny Neagle .40 .12
75 John Smoltz .60 .18
76 Roberto Alomar 1.00 .30
77 Joe Carter .40 .12
78 Mike Mussina 1.00 .30
79 B.J. Surhoff .40 .12
80 Dennis Eckersley .40 .12
81 Pedro Martinez 1.00 .30
82 Mo Vaughn .40 .12
83 Henry Rodriguez .40 .12
84 Kerry Wood 1.00 .30
85 Albert Belle .40 .12
86 Sean Casey .40 .12
87 Travis Fryman .40 .12
88 Kenny Lofton .40 .12
89 Darryl Kile .40 .12
90 Mike Lansing .40 .12
91 Bobby Bonilla .40 .12
92 Cliff Floyd .40 .12
93 Livan Hernandez .40 .12
94 Derrek Lee .40 .12
95 Moises Alou .40 .12
96 Shane Reynolds .40 .12
97 Mike Piazza 1.50 .45
98 Johnny Damon .40 .12
99 Eric Karros .40 .12
100 Hideo Nomo 1.00 .30
101 Marquis Grissom .40 .12
102 Matt Lawton .40 .12
103 Todd Walker .40 .12
104 Gary Sheffield .40 .12
105 Bernard Gilkey .40 .12
106 Rey Ordonez .40 .12
107 Chili Davis .40 .12
108 Chuck Knoblauch .40 .12
109 Charles Johnson .40 .12
110 Rickey Henderson 1.00 .30
111 Bob Abreu .40 .12
112 Doug Glanville .40 .12
113 Gregg Jefferies .40 .12
114 Al Martin .40 .12
115 Kevin Young .40 .12
116 Ron Gant .40 .12
117 Kevin Brown .60 .18
118 Ken Caminiti .40 .12
119 Joey Hamilton .40 .12
120 Jeff Kent .40 .12
121 Wade Boggs .60 .18
122 Quinton McCracken .40 .12
123 Fred McGriff .60 .18
124 Paul Sorrento .40 .12
125 Jose Canseco 1.00 .30
126 Randy Myers .40 .12
NNO Checklist 1 .40 .12
NNO Checklist 2 .40 .12

1998 Fleer Tradition Vintage '63 Classic

Randomly inserted in first and second series hobby packs, this 128-card set is parallel to the regular Vintage '63. Only 63 of these sets were produced and all cards are serial numbered in gold foil on back. All Cards are Numbered with a "C" suffix.

Nm-Mt Ex-Mt
*STARS: 12.5X TO 30X VINTAGE '63 .

1998 Fleer Tradition Decade of Excellence

Randomly inserted in hobby packs only at the rate of one in 72, this 12-card set features 1988 season photos in Fleer's 1988 card design of current players who have been in playing major league baseball for ten years or more.

Nm-Mt Ex-Mt
COMPLETE SET (12) 120.00 36.00
*RARE TRAD: 2X TO 5X BASIC DECADES
RARE TRAD. STATED ODDS 1:720 HOBBY
1 Roberto Alomar 6.00 1.80
2 Barry Bonds 15.00 4.50
3 Roger Clemens 12.00 3.60
4 David Cone 2.50 .75
5 Andres Galarraga 2.50 .75
6 Mark Grace 4.00 1.20
7 Tony Gwynn 8.00 2.40
8 Randy Johnson 6.00 1.80
9 Greg Maddux 10.00 3.00
10 Mark McGwire 15.00 4.50
11 Paul O'Neill 4.00 1.20
12 Cal Ripken 20.00 6.00

1998 Fleer Tradition Diamond Standouts

Randomly inserted in packs at the rate of one in 12, this 20-card set features color photos of great players on a diamond design silver foil background. The backs display detailed player information.

Nm-Mt Ex-Mt
COMPLETE SET (20) 50.00 15.00
1 Jeff Bagwell 1.25 .35
2 Barry Bonds 5.00 1.50
3 Roger Clemens 4.00 1.20
4 Jose Cruz Jr. .75 .23
5 Andres Galarraga .75 .23
6 Nomar Garciaparra 3.00 .90
7 Juan Gonzalez 2.00 .60
8 Ken Griffey Jr. 3.00 .90
9 Derek Jeter 5.00 1.50
10 Randy Johnson 2.00 .60
11 Chipper Jones 2.00 .60
12 Kenny Lofton .75 .23
13 Greg Maddux 3.00 .90
14 Pedro Martinez 2.00 .60
15 Mark McGwire 5.00 1.50
16 Mike Piazza 3.00 .90
17 Alex Rodriguez 3.00 .90
18 Curt Schilling 1.25 .35
19 Frank Thomas 2.00 .60
20 Larry Walker 1.25 .35

1998 Fleer Tradition Diamond Tribute

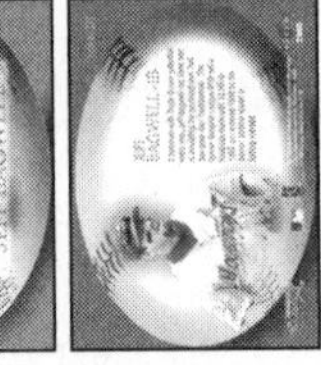

Randomly inserted in packs at a rate of one in 300, this 10-card insert set features color action photos printed on leatherette laminated stock with silver holofoil stamping.

Nm-Mt Ex-Mt
COMPLETE SET (10) 200.00 60.00
DT1 Jeff Bagwell 10.00 3.00
DT2 Roger Clemens 30.00 9.00
DT3 Nomar Garciaparra 25.00 7.50
DT4 Juan Gonzalez 15.00 4.50
DT5 Ken Griffey Jr. 25.00 7.50
DT6 Mark McGwire 40.00 12.00
DT7 Mike Piazza 25.00 7.50
DT8 Cal Ripken 50.00 15.00
DT9 Alex Rodriguez 25.00 7.50
DT10 Frank Thomas 15.00 4.50

1998 Fleer Tradition In The Clutch

Randomly inserted in packs at a rate of one in 20, this 15-card insert offers color action photos on a green holofoil background.

Nm-Mt Ex-Mt
COMPLETE SET (15) 80.00 24.00
IC1 Jeff Bagwell 2.50 .75
IC2 Barry Bonds 10.00 3.00
IC3 Roger Clemens 8.00 2.40
IC4 Jose Cruz Jr. 1.50 .45
IC5 Nomar Garciaparra 6.00 1.80
IC6 Juan Gonzalez 4.00 1.20
IC7 Ken Griffey Jr. 6.00 1.80
IC8 Tony Gwynn 5.00 1.50
IC9 Derek Jeter 10.00 3.00
IC10 Chipper Jones 4.00 1.20
IC11 Greg Maddux 6.00 1.80
IC12 Mark McGwire 10.00 3.00
IC13 Mike Piazza 6.00 1.80
IC14 Frank Thomas 4.00 1.20
IC15 Larry Walker 2.50 .75

1998 Fleer Tradition Lumber Company

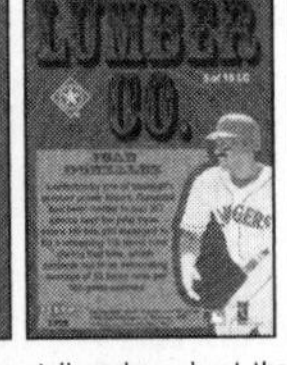

Randomly inserted in retail packs only at the rate of one in 36, this 15-card set features color photos of high-powered offensive players.

Nm-Mt Ex-Mt
COMPLETE SET (15) 120.00 36.00
1 Jeff Bagwell 4.00 1.20
2 Barry Bonds 15.00 4.50
3 Jose Cruz Jr. 2.50 .75
4 Nomar Garciaparra 10.00 3.00
5 Juan Gonzalez 6.00 1.80
6 Ken Griffey Jr. 10.00 3.00
7 Tony Gwynn 8.00 2.40
8 Chipper Jones 6.00 1.80
9 Tino Martinez 4.00 1.20
10 Mark McGwire 15.00 4.50
11 Mike Piazza 10.00 3.00
12 Cal Ripken 20.00 6.00
13 Alex Rodriguez 10.00 3.00
14 Frank Thomas 6.00 1.80
15 Larry Walker 4.00 1.20

1998 Fleer Tradition Mickey Mantle Monumental Moments

This 10 card set features highlights from Mickey Mantle's long and illustrious career with the New York Yankees. Mantle, who hit 536 Homers in his career and 18 more in the World Series is honored with these cards which were inserted one every 68 packs.

Nm-Mt Ex-Mt
COMPLETE SET (10) 150.00 45.00
COMMON CARD (1-10) 25.00 7.50
COMMON GOLD (1-10) 100.00 30.00
GOLD: RANDOM INSERTS IN SER.2 PACKS
GOLD PRINT RUN 51 SERIAL #'d SETS

1998 Fleer Tradition Power Game

Randomly inserted in packs at the rate of one in 36, this 20-card set features color action player photos of great pitchers and hitters highlighted with purple metallic foil and glossy UV coating. The backs display player statistics.

Nm-Mt Ex-Mt
COMPLETE SET (20) 120.00 36.00
1 Jeff Bagwell 4.00 1.20
2 Albert Belle 2.50 .75
3 Barry Bonds 15.00 4.50
4 Tony Clark 2.50 .75
5 Roger Clemens 12.00 3.60
6 Jose Cruz Jr. 2.50 .75
7 Andres Galarraga 2.50 .75
8 Nomar Garciaparra 10.00 3.00
9 Juan Gonzalez 6.00 1.80
10 Ken Griffey Jr. 10.00 3.00
11 Randy Johnson 6.00 1.80
12 Greg Maddux 10.00 3.00
13 Pedro Martinez 6.00 1.80
14 Tino Martinez 4.00 1.20
15 Mark McGwire 15.00 4.50
16 Mike Piazza 10.00 3.00
17 Curt Schilling 4.00 1.20
18 Frank Thomas 6.00 1.80
19 Jim Thome 6.00 1.80
20 Larry Walker 4.00 1.20

1998 Fleer Tradition Promising Forecast

Randomly inserted in packs at a rate of one in 12, this 20-card insert features color action photos on cards with flood aqueous coating, silver foil stamping and a white glow around the player's UV coated image.

Nm-Mt Ex-Mt
COMPLETE SET (20) 15.00 4.50
PF1 Rolando Arrojo 1.00 .30
PF2 Sean Casey 1.00 .30
PF3 Brad Fullmer 1.00 .30
PF4 Karim Garcia 1.00 .30
PF5 Ben Grieve 1.00 .30
PF6 Todd Helton 1.50 .45
PF7 Richard Hidalgo 1.00 .30
PF8 A.J. Hinch 1.00 .30
PF9 Paul Konerko 1.00 .30
PF10 Mark Kotsay 1.00 .30
PF11 Derrek Lee 1.00 .30
PF12 Travis Lee 1.00 .30
PF13 Eric Milton 1.00 .30
PF14 Magglio Ordonez 3.00 .90
PF15 David Ortiz 1.00 .30
PF16 Brian Rose 1.00 .30
PF17 Miguel Tejada 1.50 .45
PF18 Jason Varitek 1.00 .30
PF19 Enrique Wilson 1.00 .30
PF20 Kerry Wood 2.50 .75

1998 Fleer Tradition Rookie Sensations

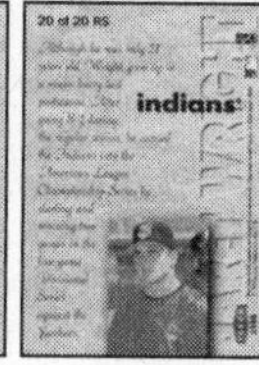

Randomly inserted in packs at the rate of one in 18, this 20-card set features gray-bordered action color images of the 1997 most promising players who were eligible for Rookie of the Year honors on multi-colored backgrounds.

	Nm-Mt	Ex-Mt
COMPLETE SET (20)	40.00	12.00
1 Mike Cameron	1.50	.45
2 Jose Cruz Jr.	1.50	.45
3 Jason Dickson	1.50	.45
4 Kelvim Escobar	1.50	.45
5 Nomar Garciaparra	6.00	1.80
6 Ben Grieve	1.50	.45
7 Vladimir Guerrero	4.00	1.20
8 Wilton Guerrero	1.50	.45
9 Jose Guillen	1.50	.45
10 Todd Helton	2.50	.75
11 Livan Hernandez	1.50	.45
12 Hideki Irabu	1.50	.45
13 Andruw Jones	1.50	.45
14 Matt Morris	1.50	.45
15 Magglio Ordonez	10.00	3.00
16 Neifi Perez	1.50	.45
17 Scott Rolen	2.50	.75
18 Fernando Tatis	1.50	.45
19 Brett Tomko	1.50	.45
20 Jaret Wright	1.50	.45

1998 Fleer Tradition Zone

Randomly inserted in packs at the rate of one in 288, this 15-card set features color photos of unstoppable players printed on cards with custom pattern rainbow foil and etching.

	Nm-Mt	Ex-Mt
COMPLETE SET (15)	250.00	75.00
1 Jeff Bagwell	10.00	3.00
2 Barry Bonds	40.00	12.00
3 Roger Clemens	30.00	9.00
4 Jose Cruz Jr.	6.00	1.80
5 Nomar Garciaparra	25.00	7.50
6 Juan Gonzalez	15.00	4.50
7 Ken Griffey Jr.	25.00	7.50
8 Tony Gwynn	20.00	6.00
9 Chipper Jones	15.00	4.50
10 Greg Maddux	25.00	7.50
11 Mark McGwire	40.00	12.00
12 Mike Piazza	25.00	7.50
13 Alex Rodriguez	25.00	7.50
14 Frank Thomas	15.00	4.50
15 Larry Walker	10.00	3.00

1998 Fleer Tradition Update

The 1998 Fleer Update set was issued exclusively in factory set form. This set, issued in November, 1998, was created in large part to get the first J.D. Drew Rookie Card on the market. The set also took advantage of the "retro" themes that were popular in 1998 and represented the return of Fleer Update factory sets that had a rich history from 1984 through 1994. In addition to the aforementioned Drew, other notable RC's in this set include Troy Glaus, Orlando Hernandez and Gabe Kapler.

	Nm-Mt	Ex-Mt
COMP.FACT.SET (100)	25.00	7.50
U1 Mark McGwire HL	1.25	.35
U2 Sammy Sosa HL	.75	.23
U3 Roger Clemens HL	1.00	.30
U4 Barry Bonds HL	1.25	.35
U5 Kerry Wood HL	.50	.15
U6 Paul Molitor HL	.30	.09
U7 Ken Griffey Jr. HL	.75	.23
U8 Cal Ripken HL	1.50	.45
U9 David Wells HL	.20	.06
U10 Alex Rodriguez HL	.75	.23
U11 Angel Pena RC	.25	.07
U12 Bruce Chen	.20	.06
U13 Craig Wilson	.20	.06
U14 O.Hernandez RC	1.25	.35
U15 Aramis Ramirez	.20	.06
U16 Aaron Boone	.20	.06
U17 Bob Henley	.20	.06
U18 Juan Guzman	.20	.06
U19 Darryl Hamilton	.20	.06
U20 Jay Payton	.20	.06
U21 Jeremy Powell	.20	.06
U22 Ben Davis	.20	.06
U23 Preston Wilson	.20	.06
U24 Jim Parque RC	.40	.12
U25 Odalis Perez RC	.60	.18
U26 Ronnie Belliard	.20	.06
U27 Royce Clayton	.20	.06
U28 George Lombard	.20	.06
U29 Tony Phillips	.20	.06
U30 F.Seguignol RC	.25	.07
U31 Armando Rios RC	.40	.12
U32 Jerry Hairston Jr. RC	.40	.12
U33 Justin Baughman RC	.25	.07
U34 Seth Greisinger	.20	.06
U35 Alex Gonzalez	.20	.06
U36 Michael Barrett	.20	.06
U37 Carlos Beltran	.20	.06
U38 Ellis Burks	.20	.06
U39 Jose Jimenez RC	.60	.18
U40 Carlos Guillen	.20	.06
U41 Marlon Anderson	.20	.06
U42 Scott Elarton	.20	.06
U43 Glenallen Hill	.20	.06
U44 Shane Monahan	.20	.06
U45 Dennis Martinez	.20	.06
U46 Carlos Febles RC	.40	.12
U47 Carlos Perez	.20	.06
U48 Wilton Guerrero	.20	.06
U49 Randy Johnson	.50	.15
U50 Brian Simmons RC	.25	.07
U51 Carlton Loewer	.20	.06
U52 Mark DeRosa RC	.40	.12
U53 Tim Young RC	.25	.07
U54 Gary Gaetti	.20	.06
U55 Eric Chavez	.30	.09
U56 Carl Pavano	.20	.06
U57 Mike Stanley	.20	.06
U58 Todd Stottlemyre	.20	.06
U59 Gabe Kapler RC	.60	.18
U60 Mike Jerzembeck RC	.25	.07
U61 Mitch Meluskey RC	.40	.12
U62 Bill Pulsipher	.20	.06
U63 Derrick Gibson	.20	.06
U64 John Rocker RC	.40	.12
U65 Calvin Pickering	.20	.06
U66 Blake Stein	.20	.06
U67 Fernando Tatis	.20	.06
U68 Gabe Alvarez	.20	.06
U69 Jeffrey Hammonds	.20	.06
U70 Adrian Beltre	.20	.06
U71 Ryan Bradley RC	.25	.07
U72 Edgard Clemente	.20	.06
U73 Rick Croushore RC	.25	.07
U74 Matt Clement	.20	.06
U75 Dermal Brown	.20	.06
U76 Paul Bako	.20	.06
U77 Placido Polanco RC	.40	.12
U78 Jay Tessmer	.20	.06
U79 Jarrod Washburn	.20	.06
U80 Kevin Witt	.20	.06
U81 Mike Metcalfe	.20	.06
U82 Daryle Ward	.20	.06
U83 Benj Sampson RC	.25	.07
U84 Mike Kinkade RC	.25	.07
U85 Randy Winn	.20	.06
U86 Jeff Shaw	.20	.06
U87 Troy Glaus RC	5.00	1.50
U88 Hideo Nomo	.50	.15
U89 Mark Grudzielanek	.20	.06
U90 Mike Frank RC	.25	.07
U91 Bobby Howry RC	.40	.12
U92 Ryan Minor RC	.25	.07
U93 Corey Koskie RC	1.25	.35
U94 Matt Anderson RC	.40	.12
U95 Joe Carter	.20	.06
U96 Paul Konerko	.20	.06
U97 Sidney Ponson	.20	.06
U98 Jeremy Giambi RC	.40	.12
U99 Jeff Kubenka RC	.25	.07
U100 J.D. Drew RC	4.00	1.20

1999 Fleer Tradition

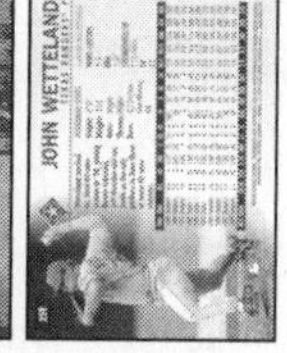

The 1999 Fleer set was issued in one series totalling 600 cards and was distributed in 10-card packs with a suggested retail price of $1.59. The fronts feature color action photos with gold foil player names. The backs carry another player photo with biographical information and career statistics. The set includes the following subsets: Franchise Futures (576-590) and Checklists (591-600).

	Nm-Mt	Ex-Mt
COMPLETE SET (600)	60.00	18.00
1 Mark McGwire	2.00	.60
2 Sammy Sosa	1.25	.35
3 Ken Griffey Jr.	1.25	.35
4 Kerry Wood	.75	.23
5 Derek Jeter	2.00	.60
6 Stan Musial	1.50	.45
7 J.D. Drew	.30	.09
8 Cal Ripken	2.50	.75
9 Alex Rodriguez	1.25	.35
10 Travis Lee	.20	.06
11 Andres Galarraga	.30	.09
12 Nomar Garciaparra	1.25	.35
13 Albert Belle	.30	.09
14 Barry Larkin	.75	.23
15 Dante Bichette	.30	.09
16 Tony Clark	.30	.09
17 Moises Alou	.30	.09
18 Rafael Palmeiro	.50	.15
19 Raul Mondesi	.30	.09
20 Vladimir Guerrero	.75	.23
21 John Olerud	.30	.09
22 Bernie Williams	.50	.15
23 Ben Grieve	.20	.06
24 Scott Rolen	.50	.15
25 Jeromy Burnitz	.30	.09
26 Ken Caminiti	.30	.09
27 Barry Bonds	2.00	.60
28 Todd Helton	.50	.15
29 Juan Gonzalez	.75	.23
30 Roger Clemens	1.50	.45
31 Andruw Jones	.30	.09
32 Mo Vaughn	.30	.09
33 Larry Walker	.50	.15
34 Frank Thomas	.75	.23
35 Manny Ramirez	.30	.09
36 Randy Johnson	.75	.23
37 Vinny Castilla	.30	.09
38 Juan Encarnacion	.20	.06
39 Jeff Bagwell	.50	.15
40 Gary Sheffield	.30	.09
41 Mike Piazza	1.25	.35
42 Richie Sexson	.30	.09
43 Tony Gwynn	1.00	.30
44 Chipper Jones	.75	.23
45 Jim Thome	.75	.23
46 Craig Biggio	.50	.15
47 Carlos Delgado	.30	.09
48 Greg Vaughn	.30	.09
49 Greg Maddux	1.25	.35
50 Troy Glaus	.50	.15
51 Roberto Alomar	.75	.23
52 Dennis Eckersley	.30	.09
53 Mike Caruso	.20	.06
54 Bruce Chen	.20	.06
55 Aaron Boone	.30	.09
56 Bartolo Colon	.30	.09
57 Derrick Gibson	.20	.06
58 Brian Anderson	.20	.06
59 Gabe Alvarez	.20	.06
60 Todd Dunwoody	.20	.06
61 Rod Beck	.20	.06
62 Derek Bell	.20	.06
63 Francisco Cordova	.20	.06
64 Johnny Damon	.30	.09
65 Adrian Beltre	.30	.09
66 Garret Anderson	.30	.09
67 Armando Benitez	.20	.06
68 Edgardo Alfonzo	.30	.09
69 Ryan Bradley	.20	.06
70 Eric Chavez	.30	.09
71 Bobby Abreu	.30	.09
72 Andy Ashby	.20	.06
73 Ellis Burks	.30	.09
74 Jeff Cirillo	.20	.06
75 Jay Buhner	.30	.09
76 Ron Gant	.30	.09
77 Rolando Arrojo	.20	.06
78 Will Clark	.75	.23
79 Chris Carpenter	.20	.06
80 Jim Edmonds	.30	.09
81 Tony Batista	.30	.09
82 Shane Andrews	.20	.06
83 Mark DeRosa	.20	.06
84 Brady Anderson	.30	.09
85 Tom Gordon	.20	.06
86 Brant Brown	.20	.06
87 Ray Durham	.30	.09
88 Ron Coomer	.20	.06
89 Bret Boone	.30	.09
90 Travis Fryman	.30	.09
91 Darryl Kile	.30	.09
92 Paul Bako	.20	.06
93 Cliff Floyd	.30	.09
94 Scott Elarton	.20	.06
95 Jeremy Giambi	.20	.06
96 Darren Dreifort	.20	.06
97 Marquis Grissom	.20	.06
98 Marty Cordova	.20	.06
99 Fernando Seguignol	.20	.06
100 Orlando Hernandez	.30	.09
101 Jose Cruz Jr.	.30	.09
102 Jason Giambi	.75	.23
103 Damion Easley	.20	.06
104 Freddy Garcia	.20	.06
105 Marlon Anderson	.20	.06
106 Kevin Brown	.50	.15
107 Joe Carter	.30	.09
108 Russ Davis	.20	.06
109 Brian Jordan	.30	.09
110 Wade Boggs	.50	.15
111 Tom Goodwin	.20	.06
112 Scott Brosius	.30	.09
113 Darin Erstad	.30	.09
114 Jay Bell	.30	.09
115 Tom Glavine	.50	.15
116 Pedro Martinez	.75	.23
117 Mark Grace	.50	.15
118 Russ Ortiz	.30	.09
119 Magglio Ordonez	.30	.09
120 Sean Casey	.30	.09
121 Rafael Roque RC	.20	.06
122 Brian Giles	.30	.09
123 Mike Lansing	.20	.06
124 David Cone	.30	.09
125 Alex Gonzalez	.20	.06
126 Carl Everett	.30	.09
127 Jeff King	.20	.06
128 Charles Johnson	.30	.09
129 Geoff Jenkins	.30	.09
130 Corey Koskie	.30	.09
131 Brad Fullmer	.20	.06
132 Al Leiter	.30	.09
133 Rickey Henderson	.75	.23
134 Rico Brogna	.20	.06
135 Jose Guillen	.30	.09
136 Matt Clement	.30	.09
137 Carlos Guillen	.30	.09
138 Orel Hershiser	.30	.09
139 Ray Lankford	.20	.06
140 Miguel Cairo	.20	.06
141 Chuck Finley	.30	.09
142 Rusty Greer	.30	.09
143 Kelvim Escobar	.20	.06
144 Ryan Klesko	.30	.09
145 Andy Benes	.30	.09
146 Eric Davis	.30	.09
147 David Wells	.30	.09
148 Trot Nixon	.50	.15
149 Jose Hernandez	.20	.06
150 Mark Johnson	.20	.06
151 Mike Frank	.20	.06
152 Joey Hamilton	.20	.06
153 David Justice	.30	.09
154 Mike Mussina	.75	.23
155 Neifi Perez	.20	.06
156 Luis Gonzalez	.30	.09
157 Livan Hernandez	.20	.06
158 Dermal Brown	.20	.06
159 Jose Lima	.20	.06
160 Eric Karros	.30	.09
161 Ronnie Belliard	.20	.06
162 Matt Lawton	.20	.06
163 Dustin Hermanson	.20	.06
164 Brian McRae	.20	.06
165 Mike Kinkade	.20	.06
166 A.J. Hinch	.20	.06
167 Doug Glanville	.20	.06
168 Hideo Nomo	.75	.23
169 Jason Kendall	.30	.09
170 Steve Finley	.30	.09
171 Jeff Kent	.30	.09
172 Ben Davis	.20	.06
173 Edgar Martinez	.50	.15
174 Eli Marrero	.20	.06
175 Quinton McCracken	.20	.06
176 Rick Helling	.20	.06
177 Tom Evans	.20	.06
178 Carl Pavano	.20	.06
179 Todd Greene	.20	.06
180 Omar Daal	.20	.06
181 George Lombard	.20	.06
182 Ryan Minor	.20	.06
183 Troy O'Leary	.20	.06
184 Robb Nen	.30	.09
185 Mickey Morandini	.20	.06
186 Robin Ventura	.30	.09
187 Pete Harnisch	.20	.06
188 Kenny Lofton	.30	.09
189 Eric Milton	.20	.06
190 Bobby Higginson	.30	.09
191 Jamie Moyer	.30	.09
192 Mark Kotsay	.20	.06
193 Shane Reynolds	.20	.06
194 Carlos Febles	.20	.06
195 Jeff Kubenka	.20	.06
196 Chuck Knoblauch	.30	.09
197 Kenny Rogers	.30	.09
198 Bill Mueller	.30	.09
199 Shane Monahan	.20	.06
200 Matt Morris	.30	.09
201 Fred McGriff	.50	.15
202 Ivan Rodriguez	.75	.23
203 Kevin Witt	.20	.06
204 Troy Percival	.30	.09
205 David Dellucci	.20	.06
206 Kevin Millwood	.30	.09
207 Jerry Hairston Jr.	.20	.06
208 Mike Stanley	.20	.06
209 Henry Rodriguez	.20	.06
210 Trevor Hoffman	.30	.09
211 Craig Wilson	.20	.06
212 Reggie Sanders	.30	.09
213 Carlton Loewer	.20	.06
214 Omar Vizquel	.30	.09
215 Gabe Kapler	.30	.09
216 Derrek Lee	.30	.09
217 Billy Wagner	.30	.09
218 Dean Palmer	.30	.09
219 Chan Ho Park	.30	.09
220 Fernando Vina	.30	.09
221 Roy Halladay	.30	.09
222 Paul Molitor	.50	.15
223 Ugueth Urbina	.20	.06
224 Rey Ordonez	.20	.06
225 Ricky Ledee	.20	.06
226 Scott Spiezio	.20	.06
227 Wendell Magee	.20	.06
228 Aramis Ramirez	.30	.09
229 Brian Simmons	.20	.06
230 Fernando Tatis	.20	.06
231 Bobby Smith	.20	.06
232 Aaron Sele	.20	.06
233 Shawn Green	.30	.09
234 Mariano Rivera	.50	.15
235 Tim Salmon	.50	.15
236 Andy Fox	.20	.06
237 Denny Neagle	.20	.06
238 John Valentin	.20	.06
239 Kevin Tapani	.20	.06
240 Paul Konerko	.30	.09
241 Robert Fick	.30	.09
242 Edgar Renteria	.30	.09
243 Brett Tomko	.20	.06
244 Daryle Ward	.20	.06
245 Carlos Beltran	.30	.09
246 Angel Pena	.20	.06
247 Steve Woodard	.20	.06
248 David Ortiz	.30	.09
249 Justin Thompson	.20	.06
250 Rondell White	.30	.09
251 Jaret Wright	.20	.06
252 Ed Sprague	.20	.06
253 Jay Payton	.20	.06
254 Mike Lowell	.30	.09
255 Orlando Cabrera	.20	.06
256 Jason Schmidt	.30	.09
257 David Segui	.20	.06
258 Paul Sorrento	.20	.06
259 John Wetteland	.30	.09
260 Devon White	.20	.06
261 Odalis Perez	.20	.06
262 Calvin Pickering	.20	.06
263 Tyler Green	.20	.06
264 Preston Wilson	.30	.09
265 Brad Radke	.30	.09
266 Walt Weiss	.20	.06
267 Tim Young	.20	.06
268 Tino Martinez	.50	.15
269 Matt Stairs	.20	.06
270 Curt Schilling	.50	.15
271 Tony Womack	.20	.06
272 Ismael Valdes	.20	.06
273 Wally Joyner	.30	.09
274 Armando Rios	.30	.09
275 Andy Pettitte	.50	.15
276 Bubba Trammell	.20	.06
277 Todd Zeile	.30	.09
278 Shannon Stewart	.30	.09
279 Matt Williams	.30	.09
280 John Rocker	.30	.09
281 B.J. Surhoff	.30	.09
282 Eric Young	.20	.06
283 Dmitri Young	.30	.09
284 John Smoltz	.50	.15
285 Todd Walker	.30	.09
286 Paul O'Neill	.50	.15
287 Blake Stein	.20	.06
288 Kevin Young	.30	.09
289 Quilvio Veras	.20	.06
290 Kirk Rueter	.20	.06
291 Randy Winn	.20	.06
292 Miguel Tejada	.30	.09
293 J.T. Snow	.30	.09
294 Michael Tucker	.20	.06
295 Jay Tessmer	.20	.06
296 Scott Erickson	.20	.06
297 Tim Wakefield	.30	.09
298 Jeff Abbott	.20	.06
299 Eddie Taubensee	.20	.06
300 Darryl Hamilton	.20	.06
301 Kevin Orie	.20	.06
302 Jose Offerman	.20	.06
303 Scott Karl	.20	.06
304 Chris Widger	.20	.06
305 Todd Hundley	.20	.06
306 Desi Relaford	.20	.06
307 Sterling Hitchcock	.20	.06
308 Delino DeShields	.20	.06
309 Alex Gonzalez	.20	.06
310 Justin Baughman	.20	.06
311 Jamey Wright	.20	.06
312 Wes Helms	.20	.06
313 Dante Powell	.20	.06
314 Jim Abbott	.50	.15
315 Manny Alexander	.20	.06
316 Harold Baines	.30	.09
317 Danny Graves	.20	.06
318 Sandy Alomar Jr.	.20	.06
319 Pedro Astacio	.20	.06
320 Jermaine Allensworth	.20	.06
321 Matt Anderson	.20	.06
322 Chad Curtis	.20	.06
323 Antonio Osuna	.20	.06
324 Brad Ausmus	.20	.06
325 Steve Trachsel	.20	.06
326 Mike Blowers	.20	.06
327 Brian Bohanon	.20	.06
328 Chris Gomez	.20	.06
329 Valerio De Los Santos	.20	.06
330 Rich Aurilia	.30	.09
331 Michael Barrett	.20	.06
332 Rick Aguilera	.20	.06
333 Adrian Brown	.20	.06
334 Bill Spiers	.20	.06
335 Matt Beech	.20	.06
336 David Bell	.20	.06
337 Juan Acevedo	.20	.06
338 Jose Canseco	.75	.23
339 Wilson Alvarez	.20	.06
340 Luis Alicea	.20	.06
341 Jason Dickson	.20	.06
342 Mike Bordick	.20	.06
343 Ben Ford	.20	.06
344 Javy Lopez	.30	.09
345 Jason Christiansen	.20	.06
346 Darren Bragg	.20	.06
347 Doug Brocail	.20	.06
348 Jeff Blauser	.20	.06
349 James Baldwin	.20	.06
350 Jeffrey Hammonds	.20	.06
351 Ricky Bottalico	.20	.06
352 Russ Branyan	.20	.06
353 Mark Brownson RC	.20	.06
354 Dave Berg	.20	.06
355 Sean Bergman	.20	.06
356 Jeff Conine	.30	.09
357 Shayne Bennett	.20	.06
358 Bobby Bonilla	.30	.09
359 Bob Wickman	.20	.06
360 Carlos Baerga	.20	.06
361 Chris Fussell	.20	.06
362 Chili Davis	.30	.09
363 Jerry Spradlin	.20	.06
364 Carlos Hernandez	.20	.06
365 Roberto Hernandez	.20	.06
366 Marvin Benard	.20	.06
367 Ken Cloude	.20	.06
368 Tony Fernandez	.20	.06
369 John Burkett	.20	.06
370 Gary DiSarcina	.20	.06
371 Alan Benes	.20	.06
372 Karim Garcia	.20	.06
373 Carlos Perez	.20	.06
374 Damon Buford	.20	.06
375 Mark Clark	.20	.06
376 Edgard Clemente	.20	.06
377 Chad Bradford RC	.20	.06
378 Frank Catalanotto	.20	.06
379 Vic Darensbourg	.20	.06
380 Sean Berry	.20	.06
381 Dave Burba	.20	.06
382 Sal Fasano	.20	.06
383 Steve Parris	.20	.06
384 Roger Cedeno	.20	.06
385 Chad Fox	.20	.06
386 Wilton Guerrero	.20	.06
387 Dennis Cook	.20	.06
388 Joe Girardi	.20	.06
389 LaTroy Hawkins	.20	.06
390 Ryan Christenson	.20	.06
391 Paul Byrd	.20	.06
392 Lou Collier	.20	.06
393 Jeff Fassero	.20	.06
394 Jim Leyritz	.20	.06
395 Shawn Estes	.20	.06
396 Mike Kelly	.20	.06
397 Rich Croushore	.20	.06
398 Royce Clayton	.20	.06
399 Rudy Seanez	.20	.06
400 Darrin Fletcher	.20	.06
401 Shigetoshi Hasegawa	.30	.09
402 Bernard Gilkey	.20	.06
403 Juan Guzman	.20	.06
404 Jeff Frye	.20	.06
405 Donovan Osborne	.20	.06
406 Alex Fernandez	.20	.06
407 Gary Gaetti	.20	.06
408 Dan Miceli	.20	.06
409 Mike Cameron	.30	.09
410 Mike Remlinger	.20	.06
411 Joey Cora	.20	.06
412 Mark Gardner	.20	.06
413 Aaron Ledesma	.20	.06
414 Jerry Dipoto	.20	.06
415 Ricky Gutierrez	.20	.06
416 John Franco	.30	.09

417 Mendy Lopez .20 .06
418 Hideki Irabu .20 .06
419 Mark Grudzielanek .20 .06
420 Bobby Hughes .20 .06
421 Pat Meares .20 .06
422 Jimmy Haynes .20 .06
423 Bob Henley .20 .06
424 Bobby Estalella .20 .06
425 Jon Lieber .20 .06
426 Giomar Guevara RC .20 .06
427 Jose Jimenez .20 .06
428 Deivi Cruz .20 .06
429 Jonathan Johnson .20 .06
430 Ken Hill .20 .06
431 Craig Grebeck .20 .06
432 Jose Rosado .20 .06
433 Danny Klassen .20 .06
434 Bobby Howry .20 .06
435 Gerald Williams .20 .06
436 Omar Olivares .20 .06
437 Chris Hoiles .20 .06
438 Seth Greisinger .20 .06
439 Scott Hatteberg .20 .06
440 Jeremi Gonzalez .20 .06
441 Wil Cordero .20 .06
442 Jeff Montgomery .20 .06
443 Chris Stynes .20 .06
444 Tony Saunders .20 .06
445 Einar Diaz .20 .06
446 Lariel Gonzalez .20 .06
447 Ryan Jackson .20 .06
448 Mike Hampton .30 .09
449 Todd Hollandsworth .20 .06
450 Gabe White .20 .06
451 John Jaha .20 .06
452 Bret Saberhagen .30 .09
453 Otis Nixon .20 .06
454 Steve Kline .20 .06
455 Butch Huskey .20 .06
456 Mike Jerzembeck .20 .06
457 Wayne Gomes .20 .06
458 Mike Macfarlane .20 .06
459 Jesus Sanchez .20 .06
460 Al Martin .20 .06
461 Dwight Gooden .50 .15
462 Ruben Rivera .20 .06
463 Pat Hentgen .20 .06
464 Jose Valentin .20 .06
465 Vladimir Nunez .20 .06
466 Charlie Hayes .20 .06
467 Jay Powell .20 .06
468 Raul Ibanez .20 .06
469 Kent Mercker .20 .06
470 John Mabry .20 .06
471 Woody Williams .20 .06
472 Roberto Kelly .20 .06
473 Jim Mecir .20 .06
474 Dave Hollins .20 .06
475 Rafael Medina .20 .06
476 Darren Lewis .20 .06
477 Felix Heredia .20 .06
478 Brian Hunter .20 .06
479 Matt Mantei .20 .06
480 Richard Hidalgo .30 .09
481 Bobby Jones .20 .06
482 Hal Morris .20 .06
483 Ramiro Mendoza .20 .06
484 Matt Luke .20 .06
485 Esteban Loaiza .30 .09
486 Mark Loretta .20 .06
487 A.J. Pierzynski .30 .09
488 Charles Nagy .20 .06
489 Kevin Sefcik .20 .06
490 Jason McDonald .20 .06
491 Jeremy Powell .20 .06
492 Scott Servais .20 .06
493 Abraham Nunez .20 .06
494 Stan Spencer .20 .06
495 Stan Javier .20 .06
496 Jose Paniagua .20 .06
497 Gregg Jefferies .20 .06
498 Gregg Olson .20 .06
499 Derek Lowe .30 .09
500 Willis Otanez .20 .06
501 Brian Moehler .20 .06
502 Glenallen Hill .20 .06
503 Bobby M. Jones .20 .06
504 Greg Norton .20 .06
505 Mike Jackson .20 .06
506 Kirt Manwaring .20 .06
507 Eric Weaver RC .20 .06
508 Mitch Meluskey .20 .06
509 Todd Jones .20 .06
510 Mike Matheny .20 .06
511 Benj Sampson .20 .06
512 Tony Phillips .20 .06
513 Mike Thurman .20 .06
514 Jorge Posada .50 .15
515 Bill Taylor .20 .06
516 Mike Sweeney .30 .09
517 Jose Silva .20 .06
518 Mark Lewis .20 .06
519 Chris Peters .20 .06
520 Brian Johnson .20 .06
521 Mike Timlin .20 .06
522 Mark McLemore .20 .06
523 Dan Plesac .20 .06
524 Kelly Stinnett .20 .06
525 Sidney Ponson .30 .09
526 Jim Parque .20 .06
527 Tyler Houston .20 .06
528 John Thomson .20 .06
529 Reggie Jefferson .20 .06
530 Robert Person .20 .06
531 Marc Newfield .20 .06
532 Javier Vazquez .30 .09
533 Terry Steinbach .20 .06
534 Turk Wendell .20 .06
535 Tim Raines .30 .09
536 Brian Meadows .20 .06
537 Mike Lieberthal .30 .09
538 Ricardo Rincon .20 .06
539 Dan Wilson .20 .06
540 John Johnstone .20 .06
541 Todd Stottlemyre .20 .06
542 Kevin Stocker .20 .06
543 Ramon Martinez .20 .06
544 Mike Simms .20 .06
545 Paul Quantrill .20 .06
546 Matt Walbeck .20 .06
547 Turner Ward .20 .06
548 Bill Pulsipher .20 .06
549 Donnie Sadler .20 .06
550 Lance Johnson .20 .06
551 Bill Simas .20 .06
552 Jeff Reed .20 .06
553 Jeff Shaw .20 .06
554 Joe Randa .20 .06
555 Paul Shuey .20 .06
556 Mike Redmond RC .20 .06
557 Sean Runyan .20 .06
558 Enrique Wilson .20 .06
559 Scott Radinsky .20 .06
560 Larry Sutton .20 .06
561 Masato Yoshii .20 .06
562 David Nilsson .20 .06
563 Mike Trombley .20 .06
564 Darryl Strawberry .50 .15
565 Dave Mlicki .20 .06
566 Placido Polanco .20 .06
567 Yorkis Perez .20 .06
568 Esteban Yan .20 .06
569 Lee Stevens .20 .06
570 Steve Sinclair .20 .06
571 Jarrod Washburn .30 .09
572 Lenny Webster .20 .06
573 Mike Sirotka .20 .06
574 Jason Varitek .30 .09
575 Terry Mulholland .20 .06
576 Adrian Beltre FF .20 .06
577 Eric Chavez FF .20 .06
578 J.D. Drew FF .20 .06
579 Juan Encarnacion FF .20 .06
580 Nomar Garciaparra FF .75 .23
581 Troy Glaus FF .30 .09
582 Ben Grieve FF .20 .06
583 Vladimir Guerrero FF .50 .15
584 Todd Helton FF .30 .09
585 Derek Jeter FF 1.00 .30
586 Travis Lee FF .20 .06
587 Alex Rodriguez FF .75 .23
588 Scott Rolen FF .30 .09
589 Richie Sexson FF .20 .06
590 Kerry Wood FF .50 .15
591 Ken Griffey Jr. CL .75 .23
592 Chipper Jones CL .50 .15
593 Alex Rodriguez CL .75 .23
594 Sammy Sosa CL .75 .23
595 Mark McGwire CL 1.00 .30
596 Cal Ripken CL 1.25 .35
597 Nomar Garciaparra CL .75 .23
598 Derek Jeter CL 1.00 .30
599 Kerry Wood CL .50 .15
600 J.D. Drew CL .20 .06
P7 J.D. Drew Promo 1.00 .30

1999 Fleer Tradition Millenium

Fleer printed 5,000 Millenium factory sets, primarily intended for sale on Shop at Home at the end of the 1999 calendar year. Each set came shrink-wrapped in an attractive factory box, of which is sealed with a gold sticker serial numbered of 5,000. Each set contains 620 cards consisting of the 600-card basic issue set plus 20 cards from the Fleer Update set (rookies U1-U10 and highlights U141-U150). The cards hailing from the Update set have been renumbered. The Update rookies are numbered 601-610 and the Update highlights are numbered 611-620. All 620 cards contain a special gold foil "Year 2000" logo.

Nm-Mt Ex-Mt
COMP.FACT.SET (620) 100.00 30.00
*STARS 1-600: 1X TO 2.5X BASIC CARDS
*ROOKIES 1-600: 1X TO 2.5X BASIC CARDS
601 Rick Ankiel 5.00 1.50
602 Peter Bergeron 1.50 .45
603 Pat Burrell 10.00 3.00
604 Eric Munson 5.00 1.50
605 Alfonso Soriano 25.00 7.50
606 Tim Hudson 15.00 4.50
607 Erubiel Durazo 5.00 1.50
608 Chad Hermansen .75 .23
609 Jeff Zimmerman 1.50 .45
610 Jesus Pena .75 .23
611 Wade Boggs HL 1.25 .35
612 Jose Canseco HL 2.00 .60
613 Roger Clemens HL 4.00 1.20
614 David Cone HL .75 .23
615 Tony Gwynn HL 2.50 .75
616 Mark McGwire HL 5.00 1.50
617 Cal Ripken HL 6.00 1.80
618 Alex Rodriguez HL 3.00 .90
619 Fernando Tatis HL .50 .15
620 Robin Ventura HL .75 .23

1999 Fleer Tradition Warning Track

Cards from this parallel set were seeded at a rate of one per retail pack. Warning Track cards can be easily identified by the red foil "Warning Track Collection" logo at the base of the card front and the W suffix numbering on the card backs.

Nm-Mt Ex-Mt
*STARS: 2.5X TO 6X BASIC CARDS ...

1999 Fleer Tradition Vintage '61

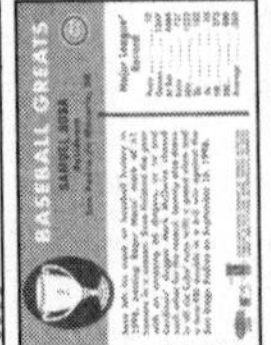

Inserted one in every hobby pack only, this 50-card set features the first 50 cards of the 1999 Fleer Tradition set in cards designed similar to the 1961 Fleer Baseball Greats set.

Nm-Mt Ex-Mt
COMPLETE SET (50) 25.00 7.50
*SINGLES: .4X TO 1X BASE CARD HI.

1999 Fleer Tradition Date With Destiny

These attractive bronze foil cards are designed to mimic the famous plaques on display at the Hall of Fame. Fleer selected ten of the games greatest active players, all of whom are well on their way to the Hall of Fame. Only 100 sets were printed (each card is serial numbered "X/100" on front) and the cards were randomly seeded into packs at an unannounced rate. Suffice to say, they're not easy to pull from packs.

Nm-Mt Ex-Mt
COMPLETE SET (10) 500.00 150.00
1 Barry Bonds 60.00 18.00
2 Roger Clemens 50.00 15.00
3 Ken Griffey Jr. 40.00 12.00
4 Tony Gwynn 30.00 9.00
5 Greg Maddux 40.00 12.00
6 Mark McGwire 60.00 18.00
7 Mike Piazza 40.00 12.00
8 Cal Ripken 80.00 24.00
9 Alex Rodriguez 40.00 12.00
10 Frank Thomas 25.00 7.50

1999 Fleer Tradition Diamond Magic

Randomly inserted in packs at the rate of one in 96, this 15-card set features color action player images printed with a special die-cut treatment on a multi-layer card for a kaleidoscope effect behind the player image.

Nm-Mt Ex-Mt
COMPLETE SET (15) 250.00 75.00
1 Barry Bonds 25.00 7.50
2 Roger Clemens 20.00 6.00
3 Nomar Garciaparra 15.00 4.50
4 Ken Griffey Jr. 15.00 4.50
5 Tony Gwynn 12.00 3.60
6 Orlando Hernandez 4.00 1.20
7 Derek Jeter 25.00 7.50
8 Randy Johnson 10.00 3.00
9 Chipper Jones 10.00 3.00
10 Greg Maddux 15.00 4.50
11 Mark McGwire 25.00 7.50
12 Alex Rodriguez 15.00 4.50
13 Sammy Sosa 15.00 4.50
14 Bernie Williams 6.00 1.80
15 Kerry Wood 10.00 3.00

1999 Fleer Tradition Going Yard

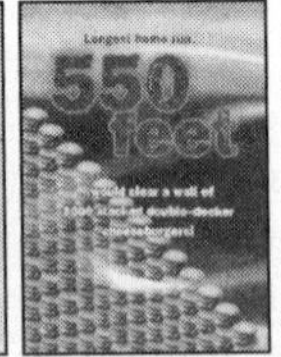

Randomly inserted in packs at the rate of one in 18, this 15-card set features color action photos of players who hit the longest home runs printed on extra wide cards to illustrate the greatness of their feats.

Nm-Mt Ex-Mt
COMPLETE SET (15) 40.00 12.00
1 Moises Alou 1.00 .30
2 Albert Belle 1.00 .30
3 Jose Canseco 2.50 .75
4 Vinny Castilla 1.00 .30
5 Andres Galarraga 1.00 .30
6 Juan Gonzalez 2.50 .75
7 Ken Griffey Jr. 4.00 1.20
8 Chipper Jones 2.50 .75
9 Mark McGwire 6.00 1.80
10 Rafael Palmeiro 1.50 .45
11 Mike Piazza 4.00 1.20
12 Alex Rodriguez 4.00 1.20
13 Sammy Sosa 4.00 1.20
14 Greg Vaughn 1.00 .30
15 Mo Vaughn 1.00 .30

1999 Fleer Tradition Golden Memories

Randomly inserted in packs at the rate of one in 54, this 15-card set features color action player photos with an embossed frame design.

Nm-Mt Ex-Mt
COMPLETE SET (15) 150.00 45.00
1 Albert Belle 2.50 .75
2 Barry Bonds 15.00 4.50

3 Roger Clemens 12.00 3.60
4 Nomar Garciaparra 10.00 3.00
5 Juan Gonzalez 6.00 1.80
6 Ken Griffey Jr. 10.00 3.00
7 Randy Johnson 6.00 1.80
8 Greg Maddux 10.00 3.00
9 Mark McGwire 15.00 4.50
10 Mike Piazza 10.00 3.00
11 Cal Ripken 20.00 6.00
12 Alex Rodriguez 10.00 3.00
13 Sammy Sosa 10.00 3.00
14 David Wells 2.50 .75
15 Kerry Wood 6.00 1.80

1999 Fleer Tradition Stan Musial Monumental Moments

Randomly inserted in packs at the rate of one in 36, this 10-card set features photos of Stan Musial during his legendary career. As a bonus to collectors, Stan signed 50 of each of these cards in this set.

Nm-Mt Ex-Mt
COMPLETE SET (10) 25.00 7.50
COMMON CARD (1-10) 2.50 .75

1999 Fleer Tradition Rookie Flashback

Randomly inserted in packs at the rate of one in six, this 15-card set features color action photos of players who were rookies during the 1998 season printed on sculpture embossed cards.

Nm-Mt Ex-Mt
COMPLETE SET (15) 10.00 3.00
1 Matt Anderson .50 .15
2 Rolando Arrojo .50 .15
3 Adrian Beltre .75 .23
4 Mike Caruso .50 .15
5 Eric Chavez .75 .23
6 J.D. Drew .75 .23
7 Juan Encarnacion .50 .15
8 Brad Fullmer .50 .15
9 Troy Glaus 1.25 .35
10 Ben Grieve .50 .15
11 Todd Helton 1.25 .35
12 Orlando Hernandez .75 .23
13 Travis Lee .50 .15
14 Richie Sexson .75 .23
15 Kerry Wood 2.00 .60

1999 Fleer Tradition Update

The 1999 Fleer Update set was issued in one series totalling 150 cards and distributed only as a factory boxed set. The fronts feature color action player photos. The backs carry player information. The set features the Season Highlights subset (Cards 141-150). Over 100 Rookie Cards are featured in this set. Among these Rookie Cards are Rick Ankiel, Josh Beckett, Pat Burrell, Tim Hudson, Eric Munson, Wily Mo Pena and Alfonso Soriano.

Nm-Mt Ex-Mt
COMP.FACT.SET (150) 40.00 12.00
U1 Rick Ankiel RC .75 .23
U2 Peter Bergeron RC .30 .09
U3 Pat Burrell RC 2.50 .75
U4 Eric Munson RC .75 .23
U5 Alfonso Soriano RC 5.00 1.50
U6 Tim Hudson RC 2.50 .75
U7 Erubiel Durazo RC .75 .23
U8 Chad Hermansen .20 .06
U9 Jeff Zimmerman RC .30 .09
U10 Jesus Pena RC .30 .09
U11 Ramon Hernandez .30 .09
U12 Trent Durrington RC .30 .09
U13 Tony Armas Jr. .20 .06
U14 Mike Fyhrie RC .30 .09
U15 Danny Kolb RC .30 .09
U16 Mike Porzio RC .30 .09
U17 Will Brunson RC .30 .09
U18 Mike Duvall RC .30 .09
U19 D.Mientkiewicz RC .75 .23
U20 Gabe Molina RC .30 .09
U21 Luis Vizcaino RC .30 .09
U22 Robinson Cancel RC .30 .09
U23 Brett Laxton RC .30 .09
U24 Joe McEwing RC .30 .09
U25 Justin Speier RC .30 .09
U26 Kip Wells RC .50 .15
U27 Armando Almanza RC .30 .09
U28 Joe Davenport RC .30 .09
U29 Yamid Haad RC .30 .09
U30 John Halama .20 .06
U31 Adam Kennedy .20 .06
U32 Micah Bowie RC .30 .09
U33 Gookie Dawkins RC .30 .09
U34 Ryan Rupe RC .30 .09
U35 B.J. Ryan RC .30 .09
U36 Chance Sanford RC .30 .09
U37 A.Shumaker RC .30 .09
U38 Ryan Glynn RC .30 .09
U39 Roosevelt Brown RC .30 .09
U40 Ben Molina RC .60 .18
U41 Scott Williamson .20 .06
U42 Eric Gagne RC 8.00 2.40
U43 John McDonald RC .30 .09
U44 Scott Sauerbeck RC .30 .09
U45 Mike Venafro RC .30 .09
U46 Edwards Guzman RC .30 .09
U47 Richard Barker RC .30 .09
U48 Braden Looper .20 .06
U49 Chad Meyers RC .30 .09
U50 Scott Strickland RC .30 .09
U51 Billy Koch .20 .06
U52 David Newhan RC .30 .09
U53 David Riske RC .30 .09
U54 Jose Santiago RC .30 .09
U55 Miguel Del Toro RC .30 .09
U56 Orber Moreno RC .30 .09
U57 Dave Roberts RC .50 .15
U58 Tim Byrdak RC .30 .09
U59 David Lee RC .30 .09
U60 Guillermo Mota RC .30 .09
U61 Wilton Veras RC .30 .09
U62 Joe Mays RC .50 .15
U63 Jose Fernandez RC .30 .09
U64 Ray King RC .30 .09
U65 Chris Petersen RC .30 .09
U66 Vernon Wells .20 .06
U67 Ruben Mateo .20 .06
U68 Ben Petrick .20 .06
U69 Chris Tremie RC .30 .09
U70 Lance Berkman .20 .06
U71 Dan Smith RC .30 .09
U72 Carlos E. Hernandez RC .30 .09
U73 Chad Harville RC .30 .09
U74 Damaso Marte RC .30 .09
U75 Aaron Myette RC .30 .09
U76 Willis Roberts RC .30 .09
U77 Erik Sabel RC .30 .09
U78 Hector Almonte RC .30 .09
U79 Kris Benson .20 .06
U80 Pat Daneker RC .30 .09
U81 Freddy Garcia RC .60 .18
U82 Byung-Hyun Kim RC 2.00 .60
U83 Wily Pena RC .75 .23
U84 Dan Wheeler RC .30 .09
U85 Tim Harikkala RC .20 .06
U86 Derrin Ebert RC .30 .09
U87 Horacio Estrada RC .30 .09
U88 Liu Rodriguez RC .30 .09
U89 J.Zimmerman RC .30 .09
U90 A.J. Burnett RC .60 .18
U91 Doug Davis RC .30 .09
U92 Rob Ramsay RC .30 .09
U93 Clay Bellinger RC .30 .09
U94 Charlie Greene RC .30 .09
U95 Bo Porter RC .30 .09
U96 Jorge Toca RC .30 .09
U97 Casey Blake RC .50 .15
U98 Amaury Garcia RC .30 .09
U99 Jose Molina RC .30 .09
U100 Melvin Mora RC 1.25 .35
U101 Joe Nathan RC .30 .09
U102 Juan Pena RC .30 .09
U103 Dave Borkowski RC .30 .09
U104 Eddie Gaillard RC .30 .09
U105 Glen Barker RC .30 .09
U106 Brett Hinchliffe RC .30 .09
U107 Carlos Lee .20 .06
U108 Rob Ryan RC .30 .09
U109 Jeff Weaver RC .50 .15
U110 Ed Yarnall .20 .06
U111 Nelson Cruz RC .30 .09
U112 C.Davidson RC .30 .09
U113 Tim Kubinski RC .30 .09
U114 Sean Spencer RC .30 .09
U115 Joe Winkelsas RC .30 .09
U116 Mike Colangelo RC .30 .09
U117 Tom Davey RC .30 .09
U118 Warren Morris .20 .06
U119 Dan Murray RC .30 .09
U120 Jose Nieves RC .30 .09
U121 Mark Quinn RC .30 .09
U122 Josh Beckett RC 15.00 4.50
U123 Chad Allen RC .30 .09
U124 Mike Figga .30 .09
U125 Beiker Graterol RC .30 .09
U126 Aaron Scheffer RC .30 .09
U127 Wiki Gonzalez RC .30 .09
U128 Ramon E.Martinez RC .30 .09
U129 Matt Riley RC 3.00 .90
U130 Chris Woodward RC .30 .09
U131 Albert Belle .20 .06
U132 Roger Cedeno .20 .06
U133 Roger Clemens 1.00 .30
U134 Brian Giles .20 .06
U135 Rickey Henderson .50 .15
U136 Randy Johnson .50 .15
U137 Brian Jordan .20 .06
U138 Paul Konerko .20 .06
U139 Hideo Nomo .50 .15
U140 Kenny Rogers .20 .06
U141 Wade Boggs HL .30 .09
U142 Jose Canseco HL .20 .06
U143 Roger Clemens HL 1.00 .30

U144 David Cone HL .20 .06
U145 Tony Gwynn HL .60 .18
U146 Mark McGwire HL 1.25 .35
U147 Cal Ripken HL 1.50 .45
U148 Alex Rodriguez HL .75 .23
U149 Fernando Tatis HL .20 .06
U150 Robin Ventura HL .20 .06

2000 Fleer Tradition

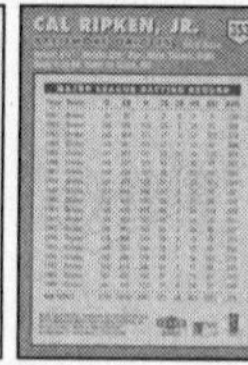

This 450-card single series set was released in February, 2000. Ten-card hobby and retail packs carried an SRP of $1.59. The basic cards are somewhat reminiscent of the 1954 Topps baseball set featuring a large headshot set against a flat color background and a small, cut-out action shot. Subsets are as follows: League Leaders (1-10), Award Winners (435-440), Division Playoffs-World Series Highlights (441-450). Dual-player prospect cards, team cards and six checklist cards (featuring a floating head image of several of the game's top stars) are also sprinkled throughout the set. In addition, a Cal Ripken promotional card was distributed to dealers and hobby media several weeks prior to the product's release. The card is easy to identify by the "PROMOTIONAL SAMPLE" text running diagonally across the front and back.

Nm-Mt Ex-Mt
COMPLETE SET (450) 50.00 15.00
1 Ken Griffey Jr .75 .23
Rafael Palmeiro
Carlos Delgado LL
2 Mark McGwire .50 .15
Sammy Sosa
Chipper Jones LL
3 Manny Ramirez .30 .09
Rafael Palmeiro
Ken Griffey Jr. LL
4 Mark McGwire .75 .23
Matt Williams
Sammy Sosa LL
5 Nomar Garciaparra .75 .23
Derek Jeter
Bernie Williams LL
6 Larry Walker .30 .09
Luis Gonzalez
Bob Abreu LL
7 Pedro Martinez .30 .09
Bartolo Colon
Mike Mussina LL
8 Mike Hampton .30 .09
Jose Lima
Greg Maddux LL
9 Pedro Martinez .30 .09
David Cone
Mike Mussina LL
10 Randy Johnson .50 .15
Kevin Millwood
Mike Hampton LL
11 Matt Mantei .30 .09
12 John Rocker .30 .09
13 Kyle Farnsworth .30 .09
14 Juan Guzman .30 .09
15 Manny Ramirez .30 .09
16 Matt Riley .30 .09
Calvin Pickering
17 Tony Clark .30 .09
18 Brian Meadows .30 .09
19 Orber Moreno .30 .09
20 Eric Karros .30 .09
21 Steve Woodard .30 .09
22 Scott Brosius .30 .09
23 Gary Bennett .30 .09
24 Jason Wood .30 .09
Dave Borkowski
25 Joe McEwing .30 .09
26 Juan Gonzalez .75 .23
27 Roy Halladay .30 .09
28 Trevor Hoffman .30 .09
29 Arizona Diamondbacks .30 .09
30 Domingo Guzman RC .30 .09
Wiki Gonzalez
31 Bret Boone .30 .09
32 Nomar Garciaparra 1.25 .35
33 Bo Porter .30 .09
34 Eddie Taubensee .30 .09
35 Pedro Astacio .30 .09
36 Derek Bell .30 .09
37 Jacque Jones .30 .09
38 Ricky Ledee .30 .09
39 Jeff Kent .30 .09
40 Matt Williams .30 .09
41 Alfonso Soriano .75 .23
D'Angelo Jimenez
42 B.J. Surhoff .30 .09
43 Denny Neagle .30 .09
44 Omar Vizquel .30 .09
45 Jeff Bagwell .50 .15
46 Mark Grudzielanek .30 .09
47 LaTroy Hawkins .30 .09
48 Orlando Hernandez .30 .09
49 Ken Griffey Jr. CL .75 .23
50 Fernando Tatis .30 .09
51 Quilvio Veras .30 .09
52 Wayne Gomes .30 .09
53 Rick Helling .30 .09
54 Shannon Stewart .30 .09
55 Dermal Brown .30 .09
Mark Quinn
56 Randy Johnson .75 .23
57 Greg Maddux 1.25 .35
58 Mike Cameron .30 .09
59 Matt Anderson .30 .09
60 Milwaukee Brewers .30 .09
61 Derrek Lee .30 .09
62 Mike Sweeney .30 .09
63 Fernando Vina .30 .09
64 Orlando Cabrera .30 .09
65 Doug Glanville .30 .09
66 Stan Spencer .30 .09
67 Ray Lankford .50 .15
68 Kelly Dransfeldt .30 .09
69 Alex Gonzalez .30 .09
70 Russ Branyan .30 .09
Danny Peoples
71 Jim Edmonds .30 .09
72 Brady Anderson .30 .09
73 Mike Stanley .30 .09
74 Travis Fryman .30 .09
75 Carlos Febles .30 .09
76 Bobby Higginson .30 .09
77 Carlos Perez .30 .09
78 Steve Cox .30 .09
Alex Sanchez
79 Dustin Hermanson .30 .09
80 Kenny Rogers .30 .09
81 Miguel Tejada .30 .09
82 Ben Davis .30 .09
83 Reggie Sanders .30 .09
84 Eric Davis .30 .09
85 J.D. Drew .30 .09
86 Ryan Rupe .30 .09
87 Bobby Smith .30 .09
88 Jose Cruz Jr. .30 .09
89 Carlos Delgado .30 .09
90 Toronto Blue Jays .30 .09
91 Denny Stark RC .40 .12
Gil Meche
92 Randy Velarde .30 .09
93 Aaron Boone .30 .09
94 Javy Lopez .30 .09
95 Johnny Damon .30 .09
96 Jon Lieber .30 .09
97 Montreal Expos .30 .09
98 Mark Kotsay .30 .09
99 Luis Gonzalez .30 .09
100 Larry Walker .50 .15
101 Adrian Beltre .30 .09
102 Alex Ochoa .30 .09
103 Michael Barrett .30 .09
104 Tampa Bay Devil Rays .30 .09
105 Rey Ordonez .30 .09
106 Derek Jeter 1.50 .45
107 Mike Lieberthal .30 .09
108 Ellis Burks .30 .09
109 Steve Finley .30 .09
110 Ryan Klesko .30 .09
111 Steve Avery .30 .09
112 Dave Veres .30 .09
113 Cliff Floyd .30 .09
114 Shane Reynolds .30 .09
115 Kevin Brown .50 .15
116 Dave Nilsson .30 .09
117 Mike Trombley .30 .09
118 Todd Walker .30 .09
119 John Olerud .30 .09
120 Chuck Knoblauch .30 .09
121 Nomar Garciaparra CL .75 .23
122 Trot Nixon .50 .15
123 Erubiel Durazo .30 .09
124 Edwards Guzman .30 .09
125 Curt Schilling .50 .15
126 Brian Jordan .30 .09
127 Cleveland Indians .30 .09
128 Benito Santiago .30 .09
129 Frank Thomas .75 .23
130 Neifi Perez .30 .09
131 Alex Fernandez .30 .09
132 Jose Lima .30 .09
133 Jorge Toca .30 .09
Melvin Mora
134 Scott Karl .30 .09
135 Brad Radke .30 .09
136 Paul O'Neill .50 .15
137 Kris Benson .30 .09
138 Colorado Rockies .30 .09
139 Jason Phillips .30 .09
140 Robb Nen .30 .09
141 Ken Hill .30 .09
142 Charles Johnson .30 .09
143 Paul Konerko .30 .09
144 Dmitri Young .30 .09
145 Justin Thompson .30 .09
146 Mark Loretta .30 .09
147 Edgardo Alfonzo .30 .09
148 Armando Benitez .30 .09
149 Octavio Dotel .30 .09
150 Wade Boggs .50 .15
151 Ramon Hernandez .30 .09
152 Freddy Garcia .30 .09
153 Edgar Martinez .50 .15
154 Ivan Rodriguez .75 .23
155 Kansas City Royals .30 .09
156 Cleatus Davidson .30 .09
Cristian Guzman
157 Andy Benes .30 .09
158 Todd Dunwoody .30 .09
159 Pedro Martinez .75 .23
160 Mike Caruso .30 .09
161 Mike Sirotka .30 .09
162 Houston Astros .30 .09
163 Darryl Kile .30 .09
164 Chipper Jones .75 .23
165 Carl Everett .30 .09
166 Geoff Jenkins .30 .09
167 Dan Perkins .30 .09
168 Andy Pettitte .50 .15
169 Francisco Cordova .30 .09
170 Jay Buhner .30 .09
171 Jay Bell .30 .09
172 Andruw Jones .30 .09
173 Bobby Howry .30 .09
174 Chris Singleton .30 .09
175 Todd Helton .50 .15
176 A.J. Burnett .30 .09
177 Marquis Grissom .30 .09
178 Eric Milton .30 .09
179 Los Angeles Dodgers .30 .09
180 Kevin Appier .30 .09
181 Brian Giles .30 .09
182 Tom Davey .30 .09
183 Mo Vaughn .30 .09
184 Jose Hernandez .30 .09
185 Jim Parque .30 .09
186 Derrick Gibson .30 .09
187 Bruce Aven .30 .09
188 Jeff Cirillo .30 .09
189 Doug Mientkiewicz .30 .09
190 Eric Chavez .30 .09
191 Al Martin .30 .09
192 Tom Glavine .50 .15
193 Butch Huskey .30 .09
194 Ray Durham .30 .09
195 Greg Vaughn .30 .09
196 Vinny Castilla .30 .09
197 Ken Caminiti .30 .09
198 Joe Mays .30 .09
199 Chicago White Sox .30 .09
200 Mariano Rivera .50 .15
201 Mark McGwire CL 1.00 .30
202 Pat Meares .30 .09
203 Andres Galarraga .30 .09
204 Tom Gordon .30 .09
205 Henry Rodriguez .30 .09
206 Brett Tomko .30 .09
207 Dante Bichette .30 .09
208 Craig Biggio .50 .15
209 Matt Lawton .30 .09
210 Tino Martinez .50 .15
211 Aaron Myette .30 .09
Josh Paul
212 Warren Morris .30 .09
213 San Diego Padres .30 .09
214 Ramon E. Martinez .30 .09
215 Troy Percival .30 .09
216 Jason Johnson .30 .09
217 Carlos Lee .30 .09
218 Scott Williamson .30 .09
219 Jeff Weaver .30 .09
220 Ronnie Belliard .30 .09
221 Jason Giambi .75 .23
222 Ken Griffey Jr. 1.25 .35
223 John Halama .30 .09
224 Brett Hinchliffe .30 .09
225 Wilson Alvarez .30 .09
226 Rolando Arrojo .30 .09
227 Ruben Mateo .30 .09
228 Rafael Palmeiro .50 .15
229 David Wells .30 .09
230 Eric Gagne .75 .23
Jeff Williams RC
231 Tim Salmon .50 .15
232 Mike Mussina .75 .23
233 Magglio Ordonez .30 .09
234 Ron Villone .30 .09
235 Antonio Alfonseca .30 .09
236 Jeromy Burnitz .30 .09
237 Ben Grieve .30 .09
238 Giomar Guevara .30 .09
239 Garret Anderson .30 .09
240 John Smoltz .50 .15
241 Mark Grace .50 .15
242 Cole Liniak .30 .09
Jose Molina
243 Damion Easley .30 .09
244 Jeff Montgomery .30 .09
245 Kenny Lofton .30 .09
246 Masato Yoshii .30 .09
247 Philadelphia Phillies .30 .09
248 Raul Mondesi .30 .09
249 Marlon Anderson .30 .09
250 Shawn Green .30 .09
251 Sterling Hitchcock .30 .09
252 Randy Wolf .30 .09
Anthony Shumaker
253 Jeff Fassero .30 .09
254 Eli Marrero .30 .09
255 Cincinnati Reds .30 .09
256 Rick Ankiel .30 .09
Adam Kennedy
257 Darin Erstad .30 .09
258 Albert Belle .30 .09
259 Bartolo Colon .30 .09
260 Bret Saberhagen .30 .09
261 Carlos Beltran .30 .09
262 Glenallen Hill .30 .09
263 Gregg Jefferies .30 .09
264 Matt Clement .30 .09
265 Miguel Del Toro .30 .09
266 Robinson Cancel .30 .09
Kevin Barker
267 San Francisco Giants .30 .09
268 Kent Bottenfield .30 .09
269 Fred McGriff .50 .15
270 Chris Carpenter .30 .09
271 Atlanta Braves .30 .09
272 Wilton Veras .40 .12
Tomo Ohka RC
273 Will Clark .75 .23
274 Troy O'Leary .30 .09
275 Sammy Sosa CL .75 .23
276 Travis Lee .30 .09
277 Sean Casey .30 .09
278 Ron Gant .30 .09
279 Roger Clemens 1.50 .45
280 Phil Nevin .30 .09
281 Mike Piazza 1.25 .35
282 Mike Lowell .30 .09
283 Kevin Millwood .30 .09
284 Joe Randa .30 .09
285 Jeff Shaw .30 .09
286 Jason Varitek .30 .09
287 Harold Baines .30 .09
288 Gabe Kapler .30 .09
289 Chuck Finley .30 .09
290 Carl Pavano .30 .09
291 Brad Ausmus .30 .09
292 Brad Fullmer .30 .09
293 Boston Red Sox .30 .09
294 Bob Wickman .30 .09
295 Billy Wagner .30 .09
296 Shawn Estes .30 .09
297 Gary Sheffield .30 .09
298 Fernando Seguignol .30 .09
299 Omar Olivares .30 .09
300 Baltimore Orioles .30 .09
301 Matt Stairs .30 .09
302 Andy Ashby .30 .09
303 Todd Greene .30 .09
304 Jesse Garcia .30 .09
305 Kerry Wood .75 .23
306 Roberto Alomar .75 .23
307 New York Mets .30 .09
308 Dean Palmer .30 .09
309 Mike Hampton .30 .09
310 Devon White .30 .09
311 Chad Hermansen .30 .09
Mike Garcia RC
312 Tim Hudson .50 .15
313 John Franco .30 .09
314 Jason Schmidt .30 .09
315 J.T. Snow .30 .09
316 Ed Sprague .30 .09
317 Chris Widger .30 .09
318 Ben Petrick .30 .09
Luther Hackman RC
319 Jose Mesa .30 .09
320 Jose Canseco .75 .23
321 John Wetteland .30 .09
322 Minnesota Twins .30 .09
323 Jeff DaVanon RC .40 .12
Brian Cooper
324 Tony Womack .30 .09
325 Rod Beck .30 .09
326 Mickey Morandini .30 .09
327 Pokey Reese .30 .09
328 Jaret Wright .30 .09
329 Glen Barker .30 .09
330 Darren Dreifort .30 .09
331 Torii Hunter .30 .09
332 Tony Armas .30 .09
Peter Bergeron
333 Hideki Irabu .30 .09
334 Desi Relaford .30 .09
335 Barry Bonds 2.00 .60
336 Gary DiSarcina .30 .09
337 Gerald Williams .30 .09
338 John Valentin .30 .09
339 David Justice .30 .09
340 Juan Encarnacion .30 .09
341 Jeremy Giambi .30 .09
342 Chan Ho Park .30 .09
343 Vladimir Guerrero .75 .23
344 Robin Ventura .50 .15
345 Bob Abreu .30 .09
346 Tony Gwynn 1.00 .30
347 Jose Jimenez .30 .09
348 Royce Clayton .30 .09
349 Kelvim Escobar .30 .09
350 Chicago Cubs .30 .09
351 Travis Dawkins .30 .09
Jason LaRue
352 Barry Larkin .75 .23
353 Cal Ripken 2.50 .75
354 Alex Rodriguez CL .75 .23
355 Todd Stottlemyre .30 .09
356 Terry Adams .30 .09
357 Pittsburgh Pirates .30 .09
358 Jim Thome .75 .23
359 Corey Lee .30 .09
Doug Davis
360 Moises Alou .30 .09
361 Todd Hollandsworth .30 .09
362 Marty Cordova .30 .09
363 David Cone .30 .09
364 Joe Nathan .30 .09
Wilson Delgado
365 Paul Byrd .30 .09
366 Edgar Renteria .30 .09
367 Rusty Greer .30 .09
368 David Segui .30 .09
369 New York Yankees .50 .15
370 Daryle Ward .30 .09
Carlos Hernandez
371 Troy Glaus .50 .15
372 Delino DeShields .30 .09
373 Jose Offerman .30 .09
374 Sammy Sosa 1.25 .35
375 Sandy Alomar Jr. .30 .09
376 Masao Kida .30 .09
377 Richard Hidalgo .30 .09
378 Ismael Valdes .30 .09
379 Ugueth Urbina .30 .09
380 Darryl Hamilton .30 .09
381 John Jaha .30 .09
382 St. Louis Cardinals .30 .09
383 Scott Sauerbeck .30 .09
384 Russ Ortiz .30 .09
385 Jamie Moyer .30 .09
386 Dave Martinez .30 .09
387 Todd Zeile .30 .09
388 Anaheim Angels .30 .09
389 Rob Ryan .30 .09
Nick Bierbrodt
390 Rickey Henderson .75 .23
391 Alex Rodriguez 1.25 .35
392 Texas Rangers .30 .09
393 Roberto Hernandez .30 .09
394 Tony Batista .30 .09
395 Oakland Athletics .30 .09
396 Randall Simon .30 .09
Dave Cortes RC
397 Gregg Olson .30 .09
398 Sidney Ponson .30 .09
399 Micah Bowie .30 .09
400 Mark McGwire 2.00 .60
401 Florida Marlins .30 .09
402 Chad Allen .30 .09
403 Casey Blake .30 .09
Vernon Wells
404 Pete Harnisch .30 .09
405 Preston Wilson .30 .09
406 Richie Sexson .30 .09
407 Rico Brogna .30 .09
408 Todd Hundley .30 .09
409 Wally Joyner .30 .09
410 Tom Goodwin .30 .09
411 Joey Hamilton .30 .09
412 Detroit Tigers .30 .09
413 Michael Tejera RC .30 .09
Ramon Castro
414 Alex Gonzalez .30 .09
415 Jermaine Dye .30 .09
416 Jose Rosado .30 .09
417 Wilton Guerrero .30 .09
418 Rondell White .30 .09
419 Al Leiter .30 .09
420 Bernie Williams .50 .15
421 A.J. Hinch .30 .09
422 Pat Burrell .50 .15
423 Scott Rolen .50 .15
424 Jason Kendall .30 .09
425 Kevin Young .30 .09
426 Eric Owens .30 .09
427 Derek Jeter CL .75 .23
428 Livan Hernandez .30 .09
429 Russ Davis .30 .09
430 Dan Wilson .30 .09
431 Quinton McCracken .30 .09
432 Homer Bush .30 .09
433 Seattle Mariners .30 .09
434 Chad Harville .30 .09
Luis Vizcaino
435 Carlos Beltran AW .30 .09
436 Scott Williamson AW .30 .09
437 Pedro Martinez AW .50 .15
438 Randy Johnson AW .50 .15
439 Ivan Rodriguez AW .50 .15
440 Chipper Jones AW .50 .15
441 Bernie Williams DIV .30 .09
442 Pedro Martinez DIV .50 .15
443 Derek Jeter DIV 1.00 .30
444 Brian Jordan DIV .30 .09
445 Todd Pratt DIV .30 .09
446 Kevin Millwood DIV .30 .09
447 Orl.Hernandez WS .30 .09
448 Derek Jeter WS 1.00 .30
449 Chad Curtis WS .30 .09
450 Roger Clemens WS .75 .23
P353 Cal Ripken Promo 3.00 .90

2000 Fleer Tradition Glossy

The 2000 Fleer Glossy set was released in early December, 2000 and features a 500-card base set. Please note that you only receive 455 of the 500 total cards that make up this set per sealed factory set. Card 451-500 are short-printed and are inserted into sets at five per factory sealed set. Cards 451-500 are serial numbered to 1000.

Nm-Mt Ex-Mt
COMP.FACT.SET (455) 60.00 18.00
*STARS 1-450: .75X TO 2X BASIC
*ROOKIES 1-450: .75X TO 2X BASIC
451 Carlos Casimiro RC 10.00 3.00
452 Adam Melhuse RC 10.00 3.00
453 Adam Bernero RC 10.00 3.00
454 Dusty Allen RC 10.00 3.00
455 Chan Perry RC 10.00 3.00
456 Damian Rolls RC 10.00 3.00
457 Josh Phelps RC 25.00 7.50
458 Barry Zito 40.00 12.00
459 Hector Ortiz RC 10.00 3.00
460 Juan Pierre RC 25.00 7.50
461 Jose Ortiz RC 10.00 3.00
462 Chad Zerbe RC 15.00 4.50
463 Julio Zuleta RC 10.00 3.00
464 Eric Byrnes 15.00 4.50
465 Wilf. Rodriguez RC 10.00 3.00
466 Wascar Serrano RC 10.00 3.00
467 Aaron McNeal RC 10.00 3.00
468 Paul Rigdon RC 10.00 3.00
469 John Snyder RC 10.00 3.00
470 J.C. Romero RC 10.00 3.00
471 Talmadge Nunnari RC 10.00 3.00
472 Mike Lamb 10.00 3.00
473 Ryan Kohlmeier RC 10.00 3.00
474 Rodney Lindsey RC 10.00 3.00
475 Elvis Pena RC 10.00 3.00
476 Alex Cabrera 10.00 3.00
477 Chris Richard 10.00 3.00
478 Pedro Feliz RC 10.00 3.00
479 Ross Gload RC 10.00 3.00
480 Timo Perez RC 10.00 3.00
481 Jason Woolf RC 10.00 3.00
482 Kenny Kelly RC 10.00 3.00
483 Sang-Hoon Lee 10.00 3.00
484 John Riedling RC 10.00 3.00
485 Chris Wakeland RC 10.00 3.00
486 Britt Reames RC 10.00 3.00
487 Greg LaRocca RC 10.00 3.00
488 Randy Keisler RC 10.00 3.00
489 Xavier Nady RC 25.00 7.50
490 Keith Ginter RC 10.00 3.00
491 Joey Nation RC 10.00 3.00
492 Kazuhiro Sasaki 15.00 4.50
493 Lesli Brea RC 10.00 3.00
494 Jace Brewer 10.00 3.00
495 Yohanny Valera RC 10.00 3.00
496 Adam Piatt 10.00 3.00
497 Nate Rolison 10.00 3.00
498 Aubrey Huff 10.00 3.00
499 Jason Tyner 10.00 3.00
500 Corey Patterson 15.00 4.50

2000 Fleer Tradition Glossy Hawaii

This is a parallel set to the regular Fleer Glossy set. Each paying participant to the Hawaii Trade Show received one of these cards at the Meet the Industry Event at the CTA booth. All of the cards in this set are given a special Hawaii Trade show logo where it says the card is a "1 of 1". Since these cards are extremely limited, no pricing information is provided.

Nm-Mt Ex-Mt
STATED PRINT RUN 1 SERIAL #'d SET

2000 Fleer Tradition Dividends

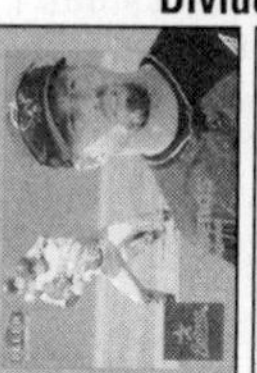

Inserted at a rate of one in six packs, these 15 cards feature some of the best players in the game.

Nm-Mt Ex-Mt
COMPLETE SET (15) 15.00 4.50
D1 Alex Rodriguez 1.25 .35
D2 Ben Grieve .30 .09
D3 Cal Ripken 2.50 .75
D4 Chipper Jones .75 .23
D5 Derek Jeter 1.50 .45
D6 Frank Thomas .75 .23

D7 Jeff Bagwell .50 .15
D8 Sammy Sosa 1.25 .35
D9 Tony Gwynn 1.00 .30
D10 Scott Rolen .50 .15
D11 Nomar Garciaparra 1.25 .35
D12 Mike Piazza 1.25 .35
D13 Mark McGwire 2.00 .60
D14 Ken Griffey Jr. 1.25 .35
D15 Juan Gonzalez .75 .23

2000 Fleer Tradition Fresh Ink

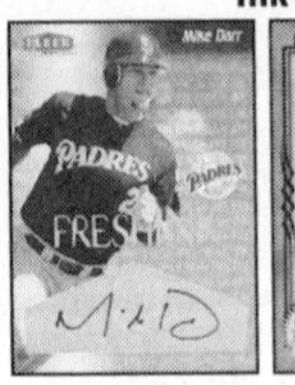

Randomly inserted into packs at one in 144 packs, this insert set features autographed cards of players such as Rick Ankiel, Sean Casey and J.D. Drew.

Nm-Mt Ex-Mt
1 Rick Ankiel 10.00 3.00
2 Carlos Beltran 15.00 4.50
3 Pat Burrell 25.00 7.50
4 Miguel Cairo 10.00 3.00
5 Sean Casey 15.00 4.50
6 Will Clark 50.00 15.00
7 Mike Darr 10.00 3.00
8 J.D. Drew 15.00 4.50
9 Erubiel Durazo 15.00 4.50
10 Carlos Febles 10.00 3.00
11 Freddy Garcia 15.00 4.50
12 Jason Grilli 10.00 3.00
13 Vladimir Guerrero 50.00 15.00
14 Tony Gwynn 50.00 15.00
15 Jerry Hairston Jr. 10.00 3.00
16 Tim Hudson 25.00 7.50
17 John Jaha 10.00 3.00
18 D'Angelo Jimenez 10.00 3.00
19 Andruw Jones 30.00 9.00
20 Gabe Kapler 10.00 3.00
21 Cesar King 10.00 3.00
22 Jason LaRue 10.00 3.00
23 Mike Lieberthal 15.00 4.50
24 Greg Maddux 120.00 36.00
25 Pedro Martinez 80.00 24.00
26 Gary Matthews Jr. 10.00 3.00
27 Orber Moreno 10.00 3.00
28 Eric Munson 15.00 4.50
29 Rafael Palmeiro 50.00 15.00
30 Jim Parque 10.00 3.00
31 Wily Pena 10.00 3.00
32 Cal Ripken 150.00 45.00
33 Alex Rodriguez 120.00 36.00
34 Tim Salmon 30.00 9.00
35 Chris Singleton 10.00 3.00
36 Alfonso Soriano 50.00 15.00
37 Ed Yarnall 10.00 3.00

2000 Fleer Tradition Grasskickers

Inserted at a rate of one in 30 packs, these 15 cards printed on rainbow holofoil feature players who put fear into their opponents.

Nm-Mt Ex-Mt
COMPLETE SET (15) 60.00 18.00
GK1 Tony Gwynn 5.00 1.50
GK2 Scott Rolen 2.50 .75
GK3 Nomar Garciaparra 6.00 1.80
GK4 Mike Piazza 6.00 1.80
GK5 Mark McGwire 10.00 3.00
GK6 Frank Thomas 4.00 1.20
GK7 Cal Ripken 12.00 3.60
GK8 Chipper Jones 4.00 1.20
GK9 Greg Maddux 6.00 1.80
GK10 Ken Griffey Jr. 6.00 1.80
GK11 Juan Gonzalez 4.00 1.20
GK12 Derek Jeter 8.00 2.40
GK13 Sammy Sosa 6.00 1.80
GK14 Roger Clemens 8.00 2.40
GK15 Alex Rodriguez 6.00 1.80

2000 Fleer Tradition Hall's Well

Inserted at a rate of one in 30 packs, these 15 cards feature players on their path to the Hall of Fame. The cards were printed on a combination of transparent plastic stock with overlays of silver foil stamping.

Nm-Mt Ex-Mt
COMPLETE SET (15) 50.00 15.00
HW1 Mark McGwire 10.00 3.00
HW2 Alex Rodriguez 6.00 1.80
HW3 Cal Ripken 12.00 3.60
HW4 Chipper Jones 4.00 1.20
HW5 Derek Jeter 8.00 2.40
HW6 Frank Thomas 4.00 1.20
HW7 Greg Maddux 6.00 1.80
HW8 Juan Gonzalez 4.00 1.20
HW9 Ken Griffey Jr. 6.00 1.80
HW10 Mike Piazza 6.00 1.80
HW11 Nomar Garciaparra 6.00 1.80
HW12 Sammy Sosa 6.00 1.80
HW13 Roger Clemens 8.00 2.40
HW14 Ivan Rodriguez 4.00 1.20
HW15 Tony Gwynn 5.00 1.50

2000 Fleer Tradition Ripken Collection

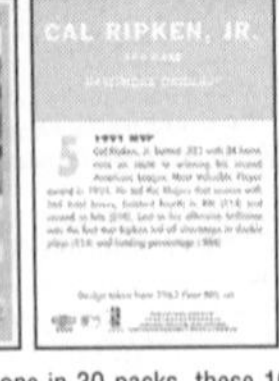

Inserted at a rate of one in 30 packs, these 10 cards feature photos of Cal Ripken Jr. in the style of vintage Fleer cards. We have identified the style of the card and the sport next to Ripken's name.

Nm-Mt Ex-Mt
COMMON CARD (1-10) 10.00 3.00

2000 Fleer Tradition Ten-4

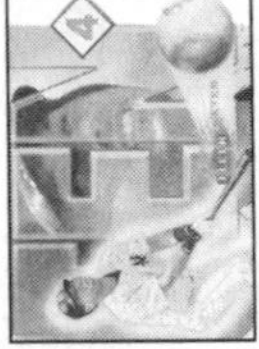
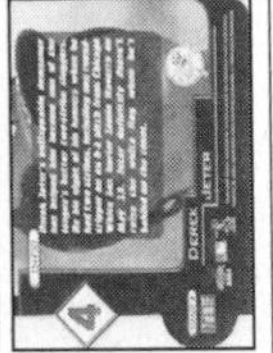

Issued at a rate of one in 18 packs, these 10 cards feature the best home run hitters highlighted on a die-cut card with silver foil stamping.

Nm-Mt Ex-Mt
COMPLETE SET (10) 25.00 7.50
TF1 Sammy Sosa 3.00 .90
TF2 Nomar Garciaparra 3.00 .90
TF3 Mike Piazza 3.00 .90
TF4 Mark McGwire 5.00 1.50
TF5 Ken Griffey Jr. 3.00 .90
TF6 Juan Gonzalez 2.00 .60
TF7 Derek Jeter 4.00 1.20
TF8 Chipper Jones 2.00 .60
TF9 Cal Ripken 6.00 1.80
TF10 Alex Rodriguez 3.00 .90

2000 Fleer Tradition Who To Watch

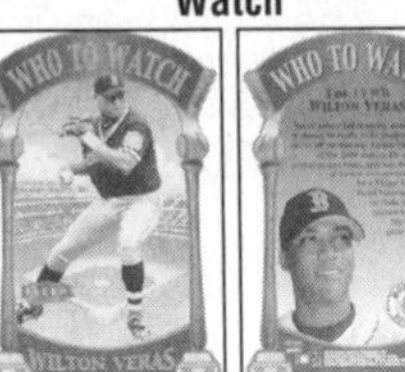

Inserted at a rate of one in three, these 15 cards feature leading prospects against a nostalgic die-cut background.

Nm-Mt Ex-Mt
COMPLETE SET (15) 5.00 1.50
WW1 Rick Ankiel .50 .15
WW2 Matt Riley .50 .15
WW3 Wilton Veras .50 .15
WW4 Ben Petrick .50 .15
WW5 Chad Hermansen .50 .15
WW6 Peter Bergeron .50 .15
WW7 Mark Quinn .50 .15
WW8 Russell Branyan .50 .15
WW9 Alfonso Soriano 1.00 .30
WW10 Randy Wolf .50 .15
WW11 Ben Davis .50 .15
WW12 Jeff DaVanon .50 .15
WW13 D'Angelo Jimenez .50 .15
WW14 Vernon Wells .50 .15
WW15 Adam Kennedy .50 .15

2000 Fleer Tradition Glossy Lumberjacks

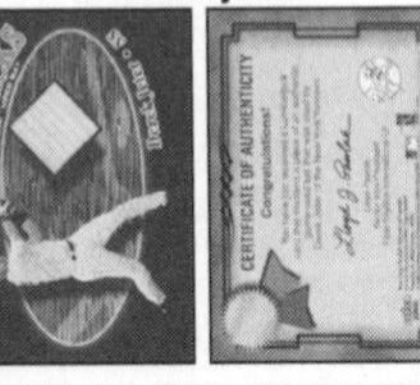

Inserted into Fleer Glossy sets at one per set, this 45-card insert set features game-used bat pieces from some of the top players in baseball. Print runs are listed below.

Nm-Mt Ex-Mt
1 Edgardo Alfonzo/145 12.00 3.60
2 Roberto Alomar/627 15.00 4.50
3 Moises Alou/529 10.00 3.00
4 Carlos Beltran/489 10.00 3.00
5 Adrian Beltre/127 12.00 3.60
6 Wade Boggs/30
7 Barry Bonds/305 40.00 12.00
8 Jeromy Burnitz/34
9 Pat Burrell/45
10 Sean Casey/50
11 Eric Chavez/259 10.00 3.00
12 Tony Clark/70 15.00 4.50
13 Carlos Delgado/70 15.00 4.50
14 J.D. Drew/135 12.00 3.60
15 Erubiel Durazo/70 15.00 4.50
16 Ray Durham/35
17 Carlos Febles/120 12.00 3.60
18 Jason Giambi/220 15.00 4.50
19 Shawn Green/429 10.00 3.00
20 Vladimir Guerrero/809 15.00 4.50
21 Derek Jeter/180 60.00 18.00
22 Chipper Jones/725 15.00 4.50
23 Gabe Kapler/160 12.00 3.60
24 Jason Kendall/34
25 Paul Konerko/70 15.00 4.50
26 Ray Lankford/35
27 Mike Lieberthal/45
28 Edgar Martinez/211 15.00 4.50
29 Raul Mondesi/458 10.00 3.00
30 Warren Morris/35
31 Magglio Ordonez/190 12.00 3.60
32 Rafael Palmeiro/49
33 Pokey Reese/110 12.00 3.60
34 Cal Ripken/235 80.00 24.00
35 Alex Rodriguez/292 40.00 12.00
36 Ivan Rodriguez/602 15.00 4.50
37 Scott Rolen/502 15.00 4.50
38 Chris Singleton/68 15.00 4.50
39 Alfonso Soriano/285 15.00 4.50
40 Frank Thomas/489 15.00 4.50
41 Jim Thome/479 15.00 4.50
42 Robin Ventura/114 12.00 3.60
43 Jose Vidro/60 15.00 4.50
44 Bernie Williams/215 15.00 4.50
45 Matt Williams/152 12.00 3.60

2000 Fleer Tradition Update

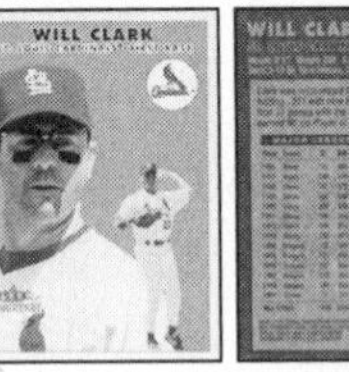

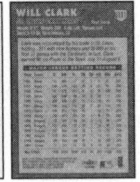

The 2000 Fleer Tradition Update set was released in October, 2000 as a 150-card factory set. The set includes 10 Season Highlight cards (1-10), and 140 cards of players that were either traded during the season or who made their major league debut (cards 11-150). Each set originally carried a suggested retail price of $29.99. Please note that card number 50 does not exist. All cards have a "U" prefix. Notable Rookie Cards include Kazuhiro Sasaki and Barry Zito. Finally, one in every 80 sets contained a Mickey Mantle game-worn jersey memorabilia card.

Nm-Mt Ex-Mt
COMP.FACT.SET (149) 20.00 6.00
1 Ken Griffey Jr. SH .75 .23
2 Cal Ripken SH 1.00 .30
3 Randy Velarde SH .30 .09
4 Fred McGriff SH .30 .09
5 Derek Jeter SH .75 .23
6 Tom Glavine SH .30 .09
7 Brent Mayne SH .30 .09
8 Alex Ochoa SH .30 .09
9 Scott Sheldon SH .30 .09
10 Randy Johnson SH .50 .15
11 Daniel Garibay RC .30 .09
12 Brad Fullmer .30 .09
13 Kazuhiro Sasaki RC 1.25 .35
14 Andy Tracy RC .30 .09
15 Bret Boone .30 .09
16 Chad Durbin RC .40 .12
17 Mark Buehrle RC 1.25 .35
18 Julio Zuleta RC .40 .12
19 Jeremy Giambi .30 .09
20 Gene Stechschulte RC .30 .09
21 Lou Pote .30 .09
Bengie Molina
22 Darrell Einertson RC .30 .09
23 Ken Griffey Jr. 1.25 .35
24 Jeff Sparks RC .30 .09
Dan Wheeler
25 Aaron Fultz RC .30 .09
26 Derek Bell .30 .09
27 Rob Bell .30 .09
D.T. Cromer
28 Robert Fick .30 .09
29 Darryl Kile .30 .09
30 Clayton Andrews .30 .09
John Bale RC
31 Dave Veres .30 .09
32 Hector Mercado RC .30 .09
33 Willie Morales RC .30 .09
34 Kelly Wunsch .30 .09
Kip Wells
35 Hideki Irabu .30 .09
36 Sean DePaula RC .30 .09
37 DeWayne Wise .30 .09
Chris Woodward
38 Curt Schilling .50 .15
39 Mark Johnson .30 .09
40 Mike Cameron .30 .09
41 Scott Sheldon .30 .09
Tom Evans
42 Brett Tomko .30 .09
43 Johan Santana RC 2.50 .75
44 Andy Benes .30 .09
45 Matt LeCroy .30 .09
Mark Redman
46 Ryan Klesko .30 .09
47 Andy Ashby .30 .09
48 Octavio Dotel .30 .09
49 Eric Byrnes RC 1.00 .30
50 Does Not Exist
51 Kenny Rogers .30 .09
52 Ben Weber RC .40 .12
53 Matt Blank .30 .09
Scott Strickland
54 Tom Goodwin .30 .09
55 Jim Edmonds Cards .30 .09
56 Derrick Turnbow RC .40 .12
57 Mark Mulder .50 .15
58 Tarrick Brock .30 .09
Ruben Quevedo
59 Danny Young RC .30 .09
60 Fernando Vina .30 .09
61 Justin Brunette RC .30 .09
62 Jimmy Anderson .30 .09
63 Reggie Sanders .30 .09
64 Adam Kennedy .30 .09
65 Jesse Garcia .30 .09
B.J. Ryan
66 Al Martin .30 .09
67 Kevin Walker RC .30 .09
68 Brad Penny .30 .09
69 B.J. Surhoff .30 .09
70 Geoff Blum .30 .09
Trace Coquillette RC
71 Jose Jimenez .30 .09
72 Chuck Finley .30 .09
73 Valerio De Los Santos .30 .09
Everett Stull
74 Terry Adams .30 .09
75 Rafael Furcal .30 .09
76 John Roskos .30 .09
Mike Darr
77 Quilvio Veras .30 .09
78 Armando Almanza .30 .09
Nate Rolison
79 Greg Vaughn .30 .09
80 Keith McDonald RC .30 .09
81 Eric Cammack RC .30 .09
82 Horacio Estrada .30 .09
Ray King
83 Kory DeHaan .30 .09
84 Kevin Hodges RC .30 .09
85 Mike Lamb RC .40 .12
86 Shawn Green .30 .09
87 Dan Reichert .30 .09
Jason Rakers
88 Adam Piatt .30 .09
89 Mike Garcia .30 .09
90 Rodrigo Lopez RC .60 .18
91 John Olerud .30 .09
92 Barry Zito RC 4.00 1.20
Terrence Long
93 Jimmy Rollins .30 .09
94 Denny Neagle .30 .09
95 Rickey Henderson .75 .23
96 Adam Eaton .30 .09
Buddy Carlyle
97 Brian O'Connor RC .30 .09
98 Andy Thompson RC .30 .09
99 Jason Boyd RC .30 .09
100 Joel Pineiro RC 4.00 1.20
Carlos Guillen
101 Raul Gonzalez RC .30 .09
102 Brandon Kolb RC .30 .09
103 Jason Maxwell .30 .09
Mike Lincoln
104 Luis Matos RC 1.50 .45
105 Morgan Burkhart RC .30 .09
106 Ismael Villegas RC .30 .09
Steve Sisco RC
107 David Justice Yankees .30 .09
108 Pablo Ozuna .30 .09
109 Jose Canseco .75 .23
110 Alex Cora .30 .09
Shawn Gilbert
111 Will Clark Cardinals .75 .23
112 Keith Luuloa .30 .09
Eric Weaver
113 Bruce Chen .30 .09
114 Adam Hyzdu .30 .09
115 Scott Forster RC .30 .09
Yovanny Lara RC
116 Allen McDill RC .30 .09
Jose Macias
117 Kevin Nicholson .30 .09
118 Israel Alcantara .30 .09
Tim Young
119 Juan Alvarez RC .30 .09
120 Julio Lugo .30 .09
Mitch Meluskey
121 B.J. Waszgis RC .30 .09
122 Jeff M. D'Amico RC .30 .09
Brett Laxton
123 Ricky Ledee .30 .09
124 Mark DeRosa .30 .09
Jason Marquis
125 Alex Cabrera RC .40 .12
126 Augie Ojeda RC .30 .09
Gary Matthews Jr.
127 Richie Sexson .30 .09
128 Santiago Perez RC .30 .09
Hector Ramirez RC
129 Rondell White .30 .09
130 Craig House RC .30 .09
131 Kevin Beirne .30 .09
Jon Garland
132 Wayne Franklin RC .30 .09
133 Henry Rodriguez .30 .09
134 Jay Payton .30 .09
Jim Mann
135 Ron Gant .30 .09
136 Paxton Crawford RC .30 .09
Sang-Hoon Lee RC
137 Kent Bottenfield .30 .09
138 Rocky Biddle RC .30 .09
139 Travis Lee .30 .09
140 Ryan Vogelsong RC .40 .12
141 Jason Conti .30 .09
Geraldo Guzman RC
142 Tim Drew .30 .09
Mark Watson RC
143 John Parrish RC .40 .12
Chris Richard RC
144 Javier Cardona RC .30 .09
Brandon Villafuerte RC
145 Tike Redman RC .40 .12
Steve Sparks RC
146 Brian Schneider .30 .09
Matt Skrmetta RC
147 Pasqual Coco RC .30 .09
148 Lorenzo Barcelo RC .30 .09
Joe Crede
149 Jace Brewer RC .40 .12
150 Milton Bradley .40 .12
Tomas De La Rosa RC
MP1 Mickey Mantle 200.00 60.00

2001 Fleer Tradition

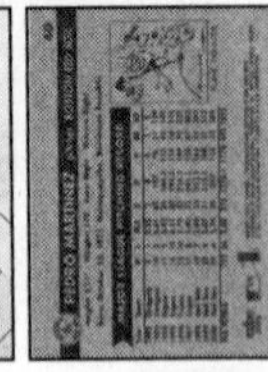

The 2001 Fleer Tradition product was released in early February, 2001 and initially featured a 450-card base set that was broken into tiers as follows: Base Veterans (1-350), Prospects (351-380), League Leaders (381-410), World Series Highlights (411-420), and Team Checklists (421-450). Each pack contained 10 cards and carried a suggested retail price of $1.99 per pack. In late October, 2001, a 485-card factory set carrying a $42.99 SRP was released. Each factory set contained the basic 450-card set plus 35 new cards (451-485) featuring a selection of rookies and prospects. Please note that there was also 100 exchange cards inserted into packs in which lucky collectors received an uncut sheet of 2001 Fleer.

Nm-Mt Ex-Mt
COMP.FACT.SET (485) 50.00 15.00
COMPLETE SET (450) 25.00 7.50
COMMON CARD (1-450) .30 .09
COMMON (451-485) .50 .15
1 Andres Galarraga .30 .09
2 Armando Rios .30 .09
3 Julio Lugo .30 .09
4 Darryl Hamilton .30 .09
5 Dave Veres .30 .09
6 Edgardo Alfonzo .30 .09
7 Brook Fordyce .30 .09
8 Eric Karros .30 .09
9 Neifi Perez .30 .09
10 Jim Edmonds .30 .09
11 Barry Larkin .75 .23
12 Trot Nixon .50 .15
13 Andy Pettitte .50 .15
14 Jose Guillen .30 .09
15 David Wells .30 .09
16 Magglio Ordonez .30 .09
17 David Segui .30 .09
17A David Segui ERR .30 .09
Card has no number on the back
18 Juan Encarnacion .30 .09
19 Robert Person .30 .09
20 Quilvio Veras .30 .09
21 Mo Vaughn .30 .09
22 B.J. Surhoff .30 .09
23 Ken Caminiti .30 .09
24 Frank Catalanotto .30 .09
25 Luis Gonzalez .30 .09
26 Pete Harnisch .30 .09
27 Alex Gonzalez .30 .09
28 Mark Quinn .30 .09
29 Luis Castillo .30 .09
30 Rick Helling .30 .09
31 Barry Bonds 2.00 .60
32 Warren Morris .30 .09
33 Aaron Boone .30 .09
34 Ricky Gutierrez .30 .09
35 Preston Wilson .30 .09
36 Erubiel Durazo .30 .09
37 Jermaine Dye .30 .09
38 John Rocker .30 .09
39 Mark Grudzielanek .30 .09
40 Pedro Martinez .75 .23
41 Phil Nevin .30 .09
42 Luis Matos .30 .09
43 Orlando Hernandez .30 .09
44 Steve Cox .30 .09
45 James Baldwin .30 .09
46 Rafael Furcal .30 .09
47 Todd Zeile .30 .09
48 Elmer Dessens .30 .09
49 Russell Branyan .30 .09
50 Juan Gonzalez .75 .23
51 Mac Suzuki .30 .09
52 Adam Kennedy .30 .09
53 Randy Velarde .30 .09
54 David Bell .30 .09
55 Royce Clayton .30 .09
56 Greg Colbrunn .30 .09
57 Rey Ordonez .30 .09
58 Kevin Millwood .30 .09
59 Fernando Vina .30 .09
60 Eddie Taubensee .30 .09
61 Enrique Wilson .30 .09
62 Jay Bell .30 .09
63 Brian Moehler .30 .09
64 Brad Fullmer .30 .09
65 Ben Petrick .30 .09
66 Orlando Cabrera .30 .09
67 Shane Reynolds .30 .09
68 Mitch Meluskey .30 .09
69 Jeff Shaw .30 .09
70 Chipper Jones .75 .23
71 Tomo Ohka .30 .09
72 Ruben Rivera .30 .09
73 Mike Sirotka .30 .09
74 Scott Rolen .50 .15
75 Glendon Rusch .30 .09
76 Miguel Tejada .30 .09
77 Brady Anderson .30 .09
78 Bartolo Colon .30 .09
79 Ron Coomer .30 .09
80 Gary DiSarcina .30 .09
81 Geoff Jenkins .30 .09
82 Billy Koch .30 .09
83 Mike Lamb .30 .09
84 Alex Rodriguez 1.25 .35
85 Denny Neagle .30 .09
86 Michael Tucker .30 .09
87 Edgar Renteria .30 .09

88 Brian Anderson .30 .09
89 Glenallen Hill .30 .09
90 Aramis Ramirez .30 .09
91 Rondell White .30 .09
92 Tony Womack .30 .09
93 Jeffrey Hammonds .30 .09
94 Freddy Garcia .30 .09
95 Bill Mueller .30 .09
96 Mike Lieberthal .30 .09
97 Michael Barrett .30 .09
98 Derrek Lee .30 .09
99 Bill Spiers .30 .09
100 Derek Lowe .30 .09
101 Javy Lopez .30 .09
102 Adrian Beltre .30 .09
103 Jim Parque .30 .09
104 Marquis Grissom .30 .09
105 Eric Chavez .30 .09
106 Todd Jones .30 .09
107 Eric Owens .30 .09
108 Roger Clemens 1.50 .45
109 Denny Hocking .30 .09
110 Roberto Hernandez .30 .09
111 Albert Belle .30 .09
112 Troy Glaus .50 .15
113 Ivan Rodriguez .75 .23
114 Carlos Guillen .30 .09
115 Chuck Finley .30 .09
116 Dmitri Young .30 .09
117 Paul Konerko .30 .09
118 Damon Buford .30 .09
119 Fernando Tatis .30 .09
120 Larry Walker .50 .15
121 Jason Kendall .30 .09
122 Matt Williams .30 .09
123 Henry Rodriguez .30 .09
124 Placido Polanco .30 .09
125 Bobby Estalella .30 .09
126 Pat Burrell .30 .09
127 Mark Loretta .30 .09
128 Moises Alou .30 .09
129 Tino Martinez .50 .15
130 Milton Bradley .30 .09
131 Todd Hundley .30 .09
132 Keith Foulke .30 .09
133 Robert Fick .30 .09
134 Cristian Guzman .30 .09
135 Rusty Greer .30 .09
136 John Olerud .30 .09
137 Mariano Rivera .50 .15
138 Jeromy Burnitz .30 .09
139 Dave Burba .30 .09
140 Ken Griffey Jr. 1.25 .35
141 Tony Gwynn 1.00 .30
142 Carlos Delgado .30 .09
143 Edgar Martinez .50 .15
144 Ramon Hernandez .30 .09
145 Pedro Astacio .30 .09
146 Ray Lankford .30 .09
147 Mike Mussina .75 .23
148 Ray Durham .30 .09
149 Lee Stevens .30 .09
150 Jay Canizaro .30 .09
151 Adrian Brown .30 .09
152 Mike Piazza 1.25 .35
153 Cliff Floyd .30 .09
154 Jose Vidro .30 .09
155 Jason Giambi .75 .23
156 Andruw Jones .30 .09
157 Robin Ventura .30 .09
158 Gary Sheffield .30 .09
159 Jeff D'Amico .30 .09
160 Chuck Knoblauch .30 .09
161 Roger Cedeno .30 .09
162 Jim Thome .75 .23
163 Peter Bergeron .30 .09
164 Kerry Wood .75 .23
165 Gabe Kapler .30 .09
166 Corey Koskie .30 .09
167 Doug Glanville .30 .09
168 Brent Mayne .30 .09
169 Scott Spiezio .30 .09
170 Steve Karsay .30 .09
171 Al Martin .30 .09
172 Fred McGriff .50 .15
173 Gabe White .30 .09
174 Alex Gonzalez .30 .09
175 Mike Darr .30 .09
176 Bengie Molina .30 .09
177 Ben Grieve .30 .09
178 Marlon Anderson .30 .09
179 Brian Giles .30 .09
180 Jose Valentin .30 .09
181 Brian Jordan .30 .09
182 Randy Johnson .75 .23
183 Ricky Ledee .30 .09
184 Russ Ortiz .30 .09
185 Mike Lowell .30 .09
186 Curtis Leskanic .30 .09
187 Bob Abreu .30 .09
188 Derek Jeter 2.00 .60
189 Lance Berkman .30 .09
190 Roberto Alomar .75 .23
191 Darin Erstad .30 .09
192 Richie Sexson .30 .09
193 Alex Ochoa .30 .09
194 Carlos Febles .30 .09
195 David Ortiz .30 .09
196 Shawn Green .30 .09
197 Mike Sweeney .30 .09
198 Vladimir Guerrero .75 .23
199 Jose Jimenez .30 .09
200 Travis Lee .30 .09
201 Rickey Henderson .75 .23
202 Bob Wickman .30 .09
203 Miguel Cairo .30 .09
204 Steve Finley .30 .09
205 Tony Batista .30 .09
206 Jamey Wright .30 .09
207 Terrence Long .30 .09
208 Trevor Hoffman .30 .09
209 John VanderWal .30 .09
210 Greg Maddux 1.25 .35
211 Tim Salmon .50 .15
212 Herbert Perry .30 .09
213 Marvin Benard .30 .09
214 Jose Offerman .30 .09
215 Jay Payton .30 .09
216 Jon Lieber .30 .09
217 Mark Kotsay .30 .09
218 Scott Brosius .30 .09
219 Scott Williamson .30 .09
220 Omar Vizquel .30 .09
221 Mike Hampton .30 .09
222 Richard Hidalgo .30 .09
223 Rey Sanchez .30 .09
224 Matt Lawton .30 .09
225 Bruce Chen .30 .09
226 Ryan Klesko .30 .09
227 Garret Anderson .30 .09
228 Kevin Brown .30 .09
229 Mike Cameron .30 .09
230 Tony Clark .30 .09
231 Curt Schilling .50 .15
232 Vinny Castilla .30 .09
233 Carl Pavano .30 .09
234 Eric Davis .30 .09
235 Darrin Fletcher .30 .09
236 Matt Stairs .30 .09
237 Octavio Dotel .30 .09
238 Mark Grace .50 .15
239 John Smoltz .50 .15
240 Matt Clement .30 .09
241 Ellis Burks .30 .09
242 Charles Johnson .30 .09
243 Jeff Bagwell .50 .15
244 Derek Bell .30 .09
245 Nomar Garciaparra 1.25 .35
246 Jorge Posada .50 .15
247 Ryan Dempster .30 .09
248 J.T. Snow .30 .09
249 Eric Young .30 .09
250 Daryle Ward .30 .09
251 Joe Randa .30 .09
252 Travis Fryman .30 .09
253 Mike Williams .30 .09
254 Jacque Jones .30 .09
255 Scott Elarton .30 .09
256 Mark McGwire 2.00 .60
257 Jay Buhner .30 .09
258 Randy Wolf .30 .09
259 Sammy Sosa 1.25 .35
260 Chan Ho Park .30 .09
261 Damion Easley .30 .09
262 Rick Ankiel .30 .09
263 Frank Thomas .75 .23
264 Kris Benson .30 .09
265 Luis Alicea .30 .09
266 Jeromy Burnitz .30 .09
267 Geoff Blum .30 .09
268 Joe Girardi .30 .09
269 Livan Hernandez .30 .09
270 Jeff Conine .30 .09
271 Danny Graves .30 .09
272 Craig Biggio .50 .15
273 Jose Canseco .75 .23
274 Tom Glavine .50 .15
275 Ruben Mateo .30 .09
276 Jeff Kent .30 .09
277 Kevin Young .30 .09
278 A.J. Burnett .30 .09
279 Dante Bichette .30 .09
280 Sandy Alomar Jr. .30 .09
281 John Wetteland .30 .09
282 Torii Hunter .30 .09
283 Jarrod Washburn .30 .09
284 Rich Aurilia .30 .09
285 Jeff Cirillo .30 .09
286 Fernando Seguignol .30 .09
287 Darren Dreifort .30 .09
288 Deivi Cruz .30 .09
289 Pokey Reese .30 .09
290 Garrett Stephenson .30 .09
291 Bret Boone .30 .09
292 Tim Hudson .30 .09
293 John Flaherty .30 .09
294 Shannon Stewart .30 .09
295 Shawn Estes .30 .09
296 Wilton Guerrero .30 .09
297 Delino DeShields .30 .09
298 David Justice .30 .09
299 Harold Baines .30 .09
300 Al Leiter .30 .09
301 Wil Cordero .30 .09
302 Antonio Alfonseca .30 .09
303 Sean Casey .30 .09
304 Carlos Beltran .30 .09
305 Brad Radke .30 .09
306 Jason Varitek .30 .09
307 Shigetoshi Hasegawa .30 .09
308 Todd Stottlemyre .30 .09
309 Raul Mondesi .30 .09
310 Mike Bordick .30 .09
311 Darryl Kile .30 .09
312 Dean Palmer .30 .09
313 Johnny Damon .30 .09
314 Todd Helton .50 .15
315 Chad Hermansen .30 .09
316 Kevin Appier .30 .09
317 Greg Vaughn .30 .09
318 Robb Nen .30 .09
319 Jose Cruz Jr. .30 .09
320 Ron Belliard .30 .09
321 Bernie Williams .50 .15
322 Melvin Mora .30 .09
323 Kenny Lofton .30 .09
324 Armando Benitez .30 .09
325 Carlos Lee .30 .09
326 Damian Jackson .30 .09
327 Eric Milton .30 .09
328 J.D. Drew .30 .09
329 Byung-Hyun Kim .30 .09
330 Chris Stynes .30 .09
331 Kazuhiro Sasaki .30 .09
332 Troy O'Leary .30 .09
333 Pat Hentgen .30 .09
334 Brad Ausmus .30 .09
335 Todd Walker .30 .09
336 Jason Isringhausen .30 .09
337 Gerald Williams .30 .09
338 Aaron Sele .30 .09
339 Paul O'Neill .50 .15
340 Cal Ripken 2.50 .75
341 Manny Ramirez .30 .09
342 Will Clark .75 .23
343 Mark Redman .30 .09
344 Bubba Trammell .30 .09
345 Troy Percival .30 .09
346 Chris Singleton .30 .09
347 Rafael Palmeiro .50 .15
348 Carl Everett .30 .09
349 Andy Benes .30 .09
350 Bobby Higginson .30 .09
351 Alex Cabrera .30 .09
352 Barry Zito .75 .23
353 Jace Brewer .30 .09
354 Paxton Crawford .30 .09
355 Oswaldo Mairena .30 .09
356 Joe Crede .30 .09
357 A.J. Pierzynski .30 .09
358 Daniel Garibay .30 .09
359 Jason Tyner .30 .09
360 Nate Rolison .30 .09
361 Scott Downs .30 .09
362 Keith Ginter .30 .09
363 Juan Pierre .30 .09
364 Adam Bernero .30 .09
365 Chris Richard .30 .09
366 Joey Nation .30 .09
367 Aubrey Huff .30 .09
368 Adam Eaton .30 .09
369 Jose Ortiz .30 .09
370 Eric Munson .30 .09
371 Matt Kinney .30 .09
372 Eric Byrnes .30 .09
373 Keith McDonald .30 .09
374 Matt Wise .30 .09
375 Timo Perez .30 .09
376 Julio Zuleta .30 .09
377 Jimmy Rollins .30 .09
378 Xavier Nady .30 .09
379 Ryan Kohlmeier .30 .09
380 Corey Patterson .30 .09
381 Todd Helton LL .30 .09
382 Moises Alou LL .30 .09
383 Vladimir Guerrero LL .50 .15
384 Luis Castillo LL .30 .09
385 Jeffrey Hammonds LL .30 .09
386 Nomar Garciaparra LL .75 .23
387 Carlos Delgado LL .30 .09
388 Darin Erstad LL .30 .09
389 Manny Ramirez LL .30 .09
390 Mike Sweeney LL .30 .09
391 Sammy Sosa LL .75 .23
392 Barry Bonds LL .75 .23
393 Jeff Bagwell LL .30 .09
394 Richard Hidalgo LL .30 .09
395 Vladimir Guerrero LL .50 .15
396 Troy Glaus LL .50 .15
397 Frank Thomas LL .50 .15
398 Carlos Delgado LL .30 .09
399 David Justice LL .30 .09
400 Jason Giambi LL .30 .09
401 Randy Johnson LL .50 .15
402 Kevin Brown LL .30 .09
403 Greg Maddux LL .75 .23
404 Al Leiter LL .30 .09
405 Mike Hampton LL .30 .09
406 Pedro Martinez LL .50 .15
407 Roger Clemens LL .75 .23
408 Mike Sirotka LL .30 .09
409 Mike Mussina LL .50 .15
410 Bartolo Colon LL .30 .09
411 Subway Series WS .50 .15
412 Jose Vizcaino WS .50 .15
413 Jose Vizcaino WS .50 .15
414 Roger Clemens WS .75 .23
415 Armando Benitez .30 .09
Edgardo Alfonzo
Timo Perez WS
416 Al Leiter WS .50 .15
417 Luis Sojo WS .50 .15
418 Yankees 3-Peat WS .75 .23
419 Derek Jeter WS 1.00 .30
420 Toast of the Town WS .50 .15
421 Rafael Furcal .30 .09
Chipper Jones
Greg Maddux
John Rocker
Tom Glavine CL
422 Armando Benitez .75 .23
Mike Piazza
Mike Hampton
Al Leiter CL
423 Ryan Dempster .50 .15
Luis Castillo
Antonio Alfonseca
Preston Wilson CL
424 Robert Person .50 .15
Scott Rolen
Randy Wolf
Bob Abreu
Doug Glanville CL
425 Vladimir Guerrero .50 .15
Peter Bergeron CL
426 Fernando Vina .30 .09
Dave Veres
Jim Edmonds
Rick Ankiel
Edgar Renteria
Darryl Kile CL
427 Danny Graves .30 .09
Ken Griffey Jr.
Sean Casey
Pokey Reese CL
428 Jon Lieber .50 .15
Sammy Sosa
Eric Young CL
429 Curtis Leskanic .50 .15
Geoff Jenkins
Jeff D'Amico
Jeromy Burnitz
Marquis Grissom CL
430 Scott Elarton .30 .09
Jeff Bagwell
Octavio Dotel
Moises Alou
Roger Cedeno CL
431 Mike Williams .50 .15
Jason Kendall
Kris Benson
Brian Giles CL
432 Livan Hernandez .30 .09
Jeff Kent
Robb Nen
Barry Bonds
Marvin Benard CL
433 Luis Gonzalez .30 .09
Steve Finley
Tony Womack
Randy Johnson CL
434 Jeff Shaw .30 .09
Gary Sheffield
Kevin Brown
Shawn Green
Chan Ho Park CL UER
B.Shaw should be J.Shaw
435 Jose Jimenez .30 .09
Todd Helton
Brian Bohanon
Tom Goodwin CL UER
C.Goodwin should be T.Goodwin
436 Trevor Hoffman .30 .09
Phil Nevin
Matt Clement
Eric Owens CL
437 Mariano Rivera .75 .23
Derek Jeter
Roger Clemens
Bernie Williams
Andy Pettitte CL
438 Pedro Martinez .50 .15
Nomar Garciaparra
Derek Lowe
Carl Everett CL
439 Ryan Kohlmeier .50 .15
Delino DeShields
Mike Mussina
Albert Belle CL
440 David Wells .30 .09
Carlos Delgado
Billy Koch
Raul Mondesi CL
441 Ramon Hernandez .30 .09
Fred McGriff
Miguel Cairo
Greg Vaughn CL
442 Mike Sirotka .50 .15
Frank Thomas
Keith Foulke
Ray Durham CL
443 Steve Karsay .30 .09
Manny Ramirez
Bartolo Colon
Roberto Alomar CL
444 Brian Moehler .30 .09
Deivi Cruz
Juan Encarnacion
Todd Jones
Bobby Higginson CL
445 Mac Suzuki .50 .15
Mike Sweeney
Johnny Damon
Jermaine Dye CL
446 Brad Radke .30 .09
Matt Lawton
Eric Milton
Jacque Jones
Cristian Guzman CL
447 Kazuhiro Sasaki .30 .09
Edgar Martinez
Aaron Sele
Rickey Henderson CL
448 Jason Isringhausen .30 .09
Jason Giambi
Tim Hudson
Randy Velarde CL
449 Shigetoshi Hasegawa .30 .09
Darin Erstad
Troy Percival
Troy Glaus CL
450 Rick Helling .30 .09
Rafael Palmeiro
John Wetteland
Luis Alicea CL
451 Albert Pujols RC 20.00 6.00
452 Ichiro Suzuki RC 10.00 3.00
453 Tsuyoshi Shinjo RC 1.50 .45
454 Johnny Estrada RC .75 .23
455 Elpidio Guzman RC .50 .15
456 Adrian Hernandez RC .50 .15
457 Rafael Soriano RC 2.00 .60
458 Drew Henson RC 1.50 .45
459 Juan Uribe RC .50 .15
460 Matt White RC .50 .15
461 Endy Chavez RC .50 .15
462 Bud Smith RC .50 .15
463 Morgan Ensberg RC 1.50 .45
464 Jay Gibbons RC 1.50 .45
465 Jackson Melian RC .50 .15
466 Junior Spivey RC 1.25 .35
467 Juan Cruz RC .50 .15
468 Wilson Betemit RC .50 .15
469 Alexis Gomez RC .50 .15
470 Mark Teixeira RC 8.00 2.40
471 Erick Almonte RC .50 .15
472 Travis Hafner RC 2.00 .60
473 Carlos Valderrama RC .50 .15
474 Brandon Duckworth RC .50 .15
475 Ryan Freel RC .50 .15
476 Wilkin Ruan RC .50 .15
477 Andres Torres RC .50 .15
478 Josh Towers RC .50 .15
479 Kyle Lohse RC 1.25 .35
480 Jason Michaels RC .50 .15
481 Alfonso Soriano .75 .23
482 C.C. Sabathia .50 .15
483 Roy Oswalt .75 .23
484 Ben Sheets UER .50 .15
Wrong team logo on the front
485 Adam Dunn .50 .15
NNO Uncut Sheet EXCH/100 2.00 .60

2001 Fleer Tradition Diamond Tributes

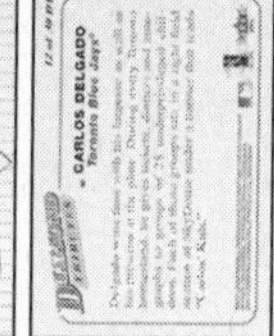

Randomly inserted into packs at one in seven, this 30-card insert is a tribute to some of the most classic players to ever step foot onto a playing field. Card backs carry a "DT" prefix.

	Nm-Mt	Ex-Mt
COMPLETE SET (30)	60.00	18.00
DT1 Jackie Robinson	2.00	.60
DT2 Mike Piazza	2.50	.75
DT3 Alex Rodriguez	2.50	.75
DT4 Barry Bonds	4.00	1.20
DT5 Nomar Garciaparra	2.50	.75
DT6 Roger Clemens	3.00	.90
DT7 Ivan Rodriguez	1.50	.45
DT8 Cal Ripken	5.00	1.50
DT9 Manny Ramirez	1.00	.30
DT10 Chipper Jones	1.50	.45
DT11 Barry Larkin	1.50	.45
DT12 Carlos Delgado	1.00	.30
DT13 J.D. Drew	1.00	.30
DT14 Carl Everett	1.00	.30
DT15 Todd Helton	1.00	.30
DT16 Greg Maddux	2.50	.75
DT17 Scott Rolen	1.00	.30
DT18 Troy Glaus	1.00	.30
DT19 Brian Giles	1.00	.30
DT20 Jeff Bagwell	1.00	.30
DT21 Sammy Sosa	2.50	.75
DT22 Randy Johnson	1.50	.45
DT23 Andruw Jones	1.00	.30
DT24 Ken Griffey Jr.	2.50	.75
DT25 Mark McGwire	4.00	1.20
DT26 Derek Jeter	4.00	1.20
DT27 Vladimir Guerrero	1.50	.45
DT28 Frank Thomas	1.50	.45
DT29 Pedro Martinez	1.50	.45
DT30 Bernie Williams	1.00	.30

2001 Fleer Tradition Grass Roots

Inserted at a rate of one every 18 packs, this 15 card set describes some of the early moments of these star players careers.

	Nm-Mt	Ex-Mt
COMPLETE SET (15)	60.00	18.00
GR1 Derek Jeter	6.00	1.80
GR2 Greg Maddux	4.00	1.20
GR3 Sammy Sosa	4.00	1.20
GR4 Alex Rodriguez	4.00	1.20
GR5 Vladimir Guerrero	2.50	.75
GR6 Scott Rolen	1.50	.45
GR7 Frank Thomas	2.50	.75
GR8 Nomar Garciaparra	4.00	1.20
GR9 Cal Ripken	8.00	2.40
GR10 Mike Piazza	4.00	1.20
GR11 Ivan Rodriguez	2.50	.75
GR12 Chipper Jones	2.50	.75
GR13 Tony Gwynn	3.00	.90
GR14 Ken Griffey Jr.	4.00	1.20
GR15 Mark McGwire	6.00	1.80

2001 Fleer Tradition Lumber Company

Randomly inserted into packs at one in 12, this 20-card insert set features players that are capable of breaking the game wide open with one swing of the bat. Card backs carry a "LC" prefix.

	Nm-Mt	Ex-Mt
COMPLETE SET (20)	50.00	15.00
LC1 Vladimir Guerrero	2.00	.60
LC2 Mo Vaughn	1.00	.30
LC3 Ken Griffey Jr.	3.00	.90
LC4 Juan Gonzalez	2.00	.60
LC5 Tony Gwynn	2.50	.75
LC6 Jim Edmonds	1.00	.30
LC7 Jason Giambi	2.00	.60
LC8 Alex Rodriguez	3.00	.90
LC9 Derek Jeter	5.00	1.50
LC10 Darin Erstad	1.00	.30
LC11 Andruw Jones	1.00	.30
LC12 Cal Ripken	6.00	1.80
LC13 Magglio Ordonez	1.00	.30
LC14 Nomar Garciaparra	3.00	.90
LC15 Chipper Jones	2.00	.60
LC16 Sean Casey	1.00	.30
LC17 Shawn Green	1.00	.30
LC18 Mike Piazza	3.00	.90
LC19 Sammy Sosa	3.00	.90
LC20 Barry Bonds	5.00	1.50

2001 Fleer Tradition Stitches in Time

Randomly inserted into packs at one in 18, this 24-card insert features Negro League greats like Josh Gibson and Satchel Paige. Card backs carry a "ST" prefix. Please note that cards ST1 and ST3 do not exist, and the card of Henry Kimbro is unnumbered.

	Nm-Mt	Ex-Mt
COMPLETE SET (24)	100.00	30.00
ST1 Does Not Exist		

ST2 Ernie Banks 5.00 1.50
ST3 Does Not Exist
ST4 Joe Black 3.00 .90
ST5 Roy Campanella 6.00 1.80
ST6 Ray Dandridge 3.00 .90
ST7 Leon Day 3.00 .90
ST8 Larry Doby 3.00 .90
ST9 Josh Gibson 5.00 1.50
ST10 Elston Howard 3.00 .90
ST11 Monte Irvin 3.00 .90
ST12 Buck Leonard 3.00 .90
ST13 Max Manning 3.00 .90
ST14 Willie Mays 10.00 3.00
ST15 Buck O'Neil 3.00 .90
ST16 Satchel Paige 10.00 3.00
ST17 Ted Radcliffe 3.00 .90
ST18 Jackie Robinson 6.00 1.80
ST19 Bill Perkins 3.00 .90
ST20 Rube Foster 5.00 1.50
ST21 Judy Johnson 3.00 .90
ST22 Oscar Charleston 3.00 .90
ST23 Pop Lloyd 3.00 .90
ST24 Artie Wilson 3.00 .90
ST25 Sam Jethroe 3.00 .90
NNO Henry Kimbro 3.00 .90

2001 Fleer Tradition Stitches in Time Autographs

Randomly inserted at one in four boxes, this seven-card insert set features authentic autographs from players like Willie Mays and Ernie Banks. Please note that these cards are not numbered and are listed below in alphabetical order. Also note that Willie Mays and Artie Wilson packed out as exchange cards with a redemption deadline of 02/01/02.

	Nm-Mt	Ex-Mt
1 Ernie Banks	60.00	18.00
2 Joe Black	30.00	9.00
3 Monte Irvin	40.00	12.00
4 Willie Mays	200.00	60.00
5 Buck O'Neil	40.00	12.00
6 Ted Radcliffe	30.00	9.00
7 Artie Wilson	30.00	9.00

2001 Fleer Tradition Stitches in Time Memorabilia

Randomly inserted at one in four boxes, this five-card insert set features actual swatches from game-used Bats or Pants from players like Willie Mays and Jackie Robinson. Please note that these cards are not numbered and are listed below in alphabetical order.

	Nm-Mt	Ex-Mt
1 Roy Campanella Bat	80.00	24.00
2 Larry Doby Bat	40.00	12.00
3 Elston Howard Bat	50.00	15.00
4 Willie Mays Pants	200.00	60.00
5 Jackie Robinson Pants	150.00	45.00

2001 Fleer Tradition Turn Back the Clock

Randomly inserted at one in four boxes, this 21-card insert set features swatches from actual game-used jerseys from players like Cal Ripken and Chipper Jones. Card backs carry a "TBC" prefix.

	Nm-Mt	Ex-Mt
TBC1 Tom Glavine	15.00	4.50
TBC2 Greg Maddux	40.00	12.00
TBC3 Sean Casey	10.00	3.00
TBC4 Pokey Reese	10.00	3.00
TBC5 Jason Giambi	15.00	4.50
TBC6 Tim Hudson	10.00	3.00
TBC7 Larry Walker	15.00	4.50
TBC8 Jeffrey Hammonds	10.00	3.00
TBC9 Scott Rolen	15.00	4.50
TBC10 Pat Burrell	10.00	3.00
TBC11 Chipper Jones	15.00	4.50
TBC12 Greg Maddux	40.00	12.00
TBC13 Troy Glaus	15.00	4.50
TBC14 Tony Gwynn	25.00	7.50
TBC15 Cal Ripken	60.00	18.00
TBC16 Tom Glavine / Greg Maddux	80.00	24.00
TBC17 Sean Casey / Pokey Reese	40.00	12.00
TBC18 Chipper Jones / Greg Maddux	100.00	30.00
TBC19 Larry Walker / Jeffrey Hammonds	40.00	12.00
TBC20 Scott Rolen / Pat Burrell	40.00	12.00
TBC21 Jason Giambi / Tim Hudson	50.00	15.00

2001 Fleer Tradition Warning Track

Randomly inserted into packs at one in 72, this 23-card insert takes a look at how today's power hitters stack up to yesterdays greats. Card backs carry a "WT" prefix. Please note, cards 2 and 5 (originally intended for Hank Aaron and Ernie Banks) were never produced, thus though numbered 1-25, the set is complete at 23 cards.

	Nm-Mt	Ex-Mt
COMPLETE SET (23)	250.00	75.00
WT1 Josh Gibson	10.00	3.00
WT2 Does Not Exist		
WT3 Willie Mays	15.00	4.50
WT4 Mark McGwire	20.00	6.00
WT5 Does Not Exist		
WT6 Barry Bonds	20.00	6.00
WT7 Jose Canseco	8.00	2.40
WT8 Ken Griffey Jr.	12.00	3.60
WT9 Cal Ripken	25.00	7.50
WT10 Rafael Palmeiro	5.00	1.50
WT11 Sammy Sosa	12.00	3.60
WT12 Juan Gonzalez	8.00	2.40
WT13 Frank Thomas	8.00	2.40
WT14 Jeff Bagwell	5.00	1.50
WT15 Gary Sheffield	5.00	1.50
WT16 Larry Walker	5.00	1.50
WT17 Mike Piazza	12.00	3.60
WT18 Larry Doby	5.00	1.50
WT19 Roy Campanella	10.00	3.00
WT20 Manny Ramirez	5.00	1.50
WT21 Chipper Jones	8.00	2.40
WT22 Alex Rodriguez	12.00	3.60
WT23 Ivan Rodriguez	8.00	2.40
WT24 Vladimir Guerrero	8.00	2.40
WT25 Nomar Garciaparra	12.00	3.60

2002 Fleer Tradition

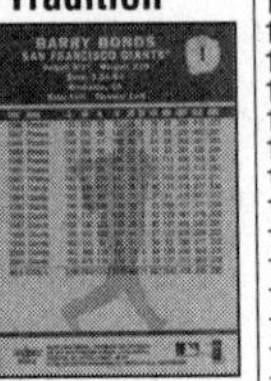

This 500 card set was issued early in 2002. This set was issued in 10 card packs and 36 packs to a box with a SRP of $1.49 per pack. The first 100 cards in this set were issued at an overall rate of one in two. In addition, cards numbered 436 through 470 featured leading prospects and cards numbered 471 through 500 featured players who had noteworthy seasons in 2001. These cards feature the 1934 Goudey-style design.

	Nm-Mt	Ex-Mt
COMPLETE SET (500)	250.00	75.00
COMP.SET w/o SP's (400)	50.00	15.00
COMMON CARD (101-500)	.30	.09
COMMON SP (1-100)	3.00	.90
COMMON CARD (436-470)	.50	.15
1 Barry Bonds SP	12.00	3.60
2 Cal Ripken SP	15.00	4.50
3 Tony Gwynn SP	6.00	1.80
4 Brad Radke SP	3.00	.90
5 Jose Ortiz SP	3.00	.90
6 Mark Mulder SP	3.00	.90
7 Jon Lieber SP	3.00	.90
8 John Olerud SP	3.00	.90
9 Phil Nevin SP	3.00	.90
10 Craig Biggio SP	3.00	.90
11 Pedro Martinez SP	5.00	1.50
12 Fred McGriff SP	3.00	.90
13 Vladimir Guerrero SP	5.00	1.50
14 Jason Giambi SP	5.00	1.50
15 Mark Kotsay SP	3.00	.90
16 Bud Smith SP	3.00	.90
17 Kevin Brown SP	3.00	.90
18 Darin Erstad SP	3.00	.90
19 Julio Franco SP	3.00	.90
20 C.C. Sabathia SP	3.00	.90
21 Larry Walker SP	3.00	.90
22 Doug Mientkiewicz SP	3.00	.90
23 Luis Gonzalez SP	3.00	.90
24 Albert Pujols SP	10.00	3.00
25 Brian Lawrence SP	3.00	.90
26 Al Leiter SP	3.00	.90
27 Mike Sweeney SP	3.00	.90
28 Jeff Weaver SP	3.00	.90
29 Matt Morris SP	3.00	.90
30 Hideo Nomo SP	5.00	1.50
31 Tom Glavine SP	3.00	.90
32 Magglio Ordonez SP	3.00	.90
33 Roberto Alomar SP	5.00	1.50
34 Roger Cedeno SP	3.00	.90
35 Greg Vaughn SP	3.00	.90
36 Chan Ho Park SP	3.00	.90
37 Rich Aurilia SP	3.00	.90
38 Tsuyoshi Shinjo SP	3.00	.90
39 Eric Young SP	3.00	.90
40 Bobby Higginson SP	3.00	.90
41 Marlon Anderson SP	3.00	.90
42 Mark Grace SP	3.00	.90
43 Steve Cox SP	3.00	.90
44 Cliff Floyd SP	3.00	.90
45 Brian Roberts SP	3.00	.90
46 Paul Konerko SP	3.00	.90
47 Brandon Duckworth SP	3.00	.90
48 Josh Beckett SP	3.00	.90
49 David Ortiz SP	3.00	.90
50 Geoff Jenkins SP	3.00	.90
51 Ruben Sierra SP	3.00	.90
52 John Franco SP	3.00	.90
53 Einar Diaz SP	3.00	.90
54 Luis Castillo SP	3.00	.90
55 Mark Quinn SP	3.00	.90
56 Shea Hillenbrand SP	3.00	.90
57 Rafael Palmeiro SP	3.00	.90
58 Paul O'Neill SP	3.00	.90
59 Andruw Jones SP	3.00	.90
60 Lance Berkman SP	3.00	.90
61 Jimmy Rollins SP	3.00	.90
62 Jose Hernandez SP	3.00	.90
63 Rusty Greer SP	3.00	.90
64 Wade Miller SP	3.00	.90
65 David Eckstein SP	3.00	.90
66 Jose Valentin SP	3.00	.90
67 Javier Vazquez SP	3.00	.90
68 Roger Clemens SP	10.00	3.00
69 Omar Vizquel SP	3.00	.90
70 Roy Oswalt SP	3.00	.90
71 Shannon Stewart SP	3.00	.90
72 Byung-Hyun Kim SP	3.00	.90
73 Jay Gibbons SP	3.00	.90
74 Barry Larkin SP	5.00	1.50
75 Brian Giles SP	3.00	.90
76 Andres Galarraga SP	3.00	.90
77 Sammy Sosa SP	8.00	2.40
78 Manny Ramirez SP	3.00	.90
79 Carlos Delgado SP	3.00	.90
80 Jorge Posada SP	3.00	.90
81 Todd Ritchie SP	3.00	.90
82 Russ Ortiz SP	3.00	.90
83 Brent Mayne SP	3.00	.90
84 Mike Mussina SP	5.00	1.50
85 Raul Mondesi SP	3.00	.90
86 Mark Loretta SP	3.00	.90
87 Tim Raines SP	3.00	.90
88 Ichiro Suzuki SP	8.00	2.40
89 Juan Pierre SP	3.00	.90
90 Adam Dunn SP	3.00	.90
91 Jason Tyner SP	3.00	.90
92 Miguel Tejada SP	3.00	.90
93 Elpidio Guzman SP	3.00	.90
94 Freddy Garcia SP	3.00	.90
95 Marcus Giles SP	3.00	.90
96 Junior Spivey SP	3.00	.90
97 Aramis Ramirez SP	3.00	.90
98 Jose Rijo SP	3.00	.90
99 Paul LoDuca SP	3.00	.90
100 Mike Cameron SP	3.00	.90
101 Alex Hernandez	.30	.09
102 Benji Gil	.30	.09
103 Benito Santiago	.30	.09
104 Bobby Abreu	.30	.09
105 Brad Penny	.30	.09
106 Calvin Murray	.30	.09
107 Chad Durbin	.30	.09
108 Chris Singleton	.30	.09
109 Chris Carpenter	.30	.09
110 David Justice	.30	.09
111 Eric Chavez	.30	.09
112 Fernando Tatis	.30	.09
113 Frank Castillo	.30	.09
114 Jason LaRue	.30	.09
115 Jim Edmonds	.30	.09
116 Joe Kennedy	.30	.09
117 Jose Jimenez	.30	.09
118 Josh Towers	.30	.09
119 Junior Herndon	.30	.09
120 Luke Prokopec	.30	.09
121 Mac Suzuki	.30	.09
122 Mark DeRosa	.30	.09
123 Marty Cordova	.30	.09
124 Michael Tucker	.30	.09
125 Michael Young	.30	.09
126 Robin Ventura	.30	.09
127 Shane Halter	.30	.09
128 Shane Reynolds	.30	.09
129 Tony Womack	.30	.09
130 A.J. Pierzynski	.30	.09
131 Aaron Rowand	.30	.09
132 Antonio Alfonseca	.30	.09
133 Arthur Rhodes	.30	.09
134 Bob Wickman	.30	.09
135 Brady Clark	.30	.09
136 Chad Hermansen	.30	.09
137 Marlon Byrd	.30	.09
138 Dan Wilson	.30	.09
139 David Cone	.30	.09
140 Dean Palmer	.30	.09
141 Denny Neagle	.30	.09
142 Derek Jeter	2.00	.60
143 Erubiel Durazo	.30	.09
144 Felix Rodriguez	.30	.09
145 Jason Hart	.30	.09
146 Jay Bell	.30	.09
147 Jeff Suppan	.30	.09
148 Jeff Zimmerman	.30	.09
149 Kerry Wood	.75	.23
150 Kerry Robinson	.30	.09
151 Kevin Appier	.30	.09
152 Michael Barrett	.30	.09
153 Mo Vaughn	.30	.09
154 Rafael Furcal	.30	.09
155 Sidney Ponson	.30	.09
156 Terry Adams	.30	.09
157 Tim Redding	.30	.09
158 Toby Hall	.30	.09
159 Aaron Sele	.30	.09
160 Bartolo Colon	.30	.09
161 Brad Ausmus	.30	.09
162 Carlos Pena	.30	.09
163 Jace Brewer	.30	.09
164 David Wells	.30	.09
165 David Segui	.30	.09
166 Derek Lowe	.30	.09
167 Derek Bell	.30	.09
168 Jason Grabowski	.30	.09
169 Johnny Damon	.30	.09
170 Jose Mesa	.30	.09
171 Juan Encarnacion	.30	.09
172 Ken Caminiti	.30	.09
173 Ken Griffey Jr.	1.25	.35
174 Luis Rivas	.30	.09
175 Mariano Rivera	.50	.15
176 Mark Grudzielanek	.30	.09
177 Mark McGwire	2.00	.60
178 Mike Bordick	.30	.09
179 Mike Hampton	.30	.09
180 Nick Bierbrodt	.30	.09
181 Paul Byrd	.30	.09
182 Robb Nen	.30	.09
183 Ryan Dempster	.30	.09
184 Ryan Klesko	.30	.09
185 Scott Spiezio	.30	.09
186 Scott Strickland	.30	.09
187 Todd Zeile	.30	.09
188 Tom Gordon	.30	.09
189 Troy Glaus	.50	.15
190 Matt Williams	.30	.09
191 Wes Helms	.30	.09
192 Jerry Hairston Jr.	.30	.09
193 Brook Fordyce	.30	.09
194 Nomar Garciaparra	1.25	.35
195 Kevin Tapani	.30	.09
196 Mark Buehrle	.30	.09
197 Dmitri Young	.30	.09
198 John Rocker	.30	.09
199 Juan Uribe	.30	.09
200 Matt Anderson	.30	.09
201 Alex Gonzalez	.30	.09
202 Julio Lugo	.30	.09
203 Roberto Hernandez	.30	.09
204 Richie Sexson	.30	.09
205 Corey Koskie	.30	.09
206 Tony Armas Jr.	.30	.09
207 Rey Ordonez	.30	.09
208 Orlando Hernandez	.30	.09
209 Pokey Reese	.30	.09
210 Mike Lieberthal	.30	.09
211 Kris Benson	.30	.09
212 Jermaine Dye	.30	.09
213 Livan Hernandez	.30	.09
214 Bret Boone	.30	.09
215 Dustin Hermanson	.30	.09
216 Placido Polanco	.30	.09
217 Jesus Colome	.30	.09
218 Alex Gonzalez	.30	.09
219 Adam Everett	.30	.09
220 Adam Piatt	.30	.09
221 Brad Fullmer	.30	.09
222 Brian Buchanan	.30	.09
223 Chipper Jones	.75	.23
224 Chuck Finley	.30	.09
225 David Bell	.30	.09
226 Jack Wilson	.30	.09
227 Jason Bere	.30	.09
228 Jeff Conine	.30	.09
229 Jeff Bagwell	.50	.15
230 Joe McEwing	.30	.09
231 Kip Wells	.30	.09
232 Mike Lansing	.30	.09
233 Neifi Perez	.30	.09
234 Omar Daal	.30	.09
235 Reggie Sanders	.30	.09
236 Shawn Wooten	.30	.09
237 Shawn Chacon	.30	.09
238 Shawn Estes	.30	.09
239 Steve Sparks	.30	.09
240 Steve Kline	.30	.09
241 Tino Martinez	.50	.15
242 Tyler Houston	.30	.09
243 Xavier Nady	.30	.09
244 Bengie Molina	.30	.09
245 Ben Davis	.30	.09
246 Casey Fossum	.30	.09
247 Chris Stynes	.30	.09
248 Danny Graves	.30	.09
249 Pedro Feliz	.30	.09
250 Darren Oliver	.30	.09
251 Dave Veres	.30	.09
252 Deivi Cruz	.30	.09
253 Desi Relaford	.30	.09
254 Devon White	.30	.09
255 Edgar Martinez	.50	.15
256 Eric Munson	.30	.09
257 Eric Karros	.30	.09
258 Homer Bush	.30	.09
259 Jason Kendall	.30	.09
260 Javy Lopez	.30	.09
261 Keith Foulke	.30	.09
262 Keith Ginter	.30	.09
263 Nick Johnson	.30	.09
264 Pat Burrell	.30	.09
265 Ricky Gutierrez	.30	.09
266 Russ Johnson	.30	.09
267 Steve Finley	.30	.09
268 Terrence Long	.30	.09
269 Tony Batista	.30	.09
270 Torii Hunter	.30	.09
271 Vinny Castilla	.30	.09
272 A.J. Burnett	.30	.09
273 Adrian Beltre	.30	.09
274 Alex Rodriguez	1.25	.35
275 Armando Benitez	.30	.09
276 Billy Koch	.30	.09
277 Brady Anderson	.30	.09
278 Brian Jordan	.30	.09
279 Carlos Febles	.30	.09
280 Daryle Ward	.30	.09
281 Eli Marrero	.30	.09
282 Garret Anderson	.30	.09
283 Jack Cust	.30	.09
284 Jacque Jones	.30	.09
285 Jamie Moyer	.30	.09
286 Jeffrey Hammonds	.30	.09
287 Jim Thome	.75	.23
288 Jon Garland	.30	.09
289 Jose Offerman	.30	.09
290 Matt Stairs	.30	.09
291 Orlando Cabrera	.30	.09
292 Ramiro Mendoza	.30	.09
293 Ray Durham	.30	.09
294 Rickey Henderson	.75	.23
295 Rob Mackowiak	.30	.09
296 Scott Rolen	.50	.15
297 Tim Hudson	.30	.09
298 Todd Helton	.50	.15
299 Tony Clark	.30	.09
300 B.J. Surhoff	.30	.09
301 Bernie Williams	.50	.15
302 Bill Mueller	.30	.09
303 Chris Richard	.30	.09
304 Craig Paquette	.30	.09
305 Curt Schilling	.50	.15
306 Damian Jackson	.30	.09
307 Derrek Lee	.30	.09
308 Eric Milton	.30	.09
309 Frank Catalanotto	.30	.09
310 J.T. Snow	.30	.09
311 Jared Sandberg	.30	.09
312 Jason Varitek	.30	.09
313 Jeff Cirillo	.30	.09
314 Jeromy Burnitz	.30	.09
315 Joe Crede	.30	.09
316 Joel Pineiro	.30	.09
317 Jose Cruz Jr.	.30	.09
318 Kevin Young	.30	.09
319 Marquis Grissom	.30	.09
320 Moises Alou	.30	.09
321 Randall Simon	.30	.09
322 Royce Clayton	.30	.09
323 Tim Salmon	.50	.15
324 Travis Fryman	.30	.09
325 Travis Lee	.30	.09
326 Vance Wilson	.30	.09
327 Jarrod Washburn	.30	.09
328 Ben Petrick	.30	.09
329 Ben Grieve	.30	.09
330 Carl Everett	.30	.09
331 Eric Byrnes	.30	.09
332 Doug Glanville	.30	.09
333 Edgardo Alfonzo	.30	.09
334 Ellis Burks	.30	.09
335 Gabe Kapler	.30	.09
336 Gary Sheffield	.30	.09
337 Greg Maddux	1.25	.35
338 J.D. Drew	.30	.09
339 Jamey Wright	.30	.09
340 Jeff Kent	.30	.09
341 Jeremy Giambi	.30	.09
342 Joe Randa	.30	.09
343 Joe Mays	.30	.09
344 Jose Macias	.30	.09
345 Kazuhiro Sasaki	.30	.09
346 Mike Kinkade	.30	.09
347 Mike Lowell	.30	.09
348 Randy Johnson	.75	.23
349 Randy Wolf	.30	.09
350 Richard Hidalgo	.30	.09
351 Ron Coomer	.30	.09
352 Sandy Alomar Jr.	.30	.09
353 Sean Casey	.30	.09
354 Trevor Hoffman	.30	.09
355 Adam Eaton	.30	.09
356 Alfonso Soriano	.50	.15
357 Barry Zito	.50	.15
358 Billy Wagner	.30	.09
359 Brent Abernathy	.30	.09
360 Bret Prinz	.30	.09
361 Carlos Beltran	.30	.09
362 Carlos Guillen	.30	.09
363 Charles Johnson	.30	.09
364 Cristian Guzman	.30	.09
365 Damion Easley	.30	.09
366 Darryl Kile	.30	.09
367 Delino DeShields	.30	.09
368 Eric Davis	.30	.09
369 Frank Thomas	.75	.23
370 Ivan Rodriguez	.75	.23
371 Jay Payton	.30	.09
372 Jeff D'Amico	.30	.09
373 John Burkett	.30	.09
374 Melvin Mora	.30	.09
375 Ramon Ortiz	.30	.09
376 Robert Person	.30	.09
377 Russell Branyan	.30	.09
378 Shawn Green	.30	.09
379 Todd Hollandsworth	.30	.09
380 Tony McKnight	.30	.09
381 Trot Nixon	.50	.15
382 Vernon Wells	.30	.09
383 Troy Percival	.30	.09
384 Albie Lopez	.30	.09
385 Alex Ochoa	.30	.09
386 Andy Pettitte	.50	.15
387 Brandon Inge	.30	.09
388 Bubba Trammell	.30	.09
389 Corey Patterson	.30	.09
390 Damian Rolls	.30	.09
391 Dee Brown	.30	.09
392 Edgar Renteria	.30	.09
393 Eric Gagne	.50	.15
394 Jason Johnson	.30	.09
395 Jeff Nelson	.30	.09
396 John Vander Wal	.30	.09
397 Johnny Estrada	.30	.09
398 Jose Canseco	.75	.23
399 Juan Gonzalez	.75	.23
400 Kevin Millwood	.30	.09
401 Lee Stevens	.30	.09
402 Matt Lawton	.30	.09
403 Mike Lamb	.30	.09
404 Octavio Dotel	.30	.09
405 Ramon Hernandez	.30	.09
406 Ruben Quevedo	.30	.09
407 Todd Walker	.30	.09
408 Troy O'Leary	.30	.09
409 Wascar Serrano	.30	.09
410 Aaron Boone	.30	.09
411 Aubrey Huff	.30	.09
412 Ben Sheets	.30	.09
413 Carlos Lee	.30	.09
414 Chuck Knoblauch	.30	.09
415 Steve Karsay	.30	.09
416 Dante Bichette	.30	.09
417 David Dellucci	.30	.09
418 Esteban Loaiza	.30	.09
419 Fernando Vina	.30	.09
420 Ismael Valdes	.30	.09
421 Jason Isringhausen	.30	.09
422 Jeff Shaw	.30	.09

423 John Smoltz .50 .15
424 Jose Vidro .30 .09
425 Kenny Lofton .30 .09
426 Mark Little .30 .09
427 Mark McLemore .30 .09
428 Marvin Benard .30 .09
429 Mike Piazza 1.25 .35
430 Pat Hentgen .30 .09
431 Preston Wilson .30 .09
432 Rick Helling .30 .09
433 Robert Fick .30 .09
434 Rondell White .30 .09
435 Adam Kennedy .30 .09
436 David Espinosa PROS .50 .15
437 Dewon Brazelton PROS .50 .15
438 Drew Henson PROS .50 .15
439 Juan Cruz PROS .50 .15
440 Jason Jennings PROS .50 .15
441 Carlos Garcia PROS .50 .15
442 Carlos Hernandez PROS .50 .15
443 Wilkin Ruan PROS .50 .15
444 Wilson Betemit PROS .50 .15
445 Horacio Ramirez PROS .50 .15
446 Danys Baez PROS .50 .15
447 Abraham Nunez PROS .50 .15
448 Josh Hamilton PROS .50 .15
449 Chris George PROS .50 .15
450 Rick Bauer PROS .50 .15
451 Donnie Bridges PROS .50 .15
452 Erick Almonte PROS .50 .15
453 Cory Aldridge PROS .50 .15
454 Ryan Drese PROS .50 .15
455 Jason Romano PROS .50 .15
456 Corky Miller PROS .50 .15
457 Rafael Soriano PROS .50 .15
458 Mark Prior PROS 2.50 .75
459 Mark Teixeira PROS 1.25 .35
460 Adrian Hernandez PROS .50 .15
461 Tim Spooneybarger PROS .50 .15
462 Bill Ortega PROS .50 .15
463 D'Angelo Jimenez PROS .50 .15
464 Andres Torres PROS .50 .15
465 Alexis Gomez PROS .50 .15
466 Angel Berroa PROS .50 .15
467 Henry Mateo PROS .50 .15
468 Endy Chavez PROS .50 .15
469 Billy Sylvester PROS .50 .15
470 Nate Frese PROS .50 .15
471 Luis Gonzalez BNR .30 .09
472 Barry Bonds BNR 2.00 .60
473 Rich Aurilia BNR .30 .09
474 Albert Pujols BNR 1.50 .45
475 Todd Helton BNR .50 .15
476 Moises Alou BNR .30 .09
477 Lance Berkman BNR .30 .09
478 Brian Giles BNR .30 .09
479 Cliff Floyd BNR .30 .09
480 Sammy Sosa BNR 1.25 .35
481 Shawn Green BNR .30 .09
482 Jon Lieber BNR .30 .09
483 Matt Morris BNR .30 .09
484 Curt Schilling BNR .50 .15
485 Randy Johnson BNR .50 .15
486 Manny Ramirez BNR .30 .09
487 Ichiro Suzuki BNR 1.25 .35
488 Juan Gonzalez BNR .75 .23
489 Derek Jeter BNR 2.00 .60
490 Alex Rodriguez BNR 1.25 .35
491 Bret Boone BNR .30 .09
492 Roberto Alomar BNR .75 .23
493 Jason Giambi BNR .75 .23
494 Rafael Palmeiro BNR .50 .15
495 Doug Mientkiewicz BNR .30 .09
496 Jim Thome BNR .50 .15
497 Freddy Garcia BNR .30 .09
498 Mark Buehrle BNR .30 .09
499 Mark Mulder BNR .30 .09
500 Roger Clemens BNR 1.50 .45

2002 Fleer Tradition Glossy

Randomly inserted into Fleer Tradition Update packs, this is a parallel of the basic Fleer Tradition set. These cards can be differentiated from the regular Fleer cards by their "glossy" sheen and have a stated print run of 200 serial numbered sets.

Nm-Mt Ex-Mt
*GLOSSY 1-100: .5X TO 1.2X BASIC..
*GLOSSY 101-435/471-500: 3X TO 8X BASIC
*GLOSSY 436-470: 2X TO 5X BASIC..

2002 Fleer Tradition Diamond Tributes

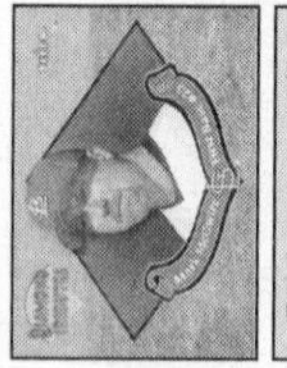
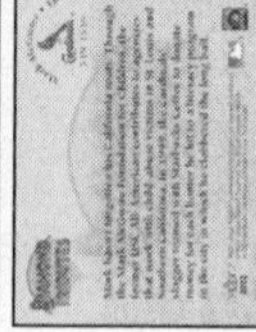

Inserted into hobby packs at stated odds of one in six and retail packs at stated odds of one in 10, these 15 cards feature players who have performed on the field of play but have also had a positive impact on the community.

	Nm-Mt	Ex-Mt
COMPLETE SET (15)	20.00	6.00
1 Cal Ripken	4.00	1.20
2 Tony Gwynn	1.50	.45
3 Derek Jeter	3.00	.90
4 Pedro Martinez	1.25	.35
5 Mark McGwire	3.00	.90
6 Sammy Sosa	2.00	.60
7 Barry Bonds	3.00	.90
8 Roger Clemens	2.50	.75
9 Mike Piazza	2.00	.60
10 Alex Rodriguez	2.00	.60
11 Randy Johnson	1.25	.35
12 Chipper Jones	1.25	.35
13 Nomar Garciaparra	2.00	.60
14 Ichiro Suzuki	2.00	.60
15 Jason Giambi	1.25	.35

2002 Fleer Tradition Grass Patch

This 10 card set is a parallel to the Grass Roots insert set. Each card in this set features not only the defensive whiz pictured but also a special game-worn jersey swatch. According to representatives at Fleer, each cards has a stated print run of 50 copies (though the cards lack any form of serial-numbering).

	Nm-Mt	Ex-Mt
1 Jeff Bagwell	40.00	12.00
2 Barry Bonds	80.00	24.00
3 Derek Jeter		
4 Greg Maddux	60.00	18.00
5 Cal Ripken	150.00	45.00
6 Alex Rodriguez	60.00	18.00
7 Ivan Rodriguez	50.00	15.00
8 Scott Rolen	40.00	12.00
9 Larry Walker	40.00	12.00
10 Bernie Williams	40.00	12.00

2002 Fleer Tradition Grass Roots

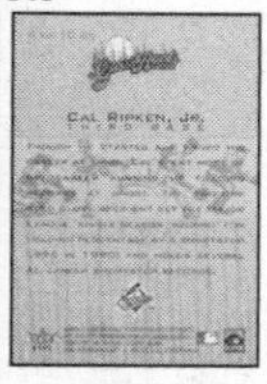

Inserted into hobby packs at stated odds of one in 18 and retail packs at stated odds of one in 20, these 10 cards feature leading defensive players.

	Nm-Mt	Ex-Mt
COMPLETE SET (10)	30.00	9.00
1 Barry Bonds	6.00	1.80
2 Alex Rodriguez	4.00	1.20
3 Derek Jeter	6.00	1.80
4 Greg Maddux	4.00	1.20
5 Ivan Rodriguez	2.50	.75
6 Cal Ripken	8.00	2.40
7 Bernie Williams	1.50	.45
8 Jeff Bagwell	1.50	.45
9 Scott Rolen	1.50	.45
10 Larry Walker	1.50	.45

2002 Fleer Tradition Heads Up

Inserted into hobby packs at stated odds of one in 36 and retail packs at stated odds of one in 40, these 10 cards feature leading players as they would look as bobbleheads.

	Nm-Mt	Ex-Mt
COMPLETE SET (10)	80.00	24.00
1 Derek Jeter	10.00	3.00
2 Ichiro Suzuki	6.00	1.80
3 Sammy Sosa	6.00	1.80
4 Mike Piazza	6.00	1.80
5 Ken Griffey Jr.	6.00	1.80
6 Alex Rodriguez	6.00	1.80
7 Barry Bonds	10.00	3.00
8 Nomar Garciaparra	6.00	1.80
9 Mark McGwire	10.00	3.00
10 Cal Ripken	12.00	3.60

2002 Fleer Tradition Lumber Company

Inserted into packs at stated odds of one in 12 hobby and one in 20 retail, these 30 cards feature superstars who can hit the ball with above average skills.

	Nm-Mt	Ex-Mt
COMPLETE SET (30)	60.00	18.00
1 Moises Alou	1.50	.45
2 Luis Gonzalez	1.50	.45
3 Todd Helton	1.50	.45
4 Mike Piazza	4.00	1.20
5 J.D. Drew	1.50	.45
6 Albert Pujols	5.00	1.50
7 Chipper Jones	2.50	.75
8 Manny Ramirez	1.50	.45
9 Miguel Tejada	1.50	.45
10 Curt Schilling	1.50	.45
11 Alex Rodriguez	4.00	1.20
12 Barry Larkin	2.50	.75
13 Nomar Garciaparra	4.00	1.20
14 Cliff Floyd	1.50	.45
15 Alfonso Soriano	1.50	.45
16 Sean Casey	1.50	.45
17 Scott Rolen	1.50	.45
18 Jose Ortiz	1.50	.45
19 Corey Patterson	1.50	.45
20 Joe Crede	1.50	.45
21 Jace Brewer	1.50	.45
22 Derek Jeter	6.00	1.80
23 Jim Thome	2.50	.75
24 Frank Thomas	2.50	.75
25 Shawn Green	1.50	.45
26 Drew Henson	1.50	.45
27 Jimmy Rollins	1.50	.45
28 David Justice	1.50	.45
29 Roberto Alomar	2.50	.75
30 Bernie Williams	1.50	.45

2002 Fleer Tradition Lumber Company Game Bat

This parallel to the Lumber Company insert set was inserted in packs at a rate of one in 72 packs. These cards feature not only the player pictured but a bat piece swatch related to that player. Jace Brewer, Sean Casey, Joe Crede, Derek Jeter, Corey Patterson and Scott Rolen were all short-prints according to representatives at Fleer.

	Nm-Mt	Ex-Mt
1 Roberto Alomar	15.00	4.50
2 Moises Alou	10.00	3.00
3 Jace Brewer SP/250	10.00	3.00
4 Sean Casey SP/250	10.00	3.00
5 Joe Crede SP/250	10.00	3.00
6 J.D. Drew	10.00	3.00
7 Cliff Floyd	10.00	3.00
8 Nomar Garciaparra	20.00	6.00
9 Luis Gonzalez	10.00	3.00
10 Shawn Green	10.00	3.00
11 Todd Helton	15.00	4.50
12 Drew Henson	10.00	3.00
13 Derek Jeter SP/250	40.00	12.00
14 Chipper Jones	15.00	4.50
15 David Justice	10.00	3.00
16 Barry Larkin	15.00	4.50
17 Jose Ortiz SP/250	10.00	3.00
18 Corey Patterson SP/250	10.00	3.00
19 Mike Piazza	15.00	4.50
20 Albert Pujols	25.00	7.50
21 Manny Ramirez	10.00	3.00
22 Alex Rodriguez	20.00	6.00
23 Scott Rolen SP/250	15.00	4.50
24 Jimmy Rollins	10.00	3.00
25 Curt Schilling	15.00	4.50
26 Alfonso Soriano	15.00	4.50
27 Miguel Tejada	10.00	3.00
28 Frank Thomas	15.00	4.50
29 Jim Thome	15.00	4.50
30 Bernie Williams	15.00	4.50

2002 Fleer Tradition This Day in History

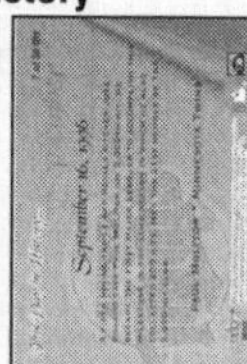

Inserted into hobby packs at stated odds of one in 18 and retail packs at stated odds of one in 24, these 29 cards feature highlights of some of the greatest days in baseball history. Please note that card number 24 (originally intended to feature Orel Hershiser) was pulled from production, thus the set is complete at 29 cards.

	Nm-Mt	Ex-Mt
COMPLETE SET (29)	150.00	45.00
1 Cal Ripken	15.00	4.50
2 Barry Bonds	12.00	3.60
3 George Brett	12.00	3.60
4 Tony Gwynn	6.00	1.80
5 Nolan Ryan	12.00	3.60
6 Reggie Jackson	3.00	.90
7 Paul Molitor	3.00	.90
8 Ichiro Suzuki	8.00	2.40
9 Alex Rodriguez	8.00	2.40
10 Don Mattingly	12.00	3.60
11 Sammy Sosa	8.00	2.40
12 Mark McGwire	12.00	3.60
13 Derek Jeter	12.00	3.60
14 Roger Clemens	10.00	3.00
15 Jim Hunter	3.00	.90
16 Greg Maddux	8.00	2.40
17 Ken Griffey Jr.	8.00	2.40
18 Gil Hodges	5.00	1.50
19 Edgar Martinez	3.00	.90
20 Mike Piazza	8.00	2.40
21 Jimmie Foxx	5.00	1.50
22 Albert Pujols	10.00	3.00
23 Chipper Jones	5.00	1.50
24 Does Not Exist		
25 Jeff Bagwell	3.00	.90
26 Nomar Garciaparra	8.00	2.40
27 Randy Johnson	5.00	1.50
28 Todd Helton	3.00	.90
29 Ted Kluszewski	3.00	.90
30 Ivan Rodriguez	5.00	1.50

2002 Fleer Tradition This Day in History Autographs

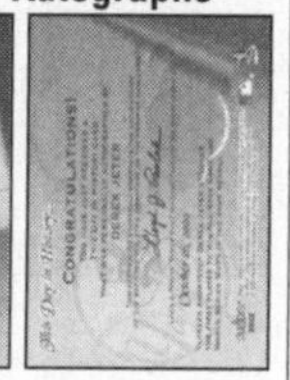

Randomly inserted into packs, these eight cards feature autographs of the player notated. Most of the players did not sign their cards in time for inclusion in this product so they were available as exchange cards. Please note that Fleer provided print run information for these cards but they are not serial numbered. Exchange cards with a redemption deadline of 01/31/03 were seeded into packs for the following players: Gwynn, R.Jackson, R.Johnson, Mattingly, Molitor and Ripken.

	Nm-Mt	Ex-Mt
1 Tony Gwynn/50		
2 Reggie Jackson/50		
3 Derek Jeter/100	120.00	36.00
4 Randy Johnson/75	80.00	24.00
5 Don Mattingly/50	120.00	36.00
6 Paul Molitor/50		
7 Albert Pujols/50	150.00	45.00
8 Cal Ripken/50	150.00	45.00

2002 Fleer Tradition This Day in History Game Used

Randomly inserted into packs, these 22 cards feature memorabilia pieces from the noted player. As these cards are printed to different amounts, we have notated that information in our checklist.

	Nm-Mt	Ex-Mt
1 Jeff Bagwell Bat/100	25.00	7.50
2 Barry Bonds Jsy/250	50.00	15.00
3 George Brett Jsy/50		
4 Roger Clemens Jsy/150	40.00	12.00
5 Jimmie Foxx Bat/250	50.00	15.00
6 Todd Helton Bat/150	25.00	7.50
7 Gil Hodges Bat/50		
8 Jim Hunter Jsy/250	25.00	7.50
10 Reggie Jackson Bat/50		
11 Derek Jeter Jsy/250	60.00	18.00
12 Randy Johnson Jsy/50		
13 Chipper Jones Bat/50		
14 Ted Kluszewski Jsy/50		
15 Greg Maddux Jsy/100	30.00	9.00
16 Don Mattingly Jsy/50		
17 Paul Molitor Bat/50		
18 Mike Piazza Bat/150	25.00	7.50
19 Albert Pujols Jsy/50		
20 Cal Ripken Jsy/50		
21 Alex Rodriguez Hat/250	40.00	12.00
22 Ivan Rodriguez Jsy/50		
23 Nolan Ryan Pants/50		

2002 Fleer Tradition Update

This 400 card set was released in October, 2003. This set was issued in 10 card packs which came 28 packs to a box and six boxes to a case with the packs having an SRP of $2. Cards numbered U1 through U100, which feature a mix of rookies and prospects, were issued at a stated rate of one per pack and are in shorter supply than the rest of the set. Other subsets include Diamond Standouts (U276-U297), All-Stars (U298-U360), Curtain Call (U361-U385) and Tale of the Tape (U386-U400).

	Nm-Mt	Ex-Mt
COMPLETE SET (400)	120.00	36.00
COMP.SET w/o SP's (300)	40.00	12.00
COMMON CARD (U101-U400)	.30	.09
COMMON CARD (U1-U100)	1.00	.30
U1 P.J. Bevis SP RC	1.00	.30
U2 Mike Crudale SP RC	1.00	.30
U3 Ben Howard SP RC	1.00	.30
U4 Travis Driskill SP RC	1.00	.30
U5 Reed Johnson SP RC	1.25	.35
U6 Kyle Kane SP RC	1.00	.30
U7 Deivis Santos SP	1.00	.30
U8 Tim Kalita SP RC	1.00	.30
U9 Brandon Puffer SP RC	1.00	.30
U10 Chris Snelling SP RC	2.50	.75
U11 Juan Brito SP RC	1.00	.30
U12 Tyler Yates SP RC	2.00	.60
U13 Victor Alvarez SP RC	1.00	.30
U14 Takahito Nomura SP RC	1.00	.30
U15 Ron Calloway SP RC	1.00	.30
U16 Satoru Komiyama SP RC	1.00	.30
U17 Julius Matos SP RC	1.00	.30
U18 Jorge Nunez SP RC	1.00	.30
U19 Anderson Machado SP RC	1.00	.30
U20 Scott Layfield SP RC	1.00	.30
U21 Aaron Cook SP RC	1.00	.30
U22 Alex Pelaez SP RC	1.00	.30
U23 Corey Thurman SP RC	1.00	.30
U24 Nelson Castro SP RC	1.00	.30
U25 Jeff Austin SP RC	1.00	.30
U26 Felix Escalona SP RC	1.00	.30
U27 Luis Ugueto SP RC	1.00	.30
U28 Jaime Cerda SP RC	1.00	.30
U29 J.J. Trujillo SP RC	1.00	.30
U30 Rodrigo Rosario SP RC	1.00	.30
U31 Jorge Padilla SP RC	1.00	.30
U32 Shawn Sedlacek SP RC	1.00	.30
U33 Nate Field SP RC	1.00	.30
U34 Earl Snyder SP RC	1.00	.30
U35 Miguel Asencio SP RC	1.00	.30
U36 Ken Huckaby SP RC	1.00	.30
U37 Valentino Pascucci SP	1.00	.30
U38 So Taguchi SP RC	1.25	.35
U39 Brian Mallette SP RC	1.00	.30
U40 Kazuhisa Ishii SP RC	3.00	.90
U41 Matt Thornton SP RC	1.00	.30
U42 Mark Corey SP RC	1.00	.30
U43 Kirk Saarloos SP RC	1.00	.30
U44 Josh Bard SP RC	1.00	.30
U45 Hansel Izquierdo SP RC	1.00	.30
U46 Rene Reyes SP RC	1.00	.30
U47 Luis Garcia SP	1.00	.30
U48 Jason Simontacchi SP RC	1.00	.30
U49 John Ennis SP RC	1.00	.30
U50 Franklyn German SP RC	1.00	.30
U51 Aaron Guiel SP RC	1.00	.30
U52 Howie Clark SP RC	1.00	.30
U53 David Ross SP RC	1.00	.30
U54 Jason Davis SP RC	2.00	.60
U55 Francis Beltran SP RC	1.00	.30
U56 Barry Wesson SP RC	1.00	.30
U57 Run. Hernandez SP RC	1.00	.30
U58 Oliver Perez SP RC	1.25	.35
U59 Ryan Bukvich SP RC	1.00	.30
U60 Steve Kent SP RC	1.00	.30
U61 Julio Mateo SP RC	1.00	.30
U62 Jason Jimenez SP RC	1.00	.30
U63 Jayson Durocher SP RC	1.00	.30
U64 Kevin Frederick SP RC	1.00	.30
U65 Kevin Gryboski SP RC	1.00	.30
U66 Edwin Almonte SP RC	1.00	.30
U67 John Foster SP RC	1.00	.30
U68 Doug Devore SP RC	1.00	.30
U69 Tom Shearn SP RC	1.00	.30
U70 Colin Young SP RC	1.00	.30
U71 Jon Adkins SP RC	1.00	.30
U72 Wilbert Nieves SP RC	1.00	.30
U73 Matt Duff SP RC	1.00	.30
U74 Carl Sadler SP RC	1.00	.30
U75 Jason Kershner SP RC	1.00	.30
U76 Brandon Backe SP RC	1.00	.30
U77 Josh Hancock SP RC	1.00	.30
U78 Chris Baker SP RC	1.00	.30
U79 Travis Hughes SP RC	1.00	.30
U80 Steve Bechler SP RC	1.00	.30
U81 Allan Simpson SP RC	1.00	.30
U82 Aaron Taylor SP RC	1.00	.30
U83 Kevin Cash SP RC	1.00	.30
U84 Chone Figgins SP RC	1.00	.30
U85 Clay Condrey SP RC	1.00	.30
U86 Shane Nance SP RC	1.00	.30
U87 Freddy Sanchez SP RC	1.00	.30
U88 Jim Rushford SP RC	1.00	.30
U89 Jeriome Robertson SP RC	1.00	.30
U90 Trey Lunsford SP RC	1.00	.30
U91 Cody McKay SP RC	1.00	.30
U92 Trey Hodges SP RC	1.00	.30
U93 Hee Seop Choi SP	1.25	.35
U94 Joe Borchard SP	1.00	.30
U95 Orlando Hudson SP	1.00	.30
U96 Carl Crawford SP	1.00	.30
U97 Mark Prior SP	5.00	1.50
U98 Brett Myers SP	1.00	.30
U99 Kenny Lofton SP	1.00	.30
U100 Cliff Floyd SP	1.00	.30
U101 Randy Winn	.30	.09
U102 Ryan Dempster	.30	.09
U103 Josh Phelps	.30	.09
U104 Marcus Giles	.30	.09
U105 Rickey Henderson	.75	.23
U106 Jose Leon	.30	.09
U107 Tino Martinez	.50	.15
U108 Greg Norton	.30	.09
U109 Odalis Perez	.30	.09
U110 J.C. Romero	.30	.09
U111 Gary Sheffield	.30	.09
U112 Ismael Valdes	.30	.09
U113 Juan Acevedo	.30	.09
U114 Ben Broussard	.30	.09
U115 Deivi Cruz	.30	.09
U116 Geronimo Gil	.30	.09
U117 Eric Hinske	.30	.09
U118 Ted Lilly	.30	.09
U119 Quinton McCracken	.30	.09
U120 Antonio Alfonseca	.30	.09
U121 Brent Abernathy	.30	.09
U122 Johnny Damon	.30	.09
U123 Francisco Cordero	.30	.09
U124 Sterling Hitchcock	.30	.09
U125 Vladimir Nunez	.30	.09
U126 Andres Galarraga	.30	.09
U127 Timo Perez	.30	.09
U128 Tsuyoshi Shinjo	.30	.09
U129 Joe Girardi	.30	.09
U130 Roberto Alomar	.75	.23
U131 Ellis Burks	.30	.09
U132 Mike DeJean	.30	.09
U133 Alex Gonzalez	.30	.09
U134 Johan Santana	.30	.09
U135 Kenny Lofton	.30	.09
U136 Juan Encarnacion	.30	.09
U137 Dewon Brazelton	.30	.09
U138 Jeromy Burnitz	.30	.09
U139 Elmer Dessens	.30	.09
U140 Juan Gonzalez	.75	.23
U141 Todd Hundley	.30	.09

U142 Tomo Ohka .30 .09
U143 Robin Ventura .30 .09
U144 Rodrigo Lopez .30 .09
U145 Ruben Sierra .30 .09
U146 Jason Phillips .30 .09
U147 Ryan Rupe .30 .09
U148 Kevin Appier .30 .09
U149 Sean Burroughs .30 .09
U150 Masato Yoshii .30 .09
U151 Juan Diaz .30 .09
U152 Tony Graffanino .30 .09
U153 Raul Ibanez .30 .09
U154 Kevin Mench .30 .09
U155 Pedro Astacio .30 .09
U156 Brent Butler .30 .09
U157 Kirk Rueter .30 .09
U158 Eddie Guardado .30 .09
U159 Hideki Irabu .30 .09
U160 Wendell Magee .30 .09
U161 Antonio Osuna .30 .09
U162 Jose Vizcaino .30 .09
U163 Danny Bautista .30 .09
U164 Vinny Castilla .30 .09
U165 Chris Singleton .30 .09
U166 Mark Redman .30 .09
U167 Olmedo Saenz .30 .09
U168 Scott Erickson .30 .09
U169 Ty Wigginton .30 .09
U170 Jason Isringhausen .30 .09
U171 Andy Van Hekken .30 .09
U172 Chris Magruder .30 .09
U173 Brandon Berger .30 .09
U174 Roger Cedeno .30 .09
U175 Kelvim Escobar .30 .09
U176 Jose Guillen .30 .09
U177 Damian Jackson .30 .09
U178 Eric Owens .30 .09
U179 Angel Berroa .30 .09
U180 Alex Cintron .30 .09
U181 Jeff Weaver .30 .09
U182 Damon Minor .30 .09
U183 Bobby Estalella .30 .09
U184 David Justice .30 .09
U185 Roy Halladay .30 .09
U186 Brian Jordan .30 .09
U187 Mike Maroth .30 .09
U188 Pokey Reese .30 .09
U189 Rey Sanchez .30 .09
U190 Hank Blalock .75 .23
U191 Jeff Cirillo .30 .09
U192 Dmitri Young .30 .09
U193 Carl Everett .30 .09
U194 Joey Hamilton .30 .09
U195 Jorge Julio .30 .09
U196 Pablo Ozuna .30 .09
U197 Jason Marquis .30 .09
U198 Dustan Mohr .30 .09
U199 Joe Borowski .30 .09
U200 Tony Clark .30 .09
U201 David Wells .30 .09
U202 Josh Fogg .30 .09
U203 Aaron Harang .30 .09
U204 John McDonald .30 .09
U205 John Stephens .30 .09
U206 Chris Reitsma .30 .09
U207 Alex Sanchez .30 .09
U208 Milton Bradley .30 .09
U209 Matt Clement .30 .09
U210 Brad Fullmer .30 .09
U211 Shigetoshi Hasegawa .30 .09
U212 Austin Kearns .30 .09
U213 Damaso Marte .30 .09
U214 Vicente Padilla .30 .09
U215 Raul Mondesi .30 .09
U216 Russell Branyan .30 .09
U217 Bartolo Colon .30 .09
U218 Moises Alou .30 .09
U219 Scott Hatteberg .30 .09
U220 Bobby Kielty .30 .09
U221 Kip Wells .30 .09
U222 Scott Stewart .30 .09
U223 Victor Martinez .30 .09
U224 Marty Cordova .30 .09
U225 Desi Relaford .30 .09
U226 Reggie Sanders .30 .09
U227 Jason Giambi .75 .23
U228 Jimmy Haynes .30 .09
U229 Billy Koch .30 .09
U230 Damian Moss .30 .09
U231 Chan Ho Park .30 .09
U232 Cliff Floyd .30 .09
U233 Todd Zeile .30 .09
U234 Jeremy Giambi .30 .09
U235 Rick Helling .30 .09
U236 Matt Lawton .30 .09
U237 Ramon Martinez .30 .09
U238 Rondell White .30 .09
U239 Scott Sullivan .30 .09
U240 Hideo Nomo .75 .23
U241 Todd Ritchie .30 .09
U242 Ramon Santiago .30 .09
U243 Jake Peavy .30 .09
U244 Brad Wilkerson .30 .09
U245 Reggie Taylor .30 .09
U246 Carlos Pena .30 .09
U247 Willis Roberts .30 .09
U248 Jason Schmidt .30 .09
U249 Mike Williams .30 .09
U250 Alan Zinter .30 .09
U251 Michael Tejera .30 .09
U252 Dave Roberts .30 .09
U253 Scott Schoeneweis .30 .09
U254 Woody Williams .30 .09
U255 John Thomson .30 .09
U256 Ricardo Rodriguez .30 .09
U257 Aaron Sele .30 .09
U258 Paul Wilson .30 .09
U259 Brett Tomko .30 .09
U260 Kenny Rogers .30 .09
U261 Mo Vaughn .30 .09
U262 John Burkett .30 .09
U263 Dennis Stark .30 .09
U264 Ray Durham .30 .09
U265 Scott Rolen .50 .15
U266 Gabe Kapler .30 .09
U267 Todd Hollandsworth .30 .09
U268 Bud Smith .30 .09
U269 Jay Payton .30 .09
U270 Tyler Houston .30 .09
U271 Brian Moehler .30 .09
U272 David Espinosa .30 .09
U273 Placido Polanco .30 .09
U274 John Patterson .30 .09
U275 Adam Hyzdu .30 .09
U276 Albert Pujols DS .75 .23
U277 Larry Walker DS .30 .09
U278 Magglio Ordonez DS .30 .09
U279 Ryan Klesko DS .30 .09
U280 Darin Erstad DS .30 .09
U281 Jeff Kent DS .30 .09
U282 Paul Lo Duca DS .30 .09
U283 Jim Edmonds DS .30 .09
U284 Chipper Jones DS .50 .15
U285 Bernie Williams DS .30 .09
U286 Pat Burrell DS .30 .09
U287 Cliff Floyd DS .30 .09
U288 Troy Glaus DS .30 .09
U289 Brian Giles DS .30 .09
U290 Jim Thome DS .50 .15
U291 Greg Maddux DS .75 .23
U292 Roberto Alomar DS .50 .15
U293 Jeff Bagwell DS .30 .09
U294 Rafael Furcal DS .30 .09
U295 Josh Beckett DS .30 .09
U296 Carlos Delgado DS .30 .09
U297 Ken Griffey Jr. DS .75 .23
U298 Jason Giambi DS .50 .15
U299 Paul Konerko AS .30 .09
U300 Mike Sweeney AS .30 .09
U301 Alfonso Soriano AS .30 .09
U302 Shea Hillenbrand AS .30 .09
U303 Tony Batista AS .30 .09
U304 Robin Ventura AS .30 .09
U305 Alex Rodriguez AS .75 .23
U306 Nomar Garciaparra AS .75 .23
U307 Derek Jeter AS 1.00 .30
U308 Miguel Tejada AS .30 .09
U309 Omar Vizquel AS .30 .09
U310 Jorge Posada AS .30 .09
U311 A.J. Pierzynski AS .30 .09
U312 Ichiro Suzuki AS .75 .23
U313 Manny Ramirez AS .30 .09
U314 Torii Hunter AS .30 .09
U315 Garret Anderson AS .30 .09
U316 Robert Fick AS .30 .09
U317 Randy Winn AS .30 .09
U318 Mark Buehrle AS .30 .09
U319 Freddy Garcia AS .30 .09
U320 Eddie Guardado AS .30 .09
U321 Roy Halladay AS .30 .09
U322 Derek Lowe AS .30 .09
U323 Pedro Martinez AS .50 .15
U324 Mariano Rivera AS .30 .09
U325 Kazuhiro Sasaki AS .30 .09
U326 Barry Zito AS .30 .09
U327 Johnny Damon AS .30 .09
U328 Ugueth Urbina AS .30 .09
U329 Todd Helton AS .30 .09
U330 Richie Sexson AS .30 .09
U331 Jose Vidro AS .30 .09
U332 Luis Castillo AS .30 .09
U333 Junior Spivey AS .30 .09
U334 Scott Rolen AS .30 .09
U335 Mike Lowell AS .30 .09
U336 Jimmy Rollins AS .30 .09
U337 Jose Hernandez AS .30 .09
U338 Mike Piazza AS .75 .23
U339 Benito Santiago AS .30 .09
U340 Sammy Sosa AS .75 .23
U341 Barry Bonds AS 1.00 .30
U342 Vladimir Guerrero AS .50 .15
U343 Lance Berkman AS .30 .09
U344 Adam Dunn AS .30 .09
U345 Shawn Green AS .30 .09
U346 Luis Gonzalez AS .30 .09
U347 Eric Gagne AS .30 .09
U348 Tom Glavine AS .30 .09
U349 Trevor Hoffman AS .30 .09
U350 Randy Johnson AS .50 .15
U351 Byung-Hyun Kim AS .30 .09
U352 Matt Morris AS .30 .09
U353 Odalis Perez AS .30 .09
U354 Curt Schilling AS .30 .09
U355 John Smoltz AS .30 .09
U356 Mike Williams AS .30 .09
U357 Andruw Jones AS .30 .09
U358 Vicente Padilla AS .30 .09
U359 Mike Remlinger AS .30 .09
U360 Robb Nen AS .30 .09
U361 Shawn Green CC .30 .09
U362 Derek Jeter CC 1.00 .30
U363 Troy Glaus CC .30 .09
U364 Ken Griffey Jr. CC .75 .23
U365 Mike Piazza CC .75 .23
U366 Jason Giambi CC .50 .15
U367 Greg Maddux CC .75 .23
U368 Albert Pujols CC .75 .23
U369 Pedro Martinez CC .50 .15
U370 Barry Zito CC .30 .09
U371 Ichiro Suzuki CC .75 .23
U372 Nomar Garciaparra CC .75 .23
U373 Vladimir Guerrero CC .50 .15
U374 Randy Johnson CC .50 .15
U375 Barry Bonds CC 1.00 .30
U376 Sammy Sosa CC .75 .23
U377 Hideo Nomo CC .75 .23
U378 Jeff Bagwell CC .30 .09
U379 Curt Schilling CC .30 .09
U380 Jim Thome CC .50 .15
U381 Todd Helton CC .30 .09
U382 Roger Clemens CC .75 .23
U383 Chipper Jones CC .50 .15
U384 Alex Rodriguez CC .75 .23
U385 Manny Ramirez CC .30 .09
U386 Barry Bonds TT 1.00 .30
U387 Jim Thome TT .50 .15
U388 Adam Dunn TT .30 .09
U389 Alex Rodriguez TT .75 .23
U390 Shawn Green TT .30 .09
U391 Jason Giambi TT .50 .15
U392 Lance Berkman TT .30 .09
U393 Pat Burrell TT .30 .09
U394 Eric Chavez TT .30 .09
U395 Mike Piazza TT .75 .23
U396 Vladimir Guerrero TT .50 .15
U397 Paul Konerko TT .30 .09
U398 Sammy Sosa TT .75 .23
U399 Richie Sexson TT .30 .09
U400 Torii Hunter TT .30 .09

2002 Fleer Tradition Update Glossy

Randomly inserted into packs, this is a parallel to the basic Fleer Tradition Update set. These cards can be differentiated from the regular cards by their "glossy" sheen on the front and each card has a stated print run of 200 serial numbered sets.

Nm-Mt Ex-Mt
*GLOSSY 1-100: 1X TO 2.5X BASIC...
*GLOSSY 101-275: 3X TO 8X BASIC..
*GLOSSY 276-400: 6X TO 15X BASIC

2002 Fleer Tradition Update Diamond Debuts

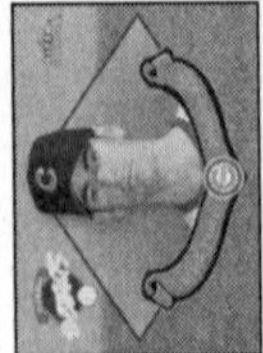

Inserted into packs at a stated rate of one in six, these 15 cards feature players who made their major league debut during the 2002 season.

	Nm-Mt	Ex-Mt
COMPLETE SET (15)	15.00	4.50
U1 Mark Prior	4.00	1.20
U2 Eric Hinske	1.00	.30
U3 Kazuhisa Ishii	3.00	.90
U4 Ben Broussard	1.00	.30
U5 Sean Burroughs	1.00	.30
U6 Austin Kearns	1.00	.30
U7 Hee Seop Choi	1.25	.35
U8 Kirk Saarloos	1.00	.30
U9 Orlando Hudson	1.00	.30
U10 So Taguchi	1.25	.35
U11 Kevin Mench	1.00	.30
U12 Carl Crawford	1.00	.30
U13 Marlon Byrd	1.00	.30
U14 Hank Blalock	2.00	.60
U15 Brett Myers	1.00	.30

2002 Fleer Tradition Update Grass Patch

Randomly inserted into packs, these seven cards feature some of the leading fielders in the game. Each card not only has a game-used memorabilia swatch on it but also has a stated print run of 50 serial numbered sets.

	Nm-Mt	Ex-Mt
1 Roberto Alomar	50.00	15.00
2 Jim Edmonds	30.00	9.00
3 Nomar Garciaparra	80.00	24.00
4 Shawn Green	30.00	9.00
5 Torii Hunter	30.00	9.00
6 Andruw Jones	30.00	9.00
7 Alfonso Soriano	40.00	12.00

2002 Fleer Tradition Update Grass Roots

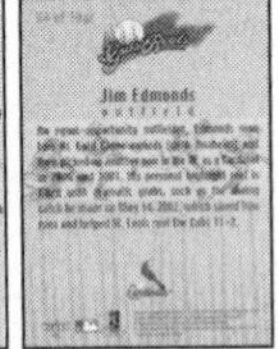

Inserted into packs at a stated rate of one in 18, this 10 card set honors some of the most exciting fielders in baseball.

	Nm-Mt	Ex-Mt
COMPLETE SET (10)	15.00	4.50
U1 Alfonso Soriano	2.00	.60
U2 Torii Hunter	2.00	.60
U3 Andruw Jones	2.00	.60
U4 Jim Edmonds	2.00	.60
U5 Shawn Green	2.00	.60
U6 Todd Helton	2.00	.60
U7 Nomar Garciaparra	4.00	1.20
U8 Roberto Alomar	2.50	.75
U9 Vladimir Guerrero	2.50	.75
U10 Ichiro Suzuki	4.00	1.20

2002 Fleer Tradition Update Heads Up

Inserted at a stated rate of one in 36, this 10 card set is designed in the style of the old Heads Up set of the 1930's.

	Nm-Mt	Ex-Mt
U1 Roger Clemens	8.00	2.40
U2 Adam Dunn	3.00	.90
U3 Kazuhisa Ishii	5.00	1.50
U4 Barry Zito	3.00	.90
U5 Pedro Martinez	4.00	1.20
U6 Alfonso Soriano	3.00	.90
U7 Mark Prior	8.00	2.40
U8 Chipper Jones	4.00	1.20
U9 Randy Johnson	4.00	1.20
U10 Lance Berkman	3.00	.90

2002 Fleer Tradition Update Heads Up Game Used Caps

Randomly inserted in packs, these cards are designed in the style of the old Heads Up cards from the 1930's. However, they are different from the regular insert set as a piece of a game-used cap is also part of the card. Each card is also printed to a stated print run of 150.

	Nm-Mt	Ex-Mt
1 Lance Berkman	20.00	6.00
2 Barry Bonds	60.00	18.00
3 Roger Clemens	50.00	15.00
4 Adam Dunn	20.00	6.00
5 Kazuhisa Ishii	25.00	7.50
6 Randy Johnson	25.00	7.50
7 Chipper Jones	25.00	7.50
8 Mike Piazza	30.00	9.00
9 Mark Prior	30.00	9.00
10 Alfonso Soriano	25.00	7.50
11 Barry Zito	25.00	7.50

2002 Fleer Tradition Update New York's Finest

Inserted into packs at stated odds of one in 83, these 15 cards honor some of the best players for either the New York Yankees or the New York Mets.

	Nm-Mt	Ex-Mt
1 Edgardo Alfonzo	8.00	2.40
2 Roberto Alomar	8.00	2.40
3 Jeromy Burnitz	8.00	2.40
4 Satoru Komiyama	8.00	2.40
5 Rey Ordonez	8.00	2.40
6 Mike Piazza	12.00	3.60
7 Mo Vaughn	8.00	2.40
8 Roger Clemens	15.00	4.50
9 Jason Giambi	8.00	2.40
10 Derek Jeter	20.00	6.00
11 Mike Mussina	8.00	2.40
12 Jorge Posada	8.00	2.40
13 Alfonso Soriano	8.00	2.40
14 Robin Ventura	8.00	2.40
15 Bernie Williams	8.00	2.40

2002 Fleer Tradition Update New York's Finest Dual Swatch

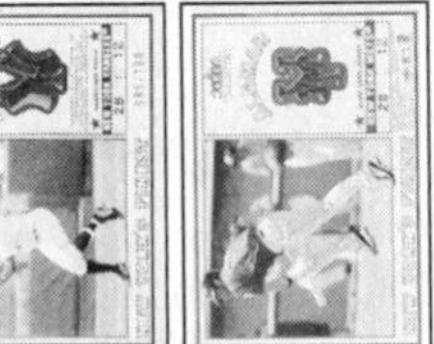

Randomly inserted into packs, these six cards feature two leading players from New York along with a game-used memorabilia piece for both players.

	Nm-Mt	Ex-Mt
1 Derek Jeter Rey Ordonez	100.00	30.00
2 Alfonso Soriano Roberto Alomar	50.00	15.00
3 Roger Clemens Mike Piazza	120.00	36.00
4 Mike Mussina Mo Vaughn	50.00	15.00
5 Bernie Williams Jeromy Burnitz	40.00	12.00
6 Robin Ventura Edgardo Alfonzo	25.00	7.50

2002 Fleer Tradition Update New York's Finest Single Swatch

Inserted into packs at stated odds of one in 112, these cards feature two star players from New York but only one memorabilia piece on each card. The player who has a memorabilia piece is listed first in our checklist along with what type of memorabilia piece is used.

	Nm-Mt	Ex-Mt
1 Derek Jeter Jsy Rey Ordonez	30.00	9.00
2 Alfonso Soriano Jsy Roberto Alomar	15.00	4.50
3 Roger Clemens Jsy Mike Piazza	20.00	6.00
4 Mike Mussina Jsy Mo Vaughn	15.00	4.50
5 Bernie Williams Jsy Jeromy Burnitz	15.00	4.50
6 Derek Jeter Jsy Satoru Komiyama	30.00	9.00
7 Robin Ventura Jsy Edgardo Alfonzo	15.00	4.50
8 Jorge Posada Jsy Mike Piazza	15.00	4.50
9 Jason Giambi Base SP Mo Vaughn	15.00	4.50
10 Alfonso Soriano Jsy Edgardo Alfonzo	15.00	4.50
11 Rey Ordonez Jsy Derek Jeter	10.00	3.00
12 Roberto Alomar Jsy Alfonso Soriano	15.00	4.50
13 Mike Piazza Jsy Roger Clemens	15.00	4.50
14 Mo Vaughn Jsy Mike Mussina	10.00	3.00
15 Jeromy Burnitz Jsy Bernie Williams	10.00	3.00
16 Satoru Komiyama Bat Derek Jeter	15.00	4.50
17 Edgardo Alfonzo Jsy Robin Ventura	10.00	3.00
18 Mike Piazza Jsy Jorge Posada	15.00	4.50
19 Mo Vaughn Jsy Jason Giambi	10.00	3.00
20 Edgardo Alfonzo Jsy Alfonso Soriano	10.00	3.00

2002 Fleer Tradition Update Plays of the Week

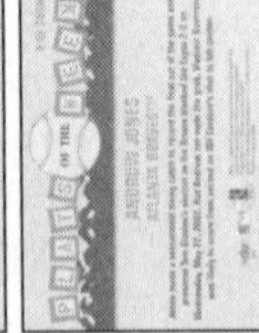

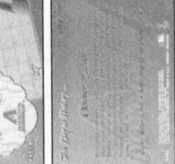

Inserted at stated odds of one in 12, these 30 cards feature some of the leading players of the 2002 season along with their highlight play of the season.

	Nm-Mt	Ex-Mt
1 Troy Glaus	1.50	.45
2 Andruw Jones	1.50	.45
3 Curt Schilling	1.50	.45
4 Manny Ramirez	1.50	.45
5 Sammy Sosa	4.00	1.20
6 Magglio Ordonez	1.50	.45
7 Ken Griffey Jr.	4.00	1.20
8 Jim Thome	2.50	.75
9 Larry Walker	1.50	.45
10 Robert Fick	1.50	.45
11 Josh Beckett	1.50	.45
12 Roy Oswalt	1.50	.45
13 Mike Sweeney	1.50	.45
14 Shawn Green	1.50	.45
15 Torii Hunter	1.50	.45
16 Vladimir Guerrero	2.50	.75
17 Mike Piazza	4.00	1.20
18 Jason Giambi	2.50	.75
19 Eric Chavez	1.50	.45
20 Pat Burrell	1.50	.45
21 Brian Giles	1.50	.45
22 Ryan Klesko	1.50	.45
23 Barry Bonds	6.00	1.80
24 Mike Cameron	1.50	.45
25 Albert Pujols	5.00	1.50
26 Alex Rodriguez	4.00	1.20
27 Carlos Delgado	1.50	.45
28 Richie Sexson	1.50	.45
29 Jay Gibbons	1.50	.45
30 Randy Winn	1.50	.45

2002 Fleer Tradition Update This Day In History

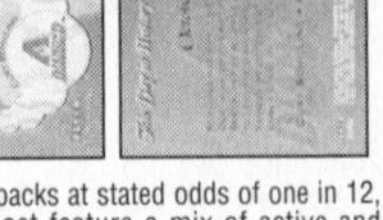

Inserted into packs at stated odds of one in 12, this 25 card set feature a mix of active and retired players along with an historical highlight that the player was involved with.

	Nm-Mt	Ex-Mt
U1 Shawn Green	1.50	.45

U2 Ozzie Smith 3.00 .90
U3 Derek Lowe 1.50 .45
U4 Ken Griffey Jr. 4.00 1.20
U5 Barry Bonds 6.00 1.80
U6 Juan Gonzalez 2.50 .75
U7 Wade Boggs 2.00 .60
U8 Mark Prior 5.00 1.50
U9 Thurman Munson 5.00 1.50
U10 Curt Schilling 1.50 .45
U11 Jason Giambi 2.50 .75
U12 Cal Ripken 10.00 3.00
U13 Craig Biggio 1.50 .45
U14 Drew Henson 1.50 .45
U15 Steve Carlton 2.00 .60
U16 Greg Maddux 4.00 1.20
U17 Adam Dunn 1.50 .45
U18 Vladimir Guerrero 2.50 .75
U19 Alex Rodriguez 4.00 1.20
U20 Carlton Fisk 2.00 .60
U21 Ichiro Suzuki 4.00 1.20
U22 Johnny Bench 3.00 .90
U23 Kazuhisa Ishii 3.00 .90
U24 Derek Jeter 6.00 1.80
U25 Jim Thome 2.50 .75

2002 Fleer Tradition Update This Day In History Autographs

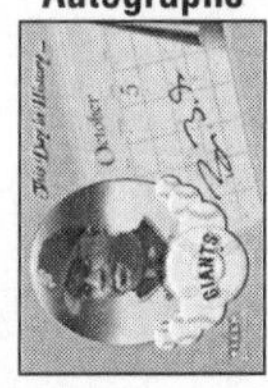

Inserted into packs at a stated rate of one in 582, this is a partial parallel to the This Day in History insert set. A few players signed an amount of cards in much shorter supply than others. Fortunately, Fleer provided the specific quantities signed for the short prints and the information is detailed in full within our checklist. In addition, an exchange card with a redemption deadline of October 31st, 2003 was seeded into packs for the Greg Maddux card.

	Nm-Mt	Ex-Mt
1 Barry Bonds SP/150	175.00	52.50
2 Mark Prior SP/64	120.00	36.00
3 Cal Ripken SP/35		
4 Drew Henson	25.00	7.50
5 Greg Maddux SP/99		
6 Derek Jeter	120.00	36.00

2002 Fleer Tradition Update This Day In History Game Used

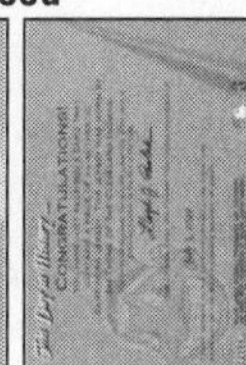

Inserted into packs at a stated rate of one in 28, these 20 cards form a partial parallel to the This Day in History insert set. These cards feature a game-used memorabilia piece of the featured player. A couple players are featured on more than one memorabilia card and we have notated that information in our checklist as well as the stated print run for the cards which were issued in notably shorter supply.

	Nm-Mt	Ex-Mt
1 Craig Biggio Bat SP/80		
2 Craig Biggio Jsy	15.00	4.50
3 Wade Boggs Jsy	15.00	4.50
4 Wade Boggs Pants	15.00	4.50
5 Barry Bonds Bat	20.00	6.00
6 Barry Bonds Jsy	20.00	6.00
7 Adam Dunn Jsy	10.00	3.00
8 Carlton Fisk Bat	15.00	4.50
9 Juan Gonzalez Bat	15.00	4.50
10 Shawn Green Jsy	10.00	3.00
11 Kazuhisa Ishii Bat	15.00	4.50
12 Derek Jeter Pants	25.00	7.50
13 Greg Maddux Jsy	15.00	4.50
14 Thurman Munson Jsy SP/40		
15 Alex Rodriguez Bat	15.00	4.50
16 Alex Rodriguez Jsy	15.00	4.50
17 Curt Schilling Jsy	15.00	4.50
18 Ozzie Smith Jsy	20.00	6.00
19 Jim Thome Bat SP/120		
20 Jim Thome Jsy	15.00	4.50

2003 Fleer Tradition

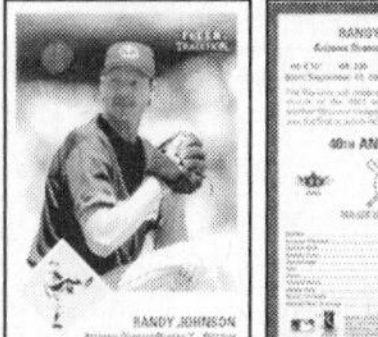

This 485 card set, deisgned in the style of 1963 Fleer, was released in January, 2003. These cards were issued in 10 card packs which were packed 40 packs to a box and 20 boxes to a case with an SRP of $1.49 per pack. The following subsets are part of the set: Cards numbered 1 through 30 are Team Leader cards, cards number 67 through 85 are Missing Link (featuring players active but not on Fleer cards in 1963) cards, cards number 417 rhrough 425 are Award Winner cards, cards number 426 through 460 are Prospect cards and cards numbered 461 through 485 are Banner Season cards. All cards numbered 1 through 100 were short printed and inserted at an rate of one per hobby pack and one per 12 retail pack. In addition, retail boxes had a special Barry Bonds pin as a box topper and a Derek Jeter promo card was issued a few weeks before this product became live so media and dealers could see what this set look like.

	Nm-Mt	Ex-Mt
COMPLETE SET (485)	150.00	45.00
COMP.SET w/o SP's (385)	40.00	12.00
COMMON CARD (1-30)	1.00	.30
COMM.SP (31-66/86-100)	1.00	.30
COMMON ML (67-85)	1.50	.45
COMMON CARD (	.30	.09
COMMON PR (426-460)	.30	.09
1 Jarrod Washburn / Troy Glaus / Garret Anderson / Ramon Ortiz TL SP	1.00	.30
2 Luis Gonzalez / Randy Johnson TL SP	1.50	.45
3 Andruw Jones / Chipper Jones / Tom Glavine / Kevin Millwood TL SP	1.50	.45
4 Tony Batista / Rodrigo Lopez TL SP	1.00	.30
5 Manny Ramirez / Nomar Garciaparra / Derek Lowe / Pedro Martinez TL SP	2.50	.75
6 Sammy Sosa / Matt Clement / Kerry Wood TL SP	2.50	.75
7 Matt Buehrle / Magglio Ordonez / Danny Wright TL SP	1.00	.30
8 Adam Dunn / Aaron Boone / Jimmy Haynes TL SP	1.00	.30
9 C.C. Sabathia / Jim Thome TL SP	1.50	.45
10 Todd Helton / Jason Jennings TL SP	1.00	.30
11 Randall Simon / Steve Sparks / Mark Redman TL SP	1.00	.30
12 Derrek Lee / Mike Lowell / A.J. Burnett TL SP	1.00	.30
13 Lance Berkman / Roy Oswalt TL SP	1.00	.30
14 Paul Byrd / Carlos Beltran TL SP	1.00	.30
15 Shawn Green / Hideo Nomo TL SP	1.50	.45
16 Richie Sexson / Ben Sheets TL SP	1.00	.30
17 Torii Hunter / Kyle Lohse / Johan Santana TL SP	1.00	.30
18 Vladimir Guerrrero / Tomo Ohka / Javier Vazquez TL SP	1.50	.45
19 Mike Piazza / Al Leiter TL SP	2.50	.75
20 Jason Giambi / David Wells / Roger Clemens TL SP	2.50	.75
21 Eric Chavez / Miguel Tejada / Barry Zito TL SP	1.00	.30
22 Pat Burrell / Vicente Padilla / Randy Wolf TL SP	1.00	.30
23 Brian Giles / Josh Fogg / Kip Wells TL SP	1.00	.30
24 Ryan Klesko / Brian Lawrence TL SP	1.00	.30
25 Barry Bonds / Russ Ortiz / Jason Schmidt TL SP	2.50	.75
26 Mike Cameron / Bret Boone / Freddy Garcia TL SP	1.00	.30
27 Albert Pujols / Matt Morris TL SP	2.50	.75
28 Aubry Huff / Randy Winn / Joe Kennedy / Tanyon Sturtze TL SP	1.00	.30
29 Alex Rodriguez / Kenny Rogers / Chan Ho Park TL SP	2.50	.75
30 Carlos Delgado / Roy Halladay TL SP	1.00	.30
31 Greg Maddux SP	4.00	1.20
32 Nick Neugebauer SP	1.00	.30
33 Larry Walker SP	1.50	.45
34 Freddy Garcia SP	1.00	.30
35 Rich Aurilia SP	1.00	.30
36 Craig Wilson SP	1.00	.30
37 Jeff Suppan SP	1.00	.30
38 Joel Pineiro SP	1.00	.30
39 Pedro Feliz SP	1.00	.30
40 Bartolo Colon SP	1.00	.30
41 Pete Walker SP	1.00	.30
42 Mo Vaughn SP	1.00	.30
43 Sidney Ponson SP	1.00	.30
44 Jason Isringhausen SP	1.00	.30
45 Hideki Irabu SP	1.00	.30
46 Pedro Martinez SP	2.50	.75
47 Tom Glavine SP	1.50	.45
48 Matt Lawton SP	1.00	.30
49 Kyle Lohse SP	1.00	.30
50 Corey Patterson SP	1.00	.30
51 Ichiro Suzuki SP UER / RBI total for 2002 incorrect	4.00	1.20
52 Wade Miller SP	1.00	.30
53 Ben Diggins SP	1.00	.30
54 Jayson Werth SP	1.00	.30
55 Masato Yoshii SP	1.00	.30
56 Mark Buehrle SP	1.00	.30
57 Drew Henson SP	1.00	.30
58 Dave Williams SP	1.00	.30
59 Juan Rivera SP	1.00	.30
60 Scott Schoeneweis SP	1.00	.30
61 Josh Beckett SP	1.50	.45
62 Vinny Castilla SP	1.00	.30
63 Barry Zito SP	1.50	.45
64 Jose Valentin SP	1.00	.30
65 Jon Lieber SP	1.00	.30
66 Jorge Padilla SP	1.00	.30
67 Luis Aparicio ML SP	1.50	.45
68 Boog Powell ML SP	2.50	.75
69 Dick Radatz ML SP	1.50	.45
70 Frank Malzone ML SP	1.50	.45
71 Lou Brock ML SP	2.50	.75
72 Billy Williams ML SP	1.50	.45
73 Early Wynn ML SP	1.50	.45
74 Jim Bunning ML SP	2.50	.75
75 Al Kaline ML SP	4.00	1.20
76 Eddie Mathews ML SP	4.00	1.20
77 Harmon Killebrew ML SP	4.00	1.20
78 Gil Hodges ML SP	2.50	.75
79 Duke Snider ML SP	2.50	.75
80 Yogi Berra ML SP	4.00	1.20
81 Whitey Ford ML SP	2.50	.75
82 Willie Stargell ML SP	2.50	.75
83 Willie McCovey ML SP	1.50	.45
84 Gaylord Perry ML SP	1.50	.45
85 Red Schoendienst ML SP	1.50	.45
86 Luis Castillo SP	1.00	.30
87 Derek Jeter SP	6.00	1.80
88 Orlando Hudson SP	1.00	.30
89 Bobby Higginson SP	1.00	.30
90 Brent Butler SP	1.00	.30
91 Brad Wilkerson SP	1.00	.30
92 Craig Biggio SP	1.50	.45
93 Marlon Anderson SP	1.00	.30
94 Ty Wigginton SP	1.00	.30
95 Hideo Nomo SP	2.50	.75
96 Barry Larkin SP	2.50	.75
97 Roberto Alomar SP	2.50	.75
98 Omar Vizquel SP	1.00	.30
99 Andres Galarraga SP	1.00	.30
100 Shawn Green SP	1.00	.30
101 Rafael Furcal	.30	.09
102 Bill Selby	.30	.09
103 Brent Abernathy	.30	.09
104 Nomar Garciaparra	1.25	.35
105 Michael Barrett	.30	.09
106 Travis Hafner	.30	.09
107 Carl Crawford	.30	.09
108 Jeff Cirillo	.30	.09
109 Mike Hampton	.30	.09
110 Kip Wells	.30	.09
111 Luis Alicea	.30	.09
112 Ellis Burks	.30	.09
113 Matt Anderson	.30	.09
114 Carlos Beltran	.30	.09
115 Paul Lo Duca	.30	.09
116 Lance Berkman	.30	.09
117 Moises Alou	.30	.09
118 Roger Cedeno	.30	.09
119 Brad Fullmer	.30	.09
120 Sean Burroughs	.30	.09
121 Eric Byrnes	.30	.09
122 Milton Bradley	.30	.09
123 Jason Giambi	.75	.23
124 Brook Fordyce	.30	.09
125 Kevin Appier	.30	.09
126 Steve Cox	.30	.09
127 Danny Bautista	.30	.09
128 Edgardo Alfonzo	.30	.09
129 Matt Clement	.30	.09
130 Robb Nen	.30	.09
131 Roy Halladay	.30	.09
132 Brian Jordan	.30	.09
133 A.J. Burnett	.30	.09
134 Aaron Cook	.30	.09
135 Paul Byrd	.30	.09
136 Ramon Ortiz	.30	.09
137 Adam Hyzdu	.30	.09
138 Rafael Soriano	.30	.09
139 Marty Cordova	.30	.09
140 Nelson Cruz	.30	.09
141 Jamie Moyer	.30	.09
142 Raul Mondesi	.30	.09
143 Josh Bard	.30	.09
144 Elmer Dessens	.30	.09
145 Rickey Henderson	.75	.23
146 Joe McEwing	.30	.09
147 Luis Rivas	.30	.09
148 Armando Benitez	.30	.09
149 Keith Foulke	.30	.09
150 Zach Day	.30	.09
151 Trey Lunsford	.30	.09
152 Bobby Abreu	.30	.09
153 Juan Cruz	.30	.09
154 Ramon Hernandez	.30	.09
155 Brandon Duckworth	.30	.09
156 Matt Ginter	.30	.09
157 Rob Mackowiak	.30	.09
158 Josh Pearce	.30	.09
159 Marlon Byrd	.30	.09
160 Todd Walker	.30	.09
161 Chad Hermansen	.30	.09
162 Felix Escalona	.30	.09
163 Ruben Mateo	.30	.09
164 Mark Johnson	.30	.09
165 Juan Pierre	.30	.09
166 Gary Sheffield	.30	.09
167 Edgar Martinez	.50	.15
168 Randy Winn	.30	.09
169 Pokey Reese	.30	.09
170 Kevin Mench	.30	.09
171 Albert Pujols	1.50	.45
172 J.T. Snow	.30	.09
173 Dean Palmer	.30	.09
174 Jay Payton	.30	.09
175 Abraham Nunez	.30	.09
176 Richie Sexson	.30	.09
177 Jose Vidro	.30	.09
178 Geoff Jenkins	.30	.09
179 Dan Wilson	.30	.09
180 John Olerud	.30	.09
181 Javy Lopez	.30	.09
182 Carl Everett	.30	.09
183 Vernon Wells	.30	.09
184 Juan Gonzalez	.75	.23
185 Jorge Posada	.50	.15
186 Mike Sweeney	.30	.09
187 Cesar Izturis	.30	.09
188 Jason Schmidt	.30	.09
189 Chris Richard	.30	.09
190 Jason Phillips	.30	.09
191 Fred McGriff	.50	.15
192 Shea Hillenbrand	.30	.09
193 Ivan Rodriguez	.75	.23
194 Mike Lowell	.30	.09
195 Neifi Perez	.30	.09
196 Kenny Lofton	.30	.09
197 A.J. Pierzynski	.30	.09
198 Larry Bigbie	.30	.09
199 Juan Uribe	.30	.09
200 Jeff Bagwell	.50	.15
201 Timo Perez	.30	.09
202 Jeremy Giambi	.30	.09
203 Deivi Cruz	.30	.09
204 Marquis Grissom	.30	.09
205 Chipper Jones	.75	.23
206 Alex Gonzalez	.30	.09
207 Steve Finley	.30	.09
208 Ben Davis	.30	.09
209 Mike Bordick	.30	.09
210 Casey Fossum	.30	.09
211 Aramis Ramirez	.30	.09
212 Aaron Boone	.30	.09
213 Orlando Cabrera	.30	.09
214 Hee Seop Choi	.30	.09
215 Jeromy Burnitz	.30	.09
216 Todd Hollandsworth	.30	.09
217 Rey Sanchez	.30	.09
218 Jose Cruz	.30	.09
219 Roosevelt Brown	.30	.09
220 Odalis Perez	.30	.09
221 Carlos Delgado	.30	.09
222 Orlando Hernandez	.30	.09
223 Adam Everett	.30	.09
224 Adrian Beltre	.30	.09
225 Ken Griffey Jr.	1.25	.35
226 Brad Penny	.30	.09
227 Carlos Lee	.30	.09
228 J.C. Romero	.30	.09
229 Ramon Martinez	.30	.09
230 Matt Morris	.30	.09
231 Ben Howard	.30	.09
232 Damon Minor	.30	.09
233 Jason Marquis	.30	.09
234 Paul Wilson	.30	.09
235 Ryan Dempster	.30	.09
236 Jeffrey Hammonds	.30	.09
237 Jaret Wright	.30	.09
238 Carlos Pena	.30	.09
239 Toby Hall	.30	.09
240 Rick Helling	.30	.09
241 Alex Escobar	.30	.09
242 Trevor Hoffman	.30	.09
243 Bernie Williams	.50	.15
244 Jorge Julio	.30	.09
245 Byung-Hyun Kim	.30	.09
246 Mike Redmond	.30	.09
247 Tony Armas	.30	.09
248 Aaron Rowand	.30	.09
249 Rusty Greer	.30	.09
250 Aaron Harang	.30	.09
251 Jeremy Fikac	.30	.09
252 Jay Gibbons	.30	.09
253 Brandon Puffer	.30	.09
254 Dewayne Wise	.30	.09
255 Chan Ho Park	.30	.09
256 David Bell	.30	.09
257 Kenny Rogers	.30	.09
258 Mark Quinn	.30	.09
259 Greg LaRocca	.30	.09
260 Reggie Taylor	.30	.09
261 Brett Tomko	.30	.09
262 Jack Wilson	.30	.09
263 Billy Wagner	.30	.09
264 Greg Norton	.30	.09
265 Tim Salmon	.50	.15
266 Joe Randa	.30	.09
267 Geronimo Gil	.30	.09
268 Johnny Damon	.30	.09
269 Robin Ventura	.30	.09
270 Frank Thomas	.75	.23
271 Terrence Long	.30	.09
272 Mark Redman	.30	.09
273 Mark Kotsay	.30	.09
274 Ben Sheets	.30	.09
275 Reggie Sanders	.30	.09
276 Mark Grace	.50	.15
277 Eddie Guardado	.30	.09
278 Julio Mateo	.30	.09
279 Bengie Molina	.30	.09
280 Bill Hall	.30	.09
281 Eric Chavez	.30	.09
282 Joe Kennedy	.30	.09
283 John Valentin	.30	.09
284 Ray Durham	.30	.09
285 Trot Nixon	.50	.15
286 Rondell White	.30	.09
287 Alex Gonzalez	.30	.09
288 Tomas Perez	.30	.09
289 Jared Sandberg	.30	.09
290 Jacque Jones	.30	.09
291 Cliff Floyd	.30	.09
292 Ryan Klesko	.30	.09
293 Morgan Ensberg	.30	.09
294 Jerry Hairston	.30	.09
295 Doug Mientkiewicz	.30	.09
296 Darin Erstad	.30	.09
297 Jeff Conine	.30	.09
298 Johnny Estrada	.30	.09
299 Mark Mulder	.30	.09
300 Jeff Kent	.30	.09
301 Roger Clemens	1.50	.45
302 Endy Chavez	.30	.09
303 Joe Crede	.30	.09
304 J.D. Drew	.30	.09
305 David Dellucci	.30	.09
306 Eli Marrero	.30	.09
307 Josh Fogg	.30	.09
308 Mike Crudale	.30	.09
309 Bret Boone	.30	.09
310 Mariano Rivera	.50	.15
311 Mike Piazza	1.25	.35
312 Jason Jennings	.30	.09
313 Jason Varitek	.30	.09
314 Vicente Padilla	.30	.09
315 Kevin Millwood	.30	.09
316 Nick Johnson	.30	.09
317 Shane Reynolds	.30	.09
318 Joe Thurston	.30	.09
319 Mike Lamb	.30	.09
320 Aaron Sele	.30	.09
321 Fernando Tatis	.30	.09
322 Randy Wolf	.30	.09
323 David Justice	.30	.09
324 Andy Pettitte	.50	.15
325 Freddy Sanchez	.30	.09
326 Scott Spiezio	.30	.09
327 Randy Johnson	.75	.23
328 Karim Garcia	.30	.09
329 Eric Milton	.30	.09
330 Jermaine Dye	.30	.09
331 Kevin Brown	.30	.09
332 Adam Pettyjohn	.30	.09
333 Jason Lane	.30	.09
334 Mark Prior	1.50	.45
335 Mike Lieberthal	.30	.09
336 Matt White	.30	.09
337 John Patterson	.30	.09
338 Marcus Giles	.30	.09
339 Kazuhisa Ishii	.30	.09
340 Willie Harris	.30	.09
341 Travis Phelps	.30	.09
342 Randall Simon	.30	.09
343 Manny Ramirez	.30	.09
344 Kerry Wood	.75	.23
345 Shannon Stewart	.30	.09
346 Mike Mussina	.75	.23
347 Joe Borchard	.30	.09
348 Tyler Walker	.30	.09
349 Preston Wilson	.30	.09
350 Damian Moss	.30	.09
351 Eric Karros	.30	.09
352 Bobby Kielty	.30	.09
353 Jason LaRue	.30	.09
354 Phil Nevin	.30	.09
355 Tony Graffanino	.30	.09
356 Antonio Alfonseca	.30	.09
357 Eddie Taubensee	.30	.09
358 Luis Ugueto	.30	.09
359 Greg Vaughn	.30	.09
360 Corey Thurman	.30	.09
361 Omar Infante	.30	.09
362 Alex Cintron	.30	.09
363 Esteban Loaiza	.30	.09
364 Tino Martinez	.50	.15
365 David Eckstein	.30	.09
366 Dave Pember RC	.30	.09
367 Damian Rolls	.30	.09
368 Richard Hidalgo	.30	.09
369 Brad Radke	.30	.09
370 Alex Sanchez	.30	.09
371 Ben Grieve	.30	.09
372 Brandon Inge	.30	.09
373 Adam Piatt	.30	.09
374 Charles Johnson	.30	.09
375 Rafael Palmeiro	.50	.15
376 Joe Mays	.30	.09
377 Derrek Lee	.30	.09
378 Fernando Vina	.30	.09
379 Andruw Jones	.30	.09
380 Troy Glaus	.50	.15
381 Bobby Hill	.30	.09
382 C.C. Sabathia	.30	.09
383 Jose Hernandez	.30	.09
384 Al Leiter	.30	.09
385 Jarrod Washburn	.30	.09
386 Cody Ransom	.30	.09
387 Matt Stairs	.30	.09
388 Edgar Renteria	.30	.09
389 Tsuyoshi Shinjo	.30	.09
390 Matt Williams	.30	.09
391 Bubba Trammell	.30	.09
392 Jason Kendall	.30	.09
393 Scott Rolen	.50	.15
394 Chuck Knoblauch	.30	.09
395 Jimmy Rollins	.30	.09
396 Gary Bennett	.30	.09
397 David Wells	.30	.09
398 Ronnie Belliard	.30	.09
399 Austin Kearns	.30	.09
400 Tim Hudson	.30	.09
401 Andy Van Hekken	.30	.09
402 Ray Lankford	.30	.09
403 Todd Helton	.50	.15
404 Jeff Weaver	.30	.09
405 Gabe Kapler	.30	.09
406 Luis Gonzalez	.30	.09
407 Sean Casey	.30	.09
408 Kazuhiro Sasaki	.30	.09
409 Mark Teixeira	.50	.15
410 Brian Giles	.30	.09
411 Robert Fick	.30	.09
412 Wilkin Ruan	.30	.09
413 Jose Rijo	.30	.09
414 Ben Broussard	.30	.09
415 Aubrey Huff	.30	.09
416 Magglio Ordonez	.30	.09
417 Barry Bonds AW	1.00	.30
418 Miguel Tejada AW	.30	.09
419 Randy Johnson AW	.50	.15
420 Barry Zito AW	.50	.15
421 Jason Jennings AW	.30	.09
422 Eric Hinske AW	.30	.09
423 Benito Santiago AW	.30	.09
424 Adam Kennedy AW	.30	.09
425 Troy Glaus AW	.30	.09
426 Brandon Phillips PR	.30	.09
427 Jake Peavy PR	.30	.09
428 Jason Romano PR	.30	.09
429 Jeriome Robertson PR	.30	.09
430 Aaron Guiel PR	.30	.09
431 Hank Blalock PR	.50	.15
432 Brad Lidge PR	.30	.09
433 Francisco Rodriguez PR	.30	.09
434 Jaime Cerda PR	.30	.09
435 Jung Bong PR	.30	.09
436 Reed Johnson PR	.30	.09
437 Rene Reyes PR	.30	.09
438 Chris Snelling PR	.30	.09
439 Miguel Olivo PR	.30	.09
440 Brian Banks PR	.30	.09
441 Eric Junge PR	.30	.09
442 Kirk Saarloos PR	.30	.09
443 Jamey Carroll PR	.30	.09
444 Josh Hancock PR	.30	.09

445 Michael Restovich PR .30 .09
446 Willie Bloomquist PR .30 .09
447 John Lackey PR .30 .09
448 Marcus Thames PR .30 .09
449 Victor Martinez PR .30 .09
450 Brett Myers PR .30 .09
451 Wes Obermueller PR .30 .09
452 Hansel Izquierdo PR .30 .09
453 Brian Tallet PR .30 .09
454 Craig Monroe PR .30 .09
455 Doug Devore PR .30 .09
456 John Buck PR .30 .09
457 Tony Alvarez PR .30 .09
458 Wily Mo Pena PR .30 .09
459 John Stephens PR .30 .09
460 Tony Torcato PR .30 .09
461 Adam Kennedy BNR .30 .09
462 Alex Rodriguez BNR .75 .23
463 Derek Lowe BNR .30 .09
464 Garret Anderson BNR .30 .09
465 Pat Burrell BNR .30 .09
466 Eric Gagne BNR .30 .09
467 Tomo Ohka BNR .30 .09
468 Josh Phelps BNR .30 .09
469 Sammy Sosa BNR .75 .23
470 Jim Thome BNR .50 .15
471 Vladimir Guerrero BNR .50 .15
472 Jason Simontacchi BNR .30 .09
473 Adam Dunn BNR .30 .09
474 Jim Edmonds BNR .30 .09
475 Barry Bonds BNR 1.00 .30
476 Paul Konerko BNR .30 .09
477 Alfonso Soriano BNR .50 .15
478 Curt Schilling BNR .30 .09
479 John Smoltz BNR .30 .09
480 Torii Hunter BNR .30 .09
481 Rodrigo Lopez BNR .30 .09
482 Miguel Tejada BNR .30 .09
483 Eric Hinske BNR .30 .09
484 Roy Oswalt BNR .30 .09
485 Junior Spivey BNR .30 .09
P1 Barry Bonds Pin 8.00 2.40
P87 Derek Jeter Promo 2.00 .60

2003 Fleer Tradition Glossy

MINT NRMT
*GLOSSY 1-100: 1.5X TO 4X BASIC...
*GLOSSY 101-485: 5X TO 12X BASIC
RANDOM IN HOBBY UPDATE PACKS.
STATED ODDS 1:24 RETAIL
STATED PRINT RUN 100 SERIAL #'d SETS

2003 Fleer Tradition Game Used

Inserted in packs at a stated rate of one in 35 hobby and one in 90 retail; these cards partially parallel the regular Fleer Tradition set. Some of these cards were issued to a shorter print run and we have notated that information next to the player's name in our checklist.

Nm-Mt Ex-Mt
*GOLD: .75X TO 2X BASIC GU
*GOLD: .6X TO 1.5X GU p/r 150-200..
*GOLD ML: .6X TO 1.5X GU p/r 150-200
*GOLD: .4X TO 1X GU p/r 50-60
GOLD RANDOM INSERTS IN PACKS..
GOLD PRINT RUN 100 SERIAL #'d SETS
2 Derek Jeter Jsy SP/150 30.00 9.00
7 Craig Biggio Bat 10.00 3.00
10 Hideo Nomo Jsy SP/200 25.00 7.50
11 Barry Larkin Jsy SP/200 15.00 4.50
22 Kazuhiro Sasaki Jsy SP/200 10.00 3.00
31 Greg Maddux Jsy 15.00 4.50
42 Mo Vaughn Jsy SP/60 15.00 4.50
46 Pedro Martinez Jsy SP/200 15.00 4.50
63 Barry Zito Jsy 10.00 3.00
67 Luis Aparicio ML Jsy SP/150 15.00 4.50
97 W.Stargell ML Pants SP/150 15.00 4.50
104 N.Garciaparra Jsy SP/200 25.00 7.50
128 Edg Alfonzo Jsy SP/200 10.00 3.00
180 John Olerud Jsy 8.00 2.40
184 Juan Gonzalez Bat SP/200 15.00 4.50
185 Jorge Posada Bat 10.00 3.00
192 Shea Hillenbrand Bat 8.00 2.40
193 Ivan Rodriguez Jsy 15.00 4.50
194 Mike Lowell Bat 8.00 2.40
200 Jeff Bagwell Jsy SP/200 15.00 4.50
205 Chipper Jones Jsy 15.00 4.50
215 Jeromy Burnitz Jsy SP/200 10.00 3.00
224 Adrian Beltre Jsy 8.00 2.40
269 Robin Ventura Jsy 8.00 2.40
270 Frank Thomas Jsy 15.00 4.50
276 Mark Grace Jsy 10.00 3.00
296 Darin Erstad Jsy 8.00 2.40
301 Roger Clemens Jsy SP/150 25.00 7.50
304 J.D. Drew Jsy 8.00 2.40
311 Mike Piazza Jsy SP/150 25.00 7.50
327 Randy Johnson Jsy SP/150 15.00 4.50
334 Mark Prior Jsy SP/200 20.00 6.00
339 Kazuhisa Ishii Jsy 8.00 2.40
343 Manny Ramirez Jsy SP/150 10.00 3.00
344 Kerry Wood Jsy SP/200 15.00 4.50
346 Mike Mussina Jsy 15.00 4.50
351 Eric Karros Jsy 8.00 2.40
375 Rafael Palmeiro Jsy 10.00 3.00
379 Andruw Jones Bat SP/150 10.00 3.00
392 Jason Kendall Pants 8.00 2.40
395 Jimmy Rollins Jsy 8.00 2.40
402 Barry Bonds AW Jsy SP/50 50.00 15.00
403 M.Tejada AW Bat SP/150 10.00 3.00
406 Jason Jennings AW Pants 8.00 2.40

2003 Fleer Tradition Black-White Goudey

Inserted randomly into hobby packs, these cards were issued in the design of the 1936

Goudey Black and White set. To honor the 1936 set further each of these cards were issued to a stated print run of 1936 serial numbered sets.

Nm-Mt Ex-Mt
*GOLD: 2.5X TO 6X BASIC B/W GOUDEY
GOLD RANDOM INSERTS IN HOBBY PACKS
GOLD PRINT RUN 36 SERIAL #'d SETS
*RED: X TO X BASIC B/W GOUDEY
RED RANDOM INSERTS IN RETAIL PACKS
RED PRINT RUN 500 SERIAL #'d SETS
1 Jim Thome 4.00 1.20
2 Derek Jeter 10.00 3.00
3 Alex Rodriguez 6.00 1.80
4 Mark Prior 8.00 2.40
5 Nomar Garciaparra 6.00 1.80
6 Curt Schilling 4.00 1.20
7 Pat Burrell 4.00 1.20
8 Frank Thomas 4.00 1.20
9 Roger Clemens 8.00 2.40
10 Chipper Jones 4.00 1.20
11 Barry Larkin 4.00 1.20
12 Hideo Nomo 4.00 1.20
13 Pedro Martinez 4.00 1.20
14 Jeff Bagwell 4.00 1.20
15 Greg Maddux 6.00 1.80
16 Vladimir Guerrero 4.00 1.20
17 Ichiro Suzuki 6.00 1.80
18 Mike Piazza 6.00 1.80
19 Drew Henson 4.00 1.20
20 Albert Pujols 8.00 2.40
21 Sammy Sosa 6.00 1.80
22 Jason Giambi 4.00 1.20
23 Randy Johnson 4.00 1.20
24 Ken Griffey Jr. 6.00 1.80
25 Barry Bonds 10.00 3.00

2003 Fleer Tradition Checklists

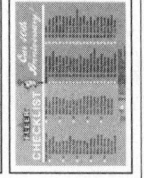

Inserted in packs at a stated rate of one in four, these 18 cards feature either Derek Jeter or Barry Bonds. These cards when matched together make up a puzzle of the featured players

Nm-Mt Ex-Mt
COMP.JETER PUZZLE (9) 8.00 2.40
COMMON JETER 1.00 .30
COMP.BONDS PUZZLE (9) 6.00 1.80
COMMON BONDS .75 .23

2003 Fleer Tradition Hardball Preview

Inserted into packs at a stated rate of one in 400 hobby and one in 480 retail, this 10 card set was issued to preview what the new Hardball set that Fleer would be releasing slightly later in 2003.

Nm-Mt Ex-Mt
1 Miguel Tejada 20.00 6.00
2 Derek Jeter 40.00 12.00
3 Mike Piazza 25.00 7.50
4 Barry Bonds 40.00 12.00
5 Mark Prior 30.00 9.00
6 Ichiro Suzuki 25.00 7.50
7 Alex Rodriguez 25.00 7.50
8 Nomar Garciaparra 25.00 7.50
9 Alfonso Soriano 20.00 6.00
10 Ken Griffey Jr. 25.00 7.50

2003 Fleer Tradition Lumber Company

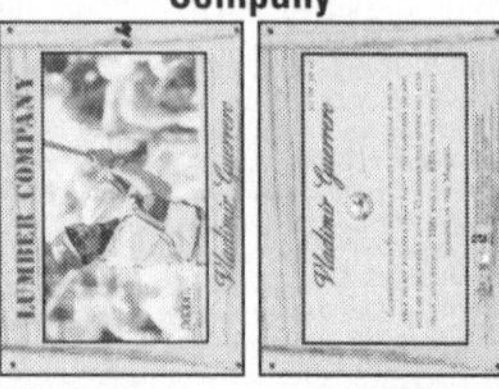

Issued at a stated rate of one in 10 hobby and one in 12 retail, these 30 cards focus on players known for the prowess with the bat.

Nm-Mt Ex-Mt
COMPLETE SET (30) 60.00 18.00
1 Mike Piazza 4.00 1.20
2 Derek Jeter 6.00 1.80
3 Alex Rodriguez 4.00 1.20
4 Miguel Tejada 1.50 .45
5 Nomar Garciaparra 4.00 1.20
6 Andruw Jones 1.50 .45
7 Pat Burrell 1.50 .45
8 Albert Pujols 5.00 1.50
9 Jeff Bagwell 1.50 .45
10 Chipper Jones 2.50 .75
11 Ichiro Suzuki 4.00 1.20
12 Alfonso Soriano 1.50 .45
13 Eric Chavez 1.50 .45
14 Brian Giles 1.50 .45
15 Shawn Green 1.50 .45
16 Jim Thome 2.50 .75
17 Lance Berkman 1.50 .45
18 Bernie Williams 1.50 .45
19 Manny Ramirez 1.50 .45
20 Vladimir Guerrero 2.50 .75
21 Carlos Delgado 1.50 .45
22 Scott Rolen 1.50 .45
23 Sammy Sosa 4.00 1.20
24 Ken Griffey Jr. 4.00 1.20
25 Barry Bonds 6.00 1.80
26 Todd Helton 1.50 .45
27 Jason Giambi 2.50 .75
28 Austin Kearns 1.50 .45
29 Jeff Kent 1.50 .45
30 Magglio Ordonez 1.50 .45

2003 Fleer Tradition Lumber Company Game Used

Inserted at a stated rate of one in 108 hobby and one in 195 retail, this is a partial parallel to the Lumber Company insert set. A few cards were issued in shorter supply and we have notated the print run information in our checklist.

Nm-Mt Ex-Mt
1 Jeff Bagwell SP/200 15.00 4.50
2 Lance Berkman SP/200 10.00 3.00
3 Barry Bonds SP/150 30.00 9.00
4 Pat Burrell SP/75 15.00 4.50
5 Eric Chavez SP/125 10.00 3.00
6 Carlos Delgado SP/200 10.00 3.00
7 Nomar Garciaparra SP/200 20.00 6.00
8 Brian Giles SP/200 10.00 3.00
9 Shawn Green SP/200 10.00 3.00
10 Todd Helton 10.00 3.00
11 Derek Jeter SP/96 40.00 12.00
12 Andruw Jones 8.00 2.40
13 Chipper Jones 15.00 4.50
14 Austin Kearns SP/75 15.00 4.50
15 Jeff Kent SP/200 10.00 3.00
16 Magglio Ordonez 8.00 2.40
17 Mike Piazza SP/200 25.00 7.50
18 Manny Ramirez 8.00 2.40
19 Alex Rodriguez 15.00 4.50
20 Scott Rolen SP/80 25.00 7.50
21 Alfonso Soriano SP/200 15.00 4.50
22 Miguel Tejada 8.00 2.40
23 Jim Thome SP/200 15.00 4.50
24 Bernie Williams 10.00 3.00

2003 Fleer Tradition Lumber Company Game Used Gold

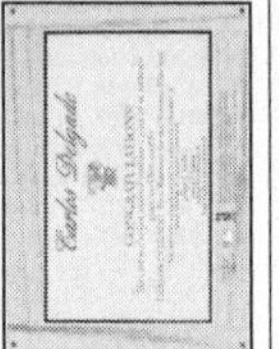

Randomly inserted in packs, this is a parallel to the Lumber Company Game Used insert set. These cards were printed to a stated print run matching the number of homers the featured player hit in 2002. If the card was issued to a stated print run of 25 or fewer, no pricing is provided due to market scarcity.

Nm-Mt Ex-Mt
1 Jeff Bagwell/31
2 Lance Berkman/42 25.00 7.50
3 Barry Bonds/46 80.00 24.00
4 Pat Burrell/37 25.00 7.50
5 Eric Chavez/34 25.00 7.50
6 Carlos Delgado/33 25.00 7.50
7 Nomar Garciaparra/24
8 Brian Giles/38 25.00 7.50
9 Shawn Green/42 25.00 7.50
10 Todd Helton/30 40.00 12.00
11 Derek Jeter/18
12 Andruw Jones/35 25.00 7.50
13 Chipper Jones/26 40.00 12.00
14 Austin Kearns/13
15 Jeff Kent/37 25.00 7.50
16 Magglio Ordonez/38 25.00 7.50
17 Mike Piazza/33 80.00 24.00
18 Manny Ramirez/33 25.00 7.50
19 Alex Rodriguez/57 50.00 15.00
20 Scott Rolen/31 40.00 12.00
21 Alfonso Soriano/39 40.00 12.00
22 Miguel Tejada/34 25.00 7.50
23 Jim Thome/52 40.00 12.00
24 Bernie Williams/19

2003 Fleer Tradition Milestones

Inserted in packs at a stated rate of one in five hobby and one in four retail, these 25 cards feature either milestones passed by active

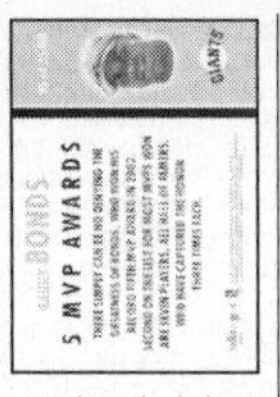

players in the 2002 season or by retired players in past seasons.

Nm-Mt Ex-Mt
COMPLETE SET (25) 30.00 9.00
1 Eddie Mathews 2.00 .60
2 Rickey Henderson 1.25 .35
3 Harmon Killebrew 2.00 .60
4 Al Kaline 2.00 .60
5 Willie McCovey 2.00 .60
6 Tom Seaver 2.00 .60
7 Reggie Jackson 2.00 .60
8 Mike Schmidt 3.00 .90
9 Nolan Ryan 4.00 1.20
10 Mike Piazza 2.00 .60
11 Randy Johnson 1.25 .35
12 Bernie Williams 1.00 .30
13 Rafael Palmeiro 1.00 .30
14 Juan Gonzalez 1.25 .35
15 Ken Griffey Jr. 2.00 .60
16 Derek Jeter 3.00 .90
17 Roger Clemens 2.50 .75
18 Roberto Alomar 1.25 .35
19 Manny Ramirez 1.00 .30
20 Luis Gonzalez 1.00 .30
21 Barry Bonds 3.00 .90
22 Nomar Garciaparra 2.00 .60
23 Fred McGriff 1.00 .30
24 Greg Maddux 2.00 .60
25 Barry Bonds 3.00 .90

2003 Fleer Tradition Milestones Game Used

Inserted at a stated rate of one in 143 hobby and one in 270 retail these 14 cards feature memorabilia cards from the some of the featured players in the Milestone set. A few of these cards were issued to a smaller print run and we have notated that information along with the print run information provided in our checklist.

Nm-Mt Ex-Mt
*GOLD: .75X TO 2X BASIC MILE
*GOLD: .6X TO 1.5X MILE SP/150-200
*GOLD: .5X TO 1.2X MILE SP/100
GOLD RANDOM INSERTS IN PACKS..
GOLD PRINT RUN 100 SERIAL #'d SETS
1 B.Bonds 5 MVP Jsy SP/200 30.00 9.00
2 B.Bonds 600 HR Bat SP/100 40.00 12.00
3 Derek Jeter Jsy SP/150 30.00 9.00
4 Greg Maddux Jsy 15.00 4.50
5 Rafael Palmeiro Jsy SP/200 15.00 4.50
6 Mike Piazza Jsy SP/100 25.00 7.50
7 Randy Johnson Jsy SP/100 15.00 4.50
8 Roberto Alomar Bat SP/200 15.00 4.50
9 Roger Clemens Jsy SP/150 25.00 7.50
10 Manny Ramirez Jsy SP/150 10.00 3.00
11 N.Garciaparra Jsy SP/100 20.00 6.00
12 Juan Gonzalez Bat SP/250 15.00 4.50
13 Fred McGriff Bat 10.00 3.00
14 Bernie Williams Jsy SP/200 15.00 4.50

2003 Fleer Tradition Standouts

Inserted in packs at a stated rate of one in 40 hobby and one in 72 retail, these 15 cards become mini-standees when the player's photo is "popped-out" of the card.

Nm-Mt Ex-Mt
1 Barry Bonds 10.00 3.00
2 Pat Burrell 5.00 1.50
3 Roger Clemens 8.00 2.40
4 Adam Dunn 5.00 1.50
5 Nomar Garciaparra 6.00 1.80
6 Ken Griffey Jr. 6.00 1.80
7 Vladimir Guerrero 5.00 1.50
8 Derek Jeter 10.00 3.00
9 Greg Maddux 6.00 1.80
10 Mike Piazza 6.00 1.80
11 Alex Rodriguez 6.00 1.80
12 Alfonso Soriano 5.00 1.50
13 Sammy Sosa 6.00 1.80
14 Ichiro Suzuki 6.00 1.80
15 Miguel Tejada 5.00 1.50

2003 Fleer Tradition Update

This 398 card set was released in October, 2003. The set was issued in 10-card packs with an $2 SRP which came 32 packs to a box and 20 boxes to a case. In addition, each sealed box

contained a 25 card "mini-box". Cards numbered 1-200 featured veterans, cards numbered 201 through 259 featured all stars, cards 260 through 275 feature interleague match-up cards while cards numbered 276 through 285 is a Tale of the Tape subset. Cards numbered 286 through 299 feature 2003 rookies and those cards were inserted at a stated rate of one in four. Cards numbered 300 through 398 feature 2003 rookies and those cards were issued as part of the 25 card mini-boxes.

MINT NRMT
COMP.SET w/o SP's (285) 40.00 18.00
COMMON CARD (1-285) .30 .14
COMMON CARD (286-299) 1.00 .45
COMMON RC (286-299) 1.00 .45
286-299 STATED ODDS 1:4 HOB/RET
COMMON CARD (300-398) 1.00 .45
COMMON RC (300-398) 1.00 .45
300-398 ISSUED IN MINI-BOXES
ONE MINI-BOX PER UPDATE BOX
25 CARDS PER MINI-BOX
1 Aaron Boone .30 .14
2 Carl Everett .30 .14
3 Eduardo Perez .30 .14
4 Jason Michaels .30 .14
5 Karim Garcia .30 .14
6 Rainer Olmedo .30 .14
7 Scott Williamson .30 .14
8 Adam Kennedy .30 .14
9 Carl Pavano .30 .14
10 Eli Marrero .30 .14
11 Jason Simontacchi .30 .14
12 Keith Foulke .30 .14
13 Preston Wilson .30 .14
14 Scott Hatteberg .30 .14
15 Adam Dunn .30 .14
16 Carlos Baerga .30 .14
17 Elmer Dessens .30 .14
18 Javier Vazquez .30 .14
19 Kenny Rogers .30 .14
20 Quinton McCracken .30 .14
21 Shane Reynolds .30 .14
22 Adam Eaton .30 .14
23 Carlos Zambrano .30 .14
24 Enrique Wilson .30 .14
25 Jeff DaVanon .30 .14
26 Kenny Lofton .30 .14
27 Ramon Castro .30 .14
28 Shannon Stewart .30 .14
29 Al Martin .30 .14
30 Carlos Guillen .30 .14
31 Eric Karros .30 .14
32 Tim Worrell .30 .14
33 Kevin Millwood .30 .14
34 Randall Simon .30 .14
35 Shawn Chacon .30 .14
36 Alex Rodriguez 1.25 .55
37 Casey Blake .30 .14
38 Eric Munson .30 .14
39 Jeff Kent .30 .14
40 Kris Benson .30 .14
41 Randy Winn .30 .14
42 Shea Hillenbrand .30 .14
43 Alfonso Soriano .50 .23
44 Chris George .30 .14
45 Eric Bruntlett .30 .14
46 Jeromy Burnitz .30 .14
47 Kyle Farnsworth .30 .14
48 Torii Hunter .30 .14
49 Sidney Ponson .30 .14
50 Andres Galarraga .30 .14
51 Chris Singleton .30 .14
52 Eric Gagne .50 .23
53 Jesse Foppert .30 .14
54 Lance Carter .30 .14
55 Ray Durham .30 .14
56 Tanyon Sturtze .30 .14
57 Andy Ashby .30 .14
58 Cliff Floyd .30 .14
59 Eric Young .30 .14
60 Jhonny Peralta RC .50 .23
61 Livan Hernandez .30 .14
62 Reggie Sanders .30 .14
63 Tim Spooneybarger .30 .14
64 Angel Berroa .30 .14
65 Coco Crisp .30 .14
66 Eric Hinske .30 .14
67 Jim Edmonds .30 .14
68 Luis Matos .30 .14
69 Rickey Henderson .75 .35
70 Todd Walker .30 .14
71 Antonio Alfonseca .30 .14
72 Corey Koskie .30 .14
73 Erubiel Durazo .30 .14
74 Jim Thome .75 .35
75 Lyle Overbay .30 .14
76 Robert Fick .30 .14
77 Todd Hollandsworth .30 .14
78 Aramis Ramirez .30 .14
79 Cristian Guzman .30 .14
80 Esteban Loaiza .30 .14
81 Jody Gerut .30 .14
82 Mark Grudzielanek .30 .14
83 Roberto Alomar .75 .35
84 Todd Hundley .30 .14
85 Mike Hampton .30 .14
86 Curt Schilling .50 .23
87 Francisco Rodriguez .30 .14
88 John Lackey .30 .14
89 Mark Redman .30 .14
90 Robin Ventura .30 .14
91 Todd Zeile .30 .14
92 B.J. Surhoff .30 .14
93 Raul Mondesi .30 .14
94 Frank Catalanotto .30 .14
95 John Smoltz .50 .23

96 Mark Ellis .30 .14
97 Rocco Baldelli 1.25 .55
98 Todd Pratt .30 .14
99 Barry Bonds 2.00 .90
100 Danny Graves .30 .14
101 Fred McGriff .50 .23
102 John Burkett .30 .14
103 Marquis Grissom .30 .14
104 Rocky Biddle .30 .14
105 Tom Glavine .50 .23
106 Bartolo Colon .30 .14
107 Darren Bragg .30 .14
108 Gabe Kapler .30 .14
109 John Franco .30 .14
110 Matt Mantei .30 .14
111 Rod Beck .30 .14
112 Tomo Ohka .30 .14
113 Ben Petrick .30 .14
114 Darren Dreifort .30 .14
115 Garret Anderson .30 .14
116 John Vander Wal .30 .14
117 Melvin Mora .30 .14
118 Rodrigo Lopez .30 .14
119 Raul Ibanez .30 .14
120 Benito Santiago .30 .14
121 David Ortiz .30 .14
122 Gary Bennett .30 .14
123 Jon Garland .30 .14
124 Michael Young .30 .14
125 Rodrigo Rosario .30 .14
126 Travis Lee .30 .14
127 Bill Mueller .30 .14
128 Derek Lowe .30 .14
129 Gil Meche .30 .14
130 Jose Guillen .30 .14
131 Miguel Cabrera 1.25 .55
132 Ron Calloway .30 .14
133 Troy Percival .30 .14
134 Billy Koch .30 .14
135 Dmitri Young .30 .14
136 Glendon Rusch .30 .14
137 Jose Jimenez .30 .14
138 Miguel Tejada .30 .14
139 John Thomson .30 .14
140 Troy O'Leary .30 .14
141 Bobby Kielty .30 .14
142 Dontrelle Willis .75 .35
143 Greg Myers .30 .14
144 Jose Vizcaino .30 .14
145 Mike MacDougal .30 .14
146 Ronnie Belliard .30 .14
147 Tyler Houston .30 .14
148 Brady Clark .30 .14
149 Edgardo Alfonzo .30 .14
150 Guillermo Mota .30 .14
151 Jose Lima .30 .14
152 Mike Williams .30 .14
153 Roy Oswalt .30 .14
154 Scott Podsednik 5.00 2.20
155 Brandon Lyon .30 .14
156 Henry Mateo .30 .14
157 Jose Macias .30 .14
158 Mike Bordick .30 .14
159 Royce Clayton .30 .14
160 Vance Wilson .30 .14
161 Brent Abernathy .30 .14
162 Horacio Ramirez .30 .14
163 Jose Reyes .50 .23
164 Nick Punto .30 .14
165 Ruben Sierra .30 .14
166 Victor Zambrano .30 .14
167 Brett Tomko .30 .14
168 Ivan Rodriguez .75 .35
169 Jose Mesa .30 .14
170 Octavio Dotel .30 .14
171 Russ Ortiz .30 .14
172 Vladimir Guerrero .75 .35
173 Brian Lawrence .30 .14
174 Jae Weong Seo .30 .14
175 Jose Cruz Jr. .30 .14
176 Pat Burrell .30 .14
177 Russell Branyan .30 .14
178 Warren Morris .30 .14
179 Brian Boehringer .30 .14
180 Jason Johnson .30 .14
181 Josh Phelps .30 .14
182 Paul Konerko .30 .14
183 Ryan Franklin .30 .14
184 Wes Helms .30 .14
185 Brooks Kieschnick .30 .14
186 Jason Davis .30 .14
187 Juan Pierre .30 .14
188 Paul Wilson .30 .14
189 Sammy Sosa 1.25 .55
190 Wil Cordero .30 .14
191 Byung-Hyun Kim .30 .14
192 Juan Encarnacion .30 .14
193 Placido Polanco .30 .14
194 Sandy Alomar Jr. .30 .14
195 Julio Lugo .30 .14
196 Junior Spivey .30 .14
197 Woody Williams .30 .14
198 Xavier Nady .30 .14
199 Mark Loretta .30 .14
200 Deivi Cruz .30 .14
201 Jorge Posada AS .30 .14
202 Carlos Delgado AS .30 .14
203 Alfonso Soriano AS .30 .14
204 Alex Rodriguez AS .75 .35
205 Troy Glaus AS .30 .14
206 Garret Anderson AS .30 .14
207 Hideki Matsui AS 2.50 1.10
208 Ichiro Suzuki AS .75 .35
209 Esteban Loaiza AS .30 .14
210 Manny Ramirez AS .30 .14
211 Roger Clemens AS .75 .35
212 Roy Halladay AS .30 .14
213 Jason Giambi AS .50 .23
214 Edgar Martinez AS .30 .14
215 Bret Boone AS .30 .14
216 Hank Blalock AS .30 .14
217 Nomar Garciaparra AS .75 .35
218 Vernon Wells AS .30 .14
219 Melvin Mora AS .30 .14
220 Magglio Ordonez AS .30 .14
221 Mike Sweeney AS .30 .14
222 Barry Zito AS .30 .14
223 Carl Everett AS .30 .14
224 Shigetoshi Hasegawa AS .30 .14
225 Jamie Moyer AS .30 .14
226 Mark Mulder AS .30 .14
227 Eddie Guardado AS .30 .14
228 Ramon Hernandez AS .30 .14
229 Keith Foulke AS .30 .14
230 Javy Lopez AS .30 .14
231 Todd Helton AS .30 .14
232 Marcus Giles AS .30 .14
233 Edgar Renteria AS .30 .14
234 Scott Rolen AS .30 .14
235 Barry Bonds AS 1.00 .45
236 Albert Pujols AS .75 .35
237 Gary Sheffield AS .30 .14
238 Jim Edmonds AS .30 .14
239 Jason Schmidt AS .30 .14
240 Mark Prior AS .75 .35
241 Dontrelle Willis AS .50 .23
242 Kerry Wood AS .50 .23
243 Kevin Brown AS .30 .14
244 Woody Williams AS .30 .14
245 Paul Lo Duca AS .30 .14
246 Richie Sexson AS .30 .14
247 Jose Vidro AS .30 .14
248 Luis Castillo AS .30 .14
249 Aaron Boone AS .30 .14
250 Mike Lowell AS .30 .14
251 Rafael Furcal AS .30 .14
252 Andruw Jones AS .30 .14
253 Preston Wilson AS .30 .14
254 John Smoltz AS .30 .14
255 Eric Gagne AS .30 .14
256 Randy Wolf AS .30 .14
257 Billy Wagner AS .30 .14
258 Luis Gonzalez AS .30 .14
259 Russ Ortiz AS .30 .14
260 Jim Thome .50 .23
Pedro Martinez IL
261 Alfonso Soriano .50 .23
Jeff Bagwell IL
262 Dontrelle Willis .75 .35
Rocco Baldelli IL
263 Carlos Delgado .50 .23
Vladimir Guerrero IL
264 Sammy Sosa .75 .35
Magglio Ordonez IL
265 Jason Giambi .50 .23
Adam Dunn IL
266 Mike Sweeney .75 .35
Albert Pujols IL
267 Barry Bonds 1.00 .45
Torii Hunter IL
268 Ichiro Suzuki .75 .35
Andruw Jones IL
269 Chipper Jones .50 .23
Hank Blalock IL
270 Mark Prior .75 .35
Vernon Wells IL
271 Nomar Garciaparra .75 .35
Scott Rolen IL
272 Alex Rodriguez .75 .35
Lance Berkman IL
273 Roger Clemens .75 .35
Kerry Wood IL
274 Derek Jeter 1.00 .45
Jose Reyes IL
275 Greg Maddux .75 .35
Barry Zito IL
276 Carlos Delgado TT .30 .14
277 J.D. Drew TT .30 .14
278 Barry Bonds TT 1.00 .45
279 Albert Pujols TT .75 .35
280 Jim Thome TT .50 .23
281 Sammy Sosa TT .75 .35
282 Alfonso Soriano TT .30 .14
283 Hideki Matsui TT 2.50 1.10
284 Mike Piazza TT .75 .35
285 Vladimir Guerrero TT .50 .23
286 Rich Harden ROO 1.50 .70
287 Chin-Hui Tsao ROO 1.00 .45
288 Edwin Jackson ROO RC 6.00 2.70
289 Chien-Ming Wang ROO RC 4.00 1.80
290 Josh Willingham ROO RC 3.00 1.35
291 Matt Kata ROO RC 2.50 1.10
292 Jose Contreras ROO RC 4.00 1.80
293 Chris Bootcheck ROO 1.00 .45
294 Javier Lopez ROO RC 1.00 .45
295 Delmon Young ROO RC 12.00 5.50
296 Pedro Liriano ROO 1.00 .45
297 Noah Lowry ROO 1.00 .45
298 Khalil Greene ROO 1.50 .70
299 Rob Bowen ROO 1.00 .45
300 Bo Hart ROO RC 4.00 1.80
301 Beau Kemp ROO RC 1.00 .45
302 Gerald Laird ROO 1.00 .45
303 Miguel Ojeda ROO RC 1.00 .45
304 Todd Wellemeyer ROO RC 1.50 .70
305 Ryan Wagner ROO RC 3.00 1.35
306 Jeff Duncan ROO RC 1.50 .70
307 Wilfredo Ledezma ROO RC 1.00 .45
308 Wes Obermueller ROO 1.00 .45
309 Bernie Castro ROO RC 1.00 .45
310 Tim Olson ROO RC 1.50 .70
311 Colin Porter ROO RC 1.00 .45
312 Francisco Cruceta ROO RC 1.00 .45
313 Guillermo Quiroz ROO RC 3.00 1.35
314 Brian Stokes ROO RC 1.00 .45
315 Robby Hammock ROO RC 1.50 .70
316 Lew Ford ROO RC 1.50 .70
317 Todd Linden ROO 1.00 .45
318 Mike Gallo ROO RC 1.00 .45
319 Francisco Rosario ROO RC 1.00 .45
320 Rosman Garcia ROO RC 1.00 .45
321 Felix Sanchez ROO RC 1.00 .45
322 Chad Gaudin ROO RC 1.00 .45
323 Phil Seibel ROO RC 1.00 .45
324 Jason Gilfillan ROO RC 1.00 .45
325 Terrmel Sledge ROO RC 1.50 .70
326 Alfredo Gonzalez ROO RC 1.00 .45
327 Josh Stewart ROO RC 1.00 .45
328 Jeremy Griffiths ROO RC 1.50 .70
329 Cory Stewart ROO RC 1.00 .45
330 Josh Hall ROO RC 1.50 .70
331 Arnie Munoz ROO RC 1.00 .45
332 Garrett Atkins ROO 1.00 .45
333 Neal Cotts ROO 1.00 .45
334 Dan Haren ROO RC 2.50 1.10
335 Shane Victorino ROO RC 1.00 .45
336 David Sanders ROO RC 1.00 .45
337 Oscar Villarreal ROO RC 1.00 .45
338 Michael Hessman ROO RC 1.00 .45
339 Andrew Brown ROO RC 1.00 .45
340 Kevin Hooper ROO 1.00 .45
341 Prentice Redman ROO RC 1.00 .45
342 Brandon Webb ROO RC 5.00 2.20
343 Jimmy Gobble ROO 1.00 .45
344 Pete LaForest ROO RC 1.50 .70
345 Chris Waters ROO RC 1.00 .45
346 Hideki Matsui ROO RC 10.00 4.50
347 Chris Capuano ROO RC 1.00 .45
348 Jon Leicester ROO RC 1.00 .45
349 Mike Nicolas ROO RC 1.00 .45
350 Nook Logan ROO RC 1.00 .45
351 Craig Brazell ROO RC 1.50 .70
352 Aaron Looper ROO RC 1.00 .45
353 D.J. Carrasco ROO RC 1.00 .45
354 Clint Barmes ROO RC 1.50 .70
355 Doug Waechter ROO RC 1.50 .70
356 Julio Manon ROO RC 1.00 .45
357 Jer. Bonderman ROO RC 2.50 1.10
358 D. Markwell ROO RC 1.00 .45
359 Dave Matranga ROO RC 1.00 .45
360 Luis Ayala ROO RC 1.00 .45
361 Jason Stanford ROO 1.00 .45
362 Roger Deago ROO RC 1.00 .45
363 Geoff Geary ROO RC 1.00 .45
364 Edgar Gonzalez ROO RC 1.00 .45
365 Michel Hernandez ROO RC 1.00 .45
366 Aquilino Lopez ROO RC 1.00 .45
367 David Manning ROO 1.00 .45
368 Carlos Mendez ROO RC 1.00 .45
369 Matt Miller ROO RC 1.00 .45
370 Mi. Nakamura ROO RC 1.00 .45
371 Mike Neu ROO RC 1.00 .45
372 Ramon Nivar ROO RC 2.00 .90
373 Kevin Ohme ROO RC 1.00 .45
374 Alex Prieto ROO RC 1.00 .45
375 Stephen Randolph ROO RC 1.00 .45
376 Brian Sweeney ROO RC 1.00 .45
377 Matt Diaz ROO RC 2.00 .90
378 Mike Gonzalez ROO 1.00 .45
379 Daniel Cabrera ROO RC 1.00 .45
380 Fernando Cabrera ROO RC 1.00 .45
381 David DeJesus ROO RC 2.00 .90
382 Mike Ryan ROO RC 1.50 .70
383 Rick Roberts ROO RC 1.00 .45
384 Seung Song ROO 1.00 .45
385 Rickie Weeks ROO RC 10.00 4.50
386 Hum. Quintero ROO RC 1.00 .45
387 Alexis Rios ROO 4.00 1.80
388 Aaron Miles ROO RC 2.50 1.10
389 Tom Gregorio ROO RC 1.00 .45
390 Anthony Ferrari ROO RC 1.00 .45
391 Kevin Correia ROO RC 1.00 .45
392 Rafael Betancourt ROO RC 1.50 .70
393 Rett Johnson ROO RC 1.50 .70
394 Richard Fischer ROO RC 1.00 .45
395 Greg Aquino ROO RC 1.00 .45
396 Daniel Garcia ROO RC 1.00 .45
397 Sergio Mitre ROO RC 2.00 .90
398 Edwin Almonte ROO 1.00 .45

2003 Fleer Tradition Update Glossy

MINT NRMT
*GLOSSY 1-285: 5X TO 12X BASIC
*GLOSSY 1-285: 3X TO 8X BASIC RC's
*GLOSSY MATSUI 207/283: 2.5X TO 6X BASIC
*GLOSSY 286-299: 1.5X TO 4X BASIC
*GLOSSY 286-299: 1.5X TO 4X BASIC RC's
*GLOSSY 300-398: 1.5X TO 4X BASIC
*GLOSSY 300-398: 1.5X TO 4X BASIC RC's
RANDOM INSERTS IN HOBBY PACKS
STATED ODDS 1:24 RETAIL
STATED PRINT RUN 100 SERIAL #'d SETS

2003 Fleer Tradition Update Diamond Debuts

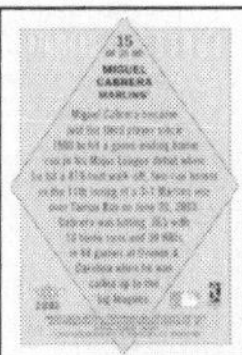

MINT NRMT
STATED ODDS 1:10 HOBBY, 1:8 RETAIL
1 Dontrelle Willis 2.50 1.10
2 Bo Hart 4.00 1.80
3 Jose Reyes 1.50 .70
4 Chin-Hui Tsao 1.00 .45
5 Brandon Webb 5.00 2.20
6 Rich Harden 1.50 .70
7 Jesse Foppert 1.00 .45
8 Rocco Baldelli 4.00 1.80
9 Hideki Matsui 10.00 4.50
10 Ron Calloway 1.00 .45
11 Jeremy Bonderman 2.50 1.10
12 Mark Teixeira 1.50 .70
13 Ryan Wagner 3.00 1.35
14 Jose Contreras 4.00 1.80
15 Miguel Cabrera 4.00 1.80
16 Lew Ford 1.50 .70
17 Jeff Duncan 1.50 .70
18 Matt Kata 2.00 .90
19 Jeremy Griffiths 1.50 .70
20 Todd Wellemeyer 1.50 .70
21 Robby Hammock 1.50 .70
22 Dave Matranga 1.00 .45
23 Laynce Nix 2.50 1.10
24 Jhonny Peralta 1.00 .45
25 Oscar Villareal 1.00 .45

2003 Fleer Tradition Update Long Gone!

MINT NRMT
RANDOM INSERTS IN HOBBY PACKS
STATED ODDS 1:72 RETAIL
1 Barry Bonds/475 12.00 5.50
2 Jason Giambi/440 5.00 2.20
3 Albert Pujols/452 10.00 4.50
4 Chipper Jones/420 5.00 2.20
5 Manny Ramirez/430 5.00 2.20

6 Sammy Sosa/536 8.00 3.60
7 Alfonso Soriano/440 5.00 2.20
8 Alex Rodriguez/430 8.00 3.60
9 Jim Thome/445 5.00 2.20
10 Vladimir Guerrero/502 5.00 2.20
11 Austin Kearns/430 5.00 2.20
12 Jeff Bagwell/420 5.00 2.20
13 Andruw Jones/430 5.00 2.20
14 Carlos Delgado/451 5.00 2.20
15 Nomar Garciaparra/440 8.00 3.60
16 Adam Dunn/464 5.00 2.20
17 Mike Piazza/450 8.00 3.60
18 Derek Jeter/410 12.00 5.50
19 Ken Griffey Jr./430 8.00 3.60
20 Hank Blalock/424 5.00 2.20

2003 Fleer Tradition Update Milestones

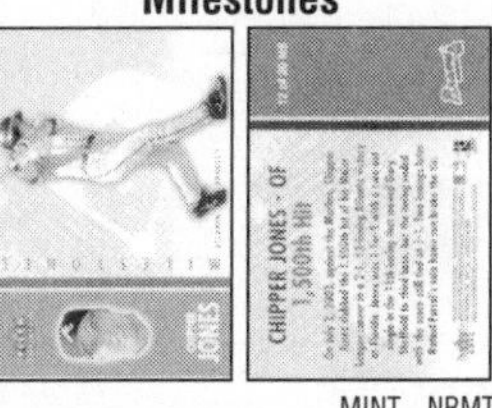

MINT NRMT
STATED ODDS 1:8 HOBBY, 1:6 RETAIL
1 Roger Clemens 4.00 1.80
2 Rafael Palmeiro 1.25 .55
3 Jeff Bagwell 1.25 .55
4 Barry Bonds 5.00 2.20
5 Sammy Sosa 3.00 1.35
6 Albert Pujols 4.00 1.80
7 Ichiro Suzuki 3.00 1.35
8 Alfonso Soriano 1.25 .55
9 Alex Rodriguez 3.00 1.35
10 Randy Johnson 2.00 .90
11 Manny Ramirez .75 .35
12 Chipper Jones 2.00 .90
13 Todd Helton 1.25 .55
14 Ken Griffey Jr. 3.00 1.35
15 Jim Thome 2.00 .90
16 Frank Thomas 2.00 .90
17 Pedro Martinez 2.00 .90
18 Hideo Nomo 2.00 .90
19 Jason Schmidt .75 .35
20 Carlos Delgado .75 .35

2003 Fleer Tradition Update Milestones Game Jersey

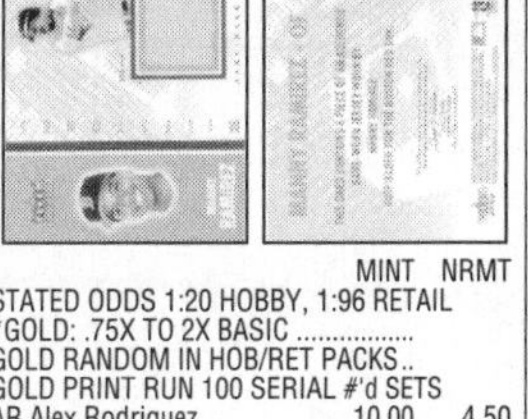

MINT NRMT
STATED ODDS 1:20 HOBBY, 1:96 RETAIL
*GOLD: .75X TO 2X BASIC
GOLD RANDOM IN HOB/RET PACKS
GOLD PRINT RUN 100 SERIAL #'d SETS
AR Alex Rodriguez 10.00 4.50
AS Alfonso Soriano 10.00 4.50
CD Carlos Delgado 8.00 3.60
CJ Chipper Jones 10.00 4.50
FT Frank Thomas 10.00 4.50
HN Hideo Nomo 10.00 4.50
JB Jeff Bagwell 10.00 4.50
JS Jason Schmidt 8.00 3.60
JT Jim Thome 10.00 4.50
MR Manny Ramirez 8.00 3.60
PM Pedro Martinez 10.00 4.50
RC Roger Clemens 15.00 6.75
RJ Randy Johnson 10.00 4.50
RP Rafael Palmeiro 10.00 4.50
SS Sammy Sosa 15.00 6.75
TH Todd Helton 10.00 4.50

2003 Fleer Tradition Update Throwback Threads

MINT NRMT
STATED ODDS 1:64 HOBBY, 1:288 RETAIL
*PATCH: 1X TO 2.5X BASIC
PATCH RANDOM INSERTS IN PACKS
PATCH PRINT RUN 100 SERIAL #'d SETS
AL Al Leiter 8.00 3.60
KM Kevin Millwood 8.00 3.60
MP Mike Piazza 15.00 6.75
TG Troy Glaus 10.00 4.50
VG Vladimir Guerrero 10.00 4.50

2003 Fleer Tradition Update Throwback Threads Dual

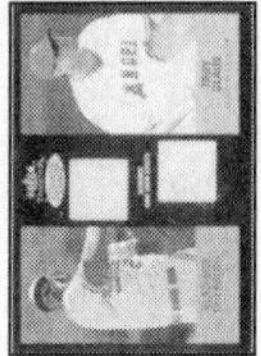

MINT NRMT
RANDOM INSERTS IN HOB/RET PACKS
STATED PRINT RUN 100 SERIAL #'d SETS
MP-AL Mike Piazza 25.00 11.00
Al Leiter
VG-TG Vladimir Guerrero 20.00 9.00
Troy Glaus

2003 Fleer Tradition Update Turn Back the Clock

MINT NRMT
STATED ODDS 1:160 HOBBY, 1:288 RETAIL
1 Yogi Berra 15.00 6.75
2 Mike Schmidt 20.00 9.00
3 Tom Seaver 10.00 4.50
4 Reggie Jackson 10.00 4.50
5 Pee Wee Reese 10.00 4.50
6 Phil Rizzuto 10.00 4.50
7 Jim Palmer 10.00 4.50
8 Robin Yount 15.00 6.75
9 Nolan Ryan 20.00 9.00
10 Al Kaline 15.00 6.75

2004 Fleer Tradition

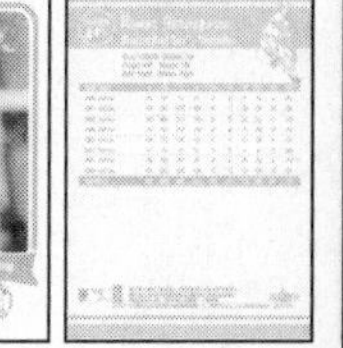

This 500-card standard-size set was released in January, 2004. The set was issued in 10 card packs which came 36 packs to a box and six boxes to a case. Cards numbered 401 through 500 were printed in lesser quantity than the first 400 cards in this set. This set has these topical subsets: Cards 1 through 10 feature World Series highlights, Cards 11-40 feature Team Leaders. In the higher numbers cards 446 through 462 feature young players in an "Standout" subset which cards 462 through 471 feature players who won major awards in 2003. The set concludes with a 30-card three player prospect set which features leading prospects for each of the major league teams.

Nm-Mt Ex-Mt
COMPLETE SET (500) 150.00 45.00
COMP.SET w/o SP's (400) 40.00 12.00
COMMON CARD (1-400) .30 .09
COMMON CARD (401-470) 1.00 .30
COMMON CARD (471-500) 1.00 .30
401-445 STATED ODDS 1:2
446-461 STATED ODDS 1:6
462-470 STATED ODDS 1:9
471-500 STATED ODDS 1:3
1 Juan Pierre WS .30 .09
2 Josh Beckett WS .50 .15
3 Ivan Rodriguez WS .75 .23
4 Miguel Cabrera WS .75 .23
5 Dontrelle Willis WS .30 .09
6 Derek Jeter WS 2.00 .60
7 Jason Giambi WS .75 .23
8 Bernie Williams WS .50 .15
9 Alfonso Soriano WS .50 .15
10 Hideki Matsui WS 1.25 .35
11 Garret Anderson .30 .09
Garret Anderson
Ramon Ortiz
John Lackey TL
12 Luis Gonzalez .30 .09
Luis Gonzalez
Brandon Webb
Curt Schilling TL
13 Javy Lopez .30 .09
Gary Sheffield
Russ Ortiz
Russ Ortiz TL
14 Tony Batista .30 .09
Jay Gibbons
Sidney Ponson
Jason Johnson TL
15 Manny Ramirez .75 .23
Nomar Garciaparra
Derek Lowe
Pedro Martinez TL
16 Sammy Sosa .75 .23
Sammy Sosa
Mark Prior
Kerry Wood TL
17 Frank Thomas .50 .15
Carlos Lee
Esteban Loaiza
Esteban Loaiza TL

18 Adam Dunn .30 .09
Sean Casey
Chris Reitsma
Paul Wilson TL
19 Jody Gerut .30 .09
Jody Gerut
C.C. Sabathia
C.C. Sabathia TL
20 Preston Wilson .30 .09
Preston Wilson
Darren Oliver
Jason Jennings TL
21 Dmitri Young .30 .09
Dmitri Young
Mike Maroth
Jeremy Bonderman TL
22 Mike Lowell .30 .09
Mike Lowell
Dontrelle Willis
Josh Beckett TL
23 Jeff Bagwell .30 .09
Jeff Bagwell
Jeriome Robertson
Wade Miller TL
24 Carlos Beltran .30 .09
Carlos Beltran
Darrell May
Darrell May TL
25 Adrian Beltre .50 .15
Shawn Green
Hideo Nomo
Kevin Brown TL
26 Richie Sexson .30 .09
Richie Sexson
Ben Sheets
Ben Sheets TL
27 Torii Hunter .30 .09
Torii Hunter
Brad Radke
Johan Santana TL
28 Vladimir Guerrero .50 .15
Orlando Cabrera
Livan Hernandez
Javier Vazquez TL
29 Cliff Floyd .30 .09
Ty Wigginton
Steve Trachsel
Al Leiter TL
30 Jason Giambi .50 .15
Jason Giambi
Andy Pettitte
Mike Mussina TL
31 Eric Chavez .30 .09
Miguel Tejada
Tim Hudson
Tim Hudson TL
32 Jim Thome .50 .15
Jim Thome
Randy Wolf
Randy Wolf TL
33 Reggie Sanders .30 .09
Reggie Sanders
Josh Fogg
Kip Wells TL
34 Ryan Klesko .30 .09
Mark Loretta
Jake Peavy
Jake Peavy TL
35 Jose Cruz Jr. .30 .09
Edgardo Alfonzo
Jason Schmidt
Jason Schmidt TL
36 Bret Boone .30 .09
Bret Boone
Jamie Moyer
Joel Pineiro TL
37 Albert Pujols .75 .23
Albert Pujols
Woody Williams
Woody Williams TL
38 Aubrey Huff .30 .09
Aubrey Huff
Victor Zambrano
Victor Zambrano TL
39 Alex Rodriguez .75 .23
Alex Rodriguez
John Thomson
John Thomson TL
40 Carlos Delgado .30 .09
Carlos Delgado
Roy Halladay
Roy Halladay TL
41 Greg Maddux 1.25 .35
42 Ben Grieve .30 .09
43 Darin Erstad .30 .09
44 Ruben Sierra .30 .09
45 Byung-Hyung Kim .30 .09
46 Freddy Garcia .30 .09
47 Richard Hidalgo .30 .09
48 Tike Redman .30 .09
49 Kevin Millwood .30 .09
50 Marquis Grissom .30 .09
51 Jae Weong Seo .30 .09
52 Wil Cordero .30 .09
53 LaTroy Hawkins .30 .09
54 Jolbert Cabrera .30 .09
55 Kevin Appier .30 .09
56 John Lackey .30 .09
57 Garret Anderson .30 .09
58 R.A. Dickey .30 .09
59 David Segui .30 .09
60 Erubiel Durazo .30 .09
61 Bobby Abreu .30 .09
62 Travis Hafner .30 .09
63 Victor Zambrano .30 .09
64 Randy Johnson .75 .23
65 Bernie Williams .50 .15
66 J.T. Snow .30 .09
67 Sammy Sosa 1.25 .35
68 Al Leiter .30 .09
69 Jason Jennings .30 .09
70 Matt Morris .30 .09
71 Mike Hampton .30 .09
72 Juan Encarnacion .30 .09
73 Alex Gonzalez .30 .09
74 Bartolo Colon .30 .09
75 Brett Myers .30 .09
76 Michael Young .30 .09
77 Ichiro Suzuki 1.25 .35
78 Jason Johnson .30 .09
79 Brad Ausmus .30 .09
80 Ted Lilly .30 .09
81 Ken Griffey Jr. 1.25 .35
82 Chone Figgins .30 .09
83 Edgar Martinez .50 .15
84 Adam Eaton .30 .09
85 Ken Harvey .30 .09
86 Francisco Rodriguez .30 .09
87 Bill Mueller .30 .09
88 Mike Maroth .30 .09
89 Charles Johnson .30 .09
90 Jhonny Peralta .30 .09
91 Kip Wells .30 .09
92 Cesar Izturis .30 .09
93 Matt Clement .30 .09
94 Lyle Overbay .30 .09
95 Kirk Rueter .30 .09
96 Cristian Guzman .30 .09
97 Garrett Stephenson .30 .09
98 Lance Berkman .30 .09
99 Brett Tomko .30 .09
100 Chris Stynes .30 .09
101 Nate Cornejo .30 .09
102 Aaron Rowand .30 .09
103 Javier Vazquez .30 .09
104 Jason Kendall .30 .09
105 Mark Redman .30 .09
106 Benito Santiago .30 .09
107 C.C. Sabathia .30 .09
108 David Wells .30 .09
109 Mark Ellis .30 .09
110 Casey Blake .30 .09
111 Sean Burroughs .30 .09
112 Carlos Beltran .30 .09
113 Ramon Hernandez .30 .09
114 Eric Hinske .30 .09
115 Luis Gonzalez .30 .09
116 Jarrod Washburn .30 .09
117 Ronnie Belliard .30 .09
118 Troy Percival .30 .09
119 Jose Valentin .30 .09
120 Chase Utley .30 .09
121 Odalis Perez .30 .09
122 Steve Finley .30 .09
123 Bret Boone .30 .09
124 Jeff Conine .30 .09
125 Josh Fogg .30 .09
126 Neifi Perez .30 .09
127 Ben Sheets .30 .09
128 Randy Winn .30 .09
129 Matt Stairs .30 .09
130 Carlos Delgado .30 .09
131 Morgan Ensberg .30 .09
132 Vinny Castilla .30 .09
133 Matt Mantei .30 .09
134 Alex Rodriguez 1.25 .35
135 Matthew LeCroy .30 .09
136 Woody Williams .30 .09
137 Frank Catalanotto .30 .09
138 Rondell White .30 .09
139 Scott Rolen .50 .15
140 Cliff Floyd .30 .09
141 Chipper Jones .75 .23
142 Robin Ventura .30 .09
143 Mariano Rivera .50 .15
144 Brady Clark .30 .09
145 Ramon Ortiz .30 .09
146 Omar Infante .30 .09
147 Mike Matheny .30 .09
148 Pedro Martinez .75 .23
149 Carlos Baerga .30 .09
150 Shannon Stewart .30 .09
151 Travis Lee .30 .09
152 Eric Byrnes .30 .09
153 Rafael Furcal .30 .09
154 B.J. Surhoff .30 .09
155 Zach Day .30 .09
156 Marlon Anderson .30 .09
157 Mark Hendrickson .30 .09
158 Mike Mussina .75 .23
159 Randall Simon .30 .09
160 Jeff DaVanon .30 .09
161 Joel Pineiro .30 .09
162 Vernon Wells .30 .09
163 Adam Kennedy .30 .09
164 Trot Nixon .50 .15
165 Rodrigo Lopez .30 .09
166 Curt Schilling .50 .15
167 Horacio Ramirez .30 .09
168 Jason Marquis .30 .09
169 Maggio Ordonez .30 .09
170 Scott Schoeneweis .30 .09
171 Andruw Jones .30 .09
172 Tino Martinez .50 .15
173 Moises Alou .30 .09
174 Kelvim Escobar .30 .09
175 Xavier Nady .30 .09
176 Ramon Martinez .30 .09
177 Pat Hentgen .30 .09
178 Austin Kearns .30 .09
179 D'Angelo Jimenez .30 .09
180 Deivi Cruz .30 .09
181 John Smoltz .50 .15
182 Toby Hall .30 .09
183 Mark Buehrle .30 .09
184 Howie Clark .30 .09
185 David Ortiz .30 .09
186 Raul Mondesi .30 .09
187 Milton Bradley .30 .09
188 Jorge Julio .30 .09
189 Victor Martinez .30 .09
190 Gabe Kapler .30 .09
191 Julio Franco .30 .09
192 Ryan Freel .30 .09
193 Brad Fullmer .30 .09
194 Joe Borowski .30 .09
195 Darren Oliver .30 .09
196 Jason Varitek .30 .09
197 Greg Myers .30 .09
198 Eric Munson .30 .09
199 Tim Wakefield .30 .09
200 Kyle Farnsworth .30 .09
201 Johnny Vander Wal .30 .09
202 Alex Escobar .30 .09
203 Sean Casey .30 .09
204 John Thomson .30 .09
205 Carlos Zambrano .30 .09
206 Kenny Lofton .30 .09
207 Marcus Giles .30 .09
208 Wade Miller .30 .09
209 Geoff Blum .30 .09
210 Jason LaRue .30 .09
211 Omar Vizquel .30 .09
212 Carlos Pena .30 .09
213 Adam Dunn .30 .09
214 Oscar Villarreal .30 .09
215 Paul Konerko .30 .09
216 Hideo Nomo .75 .23
217 Mike Sweeney .30 .09
218 Coco Crisp .30 .09
219 Shawn Chacon .30 .09
220 Brook Fordyce .30 .09
221 Josh Beckett .50 .15
222 Paul Wilson .30 .09
223 Josh Towers .30 .09
224 Geoff Jenkins .30 .09
225 Shawn Green .30 .09
226 Derek Lee .30 .09
227 Karim Garcia .30 .09
228 Preston Wilson .30 .09
229 Dane Sardinha .30 .09
230 Aramis Ramirez .30 .09
231 Doug Mientkiewicz .30 .09
232 Jay Gibbons .30 .09
233 Adam Everett .30 .09
234 Brooks Kieschnick .30 .09
235 Dmitri Young .30 .09
236 Brad Penny .30 .09
237 Todd Zeile .30 .09
238 Eric Gagne .50 .15
239 Esteban Loaiza .30 .09
240 Billy Wagner .30 .09
241 Nomar Garciaparra 1.25 .35
242 Desi Relaford .30 .09
243 Luis Rivas .30 .09
244 Andy Pettitte .50 .15
245 Ty Wigginton .30 .09
246 Edgar Gonzalez .30 .09
247 Brian Anderson .30 .09
248 Richie Sexson .30 .09
249 Russell Branyan .30 .09
250 Jose Guillen .30 .09
251 Chin-Hui Tsao .30 .09
252 Jose Hernandez .30 .09
253 Kevin Brown .30 .09
254 Pete LaForest .30 .09
255 Adrian Beltre .30 .09
256 Jacque Jones .30 .09
257 Jimmy Rollins .30 .09
258 Brandon Phillips .30 .09
259 Derek Jeter 2.00 .60
260 Carl Everett .30 .09
261 Wes Helms .30 .09
262 Kyle Lohse .30 .09
263 Jason Phillips .30 .09
264 Jake Peavy .30 .09
265 Orlando Hernandez .30 .09
266 Keith Foulke .30 .09
267 Brad Wilkerson .30 .09
268 Corey Koskie .30 .09
269 Josh Hall .30 .09
270 Bobby Higginson .30 .09
271 Andres Galarraga .30 .09
272 Alfonso Soriano .50 .15
273 Carlos Rivera .30 .09
274 Steve Trachsel .30 .09
275 David Bell .30 .09
276 Endy Chavez .30 .09
277 Jay Payton .30 .09
278 Mark Mulder .30 .09
279 Terrence Long .30 .09
280 A.J. Burnett .30 .09
281 Pokey Reese .30 .09
282 Phil Nevin .30 .09
283 Jose Contreras .30 .09
284 Jim Thome .75 .23
285 Pat Burrell .30 .09
286 Luis Castillo .30 .09
287 Juan Uribe .30 .09
288 Raul Ibanez .30 .09
289 Sidney Ponson .30 .09
290 Scott Hatteberg .30 .09
291 Jack Wilson .30 .09
292 Reggie Sanders .30 .09
293 Brian Giles .30 .09
294 Craig Biggio .50 .15
295 Kazuhisa Ishii .30 .09
296 Jim Edmonds .30 .09
297 Trevor Hoffman .30 .09
298 Ray Durham .30 .09
299 Mike Lieberthal .30 .09
300 Tim Worrell .30 .09
301 Chris George .30 .09
302 Jamie Moyer .30 .09
303 Mike Cameron .30 .09
304 Matt Kinney .30 .09
305 Aubrey Huff .30 .09
306 Brian Lawrence .30 .09
307 Carlos Guillen .30 .09
308 J.D. Drew .30 .09
309 Paul Lo Duca .30 .09
310 Tim Salmon .50 .15
311 Jason Schmidt .30 .09
312 A.J. Pierzynski .30 .09
313 Lance Carter .30 .09
314 Julio Lugo .30 .09
315 Johan Santana .30 .09
316 Laynce Nix .30 .09
317 John Olerud .30 .09
318 Robb Quinlan .30 .09
319 Scott Spiezio .30 .09
320 Tony Clark .30 .09
321 Jose Vidro .30 .09
322 Shea Hillenbrand .30 .09
323 Doug Glanville .30 .09
324 Orlando Palmeiro .30 .09
325 Juan Gonzalez .75 .23
326 Jason Giambi .75 .23
327 Junior Spivey .30 .09
328 Tom Glavine .50 .15
329 Reed Johnson .30 .09
330 David Eckstein .30 .09
331 Damian Jackson .30 .09
332 Orlando Hudson .30 .09
333 Barry Zito .50 .15
334 Robert Fick .30 .09
335 Aaron Boone .30 .09
336 Rafael Palmeiro .50 .15
337 Bobby Kielty .30 .09
338 Tony Batista .30 .09
339 Ryan Dempster .30 .09
340 Derek Lowe .30 .09
341 Alex Cintron .30 .09
342 Jermaine Dye .30 .09
343 John Burkett .30 .09
344 Javy Lopez .30 .09
345 Eric Karros .30 .09
346 Corey Patterson .30 .09
347 Josh Phelps .30 .09
348 Ryan Klesko .30 .09
349 Craig Wilson .30 .09
350 Brian Roberts .30 .09
351 Roberto Alomar .75 .23
352 Frank Thomas .75 .23
353 Gary Sheffield .30 .09
354 Alex Gonzalez .30 .09
355 Jose Cruz Jr. .30 .09
356 Jerome Williams .30 .09
357 Mark Kotsay .30 .09
358 Chris Reitsma .30 .09
359 Carlos Lee .30 .09
360 Todd Helton .50 .15
361 Gil Meche .30 .09
362 Ryan Franklin .30 .09
363 Josh Bard .30 .09
364 Juan Pierre .30 .09
365 Barry Larkin .75 .23
366 Edgar Renteria .30 .09
367 Alex Sanchez .30 .09
368 Jeff Bagwell .50 .15
369 Ben Broussard .30 .09
370 Chan-Ho Park .30 .09
371 Darrell May .30 .09
372 Roy Oswalt .30 .09
373 Craig Monroe .30 .09
374 Fred McGriff .50 .15
375 Bengie Molina .30 .09
376 Aaron Guiel .30 .09
377 Jeriome Robertson .30 .09
378 Kenny Rogers .30 .09
379 Colby Lewis .30 .09
380 Jeromy Burnitz .30 .09
381 Orlando Cabrera .30 .09
382 Joe Randa .30 .09
383 Miguel Batista .30 .09
384 Brad Radke .30 .09
385 Jeremy Giambi .30 .09
386 Vladimir Guerrero .75 .23
387 Melvin Mora .30 .09
388 Royce Clayton .30 .09
389 Danny Garcia .30 .09
390 Manny Ramirez .75 .23
391 Dave McCarty .30 .09
392 Mark Grudzielanek .30 .09
393 Mike Piazza 1.25 .35
394 Jorge Posada .50 .15
395 Tim Hudson .30 .09
396 Placido Polanco .30 .09
397 Mark Loretta .30 .09
398 Jesse Foppert .30 .09
399 Albert Pujols 1.50 .45
400 Jeremi Gonzalez .30 .09
401 Paul Bako SP 1.00 .30
402 Luis Matos SP 1.00 .30
403 Johnny Damon SP 1.00 .30
404 Kerry Wood SP 2.50 .75
405 Joe Crede SP 1.00 .30
406 Jason Davis SP 1.00 .30
407 Larry Walker SP 1.50 .45
408 Ivan Rodriguez SP 2.50 .75
409 Nick Johnson SP 1.00 .30
410 Jose Lima SP 1.00 .30
411 Brian Jordan SP 1.00 .30
412 Eddie Guardado SP 1.00 .30
413 Ron Calloway SP 1.00 .30
414 Aaron Heilman SP 1.00 .30
415 Eric Chavez SP 1.00 .30
416 Randy Wolf SP 1.00 .30
417 Jason Bay SP 1.00 .30
418 Edgardo Alfonzo SP 1.00 .30
419 Kazuhiro Sasaki SP 1.00 .30
420 Eduardo Perez SP 1.00 .30
421 Carl Crawford SP 1.00 .30
422 Troy Glaus SP 1.50 .45
423 Joaquin Benoit SP 1.00 .30
424 Russ Ortiz SP 1.00 .30
425 Larry Bigbie SP 1.00 .30
426 Todd Walker SP 1.00 .30
427 Kris Benson SP 1.00 .30
428 Sandy Alomar Jr. SP 1.00 .30
429 Jody Gerut SP 1.00 .30
430 Rene Reyes SP 1.00 .30
431 Mike Lowell SP 1.00 .30
432 Jeff Kent SP 1.00 .30
433 Mike MacDougal SP 1.00 .30
434 Dave Roberts SP 1.00 .30
435 Torii Hunter SP 1.00 .30
436 Tomo Ohka SP 1.00 .30
437 Jeremy Griffiths SP 1.00 .30
438 Miguel Tejada SP 1.00 .30
439 Vicente Padilla SP 1.00 .30
440 Bobby Hill SP 1.00 .30
441 Rich Aurilia SP 1.00 .30
442 Shigetoshi Hasegawa SP 1.00 .30
443 So Taguchi SP 1.00 .30
444 Damian Rolls SP 1.00 .30
445 Roy Halladay SP 1.00 .30
446 Rocco Baldelli SO SP 2.50 .75
447 Dontrelle Willis SO SP 1.00 .30
448 Mark Prior SO SP 5.00 1.50
449 Jason Lane SO SP 1.00 .30
450 Angel Berroa SO SP 1.00 .30
451 Jose Reyes SO SP 1.50 .45
452 Ryan Wagner SO SP 1.00 .30
453 Marlon Byrd SO SP 1.00 .30
454 Hee Seop Choi SO SP 1.00 .30
455 Brandon Webb SO SP 1.00 .30
456 Bo Hart SO SP 1.00 .30
457 Hank Blalock SO SP 1.00 .30
458 Mark Teixeira SO SP 1.00 .30
459 Hideki Matsui SO SP 4.00 1.20
460 Scott Podsednik SO SP 4.00 1.20
461 Miguel Cabrera SO SP 2.50 .75
462 Josh Beckett AW SP 1.50 .45
463 Mariano Rivera AW SP 1.50 .45
464 Ivan Rodriguez AW SP 2.50 .75
465 Alex Rodriguez AW SP 4.00 1.20
466 Albert Pujols AW SP 5.00 1.50
467 Roy Halladay AW SP 1.00 .30
468 Eric Gagne AW SP 1.50 .45
469 Angel Berroa AW SP 1.00 .30
470 Dontrelle Willis AW SP 1.00 .30
471 Chris Bootcheck 1.00 .30
Tom Gregorio
Richard Fischer SP
472 Matt Kata 1.50 .45
Tim Olson
Robby Hammock SP
473 Michael Hessman 1.00 .30
Chris Waters
Greg Aquino SP
474 Carlos Mendez 1.00 .30
Daniel Cabrera
Jeremy Guthrie SP
475 Edwin Almonte 1.00 .30
Phil Seibel
Felix Sanchez SP
476 Todd Wellemeyer 1.00 .30
Jon Leicester
Sergio Mitre SP
477 Josh Stewart 1.50 .45
Neal Cotts
Aaron Miles SP
478 Termel Sledge 1.50 .45
Josh Hall
Brandon Claussen SP
479 Francisco Cruceta 1.00 .30
Jason Stanford
Rafael Betancourt SP
480 Javier A.Lopez 1.00 .30
Garrett Atkins
Clint Barmes SP
481 Wilfredo Ledezma 1.50 .45
Nook Logan
Jeremy Bonderman SP
482 Josh Willingham 1.50 .45
Kevin Hooper
Rick Roberts SP
483 Colin Porter 1.00 .30
Mike Gallo
Dave Matranga SP
484 David DeJesus 1.50 .45
Jason Gilfillan
Jimmy Gobble SP
485 Koyie Hill 1.00 .30
Alfredo Gonzalez
Andrew Brown SP
486 Rickie Weeks 4.00 1.20
Pedro Liriano
Wes Obermueller SP
487 Alex Prieto 1.00 .30
Mike Ryan
Lew Ford SP
488 Julio Manon 1.00 .30
Luis Ayala
Seung Song SP
489 Jeff Duncan 1.50 .45
Prentice Redman
Craig Brazell SP
490 Chien-Ming Wang 1.50 .45
Michel Hernandez
Mike Gonzalez SP
491 Rich Harden 1.50 .45
Mike Neu
Geoff Geary SP
492 Diegomar Markwell 1.00 .30
Chad Gaudin
David Sanders SP
493 Beau Kemp 1.00 .30
Micheal Nakamura
D.J. Carrasco SP
494 Khalil Greene 1.50 .45
Miguel Ojeda
Bernie Castro SP
495 Noah Lowry 1.50 .45
Todd Linden
Kevin Correia SP
496 Aaron Looper 1.00 .30
Brian Sweeney
Rett Johnson SP
497 John Gall RC 1.50 .45
Dan Haren
Kevin Ohme SP
498 Delmon Young 5.00 1.50
Doug Waechter
Matt Diaz SP
499 Gerald Laird 1.00 .30
Rosman Garcia
Ramon Nivar SP
500 Alexis Rios 4.00 1.20
Guillermo Quiroz
Francisco Rosario SP

2004 Fleer Tradition Career Tributes

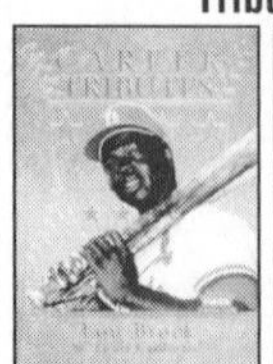

Nm-Mt Ex-Mt
PRINT RUNS B/WN 1956-1993 COPIES PER
*DIE CUT: 1.25X TO 3X BASIC...........
DIE CUT PRINTS B/WN 56-93 COPIES PER
OVERALL CAREER TRIBUTE ODDS 1:36
1 Mike Schmidt/1989 10.00 3.00
2 Nolan Ryan/1993 12.00 3.60
3 Tom Seaver/1986 5.00 1.50
4 Reggie Jackson/1987 5.00 1.50
5 Bob Gibson/1975 5.00 1.50
6 Harmon Killebrew/1975 8.00 2.40
7 Phil Rizzuto/1956 5.00 1.50
8 Lou Brock/1979 5.00 1.50
9 Eddie Mathews/1968 8.00 2.40
10 Al Kaline/1974 8.00 2.40

2004 Fleer Tradition Diamond Tributes

Nm-Mt Ex-Mt
COMPLETE SET (20) 20.00 6.00
STATED ODDS 1:6
1 Derek Jeter 4.00 1.20
2 Chipper Jones 1.50 .45
3 Vladimir Guerrero 1.50 .45
4 Kerry Wood 1.50 .45

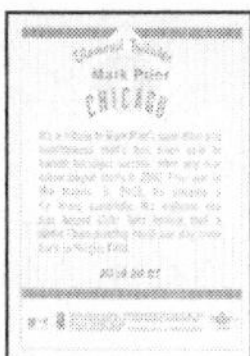

5 Jim Thome 1.50 .45
6 Nomar Garciaparra 2.50 .75
7 Alex Rodriguez 2.50 .75
8 Mike Piazza 2.50 .75
9 Jason Giambi 1.50 .45
10 Barry Zito 1.00 .30
11 Dontrelle Willis 1.00 .30
12 Albert Pujols 3.00 .90
13 Todd Helton 1.00 .30
14 Richie Sexson 1.00 .30
15 Randy Johnson 1.50 .45
16 Pedro Martinez 1.50 .45
17 Josh Beckett 1.00 .30
18 Manny Ramirez 1.00 .30
19 Roy Halladay 1.00 .30
20 Mark Prior 3.00 .90

2004 Fleer Tradition Diamond Tributes Game Jersey

Nm-Mt Ex-Mt
STATED ODDS 1:36
*PATCH: 1X TO 2.5X BASIC
PATCH RANDOM INSERTS IN PACKS
PATCH PRINT RUN 50 SERIAL #'d SETS
AP Albert Pujols 15.00 4.50
AR Alex Rodriguez 10.00 3.00
BZ Barry Zito 10.00 3.00
CJ Chipper Jones 10.00 3.00
DJ Derek Jeter 20.00 6.00
DW Dontrelle Willis 8.00 2.40
JB Josh Beckett 10.00 3.00
JG Jason Giambi 10.00 3.00
JT Jim Thome 10.00 3.00
KW Kerry Wood 10.00 3.00
MP Mike Piazza 10.00 3.00
MP2 Mark Prior 15.00 4.50
MR Manny Ramirez 8.00 2.40
NG Nomar Garciaparra 10.00 3.00
PM Pedro Martinez 10.00 3.00
RH Roy Halladay 8.00 2.40
RJ Randy Johnson 10.00 3.00
RS Richie Sexson 8.00 2.40
TH Todd Helton 10.00 3.00
VG Vladimir Guerrero 10.00 3.00

2004 Fleer Tradition Retrospection

Nm-Mt Ex-Mt
STATED ODDS 1:360
1 Rickie Weeks 20.00 6.00
2 Delmon Young 20.00 6.00
3 Torii Hunter 15.00 4.50
4 Aubrey Huff 15.00 4.50
5 Rocco Baldelli 20.00 6.00
6 Mike Lowell 15.00 4.50
7 Dontrelle Willis 15.00 4.50
8 Albert Pujols 30.00 9.00
9 Bo Hart 15.00 4.50
10 Brandon Webb 15.00 4.50

2004 Fleer Tradition Retrospection Autographs

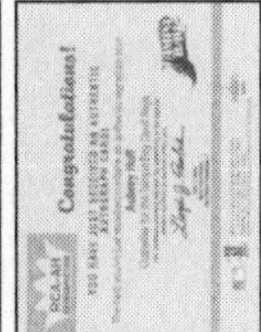

Please note that a few players did not return their autographs in time for inclusion in this product and no expiration date was set for redeeming those cards.

Nm-Mt Ex-Mt
OVERALL AUTO ODDS 1:720
STATED PRINT RUN 60 SERIAL #'d SETS
AH Aubrey Huff 25.00 7.50
AK Austin Kearns 25.00 7.50
AP Albert Pujols EXCH 120.00 36.00
BO Bo Hart 25.00 7.50
BW Brandon Webb 25.00 7.50
CP Corey Patterson 25.00 7.50
DW Dontrelle Willis 40.00 12.00
DY Delmon Young EXCH 60.00 18.00
HB Hank Blalock 40.00 12.00
JR Jose Reyes 40.00 12.00
JW Josh Willingham 25.00 7.50
MR Mike Ryan 25.00 7.50
RW Ryan Wagner EXCH 25.00 7.50
RW Rickie Weeks 50.00 15.00
SR Scott Rolen 40.00 12.00
TH Torii Hunter 25.00 7.50

2004 Fleer Tradition Retrospection Autographs Dual

Nm-Mt Ex-Mt
OVERALL AUTO ODDS 1:720
STATED PRINT RUN 19 SERIAL #'d SETS
NO PRICING DUE TO SCARCITY
EXCHANGE DEADLINE INDEFINITE
AHAK Aubrey Huff
Austin Kearns
APBH Albert Pujols
Bo Hart EXCH
BWRW Brandon Webb
Ryan Wagner EXCH
CPJR Corey Patterson
Jose Reyes
HBSR Hank Blalock
Scott Rolen
JWDW Josh Willingham
Dontrelle Willis
RWDY Rickie Weeks
Delmon Young EXCH
THMR Torii Hunter
Mike Ryan

2004 Fleer Tradition Stand Outs Game Used

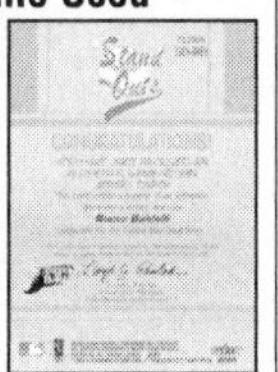

Nm-Mt Ex-Mt
STATED ODDS 1:41
GOLD RANDOM INSERTS IN PACKS
GOLD PRINTS B/WN 20-27 COPIES PER
NO GOLD PRICING DUE TO SCARCITY
AB Angel Berroa Pants 8.00 2.40
BH Bo Hart Jsy 8.00 2.40
BW Brandon Webb Pants 8.00 2.40
DW Dontrelle Willis Jsy 8.00 2.40
HB Hank Blalock Jsy 8.00 2.40
HC Hee Seop Choi Jsy 8.00 2.40
JR Jose Reyes Jsy 10.00 3.00
MB Marlon Byrd Jsy 8.00 2.40
MC Miguel Cabrera Jsy 10.00 3.00
MT Mark Teixeira Jsy 8.00 2.40
RB Rocco Baldelli Jsy 10.00 3.00

2004 Fleer Tradition This Day in History

Nm-Mt Ex-Mt
STATED ODDS 1:18
1 Josh Beckett 1.50 .45
2 Carlos Delgado 1.50 .45
3 Javy Lopez 1.50 .45
4 Greg Maddux 4.00 1.20
5 Rafael Palmeiro 1.50 .45
6 Sammy Sosa 4.00 1.20
7 Jeff Bagwell 1.50 .45
8 Frank Thomas 2.50 .75
9 Kevin Millwood 1.50 .45
10 Jose Reyes 1.50 .45
11 Rafael Furcal 1.50 .45
12 Alfonso Soriano 1.50 .45
13 Eric Gagne 1.50 .45
14 Hideki Matsui 4.00 1.20
15 Hank Blalock 1.50 .45

2004 Fleer Tradition This Day in History Game Used

Nm-Mt Ex-Mt
STATED ODDS 1:288
AS Alfonso Soriano Jsy 15.00 4.50
CD Carlos Delgado Jsy 10.00 3.00
FT Frank Thomas Jsy 15.00 4.50
GM Greg Maddux Jsy 15.00 4.50
JB Josh Beckett Jsy 15.00 4.50
JB Jeff Bagwell Jsy 15.00 4.50
JL Javy Lopez Jsy 10.00 3.00

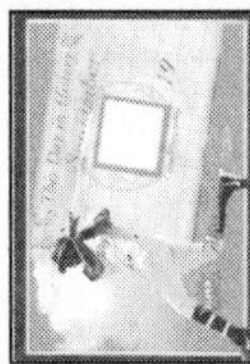

JR Jose Reyes Jsy 15.00 4.50
RP Rafael Palmeiro Jsy 15.00 4.50
SS Sammy Sosa Bat 20.00 6.00

2004 Fleer Tradition This Day in History Game Used Dual

Nm-Mt Ex-Mt
RANDOM INSERTS IN PACKS
STATED PRINT RUN 25 SERIAL #'d SETS
NO PRICING DUE TO SCARCITY
CDJR Carlos Delgado Jsy
Jose Reyes Jsy
FTJB Frank Thomas Jsy
Jeff Bagwell Jsy
JBGM Josh Beckett Jsy
Greg Maddux Jsy
JLAS Javy Lopez Jsy
Alfonso Soriano Jsy
RPSS Rafael Palmeiro Jsy
Sammy Sosa Bat

2001 Fleer Triple Crown

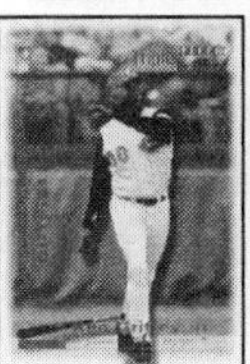
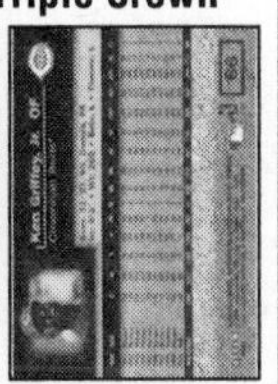

The 2001 Fleer Triple Crown product was released in January, 2001 and featured a 300-card base set. The set is broken into two subset: Base Veterans (1-250), and Prospects (251-300). Please note that Fleer created three parallels of the first 100 cards (Red, Blue, and Green). Each pack contained 10 cards and carried a suggested retail price of $1.99.

Nm-Mt Ex-Mt
COMPLETE SET (300) 30.00 9.00
COMMON CARD (1-300) .30 .09
COMMON (301-310) 5.00 1.50
1 Derek Jeter 2.00 .60
2 Vladimir Guerrero .75 .23
3 Henry Rodriguez .30 .09
4 Jason Giambi .75 .23
5 Nomar Garciaparra 1.25 .35
6 Jeff Kent .30 .09
7 Garret Anderson .30 .09
8 Todd Helton .50 .15
9 Barry Bonds 2.00 .60
10 Preston Wilson .30 .09
11 Troy Glaus .50 .15
12 Geoff Jenkins .30 .09
13 Jim Edmonds .30 .09
14 Bobby Higginson .30 .09
15 Mark Quinn .30 .09
16 Barry Larkin .75 .23
17 Richie Sexson .30 .09
18 Fernando Tatis .30 .09
19 John VanderWal .30 .09
20 Darin Erstad .30 .09
21 Shawn Green .30 .09
22 Scott Rolen .50 .15
23 Tony Batista .30 .09
24 Phil Nevin .30 .09
25 Tim Salmon .50 .15
26 Gary Sheffield .30 .09
27 Ben Grieve .30 .09
28 Jermaine Dye .30 .09
29 Andres Galarraga .30 .09
30 Adrian Beltre .30 .09
31 Rafael Palmeiro .50 .15
32 J.T. Snow .30 .09
33 Edgardo Alfonzo .30 .09
34 Paul Konerko .30 .09
35 Jim Thome .75 .23
36 Andruw Jones .30 .09
37 Mike Sweeney .30 .09
38 Jose Cruz Jr. .30 .09
39 David Ortiz .30 .09
40 Pat Burrell .30 .09
41 Chipper Jones .75 .23
42 Jeff Bagwell .50 .15
43 Raul Mondesi .30 .09
44 Rondell White .30 .09
45 Edgar Martinez .50 .15
46 Cal Ripken 2.50 .75
47 Moises Alou .30 .09
48 Shannon Stewart .30 .09
49 Tino Martinez .50 .15
50 Jason Kendall .30 .09
51 Richard Hidalgo .30 .09
52 Albert Belle .30 .09
53 Jay Payton .30 .09
54 Cliff Floyd .30 .09
55 Rusty Greer .30 .09
56 Matt Williams .30 .09
57 Sammy Sosa 1.25 .35
58 Carl Everett .30 .09
59 Carlos Delgado .30 .09
60 Jeremy Giambi .30 .09
61 Jose Canseco .75 .23
62 David Segui .30 .09
63 Jose Vidro .30 .09
64 Matt Stairs .30 .09
65 Travis Fryman .30 .09
66 Ken Griffey Jr. 1.25 .35
67 Mike Piazza 1.25 .35
68 Mark McGwire 2.00 .60
69 Craig Biggio .50 .15
70 Eric Chavez .30 .09
71 Mo Vaughn .30 .09
72 Matt Lawton .30 .09
73 Miguel Tejada .30 .09
74 Brian Giles .30 .09
75 Sean Casey .30 .09
76 Robin Ventura .30 .09
77 Ivan Rodriguez .75 .23
78 Dean Palmer .30 .09
79 Frank Thomas .75 .23
80 Bernie Williams .50 .15
81 Juan Encarnacion .30 .09
82 John Olerud .30 .09
83 Rich Aurilia .30 .09
84 Juan Gonzalez .75 .23
85 Ray Durham .30 .09
86 Steve Finley .30 .09
87 Ken Caminiti .30 .09
88 Roberto Alomar .75 .23
89 Jeromy Burnitz .30 .09
90 J.D. Drew .30 .09
91 Lance Berkman .30 .09
92 Gabe Kapler .30 .09
93 Larry Walker .50 .15
94 Alex Rodriguez 1.25 .35
95 Jeffrey Hammonds .30 .09
96 Magglio Ordonez .30 .09
97 David Justice .30 .09
98 Eric Karros .30 .09
99 Manny Ramirez .30 .09
100 Paul O'Neill .50 .15
101 Ron Gant .30 .09
102 Erubiel Durazo .30 .09
103 Jason Varitek .30 .09
104 Chan Ho Park .30 .09
105 Corey Koskie .30 .09
106 Jeff Conine .30 .09
107 Kevin Tapani .30 .09
108 Mike Lowell .30 .09
109 Tim Hudson .30 .09
110 Bobby Abreu .30 .09
111 Bret Boone .30 .09
112 David Wells .30 .09
113 Brian Jordan .30 .09
114 Mitch Meluskey .30 .09
115 Terrence Long .30 .09
116 Matt Clement .30 .09
117 Fernando Vina .30 .09
118 Luis Alicea .30 .09
119 Jay Bell .30 .09
120 Mark Grace .50 .15
121 Carlos Febles .30 .09
122 Mark Redman .30 .09
123 Kevin Jordan .30 .09
124 Pat Meares .30 .09
125 Mark McLemore .30 .09
126 Chris Singleton .30 .09
127 Trot Nixon .50 .15
128 Carlos Beltran .30 .09
129 Lee Stevens .30 .09
130 Kris Benson .30 .09
131 Jay Buhner .30 .09
132 Greg Vaughn .30 .09
133 Eric Young .30 .09
134 Tony Womack .30 .09
135 Roger Cedeno .30 .09
136 Travis Lee .30 .09
137 Marvin Benard .30 .09
138 Aaron Sele .30 .09
139 Rick Ankiel .30 .09
140 Ruben Mateo .30 .09
141 Randy Johnson .75 .23
142 Jason Tyner .30 .09
143 Mike Redmond .30 .09
144 Ron Coomer .30 .09
145 Scott Elarton .30 .09
146 Javy Lopez .30 .09
147 Carlos Lee .30 .09
148 Tony Clark .30 .09
149 Roger Clemens 1.50 .45
150 Mike Lieberthal .30 .09
151 Shawn Estes .30 .09
152 Vinny Castilla .30 .09
153 Alex Gonzalez .30 .09
154 Troy Percival .30 .09
155 Pokey Reese .30 .09
156 Todd Hollandsworth .30 .09
157 Marquis Grissom .30 .09
158 Greg Maddux 1.25 .35
159 Dante Bichette .30 .09
160 Hideo Nomo .75 .23
161 Jacque Jones .30 .09
162 Kevin Young .30 .09
163 B.J. Surhoff .30 .09
164 Eddie Taubensee .30 .09
165 Neifi Perez .30 .09
166 Orlando Hernandez .30 .09
167 Francisco Cordova .30 .09
168 Miguel Cairo .30 .09
169 Rafael Furcal .30 .09
170 Sandy Alomar Jr. .30 .09
171 Jeff Cirillo .30 .09
172 A.J. Pierzynski .30 .09
173 Fred McGriff .50 .15
174 Mike Mussina .75 .23
175 Aaron Boone .30 .09
176 Nick Johnson .30 .09
177 Kent Bottenfield .30 .09
178 Felipe Crespo .30 .09
179 Ryan Minor .30 .09
180 Charles Johnson .30 .09
181 Damion Easley .30 .09
182 Michael Barrett .30 .09
183 Doug Glanville .30 .09
184 Ben Davis .30 .09
185 Rickey Henderson .75 .23
186 Edgard Clemente .30 .09
187 Dmitri Young .30 .09
188 Tom Goodwin .30 .09
189 Mike Hampton .30 .09
190 Gerald Williams .30 .09
191 Omar Vizquel .30 .09
192 Ben Petrick .30 .09
193 Brad Radke .30 .09
194 Russ Davis .30 .09
195 Milton Bradley .30 .09
196 John Parrish .30 .09
197 Todd Hundley .30 .09
198 Carl Pavano .30 .09
199 Bruce Chen .30 .09
200 Royce Clayton .30 .09
201 Homer Bush .30 .09
202 Mark Grudzielanek .30 .09
203 Mike Lansing .30 .09
204 Daryle Ward .30 .09
205 Jeff D'Amico .30 .09
206 Ray Lankford .30 .09
207 Curt Schilling .50 .15
208 Pedro Martinez .75 .23
209 Johnny Damon .30 .09
210 Al Leiter .30 .09
211 Ruben Rivera .30 .09
212 Kazuhiro Sasaki .30 .09
213 Will Clark .75 .23
214 Rick Helling .30 .09
215 Adam Piatt .30 .09
216 Joe Girardi .30 .09
217 A.J. Burnett .30 .09
218 Mike Bordick .30 .09
219 Mike Cameron .30 .09
220 Tony Gwynn 1.00 .30
221 Deivi Cruz .30 .09
222 Bubba Trammell .30 .09
223 Scott Erickson .30 .09
224 Kerry Wood .75 .23
225 Derrek Lee .30 .09
226 Peter Bergeron .30 .09
227 Chris Gomez .30 .09
228 Al Martin .30 .09
229 Brady Anderson .30 .09
230 Ramon Martinez .30 .09
231 Darryl Kile .30 .09
232 Devon White .30 .09
233 Charlie Hayes .30 .09
234 Aramis Ramirez .30 .09
235 Mike Lamb .30 .09
236 Tom Glavine .50 .15
237 Troy O'Leary .30 .09
238 Joe Randa .30 .09
239 Dustin Hermanson .30 .09
240 Adam Kennedy .30 .09
241 Jose Valentin .30 .09
242 Derek Bell .30 .09
243 Mark Kotsay .30 .09
244 Ron Belliard .30 .09
245 Warren Morris .30 .09
246 Ozzie Guillen .30 .09
247 Andy Ashby .30 .09
248 Jose Offerman .30 .09
249 Kevin Brown .30 .09
250 Jorge Posada .50 .15
251 Alex Cabrera .30 .09
252 Chan Perry .30 .09
253 Augie Ojeda .30 .09
254 Santiago Perez .30 .09
255 Grant Roberts .30 .09
256 Dusty Allen .30 .09
257 Elvis Pena .30 .09
258 Matt Kinney .30 .09
259 Timo Perez .30 .09
260 Adam Eaton .30 .09
261 Geraldo Guzman .30 .09
262 Damian Rolls .30 .09
263 Alfonso Soriano .50 .15
264 Corey Patterson .30 .09
265 Juan Alvarez .30 .09
266 Shawn Gilbert .30 .09
267 Adam Bernero .30 .09
268 Ben Weber .30 .09
269 Tike Redman .30 .09
270 Willie Morales .30 .09
271 Tomas De la Rosa .30 .09
272 Rodney Lindsey .30 .09
273 Carlos Casimiro .30 .09
274 Jim Mann .30 .09
275 Pasqual Coco .30 .09
276 Julio Zuleta .30 .09
277 Damon Minor .30 .09
278 Jose Ortiz .30 .09
279 Eric Munson .30 .09
280 Andy Thompson .30 .09
281 Aubrey Huff .30 .09
282 Chris Richard .30 .09
283 Ross Gload .30 .09
284 Travis Dawkins .30 .09
285 Tim Drew .30 .09
286 Barry Zito .75 .23
287 Andy Tracy .30 .09
288 Julio Lugo .30 .09
289 Greg LaRocca .30 .09
290 Keith McDonald .30 .09
291 J.C. Romero .30 .09
292 Adam Melhuse .30 .09
293 Ryan Kohlmeier .30 .09
294 John Bale .30 .09
295 Eric Cammack .30 .09
296 Morgan Burkhart .30 .09
297 Kory DeHaan .30 .09
298 Mike Mahoney .30 .09
299 Hector Ortiz .30 .09
300 Talmadge Nunnari .30 .09
301 E.Guzman/2999 RC 5.00 1.50
302 D.Henson/2999 RC 6.00 1.80
303 Bud Smith/2999 RC 5.00 1.50
304 C.Valderrama/2999 RC 5.00 1.50
305 T.Shinjo/2999 RC 6.00 1.80
306 I.Suzuki/2999 RC 20.00 6.00
307 J.Melian/2999 RC 5.00 1.50
308 M.Ensberg/2999 RC 6.00 1.80
309 Albert Pujols/2999 RC 40.00 12.00
310 J.Estrada/2999 RC 5.00 1.50

2001 Fleer Triple Crown Blue

Randomly inserted exclusively into hobby packs, this 100-card set is a complete parallel of the first 100 cards in the 2001 Fleer Triple Crown base set. Please note that these cards have blue-foil lettering on the card fronts, and are individually serial numbered to each player's 2000 home run total. Cards with a print run of 15 or less are not priced.

Nm-Mt Ex-Mt
*PRINT RUN b/wn 36-50: 15X TO 40X BASIC
*PRINT RUN b/wn 26-35: 20X TO 50X BASIC
*PRINT RUN b/wn 21-25: 25X TO 60X BASIC
*PRINT RUN b/wn 16-20: 30X TO 80X BASIC

2001 Fleer Triple Crown Green

Randomly inserted exclusively into hobby packs, this 100-card set is a complete parallel of the first 100 cards in the 2001 Fleer Triple Crown base set. Please note that these cards have green-foil lettering on the card fronts, and are individually serial numbered to each player's 2000 RBI total.

Nm-Mt Ex-Mt
*PRINT RUN b/wn 121-150: 6X TO 15X BASIC
*PRINT RUN b/wn 81-120: 8X TO 20X BASIC
*PRINT RUN b/wn 66-80: 10X TO 25X BASIC
*PRINT RUN b/wn 51-65: 12.5X TO 30X BASIC
*PRINT RUN b/wn 36-50: 15X TO 40X BASIC

2001 Fleer Triple Crown Purple

Randomly inserted into retail packs, this 100-card set is a complete parallel of the first 100 cards in the 2001 Fleer Triple Crown base set. Please note that these cards have purple-foil lettering on the card fronts, and were only available in retail packs at the rate of approximately one per box.

Nm-Mt Ex-Mt
*STARS: 2.5X TO 6X BASIC CARDS ...

2001 Fleer Triple Crown Red

Randomly inserted exclusively into hobby packs, this 100-card set is a complete parallel of the first 100 cards in the 2001 Fleer Triple Crown base set. Please note that these cards have red-foil lettering on the card fronts, and are individually serial numbered to each player's 2000 batting average.

Nm-Mt Ex-Mt
*STARS: 4X TO 10X BASIC CARDS ....

2001 Fleer Triple Crown Crowning Achievements

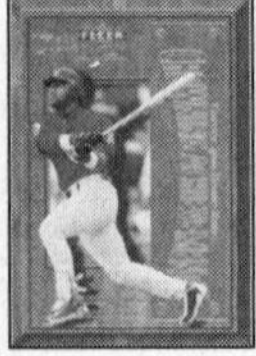

Randomly inserted into hobby packs at one in nine and retail packs at a rate of one in 12, this 15-card insert features players that have had significant achievements in their career or will reach one in 2001. Card backs carry a "CA" prefix.

	Nm-Mt	Ex-Mt
COMPLETE SET (15)	40.00	12.00
CA1 Troy Glaus	1.25	.35
CA2 Mark McGwire	5.00	1.50
CA3 Barry Larkin Andres Galarraga Craig Biggio	2.00	.60
CA4 Ken Griffey Jr.	3.00	.90
CA5 Rafael Palmeiro	1.25	.35
CA6 Alex Rodriguez	3.00	.90
CA7 Roger Clemens	4.00	1.20
CA8 Mike Piazza	3.00	.90
CA9 Cal Ripken	6.00	1.80
CA10 Randy Johnson	2.00	.60
CA11 Jeff Bagwell	1.25	.35
CA12 Sammy Sosa	3.00	.90
CA13 Greg Maddux	3.00	.90
CA14 Barry Bonds	5.00	1.50
CA15 Fred McGriff	1.25	.35

2001 Fleer Triple Crown Crowns of Gold

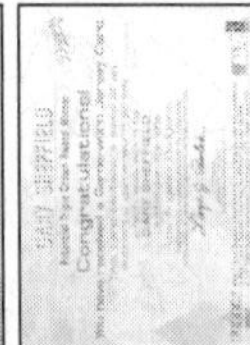

Randomly inserted exclusively into hobby packs, this 12-card insert features swatches of game-used memorabilia from players that have either won the Triple Crown award, or that will be in the running to win it. Card are listed below in alphabetical order for convenience. Out of one in every 72 packs, collectors received either a Crowns of Gold, Crowns of Gold Autograph, Feel the Game or Autographics card.

	Nm-Mt	Ex-Mt
1 Rick Ankiel Jsy	10.00	3.00
2 Steve Carlton Jsy	10.00	3.00
3 Roger Clemens Jsy	40.00	12.00
4 Carlos Delgado Bat	10.00	3.00
5 Darin Erstad Bat	10.00	3.00
6 Jimmie Foxx Bat	100.00	30.00
7 Todd Helton Bat	15.00	4.50
8 Randy Johnson Jsy	15.00	4.50
9 Frank Robinson Bat	15.00	4.50
10 Gary Sheffield Jsy	10.00	3.00
11 Frank Thomas Bat	15.00	4.50
12 Ted Williams Bat	150.00	45.00

2001 Fleer Triple Crown Crowns of Gold Autographs

Randomly inserted into packs, this four-card insert features both game-used memorabilia swatches and autographs from some of the best players in the history of baseball. This set includes Frank Robinson, Steve Carlton, Roger Clemens, and Ted Williams. Cards are listed below in alphabetical order. The Williams was an exchange and the deadline to exchange this card was February 1, 2002. Sadly, Williams was never able to sign his card and all collectors who redeemed that card were reimbursed with a significant amount of signed and memorabilia cards of their choice in it's place.

	Nm-Mt	Ex-Mt
1 Steve Carlton Jsy/72	120.00	36.00
2 Roger Clemens Jsy/98	250.00	75.00
3 Frank Robinson Bat/66	120.00	36.00
4 Ted Williams Bat/9 EXCH Williams never signed this card		

2001 Fleer Triple Crown Future Threats

Randomly inserted into hobby packs at one in seven and retail packs at a rate of one in 10, this 15-card insert features players that look to dominate starting pitching for years to come. Card backs carry a "FT" prefix.

	Nm-Mt	Ex-Mt
COMPLETE SET (15)	30.00	9.00
FT1 Derek Jeter	4.00	1.20
FT2 Alex Rodriguez	2.50	.75
FT3 Magglio Ordonez Shawn Green Andruw Jones	1.00	.30
FT4 Larry Walker	1.00	.30
FT5 Vladimir Guerrero	1.50	.45
FT6 Nomar Garciaparra	2.50	.75
FT7 Ken Griffey Jr.	2.50	.75
FT8 Barry Bonds	4.00	1.20
FT9 Chipper Jones	1.50	.45
FT10 Todd Helton	1.00	.30
FT11 Ivan Rodriguez	1.50	.45
FT12 Jeff Bagwell	1.00	.30
FT13 Frank Thomas	1.50	.45
FT14 Carlos Delgado	1.00	.30
FT15 Mike Piazza	2.50	.75

2001 Fleer Triple Crown Glamour Boys

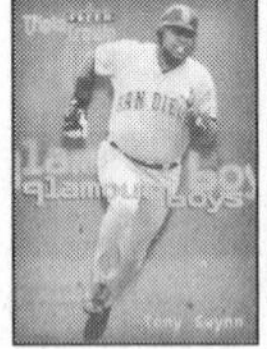

Randomly inserted into hobby packs at one in 24 and retail packs at a rate of one in 20, this 15-card insert features players that give maximum effort every game. Card backs carry a "GB" prefix.

	Nm-Mt	Ex-Mt
COMPLETE SET (15)	100.00	30.00
GB1 Derek Jeter	10.00	3.00
GB2 Vladimir Guerrero	4.00	1.20
GB3 Scott Rolen Jeff Bagwell Bernie Williams	4.00	1.20
GB4 Sammy Sosa	6.00	1.80
GB5 Ken Griffey Jr.	6.00	1.80
GB6 Mark McGwire	10.00	3.00
GB7 Ivan Rodriguez	4.00	1.20
GB8 Mike Piazza	6.00	1.80
GB9 Nomar Garciaparra	6.00	1.80
GB10 Cal Ripken	12.00	3.60
GB11 Tony Gwynn	5.00	1.50
GB12 Barry Bonds	10.00	3.00
GB13 Randy Johnson	4.00	1.20
GB14 Alex Rodriguez	6.00	1.80
GB15 Pedro Martinez	4.00	1.20

2002 Fleer Triple Crown

This set was issued in March, 2002. These cards were issued in ten-card packs with an SRP of $2.50 and had 24 packs to a box and either 6 or 16 boxes to a case. The following subsets were included in this set: Cards numbered 201-230 featured leading rookie prospects while 231-240 featured a scrapbook and cards 241-260 featured pace setters. An unnumbered Derek Jeter promo card was issued a few weeks before this product was released and is noted at the end of our listings.

	Nm-Mt	Ex-Mt
COMPLETE SET (270)	40.00	12.00
1 Mo Vaughn	.30	.09
2 Derek Jeter	2.00	.60
3 Ken Griffey Jr.	1.25	.35
4 Charles Johnson	.30	.09
5 Geoff Jenkins	.30	.09
6 Chuck Knoblauch	.30	.09
7 Jason Kendall	.30	.09
8 Jim Edmonds	.30	.09
9 David Eckstein	.30	.09
10 Carl Everett	.30	.09
11 Barry Larkin	.75	.23
12 Cliff Floyd	.30	.09
13 Ben Sheets	.30	.09
14 Jeff Conine	.30	.09
15 Brian Giles	.30	.09
16 Darryl Kile	.30	.09
17 Troy Glaus	.50	.15
18 Trot Nixon	.50	.15
19 Jim Thome	.75	.23
20 Preston Wilson	.30	.09
21 Roger Clemens	1.50	.45
22 Chad Hermansen	.30	.09
23 Matt Morris	.30	.09
24 Shawn Wooten	.30	.09
25 Manny Ramirez	.30	.09
26 Roberto Alomar	.75	.23
27 Josh Beckett	.50	.15
28 Jose Hernandez	.30	.09
29 Mike Mussina	.75	.23
30 Jack Wilson	.30	.09
31 Bud Smith	.30	.09
32 Garret Anderson	.30	.09
33 Pedro Martinez	.75	.23
34 Travis Fryman	.30	.09
35 Jeff Bagwell	.50	.15
36 Doug Mientkiewicz	.30	.09
37 Andy Pettitte	.50	.15
38 Ryan Klesko	.30	.09
39 Edgar Renteria	.30	.09
40 Mariano Rivera	.50	.15
41 Darin Erstad	.30	.09
42 Hideo Nomo	.75	.23
43 Ellis Burks	.30	.09
44 Craig Biggio	.50	.15
45 Corey Koskie	.30	.09
46 Jason Varitek	.30	.09
47 Xavier Nady	.30	.09
48 Aubrey Huff	.30	.09
49 Tim Salmon	.50	.15
50 Nomar Garciaparra	1.25	.35
51 Juan Gonzalez	.75	.23
52 Moises Alou	.30	.09
53 A.J. Pierzynski	.30	.09
54 Bernie Williams	.50	.15
55 Phil Nevin	.30	.09
56 Ben Grieve	.30	.09
57 Mark Grace	.50	.15
58 Mike Lansing	.30	.09
59 Kenny Lofton	.30	.09
60 Lance Berkman	.30	.09
61 David Ortiz	.30	.09
62 Jason Giambi	.75	.23
63 Mark Kotsay	.30	.09
64 Greg Vaughn	.30	.09
65 Junior Spivey	.30	.09
66 Fred McGriff	.50	.15
67 C.C. Sabathia	.30	.09
68 Richard Hidalgo	.30	.09
69 Torii Hunter	.30	.09
70 Jason Hart	.30	.09
71 Bubba Trammell	.30	.09
72 Jace Brewer	.30	.09
73 Matt Williams	.30	.09
74 Matt Stairs	.30	.09
75 Omar Vizquel	.30	.09
76 Daryle Ward	.30	.09
77 Joe Mays	.30	.09
78 Eric Chavez	.30	.09
79 Andres Galarraga	.30	.09
80 Rafael Palmeiro	.50	.15
81 Steve Finley	.30	.09
82 Eric Young	.30	.09
83 Todd Helton	.50	.15
84 Roy Oswalt	.30	.09
85 Eric Milton	.30	.09
86 Ramon Hernandez	.30	.09
87 Jeff Kent	.30	.09
88 Ivan Rodriguez	.75	.23
89 Luis Gonzalez	.30	.09
90 Corey Patterson	.30	.09
91 Jose Ortiz	.30	.09
92 Mike Sweeney	.30	.09
93 Cristian Guzman	.30	.09
94 Johnny Damon	.30	.09
95 Barry Bonds	2.00	.60
96 Rusty Greer	.30	.09
97 Reggie Sanders	.30	.09
98 Sammy Sosa	1.25	.35
99 Jeff Cirillo	.30	.09
100 Carlos Febles	.30	.09
101 Jose Vidro	.30	.09
102 Jermaine Dye	.30	.09
103 Rich Aurilia	.30	.09
104 Gabe Kapler	.30	.09
105 Randy Johnson	.75	.23
106 Rondell White	.30	.09
107 Ben Petrick	.30	.09
108 Joe Randa	.30	.09
109 Fernando Tatis	.30	.09
110 Tim Hudson	.30	.09
111 John Olerud	.30	.09
112 Alex Rodriguez	1.25	.35
113 Curt Schilling	.50	.15
114 Kerry Wood	.75	.23
115 Alex Ochoa	.30	.09
116 Carlos Beltran	.30	.09
117 Vladimir Guerrero	.75	.23
118 Mark Mulder	.30	.09
119 Bret Boone	.30	.09
120 Carlos Delgado	.30	.09
121 Marcus Giles	.30	.09
122 Paul Konerko	.30	.09
123 Juan Pierre	.30	.09
124 Mark Quinn	.30	.09
125 Edgardo Alfonzo	.30	.09
126 Barry Zito	.50	.15
127 Dan Wilson	.30	.09
128 Jose Cruz Jr.	.30	.09
129 Chipper Jones	.75	.23
130 Ray Durham	.30	.09
131 Larry Walker	.50	.15
132 Neifi Perez	.30	.09
133 Robin Ventura	.30	.09
134 Miguel Tejada	.30	.09
135 Edgar Martinez	.50	.15
136 Raul Mondesi	.30	.09
137 Javy Lopez	.30	.09
138 Jose Canseco	.75	.23
139 Mike Hampton	.30	.09
140 Eric Karros	.30	.09
141 Mike Piazza	1.25	.35
142 Travis Lee	.30	.09
143 Ichiro Suzuki	1.25	.35
144 Shannon Stewart	.30	.09
145 Andruw Jones	.30	.09
146 Frank Thomas	.75	.23
147 Tony Clark	.30	.09
148 Adrian Beltre	.30	.09
149 Matt Lawton	.30	.09
150 Marlon Anderson	.30	.09
151 Freddy Garcia	.30	.09
152 Brian Jordan	.30	.09
153 Carlos Lee	.30	.09
154 Eric Munson	.30	.09
155 Paul LoDuca	.30	.09
156 Jay Payton	.30	.09
157 Scott Rolen	.50	.15
158 Jamie Moyer	.30	.09
159 Tom Glavine	.50	.15
160 Magglio Ordonez	.30	.09
161 Brandon Inge	.30	.09
162 Shawn Green	.30	.09
163 Tsuyoshi Shinjo	.30	.09
164 Mike Lieberthal	.30	.09
165 Kazuhiro Sasaki	.30	.09
166 Greg Maddux	1.25	.35
167 Chris Singleton	.30	.09
168 Juan Encarnacion	.30	.09
169 Gary Sheffield	.30	.09
170 Nick Johnson	.30	.09
171 Bob Abreu	.30	.09
172 Aaron Boone	.30	.09
173 Rafael Furcal	.30	.09
174 Mark Buehrle	.30	.09
175 Bobby Higginson	.30	.09
176 Kevin Brown	.30	.09
177 Tino Martinez	.50	.15
178 Pat Burrell	.30	.09
179 Fernando Vina	.30	.09
180 Jay Gibbons	.30	.09
181 Jose Valentin	.30	.09
182 Derrek Lee	.30	.09
183 Richie Sexson	.30	.09
184 Alfonso Soriano	.50	.15
185 Jimmy Rollins	.30	.09
186 Albert Pujols	1.50	.45
187 Brady Anderson	.30	.09
188 Sean Casey	.30	.09
189 Luis Castillo	.30	.09
190 Jeromy Burnitz	.30	.09
191 Jorge Posada	.50	.15
192 Kevin Young	.30	.09
193 Eli Marrero	.30	.09
194 Shea Hillenbrand	.30	.09
195 Adam Dunn	.30	.09
196 Mike Lowell	.30	.09
197 Jeffrey Hammonds	.30	.09
198 David Justice	.30	.09
199 Aramis Ramirez	.30	.09
200 J.D. Drew	.30	.09
201 Pedro Santana FS	.25	.07
202 Endy Chavez FS	.25	.07
203 Donnie Bridges FS	.25	.07
204 Travis Phelps FS	.25	.07
205 Drew Henson FS	.50	.15
206 Angel Berroa FS	.50	.15
207 George Perez FS	.25	.07
208 Billy Sylvester FS	.25	.07
209 Juan Cruz FS	.25	.07
210 Horacio Ramirez FS	.25	.07
211 J.J. Davis FS	.25	.07
212 Cody Ransom FS	.25	.07
213 Mark Teixeira FS	1.50	.45
214 Nate Frese FS	.25	.07
215 Brian Rogers FS	.25	.07
216 Dewon Brazelton FS	.25	.07
217 Carlos Hernandez FS	.25	.07
218 Juan Rivera FS	.25	.07
219 Luis Lopez FS	.25	.07
220 Benito Baez FS	.25	.07
221 Bill Ortega FS	.25	.07
222 Dustan Mohr FS	.25	.07
223 Corky Miller FS	.25	.07
224 Tyler Walker FS	.25	.07
225 Rick Bauer FS	.25	.07
226 Mark Prior FS	2.50	.75
227 Rafael Soriano FS	.50	.15
228 Greg Miller FS	.25	.07
229 Dave Williams FS	.25	.07
230 Bert Snow FS	.25	.07
231 Barry Bonds SB	.75	.23
232 Rickey Henderson SB	.75	.23
233 Alex Rodriguez SB	.75	.23
234 Luis Gonzalez SB	.30	.09
235 Derek Jeter SB	1.00	.30
236 Bud Smith SB	.30	.09
237 Sammy Sosa SB	.75	.23
238 Jeff Bagwell SB	.30	.09
239 Jim Thome SB	.50	.15
240 Hideo Nomo SB	.50	.15
241 Greg Maddux SB	.75	.23
242 Ken Griffey Jr. SB	.75	.23
243 Curt Schilling Randy Johnson SB	.50	.15
244 Arizona Diamondbacks SB	.75	.23
245 Ichiro Suzuki SB	.75	.23
246 Albert Pujols SB	.75	.23
247 Ichiro Suzuki SB	.75	.23
248 Barry Bonds SB	.75	.23
249 Roger Clemens SB	.75	.23
250 Randy Johnson SB	.50	.15
251 Todd Helton PS	.30	.09
252 Rafael Palmeiro PS	.30	.09
253 Mike Piazza PS	.75	.23
254 Alex Rodriguez PS	.75	.23
255 Manny Ramirez PS	.30	.09
256 Ken Griffey Jr. PS	.75	.23
257 Jason Giambi PS	.50	.15
258 Chipper Jones PS	.50	.15
259 Larry Walker PS	.30	.09
260 Sammy Sosa PS	.75	.23
261 Vladimir Guerrero PS	.50	.15
262 Nomar Garciaparra PS	.75	.23
263 Randy Johnson PS	.50	.15
264 Roger Clemens PS	.75	.23
265 Ichiro Suzuki PS	.75	.23
266 Barry Bonds PS	.75	.23
267 Paul LoDuca PS	.30	.09
268 Albert Pujols PS	.75	.23
269 Derek Jeter PS	1.00	.30
270 Adam Dunn PS	.30	.09
NNO Derek Jeter Promo	3.00	.90

2002 Fleer Triple Crown Batting Average Parallel

Randomly inserted in packs and featuring green foil, this is a partial parallel to the Triple Crown insert set. Only the first 150 cards are featured in this and these have stated print runs to the players 2001 batting average. Since each card has a different print run we have notated that information in our checklist.

Nm-Mt Ex-Mt
*BATTING AVG: 4X TO 10X BASIC CARDS
PRINT RUNS: 221-350 OF EACH CARD
SEE BECKETT.COM FOR EXACT PRINT RUNS
150-CARD SKIP-NUMBERED SET.......

2002 Fleer Triple Crown Home Run Parallel

Randomly inserted in packs and featuring red foil, this is a partial parallel to the Triple Crown insert set. Only the first 150 cards are featured in this and these have stated print runs to the players 2001 home run total. Since each card has a different print run we have notated that information in our checklist. Please note that if the card had a stated print run of 15 or less no pricing is provided due to market scarcity.

Nm-Mt Ex-Mt
*PRINT RUN b/wn 66-80: 10X TO 25X
*PRINT RUN b/wn 51-65: 12.5X TO 30X
*PRINT RUN b/wn 36-50: 15X TO 40X
*PRINT RUN b/wn 26-35: 20X TO 50X
*PRINT RUN b/wn 21-25: 25X TO 60X
*PRINT RUN b/wn 16-20: 30X TO 80X
SEE BECKETT.COM FOR EXACT PRINT RUNS
150-CARD SKIP-NUMBERED SET.......

2002 Fleer Triple Crown RBI Parallel

Randomly inserted in packs and featuring blue foil, this is a partial parallel to the Triple Crown insert set. Only the first 150 cards are featured in this and these have stated print runs to the players 2001 RBI total. Since each card has a different print run we have notated that information in our checklist.

Nm-Mt Ex-Mt
*PRINT RUN b/wn 151-200: 5X TO 12X
*PRINT RUN b/wn 121-150: 6X TO 15X
*PRINT RUN b/wn 81-120: 8X TO 20X
*PRINT RUN b/wn 66-80: 10X TO 25X
*PRINT RUN b/wn 51-65: 12.5X TO 30X
*PRINT RUN b/wn 36-50: 15X TO 40X
*PRINT RUN b/wn 26-35: 20X TO 50X
*PRINT RUN b/wn 21-25: 25X TO 60X
*PRINT RUN b/wn 16-20: 30X TO 80X
SEE BECKETT.COM FOR EXACT PRINT RUNS
150-CARD SKIP-NUMBERED SET.......

2002 Fleer Triple Crown Diamond Immortality

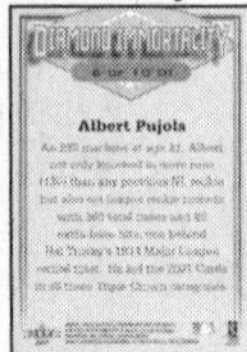

Inserted in packs at stated odds of one in 12 hobby and one in 20 retail, these 10 cards feature players who are on their way to becoming members of the Baseball Hall of Fame.

	Nm-Mt	Ex-Mt
COMPLETE SET (10)	40.00	12.00
1 Derek Jeter	6.00	1.80
2 Barry Bonds	6.00	1.80
3 Rickey Henderson	4.00	1.20
4 Roger Clemens	5.00	1.50
5 Alex Rodriguez	4.00	1.20
6 Albert Pujols	5.00	1.50
7 Nomar Garciaparra	4.00	1.20
8 Ichiro Suzuki	4.00	1.20
9 Chipper Jones	4.00	1.20
10 Ken Griffey Jr.	4.00	1.20

2002 Fleer Triple Crown Diamond Immortality Game Used

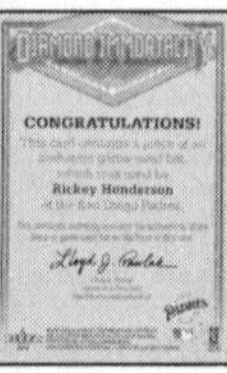

Inserted in packs at stated odds of one in 129, these eight cards are a partial parallel to the Diamond Immortality insert set. A couple of players were printed to a shorter print run and we have notated that information in our checklist with stated print run information.

	Nm-Mt	Ex-Mt
*MULTI-COLOR PATCH: .75X TO 2X BASIC		
1 Barry Bonds Pants	25.00	7.50
2 Roger Clemens Jsy	30.00	9.00
3 N.Garciaparra Jsy SP/150	40.00	12.00

4 Rickey Henderson Bat 15.00 4.50
5 Derek Jeter Bat 30.00 9.00
6 Chipper Jones Bat 15.00 4.50
7 Albert Pujols Jsy 30.00 9.00
8 Alex Rodriguez Jsy SP/400 25.00 7.50

2002 Fleer Triple Crown Home Run Kings

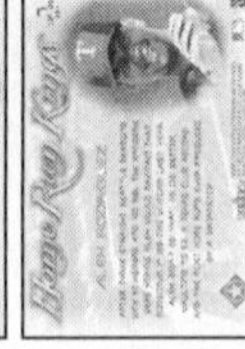

Inserted at stated odds of one in 24 hobby and one in 36 retail packs, these 25 cards feature a mix of active and retired sluggers.

	Nm-Mt	Ex-Mt
COMPLETE SET (25)	150.00	45.00
1 Ted Williams	15.00	4.50
2 Todd Helton	5.00	1.50
3 Eddie Murray	8.00	2.40
4 Jeff Bagwell	5.00	1.50
5 Babe Ruth	20.00	6.00
6 Eddie Mathews	8.00	2.40
7 Alex Rodriguez	10.00	3.00
8 Juan Gonzalez	6.00	1.80
9 Chipper Jones	6.00	1.80
10 Luis Gonzalez	5.00	1.50
11 Johnny Bench	8.00	2.40
12 Frank Thomas	6.00	1.80
13 Ernie Banks	8.00	2.40
14 Jimmie Foxx	8.00	2.40
15 Ken Griffey Jr.	10.00	3.00
16 Rafael Palmeiro	5.00	1.50
17 Sammy Sosa	10.00	3.00
18 Reggie Jackson	5.00	1.50
19 Barry Bonds	15.00	4.50
20 Willie McCovey	5.00	1.50
21 Manny Ramirez	5.00	1.50
22 Larry Walker	6.00	1.80
23 Jason Giambi	6.00	1.80
24 Mike Piazza	10.00	3.00
25 Jose Canseco	6.00	1.80

2002 Fleer Triple Crown Home Run Kings Autographs

Randomly inserted in packs, these cards are a partial parallel to the Home Run Kings insert set. Each player signed cards which matched their leading homer total for a season and we have notated that information in our checklist. All cards were exchange cards and they could be redeemed until January 31, 2003.

	Nm-Mt	Ex-Mt
1 Johnny Bench/45		
2 Barry Bonds EXCH	300.00	90.00
3 Alex Rodriguez/52 UER	150.00	45.00

Alex spelled as Aleh and Texas spelled as Tehas

2002 Fleer Triple Crown Home Run Kings Game Used

Inserted in packs at stated odds of one in 155, these 16 cards are a partial parallel to the Home Run Kings insert set. A couple of players were printed to a shorter print run and we have notated that information in our checklist with stated print run information.

*JERSEYS w/PATCH: .75X TO 2X HI COLUMN

	Nm-Mt	Ex-Mt
1 Jeff Bagwell Jsy	15.00	4.50
2 Johnny Bench Bat SP/90		
3 Barry Bonds Jsy	30.00	9.00
4 Jimmie Foxx Bat	50.00	15.00
5 Jason Giambi Jsy	15.00	4.50
6 Reggie Jackson Bat	15.00	4.50
7 Eddie Mathews Bat	15.00	4.50
8 Eddie Murray Bat	15.00	4.50
9 Rafael Palmeiro Bat	15.00	4.50
10 Mike Piazza Jsy	25.00	7.50
11 Manny Ramirez Bat SP/40		
12 Todd Helton Bat	15.00	4.50
13 Alex Rodriguez Bat	25.00	7.50
14 Babe Ruth Bat SP/27		
15 Larry Walker Bat	15.00	4.50
16 Ted Williams Jsy	100.00	30.00

2002 Fleer Triple Crown RBI Kings

Inserted at stated odds of one in 144 hobby and one in 288 retail, these 15 cards feature the leading run producers in the game today.

	Nm-Mt	Ex-Mt
COMPLETE SET (15)	200.00	60.00
1 Sammy Sosa	20.00	6.00
2 Todd Helton	10.00	3.00
3 Albert Pujols	25.00	7.50
4 Manny Ramirez	10.00	3.00
5 Luis Gonzalez	10.00	3.00
6 Shawn Green	10.00	3.00
7 Barry Bonds	30.00	9.00
8 Ken Griffey Jr.	20.00	6.00
9 Alex Rodriguez	25.00	7.50
10 Jason Giambi	12.00	3.60
11 Jeff Bagwell	10.00	3.00
12 Vladimir Guerrero	12.00	3.60
13 Juan Gonzalez	12.00	3.60
14 Chipper Jones	12.00	3.60
15 Mike Piazza	20.00	6.00

2002 Fleer Triple Crown RBI Kings Game Used

Inserted in packs at stated odds of one in 70, these 11 cards are a partial parallel to the RBI Kings insert set. A couple of cards were printed to a shorter print run and we have notated that information in our checklist with stated print run information.

	Nm-Mt	Ex-Mt
1 Jeff Bagwell Jsy	15.00	4.50
2 Barry Bonds Pants	25.00	7.50
3 Jason Giambi Jsy	15.00	4.50
4 Luis Gonzalez Bat	10.00	3.00
5 Juan Gonzalez Bat	15.00	4.50
6 Shawn Green Jsy	10.00	3.00
7 Todd Helton Jsy	15.00	4.50
8 Mike Piazza Jsy	25.00	7.50
9 Albert Pujols Bat SP/80		
10 Manny Ramirez Bat	10.00	3.00
11 Alex Rodriguez Shoe SP/500	25.00	7.50

2002 Fleer Triple Crown Season Crowns

Inserted at stated odds of one in 12 hobby and one in 20 retail, these 10 cards feature three players who are among the best at any specific category.

	Nm-Mt	Ex-Mt
COMPLETE SET (10)	40.00	12.00
1 Barry Bonds Sammy Sosa Luis Gonzalez	6.00	1.80
2 Larry Walker Nomar Garciaparra Todd Helton	4.00	1.20
3 Sammy Sosa Todd Helton Manny Ramirez	4.00	1.20
4 Pedro Martinez Derek Jeter Cal Ripken	8.00	2.40
5 Jose Canseco Barry Bonds Alex Rodriguez	6.00	1.80
6 Barry Bonds Jeff Kent Chipper Jones	5.00	1.50
7 Ichiro Suzuki Jason Giambi Ivan Rodriguez	4.00	1.20
8 Curt Schilling Tom Glavine Pedro Martinez	2.50	.75
9 Randy Johnson Pedro Martinez Greg Maddux	4.00	1.20
10 Radny Johnson Curt Schilling John Smoltz	2.50	.75

2002 Fleer Triple Crown Season Crowns Autographs

Randomly inserted in packs, these two cards are a partial parallel to the Seacon Crowns insert set. Each player signed a different number of cards Both cards were exchange cards and they could be redeemed until February 25, 2003.

	Nm-Mt	Ex-Mt
SC-BB Barry Bonds/77	300.00	90.00
SC-DJ Derek Jeter/160	200.00	60.00

2002 Fleer Triple Crown Season Crowns Game Used

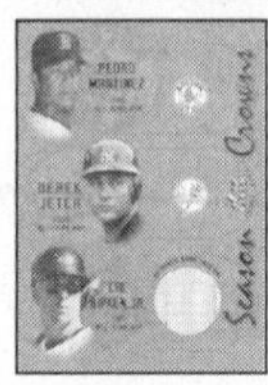

Inserted in packs at stated odds of one in 90, these 30 cards are a parallel plus to the Season Crowns insert set. Each player on each card had one piece of memorabilia attached to the card. A couple of cards were printed to a shorter print run and we have notated that information in our checklist with stated print run information.

	Nm-Mt	Ex-Mt
1A Barry Bonds HR Jsy Sammy Sosa Luis Gonzalez	30.00	9.00
1B Sammy Sosa HR Base Barry Bonds Luis Gonzalez	25.00	7.50
2A Larry Walker BA Bat Nomar Garciaparra Todd Helton	10.00	3.00
2B Nomar Garciaparra BA Jsy Larry Walker Todd Helton	25.00	7.50
2C Todd Helton BA Jsy Larry Walker Nomar Garciaparra	15.00	4.50
3A Sammy Sosa RBI Base Todd Helton Manny Ramirez	25.00	7.50
3B Todd Helton RBI Jsy Sammy Sosa Manny Ramirez	15.00	4.50
3C Manny Ramirez RBI Jsy Sammy Sosa Todd Helton	10.00	3.00
4A Pedro Martinez AS Jsy Derek Jeter Cal Ripken	15.00	4.50
4B Derek Jeter AS Pants Pedro Martinez Cal Ripken	30.00	9.00
4C Cal Ripken AS Bat SP/75 Pedro Martinez Derek Jeter	80.00	24.00
5A Jose Canseco 40/40 Jsy Barry Bonds Alex Rodriguez	15.00	4.50
5B Barry Bonds 40/40 Jsy Jose Canseco Alex Rodriguez	30.00	9.00
5C Alex Rodriguez 40/40 Jsy Jose Canseco Barry Bonds	25.00	7.50
6A Barry Bonds MVP Jsy Jeff Kent Chipper Jones	30.00	9.00
6B Jeff Kent MVP Jsy Barry Bonds Chipper Jones	10.00	3.00
7A Ichiro Suzuki MVP Base Jason Giambi Ivan Rodriguez	30.00	9.00
7B Jason Giambi MVP Jsy Ichiro Suzuki Ivan Rodriguez	15.00	4.50
7C Ivan Rodriguez MVP Jsy Ichiro Suzuki Jason Giambi	15.00	4.50
8A Curt Schilling Wins Jsy Tom Glavine Pedro Martinez	15.00	4.50
8B Tom Glavine Wins Jsy Curt Schilling Pedro Martinez	15.00	4.50
8C Pedro Martinez Wins Jsy Curt Schilling Tom Glavine	15.00	4.50
9A Randy Johnson ERA Jsy Pedro Martinez Greg Maddux	15.00	4.50
9B Pedro Martinez ERA Jsy Randy Johnson Greg Maddux	15.00	4.50
9C Greg Maddux Jersey Randy Johnson Pedro Martinez	15.00	4.50
10A Randy Johnson K's Jsy Curt Schilling John Smoltz	15.00	4.50
10B Curt Schilling K's Jsy Randy Johnson John Smoltz	15.00	4.50
10C John Smoltz K's Jersey Randy Johnson Curt Schilling	15.00	4.50

2002 Fleer Triple Crown Season Crowns Triple Swatch

Randomly inserted in packs, these eight cards are a partial parallel to the Seasons Crown insert set. These cards feature three different swatches and have a stated print run of 100 sequentially numbered sets.

	Nm-Mt	Ex-Mt
1 Barry Bonds Jsy Sammy Sosa Base Luis Gonzalez Bat	100.00	30.00
2 Larry Walker Bat Nomar Garciaparra Jsy Todd Helton Jsy	60.00	18.00
3 Sammy Sosa Base Todd Helton Jsy Manny Ramirez Jsy	60.00	18.00
6 Barry Bonds Jsy Jeff Kent Jsy Chipper Jones Bat	100.00	30.00
7 Ichiro Suzuki Base Jason Giambi Jsy Ivan Rodriguez Jsy	100.00	30.00
8 Curt Schilling Jsy Tom Glavine Jsy Pedro Martinez Jsy	60.00	18.00
9 Randy Johnson Jsy Pedro Martinez Jsy Greg Maddux Jsy	60.00	18.00
10 Randy Johnson Jsy Curt Schilling Jsy John Smoltz Jsy	60.00	18.00

2001 Fleer White Rose

This 38-card set was released along with the PT-Cruiser series of cars in 2001 in conjunction with Fleer Trading Cards and White Rose Collectibles. Please note that each card contains a "White Rose" logo in the lower corner. We are pricing the combination of the card and the cruiser on this.

	Nm-Mt	Ex-Mt
COMPLETE SET (38)	150.00	45.00
1 Cal Ripken	10.00	3.00
2 Nomar Garciaparra	5.00	1.50
3 Pedro Martinez	5.00	1.50
4 Troy Glaus	4.00	1.20
5 Frank Thomas	4.00	1.20
6 Roberto Alomar	4.00	1.20
7 Jim Thome	4.00	1.20
8 Bobby Higginson	2.00	.60
9 Jermaine Dye	2.00	.60
10 Jeromy Burnitz	2.00	.60
11 Matt Lawton	1.00	.30
12 Derek Jeter	10.00	3.00
13 Roger Clemens	6.00	1.80
14 Bernie Williams	4.00	1.20
15 Jason Giambi	4.00	1.20
16 Kazuhiro Sasaki	4.00	1.20
17 Edgar Martinez	2.50	.75
18 Alex Rodriguez	6.00	1.80
19 Ivan Rodriguez	5.00	1.50
20 Carlos Delgado	5.00	1.50
21 Chipper Jones	6.00	1.80
22 Sammy Sosa	6.00	1.80
23 Ken Griffey	6.00	1.80
24 Jeff Bagwell	5.00	1.50
25 Shawn Green	5.00	1.50
26 Vladimir Guerrero	5.00	1.50
27 Mike Piazza	6.00	1.80
28 Edgardo Alfonzo	2.00	.60
29 Pat Burrell	2.00	.60
30 Jason Kendall	2.00	.60
31 Mark McGwire	8.00	2.40
32 Jim Edmonds	2.00	.60
33 Tony Gwynn	6.00	1.80
34 Barry Bonds	6.00	1.80
35 Todd Helton	5.00	1.50
36 Preston Wilson	2.00	.60
37 Randy Johnson	5.00	1.50
38 Fred McGriff	2.00	.60

1916 Fleischmann Bread D381

This 103-card set was produced by Fleischmann Breads in 1916. These unnumbered cards are arranged here for convenience in alphabetical order; cards with tabs intact are worth 50 percent more than the prices listed below. The cards measure approximately 2 3/4" by 5 1/2" (with tab) or 2 3/4" by 4 13/16" (without tab). There is also a similar set issued by Ferguson Bread which is harder to find and is distinguished by having the photo caption written on only one line rather than two as with the Fleischmann cards.

	Ex-Mt	VG
COMPLETE SET	7000.00	3500.00
1 Babe Adams	50.00	25.00
2 Grover C. Alexander	200.00	100.00
3 Walt E. Alexander	40.00	20.00
4 Frank Allen	40.00	20.00
5 Fred Anderson	40.00	20.00
6 Dave Bancroft	80.00	40.00
7 Jack Barry	40.00	20.00
8 Beals Becker	40.00	20.00
9 Beals Becker Copyright logo more prevalent	40.00	20.00
10 Eddie Burns	40.00	20.00
11 George J. Burns	40.00	20.00
12 Bobby Byrne	40.00	20.00
13 Ray B. Caldwell	40.00	20.00
14 James Callahan P/MG	40.00	20.00
15 William Carrigan MG	40.00	20.00
16 Larry Cheney	40.00	20.00
17 Tom Clarke Photo goes to waist	40.00	20.00
18 Tom Clark Photo shows his pants	40.00	20.00
19 Ty Cobb	1500.00	750.00
20 Ray W. Collins	40.00	20.00
21 Ray Collins Copyright logo more prominent	40.00	20.00
22 Jack Coombs	60.00	30.00
23 A. Wilbur Cooper	40.00	20.00
24 George Cutshaw	40.00	20.00
25 Jake Daubert	50.00	25.00
26 Wheezer Dell	40.00	20.00
27 Bill Donovan	40.00	20.00
28 Larry Doyle	50.00	25.00
29 R.J. Egan	40.00	20.00
30 Johnny Evers	120.00	60.00
31 Ray Fisher	40.00	20.00
32 Harry Gardner (Sic)	40.00	20.00
33 Joe Gedeon	40.00	20.00
34 Larry Gilbert	40.00	20.00
35 Frank Gilhooley	40.00	20.00
36 Hank Gowdy	50.00	25.00
37 Sylvanus Gregg	40.00	20.00
38 Tom Griffith	40.00	20.00
39 Heinie Groh	50.00	25.00
40 Robert Harmon	40.00	20.00
41 Roy A. Hartzell	40.00	20.00
42 Claude Hendricks	40.00	20.00
43 Olaf Hendriksen	40.00	20.00
44 Buck Herzog P/MG	40.00	20.00
45 Hugh High	40.00	20.00
46 Dick Hoblitzell	40.00	20.00
47 Herb H. Hunter	40.00	20.00
48 Harold Janvrin	40.00	20.00
49 Hugh Jennings MG	80.00	40.00
50 John Johnston	40.00	20.00
51 Erving Kantlehner	40.00	20.00
52 Bennie Kauff	50.00	25.00
53 Ray H. Keating	40.00	20.00
54 Wade Killefer	40.00	20.00
55 Elmer Knetzer	40.00	20.00
56 Brad W. Kocher	40.00	20.00
57 Ed Konetchy	40.00	20.00
58 Fred Lauderus (Sic)	40.00	20.00
59 Dutch Leonard	50.00	25.00
60 Duffy Lewis	50.00	25.00
61 E.H.(Slim) Love	40.00	20.00
62 Albert L. Mamaux	40.00	20.00
63 Rabbit Maranville	80.00	40.00
64 Rube Marquard	80.00	40.00
65 Christy Mathewson	400.00	200.00
66 Bill McKechnie	80.00	40.00
67 Chief Meyer (Sic)	50.00	25.00
68 Otto Miller	40.00	20.00
69 Fred Mollwitz	40.00	20.00
70 Herbie Moran	40.00	20.00
71 Mike Mowrey	40.00	20.00
72 Dan Murphy	40.00	20.00
73 Art Nehf	50.00	25.00
74 Rube Oldring	40.00	20.00
75 Oliver O'Mara	40.00	20.00
76 Dode Paskert	40.00	20.00
77 D.C.Pat Ragan	40.00	20.00
78 Wm.A. Rariden	40.00	20.00
79 Davis Robertson	40.00	20.00
80 Wm. Rodgers	40.00	20.00
81 Edw.F.Rousch (Sic)	120.00	60.00
82 Nap Rucker	50.00	25.00
83 Dick Rudolph	40.00	20.00
84 Walter Schang	50.00	25.00
85 A.J.(Rube) Schauer	40.00	20.00
86 Pete Schneider	40.00	20.00
87 Ferd M. Schupp	40.00	20.00
88 Ernie Shore	50.00	25.00
89 Red Smith	40.00	20.00
90 Fred Snodgrass	50.00	25.00
91 Tris Speaker	200.00	100.00
92 George Stallings MG	40.00	20.00
93 Casey Stengel Sic, Stengle	400.00	200.00
94 Sailor Stroud	40.00	20.00
95 Amos Strunk	40.00	20.00
96 Chas.(Jeff) Tesreau	40.00	20.00
97 Chester D. Thomas	40.00	20.00
98 Chester D. Thomas Copyright logo more prominent	40.00	20.00
99 Fred Toney	40.00	20.00
100 Walter Tragresser	40.00	20.00
101 Honus Wagner	400.00	200.00
102 Carl Weilman	40.00	20.00
103 Zack Wheat	80.00	40.00
104 George Whitted	40.00	20.00
105 Arthur Wilson	40.00	20.00
106 Ivy Wingo	40.00	20.00
107 Joe Wood	60.00	30.00

2003 Flipp Sports Booklets

These booklets were issued to show, if fanned in quick order, two fast action photos of the featured player. Each player is mentioned on the outside covers and the inside covers feature biographical information as well as career statistics. Since these booklets are not numbered, we have sequenced them alphabetically.

	Nm-Mt	Ex-Mt
COMPLETE SET	60.00	18.00
1 Garrett Anderson	3.00	.90
2 Lance Berkman	4.00	1.20
3 Barry Bonds	5.00	1.50
4 Nomar Garciaparra	5.00	1.50
5 Jason Giambi	4.00	1.20
6 Troy Glaus	3.00	.90
7 Luis Gonzalez	2.50	.75
8 Torii Hunter	1.50	.45
9 Derek Jeter	10.00	3.00
10 Mike Piazza	6.00	1.80
11 Albert Pujols	6.00	1.80
12 Manny Ramirez	4.00	1.20
13 Alex Rodriguez	6.00	1.80
14 Curt Schilling Randy Johnson	4.00	1.20
15 Alfonso Soriano	3.00	.90
16 Sammy Sosa	5.00	1.50
17 Sammy Sosa Jason Giambi	4.00	1.20
18 Ichiro Suzuki	6.00	1.80
19 Mike Sweeney	2.50	.75
20 Miguel Tejada	3.00	.90

1987 Red Foley Sticker Book

The 1987 Red Foley's Best Baseball Book Ever was published by Simon and Schuster and measures 8 1/2" by 11. The book includes 130 stickers, puzzles, quizzes, how-to's, and other trivia features. The stickers appear on four insert pages in the middle of the album. Each sticker measures 1 3/8" by 1 7/8" and displays a glossy color player photo bordered in white. The stickers are to be pasted in the appropriate slots next to a trivia question about the player. The stickers are numbered on the front and checklisted below accordingly.

	Nm-Mt	Ex-Mt
COMPLETE SET (130)	12.00	4.80
1 Julio Franco	.10	.04
2 Willie Randolph	.10	.04
3 Jesse Barfield	.05	.02
4 Mike Witt	.05	.02
5 Orel Hershiser	.10	.04
6 Dwight Gooden	.25	.10
7 Dan Quisenberry	.05	.02
8 Vince Coleman	.05	.02
9 Rich Gossage	.10	.04
10 Kirk Gibson	.10	.04
11 Joaquin Andujar	.05	.02
12 David Concepcion	.10	.04
13 Andre Dawson	.50	.20
14 Tippy Martinez	.05	.02
15 Bob James	.05	.02
16 Ryne Sandberg	.75	.30
17 Bob Knepper	.05	.02
18 Bob Stanley	.05	.02
19 Jim Presley	.05	.02
20 Greg Gross	.05	.02
21 Bob Horner	.05	.02
22 Paul Molitor	.75	.30
23 Kirby Puckett	.75	.30
24 Scott Garrelts	.05	.02
25 Tony Pena	.10	.04
26 Charlie Hough	.05	.02
27 Joe Carter	.25	.10
28 Dave Winfield	.75	.30
29 Tony Fernandez	.05	.02
30 Bobby Grich	.10	.04
31 Mike Marshall	.05	.02
32 Keith Hernandez	.10	.04
33 Dennis Leonard	.05	.02
34 John Tudor	.05	.02
35 Kevin McReynolds	.05	.02
36 Lance Parrish	.10	.04
37 Carney Lansford	.10	.04
38 Buddy Bell	.10	.04
39 Tim Raines	.10	.04
40 Mike Boddicker	.05	.02
41 Carlton Fisk	.50	.20
42 Lee Smith	.25	.10
43 Glenn Davis	.05	.02
44 Jim Rice	.10	.04
45 Mark Langston	.05	.02
46 Mike Schmidt	1.00	.40
47 Dale Murphy	.50	.20
48 Cecil Cooper	.10	.04
49 Kent Hrbek	.10	.04
50 Will Clark	1.00	.40
51 Johnny Ray	.05	.02
52 Darrell Porter	.05	.02
53 Brook Jacoby	.05	.02
54 Ron Guidry	.10	.04
55 Lloyd Moseby	.05	.02
56 Donnie Moore	.05	.02
57 Fernando Valenzuela	.10	.04
58 Darryl Strawberry	.10	.04
59 Hal McRae	.10	.04
60 Tommy Herr	.05	.02
61 Steve Garvey	.25	.10
62 Alan Trammell	.25	.10
63 Jose Canseco	.50	.20
64 Pete Rose	1.00	.40
65 Jeff Reardon	.10	.04
66 Eddie Murray	.75	.30
67 Ozzie Guillen	.10	.04
68 Jody Davis	.05	.02
69 Bill Doran	.05	.02
70 Roger Clemens	1.50	.60
71 Alvin Davis	.05	.02
72 Von Hayes	.05	.02
73 Zane Smith	.05	.02
74 Ted Higuera	.05	.02
75 Tom Brunansky	.05	.02
76 Chili Davis	.25	.10
77 R.J. Reynolds	.05	.02
78 Oddibe McDowell	.05	.02
79 Brett Butler	.10	.04
80 Rickey Henderson	1.25	.50
81 Dave Stieb	.05	.02
82 Wally Joyner	.50	.20
83 Pedro Guerrero	.05	.02
84 Jesse Orosco	.10	.04
85 Steve Balboni	.05	.02
86 Willie McGee	.10	.04
87 Graig Nettles	.10	.04
88 Lou Whitaker	.10	.04
89 Jay Howell	.05	.02
90 Dave Parker	.10	.04
91 Hubie Brooks	.05	.02
92 Rick Dempsey	.10	.04
93 Neil Allen	.05	.02
94 Shawon Dunston	.05	.02
95 Jose Cruz	.10	.04
96 Wade Boggs	.75	.30
97 Danny Tartabull	.05	.02
98 Steve Bedrosian	.05	.02
99 Ken Oberkfell	.05	.02
100 Ben Oglivie	.05	.02
101 Bert Blyleven	.10	.04
102 Jeff Leonard	.05	.02
103 Rick Rhoden	.05	.02
104 Larry Parrish	.05	.02
105 Tony Bernazard	.05	.02
106 Don Mattingly	1.50	.60
107 Willie Upshaw	.05	.02
108 Reggie Jackson	.75	.30
109 Bill Madlock	.10	.04
110 Gary Carter	.75	.30
111 George Brett	1.25	.50
112 Ozzie Smith	.75	.30
113 Tony Gwynn	1.50	.60
114 Jack Morris	.10	.04
115 Dave Kingman	.10	.04
116 John Franco	.10	.04
117 Tim Wallach	.05	.02
118 Cal Ripken	3.00	1.20
119 Harold Baines	.10	.04
120 Leon Durham	.05	.02
121 Nolan Ryan	3.00	1.20
122 Dennis(Oil Can) Boyd	.05	.02
123 Matt Young	.05	.02
124 Shane Rawley	.05	.02
125 Bruce Sutter	.05	.02
126 Robin Yount	.75	.30
127 Frank Viola	.05	.02
128 Vida Blue	.10	.04
129 Rick Reuschel	.10	.04
130 Pete Incaviglia	.10	.04

1988 Red Foley Sticker Book

The 1988 Red Foley's Best Baseball Book Ever was published by Simon and Schuster and measures 8 1/2" by 11. The book includes 130 stickers (representing 104 players and 26 teams), puzzles, quizzes, how-to's, and other trivia features. The stickers appear on four insert pages in the middle of the album. Each sticker measures 1 3/8" by 1 7/8" and displays a glossy color player photo bordered in white. The stickers are to be pasted in the appropriate slots next to a trivia question about the player. The stickers are numbered on the front and present the players in alphabetical order.

	Nm-Mt	Ex-Mt
COMPLETE SET (130)	8.00	3.20
1 Mike Aldrete	.05	.02
2 Alan Ashby	.05	.02
3 Harold Baines	.10	.04
4 Floyd Bannister	.05	.02
5 Buddy Bell	.10	.04
6 George Bell	.05	.02
7 Barry Bonds	2.00	.80
8 Scott Bradley	.05	.02
9 Bob Brower	.05	.02
10 Ellis Burks	.50	.20
11 Casey Candaele	.05	.02
12 Jack Clark	.10	.04
13 Roger Clemens	1.50	.60
14 Kal Daniels	.05	.02
15 Eric Davis	.10	.04
16 Mike Davis	.05	.02
17 Andre Dawson	.25	.10
18 Rob Deer	.05	.02
19 Brian Downing	.05	.02
20 Doug Drabek	.05	.02
21 Dwight Evans	.10	.04
22 Sid Fernandez	.05	.02
23 Carlton Fisk	.40	.16
24 Scott Fletcher	.05	.02
25 Julio Franco	.10	.04
26 Gary Gaetti	.10	.04
27 Ken Gerhart	.05	.02
28 Ken Griffey	.10	.04
29 Pedro Guerrero	.05	.02
30 Billy Hatcher	.05	.02
31 Mike Heath	.05	.02
32 Neal Heaton	.05	.02
33 Tom Henke	.05	.02
34 Larry Herndon	.05	.02
35 Brian Holton	.05	.02
36 Glenn Hubbard	.05	.02
37 Bruce Hurst	.05	.02
38 Bo Jackson	.40	.16
39 Michael Jackson	.05	.02
40 Howard Johnson	.05	.02
41 Wally Joyner	.10	.04
42 Jimmy Key	.05	.02
43 Ray Knight	.05	.02
44 John Kruk	.10	.04
45 Mike Krukow	.05	.02
46 Mark Langston	.05	.02
47 Gene Larkin	.05	.02
48 Jeff Leonard	.05	.02
49 Bill Long	.05	.02
50 Fred Lynn	.05	.02
51 Dave Magadan	.05	.02
52 Joe Magrane	.05	.02
53 Don Mattingly	1.50	.60
54 Fred McGriff	.50	.20
55 Mark McGwire	2.50	1.00
56 Kevin McReynolds	.05	.02
57 Dave Meads	.05	.02
58 Keith Moreland	.05	.02
59 Dale Murphy	.25	.10
60 Juan Nieves	.05	.02
61 Paul Noce	.05	.02
62 Matt Nokes	.05	.02
63 Pete O'Brien	.05	.02
64 Paul O'Neill	.15	.06
65 Lance Parrish	.05	.02
66 Larry Parrish	.05	.02
67 Tony Pena	.10	.04
68 Terry Pendleton	.10	.04
69 Ken Phelps	.05	.02
70 Dan Plesac	.05	.02
71 Luis Polonia	.05	.02
72 Kirby Puckett	.50	.20
73 Jeff Reardon	.10	.04
74 Rick Rhoden	.05	.02
75 Dave Righetti	.05	.02
76 Cal Ripken	3.00	1.20
77 Bret Saberhagen	.10	.04
78 Benito Santiago	.10	.04
79 Mike Schmidt	1.00	.40
80 Dick Schofield	.05	.02
81 Mike Scott	.05	.02
82 John Smiley	.10	.04
83 Cory Snyder	.05	.02
84 Franklin Stubbs	.05	.02
85 B.J. Surhoff	.10	.04
86 Rick Sutcliffe	.05	.02
87 Pat Tabler	.05	.02
88 Danny Tartabull	.05	.02
89 Garry Templeton	.05	.02
90 Walt Terrell	.05	.02
91 Andre Thornton	.05	.02
92 Andy Van Slyke	.10	.04
93 Ozzie Virgil	.05	.02
94 Tim Wallach	.05	.02
95 Gary Ward	.05	.02
96 Mark Wasinger	.05	.02
97 Mitch Webster	.05	.02
98 Bob Welch	.10	.04
99 Devon White	.10	.04
100 Frank White	.10	.04
101 Ed Whitson	.05	.02
102 Bill Wilkinson	.05	.02
103 Glenn Wilson	.05	.02
104 Curt Young	.05	.02
105 Atlanta Braves	.05	.02
106 Philadelphia Phillies	.05	.02
107 San Diego Padres	.05	.02
108 San Francisco Giants	.05	.02
109 Baltimore Orioles	.05	.02
110 Detroit Tigers	.05	.02
111 Pittsburgh Pirates	.05	.02
112 Kansas City Royals	.05	.02
113 Houston Astros	.05	.02
114 Cleveland Indians	.05	.02
115 Milwaukee Brewers	.05	.02
116 St. Louis Cardinals	.05	.02
117 Chicago White Sox	.05	.02
118 Toronto Blue Jays	.05	.02
119 Boston Red Sox	.05	.02
120 Oakland A's	.05	.02
121 Chicago Cubs	.05	.02
122 Seattle Mariners	.05	.02
123 Texas Rangers	.05	.02
124 Los Angeles Dodgers	.05	.02
125 New York Yankees	.05	.02
126 New York Mets	.05	.02
127 Minnesota Twins	.05	.02
128 Montreal Expos	.05	.02
129 California Angels	.05	.02
130 Cincinnati Reds	.05	.02

1989 Red Foley Sticker Book

The 1989 Red Foley's Best Baseball Book Ever was published by Simon and Schuster and measures 8 1/2" by 11. The book includes 130 stickers, puzzles, quizzes, how-to's, and other trivia features. The stickers appear on four insert pages in the middle of the album. Each sticker measures 1 3/8" by 1 7/8" and displays a glossy color player photo bordered in white. The stickers are to be pasted in the appropriate slots next to a trivia question about the player. The stickers are numbered on the front and present the players in alphabetical order.

	Nm-Mt	Ex-Mt
COMPLETE SET (130)	15.00	6.00
1 Doyle Alexander	.05	.02
2 Luis Alicea	.05	.02
3 Roberto Alomar	1.00	.40
4 Alan Ashby	.05	.02
5 Floyd Bannister	.05	.02
6 Jesse Barfield	.05	.02
7 George Bell	.05	.02
8 Wade Boggs	.50	.20
9 Barry Bonds	1.50	.60
10 Bobby Bonilla	.10	.04
11 Chris Bosio	.05	.02
12 George Brett	1.25	.50
13 Hubie Brooks	.05	.02
14 Tom Brunansky	.05	.02
15 Tim Burke	.05	.02
16 Ivan Calderon	.05	.02
17 Tom Candiotti	.05	.02
18 Jose Canseco	.40	.16
19 Gary Carter	.50	.20
20 Joe Carter	.15	.06
21 Jack Clark	.05	.02
22 Will Clark	.50	.20
23 Roger Clemens	1.50	.60
24 David Cone	.40	.16
25 Ed Correa	.05	.02
26 Kal Daniels	.05	.02
27 Alvin Davis	.05	.02
28 Chili Davis	.10	.04
29 Eric Davis	.10	.04
30 Glenn Davis	.05	.02
31 Jody Davis	.05	.02
32 Mark Davis	.05	.02
33 Andre Dawson	.25	.10
34 Rob Deer	.05	.02
35 Jose DeLeon	.05	.02
36 Bo Diaz	.05	.02
37 Bill Doran	.05	.02
38 Shawon Dunston	.05	.02
39 Dennis Eckersley	.50	.20
40 Dwight Evans	.10	.04
41 Tony Fernandez	.10	.04
42 Brian Fisher	.05	.02
43 Carlton Fisk	.50	.20
44 Mike Flanagan	.05	.02
45 John Franco	.05	.02
46 Gary Gaetti	.10	.04
47 Andres Galarraga	.25	.10
48 Scott Garrelts	.05	.02
49 Kirk Gibson	.10	.04
50 Dan Gladden	.05	.02
51 Dwight Gooden	.10	.04
52 Pedro Guerrero	.05	.02
53 Ozzie Guillen	.10	.04
54 Tony Gwynn	1.25	.50
55 Mel Hall	.05	.02
56 Von Hayes	.05	.02
57 Keith Hernandez	.10	.04
58 Orel Hershiser	.10	.04
59 Ted Higuera	.05	.02
60 Charlie Hough	.10	.04
61 Jack Howell	.05	.02
62 Kent Hrbek	.10	.04
63 Pete Incaviglia	.05	.02
64 Bo Jackson	.25	.10
65 Brook Jacoby	.05	.02
66 Chris James	.05	.02
67 Lance Johnson	.05	.02
68 Wally Joyner	.10	.04
69 Jack Kruk	.10	.04
70 Mike LaCoss	.05	.02
71 Mark Langston	.05	.02
72 Carney Lansford	.10	.04
73 Barry Larkin	.50	.20
74 Mike LaValliere	.05	.02
75 Jose Lind	.05	.02
76 Fred Lynn	.05	.02
77 Greg Maddux	2.00	.80
78 Candy Maldonado	.05	.02
79 Don Mattingly	1.50	.60
80 Mark McGwire	2.50	1.00
81 Paul Molitor	.50	.20
82 Jack Morris	.10	.04
83 Lloyd Moseby	.05	.02
84 Dale Murphy	.25	.10
85 Eddie Murray	.50	.20
86 Matt Nokes	.05	.02
87 Pete O'Brien	.05	.02
88 Rafael Palmeiro	.40	.16
89 Melido Perez	.05	.02
90 Gerald Perry	.05	.02
91 Tim Raines	.10	.04
92 Willie Randolph	.10	.04
93 Johnny Ray	.05	.02
94 Jeff Reardon	.10	.04
95 Jody Reed	.05	.02
96 Harold Reynolds	.10	.04
97 Dave Righetti	.10	.04
98 Billy Ripken	.05	.02
99 Cal Ripken Jr.	3.00	1.20
100 Nolan Ryan	3.00	1.20
101 Juan Samuel	.05	.02
102 Benito Santiago	.10	.04
103 Steve Sax	.05	.02
104 Mike Schmidt	1.00	.40
105 Rick Schu	.05	.02
106 Mike Scott	.05	.02
107 Kevin Seitzer	.05	.02
108 Ruben Sierra	.10	.04
109 Lee Smith	.10	.04
110 Ozzie Smith	.60	.24
111 Zane Smith	.05	.02
112 Dave Stewart	.10	.04
113 Darryl Strawberry	.10	.04
114 Bruce Sutter	.05	.02
115 Bill Swift	.05	.02
116 Greg Swindell	.05	.02
117 Frank Tanana	.05	.02
118 Danny Tartabull	.05	.02
119 Milt Thompson	.05	.02
120 Robby Thompson	.05	.02
121 Alan Trammell	.15	.06
122 John Tudor	.05	.02
123 Fernando Valenzuela	.10	.04
124 Dave Valle	.05	.02
125 Frank Viola	.05	.02
126 Ozzie Virgil	.05	.02
127 Tim Wallach	.05	.02
128 Dave Winfield	.40	.16
129 Mike Witt	.05	.02
130 Robin Yount	.50	.20

1990 Red Foley Sticker Book

The 1990 Red Foley's Best Baseball Book Ever was published by Simon and Schuster and measures 8 1/2" by 11. The book includes 130 stickers (104 players and 26 teams), puzzles, quizzes, how-to's, player-team matchups, and other trivia features. The stickers appear on four insert pages in the middle of the album. Each sticker measures 1 3/8" X 1 7/8" and displays a glossy color player photo bordered in white. The stickers are to be pasted in the appropriate slots next to a trivia question about the player. The stickers are numbered on the front and present the players in alphabetical order.

	Nm-Mt	Ex-Mt
COMPLETE SET (130)	15.00	4.50
1 Allan Anderson	.05	.02
2 Scott Bailes	.05	.02
3 Jeff Ballard	.05	.02
4 Jesse Barfield	.05	.02
5 Bert Blyleven	.10	.03
6 Wade Boggs	.75	.23
7 Barry Bonds	1.50	.45
8 Chris Bosio	.05	.02
9 George Brett	1.25	.35
10 Tim Burke	.05	.02
11 Ellis Burks	.15	.04
12 Brett Butler	.10	.03
13 Ivan Calderon	.05	.02
14 Jose Canseco	.50	.15
15 Joe Carter	.10	.03
16 Jack Clark	.10	.03
17 Will Clark	.50	.15
18 Roger Clemens	1.50	.45
19 Vince Coleman	.05	.02
20 Eric Davis	.10	.03
21 Glenn Davis	.05	.02
22 Mark Davis	.05	.02
23 Andre Dawson	.25	.07
24 Rob Deer	.05	.02
25 Jose DeLeon	.05	.02
26 Jim Deshaies	.05	.02
27 Doug Drabek	.05	.02
28 Lenny Dykstra	.10	.03
29 Dennis Eckersley	.50	.15
30 Steve Farr	.05	.02
31 Tony Fernandez	.05	.02
32 Carlton Fisk	.50	.15
33 John Franco	.10	.03
34 Julio Franco	.10	.03
35 Andres Galarraga	.25	.07
36 Tom Glavine	.25	.07
37 Dwight Gooden	.10	.03
38 Mark Grace	.50	.15
39 Mike Greenwell	.05	.02
40 Ken Griffey Jr.	2.50	.75
41 Kelly Gruber	.05	.02
42 Pedro Guerrero	.05	.02
43 Tony Gwynn	1.25	.35
44 Bryan Harvey	.05	.02
45 Von Hayes	.05	.02
46 Willie Hernandez	.05	.02
47 Tommy Herr	.05	.02
48 Orel Hershiser	.10	.03
49 Jay Howell	.05	.02
50 Kent Hrbek	.10	.03
51 Bo Jackson	.25	.07
52 Steve Jeltz	.05	.02
53 Jimmy Key	.05	.02
54 Ron Kittle	.05	.02
55 Mark Langston	.05	.02
56 Carney Lansford	.10	.03
57 Barry Larkin	.40	.12
58 Jeffrey Leonard	.05	.02
59 Don Mattingly	1.50	.45
60 Fred McGriff	.25	.07
61 Mark McGwire	2.50	.75
62 Kevin McReynolds	.05	.02
63 Randy Myers	.10	.03
64 Kevin Mitchell	.05	.02
65 Paul Molitor	.50	.15
66 Mike Morgan	.05	.02
67 Dale Murphy	.25	.07
68 Eddie Murray	.50	.15
69 Matt Nokes	.05	.02
70 Greg Olson	.05	.02
71 Paul O'Neill	.15	.04
72 Rafael Palmeiro	.75	.23
73 Lance Parrish	.05	.02
74 Dan Plesac	.05	.02
75 Kirby Puckett	.50	.15
76 Jeff Reardon	.10	.03
77 Rick Reuschel	.05	.02
78 Cal Ripken	3.00	.90
79 Dave Righetti	.05	.02
80 Jeff Russell	.05	.02
81 Nolan Ryan	3.00	.90
82 Benito Santiago	.10	.03
83 Steve Sax	.05	.02
84 Mike Schooler	.05	.02
85 Mike Scott	.05	.02
86 Kevin Seitzer	.05	.02
87 Dave Smith	.05	.02
88 Lonnie Smith	.05	.02
89 Ozzie Smith	.75	.23
90 John Smoltz	.25	.07
91 Cory Snyder	.05	.02
92 Darryl Strawberry	.10	.03
93 Greg Swindell	.05	.02
94 Mickey Tettleton	.10	.03
95 Bobby Thigpen	.05	.02
96 Alan Trammell	.15	.04
97 Dave Valle	.05	.02
98 Andy Van Slyke	.10	.03
99 Tim Wallach	.05	.02
100 Jerome Walton	.05	.02
101 Lou Whitaker	.10	.03
102 Devon White	.05	.02
103 Mitch Williams	.05	.02
104 Glenn Wilson	.05	.02
105 Cleveland Indians	.05	.02
106 Texas Rangers	.05	.02
107 Cincinnati Reds	.05	.02
108 Baltimore Orioles	.05	.02
109 Boston Red Sox	.05	.02
110 Chicago White Sox	.05	.02
111 Los Angeles Dodgers	.05	.02
112 Detroit Tigers	.05	.02
113 Seattle Mariners	.05	.02
114 Toronto Blue Jays	.05	.02
115 Montreal Expos	.05	.02

116 Pittsburgh Pirates .05 .02
117 Houston Astros .05 .02
118 St. Louis Cardinals .05 .02
119 San Diego Padres .05 .02
120 California Angels .05 .02
121 New York Yankees .05 .02
122 Chicago Cubs .05 .02
123 Milwaukee Brewers .05 .02
124 Minnesota Twins .05 .02
125 San Francisco Giants .05 .02
126 Kansas City Royals .05 .02
127 Oakland A's .05 .02
128 New York Mets .05 .02
129 Philadelphia Phillies .05 .02
130 Atlanta Braves .05 .02

1991 Red Foley Stickers

The 1991 Red Foley's Best Baseball Book Ever was published by Simon and Schuster and measures 8 1/2" by 11. The 95-page book includes 130 stickers, puzzles, quizzes, how-to's, player-team matchups, and other trivia features. The stickers appear on four insert pages in the middle of the album. Each sticker measures 1 3/8" by 1 7/8" and displays a glossy color player photo bordered in white. The stickers are to be pasted in the appropriate slots throughout the sticker album. Stickers 113-130 feature All-Stars. The stickers are numbered on the front and checklisted below accordingly.

Nm-Mt Ex-Mt
COMPLETE SET (130) 20.00 6.00
1 Jim Abbott .10 .03
2 Rick Aguilera .10 .03
3 Roberto Alomar .50 .15
4 Rob Dibble .10 .03
5 Wally Backman .05 .02
6 Harold Baines .10 .03
7 Steve Bedrosian .05 .02
8 Craig Biggio .25 .07
9 Wade Boggs 1.00 .30
10 Bobby Bonilla .05 .02
11 George Brett 1.50 .45
12 Greg Brock .05 .02
13 Hubie Brooks .05 .02
14 Tom Brunansky .05 .02
15 Tim Burke .05 .02
16 Tom Candiotti .05 .02
17 Jose Canseco 1.00 .30
18 Jack Clark .10 .03
19 Will Clark .75 .23
20 Roger Clemens 2.00 .60
21 Vince Coleman .05 .02
22 Kal Daniels .05 .02
23 Glenn Davis .05 .02
24 Mark Davis .05 .02
25 Andre Dawson .50 .15
26 Rob Deer .05 .02
27 Delino DeShields .10 .03
28 Doug Drabek .05 .02
29 Shawon Dunston .05 .02
30 Len Dykstra .10 .03
31 Dennis Eckersley .50 .15
32 Kevin Elster .05 .02
33 Tony Fernandez .10 .03
34 Cecil Fielder .10 .03
35 Chuck Finley .10 .03
36 Carlton Fisk .60 .18
37 Greg Gagne .05 .02
38 Ron Gant .10 .03
39 Tom Glavine .50 .15
40 Dwight Gooden .10 .03
41 Ken Griffey Jr. 3.00 .90
42 Kelly Gruber .05 .02
43 Pedro Guerrero .05 .02
44 Ozzie Guillen .10 .03
45 Pete Harnisch .05 .02
46 Billy Hatcher .05 .02
47 Von Hayes .05 .02
48 Rickey Henderson 1.00 .30
49 Mike Henneman .05 .02
50 Kent Hrbek .10 .03
51 Pete Incaviglia .05 .02
52 Howard Johnson .05 .02
53 Randy Johnson 1.50 .45
54 Doug Jones .05 .02
55 Ricky Jordan .05 .02
56 Wally Joyner .10 .03
57 Roberto Kelly .05 .02
58 Barry Larkin .50 .15
59 Craig Lefferts .05 .02
60 Candy Maldonado .05 .02
61 Don Mattingly 2.00 .60
62 Oddibe McDowell .05 .02
63 Roger McDowell .05 .02
64 Willie McGee .10 .03
65 Fred McGriff .25 .07
66 Kevin Mitchell .05 .02
67 Mike Morgan .05 .02
68 Eddie Murray .50 .15
69 Gregg Olson .05 .02
70 Joe Orsulak .05 .02
71 Dan Petry .05 .02
72 Dan Plesac .05 .02
73 Jim Presley .05 .02
74 Kirby Puckett .50 .15
75 Tim Raines .10 .03
76 Jeff Reardon .10 .03
77 Dave Righetti .05 .02
78 Cal Ripken 4.00 1.20
79 Nolan Ryan 4.00 1.20
80 Bret Saberhagen .10 .03
81 Chris Sabo .05 .02
82 Ryne Sandberg .50 .15
83 Benito Santiago .10 .03
84 Steve Sax .05 .02
85 Mike Schooler .05 .02
86 Mike Scott .05 .02
87 Ruben Sierra .10 .03
88 Cory Snyder .05 .02
89 Dave Stieb .10 .03
90 Dave Stewart .10 .03
91 Kurt Stillwell .05 .02
92 Bobby Thigpen .05 .02
93 Alan Trammell .25 .07
94 John Tudor .05 .02
95 Dave Valle .05 .02
96 Andy Van Slyke .10 .03
97 Robin Ventura .50 .15
98 Frank Viola .05 .02
99 Tim Wallach .05 .02
100 Matt Williams .25 .07
101 Mitch Williams .05 .02
102 Dave Winfield .50 .15
103 Eric Yelding .05 .02
104 Robin Yount .75 .23
105 Steve Avery .05 .02
106 Travis Fryman .50 .15
107 Juan Gonzalez .75 .23
108 Todd Hundley .50 .15
109 Ben McDonald .05 .02
110 Jose Offerman .05 .02
111 Frank Thomas .75 .23
112 Bernie Williams .50 .15
113 Sandy Alomar Jr. AS .10 .03
114 Jack Armstrong AS .05 .02
115 Wade Boggs AS .75 .23
116 Jose Canseco AS .40 .12
117 Will Clark AS .50 .15
118 Andre Dawson AS .50 .15
119 Len Dykstra AS .10 .03
120 Ken Griffey Jr. AS 3.00 .90
121 Rickey Henderson AS 1.00 .30
122 Mark McGwire AS 3.00 .90
123 Kevin Mitchell AS .05 .02
124 Cal Ripken AS 4.00 1.20
125 Chris Sabo AS .05 .02
126 Ryne Sandberg AS .75 .23
127 Steve Sax AS .05 .02
128 Mike Scioscia AS .10 .03
129 Ozzie Smith AS 1.00 .30
130 Bob Welch AS .05 .02

1992 Red Foley Stickers

The 1992 Red Foley's Best Baseball Book Ever was published by Simon and Schuster and measures 8 1/2" by 11. The book includes 130 stickers, puzzles, quizzes, how-to's, player-team matchups, and other trivia features. The stickers appear on four insert pages in the middle of the album. Each sticker measures 1 3/8" by 1 7/8" and displays a glossy color player photo bordered in white. The stickers were to be pasted in the appropriate slots throughout the sticker album. Stickers 105-130 feature All-Stars.

Nm-Mt Ex-Mt
COMPLETE SET (130) 20.00 6.00
1 Jim Abbott .10 .03
2 Roberto Alomar .25 .07
3 Sandy Alomar Jr. .10 .03
4 Eric Anthony .05 .02
5 Kevin Appier .10 .03
6 Jack Armstrong .05 .02
7 Steve Avery .05 .02
8 Carlos Baerga .05 .02
9 Scott Bankhead .05 .02
10 George Bell .05 .02
11 Albert Belle .10 .03
12 Andy Benes .10 .03
13 Craig Biggio .15 .04
14 Wade Boggs .75 .23
15 Barry Bonds 1.50 .45
16 Bobby Bonilla .05 .02
17 Sid Bream .05 .02
18 George Brett 1.50 .45
19 Hubie Brooks .05 .02
20 Ellis Burks .10 .03
21 Brett Butler .10 .03
22 Jose Canseco .50 .15
23 Joe Carter .10 .03
24 Jack Clark .10 .03
25 Will Clark .25 .07
26 Roger Clemens 1.50 .45
27 Vince Coleman .05 .02
28 Eric Davis .10 .03
29 Glenn Davis .05 .02
30 Andre Dawson .15 .04
31 Rob Deer .05 .02
32 Delino Deshields .05 .02
33 Lenny Dykstra .10 .03
34 Scott Erickson .10 .03
35 Cecil Fielder .10 .03
36 Carlton Fisk .50 .15
37 Travis Fryman .10 .03
38 Greg Gagne .05 .02
39 Juan Gonzalez .50 .15
40 Tommy Greene .05 .02
41 Ken Griffey Jr. 2.00 .60
42 Marquis Grissom .10 .03
43 Kelly Gruber .05 .02
44 Tony Gwynn 1.00 .30
45 Dave Henderson .05 .02
46 Rickey Henderson 1.00 .30
47 Orel Hershiser .05 .02
48 Kent Hrbek .10 .03
49 Howard Johnson .05 .02
50 Felix Jose .05 .02
51 Wally Joyner .10 .03
52 Dave Justice .25 .07
53 Roberto Kelly .05 .02
54 Ray Lankford .15 .04
55 Barry Larkin .25 .07
56 Mark Lewis .05 .02
57 Kevin Maas .05 .02
58 Greg Maddux 2.00 .60
59 Dave Martinez .05 .02
60 Edgar Martinez .15 .04
61 Don Mattingly 1.50 .45
62 Ben McDonald .05 .02
63 Jack McDowell .05 .02
64 Willie McGee .10 .03
65 Fred McGriff .15 .04
66 Brian McRae .15 .04
67 Mark McGwire 2.50 .75
68 Kevin Mitchell .10 .03
69 Terry Mulholland .05 .02
70 Dale Murphy .25 .07
71 Eddie Murray .25 .07
72 John Olerud .15 .04
73 Rafael Palmeiro .50 .15
74 Terry Pendleton .05 .02
75 Luis Polonia .05 .02
76 Mark Portugal .05 .02
77 Kirby Puckett .40 .12
78 Tim Raines .10 .03
79 Harold Reynolds .10 .03
80 Billy Ripken .05 .02
81 Cal Ripken Jr. 3.00 .90
82 Nolan Ryan 3.00 .90
83 Chris Sabo .05 .02
84 Ryne Sandberg .75 .23
85 Benito Santiago .10 .03
86 Kevin Seitzer .05 .02
87 Gary Sheffield .40 .12
88 Ruben Sierra .10 .03
89 John Smiley .05 .02
90 Ozzie Smith .75 .23
91 Darryl Strawberry .10 .03
92 B.J. Surhoff .05 .02
93 Frank Thomas .50 .15
94 Alan Trammell .25 .07
95 Andy Van Slyke .05 .02
96 Greg Vaughn .10 .03
97 Frank Viola .05 .02
98 Tim Wallach .05 .02
99 Matt Williams .15 .04
100 Dave Winfield .50 .15
101 Mike Witt .05 .02
102 Eric Yelding .05 .02
103 Robin Yount .50 .15
104 Todd Zeile .05 .02
105 Roberto Alomar .40 .12
106 Sandy Alomar Jr. .10 .03
107 Wade Boggs .75 .23
108 Bobby Bonilla .10 .03
109 Ivan Calderon .05 .02
110 Will Clark .25 .07
111 Andre Dawson .15 .04
112 Cecil Fielder .10 .03
113 Carlton Fisk .50 .15
114 Tom Glavine .25 .07
115 Ken Griffey Jr. 2.50 .75
116 Tony Gwynn 1.50 .45
117 Dave Henderson .05 .02
118 Rickey Henderson 1.00 .30
119 Felix Jose .05 .02
120 Jimmy Key .05 .02
121 Tony LaRussa MG .05 .02
122 Jack Morris .10 .03
123 Lou Piniella MG .10 .03
124 Cal Ripken Jr. 3.00 .90
125 Chris Sabo .05 .02
126 Juan Samuel .05 .02
127 Ryne Sandberg .75 .23
128 Benito Santiago .10 .03
129 Ozzie Smith 1.00 .30
130 Danny Tartabull .05 .02

1993 Red Foley Stickers

The 1993 Red Foley's Best Baseball Book Ever was published by Simon and Schuster and measures 8 1/2" by 11". The book includes 130 stickers, puzzles, quizzes, how-to's, player-team matchups, and other trivia features. The stickers appear on four insert pages in the middle of the album. Each sticker measures 1 3/8" by 1 7/8" and displays a color player photo. The stickers were to be pasted in the appropriate slots throughout the sticker album. Stickers 105-130 feature All-Stars.

Nm-Mt Ex-Mt
COMPLETE SET (130) 15.00 4.50
1 Jim Abbott .10 .03
2 Roberto Alomar .25 .07
3 Sandy Alomar .10 .03
4 Steve Avery .05 .02
5 Jeff Bagwell 1.00 .30
6 Harold Baines .10 .03
7 Bret Barberie .05 .02
8 Derek Bell .05 .02
9 Jay Bell .05 .02
10 Albert Belle .10 .03
11 Andy Benes .05 .02
12 Craig Biggio .15 .04
13 Wade Boggs .60 .18
14 Barry Bonds 2.00 .60
15 Bobby Bonilla .05 .02
16 Jose Canseco .75 .23
17 Joe Carter .10 .03
18 Wes Chamberlain .05 .02
19 Will Clark .25 .07
20 Roger Clemens 2.00 .60
21 Milt Cuyler .05 .02
22 Eric Davis .10 .03
23 Delino Deshields .05 .02
24 Rob Dibble .05 .02
25 Doug Drabek .05 .02
26 Shawon Dunston .05 .02
27 Lenny Dykstra .10 .03
28 Scott Erickson .05 .02
29 Cecil Fielder .10 .03
30 Steve Finley .10 .03
31 Tom Glavine .25 .07
32 Dwight Gooden .10 .03
33 Mark Grace .15 .04
34 Ken Griffey Jr. 3.00 .90
35 Marquis Grissom .10 .03
36 Kelly Gruber .05 .02
37 Mark Gubicza .05 .02
38 Tony Gwynn 2.00 .60
39 Mel Hall .05 .02
40 Pete Harnisch .05 .02
41 Brian Harper .05 .02
42 Bryan Harvey .05 .02
43 Rickey Henderson 1.00 .30
44 Orel Hershiser .10 .03
45 Gregg Jefferies .05 .02
46 Howard Johnson .05 .02
47 Felix Jose .05 .02
48 Wally Joyner .10 .03
49 Dave Justice .25 .07
50 Roberto Kelly .05 .02
51 Chuck Knoblauch .25 .07
52 John Kruk .10 .03
53 Barry Larkin .25 .07
54 Kenny Lofton .25 .07
55 Greg Maddux 2.50 .75
56 Dennis Martinez .10 .03
57 Edgar Martinez .15 .04
58 Tino Martinez .25 .07
59 Don Mattingly 2.00 .60
60 Jack McDowell .05 .02
61 Willie McGee .10 .03
62 Fred McGriff .15 .04
63 Mark McGwire 3.00 .90
64 Brian McRae .05 .02
65 Randy Milligan .05 .02
66 Kevin Mitchell .10 .03
67 Paul Molitor .25 .07
68 Dale Murphy .15 .04
69 Mike Mussina .50 .15
70 Charles Nagy .05 .02
71 Gregg Olson .05 .02
72 Rafael Palmeiro .40 .12
73 Dean Palmer .10 .03
74 Phil Plantier .05 .02
75 Luis Polonia .05 .02
76 Kirby Puckett .75 .23
77 Tim Raines .10 .03
78 Cal Ripken Jr. 4.00 1.20
79 Bip Roberts .05 .02
80 Ivan Rodriguez 1.00 .30
81 Nolan Ryan 4.00 1.20
82 Bret Saberhagen .10 .03
83 Ryne Sandberg .60 .18
84 Deion Sanders .15 .04
85 Reggie Sanders .05 .02
86 Benito Santiago .10 .03
87 Mike Scioscia .10 .03
88 Lee Smith .10 .03
89 Ozzie Smith 1.00 .30
90 Lee Stevens .05 .02
91 Darryl Strawberry .10 .03
92 B.J. Surhoff .10 .03
93 Danny Tartabull .05 .02
94 Mickey Tettleton .05 .02
95 Frank Thomas 1.00 .30
96 Robby Thompson .05 .02
97 Alan Trammell .15 .04
98 Greg Vaughn .10 .03
99 Mo Vaughn .10 .03
100 Andy Van Slyke .05 .02
101 Robin Ventura .15 .04
102 Matt Williams .15 .04
103 Robin Yount .50 .15
104 Todd Zeile .10 .03
105 Roberto Alomar .25 .07
106 Sandy Alomar .10 .03
107 Barry Bonds 2.00 .60
108 Kevin Brown .15 .04
109 Joe Carter .10 .03
110 Will Clark .25 .07
111 Bobby Cox MG .05 .02
112 Dennis Eckersley .50 .15
113 Tony Fernandez .10 .03
114 Tom Glavine .25 .07
115 Ken Griffey Jr. 3.00 .90
116 Tony Gwynn 2.00 .60
117 Tom Kelly MG .05 .02
118 John Kruk .10 .03
119 Fred McGriff .15 .04
120 Mark McGwire 3.00 .90
121 Kirby Puckett .40 .12
122 Cal Ripken Jr. 4.00 1.20
123 Bip Roberts .05 .02
124 Ivan Rodriguez 1.00 .30
125 Gary Sheffield .40 .12
126 Ruben Sierra .10 .03
127 Ozzie Smith 1.00 .30
128 Andy Van Slyke .05 .02
129 Robin Ventura .15 .04
130 Larry Walker .10 .03

1994 Red Foley's Magazine Inserts

Bound into Red Foley's 1994 Best Baseball Book Ever, these four nine-card perforated sheets feature two-player Team Leaders cards (1-28) and single-player Superstar cards (29-36). If separated from their perforated sheets, the cards would measure the standard size. All the cards feature white-bordered color player action shots on their fronts. Each Team Leaders card has the two players' photos stacked vertically, with their names appearing to the right, and the team name and subset title appearing to the left. A colored stripe also appears on each side of the player photos. The back carries, with one stacked upon the other, each player's name, team, position, biography, and career highlights. The Superstars cards have each player's name appearing above the photo and the subset title appearing below, both accompanied by colored stripes. The back is highlighted by red stars at the top and bottom, and carries the player's name, team, position, biography, and career highlights. The cards are unnumbered and checklisted below in alphabetical order, within each subset. The two-player Team Leaders cards are listed in the order of the players on the top halves of the cards.

Nm-Mt Ex-Mt
COMPLETE SET (36) 20.00 6.00
1 Roberto Alomar .25 .07
John Olerud
2 Jeff Bagwell 1.00 .30
Doug Drabek
3 Jay Bell .25 .07
Andy Van Slyke
4 Albert Belle .50 .15
Carlos Baerga
5 Andy Benes 1.00 .30
Tony Gwynn
6 Bobby Bonilla .25 .07
Dwight Gooden
7 Jay Buhner .50 .15
Randy Johnson
8 Jose Canseco 1.00 .30
Kevin Brown
9 Will Clark .75 .23
Matt Williams
10 Cecil Fielder .50 .15
Mike Henneman
11 Mark Grace .50 .15
Randy Myers
12 Charlie Hayes .25 .07
Andres Galarraga
13 John Kruk .25 .07
Tommy Greene
14 Ray Lankford 1.00 .30
Ozzie Smith
15 Barry Larkin .50 .15
Reggie Sanders
16 Greg Maddux 1.00 .30
Tom Glavine
17 Don Mattingly .75 .23
Jim Abbott
18 Mark McGwire 1.00 .30
Dennis Eckersley
19 Brian McRae .25 .07
David Cone
20 Mike Piazza 1.00 .30
Orel Hershiser
21 Kirby Puckett 1.00 .30
Rick Aguilera
22 Cal Ripken 2.00 .60
Mike Mussina
23 Tim Salmon .25 .07
Mark Langston
24 Gary Sheffield 1.00 .30
Bryan Harvey
25 Frank Thomas 2.00 .60
Jack McDowell
26 Mo Vaughn .50 .15
Frank Viola
27 Larry Walker .50 .15
Marquis Grissom
28 Robin Yount .50 .15
Cal Eldred
29 Barry Bonds 2.50 .75
30 Joe Carter .50 .15
31 Roger Clemens 2.50 .75
32 Juan Gonzalez 1.25 .35
33 Ken Griffey Jr. 3.00 .90
34 Fred McGriff .75 .23
35 Jose Rijo .25 .07
36 Ryne Sandberg 2.50 .75

1995 Red Foley

The cards measure standard size. The cards have no numbers so we grouped both single player in alphabetical order and multi-player cards in alphabetical team order.

Nm-Mt Ex-Mt
COMPLETE SET (36) 20.00 6.00
1 Barry Bonds 2.00 .60
2 Joe Carter .50 .15
3 Roger Clemens 2.00 .60
4 Juan Gonzalez 1.25 .35
5 Ken Griffey Jr. 3.00 .90
6 Fred McGriff .75 .23
7 Cal Ripken Jr. 4.00 1.20
8 Frank Thomas 1.25 .35
9 David Justice 1.00 .30
Greg Maddux
10 Rafael Palmeiro .50 .15
Mike Mussina
11 Mo Vaughn .50 .15
Aaron Sele
12 Tim Salmon .50 .15
Chuck Finley
13 Mark Grace .50 .15
Randy Myers
14 Robin Ventura .25 .07
Wilson Alvarez
15 Barry Larkin .25 .07
Jose Rijo
16 Albert Belle .75 .23
Carlos Baerga
17 Andres Galarraga .50 .15
Dante Bichette
18 Cecil Fielder .50 .15
Travis Fryman
19 Gary Sheffield 1.00 .30
Benito Santiago
20 Jeff Bagwell .75 .23
Craig Biggio
21 Brian McRae .25 .07
David Cone
22 Mike Piazza 1.00 .30
Orel Hershiser
23 Cal Eldred .25 .07
Dave Nilsson
24 Kirby Puckett .50 .15
Rick Aguilera
25 Larry Walker .50 .15
Ken Hill
26 Barry Bonilla .25 .07
Bret Saberhagen
27 Don Mattingly 1.00 .30
Jimmy Key
28 Mark McGwire 2.00 .60
Dennis Eckersley
29 John Kruk .25 .07
Lenny Dykstra

30 Andy Van Slyke .25 .07
Al Martin
31 Gregg Jefferies .50 .15
Ozzie Smith
32 Tony Gwynn 1.00 .30
Andy Benes
33 Matt Williams .75 .23
Rod Beck
34 Jay Buhner 1.00 .30
Randy Johnson
35 Jose Canseco 1.00 .30
Will Clark
36 Roberto Alomar .25 .07
John Olerud

1996 Red Foley

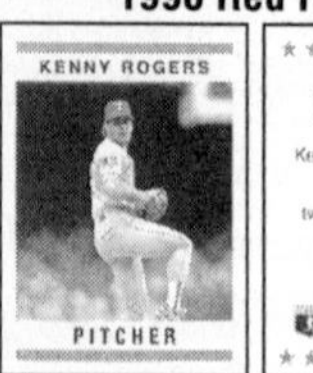

These 2" by 2 3/4" cards were issued on two pages of 16 cards each. The fronts have a photo as well as the player's identification. The backs have player information and a brief biography.

Nm-Mt Ex-Mt
COMPLETE SET (32) 25.00 7.50
1 Moises Alou .50 .15
2 Bill Pulsipher .25 .07
3 Paul O'Neill .50 .15
4 Mark McGwire 4.00 1.20
5 Len Dykstra .50 .15
6 Jay Bell .25 .07
7 Ozzie Smith 1.50 .45
8 Tony Gwynn 2.00 .60
9 Barry Bonds 2.00 .60
10 Ken Griffey Jr. 2.50 .75
11 Ivan Rodriguez 1.25 .35
12 Roberto Alomar 1.00 .30
13 Kenny Rogers .50 .15
14 Eddie Murray 1.25 .35
15 Cal Ripken Jr. 4.00 1.20
16 Rickey Henderson 1.50 .45
17 Greg Maddux 3.00 .90
18 Rafael Palmeiro 1.00 .30
19 Mo Vaughn .50 .15
20 Tim Salmon 1.00 .30
21 Sammy Sosa 2.00 .60
22 Frank Thomas 1.25 .35
23 Barry Larkin 1.00 .30
24 Carlos Baerga .25 .07
25 Larry Walker .50 .15
26 Cecil Fielder .50 .15
27 Jeff Conine .50 .15
28 Craig Biggio .75 .23
29 Wally Joyner .50 .15
30 Mike Piazza 3.00 .90
31 Kevin Seitzer .25 .07
32 Kirby Puckett 1.25 .35

1991 Foul Ball

This 36-card boxed set was produced by Eclipse Enterprises and its topic is well summarized by the blurb on the box, "Baseball's Greatest Scandals, Scoundrels and Screw-ups". The cards measure the standard size and feature Gary Cohen as writer and William Cone as artist. The fronts feature color art with white borders, while the backs have extended captions on the situation portrayed by the card.

Nm-Mt Ex-Mt
COMPLETE SET (36) 10.00 3.00
1 Foul Ball .50 .15
2 The Black Sox Scandal 1.00 .30
3 The Big Cocaine Bust .25 .07
4 The Death of a Team .25 .07
5 Pete Rose 1.00 .30
Bets on Baseball
6 Denny McLain .25 .07
Takes a Fall
7 Ty Cobb 1.00 .30
Clobbers a Fan
8 Juan Marichal .50 .15
Johnny Roseboro
9 Phil Douglas .25 .07
Kenesaw M. Landis
John McGraw
10 Beer Night at the Park .25 .07
11 Disco Demolition Night .25 .07
12 Al Campanis .25 .07
Strikes Out
13 Lenny Randle .25 .07
Frank Lucchesi
14 George Steinbrenner .50 .15
Boss George Buys It
15 The Last Stolen Base .25 .07
16 Luis Polonia .25 .07
Scores Twice
17 Charlie Finley .25 .07
Sells Out
18 Dave Pallone .25 .07
An Ump's Double Life
19 Norm Cash .25 .07
The Bat Man Tells All
20 Gaylord Perry .75 .23
A Professional Spitter
21 Dock Ellis .25 .07
Delivers A Message
22 A Major League Trade .25 .07
23 Ray Kroc .25 .07
Grabs the Mike
24 Ted Turner .25 .07
Makes the Team
25 Graig Nettles .50 .15
Bounces Out
26 The Pine Tar Game .25 .07
27 Dave Winfield 1.00 .30
Gets the Bird
28 Pascual Perez .25 .07
Goes Astray
29 Dave Stewart .25 .07
Gets Tricked
30 Wade Boggs 1.00 .30
Margo Adams
31 Two Yankee Relievers .25 .07
32 Reggie Jackson 1.00 .30
Bar Mania
33 Kiteman Grounds Out .25 .07
34 Eddie Gaedel 1.00 .30
Short Career
35 The Flying Fan .25 .07
36 Jim Bouton .50 .15
Ball Four

1887 Four Base Hits N-Unc.

The fourteen known baseball cards inscribed "Four Base Hits" were catalogued in the N690 classification for two reasons: they are identical in size and format to N690-1, and two players, Mays and Roseman, have the same pictures in both sets. Although it is known that the Charles Gross Company "farmed out" some of its insert designs to other companies, "Four Base Hits" will retain this catalog number until new evidence places them elsewhere As far as is known, the Mickey Welch card is currently unique.

Ex-Mt VG
COMPLETE SET 150000.00 75000.00
1 Tom Dailey (sic, Daly) 10000.00 5000.00
2 John Clarkson 20000.00 10000.00
3 Pat Deasley 10000.00 5000.00
4 Buck Ewing 10000.00 5000.00
5 Pete Gillespie 10000.00 5000.00
6 Frank Hankinson 10000.00 5000.00
7 Mike (King) Kelly 25000.00 12500.00
8 Al Mays 10000.00 5000.00
9 James Mutrie 10000.00 5000.00
10 James (Chief) Roseman 10000.00 5000.00
11 Marty Sullivan 10000.00 5000.00
12 George Van Haltren 10000.00 5000.00
13 John Mont. Ward 20000.00 10000.00
14 Mickey Welch 20000.00 10000.00

1996 Four Queens Chips

These cards, which cover several different series, were issued by the four queens casino in Las Vegas. These chips have the same player photo on each side and were issued in five dollar demoniations. They cover several different sets, so we have sequenced them in alphabetical order by theme.

Nm-Mt Ex-Mt
COMPLETE SET 60.00 18.00
1 Vida Blue 6.00 1.80
A's
2 John Odom 5.00 1.50
A's
3 Dick Williams MG 5.00 1.50
A's
4 Hank Bauer 6.00 1.80
Don Larsen's Perfect Game`
5 Andy Carey 5.00 1.50
Don Larsen's Perfect Game
6 Don Larsen 6.00 1.80
Perfect Game
7 Don Larsen 6.00 1.80
With other players
Perfect Game
8 Gil McDougald 6.00 1.80
Don Larsen's perfect game
9 Enos Slaughter 10.00 3.00
Don Larsen's perfect game
10 Hank Bauer 6.00 1.80
Yankees
11 Irv Noren 5.00 1.50
Yankees
12 Bill Skowron 6.00 1.80
Yankees

1980 Franchise Babe Ruth

This 80-card set measures the standard size and was manufactured by the Franchise of Bel Air, Maryland. The cards present the life of Babe Ruth and include his activities both on and off the field. The fronts have black and white photos framed by white borders. The set, which had an original print run of 1,000 sets was originally issued in complete set form and available for $8 directly from the manufacturer at the time of the issue

NM Ex
COMPLETE SET (80) 100.00 40.00
COMMON CARD (1-80) 1.50 .60

1983 Franchise Brooks Robinson

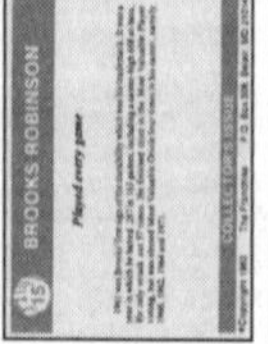

Produced by The Franchise, this 40-card standard-size set captures moments from the life and career of Brooks Robinson, the Baltimore Orioles' all-time great third baseman. On a white card face, the fronts display either posed or action black-and-white photos enclosed by an orange border stripe. Some of the front photos are horizontally oriented while others are vertically oriented. Superimposed on each card is an orange "Hall of Fame" icon. Between two orange stripes, the horizontally oriented backs feature text providing information relating to the front photo. The cards are numbered on the back in a baseball glove icon in the upper left corner.

Nm-Mt Ex-Mt
COMPLETE SET (40) 8.00 3.20
COMMON CARD (1-40) .25 .10
1 Brooks Robinson .60 .24
Title Card
7 Brooks Robinson .40 .16
Ron Hansen
Marv Breeding
Jim Gentile
First solid infield
8 Brooks Robinson .40 .16
Walt Dropo
Celebration time
9 Brooks Robinson .60 .24
Yogi Berra
Instinctive baserunner
10 Brooks Robinson .25 .10
Connie Robinson
Wedding Day
11 Brooks Robinson .25 .10
Eddie Robinson
First business partner
12 Brooks Robinson .60 .24
Luis Aparicio
Jerry Adair
Jim Gentile
Second solid infield
13 Brooks Robinson .60 .24
Al Kaline
Two Baltimore heroes
16 Brooks Robinson .40 .16
Bobby Richardson
Tony Kubek
Upsetting the Yankees
17 Brooks Robinson .40 .16
Tom Tresh
Tag out at third
18 Brooks Robinson .40 .16
Jerry Adair
Norm Siebern
Getting net results
19 Brooks Robinson .60 .24
Carl Yastrzemski
Two future MVPs
20 Brooks Robinson .75 .30
Rocky Marciano
The original Rocky
21 Brooks Robinson .60 .24
Hank Bauer
Bauer's gloveman
22 Brooks Robinson .60 .24
Luis Aparicio
Dave Johnson
Boog Powell
World Series infield
23 Brooks Robinson .60 .24
Boog Powell
Curt Blefary
Frank Robinson
Orioles' power parade
24 Brooks Robinson .60 .24
Hank Bauer
Frank Robinson
All-Star trio
25 Brooks Robinson .60 .24
Frank Robinson
Lethal lumber
26 Brooks Robinson .60 .24
Mark Belanger
Dave Johnson
Boog Powell
Belanger joins infield
27 Brooks Robinson .40 .16
Tony Oliva
Respect for Oliva
28 Brooks Robinson .60 .24
Harmon Killebrew
Out of Harm's way
29 Brooks Robinson .40 .16
Frank Lane SCOUT
Master trader
33 Brooks Robinson .60 .24
Willie Stargell
Rappin' with Willie
36 Brooks Robinson .40 .16
Lee May
Respect for teammate
37 Brooks Robinson .40 .16
Doug DeCinces
Touch of Class
39 Brooks Robinson .40 .16
Thurman Munson
Honored by Yankees
40 Brooks Robinson .60 .24
Harmon Killebrew
Two greats at third

1960 Free Press Hot Stove League Manager

Issued as inserts in the Detroit Free Press, these clippings measure approximately 5 1/2" by 6". These were issued and featured various highlights of what a manager decision was at a key part of a game. Please note that this checklist is basically complete (we still need to id card number 17) and that last addition would be greatly appreciated.

MINT NRMT
COMPLETE SET 100.00 45.00
1 Duke Snider 15.00 6.75
2 Eddie Sawyer MG 2.50 1.10
3 Elmer Valo 3.00 1.35
4 Joe Gordon MG 3.00 1.35
5 Don Blasingame 2.50 1.10
6 Paul Richards MG 2.50 1.10
7 Billy Consolo 2.50 1.10
8 Leo Kiely 2.50 1.10
9 Dave Philley 2.50 1.10
10 George Strickland MG 2.50 1.10
11 Felipe Alou 8.00 3.60
12 Al Lopez MG 5.00 2.20
13 Yogi Berra 15.00 6.75
14 Don McMahon 2.50 1.10
15 Johnny Temple 2.50 1.10
16 Solly Hemus MG 2.50 1.10
18 Bill Rigney MG 2.50 1.10
19 Bob Cerv 2.50 1.10
20 Walt Alston MG 5.00 2.20
21 Nellie Fox 8.00 3.60
22 Danny Murtaugh MG 2.50 1.10
23 Orlando Cepeda 8.00 3.60
24 George Altman 2.50 1.10

1992 French's

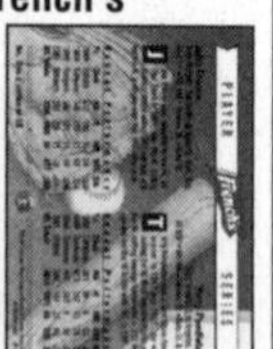

The 1992 French's Special Edition Combo Series consists of 18 two-player cards and a title/checklist card. The cards measure the standard size. Each card features one player from the American League and one player from the National League. The cards were licensed by the MLBPA and produced by MSA (Michael Schechter Associates). Collectors could obtain the title/checklist card and three free player cards through an on-pack promotion by purchasing a 16 oz. size of French's Classic Yellow Mustard (the cards were enclosed in a plastic hangtag). Alternatively, collectors could collect all 18 player cards in the series by sending in 3.00 plus 75 cents for postage and handling along with one quality seal from the 16 oz. size of French's Classic Yellow Mustard. The released production figures were 43,000 18-card sets and 4,800,000 three-card hangtags.

Nm-Mt Ex-Mt
COMPLETE SET (19) 8.00 2.40
1 Chuck Knoblauch 1.00 .30
Jeff Bagwell
2 Roger Clemens .75 .23
Tom Glavine
3 Julio Franco .25 .07
Terry Pendleton
4 Jose Canseco .50 .15
Howard Johnson
5 Scott Erickson .25 .07
John Smiley
6 Bryan Harvey .25 .07
Lee Smith
7 Kirby Puckett .75 .23
Barry Bonds
8 Robin Ventura .75 .23
Matt Williams
9 Tony Pena .25 .07
Tom Pagnozzi
10 Sandy Alomar Jr. .50 .15
Benito Santiago
11 Don Mattingly 1.00 .30
Will Clark
12 Roberto Alomar 1.00 .30
Ryne Sandberg
13 Cal Ripken 2.50 .75
Ozzie Smith
14 Wade Boggs .50 .15
Chris Sabo
15 Ken Griffey Jr. 2.00 .60
Dave Justice
16 Joe Carter 1.00 .30
Tony Gwynn
17 Rickey Henderson 1.00 .30
Darryl Strawberry
18 Jack Morris .25 .07
Steve Avery
NNO Title/Checklist Card .25 .07

1977-83 Fritsch One Year Winners

This 118-card standard-size set honors players who played roughly a season or less and were thus forgotten in baseball lore. The set was issued as three parts of one series. Cards 1-18 were issued in 1977 and feature black and white player photos, bordered in white and green. Cards 19-54 were issued in 1979 and have color player photos with white borders. Cards 55-118 were issued in 1983 and have colored photois with blue and white borders. The extended caption and Major League statistical record on the horizontally oriented backs are banded above and below by red stripes. The cards are numbered on the back in a baseball diamond in the upper left corner.

NM Ex
COMPLETE SET (118) 30.00 12.00
1 Eddie Gaedel 1.50 .60
2 Chuck Connors .75 .30
3 Joe Brovia .25 .10
4 Ross Grimsley Sr. .25 .10
5 Bob Thorpe .25 .10
6 Pete Gray .75 .30
7 Cy Buker .25 .10
8 Ted Fritsch Sr. .40 .16
9 Ron Neccai .40 .16
10 Nino Escalera .25 .10
11 Bobo Holloman .40 .16
12 Tony Roig .25 .10
13 Paul Pettit .40 .16
14 Paul Schramka .25 .10
15 Hal Trosky Jr. .40 .16
16 Floyd Wooldridge .25 .10
17 Jim Westlake .25 .10
18 Leon Brinkopf .25 .10
19 Daryl Robertson .25 .10
20 Gerry Shoen .25 .10
21 Jim Brenneman .25 .10
22 Pat House .25 .10
23 Ken Poulsen .25 .10
24 Arlo Brunsberg .25 .10
25 Jay Hankins .25 .10
26 Chuck Nieson .25 .10
27 Dick Joyce .25 .10
28 Jim Ellis .25 .10
29 John Duffie .25 .10
30 Vern Holtgrave .25 .10
31 Bill Bethea .25 .10
32 Joe Moock .25 .10
33 John Hoffman .25 .10
34 Jorge Rubio .25 .10
35 Fred Rath .25 .10
36 Jess Hickman .25 .10
37 Tom Fisher .25 .10
38 Dick Scott .25 .10
39 Jim Hibbs .25 .10
40 Paul Gilliford .25 .10
41 Bob Botz .25 .10
42 Jack Kubiszyn .25 .10
43 Rich Rusteck .25 .10
44 Roy Gleason .25 .10
45 Glenn Vaughan .25 .10
46 Bill Graham .25 .10
47 Dennis Musgraves .25 .10
48 Ron Henry .25 .10
49 Mike Jurewicz .25 .10
50 Pidge Browne .40 .16
51 Ron Keller .25 .10
52 Doug Gallagher .25 .10
53 Dave Thies .25 .10
54 Don Eaddy .25 .10
55 Don Prince .25 .10
56 Tom Granly .25 .10
57 Roy Heiser .25 .10
58 Hank Izquierdo .25 .10
59 Rex Johnston .25 .10
60 Jack Damaska .25 .10
61 John Flavin .25 .10
62 John Glenn .25 .10
63 Stan Johnson .25 .10
64 Don Choate .25 .10
65 Bill Kern .25 .10
66 Dick Luebke .25 .10
67 Glen Clark .25 .10
68 Lamar Jacobs .25 .10
69 Rick Herrscher .25 .10
70 Jim McManus .25 .10
71 Len Church .25 .10
72 Moose Stubing .25 .10
73 Cal Emery .25 .10
74 Lee Gregory .25 .10
75 Mike Page .25 .10
76 Benny Valenzuela .25 .10
77 John Papa .25 .10
78 Jim Stump .25 .10
79 Brian McCall .25 .10
80 Al Kenders .25 .10
81 Corky Withrow .25 .10
82 Verle Tiefenthaler .25 .10
83 Dave Wissman .25 .10
84 Tom Fletcher .25 .10
85 Dale Willis .25 .10
86 Larry Foster .25 .10
87 Johnnie Seale .25 .10
88 Jim Lekew .25 .10
89 Charlie Shoemaker .25 .10
90 Don Arlich .25 .10
91 George Gerberman .25 .10
92 John Preqenger .25 .10
93 Merlin Nippert .25 .10

94 Steve Demeter	.25	.10
95 John Paciorek	.40	.16
96 Larry Loughlin	.25	.10
97 Alan Brice	.25	.10
98 Chet Boak	.25	.10
99 Alan Koch	.25	.10
100 Danny Thomas	.25	.10
101 Elder White	.25	.10
102 Jim Snyder	.25	.10
103 Ted Schreiber	.25	.10
104 Evans Killeen	.25	.10
105 Ray Daviault	.25	.10
106 Larry Foss	.25	.10
107 Wayne Graham	.25	.10
108 Santiago Rosario	.25	.10
109 Bob Sprout	.25	.10
110 Tom Hughes	.25	.10
111 Em Lindbeck	.25	.10
112 Ray Blemker	.25	.10
113 Shaun Fitzmaurice	.25	.10
114 Ron Stillwell	.25	.10
115 Carl Thomas	.25	.10
116 Mike DeGerick	.25	.10
117 Jay Dahl	.25	.10
118 Al Lary	.25	.10

1988 Fritsch Baseball Card Museum

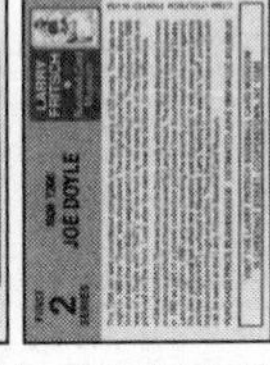

This set was issued to commemorate the opening of Larry Fritsch's Baseball Card Museum in Cooperstown, New York. This set features reprints of some of the hobby's most expensive cards.

	Nm-Mt	Ex-Mt
COMPLETE SET (8)	6.00	2.40
1 Honus Wagner T206	2.50	1.00
2 Joe Doyle T206 With and without NAT'L on front	.50	.20
3 Ty Cobb T205	2.50	1.00
4 Joe Jackson Cracker Jack	2.50	1.00
5 Eddie Plank T206	1.00	.40
6 Sherry Magee T206 With spellings Magie and Magee)	.50	.20
7 Jim Thorpe Colgan's Chips	1.50	.60
8 Baseball Card Museum Advertisement	.25	.10

1928 Fro Joy

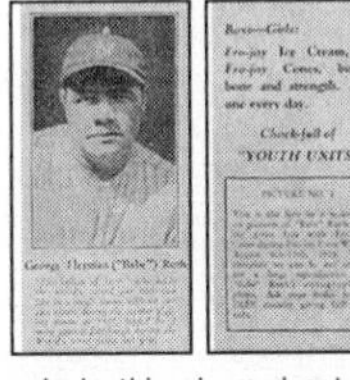

The cards in this six-card set measure approximately 2 1/16" by 4". The Fro Joy set of 1928 was designed to exploit the advertising potential of the mighty Babe Ruth. Six black and white cards explained specific baseball techniques while the reverse advertising extolled the virtues of Fro Joy ice cream and ice cream cones. Unfortunately this small set has been illegally reprinted (several times) and many of these virtually worthless fakes have been introduced into the hobby. The easiest fakes to spot are those cards (or uncut sheets) that are slightly over-sized and blue tinted; however some of the other fakes are more cleverly faithful to the original. Be very careful before purchasing Fro-Joys; obtain a qualified opinion on authenticity from an experienced dealer (preferably one who is unrelated to the dealer trying to sell you his cards). You might also show the cards (before you commit to purchase them) to an experienced printer who can advise you on the true age of the paper stock. More than one dealer has been quoted as saying that 99 percent of the Fro Joys seen are fakes. In addition, a 8 1/2" by 12" premium photo was also issued as part of the release of this promotion.

	Ex-Mt	VG
COMPLETE SET (6)	600.00	300.00
1 Babe Ruth George Herman Babe Ruth	150.00	75.00
2 Babe Ruth Look Out Mr. Pitcher	100.00	50.00
3 Babe Ruth Bang The Babe Lines one out	100.00	50.00
4 Babe Ruth When the Babe Comes Out	100.00	50.00
5 Babe Ruth Babe Ruth's Grip	100.00	50.00
6 Babe Ruth Ruth is a Crack Fielder	100.00	50.00
P1 Babe Ruth 8 1/2" by 12" premium photo	150.00	75.00

1991 Front Row Ken Griffey Jr.

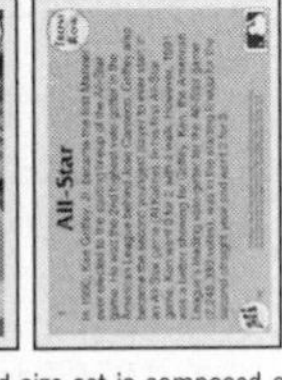

This 15-card standard-size set is composed of the ten-card insert set plus a five-card promo set. The ten-card insert set features different action shots of Ken Griffey Jr. An official certificate of authenticity included with the set gives the set serial number and production run ("X of 25,000"). These cards were randomly inserted into 1992 Front Row Baseball Draft Pick wax boxes. Except for a baseball icon on their backs marked with the word "Promo," the promo cards are identical with the first five cards in the insert set. The Promo cards in the checklist below have been numbered with a P suffix in order to avoid confusion. According to Front Row, 25,000 sets were produced. All these cards can be distinguished from the regular issue by their backs, which are gold-foil stamped with the "Front Row Collector's Club Charter Member" seal.

	Nm-Mt	Ex-Mt
COMPLETE SET (15)	15.00	4.50
COMMON CARD (1-10)	1.00	.30
COMMON PROMO (1P-5P)	1.00	.30

1992 Front Row ATG Holograms

These three standard-size hologram cards commemorate an outstanding season of three of baseball's all-time greats. The production run was 100,000 for each card. The cards are unnumbered and checklisted below in alphabetical order.

	Nm-Mt	Ex-Mt
COMPLETE SET (3)	5.00	1.50
1 Hank Aaron	2.00	.60
2 Roy Campanella	1.25	.35
3 Tom Seaver	2.00	.60

1992 Front Row Banks

This five-card standard-size set features Hall of Famer Ernie Banks. Each set includes an official certificate of authenticity that gives the production run (25,000) and the set serial number. Banks autographed the first card in 5,000 sets that were initially offered exclusively to Front Row Collector's Club Members. Cards 1-4 carry color player photos on the fronts, while card No. 5 has a black and white photo.

	Nm-Mt	Ex-Mt
COMPLETE SET (5)	4.00	1.20
COMMON CARD (1-5)	1.00	.30
1AU Ernie Banks AU	20.00	6.00

1992 Front Row Berra

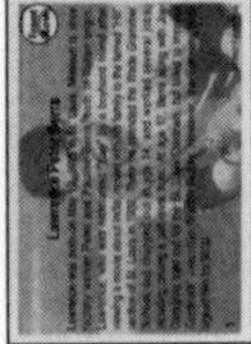

This five-card standard-size set features Hall of Famer Yogi Berra. Each set includes an official certificate of authenticity that gives the production run (25,000) and the set serial number. Berra autographed the first card in 5,000 sets that were initially offered exclusively to Front Row Collector's Club Members. Card Nos. 1 and 3 carry color player photos on the fronts, while card Nos. 2, 4 and 5 have black and white photos.

	Nm-Mt	Ex-Mt
COMPLETE SET (5)	4.00	1.20
COMMON CARD (1-5)	1.00	.30
1AU Yogi Berra AU	40.00	12.00

1992 Front Row Brooks Robinson

This five-card standard-size set features Hall of Famer Brooks Robinson. Each set includes an

official certificate of authenticity that gives the production run (25,000) and the set serial number. Robinson autographed the first card in 5,000 sets that were initially offered exclusively to Front Row Collector's Club Members.

	Nm-Mt	Ex-Mt
COMPLETE SET (5)	4.00	1.20
COMMON CARD (1-5)	1.00	.30
1AU Brooks Robinson Autograph	30.00	9.00

1992 Front Row Buck Leonard

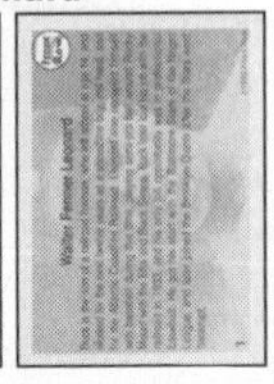

This five-card standard-size set features Hall of Famer Buck Leonard. Each set includes an official certificate of authenticity that gives the production run (25,000) and the set serial number. Leonard autographed the first card in 5,000 sets that were initially offered exclusively to Front Row Collector's Club Members.

	Nm-Mt	Ex-Mt
COMPLETE SET (5)	4.00	1.20
COMMON CARD (1-5)	1.00	.30
1AU Buck Leonard AU	30.00	9.00

1992 Front Row Dandridge

This five-card standard-size set features Hall of Famer Ray Dandridge. Each set includes an official certificate of authenticity, giving the production run (25,000) and the set serial number. Dandridge autographed the first card in 5,000 sets that were initially offered exclusively to Front Row Collector's Club Members.

	Nm-Mt	Ex-Mt
COMPLETE SET (5)	4.00	1.20
COMMON CARD (1-5)	1.00	.30
1AU Ray Dandridge AU	30.00	9.00

1992 Front Row Ford

This five-card standard-size set features Hall of Famer Whitey Ford. Each set includes an official certificate of authenticity that gives the production run (25,000) and the set serial number. Ford autographed the first card in 5,000 sets that were initially offered exclusively to Front Row Collector's Club Members.

	Nm-Mt	Ex-Mt
COMPLETE SET (5)	4.00	1.20
COMMON CARD (1-5)	1.00	.30
1AU Whitey Ford AU	40.00	12.00

1992 Front Row Griffey Club House

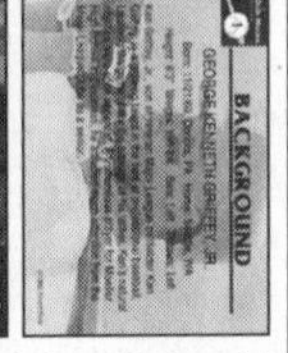

This ten-card standard-size set features full-bleed color player photos on the front. The only text on the front appears in a black square at the lower right corner, which reads "Club House Series, Ken Griffey Jr." According to Front Row, 25,000 sets were produced.

	Nm-Mt	Ex-Mt
COMPLETE SET (10)	10.00	3.00
COMMON CARD (1-10)	1.00	.30

1992 Front Row Griffey Gold

This three-card standard-size set features color player photos on the fronts bordered by 23K gold dust stamping. Each set was accompanied by a certificate of authenticity carrying the production run (20,000) and the set serial number. Front Row issued 5,000 uncut strips of the three-card set.

	Nm-Mt	Ex-Mt
COMPLETE SET (3)	15.00	4.50
COMMON CARD (1-3)	5.00	1.50

1992 Front Row Griffey Holograms

This three-card hologram standard-size set features three-dimensional shots of Ken Griffey Jr. Each set includes an official certificate of authenticity giving the set serial number and production run (50,000). All Seattle Mariner logos have been airbrushed off the cards as they were not licensed by the league or team.

	Nm-Mt	Ex-Mt
COMPLETE SET (3)	6.00	1.80
COMMON CARD (1-3)	2.00	.60

1992 Front Row Griffey Jr. Oversized Card

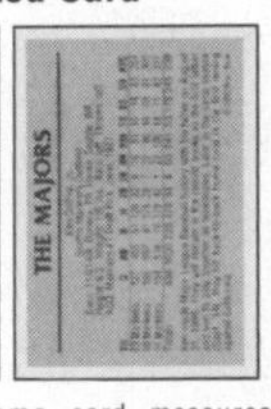

This oversized promo card measures approximately 7 1/2" X 10 1/2" and features a color action shot of Griffey at bat. The card is unnumbered.

	Nm-Mt	Ex-Mt
NNO Ken Griffey Jr.	3.00	.90

1992 Front Row Irvin

This five-card standard-size set features Hall of Famer Monte Irvin. Each set includes an official certificate of authenticity, giving the production run (25,000) and the set serial number. Irvin autographed the first card in 5,000 sets that were initially offered exclusively to Front Row Collector's Club Members. The fronts feature either black and white (cards 1-2) or color player photos (cards 3-5).

	Nm-Mt	Ex-Mt
COMPLETE SET (5)	4.00	1.20
COMMON CARD (1-5)	1.00	.30
1AU Monte Irvin AU	20.00	6.00

1992 Front Row Seaver

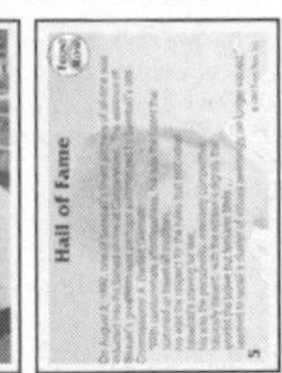

This five card set feature highlights in the career of Hall of Fame pitcher Tom Seaver. Like most of the 1992 Front Row sets, this standard-size set was issued in a quantity of 25,000 sets with 4,000 of card number 1 being autographed.

	Nm-Mt	Ex-Mt
COMPLETE SET (5)	4.00	1.20
COMMON CARD (1-5)	1.00	.30
1AU Tom Seaver AU	50.00	15.00

1992 Front Row Stargell

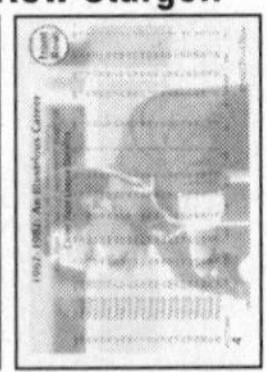

This five-card standard-size set features Hall of Famer Willie Stargell. Each set includes an official certificate of authenticity, giving the production run (25,000) and the set serial number. Stargell autographed the first card in 5,000 sets that were initially offered exclusively to Front Row Collector's Club Members.

	Nm-Mt	Ex-Mt
COMPLETE SET (5)	4.00	1.20
COMMON CARD (1-5)	1.00	.30
1AU Willie Stargell AU	20.00	6.00

1992 Front Row Thomas

This seven-card, standard-size set features on the front color player photos bordered in white. Each set includes an official certificate of authenticity that gives the production run (30,000) and the set serial number. Thomas autographed the first card in 4,000 sets that were initially offered exclusively to Front Row Collector's Club Members.

	Nm-Mt	Ex-Mt
COMPLETE SET (7)	6.00	1.80
COMMON CARD (1-7)	1.00	.30
1AU Frank Thomas AU	20.00	6.00

1992 Front Row Thomas Gold

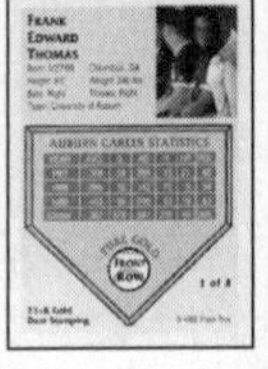

This three-card, standard-size set features color player photos on the fronts bordered by 23K gold dust stamping. Each set was accompanied by a certificate of authenticity carrying the production run (20,000) and the set serial number. Five thousand uncut strips of the three-card set were also produced.

	Nm-Mt	Ex-Mt
COMPLETE SET (3)	15.00	4.50
COMMON CARD (1-3)	5.00	1.50

1992 Front Row Tyler Green

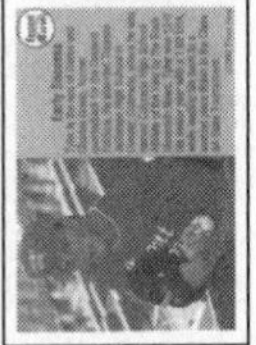

This seven card standard-size set was among the many individual player sets issued by Front Row. Each set features highlights of Travis Green's early baseball career and includes an Official Certificate of Authenticity

	Nm-Mt	Ex-Mt
COMMON PLAYER (1-7)	1.50	.45
COMMON CARD (1-7)	.25	.07

1993 Front Row Brock

The five standard-size cards comprising this set feature borderless color photos that have the Cardinals name and logo airbrushed from Brock's uniform. The set comes with a certificate of authenticity that carries the serial number out of 5,000 sets produced.

	Nm-Mt	Ex-Mt
COMPLETE SET (5)	4.00	1.20
COMMON CARD (1-5)	1.00	.30

1993 Front Row Campanella

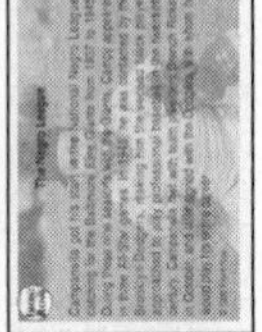

The five standard-size cards comprising this set feature borderless color photos that have

the Dodgers name and logo airbrushed from Campanella's uniform. The set comes with a certificate of authenticity that carries the serial number out of 5,000 sets produced.

Nm-Mt Ex-Mt
COMPLETE SET (5) 5.00 1.50
COMMON CARD (1-5) 1.00 .30

1993 Front Row Fingers

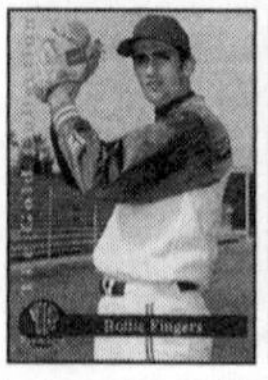

Front Row issued this five-card standard-size set as part of "The Gold Collection" line. Just 5,000 sets were produced.

Nm-Mt Ex-Mt
COMPLETE SET (5) 4.00 1.20
COMMON CARD (1-5) 1.00 .30

1993 Front Row Griffey Jr. Gold Collection

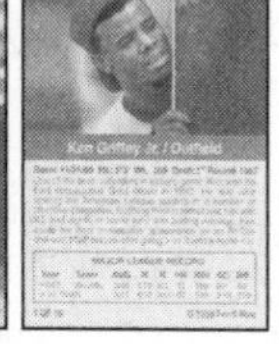

This ten-card standard-size set features borderless color action shots on its fronts.

Nm-Mt Ex-Mt
COMPLETE SET (10) 10.00 3.00
COMMON CARD (1-10) 1.00 .30

1993 Front Row Palmer

This five-card Front Row Premium standard-size set spotlights former Baltimore Orioles' pitcher Jim Palmer. Two thousand of these sets carry an authentic autograph, which appears on the first card.

Nm-Mt Ex-Mt
COMPLETE SET (5) 4.00 1.20
COMMON CARD (1-5) 1.00 .30

1993 Fun Pack

This 225-card standard-size single series set was issued by Upper Deck and targeted primarily at youngsters. Cards were distributed exclusively in hobby and retail foil fin-wrapped packs. Topical subsets featured are Stars of Tomorrow (1-9), Hot Shots (10-21), Kid Stars (22-27), Upper Deck Heroes (28-36), All-Star Advice (210-215), All-Star Fold Outs (216-220), and Checklists (221-225) and randomly numbered Glow Stars. Card numbers 37-209 are arranged alphabetically according to team names, with each team subset beginning with a Glow Star card. There are no key Rookie Cards in this set.The Hot Shot subset cards were only available in retail packs or through a as a mail-in redemption promotion available in hobby packs.

Nm-Mt Ex-Mt
COMPLETE SET (225) 60.00 18.00
1 Wil Cordero SOT .15 .04
2 Brent Gates SOT .15 .04
3 Benji Gil SOT .15 .04
4 Phil Hiatt SOT .15 .04
5 David McCarty SOT .15 .04
6 Mike Piazza SOT 2.00 .60
7 Tim Salmon SOT .50 .15
8 J.T. Snow SOT RC .75 .23
9 Kevin Young SOT .15 .04
10 Roberto Alomar HS .75 .23
11 Barry Bonds HS 2.00 .60
12 Jose Canseco HS .75 .23
13 Will Clark HS .75 .23
14 Roger Clemens HS 1.50 .45
15 Juan Gonzalez HS .50 .15
16 Ken Griffey Jr. HS 1.25 .35
17 Mark McGwire HS 2.00 .60
18 Nolan Ryan HS 2.50 .75
19 Ryne Sandberg HS 1.25 .35
20 Gary Sheffield HS .30 .09
21 Frank Thomas HS .75 .23
22 Roberto Alomar KS .30 .09
23 Roger Clemens KS .75 .23
24 Ken Griffey Jr. KS .75 .23
25 Gary Sheffield KS .15 .04
26 Nolan Ryan KS 1.25 .35
27 Frank Thomas KS .50 .15
28 Reggie Jackson HERO .30 .09
29 Roger Clemens HERO .75 .23
30 Ken Griffey Jr. HERO .75 .23
31 Bo Jackson HERO .30 .09
32 Cal Ripken Jr. HERO 1.25 .35
33 Nolan Ryan HERO 1.25 .35
34 Deion Sanders HERO .30 .09
35 Ozzie Smith HERO .75 .23
36 Frank Thomas HERO .50 .15
37 Tim Salmon GS .30 .09
38 Chili Davis .30 .09
39 Chuck Finley .30 .09
40 Mark Langston .15 .04
41 Luis Polonia .15 .04
42 Jeff Bagwell GS .30 .09
43 Jeff Bagwell .50 .15
44 Craig Biggio .50 .15
45 Ken Caminiti .30 .09
46 Doug Drabek .15 .04
47 Steve Finley .30 .09
48 Mark McGwire GS 1.00 .30
49 Dennis Eckersley .30 .09
50 Rickey Henderson .75 .23
51 Mark McGwire 2.00 .60
52 Ruben Sierra .15 .04
53 Terry Steinbach .30 .09
54 Roberto Alomar GS .30 .09
55 Roberto Alomar .75 .23
56 Joe Carter .30 .09
57 Juan Guzman .15 .04
58 Paul Molitor .50 .15
59 Jack Morris .30 .09
60 John Olerud .30 .09
61 Tom Glavine GS .30 .09
62 Steve Avery .15 .04
63 Tom Glavine .15 .04
64 David Justice .30 .09
65 Greg Maddux 1.25 .35
66 Terry Pendleton .30 .09
67 Deion Sanders .50 .15
68 John Smoltz .50 .15
69 Robin Yount GS .75 .23
70 Cal Eldred .15 .04
71 Pat Listach .15 .04
72 Greg Vaughn .30 .09
73 Robin Yount 1.25 .35
74 Ozzie Smith GS .75 .23
75 Gregg Jefferies .15 .04
76 Ray Lankford .15 .04
77 Lee Smith .30 .09
78 Ozzie Smith 1.25 .35
79 Bob Tewksbury .15 .04
80 Ryne Sandberg GS .75 .23
81 Mark Grace .50 .15
82 Mike Morgan .15 .04
83 Randy Myers .30 .09
84 Ryne Sandberg 1.25 .35
85 Sammy Sosa 1.25 .35
86 Eric Karros GS .15 .04
87 Brett Butler .30 .09
88 Orel Hershiser .30 .09
89 Eric Karros .30 .09
90 Ramon Martinez .15 .04
91 Jose Offerman .15 .04
92 Darryl Strawberry .50 .15
93 Marquis Grissom GS .15 .04
94 Delino DeShields .15 .04
95 Marquis Grissom .15 .04
96 Ken Hill .15 .04
97 Dennis Martinez .30 .09
98 Larry Walker .50 .15
99 Barry Bonds GS 1.00 .30
100 Barry Bonds 2.00 .60
101 Will Clark .75 .23
102 Bill Swift .15 .04
103 Robby Thompson .15 .04
104 Matt Williams .30 .09
105 Carlos Baerga GS .15 .04
106 Sandy Alomar Jr. .15 .04
107 Carlos Baerga .15 .04
108 Albert Belle .30 .09
109 Kenny Lofton .30 .09
110 Charles Nagy .15 .04
111 Ken Griffey Jr. GS .75 .23
112 Jay Buhner .30 .09
113 Dave Fleming .15 .04
114 Ken Griffey Jr. 1.25 .35
115 Randy Johnson .75 .23
116 Edgar Martinez .50 .15
117 Benito Santiago GS .15 .04
118 Bret Barberie .15 .04
119 Jeff Conine .30 .09
120 Brian Harvey .15 .04
121 Benito Santiago .30 .09
122 Walt Weiss .15 .04
123 Dwight Gooden GS .30 .09
124 Bobby Bonilla .30 .09
125 Vince Coleman .15 .04
126 Dwight Gooden .50 .15
127 Howard Johnson .15 .04
128 Eddie Murray .75 .23
129 Bret Saberhagen .30 .09
130 Cal Ripken Jr. GS 1.25 .35
131 Brady Anderson .30 .09
132 Mike Devereaux .15 .04
133 Ben McDonald .15 .04
134 Mike Mussina .75 .23
135 Cal Ripken Jr. 2.50 .75
136 Fred McGriff GS .30 .09
137 Andy Benes .15 .04
138 Tony Gwynn 1.00 .30
139 Fred McGriff .50 .15
140 Phil Plantier .15 .04
141 Gary Sheffield .30 .09
142 Darren Daulton GS .15 .04
143 Darren Daulton .30 .09
144 Len Dykstra .30 .09
145 Dave Hollins .15 .04
146 John Kruk .30 .09
147 Mitch Williams .15 .04
148 Andy Van Slyke GS .15 .04
149 Jay Bell .30 .09
150 Zane Smith .15 .04
151 Andy Van Slyke .30 .09
152 Tim Wakefield .30 .09
153 Juan Gonzalez GS .50 .15
154 Kevin Brown .30 .09
155 Jose Canseco .75 .23
156 Juan Gonzalez .75 .23
157 Rafael Palmeiro .50 .15
158 Dean Palmer .30 .09
159 Ivan Rodriguez .75 .23
160 Nolan Ryan 2.50 .75
161 Roger Clemens GS .75 .23
162 Roger Clemens 1.50 .45
163 Andre Dawson .30 .09
164 Mike Greenwell .15 .04
165 Tony Pena .15 .04
166 Frank Viola .30 .09
167 Barry Larkin GS .30 .09
168 Rob Dibble .30 .09
169 Roberto Kelly .15 .04
170 Barry Larkin .75 .23
171 Kevin Mitchell .15 .04
172 Bip Roberts .15 .04
173 Andres Galarraga GS .15 .04
174 Dante Bichette .30 .09
175 Jerald Clark .15 .04
176 Andres Galarraga .30 .09
177 Charlie Hayes .15 .04
178 David Nied .15 .04
179 David Cone GS .15 .04
180 Kevin Appier .30 .09
181 George Brett 2.00 .60
182 David Cone .30 .09
183 Felix Jose .15 .04
184 Wally Joyner .30 .09
185 Cecil Fielder GS .15 .04
186 Cecil Fielder .30 .09
187 Travis Fryman .30 .09
188 Tony Phillips .15 .04
189 Mickey Tettleton .15 .04
190 Lou Whitaker .30 .09
191 Kirby Puckett GS .50 .15
192 Scott Erickson .15 .04
193 Chuck Knoblauch .30 .09
194 Shane Mack .15 .04
195 Kirby Puckett .75 .23
196 Dave Winfield .30 .09
197 Frank Thomas GS .50 .15
198 George Bell .15 .04
199 Bo Jackson .75 .23
200 Jack McDowell .15 .04
201 Tim Raines .30 .09
202 Frank Thomas .75 .23
203 Robin Ventura .30 .09
204 Jim Abbott GS .30 .09
205 Jim Abbott .50 .15
206 Wade Boggs .50 .15
207 Jimmy Key .30 .09
208 Don Mattingly 2.00 .60
209 Danny Tartabull .15 .04
210 Brett Butler ASA .15 .04
211 Tony Gwynn ASA .50 .15
212 R.Henderson ASA .50 .15
213 Ramon Martinez ASA .15 .04
214 Nolan Ryan ASA 1.25 .35
215 Ozzie Smith ASA .75 .23
216 M.Grissom FOLD .15 .04
217 Dean Palmer FOLD .15 .04
218 Cal Ripken Jr. FOLD 1.25 .35
219 Deion Sanders FOLD .30 .09
220 D.Strawberry FOLD .30 .09
221 David McCarty CL .15 .04
222 Barry Bonds CL 1.00 .30
223 Juan Gonzalez CL .50 .15
224 Ken Griffey Jr. CL .75 .23
225 Frank Thomas CL .50 .15
NNO Hot Shots Card Punch .15 .04
NNO Hot Shots Card Exp. .15 .04

1993 Fun Pack All-Stars

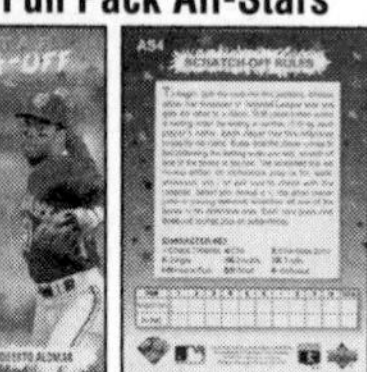

Randomly inserted in 1993 Upper Deck Fun Packs, these nine foldouts feature combinations by position for American and National leaue All-Stars. The cards measure the standard size when closed and 2 1/2" by 7" when opened. The front of each features side-by-side color action photos of an American League and a National League player.

Nm-Mt Ex-Mt
COMPLETE SET (9) 15.00 4.50
AS1 Frank Thomas 1.00 .30
Fred McGriff
AS2 Ivan Rodriguez 1.00 .30
Darren Daulton
AS3 Mark McGwire 3.00 .90
Will Clark
AS4 Roberto Alomar 2.50 .75
Ryne Sandberg
AS5 Robin Ventura .50 .15
Terry Pendleton
AS6 Cal Ripken 4.00 1.20
Ozzie Smith
AS7 Juan Gonzalez 3.00 .90
Barry Bonds
AS8 Ken Griffey Jr. 2.00 .60
Marquis Grissom
AS9 Kirby Puckett 1.50 .45
Tony Gwynn

1993 Fun Pack Mascots

Randomly inserted in 1993 Upper Deck Fun Packs, these five standard-size horizontal cards feature two mascot photos on their fronts.

Nm-Mt Ex-Mt
COMPLETE SET (5) 2.50 .75
1 Phillie Phanatic 1.00 .30
2 Pirate Parrot .50 .15
3 Fredbird .50 .15

4 BJ Birdie .50 .15
5 Youppi .50 .15

1994 Fun Pack

Issued by Upper Deck for the second straight year, the Fun Pack set consists of 240 cards. The following subsets are included in this set: Stars of Tomorrow (1-9), Standouts (175-192), Pro-Files (193-198), Headline Stars (199-207), What's the Call (208-216), Foldouts (217-225) and Fun Cards (226-234). Some dealers believe the Standout subset may be short printed. One of Michael Jordan's baseball Rookie Cards is in this set.

Nm-Mt Ex-Mt
COMPLETE SET (240) 80.00 24.00
1 Manny Ramirez .75 .23
2 Cliff Floyd .50 .15
3 Rondell White .50 .15
4 Carlos Delgado .75 .23
5 Chipper Jones 1.25 .35
6 Javier Lopez .50 .15
7 Ryan Klesko .50 .15
8 Steve Karsay .25 .07
9 Rich Becker .25 .07
10 Gary Sheffield .25 .07
11 Jeffrey Hammonds .25 .07
12 Roberto Alomar 1.25 .35
13 Brent Gates .25 .07
14 Andres Galarraga .50 .15
15 Tim Salmon .75 .23
16 Dwight Gooden .75 .23
17 Mark Grace .75 .23
18 Andy Van Slyke .50 .15
19 Juan Gonzalez 1.25 .35
20 Mickey Tettleton .25 .07
21 Roger Clemens 2.50 .75
22 Will Clark 1.25 .35
23 David Justice .50 .15
24 Ken Griffey Jr. 2.00 .60
25 Barry Bonds 3.00 .90
26 Bill Swift .25 .07
27 Fred McGriff .75 .23
28 Randy Myers .25 .07
29 Joe Carter .50 .15
30 Nigel Wilson .25 .07
31 Mike Piazza 2.00 .60
32 Dave Winfield .50 .15
33 Steve Avery .25 .07
34 Kirby Puckett 1.25 .35
35 Frank Thomas 1.25 .35
36 Aaron Sele .25 .07
37 Ricky Gutierrez .25 .07
38 Curt Schilling .75 .23
39 Mike Greenwell .25 .07
40 Andy Benes .25 .07
41 Kevin Brown .50 .15
42 Mo Vaughn .50 .15
43 Dennis Eckersley .50 .15
44 Ken Hill .25 .07
45 Cecil Fielder .50 .15
46 Bobby Jones .25 .07
47 Tom Glavine .75 .23
48 Wally Joyner .50 .15
49 Ellis Burks .50 .15
50 Jason Bere .25 .07
51 Randy Johnson 1.25 .35
52 Darryl Kile .50 .15
53 Jeff Montgomery .25 .07
54 Alex Fernandez .25 .07
55 Kevin Appier .50 .15
56 Brian McRae .25 .07
57 John Wetteland .50 .15
58 Bob Tewksbury .25 .07
59 Todd Van Poppel .25 .07
60 Ryne Sandberg 2.50 .75
61 Bret Barberie .25 .07
62 Phil Plantier .25 .07
63 Chris Hoiles .25 .07
64 Tony Phillips .25 .07
65 Salomon Torres .25 .07
66 Juan Guzman .25 .07
67 Paul O'Neill .75 .23
68 Dante Bichette .50 .15
69 Lenny Dykstra .50 .15
70 Ivan Rodriguez 1.25 .35
71 Dean Palmer .50 .15
72 Brett Butler .50 .15
73 Rick Aguilera .50 .15
74 Robby Thompson .25 .07
75 Jim Abbott .75 .23
76 Al Martin .25 .07
77 Roberto Hernandez .25 .07
78 Jay Buhner .50 .15
79 Devon White .25 .07
80 Travis Fryman .50 .15
81 Jeromy Burnitz .50 .15
82 John Burkett .25 .07
83 Orlando Merced .25 .07
84 Jose Rijo .25 .07
85 Eddie Murray 1.25 .35
86 Howard Johnson .25 .07
87 Chuck Carr .25 .07
88 Pedro Martinez 1.25 .35
89 Charlie Hayes .25 .07
90 Matt Williams .50 .15
91 Steve Finley .25 .07
92 Pat Listach .25 .07
93 Sandy Alomar Jr. .25 .07
94 Delino DeShields .25 .07
95 Rod Beck .25 .07
96 Todd Zeile UER .50 .15
(Card misnumbered 97)
97 Duane Ward UER .25 .07
(Card misnumbered 98)
98 Darryl Hamilton .25 .07
99 John Olerud .50 .15
100 Andre Dawson .50 .15
101 Ozzie Smith 2.00 .60
102 Rick Wilkins .25 .07
103 Alan Trammell .75 .23
104 Jeff Blauser .25 .07
105 Bret Boone .50 .15
106 J.T. Snow .50 .15
107 Kenny Lofton .50 .15
108 Cal Ripken Jr. 4.00 1.20
109 Carlos Baerga .25 .07
110 Bip Roberts .25 .07
111 Barry Larkin 1.25 .35
112 Mark Langston .25 .07
113 Ozzie Guillen .25 .07
114 Chad Curtis .25 .07
115 Dave Hollins .25 .07
116 Reggie Sanders .50 .15
117 Jeff Conine .50 .15
118 Mark Whiten .25 .07
119 Tony Gwynn 1.50 .45
120 John Kruk .50 .15
121 Eduardo Perez .25 .07
122 Walt Weiss .25 .07
123 Don Mattingly 3.00 .90
124 Rickey Henderson 1.25 .35
125 Mark McGwire 3.00 .90
126 Wade Boggs .75 .23
127 Bobby Bonilla .25 .07
128 Jeff King .25 .07
129 Jack McDowell .25 .07
130 Albert Belle .50 .15
131 Greg Maddux 2.00 .60
132 Dennis Martinez .50 .15
133 Jose Canseco 1.25 .35
134 Bryan Harvey .25 .07
135 Dave Fleming .25 .07
136 Larry Walker .75 .23
137 Ken Caminiti .50 .15
138 Doug Drabek .25 .07
139 Alex Gonzalez .25 .07
140 Darren Daulton .25 .07
141 Ruben Sierra .25 .07
142 Kirk Rueter .50 .15
143 Raul Mondesi .50 .15
144 Greg Vaughn .50 .15
145 Danny Tartabull .25 .07
146 Eric Karros .50 .15
147 Chuck Knoblauch .50 .15
148 Mike Mussina 1.25 .35
149 Brady Anderson .50 .15
150 Paul Molitor .75 .23
151 Bo Jackson 1.25 .35
152 Jeff Bagwell .75 .23
153 Gregg Jefferies UER .25 .07
Name spelled Greg on front
154 Rafael Palmeiro .75 .23
155 Orel Hershiser .50 .15
156 Derek Bell .25 .07
157 Jeff Kent .50 .15
158 Craig Biggio .75 .23
159 Marquis Grissom .25 .07
160 Matt Mieske .25 .07
161 Jay Bell .50 .15
162 Sammy Sosa 2.00 .60
163 Robin Ventura .50 .15
164 Deion Sanders .75 .23
165 Jimmy Key .50 .15
166 Cal Eldred .25 .07
167 David McCarty .25 .07
168 Carlos Garcia .25 .07
169 Willie Greene .25 .07
170 Michael Jordan RC 10.00 3.00
171 Roberto Mejia .25 .07
172 Phil Hiatt UER .25 .07
(Card misnumbered 72)
173 Marc Newfield .25 .07
174 Kevin Stocker .25 .07
175 Randy Johnson STA 1.25 .35
176 Ivan Rodriguez STA .75 .23
177 Frank Thomas STA 1.25 .35
178 Roberto Alomar STA 1.25 .35
179 Travis Fryman STA .50 .15
180 Cal Ripken Jr. STA 4.00 1.20
181 Juan Gonzalez STA .75 .23
182 Ken Griffey Jr. STA 2.00 .60
183 Albert Belle STA .50 .15
184 Greg Maddux STA 2.00 .60
185 Mike Piazza STA 2.00 .60
186 Fred McGriff STA .75 .23
187 R.Thompson STA .25 .07
188 Matt Williams STA .50 .15
189 Jeff Blauser STA .25 .07
190 Barry Bonds STA 3.00 .90
191 Lenny Dykstra STA .50 .15
192 David Justice STA .25 .07
193 Ken Griffey Jr. PF 1.25 .35
194 Barry Bonds PF 1.50 .45
195 Frank Thomas PF .75 .23
196 Juan Gonzalez PF .75 .23
197 Randy Johnson PF .75 .23
198 Chuck Carr PF .25 .07
199 Barry Bonds HES 3.00 .90
Juan Gonzalez
200 Ken Griffey Jr. HES 3.00 .90
Don Mattingly
201 Roberto Alomar HES 1.25 .35
Carlos Baerga
202 Dave Winfield HES 1.25 .35
Robin Yount
203 Mike Piazza HES 2.00 .60
Tim Salmon
204 Albert Belle HES 1.25 .35
Frank Thomas
205 Cliff Floyd HES .50 .15
Rondell White
206 Kirby Puckett HES 1.50 .45
Tony Gwynn
207 Roger Clemens HES 2.50 .75

Greg Maddux
208 Mike Piazza WC 1.25 .35
209 J.Canseco WC Off Head 1.25 .35
210 Frank Thomas WC .75 .23
211 Roberto Alomar WC .50 .15
212 Barry Bonds WC 1.50 .45
213 Rickey Henderson WC .75 .23
214 John Kruk WC .25 .07
215 Juan Gonzalez WC .75 .23
216 Ken Griffey Jr. WC 1.25 .35
217 R.Alomar FOLD SP 1.50 .45
218 Craig Biggio FOLD .50 .15
219 Cal Ripken Jr. FOLD 2.00 .60
220 Mike Piazza FOLD 1.25 .35
221 Brent Gates FOLD .25 .07
222 Walt Weiss FOLD .25 .07
223 Bobby Bonilla FOLD .25 .07
224 Ken Griffey Jr. FOLD 1.25 .35
225 Barry Bonds FOLD 1.50 .45
226 Barry Bonds FUN 1.50 .45
227 Joe Carter FUN .25 .07
228 Mike Greenwell FUN .25 .07
229 Ken Griffey Jr. FUN 1.25 .35
230 John Kruk FUN .25 .07
231 Mike Piazza FUN 1.25 .35
232 Kirby Puckett FUN 1.25 .35
233 John Smoltz FUN .50 .15
234 Rick Wilkins FUN .25 .07
235 Ken Griffey Jr. CL 1.25 .35
236 Frank Thomas CL .50 .15
237 Barry Bonds CL 1.50 .45
238 Mike Piazza CL 1.25 .35
239 Tim Salmon CL .50 .15
240 Juan Gonzalez CL .75 .23
P172 K.Griffey Jr. Promo 3.00 .90

1976 Funky Facts

This 40-card standard-size set is subtitled "The Wierd [sic] World of Baseball". A paper insert included with the set carries a checklist on its back. Inside a white outer border and a color inner border, the fronts feature colorful cartoon drawings. A trivia question appears above each picture in a pale yellow bar. Each back shows five trivia questions and their answers. The first question repeats the question found on card fronts.

	NM	Ex
COMPLETE SET	10.00	4.00
COMMON CARD	.25	.10

1888 G and B Chewing Gum Co E223

These cards measure approximately 1" by 2 1/8" and primarily feature players from the National League. This is one of the few nineteenth century issues which are not tobacco related. The set was issued by the G and B Chewing Gum Co and is the first set baseball issue released by a gum or candy company. The cards are unnumbered and we have sequenced them in alphabetical order. If more than one pose is known, we have put the number of said poses next to the player's name. The complete set price only includes one of each variation. Portraits are worth approximately 1.5X times the value of the drawings. Some cards were recently discovered and added to this checklist so any further additions are appreciated.

	Ex-Mt	VG
COMPLETE SET	140000.00	70000.00
1 Cap Anson	4000.00	2000.00
Card Pictures Ned Williamson		
2 Lady Baldwin (3)	2000.00	1000.00
3 Sam Barkley	2000.00	1000.00
4 Steve Brady	2000.00	1000.00
5 Bill Brown (2)	2000.00	1000.00
6 Dan Brouthers	2000.00	1000.00
7 Charlie Buffington	2000.00	1000.00
8 Oyster Burns	2500.00	1250.00
9 Bob Caruthers	2000.00	1000.00
10 John Clarkson	3500.00	1800.00
11 Pop Smith	2000.00	1000.00
12 John Coleman	2000.00	1000.00
13 Charles Comiskey	5000.00	2500.00
14 Roger Connor (2)	3500.00	1800.00
15 Ed Daily	2000.00	1000.00
16 Pat Deasley	2000.00	1000.00
17 Jim Donahue	2000.00	1000.00
18 Pat Dorgan	2000.00	1000.00
19 Dude Esterbrook	2000.00	1000.00
20 Buck Ewing	3500.00	1800.00
21 Charlie Ferguson	2500.00	1250.00
22 Frank Flint	2500.00	1250.00
23 Charles Getzein	2000.00	1000.00
24 Jack Glasscock	2000.00	1000.00
25 Kid Gleason	3000.00	1500.00
26 Frank Hankinson	2000.00	1000.00
27 Ned Hanlon	3500.00	1800.00
28 Pete Hotaling	2000.00	1000.00
29 Richard Johnston	2000.00	1000.00
30 Tim Keefe (3)	3500.00	1800.00
31 Mike Kelly (2)	6000.00	3000.00
32 August Krock	2000.00	1000.00
33 Connie Mack	6000.00	3000.00
34 Kid Madden	2000.00	1000.00
35 George Miller	2000.00	1000.00
36 John Morrill	2000.00	1000.00
37 Henry Porter	2500.00	1250.00
38 James Mutrie MG	2000.00	1000.00
39 Sam Nicoll	2000.00	1000.00
40 Tip O'Neill	2500.00	1250.00
41 Jim O'Rourke	4000.00	2000.00
42 Fred Pfeffer	2000.00	1000.00
43 Danny Richardson (2)	2000.00	1000.00
44 Yank Robinson	2000.00	1000.00
45 Chief Roseman	2000.00	1000.00
46 Jimmy Ryan (2)	3000.00	1500.00
47 William J. Sowders	2000.00	1000.00
48 Martin J. Sullivan	2000.00	1000.00
49 Billy Sunday (2)	4000.00	2000.00
50 Ezra Sutton	2000.00	1000.00
51 Mike Tiernan (2)	2000.00	1000.00
52 Sam Thompson	4000.00	2000.00
53 Lawrence Twitchell	2000.00	1000.00
54 George Van Haltren	2000.00	1000.00
55 John Montgomery Ward	4000.00	2000.00
56 Curt Welch	2500.00	1250.00
57 Mickey Welch (2)	4000.00	2000.00
58 Grasshopper Whitney	2000.00	1000.00
59 Pete Wood	2000.00	1000.00

1976 Galasso Baseball's Great Hall of Fame

These 32 cards feature players considered among the all time greats. This was the first of many collector issue sets released by Renata Galasso Inc. Many of these sets were released as premiums with orders to RGI. This set is sequenced in alphabetical order.

	NM	Ex
COMPLETE SET	25.00	10.00
1 Luke Appling	.50	.20
2 Ernie Banks	1.00	.40
3 Yogi Berra	1.00	.40
4 Roy Campanella	1.00	.40
5 Roberto Clemente	3.00	1.20
6 Alvin Dark	.25	.10
7 Joe DiMaggio	3.00	1.20
8 Bob Feller	.75	.30
9 Whitey Ford	.75	.30
10 Jimmy Foxx	1.00	.40
11 Lou Gehrig	3.00	1.20
12 Charlie Gehringer	.50	.20
13 Henry Greenberg	.50	.20
14 Gabby Hartnett	.50	.20
15 Carl Hubbell	.75	.30
16 Al Kaline	.75	.30
17 Mickey Mantle	4.00	1.60
18 Willie Mays	2.00	.80
19 Johnny Mize	.50	.20
20 Stan Musial	1.50	.60
21 Mel Ott	.50	.20
22 Satchel Paige	1.50	.60
23 Robin Roberts	.75	.30
25 Babe Ruth	4.00	1.60
26 Duke Snider	1.00	.40
27 Warren Spahn	.75	.30
28 Tris Speaker	.75	.30
29 Honus Wagner	1.00	.40
30 Ted Williams	3.00	1.20
31 Rudy York	.25	.10
32 Cy Young	1.00	.40

1977-84 Galasso Glossy Greats

This 270-card standard-size set was issued by Renata Galasso Inc. (a hobby card dealer) and originally offered as a free bonus when ordering hand-collated Topps sets. The set may be subdivided into six series with 45 cards per series, with one series being issued per year as follows: TCMA printed the first four series and Renata Galasso Inc. the last two. The fronts display black and white player photos bordered in white. The player's name, position and team for which he played appear in the bottom white border. The backs are white, printed in red and blue ink and carry a career summary and an advertisement for Renata Galasso Inc. The backs have a red baseball in each of the upper corners with the card number in the left one.

	NM	Ex
COMPLETE SET (270)	125.00	50.00
1 Joe DiMaggio	3.00	1.20
2 Ralph Kiner	.40	.16
3 Don Larsen	.30	.12
4 Robin Roberts	.40	.16
5 Roy Campanella	.75	.30
6 Smoky Burgess	.10	.04
7 Mickey Mantle	3.00	1.20
8 Willie Mays	2.00	.80
9 George Kell	.40	.16
10 Ted Williams	2.50	1.00
11 Carl Furillo	.30	.12
12 Bob Feller	.40	.16
13 Casey Stengel	.75	.30
14 Richie Ashburn	.40	.16
15 Gil Hodges	.40	.16
16 Stan Musial	2.00	.80
17 Don Newcombe	.30	.12
18 Jackie Jensen	.30	.12
19 Lou Boudreau	.40	.16
20 Jackie Robinson	2.00	.80
21 Billy Goodman	.10	.04
22 Satchel Paige	1.00	.40
23 Hoyt Wilhelm	.40	.16
24 Duke Snider	.75	.30
25 Whitey Ford	1.00	.40
26 Monte Irvin	.40	.16
27 Hank Sauer	.10	.04
28 Sal Maglie	.20	.08
29 Ernie Banks	.75	.30
30 Billy Pierce	.20	.08
31 Pee Wee Reese	.75	.30
32 Al Lopez	.40	.16
33 Allie Reynolds	.20	.08
34 Eddie Mathews	.40	.16
35 Al Rosen	.20	.08
36 Early Wynn	.40	.16
37 Phil Rizzuto	.40	.16
38 Warren Spahn	.40	.16
39 Bobby Thomson	.30	.12
40 Enos Slaughter	.40	.16
41 Roberto Clemente	2.50	1.00
42 Luis Aparicio	.40	.16
43 Roy Sievers	.10	.04
44 Hank Aaron	2.00	.80
45 Mickey Vernon	.10	.04
46 Lou Gehrig	3.00	1.20
47 Lefty O'Doul	.20	.08
48 Chuck Klein	.40	.16
49 Paul Waner	.40	.16
50 Mel Ott	.40	.16
51 Riggs Stephenson	.20	.08
52 Dizzy Dean	.40	.16
53 Frank Frisch	.40	.16
54 Red Ruffing	.40	.16
55 Lefty Grove	.40	.16
56 Heinie Manush	.40	.16
57 Jimmie Foxx	.75	.30
58 Al Simmons	.40	.16
59 Charlie Root	.10	.04
60 Goose Goslin	.40	.16
61 Mickey Cochrane	.40	.16
62 Gabby Hartnett	.40	.16
63 Joe Medwick	.40	.16
64 Ernie Lombardi	.40	.16
65 Joe Cronin	.40	.16
66 Pepper Martin	.20	.08
67 Jim Bottomley	.40	.16
68 Bill Dickey	.75	.30
69 Babe Ruth	4.00	1.60
70 Joe McCarthy MG	.30	.12
71 Doc Cramer	.10	.04
72 KiKi Cuyler	.40	.16
73 Johnny Vander Meer	.30	.12
74 Paul Derringer	.10	.04
75 Fred Fitzsimmons	.20	.08
76 Lefty Gomez	.40	.16
77 Arky Vaughan	.40	.16
78 Stan Hack	.10	.04
79 Earl Averill	.40	.16
80 Luke Appling	.40	.16
81 Mel Harder	.10	.04
82 Hank Greenberg	.40	.16
83 Schoolboy Rowe	.10	.04
84 Billy Herman	.40	.16
85 Gabby Street	.10	.04
86 Lloyd Waner	.40	.16
87 Jocko Conlon	.30	.12
88 Carl Hubbell	.75	.30
89 Checklist 1	.10	.04
90 Checklist 2	.10	.04
91 Babe Ruth	4.00	1.60
92 Rogers Hornsby	.40	.16
93 Edd Roush	.40	.16
94 George Sisler	.40	.16
95 Harry Heilmann	.40	.16
96 Tris Speaker	.75	.30
97 Burleigh Grimes	.40	.16
98 John McGraw	.75	.30
99 Eppa Rixey	.40	.16
100 Ty Cobb	3.00	1.20
101 Zack Wheat	.40	.16
102 Pie Traynor	.75	.30
103 Max Carey	.40	.16
104 Dazzy Vance	.40	.16
105 Walter Johnson	1.00	.40
106 Herb Pennock	.40	.16
107 Joe Sewell	.40	.16
108 Sam Rice	.40	.16
109 Earle Combs	.40	.16
110 Ted Lyons	.40	.16
111 Eddie Collins	.75	.30
112 Bill Terry	.40	.16
113 Hack Wilson	.40	.16
114 Rabbit Maranville	.40	.16
115 Charlie Grimm	.20	.08
116 Tony Lazzeri	.40	.16
117 Waite Hoyt	.40	.16
118 Stan Coveleski	.40	.16
119 George Kelly	.40	.16
120 Jimmie Dykes	.20	.08
121 Red Faber	.40	.16
122 Dave Bancroft	.40	.16
123 Judge Landis COMM	.30	.12
124 Branch Rickey	.30	.12
125 Jesse Haines	.40	.16
126 Carl Mays	.20	.08
127 Fred Lindstrom	.40	.16
128 Miller Huggins	.40	.16
129 Sad Sam Jones	.10	.04
130 Joe Judge	.20	.08
131 Ross Youngs	.40	.16
132 Bucky Harris	.40	.16
133 Bob Meusel	.30	.12
134 Billy Evans	.30	.12
135 Checklist 3	.10	.04
136 Ty Cobb	3.00	1.20
137 Nap Lajoie	.40	.16
138 Tris Speaker	.40	.16
139 Heinie Groh	.10	.04
140 Sam Crawford	.40	.16
141 Clyde Milan	.10	.04
142 Chief Bender	.40	.16
143 Big Ed Walsh	.40	.16
144 Walter Johnson	.75	.30
145 Connie Mack MG	.40	.16
146 Hal Chase	.30	.12
147 Hugh Duffy	.40	.16
148 Honus Wagner	.75	.30
149 Tom Connolly UMP	.30	.12
150 Clark Griffith	.30	.12
151 Zack Wheat	.40	.16
152 Christy Mathewson	.75	.30
153 Grover Cleveland Alexander	.75	.30
154 Joe Jackson	1.50	.60
155 Home Run Baker	.40	.16
156 Ed Plank	.40	.16
157 Larry Doyle	.10	.04
158 Rube Marquard	.40	.16
159 John Evers	.40	.16
160 Joe Tinker	.40	.16
161 Frank Chance	.40	.16
162 Wilbert Robinson MG	.30	.12
163 Roger Peckinpaugh	.10	.04
164 Fred Clarke	.40	.16
165 Babe Ruth	4.00	1.60
166 Wilbur Cooper	.10	.04
167 Germany Schaefer	.20	.08
168 Addie Joss	.40	.16
169 Cy Young	.40	.16
170 Ban Johnson PRES	.30	.12
171 Joe Judge	.20	.08
172 Harry Hooper	.40	.16
173 Bill Klem UMP	.30	.12
174 Ed Barrow MG	.30	.12
175 Ed Cicotte	.30	.12
176 Hughie Jennings MG	.30	.12
177 Ray Schalk	.40	.16
178 Nick Altrock	.30	.12
179 Roger Bresnahan MG	.40	.16
180 Stuffy McInnis Eddie Collins Jack Barry Frank Baker CL	.10	.04
181 Lou Gehrig	3.00	1.20
182 Eddie Collins	.40	.16
183 Art Fletcher CO	.10	.04
184 Jimmie Foxx	.40	.16
185 Lefty Gomez	.40	.16
186 Oral Hildebrand	.10	.04
187 General Crowder	.10	.04
188 Bill Dickey	.40	.16
189 Wes Ferrell	.20	.08
190 Al Simmons	.40	.16
191 Tony Lazzeri	.40	.16
192 Sam West	.10	.04
193 Babe Ruth	4.00	1.60
194 Connie Mack MG	.40	.16
195 Lefty Grove	.40	.16
196 Eddie Rommel	.10	.04
197 Ben Chapman	.10	.04
198 Joe Cronin	.40	.16
199 Rick Ferrell	.40	.16
200 Charlie Gehringer	.40	.16
201 Jimmy Dykes	.20	.08
202 Earl Averill	.40	.16
203 Pepper Martin	.20	.08
204 Bill Terry	.40	.16
205 Pie Traynor	.40	.16
206 Gabby Hartnett	.40	.16
207 Frank Frisch	.40	.16
208 Carl Hubbell	.40	.16
209 Paul Waner	.40	.16
210 Woody English	.10	.04
211 Bill Hallahan	.10	.04
212 Dick Bartell	.10	.04
213 Bill McKechnie CO	.30	.12
214 Max Carey CO	.40	.16
215 John McGraw MG	.40	.16
216 Jimmie Wilson	.10	.04
217 Chick Hafey	.40	.16
218 Chuck Klein	.40	.16
219 Lefty O'Doul	.20	.08
220 Wally Berger	.10	.04
221 Hal Schumacher	.10	.04
222 Lon Warneke	.10	.04
223 Tony Cuccinello	.10	.04
224 American League Team	.10	.04
225 National League Team	.10	.04
226 Roger Maris	.75	.30
227 Babe Ruth	4.00	1.60
228 Jackie Robinson	2.00	.80
229 Pete Gray	.40	.16
230 Ted Williams	2.50	1.00
231 Hank Aaron	2.00	.80
232 Mickey Mantle	3.00	1.20
233 Gil Hodges	.75	.30
234 Walter Johnson	.40	.16
235 Joe DiMaggio	3.00	1.20
236 Lou Gehrig	3.00	1.20
237 Stan Musial	2.00	.80
238 Mickey Cochrane	.40	.16
239 Denny McLain	.20	.08
240 Carl Hubbell	.40	.16
241 Harvey Haddix	.10	.04
242 Christy Mathewson	.40	.16
243 Johnny Vander Meer	.20	.08
244 Sandy Koufax	.75	.30
245 Willie Mays	2.00	.80
246 Don Drysdale	.40	.16
247 Bobby Richardson	.20	.08
248 Hoyt Wilhelm	.40	.16
249 Yankee Stadium	.10	.04
250 Bill Terry	.40	.16
251 Roy Campanella	.75	.30
252 Roberto Clemente	2.50	1.00
253 Casey Stengel	.40	.16
254 Ernie Banks	.75	.30
255 Bobby Thomson	.30	.12
256 Mel Ott	.40	.16
257 Tony Oliva	.20	.08
258 Satchel Paige	1.00	.40
259 Joe Jackson	1.50	.60
260 Nap Lajoie	.40	.16
261 Bill Mazeroski	.30	.12
262 Bill Wambsganss	.10	.04
263 Willie McCovey	.40	.16
264 Warren Spahn	.40	.16
265 Lefty Gomez	.40	.16
266 Dazzy Vance	.40	.16
267 Sam Crawford	.40	.16
268 Tris Speaker	.40	.16
269 Lou Brock	.75	.30
270 Cy Young	.40	.16

1984 Galasso Hall of Famers Ron Lewis

These 45 deckle edge cards measure approximately 2 3/4" by 5". The full bleed fronts have pictures of Ron Lewis oil paintings. The backs have vital statistics, a brief biography and career stats. The checklist card back says the set is numbered out of 10,000 and gives the set number. This set only covers Hall of Famers from 1936 through 1946.

	Nm-Mt	Ex-Mt
COMPLETE SET (45)	15.00	6.00
1 Ty Cobb	2.00	.80
2 Babe Ruth	2.50	1.00
3 Walter Johnson	1.00	.40
4 Christy Mathewson	1.00	.40
5 Honus Wagner	1.00	.40
6 Nap Lajoie	.75	.30
7 Tris Speaker	.75	.30
8 Cy Young	1.00	.40
9 Morgan Bulkeley	.25	.10
10 Ban Johnson	.25	.10
11 John McGraw	.50	.20
12 Connie Mack	.50	.20
13 George Wright	.25	.10
14 Grover Alexander	1.00	.40
15 Alexander Cartwright	.25	.10
16 Henry Chadwick	.25	.10
17 Eddie Collins	.75	.30
18 Lou Gehrig	2.00	.80
19 Willie Keeler	.50	.20
20 George Sisler	.50	.20
21 Cap Anson	.50	.20
22 Charles Comiskey	.50	.20
23 Candy Cummings	.50	.20
24 Buck Ewing	.50	.20
25 Charlie Radbourne	.50	.20
26 A.G. Spalding	.25	.10
27 Rogers Hornsby	1.00	.40
28 Judge Landis	.25	.10
29 Roger Bresnahan	.50	.20
30 Dan Brouthers	.50	.20
31 Fred Clarke	.50	.20
32 Jimmy Collins	.50	.20
33 Ed Delahanty	.50	.20
34 Hugh Duffy	.50	.20
35 Hughie Jennings	.50	.20
36 Mike "King" Kelly	.50	.20
37 Jim O'Rouke	.50	.20
38 Wilbert Robinson	.50	.20
39 Jesse Burkett	.50	.20
40 Frank Chance	.50	.20
41 Jack Chesbro	.50	.20
42 Johnny Evers	.50	.20
43 Joe Tinker	.50	.20
44 Eddie Plank	.50	.20
45 Galasso Hall of Fame CL	.25	.10

1984 Galasso Reggie Jackson

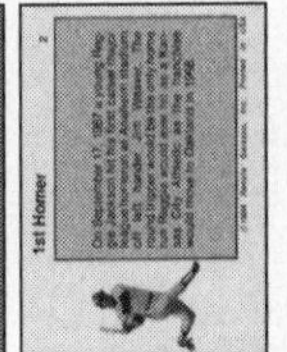

Produced by Renata Galasso, this 30-card standard-size set features color action player photos with turquoise borders. The player's first name appears in yellow script at the lower left corner. A small black-and-white cut-out photo of Jackson batting appears in the lower right corner. The horizontal backs are white and carry a pale blue box that contains career highlights. The same cut-out batting photo appears to the left of the box. The backs of card numbers 22-30 join to form a three-by-three card puzzle showing various baseball cards of Jackson against the background of his number 44 pinstriped jersey. A mini version of this set was also made, it is valued at $5 more than the regular sized set

	Nm-Mt	Ex-Mt
COMPLETE SET (30)	10.00	4.00
COMMON CARD (1-30)	.35	.14
*MINI SET: 1.5X VALUE		

1985-86 Galasso Gooden

Issued over two years, this standard-size set features then young sensation Dwight Gooden at the beginning of his career. The 1985 cards have blue borders, while the 1986 cards have yellow borders. These cards were issued by Renata Galasso, Inc. who were then among the largest baseball card dealers.

	Nm-Mt	Ex-Mt
COMPLETE SET	15.00	6.00
COMMON CARD	.25	.10
16 Dwight Gooden Hank Aaron	.75	.30

1986 Galasso Mattingly

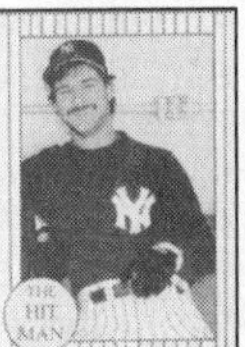

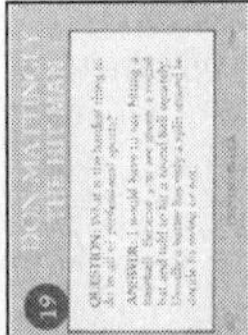

This 30 card standard-size set was issued by Renata Galasso, Inc. and featured Yankee slugger Don Mattingly. Cards numbered 1-21 feature front photos and the backs have questions/answers. The last nine cards in the set form a puzzle back.

	Nm-Mt	Ex-Mt
COMPLETE SET (30)	10.00	4.00
COMMON CARD	.50	.20

1981 Garvey Gafline

This one-card microfiche set features a small portrait of the Los Angeles Dodgers player,

Steve Garvey, printed with his biographical information and career statistics on GAFLINE 08 film.

	Nm-Mt	Ex-Mt
1 Steve Garvey	20.00	8.00

1920 Gassler's American Maid Bread D381-1

These cards measure approximately 2" by 3". The cards have a photo on most of the card with the player's name and position on the bottom. The back has an advertisment for Gassler's Bread. The cards are unnumbered and we have sequenced them alphabetically by team which are also sequenced alphabetically.

	Ex-Mt	VG
COMPLETE SET	1200.00	600.00
1 Kid Gleason MG	50.00	25.00
2 Harry Hooper	60.00	30.00
3 Dick Kerr	50.00	25.00
4 Amos Strunk	30.00	15.00
5 George Burns	30.00	15.00
6 W. L. Gardner	30.00	15.00
7 Rip Collins	30.00	15.00
8 Wm. Fewster	30.00	15.00
9 Harry Harper	30.00	15.00
10 Waite Hoyt	60.00	30.00
11 Miller Huggins MG	60.00	30.00
12 M.J. McNally	30.00	15.00
13 Bob Meusel	50.00	25.00
14 Walter Pipp	40.00	20.00
15 Jack Quinn	30.00	15.00
16 Robert Roth	30.00	15.00
17 Wally Schang	40.00	20.00
18 Aaron Ward	30.00	15.00
19 Wm. Jacobson	30.00	15.00
20 Clyde Milan	40.00	20.00
21 Walter Holke	30.00	15.00
22 P. J. Kilduff	30.00	15.00
23 Zach Wheat	60.00	30.00
24 Charles Deal	30.00	15.00
25 Charles Hollacher	30.00	15.00
26 Zeb Terry	30.00	15.00
27 Geo. J. Burns	30.00	15.00
28 Cecil Causey	30.00	15.00
29 Hugh Jennings MG	60.00	30.00
30 Arthur Nehf	40.00	20.00
31 John Rawlings	30.00	15.00
32 Bill Ryan	30.00	15.00
33 Pat Shea	30.00	15.00
34 Earl Smith	30.00	15.00
35 Frank Snyder	30.00	15.00
36 Jeff Pfeffer	30.00	15.00

1912 General Baking D304

These cards, which measure 1 3/4" by 2 1/2" feature drawings of leading players. Many of the players in this set were members of the 1911 pennant winners, leading one to believe that this set was issued sometime the next summer. Various other manufacturers also produced this set, most noticeably Brunner's Bread.

	Ex-Mt	VG
COMPLETE SET (25)	6000.00	3000.00
1 J. Frank Baker	250.00	125.00
2 Jack Barry	100.00	50.00
3 George Bell	100.00	50.00
4 Charles Bender	250.00	125.00
5 Frank Chance	300.00	150.00
6 Hal Chase	200.00	100.00
7 Ty Cobb	1000.00	500.00
8 Eddie Collins	400.00	200.00
9 Otis Crandall	100.00	50.00
10 Sam Crawford	300.00	150.00
11 John Evans	300.00	150.00
12 Arthur Fletcher	100.00	50.00
13 Charles Herzog	100.00	50.00
14 M. Kelly	100.00	50.00
15 Napoleon Lajoie	300.00	150.00
16 Rube Marquard	200.00	100.00
17 Christy Mathewson	500.00	250.00
18 Fred Merkle	100.00	50.00
19 Chief Meyers	100.00	50.00
20 Marty O'Toole	100.00	50.00
21 Nap Rucker	100.00	50.00
22 Arthur Shafer	100.00	50.00
23 Fred Tenny	100.00	50.00
24 Honus Wagner	600.00	300.00
25 Cy Young	500.00	250.00

1985 General Mills Stickers

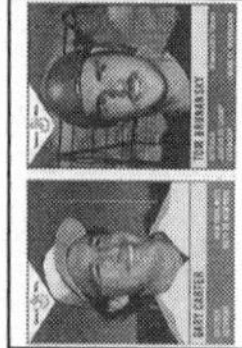

Found in boxes of Cheerios and Honey Nut Cheerios in Canada, each General Mills sticker card features two stickers, with a National League player on the left and an American League player on the right. Each sticker pair measures approximately 3 3/4" by 2 3/8" while each individual player sticker measures 1 7/8" by 2 3/8". On a white background, the fronts feature color player portraits, with the player's name in a yellow bar under the photo. The National League player's team and position (in French and English) appear in a red bar under the photo, while the American League player's team and position (also in French and English) appear in a blue bar. The players' cap team logos have been airbrushed. The General Mills logo is printed inside a triangle in the upper left corner of each sticker. The backs are blank. The set features one player per team. The pairs are valued at the sum of the individual player values. Some players are featured with more than one partner, e.g. Gary Carter is found with either Tom Brunansky or Dave Stieb and Steve Garvey is found with either George Bell or Jim Rice. The stickers are unnumbered and checklisted below in alphabetical order by National Leaguers (1-12) and American Leaguers (13-26). The number of the sticker that each player is paired with is as follows: 1/15, 1/23, 2/16, 3/13, 3/22, 4/21, 5/26, 6/19, 7/24, 8/18, 9/14, 10/25, 11/17 and 12/20.

	Nm-Mt	Ex-Mt
COMPLETE SET (26)	20.00	8.00
1 Gary Carter DP	.50	.20
2 Andre Dawson	1.00	.40
3 Steve Garvey DP	.50	.20
4 Jeff Leonard	.25	.10
5 Dale Murphy	1.00	.40
6 Terry Puhl	.25	.10
7 Johnny Ray	.25	.10
8 Ryne Sandberg	4.00	1.60
9 Mike Schmidt	2.50	1.00
10 Ozzie Smith	1.50	.60
11 Mario Soto	.25	.10
12 Fernando Valenzuela	.50	.20
13 Buddy Bell	.50	.20
14 George Brett	3.00	1.20
15 Tom Brunansky	.25	.10
16 Alvin Davis	.50	.20
17 Carlton Fisk	1.50	.60
18 Mike Hargrove	.50	.20
19 Reggie Jackson	2.00	.80
20 Dwayne Murphy	.25	.10
21 Eddie Murray	1.50	.60
22 Jim Rice	.50	.20
23 Dave Stieb	.25	.10
24 Lou Whitaker	.75	.30
25 Dave Winfield	1.50	.60
26 Robin Yount	1.50	.60

1986 General Mills Booklets

Printed on thin glossy stock, each of these six booklets measures approximately 15" by 3 13/16" when unfolded; each single player (and the complete booklet when folded) measures approximately 2 9/16" by 3 13/16". Each booklet features ten color player head shots, five on each side. The players' cap logos have been airbrushed. The sixth (non-player) panel is an entry for a contest to win a day with your favorite player at spring training in 1987. The player's statistics in English and French appear under each photo. The title card carries the booklet number in the top right corner. The set is sometimes referred to as the "Cheerios" set as it was inserted inside Cheerios cereal boxes; Cheerios is a product of General Mills. Booklets still in the original clear cellophane protective wrapping are worth an additional ten percent over the prices listed below.

	Nm-Mt	Ex-Mt
COMPLETE SET (60)	200.00	80.00
1A Wade Boggs	10.00	4.00
1B Kirk Gibson	4.00	1.60
1C Rickey Henderson	15.00	6.00
1D Don Mattingly	25.00	10.00
1E Jack Morris	4.00	1.60
1F Lance Parrish	2.00	.80
1G Jim Rice	4.00	1.60
1H Dave Righetti	2.00	.80
1I Cal Ripken	50.00	20.00
1J Lou Whitaker	6.00	2.40
2A Harold Baines	4.00	1.60
2B Phil Bradley	2.00	.80
2C George Brett	25.00	10.00
2D Carlton Fisk	10.00	4.00
2E Ozzie Guillen	6.00	2.40
2F Kent Hrbek	4.00	1.60
2G Reggie Jackson	12.00	4.80
2H Dan Quisenberry	2.00	.80
2I Bret Saberhagen	4.00	1.60
2J Frank White	2.00	.80
3A Jesse Barfield	2.00	.80
3B George Bell	2.00	.80
3C Bill Caudill	2.00	.80
3D Tony Fernandez	2.00	.80
3E Damaso Garcia	2.00	.80
3F Lloyd Moseby	2.00	.80
3G Rance Mulliniks	2.00	.80
3H Dave Stieb	4.00	1.60
3I Willie Upshaw	2.00	.80
3J Ernie Whitt	2.00	.80
4A Gary Carter	10.00	4.00
4B Jack Clark	2.00	.80
4C George Foster	2.00	.80
4D Dwight Gooden	6.00	2.40
4E Gary Matthews	2.00	.80
4F Willie McGee	4.00	1.60
4G Ryne Sandberg	20.00	8.00
4H Mike Schmidt	12.00	4.80
4I Lee Smith	4.00	1.60
4J Ozzie Smith	20.00	8.00
5A David Concepcion	4.00	1.60
5B Pedro Guerrero	2.00	.80
5C Terry Kennedy	2.00	.80
5D Dale Murphy	8.00	3.20
5E Graig Nettles	4.00	1.60
5F Dave Parker	4.00	1.60
5G Tony Perez	10.00	4.00
5H Steve Sax	2.00	.80
5I Bruce Sutter	2.00	.80
5J Fernando Valenzuela	4.00	1.60
6A Hubie Brooks	2.00	.80
6B Andre Dawson	10.00	4.00
6C Mike Fitzgerald	2.00	.80
6D Vance Law	2.00	.80
6E Tim Raines	4.00	1.60
6F Jeff Reardon	2.00	.80
6G Bryn Smith	2.00	.80
6H Jason Thompson	2.00	.80
6I Tim Wallach	2.00	.80
6J Mitch Webster	2.00	.80

1987 General Mills Booklets

Printed on thin glossy stock, each of these six booklets measures approximately 15" by 3 3/4" when unfolded; each single player (and the complete booklet when folded) measures approximately 2 9/16" by 3 3/4". Each booklet features ten color player head shots, five on each side from a respective grouping (each division and both Canadian teams). The sixth (non-player) panel is an entry for a contest to win a day with your favorite player at Spring Training in 1988. The players' cap logos have been airbrushed. Player statistics in English and French appear under each photo. The title card carries the booklet number in the top right corner. The set is sometimes referred to as the "Cheerios" set as it was inserted inside Cheerios cereal boxes; Cheerios is a product of General Mills. Booklets still in the original clear cellophane protective wrapping are worth an additional ten percent over the prices listed below.

	Nm-Mt	Ex-Mt
COMPLETE SET (60)	20.00	8.00
1A Jesse Barfield	.25	.10
1B George Bell	.25	.10
1C Tony Fernandez	.50	.20
1D Kelly Gruber	.25	.10
1E Tom Henke	.25	.10
1F Jimmy Key	.75	.30
1G Lloyd Moseby	.25	.10
1H Dave Stieb	.25	.10
1I Willie Upshaw	.25	.10
1J Ernie Whitt	.25	.10
2A Wade Boggs	1.25	.50
2B Roger Clemens	1.50	.60
2C Kirk Gibson	.50	.20
2D Rickey Henderson	1.50	.60
2E Don Mattingly	3.00	1.20
2F Jack Morris	.50	.20
2G Eddie Murray	1.25	.50
2H Pat Tabler	.25	.10
2I Dave Winfield	1.25	.50
2J Robin Yount	1.25	.50
3A Phil Bradley	.25	.10
3B George Brett	2.00	.80
3C Jose Canseco	1.50	.60
3D Carlton Fisk	1.25	.50
3E Reggie Jackson	1.25	.50
3F Wally Joyner	1.00	.40
3G Kirk McCaskill	.25	.10
3H Larry Parrish	.25	.10
3I Kirby Puckett	1.50	.60
3J Dan Quisenberry	.25	.10
4A Hubie Brooks	.25	.10
4B Mike Fitzgerald	.25	.10
4C Andres Galarraga	.75	.30
4D Vance Law	.25	.10
4E Andy McGaffigan	.25	.10
4F Bryn Smith	.25	.10
4G Jason Thompson	.25	.10
4H Tim Wallach	.25	.10
4I Mitch Webster	.25	.10
4J Floyd Youmans	.25	.10
5A Gary Carter	1.25	.50
5B Dwight Gooden	.75	.30
5C Keith Hernandez	.50	.20
5D Willie McGee	.50	.20
5E Tim Raines	.50	.20
5F R.J. Reynolds	.25	.10
5G Ryne Sandberg	1.50	.60
5H Mike Schmidt	1.25	.50
5I Ozzie Smith	2.00	.80
5J Darryl Strawberry	.50	.20
6A Kevin Bass	.25	.10
6B Eric Davis	.75	.30
6C Bill Doran	.25	.10
6D Pedro Guerrero	.25	.10
6E Tony Gwynn	2.50	1.00
6F Dale Murphy	1.00	.40
6G Dave Parker	.50	.20
6H Steve Sax	.25	.10
6I Mike Scott	.25	.10
6J Fernando Valenzuela	.50	.20

1933 George C. Miller R300

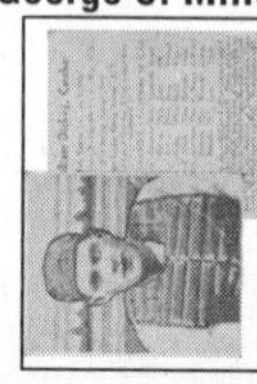

The cards in this 32-card set measure 2 1/2" by 3". This set of soft tone color baseball cards issued in 1933 by the George C. Miller Company consists of 16 players from each league. The bottom portion of the reverse contained a premium offer and many cards are found with this section cut off. Cards without the coupon are considered fair to good condition at best. The Andrews card (with coupon intact) is considered extremely scarce in relation to all other common players. Very few copies are known of the Andrews with the coupon attached.

	Ex-Mt	VG
COMPLETE SET (32)	12500.00	6200.00
1 Dale Alexander	500.00	250.00
2 Ivy Andrews	20000.00	10000.00
3 Earl Averill	800.00	400.00
4 Dick Bartell	500.00	250.00
5 Wally Berger	500.00	250.00
6 Jim Bottomley	800.00	400.00
7 Joe Cronin	800.00	400.00
8 Dizzy Dean	1000.00	500.00
9 Bill Dickey	1000.00	500.00
10 Jimmy Dykes	500.00	250.00
11 Wes Ferrell	600.00	300.00
12 Jimmy Foxx	1200.00	600.00
13 Frank Frisch	800.00	400.00
14 Charlie Gehringer	800.00	400.00
15 Goose Goslin	800.00	400.00
16 Charlie Grimm	500.00	250.00
17 Lefty Grove	1000.00	500.00
18 Chick Hafey	600.00	300.00
19 Ray Hayworth	500.00	250.00
20 Chuck Klein	800.00	400.00
21 Rabbit Maranville	800.00	400.00
22 Oscar Melillo	500.00	250.00
23 Lefty O'Doul	600.00	300.00
24 Mel Ott	1000.00	500.00
25 Carl Reynolds	500.00	250.00
26 Red Ruffing	800.00	400.00
27 Al Simmons	800.00	400.00
28 Joe Stripp	500.00	250.00
29 Bill Terry	800.00	400.00
30 Lloyd Waner	800.00	400.00
31 Paul Waner	800.00	400.00
32 Lon Warneke	500.00	250.00

1972 Gera Postcard

This postcard was given away at what was supposed to be lady umpire Bernice Gera's first game. As the only game she actually umpired in was one day later, this card features several factual errors. The postcard features a photo of Gera on top and then the basic information about the game she umpired in. Gera only umpired in one game before concluding her professional career.

	NM	Ex
1 Bernice Gera	10.00	4.00

1906 Giants Ullman's Art Frame Series

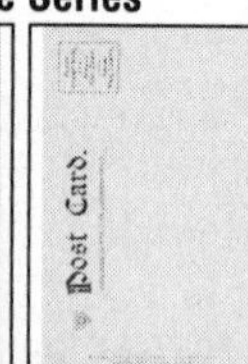

These cards, issued the year after the Giants won their first World Series, show an action view of the player or players inside a brown or green border made to resemble a picture frame. At the bottom is a gold area made to look like an identification tag for a picture containing a description of the scene and players identified. There are probably more cards in this set so additions to the checklist are appreciated.

	Ex-Mt	VG
COMPLETE SET (12)	3000.00	1500.00
1 Red Ames	250.00	125.00
2 Mike Donlin	300.00	150.00
3 George Ferguson	200.00	100.00
4 Matty Fitzgerald	200.00	100.00
5 Bill Gilbert	200.00	100.00
6 Christy Mathewson Sic, Matthewson	800.00	400.00
7 Harry Mathewson	200.00	100.00
8 Dan McGann	200.00	100.00
9 Joe McGinnity	400.00	200.00
10 John McGraw MG	400.00	200.00
11 Sammy Strang Frank Bowerman	200.00	100.00
12 Hooks Wiltse	200.00	100.00

1909 Giants Derby Cigar

These 12 blank-backed cards measure 1 3/4" by 2 3/4" and were assumed to be issued by the Derby Cigar Co. They feature members of the New York Giants and the players photo is in an oval design in the middle with the name and position at the bottom

	Ex-Mt	VG
COMPLETE SET (12)	12000.00	6000.00
1 Josh Devore	800.00	400.00
2 Larry Doyle	1000.00	500.00
3 Art Fletcher	800.00	400.00
4 Buck Herzog	800.00	400.00
5 Rube Marquard	1500.00	750.00
6 Christy Mathewson	2500.00	1250.00
7 John McGraw MG	2000.00	1000.00
8 Fred Merkle	1000.00	500.00
9 Chief Meyers	1000.00	500.00
10 Red Murray	800.00	400.00
11 Fred Snodgrass	1000.00	500.00
12 Hooks Wiltse	800.00	400.00

1932 Giants Schedule

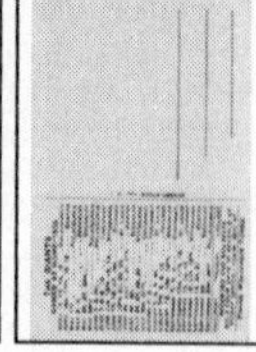

This set of the 1932 New York Giants was issued in a postcard format with a black and white action photo on the front. Player information is printed in the wide bottom margin. The back displays the team's schedule. It has been alleged that the Hubbell was counterfeited. However, many dealers believe an inordinate amount of the Hubbell's were printed and a warehouse find made them appear to be too clean to be more than 60 years old. It seems like the Hubbell commonly seen in the marketplace is just a double print and has been noted as such. Some other dealers believe the common Hubbell variety is a proof issue.

	Ex-Mt	VG
COMPLETE SET	350.00	180.00
1 Ethan Allen	10.00	5.00
2 Herman Bell	10.00	5.00
3 Hugh Critz	10.00	5.00
4 Fred Fitzsimmons	20.00	10.00
5 Chick Fullis	10.00	5.00
6 Sam Gibson	10.00	5.00
7 Fran Healy Sic, Healey	10.00	5.00
8 Frank Hogan	10.00	5.00
9 Carl Hubbell DP	25.00	12.50
10 Carl Hubbell	50.00	25.00
11 Travis Jackson	25.00	12.50
12 Len Koenecke	10.00	5.00
13 Sam Leslie	10.00	5.00
14 Dolph Luque	15.00	7.50
15 Jim Mooney	10.00	5.00
16 Bob O'Farrell	15.00	7.50
17 Mel Ott	50.00	25.00
18 Roy Parmalee	10.00	5.00
19 Bill Terry	40.00	20.00
20 Johnny Vergez	10.00	5.00
21 Bill Walker	10.00	5.00

1948 Giants Team Issue

This 26-card set, which measures 6 1/2" by 9" features black-and-white photos of the New York Giants with white borders and was issued by Harry M. Stevens, Inc. A facsimile autograph is printed across the front. The backs are blank. The cards are unnumbered and checklisted below in alphabetical order. Mel Ott was originally issued with this set but was pulled after being let go in midseason. He was replaced by Leo Durocher as manager. As far as can be determined there is an even number of Ott and Durocher cards issued. The set is considered complete with either the Ott or the Durocher card.

	NM	Ex
COMPLETE SET (26)	150.00	75.00
1 Jack Conway	4.00	2.00
2 Walker Cooper	5.00	2.50
3 Leo Durocher MG	25.00	12.50
4 Sid Gordon	4.00	2.00
5 Andy Hansen	4.00	2.00
6 Clint Hartung	4.00	2.00
7 Larry Jansen	6.00	3.00
8 Sheldon Jones	4.00	2.00
9 Monte Kennedy	4.00	2.00
10 Buddy Kerr	4.00	2.00
11 Dave Koslo	4.00	2.00
12 Thornton Lee	4.00	2.00
13 Mickey Livingston	4.00	2.00
14 Whitey Lockman	6.00	3.00
15 Jack Lohrke	4.00	2.00
16 Willard Marshall	4.00	2.00
17 Johnnie McCarthy	4.00	2.00
18 Earl McGowan	4.00	2.00
19 Johnny Mize	15.00	7.50
20 Bobo Newsom	6.00	3.00
21 Met Ott MG	25.00	12.50
22 Ray Poat	4.00	2.00
23 Bobbie Rhawn	4.00	2.00
24 Bill Rigney	6.00	3.00
25 Bob Thomson	8.00	4.00
26 Ken Trinkle	4.00	2.00
27 Wes Westrum	5.00	2.50

1949 Giants Team Issue

This 25-card set features black-and-white photos of the New York Giants with white borders and was issued by Harry M. Stevens, Inc. A facsimile autograph is printed across the front. The backs are blank. The cards are unnumbered and checklisted below in alphabetical order.

	NM	Ex
COMPLETE SET (25)	150.00	75.00
1 Hank Behrman	4.00	2.00
2 Walker Cooper	4.00	2.00
3 Leo Durocher MG	20.00	10.00
4 Fred Fitzsimmons CO	4.00	2.00
5 Frank Frisch CO	15.00	7.50
6 Augie Galan	4.00	2.00
7 Sid Gordon	4.00	2.00
8 Bert Haas	4.00	2.00
9 Andy Hansen	4.00	2.00
10 Clint Hartung	4.00	2.00
11 Bob Hofman	4.00	2.00
12 Larry Jansen	6.00	3.00
13 Sheldon Jones	4.00	2.00
14 Monte Kennedy	4.00	2.00
15 Buddy Kerr	4.00	2.00
16 Dave Koslo	4.00	2.00
17 Mickey Livingston	4.00	2.00
18 Whitey Lockman	6.00	3.00
19 Willard Marshall	4.00	2.00
20 Johnny Mize	15.00	7.50
21 Don Mueller	4.00	2.00
22 Ray Poat	4.00	2.00
23 Bobbie Rhawn	4.00	2.00
24 Bill Rigney	6.00	3.00
25 Bob Thomson	8.00	4.00

1954 Giants Jacobellis

These photos, which measure approximately 8 1/4" by 10" feature members of the 1954 New York Giants. The fronts feature the players photo, his name and on the bottom a small note that the photo was taken by Bill Jacobellis. Since these photos are unnumbered, we have sequenced them in alphabetical order.

	NM	Ex
COMPLETE SET	120.00	60.00
1 John Antonelli	12.00	6.00
2 Al Dark	12.00	6.00
3 Ruben Gomez	10.00	5.00
4 Whitey Lockman	12.00	6.00
5 Willie Mays	50.00	25.00
6 Don Mueller	10.00	5.00
7 Dusty Rhodes	10.00	5.00
8 New York Giants	20.00	10.00

1955 Giants Golden Stamps

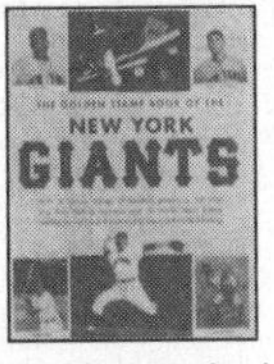

This 32-stamp set features color photos of the New York Giants and measures approximately 2" by 2 5/8". The stamps are designed to be placed in a 32-page album which measures approximately 8 3/8" by 10 15/16". The album contains black-and-white drawings of players with statistics and life stories. The stamps are unnumbered and listed below according to where they fall in the album.

	NM	Ex
COMPLETE SET (32)	100.00	50.00
1 1954 Giants Team	10.00	5.00
2 Leo Durocher MG	15.00	7.50
3 Johnny Antonelli	2.00	1.00
4 Sal Maglie	3.00	1.50
5 Ruben Gomez	2.00	1.00
6 Hoyt Wilhelm	10.00	5.00
7 Marv Grissom	2.00	1.00
8 Jim Hearn	2.00	1.00
9 Paul Giel	2.00	1.00
10 Al Corwin	2.00	1.00
11 George Spencer	2.00	1.00
12 Don Liddle	2.00	1.00
13 Windy McCall	2.00	1.00
14 Al Worthington	2.00	1.00
15 Wes Westrum	2.00	1.00
16 Whitey Lockman	2.50	1.25
17 Dave Williams	2.00	1.00
18 Hank Thompson	3.00	1.50
19 Alvin Dark	3.00	1.50
20 Monte Irvin	10.00	5.00
21 Willie Mays	25.00	12.50
22 Don Mueller	2.00	1.00
23 Dusty Rhodes	2.00	1.00
24 Ray Katt	2.00	1.00
25 Joe Amalfitano	2.00	1.00
26 Billy Gardner	2.00	1.00
27 Foster Castleman	2.00	1.00
28 Bobby Hoffman	2.00	1.00
29 Bill Taylor	2.00	1.00
30 Manager and Coaches	3.00	1.50
31 Bobby Weinstein BB	2.00	1.00
32 Polo Grounds	15.00	7.50
XX Album	4.00	2.00

1956 Giants Jay Publishing

This 12-card set of the New York Giants measures approximately 5 1/8" by 7". The fronts feature black-and-white posed player photos with the player's and team name printed below in the white border. These cards were packaged 12 to a packet and originally sold for 25 cents by mail. The backs are blank. The cards are unnumbered and checklisted below in alphabetical order.

	NM	Ex
COMPLETE SET (12)	60.00	30.00
1 Johnny Antonelli	4.00	2.00
2 Al Dark	5.00	2.50
3 Ruben Gomez	3.00	1.50
4 Monte Irvin	6.00	3.00
5 Whitey Lockman	5.00	2.50
6 Sal Maglie	5.00	2.50
7 Willie Mays	20.00	10.00
8 Don Mueller	3.00	1.50
9 Bill Rigney	4.00	2.00
10 Hank Thompson	4.00	2.00
11 Wes Westrum	3.00	1.50
12 Dave Williams	3.00	1.50

1957 Giants Jay Publishing

This 12-card set of the New York Giants measures approximately 5" by 7". The fronts feature black-and-white posed player photos with the player's and team name printed below in the white border. These cards were packaged 12 to a packet and originally sold for 25 cents by mail. The backs are blank. The cards are unnumbered and checklisted below in alphabetical order. A pre-Rookie Card of Bill White (precedes his Rookie Card by 2 years) is featured in this set.

	NM	Ex
COMPLETE SET (12)	60.00	30.00
1 Johnny Antonelli	5.00	2.50
2 Jackie Brandt	3.00	1.50
3 Eddie Bressoud	3.00	1.50
4 Ruben Gomez	3.00	1.50
5 Willie Mays	20.00	10.00
6 Don Mueller	3.00	1.50
7 Bill Rigney	4.00	2.00
8 Bill Sarni	3.00	1.50
9 Red Schoendienst	6.00	3.00
10 Daryl Spencer	3.00	1.50
11 Bill White	6.00	3.00
12 Allan Worthington	3.00	1.50

1958 Giants Jay Publishing

This 12-card set of the San Francisco Giants measures approximately 5" by 7" and features black-and-white player photos in a white border. These cards were packaged 12 to a packet. The backs are blank. The cards are unnumbered and checklisted below in alphabetical order.

	NM	Ex
COMPLETE SET (12)	50.00	25.00
1 John Antonelli	4.00	2.00
2 Curt Barclay	3.00	1.50
3 Paul Giel	3.00	1.50
4 Ruben Gomez	3.00	1.50
5 Willie Kirkland	3.00	1.50
6 Whitey Lockman	4.00	2.00
7 Willie Mays	20.00	10.00
8 Danny O'Connell	3.00	1.50
9 Hank Sauer	4.00	2.00
10 Bob Schmidt	3.00	1.50
11 Daryl Spencer	3.00	1.50
12 Al Worthington	3.00	1.50

1958 Giants S.F. Call-Bulletin

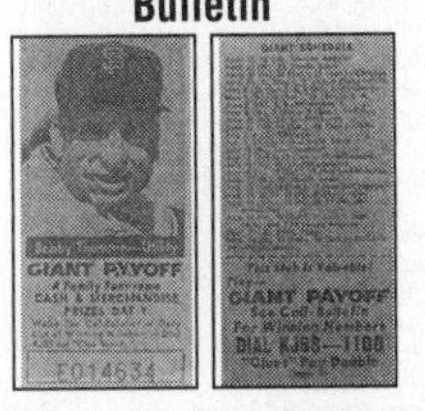

The cards in this 25-card set measure approximately 2" by 4". The 1958 San Francisco Call-Bulletin set of unnumbered cards features black print on orange paper. These cards were given away as inserts in the San Francisco Call-Bulletin newspaper. The backs of the cards list the Giants home schedule and a radio station ad. The cards are entitled "Giant Payoff" and feature San Francisco Giant players only. The bottom part of the card (tab) could be detached as a ticket stub; hence, cards with the tab intact are worth approximately double the prices listed below. The catalog designation for this set is M126. The Tom Bowers card was issued in very short supply; also Bressoud, Jablonski, and Kirkland are tougher to find than the others; all of these tougher cards are indicated as SP in the checklist below.

	NM	Ex
COMPLETE SET (25)	1400.00	700.00
COMMON CARD (1-25)	10.00	5.00
COMMON SP	125.00	60.00
1 John Antonelli	12.00	6.00
2 Curt Barclay	10.00	5.00
3 Tom Bowers SP	600.00	300.00
4 Ed Bressoud SP	125.00	60.00
5 Orlando Cepeda	50.00	25.00
6 Ray Crone	10.00	5.00
7 Jim Davenport	12.00	6.00
8 Paul Giel	20.00	10.00
9 Ruben Gomez	10.00	5.00
10 Marv Grissom	10.00	5.00
11 Ray Jablonski SP	125.00	60.00
12 Willie Kirkland SP	150.00	75.00
13 Whitey Lockman	12.00	6.00
14 Willie Mays	250.00	125.00
15 Mike McCormick	12.00	6.00
16 Stu Miller	12.00	6.00
17 Ray Monzant	10.00	5.00
18 Danny O'Connell	10.00	5.00
19 Bill Rigney MG	10.00	5.00
20 Hank Sauer	12.00	6.00
21 Bob Schmidt	10.00	5.00
22 Daryl Spencer	10.00	5.00
23 Valmy Thomas	10.00	5.00
24 Bobby Thomson	20.00	10.00
25 Al Worthington	10.00	5.00

1958-61 Giants Falstaff Beer Team Photos

This four-card set features color photos of the 1958, 1959, 1960, and 1961 San Francisco Giants teams. Each card measures approximately 6 1/4" by 9" and displays the Falstaff logo on the front. The backs carry a team promotional message.

	NM	Ex
COMPLETE SET (4)	100.00	50.00
COMMON CARD (1-4)	20.00	10.00
1 1958 Giants Team Photo	40.00	20.00
2 1959 Giants Team Photo	30.00	15.00

1959 Giants Jay Publishing

This 12-card set of the San Francisco Giants measures approximately 5" by 7" and features black-and-white player photos in a white border. These cards were packaged 12 to a packet and originally sold for 25 cents. The backs are blank. The cards are unnumbered and checklisted below in alphabetical order.

	NM	Ex
COMPLETE SET	50.00	25.00
1 Jackie Brandt	3.00	1.50
2 Orlando Cepeda	8.00	4.00
3 Jim Davenport	3.00	1.50
4 Sam Jones	3.00	1.50
5 Willie Kirkland	3.00	1.50
6 Hobie Landrith	3.00	1.50
7 Willie Mays	20.00	10.00
8 Stu Miller	3.00	1.50
9 Jack Sanford	3.00	1.50
10 Hank Sauer	4.00	2.00
11 Bob Schmidt	3.00	1.50
12 Daryl Spencer	3.00	1.50

1960 Giants Jay Publishing

This 12-card set of the San Francisco Giants measures approximately 5" by 7" and features black-and-white player photos in a white border. These cards were packaged 12 to a packet. The backs are blank. The cards are unnumbered and checklisted below in alphabetical order. Willie McCovey is featured in his Rookie Card year.

	NM	Ex
COMPLETE SET (12)	40.00	16.00
1 John Antonelli	2.50	1.00
2 Don Blasingame	2.50	1.00
3 Eddie Bressoud	2.50	1.00
4 Orlando Cepeda	6.00	2.40
5 Jim Davenport	2.50	1.00
6 Sam Jones	2.50	1.00
7 Willie Kirkland	2.50	1.00
8 Willie Mays	20.00	8.00
9 Willie McCovey	12.00	4.80
10 Mike McCormick	2.50	1.00
11 Jack Sanford	2.50	1.00
12 Bob Schmidt	2.50	1.00

1961 Giants Jay Publishing

This 12-card set of the San Francisco Giants measures approximately 5" by 7". The fronts feature black-and-white posed player photos with the player's and team name printed below in the white border. These cards were packaged 12 in a packet. The backs are blank. The cards are unnumbered and checklisted below in alphabetical order. Juan Marichal is featured in his Rookie Card year.

	NM	Ex
COMPLETE SET (12)	40.00	16.00
1 Felipe Alou	4.00	1.60
2 Don Blasingame	2.50	1.00
3 Orlando Cepeda	6.00	2.40
4 Alvin Dark MG	3.00	1.20
5 Jim Davenport	3.00	1.20
6 Sam Jones	2.50	1.00
7 Harvey Kuenn	3.00	1.20
8 Juan Marichal	15.00	6.00
9 Willie Mays	20.00	8.00
10 Mike McCormick	2.50	1.00
11 Stu Miller	2.50	1.00
12 Bob Schmidt	2.50	1.00

1962 Giants Jay Publishing

This 12-card set of the San Francisco Giants measures approximately 5" by 7". The fronts feature black-and-white posed player photos with the player's and team name printed below in the white border. These cards were packaged 12 in a packet. The backs are blank. The cards are unnumbered and checklisted below in alphabetical order.

	NM	Ex
COMPLETE SET (12)	45.00	18.00
1 Felipe Alou	4.00	1.60
2 Ed Bailey	2.50	1.00
3 Orlando Cepeda	8.00	3.20
4 Jim Davenport	3.00	1.20
5 Tom Haller	2.50	1.00
6 Chuck Hiller	2.50	1.00
7 Harvey Kuenn	3.00	1.20
8 Juan Marichal	10.00	4.00
9 Willie Mays	20.00	8.00
10 Mike McCormick	3.00	1.20
11 Stu Miller	2.50	1.00
12 Billy Pierce	4.00	1.60

1962 Giants Photo Album

Issued by the San Fransisco News Cal-Bulletin, these photos feature biographical information, a player portrait and a biography of the featured player. Each of these pages were part of a special photo album commemorating the

opening of what would be pennant winning season for the 1962 Giants. Since these photos are unnumbered, we have sequenced them in the order they appeared in the photo album. Gaylord Perry appears in this set in his Rookie Card year.

	MINT	NRMT
COMPLETE SET	200.00	90.00
1 Al Dark MG	6.00	2.70
2 Mike McCormick	6.00	2.70
3 Stu Miller	5.00	2.20
4 Jack Sanford	5.00	2.20
5 Juan Marichal	20.00	9.00
6 Bob Bolin	5.00	2.20
7 Jim Duffalo	5.00	2.20
8 Don Larsen	8.00	3.60
9 Billy O'Dell	5.00	2.20
10 Billy Pierce	8.00	3.60
11 Dick LeMay	5.00	2.20
12 Gaylord Perry	25.00	11.00
13 Ed Bailey	5.00	2.20
14 Tom Haller	5.00	2.20
15 Joe Pignatano	5.00	2.20
16 Orlando Cepeda	15.00	6.75
17 Chuck Hiller	5.00	2.20
18 Jose Pagan	5.00	2.20
19 Jim Davenport	5.00	2.20
20 Felipe Alou	10.00	4.50
21 Willie Mays	40.00	18.00
22 Harvey Kuenn	6.00	2.70
23 Willie McCovey	20.00	9.00
24 Ernie Bowman	5.00	2.20
25 Dick Phillips	5.00	2.20
26 Manny Mota	10.00	4.50

1963 Giants Jay Publishing

This 12 card set of the San Francisco Giants measures approximately 5" by 7". The fronts feature black-and-white posed player photos with the player's and team name printed below in the white border. These cards were packaged 12 in a packet. The backs are blank. The cards are unnumbered and checklisted below in alphabetical order.

	NM	Ex
COMPLETE SET (12)	40.00	16.00
1 Felipe Alou	4.00	1.60
2 Orlando Cepeda	8.00	3.20
3 Alvin Dark MG	3.00	1.20
4 Jim Davenport	3.00	1.20
5 Tom Haller	2.50	1.00
6 Chuck Hiller	2.50	1.00
7 Willie Mays	20.00	8.00
8 Willie McCovey	10.00	4.00
9 Billy O'Dell	2.50	1.00
10 Jose Pagan	2.50	1.00
11 Billy Pierce	4.00	1.60
12 Jack Sanford	2.50	1.00

1964 Giants Jay Publishing

This 12-card set of the San Francisco Giants measures approximately 5" X 7". The fronts feature black-and-white posed player photos with the player's and team name printed below in the white border. These cards were packaged 12 to a packet and originally sold for 25 cents. The backs are blank. The cards are unnumbered and checklisted below in alphabetical order.

	NM	Ex
COMPLETE SET (12)	50.00	20.00
1 Orlando Cepeda	8.00	3.20
2 Del Crandall	2.50	1.00
3 Alvin Dark MG	2.50	1.00
4 Jim Davenport	2.00	.80
5 Tom Haller	2.00	.80
6 Juan Marichal	10.00	4.00
7 Willie Mays	20.00	8.00
8 Willie McCovey	10.00	4.00
9 Billy O'Dell	2.00	.80
10 Jose Pagan	2.00	.80
11 Jack Sanford	2.00	.80
12 Bob Shaw	2.00	.80

1965 Giants Jay Publishing

This 12-card set of the San Francisco Giants measures approximately 5" by 7". The fronts feature black-and-white posed player photos with the player's and team name printed below in the white border. These cards were packaged 12 to a packet. The backs are blank. The cards are unnumbered and checklisted below in alphabetical order.

	NM	Ex
COMPLETE SET (12)	60.00	24.00
1 Jesus Alou	2.50	1.00
2 Matty Alou	3.00	1.20
3 Orlando Cepeda	6.00	2.40
4 Jim Davenport	2.00	.80
5 Herman Franks MG	2.00	.80
6 Tom Haller	2.00	.80
7 Bob Hendley	2.00	.80
8 Juan Marichal	10.00	4.00
9 Willie Mays	20.00	8.00
10 Willie McCovey	10.00	4.00
11 Jose Pagan	2.00	.80
12 Gaylord Perry	5.00	2.00

1965 Giants Team Issue

These photos, which measure approximately 5" by 7" feature members of the 1965 San Francisco Giants. The color photos take up most of the cards with the player being identified on the bottom. The backs are blank and we have sequenced them in alphabetical order.

	NM	Ex
COMPLETE SET (10)	40.00	16.00
1 Jim Davenport	2.00	.80
2 Herman Franks MG	2.00	.80
3 Tom Haller	2.00	.80
4 Jim Ray Hart	2.00	.80
5 Juan Marichal	6.00	2.40
6 Willie Mays	15.00	6.00
7 Willie McCovey	6.00	2.40
8 Lindy McDaniel	2.00	.80
9 Gaylord Perry	5.00	2.00
10 Team Photo	4.00	1.60

1970 Giants

This 12-card set is approximately 4 1/2" X 7", with the player's name and "Giants" printed on front. Cards were printed in black and white on pebbled white stock with a blank back.

	NM	Ex
COMPLETE SET (12)	30.00	12.00
1 Bobby Bonds	5.00	2.00
2 Dick Dietz	1.50	.60
3 Charles Fox MG	1.50	.60
4 Ken Henderson	1.50	.60
5 Ron Hunt	3.00	1.20
6 Hal Lanier	2.00	.80
7 Frank Linzy	1.50	.60
8 Juan Marichal	5.00	2.00
9 Willie Mays	10.00	4.00
10 Willie McCovey	5.00	2.00
11 Gaylord Perry	5.00	2.00
12 Frank Reberger	1.50	.60

1970 Giants Chevrolet Bonds

This one-card set measures approximately 3" by 5 3/4" with the top half of the card containing a black-and-white photo of Giants outfielder, Bobby Bonds. The bottom white margin was where the collector could have the player sign his Giants autograph card which was issued by Chevrolet and Nor-Cal Leasing Co. The back is blank.

	NM	Ex
1 Bobby Bonds	10.00	4.00

1971 Giants Ticketron

The 1971 Ticketron San Francisco Giants set is a ten-card set featuring members of the division-winning 1971 San Francisco Giants. The set measures approximately 3 7/8" by 6" and features an attractive full-color photo framed by white borders on the front along with a facsimile autograph. The back contains an ad for Ticketron as well as the 1971 Giants home schedule. These unnumbered cards are listed in alphabetical order for convenience.

	NM	Ex
COMPLETE SET (10)	100.00	40.00
1 Bobby Bonds	10.00	4.00
2 Dick Dietz	3.00	1.20
3 Charles Fox MG	3.00	1.20
4 Tito Fuentes	3.00	1.20
5 Ken Henderson	5.00	2.00
6 Juan Marichal	15.00	6.00

7 Willie Mays	50.00	20.00
8 Willie McCovey	15.00	6.00
9 Don McMahon	3.00	1.20
10 Gaylord Perry	15.00	6.00

1972-76 Giants Team Issue

This 18-card set features black-and-white photos of the San Francisco Giants. The cards are unnumbered and checklisted below in alphabetical order.

	NM	Ex
COMPLETE SET (18)	50.00	20.00
1 Bobby Bonds	6.00	2.40
2 Ron Bryant	2.50	1.00
3 Don Carrithers	2.50	1.00
4 Pete Falcone	2.50	1.00
5 Charlie Fox CO	2.50	1.00
6 Alan Gallagher	2.50	1.00
7 Russ Gibson	2.50	1.00
8 Ed Goodson	2.50	1.00
9 Ed Halicki	2.50	1.00
10 Jim Howarth	2.50	1.00
11 Dave Kingman	5.00	2.00
12 Garry Maddox	5.00	2.00
13 Juan Marichal	6.00	2.40
14 Willie McCovey	6.00	2.40
15 Mike Phillips	2.50	1.00
16 Bill Rigney MG	2.50	1.00
17 Chris Speier	2.50	1.00
18 Jim Willoughby	2.50	1.00

1973 Giants TCMA 1886

This set features the New York National League Team of 1886. Since these cards are not numbered, we have sequenced them in alphabetical order.

	MINT	NRMT
COMPLETE SET	15.00	6.75
1 Roger Connor	2.00	.90
2 Larry Corcoran	.50	.23
3 Tom Deasley	.50	.23
4 Mike Dorgan	.50	.23
5 Dude Esterbrook	.50	.23
6 Buck Ewing	2.00	.90
7 Joe Gerhardt	.50	.23
8 Peter Gillespie	.50	.23
9 Tim Keefe	2.00	.90
10 Jim Mutrie	.75	.35
11 Jim O'Rourke	2.00	.90
12 Daniel Richardson	.50	.23
13 John M. Ward	2.00	.90
14 Mickey Welch	2.00	.90
15 Bat Boy	.50	.23

1975 Giants

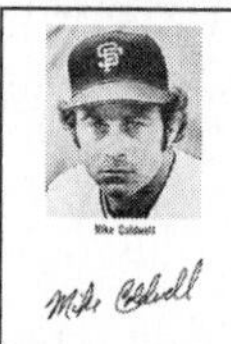

Most of the cards in this 12-card set measure approximately 3" by 5 1/2"; a few measure slightly smaller at 3" by 5". The fronts feature black-and-white portraits of members of the 1975 Giants team. The pictures are 2 1/2" by 3" and rest on a white card face accented only by the player's name printed in black below the photo and a facsimile autograph in the lower white margin. The backs are blank. The cards are unnumbered and checklisted below in alphabetical order.

	NM	Ex
COMPLETE SET (12)	10.00	4.00
1 Mike Caldwell	1.25	.50
2 Pete Falcone	1.00	.40
3 Marc Hill	1.00	.40
4 Gary Matthews	1.50	.60
5 Randy Moffitt	1.00	.40
6 Willie Montanez	1.00	.40
7 Steve Ontiveros	1.00	.40
8 Dave Rader	1.00	.40
9 Derrel Thomas	1.00	.40
10 Gary Thomasson	1.00	.40
11 Wes Westrum MG	1.00	.40
12 Charles Williams	1.00	.40

1975 Giants All-Time TCMA

This 13-card set features black-and-white photos with white borders of all-time New York Giants great players. The cards are unnumbered and checklisted below in alphabetical order.

	NM	Ex
COMPLETE SET (13)	12.00	4.80
1 Alvin Dark	.50	.20
2 Frankie Frisch	1.00	.40
3 Carl Hubbell	1.50	.60
4 Fred Lindstrom	.75	.30
5 Christy Mathewson	1.50	.60
6 Willie Mays	3.00	1.20
7 John McGraw MG	.75	.30
8 Mel Ott Name in black ink	1.50	.60
9 Mel Ott Name in red ink	1.50	.60
10 Bill Terry	1.00	.40
11 Bobby Thomson	.75	.30
12 Wes Westrum	.50	.20
13 Hoyt Wilhelm	1.00	.40

1975 Giants 1951 TCMA

This 34-card set features the 1951 New York Giants Team. The fronts display black-and-white player photos while the backs carry player statistics. The set includes two jumbo cards which measure approximately 3 1/2" by 5". The cards are unnumbered and checklisted below in alphabetical order with the jumbo cards listed last.

	NM	Ex
COMPLETE SET (34)	30.00	12.00
1 George Bamberger	.50	.20
2 Roger Bowman	.50	.20
3 Al Corwin	.50	.20
4 Al Dark	1.50	.60
5 Allen Gettel	.50	.20
6 Clint Hartung	.50	.20
7 Jim Hearn	.50	.20
8 Monte Irvin	2.00	.80
9 Larry Jansen	1.00	.40
10 Sheldon Jones	.50	.20
11 John "Spider" Jorgensen	.50	.20
12 Monte Kennedy	.50	.20
13 Alex Konikowski	.50	.20
14 Dave Koslo	.50	.20
15 Jack Kramer	.50	.20
16 Carroll "Whitey" Lockman	1.00	.40
17 Jack "Lucky" Lohrke	.50	.20
18 Sal Maglie	1.50	.60
19 Jack Maguire	.50	.20
20 Willie Mays	10.00	4.00
21 Don Mueller	1.00	.40
22 Ray Noble	.50	.20
23 Earl Rapp	.50	.20
24 Bill Rigney	.50	.20
25 George Spencer	.50	.20
26 Eddie Stanky	1.00	.40
27 Bobby Thomson	2.00	.80
28 Hank Thompson	.50	.20
29 Wes Westrum	1.00	.40
30 Davey Williams	.50	.20
31 Artie Wilson	.50	.20
32 Sal Yvars	.50	.20
33 Herman Franks CO Freddie Fitzsimmons CO Leo Durocher MG Frank Shellenback CO	1.50	.60
34 Leo Durocher MG Willie Mays	5.00	2.00

1975 Giants Team Issue

This 18-card set of the 1975 San Francisco Giants features player portraits in white borders. The cards are unnumbered and checklisted below in alphabetical order.

	NM	Ex
COMPLETE SET (18)	8.00	3.20
1 Jim Barr	.50	.20
2 Tom Bradley	.50	.20
3 Mike Caldwell	.50	.20
4 John D'Acquisto	.50	.20
5 Pete Falcone	.50	.20
6 Marc Hill	.50	.20
7 Von Joshua	.50	.20
8 Gary Matthews	1.00	.40
9 Randy Moffitt	.50	.20
10 John Motefussco	.50	.20
11 Willie Montanez	.50	.20
12 Bobby Murcer	.75	.30
13 Steve Ontiveros	.50	.20
14 Dave Radar	.50	.20
15 Chris Speier	.50	.20
16 Derrel Thomas	.50	.20
17 Wes Westrum MG	.50	.20
18 Charles Williams	.50	.20

1976 Giants Postcards

This 24-card set of the San Francisco Giants features player photos on postcard-size cards. The cards are unnumbered and checklisted below in alphabetical order.

	NM	Ex
COMPLETE SET (24)	10.00	4.00
1 Glenn Adams	.50	.20
2 Chris Arnold	.50	.20
3 Jim Barr	.50	.20
4 Mike Caldwell	.50	.20
5 John D'Acquisto	.50	.20
6 Rob Dressler	.50	.20
7 Ed Halicki	.50	.20
8 Dave Heaverlo	.50	.20
9 Larry Herndon	.50	.20
10 Marc Hill	.50	.20
11 Gary Lavelle	.50	.20
12 Gary Matthews	1.00	.40
13 Randy Moffitt	.50	.20
14 John Montefusco	.50	.20
15 Bobby Murcer	.75	.30
16 Steve Ontiveros	.50	.20
17 Dave Rader	.50	.20
18 Ken Reitz	.50	.20
19 Bill Rigney MG	.50	.20
20 Mike Sadek	.50	.20
21 Chris Speier	.50	.20
22 Derrel Thomas	.50	.20
23 Gary Thomasson	.50	.20
24 Charles Williams	.50	.20

1977 Giants

This 25-card set measures 3 1/2" by 5" and features black-and-white close-up player photos. The pictures are framed by an orange border and set on a black card face. The player's name, position and team name appear below the picture. The backs are blank. The cards are unnumbered and checklisted below in alphabetical order.

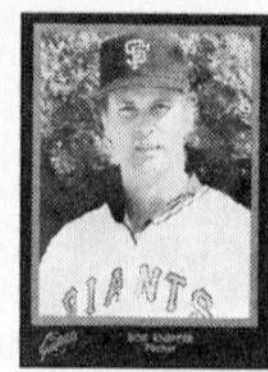

	NM	Ex
COMPLETE SET (25)	20.00	8.00
1 Joe Altobelli MG	.75	.30
2 Jim Barr	.75	.30
3 Jack Clark	2.00	.80
4 Terry Cornutt	.75	.30
5 Rob Dressler	.75	.30
6 Darrell Evans	1.50	.60
7 Frank Funk INS	.75	.30
8 Ed Halicki	.75	.30
9 Tom Haller CO	1.00	.40
10 Marc Hill	.75	.30
11 Skip James	.75	.30
12 Bob Knepper	.75	.30
13 Gary Lavelle	.75	.30
14 Bill Madlock	1.50	.60
15 Willie McCovey	3.00	1.20
16 Randy Moffitt	.75	.30
17 John Montefusco	1.00	.40
18 Marty Perez	.75	.30
19 Frank Riccelli	.75	.30
20 Mike Sadek	.75	.30
21 Hank Sauer INS	1.00	.40
22 Chris Speier	1.00	.40
23 Gary Thomasson	.75	.30
24 Tommy Toms	.75	.30
25 Bobby Winkles CO	.75	.30

1977 Giants Team Issue

This 25-card set of the 1977 San Francisco Giants features player portraits in white borders. The cards are unnumbered and checklisted below in alphabetical order.

	NM	Ex
COMPLETE SET (25)	12.00	4.80
1 Gary Alexander	.50	.20
2 Joe Altobelli MG	.50	.20
3 Rob Andrews	.50	.20
4 Jim Barr	.50	.20
5 Jack Clark	3.00	1.20
6 Terry Cornutt	.50	.20
7 Randy Elliott	.50	.20
8 Darrell Evans	1.00	.40
9 Tim Foli	.50	.20
10 Ed Halicki	.50	.20
11 Vic Harris	.50	.20
12 Dave Heaverlo	.50	.20
13 Marc Hill	.50	.20
14 Bob Knepper	.50	.20
15 Gary Lavelle	.50	.20
16 Johnnie LeMaster	.50	.20
17 Bill Madlock	.75	.30
18 Lynn McGlothen	.50	.20
19 Randy Moffitt	.50	.20
20 John Montefusco	.50	.20
21 Mike Sadek	.50	.20
22 Darrel Thomas	.50	.20
23 Gary Thomasson	.50	.20
24 Terry Whitfield	.50	.20
25 Charlie Williams	.50	.20

1978 Giants Team Issue

This 25-card set of the 1978 San Francisco Giants features player portraits in white borders. The cards are unnumbered and checklisted below in alphabetical order.

	NM	Ex
COMPLETE SET (25)	12.00	4.80
1 Joe Altobelli MG	.50	.20
2 Rob Andrews	.50	.20
3 Jim Barr	.50	.20
4 Vida Blue	1.00	.40
5 Jack Clark	1.50	.60
6 John Curtis	.50	.20
7 Darrell Evans	.75	.30
8 Ed Halicki	.50	.20
9 Vic Harris	.50	.20
10 Tom Heintzelman	.50	.20
11 Larry Herndon	.50	.20
12 Marc Hill	.50	.20
13 Mike Ivie	.50	.20
14 Skip James	.50	.20
15 Bob Knepper	.50	.20
16 Gary Lavelle	.50	.20
17 Johnnie LeMaster	.50	.20
18 Bill Madlock	1.00	.40
19 Randy Moffitt	.50	.20
20 John Montefusco	.50	.20
21 Willie McCovey	2.50	1.00
22 Lynn McGlothen	.50	.20
23 Mike Sadek	.50	.20
24 Terry Whitefield	.50	.20
25 Charlie Williams	.50	.20

1979 Giants Police

The cards in this 30-card set measure approximately 2 5/8" by 4 1/8". The 1979 Police Giants set features cards numbered by the player's uniform number. This full color set features the player's photo, the Giants' logo, and the player's name, position and number on the front of the cards. A facsimile autograph in an attractive blue ink is also contained on the front. The backs, printed in orange and black, feature Tips from the Giants, the Giants' and sponsoring radio station, KNBR, logos and a line listing the Giants, KNBR, and the San Francisco Police Department as sponsors of the set. The 15 cards which are shown with an asterisk below were available only from the Police. The other 15 cards were given away at the ballpark on June 17, 1979. These cards look very similar to the Giants police set issued in 1980, the following year. Both sets credit Dennis Desprois photographically on each card but this (1979) set seems to have a fuzzier focus on the pictures. The sets can be distinguished on the front since this set's cards have a number sign before the player's uniform number on the front. Also on the card backs the KNBR logo is usually left justified for the cards in the 1979 set whereas the 1980 set has the KNBR logo centered on the card back.

	NM	Ex
COMPLETE SET (30)	18.00	7.25
1 Dave Bristol MG	.50	.20
2 Marc Hill	.50	.20
3 Mike Sadek *	.50	.20
5 Tom Haller	.50	.20
6 Joe Altobelli CO *	.75	.30
8 Larry Shepard CO *	.75	.30
9 Heity Cruz	.50	.20
10 Johnnie LeMaster	.50	.20
12 Jim Davenport CO	.75	.30
14 Vida Blue	1.00	.40
15 Mike Ivie	.50	.20
16 Roger Metzger	.50	.20
17 Randy Moffitt	.50	.20
18 Bill Madlock	1.00	.40
21 Rob Andrews *	.50	.20
22 Jack Clark *	1.50	.60
25 Dave Roberts	.50	.20
26 John Montefusco	.75	.30
28 Ed Halicki *	.50	.20
30 John Tamargo	.50	.20
31 Larry Herndon	.50	.20
36 Bill North *	.50	.20
39 Bob Knepper *	.75	.30
40 John Curtis *	.50	.20
41 Darrell Evans *	1.50	.60
43 Tom Griffin *	.50	.20
44 Willie McCovey *	4.00	1.60
45 Terry Whitfield *	.50	.20
46 Gary Lavelle *	.50	.20
49 Max Venable *	.50	.20

1979 Giants Team Issue

Originally sold by the Giants for 20 cents each, these cards featured members of the 1979 San Francisco Giants. More cards may be known so any additions are appreciated, these cards are not numbered so we have sequenced them in alphabetical order.

	NM	Ex
COMPLETE SET	10.00	4.00
1 Rob Andrews	.50	.20
2 Vida Blue	.75	.30
3 Jack Clark	1.00	.40
4 Tom Griffin	.50	.20
5 Ed Halicki	.50	.20
6 Marc Hill	.50	.20
7 Mike Ivie	.50	.20
8 Willie McCovey	2.50	1.00
9 Roger Metzger	.50	.20
10 Greg Minton	.50	.20
11 John Montefusco	.50	.20
12 Phil Nastu	.50	.20
13 Bill North	.50	.20
14 Mike Sadek	.50	.20
15 Max Venable	.50	.20

1980 Giants Eureka Federal Savings

This eight-card set of the San Francisco Giants measures approximately 9 1/2" by 12" and features art work by Todd Alan Gold. Each card displays three color drawings of the same player, two action and one portrait. The backs are blank. These complimentary cards were available at all Eureka Federal Savings branches. The cards are unnumbered and checklisted below in alphabetical order.

	NM	Ex
COMPLETE SET (8)	10.00	4.00
1 Al Holland	1.00	.40
2 Gary Lavelle	1.00	.40
3 Johnnie LeMaster	1.00	.40
4 Milt May	1.00	.40
5 Willie McCovey	5.00	2.00
6 John Montefusco	1.00	.40
7 Bill North	1.00	.40
8 Rennie Stennett	1.00	.40

1980 Giants Greats TCMA

This 12-card standard-size set features some great Giants from both New York and San Francisco. The fronts have red borders with the player's photo inside. The player's name is printed on the bottom. The back carries a biography.

	NM	Ex
COMPLETE SET (12)	8.00	3.20
1 Willie Mays	2.50	1.00
2 Wes Westrum	.25	.10
3 Carl Hubbell	1.00	.40
4 Hoyt Wilhelm	.50	.20
5 Bobby Thomson	.50	.20
6 Frankie Frisch	.75	.30
7 Bill Terry	.75	.30
8 Alvin Dark	.50	.20
9 Mel Ott	1.25	.50
10 Christy Mathewson	1.25	.50
11 Fred Lindstrom	.50	.20
12 John McGraw MG	.75	.30

1980 Giants Police

The cards in this 31-card set measure approximately 2 5/8" by 4 1/8". The 1980 Police San Francisco Giants set features cards numbered by the player's uniform number. This full color set features the player's photo, the Giants' logo, and the player's name, number and position on the front of the cards. A facsimile autograph in an attractive blue ink is also contained on the front. The backs, printed in orange and black, feature Tips from the Giants, the Giants' and sponsoring radio station, KNBR, logos and a line listing the Giants, KNBR, and the San Francisco Police Department as sponsors of the set. The sets were given away at the ballpark on May 31, 1980.

	NM	Ex
COMPLETE SET (31)	15.00	6.00
1 Dave Bristol MG	.50	.20
2 Marc Hill	.50	.20
3 Mike Sadek	.50	.20
5 Jim Lefebvre CO	.50	.20
6 Rennie Stennett	.50	.20
7 Milt May	.50	.20
8 Vern Benson CO	.50	.20
9 Jim Wohlford	.50	.20
10 Johnnie LeMaster	.50	.20
12 Jim Davenport CO	.50	.20
14 Vida Blue	.75	.30
15 Mike Ivie	.50	.20
16 Roger Metzger	.50	.20
17 Randy Moffitt	.50	.20
19 Al Holland	.50	.20
20 Joe Strain	.50	.20
22 Jack Clark	1.00	.40
26 John Montefusco	.50	.20
28 Ed Halicki	.50	.20
31 Larry Herndon	.50	.20
32 Ed Whitson	.50	.20
36 Bill North	.50	.20
38 Greg Minton	.50	.20
39 Bob Knepper	.50	.20
41 Darrell Evans	1.00	.40
42 John Van Ornum	.50	.20
43 Tom Griffin	.50	.20
44 Willie McCovey	3.00	1.20
45 Terry Whitfield	.50	.20
46 Gary Lavelle	.50	.20
47 Don McMahon CO	.50	.20

1980 Giants Team Issue

This 30-card set of the 1980 San Francisco Giants features player portraits in white borders. The cards are unnumbered and checklisted below in alphabetical order.

	NM	Ex
COMPLETE SET (30)	18.00	7.25
1 Dave Bristol MG	.50	.20
2 Vida Blue	1.00	.40
3 Bill Bordley	.50	.20
4 Jack Clark	1.00	.40
5 Darrell Evans	1.00	.40
6 Tom Griffin	.50	.20
7 Ed Halicki	.50	.20
8 Larry Herndon	.50	.20
9 Marc Hill	.50	.20
10 Al Holland	.50	.20
11 Mike Ivie	.50	.20
12 Bob Knepper	.50	.20
13 Gary Lavelle	.50	.20
14 Johnnie LeMaster	.50	.20
15 Dennis Littlejohn	.50	.20
16 Milt May	.50	.20
17 Roger Metzger	.50	.20
18 Willie McCovey	4.00	1.60
19 Greg Minton	.50	.20
20 Randy Moffitt	.50	.20
21 John Montefusco	.50	.20
22 Rich Murray	.50	.20
23 Bill North	.50	.20
24 Allen Ripley	.50	.20
25 Mike Sadek	.50	.20
26 Rennie Stennett	.50	.20
27 Joe Strain	.50	.20
28 Terry Whitfield	.50	.20
29 Ed Whitson	.50	.20
30 Jim Wohlford	.50	.20

1981 Giants 1962 TCMA

This 35-card set was printed in 1981 by TCMA and features black-and-white photos of the

1962 San Francisco Giants team in orange borders. The backs carry player information.

	Nm-Mt	Ex-Mt
COMPLETE SET (35)	15.00	6.00
1 Alvin Dark MG	.50	.20
2 Whitey Lockman CO	.50	.20
3 Larry Jansen CO	.25	.10
4 Wes Westrum CO	.25	.10
5 Ed Bailey	.25	.10
6 Tom Haller	.25	.10
7 Harvey Kuenn	.50	.20
8 Willie Mays	5.00	2.00
9 Felipe Alou	.75	.30
10 Orlando Cepeda	1.00	.40
11 Chuck Hiller	.25	.10
12 Jose Pagan	.25	.10
13 Jim Davenport	.25	.10
14 Willie McCovey	1.00	.40
15 Matty Alou	.50	.20
16 Manny Mota	.50	.20
17 Ernie Bowman	.25	.10
18 Carl Boles	.25	.10
19 John Orsino	.25	.10
20 Joe Pignatano	.25	.10
21 Gaylord Perry	1.00	.40
22 Jim Duffalo	.25	.10
23 Dick LeMay	.25	.10
24 Bob Garibaldi	.25	.10
25 Bobby Bolin	.25	.10
26 Don Larsen	.50	.20
27 Mike McCormick	.25	.10
28 Stu Miller	.25	.10
29 Jack Sanford	.25	.10
30 Billy O'Dell	.25	.10
31 Juan Marichal	2.50	1.00
32 Billy Pierce	.75	.30
33 Dick Phillips	.25	.10
34 Cap Peterson	.25	.10
35 Bob Nieman	.25	.10

1981 Giants Team Issue

This 22-card set of the 1981 San Francisco Giants features player photos. The cards are unnumbered and checklisted below in alphabetical order.

	Nm-Mt	Ex-Mt
COMPLETE SET (22)	12.00	4.80
1 Doyle Alexander	.50	.20
2 Dave Bergman	.50	.20
3 Vida Blue	1.00	.40
4 Fred Breining	.50	.20
5 Enos Cabell	.50	.20
6 Tom Griffin	.50	.20
7 Al Holland	.50	.20
8 Gary Lavelle	.50	.20
9 Jerry Martin	.50	.20
10 Milt May	.50	.20
11 Randy Moffitt	.50	.20
12 Joe Morgan	3.00	1.20
13 Bill North	.50	.20
14 Joe Pettini	.50	.20
15 Allen Ripley	.50	.20
16 Frank Robinson MG	1.50	.60
17 Mike Sadek	.50	.20
18 Billy Smith	.50	.20
19 Rennie Stennett	.50	.20
20 Max Venable	.50	.20
21 Ed Whitson	.50	.20
22 Jim Wohlford	.50	.20

1982 Giants 25th Anniversary Team Issue

This 31-card set features photos of the 1982 San Francisco Giants. The cards are unnumbered and checklisted below in alphabetical order.

	Nm-Mt	Ex-Mt
COMPLETE SET (31)	20.00	8.00
1 Jim Barr	.50	.20
2 Dave Bergman	.50	.20
3 Fred Breining	.50	.20
4 Bob Brenly	1.50	.60
5 Jack Clark	1.00	.40
6 Jim Davenport CO	.50	.20
7 Chili Davis	3.00	1.20
8 Darrell Evans	1.00	.40
9 Alan Fowlkes	.50	.20
10 Rich Gale	.50	.20
11 Atlee Hammaker	.50	.20
12 Al Holland	.50	.20
13 Duane Kuiper	.50	.20
14 Bill Laskey	.50	.20
15 Johnnie LeMaster	.50	.20
16 Gary Lavelle	.50	.20
17 Jeff Leonard	.50	.20
18 Renie Martin	.50	.20
19 Don McMahon CO	.50	.20
20 Greg Minton	.50	.20
21 Joe Morgan	2.50	1.00
22 Tom O'Malley	.50	.20
23 Milt May	.50	.20
24 Willie McCovey	2.50	1.00
25 John Von Ornum	.50	.20
26 Frank Robinson MG	2.00	.80
27 Reggie Smith	.75	.30
28 Guy Sularz	.50	.20
29 Champ Summers	.50	.20
30 Max Venable	.50	.20
31 Jim Wohlford	.50	.20

1983 Giants Mother's

The cards in this 20-card set measure the standard size. For the first time in 30 years, Mother's Cookies issued a baseball card set. The full color set, produced by hobbyist Barry Colla, features San Francisco Giants players only. Fifteen cards were issued at the Houston Astros vs. San Francisco Giants game of August 7, 1983. Five of the cards were redeemable by sending in a coupon. The five additional cards received from redemption of the coupon were not guaranteed to be the five needed to complete the set. The fronts feature the player's photo, his name, and the Giants' logo, while the backs feature player biographies and the Mother's Cookies logo. The backs also contain a space in which to obtain the player's autograph.

	Nm-Mt	Ex-Mt
COMPLETE SET (20)	12.00	4.80
1 Frank Robinson MG	2.50	1.00
2 Jack Clark	1.50	.60
3 Chili Davis	2.00	.80
4 Johnnie LeMaster	.50	.20
5 Greg Minton	.50	.20
6 Bob Brenly	2.00	.80
7 Fred Breining	.50	.20
8 Jeff Leonard	.50	.20
9 Darrell Evans	1.50	.60
10 Tom O'Malley	.50	.20
11 Duane Kuiper	.50	.20
12 Mike Krukow	.50	.20
13 Atlee Hammaker	.50	.20
14 Gary Lavelle	.50	.20
15 Bill Laskey	.50	.20
16 Max Venable	.50	.20
17 Joel Youngblood	.50	.20
18 Dave Bergman	.50	.20
19 Mike Vail	.50	.20
20 Andy McGaffigan	.50	.20

1983 Giants Postcards

This 27-card set measuring approximately 3 1/2 by 5 1/2 features borderless glossy color photos of the San Francisco Giants. The backs display a postcard format. The cards are unnumbered and checklisted below in alphabetical order.

	Nm-Mt	Ex-Mt
COMPLETE SET (27)	15.00	6.00
1 Jim Barr	.50	.20
2 Dave Bergman	.50	.20
3 Fred Breining	.50	.20
4 Bob Brenly	1.50	.60
5 Mark Calvert	.50	.20
6 Mike Chris	.50	.20
7 Jack Clark	1.00	.40
8 Tom McCraw CO	.50	.20
Herm Starrette CO		
Danny Ozark CO		
Don Buford CO		
John Van Ornum CO		
9 Chili Davis	1.50	.60
10 Darrell Evans	.75	.30
11 Atlee Hammaker	.50	.20
12 Mike Krukow	.50	.20
13 Duane Kuiper	.50	.20
14 Bill Laskey	.50	.20
15 Gary Lavelle	.50	.20
16 Johnnie LeMaster	.50	.20
17 Jeff Leonard	.50	.20
18 Renie Martin	.50	.20
19 Milt May	.50	.20
20 Andy McGaffigan	.50	.20
21 Greg Minton	.50	.20
22 Tom O'Malley	.50	.20
23 Joe Pettini	.50	.20
24 Frank Robinson MG	1.50	.60
25 Champ Summers	.50	.20
26 Max Venable	.50	.20
27 Joel Youngblood	.50	.20

1984 Giants Mother's

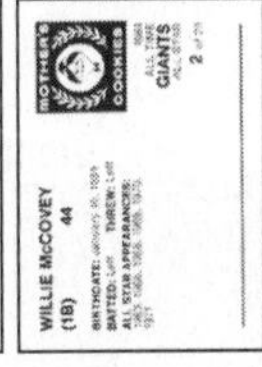

The cards in this 28-card set measure the standard-size. In 1984, the Los Angeles based Mother's Cookies Co. issued five sets of cards featuring players from major league teams. The San Francisco Giants set features previous Giant All-Star selections depicted by drawings. Similar to their 1952 and 1953 issues, the cards have rounded corners. The backs of the cards contain the Mother's Cookies logo. The cards were distributed in partial sets to fans at the respective stadiums of the teams involved. Whereas 20 cards were given to each patron, a redemption card, redeemable for eight more cards was included. Unfortunately, the eight cards received by redeeming the coupon were not necessarily the eight needed to complete a set. Hobbyist Barry Colla was involved in the production of these sets.

	Nm-Mt	Ex-Mt
COMPLETE SET (28)	15.00	6.00
1 Willie Mays	5.00	2.00
2 Willie McCovey	2.50	1.00
3 Juan Marichal	2.00	.80
4 Gaylord Perry	1.50	.60
5 Tom Haller	.25	.10
6 Jim Davenport	.25	.10
7 Jack Clark	.75	.30
8 Greg Minton	.25	.10
9 Atlee Hammaker	.25	.10
10 Gary Lavelle	.25	.10
11 Orlando Cepeda	1.00	.40
12 Bobby Bonds	.75	.30
13 John Antonelli	.25	.10
14 Bob Schmidt UER	.25	.10
(Photo actually		
Wes Westrum)		
15 Sam Jones	.25	.10
16 Mike McCormick	.25	.10
17 Ed Bailey	.25	.10
18 Stu Miller	.50	.20
19 Felipe Alou	1.00	.40
20 Jim Ray Hart	.25	.10
21 Dick Dietz	.25	.10
22 Chris Speier	.25	.10
23 Bobby Murcer	1.00	.40
24 John Montefusco	.25	.10
25 Vida Blue	.75	.30
26 Ed Whitson	.25	.10
27 Darrell Evans	.75	.30
28 Giants CL	.50	.20

1984 Giants Postcards

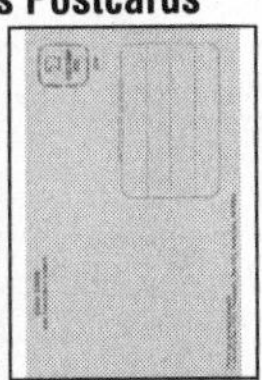

This 31-card set features glossy posed color player photos of the San Francisco Giants and measures approximately 3 7/16" by 5 1/2". The backs have a postcard format. The cards are unnumbered and checklisted below in alphabetical order.

	Nm-Mt	Ex-Mt
COMPLETE SET (31)	8.00	3.20
1 Dusty Baker	.75	.30
2 Bob Brenly	.50	.20
3 Don Buford CO	.25	.10
4 Jack Clark	.75	.30
5 Chili Davis	1.00	.40
6 Mark Davis	.25	.10
7 Altee Hammaker	.25	.10
8 Mike Krukow	.25	.10
9 Duane Kuiper	.25	.10
10 Bill Laskey	.25	.10
11 Gary Lavelle	.25	.10
12 Johnnie LeMaster	.25	.10
13 Jeff Leonard	.25	.10
14 Randy Lerch	.25	.10
15 Renie Martin	.25	.10
16 Tom McCraw CO	.25	.10
17 Greg Minton	.25	.10
18 Fran Mullins	.25	.10
19 Steve Nicosia	.25	.10
20 Al Oliver	.75	.30
21 Danny Ozark CO	.25	.10
22 John Rabb	.25	.10
23 Gene Richards	.25	.10
24 Frank Robinson MG	1.00	.40
25 Jeff Robinson	.25	.10
26 Herm Starrette CO	.25	.10
27 Scott Thompson	.25	.10
28 Manny Trillo	.25	.10
29 John Van Ornum	.25	.10
30 Frank Williams	.25	.10
31 Joel Youngblood	.25	.10

1985 Giants Mother's

The cards in this 28-card set measure the standard size. In 1985, the Los Angeles based Mother's Cookies Co. again issued five sets of cards featuring players from major league teams. The San Francisco Giants set features current players depicted by photos on cards with rounded corners. The backs of the cards contain the Mother's Cookies logo. Cards were passed out at the stadium on June 30.

	Nm-Mt	Ex-Mt
COMPLETE SET (28)	8.00	3.20
1 Jim Davenport MG	.25	.10
2 Chili Davis	1.00	.40
3 Dan Gladden	.50	.20
4 Jeff Leonard	.25	.10
5 Manny Trillo	.25	.10
6 Atlee Hammaker	.25	.10
7 Bob Brenly	.50	.20
8 Greg Minton	.25	.10
9 Bill Laskey	.25	.10
10 Vida Blue	.75	.30
11 Mike Krukow	.25	.10
12 Frank Williams	.25	.10
13 Jose Uribe	.25	.10
14 Johnnie LeMaster	.25	.10
15 Scot Thompson	.25	.10
16 Dave LaPoint	.25	.10
17 David Green	.25	.10
18 Chris Brown	.25	.10
19 Joel Youngblood	.25	.10
20 Mark Davis	.50	.20
21 Jim Gott	.25	.10
22 Doug Gwosdz	.25	.10
23 Scott Garrelts	.25	.10
24 Gary Rajsich	.25	.10
25 Rob Deer	.50	.20
26 Brad Wellman	.25	.10
27 Rocky Bridges CO	.25	.10
Chuck Hiller CO		
Tom McCraw CO		
Bob Miller CO		
Jack Mull CO		
28 Giants CL	.25	.10

1985 Giants Postcards

This 31-card set features glossy color player photos of the San Francisco Giants and measures approximately 3 1/2" by 5 1/2". The backs have a postcard format with the player's name printed in the upper left. The cards are unnumbered and checklisted below in alphabetical order.

	Nm-Mt	Ex-Mt
COMPLETE SET (31)	8.00	3.20
1 Vida Blue	.50	.20
2 Bob Brenly	.50	.20
3 Rocky Bridges CO	.25	.10
4 Chris Brown	.25	.10
5 Jim Davenport MG	.25	.10
6 Chili Davis	1.00	.40
7 Mark Davis	.25	.10
8 Rob Deer	.50	.20
9 Scott Garrelts	.25	.10
10 Dan Gladden	.50	.20
11 Jim Gott	.25	.10
12 David Green	.25	.10
13 Doug Gwosdz	.25	.10
14 Altee Hammaker	.25	.10
15 Chuck Hiller CO	.25	.10
16 Mike Krukow	.25	.10
17 Dave LaPoint	.25	.10
18 Bill Laskey	.25	.10
19 Johnnie LeMaster	.25	.10
20 Jeff Leonard	.25	.10
21 Tom McCraw CO	.25	.10
22 Bob Miller CO	.25	.10
23 Greg Minton	.25	.10
24 Jack Mull CO	.25	.10
25 Gary Rajsich	.25	.10
26 Scot Thompson	.25	.10
27 Manny Trillo	.25	.10
28 Jose Uribe	.25	.10
29 Brad Wellman	.25	.10
30 Frank Williams	.25	.10
31 Joel Youngblood	.25	.10

1986 Giants Mother's

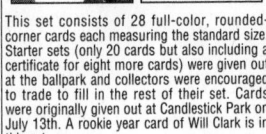

This set consists of 28 full-color, rounded-corner cards each measuring the standard size. Starter sets (only 20 cards but also including a certificate for eight more cards) were given out at the ballpark and collectors were encouraged to trade to fill in the rest of their set. Cards were originally given out at Candlestick Park on July 13th. A rookie year card of Will Clark is in this set.

	Nm-Mt	Ex-Mt
COMPLETE SET (28)	15.00	6.00
1 Roger Craig MG	.50	.20
2 Chili Davis	1.00	.40
3 Dan Gladden	.25	.10
4 Jeff Leonard	.25	.10
5 Bob Brenly	.50	.20
6 Atlee Hammaker	.25	.10
7 Will Clark	10.00	4.00
8 Greg Minton	.25	.10
9 Candy Maldonado	.25	.10
10 Vida Blue	.75	.30
11 Mike Krukow	.25	.10
12 Bob Melvin	.50	.20
13 Jose Uribe	.25	.10
14 Dan Driessen	.25	.10
15 Jeff D. Robinson	.25	.10
16 Robby Thompson	.75	.30
17 Mike LaCoss	.25	.10
18 Chris Brown	.25	.10
19 Scott Garrelts	.25	.10
20 Mark Davis	.50	.20
21 Jim Gott	.25	.10
22 Brad Wellman	.25	.10
23 Roger Mason	.25	.10
24 Bill Laskey	.25	.10
25 Brad Gulden	.25	.10
26 Joel Youngblood	.25	.10
27 Juan Berenguer	.25	.10
28 Bob Lillis CO	.25	.10
Gordy MacKenzie CO		
Bill Fahey CO		
Norm Sherry CO		
Jose Morales CO CL		

1986 Giants Postcards

This 30-card set of the San Francisco Giants features color player photos printed on postcard-size cards. The cards are unnumbered and checklisted below in alphabetical order. A rookie year card of Will Clark is in this set.

	Nm-Mt	Ex-Mt
COMPLETE SET (30)	20.00	8.00
1 Mike Aldrete	.50	.20
2 Juan Berenguer	.50	.20
3 Vida Blue	.75	.30
4 Bob Brenly	.75	.30
5 Chris Brown	.50	.20
6 Will Clark	5.00	2.00
7 Roger Craig MG	.75	.30
8 Chili Davis	1.00	.40
9 Mark Davis	.50	.20
10 Bill Fahey CO	.50	.20
11 Scott Garrelts	.50	.20
12 Dan Gladden	.50	.20
13 Jim Gott	.50	.20
14 Atlee Hammaker	.50	.20
15 Mike Krukow	.50	.20
16 Bill Laskey	.50	.20
17 Jeffrey Leonard	.50	.20
18 Bob Lillis CO	.50	.20
19 Candy Maldonado	.50	.20
20 Roger Mason	.50	.20
21 Willie Mays	2.00	.80
Willie McCovey		
22 Gordon MacKenzie CO	.50	.20
23 Bob Melvin	.75	.30
24 Greg Minton	.50	.20
25 Jose Morales CO	.50	.20
26 Jeff Robinson	.50	.20
27 Norm Sherry CO	.50	.20
28 Rob Thompson	1.00	.40
29 Jose Uribe	.50	.20
30 Brad Wellman	.50	.20

1987 Giants Mother's

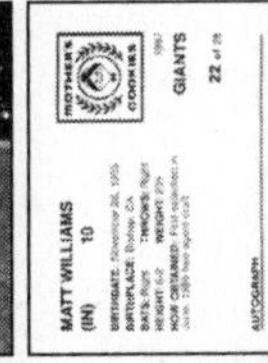

This set consists of 28 full-color, rounded-corner cards each measuring the standard size. Starter sets (only 20 cards but also including a certificate for eight more cards) were given out at the ballpark and collectors were encouraged to trade to fill in the rest of their set. Cards were originally given out at Candlestick Park on June 27th during a game against the Astros. Photos were taken by Dennis Desprois. The sets were reportedly given out free to the first 25,000 paid admissions at the game. There is an early Matt Williams card in this set.

	Nm-Mt	Ex-Mt
COMPLETE SET (28)	20.00	8.00
1 Roger Craig MG	.50	.20
2 Will Clark	5.00	2.00
3 Chili Davis	1.00	.40
4 Bob Brenly	.50	.20
5 Chris Brown	.25	.10
6 Mike Krukow	.25	.10
7 Candy Maldonado	.25	.10
8 Jeffrey Leonard	.25	.10
9 Greg Minton	.25	.10
10 Robby Thompson	.50	.20
11 Scott Garrelts	.25	.10
12 Bob Melvin	.25	.10
13 Jose Uribe	.25	.10
14 Mark Davis	.50	.20
15 Eddie Milner	.25	.10
16 Harry Spilman	.25	.10
17 Kelly Downs	.25	.10
18 Chris Speier	.25	.10
19 Jim Gott	.25	.10
20 Joel Youngblood	.25	.10
21 Mike LaCoss	.25	.10
22 Matt Williams	10.00	4.00
23 Roger Mason	.25	.10
24 Mike Aldrete	.25	.10
25 Jeff D. Robinson	.25	.10
26 Mark Grant	.25	.10
27 Don Zimmer CO	.25	.10
Bob Lillis CO		
Jose Morales CO		
Norm Sherry CO		
Bill Fahey CO		
Gordon MacKenzie CO		
28 Giants CL	.25	.10

1987 Giants Postcards

This 36-card set of the San Francisco Giants features color player photos printed on postcard-size cards. The cards are unnumbered and checklisted below in alphabetical order. A rookie year card of Matt Williams is in this set.

	Nm-Mt	Ex-Mt
COMPLETE SET (36)	25.00	10.00
1 Mike Aldrete	.50	.20
2 Randy Bockus	.50	.20
3 Bob Brenly	.75	.30
4 Chris Brown	.50	.20
5 Will Clark	3.00	1.20
6 Keith Comstock	.50	.20
7 Roger Craig MG	.75	.30
8 Chili Davis	1.00	.40
9 Mark Davis	.50	.20
10 Kelly Downs	.50	.20
11 Bill Fahey CO	.50	.20
12 Scott Garrelts	.50	.20
13 Jim Gott	.50	.20
14 Atlee Hammaker	.50	.20
15 Mike Krukow	.50	.20
16 Mike LaCoss	.50	.20

17 Jeffrey Leonard .50 .20
18 Bob Lillis CO .50 .20
19 Gordy MacKenzie CO .50 .20
20 Candy Maldonado .50 .20
21 Willie Mays 3.00 1.20
22 Willie McCovey 2.00 .80
23 Bob Melvin .75 .30
24 Eddie Milner .50 .20
25 Jose Morales CO .50 .20
26 Jon Perlman .50 .20
27 Jeff Robinson .50 .20
28 Norm Sherry CO .50 .20
29 Chris Speier .50 .20
30 Harry Spilman .50 .20
31 Robby Thompson .75 .30
32 Jose Uribe .50 .20
33 Mark Wasinger .50 .20
34 Matt Williams 6.00 2.40
35 Joel Youngblood .50 .20
36 Don Zimmer CO .75 .30

1988 Giants Mother's

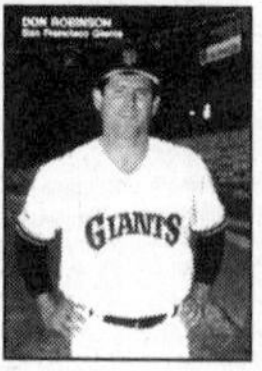

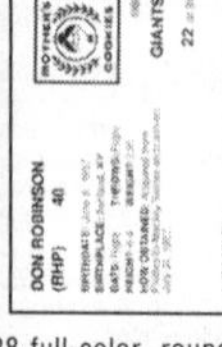

This set consists of 28 full-color, rounded-corner cards each measuring the standard size. Starter sets (only 20 cards but also including a certificate for eight more cards) were given out at the ballpark and collectors were encouraged to trade to fill in the rest of their set. Cards were originally given out at Candlestick Park on July 30th during a game. Photos were taken by Dennis Desprois. The sets were reportedly given out free to the first 35,000 paid admissions at the game.

Nm-Mt Ex-Mt
COMPLETE SET (28) 10.00 4.00
1 Roger Craig MG .50 .20
2 Will Clark 3.00 1.20
3 Kevin Mitchell .75 .30
4 Bob Brenly .50 .20
5 Mike Aldrete .25 .10
6 Mike Krukow .25 .10
7 Candy Maldonado .25 .10
8 Jeffrey Leonard .25 .10
9 Dave Dravecky .75 .30
10 Robby Thompson .25 .10
11 Scott Garrelts .25 .10
12 Bob Melvin .50 .20
13 Jose Uribe .25 .10
14 Brett Butler 1.00 .40
15 Rick Reuschel .50 .20
16 Harry Spilman .25 .10
17 Kelly Downs .25 .10
18 Chris Speier .25 .10
19 Atlee Hammaker .25 .10
20 Joel Youngblood .25 .10
21 Mike LaCoss .25 .10
22 Don Robinson .25 .10
23 Mark Wasinger .25 .10
24 Craig Lefferts .25 .10
25 Phil Garner .50 .20
26 Joe Price .25 .10
27 Dusty Baker CO .50 .20
Bill Fahey CO
Bob Lillis CO
Jose Morales CO
Gordie MacKenzie CO
Norm Sherry CO
28 Giants CL .25 .10

1988 Giants Postcards

This 35-card set of the San Francisco Giants features color player photos printed on postcard-size cards. The cards are unnumbered and checklisted below in alphabetical order.

Nm-Mt Ex-Mt
COMPLETE SET (35) 20.00 8.00
1 Mike Aldrete .50 .20
2 Dusty Baker CO .75 .30
3 Bob Brenly .75 .30
4 Brett Butler 1.00 .40
5 Candlestick Park .50 .20
6 Will Clark 1.50 .60
7 Roger Craig MG .75 .30
8 Kelly Downs .50 .20
9 Dave Dravecky .50 .20
10 Bill Fahey CO .50 .20
11 Scott Garrelts .50 .20
12 Atlee Hammaker .50 .20
13 Mike Krukow .50 .20
14 Mike LaCoss .50 .20
15 Craig Lefferts .50 .20
16 Jeffrey Leonard .50 .20
17 Bob Lillis CO .50 .20
18 Gordy MacKenzie CO .50 .20
19 Candy Maldonado .50 .20
20 Willie Mays 3.00 1.20
21 Willie McCovey 2.00 .80
22 Bob Melvin .75 .30
23 Kevin Mitchell .75 .30
24 Jose Morales CO .50 .20
25 Joe Price .50 .20
26 Rick Reuschel .75 .30
27 Don Robinson .50 .20
28 Norm Sherry CO .50 .20
29 Chris Speier .50 .20
30 Harry Spilman .50 .20
31 Robby Thompson .50 .20
32 Jose Uribe .50 .20
33 Mark Wasinger .50 .20
34 Joel Youngblood .50 .20
35 1987 NL West Champions .75 .30

1989 Giants Mother's

The 1989 Mother's Cookies San Francisco Giants set contains 28 standard-size cards with rounded corners. The fronts have borderless

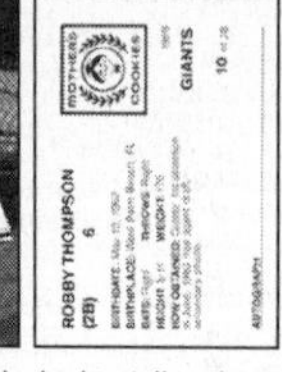

color photos, and the horizontally oriented backs have biographical information. Starter sets containing 20 of these cards were given away at a Giants home game during the 1989 season.

Nm-Mt Ex-Mt
COMPLETE SET (28) 12.00 4.80
1 Roger Craig MG .50 .20
2 Will Clark 2.50 1.00
3 Kevin Mitchell .75 .30
4 Kelly Downs .25 .10
5 Brett Butler 1.00 .40
6 Mike Krukow .25 .10
7 Candy Maldonado .25 .10
8 Terry Kennedy .25 .10
9 Dave Dravecky .75 .30
10 Robby Thompson .25 .10
11 Scott Garrelts .25 .10
12 Matt Williams 5.00 2.00
13 Jose Uribe .25 .10
14 Tracy Jones .25 .10
15 Rick Reuschel .50 .20
16 Ernest Riles .25 .10
17 Jeff Brantley .50 .20
18 Chris Speier .25 .10
19 Atlee Hammaker .25 .10
20 Ed Jurak .25 .10
21 Mike LaCoss .25 .10
22 Don Robinson .25 .10
23 Kirt Manwaring .25 .10
24 Craig Lefferts .25 .10
25 Donell Nixon .25 .10
26 Joe Price .25 .10
27 Rich Gossage .75 .30
28 Bill Fahey CO .50 .20
Dusty Baker CO
Bob Lillis CO
Wendell Kim CO
Norm Sherry CO

1990 Giants Mother's

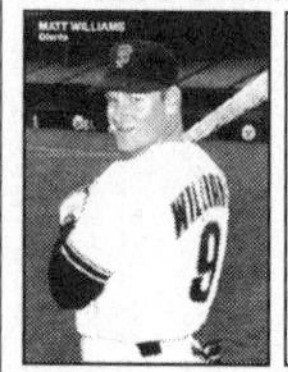

The 1990 Mother's Cookies San Francisco Giants set features cards with rounded corners measuring the standard size. The cards have full-color fronts and biographical information with no stats on the back. The Giants cards were given away at the July 29th game to the first 25,000 children 14 and under. They were distributed in 20-card random packets at the game and eight more at the redemption booths. However, both groups of cards were random and there was no guarantee of getting a complete set in the cards. The promotional idea was that the only way one could finish the set was to trade for them. The redemption certificates were to be used at the Labor Day San Francisco card show. In addition to this the Mother's A's cards were also redeemable at that show.

Nm-Mt Ex-Mt
COMPLETE SET (28) 12.00 3.60
1 Roger Craig MG .50 .15
2 Will Clark 3.00 .90
3 Gary Carter 1.25 .35
4 Kelly Downs .25 .07
5 Kevin Mitchell .75 .23
6 Steve Bedrosian .50 .15
7 Brett Butler 1.00 .30
8 Rick Reuschel .50 .15
9 Matt Williams 1.50 .45
10 Robby Thompson .25 .07
11 Mike LaCoss .25 .07
12 Terry Kennedy .25 .07
13 Atlee Hammaker .25 .07
14 Rick Leach .25 .07
15 Ernest Riles .25 .07
16 Scott Garrelts .25 .07
17 Jose Uribe .25 .07
18 Greg Litton .25 .07
19 Dave Anderson .25 .07
20 Don Robinson .25 .07
21 Dusty Baker CO .50 .15
Bob Lillis CO
Bill Fahey CO
Norm Sherry CO
Wendell Kim
22 Bill Bathe .25 .07
23 Randy O'Neal .25 .07
24 Kevin Bass .25 .07
25 Jeff Brantley .50 .15
26 John Burkett .25 .07
27 Ernie Camacho .25 .07
28 Checklist Card .25 .07

1990 Giants Smokey

This set measures 5" by 7". These cards all contain a safety message. These cards are unnumbered so we have checklisted them below in alphabetical order.

Nm-Mt Ex-Mt
COMPLETE SET (21) 12.00 3.60
1 Dusty Baker CO .75 .23
2 Steve Bedrosian .75 .23
3 Gary Carter 1.00 .30
4 Will Clark 3.00 .90
5 Roger Craig MG .50 .15
6 Kelly Downs .50 .15
7 Bill Fahey CO .50 .15
8 Scott Garrelts .50 .15
9 Atlee Hanmaker .50 .15
10 Terry Kennedy .50 .15
11 Wendell Kim CO .50 .15
12 Mike LaCoss .50 .15
13 Bob Lillis CO .50 .15
14 Greg Litton .50 .15
15 Kevin Mitchell .75 .23
16 Earnest Riles .50 .15
17 Don Robinson .50 .15
18 Norm Sherry CO .50 .15
19 Robby Thompson .50 .15
20 Jose Uribe .50 .15
21 Matt Williams 1.50 .45

1991 Giants Mother's

The 1991 Mother's Cookies San Francisco Giants set contains 28 cards with rounded corners measuring the standard size.

Nm-Mt Ex-Mt
COMPLETE SET (28) 10.00 3.00
1 Roger Craig MG .50 .15
2 Will Clark 2.50 .75
3 Steve Decker .25 .07
4 Kelly Downs .25 .07
5 Kevin Mitchell .50 .15
6 Willie McGee .50 .15
7 Bud Black .25 .07
8 Dave Righetti .50 .15
9 Matt Williams 1.25 .35
10 Robby Thompson .25 .07
11 Mike LaCoss .25 .07
12 Terry Kennedy .25 .07
13 Mark Leonard .25 .07
14 Rick Reuschel .50 .15
15 Mike Felder .25 .07
16 Scott Garrelts .25 .07
17 Jose Uribe .25 .07
18 Greg Litton .25 .07
19 Dave Anderson .25 .07
20 Don Robinson .25 .07
21 Mike Kingery .25 .07
22 Trevor Wilson .25 .07
23 Kirt Manwaring .25 .07
24 Kevin Bass .25 .07
25 Jeff Brantley .25 .07
26 John Burkett .50 .15
27 Dusty Baker CO .50 .15
Bill Fahey CO
Wendell Kim CO
Bob Lillis CO
Norm Sherry CO
28 Mark Letendre TR .25 .07
Greg Lynn TR CL

1991 Giants Pacific Gas and Electric

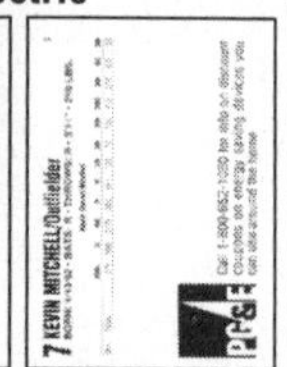

These cards were issued on six-card sheets; after perforation they measure approximately 2 1/2" by 3 1/2". One sheet was inserted in each of the first five 1991 San Francisco Giants Magazines, which were published by Woodford. The front design has color action player photos, with gray borders on a white card face. Toward the bottom of the picture are the words "San Francisco Giants," two bats, and a red banner with player information. The horizontally oriented backs are printed in black on white and include biography, Major League statistics, and various PGE (Pacific Gas and Electric) advertisements. The cards are numbered on the back in the upper right corner.

Nm-Mt Ex-Mt
COMPLETE SET (30) 20.00 6.00
1 Kevin Mitchell .75 .23
2 Robby Thompson .50 .15
3 John Burkett .50 .15
4 Kelly Downs .50 .15
5 Terry Kennedy .50 .15
6 Roger Craig MG .75 .23
7 Jeff Brantley .75 .23
8 Greg Litton .50 .15
9 Trevor Wilson .50 .15
10 Kevin Bass .50 .15
11 Matt Williams 3.00 .90
12 Jose Uribe .50 .15
13 Steve Decker .50 .15
14 Will Clark 6.00 1.80
15 Dave Righetti .75 .23
16 Mike Kingery .50 .15
17 Mike LaCoss .50 .15
18 Dave Anderson .50 .15
19 Bud Black .50 .15
20 Mike Benjamin .50 .15
21 Don Robinson .50 .15
22 Mark Leonard .50 .15
23 Willie McGee .75 .23
24 Francisco Oliveras .50 .15
25 Kirt Manwaring .50 .15
26 Rick Parker .50 .15
27 Mike Remlinger .50 .15
28 Mike Felder .50 .15
29 Scott Garrelts .50 .15
30 Tony Perezchica .50 .15

1991 Giants Postcards

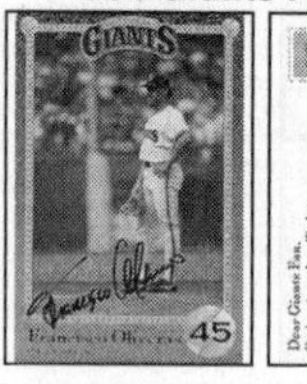

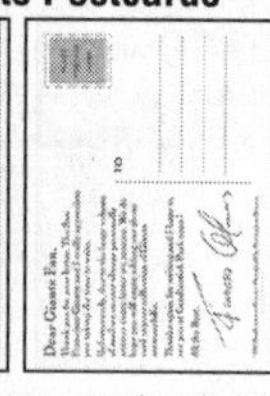

These postcards measures approximately 4" by 6" and features color player action shots on its orange and brown bordered fronts. Many of these postcards were signed in response to fans writing in for autograph requests. The postcards are unnumbered and checklisted below in alphabetical order.

Nm-Mt Ex-Mt
COMPLETE SET (2) 2.00 .60
1 Terry Kennedy 1.00 .30
2 Francisco Oliveras 1.00 .30

1991 Giants S.F. Examiner

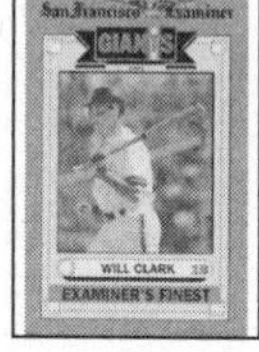

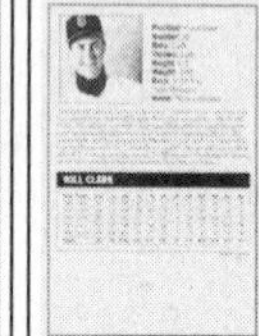

The sixteen 6" by 9" giant-sized cards in this set were issued on orange cardboard sheets measuring approximately 8 1/2" by 11" and designed for storage in a three-ring binder. The cards are unnumbered and checklisted below in alphabetical order.

Nm-Mt Ex-Mt
COMPLETE SET (16) 20.00 6.00
1 Kevin Bass 1.00 .30
2 Mike Benjamin 1.00 .30
3 Bud Black 1.00 .30
4 Jeff Brantley 1.50 .45
5 John Burkett 1.00 .30
6 Will Clark 5.00 1.50
7 Steve Decker 1.00 .30
8 Scott Garrelts 1.00 .30
9 Mike LaCoss 1.00 .30
10 Willie McGee 1.50 .45
11 Kevin Mitchell 1.50 .45
12 Dave Righetti 1.50 .45
13 Don Robinson 1.00 .30
14 Robby Thompson 1.00 .30
15 Jose Uribe 1.00 .30
16 Matt Williams 3.00 .90

1992 Giants AT and T Team Postcards

These posccards feature team photos of the first 35 years of the San Francisco Giants. These postcards are sequenced in year order.

Nm-Mt Ex-Mt
COMPLETE SET (35) 30.00 9.00
COMMON CARD (1-35) 1.00 .30
1 1958 Team Photo 2.00 .60
5 1962 Team Photo 1.50 .45
32 1989 Team Photo 1.50 .45

1992 Giants Fan Fair Fun Bucks

These "promotional buck" featured various San Francisco Giants. They are unnumbered so we have sequenced them in alphabetical order.

Nm-Mt Ex-Mt
COMPLETE SET 8.00 2.40
1 Dusty Baker 1.00 .30
2 Orlando Cepeda 2.50 .75
3 Willie Mays 5.00 1.50

1992 Giants Mother's

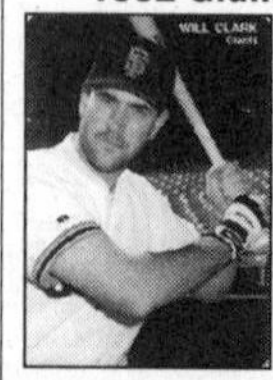

The set was sponsored by Mother's Cookies and features full-bleed color player photos of the San Francisco Giants. The 28 cards in this set have rounded corners and measure the standard size. The backs, printed in purple and red, have biographical information. The set included two coupons: one featured a mail-in offer to obtain a trading card collectors album for 3.95, while the second featured a mail-in offer to obtain an additional eight trading cards.

Nm-Mt Ex-Mt
COMPLETE SET (28) 10.00 3.00
1 Roger Craig MG .50 .15
2 Will Clark 2.50 .75
3 Bill Swift .25 .07
4 Royce Clayton .25 .07
5 John Burkett .25 .07
6 Willie McGee .50 .15
7 Bud Black .25 .07
8 Dave Righetti .50 .15
9 Matt Williams 1.50 .45
10 Robby Thompson .25 .07
11 Darren Lewis .25 .07
12 Mike Jackson .50 .15
13 Mark Leonard .25 .07
14 Rod Beck 1.50 .45
15 Mike Felder .25 .07
16 Bryan Hickerson .25 .07
17 Jose Uribe .25 .07
18 Greg Litton .25 .07
19 Cory Snyder .25 .07
20 Jim McNamara .25 .07
21 Kelly Downs .25 .07
22 Trevor Wilson .25 .07
23 Kirt Manwaring .25 .07
24 Kevin Bass .25 .07
25 Jeff Brantley .50 .15
26 Dave Burba .25 .07
27 Chris James .25 .07
28 Carlos Alfonso CO .50 .15
Dusty Baker CO
Wendell Kim CO
Bob Brenly CO
Bob Lillis CO CL

1992 Giants Pacific Gas and Electric

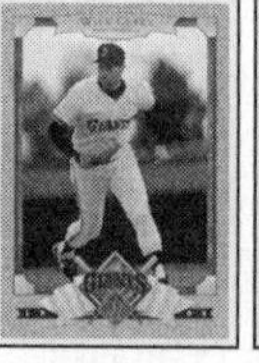

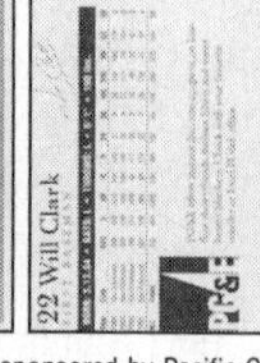

This 36-card set was sponsored by Pacific Gas and Electric and was issued in six-card perforated sheets. Each card measures approximately 2 3/4" by 3 3/4" and features on its front a brown-bordered color player action photo set off by a simulated wood picture frame. The cards are unnumbered and checklisted below in alphabetical order.

Nm-Mt Ex-Mt
COMPLETE SET (36) 25.00 7.50
1 Carlos Alfonso CO .50 .15
2 Dusty Baker CO 1.00 .30
3 Kevin Bass .50 .15
4 Rod Beck 1.50 .45
5 Mike Benjamin .50 .15
6 Bud Black .50 .15
7 Jeff Brantley .75 .23
8 Bob Brenly CO .50 .15
9 Dave Burba .50 .15
10 John Burkett .50 .15
11 Will Clark 4.00 1.20
12 Will Clark AS 2.00 .60
13 Royce Clayton .50 .15
14 Roger Craig MG .75 .23
15 Kelly Downs .50 .15
16 Mike Felder .50 .15
17 Scott Garrelts .50 .15
18 Gil Heredia .50 .15
19 Bryan Hickerson .50 .15
20 Mike Jackson .75 .23
21 Chris James .50 .15
22 Wendell Kim CO .50 .15
23 Mark Leonard .50 .15
(At bat)
24 Mark Leonard .50 .15
(Dropping bat)
25 Darren Lewis .50 .15
26 Bob Lillis CO .50 .15
27 Kirt Manwaring .50 .15
28 Willie McGee .75 .23
29 Jim McNamara .50 .15
30 Dave Righetti .75 .23
31 Cory Snyder .50 .15
32 Bill Swift .50 .15
33 Robby Thompson .50 .15
34 Jose Uribe .50 .15
35 Matt Williams 2.00 .60
36 Trevor Wilson .50 .15

1993 Giants Mother's

The 1993 Mother's Cookies Giants set consists of 28 standard-size cards with rounded corners.

Nm-Mt Ex-Mt
COMPLETE SET (28) 15.00 4.50
1 Dusty Baker MG .50 .15
2 Will Clark 3.00 .90
3 Matt Williams 1.50 .45
4 Barry Bonds 6.00 1.80
5 Bill Swift .25 .07
6 Royce Clayton .25 .07
7 John Burkett .25 .07
8 Willie McGee .50 .15
9 Kirt Manwaring .25 .07

10 Dave Righetti	.50	.15
11 Todd Benzinger	.25	.07
12 Rod Beck	1.00	.30
13 Darren Lewis	.25	.07
14 Robby Thompson	.25	.07
15 Mark Carreon	.25	.07
16 Dave Martinez	.25	.07
17 Jeff Brantley	.50	.15
18 Dave Burba	.25	.07
19 Mike Benjamin	.25	.07
20 Mike Jackson	.50	.15
21 Craig Colbert	.25	.07
22 Bud Black	.25	.07
23 Trevor Wilson	.25	.07
24 Kevin Rogers	.25	.07
25 Jeff Reed	.25	.07
26 Bryan Hickerson	.25	.07
27 Gino Minutelli	.25	.07
28 Dick Pole CO	.50	.15
Bobby Bonds CO		
Denny Sommers CO		
Wendell Kim CO		
Bob Lillis CO		
Bob Brenly CO CL		

1993 Giants Postcards

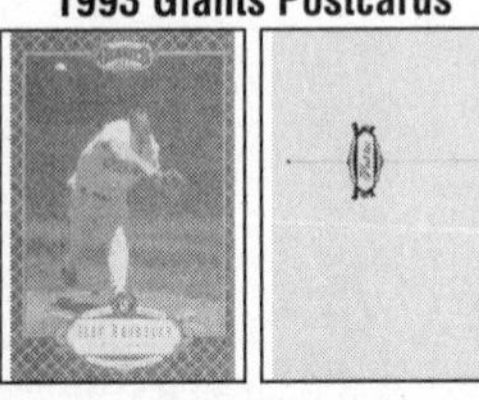

These postcards measure 4" by 6". The fronts feature black-and-white posed and action player shots. The backs are typical postcard back. The cards are unnumbered and checklisted below in alphabetical order.

	Nm-Mt	Ex-Mt
COMPLETE SET (35)	20.00	6.00
1 Dusty Baker MG	.75	.23
2 Rod Beck	1.50	.45
3 Mike Benjamin	.50	.15
4 Todd Benzinger	.50	.15
5 Buddy Black	.50	.15
6 Barry Bonds	6.00	1.80
(Catching the ball)		
7 Barry Bonds	6.00	1.80
(Running)		
8 Bobby Bonds CO	.75	.23
9 Jeff Brantley	.75	.23
10 Bob Brenly CO	.75	.23
11 Dave Burba	.50	.15
12 John Burkett	.50	.15
13 Mark Carreon	.50	.15
14 Will Clark	3.00	.90
(Batting)		
15 Will Clark	3.00	.90
(Running)		
16 Royce Clayton	.50	.15
17 Bryan Hickerson	.50	.15
18 Craig Colbert	.50	.15
19 Mike Jackson	.75	.23
20 Wendell Kim CO	.50	.15
21 Darren Lewis	.50	.15
22 Bob Lillis CO	.50	.15
23 Kirt Manwaring	.50	.15
24 Dave Martinez	.50	.15
25 Willie McGee	.75	.23
26 Luis Mercedes	.50	.15
27 Dick Pole CO	.50	.15
28 Jeff Reed	.50	.15
29 Dave Righetti	.75	.23
30 Kevin Rogers	.50	.15
31 Bill Swift	.50	.15
32 Robby Thompson	.50	.15
33 Matt Williams	1.50	.45
34 Trevor Wilson	.50	.15
35 Team Photo	.75	.23

1993 Giants Stadium Club

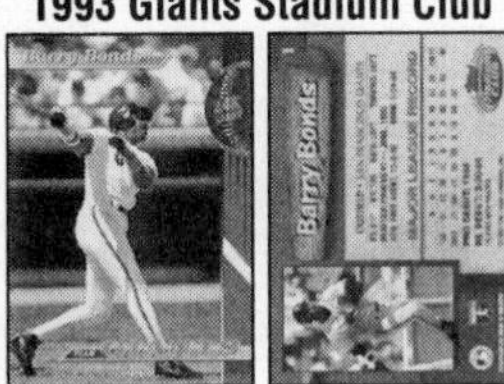

This 30-card standard-size set features the 1993 San Francisco Giants. The set was issued in hobby (plastic box) and retail (blister) form. The Barry Bonds card says 24K gold on the front. All the Bonds cards were printed that way so there is no extra value to these cards.

	Nm-Mt	Ex-Mt
COMP. FACT SET (30)	4.00	1.20
1 Barry Bonds	2.00	.60
2 Dave Righetti	.25	.07
3 Matt Williams	.75	.23
4 Royce Clayton	.10	.03
5 Salomon Torres	.10	.03
6 Kirt Manwaring	.10	.03
7 J.R. Phillips	.10	.03
8 Kevin Rogers	.10	.03
9 Will Clark	1.00	.30
10 John Burkett	.10	.03
11 Willie McGee	.25	.07
12 Rod Beck	.25	.07
13 Jeff Reed	.10	.03
14 Jeff Brantley	.25	.07
15 Steve Hosey	.10	.03
16 Chris Hancock	.10	.03
17 Adell Davenport	.10	.03
18 Mike Jackson	.25	.07
19 Dave Martinez	.10	.03
20 Bill Swift	.10	.03
21 Steve Scarsone	.10	.03
22 Trevor Wilson	.10	.03
23 Mark Carreon	.10	.03
24 Bud Black	.10	.03
25 Darren Lewis	.10	.03
26 Dan Carlson	.10	.03
27 Craig Colbert	.10	.03
28 Greg Brummett	.10	.03
29 Bryan Hickerson	.10	.03
30 Robby Thompson	.10	.03

1994 Giants AMC

Sponsored by AMC Theatres, these 24 blank-backed cards measure approximately 4 1/4" by 11" and feature white-bordered black-and-white player action photos. Some of the cards carry facsimile autographs across their photos.

	Nm-Mt	Ex-Mt
COMPLETE SET (24)	25.00	7.50
1 Dusty Baker MG	1.50	.45
2 Rod Beck	2.00	.60
3 Mike Benjamin	1.00	.30
4 Todd Benzinger	1.00	.30
5 Barry Bonds	10.00	3.00
6 John Burkett	1.00	.30
7 Mark Carreon	1.00	.30
8 Royce Clayton	1.00	.30
9 Steve Frey	1.00	.30
10 Mike Jackson	1.50	.45
11 Darren Lewis	1.00	.30
12 Kirt Manwaring	1.00	.30
13 Dave Martinez	1.00	.30
14 Willie McGee	1.50	.45
15 Rich Monteleone	1.00	.30
16 John Patterson	1.00	.30
17 Mark Portugal	1.00	.30
18 Jeff Reed	1.00	.30
19 Kevin Rogers	1.00	.30
20 Steve Scarsone	1.00	.30
21 Bill Swift	1.00	.30
22 Robby Thompson	1.00	.30
23 Salomon Torres	1.00	.30
24 Matt Williams	2.50	.75

1994 Giants KTVU-TV

This nine-card set features color player photos of the San Francisco Giants. The cards are unnumbered and checklisted below in alphabetical order.

	Nm-Mt	Ex-Mt
COMPLETE SET (9)	12.00	3.60
1 Dusty Baker MG	1.50	.45
2 Rod Beck	2.00	.60
3 Barry Bonds	6.00	1.80
4 Bobby Bonds CO	1.50	.45
5 John Burkett	1.00	.30
6 Billy Swift	1.00	.30
7 Robby Thompson	1.00	.30
8 Matt Williams	2.50	.75
9 Title Card	1.00	.30

1994 Giants Mother's

The 1994 Mother's Cookies Giants set consists of 28 standard-size cards with rounded corners.

	Nm-Mt	Ex-Mt
COMPLETE SET (28)	10.00	3.00
1 Dusty Baker MG	.50	.15
2 Robby Thompson	.25	.07
3 Barry Bonds	5.00	1.50
4 Royce Clayton	.25	.07
5 John Burkett	.25	.07
6 Bill Swift	.25	.07
7 Matt Williams	1.00	.30
8 Rod Beck	.75	.23
9 Steve Scarsone	.25	.07
10 Mark Portugal	.25	.07
11 John Patterson	.25	.07
12 Darren Lewis	.25	.07
13 Kirt Manwaring	.25	.07
14 Salomon Torres	.25	.07
15 Willie McGee	.50	.15
16 Dave Martinez	.25	.07
17 Darryl Strawberry	.50	.15
18 Steve Frey	.25	.07
19 Rich Monteleone	.25	.07
20 Todd Benzinger	.25	.07
21 Jeff Reed	.25	.07
22 Mike Benjamin	.25	.07
23 Mike Jackson	.50	.15
24 Pat Gomez	.25	.07
25 Dave Burba	.25	.07
26 Bryan Hickerson	.25	.07
27 Mark Carreon	.25	.07
28 Bobby Bonds CO	.50	.15
Bob Lillis CO		
Wendell Kim CO		
Bob Brenly CO		
Dick Pole CO		
Denny Sommers CO CL		

1994 Giants S.F. Chronicle

These three pins came attached to cards of the featured players. The brass pins carry the

player's names in black lettering, except for card No. 3, which carries the player's names on their "uniforms." The cards measure approximately 2 1/2" by 5 1/8" and feature on their fronts borderless color player photos framed by a thin white line. The cards and pins are unnumbered and checklisted below in alphabetical order.

	Nm-Mt	Ex-Mt
COMPLETE SET (3)	8.00	2.40
1 Dusty Baker MG	2.00	.60
2 Barry Bonds	5.00	1.50
3 Bill Swift	1.00	.30
John Burkett		

1994 Giants Target Bottle Caps

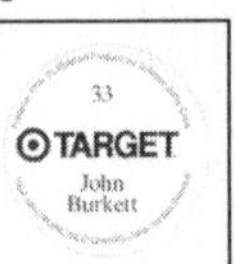

Measuring approximately 1 5/8" in diameter, these bottle caps were issued as a perforated board measuring approximately 4 3/8" by 8". Each sheet has four rows of two caps each. The fronts feature a color player portrait. The backs carry the player's name and number. The bottle caps are unnumbered and checklisted below in alphabetical order.

	Nm-Mt	Ex-Mt
COMPLETE SET	10.00	3.00
1 Dusty Baker MG	.50	.15
2 Rod Beck	.50	.15
3 Mike Benjamin	.25	.07
4 Todd Benzinger	.25	.07
5 Barry Bonds	4.00	1.20
6 Dave Burba	.25	.07
7 John Burkett	.25	.07
8 Mark Carreon	.25	.07
9 Royce Clayton	.25	.07
10 Steve Frey	.25	.07
11 Bryan Hickerson	.25	.07
12 Mike Jackson	.50	.15
13 Darren Lewis	.25	.07
14 Kirt Manwaring	.25	.07
15 Dave Martinez	.25	.07
16 Willie McGee	.50	.15
17 Tony Menendez	.25	.07
18 Rich Montelone	.25	.07
19 John Patterson	.25	.07
20 Mark Portugal	.25	.07
21 Jeff Reed	.25	.07
22 Kevin Rogers	.25	.07
23 Steve Scarsone	.25	.07
24 Bill Swift	.25	.07
25 Robby Thompson	.25	.07
26 Salomon Torres	.25	.07
27 Matt Williams	1.00	.30
28 Title Cap	.25	.07
29 BB Logo	.25	.07

1994 Giants Team Issue

These nine blank-backed photo sheets measure 8" by 10" and feature on their black-and-gold-bordered fronts with black-and-white player photos of award-winning Giants. The sheets are unnumbered and checklisted below in alphabetical order.

	Nm-Mt	Ex-Mt
COMPLETE SET (9)	12.00	3.60
1 Dusty Baker MG	1.50	.45
(Wearing sunglasses)		
2 Dusty Baker MG	1.50	.45
(Waving cap)		
3 Barry Bonds	4.00	1.20
(Dropping bat)		
4 Barry Bonds	4.00	1.20
(Running)		
5 Barry Bonds	2.00	.60
Robby Thompson		
Matt Williams		
6 Barry Bonds	2.00	.60
Kirt Manwaring		
Robby Thompson		
Matt Williams		
7 John Burkett	1.00	.30
Bill Swift		
8 Darren Lewis	1.00	.30
9 The 1993 Giants	3.00	.90
Matt Williams		
Will Clark		
Barry Bonds		
Willie McGee		

1994 Giants U.S. Playing Cards

These 56 playing standard-size cards have rounded corners, and feature color posed and

action player photos on their white-bordered fronts. The player's name and position appear near the bottom. The white and black backs carry the logos for the Giants, baseball's 125th Anniversary, MLBPA, and Bicycle Sports Collection. The set is checklisted below in playing card order by suits and assigned numbers to aces (1), jacks (11), queens (12), and kings (13).

	Nm-Mt	Ex-Mt
COMP. FACT SET (56)	4.00	1.20
1C Matt Williams	.40	.12
1D Bill Swift	.05	.02
1H Robby Thompson	.05	.02
1S Barry Bonds	1.00	.30
2C John Patterson	.05	.02
2D Luis Mercedes	.05	.02
2H Paul Faries	.05	.02
2S Salomon Torres	.05	.02
3C Steve Hosey	.05	.02
3D Mike Benjamin	.05	.02
3H Trevor Wilson	.05	.02
3S Kevin Rogers	.05	.02
4C Jeff Reed	.05	.02
4D Mark Carreon	.05	.02
4H Steve Scarsone	.05	.02
4S Todd Benzinger	.05	.02
5C Mike Jackson	.10	.03
5D Dave Burba	.05	.02
5H Bryan Hickerson	.05	.02
5S Dave Martinez	.05	.02
6C Kirt Manwaring	.05	.02
6D John Burkett	.05	.02
6H Rod Beck	.15	.04
6S Darren Lewis	.05	.02
7C Royce Clayton	.05	.02
7D Matt Williams	.40	.12
7H Barry Bonds	1.00	.30
7S Willie McGee	.10	.03
8C Robby Thompson	.05	.02
8D Salomon Torres	.05	.02
8H John Patterson	.05	.02
8S Bill Swift	.05	.02
9C Luis Mercedes	.05	.02
9D Kevin Rogers	.05	.02
9H J.R. Phillips	.05	.02
9S Paul Faries	.05	.02
10C Mike Benjamin	.05	.02
10D Todd Benzinger	.05	.02
10H Jeff Reed	.05	.02
10S Trevor Wilson	.05	.02
11C Mark Carreon	.05	.02
11D Dave Martinez	.05	.02
11H Mike Jackson	.10	.03
11S Steve Scarsone	.05	.02
12C Dave Burba	.05	.02
12D Darren Lewis	.05	.02
12H Kirt Manwaring	.05	.02
12S Bryan Hickerson	.05	.02
13C John Burkett	.05	.02
13D Willie McGee	.10	.03
13H Royce Clayton	.05	.02
13S Rod Beck	.15	.04
NNO Featured Players	.05	.02

1995 Giants Mother's

This 1995 Mother's Cookies San Francisco Giants set consists of 28 standard-size cards with rounded corners.

	Nm-Mt	Ex-Mt
COMPLETE SET (28)	10.00	3.00
1 Dusty Baker MG	.50	.15
2 Robby Thompson	.25	.07
3 Barry Bonds	4.00	1.20
4 Royce Clayton	.25	.07
5 Glenallen Hill	.25	.07
6 Terry Mulholland	.25	.07
7 Matt Williams	1.00	.30
8 Mark Portugal	.25	.07
9 John Patterson	.25	.07
10 Rod Beck	.75	.23
11 Mark Leiter	.25	.07
12 Kirt Manwaring	.25	.07
13 Steve Scarsone	.25	.07
14 Darren Lewis	.25	.07
15 Tom Lampkin	.25	.07
16 William VanLandingham	.25	.07
17 Joe Rosselli	.25	.07
18 Chris Hook	.25	.07
19 Mark Dewey	.25	.07
20 J.R. Phillips	.25	.07
21 Jeff Reed	.25	.07
22 Pat Gomez	.25	.07
23 Mike Benjamin	.25	.07
24 Trevor Wilson	.25	.07
25 Dave Burba	.25	.07
26 Jose Bautista	.25	.07
27 Mark Carreon	.25	.07
28 Dick Pole CO	.50	.15
Bobby Bonds CO		
Wendell Kim CO		
Bob Brenly CO		
Bob Lillis CO CL		

1996 Giants Mother's

This 28-card set consists of borderless posed color player portraits in stadium settings.

	Nm-Mt	Ex-Mt
COMPLETE SET (28)	8.00	2.40
1 Dusty Baker MG	.50	.15
2 Barry Bonds	4.00	1.20
3 Rod Beck	.50	.15
4 Matt Williams	1.00	.30
5 Robby Thompson	.25	.07
6 Glenallen Hill	.25	.07
7 Kirt Manwaring	.25	.07
8 Mark Carreon	.25	.07
9 Osvaldo Fernandez	.25	.07
10 J.R. Phillips	.25	.07
11 Shawon Dunston	.25	.07
12 Mark Leiter	.25	.07
13 William VanLandingham	.25	.07
14 Stan Javier	.25	.07
15 Allen Watson	.25	.07
16 Mel Hall	.25	.07
17 Doug Creek	.25	.07
18 Steve Scarsone	.25	.07
19 Mark Dewey	.25	.07
20 Mark Gardner	.25	.07
21 David McCarty	.25	.07
22 Tom Lampkin	.25	.07
23 Jeff Juden	.25	.07
24 Steve Decker	.25	.07
25 Rich DeLucia	.25	.07
26 Kim Batiste	.25	.07
27 Steve Bourgeois	.25	.07
28 Bob Lillis CO	.25	.07
Dick Pole CO		
Bobby Bonds CO		
Jim Davenport CO		
Mike Sadek CO		
Juan Lopez CO		
Wendell Kim CO		
Carlos Alfonso CO CL		

1998 Giants Mother's

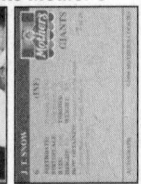

This 28-card set of the San Francisco Giants sponsored by Mother's Cookies consists of posed color player photos with rounded corners. The backs carry biographical information and the sponsor's logo on a lavender background in red and purple print. A blank slot for the player's autograph rounds out the back.

	Nm-Mt	Ex-Mt
COMPLETE SET (28)	10.00	3.00
1 Dusty Baker MG	.50	.15
2 Barry Bonds	3.00	.90
3 Shawn Estes	.25	.07
4 Jeff Kent	1.00	.30
5 Orel Hershiser	.50	.15
6 Brian Johnson	.25	.07
7 J.T. Snow	.50	.15
8 Bill Mueller	1.00	.30
9 Kirk Rueter	.25	.07
10 Darryl Hamilton	.25	.07
11 Rich Aurilia	.75	.23
12 Mark Gardner	.25	.07
13 Stan Javier	.25	.07
14 Robb Nen	.75	.23
15 Rich Rodriguez	.25	.07
16 Brent Mayne	.25	.07
17 Julian Tavarez	.25	.07
18 Rey Sanchez	.25	.07
19 Chris Jones	.25	.07
20 Charlie Hayes	.25	.07
21 Danny Darwin	.25	.07
22 Jim Poole	.25	.07
23 Marvin Benard	.25	.07
24 Steve Reed	.25	.07
25 Alex Diaz	.25	.07
26 John Johnstone	.25	.07
27 Jon Miller ANN	.50	.15
Ted Robinson ANN		
Duane Kuiper ANN		
Mike Krukow ANN		
Amaury Pi-Gonzalez ANN		
Rene De La Rosa ANN		
28 Carlos Alfonso CO	.25	.07
Gene Clines CO		
Sonny Jackson CO		
Juan Lopez CO		
Ron Perranoski CO		
Ron Wotus CO CL		

1999 Giants Keebler

This 28-card standard-size was issued by Keebler Cookies and is in the tradition of the Mothers Cookies sets. They were issued in 28 card packs with 20 of the cards being different and eight cards of the same to be used as trade bait. The borderless fronts have player portraits along with the players name and a 3Com final season logo on the bottom. The easy to read backs have biographical information about the players,

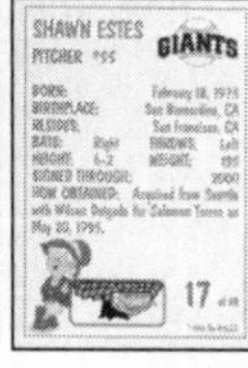

	Nm-Mt	Ex-Mt
COMPLETE SET (28)	10.00	3.00
1 Dusty Baker MG	.50	.15
2 Barry Bonds	3.00	.90
3 Jeff Kent	1.00	.30
4 Robb Nen	.75	.23
5 Bill Mueller	.75	.23
6 Russ Ortiz	.25	.07
7 Ellis Burks	.75	.23
8 Marvin Benard	.25	.07
9 Kirk Rueter	.25	.07
10 J.T.Snow	.50	.15
11 Stan Javier	.25	.07
12 Chris Brock	.25	.07
13 Charlie Hayes	.25	.07
14 Joe Nathan	.25	.07
15 Rich Rodriguez	.25	.07
16 Brent Mayne	.25	.07
17 Shawn Estes	.25	.07
18 Rich Aurilia	.75	.23
19 Mark Gardner	.25	.07
20 Scott Servais	.25	.07
21 John Johnstone	.25	.07
22 Felix Rodriguez	.25	.07
23 Armando Rios	.25	.07
24 Alan Embree	.25	.07
25 F.P. Santangelo	.25	.07
26 Jerry Spradlin	.25	.07
27 Lon Simmons ANN	.25	.07
28 Carlos Alfonso CO	.25	.07
Gene Clines CO		
Sonny Jackson CO		
Juan Lopez CO		
Ron Perranoski CO		
Ron Wotus CO CL		

1999 Giants Postcards

These postcards measure 2 13/16" by 5 1/2" and have blank backs. The cards have two different Giants logos but both styles have the Giants logo on the top with the player photo and uniform number underneath and the Pacific Bell logo on the bottom. We have sequenced these cards in alphabetical order. There is no difference in pricing for either type of Giants logo.

	Nm-Mt	Ex-Mt
COMPLETE SET	15.00	4.50
1 Rich Aurilia	1.00	.30
2 Dusty Baker MG	.75	.23
3 Marvin Benard	.50	.15
4 Barry Bonds	3.00	.90
5 Chris Brock	.50	.15
6 Ellis Burks	1.00	.30
7 Alan Embree	.50	.15
8 Shawn Estes	.50	.15
9 Mark Gardner	.50	.15
10 Charlie Hayes	.50	.15
11 Stan Javier	.50	.15
12 Jeff Kent	2.00	.60
13 Ramon E.Martinez	.50	.15
14 Brent Mayne	.50	.15
15 Bill Mueller	.50	.15
Looking Up		
16 Bill Mueller	.50	.15
Fielding		
17 Joe Nathan	.50	.15
18 Robb Nen	1.00	.30
19 Russ Ortiz	1.00	.30
20 Rich Rodriguez	.50	.15
21 Kirk Rueter	.50	.15
22 F.P. Santangelo	.50	.15
23 J.T. Snow	.75	.23
24 Scott Servais	.50	.15

2000 Giants Bonds Pac-Bell

This one card oversize set was handed out at a late-season Giants game and featured Barry Bonds. The front has the words "San Francisco Giants" on top, a black and white player photo of Bonds and on the bottom, his name, position, uniform number and "Pacific Bell" logo.

	Nm-Mt	Ex-Mt
1 Barry Bonds	5.00	1.50

2000 Giants Keebler

This 28 card standard-size set features members of the 2000 San Francisco Giants and was issued in conjuction with Keebler foods. The front of the borderless cards have a player photo with the bottom devoted to the player's name, a inagural Pacific Bell Park logo and the position. The back has vital stats.

	Nm-Mt	Ex-Mt
COMPLETE SET (28)	10.00	3.00
1 Dusty Baker MG	.50	.15
2 Barry Bonds	3.00	.90
3 Jeff Kent	1.50	.45
4 Robb Nen	.75	.23
5 J.T. Snow	.50	.15
6 Russ Ortiz	.75	.23
7 Ellis Burks	.75	.23
8 Bill Mueller	.75	.23
9 Shawn Estes	.25	.07
10 Marvin Benard	.25	.07
11 Kirk Rueter	.50	.15
12 Bobby Estalella	.25	.07
13 Livan Hernandez	.50	.15
14 Rich Aurilia	.75	.23
15 Alan Embree	.25	.07
16 Armando Rios	.25	.07
17 Felix Rodriguez	.25	.07
18 Doug Mirabelli	.25	.07
19 John Johnstone	.25	.07
20 Russ Davis	.25	.07
21 Joe Nathan	.25	.07
22 Aaron Fultz	.25	.07
23 Felipe Crespo	.25	.07
24 Mark Gardner	.25	.07
25 Ramon E. Martinez	.25	.07
26 Calvin Murray	.25	.07
27 Carlos Alfonso CO	.25	.07
Sonny Jackson CO		
Gene Clines CO		
Ron Wotus CO		
Juan Lopez CO		
Dave Righetti CO		
Robby Thompson CO		
28 Willie Mays Plaza CL	.25	.07

2001 Giants Keebler

This 28 card standard-size set features members of the 2001 San Francisco Giants and was issued in conjuction with Keebler foods. The front of the borderless cards have a player photo with the bottom devoted to the player's name, The Giants logo and the player's position. The back has vital stats.

	Nm-Mt	Ex-Mt
COMPLETE SET	12.00	3.60
1 Dusty Baker MG	.50	.15
2 Jeff Kent	1.25	.35
3 Barry Bonds	3.00	.90
4 Robb Nen	.75	.23
5 J.T. Snow	.50	.15
6 Russ Ortiz	.75	.23
7 Rich Aurilia	.75	.23
8 Benito Santiago	.50	.15
9 Shawn Estes	.25	.07
10 Marvin Benard	.25	.07
11 Kirk Rueter	.50	.15
12 Calvin Murray	.25	.07
13 Livan Hernandez	.50	.15
14 Eric Davis	.50	.15
15 Aaron Fultz	.25	.07
16 Armando Rios	.25	.07
17 Felix Rodriguez	.25	.07
18 Shawon Dunston	.25	.07
19 Mark Gardner	.25	.07
20 Ramon Martinez	.25	.07
21 Pedro Feliz	.25	.07
22 Chad Zerbe	.25	.07
23 Felipe Crespo	.25	.07
24 Tim Worrell	.25	.07
25 Edwards Guzman	.25	.07
26 Ryan Vogelsong	.25	.07
27 Brian Boehringer	.25	.07
28 Carlos Alfonso CO	.25	.07
Gene Clines CO		
Sonny Jackson CO		
Juan Lopez CO		
Dave Righetti CO		
Robby Thompson CO		
Ron Wotus CO		

2002 Giants Coke Topps

This 12-card standard-size set was available two per specially marked packs in the San Francisco Bay area. According to dealers, The Dunston and Nen cards seem to be in shorter supply. We are tagging them as SP's for now.

	Nm-Mt	Ex-Mt
COMPLETE SET	100.00	30.00
COMMON CARD	6.00	1.80
COMMON CARDS SP		
1 Jeff Kent	20.00	6.00
2 Rich Aurilia	12.00	3.60
3 J.T. Snow	6.00	1.80
4 Marvin Benard	6.00	1.80
5 Pedro Feliz	6.00	1.80
6 Shawon Dunston SP	12.00	
7 Robb Nen SP	20.00	6.00
8 Felix Rodriguez	6.00	1.80
9 Russ Ortiz	12.00	3.60
10 Kirk Rueter	10.00	3.00
11 Livan Hernandez	10.00	3.00
12 Barry Bonds	8.00	2.40

2002 Giants Keebler

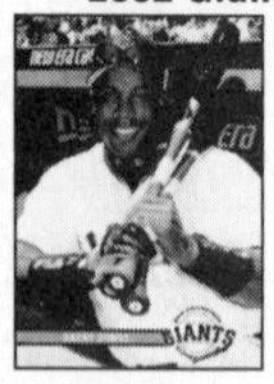

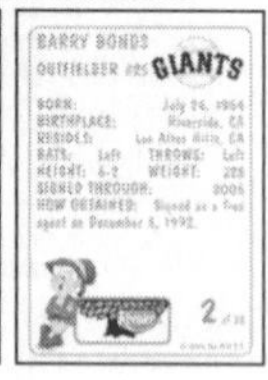

This 28 card standard-size set features the rounded corners which had been traditionally associated with Mother's Cookies sets. The packs were distributed at a game with 20 different cards and 8 duplicate cards of the same player which were designed to encourage trading to finish one's sets.

	Nm-Mt	Ex-Mt
COMPLETE SET	10.00	3.00
1 Dusty Baker MG	.75	.23
2 Barry Bonds	3.00	.90
3 Jeff Kent	1.25	.35
4 Robb Nen	.75	.23
5 J.T. Snow	.25	.07
6 Russ Ortiz	.75	.23
7 Rich Aurilia	.75	.23
8 Marvin Benard	.25	.07
9 Kirk Rueter	.50	.15
10 Benito Santiago	.50	.15
11 Jason Schmidt	1.00	.30
12 Reggie Sanders	.25	.07
13 Livan Hernandez	.50	.15
14 Tsuyoshi Shinjo	.50	.15
15 Aaron Fultz	.25	.07
16 Ramon Martinez	.25	.07
17 Felix Rodriguez	.25	.07
18 Shawon Dunston	.25	.07
19 Tim Worrell	.50	.15
20 David Bell	.25	.07
21 Pedro Feliz	.25	.07
22 Chad Zerbe	.25	.07
23 Damon Minor	.25	.07
24 Yorvit Torrealba	.25	.07
25 Jay Witasick	.25	.07
26 Ryan Jensen	.25	.07
27 Jason Christiansen	.25	.07
28 Carlos Alfonso CO	.25	.07
Gene Clines CO		
Sonny Jackson CO		
Joe Lefebvre CO		
Juan Lopez CO		
Dave Righetti CO		
Ron Wotus CO		

2003 Giants Chevron

This one card set was issued by Chevron in conjunction with the Marine Mammal Center. The front of the card features ace reliever Robb Nen along with the Lou Seal Mascot.

	MINT	NRMT
1 Robb Nen	3.00	1.35
Lou Seal		

1981 Bob Gibson Omaha Hall of Fame

This one card black and white card set, which measures 6" by 8" was issued to attendees of the program which was used to celebrate Bob Gibson's induction into the Omaha Hall of Fame.

	Nm-Mt	Ex-Mt
1 Bob Gibson	10.00	4.00

2000-01 Gold Collectibles 23K Game Used

These standard-size cards were issued by Gold Collectibles. The fronts feature a relief of the player along with a piece of game-used memorabilia. The backs have a congratulatory message about what these cards are and how they were produced. Since these cards are not numbered, we have sequenced them in alphabetical order.

	Nm-Mt	Ex-Mt
1 Hank Aaron Bat	30.00	9.00
Numbered to 1000		
2 Barry Bonds Bat	30.00	9.00
Numbered to 100		
3 Roberto Clemente Bat	40.00	12.00
Numbered to 1000		
4 Tony Gwynn Bat	30.00	9.00
Numbered to 1000		
5 Mark McGwire Bat	30.00	9.00
Numbered to 1000		
6 Cal Ripken Jr Bat	40.00	12.00
Numbered to 1000		
7 Nolan Ryan Bat	40.00	12.00
Numbered to 1000		
8 Ted Williams Bat	40.00	12.00
Numbered to 1000		
9 Barry Bonds Bat	30.00	9.00
Numbered to 750		
10 Ken Griffey Jr. Bat	30.00	9.00
Follow-Through, Numbered to 750		
11 Ken Griffey Jr. Bat	30.00	9.00
Swinging, Numbered to 750		
12 Tony Gwynn Bat	20.00	6.00
Numbered to 750		
13 Cal Ripken Jr Bat	50.00	15.00
Numbered to 750		
14 Alex Rodriguez Bat	20.00	6.00
Numbered to 750		
15 Frank Thomas Bat	20.00	6.00
Numbered to 750		
16 Bernie Williams Bat	20.00	6.00
Numbered to 750		
17 Ted Williams Bat	40.00	12.00
Numbered to 750		
18 Barry Bonds Bat	40.00	12.00
Single Season Homer run King		
19 Derek Jeter	50.00	15.00
1996 Rookie of the Year		
20 Subway Series	50.00	15.00
Bat Pieces from Derek Jeter and Mike Piazza, Numbered to 2000		

1935 Gold Medal Flour R313A

The 1935 Gold Medal Flour series was issued to jointly commemorate the World Series of 1934 which featured the Detroit Tigers and the St. Louis Cardinals as well as some other stars of the early 1930's. Each card measures approximately 3 1/4" by 5 3/8". The cards are blank backed and unnumbered. Some card have recently been discovered, which were not cards of either Tigers or Cardinals. Therefore, even more additions are possible so any additions to this checklist are appreciated

	Ex-Mt	VG
COMPLETE SET	1000.00	500.00
1 Earl Averill	60.00	30.00
2 George Blaeholder	30.00	15.00
3 Tommy Bridges	30.00	15.00
4 Irving Burns	30.00	15.00
5 Bruce Campbell	30.00	15.00
6 Tex Carleton	30.00	15.00
7 Mickey Cochrane	60.00	30.00
8 Dizzy Dean	150.00	75.00
9 Paul Dean	50.00	25.00
10 Frank Frisch	60.00	30.00
11 Goose Goslin	60.00	30.00
12 Odell Hale	30.00	15.00
13 William Hallahan	30.00	15.00
14 Mel Harder	40.00	20.00
15 Jack Knott	30.00	15.00
16 Fred Marberry	30.00	15.00
17 Pepper Martin	50.00	25.00
18 Joe Medwick	60.00	30.00
19 William Rogell	30.00	15.00
20 Joe Vosmik	30.00	15.00
21 Bill Walker	30.00	15.00
22 Jo-Jo White	30.00	15.00

1961 Golden Press

The cards in this 33-card set measure 2 1/2" by 3 1/2". The 1961 Golden Press set of full color cards features members of Baseball's Hall of Fame. The cards came in a booklet with perforations for punching the cards out of the book. The catalog designation for this set is W524. The price for the full book intact is double the complete set price listed.

	NM	Ex
COMPLETE SET (33)	150.00	60.00
1 Mel Ott	4.00	1.60
2 Grover C. Alexander	3.00	1.20
3 Babe Ruth	40.00	16.00
4 Hank Greenberg	3.00	1.20
5 Bill Terry	2.00	.80
6 Carl Hubbell	2.00	.80
7 Rogers Hornsby	4.00	1.60
8 Dizzy Dean	6.00	2.40
9 Joe DiMaggio	30.00	12.00
10 Charlie Gehringer	1.00	.40
11 Gabby Hartnett	1.00	.40
12 Mickey Cochrane	2.00	.80
13 George Sisler	1.00	.40
14 Joe Cronin	1.00	.40
15 Pie Traynor	1.00	.40
16 Lou Gehrig	30.00	12.00
17 Lefty Grove	3.00	1.20
18 Chief Bender	1.00	.40
19 Frankie Frisch	1.00	.40
20 Al Simmons	1.00	.40
21 Home Run Baker	1.00	.40
22 Jimmy Foxx	4.00	1.60
23 John McGraw	1.00	.40
24 Christy Mathewson	6.00	2.40
25 Ty Cobb	30.00	12.00
26 Dazzy Vance	1.00	.40
27 Bill Dickey	2.00	.80
28 Eddie Collins	2.00	.80
29 Walter Johnson	8.00	3.20
30 Tris Speaker	3.00	1.20
31 Nap Lajoie	3.00	1.20
32 Honus Wagner	6.00	2.40
33 Cy Young	4.00	1.60
XX Album	5.00	2.00

1990 Good Humor Ice Cream Big League Sticks

This 26-piece set of ice cream sticks are shaped like baseball bats.They carry facsimile autographs and are individually numbered and are in alphabetical order.

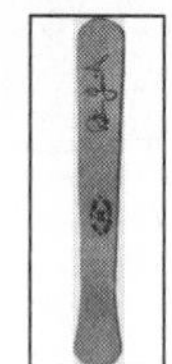

	Nm-Mt	Ex-Mt
COMPLETE SET (26)	35.00	10.50
1 Jim Abbott	.50	.15
2 George Bell	.25	.07
3 Wade Boggs	1.50	.45
4 Bobby Bonilla	.25	.07
5 Jose Canseco	1.50	.45
6 Will Clark	1.50	.45
7 Eric Davis	.50	.15
8 Carlton Fisk	1.50	.45
9 Kirk Gibson	.50	.15
10 Dwight Gooden	.50	.15
11 Ken Griffey Jr.	5.00	1.50
12 Von Hayes	.25	.07
13 Don Mattingly	4.00	1.20
14 Gregg Olson	.25	.07
15 Kirby Puckett	2.00	.60
16 Tim Raines	.50	.15
17 Nolan Ryan	8.00	2.40
18 Bret Saberhagen	.25	.07
19 Ryne Sandberg	4.00	1.20
20 Benito Santiago	.50	.15
21 Mike Scott	.25	.07
22 Lonnie Smith	.25	.07
23 Ozzie Smith	4.00	1.20
24 Cory Snyder	.25	.07
25 Alan Trammell	.75	.23
26 Robin Yount	1.50	.45
XX Album	10.00	3.00

1933 Goudey R319

The cards in this 240-card set measure approximately 2 3/8" by 2 7/8". The 1933 Goudey set, was that company's first baseball issue. The four Babe Ruth and two Lou Gehrig cards in the set are extremely popular with collectors. Card number 106, Napoleon Lajoie, was not printed in 1933, and was circulated to a limited number of collectors in 1934 upon request (it was printed along with the 1934 Goudey cards). An album was offered to house the 1933 set. Several minor leaguers are depicted. Card number 1 (Bengough) is very rarely found in mint condition; in fact, as a general rule all the first series cards are more difficult to find in Mint condition. Players with more than one card are also sometimes differentiated below by their pose: BAT (Batting), FIELD (Fielding), PIT (Pitching), THROW (Throwing). One of the Babe Ruth cards was double printed (DP) apparently in place of the Lajoie and hence is easier to obtain than the others. Due to the scarcity of the Lajoie card, the set is considered complete at 239 cards and is priced as such below. One copy of card number 106 as Leo Durocher is known to exist. The card was apparently cut from a proof sheet and is the only known copy to exist. A large window display poster which measured 5 3/8" by 11 1/4" was sent to stores and used the same Babe Ruth photo as in the Goudey Premium set. The gum used was approximately the same dimension as the actual card. At the factory each piece was scored twice so it could be snapped into three pieces. The gum had a spearmint flavor and according to collectors who remember chewing said gum, the flavor did not last very long.

	Ex-Mt	VG
COMPLETE SET (239)	40000.00	20000.00
COMMON CARD (1-52)	75.00	38.00
COMMON (41/43/53-240)	60.00	30.00
WRAP.(1-CENT, BATTER)	100.00	50.00
WRAP.(1-CENT, AD FRONT)	175.00	90.00
1 Benny Bengough	1500.00	450.00
2 Dazzy Vance	200.00	100.00
3 Hugh Critz	75.00	38.00
4 Heinie Schuble	75.00	38.00
5 Babe Herman	75.00	38.00
6 Jimmy Dykes	75.00	38.00
7 Ted Lyons	150.00	75.00
8 Roy Johnson	75.00	38.00
9 Dave Harris	75.00	38.00
10 Glenn Myatt	75.00	38.00
11 Billy Rogell	75.00	38.00
12 George Pipgras	75.00	38.00
13 Fresco Thompson	75.00	38.00
14 Henry Johnson	75.00	38.00
15 Victor Sorrell	75.00	38.00
16 George Blaeholder	75.00	38.00
17 Watson Clark	75.00	38.00
18 Muddy Ruel	75.00	38.00
19 Bill Dickey	350.00	180.00
20 Bill Terry THROW	250.00	125.00
21 Phil Collins	75.00	38.00
22 Pie Traynor	250.00	125.00
23 Kiki Cuyler	200.00	100.00
24 Horace Ford	75.00	38.00
25 Paul Waner	200.00	100.00
26 Chalmer Cissell	75.00	38.00
27 George Connally	75.00	38.00
28 Dick Bartell	75.00	38.00
29 Jimmie Foxx	600.00	300.00
30 Frank Hogan	75.00	38.00
31 Tony Lazzeri	400.00	200.00
32 Bud Clancy	75.00	38.00
33 Ralph Kress	75.00	38.00
34 Bob O'Farrell	75.00	38.00
35 Al Simmons	350.00	180.00

36 Tommy Thevenow 75.00 38.00
37 Jimmy Wilson 75.00 38.00
38 Fred Brickell 75.00 38.00
39 Mark Koenig 75.00 38.00
40 Taylor Douthit 75.00 38.00
41 Gus Mancuso 60.00 30.00
42 Eddie Collins 150.00 75.00
43 Lew Fonseca 60.00 30.00
44 Jim Bottomley 150.00 75.00
45 Larry Benton 75.00 38.00
46 Ethan Allen 75.00 38.00
47 Heinie Manush BAT 175.00 90.00
48 Marty McManus 75.00 38.00
49 Frankie Frisch 300.00 150.00
50 Ed Brandt 75.00 38.00
51 Charlie Grimm 75.00 38.00
52 Andy Cohen 75.00 38.00
53 Babe Ruth 6000.00 3000.00
54 Ray Kremer 60.00 30.00
55 Pat Malone 60.00 30.00
56 Red Ruffing 175.00 90.00
57 Earl Clark 60.00 30.00
58 Lefty O'Doul 125.00 60.00
59 Bing Miller 60.00 30.00
60 Waite Hoyt 125.00 60.00
61 Max Bishop 60.00 30.00
62 Pepper Martin 125.00 60.00
63 Joe Cronin BAT 150.00 75.00
64 Burleigh Grimes 250.00 125.00
65 Milt Gaston 60.00 30.00
66 George Grantham 60.00 30.00
67 Guy Bush 60.00 30.00
68 Horace Lisenbee 60.00 30.00
69 Randy Moore 60.00 30.00
70 Floyd (Pete) Scott 60.00 30.00
71 Robert J. Burke 60.00 30.00
72 Owen Carroll 60.00 30.00
73 Jesse Haines 125.00 60.00
74 Eppa Rixey 150.00 75.00
75 Willie Kamm 60.00 30.00
76 Mickey Cochrane 250.00 125.00
77 Adam Comorosky 60.00 30.00
78 Jack Quinn 60.00 30.00
79 Red Faber 125.00 60.00
80 Clyde Manion 60.00 30.00
81 Sam Jones 60.00 30.00
82 Dib Williams 60.00 30.00
83 Pete Jablonowski 60.00 30.00
84 Glenn Spencer 60.00 30.00
85 Heinie Sand 60.00 30.00
86 Phil Todt 60.00 30.00
87 Frank O'Rourke 60.00 30.00
88 Russell Rollings 60.00 30.00
89 Tris Speaker RET 300.00 150.00
90 Jess Petty 60.00 30.00
91 Tom Zachary 60.00 30.00
92 Lou Gehrig 2500.00 1250.00
93 John Welch 60.00 30.00
94 Bill Walker 60.00 30.00
95 Alvin Crowder 60.00 30.00
96 Willis Hudlin 60.00 30.00
97 Joe Morrissey 60.00 30.00
98 Wally Berger 75.00 38.00
99 Tony Cuccinello 75.00 38.00
100 George Uhle 60.00 30.00
101 Richard Coffman 60.00 30.00
102 Travis Jackson 150.00 75.00
103 Earle Combs 125.00 60.00
104 Fred Marberry 60.00 30.00
105 Bernie Friberg 60.00 30.00
106 Napoleon Lajoie SP 25000.00 12500.00
(Not issued until 1934)
107 Heinie Manush 125.00 60.00
108 Joe Kuhel 60.00 30.00
109 Joe Cronin 300.00 150.00
110 Goose Goslin 250.00 125.00
111 Monte Weaver 60.00 30.00
112 Fred Schulte 60.00 30.00
113 Oswald Bluege 60.00 30.00
114 Luke Sewell 75.00 38.00
115 Cliff Heathcote 60.00 30.00
116 Eddie Morgan 60.00 30.00
117 Rabbit Maranville 125.00 60.00
118 Val Picinich 60.00 30.00
119 R. Hornsby FIELD 500.00 250.00
120 Carl Reynolds 60.00 30.00
121 Walter Stewart 60.00 30.00
122 Alvin Crowder 60.00 30.00
123 Jack Russell 60.00 30.00
124 Earl Whitehill 60.00 30.00
125 Bill Terry 250.00 125.00
126 Joe Moore 60.00 30.00
127 Mel Ott 400.00 200.00
128 Chuck Klein 175.00 90.00
129 Hal Schumacher PIT 60.00 30.00
130 Fred Fitzsimmons 60.00 30.00
131 Fred Frankhouse 60.00 30.00
132 Jim Elliott 60.00 30.00
133 Fred Lindstrom 125.00 60.00
134 Sam Rice 200.00 100.00
135 Woody English 60.00 30.00
136 Flint Rhem 60.00 30.00
137 Fred(Red) Lucas 60.00 30.00
138 Herb Pennock 175.00 90.00
139 Ben Cantwell 60.00 30.00
140 Bump Hadley 60.00 30.00
141 Ray Benge 60.00 30.00
142 Paul Richards 75.00 38.00
143 Glenn Wright 60.00 30.00
144 Babe Ruth BAT DP 4000.00 2000.00
145 Rube Walberg 60.00 30.00
146 Walter Stewart PIT 60.00 30.00
147 Leo Durocher 200.00 100.00
148 Eddie Farrell 60.00 30.00
149 Babe Ruth 5000.00 2500.00
150 Ray Kolp 60.00 30.00
151 Jake Flowers 60.00 30.00
152 Zack Taylor 60.00 30.00
153 Buddy Myer 60.00 30.00
154 Jimmie Foxx 600.00 300.00
155 Joe Judge 60.00 30.00
156 Danny MacFayden 60.00 30.00
157 Sam Byrd 60.00 30.00
158 Moe Berg 400.00 200.00
159 Oswald Bluege 60.00 30.00
160 Lou Gehrig 3000.00 1500.00
161 Al Spohrer 60.00 30.00
162 Leo Mangum 60.00 30.00
163 Luke Sewell 75.00 38.00
164 Lloyd Waner 250.00 125.00
165 Joe Sewell 125.00 60.00
166 Sam West 60.00 30.00
167 Jack Russell 60.00 30.00
168 Goose Goslin 200.00 100.00
169 Al Thomas 60.00 30.00
170 Harry McCurdy 60.00 30.00
171 Charlie Jamieson 60.00 30.00
172 Billy Hargrave 60.00 30.00
173 Roscoe Holm 60.00 30.00
174 Warren(Curly) Ogden 60.00 30.00
175 Dan Howley MG 60.00 30.00
176 John Ogden 60.00 30.00
177 Walter French 60.00 30.00
178 Jackie Warner 60.00 30.00
179 Fred Leach 60.00 30.00
180 Eddie Moore 60.00 30.00
181 Babe Ruth 4000.00 2000.00
182 Andy High 60.00 30.00
183 Rube Walberg 60.00 30.00
184 Charley Berry 60.00 30.00
185 Bob Smith 60.00 30.00
186 John Schulte 60.00 30.00
187 Heinie Manush 150.00 75.00
188 Rogers Hornsby 600.00 300.00
189 Joe Cronin 200.00 100.00
190 Fred Schulte 60.00 30.00
191 Ben Chapman 75.00 38.00
192 Walter Brown 60.00 30.00
193 Lynford Lary 60.00 30.00
194 Earl Averill 200.00 100.00
195 Evar Swanson 60.00 30.00
196 Leroy Mahaffey 60.00 30.00
197 Rick Ferrell 125.00 60.00
198 Jack Burns 60.00 30.00
199 Tom Bridges 60.00 30.00
200 Bill Hallahan 60.00 30.00
201 Ernie Orsatti 60.00 30.00
202 Gabby Hartnett 250.00 125.00
203 Lon Warneke 60.00 30.00
204 Riggs Stephenson 60.00 30.00
205 Heinie Meine 60.00 30.00
206 Gus Suhr 60.00 30.00
207 Mel Ott BAT 400.00 200.00
208 Bernie James 60.00 30.00
209 Adolfo Luque 75.00 38.00
210 Spud Davis 60.00 30.00
211 Hack Wilson 400.00 200.00
212 Billy Urbanski 60.00 30.00
213 Earl Adams 60.00 30.00
214 John Kerr 60.00 30.00
215 Russ Van Atta 60.00 30.00
216 Lefty Gomez 300.00 150.00
217 Frank Crosetti 150.00 75.00
218 Wes Ferrell 75.00 38.00
219 Mule Haas UER 60.00 30.00
Name spelled Hass on front
220 Lefty Grove 500.00 250.00
221 Dale Alexander 60.00 30.00
222 Charley Gehringer 400.00 200.00
223 Dizzy Dean 600.00 300.00
224 Frank Demaree 60.00 30.00
225 Bill Jurges 60.00 30.00
226 Charley Root 60.00 30.00
227 Billy Herman 150.00 75.00
228 Tony Piet 60.00 30.00
229 Arky Vaughan 150.00 75.00
230 Carl Hubbell PIT 300.00 150.00
231 Joe Moore FIELD 60.00 30.00
232 Lefty O'Doul 125.00 60.00
233 Johnny Vergez 60.00 30.00
234 Carl Hubbell 300.00 150.00
235 Fred Fitzsimmons 60.00 30.00
236 George Davis 60.00 30.00
237 Gus Mancuso 60.00 30.00
238 Hugh Critz 60.00 30.00
239 Leroy Parmelee 60.00 30.00
240 Hal Schumacher 125.00 60.00

1933 Goudey Canadian V353

The cards in this 94-card set measure approximately 2 3/8" by 2 7/8". World Wide Gum, the Canadian subsidiary of Goudey issued this set of numbered color cards in 1933. Cards 1 to 52 contain obverses identical to the American issue, but cards 53 to 94 have a slightly different order. The fronts feature white-bordered color player drawings. The words "Big League Chewing Gum" are printed in white lettering within a red stripe near the bottom. The green ink backs are found printed in English only, or in French and English (the latter are slightly harder to find and are valued at a 25 percent premium over the prices listed below). The catalog designation for this set is V353.

Ex-Mt VG
COMPLETE SET (94) 20000.00 10000.00
1 Benny Bengough 600.00 180.00
2 Dazzy Vance 120.00 60.00
3 Hugh Critz 60.00 30.00
4 Heinie Schulbe 60.00 30.00
5 Babe Herman 100.00 50.00
6 Jimmy Dykes 80.00 40.00
7 Ted Lyons 120.00 60.00
8 Roy Johnson 60.00 30.00
9 Dave Harris 60.00 30.00
10 Glenn Myatt 60.00 30.00
11 Billy Rogell 60.00 30.00
12 George Pipgras 80.00 40.00
13 Lafayette Thompson 60.00 30.00
14 Henry Johnson 60.00 30.00
15 Victor Sorrell 60.00 30.00
16 George Blaeholder 60.00 30.00
17 Watson Clark 60.00 30.00
18 Muddy Ruel 60.00 30.00
19 Bill Dickey 400.00 200.00
20 Bill Terry 200.00 100.00
21 Phil Collins 60.00 30.00
22 Pie Traynor 120.00 60.00
23 Kiki Cuyler 120.00 60.00
24 Horace Ford 60.00 30.00
25 Paul Waner 120.00 60.00
26 Chalmer Cissell 60.00 30.00
27 George Connally 60.00 30.00
28 Dick Bartell 80.00 40.00
29 Jimmy Foxx 500.00 250.00
30 Frank Hogan 60.00 30.00
31 Tony Lazzeri 200.00 100.00
32 Bud Clancy 60.00 30.00
33 Ralph Kress 60.00 30.00
34 Bob O'Farrell 80.00 40.00
35 Al Simmons 200.00 100.00
36 Tommy Thevenow 60.00 30.00
37 Jimmy Wilson 80.00 40.00
38 Fred Bickell 60.00 30.00
39 Mark Koenig 80.00 40.00
40 Taylor Douthit 60.00 30.00
41 Gus Mancuso 60.00 30.00
42 Eddie Collins 120.00 60.00
43 Lew Fonseca 80.00 40.00
44 Jim Bottomley 120.00 60.00
45 Larry Benton 60.00 30.00
46 Ethan Allen 80.00 40.00
47 Heinie Manush 120.00 60.00
48 Marty McManus 60.00 30.00
49 Frank Frisch 120.00 60.00
50 Ed Brandt 60.00 30.00
51 Charlie Grimm 80.00 40.00
52 Andy Cohen 60.00 30.00
53 Jack Quinn 80.00 40.00
54 Urban Faber 120.00 60.00
55 Lou Gehrig 4000.00 2000.00
56 John Welch 60.00 30.00
57 Bill Walker 60.00 30.00
58 Lefty O'Doul 100.00 50.00
59 Bing Miller 80.00 40.00
60 Waite Hoyt 120.00 60.00
61 Max Bishop 80.00 40.00
62 Pepper Martin 100.00 50.00
63 Joe Cronin 120.00 60.00
64 Burleigh Grimes 120.00 60.00
65 Milt Gaston 60.00 30.00
66 George Grantham 60.00 30.00
67 Guy Bush 60.00 30.00
68 Willie Kamm 60.00 30.00
69 Mickey Cochrane 200.00 100.00
70 Adam Comorosky 60.00 30.00
71 Alvin Crowder 60.00 30.00
72 Willis Hudlin 60.00 30.00
73 Eddie Farrell 60.00 30.00
74 Leo Durocher 200.00 100.00
75 Walter Stewart 60.00 30.00
76 George Walberg 60.00 30.00
77 Glenn Wright 80.00 40.00
78 Buddy Myer 80.00 40.00
79 James(Zack) Taylor 60.00 30.00
80 George H.(Babe)Ruth 5000.00 2500.00
81 D'Arcy(Jake) Flowers 60.00 30.00
82 Ray Kolp 60.00 30.00
83 Oswald Bluege 60.00 30.00
84 Moe Berg 300.00 150.00
85 Jimmy Foxx 500.00 250.00
86 Sam Byrd 60.00 30.00
87 Danny MacFayden 60.00 30.00
88 Joe Judge 80.00 40.00
89 Joe Sewell 120.00 60.00
90 Lloyd Waner 120.00 60.00
91 Luke Sewell 80.00 40.00
92 Leo Mangum 60.00 30.00
93 George H.(Babe)Ruth 5000.00 2500.00
94 Al Spohrer 80.00 40.00

1934 Goudey R320

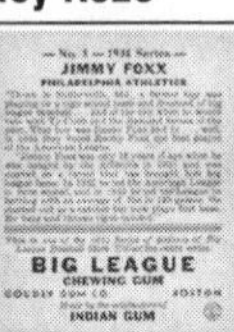

The cards in this 96-card color set measure approximately 2 3/8" by 2 7/8". Cards 1-48 are considered to be the easiest to find (although card number 1, Foxx, is very scarce in mint condition) while 73-96 are much more difficult to find. Cards of this 1934 Goudey series are slightly less abundant than cards of the 1933 Goudey set. Of the 96 cards, 84 contain a "Lou Gehrig Says" line on the front in a blue design, while 12 of the high series (80-91) contain a "Chuck Klein Says" line in a red design. These Chuck Klein cards are indicated in the checklist below by CK and are in fact the 12 National Leaguers in the high series.

Ex-Mt VG
COMPLETE SET (96) 16000.00 8000.00
COMMON CARD (1-48) 50.00 25.00
COMMON CARD (49-72) 75.00 38.00
COMMON CARD (73-96) 175.00 90.00
WRAP.(1-CENT, WHITE) 100.00 50.00
WRAP.(1-CENT, CLEAR) 100.00 50.00
1 Jimmie Foxx 750.00 220.00
2 Mickey Cochrane 175.00 90.00
3 Charlie Grimm 60.00 30.00
4 Woody English 50.00 25.00
5 Ed Brandt 50.00 25.00
6 Dizzy Dean 600.00 300.00
7 Leo Durocher 175.00 90.00
8 Tony Piet 50.00 25.00
9 Ben Chapman 60.00 30.00
10 Chuck Klein 150.00 75.00
11 Paul Waner 150.00 75.00
12 Carl Hubbell 175.00 90.00
13 Frankie Frisch 175.00 90.00
14 Willie Kamm 50.00 25.00
15 Alvin Crowder 50.00 25.00
16 Joe Kuhel 50.00 25.00
17 Hugh Critz 50.00 25.00
18 Heinie Manush 125.00 60.00
19 Lefty Grove 300.00 150.00
20 Frank Hogan 50.00 25.00
21 Bill Terry 200.00 100.00
22 Arky Vaughan 125.00 60.00
23 Charley Gehringer 200.00 100.00
24 Ray Benge 50.00 25.00
25 Roger Cramer 60.00 30.00
26 Gerald Walker 50.00 25.00
27 Luke Appling 150.00 75.00
28 Ed Coleman 50.00 25.00
29 Larry French 50.00 25.00
30 Julius Solters 50.00 25.00
31 Buck Jordan 50.00 25.00
32 Blondy Ryan 50.00 25.00
33 Frank Hurst 50.00 25.00
34 Chick Hafey 125.00 60.00
35 Ernie Lombardi 150.00 75.00
36 Walter Betts 50.00 25.00
37 Lou Gehrig 3000.00 1500.00
38 Oral Hildebrand 50.00 25.00
39 Fred Walker 50.00 25.00
40 John Stone 50.00 25.00
41 George Earnshaw 50.00 25.00
42 John Allen 50.00 25.00
43 Dick Porter 50.00 25.00
44 Tom Bridges 60.00 30.00
45 Oscar Melillo 50.00 25.00
46 Joe Stripp 50.00 25.00
47 John Frederick 50.00 25.00
48 Tex Carleton 50.00 25.00
49 Sam Leslie 75.00 38.00
50 Walter Beck 75.00 38.00
51 Rip Collins 75.00 38.00
52 Herman Bell 75.00 38.00
53 George Watkins 75.00 38.00
54 Wesley Schulmerich 75.00 38.00
55 Ed Holley 75.00 38.00
56 Mark Koenig 100.00 50.00
57 Bill Swift 75.00 38.00
58 Earl Grace 75.00 38.00
59 Joe Mowry 75.00 38.00
60 Lynn Nelson 75.00 38.00
61 Lou Gehrig 3000.00 1500.00
62 Hank Greenberg 600.00 300.00
63 Minter Hayes 75.00 38.00
64 Frank Grube 75.00 38.00
65 Cliff Bolton 75.00 38.00
66 Mel Harder 100.00 50.00
67 Bob Weiland 75.00 38.00
68 Bob Johnson 100.00 50.00
69 John Marcum 75.00 38.00
70 Pete Fox 75.00 38.00
71 Lyle Tinning 75.00 38.00
72 Arndt Jorgens 75.00 38.00
73 Ed Wells 175.00 90.00
74 Bob Boken 175.00 90.00
75 Bill Werber 175.00 90.00
76 Hal Trosky 200.00 100.00
77 Joe Vosmik 175.00 90.00
78 Pinky Higgins 200.00 100.00
79 Eddie Durham 175.00 90.00
80 Marty McManus CK 175.00 90.00
81 Bob Brown CK 175.00 90.00
82 Bill Hallahan CK 175.00 90.00
83 Jim Mooney CK 175.00 90.00
84 Paul Derringer CK 225.00 110.00
85 Adam Comorosky CK 175.00 90.00
86 Lloyd Johnson CK 175.00 90.00
87 George Darrow CK 175.00 90.00
88 Homer Peel CK 175.00 90.00
89 Linus Frey CK 175.00 90.00
90 KiKi Cuyler CK 350.00 180.00
91 Dolph Camilli CK 200.00 100.00
92 Steve Larkin 175.00 90.00
93 Fred Ostermueller 175.00 90.00
94 Red Rolfe 200.00 100.00
95 Myril Hoag 175.00 90.00
96 James DeShong 400.00 200.00

1934 Goudey Canadian V354

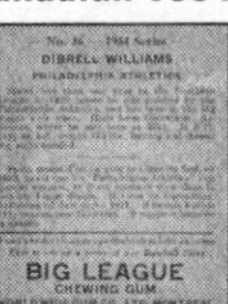

The cards in this 96-card set measure approximately 2 3/8" by 2 7/8". The 1934 Canadian Goudey set was issued by World Wide Gum Company. Cards 1 to 48 have the same format as the 1933 American Goudey issue while cards 49 to 96 have the same format as the 1934 American Goudey issue. Cards numbers 49 to 96 all have the "Lou Gehrig Says" endorsement on the front of the cards. No Chuck Klein endorsement exists as it does in the 1934 American issue. The fronts feature white-bordered color player drawings. The words "Big League Chewing Gum" are printed in white lettering within a red stripe near the bottom. The green ink backs are found printed in English only, or in French and English (the latter are slightly harder to find and are valued at a 25 percent premium over the prices listed below). The catalog designation for this set is V354.

Ex-Mt VG
COMPLETE SET (96) 13000.00 6500.00
1 Rogers Hornsby 600.00 300.00
2 Eddie Morgan 60.00 30.00
3 Val Picinich 60.00 30.00
4 Rabbit Maranville 120.00 60.00
5 Flint Rhem 60.00 30.00
6 Jim Elliott 60.00 30.00
7 Fred(Red) Lucas 60.00 30.00
8 Fred Marberry 60.00 30.00
9 Clifton Heathcote 60.00 30.00
10 Bernie Friberg 60.00 30.00
11 Woody English 60.00 30.00
12 Carl Reynolds 60.00 30.00
13 Ray Benge 60.00 30.00
14 Ben Cantwell 60.00 30.00
15 Bump Hadley 60.00 30.00
16 Herb Pennock 120.00 60.00
17 Fred Lindstrom 120.00 60.00
18 Sam Rice 120.00 60.00
19 Fred Frankhouse 60.00 30.00
20 Fred Fitzsimmons 80.00 40.00
21 Earle Combs 120.00 60.00
22 George Uhle 60.00 30.00
23 Richard Coffman 60.00 30.00
24 Travis Jackson 120.00 60.00
25 Robert J. Burke 60.00 30.00
26 Randy Moore 60.00 30.00
27 Heinie Sand 60.00 30.00
28 George (Babe) Ruth 5000.00 2500.00
29 Tris Speaker 300.00 150.00
30 Perce(Pat) Malone 60.00 30.00
31 Sam Jones 80.00 40.00
32 Eppa Rixey 120.00 60.00
33 Floyd (Pete) Scott 60.00 30.00
34 Pete Jablonowski 60.00 30.00
35 Clyde Manion 60.00 30.00
36 Dib Williams 60.00 30.00
37 Glenn Spencer 60.00 30.00
38 Ray Kremer 60.00 30.00
39 Phil Todt 60.00 30.00
40 Russell Rollings 60.00 30.00
41 Earl Clark 60.00 30.00
42 Jess Petty 60.00 30.00
43 Frank O'Rourke 60.00 30.00
44 Jesse Haines 120.00 60.00
45 Horace Lisenbee 60.00 30.00
46 Owen Carroll 60.00 30.00
47 Tom Zachary 80.00 40.00
48 Red Ruffing 120.00 60.00
49 Ray Benge 60.00 30.00
50 Woody English 60.00 30.00
51 Ben Chapman 80.00 40.00
52 Joe Kuhel 60.00 30.00
53 Bill Terry 200.00 100.00
54 Robert(Lefty) Grove 300.00 150.00
55 Dizzy Dean 800.00 400.00
56 Chuck Klein 120.00 60.00
57 Charley Gehringer 200.00 100.00
58 Jimmie Foxx 400.00 200.00
59 Mickey Cochrane 200.00 100.00
60 Willie Kamm 60.00 30.00
61 Charlie Grimm 100.00 50.00
62 Ed Brandt 60.00 30.00
63 Tony Piet 60.00 30.00
64 Frank Frisch 120.00 60.00
65 Alvin Crowder 60.00 30.00
66 Frank Hogan 60.00 30.00
67 Paul Waner 120.00 60.00
68 Heinie Manush 120.00 60.00
69 Leo Durocher 120.00 60.00
70 Arky Vaughan 120.00 60.00
71 Carl Hubbell 200.00 100.00
72 Hugh Critz 60.00 30.00
73 John(Blondy) Ryan 60.00 30.00
74 Doc Cramer 80.00 40.00
75 Baxter Jordan 60.00 30.00
76 Ed Coleman 60.00 30.00
77 Julius(Moose) Solters 60.00 30.00
78 Chick Hafey 120.00 60.00
79 Larry French 60.00 30.00
80 Frank(Don) Hurst 60.00 30.00
81 Gerald Walker 60.00 30.00
82 Ernie Lombardi 120.00 60.00
83 Walter(Huck) Betts 60.00 30.00
84 Luke Appling 120.00 60.00
85 John Frederick 60.00 30.00
86 Fred(Dixie) Walker 100.00 50.00
87 Tom Bridges 80.00 40.00
88 Dick Porter 60.00 30.00
89 John Stone 60.00 30.00
90 James(Tex) Carleton 60.00 30.00
91 Joe Stripp 60.00 30.00
92 Lou Gehrig 4000.00 2000.00
93 George Earnshaw 80.00 40.00
94 Oscar Melillo 60.00 30.00
95 Oral Hildebrand 60.00 30.00
96 John Allen 80.00 40.00

1934 Goudey Card Album

These rare 1934 Goudey American and National League Card albums were issued one per box of Big League Gum or could be had by redeeming 50 Big League wrappers to the Goudey Gum Company. The American League album is red and the National League album is blue. Each has 10 spaces allocated for each of the teams in their respective leagues and for their All-Star teams. Each team has its own biography printed in the album.

Ex-Mt VG
COMPLETE SET (2) 1000.00 500.00
1 American League 500.00 250.00
(red)
2 National League 500.00 250.00
(blue)

1934 Goudey Premiums R309-1

The most ambitious premium issue of the Goudey Gum Company was the R309-1 set of 1934. Printed on heavy cardboard, the black and white picture was embellished with a gold and frame-like border and a back stand. Each of these thick cards measures approximately 5 1/2" by 8 15/16". The Babe Ruth card seems to be more common than the other cards in this short set.

Ex-Mt VG
COMPLETE SET (4) 1200.00 600.00
1 American League 250.00 125.00
All-Stars of 1933
2 National League 250.00 125.00
All-Stars of 1933
3 World's Champions 300.00 150.00
of 1933

(New York Giants)
4 George Herman 600.00 300.00
(Babe) Ruth

1935 Goudey Premiums R309-2

The 16 cards in the R309-2 Goudey Premium set are unnumbered, glossy black and white photos on thin paper stock. Teams (1-3) and individual players (4-16) are featured in this relatively scarce premium set from 1935. The ballplayer is identified by his name rendered in longhand in the "wide pen" style of later Goudey issues. This written name is not a facsimile autograph. Each card measures approximately 5 1/2" by 9".

Ex-Mt VG
COMPLETE SET (16)............ 1500.00 750.00
COMMON TEAM (1-3)............. 80.00 40.00
COMMON CARD (4-16)............ 80.00 40.00
1 Boston Red Sox 80.00 40.00
2 Cleveland Indians.................. 80.00 40.00
3 Washington Senators............ 80.00 40.00
4 Elden Auker........................... 80.00 40.00
5 Johnny Babich........................ 80.00 40.00
6 Dick Bartell............................ 80.00 40.00
7 Lester R. Bell......................... 80.00 40.00
8 Wally Berger......................... 100.00 50.00
9 Mickey Cochrane................. 200.00 100.00
10 Ervin Fox........................... 120.00 60.00
Leon Goose Goslin
Gerald Walker
11 Lefty Gomez....................... 150.00 75.00
12 Hank Greenberg 200.00 100.00
13 Oscar Melillo 80.00 40.00
14 Mel Ott 200.00 100.00
15 Schoolboy Rowe 80.00 40.00
16 Vito Tamulis 80.00 40.00

1935 Goudey Puzzle R321

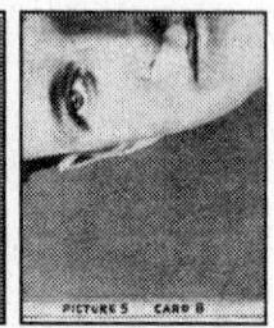

The cards in this 36-card set (the number of different front pictures) measure approximately 2 3/8" by 2 7/8". The 1935 Goudey set is sometimes called the Goudey Puzzle Set, or the Goudey 4-in-1's. There are 36 different card fronts but 114 different front/back combinations. The card number in the checklist refers to the back puzzle number, as the backs can be arranged to form a puzzle picturing a player or team. To avoid the confusion caused by two different fronts having the same back number, the rarer cards have been arbitrarily given a "1" prefix. The scarcer puzzle cards are hence all listed at the numerical end of the list below, i.e. rare puzzle 1 is listed as number 11, rare puzzle 2 is listed as 12, etc. The BLUE in the checklist refers to a card with a blue border, as most cards have a red border. The set price below includes all the cards listed. The following is the list of the puzzle back pictures: 1) Detroit Tigers; 2) Chuck Klein; 3) Frankie Frisch; 4) Mickey Cochrane; 5) Joe Cronin; 6) Jimmy Foxx; 7) Al Simmons; 8) Cleveland Indians; and 9) Washington Senators.

Ex-Mt VG
COMPLETE SET (114)........ 13500.00 6800.00
COMMON CARDS (1-9) 50.00 25.00
COMMON CARDS (11-17) 80.00 40.00
WRAP.(1-CENT, WHITE).......... 200.00 100.00
1A Frank Frisch 150.00 75.00
Dizzy Dean
Ernie Orsatti
Tex Carleton
1B Roy Mahaffey.................... 120.00 60.00
Jimmie Foxx
Dib Williams
Pinky Higgins
1C Heinie Manush 60.00 30.00
Lyn Lary
Monte Weaver
Bump Hadley
1D Mickey Cochrane 120.00 60.00
Charlie Gehringer
Tommy Bridges
Billy Rogell
1E Paul Waner......................... 100.00 50.00
Guy Bush
Waite Hoyt
Lloyd Waner
1F Burleigh Grimes................. 100.00 50.00
Chuck Klein
Kiki Cuyler
Woody English
1G Sam Leslie.......................... 50.00 25.00
Lonnie Frey
Joe Stripp
Watson Clark
1H Tony Piet............................ 60.00 30.00
Adam Comorosky
Jim Bottomley
Sparky Adams
1I George Earnshaw.............. 60.00 30.00
Jimmie Dykes
Luke Sewell
Luke Appling
1J Babe Ruth....................... 1000.00 500.00
Marty McManus
Eddie Brandt
Rabbit Maranville
1K Bill Terry 100.00 50.00
Hal Schumacher
Gus Mancuso
Travis Jackson
1L Willie Kamm........................ 60.00 30.00
Oral Hildebrand
Earl Averill
Hal Trosky
2A Frank Frisch 150.00 75.00
Dizzy Dean
Ernie Orsatti
Tex Carleton
2B Roy Mahaffey.................... 120.00 60.00
Jimmie Foxx
Dib Williams
Pinky Higgins
2C Heinie Manush 60.00 30.00
Lyn Lary
Monte Weaver
Bump Hadley
2D Mickey Cochrane 120.00 60.00
Charlie Gehringer
Tommy Bridges
Billy Rogell
2E Willie Kamm........................ 60.00 30.00
Oral Hildebrand
Earl Averill
Hal Trosky
2F George Earnshaw 60.00 30.00
Jimmie Dykes
Luke Sewell
Luke Appling
3A Babe Ruth 1000.00 500.00
Marty McManus
Eddie Brandt
Rabbit Maranville
3B Bill Terry 100.00 50.00
Hal Schumacher
Gus Mancuso
Travis Jackson
3C Paul Waner 100.00 50.00
Guy Bush
Waite Hoyt
Lloyd Waner
3D Burleigh Grimes................ 100.00 50.00
Chuck Klein
Kiki Cuyler
Woody English
3E Sam Leslie........................... 50.00 25.00
Lonnie Frey
Joe Stripp
Watson Clark
3F Tony Piet 60.00 30.00
Adam Comorosky
Jim Bottomley
Sparky Adams
4A Hugh Critz BLUE 100.00 50.00
Dick Bartell
Mel Ott
Gus Mancuso
4B Pie Traynor BLUE................ 60.00 30.00
Red Lucas
Tom Thevenow
Glenn Wright
4C Charlie Berry BLUE............. 60.00 30.00
Bobby Burke
Red Kress
Dazzy Vance
4D Red Ruffing BLUE.............. 150.00 75.00
Pat Malone
Tony Lazzeri
Bill Dickey
4E Randy Moore BLUE.............. 50.00 25.00
Shanty Hogan
Fred Frankhouse
Eddie Brandt
4F Pepper Martin BLUE............ 50.00 25.00
Bob O'Farrell
Sam Byrd
Danny MacFayden
5A Muddy Ruel........................ 100.00 50.00
Al Simmons
Willie Kamm
Mickey Cochrane
5B Willis Hudlin........................ 60.00 30.00
George Myatt
Adam Comorosky
Jim Bottomley
5C Paul Waner 100.00 50.00
Guy Bush
Waite Hoyt
Lloyd Waner
5D Sam West 50.00 25.00
Oscar Melillo
George Blaeholder
Dick Coffman
5E Sam Leslie........................... 50.00 25.00
Lonnie Frey
Joe Stripp
Watson Clark
5F Heine Schuble 60.00 30.00
Fred Marberry
Goose Goslin
General Crowder
6A Muddy Ruel........................ 100.00 50.00
Al Simmons
Willie Kamm
Mickey Cochrane
6B Willis Hudlin........................ 60.00 30.00
George Myatt
Adam Comorosky
Jim Bottomley
6C Jimmy Wilson....................... 50.00 25.00
Ethan Allen
Bubba Jonnard
Fred Brickell
6D Sam West 50.00 25.00
Oscar Melillo
George Blaeholder
Dick Coffman
6E Joe Cronin........................... 60.00 30.00
Carl Reynolds
Max Bishop
Chalmer Cissell
6F Heine Schuble 60.00 30.00
Fred Marberry
Goose Goslin
General Crowder
7A Hugh Critz BLUE 100.00 50.00
Dick Bartell
Mel Ott
Gus Mancuso
7B Pie Traynor BLUE................ 60.00 30.00
Red Lucas
Tom Thevenow
Glenn Wright
7C Charlie Berry BLUE............. 60.00 30.00
Bobby Burke
Red Kress
Dazzy Vance
7D Red Ruffing BLUE.............. 150.00 75.00
Pat Malone
Tom Lazzeri
Bill Dickey
7E Randy Moore BLUE.............. 50.00 25.00
Shanty Hogan
Fred Frankhouse
Eddie Brandt
7F Pepper Martin BLUE............ 50.00 25.00
Bob O'Farrell
Sam Byrd
Danny MacFayden
8A Mark Koenig........................ 50.00 25.00
Fred Fitzsimmons
Ray Benge
Tom Zachary
8B Minter Hayes....................... 60.00 30.00
Ted Lyons
Mule Haas
Zeke Bonura
8C Jack Burns 50.00 25.00
Rollie Hemsley
Frank Grube
Bob Weiland
8D F.Campbell.......................... 50.00 25.00
Billy Meyers
Ival Goodman
Alex Kampouris
8E Jimmy DeShong.................. 50.00 25.00
Johnny Allen
Red Rolfe
Dixie Walker
8F Pete Fox............................ 100.00 50.00
Hank Greenberg
Gee Walker
Schoolboy Rowe
8G Billy Werber........................ 60.00 30.00
Rick Ferrell
Wes Ferrell
Fritz Ostermueller
8H Joe Kuhel............................ 50.00 25.00
Earl Whitehill
Buddy Myer
John Stone
8I Joe Vosmik 50.00 25.00
Bill Knickerbocker
Mel Harder
Lefty Stewart
8J Bob Johnson 50.00 25.00
Ed Coleman
Johnny Marcum
Doc Cramer
8K Babe Herman 60.00 30.00
Gus Suhr
Tom Padden
Cy Blanton
8L Al Spohrer 50.00 25.00
Flint Rhem
Ben Cantwell
Larry Benton
8M Mark Koenig....................... 50.00 25.00
Fred Fitzsimmons
Ray Benge
Tom Zachary
9B Minter Hayes....................... 60.00 30.00
Ted Lyons
Mule Haas
Zeke Bonura
9C Jack Burns 50.00 25.00
Rollie Hemsley
Frank Grube
Bob Weiland
9D Bruce Campbell.................. 50.00 25.00
Billy Meyers
Ival Goodman
Alex Kampouris
9E Jimmy DeShong.................. 50.00 25.00
Johnny Allen
Red Rolfe
Fred Walker
9F Pete Fox............................ 100.00 50.00
Hank Greenberg
Gee Walker
Schoolboy Rowe
9G Billy Werber........................ 60.00 30.00
Rick Ferrell
Wes Ferrell
F.Ostermueller
9H Joe Kuhel............................ 50.00 25.00
Earl Whitehill
Buddy Myer
John Stone
9I Joe Vosmik 50.00 25.00
Bill Knickerbocker
Mel Harder
Lefty Stewart
9J Bob Johnson 50.00 25.00
Ed Coleman
Johnny Marcum
Doc Cramer
9K Babe Herman 60.00 30.00
Gus Suhr
Tom Padden
Cy Blanton
9L Al Spohrer 50.00 25.00
Flint Rhem
Ben Cantwell
Larry Benton
11E Jimmy Wilson.................... 80.00 40.00
Johnny Allen
Bubba Jonnard
Fred Brickell
11F Sam West........................... 80.00 40.00
Oscar Melillo
George Blaeholder
Dick Coffman
11G Joe Cronin 100.00 50.00
Carl Reynolds
Max Bishop
Chalmer Cissell
11H Heine Schuble.................. 100.00 50.00
Fred Marberry
Goose Goslin
General Crowder
11J Muddy Ruel...................... 150.00 75.00
Al Simmons
Willie Kamm
Mickey Cochrane
11K Willis Hudlin.................... 100.00 50.00
George Myatt
Adam Comorosky
Jim Bottomley
12A Hugh Critz BLUE 150.00 75.00
Dick Bartell
Mel Ott
Gus Mancuso
12B Pie Traynor BLUE............ 100.00 50.00
Red Lucas
Tommy Thevenow
Glenn Wright
12C Charlie Berry BLUE.......... 100.00 50.00
Bobby Burke
Red Kress
Dazzy Vance
12D Red Ruffing BLUE........... 250.00 125.00
Pat Malone
Tony Lazzeri
Bill Dickey
12E Randy Moore BLUE........... 80.00 40.00
Shanty Hogan
Fred Frankhouse
Eddie Brandt
12F Pepper Martin BLUE 80.00 40.00
Bob O'Farrell
Sam Byrd
Danny MacFayden
13A Muddy Ruel...................... 150.00 75.00
Al Simmons
Willie Kamm
Mickey Cochrane
13B Willis Hudlin.................... 100.00 50.00
George Myatt
Adam Comorosky
Jim Bottomley
13C Jimmy Wilson.................... 80.00 40.00
Johnny Allen
Bubba Jonnard
Fred Brickell
13D Sam West 80.00 40.00
Oscar Melillo
George Blaeholder
Dick Coffman
13E Joe Cronin....................... 100.00 50.00
Carl Reynolds
Max Bishop
Chalmer Cissell
13F Heine Schuble 100.00 50.00
Fred Marberry
Goose Goslin
General Crowder
14A Babe Ruth 1500.00 750.00
Marty McManus
Eddie Brandt
Rabbit Maranville
14B Bill Terry 150.00 75.00
Hal Schumacher
Gus Mancuso
Travis Jackson
14C Paul Waner 150.00 75.00
Guy Bush
Waite Hoyt
Lloyd Waner
14D Burleigh Grimes.............. 150.00 75.00
Chuck Klein
Kiki Cuyler
Woody English
14E Sam Leslie......................... 80.00 40.00
Lonnie Frey
Joe Stripp
Watson Clark
14F Tony Piet 100.00 50.00
Adam Comorosky
Jim Bottomley
Sparky Adams
15A Babe Ruth 1500.00 750.00
Marty McManus
Eddie Brandt
Rabbit Maranville
15B Bill Terry 150.00 75.00
Hal Schumacher
Gus Mancuso
Travis Jackson
15C Jimmy Wilson.................... 80.00 40.00
Johnny Allen
Bubba Jonnard
Fred Brickell
15D Burleigh Grimes.............. 150.00 75.00
Chuck Klein
Kiki Cuyler
Woody English
15E Joe Cronin....................... 100.00 50.00
Carl Reynolds
Max Bishop
Chalmer Cissell
15F Tony Piet 100.00 50.00
Adam Comorosky
Jim Bottomley
Sparky Adams
16A Frank Frisch 250.00 125.00
Dizzy Dean
Ernie Orsatti
Tex Carleton
16B Roy Mahaffey.................. 150.00 75.00
Jimmie Foxx
Dib Williams
Pinky Higgins
16C Heinie Manush 100.00 50.00
Lyn Lary
Monte Weaver
Bump Hadley
16D Mickey Cochrane 150.00 75.00
Charlie Gehringer
Tom Bridges
Billy Rogell
16E Willie Kamm.................... 100.00 50.00
Oral Hildebrand
Earl Averill
Hal Trosky
16F George Earnshaw 100.00 50.00
Jimmie Dykes
Luke Sewell
Luke Appling
17A Frank Frisch 250.00 125.00
Dizzy Dean
Ernie Orsatti
Tex Carleton
17B Roy Mahaffey.................. 200.00 100.00
Jimmie Foxx
Dib Williams
Pinky Higgins
17C Heinie Manush 100.00 50.00
Lyn Lary
Monte Weaver
Bump Hadley
17D Mickey Cochrane 150.00 75.00
Charlie Gehringer
Tom Bridges
Billy Rogell
17E Willie Kamm.................... 100.00 50.00
Oral Hildebrand
Earl Averill
Hal Trosky
17F George Earnshaw 100.00 50.00
Jimmie Dykes
Luke Sewell
Luke Appling

1936 Goudey B/W R322

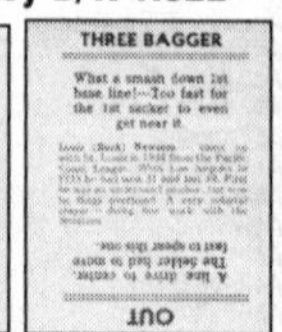

The cards in this 25-card black and white set measure approximately 2 3/8" by 2 7/8". In contrast to the color artwork of its previous sets, the 1936 Goudey set contained a simple black and white player photograph. A facsimile autograph appeared within the picture area. Each card was issued with a number of different "game situation" backs, and there may be as many as 200 different front/back combinations. This unnumbered set is checklisted and numbered below in alphabetical order for convenience. The cards were issued in penny packs which came 100 to a box.

Ex-Mt VG
COMPLETE SET (25)............ 1800.00 900.00
WRAPPER (1-CENT) 200.00 100.00
1 Wally Berger........................ 50.00 25.00
2 Zeke Bonura......................... 40.00 20.00
3 Frenchy Bordagaray 40.00 20.00
4 Bill Brubaker......................... 40.00 20.00
5 Dolph Camilli......................... 50.00 25.00
6 Clyde Castleman................... 40.00 20.00
7 Mickey Cochrane................ 200.00 100.00
8 Joe Coscarart........................ 40.00 20.00
9 Frank Crosetti....................... 75.00 38.00
10 Kiki Cuyler.......................... 80.00 40.00
11 Paul Derringer.................... 50.00 25.00
12 Jimmy Dykes....................... 50.00 25.00
13 Rick Ferrell.......................... 80.00 40.00
14 Lefty Gomez...................... 200.00 100.00
15 Hank Greenberg 250.00 125.00
16 Bucky Harris........................ 80.00 40.00
17 Rollie Hemsley 40.00 20.00
18 Pinky Higgins...................... 50.00 25.00
19 Oral Hildebrand................... 40.00 20.00
20 Chuck Klein 120.00 60.00
21 Pepper Martin 75.00 38.00
22 Bobo Newsom...................... 50.00 25.00
23 Joe Vosmik.......................... 40.00 20.00
24 Paul Waner........................ 120.00 60.00
25 Bill Werber 40.00 20.00

1936 Goudey Wide Pen Premiums R314

Each card measures approximately 3 1/4" by 5 1/2". These black and white unnumbered cards could be obtained directly from a retail outlet rather than through the mail only. Four types of this card exist. Type A contains cards, mainly individual players, with "Litho USA" in the bottom border. Type B does not have the "Litho USA" marking and comes both with and without a border. Type C cards are American players on creamy paper stock with medium thickness signatures and no "Litho USA" markings. Type D consists of Canadian players from Montreal (M) or Toronto (T) on creamy stock paper with non-glossy photos.

Ex-Mt VG
COMPLETE SET (208).......... 7000.00 3500.00
COMMON CARD (A1-A119) 15.00 7.50
COMMON CARD (B1-B25) 40.00 20.00
COMMON CARD (C1-C25) 40.00 20.00
COMMON CARD (D1-D39)........ 60.00 30.00
A1 Ethan Allen......................... 20.00 10.00
A2 Earl Averill.......................... 30.00 15.00
A3 Dick Bartell.......................... 15.00 7.50
A4 Dick Bartell.......................... 20.00 10.00
A5 Wally Berger 20.00 10.00
A6 Geo. Blaeholder................... 15.00 7.50
A7 Cy Blanton 15.00 7.50
A8 Cliff Bolton 15.00 7.50
A9 Stan Bordagaray 15.00 7.50
A10 Tommy Bridges.................. 20.00 10.00
A11 Bill Brubaker 15.00 7.50
A12 Sam Byrd............................ 15.00 7.50

A13 Dolph Camilli 20.00 10.00
A14 Clydell Castleman 15.00 7.50
(throwing)
A15 Clydell Castleman 15.00 7.50
A16 Phil Cavarretta 25.00 12.50
A17 Mickey Cochrane 40.00 20.00
A18 Earle Combs 30.00 15.00
A19 Joe Coscarart 15.00 7.50
A20 Joe Cronin 30.00 15.00
A21 Frank Crosetti 30.00 15.00
A22 Tony Cuccinello 15.00 7.50
A23 KiKi Cuyler 30.00 15.00
A24 Curt Davis 15.00 7.50
A25 Virgil Davis 15.00 7.50
A26 Paul Derringer 20.00 10.00
A27 Bill Dickey 30.00 15.00
A28 Jimmy Dykes 20.00 10.00
kneeling
A29 Rick Ferrell 30.00 15.00
A30 Wes Ferrell 25.00 12.50
A31 Lou Finney 15.00 7.50
A32 Ervin "Pete" Fox 15.00 7.50
A33 Tony Freitas 15.00 7.50
A34 Lonnie Frey 15.00 7.50
A35 Frankie Frisch 40.00 20.00
A36 Augie Galan 15.00 7.50
A37 Charley Gehringer 40.00 20.00
A38 Charlie Gelbert 15.00 7.50
A39 Lefty Gomez 40.00 20.00
A40 Goose Goslin 30.00 15.00
A41 Earl Grace 15.00 7.50
A42 Hank Greenberg 50.00 25.00
A43 Mule Haas 15.00 7.50
A44 Odell Hale 15.00 7.50
A45 Bill Hallahan 15.00 7.50
A46 Mel Harder 20.00 10.00
A47 Bucky Harris MG 30.00 15.00
A48 Gabby Hartnett 30.00 15.00
A49 Ray Hayworth 15.00 7.50
A50 Rollie Hemsley 15.00 7.50
A51 Babe Herman 25.00 12.50
A52 Frank Higgins 15.00 7.50
A53 Oral Hildebrand 15.00 7.50
A54 Myril Hoag 15.00 7.50
A55 Waite Hoyt 30.00 15.00
A56 Woody Jensen 15.00 7.50
A57 Bob Johnson 20.00 10.00
A58 Buck Jordan 15.00 7.50
A59 Alex Kampouris 15.00 7.50
A60 Chuck Klein 30.00 15.00
A61 Joe Kuhel 15.00 7.50
A62 Lyn Lary 15.00 7.50
A63 Cookie Lavagetto 20.00 10.00
A64 Sam Leslie 15.00 7.50
A64 Fred Lindstrom 30.00 15.00
A66 Ernie Lombardi 30.00 15.00
A67 Al Lopez 30.00 15.00
A68 Dan MacFayden 15.00 7.50
A69 John Marcum 15.00 7.50
A70 Pepper Martin 25.00 12.50
A71 Eric McNair 15.00 7.50
A72 Joe Medwick 30.00 15.00
A73 Gene Moore 15.00 7.50
A74 Randy Moore 15.00 7.50
A75 Terry Moore 20.00 10.00
A76 Edward Moriarty 15.00 7.50
A77 Wally Moses 15.00 7.50
A78 Buddy Myer 15.00 7.50
A79 Buck Newsom 20.00 10.00
A80 Fred Ostermueller 15.00 7.50
A81 Marvin Owen 15.00 7.50
A82 Tommy Padden 15.00 7.50
A83 Ray Pepper 15.00 7.50
A84 Tony Piet 15.00 7.50
A85 Rabbit Pytlak 15.00 7.50
A86 Rip Radcliff 15.00 7.50
A87 Bobby Reis 15.00 7.50
A88 Lew Riggs 15.00 7.50
A89 Bill Rogell 15.00 7.50
A90 Red Rolfe 20.00 10.00
A91 Schoolboy Rowe 20.00 10.00
A92 Al Schacht 25.00 12.50
A93 Luke Sewell 20.00 10.00
A94 Al Simmons 40.00 20.00
A95 John Stone 15.00 7.50
A96 Gus Suhr 15.00 7.50
A97 Joe Sullivan 15.00 7.50
A98 Bill Swift 15.00 7.50
A99 Vito Tamulis 15.00 7.50
A100 Dan Taylor 15.00 7.50
A101 Cecil Travis 15.00 7.50
A102 Hal Trosky 20.00 10.00
A103 Bill Urbanski 15.00 7.50
A104 Russ Van Atta 15.00 7.50
A105 Arky Vaughan 30.00 15.00
A106 Gerald Walker 15.00 7.50
A107 Bucky Walters 25.00 12.50
A108 Lloyd Waner 30.00 15.00
A109 Paul Waner 30.00 15.00
A110 Lon Warneke 15.00 7.50
A111 Rabbit Warstler 15.00 7.50
A112 Bill Werber 15.00 7.50
A113 Jo-Jo White 15.00 7.50
A114 Burgess Whitehead 15.00 7.50
A115 John Whitehead 15.00 7.50
A116 Whitlow Wyatt 15.00 7.50
A117 Joe DiMaggio 200.00 100.00
Joe McCarthy MG
A118 Wes Ferrell 30.00 15.00
Rick Ferrell
A119 Frank Pytlak 15.00 7.50
Steve O'Neill
B1 Mel Almada 40.00 20.00
B2 Luke Appling 80.00 40.00
B3 Henry Bonura 40.00 20.00
B4 Ben Chapman 40.00 20.00
Bill Werber
B5 Herman Clifton 40.00 20.00
B6 Roger "Doc" Cramer 50.00 25.00
B7 Joe Cronin 80.00 40.00
B8 Jimmy Dykes 50.00 25.00
B9 Ervin "Pete" Fox 40.00 20.00
B10 Jimmie Foxx 120.00 60.00
B11 Hank Greenberg 80.00 40.00
B12 Oral Hildebrand 40.00 20.00
B13 Alex Hooks 40.00 20.00
B14 Willis Hudlin 40.00 20.00
B15 Bill Knickerbocker 40.00 20.00
B16 Heinie Manush 60.00 30.00
B17 Steve O'Neill 40.00 20.00
B18 Marvin Owen 40.00 20.00
B19 Al Simmons 80.00 40.00
B20 Lem "Moose" Solters 40.00 20.00
B21 Hal Trosky (batting) 50.00 25.00
B22 Joe Vosmik 40.00 20.00
B23 Joe Vosmik(batting) 40.00 20.00
B24 Joe Vosmik(fielding) 40.00 20.00
B25 Earl Whitehill 40.00 20.00
C1 Luke Appling 80.00 40.00
batting
C2 Earl Averill 80.00 40.00
C3 Cy Blanton 40.00 20.00
C4 Zeke Bonura 40.00 20.00
batting
C5 Tom Bridges 40.00 20.00
C6 Joe DiMaggio 600.00 300.00
C7 Bobby Doerr 80.00 40.00
C8 Jimmy Dykes 40.00 20.00
throwing
C9 Bob Feller 150.00 75.00
C10 Elbie Fletcher 40.00 20.00
C11 Pete Fox (batting) 40.00 20.00
C12 Gus Galan 40.00 20.00
batting
C13 Charley Gehringer 80.00 40.00
C14 Hank Greenberg 100.00 50.00
C15 Mel Harder 60.00 30.00
C16 Gabby Hartnett 80.00 40.00
C17 Pinky Higgins 40.00 20.00
C18 Carl Hubbell 100.00 50.00
C19 Wally Moses 40.00 20.00
batting
C20 Lou Newsom 50.00 25.00
C21 Schoolboy Rowe 50.00 25.00
throwing
C22 Julius Solters 40.00 20.00
C23 Hal Trosky 50.00 25.00
C24 Joe Vosmik 40.00 20.00
kneeling
C25 Johnnie Whitehead 40.00 20.00
throwing
D1 Buddy Bates M 60.00 30.00
D2 Del Bissonette M 60.00 30.00
D3 Lincoln Blakely T 60.00 30.00
D4 Isaac J. Boone T 60.00 30.00
D5 John H. Burnett T 60.00 30.00
D6 Leon Chagnon M 60.00 30.00
D7 Gus Dugas M 60.00 30.00
D8 Henry N. Erickson 60.00 30.00
D9 Art Funk T 60.00 30.00
D10 George Granger M 60.00 30.00
D11 Thomas G. Heath 60.00 30.00
D12 Phil Hensich M 60.00 30.00
D13 LeRoy Hermann T 60.00 30.00
D14 Henry Johnson M 60.00 30.00
D15 Hal King M 60.00 30.00
D16 Charles S. Lucas T 60.00 30.00
D17 Edward S. Miller T 60.00 30.00
D18 Jake F. Mooty T 60.00 30.00
D19 Guy Moreau 60.00 30.00
D20 George Murray T 60.00 30.00
D21 Glenn Myatt M 60.00 30.00
D22 Lauri Myllykangas M 60.00 30.00
D23 Franci J. Nicholas T 60.00 30.00
D24 Bill O'Brien 60.00 30.00
D25 Thomas Oliver T 60.00 30.00
D26 James Pattison T 60.00 30.00
D27 Crip Polli M 60.00 30.00
D28 Harlin Pool T 60.00 30.00
D29 Walter Purcey T 60.00 30.00
D30 Bill Rhiel M 60.00 30.00
D31 Ben Sankey M 60.00 30.00
D32 Leslie Scarsella T 60.00 30.00
D33 Bob Seeds M 60.00 30.00
D34 Frank Shaughnessy M 60.00 30.00
D35 Harry Smythe M 60.00 30.00
D36 Ben Tate M 60.00 30.00
D37 Fresco Thompson M 80.00 40.00
D38 Charles Wilson M 60.00 30.00
D39 Francis Wistert T 60.00 30.00

1937 Goudey Knot Hole R325

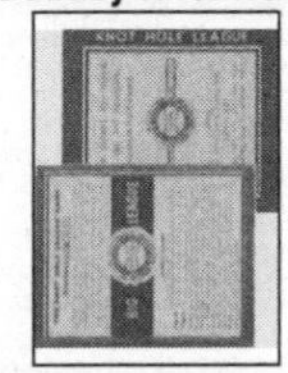

The cards in this 24-card set measure approximately 2 3/8" by 2 7/8". The 1937 "Knot Hole League Game" was another of the many innovative marketing ideas of the Goudey Gum Company. Advertised as a series of 100 game cards promising "exciting" baseball action, the set actually was limited to the 24 cards listed below.

	Ex-Mt	VG
COMPLETE SET (24)	150.00	75.00
COMMON CARD (1-24)	8.00	4.00

1937 Goudey Thum Movies R342

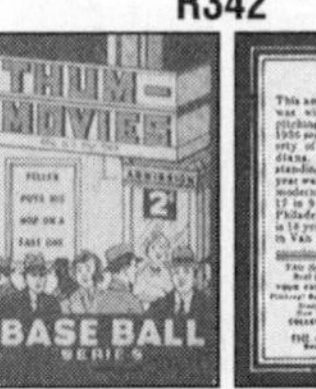

These numbered booklets are the same dimensions (2" by 3") as the R326 Flip Movies except that these are twice the thickness as they comprise both parts within a single cover. They were produced by Goudey Gum. The desirability of the set is decreased by the fact that the outside of the Thum Movie booklet does not show any picture of the player; this is in contrast to the R326 Flip Movie style which shows an inset photo of the player on the cover.

	Ex-Mt	VG
COMPLETE SET (13)	1400.00	700.00
1 John Irving Burns	80.00	40.00
2 Joe Vosmik	80.00	40.00
3 Mel Ott	150.00	75.00
4 Joe DiMaggio	400.00	200.00
5 Wally Moses	80.00	40.00
6 Van Lingle Mungo	80.00	40.00
7 Luke Appling	150.00	75.00
8 Bob Feller	150.00	75.00
9 Paul Derringer	80.00	40.00
10 Paul Waner	150.00	75.00
11 Joe Medwick	150.00	75.00
12 James Emory Foxx	150.00	75.00
13 Wally Berger	100.00	50.00

1937 Goudey Flip Movies R326

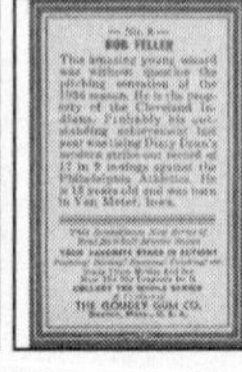

The 26 "Flip Movies" which comprise this set are a miniature version (2" by 3") of the popular penny arcade features of the period. Each movie comes in two parts, clearly labeled, and there are several cover colors as well as incorrect photos known to exist.

	Ex-Mt	VG
COMPLETE SET (13)	1250.00	600.00
1A John Irving Burns (Poles Two Bagger)	30.00	15.00
1B John Irving Burns (Poles Two Bagger)	30.00	15.00
2A Joe Vosmik (Triples)	30.00	15.00
2B Joe Vosmik (Triples)	30.00	15.00
3A Mel Ott (Puts It Over The Fence)	60.00	30.00
3B Mel Ott (Puts It Over The Fence)	60.00	30.00
4A Joe DiMaggio (Socks A Sizzling Long Drive)	200.00	100.00
4B Joe DiMaggio (Socks A Sizzling Long Drive)	200.00	100.00
5A Wally Moses (Leans Against A Fast Ball)	30.00	15.00
5B Wally Moses (Leans Against A Fast Ball)	30.00	15.00
6A Van Lingle Mungo (Tosses Fire-Ball)	30.00	15.00
6B Van Lingle Mungo (Tosses Fire-Ball)	30.00	15.00
7A Luke Appling (Gets Set For Double Play	60.00	30.00
7B Luke Appling (Gets Set For Double Play	60.00	30.00
8A Bob Feller (Puts His Hop On A Fast One)	60.00	30.00
8B Bob Feller (Puts His Hop On A Fast One)	60.00	30.00
9A Paul Derringer (Demonstrates Sharp Curve)	30.00	15.00
9B Paul Derringer (Demonstrates Sharp Curve)	30.00	15.00
10A Paul Waner (Big Poison Smacks A Triple)	60.00	30.00
10B Paul Waner (Big Poison Smacks A Triple)	60.00	30.00
11A Joe Medwick (Bats Hard Grounder)	60.00	30.00
11B Joe Medwick (Bats Hard Grounder)	60.00	30.00
12A James Emory Foxx (Smacks A Homer)	60.00	30.00
12B James Emory Foxx (Smacks A Homer)	60.00	30.00
13A Wally Berger (Puts One In The Bleachers)	40.00	20.00
13B Wally Berger (Puts One In The Bleachers)	40.00	20.00

1938 Goudey Heads Up R323

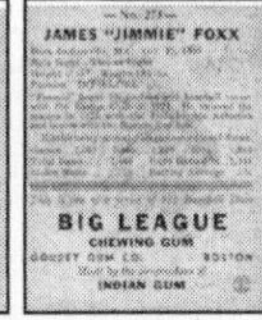

The cards in this 48-card set measure approximately 2 3/8" by 2 7/8". The 1938 Goudey set is commonly referred to as the Heads-Up set. These very popular but difficult to obtain cards came in two series of the same 24 players. The first series, numbers 241-264, is distinguished from the second series, numbers 265-288, in that the second contains etched cartoons and comments surrounding the player picture. Although the set starts with number 241, it is not a continuation of the 1933 Goudey set, but a separate set in its own right.

	Ex-Mt	VG
COMPLETE SET (48)	15000.00	7500.00
COMMON (241-264)	100.00	50.00
COMMON (265-288)	110.00	55.00
WRAP.(1-CENT, 6-FIGURE)	800.00	400.00
241 Charley Gehringer	325.00	160.00
242 Pete Fox	100.00	50.00
243 Joe Kuhel	100.00	50.00
244 Frank Demaree	100.00	50.00
245 Frank Pytlak	100.00	50.00
246 Ernie Lombardi	175.00	90.00
247 Joe Vosmik	100.00	50.00
248 Dick Bartell	100.00	50.00
249 Jimmie Foxx	400.00	200.00
250 Joe DiMaggio	3500.00	1800.00
251 Bump Hadley	100.00	50.00
252 Zeke Bonura	100.00	50.00
253 Hank Greenberg	400.00	200.00
254 Van Lingle Mungo	120.00	60.00
255 Moose Solters	100.00	50.00
256 Vernon Kennedy	100.00	50.00
257 Al Lopez	200.00	100.00
258 Bobby Doerr	250.00	125.00
259 Billy Werber	100.00	50.00
260 Rudy York	120.00	60.00
261 Rip Radcliff	100.00	50.00
262 Joe Medwick	250.00	125.00
263 Marvin Owen	100.00	50.00
264 Bob Feller	600.00	300.00
265 Charley Gehringer	350.00	180.00
266 Pete Fox	110.00	55.00
267 Joe Kuhel	110.00	55.00
268 Frank Demaree	110.00	55.00
269 Frank Pytlak	110.00	55.00
270 Ernie Lombardi	200.00	100.00
271 Joe Vosmik	110.00	55.00
272 Dick Bartell	110.00	55.00
273 Jimmie Foxx	450.00	220.00
274 Joe DiMaggio	3500.00	1800.00
275 Bump Hadley	110.00	55.00
276 Zeke Bonura	110.00	55.00
277 Hank Greenberg	450.00	220.00
278 Van Lingle Mungo	120.00	60.00
279 Moose Solters	110.00	55.00
280 Vernon Kennedy	110.00	55.00
281 Al Lopez	250.00	125.00
282 Bobby Doerr	275.00	140.00
283 Billy Werber	110.00	55.00
284 Rudy York	120.00	60.00
285 Rip Radcliff	110.00	55.00
286 Joe Medwick	275.00	140.00
287 Marvin Owen	110.00	55.00
288 Bob Feller	700.00	350.00

1939 Goudey Premiums R303A

This series of 48 paper premiums were issued in 1939 by the Goudey Company. Each premium photo measures approximately 4" by 6 3/16". This set carries the name Diamond Stars Gum on the reverse, although the National Chicle Company who produced the Diamond Stars baseball cards is in no way connected with this set. The backs contain instructions on various baseball disciplines. The color of the set is brown, not the more reddish color of sepia normally listed for this set.

	Ex-Mt	VG
COMPLETE SET (48)	1500.00	750.00
1 Luke Appling	30.00	15.00
2 Earl Averill	30.00	15.00
3 Wally Berger	25.00	12.50
4 Darrell Blanton	20.00	10.00
5 Zeke Bonura	20.00	10.00
6 Mace Brown	20.00	10.00
7 George Case	20.00	10.00
8 Ben Chapman	20.00	10.00
9 Joe Cronin	30.00	15.00
10 Frank Crosetti	25.00	12.50
11 Paul Derringer	25.00	12.50
12 Bill Dickey	40.00	20.00
13 Joe DiMaggio	250.00	125.00
14 Bob Feller	80.00	40.00
15 Jimmie Foxx	60.00	30.00
16 Charley Gehringer	40.00	20.00
17 Lefty Gomez	40.00	20.00
18 Ival Goodman	25.00	12.50
19 Joe Gordon	25.00	12.50
20 Hank Greenberg	50.00	25.00
21 Buddy Hassett	20.00	10.00
22 Jeff Heath	20.00	10.00
23 Tommy Henrich	30.00	15.00
24 Billy Herman	30.00	15.00
25 Frank Higgins	20.00	10.00
26 Fred Hutchinson	25.00	12.50
27 Bob Johnson	20.00	10.00
28 Ken Keltner	20.00	10.00
29 Mike Kreevich	20.00	10.00
30 Ernie Lombardi	30.00	15.00
31 Gus Mancuso	20.00	10.00
32 Eric McNair	20.00	10.00
33 Van Mungo	25.00	12.50
34 Buck Newsom	25.00	12.50
35 Mel Ott	40.00	20.00
36 Marvin Owen	20.00	10.00
37 Frankie Pytlak	20.00	10.00
38 Woody Rich	20.00	10.00
39 Charlie Root	20.00	10.00
40 Al Simmons	30.00	15.00
41 Jim Tabor	20.00	10.00
42 Cecil Travis	20.00	10.00
43 Hal Trosky	25.00	12.50
44 Arky Vaughan	30.00	15.00
45 Joe Vosmik	20.00	10.00
46 Lon Warneke	20.00	10.00
47 Ted Williams	250.00	125.00
48 Rudy York	25.00	12.50

1939 Goudey Premiums R303B

This set of 24 paper photos is slightly larger than its counterpart R303A and was also issued in 1939. Each premium photo measures approximately 4 3/4" by 7 5/16". The photos of R303A series are the same ones depicted on these cards, and the reverses contain "How to" instructions and the Diamond Stars Gum name. The photos are the same as R303A. This set comes in two distinct colors, black and sepia.

	Ex-Mt	VG
COMPLETE SET (24)	650.00	325.00
1 Luke Appling	25.00	12.50
2 George Case	15.00	7.50
3 Ben Chapman	15.00	7.50
4 Joe Cronin	25.00	12.50
5 Bill Dickey	30.00	15.00
6 Joe DiMaggio	200.00	100.00
7 Bob Feller	60.00	30.00
8 Jimmie Foxx	50.00	25.00
9 Lefty Gomez	30.00	15.00
10 Ival Goodman	15.00	7.50
11 Joe Gordon	20.00	10.00
12 Hank Greenberg	40.00	20.00
13 Jeff Heath	15.00	7.50
14 Billy Herman	25.00	12.50
15 Frank Higgins	15.00	7.50
16 Ken Keltner	15.00	7.50
17 Mike Kreevich	15.00	7.50
18 Ernie Lombardi	25.00	12.50
19 Gus Mancuso	15.00	7.50
20 Mel Ott	40.00	20.00
21 Al Simmons	25.00	12.50
22 Arky Vaughan	25.00	12.50
23 Joe Vosmik	15.00	7.50
24 Rudy York	20.00	10.00

1941 Goudey R324

The cards in this 33-card set measure 2 3/8" by 2 7/8". The 1941 Series of blank backed baseball cards was the last baseball issue marketed by Goudey before the war closed the door on that company for good. Each black and white player photo comes with four color backgrounds (blue, green, red, or yellow). Cards without numbers are probably miscut. Cards 21-25 are especially scarce in relation to the rest of the set. In fact the eight hardest to find cards in the set are, in order, 22, 24, 23, 25, 21, 27, 29 and 32.

	Ex-Mt	VG
COMPLETE SET (33)	2000.00	1000.00
WRAPPER (1-CENT)	200.00	100.00
1 Hugh Mulcahy	30.00	15.00
2 Harland Clift	30.00	15.00
3 Louis Chiozza	30.00	15.00
4 Warren Rosar	30.00	15.00
5 George McQuinn	30.00	15.00
6 George Dickman	30.00	15.00
7 Wayne Ambler	30.00	15.00
8 Bob Muncrief	30.00	15.00
9 Bill Dietrich	30.00	15.00
10 Taft Wright	30.00	15.00
11 Don Heffner	30.00	15.00
12 Fritz Ostermueller	30.00	15.00
13 Frank Hayes	30.00	15.00
14 John Kramer	30.00	15.00
15 Dario Lodigiani	30.00	15.00
16 George Case	30.00	15.00
17 Vito Tamulis	30.00	15.00
18 Whitlow Wyatt	40.00	20.00
19 Bill Posedel	30.00	15.00
20 Carl Hubbell	80.00	40.00
21 Harold Warstler SP	120.00	60.00
22 Joe Sullivan SP	300.00	150.00
23 Norman Young SP	200.00	100.00
24 Stanley Andrews SP	250.00	125.00
25 Morris Arnovich SP	120.00	60.00
26 Elbert Fletcher	30.00	15.00
27 Bill Crouch	60.00	30.00
28 Al Todd	30.00	15.00
29 Debs Garms	50.00	25.00
30 Jim Tobin	30.00	15.00
31 Chester Ross	30.00	15.00
32 George Coffman	40.00	20.00
33 Mel Ott	125.00	60.00

1990 Grace W/R

Produced and distributed by W/R Associates in care of Baseball Cards-N-More (Louisville, KY), the sheet has an 5 1/8" by 7" oversized color portrait of Grace in its center, surrounded on three sides by standard-size cards that trace Grace's career. The cards are unnumbered and checklisted below in chronological order.

	Nm-Mt	Ex-Mt
COMPLETE SET (9)	4.00	1.20
COMMON CARD (1-9)	.50	.15

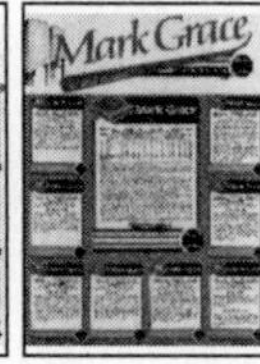

9 Mark Grace (Oversized card 5 1/8" by 7")	1.00	.30

2000 Grace Illinois Lottery

This one card post-card set features a horizontal front of Cubs star Mark Grace as well as promoting the Illinois Lottery. The back has various sponsors.

	Nm-Mt	Ex-Mt
1 Mark Grace	2.00	.60

1978 Grand Slam

Issued by Renata Galasso, Inc., these 200 cards, which measure 2 1/4" by 3 1/4" features some of the leading figures in baseball history. All the players in this set were alive at time of issue and many collectors wrote to these players to get autographs.

	NM	Ex
COMPLETE SET (200)	40.00	16.00
1 Leo Durocher	.50	.20
2 Bob Lemon	.50	.20
3 Earl Averill	.50	.20
4 Dale Alexander	.10	.04
5 Hank Greenberg	.75	.30
6 Waite Hoyt	.50	.20
7 Al Lopez	.50	.20
8 Lloyd Waner	.40	.16
9 Bob Feller	1.00	.40
10 Guy Bush	.10	.04
11 Stan Hack	.20	.08
12 Zeke Bonura	.10	.04
13 Wally Moses	.10	.04
14 Fred Fitzsimmons	.10	.04
15 Johnny Vander Meer	.20	.08
16 Riggs Stephenson	.20	.08
17 Bucky Walters	.40	.16
18 Charlie Grimm	.40	.16
19 Phil Cavarretta	.30	.12
20 Wally Berger	.20	.08
21 Joe Sewell	.40	.16
22 Edd Roush	.40	.16
23 Johnny Mize	.50	.20
24 Bill Dickey	.75	.30
25 Lou Boudreau	.50	.20
26 Bill Terry	1.00	.40
27 Willie Kamm	.10	.04
28 Charlie Gehringer	.75	.30
29 Stanley Coveleskie	.50	.20
30 Larry French	.10	.04
31 George Kelly	.30	.12
32 Terry Moore	.20	.08
33 Billy Herman	.40	.16
34 Babe Herman	.30	.12
35 Carl Hubbell	1.00	.40
36 Buck Leonard	1.00	.40
37 Gus Suhr	.10	.04
38 Burleigh Grimes	.40	.16
39 Lew Fonseca	.10	.04
40 Travis Jackson	.30	.12
41 Enos Slaughter	.50	.20
42 Fred Lindstrom	.30	.12
43 Rick Ferrell	.30	.12
44 Cookie Lavagetto	.10	.04
45 Stan Musial	2.00	.80
46 Hal Trosky	.10	.04
47 Hal Newhouser	.40	.16
48 Paul Dean	.10	.04
49 George Halas	1.00	.40
50 Jocko Conlan	.40	.16
51 Joe DiMaggio	4.00	1.60
52 Bobby Doerr	.50	.20
53 Carl Reynolds	.10	.04
54 Pete Reiser	.30	.12
55 Frank McCormick	.10	.04
56 Mel Harder	.20	.08
57 George Uhle	.10	.04
58 Doc Cramer	.10	.04
59 Taylor Douthit	.10	.04
60 Cecil Travis	.10	.04
61 James Cool Papa Bell	1.00	.40
62 Charlie Keller	.30	.12
63 Bill Hallahan	.10	.04
64 Debs Garms	.10	.04
65 Rube Marquard	.40	.16
66 Rube Walberg	.10	.04
67 Augie Galan	.20	.08
68 George Pipgras	.10	.04
69 Hal Schumacher	.10	.04
70 Dolf Camilli	.20	.08
71 Paul Richards	.10	.04
72 Judy Johnson	1.00	.40
73 Frank Crosetti	.30	.12
74 Peanuts Lowery	.10	.04
75 Walter Alston	.30	.12
76 Dutch Leonard	.10	.04
77 Barney McCosky	.10	.04
78 Joe Dobson	.10	.04
79 George Kell	.50	.20
80 Ted Lyons	.40	.16
81 Johnny Pesky	.20	.08
82 Hank Bowory	.10	.04
83 Ewell Blackwell	.10	.04
84 Pee Wee Reese	1.00	.40
85 Monte Irvin	.75	.30
86 Joe Moore	.10	.04
87 Joe Wood	.40	.16
88 Babe Dahlgren	.10	.04
89 Bibb Falk	.10	.04
90 Ed Lopat	.30	.12
91 Rip Sewell	.10	.04
92 Marty Marion	.20	.08
93 Taft Wright	.10	.04
94 Allie Reynolds	.30	.12
95 Harry Walker	.20	.08
96 Tex Hughson	.10	.04
97 George Selkirk	.10	.04
98 Dom DiMaggio	.40	.16
99 Walker Cooper	.10	.04
100 Phil Rizzuto	1.00	.40
101 Robin Robers	1.00	.40
102 Joe Adcock	.30	.12
103 Hank Bauer	.30	.12
104 Frank Baumholtz	.10	.04
105 Ray Boone	.10	.04
106 Smoky Burgess	.10	.04
107 Walt Dropo	.10	.04
108 Alvin Dark	.20	.08
109 Carl Erskine	.20	.08
110 Dick Donovan	.10	.04
111 Dee Fondy	.10	.04
112 Mike Garcia	.10	.04
113 Bob Friend	.10	.04
114 Ned Garver	.10	.04
115 Billy Goodman	.10	.04
116 Larry Jansen	.10	.04
117 Jackie Jensen	.20	.08
118 John Antonelli	.10	.04
119 Ted Kluszewski	.40	.16
120 Harvey Kuenn	.20	.08
121 Clem Labine	.10	.04
122 Red Schoendienst	.40	.16
123 Don Larsen	.30	.12
124 Vern Law	.20	.08
125 Charlie Maxwell	.10	.04
126 Wally Moon	.10	.04
127 Bob Nieman	.10	.04
128 Don Newcombe	.20	.08
129 Wally Post	.10	.04
130 Johnny Podres	.20	.08
131 Vic Raschi	.20	.08
132 Dusty Rhodes	.10	.04
133 Jim Rivera	.10	.04
134 Pete Runnels	.10	.04
135 Hank Sauer	.20	.08
136 Roy Sievers	.20	.08
137 Bobby Shantz	.20	.08
138 Curt Simmons	.10	.04
139 Bob Skinner	.10	.04
140 Bill Skowron	.30	.12
141 Warren Spahn	.75	.30
142 Gerry Staley	.10	.04
143 Frank Thomas	.20	.08
144 Bobby Thomson	.30	.12
145 Bob Turley	.10	.04
146 Vic Wertz	.10	.04
147 Bill Virdon	.10	.04
148 Gene Woodling	.10	.04
149 Eddie Yost	.10	.04
150 Sandy Koufax	2.00	.80
151 Lefty Gomez	.75	.30
152 Al Rosen	.40	.16
153 Vince DiMaggio	.20	.08
154 Bill Nicholson	.10	.04
155 Mark Koenig	.10	.04
156 Max Lanier	.10	.04
157 Ken Keltner	.10	.04
158 Whit Wyatt	.10	.04
159 Marv Owen	.10	.04
160 Red Lucas	.10	.04
161 Babe Phelps	.10	.04
162 Pete Donohue	.10	.04
163 Johnny Cooney	.10	.04
164 Glenn Wright	.10	.04
165 Willis Hudlin	.10	.04
166 Tony Cuccinello	.10	.04
167 Bill Bevans	.10	.04
168 Dave Ferriss	.10	.04
169 Whitey Kurowski	.10	.04
170 Buddy Hassett	.10	.04
171 Ossie Bluege	.10	.04
172 Hoot Evers	.10	.04
173 Thornton Lee	.10	.04
174 Spud Davis	.10	.04
175 Bob Shawkey	.30	.12
176 Smead Jolley	.10	.04
177 Andy High	.10	.04
178 George McQuinn	.10	.04
179 Mickey Vernon	.20	.08
180 Birdie Tebbetts	.10	.04
181 Jack Kramer	.10	.04
182 Don Kolloway	.10	.04
183 Claude Passeau	.10	.04
184 Frank Shea	.10	.04
185 Bob O'Farrell	.10	.04
186 Bob Johnson	.10	.04
187 Ival Goodman	.10	.04
188 Mike Kreevich	.10	.04
189 Joe Stripp	.10	.04
190 Mickey Owen	.10	.04
191 Hughie Critz	.10	.04
192 Ethan Allen	.10	.04
193 Billy Rogell	.10	.04
194 Joe Kuhel	.10	.04
195 Dale Mitchell	.20	.08
196 Eldon Auker	.10	.04
197 Johnny Beazley	.10	.04
198 Spud Chandler	.20	.08
199 Ralph Branca	.20	.08
200 Joe Cronin	.75	.30

1975-76 Great Plains Greats

This 42-card set measures approximately 2 1/2" by 3 3/4". The set was issued by the Great Plains Sports Collectors Association in conjunction with their annual show. The first series cards have the photos surrounded by a green border while the second series cards have an orange border. The Lloyd Waner card with a green border is an extra addition to the first series. The card is only available as a single when cut from an uncut sheet. Since it was not issued with the regular set, we are calling it a Short Print. Waner was never distributed since he did not sign a release form. The 1st series was available directly from the producer at time of issue for $4.25. The 2nd series was available from the producer at time of issue for $2.25. 2,000 1st series sets were printed.

	NM	Ex
COMPLETE SET (42)	20.00	8.00
1 Bob Feller	1.00	.40
2 Carl Hubbell	1.00	.40
3 Jocko Conlan	.50	.20
4 Hal Trosky	.25	.10
5 Allie Reynolds	.25	.10
6 Burleigh Grimes	.75	.30
7 Jake Beckley	.50	.20
8 Al Simmons	1.00	.40
9 Paul Waner	1.00	.40
10 Chief Bender	.75	.30
11 Fred Clarke	.50	.20
12 Jim Bottomley	.25	.10
13 Dave Bancroft	.50	.20
14 Bing Miller	.25	.10
15 Walter Johnson	1.50	.60
16 Grover Alexander	1.50	.60
17 Bob Johnson	.25	.10
18 Roger Maris	1.00	.40
19 Ken Keltner	.25	.10
20 Red Faber	.50	.20
21 Cool Papa Bell	1.00	.40
22 Yogi Berra	1.00	.40
23 Fred Lindstrom	.50	.20
24 Ray Schalk	.50	.20
25A Lloyd Waner SP	15.00	6.00
26 John Hopp	.25	.10
27 Mel Harder	.25	.10
28 Dutch Leonard	.25	.10
29 Bob O'Farrell	.25	.10
30 Cap Anson	.75	.30
31 Dazzy Vance	.50	.20
32 Red Schoendienst	.50	.20
33 George Pipgras	.25	.10
34 Harvey Kuenn	.25	.10
35 Red Ruffing	.50	.20
36 Roy Sievers	.25	.10
37 Ken Boyer	.50	.20
38 Al Smith	.25	.10
39 Casey Stengel	1.00	.40
40 Bob Gibson	.75	.30
41 Mickey Mantle	3.00	1.20
42 Denny McLain	.50	.20

1988 Grenada Baseball Stamps

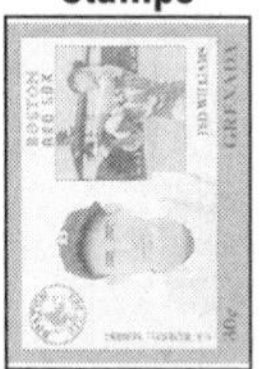

These stamps, featuring active major league stars as well as great retired players were issued by the Island of Grenada. Grenada, had previously gained recognition earlier in the decade as an island which had been invaded by U.S. forces.

	Nm-Mt	Ex-Mt
COMPLETE SET (81)	25.00	10.00
1 Johnny Bench	.50	.20
2 Dave Stieb	.05	.02
3 Reggie Jackson	.50	.20
4 Harold Baines	.10	.04
5 Wade Boggs	.25	.10
6 Pete O'Brien	.05	.02
7 Stan Musial	1.00	.40
8 Wally Joyner	.10	.04
9 Grover C. Alexander	.25	.10
10 Jose Cruz	.10	.04
11 AL Logo	.05	.02
12 Al Kaline	.25	.10
13 Chuck Klein	.10	.04
14 Don Mattingly	1.00	.40
15 Mike Witt	.05	.02
16 Mark Langston	.05	.02
17 Hubie Brooks	.05	.02
18 Harmon Killebrew	.40	.16
19 Jackie Robinson	2.00	.80
20 Dwight Gooden	.10	.04
21 Brooks Robinson	.40	.16
22 Nolan Ryan	2.00	.80
23 Mike Schmidt	.60	.24
24 Gary Gaetti	.10	.04
25 Nellie Fox	.15	.06
26 Tony Gwynn	1.00	.40
27 Dizzy Dean	.40	.16
28 Luis Aparicio	.25	.10
29 Paul Molitor	.40	.16
30 Lou Gehrig	2.00	.80
31 Jeffrey Leonard	.05	.02
32 Eric Davis	.10	.04
33 Pete Incaviglia	.05	.02
34 Steve Rogers	.05	.02
35 Ozzie Smith	.40	.16
36 Randy Jones	.05	.02
37 Gary Carter	.40	.16
38 Hank Aaron	1.50	.60
39 Gaylord Perry	.25	.10
40 Ty Cobb	1.50	.60
41 Andre Dawson	.15	.06
42 Charlie Hough	.10	.04
43 Kirby Puckett	.50	.20
44 Robin Yount	.25	.10
45 Don Drysdale	.40	.16
46 Mickey Mantle	2.00	.80
47 Roger Clemens	1.00	.40
48 Rod Carew	.40	.16
49 Ryne Sandberg	.75	.30
50 Mike Scott	.05	.02
51 Tim Raines	.10	.04
52 Willie Mays	1.00	.40
53 Bret Saberhagen	.05	.02
54 Honus Wagner	.75	.30
55 George Brett	.75	.30
56 Joe Carter	.10	.04
57 Frank Robinson	.40	.16
58 Mel Ott	.40	.16
59 Benito Santiago	.10	.04
60 Teddy Higuera	.05	.02
61 Lloyd Moseby	.05	.02
62 Bobby Bonilla	.10	.04
63 Warren Spahn	.40	.16
64 Ernie Banks	.50	.20
65 NL Logo	.05	.02
66 Julio Franco	.10	.04
67 Jack Morris	.10	.04
68 Fernando Valenzuela	.10	.04
69 Lefty Grove	.40	.16
70 Ted Williams	2.00	.80
71 Darryl Strawberry	.10	.04
72 Dale Murphy	.15	.06
73 Roberto Clemente	2.00	.80
74 Cal Ripken Jr.	2.00	.80
75 Bob Feller	.40	.16
76 George Bell	.05	.02
77 Mark McGwire	1.25	.50
78 Alvin Davis	.05	.02
79 Pete Rose	.75	.30
80 Dan Quisenberry	.05	.02
81 Babe Ruth	2.00	.80

1974 Greyhound Heroes of Base Paths

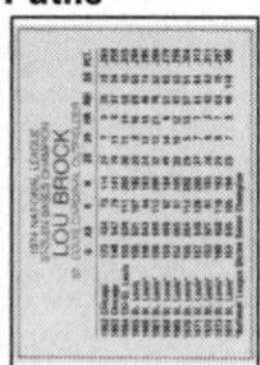

Beginning in 1965, the Greyhound Award for Stolen Bases was given to the champions in each league and the second-place finishers. The 1974 Heroes of the Base Paths pamphlet unfolds to reveal five 4" by 9" panels. The first panel is the title page and features on the back a picture of Joe Black holding the trophy. The second and third panels have on the fronts the history of the award and major league statistics pertaining to stolen bases, while the backs have an essay on the art of base stealing. Finally, the fourth and fifth panels display six player cards; after perforation, the cards measure 4" by 3". Cards 1-4 feature the AL and NL winners and the runner-ups for each league, in that order. The player cards display a black and white head shot of the player on the left half, with player information and number of stolen bases on the right half. The backs have statistics. Both sides of the cards are framed by thin brown border stripes. Cards 5-6 display black and white player photos of past winners in the AL and NL, respectively. The cards are unnumbered.

	NM	Ex
COMPLETE SET (6)	10.00	4.00
1 Bill North	1.25	.50
2 Lou Brock	4.00	1.60
3 Rod Carew	4.00	1.60
4 Davey Lopes	1.50	.60
5 Dagoberto Campaneris Tommy Harper Amos Otis Dave Nelson Billy North Don Buford Fred Patek Rod Carew	1.25	.50
6 Lou Brock Maury Wills Bobby Tolan Joe Morgan Sonny Jackson Jose Cardenal Davey Lopes	1.50	.60

1975 Greyhound Heroes of Base Paths

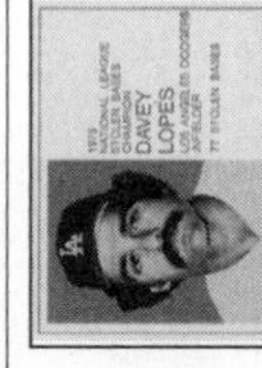

The Greyhound Award for Stolen Bases was given to the champions in each league and the second-place finishers. The 1975 Heroes of the Base Paths pamphlet unfolds to reveal five 4" by 9" panels. The first panel is the title page and features on the back a picture of Maury Wills holding the trophy. The second and third panels have on the fronts the history of the award and major league statistics pertaining to stolen bases, while backs have an essay on the art of base stealing. The fourth and fifth panels display six player cards; after perforation, cards measure approximately 4" by 3". Cards 1-4 feature the AL and NL winners and the runner-ups for each league, in that order. The player cards display a black and white head shot of the player on the left half, with player information and number of stolen bases on the right half. The backs have statistics. Both sides of the cards are framed by thin powder blue border stripes. Cards 5-6 display black and white player photos of Billy North and Davey Lopes. The cards are unnumbered.

	NM	Ex
COMPLETE SET (6)	7.50	3.00
1 Mickey Rivers	1.00	.40
2 Davey Lopes	1.25	.50
3 Claudell Washington	1.00	.40
4 Joe Morgan	4.00	1.60
5 Billy North	1.00	.40
6 Davey Lopes	1.25	.50

1976 Greyhound Heroes of Base Paths

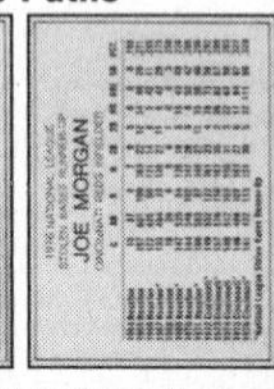

The Greyhound Award for Stolen Bases was given to the champions in each league and the second-place finishers. The 1976 Heroes of the Base Paths pamphlet unfolds to reveal five 4" by 9" panels. The first panel is the title page and features on the back a picture of Maury Wills holding the trophy. The second and third panels have on the fronts the history of the award and major league statistics pertaining to stolen bases& while the backs have an essay on the art of base stealing. The fourth and fifth panels display six player cards; after perforation, cards measure approximately 4" by 3". Cards 1-4 feature the AL and NL winners and the runner-ups for each league, in that order. The player cards display a black and white head shot of the player on the left half, with player information and number of stolen bases on the right half. The backs have statistics. Both sides of the cards are framed by thin powder reddish-brown stripes. Cards 5-6 display black and white player photos of Billy North and Davey Lopes. The cards are unnumbered.

	NM	Ex
COMPLETE SET (6)	8.00	3.20
1 Bill North	1.00	.40
2 Davey Lopes	1.25	.50
3 Ron LeFlore	1.00	.40
4 Joe Morgan	4.00	1.60
5 Billy North	1.00	.40
6 Davey Lopes	1.25	.50

1992 Griffey Arena Kid Comic Holograms

Released in September 1992, this five-card hologram standard-size set was produced by Arena Holograms. The production run was reported to be 1,700 individually numbered cases and premium gold edition cards were randomly inserted throughout. The gold versions are valued at five times the values listed below. Each foil pack contained one card in a card protector and each protector had a different color border (1-clear, 2-black, 3-red, 4-white and 5-blue).

	Nm-Mt	Ex-Mt
COMPLETE SET (5)	5.00	1.50
COMMON CARD (1-5)	1.00	.30

1991 Griffey Card Guard Promo

These standard-size cards were used as advertisements for Card Guard. The front has a color photo of Ken Griffey Jr. dressed in a tuxedo and holding a baseball card protected by Card Guard. His autograph is inscribed across the picture in gold ink. The back has an advertisement for Card Guard, highlighting its special features. There are two different angles used for Griffey's photo and we have notated each of those in our checklist

	Nm-Mt	Ex-Mt
COMPLETE SET (2)	2.00	.60
COMMON CARD	1.00	.30

1994 Griffey Dairy Queen

The 1994 Dairy Queen Ken Griffey Jr. set consists of ten standard-size cards. The cards were distributed in five-card packs at the restaurants, with the gold cards randomly inserted. The fronts feature color action shots of Griffey with the set title's logo appearing in the upper left corner of the picture. Ken Griffey's name is printed below the photo in gold block lettering beside the Dairy Queen logo. The photo is bordered in gold on some sets, and in green on others. The production run on the green-border sets was 90,000, while that of the gold-bordered sets was 10,000. The gold versions are valued at double the values listed below. Except for card number 2, the backs are in a horizontal format, with a posed or action photo on the left side. According to the information on the back, Ken Griffey Jr. personally authorized the set.

	Nm-Mt	Ex-Mt
COMPLETE SET (10)	10.00	3.00
COMMON CARD (1-10)	1.25	.35

1996 Griffey Nike

This one-card set was issued in conjunction with Nike's presendential ad campaign for Ken Griffey. The front features a black-and-white image over a white background with red printing and a top and bottom blue border containing white stars and the Nike symbol. The back displays player information.

	Nm-Mt	Ex-Mt
1 Ken Griffey	2.00	.60

1994 Griffey Nintendo

This standard-size card was inserted in packages of Nintendo's video game, Ken Griffey Jr. Presents: Major League Baseball. The front features a borderless color photo of Griffey at bat. His name, team name, and position appear in white lettering within purple and blue bars near the top. His facsimile autograph in silver ink appears vertically on the left. The horizontal back features on the left side a rear view of Griffey at bat, and on the right, his 1993 season highlights. His biography and 1993 statistics are shown within a yellow stripe across the bottom. The single card is unnumbered.

	Nm-Mt	Ex-Mt
1 Ken Griffey Jr.	3.00	.90

1977 Burleigh Grimes Daniels

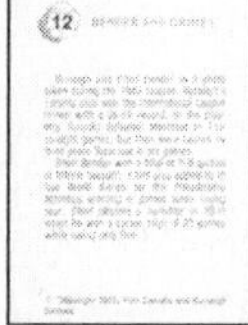

This 16-card set features black-and-white photos with blue borders of different aspects in the life of Hall of Famer and last legal spitball pitcher Burleigh Grimes. Card number 12 comes with or without an autograph. Sets were available from the producer upon release for $3.49 or in uncut sheet form for $6.49.

	NM	Ex
COMPLETE SET (16)	20.00	8.00
1 Burleigh Grimes Dodger Manager 1937-38	1.25	.50
2 Burleigh Grimes Lord Burleigh	1.25	.50
3 Burleigh Grimes Clarence Mitchell Last Spitballers	1.25	.50
4 Burleigh Grimes Rogers Hornsby John McGraw Edd Roush	1.25	.50
5 Burleigh Grimes Zack Wheat Winning Combination	1.25	.50
6 Burleigh Grimes World Champion	1.25	.50
7 Burleigh Grimes Old Stubblebeard	1.25	.50
8 Burleigh Grimes Joe McCarthy MG	1.25	.50
9 Burleigh Grimes Dazzy Vance Van Mungo Watson Clark Dodger Greats	1.25	.50
10 Burleigh Grimes Babe Ruth	1.25	.50
11 Burleigh Grimes Babe Ruth Leo Durocher Dodger Strategists	1.25	.50
12 Burleigh Grimes Chief Bender	1.25	.50
12A Burleigh Grimes AU Chief Bender	20.00	8.00
13 Burleigh Grimes Robin Roberts Number 270	1.25	.50
14 Burleigh Grimes The Origin	1.25	.50
15 Burleigh Grimes Red Faber Luke Appling Heinie Manush 1964 HOF Inductees	1.25	.50
16 Burleigh Grimes Lord Burleigh 1977	1.25	.50

1982 GS Gallery All-Time Greats

This 24-card set measure 2 1/2" by 3". Issued by long time dealer G.S. Gallery, these cards have full color pictures or drawings on the front. The backs have vital statistics and lifetime totals.

	Nm-Mt	Ex-Mt
COMPLETE SET (24)	10.00	4.00
1 Stan Musial	2.00	.80
2 Alvin Dark	.25	.10
3 Harry Walker	.25	.10
4 Dom DiMaggio	.50	.20
5 Carl Furillo	.50	.20
6 Joe DiMaggio	3.00	1.20
7 Joe Adcock	.25	.10
8 Lou Boudreau	.75	.30
9 Ted Williams	3.00	1.20
10 Phil Rizzuto	1.00	.40
11 Pee Wee Reese	1.00	.40
12 James Dykes	.25	.10
13 Nellie Fox	.75	.30
14 George Kell	.75	.30
15 Ralph Kiner	.75	.30
16 Roger Maris	1.00	.40
17 Ted Kluszewski	.50	.20
18 Wally Moon	.25	.10
19 Hank Sauer	.25	.10
20 Bob Thomson	.50	.20
21 Mel Parnell	.25	.10
22 Ewell Blackwell	.25	.10
23 Richie Ashburn	1.00	.40
24 Jackie Robinson	2.50	1.00

1973 Hall of Fame Picture Pack

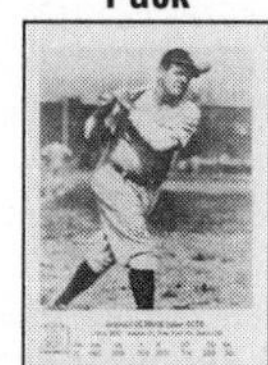

This 20-card set issued in a special envelope measures approximately 5" by 6 3/4" and features black-and-white photos of players who are in the Baseball Hall of Fame in Cooperstown, New York. Player information and statistics are printed on the front in the bottom margin. The backs are blank. The cards are unnumbered and checklisted below in alphabetical order.

	NM	Ex
COMPLETE SET (20)	35.00	14.00
1 Yogi Berra	2.50	1.00
2 Roy Campanella	2.50	1.00
3 Ty Cobb	3.00	1.20
4 Joe Cronin	1.00	.40
5 Dizzy Dean	2.00	.80
6 Joe DiMaggio	4.00	1.60
7 Bob Feller	1.00	.40
8 Lou Gehrig	4.00	1.60
9 Rogers Hornsby	1.50	.60
10 Sandy Koufax	2.50	1.00
11 Christy Mathewson	1.50	.60
12 Stan Musial	2.50	1.00
13 Satchel Paige	1.50	.60
14 Jackie Robinson	3.00	1.20
15 Babe Ruth	5.00	2.00
16 Warren Spahn	1.00	.40
17 Casey Stengel	1.00	.40
18 Honus Wagner	2.00	.80
19 Ted Williams	3.00	1.20
20 Cy Young	1.50	.60

1996-03 Hallmark Ornaments

These cards were issued as a bonus for purchasing an Hallmark Ornament. These cards all have thl Hallmark logo in the upper right. The back has a brief biography of the featured player.

	MINT	NRMT
1 Hank Aaron 1996	6.00	2.70
2 Nolan Ryan 1996	10.00	4.50
3 Mark McGwire 2000	6.00	2.70
4 Sammy Sosa 2001	5.00	2.20
5 Jason Giambi 2003	2.50	1.10

1978 Halsey Hall Recalls

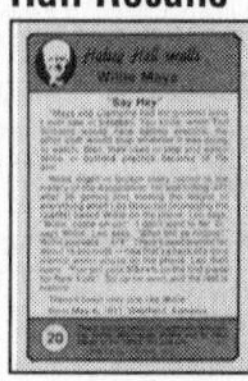

This 21-card set measures 2 1/2" by 3 3/4". The players featured were all local Minneapolis-St. Paul heroes whose exploits were remembered by local legend Halsey Hall. These sets were available upon issue from the producer for $3.50.

	NM	Ex
COMPLETE SET (21)	12.00	4.80
1 Halsey Hall	.50	.20
2 Ray Dandridge	1.00	.40
3 Bruno Haas	.25	.10
4 Fabian Gaffke	.25	.10
5 George Stumpf	.25	.10
6 Roy Campanella	2.00	.80
7 Babe Barna	.25	.10
8 Tom Sheehan	.25	.10
9 Ray Moore	.25	.10
10 Ted Williams	5.00	2.00
11 Harley Davidson	.25	.10
12 Jack Cassini	.25	.10
13 Pea Ridge Day	.25	.10
14 Oscar Roettger	.25	.10
15 Buzz Arlett	.25	.10
16 Joe Hauser	.25	.10
17 Rube Benton	.25	.10
18 Dave Barnhill	.25	.10
19 Hoyt Wilhelm	1.00	.40
20 Willie Mays	3.00	1.20
21 Nicollet Park CL	.25	.10

1998 Hamburger Helper

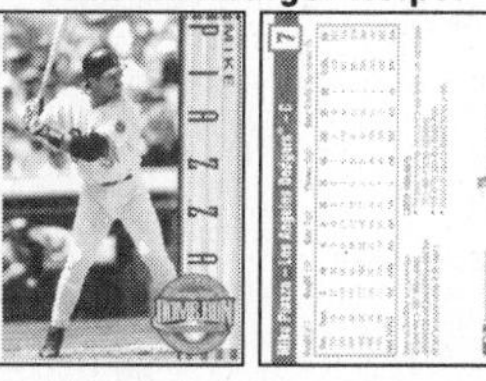

This eight-card standard-size set features color action player photos that appeared on cards which could be cut off the back of the boxes of different variations of Betty Crocker's Hamburger Helper. The backs carry player information and career statistics. There is a premium for a complete box.

	Nm-Mt	Ex-Mt
COMPLETE SET (8)	20.00	6.00
1 Mark McGwire	6.00	1.80
2 Rafael Palmeiro	2.00	.60
3 Tino Martinez	1.00	.30
4 Barry Bonds	4.00	1.20
5 Larry Walker	1.00	.30
6 Juan Gonzalez	3.00	.90
7 Mike Piazza	5.00	1.50
8 Frank Thomas	2.50	.75

1912 Hassan Triple Folders T202

The cards in this 132-card set measure approximately 2 1/4" by 5 1/4". The 1912 T202 Hassan Triple Folder issue is perhaps the most ingenious baseball card ever issued. The two end cards of each panel are full color, T205-like individual cards whereas the black and white center panel pictures an action photo or portrait. The end cards can be folded across the center panel and stored in this manner. Seventy-six different center panels are known to exist; however, many of the center panels contain more than one combination of end cards. The center panel titles are listed below in alphabetical order while the different combinations of end cards are listed below each center panel as they appear left to right on the front of the card. A total of 132 different card fronts exist. The set price below includes all panel and player combinations listed in the checklist. Back color variations (red or black) also exist. The Birmingham's Home Run card is difficult to obtain as are other cards whose center panel exists with but one combination of end cards. The Devlin with Mathewson end panels on numbers 29A and 74C picture Devlin as a Giant. Devlin is pictured as a Rustler on 29B and 74D.

	Ex-Mt	VG
COMPLETE SET (132)	35000.00 17500.00	
1A A Close Play at Home: Bobby Wallace Frank LaPorte	175.00	90.00
1B A Close Play at Home: Bobby Wallace Barney Pelty	175.00	90.00
2 A Desperate Slide: Charley O'Leary Ty Cobb	1500.00	750.00
3A A Great Batsman Cy Barger Bill Bergen	150.00	75.00
3B A Great Batsman Nap Rucker Bill Bergen	150.00	75.00
4 Ambrose McConnell at Bat Walter Blair Jack Quinn	175.00	90.00
5 A Wide Throw Saves Sam Crawford: George Mullin Oscar Stanage	200.00	100.00
6 Frank Baker Gets His Man Eddie Collins Frank Baker	400.00	200.00
7 Doc Birmingham Gets to Third Walter Johnson Gabby Street	500.00	250.00
8 Doc Birmingham Home Run Doc Birmingham Terry Turner	500.00	250.00
9 Donie Bush Just Misses Jimmy Austin Pat Moran Sherry Magee	175.00	90.00
10A Bill Carrigan Blocks His Man Harry Gaspar Larry McLean	150.00	75.00
10B Bill Carrigan Blocks His Man Heinie Wagner Bill Carrigan	150.00	75.00
11 Catching Him Napping: Rebel Oakes Roger Bresnahan	200.00	100.00
12 Caught Asleep Off First: Roger Bresnahan Robert Harmon	200.00	100.00
13A Frank Chance Beats Out a Hit Frank Chance Bill Foxen	250.00	125.00
13B Frank Chance Beats Out a Hit Matty McIntire Jimmy Archer	175.00	90.00
13C Frank Chance Beats Out a Hit Orval Overall Jimmy Archer	175.00	90.00
13D Frank Chance Beats Out a Hit John Rowan Jimmy Archer	175.00	90.00
13E Frank Chance Beats Out a Hit David Shean Frank Chance	250.00	125.00
14A Hal Chase Dives into Third Hal Chase Harry Wolter	150.00	75.00
14B Hal Chase Dives into Third George Gibson Fred Clarke	175.00	90.00
14C Hal Chase Dives into Third Deacon Phillippe George Gibson	150.00	75.00
15A Hal Chase Gets Ball Too Late Dick Egan Mike Mitchell	150.00	75.00
15B Hal Chase Gets Ball Too Late Harry Wolter Hal Chase	150.00	75.00
16A Hal Chase Guarding First Hal Chase Harry Wolter	150.00	75.00
16B Hal Chase Guarding First George Gibson Fred Clarke	175.00	90.00
16C Hal Chase Guarding First Lefty Leifield George Gibson	150.00	75.00
17 Hal Chase Ready Squeeze Play Dode Paskert Sherry Magee	175.00	90.00
18 Hal Chase Safe at Third Jack Barry Frank Baker	200.00	100.00
19 Chief Bender Waiting Chief Bender Ira Thomas	250.00	125.00
20 Fred Clarke Hikes for Home Al Bridwell Johnny Kling	200.00	100.00
21 Close at First: Neal Ball George Stovall	175.00	90.00
22A Close at the Plate Ed Walsh Fred Payne	175.00	90.00
22B Close at the Plate Doc White Fred Payne	150.00	75.00
23 Tris Speaker Close at Third Joe Wood Tris Speaker	350.00	180.00
24 Heinie Wagner Close at Third Heinie Wagner Bill Carrigan	175.00	90.00
25A Eddie Collins Easily Safe Bobby Byrne Fred Clarke	175.00	90.00
25B Eddie Collins Easily Safe Eddie Collins Frank Baker	400.00	200.00
25C Eddie Collins Easily Safe Eddie Collins Danny Murphy	250.00	125.00
26 Sam Crawford About to Smash Oscar Stanage Ed Summers	200.00	100.00
27 Birdie Cree Rolls Home Jake Daubert John Hummell	175.00	90.00
28 Davy Jones Great Slide Jim Delahanty Tom Jones	175.00	90.00
29A Art Devlin Gets His Man Art Devlin (Giants) Christy Mathewson	350.00	180.00
29B Art Devlin Gets His Man Art Devlin (Rustlers) Christy Mathewson	1000.00	500.00
29C Art Devlin Gets His Man Art Fletcher Christy Mathewson	250.00	125.00
29D Art Devlin Gets His Man Chief Meyers Christy Mathewson	400.00	200.00
30A Mike Donlin Out at First Howie Camnitz George Gibson	150.00	75.00
30B Mike Donlin Out at First Larry Doyle Fred Merkle	150.00	75.00
30C Mike Donlin Out at First Tommy Leach Chief Wilson	150.00	75.00
30D Mike Donlin Out at First Sherry Magee Red Dooin	150.00	75.00
30E Mike Donlin Out at First Deacon Phillippe George Gibson	150.00	75.00
31A Red Dooin Gets His Man Red Dooin Mickey Doolan	150.00	75.00
31B Red Dooin Gets His Man Hans Lobert Red Dooin	150.00	75.00
31C Red Dooin Gets His Man John Titus Red Dooin	150.00	75.00
32 Easy for Larry Larry Doyle Fred Merkle	175.00	90.00
33 Kid Elberfeld Beats Clyde Milan Kid Elberfeld	175.00	90.00
34 Kid Elberfeld Gets His Man Clyde Milan Kid Elberfeld	175.00	90.00
35 Hack Engle in a Close Play Tris Speaker Hack Engle	250.00	125.00
36A Johnny Evers Makes Safe Slide Jimmy Archer Johnny Evers	250.00	125.00
36B Johnny Evers Makes Safe Slide Johnny Evers Frank Chance	350.00	180.00
36C Johnny Evers Makes Safe Slide Orval Overall Jimmy Archer	175.00	90.00
36D Johnny Evers Makes Safe Slide Ed Reulbach Jimmy Archer	175.00	90.00
36E Johnny Evers Makes Safe Slide Joe Tinker Frank Chance	1000.00	500.00
37 Fast Work at Third Charley O'Leary Ty Cobb	1250.00	600.00
38A Russ Ford Putting Over Spitter	150.00	75.00

Russ Ford
Hippo Vaughn
38B Russ Ford 150.00 75.00
Putting Over Spitter
Jeff Sweeney
Russ Ford
39 Good Play at Third 1250.00 600.00
George Moriarty
Ty Cobb
40 Eddie Grant 175.00 90.00
Gets His Man
Doc Hoblitzel
Eddie Grant
41A Hal Chase Too Late 150.00 75.00
Matty McIntyre
Ambrose McConnell
41B Hal Chase Too Late 150.00 75.00
George Suggs
Larry McLean
42 Harry Lord at Third: 200.00 100.00
Ed Lennox
Joe Tinker
43 Roy Hartzell Covering 175.00 90.00
Doc Scanlon
Bill Dahlen
44 Roy Hartzell Strikes Out 175.00 90.00
Bob Groom
Dolly Gray
45 Held at Third: 175.00 90.00
Jesse Tannehill
Harry Lord
46 Jake Stahl Guarding: 175.00 90.00
Eddie Cicotte
Jake Stahl
47 Jim Delahanty at Bat: 175.00 90.00
Jim Delahanty
Davy Jones
48A Just Before the 150.00 75.00
Battle
John McGraw MG
Harry Davis pictured
Red Ames
Chief Meyers
48B Just Before the 400.00 200.00
Battle
John McGraw MG
Harry Davis
Roger Bresnahan
John McGraw MG
48C Just Before the 150.00 75.00
Battle
John McGraw MG
Harry Davis
Doc Crandall
Chief Meyers
48D Just Before the 150.00 75.00
Battle
John McGraw
Harry Davis
Josh Devore
Beals Becker
48E Just Before the 300.00 150.00
Battle
John McGraw MG
Art Fletcher
Christy Mathewson
48F Just Before the 175.00 90.00
Battle
John McGraw MG
Harry Davis
Rube Marquard
Chief Meyers
48G Just Before the 350.00 180.00
Battle
John McGraw MG
Harry Davis
John McGraw MG
Hugh -Jennings
48H Just Before the 350.00 180.00
Battle
John McGraw MG
Harry Davis
Chief Meyers
Christy Mathewson
48I Just Before the 150.00 75.00
Battle
John McGraw MG
Harry Davis
Fred Snodgrass
Red Murray
48J Just Before the 150.00 75.00
Battle
John McGraw MG
Harry Davis
Hook Wiltse
Chief Meyers
49 Jack Knight 500.00 250.00
Catches Runner
Jack Knight
Walter Johnson
50A Hans Lobert 150.00 75.00
Almost Caught
Al Bridwell
Johnny Kling
50B Hans Lobert 250.00 125.00
Almost Caught
Johnny Kling
Cy Young
50C Hans Lobert 150.00 75.00
Almost Caught
Al Mattern
Johnny Kling
50D Hans Lobert 150.00 75.00
Almost Caught
Harry Steinfeldt
Johnny Kling
51 Hans Lobert 175.00 90.00
Gets
Fred Tenney
Hans Lobert
Red Dooin
52 Harry Lord 175.00 90.00
Catches His Man
Lee Tannehill
Harry Lord
53 Ambrose McConnell 175.00 90.00
Caught
Lew Richie
Tom Needham
54 Matty McIntyre 175.00 90.00
at Bat
Matty McIntrye
Ambrose McConnell
55 George Moriarty 175.00 90.00
Spiked
Ed Willett
Oscar Stanage
56 Nearly Caught 200.00 100.00
Johnny Bates
Bob Bescher
57 Rube Oldring 175.00 90.00
Almost Home
Harry Lord
Rube Oldring
58 Germany Schaefer 175.00 90.00
on First
George McBride
Clyde Milan
59 Germany Schaefer 200.00 100.00
Steals Second
George McBride
Clark Griffith
60 Scoring from Second 175.00 90.00
Harry Lord
Rube Oldring
61A Scrambling Back 150.00 75.00
Cy Barger
Bill Bergen
61B Scrambling Back 150.00 75.00
Harry Wolter
Hal Chase
62 Tris Speaker 400.00 200.00
Almost Caught
Dots Miller
Fred Clarke
63 Tris Speaker 800.00 400.00
Rounding Third
Joe Wood
Tris Speaker
64 Tris Speaker Scores 400.00 200.00
Tris Speaker
Hack Engle
65 Jake Stahl Safe 175.00 90.00
George Stovall
Jimmy Austin
66 George Stone 175.00 90.00
About to Swing
Jimmy Sheckard
Wildfire Schulte
67A Billy Sullivan 175.00 90.00
Puts Up High One
Steve Evans
Miller Huggins
67B Billy Sullivan 150.00 75.00
Puts up High One
Dolly Gray
Bob Groom
68A Jeff Sweeney 150.00 75.00
Gets Jake Stahl
Russ Ford
Hippo Vaughn
68B Jeff Sweeney 150.00 75.00
Gets Jake Stahl
Jeff Sweeney
Russ Ford
69 Fred Tenney 175.00 90.00
Lands Safely
Bugs Raymond
Arlie Latham
70A The Athletic Infield: 175.00 90.00
Jack Barry
Frank Baker
70B The Athletic Infield 150.00 75.00
Mordecai Brown
Peaches Graham
70C The Athletic Infield 150.00 75.00
Arnold Hauser
Ed Konetchy
70D The Athletic Infield 150.00 75.00
Harry Krause
Ira Thomas
71 The Pinch Hitter 175.00 90.00
Doc Hoblitzel
Dick Egan
72 The Scissors Slide 175.00 90.00
Doc Birmingham
Terry Turner
73A Tom Jones at Bat 150.00 75.00
Art Fromme
Larry McLean
73B Tom Jones at Bat 150.00 75.00
Harry Gaspar
Larry McLean
74A Art Devlin 150.00 75.00
Too Late
Red Ames
Chief Meyers
74B Art Devlin 150.00 75.00
Too Late
Doc Crandall
Chief Meyers
74C Art Devlin 1000.00 500.00
Too Late
Art Devlin (Giants)
Christy Mathewson
74D Art Devlin 250.00 125.00
Too Late
Art Devlin (Rustlers)
Christy Mathewson
74E Art Devlin 175.00 90.00
Too Late
Rube Marquard
Chief Meyers
74F Art Devlin 150.00 75.00
Too Late
Hooks Wiltse
Chief Meyers
75A Ty Cobb 2000.00 1000.00
Steals Third
Hughie Jennings
Ty Cobb
75B Ty Cobb 2000.00 1000.00
Steals Third
George Moriarty
Ty Cobb
75C Ty Cobb Steals 1500.00 750.00
Third:
Stovall-Austin
76 Zach Wheat 250.00 125.00
Strikes Out
Bill Dahlen
Zach Wheat

1911 Helmar Stamps

Each stamp measures 1 1/8" by 1 3/8". The stamps are very thin and have an ornate, bright colorful border surrounding the black-and-white photo of the player. There are many differnet border color combinations. There is no identification of issuer to be found anywhere on the stamp. Since the stamps are unnumbered, they are listed below alphabetically within team: Boston Red Sox (1-5), Chicago White Sox (6-20), Cleveland Indians (21-26), Detroit Tigers (27-38), New York Yankees (39-51), Philadelphia A's (52-59), St. Louis Browns (60-66), Washington Senators (67-76), Boston Bees NL (77-81), Brooklyn Dodgers (82-89), Chicago Cubs (90-108), Cincinnati Reds (109-119), New York Giants (120-139), Philadelphia Phillies (140-152), Pittsburgh Pirates (153-166), and St. Louis Cardinals (166-177).

	Ex-Mt	VG
COMPLETE SET (178)	4000.00	2000.00
1 Bill Carrigan	20.00	10.00
2 Ed Cicotte	60.00	30.00
3 Hack Engle	20.00	10.00
4 Tris Speaker	40.00	20.00
5 Heine Wagner	20.00	10.00
6 Bruno Block	20.00	10.00
7 Ping Bodie	20.00	10.00
8 Nixey Callahan	20.00	10.00
9 Shano Collins	20.00	10.00
10 Patsy Dougherty	20.00	10.00
11 Bristol Lord	20.00	10.00
12 Ambrose McConnell	20.00	10.00
13 Matthew McIntyre	20.00	10.00
14 Freddy Parent	20.00	10.00
15 Jim Scott	20.00	10.00
16 William Sullivan	20.00	10.00
17 Lee Ford Tannehill	20.00	10.00
18 Ed Walsh	40.00	20.00
19 Guy White	20.00	10.00
20 Cy Young	80.00	40.00
21 Neal Ball	20.00	10.00
22 Dode Birmingham	20.00	10.00
23 George Davis	40.00	20.00
24 Napoleon Lajoie	80.00	40.00
25 Paddy Livingston	20.00	10.00
26 Terry Turner	20.00	10.00
27 Donie Bush	20.00	10.00
28 Ty Cobb	100.00	50.00
29 Sam Crawford	40.00	20.00
30 Jim Delahanty	20.00	10.00
31 Patsy Donovan	20.00	10.00
32 Hughie Jennings	40.00	20.00
33 Davy Jones	20.00	10.00
34 George Moriarty	20.00	10.00
35 George Mullin	25.00	12.50
36 Boss Schmidt	20.00	10.00
37 Oscar Strange	20.00	10.00
38 Robert Willett	20.00	10.00
39 Lew Brockett	20.00	10.00
40 Hal Chase	40.00	20.00
41 Birdie Cree	20.00	10.00
42 Ray Fisher	20.00	10.00
43 Russ Ford	20.00	10.00
44 Earl Gardner	20.00	10.00
45 Jack Quinn	25.00	12.50
46 Gabby Street	20.00	10.00
47 Ed Sweeney	20.00	10.00
48 James(Hippo) Vaughn	25.00	12.50
49 John Warhop	20.00	10.00
50 Harry Wolter	20.00	10.00
51 Harry Wolverton	20.00	10.00
52 Frank Baker	40.00	20.00
53 Jack Barry	20.00	10.00
54 Chief Bender	40.00	20.00
55 Eddie Collins	40.00	20.00
56 Harry Krause	20.00	10.00
57 Danny Murphy	20.00	10.00
58 Rube Oldring	20.00	10.00
59 Ira Thomas	20.00	10.00
60 Jimmy Austin	20.00	10.00
61 Joe Lake	20.00	10.00
62 Frank LaPorte	20.00	10.00
63 Barney Pelty	20.00	10.00
64 John Powell	20.00	10.00
65 George Stovall	20.00	10.00
66 Bobby Wallace	40.00	20.00
67 Wid Conroy	20.00	10.00
68 Dolly Gray	20.00	10.00
69 Clark Griffith	40.00	20.00
70 Bob Groom	20.00	10.00
71 Tom Hughes	20.00	10.00
72 Walter Johnson	80.00	40.00
73 John Knight	20.00	10.00
74 George McBride	20.00	10.00
75 Clyde Milan	25.00	12.50
76 Germany Schaefer	20.00	10.00
77 Al Bridwell	20.00	10.00
78 Hank Gowdy	20.00	10.00
79 Johnny Kling	20.00	10.00
80 Al Mattern	20.00	10.00
81 Ed Sweeney	20.00	10.00
82 Cy Barger	20.00	10.00
83 George Bell	20.00	10.00
84 Bill Dahlen	20.00	10.00
85 Jake Daubert	30.00	15.00
86 Tex Erwin	20.00	10.00
87 John Hummel	20.00	10.00
88 Nap Rucker	30.00	15.00
89 Zach Wheat	40.00	20.00
90 Jimmy Archer	20.00	10.00
91 Mordecai Brown	40.00	20.00
92 Frank Chance	40.00	20.00
93 Leonard(King) Cole	20.00	10.00
94 Johnny Evers	40.00	20.00
95 George(Peaches) Graham	20.00	10.00
96 Solly Hoffman	20.00	10.00
97 Ed Lennox	20.00	10.00
98 Harry McIntire	20.00	10.00
99 Tom Needham	20.00	10.00
100 Ed Reulbach	20.00	10.00
101 Lewis Richie	20.00	10.00
102 Reggie Richter	20.00	10.00
103 John Rowan	20.00	10.00
104 Frank Schulte	20.00	10.00
105 Dave Shean	20.00	10.00
106 Jimmy Sheckard	20.00	10.00
107 Joe Tinker	40.00	20.00
108 Fred Toney	20.00	10.00
109 Johnny Bates	20.00	10.00
110 Bob Bescher	20.00	10.00
111 Ed Burns	20.00	10.00
112 Fred Clarke	40.00	20.00
113 Art Fromme	20.00	10.00
114 Harry Gaspar	20.00	10.00
115 Ed Grant	20.00	10.00
116 Doc Hoblitzell	20.00	10.00
117 Larry McLean	20.00	10.00
118 Clarence Mitchell	20.00	10.00
119 George Suggs	20.00	10.00
120 Red Ames	20.00	10.00
121 Beals Becker	20.00	10.00
122 Doc Crandall	20.00	10.00
123 Art Devlin	20.00	10.00
124 Josh Devore	20.00	10.00
125 Larry Doyle	25.00	12.50
126 Louis Drucke	20.00	10.00
127 Arthur Fletcher	20.00	10.00
128 Grover Hartley	20.00	10.00
129 Buck Herzog	25.00	12.50
130 Rube Marquard	40.00	20.00
131 Christy Mathewson	80.00	40.00
132 John McGraw	40.00	20.00
133 Fred Merkle	25.00	12.50
134 John(Chief) Meyers	25.00	12.50
135 Red Murray	20.00	10.00
136 Tillie Shafer	20.00	10.00
137 Fred Snodgrass	25.00	12.50
138 John(Chief) Wilson	25.00	12.50
139 Hooks Wiltse	20.00	10.00
140 Zinn Beck	20.00	10.00
141 Red Dooin	20.00	10.00
142 Mickey Doolan	20.00	10.00
143 Tom Downey	20.00	10.00
144 Otto Knabe	20.00	10.00
145 Hans Lobert	20.00	10.00
146 Fred Luderus	20.00	10.00
147 Sherry Magee	30.00	15.00
148 Earl Moore	20.00	10.00
149 Pat Moran	20.00	10.00
150 Dode Paskert	20.00	10.00
151 William(Doc) Scanlan	20.00	10.00
152 John Titus	20.00	10.00
153 Bert Adams	20.00	10.00
154 Bobby Byrne	20.00	10.00
155 Howard Camnitz	20.00	10.00
156 Max Carey	40.00	20.00
157 Fred Clarke	40.00	20.00
158 Mike Donlin	25.00	12.50
159 John Ferry	20.00	10.00
160 George Gibson	20.00	10.00
161 Thomas Leach	20.00	10.00
162 Albert(Lefty) Leifield	20.00	10.00
163 Roy(Doc) Miller	20.00	10.00
164 Martin O'Toole	20.00	10.00
165 Michael Simon	20.00	10.00
166 John(Chief) Wilson	25.00	12.50
167 John Bliss	20.00	10.00
168 Roger Bresnahan	40.00	20.00
169 Louis Evans	20.00	10.00
170 Robert Harmon	20.00	10.00
171 Arnold Hauser	20.00	10.00
172 Miller Huggins	40.00	20.00
173 Ed Konetchy	20.00	10.00
174 Mike Mowrey	20.00	10.00
175 Ennis(Rebel) Oakes	20.00	10.00
176 Edward Phelps	20.00	10.00
177 Slim Sallee	20.00	10.00
178 Bill Steele	20.00	10.00

1989 Hershiser Socko

The 1989 Socko Orel Hershiser set contains seven unnumbered standard-size cards. The fronts are blue, green and yellow, and feature full color photos of Hershiser with the Dodger logos airbrushed out. The backs are white and include "Tips from Orel." The cards were distributed as a promotional set through Socko beverages.

	Nm-Mt	Ex-Mt
COMPLETE SET (7)	6.00	2.40
COMMON CARD (1-7)	1.00	.40

1992 High 5

This 130-decal set features five players each from the 26 Major League Baseball teams. The collector could also purchase a stadium display board to display all the decals. The decals measure the standard size. The fronts are actually reusable stickers and display color action player photos. The color of the inner border varies from card to card , while the outermost border is on all cards. The pictures are accented above and on the right by a thin color stripe. The "High 5" logo and team logo appear in the upper left and lower right corners respectively. The decals are checklisted below alphabetically within and according to teams. Stickers from expansion teams Colorado Rockies and Florida Marlins were promised for 1993. However, no 1993 set was ever issued.

	Nm-Mt	Ex-Mt
COMPLETE SET (130)	80.00	24.00
1 Mike Devereaux	.25	.07
2 Ben McDonald	.25	.07
3 Gregg Olson	.25	.07
4 Joe Orsulak	.25	.07
5 Cal Ripken	5.00	1.50
6 Wade Boggs	1.25	.35
7 Roger Clemens	2.50	.75
8 Phil Plantier	.25	.07
9 Jeff Reardon	.50	.15
10 Mo Vaughn	.75	.23
11 Jim Abbott	.50	.15
12 Chuck Finley	.25	.07
13 Brian Harvey	.25	.07
14 Mark Langston	.25	.07
15 Dave Winfield	1.25	.35
16 Carlton Fisk	1.25	.35
17 Jack McDowell	.50	.15
18 Bobby Thigpen	.25	.07
19 Frank Thomas	1.50	.45
20 Robin Ventura	.75	.23
21 Steve Avery	.25	.07
22 Ron Gant	.50	.15
23 Tom Glavine	1.25	.35
24 Dave Justice	1.00	.30
25 Terry Pendleton	.25	.07
26 George Bell	.25	.07
27 Andre Dawson	1.00	.30
28 Mark Grace	1.00	.30
29 Greg Maddux	3.00	.90
30 Ryne Sandberg	2.50	.75
31 Eric Davis	.50	.15
32 Barry Larkin	1.00	.30
33 Hal Morris	.25	.07
34 Jose Rijo	.25	.07
35 Chris Sabo	.25	.07
36 Jeff Bagwell	2.00	.60
37 Craig Biggio	1.00	.30
38 Ken Caminiti	.50	.15
39 Luis Gonzalez	1.00	.30
40 Pete Harnisch	.25	.07
41 Sandy Alomar Jr.	.50	.15
42 Carlos Baerga	.25	.07
43 Albert Belle	.50	.15
44 Alex Cole	.25	.07
45 Charles Nagy	.25	.07
46 Cecil Fielder	.50	.15
47 Travis Fryman	.50	.15
48 Tony Phillips	.25	.07
49 Alan Trammell	.75	.23
50 Lou Whitaker	.50	.15
51 Brett Butler	.50	.15
52 Lenny Harris	.25	.07
53 Ramon Martinez	.25	.07
54 Eddie Murray	1.25	.35
55 Darryl Strawberry	.50	.15
56 Ivan Calderon	.25	.07
57 Delino DeShields	.50	.15
58 Marquis Grissom	.25	.07
59 Dennis Martinez	.50	.15
60 Larry Walker	.75	.23
61 George Brett	2.50	.75
62 Jim Eisenreich	.25	.07
63 Brian McRae	.25	.07
64 Jeff Montgomery	.25	.07
65 Bret Saberhagen	.25	.07
66 Chris Bosio	.25	.07
67 Paul Molitor	1.25	.35
68 B.J. Surhoff	.50	.15
69 Greg Vaughn	.50	.15
70 Robin Yount	1.25	.35
71 David Cone	.75	.23
72 Dwight Gooden	.50	.15
73 Gregg Jefferies	.25	.07
74 Howard Johnson	.25	.07
75 Kevin McReynolds	.25	.07
76 Wes Chamberlain	.25	.07
77 Len Dykstra	.50	.15
78 John Kruk	.50	.15
79 Terry Mulholland	.25	.07
80 Mitch Williams	.25	.07
81 Rick Aguilera	.50	.15
82 Scott Erickson	.25	.07
83 Kent Hrbek	.25	.07
84 Kirby Puckett	1.25	.35
85 Kevin Tapani	.25	.07
86 Mel Hall	.25	.07
87 Roberto Kelly	.25	.07
88 Kevin Maas	.25	.07
89 Don Mattingly	2.50	.75
90 Steve Sax	.25	.07
91 Barry Bonds	2.50	.75
92 Doug Drabek	.25	.07
93 John Smiley	.25	.07
94 Zane Smith	.25	.07
95 Andy Van Slyke	.25	.07
96 Felix Jose	.25	.07
97 Ray Lankford	.50	.15
98 Lee Smith	.50	.15
99 Ozzie Smith	2.50	.75
100 Todd Zeile	.50	.15
101 Harold Baines	.75	.23
102 Jose Canseco	1.25	.35
103 Dennis Eckersley	1.25	.35
104 Dave Henderson	.25	.07
105 Rickey Henderson	1.50	.45
106 Jay Buhner	.50	.15
107 Ken Griffey Jr.	3.00	.90
108 Randy Johnson	1.50	.45
109 Edgar Martinez	.75	.23
110 Harold Reynolds	.50	.15
111 Julio Franco	.50	.15
112 Juan Gonzalez	1.25	.35
113 Rafael Palmeiro	1.00	.30
114 Nolan Ryan	5.00	1.50
115 Ruben Sierra	.50	.15
116 Roberto Alomar	1.00	.30
117 Joe Carter	.50	.15
118 Kelly Gruber	.25	.07
119 John Olerud	.75	.23
120 Devon White	.25	.07
121 Tony Fernandez	.50	.15
122 Tony Gwynn	2.50	.75
123 Bruce Hurst	.25	.07
124 Fred McGriff	.75	.23
125 Benito Santiago	.50	.15
126 Will Clark	1.25	.35
127 Willie McGee	.50	.15
128 Kevin Mitchell	.25	.07
129 Robby Thompson	.25	.07
130 Matt Williams	.75	.23

1992 High 5 Superstars

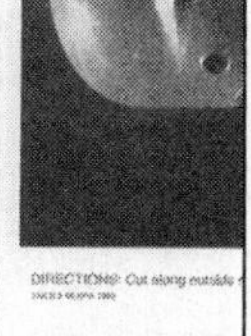

This 36-decal set features some of baseball's greatest players. Six different assortments, each featuring five player decals and one High 5 nonplayer decal, were issued (AL infielders, outfielders and pitchers as well as NL infielders, outfielders and pitchers). The decals measure the standard size. The fronts are actually reusable stickers and display color action player photos. The color of the inner border varies from decal to decal, (gradated blue, black or green) while the outermost border is white on all decals. The backs of six decals combine to form six separate 5" by 7" color close-up photos of players featured on the fronts (Clark, Griffey Jr., Justice, Ryan, Strawberry and Thomas). Each of these composite pictures includes one High 5 Superstar nonplayer decal. The decals are unnumbered and checklisted below in alphabetical order.

	Nm-Mt	Ex-Mt
COMPLETE SET (36)	40.00	12.00
1 Steve Avery	.25	.07
2 Jeff Bagwell	1.50	.45
3 Wade Boggs	1.25	.35
4 Barry Bonds	2.50	.75
5 Jose Canseco	1.25	.35
6 Joe Carter	.50	.15
7 Will Clark	1.25	.35
8 Roger Clemens	2.50	.75
9 Dennis Eckersley	1.25	.35
10 Scott Erickson	.25	.07
11 Cecil Fielder	.50	.15
12 Julio Franco	.50	.15
13 Tom Glavine	1.00	.30
14 Juan Gonzalez	1.25	.35
15 Dwight Gooden	.50	.15
16 Ron Gant	.25	.07
17 Ken Griffey Jr.	3.00	.90
18 Tony Gwynn	2.50	.75
19 Rickey Henderson	1.50	.45
20 Howard Johnson	.25	.07
21 Dave Justice	1.00	.30
22 Mark Langston	.25	.07
23 Ramon Martinez	.50	.15
24 Cal Ripken	5.00	1.50
25 Nolan Ryan	5.00	1.50
26 Ryne Sandberg	2.50	.75
27 John Smiley	.25	.07
28 Darryl Strawberry	.50	.15
29 Frank Thomas	1.50	.45
30 Matt Williams	.75	.23
31 High 5 Superstar (Part of Will Clark 5x7 Portrait)	.50	.15
32 High 5 Superstar (Part of Ken Griffey Jr. 5x7 Portrait)	2.50	.75
33 High 5 Superstar (Part of David Justice 5x7 Portrait)	.25	.07
34 High 5 Superstar (Part of Nolan Ryan 5x7 Portrait)	2.50	.75
35 High 5 Superstar (Part of Darryl Strawberry 5x7 Portrait)	.25	.07
36 High 5 Superstar (Part of Frank Thomas 5x7 Portrait)	1.00	.30

1997-98 Highland Mint Elite Series Coins

These coins are about 1.5 inches in diameter and come in a velvet display box which converts to a display stand. The announced mintages were 5000 for bronze, 2,500 for silver, and 1000 for two-tone gold (polished silver with 24K Gold plating). The first 375 of each type are also packaged in Proof Sets of all 3 coins, each with the same serial number in a special 3 coin display box.

	Nm-Mt	Ex-Mt
1 Ken Griffey Jr. G/1000	80.00	24.00
2 Ken Griffey Jr. S/2500	40.00	12.00
3 Ken Griffey Jr. B/5000	20.00	6.00
10 Chipper Jones G/1000	80.00	24.00
11 Chipper Jones S/2500	40.00	12.00
12 Chipper Jones B/5000	20.00	6.00
20 Mickey Mantle G/1000	80.00	24.00
21 Mickey Mantle S/2500	40.00	12.00
22 Mickey Mantle B/5000	20.00	6.00
30 Cal Ripken G/1000	80.00	24.00
31 Cal Ripken S/2500	40.00	12.00
32 Cal Ripken B/5000	20.00	6.00
40 Alex Rodriguez G/1000	80.00	24.00
41 Alex Rodriguez S/2500	40.00	12.00
42 Alex Rodriguez B/5000	20.00	6.00
50 Frank Thomas G/1000	80.00	24.00
51 Frank Thomas S/2500	40.00	12.00
52 Frank Thomas B/5000	20.00	6.00

1994-98 Highland Mint Magnum Series Medallions

Measuring 2 1/2" in diameter and encased in a 6" by 5" velvet box, these larger medallions feature star major leaguers. The relief on these medallions are 10 times greater than the regular medallions.

	Nm-Mt	Ex-Mt
1 Ken Griffey Jr. G/375	150.00	45.00
2 Ken Griffey Jr. S/750	100.00	30.00
3 Ken Griffey Jr. B/3000	50.00	15.00
5 Mickey Mantle G/375	150.00	45.00
6 Mickey Mantle S/750	100.00	30.00
7 Mickey Mantle B/3000	50.00	15.00
10 Cal Ripken G/375	200.00	60.00
11 Cal Ripken S/750	100.00	30.00
12 Cal Ripken B/3000	50.00	15.00
15 Alex Rodriguez S/750	100.00	30.00
16 Alex Rodriguez B/3000	50.00	15.00
19 Babe Ruth G/375	200.00	60.00
20 Babe Ruth S/750	100.00	30.00
21 Babe Ruth B/3000	50.00	15.00
25 Nolan Ryan S/750	100.00	30.00
26 Nolan Ryan B/3000	50.00	15.00
30 Frank Thomas S/750	100.00	30.00
31 Frank Thomas B/3000	50.00	15.00

1996-98 Highland Mint Mini Mint-Cards

These mini Mint-Cards are not replicas but feature Highland Mint's own design. They are one-quarter scale of regular Mint-Cards. The high relief on the fronts is four times greater than that used on regular Mint-Cards. The backs display text and statistics. Each card is individually-numbered, includes a certificate of authenticity, and is packaged in a leather display box. Mini Mint-Cards were issued as a matching set with the cards displayed side by side. Both cards carry the same serial number. The mintage is given below with reference to gold-plated on silver, silver, and bronze quantities. The suggested retail price was $300.00 for the gold, $150.00 for the silver, and $65.00 for the bronze.

	Nm-Mt	Ex-Mt
1 Ken Griffey Jr. Frank Thomas G/500	200.00	60.00
2 Ken Griffey Jr. Frank Thomas S/1000	120.00	36.00
3 Ken Griffey Jr. Frank Thomas B/5000	50.00	15.00
4 Randy Johnson Nolan Ryan G/375	200.00	60.00
5 Randy Johnson Nolan Ryan S/500	100.00	30.00
7 Randy Johnson Nolan Ryan B/2500	50.00	15.00
9 Greg Maddux Cy Young G/375	200.00	60.00
11 Greg Maddux Cy Young S/500	100.00	30.00
13 Greg Maddux Cy Young B/2500	50.00	15.00
15 Mike Piazza Roy Campanella S/500	100.00	30.00
17 Mike Piazza Roy Campanella B/2500	50.00	15.00
19 Cal Ripken Lou Gehrig G/375	300.00	90.00
21 Cal Ripken Lou Gehrig S/500	150.00	45.00
23 Cal Ripken Lou Gehrig B/2500	80.00	24.00

1994-98 Highland Mint Mint-Cards Pinnacle/UD

These Highland Mint cards are metal replicas of already issued Pinnacle and Upper Deck cards. All these standard size replicas contain approximately 4.25 ounces of metal. Suggested retail are 50.00 for bronze and 235.00 for silver. Each card includes a certificate of authenticity, and is packaged in a numbered album and a three-piece Lucite display. The cards are checklisted below alphabetically; the final mintage figures for each card are also listed.

	Nm-Mt	Ex-Mt
1 Jeff Bagwell 92/S/750	150.00	45.00
2 Jeff Bagwell 92/B/2500	50.00	15.00
3 Michael Jordan 94/G/500	500.00	150.00
4 Michael Jordan 94/S/1000	300.00	90.00
5 Michael Jordan 94/B/5000	50.00	15.00
6 Greg Maddux 92/S/750	150.00	45.00
7 Greg Maddux 92/B/2500	50.00	15.00
8 Mickey Mantle 92/G/500	500.00	150.00
9 Mickey Mantle 92/S/1000	300.00	90.00
10 Mickey Mantle 92/B/5000	50.00	15.00
11 Nolan Ryan 92/G/500	500.00	150.00
12 Nolan Ryan 92/S/1000	200.00	60.00
13 Nolan Ryan 92/B/5000	50.00	15.00

1992-94 Highland Mint Mint-Cards Topps

These cards, from the Highland Mint, measure the standard size and are exact reproductions of Topps baseball cards. Each mint-card bears a serial number on its bottom edge. These cards were originally available only in hobby stores, and were packaged in a lucite display holder within an album. Each card comes with a sequentially numbered Certificate of Authenticity. When the Highland Mint/Topps relationship was ended in 1994, the remaining unsold stock was destroyed; the final available mintage according to Highland Mint is listed below. The cards are checklisted below alphabetically.

	Nm-Mt	Ex-Mt
1 Roberto Alomar 88/S/214	150.00	45.00
2 Roberto Alomar 88/B/928	30.00	9.00
3 Ernie Banks 54/S/437	150.00	45.00
4 Ernie Banks 54/B/920	30.00	9.00
5 Johnny Bench 69/S/500	150.00	45.00
6 Johnny Bench 69/B/1384	30.00	9.00
7 Barry Bonds 86/S/596	150.00	45.00
8 Barry Bonds 86/B/2677	30.00	9.00
9 George Brett 75/S/999	150.00	45.00
10 George Brett 75/B/3560	50.00	15.00
11 Will Clark 86/S/150	250.00	75.00
12 Will Clark 86/B/1044	30.00	9.00
13 Roger Clemens 85/S/432	150.00	45.00
14 Roger Clemens 85/B/1789	30.00	9.00
15 Juan Gonzalez 90/S/365	150.00	45.00
16 Juan Gonzalez 90/B/1899	30.00	9.00
17 Ken Griffey Jr. 92/G/500	400.00	120.00
18 Ken Griffey Jr. 92/S/1000	200.00	60.00
19 Ken Griffey Jr. 92/B/5000	50.00	15.00
20 David Justice 90/S/265	150.00	45.00
21 David Justice 90/B/1396	30.00	9.00
22 Don Mattingly 84/S/414	150.00	45.00
23 Don Mattingly 84/B/1550	50.00	15.00
24 Paul Molitor 79/S/260	150.00	45.00
25 Paul Molitor 79/B/639	50.00	15.00
26 Mike Piazza 93/G/374	300.00	90.00
27 Mike Piazza 93/S/750	150.00	45.00
28 Mike Piazza 93/B/2500	40.00	12.00
29 Kirby Puckett 85/S/359	150.00	45.00
30 Kirby Puckett 85/B/1723	40.00	12.00
31 Cal Ripken 92/S/1000	250.00	75.00
32 Cal Ripken 92/B/4065	80.00	24.00
33 Brooks Robinson 57/S/796	150.00	45.00
34 Brooks Robinson 57/B/2043	30.00	9.00
35 Nolan Ryan 92/S/999	400.00	120.00
36 Nolan Ryan 92/B/5000	120.00	36.00
37 Tim Salmon 93/S/264	150.00	45.00
38 Tim Salmon 93/B/768	30.00	9.00
39 Ryne Sandberg 92/S/430	150.00	45.00
40 Ryne Sandberg 92/B/1932	40.00	12.00
41 Deion Sanders 89/S/187	150.00	45.00
42 Deion Sanders 89/B/668	30.00	9.00
43 Mike Schmidt 74/S/500	150.00	45.00
44 Mike Schmidt 74/B/1641	30.00	9.00
45 Ozzie Smith 79/S/211	200.00	60.00
46 Ozzie Smith 79/B/1088	50.00	15.00
47 Frank Thomas 92/G/500	400.00	120.00
48 Frank Thomas 92/S/1000	250.00	75.00
49 Frank Thomas 92/B/5000	50.00	15.00
50 Dave Winfield 74/S/266	150.00	45.00
51 Dave Winfield 74/B/1216	30.00	9.00
52 Carl Yastrzemski 60/S/500	150.00	45.00
53 Carl Yastrzemski 60/B/1072	30.00	9.00
54 Robin Yount 75/S/349	150.00	45.00
55 Robin Yount 75/B/1564	30.00	9.00

1992-98 Highland Mint Mint-Coins

Each of these one-troy ounce medallions is individualy numbered and accompanied by a certificate of authenticity. The fronts feature players' likenesses, names, uniform numbers and signatures; the backs show the MLBPA logo and statistics. The suggested retail prices range from $19.95 to $24.95 for silver. Nine of the silver coins (Belle, Boggs, Canseco, Clark, Gwynn, Jones, Nomo, Puckett, and Smith) were also issued as a set, protected in a cherry box and accompanied by a special certificate of authenticity featuring copies of player autographs. Just 500 of these sets were produced and all the medallions in each set carry the same serial number. These medallions represent the first 500 serial numbers from the original minting. The suggested retail price for the special set was $280. The quantities issued are listed separately for each type of metal.

	Nm-Mt	Ex-Mt
0 Roberto Alomar S/5000	20.00	6.00
1 Jeff Bagwell S/5000	15.00	4.50
2 Jeff Bagwell B/25000	10.00	3.00
5 Albert Belle S/5000	15.00	4.50
10 Wade Boggs S/5000	15.00	4.50
15 Barry Bonds G/1500	30.00	9.00
16 Barry Bonds S/5000	15.00	4.50
20 Jose Canseco S/5000	15.00	4.50
25 Will Clark S/5000	15.00	4.50
30 Roger Clemens G/1500	30.00	9.00
31 Roger Clemens S/5000	15.00	4.50
32 Roberto Clemente S/2500	20.00	6.00
33 Jose Cruz Jr. S/5000	15.00	4.50
35 Cecil Fielder S/5000	15.00	4.50
40 Ken Griffey Jr. G/1500	50.00	15.00
41 Ken Griffey Jr. S/5000	30.00	9.00
42 Ken Griffey Jr. B/25000	10.00	3.00
45 Tony Gwynn S/5000	15.00	4.50
48 Hideki Irabu S/5000	15.00	4.50
50 Derek Jeter G/1500	40.00	12.00
51 Derek Jeter S/5000	15.00	4.50
52 Derek Jeter B/25000	10.00	3.00
55 Andruw Jones S/5000	15.00	4.50
60 Chipper Jones G/1500	40.00	12.00
61 Chipper Jones S/5000	15.00	4.50
62 Chipper Jones B/25000	10.00	3.00
65 Greg Maddux G/1500	40.00	12.00
66 Greg Maddux S/5000	20.00	6.00
67 Greg Maddux B/25000	10.00	3.00
69 Mickey Mantle B/25000	10.00	3.00
70 Don Mattingly S/5000	20.00	6.00
71 Don Mattingly B/25000	10.00	3.00
72 Mark McGwire S/5000	15.00	4.50
75 Raul Mondesi S/5000	15.00	4.50
80 Eddie Murray S/5000	15.00	4.50
85 Hideo Nomo G/1500	40.00	12.00
86 Hideo Nomo S/5000	15.00	4.50
90 Mike Piazza G/1500	40.00	12.00
91 Mike Piazza S/5000	15.00	4.50
92 Mike Piazza B/25000	10.00	3.00
95 Kirby Puckett G/1500	40.00	12.00
96 Kirby Puckett S/5000	10.00	3.00
100 Cal Ripken G/1500	50.00	15.00
101 Cal Ripken S/5000	30.00	9.00
102 Cal Ripken B/15000	10.00	3.00
103 Cal Ripken B/25000	10.00	3.00
105 Alex Rodriguez G/1500	40.00	12.00
106 Alex Rodriguez S/5000	15.00	4.50
107 Alex Rodriguez B/25000	10.00	3.00
109 Ryne Sandberg S/5000	15.00	4.50
110 Ozzie Smith S/5000	15.00	4.50
115 Frank Thomas G/1500	40.00	12.00
116 Frank Thomas S/5000	30.00	9.00
117 Frank Thomas B/25000	10.00	3.00
120 Mo Vaughn S/5000	15.00	4.50

1999 Hillshire Farms Home Run Heroes Autographs

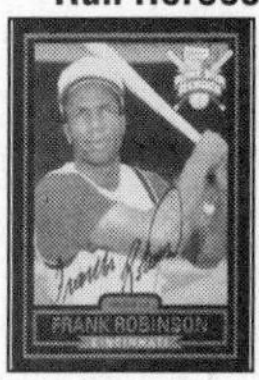

Available through a wrapper redemption offer from Hillshire Meats, these four standard-size cards feature autographs of retired Hall of Famers. The black-bordered photos have the player photo along with the "Hilshire Farms" logo and the players name on the bottom. The back has biographical information, career stats and a blurb. These cards came with an certificate of authenticity. Since these cards are unnumbered, we have sequenced them in alphabetical order.

	Nm-Mt	Ex-Mt
COMPLETE SET	25.00	7.50
1 Ernie Banks	5.00	1.50
2 Harmon Killebrew	5.00	1.50
3 Frank Robinson	5.00	1.50
4 Willie Stargell	10.00	3.00

1958 Hires

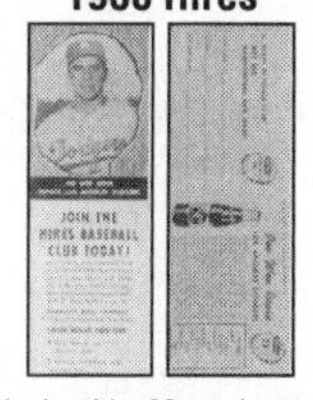

The cards in this 66-card set measure approximately 2 5/16" by 3 1/2" or 2 5/16" by 7" with tabs. The 1958 Hires Root Beer set of numbered, colored cards was issued with detachable coupons as inserts with Hires Root Beer cartons. Cards with the coupon still intact are worth 2.5 times the prices listed below. The card front picture is surrounded by a wood grain effect which makes it look like the player is seen through a knot hole. The numbering of this set is rather strange in that it begins with 10 and skips 69.

	NM	Ex
COMPLETE SET (66)	1600.00	800.00
10 Richie Ashburn	80.00	40.00
11 Chico Carrasquel	15.00	7.50
12 Dave Philley	15.00	7.50
13 Don Newcombe	20.00	10.00
14 Wally Post	15.00	7.50
15 Rip Repulski	15.00	7.50
16 Chico Fernandez	15.00	7.50
17 Larry Doby	40.00	20.00
18 Hector Brown	15.00	7.50
19 Danny O'Connell	15.00	7.50
20 Granny Hamner	15.00	7.50
21 Dick Groat	20.00	10.00
22 Ray Narleski	15.00	7.50
23 Pee Wee Reese	80.00	40.00
24 Bob Friend	15.00	7.50
25 Willie Mays	250.00	125.00
26 Bob Nieman	15.00	7.50
27 Frank Thomas	20.00	10.00
28 Curt Simmons	20.00	10.00
29 Stan Lopata	15.00	7.50
30 Bob Skinner	15.00	7.50
31 Ron Kline	15.00	7.50
32 Willie Miranda	15.00	7.50
33 Bobby Avila	15.00	7.50
34 Clem Labine	20.00	10.00
35 Ray Jablonski	15.00	7.50
36 Bill Mazeroski	50.00	25.00
37 Billy Gardner	15.00	7.50
38 Pete Runnels	15.00	7.50
39 Jack Sanford	15.00	7.50
40 Dave Sisler	15.00	7.50
41 Don Zimmer	20.00	10.00
42 Johnny Podres	20.00	10.00
43 Dick Farrell	15.00	7.50
44 Hank Aaron	250.00	125.00
45 Bill Virdon	15.00	7.50
46 Bobby Thomson	20.00	10.00
47 Willard Nixon	15.00	7.50
48 Billy Loes	15.00	7.50
49 Hank Sauer	20.00	10.00
50 Johnny Antonelli	20.00	10.00
51 Daryl Spencer	15.00	7.50
52 Ken Lehman	15.00	7.50
53 Sammy White	15.00	7.50
54 Charley Neal	15.00	7.50
55 Don Drysdale	80.00	40.00
56 Jackie Jensen	40.00	20.00
57 Ray Katt	15.00	7.50
58 Frank Sullivan	15.00	7.50
59 Roy Face	20.00	10.00
60 Willie Jones	15.00	7.50
61 Duke Snider	80.00	40.00
62 Whitey Lockman	15.00	7.50
63 Gino Cimoli	15.00	7.50
64 Marv Grissom	15.00	7.50
65 Gene Baker	15.00	7.50
66 George Zuverink	15.00	7.50
67 Ted Kluszewski	40.00	20.00
68 Jim Busby	15.00	7.50
69 Not Issued		
70 Curt Barclay	15.00	7.50
71 Hank Foiles	15.00	7.50
72 Gene Stephens	15.00	7.50
73 Al Worthington	15.00	7.50
74 Al Walker	15.00	7.50
75 Bob Boyd	15.00	7.50
76 Al Pilarcik	15.00	7.50

1958 Hires Test

The cards in this eight-card test set measure approximately 2 5/16" by 3 1/2" or 2 5/16" by 7" with tabs. The 1958 Hires Root Beer test set features unnumbered, color cards. The card front photos are shown on a yellow or orange back ground instead of the wood grain background used in the Hires regular set. The cards contain a detachable coupon just as the regular Hires issue does. Cards were test marketed on a very limited basis in a few cities. Cards with the coupon still intact are especially tough to find and are worth triple the prices in the checklist below. The checklist below is ordered alphabetically.

	NM	Ex
COMPLETE SET (8)	1500.00	750.00
1 Johnny Antonelli	150.00	75.00
2 Jim Busby	125.00	60.00
3 Chico Fernandez	125.00	60.00
4 Bob Friend	150.00	75.00
5 Vern Law	150.00	75.00
6 Stan Lopata	125.00	60.00
7 Willie Mays	800.00	400.00
8 Al Pilarcik	125.00	60.00

1992 Hit The Books Bookmarks

These bookmarks were produced of leading major leaguers. The purpose was to increase interest in reading and visiting local libraries. These bookmarks are unnumbered and we have sequenced them in alphabetical order.

	Nm-Mt	Ex-Mt
COMPLETE SET (36)	50.00	15.00
1 Jim Abbott	1.25	.35
2 Sandy Alomar	1.25	.35
3 Jay Bell	1.00	.30
4 Craig Biggio	1.50	.45
5 Mike Boddicker	1.00	.30
6 Bobby Bonilla	1.00	.30
7 George Brett	4.00	1.20
8 Brett Butler	1.25	.35
9 Joe Carter	1.25	.35
10 Will Clark	2.00	.60
11 Colorado Rockies	1.00	.30
12 Andre Dawson	1.50	.45
13 Cecil Fielder	1.25	.35
14 Florida Marlins	1.00	.30
15 Ozzie Guillen	1.25	.35
16 Tony Gwynn	4.00	1.20
17 Howard Johnson	1.00	.30
18 Dave Justice	2.00	.60
19 Mark Langston	1.00	.30
20 Barry Larkin	2.00	.60
21 Don Mattingly	4.00	1.20
22 Ben McDonald	1.00	.30
23 Paul Molitor	2.50	.75
24 Dale Murphy	1.50	.45
25 Tony Pena	1.00	.30
26 Kirby Puckett	3.00	.90
27 Harold Reynolds	1.25	.35
28 Cal Ripken	8.00	2.40
29 Chris Sabo	1.00	.30
30 Ryne Sandberg	4.00	1.20
31 Mike Scioscia	1.25	.35
32 Ruben Sierra	1.25	.35
33 Ozzie Smith	4.00	1.20
34 Dave Stewart	1.00	.30
35 Andy Van Slyke	1.00	.30
36 Tim Wallach	1.00	.30

1981-01 HOF Metal

These standard-size blank-backed cards, made of metal, duplicates the Hall of Fame plaques of these baseball immortals. These cards were issued in a continuing series from 1981 to the present. It is believed that all players inducted through 1989 were made in this set, further information is greatly appreciated.

	Nm-Mt	Ex-Mt
COMPLETE SET	1500.00	600.00
1 Hank Aaron	40.00	16.00
2 Grover C. Alexander	25.00	10.00
3 Walter Alston	12.00	4.80
4 Cap Anson	20.00	8.00
5 Johnny Bench	20.00	8.00
6 Chief Bender	12.00	4.80
7 Yogi Berra	25.00	10.00
8 Lou Brock	20.00	8.00
9 Morgan Bulkeley	10.00	4.00
10 Roy Campanella	30.00	12.00
11 Max Carey	12.00	4.80
12 Roberto Clemente	50.00	20.00
13 Ty Cobb	40.00	16.00
14 Mickey Cochrane	20.00	8.00
15 Eddie Collins	25.00	10.00
16 Charles Comiskey	12.00	4.80
17 Jocko Conlan	10.00	4.00
18 Stan Coveleski	12.00	4.80
19 Dizzy Dean	20.00	8.00
20 Bill Dickey	20.00	8.00
21 Martin Dihigo	20.00	8.00
22 Joe DiMaggio	50.00	20.00
23 Bobby Doerr	12.00	4.80
24 Don Drysdale	20.00	8.00
25 Bob Feller	25.00	10.00
26 Rick Ferrell	10.00	4.00
27 Whitey Ford	25.00	10.00
28 Jimmie Foxx	25.00	10.00
29 Lou Gehrig	40.00	16.00
30 Charlie Gehringer	20.00	8.00

31 Bob Gibson	20.00	8.00
32 Josh Gibson	30.00	12.00
33 Hank Greenberg	30.00	12.00
34 William Harridge	10.00	4.00
35 Carl Hubbell	20.00	8.00
36 Catfish Hunter	20.00	8.00
37 Walter Johnson	30.00	12.00
38 Al Kaline	25.00	10.00
39 Chuck Klein	12.00	4.80
40 Nap Lajoie	20.00	8.00
41 Kenesaw Landis	12.00	4.80
42 Bob Lemon	20.00	8.00
43 Buck Leonard	12.00	4.80
44 Connie Mack	20.00	8.00
45 Mickey Mantle	50.00	20.00
46 Christy Mathewson	25.00	10.00
47 Stan Musial	25.00	10.00
48 Kid Nichols	12.00	4.80
49 Mel Ott	15.00	6.00
50 Satchel Paige	30.00	12.00
51 Eddie Plank	12.00	4.80
52 Charles Radbourne	10.00	4.00
53 Pee Wee Reese	25.00	10.00
54 Robin Roberts	20.00	8.00
55 Brooks Robinson	20.00	8.00
56 Frank Robinson	20.00	8.00
57 Jackie Robinson	50.00	20.00
58 Babe Ruth	50.00	20.00
59 Red Schoendienst	12.00	4.80
60 Enos Slaughter	12.00	4.80
61 Al Simmons	15.00	6.00
62 Warren Spahn	20.00	8.00
63 Tris Speaker	25.00	10.00
64 Casey Stengel	25.00	10.00
65 Joe Tinker	12.00	4.80
66 Pie Traynor	15.00	6.00
67 Dazzy Vance	12.00	4.80
68 Honus Wagner	30.00	12.00
69 Bobby Wallace	12.00	4.80
70 John Montgomery Ward	12.00	4.80
71 George Weiss	10.00	4.00
72 Zach Wheat	12.00	4.80
73 Hoyt Wilhelm	12.00	4.80
74 Billy Williams	12.00	4.80
75 Early Wynn	15.00	6.00
76 Cy Young	25.00	10.00

1989 HOF Sticker Book

These stickers honor members of the baseball Hall of Fame. They are numbered in order of position played: First Base (1-9), Second Base (10-13), Shortstop (14-21), Third Base (22-26), Outfield (27-53), Catcher (54-58), Pitcher (59-84), Manager (85-89) and Builders (90-100).

	Nm-Mt	Ex-Mt
COMPLETE SET (100)	25.00	10.00
1 Lou Gehrig	2.00	.80
2 Bill Terry	.75	.30
3 Johnny Mize	.50	.20
4 Willie McCovey	.50	.20
5 Cap Anson	.75	.30
6 Ernie Banks	.75	.30
7 Dan Brouthers	.25	.10
8 George Kelly	.25	.10
9 Roger Connor	.25	.10
10 Nap Lajoie	.75	.30
11 Bobby Doerr	.25	.10
12 Jackie Robinson	2.00	.80
13 Frankie Frisch	.50	.20
14 Honus Wagner	.75	.30
15 George Wright	.25	.10
16 Hughie Jennings	.25	.10
17 Rabbit Maranville	.25	.10
18 Luis Aparicio	.50	.20
19 Joe Cronin	.50	.20
20 Dave Bancroft	.25	.10
21 Arky Vaughan	.25	.10
22 Joe Sewell	.25	.10
23 Jimmy Collins	.25	.10
24 George Kell	.25	.10
25 Eddie Mathews	.50	.20
26 Ray Dandridge	.25	.10
27 Willie Stargell	.50	.20
28 Ted Williams	2.00	.80
29 Billy Williams	.50	.20
30 Stan Musial	1.50	.60
31 Ed Delahanty	.25	.10
32 Monte Irvin	.25	.10
33 Jesse Burkett	.25	.10
34 Chick Hafey	.25	.10
35 Joe Kelley	.25	.10
36 Heinie Manush	.25	.10
37 Ty Cobb	1.50	.60
38 Max Carey	.25	.10
39 Joe DiMaggio	2.00	.80
40 Mickey Mantle	2.00	.80
41 Tris Speaker	.75	.30
42 Lloyd Waner	.25	.10
43 Billy Hamilton	.25	.10
44 Hank Aaron	1.50	.60
45 Paul Waner	.50	.20
46 Roberto Clemente	2.00	.80
47 Babe Ruth	2.00	.80
48 Chuck Klein	.25	.10
49 Mel Ott	.50	.20
50 Sam Crawford	.25	.10
51 Willie Keeler	.25	.10
52 Harry Hooper	.25	.10
53 Elmer Flick	.25	.10
54 Roy Campanella	.75	.30
55 Roger Bresnahan	.25	.10
56 Mickey Cochrane	.50	.20
57 Buck Ewing	.25	.10
58 Ernie Lombardi	.25	.10
59 Cy Young	.75	.30
60 Mordecai Brown	.25	.10
61 Red Faber	.25	.10
62 Bob Feller	.75	.30
63 Martin Dihigo	.25	.10
64 Candy Cummings	.25	.10
65 Christy Mathewson	.75	.30
66 Rube Marquard	.25	.10
67 Herb Pennock	.25	.10
68 Bob Lemon	.25	.10
69 Eppa Rixey	.25	.10
70 Whitey Ford	.75	.30
71 Waite Hoyt	.25	.10
72 Grover Alexander	.75	.30
73 Dazzy Vance	.25	.10
74 Lefty Grove	.50	.20
75 Carl Hubbell	.50	.20
76 Lefty Gomez	.25	.10
77 Ed Walsh	.25	.10
78 Eddie Plank	.25	.10
79 Sandy Koufax	.75	.30
80 Pud Galvin	.25	.10
81 Hoyt Wilhelm	.25	.10
82 Catfish Hunter	.25	.10
83 Red Ruffing	.25	.10
84 Warren Spahn	.50	.20
85 Connie Mack	.50	.20
86 Wilbert Robinson	.10	.04
87 Joe McCarthy	.10	.04
88 Bill McKechnie	.10	.04
89 John McGraw	.50	.20
90 Alexander Cartwright	.10	.04
91 Branch Rickey	.10	.04
92 Warren Giles	.10	.04
93 Tom Yawkey	.10	.04
94 Ed Barrow	.10	.04
95 Kenesaw Landis	.10	.04
96 Ban Johnson	.10	.04
97 Happy Chandler	.10	.04
98 Jocko Conlan	.10	.04
99 Cal Hubbard	.10	.04
100 Billy Evans	.10	.04

1990 HOF Sticker Book

Unlike the previous year when all the people pictured were in the Hall of Fame, this year's version features a mix of players in the Hall or players who participated in special events. These stickers are sequenced in chronological order.

	Nm-Mt	Ex-Mt
COMPLETE SET (100)	25.00	7.50
1 George Bradley	.20	.06
2 Old Hoss Radbourn	.40	.12
3 Guy Hecker	.20	.06
4 Tim Keefe	.40	.12
5 Curt Welch	.20	.06
6 George Gore	.20	.06
7 Tip O'Neill	.20	.06
8 Hugh Duffy	.40	.12
9 Cap Anson	.75	.23
10 Christy Mathewson	.75	.23
11 Joe McGinnity	.40	.12
12 Ed Reulbach	.20	.06
13 Jack Taylor	.20	.06
14 Cy Young	.75	.23
15 Ernie Shore	.20	.06
16 Smokey Joe Wood	.20	.06
17 Fred Toney Hippo Vaughn	.20	.06
18 Chief Wilson	.20	.06
19 Ty Cobb	1.50	.45
20 Fielder Jones	.20	.06
21 George Stallings MG	.20	.06
22 Leon Cadore Joe Oeschger	.20	.06
23 George Sisler	.60	.18
24 Bill Wambsganss	.20	.06
25 Babe Ruth	2.50	.75
26 Jim Bottomley	.40	.12
27 Rogers Hornsby	.75	.23
28 Walter Johnson	.75	.23
29 Hack Wilson	.40	.12
30 Wes Ferrell	.20	.06
31 Lefty Grove	.60	.18
32 Carl Hubbell	.60	.18
33 Joe Sewell	.20	.06
34 Johnny Frederick	.20	.06
35 Rudy York	.20	.06
36 Johnny Vander Meer	.20	.06
37 Pinky Higgins	.20	.06
38 Lou Gehrig	2.00	.60
39 Joe DiMaggio	2.00	.60
40 Ted Williams	2.00	.60
41 Jim Tobin	.20	.06
42 Hal Newhouser	.40	.12
43 Cookie Lavagetto	.20	.06
44 Jim Konstanty	.20	.06
45 Connie Mack MG	.60	.18
46 Bobby Thomson	.20	.06
47 Bobo Holloman	.20	.06
48 Gene Stephens	.20	.06
49 Mickey Mantle	2.00	.60
50 Joe Adcock	.20	.06
51 Stan Musial	1.50	.45
52 Al Kaline	.60	.18
53 Dale Long	.20	.06
54 Don Larsen	.20	.06
55 Dave Philley	.20	.06
56 Vic Power	.20	.06
57 Harvey Haddix	.20	.06
58 Roy Face	.20	.06
59 Larry Sherry	.20	.06
60 Casey Stengel MG	.60	.18
61 Bobby Richardson	.20	.06
62 Bill Mazeroski	.40	.12
63 Roger Maris	.20	.06
64 Bill Fischer	.20	.06
65 Willie Mays	1.50	.45
66 Maury Wills	.20	.06
67 Bert Campaneris	.20	.06
68 Warren Spahn	.60	.18
69 Sandy Koufax	.75	.23
70 Tony Cloninger	.20	.06
71 Carl Yastrzemski	.75	.23
72 Denny McLain	.20	.06
73 Don Drysdale	.60	.18
74 Bob Gibson	.60	.18
75 Frank Howard	.20	.06
76 Tom Seaver	.75	.23
77 Nolan Ryan	2.00	.60
78 Steve Carlton	.75	.23
79 Mike Marshall	.20	.06
80 Nate Colbert	.20	.06
81 Hank Aaron	1.50	.45
82 Rennie Stennett	.20	.06
83 Fred Lynn	.20	.06
84 Pete Rose	.75	.23
85 Pedro Guerrero	.20	.06
86 Lou Brock	.60	.18
87 Rickey Henderson	.60	.18
88 Reggie Jackson	.75	.23
89 Bob Horner	.20	.06
90 Don Mattingly	.75	.23
91 Mark McGwire	2.00	.60
92 Benito Santiago	.20	.06
93 George Brett	1.50	.45
94 Mike Schmidt	.75	.23
95 Jose Canseco	.60	.18
96 Andre Dawson	.40	.12
97 Ron Guidry	.20	.06
98 Dwight Gooden	.40	.12
99 Orel Hershiser	.40	.12
100 Vince Coleman	.20	.06

1977 Holiday Inn Discs

The popular hotel chain was the distributor of these Discs in 1977. They are reasonably difficult to obtain within the hobby.

	NM	Ex
COMPLETE SET (70)	500.00	200.00
1 Sal Bando	2.00	.80
2 Buddy Bell	4.00	1.60
3 Johnny Bench	25.00	10.00
4 Lou Brock	20.00	8.00
5 Larry Bowa	4.00	1.60
6 Steve Braun	2.00	.80
7 George Brett	40.00	16.00
8 Jeff Burroughs	2.00	.80
9 Campy Campaneris	4.00	1.60
10 John Candelaria	2.00	.80
11 Jose Cardenal	2.00	.80
12 Rod Carew	20.00	8.00
13 Steve Carlton	20.00	8.00
14 Dave Cash	2.00	.80
15 Cesar Cedeno	2.00	.80
16 Ron Cey	4.00	1.60
17 Dave Concepcion	6.00	2.40
18 Dennis Eckersley	20.00	8.00
19 Mark Fidrych	20.00	8.00
20 Rollie Fingers	12.00	4.80
21 Carlton Fisk	20.00	8.00
22 George Foster	6.00	2.40
23 Wayne Garland	2.00	.80
24 Ralph Garr	4.00	1.60
25 Steve Garvey	8.00	3.20
26 Cesar Geronimo	2.00	.80
27 Bobby Grich	4.00	1.60
28 Ken Griffey	6.00	2.40
29 Don Gullett	2.00	.80
30 Mike Hargrove	4.00	1.60
31 Al Hrabosky	2.00	.80
32 Catfish Hunter	12.00	4.80
33 Reggie Jackson	30.00	12.00
34 Randy Jones	2.00	.80
35 Dave Kingman	8.00	3.20
36 Jerry Koosman	4.00	1.60
37 Dave LaRoche	2.00	.80
38 Greg Luzinski	6.00	2.40
39 Fred Lynn	4.00	1.60
40 Bill Madlock	4.00	1.60
41 Rick Manning	2.00	.80
42 Jon Matlack	2.00	.80
43 John Mayberry	2.00	.80
44 Hal McRae	4.00	1.60
45 Andy Messersmith	2.00	.80
46 Rick Monday	2.00	.80
47 John Montefusco	2.00	.80
48 Joe Morgan	12.00	4.80
49 Thurman Munson	8.00	3.20
50 Bobby Murcer	6.00	2.40
51 Bill North	2.00	.80
52 Jim Palmer	12.00	4.80
53 Tony Perez	12.00	4.80
54 Jerry Reuss	2.00	.80
55 Brooks Robinson	20.00	8.00
56 Pete Rose	30.00	12.00
57 Joe Rudi	2.00	.80
58 Nolan Ryan	50.00	20.00
59 Manny Sanguillen	2.00	.80
60 Mike Schmidt	30.00	12.00
61 Tom Seaver	30.00	12.00
62 Bill Singer	2.00	.80
63 Willie Stargell	12.00	4.80
64 Rusty Staub	6.00	2.40
65 Luis Tiant	4.00	1.60
66 Bob Watson	4.00	1.60
67 Butch Wynegar	2.00	.80
68 Carl Yastrzemski	20.00	8.00
69 Robin Yount	25.00	10.00
70 Richie Zisk	2.00	.80

1960 Home Run Derby

This 20-card set was produced in 1960 by American Motors to publicize a TV program. Though the show was filmed in the 1959 off season, it appears that the set was released in early 1960. This is based on the fact that Rocky Colavito was traded to the Tigers in April, 1960

and his card in the set lists him with the Tigers while showing him in his Indians uniform. The cards are black and white and blank backed. The cards measure approximately 3 1/8" by 5 1/4". The cards are unnumbered and are ordered alphabetically below for convenience. During 1988, the 19 player cards in this set were publicly reprinted.

	NM	Ex
COMPLETE SET (20)	3000.00	1200.00
1 Hank Aaron	500.00	200.00
2 Bob Allison	60.00	24.00
3 Ernie Banks	200.00	80.00
4 Ken Boyer	80.00	32.00
5 Bob Cerv	60.00	24.00
6 Rocky Colavito Listed at Detroit Tigers but wearing Indians uniform	120.00	47.50
7 Gil Hodges	120.00	47.50
8 Jackie Jensen	80.00	32.00
9 Al Kaline	200.00	80.00
10 Harmon Killebrew	200.00	80.00
11 Jim Lemon	60.00	24.00
12 Mickey Mantle	1500.00	600.00
13 Eddie Mathews	200.00	80.00
14 Willie Mays	500.00	200.00
15 Wally Post	60.00	24.00
16 Frank Robinson	200.00	80.00
17 Mark Scott ANN	60.00	24.00
18 Duke Snider	200.00	80.00
19 Dick Stuart	60.00	24.00
20 Gus Triandos	60.00	24.00

1999 Home Run Heroes

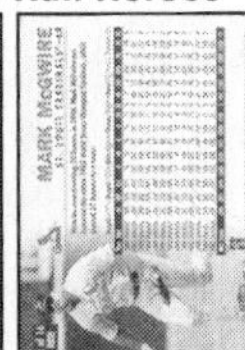

All four MLB licensed card manufacturers participated in this cross-company retail promotion to honor baseball's best sluggers. The cards were distributed at large retail shops like Wal-Mart in March and April of 1999. Each manufacturer selected four players of their choice. Cards 1-4 were issued by Fleer/SkyBox, 5-8 were issued by Upper Deck, cards 9-12 were issued by Topps and 13-16 issued by Pacific. Each card shares similar design elements to the base brand they're sourced from, but all have been given a bold unifying, gold foil strip stating "HOME RUN HEROES" on the right side of the card front.

	Nm-Mt	Ex-Mt
COMPLETE SET (16)	60.00	18.00
1 Mark McGwire Fleer	6.00	1.80
2 Sammy Sosa Sports Illustrated	4.00	1.20
3 Mike Piazza SkyBox Thunder	4.00	1.20
4 Nomar Garciaparra Skybox Thunder	4.00	1.20
5 Mark McGwire Upper Deck	6.00	1.80
6 Sammy Sosa Upper Deck	4.00	1.20
7 Ken Griffey Jr. Upper Deck	4.00	1.20
8 Frank Thomas Upper Deck	2.00	.60
9 Mark McGwire Topps Chrome	6.00	1.80
10 Sammy Sosa Topps Chrome	4.00	1.20
11 Alex Rodriguez Topps Chrome	4.00	1.20
12 Vladimir Guerrero Topps Chrome	2.00	.60
13 Mark McGwire Pacific	6.00	1.80
14 Sammy Sosa Pacific	4.00	1.20
15 Juan Gonzalez Pacific	2.00	.60
16 Manny Ramirez Pacific	2.00	.60

1991 Homers Cookies Classics

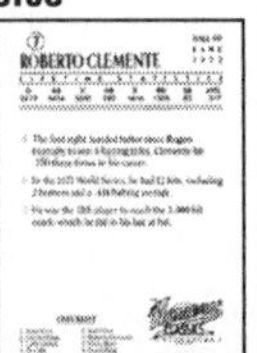

This nine-card standards-size set was sponsored by Legend Food Products in honor of Hall of Famers in baseball history. One free card was randomly inserted in each box of Homers Baseball Cookies. The cards have vintage sepia-toned player photos, with bronze borders on a white card face. The player's name appears in a bronze stripe overlaying the bottom edge of the picture. In black print on white, the back presents lifetime statistics, career highlights, and a checklist for the set.

	Nm-Mt	Ex-Mt
COMPLETE SET (9)	9.00	2.70
1 Babe Ruth	3.00	.90
2 Satchel Paige	1.50	.45
3 Lefty Gomez	1.00	.30
4 Ty Cobb	1.50	.45
5 Cy Young	1.25	.35
6 Bob Feller	1.25	.35
7 Roberto Clemente	2.00	.60
8 Dizzy Dean	1.25	.35
9 Lou Gehrig	2.00	.60

1927 Honey Boy Ice Cream

These 21 cards, which measure approximately 1 5/8" by 2 /38" feature a mix of major and minor league players.Honey Boy was a Canadian product. Some collectors refer to this set as the "Purity" set since that was the specific brand that these cards were inserted in. The first half of this set is dedicated to Canadian players while the second half is devoted to major leaguers. The cards were redeemable for a "brick" of Honey Boy Ice Cream. When all 21 cards were accumulated and sent in, the cards were then given a punch hole and returned to the lucky collector along with the brick.

	Ex-Mt	VG
COMPLETE SET (21)	30000.00	15000.00
COMMON MINORS (1-9)	500.00	250.00
COMMON MAJORS (10-21)	1500.00	750.00
1 Steamer Maxwell Arenas	500.00	250.00
2 Cecil Brown Dominion Express	500.00	250.00
3 Carson McVey Transcona	500.00	250.00
4 Sam Perlman Tigers	500.00	250.00
5 Snake Siddle Arenas	500.00	250.00
6 Eddie Cass Columbus	500.00	250.00
7 Jimmy Bradley Columbus	500.00	250.00
8 Gordon Caslake Dominion Express	500.00	250.00
9 Ward McVey Tigers	500.00	250.00
10 Tris Speaker	3000.00	1500.00
11 George Sisler	3000.00	1500.00
12 Emil Meusel	1500.00	750.00
13 Edd Roush	2500.00	1250.00
14 Babe Ruth	5000.00	2500.00
15 Harry Heilmann	2500.00	1250.00
16 Heinie Groh	1500.00	750.00
17 Eddie Collins	3000.00	1500.00
18 Grover Alexander	3000.00	1500.00
19 Dave Bancroft	2500.00	1250.00
20 Frank Frisch	3000.00	1500.00
21 George Burns	1500.00	750.00

1905 Carl Horner Cabinets

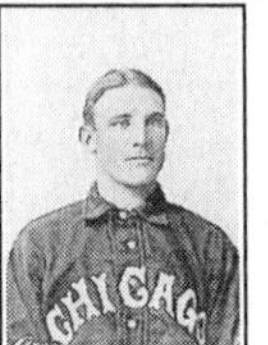

These portraits, which measure an approximate 5 1/2" by 7" feature photographs which were also used in the W600 set. The players name is on the bottom. These are rarely seen in the secondary market and since several cards were discovered recently, it is believed that there should be many additions to this checklists. Since these are unnumbered, we have sequenced them in alphabetical order.

	Ex-Mt	VG
COMPLETE SET	8000.00	4000.00
1 Nick Altrock	300.00	150.00
2 Frank Arrelanes	300.00	150.00
3 Jake Beckley	600.00	300.00
4 Roger Bresnahan	600.00	300.00
5 Bill Dahlen	300.00	150.00
6 Kid Elberfeld	300.00	150.00
7 Rube Ellis	300.00	150.00
8 Billy Gilbert	300.00	150.00
9 Danny Green	300.00	150.00
10 Addie Joss	800.00	400.00
11 Rube Kroh	300.00	150.00
12 Joe McGinnity	600.00	300.00
13 Harry Niles	300.00	150.00
14 George Stovall	300.00	150.00
15 Joe Tinker	800.00	400.00
16 Vic Willis	600.00	300.00
17 Hooks Wiltse	300.00	150.00
18 Cy Young	1500.00	750.00

1975 Hostess

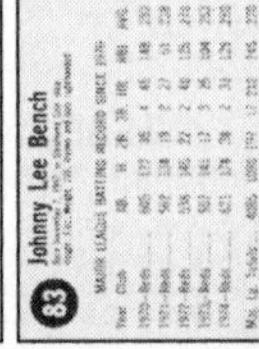

The cards in this 150-card set measure approximately 2 1/4" by 3 1/4" individually or 3 1/4" by 7 1/4" as panels of three. The 1975 Hostess set was issued in panels of three cards each on the backs of family-size packages of Hostess cakes. Card number 125, Bill Madlock, was listed correctly as an infielder and incorrectly as a pitcher. Number 11, Burt Hooton, and number 89, Doug Rader, are spelled two different ways. Some panels are more difficult to find than others as they were issued only on the backs of less popular Hostess products. These scarcer cards are shown with SP in the checklist. Although complete panel prices are not explicitly listed, they would generally have a value of 20-30 percent greater than the sum of the values of the individual players on that panel. One of the more interesting cards in the set is that of Robin Yount; Hostess issued one of the few Yount cards available in 1975, his rookie year for cards. An album to hold these cards was issued. The albums were originally intended to be given out in grocery stores. However, most seemingly were distributed through Hostess stores.

	NM	Ex
COMP.INDIV.SET (150)	250.00	100.00
COMMON CARD (1-150)	.50	.20
COMMON SP	.75	.30
1 Bob Tolan	.50	.20
2 Cookie Rojas	.50	.20
3 Darrell Evans	.75	.30
4 Sal Bando	.75	.30
5 Joe Morgan	4.00	1.60
6 Mickey Lolich	.75	.30
7 Don Sutton	4.00	1.60
8 Bill Melton	.50	.20
9 Tim Foli	.50	.20
10 Joe Lahoud	.50	.20
11A Burt Hooton ERR Misspelled Bert Hooten on card	1.00	.40
11B Burt Hooton COR	1.00	.40
12 Paul Blair	.50	.20
13 Jim Barr	.50	.20
14 Toby Harrah	.50	.20
15 John Milner	.50	.20
16 Ken Holtzman	.50	.20
17 Cesar Cedeno	.50	.20
18 Dwight Evans	1.50	.60
19 Willie McCovey	3.00	1.20
20 Tony Oliva	1.50	.60
21 Manny Sanguillen	.50	.20
22 Mickey Rivers	.50	.20
23 Lou Brock	4.00	1.60
24 Graig Nettles UER Craig on front	1.50	.60
25 Jim Wynn	.50	.20
26 George Scott	.50	.20
27 Greg Luzinski	1.00	.40
28 Bert Campaneris	.75	.30
29 Pete Rose	10.00	4.00
30 Buddy Bell	1.00	.40
31 Gary Matthews	.75	.30
32 Freddie Patek	.50	.20
33 Mike Lum	.50	.20
34 Ellie Rodriguez	.50	.20
35 Milt May UER Photo actually Lee May	.50	.20
36 Willie Horton	.75	.30
37 Dave Winfield	20.00	8.00
38 Tom Grieve	.50	.20
39 Barry Foote	.50	.20
40 Joe Rudi	.50	.20
41 Bake McBride	.50	.20
42 Mike Cuellar	.50	.20
43 Garry Maddox	.50	.20
44 Carlos May	.50	.20
45 Bud Harrelson	.50	.20
46 Dave Chalk	.50	.20
47 Dave Concepcion	1.50	.60
48 Carl Yastrzemski	5.00	2.00
49 Steve Garvey	2.50	1.00
50 Amos Otis	.50	.20
51 Rick Reuschel	.50	.20
52 Rollie Fingers	3.00	1.20
53 Bob Watson	.75	.30
54 John Ellis	.50	.20
55 Bob Bailey	.50	.20
56 Rod Carew	5.00	2.00
57 Rich Hebner	.50	.20
58 Nolan Ryan	40.00	16.00
59 Reggie Smith	.75	.30
60 Joe Coleman	.50	.20
61 Ron Cey	.75	.30
62 Darrell Porter	.75	.30
63 Steve Carlton	5.00	2.00
64 Gene Tenace	.50	.20
65 Jose Cardenal	.50	.20
66 Bill Lee	.50	.20
67 Dave Lopes	.75	.30
68 Wilbur Wood	.50	.20
69 Steve Renko	.50	.20
70 Joe Torre	1.50	.60
71 Ted Sizemore	.50	.20
72 Bobby Grich	.75	.30
73 Chris Speier	.50	.20
74 Bert Blyleven	1.00	.40
75 Tom Seaver	10.00	4.00
76 Nate Colbert	.50	.20
77 Don Kessinger	.50	.20
78 George Medich	.50	.20
79 Andy Messersmith SP	.75	.30
80 Robin Yount SP	40.00	16.00
81 Al Oliver SP	1.00	.40
82 Bill Singer SP	.75	.30
83 Johnny Bench SP	12.00	4.80
84 Gaylord Perry SP	4.00	1.60
85 Dave Kingman SP	2.00	.80
86 Ed Herrmann SP	.75	.30
87 Ralph Garr SP	.75	.30
88 Reggie Jackson SP	12.00	4.80
89A Doug Rader ERR SP Misspelled Radar	1.50	.60
89B Doug Rader COR SP	6.00	2.40
90 Elliott Maddox SP	.75	.30
91 Bill Russell SP	1.50	.60
92 John Mayberry SP	.75	.30
93 Dave Cash SP	.75	.30
94 Jeff Burroughs SP	.75	.30
95 Ted Simmons SP	2.00	.80
96 Joe Decker SP	.75	.30
97 Bill Buckner SP	1.50	.60
98 Bobby Darwin SP	.75	.30
99 Phil Niekro SP	4.00	1.60
100 Jim Sundberg	.50	.20
101 Greg Gross	.50	.20
102 Luis Tiant	1.00	.40
103 Glenn Beckert	.50	.20
104 Hal McRae	.75	.30
105 Mike Jorgensen	.50	.20
106 Mike Hargrove	1.50	.60
107 Don Gullett	.75	.30
108 Tito Fuentes	.50	.20
109 John Grubb	.50	.20
110 Jim Kaat	1.00	.40
111 Felix Millan	.50	.20
112 Don Money	.50	.20
113 Rick Monday	.50	.20
114 Dick Bosman	.50	.20
115 Roger Metzger	.50	.20
116 Fergie Jenkins	3.00	1.20
117 Dusty Baker	1.00	.40
118 Billy Champion SP	.75	.30
119 Bob Gibson SP	5.00	2.00
120 Bill Freehan SP	1.00	.40
121 Cesar Geronimo	.50	.20
122 Jorge Orta	.50	.20
123 Cleon Jones	.50	.20
124 Steve Busby	.50	.20
125A Bill Madlock ERR Pitcher	1.50	.60
125B Bill Madlock COR Infielder	1.50	.60
126 Jim Palmer	4.00	1.60
127 Tony Perez	2.50	1.00
128 Larry Hisle	.50	.20
129 Rusty Staub	1.00	.40
130 Hank Aaron SP	20.00	8.00
131 Rennie Stennett SP	.75	.30
132 Rico Petrocelli SP	1.00	.40
133 Mike Schmidt	20.00	8.00
134 Sparky Lyle	1.00	.40
135 Willie Stargell	3.00	1.20
136 Ken Henderson	.50	.20
137 Willie Montanez	.50	.20
138 Thurman Munson	3.00	1.20
139 Richie Zisk	.50	.20
140 George Hendrick	.50	.20
141 Bobby Murcer	.75	.30
142 Lee May	.50	.20
143 Carlton Fisk	10.00	4.00
144 Brooks Robinson	5.00	2.00
145 Bobby Bonds	1.50	.60
146 Gary Sutherland	.50	.20
147 Oscar Gamble	.50	.20
148 Jim Hunter	4.00	1.60
149 Tug McGraw	1.00	.40
150 Dave McNally	.75	.30
XX Album	8.00	3.20

1975 Hostess Twinkie

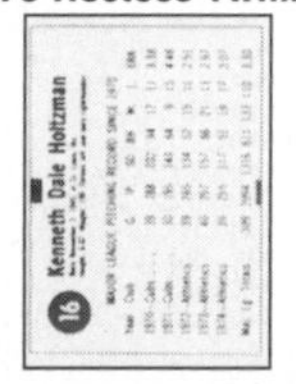

The cards in this 60-card set measure approximately 2 1/4" by 3 1/4". The 1975 Hostess Twinkie set was issued on a limited basis in the far western part of the country. The set contains the same numbers as the regular set to number 36; however, the set is skip numbered after number 36. The cards were issued as the backs for 25-cent Twinkies packs. The fronts are indistinguishable from the regular Hostess cards; however the card backs are different in that the Twinkie cards have a thick black bar in the middle of the reverse. The cards are frequently found with product stains. One of the more interesting cards in the set is that of Robin Yount; Hostess issued one of the few Yount cards available in 1975, his rookie year for cards.

	NM	Ex
COMPLETE SET (60)	150.00	60.00
1 Bob Tolan	1.00	.40
2 Cookie Rojas	1.00	.40
3 Darrell Evans	1.50	.60
4 Sal Bando	1.50	.60
5 Joe Morgan	6.00	2.40
6 Mickey Lolich	2.00	.80
7 Don Sutton	5.00	2.00
8 Bill Melton	1.00	.40
9 Tim Foli	1.00	.40
10 Joe Lahoud	1.00	.40
11 Burt Hooton UER (Misspelled Bert Hooten on card)	1.00	.40
12 Paul Blair	1.00	.40
13 Jim Barr	1.00	.40
14 Toby Harrah	1.00	.40
15 John Milner	1.00	.40
16 Ken Holtzman	1.00	.40
17 Cesar Cedeno	1.00	.40
18 Dwight Evans	2.50	1.00
19 Willie McCovey	5.00	2.00
20 Tony Oliva	2.00	.80
21 Manny Sanguillen	1.00	.40
22 Mickey Rivers	1.00	.40
23 Lou Brock	6.00	2.40
24 Graig Nettles UER (Craig on front)	2.50	1.00
25 Jim Wynn	1.50	.60
26 George Scott	1.00	.40
27 Greg Luzinski	1.50	.60
28 Bert Campaneris	1.50	.60
29 Pete Rose	15.00	6.00
30 Buddy Bell	2.00	.80
31 Gary Matthews	1.50	.60
32 Freddie Patek	1.00	.40
33 Mike Lum	1.00	.40
34 Ellie Rodriguez	1.00	.40
35 Milt May UER (Lee May picture)	1.00	.40
36 Willie Horton	1.50	.60
40 Joe Rudi	1.50	.60
43 Garry Maddox	1.00	.40
46 Dave Chalk	1.00	.40
49 Steve Garvey	4.00	1.60
52 Rollie Fingers	5.00	2.00
58 Nolan Ryan	50.00	20.00
61 Ron Cey	2.00	.80
64 Gene Tenace	1.00	.40
65 Jose Cardenal	1.00	.40
67 Dave Lopes	2.00	.80
68 Wilbur Wood	1.00	.40
73 Chris Speier	1.00	.40
77 Don Kessinger	1.00	.40
79 Andy Messersmith	1.00	.40
80 Robin Yount	35.00	14.00
82 Bill Singer	1.00	.40
103 Glenn Beckert	1.00	.40
110 Jim Kaat	2.00	.80
112 Don Money	1.50	.60
113 Rick Monday	1.50	.60
122 Jorge Orta	1.00	.40
125 Bill Madlock	2.00	.80
130 Hank Aaron	20.00	8.00
136 Ken Henderson	1.00	.40
XX Checklist	25.00	10.00

1976 Hostess

The cards in this 150-card set measure approximately 2 1/4" by 3 1/4" individually or 3 1/4" by 7 1/4" as panels of three. The 1976 Hostess set contains full-color, numbered cards issued in panels of three cards each on family-size packages of Hostess cakes. Scarcer panels (those only found on less popular Hostess products) are listed in the checklist below with SP. Complete panels of three have a value 20-30 percent more than the sum of the individual cards on the panel. Nine additional numbers (151-159) were apparently planned but never actually issued. These exist as proof cards and are quite scarce, e.g., 151 Ferguson Jenkins (even though he already appears in the set as card number 138), 152 Mike Cuellar, 153 Tom Murphy, 154 Al Cowens, 155 Barry Foote, 156 Steve Carlton, 157 Richie Zisk, 158 Ken Holtzman, and 159 Cliff Johnson. One of the more interesting cards in the set is that of Dennis Eckersley; Hostess issued one of the few Eckersley cards available in 1976, his rookie year for cards. An album to hold these cards were issued.

	NM	Ex
COMP.INDIV.SET (150)	300.00	120.00
COMMON CARD (1-150)	.50	.20
COMMON SP	.75	.30
1 Fred Lynn	1.50	.60
2 Joe Morgan	4.00	1.60
3 Phil Niekro	4.00	1.60
4 Gaylord Perry	3.00	1.20
5 Bob Watson	.75	.30
6 Bill Freehan	.75	.30
7 Lou Brock	4.00	1.60
8 Al Fitzmorris	.50	.20
9 Rennie Stennett	.50	.20
10 Tony Oliva	1.50	.60
11 Robin Yount	20.00	8.00
12 Rick Manning	.50	.20
13 Bobby Grich	.75	.30
14 Terry Forster	.50	.20
15 Dave Kingman	1.00	.40
16 Thurman Munson	3.00	1.20
17 Rick Reuschel	.50	.20
18 Bobby Bonds	1.50	.60
19 Steve Garvey	2.50	1.00
20 Vida Blue	.75	.30
21 Dave Rader	.50	.20
22 Johnny Bench	8.00	3.20
23 Luis Tiant	.75	.30
24 Darrell Evans	.75	.30
25 Larry Dierker	.50	.20
26 Willie Horton	.75	.30
27 John Ellis	.50	.20
28 Al Cowens	.50	.20
29 Jerry Reuss	.50	.20
30 Reggie Smith	.75	.30
31 Bobby Darwin SP	.75	.30
32 Fritz Peterson SP	.75	.30
33 Rod Carew SP	10.00	4.00
34 Carlos May SP	.75	.30
35 Tom Seaver SP	15.00	6.00
36 Brooks Robinson SP	10.00	4.00
37 Jose Cardenal	.50	.20
38 Ron Blomberg	.50	.20
39 Leroy Stanton	.50	.20
40 Dave Cash	.50	.20
41 John Montefusco	.50	.20
42 Bob Tolan	.50	.20
43 Carl Morton	.50	.20
44 Rick Burleson	.50	.20
45 Don Gullett	.50	.20
46 Vern Ruhle	.50	.20
47 Cesar Cedeno	.75	.30
48 Toby Harrah	.50	.20
49 Willie Stargell	3.00	1.20
50 Al Hrabosky	.50	.20
51 Amos Otis	.50	.20
52 Bud Harrelson	.50	.20
53 Jim Hughes	.50	.20
54 George Scott	.50	.20
55 Mike Vail SP	.75	.30
56 Jim Palmer SP	6.00	2.40
57 Jorge Orta SP	.75	.30
58 Chris Chambliss SP	1.00	.40
59 Dave Chalk SP	.75	.30
60 Ray Burris SP	.75	.30
61 Bert Campaneris SP	1.00	.40
62 Gary Carter SP	15.00	6.00
63 Ron Cey SP	1.50	.60
64 Carlton Fisk SP	15.00	6.00
65 Marty Perez SP	.75	.30
66 Pete Rose SP	20.00	8.00
67 Roger Metzger SP	.75	.30
68 Jim Sundberg SP	.75	.30
69 Ron LeFlore SP	.75	.30
70 Ted Sizemore SP	.75	.30
71 Steve Busby SP	.75	.30
72 Manny Sanguillen SP	.75	.30
73 Larry Hisle SP	.75	.30
74 Pete Broberg SP	.75	.30
75 Boog Powell SP	2.00	.80
76 Ken Singleton SP	1.00	.40
77 Goose Gossage SP	2.00	.80
78 Jerry Grote SP	.75	.30
79 Nolan Ryan SP	50.00	20.00
80 Rick Monday SP	1.00	.40
81 Graig Nettles SP	2.00	.80
82 Chris Speier	.50	.20
83 Dave Winfield	12.00	4.80
84 Mike Schmidt	15.00	6.00
85 Buzz Capra	.50	.20
86 Tony Perez	2.50	1.00
87 Dwight Evans	1.50	.60
88 Mike Hargrove	.75	.30
89 Joe Coleman	.50	.20
90 Greg Gross	.50	.20
91 John Mayberry UER Card stats has him playing for the Astros	.50	.20
92 John Candelaria	.75	.30
93 Bake McBride	.50	.20
94 Hank Aaron	15.00	6.00
95 Buddy Bell	.75	.30
96 Steve Braun	.50	.20
97 Jon Matlack	.50	.20
98 Lee May	.50	.20
99 Wilbur Wood	.50	.20
100 Bill Madlock	.75	.30
101 Frank Tanana	.75	.30
102 Mickey Rivers	.50	.20
103 Mike Ivie	.50	.20
104 Rollie Fingers	3.00	1.20
105 Dave Lopes	.75	.30
106 George Foster	1.00	.40
107 Denny Doyle	.50	.20
108 Earl Williams	.50	.20
109 Tom Veryzer	.50	.20
110 J.R. Richard	.50	.20
111 Jeff Burroughs	.50	.20
112 Al Oliver	.75	.30
113 Ted Simmons	1.00	.40
114 George Brett	40.00	16.00
115 Frank Duffy	.50	.20
116 Bert Blyleven	1.00	.40
117 Darrell Porter	.50	.20
118 Don Baylor	1.00	.40
119 Bucky Dent	.75	.30
120 Felix Millan	.50	.20
121 Mike Cuellar	.50	.20
122 Gene Tenace	.50	.20
123 Bobby Murcer	.75	.30
124 Willie McCovey	3.00	1.20
125 Greg Luzinski	.75	.30
126 Larry Parrish	.50	.20
127 Jim Rice	2.00	.80
128 Dave Concepcion	1.00	.40
129 Jim Wynn	.50	.20
130 Tom Grieve	.50	.20
131 Mike Cosgrove	.50	.20
132 Dan Meyer	.50	.20
133 Dave Parker	2.00	.80
134 Don Kessinger	.50	.20
135 Hal McRae	.75	.30
136 Don Money	.50	.20
137 Dennis Eckersley	20.00	8.00
138 Fergie Jenkins	3.00	1.20
139 Mike Torrez	.50	.20
140 Jerry Morales	.50	.20
141 Jim Hunter	3.00	1.20
142 Gary Matthews	.50	.20
143 Randy Jones	.50	.20
144 Mike Jorgensen	.50	.20
145 Larry Bowa	.75	.30
146 Reggie Jackson	10.00	4.00
147 Steve Yeager	.50	.20
148 Dave May	.50	.20
149 Carl Yastrzemski	6.00	2.40
150 Cesar Geronimo	.50	.20
XX Album	8.00	3.20

1976 Hostess Twinkie

The cards in this 60-card set measure approximately 2 1/4" by 3 1/4". The 1976 Hostess Twinkies set contains the first 60 cards of the 1976 Hostess set. These cards were issued as backs on 25-cent Twinkie packages as in the 1975 Twinkies set. The fronts are indistinguishable from the regular Hostess cards; however the card backs are different in that the Twinkie cards have a thick black bar in the middle of the reverse. The cards are frequently found with product stains.

	NM	Ex
COMPLETE SET (60)	125.00	50.00
1 Fred Lynn	2.50	1.00
2 Joe Morgan	6.00	2.40
3 Phil Niekro	5.00	2.00
4 Gaylord Perry	5.00	2.00
5 Bob Watson	1.50	.60
6 Bill Freehan	1.50	.60
7 Lou Brock	5.00	2.00
8 Al Fitzmorris	1.00	.40
9 Rennie Stennett	1.00	.40
10 Tony Oliva	2.50	1.00
11 Robin Yount	15.00	6.00
12 Rick Manning	1.00	.40
13 Bobby Grich	1.50	.60
14 Terry Forster	1.00	.40
15 Dave Kingman	2.50	1.00
16 Thurman Munson	6.00	2.40
17 Rick Reuschel	1.50	.60
18 Bobby Bonds	2.50	1.00
19 Steve Garvey	6.00	2.40
20 Vida Blue	2.00	.80
21 Dave Rader	1.00	.40
22 Johnny Bench	10.00	4.00
23 Luis Tiant	1.50	.60
24 Darrell Evans	1.50	.60
25 Larry Dierker	1.00	.40
26 Willie Horton	1.50	.60
27 John Ellis	1.00	.40
28 Al Cowens	1.00	.40
29 Jerry Reuss	1.50	.60
30 Reggie Smith	1.50	.60
31 Bobby Darwin	1.00	.40
32 Fritz Peterson	1.00	.40
33 Rod Carew	6.00	2.40
34 Carlos May	1.00	.40
35 Tom Seaver	10.00	4.00
36 Brooks Robinson	6.00	2.40
37 Jose Cardenal	1.00	.40
38 Ron Blomberg	1.00	.40
39 Leroy Stanton	1.00	.40
40 Dave Cash	1.00	.40
41 John Montefusco	1.00	.40
42 Bob Tolan	1.00	.40
43 Carl Morton	1.00	.40
44 Rick Burleson	1.50	.60
45 Don Gullett	1.50	.60
46 Vern Ruhle	1.00	.40
47 Cesar Cedeno	1.50	.60
48 Toby Harrah	1.50	.60
49 Willie Stargell	5.00	2.00
50 Al Hrabosky	1.50	.60
51 Amos Otis	1.50	.60
52 Bud Harrelson	1.50	.60
53 Jim Hughes	1.50	.60
54 George Scott	1.50	.60
55 Mike Vail	1.50	.60
56 Jim Palmer	5.00	2.00
57 Jorge Orta	1.00	.40
58 Chris Chambliss	2.00	.80
59 Dave Chalk	1.00	.40
60 Ray Burris	1.00	.40

1977 Hostess

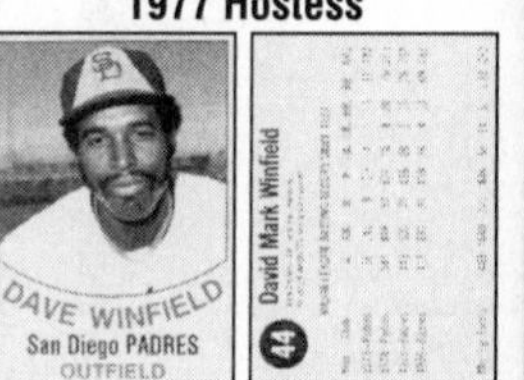

The cards in this 150-card set measure approximately 2 1/4" by 3 1/4" individually or 3 1/4" by 7 1/4" as panels of three. The 1977 Hostess set contains full-color, numbered cards issued in panels of three cards each with Hostess family-size cake products. Scarcer cards are listed in the checklist below with SP. Although complete panel prices are not explicitly listed below, they would generally have a value 20-30 percent greater than the sum of the individual players on the panel. There were ten additional cards proofed, but not produced or distributed; they are 151 Ed Kranepool, 152 Ross Grimsley, 153 Ken Brett, 154 Rowland Office, 155 Rick Wise, 156 Paul Splittorff, 157 Gerald Augustine, 158 Ken Forsch, 159 Jerry Reuss (Reuss is also number 119 in the set), and 160 Nelson Briles. There is also a variation set only that was available one card per Twinkie package. Common cards in this Twinkie set are worth double the prices listed below, although the stars are only worth about 25 percent more. The Twinkie cards are distinguished by the thick printing bar or band printed on the card backs just below the statistics. An album to hold these cards were issued.

	NM	Ex
COMP.INDIV.SET (150)	250.00	100.00
COMMON CARD (1-150)	.50	.20
COMMON SP	.75	.30
1 Jim Palmer	4.00	1.60
2 Joe Morgan	4.00	1.60
3 Reggie Jackson	10.00	4.00
4 Carl Yastrzemski	6.00	2.40
5 Thurman Munson	3.00	1.20
6 Johnny Bench	8.00	3.20
7 Tom Seaver	8.00	3.20
8 Pete Rose	10.00	4.00
9 Rod Carew	4.00	1.60
10 Luis Tiant	.75	.30
11 Phil Garner	.75	.30
12 Sixto Lezcano	.50	.20
13 Mike Torrez	.50	.20
14 Dave Lopes	.75	.30
15 Doug DeCinces	.50	.20
16 Jim Spencer	.50	.20
17 Hal McRae	.75	.30
18 Mike Hargrove	.75	.30
19 Willie Montanez SP	.75	.30
20 Roger Metzger SP	.75	.30
21 Dwight Evans SP	2.00	.80
22 Steve Rogers SP	.75	.30
23 Jim Rice SP	2.50	1.00
24 Pete Falcone SP	.75	.30
25 Greg Luzinski SP	1.50	.60
26 Randy Jones SP	.75	.30
27 Willie Stargell SP	5.00	2.00
28 John Hiller SP	.75	.30
29 Bobby Murcer SP	2.00	.80
30 Rick Monday SP	1.00	.40
31 John Montefusco SP	.75	.30
32 Lou Brock SP	5.00	2.00
33 Bill North SP	.75	.30

Card	NM	Ex
34 Robin Yount SP	25.00	10.00
35 Steve Garvey SP	5.00	2.00
36 George Brett SP	35.00	14.00
37 Toby Harrah SP	.75	.30
38 Jerry Royster SP	.75	.30
39 Bob Watson SP	1.00	.40
40 George Foster	.75	.30
41 Gary Carter	4.00	1.60
42 John Denny	.50	.20
43 Mike Schmidt SP	12.00	4.80
44 Dave Winfield	10.00	4.00
45 Al Oliver	.75	.30
46 Mark Fidrych	3.00	1.20
47 Larry Herndon	.50	.20
48 Dave Goltz	.50	.20
49 Jerry Morales	.50	.20
50 Ron LeFlore	.50	.20
51 Fred Lynn	.75	.30
52 Vida Blue	.75	.30
53 Rick Manning	.50	.20
54 Bill Buckner	.75	.30
55 Lee May	.75	.30
56 John Mayberry	.50	.20
57 Darrel Chaney	.50	.20
58 Cesar Cedeno	.75	.30
59 Ken Griffey	1.00	.40
60 Dave Kingman	1.00	.40
61 Ted Simmons	1.00	.40
62 Larry Bowa	.75	.30
63 Frank Tanana	.75	.30
64 Jason Thompson	.50	.20
65 Ken Brett	.50	.20
66 Roy Smalley	.50	.20
67 Ray Burris	.50	.20
68 Rick Burleson	.50	.20
69 Buddy Bell	.75	.30
70 Don Sutton	4.00	1.60
71 Mark Belanger	.50	.20
72 Dennis Leonard	.50	.20
73 Gaylord Perry	3.00	1.20
74 Dick Ruthven	.50	.20
75 Jose Cruz	.75	.30
76 Cesar Geronimo	.50	.20
77 Jerry Koosman	.75	.30
78 Garry Templeton	.50	.20
79 Jim Hunter	3.00	1.20
80 John Candelaria	.50	.20
81 Nolan Ryan	40.00	16.00
82 Rusty Staub	.75	.30
83 Jim Barr	.50	.20
84 Butch Wynegar	.75	.30
85 Jose Cardenal	.50	.20
86 Claudell Washington	.50	.20
87 Bill Travers	.50	.20
88 Rick Waits	.50	.20
89 Ron Cey	.75	.30
90 Al Bumbry	.50	.20
91 Bucky Dent	.75	.30
92 Amos Otis	.50	.20
93 Tom Grieve	.50	.20
94 Enos Cabell	.50	.20
95 Dave Concepcion	1.00	.40
96 Felix Millan	.50	.20
97 Bake McBride	.50	.20
98 Chris Chambliss	.75	.30
99 Butch Metzger	.50	.20
100 Rennie Stennett	.50	.20
101 Dave Roberts	.50	.20
102 Lyman Bostock	.75	.30
103 Rick Reuschel	.50	.20
104 Carlton Fisk	10.00	4.00
105 Jim Slaton	.50	.20
106 Dennis Eckersley	8.00	3.20
107 Ken Singleton	.50	.20
108 Ralph Garr	.50	.20
109 Freddie Patek SP	.75	.30
110 Jim Sundberg SP	.75	.30
111 Phil Niekro SP	5.00	2.00
112 J.R. Richard SP	.75	.30
113 Gary Nolan SP	.75	.30
114 Jon Matlack SP	.75	.30
115 Keith Hernandez SP	2.00	.80
116 Graig Nettles SP	1.50	.60
117 Steve Carlton SP	8.00	3.20
118 Bill Madlock SP	1.00	.40
119 Jerry Reuss SP	1.00	.40
120 Aurelio Rodriguez SP	.75	.30
121 Dan Ford SP	.75	.30
122 Ray Fosse SP	.75	.30
123 George Hendrick SP	.75	.30
124 Alan Ashby	.50	.20
125 Joe Lis	.50	.20
126 Sal Bando	.50	.20
127 Richie Zisk	.50	.20
128 Rich Gossage	1.50	.60
129 Don Baylor	.75	.30
130 Dave McKay	.50	.20
131 Bob Grich	.75	.30
132 Dave Pagan	.50	.20
133 Dave Cash	.50	.20
134 Steve Braun	.50	.20
135 Dan Meyer	.50	.20
136 Bill Stein	.50	.20
137 Rollie Fingers	3.00	1.20
138 Brian Downing	.50	.20
139 Bill Singer	.50	.20
140 Doyle Alexander	.50	.20
141 Gene Tenace	.50	.20
142 Gary Matthews	.50	.20
143 Don Gullett	.50	.20
144 Wayne Garland	.50	.20
145 Pete Broberg	.50	.20
146 Joe Rudi	.50	.20
147 Glenn Abbott	.50	.20
148 George Scott	.50	.20
149 Bert Campaneris	.50	.20
150 Andy Messersmith	.50	.20
XX Album	8.00	3.20

1978 Hostess

The cards in this 150-card set measure approximately 2 1/4" by 3 1/4" individually or 3 1/4" by 7 1/4" as panels of three. The 1978 Hostess set contains full-color, numbered cards issued in panels of three cards each on family packages of Hostess cake products. Scarcer cards are listed in the checklist with SP. The 1978 Hostess panels are considered by some collectors to be somewhat more difficult to obtain than Hostess panels of other years.

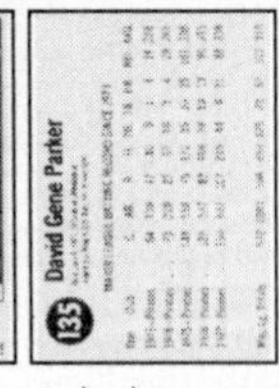

Although complete panel prices are not explicitly listed below, they would generally have a value 20-25 percent greater than the sum of the individual players on the panel. There is additional interest in Eddie Murray number 31, since this card corresponds to his rookie year in cards. An album to hold all these cards were issued. There was an album issued for these cards. It is priced below.

	NM	Ex
COMP.INDIV.SET (150)	250.00	100.00
COMMON CARD (1-150)	.50	.20
COMMON SP	.75	.30
1 Butch Hobson	.50	.20
2 George Foster	.75	.30
3 Bob Forsch	.50	.20
4 Tony Perez	1.50	.60
5 Bruce Sutter	1.50	.60
6 Hal McRae	.75	.30
7 Tommy John	1.50	.60
8 Greg Luzinski	.75	.30
9 Enos Cabell	.50	.20
10 Doug DeCinces	.50	.20
11 Willie Stargell	3.00	1.20
12 Ed Halicki	.50	.20
13 Larry Hisle	.50	.20
14 Jim Slaton	.50	.20
15 Buddy Bell	.75	.30
16 Earl Williams	.50	.20
17 Glenn Abbott	.50	.20
18 Dan Ford	.50	.20
19 Gary Matthews	.50	.20
20 Eric Soderholm	.50	.20
21 Bump Wills	.50	.20
22 Keith Hernandez	1.50	.60
23 Dave Cash	.50	.20
24 George Scott	.50	.20
25 Ron Guidry	1.50	.60
26 Dave Kingman	1.00	.40
27 George Brett	25.00	10.00
28 Bob Watson SP	1.00	.40
29 Bob Boone SP	1.50	.60
30 Reggie Smith SP	1.00	.40
31 Eddie Murray SP	40.00	16.00
32 Gary Lavelle SP	.75	.30
33 Rennie Stennett SP	.75	.30
34 Duane Kuiper SP	.75	.30
35 Sixto Lezcano SP	.75	.30
36 Dave Rozema SP	.75	.30
37 Butch Wynegar SP	.75	.30
38 Mitchell Page SP	.75	.30
39 Bill Stein SP	.75	.30
40 Elliott Maddox	.50	.20
41 Mike Hargrove	.75	.30
42 Bobby Bonds	1.50	.60
43 Garry Templeton	.50	.20
44 Johnny Bench	8.00	3.20
45 Jim Rice	2.00	.80
46 Bill Buckner	.75	.30
47 Reggie Jackson	8.00	3.20
48 Freddie Patek	.50	.20
49 Steve Carlton	4.00	1.60
50 Cesar Cedeno	.75	.30
51 Steve Yeager	.50	.20
52 Phil Garner	.50	.20
53 Lee May	.75	.30
54 Darrell Evans	.75	.30
55 Steve Kemp	.50	.20
56 Dusty Baker	.75	.30
57 Ray Fosse	.50	.20
58 Manny Sanguillen	.50	.20
59 Tom Johnson	.50	.20
60 Lee Stanton	.50	.20
61 Jeff Burroughs	.50	.20
62 Bobby Grich	.75	.30
63 Dave Winfield	8.00	3.20
64 Dan Driessen	.50	.20
65 Ted Simmons	1.00	.40
66 Jerry Remy	.50	.20
67 Al Cowens	.50	.20
68 Sparky Lyle	.75	.30
69 Manny Trillo	.50	.20
70 Don Sutton	3.00	1.20
71 Larry Bowa	.75	.30
72 Jose Cruz	.75	.30
73 Willie McCovey	3.00	1.20
74 Bert Blyleven	1.00	.40
75 Ken Singleton	.50	.20
76 Bill North	.50	.20
77 Jason Thompson	.50	.20
78 Dennis Eckersley	5.00	2.00
79 Jim Sundberg	.50	.20
80 Jerry Koosman	.75	.30
81 Bruce Bochte	.50	.20
82 George Hendrick	.50	.20
83 Nolan Ryan	40.00	16.00
84 Roy Howell	.50	.20
85 Roger Metzger	.50	.20
86 Doc Medich	.50	.20
87 Joe Morgan	4.00	1.60
88 Dennis Leonard	.50	.20
89 Willie Randolph	1.00	.40
90 Bobby Murcer	.75	.30
91 Rick Manning	.50	.20
92 J.R. Richard	.50	.20
93 Ron Cey	.75	.30
94 Sal Bando	.50	.20
95 Ron LeFlore	.50	.20
96 Dave Goltz	.50	.20
97 Dan Meyer	.50	.20
98 Chris Chambliss	.75	.30
99 Biff Pocoroba	.50	.20
100 Oscar Gamble	.50	.20
101 Frank Tanana	.75	.30
102 Len Randle	.50	.20
103 Tommy Hutton	.50	.20
104 John Candelaria	.50	.20
105 Jorge Orta	.50	.20
106 Ken Reitz	.50	.20
107 Bill Campbell	.50	.20
108 Dave Concepcion	1.00	.40
109 Joe Ferguson	.50	.20
110 Mickey Rivers	.75	.30
111 Paul Splittorff	.50	.20
112 Dave Lopes	.50	.20
113 Mike Schmidt	10.00	4.00
114 Joe Rudi	.50	.20
115 Milt May	.50	.20
116 Jim Palmer	4.00	1.60
117 Bill Madlock	.75	.30
118 Roy Smalley	.50	.20
119 Cecil Cooper	.75	.30
120 Rick Langford	.50	.20
121 Ruppert Jones	.50	.20
122 Phil Niekro	3.00	1.20
123 Toby Harrah	.50	.20
124 Chet Lemon	.50	.20
125 Gene Tenace	.50	.20
126 Steve Henderson	.50	.20
127 Mike Torrez	.50	.20
128 Pete Rose	10.00	4.00
129 John Denny	.50	.20
130 Darrell Porter	.50	.20
131 Rick Reuschel	.50	.20
132 Graig Nettles	1.00	.40
133 Garry Maddox	.50	.20
134 Mike Flanagan	.50	.20
135 Dave Parker	1.50	.60
136 Terry Whitfield	.50	.20
137 Wayne Garland	.50	.20
138 Robin Yount	15.00	6.00
139 Gaylord Perry	3.00	1.20
140 Rod Carew	4.00	1.60
141 Wayne Gross	.50	.20
142 Barry Bonnell	.50	.20
143 Willie Montanez	.50	.20
144 Rollie Fingers	3.00	1.20
145 Lyman Bostock	.75	.30
146 Gary Carter	3.00	1.20
147 Ron Blomberg	.50	.20
148 Bob Bailor	.50	.20
149 Tom Seaver	6.00	2.40
150 Thurman Munson	3.00	1.20
XX Album	8.00	3.20

1979 Hostess

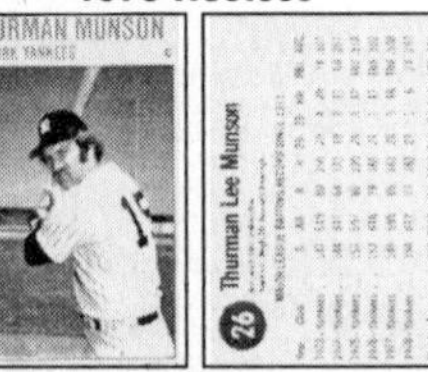

The cards in this 150-card set measure approximately 2 1/4" by 3 1/4" individually or 3 1/4" by 7 1/4" as panels of three. The 1979 Hostess set contains full color, numbered cards issued in panels of three cards each on the backs of family sized Hostess cake products. Scarcer cards are listed in the checklist below with SP. Although complete panel prices are not explicitly listed below they would generally have a value 20-25 percent greater than the sum of the individual players on the panel. The collectors who don't consider 1978 to be the most difficult Hostess to acquire, believe that 1979's are the toughest to get. The shelf life on the 1979's seemed to be slightly shorter than other years.There is additional interest in Ozzie Smith (102) since this card corresponds to his rookie year in cards. An album to hold these cards were issued.

	NM	Ex
COMP.INDIV.SET (150)	250.00	100.00
COMMON CARD (1-150)	.50	.20
COMMON SP	.75	.30
1 John Denny	.50	.20
2 Jim Rice	1.50	.60
3 Doug Bair	.50	.20
4 Darrell Porter	.50	.20
5 Ross Grimsley	.50	.20
6 Bobby Murcer	.75	.30
7 Lee Mazzilli	.50	.20
8 Steve Garvey	2.00	.80
9 Mike Schmidt	10.00	4.00
10 Terry Whitfield	.50	.20
11 Jim Palmer	4.00	1.60
12 Omar Moreno	.50	.20
13 Duane Kuiper	.50	.20
14 Mike Caldwell	.50	.20
15 Steve Kemp	.50	.20
16 Dave Goltz	.50	.20
17 Mitchell Page	.50	.20
18 Bill Stein	.50	.20
19 Gene Tenace	.50	.20
20 Jeff Burroughs	.50	.20
21 Francisco Barrios	.50	.20
22 Mike Torrez	.50	.20
23 Ken Reitz	.50	.20
24 Gary Carter	3.00	1.20
25 Al Hrabosky	.50	.20
26 Thurman Munson	3.00	1.20
27 Bill Buckner	.75	.30
28 Ron Cey SP	1.00	.40
29 J.R. Richard SP	1.00	.40
30 Greg Luzinski SP	1.00	.40
31 Ed Ott SP	.75	.30
32 Dennis Martinez SP	3.00	1.20
33 Darrell Evans SP	1.00	.40
34 Ron LeFlore	.50	.20
35 Rick Waits	.50	.20
36 Cecil Cooper	.75	.30
37 Leon Roberts	.50	.20
38 Rod Carew	4.00	1.60
39 John Henry Johnson	.50	.20
40 Chet Lemon	.50	.20
41 Craig Swan	.50	.20
42 Gary Matthews	.50	.20
43 Lamar Johnson	.50	.20
44 Ted Simmons	.75	.30
45 Ken Griffey	.75	.30
46 Fred Patek	.50	.20
47 Frank Tanana	.75	.30
48 Goose Gossage	1.00	.40
49 Burt Hooton	.50	.20
50 Ellis Valentine	.50	.20
51 Ken Forsch	.50	.20
52 Bob Knepper	.50	.20
53 Dave Parker	1.50	.60
54 Doug DeCinces	.50	.20
55 Robin Yount	10.00	4.00
56 Rusty Staub	.75	.30
57 Gary Alexander	.50	.20
58 Julio Cruz	.50	.20
59 Matt Keough	.50	.20
60 Roy Smalley	.50	.20
61 Joe Morgan	4.00	1.60
62 Phil Niekro	3.00	1.20
63 Don Baylor	.75	.30
64 Dwight Evans	1.00	.40
65 Tom Seaver	6.00	2.40
66 George Hendrick	.50	.20
67 Rick Reuschel	.50	.20
68 George Brett	15.00	6.00
69 Lou Piniella	.75	.30
70 Enos Cabell	.50	.20
71 Steve Carlton	4.00	1.60
72 Reggie Smith	.75	.30
73 Rick Dempsey SP	1.00	.40
74 Vida Blue SP	1.50	.60
75 Phil Garner SP	.75	.30
76 Rick Manning SP	.75	.30
77 Mark Fidrych SP	2.50	1.00
78 Mario Guerrero SP	.75	.30
79 Bob Stinson SP	.75	.30
80 Al Oliver SP	1.50	.60
81 Doug Flynn SP	.75	.30
82 John Mayberry	.50	.20
83 Gaylord Perry	3.00	1.20
84 Joe Rudi	.50	.20
85 Dave Concepcion	1.00	.40
86 John Candelaria	.50	.20
87 Pete Vuckovich	.50	.20
88 Ivan DeJesus	.50	.20
89 Ron Guidry	1.00	.40
90 Hal McRae	.75	.30
91 Cesar Cedeno	.50	.20
92 Don Sutton	3.00	1.20
93 Andre Thornton	.50	.20
94 Roger Erickson	.50	.20
95 Larry Hisle	.50	.20
96 Jason Thompson	.50	.20
97 Jim Sundberg	.50	.20
98 Bob Horner	.75	.30
99 Ruppert Jones	.50	.20
100 Willie Montanez	.50	.20
101 Nolan Ryan	40.00	16.00
102 Ozzie Smith	40.00	16.00
103 Eric Soderholm	.50	.20
104 Willie Stargell	3.00	1.20
105A Bob Bailor ERR	.75	.30
(Reverse negative)		
105B Bob Bailor COR	1.50	.60
106 Carlton Fisk	8.00	3.20
107 George Foster	.75	.30
108 Keith Hernandez	1.50	.60
109 Dennis Leonard	.50	.20
110 Graig Nettles	1.00	.40
111 Jose Cruz	.75	.30
112 Bobby Grich	.75	.30
113 Bob Boone	.75	.30
114 Dave Lopes	.50	.20
115 Eddie Murray	15.00	6.00
116 Jack Clark	1.00	.40
117 Lou Whitaker	4.00	1.60
118 Miguel Dilone	.50	.20
119 Sal Bando	.50	.20
120 Reggie Jackson	10.00	4.00
121 Dale Murphy	8.00	3.20
122 Jon Matlack	.50	.20
123 Bruce Bochte	.50	.20
124 John Stearns	.50	.20
125 Dave Winfield	8.00	3.20
126 Jorge Orta	.50	.20
127 Garry Templeton	.50	.20
128 Johnny Bench	6.00	2.40
129 Butch Hobson	.50	.20
130 Bruce Sutter	.75	.30
131 Bucky Dent	.75	.30
132 Amos Otis	.50	.20
133 Bert Blyleven	1.00	.40
134 Larry Bowa	.75	.30
135 Ken Singleton	.50	.20
136 Sixto Lezcano	.50	.20
137 Roy Howell	.50	.20
138 Bill Madlock	.75	.30
139 Dave Revering	.50	.20
140 Richie Zisk	.50	.20
141 Butch Wynegar	.50	.20
142 Alan Ashby	.50	.20
143 Sparky Lyle	.75	.30
144 Pete Rose	10.00	4.00
145 Dennis Eckersley	2.50	1.00
146 Dave Kingman	1.00	.40
147 Buddy Bell	.75	.30
148 Mike Hargrove	.75	.30
149 Jerry Koosman	.75	.30
150 Toby Harrah	.50	.20
XX Album	8.00	3.20

1987 Hostess Stickers

This set of 30 small, full-color stickers was produced in Canada by Hostess Potato Chips and distributed in bags of potato chips. Each sticker was loosely wrapped in cellophane (to protect against potato chip stains) and measures approximately 1 3/8" by 1 3/4" with rounded corners. The backs of the stickers contain the player's name, team and position in English as well as in French. They are numbered on the front in the lower left corner. The first six cards are Blue Jays and Expos; the rest of the set consists of one player per American team.

	Nm-Mt	Ex-Mt
COMPLETE SET (30)	40.00	16.00
1 Jesse Barfield	.50	.20
2 Ernie Whitt	.50	.20
3 George Bell	.50	.20
4 Hubie Brooks	.50	.20
5 Tim Wallach	.50	.20
6 Floyd Youmans	.50	.20
7 Dale Murphy	1.50	.60
8 Ryne Sandberg	5.00	2.00
9 Eric Davis	1.00	.40
10 Mike Scott	.50	.20
11 Fernando Valenzuela	.75	.30
12 Gary Carter	2.00	.80
13 Mike Schmidt	2.50	1.00
14 Tony Pena	.75	.30
15 Ozzie Smith	5.00	2.00
16 Tony Gwynn	5.00	2.00
17 Mike Krukow	.50	.20
18 Eddie Murray	3.00	1.20
19 Wade Boggs	2.00	.80
20 Wally Joyner	1.50	.60
21 Harold Baines	.75	.30
22 Brook Jacoby	.50	.20
23 Lou Whitaker	.75	.30
24 George Brett	5.00	2.00
25 Robin Yount	2.00	.80
26 Kirby Puckett	2.50	1.00
27 Don Mattingly	5.00	2.00
28 Jose Canseco	2.00	.80
29 Phil Bradley	.50	.20
30 Pete O'Brien	.50	.20

1993 Hostess

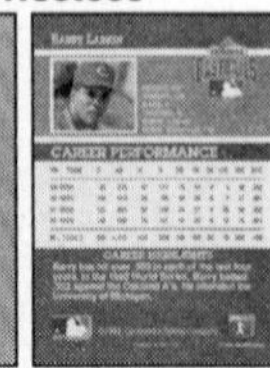

These standard-size cards were free with the purchase of packages of Hostess Baseballs, a new snack food. The frosted yellow cakes have creamy filling and were decorated with red icing to resemble the stitching of a baseball. Each two-cake snack pack contained one three-card pack and cost 85 cents, while each eight-cake family pack contained two packs and cost 2.99. The cards were issued in two series (1-16 and 17-32), the first being available nationally beginning on April 12 and the second series beginning mid-season. A checklist was included on the back of each family pack.

	Nm-Mt	Ex-Mt
COMPLETE SET (32)	6.00	1.80
1 Andy Van Slyke	.10	.03
2 Ryne Sandberg	.50	.15
3 Bobby Bonilla	.10	.03
4 John Kruk	.20	.06
5 Ray Lankford	.20	.06
6 Gary Sheffield	.50	.15
7 Darryl Strawberry	.20	.06
8 Barry Larkin	.40	.12
9 Terry Pendleton	.10	.03
10 Jose Canseco	.50	.15
11 Dennis Eckersley	.50	.15
12 Brian McRae	.10	.03
13 Frank Thomas	.50	.15
14 Roberto Alomar	.40	.12
15 Carlos Baerga	.10	.03
16 Cecil Fielder	.20	.06
17 Will Clark	.40	.12
18 Andres Galarraga	.40	.12
19 Jeff Bagwell	.40	.12
20 Brett Butler	.20	.06
21 Benito Santiago	.20	.06
22 Tom Glavine	.40	.12
23 Rickey Henderson	.50	.15
24 Wally Joyner	.20	.06
25 Ken Griffey Jr.	1.00	.30
26 Cal Ripken	1.50	.45
27 Roger Clemens	.75	.23
28 Don Mattingly	.75	.23
29 Kirby Puckett	.50	.15
30 Larry Walker	.20	.06
31 Jack McDowell	.10	.03
32 Pat Listach	.10	.03

1990 Hottest 50 Players Stickers

Issued by Publications International, this sticker album measures 8 1/4" by 10 7/8" and includes 50 giant player stickers and 6 bonus stadium stickers. The oversized stickers measure 4 1/8 by 5 1/2" and feature glossy color action player photos inside a white border. The NL players stickers have a red stripe at the top and a blue stripe at the bottom, while the AL Rookies stickers have a blue stripe at the top and a red stripe at the bottom. The 32-page sticker album has slots for two stickers per page and presents career summary, biography, and statistics out to the side. The stickers are unnumbered and checklisted below in alphabetical order.

	Nm-Mt	Ex-Mt
COMPLETE SET (56)	35.00	10.50
1 George Bell	.25	.07
2 Wade Boggs	2.00	.60
3 Bobby Bonilla	.25	.07
4 Jose Canseco	1.50	.45
5 Joe Carter	.50	.15
6 Will Clark	1.50	.45
7 Roger Clemens	4.00	1.20
8 Alvin Davis	.25	.07
9 Eric Davis	.50	.15
10 Glenn Davis	.25	.07
11 Mark Davis	.25	.07
12 Carlton Fisk	2.00	.60
13 John Franco	.50	.15
14 Gary Gaetti	.25	.07
15 Andres Galarraga	1.00	.30
16 Dwight Gooden	.50	.15
17 Mark Grace	1.00	.30
18 Pedro Guerrero	.25	.07
19 Tony Gwynn	4.00	1.20
20 Rickey Henderson	2.50	.75
21 Orel Hershiser	.50	.15
22 Bo Jackson	1.00	.30
23 Ricky Jordan	.25	.07

24 Wally Joyner .50 .15
25 Don Mattingly 4.00 1.20
26 Fred McGriff .75 .23
27 Kevin Mitchell .25 .07
28 Paul Molitor 1.25 .35
29 Dale Murphy 1.00 .30
30 Eddie Murray 1.25 .35
31 Kirby Puckett 2.00 .60
32 Tim Raines .50 .15
33 Harold Reynolds .50 .15
34 Cal Ripken Jr. 8.00 2.40
35 Nolan Ryan 8.00 2.40
36 Bret Saberhagen .50 .15
37 Ryne Sandberg 4.00 1.20
38 Steve Sax .25 .07
39 Mike Scott .25 .07
40 Ruben Sierra .50 .15
41 Ozzie Smith 4.00 1.20
42 John Smoltz 1.00 .30
43 Darryl Strawberry .50 .15
44 Greg Swindell .25 .07
45 Mickey Tettleton .50 .15
46 Alan Trammell .75 .23
47 Andy Van Slyke .50 .15
48 Lou Whitaker .50 .15
49 Devon White .25 .07
50 Robin Yount 2.00 .60
51 Dodger Stadium .25 .07
52 Jack Murphy Stadium .25 .07
53 Shea Stadium .25 .07
54 Three Rivers Stadium .25 .07
55 Tiger Stadium .25 .07
56 Yankee Stadium .25 .07

1990 Hottest 50 Rookies Stickers

Issued by Publications International, this sticker album measures 8 1/4" by 10 7/8" and includes 50 giant rookie stickers and 6 bonus stadium stickers. The oversized stickers measure 4 1/8 by 5 1/2" and feature glossy color action player photos inside a white border. The NL Rookie stickers have a red stripe at the top and a blue stripe at the bottom, while the AL Rookie stickers have a blue stripe at the top and a red stripe at the bottom. The 32-page sticker album has slots for two stickers per page and presents career summary, biography, and statistics out to the side. The stickers are unnumbered and checklisted below in alphabetical order.

Nm-Mt Ex-Mt
COMPLETE SET (56) 30.00 9.00
1 Jim Abbott .50 .15
2 Sandy Alomar Jr. .50 .15
3 Kent Anderson .25 .07
4 Eric Anthony .25 .07
5 Jeff Ballard .25 .07
6 Albert Belle .50 .15
7 Andy Benes .25 .07
8 Lance Blankenship .25 .07
9 Jeff Brantley .50 .15
10 Cris Carpenter .25 .07
11 Mark Carreon .25 .07
12 Dennis Cook .25 .07
13 Scott Coolbaugh .25 .07
14 Luis de los Santos .25 .07
15 Junior Felix .25 .07
16 Mark Gardner .25 .07
17 German Gonzalez .25 .07
18 Tom Gordon .50 .15
19 Ken Griffey Jr. 5.00 1.50
20 Marquis Grissom .75 .23
21 Charlie Hayes .25 .07
22 Gregg Jefferies .25 .07
23 Randy Johnson 4.00 1.20
24 Felix Jose .25 .07
25 Jeff King .25 .07
26 Randy Kramer .25 .07
27 Derek Lilliquist .25 .07
28 Greg Litton .25 .07
29 Kelly Mann .25 .07
30 Ramon Martinez .50 .15
31 Luis Medina .25 .07
32 Hal Morris .25 .07
33 Joe Oliver .25 .07
34 Gregg Olson .50 .15
35 Dean Palmer 1.00 .30
36 Carlos Quintana .25 .07
37 Kevin Ritz .25 .07
38 Deion Sanders 1.50 .45
39 Scott Scudder .25 .07
40 Steve Searcy .25 .07
41 Gary Sheffield 2.00 .60
42 Dwight Smith .25 .07
43 Sammy Sosa 8.00 2.40
44 Greg Vaughn .50 .15
45 Robin Ventura 1.00 .30
46 Jerome Walton .25 .07
47 Dave West .25 .07
48 John Wetteland 1.00 .30
49 Eric Yelding .25 .07
50 Todd Zeile .50 .15
51 Dodger Stadium .25 .07
52 Jack Murphy Stadium .25 .07
53 Shea Stadium .25 .07
54 Three Rivers Stadium .25 .07
55 Tiger Stadium .25 .07
56 Yankee Stadium .25 .07

1970 House of Jazz

This 33-card set features black-and-white photos of great baseball players and measures approximately 2 1/2" by 3 1/2". The cards were originally issued as a premium with record purchases by a specialty record store in Glenside, PA and was distriubted in seven different series. Originally planned as a 35-card set, the cards of Stan Lopata and Mickey Mantle, planned for the second series, were lost or destroyed in production. No more than 100 of each card was ever printed. The cards are unnumbered and checklisted below in alphabetical order.

NM Ex
COMPLETE SET (33) 350.00 140.00
1 Bill Antonelli 2.00 .80
2 Rich Ashburn 10.00 4.00
3 Ernie Banks 10.00 4.00
4 Hank Bauer 3.00 1.20
5 Joe DiMaggio 40.00 16.00
6 Bobby Doerr 4.00 1.60
7 Herman Franks 2.00 .80
8 Lou Gehrig 40.00 16.00
9 Granny Hamner 2.00 .80
10 Al Kaline 10.00 4.00
11 Harmon Killebrew 10.00 4.00
12 Jim Konstanty 2.50 1.00
13 Bob Lemon 4.00 1.60
14 Ed Lopat 2.50 1.00
15 Harry Lowrey 2.00 .80
16 Phil Marchildon 2.00 .80
17 Walt Masterson 2.00 .80
18 Eddie Mathews 10.00 4.00
19 Willie Mays 30.00 12.00
20 Don Newcombe 3.00 1.20
21 Joe Nuxhall 2.00 .80
22 Satchel Paige 30.00 12.00
23 Roy Partee 2.00 .80
24 Jackie Robinson 40.00 16.00
25 Babe Ruth 50.00 20.00
26 Carl Scheib 2.00 .80
27 Bobby Shantz 2.50 1.00
28 Burt Shotton 2.00 .80
29 Duke Snider 15.00 6.00
30 Warren Spahn 10.00 4.00
31 Johnny Temple 2.00 .80
32 Ted Williams 40.00 16.00
33 Early Wynn 10.00 4.00

1988 Houston Show

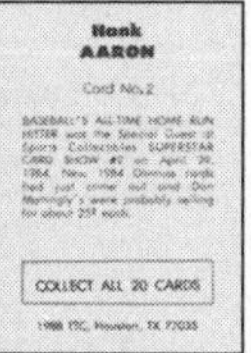

This 20-card set measures approximately 2 1/4" by 3 1/4". On a white card face, the fronts feature black-and-white player photos accented by a purple picture frame. A white star appears at each corner of the frame, and a row of purple stars edges the pictures on the left and right sides. The backs carry the player's name, the card number, a career summary, and "1988 TTC, Houston TX 77035" as a tagline.

Nm-Mt Ex-Mt
COMPLETE SET (20) 30.00 12.00
1 Brooks Robinson 2.00 .80
2 Hank Aaron 8.00 3.20
3 Gaylord Perry 1.00 .40
4 Stan Musial 6.00 2.40
5 Willie Mays 8.00 3.20
6 Ernie Banks 3.00 1.20
7 Rod Carew 2.00 .80
8 Duke Snider 2.00 .80
9 Mickey Mantle 15.00 6.00
10 Lou Brock 2.00 .80
11 Yogi Berra 2.00 .80
12 Nolan Ryan 12.00 4.80
13 Roger Clemens 4.00 1.60
14 Jose Cruz .50 .20
15 Gerald Young .25 .10
16 Enos Slaughter 1.00 .40
17 Glenn Davis .25 .10
18 J.R. Richard .25 .10
19 Fergie Jenkins 1.00 .40
20 Pete Incaviglia .25 .10

1979 Elston Howard Sausage

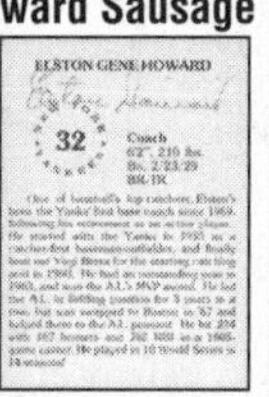

This one-card set features a small black-and-white head photo of Elston Howard of the New York Yankees on a black card with white printing. The white back displays information about the player. Some of the cards were personally autographed. The card was used as a business card advertising Elston Howard's Sausage, a division of Piedmont Provision Co.

NM Ex
1 Elston Howard 10.00 4.00

1953-59 Howard Photo Service PC751

The Howard Photo Service late 1950's postcard set was, until recently, thought to contain only the Bob Turley card. However, the recently discovered cards indicates that additional cards may be found in the future. These black and white postcards were issued in New York.

NM Ex
COMPLETE SET (5) 50.00 25.00
1 Ned Garver 10.00 5.00
2 Billy Hitchcock 10.00 5.00
3 Dave Madison 10.00 5.00
4 Willie Mays 40.00 20.00
5 Bob Turley 15.00 7.50

1997 Howard University Robinson

This one-card set measures approximately 4 1/4" by 6" and features a black-and-white action photo of Jackie Robinson. The back displays information about some important events in the history of African Americans in athletics.

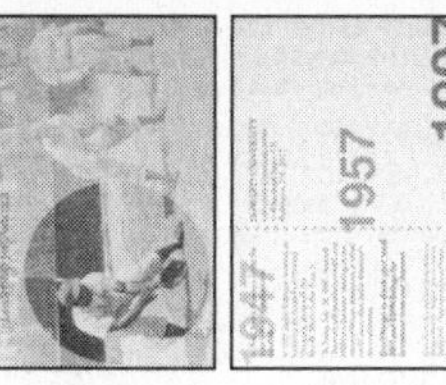

Nm-Mt Ex-Mt
1 Jackie Robinson 3.00 .90

1993 Hoyle

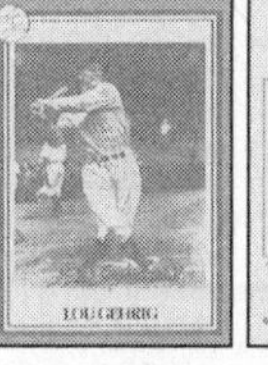

One of these nine cards was inserted in specially marked Hoyle Official Playing Card decks. The back of the card box contains a checklist for all nine cards and an opening at the bottom, where the name of the player whose card is inserted in the pack appears. The cards measure the standard size and have rounded corners. On a grey background, the fronts feature black-and-white action player photos with black and white borders. The player's name appears in a white bar under the photo, while a facsimile autograph printed on the lower portion of the photo. The backs carry a player biography and stats. The cards are unnumbered and checklisted below in alphabetical order.

Nm-Mt Ex-Mt
COMPLETE SET (9) 10.00 3.00
1 Ty Cobb 2.00 .60
2 Dizzy Dean 1.00 .30
3 Lou Gehrig 2.00 .60
4 Walter Johnson 1.25 .35
5 Satchel Paige 1.25 .35
6 Babe Ruth 2.00 .60
7 Casey Stengel 1.00 .30
8 Honus Wagner 1.25 .35
9 Cy Young 1.25 .35

1993 Humpty Dumpty Canadian

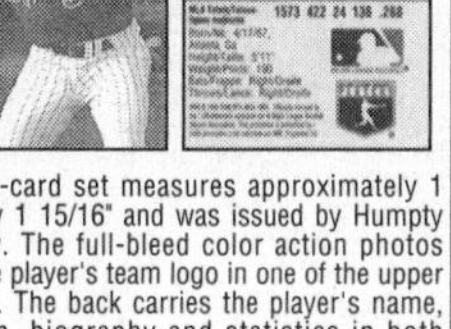

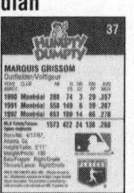

This 51-card set measures approximately 1 7/16" by 1 15/16" and was issued by Humpty Dumpty. The full-bleed color action photos have the player's team logo in one of the upper corners. The back carries the player's name, position, biography and statistics in both French and English. The Humpty Dumpty logo appears at the top over a navy blue border. The cards are numbered on the back.

Nm-Mt Ex-Mt
COMPLETE SET (51) 35.00 10.50
1 Cal Ripken 5.00 1.50
2 Mike Mussina 1.00 .30
3 Roger Clemens 2.50 .75
4 Chuck Finley .50 .15
5 Sandy Alomar Jr. .50 .15
6 Frank Thomas 1.25 .35
7 Robin Ventura .75 .23
8 Cecil Fielder .50 .15
9 George Brett 2.50 .75
10 Cal Eldred .25 .07
11 Kirby Puckett 1.25 .35
12 Dave Winfield 1.25 .35
13 Jim Abbott .25 .07
14 Rickey Henderson 1.50 .45
15 Ken Griffey Jr. 3.00 .90
16 Nolan Ryan 5.00 1.50
17 Ivan Rodriguez 1.25 .35
18 Paul Molitor 1.25 .35
19 John Olerud .75 .23
20 Joe Carter .50 .15
21 Jack Morris .50 .15
22 Roberto Alomar 1.00 .30
23 Pat Borders .25 .07
24 Devon White .25 .07
25 Juan Guzman .25 .07
26 Steve Avery .25 .07
27 John Smoltz .75 .23
28 Mark Grace 1.00 .30
29 Jose Rijo .25 .07
30 David Nied .25 .07
31 Benito Santiago .50 .15
32 Jeff Bagwell 1.50 .45
33 Tim Wallach .25 .07
34 Eric Karros .50 .15
35 Delino DeShields .25 .07
36 Wilfredo Cordero .25 .07
37 Marquis Grissom .50 .15
38 Ken Hill .25 .07
39 Moises Alou .50 .15
40 Chris Nabholz .25 .07
41 Dennis Martinez .50 .15
42 Larry Walker .75 .23
43 Bobby Bonilla .25 .07
44 Len Dykstra .50 .15
45 Tim Wakefield 1.00 .30
46 Andy Van Slyke .25 .07
47 Tony Gwynn 2.50 .75
48 Fred McGriff .75 .23
49 Barry Bonds 2.50 .75
50 Ozzie Smith 2.50 .75
51 Checklist 1-51 .25 .07
xx Album 5.00 1.50

1987 Hygrade All-Time Greats

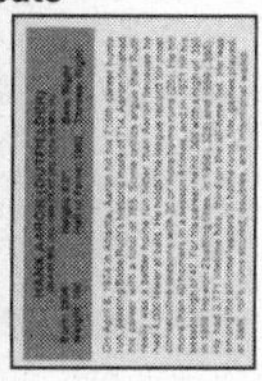

This 50-card set features some of the best players in Baseball of all time. The fronts carry a color player photo in a green border. A small gold oval in the lower left indicates the player's playing years. The backs display player information and why the player is one of the all-time greats. It is believed that these cards were actually issued at a couple different times, therefore cropping differences may exist for all players. The cards are unnumbered and checklisted below in alphabetical order. The cards we have listed as 51 through 100 have a heavier stock of cardboard.

Nm-Mt Ex-Mt
COMPLETE SET 30.00 12.00
1 Hank Aaron 1.00 .40
2 Grover Alexander .50 .20
3 Luke Appling .10 .04
4 Ernie Banks .50 .20
5 Yogi Berra .50 .20
6 Three Finger Brown .10 .04
7 Roy Campanella .50 .20
8 Roberto Clemente 1.00 .40
9 Ty Cobb 1.00 .40
10 Mickey Cochrane .25 .10
11 Eddie Collins .25 .10
12 Sam Crawford .25 .10
13 Joe Cronin .10 .04
14 Bill Dickey .25 .10
15 Joe DiMaggio 1.00 .40
16 Bob Feller .25 .10
17 Whitey Ford .50 .20
18 Jimmie Foxx .50 .20
19 Frankie Frisch .10 .04
20 Lou Gehrig 1.00 .40
21 Charlie Gehringer .10 .04
22 Hank Greenberg .50 .20
23 Lefty Grove .25 .10
24 Gabby Hartnett .10 .04
25 Rogers Hornsby .50 .20
26 Carl Hubbell .50 .20
27 Walter Johnson .75 .30
28 Jim Kaat .10 .04
Chi White Sox
29 Ralph Kiner .10 .04
30 Don Larsen .10 .04
31 Mickey Mantle 1.50 .60
32 Christy Mathewson .10 .04
33 Willie Mays 1.00 .40
34 Stan Musial .50 .20
35 Mel Ott .10 .04
36 Brooks Robinson .50 .20
37 Jackie Robinson 1.00 .40
38 Babe Ruth 1.50 .60
39 Al Simmons .10 .04
40 George Sisler .10 .04
41 Duke Snider .50 .20
42 Tris Speaker .10 .04
43 Bill Terry .10 .04
44 Pie Traynor .25 .10
45 Ed Walsh .10 .04
46 Paul Waner .25 .10
47 Billy Williams .25 .10
48 Ted Williams 1.00 .40
49 Maury Wills .10 .04
50 Ross Youngs .10 .04
51 Joe Adcock .10 .04
52 Dick Allen .10 .04
53 Luis Aparicio .25 .10
54 Richie Ashburn .25 .10
55 Hank Bauer .10 .04
56 Johnny Bench .75 .30
57 Lou Boudreau .25 .10
58 Lou Brock .25 .10
59 Jim Bunning .25 .10
60 Rod Carew .75 .30
61 Orlando Cepeda .25 .10
62 Rocky Colavito .50 .20
63 Larry Doby .25 .10
64 Don Drysdale .75 .30
65 Leo Durocher .25 .10
66 Carl Erskine .10 .04
67 Curt Flood .10 .04
68 Carl Furillo .10 .04
69 Gil Hodges .25 .10
70 Catfish Hunter .50 .20
71 Monte Irvin .25 .10
72 Fergie Jenkins .25 .10
73 Jim Kaat .25 .10
St. Louis
74 George Kell .25 .10
75 Ted Kluszewski .25 .10
76 Bob Lemon .25 .10
77 Ernie Lombardi .25 .10
78 Eddie Lopat .10 .04
79 Juan Marichal .50 .20
80 Roger Maris .50 .20
81 Billy Martin .25 .10
82 Eddie Mathews .75 .30
83 Bill Mazeroski .25 .10
84 Joe Morgan .75 .30
85 Thurman Munson 1.00 .40
86 Tony Oliva .25 .10
87 Jim Palmer .50 .20
88 Gaylord Perry .25 .10
89 Boog Powell .25 .10
90 Pee Wee Reese 1.00 .40
91 Robin Roberts .25 .10
92 Tom Seaver 1.00 .40
93 Bobby Shantz .25 .10
94 Enos Slaughter .25 .10
95 Duke Snider 1.00 .40
96 Willie Stargell .75 .30
97 Bobby Thomson .25 .10
98 Hoyt Wilhelm .25 .10
99 Early Wynn .25 .10
100 Carl Yastrzemski .50 .20

1996 Illinois Lottery

This five-card set consists of legendary Chicago Cubs and White Sox players and also included St. Louis Cardinals player, Red Schoendeinst. The cards are actually real Illinois scratch-off lottery ticket stubs and can be found scratched or unscratched. The cards are unnumbered and checklisted below in alphabetical order.

Nm-Mt Ex-Mt
COMPLETE SET (5) 5.00 1.50
1 Ernie Banks 2.00 .60
2 Carlton Fisk 2.00 .60
3 Minnie Minoso 1.00 .30
4 Red Schoendeinst 1.25 .35
5 Billy Williams 1.50 .45

2000 Impact

The 2000 Impact product (produced by Fleer) was released in July, 2000 as a 200-card set. The set features 175 veteran players and 25 prospect cards. Each pack contained 10 cards, and carried a suggested retail price of $.99. Despite the obvious need for the hobby to offer affordable packs to children and other newer collectors, this product was largely met with indifference in the secondary market.

Nm-Mt Ex-Mt
COMPLETE SET (200) 15.00 4.50
1 Cal Ripken 1.50 .45
2 Jose Canseco .50 .15
3 Manny Ramirez .20 .06
4 Bernie Williams .30 .09
5 Troy Glaus .30 .09
6 Jeff Bagwell .30 .09
7 Corey Koskie .20 .06
8 Barry Larkin .50 .15
9 Mark Quinn .20 .06
10 Russ Ortiz .20 .06
11 Tim Salmon .30 .09
12 Preston Wilson .20 .06
13 Mo Vaughn .20 .06
14 Ray Lankford .20 .06
15 Sterling Hitchcock .20 .06
16 Al Leiter .20 .06
17 Jim Morris 1.25 .35
18 Freddy Garcia .20 .06
19 Adrian Beltre .20 .06
20 Eric Chavez .20 .06
21 Robinson Cancel .20 .06
22 Edgar Renteria .20 .06
23 John Jaha .20 .06
24 Chuck Finley .20 .06
25 Andres Galarraga .20 .06
26 Paul Byrd .20 .06
27 John Halama .20 .06
28 Eric Karros .20 .06
29 Mike Piazza .75 .23
30 Ryan Rupe .20 .06
31 Frank Thomas .50 .15
32 Randy Velarde .20 .06
33 Bobby Abreu .20 .06
34 Randy Johnson .50 .15
35 Matt Williams .20 .06
36 Tony Gwynn .60 .18
37 Dean Palmer .20 .06
38 Aaron Sele .20 .06
39 Rondell White .20 .06
40 Erubiel Durazo .20 .06
41 Curt Schilling .30 .09
42 Kip Wells .20 .06
43 Craig Biggio .30 .09
44 Tom Glavine .30 .09
45 Trevor Hoffman .20 .06
46 Greg Vaughn .20 .06
47 Edgar Martinez .30 .09
48 Maggio Ordonez .20 .06
49 Mark Mulder .30 .09
50 John Rocker .20 .06
51 Kenny Rogers .20 .06
52 Gary Sheffield .20 .06
53 Brian Simmons .20 .06
54 Tony Womack .20 .06
55 Ken Caminiti .20 .06
56 Jeff Cirillo .20 .06
57 Ray Durham .20 .06
58 Mike Lieberthal .20 .06
59 Ruben Mateo .20 .06
60 Mike Cameron .20 .06
61 Rusty Greer .20 .06
62 Alex Rodriguez .75 .23
63 Robin Ventura .20 .06

2000 Impact

64 Pokey Reese .20 .06
65 Jose Lima .20 .06
66 Neifi Perez .20 .06
67 Rafael Palmeiro .30 .09
68 Scott Rolen .30 .09
69 Mike Hampton .20 .06
70 Sammy Sosa .75 .23
71 Mike Stanley .20 .06
72 Dan Wilson .20 .06
73 Kerry Wood .50 .15
74 Mike Mussina .50 .15
75 Masato Yoshii .20 .06
76 Peter Bergeron .20 .06
77 Carlos Delgado .20 .06
78 Juan Encarnacion .20 .06
79 Nomar Garciaparra .75 .23
80 Jason Kendall .20 .06
81 Pedro Martinez .50 .15
82 Darin Erstad .20 .06
83 Larry Walker .30 .09
84 Rick Ankiel .20 .06
85 Scott Erickson .20 .06
86 Roger Clemens 1.00 .30
87 Matt Lawton .20 .06
88 Jon Lieber .20 .06
89 Shane Reynolds .20 .06
90 Ivan Rodriguez .50 .15
91 Pat Burrell .30 .09
92 Kent Bottenfield .20 .06
93 David Cone .20 .06
94 Mark Grace .30 .09
95 Paul Konerko .20 .06
96 Eric Milton .20 .06
97 Lee Stevens .20 .06
98 B.J. Surhoff .20 .06
99 Billy Wagner .20 .06
100 Ken Griffey Jr. .75 .23
101 Randy Wolf .20 .06
102 Henry Rodriguez .20 .06
103 Carlos Beltran .20 .06
104 Rich Aurilia .20 .06
105 Chipper Jones .50 .15
106 Homer Bush .20 .06
107 Johnny Damon .20 .06
108 J.D. Drew .20 .06
109 Orlando Hernandez .20 .06
110 Brad Radke .20 .06
111 Wilton Veras .20 .06
112 Dmitri Young .20 .06
113 Jermaine Dye .20 .06
114 Kris Benson .20 .06
115 Derek Jeter 1.25 .35
116 Cole Liniak .20 .06
117 Jim Thome .50 .15
118 Pedro Astacio .20 .06
119 Carlos Febles .20 .06
120 Darryl Kile .20 .06
121 Alfonso Soriano .50 .15
122 Michael Barrett .20 .06
123 Ellis Burks .20 .06
124 Chad Hermansen .20 .06
125 Trot Nixon .30 .09
126 Bobby Higginson .20 .06
127 Rick Helling .20 .06
128 Chris Carpenter .20 .06
129 Vinny Castilla .20 .06
130 Brian Giles .20 .06
131 Todd Helton .30 .09
132 Jason Varitek .20 .06
133 Rob Ducey .20 .06
134 Octavio Dotel .20 .06
135 Adam Kennedy .20 .06
136 Jeff Kent .20 .06
137 Aaron Boone .20 .06
138 Todd Walker .20 .06
139 Jeromy Burnitz .20 .06
140 Roberto Hernandez .20 .06
141 Matt LeCroy .20 .06
142 Ugueth Urbina .20 .06
143 David Wells .20 .06
144 Luis Gonzalez .20 .06
145 Andruw Jones .20 .06
146 Juan Gonzalez .50 .15
147 Moises Alou .20 .06
148 Michael Tejera .20 .06
149 Brian Jordan .20 .06
150 Mark McGwire 1.25 .35
151 Shawn Green .20 .06
152 Jay Bell .20 .06
153 Fred McGriff .30 .09
154 Rey Ordonez .20 .06
155 Matt Stairs .20 .06
156 A.J. Burnett .20 .06
157 Omar Vizquel .20 .06
158 Damion Easley .20 .06
159 Dante Bichette .20 .06
160 Javy Lopez .20 .06
161 Fernando Seguignol .20 .06
162 Richie Sexson .20 .06
163 Vladimir Guerrero .50 .15
164 Kevin Young .20 .06
165 Josh Beckett .60 .18
166 Albert Belle .20 .06
167 Cliff Floyd .20 .06
168 Gabe Kapler .20 .06
169 Nick Johnson .20 .06
170 Raul Mondesi .20 .06
171 Warren Morris .20 .06
172 Kenny Lofton .20 .06
173 Reggie Sanders .20 .06
174 Mike Sweeney .20 .06
175 Robert Fick .20 .06
176 Barry Bonds 1.25 .35
177 Luis Castillo .20 .06
178 Roger Cedeno .20 .06
179 Jim Edmonds .20 .06
180 Geoff Jenkins .20 .06
181 Adam Piatt .20 .06
182 Phil Nevin .20 .06
183 Roberto Alomar .50 .15
184 Kevin Brown .20 .06
185 D.T. Cromer .20 .06
186 Jason Giambi .50 .15
187 Fernando Tatis .20 .06
188 Brady Anderson .20 .06
189 Tony Clark .20 .06
190 Alex Fernandez .20 .06
191 Matt Blank .20 .06
192 Greg Maddux .75 .23
193 Kevin Millwood .20 .06
194 Jason Schmidt .20 .06
195 Shannon Stewart .20 .06
196 Rolando Arrojo .20 .06
197 Darren Dreifort .20 .06
198 Ben Grieve .20 .06
199 Bartolo Colon .20 .06
200 Sean Casey .20 .06

2000 Impact Genuine Coverage

Randomly inserted into packs at a rate of one in 720 hobby and one in 2500 retail, this insert set features swatches of game-used batting gloves incorporated directly into the card. They are some of the toughest memorabilia cards to located on the secondary market and share a very similar design to other Genuine Coverage memorabilia cards issued in 2000 SkyBox packs.

	Nm-Mt	Ex-Mt
1 Bob Abreu	15.00	4.50
2 Glen Barker	15.00	4.50
3 Barry Bonds	80.00	24.00
4 Jose Cruz Jr.	15.00	4.50
5 Ben Davis	15.00	4.50
6 Jason Giambi	25.00	7.50
7 Trevor Hoffman	15.00	4.50
8 Jacque Jones	15.00	4.50
9 Jason LaRue	15.00	4.50
10 Matt Lawton	15.00	4.50
11 Carlos Lee	15.00	4.50
12 Cole Liniak	15.00	4.50
13 Joe Nathan	15.00	4.50
14 Magglio Ordonez	15.00	4.50
15 Rafael Palmeiro	25.00	7.50
16 Alex Rodriguez	60.00	18.00
17 Shannon Stewart	15.00	4.50
18 Mike Sweeney	15.00	4.50

2000 Impact Mighty Fine in '99

Inserted at one per pack, this 40-card insert set features players that had outstanding seasons in 1999. The first 25 cards from this set feature members of the World Champion 1999 New York Yankees squad. Card backs carry a "MF" prefix.

	Nm-Mt	Ex-Mt
COMPLETE SET (40)	15.00	4.50
MF1 Clay Bellinger	.30	.09
MF2 Scott Brosius	.30	.09
MF3 Roger Clemens	1.50	.45
MF4 David Cone	.30	.09
MF5 Chad Curtis	.30	.09
MF6 Chili Davis	.30	.09
MF7 Joe Girardi	.30	.09
MF8 Jason Grimsley	.30	.09
MF9 Orlando Hernandez	.30	.09
MF10 Hideki Irabu	.30	.09
MF11 Derek Jeter	2.00	.60
MF12 Chuck Knoblauch	.30	.09
MF13 Ricky Ledee	.30	.09
MF14 Jim Leyritz	.30	.09
MF15 Tino Martinez	.30	.09
MF16 Ramiro Mendoza	.30	.09
MF17 Jeff Nelson	.30	.09
MF18 Paul O'Neill	.30	.09
MF19 Andy Pettitte	.30	.09
MF20 Jorge Posada	.30	.09
MF21 Mariano Rivera	.30	.09
MF22 Luis Sojo	.30	.09
MF23 Mike Stanton	.30	.09
MF24 Allen Watson	.30	.09
MF25 Bernie Williams	.50	.15
MF26 Chipper Jones	.75	.23
MF27 Ivan Rodriguez	.75	.23
MF28 Randy Johnson	.75	.23
MF29 Pedro Martinez	.75	.23
MF30 Scott Williamson	.30	.09
MF31 Carlos Beltran	.30	.09
MF32 Mark McGwire	2.00	.60
MF33 Ken Griffey Jr.	1.25	.35
MF34 Robin Ventura	.30	.09
MF35 Tony Gwynn	1.00	.30
MF36 Wade Boggs	.75	.23
MF37 Cal Ripken	2.50	.75
MF38 Jose Canseco	.75	.23
MF39 Alex Rodriguez	1.25	.35
MF40 Fernando Tatis	.30	.09

2000 Impact Point of Impact

Randomly inserted into packs at one in 30, this insert set features 10 of the major league's top homerun hitters. Card backs carry a "PI" prefix.

	Nm-Mt	Ex-Mt
COMPLETE SET (10)	50.00	15.00
PI1 Ken Griffey Jr.	4.00	1.20
PI2 Mark McGwire	6.00	1.80
PI3 Sammy Sosa	4.00	1.20
PI4 Jeff Bagwell	1.50	.45
PI5 Derek Jeter	6.00	1.80
PI6 Chipper Jones	2.50	.75
PI7 Nomar Garciaparra	4.00	1.20
PI8 Cal Ripken	8.00	2.40
PI9 Barry Bonds	6.00	1.80
PI10 Alex Rodriguez	4.00	1.20

2000 Impact Tattoos

Randomly inserted into packs at one in four, this 30-card insert set features team-logo tattoos of all thirty major league teams.

	Nm-Mt	Ex-Mt
COMPLETE SET (30)	10.00	3.00
1 Anaheim Angels	.50	.15
2 Arizona Diamondbacks	.50	.15
3 Atlanta Braves	.50	.15
4 Baltimore Orioles	.50	.15
5 Boston Red Sox	.50	.15
6 Chicago Cubs	.50	.15
7 Chicago White Sox	.50	.15
8 Cincinnati Reds	.50	.15
9 Cleveland Indians	.50	.15
10 Colorado Rockies	.50	.15
11 Detroit Tigers	.50	.15
12 Florida Marlins	.50	.15
13 Houston Astros	.50	.15
14 Kansas City Royals	.50	.15
15 Los Angeles Dodgers	.50	.15
16 Milwaukee Brewers	.50	.15
17 Minnesota Twins	.50	.15
18 Montreal Expos	.50	.15
19 New York Mets	.50	.15
20 New York Yankees	.50	.15
21 Oakland Athletics	.50	.15
22 Philadelphia Phillies	.50	.15
23 Pittsburgh Pirates	.50	.15
24 San Diego Padres	.50	.15
25 San Francisco Giants	.50	.15
26 Seattle Mariners	.50	.15
27 St. Louis Cardinals	.50	.15
28 Tampa Bay Devil Rays	.50	.15
29 Texas Rangers	.50	.15
30 Toronto Blue Jays	.50	.15

1905 Indians Souvenir Postcard Shop of Cleveland PC785

These distinguished looking black and white cards measures 3 1/4" by 5 1/2" and is similar to PC 782 in appearance and it was also issued in 1905. The Souvenir Postcard Shop of Cleveland identification appears on the front of the card. The backs are devoid of company identification.

	Ex-Mt	VG
COMPLETE SET	3500.00	1800.00
1 Harry Bay	150.00	75.00
2 Harry Bemis	150.00	75.00
3 Bill Bernhard	150.00	75.00
4 Bill Bradley	150.00	75.00
5 Fred Buelow	150.00	75.00
6 Chuck Carr	150.00	75.00
7 Frank Donahue	150.00	75.00
8 Elmer Flick	250.00	125.00
9 Otto Hess	150.00	75.00
10 Jay Jackson	150.00	75.00
11 Addie Joss	250.00	125.00
12 Nick Kahl	150.00	75.00
13 Nap Lajoie	1000.00	500.00
14 Earl Moore	150.00	75.00
15 Robert Rhoads	150.00	75.00
16 George Stovall	200.00	100.00
17 Terry Turner	200.00	100.00
18 Ernest Vinson	150.00	75.00

1947 Indians Team Issue

These 26 photos measure 6" by 8 1/2". They have player photos and a facsimile autograph. All of this is framed by white borders. The backs are blank and we have sequenced these photos in alphabetical order.

	Ex-Mt	VG
COMPLETE SET (26)	100.00	50.00
1 Don Black	3.00	1.50
2 Eddie Bockman	3.00	1.50
3 Lou Boudreau P/MG	10.00	5.00
4 Jack Conway	3.00	1.50
5 Larry Doby	10.00	5.00
6 Hank Edwards	3.00	1.50
7 Red Embree	3.00	1.50
8 Bob Feller	15.00	7.50
9 Les Fleming	3.00	1.50
10 Allen Gettel	3.00	1.50
11 Joe Gordon	6.00	3.00
12 Steve Gromek	3.00	1.50
13 Mel Harder	5.00	2.50
14 Jim Hegan	4.00	2.00
15 Ken Keltner	4.00	2.00
16 Ed Klieman	3.00	1.50
17 Bob Lemon	10.00	5.00
18 Al Lopez	10.00	5.00
19 George "Catfish" Metkovich	3.00	1.50
20 Dale Mitchell	4.00	2.00
21 Hal Peck	3.00	1.50
22 Eddie Robinson	3.00	1.50
23 Hank Ruszkowksi	3.00	1.50
24 Pat Seerey	3.00	1.50
25 Bryan Stephens	3.00	1.50
26 Les Willis	3.00	1.50

1947 Indians Van Patrick PC-761

This set of 26 black and white postcards was issued in 1947 and features only Cleveland Indians. The cards were obtained by writing to Van Patrick, then the Cleveland announcer. The backs of the postcards features the name of the player on the front in a short note from Van Patrick. Two cards of Bob Feller exist; they are noted in the listings below. According to advanced postcard collectors, it is possible that other members of the 47 Indians have cards as well but they have yet to be discovered.

	Ex-Mt	VG
COMPLETE SET	900.00	450.00
1 Don Black	30.00	15.00
2 Eddie Bockman	30.00	15.00
3 Lou Boudreau P/MG	60.00	30.00
4 Jack Conway	30.00	15.00
5 Hank Edwards	30.00	15.00
6 Red Embree	30.00	15.00
7A Bob Feller Pitching, abode wall	80.00	40.00
7B Bob Feller Pitching, Leg up, fuzzy card back	80.00	40.00
8 Les Fleming	30.00	15.00
9 Al Gettel	30.00	15.00
10 Joe Gordon	50.00	25.00
11 Steve Gromek	30.00	15.00
12 Mel Harder	50.00	25.00
13 Jim Hegan	40.00	20.00
14 Ken Keltner	30.00	15.00
15 Eddie Klieman	30.00	15.00
16 Bob Lemon	60.00	30.00
17 Al Lopez	60.00	30.00
18 George Metkovich	30.00	15.00
19 Dale Mitchell	30.00	15.00
20 Hal Peck	30.00	15.00
21 Eddie Robinson	30.00	15.00
22 Hank Ruszowski	30.00	15.00
23 Pat Seerey	30.00	15.00
24 Bryan Stephens	30.00	15.00
25 Les Willis	30.00	15.00

1948 Indians Team Issue

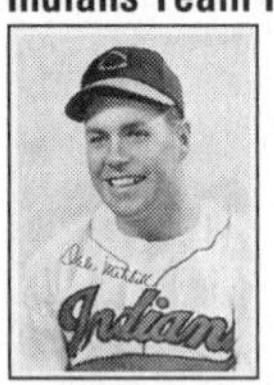

This set commemorates the members of the World Champion 1948 Cleveland Indians. The black and white photos measure approximately 6 1/2" by 9" and are blank backed. We have arranged this checklist in alphabetical order.

	NM	Ex
COMPLETE SET (31)	200.00	100.00
1 Gene Bearden	5.00	2.50
2 Johnny Berardino	15.00	7.50
3 Don Black	4.00	2.00
4 Lou Boudreau P/MG	15.00	7.50
5 Russ Christopher	4.00	2.00
6 Allie Clark	4.00	2.00
7 Larry Doby	20.00	10.00
8 Hank Edwards	4.00	2.00
9 Bob Feller	20.00	10.00
10 Joe Gordon	6.00	3.00
11 Hank Greenberg GM In Uniform	25.00	12.50
12 Hank Greenberg GM In Street Clothes	20.00	10.00
13 Steve Gromek	4.00	2.00
14 Mel Harder	6.00	3.00
15 Jim Hegan	5.00	2.50
16 Walt Judnich	4.00	2.00
17 Ken Keltner	4.00	2.00
18 Bob Kennedy	5.00	2.50
19 Ed Klieman	4.00	2.00
20 Bob Lemon	8.00	4.00
21 Bill McKechnie CO	8.00	4.00
22 Dale Mitchell	5.00	2.50
23 Bob Muncrief	4.00	2.00
24 Satchel Paige	25.00	12.50
25 Hal Peck	4.00	2.00
26 Eddie Robinson	4.00	2.00
27 Muddy Ruel CO	4.00	2.00
28 Joe Tipton	4.00	2.00
29 Thurman Tucker	4.00	2.00
30 Bill Veeck OWN	8.00	4.00
31 Sam Zoldak	4.00	2.00

1949 Indians Team Issue

These 30 photos measure approximatley 6 1/2" by 9". They feature members of the 1949 Cleveland Indians. The black and white photos are framed by white borders. The backs are blank and we have sequenced this set in alphabetical order. This set was available from the Cleveland Indians for 50 cents at time of issue.

	NM	Ex
COMPLETE SET (30)	200.00	100.00
1 Bob Avila	6.00	3.00
2 Al Benton	4.00	2.00
3 Gene Bearden	4.00	2.00
4 John Berardino	8.00	4.00
5 Ray Boone	6.00	3.00
6 Lou Boudreau P/MG	20.00	10.00
7 Allie Clark	4.00	2.00
8 Larry Doby	20.00	10.00
9 Bob Feller	20.00	10.00
10 Mike Garcia	6.00	3.00
11 Joe Gordon	8.00	4.00
12 Hank Greenberg GM	20.00	10.00
13 Steve Gromek	4.00	2.00
14 Jim Hegan	6.00	3.00
15 Ken Keltner	6.00	3.00
16 Bob Kennedy	4.00	2.00
17 Bob Lemon	15.00	7.50
18 Dale Mitchell	6.00	3.00
19 Satchel Paige	25.00	12.50
20 Frank Papish	4.00	2.00
21 Hal Peck	4.00	2.00
22 Al Rosen	10.00	5.00
23 Mike Tresh	4.00	2.00
24 Thurman Tucker	4.00	2.00
25 Bill Veeck OWN	10.00	5.00
26 Mickey Vernon	8.00	4.00
27 Early Wynn	15.00	7.50
28 Sam Zoldak	4.00	2.00
29 George Susce CO Muddy Ruel CO Bill McKechnie CO Steve O'Neill CO Mel Harder CO	6.00	3.00
30 Cleveland Stadium	15.00	7.50

1950 Indians Num Num

This issue features members of the 1950 Cleveland Indians. The black and white photos measure 6 1/2" by 9". Complete sets were sent out by Num Num in special envelopes. Some backs feature a redemption offer for other photos. We have checklisted the set alphabetically.

	NM	Ex
COMPLETE SET (23)	800.00	400.00
1 Bob Avila	30.00	15.00
2 Gene Bearden	25.00	12.50
3 Al Benton	25.00	12.50
4 Ray Boone	30.00	15.00
5 Lou Boudreau P/MG	50.00	25.00
6 Allie Clark	25.00	12.50
7 Larry Doby	50.00	25.00
8 Luke Easter	40.00	20.00
9 Bob Feller	100.00	50.00
10 Mike Garcia	30.00	15.00
11 Joe Gordon	80.00	40.00
12 Steve Gromek	25.00	12.50
13 Jim Hegan	30.00	15.00
14 Bob Kennedy	30.00	15.00
15 Bob Lemon	50.00	25.00
16 Dale Mitchell	30.00	15.00
17 Ray Murray	25.00	12.50
18 Chick Pieretti	25.00	12.50
19 Al Rosen	40.00	20.00
20 Mike Tresh	25.00	12.50
21 Thurman Tucker	25.00	12.50
22 Early Wynn	50.00	25.00
23 Sam Zoldak	25.00	12.50

1950 Indians Team Issue

These 26 black and white photos measure approximately 6 1/2" by 9". They feature members of the Cleveland Indians. The photos are surrounded by a white border and have facsimile autogrpahs. The photos are unnumbered and we have sequenced them in alphabetical order.

	NM	Ex
COMPLETE SET (27)	150.00	75.00
1 Bob Avila	5.00	2.50
2 Gene Bearden	3.00	1.50
3 Al Benton	3.00	1.50
4 Ray Boone	5.00	2.50
5 Lou Boudreau P/MG	12.00	6.00
6 Allie Clark	3.00	1.50
7 Larry Doby	20.00	10.00
8 Luke Easter	6.00	3.00
9 Bob Feller	20.00	10.00
10 Jess Flores	3.00	1.50
11 Mike Garcia	5.00	2.50
12 Joe Gordon	6.00	3.00
13 Hank Greenberg GM	25.00	12.50
14 Steve Gromek	3.00	1.50
15 Jim Hegan	5.00	2.50
16 Bob Kennedy	5.00	2.50
17 Bob Lemon	12.00	6.00
18 Dale Mitchell	5.00	2.50
19 Ray Murray	3.00	1.50
20 Chick Pieretti	3.00	1.50
21 Al Rosen	6.00	3.00
22 Dick Rozek	3.00	1.50
23 Ellis Ryan OWN	3.00	1.50
24 Thurman Tucker	3.00	1.50
25 Early Wynn	15.00	7.50
26 Sam Zoldak	3.00	1.50
27 Cleveland Stadium	25.00	12.50

1951 Indians Hage's

This seven-card set of the Cleveland Indians was issued by Hage's Ice Cream and features green-and-brown tinted player photos printed on black-backed cards. The cards are unnumbered and checklisted below in alphabetical order.

	NM	Ex
COMPLETE SET (7)	125.00	60.00
1 Ray Boone	20.00	10.00
2 Allie Clark	15.00	7.50
3 Luke Easter	20.00	10.00
4 Jesse Flores	15.00	7.50
5 Al Olsen	15.00	7.50
6 Al Rosen	25.00	12.50
7 George Zuverink	15.00	7.50

1951 Indians Team Issue

These 6 1/2" by 9" photos were issued by the Cleveland Indians and featured members of the 1951 Indians. The black and white photos are surrounded by a white border and have fascimile autographs. The photos are unnumbered and we have sequenced them in alphabetical order. This list may be incomplete and any additions are welcome.

	NM	Ex
COMPLETE SET	200.00	100.00
1 Bobby Avila	6.00	3.00
2 Johnny Beardino	8.00	4.00
3 Lou Boudreau Batting	10.00	5.00
4 Lou Boudreau Throwing	10.00	5.00
5 Ray Boone	5.00	2.50
6 Lou Brissie	5.00	2.50
7 Allie Clark	5.00	2.50
8 Merrill Combs	5.00	2.50
9 Bob Chakales	5.00	2.50
10 Sam Chapman	5.00	2.50
11 Larry Doby	10.00	5.00
12 Luke Easter	5.00	2.50
13 Red Fahr	5.00	2.50
14 Bob Feller	12.00	6.00
15 Jess Flores	5.00	2.50
16 Mike Garcia	6.00	3.00
17 Joe Gordon	8.00	4.00
18 Steve Gromek	5.00	2.50
19 Jim Hegan	6.00	3.00
20 Bob Kennedy	6.00	3.00
21 Bob Lemon Facing Straight Ahead	10.00	5.00
22 Bob Lemon Facing Left	10.00	5.00
23 Dale Mitchell	6.00	3.00
24 Ray Murray	5.00	2.50
25 Al Rosen	8.00	4.00
26 Dick Rozek	5.00	2.50
27 Harry Simpson	5.00	2.50
28 Snuffy Stirnweiss	5.00	2.50
29 Thurman Tucker	5.00	2.50
30 Mickey Vernon	6.00	3.00
31 Early Wynn	10.00	5.00
32 Sam Zoldak	5.00	2.50

1952 Indians Num Num

The cards in this 20-card set measure approximately 3 1/2" by 4 1/2". The 1952 Num Num Potato Chips issue features black and white, numbered cards of the Cleveland Indians. Cards came with and without coupons (tabs). The cards were issued without coupons directly by the Cleveland baseball club. When the complete set was obtained the tabs were cut off and exchanged for an autographed baseball. Card Number 16, Kennedy, is rather scarce. Cards with the tabs still intact are worth approximately double the values listed below. The catalog designation for this set is F337-2.

	NM	Ex
COMPLETE SET (20)	1000.00	500.00
COMMON CARD (1-20)	25.00	12.50
COMMON SP	400.00	200.00
1 Lou Brissie	25.00	12.50
2 Jim Hegan	30.00	15.00
3 Birdie Tebbetts	30.00	15.00
4 Bob Lemon	50.00	25.00
5 Bob Feller	150.00	75.00
6 Early Wynn	50.00	25.00
7 Mike Garcia	30.00	15.00
8 Steve Gromek	25.00	12.50
9 Bob Chakales	25.00	12.50
10 Al Rosen	40.00	20.00
11 Dick Rozek	25.00	12.50
12 Luke Easter	30.00	15.00
13 Ray Boone	30.00	15.00
14 Bobby Avila	30.00	15.00
15 Dale Mitchell	30.00	15.00
16 Bob Kennedy SP	400.00	200.00
17 Harry Simpson	25.00	12.50
18 Larry Doby	50.00	25.00
19 Sam Jones	30.00	15.00
20 Al Lopez MG	50.00	25.00

1953 Indians Team Issue

These photos which measure approximately 6" by 9" feature members of the 1953 Indians. The black and white photos are produced with a glossy paper and have fascimile autographs. Since these cards are unnumbered, we have sequenced them in alphabetical order.

	NM	Ex
COMPLETE SET	100.00	50.00
1 Al Aber	5.00	2.50
2 Bob Avila	6.00	3.00
3 Ray Boone	5.00	2.50
4 Larry Doby	10.00	5.00
5 Luke Easter	5.00	2.50
6 Bob Feller	12.00	6.00
7 Mike Garcia	6.00	3.00
8 Bill Glynn	5.00	2.50
9 Jim Hegan	5.00	2.50
10 Bob Hooper	5.00	2.50
11 Dave Hoskins	5.00	2.50
12 Bob Kennedy	5.00	2.50
13 Bob Lemon	10.00	5.00
14 Jim Lemon	5.00	2.50
15 Al Lopez MG	10.00	5.00
16 Dale Mitchell	5.00	2.50
17 Al Rosen	8.00	4.00
18 Harry Simpson	5.00	2.50
19 George Strickland	5.00	2.50
20 Early Wynn	10.00	5.00

1954 Indians Team Issue

These photos, which measure approximately 6" by 8 3/4" feature members of the American League champions Cleveland Indians. These photos are similar to the 1953 Indians in style but are slightly smaller and are printed on heavier paper. Since these are unnumbered, we have sequenced them in alphabetical order.

	NM	Ex
COMPLETE SET	150.00	75.00
1 Bob Avila	5.00	2.50
2 Sam Dente	5.00	2.50
3 Larry Doby	10.00	5.00
4 Bob Feller	12.00	6.00
5 Mike Garcia	6.00	3.00
6 Bill Glynn	5.00	2.50
7 Jim Hegan	5.00	2.50
8 Bob Hooper	5.00	2.50
9 Dave Hoskins	5.00	2.50
10 Art Houtemann	5.00	2.50
11 Bob Lemon	10.00	5.00
12 Al Lopez MG	10.00	5.00
13 Hank Majeski	5.00	2.50
14 Dale Mitchell	5.00	2.50
15 Don Mossi	8.00	4.00
16 Hal Naragon	5.00	2.50
17 Ray Narleski	6.00	3.00
18 Hal Newhouser	10.00	5.00
19 Dave Philley	5.00	2.50
20 Dave Pope	5.00	2.50
21 Rudy Regalado	5.00	2.50
22 Al Rosen	8.00	4.00
23 Al Smith	5.00	2.50
24 George Strickland	5.00	2.50
25 Vic Wertz	5.00	2.50
26 Wally Westlake	5.00	2.50
27 Early Wynn	10.00	5.00

1955 Indians Team Issue

These cards which measure appromixately 6" by 8 3/4" feature members of the 1955 Indians. Most of these cards have fascimile autographs printed on them except for Foiles, Kiner, Score and Wertz. This checklist comes from a set purchased from the Indians in July, 1955 so there might have been additions both before and after these were issued. Since these cards are unnumbered, we have sequenced them in alphabetical order.

	NM	Ex
COMPLETE SET	120.00	60.00
1 Bob Avila	6.00	3.00
2 Sam Dente	5.00	2.50
3 Larry Doby	10.00	5.00
4 Bob Feller	12.00	6.00
5 Hank Foiles	5.00	2.50
6 Mike Garcia	6.00	3.00
7 Jim Hegan	5.00	2.50
8 Art Houtteman	5.00	2.50
9 Ralph Kiner	10.00	5.00
10 Bob Lemon	10.00	5.00
11 Dale Mitchell	5.00	2.50
12 Don Mossi	6.00	3.00
13 Hal Naragon	5.00	2.50
14 Ray Narleski	5.00	2.50
15 Dave Philley	5.00	2.50
16 Al Rosen	8.00	4.00
17 Herb Score	10.00	5.00
18 Al Smith	5.00	2.50
19 George Strickland	5.00	2.50
20 Vic Wertz	5.00	2.50
21 Wally Westlake	5.00	2.50
22 Early Wynn	10.00	5.00

1955 Indians Golden Stamps

This 32-stamp set features color photos of the Cleveland Indians and measures approximately 2" by 2 5/8". The stamps are designed to be placed in a 32-page album which measures approximately 8 3/8" by 10 15/16". The album contains black-and-white drawings of players with statistics and life stories. The stamps are unnumbered and listed below according to where they fall in the album.

	NM	Ex
COMPLETE SET (32)	50.00	25.00
1 Al Lopez MG	5.00	2.50
2 Bob Lemon	10.00	5.00
3 Early Wynn	10.00	5.00
4 Mike Garcia	3.00	1.50
5 Bob Feller	15.00	7.50
6 Art Houtteman	2.00	1.00
7 Herb Score	5.00	2.50
8 Don Mossi	4.00	2.00
9 Ray Narleski	2.00	1.00
10 Jim Hegan	3.00	1.50
11 Vic Wertz	2.00	1.00
12 Bobby Avila	2.00	1.00
13 George Strickland	2.00	1.00
14 Al Rosen	4.00	2.00
15 Larry Doby	10.00	5.00
16 Ralph Kiner	5.00	2.50
17 Al Smith	2.00	1.00
18 Wally Westlake	2.00	1.00
19 Hal Naragon	2.00	1.00
20 Hank Foiles	2.00	1.00
21 Hank Majeski	2.00	1.00
22 Bill Wight	2.00	1.00
23 Sam Dente	2.00	1.00
24 Dave Pope	2.00	1.00
25 Dave Philley	2.00	1.00
26 Dale Mitchell	3.00	1.50
27 Hank Greenberg GM	15.00	7.50
28 Mel Harder CO	3.00	1.50
29 Ralph Kress CO	2.00	1.00
30 Tony Cuccinello CO	2.00	1.00
31 Bill Lobe CO	2.00	1.00
32 Cleveland Stadium	10.00	5.00
XX Album	5.00	2.50

1955-56 Indians Carling Black Label

This ten-card, approximately 8 1/2" by 12", set was issued by Carling Beer and celebrated members of the (then) perennial contending Cleveland Indians. These cards feature a black and white photo with the printed name of the player inserted in the photo. Underneath the photo is a joint advertisement for Carling Black Label Beer and The Cleveland Indians. The set looks like it could be easily replicated and may indeed have been reprinted. The checklist for this unnumbered set is ordered alphabetically.

	NM	Ex
COMPLETE SET (10)	100.00	50.00
1 Bob Feller	30.00	15.00
2 Mike Garcia	10.00	5.00
3 Jim Hegan	10.00	5.00
4 Art Houtteman	8.00	4.00
5 Ralph Kiner	15.00	7.50
6 Bob Lemon	15.00	7.50
7 Al Rosen	12.00	6.00
8 Herb Score	15.00	7.50
9 Al Smith	8.00	4.00
10 George Strickland	8.00	4.00
11 Early Wynn	15.00	7.50

1956 Indians Team Issue

These cards, which measure approximately 6" by 9" feature members of the 1956 Cleveland Indians. Similar to the 1955 set and many of the photos were also repeats from the 1955 set. This set was produced early in the season so additions to this checklist is appreciated. These cards are not numbered, so we have sequenced them in alphabetical order. Rocky Colavito appears in this set before his Rookie Card year.

	NM	Ex
COMPLETE SET	120.00	60.00
1 Earl Averill	5.00	2.50
2 Bob Avila	6.00	3.00
3 Rocky Colavito	20.00	10.00
4 Bob Feller	12.00	6.00
5 Mike Garcia	6.00	3.00
6 Jim Hegan	5.00	2.50
7 Art Houtemann	5.00	2.50
8 Bob Lemon	10.00	5.00
9 Al Lopez MG	10.00	5.00
10 Sam Mele	5.00	2.50
11 Dale Mitchell	5.00	2.50
12 Don Mossi	6.00	3.00
13 Ray Narleski	5.00	2.50
14 Rudy Regalado	5.00	2.50
15 Al Rosen	8.00	4.00
16 Al Smith	5.00	2.50
17 George Strickland	5.00	2.50
18 Gene Woodling	5.00	2.50
19 Early Wynn	10.00	5.00

1956 Indians Team Issue Mail

Unlike the other 1956 Indians Team Issue, this set was available to mail order customers. Thes cards, which measure approximately 6 1/2" by 9" are slightly thinner in card stock than the other Indian team issue. Rocky Colavito appears in this photo set a year before his Topps Rookie Card was issued.

	NM	Ex
COMPLETE SET	150.00	75.00
1 Earl Averill	5.00	2.50
2 Bob Avila	6.00	3.00
3 Jim Busby	5.00	2.50
4 Chico Carrasquel	5.00	2.50
5 Rocky Colavito	15.00	7.50
6 Bud Daley	5.00	2.50
7 Bob Feller	12.00	6.00
8 Mike Garcia	6.00	3.00
9 Mel Harder CO Bill Lobe CO Tony Cuccinello CO Red Kress CO	5.00	2.50
10 Jim Hegan	5.00	2.50
11 Kenny Kuhn	5.00	2.50
12 Bob Lemon	10.00	5.00
13 Al Lopez MG	10.00	5.00
14 Sam Mele	5.00	2.50
15 Dale Mitchell	5.00	2.50
16 Don Mossi	6.00	3.00
17 Hal Naragon	5.00	2.50
18 Ray Narleski	5.00	2.50
19 Al Rosen	8.00	4.00
20 Herb Score	8.00	4.00
21 Al Smith	5.00	2.50
22 George Strickland	5.00	2.50
23 Vic Wertz	5.00	2.50
24 Gene Woodling	5.00	2.50
25 Early Wynn	10.00	5.00

1957 Indians Sohio

The 1957 Sohio Cleveland Indians set consists of 18 perforated photos; originally issued in strips of three cards, which after perforation measure approximately 5" by 7". These black and white cards were issued with facsimile autographs on the front which were designed to be pasted into a special photo album issued by SOHIO (Standard Oil of Ohio). The set features one of the earliest Roger Maris cards which even predates his 1958 Topps rookie card. In addition, the Rocky Colavito card is popular as well as 1957 was Rocky's rookie year for cards. These unnumbered cards are listed below in alphabetical order for convenience. It has been alleged that counterfeits of this set have been recently produced.

	NM	Ex
COMPLETE SET (18)	300.00	150.00
1 Bob Avila	6.00	3.00
2 Jim Busby	4.00	2.00
3 Chico Carrasquel	4.00	2.00
4 Rocky Colavito	60.00	30.00
5 Mike Garcia	6.00	3.00
6 Jim Hegan	4.00	2.00
7 Bob Lemon	30.00	15.00
8 Roger Maris	150.00	75.00
9 Don Mossi	6.00	3.00
10 Ray Narleski	4.00	2.00
11 Russ Nixon	4.00	2.00
12 Herb Score	8.00	4.00
13 Al Smith	4.00	2.00
14 George Strickland	4.00	2.00
15 Bob Usher	4.00	2.00
16 Vic Wertz	6.00	3.00
17 Gene Woodling	6.00	3.00
18 Early Wynn	30.00	15.00

1957 Indians Team Issue

This 29-card set of the Cleveland Indians features black-and-white player photos measuring approximately 6 1/2" by 9". The backs are blank. The cards are unnumbered and checklisted below in alphabetical order.

	NM	Ex
COMPLETE SET (29)	125.00	60.00
1 Joe Altobelli	3.00	1.50
2 Bob Avila	4.00	2.00
3 Alfonso Carrasquel	3.00	1.50
4 Rocky Colavito	10.00	5.00
5 Bud Daley	3.00	1.50
6 Kerby Ferrell MG	3.00	1.50
7 Mike Garcia	3.00	1.50
8 Mel Harder CO Red Kress CO Kerby Ferrell CO Eddie Stanky CO	4.00	2.00
9 Jim Hegan	3.00	1.50
10 Art Houtteman	3.00	1.50
11 Kenny Kuhn	3.00	1.50
12 Bob Lemon	10.00	5.00
13 Roger Maris	25.00	12.50
14 Don Mossi	4.00	2.00
15 Hal Naragon	3.00	1.50
16 Ray Narleski	3.00	1.50
17 Russ Nixon	3.00	1.50
18 Stan Pitula	3.00	1.50
19 Lawrence Raines	3.00	1.50
20 Herb Score	5.00	2.50
21 Al Smith	3.00	1.50
22 George Strickland	3.00	1.50
23 Dick Tomanek	3.00	1.50
24 Bob Usher	3.00	1.50
25 Preston Ward	3.00	1.50
26 Vic Wertz	4.00	2.00
27 Dick Williams	5.00	2.50
28 Gene Woodling	4.00	2.00
29 Early Wynn	10.00	5.00

1958 Indians Team Issue

This 30-card set of the Cleveland Indians features black-and-white player photos measuring approximately 6 1/2" by 9" with white borders and facsimile autographs. The backs are blank. The first 24 cards were issued in the set in May. The last five cards were found in the August set with several of the other players dropped. The set could be obtained by mail for 50 cents from the club.

	NM	Ex
COMPLETE SET (30)	125.00	60.00
1 Bob Avila	4.00	2.00
2 Bobby Bragan MG	3.00	1.50
3 Dick Brown	3.00	1.50
4 Alfonso(Chico) Carrasquel	3.00	1.50
5 Rocky Colavito	6.00	3.00
6 Larry Doby	10.00	5.00
7 Mike Garcia	4.00	2.00
8 Gary Geiger	3.00	1.50
9 Jim Grant	3.00	1.50
10 Bill Harrell	3.00	1.50
11 Red Kress CO Bobby Bragan MG Eddie Stanky CO Mel Harder CO	4.00	2.00
12 Roger Maris	20.00	10.00
13 Cal McLish	3.00	1.50
14 Minnie Minoso	6.00	3.00
15 Bill Moran	3.00	1.50
16 Don Mossi	4.00	2.00
17 Ray Narleski	3.00	1.50
18 Russ Nixon	3.00	1.50
19 J.W. Porter	3.00	1.50
20 Herb Score	5.00	2.50
21 Dick Tomanek	3.00	1.50
22 Mickey Vernon	4.00	2.00
23 Preston Ward	3.00	1.50
24 Hoyt Wilhelm	10.00	5.00
25 Gary Bell	3.00	1.50
26 Rocky Colavito	15.00	7.50
27 Woodie Held	4.00	2.00
28 Bill Hunter	3.00	1.50
29 Don Mossi	4.00	2.00
30 Vic Power	6.00	3.00

1959 Indians

This set features black-and-white photos of the 1959 Cleveland Indians and measures approximately 6 1/2" by 9". Some of the photos have a facsimile autograph identifying the player while others have the player's name printed in a small bar in a bottom corner. The backs are blank. The cards are unnumbered and checklisted below in alphabetical order.

	NM	Ex
COMPLETE SET (26)	80.00	40.00
1 Gary Bell	3.00	1.50
2 Jim Bolger	3.00	1.50
3 Dick Brodowski	3.00	1.50
4 Al Cicotte	3.00	1.50
5 Rocky Colavito	10.00	5.00
6 Don Ferrarese	3.00	1.50
7 Tito Francona	4.00	2.00
8 Mike Garcia	4.00	2.00
9 Joe Gordon MG	5.00	2.50
10 Jim Grant	3.00	1.50
11 Mel Harder CO	4.00	2.00
12 Carroll Hardy	3.00	1.50
13 Woodie Held	3.00	1.50
14 Frank Lane GM	3.00	1.50
15 Billy Martin	10.00	5.00
16 Cal McLish	3.00	1.50
17 Minnie Minoso	6.00	3.00
18 Hal Naragon	3.00	1.50
19 Russ Nixon	3.00	1.50
20 Jim Perry	4.00	2.00
21 Jim Piersall	5.00	2.50
22 Vic Power	4.00	2.00
23 Herb Score	5.00	2.50
24 George Strickland	3.00	1.50
25 Mickey Vernon	4.00	2.00
26 Ray Webster	3.00	1.50

1960 Indians Jay Publishing

This 12-card set of the Cleveland Indians measures approximately 5" by 7". The fronts feature black-and-white posed player photos with the player's and team name printed below in the white border. These cards were packaged 12 to a packet and originally sold for 25 cents. The backs are blank. The cards are unnumbered and checklisted below in alphabetical order.

	NM	Ex
COMPLETE SET (12)	30.00	12.00
1 Tito Francona	3.00	1.20
2 Jim Grant	2.50	1.00
3 Woody Held	2.50	1.00
4 Harvey Kuenn	3.00	1.20
5 Barry Latman	2.50	1.00
6 Russ Nixon	2.50	1.00
7 Bubba Phillips	2.50	1.00

8 Jimmy Piersall	4.00	1.60
9 Vic Power	3.00	1.20
10 John Romano	2.50	1.00
11 George Strickland	2.50	1.00
12 John Temple	2.50	1.00

1961 Indians Team Issue

These black-backed photos, which measure approximately 6" by 9" feature members of the 1961 Cleveland Indians. These photos are unnumbered and are sequenced in alphabetical order. This list is probably incomplete, so any additions are appreciated.

	NM	Ex
COMPLETE SET	15.00	6.00
1 John Antonelli	2.50	1.00
2 Gary Bell	2.00	.80
3 Tito Francona	2.00	.80
4 Woodie Held	2.00	.80
5 Bubba Phillips	2.00	.80
6 Vic Power	2.00	.80
7 John Romano	2.00	.80
8 Dick Stigman	2.00	.80
9 John Temple	2.00	.80

1962 Indians Jay Publishing

This 12-card set of the Cleveland Indians measures approximately 5" by 7". The fronts feature black-and-white posed player photos with the player's and team name printed below in the white border. These cards were packaged 12 to a packet. The backs are blank. The cards are unnumbered and checklisted below in alphabetical order.

	NM	Ex
COMPLETE SET (12)	30.00	12.00
1 Gary Bell	2.50	1.00
2 Dick Donovan	2.50	1.00
3 Tito Francona	3.00	1.20
4 Jim Grant	3.00	1.20
5 Woody Held	3.00	1.20
6 Willie Kirkland	2.50	1.00
7 Barry Latman	2.50	1.00
8 Mel McGaha MG	2.50	1.00
9 Bob Nieman	2.50	1.00
10 Bubba Phillips	2.50	1.00
11 Pedro Ramos	2.50	1.00
12 John Romano	2.50	1.00

1963 Indians Jay Publishing

This 12-card set of the Cleveland Indians measures approximately 5" by 7". The fronts feature black-and-white posed player photos with the player's and team name printed below in the white border. These cards were packaged 12 to a packet. The backs are blank. The cards are unnumbered and checklisted below in alphabetical order.

	NM	Ex
COMPLETE SET (12)	25.00	10.00
1 Joe Adcock	3.00	1.20
2 Gary Bell	2.00	.80
3 Vic Davalillo	2.00	.80
4 Mike De La Hoz	2.00	.80
5 Dick Donovan	2.00	.80
6 Tito Francona	2.50	1.00
7 Jim Grant	2.50	1.00
8 Woody Held	2.00	.80
9 Willie Kirkland	2.00	.80
10 Barry Latman	2.00	.80
11 John Romano	2.00	.80
12 Birdie Tebbetts MG	2.50	1.00

1964 Indians Jay Publishing

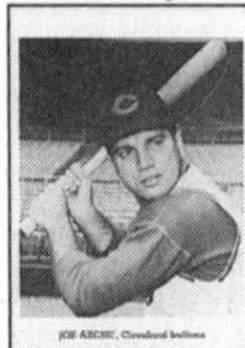

This 12-card set of the Cleveland Indians measures approximately 5" by 7". The fronts feature black-and-white posed player photos with the player's and team name printed below in the white border. These cards were packaged 12 to a packet. The backs are blank. The cards are unnumbered and checklisted below in alphabetical order.

	NM	Ex
COMPLETE SET (12)	25.00	10.00
1 Max Alvis	2.50	1.00
2 Joe Azcue	2.00	.80
3 Vic Davalillo	2.00	.80
4 Dick Donovan	2.00	.80
5 Tito Francona	2.50	1.00
6 Jim Grant	2.50	1.00
7 Woody Held	2.00	.80
8 Jack Kralick	2.00	.80
9 Pedro Ramos	2.00	.80
10 John Romano	2.00	.80
11 Al Smith	2.00	.80
12 Birdie Tebbetts MG	2.50	1.00

1965 Indians Jay Publishing

This 12-card set of the Cleveland Indians measures approximately 5" by 7". The fronts feature black-and-white posed player photos with the player's and team name printed below in the white border. These cards were packaged 12 to a packet. The backs are blank. The cards are unnumbered and checklisted below in alphabetical order. Luis Tiant appears in his Rookie Card season.

	NM	Ex
COMPLETE SET (12)	25.00	10.00
1 Max Alvis	2.00	.80
2 Gary Bell	2.00	.80
3 Larry Brown	2.00	.80
4 Rocky Colavito	4.00	1.60
5 Dick Donovan	2.00	.80
6 Chuck Hinton	2.00	.80
7 Jack Kralick	2.00	.80
8 Sam McDowell	3.00	1.20
9 Birdie Tebbetts MG	2.00	.80
10 Ralph Terry	2.50	1.00
11 Luis Tiant	4.00	1.60
12 Leon Wagner	2.00	.80

1966 Indians Photos

These photos, which measure 8" by 10" feature members of the 1966 Cleveland Indians. Since these photos are unnumbered, we have sequenced them in alphabetical order.

	NM	Ex
COMPLETE SET	25.00	10.00
1 Max Alvis	3.00	1.20
2 Gary Bell	3.00	1.20
3 Del Crandall	3.00	1.20
4 Sam McDowell	5.00	2.00
5 Duke Sims	3.00	1.20
6 Birdie Tebbetts MG Early Wynn CO George Strickland CO Reggie Otero CO	4.00	1.60
7 Luis Tiant	6.00	2.40
8 Leon Wagner	3.00	1.20

1966 Indians Team Issue

This 12-card set of the Cleveland Indians measures approximately 4 7/8" by 7 1/8" and features black-and-white player photos in a white border. These cards were packaged 12 to a packet and originally sold for 25 cents. The backs are blank. The cards are unnumbered and checklisted below in alphabetical order.

	NM	Ex
COMPLETE SET (12)	30.00	12.00
1 Max Alvis	2.00	.80
2 Joe Azcue	2.00	.80
3 Rocky Colavito	4.00	1.60
4 Vic Davalillo	2.50	1.00
5 Chuck Hinton	2.00	.80
6 Dick Howser	2.50	1.00
7 Jack Kralick	2.00	.80
8 Sam McDowell	3.00	1.20
9 Don McMahon	2.00	.80
10 Birdie Tebbetts MG	2.00	.80
11 Luis Tiant	4.00	1.60
12 Leon Wagner	2.00	.80

1970 Indians

This 12-card set of the Cleveland Indians measures approximately 4 1/4" by 7" and features white-bordered black-and-white player photos. The player's name and team are printed in the wide top margin. The backs are blank. The cards are unnumbered and checklisted below in alphabetical order.

	NM	Ex
COMPLETE SET (12)	20.00	8.00
1 Buddy Bradford	1.50	.60
2 Larry Brown	1.50	.60
3 Alvin Dark MG	2.00	.80
4 Ray Fosse	2.00	.80
5 Steve Hargan	1.50	.60
6 Ken Harrelson	2.50	1.00
7 Dennis Higgins	1.50	.60
8 Sam McDowell	2.50	1.00
9 Graig Nettles	3.00	1.20
10 Vada Pinson	3.00	1.20
11 Ken Suarez	1.50	.60
12 Ted Uhlaender	1.50	.60

1971 Indians

These 12 cards featuring members of the Cleveland Indians measure approximately 7" by 8 3/4" with the fronts having white-bordered color player photos. The player's name and team is printed in black in the white margin below the picture. The backs are blank. The cards are unnumbered and checklisted below in alphabetical order.

	NM	Ex
COMPLETE SET (12)	20.00	8.00
1 Buddy Bradford	1.50	.60
2 Alvin Dark MG	2.50	1.00
3 Steve Dunning	1.50	.60
4 Ray Fosse	2.00	.80
5 Steve Hargan	1.50	.60
6 Ken Harrelson	2.50	1.00
7 Chuck Hinton	1.50	.60
8 Ray Lamb	1.50	.60
9 Sam McDowell	3.00	1.20
10 Vada Pinson	3.00	1.20
11 Ken Suarez	1.50	.60
12 Ted Uhlaender	1.50	.60

1972 Indians Brown Derby Poster

Issued through the Brown Derby restaurant chain, these posters measured 22" by 27" and featured members of the 1972 Cleveland Indians. They were apparently issued each Sunday, but incomplete information is known as to which players were actually produced for this set or whether all 16 players which were supposed to be issued were issued. Since these cards are not numbered, we have sequenced them in alphabetical information. Obviously, more information on this set would be greatly appreciated.

	NM	Ex
COMPLETE SET	40.00	16.00
1 Chris Chambliss	8.00	3.20
2 Ray Fosse	5.00	2.00
3 Roy Foster	5.00	2.00
4 Graig Nettles	8.00	3.20
5 Gaylord Perry	12.00	4.80
6 Dick Tidrow	5.00	2.00
7 Del Unser	5.00	2.00

1973 Indians Team Issue

This set features color photos of the 1973 Cleveland Indians printed on postcard-size cards with postcard backs. The cards are unnumbered and checklisted below in alphabetical order. Four of the cards had numbers on them, and these numbers are listed after the player's names. These cards were published by Cleveland Sports Pro Enterprises and the photos were taken by Axel Studios. A collector could order these postcards, as they were issued in 25-card sets and evolved during the year from the producer for $3 per set.

	NM	Ex
COMPLETE SET	30.00	12.00
1 Dwain Anderson 332	1.00	.40
2 Ken Aspromonte MG	1.00	.40
3 Fred Beene 322	1.00	.40
4 Buddy Bell	2.50	1.00
5 Dick Bosman	1.00	.40
6 Jack Brohamer	1.00	.40
7 Leo Cardenas	1.00	.40
8 Chris Chambliss	2.00	.80
9 Frank Duffy	1.00	.40
10 Dave Duncan	1.00	.40
11 John Ellis	1.00	.40
12 Ed Farmer	1.00	.40
13 Oscar Gamble	1.50	.60
14 George Hendrick	1.50	.60
15 Tom Hilgendorf	1.00	.40
16 Jerry Johnson	1.00	.40
17 Ray Lamb	1.00	.40
18 Ron Lolich	1.00	.40
19 John Lowenstein	1.00	.40
20 Steve Mingori	1.00	.40
21 Tony Pacheco CO 327	1.00	.40
22 Gaylord Perry	4.00	1.60
23 Tom Ragland	1.00	.40
24 Warren Spahn CO	4.00	1.60
25 Charlie Spikes	1.00	.40
26 Brent Strom	1.00	.40
27 Dick Tidrow	1.00	.40
28 Rosendo"Rusty" Torres 342	1.00	.40
29 Rusty Torres UER (Back says Leo Cardenas)	1.00	.40
30 Milt Wilcox	1.00	.40
31 Walt Williams	1.00	.40

1974 Indians Team Issue

These postcards feature players who made their debut with the Indians in 1974. Many of the 1973 players also appeared in 1974 but they are not listed here. Since these cards are not numbered, we have sequenced them in alphabetical order.

	NM	Ex
COMPLETE SET	20.00	8.00
1 Luis Alvarado	1.00	.40
2 Dwain Anderson	1.00	.40
3 Steve Arlin	1.00	.40
4 Alan Ashby	1.00	.40
5 Fred Beene	1.00	.40
6 Ossie Blanco	1.00	.40
7 Clay Bryant	1.00	.40
8 Tom Buskey	1.00	.40
9 Ed Crosby	1.00	.40
10 Larry Doby CO	2.50	1.00
11 Bruce Ellingsen	1.00	.40
12 Bob Johnson	1.00	.40
13 Steve Kline	1.00	.40
14 Leron Lee	1.00	.40
15 Joe Lis	1.00	.40
16 Tony Pacheco CO	1.00	.40
17 Jim Perry	1.50	.60
18 Fritz Peterson	1.00	.40
19 Ken Sanders	1.00	.40

1975 Indians 1954 TCMA

The 39-card set of the 1954 Cleveland Indians features black-and-white player photos in white borders. The backs carry player statistics for 1954. The cards are unnumbered and checklisted below in alphabetical order with cards 37, 38, and 39 being jumbo cards.

	NM	Ex
COMPLETE SET (39)	30.00	12.00
1 Bobby Avila	1.00	.40
2 Bob Chakales	.50	.20
3 Tony Cuccinello CO	.50	.20
4 Sam Dente	.50	.20
5 Larry Doby	3.00	1.20
6 Luke Easter	.50	.20
7 Bob Feller	5.00	2.00
8 Mike Garcia	.50	.20
9 Joe Ginsberg	.50	.20
10 Billy Glynn	.50	.20
11 Mickey Grasso	.50	.20
12 Mel Harder CO	1.00	.40
13 Jim Hegan	1.00	.40
14 Bob Hooper	.50	.20
15 Dave Hoskins	.50	.20
16 Art Houtteman	.50	.20
17 Bob Kennedy	.50	.20
18 Bob Lemon	2.00	.80
19 Al Lopez MG	1.50	.60
20 Hank Majeski	.50	.20
21 Dale Mitchell	1.00	.40
22 Don Mossi	1.50	.60
23 Hal Naragon	.50	.20
24 Ray Narleski	.50	.20
25 Rocky Nelson	.50	.20
26 Hal Newhouser	2.00	.80
27 Dave Philley	.50	.20
28 Dave Pope	.50	.20
29 Rudy Regaldo	.50	.20
30 Al Rosen	2.00	.80
31 Jose Santiago	.50	.20
32 Al Smith	.50	.20
33 George Strickland	.50	.20
34 Vic Wertz	.50	.20
35 Wally Westlake	.50	.20
36 Early Wynn	1.00	.40
37 Dave Pope Dave Philley Larry Doby Al Smith	1.00	.40
38 Bill Lobe CO Tony Cuccinello CO Red Kress CO Mel Harder CO Al Lopez MG	1.00	.40
39 Early Wynn Bob Lemon Bob Hooper Art Houtteman Jose Santiago Ray Narleski Mike Garcia Hal Newhouser Al Lopez MG Don Mossi Bob Feller	2.00	.80

1975 Indians JB Robinson

This seven-card set was issued by JB Robinson Jewelers and features 8 1/2" by 8 1/2" color photos of the Cleveland Indians. The cards are unnumbered and checklisted below in alphabetical order.

	NM	Ex
COMPLETE SET (7)	12.00	4.80
1 Buddy Bell	2.50	1.00
2 Jack Brohamer	1.00	.40
3 Rico Carty	2.00	.80
4 Frank Duffy	1.00	.40
5 Oscar Gamble	1.50	.60
6 Boog Powell	2.50	1.00
7 Frank Robinson P/MG	2.50	1.00

1975 Indians Postcards

This 25-card set of the Cleveland Indians features player photos on postcard-size cards. The cards are unnumbered and checklisted below in alphabetical order.

	NM	Ex
COMPLETE SET (25)	12.00	4.80
1 Alan Ashby	.75	.30
2 Fred Beene	.50	.20
3 Buddy Bell	1.50	.60
4 Ken Berry	.50	.20
5 Dick Bosman	.50	.20
6 Jack Brohamer	.50	.20
7 Tom Buskey	.50	.20
8 Rico Carty	.75	.30
9 Ed Crosby	.50	.20
10 Frank Duffy	.50	.20
11 John Ellis	.50	.20
12 Oscar Gamble	.75	.30
13 George Hendrick	.75	.30
14 Don Hood	.50	.20
15 Jim Kern	.50	.20
16 Dave LaRoche	.50	.20
17 Leron Lee	.50	.20
18 John Lowenstein	.50	.20
19 Gaylord Perry	2.00	.80
20 Jim Perry	.75	.30
21 Fritz Peterson	.50	.20
22 John"Boog" Powell	1.50	.60
23 Frank Robinson P/MG	2.00	.80
24 Charlie Spikes	.50	.20
25 Coaching Staff	.50	.20

1976 Indians Team Issue

This nine-card set of the Cleveland Indians features color player photos printed on postcard-size cards. The cards are unnumbered and checklisted below in alphabetical order.

	NM	Ex
COMPLETE SET (9)	8.00	3.20
1 Larvell Banks	.50	.20
2 Tom Buskey	.50	.20
3 Dennis Eckersley	5.00	2.00
4 Ray Fosse	.50	.20
5 Don Hood	.50	.20
6 Dave LaRoche	.50	.20
7 Boog Powell	1.50	.60
8 Ron Pruitt	.50	.20
9 Stan Thomas	.50	.20

1977 Indians 1920 TCMA

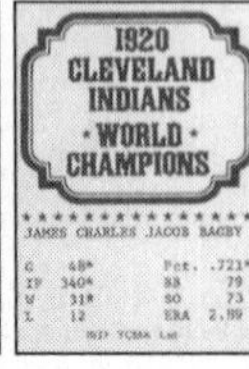

This 22-card set commemorates the 1920 World Champion Cleveland Indians. The fronts feature black-and-white player photos, while the backs display player statistics. One jumbo card measuring approximately 3 3/4" by 5" carries a story about the 1920 Cleveland Indians Team. The cards are unnumbered and checklisted below in alphabetical order with the jumbo card listed as number 22.

	NM	Ex
COMPLETE SET (22)	20.00	8.00
1 Jim Bagby	1.00	.40
2 George Burns	.50	.20
3 Ray Caldwell	.50	.20
4 Ray Chapman	1.50	.60
5 Stan Coleleski	2.00	.80
6 Joe Evans	.50	.20
7 Larry Gardner	.50	.20
8 Jack Graney	.50	.20
9 Charlie Jamieson	.50	.20
10 Wheeler "Doc" Johnston	.50	.20
11 Harry Lunte	.50	.20
12 John "Duster" Mails	.50	.20
13 Guy Morton	.50	.20
14 Les Nunamaker	.50	.20
15 Steve O'Neill	1.00	.40
16 Joe Sewell	2.00	.80
17 Elmer Smith	.50	.20
18 Tris Speaker P/MG	5.00	2.00
19 George Uhle	.50	.20
20 Bill Wambsganss	1.50	.60
21 Joe Wood	1.50	.60
22 Wilbert Robinson MG Tris Speaker	2.00	.80

1977 Indians Team Issue

This 25-card set features black-and-white, glossy photos of the Cleveland Indians printed on postcard-size cards. Jim Bibby's card (number 1) is the only color photo. The cards are unnumbered and checklisted below in alphabetical order.

	NM	Ex
COMPLETE SET (25)	15.00	6.00
1 Jim Bibby	1.00	.40
2 Larvell Blanks	.50	.20
3 Bruce Bochte	.50	.20
4 Tom Buskey	.50	.20
5 Rico Carty	.75	.30
6 Rocky Colavito CO	1.50	.60
7 Pat Dobson	.50	.20
8 Frank Duffy	.50	.20
9 Dennis Eckersley	3.00	1.20
10 Al Fitzmorris	.50	.20
11 Ray Fosse	.50	.20
12 Fred Kendall	.50	.20
13 Jim Kern	.50	.20
14 Dave LaRoche	.50	.20
15 John Lowenstein	.50	.20
16 Rick Manning	.50	.20
17 Bill Melton	.50	.20
18 Sid Monge	.50	.20
19 Jim Norris	.50	.20
20 Joe Nossek CO	.50	.20
21 Ron Pruitt	.50	.20
22 Frank Robinson MG	1.50	.60
23 Andre Thornton	1.00	.40
24 Jeff Torborg CO	.50	.20
25 Rick Waits	.50	.20

1978 Indians Team Issue

This 31-card set of the Cleveland Indians features black-and-white photos on postcard-size cards. The cards are unnumbered and checklisted below in alphabetical order.

	NM	Ex
COMPLETE SET (31)	12.00	4.80
1 Buddy Bell	1.00	.40
2 Larvell Blanks	.50	.20
3 Wayne Cage	.50	.20
4 David Clyde	.50	.20

5 Rocky Colavito CO 1.50 .60
6 Ted Cox .50 .20
7 Paul Dade .50 .20
8 Bo Diaz .50 .20
9 Dave Duncan CO .50 .20
10 Al Fitzmorris .50 .20
11 Wayne Garland .50 .20
12 Johnny Grubb .50 .20
13 Harvey Haddix CO .50 .20
14 Ron Hassey .50 .20
15 Don Hood .50 .20
16 Willie Horton .75 .30
17 Jim Kern .50 .20
18 Dennis Kinney .50 .20
19 Duane Kuiper .50 .20
20 Rick Manning .50 .20
21 Sid Monge .50 .20
22 Jim Norris .50 .20
23 Joe Nossek CO .50 .20
24 Mike Paxton .50 .20
25 Ron Pruitt .50 .20
26 Horace Speed .50 .20
27 Andre Thornton 1.00 .40
28 Jeff Torborg MG .50 .20
29 Tom Veryzer .50 .20
30 Rick Waits .50 .20
31 Rick Wise .50 .20

1979 Indians Team Issue

These cards are similar to the other Indians team issues around this period. These cards are black and white with a light paper stock. These cards are unnumbered so we have sequenced them in alphabetical order.

NM Ex
COMPLETE SET 15.00 6.00
1 Gary Alexander .50 .20
2 Del Alston .50 .20
3 Larry Anderson .50 .20
4 Len Barker .50 .20
5 Bobby Bonds 1.00 .40
6 Wayne Cage .50 .20
7 David Clyde .50 .20
8 Ted Cox .50 .20
9 Victor Cruz .50 .20
10 Paul Dade .50 .20
11 Bo Diaz .50 .20
12 Dave Duncan .50 .20
13 Dave Garcia MG .50 .20
14 Wayne Garland .50 .20
15 Mike Hargrove .75 .30
16 Toby Harrah .75 .30
17 Chuck Hartenstein .50 .20
18 Don Hood .50 .20
19 Cliff Johnson .50 .20
20 Duane Kuiper .50 .20
21 Rick Manning .50 .20
22 Sid Monge .50 .20
23 Joe Nossek .50 .20
24 Mike Paxton .50 .20
25 Paul Reuschel .50 .20
26 Ron Pruitt .50 .20
27 Dave Rosello .50 .20
28 Horace Speed .50 .20
29 Dan Spillner .50 .20
30 Andre Thornton .75 .30
31 Jeff Torborg MG .50 .20
32 Tom Veryzer .50 .20
33 Rick Waits .50 .20
34 Eric Wilkins .50 .20
35 Rick Wise .50 .20

1980 Indians Team Issue

This 31-card set of the Cleveland Indians features black-and-white player photos printed on postcard-size cards. The cards are unnumbered and checklisted below in alphabetical order. The postcards numbered from 32 through 38 were late additions as the Indians made player moves during the season

NM Ex
COMPLETE SET (31) 15.00 6.00
1 Gary Alexander .50 .20
2 Del Alston .50 .20
3 Len Barker .50 .20
5 Victor Cruz .50 .20
6 John Denny .50 .20
6 Joe Charboneau 1.50 .60
7 Bo Diaz .50 .20
8 Dave Duncan CO .50 .20
9 Jerry Dybzinski .50 .20
10 Dave Garcia MG .50 .20
11 Wayne Garland .50 .20
12 Mike Hargrove 1.00 .40
13 Toby Harrah .75 .30
14 Ron Hassey .50 .20
15 Cliff Johnson .50 .20
16 Duane Kuiper .50 .20
17 Rick Manning .50 .20
18 Tom McCraw CO .50 .20
19 Sid Monge .50 .20
20 Andres Mora .50 .20
21 Joe Nossek CO .50 .20
22 Jorge Orta .50 .20
23 Bob Owchinko .50 .20
24 Ron Pruitt .50 .20
25 Dave Rosello .50 .20
26 Dennis Sommers CO .50 .20
27 Dan Spillner .50 .20
28 Mike Stanton .50 .20
29 Andre Thornton .75 .30
30 Tom Veryzer .50 .20
31 Rick Waits .50 .20
32 Baseball Bug .50 .20
33 Alan Bannister .50 .20
34 Jack Brohamer .50 .20
35 Miguel Dilone .50 .20
36 Gary Gray .50 .20
37 Ross Grimsley .50 .20
38 Sandy Withol .50 .20

1982 Indians

This 36-card set measures approximately 3 1/2" by 5 1/2" and feature black and white player portraits in a white border with the player's name, position and team name in the bottom margin. The backs are blank. The cards are unnumbered and checklisted below in

alphabetical order. This issue features members of the 1982 Clevleland Indians.

Nm-Mt Ex-Mt
COMPLETE SET (36) 15.00 6.00
1 Bud Anderson .50 .20
2 Chris Bando .50 .20
3 Alan Bannister .50 .20
4 Len Barker .50 .20
5 Bert Blyleven 1.00 .40
6 John Bohnet .50 .20
7 Carmelo Castillo .50 .20
8 Joe Charboneau .75 .30
9 Rodney Craig .50 .20
10 John Denny .50 .20
11 Miguel Dilone .50 .20
12 Jerry Dybzinski .50 .20
13 Dave Garcia MG .50 .20
14 Gordy Glaser .50 .20
15 Ed Glynn .50 .20
16 Johnny Goryl CO .50 .20
17 Mike Hargrove 1.00 .40
18 Toby Harrah .75 .30
19 Ron Hassey .50 .20
20 Von Hayes .75 .30
21 Neal Heaton .50 .20
22 Dennis Lewallyn .50 .20
23 Rick Manning .50 .20
24 Bake McBride .50 .20
25 Tommy McCraw CO .50 .20
26 Bill Nahorodny .50 .20
27 Karl Pagel .50 .20
28 Jack Perconte .50 .20
29 Mel Queen CO .50 .20
30 Dennis Sommers CO .50 .20
31 Lary Sorensen .50 .20
32 Dan Spillner .50 .20
33 Rick Sutcliffe 1.00 .40
34 Andre Thornton .75 .30
35 Rick Waits .50 .20
36 Eddie Whitson .50 .20

1982 Indians Burger King

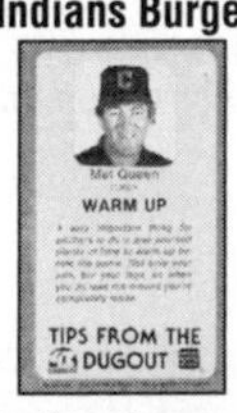

The cards in this 12-card set measure approximately 3" by 5". Tips From The Dugout is the series title of this set issued on a one card per week basis by the Burger King chain in the Cleveland area. Each card contains a black and white photo of manager Dave Garcia or coaches Goryl, McCraw, Queen and Sommers, under whom appears a paragraph explaining some aspect of inside baseball. The photo and "Tip" are set upon a large yellow area surrounded by green borders. The cards are not numbered and are blank-backed. The logos of Burger King and WUAB-TV appear at the base of the card.

Nm-Mt Ex-Mt
COMPLETE SET (12) 12.00 4.80
1 Dave Garcia MG 1.00 .40
2 Dave Garcia MG 1.00 .40
3 Johnny Goryl CO 1.00 .40
4 Johnny Goryl CO 1.00 .40
5 Tom McCraw CO 1.00 .40
6 Tom McCraw CO 1.00 .40
7 Tom McCraw CO 1.00 .40
8 Mel Queen CO 1.00 .40
9 Mel Queen CO 1.00 .40
10 Dennis Sommers CO 1.00 .40
11 Dennis Sommers CO 1.00 .40
12 Dennis Sommers CO 1.00 .40

1982 Indians Wheaties

The cards in this 30-card set measure approximately 2 13/16" by 4 1/8". This set of Cleveland Indians baseball players was co-produced by the Indians baseball club and Wheaties, whose respective logos appear on the front of every card. The cards were given away in groups of 10 as a promotion during games on May 30 (1-10), June 19 (11-20) and July 16, 1982 (21-30). The manager (MG), four coaches (CO), and 25 players are featured in a simple format of a color picture, player name and position. The cards are not numbered and the backs contain a Wheaties ad. The set was later sold at the Cleveland Indians gift shop. The cards are ordered below alphabetically within groups of ten as they were issued.

Nm-Mt Ex-Mt
COMPLETE SET (30) 15.00 6.00
1 Bert Blyleven 1.00 .40
2 Joe Charboneau .75 .30
3 Jerry Dybzinski .50 .20
4 Dave Garcia MG .50 .20
5 Toby Harrah .75 .30
6 Ron Hassey .50 .20
7 Dennis Lewallyn .50 .20
8 Rick Manning .50 .20
9 Tommy McCraw CO .50 .20
10 Rick Waits .50 .20
11 Chris Bando .50 .20
12 Len Barker .75 .30
13 Tom Brennan .50 .20
14 Rodney Craig .50 .20
15 Mike Fischlin .50 .20
16 Johnny Goryl CO .50 .20
17 Mel Queen CO .50 .20
18 Lary Sorensen .50 .20
19 Andre Thornton 1.00 .40
20 Eddie Whitson .50 .20
21 Alan Bannister .50 .20
22 John Denny .50 .20
23 Miguel Dilone .50 .20
24 Mike Hargrove 1.00 .40
25 Von Hayes 1.00 .40
26 Bake McBride .50 .20
27 Jack Perconte .50 .20
28 Dennis Sommers CO .50 .20
29 Dan Spillner .50 .20
30 Rick Sutcliffe 1.00 .40

1983 Indians Postcards

These postcards feature members of the 1983 Cleveland Indians. They are unnumbered and we have sequenced them in alphabetical order.

Nm-Mt Ex-Mt
COMPLETE SET 10.00 4.00
1 Bud Anderson .25 .10
2 Jay Baller .25 .10
3 Chris Bando .25 .10
4 Alan Bannister .25 .10
5 Len Barker .25 .10
6 Bert Blyleven .75 .30
7 Carmelo Castillo .25 .10
8 Wil Culmer .25 .10
9 Miguel Dilone .25 .10
10 Jerry Dybzinski .25 .10
11 Jim Essian .25 .10
12 Juan Eichelberger .25 .10
13 Mike Ferraro MG .25 .10
14 Mike Fischlin .25 .10
15 Julio Franco 2.00 .80
16 Ed Glynn .25 .10
17 Mike Hargrove .75 .30
18 Toby Harrah .50 .20
19 Ron Hassey .25 .10
20 Neal Heaton .25 .10
21 Rick Manning .25 .10
22 Bake McBride .25 .10
23 Don McMahon CO .25 .10
24 Ed Napoleon CO .25 .10
25 Karl Pagel .25 .10
26 Jack Perconte .25 .10
27 Broderick Perkins .25 .10
28 Jerry Reed .25 .10
29 Kevin Rhomberg .25 .10
30 Ramon Romero .25 .10
31 Dennis Sommers CO .25 .10
32 Lary Sorensen .25 .10
33 Dan Spillner .25 .10
34 Rick Sutcliffe .50 .20
35 Andre Thornton .75 .30
36 Manny Trillo .50 .20
37 Otto Velez .25 .10
38 George Vuckovich .25 .10
39 Rick Waits .25 .10

1983 Indians Wheaties

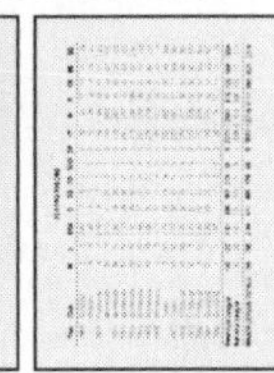

The cards in this 32-card set measure approximately 2 13/16" by 4 1/8". The full color set of 1983 Wheaties Indians is quite similar to the Wheaties set of 1982. The backs, however, are significantly different. They contain complete career playing records of the players. The complete sets were given away at the ball park on May 15, 1983. The set was later made available at the Indians Gift Shop. The manager (MG) and several coaches (CO) are included in the set. The cards below are ordered alphabetically by the subject's name.

Nm-Mt Ex-Mt
COMPLETE SET (32) 10.00 4.00
1 Bud Anderson .25 .10
2 Jay Baller .25 .10
3 Chris Bando .25 .10
4 Alan Bannister .25 .10
5 Len Barker .50 .20
6 Bert Blyleven 1.00 .40
7 Wil Culmer .25 .10
8 Miguel Dilone .25 .10
9 Juan Eichelberger .25 .10
10 Jim Essian .25 .10
11 Mike Ferraro MG .25 .10
12 Mike Fischlin .25 .10
13 Julio Franco 1.50 .60
14 Ed Glynn .25 .10
15 Johnny Goryl CO .25 .10
16 Mike Hargrove .75 .30
17 Toby Harrah .50 .20
18 Ron Hassey .25 .10
19 Neal Heaton .25 .10
20 Rick Manning .25 .10
21 Bake McBride .25 .10
22 Don McMahon CO .25 .10
23 Ed Napoleon CO .25 .10
24 Broderick Perkins .25 .10
25 Dennis Sommers CO .25 .10
26 Lary Sorensen .25 .10
27 Dan Spillner .25 .10
28 Rick Sutcliffe 1.00 .40
29 Andre Thornton .75 .30
30 Manny Trillo .50 .20
31 George Vukovich .25 .10
32 Rick Waits .25 .10

1984 Indians

This 33-card set of the Cleveland Indians measures approximately 3 1/2" by 5 1/2" and features black-and-white player portraits in a white border. The player's name, position, and team are printed in the wide bottom margin. The backs are blank. The cards are unnumbered and checklisted below in alphabetical order.

Nm-Mt Ex-Mt
COMPLETE SET (33) 10.00 4.00
1 Luis Aponte .25 .10
2 Chris Bando .25 .10
3 Rick Behenna .25 .10
4 Tony Bernazard .25 .10
5 Bert Blyleven 1.00 .40
6 Bobby Bonds CO .75 .30
7 Brett Butler 1.50 .60
8 Ernie Camacho .25 .10
9 Carmelo Castillo .25 .10
10 Pat Corrales MG .25 .10
11 Jamie Easterly .25 .10
12 Mike Fischlin .25 .10
13 Julio Franco 1.50 .60
14 George Frazier .25 .10
15 Johnny Goryl CO .25 .10
16 Mike Hargrove .75 .30
17 Ron Hassey .25 .10
18 Neal Heaton .25 .10
19 Brook Jacoby .50 .20
20 Mike Jeffcoat .25 .10
21 Don McMahon CO .25 .10
22 Ed Napoleon CO .25 .10
23 Otis Nixon 1.00 .40
24 Broderick Perkins .25 .10
25 Kevin Rhomberg .25 .10
26 Dan Spillner .25 .10
27 Dennis Sommers .25 .10
28 Rick Sutcliffe .50 .20
29 Pat Tabler .25 .10
30 Andre Thornton .75 .30
31 George Vukovich .25 .10
32 Tom Waddell .25 .10
33 Jerry Willard .25 .10

1984 Indians Wheaties

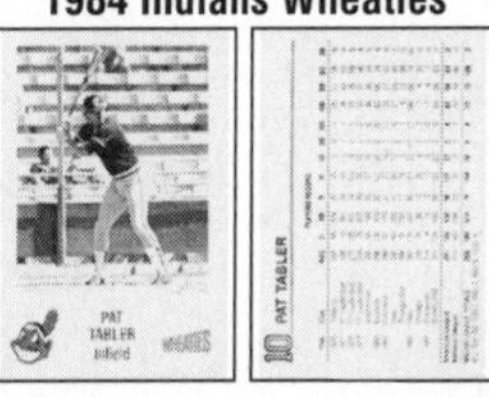

The cards in this 29-card set measure approximately 2 13/16" by 4 1/8". For the third straight year, Wheaties distributed a set of Cleveland Indians baseball cards. These oversized cards were passed out at a Baseball Card Day at the Cleveland Stadium. Similar in appearance to the cards of the past two years, both the Indians and the Wheaties logos appear on the obverse, along with the name, team and position. Cards are numbered on the back by the player's uniform number.

Nm-Mt Ex-Mt
COMPLETE SET (29) 10.00 4.00
2 Brett Butler 1.00 .40
4 Tony Bernazard .25 .10
8 Carmelo Castillo .25 .10
10 Pat Tabler .25 .10
13 Ernie Camacho .25 .10
14 Julio Franco 1.00 .40
15 Broderick Perkins .25 .10
16 Jerry Willard .25 .10
18 Pat Corrales MG .25 .10
21 Mike Hargrove .75 .30
22 Mike Fischlin .25 .10
23 Chris Bando .25 .10
24 George Vukovich .25 .10
26 Brook Jacoby .50 .20
27 Steve Farr .50 .20
28 Bert Blyleven 1.00 .40
29 Andre Thornton .75 .30
30 Joe Carter 5.00 2.00
31 Steve Comer .25 .10
33 Roy Smith .25 .10
34 Mel Hall .50 .20
36 Jamie Easterly .25 .10
37 Don Schulze .25 .10
38 Luis Aponte .25 .10
44 Neal Heaton .25 .10
46 Mike Jeffcoat .25 .10
54 Tom Waddell .25 .10
NNO John Goryl CO .50 .20
Dennis Sommers CO
Ed Napoleon CO
Bobby Bonds CO
Don McMahon CO
NNO Tom-E-Hawk (Mascot) .25 .10

1985 Indians

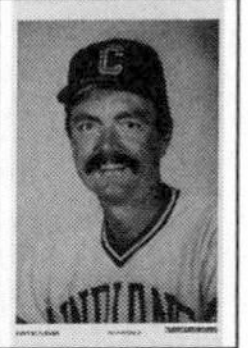

This 36-card set of the Cleveland Indians measures approximately 3 1/2" by 5 1/2" and features white-bordered, black-and-white player photos. The player's name, position and team are printed in the wide bottom margin. The backs are blank. The cards are unnumbered and checklisted below in alphabetical order.

Nm-Mt Ex-Mt
COMPLETE SET (36) 10.00 4.00
1 Chris Bando .25 .10
2 Rick Behenna .25 .10
3 Butch Benton .25 .10
4 Tony Bernazard .25 .10
5 Bert Blyleven 1.00 .40
6 Bobby Bonds CO .75 .30
7 Brett Butler 1.00 .40
8 Ernie Camacho .25 .10
9 Joe Carter 2.50 1.00
10 Carmen Castillo .25 .10
11 Pat Corrales MG .25 .10
12 Jamie Easterly .25 .10
13 Mike Fischlin .25 .10
14 Julio Franco 1.00 .40
15 John Goryl CO .25 .10
16 Mel Hall .25 .10
17 Mike Hargrove .75 .30
18 Neal Heaton .25 .10
19 Brook Jacoby .25 .10
20 Mike Jeffcoat .25 .10
21 Don McMahon CO .25 .10
22 Ed Napoleon CO .25 .10
23 Otis Nixon 1.00 .40
24 Geno Petralli .25 .10
25 Ramon Romero .25 .10
26 Vern Ruhle .25 .10
27 Don Schulze .25 .10
28 Jim Siwy .25 .10
29 Roy Smith .25 .10
30 Dennis Sommers CO .25 .10
31 Pat Tabler .25 .10
32 Andre Thornton .75 .30
33 Dave Von Ohlen .25 .10
34 George Vukovich .25 .10
35 Tom Waddell .25 .10
36 Jerry Willard .25 .10

1985 Indians Polaroid

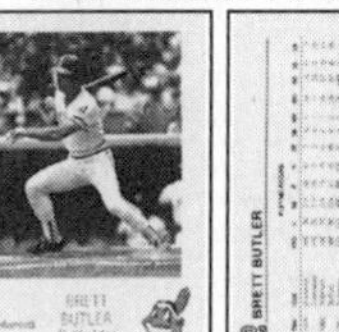

This 32-card set features cards (each measuring approximately 2 13/16" by 4 1/8") of the Cleveland Indians. The cards are unnumbered except for uniform number, as they are listed below. The set was also sponsored by J.C. Penney and was distributed at the stadium to fans in attendance on Baseball Card Day.

Nm-Mt Ex-Mt
COMPLETE SET (32) 18.00 7.25
2 Brett Butler 1.00 .40
4 Tony Bernazard .50 .20
8 Carmen Castillo .50 .20
10 Pat Tabler .50 .20
12 Benny Ayala .50 .20
13 Ernie Camacho .50 .20
14 Julio Franco 1.00 .40
16 Jerry Willard .50 .20
18 Pat Corrales MG .50 .20
20 Otis Nixon 1.50 .60
21 Mike Hargrove 1.00 .40
22 Mike Fischlin .50 .20
23 Chris Bando .50 .20
24 George Vukovich .50 .20
26 Brook Jacoby .75 .30
27 Mel Hall .75 .30
28 Bert Blyleven 1.00 .40
29 Andre Thornton 1.00 .40
30 Joe Carter 6.00 2.40
32 Rick Behenna .50 .20
33 Roy Smith .50 .20
35 Jerry Reed .50 .20
36 Jamie Easterly .50 .20
38 Dave Von Ohlen .50 .20
41 Rich Thompson .50 .20
43 Bryan Clark .50 .20
44 Neal Heaton .50 .20
48 Vern Ruhle .50 .20
49 Jeff Barkley .50 .20
50 Ramon Romero .50 .20
54 Tom Waddell .50 .20
NNO Bobby Bonds CO .75 .30
John Goryl CO
Don McMahon CO
Ed Napoleon CO
Dennis Sommers CO

1986 Indians Greats TCMA

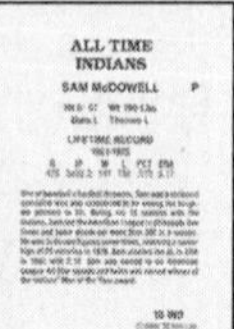

This 12-card standard-size set features some of the best all-time Cleveland Indians. The cards feature the player photo, his name and position on the front. The backs have vital statistics, a biography and career totals.

Nm-Mt Ex-Mt
COMPLETE SET (12) 6.00 2.40
1 Hal Trosky .25 .10

2 Nap Lajoie 1.00 .40
3 Lou Boudreau .75 .30
4 Al Rosen .25 .10
5 Joe Jackson 2.00 .80
6 Tris Speaker 1.00 .40
7 Larry Doby .75 .30
8 Jim Hegan .25 .10
9 Cy Young 1.00 .40
10 Sam McDowell .25 .10
11 Ray Narleski .25 .10
12 Al Lopez MG .50 .20

1986 Indians Oh Henry

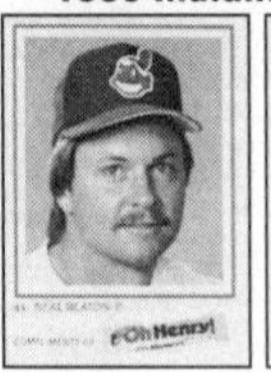

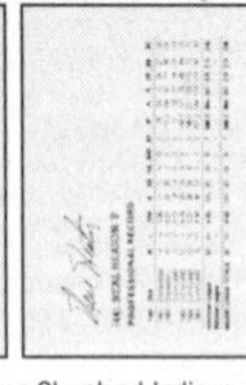

This 30-card set features Cleveland Indians and was distributed at the stadium to fans in attendance on Baseball Card Day. The cards were printed in one folded sheet which was perforated for easy separation into individual cards. The cards have white borders with a blue frame around each photo. The card backs include detailed career year-by-year statistics. The individual cards measure approximately 2 1/4" by 3 1/8" and have full-color fronts.

Nm-Mt Ex-Mt
COMPLETE SET (30) 15.00 6.00
2 Brett Butler 1.50 .60
4 Tony Bernazard .25 .10
6 Andy Allanson .25 .10
7 Pat Corrales MG .25 .10
8 Carmen Castillo .25 .10
10 Pat Tabler .25 .10
13 Ernie Camacho .25 .10
14 Julio Franco 1.00 .40
15 Dan Rohn .25 .10
18 Ken Schrom .25 .10
20 Otis Nixon 1.00 .40
22 Fran Mullins .25 .10
23 Chris Bando .25 .10
24 Ed Williams .25 .10
26 Brook Jacoby .50 .20
27 Mel Hall .25 .10
29 Andre Thornton 1.00 .40
30 Joe Carter 5.00 2.00
35 Phil Niekro 2.50 1.00
36 Jamie Easterly .25 .10
37 Don Schulze .25 .10
42 Rick Yett .25 .10
43 Scott Bailes .25 .10
44 Neal Heaton .25 .10
46 Jim Kern .25 .10
48 Dickie Noles .25 .10
49 Tom Candiotti 1.00 .40
53 Reggie Ritter .25 .10
54 Tom Waddell .25 .10
NNO Jack Aker CO .50 .20
Bobby Bonds CO
Doc Edwards CO
John Goryl CO

1986 Indians Team Issue

This 52-card set measures approximately 3 1/2" by 5 1/2" and features black-and-white player portraits in a white border with the player's name, position, and team name in the bottom margin. The backs are black. The set is large as players changed during the season, and their cards were added to the set. The cards are unnumbered and checklisted below in alphabetical order.

Nm-Mt Ex-Mt
COMPLETE SET (52) 15.00 6.00
1 Jack Aker CO .25 .10
2 Andy Allanson .25 .10
3 Scott Bailes .25 .10
4 Chris Bando .25 .10
5 Jay Bell 1.50 .60
6 Tony Bernazard .25 .10
7 Bobby Bonds CO .50 .20
8 Bernardo Brito .25 .10
9 Kevin Buckley .25 .10
10 John Butcher .25 .10
11 Brett Butler .75 .30
12 Ernie Camacho .25 .10
13 Tom Candiotti .25 .10
14 Joe Carter 1.50 .60
15 Carmen Castillo .25 .10
16 Dave Clark .25 .10
17 Pat Corrales MG .25 .10
18 Keith Creel .25 .10
19 Jamie Easterly .25 .10
20 Doc Edwards CO .25 .10
21 Julio Franco 1.00 .40
22 Vic Garcia .25 .10
23 Johnny Goryl CO .25 .10
24 Mel Hall .25 .10
25 Neal Heaton .25 .10
26 Brook Jacoby .25 .10
27 Jim Kern .25 .10
28 Fran Mullins .25 .10
29 Phil Niekro 1.50 .60
30 Otis Nixon 1.00 .40
31 Junior Noboa .25 .10
32 Dickie Noles .25 .10
33 Bryan Oelkers .25 .10
34 Craig Pippin .25 .10
35 Reggie Ritter .25 .10
36 Scott Roberts .25 .10
37 Dan Rohn .25 .10
38 Jose Roman .25 .10
39 Miguel Roman .25 .10
40 Ken Schrom .25 .10
41 Don Schulze .25 .10
42 Cory Snyder .50 .20
43 Dain Syverson .25 .10
44 Pat Tabler .25 .10
45 Andre Thornton .75 .30
46 Tom Waddell .25 .10
47 Curt Wardle .25 .10
48 Randy Washington .25 .10
49 Jim Weaver .25 .10
50 Ed Williams .25 .10
51 Jim Wilson .25 .10
52 Rich Yett .25 .10

1987 Indians Gatorade

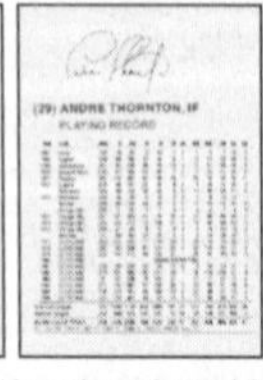

Gatorade sponsored this perforated set of 30 full-color cards of the Cleveland Indians. The cards measure approximately 2 1/8" by 3" (or 3 1/8") and feature the Gatorade logo prominently on the fronts of the cards. The cards were distributed as a tri-folded sheet (each part approximately 9 5/8" by 11 3/16") on April 25th at the stadium during the game against the Yankees. The large team photo is approximately 11 3/16" by 9 5/8". Card backs for the individual players contain year-by-year stats for that player. The cards are referenced and listed below by uniform number.

Nm-Mt Ex-Mt
COMPLETE SET (30) 10.00 4.00
2 Brett Butler 1.00 .40
4 Tony Bernazard .25 .10
6 Andy Allanson .25 .10
7 Pat Corrales MG .25 .10
8 Carmen Castillo .25 .10
10 Pat Tabler .25 .10
11 Jamie Easterly .25 .10
12 Dave Clark .25 .10
13 Ernie Camacho .25 .10
14 Julio Franco 1.00 .40
17 Junior Noboa .25 .10
18 Ken Schrom .25 .10
20 Otis Nixon .50 .20
21 Greg Swindell .50 .20
22 Frank Wills .25 .10
23 Chris Bando .25 .10
24 Rick Dempsey .50 .20
26 Brook Jacoby .50 .20
27 Mel Hall .25 .10
28 Cory Snyder .50 .20
29 Andre Thornton .75 .30
30 Joe Carter 4.00 1.60
35 Phil Niekro 2.00 .80
36 Ed VandeBerg .25 .10
42 Rich Yett .25 .10
43 Scott Bailes .25 .10
46 Doug Jones .75 .30
49 Tom Candiotti .75 .30
54 Tom Waddell .25 .10
NNO Bobby Bonds CO .50 .20
John Goryl CO
Pat Corrales MG
Doc Edwards CO
Jack Aker CO
NNO Team Photo 3.00 1.20
(Large size)

1988 Indians Gatorade

This set was distributed as 30 perforated player cards attached to a large team photo of the Cleveland Indians. The cards measure approximately 2 1/4" by 3". Card backs are oriented either horizontally or vertically. Card backs are printed in red, blue, and black on white card stock. Card backs contain a facsimile autograph of the player. Cards are not arranged on the sheet in any order. The cards are unnumbered except for uniform number, which is given on the front and back of each card. The cards are referenced and listed below by uniform number. The Gatorade logo is on the front of every card in the lower right corner.

Nm-Mt Ex-Mt
COMPLETE SET (30) 8.00 3.20
2 Tom Spencer CO .25 .10
6 Andy Allanson .25 .10
7 Luis Isaac CO .25 .10
8 Carmen Castillo .25 .10
9 Charlie Manuel CO .25 .10
10 Pat Tabler .25 .10
11 Doug Jones .50 .20
14 Julio Franco 1.00 .40
15 Ron Washington .25 .10
16 Jay Bell 2.00 .80
17 Bill Laskey .25 .10
20 Willie Upshaw .25 .10
21 Greg Swindell .25 .10
23 Chris Bando .25 .10
25 Dave Clark .25 .10
26 Brook Jacoby .25 .10
27 Mel Hall .25 .10
28 Cory Snyder .25 .10
30 Joe Carter 3.00 1.20
31 Dan Schatzeder .25 .10
32 Doc Edwards MG .25 .10
33 Ron Kittle .25 .10
35 Mark Wiley CO .25 .10
42 Rich Yett .25 .10
43 Scott Bailes .25 .10
45 John Goryl CO .25 .10
47 Jeff Kaiser .25 .10
49 Tom Candiotti .50 .20
50 Jeff Dedmon .25 .10
52 John Farrell .25 .10
NNO Team Photo 2.50 1.00
(Large size)

1988 Indians Team Issue

This 40-card set of the Cleveland Indians features black-and-white player photos printed on postcard-size cards. The cards are unnumbered and checklisted below in alphabetical order

Nm-Mt Ex-Mt
COMPLETE SET (40) 20.00 8.00
1 Darrel Akerfelds .50 .20
2 Andy Allanson .50 .20
3 Scott Bailes .50 .20
4 Chris Bando .50 .20
5 Jay Bell 1.00 .40
6 Bud Black .50 .20
7 Tom Candiotti .75 .30
8 Joe Carter 1.50 .60
9 Carmen Castillo .50 .20
10 Dave Clark .50 .20
11 Doc Edwards MG .50 .20
12 John Farrell .50 .20
13 Julio Franco 1.50 .60
14 Terry Francona .75 .30
15 Don Gordon .50 .20
16 Johnny Goryl CO .50 .20
17 Mel Hall .50 .20
18 Brad Havens .50 .20
19 Tommy Hinzo .50 .20
20 Luis Isaac CO .50 .20
21 Brook Jacoby .50 .20
22 Doug Jones .75 .30
23 Ron Kittle .50 .20
24 Bill Laskey .50 .20
25 Don Lovell .50 .20
26 Charlie Manuel CO .50 .20
27 Jon Perlman .50 .20
28 Domingo Ramos .50 .20
29 Rick Rodriguez .50 .20
30 Dan Schatzeder .50 .20
31 Charlie Scott .50 .20
32 Cory Snyder .75 .30
33 Tom Spencer CO .50 .20
34 Greg Swindell .75 .30
35 Pat Tabler .50 .20
36 Willie Upshaw .50 .20
37 Ron Washington .50 .20
38 Mark Wiley CO .50 .20
39 Eddie Williams .50 .20
40 Rich Yett .50 .20

1989 Indians Team Issue

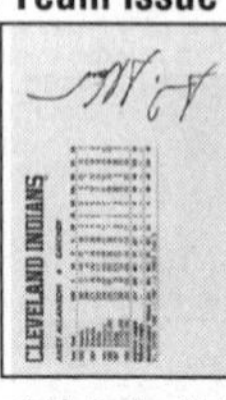

This 28-card set was available in the giftshop and was given away at the ballpark on May 13. The cards measure 2 7/8" by 4 1/4" and are printed on thin card stock. On a white card face, the fronts feature color player photos with a white inner border and red outer border. "The Tribe" logo is printed in the upper left corner, while player information is printed in the lower border. The backs carry the team name in red, while seasonal and career statistics and facsimile autograph are in blue. The cards are unnumbered and checklisted below in alphabetical order.

Nm-Mt Ex-Mt
COMPLETE SET (28) 8.00 3.20
1 Luis Aguayo .25 .10
2 Andy Allanson .25 .10
3 Keith Atherton .25 .10
4 Scott Bailes .25 .10
5 Bud Black .25 .10
6 Jerry Browne .25 .10
7 Tom Candiotti .25 .10
8 Joe Carter 2.50 1.00
9 Dave Clark .25 .10
10 Doc Edwards MG .25 .10
11 John Farrell .25 .10
12 Felix Fermin .25 .10
13 Brad Havens .25 .10
14 Brook Jacoby .25 .10
15 Doug Jones .50 .20
16 Pat Keedy .25 .10
17 Brad Komminsk .25 .10
18 Oddibe McDowell .25 .10
19 Luis Medina .25 .10
20 Rod Nichols .25 .10
21 Pete O'Brien .25 .10
22 Jesse Orosco .50 .20
23 Joe Skalski .25 .10
24 Joel Skinner .25 .10
25 Cory Snyder .25 .10
26 Greg Swindell .25 .10
27 Rich Yett .25 .10
28 Jim Davenport CO .25 .10
Luis Isaac CO
Charlie Manuel CO
Tom Spencer CO
Mark Wiley CO

1990 Indians Team Issue

This 46-card set was available in the Indians giftshop for sale. The cards are unnumbered and we have checklisted them below in alphabetical order.

Nm-Mt Ex-Mt
COMPLETE SET (46) 10.00 3.00
1 Beau Allred .25 .07
2 Sandy Alomar Jr. 1.00 .30
3 Carlos Baerga 1.00 .30
4 Kevin Bearse .25 .07
5 Joey Belle 2.00 .60
6 Bud Black .25 .07
7 Tom Brookens .25 .07
8 Jerry Browne .25 .07
9 Tom Candiotti .25 .07
10 Colin Charland .25 .07
11 Rich Dauer CO .25 .07
12 John Farrell .25 .07
13 Felix Fermin .25 .07
14 Cecilio Guante .25 .07
15 Mike Hargrove CO .50 .15
16 Keith Hernandez .50 .15
17 Luis Isaac CO .25 .07
18 Brook Jacoby .25 .07
19 Dion James .25 .07
20 Chris James .25 .07
21 Doug Jones .50 .15
22 Carl Keliipuleoli .25 .07
23 Tom Lampkin .25 .07
24 Tom Magrann .25 .07
25 Candy Maldonado .25 .07
26 Jeff Manto .25 .07
27 John McNamara MG .25 .07
28 Jose Morales CO .25 .07
29 Rod Nichols .25 .07
30 Al Nipper .25 .07
31 Steve Olin .25 .07
32 Jesse Orosco .50 .15
33 Doug Robertson .25 .07
34 Rudy Seanez .25 .07
35 Jeff Shaw .75 .23
36 Doug Sisk .25 .07
37 Joe Skalski .25 .07
38 Joel Skinner .25 .07
39 Cory Snyder .25 .07
40 Greg Swindell .25 .07
41 Sergio Valdez .25 .07
42 Mike Walker .25 .07
43 Mitch Webster .25 .07
44 Kevin Wickander .25 .07
45 Mark Wiley CO .25 .07
46 Billy Williams CO .75 .23

1991 Indians Fan Club/McDonald's

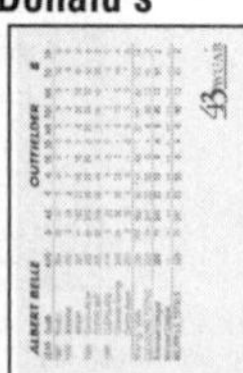

This 30-card set was sponsored by McDonald's and Channel 43 (WUAB). The cards are printed on thin card stock and measure approximately 2 7/8" by 4 1/4". The cards are unnumbered and checklisted below in alphabetical order.

Nm-Mt Ex-Mt
COMPLETE SET (30) 15.00 4.50
1 Beau Allred .50 .15
2 Sandy Alomar .75 .23
3 Carlos Baerga .75 .23
4 Albert Belle 1.50 .45
5 Jerry Browne .50 .15
6 Tom Candiotti .75 .23
7 Alex Cole .50 .15
8 Bruce Egloff .50 .15
9 Jose Escobar .50 .15
10 Felix Fermin .50 .15
11 Brook Jacoby .50 .15
12 John Farrell .50 .15
13 Shawn Hillegas .50 .15
14 Mike Huff .50 .15
15 Chris James .50 .15
16 Doug Jones .75 .23
17 Eric King .50 .15
18 Jeff Manto .50 .15
19 John McNamara MG .50 .15
20 Charles Nagy .75 .23
21 Rod Nichols .50 .15
22 Steve Olin .50 .15
23 Jesse Orosco .75 .23
24 Dave Otto .50 .15
25 Joel Skinner .50 .15
26 Greg Swindell .50 .15
27 Mike Walker .50 .15
28 Turner Ward .50 .15
29 Mitch Webster .50 .15
30 Billy Williams CO .75 .23
Jose Morales CO
Rich Dauer CO
Mike Hargrove CO
Luis Isaac CO
Mark Wiley CO

1992 Indians Fan Club/McDonald's

This 30-card set was sponsored by McDonald's and WUAB Channel 43. The cards are printed on thin card stock and measure approximately 2 7/8" by 4 1/4". The cards are unnumbered and checklisted below in alphabetical order. The set was also produced as a team issue set which is distinguished by the Chief Wahoo mascot logo replacing the McDonald's logo and the removal of the WUAB references. The value for either set is identical.

Nm-Mt Ex-Mt
COMPLETE SET (30) 18.00 5.50
1 Sandy Alomar Jr. .75 .23
2 Jack Armstrong .50 .15
3 Brad Arnsberg .50 .15
4 Carlos Baerga .75 .23
5 Eric Bell .50 .15
6 Albert Belle 1.50 .45
7 Alex Cole .50 .15
8 Dennis Cook .50 .15
9 Felix Fermin .50 .15
10 Mike Hargrove MG .75 .23
11 Glenallen Hill .50 .15
12 Thomas Howard .50 .15
13 Brook Jacoby .50 .15
14 Reggie Jefferson .50 .15
15 Mark Lewis .50 .15
16 Derek Lilliquist .50 .15
17 Kenny Lofton 2.00 .60
18 Charles Nagy .50 .15
19 Rod Nichols .50 .15
20 Steve Olin .50 .15
21 Junior Ortiz .50 .15
22 Dave Otto .50 .15
23 Tony Perezchica .50 .15
24 Ted Power .50 .15
25 Scott Scudder .50 .15
26 Joel Skinner .50 .15
27 Paul Sorrento .75 .23
28 Jim Thome 4.00 1.20
29 Mark Whiten .50 .15
30 Jeff Newman CO .50 .15
Rick Adair CO
Ken Bolek CO
Dom Chiti CO
Ron Clark CO
Jose Morales CO
Dave Nelson CO

1993 Indians WUAB-TV

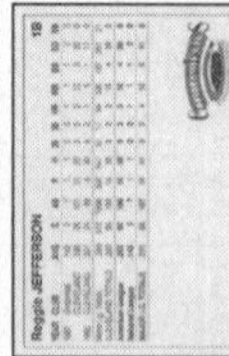

This 34-card team-issued set was available in the Indians giftshop. The WUAB Channel 43 logo appears on only one card, that of Slider, the Tribe's mascot. The cards are unnumbered and checklisted below in alphabetical order. A McDonalds version is produced with two extra cards. The two extra cards are in the version not available at the ball park.

Nm-Mt Ex-Mt
COMPLETE SET (34) 12.00 3.60
1 Sandy Alomar Jr. .50 .15
2 Carlos Baerga .50 .15
3 Albert Belle 1.00 .30
4 Mike Bielecki .25 .07
5 Mike Christopher .25 .07
6 Mark Clark .25 .07
7 Dennis Cook .25 .07
8 Alvaro Espinoza .25 .07
9 Felix Fermin .25 .07
10 Mike Hargrove MG .25 .07
11 Glenallen Hill .25 .07
12 Thomas Howard .25 .07
13 Reggie Jefferson .25 .07
14 Wayne Kirby .25 .07
15 Tom Kramer .25 .07
16 Mark Lewis .25 .07
17 Derek Lilliquist .25 .07
18 Kenny Lofton 1.50 .45
19 Carlos Martinez .25 .07
20 Jose Mesa .50 .15
21 Jeff Mutis .25 .07
22 Charles Nagy .25 .07
23 Bob Ojeda .25 .07
24 Junior Ortiz .25 .07
25 Eric Plunk .25 .07
26 Ted Power .25 .07
27 Scott Scudder .25 .07
28 Joel Skinner .25 .07
29 Paul Sorrento .25 .07
30 Jim Thome 2.00 .60
31 Jeff Treadway .25 .07
32 Kevin Wickander .25 .07
33 Rick Adair CO .25 .07
Ken Bolke CO
Dom Chiti CO
Ron Clark CO
Jose Morales CO
Dave Nelson CO
Jeff Newman CO
34 Slider (Mascot) .25 .07
and Liz (WUAB)
35 Ronald McDonald .25 .07
Mascot
36 Fan Club Welcome .25 .07

1996 Indians Fleer

This 20-card standard-size set was issued by Fleer as a test to see how regional team issues would sell. These cards are different from the regular 1996 Fleer issues as the 10-card packs feature the Indians logo. The cards have silver-foil and are issued with UV coating and they are numbered "X" of 20. The set is sequenced in alphabetical order.

Nm-Mt Ex-Mt
COMPLETE SET (20) 4.00 1.20
1 Sandy Alomar Jr. .20 .06

2 Paul Assenmacher .10 .03
3 Carlos Baerga .20 .06
4 Albert Belle .20 .06
5 Orel Hershiser .20 .06
6 Kenny Lofton .30 .09
7 Dennis Martinez .20 .06
8 Jose Mesa .20 .06
9 Eddie Murray .50 .15
10 Charles Nagy .10 .03
11 Tony Pena .20 .06
12 Herb Perry .10 .03
13 Eric Plunk .10 .03
14 Jim Poole .10 .03
15 Manny Ramirez .75 .23
16 Julian Tavarez .10 .03
17 Jim Thome .75 .23
18 Omar Vizquel .50 .15
19 Indians Logo .10 .03
20 Indians CL .10 .03

1996 Indians Upper Deck

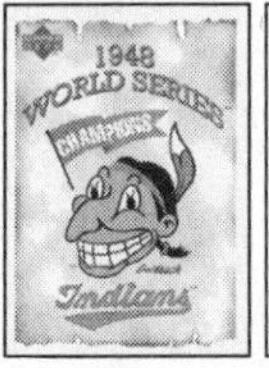

This one card standard-size set features the Indians logo on the front and commemorates their achievement in winning the 1948 World Championship. The back describes the history of the logo of the vintage Indians from that Bill Veeck/Lou Boudreau era. It was available in the Cleveland area as a stand alone card.

Nm-Mt Ex-Mt
1 Cleveland Indians Logo 5.00 1.50

1997 Indians Score

This 15-card set of the Cleveland Indians was issued in five-card packs with a suggested retail price of $1.30 each. The fronts feature color player photos with special team specific color foil stamping. The backs carry player information. Only 100 cases were made for each team. Platinum parallel cards were inserted at a rate of 1:6, Premier parallel cards at a rate of 1:31. A card of Brian Giles in his Rookie Card year is a featured card in this set.

Nm-Mt Ex-Mt
COMPLETE SET (15) 6.00 1.80
*PLATINUM: 5X BASIC CARDS
*PREMIER: 20X BASIC CARDS
1 Albert Belle .40 .12
2 Jack McDowell .25 .07
3 Jim Thome 1.00 .30
4 Dennis Martinez .40 .12
5 Julio Franco .40 .12
6 Omar Vizquel .75 .23
7 Kenny Lofton .60 .18
8 Manny Ramirez 1.00 .30
9 Sandy Alomar Jr. .40 .12
10 Charles Nagy .25 .07
11 Kevin Seitzer .25 .07
12 Mark Carreon .25 .07
13 Jeff Kent .75 .23
14 Danny Graves .40 .12
15 Brian Giles 2.00 .60

1997 Indians Score Update

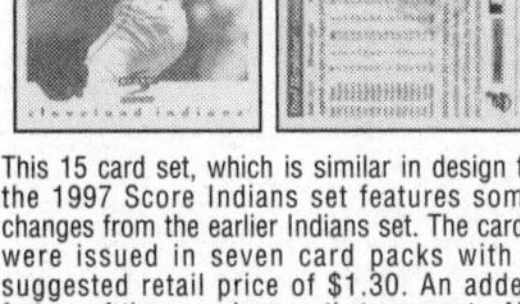

This 15 card set, which is similar in design to the 1997 Score Indians set features some changes from the earlier Indians set. The cards were issued in seven card packs with a suggested retail price of $1.30. An added feature of these packs was that passes to All-Star fanfest were randomly included in the packs. A parallel Tribe collection card was included one every six packs. Brian Giles appears in his Rookie Card season.

Nm-Mt Ex-Mt
COMPLETE SET (15) 5.00 1.50
*TRIBE COLLECTION: 5X BASIC CARDS
1 Matt Williams .60 .18
2 Jack McDowell .25 .07
3 Jim Thome 1.00 .30
4 Chad Ogea .25 .07
5 Julio Franco .40 .12
6 Omar Vizquel .75 .23
7 Kenny Lofton .60 .18
8 Manny Ramirez 1.00 .30
9 Sandy Alomar Jr. .40 .12
10 Charles Nagy .25 .07
11 Kevin Seitzer .25 .07
12 Orel Hershiser .40 .12
13 Paul Assenmacher .25 .07
14 Eric Plunk .25 .07
15 Brian Giles 2.00 .60

1998 Indians Score

This 15-card set was issued in special retail packs and features color photos of the Cleveland Indians team. The backs carry player information. A special platinum parallel set was also issued and randomly inserted in packs.

Nm-Mt Ex-Mt
COMPLETE SET (15) 6.00 1.80
*PLATINUM: 5X BASIC CARDS
1 Jack McDowell .25 .07
2 Jim Thome 1.25 .35
3 Brian Anderson .25 .07
4 Sandy Alomar Jr. .50 .15
5 Omar Vizquel 1.00 .30
6 Brian Giles 1.00 .30
7 Charles Nagy .25 .07
8 Mike Jackson .50 .15
9 David Justice 1.00 .30
10 Jeff Juden .25 .07
11 Matt Williams .75 .23
12 Marquis Grissom .50 .15
13 Tony Fernandez .50 .15
14 Bartolo Colon 1.00 .30
15 Jaret Wright .25 .07

2001 Indians Postcards

This 37-card set was published by Barry Colla. The cards measure at 3 1/2" x 5 1/2". They are numbered on the back. Bios are also found on the back. All cards have an "01" to signify year of issue to go with their number.

Nm-Mt Ex-Mt
COMPLETE SET (37) 12.00 3.60
1 Roberto Alomar 1.00 .30
2 Russ Branyan .50 .15
3 Dave Burba .25 .07
4 Ellis Burks .50 .15
5 Bartolo Colon 1.00 .30
6 Einar Diaz .25 .07
7 Chuck Finley .50 .15
8 Travis Fryman .50 .15
9 Juan Gonzalez 1.00 .30
10 Steve Karsay .25 .07
11 Kenny Lofton 1.00 .30
12 Charles Nagy .25 .07
13 Jim Thome 1.50 .45
14 Omar Vizquel 1.00 .30
15 Bob Wickman .25 .07
16 Jaret Wright .25 .07
17 Jolbert Cabrera .25 .07
18 Wil Cordero .25 .07
19 Marty Cordova .25 .07
20 Jacob Cruz .25 .07
21 Tim Drew .25 .07
22 John McDonald .25 .07
23 Steve Reed .25 .07
24 Ricardo Rincon .25 .07
25 C.C. Sabathia 1.00 .30
26 Paul Shuey .25 .07
27 Justin Speier .25 .07
28 Eddie Taubensee .25 .07
29 Steve Woodard .25 .07
30 Charlie Manuel MG .25 .07
31 Luis Isaac CO .25 .07
32 Clarence Jones CO .25 .07
33 Grady Little CO .25 .07
34 Dick Pole CO .25 .07
35 Joel Skinner CO .25 .07
36 Ted Uhlaender CO .25 .07
37 Dan Williams CO .25 .07

2003 Indians Postcards

These postcards feature photos taken by noted sports photographer Barry Colla. Each of these cards featuring numbering ending in 03 and we have catalogued these cards by the 1st two numbers used on these cards.

MINT NRMT
COMPLETE SET 20.00 9.00
33 Brady Anderson .75 .35
34 Brian Anderson .50 .23
35 Danny Baez .75 .35
36 Josh Bard .50 .23
37 Milton Bradley 1.00 .45
38 Ellis Burks .75 .35
39 Karim Garcia .75 .35
40 Travis Hafner .75 .35
41 Matt Lawton .50 .23
42 John McDonald .50 .23
43 Brandon Phillips .75 .35
44 C.C. Sabathia 1.50 .70
45 Omar Vizquel 1.50 .70
46 Jason Bere .50 .23
47 Casey Blake .50 .23
48 Ben Broussard .50 .23
49 Jason Davis .50 .23
50 Ricky Gutierrez .50 .23
51 Tim Laker .50 .23
52 Cliff Lee .50 .23
53 Terry Mulholland .50 .23
54 David Riske .50 .23
55 Ricardo Rodriguez .50 .23
56 Carl Sadler .50 .23
57 Jose Santiago .50 .23
58 Bill Selby .50 .23
59 Shane Spencer .50 .23
60 Billy Traber .50 .23
61 Eric Wedge MG .50 .23
62 Jake Westbrook .50 .23
63 Bob Wickman .50 .23
64 Mark Wohlers .50 .23
65 Buddy Bell CO .50 .23
66 Jeff Datz CO .50 .23
67 Luis Isaac CO .50 .23
68 Dave Keller CO .50 .23
69 Eddie Murray CO 1.50 .70
70 Joel Skinner CO .50 .23
71 Dan Williams CO .50 .23
72 Carl Willis CO .50 .23

1997 Infinity HOF Fantasy Camp

These standard-size cards are from a 1997 Hall Of Fame Fantasy Camp, and was sponsored by INFINITI. They were giveaways at the camp to the particiapants.

Nm-Mt Ex-Mt
COMPLETE SET 20.00 6.00
1 Harmon Killebrew 10.00 3.00
2 Brooks Robinson 10.00 3.00

1976 Isaly Discs

These discs have the same design as the Crane Discs. These discs are valued the same as Crane Discs and are easily available within the hobby.

NM Ex
COMPLETE SET (70) 20.00 8.00
2 Johnny Bench 1.50 .60
3 Vida Blue .25 .10
4 Larry Bowa .25 .10
5 Lou Brock 1.50 .60
6 Jeff Burroughs .10 .04
7 John Candelaria .10 .04
8 Jose Cardenal .10 .04
9 Rod Carew 1.50 .60
10 Steve Carlton 1.50 .60
11 Dave Cash .10 .04
12 Cesar Cedeno .25 .10
13 Ron Cey .25 .10
14 Carlton Fisk 2.00 .80
15 Tito Fuentes .10 .04
16 Steve Garvey .75 .30
17 Ken Griffey .25 .10
18 Don Gullett .10 .04
19 Willie Horton .10 .04
20 Al Hrabosky .10 .04
21 Catfish Hunter 1.50 .60
22A Reggie Jackson 5.00 2.00
Oakland Athletics
22B Reggie Jackson 1.50 .60
Baltimore Orioles
23 Randy Jones .10 .04
24 Jim Kaat .50 .20
25 Don Kessinger .10 .04
26 Dave Kingman .50 .20
27 Jerry Koosman .25 .10
28 Mickey Lolich .25 .10
29 Greg Luzinski .50 .20
30 Fred Lynn .50 .20
31 Bill Madlock .25 .10
32A Carlos May .75 .30
Chicago White Sox
32B Carlos May .10 .04
New York Yankees
33 John Mayberry .10 .04
34 Bake McBride .10 .04
35 Doc Medich .10 .04
36A Andy Messersmith .75 .30
Los Angeles Dodgers
36B Andy Messersmith .10 .04
Atlanta Braves
37 Rick Monday .10 .04
38 John Montefusco .10 .04
39 Jerry Morales .10 .04
40 Joe Morgan 1.50 .60
41 Thurman Munson .75 .30
42 Bobby Murcer .50 .20
43 Al Oliver .50 .20
44 Jim Palmer 1.50 .60
45 Dave Parker .75 .30
46 Tony Perez .75 .30
47 Jerry Reuss .10 .04
48 Brooks Robinson 1.50 .60
49 Frank Robinson 1.50 .60
50 Steve Rogers .10 .04
51 Pete Rose 2.00 .80
52 Nolan Ryan 4.00 1.60
53 Manny Sanguillen .10 .04
54 Mike Schmidt 2.50 1.00
55 Tom Seaver 2.00 .80
56 Ted Simmons .50 .20
57 Reggie Smith .25 .10
58 Willie Stargell 1.50 .60
59 Rusty Staub .50 .20
60 Rennie Stennett .10 .04
61 Don Sutton 1.50 .60
62A Andre Thornton .75 .30
Chicago Cubs
62B Andre Thornton .10 .04
Montreal Expos
63 Luis Tiant .50 .20
64 Joe Torre .75 .30
65 Mike Tyson .10 .04
66 Bob Watson .25 .10
67 Wilbur Wood .10 .04
68 Jimmy Wynn .10 .04
69 Carl Yastrzemski 1.50 .60
70 Richie Zisk .10 .04

1910 J.H. Dockman All-Star Baseball E-Unc.

Produced by J.H. Dockman and Son, this unattractive issue is actually the sides of a candy package. The package measures approximately 1 7/8" by 3 3/8" and is 3/4" thick. Each package features two players, crudely drawn, one on each side. The words "All Star Baseball Package" appear on the side of the package and at the top of each player panel. The other side panel displays the words, "Candy and Gift." The end panel indicates a serial number, Dockman's name and reference to the Food and Drugs Act of 1906. A complete box is worth four times the individual value.

Ex-Mt VG
COMPLETE SET (16) 1200.00 600.00
1 Henry Beckendorf 60.00 30.00
2 Roger Bresnahan 100.00 50.00
3 Al Burch 60.00 30.00
4 Frank Chance 150.00 75.00
5 Wid Conroy 60.00 30.00
6 Jack Coombs 80.00 40.00
7 George Gibson 60.00 30.00
8 Doc Hoblitzel 60.00 30.00
9 Johnny Kling 60.00 30.00
10 Frank LaPorte 60.00 30.00
11 Connie Mack MG 200.00 100.00
12 Christy Mathewson 300.00 150.00
13 Matthew McIntyre 60.00 30.00
14 Jimmy Sheckard 60.00 30.00
15 Al Schweitzer 60.00 30.00
16 Harry Wolter 60.00 30.00

1950-54 J.J.K. Copyart Photographers

This set measures 3 1/2" by 5 1/2" and features New York Giants, Boston Braves, Philadelphia Phillies and one Brooklyn Dodger. The postcards are black and white glossy photos with no company identification on the back.

NM Ex
COMPLETE SET (24) 200.00 100.00
1 Johnny Antonelli (2) 6.00 3.00
2 Sam Calderone 5.00 2.50
3 Del Crandall 6.00 3.00
4 Del Ennis 5.00 2.50
5 Jim Hearn (2) 5.00 2.50
6 Tommy Holmes 6.00 3.00
7 Larry Jansen 6.00 3.00
8 Whitey Lockman (2) 5.00 2.50
9 Williard Marhsall 5.00 2.50
10 Eddie Mathews 20.00 10.00
11 Don Mueller 5.00 2.50
12 Danny O'Connell 5.00 2.50
13 Bill Rigney 6.00 3.00
14 Robin Roberts 15.00 7.50
15 Jackie Robinson 50.00 25.00
16 Hank Sauer 6.00 3.00
17 Red Schoendienst 15.00 7.50
18 Curt Simmons 6.00 3.00
19 Sibby Sisti 5.00 2.50
20 Eddie Stanky 10.00 5.00
Boston Braves
21 Eddie Stanly 10.00 5.00
New York Giants
22 Wes Westrum 5.00 2.50
23 Hoyt Wilhelm 15.00 7.50
24 Al Worthington 5.00 2.50

2001 Joe Jackson Ebay

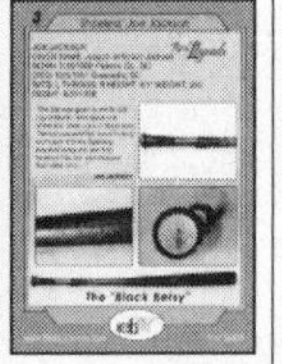

This three-card set was produced as a promotion for the 2001 Joe Jackson special memorabilia auction sold via Ebay. This three-card set features different drawings of Jackson and his memorablia. This set was produced by RealLegends.Com and each card is numbered "1 of 5000".

MINT NRMT
COMPLETE SET 15.00 6.75
COMMON CARD 5.00 2.20

1969 Reggie Jackson Regiment

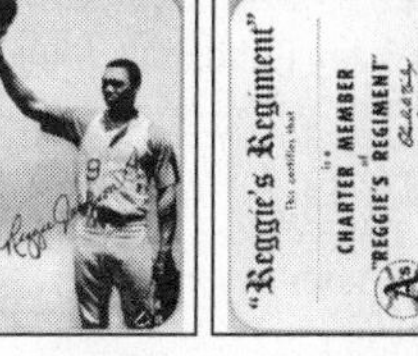

This one card set was issued during the early days of Reggie Jackson's career. It was issued as a ballpark promotion during his sensational first half of the 1969 season in which he hit 37 homers.

NM Ex
1 Reggie Jackson 30.00 12.00

1981 Reggie Jackson Accel

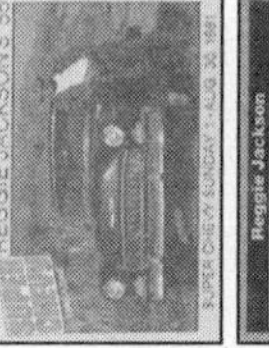

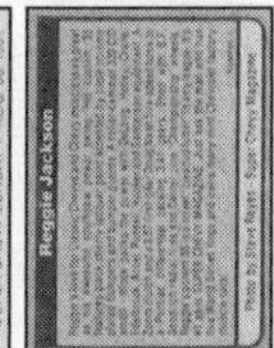

This three-card standard-size set features baseball great Reggie Jackson in front of some of his prize automobiles. The fronts feature Jackson posed with the cars. The backs have details about the cars. According ro reports at the time, approximately 7,000 sets were printed.

Nm-Mt Ex-Mt
COMPLETE SET (3) 20.00 8.00
COMMON CARD (1-3) 8.00 3.20

1997 Reggie Jackson Viking

This one card was issued by Viking Computer Memory as part of their commemorative card series to honor people who were used as spokespersons for them. This particular card features a pose of Reggie Jackson in his airbrushed Yankee uniform on the front and the back has a writeup about reggie along with a posed shot and an action shot. There might be more cards Viking did so any additions to this checklist are appreciated

Nm-Mt Ex-Mt
2 Reggie Jackson 10.00 3.00

1959 Jay Publishing All-Stars

The 23 blank-backed photos comprising the 1958 Jay Publishing All-Stars set measure 5" by 7" and feature white-bordered black-and-white posed player shots. The player's name appears in black lettering within the bottom white margin. The pictures are unnumbered and checklisted below in alphabetical order.

NM Ex
COMPLETE SET (23) 150.00 75.00
1 Henry Aaron 20.00 10.00
2 Luis Aparicio 8.00 4.00
3 Bob Cerv 2.00 1.00
4 Delmar Crandall 2.00 1.00
5 Whitey Ford 8.00 4.00
6 Nelson Fox 8.00 4.00
7 Bob Friend 2.00 1.00
8 Fred Haney MG 2.00 1.00
9 Jack Jensen 3.00 1.50
10 Frank Malzone 2.00 1.00
11 Mickey Mantle 40.00 20.00
12 Willie Mays 20.00 10.00
Bill White in Background
12 Bill Mazeroski 6.00 3.00
13 Roy McMillan 2.00 1.00
14 Stan Musial 15.00 7.50
15 Bill Pierce 2.00 1.00
16 Robin Roberts 8.00 4.00
17 Bob Skinner 2.00 1.00
18 Bill Skowron 3.00 1.50
19 Warren Spahn 8.00 4.00
20 Casey Stengel MG 8.00 4.00
21 Frank Thomas 2.00 1.00
22 Gus Triandos 2.00 1.00
23 Bob Turley 2.00 1.00

1958 Jay Publishing All-Time Greats

This 10-card set features glossy black-and-white photos of Baseball's all-time great players. The backs are blank. The cards are unnumbered and checklisted below in alphabetical order.

NM Ex
COMPLETE SET (10) 70.00 35.00
1 Ty Cobb 15.00 7.50
2 Joe DiMaggio 15.00 7.50
3 Lou Gehrig 15.00 7.50

Card	NM	Ex
4 Rogers Hornsby Spelled Roger	5.00	2.50
5 Carl Hubbell	2.00	1.00
6 Connie Mack	2.00	1.00
7 Christy Mathewson	4.00	2.00
8 Johnny Mize	2.00	1.00
9 Babe Ruth	20.00	10.00
10 Casey Stengel	4.00	2.00

1958 Jay Publishing Sluggers

This 10-card set features glossy black-and-white photos of some of Baseball's great hitters. The backs are blank. The cards are unnumbered and checklisted below in alphabetical order.

	NM	Ex
COMPLETE SET (10)	100.00	50.00
1 Hank Aaron	15.00	7.50
2 Larry Berra	8.00	4.00
3 Nelson Fox	5.00	2.50
4 Al Kaline	6.00	3.00
5 Mickey Mantle	25.00	12.50
6 Ed Mathews	6.00	3.00
7 Willie Mays	15.00	7.50
8 Stan Musial	10.00	5.00
9 Duke Snider	8.00	4.00
10 Ted Williams	20.00	10.00

1962 Jello

The cards in this 200-card (only 197 were ever issued) set measure 2 1/2" by 3 3/8". The 1962 Jello set has the same checklist as the Post Cereal set of the same year, but is considered by some to be a test issue. The cards are grouped numerically by team. For example: New York Yankees (1-13), Detroit (14-26), Baltimore (27-36), Cleveland (37-45), Chicago White Sox (46-55), Boston (56-64), Washington (65-73), Los Angeles Angels (74-82), Minnesota (83-91), Kansas City (92-100), Los Angeles Dodgers (101-115), Cincinnati (116-130), San Francisco (131-144), Milwaukee (145-157), St. Louis (158-168), Pittsburgh (169-181), Chicago Cubs (182-191), and Philadelphia (192-200). Although the players and numbers are identical in both sets, the Jello series has its own list of scarce and difficult cards. Numbers 29, 82 and 176 were never issued. A Jello card is easily distinguished from its counterpart in Post by the absence of the Post logo. The catalog designation for this set is F229-1.

	NM	Ex
COMPLETE SET (197)	5000.00	2000.00
1 Bill Skowron	25.00	10.00
2 Bobby Richardson	25.00	10.00
3 Cletis Boyer	12.00	4.80
4 Tony Kubek	20.00	8.00
5 Mickey Mantle	1000.00	400.00
6 Roger Maris	200.00	80.00
7 Yogi Berra	120.00	47.50
8 Elston Howard	12.00	4.80
9 Whitey Ford	80.00	32.00
10 Ralph Terry	10.00	4.00
11 John Blanchard	10.00	4.00
12 Luis Arroyo	10.00	4.00
13 Bill Stafford	15.00	6.00
14 Norm Cash	12.00	4.80
15 Jake Wood	6.00	2.40
16 Steve Boros	6.00	2.40
17 Chico Fernandez	6.00	2.40
18 Bill Bruton	6.00	2.40
19 Ken Aspromonte	6.00	2.40
20 Al Kaline	60.00	24.00
21 Dick Brown	6.00	2.40
22 Frank Lary	6.00	2.40
23 Don Mossi	10.00	4.00
24 Phil Regan	6.00	2.40
25 Charley Maxwell	6.00	2.40
26 Jim Bunning	30.00	12.00
27 Jim Gentile	10.00	4.00
28 Marv Breeding	6.00	2.40
29 Not issued		
30 Ron Hansen	6.00	2.40
31 Jackie Brandt	25.00	10.00
32 Dick Williams	12.00	4.80
33 Gus Triandos	6.00	2.40
34 Milt Pappas	6.00	2.40
35 Hoyt Wilhelm	50.00	20.00
36 Chuck Estrada	6.00	2.40
37 Vic Power	6.00	2.40
38 Johnny Temple	6.00	2.40
39 Bubba Phillips	25.00	10.00
40 Tito Francona	6.00	2.40
41 Willie Kirkland	6.00	2.40
42 John Romano	6.00	2.40
43 Jim Perry	10.00	4.00
44 Woodie Held	6.00	2.40
45 Chuck Essegian	6.00	2.40
46 Roy Sievers	6.00	2.40
47 Nellie Fox	35.00	14.00
48 Al Smith	6.00	2.40
49 Luis Aparicio	40.00	16.00
50 Jim Landis	6.00	2.40
51 Minnie Minoso	25.00	10.00
52 Andy Carey	25.00	10.00
53 Sherman Lollar	6.00	2.40
54 Billy Pierce	10.00	4.00
55 Early Wynn	30.00	12.00
56 Chuck Schilling	25.00	10.00
57 Pete Runnels	10.00	4.00
58 Frank Malzone	10.00	4.00
59 Don Buddin	10.00	4.00
60 Gary Geiger	25.00	10.00
61 Carl Yastrzemski	300.00	120.00
62 Jackie Jensen	30.00	12.00
63 Jim Pagliaroni	25.00	10.00
64 Don Schwall	10.00	4.00
65 Dale Long	10.00	4.00
66 Chuck Cottier	10.00	4.00
67 Billy Klaus	25.00	10.00
68 Coot Veal	10.00	4.00
69 Marty Keough	40.00	16.00
70 Willie Tasby	40.00	16.00
71 Gene Woodling	10.00	4.00
72 Gene Green	40.00	16.00
73 Dick Donovan	10.00	4.00
74 Steve Bilko	10.00	4.00
75 Rocky Bridges	25.00	10.00
76 Eddie Yost	15.00	6.00
77 Leon Wagner	12.00	4.80
78 Albie Pearson	10.00	4.00
79 Ken Hunt	15.00	6.00
80 Earl Averill	40.00	16.00
81 Ryne Duren	12.00	4.80
82 Not issued		
83 Bob Allison	10.00	4.00
84 Billy Martin	30.00	12.00
85 Harmon Killebrew	50.00	20.00
86 Zoilo Versalles	10.00	4.00
87 Lenny Green	30.00	12.00
88 Bill Tuttle	6.00	2.40
89 Jim Lemon	6.00	2.40
90 Earl Battey	25.00	10.00
91 Camilo Pascual	6.00	2.40
92 Norm Siebern	10.00	4.00
93 Jerry Lumpe	10.00	4.00
94 Dick Howser	12.00	4.80
95 Gene Stephens	40.00	16.00
96 Leo Posada	12.00	4.80
97 Joe Pignatano	10.00	4.00
98 Jim Archer	10.00	4.00
99 Haywood Sullivan	25.00	10.00
100 Art Ditmar	10.00	4.00
101 Gil Hodges	50.00	20.00
102 Charlie Neal	10.00	4.00
103 Daryl Spencer	10.00	4.00
104 Maury Wills	30.00	12.00
105 Tommy Davis	15.00	6.00
106 Willie Davis	15.00	6.00
107 Johnny Roseboro	40.00	16.00
108 John Podres	15.00	6.00
109 Sandy Koufax	120.00	47.50
110 Don Drysdale	60.00	24.00
111 Larry Sherry	25.00	10.00
112 Jim Gilliam	30.00	12.00
113 Norm Larker	40.00	16.00
114 Duke Snider	80.00	32.00
115 Stan Williams	25.00	10.00
116 Gordy Coleman	80.00	32.00
117 Don Blasingame	25.00	10.00
118 Gene Freese	40.00	16.00
119 Ed Kasko	40.00	16.00
120 Gus Bell	30.00	12.00
121 Vada Pinson	15.00	6.00
122 Frank Robinson	40.00	16.00
123 Bob Purkey	10.00	4.00
124 Joey Jay	10.00	4.00
125 Jim Brosnan	10.00	4.00
126 Jim O'Toole	10.00	4.00
127 Jerry Lynch	10.00	4.00
128 Wally Post	10.00	4.00
129 Ken Hunt	10.00	4.00
130 Jerry Zimmerman	10.00	4.00
131 Willie McCovey	60.00	24.00
132 Jose Pagan	30.00	12.00
133 Felipe Alou	15.00	6.00
134 Jim Davenport	12.00	4.80
135 Harvey Kuenn	15.00	6.00
136 Orlando Cepeda	30.00	12.00
137 Ed Bailey	10.00	4.00
138 Sam Jones	10.00	4.00
139 Mike McCormick	10.00	4.00
140 Juan Marichal	80.00	32.00
141 Jack Sanford	10.00	4.00
142 Willie Mays	250.00	100.00
143 Stu Miller	60.00	24.00
144 Joe Amalfitano	10.00	4.00
145 Joe Adcock	10.00	4.00
146 Frank Bolling	6.00	2.40
147 Eddie Mathews	50.00	20.00
148 Roy McMillan	6.00	2.40
149 Hank Aaron	200.00	80.00
150 Gino Cimoli	25.00	10.00
151 Frank Thomas	10.00	4.00
152 Joe Torre	20.00	8.00
153 Lew Burdette	12.00	4.80
154 Bob Buhl	6.00	2.40
155 Carlton Willey	6.00	2.40
156 Lee Maye	25.00	10.00
157 Al Spangler	40.00	16.00
158 Bill White	60.00	24.00
159 Ken Boyer	25.00	10.00
160 Joe Cunningham	10.00	4.00
161 Carl Warwick	10.00	4.00
162 Carl Sawatski	6.00	2.40
163 Lindy McDaniel	6.00	2.40
164 Ernie Broglio	10.00	4.00
165 Larry Jackson	6.00	2.40
166 Curt Flood	30.00	12.00
167 Curt Simmons	30.00	12.00
168 Alex Grammas	25.00	10.00
169 Dick Stuart	6.00	2.40
170 Bill Mazeroski	30.00	12.00
171 Don Hoak	10.00	4.00
172 Dick Groat	12.00	4.80
173 Roberto Clemente	300.00	120.00
174 Bob Skinner	25.00	10.00
175 Bill Virdon	30.00	12.00
176 Not issued		
177 Roy Face	12.00	4.80
178 Bob Friend	6.00	2.40
179 Vern Law	30.00	12.00
180 Harvey Haddix	35.00	14.00
181 Hal Smith	25.00	10.00
182 Ed Bouchee	25.00	10.00
183 Don Zimmer	12.00	4.80
184 Ron Santo	20.00	8.00
185 Andre Rodgers	6.00	2.40
186 Richie Ashburn	40.00	16.00
187 George Altman	6.00	2.40
188 Ernie Banks	40.00	16.00
189 Sam Taylor	6.00	2.40
190 Don Elston	6.00	2.40
191 Jerry Kindall	20.00	8.00
192 Pancho Herrera	6.00	2.40
193 Tony Taylor	10.00	4.00
194 Ruben Amaro	20.00	8.00
195 Don Demeter	6.00	2.40
196 Bobby Gene Smith	6.00	2.40
197 Clay Dalrymple	6.00	2.40
198 Robin Roberts	30.00	12.00
199 Art Mahaffey	6.00	2.40
200 John Buzhardt	6.00	2.40

1963 Jello

The cards in this 200-card set measure 2 1/2" by 3 3/8". The 1963 Jello set contains the same players and numbers as the Post Cereal set of the same year. The players are grouped by team with American Leaguers comprising 1-100 and National Leaguers 101-200. The ordering of teams is as follows: Minnesota (1-11), New York Yankees, Los Angeles Angels (24-34), Chicago White Sox (35-45), Detroit (46-56), Baltimore (57-66), Cleveland (67-76), Boston (77-84), Kansas City (85-92), Washington (93-100), San Francisco (101-112), Los Angeles Dodgers (113-124), Cincinnati (125-136), Pittsburgh (137-147), Milwaukee (148-157), St. Louis (158-168), Chicago Cubs (169-176), Philadelphia (177-184), Houston (185-192) and New York Mets (193-200). As in 1962, the Jello series has its own list of scarcities (many resulting from an unpopular package size). Since the Post Cereal logo was removed from the 1963 cereal set, Jello cards are primarily distinguishable by (1) smaller card size and (2) smaller print. The catalog designation is F229-2.

	NM	Ex
COMPLETE SET (200)	3000.00	1200.00
1 Vic Power	4.00	1.60
2 Bernie Allen	20.00	8.00
3 Zoilo Versalles	25.00	10.00
4 Rich Rollins	4.00	1.60
5 Harmon Killebrew	15.00	6.00
6 Lenny Green	25.00	10.00
7 Bob Allison	6.00	2.40
8 Earl Battey	15.00	6.00
9 Camilo Pascual	6.00	2.40
10 Jim Kaat	50.00	20.00
11 Jack Kralick	4.00	1.60
12 Bill Skowron	25.00	10.00
13 Bobby Richardson	8.00	3.20
14 Cletis Boyer	6.00	2.40
15 Mickey Mantle	250.00	100.00
16 Roger Maris	100.00	40.00
17 Yogi Berra	30.00	12.00
18 Elston Howard	50.00	20.00
19 Whitey Ford	20.00	8.00
20 Ralph Terry	4.00	1.60
21 John Blanchard	15.00	6.00
22 Bill Stafford	20.00	8.00
23 Tom Tresh	10.00	4.00
24 Steve Bilko	4.00	1.60
25 Bill Moran	4.00	1.60
26 Joe Koppe	4.00	1.60
27 Felix Torres	4.00	1.60
28 Leon Wagner	4.00	1.60
29 Albie Pearson	4.00	1.60
30 Lee Thomas	4.00	1.60
31 Bob Rodgers	20.00	8.00
32 Dean Chance	8.00	3.20
33 Ken McBride	20.00	8.00
34 George Thomas	20.00	8.00
35 Joe Cunningham	20.00	8.00
36 Nellie Fox	10.00	4.00
37 Luis Aparicio	10.00	4.00
38 Al Smith	6.00	2.40
39 Floyd Robinson	4.00	1.60
40 Jim Landis	4.00	1.60
41 Charlie Maxwell	4.00	1.60
42 Sherman Lollar	6.00	2.40
43 Early Wynn	10.00	4.00
44 Juan Pizarro	20.00	8.00
45 Ray Herbert	25.00	10.00
46 Norm Cash	8.00	3.20
47 Steve Boros	30.00	12.00
48 Dick McAuliffe	8.00	3.20
49 Bill Bruton	20.00	8.00
50 Rocky Colavito	10.00	4.00
51 Al Kaline	15.00	6.00
52 Dick Brown	20.00	8.00
53 Jim Bunning	10.00	4.00
54 Hank Aguirre	4.00	1.60
55 Frank Lary	20.00	8.00
56 Don Mossi	25.00	10.00
57 Jim Gentile	8.00	3.20
58 Jackie Brandt	6.00	2.40
59 Brooks Robinson	15.00	6.00
60 Ron Hansen	4.00	1.60
61 Jerry Adair	40.00	16.00
62 Boog Powell	8.00	3.20
63 Russ Snyder	25.00	10.00
64 Steve Barber	6.00	2.40
65 Milt Pappas	20.00	8.00
66 Robin Roberts	12.00	4.80
67 Tito Francona	4.00	1.60
68 Jerry Kindall	20.00	8.00
69 Woody Held	4.00	1.60
70 Bubba Phillips	4.00	1.60
71 Chuck Essegian	4.00	1.60
72 Willie Kirkland	20.00	8.00
73 Al Luplow	4.00	1.60
74 Ty Cline	40.00	16.00
75 Dick Donovan	4.00	1.60
76 John Romano	4.00	1.60
77 Pete Runnels	8.00	3.20
78 Ed Bressoud	20.00	8.00
79 Frank Malzone	6.00	2.40
80 Carl Yastrzemski	80.00	32.00
81 Gary Geiger	6.00	2.40
82 Lou Clinton	20.00	8.00
83 Earl Wilson	6.00	2.40
84 Bill Monbouquette	4.00	1.60
85 Norm Siebern	4.00	1.60
86 Jerry Lumpe	4.00	1.60
87 Manny Jimenez	4.00	1.60
88 Gino Cimoli	6.00	2.40
89 Ed Charles	40.00	16.00
90 Ed Rakow	6.00	2.40
91 Bobby Del Greco	40.00	16.00
92 Haywood Sullivan	20.00	8.00
93 Chuck Hinton	4.00	1.60
94 Ken Retzer	20.00	8.00
95 Harry Bright	20.00	8.00
96 Bob Johnson	6.00	2.40
97 Dave Stenhouse	15.00	6.00
98 Chuck Cottier	6.00	2.40
99 Tom Cheney	6.00	2.40
100 Claude Osteen	25.00	10.00
101 Orlando Cepeda	10.00	4.00
102 Chuck Hiller	15.00	6.00
103 Jose Pagan	20.00	8.00
104 Jim Davenport	4.00	1.60
105 Harvey Kuenn	6.00	2.40
106 Willie Mays	100.00	40.00
107 Felipe Alou	8.00	3.20
108 Tom Haller	6.00	2.40
109 Juan Marichal	10.00	4.00
110 Jack Sanford	4.00	1.60
111 Bill O'Dell	4.00	1.60
112 Willie McCovey	120.00	47.50
113 Lee Walls	20.00	8.00
114 Jim Gilliam	30.00	12.00
115 Maury Wills	8.00	3.20
116 Ron Fairly	6.00	2.40
117 Tommy Davis	6.00	2.40
118 Duke Snider	12.00	4.80
119 Willie Davis	6.00	2.40
120 John Roseboro	4.00	1.60
121 Sandy Koufax	40.00	16.00
122 Stan Williams	4.00	1.60
123 Don Drysdale	10.00	4.00
124 Daryl Spencer	4.00	1.60
125 Gordy Coleman	6.00	2.40
126 Don Blasingame	20.00	8.00
127 Leo Cardenas	4.00	1.60
128 Eddie Kasko	20.00	8.00
129 Jerry Lynch	4.00	1.60
130 Vada Pinson	10.00	4.00
131 Frank Robinson	12.00	4.80
132 Johnny Edwards	20.00	8.00
133 Joey Jay	4.00	1.60
134 Bob Purkey	4.00	1.60
135 Marty Keough	40.00	16.00
136 Jim O'Toole	20.00	8.00
137 Dick Stuart	4.00	1.60
138 Bill Mazeroski	10.00	4.00
139 Dick Groat	6.00	2.40
140 Don Hoak	4.00	1.60
141 Bob Skinner	4.00	1.60
142 Bill Virdon	6.00	2.40
143 Roberto Clemente	120.00	47.50
144 Smoky Burgess	8.00	3.20
145 Bob Friend	4.00	1.60
146 Al McBean	25.00	10.00
147 Roy Face	6.00	2.40
148 Joe Adcock	6.00	2.40
149 Frank Bolling	4.00	1.60
150 Roy McMillan	6.00	2.40
151 Eddie Mathews	15.00	6.00
152 Hank Aaron	100.00	40.00
153 Del Crandall	25.00	10.00
154 Bob Shaw	6.00	2.40
155 Lew Burdette	6.00	2.40
156 Joe Torre	50.00	20.00
157 Tony Cloninger	40.00	16.00
158 Bill White	10.00	4.00
159 Julian Javier	20.00	8.00
160 Ken Boyer	10.00	4.00
161 Julio Gotay	25.00	10.00
162 Curt Flood	6.00	2.40
163 Charlie James	50.00	20.00
164 Gene Oliver	25.00	10.00
165 Ernie Broglio	4.00	1.60
166 Bob Gibson	100.00	40.00
167 Lindy McDaniel	20.00	8.00
168 Ray Washburn	6.00	2.40
169 Ernie Banks	15.00	6.00
170 Ron Santo	8.00	3.20
171 George Altman	4.00	1.60
172 Billy Williams	80.00	32.00
173 Andre Rodgers	25.00	10.00
174 Ken Hubbs	8.00	3.20
175 Don Landrum	20.00	8.00
176 Dick Bertell	20.00	8.00
177 Roy Sievers	6.00	2.40
178 Tony Taylor	25.00	10.00
179 Johnny Callison	6.00	2.40
180 Don Demeter	4.00	1.60
181 Tony Gonzalez	20.00	8.00
182 Wes Covington	20.00	8.00
183 Art Mahaffey	4.00	1.60
184 Clay Dalrymple	6.00	2.40
185 Al Spangler	4.00	1.60
186 Roman Mejias	4.00	1.60
187 Bob Aspromonte	30.00	12.00
188 Norm Larker	4.00	1.60
189 Johnny Temple	4.00	1.60
190 Carl Warwick	20.00	8.00
191 Bob Lillis	20.00	8.00
192 Dick Farrell	40.00	16.00
193 Gil Hodges	12.00	4.80
194 Marv Throneberry	6.00	2.40
195 Charlie Neal	25.00	10.00
196 Frank Thomas	6.00	2.40
197 Richie Ashburn	10.00	4.00
198 Felix Mantilla	20.00	8.00
199 Rod Kanehl	20.00	8.00
200 Roger Craig	30.00	12.00

2003 Jewish Major Leaguers

Issued by the American Jewish Historical Society, this set cost $100 to purchase directly from the organization. These cards have black borders, the term "Jewish Major Leaguer" at the top and the player's name on the bottom. The horizontal backs have biographical information as well as informational blurb.

	MINT	NRMT
COMPLETE SET	100.00	45.00
*GOLD CARDS: 1.5X TO 4X BASIC CARDS		
GOLD CARDS: 500 SERIAL #D SETS..		
*SILVER CARDS: .75X TO 2X BASIC CARDS		
SILVER CARDS: 1500 SERIAL #'D SETS		
1 Sandy Koufax	15.00	6.75
2 Harry Danning	1.50	.70
3 Hank Greenberg	10.00	4.50
4 Andy Cohen	1.00	.45
5 Al Rosen	2.50	1.10
6 Buddy Myer	1.50	.70
7 Sid Gordon	1.50	.70
8 Shawn Green	8.00	3.60
9 Morrie Arnovich	1.00	.45
10 Lipman Pike	1.00	.45
11 Nate Berkenstock	1.00	.45
12 Jacob Pike	1.00	.45
13 Jake Goodman	1.00	.45
14 Ike Samuls	1.00	.45
15 Leo Fishel	1.00	.45
16 Bill Cristall	1.00	.45
17 Harry Kane	1.00	.45
18 Barney Pelty	1.00	.45
19 Moxie Manuel	1.00	.45
20 Phil Cooney	1.00	.45
21 Guy Zinn	1.00	.45
22 Ed Mensor	1.00	.45
23 Erskine Mayer	1.00	.45
24 Henry Bostick	1.00	.45
25 Sam Mayer	1.00	.45
26 Sammy Bohne	1.00	.45
27 Jake Pitler	1.00	.45
28 Bob Berman	1.00	.45
29 Eddie Corey	1.00	.45
30 Jesse Baker	1.00	.45
31 Al Schacht	2.00	.90
32 Sam Fishburn	1.00	.45
33 Reuben Ewing	1.00	.45
34 Heinie Scheer	1.00	.45
35 Lou Rosenberg	1.00	.45
36 Moe Berg	5.00	2.20
37 Joe Bennett	1.00	.45
38 Moses Solomon	1.00	.45
39 Happy Foreman	1.00	.45
40 Si Rosenthal	1.00	.45
41 Ike Danning	1.00	.45
42 Jonah Goldman	1.00	.45
43 Ed Wineapple	1.00	.45
44 Jimmie Reese	1.50	.70
45 Harry Rosenberg	1.00	.45
46 Jim Levey	1.00	.45
47 Alta Cohen	1.00	.45
48 Max Rosenfeld	1.00	.45
49 Lou Brower	1.00	.45
50 Izzy Goldstein	1.00	.45
51 Milt Galatzer	1.00	.45
52 Phil Weintraub	1.00	.45
53 Cy Malis	1.00	.45
54 Syd Cohen	1.00	.45
55 Fred Sington	1.00	.45
56 Harry Eisenstat	1.00	.45
57 Chick Starr	1.00	.45
58 Goody Rosen	1.00	.45
59 Harry Chozen	1.00	.45
60 Eddie Feinberg	1.00	.45
61 Sam Nahem	1.00	.45
62 Dick Conger	1.00	.45
63 Murray Franklin	1.00	.45
64 Harry Feldman	1.00	.45
65 Harry Shuman	1.00	.45
66 Eddie Turchin	1.00	.45
67 Cy Block	1.00	.45
68 Hal Schacker	1.00	.45
69 Mike Schemer	1.00	.45
70 Herb Karpel	1.00	.45
71 Bud Swartz	1.00	.45
72 Mickey Rutner	1.00	.45
73 Marv Rotblatt	1.00	.45
74 Joe Ginsberg	1.00	.45
75 Cal Abrams	1.00	.45
76 Saul Rogovin	1.00	.45
77 Sid Schacht	1.00	.45
78 Lou Limmer	1.00	.45
79 Duke Markell	1.00	.45
80 Al Richter	1.00	.45
81 Al Federoff	1.00	.45
82 Herb Gorman	1.00	.45
83 Moe Savransky	1.00	.45
84 Hy Cohen	1.00	.45
85 Al Silvera	1.00	.45
86 Barry Latman	1.00	.45
87 Ed Mayer	1.00	.45
88 Larry Sherry	1.00	.45
89 Don Taussig	1.00	.45
90 Norm Sherry	1.00	.45
91 Randy Cardinal	1.00	.45
92 Alan Koch	1.00	.45
93 Larry Yellen	1.00	.45
94 Steve Hertz	1.00	.45
95 Art Shamsky	1.00	.45
96 Richie Scheinblum	1.00	.45
97 Greg Goossen	1.00	.45
98 Norm Miller	1.00	.45
99 Ken Holtzman	1.00	.45
100 Mike Epstein	1.00	.45
101 Ron Blomberg	1.00	.45
102 Lloyd Allen	1.00	.45
103 Dave Roberts	1.00	.45
104 Elliott Maddox	1.00	.45
105 Steve Stone	1.50	.70
106 Steve Yeager	1.00	.45
107 Skip Jutze	1.00	.45
108 Dick Sharon	1.00	.45
109 Jeff Newman	1.00	.45
110 Ross Baumgarten	1.00	.45
111 Jeff Stember	1.00	.45
112 Steve Ratzer	1.00	.45
113 Bob Tufts	1.00	.45
114 Larry Rothschild	1.00	.45
115 Mark Gilbert	1.00	.45
116 Steve Rosenberg	1.00	.45
117 Roger Samuels	1.00	.45
118 Steve Wapnick	1.00	.45
119 Scott Radinsky	1.00	.45
120 Ruben Amaro Jr.	1.00	.45
121 Wayne Rosenthal	1.00	.45
122 Eddie Zosky	1.00	.45

123 Jesse Levis 1.00 .45
124 Brad Ausmus 1.00 .45
125 Eric Helfand 1.00 .45
126 Mike Lieberthal 1.00 .45
127 Andy Lorraine 1.00 .45
128 Brian Kowitz 1.00 .45
129 Brian Bark 1.00 .45
130 Mike Milchin 1.00 .45
131 Al Levine 1.00 .45
132 Micah Franklin 1.00 .45
133 Mike Saipe 1.00 .45
134 Keith Glauber 1.00 .45
135 Gabe Kapler 1.00 .45
136 Scott Schoeneweis 1.00 .45
137 David Newhan 1.00 .45
138 Jason Marquis 1.50 .70
139 Frank Charles 1.00 .45
140 Tony Cogan 1.00 .45
141 Justin Wayne 1.50 .70
142 Matt Ford 1.00 .45
143 Header Card 1.00 .45
144 Information Card 1.00 .45
145 Leader Card 1.00 .45
146 Leader Card 1.00 .45
147 Checklist Card 1.00 .45
148 Checklist Card 1.00 .45
149 George Brace 1.00 .45

1991 Jimmy Dean

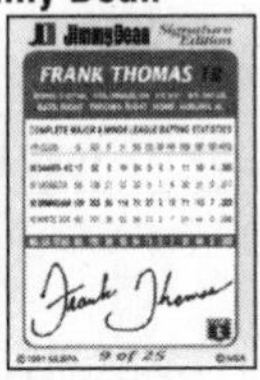

Michael Schechter Associates (MSA) produced this 25-card standard-size set on behalf of Jimmy Dean Sausage. Since these player photos were not expressly licensed by Major League Baseball, the team logos have been airbrushed out. During the promotion, uncut sheets were offered by the company through a mail-in offer involving Jimmy Dean proofs of purchase.

	Nm-Mt	Ex-Mt
COMPLETE SET (25)	12.00	3.60
1 Will Clark	.50	.15
2 Ken Griffey Jr.	1.25	.35
3 Dale Murphy	.40	.12
4 Barry Bonds	1.00	.30
5 Darryl Strawberry	.20	.06
6 Ryne Sandberg	.75	.23
7 Gary Sheffield	.50	.15
8 Sandy Alomar Jr.	.20	.06
9 Frank Thomas	.50	.15
10 Barry Larkin	.40	.12
11 Kirby Puckett	.50	.15
12 George Brett	1.00	.30
13 Kevin Mitchell	.10	.03
14 Dave Justice	.40	.12
15 Cal Ripken	2.00	.60
16 Craig Biggio	.30	.09
17 Rickey Henderson	.60	.18
18 Roger Clemens	1.00	.30
19 Jose Canseco	.50	.15
20 Ozzie Smith	1.00	.30
21 Cecil Fielder	.20	.06
22 Dave Winfield	.50	.15
23 Kevin Maas	.10	.03
24 Nolan Ryan	2.00	.60
25 Dwight Gooden	.20	.06

1992 Jimmy Dean

Michael Schechter Associates (MSA) produced this 18-card standard-size set for Jimmy Dean. In a cello pack, three free cards were included in any Jimmy Dean Sandwich, Flapsticks, or Links/Patties Breakfast Sausage.

	Nm-Mt	Ex-Mt
COMPLETE SET (18)	8.00	2.40
1 Jim Abbott	.20	.06
2 Barry Bonds	1.00	.30
3 Jeff Bagwell	.75	.23
4 Frank Thomas	.50	.15
5 Steve Avery	.10	.03
6 Chris Sabo	.10	.03
7 Will Clark	.50	.15
8 Don Mattingly	1.00	.30
9 Darryl Strawberry	.20	.06
10 Roger Clemens	1.00	.30
11 Ken Griffey Jr.	1.25	.35
12 Chuck Knoblauch	.40	.12
13 Tony Gwynn	1.00	.30
14 Juan Gonzalez	.40	.12
15 Cecil Fielder	.20	.06
16 Bobby Bonilla	.10	.03
17 Wes Chamberlain	.10	.03
18 Ryne Sandberg	1.00	.30

1992 Jimmy Dean Living Legends

This six-card standard-size set was produced by MSA (Michael Schechter Associates) and features future candidates for the Hall of Fame. Collectors could obtain the complete set through a mail-in offer detailed on packages of Jimmy Dean Breakfast Sausage or Smoked Sausage. While supplies lasted, the sets could be obtained by sending in three UPC proofs of

purchase from Jimmy Dean Sausage plus 1.00 for shipping and handling. Reportedly 105,000 sets were printed.

	Nm-Mt	Ex-Mt
COMPLETE SET (6)	15.00	4.50
1 George Brett	2.50	.75
2 Carlton Fisk	1.50	.45
3 Ozzie Smith	1.50	.45
4 Robin Yount	1.50	.45
5 Cal Ripken	5.00	1.50
6 Nolan Ryan	5.00	1.50

1992 Jimmy Dean Rookie Stars

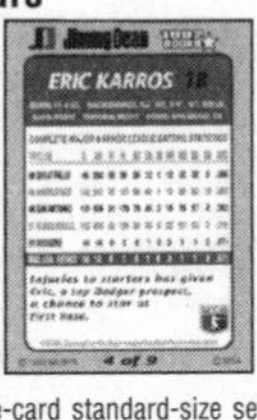

The players in this nine-card standard-size set were chosen based on actual 1992 first-half performance. Three free cards were included in specially marked packages of Jimmy Dean Sausage, Chicken Biscuits, Steak Biscuits, and MiniBurgers. Oversized 7" by 9 3/4" versions of the cards, featuring a Rookie Star front on one side and a Living Legend front on the other, were placed at point of purchase for promotional purchases.

	Nm-Mt	Ex-Mt
COMPLETE SET (9)	4.00	1.20
1 Andy Stankiewicz	.15	.04
2 Pat Listach	.15	.04
3 Brian Jordan	1.00	.30
4 Eric Karros	.75	.23
5 Reggie Sanders	.15	.04
6 Dave Fleming	.15	.04
7 Donovan Osborne	.15	.04
8 Kenny Lofton	1.50	.45
9 Moises Alou	.75	.23

1993 Jimmy Dean

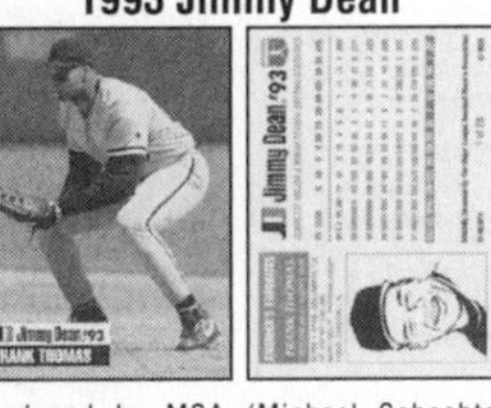

Produced by MSA (Michael Schechter Associates) for Jimmy Dean, these 28 cards measure the standard size. Eighteen cards were distributed in packs of three inside certain packages of Jimmy Dean products. The remaining ten cards were a special issue subset that could only be obtained through redemption of UPC symbols from Jimmy Dean Roll Sausage.

	Nm-Mt	Ex-Mt
COMPLETE SET (28)	10.00	3.00
1 Frank Thomas	1.00	.30
2 Barry Larkin	.75	.23
3 Cal Ripken	3.00	.90
4 Andy Van Slyke	.25	.07
5 Darren Daulton	.40	.12
6 Don Mattingly	1.50	.45
7 Roger Clemens	1.50	.45
8 Juan Gonzalez	1.00	.30
9 Mark Langston	.25	.07
10 Barry Bonds	1.50	.45
11 Ken Griffey Jr.	2.00	.60
12 Cecil Fielder	.40	.12
13 Kirby Puckett	1.00	.30
14 Tom Glavine	.60	.18
15 George Brett	1.50	.45
16 Nolan Ryan	3.00	.90
17 Eddie Murray	1.00	.30
18 Gary Sheffield	1.00	.30
19 Doug Drabek	.25	.07
20 Ray Lankford	.40	.12
21 Benito Santiago	.40	.12
22 Mark McGwire	2.50	.75
23 Kenny Lofton	1.00	.30
24 Eric Karros	.60	.18
25 Ryne Sandberg	1.25	.35
26 Charlie Hayes	.25	.07
27 Mike Mussina	.75	.23
28 Pat Listach	.25	.07

1993 Jimmy Dean Rookies

This nine-card standard-size set displays a cutout photo of the player superimposed on a gray studio background. The cards are numbered in alphabetical order.

	Nm-Mt	Ex-Mt
COMPLETE SET (9)	5.00	1.50
1 Rich Amaral	.10	.03
2 Vinny Castilla	.40	.12
3 Jeff Conine	.10	.03
4 Brent Gates	.10	.03
5 Wayne Kirby	.10	.03
6 Mike Lansing	.20	.06

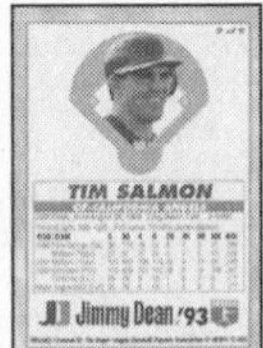

7 David Nied	.10	.03
8 Mike Piazza	3.00	.90
9 Tim Salmon	1.50	.45

1995 Jimmy Dean All-Time Greats

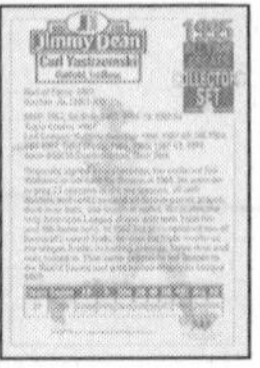

This six-card standard-size set was cosponsored by Jimmy Dean Foods and the Major League Baseball Players Alumni Association. The cards were individually cello wrapped and inserted inside packages, and an accompanying paper insert featured coupons and a mail-in offer. (The mail-in offer was also found on boxes of Jimmy Dean Breakfast foods.) For two proofs-of-purchase plus $7.00, the collector received one autographed card featuring Billy Williams, Al Kaline, or Jim "Catfish" Hunter. Expiring December 31, 1995, the offer was limited to 12 baseball cards per original order form. The cards are checklisted below in alphabetical order.

	Nm-Mt	Ex-Mt
COMPLETE SET (6)	5.00	1.50
1 Rod Carew	1.00	.30
2 Jim(Catfish) Hunter	1.00	.30
3 Al Kaline	1.00	.30
4 Mike Schmidt	2.00	.60
5 Billy Williams	1.00	.30
6 Carl Yastrzemski	1.50	.45
NNO Jim(Catfish)Hunter AU	30.00	9.00
NNO Billy Williams AU	20.00	6.00
NNO Al Kaline AU	20.00	6.00

1997 Jimmy Dean

This two-card set was distributed through Jimmy Dean Products and could be obtained by sending in $12.95 and two UPCs from these products. All cards in this limited edition are autographed. The fronts feature black-and-white action player photos in a gold margin with a thin white inside border and green diamonds at the corners. The backs carry player information and career statistics. The cards are unnumbered and checklisted below in alphabetical order.

	Nm-Mt	Ex-Mt
COMPLETE SET (2)	30.00	9.00
1 Yogi Berra AU	15.00	4.50
2 Brooks Robinson AU	15.00	4.50

1959 Jimmy Fund Membership Card

This one card "set" is presumed to be issued in 1959 and features a photo of the Jimmy Fund building on the front. The back contains a "photo" of Ted Williams along with a statement thanking the member for their support of the Jimmy Fund.

	NM	Ex
1 Jimmy Fund Building	8.00	4.00

1976 Jimmy Fund

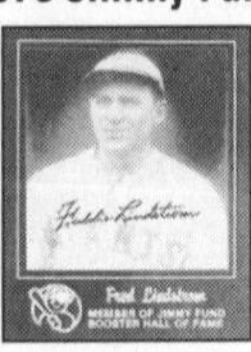

These oversize cards were issued in 1976 and featured members of the Baseball Hall of Fame. These cards are rarely seen and have black and white photos on the front with the players names and their Jimmy Fund affiliation on the bottom. As far as is known, the only players issued are in the Hall of Fame. As the cards are blank backed and unnumbered we have sequenced them in alphabetical order. There may be additions to this checklist so any additional information is appreciated.

	NM	Ex
COMPLETE SET	600.00	240.00
1 Cool Papa Bell	50.00	20.00
2 Jocko Conlon UER	50.00	20.00
Spelled Conlin		
3 Stan Coveleskie	50.00	20.00
4 Charlie Gehringer	60.00	24.00
5 Hank Greenberg	80.00	32.00
6 Burleigh Grimes	50.00	20.00
7 Waite Hoyt	50.00	20.00
8 Monte Irvin	60.00	24.00
9 George Kelly	50.00	20.00
10 Sandy Koufax	150.00	60.00
11 Fred Lindstrom	50.00	20.00

1991 Walter Johnson Postcard

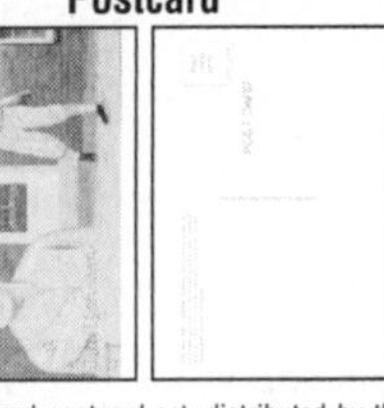

This one card postcard set, distributed by the Coffeyville Historical Sociey, features all time great Walter Johnson. The front is a picture of the Walter Johnson Mural and was commissioned by the Coffeyville Historical Society.

	MINT	NRMT
1 Walter Johnson	3.00	1.35

1976 Jerry Jonas Promotion Cards

These eight cards were issued by Jerry Jonas Promotions as part of an attempt to secure a major league liscense. These cards were presented at the World Series meetings in 1975. These cards, featuring all time greats, were in the format of the regular 1975 Topps issue. The set is also sometimes found as an uncut sheet of all eight players. According to published reports no more than 100 sets of these were printed.

	NM	Ex
COMPLETE SET	600.00	240.00
1 Sandy Koufax	100.00	40.00
2 Mel Ott	60.00	24.00
3 Willie Mays	150.00	60.00
4 Stan Musial	100.00	40.00
5 Rogers Hornsby	50.00	20.00
6 Honus Wagner	80.00	32.00
7 Grover Alexander	80.00	32.00
8 Robin Roberts	60.00	24.00

1997 Chipper Jones Police

This one-card set features a color photo of the Atlanta Braves player, Chipper Jones, with a member of the Covington Police Department. The back displays information about both pictured men and a Safety Message.

	Nm-Mt	Ex-Mt
1 Chipper Jones	3.00	.90
Wayne Digby		

1911 Jones, Keyser and Arras Cabinets

These 4 3/4" by 7 1/4" cabinets were issued in 1911 from this New York City based company. The fronts feature a player photo with the image number on the bottom of the photo and the players name on the bottom of the card. There may be more cabinets in this set so any additional information is appreciated.

	Ex-Mt	VG
COMPLETE SET	12000.00	6000.00
301 Russ Ford	150.00	75.00
303 Jack Warhop	150.00	75.00
304 Bill Dahlen MG	150.00	75.00
306 Zack Wheat	300.00	150.00
307 Al Bridwell	150.00	75.00
308 Red Murray	150.00	75.00
310 Fred Snodgrass	200.00	100.00
311 Red Ames	150.00	75.00
312 Fred Merkle	250.00	125.00
313 Art Devlin	150.00	75.00
314 Hooks Wiltse	150.00	75.00
315 Josh Devore	150.00	75.00
316 Eddie Collins	500.00	250.00
317 Ed Reulbach	150.00	75.00
318 Jimmy Sheckard	150.00	75.00
320 Wildfire Schulte	200.00	100.00
321 Solly Hofman	150.00	75.00
322 Bill Bergen	150.00	75.00
323 George Bell	150.00	75.00
325 Fred Clarke MG	300.00	150.00
326 Clark Griffith MG	300.00	150.00
327 Roger Bresnahan	300.00	150.00
328 Fred Tenney	150.00	75.00
329 Harry Lord	150.00	75.00
331 Walter Johnson	800.00	400.00
332 Nap Lajoie	600.00	300.00
333 Joe Tinker	500.00	250.00
334 Mordecai Brown	300.00	150.00
336 Jimmy Archer	150.00	75.00
340 Hal Chase	250.00	125.00
341 Larry Doyle	200.00	100.00
342 Chief Meyers	200.00	100.00
343 Christy Mathewson	800.00	400.00
344 Bugs Raymond	150.00	75.00
345 John McGraw MG	600.00	300.00
346 Honus Wagner	800.00	400.00
347 Ty Cobb	1200.00	600.00
348 Johnnie Evers	500.00	250.00
349 Frank Chance	500.00	250.00

1886-88 Joseph Hall Cabinets

In 1888, Joseph Hall produced a 14-card set of cabinets. The cabinet cards feature major league team photos. The horiztontal cabinets measure 6 1/2" by 4 1/4". The cards have says Joseph Hall directly under the team photo.

	Ex-Mt	VG
COMPLETE SET	80000.00	40000.00
1 Baltimore, 1888	6000.00	3000.00
2 Boston, 1888	10000.00	5000.00
3 Brooklyn, 1888	6000.00	3000.00
4 Chicago, 1888	10000.00	5000.00
5 Cincinnati, 1888	6000.00	3000.00
6 Cleveland, 1888	6000.00	3000.00
7 Detroit, 1888	8000.00	4000.00
8 Indianapolis, 1888	6000.00	3000.00
9 Kansas City, 1888	6000.00	3000.00
10 Louisville, 1888	6000.00	3000.00
11 New York, 1888	6000.00	3000.00
12 Athletic, 1888	8000.00	4000.00
13 St. Louis, 1888	6000.00	3000.00
14 Washington, 1888	6000.00	3000.00

1910 Ju Ju Drums E286

These round "cards" have a diameter measure of 1 7/16". They were issued by Ju Ju Drums gum. The set can be dated to 1910 by the inclusion of Elmer Zacher who had his only major league season that year. These cards are unnumbered and we have sequenced them in alphabetical order.

	Ex-Mt	VG
COMPLETE SET (43)	15000.00	7500.00
1 Eddie Ainsmith	200.00	100.00
2 Jimmy Austin	200.00	100.00
3 Chief Bender	400.00	200.00
4 Bruno Block	200.00	100.00
5 Jimmy Burke	200.00	100.00
6 Donie Bush	200.00	100.00
7 Frank Chance	500.00	250.00
8 Harry Cheek	200.00	100.00
9 Eddie Cicotte	400.00	200.00
10 Ty Cobb	2500.00	1250.00
11 King Cole	200.00	100.00
12 Jack Coombs	400.00	200.00
13 Bill Dahlen	200.00	100.00
14 Bert Daniels	200.00	100.00
15 George Davis	400.00	200.00
16 Larry Doyle	250.00	125.00
17 Rube Ellis	200.00	100.00
18 George Ferguson	200.00	100.00
19 Russ Ford	200.00	100.00
20 Robert Harmon	200.00	100.00
21 Robert Hyatt	200.00	100.00
22 William Killefer	200.00	100.00
23 Arthur Krueger	200.00	100.00
24 Thomas Leach	250.00	125.00
25 Christy Mathewson	1200.00	600.00
26 John McGraw	600.00	300.00
27 Deacon McGuire	200.00	100.00
28 Chief Meyers	250.00	125.00
29 Roy Miller	200.00	100.00
30 George Mullin	250.00	125.00
31 Tom Needham	200.00	100.00
32 Rube Oldring	200.00	100.00
33 Barney Pelty	200.00	100.00
34 Ed Reulbach	250.00	125.00
35 John Rowan	200.00	100.00
36 David Shean	200.00	100.00
37 Tris Speaker	800.00	400.00
38 Ed Sweeney	200.00	100.00
39 Jimmy Walsh	200.00	100.00
40 Honus Wagner	1200.00	600.00
41 Doc White	200.00	100.00
42 Ralph Works	200.00	100.00
43 Elmer Zacher	200.00	100.00

1893 Just So

These 14 cards measure 2 1/2" by 3 7/8" and feature members of the Cleveland Spiders. So far, these cards have been checklisted but others may exist. We have sequenced these cards in alphabetical order. The earliest known Cy Young card is in this set.

	Ex-Mt	VG
COMPLETE SET (13)	150000.00	75000.00
1 Frank Boyd	10000.00	5000.00
2 Jesse Burkett	20000.00	10000.00
3 Cupid Childs	10000.00	5000.00
4 John Clarkson	20000.00	10000.00
5 George Cuppy	10000.00	5000.00
6 George Davis	20000.00	10000.00
7 Charlie Hastings	10000.00	5000.00
8 Ed McKean	10000.00	5000.00
9 Jack O'Connor	10000.00	5000.00
10 Patsy Tebeau	12000.00	6000.00
11 Jake Virtue	10000.00	5000.00
12 Tom Williams	10000.00	5000.00
13 Cy Young	40000.00	20000.00
14 Chief Zimmer	10000.00	5000.00

1982 K-Mart

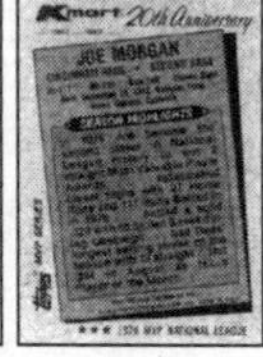

The cards in this 44-card set measure the standard size. This set was mass produced by Topps for K-Mart's 20th Anniversary Celebration and distributed in a custom box. The set features Topps cards of National and American League MVP's from 1962 through 1981. The backs highlight individual MVP winning performances. The dual National League MVP winners of 1979 and special cards commemorating the accomplishments of Drysdale (scoreless consecutive innings pitched streak), Aaron (home run record), and Rose (National League most hits lifetime record) round out the set. The 1975 Fred Lynn card is an original construction from the multi-player "Rookie Outfielders" card of Lynn of 1975. The Maury Wills card number 2, similarly, was created after the fact as Maury was not originally included in the 1962 Topps set. Topps had solved the same problem in essentially the same way in their 1975 set on card number 200.

	Nm-Mt	Ex-Mt
COMP.FACT SET (44)	2.00	.80
1 Mickey Mantle: 62AL	.75	.30
2 Maury Wills: 62NL	.10	.04
3 Elston Howard: 63AL	.05	.02
4 Sandy Koufax: 63NL	.25	.10
5 Brooks Robinson: 64AL	.10	.04
6 Ken Boyer: 64NL	.05	.02
7 Zoilo Versalles: 65AL	.05	.02
8 Willie Mays: 65NL	.50	.20
9 Frank Robinson: 66AL	.10	.04
10 Bob Clemente: 66NL	.50	.20
11 Carl Yastrzemski: 67AL	.10	.04
12 Orlando Cepeda: 67NL	.05	.02
13 Denny McLain: 68AL	.05	.02
14 Bob Gibson: 68NL	.10	.04
15 H.Killebrew 69AL	.10	.04
16 Willie McCovey: 69NL	.10	.04
17 Boog Powell: 70AL	.05	.02
18 Johnny Bench: 70NL	.10	.04
19 Vida Blue: 71AL	.05	.02
20 Joe Torre: 71NL	.05	.02
21 Rich Allen: 72AL	.05	.02
22 Johnny Bench: 72NL	.10	.04
23 Reggie Jackson: 73AL	.15	.06
24 Pete Rose: 73NL	.25	.10
25 Jeff Burroughs: 74AL	.05	.02
26 Steve Garvey: 74NL	.05	.02
27 Fred Lynn: 75AL	.10	.04
28 Joe Morgan: 75NL	.10	.04
29 T.Munson 76AL	.05	.02
30 Joe Morgan: 76NL	.10	.04
31 Rod Carew: 77AL	.10	.04
32 George Foster: 77NL	.05	.02
33 Jim Rice: 78AL	.10	.04
34 Dave Parker: 78NL	.10	.04
35 Don Baylor: 79AL	.05	.02
36 Keith Hernandez: 79NL	.05	.02
37 Willie Stargell: 79NL	.10	.04
38 George Brett: 80AL	.40	.16
39 Mike Schmidt: 80NL	.15	.06
40 Rollie Fingers: 81AL	.10	.04
41 Mike Schmidt: 81NL	.15	.06
42 Don Drysdale '68 HL	.10	.04
43 Hank Aaron '74 HL	.50	.20
44 Pete Rose '81 HL	.15	.06

1987 K-Mart

Topps produced this 33-card boxed standard-size set for K-Mart. The set celebrates K-Mart's 25th anniversary and is subtitled, "Stars of the Decades." Card fronts feature a color photo of the player oriented diagonally. Card backs provide statistics for the player's best decade. The set numbering is arranged alphabetically within decade groups: 1960s (1-11), 1970s (12-22), and 1980s (23-33).

	Nm-Mt	Ex-Mt
COMP. FACT SET (33)	4.00	1.60
1 Hank Aaron	.75	.30
2 Roberto Clemente	1.00	.40
3 Bob Gibson	.15	.06
4 Harmon Killebrew	.15	.06
5 Mickey Mantle	2.00	.80
6 Juan Marichal	.15	.06
7 Roger Maris	.25	.10
8 Willie Mays	.75	.30
9 Brooks Robinson	.15	.06
10 Frank Robinson	.15	.06
11 Carl Yastrzemski	.15	.06
12 Johnny Bench	.25	.10
13 Lou Brock	.25	.10
14 Rod Carew	.25	.10
15 Steve Carlton	.25	.10
16 Reggie Jackson	.40	.16
17 Jim Palmer	.25	.10
18 Jim Rice	.10	.04
19 Pete Rose	.50	.20
20 Nolan Ryan	2.00	.80
21 Tom Seaver	.40	.16
22 Willie Stargell	.25	.10
23 Wade Boggs	.40	.16
24 George Brett	.75	.30
25 Gary Carter	.30	.12
26 Dwight Gooden	.15	.06
27 Rickey Henderson	.40	.16
28 Don Mattingly	.75	.30
29 Dale Murphy	.25	.10
30 Eddie Murray	.30	.12
31 Mike Schmidt	.50	.20
32 Darryl Strawberry	.10	.04
33 Fernando Valenzuela	.10	.04

1988 K-Mart

Topps produced this 33-card standard-sized boxed set exclusively for K-Mart. The set is subtitled, "Memorable Moments." Card fronts feature a color photo of the player with the K-Mart logo in lower right corner. Card backs provide details for that player's "memorable moment." The set is packaged in a bright yellow and green box with a checklist on the back panel of the box. The cards in the set were numbered by K-Mart essentially in alphabetical order.

	Nm-Mt	Ex-Mt
COMP. FACT SET (33)	4.00	1.60
1 George Bell	.05	.02
2 Wade Boggs	.40	.16
3 George Brett	.75	.30
4 Jose Canseco	.50	.20
5 Jack Clark	.10	.04
6 Will Clark	.50	.20
7 Roger Clemens	.75	.30
8 Vince Coleman	.05	.02
9 Andre Dawson	.20	.08
10 Dwight Gooden	.10	.04
11 Pedro Guerrero	.05	.02
12 Tony Gwynn	1.00	.40
13 Rickey Henderson	.60	.24
14 Keith Hernandez	.10	.04
15 Don Mattingly	1.00	.40
16 Mark McGwire	1.50	.60
17 Paul Molitor	.50	.20
18 Dale Murphy	.20	.08
19 Tim Raines	.10	.04
20 Dave Righetti	.05	.02
21 Cal Ripken	2.00	.80
22 Pete Rose	.50	.20
23 Nolan Ryan	2.00	.80
24 Benito Santiago	.10	.04
25 Mike Schmidt	.50	.20
26 Mike Scott	.05	.02
27 Kevin Seitzer	.05	.02
28 Ozzie Smith	1.00	.40
29 Darryl Strawberry	.10	.04
30 Rick Sutcliffe	.05	.02
31 Fernando Valenzuela	.10	.04
32 Todd Worrell	.05	.02
33 Robin Yount	.40	.16

1989 K-Mart

The 1989 K-Mart Dream Team set contains 33 standard-size glossy cards. The fronts are blue. The cards were distributed as a boxed set through K-Mart stores. The set features 11 major league rookies of 1988 plus 11 "American League Rookies of the '80s" and 11 "National League Rookies of the '80s". The complete subject list for the set is provided on the back panel of the custom box.

	Nm-Mt	Ex-Mt
COMP. FACT SET (33)	3.00	1.20
1 Mark Grace	.75	.30
2 Ron Gant	.10	.04
3 Chris Sabo	.05	.02
4 Walt Weiss	.05	.02
5 Jay Buhner	.20	.08
6 Cecil Espy	.05	.02
7 Dave Gallagher	.05	.02
8 Damon Berryhill	.05	.02
9 Tim Belcher	.05	.02
10 Paul Gibson	.05	.02
11 Gregg Jefferies	.05	.02
12 Don Mattingly	.75	.30
13 Harold Reynolds	.10	.04
14 Wade Boggs	.40	.16
15 Cal Ripken	1.50	.60
16 Kirby Puckett	.40	.16
17 George Bell	.05	.02
18 Jose Canseco	.50	.20
19 Terry Steinbach	.05	.02
20 Roger Clemens	.75	.30
21 Mark Langston	.05	.02
22 Harold Baines	.10	.04
23 Will Clark	.40	.16
24 Ryne Sandberg	.60	.24
25 Tim Wallach	.05	.02
26 Shawon Dunston	.05	.02
27 Tim Raines	.10	.04
28 Darryl Strawberry	.10	.04
29 Tony Gwynn	.75	.30
30 Tony Pena	.10	.04
31 Dwight Gooden	.10	.04
32 Fernando Valenzuela	.10	.04
33 Pedro Guerrero	.05	.02

1990 K-Mart

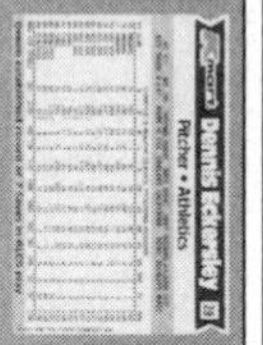

The 1990 K-Mart Superstars set is a 33-card, standard-size set issued for the K-Mart chain by the Topps Company. This set was issued with a piece of gum in the custom set box.

	Nm-Mt	Ex-Mt
COMP. FACT SET (33)	5.00	1.50
1 Will Clark	.40	.12
2 Ryne Sandberg	.75	.23
3 Howard Johnson	.05	.02
4 Ozzie Smith	.75	.23
5 Tony Gwynn	1.00	.30
6 Kevin Mitchell	.05	.02
7 Jerome Walton	.05	.02
8 Craig Biggio	.50	.15
9 Mike Scott	.05	.02
10 Dwight Gooden	.10	.03
11 Sid Fernandez	.05	.02
12 Joe Magrane	.05	.02
13 Jay Howell	.05	.02
14 Mark Davis	.05	.02
15 Pedro Guerrero	.05	.02
16 Glenn Davis	.05	.02
17 Don Mattingly	1.00	.30
18 Julio Franco	.10	.03
19 Wade Boggs	.40	.12
20 Cal Ripken	2.00	.60
21 Jose Canseco	.40	.12
22 Kirby Puckett	.50	.15
23 Rickey Henderson	.60	.18
24 Mickey Tettleton	.10	.03
25 Nolan Ryan	2.00	.60
26 Bret Saberhagen	.10	.03
27 Jeff Ballard	.05	.02
28 Chuck Finley	.10	.03
29 Dennis Eckersley	.40	.12
30 Dan Plesac	.05	.02
31 Fred McGriff	.20	.06
32 Mark McGwire	1.50	.45
33 Tony LaRussa MG and Roger Craig MG	.10	.03

1955 Kahn's

The cards in this six-card set measure 3 1/4" X 4". The 1955 Kahn's Wieners set received very limited distribution. The cards were supposedly given away at an amusement park. The set portrays the players in street clothes rather than in uniform and hence are sometimes referred to as "street clothes" Kahn's. All Kahn's sets from 1955 through 1963 are black and white and contain a 1/2" tab. Cards with the tab still intact are worth approximately 50 percent more than cards without the tab. Cards feature a facsimile autograph of the player on the front. Cards are blank-backed. Only Cincinnati Redlegs players are featured.

	NM	Ex
COMPLETE SET (6)	3000.00	1500.00
1 Gus Bell	600.00	300.00
2 Ted Kluszewski	750.00	375.00
3 Roy McMillan	450.00	220.00
4 Joe Nuxhall	500.00	250.00
5 Wally Post	450.00	220.00
6 Johnny Temple	450.00	220.00

1956 Kahn's

The cards in this 15-card set measure 3 1/4" X 4". The 1956 Kahn's set was the first set to be issued with Kahn's meat products. The cards are blank backed. The set is distinguished by the old style, short sleeve shirts on the players and the existence of backgounds (Kahn's cards

of later years utilize a blank background). Cards which have the tab still intact are worth approximately 50 percent more than cards without the tab. Only Cincinnati Redlegs players are featured. The cards are listed and numbered below in alphabetical order by the subject's name. This set contains a very early Frank Robinson card.

	NM	Ex
COMPLETE SET (15)	1600.00	800.00
1 Ed Bailey	80.00	40.00
2 Gus Bell	100.00	50.00
3 Joe Black	120.00	60.00
4 Smoky Burgess	100.00	50.00
5 Art Fowler	80.00	40.00
6 Herschel Freeman	80.00	40.00
7 Ray Jablonski	80.00	40.00
8 John Klippstein	80.00	40.00
9 Ted Kluszewski	200.00	100.00
10 Brooks Lawrence	100.00	50.00
11 Roy McMillan	100.00	50.00
12 Joe Nuxhall	100.00	50.00
13 Wally Post	100.00	50.00
14 Frank Robinson	500.00	250.00
15 Johnny Temple	100.00	50.00

1957 Kahn's

The cards in this 29-card set measure 3 1/4" by 4". The 1957 Kahn's Wieners set contains black and white, blank backed, unnumbered cards. The set features only the Cincinnati Redlegs and Pittsburgh Pirates. The cards feature a light background. Each card features a facsimile autograph of the player on the front. The Groat card exists with a "Richard Groat" autograph and also exists with the printed name "Dick Groat" on the card. The set price inlcudes both Groats. The catalog designation is F155-3. The cards are listed and numbered below in alphabetical order by the subject's name. A Bill Mazeroski card was printed during this, his Rookie Card season.

	NM	Ex
COMPLETE SET (29)	3000.00	1500.00
1 Tom Acker	60.00	30.00
2 Ed Bailey	60.00	30.00
3 Gus Bell	80.00	40.00
4 Smoky Burgess	80.00	40.00
5 Roberto Clemente	1000.00	500.00
6 George Crowe	60.00	30.00
7 Roy Face	100.00	50.00
8 Herschel Freeman	60.00	30.00
9 Bob Friend	80.00	40.00
10 Dick Groat	100.00	50.00
11 Richard Groat	200.00	100.00
12 Don Gross	60.00	30.00
13 Warren Hacker	60.00	30.00
14 Don Hoak	80.00	40.00
15 Hal Jeffcoat	60.00	30.00
16 Ron Kline	60.00	30.00
17 John Klippstein	60.00	30.00
18 Ted Kluszewski	200.00	100.00
19 Brooks Lawrence	80.00	40.00
20 Dale Long	60.00	30.00
21 Bill Mazeroski	250.00	125.00
22 Roy McMillan	80.00	40.00
23 Joe Nuxhall	60.00	30.00
24 Wally Post	80.00	40.00
25 Frank Robinson	400.00	200.00
26 John Temple	80.00	40.00
27 Frank Thomas	60.00	30.00
28 Bob Thurman	60.00	30.00
29 Lee Walls	60.00	30.00

1958 Kahn's

The cards in this 29-card set measure approximately 3 1/4" X 4". The 1958 Kahn's Wieners set of unnumbered, black and white cards features Cincinnati Redlegs, Philadelphia Phillies and Pittsburgh Pirates. The backs present a story for each player entitled "My Greatest Thrill in Baseball". A method of distinguishing 1958 Kahn's from 1959 Kahn's is that the word Wieners is found on the front of the 1958 but not on the front of the 1959 cards. Cards of Wally Post, Charlie Rabe and Frank Thomas are somewhat more difficult to find and are designated SP in the checklist below. The cards are listed and numbered below in alphabetical order by the subject's name.

	NM	Ex
COMPLETE SET (29)	3200.00	1600.00
COMMON CARD (1-29)	50.00	25.00
COMMON SP	300.00	150.00
1 Ed Bailey	50.00	25.00
2 Gene Baker	50.00	25.00
3 Gus Bell	60.00	30.00
4 Smoky Burgess	60.00	30.00
5 Roberto Clemente	800.00	400.00
6 George Crowe	60.00	30.00
7 Roy Face	80.00	40.00
8 Hank Foiles	50.00	25.00
9 Dee Fondy	50.00	25.00
10 Bob Friend	60.00	30.00
11 Dick Groat	80.00	40.00
12 Harvey Haddix	60.00	30.00
13 Don Hoak	50.00	25.00
14 Hal Jeffcoat	50.00	25.00
15 Ron Kline	50.00	25.00
16 Ted Kluszewski	125.00	60.00
17 Vernon Law	60.00	30.00
18 Brooks Lawrence	60.00	30.00
19 Bill Mazeroski	125.00	60.00
20 Roy McMillan	60.00	30.00
21 Joe Nuxhall	60.00	30.00
22 Wally Post SP	350.00	180.00
23 John Powers	50.00	25.00
24 Bob Purkey	50.00	25.00
25 Charlie Rabe SP	300.00	150.00
26 Frank Robinson	250.00	125.00
27 Bob Skinner	50.00	25.00
28 Johnny Temple	60.00	30.00
29 Frank Thomas SP	350.00	180.00

1959 Kahn's

The cards in this 38-card set measure approximately 3 1/4" X 4". The 1959 Kahn's set features members of the Cincinnati Reds, Cleveland Indians and Pittsburgh Pirates. Backs feature stories entitled "The Toughest Play I have to Make," or "The Toughest Batter I Have To Face." The Brodowski card is very scarce while Haddix, Held and McLish are considered quite difficult to obtain; these scarcities are designated SP in the checklist below. The cards are listed and numbered below in alphabetical order by the subject's name.

	NM	Ex
COMPLETE SET (38)	4500.00	2200.00
COMMON CARD (1-38)	50.00	25.00
COMMON SP	400.00	200.00
1 Ed Bailey	50.00	25.00
2 Gary Bell	50.00	25.00
3 Gus Bell	60.00	30.00
4 Dick Brodowski SP	600.00	300.00
5 Smoky Burgess	60.00	30.00
6 Roberto Clemente	800.00	400.00
7 Rocky Colavito	125.00	60.00
8 Roy Face	80.00	40.00
9 Bob Friend	60.00	30.00
10 Joe Gordon MG	60.00	30.00
11 Jim Grant	60.00	30.00
12 Dick Groat	80.00	40.00
13 Harvey Haddix SP (Blank back)	400.00	200.00
14 Woodie Held SP	400.00	200.00
15 Don Hoak	50.00	25.00
16 Ron Kline	50.00	25.00
17 Ted Kluszewski	125.00	60.00
18 Vernon Law	60.00	30.00
19 Jerry Lynch	50.00	25.00
20 Billy Martin	125.00	60.00
21 Bill Mazeroski	125.00	60.00
22 Cal McLish SP	400.00	200.00
23 Roy McMillan	50.00	25.00
24 Minnie Minoso	100.00	50.00
25 Russ Nixon	50.00	25.00
26 Joe Nuxhall	60.00	30.00
27 Jim Perry	80.00	40.00
28 Vada Pinson	100.00	50.00
29 Vic Power	50.00	25.00
30 Bob Purkey	50.00	25.00
31 Frank Robinson	200.00	100.00
32 Herb Score	80.00	40.00
33 Bob Skinner	50.00	25.00
34 George Strickland	50.00	25.00
35 Dick Stuart	60.00	30.00
36 Johnny Temple	50.00	25.00
37 Frank Thomas	60.00	30.00
38 George Witt	50.00	25.00

1960 Kahn's

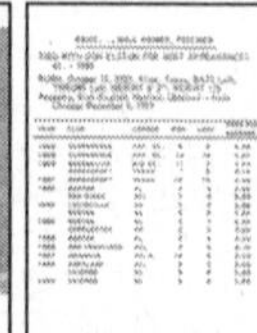

The cards in this 42-card set measure 3 1/4" X 4". The 1960 Kahn's set features players of the Chicago Cubs, Chicago White Sox, Cincinnati Redlegs, Cleveland Indians, Pittsburgh Pirates and St. Louis Cardinals. The backs give vital player information and records through the 1959 season. Kline appears with either St. Louis or Pittsburgh. The set price includes both Kline's. The Harvey Kuenn card in this set appears with a blank back and is scarce. The cards are listed and numbered below in alphabetical order by the subject's name.

	NM	Ex
COMPLETE SET (43)	2000.00	800.00
1 Ed Bailey	25.00	10.00
2 Gary Bell	25.00	10.00
3 Gus Bell	30.00	12.00
4 Smoky Burgess	30.00	12.00
5 Gino Cimoli	25.00	10.00
6 Roberto Clemente	500.00	200.00
7 Roy Face	30.00	12.00
8 Tito Francona	25.00	10.00
9 Bob Friend	30.00	12.00
10 Jim Grant	30.00	12.00
11 Dick Groat	40.00	16.00
12 Harvey Haddix	30.00	12.00
13 Woodie Held	25.00	10.00
14 Bill Henry	25.00	10.00
15 Don Hoak	25.00	10.00
16 Jay Hook	25.00	10.00
17 Eddie Kasko	25.00	10.00
18A Ron Kline (Pittsburgh)	50.00	20.00
18B Ron Kline (St. Louis)	50.00	20.00
19 Ted Kluszewski	60.00	24.00
20 Harvey Kuenn SP (Blank back)	400.00	160.00
21 Vernon Law	30.00	12.00
22 Brooks Lawrence	30.00	12.00
23 Jerry Lynch	25.00	10.00
24 Billy Martin	60.00	24.00
25 Bill Mazeroski	60.00	24.00
26 Cal McLish	25.00	10.00
27 Roy McMillan	25.00	10.00
28 Don Newcombe	40.00	16.00
29 Russ Nixon	25.00	10.00
30 Joe Nuxhall	30.00	12.00
31 Jim O'Toole	25.00	10.00
32 Jim Perry	30.00	12.00
33 Vada Pinson	50.00	20.00
34 Vic Power	25.00	10.00
35 Bob Purkey	25.00	10.00
36 Frank Robinson	150.00	60.00
37 Herb Score	30.00	12.00
38 Bob Skinner	25.00	10.00
39 Dick Stuart	30.00	12.00
40 Johnny Temple	30.00	12.00
41 Frank Thomas	30.00	12.00
42 Lee Walls	25.00	10.00

1961 Kahn's

The cards in this 43-card set measure approximately 3 1/4" X 4". The 1961 Kahn's Wieners set of black and white, unnumbered cards features members of the Cincinnati Reds, Cleveland Indians and Pittsburgh Pirates. This year was the first year Kahn's made complete sets available to the public; hence they are more available, especially in the better condition grades than the Kahn's of the previous years. The backs give vital player information and year by year career statistics through 1960. The catalog designation is F155-7. The cards are listed and numbered below in alphabetical order by the subject's name.

	NM	Ex
COMPLETE SET (43)	850.00	350.00
1 John Antonelli	12.00	4.80
2 Ed Bailey	12.00	4.80
3 Gary Bell	12.00	4.80
4 Gus Bell	15.00	6.00
5 Jim Brosnan	15.00	6.00
6 Smoky Burgess	15.00	6.00
7 Gino Cimoli	12.00	4.80
8 Roberto Clemente	400.00	160.00
9 Gordie Coleman	12.00	4.80
10 Jimmy Dykes MG	15.00	6.00
11 Roy Face	15.00	6.00
12 Tito Francona	12.00	4.80
13 Gene Freese	12.00	4.80
14 Bob Friend	15.00	6.00
15 Jim Grant	15.00	6.00
16 Dick Groat	15.00	6.00
17 Harvey Haddix	15.00	6.00
18 Woodie Held	12.00	4.80
19 Don Hoak	12.00	4.80
20 Jay Hook	12.00	4.80
21 Joey Jay	12.00	4.80
22 Eddie Kasko	12.00	4.80
23 Willie Kirkland	12.00	4.80
24 Vernon Law	15.00	6.00
25 Jerry Lynch	12.00	4.80
26 Jim Maloney	20.00	8.00
27 Bill Mazeroski	40.00	16.00
28 Wilmer Mizell	15.00	6.00
29 Rocky Nelson	12.00	4.80
30 Jim O'Toole	12.00	4.80
31 Jim Perry	15.00	6.00
32 Bubba Phillips	12.00	4.80
33 Vada Pinson	30.00	12.00
34 Wally Post	12.00	4.80
35 Vic Power	12.00	4.80
36 Bob Purkey	12.00	4.80
37 Frank Robinson	100.00	40.00
38 John Romano	12.00	4.80
39 Dick Schofield	12.00	4.80
40 Bob Skinner	12.00	4.80
41 Hal Smith	12.00	4.80
42 Dick Stuart	15.00	6.00
43 Johnny Temple	12.00	4.80

1962 Kahn's

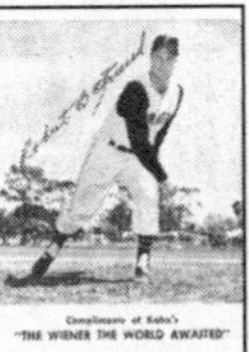

The cards in this 38-card set measure approximately 3 1/4" X 4". The 1962 Kahn's Wieners set of black and white, unnumbered cards features Cincinnati, Cleveland, Minnesota and Pittsburgh players. Card numbers 1 Bell, 33 Power and 34 Purkey exist in two different forms; these variations are listed in the checklist below. The backs of the cards contain career information. The catalog designation is F155-8. The set price below includes the set with all variation cards. The cards are listed and numbered below in alphabetical order by the subject's name.

	NM	Ex
COMPLETE SET (41)	1200.00	475.00
1A Gary Bell (With fat man)	100.00	40.00
1B Gary Bell (No fat man)	40.00	16.00
2 Jim Brosnan	15.00	6.00
3 Smoky Burgess	15.00	6.00
4 Chico Cardenas	15.00	6.00
5 Roberto Clemente	250.00	100.00
6 Ty Cline	10.00	4.00
7 Gordon Coleman	15.00	6.00
8 Dick Donovan	10.00	4.00
9 John Edwards	10.00	4.00
10 Tito Francona	10.00	4.00
11 Gene Freese	10.00	4.00
12 Bob Friend	15.00	6.00
13 Joe Gibbon	100.00	40.00
14 Jim Grant	15.00	6.00
15 Dick Groat	20.00	8.00
16 Harvey Haddix	15.00	6.00
17 Woodie Held	10.00	4.00
18 Bill Henry	10.00	4.00
19 Don Hoak	10.00	4.00
20 Ken Hunt	10.00	4.00
21 Joey Jay	10.00	4.00
22 Eddie Kasko	10.00	4.00
23 Willie Kirkland	10.00	4.00
24 Barry Latman	10.00	4.00
25 Jerry Lynch	10.00	4.00
26 Jim Maloney	20.00	8.00
27 Bill Mazeroski	30.00	12.00
28 Jim O'Toole	10.00	4.00
29 Jim Perry	15.00	6.00
30 Bubba Phillips	10.00	4.00
31 Vada Pinson	20.00	8.00
32 Wally Post	10.00	4.00
33A Vic Power (Indians)	40.00	16.00
33B Vic Power (Twins)	100.00	40.00
34A Bob Purkey (With autograph)	40.00	16.00
34B Bob Purkey (No autograph)	100.00	40.00
35 Frank Robinson	100.00	40.00
36 John Romano	10.00	4.00
37 Dick Stuart	15.00	6.00
38 Bill Virdon	20.00	8.00

1963 Kahn's

The cards in this 30-card set measure approximately 3 1/4" X 4". The 1963 Kahn's Wieners set of black and white, unnumbered cards features players from Cincinnati, Cleveland, St. Louis, Pittsburgh and the New York Yankees. The cards feature a white border around the picture of the players. The backs contain career information. The catalog designation for this set is F155-10. The cards are listed and numbered below in alphabetical order by the subject's name.

	NM	Ex
COMPLETE SET (30)	600.00	240.00
1 Bob Bailey	10.00	4.00
2 Don Blasingame	10.00	4.00
3 Clete Boyer	15.00	6.00
4 Smoky Burgess	12.00	4.80
5 Chico Cardenas	12.00	4.80
6 Roberto Clemente	250.00	100.00
7 Donn Clendenon	12.00	4.80
8 Gordon Coleman	12.00	4.80
9 John Edwards	10.00	4.00
10 Gene Freese	10.00	4.00
11 Bob Friend	12.00	4.80
12 Joe Gibbon	10.00	4.00
13 Dick Groat	15.00	6.00
14 Harvey Haddix	12.00	4.80
15 Elston Howard	25.00	10.00
16 Joey Jay	10.00	4.00
17 Eddie Kasko	10.00	4.00
18 Tony Kubek	30.00	12.00
19 Jerry Lynch	10.00	4.00
20 Jim Maloney	15.00	6.00
21 Bill Mazeroski	30.00	12.00
22 Joe Nuxhall	12.00	4.80
23 Jim O'Toole	10.00	4.00
24 Vada Pinson	20.00	8.00
25 Bob Purkey	10.00	4.00
26 Bobby Richardson	30.00	12.00
27 Frank Robinson	100.00	40.00
28 Bill Stafford	10.00	4.00
29 Ralph Terry	12.00	4.80
30 Bill Virdon	12.00	4.80

1964 Kahn's

The cards in this 31-card set measure 3" X 3 1/2". The 1964 Kahn's set marks the beginning of the full color cards and the elimination of the tabs which existed on previous Kahn's cards. The set of unnumbered cards contains player information through the 1963 season on the backs. The set features Cincinnati, Cleveland and Pittsburgh players. The cards are listed and numbered below in alphabetical order by the subject's name. An early card of Pete Rose highlights this set.

	NM	Ex
COMPLETE SET (31)	1000.00	400.00
1 Max Alvis	10.00	4.00
2 Bob Bailey	10.00	4.00
3 Chico Cardenas	12.00	4.80
4 Roberto Clemente	250.00	100.00
5 Donn Clendenon	12.00	4.80
6 Vic Davalillo	10.00	4.00
7 Dick Donovan	10.00	4.00
8 John Edwards	10.00	4.00
9 Bob Friend	12.00	4.80
10 Jim Grant	12.00	4.80
11 Tommy Harper	12.00	4.80
12 Woodie Held	12.00	4.80
13 Joey Jay	10.00	4.00
14 Jack Kralick	10.00	4.00
15 Jerry Lynch	10.00	4.00
16 Jim Maloney	12.00	4.80
17 Bill Mazeroski	25.00	10.00
18 Alvin McBean	10.00	4.00
19 Joe Nuxhall	12.00	4.80
20 Jim Pagliaroni	10.00	4.00
21 Vada Pinson	20.00	8.00
22 Bob Purkey	10.00	4.00
23 Pedro Ramos	10.00	4.00
24 Frank Robinson	100.00	40.00
25 John Romano	10.00	4.00
26 Pete Rose	400.00	160.00
27 John Tsitouris	10.00	4.00
28 Bob Veale	12.00	4.80
29 Bill Virdon	12.00	4.80
30 Leon Wagner	10.00	4.00
31 Fred Whitfield	10.00	4.00

1965 Kahn's

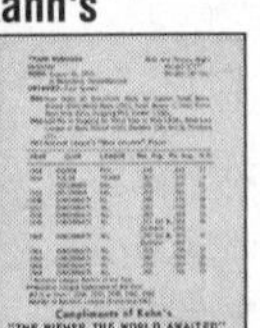

The cards in this 45-card set measure 3" X 3 1/2". The 1965 Kahn's set contains full-color, unnumbered cards. The set features Cincinnati, Cleveland, Pittsburgh and Milwaukee players. Backs contain statistical information through the 1964 season. The cards are listed and numbered below in alphabetical order by the subject's name.

	NM	Ex
COMPLETE SET (45)	1000.00	400.00
1 Henry Aaron	150.00	60.00
2 Max Alvis	12.00	4.80
3 Joe Azcue	10.00	4.00
4 Bob Bailey	10.00	4.00
5 Frank Bolling	10.00	4.00
6 Chico Cardenas	12.00	4.80
7 Rico Carty	15.00	6.00
8 Donn Clendenon	12.00	4.80
9 Tony Cloninger	12.00	4.80
10 Gordon Coleman	10.00	4.00
11 Vic Davalillo	10.00	4.00
12 John Edwards	10.00	4.00
13 Sammy Ellis	10.00	4.00
14 Bob Friend	12.00	4.80
15 Tommy Harper	12.00	4.80
16 Chuck Hinton	10.00	4.00
17 Dick Howser	12.00	4.80
18 Joey Jay	10.00	4.00
19 Deron Johnson	12.00	4.80
20 Jack Kralick	10.00	4.00
21 Denver LeMaster	10.00	4.00
22 Jerry Lynch	10.00	4.00
23 Jim Maloney	15.00	6.00
24 Lee Maye	10.00	4.00
25 Bill Mazeroski	25.00	10.00
26 Alvin McBean	10.00	4.00
27 Bill McCool	10.00	4.00
28 Sam McDowell	15.00	6.00
29 Don McMahon	10.00	4.00
30 Denis Menke	10.00	4.00
31 Joe Nuxhall	12.00	4.80
32 Gene Oliver	10.00	4.00
33 Jim O'Toole	10.00	4.00
34 Jim Pagliaroni	10.00	4.00
35 Vada Pinson	20.00	8.00
36 Frank Robinson	100.00	40.00
37 Pete Rose	200.00	80.00
38 Willie Stargell	100.00	40.00
39 Ralph Terry	12.00	4.80
40 Luis Tiant	20.00	8.00
41 Joe Torre	25.00	10.00
42 John Tsitouris	10.00	4.00
43 Bob Veale	12.00	4.80
44 Bill Virdon	12.00	4.80
45 Leon Wagner	10.00	4.00

1966 Kahn's

The cards in this 32-card set measure 2 13/16" X 4". 1966 Kahn's full-color, unnumbered set features players from Atlanta, Cincinnati, Cleveland and Pittsburgh. The set is identified by yellow and white vertical stripes and the name Kahn's written in red across a red rose at the top. The cards contain a 1 5/16" ad in the form of a tab. Cards with the ad (tab) are worth twice as much as cards without the ad. (double the prices below) The cards are listed and numbered below in alphabetical order by the subject's name.

	NM	Ex
COMPLETE SET (32)	600.00	240.00
1 Henry Aaron Portrait, no windbreaker under jersey	125.00	50.00
2 Felipe Alou: Braves Full pose batting screen in background	20.00	8.00
3 Max Alvis: Indians Kneeling full pose with bat no patch on jersey	10.00	4.00
4 Bob Bailey	10.00	4.00
5 Wade Blasingame	10.00	4.00
6 Frank Bolling	10.00	4.00
7 Chico Cardenas: Reds Fielding feet at base	12.00	4.80
8 Roberto Clemente	150.00	60.00
9 Tony Cloninger: Braves Pitching foulpole in background	12.00	4.80
10 Vic Davalillo	10.00	4.00
11 John Edwards: Reds Catching	10.00	4.00
12 Sam Ellis: Reds White hat	10.00	4.00
13 Pedro Gonzalez	10.00	4.00
14 Tommy Harper: Reds Arm cocked	12.00	4.80
15 Deron Johnson: Reds Batting with batting cage in background	12.00	4.80
16 Mack Jones	10.00	4.00
17 Denver Lemaster	10.00	4.00
18 Jim Maloney: Reds Pitching white hat	12.00	4.80
19 Bill Mazeroski: Pirates Throwing	25.00	10.00
20 Bill McCool: Reds White hat	10.00	4.00
21 Sam McDowell Indians, Kneeling	12.00	4.80
22 Denis Menke: Braves White windbreaker under jersey	10.00	4.00
23 Joe Nuxhall	12.00	4.80
24 Jim Pagliaroni: Pirates Catching	10.00	4.00
25 Milt Pappas	12.00	4.80
26 Vada Pinson: Reds (Fielding ball on ground	20.00	8.00
27 Pete Rose: Reds With glove	125.00	50.00
28 Sonny Siebert: Indians Pitching signature at feet	12.00	4.80
29 Willie Stargell: Pirates Batting clouds in sky	50.00	20.00
30 Joe Torre: Braves Catching with hand on mask	25.00	10.00
31 Bob Veale: Pirates Hands at knee with glasses	12.00	4.80
32 Fred Whitfield	10.00	4.00

1967 Kahn's

The cards in this 41-player set measure 2 13/16" X 4". The 1967 Kahn's set of full-color, unnumbered cards is almost identical in style to the 1966 issue. Different meat products had different background colors (yellow and white stripes, red and white stripes, etc.). The set features players from Atlanta, Cincinnati, Cleveland, New York Mets and Pittsburgh. Cards with the ads (see 1966 set) are worth twice as much as cards without the ad, i.e., double the prices below. The complete set price below includes all variations. The cards are listed and numbered below in alphabetical order by the subject's name. Examples have been seen in which the top borders have a very small indentation.

	NM	Ex
COMPLETE SET (51)	800.00	325.00
1A Henry Aaron: Braves (Swinging pose, batting glove, ball, and hat on ground)	100.00	40.00
1B Henry Aaron: Braves (Swinging pose, batting glove, ball, and hat on ground; Cut Along Dotted Lines printed on lower tab)	125.00	50.00
2 Gene Alley: Pirates (Portrait)	10.00	4.00
3 Felipe Alou: Braves (Full pose, bat on shoulder)	15.00	6.00
4A Matty Alou: Pirates (Portrait with bat, Matio Rojas Alou"; yellow stripes)	10.00	4.00
4B Matty Alou: Pirates (Portrait with bat Matio Rojas Alou"; red stripes)	12.00	4.80
5 Max Alvis: Indians (Fielding, hands on knees)	8.00	3.20
6A Ken Boyer (Batting righthanded; autograph at waist)	12.00	4.80
6B Ken Boyer (Batting righthanded; autograph at shoulders; Cut Along Dotted Lines printed on lower tab)	15.00	6.00
7 Chico Cardenas: Reds (Fielding hand on knee)	10.00	4.00
8 Rico Carty	10.00	4.00
9 Tony Cloninger: Braves (Pitching, no foul-pole in background)	10.00	4.00
10 Tommy Davis	10.00	4.00
11 John Edwards: Reds (Kneeling with bat)	8.00	3.20
12A Sam Ellis: Reds (All red hat)	8.00	3.20
12B Sam Ellis: Reds (All red hat; Cut Along Dotted Lines printed on lower tab)	10.00	4.00
13 Jack Fisher	8.00	3.20
14 Steve Hargan: Indians (Pitching, no clouds blue sky)	8.00	3.20
15 Tommy Harper: Reds (Fielding, glove on ground)	10.00	4.00
16A Tommy Helms (Batting righthanded; top of bat visible)	10.00	4.00
16B Tommy Helms (Batting righthanded; bat chopped above hat; Cut Along Dotted Lines printed on lower tab)	12.00	4.80
17 Deron Johnson: Reds (Batting, blue sky)	10.00	4.00
18 Ken Johnson	8.00	3.20
19 Cleon Jones	10.00	4.00
20A Ed Kranepool (Ready for throw; yellow stripes)	10.00	4.00
20B Ed Kranepool (Ready for throw; red stripes)	10.00	4.00
21A Jim Maloney: Reds (Pitching, red hat, follow thru delivery; yellow stripes)	10.00	4.00
21B Jim Maloney: Reds (Pitching, red hat, follow thru delivery; red stripes)	12.00	4.80
22 Lee May: Reds (Hands on knee)	10.00	4.00
23A Bill Mazeroski: Pirates (Portrait; autograph below waist)	20.00	8.00
23B Bill Mazeroski: Pirates (Portrait; autograph above waist; Cut Along Dotted Lines printed on lower tab)	25.00	10.00
24 Bill McCool: Reds (Red hat, left hand out)	8.00	3.20
25 Sam McDowell: Indians (Pitching, left hand under glove)	12.00	4.80
26 Denis Menke: Braves (Blue sleeves)	8.00	3.20
27 Jim Pagliaroni: Pirates (Catching no chest protector)	8.00	3.20
28 Don Pavletich	8.00	3.20
29 Tony Perez: Reds (Throwing)	40.00	16.00
30 Vada Pinson: Reds (Ready to throw)	15.00	6.00
31 Dennis Ribant	8.00	3.20
32 Pete Rose: Reds (Batting)	100.00	40.00
33 Art Shamsky: Reds	8.00	3.20
34 Bob Shaw	8.00	3.20
35 Sonny Siebert: Indians (Pitching signature at knees)	8.00	3.20
36 Willie Stargell: Pirates (Batting no clouds)	40.00	16.00
37A Joe Torre: Braves (Catching, mask on ground)	15.00	6.00
37B Joe Torre: Braves (Catching, mask on ground; Cut Along Dotted Lines printed on lower tab)	25.00	10.00
38 Bob Veale: Pirates (Portrait, hands not shown)	8.00	3.20
39 Leon Wagner: Indians (Fielding)	8.00	3.20
40A Fred Whitfield (Batting lefthanded)	8.00	3.20
40B Fred Whitfield (Batting lefthanded; Cut Along Dotted Lines	8.00	3.20

printed on lower tab)
41 Woody Woodward................ 8.00 3.20

1968 Kahn's

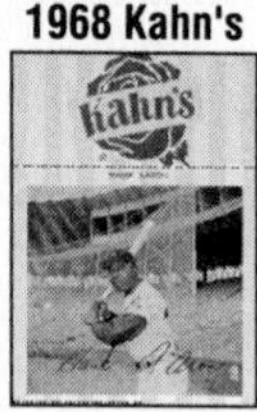

The cards in this 50-piece set contain two different sizes. The smaller of the two sizes, which contains 12 cards, is 2 13/16" X 3 1/4" with the ad tab and 2 13/16" X 1 7/8" without the ad tab. The larger size, which contains 38 cards, measures 2 13/16" X 3 7/8" with the ad tab and 2 13/16" X 2 11/16" without the ad tab. The 1968 Kahn's set of full-color, blank backed, unnumbered cards features players from Atlanta, Chicago Cubs, Chicago White Sox, Cincinnati, Cleveland, Detroit, New York Mets and Pittsburgh. In the set of 12, listed with the letter A in the checklist, Maloney exists with either yellow or yellow and green stripes at the top of the card. The large set of 38, listed with a letter B in the checklist, contains five cards which exist in two variations. The variations in this large set have either yellow or red stripes at the top of the cards, with Maloney being an exception. Maloney has either a yellow stripe or a Blue Mountain ad at the top. Cards with the ad tabs (see other Kahn's sets) are worth twice as much as cards without the ad, i.e., double the prices below. The cards are listed and numbered below in alphabetical order (within each subset) by the subject's name. The set features a card of Johnny Bench in his Rookie Card year.

NM Ex
COMPLETE SET (50)............ 1000.00 400.00
A1 Hank Aaron....................... 100.00 40.00
A2 Gene Alley........................... 10.00 4.00
A3 Max Alvis.............................. 8.00 3.20
A4 Clete Boyer.......................... 12.00 4.80
A5 Chico Cardenas.................... 10.00 4.00
A6 Bill Freehan.......................... 12.00 4.80
A7 Jim Maloney (2).................... 12.00 4.80
A8 Lee May................................. 12.00 4.80
A9 Bill Mazeroski........................ 25.00 10.00
A10 Vada Pinson......................... 15.00 6.00
A11 Joe Torre............................. 20.00 8.00
A12 Bob Veale............................ 10.00 4.00
B1 Hank Aaron: Braves........... 100.00 40.00
Full pose
batting
bat cocked
B2 Tommy Agee......................... 10.00 4.00
B3 Gene Alley: Pirates................ 8.00 3.20
Fielding, full pose
B4 Felipe Alou.......................... 15.00 6.00
Full pose
batting, swinging
player in background
B5 Matty Alou: Pirates.............. 10.00 4.00
Portrait with bat
Matio Alou (2)
B6 Max Alvis............................... 8.00 3.20
Fielding
glove on ground
B7 Gerry Arrigo: Reds................ 8.00 3.20
Pitching
followthru delivery
B8 John Bench......................... 300.00 120.00
B9 Clete Boyer........................... 12.00 4.80
B10 Larry Brown.......................... 8.00 3.20
B11 Leo Cardenas: Reds........... 10.00 4.00
Leaping in the air
B12 Bill Freehan......................... 12.00 4.80
B13 Steve Hargan:...................... 8.00 3.20
Indians
Pitching
clouds in background
B14 Joel Horlen........................... 8.00 3.20
White Sox
Portrait
B15 Tony Horton: Indians......... 12.00 4.80
Portrait
signed Anthony
B16 Willie Horton....................... 12.00 4.80
B17 Fergie Jenkins..................... 40.00 16.00
B18 Deron Johnson:................... 10.00 4.00
Braves
B19 Mack Jones: Reds................ 8.00 3.20
B20 Bob Lee................................ 8.00 3.20
B21 Jim Maloney: Reds............ 12.00 4.80
Red hat
pitching hands up (2)
B22 Lee May: Reds.................... 10.00 4.00
Batting
B23 Bill Mazeroski:.................... 25.00 10.00
Pirates
Fielding
hands in front
of body
B24 Dick McAuliffe...................... 8.00 3.20
B25 Bill McCool........................... 8.00 3.20
Red hat
left hand down
B26 Sam McDowell:................... 12.00 4.80
Indians
Pitching
left hand over glove (2)
B27 Tony Perez......................... 30.00 12.00
Fielding ball in glove (2)
B28 Gary Peters.......................... 8.00 3.20
White Sox
Portrait
B29 Vada Pinson: Reds............ 12.00 4.80
Batting
B30 Chico Ruiz............................ 8.00 3.20
B31 Ron Santo: Cubs................ 25.00 10.00
Batting
follow thru (2)
B32 Art Shamsky: Mets.............. 8.00 3.20
B33 Luis Tiant: Indians............. 15.00 6.00
Hands over head
B34 Joe Torre: Braves.............. 20.00 8.00
Batting
B35 Bob Veale: Pirates............... 8.00 3.20
Hands chest high
B36 Leon Wagner: Indians.......... 8.00 3.20
Batting
B37 Billy Williams: Cubs.......... 40.00 16.00
Bat behind back
B38 Earl Wilson.......................... 8.00 3.20

1969 Kahn's

The cards in this 25-piece set contain two different sizes. The three small cards (see 1968 description) measure 2 13/16" X 3 1/4" and the 22 large cards (see 1968 description) measure 2 13/16" X 3 15/16". The 1969 Kahn's Wieners set of full-color, unnumbered cards features players from Atlanta, Chicago Cubs, Chicago White Sox, Cincinnati, Cleveland, Pittsburgh and St. Louis. The small cards have the letter A in the checklist while the large cards have the letter B in the checklist. Four of the larger cards exist in two variations (red or yellow color stripes at the top of the card). These variations are identified in the checklist below. Cards with the ad tabs (see other Kahn's sets) are worth twice as much as cards without the ad, i.e., double the prices below. The cards are listed and numbered below in alphabetical order (within each subset) by the subject's name.

NM Ex
COMPLETE SET (25)............. 450.00 180.00
A1 Hank Aaron....................... 100.00 40.00
Portrait
A2 Jim Maloney....................... 10.00 4.00
Pitching
hands at side
A3 Tony Perez......................... 25.00 10.00
Glove on
B1 Hank Aaron....................... 100.00 40.00
B2 Matty Alou......................... 10.00 4.00
Batting
B3 Max Alvis............................. 8.00 3.20
69 patch
B4 Gerry Arrigo......................... 8.00 3.20
Leg up
B5 Steve Blass........................ 10.00 4.00
B6 Clay Carroll.......................... 8.00 3.20
B7 Tony Cloninger: Reds........... 8.00 3.20
B8 George Culver...................... 8.00 3.20
B9 Joel Horlen......................... 10.00 4.00
Pitching
B10 Tony Horton...................... 12.00 4.80
Batting
B11 Alex Johnson..................... 10.00 4.00
B12 Jim Maloney...................... 10.00 4.00
B13 Lee May............................ 10.00 4.00
Foot on bag (2)
B14 Bill Mazeroski.................... 25.00 10.00
Hands on knees (2)
B15 Sam McDowell................... 10.00 4.00
Leg up (2)
B16 Tony Perez........................ 30.00 12.00
B17 Gary Peters........................ 8.00 3.20
Pitching
B18 Ron Santo......................... 20.00 8.00
Emblem (2)
B19 Luis Tiant.......................... 15.00 6.00
Glove at knee
B20 Joe Torre: Cardinals.......... 20.00 8.00
B21 Bob Veale......................... 10.00 4.00
Hands at knees
no glasses
B22 Billy Williams.................... 30.00 12.00
Bat behind head

1985 Kahn's Commemorative Coins

Issued in conjunction with Hillshire Farms, this three card and coin set features all-time leading hitters Carl Yastrzemski and Pete Rose. The cards measure 3 3/4" by 5 1/2" and give highlights of each player's career. The coin is attached to the card is titled "Cooperstown Collection".

Nm-Mt Ex-Mt
COMPLETE SET (3)................. 15.00 6.00
1 Johnny Bench......................... 8.00 3.20
2 Pete Rose............................ 10.00 4.00
3 Carl Yastrzemski.................... 5.00 2.00

1989 Kahn's Cooperstown

The 1989 Kahn's Cooperstown set contains 11 standard-size cards. This set is sometimes referenced as Hillshire Farms or Kahn's Cooperstown Collection. All players included in the set are members (for the most part they are recent inductees) of the Hall of Fame. The pictures are actually paintings and are surrounded by gold borders. The fronts resemble plaques and also have facsimile autographs. The cards were available from the company via a send-in offer. A set of cards was available in return for three proofs of purchase (and $1 postage and handling) from Hillshire Farms. The last card in the set is actually a coupon card for Kahn's products; this card is not even considered part of the set by some collectors. A related promotion offered two coin cards (coins laminated on cards) featuring Johnny Bench and Carl Yastrzemski. Coin cards are 5 1/2" X 3 3/4" and are blank backed.

Nm-Mt Ex-Mt
COMPLETE SET (12)................... 5.00 2.00
1 Cool Papa Bell............................ .50 .20
2 Johnny Bench.......................... 1.00 .40
3 Lou Brock.................................. .75 .30
4 Whitey Ford................................ .75 .30
5 Bob Gibson................................. .75 .30
6 Billy Herman................................ .50 .20
7 Harmon Killebrew......................... .75 .30
8 Eddie Mathews............................ .75 .30
9 Brooks Robinson....................... 1.00 .40
10 Willie Stargell.......................... 1.00 .40
11 Carl Yastrzemski...................... 1.00 .40
12 Coupon Card.............................. .25 .10

1887 Kalamazoo Bats N690-1

The Charles Gross Company of Philadelphia marketed this series of baseball players in 1887 in packages of tobacco with the intriguing name Kalamazoo Bats. This name involved a two-fold meaning since the word "bat" also referred to a wad of tobacco. There are 61 sepia photographs of baseball players known; most cards are blank backed although some are found with a list of premiums printed on the reverse. A Tom McLaughlin card was found recently, so this checklist may not be complete and all additions are appreciated.

Ex-Mt VG
COMPLETE SET (60)......... 150000.00
75000.00
COMMON PHILADELPHIA.... 1200.00 600.00
COMMON N.Y. GIANTS......... 4000.00 2000.00
COMMON METS.................. 6000.00 3000.00
1 George Andrews: Phila........ 1200.00 600.00
2 Charlie Bastian.................. 1200.00 600.00
Denny Lyons:
Philadelphia
3 Louis Bierbauer:................ 1200.00 600.00
Athletics
4 Louis Bierbauer................. 1200.00 600.00
Gallagher:
Athletics
5 Charlie Buffington:............. 1200.00 600.00
Philadelphia
6 Dan Casey: Phila............... 1200.00 600.00
7 Jack Clements: Phila.......... 1200.00 600.00
8 Roger Connor: New York.... 8000.00 4000.00
9 Larry Corcoran:................. 4000.00 2000.00
New York
10 Ed Cushman..................... 6000.00 3000.00
11 Pat Deasley..................... 4000.00 2000.00
12 Devlin: Phila..................... 1200.00 600.00
13 Jim Donahue: Mets........... 6000.00 3000.00
14 Mike Dorgan: New York.... 4000.00 2000.00
15 Dude Esterbrooke (sic):.... 6000.00 3000.00
Mets
16 Buck Ewing..................... 4000.00 2000.00
New York
17 Sid Farrar: Phila.............. 1500.00 750.00
18 Charlie Ferguson.............. 1200.00 600.00
Philadelphia
19 Jim Fogarty: Phila............ 1200.00 600.00
20 Jim Fogarty..................... 1200.00 600.00
James McGuire:
Philadelphia
21 Elmer E. Foster: Mets....... 6000.00 3000.00
22 Gibson: Philadelphia......... 1200.00 600.00
23 Pete Gillespie:.................. 4000.00 2000.00
New York
24 Tom Gunning: Phila.......... 1200.00 600.00
25 Art Irwin: Phila................. 1200.00 600.00
26 Art Irwin (Capt.)............... 1200.00 600.00
Al Maul:
Philadelphia
27 Tim Keefe........................ 6000.00 3000.00
28 Ted Larkin: Athletics........ 1200.00 600.00
29 Jack Lynch: Mets............. 6000.00 3000.00
30 Denny Lyons: Phila.......... 1200.00 600.00
31 Denny Lyons................... 1200.00 600.00
Billy Taylor:
Philadelphia
32 Fred Mann: Athletics........ 1200.00 600.00
33 Charlie Mason MG........... 1200.00 600.00
34 Bobby Mathews:.............. 1200.00 600.00
Athletics
35 Al Maul: Philadelphia........ 1200.00 600.00
36 Al Mays: Mets.................. 6000.00 3000.00
37 Jim McGarr..................... 1200.00 600.00
38 James McGuire................ 1200.00 600.00
one hand at chin throwing
Philadelphia
39 James McGuire................ 1200.00 600.00
both hands at chin catching
Philadelphia
40 Tom McLaughlin............... 6000.00 3000.00
Mets
41 Jocko Milligan.................. 1200.00 600.00
Henry Larkin:
Athletics
42 Joe Mulvey: Phila............. 1200.00 600.00
43 Jack Nelson: Mets............ 6000.00 3000.00
44 Jim O'Rourke................... 8000.00 4000.00
New York
45 Dave Orr: Mets................ 6000.00 3000.00
46 Tom Poorman.................. 1200.00 600.00
47 Danny Richardson........... 4000.00 2000.00
New York
48 Wilbert Robinson:............ 2500.00 1250.00
Athletics
49 Wilbert Robinson............. 2000.00 1000.00
Fred Mann: Athletics
50 James(Chief)Roseman:.... 6000.00 3000.00
Mets
51 Harry Stowe (sic.............. 3000.00 1500.00
Stovey) (hands at
hips standing):
Athletics
52 Harry Stowe (sic.............. 3000.00 1500.00
Stovey)(hands raised
catching):Athletics
53 Harry Stowe (sic)............ 2500.00 1250.00
Jocko Milligan
Athletics
54 George Townsend:........... 1200.00 600.00
Athletics
55 George Townsend............ 1200.00 600.00
Jocko Milligan
Athletics
56 John M. Ward................. 6000.00 3000.00
57 Mickey Welch.................. 6000.00 3000.00
58 Gus Weyhing.................. 1200.00 600.00
59 Pete Wood: Phila............ 1200.00 600.00
60 Harry Wright:.................. 5000.00 2500.00
Phila.-Mgr.
61 New York....................... 1200.00 600.00
Players Composite

1887 Kalamazoo Teams N690-2

Like the cards of set N690-1, the team cards of this set are sepia photographs and are blank-backed. There are only six teams known at the present time, and the cards themselves are slightly larger than those of the individual ballplayers in N690-1. They also appear to have been issued in 1887. There are only two copies known of the Pittsburg card and we are not pricing that card due to market scarcity.

Ex-Mt VG
COMPLETE SET (6)............ 40000.00
20000.00
1 Athletics Club.................... 4000.00 2000.00
2 Baltimore B.B.C.............. 10000.00 5000.00
3 Boston B.B.C................... 5000.00 2500.00
4 Detroit B.B.C.................... 8000.00 4000.00
5 Philadelphia B.B.C........... 5000.00 2500.00
6 Pittsburg B.B.C.............. 10000.00 5000.00

1974 Kaline Sun-Glo Pop

Sun-Glo Pop issued this card attached to a bottle of pop. The bright green card has a black and white portrait of Al Kaline (not in uniform) with his name printed in black script lettering below followed by the words "drinks Sun-Glo pop". The back is blank.

NM Ex
1 Al Kaline............................. 10.00 4.00

1910 Kallis and Dane

These two 6 1/2" by 5 1/2" blank backed cards were produced by Kallis and Dane printers and featured pictures and highlights from the 1910 World Series. Any additions to the checklist as well as comments are greatly appreciated.

Ex-Mt VG
COMPLETE SET..................... 400.00 200.00
1 Johnny Evers...................... 300.00 150.00
Stealing Home
Harry Steinfeldt at bat
2 Paddy Livingston................. 100.00 50.00
Cutting off a Run
Connie Mack MG inset photo

1985 KAS Discs

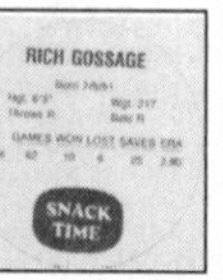

This set was apparently a test issue for the next year's more mass-produced set. Although this set is rarely seen in the secondary market, a few dealers in the mid 1980's got a small supply of this set. Typical of MSA sets all the team insignias are air-brushed out. This set was also issued in a proof square form and those cards are valued at twice the listed prices.

Nm-Mt Ex-Mt
COMPLETE SET..................... 200.00 80.00
1 Steve Carlton....................... 15.00 6.00
2 Jack Clark............................. 5.00 2.00
3 Rich Gossage....................... 8.00 3.20
4 Tony Gwynn....................... 30.00 12.00
5 Keith Hernandez.................. 8.00 3.20
6 Bob Horner.......................... 5.00 2.00
7 Kent Hrbek.......................... 5.00 2.00
8 Willie McGee....................... 6.00 2.40
9 Dan Quisenberry.................. 5.00 2.00
10 Cal Ripken........................ 50.00 20.00
11 Ryne Sandberg.................. 25.00 10.00
12 Mike Schmidt.................... 20.00 8.00
13 Tom Seaver...................... 20.00 8.00
14 Ozzie Smith...................... 25.00 10.00
15 Rick Sutcliffe..................... 5.00 2.00
16 Bruce Sutter...................... 5.00 2.00
17 Alan Trammell.................... 8.00 3.20
18 Fernando Valenzuela.......... 6.00 2.40
19 Willie Wilson....................... 5.00 2.00
20 Dave Winfield.................... 15.00 6.00

1986 Kay-Bee

This 33-card, standard-sized set was produced by Topps but manufactured in Northern Ireland. This boxed set retailed in Kay-Bee stores for $1.99; the checklist was listed on the back of the box. The set is subtitled "Young Superstars of Baseball" and does indeed feature many young players. The cards are numbered on the back; the set card numbering is in alphabetical order by player's name.

Nm-Mt Ex-Mt
COMP. FACT SET (33)................ 4.00 1.60
1 Rick Aguilera............................ .15 .06
2 Chris Brown.............................. .05 .02
3 Tom Browning........................... .05 .02
4 Tom Brunansky.......................... .05 .02
5 Vince Coleman.......................... .15 .06
6 Ron Darling............................... .05 .02
7 Alvin Davis................................ .05 .02
8 Mariano Duncan......................... .15 .06
9 Shawon Dunston........................ .10 .04
10 Sid Fernandez.......................... .05 .02
11 Tony Fernandez........................ .05 .02
12 Brian Fisher............................. .05 .02
13 John Franco............................. .20 .08
14 Julio Franco............................. .20 .08
15 Dwight Gooden......................... .20 .08
16 Ozzie Guillen........................... .20 .08
17 Tony Gwynn........................... 1.00 .40
18 Jimmy Key............................... .20 .08
19 Don Mattingly......................... 1.00 .40
20 Oddibe McDowell...................... .05 .02
21 Roger McDowell........................ .10 .04
22 Dan Pasqua............................. .05 .02
23 Terry Pendleton........................ .10 .04
24 Jim Presley.............................. .05 .02
25 Kirby Puckett............................ .50 .20
26 Earnie Riles.............................. .05 .02
27 Bret Saberhagen....................... .20 .08
28 Mark Salas............................... .05 .02
29 Juan Samuel............................. .05 .02
30 Jeff Stone................................. .05 .02
31 Darryl Strawberry...................... .10 .04
32 Andy Van Slyke......................... .10 .04
33 Frank Viola............................... .15 .06

1987 Kay-Bee

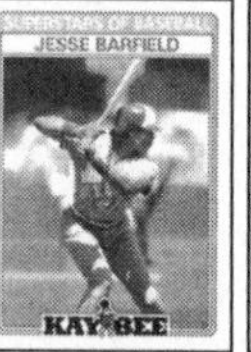

This small 33-card boxed standard-size set was produced by Topps for Kay-Bee Toy Stores. The set is subtitled "Super Stars of Baseball" and has full-color fronts. The card backs are printed in blue and black on white card stock. The checklist for the set is printed on the back panel of the yellow box. The set card numbering is alphabetical by player's name.

Nm-Mt Ex-Mt
COMP. FACT SET (33)................ 4.00 1.60
1 Harold Baines............................ .10 .04
2 Jesse Barfield............................ .05 .02
3 Don Baylor................................ .10 .04
4 Wade Boggs.............................. .40 .16
5 George Brett.............................. .75 .30
6 Hubie Brooks............................. .05 .02
7 Jose Canseco............................ .50 .20
8 Gary Carter............................... .50 .20
9 Joe Carter................................. .20 .08
10 Roger Clemens...................... 1.00 .40
11 Vince Coleman......................... .05 .02
12 Glenn Davis............................. .05 .02
13 Dwight Gooden........................ .15 .06
14 Pedro Guerrero........................ .05 .02
15 Tony Gwynn.......................... 1.00 .40
16 Rickey Henderson.................... .75 .30
17 Keith Hernandez...................... .15 .06
18 Wally Joyner........................... .20 .08
19 Don Mattingly........................ 1.00 .40
20 Jack Morris.............................. .10 .04
21 Dale Murphy............................ .20 .08
22 Eddie Murray........................... .40 .16
23 Dave Parker............................. .10 .04
24 Kirby Puckett........................... .50 .20
25 Tim Raines.............................. .10 .04
26 Jim Rice.................................. .10 .04
27 Dave Righetti........................... .05 .02
28 Ryne Sandberg........................ .75 .30

29 Mike Schmidt .50 .20
30 Mike Scott .05 .02
31 Darryl Strawberry .10 .04
32 Fernando Valenzuela .10 .04
33 Dave Winfield .40 .16

1988 Kay-Bee

This small 33-card boxed standard-size set was produced by Topps for Kay-Bee Toy Stores. The set is subtitled "Superstars of Baseball" and have full-color fronts. The card backs are printed in blue and green on white card stock. The checklist for the set is printed on the back panel of the box. The set card numbering is alphabetical by player's name.

	Nm-Mt	Ex-Mt
COMP. FACT SET (33)	5.00	2.00
1 George Bell	.05	.02
2 Wade Boggs	.50	.20
3 Jose Canseco	.50	.20
4 Joe Carter	.20	.08
5 Jack Clark	.10	.04
6 Alvin Davis	.05	.02
7 Eric Davis	.10	.04
8 Andre Dawson	.20	.08
9 Darrell Evans	.10	.04
10 Dwight Evans	.10	.04
11 Gary Gaetti	.10	.04
12 Pedro Guerrero	.05	.02
13 Tony Gwynn	1.00	.40
14 Howard Johnson	.05	.02
15 Wally Joyner	.15	.06
16 Don Mattingly	1.00	.40
17 Willie McGee	.10	.04
18 Mark McGwire	1.50	.60
19 Paul Molitor	.50	.20
20 Dale Murphy	.20	.08
21 Dave Parker	.10	.04
22 Lance Parrish	.05	.02
23 Kirby Puckett	.50	.20
24 Tim Raines	.10	.04
25 Cal Ripken	2.00	.80
26 Juan Samuel	.05	.02
27 Mike Schmidt	.50	.20
28 Ruben Sierra	.10	.04
29 Darryl Strawberry	.10	.04
30 Danny Tartabull	.05	.02
31 Alan Trammell	.15	.06
32 Tim Wallach	.05	.02
33 Dave Winfield	.40	.16

1989 Kay-Bee

The 1989 Kay-Bee set contains 33 standard-size glossy cards. The fronts have magenta and yellow borders. The horizontally oriented backs are brown and yellow. The cards were distributed as boxed sets through Kay-Bee toy stores. The set card numbering is alphabetical by player's name.

	Nm-Mt	Ex-Mt
COMP. FACT SET (33)	5.00	2.00
1 Wade Boggs	.30	.12
2 George Brett	.75	.30
3 Jose Canseco	.50	.20
4 Gary Carter	.50	.20
5 Jack Clark	.05	.02
6 Will Clark	.40	.16
7 Roger Clemens	.75	.30
8 Eric Davis	.10	.04
9 Andre Dawson	.25	.10
10 Dwight Evans	.10	.04
11 Carlton Fisk	.40	.16
12 Andres Galarraga	.30	.12
13 Kirk Gibson	.10	.04
14 Dwight Gooden	.10	.04
15 Mike Greenwell	.05	.02
16 Pedro Guerrero	.05	.02
17 Tony Gwynn	1.00	.40
18 Rickey Henderson	.40	.16
19 Orel Hershiser	.10	.04
20 Don Mattingly	.75	.30
21 Mark McGwire	1.50	.60
22 Dale Murphy	.25	.10
23 Eddie Murray	.30	.12
24 Kirby Puckett	.50	.20
25 Tim Raines	.10	.04
26 Ryne Sandberg	.60	.24
27 Mike Schmidt	.40	.16
28 Ozzie Smith	.75	.30
29 Darryl Strawberry	.10	.04
30 Alan Trammell	.15	.06
31 Frank Viola	.05	.02
32 Dave Winfield	.30	.12
33 Robin Yount	.25	.10

1990 Kay-Bee

The 1990 Kay-Bee Kings of Baseball set is a standard-size 33-card set sequenced alphabetically that Topps produced for the Kay-Bee toy store chain. A solid red border inside a purple white striped box is the major design feature of this set. The set card numbering is alphabetical by player's name.

	Nm-Mt	Ex-Mt
COMP. FACT SET (33)	6.00	1.80
1 Doyle Alexander	.05	.02
2 Bert Blyleven	.10	.03
3 Wade Boggs	.50	.15
4 George Brett	1.00	.30
5 John Candelaria	.05	.02
6 Gary Carter	.40	.12
7 Vince Coleman	.05	.02
8 Andre Dawson	.20	.06
9 Dennis Eckersley	.40	.12
10 Darrell Evans	.10	.03
11 Dwight Evans	.10	.03
12 Carlton Fisk	.40	.12
13 Ken Griffey Sr.	.05	.02
14 Tony Gwynn	1.00	.30
15 Rickey Henderson	.60	.18
16 Keith Hernandez	.10	.03
17 Charlie Hough	.05	.02
18 Don Mattingly	1.00	.30
19 Jack Morris	.10	.03
20 Dale Murphy	.20	.06
21 Eddie Murray	.40	.12
22 Dave Parker	.10	.03
23 Kirby Puckett	.75	.23
24 Tim Raines	.10	.03
25 Rick Reuschel	.05	.02
26 Jerry Reuss	.05	.02
27 Jim Rice	.10	.03
28 Nolan Ryan	2.00	.60
29 Ozzie Smith	1.00	.30
30 Frank Tanana	.05	.02
31 Willie Wilson	.05	.02
32 Dave Winfield	.50	.15
33 Robin Yount	.50	.15

1970 Kellogg's

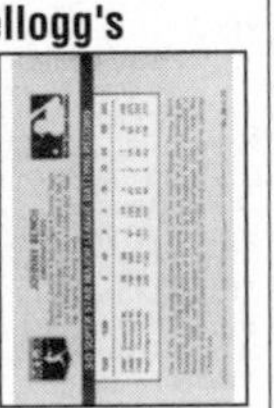

The cards in this 75-card set measure approximately 2 1/4" by 3 1/2". The 1970 Kellogg's set was Kellogg's first venture into the baseball card producing field. The design incorporates a brilliant color photo of the player set against an indistinct background, which is then covered with a layer of plastic to simulate a 3-D look. Some veteran card dealers consider cards 16-30 to be in shorter supply than the other cards in the set. The cards were individually inserted one per specially marked boxes of Kellogg's cereal. Cards still found with the wrapper intact are valued 50 percent greater than the values listed below. Kellogg's also distributed six-card packs which were available when collectors bought two card team patches. These packs, are still occassionally seen in the hobby and have a current value of $35.

	NM	Ex
COMPLETE SET (75)	250.00	100.00
1 Ed Kranepool	1.50	.60
2 Pete Rose	15.00	6.00
3 Cleon Jones	1.50	.60
4 Willie McCovey	6.00	2.40
5 Mel Stottlemyre	1.50	.60
6 Frank Howard	1.50	.60
7 Tom Seaver	15.00	6.00
8 Don Sutton	5.00	2.00
9 Jim Wynn	1.50	.60
10 Jim Maloney	1.00	.40
11 Tommie Agee	1.50	.60
12 Willie Mays	20.00	8.00
13 Juan Marichal	5.00	2.00
14 Dave McNally	1.50	.60
15 Frank Robinson	8.00	3.20
16 Carlos May	1.00	.40
17 Bill Singer	1.00	.40
18 Rick Reichardt	1.00	.40
19 Boog Powell	2.00	.80
20 Gaylord Perry	6.00	2.40
21 Brooks Robinson	12.00	4.80
22 Luis Aparicio	5.00	2.00
23 Joel Horlen	1.00	.40
24 Mike Epstein	1.00	.40
25 Tom Haller	1.00	.40
26 Willie Crawford	1.00	.40
27 Roberto Clemente	30.00	12.00
28 Matty Alou	1.00	.40
29 Willie Stargell	8.00	3.20
30 Tim Cullen	1.00	.40
31 Randy Hundley	1.00	.40
32 Reggie Jackson	20.00	8.00
33 Rich Allen	2.50	1.00
34 Tim McCarver	2.00	.80
35 Ray Culp	1.00	.40
36 Jim Fregosi	1.00	.40
37 Billy Williams	5.00	2.00
38 Johnny Odom	1.00	.40
39 Bert Campaneris	1.50	.60
40 Ernie Banks	10.00	4.00
41 Chris Short	1.00	.40
42 Ron Santo	2.00	.80
43 Glenn Beckert	1.50	.60
44 Lou Brock	6.00	2.40
45 Larry Hisle	1.00	.40
46 Reggie Smith	1.50	.60
47 Rod Carew	8.00	3.20
48 Curt Flood	1.50	.60
49 Jim Lonborg	1.00	.40
50 Sam McDowell	1.50	.60
51 Sal Bando	1.50	.60
52 Al Kaline	10.00	4.00
53 Gary Nolan	1.00	.40
54 Rico Petrocelli	1.50	.60
55 Ollie Brown	1.00	.40
56 Luis Tiant	1.50	.60
57 Bill Freehan	1.50	.60
58 Johnny Bench	20.00	8.00
59 Joe Pepitone	1.50	.60
60 Bobby Murcer	1.50	.60
61 Harmon Killebrew	8.00	3.20
62 Don Wilson	1.00	.40
63 Tony Oliva	2.50	1.00
64 Jim Perry	1.00	.40
65 Mickey Lolich	1.50	.60
66 Jose Laboy	1.00	.40
67 Dean Chance	1.00	.40
68 Ken Harrelson	1.50	.60
69 Willie Horton	1.50	.60
70 Wally Bunker	1.00	.40
71A Bob Gibson ERR (1959 innings pitched is blank)	6.00	2.40
71B Bob Gibson COR (1959 innings is 76)	6.00	2.40
72 Joe Morgan	5.00	2.00
73 Denny McLain	1.50	.60
74 Tommy Harper	1.00	.40
75 Don Mincher	1.00	.40

1971 Kellogg's

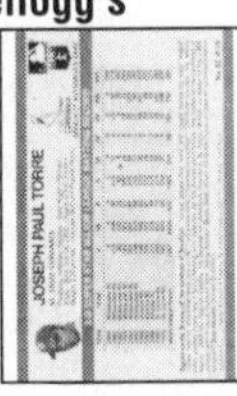

The cards in this 75-card set measure approximately 2 1/4" by 3 1/2". The 1971 set of 3-D cards marketed by the Kellogg Company is the scarcest of all that company's issues. It was distributed as single cards, one in each package of cereal, without the usual complete set mail-in offer. In addition, card dealers were unable to obtain this set in quantity, as they have in other years. All the cards are available with and without the year 1970 before XOGRAPH on the back in the lower left corner; the version without carries a slight premium for most numbers. Prices listed below are for the more common variety with the year 1970. Cards still found with the wrapper intact are valued 50 percent greater than the values listed below.

	NM	Ex
COMP.MASTER SET (92)	1200.00	475.00
COMPLETE SET (75)	1000.00	400.00
1 Wayne Simpson	8.00	3.20
2 Tom Seaver	40.00	16.00
3 Jim Perry	10.00	4.00
4 Bob Robertson	8.00	3.20
5 Roberto Clemente	60.00	24.00
6 Gaylord Perry	20.00	8.00
7 Felipe Alou	10.00	4.00
8 Denis Menke	8.00	3.20
9A Don Kessinger (No 1970 date)	10.00	4.00
9B Don Kessinger ERR (Dated 1970; hits 167; avg. .265)	10.00	4.00
9C Don Kessinger COR (Dated1970; hits 168; avg. .266)	10.00	4.00
10 Willie Mays	50.00	20.00
11 Jim Hickman	8.00	3.20
12 Tony Oliva	15.00	6.00
13 Manny Sanguillen	8.00	3.20
14 Frank Howard	10.00	4.00
15 Frank Robinson	25.00	10.00
16 Willie Davis	10.00	4.00
17 Lou Brock	25.00	10.00
18 Cesar Tovar	8.00	3.20
19 Luis Aparicio	20.00	8.00
20 Boog Powell	12.00	4.80
21 Dick Selma	8.00	3.20
22 Danny Walton	8.00	3.20
23 Carl Morton	8.00	3.20
24 Sonny Siebert	8.00	3.20
25 Jim Merritt	8.00	3.20
26 Jose Cardenal	8.00	3.20
27 Don Mincher	8.00	3.20
28A Clyde Wright (No 1970 date; team logo is Angels crest)	12.00	4.80
28B Clyde Wright ((No 1970 date; team logo is California outline with Angels written inside)	12.00	4.80
28C Clyde Wright (Dated 1970; team logo is California state outline)	10.00	4.00
29 Les Cain	8.00	3.20
30 Danny Cater	8.00	3.20
31 Don Sutton	20.00	8.00
32 Chuck Dobson	8.00	3.20
33 Willie McCovey	25.00	10.00
34 Mike Epstein	8.00	3.20
35 Paul Blair	8.00	3.20
36A Gary Nolan (No 1970 date)	10.00	4.00
36B Gary Nolan (Dated 1970; 1970; BB 95, SO 177)	10.00	4.00
36C Gary Nolan (Dated 1970; 1970; BB 96, SO 181)	10.00	4.00
37 Sam McDowell	10.00	4.00
38 Amos Otis	10.00	4.00
39 Ray Fosse	8.00	3.20
40 Mel Stottlemyre	10.00	4.00
41 Clarence Gaston	8.00	3.20
42 Dick Dietz	8.00	3.20
43 Roy White	8.00	3.20
44 Al Kaline	30.00	12.00
45 Carlos May	8.00	3.20
46 Tommie Agee	8.00	3.20
47 Tommy Harper	8.00	3.20
48 Larry Dierker	8.00	3.20
49 Mike Cuellar	10.00	4.00
50 Ernie Banks	30.00	12.00
51 Bob Gibson	25.00	10.00
52 Reggie Smith	10.00	4.00
53 Matty Alou	10.00	4.00
54A Alex Johnson (No 1970 date; team logo is Angels crest)	12.00	4.80
54B Alex Johnson (No 1970 date; team logo is California state outline)	12.00	4.80
54C Alex Johnson (Dated 1970; team logo is California state outline)	10.00	4.00
55 Harmon Killebrew	25.00	10.00
56 Bill Grabarkewitz	8.00	3.20
57 Rich Allen	12.00	4.80
58 Tony Perez	20.00	8.00
59 Dave McNally	10.00	4.00
60 Jim Palmer	25.00	10.00
61 Billy Williams	20.00	8.00
62 Joe Torre	15.00	6.00
63 Jim Northrup	10.00	4.00
64A Jim Fregosi (No 1970 date; team logo is Angels crest)	12.00	4.80
64B Jim Fregosi (No 1970 date; team logo is California state outline)	12.00	4.80
64C Jim Fregosi (Dated1970; 1970; Hits 166, avg. .276)	10.00	4.00
64D Jim Fregosi (Dated1970; 1970; Hits 167, avg. .278)	10.00	4.00
65 Pete Rose	50.00	20.00
66A Bud Harrelson (No 1970 date)	10.00	4.00
66B Bud Harrelson ERR (Dated 1970; 1970 RBI 43)	10.00	4.00
66C Bud Harrelson COR (Dated 1970; 1970 RBI 42)	10.00	4.00
67 Tony Taylor	10.00	4.00
68 Willie Stargell	20.00	8.00
69 Tony Horton	12.00	4.80
70A Claude Osteen ERR (No 1970 date; card number missing)	12.00	4.80
70B Claude Osteen COR (No 1970 date; card number present)	12.00	4.80
70C Claude Osteen COR (Dated 1970)	10.00	4.00
71 Glenn Beckert	8.00	3.20
72 Nate Colbert	8.00	3.20
73A Rick Monday (No 1970 date)	10.00	4.00
73B Rick Monday ERR (Dated 1970; 1970; AB 377, avg. .289)	10.00	4.00
73C Rick Monday COR (Dated 1970; 1970; AB 376, avg. .290)	10.00	4.00
74 Tommy John	12.00	4.80
75 Chris Short	8.00	3.20

1972 Kellogg's

The cards in this 54-card set measure approximately 2 1/8" by 3 1/4". The dimensions of the cards in the 1972 Kellogg's set were reduced in comparison to those of the 1971 series. In addition, the length of the set was set at 54 cards rather than the 75 of the previous year. The cards of this Kellogg's set are characterized by the diagonal bands found on the obverse. Cards still found with the wrapper intact are valued 50 percent greater than the values listed below.

	NM	Ex
COMP.MASTER SET (75)	200.00	80.00
COMPLETE SET (54)	100.00	40.00
1A Tom Seaver ERR (1970 ERA 2.85)	20.00	8.00
1B Tom Seaver COR (1970 ERA 2.81)	10.00	4.00
2 Amos Otis	1.00	.40
3A Willie Davis ERR (Lifetime runs 842)	2.00	.80
3B Willie Davis COR (Lifetime runs 841)	1.00	.40
4 Wilbur Wood	1.00	.40
5 Bill Parsons	1.00	.40
6 Pete Rose	15.00	6.00
7A Willie McCovey ERR (Lifetime HR 360)	8.00	3.20
7B Willie McCovey COR (Lifetime HR 370)	4.00	1.60
8 Ferguson Jenkins	4.00	1.60
9A Vida Blue ERR (Lifetime ERA 2.35)	2.00	.80
9B Vida Blue COR (Lifetime ERA 2.31)	1.00	.40
10 Joe Torre	2.00	.80
11 Merv Rettenmund	1.00	.40
12 Bill Melton	1.00	.40
13A Jim Palmer ERR (Lifetime games 170)	10.00	4.00
13B Jim Palmer COR (Lifetime games 168)	5.00	2.00
14 Doug Rader	1.00	.40
15A Dave Roberts ERR (NL missing in bio)	2.00	.80
15B Dave Roberts COR (NL in bio, line 2)	1.00	.40
16 Bobby Murcer	1.50	.60
17 Wes Parker	1.00	.40
18A Joe Coleman ERR (Lifetime BB 294)	2.00	.80
18B Joe Coleman COR (Lifetime BB 393)	1.00	.40
19 Manny Sanguillen	1.00	.40
20 Reggie Jackson	10.00	4.00
21 Ralph Garr	1.00	.40
22 Jim Hunter	4.00	1.60
23 Rick Wise	1.00	.40
24 Glenn Beckert	1.00	.40
25 Tony Oliva	2.50	1.00
26A Bob Gibson ERR (Lifetime SO 2577)	8.00	3.20
26B Bob Gibson COR (Lifetime SO 2578)	4.00	1.60
27A Mike Cuellar ERR (1971 ERA 3.80)	2.00	.80
27B Mike Cuellar COR (1971 ERA 3.08)	1.00	.40
28 Chris Speier	1.00	.40
29A Dave McNally ERR (Lifetime ERA 3.18)	2.00	.80
29B Dave McNally COR (Lifetime ERA 3.15)	1.00	.40
30 Leo Cardenas	1.00	.40
31A Bill Freehan ERR (Lifetime runs 497)	2.00	.80
31B Bill Freehan COR (Lifetime runs 500)	1.00	.40
32A Bud Harrelson ERR (Lifetime hits 634)	2.00	.80
32B Bud Harrelson COR (Lifetime hits 624)	1.00	.40
33A Sam McDowell ERR (Bio line 3 has less than 200)	2.00	.80
33B Sam McDowell COR (Bio line 3 has less than 225)	1.00	.40
34A Claude Osteen ERR (1971 ERA 3.25)	2.00	.80
34B Claude Osteen COR (1971 ERA 3.51)	1.00	.40
35 Reggie Smith	1.50	.60
36 Sonny Siebert	1.00	.40
37 Lee May	1.50	.60
38 Mickey Lolich	1.50	.60
39A Cookie Rojas ERR (Lifetime 2B 149)	2.00	.80
39B Cookie Rojas COR (Lifetime 2B 150)	1.00	.40
40A Dick Drago ERR (Bio line 3 has Poyals)	2.00	.80
40B Dick Drago COR (Bio line 3 has Royals)	1.00	.40
41 Nate Colbert	1.00	.40
42 Andy Messersmith	1.00	.40
43A Dave Johnson ERR (Lifetime AB 3110, avg. .262)	2.00	.80
43B Dave Johnson COR (Lifetime AB 3113, avg. .264)	1.50	.60
44 Steve Blass	1.00	.40
45 Bob Robertson	1.00	.40
46A Billy Williams ERR (Bio has "missed only one game")	6.00	2.40
46B Billy Williams COR (Bio has that line eliminated)	4.00	1.60
47 Juan Marichal	4.00	1.60
48 Lou Brock	4.00	1.60
49 Roberto Clemente	20.00	8.00
50 Mel Stottlemyre	1.00	.40
51 Don Wilson	1.00	.40
52A Sal Bando ERR (Lifetime RBI 355)	2.00	.80
52B Sal Bando COR (Lifetime RBI 356)	1.00	.40
53A Willie Stargell ERR (Lifetime 2B 197)	8.00	3.20
53B Willie Stargell COR (Lifetime 2B 196)	4.00	1.60
54A Willie Mays ERR (Lifetime RBI 1855)	25.00	10.00
54B Willie Mays COR (Lifetime RBI 1856)	12.00	4.80

1972 Kellogg's ATG

The cards in this 15-card set measure 2 1/4" by 3 1/2". The 1972 All-Time Greats 3-D set was issued with Kellogg's Danish Go Rounds. The set contains two different cards of Babe Ruth. The set is a reissue of a 1970 set issued by Rold Gold Pretzels to commemorate baseball's first 100 years. The Rold Gold cards are copyrighted 1970 on the reverse and are valued at approximately double the prices listed below.

	NM	Ex
COMPLETE SET (15)	35.00	14.00
1 Walter Johnson	2.50	1.00
2 Rogers Hornsby	1.50	.60
3 John McGraw	1.50	.60
4 Mickey Cochrane	1.50	.60
5 George Sisler	1.50	.60
6 Babe Ruth	10.00	4.00
7 Lefty Grove	1.50	.60
8 Pie Traynor	1.00	.40
9 Honus Wagner	2.50	1.00
10 Eddie Collins	1.00	.40
11 Tris Speaker	1.50	.60
12 Cy Young	2.50	1.00
13 Lou Gehrig	8.00	3.20
14 Babe Ruth	10.00	4.00
15 Ty Cobb	8.00	3.20

1973 Kellogg's 2D

The cards in this 54-card set measure approximately 2 1/4" by 3 1/2". The 1973

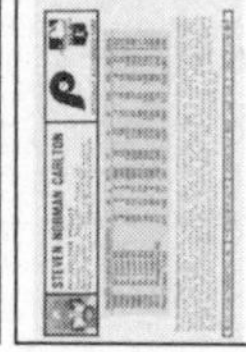

Kellogg's set is the only non-3D set produced by the Kellogg Company. Apparently Kellogg's decided to have the cards produced through Visual Panographics rather than by Xograph, as in the other years. The complete set could be obtained from the company through a box-top redemption procedure. The card size is slightly larger than the previous year. According to published reports at the time, the redemption for this set cost either $1.50 and one Raisin Bran box top or $1.25 and two Raisin Bran box tops.

	NM	Ex
COMPLETE SET (54)	80.00	32.00
1 Amos Otis	.75	.30
2 Ellie Rodriguez	.50	.20
3 Mickey Lolich	.75	.30
4 Tony Oliva	1.50	.60
5 Don Sutton	3.00	1.20
6 Pete Rose	12.00	4.80
7 Steve Carlton	5.00	2.00
8 Bobby Bonds	1.50	.60
9 Wilbur Wood	.50	.20
10 Billy Williams	4.00	1.60
11 Steve Blass	.50	.20
12 Jon Matlack	.50	.20
13 Cesar Cedeno	.75	.30
14 Bob Gibson	4.00	1.60
15 Sparky Lyle	1.00	.40
16 Nolan Ryan	25.00	10.00
17 Jim Palmer	5.00	2.00
18 Ray Fosse	.50	.20
19 Bobby Murcer	.75	.30
20 Jim Hunter	3.00	1.20
21 Tom McCraw	.50	.20
22 Reggie Jackson	10.00	4.00
23 Bill Stoneman	.50	.20
24 Lou Piniella	1.00	.40
25 Willie Stargell	5.00	2.00
26 Dick Allen	1.50	.60
27 Carlton Fisk	12.00	4.80
28 Ferguson Jenkins	4.00	1.60
29 Phil Niekro	4.00	1.60
30 Gary Nolan	.50	.20
31 Joe Torre	1.50	.60
32 Bobby Tolan	.50	.20
33 Nate Colbert	.50	.20
34 Joe Morgan	4.00	1.60
35 Bert Blyleven	1.00	.40
36 Joe Rudi	.75	.30
37 Ralph Garr	.50	.20
38 Gaylord Perry	4.00	1.60
39 Bobby Grich	.75	.30
40 Lou Brock	4.00	1.60
41 Pete Broberg	.50	.20
42 Manny Sanguillen	.50	.20
43 Willie Davis	.75	.30
44 Dave Kingman	1.50	.60
45 Carlos May	.50	.20
46 Tom Seaver	10.00	4.00
47 Mike Cuellar	.50	.20
48 Joe Coleman	.50	.20
49 Claude Osteen	.50	.20
50 Steve Kline	.50	.20
51 Rod Carew	5.00	2.00
52 Al Kaline	6.00	2.40
53 Larry Dierker	.50	.20
54 Ron Santo	1.00	.40

1974 Kellogg's

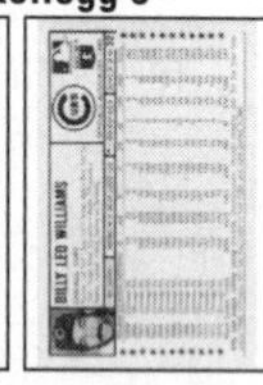

The cards in this 54-card set measure 2 1/8" by 3 1/4". In 1974 the Kellogg's set returned to its 3-D format; it also returned to the smaller-size card. Complete sets could be obtained from the company through a box-top offer. The cards are numbered on the back. Cards still found with the wrapper intact are valued 25 percent greater than the values listed below.

	NM	Ex
COMPLETE SET (54)	60.00	24.00
1 Bob Gibson	3.00	1.20
2 Rick Monday	.50	.20
3 Joe Coleman	.50	.20
4 Bert Campaneris	.75	.30
5 Carlton Fisk	6.00	2.40
6 Jim Palmer	3.00	1.20
7A Ron Santo ERR	6.00	2.40
Chicago Cubs		
7B Ron Santo COR	.75	.30
Chicago White Sox		
8 Nolan Ryan	20.00	8.00
9 Greg Luzinski	.75	.30
10 Buddy Bell	.75	.30
11 Bob Watson	.75	.30
12 Bill Singer	.50	.20
13 Dave May	.50	.20
14 Jim Brewer	.50	.20
15 Manny Sanguillen	.50	.20
16 Jeff Burroughs	.75	.30
17 Amos Otis	.50	.20
18 Ed Goodson	.50	.20
19 Nate Colbert	.50	.20
20 Reggie Jackson	10.00	4.00
21 Ted Simmons	1.00	.40
22 Bobby Murcer	.75	.30
23 Willie Horton	.75	.30
24 Orlando Cepeda	3.00	1.20
25 Ron Hunt	.50	.20
26 Wayne Twitchell	.50	.20
27 Ron Fairly	.50	.20
28 Johnny Bench	6.00	2.40
29 John Mayberry	.50	.20
30 Rod Carew	4.00	1.60
31 Ken Holtzman	.50	.20
32 Billy Williams	3.00	1.20
33 Dick Allen	1.50	.60
34A Wilbur Wood ERR	3.00	1.20
(1973 K 198)		
34B Wilbur Wood COR	.50	.20
(1973 K 199)		
35 Danny Thompson	.50	.20
36 Joe Morgan	3.00	1.20
37 Willie Stargell	3.00	1.20
38 Pete Rose	10.00	4.00
39 Bobby Bonds	1.50	.60
40 Chris Speier	.50	.20
41 Sparky Lyle	.75	.30
42 Cookie Rojas	.50	.20
43 Tommy Davis	.50	.20
44 Jim Hunter	3.00	1.20
45 Willie Davis	.50	.20
46 Bert Blyleven	.75	.30
47 Pat Kelly	.50	.20
48 Ken Singleton	.50	.20
49 Manny Mota	.75	.30
50 Dave Johnson	1.00	.40
51 Sal Bando	.75	.30
52 Tom Seaver	10.00	4.00
53 Felix Millan	.50	.20
54 Ron Blomberg	.50	.20

1975 Kellogg's

The cards in this 57-card set measure approximately 2 1/8" by 3 1/4". The 1975 Kellogg's 3-D set could be obtained card by card in cereal boxes or as a set from a box-top offer from the company. Card number 44, Jim Hunter, exists with the A's emblem or the Yankees emblem on the back of the card. Cards still found with the wrapper intact are valued 25 percent greater than the values listed below. This set was available from Kellogg's for 2 box tops and a $2 charge.

	NM	Ex
COMPLETE SET (57)	160.00	65.00
1 Roy White	1.50	.60
2 Ross Grimsley	1.00	.40
3 Reggie Smith	1.50	.60
4A Bob Grich ERR	1.50	.60
Bio last line begins		
1973 work		
4B Bob Grich COR	3.00	1.20
Bio last line begins		
because his fielding		
5 Greg Gross	1.00	.40
6 Bob Watson	1.50	.60
7 Johnny Bench	10.00	4.00
8 Jeff Burroughs	1.00	.40
9 Elliott Maddox	1.00	.40
10 Jon Matlack	1.00	.40
11 Pete Rose	20.00	8.00
12 Lee Stanton	1.00	.40
13 Bake McBride	1.00	.40
14 Jorge Orta	1.00	.40
15 Al Oliver	1.50	.60
16 John Briggs	1.00	.40
17 Steve Garvey	5.00	2.00
18 Brooks Robinson	8.00	3.20
19 John Hiller	1.00	.40
20 Lynn McGlothen	1.00	.40
21 Cleon Jones	1.00	.40
22 Fergie Jenkins	4.00	1.60
23 Bill North	1.00	.40
24 Steve Busby	1.00	.40
25 Richie Zisk	1.00	.40
26 Nolan Ryan	40.00	16.00
27 Joe Morgan	5.00	2.00
28 Joe Rudi	1.50	.60
29 Jose Cardenal	1.00	.40
30 Andy Messersmith	1.00	.40
31 Willie Montanez	1.00	.40
32 Bill Buckner	1.50	.60
33 Rod Carew	8.00	3.20
34 Lou Piniella	1.50	.60
35 Ralph Garr	1.00	.40
36 Mike Marshall	1.50	.60
37 Garry Maddox	1.00	.40
38 Dwight Evans	2.00	.80
39 Lou Brock	8.00	3.20
40 Ken Singleton	1.00	.40
41 Steve Braun	1.00	.40
42 Rich Allen	2.50	1.00
43 John Grubb	1.00	.40
44A Jim Hunter	5.00	2.00
Oakland A's team		
logo on back		
44B Jim Hunter	15.00	6.00
New York Yankees		
team logo on back		
45 Gaylord Perry	4.00	1.60
46 George Hendrick	1.00	.40
47 Sparky Lyle	1.50	.60
48 Dave Cash	1.00	.40
49 Luis Tiant	1.50	.60
50 Cesar Geronimo	1.00	.40
51 Carl Yastrzemski	10.00	4.00
52 Ken Brett	1.00	.40
53 Hal McRae	1.50	.60
54 Reggie Jackson	15.00	6.00
55 Rollie Fingers	5.00	2.00
56 Mike Schmidt	25.00	10.00
57 Richie Hebner	1.00	.40

1976 Kellogg's

The cards in this 57-card set measure approximately 2 1/8" by 3 1/4". The 1976 Kellogg's 3-D set could be obtained card by card in cereal boxes or as a set from the company for box-tops. Card numbers 1-3 (marked in the checklist below with SP) were apparently printed apart from the other 54 and are in shorter supply. Cards still found with the wrapper intact are valued 25 percent greater than the values listed below.

	NM	Ex
COMP.MASTER SET (68)	150.00	60.00
COMPLETE SET (57)	75.00	30.00
COMMON CARD (4-57)	.50	.20
SHORT PRINT COMMONS	10.00	4.00
1 Steve Hargan SP	10.00	4.00
2 Claudell Washington SP	10.00	4.00
3 Don Gullett SP	10.00	4.00
4 Randy Jones	.50	.20
5 Jim Hunter	3.00	1.20
6A Clay Carroll	3.00	1.20
Team logo		
Cincinnati Reds on back		
6B Clay Carroll	1.00	.40
Team logo		
Chicago White Sox on back		
7 Joe Rudi	.50	.20
8 Reggie Jackson	6.00	2.40
9 Felix Millan	.50	.20
10 Jim Rice	3.00	1.20
11 Bert Blyleven	.75	.30
12 Ken Singleton	.50	.20
13 Don Sutton	2.50	1.00
14 Joe Morgan	3.00	1.20
15 Dave Parker	2.00	.80
16 Dave Cash	.50	.20
17 Ron LeFlore	.50	.20
18 Greg Luzinski	.75	.30
19 Dennis Eckersley	15.00	6.00
20 Bill Madlock	.50	.20
21 George Scott	.50	.20
22 Willie Stargell	3.00	1.20
23 Al Hrabosky	.50	.20
24 Carl Yastrzemski	6.00	2.40
25A Jim Kaat	3.00	1.20
Team logo		
Chicago White Sox on back		
25B Jim Kaat	1.50	.60
Team logo		
Philadelphia Phillies on back		
26 Marty Perez	.50	.20
27 Bob Watson	.75	.30
28 Eric Soderholm	.50	.20
29 Bill Lee	.50	.20
30A Frank Tanana ERR	1.00	.40
1975 ERA 2.63		
30B Frank Tanana COR	.75	.30
1975 ERA 2.62		
31 Fred Lynn	1.00	.40
32A Tom Seaver ERR	7.50	3.00
1967 Pct. 552		
with no decimal point)		
32B Tom Seaver COR	7.50	3.00
1967 Pct. .552		
33 Steve Busby	.50	.20
34 Gary Carter	4.00	1.60
35 Rick Wise	.50	.20
36 Johnny Bench	6.00	2.40
37 Jim Palmer	3.00	1.20
38 Bobby Murcer	.75	.30
39 Von Joshua	.50	.20
40 Lou Brock	4.00	1.60
41A Mickey Rivers	2.00	.80
No line in bio about Yankees		
41B Mickey Rivers	.75	.30
Bio has "Yankees obtained ..."		
42 Manny Sanguillen	.50	.20
43 Jerry Reuss	.50	.20
44 Ken Griffey	1.00	.40
45A Jorge Orta ERR	.75	.30
Lifetime AB 1615		
45B Jorge Orta COR	.75	.30
Lifetime AB 1616		
46 John Mayberry	.50	.20
47A Vida Blue	.75	.30
Bio "struck out more batters"		
47B Vida Blue	.75	.30
Bio "pitched more innings"		
48 Rod Carew	4.00	1.60
49A Jon Matlack ERR	.75	.30
1975 ER 87		
49B Jon Matlack COR	.75	.30
1975 ER 86		
50 Boog Powell	1.00	.40
51A Mike Hargrove ERR	1.00	.40
Lifetime AB 935		
51B Mike Hargrove COR	1.00	.40
Lifetime AB 934		
52A Paul Lindblad ERR	.75	.30
1975 ERA 2.43		
52B Paul Lindblad COR	.75	.30
1975 ERA 2.72		
53 Thurman Munson	4.00	1.60
54 Steve Garvey	2.50	1.00
55 Pete Rose	12.00	4.80
56A Greg Gross ERR	.75	.30
Lifetime games 334		
56B Greg Gross COR	.75	.30
Lifetime games 302		
57 Ted Simmons	1.00	.40

1977 Kellogg's

The cards in this 57-card set measure approximately 2 1/8" by 3 1/4". The 1977 Kellogg's series of 3-D baseball player cards

could be obtained card by card from cereal boxes or by sending in box-tops and money. Each player's picture appears in miniature form on the reverse, an idea begun in 1971 and replaced in subsequent years by the use of a picture of the Kellogg's mascot. Cards still found with the wrapper intact are valued 25 percent greater than the values listed below.

	NM	Ex
COMPLETE SET (57)	50.00	20.00
1 George Foster	.75	.30
2 Bert Campaneris	.50	.20
3 Fergie Jenkins	3.00	1.20
4 Dock Ellis	.50	.20
5 John Montefusco	.50	.20
6 George Brett	20.00	8.00
7 John Candelaria	.50	.20
8 Fred Norman	.50	.20
9 Bill Travers	.50	.20
10 Hal McRae	.75	.30
11 Doug Rau	.50	.20
12 Greg Luzinski	.75	.30
13 Ralph Garr	.50	.20
14 Steve Garvey	2.00	.80
15 Rick Manning	.50	.20
16A Lyman Bostock ERR	3.00	1.20
(Dock Ellis photo		
on back)		
16B Lyman Bostock COR	.75	.30
17 Randy Jones	.50	.20
18 Ron Cey	.75	.30
19 Dave Parker	1.50	.60
20 Pete Rose	8.00	3.20
21A Wayne Garland	.50	.20
(No trade to Cleve-		
land is mentioned)		
21B Wayne Garland	1.50	.60
(Trade mentioned		
bio ends "now flip		
for Cleveland)		
22 Bill North	.50	.20
23 Thurman Munson	3.00	1.20
24 Tom Poquette	.50	.20
25 Ron LeFlore	.50	.20
26 Mark Fidrych	5.00	2.00
27 Sixto Lezcano	.50	.20
28 Dave Winfield	8.00	3.20
29 Jerry Koosman	.75	.30
30 Mike Hargrove	.75	.30
31 Willie Montanez	.50	.20
32 Don Stanhouse	.50	.20
33 Jay Johnstone	.50	.20
34 Bake McBride	.50	.20
35 Dave Kingman	1.50	.60
36 Fred Patek	.50	.20
37 Garry Maddox	.50	.20
38A Ken Reitz	.50	.20
(No trade mentioned)		
38B Ken Reitz	1.50	.60
(Trade mentioned)		
39 Bobby Grich	.75	.30
40 Cesar Geronimo	.50	.20
41 Jim Lonborg	.50	.20
42 Ed Figueroa	.50	.20
43 Bill Madlock	.75	.30
44 Jerry Remy	.50	.20
45 Frank Tanana	.75	.30
46 Al Oliver	.75	.30
47 Charlie Hough	.75	.30
48 Lou Piniella	.75	.30
49 Ken Griffey	1.50	.60
50 Jose Cruz	.75	.30
51 Rollie Fingers	3.00	1.20
52 Chris Chambliss	.75	.30
53 Rod Carew	5.00	2.00
54 Andy Messersmith	.50	.20
55 Mickey Rivers	.75	.30
56 Butch Wynegar	.50	.20
57 Steve Carlton	5.00	2.00

1978 Kellogg's

The cards in this 57-card set measure 2 1/8" by 3 1/4". This 1978 3-D Kellogg's series marks the first year in which Tony the Tiger appears on the reverse of each card next to the team and MLB logos. Once again the set could be obtained as individually wrapped cards in cereal boxes or as a set via a mail-in offer. The key card in the set is Eddie Murray, as it was one of Murray's few card issues in 1978, the year of his Topps Rookie Card. Cards still found with the wrapper intact are valued 25 percent greater than the values listed below.

	NM	Ex
COMPLETE SET (57)	50.00	20.00
1 Steve Carlton	3.00	1.20
2 Bucky Dent	.75	.30
3 Mike Schmidt	6.00	2.40
4 Ken Griffey	1.00	.40
5 Al Cowens	.50	.20
6 George Brett	15.00	6.00
7 Lou Brock	3.00	1.20
8 Goose Gossage	1.00	.40
9 Tom Johnson	.50	.20
10 George Foster	.75	.30
11 Dave Winfield	4.00	1.60
12 Dan Meyer	.50	.20
13 Chris Chambliss	.75	.30
14 Paul Dade	.50	.20
15 Jeff Burroughs	.50	.20
16 Jose Cruz	.75	.30
17 Mickey Rivers	.75	.30
18 John Candelaria	.50	.20
19 Ellis Valentine	.50	.20
20 Hal McRae	.50	.20
21 Dave Rozema	.50	.20
22 Lenny Randle	.50	.20
23 Willie McCovey	3.00	1.20
24 Ron Cey	.75	.30
25 Eddie Murray	20.00	8.00
26 Larry Bowa	.75	.30
27 Tom Seaver	5.00	2.00
28 Garry Maddox	.50	.20
29 Rod Carew	4.00	1.60
30 Thurman Munson	2.50	1.00
31 Garry Templeton	.75	.30
32 Eric Soderholm	.50	.20
33 Greg Luzinski	.75	.30
34 Reggie Smith	.75	.30
35 Dave Goltz	.50	.20
36 Tommy John	1.00	.40
37 Ralph Garr	.50	.20
38 Alan Bannister	.50	.20
39 Bob Bailor	.50	.20
40 Reggie Jackson	4.00	1.60
41 Cecil Cooper	.75	.30
42 Burt Hooton	.50	.20
43 Sparky Lyle	.75	.30
44 Steve Ontiveros	.50	.20
45 Rick Reuschel	.50	.20
46 Lyman Bostock	.75	.30
47 Mitchell Page	.50	.20
48 Bruce Sutter	1.00	.40
49 Jim Rice	1.50	.60
50 Ken Forsch	.50	.20
51 Nolan Ryan	15.00	6.00
52 Dave Parker	1.00	.40
53 Bert Blyleven	.75	.30
54 Frank Tanana	.75	.30
55 Ken Singleton	.50	.20
56 Mike Hargrove	.75	.30
57 Don Sutton	2.50	1.00

1979 Kellogg's

The cards in this 60-card set measure approximately 1 15/16" by 3 1/4". The 1979 edition of Kellogg's 3-D baseball cards have a 3/16" reduced width from the previous year; a nicely designed curved panel above the picture gives this set a distinctive appearance. The set contains the largest number of cards issued in a Kellogg's set since the 1971 series. Three different press runs produced numerous variations in this set. The first two printings were included in cereal boxes, while the third printing was for the complete set mail-in offer. Forty-seven cards have three variations, while thirteen cards (4, 6, 9, 15, 19, 20, 30, 33, 41, 43, 45, 51, and 54) are unchanged from the second and third printings. The three printings may be distinguished by the placement of the registered symbol by Tony the Tiger and by team logos. In the third printing, four cards (16, 18, 22, 44) show the "P" team logo (no registered symbol), and card numbers 56 and 57 omit the registered symbol by Tony. Cards still found with the wrapper intact are valued 25 percent greater than the values listed below. The set was available from Kellogg's for two boxtops and $2 and the offer was available until April 30, 1980.

	NM	Ex
COMPLETE SET (60)	30.00	12.00
1 Bruce Sutter	.50	.20
2 Ted Simmons	.50	.20
3 Ross Grimsley	.25	.10
4 Wayne Nordhagen	.25	.10
5 Jim Palmer	3.00	1.20
6 John Henry Johnson	.25	.10
7 Jason Thompson	.25	.10
8 Pat Zachry	.25	.10
9 Dennis Eckersley	3.00	1.20
10 Paul Splittorff	.25	.10
11 Ron Guidry	.75	.30
12 Jeff Burroughs	.25	.10
13 Rod Carew	3.00	1.20
14A Buddy Bell	1.50	.60
(No trade mentioned)		
14B Buddy Bell	.50	.20
(Traded to Rangers)		
15 Jim Rice	1.00	.40
16 Garry Maddox	.25	.10
17 Willie McCovey	2.00	.80
18 Steve Carlton	3.00	1.20
19 J.R. Richard	.25	.10
20 Paul Molitor	6.00	2.40
21 Dave Parker	.75	.30
22 Pete Rose	5.00	2.00
23 Vida Blue	.50	.20
24 Richie Zisk	.25	.10
25 Darrell Porter	.25	.10
26 Dan Driessen	.25	.10
27 Geoff Zahn	.25	.10
28 Phil Niekro	2.00	.80
29 Tom Seaver	4.00	1.60
30 Fred Lynn	.50	.20
31 Bill Bonham	.25	.10
32 George Foster	.50	.20
33 Terry Puhl	.25	.10
34 John Candelaria	.25	.10
35 Bob Knepper	.25	.10

36 Fred Patek	.25	.10
37 Chris Chambliss	.50	.20
38 Bob Forsch	.25	.10
39 Ken Griffey	.50	.20
40 Jack Clark	.50	.20
41 Dwight Evans	.50	.20
42 Lee Mazzilli	.25	.10
43 Mario Guerrero	.25	.10
44 Larry Bowa	.50	.20
45 Carl Yastrzemski	4.00	1.60
46 Reggie Jackson	4.00	1.60
47 Rick Reuschel	.25	.10
48 Mike Flanagan	.25	.10
49 Gaylord Perry	2.00	.80
50 George Brett	10.00	4.00
51 Craig Reynolds	.25	.10
52 Dave Lopes	.50	.20
53 Bill Almon	.25	.10
54 Roy Howell	.25	.10
55 Frank Tanana	.25	.10
56 Doug Rau	.25	.10
57 Rick Monday	.25	.10
58 Jon Matlack	.25	.10
59 Ron Jackson	.25	.10
60 Jim Sundberg	.25	.10

1980 Kellogg's

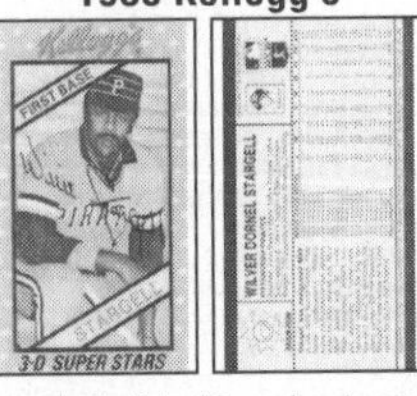

The cards in this 60-card set measure approximately 1 7/8" by 3 1/4". The 1980 Kellogg's 3-D set is quite similar to, but smaller (narrower) than, the other recent Kellogg's issues. Sets could be obtained card by card from cereal boxes or as a set from a box-top offer from the company. Cards still found with the wrapper intact are valued 25 percent greater than the values listed below.

	NM	Ex
COMPLETE SET (60)	25.00	10.00
1 Ross Grimsley	.25	.10
2 Mike Schmidt	4.00	1.60
3 Mike Flanagan	.25	.10
4 Ron Guidry	.50	.20
5 Bert Blyleven	.50	.20
6 Dave Kingman	.75	.30
7 Jeff Newman	.25	.10
8 Steve Rogers	.25	.10
9 George Brett	8.00	3.20
10 Bruce Sutter	.50	.20
11 Gorman Thomas	.25	.10
12 Darrell Porter	.25	.10
13 Roy Smalley	.25	.10
14 Steve Carlton	2.00	.80
15 Jim Palmer	2.00	.80
16 Bob Bailor	.25	.10
17 Jason Thompson	.25	.10
18 Graig Nettles	.50	.20
19 Ron Cey	.50	.20
20 Nolan Ryan	8.00	3.20
21 Ellis Valentine	.25	.10
22 Larry Hisle	.25	.10
23 Dave Parker	.75	.30
24 Eddie Murray	4.00	1.60
25 Willie Stargell	2.00	.80
26 Reggie Jackson	4.00	1.60
27 Carl Yastrzemski	3.00	1.20
28 Andre Thornton	.25	.10
29 Dave Lopes	.50	.20
30 Ken Singleton	.25	.10
31 Steve Garvey	1.00	.40
32 Dave Winfield	2.00	.80
33 Steve Kemp	.25	.10
34 Claudell Washington	.25	.10
35 Pete Rose	4.00	1.60
36 Cesar Cedeno	.25	.10
37 John Stearns	.25	.10
38 Lee Mazzilli	.25	.10
39 Larry Bowa	.50	.20
40 Fred Lynn	.50	.20
41 Carlton Fisk	4.00	1.60
42 Vida Blue	.50	.20
43 Keith Hernandez	.50	.20
44 Jim Rice	1.00	.40
45 Ted Simmons	.50	.20
46 Chet Lemon	.25	.10
47 Ferguson Jenkins	2.00	.80
48 Gary Matthews	.50	.20
49 Tom Seaver	4.00	1.60
50 George Foster	.50	.20
51 Phil Niekro	2.00	.80
52 Johnny Bench	3.00	1.20
53 Buddy Bell	.50	.20
54 Lance Parrish	.50	.20
55 Joaquin Andujar	.25	.10
56 Don Baylor	.75	.30
57 Jack Clark	.50	.20
58 J.R. Richard	.25	.10
59 Bruce Bochte	.25	.10
60 Rod Carew	3.00	1.20

1981 Kellogg's

The cards in this 66-card set measure 2 1/2" by 3 1/2". The 1981 Kellogg's set witnessed an increase in both the size of the card and the size of the set. For the first time, cards were not packed in cereal packages but available only by mail-in procedure. The offer for the card set was advertised on boxes of Kellogg's Corn Flakes. The cards were printed on a different stock than in previous years, presumably to prevent the cracking problem which has plagued all Kellogg's 3-D issues. At the end of the promotion, the remainder of the sets not distributed (to cereal-eaters), were "sold" into the organized hobby, thus creating a situation where the set is relatively plentiful compared to other years of Kellogg's. Cards from this set may be found without the laminated finish that creates the 3D effect.

	Nm-Mt	Ex-Mt
COMPLETE SET (66)	15.00	6.00
1 George Foster	.20	.08
2 Jim Palmer	1.00	.40
3 Reggie Jackson	1.50	.60
4 Al Oliver	.20	.08
5 Mike Schmidt	2.00	.80
6 Nolan Ryan	4.00	1.60
7 Bucky Dent	.20	.08
8 George Brett	4.00	1.60
9 Jim Rice	.30	.12
10 Steve Garvey	.50	.20
11 Willie Stargell	.75	.30
12 Phil Niekro	1.00	.40
13 Dave Parker	.30	.12
14 Cesar Cedeno	.10	.04
15 Don Baylor	.20	.08
16 J.R. Richard	.10	.04
17 Tony Perez	.75	.30
18 Eddie Murray	2.00	.80
19 Chet Lemon	.10	.04
20 Ben Oglivie	.10	.04
21 Dave Winfield	1.50	.60
22 Joe Morgan	.75	.30
23 Vida Blue	.20	.08
24 Willie Wilson	.10	.04
25 Steve Henderson	.10	.04
26 Rod Carew	1.00	.40
27 Garry Templeton	.10	.04
28 Dave Concepcion	.20	.08
29 Dave Lopes	.20	.08
30 Ken Landreaux	.10	.04
31 Keith Hernandez	.20	.08
32 Cecil Cooper	.20	.08
33 Rickey Henderson	4.00	1.60
34 Frank White	.20	.08
35 George Hendrick	.10	.04
36 Reggie Smith	.20	.08
37 Tug McGraw	.20	.08
38 Tom Seaver	1.50	.60
39 Ken Singleton	.10	.04
40 Fred Lynn	.20	.08
41 Rich Gossage	.30	.12
42 Terry Puhl	.10	.04
43 Larry Bowa	.20	.08
44 Phil Garner	.10	.04
45 Ron Guidry	.20	.08
46 Lee Mazzilli	.10	.04
47 Dave Kingman	.30	.12
48 Carl Yastrzemski	1.00	.40
49 Rick Burleson	.10	.04
50 Steve Carlton	1.00	.40
51 Alan Trammell	.75	.30
52 Tommy John	.30	.12
53 Paul Molitor	2.00	.80
54 Joe Charboneau	.50	.20
55 Rick Langford	.10	.04
56 Bruce Sutter	.20	.08
57 Robin Yount	1.50	.60
58 Steve Stone	.10	.04
59 Larry Gura	.10	.04
60 Mike Flanagan	.10	.04
61 Bob Horner	.10	.04
62 Bruce Bochte	.10	.04
63 Pete Rose	2.00	.80
64 Buddy Bell	.20	.08
65 Johnny Bench	1.50	.60
66 Mike Hargrove	.20	.08

1982 Kellogg's

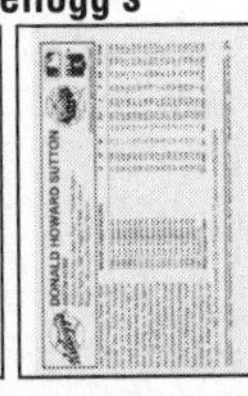

The cards in this 64-card set measure 2 1/8" by 3 1/4". The 1982 version of 3-D cards prepared for the Kellogg Company by Visual Panographics, Inc., is not only smaller in physical dimensions from the 1981 series (which was standard card size at 2 1/2" by 3 1/2") but is also two cards shorter in length (64 in '82 and 66 in '81). In addition, while retaining the policy of not inserting single cards into cereal packages and offering the sets through box-top mail-ins only, the Kellogg Company accepted box tops from four types of cereals, as opposed to only one type the previous year. Each card features a color 3-D ballplayer picture with a vertical line of white stars on each side set upon a blue background. The player's name and the word Kellogg's are printed in red on the obverse, and the card number is found on the bottom right of the reverse. Every card in the set has a statistical procedural error that was never corrected. All seasonal averages were added up and then divided by the number of seasons played.

	Nm-Mt	Ex-Mt
COMPLETE SET (64)	15.00	6.00
1 Richie Zisk	.10	.04
2 Bill Buckner	.20	.08
3 George Brett	4.00	1.60
4 Rickey Henderson	3.00	1.20
5 Jack Morris	.30	.12
6 Ozzie Smith	3.00	1.20
7 Rollie Fingers	.75	.30
8 Tom Seaver	1.50	.60
9 Fernando Valuenzuela	.50	.20
10 Hubie Brooks	.10	.04
11 Nolan Ryan	4.00	1.60
12 Dave Winfield	1.00	.40
13 Bob Horner	.10	.04
14 Reggie Jackson	1.50	.60
15 Burt Hooton	.10	.04
16 Mike Schmidt	2.00	.80
17 Bruce Sutter	.20	.08
18 Pete Rose	2.00	.80
19 Dave Kingman	.30	.12
20 Neil Allen	.10	.04
21 Don Sutton	.75	.30
22 Dave Concepcion	.20	.08
23 Keith Hernandez	.20	.08
24 Gary Carter	.75	.30
25 Carlton Fisk	1.50	.60
26 Ron Guidry	.20	.08
27 Steve Carlton	1.00	.40
28 Robin Yount	1.50	.60
29 John Castino	.10	.04
30 Johnny Bench	1.00	.40
31 Bob Knepper	.10	.04
32 Rich Gossage	.20	.08
33 Buddy Bell	.20	.08
34 Art Howe	.20	.08
35 Tony Armas	.10	.04
36 Phil Niekro	.75	.30
37 Len Barker	.10	.04
38 Bob Grich	.20	.08
39 Steve Kemp	.10	.04
40 Kirk Gibson	.50	.20
41 Carney Lansford	.10	.04
42 Jim Palmer	1.00	.40
43 Carl Yastrzemski	1.00	.40
44 Rick Burleson	.10	.04
45 Dwight Evans	.20	.08
46 Ron Cey	.20	.08
47 Steve Garvey	.50	.20
48 Dave Parker	.30	.12
49 Mike Easler	.10	.04
50 Dusty Baker	.20	.08
51 Rod Carew	1.00	.40
52 Chris Chambliss	.20	.08
53 Tim Raines	.50	.20
54 Chet Lemon	.10	.04
55 Bill Madlock	.20	.08
56 George Foster	.20	.08
57 Dwayne Murphy	.10	.04
58 Ken Singleton	.10	.04
59 Mike Norris	.10	.04
60 Cecil Cooper	.20	.08
61 Al Oliver	.20	.08
62 Willie Wilson	.10	.04
63 Vida Blue	.20	.08
64 Eddie Murray	2.00	.80

1983 Kellogg's

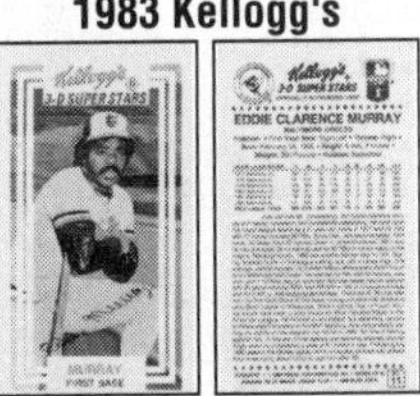

The cards in this 60-card set measure approximately 1 7/8" by 3 1/4". For the 14th year in a row and final year, the Kellogg Company issued a card set of Major League players. The set of 3-D cards contains the photo, player's autograph, Kellogg's logo, and name and position of the player on the front of the card. The backs feature the player's team logo, career statistics, player biography, and a narrative on the player's career. Every card in the set has a statistical procedural error that was never corrected. All seasonal averages were added up and then divided by the number of seasons played.

	Nm-Mt	Ex-Mt
COMPLETE SET (60)	15.00	6.00
1 Rod Carew	1.00	.40
2 Rollie Fingers	.75	.30
3 Reggie Jackson	1.50	.60
4 George Brett	3.00	1.20
5 Hal McRae	.20	.08
6 Pete Rose	1.50	.60
7 Fernando Valenzuela	.30	.12
8 Rickey Henderson	2.00	.80
9 Carl Yastrzemski	1.00	.40
10 Rich Gossage	.20	.08
11 Eddie Murray	1.50	.60
12 Buddy Bell	.20	.08
13 Jim Rice	.30	.12
14 Robin Yount	1.00	.40
15 Dave Winfield	1.00	.40
16 Harold Baines	.75	.30
17 Garry Templeton	.10	.04
18 Bill Madlock	.20	.08
19 Pete Vuckovich	.10	.04
20 Pedro Guerrero	.20	.08
21 Ozzie Smith	2.00	.80
22 George Foster	.20	.08
23 Willie Wilson	.10	.04
24 Johnny Ray	.10	.04
25 George Hendrick	.10	.04
26 Andre Thornton	.10	.04
27 Leon Durham	.10	.04
28 Cecil Cooper	.20	.08
29 Don Baylor	.20	.08
30 Lonnie Smith	.10	.04
31 Nolan Ryan	3.00	1.20
32 Dan Quisenberry UER Name spelled Quiesenberry on front	.20	.08
33 Len Barker	.10	.04
34 Neil Allen	.10	.04
35 Jack Morris	.20	.08
36 Dave Stieb	.20	.08
37 Bruce Sutter	.20	.08
38 Jim Sundberg	.20	.08
39 Jim Palmer	1.00	.40
40 Lance Parrish	.20	.08
41 Floyd Bannister	.10	.04
42 Larry Gura	.10	.04
43 Britt Burns	.10	.04
44 Toby Harrah	.10	.04
45 Steve Carlton	1.00	.40
46 Greg Minton	.10	.04
47 Gorman Thomas	.10	.04
48 Jack Clark	.20	.08
49 Keith Hernandez	.20	.08
50 Greg Luzinski	.20	.08
51 Fred Lynn	.20	.08
52 Dale Murphy	.75	.30
53 Kent Hrbek	.20	.08
54 Bob Horner	.10	.04
55 Gary Carter	.60	.24
56 Carlton Fisk	1.00	.40
57 Dave Concepcion	.20	.08
58 Mike Schmidt	1.50	.60
59 Bill Buckner	.20	.08
60 Bob Grich	.20	.08

1991 Kellogg's 3D

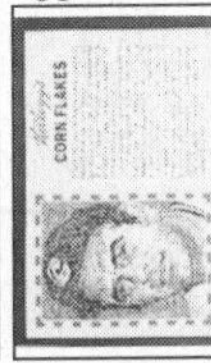

Sportflics/Optigraphics produced this 15-card set for Kellogg's, and the cards measure approximately 2 1/2" by 3 5/16". The fronts have a three-dimensional image that alternates between a posed or action color shot and a head and shoulders close-up. The card face is aqua blue, with white stripes (that turn pink) and white borders. In red and dark blue print, the horizontally oriented backs have a facial drawing of the player on the left half, and career summary on the right half. The cards are numbered on the back. The cards were inserted in specially marked boxes (18 oz. and 24 oz. only) of Kellogg's Corn Flakes. In addition, the complete set and a blue display rack were available through a mail-in offer for 4.95 and two UPC symbols.

	Nm-Mt	Ex-Mt
COMPLETE SET (15)	10.00	3.00
1 Gaylord Perry	.75	.23
2 Hank Aaron	1.50	.45
3 Willie Mays	1.50	.45
4 Ernie Banks	1.50	.45
5 Bob Gibson	.75	.23
6 Harmon Killebrew	.75	.23
7 Rollie Fingers	.75	.23
8 Steve Carlton	1.00	.30
9 Billy Williams	.75	.23
10 Lou Brock	1.00	.30
11 Yogi Berra	1.50	.45
12 Warren Spahn	1.00	.30
13 Boog Powell	.50	.15
14 Don Baylor	.50	.15
15 Ralph Kiner	.75	.23

1991 Kellogg's Legends Spanish

This 11-card "Hispanic Legends of Baseball" set was sponsored by Kellogg's and celebrates ten Hispanic greats from Major League Baseball. The cards were inserted in boxes of Kellogg's Corn Flakes, Frosted Flakes, and Fruit Loops in selected geographic areas. The cards measure the standard size. The fronts feature color player photos bordered in white. The pictures are accented above and on the left by red, orange, and yellow border stripes. The set name appears on a home plate icon at the upper left corner, while the player's name appears in a white bar that cuts across the picture. On the bilingual (Spanish and English) backs, the biographical and statistical information are vertically oriented on the left portion, while a black and white head shot and player profile fill out the remainder of the back. The cards are unnumbered and checklisted below in alphabetical order. This set also comes saying "Kellogs Legends of Baseball" in English on the front with an English only back.

	Nm-Mt	Ex-Mt
COMPLETE SET (11)	15.00	4.50
1 Bert Campaneris	.75	.23
2 Rod Carew	3.00	.90
3 Rico Carty	.75	.23
4 Cesar Cedeno	.75	.23
5 Orlando Cepeda	1.50	.45
6 Roberto Clemente	12.00	3.60
7 Mike Cuellar	.75	.23
8 Ed Figueroa	.50	.15
9 Minnie Minoso	1.50	.45
10 Manny Sanguillen	.50	.15
NNO Title Card	.50	.15

1991 Kellogg's Stand Ups

This set was sponsored by Kellogg's in honor of six retired baseball stars as part of a promotion entitled "Baseball Greats." Six different stars are featured on the backs of (specially marked 7 oz. and 12 oz.) Kellogg's Corn Flakes boxes. Since there were two different size boxes, there are two sizes of each card, the larger is approximately 9 1/4" by 6" coming from the 12 oz. box. The color action

portraits can be cut out and stood up for display, and career highlights appear to the right of the stand up. The boxes are unnumbered and checklisted below in alphabetical order. All six of these players were also included in the 15-card Kellogg's 3D Baseball Greats set. The complete set price below includes either the small or the large package cards but not both.

	Nm-Mt	Ex-Mt
COMPLETE SET (6)	10.00	3.00
1 Hank Aaron	4.00	1.20
2 Ernie Banks	3.00	.90
3 Yogi Berra	3.00	.90
4 Lou Brock	2.00	.60
5 Steve Carlton	2.00	.60
6 Bob Gibson	2.50	.75

1992 Kellogg's All-Stars

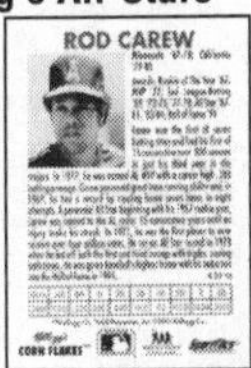

This ten-card standard-size set was produced by Optigraphics Corp. (Grand Prairie, TX) for Kellogg's and features retired baseball stars. One card was protected by a cello pack and inserted into Kellogg's cereal boxes. In the U.S., the cards were inserted in boxes of Corn Flakes, while in Canada they were inserted in Frosted Flakes and some other cereals. The complete set and a baseball display board to hold the collection were available through a mail-in offer for 4.75 and two UPC symbols from the side panel of Corn Flakes boxes (in Canada, for 7.99 and three tokens; one token was found on the side panel of each cereal box). The front of the "Double Action" cards have a three-dimensional image that alternates between two action shots and gives the impression of a batter or pitcher in motion. The pictures are bordered in red, white, and blue. The backs carry a black and white close-up photo, summary of the player's career (teams and years he played for them), awards, and career highlights. The Canadian Frosted Flakes cards are valued at two times the values listed below. The box back pictures both images of the Seaver card. While these pictures resemble the actual card, they are not standard-size or even rectangulary shaped.

	Nm-Mt	Ex-Mt
COMPLETE SET (10)	6.00	1.80
1 Willie Stargell	.75	.23
2 Tony Perez	.50	.15
3 Jim Palmer	1.00	.30
4 Rod Carew	1.00	.30
5 Tom Seaver	1.50	.45
6 Phil Niekro	.75	.23
7 Bill Madlock	.25	.07
8 Jim Rice	.50	.15
9 Dan Quisenberry	.25	.07
10 Mike Schmidt	2.00	.60

1992 Kellogg's Frosted Flakes Box Back

Some specially marked backs of Frosted Flakes show a team photo of the 1992 World Champion Toronto Blue Jays with facsimile autographs. The back is blank-backed and mesaures 7 1/2" by 11 1/8" The front features a green-bordered color team photo. All the text is billingual (French and English).

	Nm-Mt	Ex-Mt
1 Toronto Blue Jays Team Photo (With facsimile autographs)	20.00	6.00

1994 Kellogg's Clemente

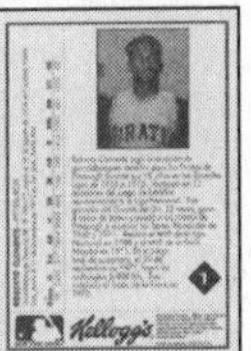

Protected by a clear plastic cello pack, these three standard-size cards were inserted into Kellogg's Corn Flakes cereal boxes in Puerto Rico, one card per box. The 18-ounce boxes commemorate the 20th anniversary of Clemente's 3,000th hit, the foundation of the Ciudad Deportiva Roberto Clemente, and his unexpected death. The fronts feature color action player photos bordered in white. The pictures are accented by green, blue and red stripes. The player's name and number are printed inside a yellow bar on the bottom of the photo. The team logo appears in the upper right corner, while the set name appears on a home plate icon at the upper left corner. On the backs, the biographical and statistical information are vertically oriented on the left portion, while a black-and-white head shot and player profile fill out the remainder. All text is in Spanish.

	Nm-Mt	Ex-Mt
COMPLETE SET (3)	250.00	75.00
COMMON CARD (1-3)	80.00	24.00

1988 Kenner Starting Lineup Unissued

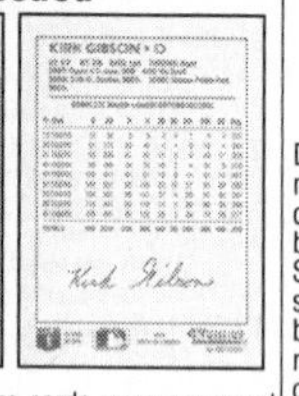

These ten standard-size cards were supposed to be included (along with the accompanying statues) in the 1988 Kenner release. Most of these players were traded either after production of the cards or were released by the teams they were then playing for. Please keep us informed of any other interesting Kenner cards which may never have made the market. These cards are not numbered so we have sequenced them in alphabetical order

	Nm-Mt	Ex-Mt
COMPLETE SET (9)	125.00	50.00
1 Phil Bradley	10.00	4.00
2 Chili Davis	15.00	6.00
3 Mike Davis	10.00	4.00
4 Richard Dotson	10.00	4.00
5 Kirk Gibson	25.00	10.00
6 Goose Gossage	20.00	8.00
7 Ray Knight	10.00	4.00
8 Lee Smith	15.00	6.00
9 Bob Welch	10.00	4.00
10 Glenn Wilson	10.00	4.00

1987 Key Food Discs

This set is a parallel to the 1987 MSA Iced Tea Discs. They say Key Food on the front and are valued the same as the regular discs.

	Nm-Mt	Ex-Mt
COMPLETE SET (20)	7.50	3.00
1 Darryl Strawberry	.25	.10
2 Roger Clemens	1.25	.50
3 Ron Darling	.10	.04
4 Keith Hernandez	.25	.10
5 Tony Pena	.25	.10
6 Don Mattingly	1.25	.50
7 Eric Davis	.25	.10
8 Gary Carter	.75	.30
9 Dave Winfield	.75	.30
10 Wally Joyner	.75	.30
11 Mike Schmidt	.75	.30
12 Robby Thompson	.10	.04
13 Wade Boggs	.75	.30
14 Cal Ripken	2.50	1.00
15 Dale Murphy	.50	.20
16 Tony Gwynn	2.00	.80
17 Jose Canseco	.50	.20
18 Rickey Henderson	1.00	.40
19 Lance Parrish	.10	.04
20 Dave Righetti	.10	.04

1988 Key Food Discs

For the second year, Key Foods was one of the title sponsors of the MSA Iced Tea Discs. The words Key Foods are on the front. They are valued the same as the regular discs.

	Nm-Mt	Ex-Mt
COMPLETE SET (20)	10.00	4.00
1 Wade Boggs	1.00	.40
2 Ellis Burks	.75	.30
3 Don Mattingly	2.00	.80
4 Mark McGwire	3.00	1.20
5 Matt Nokes	.10	.04
6 Kirby Puckett	1.00	.40
7 Billy Ripken	.10	.04
8 Kevin Seitzer	.10	.04
9 Roger Clemens	2.00	.80
10 Will Clark	.75	.30
11 Vince Coleman	.10	.04
12 Eric Davis	.25	.10
13 Dave Magadan	.10	.04
14 Dale Murphy	.50	.20
15 Benito Santiago	.25	.10
16 Mike Schmidt	.75	.30
17 Darryl Strawberry	.25	.10
18 Steve Bedrosian	.10	.04
19 Dwight Gooden	.25	.10
20 Fernando Valenzuela	.25	.10

1989 Key Food Discs

For the third year, the MSA Iced Tea Discs were also issued by the Key Foods brand. These discs, parallel to the MSA Iced Tea discs are valued the same as those discs.

	Nm-Mt	Ex-Mt
COMPLETE SET (20)	40.00	16.00
1 Don Mattingly	6.00	2.40
2 Dave Cone	1.00	.40
3 Mark McGwire	10.00	4.00
4 Will Clark	4.00	1.60
5 Darryl Strawberry	2.00	.80
6 Dwight Gooden	2.00	.80
7 Wade Boggs	4.00	1.60
8 Roger Clemens	6.00	2.40
9 Benito Santiago	2.00	.80
10 Orel Hershiser	2.00	.80
11 Eric Davis	2.00	.80
12 Kirby Puckett	5.00	2.00
13 Dave Winfield	4.00	1.60
14 Andre Dawson	4.00	1.60
15 Steve Bedrosian	1.00	.40
16 Cal Ripken	12.00	4.80
17 Andy Van Slyke	1.00	.40
18 Jose Canseco	4.00	1.60
19 Jose Oquendo	1.00	.40
20 Dale Murphy	3.00	1.20

1983 KG Glossy

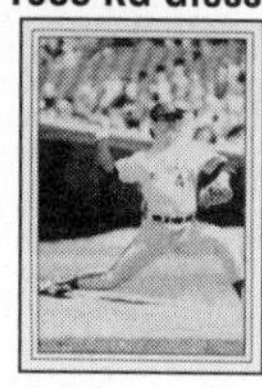

Despite being similar to the 1983 Topps Glossy mail-away set and it is possible that these cards were issued as a test for that set. It is believed that these cards were issued by KG. Since the cards are unnumbered, we have sequenced them in alphabetical order. It is believed that these cards were printed and test released in Michigan. Any further information on this issue is appreciated.

	Nm-Mt	Ex-Mt
COMPLETE SET (22)	30.00	12.00
1 Wade Boggs	5.00	2.00
2 George Brett	2.50	1.00
3 Rod Carew	1.50	.60
4 Steve Carlton	1.50	.60
5 Gary Carter	1.25	.50
6 Steve Garvey	.75	.30
7 Reggie Jackson	1.50	.60
8 Ron Kittle	.50	.20
9 Bill Madlock	.50	.20
10 Dale Murphy	1.00	.40
11 Eddie Murray	1.25	.50
12 Jim Palmer	1.25	.50
13 Lance Parrish	.50	.20
14 Cal Ripken	5.00	2.00
15 Pete Rose	2.00	.80
16 Steve Sax	.50	.20
17 Mike Schmidt	1.25	.50
18 Tom Seaver	1.50	.60
19 Fernando Valenzuela	1.00	.40
20 Dave Winfield	1.25	.50
21 Carl Yastrzemski	1.25	.50
22 Robin Yount	1.25	.50

1988 King-B Discs

In 1988 King-B Quality Meat Products (Beef Jerky) introduced a set of 24 discs produced in conjunction with the Major League Baseball Players Association and Mike Schechter Associates. A single disc was inserted inside each specially marked package. The discs are numbered on the back and have a medium blue border on the front. Discs are approximately 2 3/8" in diameter. The disc backs contain very sparse personal or statistical information about the player and are printed in blue on white stock.

	Nm-Mt	Ex-Mt
COMPLETE SET (24)	100.00	40.00
1 Mike Schmidt	4.00	1.60
2 Dale Murphy	2.50	1.00
3 Kirby Puckett	4.00	1.60
4 Ozzie Smith	8.00	3.20
5 Tony Gwynn	10.00	4.00
6 Mark McGwire	12.00	4.80
7 George Brett	10.00	4.00
8 Darryl Strawberry	1.50	.60
9 Wally Joyner	1.50	.60
10 Cory Snyder	1.00	.40
11 Barry Bonds	15.00	6.00
12 Darrell Evans	1.50	.60
13 Mike Scott	1.00	.40
14 Andre Dawson	2.50	1.00
15 Don Mattingly	8.00	3.20
16 Candy Maldonado	1.00	.40
17 Alvin Davis	1.00	.40
18 Carlton Fisk	4.00	1.60
19 Fernando Valenzuela	1.50	.60
20 Roger Clemens	8.00	3.20
21 Larry Parrish	1.00	.40
22 Eric Davis	1.50	.60
23 Paul Molitor	4.00	1.60
24 Cal Ripken	15.00	6.00

1989 King-B Discs

The 1989 King-B Disc set contains 24 discs, each measuring approximately 2 3/4" in diameter. The set was prepared by MSA; there are no team logos featured on the disc. The year and lifetime statistics are featured for each player on the back of the disc. The discs were issued one per small cannister of Beef Jerky. It has been estimated that five million discs were produced for this set.

	Nm-Mt	Ex-Mt
COMPLETE SET (24)	30.00	12.00
1 Kirk Gibson	.50	.20
2 Eddie Murray	2.00	.80
3 Wade Boggs	1.50	.60
4 Mark McGwire	8.00	3.20
5 Ryne Sandberg	3.00	1.20
6 Ozzie Guillen	.50	.20
7 Chris Sabo	.25	.10
8 Joe Carter	.75	.30
9 Alan Trammell	.75	.30
10 Nolan Ryan	12.00	4.80
11 Bo Jackson	2.00	.80
12 Orel Hershiser	.50	.20
13 Robin Yount	2.00	.80
14 Frank Viola	.25	.10
15 Darryl Strawberry	.50	.20
16 Dave Winfield	2.00	.80
17 Jose Canseco	2.00	.80
18 Von Hayes	.25	.10
19 Andy Van Slyke	.50	.20
20 Pedro Guerrero	.25	.10
21 Tony Gwynn	6.00	2.40
22 Will Clark	2.00	.80
23 Danny Jackson	.25	.10
24 Pete Incaviglia	.25	.10

1990 King-B Discs

The 1990 King-B Disc set contains 24 discs, each measuring approximately 2 3/4" inches in diameter. The set was prepared by MSA; there are no team logos featured on the disc. The discs were issued one per small cannister of Beef Jerky.

	Nm-Mt	Ex-Mt
COMPLETE SET (24)	30.00	9.00
1 Mike Scott	.25	.07
2 Kevin Mitchell	.25	.07
3 Tony Gwynn	5.00	1.50
4 Ozzie Smith	4.00	1.20
5 Kirk Gibson	.50	.15
6 Tim Raines	.50	.15
7 Von Hayes	.25	.07
8 Bobby Bonilla	.25	.07
9 Wade Boggs	2.00	.60
10 Chris Sabo	.25	.07
11 Dale Murphy	1.00	.30
12 Cory Snyder	.25	.07
13 Fred McGriff	1.50	.45
14 Don Mattingly	5.00	1.50
15 Jerome Walton	.25	.07
16 Ken Griffey Jr.	8.00	2.40
17 Bo Jackson	.50	.15
18 Robin Yount	1.25	.35
19 Rickey Henderson	2.50	.75
20 Jim Abbott	.75	.23
21 Kirby Puckett	1.50	.45
22 Nolan Ryan	10.00	3.00
23 Gregg Olson	.25	.07
24 Lou Whitaker	.50	.15

1991 King-B Discs

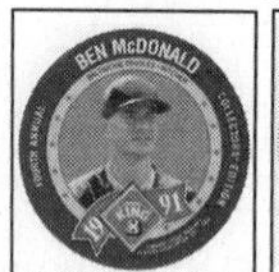

This was the fourth season that MSA issued discs as inserts in King-B meat products. These discs, which measure approximately 2 3/4" in diameter, feature leading major leaguers.

	Nm-Mt	Ex-Mt
COMPLETE SET (24)	20.00	6.00
1 Willie McGee	.50	.15
2 Kevin Seitzer	.25	.07
3 Kevin Maas	.25	.07
4 Ben McDonald	.25	.07
5 Rickey Henderson	2.50	.75
6 Ken Griffey Jr.	5.00	1.50
7 John Olerud	.75	.23
8 Dwight Gooden	.50	.15
9 Ruben Sierra	.50	.15
10 Luis Polonia	.25	.07
11 Wade Boggs	2.00	.60
12 Ramon Martinez	.25	.07
13 Craig Biggio	1.50	.45
14 Cecil Fielder	.50	.15
15 Will Clark	1.50	.45
16 Matt Williams	1.00	.30
17 Sandy Alomar Jr.	.50	.15
18 Dave Justice	1.00	.30
19 Ryne Sandberg	3.00	.90
20 Benito Santiago	.25	.07
21 Barry Bonds	5.00	1.50
22 Carlton Fisk	1.50	.45
23 Kirby Puckett	1.50	.45
24 Jose Rijo	.25	.07

1992 King-B Discs

These discs, which measure approximately 2 3/4" in diameter, feature top major league stars. These discs, inserted in beef jerky containers, were issued in conjunction with Michael Schecter Associates.

	Nm-Mt	Ex-Mt
COMPLETE SET (24)	12.00	3.60
1 Terry Pendleton	.10	.03
2 Chris Sabo	.10	.03
3 Frank Thomas	.75	.23
4 Todd Zeile	.20	.06
5 Bobby Bonilla	.10	.03
6 Howard Johnson	.10	.03
7 Nolan Ryan	3.00	.90
8 Ken Griffey Jr.	1.50	.45
9 Roger Clemens	1.50	.45
10 Tony Gwynn	1.50	.45
11 Steve Avery	.10	.03
12 Cal Ripken	3.00	.90
13 Danny Tartabull	.10	.03
14 Paul Molitor	.75	.23
15 Willie McGee	.20	.06
16 Wade Boggs	1.00	.30
17 Cecil Fielder	.20	.06
18 Jack Morris	.20	.06
19 Ryne Sandberg	1.25	.35
20 Kirby Puckett	.75	.23
21 Craig Biggio	.40	.12
22 Harold Baines	.30	.09
23 Scott Erickson	.10	.03
24 Joe Carter	.20	.06

1993 King-B Discs

These discs marked the sixth consecutive season that Michael Schecter Associates in conjunction with King-B meat products produced a 24 disc set. This set measure approximately 2 3/4" in diameter and features major league stars.

	Nm-Mt	Ex-Mt
COMPLETE SET (24)	8.00	2.40
1 Barry Bonds	1.00	.30
2 Ken Griffey Jr.	1.25	.35
3 Cal Ripken	2.00	.60
4 Frank Thomas	.50	.15
5 Steve Avery	.10	.03
6 Benito Santiago	.20	.06
7 Luis Polonia	.10	.03
8 Jose Rijo	.10	.03
9 George Brett	1.00	.30
10 Darren Daulton	.20	.06
11 Cecil Fielder	.20	.06
12 Ozzie Smith	.75	.23
13 Joe Carter	.20	.06
14 Dwight Gooden	.20	.06
15 Tom Henke	.10	.03
16 Brett Butler	.20	.06
17 Nolan Ryan	2.00	.60
18 Sandy Alomar	.20	.06
19 Tom Glavine	.50	.15
20 Rafael Palmeiro	.50	.15
21 Roger Clemens	1.00	.30
22 Ryne Sandberg	.75	.23
23 Doug Drabek	.10	.03
24 Chuck Knoblauch	.40	.12

1994 King-B Discs

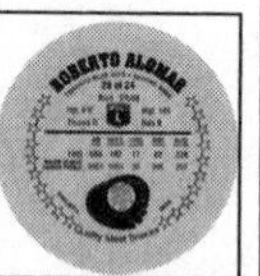

The 1994 King-B set contains 24 round cards each measuring approximately 2 7/8" in diameter.

	Nm-Mt	Ex-Mt
COMPLETE SET (24)	5.00	1.50
1 Fred McGriff	.30	.09
2 Paul Molitor	.60	.18
3 Jack McDowell	.10	.03
4 Darren Daulton	.20	.06
5 Wade Boggs	.50	.15
6 Ken Griffey Jr.	1.25	.35
7 Tim Salmon	.40	.12
8 Dennis Eckersley	.60	.18
9 Albert Belle	.20	.06
10 Travis Fryman	.20	.06
11 Chris Hoiles	.10	.03
12 Kirby Puckett	.50	.15
13 John Olerud	.30	.09
14 Frank Thomas	.50	.15
15 Lenny Dykstra	.20	.06
16 Andres Galarraga	.40	.12
17 Barry Larkin	.40	.12
18 Greg Maddux	1.00	.30
19 Mike Piazza	1.00	.30
20 Roberto Alomar	.40	.12
21 Robin Ventura	.40	.12
22 Ryne Sandberg	.75	.23
23 Andy Van Slyke	.20	.06
24 Barry Bonds	1.00	.30

1995 King-B Discs

This was the eighth year that King-B, in conjunction with MSA enterprises, issued discs. The players featured are among the best in baseball. The backs have season and career stats as well as vital statistics.

	Nm-Mt	Ex-Mt
COMPLETE SET (24)	20.00	6.00
1 Roberto Alomar	.50	.15
2 Jeff Bagwell	1.25	.35
3 Wade Boggs	1.25	.35
4 Barry Bonds	2.50	.75
5 Joe Carter	.20	.06
6 Mariano Duncan	.10	.03
7 Len Dykstra	.20	.06
8 Andres Galarraga	.50	.15
9 Matt Williams	.30	.09
10 Raul Mondesi	.20	.06
11 Ken Griffey Jr.	3.00	.90
12 Gregg Jefferies	.10	.03
13 Fred McGriff	.30	.09
14 Paul Molitor	1.00	.30
15 Dave Justice	.50	.15
16 Mike Piazza	3.00	.90
17 Kirby Puckett	1.25	.35
18 Cal Ripken	5.00	1.50
19 Ivan Rodriguez	1.00	.30
20 Ozzie Smith	1.50	.45
21 Gary Sheffield	.75	.23
22 Frank Thomas	.75	.23
23 Greg Maddux	3.00	.90
24 Jimmy Key	.20	.06

1996 King-B Discs

The 1996 King-B set consists of 24 round cards measuring approximately 2 7/8" in diameter. The fronts feature a color player photo with airbrushed uniforms. The year 1996 is on the left side, while the player's name and 9th annual Collectors edition appears on the bottom. The back has vital statistics, season and career statistics.

	Nm-Mt	Ex-Mt
COMPLETE SET (24)	20.00	6.00
1 Roger Clemens	2.50	.75
2 Mo Vaughn	.25	.07
3 Dante Bichette	.25	.07
4 Jeff Bagwell	1.25	.35
5 Randy Johnson	1.25	.35
6 Ken Griffey Jr.	2.50	.75
7 Kirby Puckett	.75	.23
8 Orel Hershiser	.25	.07
9 Albert Belle	.25	.07
10 Tony Gwynn	2.50	.75
11 Tom Glavine	.75	.23
12 Jim Abbott	.25	.07
13 Andres Galarraga	.75	.23
14 Frank Thomas	.75	.23
15 Barry Larkin	.75	.23
16 Mike Piazza	3.00	.90
17 Matt Williams	.50	.15
18 Greg Maddux	3.00	.90
19 Hideo Nomo	2.50	.75
20 Roberto Alomar	.75	.23
21 Ivan Rodriguez	1.00	.30
22 Cal Ripken	5.00	1.50
23 Barry Bonds	2.50	.75
24 Mark McGwire	3.00	.90

1997 King-B Discs

This 28-card set of rounded cards measures approximately 2 5/16" in diameter. The fronts feature color action player images on a black-and-gold marblized background. The backs carry player information and career statistics on a black-and-white player photo background. This set marks the 10th Anniversary of the King-B Discs.

	Nm-Mt	Ex-Mt
COMPLETE SET (28)	20.00	6.00
1 Brady Anderson	.40	.12
2 Barry Bonds	2.50	.75
3 Travis Fryman	.40	.12
4 Rey Ordonez	.20	.06
5 Kenny Lofton	.60	.18
6 Mark McGwire	3.00	.90
7 Jeff Bagwell	1.25	.35
8 Roger Clemens	2.50	.75
9 Juan Gonzalez	1.00	.30
10 Mike Piazza	3.00	.90
11 Tim Salmon	.75	.23
12 Jeff Montgomery	.20	.06
13 Joe Carter	.40	.12
14 David Cone	.75	.23
15 Frank Thomas	1.00	.30
16 Mickey Morandini	.20	.06
17 Ray Lankford	.40	.12
18 Pedro Martinez	1.25	.35
19 Tom Glavine	1.00	.30
20 Chuck Knoblauch	.75	.23
21 Dan Wilson	.20	.06
22 Gary Sheffield	1.00	.30
23 Dante Bichette	.20	.06
24 Al Martin	.20	.06
25 Barry Larkin	.75	.23
26 Ryne Sandberg	1.50	.45
27 Steve Finley	.40	.12
28 Matt Mieske	.20	.06

1998 King-B Discs

These 28 discs were issued in 1998 with King-B and honored some of the leading players in baseball. For the first time, this set was issued in conjuction with Pacific Trading Cards.

	Nm-Mt	Ex-Mt
COMPLETE SET	15.00	4.50
1 Brady Anderson	.20	.06

2 Barry Bonds 2.50 .75
3 Tony Clark .10 .03
4 Rey Ordonez .10 .03
5 Travis Fryman .20 .06
6 Jason Giambi 1.00 .30
7 Jeff Bagwell 1.25 .35
8 Tim Naehring .10 .03
9 Juan Gonzalez 1.25 .35
10 Mike Piazza 3.00 .90
11 Tim Salmon .50 .15
12 Jeff Montgomery .10 .03
13 Tom Glavine .50 .15
14 Chuck Knoblauch .20 .06
15 Dan Wilson .10 .03
16 Gary Sheffield .75 .23
17 Dante Bichette .10 .03
18 Al Martin .10 .03
19 Roger Clemens 2.50 .75
20 David Cone .50 .15
21 Frank Thomas 1.00 .30
22 Mike Lieberthal .20 .06
23 Ray Lankford .20 .06
24 Rondell White .20 .06
25 Barry Larkin .50 .15
26 Matt Mieske .10 .03
27 Steve Finley .20 .06
28 Fernando Vina .10 .03

1999 King-B Discs

For the 12th consecutive year, King-B issued discs with their products. This set features some of the leading players in Baseball. This set was issued in conjunction with Pacific Trading Cards and features a color photo on the front and a black and white player photo on the back.

Nm-Mt Ex-Mt
COMPLETE SET 20.00 6.00
1 Brady Anderson .20 .06
2 Barry Bonds 2.50 .75
3 Scott Rolen .60 .18
4 Tony Clark .10 .03
5 Jeff Bagwell 1.25 .35
6 Roberto Alomar .60 .18
7 Mark Kotsay .10 .03
8 Juan Gonzalez 1.00 .30
9 Tim Salmon .20 .06
10 Tom Glavine .75 .23
11 Frank Thomas 1.25 .35
12 Dan Wilson .10 .03
13 Dante Bichette .10 .03
14 Mickey Morandini .10 .03
15 Fred McGriff .40 .12
16 Andy Benes .10 .03
17 Al Martin .10 .03
17 Jeff Montgomery .10 .03
18 Pedro Martinez 1.25 .35
19 Barry Larkin .60 .18
20 Carlos Delgado 1.25 .35
21 Mike Myers .10 .03
22 Ray Lankford .20 .06
23 Brad Radke .10 .03
25 Raul Mondesi .20 .06
26 Ugueth Urbina .10 .03
27 Derek Jeter 5.00 1.50
28 Ben Grieve .20 .06
29 Mike Piazza 3.00 .90
30 Wally Joyner .10 .03

2000 King-B Discs

For the 13th consecutive year, King-B issued discs with their products. This set features some of the leading players in Baseball. This set was issued in conjunction with Pacific Trading Cards and features a color photo on the front and a black and white player photo on the back.

Nm-Mt Ex-Mt
COMPLETE SET (30) 20.00 6.00
1 Nomar Garciaparra 2.00 .60
2 Larry Walker .20 .06
3 Manny Ramirez 1.00 .30
4 Carlos Beltran .60 .18
5 Mark McGwire 3.00 .90
6 Jeromy Burnitz .20 .06
7 Carlos Delgado 1.25 .35
8 Tom Glavine .75 .23
9 Shawn Green .60 .18
10 Mark Kotsay .10 .03
11 Warren Morris .10 .03
12 Fred McGriff .40 .12
13 Brady Anderson .20 .06
14 Jeff Bagwell 1.25 .35
15 Tony Clark .10 .03
16 Ben Grieve .10 .03
17 Vladimir Guerrero 1.50 .45
18 Tony Gwynn 2.50 .75
19 Derek Jeter 5.00 1.50
20 Barry Larkin .60 .18
21 Rafael Palmeiro .75 .23
22 Mike Piazza 3.00 .90
23 Brad Radke .10 .03
24 Scott Rolen .20 .06
25 Tim Salmon .20 .06
26 Frank Thomas 1.25 .35
27 Mark Grace .60 .18
28 Jeff Kent .60 .18
29 Dan Wilson .10 .03
30 Jay Bell .10 .03

2001 King-B Discs

These 30 discs represent the 14th straight years that these discs were inserted into King-B products. Unlike previous years, these discs are not sequentially numbered; rather they are all numbered as 1 of 30; so we have sequenced this set in alphabetical order.

Nm-Mt Ex-Mt
COMPLETE SET (30) 20.00 6.00
1 Brady Anderson .20 .06
2 Jeff Bagwell 1.25 .35
3 Jay Bell .10 .03
4 Carlos Beltran .60 .18
5 Jeromy Burnitz .20 .06
6 Tony Clark .10 .03
7 Carlos Delgado 1.25 .35
8 Nomar Garciaparra 2.00 .60
9 Tom Glavine .75 .23
10 Mark Grace .60 .18
11 Shawn Green .60 .18
12 Ben Grieve .20 .06
13 Vladimir Guerrero 1.25 .35
14 Tony Gwynn 2.50 .75
15 Barry Larkin .60 .18
16 Derek Jeter 5.00 1.50
17 Jeff Kent .60 .18
18 Mark Kotsay .10 .03
19 Fred McGriff .40 .12
20 Mark McGwire 3.00 .90
21 Warren Morris .10 .03
22 Rafael Palmeiro .75 .23
23 Mike Piazza 3.00 .90
24 Brad Radke .10 .03
25 Manny Ramirez 1.00 .30
26 Scott Rolen .60 .18
27 Tim Salmon .20 .06
28 Frank Thomas 1.25 .35
29 Larry Walker .60 .18
30 Dan Wilson .10 .03

2002 King-B Discs

For the 15th consecutive year (and what turned out to be the final year for this promotion) the King-B company has included these discs as premiums in their products. These discs were produced for King-B by Donruss.

Nm-Mt Ex-Mt
COMPLETE SET (28) 20.00 6.00
1 Randy Johnson 1.25 .35
2 Curt Schilling .75 .23
3 Chipper Jones 1.50 .45
4 Greg Maddux 2.00 .60
5 John Burkett .20 .06
6 Manny Ramirez 1.00 .30
7 Barry Larkin .60 .18
8 Roberto Alomar .75 .23
9 Chuck Finley .40 .12
10 Jim Thome 1.00 .30
11 Juan Gonzalez .75 .23
12 Larry Walker .40 .12
13 Charles Johnson .20 .06
14 Moises Alou .40 .12
15 Gary Sheffield .75 .23
16 Chan Ho Park .40 .12
17 Vladimir Guerrero 1.25 .35
18 Roger Clemens 2.00 .60
19 Mariano Rivera .75 .23
20 Jason Giambi 1.25 .35
21 Rich Aurilia .40 .12
22 Jeff Kent .60 .18
23 Edgar Martinez .60 .18
24 Kazuhiro Sasaki .40 .12
25 Bret Boone .40 .12
26 John Olerud .40 .12
27 Greg Vaughn .40 .12
28 Ivan Rodriguez 1.25 .35

1985 Kitty Clover Discs

Very similar to the KAS test set, there was a Kitty Clover test set as well. The player selection is the same as the KAS test set. According to informed sources, 2000 sets were produced of this issue. The team insignias are all air-brushed out. Square corner proof versions exist and are double the prices listed below.

Nm-Mt Ex-Mt
COMPLETE SET 750.00 300.00
1 Steve Carlton 40.00 16.00
2 Jack Clark 15.00 6.00
3 Rich Gossage 15.00 6.00
4 Tony Gwynn 100.00 40.00
5 Keith Hernandez 20.00 8.00
6 Bob Horner 15.00 6.00
7 Kent Hrbek 15.00 6.00
8 Willie McGee 20.00 8.00
9 Dan Quisenberry 15.00 6.00
10 Cal Ripken 200.00 80.00
11 Ryne Sandberg 100.00 40.00
12 Mike Schmidt 80.00 32.00
13 Tom Seaver 80.00 32.00
14 Ozzie Smith 100.00 40.00
15 Rick Sutcliffe 15.00 6.00
16 Bruce Sutter 15.00 6.00
17 Alan Trammell 40.00 16.00
18 Fernando Valenzuela 20.00 8.00
19 Willie Wilson 15.00 6.00
20 Dave Winfield 50.00 20.00

1962 Kluszewski Charcoal Steak House

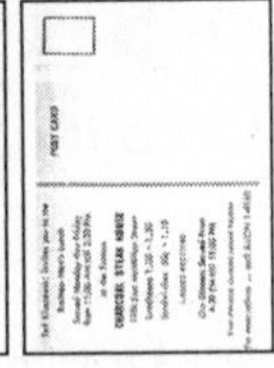

This one card postcard set features former Cincinnati Reds slugger Ted Kluszewski. The front features a photo of Klu wearing an Los Angeles Angels cap while the back features information about the Charcoal Steak House. Please note that the date of this card is noted by the cap that big Klu is wearing.

MINT NRMT
1 Ted Kluszewski 30.00 13.50

1992 Kodak Celebration Denver

Issued by Kodak to promote the Kodak Celebration of Baseball Fan Fair in Denver, August 14-16, 1992, this four-card standard-size set (plus one free admission coupon card) features Major League Baseball Players Alumni who were scheduled to appear at the show. Aside from the Jenkins card, which features a color painting of him, the fronts carry white-bordered color player action photos. The cards are unnumbered and checklisted below in alphabetical order.

Nm-Mt Ex-Mt
COMPLETE SET (5) 12.00 3.60
1 Orlando Cepeda 2.50 .75
2 Ferguson Jenkins Art 4.00 1.20
3 Graig Nettles 2.00 .60
4 Brooks Robinson 5.00 1.50
5 Admission Coupon Card 1.00 .30

1999 Kodak Cooperstown Collection

These six photos were produced by Kodak and featured leading players in history. These "moving" photos of which there are two on each card along with a portrait shot were issued in a specialty box. In addition, the materials you needed for a stand so the card so be displayed better were included in the box. The backs are blank. As the items are unnumbered we have sequenced them in alphabetical order.

Nm-Mt Ex-Mt
COMPLETE SET (6) 60.00 18.00
1 Hank Aaron 10.00 3.00
2 Lou Gehrig 12.00 3.60
3 Reggie Jackson 10.00 3.00
4 Mickey Mantle 15.00 4.50
5 Jackie Robinson 12.00 3.60
6 Babe Ruth 15.00 4.50

1998 Kodak Mantle

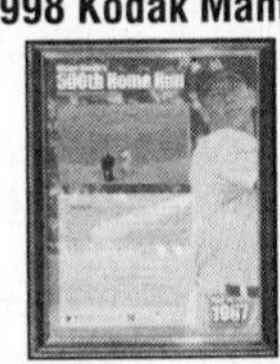

This one card oversize set was issued to commemorative Mickey Mantle's 500 homer. The card is isssued in a nice frame and the top part is a magic motion of Mantle's swing against Stu Miller which placed him into the 500 club. The back has highlights of Mantle's career along with complete statistics.

Nm-Mt Ex-Mt
1 Mickey Mantle 10.00 3.00

2000 Kodak Motion Cards

These cards features 2 to 3 seconds of full motion taken from Major League footage. The fronts have a player portrait, and a large moving photo and then in the corner a smaller moving photo. The cards are titled "Player Collection" on the top and that note changes into Card number "x of 6".

Nm-Mt Ex-Mt
COMPLETE SET (6) 60.00 18.00
1 Ken Griffey Jr. 12.00 3.60
2 Mark McGwire 15.00 4.50

3 Sammy Sosa 10.00 3.00
4 Derek Jeter 15.00 4.50
5 Mike Piazza 12.00 3.60
6 Alex Rodriguez 12.00 3.60

1985 Kondritz Trading Cards Vince Coleman

This 20 standard-size set was issued to honor Cardinal star rookie Vince Coleman who established an major league record for rookie steals.

Nm-Mt Ex-Mt
COMPLETE SET (20) 8.00 3.20
COMMON CARD (1-20) .50 .20

1986 Kondritz Trading Cards Ozzie Smith

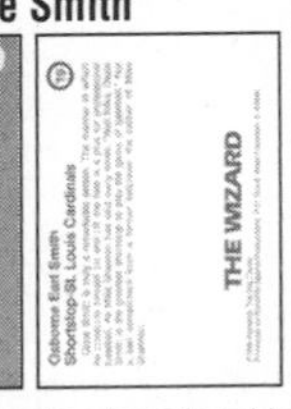

This 20-card standard-size set was issued by Kondritz trading card to commemorate the career of Ozzie Smith. These 20 cards are all red bordered and say Ozzie Smith on the top with the nickname "Oz" in a white circle in the top right corner. The backs have various descriptions about his career.

Nm-Mt Ex-Mt
COMPLETE SET (20) 15.00 6.00
COMMON CARD (1-20) .75 .30

1921 Koester's Bread World Series Issue D383

Issued in conjunction with the first all New York World Series, these cards feature members of the Giants and Yankees. The cards measure approximately 2" by 3 1/2" and are unnumbered. Therefore, we have sequenced them in alphabetical order by team. The following players are not known in the E121 issue: Ferguson, Mitchell, O'Leary, Barnes, Berry, Brown, Burkett, Cunningham and Stengel. These players sell at a premium over the other regular cards in this set.

Ex-Mt VG
COMPLETE SET 3000.00 1500.00
1 Dave Bancroft 100.00 50.00
2 Jesse Barnes 50.00 25.00
3 Joe Berry 50.00 25.00
4 Eddie Brown 50.00 25.00
5 Jesse Burkett CO 100.00 50.00
6 George Burns 50.00 25.00
7 Red Causey 50.00 25.00
8 Bill Cunningham 50.00 25.00
9 Phil Douglas 50.00 25.00
10 Frank Frisch 100.00 50.00
11 Alex Gaston 50.00 25.00
12 Mike Gonzalez 50.00 25.00
13 Hugh Jennings CO 100.00 50.00
14 George Kelly 100.00 50.00
15 John McGraw MG 100.00 50.00
16 Irish Meusel 50.00 25.00
17 Art Nehf 80.00 40.00
18 Johnny Rawlings 50.00 25.00
19 Rosy Ryan 50.00 25.00
20 Slim Sallee 50.00 25.00
21 Red Shea 50.00 25.00
22 Earl Smith 50.00 25.00
23 Frank Snyder 50.00 25.00
24 Casey Stengel 150.00 75.00
25 Fred Toney 50.00 25.00
26 Ross Youngs 100.00 50.00
27 Frank Baker 100.00 50.00
28 Ping Bodie 60.00 30.00
29 Rip Collins 50.00 25.00
30 Al DeVormer 50.00 25.00
31 Alex Ferguson 50.00 25.00
32 Chick Fewster 50.00 25.00
33 Harry Harper 50.00 25.00
34 Chicken Hawks 50.00 25.00
35 Fred Hofmann 50.00 25.00
36 Waite Hoyt 100.00 50.00
37 Miller Huggins MG 100.00 50.00
38 Carl Mays 80.00 40.00
39 Mike McNally 50.00 25.00
40 Bob Meusel 80.00 40.00
41 Elmer Miller 50.00 25.00
42 Johnny Mitchell 50.00 25.00
43 Charlie O'Leary CO 50.00 25.00
44 Roger Peckinpaugh 80.00 40.00
45 Bill Piercy 50.00 25.00
46 Jack Quinn 80.00 40.00

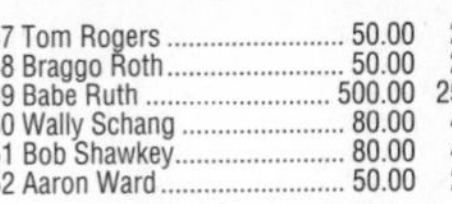
47 Tom Rogers 50.00 25.00
48 Braggo Roth 50.00 25.00
49 Babe Ruth 500.00 250.00
50 Wally Schang 80.00 40.00
51 Bob Shawkey 80.00 40.00
52 Aaron Ward 50.00 25.00

1987 Kraft Foods

Specially marked boxes of 1987 Kraft Macaroni featured a pair of cards. The individual cards measure approximately 2 1/4" by 3 1/2" and are printed in color. The player's team insignia are airbrushed out as the set was only licensed by the Major League Baseball Players Association. The cards are blank backed and are numbered in the lower right corner of the card. The set is subtitled "Home Plate Heroes." The cards on the box provide a dotted blue line as a guide for accurately cutting the cards from the box. There were many different two-card panels. Panel prices are based on the sum of the individual player's values making up that particular panel.

Nm-Mt Ex-Mt
COMPLETE SET (48) 25.00 10.00
1 Eddie Murray 1.00 .40
2 Dale Murphy .75 .30
3 Cal Ripken 4.00 1.60
4 Mike Scott .10 .04
5 Jim Rice .25 .10
6 Jody Davis .10 .04
7 Wade Boggs 1.25 .50
8 Ryne Sandberg 2.00 .80
9 Wally Joyner .75 .30
10 Eric Davis .50 .20
11 Ozzie Guillen .25 .10
12 Tony Pena .25 .10
13 Harold Baines .50 .20
14 Johnny Ray .10 .04
15 Joe Carter .75 .30
16 Ozzie Smith 2.00 .80
17 Cory Snyder .10 .04
18 Vince Coleman .10 .04
19 Kirk Gibson .25 .10
20 Steve Garvey .50 .20
21 George Brett 2.50 1.00
22 John Tudor .10 .04
23 Robin Yount 1.00 .40
24 Von Hayes .10 .04
25 Kent Hrbek .25 .10
26 Darryl Strawberry .25 .10
27 Kirby Puckett 1.00 .40
28 Ron Darling .10 .04
29 Don Mattingly 2.00 .80
30 Mike Schmidt 1.00 .40
31 Rickey Henderson 1.50 .60
32 Fernando Valenzuela .25 .10
33 Dave Winfield 1.00 .40
34 Pete Rose 1.50 .60
35 Jose Canseco 1.50 .60
36 Glenn Davis .10 .04
37 Alvin Davis .10 .04
38 Steve Sax .10 .04
39 Pete Incaviglia .25 .10
40 Jeff Reardon .25 .10
41 Jesse Barfield .10 .04
42 Hubie Brooks .10 .04
43 George Bell .10 .04
44 Tony Gwynn 2.00 .80
45 Roger Clemens 3.00 1.20
46 Chili Davis .50 .20
47 Mike Witt .10 .04
48 Nolan Ryan 4.00 1.60

1993 Kraft

The Kraft Singles Superstars '93 Collector's series consists of 30 pop-up cards. One card was inserted in each specially marked 12-oz., 16-oz., and 3-lb. Kraft Singles package until June. Boxed sets of all the cards could be purchased through a mail-in form enclosed with each card for 1.75 plus proof-of-purchase points from Kraft Singles packages. Also a collector's album could be purchased for 4.75 plus 36 proof-of-purchase points. The standard-size cards feature a color action photo of the player in a batting stance, and these pictures are bordered by either blue (1-15) on American League cards or green (16-30) on National League cards. The cards are numbered on the front at the lower left corner following alphabetical order by league.

Nm-Mt Ex-Mt
COMPLETE SET (30) 20.00 6.00
1 Jim Abbott .50 .15
2 Roberto Alomar 1.00 .30
3 Sandy Alomar .50 .15
4 George Brett 4.00 1.20
5 Roger Clemens 4.00 1.20
6 Dennis Eckersley 1.50 .45
7 Cecil Fielder .50 .15
8 Ken Griffey Jr. 4.00 1.20
9 Don Mattingly 4.00 1.20
10 Mark McGwire 6.00 1.80

11 Kirby Puckett 1.50 .45
12 Cal Ripken 8.00 2.40
13 Nolan Ryan 8.00 2.40
14 Robin Ventura 1.00 .30
15 Robin Yount 1.25 .35
16 Bobby Bonilla .25 .07
17 Ken Caminiti .25 .07
18 Will Clark 1.25 .35
19 Darren Daulton .50 .15
20 Doug Drabek .25 .07
21 Delino DeShields .25 .07
22 Tom Glavine 1.50 .45
23 Tony Gwynn 4.00 1.20
24 Orel Hershiser .50 .15
25 Barry Larkin 1.00 .30
26 Terry Pendleton .25 .07
27 Ryne Sandberg 2.00 .60
28 Gary Sheffield 1.25 .35
29 Lee Smith .50 .15
30 Andy Van Slyke .25 .07

1994 Kraft

The 1994 Kraft Singles Superstars set consists of 30 pop-up cards measuring approximately 2 1/2" by 3 3/8" and features "The Single Best Day" of 15 players from the American (1-15) and National (16-30) Leagues. One card was inserted in each specially marked 16-oz. and 3-lb. Kraft Singles package available in April and May. On-pack and in-store point-of-purchase mail-in offers enabled consumers to order a boxed American and/or National League 15-card set for $1.95 plus proof-of-purchase for each set. The cards are numbered on the back at the upper right, following alphabetical order by league.

Nm-Mt Ex-Mt
COMPLETE SET (30) 20.00 6.00
1 Carlos Baerga .50 .15
2 Dennis Eckersley 1.25 .35
3 Cecil Fielder .50 .15
4 Juan Gonzalez 1.00 .30
5 Ken Griffey Jr. 2.50 .75
6 Mark Langston .25 .07
7 Brian McRae .25 .07
8 Paul Molitor 1.00 .30
9 Kirby Puckett 2.50 .75
10 Cal Ripken 5.00 1.50
11 Danny Tartabull .25 .07
12 Frank Thomas 1.25 .35
13 Greg Vaughn .25 .07
14 Mo Vaughn .50 .15
15 Dave Winfield 1.25 .35
16 Jeff Bagwell 1.25 .35
17 Barry Bonds 2.50 .75
18 Bobby Bonilla .25 .07
19 Delino DeShields .25 .07
20 Lenny Dykstra .50 .15
21 Andres Galarraga 1.00 .30
22 Tom Glavine 1.00 .30
23 Mark Grace 1.00 .30
24 Tony Gwynn 2.50 .75
25 David Justice 1.00 .30
26 Barry Larkin 1.00 .30
27 Mike Piazza 3.00 .90
28 Gary Sheffield 1.25 .35
29 Ozzie Smith 2.00 .60
30 Andy Van Slyke .25 .07

1995 Kraft

Consisting of 30 standard-size cards, the 1995 Kraft Singles Superstars Pop-up Action cards were included in specially-marked 12-ounce and 16-ounce packages of Kraft singles. One card was inserted in each package. The set could also be obtained through the mail by filling out the mail-in order form and sending in 36 Kraft Singles purchase points and $1.95 for each 15-card League set. The cards are arranged in alphabetical order within American (1-15) and National (16-30) Leagues.

Nm-Mt Ex-Mt
COMPLETE SET (30) 25.00 7.50
1 Roberto Alomar 1.00 .30
2 Joe Carter .50 .15
3 Cecil Fielder .50 .15
4 Juan Gonzalez 1.00 .30
5 Ken Griffey Jr. 3.00 .90
6 Jimmy Key .50 .15
7 Chuck Knoblauch 1.00 .30
8 Kenny Lofton 1.00 .30
9 Mike Mussina 1.00 .30
10 Paul O'Neill .50 .15
11 Kirby Puckett 2.00 .60
12 Cal Ripken 5.00 1.50
13 Ivan Rodriguez 1.25 .35
14 Frank Thomas 1.25 .35
15 Mo Vaughn .50 .15
16 Moises Alou .50 .15
17 Jeff Bagwell 1.25 .35
18 Barry Bonds 2.50 .75
19 Jeff Conine .50 .15
20 Len Dykstra .50 .15
21 Andres Galarraga 1.00 .30
22 Tony Gwynn 2.50 .75
23 Gregg Jefferies .25 .07
24 Barry Larkin 1.00 .30
25 Greg Maddux 3.00 .90
26 Mike Piazza 3.00 .90
27 Bret Saberhagen .50 .15
28 Ozzie Smith 2.00 .60
29 Sammy Sosa 2.50 .75
30 Matt Williams .75 .23

1992 L and K Decals

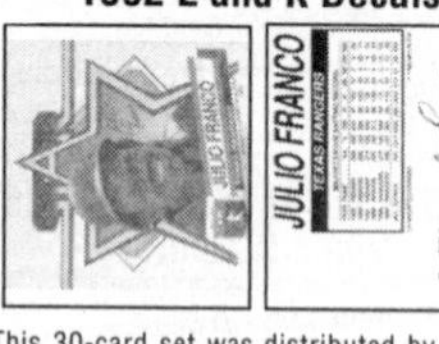

This 30-card set was distributed by Moore Sports Ltd. of New York and features color player head photos inside a large star printed as decals. The set was issued on uncut sheets which could be cut and used on various items such as mugs, mini-plates, glasses, etc. The back decal contains player statistics. Supposedly there were only 50 sheets produced with extra backs for some of the players and missing backs for others. The decals are unnumbered and checklisted below in alphabetical order.

Nm-Mt Ex-Mt
COMPLETE SET (30) 500.00 150.00
1 Wade Boggs 15.00 4.50
2 Barry Bonds 30.00 9.00
3 George Brett 30.00 9.00
4 Will Clark 15.00 4.50
5 Jose Canseco 12.00 3.60
6 Roger Clemens 30.00 9.00
7 David Cone 8.00 2.40
8 Andre Dawson 12.00 3.60
9 Rob Dibble 6.00 1.80
10 Lenny Dykstra 8.00 2.40
11 Cecil Fielder 8.00 2.40
12 Julio Franco 8.00 2.40
13 Doc Gooden 8.00 2.40
14 Ken Griffey Jr. 50.00 15.00
15 Ken Griffey Sr. 6.00 1.80
16 Tony Gwynn 30.00 9.00
17 Rickey Henderson 20.00 6.00
18 Orel Hershiser 8.00 2.40
19 Howard Johnson 6.00 1.80
20 Dave Justice 12.00 3.60
21 Don Mattingly 30.00 9.00
22 Fred McGriff 10.00 3.00
23 Cal Ripken 60.00 18.00
24 Nolan Ryan 60.00 18.00
25 Ryan Sandberg 15.00 4.50
26 Steve Sax 6.00 1.80
27 Ozzie Smith 30.00 9.00
28 Darryl Strawberry 8.00 2.40
29 Frank Viola 6.00 1.80
30 Dave Winfield 15.00 4.50

1911 L1 Leathers

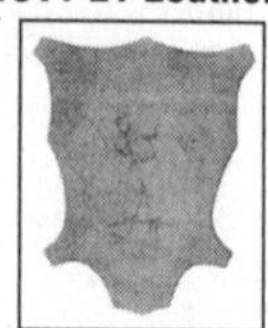

This highly prized set of baseball player pictures on a piece of leather shaped to resemble the hide of a small animal was issued during the 1911 time period. Each "leather" measures 10" by 12". While the pictures are those of the T3 Turkey Red card premium set, only the most popular players of the time are depicted. The cards are numbered at the bottom part of the leather away from the central image.

Ex-Mt VG
COMPLETE SET (25) 50000.00 25000.00
111 Rube Marquard 2000.00 1000.00
112 Marty O'Toole 1000.00 500.00
113 Rube Benton 1000.00 500.00
114 Grover C. Alexander 2500.00 1250.00
115 Russ Ford 1000.00 500.00
116 John McGraw MG 2000.00 1000.00
117 Nap Rucker 1200.00 600.00
118 Mike Mitchell 1000.00 500.00
119 Chief Bender 2000.00 1000.00
120 Frank Baker 2000.00 1000.00
121 Napoleon Lajoie 2000.00 1000.00
122 Joe Tinker 2000.00 1000.00
123 Sherry Magee 1000.00 500.00
124 Howie Camnitz 1000.00 500.00
125 Eddie Collins 2000.00 1000.00
126 Red Dooin 1000.00 500.00
127 Ty Cobb 10000.00 5000.00
128 Hugh Jennings MG 2000.00 1000.00
129 Roger Bresnahan 2000.00 1000.00
130 Jake Stahl 1000.00 500.00
131 Tris Speaker 2000.00 1000.00
132 Ed Walsh 1000.00 500.00
133 Christy Mathewson 5000.00 2500.00
134 Johnny Evers 2000.00 1000.00
135 Walter Johnson 6000.00 3000.00

1996-97 Las Vegas Club Chips

These two chips were issued by the Las Veagas Club and featured various baseball legends on them. They were issued in $10 demonations.

Nm-Mt Ex-Mt
COMPLETE SET 35.00 10.50
1 Bob Feller 10.00 3.00
Issued in 1996
2 Dizzy Dean 10.00 3.00

1997
3 Lou Gehrig 15.00 4.50
Bath Ruth
1997

1968 Laughlin World Series

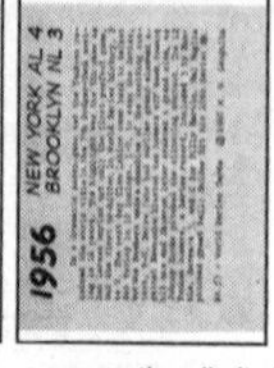

This set of 64 cards was apparently a limited test issue by sports artist R.G. Laughlin for the World Series set concept that was mass marketed by Fleer two and three years later. The cards are slightly oversized, (2 3/4" by 3 1/2") and are black and white on the front and red and white on the back. All the years are represented except for 1904 when no World Series was played. In the list below, the winning series team is listed first. According to an ad placed by Mr. Laughlin, only 300 of these sets were produced.

NM Ex
COMPLETE SET (64) 150.00 60.00
1 1903 Red Sox/Pirates 2.00 .80
Deacon Phillippe
2 1905 Giants/A's 3.00 1.20
(Christy Mathewson)
3 1906 White Sox/Cubs 2.00 .80
4 1907 Cubs/Tigers 2.00 .80
5 1908 Cubs/Tigers 4.00 1.60
(Joe Tinker
Johnny Evers
and Frank Chance)
6 1909 Pirates/Tigers 4.00 1.60
(Honus Wagner
Ty Cobb)
7 1910 A's/Cubs 2.00 .80
8 1911 A's/Giants 3.00 1.20
John McGraw MG
9 1912 Red Sox/Giants 2.00 .80
10 1913 A's/Giants 2.00 .80
11 1914 Braves/A's 2.00 .80
12 1915 Red Sox/Phillies 8.00 3.20
(Babe Ruth)
13 1916 Red Sox/Dodgers 8.00 3.20
(Babe Ruth)
14 1917 White Sox/Giants 2.00 .80
15 1918 Red Sox/Cubs 2.00 .80
16 1919 Reds/White Sox 4.00 1.60
17 1920 Indians/Dodgers 2.00 .80
Bill Wambsganss
18 1921 Giants/Yankees 2.50 1.00
(Waite Hoyt)
19 1922 Giants/Yankees 2.50 1.00
Frank Frisch
Heinie Groh
20 1923 Yankees/Giants 8.00 3.20
(Babe Ruth)
21 1924 Senators/Giants 2.00 .80
22 1925 Pirates/Senators 4.00 1.60
(Walter Johnson)
23 1926 Cardinals/Yankees 3.00 1.20
Grover C. Alexander
Tony Lazzeri
24 1927 Yankees/Pirates 2.50 1.00
25 1928 Yankees/Cardinals 7.50 3.00
Babe Ruth
Lou Gehrig
26 1929 A's/Cubs 2.00 .80
27 1930 A's/Cardinals 2.00 .80
28 1931 Cardinals/A's 2.50 1.00
(Pepper Martin)
29 1932 Yankees/Cubs 8.00 3.20
(Babe Ruth)
30 1933 Giants/Senators 3.00 1.20
(Mel Ott)
31 1934 Cardinals/Tigers 4.00 1.60
Dizzy Dean
Paul Dean
32 1935 Tigers/Cubs 2.00 .80
33 1936 Yankees/Giants 2.00 .80
34 1937 Yankees/Giants 2.50 1.00
(Carl Hubbell)
35 1938 Yankees/Cubs 2.00 .80
36 1939 Yankees/Reds 4.00 1.60
(Joe DiMaggio)
37 1940 Reds/Tigers 2.00 .80
38 1941 Yankees/Dodgers 2.50 1.00
(Mickey Owen)
39 1942 Cardinals/Yankees 2.00 .80
40 1943 Yankees/Cardinals 2.50 1.00
Joe McCarthy MG
41 1944 Cardinals/Browns 2.00 .80
42 1945 Tigers/Cubs 3.00 1.20
(Hank Greenberg)
43 1946 Cardinals/Red Sox 3.00 1.20
(Enos Slaughter)
44 1947 Yankees/Dodgers 2.50 1.00
(Al Gionfriddo)
45 1948 Indians/Braves 3.00 1.20
(Bob Feller)
46 1949 Yankees/Dodgers 2.50 1.00
Allie Reynolds
Preacher Roe
47 1950 Yankees/Phillies 2.00 .80
48 1951 Yankees/Giants 2.00 .80
49 1952 Yankees/Dodgers 3.00 1.20
Johnny Mize
Duke Snider
50 1953 Yankees/Dodgers 3.00 1.20
Casey Stengel MG
51 1954 Giants/Indians 2.00 .80
(Dusty Rhodes)
52 1955 Dodgers/Yankees 2.50 1.00
(Johnny Podres)
53 1956 Yankees/Dodgers 2.50 1.00
(Don Larsen)
54 1957 Braves/Yankees 2.00 .80
(Lew Burdette)
55 1958 Yankees/Braves 2.00 .80
(Hank Bauer)
56 1959 Dodgers/Wh.Sox 2.00 .80
(Larry Sherry)
57 1960 Pirates/Yankees 2.50 1.00
58 1961 Yankees/Reds 3.00 1.20
(Whitey Ford)
59 1962 Yankees/Giants 2.00 .80
60 1963 Dodgers/Yankees 3.00 1.20
(Sandy Koufax)
61 1964 Cardinals/Yankees 8.00 3.20
(Mickey Mantle)
62 1965 Dodgers/Twins 3.00 1.20
Sandy Koufax
63 1966 Orioles/Dodgers 2.00 .80
64 1967 Cardinals/Red Sox 3.00 1.20
(Bob Gibson)

1972 Laughlin Great Feats

This 51 card-set is printed on white card stock. Sports artist R.G. Laughlin is copyrighted only on the unnumbered title card but not on each card. The obverses are line drawings in black and white inside a red border. The cards measure 2 9/16" by 3 9/16". The set features "Great Feats" from baseball's past. The cards are blank backed and hence are numbered and captioned on the front. There is a variation set with a blue border and colored in flesh tones in the players pictured; this variation is a little more attractive and hence is valued a little higher. The blue-bordered variation set has larger type in the captions; in fact, the type has been reset and there are some minor wording differences. The blue-bordered set is also 1/16" wider. These sets were originally available from the artist for $3.25.

NM Ex
COMPLETE SET (51) 45.00 18.00
1 Joe DiMaggio 5.00 2.00
2 Walter Johnson 1.50 .60
3 Rudy York .50 .20
4 Sandy Koufax 1.50 .60
5 George Sisler .75 .30
6 Iron Man McGinnity .75 .30
7 Johnny VanderMeer .50 .20
8 Lou Gehrig 5.00 2.00
9 Max Carey .75 .30
10 Ed Delahanty .75 .30
11 Pinky Higgins .50 .20
12 Jack Chesbro .75 .30
13 Jim Bottomley .75 .30
14 Rube Marquard .75 .30
15 Rogers Hornsby 1.00 .40
16 Lefty Grove 1.00 .40
17 Johnny Mize .75 .30
18 Lefty Gomez .75 .30
19 Jimmie Foxx 1.00 .40
20 Casey Stengel 1.00 .40
21 Dazzy Vance .75 .30
22 Jerry Lynch .50 .20
23 Hughie Jennings .75 .30
24 Stan Musial 2.00 .80
25 Christy Mathewson 1.50 .60
26 Roy Face .50 .20
27 Hack Wilson .75 .30
28 Smoky Burgess .50 .20
29 Cy Young 1.50 .60
30 Wilbert Robinson .75 .30
31 Wee Willie Keeler .75 .30
32 Babe Ruth 5.00 2.00
33 Mickey Mantle 6.00 2.40
34 Hub Leonard .50 .20
35 Ty Cobb 4.00 1.60
36 Carl Hubbell .75 .30
37 Joe Oeschger and .50 .20
Leon Cadore
38 Don Drysdale .75 .30
39 Fred Toney and .50 .20
Hippo Vaughn
40 Joe Sewell .75 .30
41 Grover C. Alexander 1.00 .40
42 Joe Adcock .50 .20
43 Eddie Collins 1.00 .40
44 Bob Feller 1.50 .60
45 Don Larsen .50 .20
46 Dave Philley .50 .20
47 Bill Fischer .50 .20
48 Dale Long .50 .20
49 Bill Wambsganss .50 .20
50 Roger Maris 1.50 .60
NNO Title Card 1.00 .40

1974 Laughlin All-Star Games

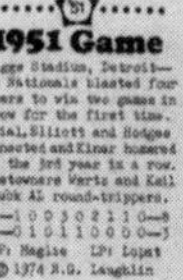

This 40-card set is printed on white card stock. Sports artist R.G. Laughlin is copyrighted at the bottom of the reverse of each card. The obverses are line drawings primarily in red, light blue, black and white inside a white border. The cards measure approximately 2 11/16" by 3 3/8". The set features memorable moments from each year's All-Star Game. The cards are numbered on the back according to the last two digits of the year and captioned on the front. The backs are printed in blue on white stock. There is no card No. 45 in the set as there was no All-Star Game played in 1945 because of World War II. This set was available from Bob Laughlin for $3.50.

NM Ex
COMPLETE SET (40) 40.00 16.00
33 Babe Ruth 6.00 2.40
Homer
34 Carl Hubbell 1.00 .40
Fans Five
35 Jimmie Foxx 1.00 .40
Smashes Homer
36 Dizzy Dean 1.00 .40
Fogs 'Em
37 Ducky Medwick .75 .30
Four Hits
38 John VanderMeer .75 .30
No-Hit
39 Joe DiMaggio 4.00 1.60
Homers
40 Max West's .50 .20
3-Run Shot
41 Arky Vaughan .75 .30
Busts Two
42 Rudy York .50 .20
2-Run Smash
43 Bobby Doerr .75 .30
3-Run Blast
44 Phil Cavarretta .50 .20
Reaches
46 Ted Williams 4.00 1.60
Field Day
47 Johnny Mize .75 .30
Plants One
48 Vic Raschi .50 .20
Pitches
49 Jackie Robinson 3.00 1.20
Scores
50 Red Schoendienst .75 .30
Breaks
51 Ralph Kiner .75 .30
Homers
52 Hank Sauer .50 .20
Shot
53 Enos Slaughter .75 .30
Hustles
54 Al Rosen .50 .20
Hits
55 Stan Musial 2.00 .80
Homer
56 Ken Boyer .50 .20
Super
57 Al Kaline 1.00 .40
Hits
58 Nellie Fox .75 .30
Gets Two
59 Frank Robinson 1.00 .40
Perfect
60 Willie Mays 3.00 1.20
3-for-4
61 Jim Bunning .75 .30
Hitless
62 Roberto Clemente 4.00 1.60
Perfect
63 Dick Radatz .50 .20
Monster Strikeouts
64 John Callison .50 .20
Homer
65 Willie Stargell .75 .30
Big Day
66 Brooks Robinson 1.00 .40
Hits
67 Fergie Jenkins .75 .30
Fans Six
68 Tom Seaver 2.00 .80
Terrific
69 Willie McCovey .75 .30
Belts Two
70 Carl Yatrzemski 1.00 .40
Four Hits
71 Reggie Jackson 2.00 .80
Unloads
72 Henry Aaron 3.00 1.20
Hammers
73 Bobby Bonds .75 .30
Perfect

1974 Laughlin Old Time Black Stars

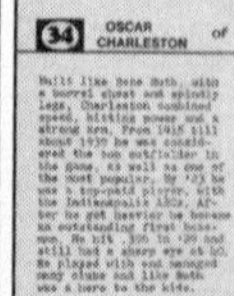

This 36-card set is printed on flat (non-glossy) white card stock. Sports artist R.G. Laughlin's work is evident but there are no copyright notices or any mention of him anywhere on any of the cards in this set. The obverses are line drawings in tan and brown. The cards measure approximately 2 5/8" by 3 1/2". The set features outstanding black players form the past. The backs are printed in brown on white stock. These sets were available from Bob Laughlin for $3.

NM Ex
COMPLETE SET (36) 50.00 20.00
1 Smokey Joe Williams 2.50 1.00
2 Rap Dixon 1.00 .40
3 Oliver Marcelle 1.00 .40
4 Bingo DeMoss 1.50 .60
5 Willie Foster 1.50 .60

6 John Beckwith 1.00 .40
7 Floyd(Jelly) Gardner 1.00 .40
8 Josh Gibson 6.00 2.40
9 Jose Mendez 1.00 .40
10 Pete Hill 1.00 .40
11 Buck Leonard 4.00 1.60
12 Jud Wilson 1.00 .40
13 Willie Wells 2.00 .80
14 Jimmie Lyons 1.00 .40
15 Satchel Paige 6.00 2.40
16 Louis Santop 1.00 .40
17 Frank Grant 1.00 .40
18 Christobel Torrienti 1.50 .60
19 Bullet Rogan 1.50 .60
20 Dave Malarcher 1.50 .60
21 Spot Poles 1.00 .40
22 Home Run Johnson 1.00 .40
23 Charlie Grant 1.00 .40
24 Cool Papa Bell 4.00 1.60
25 Cannonball Dick Redding 1.00 .40
26 Ray Dandridge 2.50 1.00
27 Biz Mackey 2.00 .80
28 Fats Jenkins 1.00 .40
29 Martin Dihigo 4.00 1.60
30 Mule Suttles 1.00 .40
31 Bill Monroe 1.00 .40
32 Dan McClellan 1.00 .40
33 John Henry Lloyd 4.00 1.60
34 Oscar Charleston 4.00 1.60
35 Andrew(Rube) Foster 4.00 1.60
36 William(Judy) Johnson 4.00 1.60

1974 Laughlin Sportslang

This 41-card set is printed on white card stock. Sports artist R.G. Laughlin 1974 is copyrighted at the bottom of every reverse. The obverses are drawings in red and blue on a white enamel card stock. The cards measure approximately 2 3/4" by 3 3/8". The set actually features the slang of several sports, not just baseball. The cards are numbered on the back and captioned on the front. The card back also provides an explanation of the slang term pictured on the card front.

	NM	Ex
COMPLETE SET (41)	8.00	3.20
COMMON CARD (1-41)	.25	.10

1975 Laughlin Batty Baseball

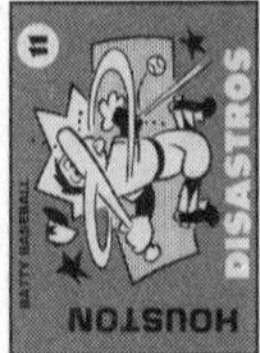

This-25 card set is printed on white card stock. Sports artist R.G. Laughlin 1975 is copyrighted on the title card. The obverses are line drawings primarily in orange, black and white. The cards measure 2 9/16" X 3 7/16". The set features a card for each team with a depiction of a fractured nickname for the team. The cards are numbered on the front. The backs are blank on white stock.

	NM	Ex
COMPLETE SET (25)	50.00	20.00
COMMON CARD (1-24)	2.50	1.00

1976 Laughlin Diamond Jubilee

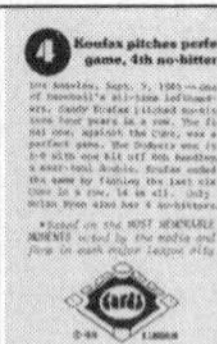

This 32-card set is printed on non-glossy white card stock. Sports artist R.Laughlin 1976 is copyrighted at the bottom of the reverse of each card. The obverses are line drawings primarily in red, blue, black and white inside a red border. The cards measure approximately 2 13/16" by 3 15/16". The set features memorable moments voted by the media and fans in each major league city. The cards are numbered on the back and captioned on the front and the back. The backs are printed in dark blue on white stock. The set was available from the artist for $3.50.

	NM	Ex
COMPLETE SET (32)	80.00	32.00
1 Nolan Ryan	30.00	12.00
2 Ernie Banks	1.50	.60
3 Mickey Lolich	.50	.20
4 Sandy Koufax	3.00	1.20
5 Frank Robinson	1.50	.60
6 Bill Mazeroski	.75	.30
7 Jim Hunter	.75	.30
8 Hank Aaron	5.00	2.00
9 Carl Yastrzemski	1.50	.60
10 Jim Bunning	.75	.30
11 Brooks Robinson	1.50	.60
12 John VanderMeer	.75	.30
13 Harmon Killebrew	1.50	.60
14 Lou Brock	1.50	.60
15 Steve Busby	.50	.20
16 Nate Colbert	.50	.20
17 Don Larsen	.75	.30
18 Willie Mays	3.00	1.20
19 David Clyde	.50	.20
20 Mack Jones	.50	.20
21 Mike Hegan	.50	.20
22 Jerry Koosman	.50	.20
23 Early Wynn	.75	.30
24 Nellie Fox	.75	.30
25 Joe DiMaggio	6.00	2.40
26 Jackie Robinson	4.00	1.60
27 Ted Williams	6.00	2.40
28 Lou Gehrig	6.00	2.40
29 Bobby Thomson	.75	.30
30 Roger Maris	1.50	.60
31 Harvey Haddix	.50	.20
32 Babe Ruth	8.00	3.20

1976 Laughlin Indianapolis Clowns

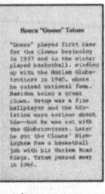

This 42-card set was issued to commemorate the Indianapolis Clowns, a black team that began touring in 1929 and played many games for charity. The cards measure 2 5/8" by 4 1/4". The front design has blackand-white player photos inside a white frame against a light blue card face. The team name is printed in red and white above the picture. In red courier-style print on white, the backs present extended captions. The cards are numbered on the front.

	NM	Ex
COMPLETE SET (42)	40.00	16.00
1 Ed Hamman Ed the Clown	1.50	.60
2 Dero Austin	1.00	.40
3 James Williams Nickname Natureboy	1.00	.40
4 Sam Brison Nickname Birmingham	1.00	.40
5 Richard King Nickname King Tut	1.00	.40
6 Syd Pollock Founder	1.00	.40
7 Nataniel(Lefty) Small	1.00	.40
8 Grant Greene Nickname Double Duty	1.00	.40
9 Nancy Miller Lady umpire	1.00	.40
10 Billy Vaughn	1.00	.40
11 Sam Brison Putout for Sam	1.00	.40
12 Ed Hamman	1.50	.60
13 Dero Austin Home delivery	1.00	.40
14 Steve(Nub) Anderson	1.00	.40
15 Joe Cherry	1.00	.40
16 Reece(Goose) Tatum	4.00	1.60
17 James Williams Natureboy	1.00	.40
18 Byron Purnell	1.00	.40
19 Bat boy	1.00	.40
20 Spec BeBop	1.00	.40
21 Satchel Paige	5.00	2.00
22 Prince Jo Henry	1.00	.40
23 Ed Hamman Syd Pollock	1.00	.40
24 Paul Casanova	1.50	.60
25 Steve(Nub) Anderson Nub singles	1.00	.40
26 Comiskey Park	1.50	.60
27 Toni Stone Second basewoman	2.50	1.00
28 Dero Austin Small target	1.00	.40
29 Sam Brison and Natureboy Williams Calling Dr. Kildare	1.00	.40
30 Oscar Charleston	2.50	1.00
31 Richard King King Tut	1.00	.40
32 Ed Hamman Joe Cherry Hal King Ed and prospects	1.00	.40
33 In style Team bus	1.00	.40
34 Hank Aaron	5.00	2.00
35 The Great Yogi	2.50	1.00
36 W.H.(Chauff) Wilson	1.00	.40
37 Sam Brison Sonny Jackson Doin' their thing	1.50	.60
38 Billy Vaughn The hard way	1.00	.40
39 James Williams 1B the easy way	1.00	.40
40 Ed Hamman Casey Stengel Casey and Ed	2.50	1.00
xx Title Card	1.00	.40
xx Baseball Laff Book	1.00	.40

1977 Laughlin Erorrs

This set of 39 blank-backed cards is printed on white card stock and measures 2 5/8" by 3 3/4". Sports artist R.G. Laughlin has created illustrations for actual errors made on baseball cards over the years, a sampling of the hundreds of mistakes that found their way into print. The illustrations are bordered in green with "Erorrs" (incorrect spelling intentional) in wide white script at the top of the cards. Each card lists the year, card make and number

depicted in the line drawing. The cards are unnumbered and checklisted below in chronological order. This set was available from the artist for $3 at the time of issue.

	NM	Ex
COMPLETE SET (39)	30.00	12.00
COMMON CARD (1-39)	1.00	.40

1978 Laughlin Long Ago Black Stars

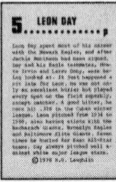

This set of 36 cards is printed on non-glossy white card stock. Sports artist R.G. Laughlin's work is evident and the reverse of each card indicates copyright by R.G. Laughlin 1978. The obverses are line drawings in light and dark green. The cards measure 2 5/8" by 3 1/2". The set features outstanding black players form the past. The cards are numbered on the back. The backs are printed in black on white stock. This is not a reissue of the similar Laughlin set from 1974 Old Time Black Stars but is actually in effect a second series with all new players and was available from Mr. Laughlin at time of issue for $3.75.

	NM	Ex
COMPLETE SET (36)	50.00	20.00
1 Ted Trent	2.00	.80
2 Larry Brown	1.50	.60
3 Newt Allen	3.00	1.20
4 Norman Stearns	1.50	.60
5 Leon Day	6.00	2.40
6 Dick Lundy	1.50	.60
7 Bruce Petway	2.00	.80
8 Bill Drake	1.50	.60
9 Chaney White	1.50	.60
10 Webster McDonald	1.50	.60
11 Tommy Butts	1.50	.60
12 Ben Taylor	1.50	.60
13 James(Joe) Greene	1.50	.60
14 Dick Seay	1.50	.60
15 Sammy Hughes	1.50	.60
16 Ted Page	4.00	1.60
17 Willie Cornelius	1.50	.60
18 Pat Patterson	1.50	.60
19 Frank Wickware	1.50	.60
20 Albert Haywood	1.50	.60
21 Bill Holland	1.50	.60
22 Sol White	1.50	.60
23 Chet Brewer	3.00	1.20
24 Crush Holloway	1.50	.60
25 George Johnson	1.50	.60
26 George Scales	1.50	.60
27 Dave Brown	1.50	.60
28 John Donaldson	1.50	.60
29 William Johnson	4.00	1.60
30 Bill Yancey	3.00	1.20
31 Sam Bankhead	2.00	.80
32 Leroy Matlock	1.50	.60
33 Quincy Troupe	2.00	.80
34 Hilton Smith	5.00	2.00
35 Jim Crutchfield	2.00	.80
36 Ted Radcliffe	3.00	1.20

1980 Laughlin 300/400/500

This square (approximately 3 1/4" square) set of 30 players features members of the 300/400/500 club, namely 300 pitching wins, batting .400 or better, or hitting 500 homers since 1900. Cards are blank backed but are numbered on the front. The cards feature the artwork of R.G. Laughlin for the player's body connected to an out of proportion head shot stock photo. This creates an effect faintly reminiscent of the Goudey Heads Up cards.

	NM	Ex
COMPLETE SET (30)	30.00	12.00
1 Title Card	.50	.20
2 Babe Ruth	4.00	1.60
3 Walter Johnson	1.00	.40
4 Ty Cobb	1.50	.60
5 Christy Mathewson	1.50	.60
6 Ted Williams	3.00	1.20
7 Bill Terry	.50	.20
8 Grover C. Alexander	.75	.30
9 Napoleon Lajoie	.75	.30
10 Willie Mays	1.50	.60
11 Cy Young	1.00	.40
12 Mel Ott	.75	.30
13 Joe Jackson	1.50	.60
14 Harmon Killebrew	.75	.30
15 Warren Spahn	.75	.30
16 Hank Aaron	2.50	1.00
17 Rogers Hornsby	1.50	.60
18 Mickey Mantle	4.00	1.60
19 Lefty Grove	.75	.30
20 Ted Williams	1.50	.60
21 Jimmie Foxx	1.00	.40
22 Eddie Plank	.50	.20
23 Frank Robinson	.75	.30
24 George Sisler	.50	.20
25 Eddie Mathews	.75	.30
26 Early Wynn	.50	.20
27 Ernie Banks	1.00	.40
28 Harry Heilmann	.50	.20
29 Lou Gehrig	2.50	1.00
30 Willie McCovey	.75	.30

1980 Laughlin Famous Feats

This set of 40 standard-size cards is printed on white card stock. Sports artist R.G. Laughlin 1980 is copyrighted at the bottom of every obverse. The obverses are line drawings primarily in many colors. The set is subtitled "Second Series" of Famous Feats. The cards are numbered on the front. The backs are blank on white stock.

	NM	Ex
COMPLETE SET (40)	15.00	6.00
1 Honus Wagner	.75	.30
2 Herb Pennock	.40	.16
3 Al Simmons	.40	.16
4 Hack Wilson	.40	.16
5 Dizzy Dean	.60	.24
6 Chuck Klein	.40	.16
7 Nellie Fox	.40	.16
8 Lefty Grove	.60	.24
9 George Sisler	.40	.16
10 Lou Gehrig	1.50	.60
11 Rube Waddell	.40	.16
12 Max Carey	.40	.16
13 Thurman Munson	.60	.24
14 Mel Ott	.60	.24
15 Doc White	.20	.08
16 Babe Ruth	2.00	.80
17 Schoolboy Rowe	.20	.08
18 Jackie Robinson	1.25	.50
19 Joe Medwick	.40	.16
20 Casey Stengel	.75	.30
21 Roberto Clemente	1.50	.60
22 Christy Mathewson	.75	.30
23 Jimmie Foxx	.60	.24
24 Joe Jackson	1.25	.50
25 Walter Johnson	.75	.30
26 Tony Lazzeri	.40	.16
27 Hugh Casey	.20	.08
28 Ty Cobb	1.50	.60
29 Stuffy McInnis	.20	.08
30 Cy Young	.60	.24
31 Lefty O'Doul	.20	.08
32 Eddie Collins	.40	.16
33 Joe McCarthy	.40	.16
34 Ed Walsh	.40	.16
35 George Burns	.20	.08
36 Walt Dropo	.20	.08
37 Connie Mack	.60	.24
38 Babe Adams	.20	.08
39 Rogers Hornsby	.60	.24
40 Grover C. Alexander	.60	.24

1914 Lawrence Semon Postcards

These seven postcards were produced by photographer Lawrence Semon. These postcards feature a large photo of the player using most of the space of the card with the players name and some information on the bottom. Six additions to this checklist were discovered in recent years -- so there might be more and additions to this checklist are welcome.

	Ex-Mt	VG
COMPLETE SET	4000.00	2000.00
1 George Burns	200.00	100.00
2 Frank Chance	400.00	200.00
3 Ty Cobb	1200.00	600.00
4 Walter Johnson	800.00	400.00
5 Connie Mack MG	600.00	300.00
6 Rube Marquard	400.00	200.00
7 John McGraw MG	600.00	300.00

1949 Leaf

The cards in this 98-card set measure 2 3/8" by 2 7/8". The 1949 Leaf set was the first post-war baseball series issued in color. This effort was not entirely successful due to a lack of refinement which resulted in many color variations and cards out of register. In addition, the set was skip numbered from 1-168, with 49 of the 98 cards printed in limited quantities (marked with SP in the checklist). Cards 102 and 136 have variations, and cards are sometimes found with overprinted, incorrect or blank backs. Some cards were produced with a 1948 copyright date but overwhelming evidence seemed to indicate that this set was not actually released until early in 1949. An album to hold these cards was available as a premium. The album could only be obtained by sending in five wrappers and 25 cents. Since so few albums appear on the secondary market, no value is attached to them. Notable Rookie Cards in this set include Stan Musial, Satchel Paige, and Jackie Robinson.

	NM	Ex
COMPLETE SET (98)	30000.00	15000.00
COMMON CARD (1-168)	25.00	12.50
COMMON SP's	300.00	150.00
WRAPPER (1-CENT)	160.00	80.00
1 Joe DiMaggio	3000.00	1200.00
3 Babe Ruth	2500.00	1250.00
4 Stan Musial	1000.00	500.00
5 Virgil Trucks SP RC	400.00	200.00
8 S.Paige SP RC !	12000.00	6000.00
10 Dizzy Trout	40.00	20.00
11 Phil Rizzuto	350.00	180.00
13 Cass Michaels SP	300.00	150.00
14 Billy Johnson	40.00	20.00
17 Frank Overmire	25.00	12.50
19 Johnny Wyrostek SP	300.00	150.00
20 Hank Sauer SP	400.00	200.00
22 Al Evans	25.00	12.50
26 Sam Chapman	40.00	20.00
27 Mickey Harris	25.00	12.50
28 Jim Hegan RC	40.00	20.00
29 Elmer Valo RC	40.00	20.00
30 Billy Goodman SP RC	400.00	200.00
31 Lou Brissie	25.00	12.50
32 Warren Spahn	350.00	180.00
33 Peanuts Lowrey SP	300.00	150.00
36 Al Zarilla SP	300.00	150.00
38 Ted Kluszewski RC	200.00	100.00
39 Ewell Blackwell	60.00	30.00
42 Kent Peterson	25.00	12.50
43 Ed Stevens SP	300.00	150.00
45 Ken Keltner SP	300.00	150.00
46 Johnny Mize	100.00	50.00
47 George Vico	25.00	12.50
48 Johnny Schmitz SP	300.00	150.00
49 Del Ennis RC	60.00	30.00
50 Dick Wakefield	25.00	12.50
51 Al Dark SP RC	500.00	250.00
53 Johnny VanderMeer	100.00	50.00
54 Bobby Adams SP	300.00	150.00
55 Tommy Henrich SP	500.00	250.00
56 Larry Jansen RC UER (Misspelled Jensen)	40.00	20.00
57 Bob McCall	25.00	12.50
59 Luke Appling	100.00	50.00
61 Jake Early	25.00	12.50
62 Eddie Joost SP	300.00	150.00
63 Barney McCosky SP	300.00	150.00
65 Robert Elliott RC UER (Misspelled Elliot on card front)	100.00	50.00
66 Orval Grove SP	300.00	150.00
68 Eddie Miller SP	300.00	150.00
70 Honus Wagner CO	350.00	180.00
72 Hank Edwards	25.00	12.50
73 Pat Seerey	25.00	12.50
75 Dom DiMaggio SP	600.00	300.00
76 Ted Williams	1200.00	600.00
77 Roy Smalley RC	25.00	12.50
78 Hoot Evers SP	300.00	150.00
79 Jackie Robinson RC	1500.00	750.00
81 Whitey Kurowski SP	300.00	150.00
82 Johnny Lindell	40.00	20.00
83 Bobby Doerr	100.00	50.00
84 Sid Hudson	25.00	12.50
85 Dave Philley SP RC	400.00	200.00
86 Ralph Weigel	25.00	12.50
88 Frank Gustine SP	300.00	150.00
91 Ralph Kiner	200.00	100.00
93 Bob Feller SP	2000.00	1000.00
95 George Stirnweiss RC	40.00	20.00
97 Marty Marion	60.00	30.00
98 Hal Newhouser SP RC	600.00	300.00
102A Gene Hermansk ERR	250.00	125.00
102B G.Hermanski COR	40.00	20.00
104 Eddie Stewart SP	300.00	150.00
106 Lou Boudreau	100.00	50.00
108 Matt Batts SP	300.00	150.00
111 Jerry Priddy	25.00	12.50
113 Dutch Leonard SP	300.00	150.00
117 Joe Gordon	40.00	20.00
120 George Kell SP RC	600.00	300.00
121 Johnny Pesky SP RC	400.00	200.00
123 Cliff Fannin SP	300.00	150.00
125 Andy Pafko RC	25.00	12.50
127 Enos Slaughter SP	800.00	400.00
128 Buddy Rosar	25.00	12.50
129 Kirby Higbe SP	300.00	150.00
131 Sid Gordon SP	300.00	150.00
133 Tommy Holmes SP	500.00	250.00
136A Cliff Aberson (Full sleeve)	25.00	12.50
136B Cliff Aberson (Short sleeve)	250.00	125.00
137 Harry Walker SP	400.00	200.00
138 Larry Doby SP RC	700.00	350.00
139 Johnny Hopp RC	25.00	12.50
142 D.Murtaugh SP RC	400.00	200.00
143 Dick Sisler SP	300.00	150.00
144 Bob Dillinger SP	300.00	150.00
146 Pete Reiser SP	500.00	250.00
149 Hank Majeski SP	300.00	150.00
153 Floyd Baker SP	300.00	150.00
158 H. Brecheen SP RC	400.00	200.00
159 Mizell Platt	25.00	12.50
160 Bob Scheffing SP	300.00	150.00
161 Vern Stephens SP RC	400.00	200.00
163 F.Hutchinson SP RC	400.00	200.00
165 Dale Mitchell SP RC	400.00	200.00
168 P.Cavarretta SP UER	500.00	200.00

Name spelled Cavaretta
NNO Album

1949 Leaf Premiums

This set of eight large, blank-backed premiums is rather scarce. They were issued as premiums with the 1949 Leaf Gum set. The catalog designation is R401-4. The set is subtitled "Baseball's Immortals" and there is no reference anywhere on the premium to Leaf, the issuing company. These large photos measure approximately 5 1/2" x 7 3/16" and are printed on thin paper.

NM Ex
COMPLETE SET (8) 2250.00 1100.00
1 Grover C. Alexander 200.00 100.00
2 Mickey Cochrane 200.00 100.00
3 Lou Gehrig 500.00 250.00
4 Walter Johnson 300.00 150.00
5 Christy Mathewson 300.00 150.00
6 John McGraw 200.00 100.00
7 Babe Ruth 800.00 400.00
8 Ed Walsh 150.00 75.00

1960 Leaf

The cards in this 144-card set measure the standard size. The 1960 Leaf set was issued in a regular gum package style but with a marble instead of gum. The series was a joint production by Sports Novelties, Inc., and Leaf, two Chicago-based companies. Cards 73-144 are more difficult to find than the lower numbers. Photo variations exist (probably proof cards) for the seven cards listed with an asterisk and there is a well-known error card, number 25 showing Brooks Lawrence (in a Reds uniform) with Jim Grant's name on front, and Grant's biography and record on back. The corrected version with Grant's photo is the more difficult variety. The only notable Rookie Card in this set is Dallas Green. The complete set price below includes both versions of Jim Grant.

NM Ex
COMPLETE SET (144) 1750.00 700.00
COMMON CARD (1-72) 3.00 1.20
COMMON CARD (73-144) 30.00 12.00
WRAPPER 50.00 20.00
1 Luis Aparicio * 25.00 6.25
2 Woody Held 3.00 1.20
3 Frank Lary 4.00 1.60
4 Camilo Pascual 5.00 2.00
5 Pancho Herrera 3.00 1.20
6 Felipe Alou 8.00 3.20
7 Benjamin Daniels 3.00 1.20
8 Roger Craig 5.00 2.00
9 Eddie Kasko 3.00 1.20
10 Bob Grim 4.00 1.60
11 Jim Busby 4.00 1.60
12 Ken Boyer 8.00 3.20
13 Bob Boyd 3.00 1.20
14 Sam Jones 4.00 1.60
15 Larry Jackson 4.00 1.60
16 Elroy Face 4.00 1.60
17 Walt Moryn * 3.00 1.20
18 Jim Gilliam 5.00 2.00
19 Don Newcombe 5.00 2.00
20 Glen Hobbie 3.00 1.20
21 Pedro Ramos 4.00 1.60
22 Ryne Duren 3.00 1.20
23 Joey Jay * 4.00 1.60
24 Lou Berberet 3.00 1.20
25A Jim Grant ERR 15.00 6.00
(Photo actually
Brooks Lawrence)
25B Jim Grant COR 25.00 10.00
26 Tom Borland 3.00 1.20
27 Brooks Robinson 40.00 16.00
28 Jerry Adair 3.00 1.20
29 Ron Jackson 3.00 1.20
30 George Strickland 3.00 1.20
31 Rocky Bridges 3.00 1.20
32 Bill Tuttle 4.00 1.60
33 Ken Hunt 3.00 1.20
34 Hal Griggs 3.00 1.20
35 Jim Coates * 3.00 1.20
36 Brooks Lawrence 3.00 1.20
37 Duke Snider 40.00 16.00
38 Al Spangler 3.00 1.20
39 Jim Owens 3.00 1.20
40 Bill Virdon 5.00 2.00
41 Ernie Broglio 3.00 1.20
42 Andre Rodgers 3.00 1.20
43 Julio Becquer 4.00 1.60
44 Tony Taylor 4.00 1.60
45 Jerry Lynch 4.00 1.60
46 Cletis Boyer 8.00 3.20
47 Jerry Lumpe 3.00 1.20
48 Charlie Maxwell 4.00 1.60
49 Jim Perry 4.00 1.60
50 Danny McDevitt 3.00 1.20
51 Juan Pizarro 3.00 1.20
52 Dallas Green RC 8.00 3.20
53 Bob Friend 4.00 1.60
54 Jack Sanford 4.00 1.60
55 Jim Rivera 3.00 1.20
56 Ted Wills 3.00 1.20
57 Milt Pappas 4.00 1.60
58 Hal Smith * 3.00 1.20
59 Bobby Avila 3.00 1.20
60 Clem Labine 5.00 2.00
61 Norman Rehm * 3.00 1.20
62 John Gabler 4.00 1.60
63 John Tsitouris 3.00 1.20
64 Dave Sisler 3.00 1.20
65 Vic Power 4.00 1.60
66 Earl Battey 3.00 1.20
67 Bob Purkey 3.00 1.20
68 Moe Drabowsky 4.00 1.60
69 Hoyt Wilhelm 15.00 6.00
70 Humberto Robinson 3.00 1.20
71 Whitey Herzog 8.00 3.20
72 Dick Donovan * 3.00 1.20
73 Gordon Jones 30.00 12.00
74 Joe Hicks 30.00 12.00
75 Ray Culp RC 40.00 16.00
76 Dick Drott 30.00 12.00
77 Bob Duliba 30.00 12.00
78 Art Ditmar 30.00 12.00
79 Steve Korcheck 30.00 12.00
80 Henry Mason 30.00 12.00
81 Harry Simpson 30.00 12.00
82 Gene Green 30.00 12.00
83 Bob Shaw 30.00 12.00
84 Howard Reed 30.00 12.00
85 Dick Stigman 30.00 12.00
86 Rip Repulski 30.00 12.00
87 Seth Morehead 30.00 12.00
88 Camilo Carreon 30.00 12.00
89 John Blanchard 40.00 16.00
90 Billy Hoeft 30.00 12.00
91 Fred Hopke 30.00 12.00
92 Joe Martin 30.00 12.00
93 Wally Shannon 30.00 12.00
94 Hal R. Smith 40.00 16.00
Hal W. Smith
95 Al Schroll 30.00 12.00
96 John Kucks 30.00 12.00
97 Tom Morgan 30.00 12.00
98 Willie Jones 30.00 12.00
99 Marshall Renfroe 30.00 12.00
100 Willie Tasby 30.00 12.00
101 Irv Noren 30.00 12.00
102 Russ Snyder 30.00 12.00
103 Bob Turley 40.00 16.00
104 Jim Woods 30.00 12.00
105 Ronnie Kline 30.00 12.00
106 Steve Bilko 30.00 12.00
107 Elmer Valo 30.00 12.00
108 Tom McAvoy 30.00 12.00
109 Stan Williams 30.00 12.00
110 Earl Averill Jr. 30.00 12.00
111 Lee Walls 30.00 12.00
112 Paul Richards MG 30.00 12.00
113 Ed Sadowski 30.00 12.00
114 Stover McIlwain 30.00 12.00
115 Chuck Tanner UER 40.00 16.00
(Photo actually
Ken Kuhn)
116 Lou Klimchock 30.00 12.00
117 Neil Chrisley 30.00 12.00
118 John Callison 50.00 20.00
119 Hal Smith 30.00 12.00
120 Carl Sawatski 30.00 12.00
121 Frank Leja 30.00 12.00
122 Earl Torgeson 30.00 12.00
123 Art Schult 30.00 12.00
124 Jim Brosnan 30.00 12.00
125 Sparky Anderson 60.00 24.00
126 Joe Pignatano 30.00 12.00
127 Rocky Nelson 30.00 12.00
128 Orlando Cepeda 80.00 32.00
129 Daryl Spencer 30.00 12.00
130 Ralph Lumenti 30.00 12.00
131 Sam Taylor 30.00 12.00
132 Harry Brecheen CO 40.00 16.00
133 Johnny Groth 30.00 12.00
134 Wayne Terwilliger 30.00 12.00
135 Kent Hadley 30.00 12.00
136 Faye Throneberry 30.00 12.00
137 Jack Meyer 30.00 12.00
138 Chuck Cottier RC 30.00 12.00
139 Joe DeMaestri 30.00 12.00
140 Gene Freese 30.00 12.00
141 Curt Flood 50.00 20.00
142 Gino Cimoli 30.00 12.00
143 Clay Dalrymple 30.00 12.00
144 Jim Bunning 80.00 20.00

1985 Leaf/Donruss

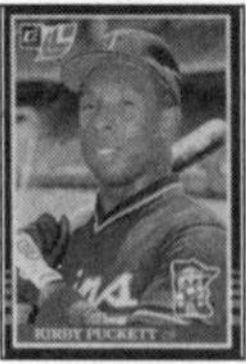

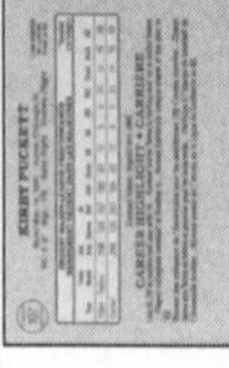

This standard-size set of cards was produced in an effort to establish a Canadian baseball card market much as Topps' affiliate O-Pee-Chee had done. The Donruss Company in conjunction with its new parent Leaf Company issued this set to the Canadian market. The set was later released in the United States through hobby dealer channels. The cards were issued in wax packs. A piece of a large Lou Gehrig puzzle was inserted in each pack. Aside from card number differences the cards are essentially the same as the Donruss U.S. regular issue of the cards of the same players; however the backs are in both French and English. Two cards, Dick Perez artwork of Tim Raines (252) and Dave Stieb (251), are called Canadian Greats (CG) and are not contained in the Donruss U.S. set. As in most Canadian sets, the players featured are heavily biased towards Canadian teams and those American teams closest to the Canadian border. Diamond Kings (numbers 1-26 denoted DK) and Rated Rookies (number 27 denoted RR) are included just as in the American set. Those players selected for and included as Diamond Kings do not have a regular card in the set. The player cards are numbered on the back. The checklist cards (listed at the end of the list below) are numbered one, two and three (but are not given a traditional card number); the Diamond Kings checklist card is unnumbered; and the Lou Gehrig puzzle card is mistakenly numbered 635. Key cards in this set include Roger Clemens and Dwight Gooden in their Rookie Card year.

Nm-Mt Ex-Mt
COMPLETE SET (264) 50.00 20.00
1 Ryne Sandberg DK 2.00 .80
2 Doug DeCinces DK .05 .02
3 Richard Dotson DK .05 .02
4 Bert Blyleven DK .10 .04
5 Lou Whitaker DK .15 .06
6 Dan Quisenberry DK .05 .02
7 Don Mattingly DK 3.00 1.20
8 Carney Lansford DK .05 .02
9 Frank Tanana DK .05 .02
10 Willie Upshaw DK .05 .02
11 C.Washington DK .05 .02
12 Mike Marshall DK .05 .02
13 Joaquin Andujar DK .05 .02
14 Cal Ripken DK 4.00 1.60
15 Jim Rice DK .10 .04
16 Don Sutton DK .40 .16
17 Frank Viola DK .10 .04
18 Alvin Davis DK .05 .02
19 Mario Soto DK .05 .02
20 Jose Cruz DK .10 .04
21 Charlie Lea DK .05 .02
22 Jesse Orosco DK .10 .04
23 Juan Samuel DK .05 .02
24 Tony Pena DK .10 .04
25 Tony Gwynn DK 5.00 2.00
26 Bob Brenly DK .10 .04
27 Steve Kiefer RR .05 .02
28 Joe Morgan .50 .20
29 Luis Leal .05 .02
30 Dan Gladden .10 .04
31 Shane Rawley .05 .02
32 Mark Clear .05 .02
33 Terry Kennedy .05 .02
34 Hal McRae .10 .04
35 Mickey Rivers .05 .02
36 Tom Brunansky .05 .02
37 LaMarr Hoyt .05 .02
38 Orel Hershiser 1.50 .60
39 Chris Bando .05 .02
40 Lee Lacy .05 .02
41 Lance Parrish .10 .04
42 George Foster .10 .04
43 Kevin McReynolds .05 .02
44 Robin Yount .50 .20
45 Craig McMurtry .05 .02
46 Mike Witt .05 .02
47 Gary Redus .05 .02
48 Dennis Rasmussen .05 .02
49 Gary Woods .05 .02
50 Phil Bradley .10 .04
51 Steve Bedrosian .05 .02
52 Duane Walker .05 .02
53 Geoff Zahn .05 .02
54 Dave Stieb .05 .02
55 Pascual Perez .05 .02
56 Mark Langston .20 .08
57 Bob Dernier .05 .02
58 Joe Cowley .05 .02
59 Dan Schatzeder .05 .02
60 Ozzie Smith 1.50 .60
61 Bob Knepper .05 .02
62 Keith Hernandez .10 .04
63 Rick Rhoden .05 .02
64 Alejandro Pena .05 .02
65 Damaso Garcia .05 .02
66 Chili Davis .10 .04
67 Al Oliver .10 .04
68 Alan Wiggins .05 .02
69 Darryl Motley .05 .02
70 Gary Ward .05 .02
71 John Butcher .05 .02
72 Scott McGregor .05 .02
73 Bruce Hurst .05 .02
74 Dwayne Murphy .05 .02
75 Greg Luzinski .10 .04
76 Pat Tabler .05 .02
77 Chet Lemon .05 .02
78 Jim Sundberg .05 .02
79 Wally Backman .05 .02
80 Terry Puhl .05 .02
81 Storm Davis .05 .02
82 Jim Wohlford .05 .02
83 Willie Randolph .10 .04
84 Ron Cey .10 .04
85 Jim Beattie .05 .02
86 Rafael Ramirez .05 .02
87 Cesar Cedeno .10 .04
88 Bobby Grich .10 .04
89 Jason Thompson .05 .02
90 Steve Sax .05 .02
91 Tony Fernandez .20 .08
92 Jeff Leonard .05 .02
93 Von Hayes .05 .02
94 Steve Garvey .20 .08
95 Steve Balboni .05 .02
96 Larry Parrish .05 .02
97 Tim Teufel .05 .02
98 Sammy Stewart .05 .02
99 Roger Clemens RC 20.00 8.00
100 Steve Kemp .05 .02
101 Tom Seaver .75 .30
102 Andre Thornton .05 .02
103 Kirk Gibson .15 .06
104 Ted Simmons .10 .04
105 David Palmer .05 .02
106 Roy Lee Jackson .05 .02
107 Kirby Puckett RC 5.00 2.00
108 Charlie Hough .10 .04
109 Mike Boddicker .05 .02
110 Willie Wilson .05 .02
111 Tim Lollar .05 .02
112 Tony Armas .05 .02
113 Steve Carlton .50 .20
114 Gary Lavelle .05 .02
115 Cliff Johnson .05 .02
116 Ray Burris .05 .02
117 Rudy Law .05 .02
118 Mike Scioscia .15 .06
119 Kent Tekulve UER .10 .04
(Telukve on back)
120 George Vukovich .05 .02
121 Barbaro Garbey .05 .02
122 Mookie Wilson .10 .04
123 Ben Oglivie .05 .02
124 Jerry Mumphrey .05 .02
125 Willie McGee .10 .04
126 Jeff Reardon .10 .04
127 Dave Winfield .75 .30
128 Lee Smith .15 .06
129 Ken Phelps .05 .02
130 Rick Camp .05 .02
131 Dave Concepcion .10 .04
132 Rod Carew .50 .20
133 Andre Dawson .20 .08
134 Doyle Alexander .05 .02
135 Miguel Dilone .05 .02
136 Jim Gott .05 .02
137 Eric Show .05 .02
138 Phil Niekro .20 .08
139 Rick Sutcliffe .05 .02
140 Dave Winfield 1.50 .60
Don Mattingly
141 Ken Oberkfell .05 .02
142 Jack Morris .10 .04
143 Lloyd Moseby .05 .02
144 Pete Rose 1.25 .50
145 Gary Gaetti .10 .04
146 Don Baylor .10 .04
147 Bobby Meacham .05 .02
148 Frank White .10 .04
149 Mark Thurmond .05 .02
150 Dwight Evans .10 .04
151 Al Holland .05 .02
152 Joel Youngblood .05 .02
153 Rance Mulliniks .05 .02
154 Bill Caudill .05 .02
155 Carlton Fisk .75 .30
156 Rick Honeycutt .05 .02
157 John Candelaria .05 .02
158 Alan Trammell .15 .06
159 Darryl Strawberry .20 .08
160 Aurelio Lopez .05 .02
161 Enos Cabell .05 .02
162 Dion James .05 .02
163 Bruce Sutter .10 .04
164 Razor Shines .05 .02
165 Butch Wynegar .05 .02
166 Rich Bordi .05 .02
167 Spike Owen .05 .02
168 Chris Chambliss .05 .02
169 Dave Parker .10 .04
170 Reggie Jackson .75 .30
171 Bryn Smith .05 .02
172 Dave Collins .05 .02
173 Dave Engle .05 .02
174 Buddy Bell .05 .02
175 Mike Flanagan .05 .02
176 George Brett 2.50 1.00
177 Graig Nettles .10 .04
178 Jerry Koosman .05 .02
179 Wade Boggs 1.50 .60
180 Jody Davis .05 .02
181 Ernie Whitt .05 .02
182 Dave Kingman .10 .04
183 Vance Law .05 .02
184 Fernando Valenzuela .10 .04
185 Bill Madlock .05 .02
186 Brett Butler .10 .04
187 Doug Sisk .05 .02
188 Dan Petry .05 .02
189 Joe Niekro .05 .02
190 Rollie Fingers .20 .08
191 David Green .05 .02
192 Steve Rogers .05 .02
193 Ken Griffey .10 .04
194 Scott Sanderson .05 .02
195 Barry Bonnell .05 .02
196 Bruce Benedict .05 .02
197 Keith Moreland .05 .02
198 Fred Lynn .10 .04
199 Tim Wallach .05 .02
200 Kent Hrbek .10 .04
201 Pete O'Brien .05 .02
202 Bud Black .05 .02
203 Eddie Murray 1.50 .60
204 Goose Gossage .10 .04
205 Mike Schmidt 1.25 .50
206 Mike Easler .05 .02
207 Jack Clark .10 .04
208 Rickey Henderson 1.25 .50
209 Jesse Barfield .05 .02
210 Ron Kittle .05 .02
211 Pedro Guerrero .05 .02
212 Johnny Ray .05 .02
213 Julio Franco .10 .04
214 Hubie Brooks .05 .02
215 Darrell Evans .10 .04
216 Nolan Ryan 5.00 2.00
217 Jim Gantner .05 .02
218 Tim Raines .10 .04
219 Dave Righetti .05 .02
220 Gary Matthews .05 .02
221 Jack Perconte .05 .02
222 Dale Murphy .20 .08
223 Brian Downing .05 .02
224 Mickey Hatcher .05 .02
225 Lonnie Smith .05 .02
226 Jorge Orta .05 .02
227 Milt Wilcox .05 .02
228 John Denny .05 .02
229 Marty Barrett .05 .02
230 Alfredo Griffin .05 .02
231 Harold Baines .15 .06
232 Bill Russell .05 .02
233 Marvell Wynne .05 .02
234 Dwight Gooden 1.50 .60
235 Willie Hernandez .05 .02
236 Bill Gullickson .05 .02
237 Ron Guidry .10 .04
238 Leon Durham .05 .02
239 Al Cowens .05 .02
240 Bob Horner .05 .02
241 Gary Carter .50 .20
242 Glenn Hubbard .05 .02
243 Steve Trout .05 .02
244 Jay Howell .05 .02
245 Terry Francona .10 .04
246 Cecil Cooper .10 .04
247 Larry McWilliams .05 .02
248 George Bell .05 .02
249 Larry Herndon .05 .02
250 Ozzie Virgil .05 .02
251 Dave Stieb CG .10 .04
252 Tim Raines CG .20 .08
253 Ricky Horton .05 .02
254 Bill Buckner .10 .04
255 Dan Driessen .05 .02
256 Ron Darling .05 .02
257 Doug Flynn .05 .02
258 Darrell Porter .05 .02
259 George Hendrick .05 .02
260 Checklist DK 1-26 .05 .02
(Unnumbered)
261 Checklist 27-106 .05 .02
(Unnumbered)
262 Checklist 107-178 .05 .02
(Unnumbered)
263 Checklist 179-259 .05 .02
(Unnumbered)
635 Lou Gehrig .20 .08
Puzzle Card UER
(Misnumbered)

1986 Leaf/Donruss

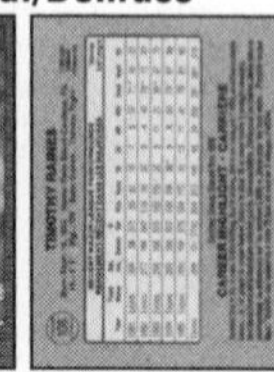

This 264-card standard-size set was issued with a puzzle of Hank Aaron. Except for the numbering, the company logo and the bilingual backs, the cards are essentially the same as the Donruss U.S. regular issue cards of the same players. On a light blue background, the horizontal backs carry player biography, statistics and career highlights in French and English. Two cards, Dick Perez artwork of Jesse Barfield (254) and Jeff Reardon (214), are called Canadian Greats (CG) and are not contained in the Donruss U.S. set. Diamond Kings (numbers 1-26, denoted DK) and Rated Rookies (numbers 27-29, denoted RR) are included just as in the American set. The cards are numbered on the back. As in most Canadian sets, the players featured are heavily biased toward Canadian teams and those American teams closest to the Canadian border. Those players selected for and included as Diamond Kings do not have a regular card in the set. The checklist cards (listed at the end of the list below) are numbered one, two and three (but are not given a traditional card number); the Diamond Kings checklist card is also unnumbered. Two key cards in this set are Andres Galarraga and Fred McGriff, who are Rookie Cards in the 1986 Donruss set.

Nm-Mt Ex-Mt
COMPLETE SET (264) 20.00 8.00
1 Kirk Gibson DK .20 .08
2 Goose Gossage DK .15 .06
3 Willie McGee DK .10 .04
4 George Bell DK .05 .02
5 Tony Armas DK .05 .02
6 Chili Davis DK .10 .04
7 Cecil Cooper DK .10 .04
8 Mike Boddicker DK .05 .02
9 Davey Lopes DK .05 .02
10 Bill Doran DK .05 .02
11 Bret Saberhagen DK .10 .04
12 Brett Butler DK .10 .04
13 Harold Baines DK .15 .06
14 Mike Davis DK .05 .02
15 Tony Perez DK .40 .16
16 Willie Randolph DK .10 .04
17 Bob Boone DK .10 .04
18 Orel Hershiser DK .15 .06
19 Johnny Ray DK .05 .02
20 Gary Ward DK .05 .02
21 Rick Mahler DK .05 .02
22 Phil Bradley DK .05 .02
23 Jerry Koosman DK .10 .04
24 Tom Brunansky DK .05 .02
25 Andre Dawson DK .20 .08
26 Dwight Gooden DK .20 .08
27 A.Galarraga RR RC 5.00 2.00
28 Fred McGriff RR RC 5.00 2.00
29 Dave Shipanoff RR .05 .02
30 Danny Jackson .05 .02
31 Robin Yount .40 .16
32 Mike Fitzgerald .05 .02
33 Lou Whitaker .10 .04
34 Alfredo Griffin .05 .02
35 Oil Can Boyd .05 .02
36 Ron Guidry .10 .04
37 Rickey Henderson .75 .30
38 Jack Morris .10 .04
39 Brian Downing .05 .02
40 Mike Marshall .05 .02
41 Tony Gwynn 1.50 .60
42 George Brett 1.25 .50
43 Jim Gantner .05 .02
44 Hubie Brooks .05 .02
45 Tony Fernandez .10 .04
46 Oddibe McDowell .05 .02
47 Ozzie Smith 1.00 .40
48 Ken Griffey .10 .04
49 Jose Cruz .10 .04
50 Mariano Duncan .10 .04
51 Mike Schmidt .60 .24
52 Pat Tabler .05 .02
53 Pete Rose .60 .24
54 Frank White .10 .04
55 Carney Lansford .05 .02
56 Steve Garvey .20 .08
57 Vance Law .05 .02
58 Tony Pena .10 .04
59 Wayne Tolleson .05 .02

60 Dale Murphy .20 .08
61 LaMarr Hoyt .05 .02
62 Ryne Sandberg 1.00 .40
63 Gary Carter .50 .20
64 Lee Smith .15 .06
65 Alvin Davis .05 .02
66 Edwin Nunez .05 .02
67 Kent Hrbek .10 .04
68 Dave Stieb .10 .04
69 Kirby Puckett 1.25 .50
70 Paul Molitor .60 .24
71 Glenn Hubbard .05 .02
72 Lloyd Moseby .05 .02
73 Mike Smithson .05 .02
74 Jeff Leonard .05 .02
75 Danny Darwin .05 .02
76 Kevin McReynolds .05 .02
77 Bill Buckner .10 .04
78 Ron Oester .05 .02
79 Tommy Herr .05 .02
80 Mike Pagliarulo .05 .02
81 Ron Romanick .05 .02
82 Brook Jacoby .05 .02
83 Eddie Murray .75 .30
84 Gary Pettis .05 .02
85 Chet Lemon .05 .02
86 Toby Harrah .05 .02
87 Mike Scioscia .15 .06
88 Bert Blyleven .10 .04
89 Dave Righetti .05 .02
90 Bob Knepper .05 .02
91 Fernando Valenzuela .10 .04
92 Dave Dravecky .10 .04
93 Julio Franco .10 .04
94 Keith Moreland .05 .02
95 Darryl Motley .05 .02
96 Jack Clark .10 .04
97 Tim Wallach .05 .02
98 Steve Balboni .05 .02
99 Storm Davis .05 .02
100 Jay Howell .05 .02
101 Alan Trammell .15 .06
102 Willie Hernandez .05 .02
103 Don Mattingly 1.50 .60
104 Lee Lacy .05 .02
105 Pedro Guerrero .05 .02
106 Willie Wilson .05 .02
107 Craig Reynolds .05 .02
108 Tim Raines .10 .04
109 Shane Rawley .05 .02
110 Larry Parrish .05 .02
111 Eric Show .05 .02
112 Mike Witt .05 .02
113 Dennis Eckersley .50 .20
114 Mike Moore .05 .02
115 Vince Coleman .10 .04
116 Damaso Garcia .05 .02
117 Steve Carlton .40 .16
118 Floyd Bannister .05 .02
119 Mario Soto .05 .02
120 Fred Lynn .10 .04
121 Bob Horner .05 .02
122 Rick Sutcliffe .05 .02
123 Walt Terrell .05 .02
124 Keith Hernandez .10 .04
125 Dave Winfield .50 .20
126 Frank Viola .10 .04
127 Dwight Evans .10 .04
128 Willie Upshaw .05 .02
129 Andre Thornton .05 .02
130 Donnie Moore .05 .02
131 Darryl Strawberry .10 .04
132 Nolan Ryan 2.50 1.00
133 Garry Templeton .05 .02
134 John Tudor .05 .02
135 Dave Parker .10 .04
136 Larry McWilliams .05 .02
137 Terry Pendleton .10 .04
138 Terry Puhl .05 .02
139 Bob Dernier .05 .02
140 Ozzie Guillen RC* .20 .08
141 Jim Clancy .05 .02
142 Cal Ripken 2.50 1.00
143 Mickey Hatcher .05 .02
144 Dan Petry .05 .02
145 Rich Gedman .05 .02
146 Jim Rice .10 .04
147 Butch Wynegar .05 .02
148 Donnie Hill .05 .02
149 Jim Sundberg .05 .02
150 Joe Hesketh .05 .02
151 Chris Codiroli .05 .02
152 Charlie Hough .10 .04
153 Herm Winningham .05 .02
154 Dave Rozema .05 .02
155 Don Slaught .05 .02
156 Juan Beniquez .05 .02
157 Ted Higuera .05 .02
158 Andy Hawkins .05 .02
159 Don Robinson .05 .02
160 Glenn Wilson .05 .02
161 Earnest Riles .05 .02
162 Nick Esasky .05 .02
163 Carlton Fisk .40 .16
164 Claudell Washington .05 .02
165 Scott McGregor .05 .02
166 Nate Snell .05 .02
167 Ted Simmons .10 .04
168 Wade Boggs .50 .20
169 Marty Barrett .05 .02
170 Bud Black .05 .02
171 Charlie Leibrandt .05 .02
172 Charlie Lea .05 .02
173 Reggie Jackson .50 .20
174 Bryn Smith .05 .02
175 Glenn Davis .05 .02
176 Von Hayes .05 .02
177 Danny Cox .05 .02
178 Sammy Khalifa .05 .02
179 Tom Browning .05 .02
180 Scott Garrelts .05 .02
181 Shawon Dunston .10 .04
182 Doyle Alexander .05 .02
183 Jim Presley .05 .02
184 Al Cowens .05 .02
185 Mark Salas .05 .02
186 Tom Niedenfuer .05 .02
187 Dave Henderson .05 .02
188 Lonnie Smith .05 .02
189 Bruce Bochte .05 .02
190 Leon Durham .05 .02
191 Terry Francona .05 .02
192 Bruce Sutter .10 .04
193 Steve Crawford .05 .02
194 Bob Brenly .10 .04
195 Dan Pasqua .05 .02
196 Juan Samuel .05 .02
197 Floyd Rayford .05 .02
198 Tim Burke .05 .02
199 Ben Oglivie .05 .02
200 Don Carman .05 .02
201 Lance Parrish .10 .04
202 Terry Forster .05 .02
203 Neal Heaton .05 .02
204 Ivan Calderon .05 .02
205 Jorge Orta .05 .02
206 Tom Henke .05 .02
207 Rick Reuschel .10 .04
208 Dan Quisenberry .10 .04
209 Pete Rose HL 1.25 .50
210 Floyd Youmans .05 .02
211 Tom Filer .05 .02
212 R.J. Reynolds .05 .02
213 Gorman Thomas .05 .02
214 Jeff Reardon CG .10 .04
215 Chris Brown .05 .02
216 Rick Aguilera .15 .06
217 Ernie Whitt .05 .02
218 Joe Orsulak .05 .02
219 Jimmy Key .15 .06
220 Atlee Hammaker .05 .02
221 Ron Darling .10 .04
222 Zane Smith .05 .02
223 Bob Welch .10 .04
224 Reid Nichols .05 .02
225 Vince Coleman .10 .04
Willie McGee
226 Mark Gubicza .05 .02
227 Tim Birtsas .05 .02
228 Mike Hargrove .10 .04
229 Randy St. Claire .05 .02
230 Larry Herndon .05 .02
231 Dusty Baker .10 .04
232 Mookie Wilson .10 .04
233 Jeff Lahti .05 .02
234 Tom Seaver .50 .20
235 Mike Scott .05 .02
236 Don Sutton .40 .16
237 Roy Smalley .05 .02
238 Bill Madlock .10 .04
239 Charlie Hudson .05 .02
Charles on both sides
240 John Franco .20 .08
241 Frank Tanana .10 .04
242 Sid Fernandez .05 .02
243 Phil Niekro .20 .08
Joe Niekro
244 Dennis Lamp .05 .02
245 Gene Nelson .05 .02
246 Terry Harper .05 .02
247 Vida Blue .10 .04
248 Roger McDowell .20 .08
249 Tony Bernazard .05 .02
250 Cliff Johnson .05 .02
251 Hal McRae .10 .04
252 Garth Iorg .05 .02
253 Mitch Webster .05 .02
254 Jesse Barfield CG .10 .04
255 Dan Driessen .05 .02
256 Mike Brown .05 .02
257 Ron Kittle .05 .02
258 Bo Diaz .05 .02
259 Hank Aaron Puzzle .20 .08
260 Pete Rose KING 1.25 .50
261 Checklist DK 1-26 .05 .02
Unnumbered
262 Checklist 27-106 .05 .02
Unnumbered
263 Checklist 107-186 .05 .02
Unnumbered
264 Checklist 187-260 .05 .02
Unnumbered

1987 Leaf/Donruss

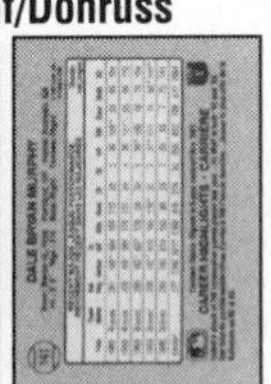

This 264-card standard-size set was issued with a puzzle of Roberto Clemente. Except for the numbering, the company logo and the bilingual backs, the cards are essentially the same as the Donruss U.S. regular issue cards of the same players. On a golden background, the horizontal backs carry player biography, statistics and career highlights in French and English. Two cards, Dick Perez artwork of Floyd Youmans (65) and Mark Eichhorn (173), are called Canadian Greats (CG) and are not contained in the Donruss U.S. set. Diamond Kings (numbers 1-26, denoted DK) and Rated Rookies (numbers 28-47, denoted RR) are included just as in the American set. The players featured in this set are heavily biased toward Canadian teams and those American teams closest to the Canadian border. Players appearing in their Rookie Card year include Will Clark, Wally Joyner and Greg Maddux. There is also a early Mark McGwire card in this set.

Nm-Mt Ex-Mt
COMPLETE SET (264) 50.00 20.00
1 Wally Joyner DK .20 .08
2 Roger Clemens DK 1.00 .40
3 Dale Murphy DK .20 .08
4 Darryl Strawberry DK .10 .04
5 Ozzie Smith DK .50 .20
6 Jose Canseco DK .60 .24
7 Charlie Hough DK .05 .02
8 Brook Jacoby DK .05 .02
9 Fred Lynn DK .10 .04
10 Rick Rhoden DK .05 .02
11 Chris Brown DK .05 .02
12 Von Hayes DK .05 .02
13 Jack Morris DK .10 .04
14 Kevin McReynolds DK .05 .02
15 George Brett DK .60 .24
16 Ted Higuera DK .05 .02
17 Hubie Brooks DK .05 .02
18 Mike Scott DK .05 .02
19 Kirby Puckett DK .25 .10
20 Dave Winfield DK .30 .12
21 Lloyd Moseby DK .05 .02
22 Eric Davis DK .15 .06
23 Jim Presley DK .05 .02
24 Keith Moreland DK .05 .02
25 Greg Walker DK .05 .02
26 Steve Sax DK .05 .02
27 DK Checklist 1-26 .05 .02
28 B.J. Surhoff RR RC .50 .20
29 Randy Myers RR RC .20 .08
30 Ken Gerhart RR .05 .02
31 Benito Santiago RR .15 .06
32 Greg Swindell RR RC .10 .04
33 Mike Birkbeck RR .05 .02
34 Terry Steinbach RR RC .20 .08
35 Bo Jackson RR RC 1.50 .60
36 Greg Maddux RR RC 10.00 4.00
37 Jim Lindeman RR .05 .02
38 Devon White RR RC .30 .12
39 Eric Bell RR .05 .02
40 Will Fraser RR .05 .02
41 Jerry Browne RR .05 .02
42 Chris James RR .05 .02
43 Rafael Palmeiro RR RC 5.00 2.00
44 Pat Dodson RR .05 .02
45 Duane Ward RR .10 .04
46 Mark McGwire RR 10.00 4.00
47 Bruce Fields RR .05 .02
48 Jody Davis .05 .02
49 Roger McDowell .05 .02
50 Jose Guzman .05 .02
51 Oddibe McDowell .05 .02
52 Harold Baines .15 .06
53 Dave Righetti .05 .02
54 Moose Haas .05 .02
55 Mark Langston .05 .02
56 Kirby Puckett .50 .20
57 Dwight Evans .10 .04
58 Willie Randolph .10 .04
59 Wally Backman .05 .02
60 Bryn Smith .05 .02
61 Tim Wallach .05 .02
62 Joe Hesketh .05 .02
63 Garry Templeton .05 .02
64 Robby Thompson .10 .04
65 Floyd Youmans CG .10 .04
66 Ernest Riles .05 .02
67 Robin Yount .40 .16
68 Darryl Strawberry .10 .04
69 Ernie Whitt .05 .02
70 Dave Winfield .40 .16
71 Paul Molitor .40 .16
72 Dave Stieb .10 .04
73 Tom Henke .05 .02
74 Frank Viola .05 .02
75 Scott Garrelts .05 .02
76 Mike Boddicker .05 .02
77 Keith Moreland .05 .02
78 Lou Whitaker .10 .04
79 Dave Parker .10 .04
80 Lee Smith .15 .06
81 Tom Candiotti .05 .02
82 Greg A. Harris .05 .02
83 Fred Lynn .10 .04
84 Dwight Gooden .10 .04
85 Ron Darling .05 .02
86 Mike Krukow .05 .02
87 Spike Owen .05 .02
88 Len Dykstra .15 .06
89 Rick Aguilera .10 .04
90 Jim Clancy .05 .02
91 Joe Johnson .05 .02
92 Damaso Garcia .05 .02
93 Sid Fernandez .05 .02
94 Bob Ojeda .05 .02
95 Ted Higuera .05 .02
96 George Brett 1.00 .40
97 Willie Wilson .10 .04
98 Cal Ripken 2.50 1.00
99 Kent Hrbek .10 .04
100 Bert Blyleven .10 .04
101 Ron Guidry .10 .04
102 Andy Allanson .05 .02
103 Dave Henderson .05 .02
104 Kirk Gibson .10 .04
105 Lloyd Moseby .05 .02
106 Tony Fernandez .10 .04
107 Lance Parrish .10 .04
108 Ozzie Smith .60 .24
109 Gary Carter .50 .20
110 Eddie Murray .50 .20
111 Mike Witt .05 .02
112 Bobby Witt .10 .04
113 Willie McGee .10 .04
114 Steve Garvey .15 .06
115 Glenn Davis .05 .02
116 Jose Cruz .10 .04
117 Ozzie Guillen .10 .04
118 Alvin Davis .05 .02
119 Jose Rijo .05 .02
120 Bill Madlock .10 .04
121 Tommy Herr .05 .02
122 Mike Schmidt .60 .24
123 Mike Scioscia .15 .06
124 Terry Pendleton .10 .04
125 Leon Durham .05 .02
126 Alan Trammell .15 .06
127 Jesse Barfield .05 .02
128 Shawon Dunston .05 .02
129 Pete Rose .60 .24
130 Von Hayes .05 .02
131 Julio Franco .10 .04
132 Juan Samuel .05 .02
133 Joe Carter .20 .08
134 Brook Jacoby .05 .02
135 Jack Morris .10 .04
136 Bob Horner .05 .02
137 Calvin Schiraldi .05 .02
138 Tom Browning .05 .02
139 Shane Rawley .05 .02
140 Mario Soto .05 .02
141 Dale Murphy .20 .08
142 Hubie Brooks .05 .02
143 Jeff Reardon .10 .04
144 Will Clark 2.00 .80
145 Ed Correa .05 .02
146 Glenn Wilson .05 .02
147 Johnny Ray .05 .02
148 Fernando Valenzuela .10 .04
149 Tim Raines .10 .04
150 Don Mattingly 1.25 .50
151 Jose Canseco .60 .24
152 Gary Pettis .05 .02
153 Don Sutton .40 .16
154 Jim Presley .05 .02
155 Checklist 28-105 .05 .02
156 Dale Sveum .05 .02
157 Cory Snyder .05 .02
158 Jeff Sellers .05 .02
159 Denny Walling .05 .02
160 Danny Cox .05 .02
161 Bob Forsch .05 .02
162 Joaquin Andujar .05 .02
163 Roberto Clemente .20 .08
Puzzle Card
164 Paul Assenmacher .10 .04
165 Marty Barrett .05 .02
166 Ray Knight .05 .02
167 Rafael Santana .05 .02
168 Bruce Ruffin .05 .02
169 Buddy Bell .10 .04
170 Kevin Mitchell .20 .08
171 Ken Oberkfell .05 .02
172 Gene Garber .05 .02
173 Mark Eichhorn CG .10 .04
174 Don Carman .05 .02
175 Jesse Orosco .10 .04
176 Mookie Wilson .10 .04
177 Gary Ward .05 .02
178 John Franco .10 .04
179 Eric Davis .15 .06
180 Walt Terrell .05 .02
181 Phil Niekro .40 .16
182 Pat Tabler .05 .02
183 Brett Butler .10 .04
184 George Bell .05 .02
185 Pete Incaviglia .10 .04
186 Pete O'Brien .05 .02
187 Jimmy Key .15 .06
188 Frank White .10 .04
189 Mike Pagliarulo .05 .02
190 Roger Clemens 1.25 .50
191 Rickey Henderson .75 .30
192 Mike Easler .05 .02
193 Wade Boggs .40 .16
194 Vince Coleman .05 .02
195 Charlie Kerfeld .05 .02
196 Dickie Thon .05 .02
197 Bill Doran .05 .02
198 Alfredo Griffin .05 .02
199 Carlton Fisk .40 .16
200 Phil Bradley .05 .02
201 Reggie Jackson .50 .20
202 Bob Boone .10 .04
203 Steve Sax .05 .02
204 Tom Niedenfuer .05 .02
205 Tim Burke .05 .02
206 Floyd Youmans .05 .02
207 Jay Tibbs .05 .02
208 Chili Davis .15 .06
209 Larry Parrish .05 .02
210 John Cerutti .05 .02
211 Kevin Bass .05 .02
212 Andre Dawson .20 .08
213 Bob Sebra .05 .02
214 Kevin McReynolds .05 .02
215 Jim Morrison .05 .02
216 Candy Maldonado .05 .02
217 John Kruk .20 .08
218 Todd Worrell .10 .04
219 Barry Bonds RC* 20.00 8.00
220 Andy McGaffigan .05 .02
221 Andres Galarraga .40 .16
222 Mike Fitzgerald .05 .02
223 Kirk McCaskill .05 .02
224 Dave Smith .05 .02
225 Ruben Sierra RC .50 .20
226 Scott Fletcher .05 .02
227 Chet Lemon .05 .02
228 Dan Petry .05 .02
229 Mark Eichhorn .05 .02
230 Cecil Cooper .10 .04
231 Willie Upshaw .05 .02
232 Don Baylor .10 .04
233 Keith Hernandez .10 .04
234 Ryne Sandberg .75 .30
235 Tony Gwynn 1.25 .50
236 Chris Brown .05 .02
237 Pedro Guerrero .05 .02
238 Mark Gubicza .05 .02
239 Sid Bream .05 .02
240 Joe Cowley .05 .02
241 Bill Buckner .10 .04
242 John Candelaria .05 .02
243 Scott McGregor .05 .02
244 Tom Brunansky .05 .02
245 Gary Gaetti .10 .04
246 Orel Hershiser .10 .04
247 Jim Rice .10 .04
248 Oil Can Boyd .05 .02
249 Bob Knepper .05 .02
250 Danny Tartabull .05 .02
251 John Cangelosi .05 .02
252 Wally Joyner RC* .50 .20
253 Bruce Hurst .05 .02
254 Rich Gedman .05 .02
255 Jim Deshaies .05 .02
256 Tony Pena .10 .04
257 Nolan Ryan 2.50 1.00
258 Mike Scott .05 .02
259 Checklist 106-183 .05 .02
260 Dennis Rasmussen .05 .02
261 Bret Saberhagen .10 .04
262 Steve Balboni .05 .02
263 Tom Seaver .40 .16
264 Checklist 184-264 .05 .02

1987 Leaf Special Olympics

This set is also known as the Candy City team as that is the logo which appears on the front

of the card. This set was issued for the proceeds of the set to go to the Special Olympics. The set was in the style of the 1983 Donruss Hall of Fame Heroes set and the only additions were generic cards about various sports. The cards are standard size. These cards were issued in special three card packs which contained two baseball players and one special olympics card. A collector could receive the entire 18 card set by mailing $1 as a donation.

Nm-Mt Ex-Mt
COMPLETE SET (18) 10.00 4.00
COMMON CARD (H1-H12) .25 .10
COMMON CARD (S1-S6) .10 .04
H1 Mickey Mantle 4.00 1.60
H2 Yogi Berra .75 .30
H3 Roy Campanella .75 .30
H4 Stan Musial 1.50 .60
H5 Ted Williams 2.00 .80
H6 Duke Snider .75 .30
H7 Hank Aaron 1.50 .60
H8 Pee Wee Reese .75 .30
H9 Brooks Robinson .50 .20
H10 Al Kaline .50 .20
H11 Willie McCovey .25 .10
H12 Cool Papa Bell .25 .10
S1 Basketball .30 .12
S2 Softball .50 .20
S3 Track And Field .50 .20
S4 Soccer .20 .08
S5 Gymnastics .50 .20
S6 VII International .50 .20
Summer Games

1988 Leaf/Donruss

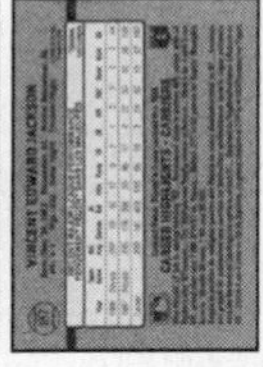

This 264-card standard-size set was issued with a puzzle of Stan Musial. Except for the numbering, the company logo and the bilingual backs, the cards are essentially the same as the Donruss U.S. regular issue cards of the same players. On a light blue background, the horizontal backs carry player biography, statistics, and career highlights in French and English. Two cards, Dick Perez artwork of George Bell (213) and Tim Wallach (255), are called Canadian Greats (CG) and are not contained in the Donruss U.S. set. Diamond Kings (numbers 1-26, denoted DK) and Rated Rookies (numbers 28-47, denoted RR) are included just as in the American set. There are also bonus cards of the two Canadian teams' MVP's, George Bell and Tim Raines, as in the Donruss American set. The players featured are heavily biased toward Canadian teams and those American teams closest to the Canadian border. Players appearing in their Rookie Card year include Roberto Alomar and Mark Grace.

Nm-Mt Ex-Mt
COMPLETE SET (264) 15.00 6.00
1 Mark McGwire DK 2.00 .80
2 Tim Raines DK .10 .04
3 Benito Santiago DK .10 .04
4 Alan Trammell DK .15 .06
5 Danny Tartabull DK .05 .02
6 Ron Darling DK .05 .02
7 Paul Molitor DK .40 .16
8 Devon White DK .05 .02
9 Andre Dawson DK .20 .08
10 Julio Franco DK .10 .04
11 Scott Fletcher DK .05 .02
12 Tony Fernandez DK .10 .04
13 Shane Rawley DK .05 .02
14 Kal Daniels DK .05 .02
15 Jack Clark DK .10 .04
16 Dwight Evans DK .05 .02
17 Tommy John DK .10 .04
18 Andy Van Slyke DK .05 .02
19 Gary Gaetti DK .10 .04
20 Mark Langston DK .05 .02
21 Will Clark DK .40 .16
22 Glenn Hubbard DK .05 .02
23 Billy Hatcher DK .05 .02
24 Bob Welch DK .05 .02
25 Ivan Calderon DK .05 .02
26 Cal Ripken DK 1.50 .60
27 DK Checklist 1-26 .05 .02
28 Mackey Sasser RR RC .05 .02
29 Jeff Treadway RR .05 .02
30 Mike Campbell RR .05 .02
31 Lance Johnson RR RC .15 .06
32 Nelson Liriano RR .05 .02
33 Shawn Abner RR .05 .02
34 Roberto Alomar RR RC 2.00 .80
35 Shawn Hillegas RR .05 .02
36 Joey Meyer RR .05 .02
37 Kevin Elster RR .05 .02
38 Jose Lind RR RC .05 .02
39 Kirt Manwaring RR RC .05 .02
40 Mark Grace RR RC 2.00 .80
41 Jody Reed RR RC .05 .02
42 John Farrell RR .05 .02
43 Al Leiter RR RC .40 .16

44 Gary Thurman RR .05 .02
45 Vicente Palacios RR .05 .02
46 Eddie Williams RR .05 .02
47 Jack McDowell RR RC .20 .08
48 Dwight Gooden .10 .04
49 Mike Witt .05 .02
50 Wally Joyner .15 .06
51 Brook Jacoby .05 .02
52 Bert Blyleven .10 .04
53 Ted Higuera .05 .02
54 Mike Scott .05 .02
55 Jose Guzman .05 .02
56 Roger Clemens .75 .30
57 Dave Righetti .05 .02
58 Benito Santiago .10 .04
59 Ozzie Guillen .10 .04
60 Matt Nokes .05 .02
61 Fernando Valenzuela .10 .04
62 Orel Hershiser .10 .04
63 Sid Fernandez .05 .02
64 Ozzie Virgil .05 .02
65 Wade Boggs .40 .16
66 Floyd Youmans .05 .02
67 Jimmy Key .10 .04
68 Bret Saberhagen .10 .04
69 Jody Davis .05 .02
70 Shawon Dunston .05 .02
71 Julio Franco .10 .04
72 Danny Cox .05 .02
73 Jim Clancy .05 .02
74 Mark Eichhorn .05 .02
75 Scott Bradley .05 .02
76 Charlie Leibrandt .05 .02
77 Nolan Ryan 1.50 .60
78 Ron Darling .05 .02
79 John Franco .10 .04
80 Dave Stieb .05 .02
81 Mike Fitzgerald .05 .02
82 Steve Bedrosian .05 .02
83 Dale Murphy .20 .08
84 Tim Burke .05 .02
85 Jack Morris .10 .04
86 Greg Walker .05 .02
87 Kevin Mitchell .10 .04
88 Doug Drabek .05 .02
89 Charlie Hough .10 .04
90 Tony Gwynn .75 .30
91 Rick Sutcliffe .05 .02
92 Shane Rawley .05 .02
93 George Brett .60 .24
94 Frank Viola .05 .02
95 Tony Pena .05 .02
96 Jim Deshaies .05 .02
97 Mike Scioscia .10 .04
98 Rick Rhoden .05 .02
99 Terry Kennedy .05 .02
100 Cal Ripken 1.50 .60
101 Pedro Guerrero .05 .02
102 Andy Van Slyke .10 .04
103 Willie McGee .10 .04
104 Mike Kingery .05 .02
105 Kevin Seitzer .05 .02
106 Robin Yount .40 .16
107 Tracy Jones .05 .02
108 Dave Magadan .05 .02
109 Mel Hall .05 .02
110 Billy Hatcher .05 .02
111 Todd Benzinger .05 .02
112 Mike LaValliere .05 .02
113 Barry Bonds 1.00 .40
114 Tim Raines .10 .04
115 Ozzie Smith .50 .20
116 Dave Winfield .40 .16
117 Keith Hernandez .10 .04
118 Jeffrey Leonard .05 .02
119 Larry Parrish .05 .02
120 Robby Thompson .05 .02
121 Andres Galarraga .20 .08
122 Mickey Hatcher .05 .02
123 Mark Langston .05 .02
124 Mike Schmidt .60 .24
125 Cory Snyder .05 .02
126 Andre Dawson .20 .08
127 Devon White .05 .02
128 Vince Coleman .05 .02
129 Bryn Smith .05 .02
130 Lance Parrish .05 .02
131 Willie Upshaw .05 .02
132 Pete O'Brien .05 .02
133 Tony Fernandez .10 .04
134 Billy Ripken .05 .02
135 Len Dykstra .10 .04
136 Kirk Gibson .10 .04
137 Kevin Bass .05 .02
138 Jose Canseco .50 .20
139 Kent Hrbek .10 .04
140 Lloyd Moseby .05 .02
141 Marty Barrett .05 .02
142 Carmelo Martinez .05 .02
143 Tom Foley .05 .02
144 Kirby Puckett .30 .12
145 Rickey Henderson .60 .24
146 Juan Samuel .05 .02
147 Pete Incaviglia .05 .02
148 Greg Brock .05 .02
149 Eric Davis .10 .04
150 Kal Daniels .05 .02
151 Bob Boone .10 .04
152 John Cerutti .05 .02
153 Mike Greenwell .05 .02
154 Oddibe McDowell .05 .02
155 Scott Fletcher .05 .02
156 Gary Carter .40 .16
157 Harold Baines .10 .04
158 Greg Swindell .05 .02
159 Mark McLemore .10 .04
160 Keith Moreland .05 .02
161 Jim Gantner .05 .02
162 Willie Randolph .10 .04
163 Fred Lynn .05 .02
164 B.J. Surhoff .10 .04
165 Ken Griffey .10 .04
166 Chet Lemon .05 .02
167 Alan Trammell .15 .06
168 Paul Molitor .40 .16
169 Lou Whitaker .10 .04
170 Will Clark .40 .16
171 Dwight Evans .10 .04
172 Eddie Murray .40 .16
173 Darrell Evans .10 .04
174 Ellis Burks .40 .16
175 Ivan Calderon .05 .02
176 John Kruk .10 .04
177 Don Mattingly .75 .30
178 Dick Schofield .05 .02
179 Bruce Hurst .05 .02
180 Ron Guidry .10 .04
181 Jack Clark .10 .04
182 Franklin Stubbs .05 .02
183 Bill Doran .05 .02
184 Joe Carter .20 .08
185 Steve Sax .05 .02
186 Glenn Davis .05 .02
187 Bo Jackson .40 .16
188 Bobby Bonilla .05 .02
189 Willie Wilson .05 .02
190 Danny Tartabull .05 .02
191 Bo Diaz .05 .02
192 Buddy Bell .10 .04
193 Tim Wallach .05 .02
194 Mark McGwire 1.50 .60
195 Carney Lansford .10 .04
196 Alvin Davis .05 .02
197 Von Hayes .05 .02
198 Mitch Webster .05 .02
199 Casey Candaele .05 .02
200 Gary Gaetti .10 .04
201 Tommy Herr .05 .02
202 Wally Backman .05 .02
203 Brian Downing .05 .02
204 Rance Mulliniks .05 .02
205 Craig Reynolds .05 .02
206 Ruben Sierra .10 .04
207 Ryne Sandberg .60 .24
208 Carlton Fisk .40 .16
209 Checklist 28-107 .05 .02
210 Gerald Young .05 .02
211 Tim Raines MVP .15 .06
(Bonus card pose)
212 John Tudor .05 .02
213 George Bell CG .10 .04
214 George Bell MVP .10 .04
(Bonus card pose)
215 Jim Rice .10 .04
216 Gerald Perry .05 .02
217 Dave Stewart .10 .04
218 Jose Uribe .05 .02
219 Rick Reuschel .10 .04
220 Darryl Strawberry .10 .04
221 Chris Brown .05 .02
222 Ted Simmons .10 .04
223 Lee Mazzilli .05 .02
224 Denny Walling .05 .02
225 Jesse Barfield .05 .02
226 Barry Larkin .50 .20
227 Harold Reynolds .10 .04
228 Kevin McReynolds .05 .02
229 Todd Worrell .10 .04
230 Tommy John .10 .04
231 Rick Aguilera .10 .04
232 Bill Madlock .10 .04
233 Roy Smalley .05 .02
234 Jeff Musselman .05 .02
235 Mike Dunne .05 .02
236 Jerry Browne .05 .02
237 Sam Horn .05 .02
238 Howard Johnson .05 .02
239 Candy Maldonado .05 .02
240 Nick Esasky .05 .02
241 Geno Petralli .05 .02
242 Herm Winningham .05 .02
243 Roger McDowell .05 .02
244 Brian Fisher .05 .02
245 John Marzano .05 .02
246 Terry Pendleton .10 .04
247 Rick Leach .05 .02
248 Pascual Perez .05 .02
249 Mookie Wilson .10 .04
250 Ernie Whitt .05 .02
251 Ron Kittle .05 .02
252 Oil Can Boyd .05 .02
253 Jim Gott .05 .02
254 George Bell .05 .02
255 Tim Wallach CG .10 .04
256 Luis Polonia .05 .02
257 Hubie Brooks .05 .02
258 Mickey Brantley .05 .02
259 Gregg Jefferies RC .10 .04
260 Johnny Ray .05 .02
261 Checklist 108-187 .05 .02
262 Dennis Martinez .10 .04
263 Stan Musial .20 .08
Puzzle Card
264 Checklist 188-264 .05 .02

1990 Leaf Previews

The 1990 Leaf Previews set contains standard-size cards which were mailed to dealers to announce the 1990 version of Donruss' second major set of the year marketed as an upscale alternative under their Leaf name. This 12-card set was presented in the same style as the other Leaf cards were done in except that "Special Preview" was imprinted in white on the back. The cards were released in two series of 264 and the first series was not released until mid-season.

	Nm-Mt	Ex-Mt
COMPLETE SET (12)	500.00	150.00
1 Steve Sax	15.00	4.50
2 Joe Carter	25.00	7.50
3 Dennis Eckersley	60.00	18.00
4 Ken Griffey Jr.	125.00	38.00
5 Barry Larkin	50.00	15.00
6 Mark Langston	15.00	4.50
7 Eric Anthony	15.00	4.50
8 Robin Ventura	50.00	15.00
9 Greg Vaughn	25.00	7.50
10 Bobby Bonilla	15.00	4.50
11 Gary Gaetti	25.00	7.50
12 Ozzie Smith	100.00	30.00

1990 Leaf

The 1990 Leaf set was the first premium set introduced by Donruss and represents one of the more significant products issued in the 1990's. The cards were issued in 15-card foil wrapped packs and were not available in factory sets. Each pack also contained one three-piece puzzle panel of a 63-piece Yogi

Berra "Donruss Hall of Fame Diamond King" puzzle. This set, which was produced on high quality paper stock, was issued in two separate series of 264 standard-size cards each. The second series was issued approximately six weeks after the release of the first series. The cards feature full-color photos on both the front and back. Rookie Cards in the set include David Justice, John Olerud, Sammy Sosa, Frank Thomas and Larry Walker.

	Nm-Mt	Ex-Mt
COMPLETE SET (528)	100.00	30.00
COMPLETE SERIES 1 (264)	60.00	18.00
COMPLETE SERIES 2 (264)	40.00	12.00
COMP. BERRA PUZZLE	1.00	.30

1 Introductory Card .40 .12
2 Mike Henneman .40 .12
3 Steve Bedrosian .40 .12
4 Mike Scott .40 .12
5 Allan Anderson .40 .12
6 Rick Sutcliffe .60 .18
7 Gregg Olson .60 .18
8 Kevin Elster .40 .12
9 Pete O'Brien .40 .12
10 Carlton Fisk 1.00 .30
11 Joe Magrane .40 .12
12 Roger Clemens 3.00 .90
13 Tom Glavine 1.00 .30
14 Tom Gordon .60 .18
15 Todd Benzinger .40 .12
16 Hubie Brooks .40 .12
17 Roberto Kelly .40 .12
18 Barry Larkin 1.50 .45
19 Mike Boddicker .40 .12
20 Roger McDowell .40 .12
21 Nolan Ryan 5.00 1.50
22 John Farrell .40 .12
23 Bruce Hurst .40 .12
24 Wally Joyner .60 .18
25 Greg Maddux 6.00 1.80
26 Chris Bosio .40 .12
27 John Cerutti .40 .12
28 Tim Burke .40 .12
29 Dennis Eckersley .60 .18
30 Glenn Davis .40 .12
31 Jim Abbott 1.00 .30
32 Mike LaValliere .40 .12
33 Andres Thomas .40 .12
34 Lou Whitaker .60 .18
35 Alvin Davis .40 .12
36 Melido Perez .40 .12
37 Craig Biggio 1.00 .30
38 Rick Aguilera .60 .18
39 Pete Harnisch .60 .18
40 David Cone .60 .18
41 Scott Garrelts .40 .12
42 Jay Howell .40 .12
43 Eric King .40 .12
44 Pedro Guerrero .40 .12
45 Mike Bielecki .40 .12
46 Bob Boone .60 .18
47 Kevin Brown .60 .18
48 Jerry Browne .40 .12
49 Mike Scioscia .40 .12
50 Chuck Cary .40 .12
51 Wade Boggs 1.00 .30
52 Von Hayes .40 .12
53 Tony Fernandez .40 .12
54 Dennis Martinez .60 .18
55 Tom Candiotti .40 .12
56 Andy Benes .60 .18
57 Rob Dibble .60 .18
58 Chuck Crim .40 .12
59 John Smoltz 1.50 .45
60 Mike Heath .40 .12
61 Kevin Gross .40 .12
62 Mark McGwire 4.00 1.20
63 Bert Blyleven .60 .18
64 Bob Walk .40 .12
65 Mickey Tettleton .40 .12
66 Sid Fernandez .40 .12
67 Terry Kennedy .40 .12
68 Fernando Valenzuela .60 .18
69 Don Mattingly 4.00 1.20
70 Paul O'Neill 1.00 .30
71 Robin Yount 2.50 .75
72 Bret Saberhagen .60 .18
73 Geno Petralli .40 .12
74 Brook Jacoby .40 .12
75 Roberto Alomar 1.50 .45
76 Devon White .40 .12
77 Jose Lind .40 .12
78 Pat Combs .40 .12
79 Dave Stieb .60 .18
80 Tim Wallach .40 .12
81 Dave Stewart .60 .18
82 Eric Anthony RC .40 .12
83 Randy Bush .40 .12
84 Rickey Henderson CL .60 .18
85 Jaime Navarro .40 .12
86 Tommy Gregg .40 .12
87 Frank Tanana .40 .12
88 Omar Vizquel 1.50 .45
89 Ivan Calderon .40 .12
90 Vince Coleman .40 .12
91 Barry Bonds 4.00 1.20
92 Randy Milligan .40 .12
93 Frank Viola .40 .12
94 Matt Williams .60 .18
95 Alfredo Griffin .40 .12
96 Steve Sax .40 .12
97 Gary Gaetti .60 .18
98 Ryne Sandberg 3.00 .90
99 Danny Tartabull .40 .12
100 Rafael Palmeiro 1.00 .30
101 Jesse Orosco .40 .12
102 Garry Templeton .40 .12
103 Frank DiPino .40 .12
104 Tony Pena .40 .12
105 Dickie Thon .40 .12
106 Kelly Gruber .40 .12
107 Marquis Grissom RC 1.00 .30
108 Jose Canseco 1.50 .45
109 Mike Blowers RC .40 .12
110 Tom Browning .40 .12
111 Greg Vaughn .60 .18
112 Oddibe McDowell .40 .12
113 Gary Ward .40 .12
114 Jay Buhner .60 .18
115 Eric Show .40 .12
116 Bryan Harvey .40 .12
117 Andy Van Slyke .60 .18
118 Jeff Ballard .40 .12
119 Barry Lyons .40 .12
120 Kevin Mitchell .40 .12
121 Mike Gallego .40 .12
122 Dave Smith .40 .12
123 Kirby Puckett 1.50 .45
124 Jerome Walton .40 .12
125 Bo Jackson 1.50 .45
126 Harold Baines .60 .18
127 Scott Bankhead .40 .12
128 Ozzie Guillen .40 .12
129 Jose Oquendo UER .40 .12
(League misspelled as Legue)
130 John Dopson .40 .12
131 Charlie Hayes .40 .12
132 Fred McGriff 1.50 .45
133 Chet Lemon .40 .12
134 Gary Carter 1.00 .30
135 Rafael Ramirez .40 .12
136 Shane Mack .40 .12
137 Mark Grace UER 1.00 .30
(Card back has OB:L, should be B:L)
138 Phil Bradley .40 .12
139 Dwight Gooden 1.00 .30
140 Harold Reynolds .60 .18
141 Scott Fletcher .40 .12
142 Ozzie Smith 2.50 .75
143 Mike Greenwell .40 .12
144 Pete Smith .40 .12
145 Mark Gubicza .40 .12
146 Chris Sabo .40 .12
147 Ramon Martinez .40 .12
148 Tim Leary .40 .12
149 Randy Myers .60 .18
150 Jody Reed .40 .12
151 Bruce Ruffin .40 .12
152 Jeff Russell .40 .12
153 Doug Jones .40 .12
154 Tony Gwynn 2.00 .60
155 Mark Langston .40 .12
156 Mitch Williams .40 .12
157 Gary Sheffield 1.50 .45
158 Tom Henke .40 .12
159 Oil Can Boyd .40 .12
160 Rickey Henderson 1.50 .45
161 Bill Doran .40 .12
162 Chuck Finley .60 .18
163 Jeff King .40 .12
164 Nick Esasky .40 .12
165 Cecil Fielder .60 .18
166 Dave Valle .40 .12
167 Robin Ventura 1.50 .45
168 Jim Deshaies .40 .12
169 Juan Berenguer .40 .12
170 Craig Worthington .40 .12
171 Gregg Jefferies .60 .18
172 Will Clark 1.50 .45
173 Kirk Gibson .60 .18
174 Carlton Fisk CL .60 .18
175 Bobby Thigpen .40 .12
176 John Tudor .40 .12
177 Andre Dawson .60 .18
178 George Brett 4.00 1.20
179 Steve Buechele .40 .12
180 Joey Belle 1.50 .45
181 Eddie Murray 1.50 .45
182 Bob Geren .40 .12
183 Rob Murphy .40 .12
184 Tom Herr .40 .12
185 George Bell .40 .12
186 Spike Owen .40 .12
187 Cory Snyder .40 .12
188 Fred Lynn .40 .12
189 Eric Davis .60 .18
190 Dave Parker .60 .18
191 Jeff Blauser .40 .12
192 Matt Nokes .40 .12
193 Delino DeShields RC 1.00 .30
194 Scott Sanderson .40 .12
195 Lance Parrish .40 .12
196 Bobby Bonilla .60 .18
197 Cal Ripken UER 5.00 1.50
(Reistertown, should be Reisterstown)
198 Kevin McReynolds .40 .12
199 Robby Thompson .40 .12
200 Tim Belcher .40 .12
201 Jesse Barfield .40 .12
202 Mariano Duncan .40 .12
203 Bill Spiers .40 .12
204 Frank White .60 .18
205 Julio Franco .40 .12
206 Greg Swindell .40 .12
207 Benito Santiago .60 .18
208 Johnny Ray .40 .12
209 Gary Redus .40 .12
210 Jeff Parrett .40 .12
211 Jimmy Key .60 .18
212 Tim Raines .60 .18
213 Carney Lansford .60 .18
214 Gerald Young .40 .12
215 Gene Larkin .40 .12
216 Dan Plesac .40 .12
217 Lonnie Smith .40 .12
218 Alan Trammell 1.00 .30
219 Jeffrey Leonard .40 .12
220 Sammy Sosa RC 50.00 15.00
221 Todd Zeile .60 .18
222 Bill Landrum .40 .12
223 Mike Devereaux .40 .12
224 Mike Marshall .40 .12
225 Jose Uribe .40 .12
226 Juan Samuel .40 .12
227 Mel Hall .40 .12
228 Kent Hrbek .60 .18
229 Shawon Dunston .40 .12
230 Kevin Seitzer .40 .12
231 Pete Incaviglia .40 .12
232 Sandy Alomar Jr. .60 .18
233 Bip Roberts .40 .12
234 Scott Terry .40 .12
235 Dwight Evans .60 .18
236 Ricky Jordan .40 .12
237 John Olerud RC 5.00 1.50
238 Zane Smith .40 .12
239 Walt Weiss .40 .12
240 Alvaro Espinoza .40 .12
241 Billy Hatcher .40 .12
242 Paul Molitor 1.00 .30
243 Dale Murphy 1.50 .45
244 Dave Bergman .40 .12
245 Ken Griffey Jr. 6.00 1.80
246 Ed Whitson .40 .12
247 Kirk McCaskill .40 .12
248 Jay Bell .60 .18
249 Ben McDonald RC 1.00 .30
250 Darryl Strawberry 1.00 .30
251 Brett Butler .60 .18
252 Terry Steinbach .40 .12
253 Ken Caminiti 1.50 .45
254 Dan Gladden .40 .12
255 Dwight Smith .40 .12
256 Kurt Stillwell .40 .12
257 Ruben Sierra .40 .12
258 Mike Schooler .40 .12
259 Lance Johnson .40 .12
260 Terry Pendleton .60 .18
261 Ellis Burks 1.00 .30
262 Len Dykstra .60 .18
263 Mookie Wilson .60 .18
264 Nolan Ryan CL UER 1.50 .45
No TM after Ranger logo
265 Nolan Ryan 2.50 .75
No Hit King
266 Brian DuBois .40 .12
267 Don Robinson .40 .12
268 Glenn Wilson .40 .12
269 Kevin Tapani RC 1.00 .30
270 Marvell Wynne .40 .12
271 Bill Ripken .40 .12
272 Howard Johnson .40 .12
273 Brian Holman .40 .12
274 Dan Pasqua .40 .12
275 Ken Dayley .40 .12
276 Jeff Reardon .60 .18
277 Jim Presley .40 .12
278 Jim Eisenreich .40 .12
279 Danny Jackson .40 .12
280 Orel Hershiser .60 .18
281 Andy Hawkins .40 .12
282 Jose Rijo .40 .12
283 Luis Rivera .40 .12
284 John Kruk .60 .18
285 Jeff Huson RC .40 .12
286 Joel Skinner .40 .12
287 Jack Clark .60 .18
288 Chili Davis .60 .18
289 Joe Girardi 1.00 .30
290 B.J. Surhoff .60 .18
291 Luis Sojo .40 .12
292 Tom Foley .40 .12
293 Mike Moore .40 .12
294 Ken Oberkfell .40 .12
295 Luis Polonia .40 .12
296 Doug Drabek .40 .12
297 Dave Justice RC 5.00 1.50
298 Paul Gibson .40 .12
299 Edgar Martinez 1.00 .30
300 F.Thomas RC UER 25.00 7.50
No B in front of birthdate
301 Eric Yelding .40 .12
302 Greg Gagne .40 .12
303 Brad Komminsk .40 .12
304 Ron Darling .40 .12
305 Kevin Bass .40 .12
306 Jeff Hamilton .40 .12
307 Ron Karkovice .40 .12
308 Milt Thompson UER .60 .18
(Ray Lankford pictured on card back)
309 Mike Harkey .40 .12
310 Mel Stottlemyre Jr. .40 .12
311 Kenny Rogers .60 .18
312 Mitch Webster .40 .12
313 Kal Daniels .40 .12
314 Matt Nokes .40 .12
315 Dennis Lamp .40 .12
316 Ken Howell .40 .12
317 Glenallen Hill .40 .12
318 Dave Martinez .40 .12
319 Chris James .40 .12
320 Mike Pagliarulo .40 .12
321 Hal Morris .40 .12
322 Rob Deer .40 .12
323 Greg Olson .40 .12
324 Tony Phillips .40 .12
325 Larry Walker RC 10.00 3.00
326 Ron Hassey .40 .12
327 Jack Howell .40 .12
328 John Smiley .40 .12
329 Steve Finley .60 .18
330 Dave Magadan .40 .12
331 Greg Litton .40 .12
332 Mickey Hatcher .40 .12
333 Lee Guetterman .40 .12
334 Norm Charlton .40 .12
335 Edgar Diaz .40 .12
336 Willie Wilson .40 .12
337 Bobby Witt .40 .12
338 Candy Maldonado .40 .12
339 Craig Lefferts .40 .12
340 Dante Bichette 1.50 .45
341 Wally Backman .40 .12
342 Dennis Cook .40 .12
343 Pat Borders .40 .12
344 Wallace Johnson .40 .12
345 Willie Randolph .60 .18
346 Danny Darwin .40 .12
347 Al Newman .40 .12
348 Mark Knudson .40 .12
349 Joe Boever .40 .12
350 Larry Sheets .40 .12
351 Mike Jackson .40 .12
352 Wayne Edwards .40 .12
353 Bernard Gilkey RC 1.00 .30

354 Don Slaught .40 .12
355 Joe Orsulak .40 .12
356 John Franco .60 .18
357 Jeff Brantley .40 .12
358 Mike Morgan .40 .12
359 Deion Sanders 1.50 .45
360 Terry Leach .40 .12
361 Les Lancaster .40 .12
362 Storm Davis .40 .12
363 Scott Coolbaugh .40 .12
364 Ozzie Smith CL 1.00 .30
365 Cecilio Guante .40 .12
366 Joey Cora .60 .18
367 Willie McGee .60 .18
368 Jerry Reed .40 .12
369 Darren Daulton .60 .18
370 Manny Lee .40 .12
371 Mark Gardner .40 .12
372 Rick Honeycutt .40 .12
373 Steve Balboni .40 .12
374 Jack Armstrong .40 .12
375 Charlie O'Brien .40 .12
376 Ron Gant .60 .18
377 Lloyd Moseby .40 .12
378 Gene Harris .40 .12
379 Joe Carter .60 .18
380 Scott Bailes .40 .12
381 R.J. Reynolds .40 .12
382 Bob Melvin .40 .12
383 Tim Teufel .40 .12
384 John Burkett .40 .12
385 Felix Jose .40 .12
386 Larry Andersen .40 .12
387 David West .40 .12
388 Luis Salazar .40 .12
389 Mike Macfarlane .40 .12
390 Charlie Hough .60 .18
391 Greg Briley .40 .12
392 Donn Pall .40 .12
393 Bryn Smith .40 .12
394 Carlos Quintana .40 .12
395 Steve Lake .40 .12
396 Mark Whiten RC 1.00 .30
397 Edwin Nunez .40 .12
398 Rick Parker .40 .12
399 Mark Portugal .40 .12
400 Roy Smith .40 .12
401 Hector Villanueva .40 .12
402 Bob Milacki .40 .12
403 Alejandro Pena .40 .12
404 Scott Bradley .40 .12
405 Ron Kittle .40 .12
406 Bob Tewksbury .40 .12
407 Wes Gardner .40 .12
408 Ernie Whitt .40 .12
409 Terry Shumpert .40 .12
410 Tim Layana .40 .12
411 Chris Gwynn .40 .12
412 Jeff D. Robinson .40 .12
413 Scott Scudder .40 .12
414 Kevin Romine .40 .12
415 Jose DeJesus .40 .12
416 Mike Jeffcoat .40 .12
417 Rudy Seanez .40 .12
418 Mike Dunne .40 .12
419 Dick Schofield .40 .12
420 Steve Wilson .40 .12
421 Bill Krueger .40 .12
422 Junior Felix .40 .12
423 Drew Hall .40 .12
424 Curt Young .40 .12
425 Franklin Stubbs .40 .12
426 Dave Winfield .60 .18
427 Rick Reed RC 1.00 .30
428 Charlie Leibrandt .40 .12
429 Jeff M. Robinson .40 .12
430 Erik Hanson .40 .12
431 Barry Jones .40 .12
432 Alex Trevino .40 .12
433 John Moses .40 .12
434 Dave Johnson .40 .12
435 Mackey Sasser .40 .12
436 Rick Leach .40 .12
437 Lenny Harris .40 .12
438 Carlos Martinez .40 .12
439 Rex Hudler .40 .12
440 Domingo Ramos .40 .12
441 Gerald Perry .40 .12
442 Jeff Russell .40 .12
443 Carlos Baerga RC 1.00 .30
444 Will Clark CL .60 .18
445 Stan Javier .40 .12
446 Kevin Maas RC 1.00 .30
447 Tom Brunansky .40 .12
448 Carmelo Martinez .40 .12
449 Willie Blair RC .40 .12
450 Andres Galarraga .60 .18
451 Bud Black .40 .12
452 Greg W. Harris .40 .12
453 Joe Oliver .40 .12
454 Greg Brock .40 .12
455 Jeff Treadway .40 .12
456 Lance McCullers .40 .12
457 Dave Schmidt .40 .12
458 Todd Burns .40 .12
459 Max Venable .40 .12
460 Neal Heaton .40 .12
461 Mark Williamson .40 .12
462 Keith Miller .40 .12
463 Mike LaCoss .40 .12
464 Jose Offerman RC 1.00 .30
465 Jim Leyritz RC 1.00 .30
466 Glenn Braggs .40 .12
467 Ron Robinson .40 .12
468 Mark Davis .40 .12
469 Gary Pettis .40 .12
470 Keith Hernandez 1.00 .30
471 Dennis Rasmussen .40 .12
472 Mark Eichhorn .40 .12
473 Ted Power .40 .12
474 Terry Mulholland .40 .12
475 Todd Stottlemyre .60 .18
476 Jerry Goff .40 .12
477 Gene Nelson .40 .12
478 Rich Gedman .40 .12
479 Brian Harper .40 .12
480 Mike Felder .40 .12
481 Steve Avery 1.50 .45
482 Jack Morris .60 .18
483 Randy Johnson 2.50 .75
484 Scott Radinsky RC .40 .12
485 Jose DeLeon .40 .12
486 Stan Belinda RC .40 .12
487 Brian Holton .40 .12
488 Mark Carreon .40 .12
489 Trevor Wilson .40 .12
490 Mike Sharperson .40 .12
491 Alan Mills RC .40 .12
492 John Candelaria .40 .12
493 Paul Assenmacher .40 .12
494 Steve Crawford .40 .12
495 Brad Arnsberg .40 .12
496 Sergio Valdez .40 .12
497 Mark Parent .40 .12
498 Tom Pagnozzi .40 .12
499 Greg A. Harris .40 .12
500 Randy Ready .40 .12
501 Duane Ward .40 .12
502 Nelson Santovenia .40 .12
503 Joe Klink .40 .12
504 Eric Plunk .40 .12
505 Jeff Reed .40 .12
506 Ted Higuera .40 .12
507 Joe Hesketh .40 .12
508 Dan Petry .40 .12
509 Matt Young .40 .12
510 Jerald Clark .40 .12
511 John Orton .40 .12
512 Scott Ruskin .40 .12
513 Chris Hoiles RC 1.00 .30
514 Daryl Boston .40 .12
515 Francisco Oliveras .40 .12
516 Ozzie Canseco .40 .12
517 Xavier Hernandez RC .40 .12
518 Fred Manrique .40 .12
519 Shawn Boskie RC .40 .12
520 Jeff Montgomery .60 .18
521 Jack Daugherty .40 .12
522 Keith Comstock .40 .12
523 Greg Hibbard RC .40 .12
524 Lee Smith .60 .18
525 Dana Kiecker .40 .12
526 Darrel Akerfelds .40 .12
527 Greg Myers .40 .12
528 Ryne Sandberg CL 1.50 .45

1991 Leaf Previews

The 1991 Leaf Previews set consists of 26 standard-size cards. Cards from this set were issued as inserts (four at a time) inside specially marked 1991 Donruss hobby factory sets. The front design has color action player photos, with white and silver borders.

Nm-Mt Ex-Mt
COMPLETE SET (26) 40.00 12.00
1 Dave Justice 1.00 .30
2 Ryne Sandberg 4.00 1.20
3 Barry Larkin 2.50 .75
4 Craig Biggio 1.50 .45
5 Ramon Martinez .50 .15
6 Tim Wallach .50 .15
7 Dwight Gooden 1.50 .45
8 Len Dykstra 1.00 .30
9 Barry Bonds 6.00 1.80
10 Ray Lankford .50 .15
11 Tony Gwynn 3.00 .90
12 Will Clark 2.50 .75
13 Leo Gomez .50 .15
14 Wade Boggs 1.50 .45
15 Chuck Finley UER 1.00 .30
(Position on card back is First Base)
16 Carlton Fisk 1.50 .45
17 Sandy Alomar Jr. .50 .15
18 Cecil Fielder 1.00 .30
19 Bo Jackson 1.00 .30
20 Paul Molitor 1.50 .45
21 Kirby Puckett 2.50 .75
22 Don Mattingly 6.00 1.80
23 Rickey Henderson 2.50 .75
24 Tino Martinez 1.00 .30
25 Nolan Ryan 10.00 3.00
26 Dave Stieb .50 .15

1991 Leaf

This 528-card standard size set was issued by Donruss in two separate series of 264 cards. Cards were exclusively issued in foil packs. The front design has color action player photos, with white and silver borders. A thicker stock was used for these (then) premium level cards. Production for the 1991 set was greatly increased due to the huge demand for the benchmark 1990 Leaf set. However, the 1991 cards were met with modest enthusiasm due to a weak selection of Rookie Cards and superior competition from brands like 1991 Stadium Club.

Nm-Mt Ex-Mt
COMPLETE SET (528) 15.00 4.50
COMP. SERIES 1 (264) 5.00 1.50
COMP. SERIES 2 (264) 10.00 3.00
COMP. KILLEBREW PUZZLE 1.00 .30
1 The Leaf Card .10 .03
2 Kurt Stillwell .10 .03
3 Bobby Witt .10 .03
4 Tony Phillips .10 .03
5 Scott Garrelts .10 .03
6 Greg Swindell .10 .03
7 Billy Ripken .10 .03
8 Dave Martinez .10 .03
9 Kelly Gruber .10 .03
10 Juan Samuel .10 .03
11 Brian Holman .10 .03
12 Craig Biggio .30 .09
13 Lonnie Smith .10 .03
14 Ron Robinson .10 .03
15 Mike LaValliere .10 .03
16 Mark Davis .10 .03
17 Jack Daugherty .10 .03
18 Mike Henneman .10 .03
19 Mike Greenwell .10 .03
20 Dave Magadan .10 .03
21 Mark Williamson .10 .03
22 Marquis Grissom .10 .03
23 Pat Borders .10 .03
24 Mike Scioscia .10 .03
25 Shawon Dunston .10 .03
26 Randy Bush .10 .03
27 John Smoltz .30 .09
28 Chuck Crim .10 .03
29 Don Slaught .10 .03
30 Mike Macfarlane .10 .03
31 Wally Joyner .20 .06
32 Pat Combs .10 .03
33 Tony Pena .10 .03
34 Howard Johnson .10 .03
35 Leo Gomez .10 .03
36 Spike Owen .10 .03
37 Eric Davis .20 .06
38 Roberto Kelly .10 .03
39 Jerome Walton .10 .03
40 Shane Mack .10 .03
41 Kent Mercker .10 .03
42 B.J. Surhoff .20 .06
43 Jerry Browne .10 .03
44 Lee Smith .20 .06
45 Chuck Finley .20 .06
46 Terry Mulholland .10 .03
47 Tom Bolton .10 .03
48 Tom Herr .10 .03
49 Jim Deshaies .10 .03
50 Walt Weiss .10 .03
51 Hal Morris .10 .03
52 Lee Guetterman .10 .03
53 Paul Assenmacher .10 .03
54 Brian Harper .10 .03
55 Paul Gibson .10 .03
56 John Burkett .10 .03
57 Doug Jones .10 .03
58 Jose Oquendo .10 .03
59 Dick Schofield .10 .03
60 Dickie Thon .10 .03
61 Ramon Martinez .10 .03
62 Jay Buhner .20 .06
63 Mark Portugal .10 .03
64 Bob Welch .10 .03
65 Chris Sabo .10 .03
66 Chuck Cary .10 .03
67 Mark Langston .10 .03
68 Joe Boever .10 .03
69 Jody Reed .10 .03
70 Alejandro Pena .10 .03
71 Jeff King .10 .03
72 Tom Pagnozzi .10 .03
73 Joe Oliver .10 .03
74 Mike Witt .10 .03
75 Hector Villanueva .10 .03
76 Dan Gladden .10 .03
77 Dave Justice .20 .06
78 Mike Gallego .10 .03
79 Tom Candiotti .10 .03
80 Ozzie Smith .75 .23
81 Luis Polonia .10 .03
82 Randy Ready .10 .03
83 Greg A. Harris .10 .03
84 David Justice CL .10 .03
85 Kevin Mitchell .10 .03
86 Mark McLemore .10 .03
87 Terry Steinbach .10 .03
88 Tom Browning .10 .03
89 Matt Nokes .10 .03
90 Mike Harkey .10 .03
91 Omar Vizquel .20 .06
92 Dave Bergman .10 .03
93 Matt Williams .20 .06
94 Steve Olin .10 .03
95 Craig Wilson .10 .03
96 Dave Stieb .10 .03
97 Ruben Sierra .10 .03
98 Jay Howell .10 .03
99 Scott Bradley .10 .03
100 Eric Yelding .10 .03
101 Rickey Henderson .50 .15
102 Jeff Reed .10 .03
103 Jimmy Key .20 .06
104 Terry Shumpert .10 .03
105 Kenny Rogers .20 .06
106 Cecil Fielder .20 .06
107 Robby Thompson .10 .03
108 Alex Cole .10 .03
109 Randy Milligan .10 .03
110 Andres Galarraga .20 .06
111 Bill Spiers .10 .03
112 Kal Daniels .10 .03
113 Henry Cotto .10 .03
114 Casey Candaele .10 .03
115 Jeff Blauser .10 .03
116 Robin Yount .75 .23
117 Ben McDonald .10 .03
118 Bret Saberhagen .20 .06
119 Juan Gonzalez .50 .15
120 Lou Whitaker .20 .06
121 Ellis Burks .20 .06
122 Charlie O'Brien .10 .03
123 John Smiley .10 .03
124 Tim Burke .10 .03
125 John Olerud .20 .06
126 Eddie Murray .50 .15
127 Greg Maddux .75 .23
128 Kevin Tapani .10 .03
129 Ron Gant .20 .06
130 Jay Bell .20 .06
131 Chris Hoiles .10 .03
132 Tom Gordon .10 .03
133 Kevin Seitzer .10 .03
134 Jeff Huson .10 .03
135 Jerry Don Gleaton .10 .03
136 Jeff Brantley UER .10 .03
(Photo actually Rick Leach on back)
137 Felix Fermin .10 .03
138 Mike Devereaux .10 .03
139 Delino DeShields .20 .06
140 David Wells .20 .06
141 Tim Crews .10 .03
142 Erik Hanson .10 .03
143 Mark Davidson .10 .03
144 Tommy Gregg .10 .03
145 Jim Gantner .10 .03
146 Jose Lind .10 .03
147 Danny Tartabull .10 .03
148 Geno Petralli .10 .03
149 Travis Fryman .20 .06
150 Tim Naehring .10 .03
151 Kevin McReynolds .10 .03
152 Joe Orsulak .10 .03
153 Steve Frey .10 .03
154 Duane Ward .10 .03
155 Stan Javier .10 .03
156 Damon Berryhill .10 .03
157 Gene Larkin .10 .03
158 Greg Olson .10 .03
159 Mark Knudson .10 .03
160 Carmelo Martinez .10 .03
161 Storm Davis .10 .03
162 Jim Abbott .30 .09
163 Len Dykstra .20 .06
164 Tom Brunansky .10 .03
165 Dwight Gooden .30 .09
166 Jose Mesa .10 .03
167 Oil Can Boyd .10 .03
168 Barry Larkin .50 .15
169 Scott Sanderson .10 .03
170 Mark Grace .30 .09
171 Mark Guthrie .10 .03
172 Tom Glavine .30 .09
173 Gary Sheffield .20 .06
174 Roger Clemens CL .50 .15
175 Chris James .10 .03
176 Milt Thompson .10 .03
177 Donnie Hill .10 .03
178 Wes Chamberlain RC .10 .03
179 John Marzano .10 .03
180 Frank Viola .20 .06
181 Eric Anthony .10 .03
182 Jose Canseco .50 .15
183 Scott Scudder .10 .03
184 Dave Eiland .10 .03
185 Luis Salazar .10 .03
186 Pedro Munoz RC .10 .03
187 Steve Searcy .10 .03
188 Don Robinson .10 .03
189 Sandy Alomar Jr. .10 .03
190 Jose DeLeon .10 .03
191 John Orton .10 .03
192 Darren Daulton .20 .06
193 Mike Morgan .10 .03
194 Greg Briley .10 .03
195 Karl Rhodes .10 .03
196 Harold Baines .20 .06
197 Bill Doran .10 .03
198 Alvaro Espinoza .10 .03
199 Kirk McCaskill .10 .03
200 Jose DeJesus .10 .03
201 Jack Clark .20 .06
202 Daryl Boston .10 .03
203 Randy Tomlin RC .10 .03
204 Pedro Guerrero .20 .06
205 Billy Hatcher .10 .03
206 Tim Leary .10 .03
207 Ryne Sandberg .75 .23
208 Kirby Puckett .50 .15
209 Charlie Leibrandt .10 .03
210 Rick Honeycutt .10 .03
211 Joel Skinner .10 .03
212 Rex Hudler .10 .03
213 Bryan Harvey .10 .03
214 Charlie Hayes .10 .03
215 Matt Young .10 .03
216 Terry Kennedy .10 .03
217 Carl Nichols .10 .03
218 Mike Moore .10 .03
219 Paul O'Neill .30 .09
220 Steve Sax .10 .03
221 Shawn Boskie .10 .03
222 Rich DeLucia .10 .03
223 Lloyd Moseby .10 .03
224 Mike Kingery .10 .03
225 Carlos Baerga .10 .03
226 Bryn Smith .10 .03
227 Todd Stottlemyre .10 .03
228 Julio Franco .20 .06
229 Jim Gott .10 .03
230 Mike Schooler .10 .03
231 Steve Finley .20 .06
232 Dave Henderson .10 .03
233 Luis Quinones .10 .03
234 Mark Whiten .10 .03
235 Brian McRae RC .20 .06
236 Rich Gossage .20 .06
237 Rob Deer .10 .03
238 Will Clark .50 .15
239 Albert Belle .20 .06
240 Bob Melvin .10 .03
241 Larry Walker .50 .15
242 Dante Bichette .20 .06
243 Orel Hershiser .20 .06
244 Pete O'Brien .10 .03
245 Pete Harnisch .10 .03
246 Jeff Treadway .10 .03
247 Julio Machado .10 .03
248 Dave Johnson .10 .03
249 Kirk Gibson .20 .06
250 Kevin Brown .20 .06
251 Milt Cuyler .10 .03
252 Jeff Reardon .20 .06
253 David Cone .20 .06
254 Gary Redus .10 .03
255 Junior Noboa .10 .03
256 Greg Myers .10 .03
257 Dennis Cook .10 .03
258 Joe Girardi .10 .03
259 Allan Anderson .10 .03
260 Paul Marak .10 .03
261 Barry Bonds 1.25 .35
262 Juan Bell .10 .03
263 Russ Morman .10 .03
264 George Brett CL .50 .15
265 Jerald Clark .10 .03
266 Dwight Evans .20 .06
267 Roberto Alomar .50 .15
268 Danny Jackson .10 .03
269 Brian Downing .10 .03
270 John Cerutti .10 .03
271 Robin Ventura .20 .06
272 Gerald Perry .10 .03
273 Wade Boggs .30 .09
274 Dennis Martinez .20 .06
275 Andy Benes .10 .03
276 Tony Fossas .10 .03
277 Franklin Stubbs .10 .03
278 John Kruk .20 .06
279 Kevin Gross .10 .03
280 Von Hayes .10 .03
281 Frank Thomas .50 .15
282 Rob Dibble .20 .06
283 Mel Hall .10 .03
284 Rick Mahler .10 .03
285 Dennis Eckersley .20 .06
286 Bernard Gilkey .10 .03
287 Dan Plesac .10 .03
288 Jason Grimsley .10 .03
289 Mark Lewis .10 .03
290 Tony Gwynn .60 .18
291 Jeff Russell .10 .03
292 Curt Schilling .30 .09
293 Pascual Perez .10 .03
294 Jack Morris .20 .06
295 Hubie Brooks .10 .03
296 Alex Fernandez .10 .03
297 Harold Reynolds .20 .06
298 Craig Worthington .10 .03
299 Willie Wilson .10 .03
300 Mike Maddux .10 .03
301 Dave Righetti .20 .06
302 Paul Molitor .30 .09
303 Gary Gaetti .20 .06
304 Terry Pendleton .20 .06
305 Kevin Elster .10 .03
306 Scott Fletcher .10 .03
307 Jeff Robinson .10 .03
308 Jesse Barfield .10 .03
309 Mike LaCoss .10 .03
310 Andy Van Slyke .20 .06
311 Glenallen Hill .10 .03
312 Bud Black .10 .03
313 Kent Hrbek .20 .06
314 Tim Teufel .10 .03
315 Tony Fernandez .10 .03
316 Beau Allred .10 .03
317 Curtis Wilkerson .10 .03
318 Bill Sampen .10 .03
319 Randy Johnson .60 .18
320 Mike Heath .10 .03
321 Sammy Sosa 1.00 .30
322 Mickey Tettleton .10 .03
323 Jose Vizcaino .10 .03
324 John Candelaria .10 .03
325 Dave Howard .10 .03
326 Jose Rijo .10 .03
327 Todd Zeile .10 .03
328 Gene Nelson .10 .03
329 Dwayne Henry .10 .03
330 Mike Boddicker .10 .03
331 Ozzie Guillen .10 .03
332 Sam Horn .10 .03
333 Wally Whitehurst .10 .03
334 Dave Parker .20 .06
335 George Brett 1.25 .35
336 Bobby Thigpen .10 .03
337 Ed Whitson .10 .03
338 Ivan Calderon .10 .03
339 Mike Pagliarulo .10 .03
340 Jack McDowell .10 .03
341 Dana Kiecker .10 .03
342 Fred McGriff .30 .09
343 Mark Lee RC .10 .03
344 Alfredo Griffin .10 .03
345 Scott Bankhead .10 .03
346 Darrin Jackson .10 .03
347 Rafael Palmeiro .30 .09
348 Steve Farr .10 .03
349 Hensley Meulens .10 .03
350 Danny Cox .10 .03
351 Alan Trammell .30 .09
352 Edwin Nunez .10 .03
353 Joe Carter .20 .06
354 Eric Show .10 .03
355 Vance Law .10 .03
356 Jeff Gray .10 .03
357 Bobby Bonilla .20 .06
358 Ernest Riles .10 .03
359 Ron Hassey .10 .03
360 Willie McGee .20 .06
361 Mackey Sasser .10 .03
362 Glenn Braggs .10 .03
363 Mario Diaz .10 .03
364 Barry Bonds CL .60 .18
365 Kevin Bass .10 .03
366 Pete Incaviglia .10 .03
367 Luis Sojo UER .10 .03
(1989 stats interspersed with 1990's)
368 Lance Parrish .20 .06
369 Mark Leonard .10 .03
370 Heath. Slocumb RC .20 .06
371 Jimmy Jones .10 .03
372 Ken Griffey Jr. 1.00 .30
373 Chris Hammond .10 .03
374 Chili Davis .20 .06
375 Joey Cora .10 .03
376 Ken Hill .10 .03
377 Darryl Strawberry .30 .09
378 Ron Darling .10 .03
379 Sid Bream .10 .03
380 Bill Swift .10 .03
381 Shawn Abner .10 .03
382 Eric King .10 .03
383 Mickey Morandini .10 .03
384 Carlton Fisk .30 .09
385 Steve Lake .10 .03
386 Mike Jeffcoat .10 .03
387 Darren Holmes RC .20 .06
388 Tim Wallach .10 .03
389 George Bell .10 .03
390 Craig Lefferts .10 .03
391 Ernie Whitt .10 .03
392 Felix Jose .10 .03
393 Kevin Maas .10 .03
394 Devon White .10 .03
395 Otis Nixon .10 .03
396 Chuck Knoblauch .20 .06
397 Scott Coolbaugh .10 .03
398 Glenn Davis .10 .03
399 Manny Lee .10 .03

400 Andre Dawson .20 .06
401 Scott Chiamparino .10 .03
402 Bill Gullickson .10 .03
403 Lance Johnson .10 .03
404 Juan Agosto .10 .03
405 Danny Darwin .10 .03
406 Barry Jones .10 .03
407 Larry Andersen .10 .03
408 Luis Rivera .10 .03
409 Jaime Navarro .10 .03
410 Roger McDowell .10 .03
411 Brett Butler .20 .06
412 Dale Murphy .50 .15
413 Tim Raines UER .20 .06
(Listed as hitting .500 in 1980, should be .050)
414 Norm Charlton .10 .03
415 Greg Cadaret .10 .03
416 Chris Nabholz .10 .03
417 Dave Stewart .20 .06
418 Rich Gedman .10 .03
419 Willie Randolph .20 .06
420 Mitch Williams .10 .03
421 Brook Jacoby .10 .03
422 Greg W. Harris .10 .03
423 Nolan Ryan 2.00 .60
424 Dave Rohde .10 .03
425 Don Mattingly 1.25 .35
426 Greg Gagne .10 .03
427 Vince Coleman .10 .03
428 Dan Pasqua .10 .03
429 Alvin Davis .10 .03
430 Cal Ripken 1.50 .45
431 Jamie Quirk .10 .03
432 Benito Santiago .20 .06
433 Jose Uribe .10 .03
434 Candy Maldonado .10 .03
435 Junior Felix .10 .03
436 Deion Sanders .30 .09
437 John Franco .20 .06
438 Greg Hibbard .10 .03
439 Floyd Bannister .10 .03
440 Steve Howe .10 .03
441 Steve Decker .10 .03
442 Vicente Palacios .10 .03
443 Pat Tabler .10 .03
444 Darryl Strawberry CL .10 .03
445 Mike Felder .10 .03
446 Al Newman .10 .03
447 Chris Donnels .10 .03
448 Rich Rodriguez .10 .03
449 Turner Ward RC .20 .06
450 Bob Walk .10 .03
451 Gilberto Reyes .10 .03
452 Mike Jackson .10 .03
453 Rafael Belliard .10 .03
454 Wayne Edwards .10 .03
455 Andy Allanson .10 .03
456 Dave Smith .10 .03
457 Gary Carter .30 .09
458 Warren Cromartie .10 .03
459 Jack Armstrong .10 .03
460 Bob Tewksbury .10 .03
461 Joe Klink .10 .03
462 Xavier Hernandez .10 .03
463 Scott Radinsky .10 .03
464 Jeff Robinson .10 .03
465 Gregg Jefferies .10 .03
466 Denny Neagle RC .50 .15
467 Carmelo Martinez .10 .03
468 Donn Pall .10 .03
469 Bruce Hurst .10 .03
470 Eric Bullock .10 .03
471 Rick Aguilera .20 .06
472 Charlie Hough .20 .06
473 Carlos Quintana .10 .03
474 Marty Barrett .10 .03
475 Kevin D. Brown .10 .03
476 Bobby Ojeda .10 .03
477 Edgar Martinez .30 .09
478 Bip Roberts .10 .03
479 Mike Flanagan .10 .03
480 John Habyan .10 .03
481 Larry Casian .10 .03
482 Wally Backman .10 .03
483 Doug Dascenzo .10 .03
484 Rick Dempsey .10 .03
485 Ed Sprague .10 .03
486 Steve Chitren .10 .03
487 Mark McGwire 1.25 .35
488 Roger Clemens 1.00 .30
489 Orlando Merced RC .10 .03
490 Rene Gonzales .10 .03
491 Mike Stanton .10 .03
492 Al Osuna RC .10 .03
493 Rick Cerone .10 .03
494 Mariano Duncan .10 .03
495 Zane Smith .10 .03
496 John Morris .10 .03
497 Frank Tanana .10 .03
498 Junior Ortiz .10 .03
499 Dave Winfield .20 .06
500 Gary Varsho .10 .03
501 Chico Walker .10 .03
502 Ken Caminiti .20 .06
503 Ken Griffey Sr. .20 .06
504 Randy Myers .10 .03
505 Steve Bedrosian .10 .03
506 Cory Snyder .10 .03
507 Cris Carpenter .10 .03
508 Tim Belcher .10 .03
509 Jeff Hamilton .10 .03
510 Steve Avery .10 .03
511 Dave Valle .10 .03
512 Tom Lampkin .10 .03
513 Shawn Hillegas .10 .03
514 Reggie Jefferson .10 .03
515 Ron Karkovice .10 .03
516 Doug Drabek .10 .03
517 Tom Henke .10 .03
518 Chris Bosio .10 .03
519 Gregg Olson .10 .03
520 Bob Scanlan .10 .03
521 Alonzo Powell .10 .03
522 Jeff Ballard .10 .03
523 Ray Lankford .10 .03
524 Tommy Greene .10 .03
525 Mike Timlin RC .20 .06
526 Juan Berenguer .10 .03
527 Scott Erickson .10 .03
528 Sandy Alomar Jr. CL .10 .03

1991 Leaf Gold Rookies

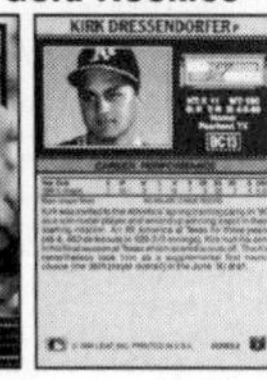

This 26-card standard size set was issued by Leaf as an insert to their 1991 Leaf regular issue.The first twelve cards were issued as random inserts in with the first series of 1991 Leaf foil packs. The rest were issued as random inserts in with the second series. The set features a selection of rookie prospects. The earliest Leaf Gold Rookie cards issued with the first series can sometimes be found with erroneous regular numbered backs 265 through 276 instead of the correct BC1 through BC12. These numbered variations are very tough to find.

Nm-Mt Ex-Mt
COMPLETE SET (26) 15.00 4.50
*265-276 ERR: 4X TO 10X BASIC GR.
265-276 ERR RANDOM IN EARLY PACKS
BC1 Scott Leius 1.00 .30
BC2 Luis Gonzalez 3.00 .90
BC3 Wil Cordero 1.00 .30
BC4 Gary Scott 1.00 .30
BC5 Willie Banks 1.00 .30
BC6 Arthur Rhodes 1.00 .30
BC7 Mo Vaughn 1.00 .30
BC8 Henry Rodriguez 1.00 .30
BC9 Todd Van Poppel 1.00 .30
BC10 Reggie Sanders 1.50 .45
BC11 Rico Brogna 1.00 .30
BC12 Mike Mussina 3.00 .90
BC13 Kirk Dressendorfer 1.00 .30
BC14 Jeff Bagwell 4.00 1.20
BC15 Pete Schourek 1.00 .30
BC16 Wade Taylor 1.00 .30
BC17 Pat Kelly 1.00 .30
BC18 Tim Costo 1.00 .30
BC19 Roger Salkeld 1.00 .30
BC20 Andujar Cedeno 1.00 .30
BC21 Ryan Klesko UER 2.00 .60
(1990 Sumter BA .289; should be .368)
BC22 Mike Huff 1.00 .30
BC23 Anthony Young 1.00 .30
BC24 Eddie Zosky 1.00 .30
BC25 Nolan Ryan DP UER 2.00 .60
No Hitter 7
(Word other repeated in 7th line)
BC26 R.Henderson DP 1.50 .45
Record Steal

1992 Leaf Previews

Four Leaf Preview standard-size cards were included in each 1992 Donruss hobby factory set. The cards were intended to show collectors and dealers the style of the 1992 Leaf set. The fronts carry glossy color player photos framed by silver borders.

Nm-Mt Ex-Mt
COMPLETE SET (26) 50.00 15.00
1 Steve Avery .30 .09
2 Ryne Sandberg 4.00 1.20
3 Chris Sabo .30 .09
4 Jeff Bagwell 2.50 .75
5 Darryl Strawberry 1.50 .45
6 Bret Barberie .30 .09
7 Howard Johnson .30 .09
8 John Kruk 1.00 .30
9 Andy Van Slyke 1.00 .30
10 Felix Jose .30 .09
11 Fred McGriff 1.50 .45
12 Will Clark 2.50 .75
13 Cal Ripken 8.00 2.40
14 Phil Plantier .30 .09
15 Lee Stevens .30 .09
16 Frank Thomas 2.50 .75
17 Mark Whiten .30 .09
18 Cecil Fielder 1.00 .30
19 George Brett 6.00 1.80
20 Robin Yount 4.00 1.20
21 Scott Erickson .30 .09
22 Don Mattingly 6.00 1.80
23 Jose Canseco 2.50 .75
24 Ken Griffey Jr. 4.00 1.20
25 Nolan Ryan 10.00 3.00
26 Joe Carter 1.00 .30

1992 Leaf Gold Previews

These Leaf Gold Preview cards were sent to members of the Donruss/Leaf Dealer Network who ordered 1992 Donruss Factory sets. For each set ordered, dealers received one two-card pack. These cards showed the style of the new 1992 Leaf Gold cards which would be included one per pack in the forthcoming set. The cards measure the standard size. The fronts feature color action player photos inside a gold foil picture frame and a black outer border.

Nm-Mt Ex-Mt
COMPLETE SET (33) 80.00 24.00
1 Steve Avery 1.00 .30
2 Ryne Sandberg 5.00 1.50
3 Chris Sabo 1.00 .30
4 Jeff Bagwell 5.00 1.50
5 Darryl Strawberry 1.50 .45
6 Bret Barberie 1.00 .30
7 Howard Johnson 1.00 .30
8 John Kruk 1.50 .45
9 Andy Van Slyke 1.50 .45
10 Felix Jose 1.00 .30
11 Fred McGriff 2.00 .60
12 Will Clark 4.00 1.20
13 Cal Ripken 20.00 6.00
14 Phil Plantier 1.00 .30
15 Lee Stevens 1.00 .30
16 Frank Thomas 4.00 1.20
17 Mark Whiten 1.00 .30
18 Cecil Fielder 1.50 .45
19 George Brett 10.00 3.00
20 Robin Yount 4.00 1.20
21 Scott Erickson 1.00 .30
22 Don Mattingly 10.00 3.00
23 Jose Canseco 4.00 1.20
24 Ken Griffey Jr. 12.00 3.60
25 Nolan Ryan 20.00 6.00
26 Joe Carter 1.50 .45
27 Deion Sanders 2.50 .75
28 Dean Palmer 1.50 .45
29 Andy Benes 1.50 .45
30 Gary DiSarcina 1.00 .30
31 Chris Hoiles 1.00 .30
32 Mark McGwire 15.00 4.50
33 Reggie Sanders 1.00 .30

1992 Leaf

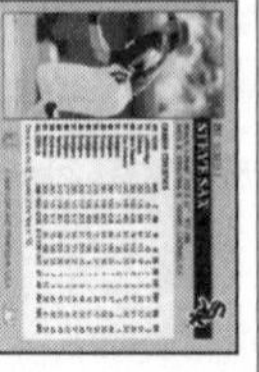

The 1992 Leaf set consists of 528 cards, issued in two separate 264-card series. Cards were distributed in first and second series 15-card foil packs. Each pack contained a selection of basic cards and one black gold parallel card. The basic card fronts feature color action player photos on a silver card face. The player's name appears in a black bar edged at the bottom by a thin red stripe. The team logo overlaps the bar at the right corner. Rookie Cards in this set include Brian Jordan and Jeff Kent.

Nm-Mt Ex-Mt
COMPLETE SET (528) 15.00 4.50
COMP. SERIES 1 (264) 5.00 1.50
COMP. SERIES 2 (264) 10.00 3.00
1 Jim Abbott .25 .07
2 Cal Eldred .05 .02
3 Bud Black .05 .02
4 Dave Howard .05 .02
5 Luis Sojo .05 .02
6 Gary Scott .05 .02
7 Joe Oliver .05 .02
8 Chris Gardner .05 .02
9 Sandy Alomar Jr. .05 .02
10 Greg W. Harris .05 .02
11 Doug Drabek .05 .02
12 Darryl Hamilton .05 .02
13 Mike Mussina .40 .12
14 Kevin Tapani .05 .02
15 Ron Gant .15 .04
16 Mark McGwire 1.00 .30
17 Robin Ventura .15 .04
18 Pedro Guerrero .15 .04
19 Roger Clemens .75 .23
20 Steve Farr .05 .02
21 Frank Tanana .05 .02
22 Joe Hesketh .05 .02
23 Erik Hanson .05 .02
24 Greg Cadaret .05 .02
25 Rex Hudler .05 .02
26 Mark Grace .25 .07
27 Kelly Gruber .05 .02
28 Jeff Bagwell .40 .12
29 Darryl Strawberry .25 .07
30 Dave Smith .05 .02
31 Kevin Appier .15 .04
32 Steve Chitren .05 .02
33 Kevin Gross .05 .02
34 Rick Aguilera .15 .04
35 Juan Guzman .05 .02
36 Joe Orsulak .05 .02
37 Tim Raines .15 .04
38 Harold Reynolds .15 .04
39 Charlie Hough .15 .04
40 Tony Phillips .05 .02
41 Nolan Ryan 1.50 .45
42 Vince Coleman .05 .02
43 Andy Van Slyke .15 .04
44 Tim Burke .05 .02
45 Luis Polonia .05 .02
46 Tom Browning .05 .02
47 Willie McGee .15 .04
48 Gary DiSarcina .05 .02
49 Mark Lewis .05 .02
50 Phil Plantier .05 .02
51 Doug Dascenzo .05 .02
52 Cal Ripken 1.25 .35
53 Pedro Munoz .05 .02
54 Carlos Hernandez .05 .02
55 Jerald Clark .05 .02
56 Jeff Brantley .05 .02
57 Don Mattingly 1.00 .30
58 Roger McDowell .05 .02
59 Steve Avery .05 .02
60 John Olerud .15 .04
61 Bill Gullickson .05 .02
62 Juan Gonzalez .40 .12
63 Felix Jose .05 .02
64 Robin Yount .60 .18
65 Greg Briley .05 .02
66 Steve Finley .15 .04
67 Frank Thomas CL .25 .07
68 Tom Gordon .05 .02
69 Rob Dibble .15 .04
70 Glenallen Hill .05 .02
71 Calvin Jones .05 .02
72 Joe Girardi .05 .02
73 Barry Larkin .40 .12
74 Andy Benes .05 .02
75 Milt Cuyler .05 .02
76 Kevin Bass .05 .02
77 Pete Harnisch .05 .02
78 Wilson Alvarez .05 .02
79 Mike Devereaux .05 .02
80 Doug Henry RC .10 .03
81 Orel Hershiser .15 .04
82 Shane Mack .05 .02
83 Mike Macfarlane .05 .02
84 Thomas Howard .05 .02
85 Alex Fernandez .05 .02
86 Reggie Jefferson .05 .02
87 Leo Gomez .05 .02
88 Mel Hall .05 .02
89 Mike Greenwell .05 .02
90 Jeff Russell .05 .02
91 Steve Buechele .05 .02
92 David Cone .15 .04
93 Kevin Reimer .05 .02
94 Mark Lemke .05 .02
95 Bob Tewksbury .05 .02
96 Zane Smith .05 .02
97 Mark Eichhorn .05 .02
98 Kirby Puckett .40 .12
99 Paul O'Neill .25 .07
100 Dennis Eckersley .15 .04
101 Duane Ward .05 .02
102 Matt Nokes .05 .02
103 Mo Vaughn .15 .04
104 Pat Kelly .05 .02
105 Ron Karkovice .05 .02
106 Bill Spiers .05 .02
107 Gary Gaetti .15 .04
108 Mackey Sasser .05 .02
109 Robby Thompson .05 .02
110 Marvin Freeman .05 .02
111 Jimmy Key .15 .04
112 Dwight Gooden .25 .07
113 Charlie Leibrandt .05 .02
114 Devon White .05 .02
115 Charles Nagy .05 .02
116 Rickey Henderson .40 .12
117 Paul Assenmacher .05 .02
118 Junior Felix .05 .02
119 Julio Franco .15 .04
120 Norm Charlton .05 .02
121 Scott Servais .05 .02
122 Gerald Perry .05 .02
123 Brian McRae .05 .02
124 Don Slaught .05 .02
125 Juan Samuel .05 .02
126 Harold Baines .15 .04
127 Scott Livingstone .05 .02
128 Jay Buhner .15 .04
129 Darrin Jackson .05 .02
130 Luis Mercedes .05 .02
131 Brian Harper .05 .02
132 Howard Johnson .05 .02
133 Nolan Ryan CL .40 .12
134 Dante Bichette .15 .04
135 Dave Righetti .15 .04
136 Jeff Montgomery .05 .02
137 Joe Grahe .05 .02
138 Delino DeShields .05 .02
139 Jose Rijo .05 .02
140 Ken Caminiti .15 .04
141 Steve Olin .05 .02
142 Kurt Stillwell .05 .02
143 Jay Bell .15 .04
144 Jaime Navarro .05 .02
145 Ben McDonald .05 .02
146 Greg Gagne .05 .02
147 Jeff Blauser .05 .02
148 Carney Lansford .15 .04
149 Ozzie Guillen .05 .02
150 Milt Thompson .05 .02
151 Jeff Reardon .15 .04
152 Scott Sanderson .05 .02
153 Cecil Fielder .15 .04
154 Greg A. Harris .05 .02
155 Rich DeLucia .05 .02
156 Roberto Kelly .05 .02
157 Bryn Smith .05 .02
158 Chuck McElroy .05 .02
159 Tom Henke .05 .02
160 Luis Gonzalez .25 .07
161 Steve Wilson .05 .02
162 Shawn Boskie .05 .02
163 Mark Davis .05 .02
164 Mike Moore .05 .02
165 Mike Scioscia .05 .02
166 Scott Erickson .05 .02
167 Todd Stottlemyre .05 .02
168 Alvin Davis .05 .02
169 Greg Hibbard .05 .02
170 David Valle .05 .02
171 Dave Winfield .15 .04
172 Alan Trammell .25 .07
173 Kenny Rogers .15 .04
174 John Franco .15 .04
175 Jose Lind .05 .02
176 Pete Schourek .05 .02
177 Von Hayes .05 .02
178 Chris Hammond .05 .02
179 John Burkett .05 .02
180 Dickie Thon .05 .02
181 Joel Skinner .05 .02
182 Scott Cooper .05 .02
183 Andre Dawson .15 .04
184 Billy Ripken .05 .02
185 Kevin Mitchell .05 .02
186 Brett Butler .15 .04
187 Tony Fernandez .05 .02
188 Cory Snyder .05 .02
189 John Habyan .05 .02
190 Dennis Martinez .15 .04
191 John Smoltz .25 .07
192 Greg Myers .05 .02
193 Rob Deer .05 .02
194 Ivan Rodriguez .40 .12
195 Ray Lankford .05 .02
196 Bill Wegman .05 .02
197 Edgar Martinez .25 .07
198 Darryl Kile .15 .04
199 Cal Ripken CL .40 .12
200 Brent Mayne .05 .02
201 Larry Walker .25 .07
202 Carlos Baerga .05 .02
203 Russ Swan .05 .02
204 Mike Morgan .05 .02
205 Hal Morris .05 .02
206 Tony Gwynn .50 .15
207 Mark Leiter .05 .02
208 Kirt Manwaring .05 .02
209 Al Osuna .05 .02
210 Bobby Thigpen .05 .02
211 Chris Hoiles .05 .02
212 B.J. Surhoff .15 .04
213 Lenny Harris .05 .02
214 Scott Leius .05 .02
215 Gregg Jefferies .05 .02
216 Bruce Hurst .05 .02
217 Steve Sax .05 .02
218 Dave Otto .05 .02
219 Sam Horn .05 .02
220 Charlie Hayes .05 .02
221 Frank Viola .15 .04
222 Jose Guzman .05 .02
223 Gary Redus .05 .02
224 Dave Gallagher .05 .02
225 Dean Palmer .15 .04
226 Greg Olson .05 .02
227 Jose DeLeon .05 .02
228 Mike LaValliere .05 .02
229 Mark Langston .05 .02
230 Chuck Knoblauch .15 .04
231 Bill Doran .05 .02
232 Dave Henderson .05 .02
233 Roberto Alomar .40 .12
234 Scott Fletcher .05 .02
235 Tim Naehring .05 .02
236 Mike Gallego .05 .02
237 Lance Johnson .05 .02
238 Paul Molitor .25 .07
239 Dan Gladden .05 .02
240 Willie Randolph .15 .04
241 Will Clark .40 .12
242 Sid Bream .05 .02
243 Derek Bell .15 .04
244 Bill Pecota .05 .02
245 Terry Pendleton .15 .04
246 Randy Ready .05 .02
247 Jack Armstrong .05 .02
248 Todd Van Poppel .05 .02
249 Shawon Dunston .05 .02
250 Bobby Rose .05 .02
251 Jeff Huson .05 .02
252 Bip Roberts .05 .02
253 Doug Jones .05 .02
254 Lee Smith .15 .04
255 George Brett 1.00 .30
256 Randy Tomlin .05 .02
257 Todd Benzinger .05 .02
258 Dave Stewart .15 .04
259 Mark Carreon .05 .02
260 Pete O'Brien .05 .02
261 Tim Teufel .05 .02
262 Bob Milacki .05 .02
263 Mark Guthrie .05 .02
264 Darrin Fletcher .05 .02
265 Omar Vizquel .15 .04
266 Chris Bosio .05 .02
267 Jose Canseco .40 .12
268 Mike Boddicker .05 .02
269 Lance Parrish .15 .04
270 Jose Vizcaino .05 .02
271 Chris Sabo .05 .02
272 Royce Clayton .05 .02
273 Marquis Grissom .05 .02
274 Fred McGriff .25 .07
275 Barry Bonds 1.00 .30
276 Greg Vaughn .15 .04
277 Gregg Olson .05 .02
278 Dave Hollins .05 .02
279 Tom Glavine .25 .07
280 Bryan Hickerson UER .05 .02
Name spelled Brian on front
281 Scott Radinsky .05 .02
282 Omar Olivares .05 .02
283 Ivan Calderon .05 .02
284 Kevin Maas .05 .02
285 Mickey Tettleton .05 .02
286 Wade Boggs .25 .07
287 Stan Belinda .05 .02
288 Bret Barberie .05 .02
289 Jose Oquendo .05 .02
290 Frank Castillo .05 .02
291 Dave Stieb .05 .02
292 Tommy Greene .05 .02
293 Eric Karros .15 .04
294 Greg Maddux .60 .18
295 Jim Eisenreich .05 .02
296 Rafael Palmeiro .25 .07
297 Ramon Martinez .05 .02
298 Tim Wallach .05 .02
299 Jim Thome .40 .12
300 Chito Martinez .05 .02
301 Mitch Williams .05 .02
302 Randy Johnson .40 .12
303 Carlton Fisk .25 .07
304 Travis Fryman .15 .04
305 Bobby Witt .05 .02
306 Dave Magadan .05 .02
307 Alex Cole .05 .02
308 Bobby Bonilla .15 .04
309 Bryan Harvey .05 .02
310 Rafael Belliard .05 .02
311 Mariano Duncan .05 .02
312 Chuck Crim .05 .02
313 John Kruk .15 .04
314 Ellis Burks .15 .04
315 Craig Biggio .25 .07
316 Glenn Davis .05 .02
317 Ryne Sandberg .60 .18
318 Mike Sharperson .05 .02
319 Rich Rodriguez .05 .02
320 Lee Guetterman .05 .02
321 Benito Santiago .15 .04
322 Jose Offerman .05 .02
323 Tony Pena .05 .02
324 Pat Borders .05 .02
325 Mike Henneman .05 .02
326 Kevin Brown .15 .04
327 Chris Nabholz .05 .02
328 Franklin Stubbs .05 .02
329 Tino Martinez .25 .07
330 Mickey Morandini .05 .02
331 Ryne Sandberg CL .40 .12
332 Mark Gubicza .05 .02
333 Bill Landrum .05 .02
334 Mark Whiten .05 .02
335 Darren Daulton .15 .04
336 Rick Wilkins .05 .02
337 Brian Jordan RC .75 .23
338 Kevin Ward .05 .02
339 Ruben Amaro .05 .02
340 Trevor Wilson .05 .02
341 Andujar Cedeno .05 .02
342 Michael Huff .05 .02
343 Brady Anderson .15 .04

Card	Nm-Mt	Ex-Mt
344 Craig Grebeck	.05	.02
345 Bob Ojeda	.05	.02
346 Mike Pagliarulo	.05	.02
347 Terry Shumpert	.05	.02
348 Dann Bilardello	.05	.02
349 Frank Thomas	.40	.12
350 Albert Belle	.15	.04
351 Jose Mesa	.05	.02
352 Rich Monteleone	.05	.02
353 Bob Walk	.05	.02
354 Monty Fariss	.05	.02
355 Luis Rivera	.05	.02
356 Anthony Young	.05	.02
357 Geno Petralli	.05	.02
358 Otis Nixon	.05	.02
359 Tom Pagnozzi	.05	.02
360 Reggie Sanders	.15	.04
361 Lee Stevens	.05	.02
362 Kent Hrbek	.15	.04
363 Orlando Merced	.05	.02
364 Mike Bordick	.05	.02
365 Dion James UER (Blue Jays logo on card back)	.05	.02
366 Jack Clark	.15	.04
367 Mike Stanley	.05	.02
368 Randy Velarde	.05	.02
369 Dan Pasqua	.05	.02
370 Pat Listach RC	.25	.07
371 Mike Fitzgerald	.05	.02
372 Tom Foley	.05	.02
373 Matt Williams	.15	.04
374 Brian Hunter	.05	.02
375 Joe Carter	.15	.04
376 Bret Saberhagen	.15	.04
377 Mike Stanton	.05	.02
378 Hubie Brooks	.05	.02
379 Eric Bell	.05	.02
380 Walt Weiss	.05	.02
381 Danny Jackson	.05	.02
382 Manuel Lee	.05	.02
383 Ruben Sierra	.05	.02
384 Greg Swindell	.05	.02
385 Ryan Bowen	.05	.02
386 Kevin Ritz	.05	.02
387 Curtis Wilkerson	.05	.02
388 Gary Varsho	.05	.02
389 Dave Hansen	.05	.02
390 Bob Welch	.05	.02
391 Lou Whitaker	.15	.04
392 Ken Griffey Jr.	.60	.18
393 Mike Maddux	.05	.02
394 Arthur Rhodes	.05	.02
395 Chili Davis	.15	.04
396 Eddie Murray	.40	.12
397 Robin Yount CL	.25	.07
398 Dave Cochrane	.05	.02
399 Kevin Seitzer	.05	.02
400 Ozzie Smith	.60	.18
401 Paul Sorrento	.05	.02
402 Les Lancaster	.05	.02
403 Junior Noboa	.05	.02
404 David Justice	.15	.04
405 Andy Ashby	.05	.02
406 Danny Tartabull	.05	.02
407 Bill Swift	.05	.02
408 Craig Lefferts	.05	.02
409 Tom Candiotti	.05	.02
410 Lance Blankenship	.05	.02
411 Jeff Tackett	.05	.02
412 Sammy Sosa	.60	.18
413 Jody Reed	.05	.02
414 Bruce Ruffin	.05	.02
415 Gene Larkin	.05	.02
416 John Vander Wal RC	.25	.07
417 Tim Belcher	.05	.02
418 Steve Frey	.05	.02
419 Dick Schofield	.05	.02
420 Jeff King	.05	.02
421 Kim Batiste	.05	.02
422 Jack McDowell	.05	.02
423 Damon Berryhill	.05	.02
424 Gary Wayne	.05	.02
425 Jack Morris	.15	.04
426 Moises Alou	.15	.04
427 Mark McLemore	.05	.02
428 Juan Guerrero	.05	.02
429 Scott Scudder	.05	.02
430 Eric Davis	.15	.04
431 Joe Slusarski	.05	.02
432 Todd Zeile	.05	.02
433 Dwayne Henry	.05	.02
434 Cliff Brantley	.05	.02
435 Butch Henry RC	.10	.03
436 Todd Worrell	.05	.02
437 Bob Scanlan	.05	.02
438 Wally Joyner	.15	.04
439 John Flaherty	.05	.02
440 Brian Downing	.05	.02
441 Darren Lewis	.05	.02
442 Gary Carter	.25	.07
443 Wally Ritchie	.05	.02
444 Chris Jones	.05	.02
445 Jeff Kent RC	1.50	.45
446 Gary Sheffield	.15	.04
447 Ron Darling	.05	.02
448 Deion Sanders	.25	.07
449 Andres Galarraga	.15	.04
450 Chuck Finley	.15	.04
451 Derek Lilliquist	.05	.02
452 Carl Willis	.05	.02
453 Wes Chamberlain	.05	.02
454 Roger Mason	.05	.02
455 Spike Owen	.05	.02
456 Thomas Howard	.05	.02
457 Dave Martinez	.05	.02
458 Pete Incaviglia	.05	.02
459 Keith A. Miller	.05	.02
460 Mike Fetters	.05	.02
461 Paul Gibson	.05	.02
462 George Bell	.05	.02
463 Bobby Bonilla CL	.05	.02
464 Terry Mulholland	.05	.02
465 Storm Davis	.05	.02
466 Gary Pettis	.05	.02
467 Randy Bush	.05	.02
468 Ken Hill	.05	.02
469 Rheal Cormier	.05	.02
470 Andy Stankiewicz	.05	.02
471 Dave Burba	.05	.02
472 Henry Cotto	.05	.02
473 Dale Sveum	.05	.02
474 Rich Gossage	.15	.04
475 William Suero	.05	.02
476 Doug Strange	.05	.02
477 Bill Krueger	.05	.02
478 John Wetteland	.15	.04
479 Melido Perez	.05	.02
480 Lonnie Smith	.05	.02
481 Mike Jackson	.05	.02
482 Mike Gardiner	.05	.02
483 David Wells	.15	.04
484 Barry Jones	.05	.02
485 Scott Bankhead	.05	.02
486 Terry Leach	.05	.02
487 Vince Horsman	.05	.02
488 Dave Eiland	.05	.02
489 Alejandro Pena	.05	.02
490 Julio Valera	.05	.02
491 Joe Boever	.05	.02
492 Paul Miller RC	.05	.02
493 Archi Cianfrocco RC	.10	.03
494 Dave Fleming	.05	.02
495 Kyle Abbott	.05	.02
496 Chad Kreuter	.05	.02
497 Chris James	.05	.02
498 Donnie Hill	.05	.02
499 Jacob Brumfield	.05	.02
500 Ricky Bones	.05	.02
501 Terry Steinbach	.05	.02
502 Bernard Gilkey	.05	.02
503 Dennis Cook	.05	.02
504 Len Dykstra	.15	.04
505 Mike Bielecki	.05	.02
506 Bob Kipper	.05	.02
507 Jose Melendez	.05	.02
508 Rick Sutcliffe	.15	.04
509 Ken Patterson	.05	.02
510 Andy Allanson	.05	.02
511 Al Newman	.05	.02
512 Mark Gardner	.05	.02
513 Jeff Schaefer	.05	.02
514 Jim McNamara	.05	.02
515 Peter Hoy	.05	.02
516 Curt Schilling	.25	.07
517 Kirk McCaskill	.05	.02
518 Chris Gwynn	.05	.02
519 Sid Fernandez	.05	.02
520 Jeff Parrett	.05	.02
521 Scott Ruskin	.05	.02
522 Kevin McReynolds	.05	.02
523 Rick Cerone	.05	.02
524 Jesse Orosco	.05	.02
525 Troy Afenir	.05	.02
526 John Smiley	.05	.02
527 Dale Murphy	.40	.12
528 Leaf Set Card	.05	.02

1992 Leaf Black Gold

This 528-card standard-size set was issued in two 264-card series. These Black Gold cards were inserted one per foil pack. The cards are similar to the regular issue Leaf cards, except that the card face is black rather than silver and accented by a gold foil inner border. Likewise, the horizontal backs have a gold rather than a silver background. The set is noteworthy as one of the earliest pack-distributed parallel issues in the hobby.

	Nm-Mt	Ex-Mt
COMPLETE SET (528)	60.00	18.00
COMP. SERIES 1 (264)	20.00	6.00
COMP. SERIES 2 (264)	40.00	12.00

*B.GOLD STARS: 2X TO 5X BASIC CARDS
*B.GOLD RC'S: 1.25X TO 3X BASIC CARDS

1992 Leaf Gold Rookies

This 24-card standard-size set honors 1992's most promising newcomers. The first 12 cards were randomly inserted in Leaf series I foil packs, while the second 12 cards were featured only in series II packs. The fronts display full-bleed color action photos highlighted by gold foil border stripes. A gold foil diamond appears at the corners of the picture frame, and the player's name appears in a black bar that extends between the bottom two diamonds. An early Pedro Martinez insert is the key card in this set.

	Nm-Mt	Ex-Mt
COMPLETE SET (24)	25.00	7.50
COMPLETE SERIES 1 (12)	20.00	6.00
COMPLETE SERIES 2 (12)	5.00	1.50
BC1 Chad Curtis	1.00	.30
BC2 Brent Gates	1.00	.30
BC3 Pedro Martinez	8.00	2.40
BC4 Kenny Lofton	1.50	.45
BC5 Turk Wendell	1.00	.30
BC6 Mark Hutton	1.00	.30
BC7 Todd Hundley	1.00	.30
BC8 Matt Stairs	1.00	.30
BC9 Eddie Taubensee	1.00	.30
BC10 David Nied	1.00	.30
BC11 Salomon Torres	1.00	.30
BC12 Bret Boone	2.00	.60
BC13 Johnny Ruffin	1.00	.30
BC14 Ed Martel	1.00	.30
BC15 Rick Trlicek	1.00	.30
BC16 Raul Mondesi	2.00	.60
BC17 Pat Mahomes	1.00	.30
BC18 Dan Wilson	1.00	.30
BC19 Donovan Osborne	1.00	.30
BC20 Dave Silvestri	1.00	.30
BC21 Gary DiSarcina	1.00	.30
BC22 Denny Neagle	1.00	.30
BC23 Steve Hosey	1.00	.30
BC24 John Doherty	1.00	.30

1993 Leaf

The 1993 Leaf baseball set consists of three series of 220, 220, and 110 standard-size cards, respectively. Cards were distributed in 14-card foil packs, jumbo packs and magazine packs. Rookie Cards in this set include J.T. Snow. White Sox slugger (and at that time, Leaf Representative) Frank Thomas signed 3,500 cards, which were randomly seeded into packs. In addition, a special card commemorating Dave Winfield's 3,000 hit was also seeded into packs. Both cards are listed at the end of our checklist but are not considered part of the 550-card basic set.

	Nm-Mt	Ex-Mt
COMPLETE SET (550)	35.00	10.50
COMP. SERIES 1 (220)	15.00	4.50
COMP. SERIES 2 (220)	15.00	4.50
COMPLETE UPDATE (110)	5.00	1.50
1 Ben McDonald	.15	.04
2 Sid Fernandez	.15	.04
3 Juan Guzman	.15	.04
4 Curt Schilling	.50	.15
5 Ivan Rodriguez	.75	.23
6 Don Slaught	.15	.04
7 Terry Steinbach	.15	.04
8 Todd Zeile	.15	.04
9 Andy Stankiewicz	.15	.04
10 Tim Teufel	.15	.04
11 Marvin Freeman	.15	.04
12 Jim Austin	.15	.04
13 Bob Scanlan	.15	.04
14 Rusty Meacham	.15	.04
15 Casey Candaele	.15	.04
16 Travis Fryman	.30	.09
17 Jose Offerman	.15	.04
18 Albert Belle	.30	.09
19 John Vander Wal	.15	.04
20 Dan Pasqua	.15	.04
21 Frank Viola	.30	.09
22 Terry Mulholland	.15	.04
23 Gregg Olson	.15	.04
24 Randy Tomlin	.15	.04
25 Todd Stottlemyre	.15	.04
26 Jose Oquendo	.15	.04
27 Julio Franco	.30	.09
28 Tony Gwynn	1.00	.30
29 Ruben Sierra	.15	.04
30 Robby Thompson	.15	.04
31 Jim Bullinger	.15	.04
32 Rick Aguilera	.15	.04
33 Scott Servais	.15	.04
34 Cal Eldred	.15	.04
35 Mike Piazza	2.00	.60
36 Brent Mayne	.15	.04
37 Wil Cordero	.15	.04
38 Milt Cuyler	.15	.04
39 Howard Johnson	.15	.04
40 Kenny Lofton	.30	.09
41 Alex Fernandez	.15	.04
42 Denny Neagle	.30	.09
43 Tony Pena	.15	.04
44 Bob Tewksbury	.15	.04
45 Glenn Davis	.15	.04
46 Fred McGriff	.50	.15
47 John Olerud	.30	.09
48 Steve Hosey	.15	.04
49 Rafael Palmeiro	.50	.15
50 David Justice	.30	.09
51 Pete Harnisch	.15	.04
52 Sam Militello	.15	.04
53 Orel Hershiser	.30	.09
54 Pat Mahomes	.15	.04
55 Greg Colbrunn	.15	.04
56 Greg Vaughn	.30	.09
57 Vince Coleman	.15	.04
58 Brian McRae	.15	.04
59 Len Dykstra	.30	.09
60 Dan Gladden	.15	.04
61 Ted Power	.15	.04
62 Donovan Osborne	.15	.04
63 Ron Karkovice	.15	.04
64 Frank Seminara	.15	.04
65 Bob Zupcic	.15	.04
66 Kirt Manwaring	.15	.04
67 Mike Devereaux	.15	.04
68 Mark Lemke	.15	.04
69 Devon White	.15	.04
70 Sammy Sosa	1.25	.35
71 Pedro Astacio	.15	.04
72 Dennis Eckersley	.30	.09
73 Chris Nabholz	.15	.04
74 Melido Perez	.15	.04
75 Todd Hundley	.15	.04
76 Kent Hrbek	.30	.09
77 Mickey Morandini	.15	.04
78 Tim McIntosh	.15	.04
79 Andy Van Slyke	.30	.09
80 Kevin McReynolds	.15	.04
81 Mike Henneman	.15	.04
82 Greg W. Harris	.15	.04
83 Sandy Alomar Jr.	.15	.04
84 Mike Jackson	.15	.04
85 Ozzie Guillen	.15	.04
86 Jeff Blauser	.15	.04
87 John Valentin	.15	.04
88 Rey Sanchez	.15	.04
89 Rick Sutcliffe	.30	.09
90 Luis Gonzalez	.30	.09
91 Jeff Fassero	.15	.04
92 Kenny Rogers	.30	.09
93 Bret Saberhagen	.30	.09
94 Bob Welch	.15	.04
95 Darren Daulton	.30	.09
96 Mike Gallego	.15	.04
97 Orlando Merced	.15	.04
98 Chuck Knoblauch	.30	.09
99 Bernard Gilkey	.15	.04
100 Billy Ashley	.15	.04
101 Kevin Appier	.30	.09
102 Jeff Brantley	.15	.04
103 Bill Gullickson	.15	.04
104 John Smoltz	.50	.15
105 Paul Sorrento	.15	.04
106 Steve Buechele	.15	.04
107 Steve Sax	.15	.04
108 Andujar Cedeno	.15	.04
109 Billy Hatcher	.15	.04
110 Checklist	.15	.04
111 Alan Mills	.15	.04
112 John Franco	.30	.09
113 Jack Morris	.30	.09
114 Mitch Williams	.15	.04
115 Nolan Ryan	3.00	.90
116 Jay Bell	.30	.09
117 Mike Bordick	.15	.04
118 Geronimo Pena	.15	.04
119 Danny Tartabull	.15	.04
120 Checklist	.15	.04
121 Steve Avery	.15	.04
122 Ricky Bones	.15	.04
123 Mike Morgan	.15	.04
124 Jeff Montgomery	.15	.04
125 Jeff Bagwell	.50	.15
126 Tony Phillips	.15	.04
127 Lenny Harris	.15	.04
128 Glenallen Hill	.15	.04
129 Marquis Grissom	.15	.04
130 Gerald Williams UER (Bernie Williams picture and stats)	.15	.04
131 Greg A. Harris	.15	.04
132 Tommy Greene	.15	.04
133 Chris Hoiles	.15	.04
134 Bob Walk	.15	.04
135 Duane Ward	.15	.04
136 Tom Pagnozzi	.15	.04
137 Jeff Huson	.15	.04
138 Kurt Stillwell	.15	.04
139 Dave Henderson	.15	.04
140 Darrin Jackson	.15	.04
141 Frank Castillo	.15	.04
142 Scott Erickson	.15	.04
143 Darryl Kile	.30	.09
144 Bill Wegman	.15	.04
145 Steve Wilson	.15	.04
146 George Brett	2.00	.60
147 Moises Alou	.30	.09
148 Lou Whitaker	.30	.09
149 Chico Walker	.15	.04
150 Jerry Browne	.15	.04
151 Kirk McCaskill	.15	.04
152 Zane Smith	.15	.04
153 Matt Young	.15	.04
154 Lee Smith	.30	.09
155 Leo Gomez	.15	.04
156 Dan Walters	.15	.04
157 Pat Borders	.15	.04
158 Matt Williams	.30	.09
159 Dean Palmer	.30	.09
160 John Patterson	.15	.04
161 Doug Jones	.15	.04
162 John Habyan	.15	.04
163 Pedro Martinez	1.50	.45
164 Carl Willis	.15	.04
165 Darrin Fletcher	.15	.04
166 B.J. Surhoff	.30	.09
167 Eddie Murray	.75	.23
168 Keith Miller	.15	.04
169 Ricky Jordan	.15	.04
170 Juan Gonzalez	.75	.23
171 Charles Nagy	.15	.04
172 Mark Clark	.15	.04
173 Bobby Thigpen	.15	.04
174 Tim Scott	.15	.04
175 Scott Cooper	.15	.04
176 Royce Clayton	.15	.04
177 Brady Anderson	.30	.09
178 Sid Bream	.15	.04
179 Derek Bell	.15	.04
180 Otis Nixon	.15	.04
181 Kevin Gross	.15	.04
182 Ron Darling	.15	.04
183 John Wetteland	.30	.09
184 Mike Stanley	.15	.04
185 Jeff Kent	.75	.23
186 Brian Harper	.15	.04
187 Mariano Duncan	.15	.04
188 Robin Yount	1.25	.35
189 Al Martin	.15	.04
190 Eddie Zosky	.15	.04
191 Mike Munoz	.15	.04
192 Andy Benes	.15	.04
193 Dennis Cook	.15	.04
194 Bill Swift	.15	.04
195 Frank Thomas	.75	.23
195A Frank Thomas (Franklin visible on batting glove)	1.25	.35
196 Damon Berryhill	.15	.04
197 Mike Greenwell	.15	.04
198 Mark Grace	.50	.15
199 Darryl Hamilton	.15	.04
200 Derrick May	.15	.04
201 Ken Hill	.15	.04
202 Kevin Brown	.30	.09
203 Dwight Gooden	.50	.15
204 Bobby Witt	.15	.04
205 Juan Bell	.15	.04
206 Kevin Maas	.15	.04
207 Jeff King	.15	.04
208 Scott Leius	.15	.04
209 Rheal Cormier	.15	.04
210 Darryl Strawberry	.50	.15
211 Tom Gordon	.15	.04
212 Bud Black	.15	.04
213 Mickey Tettleton	.15	.04
214 Pete Smith	.15	.04
215 Felix Fermin	.15	.04
216 Rick Wilkins	.15	.04
217 George Bell	.15	.04
218 Eric Anthony	.15	.04
219 Pedro Munoz	.15	.04
220 Checklist	.15	.04
221 Lance Blankenship	.15	.04
222 Deion Sanders	.50	.15
223 Craig Biggio	.50	.15
224 Ryne Sandberg	1.25	.35
225 Ron Gant	.30	.09
226 Tom Brunansky	.15	.04
227 Chad Curtis	.15	.04
228 Joe Carter	.30	.09
229 Brian Jordan	.30	.09
230 Brett Butler	.30	.09
231 Frank Bolick	.15	.04
232 Rod Beck	.15	.04
233 Carlos Baerga	.15	.04
234 Eric Karros	.30	.09
235 Jack Armstrong	.15	.04
236 Bobby Bonilla	.30	.09
237 Don Mattingly	2.00	.60
238 Jeff Gardner	.15	.04
239 Dave Hollins	.15	.04
240 Steve Cooke	.15	.04
241 Jose Canseco	.75	.23
242 Ivan Calderon	.15	.04
243 Tim Belcher	.15	.04
244 Freddie Benavides	.15	.04
245 Roberto Alomar	.75	.23
246 Rob Deer	.15	.04
247 Will Clark	.75	.23
248 Mike Felder	.15	.04
249 Harold Baines	.30	.09
250 David Cone	.30	.09
251 Mark Guthrie	.15	.04
252 Ellis Burks	.30	.09
253 Jim Abbott	.50	.15
254 Chili Davis	.30	.09
255 Chris Bosio	.15	.04
256 Bret Barberie	.15	.04
257 Hal Morris	.15	.04
258 Dante Bichette	.30	.09
259 Storm Davis	.15	.04
260 Gary DiSarcina	.15	.04
261 Ken Caminiti	.30	.09
262 Paul Molitor	.50	.15
263 Joe Oliver	.15	.04
264 Pat Listach	.15	.04
265 Gregg Jefferies	.15	.04
266 Jose Guzman	.15	.04
267 Eric Davis	.30	.09
268 Delino DeShields	.15	.04
269 Barry Bonds	2.00	.60
270 Mike Bielecki	.15	.04
271 Jay Buhner	.30	.09
272 Scott Pose RC	.15	.04
273 Tony Fernandez	.15	.04
274 Chito Martinez	.15	.04
275 Phil Plantier	.15	.04
276 Pete Incaviglia	.15	.04
277 Carlos Garcia	.15	.04
278 Tom Henke	.15	.04
279 Roger Clemens	1.50	.45
280 Rob Dibble	.30	.09
281 Daryl Boston	.15	.04
282 Greg Gagne	.15	.04
283 Cecil Fielder	.30	.09
284 Carlton Fisk	.50	.15
285 Wade Boggs	.50	.15
286 Damion Easley	.15	.04
287 Norm Charlton	.15	.04
288 Jeff Conine	.30	.09
289 Roberto Kelly	.15	.04
290 Jerald Clark	.15	.04
291 Rickey Henderson	.75	.23
292 Chuck Finley	.30	.09
293 Doug Drabek	.15	.04
294 Dave Stewart	.30	.09
295 Tom Glavine	.50	.15
296 Jaime Navarro	.15	.04
297 Ray Lankford	.15	.04
298 Greg Hibbard	.15	.04
299 Jody Reed	.15	.04
300 Dennis Martinez	.30	.09
301 Dave Martinez	.15	.04
302 Reggie Jefferson	.15	.04
303 John Cummings RC	.15	.04
304 Orestes Destrade	.15	.04
305 Mike Maddux	.15	.04
306 David Segui	.15	.04
307 Gary Sheffield	.30	.09
308 Danny Jackson	.15	.04
309 Craig Lefferts	.15	.04
310 Andre Dawson	.30	.09
311 Barry Larkin	.75	.23
312 Alex Cole	.15	.04
313 Mark Gardner	.15	.04
314 Kirk Gibson	.30	.09
315 Shane Mack	.15	.04
316 Bo Jackson	.75	.23
317 Jimmy Key	.30	.09
318 Greg Myers	.15	.04
319 Ken Griffey Jr.	1.25	.35
320 Monty Fariss	.15	.04
321 Kevin Mitchell	.15	.04
322 Andres Galarraga	.30	.09
323 Mark McGwire	2.00	.60
324 Mark Langston	.15	.04
325 Steve Finley	.30	.09
326 Greg Maddux	1.25	.35
327 Dave Nilsson	.15	.04
328 Ozzie Smith	1.25	.35
329 Candy Maldonado	.15	.04
330 Checklist	.15	.04
331 Tim Pugh RC	.15	.04
332 Joe Girardi	.15	.04
333 Junior Felix	.15	.04
334 Greg Swindell	.15	.04
335 Ramon Martinez	.15	.04
336 Sean Berry	.15	.04
337 Joe Orsulak	.15	.04
338 Wes Chamberlain	.15	.04
339 Stan Belinda	.15	.04
340 Checklist UER (306 Luis Mercedes)	.15	.04
341 Bruce Hurst	.15	.04
342 John Burkett	.15	.04
343 Mike Mussina	.75	.23
344 Scott Fletcher	.15	.04
345 Rene Gonzales	.15	.04
346 Roberto Hernandez	.15	.04
347 Carlos Martinez	.15	.04
348 Bill Krueger	.15	.04
349 Felix Jose	.15	.04
350 John Jaha	.15	.04

351 Willie Banks .15 .04
352 Matt Nokes .15 .04
353 Kevin Seitzer .15 .04
354 Erik Hanson .15 .04
355 David Hulse RC .15 .04
356 Domingo Martinez RC .15 .04
357 Greg Olson .15 .04
358 Randy Myers .15 .04
359 Tom Browning .15 .04
360 Charlie Hayes .15 .04
361 Bryan Harvey .15 .04
362 Eddie Taubensee .15 .04
363 Tim Wallach .15 .04
364 Mel Rojas .15 .04
365 Frank Tanana .15 .04
366 John Kruk .30 .09
367 Tim Laker RC .15 .04
368 Rich Rodriguez .15 .04
369 Darren Lewis .15 .04
370 Harold Reynolds .30 .09
371 Jose Melendez .15 .04
372 Joe Grahe .15 .04
373 Lance Johnson .15 .04
374 Jose Mesa .15 .04
375 Scott Livingstone .15 .04
376 Wally Joyner .30 .09
377 Kevin Reimer .15 .04
378 Kirby Puckett .75 .23
379 Paul O'Neill .50 .15
380 Randy Johnson .75 .23
381 Manuel Lee .15 .04
382 Dick Schofield .15 .04
383 Darren Holmes .15 .04
384 Charlie Hough .30 .09
385 John Orton .15 .04
386 Edgar Martinez .50 .15
387 Terry Pendleton .30 .09
388 Dan Plesac .15 .04
389 Jeff Reardon .30 .09
390 David Nied .15 .04
391 Dave Magadan .15 .04
392 Larry Walker .50 .15
393 Ben Rivera .15 .04
394 Lonnie Smith .15 .04
395 Craig Shipley .15 .04
396 Willie McGee .30 .09
397 Arthur Rhodes .15 .04
398 Mike Stanton .15 .04
399 Luis Polonia .15 .04
400 Jack McDowell .15 .04
401 Mike Moore .15 .04
402 Jose Lind .15 .04
403 Bill Spiers .15 .04
404 Kevin Tapani .15 .04
405 Spike Owen .15 .04
406 Tino Martinez .50 .15
407 Charlie Leibrandt .15 .04
408 Ed Sprague .15 .04
409 Bryn Smith .15 .04
410 Benito Santiago .30 .09
411 Jose Rijo .15 .04
412 Pete O'Brien .15 .04
413 Willie Wilson .15 .04
414 Bip Roberts .15 .04
415 Eric Young .15 .04
416 Walt Weiss .15 .04
417 Milt Thompson .15 .04
418 Chris Sabo .15 .04
419 Scott Sanderson .15 .04
420 Tim Raines .30 .09
421 Alan Trammell .50 .15
422 Mike Macfarlane .15 .04
423 Dave Winfield .30 .09
424 Bob Wickman .15 .04
425 David Valle .15 .04
426 Gary Redus .15 .04
427 Turner Ward .15 .04
428 Reggie Sanders .30 .09
429 Todd Worrell .15 .04
430 Julio Valera .15 .04
431 Cal Ripken Jr. 2.50 .75
432 Mo Vaughn .30 .09
433 John Smiley .15 .04
434 Omar Vizquel .30 .09
435 Billy Ripken .15 .04
436 Cory Snyder .15 .04
437 Carlos Quintana .15 .04
438 Omar Olivares .15 .04
439 Robin Ventura .30 .09
440 Checklist .15 .04
441 Kevin Higgins .15 .04
442 Carlos Hernandez .15 .04
443 Dan Peltier .15 .04
444 Derek Lilliquist .15 .04
445 Tim Salmon .50 .15
446 Sherman Obando RC .15 .04
447 Pat Kelly .15 .04
448 Todd Van Poppel .15 .04
449 Mark Whiten .15 .04
450 Checklist .15 .04
451 Pat Meares RC .30 .09
452 Tony Tarasco RC .15 .04
453 Chris Gwynn .15 .04
454 Armando Reynoso .15 .04
455 Danny Darwin .15 .04
456 Willie Greene .15 .04
457 Mike Blowers .15 .04
458 Kevin Roberson RC .15 .04
459 Graeme Lloyd RC .30 .09
460 David West .15 .04
461 Joey Cora .15 .04
462 Alex Arias .15 .04
463 Chad Kreuter .15 .04
464 Mike Lansing RC .30 .09
465 Mike Timlin .15 .04
466 Paul Wagner .15 .04
467 Mark Portugal .15 .04
468 Jim Leyritz .15 .04
469 Ryan Klesko .30 .09
470 Mario Diaz .15 .04
471 Guillermo Velasquez .15 .04
472 Fernando Valenzuela .30 .09
473 Raul Mondesi .30 .09
474 Mike Pagliarulo .15 .04
475 Chris Hammond .15 .04
476 Torey Lovullo .15 .04
477 Trevor Wilson .15 .04
478 Marcos Armas RC .15 .04
479 Dave Gallagher .15 .04
480 Jeff Treadway .15 .04
481 Jeff Branson .15 .04
482 Dickie Thon .15 .04
483 Eduardo Perez .15 .04
484 David Wells .30 .09
485 Brian Williams .15 .04
486 Domingo Cedeno RC .15 .04
487 Tom Candiotti .15 .04
488 Steve Frey .15 .04
489 Greg McMichael RC .15 .04
490 Marc Newfield .15 .04
491 Larry Andersen .15 .04
492 Damon Buford .15 .04
493 Ricky Gutierrez .15 .04
494 Jeff Russell .15 .04
495 Vinny Castilla .30 .09
496 Wilson Alvarez .15 .04
497 Scott Bullett .15 .04
498 Larry Casian .15 .04
499 Jose Vizcaino .15 .04
500 J.T. Snow RC .75 .23
501 Bryan Hickerson .15 .04
502 Jeremy Hernandez .15 .04
503 Jeromy Burnitz .30 .09
504 Steve Farr .15 .04
505 J. Owens RC .15 .04
506 Craig Paquette .15 .04
507 Jim Eisenreich .15 .04
508 Matt Whiteside RC .15 .04
509 Luis Aquino .15 .04
510 Mike LaValliere .15 .04
511 Jim Gott .15 .04
512 Mark McLemore .15 .04
513 Randy Milligan .15 .04
514 Gary Gaetti .30 .09
515 Lou Frazier RC .15 .04
516 Rich Amaral .15 .04
517 Gene Harris .15 .04
518 Aaron Sele .15 .04
519 Mark Wohlers .15 .04
520 Scott Kamieniecki .15 .04
521 Kent Mercker .15 .04
522 Jim Deshaies .15 .04
523 Kevin Stocker .15 .04
524 Jason Bere .15 .04
525 Tim Bogar RC .15 .04
526 Brad Pennington .15 .04
527 Curt Leskanic RC .15 .04
528 Wayne Kirby .15 .04
529 Tim Costo .15 .04
530 Doug Henry .15 .04
531 Trevor Hoffman .30 .09
532 Kelly Gruber .15 .04
533 Mike Harkey .15 .04
534 John Doherty .15 .04
535 Erik Pappas .15 .04
536 Brent Gates .15 .04
537 Roger McDowell .15 .04
538 Chris Haney .15 .04
539 Blas Minor .15 .04
540 Pat Hentgen .15 .04
541 Chuck Carr .15 .04
542 Doug Strange .15 .04
543 Xavier Hernandez .15 .04
544 Paul Quantrill .15 .04
545 Anthony Young .15 .04
546 Bret Boone .50 .15
547 Dwight Smith .15 .04
548 Bobby Munoz .15 .04
549 Russ Springer .15 .04
550 Roger Pavlik .15 .04
DW Dave Winfield 1.00 .30
3000 Hits
FT Frank Thomas AU/3500 60.00 18.00
(Certified autograph)

1993 Leaf Fasttrack

These 20 standard-size cards, featuring a selection of talented young stars, were randomly inserted into 1993 Leaf retail packs; the first ten were series I inserts, the second ten were series II inserts.

	Nm-Mt	Ex-Mt
COMPLETE SET (20)	60.00	18.00
COMPLETE SERIES 1 (10)	40.00	12.00
COMPLETE SERIES 2 (10)	30.00	9.00
1 Frank Thomas	10.00	3.00
2 Tim Wakefield	2.00	.60
3 Kenny Lofton	4.00	1.20
4 Mike Mussina	10.00	3.00
5 Juan Gonzalez	10.00	3.00
6 Chuck Knoblauch	4.00	1.20
7 Eric Karros	4.00	1.20
8 Ray Lankford	2.00	.60
9 Juan Guzman	2.00	.60
10 Pat Listach	2.00	.60
11 Carlos Baerga	2.00	.60
12 Felix Jose	2.00	.60
13 Steve Avery	2.00	.60
14 Robin Ventura	4.00	1.20
15 Ivan Rodriguez	10.00	3.00
16 Cal Eldred	2.00	.60
17 Jeff Bagwell	6.00	1.80
18 David Justice	4.00	1.20
19 Travis Fryman	4.00	1.20
20 Marquis Grissom	2.00	.60

1993 Leaf Gold All-Stars

These 30 standard-size dual-sided cards feature members of the American and National league All-Star squads. The first 20 were inserted one per 1993 Leaf jumbo packs; the first ten were series I inserts, the second ten were series II inserts. The final ten cards were randomly inserted in 1993 Leaf Update packs.

	Nm-Mt	Ex-Mt
COMPLETE REG.SET (20)	40.00	12.00
COMP. UPDATE SET (10)	12.00	3.60
R1 Ivan Rodriguez / Darren Daulton	1.25	.35
R2 Don Mattingly / Fred McGriff	3.00	.90
R3 Cecil Fielder / Jeff Bagwell	.75	.23
R4 Carlos Baerga / Ryne Sandberg	2.00	.60
R5 Chuck Knoblauch / Delino DeShields	.50	.15
R6 Robin Ventura / Terry Pendleton	.50	.15
R7 Ken Griffey Jr. / Andy Van Slyke	2.00	.60
R8 Joe Carter / Dave Justice	.50	.15
R9 Jose Canseco / Tony Gwynn	1.50	.45
R10 Dennis Eckersley / Rob Dibble	.50	.15
R11 Mark McGwire / Will Clark	3.00	.90
R12 Frank Thomas / Mark Grace	1.25	.35
R13 Roberto Alomar / Craig Biggio	.75	.23
R14 Cal Ripken / Barry Larkin	4.00	1.20
R15 Edgar Martinez / Gary Sheffield	.75	.23
R16 Juan Gonzalez / Barry Bonds	3.00	.90
R17 Kirby Puckett / Marquis Grissom	1.25	.35
R18 Jim Abbott / Tom Glavine	.75	.23
R19 Nolan Ryan / Greg Maddux	5.00	1.50
R20 Roger Clemens / Doug Drabek	2.50	.75
U1 Mark Langston / Terry Mulholland	.25	.07
U2 Ivan Rodriguez / Darren Daulton	1.25	.35
U3 John Olerud / John Kruk	.50	.15
U4 Roberto Alomar / Ryne Sandberg	2.00	.60
U5 Wade Boggs / Gary Sheffield	.75	.23
U6 Cal Ripken / Barry Larkin	4.00	1.20
U7 Kirby Puckett / Barry Bonds	1.25	.35
U8 Ken Griffey Jr. / Marquis Grissom	2.00	.60
U9 Joe Carter / David Justice	.50	.15
U10 Paul Molitor / Mark Grace	.75	.23

1993 Leaf Gold Rookies

These cards of promising newcomers were randomly inserted into 1993 Leaf packs; the first ten in series I, the last ten in series II, and five in the Update product. Leaf produced jumbo (3 1/2 by 5 inch) versions for retail repacks; they are valued at approximately double the prices below.

	Nm-Mt	Ex-Mt
COMPLETE REG.SET (20)	30.00	9.00
COMP. UPDATE SET (5)	20.00	6.00
*JUMBOS:2X BASIC GOLD ROOKIES .		
JUMBOS DIST.IN RETAIL PACKS		
R1 Kevin Young	2.00	.60
R2 Wil Cordero	1.00	.30
R3 Mark Kiefer	1.00	.30
R4 Gerald Williams	1.00	.30
R5 Brandon Wilson	1.00	.30
R6 Greg Gohr	1.00	.30
R7 Ryan Thompson	1.00	.30
R8 Tim Wakefield	2.00	.60
R9 Troy Neel	1.00	.30
R10 Tim Salmon	3.00	.90
R11 Kevin Rogers	1.00	.30
R12 Rod Bolton	1.00	.30
R13 Ken Ryan	1.00	.30
R14 Phil Hiatt	1.00	.30
R15 Rene Arocha	2.00	.60
R16 Nigel Wilson	1.00	.30
R17 J.T. Snow	5.00	1.50
R18 Benji Gil	1.00	.30
R19 Chipper Jones	5.00	1.50
R20 Darrell Sherman	1.00	.30
U1 Allen Watson	1.00	.30
U2 Jeffrey Hammonds	1.00	.30
U3 David McCarty	1.00	.30
U4 Mike Piazza	10.00	3.00
U5 Roberto Mejia	1.00	.30

1993 Leaf Heading for the Hall

Randomly inserted into 1993 Leaf series 1 and 2 packs, this ten-card standard-size set features potential Hall of Famers. Cards 1-5 were series I inserts and cards 6-10 were series II inserts.

	Nm-Mt	Ex-Mt
COMPLETE SET (10)	30.00	9.00
COMPLETE SERIES 1 (5)	20.00	6.00
COMPLETE SERIES 2 (5)	10.00	3.00
1 Nolan Ryan	12.00	3.60
2 Tony Gwynn	4.00	1.20
3 Robin Yount	5.00	1.50
4 Eddie Murray	3.00	.90
5 Cal Ripken	10.00	3.00
6 Roger Clemens	6.00	1.80
7 George Brett	8.00	2.40
8 Ryne Sandberg	5.00	1.50
9 Kirby Puckett	3.00	.90
10 Ozzie Smith	5.00	1.50

1993 Leaf Special Edition

This two card set, which measured 5" by 7" was issued by Donruss/Leaf and featured two of the hottest players in baseball at that time. Each of these cards were serial numbered to 10,000 on the back.

	MINT	NRMT
COMPLETE SET	6.00	2.70
1 Frank Thomas	2.50	1.10
2 Barry Bonds	5.00	2.20

1993 Leaf Thomas

This ten-card standard-size set spotlights Chicago White Sox slugger and Donruss/Leaf spokesperson Frank Thomas and were randomly inserted into all forms of Leaf packs. Five cards were inserted in each of the two series. Jumbo (5" by 7") versions of these cards were issued one per box of Leaf Update. The Jumbos are individually numbered out of 7,500.

	Nm-Mt	Ex-Mt
COMMON (1-10)	2.00	.60

*JUMBOS: .6X TO 1.5X BASIC THOMAS
ONE JUMBO CARD PER UPDATE BOX

1994 Leaf Promos

Issued to herald the release of the 1994 Leaf set, these nine promo cards measure the standard size and parallel the corresponding regular issue 1994 Leaf cards. The "Promotional Sample" disclaimer appears diagonally on the front and back. The cards are numbered on the back as "X of 9."

	Nm-Mt	Ex-Mt
COMPLETE SET (9)	15.00	4.50
1 Roberto Alomar	1.00	.30
2 Darren Daulton	.50	.15
3 Ken Griffey Jr.	3.00	.90
4 David Justice	1.00	.30
5 Don Mattingly	2.50	.75
6 Mike Piazza	3.00	.90
7 Cal Ripken	5.00	1.50
8 Ryne Sandberg	2.00	.60
9 Frank Thomas	1.50	.45

1994 Leaf

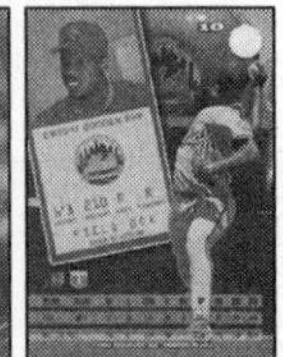

The 1994 Leaf baseball set consists of two series of 220 standard-size cards for a total of 440. Randomly seeded "Super Packs" contained complete insert sets. Cards featuring players from the Texas Rangers, Cleveland Indians, Milwaukee Brewers and Houston Astros were held out of the first series in order to have up-to-date photography in each team's new uniforms. A limited number of players from the San Francisco Giants are featured in the first series because of minor modifications to the team's uniforms. Randomly inserted in hobby packs at a rate of one in 36 was a stamped version of Frank Thomas' 1990 Leaf rookie card.

	Nm-Mt	Ex-Mt
COMPLETE SET (440)	24.00	7.25
COMP. SERIES 1 (220)	12.00	3.60
COMP. SERIES 2 (220)	12.00	3.60
1 Cal Ripken Jr.	2.50	.75
2 Tony Tarasco	.15	.04
3 Joe Girardi	.15	.04
4 Bernie Williams	.50	.15
5 Chad Kreuter	.15	.04
6 Troy Neel	.15	.04
7 Tom Pagnozzi	.15	.04
8 Kirk Rueter	.30	.09
9 Chris Bosio	.15	.04
10 Dwight Gooden	.50	.15
11 Mariano Duncan	.15	.04
12 Jay Bell	.30	.09
13 Lance Johnson	.15	.04
14 Richie Lewis	.15	.04
15 Dave Martinez	.15	.04
16 Orel Hershiser	.30	.09
17 Rob Butler	.15	.04
18 Glenallen Hill	.15	.04
19 Chad Curtis	.15	.04
20 Mike Stanton	.15	.04
21 Tim Wallach	.15	.04
22 Milt Thompson	.15	.04
23 Kevin Young	.15	.04
24 John Smiley	.15	.04
25 Jeff Montgomery	.15	.04
26 Robin Ventura	.30	.09
27 Scott Lydy	.15	.04
28 Todd Stottlemyre	.15	.04
29 Mark Whiten	.15	.04
30 Robby Thompson	.15	.04
31 Bobby Bonilla	.30	.09
32 Andy Ashby	.15	.04
33 Greg Myers	.15	.04
34 Billy Hatcher	.15	.04
35 Brad Holman	.15	.04
36 Mark McLemore	.15	.04
37 Scott Sanders	.15	.04
38 Jim Abbott	.50	.15
39 David Wells	.30	.09
40 Roberto Kelly	.15	.04
41 Jeff Conine	.30	.09
42 Sean Berry	.15	.04
43 Mark Grace	.50	.15
44 Eric Young	.15	.04
45 Rick Aguilera	.15	.04
46 Chipper Jones	.75	.23
47 Mel Rojas	.15	.04
48 Ryan Thompson	.15	.04
49 Al Martin	.15	.04
50 Cecil Fielder	.30	.09
51 Pat Kelly	.15	.04
52 Kevin Tapani	.15	.04
53 Tim Costo	.15	.04
54 Dave Hollins	.15	.04
55 Kirt Manwaring	.15	.04
56 Gregg Jefferies	.15	.04
57 Ron Darling	.15	.04
58 Bill Haselman	.15	.04
59 Phil Plantier	.15	.04
60 Frank Viola	.30	.09
61 Todd Zeile	.15	.04
62 Bret Barberie	.15	.04
63 Roberto Mejia	.15	.04
64 Chuck Knoblauch	.30	.09
65 Jose Lind	.15	.04
66 Brady Anderson	.30	.09
67 Ruben Sierra	.15	.04
68 Jose Vizcaino	.15	.04
69 Joe Grahe	.15	.04
70 Kevin Appier	.30	.09
71 Wilson Alvarez	.15	.04
72 Tom Candiotti	.15	.04
73 John Burkett	.15	.04
74 Anthony Young	.15	.04
75 Scott Cooper	.15	.04
76 Nigel Wilson	.15	.04
77 John Valentin	.15	.04
78 David McCarty	.15	.04
79 Archi Cianfrocco	.15	.04
80 Lou Whitaker	.30	.09
81 Dante Bichette	.30	.09
82 Mark Dewey	.15	.04
83 Danny Jackson	.15	.04
84 Harold Baines	.30	.09
85 Todd Benzinger	.15	.04
86 Damion Easley	.15	.04
87 Danny Cox	.15	.04
88 Jose Bautista	.15	.04
89 Mike Lansing	.15	.04
90 Phil Hiatt	.15	.04
91 Tim Pugh	.15	.04
92 Tino Martinez	.50	.15
93 Raul Mondesi	.30	.09
94 Greg Maddux	1.25	.35
95 Al Leiter	.30	.09
96 Benito Santiago	.30	.09
97 Lenny Dykstra	.30	.09
98 Sammy Sosa	1.50	.45
99 Tim Bogar	.15	.04
100 Checklist	.15	.04
101 Deion Sanders	.50	.15
102 Bobby Witt	.15	.04
103 Wil Cordero	.15	.04
104 Rich Amaral	.15	.04
105 Mike Mussina	.75	.23
106 Reggie Sanders	.30	.09
107 Ozzie Guillen	.15	.04
108 Paul O'Neill	.50	.15
109 Tim Salmon	.50	.15
110 Rheal Cormier	.15	.04
111 Billy Ashley	.15	.04
112 Jeff Kent	.30	.09
113 Derek Bell	.15	.04
114 Danny Darwin	.15	.04
115 Chip Hale	.15	.04
116 Tim Raines	.30	.09
117 Ed Sprague	.15	.04
118 Darrin Fletcher	.15	.04
119 Darren Holmes	.15	.04
120 Alan Trammell	.50	.15
121 Don Mattingly	2.00	.60
122 Greg Gagne	.15	.04
123 Jose Offerman	.15	.04
124 Joe Orsulak	.15	.04

125 Jack McDowell .15 .04
126 Barry Larkin .75 .23
127 Ben McDonald .15 .04
128 Mike Bordick .15 .04
129 Devon White .15 .04
130 Mike Perez .15 .04
131 Jay Buhner .30 .09
132 Phil Leftwich RC .15 .04
133 Tommy Greene .15 .04
134 Charlie Hayes .15 .04
135 Don Slaught .15 .04
136 Mike Gallego .15 .04
137 Dave Winfield .30 .09
138 Steve Avery .15 .04
139 Derrick May .15 .04
140 Bryan Harvey .15 .04
141 Wally Joyner .30 .09
142 Andre Dawson .30 .09
143 Andy Benes .15 .04
144 John Franco .30 .09
145 Jeff King .15 .04
146 Joe Oliver .15 .04
147 Bill Gullickson .15 .04
148 Armando Reynoso .15 .04
149 Dave Fleming .15 .04
150 Checklist .15 .04
151 Todd Van Poppel .15 .04
152 Bernard Gilkey .15 .04
153 Kevin Gross .15 .04
154 Mike Devereaux .15 .04
155 Tim Wakefield .30 .09
156 Andres Galarraga .30 .09
157 Pat Meares .15 .04
158 Jim Leyritz .15 .04
159 Mike Macfarlane .15 .04
160 Tony Phillips .15 .04
161 Brent Gates .15 .04
162 Mark Langston .15 .04
163 Allen Watson .15 .04
164 Randy Johnson .75 .23
165 Doug Brocail .15 .04
166 Rob Dibble .30 .09
167 Roberto Hernandez .15 .04
168 Felix Jose .15 .04
169 Steve Cooke .15 .04
170 Darren Daulton .30 .09
171 Eric Karros .30 .09
172 Geronimo Pena .15 .04
173 Gary DiSarcina .15 .04
174 Marquis Grissom .15 .04
175 Joey Cora .15 .04
176 Jim Eisenreich .15 .04
177 Brad Pennington .15 .04
178 Terry Steinbach .15 .04
179 Pat Borders .15 .04
180 Steve Buechele .15 .04
181 Jeff Fassero .15 .04
182 Mike Greenwell .15 .04
183 Mike Henneman .15 .04
184 Ron Karkovice .15 .04
185 Pat Hentgen .15 .04
186 Jose Guzman .15 .04
187 Brett Butler .30 .09
188 Charlie Hough .30 .09
189 Terry Pendleton .30 .09
190 Melido Perez .15 .04
191 Orestes Destrade .15 .04
192 Mike Morgan .15 .04
193 Joe Carter .30 .09
194 Jeff Blauser .15 .04
195 Chris Hoiles .15 .04
196 Ricky Gutierrez .15 .04
197 Mike Moore .15 .04
198 Carl Willis .15 .04
199 Aaron Sele .15 .04
200 Checklist .15 .04
201 Tim Naehring .15 .04
202 Scott Livingstone .15 .04
203 Luis Alicea .15 .04
204 Torey Lovullo .15 .04
205 Jim Gott .15 .04
206 Bob Wickman .15 .04
207 Greg McMichael .15 .04
208 Scott Brosius .30 .09
209 Chris Gwynn .15 .04
210 Steve Sax .15 .04
211 Dick Schofield .15 .04
212 Robb Nen .30 .09
213 Ben Rivera .15 .04
214 Vinny Castilla .30 .09
215 Jamie Moyer .30 .09
216 Wally Whitehurst .15 .04
217 Frank Castillo .15 .04
218 Mike Blowers .15 .04
219 Tim Scott .15 .04
220 Paul Wagner .15 .04
221 Jeff Bagwell .50 .15
222 Ricky Bones .15 .04
223 Sandy Alomar Jr. .15 .04
224 Rod Beck .15 .04
225 Roberto Alomar .75 .23
226 Jack Armstrong .15 .04
227 Scott Erickson .15 .04
228 Rene Arocha .15 .04
229 Eric Anthony .15 .04
230 Jeromy Burnitz .30 .09
231 Kevin Brown .30 .09
232 Tim Belcher .15 .04
233 Bret Boone .30 .09
234 Dennis Eckersley .30 .09
235 Tom Glavine .50 .15
236 Craig Biggio .50 .15
237 Pedro Astacio .15 .04
238 Ryan Bowen .15 .04
239 Brad Ausmus .15 .04
240 Vince Coleman .15 .04
241 Jason Bere .15 .04
242 Ellis Burks .30 .09
243 Wes Chamberlain .15 .04
244 Ken Caminiti .30 .09
245 Willie Banks .15 .04
246 Sid Fernandez .15 .04
247 Carlos Baerga .15 .04
248 Carlos Garcia .15 .04
249 Jose Canseco .75 .23
250 Alex Diaz .15 .04
251 Albert Belle .30 .09
252 Moises Alou .30 .09
253 Bobby Ayala .15 .04
254 Tony Gwynn 1.00 .30
255 Roger Clemens 1.50 .45
256 Eric Davis .30 .09
257 Wade Boggs .50 .15
258 Chili Davis .30 .09
259 Rickey Henderson .75 .23
260 Andujar Cedeno .15 .04
261 Cris Carpenter .15 .04
262 Juan Guzman .15 .04
263 David Justice .30 .09
264 Barry Bonds 2.00 .60
265 Pete Incaviglia .15 .04
266 Tony Fernandez .15 .04
267 Cal Eldred .15 .04
268 Alex Fernandez .15 .04
269 Kent Hrbek .30 .09
270 Steve Farr .15 .04
271 Doug Drabek .15 .04
272 Brian Jordan .30 .09
273 Xavier Hernandez .15 .04
274 David Cone .30 .09
275 Brian Hunter .15 .04
276 Mike Harkey .15 .04
277 Delino DeShields .15 .04
278 David Hulse .15 .04
279 Mickey Tettleton .15 .04
280 Kevin McReynolds .15 .04
281 Darryl Hamilton .15 .04
282 Ken Hill .15 .04
283 Wayne Kirby .15 .04
284 Chris Hammond .15 .04
285 Mo Vaughn .30 .09
286 Ryan Klesko .30 .09
287 Rick Wilkins .15 .04
288 Bill Swift .15 .04
289 Rafael Palmeiro .50 .15
290 Brian Harper .15 .04
291 Chris Turner .15 .04
292 Luis Gonzalez .30 .09
293 Kenny Rogers .30 .09
294 Kirby Puckett .75 .23
295 Mike Stanley .15 .04
296 Carlos Reyes RC .15 .04
297 Charles Nagy .15 .04
298 Reggie Jefferson .15 .04
299 Bip Roberts .15 .04
300 Darrin Jackson .15 .04
301 Mike Jackson .15 .04
302 Dave Nilsson .15 .04
303 Ramon Martinez .15 .04
304 Bobby Jones .15 .04
305 Johnny Ruffin .15 .04
306 Brian McRae .15 .04
307 Bo Jackson .75 .23
308 Dave Stewart .30 .09
309 John Smoltz .50 .15
310 Dennis Martinez .30 .09
311 Dean Palmer .30 .09
312 David Nied .15 .04
313 Eddie Murray .75 .23
314 Darryl Kile .30 .09
315 Rick Sutcliffe .30 .09
316 Shawon Dunston .15 .04
317 John Jaha .15 .04
318 Salomon Torres .15 .04
319 Gary Sheffield .30 .09
320 Curt Schilling .50 .15
321 Greg Vaughn .30 .09
322 Jay Howell .15 .04
323 Todd Hundley .15 .04
324 Chris Sabo .15 .04
325 Stan Javier .15 .04
326 Willie Greene .15 .04
327 Hipolito Pichardo .15 .04
328 Doug Strange .15 .04
329 Dan Wilson .15 .04
330 Checklist .15 .04
331 Omar Vizquel .30 .09
332 Scott Servais .15 .04
333 Bob Tewksbury .15 .04
334 Matt Williams .30 .09
335 Tom Foley .15 .04
336 Jeff Russell .15 .04
337 Scott Leius .15 .04
338 Ivan Rodriguez .75 .23
339 Kevin Seitzer .15 .04
340 Jose Rijo .15 .04
341 Eduardo Perez .15 .04
342 Kirk Gibson .30 .09
343 Randy Milligan .15 .04
344 Edgar Martinez .50 .15
345 Fred McGriff .50 .15
346 Kurt Abbott RC .30 .09
347 John Kruk .30 .09
348 Mike Felder .15 .04
349 Dave Staton .15 .04
350 Kenny Lofton .30 .09
351 Graeme Lloyd .15 .04
352 David Segui .15 .04
353 Danny Tartabull .15 .04
354 Bob Welch .15 .04
355 Duane Ward .15 .04
356 Karl Rhodes .15 .04
357 Lee Smith .30 .09
358 Chris James .15 .04
359 Walt Weiss .15 .04
360 Pedro Munoz .15 .04
361 Paul Sorrento .15 .04
362 Todd Worrell .15 .04
363 Bob Hamelin .15 .04
364 Julio Franco .30 .09
365 Roberto Petagine .15 .04
366 Willie McGee .30 .09
367 Pedro Martinez .75 .23
368 Ken Griffey Jr. 1.25 .35
369 B.J. Surhoff .30 .09
370 Kevin Mitchell .15 .04
371 John Doherty .15 .04
372 Manuel Lee .15 .04
373 Terry Mulholland .15 .04
374 Zane Smith .15 .04
375 Otis Nixon .15 .04
376 Jody Reed .15 .04
377 Doug Jones .15 .04
378 John Olerud .30 .09
379 Greg Swindell .15 .04
380 Checklist .15 .04
381 Royce Clayton .15 .04
382 Jim Thome .75 .23
383 Steve Finley .30 .09
384 Ray Lankford .15 .04
385 Henry Rodriguez .15 .04
386 Dave Magadan .15 .04
387 Gary Redus .15 .04
388 Orlando Merced .15 .04
389 Tom Gordon .15 .04
390 Luis Polonia .15 .04
391 Mark McGwire 2.00 .60
392 Mark Lemke .15 .04
393 Doug Henry .15 .04
394 Chuck Finley .30 .09
395 Paul Molitor .50 .15
396 Randy Myers .15 .04
397 Larry Walker .50 .15
398 Pete Harnisch .15 .04
399 Darren Lewis .15 .04
400 Frank Thomas .75 .23
401 Jack Morris .30 .09
402 Greg Hibbard .15 .04
403 Jeffrey Hammonds .15 .04
404 Will Clark .75 .23
405 Travis Fryman .30 .09
406 Scott Sanderson .15 .04
407 Gene Harris .15 .04
408 Chuck Carr .15 .04
409 Ozzie Smith 1.25 .35
410 Kent Mercker .15 .04
411 Andy Van Slyke .30 .09
412 Jimmy Key .30 .09
413 Pat Mahomes .15 .04
414 John Wetteland .30 .09
415 Todd Jones .15 .04
416 Greg Harris .15 .04
417 Kevin Stocker .15 .04
418 Juan Gonzalez .75 .23
419 Pete Smith .15 .04
420 Pat Listach .15 .04
421 Trevor Hoffman .30 .09
422 Scott Fletcher .15 .04
423 Mark Lewis .15 .04
424 Mickey Morandini .15 .04
425 Ryne Sandberg 1.25 .35
426 Erik Hanson .15 .04
427 Gary Gaetti .30 .09
428 Harold Reynolds .30 .09
429 Mark Portugal .15 .04
430 David Valle .15 .04
431 Mitch Williams .15 .04
432 Howard Johnson .15 .04
433 Hal Morris .15 .04
434 Tom Henke .15 .04
435 Shane Mack .15 .04
436 Mike Piazza 1.50 .45
437 Bret Saberhagen .30 .09
438 Jose Mesa .15 .04
439 Jaime Navarro .15 .04
440 Checklist .15 .04
A300 Frank Thomas .75 .23
Leaf 5th Anniversary

1994 Leaf Clean-Up Crew

Inserted in magazine jumbo packs at a rate of one in 12, this 12-card set was issued in two series of six.

	Nm-Mt	Ex-Mt
COMPLETE SET (12)	30.00	9.00
COMPLETE SERIES 1 (6)	10.00	3.00
COMPLETE SERIES 2 (6)	20.00	6.00
1 Larry Walker	5.00	1.50
2 Andres Galarraga	3.00	.90
3 Dave Hollins	1.50	.45
4 Bobby Bonilla	3.00	.90
5 Cecil Fielder	3.00	.90
6 Danny Tartabull	1.50	.45
7 Juan Gonzalez	8.00	2.40
8 Joe Carter	3.00	.90
9 Fred McGriff	5.00	1.50
10 Matt Williams	3.00	.90
11 Albert Belle	3.00	.90
12 Harold Baines	3.00	.90

1994 Leaf Gamers

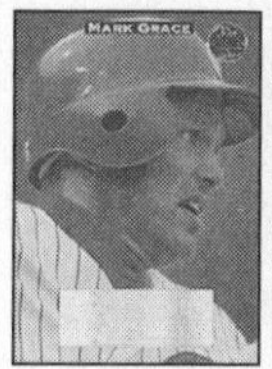

A close-up photo of the player highlights this 12-card standard-size set that was issued in two series of six. They were randomly inserted in jumbo packs at a rate of one in eight.

	Nm-Mt	Ex-Mt
COMPLETE SET (12)	80.00	24.00
COMPLETE SERIES 1 (6)	40.00	12.00
COMPLETE SERIES 2 (6)	40.00	12.00
1 Ken Griffey Jr.	10.00	3.00
2 Lenny Dykstra	2.50	.75
3 Juan Gonzalez	6.00	1.80
4 Don Mattingly	15.00	4.50
5 David Justice	2.50	.75
6 Mark Grace	4.00	1.20
7 Frank Thomas	6.00	1.80
8 Barry Bonds	15.00	4.50
9 Kirby Puckett	6.00	1.80
10 Will Clark	6.00	1.80
11 John Kruk	2.50	.75
12 Mike Piazza	12.00	3.60

1994 Leaf Gold Rookies

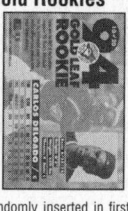

This set, which was randomly inserted in first series packs at a rate of one in 18 and second series packs at a rate of one in twelve, features 20 of the hottest young stars in the majors.

	Nm-Mt	Ex-Mt
COMPLETE SERIES 1 (10)	10.00	3.00
COMPLETE SERIES 2 (10)	5.00	1.50
1 Javier Lopez	1.50	.45
2 Rondell White	1.50	.45
3 Butch Huskey	1.00	.30
4 Midre Cummings	1.00	.30
5 Scott Ruffcorn	1.00	.30
6 Manny Ramirez	2.50	.75
7 Danny Bautista	1.00	.30
8 Russ Davis	1.00	.30
9 Steve Karsay	1.00	.30
10 Carlos Delgado	2.50	.75
11 Bob Hamelin	1.00	.30
12 Marcus Moore	1.00	.30
13 Miguel Jimenez	1.00	.30
14 Matt Walbeck	1.00	.30
15 James Mouton	1.00	.30
16 Rich Becker	1.00	.30
17 Brian Anderson	1.50	.45
18 Cliff Floyd	1.50	.45
19 Steve Trachsel	1.00	.30
20 Hector Carrasco	1.00	.30

1994 Leaf Gold Stars

Randomly inserted in all packs at a rate of one in 90, the 15 standard-size cards in this set are individually numbered and limited to 10,000 per player. The cards were issued in two series with eight cards in series one and seven in series two. They are numbered "X/10,000".

	Nm-Mt	Ex-Mt
COMPLETE SET (15)	150.00	45.00
COMPLETE SERIES 1 (8)	100.00	30.00
COMPLETE SERIES 2 (7)	50.00	15.00
1 Roberto Alomar	12.00	3.60
2 Barry Bonds	30.00	9.00
3 David Justice	5.00	1.50
4 Ken Griffey Jr.	20.00	6.00
5 Lenny Dykstra	5.00	1.50
6 Don Mattingly	30.00	9.00
7 Andres Galarraga	5.00	1.50
8 Greg Maddux	20.00	6.00
9 Carlos Baerga	2.50	.75
10 Paul Molitor	8.00	2.40
11 Frank Thomas	12.00	3.60
12 John Olerud	5.00	1.50
13 Juan Gonzalez	12.00	3.60
14 Fred McGriff	8.00	2.40
15 Jack McDowell	2.50	.75

1994 Leaf MVP Contenders

This 30-card standard-size set contains 15 players from each league who were projected to be 1994 MVP hopefuls. These unnumbered cards were randomly inserted in all second series packs at a rate of one in 36. If the player appearing on the card was named his league's MVP (Frank Thomas American League and Jeff Bagwell National League), the card could be redeemed for a 5" x 7" Frank Thomas card individually numbered out of 20,000. The backs contain all the rules and read "1 of 10,000". The expiration for redeeming Thomas and Bagwell cards was Jan. 19, 1995.

	Nm-Mt	Ex-Mt
COMPLETE SET (30)	150.00	45.00
*GOLD: SAME PRICE AS BASIC MVPS		
ONE GOLD SET PER A12 OR N2 VIA MAIL		
ONE THOMAS J400 PER A12 OR N2 VIA MAIL		
THOMAS J400 PRINT RUN 20,000 #'d CARDS		
A1 Albert Belle	3.00	.90
A2 Jose Canseco	8.00	2.40
A3 Joe Carter	3.00	.90
A4 Will Clark	8.00	2.40
A5 Cecil Fielder	3.00	.90
A6 Juan Gonzalez	8.00	2.40
A7 Ken Griffey Jr.	12.00	3.60
A8 Paul Molitor	5.00	1.50
A9 Rafael Palmeiro	5.00	1.50
A10 Kirby Puckett	8.00	2.40
A11 Cal Ripken Jr.	25.00	7.50
A12 Frank Thomas W	6.00	1.80
A13 Mo Vaughn	3.00	.90
A14 Carlos Baerga	1.50	.45
A15 AL Bonus Card	1.50	.45
N1 Gary Sheffield	3.00	.90
N2 Jeff Bagwell W	4.00	1.20
N3 Dante Bichette	3.00	.90
N4 Barry Bonds	20.00	6.00
N5 Darren Daulton	3.00	.90
N6 Andres Galarraga	3.00	.90
N7 Gregg Jefferies	1.50	.45
N8 David Justice	3.00	.90
N9 Ray Lankford	1.50	.45
N10 Fred McGriff	5.00	1.50
N11 Barry Larkin	8.00	2.40
N12 Mike Piazza	15.00	4.50
N13 Deion Sanders	5.00	1.50
N14 Matt Williams	3.00	.90
N15 NL Bonus Card	1.50	.45
J400 F.Thomas Jumbo	6.00	1.80

1994 Leaf Power Brokers

Inserted in second series retail and hobby foil packs at a rate of one in 12, this 10-card standard-size set spotlights top sluggers.

	Nm-Mt	Ex-Mt
COMPLETE SET (10)	20.00	6.00
1 Frank Thomas	2.00	.60
2 David Justice	.75	.23
3 Barry Bonds	5.00	1.50
4 Juan Gonzalez	2.00	.60
5 Ken Griffey Jr.	3.00	.90
6 Mike Piazza	4.00	1.20
7 Cecil Fielder	.75	.23
8 Fred McGriff	1.25	.35
9 Joe Carter	.75	.23
10 Albert Belle	.75	.23

1994 Leaf Slideshow

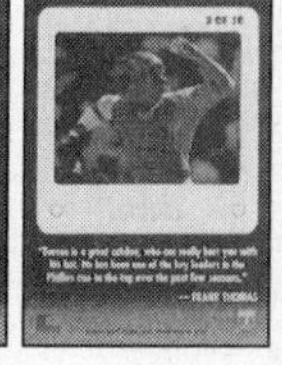

Randomly inserted in first and second series packs at a rate of one in 54, these ten standard-size cards simulate mounted photographic slides, but the images of the players are actually printed on acetate.

	Nm-Mt	Ex-Mt
COMPLETE SET (10)	50.00	15.00
COMPLETE SERIES 1 (5)	25.00	7.50
COMPLETE SERIES 2 (5)	25.00	7.50
1 Frank Thomas	5.00	1.50
2 Mike Piazza	10.00	3.00
3 Darren Daulton	2.00	.60
4 Ryne Sandberg	8.00	2.40
5 Roberto Alomar	5.00	1.50
6 Barry Bonds	12.00	3.60
7 Juan Gonzalez	5.00	1.50
8 Tim Salmon	3.00	.90
9 Ken Griffey Jr.	8.00	2.40
10 David Justice	2.00	.60

1994 Leaf Statistical Standouts

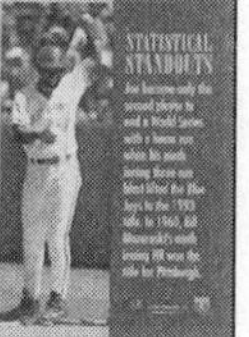

Inserted in retail and hobby foil packs at a rate of one in 12, this 10-card standard-size set features players that had significant statistical achievements in 1993. For example: Cal Ripken's home run record for a shortstop.

	Nm-Mt	Ex-Mt
COMPLETE SET (10)	15.00	4.50
1 Frank Thomas	1.25	.35
2 Barry Bonds	3.00	.90
3 Juan Gonzalez	1.25	.35
4 Mike Piazza	2.50	.75
5 Greg Maddux	2.00	.60
6 Ken Griffey Jr.	2.00	.60
7 Joe Carter	.50	.15
8 Dave Winfield	.50	.15
9 Tony Gwynn	1.50	.45
10 Cal Ripken	4.00	1.20

1995 Leaf Promos

These nine standard-size cards were issued to preview the 1995 Leaf set.

	Nm-Mt	Ex-Mt
COMPLETE SET (9)	15.00	4.50
1 Jeff Bagwell	1.50	.45
2 Wade Boggs	1.50	.45
3 Joe Carter	.75	.23
4 Greg Maddux	3.00	.90
5 Raul Mondesi	.75	.23
6 Kirby Puckett	2.50	.75
7 Cal Ripken	5.00	1.50

8 Frank Thomas 1.50 .45
9 Matt Williams 1.00 .30

1995 Leaf

The 1995 Leaf set was issued in two series of 200 standard-size cards for a total of 400. Full-bleed fronts contain diamond-shaped player hologram in the upper left. The team name is done in silver foil up the left side. Peculiar backs contain two photos, the card number within a stamp or seal like emblem in the upper right and '94 and career stats graph toward bottom left. Hideo Nomo is the only key Rookie Card in this set.

	Nm-Mt	Ex-Mt
COMPLETE SET (400)	40.00	12.00
COMP. SERIES 1 (200)	15.00	4.50
COMP. SERIES 2 (200)	25.00	7.50
1 Frank Thomas	.75	.23
2 Carlos Garcia	.15	.04
3 Todd Hundley	.15	.04
4 Damion Easley	.15	.04
5 Roberto Mejia	.15	.04
6 John Mabry	.15	.04
7 Aaron Sele	.15	.04
8 Kenny Lofton	.30	.09
9 John Doherty	.15	.04
10 Joe Carter	.30	.09
11 Mike Lansing	.15	.04
12 John Valentin	.15	.04
13 Ismael Valdes	.15	.04
14 Dave McCarty	.15	.04
15 Melvin Nieves	.15	.04
16 Bobby Jones	.15	.04
17 Trevor Hoffman	.30	.09
18 John Smoltz	.50	.15
19 Leo Gomez	.15	.04
20 Roger Pavlik	.15	.04
21 Dean Palmer	.30	.09
22 Rickey Henderson	.75	.23
23 Eddie Taubensee	.15	.04
24 Damon Buford	.15	.04
25 Mark Wohlers	.15	.04
26 Jim Edmonds	.30	.09
27 Wilson Alvarez	.15	.04
28 Matt Williams	.30	.09
29 Jeff Montgomery	.15	.04
30 Shawon Dunston	.15	.04
31 Tom Pagnozzi	.15	.04
32 Jose Lind	.15	.04
33 Royce Clayton	.15	.04
34 Cal Eldred	.15	.04
35 Chris Gomez	.15	.04
36 Henry Rodriguez	.15	.04
37 Dave Fleming	.15	.04
38 Jon Lieber	.15	.04
39 Scott Servais	.15	.04
40 Wade Boggs	.50	.15
41 John Olerud	.30	.09
42 Eddie Williams	.15	.04
43 Paul Sorrento	.15	.04
44 Ron Karkovice	.15	.04
45 Kevin Foster	.15	.04
46 Miguel Jimenez	.15	.04
47 Reggie Sanders	.30	.09
48 Rondell White	.30	.09
49 Scott Leius	.15	.04
50 Jose Valentin	.15	.04
51 Wm. VanLandingham	.15	.04
52 Denny Hocking	.15	.04
53 Jeff Fassero	.15	.04
54 Chris Hoiles	.15	.04
55 Walt Weiss	.15	.04
56 Geronimo Berroa	.15	.04
57 Rich Rowland	.15	.04
58 Dave Weathers	.15	.04
59 Sterling Hitchcock	.15	.04
60 Raul Mondesi	.30	.09
61 Rusty Greer	.30	.09
62 David Justice	.30	.09
63 Cecil Fielder	.30	.09
64 Brian Jordan	.30	.09
65 Mike Lieberthal	.30	.09
66 Rick Aguilera	.15	.04
67 Chuck Finley	.30	.09
68 Andy Ashby	.15	.04
69 Alex Fernandez	.15	.04
70 Ed Sprague	.15	.04
71 Steve Buechele	.15	.04
72 Willie Greene	.15	.04
73 Dave Nilsson	.15	.04
74 Bret Saberhagen	.30	.09
75 Jimmy Key	.30	.09
76 Darren Lewis	.15	.04
77 Steve Cooke	.15	.04
78 Kirk Gibson	.30	.09
79 Ray Lankford	.15	.04
80 Paul O'Neill	.50	.15
81 Mike Bordick	.15	.04
82 Wes Chamberlain	.15	.04
83 Rico Brogna	.15	.04
84 Kevin Appier	.30	.09
85 Juan Guzman	.15	.04
86 Kevin Seitzer	.15	.04
87 Mickey Morandini	.15	.04
88 Pedro Martinez	.75	.23
89 Matt Mieske	.15	.04
90 Tino Martinez	.50	.15
91 Paul Shuey	.15	.04
92 Bip Roberts	.15	.04
93 Chili Davis	.30	.09
94 Deion Sanders	.50	.15
95 Darrell Whitmore	.15	.04
96 Joe Orsulak	.15	.04
97 Bret Boone	.30	.09
98 Kent Mercker	.15	.04
99 Scott Livingstone	.15	.04
100 Brady Anderson	.30	.09
101 James Mouton	.15	.04
102 Jose Rijo	.15	.04
103 Bobby Munoz	.15	.04
104 Ramon Martinez	.15	.04
105 Bernie Williams	.50	.15
106 Troy Neel	.15	.04
107 Ivan Rodriguez	.75	.23
108 Salomon Torres	.15	.04
109 Johnny Ruffin	.15	.04
110 Darryl Kile	.30	.09
111 Bobby Ayala	.15	.04
112 Ron Darling	.15	.04
113 Jose Lima	.15	.04
114 Joey Hamilton	.15	.04
115 Greg Maddux	1.25	.35
116 Greg Colbrunn	.15	.04
117 Ozzie Guillen	.15	.04
118 Brian Anderson	.15	.04
119 Jeff Bagwell	.50	.15
120 Pat Listach	.15	.04
121 Sandy Alomar Jr.	.15	.04
122 Jose Vizcaino	.15	.04
123 Rick Helling	.15	.04
124 Allen Watson	.15	.04
125 Pedro Munoz	.15	.04
126 Craig Biggio	.50	.15
127 Kevin Stocker	.15	.04
128 Wil Cordero	.15	.04
129 Rafael Palmeiro	.50	.15
130 Gar Finnvold	.15	.04
131 Darren Hall	.15	.04
132 Heathcliff Slocumb	.15	.04
133 Darrin Fletcher	.15	.04
134 Cal Ripken	2.50	.75
135 Dante Bichette	.30	.09
136 Don Slaught	.15	.04
137 Pedro Astacio	.15	.04
138 Ryan Thompson	.15	.04
139 Greg Gohr	.15	.04
140 Javier Lopez	.30	.09
141 Lenny Dykstra	.30	.09
142 Pat Rapp	.15	.04
143 Mark Kiefer	.15	.04
144 Greg Gagne	.15	.04
145 Eduardo Perez	.15	.04
146 Felix Fermin	.15	.04
147 Jeff Frye	.15	.04
148 Terry Steinbach	.15	.04
149 Jim Eisenreich	.15	.04
150 Brad Ausmus	.15	.04
151 Randy Myers	.15	.04
152 Rick White	.15	.04
153 Mark Portugal	.15	.04
154 Delino DeShields	.15	.04
155 Scott Cooper	.15	.04
156 Pat Hentgen	.15	.04
157 Mark Gubicza	.15	.04
158 Carlos Baerga	.15	.04
159 Joe Girardi	.15	.04
160 Rey Sanchez	.15	.04
161 Todd Jones	.15	.04
162 Luis Polonia	.15	.04
163 Steve Trachsel	.15	.04
164 Roberto Hernandez	.15	.04
165 John Patterson	.15	.04
166 Rene Arocha	.15	.04
167 Will Clark	.75	.23
168 Jim Leyritz	.15	.04
169 Todd Van Poppel	.15	.04
170 Robb Nen	.30	.09
171 Midre Cummings	.15	.04
172 Jay Buhner	.30	.09
173 Kevin Tapani	.15	.04
174 Mark Lemke	.15	.04
175 Marcus Moore	.15	.04
176 Wayne Kirby	.15	.04
177 Rich Amaral	.15	.04
178 Lou Whitaker	.30	.09
179 Jay Bell	.30	.09
180 Rick Wilkins	.15	.04
181 Paul Molitor	.50	.15
182 Gary Sheffield	.30	.09
183 Kirby Puckett	.75	.23
184 Cliff Floyd	.30	.09
185 Darren Oliver	.15	.04
186 Tim Naehring	.15	.04
187 John Hudek	.15	.04
188 Eric Young	.15	.04
189 Roger Salkeld	.15	.04
190 Kirt Manwaring	.15	.04
191 Kurt Abbott	.15	.04
192 David Nied	.15	.04
193 Todd Zeile	.15	.04
194 Wally Joyner	.30	.09
195 Dennis Martinez	.30	.09
196 Billy Ashley	.15	.04
197 Ben McDonald	.15	.04
198 Bob Hamelin	.15	.04
199 Chris Turner	.15	.04
200 Lance Johnson	.15	.04
201 Willie Banks	.15	.04
202 Juan Gonzalez	.75	.23
203 Scott Sanders	.15	.04
204 Scott Brosius	.30	.09
205 Curt Schilling	.50	.15
206 Alex Gonzalez	.15	.04
207 Travis Fryman	.30	.09
208 Tim Raines	.30	.09
209 Steve Avery	.15	.04
210 Hal Morris	.15	.04
211 Ken Griffey Jr.	1.25	.35
212 Ozzie Smith	1.25	.35
213 Chuck Carr	.15	.04
214 Ryan Klesko	.30	.09
215 Robin Ventura	.30	.09
216 Luis Gonzalez	.30	.09
217 Ken Ryan	.15	.04
218 Mike Piazza	1.25	.35
219 Matt Walbeck	.15	.04
220 Jeff Kent	.30	.09
221 Orlando Miller	.15	.04
222 Kenny Rogers	.30	.09
223 J.T. Snow	.30	.09
224 Alan Trammell	.50	.15
225 John Franco	.30	.09
226 Gerald Williams	.15	.04
227 Andy Benes	.15	.04
228 Dan Wilson	.15	.04
229 Dave Hollins	.15	.04
230 Vinny Castilla	.30	.09
231 Devon White	.30	.09
232 Fred McGriff	.50	.15
233 Quilvio Veras	.15	.04
234 Tom Candiotti	.15	.04
235 Jason Bere	.15	.04
236 Mark Langston	.15	.04
237 Mel Rojas	.15	.04
238 Chuck Knoblauch	.30	.09
239 Bernard Gilkey	.15	.04
240 Mark McGwire	2.00	.60
241 Kirk Rueter	.15	.04
242 Pat Kelly	.15	.04
243 Ruben Sierra	.15	.04
244 Randy Johnson	.75	.23
245 Shane Reynolds	.15	.04
246 Danny Tartabull	.15	.04
247 Darryl Hamilton	.15	.04
248 Danny Bautista	.15	.04
249 Tom Gordon	.15	.04
250 Tom Glavine	.50	.15
251 Orlando Merced	.15	.04
252 Eric Karros	.30	.09
253 Benji Gil	.15	.04
254 Sean Bergman	.15	.04
255 Roger Clemens	1.50	.45
256 Roberto Alomar	.75	.23
257 Benito Santiago	.30	.09
258 Robby Thompson	.15	.04
259 Marvin Freeman	.15	.04
260 Jose Offerman	.15	.04
261 Greg Vaughn	.30	.09
262 David Segui	.15	.04
263 Geronimo Pena	.15	.04
264 Tim Salmon	.50	.15
265 Eddie Murray	.75	.23
266 Mariano Duncan	.15	.04
267 Hideo Nomo RC	1.50	.45
268 Derek Bell	.15	.04
269 Mo Vaughn	.30	.09
270 Jeff King	.15	.04
271 Edgar Martinez	.50	.15
272 Sammy Sosa	1.25	.35
273 Scott Ruffcorn	.15	.04
274 Darren Daulton	.30	.09
275 John Jaha	.15	.04
276 Andres Galarraga	.30	.09
277 Mark Grace	.50	.15
278 Mike Moore	.15	.04
279 Barry Bonds	2.00	.60
280 Manny Ramirez	.30	.09
281 Ellis Burks	.30	.09
282 Greg Swindell	.15	.04
283 Barry Larkin	.75	.23
284 Albert Belle	.30	.09
285 Shawn Green	.30	.09
286 John Roper	.15	.04
287 Scott Erickson	.15	.04
288 Moises Alou	.30	.09
289 Mike Blowers	.15	.04
290 Brent Gates	.15	.04
291 Sean Berry	.15	.04
292 Mike Stanley	.15	.04
293 Jeff Conine	.30	.09
294 Tim Wallach	.15	.04
295 Bobby Bonilla	.30	.09
296 Bruce Ruffin	.15	.04
297 Chad Curtis	.15	.04
298 Mike Greenwell	.15	.04
299 Tony Gwynn	1.00	.30
300 Russ Davis	.15	.04
301 Danny Jackson	.15	.04
302 Pete Harnisch	.15	.04
303 Don Mattingly	2.00	.60
304 Rheal Cormier	.15	.04
305 Larry Walker	.50	.15
306 Hector Carrasco	.15	.04
307 Jason Jacome	.15	.04
308 Phil Plantier	.15	.04
309 Harold Baines	.30	.09
310 Mitch Williams	.15	.04
311 Charles Nagy	.15	.04
312 Ken Caminiti	.30	.09
313 Alex Rodriguez	2.00	.60
314 Chris Sabo	.15	.04
315 Gary Gaetti	.30	.09
316 Andre Dawson	.30	.09
317 Mark Clark	.15	.04
318 Vince Coleman	.15	.04
319 Brad Clontz	.15	.04
320 Steve Finley	.30	.09
321 Doug Drabek	.15	.04
322 Mark McLemore	.15	.04
323 Stan Javier	.15	.04
324 Ron Gant	.30	.09
325 Charlie Hayes	.15	.04
326 Carlos Delgado	.30	.09
327 Ricky Bottalico	.15	.04
328 Rod Beck	.15	.04
329 Mark Acre	.15	.04
330 Chris Bosio	.15	.04
331 Tony Phillips	.15	.04
332 Garret Anderson	.30	.09
333 Pat Meares	.15	.04
334 Todd Worrell	.15	.04
335 Marquis Grissom	.15	.04
336 Brent Mayne	.15	.04
337 Lee Tinsley	.15	.04
338 Terry Pendleton	.30	.09
339 David Cone	.30	.09
340 Tony Fernandez	.15	.04
341 Jim Bullinger	.15	.04
342 Armando Benitez	.30	.09
343 John Smiley	.15	.04
344 Dan Miceli	.15	.04
345 Charles Johnson	.30	.09
346 Lee Smith	.30	.09
347 Brian McRae	.15	.04
348 Jim Thome	.75	.23
349 Jose Oliva	.15	.04
350 Terry Mulholland	.15	.04
351 Tom Henke	.15	.04
352 Dennis Eckersley	.30	.09
353 Sid Fernandez	.15	.04
354 Paul Wagner	.15	.04
355 John Dettmer	.15	.04
356 John Wetteland	.30	.09
357 John Burkett	.15	.04
358 Marty Cordova	.15	.04
359 Norm Charlton	.15	.04
360 Mike Devereaux	.15	.04
361 Alex Cole	.15	.04
362 Brett Butler	.30	.09
363 Mickey Tettleton	.15	.04
364 Al Martin	.15	.04
365 Tony Tarasco	.15	.04
366 Pat Mahomes	.15	.04
367 Gary DiSarcina	.15	.04
368 Bill Swift	.15	.04
369 Chipper Jones	.75	.23
370 Orel Hershiser	.30	.09
371 Kevin Gross	.15	.04
372 Dave Winfield	.30	.09
373 Andujar Cedeno	.15	.04
374 Jim Abbott	.50	.15
375 Glenallen Hill	.15	.04
376 Otis Nixon	.15	.04
377 Roberto Kelly	.15	.04
378 Chris Hammond	.15	.04
379 Mike Macfarlane	.15	.04
380 J.R. Phillips	.15	.04
381 Luis Alicea	.15	.04
382 Bret Barberie	.15	.04
383 Tom Goodwin	.15	.04
384 Mark Whiten	.15	.04
385 Jeffrey Hammonds	.15	.04
386 Omar Vizquel	.30	.09
387 Mike Mussina	.75	.23
388 Ricky Bones	.15	.04
389 Steve Ontiveros	.15	.04
390 Jeff Blauser	.15	.04
391 Jose Canseco	.75	.23
392 Bob Tewksbury	.15	.04
393 Jacob Brumfield	.15	.04
394 Doug Jones	.15	.04
395 Ken Hill	.15	.04
396 Pat Borders	.15	.04
397 Carl Everett	.30	.09
398 Gregg Jefferies	.15	.04
399 Jack McDowell	.15	.04
400 Denny Neagle	.30	.09

1995 Leaf 300 Club

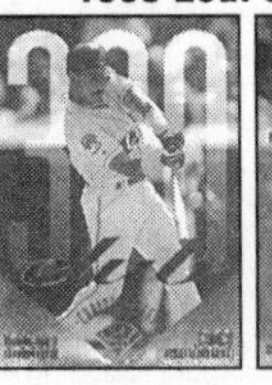

Randomly inserted in first and second series mini and retail packs at a rate of one every 12 packs, this set depicts all 18 players who had a career average of .300 or better entering the 1995 campaign. Full-bleed backs list the 18 players and their averages to that point.

	Nm-Mt	Ex-Mt
COMPLETE SET (18)	100.00	30.00
COMPLETE SERIES 1 (9)	35.00	10.50
COMPLETE SERIES 2 (9)	65.00	19.50
1 Frank Thomas	6.00	1.80
2 Paul Molitor	4.00	1.20
3 Mike Piazza	10.00	3.00
4 Moises Alou	2.50	.75
5 Mike Greenwell	1.25	.35
6 Will Clark	6.00	1.80
7 Hal Morris	1.25	.35
8 Edgar Martinez	4.00	1.20
9 Carlos Baerga	1.25	.35
10 Ken Griffey Jr.	10.00	3.00
11 Wade Boggs	4.00	1.20
12 Jeff Bagwell	4.00	1.20
13 Tony Gwynn	8.00	2.40
14 John Kruk	1.25	.35
15 Don Mattingly	15.00	4.50
16 Mark Grace	4.00	1.20
17 Kirby Puckett	6.00	1.80
18 Kenny Lofton	2.50	.75

1995 Leaf Checklists

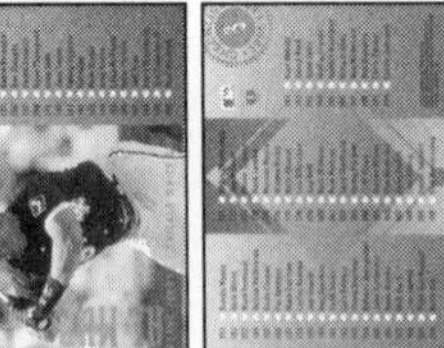

Four checklist cards were randomly inserted in either series for a total of eight standard-size cards. The set was composed of major award winners from the 1994 season.

	Nm-Mt	Ex-Mt
COMPLETE SERIES 1 (4)	1.50	.45
COMPLETE SERIES 2 (4)	3.00	.90
1 Bob Hamelin UER (Name spelled Hamlin)	.15	.04
2 David Cone	.30	.09
3 Frank Thomas	.75	.23
4 Paul O'Neill	.50	.15
5 Raul Mondesi	.30	.09
6 Greg Maddux	1.25	.35
7 Tony Gwynn	1.00	.30
8 Jeff Bagwell	.50	.15

1995 Leaf Cornerstones

Cards from this six-card standard-size set were randomly inserted in first series packs. Horizontally designed, leading first and thrid basemen from the same team are featured.

	Nm-Mt	Ex-Mt
COMPLETE SET (6)	8.00	2.40
1 Frank Thomas Robin Ventura	1.50	.45
2 Cecil Fielder Travis Fryman	.60	.18
3 Don Mattingly Wade Boggs	4.00	1.20
4 Jeff Bagwell Ken Caminiti	1.00	.30
5 Will Clark Dean Palmer	1.50	.45
6 J.R. Phillips Matt Williams	.60	.18

1995 Leaf Gold Rookies

Inserted in every other first series pack, this 16-card standard-size set showcases those that were expected to have an impact in 1995.

	Nm-Mt	Ex-Mt
COMPLETE SET (16)	6.00	1.80
1 Alex Rodriguez	3.00	.90
2 Garret Anderson	.50	.15
3 Shawn Green	.50	.15
4 Armando Benitez	.50	.15
5 Darren Dreifort	.25	.07
6 Orlando Miller	.25	.07
7 Jose Oliva	.25	.07
8 Ricky Bottalico	.25	.07
9 Charles Johnson	.50	.15
10 Brian L.Hunter	.50	.15
11 Ray McDavid	.25	.07
12 Chan Ho Park	.25	.07
13 Mike Kelly	.25	.07
14 Cory Bailey	.25	.07
15 Alex Gonzalez	.25	.07
16 Andrew Lorraine	.25	.07

1995 Leaf Gold Stars

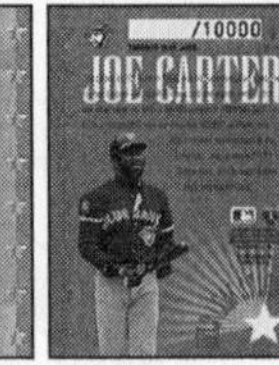

Randomly inserted in first and second series packs at a rate of one in 110, this 14-card standard-size set (eight first series, six second series) showcases some of the game's superstars.Individually numbered on back out of 10,000, the cards feature fronts that have a player photo superimposed metallic, refractive background.

	Nm-Mt	Ex-Mt
COMPLETE SET (14)	160.00	47.50
COMPLETE SERIES 1 (8)	80.00	24.00
COMPLETE SERIES 2 (6)	80.00	24.00
1 Jeff Bagwell	6.00	1.80
2 Albert Belle	4.00	1.20
3 Tony Gwynn	12.00	3.60
4 Ken Griffey Jr.	15.00	4.50
5 Barry Bonds	25.00	7.50
6 Don Mattingly	25.00	7.50
7 Raul Mondesi	4.00	1.20
8 Joe Carter	4.00	1.20
9 Greg Maddux	15.00	4.50
10 Frank Thomas	10.00	3.00
11 Mike Piazza	15.00	4.50
12 Jose Canseco	10.00	3.00
13 Kirby Puckett	10.00	3.00
14 Matt Williams	4.00	1.20

1995 Leaf Great Gloves

This 16-card standard-size set was randomly inserted in series two packs at a rate of one every two packs. The cards are numbered "X" of 16 in the upper right.

	Nm-Mt	Ex-Mt
COMPLETE SET (16)	10.00	3.00
1 Jeff Bagwell	.50	.15
2 Roberto Alomar	.75	.23
3 Barry Bonds	2.00	.60
4 Wade Boggs	.50	.15
5 Andres Galarraga	.30	.09
6 Ken Griffey Jr.	1.25	.35
7 Marquis Grissom	.15	.04
8 Kenny Lofton	.30	.09
9 Barry Larkin	.75	.23
10 Don Mattingly	2.00	.60
11 Greg Maddux	1.25	.35
12 Kirby Puckett	.75	.23
13 Ozzie Smith	1.25	.35
14 Cal Ripken Jr.	2.50	.75
15 Matt Williams	.30	.09
16 Ivan Rodriguez	.75	.23

1995 Leaf Heading for the Hall

This eight-card standard-size set was randomly inserted into series two hobby packs. The cards are individually numbered out of 5,000 as well.

	Nm-Mt	Ex-Mt
COMPLETE SET (8)	150.00	45.00
1 Frank Thomas	12.00	3.60
2 Ken Griffey Jr.	20.00	6.00
3 Jeff Bagwell	8.00	2.40
4 Barry Bonds	30.00	9.00
5 Kirby Puckett	12.00	3.60
6 Cal Ripken	40.00	12.00
7 Tony Gwynn	15.00	4.50
8 Paul Molitor	8.00	2.40

1995 Leaf Opening Day

This eight-card standard-size set was available through a wrapper mail-in offer. Upon receipt of eight 1995 Leaf, Studio or Donruss wrappers, a collector received this set. Besides the wrappers, the set cost $2 in shipping and handling and the final deadline was Aug. 31, 1995. The fronts have the words "1995 Opening Day" on the left with the player's picture and name on the right. The "Leaf 95" logo is in the upper right corner. All photos were taken on opening day including shots of Larry Walker as a Colorado Rockie and Jose Canseco in his Boston Red Sox debut. The cards are numbered "X" of 8 in the upper right corner.

	Nm-Mt	Ex-Mt
COMPLETE SET (8)	10.00	3.00
1 Frank Thomas	.75	.23
2 Jeff Bagwell	1.00	.30
3 Barry Bonds	1.50	.45
4 Ken Griffey Jr.	2.50	.75
5 Mike Piazza	2.00	.60
6 Cal Ripken	3.00	.90
7 Jose Canseco	.50	.15
8 Larry Walker	.40	.12

1995 Leaf Slideshow

This 16-card standard-size set was issued eight per series and randomly inserted at a rate of one per 30 hobby packs and one per 36 retail packs. The eight cards in the first series are numbered 1A-8A and repeated with different photos in the second series as 1B-8B. Both versions carry the same value.

	Nm-Mt	Ex-Mt
COMPLETE SET (16)	80.00	24.00
COMPLETE SERIES 1 (8)	40.00	12.00
COMPLETE SERIES 2 (8)	40.00	12.00
1A Raul Mondesi	1.50	.45
2A Frank Thomas	4.00	1.20
3A Fred McGriff	2.50	.75
4A Cal Ripken	12.00	3.60
5A Jeff Bagwell	2.50	.75
6A Will Clark	4.00	1.20
7A Matt Williams	1.50	.45
8A Ken Griffey Jr.	6.00	1.80

1995 Leaf Statistical Standouts Promos

One of nine different Staistical Standouts Promo cards was inserted into 1995 Leaf dealer order forms and hobby media press releases. The cards parallel the standard Statistical Standouts inserts except for the clipped upper right corner and lack of serial numbering on back.

	Nm-Mt	Ex-Mt
COMPLETE SET	25.00	7.50
1 Joe Carter	1.00	.30
2 Ken Griffey Jr.	6.00	1.80
3 Don Mattingly	4.00	1.20
4 Fred McGriff	1.50	.45
5 Paul Molitor	2.50	.75
6 Kirby Puckett	2.50	.75
7 Cal Ripken	8.00	2.40
8 Frank Thomas	2.50	.75
9 Matt Williams	2.00	.60

1995 Leaf Statistical Standouts

Randomly inserted in first series hobby packs at a rate of one in 70, this set features nine players who stood out from the rest statistically.

	Nm-Mt	Ex-Mt
COMPLETE SET (9)	150.00	45.00
1 Joe Carter	8.00	2.40
2 Ken Griffey Jr.	25.00	7.50
3 Don Mattingly	40.00	12.00
4 Fred McGriff	10.00	3.00
5 Paul Molitor	10.00	3.00
6 Kirby Puckett	15.00	4.50
7 Cal Ripken	50.00	15.00
8 Frank Thomas	15.00	4.50
9 Matt Williams	8.00	2.40

1995 Leaf Thomas

This six-card standard-size set was randomly inserted into series two packs at a rate of one in eighteen.

	Nm-Mt	Ex-Mt
COMPLETE SET (6)	15.00	4.50
COMMON CARD (1-6)	2.00	.60

1995 Leaf Thomas Akklaim

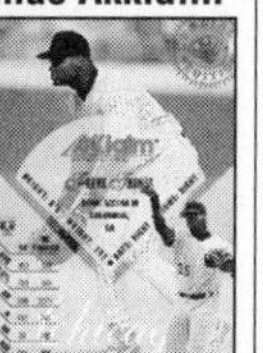

This one-card set features a borderless action photo of Frank Thomas with a small head photo in the upper left inside a baseball diamond frame. The front displays the words "Big Hurt" in big block silver foil lettering. The back shows player information and career statistics on a player picture background.

	Nm-Mt	Ex-Mt
1 Frank Thomas	5.00	1.50

1996 Leaf

The 1996 Leaf set was issued in one series totalling 220 cards. The fronts feature color action player photos with silver foil printing and lines forming a border on the left and bottom. The backs display another player photo with 1995 season and career statistics. Card number 210 is a checklist for the insert sets and cards number 211-220 feature rookies. The fronts of these 10 cards are different in design from the first 200 with a color action player cut-out over a green-shadow background of the same picture and gold lettering.

	Nm-Mt	Ex-Mt
COMPLETE SET (220)	20.00	6.00
1 John Smoltz	.50	.15
2 Dennis Eckersley	.30	.09
3 Delino DeShields	.30	.09
4 Cliff Floyd	.30	.09
5 Chuck Finley	.30	.09
6 Cecil Fielder	.30	.09
7 Tim Naehring	.30	.09
8 Carlos Perez	.30	.09
9 Brad Ausmus	.30	.09
10 Matt Lawton RC	.40	.12
11 Alan Trammell	.50	.15
12 Steve Finley	.30	.09
13 Paul O'Neill	.50	.15
14 Gary Sheffield	.30	.09
15 Mark McGwire	2.00	.60
16 Bernie Williams	.50	.15
17 Jeff Montgomery	.30	.09
18 Chan Ho Park	.30	.09
19 Greg Vaughn	.30	.09
20 Jeff Kent	.30	.09
21 Cal Ripken	2.50	.75
22 Charles Johnson	.30	.09
23 Eric Karros	.30	.09
24 Alex Rodriguez	1.50	.45
25 Chris Snopek	.30	.09
26 Jason Isringhausen	.30	.09
27 Chili Davis	.30	.09
28 Chipper Jones	.75	.23
29 Bret Saberhagen	.30	.09
30 Tony Clark	.30	.09
31 Marty Cordova	.30	.09
32 Dwayne Hosey	.30	.09
33 Fred McGriff	.50	.15
34 Deion Sanders	.50	.15
35 Orlando Merced	.30	.09
36 Brady Anderson	.30	.09
37 Ray Lankford	.30	.09
38 Manny Ramirez	.30	.09
39 Alex Fernandez	.30	.09
40 Greg Colbrunn	.30	.09
41 Ken Griffey, Jr.	1.25	.35
42 Mickey Morandini	.30	.09
43 Chuck Knoblauch	.30	.09
44 Quinton McCracken	.30	.09
45 Tim Salmon	.50	.15
46 Jose Mesa	.30	.09
47 Marquis Grissom	.30	.09
48 Greg Maddux Randy Johnson CL	.30	.09
49 Raul Mondesi	.30	.09
50 Mark Grudzielanek	.30	.09
51 Ray Durham	.30	.09
52 Matt Williams	.30	.09
53 Bob Hamelin	.30	.09
54 Lenny Dykstra	.30	.09
55 Jeff King	.30	.09
56 LaTroy Hawkins	.30	.09
57 Terry Pendleton	.30	.09
58 Kevin Stocker	.30	.09
59 Ozzie Timmons	.30	.09
60 David Justice	.30	.09
61 Ricky Bottalico	.30	.09
62 Andy Ashby	.30	.09
63 Larry Walker	.50	.15
64 Jose Canseco	.75	.23
65 Bret Boone	.30	.09
66 Shawn Green	.30	.09
67 Chad Curtis	.30	.09
68 Travis Fryman	.30	.09
69 Roger Clemens	1.50	.45
70 David Bell	.30	.09
71 Rusty Greer	.30	.09
72 Bob Higginson	.30	.09
73 Joey Hamilton	.30	.09
74 Kevin Seitzer	.30	.09
75 Julian Tavarez	.30	.09
76 Troy Percival	.30	.09
77 Kirby Puckett	.75	.23
78 Barry Bonds	2.00	.60
79 Michael Tucker	.30	.09
80 Paul Molitor	.50	.15
81 Carlos Garcia	.30	.09
82 Johnny Damon	.30	.09
83 Mike Hampton	.30	.09
84 Ariel Prieto	.30	.09
85 Tony Tarasco	.30	.09
86 Pete Schourek	.30	.09
87 Tom Glavine	.50	.15
88 Rondell White	.30	.09
89 Jim Edmonds	.30	.09
90 Robby Thompson	.30	.09
91 Wade Boggs	.50	.15
92 Pedro Martinez	.75	.23
93 Gregg Jefferies	.30	.09
94 Albert Belle	.30	.09
95 Benji Gil	.30	.09
96 Denny Neagle	.30	.09
97 Mark Langston	.30	.09
98 Sandy Alomar Jr.	.30	.09
99 Tony Gwynn	1.00	.30
100 Todd Hundley	.30	.09
101 Dante Bichette	.30	.09
102 Eddie Murray	.75	.23
103 Lyle Mouton	.30	.09
104 John Jaha	.30	.09
105 Barry Larkin Mo Vaughn CL	.30	.09
106 Jon Nunnally	.30	.09
107 Juan Gonzalez	.75	.23
108 Kevin Appier	.30	.09
109 Brian McRae	.30	.09
110 Lee Smith	.30	.09
111 Tim Wakefield	.30	.09
112 Sammy Sosa	1.25	.35
113 Jay Buhner	.30	.09
114 Garret Anderson	.30	.09
115 Edgar Martinez	.50	.15
116 Edgardo Alfonzo	.30	.09
117 Billy Ashley	.30	.09
118 Joe Carter	.30	.09
119 Javy Lopez	.30	.09
120 Bobby Bonilla	.30	.09
121 Ken Caminiti	.30	.09
122 Barry Larkin	.75	.23
123 Shannon Stewart	.30	.09
124 Orel Hershiser	.30	.09
125 Jeff Conine	.30	.09
126 Mark Grace	.50	.15
127 Kenny Lofton	.30	.09
128 Luis Gonzalez	.30	.09
129 Rico Brogna	.30	.09
130 Mo Vaughn	.30	.09
131 Brad Radke	.30	.09
132 Jose Herrera	.30	.09
133 Rick Aguilera	.30	.09
134 Gary DiSarcina	.30	.09
135 Andres Galarraga	.30	.09
136 Carl Everett	.30	.09
137 Steve Avery	.30	.09
138 Vinny Castilla	.30	.09
139 Dennis Martinez	.30	.09
140 John Wetteland	.30	.09
141 Alex Gonzalez	.30	.09
142 Brian Jordan	.30	.09
143 Todd Hollandsworth	.30	.09
144 Terrell Wade	.30	.09
145 Wilson Alvarez	.30	.09
146 Reggie Sanders	.30	.09
147 Will Clark	.75	.23
148 Hideo Nomo	.75	.23
149 J.T.Snow	.30	.09
150 Frank Thomas	.75	.23
151 Ivan Rodriguez	.75	.23
152 Jay Bell	.30	.09
153 Hideo Nomo CL Marty Cordova	.30	.09
154 David Cone	.30	.09
155 Roberto Alomar	.75	.23
156 Carlos Delgado	.30	.09
157 Carlos Baerga	.30	.09
158 Geronimo Berroa	.30	.09
159 Joe Vitiello	.30	.09
160 Terry Steinbach	.30	.09
161 Doug Drabek	.30	.09
162 David Segui	.30	.09
163 Ozzie Smith	1.25	.35
164 Kurt Abbott	.30	.09
165 Randy Johnson	.75	.23
166 John Valentin	.30	.09
167 Mickey Tettleton	.30	.09
168 Ruben Sierra	.30	.09
169 Jim Thome	.75	.23
170 Mike Greenwell	.30	.09
171 Quilvio Veras	.30	.09
172 Robin Ventura	.30	.09
173 Bill Pulsipher	.30	.09
174 Rafael Palmeiro	.50	.15
175 Hal Morris	.30	.09
176 Ryan Klesko	.30	.09
177 Eric Young	.30	.09
178 Shane Andrews	.30	.09
179 Brian L.Hunter	.30	.09
180 Brett Butler	.30	.09
181 John Olerud	.30	.09
182 Moises Alou	.30	.09
183 Glenallen Hill	.30	.09
184 Ismael Valdes	.30	.09
185 Andy Pettitte	.50	.15
186 Yamil Benitez	.30	.09
187 Jason Bere	.30	.09
188 Dean Palmer	.30	.09
189 Jimmy Haynes	.30	.09
190 Trevor Hoffman	.30	.09
191 Mike Mussina	.75	.23
192 Greg Maddux	1.25	.35
193 Ozzie Guillen	.30	.09
194 Pat Listach	.30	.09
195 Derek Bell	.30	.09
196 Darren Daulton	.30	.09
197 John Mabry	.30	.09
198 Ramon Martinez	.30	.09
199 Jeff Bagwell	.50	.15
200 Mike Piazza	1.25	.35
201 Al Martin	.30	.09
202 Aaron Sele	.30	.09
203 Ed Sprague	.30	.09
204 Rod Beck	.30	.09
205 Tony Gwynn Edgar Martinez CL	.30	.09
206 Mike Lansing	.30	.09
207 Craig Biggio	.50	.15
208 Jeffrey Hammonds	.30	.09
209 Dave Nilsson	.30	.09
210 Dante Bichette Albert Belle CL	.30	.09
211 Derek Jeter	2.00	.60
212 Alan Benes	.30	.09
213 Jason Schmidt	.30	.09
214 Alex Ochoa	.30	.09
215 Ruben Rivera	.30	.09
216 Roger Cedeno	.30	.09
217 Jeff Suppan	.30	.09
218 Billy Wagner	.30	.09
219 Mark Loretta	.30	.09
220 Karim Garcia	.30	.09

1996 Leaf Bronze Press Proofs

This 220-card Bronze set is parallel to the regular Leaf set and between the three types of press proofs were inserted at a rate of one in 10 packs. Similar in design to the regular set, 2,000 non-serial numbered Bronze sets were produced and feature a special holographic foil.

Nm-Mt Ex-Mt

*STARS: 4X TO 10X BASIC CARDS ....
*ROOKIES: 2.5X TO 6X BASIC CARDS

1996 Leaf Gold Press Proofs

This 220-card Gold set is parallel to the regular Leaf set. Only five hundred sets were produced and they were randomly inserted into packs. One in every ten packs contained either a Bronze, Gold or Silver Press Proof. Collectors need to be careful as the Bronze and the Gold press proofs look very similar. 500 non-serial numbered sets were produced.

Nm-Mt Ex-Mt

*STARS: 12.5X TO 30X BASIC CARDS
*ROOKIES: 8X TO 20X BASIC CARDS

1996 Leaf Silver Press Proofs

This 220-card Silver set is also a parallel to the regular Leaf issue. One thousand sets were produced and the cards were randomly inserted into packs. One in every 10 packs contains either a bronze, gold or silver press proof. 1,000 non-serial numbered sets were produced.

Nm-Mt Ex-Mt

*STARS: 8X TO 20X BASIC CARDS....
*ROOKIES: 5X TO 12X BASIC CARDS

1996 Leaf All-Star Game MVP Contenders

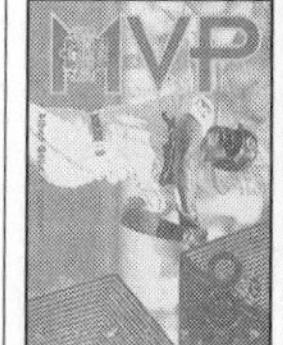

This 20 card set features possible contenders for the MVP at the 1996 All-Star Game held in Philadelphia. The cards were randomly inserted into packs. If the player on the front of the card won the MVP Award (which turned out to be Mike Piazza), the holder could send it in for a special Gold MVP Contenders set of which only 5,000 were produced. The fronts display a color action player photo. The backs carry the instructions on how to redeem the card. The expiration date for the redemption was August 15th, 1996. The Piazza card when returned with the redemption set had a hole in it to indicate the set had been redeemed.

	Nm-Mt	Ex-Mt
COMPLETE SET (20	40.00	12.00
1 Frank Thomas	1.50	.45
2 Mike Piazza W	4.00	1.20
3 Sammy Sosa	2.50	.75
4 Cal Ripken	5.00	1.50
5 Jeff Bagwell	1.00	.30
6 Reggie Sanders	.60	.18
7 Mo Vaughn	.60	.18
8 Tony Gwynn	2.00	.60
9 Dante Bichette	.60	.18
10 Tim Salmon	1.00	.30
11 Chipper Jones	1.50	.45
12 Kenny Lofton	.60	.18
13 Manny Ramirez	.60	.18
14 Barry Bonds	4.00	1.20
15 Raul Mondesi	.60	.18
16 Kirby Puckett	1.50	.45
17 Albert Belle	.60	.18
18 Ken Griffey Jr.	2.50	.75
19 Greg Maddux	2.50	.75
20 Bonus Card	.60	.18

1996 Leaf Gold Stars

Randomly inserted in hobby and retail packs at a rate of one in 190, this 15-card set honors some of the games great players on 22 karat gold trim cards. Only 2,500 cards of each player were printed and are individually numbered.

	Nm-Mt	Ex-Mt
COMPLETE SET (15)	300.00	90.00
1 Frank Thomas	20.00	6.00
2 Dante Bichette	8.00	2.40
3 Sammy Sosa	30.00	9.00
4 Ken Griffey Jr.	30.00	9.00
5 Mike Piazza	30.00	9.00
6 Tim Salmon	12.00	3.60
7 Hideo Nomo	20.00	6.00
8 Cal Ripken	60.00	18.00
9 Chipper Jones	20.00	6.00
10 Albert Belle	8.00	2.40
11 Tony Gwynn	25.00	7.50
12 Mo Vaughn	8.00	2.40
13 Barry Larkin	20.00	6.00
14 Manny Ramirez	8.00	2.40
15 Greg Maddux	30.00	9.00

1996 Leaf Hats Off

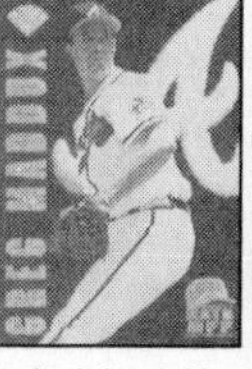

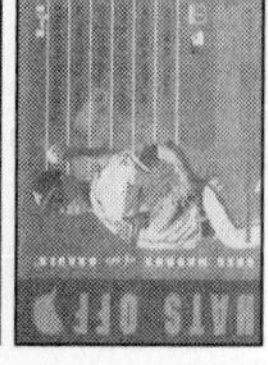

Randomly inserted in retail packs only at a rate of one in 72, this eight-card set was printed and embossed on a wool-like material with the feel of a Major League ball cap. Only 5,000 of each player was produced and is individually numbered.

	Nm-Mt	Ex-Mt
COMPLETE SET (8)	100.00	30.00
1 Cal Ripken	30.00	9.00
2 Barry Larkin	10.00	3.00
3 Frank Thomas	10.00	3.00
4 Mo Vaughn	4.00	1.20
5 Ken Griffey Jr.	15.00	4.50
6 Hideo Nomo	10.00	3.00
7 Albert Belle	4.00	1.20
8 Greg Maddux	15.00	4.50

1996 Leaf Picture Perfect Promos

One of twelve different Picture Perfect Promo cards was inserted into 1996 Leaf dealer order forms and hobby media press releases. The cards parallel the standard Picture Perfect inserts except for the text "promotional card" running diagonally across the front of the card and "PROMO/5000" text on back.

	Nm-Mt	Ex-Mt
COMPLETE SET (12)	80.00	24.00
1 Frank Thomas	4.00	1.20
2 Cal Ripken	20.00	6.00
3 Greg Maddux	12.00	3.60
4 Manny Ramirez	5.00	1.50
5 Chipper Jones	10.00	3.00
6 Tony Gwynn	10.00	3.00
7 Ken Griffey Jr.	12.00	3.60
8 Albert Belle	1.00	.30
9 Jeff Bagwell	5.00	1.50
10 Mike Piazza	12.00	3.60
11 Mo Vaughn	1.00	.30
12 Barry Bonds	10.00	3.00

1996 Leaf Picture Perfect

Randomly inserted in hobby (1-6) and retail (7-12) packs at a rate of one in 140, this 12-card set is printed on real wood with gold foil trim. The fronts feature a color player action framed photo. The backs carry another player photo with player information. Only 5,000 of each card were printed and each is individually numbered.

	Nm-Mt	Ex-Mt
COMPLETE SET (12)	150.00	45.00
1 Frank Thomas	10.00	3.00
2 Cal Ripken	30.00	9.00
3 Greg Maddux	15.00	4.50
4 Manny Ramirez	4.00	1.20
5 Chipper Jones	10.00	3.00
6 Tony Gwynn	12.00	3.60
7 Ken Griffey Jr.	15.00	4.50
8 Albert Belle	4.00	1.20
9 Jeff Bagwell	6.00	1.80
10 Mike Piazza	15.00	4.50
11 Mo Vaughn	4.00	1.20
12 Barry Bonds	25.00	7.50

1996 Leaf Statistical Standouts

Randomly inserted in hobby packs only at a rate of one in 210, this eight-card set features players who stood out statistically. The cards were printed on a material with the feel of the leather that's between the seams or stitches of a baseball. Only 2,500 of each card was printed and each is numbered individually on the back.

	Nm-Mt	Ex-Mt
COMPLETE SET (8)	150.00	45.00
1 Cal Ripken	50.00	15.00
2 Tony Gwynn	20.00	6.00
3 Frank Thomas	15.00	4.50
4 Ken Griffey Jr.	25.00	7.50
5 Hideo Nomo	15.00	4.50
6 Greg Maddux	25.00	7.50
7 Albert Belle	6.00	1.80
8 Chipper Jones	15.00	4.50

1996 Leaf Thomas Greatest Hits

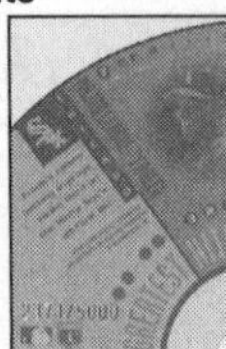

Randomly inserted in hobby (1-4) and retail (5-7) packs at a rate of one in 210, this eight-card set was printed on die-cut plastic to simulate a compact disc. The cards feature the statistical highlights of Frank Thomas. The wrapper displays the details for the special mail-in offer to obtain card number 8. Five thousand sets were printed.

	Nm-Mt	Ex-Mt
COMMON CARD (1-7)	12.00	3.60
COMMON EXCHANGE (8)	15.00	4.50

1996 Leaf Total Bases Promos

One of twelve different Total Bases Promo cards was inserted into 1996 Leaf dealer order forms and hobby media press releases. The cards parallel the standard Total Bases inserts except for the text "promotional card" running diagonally across the front of the card and "PROMO/5000" text on back.

	Nm-Mt	Ex-Mt
COMPLETE SET (12)	30.00	9.00
1 Frank Thomas	2.50	.75
2 Albert Belle	1.00	.30
3 Rafael Palmeiro	2.00	.60
4 Barry Bonds	4.00	1.20
5 Kirby Puckett	2.50	.75
6 Joe Carter	1.00	.30
7 Paul Molitor	2.50	.75
8 Fred McGriff	1.50	.45
9 Ken Griffey Jr.	5.00	1.50
10 Carlos Baerga	1.00	.30
11 Juan Gonzalez	2.50	.75
12 Cal Ripken	8.00	2.40

1996 Leaf Total Bases

Randomly inserted in hobby packs only at a rate of one in 72, this 12-card set is printed on canvas and features the top offensive stars. Only 5,000 of each card was printed and are individually numbered. The fronts carry a color

action player cut-out over a base background. The backs display another player photo and 1995 stats.

	Nm-Mt	Ex-Mt
COMPLETE SET (12)	100.00	30.00
1 Frank Thomas	8.00	2.40
2 Albert Belle	3.00	.90
3 Rafael Palmeiro	5.00	1.50
4 Barry Bonds	20.00	6.00
5 Kirby Puckett	8.00	2.40
6 Joe Carter	3.00	.90
7 Paul Molitor	5.00	1.50
8 Fred McGriff	5.00	1.50
9 Ken Griffey Jr.	12.00	3.60
10 Carlos Baerga	3.00	.90
11 Juan Gonzalez	8.00	2.40
12 Cal Ripken	25.00	7.50

1997 Leaf

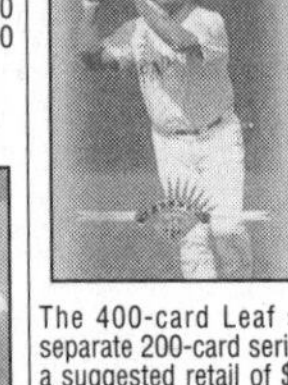

The 400-card Leaf set was issued in two separate 200-card series. 10-card packs carried a suggested retail of $2.99. Each card features color action player photos with foil enhancement. The backs carry another player photo and season and career statistics. The set contains the following subsets: Legacy (188-197/348-367), Checklists (198-200/398-400) and Gamers (368-397). Rookie Cards in this set include Jose Cruz Jr., Brian Giles and Hideki Irabu. In a tie in with the 50th anniversary of Jackie Robinson's major league debut, Donruss/Leaf also issued some collectible items. They made 42 all-leather jackets (issued to match Robinson's uniform number). There were also 311 leather jackets produced (to match Robinson's career batting average). 1,500 lithographs were also produced of which Rachel Robinson (Jackie's widow) signed 500 of them.

	Nm-Mt	Ex-Mt
COMPLETE SET (400)	40.00	12.00
COMP. SERIES 1 (200)	20.00	6.00
COMP. SERIES 2 (200)	20.00	6.00
1 Wade Boggs	.50	.15
2 Brian McRae	.30	.09
3 Jeff D'Amico	.30	.09
4 George Arias	.30	.09
5 Billy Wagner	.30	.09
6 Ray Lankford	.30	.09
7 Will Clark	.75	.23
8 Edgar Renteria	.30	.09
9 Alex Ochoa	.30	.09
10 Roberto Hernandez	.30	.09
11 Joe Carter	.30	.09
12 Gregg Jefferies	.30	.09
13 Mark Grace	.50	.15
14 Roberto Alomar	.75	.23
15 Joe Randa	.30	.09
16 Alex Rodriguez	1.25	.35
17 Tony Gwynn	1.00	.30
18 Steve Gibralter	.30	.09
19 Scott Stahoviak	.30	.09
20 Matt Williams	.30	.09
21 Quinton McCracken	.30	.09
22 Ugueth Urbina	.30	.09
23 Jermaine Allensworth	.30	.09
24 Paul Molitor	.50	.15
25 Carlos Delgado	.30	.09
26 Bob Abreu	.30	.09
27 John Jaha	.30	.09
28 Rusty Greer	.30	.09
29 Kimera Bartee	.30	.09
30 Ruben Rivera	.30	.09
31 Jason Kendall	.30	.09
32 Lance Johnson	.30	.09
33 Robin Ventura	.30	.09
34 Kevin Appier	.30	.09
35 John Mabry	.30	.09
36 Ricky Otero	.30	.09
37 Mike Lansing	.30	.09
38 Mark McGwire	2.00	.60
39 Tim Naehring	.30	.09
40 Tom Glavine	.50	.15
41 Rey Ordonez	.30	.09
42 Tony Clark	.30	.09
43 Rafael Palmeiro	.50	.15
44 Pedro Martinez	.75	.23
45 Keith Lockhart	.30	.09
46 Dan Wilson	.30	.09
47 John Wetteland	.30	.09
48 Chan Ho Park	.30	.09
49 Gary Sheffield	.30	.09
50 Shawn Estes	.30	.09
51 Royce Clayton	.30	.09
52 Jaime Navarro	.30	.09
53 Raul Casanova	.30	.09
54 Jeff Bagwell	.50	.15
55 Barry Larkin	.75	.23
56 Charles Nagy	.30	.09
57 Ken Caminiti	.30	.09
58 Todd Hollandsworth	.30	.09
59 Pat Hentgen	.30	.09
60 Jose Valentin	.30	.09
61 Frank Rodriguez	.30	.09
62 Mickey Tettleton	.30	.09
63 Marty Cordova	.30	.09
64 Cecil Fielder	.30	.09
65 Barry Bonds	2.00	.60
66 Scott Servais	.30	.09
67 Ernie Young	.30	.09
68 Wilson Alvarez	.30	.09
69 Mike Grace	.30	.09
70 Shane Reynolds	.30	.09
71 Henry Rodriguez	.30	.09
72 Eric Karros	.30	.09
73 Mark Langston	.30	.09
74 Scott Karl	.30	.09
75 Trevor Hoffman	.30	.09
76 Orel Hershiser	.30	.09
77 John Smoltz	.50	.15
78 Raul Mondesi	.30	.09
79 Jeff Brantley	.30	.09
80 Donne Wall	.30	.09
81 Joey Cora	.30	.09
82 Mel Rojas	.30	.09
83 Chad Mottola	.30	.09
84 Omar Vizquel	.30	.09
85 Greg Maddux	1.25	.35
86 Jamey Wright	.30	.09
87 Chuck Finley	.30	.09
88 Brady Anderson	.30	.09
89 Alex Gonzalez	.30	.09
90 Andy Benes	.30	.09
91 Reggie Jefferson	.30	.09
92 Paul O'Neill	.50	.15
93 Javier Lopez	.30	.09
94 Mark Grudzielanek	.30	.09
95 Marc Newfield	.30	.09
96 Kevin Ritz	.30	.09
97 Fred McGriff	.50	.15
98 Dwight Gooden	.50	.15
99 Hideo Nomo	.75	.23
100 Steve Finley	.30	.09
101 Juan Gonzalez	.75	.23
102 Jay Buhner	.30	.09
103 Paul Wilson	.30	.09
104 Alan Benes	.30	.09
105 Manny Ramirez	.30	.09
106 Kevin Elster	.30	.09
107 Frank Thomas	.75	.23
108 Orlando Miller	.30	.09
109 Ramon Martinez	.30	.09
110 Kenny Lofton	.30	.09
111 Bernie Williams	.50	.15
112 Robby Thompson	.30	.09
113 Bernard Gilkey	.30	.09
114 Ray Durham	.30	.09
115 Jeff Cirillo	.30	.09
116 Brian Jordan	.30	.09
117 Rich Becker	.30	.09
118 Al Leiter	.30	.09
119 Mark Johnson	.30	.09
120 Ellis Burks	.30	.09
121 Sammy Sosa	1.25	.35
122 Willie Greene	.30	.09
123 Michael Tucker	.30	.09
124 Eddie Murray	.75	.23
125 Joey Hamilton	.30	.09
126 Antonio Osuna	.30	.09
127 Bobby Higginson	.30	.09
128 Tomas Perez	.30	.09
129 Tim Salmon	.50	.15
130 Mark Wohlers	.30	.09
131 Charles Johnson	.30	.09
132 Randy Johnson	.75	.23
133 Brooks Kieschnick	.30	.09
134 Al Martin	.30	.09
135 Dante Bichette	.30	.09
136 Andy Pettitte	.50	.15
137 Jason Giambi	.75	.23
138 James Baldwin	.30	.09
139 Ben McDonald	.30	.09
140 Shawn Green	.30	.09
141 Geronimo Berroa	.30	.09
142 Jose Offerman	.30	.09
143 Curtis Pride	.30	.09
144 Terrell Wade	.30	.09
145 Ismael Valdes	.30	.09
146 Mike Mussina	.75	.23
147 Mariano Rivera	.50	.15
148 Ken Hill	.30	.09
149 Darin Erstad	.30	.09
150 Jay Bell	.30	.09
151 Mo Vaughn	.30	.09
152 Ozzie Smith	1.25	.35
153 Jose Mesa	.30	.09
154 Osvaldo Fernandez	.30	.09
155 Vinny Castilla	.30	.09
156 Jason Isringhausen	.30	.09
157 B.J. Surhoff	.30	.09
158 Robert Perez	.30	.09
159 Ron Coomer	.30	.09
160 Darren Oliver	.30	.09
161 Mike Mohler	.30	.09
162 Russ Davis	.30	.09
163 Bret Boone	.30	.09
164 Ricky Bottalico	.30	.09
165 Derek Jeter	2.00	.60
166 Orlando Merced	.30	.09
167 John Valentin	.30	.09
168 Andruw Jones	.30	.09
169 Angel Echevarria	.30	.09
170 Todd Walker	.30	.09
171 Desi Relaford	.30	.09
172 Trey Beamon	.30	.09
173 Brian Giles RC	1.50	.45
174 Scott Rolen	.50	.15
175 Shannon Stewart	.30	.09
176 Dmitri Young	.30	.09
177 Justin Thompson	.30	.09
178 Trot Nixon	.50	.15
179 Josh Booty	.30	.09
180 Robin Jennings	.30	.09
181 Marvin Benard	.30	.09
182 Luis Castillo	.30	.09
183 Wendell Magee	.30	.09
184 Vladimir Guerrero	.75	.23
185 Nomar Garciaparra	1.25	.35
186 Ryan Hancock	.30	.09
187 Mike Cameron	.30	.09
188 Cal Ripken LG	1.25	.35
189 Chipper Jones LG	.50	.15
190 Albert Belle LG	.30	.09
191 Mike Piazza LG	.75	.23
192 Chuck Knoblauch LG	.30	.09
193 Ken Griffey Jr. LG	.75	.23
194 Ivan Rodriguez LG	.50	.15
195 Jose Canseco LG	.30	.09
196 Ryne Sandberg LG	.75	.23
197 Jim Thome LG	.30	.09
198 Andy Pettitte CL	.30	.09
199 Andruw Jones CL	.30	.09
200 Derek Jeter CL	1.00	.30
201 Chipper Jones	.75	.23
202 Albert Belle	.30	.09
203 Mike Piazza	1.25	.35
204 Ken Griffey Jr.	1.25	.35
205 Ryne Sandberg	1.25	.35
206 Jose Canseco	.75	.23
207 Chili Davis	.30	.09
208 Roger Clemens	1.50	.45
209 Deion Sanders	.50	.15
210 Darryl Hamilton	.30	.09
211 Jermaine Dye	.30	.09
212 Matt Williams	.30	.09
213 Kevin Elster	.30	.09
214 John Wetteland	.30	.09
215 Garret Anderson	.30	.09
216 Kevin Brown	.30	.09
217 Matt Lawton	.30	.09
218 Cal Ripken	2.50	.75
219 Moises Alou	.30	.09
220 Chuck Knoblauch	.30	.09
221 Ivan Rodriguez	.75	.23
222 Travis Fryman	.30	.09
223 Jim Thome	.75	.23
224 Eddie Murray	.75	.23
225 Eric Young	.30	.09
226 Ron Gant	.30	.09
227 Tony Phillips	.30	.09
228 Reggie Sanders	.30	.09
229 Johnny Damon	.30	.09
230 Bill Pulsipher	.30	.09
231 Jim Edmonds	.30	.09
232 Melvin Nieves	.30	.09
233 Ryan Klesko	.30	.09
234 David Cone	.30	.09
235 Derek Bell	.30	.09
236 Julio Franco	.30	.09
237 Juan Guzman	.30	.09
238 Larry Walker	.50	.15
239 Delino DeShields	.30	.09
240 Troy Percival	.30	.09
241 Andres Galarraga	.30	.09
242 Rondell White	.30	.09
243 John Burkett	.30	.09
244 J.T. Snow	.30	.09
245 Alex Fernandez	.30	.09
246 Edgar Martinez	.50	.15
247 Craig Biggio	.50	.15
248 Todd Hundley	.30	.09
249 Jimmy Key	.30	.09
250 Cliff Floyd	.30	.09
251 Jeff Conine	.30	.09
252 Curt Schilling	.50	.15
253 Jeff King	.30	.09
254 Tino Martinez	.50	.15
255 Carlos Baerga	.30	.09
256 Jeff Fassero	.30	.09
257 Dean Palmer	.30	.09
258 Robb Nen	.30	.09
259 Sandy Alomar Jr.	.30	.09
260 Carlos Perez	.30	.09
261 Rickey Henderson	.75	.23
262 Bobby Bonilla	.30	.09
263 Darren Daulton	.30	.09
264 Jim Leyritz	.30	.09
265 Dennis Martinez	.30	.09
266 Butch Huskey	.30	.09
267 Joe Vitiello	.30	.09
268 Steve Trachsel	.30	.09
269 Glenallen Hill	.30	.09
270 Terry Steinbach	.30	.09
271 Mark McLemore	.30	.09
272 Devon White	.30	.09
273 Jeff Kent	.30	.09
274 Tim Raines	.30	.09
275 Carlos Garcia	.30	.09
276 Hal Morris	.30	.09
277 Gary Gaetti	.30	.09
278 John Olerud	.30	.09
279 Wally Joyner	.30	.09
280 Brian Hunter	.30	.09
281 Steve Karsay	.30	.09
282 Denny Neagle	.30	.09
283 Jose Herrera	.30	.09
284 Todd Stottlemyre	.30	.09
285 Bip Roberts	.30	.09
286 Kevin Seitzer	.30	.09
287 Benji Gil	.30	.09
288 Dennis Eckersley	.30	.09
289 Brad Ausmus	.30	.09
290 Otis Nixon	.30	.09
291 Darryl Strawberry	.50	.15
292 Marquis Grissom	.30	.09
293 Darryl Kile	.30	.09
294 Quilvio Veras	.30	.09
295 Tom Goodwin	.30	.09
296 Benito Santiago	.30	.09
297 Mike Bordick	.30	.09
298 Roberto Kelly	.30	.09
299 David Justice	.30	.09
300 Carl Everett	.30	.09
301 Mark Whiten	.30	.09
302 Aaron Sele	.30	.09
303 Darren Dreifort	.30	.09
304 Bobby Jones	.30	.09
305 Fernando Vina	.30	.09
306 Ed Sprague	.30	.09
307 Andy Ashby	.30	.09
308 Tony Fernandez	.30	.09
309 Roger Pavlik	.30	.09
310 Mark Clark	.30	.09
311 Mariano Duncan	.30	.09
312 Tyler Houston	.30	.09
313 Eric Davis	.30	.09
314 Greg Vaughn	.30	.09
315 David Segui	.30	.09
316 Dave Nilsson	.30	.09
317 F.P. Santangelo	.30	.09
318 Wilton Guerrero	.30	.09
319 Jose Guillen	.30	.09
320 Kevin Orie	.30	.09
321 Derrek Lee	.30	.09
322 Bubba Trammell RC	.40	.12
323 Pokey Reese	.30	.09
324 Hideki Irabu RC	.40	.12
325 Scott Spiezio	.30	.09
326 Bartolo Colon	.30	.09
327 Damon Mashore	.30	.09
328 Ryan McGuire	.30	.09
329 Chris Carpenter	.30	.09
330 Jose Cruz Jr. RC	1.25	.35
331 Todd Greene	.30	.09
332 Brian Moehler	.30	.09
333 Mike Sweeney	.30	.09
334 Neifi Perez	.30	.09
335 Matt Morris	.30	.09
336 Marvin Benard	.30	.09
337 Karim Garcia	.30	.09
338 Jason Dickson	.30	.09
339 Brant Brown	.30	.09
340 Jeff Suppan	.30	.09
341 Deivi Cruz RC	.40	.12
342 Antone Williamson	.30	.09
343 Curtis Goodwin	.30	.09
344 Brooks Kieschnick	.30	.09
345 Tony Womack RC	.40	.12
346 Rudy Pemberton	.30	.09
347 Todd Dunwoody	.30	.09
348 Frank Thomas LG	.50	.15
349 Andruw Jones LG	.30	.09
350 Alex Rodriguez LG	.75	.23
351 Greg Maddux LG	.75	.23
352 Jeff Bagwell LG	.30	.09
353 Juan Gonzalez LG	.50	.15
354 Barry Bonds LG	.75	.23
355 Mark McGwire LG	1.00	.30
356 Tony Gwynn LG	.50	.15
357 Gary Sheffield LG	.30	.09
358 Derek Jeter LG	1.00	.30
359 Manny Ramirez LG	.30	.09
360 Hideo Nomo LG	.30	.09
361 Sammy Sosa LG	.75	.23
362 Paul Molitor LG	.30	.09
363 Kenny Lofton LG	.30	.09
364 Eddie Murray LG	.50	.15
365 Barry Larkin LG	.30	.09
366 Roger Clemens LG	.75	.23
367 John Smoltz LG	.30	.09
368 Alex Rodriguez GM	.75	.23
369 Frank Thomas GM	.50	.15
370 Cal Ripken GM	1.25	.35
371 Ken Griffey Jr. GM	.75	.23
372 Greg Maddux GM	.75	.23
373 Mike Piazza GM	.75	.23
374 Chipper Jones GM	.50	.15
375 Albert Belle GM	.30	.09
376 Chuck Knoblauch GM	.30	.09
377 Brady Anderson GM	.30	.09
378 David Justice GM	.30	.09
379 Randy Johnson GM	.50	.15
380 Wade Boggs GM	.30	.09
381 Kevin Brown GM	.30	.09
382 Tom Glavine GM	.30	.09
383 Raul Mondesi GM	.30	.09
384 Ivan Rodriguez GM	.50	.15
385 Larry Walker GM	.30	.09
386 Bernie Williams GM	.30	.09
387 Rusty Greer GM	.30	.09
388 Rafael Palmeiro GM	.30	.09
389 Matt Williams GM	.30	.09
390 Eric Young GM	.30	.09
391 Fred McGriff GM	.30	.09
392 Ken Caminiti GM	.30	.09
393 Roberto Alomar GM	.30	.09
394 Brian Jordan GM	.30	.09
395 Mark Grace GM	.30	.09
396 Jim Edmonds GM	.30	.09
397 Deion Sanders GM	.30	.09
398 Vladimir Guerrero CL	.50	.15
399 Darin Erstad CL	.30	.09
400 N. Garciaparra CL	.75	.23
NNO J.Robinson Reprint	25.00	7.50

1997 Leaf Fractal Matrix

Randomly inserted in packs, this 400-card set is parallel to the regular Leaf issue and features color player photos with either a bronze, silver or gold finish. Only 200 cards are bronze, 120 cards are silver, and 80 cards are gold. No card is available in more than one of the colors. In a convoluted effort, the fractal matrix parallel concept split the 400 card set into nine different tiered levels of parallels, each with print runs that varied from as many of several thousand of some cards (mostly the Bronze cards) to less than a few hundred of other cards (In the Gold X subset). Cards were split into colors (Bronze, Gold and Silver) and axis (X, Y and Z). Cards are listed in our checklist with color and axis designation. Unfortunately, the designers at Leaf failed to create any notable markings to differentiate the X, Y and Z axis for all the cards in this set. Leaf did issue an axis schematic on the back of the 1997 boxes and we've carefully incorporated that information into our checklist for accurate reference.

	Nm-Mt	Ex-Mt
*BRONZE: 1.5X TO 4X BASIC CARDS.		
*SILVER: 2X TO 5X BASIC CARDS		
*SILVER ROOKIES: .6X TO 1.5X BASIC		
*GOLD Y/Z: 3X TO 8X BASIC CARDS..		
*GOLD X: 6X TO 15X BASIC CARDS...		
*GOLD X RC's: 2X TO 5X BASIC CARDS		
RANDOM INSERTS IN PACKS		
SEE WEBSITE FOR AXIS SCHEMATIC.		

1997 Leaf Fractal Matrix Die Cuts

This 400-card set is parallel to the regular set and features three different die-cut versions in three different finishes. 200 of the 400-card set are produced in the X-Axis cut with 150 of those bronze, 40 of those silver, and 10 of those gold. 120 of the 400-card set are available in type Y-Axis cut with 40 of those bronze, 60 silver, and 20 gold. Eighty of the 200-card set are produced in the Z-Axis cut with 10 of those bronze, 20 of those silver and 50 of those gold. No card was available in more than one color nor in more than one die-cut version. Unlike the non die-cut Fractal Matrix cards, these Die Cut parallels have distinguishable axis groupings based on the shape of the die cut edges.

	Nm-Mt	Ex-Mt
*X-AXIS: 2X TO 5X BASIC CARDS......		
*X-AXIS ROOKIES: 1.25X TO 3X BASIC		
*Y-AXIS: 3X TO 8X BASIC CARDS......		
*Y-AXIS ROOKIES: .75X TO 2X BASIC		
*Z-AXIS: 2.5X TO 6X BASIC CARDS ...		
RANDOM INSERTS IN PACKS		
SEE WEBSITE FOR AXIS SCHEMATIC.		

1997 Leaf Banner Season

Randomly inserted in series one magazine packs, this 15-card set features color action player photos on die-cut cards and is printed on canvas card stock. Only 2500 of each card was produced and are sequentially numbered.

	Nm-Mt	Ex-Mt
COMPLETE SET (15)	120.00	36.00
1 Jeff Bagwell	8.00	2.40
2 Ken Griffey Jr.	20.00	6.00
3 Juan Gonzalez	12.00	3.60
4 Frank Thomas	12.00	3.60
5 Alex Rodriguez	20.00	6.00
6 Kenny Lofton	5.00	1.50
7 Chuck Knoblauch	5.00	1.50
8 Mo Vaughn	5.00	1.50
9 Chipper Jones	12.00	3.60
10 Ken Caminiti	5.00	1.50
11 Craig Biggio	8.00	2.40
12 John Smoltz	8.00	2.40
13 Pat Hentgen	5.00	1.50
14 Derek Jeter	30.00	9.00
15 Todd Hollandsworth	5.00	1.50

1997 Leaf Dress for Success

Randomly inserted in series one retail packs, this 18-card retail only set features color player photos prined on a jersey-simulated, nylon card stock and is accented with flocking on the team logo and gold-foil stamping. Only 3,500 of each card were produced and are sequentially numbered.

	Nm-Mt	Ex-Mt
COMPLETE SET (18)	40.00	12.00
1 Greg Maddux	3.00	.90
2 Cal Ripken	6.00	1.80
3 Albert Belle	.75	.23
4 Frank Thomas	2.00	.60
5 Dante Bichette	.75	.23
6 Gary Sheffield	.75	.23
7 Jeff Bagwell	1.25	.35
8 Mike Piazza	3.00	.90
9 Mark McGwire	5.00	1.50
10 Ken Caminiti	.75	.23
11 Alex Rodriguez	3.00	.90
12 Ken Griffey Jr.	3.00	.90
13 Juan Gonzalez	2.00	.60
14 Brian Jordan	.75	.23
15 Mo Vaughn	.75	.23
16 Ivan Rodriguez	2.00	.60
17 Andruw Jones	.75	.23
18 Chipper Jones	2.00	.60

1997 Leaf Get-A-Grip

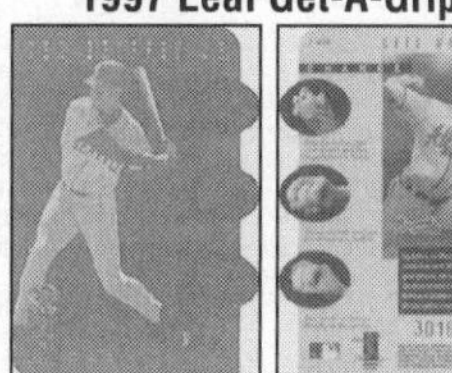

Randomly inserted in series one hobby packs, this 16-card double player insert set features color player photos of some of the current top pitchers matched against some of the league's current power hitters. The set is printed on full-silver, ploy-laminated card stock with gold-foil stamping. Only 3,500 of each card was produced and are sequentially numbered.

	Nm-Mt	Ex-Mt
COMPLETE SET (16)	150.00	45.00
1 Ken Griffey Jr.	12.00	3.60
Greg Maddux		
2 John Smoltz	8.00	2.40
Frank Thomas		
3 Mike Piazza	12.00	3.60
Andy Pettitte		
4 Randy Johnson	8.00	2.40
Chipper Jones		
5 Tom Glavine	12.00	3.60
Alex Rodriguez		
6 Pat Hentgen	5.00	1.50
Jeff Bagwell		
7 Kevin Brown	8.00	2.40
Juan Gonzalez		
8 Barry Bonds	20.00	6.00
Mike Mussina		
9 Hideo Nomo	8.00	2.40
Albert Belle		
10 Troy Percival	3.00	.90
Andruw Jones		
11 Roger Clemens	15.00	4.50
Brian Jordan		
12 Paul Wilson	8.00	2.40
Ivan Rodriguez		
13 Andy Benes	3.00	.90
Mo Vaughn		
14 Al Leiter	20.00	6.00
Derek Jeter		
15 Bill Pulsipher	25.00	7.50
Cal Ripken		
16 Mariano Rivera	5.00	1.50
Ken Caminiti		

1997 Leaf Gold Stars

Randomly inserted in all series two packs, this 36-card set features color action images of some of Baseball's hottest names with actual 24kt. gold foil stamping. Only 2,500 of each card were produced and are sequentially numbered.

	Nm-Mt	Ex-Mt
COMPLETE SET (36)	500.00	150.00
1 Frank Thomas	8.00	2.40
2 Alex Rodriguez	12.00	3.60
3 Ken Griffey Jr.	12.00	3.60
4 Andruw Jones	3.00	.90
5 Chipper Jones	8.00	2.40
6 Jeff Bagwell	5.00	1.50
7 Derek Jeter	20.00	6.00
8 Deion Sanders	5.00	1.50
9 Ivan Rodriguez	8.00	2.40
10 Juan Gonzalez	8.00	2.40
11 Greg Maddux	12.00	3.60
12 Andy Pettitte	5.00	1.50
13 Roger Clemens	15.00	4.50
14 Hideo Nomo	8.00	2.40
15 Tony Gwynn	10.00	3.00
16 Barry Bonds	20.00	6.00
17 Kenny Lofton	3.00	.90
18 Paul Molitor	5.00	1.50
19 Jim Thome	8.00	2.40
20 Albert Belle	3.00	.90
21 Cal Ripken	25.00	7.50
22 Mark McGwire	20.00	6.00
23 Barry Larkin	8.00	2.40
24 Mike Piazza	12.00	3.60
25 Darin Erstad	3.00	.90
26 Chuck Knoblauch	3.00	.90
27 Vladimir Guerrero	8.00	2.40
28 Tony Clark	3.00	.90
29 Scott Rolen	5.00	1.50
30 Nomar Garciaparra	12.00	3.60
31 Eric Young	3.00	.90
32 Ryne Sandberg	12.00	3.60
33 Roberto Alomar	8.00	2.40
34 Eddie Murray	8.00	2.40
35 Rafael Palmeiro	5.00	1.50
36 Jose Guillen	3.00	.90

1997 Leaf Knot-Hole Gang Samples

One of twelve different sample cards was distributed to dealers and hobby media prior to the release of 1997 Leaf to preview the set. The cards are marked "PROMO/5000" on back and are straight parallels to the basic Knot-Hole Gang insert cards.

	Nm-Mt	Ex-Mt
COMPLETE SET (12)	40.00	12.00
1 Chuck Knoblauch	1.50	.45
2 Ken Griffey Jr.	5.00	1.50
3 Frank Thomas	2.50	.75
4 Tony Gwynn	4.00	1.20
5 Mike Piazza	6.00	1.80
6 Jeff Bagwell	2.50	.75
7 Rusty Greer	2.00	.60
8 Cal Ripken	8.00	2.40
9 Chipper Jones	5.00	1.50
10 Ryan Klesko	1.00	.30
11 Barry Larkin	2.00	.60
12 Paul Molitor	2.50	.75

1997 Leaf Knot-Hole Gang

This 12-card insert set, randomly seeded into first series hobby packs, features color action player photos printed on wooden card stock. The die-cut card resembles a wooden fence with the player being seen in action through a knot hole. Only 5,000 of this set was produced and is sequentially numbered.

	Nm-Mt	Ex-Mt
COMPLETE SET (12)	50.00	15.00
1 Chuck Knoblauch	1.50	.45
2 Ken Griffey Jr.	6.00	1.80
3 Frank Thomas	4.00	1.20
4 Tony Gwynn	5.00	1.50
5 Mike Piazza	6.00	1.80
6 Jeff Bagwell	2.50	.75
7 Rusty Greer	1.50	.45
8 Cal Ripken	12.00	3.60
9 Chipper Jones	4.00	1.20
10 Ryan Klesko	1.50	.45
11 Barry Larkin	4.00	1.20
12 Paul Molitor	2.50	.75

1997 Leaf Leagues of the Nation

Randomly inserted in all series two packs, this 15-card set celebrates the first season of interleague play with double-sided, die-cut cards that highlight some of the best interleague match-ups. Using flocking technology, the cards display color action player photos with the place and date of the game where the match-up between the pictured players took place. Only 2,500 of each card were produced and are sequentially numbered.

	Nm-Mt	Ex-Mt
COMPLETE SET (15)	300.00	90.00
1 Juan Gonzalez	30.00	9.00
Barry Bonds		
2 Cal Ripken	40.00	12.00
Chipper Jones		
3 Mark McGwire	30.00	9.00
Ken Caminiti		
4 Derek Jeter	30.00	9.00
Kenny Lofton		
5 Ivan Rodriguez	20.00	6.00
Mike Piazza		
6 Ken Griffey Jr.	20.00	6.00
Larry Walker		
7 Frank Thomas	20.00	6.00
Sammy Sosa		
8 Paul Molitor	8.00	2.40
Barry Larkin		
9 Albert Belle	5.00	1.50
Deion Sanders		
10 Matt Williams	8.00	2.40
Jeff Bagwell		
11 Mo Vaughn	5.00	1.50
Gary Sheffield		
12 Alex Rodriguez	20.00	6.00
Tony Gwynn		
13 Tino Martinez	8.00	2.40
Scott Rolen		
14 Darin Erstad	5.00	1.50
Wilton Guerrero		
15 Tony Clark	12.00	3.60
Vladimir Guerrero		

1997 Leaf Statistical Standouts

This 15-card insert set, randomly seeded into all first series packs, showcases some of the league's statistical leaders and is printed on full-leather, die-cut, foil-stamped card stock. The player's statistics are displayed beside a color player photo. Only 1,000 of this set were produced and are sequentially numbered.

	Nm-Mt	Ex-Mt
COMPLETE SET (15)	400.00	120.00
1 Albert Belle	8.00	2.40
2 Juan Gonzalez	20.00	6.00
3 Ken Griffey Jr.	30.00	9.00
4 Alex Rodriguez	30.00	9.00
5 Frank Thomas	20.00	6.00
6 Chipper Jones	20.00	6.00
7 Greg Maddux	30.00	9.00
8 Mike Piazza	30.00	9.00
9 Cal Ripken	60.00	18.00
10 Mark McGwire	50.00	15.00
11 Barry Bonds	50.00	15.00
12 Derek Jeter	50.00	15.00
13 Ken Caminiti	8.00	2.40
14 John Smoltz	12.00	3.60
15 Paul Molitor	12.00	3.60

1997 Leaf Thomas Collection

Randomly inserted in all series two packs, this six-card set commemorates the multi-faceted talents of first baseman and at the time, Leaf Company spokesman, Frank Thomas with actual pieces of his game-used hats, jerseys (home and away), sweatbands, batting gloves or bats embedded in the cards. Only 100 of each card were produced and are sequentially numbered. This set, along with the 1997 Upper Deck Game Jersey inserts, represents one of the earliest forays by an mlb-licensed manufactuer into game-used memorabilia inserts.

	Nm-Mt	Ex-Mt
1 Frank Thomas	150.00	45.00
Game Hat/Blue Text		
2 Frank Thomas	150.00	45.00
Home Jersey/Orange Text		
3 Frank Thomas	150.00	45.00
Batting Glove/Yellow Text		
4 Frank Thomas	150.00	45.00
Bat/Green Text		
5 Frank Thomas	150.00	45.00
Sweatband/Purple Text		
6 Frank Thomas	150.00	45.00
Away Jersey/Red Text		

1997 Leaf Warning Track

Randomly inserted in all series two packs, this 18-card set features color action photos of outstanding outfielders printed on embossed canvas card stock. Only 3,500 of each card were produced and are sequentially numbered.

	Nm-Mt	Ex-Mt
COMPLETE SET (18)	100.00	30.00
1 Ken Griffey Jr.	12.00	3.60
2 Albert Belle	3.00	.90
3 Barry Bonds	20.00	6.00
4 Andruw Jones	3.00	.90
5 Kenny Lofton	3.00	.90
6 Tony Gwynn	10.00	3.00
7 Manny Ramirez	3.00	.90
8 Rusty Greer	3.00	.90
9 Bernie Williams	5.00	1.50
10 Gary Sheffield	3.00	.90
11 Juan Gonzalez	8.00	2.40
12 Raul Mondesi	3.00	.90
13 Brady Anderson	3.00	.90
14 Rondell White	3.00	.90
15 Sammy Sosa	12.00	3.60
16 Deion Sanders	5.00	1.50
17 Dave Justice	3.00	.90
18 Jim Edmonds	3.00	.90

1997 Leaf Thomas Info

This card was put into the front of every 12 card Leaf Blister pack. The front has an action photo of Thomas while the back explains more about the 97 Leaf Product. The card is a stand alone and not inserted in the unopened part of the pack. The blister pack retailed for $2.99.

	Nm-Mt	Ex-Mt
1 Frank Thomas	2.00	.60

1997 Leaf Thomas Leukemia

This four-card set was produced by Donruss for the Frank Thomas Charitable Foundation. The cards feature borderless color photos of Frank Thomas, who lost a sister to Leukemia, with other people who have some connection to the illness. The back of card number 1 displays a portrait of a Leukemia victim. All proceeds from the sale of the set went to the Foundation. The cards could be ordered by mail from Big Heart Charity Card for $20 each. Only 2500 of each card was produced and are sequentially numbered.

	Nm-Mt	Ex-Mt
COMPLETE SET (4)	100.00	30.00
COMMON CARD (1-4)	25.00	7.50
1 Frank Thomas	30.00	9.00
Rod Carew		
Michelle Carew(on back)		

1998 Leaf

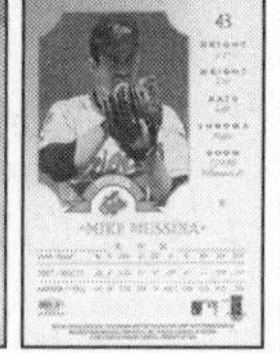

The 1998 Leaf set was issued in one series totalling 200 cards. The 10-card packs carried a suggested retail price of $2.99. The set contains the topical subsets: Curtain Calls (148-157), Gold Leaf Stars (158-177), and Gold Leaf Rookies (178-197). All three subsets are short-printed in relation to cards from 1-147 and 201. Those short prints represent one of the early efforts by a manufacturer to incorportate short-print subsets cards into a basic issue set. The product went live in mid-March, 1998. Card number 42 does not exist as Leaf retired the number in honor of Jackie Robinson.

	Nm-Mt	Ex-Mt
COMPLETE SET (200)	60.00	18.00
COMP.SET w/o SP's (147)	15.00	4.50
COMMON CARD (1-201)	.30	.09
COMMON SP (148-197)	1.50	.45
1 Rusty Greer	.30	.09
2 Tino Martinez	.50	.15
3 Bobby Bonilla	.30	.09
4 Jason Giambi	.75	.23
5 Matt Morris	.30	.09
6 Craig Counsell	.30	.09
7 Reggie Jefferson	.30	.09
8 Brian Rose	.30	.09
9 Ruben Rivera	.30	.09
10 Shawn Estes	.30	.09
11 Tony Gwynn	1.00	.30
12 Jeff Abbott	.30	.09
13 Jose Cruz Jr.	.30	.09
14 Francisco Cordova	.30	.09
15 Ryan Klesko	.30	.09
16 Tim Salmon	.50	.15
17 Brett Tomko	.30	.09
18 Matt Williams	.30	.09
19 Joe Carter	.30	.09
20 Harold Baines	.30	.09
21 Gary Sheffield	.30	.09
22 Charles Johnson	.30	.09
23 Aaron Boone	.30	.09
24 Eddie Murray	.75	.23
25 Matt Stairs	.30	.09
26 David Cone	.30	.09
27 Jon Nunnally	.30	.09
28 Chris Stynes	.30	.09
29 Enrique Wilson	.30	.09
30 Randy Johnson	.75	.23
31 Garret Anderson	.30	.09
32 Manny Ramirez	.30	.09
33 Jeff Suppan	.30	.09
34 Rickey Henderson	.75	.23
35 Scott Spiezio	.30	.09
36 Rondell White	.30	.09
37 Todd Greene	.30	.09
38 Delino DeShields	.30	.09
39 Kevin Brown	.50	.15
40 Chili Davis	.30	.09
41 Jimmy Key	.30	.09
43 Mike Mussina	.75	.23
44 Joe Randa	.30	.09
45 Chan Ho Park	.30	.09
46 Brad Radke	.30	.09
47 Geronimo Berroa	.30	.09
48 Wade Boggs	.50	.15
49 Kevin Appier	.30	.09
50 Moises Alou	.30	.09
51 David Justice	.30	.09
52 Ivan Rodriguez	.75	.23
53 J.T. Snow	.30	.09
54 Brian Giles	.30	.09
55 Will Clark	.75	.23
56 Justin Thompson	.30	.09
57 Javier Lopez	.30	.09
58 Hideki Irabu	.30	.09
59 Mark Grudzielanek	.30	.09
60 Abraham Nunez	.30	.09
61 Todd Hollandsworth	.30	.09
62 Jay Bell	.30	.09
63 Nomar Garciaparra	1.25	.35
64 Vinny Castilla	.30	.09
65 Lou Collier	.30	.09
66 Kevin Orie	.30	.09
67 John Valentin	.30	.09
68 Robin Ventura	.30	.09
69 Denny Neagle	.30	.09
70 Tony Womack	.30	.09
71 Dennis Reyes	.30	.09
72 Wally Joyner	.30	.09
73 Kevin Brown	.50	.15
74 Ray Durham	.30	.09
75 Mike Cameron	.30	.09
76 Dante Bichette	.30	.09
77 Jose Guillen	.30	.09
78 Carlos Delgado	.30	.09
79 Paul Molitor	.50	.15
80 Jason Kendall	.30	.09
81 Mark Bellhorn	.30	.09
82 Damian Jackson	.30	.09
83 Bill Mueller	.30	.09
84 Kevin Young	.30	.09
85 Curt Schilling	.50	.15
86 Jeffrey Hammonds	.30	.09
87 Sandy Alomar Jr.	.30	.09
88 Bartolo Colon	.30	.09
89 Wilton Guerrero	.30	.09
90 Bernie Williams	.50	.15
91 Deion Sanders	.50	.15
92 Mike Piazza	1.25	.35
93 Butch Huskey	.30	.09
94 Edgardo Alfonzo	.30	.09
95 Alan Benes	.30	.09
96 Craig Biggio	.50	.15
97 Mark Grace	.50	.15
98 Shawn Green	.30	.09
99 Derrek Lee	.30	.09
100 Ken Griffey Jr.	1.25	.35
101 Tim Raines	.30	.09
102 Pokey Reese	.30	.09
103 Lee Stevens	.30	.09
104 Shannon Stewart	.30	.09
105 John Smoltz	.50	.15
106 Frank Thomas	.75	.23
107 Jeff Fassero	.30	.09
108 Jay Buhner	.30	.09
109 Jose Canseco	.75	.23
110 Omar Vizquel	.30	.09
111 Travis Fryman	.30	.09
112 Dave Nilsson	.30	.09
113 John Olerud	.30	.09
114 Larry Walker	.50	.15

115 Jim Edmonds .30 .09
116 Bobby Higginson .30 .09
117 Todd Hundley .30 .09
118 Paul O'Neill .50 .15
119 Bip Roberts .30 .09
120 Ismael Valdes .30 .09
121 Pedro Martinez .75 .23
122 Jeff Cirillo .30 .09
123 Andy Benes .30 .09
124 Bobby Jones .30 .09
125 Brian Hunter .30 .09
126 Darryl Kile .30 .09
127 Pat Hentgen .30 .09
128 Marquis Grissom .30 .09
129 Eric Davis .30 .09
130 Chipper Jones .75 .23
131 Edgar Martinez .50 .15
132 Andy Pettitte .50 .15
133 Cal Ripken 2.50 .75
134 Scott Rolen .50 .15
135 Ron Coomer .30 .09
136 Luis Castillo .30 .09
137 Fred McGriff .50 .15
138 Neifi Perez .30 .09
139 Eric Karros .30 .09
140 Alex Fernandez .30 .09
141 Jason Dickson .30 .09
142 Lance Johnson .30 .09
143 Ray Lankford .30 .09
144 Sammy Sosa 1.25 .35
145 Eric Young .30 .09
146 Bubba Trammell .30 .09
147 Todd Walker .30 .09
148 Mo Vaughn CC 1.50 .45
149 Jeff Bagwell CC 2.50 .75
150 Kenny Lofton CC 1.50 .45
151 Raul Mondesi CC 1.50 .45
152 Mike Piazza CC 6.00 1.80
153 Chipper Jones CC 4.00 1.20
154 Larry Walker CC 2.50 .75
155 Greg Maddux CC 6.00 1.80
156 Ken Griffey Jr. CC 6.00 1.80
157 Frank Thomas CC 4.00 1.20
158 Darin Erstad GLS 1.50 .45
159 Roberto Alomar GLS 4.00 1.20
160 Albert Belle GLS 1.50 .45
161 Jim Thome GLS 4.00 1.20
162 Tony Clark GLS 1.50 .45
163 Chuck Knoblauch GLS 1.50 .45
164 Derek Jeter GLS 10.00 3.00
165 Alex Rodriguez GLS 6.00 1.80
166 Tony Gwynn GLS 5.00 1.50
167 Roger Clemens GLS 8.00 2.40
168 Barry Larkin GLS 4.00 1.20
169 Andres Galarraga GLS 1.50 .45
170 Vlad. Guerrero GLS 4.00 1.20
171 Mark McGwire GLS 10.00 3.00
172 Barry Bonds GLS 10.00 3.00
173 Juan Gonzalez GLS 4.00 1.20
174 Andruw Jones GLS 1.50 .45
175 Paul Molitor GLS 2.50 .75
176 Hideo Nomo GLS 4.00 1.20
177 Cal Ripken GLS 12.00 3.60
178 Brad Fullmer GLR 1.50 .45
179 Jaret Wright GLR 1.50 .45
180 Bobby Estalella GLR 1.50 .45
181 Ben Grieve GLR 1.50 .45
182 Paul Konerko GLR 1.50 .45
183 David Ortiz GLR 1.50 .45
184 Todd Helton GLR 2.50 .75
185 J.Encarnacion GLR 1.50 .45
186 Miguel Tejada GLR 2.50 .75
187 Jacob Cruz GLR 1.50 .45
188 Mark Kotsay GLR 1.50 .45
189 Fernando Tatis GLR 1.50 .45
190 Ricky Ledee GLR 1.50 .45
191 Richard Hidalgo GLR 1.50 .45
192 Richie Sexson GLR 1.50 .45
193 Luis Ordaz GLR 1.50 .45
194 Eli Marrero GLR 1.50 .45
195 Livan Hernandez GLR 1.50 .45
196 Homer Bush GLR 1.50 .45
197 Raul Ibanez GLR 1.50 .45
198 Nomar Garciaparra CL .75 .23
199 Scott Rolen CL .30 .09
200 Jose Cruz Jr. CL .30 .09
201 Al Martin .30 .09

1998 Leaf Fractal Diamond Axis

Randomly inserted in packs, this 200-card set is parallel to the Leaf base set. Each card features die cut edges and blue foil fronts. Only 50 serially numbered sets were produced. Card number 42 does not exist.

Nm-Mt Ex-Mt
*STARS 1-147/198-201: 15X TO 40X BASIC
*SP STARS 148-197: 3X TO 8X BASIC SP'S

1998 Leaf Fractal Matrix

Randomly inserted in packs, this 200-card set is parallel to the Leaf base set and features color player photos with either a bronze, silver or gold finish. Only 100 cards are bronze, 60 are silver, and 40 are gold. No card is available in more than one of the colors. The set is broken into nine tiers based on three colors (Bronze, Gold and Silver) and three axis (X, Y and Z). Unlike the previous year, the 1998 cards carry an axis-logo on the card front, allowing collectors to identify the specific tier. It's estimated that print runs range from as few as 50 to as many of 2000 of each card.

Nm-Mt Ex-Mt
*BRONZE 1-147/198-201: 1.5X TO 4X BASIC
*BRONZE 148-197: .3X TO .8X BASIC
BRONZE X STATED PRINT RUN 1600 SETS
BRONZE Y STATED PRINT RUN 1800 SETS
BRONZE Z STATED PRINT RUN 1900 SETS
*SILVER 1-147/198-201: 3X TO 8X BASIC
*SILVER: 148-197: .6X TO 1.5X BASIC
SILVER X STATED PRINT RUN 600 SETS
SILVER Y STATED PRINT RUN 800 SETS
SILVER Z STATED PRINT RUN 900 SETS
*GOLD 1-147/198-201: 5X TO 12X BASIC
*GOLD: 148-197: 1X TO 2.5X BASIC
GOLD X STATED PRINT RUN 100 SETS
GOLD Y STATED PRINT RUN 300 SETS
GOLD Z STATED PRINT RUN 400 SETS
RANDOM INSERTS IN PACKS
CARD NUMBER 42 DOES NOT EXIST.

1998 Leaf Fractal Matrix Die Cuts

Randomly inserted in packs, this 200-card set is parallel to the regular set and features three different die-cut versions in three different finishes. Only 100 of the set are produced in the x-axis cut with 75 of those bronze, 20 silver, and five gold. Only 60 are available in the type y-axis cut with 20 of those bronze, 30 silver, and 10 gold. Only 40 are produced in the z-axis cut with five bronze, 10 silver and 25 gold. No card is available in more than one color nor in more than one die-cut version. Card number 42 does not exist.

Nm-Mt Ex-Mt
*X-AXIS 1-147/198-201: 5X TO 12X BASIC
*X-AXIS 148-197: 1X TO 2.5X BASIC
X-AXIS STATED PRINT RUN 400 SETS
*Y-AXIS 1-147/198-201: 8X TO 20X BASIC
*Y-AXIS 148-197: 1.5X TO 4X BASIC
Y-AXIS STATED PRINT RUN 200 SETS
*Z-AXIS 1-147/198-201: 12.5X TO 30X BASIC
*Z-AXIS 148-197: 2.5X TO 6X BASIC
Z-AXIS STATED PRINT RUN 100 SETS
RANDOM INSERTS IN PACKS
CARD NUMBER 42 DOES NOT EXIST.
SEE WEBSITE FOR AXIS SCHEMATIC.

1998 Leaf Crusade Green

As part of the 1998 Donruss/Leaf Crusade insert program, 30 cards were exclusively issued in 1998 Leaf Packs. Please refer to 1998 Donruss Crusade for further information.

Nm-Mt Ex-Mt
PLEASE SEE 1998 DONRUSS CRUSADE

1998 Leaf Heading for the Hall Samples

To preview the 1998 Leaf product, all dealer wholesale order forms contained one of these twenty different samples. The cards differ from the basic Heading for the Hall inserts in two ways: the large "SAMPLE" text printed diagonally across the card back and the lack of serial numbering on back.

Nm-Mt Ex-Mt
COMPLETE SET (20) 80.00 24.00
1 Roberto Alomar 2.00 .60
2 Jeff Bagwell 3.00 .90
3 Albert Belle 1.00 .30
4 Wade Boggs 4.00 1.20
5 Barry Bonds 5.00 1.50
6 Roger Clemens 5.00 1.50
7 Juan Gonzalez 2.00 .60
8 Ken Griffey Jr. 6.00 1.80
9 Tony Gwynn 5.00 1.50
10 Barry Larkin 2.00 .60
11 Kenny Lofton 1.50 .45
12 Greg Maddux 6.00 1.80
13 Mark McGwire 8.00 2.40
14 Paul Molitor 2.50 .75
15 Eddie Murray 2.00 .60
16 Mike Piazza 8.00 2.40
17 Cal Ripken 10.00 3.00
18 Ivan Rodriguez 3.00 .90
19 Ryne Sandberg 4.00 1.20
20 Frank Thomas 3.00 .90

1998 Leaf Heading for the Hall

This 20 card set was randomly inserted into 1998 Leaf packs. The fronts have a design similar to the Hall of Fame packs. The player's name and team is at top. The back has another photo along with a brief blurb. The cards are numbered "X of 3500" on the back as well.

Nm-Mt Ex-Mt
COMPLETE SET (20) 150.00 45.00
1 Roberto Alomar 8.00 2.40
2 Jeff Bagwell 5.00 1.50
3 Albert Belle 3.00 .90
4 Wade Boggs 5.00 1.50
5 Barry Bonds 20.00 6.00
6 Roger Clemens 15.00 4.50
7 Juan Gonzalez 8.00 2.40
8 Ken Griffey Jr. 12.00 3.60
9 Tony Gwynn 10.00 3.00
10 Barry Larkin 8.00 2.40
11 Kenny Lofton 3.00 .90
12 Greg Maddux 12.00 3.60
13 Mark McGwire 20.00 6.00
14 Paul Molitor 5.00 1.50
15 Eddie Murray 8.00 2.40
16 Mike Piazza 12.00 3.60
17 Cal Ripken 25.00 7.50
18 Ivan Rodriguez 8.00 2.40
19 Ryne Sandberg 12.00 3.60
20 Frank Thomas 8.00 2.40

1998 Leaf State Representatives

This 30 card set was randomly inserted into packs. The fronts have the words "State Representatives" on the top with the player's name and team on the bottom. The player's photo has a metallic sheen to it as he is pictured against a state outline. The back has a small player portrait along with some information about the player. The cards are serial numbered "X of 5,000" on the back.

Nm-Mt Ex-Mt
COMPLETE SET (30) 150.00 45.00
1 Ken Griffey Jr. 10.00 3.00
2 Frank Thomas 6.00 1.80
3 Alex Rodriguez 10.00 3.00
4 Cal Ripken 20.00 6.00
5 Chipper Jones 6.00 1.80
6 Andruw Jones 2.50 .75
7 Scott Rolen 4.00 1.20
8 Nomar Garciaparra 10.00 3.00
9 Tim Salmon 4.00 1.20
10 Manny Ramirez 2.50 .75
11 Jose Cruz Jr. 2.50 .75
12 Vladimir Guerrero 6.00 1.80
13 Tino Martinez 4.00 1.20
14 Larry Walker 4.00 1.20
15 Mo Vaughn 2.50 .75
16 Jim Thome 6.00 1.80
17 Tony Clark 2.50 .75
18 Derek Jeter 15.00 4.50
19 Juan Gonzalez 6.00 1.80
20 Jeff Bagwell 4.00 1.20
21 Ivan Rodriguez 6.00 1.80
22 Mark McGwire 15.00 4.50
23 David Justice 2.50 .75
24 Chuck Knoblauch 2.50 .75
25 Andy Pettitte 4.00 1.20
26 Raul Mondesi 2.50 .75
27 Randy Johnson 6.00 1.80
28 Greg Maddux 10.00 3.00
29 Bernie Williams 4.00 1.20
30 Rusty Greer 2.50 .75

1998 Leaf Statistical Standouts

These 24 horizontal cards feature leading players. The front of the card has the players photo against a background of a glove and ball. The ball has been signed by that player. The card's front feels like leather and the words "Statistical Standouts" is printed on the side. The backs have year and career stats on the back along with another player photo. The cards are serial numbered "X of 2500" on the back.

Nm-Mt Ex-Mt
COMPLETE SET (24) 250.00 75.00
*DIE CUTS: .75X TO 2X BASIC STAT.STAND.
DIE CUT PRINT RUN 250 SERIAL #'d SETS
RANDOM INSERTS IN PACKS
1 Frank Thomas 10.00 3.00
2 Ken Griffey Jr. 15.00 4.50
3 Alex Rodriguez 15.00 4.50
4 Mike Piazza 15.00 4.50
5 Greg Maddux 15.00 4.50
6 Cal Ripken 30.00 9.00
7 Chipper Jones 10.00 3.00
8 Juan Gonzalez 10.00 3.00
9 Jeff Bagwell 6.00 1.80
10 Mark McGwire 25.00 7.50
11 Tony Gwynn 12.00 3.60
12 Mo Vaughn 4.00 1.20
13 Nomar Garciaparra 15.00 4.50
14 Jose Cruz Jr. 4.00 1.20
15 Vladimir Guerrero 10.00 3.00
16 Scott Rolen 6.00 1.80
17 Andy Pettitte 6.00 1.80
18 Randy Johnson 10.00 3.00
19 Larry Walker 6.00 1.80
20 Kenny Lofton 4.00 1.20
21 Tony Clark 4.00 1.20
22 David Justice 4.00 1.20
23 Derek Jeter 25.00 7.50
24 Barry Bonds 25.00 7.50

2002 Leaf Samples

Issued one per sealed copy of Beckett Baseball Card Monthly issue number 205, this is a partial parallel to the 2002 Leaf Set. Only the first 150 cards of the 2002 Leaf set were issued in this format.

Nm-Mt Ex-Mt
*SAMPLES: 1.5X TO 4X BASIC

2002 Leaf

This 200 card set was issued in late winter, 2002. This set was distributed in four card packs with an SRP of $3 which were sent in 24 packs to a box with 20 boxes to a case. Cards numbered from 151-200, which were inserted at a stated rate of one in six, featured 50 of the leading rookie prospects entering the 2002 season. Card number 42, which Leaf had previously retired in honor of Jackie Robinson, was originally intended to feature a short-print card honoring the sensational rookie season of Ichiro Suzuki. However, Leaf decided to continue honoring Robinson and never went through with printing card 42. Cards numbered 201 and 202 feature Japanese imports So Taguchi and Kazuhisa Ishii, both of which were short-printed in relation to the other prospect cards 151-200. The cards production runs were announced by the manufacturer as 250 copies for Ishii and 500 for Taguchi.

Nm-Mt Ex-Mt
COMP.SET w/o SP's (149) 25.00 7.50
COMMON (1-41/43-150) .30 .09
COMMON CARD (151-200) 4.00 1.20
1 Tim Salmon .50 .15
2 Troy Glaus .50 .15
3 Curt Schilling .50 .15
4 Luis Gonzalez .30 .09
5 Mark Grace .50 .15
6 Matt Williams .30 .09
7 Randy Johnson .75 .23
8 Tom Glavine .50 .15
9 Brady Anderson .30 .09
10 Hideo Nomo .75 .23
11 Pedro Martinez .75 .23
12 Corey Patterson .30 .09
13 Paul Konerko .30 .09
14 Jon Lieber .30 .09
15 Carlos Lee .30 .09
16 Magglio Ordonez .30 .09
17 Adam Dunn .30 .09
18 Ken Griffey Jr. 1.25 .35
19 C.C. Sabathia .30 .09
20 Jim Thome .75 .23
21 Juan Gonzalez .75 .23
22 Kenny Lofton .30 .09
23 Juan Encarnacion .30 .09
24 Tony Clark .30 .09
25 A.J. Burnett .30 .09
26 Josh Beckett .50 .15
27 Lance Berkman .30 .09
28 Eric Karros .30 .09
29 Shawn Green .30 .09
30 Brad Radke .30 .09
31 Joe Mays .30 .09
32 Javier Vazquez .30 .09
33 Alfonso Soriano .50 .15
34 Jorge Posada .50 .15
35 Eric Chavez .30 .09
36 Mark Mulder .30 .09
37 Miguel Tejada .30 .09
38 Tim Hudson .30 .09
39 Bob Abreu .30 .09
40 Pat Burrell .30 .09
41 Ryan Klesko .30 .09
43 John Olerud .30 .09
44 Ellis Burks .30 .09
45 Mike Cameron .30 .09
46 Jim Edmonds .30 .09
47 Ben Grieve .30 .09
48 Carlos Pena .30 .09
49 Alex Rodriguez 1.25 .35
50 Raul Mondesi .30 .09
51 Billy Koch .30 .09
52 Manny Ramirez .30 .09
53 Darin Erstad .30 .09
54 Troy Percival .30 .09
55 Andruw Jones .30 .09
56 Chipper Jones .75 .23
57 David Segui .30 .09
58 Chris Stynes .30 .09
59 Trot Nixon .50 .15
60 Sammy Sosa 1.25 .35
61 Kerry Wood .75 .23
62 Frank Thomas .75 .23
63 Barry Larkin .75 .23
64 Bartolo Colon .30 .09
65 Kazuhiro Sasaki .30 .09
66 Roberto Alomar .75 .23
67 Mike Hampton .30 .09
68 Roger Cedeno .30 .09
69 Cliff Floyd .30 .09
70 Mike Lowell .30 .09
71 Billy Wagner .30 .09
72 Craig Biggio .50 .15
73 Jeff Bagwell .50 .15
74 Carlos Beltran .30 .09
75 Mark Quinn .30 .09
76 Mike Sweeney .30 .09
77 Gary Sheffield .30 .09
78 Kevin Brown .30 .09
79 Paul LoDuca .30 .09
80 Ben Sheets .30 .09
81 Jeromy Burnitz .30 .09
82 Richie Sexson .30 .09
83 Corey Koskie .30 .09
84 Eric Milton .30 .09
85 Jose Vidro .30 .09
86 Mike Piazza 1.25 .35
87 Robin Ventura .30 .09
88 Andy Pettitte .50 .15
89 Mike Mussina .75 .23
90 Orlando Hernandez .30 .09
91 Roger Clemens 1.50 .45
92 Barry Zito .50 .15
93 Jermaine Dye .30 .09
94 Jimmy Rollins .30 .09
95 Jason Kendall .30 .09
96 Rickey Henderson .75 .23
97 Andres Galarraga .30 .09
98 Bret Boone .30 .09
99 Freddy Garcia .30 .09
100 J.D. Drew .30 .09
101 Jose Cruz Jr. .30 .09
102 Greg Maddux 1.25 .35
103 Javy Lopez .30 .09
104 Nomar Garciaparra 1.25 .35
105 Fred McGriff .50 .15
106 Keith Foulke .30 .09
107 Ray Durham .30 .09
108 Sean Casey .30 .09
109 Todd Walker .30 .09
110 Omar Vizquel .30 .09
111 Travis Fryman .30 .09
112 Larry Walker .50 .15
113 Todd Helton .50 .15
114 Bobby Higginson .30 .09
115 Charles Johnson .30 .09
116 Moises Alou .30 .09
117 Richard Hidalgo .30 .09
118 Roy Oswalt .30 .09
119 Neifi Perez .30 .09
120 Adrian Beltre .30 .09
121 Chan Ho Park .30 .09
122 Geoff Jenkins .30 .09
123 Doug Mientkiewicz .30 .09
124 Torii Hunter .30 .09
125 Vladimir Guerrero .75 .23
126 Matt Lawton .30 .09
127 Tsuyoshi Shinjo .30 .09
128 Bernie Williams .50 .15
129 Derek Jeter 2.00 .60
130 Mariano Rivera .50 .15
131 Tino Martinez .50 .15
132 Jason Giambi .75 .23
133 Scott Rolen .50 .15
134 Brian Giles .30 .09
135 Phil Nevin .30 .09
136 Trevor Hoffman .30 .09
137 Barry Bonds 2.00 .60
138 Jeff Kent .30 .09
139 Shannon Stewart .30 .09
140 Shawn Estes .30 .09
141 Edgar Martinez .50 .15
142 Ichiro Suzuki 1.25 .35
143 Albert Pujols 1.50 .45
144 Bud Smith .30 .09
145 Matt Morris .30 .09
146 Frank Catalanotto .30 .09
147 Gabe Kapler .30 .09
148 Ivan Rodriguez .75 .23
149 Rafael Palmeiro .50 .15
150 Carlos Delgado .30 .09
151 Marlon Byrd ROO 4.00 1.20
152 Alex Herrera ROO 4.00 1.20
153 Brandon Backe ROO RC 4.00 1.20
154 Jorge De La Rosa ROO RC 4.00 1.20
155 Corky Miller ROO 4.00 1.20
156 Dennis Tankersley ROO 4.00 1.20
157 Kyle Kane ROO RC 4.00 1.20
158 Justin Duchscherer ROO 4.00 1.20
159 Brian Mallette ROO RC 4.00 1.20
160 Eric Hinske ROO 4.00 1.20
161 Jason Lane ROO 4.00 1.20
162 Hee Seop Choi ROO 5.00 1.50
163 Juan Cruz ROO 4.00 1.20
164 Rodrigo Rosario ROO RC 4.00 1.20
165 Matt Guerrier ROO 4.00 1.20
166 And. Machado ROO RC 4.00 1.20
167 Geronimo Gil ROO 4.00 1.20
168 Dewon Brazelton ROO 4.00 1.20
169 Mark Prior ROO 15.00 4.50
170 Bill Hall ROO 4.00 1.20
171 Jorge Padilla ROO RC 4.00 1.20
172 Josh Pearce ROO 4.00 1.20
173 Allan Simpson ROO RC 4.00 1.20
174 Doug Devore ROO RC 4.00 1.20
175 Luis Garcia ROO 4.00 1.20
176 Angel Berroa ROO 4.00 1.20
177 Steve Bechler ROO RC 4.00 1.20
178 Antonio Perez ROO 4.00 1.20
179 Mark Teixeira ROO 8.00 2.40
180 Mark Ellis ROO 4.00 1.20
181 Michael Cuddyer ROO 4.00 1.20
182 Michael Rivera ROO 4.00 1.20
183 Raul Chavez ROO RC 4.00 1.20
184 Juan Pena ROO 4.00 1.20
185 Austin Kearns ROO 4.00 1.20
186 Ryan Ludwick ROO 4.00 1.20
187 Ed Rogers ROO 4.00 1.20
188 Wilson Betemit ROO 4.00 1.20
189 Nick Neugebauer ROO 4.00 1.20
190 Tom Shearn ROO RC 4.00 1.20
191 Eric Cyr ROO 4.00 1.20
192 Victor Martinez ROO 4.00 1.20
193 Brandon Berger ROO 4.00 1.20
194 Erik Bedard ROO 4.00 1.20
195 Franklyn German ROO RC 4.00 1.20
196 Joe Thurston ROO 4.00 1.20
197 John Buck ROO 4.00 1.20
198 Jeff Deardorff ROO 4.00 1.20
199 Ryan Jamison ROO 4.00 1.20
200 Alfredo Amezaga ROO 4.00 1.20
201 So Taguchi ROO/500 RC 15.00 4.50
202 Kazuhisa Ishii ROO/250 RC 25.00 7.50

2002 Leaf Autographs

Taguchi signed 50 serial numbered cards and Ishii signed 25 serial numbered cards. The Taguchi autographs were distributed in packs but an exchange card with a deadline of October 1st, 2003 was seeded into packs for the Ishii autographs. Each card is a straight parallel of the basic RC's except for a signed silver foil sticker placed over the front and foil serial-numbering on back.

Nm-Mt Ex-Mt
201 So Taguchi /50
202 Kazuhisa Ishii/25

2002 Leaf Lineage

Inserted in hobby packs at stated odds of one in 12, this is a mini-parallel of the 2002 Leaf set. Only the first 150 cards from the set are featured and the set is split up into three sections: Cards numbered 1-50 feature 1999 replicas, while cards numbered from 51-100 feature 2000 replicas and cards numbered from 101-150 feature 2001 replicas.

Nm-Mt Ex-Mt
*LINEAGE: 3X TO 8X BASIC CARDS

2002 Leaf Lineage Century

Randomly Iserted in hobby packs, this is a mini-parallel of the 2002 Leaf set. Only the first 150 cards from this set are featured and the set is split up into three sections: Cards numbered 1-50 feature 1999 replicas, while cards numbered from 51-100 feature 2000 replicas and cards numbered from 101-150 feature 2001 replicas. These cards are serial numbered to 100.

Nm-Mt Ex-Mt
*CENTURY: 8X TO 20X BASIC CARDS

2002 Leaf Press Proofs Blue

Inserted at stated odds of one in 24 retail packs, this is a partial parallel of the 2002 Leaf set and featured the first 150 cards from that set.

	Nm-Mt	Ex-Mt
*BLUE: 6X TO 15X BASIC CARDS		

2002 Leaf Press Proofs Platinum

Randomly inserted in hobby packs, this is a mini-parallel of the 2002 Leaf set. Only the first 150 cards from the basic Leaf set and cards 201 and 202 are featured in this parallel. All cards except for card 202 are serial numbered to 25. Only ten serial-numbered copies of card number 202 (featuring Japanese pitcher Kazuhisa Ishii) were produced.

	Nm-Mt	Ex-Mt
*PLATINUM: 30X TO 80X BASIC CARDS		
201-202 NOT PRICED DUE TO SCARCITY		

2002 Leaf Press Proofs Red

Issued at stated odds of one in 12 retail packs, this set parallels the first 150 cards of the 2002 Leaf set. In addition, the two cards of Japanese imports So Taguchi and Kazuhisa Ishii are printed to stated print runs of 500 and 250 respectively.

	Nm-Mt	Ex-Mt
*RED 1-150: 3X TO 8X BASIC CARDS		
201 So Taguchi/500	15.00	4.50
202 Kazuhisa Ishii/250	25.00	7.50

2002 Leaf Burn and Turn

Issued at stated odds of one in 96 hobby and one in 120 retail packs, these 10 cards feature most of the leading double play duos in major league baseball.

	Nm-Mt	Ex-Mt
COMPLETE SET (10)	100.00	30.00
1 Fernando Vina	8.00	2.40
Edgar Renteria		
2 Alex Rodriguez	15.00	4.50
Mike Young		
3 Derek Jeter	25.00	7.50
Alfonso Soriano		
4 Carlos Guillen	8.00	2.40
Bret Boone		
5 Jose Vidro	8.00	2.40
Orlando Cabrera		
6 Barry Larkin	10.00	3.00
Todd Walker		
7 Carlos Febles	8.00	2.40
Neifi Perez		
8 Jeff Kent	8.00	2.40
Rich Aurilia		
9 Craig Biggio	8.00	2.40
Julio Lugo		
10 Miguel Tejada	8.00	2.40
Mark Ellis		

2002 Leaf Clean Up Crew

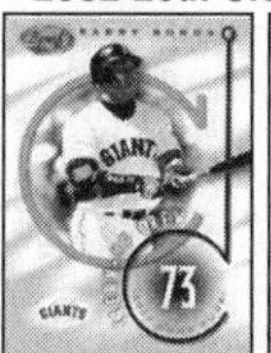
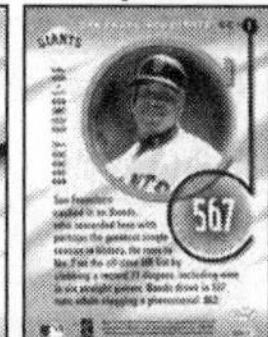

Issued at stated odds of one in 192 hobby and one in 240 retail packs, these 15 cards feature leading sluggers of the game. The cards are set on conventional cardboard with silver foil stamping.

	Nm-Mt	Ex-Mt
COMPLETE SET (15)	200.00	60.00
1 Barry Bonds	30.00	9.00
2 Sammy Sosa	20.00	6.00
3 Luis Gonzalez	10.00	3.00
4 Richie Sexson	10.00	3.00
5 Jim Thome	12.00	3.60
6 Chipper Jones	12.00	3.60
7 Alex Rodriguez	20.00	6.00
8 Troy Glaus	10.00	3.00
9 Rafael Palmeiro	10.00	3.00
10 Lance Berkman	10.00	3.00
11 Mike Piazza	20.00	6.00
12 Jason Giambi	12.00	3.60
13 Todd Helton	10.00	3.00
14 Shawn Green	10.00	3.00
15 Carlos Delgado	10.00	3.00

2002 Leaf Clubhouse Signatures Bronze

Randomly inserted in packs, these 33 cards feature a mix of signed cards of retired legends, superstar veterans and future stars. Each of these cards is serial numbered and we have listed the print run in our checklist. Cards with a print run of 100 or fewer are not priced due to market scarcity.

	Nm-Mt	Ex-Mt
1 Adam Dunn/200	25.00	7.50
2 Alan Trammell/75		
3 Alfonso Soriano/75		
4 Andre Dawson/100		
5 Aramis Ramirez/250	15.00	4.50
6 Austin Kearns/300	15.00	4.50
7 Barry Zito/100	40.00	12.00
8 Billy Williams/150	15.00	4.50
9 Bob Feller/250	25.00	7.50
10 Bud Smith/200	15.00	4.50
11 Don Mattingly/25		
12 Edgar Martinez/50		
13 J.D. Drew/25		
14 Jason Lane/250	15.00	4.50
15 Jermaine Dye/125	20.00	6.00
16 Joe Crede/200	15.00	4.50
17 Joe Mays/200	15.00	4.50
18 Johnny Estrada/250	15.00	4.50
19 Mark Ellis/300	15.00	4.50
20 Mark Mulder/50		
21 Marlon Byrd/200	15.00	4.50
22 Ozzie Smith/25		
23 Paul LoDuca/300	15.00	4.50
24 Phil Rizzuto/25		
25 Robert Fick/300	15.00	4.50
26 Ron Santo/300	25.00	7.50
27 Roy Oswalt/300	15.00	4.50
28 Ryne Sandberg/25		
29 Steve Garvey/200	15.00	4.50
30 Terrence Long/250	15.00	4.50
31 Tim Redding/300	15.00	4.50
32 Wilson Betemit/150	15.00	4.50
33 Xavier Nady/200	15.00	4.50

2002 Leaf Clubhouse Signatures Gold

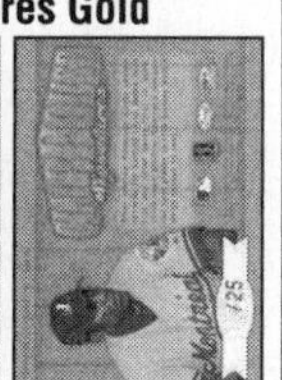

Randomly inserted in packs, these 48 cards feature a mix of signed cards of retired legends, superstar veterans and future stars. Each of these cards is serial numbered to 25. An exchange card with a redemption deadline of October 1st, 2003 was seeded into packs for the Ozzie Smith card. Due to market scarcity, no pricing is provided for these cards.

	Nm-Mt	Ex-Mt
1 Adam Dunn		
2 Alan Trammell		
3 Alfonso Soriano		
4 Andre Dawson		
5 Aramis Ramirez		
6 Austin Kearns		
7 Barry Zito		
8 Billy Williams		
9 Bob Feller		
10 Bud Smith		
11 Cal Ripken		
12 Chan Ho Park		
13 Don Mattingly		
14 Edgar Martinez		
15 Eric Chavez		
16 J.D. Drew		
17 Jason Lane		
18 Javier Vazquez		
19 Jermaine Dye		
20 Joe Crede		
21 Joe Mays		
22 Johnny Estrada		
23 Josh Beckett		
24 Kirby Puckett		
25 Luis Gonzalez		
26 Mark Ellis		
27 Mark Mulder		
28 Marlon Byrd		
29 Miguel Tejada		
30 Mike Schmidt		
31 Orel Hershiser		
32 Ozzie Smith		
33 Paul LoDuca		
34 Phil Rizzuto		
35 Rich Aurilia		
36 Robert Fick		
37 Roger Clemens		
38 Ron Santo		
39 Roy Oswalt		
40 Ryne Sandberg		
41 Sean Casey		
42 Steve Garvey		
43 Terrence Long		
44 Tim Redding		
45 Todd Helton		
46 Vladimir Guerrero		
47 Wilson Betemit		
48 Xavier Nady		

2002 Leaf Clubhouse Signatures Silver

Randomly inserted in packs, these 37 cards feature a mix of signed cards of retired legends, superstar veterans and future stars. Each of these cards is serial numbered and we have listed the print run in our checklist. Cards with a stated print run of 25 or fewer are not priced due to market scarcity.

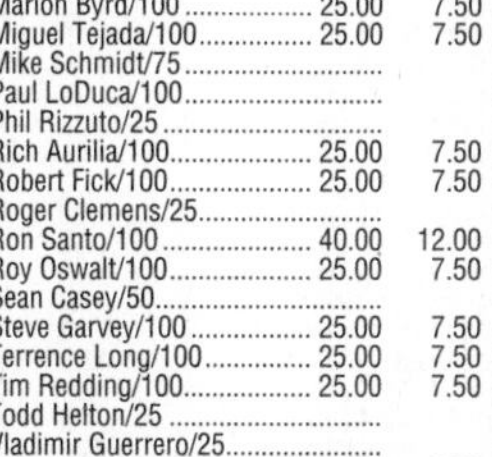

	Nm-Mt	Ex-Mt
1 Adam Dunn/75	40.00	12.00
2 Andre Dawson/100		
3 Aramis Ramirez/100	25.00	7.50
4 Austin Kearns/100	25.00	7.50
5 Barry Zito/100	40.00	12.00
6 Billy Williams/100	25.00	7.50
7 Bob Feller/100	40.00	12.00
8 Bud Smith/100	25.00	7.50
9 Cal Ripken/25		
10 Edgar Martinez/100	40.00	12.00
11 Eric Chavez/100	25.00	7.50
12 Jason Lane/100	25.00	7.50
13 Jermaine Dye/100	25.00	7.50
14 Joe Crede/50	25.00	7.50
15 Joe Mays/50	25.00	7.50
16 Johnny Estrada/100	25.00	7.50
17 Javier Vazquez/100	25.00	7.50
18 Mark Ellis/100	25.00	7.50
19 Mark Mulder/100	40.00	12.00
20 Marlon Byrd/100	25.00	7.50
21 Miguel Tejada/100	25.00	7.50
22 Mike Schmidt/75		
23 Paul LoDuca/100		
24 Phil Rizzuto/25		
25 Rich Aurilia/100	25.00	7.50
26 Robert Fick/100	25.00	7.50
27 Roger Clemens/25		
28 Ron Santo/100	40.00	12.00
29 Roy Oswalt/100	25.00	7.50
30 Sean Casey/50		
31 Steve Garvey/100	25.00	7.50
32 Terrence Long/100	25.00	7.50
33 Tim Redding/100	25.00	7.50
34 Todd Helton/25		
35 Vladimir Guerrero/25		
36 Wilson Betemit/100	25.00	7.50
37 Xavier Nady/100	25.00	7.50

2002 Leaf Cornerstones

Randomly inserted in packs, these 10 cards feature some of the elite perfomers with dual-player game-worn jersey swatches. These cards are serial numbered to 50. Due to market scarcity, no pricing is provided for these cards.

	Nm-Mt	Ex-Mt
1 Andruw Jones		
Chipper Jones		
2 Craig Biggio		
Jeff Bagwell		
3 Ivan Rodriguez		
Rafael Palmeiro		
4 Curt Schilling		
Randy Johnson		
5 Gary Sheffield		
Shawn Green		
6 Larry Walker		
Todd Helton		
7 Carlos Delgado		
Shannon Stewart		
8 Omar Vizquel		
Jim Thome		
9 Vladimir Guerrero		
Jose Vidro		
10 Bernie Williams		
Roger Clemens		

2002 Leaf Future 500 Club

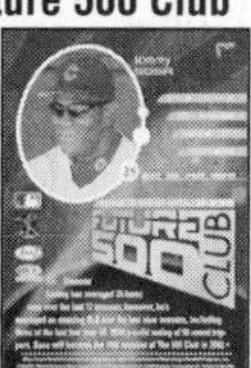

Inserted at stated odds of one in 64 hobby and one in 103 retail, these 10 cards honor players who appear to have good chances of reaching the 500 career homer mark. These cards have holo-foil stamping as well as the year that the player is projected to arrive at the 500 homer club.

	Nm-Mt	Ex-Mt
COMPLETE SET (10)	80.00	24.00
1 Sammy Sosa	10.00	3.00
2 Mike Piazza	10.00	3.00
3 Alex Rodriguez	10.00	3.00
4 Chipper Jones	6.00	1.80
5 Jeff Bagwell	5.00	1.50
6 Carlos Delgado	5.00	1.50
7 Shawn Green	5.00	1.50
8 Ken Griffey Jr.	10.00	3.00
9 Rafael Palmeiro	5.00	1.50
10 Vladimir Guerrero	6.00	1.80

2002 Leaf Game Collection

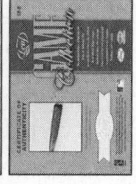

Inserted into retail packs at stated odds of one in 62, these 46 cards feature game-used memorabilia from the featured player. Some cards were printed in shorter quantities and we have provided those stated print runs in our checklist. For cards with a stated print run of 25 or fewer, no pricing is provided due to market scarcity.

	Nm-Mt	Ex-Mt
AB-B Adrian Beltre Bat	10.00	3.00
AD-BG Adam Dunn Btg Glv SP/25		
AG-B Andres Galarraga Bat	10.00	3.00
AJ-B Andruw Jones Bat SP/300	15.00	4.50
BG-B Brian Giles Bat	10.00	3.00
BH-B Bobby Higginson Bat	10.00	3.00
BS-H Ben Sheets Hat SP/25		
BW-S Bernie Williams Shoes SP/25		
BZ-FG Barry Zito Fld Glv SP/25		
CB-B Carlos Beltran Bat	10.00	3.00
CB-IB Craig Biggio Bat	15.00	4.50
CF-B Carlton Fisk Bat	15.00	4.50
CK-B Chuck Knoblauch Bat	10.00	3.00
CP-S Corey Patterson Shoes SP/25		
EM-B Eddie Murray Bat SP/250	25.00	7.50
GJ-P Geoff Jenkins Pants	10.00	3.00
IR-BG Ivan Rodriguez Btg Glv SP/25		
JB-B Jeff Bagwell Bat SP/100		
JD-H Johnny Damon Hat SP/25		
JE-B Juan Encarnacion Bat	10.00	3.00
JG-B Juan Gonzalez Bat	15.00	4.50
KL-B Kenny Lofton Bat	10.00	3.00
KW-S Kerry Wood Shoes SP/25		
LB-BG Lance Berkman Btg Glv SP/25		
LW-B Larry Walker Bat SP/50		
MB-BG Marlon Byrd Btg Glv SP/25		
MG-B Mark Grace Bat SP/200	25.00	7.50
MM-FG Mike Mussina Fld Glv SP/25		
MO-B Magglio Ordonez Bat SP/150	15.00	4.50
MP-B Mike Piazza Bat SP/100		
PB-B Pat Burrell Bat SP/100		
RA-B Roberto Alomar Bat	15.00	4.50
RD-B Ray Durham Bat	10.00	3.00
RG-B Rusty Greer Bat	10.00	3.00
RJ-FG Randy Johnson Fld Glv SP/25		
RP-B Rafael Palmeiro Bat	15.00	4.50
RP-BG Rafael Palmeiro Btg Glv SP/25		
RV-B Robin Ventura Bat	10.00	3.00
SC-B Sean Casey Bat	10.00	3.00
SR-B Scott Rolen Bat SP/250	25.00	7.50
SS-H Shannon Stewart Hat SP/25		
TC-B Tony Clark Bat	10.00	3.00
TG-BG Tony Gwynn Btg Glv SP/25		
TH-B Todd Helton Bat	15.00	4.50
TN-B Trot Nixon Bat	15.00	4.50
WB-B Wade Boggs Bat	15.00	4.50

2002 Leaf Gold Rookies

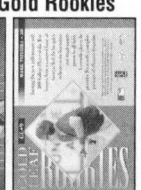

Inserted at stated rate of one in 24 hobby or retail packs, these 10 cards feature the leading prospects entering the 2002 season. These cards are spotlighted on mirror board with gold foil.

	Nm-Mt	Ex-Mt
COMPLETE SET (10)	50.00	15.00
1 Josh Beckett	4.00	1.20
2 Marlon Byrd	4.00	1.20
3 Dennis Tankersley	4.00	1.20
4 Jason Lane	4.00	1.20
5 Dewon Brazelton	4.00	1.20
6 Mark Prior	12.00	3.60
7 Bill Hall	4.00	1.20
8 Angel Berroa	4.00	1.20
9 Mark Teixeira	6.00	1.80
10 John Buck	4.00	1.20

2002 Leaf Heading for the Hall

Inserted at stated odds of one in 64 hobby and one in 240 retail, these 10 cards feature active or retired players who are virtually insured enshirement in the Baseball Hall of Fame.

	Nm-Mt	Ex-Mt
COMPLETE SET (10)	80.00	24.00
1 Greg Maddux	10.00	3.00
2 Ozzie Smith	10.00	3.00
3 Andre Dawson	5.00	1.50
4 Dennis Eckersley	5.00	1.50
5 Roberto Alomar	6.00	1.80
6 Cal Ripken	20.00	6.00
7 Roger Clemens	12.00	3.60
8 Tony Gwynn	8.00	2.40
9 Alex Rodriguez	10.00	3.00
10 Jeff Bagwell	5.00	1.50

2002 Leaf Heading for the Hall Autographs

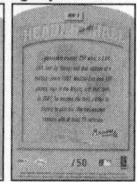

Randomly inserted in hobby packs, these cards parallel the Leaf Heading to the Hall insert set. Each player signed 50 cards for this product. These cards can also be differentiated from the regular cards as these cards are also die cut. No pricing is provided due to market scarcity.

	Nm-Mt	Ex-Mt
1 Greg Maddux		
2 Ozzie Smith		
3 Andre Dawson		
4 Dennis Eckersley		
5 Roberto Alomar		
6 Cal Ripken		
7 Roger Clemens		
8 Tony Gwynn		
9 Alex Rodriguez		
10 Jeff Bagwell		

2002 Leaf League of Nations

Inserted at stated odds of one in 60, these 10 cards feature players from foreign countries. These cards are highlighted with holo-foil and color tint relating to their homeland colors.

	Nm-Mt	Ex-Mt
1 Ichiro Suzuki	10.00	3.00
2 Tsuyoshi Shinjo	5.00	1.50
3 Chan Ho Park	5.00	1.50
4 Larry Walker	5.00	1.50
5 Andruw Jones	5.00	1.50
6 Hideo Nomo	12.00	3.60
7 Byung-Hyun Kim	5.00	1.50
8 Sun-Woo Kim	5.00	1.50
9 Orlando Hernandez	5.00	1.50
10 Luke Prokopec	5.00	1.50

2002 Leaf Retired Number Jerseys

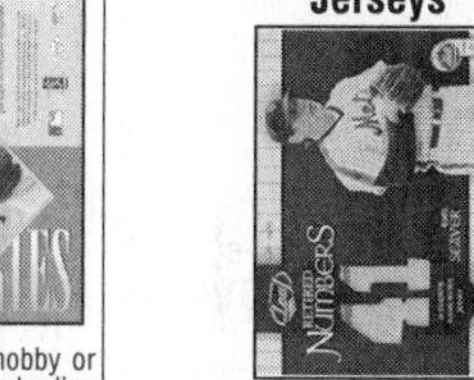

Randomly inserted in packs, these five cards feature jersey swatches from players who have had their uniform numbers retired. This insert set is sequentially numbered to the player's jersey number. We have listed each print run in our checklist below. Please note that these cards are not priced due to market scarcity.

	Nm-Mt	Ex-Mt
RN1 Mike Schmidt/20		
RN2 Tom Seaver/41		
RN3 Rod Carew/29		
RN4 Ted Williams/9		
RN5 Johnny Bench/5		

2002 Leaf Rookie Reprints

Randomly inserted in packs, these six cards feature reprints sequentially numbered to the card's original year of issue. We have listed those print runs in our checklist.

	Nm-Mt	Ex-Mt
1 Roger Clemens/1985	15.00	4.50
2 Kirby Puckett/1985	8.00	2.40
3 Andres Galarraga/1986	5.00	1.50
4 Fred McGriff/1986	5.00	1.50
5 Sammy Sosa/1990	12.00	3.60
6 Frank Thomas/1990	8.00	2.40

2002 Leaf Shirt Off My Back

Inserted at stated odds of one in 29 hobby packs, these 60 cards feature a game-worn jersey swatch from either an active or retired star. Some cards were printed in shorter quantity than others, we have noted those cards with their stated print runs in our checklist. Cards with a stated print run of 50 or fewer are not priced due to market scarcity.

	Nm-Mt	Ex-Mt
*MULTI-COLOR PATCH 1.25X TO 3X HI		
AB A.J. Burnett	10.00	3.00
AK Al Kaline SP/100	40.00	12.00
AP Andy Pettitte SP/50	50.00	15.00
AR Alex Rodriguez SP/150	40.00	12.00
BJA Bo Jackson SP/25		
BL Barry Larkin	15.00	4.50
BR Brad Radke	10.00	3.00
CB Carlos Beltran	10.00	3.00
CD Carlos Delgado	10.00	3.00
CF Cliff Floyd	10.00	3.00
CHP Chan Ho Park SP/100	25.00	7.50
CJ Chipper Jones SP/100	40.00	12.00
CL Carlos Lee	10.00	3.00
CR Cal Ripken SP/50	150.00	45.00
CS Curt Schilling SP/150	40.00	12.00
DE Darin Erstad SP/100	25.00	7.50
DM Don Mattingly SP/100	60.00	18.00
DW Dave Winfield SP/150	25.00	7.50
EK Eric Karros	10.00	3.00
EM Edgar Martinez SP/150	40.00	12.00
FG Freddy Garcia SP/100	25.00	7.50
GB George Brett SP/100	60.00	18.00
GM Greg Maddux SP/100	40.00	12.00
HN Hideo Nomo SP/100	40.00	12.00
JB Jeff Bagwell SP/100	40.00	12.00
JBU Jeromy Burnitz	10.00	3.00
JL Javy Lopez	10.00	3.00
JO John Olerud	10.00	3.00
JS John Smoltz	15.00	4.50
KB Kevin Brown SP/100	25.00	7.50
KM Kevin Millwood	10.00	3.00
KP Kirby Puckett SP/100	40.00	12.00
KS Kazuhiro Sasaki SP/100	25.00	7.50
LB Lance Berkman SP/300	25.00	7.50
LG Luis Gonzalez	10.00	3.00
LW Larry Walker SP/50	50.00	15.00
MB Michael Barrett	10.00	3.00
MBU Mark Buehrle	10.00	3.00
MH Mike Hampton	10.00	3.00
MO Magglio Ordonez	10.00	3.00
MP Mike Piazza SP/150	40.00	12.00
MR Manny Ramirez SP/100	25.00	7.50
MS Mike Sweeney	10.00	3.00
MT Miguel Tejada	10.00	3.00
MW Matt Williams	10.00	3.00
NG Nomar Garciaparra SP/25		
PM Pedro Martinez SP/100	40.00	12.00
RA Roberto Alomar SP/250	15.00	4.50
RD Ryan Dempster	10.00	3.00
RJ Randy Johnson SP/100	40.00	12.00
RP Rafael Palmeiro	15.00	4.50
RS Richie Sexson	10.00	3.00
SR Scott Rolen SP/250	40.00	12.00
TG Tony Gwynn SP/100	40.00	12.00
TG Tom Glavine	15.00	4.50
TGL Troy Glaus SP/275	40.00	12.00
TH Todd Helton	15.00	4.50
TH Tim Hudson	10.00	3.00
TP Troy Percival	10.00	3.00
TS Tsuyoshi Shinjo SP/100	25.00	7.50

2002 Leaf Hawaii So Taguchi Promo

This card was handed out at the 2002 Hawaii Trade Conference in an effort to preview the then-upcoming Leaf brand. The card is identical in design to the standard Taguchi RC distributed in Leaf packs barring the silver foil Hawaii Trade Conference logo on front and foil-stamped serial-numbering on back. Only fifty copies were produced and according to representatives at Playoff, approximately 25-35 copies were distributed at the show.

	Nm-Mt	Ex-Mt
201 So Taguchi	100.00	30.00

2003 Leaf Samples

Issued one per Beckett Baseball Card Magazine, these cards previewed the 2003 Leaf set. These cards have the word "sample" printed in silver on the back.

	Nm-Mt	Ex-Mt
*SAMPLES: 1.5X TO 4X BASIC CARDS		

2003 Leaf

This 329-card set was issued in two separate releases. The primary Leaf product - containing cards 1-320 from the basic set - was released in February, 2003. This product was issued in 10-card packs with an SRP of $3 per pack. These packs were issued in 24 pack boxes which came 20 boxes to a case. This set includes the following subsets: Passing the Torch (251 to 270) and a Rookies subset (271-320). Jose Contreras, the cuban refugee signed to a large free-agent contract, had his very first card in this set. Cards 321-329 were issued within packs of DLP Rookies and Traded in December, 2003. There is no card number 42 as both Bobby Higginson and Carlos Pena share card number 41.

	Nm-Mt	Ex-Mt
COMP.LO SET (320)	40.00	12.00
COMP.UPDATE SET (9)	8.00	2.40
COMMON CARD (1-270)	.30	.09
COMMON CARD (271-320)	.50	.15
COMMON CARD (321-329)	.50	.15
1 Brad Fullmer	.30	.09
2 Darin Erstad	.30	.09
3 David Eckstein	.30	.09
4 Garret Anderson	.30	.09
5 Jarrod Washburn	.30	.09
6 Kevin Appier	.30	.09
7 Tim Salmon	.50	.15
8 Troy Glaus	.50	.15
9 Troy Percival	.30	.09
10 Buddy Groom	.30	.09
11 Jay Gibbons	.30	.09
12 Jeff Conine	.30	.09
13 Marty Cordova	.30	.09
14 Melvin Mora	.30	.09
15 Rodrigo Lopez	.30	.09
16 Tony Batista	.30	.09
17 Jorge Julio	.30	.09
18 Cliff Floyd	.30	.09
19 Derek Lowe	.30	.09
20 Jason Varitek	.30	.09
21 Johnny Damon	.30	.09
22 Manny Ramirez	.30	.09
23 Nomar Garciaparra	1.25	.35
24 Pedro Martinez	.75	.23
25 Rickey Henderson	.75	.23
26 Shea Hillenbrand	.30	.09
27 Trot Nixon	.50	.15
28 Carlos Lee	.30	.09
29 Frank Thomas	.75	.23
30 Jose Valentin	.30	.09
31 Magglio Ordonez	.30	.09
32 Mark Buehrle	.30	.09
33 Paul Konerko	.30	.09
34 C.C. Sabathia	.30	.09
35 Danys Baez	.30	.09
36 Ellis Burks	.30	.09
37 Jim Thome	.75	.23
38 Omar Vizquel	.30	.09
39 Ricky Gutierrez	.30	.09
40 Travis Fryman	.30	.09
41A Bobby Higginson	.30	.09
41B Carlos Pena	.30	.09
43 Juan Acevedo	.30	.09
44 Mark Redman	.30	.09
45 Randall Simon	.30	.09
46 Robert Fick	.30	.09
47 Steve Sparks	.30	.09
48 Carlos Beltran	.30	.09
49 Joe Randa	.30	.09
50 Michael Tucker	.30	.09
51 Mike Sweeney	.30	.09
52 Paul Byrd	.30	.09
53 Raul Ibanez	.30	.09
54 Runelvys Hernandez	.30	.09
55 A.J. Pierzynski	.30	.09
56 Brad Radke	.30	.09
57 Corey Koskie	.30	.09
58 Cristian Guzman	.30	.09
59 David Ortiz	.30	.09
60 Doug Mientkiewicz	.30	.09
61 Dustan Mohr	.30	.09
62 Eddie Guardado	.30	.09
63 Jacque Jones	.30	.09
64 Torii Hunter	.30	.09
65 Alfonso Soriano	.50	.15
66 Andy Pettitte	.50	.15
67 Bernie Williams	.50	.15
68 David Wells	.30	.09
69 Derek Jeter	2.00	.60
70 Jason Giambi	.75	.23
71 Jeff Weaver	.30	.09
72 Jorge Posada	.50	.15
73 Mike Mussina	.75	.23
74 Nick Johnson	.30	.09
75 Raul Mondesi	.30	.09
76 Robin Ventura	.30	.09
77 Roger Clemens	1.50	.45
78 Barry Zito	.50	.15
79 Billy Koch	.30	.09
80 David Justice	.30	.09
81 Eric Chavez	.30	.09
82 Jermaine Dye	.30	.09
83 Mark Mulder	.30	.09
84 Miguel Tejada	.30	.09
85 Ray Durham	.30	.09
86 Scott Hatteberg	.30	.09
87 Ted Lilly	.30	.09
88 Tim Hudson	.30	.09
89 Bret Boone	.30	.09
90 Carlos Guillen	.30	.09
91 Chris Snelling	.30	.09
92 Dan Wilson	.30	.09
93 Edgar Martinez	.50	.15
94 Freddy Garcia	.30	.09
95 Ichiro Suzuki	1.25	.35
96 Jamie Moyer	.30	.09
97 Joel Pineiro	.30	.09
98 John Olerud	.30	.09
99 Mark McLemore	.30	.09
100 Mike Cameron	.30	.09
101 Kazuhiro Sasaki	.30	.09
102 Aubrey Huff	.30	.09
103 Ben Grieve	.30	.09
104 Joe Kennedy	.30	.09
105 Paul Wilson	.30	.09
106 Randy Winn	.30	.09
107 Steve Cox	.30	.09
108 Alex Rodriguez	1.25	.35
109 Chan Ho Park	.30	.09
110 Hank Blalock	.50	.15
111 Herbert Perry	.30	.09
112 Ivan Rodriguez	.75	.23
113 Juan Gonzalez	.75	.23
114 Kenny Rogers	.30	.09
115 Kevin Mench	.30	.09
116 Rafael Palmeiro	.50	.15
117 Carlos Delgado	.30	.09
118 Eric Hinske	.30	.09
119 Jose Cruz	.30	.09
120 Josh Phelps	.30	.09
121 Roy Halladay	.30	.09
122 Shannon Stewart	.30	.09
123 Vernon Wells	.30	.09
124 Curt Schilling	.50	.15
125 Junior Spivey	.30	.09
126 Luis Gonzalez	.30	.09
127 Mark Grace	.50	.15
128 Randy Johnson	.75	.23
129 Steve Finley	.30	.09
130 Tony Womack	.30	.09
131 Andruw Jones	.30	.09
132 Chipper Jones	.75	.23
133 Gary Sheffield	.30	.09
134 Greg Maddux	1.25	.35
135 John Smoltz	.50	.15
136 Kevin Millwood	.30	.09
137 Rafael Furcal	.30	.09
138 Tom Glavine	.50	.15
139 Alex Gonzalez	.30	.09
140 Corey Patterson	.30	.09
141 Fred McGriff	.50	.15
142 Jon Lieber	.30	.09
143 Kerry Wood	.75	.23
144 Mark Prior	1.50	.45
145 Matt Clement	.30	.09
146 Moises Alou	.30	.09
147 Sammy Sosa	1.25	.35
148 Aaron Boone	.30	.09
149 Adam Dunn	.30	.09
150 Austin Kearns	.30	.09
151 Barry Larkin	.75	.23
152 Danny Graves	.30	.09
153 Elmer Dessens	.30	.09
154 Ken Griffey Jr.	1.25	.35
155 Sean Casey	.30	.09
156 Todd Walker	.30	.09
157 Gabe Kapler	.30	.09
158 Jason Jennings	.30	.09
159 Jay Payton	.30	.09
160 Larry Walker	.50	.15
161 Mike Hampton	.30	.09
162 Todd Helton	.50	.15
163 Todd Zeile	.30	.09
164 A.J. Burnett	.30	.09
165 Derrek Lee	.30	.09
166 Josh Beckett	.50	.15
167 Juan Encarnacion	.30	.09
168 Luis Castillo	.30	.09
169 Mike Lowell	.30	.09
170 Preston Wilson	.30	.09
171 Billy Wagner	.30	.09
172 Craig Biggio	.50	.15
173 Daryle Ward	.30	.09
174 Jeff Bagwell	.50	.15
175 Lance Berkman	.30	.09
176 Octavio Dotel	.30	.09
177 Richard Hidalgo	.30	.09
178 Roy Oswalt	.30	.09
179 Adrian Beltre	.30	.09
180 Eric Gagne	.50	.15
181 Eric Karros	.30	.09
182 Hideo Nomo	.75	.23
183 Kazuhisa Ishii	.30	.09
184 Kevin Brown	.30	.09
185 Mark Grudzielanek	.30	.09
186 Odalis Perez	.30	.09
187 Paul Lo Duca	.30	.09
188 Shawn Green	.30	.09
189 Alex Sanchez	.30	.09
190 Ben Sheets	.30	.09
191 Jeffrey Hammonds	.30	.09
192 Jose Hernandez	.30	.09
193 Takahito Nomura	.30	.09
194 Richie Sexson	.30	.09
195 Andres Galarraga	.30	.09
196 Bartolo Colon	.30	.09
197 Brad Wilkerson	.30	.09
198 Javier Vazquez	.30	.09
199 Jose Vidro	.30	.09
200 Michael Barrett	.30	.09
201 Tomo Ohka	.30	.09
202 Vladimir Guerrero	.75	.23
203 Al Leiter	.30	.09
204 Armando Benitez	.30	.09
205 Edgardo Alfonzo	.30	.09
206 Mike Piazza	1.25	.35
207 Mo Vaughn	.30	.09
208 Pedro Astacio	.30	.09
209 Roberto Alomar	.75	.23
210 Roger Cedeno	.30	.09
211 Timo Perez	.30	.09
212 Bobby Abreu	.30	.09
213 Jimmy Rollins	.30	.09
214 Mike Lieberthal	.30	.09
215 Pat Burrell	.30	.09
216 Randy Wolf	.30	.09
217 Travis Lee	.30	.09
218 Vicente Padilla	.30	.09
219 Aramis Ramirez	.30	.09
220 Brian Giles	.30	.09
221 Craig Wilson	.30	.09
222 Jason Kendall	.30	.09
223 Josh Fogg	.30	.09
224 Kevin Young	.30	.09
225 Kip Wells	.30	.09
226 Mike Williams	.30	.09
227 Brett Tomko	.30	.09
228 Brian Lawrence	.30	.09
229 Mark Kotsay	.30	.09
230 Oliver Perez	.30	.09
231 Phil Nevin	.30	.09
232 Ryan Klesko	.30	.09
233 Sean Burroughs	.30	.09
234 Trevor Hoffman	.30	.09
235 Barry Bonds	2.00	.60
236 Benito Santiago	.30	.09
237 Jeff Kent	.30	.09
238 Kirk Rueter	.30	.09
239 Livan Hernandez	.30	.09
240 Kenny Lofton	.30	.09
241 Rich Aurilia	.30	.09
242 Russ Ortiz	.30	.09
243 Albert Pujols	1.50	.45
244 Edgar Renteria	.30	.09
245 J.D. Drew	.30	.09
246 Jason Isringhausen	.30	.09
247 Jim Edmonds	.30	.09
248 Matt Morris	.30	.09
249 Tino Martinez	.50	.15
250 Scott Rolen	.50	.15
251 Curt Schilling PT	.30	.09
252 Ivan Rodriguez PT	.50	.15
253 Mike Piazza PT	.75	.23
254 Sammy Sosa PT	.75	.23
255 Matt Williams PT	.30	.09
256 Frank Thomas PT	.50	.15
257 Barry Bonds PT	1.00	.30
258 Roger Clemens PT	.75	.23
259 Rickey Henderson PT	.75	.23
260 Ken Griffey Jr. PT	.75	.23
261 Greg Maddux PT	.75	.23
262 Randy Johnson PT	.50	.15
263 Jeff Bagwell PT	.30	.09
264 Roberto Alomar PT	.50	.15
265 Tom Glavine PT	.30	.09
266 Juan Gonzalez PT	.50	.15
267 Mark Grace PT	.30	.09
268 Mike Mussina PT	.50	.15
269 Ryan Klesko PT	.30	.09
270 Fred McGriff PT	.30	.09
271 Joe Borchard ROO	.40	.12
272 Chris Snelling ROO	.40	.12
273 Brian Tallet ROO	.50	.15
274 Cliff Lee ROO	.40	.12
275 Freddy Sanchez ROO	.50	.15
276 Chone Figgins ROO	.50	.15
277 Kevin Cash ROO	.50	.15
278 Josh Bard ROO	.50	.15
279 Jeriome Robertson ROO	.50	.15
280 Jeremy Hill ROO	.50	.15
281 Shane Nance ROO	.50	.15
282 Jeff Baker ROO	.50	.15
283 Trey Hodges ROO	.50	.15
284 Eric Eckenstahler ROO	.50	.15
285 Jim Rushford ROO	.50	.15
286 Carlos Rivera ROO	.50	.15
287 Josh Bonifay ROO	.40	.12
288 Garrett Atkins ROO	.40	.12
289 Nic Jackson ROO	.50	.15
290 Corwin Malone ROO	.50	.15
291 Jimmy Gobble ROO	.40	.12
292 Josh Wilson ROO	.50	.15
293 Clint Barmes ROO RC	.60	.18
294 Jon Adkins ROO	.50	.15
295 Tim Kalita ROO	.50	.15
296 Nelson Castro ROO	.50	.15
297 Colin Young ROO	.50	.15
298 Adrian Burnside ROO	.50	.15
299 Luis Martinez ROO	.50	.15
300 Terrmel Sledge ROO RC	.60	.18
301 Todd Donovan ROO	.50	.15
302 Jeremy Ward ROO	.50	.15
303 Wilson Valdez ROO	.50	.15
304 Jose Contreras ROO RC	1.00	.30
305 Marshall McDougall ROO	.50	.15
306 Mitch Wylie ROO	.50	.15
307 Ron Calloway ROO	.50	.15
308 Jose Valverde ROO	.50	.15
309 Jason Davis ROO	.40	.12
310 Scotty Layfield ROO	.50	.15
311 Matt Thornton ROO	.50	.15
312 Adam Walker ROO	.50	.15
313 Gustavo Chacin ROO	.50	.15
314 Ron Chiavacci ROO	.50	.15
315 Wilbert Nieves ROO	.50	.15
316 Cliff Bartosh ROO	.50	.15
317 Mike Gonzalez ROO	.50	.15
318 Jeremy Guthrie ROO	.50	.15
319 Eric Junge ROO	.50	.15
320 Ben Kozlowski ROO	.50	.15
321 Hideki Matsui ROO RC	2.00	.60
322 Ramon Nivar ROO RC	.50	.15
323 Adam Loewen ROO RC	1.25	.35
324 Brandon Webb ROO RC	1.25	.35
325 Chien-Ming Wang ROO RC	1.00	.30
326 Delmon Young ROO RC	3.00	.90
327 Ryan Wagner ROO RC	.75	.23
328 Dan Haren ROO RC	.60	.18
329 Rickie Weeks ROO RC	2.50	.75

2003 Leaf Autographs

This nine card set was issued in two separate series. Card 304 features Yankees rookie Jose Contreras and was distrbuted within standard 2003 Leaf packs. The remaining eight cards from this set were randomly seeded into packs of 2003 DLP Rookies and Traded. Print runs range from 10-100 copies per and all cards are serial numbered.

	Nm-Mt	Ex-Mt
304 Jose Contreras ROO/100	40.00	12.00
322 Ramon Nivar ROO/100	20.00	6.00
323 Adam Loewen ROO/100	40.00	12.00
324 Brandon Webb ROO/100	40.00	12.00
325 Chien-Ming Wang ROO/50	60.00	18.00
326 Delmon Young ROO/25		
327 Ryan Wagner ROO/100	25.00	7.50
328 Dan Haren ROO/100	20.00	6.00
329 Rickie Weeks ROO/10		

2003 Leaf Chicago Collection

This set, which parallels the 2003 Leaf set was issued at the March, 2003 Chicago Sun Times show as part of a show special. Any collector who opened three packs of a Playoff/Donruss product at the Donruss booth received one of these cards as a redemption for the wrappers. These cards were issued to a stated print run of five serial numbered sets and no pricing is available due to market scarcity.

	Nm-Mt	Ex-Mt
DISTRIBUTED AT CHICAGO SPORTSFEST		
STATED PRINT RUN 5 SERIAL #'d SETS		
NO PRICING DUE TO SCARCITY		

2003 Leaf Press Proofs Blue

Randomly inserted into packs, this is a parallel to the Leaf Set. Cards 321-329 were randomly seeded into packs of DLP Rookies and Traded. These cards feature a blue foil logo and were issued to a stated print run of 50 serial numbered sets.

	Nm-Mt	Ex-Mt
*BLUE 1-250: &&6X TO &&15X BASIC		
*BLUE 251-270: &&10X TO &&25X BASIC		
*BLUE 271-320: &&4X TO &&10X BASIC		
*BLUE 271-320: 4X TO 10X BASIC RC's		
*BLUE 321-329: 6X TO 15X BASIC		

2003 Leaf Press Proofs Red

Inserted in packs at a stated rate of one in 12, this is a complete parallel to the Leaf Set. Cards 321-329 were randomly seeded into packs of DLP Rookies and Traded - and unlike the first 320 cards - are serial numbered to 100 copies per. These cards feature the words Press Proof printed in red foil on each card front.

	Nm-Mt	Ex-Mt
*RED 1-250: 2.5X TO 6X BASIC		
*RED 251-270: 4X TO 10X BASIC		
*RED 271-320: 2.5X TO 6X BASIC		
*RED 271-320: 2X TO 5X BASIC RC's		
*RED 321-329: 4X TO 10X BASIC RC's		

2003 Leaf 60

This 50 card insert set was issued at a stated rate of one in eight packs. These cards were designed in the style of the 1960 Leaf set and feature black and white photos.

	Nm-Mt	Ex-Mt
*FOIL: 2X TO 5X BASIC CARDS		
FOIL RANDOM INSERTS IN PACKS		
FOIL PRINT RUN 60 SERIAL #'d SETS		
1 Troy Glaus	3.00	.90
2 Curt Schilling	3.00	.90
3 Randy Johnson	4.00	1.20
4 Andruw Jones	3.00	.90
5 Chipper Jones	4.00	1.20
6 Greg Maddux	6.00	1.80
7 Tom Glavine	3.00	.90
8 Manny Ramirez	3.00	.90
9 Nomar Garciaparra	6.00	1.80
10 Pedro Martinez	4.00	1.20
11 Rickey Henderson	4.00	1.20
12 Sammy Sosa	6.00	1.80
13 Frank Thomas	4.00	1.20
14 Magglio Ordonez	3.00	.90
15 Mark Buehrle	3.00	.90
16 Adam Dunn	3.00	.90
17 Ken Griffey Jr.	6.00	1.80
18 Jim Thome	4.00	1.20
19 Omar Vizquel	3.00	.90
20 Larry Walker	3.00	.90
21 Todd Helton	3.00	.90
22 Lance Berkman	3.00	.90
23 Roy Oswalt	3.00	.90
24 Mike Sweeney	3.00	.90
25 Hideo Nomo	4.00	1.20
26 Kazuhisa Ishii	3.00	.90
27 Shawn Green	3.00	.90
28 Torii Hunter	3.00	.90
29 Vladimir Guerrero	4.00	1.20
30 Mike Piazza	6.00	1.80
31 Alfonso Soriano	3.00	.90
32 Bernie Williams	3.00	.90
33 Derek Jeter	10.00	3.00
34 Jason Giambi	4.00	1.20
35 Roger Clemens	8.00	2.40
36 Barry Zito	3.00	.90
37 Miguel Tejada	3.00	.90
38 Pat Burrell	3.00	.90
39 Ryan Klesko	3.00	.90
40 Barry Bonds	10.00	3.00
41 Jeff Kent	3.00	.90
42 Ichiro Suzuki	6.00	1.80
43 John Olerud	3.00	.90
44 Albert Pujols	8.00	2.40
45 Jim Edmonds	3.00	.90
46 Scott Rolen	3.00	.90
47 Alex Rodriguez	6.00	1.80
48 Ivan Rodriguez	4.00	1.20
49 Rafael Palmeiro	3.00	.90
50 Roy Halladay	3.00	.90

2003 Leaf Certified Samples

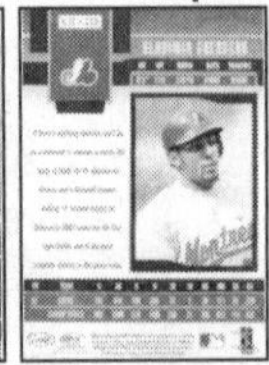

Inserted in packs at a stated rate of one in 23, this 15-card insert set previews the upcoming Leaf Certified set. These cards were printed on metalized film board.

	Nm-Mt	Ex-Mt
*MIRROR RED: 1.5X TO 4X BASIC		
MIRROR RED PRINT RUN 150 #'d SETS		
*MIRROR BLUE: 1X TO 2.5X BASIC		

MIRROR BLUE PRINT RUN 75 #'d SETS
MIRROR GOLD PRINT RUN 25 #'d SETS
MIRROR GOLD TOO SCARCE TO PRICE
MIRROR CARDS RANDOM INSERTS IN PACKS
1 Derek Jeter 10.00 3.00
2 Greg Maddux 6.00 1.80
3 Mike Piazza 6.00 1.80
4 Barry Bonds 10.00 3.00
5 Lance Berkman 3.00 .90
6 Alex Rodriguez 6.00 1.80
7 Alfonso Soriano 3.00 .90
8 Ichiro Suzuki 6.00 1.80
9 Sammy Sosa 6.00 1.80
10 Vladimir Guerrero 4.00 1.20
11 Albert Pujols 8.00 2.40
12 Pedro Martinez 4.00 1.20
13 Randy Johnson 4.00 1.20
14 Nomar Garciaparra 6.00 1.80
15 Barry Zito 3.00 .90

2003 Leaf Clean Up Crew

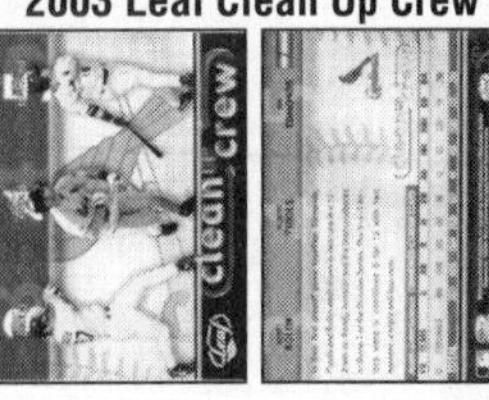

Inserted in packs at a stated rate of one in 49, these ten cards feature the middle of the lineup for ten different major league teams.

Nm-Mt Ex-Mt
1 Alex Rodriguez 6.00 1.80
Rafael Palmeiro
Ivan Rodriguez
2 Nomar Garciaparra 6.00 1.80
Manny Ramirez
Cliff Floyd
3 Jason Giambi 4.00 1.20
Bernie Williams
Jorge Posada
4 Rich Aurilla 10.00 3.00
Jeff Kent
Barry Bonds
5 Larry Walker 4.00 1.20
Todd Helton
Jay Payton
6 Lance Berkman 4.00 1.20
Jeff Bagwell
Darryl Ward
7 Scott Rolen 8.00 2.40
Albert Pujols
Jim Edmonds
8 Gary Sheffield 4.00 1.20
Chipper Jones
Andruw Jones
9 Miguel Tejada 4.00 1.20
Eric Chavez
Jermaine Dye
10 Sammy Sosa 6.00 1.80
Moises Alou
Fred McGriff

2003 Leaf Clean Up Crew Materials

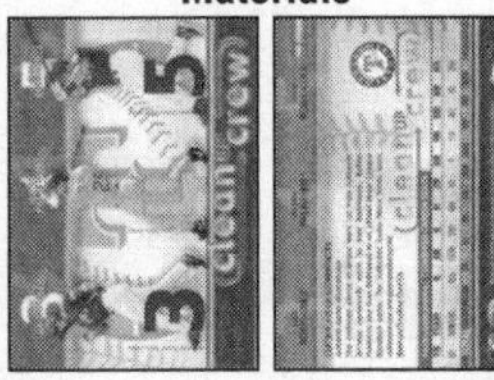

Randomly inserted into packs, this is a parallel to the Clean Up Crew set. These cards feature a memorabilia piece from each of the three players featured and these cards were issued to a stated print run of 25 serial numbered sets.

Nm-Mt Ex-Mt
1 Alex Rodriguez Jsy 40.00 12.00
Rafael Palmeiro Jsy
Ivan Rodriguez Jsy
2 Nomar Garciaparra Jsy 40.00 12.00
Manny Ramirez Jsy
Cliff Floyd Bat
3 Jason Giambi Ball 40.00 12.00
Bernie Williams Ball
Jorge Posada Ball
4 Rich Aurilla Ball 60.00 18.00
Jeff Kent Ball
Barry Bonds Ball
5 Larry Walker Jsy 40.00 12.00
Todd Helton Jsy
Jay Payton Jsy
6 Lance Berkman Jsy 40.00 12.00
Jeff Bagwell Jsy
Daryle Ward Bat
7 Scott Rolen Bat 60.00 18.00
Albert Pujols Ball
Jim Edmonds Base
8 Gary Sheffield Bat 40.00 12.00
Chipper Jones Jsy
Andruw Jones Jsy
9 Miguel Tejada Jsy 25.00 7.50
Eric Chavez Jsy
Jermaine Dye Bat
10 Sammy Sosa Ball 40.00 12.00
Moises Alou Ball
Fred McGriff Ball

2003 Leaf Clubhouse Signatures Bronze

Randomly inserted into packs, these 24 cards feature authentic signatures of the players. Some of these cards were issued to a smaller quantity and we have notated that information

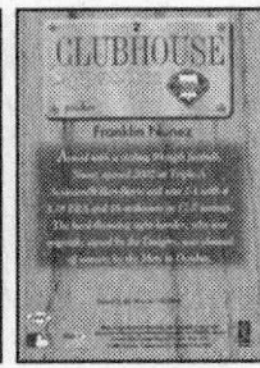

and the stated print run information next to the player's name in our checklist. Please note that for cards with a print run of 25 or fewer, no pricing is provided due to market scarcity..

Nm-Mt Ex-Mt
1 Edwin Almonte 10.00 3.00
2 Jeff Baker SP/100 10.00 3.00
3 Josh Bard 10.00 3.00
4 Angel Berroa SP/100 15.00 4.50
5 Joe Crede SP/25
6 Andre Dawson SP/50 40.00 12.00
7 Bobby Doerr SP/100 25.00 7.50
8 Adam Dunn SP/10
9 Doc Gooden SP/100 60.00 18.00
10 Drew Henson SP/50 50.00 15.00
11 Eric Hinske 10.00 3.00
12 Torii Hunter SP/75 40.00 12.00
13 Omar Infante 10.00 3.00
14 Brian Lawrence 10.00 3.00
15 Kevin Mench 10.00 3.00
16 Jack Morris SP/100 25.00 7.50
17 Franklin Nunez 10.00 3.00
18 Magglio Ordonez SP/50 40.00 12.00
19 Corey Patterson SP/100 15.00 4.50
20 Jhonny Peralta 15.00 4.50
21 J.C. Romero 10.00 3.00
22 Chris Snelling SP/100 15.00 4.50
23 Alfonso Soriano SP/25
24 Brian Tallet SP/100 10.00 3.00

2003 Leaf Clubhouse Signatures Gold

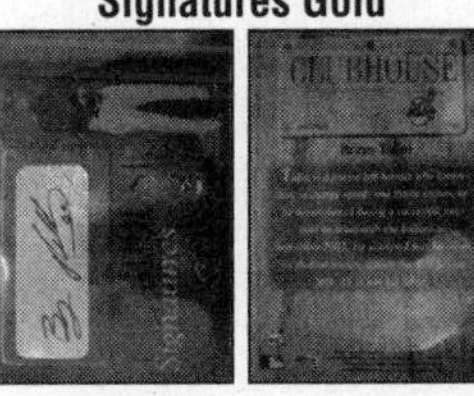

This is a parallel to the Leaf Clubhouse Signatures set. These cards were issued to a stated print run of 25 serial numbered sets and no pricing is provided due to market scarcity.

Nm-Mt Ex-Mt
1 Edwin Almonte
2 Jeff Baker
3 Josh Bard
4 Angel Berroa
5 Joe Crede
6 Andre Dawson
7 Bobby Doerr
8 Adam Dunn
9 Doc Gooden
10 Vladimir Guerrero
11 Drew Henson
12 Eric Hinske
13 Torii Hunter
14 Omar Infante
15 Brian Lawrence
16 Kevin Mench
17 Jack Morris
18 Franklin Nunez
19 Magglio Ordonez
20 Corey Patterson
21 Jhonny Peralta
22 J.C. Romero
23 Chris Snelling
24 Alfonso Soriano
25 Brian Tallet

2003 Leaf Clubhouse Signatures Silver

Randomly inserted into packs, this is a parallel to the Leaf Clubhouse Signatures set. These cards were issued to a stated print run of 100 serial numbered sets except for Andre Dawson who was issued to a stated print run of 25 serial numbered sets.

Nm-Mt Ex-Mt
1 Edwin Almonte 10.00 3.00
2 Jeff Baker 10.00 3.00
3 Josh Bard 10.00 3.00
4 Angel Berroa 15.00 4.50
5 Andre Dawson SP/25
6 Bobby Doerr 25.00 7.50
7 Doc Gooden 60.00 18.00
8 Drew Henson 25.00 7.50
9 Eric Hinske 10.00 3.00
10 Torii Hunter 50.00 15.00
11 Omar Infante 10.00 3.00
12 Brian Lawrence 10.00 3.00
13 Kevin Mench 10.00 3.00
14 Jack Morris 25.00 7.50
15 Franklin Nunez 10.00 3.00
16 Magglio Ordonez 25.00 7.50
17 Jhonny Peralta 15.00 4.50
18 J.C. Romero 10.00 3.00
19 Chris Snelling 15.00 4.50
20 Brian Tallet 10.00 3.00

2003 Leaf Game Collection

Randomly inserted into packs, this set displays one swatch of game-used materials. These cards were issued to a stated print run of 150 serial numbered sets.

Nm-Mt Ex-Mt
1 Miguel Tejada Hat 10.00 3.00
2 Shannon Stewart Hat 10.00 3.00
3 Mike Schmidt Jacket 50.00 15.00
4 Nolan Ryan Jacket 80.00 24.00
5 Rafael Palmeiro Fld Glv 25.00 7.50
6 Andruw Jones Shoe 10.00 3.00
7 Bernie Williams Shoe 15.00 4.50
8 Ivan Rodriguez Shoe 15.00 4.50
9 Lance Berkman Shoe 10.00 3.00
10 Magglio Ordonez Shoe 10.00 3.00
11 Roy Oswalt Fld Glv 15.00 4.50
12 Andy Pettitte Shoe 15.00 4.50
13 Vladimir Guerrero Fld Glv 40.00 12.00
14 Jason Jennings Fld Glv 15.00 4.50
15 Mike Sweeney Shoe 10.00 3.00
16 Joe Borchard Shoe 10.00 3.00
17 Mark Prior Shoe 25.00 7.50
18 Gary Carter Jacket 15.00 4.50
19 Austin Kearns Fld Glv 15.00 4.50
20 Ryan Klesko Fld Glv 15.00 4.50

2003 Leaf Gold Rookies

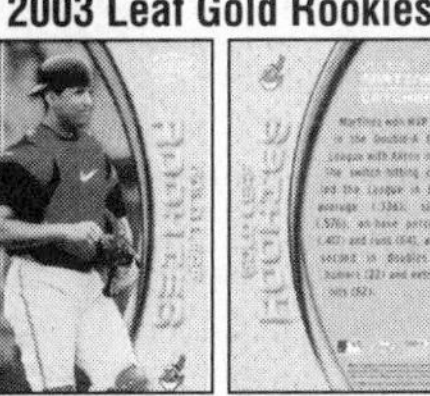

Issued at a stated rate of one in 24, this 10 card set features some of the leading candidates for Rookie of the Year. These cards were issued on a special foil board.

Nm-Mt Ex-Mt
MIRROR GOLD RANDOM INSERTS IN PACKS
MIRROR GOLD PRINT RUN 25 #'d SETS
MIRROR GOLD TOO SCARCE TO PRICE
1 Joe Borchard 3.00 .90
2 Chone Figgins 3.00 .90
3 Alexis Gomez 3.00 .90
4 Chris Snelling 3.00 .90
5 Cliff Lee 3.00 .90
6 Victor Martinez 3.00 .90
7 Hee Seop Choi 3.00 .90
8 Michael Restovich 3.00 .90
9 Anderson Machado 3.00 .90
10 Drew Henson 3.00 .90

2003 Leaf Hard Hats

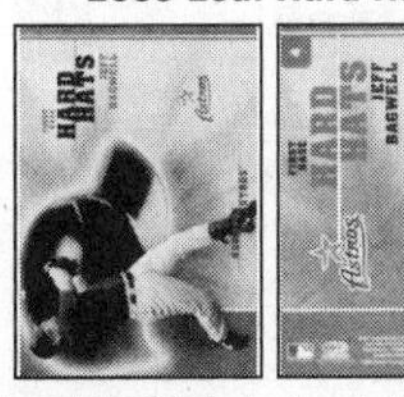

Issued at a stated rate of one in 13, these 12 cards feature the 1997 Studio design set against a rainbow board.

Nm-Mt Ex-Mt
1 Alex Rodriguez 4.00 1.20
2 Bernie Williams 2.00 .60
3 Ivan Rodriguez 2.50 .75
4 Jeff Bagwell 2.00 .60
5 Rafael Furcal 2.00 .60
6 Rafael Palmeiro 2.00 .60
7 Tony Gwynn 3.00 .90
8 Vladimir Guerrero 2.50 .75
9 Adrian Beltre 2.00 .60
10 Shawn Green 2.00 .60
11 Andruw Jones 2.00 .60
12 George Brett 6.00 1.80

2003 Leaf Hard Hats Batting Helmets

Randomly inserted into packs, this is a parallel to the Hard Hats insert set. These cards feature a swatch of a game-worn batting helmet embedded on the card and these cards were issued to a stated print run of 100 serial numbered sets.

Nm-Mt Ex-Mt
1 Alex Rodriguez 60.00 18.00
2 Bernie Williams 40.00 12.00
3 Ivan Rodriguez 40.00 12.00
4 Jeff Bagwell 40.00 12.00
5 Rafael Furcal 25.00 7.50
6 Rafael Palmeiro 40.00 12.00
7 Tony Gwynn 50.00 15.00
8 Vladimir Guerrero 40.00 12.00
9 Adrian Beltre 25.00 7.50
10 Shawn Green 25.00 7.50
11 Andruw Jones 25.00 7.50
12 George Brett 120.00 36.00

2003 Leaf Home/Away

Issued at a stated rate of one in 34, these 20 cards feature either home or away stats for these 10 featured players. The last three year of stats are featured on the cards.

Nm-Mt Ex-Mt
1A Andruw Jones A 4.00 1.20
1H Andruw Jones H 4.00 1.20
2A Cal Ripken A 15.00 4.50
2H Cal Ripken H 15.00 4.50
3A Edgar Martinez A 4.00 1.20
3H Edgar Martinez H 4.00 1.20
4A Jim Thome A 5.00 1.50
4H Jim Thome H 5.00 1.50
5A Larry Walker A 4.00 1.20
5H Larry Walker H 4.00 1.20
6A Nomar Garciaparra A 8.00 2.40
6H Nomar Garciaparra H 8.00 2.40
7A Mark Prior A 10.00 3.00
7H Mark Prior H 10.00 3.00
8A Mike Piazza A 8.00 2.40
8H Mike Piazza H 8.00 2.40
9A Vladimir Guerrero A 5.00 1.50
9H Vladimir Guerrero H 5.00 1.50
10A Chipper Jones A 5.00 1.50
10H Chipper Jones H 5.00 1.50

2003 Leaf Home/Away Materials

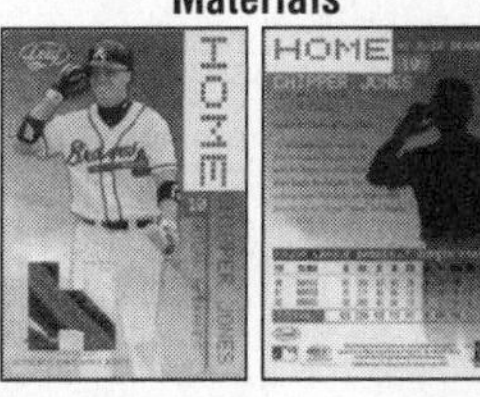

Randomly inserted into packs, this is a parallel to the Home/Away set. These cards feature jersey swatches displayed on the front and these cards were issued to a stated print run of 250 serial numbered sets.

Nm-Mt Ex-Mt
1A Andruw Jones A 10.00 3.00
1H Andruw Jones H 10.00 3.00
2A Cal Ripken A 60.00 18.00
2H Cal Ripken H 60.00 18.00
3A Edgar Martinez A 15.00 4.50
3H Edgar Martinez H 15.00 4.50
4A Jim Thome A 15.00 4.50
4H Jim Thome H 15.00 4.50
5A Larry Walker A 15.00 4.50
5H Larry Walker H 15.00 4.50
6A Nomar Garciaparra A 20.00 6.00
6H Nomar Garciaparra H 20.00 6.00
7A Mark Prior A 20.00 6.00
7H Mark Prior H 20.00 6.00
8A Mike Piazza A 20.00 6.00
8H Mike Piazza H 20.00 6.00
9A Vladimir Guerrero A 15.00 4.50
9H Vladimir Guerrero H 15.00 4.50
10A Chipper Jones A 15.00 4.50
10H Chipper Jones H 15.00 4.50

2003 Leaf Maple and Ash

Randomly inserted into packs, these cards feature faux wood grain and also have a game-used bat piece. These cards were issued to a stated print run of 400 serial numbered sets.

Nm-Mt Ex-Mt
1 Jorge Posada 15.00 4.50
2 Mike Piazza 20.00 6.00
3 Alex Rodriguez 20.00 6.00
4 Jeff Bagwell 15.00 4.50
5 Joe Borchard 10.00 3.00
6 Miguel Tejada 10.00 3.00
7 Adam Dunn 10.00 3.00
8 Jim Thome 15.00 4.50
9 Lance Berkman 10.00 3.00
10 Torii Hunter 10.00 3.00
11 Carlos Delgado 10.00 3.00
12 Reggie Jackson 15.00 4.50
13 Juan Gonzalez 15.00 4.50
14 Vladimir Guerrero 15.00 4.50
15 Richie Sexson 10.00 3.00

2003 Leaf Number Off My Back

Randomly inserted in packs, these cards feature a swatch from a game-worn jersey number. These cards were issued to a stated print run of 50 serial numbered sets.

Nm-Mt Ex-Mt
1 Carlos Delgado 25.00 7.50
2 Don Mattingly 150.00 45.00
3 Todd Helton 40.00 12.00
4 Vernon Wells 25.00 7.50
5 Bernie Williams 40.00 12.00
6 Luis Gonzalez 25.00 7.50
7 Kerry Wood 40.00 12.00
8 Eric Chavez 25.00 7.50
9 Shawn Green 25.00 7.50
10 Roy Oswalt 25.00 7.50
11 Nomar Garciaparra 60.00 18.00
12 Robin Yount 100.00 30.00
13 Troy Glaus 40.00 12.00
14 C.C. Sabathia 25.00 7.50
15 Alex Rodriguez 60.00 18.00
16 Mark Mulder 25.00 7.50
17 Will Clark 100.00 30.00
18 Alfonso Soriano 40.00 12.00
19 Andy Pettitte 40.00 12.00
20 Curt Schilling 40.00 12.00

2003 Leaf Shirt Off My Back

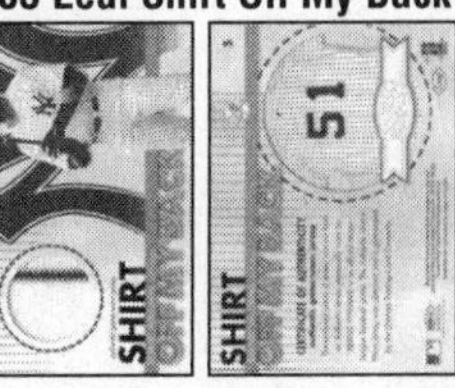

Randomly inserted into packs, this 20-card insert set features one swatch of game-worn jersey of the featured player. These cards were issued to a stated print run of 500 serial numbered sets.

Nm-Mt Ex-Mt
1 Carlos Delgado 8.00 2.40
2 Don Mattingly 25.00 7.50
3 Todd Helton 10.00 3.00
4 Vernon Wells 8.00 2.40
5 Bernie Williams 10.00 3.00
6 Luis Gonzalez 8.00 2.40
7 Kerry Wood 10.00 3.00
8 Eric Chavez 8.00 2.40
9 Shawn Green 8.00 2.40
10 Roy Oswalt 8.00 2.40
11 Nomar Garciaparra 15.00 4.50
12 Robin Yount 15.00 4.50
13 Troy Glaus 10.00 3.00
14 C.C. Sabathia 8.00 2.40
15 Alex Rodriguez 10.00 3.00
16 Mark Mulder 8.00 2.40
17 Will Clark 15.00 4.50
18 Alfonso Soriano 10.00 3.00
19 Andy Pettitte 10.00 3.00
20 Curt Schilling 10.00 3.00

2003 Leaf Slick Leather

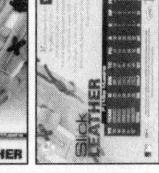

Issued at a stated rate of one in 21, this 15-card insert set features the most skilled fielders on cards featuring faux leather grain.

Nm-Mt Ex-Mt
1 Omar Vizquel 3.00 .90
2 Roberto Alomar 4.00 1.20
3 Ivan Rodriguez 4.00 1.20
4 Greg Maddux 6.00 1.80
5 Scott Rolen 3.00 .90
6 Todd Helton 3.00 .90
7 Andruw Jones 3.00 .90
8 Jim Edmonds 3.00 .90
9 Barry Bonds 10.00 3.00
10 Eric Chavez 3.00 .90
11 Ichiro Suzuki 6.00 1.80
12 Mike Mussina 4.00 1.20
13 John Olerud 3.00 .90
14 Torii Hunter 3.00 .90
15 Larry Walker 3.00 .90

2004 Leaf

This 301-card standard-size set was released in January, 2004. The set was issued in six-card packs with an $3 SRP which came 24 packs to a box and six boxes to a case. The first 200 cards were printed in higher quantities than the last 101 cards in this set. Cards numbered 201 through 251 feature 50 of the leading prospects. Cards numbered 252 through 271

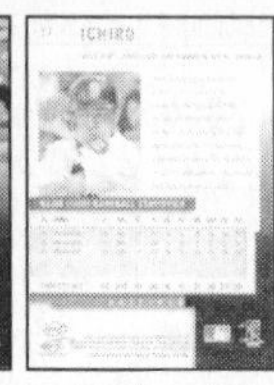

feature 20 players in a Passing Through Time subset while the final 30 cards of the set feature team checklists. Card number 42 was not issued as this product does not use that number in honor of Jackie Robinson.

Nm-Mt Ex-Mt
COMPLETE SET (301) 100.00 30.00
COMP.SETw/o SP's (200) 25.00 7.50
COMMON CARD (1-201) .30 .09
COMMON CARD (202-251) 1.00 .30
COMMON CARD (252-301) 1.00 .30
202-301 RANDOM INSERTS IN PACKS
CARD 42 DOES NOT EXIST
1 Darin Erstad .30 .09
2 Garret Anderson .30 .09
3 Jarrod Washburn .30 .09
4 Kevin Appier .30 .09
5 Tim Salmon .50 .15
6 Troy Glaus .50 .15
7 Troy Percival .30 .09
8 Jason Johnson .30 .09
9 Jay Gibbons .30 .09
10 Melvin Mora .30 .09
11 Sidney Ponson .30 .09
12 Tony Batista .30 .09
13 Derek Lowe .30 .09
14 Robert Person .30 .09
15 Manny Ramirez .30 .09
16 Nomar Garciaparra 1.25 .35
17 Pedro Martinez .75 .23
18 Jorge De La Rosa .30 .09
19 Bartolo Colon .30 .09
20 Carlos Lee .30 .09
21 Esteban Loaiza .30 .09
22 Frank Thomas .75 .23
23 Joe Crede .30 .09
24 Magglio Ordonez .30 .09
25 Ryan Ludwick .30 .09
26 Luis Garcia .30 .09
27 Brandon Phillips .30 .09
28 C.C Sabathia .30 .09
29 Jhonny Peralta .30 .09
30 Josh Bard .30 .09
31 Omar Vizquel .30 .09
32 Fernando Rodney .30 .09
33 Mike Maroth .30 .09
34 Bobby Higginson .30 .09
35 Omar Infante .30 .09
36 Dmitri Young .30 .09
37 Eric Munson .30 .09
38 Jeremy Bonderman .30 .09
39 Carlos Beltran .30 .09
40 Jeremy Affeldt .30 .09
41 Dee Brown .30 .09
42 Does Not Exist
43 Mike Sweeney .30 .09
44 Brent Abernathy .30 .09
45 Runelvys Hernandez .30 .09
46 A.J. Pierzynski .30 .09
47 Corey Koskie .30 .09
48 Cristian Guzman .30 .09
49 Jacque Jones .30 .09
50 Kenny Rogers .30 .09
51 J.C. Romero .30 .09
52 Torii Hunter .30 .09
53 Alfonso Soriano .50 .15
54 Bernie Williams .50 .15
55 David Wells .30 .09
56 Derek Jeter 2.00 .60
57 Hideki Matsui 1.25 .35
58 Jason Giambi .75 .23
59 Jorge Posada .50 .15
60 Jose Contreras .30 .09
61 Mike Mussina .75 .23
62 Nick Johnson .30 .09
63 Roger Clemens 1.50 .45
64 Barry Zito .50 .15
65 Justin Duchscherer .30 .09
66 Eric Chavez .30 .09
67 Erubial Durazo .30 .09
68 Miguel Tejada .30 .09
69 Mark Mulder .30 .09
70 Terrence Long .30 .09
71 Tim Hudson .30 .09
72 Bret Boone .30 .09
73 Dan Wilson .30 .09
74 Edgar Martinez .50 .15
75 Freddy Garcia .30 .09
76 Rafael Soriano .30 .09
77 Ichiro Suzuki 1.25 .35
78 Jamie Moyer .30 .09
79 John Olerud .30 .09
80 Kazuhiro Sasaki .30 .09
81 Aubrey Huff .30 .09
82 Carl Crawford .30 .09
83 Joe Kennedy .30 .09
84 Rocco Baldelli .75 .23
85 Toby Hall .30 .09
86 Alex Rodriguez 1.25 .35
87 Kevin Mench .30 .09
88 Hank Blalock .30 .09
89 Juan Gonzalez .75 .23
90 Mark Teixeira .30 .09
91 Rafael Palmeiro .50 .15
92 Carlos Delgado .30 .09
93 Eric Hinske .30 .09
94 Josh Phelps .30 .09
95 Brian Bowles .30 .09
96 Roy Halladay .30 .09
97 Shannon Stewart .30 .09
98 Vernon Wells .30 .09
99 Curt Schilling .50 .15
100 Junior Spivey .30 .09
101 Luis Gonzalez .30 .09
102 Lyle Overbay .30 .09
103 Mark Grace .50 .15
104 Randy Johnson .75 .23
105 Shea Hillenbrand .30 .09
106 Andruw Jones .30 .09
107 Chipper Jones .75 .23
108 Gary Sheffield .30 .09
109 Greg Maddux 1.25 .35
110 Javy Lopez .30 .09
111 John Smoltz .50 .15
112 Marcus Giles .30 .09
113 Rafael Furcal .30 .09
114 Corey Patterson .30 .09
115 Juan Cruz .30 .09
116 Kerry Wood .75 .23
117 Mark Prior 1.50 .45
118 Moises Alou .30 .09
119 Sammy Sosa 1.25 .35
120 Aaron Boone .30 .09
121 Adam Dunn .30 .09
122 Austin Kearns .30 .09
123 Barry Larkin .75 .23
124 Ken Griffey Jr. 1.25 .35
125 Brian Reith .30 .09
126 Wily Mo Pena .30 .09
127 Jason Jennings .30 .09
128 Jay Payton .30 .09
129 Larry Walker .50 .15
130 Preston Wilson .30 .09
131 Todd Helton .50 .15
132 Dontrelle Willis .30 .09
133 Ivan Rodriguez .75 .23
134 Josh Beckett .50 .15
135 Juan Encarnacion .30 .09
136 Mike Lowell .30 .09
137 Craig Biggio .50 .15
138 Jeff Bagwell .50 .15
139 Jeff Kent .30 .09
140 Lance Berkman .30 .09
141 Richard Hidalgo .30 .09
142 Roy Oswalt .30 .09
143 Eric Gagne .50 .15
144 Fred McGriff .50 .15
145 Hideo Nomo .75 .23
146 Kazuhisa Ishii .30 .09
147 Kevin Brown .30 .09
148 Paul Lo Duca .30 .09
149 Shawn Green .30 .09
150 Ben Sheets .30 .09
151 Geoff Jenkins .30 .09
152 Rey Sanchez .30 .09
153 Richie Sexson .30 .09
154 Wes Helms .30 .09
155 Shane Nance .30 .09
156 Fernando Tatis .30 .09
157 Javier Vazquez .30 .09
158 Jose Vidro .30 .09
159 Orlando Cabrera .30 .09
160 Henry Mateo .30 .09
161 Vladimir Guerrero .75 .23
162 Zach Day .30 .09
163 Edwin Almonte .30 .09
164 Al Leiter .30 .09
165 Cliff Floyd .30 .09
166 Jae Weong Seo .30 .09
167 Mike Piazza 1.25 .35
168 Roberto Alomar .75 .23
169 Tom Glavine .50 .15
170 Bobby Abreu .30 .09
171 Brandon Duckworth .30 .09
172 Jim Thome .75 .23
173 Kevin Millwood .30 .09
174 Pat Burrell .30 .09
175 Aramis Ramirez .30 .09
176 Jack Wilson .30 .09
177 Brian Giles .30 .09
178 Jason Kendall .30 .09
179 Kenny Lofton .30 .09
180 Kip Wells .30 .09
181 Kris Benson .30 .09
182 Albert Pujols 1.50 .45
183 J.D. Drew .30 .09
184 Jim Edmonds .30 .09
185 Matt Morris .30 .09
186 Scott Rolen .50 .15
187 Woody Williams .30 .09
188 Cliff Bartosh .30 .09
189 Brian Lawrence .30 .09
190 Ryan Klesko .30 .09
191 Sean Burroughs .30 .09
192 Xavier Nady .30 .09
193 Dennis Tankersley .30 .09
194 Donaldo Mendez .30 .09
195 Barry Bonds 2.00 .60
196 Benito Santiago .30 .09
197 Edgardo Alfonzo .30 .09
198 Cody Ransom .30 .09
199 Jason Schmidt .30 .09
200 Rich Aurilia .30 .09
201 Ken Harvey .30 .09
202 Adam Loewen ROO 2.00 .60
203 Alfredo Gonzalez ROO 1.00 .30
204 Arnie Munoz ROO 1.00 .30
205 Andrew Brown ROO 1.00 .30
206 Josh Hall ROO 1.00 .30
207 Josh Stewart PROS 1.00 .30
208 Clint Barmes PROS 1.00 .30
209 Brandon Webb PROS 2.00 .60
210 Chien-Ming Wang PROS 2.00 .60
211 Edgar Gonzalez PROS 1.00 .30
212 Alejandro Machado PROS 1.00 .30
213 Jeremy Griffiths PROS 1.00 .30
214 Craig Brazell PROS 1.00 .30
215 Daniel Cabrera PROS 1.00 .30
216 Fernando Cabrera PROS 1.00 .30
217 Termel Sledge PROS 1.00 .30
218 Rob Hammock PROS 1.00 .30
219 Francisco Rosario PROS 1.00 .30
220 Francisco Cruceta PROS 1.00 .30
221 Rett Johnson PROS 1.00 .30
222 Guillermo Quiroz PROS 2.00 .60
223 Hong-Chih Kuo PROS 2.00 .60
224 Ian Ferguson PROS 1.00 .30
225 Tim Olson PROS 1.00 .30
226 Todd Wellemeyer PROS 1.00 .30
227 Rich Fischer PROS 1.00 .30
228 Phil Seibel PROS 1.00 .30
229 Joe Valentine PROS 1.00 .30
230 Matt Kata PROS 2.00 .60
231 Michael Hessman PROS 1.00 .30
232 Michel Hernandez PROS 1.00 .30
233 Doug Waechter PROS 1.00 .30
234 Prentice Redman PROS 1.00 .30
235 Nook Logan PROS 1.00 .30
236 Oscar Villarreal PROS 1.00 .30
237 Pete LaForest PROS 1.00 .30
238 Matt Bruback PROS 1.00 .30
239 Josh Willingham PROS 2.00 .60
240 Greg Aquino PROS 1.00 .30
241 Lew Ford PROS 1.00 .30
242 Jeff Duncan PROS 1.00 .30
243 Chris Waters PROS 1.00 .30
244 Miguel Ojeda PROS 1.00 .30
245 Rosman Garcia PROS 1.00 .30
246 Felix Sanchez PROS 1.00 .30
247 Jon Leicester PROS 1.00 .30
248 Roger Deago PROS 1.00 .30
249 Mike Ryan PROS 1.00 .30
250 Chris Capuano PROS 1.00 .30
251 Matt White PROS 1.00 .30
252 Bernie Williams PTT 1.00 .30
253 Mark Grace PTT 1.00 .30
254 Chipper Jones PTT 1.50 .45
255 Greg Maddux PTT 2.50 .75
256 Sammy Sosa PTT 2.50 .75
257 Mike Mussina PTT 1.50 .45
258 Tim Salmon PTT 1.00 .30
259 Barry Larkin PTT 1.50 .45
260 Randy Johnson PTT 1.50 .45
261 Jeff Bagwell PTT 1.50 .45
262 Roberto Alomar PTT 1.50 .45
263 Tom Glavine PTT 1.00 .30
264 Roger Clemens PTT 3.00 .90
265 Barry Bonds PTT 4.00 1.20
266 Ivan Rodriguez PTT 1.50 .45
267 Pedro Martinez PTT 1.50 .45
268 Ken Griffey Jr. PTT 2.50 .75
269 Jim Thome PTT 1.50 .45
270 Frank Thomas PTT 1.50 .45
271 Mike Piazza PTT 2.50 .75
272 Troy Glaus TC 1.00 .30
273 Melvin Mora TC 1.00 .30
274 Nomar Garciaparra TC 2.50 .75
275 Magglio Ordonez TC 1.00 .30
276 Omar Vizquel TC 1.00 .30
277 Dmitri Young TC 1.00 .30
278 Mike Sweeney TC 1.00 .30
279 Torii Hunter TC 1.00 .30
280 Derek Jeter TC 4.00 1.20
281 Barry Zito TC 1.00 .30
282 Ichiro Suzuki TC 2.50 .75
283 Rocco Baldelli TC 1.50 .45
284 Alex Rodriguez TC 2.50 .75
285 Carlos Delgado TC 1.00 .30
286 Randy Johnson TC 1.50 .45
287 Greg Maddux TC 2.50 .75
288 Sammy Sosa TC 2.50 .75
289 Ken Griffey Jr. TC 2.50 .75
290 Todd Helton TC 1.00 .30
291 Ivan Rodriguez TC 1.50 .45
292 Jeff Bagwell TC 1.00 .30
293 Hideo Nomo TC 1.50 .45
294 Richie Sexson TC 1.00 .30
295 Vladimir Guerrero TC 1.50 .45
296 Mike Piazza TC 2.50 .75
297 Jim Thome TC 1.50 .45
298 Jason Kendall TC 1.00 .30
299 Albert Pujols TC 3.00 .90
300 Ryan Klesko TC 1.00 .30
301 Barry Bonds TC 4.00 1.20

2004 Leaf Autographs

Nm-Mt Ex-Mt
RANDOM INSERTS IN PACKS
SP INFO PROVIDED BY DONRUSS
SP'S ARE NOT SERIAL-NUMBERED
14 Robert Person 10.00 3.00
18 Jorge De La Rosa 10.00 3.00
25 Ryan Ludwick 10.00 3.00
26 Luis Garcia 10.00 3.00
29 Jhonny Peralta 10.00 3.00
30 Josh Bard 10.00 3.00
32 Fernando Rodney 10.00 3.00
33 Mike Maroth 10.00 3.00
35 Omar Infante 10.00 3.00
37 Eric Munson SP/9
41 Dee Brown 10.00 3.00
44 Brent Abernathy SP 15.00 4.50
51 J.C. Romero 10.00 3.00
65 Justin Duchscherer 15.00 4.50
70 Terrence Long SP 25.00 7.50
76 Rafael Soriano 10.00 3.00
85 Toby Hall SP 15.00 4.50
87 Kevin Mench 10.00 3.00
95 Brian Bowles 10.00 3.00
115 Juan Cruz 10.00 3.00
125 Brian Reith 10.00 3.00
126 Wily Mo Pena 10.00 3.00
127 Jason Jennings 10.00 3.00
150 Ben Sheets SP/17
155 Shane Nance 10.00 3.00
160 Henry Mateo SP 15.00 4.50
163 Edwin Almonte 10.00 3.00
171 Brandon Duckworth 10.00 3.00
176 Jack Wilson 10.00 3.00
180 Kip Wells 10.00 3.00
188 Cliff Bartosh 10.00 3.00
189 Brian Lawrence 10.00 3.00
193 Dennis Tankersley 10.00 3.00
194 Donaldo Mendez 10.00 3.00
198 Cody Ransom SP 15.00 4.50
247 Jon Leicester PROS SP 15.00 4.50

2004 Leaf Press Proofs Blue

Nm-Mt Ex-Mt
*BLUE 1-201: 4X TO 10X BASIC
*BLUE 202-251: 1.25X TO 3X BASIC
*BLUE 252-301: 2X TO 5X BASIC
RANDOM INSERTS IN PACKS
STATED PRINT RUN 100 SERIAL #'d SETS

2004 Leaf Press Proofs Gold

Nm-Mt Ex-Mt
RANDOM INSERTS IN PACKS
STATED PRINT RUN 25 SERIAL #'d SETS
NO PRICING DUE TO SCARCITY

2004 Leaf Press Proofs Red

Nm-Mt Ex-Mt
*RED 1-201: 2X TO 5X BASIC
*RED 202-251: .6X TO 1.5X BASIC
*RED 252-301: 1X TO 2.5X BASIC
STATED ODDS 1:8

2004 Leaf Press Proofs Silver

Nm-Mt Ex-Mt
*SILVER 1-201: 6X TO 15X BASIC
*SILVER 202-251: 2X TO 5X BASIC
*SILVER 252-301: 3X TO 8X BASIC
RANDOM INSERTS IN PACKS
STATED PRINT RUN 50 SERIAL #'d SETS

2004 Leaf Clean Up Crew

Nm-Mt Ex-Mt
STATED ODDS 1:49
1 Sammy Sosa 6.00 1.80
Moises Alou
Hee Seop Choi
2 Jason Giambi 6.00 1.80
Alfonso Soriano
Hideki Matsui
3 Vernon Wells 4.00 1.20
Carlos Delgado
Josh Phelps
4 Alex Rodriguez 6.00 1.80
Juan Gonzalez
Hank Blalock
5 Gary Sheffield 4.00 1.20
Chipper Jones
Andruw Jones
6 Ken Griffey Jr. 6.00 1.80
Austin Kearns
Aaron Boone
7 Albert Pujols 8.00 2.40
Jim Edmonds
Scott Rolen
8 Jeff Bagwell 4.00 1.20
Lance Berkman
Jeff Kent
9 Todd Helton 4.00 1.20
Preston Wilson
Larry Walker
10 Miguel Tejada 4.00 1.20
Erubial Durazo
Eric Chavez

2004 Leaf Clean Up Crew Materials

Nm-Mt Ex-Mt
RANDOM INSERTS IN PACKS
STATED PRINT RUN 50 SERIAL #'d SETS
1 Sammy Sosa Bat 40.00 12.00
Moises Alou Bat
Hee Seop Choi Jsy
2 Alfonso Soriano Base 60.00 18.00
Jason Giambi Base
Hideki Matsui Base
3 Vernon Wells Jsy 25.00 7.50
Carlos Delgado Jsy
Josh Phelps Jsy
4 Alex Rodriguez Bat 40.00 12.00
Juan Gonzalez Bat
Hank Blalock Bat
5 Gary Sheffield Jsy 40.00 12.00
Chipper Jones Jsy
Andruw Jones Bat
6 Ken Griffey Jr. Base 40.00 12.00
Austin Kearns Base
Aaron Boone Base
7 Albert Pujols Bat 50.00 15.00
Jim Edmonds Jsy
Scott Rolen Bat
8 Jeff Bagwell Bat 40.00 12.00
Lance Berkman Bat
Jeff Kent Jsy
9 Todd Helton Bat 40.00 12.00
Preston Wilson Bat
Larry Walker Jsy
10 Miguel Tejada Jsy 25.00 7.50
Erubial Durazo Bat
Eric Chavez Jsy

2004 Leaf Cornerstones

Nm-Mt Ex-Mt
STATED ODDS 1:78
1 Alex Rodriguez 8.00 2.40
Hank Blalock
2 Kerry Wood 10.00 3.00
Mark Prior
3 Roger Clemens 10.00 3.00
Alfonso Soriano
4 Nomar Garicaparra 8.00 2.40

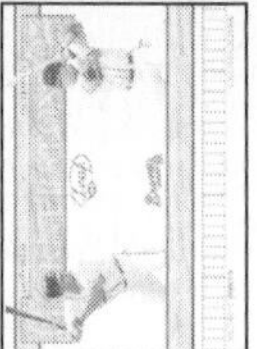

Manny Ramirez
5 Austin Kearns 5.00 1.50
Adam Dunn
6 Tom Glavine 8.00 2.40
Mike Piazza
7 Andruw Jones 5.00 1.50
Chipper Jones
8 Albert Pujols 10.00 3.00
Scott Rolen
9 Curt Schilling 5.00 1.50
Randy Johnson
10 Hideo Nomo 5.00 1.50
Kazuhisa Ishii

2004 Leaf Cornerstones Materials

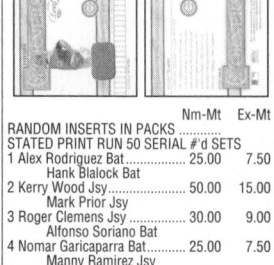

Nm-Mt Ex-Mt
RANDOM INSERTS IN PACKS
STATED PRINT RUN 50 SERIAL #'d SETS
1 Alex Rodriguez Bat 25.00 7.50
Hank Blalock Bat
2 Kerry Wood Jsy 50.00 15.00
Mark Prior Jsy
3 Roger Clemens Jsy 30.00 9.00
Alfonso Soriano Bat
4 Nomar Garicaparra Bat 25.00 7.50
Manny Ramirez Jsy
5 Austin Kearns Bat 15.00 4.50
Adam Dunn Jsy
6 Tom Glavine Jsy
Mike Piazza Bat
7 Andruw Jones Bat 25.00 7.50
Chipper Jones Jsy
8 Albert Pujols Bat 50.00 15.00
Scott Rolen Bat
9 Curt Schilling Jsy 25.00 7.50
Randy Johnson Jsy
10 Hideo Nomo Jsy 25.00 7.50
Kazuhisa Ishii Jsy

2004 Leaf Exhibits 1947-66 Made by Donruss-Playoff Print

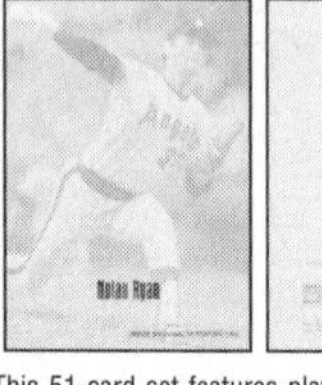

This 51-card set features players in the design of the old exhibit company cards issued from 1921 through 1964. Please note that there were more than 40 varieties for each of these cards issued and we have notated what the multipier is for each card.

MINT NRMT
STATED PRINT RUN 66 SERIAL #'d SETS
*1921 ACTIVE: .75X TO 2X
*1921 RETIRED: 1X TO 2.5X
1921 PRINT RUN 21 #'d SETS
*1921 AML ACTIVE: .75X TO 2X
*1921 AML RETIRED: 1X TO 2.5X
1921 AL P.RUN 21 #'d SETS
*1925 L ACTIVE: .75X TO 2X
*1925 L RETIRED: 1X TO 2.5X
1925 L PRINT RUN 25 #'d SETS
*1925 R ACTIVE: .75X TO 2X
*1925 R RETIRED: 1X TO 2.5X
1925 R PRINT RUN25 #'d SETS
*1926 B ACTIVE: .75X TO 2X
*1926 B RETIRED: 1X TO 2.5X
1926 B PRINT RUN 26 #'d SETS
*1926 BDP ACTIVE: .75X TO 2X
*1926 BDP RETIRED: 1X TO 2.5X
1926 BDP PRINT RUN 26 #'d SETS
*1926 U ACTIVE: .75X TO 2X
*1926 U RETIRED: 1X TO 2.5X
1926 U PRINT RUN 26 #'d SETS
*1926 UDP ACTIVE: .75X TO 2X
*1926 UDP RETIRED: 1X TO 2.5X
1926 UDP PRINT RUN 26 #'d SETS
*1927 ACTIVE: .75X TO 2X
*1927 RETIRED: 1X TO 2.5X
1927 PRINT RUN 27 #'d SETS
*1927 DP ACTIVE: .75X TO 2X
*1927 DP RETIRED: 1X TO 2.5X
1927 DP PRINT RUN 27 #'d SETS
*1939-46 BOLL: .5X TO 1.2X
1939-46 BOLL PRINT RUN 46 #'d SETS
*1939-46 BOLR: .5X TO 1.2X
1939-46 BOLR PRINT RUN 46 #'d SETS
*1939-46 BWL: .5X TO 1.2X
1939-46 BWL PRINT RUN 46 #'d SETS
*1939-46 BWR: .5X TO 1.2X
1939-46 BWR PRINT RUN 46 #'d SETS
*1939-46 CL: .5X TO 1.2X

1939-46 CL PRINT RUN 46 #'d SETS.
*1939-46 CR: .5X TO 1.2X
1939-46 CR PRINT RUN 46 #'d SETS.
*1939-46 CYL: .5X TO 1.2X
1939-46 CYL PRINT RUN 46 #'d SETS
*1939-46 CYR: .5X TO 1.2X
1939-46 CYR PRINT RUN 46 #'d SETS
*1939-46 SL: .5X TO 1.2X
1939-46 SL PRINT RUN 46 #'d SETS.
*1939-46 SR: .5X TO 1.2X
1939-46 SR PRINT RUN 46 #'d SETS.
*1939-46 SYL: .5X TO 1.2X
1939-46 SYL PRINT RUN 46 #'d SETS
*1939-46 SYR: .5X TO 1.2X
1939-46 SYR PRINT RUN 46 #'d SETS
*1939-46 TYL: .5X TO 1.2X
1939-46 TYL PRINT RUN 46 #'d SETS
*1939-46 TYR: .5X TO 1.2X
1939-46 TYR PRINT RUN 46 #'d SETS
*1939-46 VBWL: .5X TO 1.2X
1939-46 VBWL PRINT RUN 46 #'d SETS
*1939-46 VBWR: .5X TO 1.2X
1939-46 VBWR PRINT RUN 46 #'d SETS
*1939-46 VTYL: .5X TO 1.2X
1939-46 VTYL PRINT RUN 46 #'d SETS
*1939-46 VTYR: .5X TO 1.2X
1939-46 VTYR PRINT RUN 46 #'d SETS
*1939-46 YTL: .5X TO 1.2X
1939-46 YTL PRINT RUN 46 #'d SETS
*1939-46 YTR: .5X TO 1.2X
1939-46 YTR PRINT RUN 46 #'d SETS
*1947-66 DP SIG: .4X TO 1X
1947-66 DP SIG PRINT RUN 66 #'d SETS
*1947-66 MPRI: .4X TO 1X
1947-66 MPRI PRINT RUN 66 #'d SETS
*1947-66 MSIG: .4X TO 1X
1947-66 MSIG PRINT RUN 66 #'d SETS
*1947-66 PDPPRI: .4X TO 1X
1947-66 PDPPRI PRINT RUN 66 #'d SETS
*1947-66 PDPSIG: .4X TO 1X
1947-66 PDPSIG PRINT RUN 66 #'d SETS
*1947-66 PPRI: .4X TO 1X
1947-66 PPRI PRINT RUN 66 #'d SETS
*1947-66 PSIG: .4X TO 1X
1947-66 PSIG PRINT RUN 66 #'d SETS
*1962-63 NSNL: .4X TO 1X
1962-63 NSNL PRINT RUN 63 #'d SETS
*1962-63 NSNR: .4X TO 1X
1962-63 NSNR PRINT RUN 63 #'d SETS
*1962-63 SBNL: .4X TO 1X
1962-63 SBNL PRINT RUN 63 #'d SETS
*1962-63 SBNR: .4X TO 1X
1962-63 SBNR PRINT RUN 63 #'d SETS
*1962-63 SRNL: .4X TO 1X
1962-63 SRNL PRINT RUN 63 #'d SETS
*1962-63 SRNR: .4X TO 1X
1962-63 SRNR PRINT RUN 63 #'d SETS
RANDOM INSERTS IN PACKS
SEE CARD BACKS FOR ABBREV.LEGEND

Card		
1 Adam Dunn	5.00	2.20
2 Albert Pujols	12.00	5.50
3 Alex Rodriguez	10.00	4.50
4 Alfonso Soriano	5.00	2.20
5 Andruw Jones	5.00	2.20
6A Barry Bonds	15.00	6.75
6B Nolan Ryan Mets	10.00	4.50
7 Barry Larkin	8.00	3.60
8 Barry Zito	5.00	2.20
9 Cal Ripken	20.00	9.00
10 Chipper Jones	8.00	3.60
11 Dale Murphy	10.00	4.50
12 Derek Jeter	15.00	6.75
13 Don Mattingly	15.00	6.75
14 Ernie Banks	10.00	4.50
15 Frank Thomas	8.00	3.60
16 George Brett	15.00	6.75
17 Greg Maddux	10.00	4.50
18 Hank Blalock	5.00	2.20
19 Hideo Nomo	8.00	3.60
20 Ichiro Suzuki	10.00	4.50
21 Jason Giambi	8.00	3.60
22 Jim Thome	8.00	3.60
23 Juan Gonzalez	8.00	3.60
24 Ken Griffey Jr.	10.00	4.50
25 Kirby Puckett	10.00	4.50
26 Mark Prior	12.00	5.50
27 Mike Mussina	8.00	3.60
28 Mike Piazza	10.00	4.50
29 Mike Schmidt	12.00	5.50
30 Nolan Ryan Angels	10.00	4.50
31 Nolan Ryan Astros	10.00	4.50
32 Nolan Ryan Rangers	10.00	4.50
33 Nomar Garciaparra	10.00	4.50
34 Ozzie Smith	10.00	4.50
35 Pedro Martinez	8.00	3.60
36 Randy Johnson	8.00	3.60
37 Reggie Jackson Yanks	8.00	3.60
38 Reggie Jackson A's	8.00	3.60
39 Rickey Henderson	8.00	3.60
40 Roberto Alomar	8.00	3.60
41 Roberto Clemente	12.00	5.50
42 Rod Carew	8.00	3.60
43 Roger Clemens	12.00	5.50
44 Sammy Sosa	10.00	4.50
45 Stan Musial	10.00	4.50
46 Tom Glavine	5.00	2.20
47 Tom Seaver	8.00	3.60
48 Tony Gwynn	10.00	4.50
49 Vladimir Guerrero	8.00	3.60
50 Yogi Berra	10.00	4.50

2004 Leaf Gamers

	MINT	NRMT

STATED ODDS 1:19
*QUANTUM: 1X TO 2.5X BASIC
QUANTUM RANDOM INSERTS IN PACKS
QUANTUM PRINT RUN 100 #'d SETS.

Card		
1 Albert Pujols	6.00	2.70
2 Alex Rodriguez	5.00	2.20
3 Alfonso Soriano	3.00	1.35
4 Barry Bonds	8.00	3.60
5 Barry Zito	3.00	1.35
6 Chipper Jones	3.00	1.35
7 Derek Jeter	8.00	3.60
8 Greg Maddux	5.00	2.20
9 Ichiro Suzuki	5.00	2.20
10 Jason Giambi	3.00	1.35
11 Jeff Bagwell	3.00	1.35
12 Ken Griffey Jr.	5.00	2.20
13 Manny Ramirez	2.00	.90
14 Mark Prior	6.00	2.70
15 Mike Piazza	5.00	2.20
16 Nomar Garciaparra	5.00	2.20
17 Pedro Martinez	3.00	1.35
18 Randy Johnson	3.00	1.35
19 Roger Clemens	6.00	2.70
20 Sammy Sosa	5.00	2.20

2004 Leaf Gold Rookies

STATED ODDS 1:23
MIRROR GOLD RANDOM INSERTS IN PACKS
MIRROR GOLD PRINT RUN 25 #'d SETS
MIRROR GOLD TOO SCARCE TO PRICE

	MINT	NRMT
1 Adam Loewen	3.00	1.35
2 Rickie Weeks	8.00	3.60
3 Khalil Greene	3.00	1.35
4 Chad Tracy	3.00	1.35
5 Alexis Rios	5.00	2.20
6 Craig Brazell	3.00	1.35
7 Clint Barmes	3.00	1.35
8 Pete LaForest	3.00	1.35
9 Alfredo Gonzalez	3.00	1.35
10 Arnie Munoz	3.00	1.35

2004 Leaf Home/Away

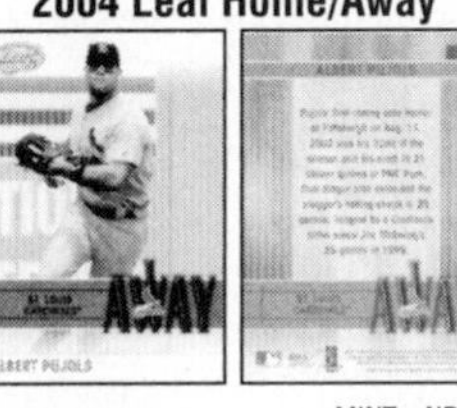

STATED ODDS 1:35

	MINT	NRMT
1A Greg Maddux A	8.00	3.60
1H Greg Maddux H	8.00	3.60
2A Sammy Sosa A	8.00	3.60
2H Sammy Sosa H	8.00	3.60
3A Alex Rodriguez A	8.00	3.60
3H Alex Rodriguez H	8.00	3.60
4A Albert Pujols A	10.00	4.50
4H Albert Pujols H	10.00	4.50
5A Jason Giambi A	5.00	2.20
5H Jason Giambi H	5.00	2.20
6A Chipper Jones A	5.00	2.20
6H Chipper Jones H	5.00	2.20
7A Vladimir Guerrero A	5.00	2.20
7H Vladimir Guerrero H	5.00	2.20
8A Mike Piazza A	8.00	3.60
8H Mike Piazza H	8.00	3.60
9A Nomar Garciaparra A	8.00	3.60
9H Nomar Garciaparra H	8.00	3.60
10A Austin Kearns A	4.00	1.80
10H Austin Kearns H	4.00	1.80

2004 Leaf Home/Away Jerseys

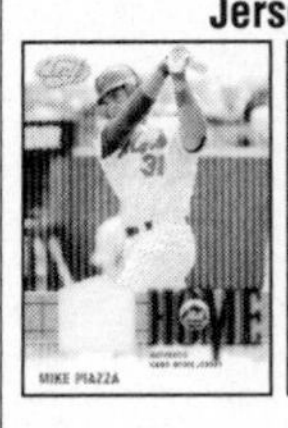

STATED ODDS 1:119
*PRIME: 1.25X TO 3X BASIC
PRIME RANDOM INSERTS IN PACKS.
PRIME PRINT RUN 50 #'d SETS

	MINT	NRMT
1A Greg Maddux A	10.00	4.50
1H Greg Maddux H	10.00	4.50
2A Sammy Sosa A	15.00	6.75
2H Sammy Sosa H	15.00	6.75
3A Alex Rodriguez A	10.00	4.50
3H Alex Rodriguez H	10.00	4.50
4A Albert Pujols A	15.00	6.75
4H Albert Pujols H	15.00	6.75
5A Jason Giambi A	10.00	4.50
5H Jason Giambi H	10.00	4.50
6A Chipper Jones A	10.00	4.50
6H Chipper Jones H	10.00	4.50
7A Vladimir Guerrero A	10.00	4.50
7H Vladimir Guerrero H	10.00	4.50
8A Mike Piazza A	10.00	4.50
8H Mike Piazza H	10.00	4.50
9A Nomar Garciaparra A	10.00	4.50
9H Nomar Garciaparra H	10.00	4.50
10A Austin Kearns A	8.00	3.60
10H Austin Kearns H	8.00	3.60

2004 Leaf Limited Previews

*GOLD: 1.25X TO 3X BASIC
GOLD PRINT RUN 50 SERIAL #'d SETS
*SILVER: .75X TO 2X BASIC
SILVER PRINT RUN 100 SERIAL #'d SETS
RANDOM INSERTS IN PACKS

	MINT	NRMT
1 Derek Jeter	10.00	4.50
2 Barry Zito	4.00	1.80
3 Ichiro Suzuki	6.00	2.70
4 Pedro Martinez	4.00	1.80
5 Alfonso Soriano	4.00	1.80
6 Alex Rodriguez	6.00	2.70
7 Greg Maddux	6.00	2.70
8 Mike Piazza	6.00	2.70
9 Mark Prior	8.00	3.60
10 Albert Pujols	8.00	3.60
11 Sammy Sosa	6.00	2.70
12 Ken Griffey Jr.	6.00	2.70
13 Nomar Garciaparra	6.00	2.70
14 Randy Johnson	4.00	1.80
15 Jason Giambi	4.00	1.80
16 Barry Bonds	10.00	4.50
17 Manny Ramirez	4.00	1.80
18 Chipper Jones	4.00	1.80
19 Jeff Bagwell	4.00	1.80
20 Roger Clemens	8.00	3.60

2004 Leaf MVP Winners

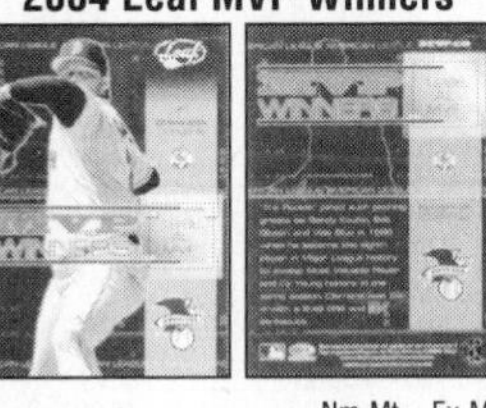

STATED ODDS 1:11
*GOLD: .6X TO 1.5X BASIC
GOLD RANDOM INSERTS IN PACKS
GOLD PRINT RUN 500 SERIAL #'d SETS

	Nm-Mt	Ex-Mt
1 Stan Musial	4.00	1.20
2 Ernie Banks	3.00	.90
3 Roberto Clemente	5.00	1.50
4 George Brett	6.00	1.80
5 Mike Schmidt	5.00	1.50
6 Cal Ripken 83	8.00	2.40
7 Dale Murphy	3.00	.90
8 Ryne Sandberg	5.00	1.50
9 Don Mattingly	6.00	1.80
10 Roger Clemens	5.00	1.50
11 Rickey Henderson	3.00	.90
12 Cal Ripken 91	8.00	2.40
13 Barry Bonds 92	6.00	1.80
14 Barry Bonds 93	6.00	1.80
15 Frank Thomas	3.00	.90
16 Ken Griffey Jr.	4.00	1.20
17 Sammy Sosa	4.00	1.20
18 Chipper Jones	3.00	.90
19 Jason Giambi	3.00	.90
20 Ichiro Suzuki	4.00	1.20

2004 Leaf Picture Perfect

STATED ODDS 1:37

	MINT	NRMT
1 Albert Pujols	10.00	4.50
2 Alex Rodriguez	8.00	3.60
3 Alfonso Soriano	5.00	2.20
4 Austin Kearns	3.00	1.35
5 Carlos Delgado	3.00	1.35
6 Chipper Jones	5.00	2.20
7 Hank Blalock	3.00	1.35
8 Jason Giambi	5.00	2.20
9 Jeff Bagwell	5.00	2.20
10 Jim Thome	5.00	2.20
11 Manny Ramirez	3.00	1.35
12 Mike Piazza	8.00	3.60
13 Nomar Garciaparra	8.00	3.60
14 Sammy Sosa	8.00	3.60
15 Todd Helton	5.00	2.20

2004 Leaf Picture Perfect Bats

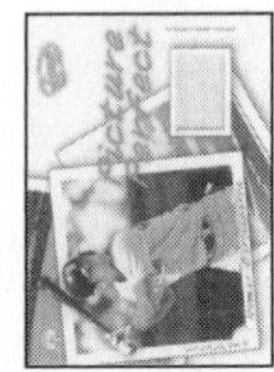

STATED ODDS 1:437

	MINT	NRMT
1 Albert Pujols	15.00	6.75
2 Alex Rodriguez	10.00	4.50
3 Alfonso Soriano	10.00	4.50
4 Austin Kearns	8.00	3.60
5 Carlos Delgado	8.00	3.60
6 Chipper Jones	10.00	4.50
7 Hank Blalock	8.00	3.60
8 Jason Giambi	10.00	4.50
9 Jeff Bagwell	10.00	4.50
10 Jim Thome	10.00	4.50
11 Manny Ramirez	8.00	3.60
12 Mike Piazza	10.00	4.50
13 Nomar Garciaparra	10.00	4.50
14 Sammy Sosa	15.00	6.75
15 Todd Helton	10.00	4.50

2004 Leaf Recollection Autographs

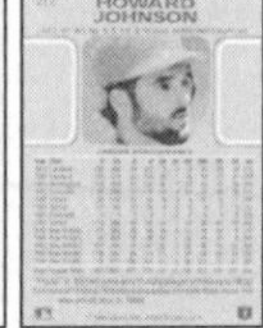

RANDOM INSERTS IN PACKS
PRINT RUNS B/WN 1-31 COPIES PER
NO PRICING ON QTY OF 25 OR LESS.
ALL CARDS ARE 1990 LEAF BUYBACKS

	MINT	NRMT
3 Jesse Barfield 90/29	30.00	13.50
15 Charlie Hough 90/31	20.00	9.00

2004 Leaf Shirt Off My Back

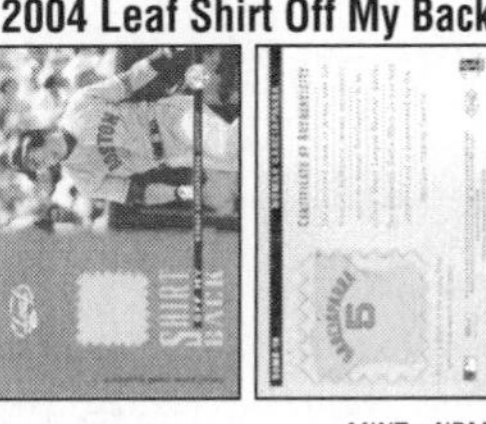

STATED ODDS 1:47

	MINT	NRMT
1 Shawn Green	8.00	3.60
2 Andruw Jones	8.00	3.60
3 Ivan Rodriguez	10.00	4.50
4 Hideo Nomo	10.00	4.50
5 Don Mattingly	20.00	9.00
6 Mark Prior	15.00	6.75
7 Alfonso Soriano	10.00	4.50
8 Richie Sexson	8.00	3.60
9 Vernon Wells	8.00	3.60
10 Nomar Garciaparra	10.00	4.50
11 Jason Giambi	10.00	4.50
12 Austin Kearns	8.00	3.60
13 Chipper Jones	10.00	4.50
14 Rickey Henderson	10.00	4.50
15 Alex Rodriguez	10.00	4.50
16 Garret Anderson	8.00	3.60
17 Vladimir Guerrero	10.00	4.50
18 Sammy Sosa	15.00	6.75
19 Mike Piazza	10.00	4.50
20 David Wells	8.00	3.60
21 Scott Rolen	10.00	4.50
22 Adam Dunn	8.00	3.60
23 Carlos Delgado	8.00	3.60
24 Greg Maddux	10.00	4.50
25 Hank Blalock	8.00	3.60

2004 Leaf Shirt Off My Back Jersey Number Patch

RANDOM INSERTS IN PACKS
STATED PRINT RUN 50 SERIAL #'d SETS
BLALOCK PRINT RUN 32 SERIAL #'d CARDS
SOSA PRINT RUN 42 SERIAL #'d CARDS

	MINT	NRMT
1 Shawn Green	15.00	6.75
2 Andruw Jones	15.00	6.75
3 Ivan Rodriguez	25.00	11.00
4 Hideo Nomo	25.00	11.00
5 Don Mattingly	40.00	18.00
6 Mark Prior	40.00	18.00
7 Alfonso Soriano	25.00	11.00
8 Richie Sexson	15.00	6.75
9 Vernon Wells	15.00	6.75
10 Nomar Garciaparra	30.00	13.50
11 Jason Giambi	25.00	11.00
12 Austin Kearns	15.00	6.75
13 Chipper Jones	25.00	11.00
14 Rickey Henderson	25.00	11.00
15 Alex Rodriguez	30.00	13.50
16 Garret Anderson	15.00	6.75
17 Vladimir Guerrero	25.00	11.00
18 Sammy Sosa/42	40.00	18.00
19 Mike Piazza	30.00	13.50
20 David Wells	15.00	6.75
21 Scott Rolen	25.00	11.00
22 Adam Dunn	15.00	6.75
23 Carlos Delgado	15.00	6.75
24 Greg Maddux	30.00	13.50
25 Hank Blalock/32	15.00	6.75

2004 Leaf Shirt Off My Back Jersey Number Patch Autographs

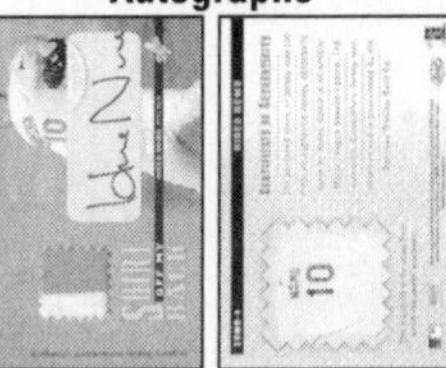

	MINT	NRMT

RANDOM INSERTS IN PACKS
STATED PRINT RUN 5 SERIAL #'d SETS
NO PRICING DUE TO SCARCITY

2004 Leaf Shirt Off My Back Team Logo Patch

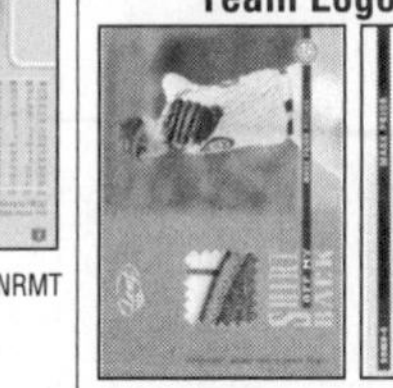

RANDOM INSERTS IN PACKS
PRINT RUNS B/WN 7-75 COPIES PER
NO PRICING ON QTY OF 25 OR LESS.

	Nm-Mt	Ex-Mt
1 Shawn Green/41	20.00	6.00
2 Andruw Jones/75	15.00	4.50
3 Ivan Rodriguez/75	25.00	7.50
4 Hideo Nomo/74	30.00	9.00
5 Don Mattingly/7		
6 Mark Prior/46	40.00	12.00
7 Alfonso Soriano/28	40.00	12.00
8 Richie Sexson/38	20.00	6.00
9 Vernon Wells/74	15.00	4.50
10 Nomar Garciaparra/75	30.00	9.00
11 Jason Giambi/26	40.00	12.00
12 Austin Kearns/32	25.00	7.50
13 Chipper Jones/75	25.00	7.50
14 Rickey Henderson/40	30.00	9.00
15 Alex Rodriguez/75	30.00	9.00
16 Garret Anderson/71	15.00	4.50
17 Vladimir Guerrero/55	25.00	7.50
18 Sammy Sosa/39	40.00	12.00
19 Mike Piazza/75	30.00	9.00
20 David Wells/74	15.00	4.50
21 Scott Rolen/29	40.00	12.00
22 Adam Dunn/32	25.00	7.50
23 Carlos Delgado/56	15.00	4.50
24 Greg Maddux/75	30.00	9.00
25 Hank Blalock/62	15.00	4.50

2004 Leaf Shirt Off My Back Team Logo Patch Autographs

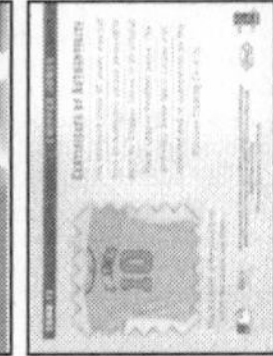

	Nm-Mt	Ex-Mt

RANDOM INSERTS IN PACKS
STATED PRINT RUN 5 SERIAL #'d SETS
NO PRICING DUE TO SCARCITY

2004 Leaf Sunday Dress

STATED ODDS 1:17

	Nm-Mt	Ex-Mt
1 Frank Thomas	2.50	.75
2 Barry Zito	2.00	.60
3 Mike Piazza	4.00	1.20
4 Mark Prior	5.00	1.50
5 Jeff Bagwell	2.00	.60
6 Roy Oswalt	2.00	.60
7 Todd Helton	2.00	.60
8 Magglio Ordonez	2.00	.60
9 Alex Rodriguez	4.00	1.20
10 Manny Ramirez	2.00	.60

2004 Leaf Sunday Dress Jerseys

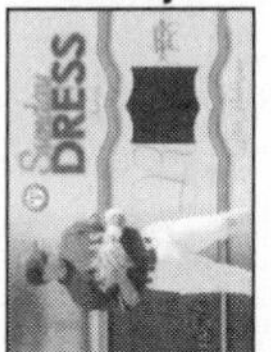

Nm-Mt Ex-Mt
STATED ODDS 1:119
*PRIME: .75X TO 2X BASIC
PRIME RANDOM INSERTS IN PACKS.
PRIME PRINT RUN 100 SERIAL #'d SETS
1 Frank Thomas 10.00 3.00
2 Barry Zito 10.00 3.00
3 Mike Piazza 10.00 3.00
4 Mark Prior 15.00 4.50
5 Jeff Bagwell 10.00 3.00
6 Roy Oswalt 8.00 2.40
7 Todd Helton 10.00 3.00
8 Magglio Ordonez 8.00 2.40
9 Alex Rodriguez 10.00 3.00
10 Manny Ramirez 8.00 2.40

2001 Leaf Certified Materials

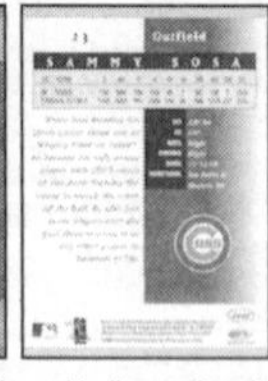

This 160 card set was issued in five card packs. Cards numbered 111-160 feature young players along with a piece of game-used memorabilia. These cards are serial numbered to 200.

Nm-Mt Ex-Mt
COMP.SET w/o SP's (110) 40.00 12.00
COMMON CARD (1-110) 1.00 .30
COMMON (111-160) 20.00 6.00
1 Alex Rodriguez 4.00 1.20
2 Barry Bonds 6.00 1.80
3 Cal Ripken 8.00 2.40
4 Chipper Jones 2.50 .75
5 Derek Jeter 6.00 1.80
6 Troy Glaus 1.50 .45
7 Frank Thomas 2.50 .75
8 Greg Maddux 4.00 1.20
9 Ivan Rodriguez 2.50 .75
10 Jeff Bagwell 1.50 .45
11 Eric Karros 1.00 .30
12 Todd Helton 1.50 .45
13 Ken Griffey Jr. 4.00 1.20
14 Manny Ramirez 1.00 .30
15 Mark McGwire 6.00 1.80
16 Mike Piazza 4.00 1.20
17 Nomar Garciaparra 4.00 1.20
18 Pedro Martinez 2.50 .75
19 Randy Johnson 2.50 .75
20 Rick Ankiel 1.00 .30
21 Rickey Henderson 2.50 .75
22 Roger Clemens 5.00 1.50
23 Sammy Sosa 4.00 1.20
24 Tony Gwynn 3.00 .90
25 Vladimir Guerrero 2.50 .75
26 Kazuhiro Sasaki 1.00 .30
27 Roberto Alomar 2.50 .75
28 Barry Zito 2.50 .75
29 Pat Burrell 1.00 .30
30 Harold Baines 1.00 .30
31 Carlos Delgado 1.00 .30
32 J.D. Drew 1.00 .30
33 Jim Edmonds 1.00 .30
34 Darin Erstad 1.00 .30
35 Jason Giambi 2.50 .75
36 Tom Glavine 1.50 .45
37 Juan Gonzalez 2.50 .75
38 Mark Grace 1.50 .45
39 Shawn Green 1.00 .30
40 Tim Hudson 1.00 .30
41 Andruw Jones 1.00 .30
42 Jeff Kent 1.00 .30
43 Barry Larkin 2.50 .75
44 Rafael Furcal 1.00 .30
45 Mike Mussina 2.50 .75
46 Hideo Nomo 2.50 .75
47 Rafael Palmeiro 1.50 .45
48 Scott Rolen 1.50 .45
49 Gary Sheffield 1.00 .30
50 Bernie Williams 1.50 .45
51 Bob Abreu 1.00 .30
52 Edgardo Alfonzo 1.00 .30
53 Edgar Martinez 1.50 .45
54 Magglio Ordonez 1.00 .30
55 Kerry Wood 2.50 .75
56 Adrian Beltre 1.00 .30
57 Lance Berkman 1.00 .30
58 Kevin Brown 1.00 .30
59 Sean Casey 1.00 .30
60 Eric Chavez 1.00 .30
61 Bartolo Colon 1.00 .30
62 Johnny Damon 1.00 .30
63 Jermaine Dye 1.00 .30
64 Juan Encarnacion UER 1.00 .30
Card has him playing for Detroit Lions
65 Carl Everett 1.00 .30
66 Brian Giles 1.00 .30
67 Mike Hampton 1.00 .30
68 Richard Hidalgo 1.00 .30
69 Geoff Jenkins 1.00 .30
70 Jacque Jones 1.00 .30
71 Jason Kendall 1.00 .30
72 Ryan Klesko 1.00 .30
73 Chan Ho Park 1.00 .30
74 Richie Sexson 1.00 .30
75 Mike Sweeney 1.00 .30
76 Fernando Tatis 1.00 .30
77 Miguel Tejada 1.00 .30
78 Jose Vidro 1.00 .30
79 Larry Walker 1.50 .45
80 Preston Wilson 1.00 .30
81 Craig Biggio 1.50 .45
82 Fred McGriff 1.50 .45
83 Jim Thome 2.50 .75
84 Garret Anderson 1.00 .30
85 Russell Branyan 1.00 .30
86 Tony Batista 1.00 .30
87 Terrence Long 1.00 .30
88 Deion Sanders 1.50 .45
89 Rusty Greer 1.00 .30
90 Orlando Hernandez 1.00 .30
91 Gabe Kapler 1.00 .30
92 Paul Konerko 1.00 .30
93 Carlos Lee 1.00 .30
94 Kenny Lofton 1.00 .30
95 Raul Mondesi 1.00 .30
96 Jorge Posada 1.50 .45
97 Tim Salmon 1.50 .45
98 Greg Vaughn 1.00 .30
99 Mo Vaughn 1.00 .30
100 Omar Vizquel 1.00 .30
101 Ray Durham 1.00 .30
102 Jeff Cirillo 1.00 .30
103 Dean Palmer 1.00 .30
104 Ryan Dempster 1.00 .30
105 Carlos Beltran 1.00 .30
106 Timo Perez 1.00 .30
107 Robin Ventura 1.00 .30
108 Andy Pettitte 1.50 .45
109 Aramis Ramirez 1.00 .30
110 Phil Nevin 1.00 .30
111 Alex Escobar FF 20.00 6.00
112 Johnny Estrada FF RC 25.00 7.50
113 Pedro Feliz FF 20.00 6.00
114 Nate Frese FF RC 20.00 6.00
115 Joe Kennedy FF RC 20.00 6.00
116 B. Larson FF RC 20.00 6.00
117 Alexis Gomez FF RC 20.00 6.00
118 Jason Hart FF 20.00 6.00
119 Jason Michaels FF RC 20.00 6.00
120 Marcus Giles FF 20.00 6.00
121 C. Parker FF RC 20.00 6.00
122 Jackson Melian FF RC 20.00 6.00
123 D. Mendez FF RC 20.00 6.00
124 A. Hernandez FF RC 20.00 6.00
125 Bud Smith FF RC 20.00 6.00
126 Jose Mieses FF RC 20.00 6.00
127 Roy Oswalt FF 25.00 7.50
128 Eric Munson FF 20.00 6.00
129 Xavier Nady FF 20.00 6.00
130 H. Ramirez FF RC 25.00 7.50
131 Abraham Nunez FF 20.00 6.00
132 Jose Ortiz FF 20.00 6.00
133 Jeremy Owens FF RC 20.00 6.00
134 Claudio Vargas FF RC 20.00 6.00
135 R. Rodriguez FF RC 20.00 6.00
136 Aubrey Huff FF 20.00 6.00
137 Ben Sheets FF 20.00 6.00
138 Adam Dunn FF 20.00 6.00
139 Andres Torres FF RC 20.00 6.00
140 Elpidio Guzman FF RC 20.00 6.00
141 Jay Gibbons FF RC 25.00 7.50
142 Wilkin Ruan FF RC 20.00 6.00
143 T. Shinjo FF RC 25.00 7.50
144 Alfonso Soriano FF 25.00 7.50
145 Josh Towers FF RC 20.00 6.00
146 Ichiro Suzuki FF RC 120.00 36.00
147 Juan Uribe FF RC 20.00 6.00
148 Joe Crede FF 20.00 6.00
149 C. Valderrama FF RC 20.00 6.00
150 Matt White FF RC 20.00 6.00
151 Dee Brown FF 20.00 6.00
152 Juan Cruz FF RC 20.00 6.00
153 Cory Aldridge FF RC 20.00 6.00
154 Wilmy Caceres FF RC 20.00 6.00
155 Josh Beckett FF 25.00 7.50
156 Wilson Betemit FF RC 20.00 6.00
157 Corey Patterson FF 20.00 6.00
158 Albert Pujols FF RC 150.00 45.00
159 Rafael Soriano FF RC 30.00 9.00
160 Jack Wilson FF RC 20.00 6.00

2001 Leaf Certified Materials Mirror Gold

Randomly inserted into packs, these 160 cards parallel the basic Leaf Certified Material set. Each card is serial numbered to 25.

Nm-Mt Ex-Mt
*STARS 1-110: 10X TO 25X BASIC CARDS

2001 Leaf Certified Materials Mirror Red

Randomly inserted into packs, these 160 cards parallel the basic Leaf Certified Material set. Each card is serial numbered to 75. An exchange card with a redemption deadline of November 1st, 2003 was seeded into packs for card 125 Bud Smith.

Nm-Mt Ex-Mt
*STARS 1-110: 4X TO 10X BASIC CARDS
111 Alex Escobar FF AU 25.00 7.50
112 Johnny Estrada FF AU 40.00 12.00
113 Pedro Feliz FF AU 25.00 7.50
114 Nate Frese FF AU 25.00 7.50
115 Joe Kennedy FF 20.00 6.00
116 B. Larson FF AU 25.00 7.50
117 Alexis Gomez FF AU 25.00 7.50
118 Jason Hart FF AU 25.00 7.50
119 Jason Michaels FF AU 25.00 7.50
120 Marcus Giles FF AU 25.00 7.50
121 C. Parker FF AU 25.00 7.50
122 Jackson Melian FF 20.00 6.00
123 D. Mendez FF AU 25.00 7.50
124 A. Hernandez FF AU 25.00 7.50
125 B. Smith FF AU EXCH 25.00 7.50
126 Jose Mieses FF AU 25.00 7.50
127 Roy Oswalt FF AU 40.00 12.00
128 Eric Munson FF 20.00 6.00
129 Xavier Nady FF AU 25.00 7.50
130 H. Ramirez FF AU 60.00 18.00
131 A. Nunez FF AU 25.00 7.50
132 Jose Ortiz FF AU 25.00 7.50
133 Jeremy Owens FF AU 25.00 7.50
134 Claudio Vargas FF AU 25.00 7.50
135 R. Rodriguez FF AU 25.00 7.50
136 Aubrey Huff FF AU 25.00 7.50
137 Ben Sheets FF AU 25.00 7.50
138 Adam Dunn FF AU 40.00 12.00
139 Andres Torres FF AU 25.00 7.50
140 Elpidio Guzman FF AU 25.00 7.50
141 Jay Gibbons FF AU 40.00 12.00
142 Wilkin Ruan FF AU 25.00 7.50
143 Tsuyoshi Shinjo FF 40.00 12.00
144 A. Soriano FF AU 80.00 24.00
145 Josh Towers FF AU 25.00 7.50
146 Ichiro Suzuki FF 200.00 60.00
147 Juan Uribe FF AU 25.00 7.50
148 Joe Crede FF AU 25.00 7.50
149 C. Valderrama FF AU 25.00 7.50
150 Matt White FF AU 25.00 7.50
151 Dee Brown FF AU 25.00 7.50
152 Juan Cruz FF AU 25.00 7.50
153 Cory Aldridge FF AU 25.00 7.50
154 Wilmy Caceres FF AU 25.00 7.50
155 Josh Beckett FF AU 50.00 15.00
156 Wilson Betemit FF AU 25.00 7.50
157 C. Patterson FF AU 25.00 7.50
158 Albert Pujols FF AU 300.00 90.00
159 Rafael Soriano FF AU 50.00 15.00
160 Jack Wilson FF AU 25.00 7.50

2001 Leaf Certified Materials Fabric of the Game

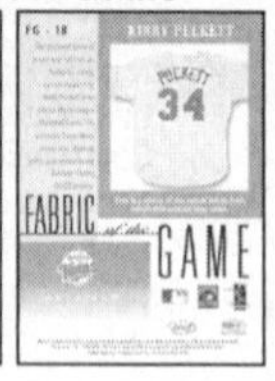

Randomly inserted into packs, 118 players are featured in this set. Each player has a base card as well as cards serial numbered to a key career stat, jersey number, a key seasonal stat or a Century card. All the Century cards are serial numbered to 21. Certain players had less basic cards issued, these cards are notated with an SP and according to the manufacturer less than 100 of these cards were produced. In addition, exchange cards with a redemption deadline of November 1st, 2003 were seeded into packs for the following: Jeff Bagwell CE AU, Ernie Banks JN AU, Roger Clemens JN AU, Vladimir Guerrero JN AU, Tony Gwynn CE AU, Don Mattingly CE AU, Kirby Puckett JN AU, Nolan Ryan CE AU, Ryne Sandberg CE AU and Mike Schmidt JN AU.

Nm-Mt Ex-Mt
1BA Lou Gehrig SP
1CE Lou Gehrig/21
1CR Lou Gehrig/23
1JN Lou Gehrig/4
1SN Lou Gehrig/184 250.00 75.00
2BA Babe Ruth SP
2CE Babe Ruth/21
2CR Babe Ruth/136 300.00 90.00
2JN Babe Ruth/3
2SN Babe Ruth/60 500.00 150.00
3BA Stan Musial SP 80.00 24.00
3CE Stan Musial/21
3CR Stan Musial/177 50.00 15.00
3JN Stan Musial/6
3SN Stan Musial/39 120.00 36.00
4BA Nolan Ryan 50.00 15.00
4CE Nolan Ryan AU/21
4CR Nolan Ryan/61 100.00 30.00
4JN Nolan Ryan/34 120.00 36.00
4SN Nolan Ryan/22
5BA Roberto Clemente SP
5CE Roberto Clemente/21
5CR R. Clemente/166 120.00 36.00
5JN Roberto Clemente/21
5SN Roberto Clemente/29 300.00 90.00
6BA Al Kaline SP 40.00 12.00
6CE Al Kaline/21
6CR Al Kaline/137 40.00 12.00
6JN Al Kaline/6
6SN Al Kaline/29 80.00 24.00
7BA Brooks Robinson 25.00 7.50
7CE Brooks Robinson/21
7CR Brooks Robinson/68 40.00 12.00
7JN Brooks Robinson/5
7SN Brooks Robinson/28 80.00 24.00
8BA Mel Ott 50.00 15.00
8CE Mel Ott/21
8CR Mel Ott/72 60.00 18.00
8JN Mel Ott/4
8SN Mel Ott/42 80.00 24.00
9BA Dave Winfield SP 25.00 7.50
9CE Dave Winfield/21
9CR Dave Winfield/88 25.00 7.50
9JN Dave Winfield/31 40.00 12.00
9SN Dave Winfield/37 40.00 12.00
10BA Eddie Mathews SP 40.00 12.00
10CE Eddie Mathews/21
10CR Eddie Mathews/72 40.00 12.00
10JN Eddie Mathews/41 60.00 18.00
10SN Eddie Mathews/47 60.00 18.00
11BA Ernie Banks 25.00 7.50
11CE Ernie Banks/21
11CR Ernie Banks/50 40.00 12.00
11JN Ernie Banks AU/14
11SN Ernie Banks/47 60.00 18.00
12BA Frank Robinson SP 40.00 12.00
12CE Frank Robinson/21
12CR Frank Robinson/72 40.00 12.00
12JN Frank Robinson/20
12SN Frank Robinson/49 60.00 18.00
13BA George Brett SP 80.00 24.00
13CE George Brett/21
13CR George Brett/137 50.00 15.00
13JN George Brett/5
13SN George Brett/30 120.00 36.00
14BA Hank Aaron SP 120.00 36.00
14CE Hank Aaron/21
14CR Hank Aaron/98 80.00 24.00
14JN Hank Aaron/44 200.00 60.00
14SN Hank Aaron/47 150.00 45.00
15BA Harmon Killebrew 25.00 7.50
15CE Harmon Killebrew/21
15CR Harmon Killebrew/24
15JN Harmon Killebrew/3
15SN H. Killebrew/49 60.00 18.00
16BA Joe Morgan SP 25.00 7.50
16CE Joe Morgan/21
16CR Joe Morgan/96 25.00 7.50
16JN Joe Morgan/8
16SN Joe Morgan/27 50.00 15.00
17BA Johnny Bench 25.00 7.50
17CE Johnny Bench/21
17CR Johnny Bench/68 40.00 12.00
17JN Johnny Bench/5
17SN Johnny Bench/45 60.00 18.00
18BA Kirby Puckett SP 40.00 12.00
18CE Kirby Puckett/21
18CR Kirby Puckett/134 40.00 12.00
18JN Kirby Puckett AU/34 200.00 60.00
18SN Kirby Puckett/31 80.00 24.00
19BA Mike Schmidt SP 50.00 15.00
19CE Mike Schmidt/21
19CR Mike Schmidt/59 60.00 18.00
19JN Mike Schmidt AU/20
19SN Mike Schmidt/48 80.00 24.00
20BA Phil Rizzuto SP 40.00 12.00
20CE Phil Rizzuto/21
20CR Phil Rizzuto/149 40.00 12.00
20JN Phil Rizzuto/10
20SN Phil Rizzuto/7
21BA Reggie Jackson SP 40.00 12.00
21CE Reggie Jackson/21
21CR Reggie Jackson/49 60.00 18.00
21JN Reggie Jackson/44 60.00 18.00
21SN Reggie Jackson/47 60.00 18.00
22BA Jim Hunter 25.00 7.50
22CE Jim Hunter/21
22CR Jim Hunter/42 60.00 18.00
22JN Jim Hunter/27 80.00 24.00
22SN Jim Hunter/25
23BA Rod Carew SP 40.00 12.00
23CE Rod Carew/21
23CR Rod Carew/92 40.00 12.00
23JN Rod Carew/29 80.00 24.00
23SN Rod Carew/100 40.00 12.00
24BA Bob Feller 25.00 7.50
24CE Bob Feller/21
24CR Bob Feller/44 60.00 18.00
24JN Bob Feller/19
24SN Bob Feller/36 60.00 18.00
25BA Lou Brock SP 40.00 12.00
25CE Lou Brock/21
25CR Lou Brock/141 40.00 12.00
25JN Lou Brock/20
25SN Lou Brock/21
26BA Tom Seaver SP 40.00 12.00
26CE Tom Seaver/21
26CR Tom Seaver/61 40.00 12.00
26JN Tom Seaver/41 60.00 18.00
26SN Tom Seaver/25
27BA Paul Molitor SP 40.00 12.00
27CE Paul Molitor/21
27CR Paul Molitor/114 40.00 12.00
27JN Paul Molitor/4
27SN Paul Molitor/41 60.00 18.00
28BA Willie McCovey SP 25.00 7.50
28CE Willie McCovey/21
28CR Willie McCovey/18
28JN Willie McCovey/44 40.00 12.00
28SN Willie McCovey/126 25.00 7.50
29BA Yogi Berra 25.00 7.50
29CE Yogi Berra/21
29CR Yogi Berra/49 60.00 18.00
29JN Yogi Berra/35 80.00 24.00
29SN Yogi Berra/30 80.00 24.00
30BA Don Drysdale SP 40.00 12.00
30CE Don Drysdale/21
30CR Don Drysdale/49 60.00 18.00
30JN Don Drysdale/53 40.00 12.00
30SN Don Drysdale/25
31BA Duke Snider SP 40.00 12.00
31CE Duke Snider/21
31CR Duke Snider/99 40.00 12.00
31JN Duke Snider/4
31SN Duke Snider/43 60.00 18.00
32BA Does Not Exist
32CE Does Not Exist
32CR Does Not Exist
32JN Does Not Exist
32SN Does Not Exist
33BA Orlando Cepeda 15.00 4.50
33CE Orlando Cepeda/21
33CR Orlando Cepeda/27 50.00 15.00
33JN Orlando Cepeda/30 50.00 15.00
33SN Orlando Cepeda/46 40.00 12.00
34BA Casey Stengel SP 40.00 12.00
34CE Casey Stengel/21
34CR Casey Stengel/10
34JN Casey Stengel/37 60.00 18.00
34SN Casey Stengel/103 40.00 12.00
35BA Robin Yount SP 40.00 12.00
35CE Robin Yount/21
35CR Robin Yount/126 40.00 12.00
35JN Robin Yount/19
35SN Robin Yount/29 80.00 24.00
36BA Eddie Murray 25.00 7.50
36CE Eddie Murray/21
36CR Eddie Murray/35 80.00 24.00
36JN Eddie Murray/22
36SN Eddie Murray/33 80.00 24.00
37BA Jim Palmer 15.00 4.50
37CE Jim Palmer/21
37CR Jim Palmer/53 25.00 7.50
37JN Jim Palmer/22
37SN Jim Palmer/23
38BA Juan Marichal 15.00 4.50
38CE Juan Marichal/21
38CR Juan Marichal/52 25.00 7.50
38JN Juan Marichal/27 50.00 15.00
38SN Juan Marichal/26 50.00 15.00
39BA Willie Stargell 25.00 7.50
39CE Willie Stargell/21
39CR Willie Stargell/55 40.00 12.00
39JN Willie Stargell/8
39SN Willie Stargell/48 60.00 18.00
40BA Ted Williams SP 150.00 45.00
40CE Ted Williams/21
40CR Ted Williams/71 150.00 45.00
40JN Ted Williams/9
40SN Ted Williams/43 200.00 60.00
41BA Cal Ripken 40.00 12.00
41CE Cal Ripken/21
41CR Cal Ripken/277 50.00 15.00
41JN Cal Ripken/8
41SN Cal Ripken/114 100.00 30.00
42BA V. Guerrero SP 25.00 7.50
42CE Vladimir Guerrero/21
42CR V. Guerrero/322 15.00 4.50
42JN Vladimir Guerrero AU/27 EXCH
42SN V. Guerrero/44 50.00 15.00
43BA Greg Maddux 25.00 7.50
43CE Greg Maddux/21
43CR Greg Maddux/240 25.00 7.50
43JN Greg Maddux/31 80.00 24.00
43SN Greg Maddux/20
44BA Barry Bonds 30.00 9.00
44CE Barry Bonds/21
44CR Barry Bonds/289 40.00 12.00
44JN Barry Bonds/25
44SN Barry Bonds/49 100.00 30.00
45BA Pedro Martinez 15.00 4.50
45CE Pedro Martinez/21
45CR Pedro Martinez/268 15.00 4.50
45JN Pedro Martinez/45 50.00 15.00
45SN Pedro Martinez/23
46BA Ivan Rodriguez 15.00 4.50
46CE Ivan Rodriguez/21
46CR Ivan Rodriguez/304 15.00 4.50
46JN Ivan Rodriguez/7
46SN Ivan Rodriguez/35 60.00 18.00
47BA Roger Maris 50.00 15.00
47CE Roger Maris/21
47CR Roger Maris/275 50.00 15.00
47JN Roger Maris/3
47SN Roger Maris/61 100.00 30.00
48BA Randy Johnson 15.00 4.50
48CE Randy Johnson/21
48CR Randy Johnson/179 15.00 4.50
48JN Randy Johnson/51 40.00 12.00
48SN Randy Johnson/20
49BA Roger Clemens 25.00 7.50
49CE Roger Clemens/21
49CR Roger Clemens/260 30.00 9.00
49JN Roger Clemens AU/22
49SN Roger Clemens/24
50BA Todd Helton 15.00 4.50
50CE Todd Helton/21
50CR Todd Helton/334 15.00 4.50
50JN Todd Helton/17
50SN Todd Helton/42 50.00 15.00
51BA Tony Gwynn 15.00 4.50
51CE Tony Gwynn AU/21
51CR Tony Gwynn/134 40.00 12.00
51JN Tony Gwynn/19
51SN Tony Gwynn/119 40.00 12.00
52BA Troy Glaus 15.00 4.50
52CE Troy Glaus/21
52CR Troy Glaus/256 15.00 4.50
52JN Troy Glaus/25
52SN Troy Glaus/47 50.00 15.00
53BA Phil Niekro 15.00 4.50
53CE Phil Niekro/21
53CR Phil Niekro/245 15.00 4.50
53JN Phil Niekro/35 50.00 15.00
53SN Phil Niekro/23
54BA Don Sutton 15.00 4.50
54CE Don Sutton/21
54CR Don Sutton/178 15.00 4.50
54JN Don Sutton/20
54SN Don Sutton/21
55BA Frank Thomas 15.00 4.50
55CE Frank Thomas/21
55CR Frank Thomas/321 15.00 4.50
55JN Frank Thomas/35 60.00 18.00
55SN Frank Thomas/43 50.00 15.00
56BA Jeff Bagwell 15.00 4.50
56CE Jeff Bagwell AU/21
56CR Jeff Bagwell/305 15.00 4.50
56JN Jeff Bagwell/5
56SN Jeff Bagwell/135 25.00 7.50
57BA Rickey Henderson 15.00 4.50
57CE Rickey Henderson/21
57CR R. Henderson/282 15.00 4.50
57JN R. Henderson/35 60.00 18.00
57SN R. Henderson/28 60.00 18.00
58BA Darin Erstad SP 15.00 4.50
58CE Darin Erstad/21
58CR Darin Erstad/301 10.00 3.00
58JN Darin Erstad/17
58SN Darin Erstad/100 15.00 4.50
59BA Andruw Jones 10.00 3.00
59CE Andruw Jones/21
59CR Andruw Jones/272 10.00 3.00
59JN Andruw Jones/25
59SN Andruw Jones/36 30.00 9.00
60BA Roberto Alomar 15.00 4.50
60CE Roberto Alomar/21
60CR Roberto Alomar/170 15.00 4.50
60JN Roberto Alomar/12
60SN Roberto Alomar/120 25.00 7.50
61BA Mike Piazza SP 40.00 12.00
61CE Mike Piazza/21
61CR Mike Piazza/328 25.00 7.50
61JN Mike Piazza/31 80.00 24.00
61SN Mike Piazza/40 80.00 24.00
62BA Chipper Jones 15.00 4.50
62CE Chipper Jones/21
62CR Chipper Jones/189 15.00 4.50
62JN Chipper Jones/10
62SN Chipper Jones/45 50.00 15.00
63BA Shawn Green 10.00 3.00
63CE Shawn Green/21
63CR Shawn Green/143 15.00 4.50
63JN Shawn Green/15
63SN Shawn Green/123 15.00 4.50
64BA Don Mattingly SP 80.00 24.00
64CE Don Mattingly AU/21
64CR Don Mattingly/222 40.00 12.00
64JN Don Mattingly/23
64SN Don Mattingly/145 60.00 18.00
65BA Rafael Palmeiro 15.00 4.50
65CE Rafael Palmeiro/21
65CR Rafael Palmeiro/296 15.00 4.50
65JN Rafael Palmeiro/25
65SN Rafael Palmeiro/47 50.00 15.00
66BA Wade Boggs 25.00 7.50
66CE Wade Boggs/21
66CR Wade Boggs/116 40.00 12.00
66JN Wade Boggs/26 80.00 24.00
66SN Wade Boggs/89 40.00 12.00
67BA Hoyt Wilhelm 15.00 4.50
67CE Hoyt Wilhelm/21
67CR Hoyt Wilhelm/143 25.00 7.50
67JN Hoyt Wilhelm/31 50.00 15.00
67SN Hoyt Wilhelm/27 50.00 15.00
68BA Andre Dawson 15.00 4.50
68CE Andre Dawson/21
68CR Andre Dawson/314 15.00 4.50
68JN Andre Dawson/8
68SN Andre Dawson/49 40.00 12.00
69BA Ryne Sandberg 40.00 12.00
69CE Ryne Sandberg AU/21
69CR Ryne Sandberg/282 25.00 7.50
69JN Ryne Sandberg/23
69SN Ryne Sandberg/40 80.00 24.00
70BA N.Garciaparra SP 40.00 12.00
70CE Nomar Garciaparra/21

70CR N.Garciaparra/333 25.00 7.50
70JN Nomar Garciaparra/5
70SN N.Garciaparra/35 100.00 30.00
71BA Tom Glavine 15.00 4.50
71CE Tom Glavine/21
71CR Tom Glavine/208 15.00 4.50
71JN Tom Glavine/47 50.00 15.00
71SN Tom Glavine/247 15.00 4.50
72BA Magglio Ordonez 10.00 3.00
72CE Magglio Ordonez/21
72CR M.Ordonez/301 10.00 3.00
72JN Magglio Ordonez/30 40.00 12.00
72SN Magglio Ordonez/126 15.00 4.50
73BA Bernie Williams 15.00 4.50
73CE Bernie Williams/21
73CR Bernie Williams/304 15.00 4.50
73JN Bernie Williams/51 40.00 12.00
73SN Bernie Williams/30 60.00 18.00
74BA Jim Edmonds 10.00 3.00
74CE Jim Edmonds/21
74CR Jim Edmonds/291 10.00 3.00
74JN Jim Edmonds/15
74SN Jim Edmonds/108 15.00 4.50
75BA Hideo Nomo 50.00 15.00
75CE Hideo Nomo/21
75CR Hideo Nomo/69 100.00 30.00
75JN Hideo Nomo/11
75SN Hideo Nomo/16
76BA Barry Larkin 15.00 4.50
76CE Barry Larkin/21
76CR Barry Larkin/300 15.00 4.50
76JN Barry Larkin/11
76SN Barry Larkin/33 60.00 18.00
77BA Scott Rolen 15.00 4.50
77CE Scott Rolen/21
77CR Scott Rolen/284 15.00 4.50
77JN Scott Rolen/17
77SN Scott Rolen/31 60.00 18.00
78BA Miguel Tejada 10.00 3.00
78CE Miguel Tejada/21
78CR Miguel Tejada/253 10.00 3.00
78JN Miguel Tejada/4
78SN Miguel Tejada/30 40.00 12.00
79BA Freddy Garcia 10.00 3.00
79CE Freddy Garcia/21
79CR Freddy Garcia/249 10.00 3.00
79JN Freddy Garcia/34 40.00 12.00
79SN Freddy Garcia/170 10.00 3.00
80BA Edgar Martinez 15.00 4.50
80CE Edgar Martinez/21
80CR Edgar Martinez/320 15.00 4.50
80JN Edgar Martinez/11
80SN Edgar Martinez/37 50.00 15.00
81BA Edgardo Alfonzo 10.00 3.00
81CE Edgardo Alfonzo/21
81CR E. Alfonzo/296 10.00 3.00
81JN Edgardo Alfonzo/13
81SN E. Alfonzo/108 15.00 4.50
82BA Steve Garvey 15.00 4.50
82CE Steve Garvey/21
82CR Steve Garvey/272 15.00 4.50
82JN Steve Garvey/6
82SN Steve Garvey/33 50.00 15.00
83BA Larry Walker 15.00 4.50
83CE Larry Walker/21
83CR Larry Walker/311 15.00 4.50
83JN Larry Walker/12
83SN Larry Walker/49 50.00 15.00
84BA A.J. Burnett 10.00 3.00
84CE A.J. Burnett/21
84CR A.J. Burnett/90 15.00 4.50
84JN A.J. Burnett/43 30.00 9.00
84SN A.J. Burnett/57 25.00 7.50
85BA Richie Sexson 10.00 3.00
85CE Richie Sexson/21
85CR Richie Sexson/242 10.00 3.00
85JN Richie Sexson/11
85SN Richie Sexson/116 15.00 4.50
86BA Mark Mulder 10.00 3.00
86CE Mark Mulder/21
86CR Mark Mulder/88 15.00 4.50
86JN Mark Mulder/20
86SN Mark Mulder/9
87BA Kerry Wood 15.00 4.50
87CE Kerry Wood/21
87CR Kerry Wood/21
87JN Kerry Wood/34 60.00 18.00
87SN Kerry Wood/233 15.00 4.50
88BA Sean Casey 10.00 3.00
88CE Sean Casey/21
88CR Sean Casey/312 10.00 3.00
88JN Sean Casey/21
88SN Sean Casey/25
89BA Jermaine Dye SP 15.00 4.50
89CE Jermaine Dye/21
89CR Jermaine Dye/286 10.00 3.00
89JN Jermaine Dye/24
89SN Jermaine Dye/118 15.00 4.50
90BA Kevin Brown SP 15.00 4.50
90CE Kevin Brown/21
90CR Kevin Brown/170 10.00 3.00
90JN Kevin Brown/27 40.00 12.00
90SN Kevin Brown/257 10.00 3.00
91BA Craig Biggio 15.00 4.50
91CE Craig Biggio/21
91CR Craig Biggio/291 15.00 4.50
91JN Craig Biggio/7
91SN Craig Biggio/88 25.00 7.50
92BA Mike Sweeney SP 15.00 4.50
92CE Mike Sweeney/21
92CR Mike Sweeney/302 10.00 3.00
92JN Mike Sweeney/29 40.00 12.00
92SN Mike Sweeney/144 15.00 4.50
93BA Jim Thome 15.00 4.50
93CE Jim Thome/21
93CR Jim Thome/233 15.00 4.50
93JN Jim Thome/25
93SN Jim Thome/40 50.00 15.00
94BA Al Leiter 10.00 3.00
94CE Al Leiter/21
94CR Al Leiter/106 15.00 4.50
94JN Al Leiter/22
94SN Al Leiter/247 10.00 3.00
95BA Barry Zito 15.00 4.50
95CE Barry Zito/21
95CR Barry Zito/272 15.00 4.50
95JN Barry Zito/75 25.00 7.50
95SN Barry Zito/78 25.00 7.50
96BA Rafael Furcal 10.00 3.00
96CE Rafael Furcal/21
96CR Rafael Furcal/295 10.00 3.00
96JN Rafael Furcal/1
96SN Rafael Furcal/37 30.00 9.00
97BA J.D. Drew 10.00 3.00
97CE J.D. Drew/21
97CR J.D. Drew/276 10.00 3.00
97JN J.D. Drew/7
97SN J.D. Drew/18
98BA Andres Galarraga 10.00 3.00
98CE Andres Galarraga/21
98CR A. Galarraga/291 10.00 3.00
98JN Andres Galarraga/14
98SN A. Galarraga/150 10.00 3.00
99BA Kazuhiro Sasaki 10.00 3.00
99CE Kazuhiro Sasaki/21
99CR Kazuhiro Sasaki/266 10.00 3.00
99JN Kazuhiro Sasaki/22
99SN Kazuhiro Sasaki/45 30.00 9.00
100BA Chan Ho Park 10.00 3.00
100CE Chan Ho Park/21
100CR Chan Ho Park/65 25.00 7.50
100JN Chan Ho Park/61 25.00 7.50
100SN Chan Ho Park/217 10.00 3.00
101BA Eric Milton 10.00 3.00
101CE Eric Milton/21
101CR Eric Milton/28 40.00 12.00
101JN Eric Milton/21
101SN Eric Milton/163 10.00 3.00
102BA Carlos Lee 10.00 3.00
102CE Carlos Lee/21
102CR Carlos Lee/297 10.00 3.00
102JN Carlos Lee/45 30.00 9.00
102SN Carlos Lee/24
103BA Preston Wilson 10.00 3.00
103CE Preston Wilson/21
103CR P. Wilson/266 10.00 3.00
103JN Preston Wilson/44 30.00 9.00
103SN Preston Wilson/31 40.00 12.00
104BA Adrian Beltre 10.00 3.00
104CE Adrian Beltre/21
104CR Adrian Beltre/272 10.00 3.00
104JN Adrian Beltre/29 40.00 12.00
104SN Adrian Beltre/85 15.00 4.50
105BA Luis Gonzalez 10.00 3.00
105CE Luis Gonzalez/21
105CR Luis Gonzalez/281 10.00 3.00
105JN Luis Gonzalez/20
105SN Luis Gonzalez/114 15.00 4.50
106BA Kenny Lofton 10.00 3.00
106CE Kenny Lofton/21
106CR Kenny Lofton/306 10.00 3.00
106JN Kenny Lofton/7
106SN Kenny Lofton/15
107BA Shannon Stewart 10.00 3.00
107CE Shannon Stewart/21
107CR S. Stewart/297 10.00 3.00
107JN Shannon Stewart/24
107SN Shannon Stewart/21
108BA Javy Lopez 10.00 3.00
108CE Javy Lopez/21
108CR Javy Lopez/290 10.00 3.00
108JN Javy Lopez/8
108SN Javy Lopez/106 15.00 4.50
109BA Raul Mondesi 10.00 3.00
109CE Raul Mondesi/21
109CR Raul Mondesi/286 10.00 3.00
109JN Raul Mondesi/43 30.00 9.00
109SN Raul Mondesi/33 40.00 12.00
110BA Mark Grace 15.00 4.50
110CE Mark Grace/21
110CR Mark Grace/308 15.00 4.50
110JN Mark Grace/17
110SN Mark Grace/51 40.00 12.00
111BA Curt Schilling 15.00 4.50
111CE Curt Schilling/21
111CR Curt Schilling/110 25.00 7.50
111JN Curt Schilling/38 50.00 15.00
111SN Curt Schilling/235 15.00 4.50
112BA Cliff Floyd 10.00 3.00
112CE Cliff Floyd/21
112CR Cliff Floyd/275 10.00 3.00
112JN Cliff Floyd/30 40.00 12.00
112SN Cliff Floyd/22
113BA Moises Alou 10.00 3.00
113CE Moises Alou/21
113CR Moises Alou/303 10.00 3.00
113JN Moises Alou/18
113SN Moises Alou/124 15.00 4.50
114BA Aaron Sele 10.00 3.00
114CE Aaron Sele/21
114CR Aaron Sele/92 15.00 4.50
114JN Aaron Sele/30 40.00 12.00
114SN Aaron Sele/19
115BA Jose Cruz Jr. 10.00 3.00
115CE Jose Cruz Jr./21
115CR Jose Cruz Jr./245 10.00 3.00
115JN Jose Cruz Jr./23
115SN Jose Cruz Jr./31 40.00 12.00
116BA John Olerud 10.00 3.00
116CE John Olerud/21
116CR John Olerud/186 10.00 3.00
116JN John Olerud/5
116SN John Olerud/107 15.00 4.50
117BA Jose Vidro 10.00 3.00
117CE Jose Vidro/21
117CR Jose Vidro/296 10.00 3.00
117JN Jose Vidro/3
117SN Jose Vidro/24
118BA John Smoltz 15.00 4.50
118CE John Smoltz/21
118CR John Smoltz/335 15.00 4.50
118JN John Smoltz/29 60.00 18.00
118SN John Smoltz/24

2002 Leaf Certified

This 200-card set was released in early September, 2002. It was issued in five card packs which came 12 packs to a box and six boxes to a case. The first 150 card featured veteran stars while the final 50 cards features rookies and prospects along with a game-used memorabilia piece for each of them. Those final fifty cards have a stated print run of 500 serial numbered sets.

Nm-Mt Ex-Mt
COMP.SET w/o SP's (150) 80.00 24.00
COMMON CARD (1-150) 1.00 .30
COMMON CARD (151-200) 10.00 3.00
1 Alex Rodriguez 4.00 1.20
2 Luis Gonzalez 1.00 .30
3 Javier Vazquez 1.00 .30
4 Juan Uribe 1.00 .30
5 Ben Sheets 1.00 .30
6 George Brett 6.00 1.80
7 Magglio Ordonez 1.00 .30
8 Randy Johnson 2.50 .75
9 Joe Kennedy 1.00 .30
10 Richie Sexson 1.00 .30
11 Larry Walker 1.50 .45
12 Lance Berkman 1.00 .30
13 Jose Cruz Jr. 1.00 .30
14 Doug Davis 1.00 .30
15 Cliff Floyd 1.00 .30
16 Ryan Klesko 1.00 .30
17 Troy Glaus 1.50 .45
18 Robert Person 1.00 .30
19 Bartolo Colon 1.00 .30
20 Adam Dunn 1.00 .30
21 Kevin Brown 1.00 .30
22 John Smoltz 1.50 .45
23 Edgar Martinez 1.50 .45
24 Eric Karros 1.00 .30
25 Tony Gwynn 3.00 .90
26 Mark Mulder 1.00 .30
27 Don Mattingly 6.00 1.80
28 Brandon Duckworth 1.00 .30
29 C.C. Sabathia 1.00 .30
30 Nomar Garciaparra 4.00 1.20
31 Adam Johnson 1.00 .30
32 Miguel Tejada 1.00 .30
33 Ryne Sandberg 5.00 1.50
34 Roger Clemens 5.00 1.50
35 Edgardo Alfonzo 1.00 .30
36 Jason Jennings 1.00 .30
37 Todd Helton 1.50 .45
38 Nolan Ryan 6.00 1.80
39 Paul LoDuca 1.00 .30
40 Cal Ripken 8.00 2.40
41 Terrence Long 1.00 .30
42 Mike Sweeney 1.00 .30
43 Carlos Lee 1.00 .30
44 Ben Grieve 1.00 .30
45 Tony Armas Jr. 1.00 .30
46 Joe Mays 1.00 .30
47 Jeff Kent 1.00 .30
48 Andy Pettitte 1.50 .45
49 Kirby Puckett 2.50 .75
50 Aramis Ramirez 1.00 .30
51 Tim Redding 1.00 .30
52 Freddy Garcia 1.00 .30
53 Javy Lopez 1.00 .30
54 Mike Schmidt 6.00 1.80
55 Wade Miller 1.00 .30
56 Ramon Ortiz 1.00 .30
57 Ray Durham 1.00 .30
58 J.D. Drew 1.00 .30
59 Bret Boone 1.00 .30
60 Mark Buehrle 1.00 .30
61 Geoff Jenkins 1.00 .30
62 Greg Maddux 4.00 1.20
63 Mark Grace 1.50 .45
64 Toby Hall 1.00 .30
65 A.J. Burnett 1.00 .30
66 Bernie Williams 1.50 .45
67 Roy Oswalt 1.00 .30
68 Shannon Stewart 1.00 .30
69 Barry Zito 1.50 .45
70 Juan Pierre 1.00 .30
71 Preston Wilson 1.00 .30
72 Rafael Furcal 1.00 .30
73 Sean Casey 1.00 .30
74 John Olerud 1.00 .30
75 Paul Konerko 1.00 .30
76 Vernon Wells 1.00 .30
77 Juan Gonzalez 2.50 .75
78 Ellis Burks 1.00 .30
79 Jim Edmonds 1.00 .30
80 Robert Fick 1.00 .30
81 Michael Cuddyer 1.00 .30
82 Tim Hudson 1.00 .30
83 Phil Nevin 1.00 .30
84 Curt Schilling 1.50 .45
85 Juan Cruz 1.00 .30
86 Jeff Bagwell 1.50 .45
87 Raul Mondesi 1.00 .30
88 Bud Smith 1.00 .30
89 Omar Vizquel 1.00 .30
90 Vladimir Guerrero 2.50 .75
91 Garret Anderson 1.00 .30
92 Mike Piazza 4.00 1.20
93 Josh Beckett 1.50 .45
94 Carlos Delgado 1.00 .30
95 Kazuhiro Sasaki 1.00 .30
96 Chipper Jones 2.50 .75
97 Jacque Jones 1.00 .30
98 Pedro Martinez 2.50 .75
99 Marcus Giles 1.00 .30
100 Craig Biggio 1.50 .45
101 Orlando Cabrera 1.00 .30
102 Al Leiter 1.00 .30
103 Michael Barrett 1.00 .30
104 Hideo Nomo 2.50 .75
105 Mike Mussina 2.50 .75
106 Jeremy Giambi 1.00 .30
107 Cristian Guzman 1.00 .30
108 Frank Thomas 2.50 .75
109 Carlos Beltran 1.00 .30
110 Jorge Posada 1.50 .45
111 Roberto Alomar 2.50 .75
112 Bob Abreu 1.00 .30
113 Robin Ventura 1.00 .30
114 Pat Burrell 1.00 .30
115 Kenny Lofton 1.00 .30
116 Adrian Beltre 1.00 .30
117 Gary Sheffield 1.00 .30
118 Jermaine Dye 1.00 .30
119 Manny Ramirez 1.00 .30
120 Brian Giles 1.00 .30
121 Tsuyoshi Shinjo 1.00 .30
122 Rafael Palmeiro 1.50 .45
123 Mo Vaughn UER 1.00 .30
Yankee Logo on back
124 Kerry Wood 2.50 .75
125 Moises Alou 1.00 .30
126 Rickey Henderson 2.50 .75
127 Corey Patterson 1.00 .30
128 Jim Thome 2.50 .75
129 Richard Hidalgo 1.00 .30
130 Darin Erstad 1.00 .30
131 Johnny Damon 1.00 .30
132 Juan Encarnacion 1.00 .30
133 Scott Rolen 1.50 .45
134 Tom Glavine 1.50 .45
135 Ivan Rodriguez 2.50 .75
136 Jay Gibbons 1.00 .30
137 Trot Nixon 1.50 .45
138 Nick Neugebauer 1.00 .30
139 Barry Larkin 2.50 .75
140 Andruw Jones 1.00 .30
141 Shawn Green 1.00 .30
142 Jose Vidro 1.00 .30
143 Derek Jeter 6.00 1.80
144 Ichiro Suzuki 4.00 1.20
145 Ken Griffey Jr. 4.00 1.20
146 Barry Bonds 6.00 1.80
147 Albert Pujols 5.00 1.50
148 Sammy Sosa 4.00 1.20
149 Jason Giambi 2.50 .75
150 Alfonso Soriano 1.50 .45
151 Drew Henson NG Bat 10.00 3.00
152 Luis Garcia NG Bat 10.00 3.00
153 Geronimo Gil NG Jsy 10.00 3.00
154 Corky Miller NG Jsy 10.00 3.00
155 Mike Rivera NG Bat 10.00 3.00
156 Mark Ellis NG Jsy 10.00 3.00
157 Josh Pearce NG Bat 10.00 3.00
158 Ryan Ludwick NG Bat 10.00 3.00
159 So Taguchi NG Bat RC 15.00 4.50
160 Cody Ransom NG Jsy 10.00 3.00
161 Jeff Deardorff NG Bat 10.00 3.00
162 Fr. German NG Bat RC 10.00 3.00
163 Ed Rogers NG Jsy 10.00 3.00
164 Eric Cyr NG Jsy 10.00 3.00
165 Victor Alvarez NG Jsy RC 10.00 3.00
166 Victor Martinez NG Jsy 10.00 3.00
167 Brandon Berger NG Jsy 10.00 3.00
168 Juan Diaz NG Jsy 10.00 3.00
169 Kevin Frederick NG Jsy RC 10.00 3.00
170 Earl Snyder NG Bat RC 10.00 3.00
171 Morgan Ensberg NG Bat 10.00 3.00
172 Ryan Jamison NG Jsy 10.00 3.00
173 Rod. Rosario NG Jsy RC 10.00 3.00
174 Willie Harris NG Bat 10.00 3.00
175 Ramon Vazquez NG Bat 10.00 3.00
176 Kazuhisa Ishii NG Bat RC 20.00 6.00
177 Hank Blalock NG Jsy 15.00 4.50
178 Mark Prior NG Bat 25.00 7.50
179 Dewon Brazelton NG Jsy 10.00 3.00
180 Doug Devore NG Jsy RC 10.00 3.00
181 Jorge Padilla NG Bat RC 10.00 3.00
182 Mark Teixeira NG Jsy 15.00 4.50
183 Orlando Hudson NG Bat 10.00 3.00
184 John Buck NG Jsy 10.00 3.00
185 Erik Bedard NG Jsy 10.00 3.00
186 Allan Simpson NG Jsy RC 10.00 3.00
187 Travis Hafner NG Jsy 10.00 3.00
188 Jason Lane NG Jsy 10.00 3.00
189 Marlon Byrd NG Jsy 10.00 3.00
190 Joe Thurston NG Jsy 10.00 3.00
191 Brandon Backe NG Jsy RC 10.00 3.00
192 Josh Phelps NG Jsy 10.00 3.00
193 Bill Hall NG Bat 10.00 3.00
194 Chris Snelling NG Bat RC 15.00 4.50
195 Austin Kearns NG Jsy 10.00 3.00
196 Antonio Perez NG Bat 10.00 3.00
197 Angel Berroa NG Bat 10.00 3.00
198 Andy Machado NG Jsy RC 10.00 3.00
199 Alfredo Amezaga NG Jsy 10.00 3.00
200 Eric Hinske NG Bat 10.00 3.00

2002 Leaf Certified Mirror Blue

Randomly inserted in packs, this is a parallel to the Leaf Certified set. These cards used blue tint and foil and are printed to a stated print run of 75 serial numbered sets.

Nm-Mt Ex-Mt
*MIRROR BLUE 1-150: .6X TO 1.5X MIR.RED
*MIRROR BLUE 151-200: .6X TO 1.5X MIR.RED

2002 Leaf Certified Mirror Red

Randomly inserted in packs, this is a parallel to the Leaf Certified set. These cards used red tint and foil and are printed to a stated print run of 150 serial numbered set.

Nm-Mt Ex-Mt
1 Alex Rodriguez Jsy 25.00 7.50
2 Luis Gonzalez Jsy 10.00 3.00
3 Javier Vazquez Jsy 10.00 3.00
4 Juan Uribe Jsy 10.00 3.00
5 Ben Sheets Jsy 10.00 3.00
6 George Brett Jsy 60.00 18.00
7 Magglio Ordonez Jsy 10.00 3.00
8 Randy Johnson Jsy 20.00 6.00
9 Joe Kennedy Jsy 10.00 3.00
10 Richie Sexson Jsy 10.00 3.00
11 Larry Walker Jsy 15.00 4.50
12 Lance Berkman Jsy 15.00 4.50
13 Jose Cruz Jr. Jsy 10.00 3.00
14 Doug Davis Jsy 10.00 3.00
15 Cliff Floyd Jsy 10.00 3.00
16 Ryan Klesko Bat SP/100 10.00 3.00
17 Troy Glaus Jsy 15.00 4.50
18 Robert Person Jsy 10.00 3.00
19 Bartolo Colon Jsy 10.00 3.00
20 Adam Dunn Jsy 10.00 3.00
21 Kevin Brown Jsy 10.00 3.00
22 John Smoltz Jsy 15.00 4.50
23 Edgar Martinez Jsy 15.00 4.50
24 Eric Karros Jsy 10.00 3.00
25 Tony Gwynn Jsy 25.00 7.50
26 Mark Mulder Jsy 10.00 3.00
27 Don Mattingly Jsy 60.00 18.00
28 Brandon Duckworth Jsy 10.00 3.00
29 C.C. Sabathia Jsy 10.00 3.00
30 Nomar Garciaparra Jsy 25.00 7.50
31 Adam Johnson Jsy 10.00 3.00
32 Miguel Tejada Jsy 10.00 3.00
33 Ryne Sandberg Jsy 50.00 15.00
34 Roger Clemens Jsy 40.00 12.00
35 Edgardo Alfonzo Jsy 10.00 3.00
36 Jason Jennings Jsy 10.00 3.00
37 Todd Helton Jsy 15.00 4.50
38 Nolan Ryan Jsy 80.00 24.00
39 Paul LoDuca Jsy 10.00 3.00
40 Cal Ripken Jsy 80.00 24.00
41 Terrence Long Jsy 10.00 3.00
42 Mike Sweeney Jsy 10.00 3.00
43 Carlos Lee Jsy 10.00 3.00
44 Ben Grieve Jsy 10.00 3.00
45 Tony Armas Jr. Jsy 10.00 3.00
46 Joe Mays Jsy 10.00 3.00
47 Jeff Kent Jsy 10.00 3.00
48 Andy Pettitte Jsy 15.00 4.50
49 Kirby Puckett Jsy 20.00 6.00
50 Aramis Ramirez Jsy 10.00 3.00
51 Tim Redding Jsy 10.00 3.00
52 Freddy Garcia Jsy 10.00 3.00
53 Javy Lopez Jsy 10.00 3.00
54 Mike Schmidt Jsy 50.00 15.00
55 Wade Miller Jsy 10.00 3.00
56 Ramon Ortiz Jsy 10.00 3.00
57 Ray Durham Jsy 10.00 3.00
58 J.D. Drew Jsy 10.00 3.00
59 Bret Boone Jsy 10.00 3.00
60 Mark Buehrle Jsy 10.00 3.00
61 Geoff Jenkins Jsy 10.00 3.00
62 Greg Maddux Jsy 25.00 7.50
63 Mark Grace Jsy 15.00 4.50
64 Toby Hall Jsy 10.00 3.00
65 A.J. Burnett Jsy 10.00 3.00
66 Bernie Williams Jsy 15.00 4.50
67 Roy Oswalt Jsy 10.00 3.00
68 Shannon Stewart Jsy 10.00 3.00
69 Barry Zito Jsy 15.00 4.50
70 Juan Pierre Jsy 10.00 3.00
71 Preston Wilson Jsy 10.00 3.00
72 Rafael Furcal Jsy 10.00 3.00
73 Sean Casey Jsy 10.00 3.00
74 John Olerud Jsy 10.00 3.00
75 Paul Konerko Jsy 15.00 4.50
76 Vernon Wells Jsy 10.00 3.00
77 Juan Gonzalez Jsy 20.00 6.00
78 Ellis Burks Jsy 10.00 3.00
79 Jim Edmonds Jsy 10.00 3.00
80 Robert Fick Jsy 10.00 3.00
81 Michael Cuddyer Jsy 10.00 3.00
82 Tim Hudson Jsy 10.00 3.00
83 Phil Nevin Jsy 10.00 3.00
84 Curt Schilling Jsy 15.00 4.50
85 Juan Cruz Jsy 10.00 3.00
86 Jeff Bagwell Jsy 15.00 4.50
87 Raul Mondesi Jsy 10.00 3.00
88 Bud Smith Jsy 10.00 3.00
89 Omar Vizquel Jsy 10.00 3.00
90 Vladimir Guerrero Jsy 20.00 6.00
91 Garret Anderson Jsy 10.00 3.00
92 Mike Piazza Jsy 25.00 7.50
93 Josh Beckett Jsy 15.00 4.50
94 Carlos Delgado Jsy 10.00 3.00
95 Kazuhiro Sasaki Jsy 10.00 3.00
96 Chipper Jones Jsy 20.00 6.00
97 Jacque Jones Jsy 10.00 3.00
98 Pedro Martinez Jsy 20.00 6.00
99 Marcus Giles Jsy 10.00 3.00
100 Craig Biggio Jsy 15.00 4.50
101 Orlando Cabrera Jsy 10.00 3.00
102 Al Leiter Jsy 10.00 3.00
103 Michael Barrett Jsy 10.00 3.00
104 Hideo Nomo Jsy 80.00 24.00
105 Mike Mussina Jsy 50.00 15.00
106 Jeremy Giambi Jsy 10.00 3.00
107 Cristian Guzman Jsy 10.00 3.00
108 Frank Thomas Jsy 20.00 6.00
109 Carlos Beltran Bat 10.00 3.00
110 Jorge Posada Bat 15.00 4.50
111 Roberto Alomar Bat 20.00 6.00
112 Bob Abreu Bat 10.00 3.00
113 Robin Ventura Bat 10.00 3.00
114 Pat Burrell Bat 10.00 3.00
115 Kenny Lofton Bat 10.00 3.00
116 Adrian Beltre Bat 10.00 3.00
117 Gary Sheffield Bat 10.00 3.00
118 Jermaine Dye Bat 10.00 3.00
119 Manny Ramirez Bat 10.00 3.00
120 Brian Giles Bat 10.00 3.00
121 Tsuyoshi Shinjo Bat 10.00 3.00
122 Rafael Palmeiro Bat 15.00 4.50
123 Mo Vaughn Bat 10.00 3.00
124 Kerry Wood Bat 20.00 6.00
125 Moises Alou Bat 10.00 3.00
126 Rickey Henderson Bat 20.00 6.00
127 Corey Patterson Bat 10.00 3.00
128 Jim Thome Bat 20.00 6.00
129 Richard Hidalgo Bat 10.00 3.00
130 Darin Erstad Bat 10.00 3.00
131 Johnny Damon Bat 10.00 3.00
132 Juan Encarnacion Bat 10.00 3.00
133 Scott Rolen Bat 15.00 4.50
134 Tom Glavine Bat 15.00 4.50
135 Ivan Rodriguez Bat 20.00 6.00
136 Jay Gibbons Bat 10.00 3.00
137 Trot Nixon Bat 15.00 4.50
138 Nick Neugebauer Bat 10.00 3.00
139 Barry Larkin Bat 20.00 6.00
140 Andruw Jones Bat 10.00 3.00
141 Shawn Green Bat 10.00 3.00
142 Jose Vidro Jsy 10.00 3.00
143 Derek Jeter Base 30.00 9.00
144 Ichiro Suzuki Base 25.00 7.50
145 Ken Griffey Jr. Base 20.00 6.00
146 Barry Bonds Base 30.00 9.00
147 Albert Pujols Base 20.00 6.00
148 Sammy Sosa Base 15.00 4.50
149 Jason Giambi Base 20.00 6.00
150 Alfonso Soriano Jsy 15.00 4.50
151 Drew Henson NG Bat 10.00 3.00
152 Luis Garcia NG Bat 10.00 3.00
153 Geronimo Gil NG Jsy 10.00 3.00
154 Corky Miller NG Jsy 10.00 3.00
155 Mike Rivera NG Bat 10.00 3.00
156 Mark Ellis NG Jsy 10.00 3.00
157 Josh Pearce NG Bat 10.00 3.00

158 Ryan Ludwick NG Bat 10.00 3.00
159 So Taguchi NG Bat 15.00 4.50
160 Cody Ransom NG Jsy 10.00 3.00
161 Jeff Deardorff NG Bat 10.00 3.00
162 Franklyn German NG Bat 10.00 3.00
163 Ed Rogers NG Jsy 10.00 3.00
164 Eric Cyr NG Jsy 10.00 3.00
165 Victor Alvarez NG Jsy 10.00 3.00
166 Victor Martinez NG Jsy 10.00 3.00
167 Brandon Berger NG Jsy 10.00 3.00
168 Juan Diaz NG Jsy 10.00 3.00
169 Kevin Frederick NG Jsy 10.00 3.00
170 Earl Snyder NG Bat 10.00 3.00
171 Morgan Ensberg NG Bat 10.00 3.00
172 Ryan Jamison NG Jsy 10.00 3.00
173 Rodrigo Rosario NG Jsy 10.00 3.00
174 Willie Harris NG Bat 10.00 3.00
175 Ramon Vazquez NG Bat 10.00 3.00
176 Kazuhisa Ishii NG Bat 20.00 6.00
177 Hank Blalock NG Jsy 15.00 4.50
178 Mark Prior NG Bat 25.00 7.50
179 Dewon Brazelton NG Jsy 10.00 3.00
180 Doug Devore NG Jsy 10.00 3.00
181 Jorge Padilla NG Jsy 10.00 3.00
182 Mark Teixeira NG Jsy 15.00 4.50
183 Orlando Hudson NG Bat 10.00 3.00
184 John Buck NG Jsy 10.00 3.00
185 Erik Bedard NG Jsy 10.00 3.00
186 Allan Simpson NG Jsy 10.00 3.00
187 Travis Hafner NG Jsy 10.00 3.00
188 Jason Lane NG Jsy 10.00 3.00
189 Marlon Byrd NG Jsy 10.00 3.00
190 Joe Thurston NG Jsy 10.00 3.00
191 Brandon Backe NG Jsy 10.00 3.00
192 Josh Phelps NG Jsy 10.00 3.00
193 Bill Hall NG Bat 10.00 3.00
194 Chris Snelling NG Bat 15.00 4.50
195 Austin Kearns NG Jsy 10.00 3.00
196 Antonio Perez NG Bat 10.00 3.00
197 Angel Berroa NG Bat 10.00 3.00
198 Anderson Machado NG Jsy 10.00 3.00
199 Alfredo Amezaga NG Jsy 10.00 3.00
200 Eric Hinske NG Bat 10.00 3.00

2002 Leaf Certified All-Certified Team

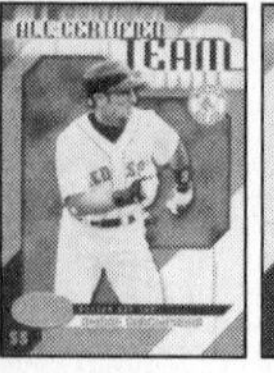
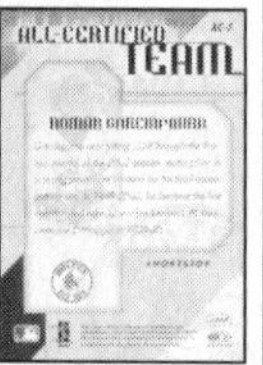

Inserted at stated odds of one in 17, these 25 card feature major stars using mirror board and gold foil stamping.

Nm-Mt Ex-Mt
COMPLETE SET (25) 100.00 30.00
*BLUE: 2X TO 5X BASIC ALL-CERT.TEAM
BLUE: RANDOM INSERTS IN PACKS..
BLUE PRINT RUN 50 SERIAL #'d SETS
GOLD: RANDOM INSERTS IN PACKS.
GOLD PRINT RUN 25 SERIAL #'d SETS
NO GOLD PRICING DUE TO SCARCITY
*RED: 1.25X TO 3X BASIC ALL-CERT.TEAM
RED: RANDOM INSERTS IN PACKS....
RED PRINT RUN 75 SERIAL #'d SETS
1 Ichiro Suzuki 6.00 1.80
2 Alex Rodriguez 6.00 1.80
3 Sammy Sosa 6.00 1.80
4 Jeff Bagwell 3.00 .90
5 Greg Maddux 6.00 1.80
6 Todd Helton 3.00 .90
7 Nomar Garciaparra 6.00 1.80
8 Ken Griffey Jr. 6.00 1.80
9 Roger Clemens 8.00 2.40
10 Adam Dunn 3.00 .90
11 Chipper Jones 4.00 1.20
12 Hideo Nomo 4.00 1.20
13 Lance Berkman 3.00 .90
14 Barry Bonds 10.00 3.00
15 Manny Ramirez 3.00 .90
16 Jason Giambi 4.00 1.20
17 Rickey Henderson 4.00 1.20
18 Randy Johnson 4.00 1.20
19 Derek Jeter 10.00 3.00
20 Kazuhisa Ishii 5.00 1.50
21 Frank Thomas 4.00 1.20
22 Mike Piazza 6.00 1.80
23 Albert Pujols 8.00 2.40
24 Pedro Martinez 4.00 1.20
25 Vladimir Guerrero 4.00 1.20

2002 Leaf Certified Fabric of the Game

Randomly inserted in packs, these 703 cards feature a game-used swatch and are broken up into the following categories. There is a base card which has a stated print run of anywhere from five to 100 copies and cut into a design of a base. There is also pattern which have a stated print run of five to 50 copies with the swatch cut into the shape of the player's position. There is also a jersey subset which is cut into the shape of the player's uniform number. These cards range anywhere from a stated print run to anywhere from one to 75 serial numbered cards. There is also the debut year subset which has a stated print run of anywhere from 14 to 101 serial numbered cards. In addition, an unnannouced subset featured either information about the player's induction into the Hall of Fame or their nickname. These cards mostly have stated print runs of 25 or less and therefore are not priced due to market scarcity.

Nm-Mt Ex-Mt
1BA Bobby Doerr/10
1DY Bobby Doerr/37 30.00 9.00
1IN Bobby Doerr HOF 86/4
1JN Bobby Doerr/1
1PS Bobby Doerr/25
1INA Bobby Doerr HOF 86 AU/1
2BA Ozzie Smith/15
2DY Ozzie Smith/78 40.00 12.00
2JN Ozzie Smith/1
2PS Ozzie Smith/15
2INA Ozzie Smith HOF 02 AU/5
3BA Pee Wee Reese/5
3DY Pee Wee Reese/40 50.00 15.00
3IN Pee Wee Reese HOF 84/5
3JN Pee Wee Reese/1
3PS Pee Wee Reese/10
4BA Tommy Lasorda/80 15.00 4.50
4DY Tommy Lasorda/54 25.00 7.50
4IN Tommy Lasorda HOF 97/20
4JN Tommy Lasorda/2
4PS Tommy Lasorda/50 25.00 7.50
5BA Red Schoendienst/5
5DY Red Schoendienst/45 30.00 9.00
5IN Red Schoendienst HOF 89/5
5JN Red Schoendienst/2
5PS Red Schoendienst/10
6BA Lou Gehrig/5
6DY Lou Gehrig/23
6IN Lou Gehrig HOF 39/5
6JN Lou Gehrig/4
6PS Lou Gehrig/10
7BA Harmon Killebrew/10
7DY Harmon Killebrew/54 40.00 12.00
7JN Harmon Killebrew/3
7PS Harmon Killebrew/20
7INA Harmon Killebrew HOF 84 AU/5
8BA Roger Maris A's/10
8DY Roger Maris A's/57 80.00 24.00
8JN Roger Maris A's/3
8PS Roger Maris A's/10
9BA Babe Ruth/5
9DY Babe Ruth/14
9IN Babe Ruth HOF 36/5
9JN Babe Ruth/3
9PS Babe Ruth/10
10BA Mel Ott/5
10DY Mel Ott/26 100.00 30.00
10IN Mel Ott HOF 51/5
10JN Mel Ott/4
10PS Mel Ott/10
11BA Paul Molitor/100 25.00 7.50
11DY Paul Molitor/78 25.00 7.50
11JN Paul Molitor/4
11PS Paul Molitor/50 40.00 12.00
12BA Duke Snider/5
12DY Duke Snider/47 50.00 15.00
12JN Duke Snider/4
12PS Duke Snider/10
12INA Duke Snider HOF 80 AU/5
13BA Brooks Robinson/5
13DY Brooks Robinson/55 40.00 12.00
13JN Brooks Robinson/5
13PS Brooks Robinson/10
13INA Brooks Robinson HOF 83 AU/5
14BA George Brett/40 80.00 24.00
14DY George Brett/73 60.00 18.00
14IN George Brett HOF 99/5
14JN George Brett/5
14PS George Brett/25
14INA George Brett HOF 99 AU/5
15BA Johnny Bench/80 25.00 7.50
15DY Johnny Bench/67 40.00 12.00
15IN Johnny Bench HOF 89/15
15JN Johnny Bench/5
15PS Johnny Bench/50 40.00 12.00
15INA Johnny Bench HOF 89 AU/5
16BA Lou Boudreau/5
16DY Lou Boudreau/38 30.00 9.00
16IN Lou Boudreau HOF 70/5
16JN Lou Boudreau/5
16PS Lou Boudreau/10
17BA Stan Musial/5
17DY Stan Musial/41 80.00 24.00
17JN Stan Musial/6
17PS Stan Musial/10
17INA Stan Musial HOF 69 AU/5
18BA Al Kaline/5
18DY Al Kaline/53 40.00 12.00
18JN Al Kaline/6
18PS Al Kaline/10
18INA Al Kaline HOF 80 AU/5
19BA Steve Garvey/100 15.00 4.50
19DY Steve Garvey/69 25.00 7.50
19JN Steve Garvey/6
19PS Steve Garvey/45 30.00 9.00
20BA Nomar Garciaparra/100 30.00 9.00
20DY Nomar Garciaparra/96 30.00 9.00
20PS Nomar Garciaparra/50 40.00 12.00
20JNA Nomar Garciaparra AU /5
21BA Joe Morgan/80 15.00 4.50
21DY Joe Morgan/63 25.00 7.50
21IN Joe Morgan HOF 90/15
21JN Joe Morgan/8
21PS Joe Morgan/50 25.00 7.50
21INA Joe Morgan HOF 90 AU/5
22BA Willie Stargell/5
22DY Willie Stargell/62 40.00 12.00
22IN Willie Stargell HOF 88/5
22JN Willie Stargell/8
22PS Willie Stargell/10
23BA Andre Dawson/80 15.00 4.50
23DY Andre Dawson/76 15.00 4.50
23IN Andre Dawson Hawk/15
23JN Andre Dawson/8
23PS Andre Dawson/50 25.00 7.50
23INA Andre Dawson Hawk AU/5
24BA Gary Carter/100 25.00 7.50
24DY Gary Carter/74 40.00 12.00
24JN Gary Carter/8
24PS Gary Carter/50 40.00 12.00
25BA Reggie Jackson A's/10
25DY Reggie Jackson A's/67 40.00 12.00
25JN Reggie Jackson A's/9
25PS Reggie Jackson A's/25
25INA Reggie Jackson A's HOF 93 AU/5
26BA Ted Williams/5
26DY Ted Williams/39
26IN Ted Williams HOF 66/5
26JN Ted Williams/9
26PS Ted Williams/10
27BA Phil Rizzuto/5
27DY Phil Rizzuto/41 50.00 15.00
27JN Phil Rizzuto/10
27PS Phil Rizzuto/10
27INA Phil Rizzuto HOF 94 AU/5
28BA Luis Aparicio/5
28DY Luis Aparicio/56 25.00 7.50
28JN Luis Aparicio/11
28PS Luis Aparicio/10
28INA Luis Aparicio HOF 84 AU/5
29BA Robin Yount/80 40.00 12.00
29DY Robin Yount/74 40.00 12.00
29IN Robin Yount HOF 99/15
29JN Robin Yount/19
29PS Robin Yount/50 40.00 12.00
29INA Robin Yount HOF 99 AU/5
30BA Tony Gwynn/100 25.00 7.50
30DY Tony Gwynn/82 25.00 7.50
30JN Tony Gwynn/14
30PS Tony Gwynn/50 40.00 12.00
30JNA Tony Gwynn AU/5
31BA Ernie Banks/5
31DY Ernie Banks/53 40.00 12.00
31JN Ernie Banks/14
31PS Ernie Banks/10
31INA Ernie Banks HOF 77 AU/5
32BA Joe Torre/50 25.00 7.50
32DY Joe Torre/60 25.00 7.50
32JN Joe Torre/15
32PS Joe Torre/25
33BA Bo Jackson/100 25.00 7.50
33DY Bo Jackson/86 25.00 7.50
33JN Bo Jackson/16
33PS Bo Jackson/35 60.00 18.00
34BA Alfonso Soriano/80 25.00 7.50
34DY Alfonso Soriano/99 25.00 7.50
34JN Alfonso Soriano/12
34PS Alfonso Soriano/50 40.00 12.00
35BA Cal Ripken/80 80.00 24.00
35DY Cal Ripken/81 80.00 24.00
35IN Cal Ripken Iron Man/15
35JN Cal Ripken/8
35PS Cal Ripken/50 100.00 30.00
35INA Cal Ripken Iron Man AU/5
36BA Miguel Tejada/100 15.00 4.50
36DY Miguel Tejada/97 15.00 4.50
36JN Miguel Tejada/4
36PS Miguel Tejada/50 25.00 7.50
37BA Alex Rodriguez M's/100 25.00 7.50
37DY Alex Rodriguez M's/94 25.00 7.50
37JN Alex Rodriguez M's/3
37PS Alex Rodriguez M's/50 40.00 12.00
38BA Mike Schmidt/80 50.00 15.00
38DY Mike Schmidt/72 50.00 15.00
38IN Mike Schmidt HOF 95/15
38JN Mike Schmidt/20
38PS Mike Schmidt/50 60.00 18.00
38INA Mike Schmidt HOF 95 AU/5
39BA Lou Brock/5
39DY Lou Brock/61 40.00 12.00
39JN Lou Brock/20
39PS Lou Brock/10
39INA Lou Brock HOF 85 AU/5
40BA Don Sutton/80 15.00 4.50
40DY Don Sutton/66 25.00 7.50
40IN Don Sutton HOF 98/15
40JN Don Sutton/20
40PS Don Sutton/50 25.00 7.50
40INA Don Sutton HOF 98 AU/5
41BA Roberto Clemente/5
41DY Roberto Clemente/55 150.00 45.00
41IN Roberto Clemente HOF 73/5
41JN Roberto Clemente/21
41PS Roberto Clemente/10
42BA Jim Palmer/20
42DY Jim Palmer/65 25.00 7.50
42JN Jim Palmer/22
42PS Jim Palmer/15
42INA Jim Palmer HOF 90 AU/5
43BA Don Mattingly/40 100.00 30.00
43DY Don Mattingly/82 60.00 18.00
43IN Don Mattingly Donnie BB/5
43JN Don Mattingly/23
43PS Don Mattingly/25
43INA Don Mattingly Donnie BB AU/5.
44BA Ryne Sandberg 40 80.00 24.00
44DY Ryne Sandberg/81 60.00 18.00
44IN Ryne Sandberg Ryno/5
44JN Ryne Sandberg/23
44PS Ryne Sandberg/25
44INA Ryne Sandberg Ryno AU/5
45BA Early Wynn/5
45DY Early Wynn/39 30.00 9.00
45IN Early Wynn HOF 72/5
45JN Early Wynn/24
45PS Early Wynn/10
46BA Mike Piazza Dodgers/100. 25.00 7.50
46DY Mike Piazza Dodgers/92 25.00 7.50
46JN Mike Piazza Dodgers/31 50.00 15.00
46PS Mike Piazza Dodgers/50 30.00 9.00
47BA Wade Boggs/100 25.00 7.50
47DY Wade Boggs/82 25.00 7.50
47JN Wade Boggs/26 60.00 18.00
47PS Wade Boggs/45 50.00 15.00
48BA Catfish Hunter/10
48DY Catfish Hunter/65 40.00 12.00
48IN Catfish Hunter HOF 87/5
48JN Catfish Hunter/27 60.00 18.00
48PS Catfish Hunter/25
49BA Juan Marichal/20
49DY Juan Marichal/60 25.00 7.50
49JN Juan Marichal/27 40.00 12.00
49PS Juan Marichal/15
49INA Juan Marichal HOF 83 AU/5
50BA Carlton Fisk Red Sox/80 25.00 7.50
50DY Carlton Fisk Red Sox/69 40.00 12.00
50IN Carlton Fisk Red Sox HOF 00/15.
50JN Carlton Fisk Red Sox/27 60.00 18.00
50PS Carlton Fisk Red Sox/50 40.00 12.00
50INA Carlton Fisk Red Sox HOF 00 AU/5
51BA Curt Schilling/100 25.00 7.50
51DY Curt Schilling/88 25.00 7.50
51JN Curt Schilling/38 50.00 15.00
51PS Curt Schilling/50 40.00 12.00
52BA Rod Carew Angels/80 25.00 7.50
52DY Rod Carew Angels/67 40.00 12.00
52IN Rod Carew Angels HOF 91/15
52JN Rod Carew Angels/29
52PS Rod Carew Angels/50 40.00 12.00
52INA Rod Carew Angels HOF 91 AU/5
53BA Rod Carew Twins/10
53DY Rod Carew Twins/67 40.00 12.00
53JN Rod Carew Twins/29
53PS Rod Carew Twins/25
53INA Rod Carew Twins HOF 91 AU/5
54BA Joe Carter/100 15.00 4.50
54DY Joe Carter/83 15.00 4.50
54JN Joe Carter/29 40.00 12.00
54PS Joe Carter/50 25.00 7.50
55BA Nolan Ryan Angels/5
55DY Nolan Ryan Angels/66 80.00 24.00
55IN Nolan Ryan Angels HOF 99/5
55JN Nolan Ryan Angels/30
55PS Nolan Ryan Angels/10
55INA Nolan Ryan Angels HOF 99 AU/5
56BA Orlando Cepeda/80 15.00 4.50
56DY Orlando Cepeda/58 25.00 7.50
56IN Orlando Cepeda HOF 99/15
56JN Orlando Cepeda/30 40.00 12.00
56PS Orlando Cepeda/50 25.00 7.50
56INA Orlando Cepeda HOF 99 AU/5
57BA Dave Winfield/80 15.00 4.50
57DY Dave Winfield/73 25.00 7.50
57IN Dave Winfield HOF 01/15
57JN Dave Winfield/31 40.00 12.00
57PS Dave Winfield/50 25.00 7.50
57INA Dave Winfield HOF 01 AU/5
58BA Hoyt Wilhelm/80 15.00 4.50
58DY Hoyt Wilhelm/52 25.00 7.50
58IN Hoyt Wilhelm HOF 85/15
58JN Hoyt Wilhelm/31 40.00 12.00
58PS Hoyt Wilhelm/50 25.00 7.50
58INA Hoyt Wilhelm HOF 85 AU/5
59BA Steve Carlton/80 15.00 4.50
59DY Steve Carlton/65 25.00 7.50
59IN Steve Carlton HOF 94/15
59JN Steve Carlton/32 40.00 12.00
59PS Steve Carlton/50 25.00 7.50
59INA Steve Carlton HOF 94 AU/5
60BA Eddie Murray/100 25.00 7.50
60DY Eddie Murray/77 25.00 7.50
60JN Eddie Murray/33 60.00 18.00
60PS Eddie Murray/50 40.00 12.00
61BA Nolan Ryan Rangers/40. 100.00 30.00
61DY Nolan Ryan Rangers/66 80.00 24.00
61IN Nolan Ryan Rangers HOF 99/5
61JN Nolan Ryan Rangers/34 . 100.00 30.00
61PS Nolan Ryan Rangers/25
61INA Nolan Ryan Rangers HOF 99 AU/5
62BA Nolan Ryan Astros/40 100.00 30.00
62DY Nolan Ryan Astros/66 80.00 24.00
62IN Nolan Ryan Astros HOF 99/5
62JN Nolan Ryan Astros/34 100.00 30.00
62PS Nolan Ryan Astros/25
62INA Nolan Ryan Astros HOF 99 AU/5
63BA Kirby Puckett/40 50.00 15.00
63DY Kirby Puckett/84 25.00 7.50
63IN Kirby Puckett HOF 01/5
63JN Kirby Puckett/34 60.00 18.00
63PS Kirby Puckett/25
63INA Kirby Puckett HOF 01 AU/5
64BA Yogi Berra/5
64DY Yogi Berra/46 50.00 15.00
64JN Yogi Berra/35 60.00 18.00
64PS Yogi Berra/10
64INA Yogi Berra HOF 72 AU/5
65BA Phil Niekro/80 15.00 4.50
65DY Phil Niekro/64 25.00 7.50
65IN Phil Niekro HOF 97/15
65JN Phil Niekro/35 40.00 12.00
65PS Phil Niekro/50 25.00 7.50
65INA Phil Niekro HOF 97 AU/5
66BA Gaylord Perry/80 15.00 4.50
66DY Gaylord Perry/62 25.00 7.50
66IN Gaylord Perry HOF 91/20
66JN Gaylord Perry/36 30.00 9.00
66PS Gaylord Perry/50 25.00 7.50
67BA Pedro Martinez Expos/100 25.00 7.50
67DY Pedro Martinez Expos/92. 25.00 7.50
67JN Pedro Martinez Expos/45. 50.00 15.00
67PS Pedro Martinez Expos/50. 40.00 12.00
68BA Alex Rodriguez Rgr/100 25.00 7.50
68DY Alex Rodriguez Rgr/94 25.00 7.50
68PS Alex Rodriguez Rgr/50 40.00 12.00
68JNA Alex Rodriguez Rgr AU/3
69BA Dave Parker/100 15.00 4.50
69DY Dave Parker/73 25.00 7.50
69JN Dave Parker/39 30.00 9.00
69PS Dave Parker/50 25.00 7.50
70BA Darin Erstad/100 15.00 4.50
70DY Darin Erstad/96 15.00 4.50
70JN Darin Erstad 17
70PS Darin Erstad/50 25.00 7.50
71BA Eddie Mathews/5
71DY Eddie Mathews/52 40.00 12.00
71IN Eddie Mathews HOF 78/5
71JN Eddie Mathews/41 50.00 15.00
71PS Eddie Mathews/10
72BA Tom Seaver Mets/5
72DY Tom Seaver Mets/67 40.00 12.00
72JN Tom Seaver Mets/41 50.00 15.00
72PS Tom Seaver Mets/10
72INA Tom Seaver Mets HOF 92 AU/5
73BA Tom Seaver Reds/10
73DY Tom Seaver Reds/67 40.00 12.00
73JN Tom Seaver Reds/41 50.00 15.00
73PS Tom Seaver Reds/25
73INA Tom Seaver Reds HOF 92 AU/5
74BA Jackie Robinson/5
74DY Jackie Robinson/47 100.00 30.00
74IN Jackie Robinson HOF 62/5
74JN Jackie Robinson/42 100.00 30.00
74PS Jackie Robinson/10
75BA Randy Johnson M's/80 25.00 7.50
75DY Randy Johnson M's/88 25.00 7.50
75IN Randy Johnson M's Big Unit/20.
75JN Randy Johnson M's/51 40.00 12.00
75PS Randy Johnson M's/50 40.00 12.00
76BA Reggie Jackson Yanks/10
76DY Reggie Jackson Yanks/67 40.00 12.00
76JN Reggie Jackson Yanks/44 50.00 15.00
76PS Reggie Jackson Yanks/25
76INA Reggie Jackson Yanks HOF 93 AU/5
77BA Reggie Jackson Angels/80 25.00 7.50
77DY Reggie Jackson Angels/67 40.00 12.00
77IN Reggie Jackson Angels HOF 93/15
77JN Reggie Jackson Angels/44 50.00 15.00
77PS Reggie Jackson Angels/50 40.00 12.00
77INA Reggie Jackson Angels HOF 93 AU/5
78BA Willie McCovey/80 15.00 4.50
78DY Willie McCovey/59 25.00 7.50
78IN Willie McCovey HOF 86/15
78JN Willie McCovey/44 30.00 9.00
78PS Willie McCovey/50 25.00 7.50
78INA Willie McCovey HOF 86 AU/5
79BA Eric Davis/100 15.00 4.50
79DY Eric Davis/84 15.00 4.50
79JN Eric Davis/34 40.00 12.00
79PS Eric Davis/50 25.00 7.50
79JNA Eric Davis AU/10
80BA Carlos Delgado/95 15.00 4.50
80DY Carlos Delgado/93 15.00 4.50
80JN Carlos Delgado/25
80PS Carlos Delgado/25
81BA Dale Murphy/100 25.00 7.50
81DY Dale Murphy/76 25.00 7.50
81PS Dale Murphy/50 40.00 12.00
81JNA Dale Murphy AU/3
82BA Brian Giles/100 15.00 4.50
82DY Brian Giles/95 15.00 4.50
82JN Brian Giles/24
82PS Brian Giles/50 25.00 7.50
83BA Kazuhiro Sasaki/100 15.00 4.50
83DY Kazuhiro Sasaki/100 15.00 4.50
83JN Kazuhiro Sasaki/22
83PS Kazuhiro Sasaki 50 25.00 7.50
84BA Phil Nevin/100 15.00 4.50
84DY Phil Nevin/95 15.00 4.50
84JN Phil Nevin/23
84PS Phil Nevin/50 25.00 7.50
85BA Frank Thomas/80 25.00 7.50
85DY Frank Thomas/90 25.00 7.50
85IN Frank Thomas Big Hurt/15
85JN Frank Thomas/35 60.00 18.00
85PS Frank Thomas/50 40.00 12.00
85INA Frank Thomas Big Hurt AU/5
86BA Raul Mondesi/100 15.00 4.50
86DY Raul Mondesi/93 15.00 4.50
86JN Raul Mondesi/43 30.00 9.00
86PS Raul Mondesi/50 25.00 7.50
87BA Don Drysdale/5
87DY Don Drysdale/56 40.00 12.00
87IN Don Drysdale HOF 84/5
87JN Don Drysdale/53 40.00 12.00
87PS Don Drysdale/10
88BA Gary Sheffield/100 15.00 4.50
88DY Gary Sheffield/88 15.00 4.50
88JN Gary Sheffield/10
88PS Gary Sheffield/50 25.00 7.50
89BA Andy Pettitte/100 25.00 7.50
89DY Andy Pettitte/95 25.00 7.50
89JN Andy Pettitte/46 50.00 15.00
89PS Andy Pettitte/50 40.00 12.00
90BA Lance Berkman/45 30.00 9.00
90DY Lance Berkman/99 15.00 4.50
90JN Lance Berkman/12
90PS Lance Berkman/25
90JNA Lance Berkman AU/5
91BA Paul Lo Duca/100 15.00 4.50
91DY Paul Lo Duca/98 15.00 4.50
91JN Paul Lo Duca/16
91PS Paul Lo Duca/50 25.00 7.50
92BA Kevin Brown/25
92DY Kevin Brown/86 15.00 4.50
92JN Kevin Brown/27 40.00 12.00
92PS Kevin Brown/25
93BA Jim Thome/100 25.00 7.50
93DY Jim Thome/91 25.00 7.50
93JN Jim Thome/20
93PS Jim Thome/50 40.00 12.00
93JNA Jim Thome AU/5
94BA Mike Sweeney/100 15.00 4.50
94DY Mike Sweeney/95 15.00 4.50
94JN Mike Sweeney/29 40.00 12.00
94PS Mike Sweeney/50 25.00 7.50
95BA Pedro Martinez Red Sox/100 25.00 7.50
95DY Pedro Martinez Red Sox/92 25.00 7.50
95JN Pedro Martinez Red Sox/45 50.00 15.00
95PS Pedro Martinez Red Sox/45 50.00 15.00
96BA Cliff Floyd/100 15.00 4.50
96DY Cliff Floyd/93 15.00 4.50
96JN Cliff Floyd/30 40.00 12.00
96PS Cliff Floyd/50 25.00 7.50
97BA Larry Walker/100 25.00 7.50
97DY Larry Walker/89 25.00 7.50
97JN Larry Walker/33 60.00 18.00
97PS Larry Walker/50 40.00 12.00
98BA Ivan Rodriguez/80 25.00 7.50
98DY Ivan Rodriguez/91 25.00 7.50
98IN Ivan Rodriguez Pudge/15
98JN Ivan Rodriguez/7
98PS Ivan Rodriguez/50 40.00 12.00
98INA Ivan Rodriguez Pudge AU/5
99BA Aramis Ramirez/100 15.00 4.50
99DY Aramis Ramirez/98 15.00 4.50
99JN Aramis Ramirez/16
99PS Aramis Ramirez/50 25.00 7.50
100BA Roberto Alomar/100 25.00 7.50
100DY Roberto Alomar/88 25.00 7.50
100JN Roberto Alomar/12
100PS Roberto Alomar/50 40.00 12.00
101BA Ben Sheets/100 15.00 4.50
101DY Ben Sheets/101 15.00 4.50
101JN Ben Sheets/15
101PS Ben Sheets/50 25.00 7.50
102BA Adam Dunn/5
102DY Adam Dunn/101 15.00 4.50
102JN Adam Dunn/39 30.00 9.00
102PS Adam Dunn/5
102JNA Adam Dunn AU/5
103BA Hideo Nomo/15
103DY Hideo Nomo/95 40.00 12.00
103JN Hideo Nomo/11
103PS Hideo Nomo/20
104BA C.C. Sabathia/50 25.00 7.50
104DY C.C. Sabathia/101 15.00 4.50
104JN C.C. Sabathia/52 25.00 7.50
104PS C.C. Sabathia/50 25.00 7.50
105BA R.Henderson A's/100 25.00 7.50
105DY Rickey Henderson A's/79 25.00 7.50
105JN R.Henderson A's/30 60.00 18.00
105PS Rickey Henderson A's/50 40.00 12.00
105JNA Rickey Henderson A's AU/5
106BA Carlton Fisk W.Sox/80 25.00 7.50
106DY Carlton Fisk W.Sox/69 40.00 12.00
106IN Carlton Fisk W.Sox HOF 00/15
106JN Carlton Fisk W.Sox/72 40.00 12.00

106PS Carlton Fisk W.Sox/50 40.00 12.00
106INA Carlton Fisk W.Sox HOF 00 AU/5
107BA Chan Ho Park/100 15.00 4.50
107DY Chan Ho Park/94 15.00 4.50
107JN Chan Ho Park/61 25.00 7.50
107PS Chan Ho Park/50 25.00 7.50
108BA Mike Mussina/100 25.00 7.50
108DY Mike Mussina/91 25.00 7.50
108JN Mike Mussina 35 60.00 18.00
108PS Mike Mussina/50 40.00 12.00
109BA Mark Mulder/100 15.00 4.50
109DY Mark Mulder/100 15.00 4.50
109JN Mark Mulder/20
109PS Mark Mulder/35 40.00 12.00
110BA Tsuyoshi Shinjo/100 15.00 4.50
110DY Tsuyoshi Shinjo/101 15.00 4.50
110JN Tsuyoshi Shinjo/5
110PS Tsuyoshi Shinjo/30 40.00 12.00
111BA Pat Burrell/100 15.00 4.50
111DY Pat Burrell/100 15.00 4.50
111JN Pat Burrell/5
111PS Pat Burrell/50 25.00 7.50
112BA Edgar Martinez/100 25.00 7.50
112DY Edgar Martinez/87 25.00 7.50
112JN Edgar Martinez/11
112PS Edgar Martinez/50 40.00 12.00
113BA Barry Larkin/100 25.00 7.50
113DY Barry Larkin/86 25.00 7.50
113JN Barry Larkin/11
113PS Barry Larkin/50 40.00 12.00
114BA Jeff Kent/100 15.00 4.50
114DY Jeff Kent/92 15.00 4.50
114JN Jeff Kent/21
114PS Jeff Kent/50 25.00 7.50
115BA Chipper Jones/100 25.00 7.50
115DY Chipper Jones/93 25.00 7.50
115JN Chipper Jones/10
115PS Chipper Jones/50 40.00 12.00
116BA Magglio Ordonez/100 15.00 4.50
116DY Magglio Ordonez/97 15.00 4.50
116JN Magglio Ordonez/30 40.00 12.00
116PS Magglio Ordonez/50 25.00 7.50
117BA Jim Edmonds/100 15.00 4.50
117DY Jim Edmonds/93 15.00 4.50
117JN Jim Edmonds/15
117PS Jim Edmonds/50 25.00 7.50
118BA Andruw Jones/100 15.00 4.50
118DY Andruw Jones/96 15.00 4.50
118JN Andruw Jones/25
118PS Andruw Jones/45 30.00 9.00
119BA Jose Canseco/100 25.00 7.50
119DY Jose Canseco/85 25.00 7.50
119JN Jose Canseco/23
119PS Jose Canseco/50 40.00 12.00
119JNA Jose Canseco AU/10
120BA Manny Ramirez/100 15.00 4.50
120DY Manny Ramirez/93 15.00 4.50
120JN Manny Ramirez/24
120PS Manny Ramirez/50 25.00 7.50
121BA Sean Casey/100 15.00 4.50
121DY Sean Casey/97 15.00 4.50
121JN Sean Casey/21
121PS Sean Casey/50 25.00 7.50
122BA Bret Boone/100 15.00 4.50
122DY Bret Boone/92 15.00 4.50
122JN Bret Boone/29 40.00 12.00
122PS Bret Boone/50 25.00 7.50
123BA Tim Hudson/100 15.00 4.50
123DY Tim Hudson/99 15.00 4.50
123JN Tim Hudson/15
123PS Tim Hudson/50 25.00 7.50
124BA Craig Biggio/100 25.00 7.50
124DY Craig Biggio/88 25.00 7.50
124JN Craig Biggio/7
124PS Craig Biggio/50 40.00 12.00
125BA Mike Piazza Mets/100 25.00 7.50
125DY Mike Piazza Mets/92 25.00 7.50
125JN Mike Piazza Mets/31 50.00 15.00
125PS Mike Piazza Mets/50 30.00 9.00
126BA Jack Morris/100 15.00 4.50
126DY Jack Morris/77 15.00 4.50
126JN Jack Morris/47 30.00 9.00
126PS Jack Morris/25
127BA Roy Oswalt/100 15.00 4.50
127DY Roy Oswalt/101 15.00 4.50
127JN Roy Oswalt/39 30.00 9.00
127PS Roy Oswalt/50 25.00 7.50
127JNA Roy Oswalt AU/5
128BA Shawn Green/100 15.00 4.50
128DY Shawn Green/93 15.00 4.50
128JN Shawn Green/15
128PS Shawn Green/50 25.00 7.50
129BA Carlos Beltran/100 15.00 4.50
129DY Carlos Beltran/98 15.00 4.50
129JN Carlos Beltran/15
129PS Carlos Beltran/50 25.00 7.50
130BA Todd Helton/100 25.00 7.50
130DY Todd Helton/97 25.00 7.50
130JN Todd Helton/17
130PS Todd Helton/50 40.00 12.00
131BA Barry Zito/75 25.00 7.50
131DY Barry Zito/100 25.00 7.50
131JN Barry Zito/75 25.00 7.50
131PS Barry Zito/30 60.00 18.00
132BA J.D. Drew/100 15.00 4.50
132DY J.D. Drew/98 15.00 4.50
132JN J.D. Drew/7
132PS J.D. Drew/50 25.00 7.50
133BA Mark Grace/100 25.00 7.50
133DY Mark Grace 88 25.00 7.50
133JN Mark Grace/17
133PS Mark Grace/50 40.00 12.00
134BA R.Henderson Mets/100 25.00 7.50
134DY R.Henderson Mets/79 25.00 7.50
134JN Rickey Henderson Mets/24
134PS R.Henderson Mets/50 40.00 12.00
135BA Greg Maddux/100 25.00 7.50
135DY Greg Maddux/86 25.00 7.50
135JN Greg Maddux/31
135PS Greg Maddux/50 30.00 9.00
136BA Garret Anderson/100 15.00 4.50
136DY Garret Anderson/94 15.00 4.50
136JN Garret Anderson/16
136PS Garret Anderson/50 25.00 7.50
137BA Rafael Palmeiro/100 25.00 7.50
137DY Rafael Palmeiro/86 25.00 7.50
137JN Rafael Palmeiro/20
137PS Rafael Palmeiro/50 40.00 12.00
137JNA Rafael Palmeiro AU/5
138BA Luis Gonzalez/50 25.00 7.50
138DY Luis Gonzalez/90 15.00 4.50
138JN Luis Gonzalez/20
138PS Luis Gonzalez/45 30.00 9.00
139BA Nick Johnson/100 15.00 4.50
139DY Nick Johnson/101 15.00 4.50
139JN Nick Johnson/26 40.00 12.00
139PS Nick Johnson/50 25.00 7.50
139JNA Nick Johnson AU/10
140BA Vladimir Guerrero/80 25.00 7.50
140DY Vladimir Guerrero/96 25.00 7.50
140JN Vladimir Guerrero/22
140PS Vladimir Guerrero/50 40.00 12.00
140JNA Vladimir Guerrero AU/5
141BA Mark Buehrle/20
141DY Mark Buehrle/100 15.00 4.50
141JN Mark Buehrle/56 25.00 7.50
141PS Mark Buehrle/20
142BA Troy Glaus/100 25.00 7.50
142DY Troy Glaus/98 25.00 7.50
142JN Troy Glaus/25
142PS Troy Glaus/50 40.00 12.00
143BA Juan Gonzalez/100 25.00 7.50
143DY Juan Gonzalez/89 25.00 7.50
143JN Juan Gonzalez/22
143PS Juan Gonzalez/50 40.00 12.00
144BA Kerry Wood/100 25.00 7.50
144DY Kerry Wood/98 25.00 7.50
144JN Kerry Wood/34 60.00 18.00
144PS Kerry Wood/50 40.00 12.00
145BA Roger Clemens/80 40.00 12.00
145DY Roger Clemens/84 40.00 12.00
145IN Roger Clemens Rocket/16
145JN Roger Clemens/20
145PS Roger Clemens/50 60.00 18.00
145INA Roger Clemens Rocket AU/5
146BA Bob Abreu/100 15.00 4.50
146DY Bob Abreu/96 15.00 4.50
146JN Bob Abreu/53 25.00 7.50
146PS Bob Abreu/50 25.00 7.50
147BA Bernie Williams/95 25.00 7.50
147DY Bernie Williams/91 25.00 7.50
147JN Bernie Williams/51 40.00 12.00
147PS Bernie Williams/25
148BA Tom Glavine/100 25.00 7.50
148DY Tom Glavine/87 25.00 7.50
148JN Tom Glavine/47 50.00 15.00
148PS Tom Glavine/50 40.00 12.00
149BA Jorge Posada/100 25.00 7.50
149DY Jorge Posada/95 25.00 7.50
149JN Jorge Posada/20
149PS Jorge Posada/50 40.00 12.00
150BA R.Johnson D'Backs/80 25.00 7.50
150DY R.Johnson D'Backs/88 25.00 7.50
150IN Randy Johnson D'Backs Big Unit/20
150JN R.Johnson D'Backs/51 40.00 12.00
150PS R.Johnson D'Backs/50 40.00 12.00

2002 Leaf Certified Skills

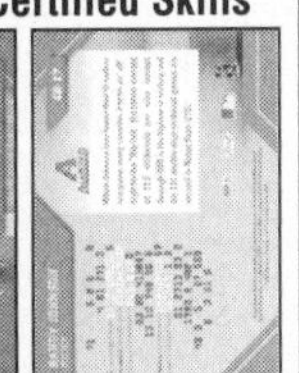

Inserted at stated odds of one in 17, these 20 cards feature players who have have already established excellent stats be it for a game, season or career. These cards are produced on mirror board with silver foil stamping.

	Nm-Mt	Ex-Mt
COMPLETE SET (20)	120.00	36.00
*BLUE: 1.25X TO 3X BASIC SKILLS		
BLUE: RANDOM INSERTS IN PACKS		
BLUE PRINT RUN 75 SERIAL #'d SETS		
GOLD: RANDOM INSERTS IN PACKS		
GOLD PRINT RUN 25 SERIAL #'d SETS		
NO GOLD PRICING DUE TO SCARCITY		
*RED: .75X TO 2X BASIC SKILLS		
RED: RANDOM INSERTS IN PACKS		
RED PRINT RUN 150 SERIAL #'d SETS		
1 Barry Bonds	10.00	3.00
2 Greg Maddux	6.00	1.80
3 Rickey Henderson	4.00	1.20
4 Ichiro Suzuki	6.00	1.80
5 Pedro Martinez	4.00	1.20
6 Kazuhisa Ishii	5.00	1.50
7 Alex Rodriguez	6.00	1.80
8 Mike Piazza	6.00	1.80
9 Sammy Sosa	6.00	1.80
10 Derek Jeter	10.00	3.00
11 Albert Pujols	8.00	2.40
12 Roger Clemens	8.00	2.40
13 Mark Prior	8.00	2.40
14 Chipper Jones	4.00	1.20
15 Ken Griffey Jr.	6.00	1.80
16 Frank Thomas	4.00	1.20
17 Randy Johnson	4.00	1.20
18 Vladimir Guerrero	4.00	1.20
19 Nomar Garciaparra	6.00	1.80
20 Jeff Bagwell	3.00	.90

2003 Leaf Certified Materials

This 259-card set was issued in two separate series. The primary Leaf Certified Materials brand - containing cards 1-250 from the basic set - was released in August, 2003. The set was issued in seven card packs with an $10 SRP which were packaged 10 to a box and 20 boxes to a case. Cards numbered 1 through 200 feature veterans. Cards numbered 201 through 205 featured some baseball legends while cards numbered 206 through 250 are entitled New Generation and feature top prospects and rookies. Those cards, with the exception of card 220 were issued to a stated print run of 400 serial numbered sets. Card 220, featuring Jose Contreras, was issued to a stated print run of 100 serial numbered sets. Cards 251-259 were randomly seeded into packs of DLP Rookies and Traded of which was distributed in December, 2003. The nine update cards carry on the New Generation subset featuring top prospects, and like the earlier cards feature certified autographs. Serial numbered print runs for these update cards range from 100-250 copies per.

	MINT	NRMT
COMP.LO SET w/o SP's (200)	60.00	27.00
COMMON CARD (1-200)	1.00	.45
COMMON CARD (201-205)	10.00	4.50
COMMON CARD (206-250)	10.00	4.50
201-250 RANDOM INSERTS IN PACKS		
COM.(251-259) p/r 150-250	10.00	4.50
1 Troy Glaus	1.50	.70
2 Alfredo Amezaga	1.00	.45
3 Garret Anderson	1.00	.45
4 Nolan Ryan Angels	6.00	2.70
5 Darin Erstad	1.00	.45
6 Junior Spivey	1.00	.45
7 Randy Johnson	2.50	1.10
8 Curt Schilling	1.50	.70
9 Luis Gonzalez	1.00	.45
10 Steve Finley	1.00	.45
11 Matt Williams	1.00	.45
12 Greg Maddux	4.00	1.80
13 Chipper Jones	2.50	1.10
14 Gary Sheffield	1.00	.45
15 Adam LaRoche	1.50	.70
16 Andruw Jones	1.00	.45
17 Robert Fick	1.00	.45
18 John Smoltz	1.50	.70
19 Javy Lopez	1.00	.45
20 Jay Gibbons	1.00	.45
21 Geronimo Gil	1.00	.45
22 Cal Ripken	8.00	3.60
23 Nomar Garciaparra	4.00	1.80
24 Pedro Martinez	2.50	1.10
25 Freddy Sanchez	1.00	.45
26 Rickey Henderson	2.50	1.10
27 Manny Ramirez	1.00	.45
28 Casey Fossum	1.00	.45
29 Sammy Sosa	4.00	1.80
30 Kerry Wood	2.50	1.10
31 Corey Patterson	1.00	.45
32 Nic Jackson	1.00	.45
33 Mark Prior	5.00	2.20
34 Juan Cruz	1.00	.45
35 Steve Smyth	1.00	.45
36 Magglio Ordonez	1.00	.45
37 Joe Borchard	1.00	.45
38 Frank Thomas	2.50	1.10
39 Mark Buehrle	1.00	.45
40 Joe Crede	1.00	.45
41 Carlos Lee	1.00	.45
42 Paul Konerko	1.00	.45
43 Adam Dunn	1.00	.45
44 Corky Miller	1.00	.45
45 Brandon Larson	1.00	.45
46 Ken Griffey Jr.	4.00	1.80
47 Barry Larkin	2.50	1.10
48 Sean Casey	1.00	.45
49 Wily Mo Pena	1.00	.45
50 Austin Kearns	1.00	.45
51 Victor Martinez	1.00	.45
52 Brian Tallet	1.00	.45
53 Cliff Lee	1.00	.45
54 Jeremy Guthrie	1.00	.45
55 C.C. Sabathia	1.00	.45
56 Ricardo Rodriguez	1.00	.45
57 Omar Vizquel	1.00	.45
58 Travis Hafner	1.00	.45
59 Todd Helton	1.50	.70
60 Jason Jennings	1.00	.45
61 Jeff Baker	1.00	.45
62 Larry Walker	1.50	.70
63 Travis Chapman	1.00	.45
64 Mike Maroth	1.00	.45
65 Josh Beckett	1.50	.70
66 Ivan Rodriguez	2.50	1.10
67 Brad Penny	1.00	.45
68 A.J. Burnett	1.00	.45
69 Craig Biggio	1.50	.70
70 Roy Oswalt	1.00	.45
71 Jason Lane	1.00	.45
72 Nolan Ryan Astros	6.00	2.70
73 Wade Miller	1.00	.45
74 Richard Hidalgo	1.00	.45
75 Jeff Bagwell	1.50	.70
76 Lance Berkman	1.00	.45
77 Rodrigo Rosario	1.00	.45
78 Jeff Kent	1.00	.45
79 John Buck	1.00	.45
80 Angel Berroa	1.00	.45
81 Mike Sweeney	1.00	.45
82 Mac Suzuki	1.00	.45
83 Alexis Gomez	1.00	.45
84 Carlos Beltran	1.00	.45
85 Runelvys Hernandez	1.00	.45
86 Hideo Nomo	2.50	1.10
87 Paul Lo Duca	1.00	.45
88 Cesar Izturis	1.00	.45
89 Kazuhisa Ishii	1.00	.45
90 Shawn Green	1.00	.45
91 Joe Thurston	1.00	.45
92 Adrian Beltre	1.00	.45
93 Kevin Brown	1.00	.45
94 Richie Sexson	1.00	.45
95 Ben Sheets	1.00	.45
96 Takahito Nomura	1.00	.45
97 Geoff Jenkins	1.00	.45
98 Bill Hall	1.00	.45
99 Torii Hunter	1.00	.45
100 A.J. Pierzynski	1.00	.45
101 Michael Cuddyer	1.00	.45
102 Jose Morban	1.00	.45
103 Brad Radke	1.00	.45
104 Jacque Jones	1.00	.45
105 Eric Milton	1.00	.45
106 Joe Mays	1.00	.45
107 Adam Johnson	1.00	.45
108 Javier Vazquez	1.00	.45
109 Vladimir Guerrero	2.50	1.10
110 Jose Vidro	1.00	.45
111 Michael Barrett	1.00	.45
112 Orlando Cabrera	1.00	.45
113 Tom Glavine	1.50	.70
114 Roberto Alomar	2.50	1.10
115 Tsuyoshi Shinjo	1.00	.45
116 Cliff Floyd	1.00	.45
117 Mike Piazza	4.00	1.80
118 Al Leiter	1.00	.45
119 Don Mattingly	6.00	2.70
120 Roger Clemens	5.00	2.20
121 Derek Jeter	6.00	2.70
122 Alfonso Soriano	1.50	.70
123 Drew Henson	1.00	.45
124 Brandon Claussen	1.00	.45
125 Christian Parker	1.00	.45
126 Jason Giambi	2.50	1.10
127 Mike Mussina	2.50	1.10
128 Bernie Williams	1.50	.70
129 Jason Anderson	1.00	.45
130 Nick Johnson	1.00	.45
131 Jorge Posada	1.50	.70
132 Andy Pettitte	1.50	.70
133 Barry Zito	1.50	.70
134 Miguel Tejada	1.00	.45
135 Eric Chavez	1.00	.45
136 Tim Hudson	1.00	.45
137 Mark Mulder	1.00	.45
138 Terrence Long	1.00	.45
139 Mark Ellis	1.00	.45
140 Jim Thome	2.50	1.10
141 Pat Burrell	1.00	.45
142 Marlon Byrd	1.00	.45
143 Bobby Abreu	1.00	.45
144 Brandon Duckworth	1.00	.45
145 Robert Person	1.00	.45
146 Anderson Machado	1.00	.45
147 Aramis Ramirez	1.00	.45
148 Jack Wilson	1.00	.45
149 Carlos Rivera	1.00	.45
150 Jose Castillo	1.00	.45
151 Walter Young	1.00	.45
152 Brian Giles	1.00	.45
153 Jason Kendall	1.00	.45
154 Ryan Klesko	1.00	.45
155 Mike Rivera	1.00	.45
156 Sean Burroughs	1.00	.45
157 Brian Lawrence	1.00	.45
158 Xavier Nady	1.00	.45
159 Dennis Tankersley	1.00	.45
160 Phil Nevin	1.00	.45
161 Barry Bonds	6.00	2.70
162 Kenny Lofton	1.00	.45
163 Rich Aurilia	1.00	.45
164 Ichiro Suzuki	4.00	1.80
165 Edgar Martinez	1.50	.70
166 Chris Snelling	1.00	.45
167 Rafael Soriano	1.00	.45
168 John Olerud	1.00	.45
169 Bret Boone	1.00	.45
170 Freddy Garcia	1.00	.45
171 Aaron Sele	1.00	.45
172 Kazuhiro Sasaki	1.00	.45
173 Albert Pujols	5.00	2.20
174 Scott Rolen	1.50	.70
175 So Taguchi	1.00	.45
176 Jim Edmonds	1.00	.45
177 Edgar Renteria	1.00	.45
178 J.D. Drew	1.00	.45
179 Antonio Perez	1.00	.45
180 Dewon Brazelton	1.00	.45
181 Aubrey Huff	1.00	.45
182 Toby Hall	1.00	.45
183 Ben Grieve	1.00	.45
184 Joe Kennedy	1.00	.45
185 Alex Rodriguez	4.00	1.80
186 Rafael Palmeiro	1.50	.70
187 Hank Blalock	1.50	.70
188 Mark Teixeira	1.50	.70
189 Juan Gonzalez	2.50	1.10
190 Kevin Mench	1.00	.45
191 Nolan Ryan Rgr	6.00	2.70
192 Doug Davis	1.00	.45
193 Eric Hinske	1.00	.45
194 Vinny Chulk	1.00	.45
195 Alexis Rios	4.00	1.80
196 Carlos Delgado	1.00	.45
197 Shannon Stewart	1.00	.45
198 Josh Phelps	1.00	.45
199 Vernon Wells	1.00	.45
200 Roy Halladay	1.00	.45
201 Babe Ruth RET	20.00	9.00
202 Lou Gehrig RET	12.00	5.50
203 Jackie Robinson RET	12.00	5.50
204 Ty Cobb RET	15.00	6.75
205 Thurman Munson RET	10.00	4.50
206 Pr. Redman NG AU RC	10.00	4.50
207 Craig Brazell NG AU RC	15.00	6.75
208 Nook Logan NG AU RC	10.00	4.50
209 Hong-Chih Kuo NG AU RC	25.00	11.00
210 Matt Kata NG AU RC	15.00	6.75
211 C.Wang NG AU RC	40.00	18.00
212 Alej Machado NG AU RC	10.00	4.50
213 Mike Hessman NG AU RC	10.00	4.50
214 Franc Rosario NG AU RC	10.00	4.50
215 Pedro Liriano NG AU	10.00	4.50
216 J.Bonderman NG AU RC	20.00	9.00
217 Oscar Villarreal NG AU RC	10.00	4.50
218 Arnie Munoz NG AU RC	10.00	4.50
219 Tim Olson NG AU RC	15.00	6.75
220 J.Contreras NG AU/100 RC	50.00	22.00
221 Franc Cruceta NG AU RC	10.00	4.50
222 John Webb NG AU	10.00	4.50
223 Phil Seibel NG AU RC	10.00	4.50
224 Aaron Looper NG AU RC	10.00	4.50
225 Brian Stokes NG AU RC	10.00	4.50
226 G.Quiroz NG AU RC	20.00	9.00
227 Fern Cabrera NG AU RC	10.00	4.50
228 Josh Hall NG AU RC	15.00	6.75
229 Diego Markwell NG AU RC	10.00	4.50
230 Andrew Brown NG AU RC	10.00	4.50
231 Doug Waechter NG AU RC	15.00	6.75
232 Felix Sanchez NG AU RC	10.00	4.50
233 Gerardo Garcia NG AU	10.00	4.50
234 Matt Bruback NG AU RC	10.00	4.50
235 Mi. Hernandez NG AU RC	10.00	4.50
236 Rett Johnson NG AU RC	15.00	6.75
237 Ryan Cameron NG AU RC	10.00	4.50
238 Rob Hammock NG AU RC	15.00	6.75
239 Clint Barmes NG AU RC	15.00	6.75
240 Brandon Webb NG AU RC	40.00	18.00
241 Jon Leicester NG AU RC	10.00	4.50
242 Shane Bazzell NG AU RC	10.00	4.50
243 Joe Valentine NG AU RC	10.00	4.50
244 Josh Stewart NG AU RC	10.00	4.50
245 Pete LaForest NG AU RC	15.00	6.75
246 Shane Victorino NG AU RC	10.00	4.50
247 Terrmel Sledge NG AU RC	15.00	6.75
248 Lew Ford NG AU RC	15.00	6.75
249 T.Wellemeyer NG AU RC	15.00	6.75
250 Hideki Matsui NG RC	25.00	11.00
251 Adam Loewen NG AU/250 RC	40.00	18.00
252 Dan Haren NG AU/250 RC	20.00	9.00
253 Dontrelle Willis NG AU/150	30.00	13.50
254 Ramon Nivar NG AU/250 RC	20.00	9.00
255 Chad Gaudin NG AU/250 RC	10.00	4.50
256 Kevin Correia NG AU/150 RC	10.00	4.50
257 Rickie Weeks NG AU/100 RC	100.00	45.00
258 Ryan Wagner NG AU/250 RC	25.00	11.00
259 Delm Young NG AU/100 RC	100.00	45.00

2003 Leaf Certified Materials Mirror Black

	MINT	NRMT
1-250 RANDOM INSERTS IN PACKS		
251-259 RANDOM IN DLP R/T PACKS		
STATED PRINT RUN 1 SERIAL #'d SET		
NO PRICING DUE TO SCARCITY		

2003 Leaf Certified Materials Mirror Black Autographs

	MINT	NRMT
1-250 RANDOM INSERTS IN PACKS		
251-259 RANDOM IN DLP R/T PACKS		
STATED PRINT RUN 1 SERIAL #'d SET		
NO PRICING DUE TO SCARCITY		

2003 Leaf Certified Materials Mirror Black Materials

	MINT	NRMT
RANDOM INSERTS IN PACKS		
STATED PRINT RUN 1 SERIAL #'d SET		
NO PRICING DUE TO SCARCITY		

2003 Leaf Certified Materials Mirror Blue

	MINT	NRMT
*BLUE 1-200: 3X TO 8X BASIC		
*BLUE 201-205: 1X TO 2.5X BASIC		
*BLUE 206-219/221-249: .3X TO .8X BASIC		
*BLUE 220: .2X TO .5X BASIC 220		
*BLUE 250: .75X TO 2X BASIC 250		
*BLUE 251-259: .3X TO .8X BASIC p/r 250		
*BLUE 251-259: .2X TO .5X BASIC p/r 100-150		
1-250 RANDOM INSERTS IN PACKS		
251-259 RANDOM IN DLP R/T PACKS		
STATED PRINT RUN 50 SERIAL #'d SETS		

2003 Leaf Certified Materials Mirror Blue Autographs

	MINT	NRMT
1-250 RANDOM INSERTS IN PACKS		
251-259 RANDOM IN DLP R/T PACKS		
PRINT RUNS B/WN 5-50 COPIES PER		
NO PRICING ON QTY OF 25 OR LESS.		
2 Alfredo Amezaga/50	15.00	6.75
3 Garret Anderson/10		
4 Nolan Ryan Angels/5		
6 Junior Spivey/50	15.00	6.75
15 Adam LaRoche/50	40.00	18.00
17 Robert Fick/10		
20 Jay Gibbons/50	25.00	11.00
21 Geronimo Gil/50	15.00	6.75
22 Cal Ripken/5		
25 Freddy Sanchez/17		
28 Casey Fossum/50	15.00	6.75
31 Corey Patterson/5		
32 Nic Jackson/50	15.00	6.75
33 Mark Prior/50	150.00	70.00
34 Juan Cruz/50	15.00	6.75
35 Steve Smyth/50	15.00	6.75
37 Joe Borchard/50	25.00	11.00
39 Mark Buehrle/50	25.00	11.00
40 Joe Crede/30	15.00	6.75
41 Carlos Lee/5		
45 Brandon Larson/50	15.00	6.75
49 Wily Mo Pena/50	15.00	6.75
51 Victor Martinez/50	25.00	11.00
52 Brian Tallet/50	15.00	6.75
53 Cliff Lee/50	15.00	6.75
54 Jeremy Guthrie/50	15.00	6.75
55 C.C. Sabathia/4		
56 Ricardo Rodriguez/50	15.00	6.75
60 Jason Jennings/50	15.00	6.75
61 Jeff Baker/50	15.00	6.75
63 Travis Chapman/50	15.00	6.75

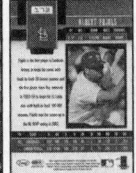

64 Mike Maroth/50 15.00 6.75
70 Roy Oswalt/50 25.00 11.00
71 Jason Lane/50 15.00 6.75
72 Nolan Ryan Astros/5
73 Wade Miller/50 25.00 11.00
74 Richard Hidalgo/5
77 Rodrigo Rosario/50 15.00 6.75
79 John Buck/10
80 Angel Berroa/50 25.00 11.00
81 Mike Sweeney/5
82 Mac Suzuki/50 25.00 11.00
83 Alexis Gomez/10
85 Runelvys Hernandez/50 15.00 6.75
86 Hideo Nomo/15
87 Paul Lo Duca/10
88 Cesar Izturis/50 15.00 6.75
89 Kazuhisa Ishii/5
91 Joe Thurston/50 15.00 6.75
94 Richie Sexson/5
95 Ben Sheets/5
96 Takahito Nomura/10
98 Bill Hall/30 15.00 6.75
100 A.J. Pierzynski/5
102 Jose Morban/50 15.00 6.75
107 Adam Johnson/50 15.00 6.75
108 Javier Vazquez/10
110 Jose Vidro/10
116 Cliff Floyd/5
117 Mike Piazza/15
119 Don Mattingly/5
122 Alfonso Soriano/10
123 Drew Henson/5
124 Brandon Claussen/50 25.00 11.00
125 Christian Parker/50 15.00 6.75
129 Jason Anderson/50 15.00 6.75
130 Nick Johnson/10
133 Barry Zito/5
134 Miguel Tejada/5
135 Eric Chavez/5
136 Tim Hudson/5
138 Terrence Long/50 25.00 11.00
142 Marlon Byrd/50 25.00 11.00
143 Bobby Abreu/5
144 Brandon Duckworth/50 15.00 6.75
145 Robert Person/50 15.00 6.75
146 Anderson Machado/50 15.00 6.75
147 Aramis Ramirez/8
148 Jack Wilson/50 15.00 6.75
149 Carlos Rivera/50 15.00 6.75
150 Jose Castillo/50 25.00 11.00
151 Walter Young/50 15.00 6.75
154 Ryan Klesko/5
155 Mike Rivera/50 15.00 6.75
157 Brian Lawrence/50 15.00 6.75
158 Xavier Nady/50 15.00 6.75
159 Dennis Tankersley/50 15.00 6.75
165 Edgar Martinez/5
166 Chris Snelling/50 25.00 11.00
167 Rafael Soriano/50 15.00 6.75
170 Freddy Garcia/5
173 Albert Pujols/5
176 Jim Edmonds/10
179 Antonio Perez/50 15.00 6.75
180 Dewon Brazelton/50 15.00 6.75
181 Aubrey Huff/50 25.00 11.00
182 Toby Hall/50 15.00 6.75
184 Joe Kennedy/50 15.00 6.75
187 Hank Blalock/50 40.00 18.00
188 Mark Teixeira/50 40.00 18.00
189 Juan Gonzalez/10
190 Kevin Mench/50 15.00 6.75
191 Nolan Ryan Rgr/5
193 Eric Hinske/50 15.00 6.75
194 Vinny Chulk/50 15.00 6.75
195 Alexis Rios/50 60.00 27.00
197 Shannon Stewart/10
206 Prentice Redman NG/50 15.00 6.75
207 Craig Brazell NG/50 25.00 11.00
208 Nook Logan NG/50 15.00 6.75
209 Hong-Chih Kuo NG/40 50.00 22.00
210 Matt Kata NG/50 40.00 18.00
211 Chien-Ming Wang NG/40 80.00 36.00
212 Alejandro Machado NG/50 15.00 6.75
213 Michael Hessman NG/50 15.00 6.75
214 Francisco Rosario NG/50 15.00 6.75
215 Pedro Liriano NG/50 15.00 6.75
216 Jeremy Bonderman NG/50 40.00 18.00
217 Oscar Villarreal NG/50 15.00 6.75
218 Arnie Munoz NG/50 15.00 6.75
219 Tim Olson NG/50 25.00 11.00
220 Jose Contreras NG/15
221 Francisco Cruceta NG/50 15.00 6.75
222 John Webb NG/50 15.00 6.75
223 Phil Seibel NG/50 15.00 6.75
224 Aaron Looper NG/50 15.00 6.75
225 Brian Stokes NG/50 15.00 6.75
226 Guillermo Quiroz NG/50 40.00 18.00
227 Fernando Cabrera NG/50 15.00 6.75
228 Josh Hall NG/50 25.00 11.00
229 Diegomar Markwell NG/50 15.00 6.75
230 Andrew Brown NG/50 15.00 6.75
231 Doug Waechter NG/50 25.00 11.00
232 Felix Sanchez NG/50 15.00 6.75
233 Gerardo Garcia NG/50 15.00 6.75
234 Matt Bruback NG/50 15.00 6.75
235 Michel Hernandez NG/50 15.00 6.75
236 Rett Johnson NG/50 25.00 11.00
237 Ryan Cameron NG/50 15.00 6.75
238 Rob Hammock NG/50 25.00 11.00
239 Clint Barmes NG/50 25.00 11.00
240 Brandon Webb NG/50 80.00 36.00
241 Jon Leicester NG/50 15.00 6.75
242 Shane Bazzell NG/50 15.00 6.75
243 Joe Valentine NG/50 15.00 6.75
244 Josh Stewart NG/50 15.00 6.75
245 Pete LaForest NG/50 25.00 11.00
246 Shane Victorino NG/50 15.00 6.75
247 Terrmel Sledge NG/50 25.00 11.00
248 Lew Ford NG/50 25.00 11.00
249 Todd Wellemeyer NG/50 25.00 11.00
251 Adam Loewen NG/50 80.00 36.00
252 Dan Haren NG/50 40.00 18.00
253 Dontrelle Willis NG/25
254 Ramon Nivar NG/50 40.00 18.00
255 Chad Gaudin NG/50 15.00 6.75
256 Kevin Correia NG/25
257 Rickie Weeks NG/15
258 Ryan Wagner NG/50 40.00 18.00
259 Delmon Young NG/25

2003 Leaf Certified Materials Mirror Blue Materials

MINT NRMT
RANDOM INSERTS IN PACKS
PRINT RUNS B/WN 10-100 COPIES PER
NO PRICING ON QTY OF 25 OR FEWER
1 Troy Glaus Jsy/100 15.00 6.75
2 Alfredo Amezaga Jsy/100 10.00 4.50
3 Garret Anderson Bat/100 10.00 4.50
4 Nolan Ryan Angels Jsy/15
5 Darin Erstad Bat/100 10.00 4.50
6 Junior Spivey Bat/100 10.00 4.50
7 Randy Johnson Jsy/100 15.00 6.75
8 Curt Schilling Jsy/100 15.00 6.75
9 Luis Gonzalez Jsy/100 10.00 4.50
10 Steve Finley Jsy/100 10.00 4.50
11 Matt Williams Jsy/100 10.00 4.50
12 Greg Maddux Jsy/100 25.00 11.00
13 Chipper Jones Jsy/50 25.00 11.00
14 Gary Sheffield Bat/100 10.00 4.50
15 Adam LaRoche Bat/100 15.00 6.75
16 Andruw Jones Jsy/100 10.00 4.50
17 Robert Fick Bat/100 10.00 4.50
18 John Smoltz Jsy/100 15.00 6.75
19 Javy Lopez Jsy/100 10.00 4.50
20 Jay Gibbons Jsy/100 10.00 4.50
21 Geronimo Gil Jsy/100 10.00 4.50
22 Cal Ripken Jsy/15
23 Nomar Garciaparra Jsy/100 30.00 13.50
24 Pedro Martinez Jsy/100 15.00 6.75
25 Freddy Sanchez Bat/100 10.00 4.50
26 Rickey Henderson Bat/100 15.00 6.75
27 Manny Ramirez Jsy/100 10.00 4.50
28 Casey Fossum Jsy/100 10.00 4.50
29 Sammy Sosa Jsy/100 30.00 13.50
30 Kerry Wood Jsy/100 15.00 6.75
31 Corey Patterson Bat/100 10.00 4.50
32 Nic Jackson Bat/100 10.00 4.50
33 Mark Prior Jsy/100 30.00 13.50
34 Juan Cruz Jsy/100 10.00 4.50
35 Steve Smyth Jsy/100 10.00 4.50
36 Magglio Ordonez Jsy/100 10.00 4.50
37 Joe Borchard Jsy/100 10.00 4.50
38 Frank Thomas Jsy/100 15.00 6.75
39 Mark Buehrle Jsy/100 10.00 4.50
40 Joe Crede Hat/100 10.00 4.50
41 Carlos Lee Jsy/100 10.00 4.50
42 Paul Konerko Jsy/100 10.00 4.50
43 Adam Dunn Jsy/100 10.00 4.50
45 Brandon Larson Spikes/40 15.00 6.75
46 Ken Griffey Jr. Base/100 25.00 11.00
47 Barry Larkin Jsy/100 15.00 6.75
48 Sean Casey Bat/100 10.00 4.50
49 Wily Mo Pena Bat/100 10.00 4.50
50 Austin Kearns Jsy/100 10.00 4.50
51 Victor Martinez Jsy/100 10.00 4.50
55 C.C. Sabathia Jsy/100 10.00 4.50
56 Ricardo Rodriguez Bat/100 10.00 4.50
57 Omar Vizquel Jsy/100 10.00 4.50
58 Travis Hafner Bat/100 10.00 4.50
59 Todd Helton Jsy/100 15.00 6.75
60 Jason Jennings Jsy/100 10.00 4.50
62 Larry Walker Jsy/100 15.00 6.75
63 Travis Chapman Bat/100 10.00 4.50
64 Mike Maroth Jsy/100 10.00 4.50
65 Josh Beckett Jsy/100 15.00 6.75
66 Ivan Rodriguez Bat/100 15.00 6.75
67 Brad Penny Jsy/100 10.00 4.50
68 A.J. Burnett Jsy/100 10.00 4.50
69 Craig Biggio Jsy/100 15.00 6.75
70 Roy Oswalt Jsy/100 10.00 4.50
71 Jason Lane Jsy/100 10.00 4.50
72 Nolan Ryan Astros Jsy/15
73 Wade Miller Jsy/100 10.00 4.50
74 Richard Hidalgo Pants/100 10.00 4.50
75 Jeff Bagwell Jsy/100 15.00 6.75
76 Lance Berkman Jsy/100 10.00 4.50
77 Rodrigo Rosario Jsy/100 10.00 4.50
78 Jeff Kent Bat/100 10.00 4.50
79 John Buck Jsy/100 10.00 4.50
80 Angel Berroa Bat/100 10.00 4.50
81 Mike Sweeney Jsy/100 10.00 4.50
84 Carlos Beltran Jsy/100 10.00 4.50
86 Hideo Nomo Jsy/100 40.00 18.00
87 Paul Lo Duca Jsy/100 10.00 4.50
88 Cesar Izturis Pants/100 10.00 4.50
89 Kazuhisa Ishii Jsy/100 10.00 4.50
90 Shawn Green Jsy/100 10.00 4.50
91 Joe Thurston Jsy/100 10.00 4.50
92 Adrian Beltre Bat/100 10.00 4.50
93 Kevin Brown Jsy/100 10.00 4.50
94 Richie Sexson Jsy/100 10.00 4.50
95 Ben Sheets Jsy/100 10.00 4.50
97 Geoff Jenkins Jsy/100 10.00 4.50
98 Bill Hall Bat/100 10.00 4.50
99 Torii Hunter Jsy/100 10.00 4.50
101 Michael Cuddyer Jsy/100 10.00 4.50
102 Jose Morban Bat/100 10.00 4.50
103 Brad Radke Jsy/100 10.00 4.50
104 Jacque Jones Jsy/100 10.00 4.50
105 Eric Milton Jsy/100 10.00 4.50
106 Joe Mays Jsy/100 10.00 4.50
107 Adam Johnson Jsy/100 10.00 4.50
108 Javier Vazquez Jsy/100 10.00 4.50
109 Vladimir Guerrero Jsy/100 15.00 6.75
110 Jose Vidro Jsy/100 10.00 4.50
111 Michael Barrett Jsy/40 15.00 6.75
112 Orlando Cabrera Jsy/100 10.00 4.50
113 Tom Glavine Bat/100 15.00 6.75
114 Roberto Alomar Bat/100 15.00 6.75
115 Tsuyoshi Shinjo Jsy/100 10.00 4.50
116 Cliff Floyd Bat/100 10.00 4.50
117 Mike Piazza Jsy/100 25.00 11.00
118 Al Leiter Jsy/100 10.00 4.50
119 Don Mattingly Jsy/15
120 Roger Clemens Jsy/100 30.00 13.50
121 Derek Jeter Base/100 30.00 13.50
122 Alfonso Soriano Jsy/100 15.00 6.75
123 Drew Henson Bat/100 10.00 4.50
124 Brandon Claussen Hat/40 15.00 6.75
125 Christian Parker Pants/100 10.00 4.50
126 Jason Giambi Jsy/100 15.00 6.75
127 Mike Mussina Jsy/40 25.00 11.00
128 Bernie Williams Jsy/100 15.00 6.75
130 Nick Johnson Jsy/100 10.00 4.50
131 Jorge Posada Jsy/100 15.00 6.75
132 Andy Pettitte Jsy/100 15.00 6.75
133 Barry Zito Jsy/100 15.00 6.75
134 Miguel Tejada Jsy/100 10.00 4.50
135 Eric Chavez Jsy/100 10.00 4.50
136 Tim Hudson Jsy/100 10.00 4.50
137 Mark Mulder Jsy/100 10.00 4.50
138 Terrence Long Jsy/100 10.00 4.50
139 Mark Ellis Jsy/100 10.00 4.50
140 Jim Thome Bat/100 15.00 6.75
141 Pat Burrell Bat/100 10.00 4.50
142 Marlon Byrd Jsy/100 10.00 4.50
143 Bobby Abreu Jsy/100 10.00 4.50
144 Brandon Duckworth Jsy/100 10.00 4.50
145 Robert Person Jsy/100 10.00 4.50
146 Anderson Machado Jsy/100 10.00 4.50
147 Aramis Ramirez Jsy/100 10.00 4.50
148 Jack Wilson Bat/100 10.00 4.50
150 Jose Castillo Bat/100 10.00 4.50
151 Walter Young Bat/100 10.00 4.50
152 Brian Giles Bat/100 10.00 4.50
153 Jason Kendall Jsy/100 10.00 4.50
154 Ryan Klesko Jsy/50 15.00 6.75
155 Mike Rivera Bat/100 10.00 4.50
157 Brian Lawrence Bat/100 10.00 4.50
158 Xavier Nady Hat/40 15.00 6.75
159 Dennis Tankersley Jsy/100 10.00 4.50
160 Phil Nevin Jsy/100 10.00 4.50
161 Barry Bonds Base/100 30.00 13.50
162 Kenny Lofton Bat/100 10.00 4.50
163 Rich Aurilia Jsy/100 10.00 4.50
164 Ichiro Suzuki Base/100 30.00 13.50
165 Edgar Martinez Jsy/100 15.00 6.75
166 Chris Snelling Bat/100 10.00 4.50
167 Rafael Soriano Jsy/100 10.00 4.50
168 John Olerud Jsy/100 10.00 4.50
169 Bret Boone Jsy/100 10.00 4.50
170 Freddy Garcia Jsy/100 10.00 4.50
171 Aaron Sele Jsy/100 10.00 4.50
172 Kazuhiro Sasaki Jsy/100 10.00 4.50
173 Albert Pujols Jsy/100 40.00 18.00
174 Scott Rolen Bat/100 15.00 6.75
175 So Taguchi Jsy/100 10.00 4.50
176 Jim Edmonds Jsy/100 10.00 4.50
177 Edgar Renteria Jsy/100 10.00 4.50
178 J.D. Drew Jsy/100 10.00 4.50
179 Antonio Perez Bat/100 10.00 4.50
180 Dewon Brazelton Jsy/100 10.00 4.50
181 Aubrey Huff Jsy/50 15.00 6.75
182 Toby Hall Jsy/100 10.00 4.50
183 Ben Grieve Jsy/100 10.00 4.50
184 Joe Kennedy Jsy/100 10.00 4.50
185 Alex Rodriguez Jsy/100 30.00 13.50
186 Rafael Palmeiro Jsy/100 15.00 6.75
187 Hank Blalock Jsy/100 15.00 6.75
188 Mark Teixeira Jsy/100 15.00 6.75
189 Juan Gonzalez Bat/100 15.00 6.75
190 Kevin Mench Jsy/100 10.00 4.50
191 Nolan Ryan Rgr Jsy/15
192 Doug Davis Jsy/100 10.00 4.50
193 Eric Hinske Jsy/100 10.00 4.50
196 Carlos Delgado Jsy/100 10.00 4.50
197 Shannon Stewart Jsy/100 10.00 4.50
198 Josh Phelps Jsy/100 10.00 4.50
199 Vernon Wells Jsy/100 10.00 4.50
200 Roy Halladay Jsy/100 10.00 4.50
201 Babe Ruth RET Pants/10
202 Lou Gehrig RET Pants/10
203 Jackie Robinson RET Jsy/10
204 Ty Cobb RET Pants/10
205 Thurman Munson RET Jsy/10

2003 Leaf Certified Materials Mirror Emerald

MINT NRMT
1-250 RANDOM INSERTS IN PACKS
251-259 RANDOM IN DLP R/T PACKS
STATED PRINT RUN 5 SERIAL #'d SETS
NO PRICING DUE TO SCARCITY

2003 Leaf Certified Materials Mirror Emerald Autographs

MINT NRMT
1-250 RANDOM INSERTS IN PACKS
251-259 RANDOM IN DLP R/T PACKS
STATED PRINT RUN 5 SERIAL #'d SETS
NO PRICING DUE TO SCARCITY

2003 Leaf Certified Materials Mirror Emerald Materials

MINT NRMT
RANDOM INSERTS IN PACKS
STATED PRINT RUN 5 SERIAL #'d SETS
NO PRICING DUE TO SCARCITY

2003 Leaf Certified Materials Mirror Gold

MINT NRMT
1-250 RANDOM INSERTS IN PACKS
251-259 RANDOM IN DLP R/T PACKS
STATED PRINT RUN 25 SERIAL #'d SETS
NO PRICING DUE TO SCARCITY

2003 Leaf Certified Materials Mirror Gold Autographs

MINT NRMT
1-250 RANDOM INSERTS IN PACKS
251-259 RANDOM IN DLP R/T PACKS
PRINT RUNS B/WN 5-25 COPIES PER
NO PRICING DUE TO SCARCITY

2003 Leaf Certified Materials Mirror Gold Materials

MINT NRMT
RANDOM INSERTS IN PACKS
PRINT RUNS B/WN 5-25 COPIES PER
NO PRICING DUE TO SCARCITY

2003 Leaf Certified Materials Mirror Red

MINT NRMT
*ACTIVE RED 1-200: 2X TO 5X BASIC
*RETIRED RED 1-200: 2.5X TO 6X BASIC
*RED 201-205: .75X TO 2X BASIC
*RED 206-219/221-250: .2X TO .5X BASIC
*RED 220: .12X TO .3X BASIC 220
*RED 250: .5X TO 1.2X BASIC 250
*RED 251-259: .2X TO .5X BASIC p/r 250
*RED 251-259: .15X TO .4X BASIC p/r 100-150
1-250 RANDOM INSERTS IN PACKS
251-259 RANDOM IN DLP R/T PACKS
STATED PRINT RUN 100 SERIAL #'d SETS

2003 Leaf Certified Materials Mirror Red Autographs

MINT NRMT
1-250 RANDOM INSERTS IN PACKS
251-259 RANDOM IN DLP R/T PACKS
PRINT RUNS B/WN 5-100 COPIES PER
NO PRICING ON QTY OF 25 OR LESS.
2 Alfredo Amezaga/100 15.00 6.75
3 Garret Anderson/10
4 Nolan Ryan Angels/5
6 Junior Spivey/15
15 Adam LaRoche/100 40.00 18.00
17 Robert Fick/15
20 Jay Gibbons/100 25.00 11.00
21 Geronimo Gil/15
22 Cal Ripken/5
25 Freddy Sanchez/100 15.00 6.75
28 Casey Fossum/50 15.00 6.75
31 Corey Patterson/6
32 Nic Jackson/100 15.00 6.75
33 Mark Prior/15
34 Juan Cruz/15
35 Steve Smyth/94 15.00 6.75
37 Joe Borchard/15
39 Mark Buehrle/15
40 Joe Crede/15
45 Brandon Larson/100 15.00 6.75
49 Wily Mo Pena/100 15.00 6.75
51 Victor Martinez/15
52 Brian Tallet/15
53 Cliff Lee/15
54 Jeremy Guthrie/15
56 Ricardo Rodriguez/100 15.00 6.75
60 Jason Jennings/15
61 Jeff Baker/15
63 Travis Chapman/100 15.00 6.75
64 Mike Maroth/100 15.00 6.75
70 Roy Oswalt/15
71 Jason Lane/100 15.00 6.75
72 Nolan Ryan Astros/5
73 Wade Miller/15
74 Richard Hidalgo/10
77 Rodrigo Rosario/100 15.00 6.75
79 John Buck/15
80 Angel Berroa/15
81 Mike Sweeney/10
82 Mac Suzuki/15
83 Alexis Gomez/15
85 Runelvys Hernandez/100 15.00 6.75
86 Hideo Nomo/16
87 Paul Lo Duca/15
88 Cesar Izturis/100 15.00 6.75
89 Kazuhisa Ishii/5
91 Joe Thurston/100 15.00 6.75
94 Richie Sexson/10
95 Ben Sheets/10
96 Takahito Nomura/15
98 Bill Hall/100 15.00 6.75
100 A.J. Pierzynski/10
102 Jose Morban/100 15.00 6.75
106 Joe Mays/9
107 Adam Johnson/15
108 Javier Vazquez/15
110 Jose Vidro/15
116 Cliff Floyd/10
117 Mike Piazza/20
119 Don Mattingly/5
122 Alfonso Soriano/15
123 Drew Henson/10
124 Brandon Claussen/60 25.00 11.00
125 Christian Parker/15
129 Jason Anderson/100 15.00 6.75
130 Nick Johnson/15
133 Barry Zito/10
134 Miguel Tejada/10
135 Eric Chavez/10
136 Tim Hudson/10
138 Terrence Long/15
141 Pat Burrell/6
142 Marlon Byrd/100 25.00 11.00
143 Bobby Abreu/10
144 Brandon Duckworth/15
145 Robert Person/15
146 Anderson Machado/100 15.00 6.75
148 Jack Wilson/15
149 Carlos Rivera/100 15.00 6.75
150 Jose Castillo/100 25.00 11.00
151 Walter Young/100 15.00 6.75
152 Brian Giles/15
154 Ryan Klesko/10
155 Mike Rivera/100 15.00 6.75
157 Brian Lawrence/100 15.00 6.75
158 Xavier Nady Hat/15
159 Dennis Tankersley/15
165 Edgar Martinez/10
166 Chris Snelling/100 25.00 11.00
167 Rafael Soriano/15
170 Freddy Garcia/15
173 Albert Pujols/10
176 Jim Edmonds/10
179 Antonio Perez/15
180 Dewon Brazelton/15
181 Aubrey Huff/15
182 Toby Hall/15
184 Joe Kennedy/15
187 Hank Blalock/15
188 Mark Teixeira/15
189 Juan Gonzalez/10
190 Kevin Mench/100 15.00 6.75
191 Nolan Ryan Rgr/5
193 Eric Hinske/100 15.00 6.75
194 Vinny Chulk/100 15.00 6.75
195 Alexis Rios/100 50.00 22.00
197 Shannon Stewart/15
206 Prentice Redman NG/100 10.00 4.50
207 Craig Brazell NG/100 15.00 6.75
208 Nook Logan NG/100 10.00 4.50
209 Hong-Chih Kuo NG/50 40.00 18.00
210 Matt Kata NG/100 25.00 11.00
211 Chien-Ming Wang NG/50 80.00 36.00
212 Alejandro Machado NG/100 10.00 4.50
213 Michael Hessman NG/100 10.00 4.50
214 Francisco Rosario NG/100 10.00 4.50
215 Pedro Liriano NG/100 10.00 4.50
216 Jeremy Bonderman NG/100 25.00 11.00
217 Oscar Villarreal NG/100 10.00 4.50
218 Arnie Munoz NG/100 10.00 4.50
219 Tim Olson NG/100 15.00 6.75
220 Jose Contreras NG/5
221 Francisco Cruceta NG/100 10.00 4.50
222 John Webb NG/100 10.00 4.50
223 Phil Seibel NG/100 10.00 4.50
224 Aaron Looper NG/100 10.00 4.50
225 Brian Stokes NG/100 10.00 4.50
226 Guillermo Quiroz NG/100 25.00 11.00
227 Fernando Cabrera NG/100 10.00 4.50
228 Josh Hall NG/100 15.00 6.75
229 Diegomar Markwell NG/100 10.00 4.50
230 Andrew Brown NG/100 10.00 4.50
231 Doug Waechter NG/100 15.00 6.75
232 Felix Sanchez NG/100 10.00 4.50
233 Gerardo Garcia NG/100 10.00 4.50
234 Matt Bruback NG/100 10.00 4.50
235 Michel Hernandez NG/100 10.00 4.50
236 Rett Johnson NG/100 15.00 6.75
237 Ryan Cameron NG/100 10.00 4.50
238 Rob Hammock NG/100 15.00 6.75
239 Clint Barmes NG/100 15.00 6.75
240 Brandon Webb NG/100 50.00 22.00
241 Jon Leicester NG/100 10.00 4.50
242 Shane Bazzell NG/100 10.00 4.50
243 Joe Valentine NG/100 10.00 4.50
244 Josh Stewart NG/100 10.00 4.50
245 Pete LaForest NG/100 15.00 6.75
246 Shane Victorino NG/100 10.00 4.50
247 Terrmel Sledge NG/100 15.00 6.75
248 Lew Ford NG/100 15.00 6.75
249 Todd Wellemeyer NG/100 15.00 6.75
251 Adam Loewen NG/100 50.00 22.00
252 Dan Haren NG/100 25.00 11.00
253 Dontrelle Willis NG/50 40.00 18.00
254 Ramon Nivar NG/100 25.00 11.00
255 Chad Gaudin NG/100 10.00 4.50
256 Kevin Correia NG/100 10.00 4.50
257 Rickie Weeks NG/25
258 Ryan Wagner NG/100 25.00 11.00
259 Delmon Young NG/50 100.00 45.00

2003 Leaf Certified Materials Mirror Red Materials

MINT NRMT
RANDOM INSERTS IN PACKS
PRINT RUNS B/WN 15-250 COPIES PER
NO PRICING ON QTY OF 25 OR LESS.
1 Troy Glaus Jsy/250 10.00 4.50
2 Alfredo Amezaga Jsy/100 10.00 4.50
3 Garret Anderson Bat/250 8.00 3.60
4 Nolan Ryan Angels Jsy/35 80.00 36.00
5 Darin Erstad Bat/250 8.00 3.60
6 Junior Spivey Bat/250 8.00 3.60
7 Randy Johnson Jsy/250 10.00 4.50
8 Curt Schilling Jsy/250 10.00 4.50
9 Luis Gonzalez Jsy/250 8.00 3.60
10 Steve Finley Jsy/250 8.00 3.60
11 Matt Williams Jsy/100 10.00 4.50
12 Greg Maddux Jsy/250 20.00 9.00
13 Chipper Jones Jsy/250 10.00 4.50
14 Gary Sheffield Bat/125 10.00 4.50
15 Adam LaRoche Bat/250 10.00 4.50
16 Andruw Jones Jsy/250 8.00 3.60
17 Robert Fick Bat/250 8.00 3.60
18 John Smoltz Jsy/250 10.00 4.50
19 Javy Lopez Jsy/250 8.00 3.60
20 Jay Gibbons Jsy/250 8.00 3.60
21 Geronimo Gil Jsy/250 8.00 3.60
22 Cal Ripken Jsy/35 120.00 55.00
23 Nomar Garciaparra Jsy/250 25.00 11.00
24 Pedro Martinez Jsy/250 10.00 4.50
25 Freddy Sanchez Bat/250 8.00 3.60
26 Rickey Henderson Bat/250 10.00 4.50
27 Manny Ramirez Jsy/250 8.00 3.60
28 Casey Fossum Jsy/250 8.00 3.60
29 Sammy Sosa Jsy/250 25.00 11.00
30 Kerry Wood Jsy/250 10.00 4.50
31 Corey Patterson Bat/250 8.00 3.60
32 Nic Jackson Bat/250 8.00 3.60
33 Mark Prior Jsy/250 25.00 11.00
34 Juan Cruz Jsy/250 8.00 3.60
35 Steve Smyth Jsy/250 8.00 3.60
36 Magglio Ordonez Jsy/250 8.00 3.60
37 Joe Borchard Jsy/250 8.00 3.60
38 Frank Thomas Jsy/250 10.00 4.50
39 Mark Buehrle Jsy/250 8.00 3.60
40 Joe Crede Hat/100 10.00 4.50
41 Carlos Lee Jsy/250 8.00 3.60

42 Paul Konerko Jsy/250 8.00 3.60
43 Adam Dunn Jsy/250 8.00 3.60
45 Brandon Larson Spikes/150 8.00 3.60
46 Ken Griffey Jr. Base/250 20.00 9.00
47 Barry Larkin Jsy/250 10.00 4.50
48 Sean Casey Bat/250 8.00 3.60
49 Wily Mo Pena Bat/250 8.00 3.60
50 Austin Kearns Jsy/250 8.00 3.60
51 Victor Martinez Jsy/100 10.00 4.50
55 C.C. Sabathia Jsy/250 8.00 3.60
56 Ricardo Rodriguez Bat/250 8.00 3.60
57 Omar Vizquel Jsy/250 8.00 3.60
58 Travis Hafner Bat/250 8.00 3.60
59 Todd Helton Jsy/250 10.00 4.50
60 Jason Jennings Jsy/250 8.00 3.60
62 Larry Walker Jsy/250 10.00 4.50
63 Travis Chapman Bat/250 8.00 3.60
64 Mike Maroth Jsy/250 8.00 3.60
65 Josh Beckett Jsy/250 10.00 4.50
66 Ivan Rodriguez Bat/250 10.00 4.50
67 Brad Penny Jsy/250 8.00 3.60
68 A.J. Burnett Jsy/250 8.00 3.60
69 Craig Biggio Jsy/250 10.00 4.50
70 Roy Oswalt Jsy/250 8.00 3.60
71 Jason Lane Jsy/250 8.00 3.60
72 Nolan Ryan Astros Jsy/35 80.00 36.00
73 Wade Miller Jsy/250 8.00 3.60
74 Richard Hidalgo Pants/250 8.00 3.60
75 Jeff Bagwell Jsy/250 10.00 4.50
76 Lance Berkman Jsy/250 8.00 3.60
77 Rodrigo Rosario Jsy/250 8.00 3.60
78 Jeff Kent Bat/250 8.00 3.60
79 John Buck Jsy/250 8.00 3.60
80 Angel Berroa Bat/250 10.00 4.50
81 Mike Sweeney Jsy/250 8.00 3.60
84 Carlos Beltran Jsy/250 8.00 3.60
86 Hideo Nomo Jsy/250 30.00 13.50
87 Paul Lo Duca Jsy/250 8.00 3.60
88 Cesar Izturis Pants/250 8.00 3.60
89 Kazuhisa Ishii Jsy/250 8.00 3.60
90 Shawn Green Jsy/250 8.00 3.60
91 Joe Thurston Jsy/250 8.00 3.60
92 Adrian Beltre Bat/250 8.00 3.60
93 Kevin Brown Jsy/250 8.00 3.60
94 Richie Sexson Jsy/250 8.00 3.60
95 Ben Sheets Jsy/250 8.00 3.60
97 Geoff Jenkins Jsy/250 8.00 3.60
98 Bill Hall Bat/250 8.00 3.60
99 Torii Hunter Jsy/250 8.00 3.60
101 Michael Cuddyer Jsy/250 8.00 3.60
102 Jose Morban Bat/250 8.00 3.60
103 Brad Radke Jsy/250 8.00 3.60
104 Jacque Jones Jsy/250 8.00 3.60
105 Eric Milton Jsy/250 8.00 3.60
106 Joe Mays Jsy/250 8.00 3.60
107 Adam Johnson Jsy/250 8.00 3.60
108 Javier Vazquez Jsy/250 8.00 3.60
109 Vladimir Guerrero Jsy/250 10.00 4.50
110 Jose Vidro Jsy/250 8.00 3.60
111 Michael Barrett Jsy/50 15.00 6.75
112 Orlando Cabrera Jsy/250 8.00 3.60
113 Tom Glavine Bat/250 10.00 4.50
114 Roberto Alomar Bat/250 10.00 4.50
115 Tsuyoshi Shinjo Jsy/250 8.00 3.60
116 Cliff Floyd Bat/250 8.00 3.60
117 Mike Piazza Jsy/250 20.00 9.00
118 Al Leiter Jsy/250 8.00 3.60
119 Don Mattingly Jsy/35 80.00 36.00
120 Roger Clemens Jsy/250 25.00 11.00
121 Derek Jeter Base/250 25.00 11.00
122 Alfonso Soriano Jsy/250 10.00 4.50
123 Drew Henson Bat/250 8.00 3.60
124 Brandon Claussen Hat/50 15.00 6.75
125 Christian Parker Pants/250 8.00 3.60
126 Jason Giambi Jsy/250 10.00 4.50
127 Mike Mussina Jsy/250 10.00 4.50
128 Bernie Williams Jsy/250 10.00 4.50
130 Nick Johnson Jsy/250 8.00 3.60
131 Jorge Posada Jsy/250 10.00 4.50
132 Andy Pettitte Jsy/250 10.00 4.50
133 Barry Zito Jsy/250 10.00 4.50
134 Miguel Tejada Jsy/250 8.00 3.60
135 Eric Chavez Jsy/250 8.00 3.60
136 Tim Hudson Jsy/250 8.00 3.60
137 Mark Mulder Jsy/250 8.00 3.60
138 Terrence Long Jsy/250 8.00 3.60
139 Mark Ellis Jsy/250 8.00 3.60
140 Jim Thome Bat/250 10.00 4.50
141 Pat Burrell Bat/250 8.00 3.60
142 Marlon Byrd Jsy/250 8.00 3.60
143 Bobby Abreu Jsy/250 8.00 3.60
144 Brandon Duckworth Jsy/250 8.00 3.60
145 Robert Person Jsy/250 8.00 3.60
146 Anderson Machado Jsy/250 8.00 3.60
147 Aramis Ramirez Jsy/250 8.00 3.60
148 Jack Wilson Bat/250 8.00 3.60
150 Jose Castillo Bat/250 8.00 3.60
151 Walter Young Bat/250 8.00 3.60
152 Brian Giles Bat/250 8.00 3.60
153 Jason Kendall Jsy/250 8.00 3.60
154 Ryan Klesko Jsy/25
155 Mike Rivera Bat/250 8.00 3.60
157 Brian Lawrence Bat/250 8.00 3.60
158 Xavier Nady Hat/60 15.00 6.75
159 Dennis Tankersley Jsy/250 8.00 3.60
160 Phil Nevin Jsy/250 8.00 3.60
161 Barry Bonds Base/250 25.00 11.00
162 Kenny Lofton Bat/250 8.00 3.60
163 Rich Aurilia Jsy/250 8.00 3.60
164 Ichiro Suzuki Base/250 25.00 11.00
165 Edgar Martinez Jsy/100 15.00 6.75
166 Chris Snelling Bat/250 8.00 3.60
167 Rafael Soriano Jsy/250 8.00 3.60
168 John Olerud Jsy/250 8.00 3.60
169 Bret Boone Jsy/250 8.00 3.60
170 Freddy Garcia Jsy/250 8.00 3.60
171 Aaron Sele Jsy/250 8.00 3.60
172 Kazuhiro Sasaki Jsy/250 8.00 3.60
173 Albert Pujols Jsy/250 30.00 13.50
174 Scott Rolen Bat/250 10.00 4.50
175 So Taguchi Jsy/250 8.00 3.60
176 Jim Edmonds Jsy/250 8.00 3.60
177 Edgar Renteria Jsy/250 8.00 3.60
178 J.D. Drew Jsy/250 8.00 3.60
179 Antonio Perez Bat/250 8.00 3.60
180 Dewon Brazelton Jsy/250 8.00 3.60
181 Aubrey Huff Jsy/50 15.00 6.75
182 Toby Hall Jsy/250 8.00 3.60
183 Ben Grieve Jsy/100 10.00 4.50
184 Joe Kennedy Jsy/250 8.00 3.60
185 Alex Rodriguez Jsy/250 25.00 11.00
186 Rafael Palmeiro Jsy/250 10.00 4.50
187 Hank Blalock Jsy/250 10.00 4.50
188 Mark Teixeira Jsy/250 10.00 4.50
189 Juan Gonzalez Bat/250 10.00 4.50
190 Kevin Mench Jsy/250 8.00 3.60
191 Nolan Ryan Rgr Jsy/35 80.00 36.00
192 Doug Davis Jsy/250 8.00 3.60
193 Eric Hinske Jsy/250 8.00 3.60
196 Carlos Delgado Jsy/250 8.00 3.60
197 Shannon Stewart Jsy/250 8.00 3.60
198 Josh Phelps Jsy/250 8.00 3.60
199 Vernon Wells Jsy/250 8.00 3.60
200 Roy Halladay Jsy/250 8.00 3.60
201 Babe Ruth RET Pants/15
202 Lou Gehrig RET Pants/15
203 Jackie Robinson RET Jsy/15
204 Ty Cobb RET Pants/15
205 Thurman Munson RET Jsy/15

2003 Leaf Certified Materials Fabric of the Game

Randomly inserted into packs, these 900 cards feature six versions of 150 different cards. The set is broken down into BA (designed like a Base); DY (indicating the year the team was 1st known by their current nomenclature); IN (inscription; JN (Jersey Number); JY (Jersey Year that this jersey was used in) and PS (Position). We have put the stated print run next to the player's name in our checklist.

MINT NRMT
PRINT RUNS BETWEEN 1-102 COPIES PER
NO PRICING ON QTY OF 25 OR LESS.

1BA Bobby Doerr BA/50 20.00 9.00
1DY Bobby Doerr DY/7
1IN Bobby Doerr IN/25
1JN Bobby Doerr JN/1
1JY Bobby Doerr JY/39 25.00 11.00
1PS Bobby Doerr PS/50 20.00 9.00
2BA Ozzie Smith BA/100 40.00 18.00
2DY Ozzie Smith DY/1
2IN Ozzie Smith IN/50 50.00 22.00
2JN Ozzie Smith JN/1
2JY Ozzie Smith JY/88 40.00 18.00
2PS Ozzie Smith PS/50 50.00 22.00
3BA Pee Wee Reese BA/20
3DY Pee Wee Reese DY/32 40.00 18.00
3IN Pee Wee Reese IN/15
3JN Pee Wee Reese JN/1
3JY Pee Wee Reese JY/58 25.00 11.00
3PS Pee Wee Reese PS/20
4BA Jeff Bagwell Pants BA/100 15.00 6.75
4DY Jeff Bagwell Pants DY/65 20.00 9.00
4IN Jeff Bagwell Pants IN/50 20.00 9.00
4JN Jeff Bagwell Pants JN/5
4JY Jeff Bagwell Pants JY/98 15.00 6.75
4PS Jeff Bagwell Pants PS/50 20.00 9.00
5BA Tommy Lasorda BA/100 15.00 6.75
5DY Tommy Lasorda DY/58 20.00 9.00
5IN Tommy Lasorda IN/25
5JN Tommy Lasorda JN/2
5JY Tommy Lasorda JY/84 15.00 6.75
5PS Tommy Lasorda PS/50 20.00 9.00
6BA Red Schoendienst BA/25
6DY Red Schoendienst DY/1
6IN Red Schoendienst IN/15
6JN Red Schoendienst JN/2
6JY Red Schoendienst JY/55 20.00 9.00
6PS Red Schoendienst PS/50 20.00 9.00
7BA Harmon Killebrew BA/50 40.00 18.00
7DY Harmon Killebrew DY/61 40.00 18.00
7IN Harmon Killebrew IN/50 40.00 18.00
7JN Harmon Killebrew JN/3
7JY Harmon Killebrew JY/71 40.00 18.00
7PS Harmon Killebrew PS/50 40.00 18.00
8BA Roger Maris BA/25
8DY Roger Maris DY/55 80.00 36.00
8IN Roger Maris IN/20
8JN Roger Maris JN/3
8JY Roger Maris JY/58 80.00 36.00
8PS Roger Maris PS/50 80.00 36.00
9BA Alex Rodriguez M's BA/100 25.00 11.00
9DY Alex Rodriguez M's DY/77 25.00 11.00
9IN Alex Rodriguez M's IN/50 40.00 18.00
9JN Alex Rodriguez M's JN/3
9JY Alex Rodriguez M's JY/99 25.00 11.00
9PS Alex Rodriguez M's PS/50 40.00 18.00
10BA Alex Rodriguez Rgr BA/100 25.00 11.00
10DY Alex Rodriguez Rgr DY/72 25.00 11.00
10IN Alex Rodriguez Rgr IN/50 40.00 18.00
10JN Alex Rodriguez Rgr JN/3
10JY Alex Rodriguez Rgr JY/101 25.00 11.00
10PS Alex Rodriguez Rgr PS/50 40.00 18.00
11BA Dale Murphy BA/50 40.00 18.00
11DY Dale Murphy DY/66 40.00 18.00
11IN Dale Murphy IN/50 40.00 18.00
11JN Dale Murphy JN/3
11JY Dale Murphy JY/85 30.00 13.50
11PS Dale Murphy PS/50 40.00 18.00
12BA Alan Trammell BA/100 20.00 9.00
12DY Alan Trammell DY/1
12IN Alan Trammell IN/50 25.00 11.00
12JN Alan Trammell JN/3
12JY Alan Trammell JY/90 20.00 9.00
12PS Alan Trammell PS/50 25.00 11.00
13BA Babe Ruth Pants BA/10
13DY Babe Ruth Pants DY/13
13IN Babe Ruth Pants IN/10
13JN Babe Ruth Pants JN/3
13JY Babe Ruth Pants JY/30 350.00 160.00
13PS Babe Ruth Pants PS/10
14BA Lou Gehrig BA/10
14DY Lou Gehrig DY/13
14IN Lou Gehrig IN/10
14JN Lou Gehrig JN/4
14JY Lou Gehrig JY/38 300.00 135.00
14PS Lou Gehrig PS/10
15BA Babe Ruth BA/10
15DY Babe Ruth DY/13
15IN Babe Ruth IN/10
15JN Babe Ruth JN/3
15JY Babe Ruth JY/30 400.00 180.00
15PS Babe Ruth PS/10
16BA Mel Ott BA/10
16DY Mel Ott DY/1
16IN Mel Ott IN/10
16JN Mel Ott JN/4
16JY Mel Ott JY/46 50.00 22.00
16PS Mel Ott PS/10
17BA Paul Molitor BA/100 20.00 9.00
17DY Paul Molitor DY/70 25.00 11.00
17IN Paul Molitor IN/50 25.00 11.00
17JN Paul Molitor JN/4
17JY Paul Molitor JY/84 20.00 9.00
17PS Paul Molitor PS/50 25.00 11.00
18BA Duke Snider BA/15
18DY Duke Snider DY/58 40.00 18.00
18IN Duke Snider IN/15
18JN Duke Snider JN/4
18JY Duke Snider JY/62 40.00 18.00
18PS Duke Snider PS/15
19BA Miguel Tejada BA/50 15.00 6.75
19DY Miguel Tejada DY/68 15.00 6.75
19IN Miguel Tejada IN/50 15.00 6.75
19JN Miguel Tejada JN/4
19JY Miguel Tejada JY/99 10.00 4.50
19PS Miguel Tejada PS/50 15.00 6.75
20BA Lou Gehrig Pants BA/10
20DY Lou Gehrig Pants DY/13
20IN Lou Gehrig Pants IN/10
20JN Lou Gehrig Pants JN/4
20JY Lou Gehrig Pants JY/38 250.00 110.00
20PS Lou Gehrig Pants PS/10
21BA Brooks Robinson BA/15
21DY Brooks Robinson DY/54 40.00 18.00
21IN Brooks Robinson IN/15
21JN Brooks Robinson JN/5
21JY Brooks Robinson JY/66 40.00 18.00
21PS Brooks Robinson PS/15
22BA George Brett BA/50 80.00 36.00
22DY George Brett DY/69 80.00 36.00
22IN George Brett IN/50 80.00 36.00
22JN George Brett JN/5
22JY George Brett JY/91 60.00 27.00
22PS George Brett PS/50 80.00 36.00
23BA Johnny Bench BA/50 40.00 18.00
23DY Johnny Bench DY/59 40.00 18.00
23IN Johnny Bench IN/50 40.00 18.00
23JN Johnny Bench JN/5
23JY Johnny Bench JY/81 30.00 13.50
23PS Johnny Bench PS/50 40.00 18.00
24BA Lou Boudreau BA/15
24DY Lou Boudreau DY/15
24IN Lou Boudreau IN/15
24JN Lou Boudreau JN/5
24JY Lou Boudreau JY/48 25.00 11.00
24PS Lou Boudreau PS/15
25BA Nomar Garciaparra BA/100 30.00 13.50
25DY Nomar Garciaparra DY/7
25IN Nomar Garciaparra IN/50 40.00 18.00
25JN Nomar Garciaparra JN/5
25JY Nomar Garciaparra JY/100 30.00 13.50
25PS Nomar Garciaparra PS/50 40.00 18.00
26BA Tsuyoshi Shinjo BA/50 15.00 6.75
26DY Tsuyoshi Shinjo DY/62 15.00 6.75
26IN Tsuyoshi Shinjo IN/25
26JN Tsuyoshi Shinjo JN/5
26JY Tsuyoshi Shinjo JY/101 10.00 4.50
26PS Tsuyoshi Shinjo PS/25
27BA Pat Burrell BA/100 10.00 4.50
27DY Pat Burrell DY/46 20.00 9.00
27IN Pat Burrell IN/25
27JN Pat Burrell JN/5
27JY Pat Burrell JY/101 10.00 4.50
27PS Pat Burrell PS/25
28BA Albert Pujols BA/100 40.00 18.00
28DY Albert Pujols DY/1
28IN Albert Pujols IN/50 50.00 22.00
28JN Albert Pujols JN/5
28JY Albert Pujols JY/101 40.00 18.00
28PS Albert Pujols PS/50 50.00 22.00
29BA Stan Musial BA/10
29DY Stan Musial DY/1
29IN Stan Musial IN/10
29JN Stan Musial JN/6
29JY Stan Musial JY/43 80.00 36.00
29PS Stan Musial PS/10
30BA Al Kaline BA/20
30DY Al Kaline DY/1
30IN Al Kaline IN/15
30JN Al Kaline JN/6
30JY Al Kaline JY/64 40.00 18.00
30PS Al Kaline PS/15
31BA Ivan Rodriguez BA/100 15.00 6.75
31DY Ivan Rodriguez DY/72 25.00 11.00
31IN Ivan Rodriguez IN/50 25.00 11.00
31JN Ivan Rodriguez JN/7
31JY Ivan Rodriguez JY/101 15.00 6.75
31PS Ivan Rodriguez PS/50 25.00 11.00
32BA Craig Biggio BA/100 15.00 6.75
32DY Craig Biggio DY/65 20.00 9.00
32IN Craig Biggio IN/25
32JN Craig Biggio JN/7
32JY Craig Biggio JY/101 15.00 6.75
32PS Craig Biggio PS/50 20.00 9.00
33BA Joe Morgan BA/10
33DY Joe Morgan DY/59 20.00 9.00
33IN Joe Morgan IN/10
33JN Joe Morgan JN/8
33JY Joe Morgan JY/74 20.00 9.00
33PS Joe Morgan PS/10
34BA Willie Stargell BA/50 25.00 11.00
34DY Willie Stargell DY/1
34IN Willie Stargell IN/15
34JN Willie Stargell JN/8
34JY Willie Stargell JY/68 25.00 11.00
34PS Willie Stargell PS/50 25.00 11.00
35BA Andre Dawson BA/100 15.00 6.75
35DY Andre Dawson DY/7
35IN Andre Dawson IN/50 20.00 9.00
35JN Andre Dawson JN/8
35JY Andre Dawson JY/87 15.00 6.75
35PS Andre Dawson PS/50 20.00 9.00
36BA Gary Carter BA/100 20.00 9.00
36DY Gary Carter DY/62 25.00 11.00
36IN Gary Carter IN/50 25.00 11.00
36JN Gary Carter JN/8
36JY Gary Carter JY/85 20.00 9.00
36PS Gary Carter PS/50 25.00 11.00
37BA Cal Ripken BA/50 80.00 36.00
37DY Cal Ripken DY/54 80.00 36.00
37IN Cal Ripken IN/50 80.00 36.00
37JN Cal Ripken JN/8
37JY Cal Ripken JY/101 60.00 27.00
37PS Cal Ripken PS/50 80.00 36.00
38BA Enos Slaughter BA/15
38DY Enos Slaughter DY/1
38IN Enos Slaughter IN/15
38JN Enos Slaughter JN/9
38JY Enos Slaughter JY/53 40.00 18.00
38PS Enos Slaughter PS/25
39BA Reggie Jackson A's BA/50 25.00 11.00
39DY Reggie Jackson A's DY/68 25.00 11.00
39IN Reggie Jackson A's IN/25
39JN Reggie Jackson A's JN/9
39JY Reggie Jackson A's JY/75 25.00 11.00
39PS Reggie Jackson A's PS/50 25.00 11.00
40BA Phil Rizzuto BA/20
40DY Phil Rizzuto DY/13
40IN Phil Rizzuto IN/15
40JN Phil Rizzuto JN/10
40JY Phil Rizzuto JY/47 30.00 13.50
40PS Phil Rizzuto PS/15
41BA Chipper Jones BA/100 15.00 6.75
41DY Chipper Jones DY/66 25.00 11.00
41IN Chipper Jones IN/50 25.00 11.00
41JN Chipper Jones JN/10
41JY Chipper Jones JY/101 15.00 6.75
41PS Chipper Jones PS/50 25.00 11.00
42BA H.Nomo Dodgers BA/100 40.00 18.00
42DY H.Nomo Dodgers DY/58 50.00 22.00
42IN H.Nomo Dodgers IN/50 50.00 22.00
42JN H.Nomo Dodgers JN/16
42JY H.Nomo Dodgers JY/95 40.00 18.00
42PS H.Nomo Dodgers PS/50 50.00 22.00
43BA Luis Aparicio BA/25
43DY Luis Aparicio DY/4
43IN Luis Aparicio IN/15
43JN Luis Aparicio JN/11
43JY Luis Aparicio JY/69 20.00 9.00
43PS Luis Aparicio PS/20
44BA H.Nomo R.Sox BA/100 40.00 18.00
44DY H.Nomo R.Sox DY/7
44IN H.Nomo R.Sox IN/50 50.00 22.00
44JN H.Nomo R.Sox JN/11
44JY H.Nomo R.Sox JY/101 40.00 18.00
44PS H.Nomo R.Sox PS/50 50.00 22.00
45BA Edgar Martinez BA/100 15.00 6.75
45DY Edgar Martinez DY/77 15.00 6.75
45IN Edgar Martinez IN/25
45JN Edgar Martinez JN/11
45JY Edgar Martinez JY/100 15.00 6.75
45PS Edgar Martinez PS/50 20.00 9.00
46BA Barry Larkin BA/100 15.00 6.75
46DY Barry Larkin DY/59 25.00 11.00
46IN Barry Larkin IN/25
46JN Barry Larkin JN/11
46JY Barry Larkin JY/100 15.00 6.75
46PS Barry Larkin PS/50 25.00 11.00
47BA Alfonso Soriano BA/100 15.00 6.75
47DY Alfonso Soriano DY/13
47IN Alfonso Soriano IN/50 20.00 9.00
47JN Alfonso Soriano JN/12
47JY Alfonso Soriano JY/102 15.00 6.75
47PS Alfonso Soriano PS/50 20.00 9.00
48BA Wade Boggs Rays BA/100 20.00 9.00
48DY Wade Boggs Rays DY/98 20.00 9.00
48IN Wade Boggs Rays IN/50 25.00 11.00
48JN Wade Boggs Rays JN/12
48JY Wade Boggs Rays JY/99 20.00 9.00
48PS Wade Boggs Rays PS/50 25.00 11.00
49BA Wade Boggs Yanks BA/50 25.00 11.00
49DY Wade Boggs Yanks DY/13
49IN Wade Boggs Yanks IN/50 25.00 11.00
49JN Wade Boggs Yanks JN/12
49JY Wade Boggs Yanks JY/94 20.00 9.00
49PS Wade Boggs Yanks PS/50 25.00 11.00
50BA Ernie Banks BA/15
50DY Ernie Banks DY/7
50IN Ernie Banks IN/15
50JN Ernie Banks JN/14
50JY Ernie Banks JY/68 40.00 18.00
50PS Ernie Banks PS/15
51BA Joe Torre BA/50 25.00 11.00
51DY Joe Torre DY/66 25.00 11.00
51IN Joe Torre IN/50 25.00 11.00
51JN Joe Torre JN/15
51JY Joe Torre JY/66 25.00 11.00
51PS Joe Torre PS/50 25.00 11.00
52BA Tim Hudson BA/100 10.00 4.50
52DY Tim Hudson DY/68 15.00 6.75
52IN Tim Hudson IN/25
52JN Tim Hudson JN/15
52JY Tim Hudson JY/101 10.00 4.50
52PS Tim Hudson PS/50 15.00 6.75
53BA Shawn Green BA/100 10.00 4.50
53DY Shawn Green DY/58 15.00 6.75
53IN Shawn Green IN/25
53JN Shawn Green JN/15
53JY Shawn Green JY/102 10.00 4.50
53PS Shawn Green PS/50 15.00 6.75
54BA Carlos Beltran BA/100 10.00 4.50
54DY Carlos Beltran DY/69 15.00 6.75
54IN Carlos Beltran IN/25
54JN Carlos Beltran JN/15
54JY Carlos Beltran JY/101 10.00 4.50
54PS Carlos Beltran PS/50 15.00 6.75
55BA Bo Jackson BA/50 40.00 18.00
55DY Bo Jackson DY/69 40.00 18.00
55IN Bo Jackson IN/25
55JN Bo Jackson JN/16
55JY Bo Jackson JY/90 30.00 13.50
55PS Bo Jackson PS/50 40.00 18.00
56BA Hal Newhouser BA/50 20.00 9.00
56DY Hal Newhouser DY/15
56IN Hal Newhouser IN/25
56JN Hal Newhouser JN/16
56JY Hal Newhouser JY/55 20.00 9.00
56PS Hal Newhouser PS/50 20.00 9.00
57BA Jason Giambi A's BA/100 15.00 6.75
57DY Jason Giambi A's DY/68 25.00 11.00
57IN Jason Giambi A's IN/50 25.00 11.00
57JN Jason Giambi A's JN/16
57JY Jason Giambi A's JY/101 15.00 6.75
57PS Jason Giambi A's PS/50 25.00 11.00
58BA Lance Berkman BA/100 10.00 4.50
58DY Lance Berkman DY/65 15.00 6.75
58IN Lance Berkman IN/50 15.00 6.75
58JN Lance Berkman JN/17
58JY Lance Berkman JY/102 10.00 4.50
58PS Lance Berkman PS/50 15.00 6.75
59BA Todd Helton BA/100 15.00 6.75
59DY Todd Helton DY/93 15.00 6.75
59IN Todd Helton IN/25
59JN Todd Helton JN/17
59JY Todd Helton JY/100 15.00 6.75
59PS Todd Helton PS/50 20.00 9.00
60BA Mark Grace BA/100 15.00 6.75
60DY Mark Grace DY/7
60IN Mark Grace IN/25
60JN Mark Grace JN/17
60JY Mark Grace JY/95 15.00 6.75
60PS Mark Grace PS/50 20.00 9.00
61BA Fred Lynn BA/100 15.00 6.75
61DY Fred Lynn DY/7
61IN Fred Lynn IN/25
61JN Fred Lynn JN/19
61JY Fred Lynn JY/75 20.00 9.00
61PS Fred Lynn PS/50 20.00 9.00
62BA Bob Feller BA/10
62DY Bob Feller DY/15
62IN Bob Feller IN/10
62JN Bob Feller JN/19
62JY Bob Feller JY/52 50.00 22.00
62PS Bob Feller PS/10
63BA Robin Yount BA/100 40.00 18.00
63DY Robin Yount DY/70 50.00 22.00
63IN Robin Yount IN/50 50.00 22.00
63JN Robin Yount JN/19
63JY Robin Yount JY/88 40.00 18.00
63PS Robin Yount PS/50 50.00 22.00
64BA Tony Gwynn BA/100 25.00 11.00
64DY Tony Gwynn DY/69 30.00 13.50
64IN Tony Gwynn IN/50 30.00 13.50
64JN Tony Gwynn JN/19
64JY Tony Gwynn JY/99 30.00 13.50
64PS Tony Gwynn PS/50 25.00 11.00
65BA Tony Gwynn Pants BA/100 25.00 11.00
65DY Tony Gwynn Pants DY/69 30.00 13.50
65IN Tony Gwynn Pants IN/50 30.00 13.50
65JN Tony Gwynn Pants JN/19
65JY Tony Gwynn Pants JY/99 25.00 11.00
65PS Tony Gwynn Pants PS/50 30.00 13.50
66BA Frank Robinson BA/10
66DY Frank Robinson DY/54 25.00 11.00
66IN Frank Robinson IN/10
66JN Frank Robinson JN/20
66JY Frank Robinson JY/70 25.00 11.00
66PS Frank Robinson PS/10
67BA Mike Schmidt BA/50 50.00 22.00
67DY Mike Schmidt DY/46 50.00 22.00
67IN Mike Schmidt IN/50 50.00 22.00
67JN Mike Schmidt JN/20
67JY Mike Schmidt JY/81 40.00 18.00
67PS Mike Schmidt PS/50 50.00 22.00
68BA Lou Brock BA/20
68DY Lou Brock DY/1
68IN Lou Brock IN/15
68JN Lou Brock JN/20
68JY Lou Brock JY/66 25.00 11.00
68PS Lou Brock PS/15
69BA Don Sutton BA/50 20.00 9.00
69DY Don Sutton DY/58 20.00 9.00
69IN Don Sutton IN/25
69JN Don Sutton JN/20
69JY Don Sutton JY/72 20.00 9.00
69PS Don Sutton PS/25
70BA Mark Mulder BA/100 10.00 4.50
70DY Mark Mulder DY/68 15.00 6.75
70IN Mark Mulder IN/25
70JN Mark Mulder JN/20
70JY Mark Mulder JY/101 10.00 4.50
70PS Mark Mulder PS/50 15.00 6.75
71BA Luis Gonzalez BA/100 10.00 4.50
71DY Luis Gonzalez DY/98 10.00 4.50
71IN Luis Gonzalez IN/25
71JN Luis Gonzalez JN/20
71JY Luis Gonzalez JY/101 10.00 4.50
71PS Luis Gonzalez PS/50 15.00 6.75
72BA Jorge Posada BA/100 15.00 6.75
72DY Jorge Posada DY/13
72IN Jorge Posada IN/25
72JN Jorge Posada JN/20
72JY Jorge Posada JY/101 15.00 6.75
72PS Jorge Posada PS/50 20.00 9.00
73BA Sammy Sosa BA/100 30.00 13.50
73DY Sammy Sosa DY/7
73IN Sammy Sosa IN/50 40.00 18.00
73JN Sammy Sosa JN/21
73JY Sammy Sosa JY/101 30.00 13.50
73PS Sammy Sosa PS/50 40.00 18.00
74BA Roberto Alomar BA/100 15.00 6.75
74DY Roberto Alomar DY/62 25.00 11.00
74IN Roberto Alomar IN/25
74JN Roberto Alomar JN/12
74JY Roberto Alomar JY/102 15.00 6.75
74PS Roberto Alomar PS/50 25.00 11.00
75BA Roberto Clemente BA/10
75DY Roberto Clemente DY/1
75IN Roberto Clemente IN/10
75JN Roberto Clemente JN/21
75JY Roberto Clemente JY/69 120.00 55.00
75PS Roberto Clemente PS/10
76BA Jeff Kent BA/100 10.00 4.50
76DY Jeff Kent DY/58 15.00 6.75
76IN Jeff Kent IN/25
76JN Jeff Kent JN/21
76JY Jeff Kent JY/101 10.00 4.50
76PS Jeff Kent PS/50 15.00 6.75
77BA Sean Casey BA/20
77DY Sean Casey DY/59 15.00 6.75
77IN Sean Casey IN/25
77JN Sean Casey JN/21
77JY Sean Casey JY/100 10.00 4.50
77PS Sean Casey PS/25
78BA R.Clemens R.Sox BA/50 40.00 18.00
78DY R.Clemens R.Sox DY/7
78IN R.Clemens R.Sox IN/50 40.00 18.00
78JN R.Clemens R.Sox JN/21
78JY R.Clemens R.Sox JY/95 30.00 13.50
78PS R.Clemens R.Sox PS/50 25.00 11.00
79BA Warren Spahn BA/20
79DY Warren Spahn DY/53 40.00 18.00
79IN Warren Spahn IN/15
79JN Warren Spahn JN/21

79JY Warren Spahn JY/58........ 40.00 18.00
79PS Warren Spahn PS/15................
80BA R.Clemens Yanks BA/100 30.00 13.50
80DY R.Clemens Yanks DY/13...........
80IN R.Clemens Yanks IN/50.... 40.00 18.00
80JN R.Clemens Yanks JN/22............
80JY R.Clemens Yanks JY/102. 30.00 13.50
80PS R.Clemens Yanks PS/50.. 40.00 18.00
81BA Jim Palmer BA/50............ 25.00 11.00
81DY Jim Palmer DY/54 .... 25.00 11.00
81IN Jim Palmer IN/25......................
81JN Jim Palmer JN/22 ....
81JY Jim Palmer JY/69............ 25.00 11.00
81PS Jim Palmer PS/50............ 25.00 11.00
82BA Juan Gonzalez BA/50 .... 25.00 11.00
82DY Juan Gonzalez DY/15................
82IN Juan Gonzalez IN/25..................
82JN Juan Gonzalez JN/22..................
82JY Juan Gonzalez JY/101 ...... 15.00 6.75
82PS Juan Gonzalez PS/50 .... 25.00 11.00
83BA Will Clark BA/100............. 30.00 13.50
83DY Will Clark DY/58 .... 40.00 18.00
83IN Will Clark IN/25.........................
83JN Will Clark JN/22 ....
83JY Will Clark JY/88................ 30.00 13.50
83PS Will Clark PS/50............... 40.00 18.00
84BA Don Mattingly BA/50........ 60.00 27.00
84DY Don Mattingly DY/13 ....
84IN Don Mattingly IN/50 .... 60.00 27.00
84JN Don Mattingly JN/23..................
84JY Don Mattingly JY/93......... 50.00 22.00
84PS Don Mattingly PS/50........ 60.00 27.00
85BA Ryne Sandberg BA/40...... 80.00 36.00
85DY Ryne Sandberg DY/7 ....
85IN Ryne Sandberg IN/50 .... 80.00 36.00
85JN Ryne Sandberg JN/23.................
85JY Ryne Sandberg JY/85....... 50.00 22.00
85PS Ryne Sandberg PS/50...... 80.00 36.00
86BA Early Wynn BA/20......................
86DY Early Wynn DY/15 ....
86IN Early Wynn IN/15........................
86JN Early Wynn JN/24 ....
86JY Early Wynn JY/55............. 20.00 9.00
86PS Early Wynn PS/15......................
87BA Manny Ramirez BA/50 ..... 15.00 6.75
87DY Manny Ramirez DY/7................
87IN Manny Ramirez IN/25.................
87JN Manny Ramirez JN/24................
87JY Manny Ramirez JY/102.... 10.00 4.50
87PS Manny Ramirez PS/50 ..... 15.00 6.75
88BA R.Henderson Mets BA/100 15.00 6.75
88DY R.Henderson Mets DY/62 25.00 11.00
88IN R.Henderson Mets IN/50.. 25.00 11.00
88JN R.Henderson Mets JN/24..........
88JY R.Henderson Mets JY/99 . 15.00 6.75
88PS R.Henderson Mets PS/50 25.00 11.00
89BA R.Henderson Padres BA/100 15.00 6.75
89DY R.Henderson Padres DY/69 25.00 11.00
89IN R.Henderson Padres IN/25 ....
89JN R.Henderson Padres JN/24........
89JY R.Henderson Padres JY/102 15.00 6.75
89PS R.Henderson Padres PS/50 25.00 11.00
90BA Jason Giambi Yanks BA/100 15.00 6.75
90DY Jason Giambi Yanks DY/13 ....
90IN Jason Giambi Yanks IN/50 25.00 11.00
90JN Jason Giambi Yanks JN/25 ....
90JY Jason Giambi Yanks JY/102 15.00 6.75
90PS Jason Giambi Yanks PS/50 25.00 11.00
91BA Carlos Delgado BA/100.... 10.00 4.50
91DY Carlos Delgado DY/77 ..... 10.00 4.50
91IN Carlos Delgado IN/25..................
91JN Carlos Delgado JN/25 ....
91JY Carlos Delgado JY/100..... 10.00 4.50
91PS Carlos Delgado PS/50...... 15.00 6.75
92BA Jim Thome BA/100 .... 15.00 6.75
92DY Jim Thome DY/15.......................
92IN Jim Thome IN/25.........................
92JN Jim Thome JN/25.........................
92JY Jim Thome JY/102........... 15.00 6.75
92PS Jim Thome PS/50 .... 25.00 11.00
93BA Andruw Jones BA/100 ..... 10.00 4.50
93DY Andruw Jones DY/66....... 15.00 6.75
93IN Andruw Jones IN/25....................
93JN Andruw Jones JN/25...................
93JY Andruw Jones JY/101 ...... 10.00 4.50
93PS Andruw Jones PS/50 .... 15.00 6.75
94BA Rafael Palmeiro BA/100... 15.00 6.75
94DY Rafael Palmeiro DY/72..... 20.00 9.00
94IN Rafael Palmeiro IN/25................
94JN Rafael Palmeiro JN/25 ....
94JY Rafael Palmeiro JY/102.... 15.00 6.75
94PS Rafael Palmeiro PS/50..... 20.00 9.00
95BA Troy Glaus BA/100........... 15.00 6.75
95DY Troy Glaus DY/97 .... 15.00 6.75
95IN Troy Glaus IN/50............... 20.00 9.00
95JN Troy Glaus JN/25 ....
95JY Troy Glaus JY/100............ 15.00 6.75
95PS Troy Glaus PS/50............. 20.00 9.00
96BA Wade Boggs R.Sox BA/100 20.00 9.00
96DY Wade Boggs R.Sox DY/7 ....
96IN Wade Boggs R.Sox IN/50 . 25.00 11.00
96JN Wade Boggs R.Sox JN/26 50.00 22.00
96JY Wade Boggs R.Sox JY/86 20.00 9.00
96PS Wade Boggs R.Sox PS/50 25.00 11.00
97BA Catfish Hunter BA/50 .... 25.00 11.00
97DY Catfish Hunter DY/68....... 25.00 11.00
97IN Catfish Hunter IN/25...................
97JN Catfish Hunter JN/27........ 40.00 18.00
97JY Catfish Hunter JY/68 .... 25.00 11.00
97PS Catfish Hunter PS/50 .... 25.00 11.00
98BA Juan Marichal BA/50........ 20.00 9.00
98DY Juan Marichal DY/58 .... 20.00 9.00
98IN Juan Marichal IN/25 ....
98JN Juan Marichal JN/27 .... 30.00 13.50
98JY Juan Marichal JY/67......... 20.00 9.00
98PS Juan Marichal PS/50........ 20.00 9.00
99BA Carlton Fisk R.Sox BA/50. 25.00 11.00
99DY Carlton Fisk R.Sox DY/7 ....
99IN Carlton Fisk R.Sox IN/25............
99JN Carlton Fisk R.Sox JN/27 . 40.00 18.00
99JY Carlton Fisk R.Sox JY/80.. 20.00 9.00
99PS Carlton Fisk R.Sox PS/50. 25.00 11.00
100BA Vladimir Guerrero BA/100 15.00 6.75
100DY Vladimir Guerrero DY/69 25.00 11.00
100IN Vladimir Guerrero IN/25 ....
100JN Vladimir Guerrero JN/27 50.00 22.00
100JY Vladimir Guerrero JY/101 15.00 6.75
100PS Vladimir Guerrero PS/50 25.00 11.00
101BA Rod Carew Angels BA/50 20.00 9.00
101DY Rod Carew Angels DY/65 25.00 11.00
101IN Rod Carew Angels IN/25..........
101JN Rod Carew Angels JN/29 40.00 18.00
101JY Rod Carew Angels JY/85 20.00 9.00
101PS Rod Carew Angels PS/50 25.00 11.00
102BA Rod Carew Twins BA/50 25.00 11.00
102DY Rod Carew Twins DY/61 25.00 11.00
102IN Rod Carew Twins IN/25............
102JN Rod Carew Twins JN/29. 40.00 18.00
102JY Rod Carew Twins JY/71 . 25.00 11.00
102PS Rod Carew Twins PS/50 25.00 11.00
103BA Joe Carter BA/50........... 20.00 9.00
103DY Joe Carter DY/77 .... 15.00 6.75
103IN Joe Carter IN/25 ....
103JN Joe Carter JN/29 .... 30.00 13.50
103JY Joe Carter JY/94............ 15.00 6.75
103PS Joe Carter PS/25......................
104BA Mike Sweeney BA/100 ... 10.00 4.50
104DY Mike Sweeney DY/69..... 15.00 6.75
104IN Mike Sweeney IN/25.................
104JN Mike Sweeney JN/29...... 30.00 13.50
104JY Mike Sweeney JY/101 .... 10.00 4.50
104PS Mike Sweeney PS/50 ..... 15.00 6.75
105BA Nolan Ryan Angels BA/25 ....
105DY Nolan Ryan Angels DY/65 60.00 27.00
105IN Nolan Ryan Angels IN/25..........
105JN Nolan Ryan Angels JN/30 80.00 36.00
105JY N.Ryan Angels JY/70 UER 60.00 27.00
Jersey year is credited to 1970; Ryan did not arrive in California till 1972
105PS Nolan Ryan Angels PS/50 60.00 27.00
106BA Orlando Cepeda BA/50... 20.00 9.00
106DY Orlando Cepeda DY/58 .. 20.00 9.00
106IN Orlando Cepeda IN/50..... 20.00 9.00
106JN Orlando Cepeda JN/30 ... 30.00 13.50
106JY Orlando Cepeda JY/65.... 20.00 9.00
106PS Orlando Cepeda PS/50... 20.00 9.00
107BA Magglio Ordonez BA/100 10.00 4.50
107DY Magglio Ordonez DY/4............
107IN Magglio Ordonez IN/25............
107JN Magglio Ordonez JN/30 . 30.00 13.50
107JY Magglio Ordonez JY/102 10.00 4.50
107PS Magglio Ordonez PS/50. 15.00 6.75
108BA Hoyt Wilhelm BA/50....... 20.00 9.00
108DY Hoyt Wilhelm DY/4 ....
108IN Hoyt Wilhelm IN/25 ....
108JN Hoyt Wilhelm JN/31 .... 30.00 13.50
108JY Hoyt Wilhelm JY/68 .... 20.00 9.00
108PS Hoyt Wilhelm PS/50....... 20.00 9.00
109BA Mike Piazza BA/100 .... 25.00 11.00
109DY Mike Piazza DY/62.......... 30.00 13.50
109IN Mike Piazza IN/50 .... 30.00 13.50
109JN Mike Piazza JN/31 .... 50.00 22.00
109JY Mike Piazza JY/100 .... 25.00 11.00
109PS Mike Piazza PS/50 .... 30.00 13.50
110BA Greg Maddux BA/100..... 25.00 11.00
110DY Greg Maddux DY/66 ...... 30.00 13.50
110IN Greg Maddux IN/50 .... 30.00 13.50
110JN Greg Maddux JN/31 .... 50.00 22.00
110JY Greg Maddux JY/102 ..... 25.00 11.00
110PS Greg Maddux PS/50....... 30.00 13.50
111BA Mark Prior BA/100......... 30.00 13.50
111DY Mark Prior DY/7.......................
111IN Mark Prior IN/50............. 40.00 18.00
111JN Mark Prior JN/22 ....
111JY Mark Prior JY/102.......... 30.00 13.50
111PS Mark Prior PS/50........... 40.00 18.00
112BA Torii Hunter BA/100....... 10.00 4.50
112DY Torii Hunter DY/61......... 15.00 6.75
112IN Torii Hunter IN/50........... 15.00 6.75
112JN Torii Hunter JN/48 .... 20.00 9.00
112JY Torii Hunter JY/101 .... 10.00 4.50
112PS Torii Hunter PS/50......... 15.00 6.75
113BA Steve Carlton BA/100..... 15.00 6.75
113DY Steve Carlton DY/46 ...... 25.00 11.00
113IN Steve Carlton IN/50......... 20.00 9.00
113JN Steve Carlton JN/32 .... 30.00 13.50
113JY Steve Carlton JY/81........ 15.00 6.75
113PS Steve Carlton PS/50....... 20.00 9.00
114BA Jose Canseco BA/100.... 30.00 13.50
114DY Jose Canseco DY/68...... 40.00 18.00
114IN Jose Canseco IN/50........ 40.00 18.00
114JN Jose Canseco JN/33....... 60.00 27.00
114JY Jose Canseco JY/89....... 30.00 13.50
114PS Jose Canseco PS/50 ...... 40.00 18.00
115BA Nolan Ryan Rgr BA/50... 60.00 27.00
115DY Nolan Ryan Rgr DY/72 .. 60.00 27.00
115IN Nolan Ryan Rgr IN/50..... 60.00 27.00
115JN Nolan Ryan Rgr JN/34 ... 80.00 36.00
115JY Nolan Ryan Rgr JY/90.... 60.00 27.00
115PS Nolan Ryan Rgr PS/50... 60.00 27.00
116BA Nolan Ryan Astros BA/50 60.00 27.00
116DY Nolan Ryan Astros DY/65 60.00 27.00
116IN Nolan Ryan Astros IN/25 ....
116JN Nolan Ryan Astros JN/34 80.00 36.00
116JY Nolan Ryan Astros JY/84 60.00 27.00
116PS Nolan Ryan Astros PS/50 60.00 27.00
117BA Ty Cobb Pants BA/25...............
117DY Ty Cobb Pants DY/1 ....
117IN Ty Cobb Pants IN/25.................
117JN Ty Cobb Pants JN/1 ....
117JY Ty Cobb Pants JY/27.... 200.00 90.00
117PS Ty Cobb Pants PS/10...............
118BA Kerry Wood BA/100....... 15.00 6.75
118DY Kerry Wood DY/7......................
118IN Kerry Wood IN/25.....................
118JN Kerry Wood JN/34 .... 50.00 22.00
118JY Kerry Wood JY/101........ 15.00 6.75
118PS Kerry Wood PS/50......... 25.00 11.00
119BA M.Mussina Yanks BA/50 25.00 11.00
119DY M.Mussina Yanks DY/13 ....
119IN M.Mussina Yanks IN/25...........
119JN M.Mussina Yanks JN/35 50.00 22.00
119JY M.Mussina Yanks JY/101 15.00 6.75
119PS M.Mussina Yanks PS/50 25.00 11.00
120BA Yogi Berra BA/10.....................
120DY Yogi Berra DY/13.....................
120IN Yogi Berra IN/10.......................
120JN Yogi Berra JN/35............ 50.00 22.00
120JY Yogi Berra JY/47 .... 40.00 18.00
120PS Yogi Berra PS/10 ....
121BA Thurman Munson BA/25.........
121DY Thurman Munson DY/13 ....
121IN Thurman Munson IN/25 ....
121JN Thurman Munson JN/15 ....
121JY Thurman Munson JY/79. 40.00 18.00
121PS Thurman Munson PS/5...........
122BA Frank Thomas BA/100 ... 15.00 6.75
122DY Frank Thomas DY/4 ....
122IN Frank Thomas IN/25 ....
122JN Frank Thomas JN/35...... 50.00 22.00
122JY Frank Thomas JY/94 ...... 15.00 6.75
122PS Frank Thomas PS/50 ..... 25.00 11.00
123BA R.Henderson A's BA/50 . 25.00 11.00
123DY R.Henderson A's DY/68. 25.00 11.00
123IN R.Henderson A's IN/25............
123JN R.Henderson A's JN/35.. 50.00 22.00
123JY R.Henderson A's JY/80.. 15.00 6.75
123PS R.Henderson A's PS/50 . 25.00 11.00
124BA M.Muss O's Pants BA/100 15.00 6.75
124DY M.Muss O's Pants DY/54 25.00 11.00
124IN M.Muss O's Pants IN/25..........
124JN M.Muss O's Pants JN/35 50.00 22.00
124JY M.Muss O's Pants JY/97 15.00 6.75
124PS M.Muss O's Pants PS/50 25.00 11.00
125BA Gaylord Perry BA/100 .... 15.00 6.75
125DY Gaylord Perry DY/77...... 15.00 6.75
125IN Gaylord Perry IN/25.................
125JN Gaylord Perry JN/36....... 25.00 11.00
125JY Gaylord Perry JY/82 .... 15.00 6.75
125PS Gaylord Perry PS/50 ...... 20.00 9.00
126BA Nick Johnson BA/100 .... 10.00 4.50
126DY Nick Johnson DY/13................
126IN Nick Johnson IN/25 ....
126JN Nick Johnson JN/36....... 20.00 9.00
126JY Nick Johnson JY/102 ..... 10.00 4.50
126PS Nick Johnson PS/50 ...... 15.00 6.75
127BA Curt Schilling BA/100 .... 15.00 6.75
127DY Curt Schilling DY/98 ...... 15.00 6.75
127IN Curt Schilling IN/25 ....
127JN Curt Schilling JN/38....... 25.00 11.00
127JY Curt Schilling JY/102 ..... 15.00 6.75
127PS Curt Schilling PS/50 ...... 20.00 9.00
128BA Dave Parker BA/100....... 15.00 6.75
128DY Dave Parker DY/1 ....
128IN Dave Parker IN/25....................
128JN Dave Parker JN/39 .... 25.00 11.00
128JY Dave Parker JY/80.......... 15.00 6.75
128PS Dave Parker PS/50......... 20.00 9.00
129BA Eddie Mathews BA/15.............
129DY Eddie Mathews DY/53 ... 40.00 18.00
129IN Eddie Mathews IN/15...............
129JN Eddie Mathews JN/41 .... 40.00 18.00
129JY Eddie Mathews JY/59..... 40.00 18.00
129PS Eddie Mathews PS/15.............
130BA Tom Seaver Mets BA/10 ....
130DY Tom Seaver Mets DY/62 25.00 11.00
130IN Tom Seaver Mets IN/10...........
130JN Tom Seaver Mets JN/41. 30.00 13.50
130JY Tom Seaver Mets JY/69 . 25.00 11.00
130PS Tom Seaver Mets PS/10 ....
131BA Tom Seaver Reds BA/10..........
131DY Tom Seaver Reds DY/59 25.00 11.00
131IN Tom Seaver Reds IN/10............
131JN Tom Seaver Reds JN/41 30.00 13.50
131JY Tom Seaver Reds JY/78. 20.00 9.00
131PS Tom Seaver Reds PS/22 ....
132BA Jackie Robinson BA/10............
132DY Jackie Robinson DY/32 ....
132IN Jackie Robinson IN/10..............
132JN Jackie Robinson JN/42 100.00 45.00
132JY Jackie Robinson JY/52... 80.00 36.00
132PS Jackie Robinson PS/10............
133BA R.Jackson Angels BA/100 20.00 9.00
133DY R.Jackson Angels DY/65 25.00 11.00
133IN R.Jackson Angels IN/50.. 25.00 11.00
133JN R.Jackson Angels JN/44 30.00 13.50
133JY R.Jackson Angels JY/80. 20.00 9.00
133PS R.Jackson Angels PS/50 25.00 11.00
134BA Willie McCovey BA/100.. 20.00 9.00
134DY Willie McCovey DY/58 ... 25.00 11.00
134IN Willie McCovey IN/25 ....
134JN Willie McCovey JN/44 .... 30.00 13.50
134JY Willie McCovey JY/77..... 20.00 9.00
134PS Willie McCovey PS/50.... 25.00 11.00
135BA Eric Davis BA/100 .... 15.00 6.75
135DY Eric Davis DY/59............ 20.00 9.00
135IN Eric Davis IN/25.......................
135JN Eric Davis JN/44............ 25.00 11.00
135JY Eric Davis JY/89............. 15.00 6.75
135PS Eric Davis PS/50 .... 20.00 9.00
136BA Adam Dunn BA/100 .... 10.00 4.50
136DY Adam Dunn DY/59......... 15.00 6.75
136IN Adam Dunn IN/25.....................
136JN Adam Dunn JN/44.......... 20.00 9.00
136JY Adam Dunn JY/102 .... 10.00 4.50
136PS Adam Dunn PS/50 .... 15.00 6.75
137BA Roy Oswalt BA/100........ 10.00 4.50
137DY Roy Oswalt DY/65 .... 15.00 6.75
137IN Roy Oswalt IN/50............ 15.00 6.75
137JN Roy Oswalt JN/44 .... 20.00 9.00
137JY Roy Oswalt JY/102.......... 10.00 4.50
137PS Roy Oswalt PS/50.......... 15.00 6.75
138BA P.Martinez Expos BA/50 25.00 11.00
138DY P.Martinez Expos DY/69 25.00 11.00
138IN P.Martinez Expos IN/25 ....
138JN P.Martinez Expos JN/45. 40.00 18.00
138JY P.Martinez Expos JY/95 . 15.00 6.75
138PS P.Martinez Expos PS/50 25.00 11.00
139BA P.Martinez R.Sox BA/100 15.00 6.75
139DY P.Martinez R.Sox DY/7 ....
139IN P.Martinez R.Sox IN/50 .. 25.00 11.00
139JN P.Martinez R.Sox JN/45. 40.00 18.00
139JY P.Martinez R.Sox JY/102 15.00 6.75
139PS P.Martinez R.Sox PS/50 25.00 11.00
140BA Andy Pettitte BA/100...... 15.00 6.75
140DY Andy Pettitte DY/13 ....
140IN Andy Pettitte IN/25 ....
140JN Andy Pettitte JN/46 .... 25.00 11.00
140JY Andy Pettitte JY/97.......... 15.00 6.75
140PS Andy Pettitte PS/50....... 20.00 9.00
141BA Jack Morris BA/100 .... 15.00 6.75
141DY Jack Morris DY/1.....................
141IN Jack Morris IN/50........... 20.00 9.00
141JN Jack Morris JN/47.......... 25.00 11.00
141JY Jack Morris JY/85 .... 15.00 6.75
141PS Jack Morris PS/50 .... 20.00 9.00
142BA Tom Glavine BA/100...... 15.00 6.75
142DY Tom Glavine DY/66........ 20.00 9.00
142IN Tom Glavine IN/25....................
142JN Tom Glavine JN/47......... 25.00 11.00
142JY Tom Glavine JY/100 .... 15.00 6.75
142PS Tom Glavine PS/50 .... 20.00 9.00
143BA R.Johnson M's BA/100.. 15.00 6.75
143DY R.Johnson M's DY/77 ... 15.00 6.75
143IN R.Johnson M's IN/50...... 25.00 11.00
143JN R.Johnson M's JN/51 .... 25.00 11.00
143JY R.Johnson M's JY/98..... 15.00 6.75
143PS R.Johnson M's PS/50.... 25.00 11.00
144BA Bernie Williams BA/100 . 15.00 6.75
144DY Bernie Williams DY/13.............
144IN Bernie Williams IN/50..... 20.00 9.00
144JN Bernie Williams JN/51.... 20.00 9.00
144JY Bernie Williams JY/100.. 15.00 6.75
144PS Bernie Williams PS/50 ... 20.00 9.00
145BA R.Johnson D'backs BA/50 25.00 11.00
145DY R.Johnson D'backs DY/98 15.00 6.75
145IN R.Johnson D'backs IN/50 25.00 11.00
145JN R.Johnson D'backs JN/51 25.00 11.00
145JY R.Johnson D'backs JY/102 15.00 6.75
145PS R.Johnson D'backs PS/50 25.00 11.00
146BA Don Drysdale BA/15................
146DY Don Drysdale DY/58 ...... 40.00 18.00
146IN Don Drysdale IN/25 ....
146JN Don Drysdale JN/53 .... 40.00 18.00
146JY Don Drysdale JY/64 .... 40.00 18.00
146PS Don Drysdale PS/25................
147BA Mark Buehrle BA/100..... 10.00 4.50
147DY Mark Buehrle DY/4 ....
147IN Mark Buehrle IN/25..................
147JN Mark Buehrle JN/56 .... 15.00 6.75
147JY Mark Buehrle JY/101...... 10.00 4.50
147PS Mark Buehrle PS/50....... 15.00 6.75
148BA Chan Ho Park BA/100 .... 15.00 6.75
148DY Chan Ho Park DY/58...... 20.00 9.00
148IN Chan Ho Park IN/25 ....
148JN Chan Ho Park JN/61....... 20.00 9.00
148JY Chan Ho Park JY/101 ..... 15.00 6.75
148PS Chan Ho Park PS/50 ...... 20.00 9.00
149BA Carlton Fisk W.Sox BA/100 20.00 9.00
149DY Carlton Fisk W.Sox DY/4 ....
149IN Carlton Fisk W.Sox IN/50 25.00 11.00
149JN Carlton Fisk W.Sox JN/72 25.00 11.00
149JY Carlton Fisk W.Sox JY/92 20.00 9.00
149PS Carlton Fisk W.Sox PS/50 25.00 11.00
150BA Barry Zito BA/100 .... 15.00 6.75
150DY Barry Zito DY/68............ 20.00 9.00
150IN Barry Zito IN/25......................
150JN Barry Zito JN/75............. 20.00 9.00
150JY Barry Zito JY/101 .... 15.00 6.75
150PS Barry Zito PS/50 .... 20.00 9.00

2003 Leaf Certified Materials Fabric of the Game Autographs

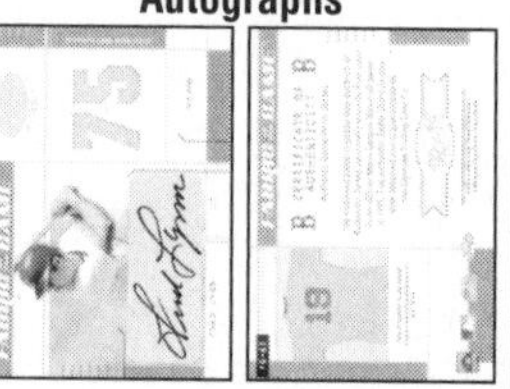

This is a partial parallel to the Fabric of the Game insert set. Each of these cards were signed, using Donruss/Playoff "band-aid" autographs to a stated print run of five or fewer cards. We have put the announced print run next to the player's name in our checklist and please note there is no pricing due to market scarcity. In addition, because of the use of stickered autographs, please note that autographs of deceased players such as Enos Slaughter and Hoyt Wilhelm are included in this set.

MINT NRMT
RANDOM INSERTS IN PACKS ....
CARDS DISPLAY CUMULATIVE PRINT RUNS
ACTUAL PRINT RUNS B/WN 1-5 COPIES PER
SKIP-NUMBERED 302-CARD SET.......
NO PRICING DUE TO SCARCITY.........

1998 Leaf Fractal Foundations

The 1998 Leaf Fractal Foundations set was issued in one series totalling 200 cards. The cards are an upgraded parallel from the 1998 leaf set and the fronts feature color player photos printed on foil board. Each card is sequentially numbered to 3,999. Card number 42 does not exist.

Nm-Mt Ex-Mt
COMPLETE SET (200)............. 150.00 45.00
1 Rusty Greer.............................. 2.00 .60
2 Tino Martinez .... 3.00 .90
3 Bobby Bonilla........................... 2.00 .60
4 Jason Giambi 5.00 1.50
5 Matt Morris .... 2.00 .60
6 Craig Counsell.......................... 2.00 .60
7 Reggie Jefferson .... 2.00 .60
8 Brian Rose................................ 2.00 .60
9 Ruben Rivera............................ 2.00 .60
10 Shawn Estes........................... 2.00 .60
11 Tony Gwynn 6.00 1.80
12 Jeff Abbott .... 2.00 .60
13 Jose Cruz Jr. .... 2.00 .60
14 Francisco Cordova.................. 2.00 .60
15 Ryan Klesko .... 2.00 .60
16 Tim Salmon............................ 3.00 .90
17 Brett Tomko .... 2.00 .60
18 Matt Williams .... 2.00 .60
19 Joe Carter............................... 2.00 .60
20 Harold Baines......................... 2.00 .60
21 Gary Sheffield......................... 2.00 .60
22 Charles Johnson .... 2.00 .60
23 Aaron Boone .... 2.00 .60
24 Eddie Murray.......................... 5.00 1.50
25 Matt Stairs.............................. 2.00 .60
26 David Cone............................. 2.00 .60
27 Jon Nunnally .... 2.00 .60
28 Chris Stynes............................ 2.00 .60
29 Enrique Wilson........................ 2.00 .60
30 Randy Johnson 5.00 1.50
31 Garret Anderson..................... 2.00 .60
32 Manny Ramirez...................... 2.00 .60
33 Jeff Suppan............................ 2.00 .60
34 Rickey Henderson 5.00 1.50
35 Scott Spiezio .... 2.00 .60
36 Rondell White......................... 2.00 .60
37 Todd Greene........................... 2.00 .60
38 Delino DeShields .... 2.00 .60
39 Kevin Brown........................... 3.00 .90
40 Chili Davis .... 2.00 .60
41 Jimmy Key .... 2.00 .60
43 Mike Mussina.......................... 5.00 1.50
44 Joe Randa .... 2.00 .60
45 Chan Ho Park .... 2.00 .60
46 Brad Radke............................. 2.00 .60
47 Geronimo Berroa.................... 2.00 .60
48 Wade Boggs............................ 3.00 .90
49 Kevin Appier .... 2.00 .60
50 Moises Alou .... 2.00 .60
51 David Justice........................... 2.00 .60
52 Ivan Rodriguez 5.00 1.50
53 J.T. Snow .... 2.00 .60
54 Brian Giles.............................. 2.00 .60
55 Will Clark................................ 5.00 1.50
56 Justin Thompson .... 2.00 .60
57 Javier Lopez .... 2.00 .60
58 Hideki Irabu............................ 2.00 .60
59 Mark Grudzielanek................. 2.00 .60
60 Abraham Nunez...................... 2.00 .60
61 Todd Hollandsworth............... 2.00 .60
62 Jay Bell................................... 2.00 .60
63 Nomar Garciaparra................. 8.00 2.40
64 Vinny Castilla.......................... 2.00 .60
65 Lou Collier.............................. 2.00 .60
66 Kevin Orie.............................. 2.00 .60
67 John Valentin .... 2.00 .60
68 Robin Ventura .... 2.00 .60
69 Denny Neagle......................... 2.00 .60
70 Tony Womack .... 2.00 .60
71 Dennis Reyes .... 2.00 .60
72 Wally Joyner .... 2.00 .60
73 Kevin Brown........................... 3.00 .90
74 Ray Durham .... 2.00 .60
75 Mike Cameron........................ 2.00 .60
76 Dante Bichette........................ 2.00 .60
77 Jose Guillen............................ 2.00 .60
78 Carlos Delgado....................... 2.00 .60
79 Paul Molitor............................ 3.00 .90
80 Jason Kendall......................... 2.00 .60
81 Mark Bellhorn......................... 2.00 .60
82 Damian Jackson..................... 2.00 .60
83 Bill Mueller .... 2.00 .60
84 Kevin Young........................... 2.00 .60
85 Curt Schilling.......................... 3.00 .90
86 Jeffrey Hammonds................. 2.00 .60
87 Sandy Alomar Jr..................... 2.00 .60
88 Bartolo Colon .... 2.00 .60
89 Wilton Guerrero...................... 2.00 .60
90 Bernie Williams .... 3.00 .90
91 Deion Sanders........................ 3.00 .90
92 Mike Piazza 8.00 2.40
93 Butch Huskey .... 2.00 .60
94 Edgardo Alfonzo..................... 2.00 .60
95 Alan Benes .... 2.00 .60
96 Craig Biggio............................ 3.00 .90
97 Mark Grace............................. 3.00 .90
98 Shawn Green.......................... 2.00 .60
99 Derrek Lee.............................. 2.00 .60
100 Ken Griffey Jr. 8.00 2.40
101 Tim Raines .... 2.00 .60
102 Pokey Reese......................... 2.00 .60
103 Lee Stevens.......................... 2.00 .60
104 Shannon Stewart.................. 2.00 .60
105 John Smoltz .... 3.00 .90
106 Frank Thomas 5.00 1.50
107 Jeff Fassero.......................... 2.00 .60
108 Jay Buhner .... 2.00 .60
109 Jose Canseco 5.00 1.50
110 Omar Vizquel........................ 2.00 .60
111 Travis Fryman .... 2.00 .60
112 Dave Nilsson .... 2.00 .60
113 John Olerud.......................... 2.00 .60
114 Larry Walker......................... 3.00 .90
115 Jim Edmonds........................ 2.00 .60
116 Bobby Higginson.................. 2.00 .60
117 Todd Hundley....................... 2.00 .60
118 Paul O'Neill.......................... 3.00 .90
119 Bip Roberts .... 2.00 .60
120 Ismael Valdes....................... 2.00 .60
121 Pedro Martinez..................... 5.00 1.50
122 Jeff Cirillo............................ 2.00 .60
123 Andy Benes .... 2.00 .60
124 Bobby Jones .... 2.00 .60
125 Brian Hunter......................... 2.00 .60
126 Darryl Kile .... 2.00 .60
127 Pat Hentgen.......................... 2.00 .60
128 Marquis Grissom.................. 2.00 .60
129 Eric Davis .... 2.00 .60
130 Chipper Jones 5.00 1.50
131 Edgar Martinez..................... 3.00 .90
132 Andy Pettitte......................... 3.00 .90
133 Cal Ripken.......................... 15.00 4.50
134 Scott Rolen .... 3.00 .90
135 Ron Coomer.......................... 2.00 .60
136 Luis Castillo.......................... 2.00 .60
137 Fred McGriff......................... 3.00 .90
138 Neifi Perez........................... 2.00 .60
139 Eric Karros .... 2.00 .60
140 Alex Fernandez..................... 2.00 .60
141 Jason Dickson....................... 2.00 .60
142 Lance Johnson...................... 2.00 .60
143 Ray Lankford......................... 2.00 .60
144 Sammy Sosa......................... 8.00 2.40
145 Eric Young............................ 2.00 .60
146 Bubba Trammell................... 2.00 .60
147 Todd Walker......................... 2.00 .60
148 Mo Vaughn CC .... 2.00 .60
149 Jeff Bagwell CC .... 3.00 .90
150 Kenny Lofton CC .... 2.00 .60
151 Raul Mondesi CC.................. 2.00 .60
152 Mike Piazza CC.................... 8.00 2.40
153 Chipper Jones CC................. 5.00 1.50
154 Larry Walker CC .... 3.00 .90
155 Greg Maddux CC 8.00 2.40
156 Ken Griffey Jr. CC................. 8.00 2.40
157 Frank Thomas CC................. 5.00 1.50
158 Darin Erstad GLS.................. 2.00 .60
159 Roberto Alomar GLS 5.00 1.50
160 Albert Belle GLS .... 2.00 .60
161 Jim Thome GLS 5.00 1.50
162 Tony Clark GLS .... 2.00 .60
163 Chuck Knoblauch GLS.......... 2.00 .60

Card	Nm-Mt	Ex-Mt
164 Derek Jeter GLS	12.00	3.60
165 Alex Rodriguez GLS	8.00	2.40
166 Tony Gwynn GLS	6.00	1.80
167 Roger Clemens GLS	10.00	3.00
168 Barry Larkin GLS	5.00	1.50
169 A. Galarraga GLS	2.00	.60
170 Vlad. Guerrero GLS	5.00	1.50
171 Mark McGwire GLS	12.50	3.70
172 Barry Bonds GLS	12.00	3.60
173 Juan Gonzalez GLS	5.00	1.50
174 Andruw Jones GLS	2.00	.60
175 Paul Molitor GLS	3.00	.90
176 Hideo Nomo GLS	5.00	1.50
177 Cal Ripken GLS	15.00	4.50
178 Brad Fullmer GLR	2.00	.60
179 Jaret Wright GLR	2.00	.60
180 Bobby Estalella GLR	2.00	.60
181 Ben Grieve GLR	2.00	.60
182 Paul Konerko GLR	2.00	.60
183 David Ortiz GLR	2.00	.60
184 Todd Helton GLR	3.00	.90
185 J.Encarnacion GLR	2.00	.60
186 Miguel Tejada GLR	3.00	.90
187 Jacob Cruz GLR	2.00	.60
188 Mark Kotsay GLR	2.00	.60
189 Fernando Tatis GLR	2.00	.60
190 Ricky Ledee GLR	2.00	.60
191 Richard Hidalgo GLR	2.00	.60
192 Richie Sexson GLR	2.00	.60
193 Luis Ordaz GLR	2.00	.60
194 Eli Marrero GLR	2.00	.60
195 Livan Hernandez GLR	2.00	.60
196 Homer Bush GLR	2.00	.60
197 Raul Ibanez GLR	2.00	.60
198 N. Garciaparra CL	5.00	1.50
199 Scott Rolen CL	2.00	.60
200 Jose Cruz Jr. CL	2.00	.60
201 Al Martin	2.00	.60

1998 Leaf Fractal Materials

Inserted at a rate of one per pack, cards from this 200-card set parallel the base Leaf Fractal Foundation set. The cards are printed on real "feel of the game" materials including wood, nylon, plastic and leather. Of the 100 cards printed on plastic, only 3,250 of each card was made; of the 50 on leather, 1000 were made; only 500 of the 30 printed on nylon were made; and of the 20 printed on wood, only 250 of each were made. All the cards are sequentially numbered. Card number 42 does not exist.

Nm-Mt Ex-Mt

*PLASTIC: .25X TO .6X BASIC CARDS
PLASTIC X PRINT 3050 SERIAL #'d SETS
PLASTIC Y PRINT 3150 SERIAL #'d SETS
PLASTIC Z PRINT 3200 SERIAL #'d SETS
*LEATHER: .5X TO 1.25X BASIC CARDS
LEATHER X PRINT RUN 800 SERIAL #'d SETS
LEATHER Y PRINT RUN 900 SERIAL #'d SETS
LEATHER Z PRINT RUN 950 SERIAL #'d SETS
*NYLON: 1X TO 2.5X BASIC CARDS...
NYLON X PRINT RUN 300 SERIAL #'d SETS
NYLON Y PRINT RUN 400 SERIAL #'d SETS
NYLON Z PRINT RUN 450 SERIAL #'d SETS
*WOOD Y/Z: 1.25X TO 3X BASIC CARDS
*WOOD X: 6X TO 15X BASIC CARDS .
WOOD X PRINT RUN 50 SERIAL #'d SETS
WOOD Y PRINT RUN 150 SERIAL #'d SETS
WOOD Z PRINT RUN 200 SERIAL #'d SETS
CARD NUMBER 42 DOES NOT EXIST.

1998 Leaf Fractal Materials Die Cuts

This 200-card set is a die-cut parallel version of the Leaf Fractal Materials set. The first 200 cards of 75 players printed on plastic, 15 printed on leather, five printed on nylon, and five printed on wood have a die-cut x-axis background. The first 100 cards of 20 players printed on plastic, 25 printed on leather, 10 printed on nylon and five printed on wood have a die-cut y-axis background. The first 50 cards of five players printed on plastic, 10 printed on leather, 15 printed on nylon, and 10 printed on wood have a die-cut z-axis background. Each card is sequentially numbered. Card number 42 does not exist. Only 200 of each x-axis were produced, 100 of each y-axis and 50 of each z-axis were produced. Serial numbering on the actual cards is misleading because the non die cut Fractal Materials and the Die-Cut Fractal Materials were numbered prior to being die cut.

Nm-Mt Ex-Mt

*X-AXIS: 1.25X TO 3X BASIC CARDS.
X-AXIS PRINT RUN 200 SERIAL #'d SETS
*Y-AXIS: 2X TO 5X BASIC CARDS......
Y-AXIS PRINT RUN 100 SERIAL #'d SETS
*Z-AXIS: 2.5X TO 6X BASIC CARDS ...
Z-AXIS PRINT RUN 50 SERIAL #'d SETS
CARD NUMBER 42 DOES NOT EXIST .

1998 Leaf Fractal Materials Z2 Axis

This 200-card set is parallel to the base set and features full die-cut cards. Each card is sequentially numbered to 20. Card number 42 does not exist.

Nm-Mt Ex-Mt

*STARS: 5X TO 12X BASIC FOUNDATION

1998 Leaf Fractal Materials Samples

To preview the 1998 Leaf Fractal Materials product, one of fifty different sample cards was included in each dealer wholesale order form. The 50-card leather subset (within the 200-card Fractal Materials set) was used as the basis for this promotional issue, resulting in a skipped numbering system. These sample cards differ from the standard leather Fractal Materials cards in two significant ways: the large "SAMPLE" text running diagonally across the back of the card and the lack of serial numbering on back.

Card	Nm-Mt	Ex-Mt
COMPLETE SET (50)	500.00	150.00
5 Matt Morris	10.00	3.00
9 Ruben Rivera	4.00	1.20
10 Shawn Estes	4.00	1.20
15 Ryan Klesko	10.00	3.00
17 Brett Tomko	4.00	1.20
22 Charles Johnson	6.00	1.80
33 Jeff Suppan	4.00	1.20
36 Rondell White	6.00	1.80
39 Kevin Brown	10.00	3.00
53 J.T. Snow	6.00	1.80
55 Will Clark	15.00	4.50
58 Hideki Irabu	4.00	1.20
66 Kevin Orie	4.00	1.20
70 Tony Womack	4.00	1.20
71 Dennis Reyes	4.00	1.20
76 Dante Bichette	4.00	1.20
78 Carlos Delgado	15.00	4.50
81 Mark Bellhorn	4.00	1.20
87 Sandy Alomar Jr.	6.00	1.80
89 Wilton Guerrero	4.00	1.20
93 Butch Huskey	4.00	1.20
94 Edgardo Alfonzo	12.00	3.60
95 Alan Benes	4.00	1.20
97 Mark Grace	15.00	4.50
98 Shawn Green	12.00	3.60
99 Derrek Lee	10.00	3.00
105 John Smoltz	6.00	1.80
108 Jay Buhner	6.00	1.80
109 Jose Canseco	15.00	4.50
116 Bobby Higginson	6.00	1.80
117 Todd Hundley	6.00	1.80
136 Luis Castillo	6.00	1.80
137 Fred McGriff	10.00	3.00
138 Neifi Perez	4.00	1.20
146 Bubba Trammell	4.00	1.20
147 Todd Walker	6.00	1.80
158 Darin Erstad	12.00	3.60
160 Albert Belle	6.00	1.80
161 Jim Thome	12.00	3.60
162 Tony Clark	4.00	1.20
163 Chuck Knoblauch	6.00	1.80
167 Roger Clemens	30.00	9.00
170 Vladimir Guerrero	20.00	6.00
171 Mark McGwire	50.00	15.00
172 Barry Bonds	30.00	9.00
176 Hideo Nomo	100.00	30.00
189 Fernando Tatis	4.00	1.20
194 Eli Marrero	4.00	1.20
195 Livan Hernandez	6.00	1.80
201 Al Martin	4.00	1.20

1994 Leaf Limited

This 160-card standard-size set was issued exclusively to hobby dealers. The set is organized alphabetically within teams with AL preceding NL.

Card	Nm-Mt	Ex-Mt
COMPLETE SET (160)	80.00	24.00
1 Jeffrey Hammonds	.50	.15
2 Ben McDonald	.50	.15
3 Mike Mussina	2.50	.75
4 Rafael Palmeiro	1.50	.45
5 Cal Ripken Jr.	8.00	2.40
6 Lee Smith	1.00	.30
7 Roger Clemens	5.00	1.50
8 Scott Cooper	.50	.15
9 Andre Dawson	1.00	.30
10 Mike Greenwell	.50	.15
11 Aaron Sele	.50	.15
12 Mo Vaughn	1.00	.30
13 Brian Anderson RC	1.00	.30
14 Chad Curtis	.50	.15
15 Chili Davis	1.00	.30
16 Gary DiSarcina	.50	.15
17 Mark Langston	.50	.15
18 Tim Salmon	1.50	.45
19 Wilson Alvarez	.50	.15
20 Jason Bere	.50	.15
21 Julio Franco	1.00	.30
22 Jack McDowell	.50	.15
23 Tim Raines	1.00	.30
24 Frank Thomas	2.50	.75
25 Robin Ventura	1.00	.30
26 Carlos Baerga	.50	.15
27 Albert Belle	1.00	.30
28 Kenny Lofton	1.00	.30
29 Eddie Murray	2.50	.75
30 Manny Ramirez	1.50	.45
31 Cecil Fielder	1.00	.30
32 Travis Fryman	1.00	.30
33 Mickey Tettleton	.50	.15
34 Alan Trammell	1.50	.45
35 Lou Whitaker	1.00	.30
36 David Cone	1.00	.30
37 Gary Gaetti	1.00	.30
38 Greg Gagne	.50	.15
39 Bob Hamelin	.50	.15
40 Wally Joyner	1.00	.30
41 Brian McRae	.50	.15
42 Ricky Bones	.50	.15
43 Brian Harper	.50	.15
44 John Jaha	.50	.15
45 Pat Listach	.50	.15
46 Dave Nilsson	.50	.15
47 Greg Vaughn	1.00	.30
48 Kent Hrbek	1.00	.30
49 Chuck Knoblauch	1.00	.30
50 Shane Mack	.50	.15
51 Kirby Puckett	2.50	.75
52 Dave Winfield	1.00	.30
53 Jim Abbott	1.50	.45
54 Wade Boggs	1.50	.45
55 Jimmy Key	1.00	.30
56 Don Mattingly	6.00	1.80
57 Paul O'Neill	1.50	.45
58 Danny Tartabull	.50	.15
59 Dennis Eckersley	1.00	.30
60 Rickey Henderson	2.50	.75
61 Mark McGwire	6.00	1.80
62 Troy Neel	.50	.15
63 Ruben Sierra	.50	.15
64 Eric Anthony	.50	.15
65 Jay Buhner	1.00	.30
66 Ken Griffey Jr.	4.00	1.20
67 Randy Johnson	2.50	.75
68 Edgar Martinez	1.50	.45
69 Tino Martinez	1.50	.45
70 Jose Canseco	2.50	.75
71 Will Clark	2.50	.75
72 Juan Gonzalez	2.50	.75
73 Dean Palmer	1.00	.30
74 Ivan Rodriguez	2.50	.75
75 Roberto Alomar	2.50	.75
76 Joe Carter	1.00	.30
77 Carlos Delgado	1.50	.45
78 Paul Molitor	1.50	.45
79 John Olerud	1.00	.30
80 Devon White	.50	.15
81 Steve Avery	.50	.15
82 Tom Glavine	1.50	.45
83 David Justice	1.00	.30
84 Roberto Kelly	.50	.15
85 Ryan Klesko	1.00	.30
86 Javier Lopez	1.00	.30
87 Greg Maddux	4.00	1.20
88 Fred McGriff	1.50	.45
89 Shawon Dunston	.50	.15
90 Mark Grace	1.50	.45
91 Derrick May	.50	.15
92 Sammy Sosa	4.00	1.20
93 Rick Wilkins	.50	.15
94 Bret Boone	1.00	.30
95 Barry Larkin	2.50	.75
96 Kevin Mitchell	.50	.15
97 Hal Morris	.50	.15
98 Deion Sanders	1.50	.45
99 Reggie Sanders	1.00	.30
100 Dante Bichette	1.00	.30
101 Ellis Burks	1.00	.30
102 Andres Galarraga	1.00	.30
103 Joe Girardi	.50	.15
104 Charlie Hayes	.50	.15
105 Chuck Carr	.50	.15
106 Jeff Conine	1.00	.30
107 Bryan Harvey	.50	.15
108 Benito Santiago	1.00	.30
109 Gary Sheffield	1.00	.30
110 Jeff Bagwell	1.50	.45
111 Craig Biggio	1.50	.45
112 Ken Caminiti	1.00	.30
113 Andujar Cedeno	.50	.15
114 Doug Drabek	.50	.15
115 Luis Gonzalez	1.00	.30
116 Brett Butler	1.00	.30
117 Delino DeShields	.50	.15
118 Eric Karros	1.00	.30
119 Raul Mondesi	1.00	.30
120 Mike Piazza	5.00	1.50
121 Henry Rodriguez	.50	.15
122 Tim Wallach	.50	.15
123 Moises Alou	1.00	.30
124 Cliff Floyd	1.00	.30
125 Marquis Grissom	.50	.15
126 Ken Hill	.50	.15
127 Larry Walker	1.50	.45
128 John Wetteland	1.00	.30
129 Bobby Bonilla	1.00	.30
130 John Franco	1.00	.30
131 Jeff Kent	1.00	.30
132 Bret Saberhagen	1.00	.30
133 Ryan Thompson	.50	.15
134 Darren Daulton	1.00	.30
135 Mariano Duncan	.50	.15
136 Lenny Dykstra	1.00	.30
137 Danny Jackson	.50	.15
138 John Kruk	1.00	.30
139 Jay Bell	1.00	.30
140 Jeff King	.50	.15
141 Al Martin	.50	.15
142 Orlando Merced	.50	.15
143 Andy Van Slyke	1.00	.30
144 Bernard Gilkey	.50	.15
145 Gregg Jefferies	.50	.15
146 Ray Lankford	.50	.15
147 Ozzie Smith	4.00	1.20
148 Mark Whiten	.50	.15
149 Todd Zeile	.50	.15
150 Derek Bell	.50	.15
151 Andy Benes	.50	.15
152 Tony Gwynn	3.00	.90
153 Phil Plantier	.50	.15
154 Bip Roberts	.50	.15
155 Rod Beck	.50	.15
156 Barry Bonds	6.00	1.80
157 John Burkett	.50	.15
158 Royce Clayton	.50	.15
159 Bill Swift	.50	.15
160 Matt Williams	1.00	.30

1994 Leaf Limited Gold All-Stars

Randomly inserted in packs at a rate of one in seven, this 18-card standard-size set features the starting players at each position in both the National and American leagues for the 1994 All-Star Game. They are identical in design to the basic Limited product except for being gold and individually numbered out of 10,000.

Card	Nm-Mt	Ex-Mt
COMPLETE SET (18)	40.00	12.00
1 Frank Thomas	2.00	.60
2 Gregg Jefferies	.40	.12
3 Roberto Alomar	2.00	.60
4 Mariano Duncan	.40	.12
5 Wade Boggs	1.25	.35
6 Matt Williams	.75	.23
7 Cal Ripken Jr.	6.00	1.80
8 Ozzie Smith	3.00	.90
9 Kirby Puckett	2.00	.60
10 Barry Bonds	5.00	1.50
11 Ken Griffey Jr.	3.00	.90
12 Tony Gwynn	2.50	.75
13 Joe Carter	.75	.23
14 David Justice	.75	.23
15 Ivan Rodriguez	2.00	.60
16 Mike Piazza	4.00	1.20
17 Jimmy Key	.75	.23
18 Greg Maddux	3.00	.90

1994 Leaf Limited Rookies

This 80-card standard-size premium set was issued by Donruss exclusively to hobby dealers. The set showcases top rookies and prospects of 1994. Rookie Cards in this set include Armando Benitez, Rusty Greer and Chan Ho Park.

Card	Nm-Mt	Ex-Mt
COMPLETE SET (80)	25.00	7.50
1 Charles Johnson	.75	.23
2 Rico Brogna	.40	.12
3 Melvin Nieves	.40	.12
4 Rich Becker	.40	.12
5 Russ Davis	.40	.12
6 Matt Mieske	.40	.12
7 Paul Shuey	.40	.12
8 Hector Carrasco	.40	.12
9 J.R. Phillips	.40	.12
10 Scott Ruffcorn	.40	.12
11 Kurt Abbott RC	.75	.23
12 Danny Bautista	.40	.12
13 Rick White	.40	.12
14 Steve Dunn	.40	.12
15 Joe Ausanio	.40	.12
16 Salomon Torres	.40	.12
17 Ricky Bottalico RC	.75	.23
18 Johnny Ruffin	.40	.12
19 Kevin Foster RC	.40	.12
20 W.VanLandingham RC	.40	.12
21 Troy O'Leary	.40	.12
22 Mark Acre RC	.40	.12
23 Norberto Martin	.40	.12
24 Jason Jacome RC	.40	.12
25 Steve Trachsel	.40	.12
26 Denny Hocking	.40	.12
27 Mike Lieberthal	.75	.23
28 Gerald Williams	.40	.12
29 John Mabry RC	.75	.23
30 Greg Blosser	.40	.12
31 Carl Everett	.75	.23
32 Steve Karsay	.40	.12
33 Jose Valentin	.40	.12
34 Jon Lieber	.40	.12
35 Chris Gomez	.40	.12
36 Jesus Tavarez RC	.40	.12
37 Tony Longmire	.40	.12
38 Luis Lopez	.40	.12
39 Matt Walbeck	.40	.12
40 Rikkert Faneyte RC	.40	.12
41 Shane Reynolds	.40	.12
42 Joey Hamilton	.40	.12
43 Ismael Valdes RC	.75	.23
44 Danny Miceli	.40	.12
45 Darren Bragg RC	.40	.12
46 Alex Gonzalez	.40	.12
47 Rick Helling	.40	.12
48 Jose Oliva	.40	.12
49 Jim Edmonds	1.25	.35
50 Miguel Jimenez	.40	.12
51 Tony Eusebio	.40	.12
52 Shawn Green	2.00	.60
53 Billy Ashley	.40	.12
54 Rondell White	.75	.23
55 Cory Bailey RC	.40	.12
56 Tim Davis	.40	.12
57 John Hudek RC	.40	.12
58 Darren Hall	.40	.12
59 Darren Dreifort	.40	.12
60 Mike Kelly	.40	.12
61 Marcus Moore	.40	.12
62 Garret Anderson	2.00	.60
63 Brian L. Hunter	.40	.12
64 Mark Smith	.40	.12
65 Garey Ingram RC	.40	.12
66 Rusty Greer RC	2.00	.60
67 Marc Newfield	.40	.12
68 Gar Finnvold	.40	.12
69 Paul Spoljaric	.40	.12
70 Ray McDavid	.40	.12
71 Orlando Miller	.40	.12
72 Jorge Fabregas	.40	.12
73 Ray Holbert	.40	.12
74 Armando Benitez RC	2.00	.60
75 Ernie Young RC	.75	.23
76 James Mouton	.40	.12
77 Robert Perez RC	.40	.12
78 Chan Ho Park RC	3.00	.90
79 Roger Salkeld	.40	.12
80 Tony Tarasco	.40	.12

1994 Leaf Limited Rookies Phenoms

This 10-card standard-size set was randomly inserted in Leaf Limited Rookies packs at a rate of approximately of one in twelve. This set showcases top 1994 rookies especially Alex Rodriguez. The fronts are designed much like the Limited Rookies basic set cards except the card is comprised of gold foil instead of silver on the front. Gold backs are also virtually identical to the Limited Rookies in terms of content and layout. The cards are individually numbered on back out of 5,000. The Rodriguez card, primarily because of it's status as one of A-Rod's earliest serial-numbered MLB-liscensed issues (coupled with high-end production qualities and a known print run) has become one of the more desirable cards issued in the 1990's. Collectors should take caution of trimmed copies when purchasing this card in "raw" form.

Card	Nm-Mt	Ex-Mt
COMPLETE SET (10)	200.00	60.00
1 Raul Mondesi	8.00	2.40
2 Bob Hamelin	5.00	1.50
3 Midre Cummings	5.00	1.50
4 Carlos Delgado	10.00	3.00
5 Cliff Floyd	8.00	2.40
6 Jeffrey Hammonds	5.00	1.50
7 Ryan Klesko	8.00	2.40
8 Javier Lopez	8.00	2.40
9 Manny Ramirez	10.00	3.00
10 Alex Rodriguez	250.00	75.00

1995 Leaf Limited

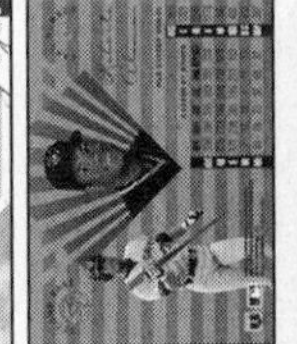

This 192 standard-size card set was issued in two series. Each series contained 96 cards. These cards were issued in six-box cases with 20 packs per box and five cards per pack. Forty-five thousand boxes of each series was produced. Rookie Cards in this set include Bob Higginson and Hideo Nomo.

Card	Nm-Mt	Ex-Mt
COMPLETE SET (192)	40.00	12.00
COMPLETE SERIES 1 (96)	20.00	6.00
COMPLETE SERIES 2 (96)	20.00	6.00
1 Frank Thomas	1.25	.35
2 Geronimo Berroa	.25	.07
3 Tony Phillips	.25	.07
4 Roberto Alomar	1.25	.35
5 Steve Avery	.25	.07
6 Darryl Hamilton	.25	.07
7 Scott Cooper	.25	.07
8 Mark Grace	.75	.23
9 Billy Ashley	.25	.07
10 Wil Cordero	.25	.07
11 Barry Bonds	3.00	.90
12 Kenny Lofton	.50	.15
13 Jay Buhner	.50	.15
14 Alex Rodriguez	3.00	.90
15 Bobby Bonilla	.50	.15
16 Brady Anderson	.50	.15
17 Ken Caminiti	.50	.15
18 Charlie Hayes	.25	.07
19 Jay Bell	.50	.15
20 Will Clark	1.25	.35
21 Jose Canseco	1.25	.35
22 Bret Boone	.50	.15
23 Dante Bichette	.50	.15
24 Kevin Appier	.50	.15
25 Chad Curtis	.25	.07
26 Marty Cordova	.25	.07
27 Jason Bere	.25	.07
28 Jimmy Key	.50	.15
29 Rickey Henderson	1.25	.35
30 Tim Salmon	.75	.23
31 Joe Carter	.50	.15
32 Tom Glavine	.75	.23
33 Pat Listach	.25	.07
34 Brian Jordan	.50	.15
35 Brian McRae	.25	.07
36 Eric Karros	.50	.15
37 Pedro Martinez	1.25	.35
38 Royce Clayton	.25	.07
39 Eddie Murray	1.25	.35
40 Randy Johnson	1.25	.35
41 Jeff Conine	.50	.15
42 Brett Butler	.50	.15
43 Jeffrey Hammonds	.25	.07
44 Andujar Cedeno	.25	.07
45 Dave Hollins	.25	.07
46 Jeff King	.25	.07
47 Benji Gil	.25	.07
48 Roger Clemens	2.50	.75
49 Barry Larkin	1.25	.35
50 Joe Girardi	.25	.07
51 Bob Hamelin	.25	.07
52 Travis Fryman	.50	.15
53 Chuck Knoblauch	.50	.15
54 Ray Durham	.50	.15
55 Don Mattingly	3.00	.90
56 Ruben Sierra	.25	.07
57 J.T. Snow	.50	.15

58 Derek Bell .25 .07
59 David Cone .50 .15
60 Marquis Grissom .25 .07
61 Kevin Seitzer .25 .07
62 Ozzie Smith 2.00 .60
63 Rick Wilkins .25 .07
64 Hideo Nomo RC 2.50 .75
65 Tony Tarasco .25 .07
66 Manny Ramirez .50 .15
67 Charles Johnson .50 .15
68 Craig Biggio .75 .23
69 Bobby Jones .25 .07
70 Mike Mussina 1.25 .35
71 Alex Gonzalez .25 .07
72 Gregg Jefferies .25 .07
73 Rusty Greer .50 .15
74 Mike Greenwell .25 .07
75 Hal Morris .25 .07
76 Paul O'Neill .75 .23
77 Luis Gonzalez .50 .15
78 Chipper Jones 1.25 .35
79 Mike Piazza 2.00 .60
80 Rondell White .50 .15
81 Glenallen Hill .25 .07
82 Shawn Green .50 .15
83 Bernie Williams .75 .23
84 Jim Thome 1.25 .35
85 Terry Pendleton .50 .15
86 Rafael Palmeiro .75 .23
87 Tony Gwynn 1.50 .45
88 Mickey Tettleton .25 .07
89 John Valentin .25 .07
90 Deion Sanders .75 .23
91 Larry Walker .75 .23
92 Michael Tucker .25 .07
93 Alan Trammell .75 .23
94 Tim Raines .50 .15
95 David Justice .50 .15
96 Tino Martinez .75 .23
97 Cal Ripken Jr. 4.00 1.20
98 Deion Sanders .75 .23
99 Darren Daulton .50 .15
100 Paul Molitor .75 .23
101 Randy Myers .25 .07
102 Wally Joyner .50 .15
103 Carlos Perez RC .50 .15
104 Brian Hunter .25 .07
105 Wade Boggs .75 .23
106 Bob Higginson RC 1.25 .35
107 Jeff Kent .50 .15
108 Jose Offerman .25 .07
109 Dennis Eckersley .50 .15
110 Dave Nilsson .25 .07
111 Chuck Finley .50 .15
112 Devon White .50 .15
113 Bip Roberts .25 .07
114 Ramon Martinez .25 .07
115 Greg Maddux 2.00 .60
116 Curtis Goodwin .25 .07
117 John Jaha .25 .07
118 Ken Griffey Jr. 2.00 .60
119 Geronimo Pena .25 .07
120 Shawon Dunston .25 .07
121 Ariel Prieto RC .25 .07
122 Kirby Puckett 1.25 .35
123 Carlos Baerga .25 .07
124 Todd Hundley .25 .07
125 Tim Naehring .25 .07
126 Gary Sheffield .50 .15
127 Dean Palmer .50 .15
128 Rondell White .50 .15
129 Greg Gagne .25 .07
130 Jose Rijo .25 .07
131 Ivan Rodriguez 1.25 .35
132 Jeff Bagwell .75 .23
133 Greg Vaughn .50 .15
134 Chili Davis .50 .15
135 Al Martin .25 .07
136 Kenny Rogers .50 .15
137 Aaron Sele .25 .07
138 Raul Mondesi .50 .15
139 Cecil Fielder .50 .15
140 Tim Wallach .25 .07
141 Andres Galarraga .50 .15
142 Lou Whitaker .50 .15
143 Jack McDowell .25 .07
144 Matt Williams .50 .15
145 Ryan Klesko .50 .15
146 Carlos Garcia .25 .07
147 Albert Belle .50 .15
148 Ryan Thompson .25 .07
149 Roberto Kelly .25 .07
150 Edgar Martinez .75 .23
151 Robby Thompson .25 .07
152 Mo Vaughn .50 .15
153 Todd Zeile .25 .07
154 Harold Baines .50 .15
155 Phil Plantier .25 .07
156 Mike Stanley .25 .07
157 Ed Sprague .25 .07
158 Moises Alou .50 .15
159 Quilvio Veras .25 .07
160 Reggie Sanders .50 .15
161 Delino DeShields .25 .07
162 Rico Brogna .25 .07
163 Greg Colbrunn .25 .07
164 Steve Finley .50 .15
165 Orlando Merced .25 .07
166 Mark McGwire 3.00 .90
167 Garret Anderson .50 .15
168 Paul Sorrento .25 .07
169 Mark Langston .25 .07
170 Danny Tartabull .25 .07
171 Vinny Castilla .50 .15
172 Javier Lopez .50 .15
173 Bret Saberhagen .50 .15
174 Eddie Williams .25 .07
175 Scott Leius .25 .07
176 Juan Gonzalez 1.25 .35
177 Gary Gaetti .50 .15
178 Jim Edmonds .50 .15
179 John Olerud .50 .15
180 Lenny Dykstra .50 .15
181 Ray Lankford .25 .07
182 Ron Gant .50 .15
183 Doug Drabek .25 .07
184 Fred McGriff .75 .23
185 Andy Benes .25 .07
186 Kurt Abbott .25 .07
187 Bernard Gilkey .25 .07
188 Sammy Sosa 2.00 .60
189 Lee Smith .50 .15
190 Dennis Martinez .50 .15
191 Ozzie Guillen .25 .07
192 Robin Ventura .50 .15

1995 Leaf Limited Gold

These 24 standard-size quasi-parallel cards were inserted one per series one pack. Players from both series were included in this set. While using the same design as the regular issue, they are distinguished by different photos, different numbers and gold holographic foil.

Nm-Mt Ex-Mt
1 Frank Thomas 1.25 .35
2 Jeff Bagwell .75 .23
3 Raul Mondesi .50 .15
4 Barry Bonds 3.00 .90
5 Albert Belle .50 .15
6 Ken Griffey Jr. 2.00 .60
7 Cal Ripken UER 4.00 1.20
Name spelled Ripkin on card
8 Will Clark 1.25 .35
9 Jose Canseco 1.25 .35
10 Larry Walker .75 .23
11 Kirby Puckett 1.25 .35
12 Don Mattingly 3.00 .90
13 Tim Salmon .75 .23
14 Roberto Alomar 1.25 .35
15 Greg Maddux 2.00 .60
16 Mike Piazza 2.00 .60
17 Matt Williams .50 .15
18 Kenny Lofton .50 .15
19 Alex Rodriguez UER 3.00 .90
Name spelled Rodriquez on card
20 Tony Gwynn 1.50 .45
21 Mo Vaughn .50 .15
22 Chipper Jones 1.25 .35
23 Manny Ramirez .50 .15
24 Deion Sanders .75 .23

1995 Leaf Limited Bat Patrol

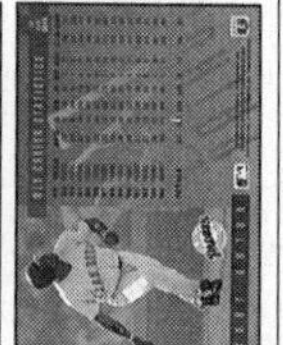

These 24 standard-size cards were inserted one per series two pack. The cards are numbered in the upper right corner as "X" of 24.

Nm-Mt Ex-Mt
COMPLETE SET (24) 25.00 7.50
1 Frank Thomas 1.25 .35
2 Tony Gwynn 1.50 .45
3 Wade Boggs .75 .23
4 Larry Walker .75 .23
5 Ken Griffey, Jr. 2.00 .60
6 Jeff Bagwell .75 .23
7 Manny Ramirez .50 .15
8 Mark Grace .75 .23
9 Kenny Lofton .50 .15
10 Mike Piazza 2.00 .60
11 Will Clark 1.25 .35
12 Mo Vaughn .50 .15
13 Carlos Baerga .25 .07
14 Rafael Palmeiro .75 .23
15 Barry Bonds 3.00 .90
16 Kirby Puckett 1.25 .35
17 Roberto Alomar 1.25 .35
18 Barry Larkin 1.25 .35
19 Eddie Murray 1.25 .35
20 Tim Salmon .75 .23
21 Don Mattingly 3.00 .90
22 Fred McGriff .75 .23
23 Albert Belle .50 .15
24 Dante Bichette .50 .15

1995 Leaf Limited Lumberjacks

These eight standard-size cards were randomly inserted into second series packs. The cards are individually numbered out of 5,000. The fronts feature a player photo surrounded by his name, the word "Lumberjacks" and "Handcrafted" in a semi-circular pattern on a simulated wood grain stock. Please note, these cards do not feature elements of game-used material.

Nm-Mt Ex-Mt
COMPLETE SET (16) 200.00 60.00
COMPLETE SERIES 1 (8) 100.00 30.00
COMPLETE SERIES 2 (8) 100.00 30.00
1 Albert Belle 4.00 1.20
2 Barry Bonds 25.00 7.50
3 Juan Gonzalez 10.00 3.00
4 Ken Griffey Jr. 15.00 4.50
5 Fred McGriff 6.00 1.80
6 Mike Piazza 15.00 4.50
7 Kirby Puckett 10.00 3.00
8 Mo Vaughn 4.00 1.20
9 Frank Thomas 10.00 3.00
10 Jeff Bagwell 6.00 1.80
11 Matt Williams 4.00 1.20
12 Jose Canseco 10.00 3.00
13 Raul Mondesi 4.00 1.20
14 Manny Ramirez 4.00 1.20
15 Cecil Fielder 4.00 1.20
16 Cal Ripken 30.00 9.00

1996 Leaf Limited

The 1996 Leaf Limited set was issued exclusively to hobby outlets with a maximum production run of 45,000 boxes. Each box contained two smaller mini-boxes, enabling the dealer to use his imagination in the marketing of this product. The five-card packs carried a suggested retail price of $3.24. Each Master Box was sequentially- numbered via a box topper. If this number matched the 1996 year-ending stats, the collector and the dealer both had a chance to win prizes such as a Frank Thomas game-used bat, autographed batting glove, or a "Two Biggest Weapons" poster. The collector would return the winning box number to the hobby shop, and the dealer would mail it to Donruss with both receiving the same prize. The card fronts displayed color player photos with another photo and player information on the backs.

Nm-Mt Ex-Mt
COMPLETE SET (90) 50.00 15.00
1 Ivan Rodriguez 1.50 .45
2 Roger Clemens 3.00 .90
3 Gary Sheffield .60 .18
4 Tino Martinez 1.00 .30
5 Sammy Sosa 2.50 .75
6 Reggie Sanders .60 .18
7 Ray Lankford .60 .18
8 Manny Ramirez .60 .18
9 Jeff Bagwell 1.00 .30
10 Greg Maddux 2.50 .75
11 Ken Griffey Jr. 2.50 .75
12 Rondell White .60 .18
13 Mike Piazza 2.50 .75
14 Marc Newfield .60 .18
15 Cal Ripken 5.00 1.50
16 Carlos Delgado .60 .18
17 Tim Salmon 1.00 .30
18 Andres Galarraga .60 .18
19 Chuck Knoblauch .60 .18
20 Matt Williams .60 .18
21 Mark McGwire 4.00 1.20
22 Ben McDonald .60 .18
23 Frank Thomas 1.50 .45
24 Johnny Damon .60 .18
25 Gregg Jefferies .60 .18
26 Travis Fryman .60 .18
27 Chipper Jones 1.50 .45
28 David Cone .60 .18
29 Kenny Lofton .60 .18
30 Mike Mussina 1.50 .45
31 Alex Rodriguez 3.00 .90
32 Carlos Baerga .60 .18
33 Brian Hunter .60 .18
34 Juan Gonzalez 1.50 .45
35 Bernie Williams 1.00 .30
36 Wally Joyner .60 .18
37 Fred McGriff 1.00 .30
38 Randy Johnson 1.50 .45
39 Marty Cordova .60 .18
40 Garret Anderson .60 .18
41 Albert Belle .60 .18
42 Edgar Martinez 1.00 .30
43 Barry Larkin 1.50 .45
44 Paul O'Neill 1.00 .30
45 Cecil Fielder .60 .18
46 Rusty Greer .60 .18
47 Mo Vaughn .60 .18
48 Dante Bichette .60 .18
49 Ryan Klesko .60 .18
50 Roberto Alomar 1.50 .45
51 Raul Mondesi .60 .18
52 Robin Ventura .60 .18
53 Tony Gwynn 2.00 .60
54 Mark Grace 1.00 .30
55 Jim Thome 1.50 .45
56 Jason Giambi 1.50 .45
57 Tom Glavine 1.00 .30
58 Jim Edmonds .60 .18
59 Pedro Martinez 1.50 .45
60 Charles Johnson .60 .18
61 Wade Boggs 1.00 .30
62 Orlando Merced .60 .18
63 Craig Biggio 1.00 .30
64 Brady Anderson .60 .18
65 Hideo Nomo 1.50 .45
66 Ozzie Smith 2.50 .75
67 Eddie Murray 1.50 .45
68 Will Clark 1.50 .45
69 Jay Buhner .60 .18
70 Kirby Puckett 1.50 .45
71 Barry Bonds 4.00 1.20
72 Ray Durham .60 .18
73 Sterling Hitchcock .60 .18
74 John Smoltz 1.00 .30
75 Andre Dawson .60 .18
76 Joe Carter .60 .18
77 Ryne Sandberg 2.50 .75
78 Rickey Henderson 1.50 .45
79 Brian Jordan .60 .18
80 Greg Vaughn .60 .18
81 Andy Pettitte 1.00 .30
82 Dean Palmer .60 .18
83 Paul Molitor 1.00 .30
84 Rafael Palmeiro 1.00 .30
85 Henry Rodriguez .60 .18
86 Larry Walker 1.00 .30
87 Ismael Valdes .60 .18
88 Derek Bell .60 .18
89 J.T. Snow .60 .18
90 Jack McDowell .60 .18

1996 Leaf Limited Gold

Randomly inserted into one in every 11 packs, cards from this 90-card insert set parallel the regular Leaf Limited issue. Similar in design, it differs from the regular set with its gold holographic foil treatment.

Nm-Mt Ex-Mt
*STARS: 2.5X TO 6X BASIC CARDS ...

1996 Leaf Limited Lumberjacks Samples

One of ten different Leaf Limited Lumberjacks Samples cards was inserted into 1996 Leaf Limited dealer order forms and hobby media press releases. The cards parallel the standard Lumberjacks inserts except for the text "sample card" running diagonally across the front and back of the card and "PROMO/5000" text on back.

Nm-Mt Ex-Mt
COMPLETE SET (10) 80.00 24.00
1 Ken Griffey Jr. 10.00 3.00
2 Sammy Sosa 8.00 2.40
3 Cal Ripken 15.00 4.50
4 Frank Thomas 4.00 1.20
5 Alex Rodriguez 10.00 3.00
6 Mo Vaughn 3.00 .90
7 Chipper Jones 8.00 2.40
8 Mike Piazza 10.00 3.00
9 Jeff Bagwell 4.00 1.20
10 Mark McGwire 12.00 3.60

1996 Leaf Limited Lumberjacks

Printed with maple stock that puts wood grains on both sides (but does not incorporate game-used bat chips), this 10-card insert set features the league's top sluggers. The fronts carry color player photos with player information and statistics on the backs. Only 5,000 sets were produced and each card is individually numbered.

Nm-Mt Ex-Mt
COMPLETE SET (10) 120.00 36.00
*BLACK: 1.5X TO 4X BASIC LUMBERJACK
BLACK PRINT RUN 500 SERIAL #'d SETS
1 Ken Griffey Jr. 12.00 3.60
2 Sammy Sosa 12.00 3.60
3 Cal Ripken 25.00 7.50
4 Frank Thomas 8.00 2.40
5 Alex Rodriguez 15.00 4.50
6 Mo Vaughn 3.00 .90
7 Chipper Jones 8.00 2.40
8 Mike Piazza 12.00 3.60
9 Jeff Bagwell 5.00 1.50
10 Mark McGwire 20.00 6.00

1996 Leaf Limited Pennant Craze Promos

Issued to promote the Leaf Limited Pennant Craze insert set, these cards are differentiated from the regular Leaf Limited insert cards as they are numbered 0000/2500 on the back.

Nm-Mt Ex-Mt
COMPLETE SET (10) 40.00 12.00
1 Juan Gonzalez 2.50 .75
2 Cal Ripken 10.00 3.00
3 Frank Thomas 2.50 .75
4 Ken Griffey Jr. 6.00 1.80
5 Albert Belle 1.00 .30
6 Greg Maddux 6.00 1.80
7 Paul Molitor 2.50 .75
8 Alex Rodriguez 6.00 1.80
9 Barry Bonds 5.00 1.50
10 Chipper Jones 5.00 1.50

1996 Leaf Limited Pennant Craze

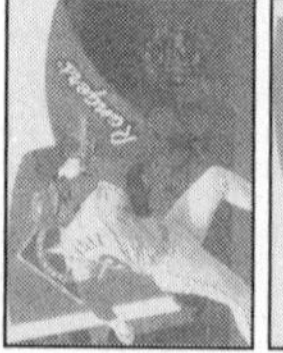

This 10-card insert set features 10 superstars who have a thirst for the pennant. A special flocking technique puts the felt feel of a pennant on a die cut card. Only 2,500 sets were produced and are individually numbered.

Nm-Mt Ex-Mt
COMPLETE SET (10) 200.00 60.00
1 Juan Gonzalez 15.00 4.50
2 Cal Ripken 50.00 15.00
3 Frank Thomas 15.00 4.50
4 Ken Griffey Jr. 25.00 7.50
5 Albert Belle 6.00 1.80
6 Greg Maddux 25.00 7.50
7 Paul Molitor 10.00 3.00
8 Alex Rodriguez 30.00 9.00
9 Barry Bonds 40.00 12.00
10 Chipper Jones 15.00 4.50

1996 Leaf Limited Rookies

Randomly inserted in packs at a rate of one in seven, this 10-card set printed in silver holographic foil features some of the hottest rookies of the year. A first year card of Darin Erstad is in this set.

Nm-Mt Ex-Mt
COMPLETE SET (10) 40.00 12.00
*GOLD: 1X TO 2.5X BASIC ROOKIES..
GOLD: RANDOM INSERTS IN PACKS .
1 Alex Ochoa 1.00 .30
2 Darin Erstad 6.00 1.80
3 Ruben Rivera 1.00 .30
4 Derek Jeter 15.00 4.50
5 Jermaine Dye 2.00 .60
6 Jason Kendall 2.00 .60
7 Mike Grace 1.00 .30
8 Andruw Jones 6.00 1.80
9 Rey Ordonez 1.00 .30
10 George Arias 1.00 .30

2001 Leaf Limited

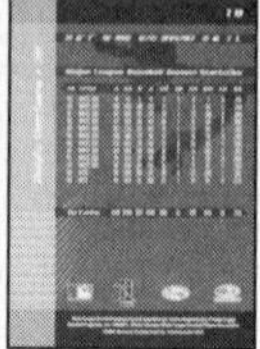

This hobby-exclusive product was released in mid-December 2001, and featured a 375-card base set that was broken into tiers as follows: 150 Base Veterans, 50 Lumberjacks (numbered to either 500, 250, or 100), 100 Rookies (numbered to either 1500 or 1000), 25 Autographed Rookies (numbered to 1000, 750, or 500), and 50 Memorabilia Rookies (see print runs below). Each pack contained three cards, and carried a $6.99 S.R.P..

Nm-Mt Ex-Mt
COMP.SET w/o SP'S (150) 100.00 30.00
COMMON CARD (1-150) 1.00 .30
COMMON LUM/500 (151-200) 8.00 2.40
COMMON LUM/250 (151-200) 10.00 3.00
COMMON LUM/100 (151-200) 25.00 7.50
COMMON (201-250) 5.00 1.50
COMMON (251-300) 5.00 1.50
COMMON (301-325) 10.00 3.00
COMMON BASE (326-375) 15.00 4.50
COMMON BAT (326-375) 8.00 2.40
COMMON HAT (326-375) 25.00 7.50
COMMON JSY (326-375) 8.00 2.40
COMMON PANTS (326-375) 8.00 2.40
COMMON SPIKES (326-375) 25.00 7.50
1 Curt Schilling 1.50 .45
2 Craig Biggio 1.50 .45
3 Brian Giles 1.00 .30
4 Scott Brosius 1.00 .30
5 Barry Larkin 2.50 .75
6 Bartolo Colon 1.00 .30
7 John Olerud 1.00 .30
8 Cal Ripken 8.00 2.40
9 Moises Alou 1.00 .30
10 Barry Zito 2.50 .75
11 Ken Griffey Jr. 4.00 1.20
12 Garret Anderson 1.00 .30
13 Andy Pettitte 1.50 .45
14 Jim Edmonds 1.00 .30
15 Tom Glavine 1.50 .45
16 Jose Canseco 2.50 .75
17 Fred McGriff 1.50 .45
18 Robin Ventura 1.00 .30
19 Tony Gwynn 3.00 .90
20 Jeff Cirillo 1.00 .30
21 Brad Radke 1.00 .30
22 Ellis Burks 1.00 .30
23 Scott Rolen 1.50 .45
24 Rickey Henderson 2.50 .75
25 Edgar Martinez 1.50 .45
26 Kerry Wood 2.50 .75
27 Al Leiter 1.00 .30
28 Jose Cruz Jr. 1.00 .30
29 Sean Casey 1.00 .30
30 Eric Chavez 1.00 .30
31 Jarrod Washburn 1.00 .30
32 Gary Sheffield 1.00 .30
33 Jermaine Dye 1.00 .30
34 Bernie Williams 1.50 .45
35 Tony Armas Jr. 1.00 .30
36 Carlos Beltran 1.00 .30
37 Geoff Jenkins 1.00 .30
38 Shawn Green 1.00 .30
39 Ryan Klesko 1.00 .30
40 Richie Sexson 1.00 .30
41 Pat Burrell 1.00 .30
42 J.D. Drew 1.00 .30
43 Larry Walker 1.50 .45
44 Andres Galarraga 1.00 .30
45 Tino Martinez 1.50 .45
46 Rafael Furcal 1.00 .30
47 Cristian Guzman 1.00 .30
48 Omar Vizquel 1.00 .30
49 Bret Boone 1.00 .30
50 Wade Miller 1.00 .30
51 Eric Milton 1.00 .30
52 Gabe Kapler 1.00 .30
53 Johnny Damon 1.00 .30
54 Shannon Stewart 1.00 .30
55 Kenny Lofton 1.00 .30
56 Raul Mondesi 1.00 .30
57 Jorge Posada 1.50 .45
58 Mark Grace 1.50 .45
59 Robert Fick 1.00 .30
60 Phil Nevin 1.00 .30
61 Mike Mussina 2.50 .75
62 Joe Mays 1.00 .30
63 Todd Helton 1.50 .45

64 Tim Hudson 1.00 .30
65 Manny Ramirez 1.00 .30
66 Sammy Sosa 4.00 1.20
67 Darin Erstad 1.00 .30
68 Roberto Alomar 2.50 .75
69 Jeff Bagwell 1.50 .45
70 Mark McGwire 6.00 1.80
71 Jason Giambi 2.50 .75
72 Cliff Floyd 1.00 .30
73 Barry Bonds 6.00 1.80
74 Juan Gonzalez 2.50 .75
75 Jeremy Giambi 1.00 .30
76 Carlos Lee 1.00 .30
77 Randy Johnson 2.50 .75
78 Frank Thomas 2.50 .75
79 Carlos Delgado 1.00 .30
80 Pedro Martinez 2.50 .75
81 Rusty Greer 1.00 .30
82 Brian Jordan 1.00 .30
83 Vladimir Guerrero 2.50 .75
84 Mike Sweeney 1.00 .30
85 Jose Vidro 1.00 .30
86 Paul LoDuca 1.00 .30
87 Matt Morris 1.00 .30
88 Adrian Beltre 1.00 .30
89 Aramis Ramirez 1.00 .30
90 Derek Jeter 6.00 1.80
91 Rich Aurilia 1.00 .30
92 Freddy Garcia 1.00 .30
93 Preston Wilson 1.00 .30
94 Greg Maddux 4.00 1.20
95 Miguel Tejada 1.00 .30
96 Luis Gonzalez 1.00 .30
97 Torii Hunter 1.00 .30
98 Nomar Garciaparra 4.00 1.20
99 Jamie Moyer 1.00 .30
100 Javier Vazquez 1.00 .30
101 Ben Grieve 1.00 .30
102 Mike Piazza 4.00 1.20
103 Paul O'Neill 1.50 .45
104 Terrence Long 1.00 .30
105 Charles Johnson 1.00 .30
106 Rafael Palmeiro 1.50 .45
107 David Cone 1.00 .30
108 Alex Rodriguez 4.00 1.20
109 John Burkett 1.00 .30
110 Chipper Jones 2.50 .75
111 Ryan Dempster 1.00 .30
112 Bobby Abreu 1.00 .30
113 Brad Fullmer 1.00 .30
114 Kazuhiro Sasaki 1.00 .30
115 Mariano Rivera 1.50 .45
116 Edgardo Alfonzo 1.00 .30
117 Ray Durham 1.00 .30
118 Richard Hidalgo 1.00 .30
119 Jeff Weaver 1.00 .30
120 Paul Konerko 1.00 .30
121 Jon Lieber 1.00 .30
122 Mike Hampton 1.00 .30
123 Mike Cameron 1.00 .30
124 Kevin Brown 1.00 .30
125 Doug Mientkiewicz 1.00 .30
126 Jim Thome 2.50 .75
127 Corey Koskie 1.00 .30
128 Trot Nixon 1.50 .45
129 Darryl Kile 1.00 .30
130 Ivan Rodriguez 2.50 .75
131 Carl Everett 1.00 .30
132 Jeff Kent 1.00 .30
133 Rondell White 1.00 .30
134 Chan Ho Park 1.00 .30
135 Robert Person 1.00 .30
136 Troy Glaus 1.50 .45
137 Aaron Sele 1.00 .30
138 Roger Clemens 5.00 1.50
139 Tony Clark 1.00 .30
140 Mark Buehrle 1.00 .30
141 David Justice 1.00 .30
142 Magglio Ordonez 1.00 .30
143 Bobby Higginson 1.00 .30
144 Hideo Nomo 2.50 .75
145 Tim Salmon 1.50 .45
146 Mark Mulder 1.00 .30
147 Troy Percival 1.00 .30
148 Lance Berkman 1.00 .30
149 Russ Ortiz 1.00 .30
150 Andruw Jones 1.00 .30
151 Mike Piazza LUM/500 15.00 4.50
152 M.Ramirez LUM/500 8.00 2.40
153 B.Williams LUM/500 10.00 3.00
154 N.Garciaparra LUM/500 15.00 4.50
155 A.Galarraga LUM/500 8.00 2.40
156 K.Lofton LUM/500 8.00 2.40
157 Scott Rolen LUM/250 15.00 4.50
158 Jim Thome LUM/500 10.00 3.00
159 Darin Erstad LUM/500 8.00 2.40
160 G.Anderson LUM/500 8.00 2.40
161 A.Jones LUM/500 8.00 2.40
162 J.Gonzalez LUM/500 10.00 3.00
163 R.Palmeiro LUM/500 10.00 3.00
164 M.Ordonez LUM/500 8.00 2.40
165 Jeff Bagwell LUM/250 15.00 4.50
166 Eric Chavez LUM/500 8.00 2.40
167 Brian Giles LUM/500 8.00 2.40
168 A.Beltre LUM/500 8.00 2.40
169 T.Gwynn LUM/500 15.00 4.50
170 S.Green LUM/500 8.00 2.40
171 Todd Helton LUM/500 10.00 3.00
172 Troy Glaus LUM/100 40.00 12.00
173 L.Berkman LUM/500 8.00 2.40
174 I.Rodriguez LUM/500 10.00 3.00
175 Sean Casey LUM/500 8.00 2.40
176 A.Ramirez LUM/100 25.00 7.50
177 J.D. Drew LUM/500 8.00 2.40
178 Barry Bonds LUM/250 30.00 9.00
179 Barry Larkin LUM/500 10.00 3.00
180 Cal Ripken LUM/500 40.00 12.00
181 F.Thomas LUM/500 10.00 3.00
182 Craig Biggio LUM/250 15.00 4.50
183 Carlos Lee LUM/500 8.00 2.40
184 C. Jones LUM/500 10.00 3.00
185 Miguel Tejada LUM/250 10.00 3.00
186 Jose Vidro LUM/500 8.00 2.40
187 T.Long LUM/500 8.00 2.40
188 Moises Alou LUM/500 8.00 2.40
189 Trot Nixon LUM/500 10.00 3.00
190 S.Stewart LUM/500 8.00 2.40
191 Ryan Klesko LUM/500 8.00 2.40
192 C.Beltran LUM/500 8.00 2.40
193 V.Guerrero LUM/500 10.00 3.00
194 E.Martinez LUM/500 10.00 3.00
195 L.Gonzalez LUM/500 8.00 2.40
196 R.Hidalgo LUM/500 8.00 2.40
197 R.Alomar LUM/500 10.00 3.00
198 M.Sweeney LUM/100 25.00 7.50
199 B.Abreu LUM/250 10.00 3.00
200 Cliff Floyd LUM/500 8.00 2.40
201 Jackson Melian RC 5.00 1.50
202 Jason Jennings 5.00 1.50
203 Toby Hall 5.00 1.50
204 Jason Karnuth RC 5.00 1.50
205 Jason Smith RC 5.00 1.50
206 Mike Maroth RC 5.00 1.50
207 Sean Douglass RC 5.00 1.50
208 Adam Johnson 5.00 1.50
209 Luke Hudson RC 5.00 1.50
210 Nick Maness RC 5.00 1.50
211 Les Walrond RC 5.00 1.50
212 Travis Phelps RC 5.00 1.50
213 Carlos Garcia RC 5.00 1.50
214 Bill Ortega RC 5.00 1.50
215 Gene Altman RC 5.00 1.50
216 Nate Frese RC 5.00 1.50
217 Bob File RC 5.00 1.50
218 Steve Green RC 5.00 1.50
219 Kris Keller RC 5.00 1.50
220 Matt White RC 5.00 1.50
221 Nate Teut RC 5.00 1.50
222 Nick Johnson 5.00 1.50
223 Jeremy Fikac RC 5.00 1.50
224 Abraham Nunez 5.00 1.50
225 Mike Penney RC 5.00 1.50
226 Roy Smith RC 5.00 1.50
227 Tim Christman RC 5.00 1.50
228 Carlos Pena 5.00 1.50
229 Joe Beimel RC 5.00 1.50
230 Mike Koplove RC 5.00 1.50
231 Scott MacRae RC 5.00 1.50
232 Kyle Lohse RC 8.00 2.40
233 Jerrod Riggan RC 5.00 1.50
234 Scott Podsednik RC 25.00 7.50
235 Winston Abreu RC 5.00 1.50
236 Ryan Freel RC 5.00 1.50
237 Ken Vining RC 5.00 1.50
238 Bret Prinz RC 5.00 1.50
239 Paul Phillips RC 5.00 1.50
240 Josh Fogg RC 5.00 1.50
241 Saul Rivera RC 5.00 1.50
242 Esix Snead RC 5.00 1.50
243 John Grabow RC 5.00 1.50
244 Tony Cogan RC 5.00 1.50
245 Pedro Santana RC 5.00 1.50
246 Jack Cust 5.00 1.50
247 Joe Crede 5.00 1.50
248 Juan Moreno RC 5.00 1.50
249 Kevin Joseph RC 5.00 1.50
250 Scott Stewart RC 5.00 1.50
251 Rob Mackowiak RC 5.00 1.50
252 Luis Pineda RC 5.00 1.50
253 Bert Snow RC 5.00 1.50
254 Dustan Mohr RC 5.00 1.50
255 Justin Kaye RC 5.00 1.50
256 Chad Paronto RC 5.00 1.50
257 Nick Punto RC 5.00 1.50
258 Brian Roberts RC 5.00 1.50
259 Eric Hinske RC 8.00 2.40
260 Victor Zambrano RC 8.00 2.40
261 Juan Pena RC 5.00 1.50
262 Rick Bauer RC 5.00 1.50
263 Jorge Julio RC 5.00 1.50
264 Craig Monroe RC 5.00 1.50
265 Stubby Clapp RC 5.00 1.50
266 Martin Vargas RC 5.00 1.50
267 Josue Perez RC 5.00 1.50
268 Cody Ransom RC 5.00 1.50
269 Will Ohman RC 5.00 1.50
270 Juan Diaz RC 5.00 1.50
271 Ramon Vazquez RC 5.00 1.50
272 Grant Balfour RC 5.00 1.50
273 Ryan Jensen RC 5.00 1.50
274 Benito Baez RC 5.00 1.50
275 Angel Santos RC 5.00 1.50
276 Brian Reith RC 5.00 1.50
277 Brandon Lyon RC 5.00 1.50
278 Erik Hiljus RC 5.00 1.50
279 Brandon Knight RC 5.00 1.50
280 Jose Acevedo RC 5.00 1.50
281 Cesar Crespo RC 5.00 1.50
282 Kevin Olsen RC 5.00 1.50
283 Duaner Sanchez RC 5.00 1.50
284 Endy Chavez RC 5.00 1.50
285 Blaine Neal RC 5.00 1.50
286 Brett Jodie RC 5.00 1.50
287 Brad Voyles RC 5.00 1.50
288 Doug Nickle RC 5.00 1.50
289 Junior Spivey RC 8.00 2.40
290 Henry Mateo RC 5.00 1.50
291 Xavier Nady 5.00 1.50
292 Lance Davis RC 5.00 1.50
293 Willie Harris RC 5.00 1.50
294 Mark Lukasiewicz RC 5.00 1.50
295 Ryan Drese RC 5.00 1.50
296 Morgan Ensberg RC 12.00 3.60
297 Jose Mieses RC 5.00 1.50
298 Jason Michaels RC 5.00 1.50
299 Kris Foster RC 5.00 1.50
300 J.Duchscherer RC 5.00 1.50
301 Elpidio Guzman AU RC 10.00 3.00
302 Cory Aldridge AU RC 10.00 3.00
303 A.Berroa AU/500 RC 40.00 12.00
304 Travis Hafner AU RC 25.00 7.50
305 H.Ramirez AU RC 15.00 4.50
306 Juan Uribe AU RC 10.00 3.00
307 M.Prior AU/500 RC 250.00 75.00
308 B.Larson AU RC 10.00 3.00
309 N.Neugebauer AU/750 10.00 3.00
310 Zach Day AU/750 RC 15.00 4.50
311 Jeremy Owens AU RC 10.00 3.00
312 D.Brazelton AU/500 RC 15.00 4.50
313 B.Duckworth AU/750 RC 10.00 3.00
314 A.Hernandez AU RC 10.00 3.00
315 M.Teixeira AU/500 RC 120.00 36.00
316 Brian Rogers AU RC 10.00 3.00
317 D.Brous AU/750 RC 10.00 3.00
318 Geronimo Gil AU RC 10.00 3.00
319 Erick Almonte AU RC 10.00 3.00
320 Claudio Vargas AU RC 10.00 3.00
321 Wilkin Ruan AU RC 10.00 3.00
322 David Williams AU RC 10.00 3.00
323 Alexis Gomez AU RC 10.00 3.00
324 Mike Rivera AU RC 10.00 3.00
325 B.Berger AU RC 10.00 3.00
326 Keith Ginter Bat/125 25.00 7.50
327 Brandon Inge Bat/700 8.00 2.40
328 B.Abernathy Bat/700 8.00 2.40
329 B.Sylvester Bat/700 RC 8.00 2.40
330 B.Miadich Jsy/500 RC 8.00 2.40
331 T.Shinjo Jsy/500 RC 15.00 4.50
332 E.Valent Spikes/125 25.00 7.50
333 Dee Brown Jsy/500 8.00 2.40
334 A.Torres Spikes/125 RC 25.00 7.50
335 Timo Perez Bat/700 8.00 2.40
336 C.Izturis Pants/650 8.00 2.40
337 P.Feliz Spikes/125 25.00 7.50
338 Jason Hart Bat/200 10.00 3.00
339 G.Miller Bat/700 RC 8.00 2.40
340 Eric Munson Bat/700 8.00 2.40
341 Aubrey Huff Jsy/450 8.00 2.40
342 W.Caceres Bat/700 RC 8.00 2.40
343 A.Escobar Pants/650 8.00 2.40
344 B.Lawrence Bat/700 RC 8.00 2.40
345 Adam Pettyjohn Pants/650 RC 8.00 2.40
346 D.Mendez Bat/700 RC 8.00 2.40
347 Carlos Valderrama Jsy/250 RC 10.00 3.00
348 C.Parker Pants/650 RC 8.00 2.40
349 C.Miller Jsy/500 RC 8.00 2.40
350 M.Cuddyer Jsy/500 8.00 2.40
351 Adam Dunn Bat/500 15.00 4.50
352 J.Beckett Pants/650 10.00 3.00
353 Juan Cruz Jsy/500 RC 8.00 2.40
354 Ben Sheets Jsy/400 8.00 2.40
355 Roy Oswalt Bat/100 40.00 12.00
356 R.Soriano Pants/650 RC 15.00 4.50
357 R.Rodriguez Pants/650 RC 8.00 2.40
358 J.Rollins Base/300 15.00 4.50
359 C.C. Sabathia Jsy/500 8.00 2.40
360 B.Smith Jsy/500 RC 8.00 2.40
361 Jose Ortiz Hat/100 25.00 7.50
362 Marcus Giles Jsy/400 8.00 2.40
363 J.Wilson Hat/100 RC 25.00 7.50
364 W.Betemit Hat/100 RC 25.00 7.50
365 C.Patterson Pants/650 8.00 2.40
366 J.Gibbons Spikes/125 RC 60.00 18.00
367 A.Pujols Jsy/250 RC 150.00 45.00
368 J.Kennedy Hat/100 RC 25.00 7.50
369 A.Soriano Hat/100 40.00 12.00
370 D.James Pants/650 RC 8.00 2.40
371 J.Towers Pants/650 RC 8.00 2.40
372 J.Affeldt Pants/650 RC 10.00 3.00
373 Tim Redding Jsy/500 8.00 2.40
374 I.Suzuki Base/100 RC 500.00 150.00
375 J.Estrada Bat/100 RC 40.00 12.00

2003 Leaf Limited

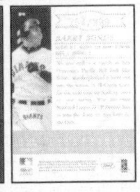

This 204 card set was issued in two separate series. The primary Leaf Limited product - containing cards 1-200 from the basic set - was released in September, 2003. The set was issued in four card packs with an $70 SRP which came four packs to a box and 10 boxes to a case. The first 150 cards feature active veteran players and were issued to a stated print run of 999 serial numbered sets. Cards numbered 151 through 170 feature retired greats and were randomly inserted into packs and issued to a stated print run of 399 serial numbered sets. Cards numbered 171 through 200 are entitled Phenoms and feature rookie players, most of whom signed their cards and most of those cards were issued to a stated print run of 99 serial numbered sets. Cards number 174 and 199 are not autographed and those cards just feature game-used pieces of memorabilia. Cards 201-204 were randomly seeded within packs of DLP Rookies and Traded released in December, 2003. Each of these Update cards was signed by the featured athltete, serial-numbered to 99 copies and continued the Phenoms subset established in cards 171-200.

MINT NRMT
COMMON CARD (1-151) 3.00 1.35
1-151 PRINT RUN 999 SERIAL #'d SETS
COMMON CARD (151-170) 6.00 2.70
151-170 RANDOM INSERTS IN PACKS
151-170 PRINT RUN 399 SERIAL #'d SETS
COMMON AU GU (171-200) 20.00 9.00
AU GU 171-200 PRINT 99 SERIAL #'d SETS
GU 174/199 PRINT RUN 99 SERIAL #'d SETS
COMMON AU (171-204) p/r 99. 15.00 6.75
AU 171-204 PRINT B/WN 49-99 COPIES PER
171-200 RANDOM INSERTS IN PACKS
201-204 RANDOM IN DLP R/T PACKS
A EQUALS AWAY UNIFORM IMAGE
H EQUALS HOME UNIFORM IMAGE

1 Derek Jeter Btg 10.00 4.50
2 Eric Chavez 3.00 1.35
3 Alex Rodriguez Rgr A 6.00 2.70
4 Miguel Tejada Fldg 3.00 1.35
5 Nomar Garciaparra H 6.00 2.70
6 Jeff Bagwell H 3.00 1.35
7 Jim Thome Phils A 4.00 1.80
8 Pat Burrell w/Bat 3.00 1.35
9 Albert Pujols H 8.00 3.60
10 Juan Gonzalez Rgr Btg 4.00 1.80
11 Shawn Green Jays 3.00 1.35
12 Craig Biggio H 3.00 1.35
13 Chipper Jones H 4.00 1.80
14 H.Nomo Dodgers 4.00 1.80
15 Vernon Wells 3.00 1.35
16 Gary Sheffield 3.00 1.35
17 Barry Larkin 4.00 1.80
18 Josh Beckett White 3.00 1.35
19 Edgar Martinez A 3.00 1.35
20 I.Rodriguez Marlins 4.00 1.80
21 Jeff Kent Astros 3.00 1.35
22 Roberto Alomar Mets A 4.00 1.80
23 Alfonso Soriano A 3.00 1.35
24 Jim Thome Indians H 4.00 1.80
25 J.Gonzalez Indians Btg 4.00 1.80
26 Carlos Beltran 3.00 1.35
27 S.Green Dodgers H 3.00 1.35
28 Tim Hudson H 3.00 1.35
29 Deion Sanders 3.00 1.35
30 Rafael Palmeiro O's 3.00 1.35
31 Todd Helton H 3.00 1.35
32 L.Berkman No Socks 3.00 1.35
33 M.Mussina Yanks H 4.00 1.80
34 Kazuhisa Ishii H 3.00 1.35
35 Pat Burrell Run 3.00 1.35
36 Miguel Tejada Btg 3.00 1.35
37 J.Gonzalez Rgr Stand 4.00 1.80
38 Roberto Alomar Mets H 4.00 1.80
39 R.Alom Indians Bunt 4.00 1.80
40 Luis Gonzalez 3.00 1.35
41 Jorge Posada 3.00 1.35
42 Mark Mulder Leg 3.00 1.35
43 Sammy Sosa H 6.00 2.70
44 Mark Prior H 8.00 3.60
45 R.Clemens Yanks H 8.00 3.60
46 Tom Glavine Mets H 3.00 1.35
47 Mark Teixeira A 3.00 1.35
48 Manny Ramirez H 3.00 1.35
49 Frank Thomas Swing 4.00 1.80
50 Troy Glaus White 3.00 1.35
51 Andruw Jones H 3.00 1.35
52 J.Giambi Yanks H 4.00 1.80
53 Jim Thome Phils H 4.00 1.80
54 Barry Bonds H 10.00 4.50
55 R.Palmeiro Rgr A 3.00 1.35
56 Edgar Martinez H 3.00 1.35
57 Vladimir Guerrero H 4.00 1.80
58 Roberto Alomar O's 4.00 1.80
59 Mike Sweeney 3.00 1.35
60 Magglio Ordonez A 3.00 1.35
61 Ken Griffey Jr. Btg 6.00 2.70
62 Craig Biggio A 3.00 1.35
63 Greg Maddux H 6.00 2.70
64 Mike Piazza Mets H 6.00 2.70
65 T.Glavine Braves A 3.00 1.35
66 Kerry Wood H 4.00 1.80
67 Frank Thomas Arms 4.00 1.80
68 M.Mussina Yanks A 4.00 1.80
69 Nick Johnson H 3.00 1.35
70 Bernie Williams H 3.00 1.35
71 Scott Rolen 3.00 1.35
72 C.Schill D'backs Leg 3.00 1.35
73 Adam Dunn A 3.00 1.35
74 Roy Oswalt A 3.00 1.35
75 P.Martinez Sox H 4.00 1.80
76 Tom Glavine Mets A 3.00 1.35
77 Torii Hunter Swing 3.00 1.35
78 Austin Kearns 3.00 1.35
79 R.Johnson D'backs A 4.00 1.80
80 Bernie Williams A 3.00 1.35
81 Ichiro Suzuki Btg 6.00 2.70
82 Kerry Wood A 4.00 1.80
83 Kazuhisa Ishii A 3.00 1.35
84 R.Johnson Astros 4.00 1.80
85 Nick Johnson A 3.00 1.35
86 J.Beckett Pinstripe 3.00 1.35
87 Curt Schilling Phils 3.00 1.35
88 Mike Mussina O's 4.00 1.80
89 P.Martinez Dodgers 4.00 1.80
90 Barry Zito A 3.00 1.35
91 Jim Edmonds 3.00 1.35
92 R.Henderson Sox 4.00 1.80
93 R.Henderson Padres 4.00 1.80
94 R.Henderson M's 4.00 1.80
95 R.Henderson Mets 4.00 1.80
96 R.Henderson Jays 4.00 1.80
97 R.Johnson M's Arm Up 4.00 1.80
98 Mark Grace 3.00 1.35
99 P.Martinez Expos 4.00 1.80
100 Hee Seop Choi 3.00 1.35
101 Ivan Rodriguez Rgr 3.00 1.35
102 Jeff Kent Giants 3.00 1.35
103 Hideo Nomo Sox 4.00 1.80
104 Hideo Nomo Mets 4.00 1.80
105 Mike Piazza Dodgers 6.00 2.70
106 T.Glavine Braves H 3.00 1.35
107 R.Alom Indians Swing 4.00 1.80
108 Roger Clemens Sox 8.00 3.60
109 Jason Giambi A's H 4.00 1.80
110 Jim Thome Indians A 4.00 1.80
111 Alex Rodriguez M's H 6.00 2.70
112 J.Gonz Indians Hands 4.00 1.80
113 Torii Hunter Crouch 3.00 1.35
114 Roy Oswalt H 3.00 1.35
115 C.Schill D'backs Throw 3.00 1.35
116 Magglio Ordonez H 3.00 1.35
117 R.Palmeiro Rgr H 3.00 1.35
118 Andruw Jones A 3.00 1.35
119 Manny Ramirez A 3.00 1.35
120 Mark Teixeira H 3.00 1.35
121 Mark Mulder Stance 3.00 1.35
122 Garret Anderson 3.00 1.35
123 Tim Hudson A 3.00 1.35
124 Todd Helton A 3.00 1.35
125 Troy Glaus Pinstripe 3.00 1.35
126 Derek Jeter Run 10.00 4.50
127 Barry Bonds A 10.00 4.50
128 Greg Maddux A 6.00 2.70
129 R.Clemens Yanks A 8.00 3.60
130 Nomar Garciaparra A 6.00 2.70
131 Mike Piazza Mets A 6.00 2.70
132 Alex Rodriguez Rgr H 6.00 2.70
133 Ichiro Suzuki Run 6.00 2.70
134 R.Johnson D'backs H 4.00 1.80
135 Sammy Sosa A 6.00 2.70
136 Ken Griffey Jr. Fldg 6.00 2.70
137 Alfonso Soriano H 3.00 1.35
138 J.Giambi Yanks A 4.00 1.80
139 Albert Pujols A 8.00 3.60
140 Chipper Jones A 4.00 1.80
141 Adam Dunn H 3.00 1.35
142 P.Martinez Sox A 4.00 1.80
143 Vladimir Guerrero A 4.00 1.80
144 Mark Prior A 8.00 3.60
145 Barry Zito H 3.00 1.35
146 Jeff Bagwell A 3.00 1.35
147 Lance Berkman Socks 3.00 1.35
148 S.Green Dodgers A 3.00 1.35
149 Jason Giambi A's A 4.00 1.80
150 R.Johnson M's Arm Out 4.00 1.80
151 Alex Rodriguez M's A 6.00 2.70
152 Babe Ruth 15.00 6.75
153 Ty Cobb 8.00 3.60
154 Jackie Robinson 8.00 3.60
155 Lou Gehrig 10.00 4.50
156 Thurman Munson 8.00 3.60
157 Roberto Clemente 12.00 5.50
158 Nolan Ryan Rgr 12.00 5.50
159 Nolan Ryan Angels 12.00 5.50
160 Nolan Ryan Astros 12.00 5.50
161 Cal Ripken 20.00 9.00
162 Don Mattingly 15.00 6.75
163 Stan Musial 10.00 4.50
164 Tony Gwynn 8.00 3.60
165 Yogi Berra 6.00 2.70
166 Johnny Bench 6.00 2.70
167 Mike Schmidt 12.00 5.50
168 George Brett 15.00 6.75
169 Ryne Sandberg 12.00 5.50
170 Ernie Banks 6.00 2.70
171 J.Bonder A PH AU Jsy RC 30.00 13.50
172 J.Contreras A PH AU RC 50.00 22.00
173 C.Wang PH AU RC 60.00 27.00
174 H.Matsui H PH Base RC 50.00 22.00
175 Hong-Chih Kuo PH AU Bat RC 40.00 18.00
176 B.Webb A PH AU Bat RC 50.00 22.00
177 Rich Fischer PH AU RC 15.00 6.75
178 R.Hammock PH AU Bat RC 25.00 11.00
179 T.Welle Stance PH AU/49 RC 25.00 11.00
180 P.Redman PH AU Bat RC 20.00 9.00
181 Nook Logan PH AU RC 15.00 6.75
182 Craig Brazell PH AU RC 20.00 9.00
183 Tim Olson PH AU Bat RC 25.00 11.00
184 Matt Kata PH AU Bat RC 25.00 11.00
185 Alej Machado PH AU RC 15.00 6.75
186 Mike Hessman PH AU RC 15.00 6.75
187 Oscar Villarreal PH AU RC 15.00 6.75
188 G.Quiroz PH AU Bat RC 40.00 18.00
189 M.Hernandez PH AU RC 15.00 6.75
190 C.Barmes H PH AU Bat RC 25.00 11.00
191 P.LaForest PH AU Bat RC 25.00 11.00
192 Adam Loewen PH AU RC 80.00 36.00
193 T.Sledge PH AU Bat RC 25.00 11.00
194 Lew Ford PH AU Bat RC 25.00 11.00
195 T.Welle Throw PH AU/49 RC 25.00 11.00
196 C.Barmes A PH AU Bat RC 25.00 11.00
197 J.Bonder H PH AU Jsy RC 30.00 13.50
198 B.Webb H PH AU Jsy RC 50.00 22.00
199 H.Matsui A PH Base RC 50.00 22.00
200 J.Contreras H PH AU RC 50.00 22.00
201 Delmon Young PH AU RC 120.00 55.00
202 Rickie Weeks PH AU RC 120.00 55.00
203 Edwin Jackson PH AU RC 100.00 45.00
204 Dan Haren PH AU RC 30.00 13.50

2003 Leaf Limited Gold Spotlight

MINT NRMT
*GOLD 1-151: 1.5X TO 4X BASIC
*GOLD 152-170: 1.25X TO 3X BASIC
1-170 PRINT RUN 50 SERIAL #'d SETS
171-204 PRINT RUN 25 SERIAL #'d SETS
179/195/202 PRINT RUN 10 SERIAL #'d PER
171-204 NO PRICING DUE TO SCARCITY
1-200 RANDOM INSERTS IN PACKS
201-204 RANDOM IN DLP R/T PACKS

2003 Leaf Limited Silver Spotlight

MINT NRMT
*SILVER 1-151: .75X TO 2X BASIC
*SILVER 152-170: .6X TO 1.5X BASIC
1-170 PRINT RUN 100 SERIAL #'d SETS
*SILVER AU GU 171-200: .5X TO 1.2X
*SILVER GU 174/199: .6X TO 1.5X
*SILVER AU 171-204 p/r 50: .5X TO 1.2X
171-204 PRINT RUN 50 SERIAL #'d SETS
179/195 PRINT 29 SERIAL #'d COPIES PER
CARD 202 PRINT RUN 25 SERIAL #'d COPIES
NO PRICING ON QTY OF 29 OR LESS.
1-200 RANDOM INSERTS IN PACKS
201-204 RANDOM IN DLP R/T PACKS

2003 Leaf Limited Moniker

MINT NRMT
RANDOM INSERTS IN PACKS
PRINT RUNS B/WN 1-10 COPIES PER
NO PRICING DUE TO SCARCITY

2003 Leaf Limited Moniker Bat

MINT NRMT
RANDOM INSERTS IN PACKS
PRINT RUNS B/WN 1-25 COPIES PER
NO PRICING ON QTY OF 10 OR LESS.

2003 Leaf Limited Moniker Jersey

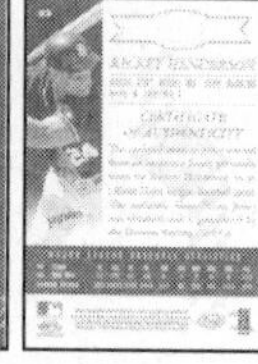

MINT NRMT
RANDOM INSERTS IN PACKS
PRINT RUNS B/WN 1-25 COPIES PER
NO PRICING ON QTY OF 10 OR LESS.

2003 Leaf Limited Moniker Jersey Number

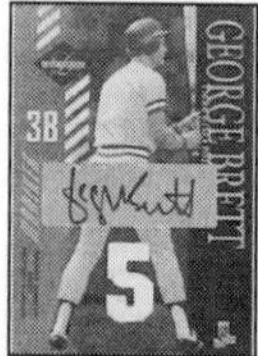
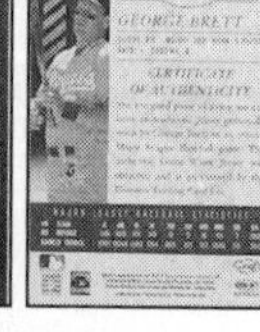

MINT NRMT
RANDOM INSERTS IN PACKS ....
PRINT RUNS B/WN 1-25 COPIES PER
NO PRICING ON QTY OF 10 OR LESS.

2003 Leaf Limited Moniker Jersey Position

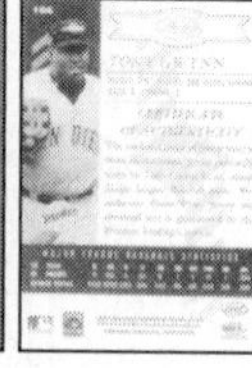

MINT NRMT
RANDOM INSERTS IN PACKS ....
PRINT RUNS B/WN 1-25 COPIES PER
NO PRICING ON QTY OF 10 OR LESS.

2003 Leaf Limited Threads

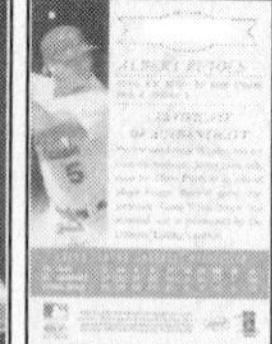

MINT NRMT
RANDOM INSERTS IN PACKS ....
PRINT RUNS B/WN 5-100 COPIES PER
NO PRICING ON QTY OF 10 OR LESS.
1 Derek Jeter Btg Base/50 .... 40.00 18.00
2 Eric Chavez/25 .... 15.00 6.75
3 Alex Rodriguez Rgr A/100 .... 15.00 6.75
4 Miguel Tejada Fldg/50 .... 10.00 4.50
5 Nomar Garciaparra H/100 .... 15.00 6.75
6 Jeff Bagwell H/50 .... 15.00 6.75
7 Jim Thome Phils A/50 .... 15.00 6.75
8 Pat Burrell w/Bat/25 .... 15.00 6.75
9 Albert Pujols H/100 .... 25.00 11.00
10 Juan Gonzalez Rgr Btg/25 .... 25.00 11.00
11 Shawn Green Jays/25 .... 15.00 6.75
12 Craig Biggio H/25 .... 25.00 11.00
13 Chipper Jones H/50 .... 15.00 6.75
14 H.Nomo Dodgers/100 .... 20.00 9.00
15 Vernon Wells/25 .... 15.00 6.75
16 Gary Sheffield/25 .... 15.00 6.75
17 Barry Larkin/25 .... 25.00 11.00
18 Josh Beckett White/25 .... 25.00 11.00
19 Edgar Martinez A/25 .... 25.00 11.00
20 I.Rodriguez Marlins/25 .... 25.00 11.00
21 Jeff Kent Astros/25 .... 15.00 6.75
22 Roberto Alomar Mets A/25 ... 25.00 11.00
23 Alfonso Soriano A/100 .... 10.00 4.50
24 Jim Thome Indians H/25 ...... 25.00 11.00
25 J.Gonzalez Indians Btg/25 .... 25.00 11.00
26 Carlos Beltran/25 .... 15.00 6.75
27 S.Green Dodgers H/50 .... 10.00 4.50
28 Tim Hudson H/25 .... 15.00 6.75
29 Deion Sanders/25 .... 25.00 11.00
30 Rafael Palmeiro O's/25 .... 25.00 11.00
31 Todd Helton H/50 .... 15.00 6.75
32 L.Berkman No Socks/25 .... 15.00 6.75
33 M.Mussina Yanks H/50 .... 15.00 6.75
34 Kazuhisa Ishii H/50 .... 10.00 4.50
35 Pat Burrell Run/25 .... 15.00 6.75
36 Miguel Tejada Btg/50 .... 10.00 4.50
37 J.Gonzalez Rgr Stand/25 ...... 25.00 11.00
38 Roberto Alomar Mets H/25 .. 25.00 11.00
39 R.Alom Indians Bunt/25 .... 25.00 11.00
40 Luis Gonzalez/25 .... 15.00 6.75
41 Jorge Posada/50 .... 15.00 6.75
42 Mark Mulder Leg/25 .... 15.00 6.75
43 Sammy Sosa H/100 .... 20.00 9.00
44 Mark Prior H/50 .... 30.00 13.50
45 R.Clemens Yanks H/100 .... 15.00 6.75
46 Tom Glavine Mets H/25 .... 25.00 11.00
47 Mark Teixeira A/25 .... 25.00 11.00
48 Manny Ramirez H/50 .... 10.00 4.50
49 Frank Thomas Swing/25 .... 25.00 11.00
50 Troy Glaus White/50 .... 15.00 6.75
51 Andruw Jones H/50 .... 10.00 4.50
52 J.Giambi Yanks H/100 .... 10.00 4.50
53 Jim Thome Phils H/50 .... 15.00 6.75
54 Barry Bonds H Base/50 .... 40.00 18.00
55 R.Palmeiro Rgr A/25 .... 25.00 11.00
56 Edgar Martinez H/25 .... 25.00 11.00
57 Vladimir Guerrero H/50 .... 15.00 6.75
58 Roberto Alomar O's/25 .... 25.00 11.00
59 Mike Sweeney/25 .... 15.00 6.75
60 Magglio Ordonez A/25 .... 15.00 6.75
62 Craig Biggio A/25 .... 25.00 11.00
63 Greg Maddux H/100 .... 15.00 6.75
64 Mike Piazza Mets H/100 .... 15.00 6.75
65 T.Glavine Braves A/25 .... 25.00 11.00
66 Kerry Wood H/25 .... 25.00 11.00
67 Frank Thomas Arms/25 .... 25.00 11.00
68 M.Mussina Yanks A/50 .... 15.00 6.75
69 Nick Johnson H/25 .... 15.00 6.75
70 Bernie Williams H/50 .... 15.00 6.75
71 Scott Rolen/25 .... 25.00 11.00
72 C.Schill D'backs Leg/25 .... 25.00 11.00
73 Adam Dunn A/50 .... 10.00 4.50
74 Roy Oswalt A/25 .... 15.00 6.75
75 P.Martinez Sox H/50 .... 15.00 6.75
76 Tom Glavine Mets A/25 .... 25.00 11.00
77 Torii Hunter Swing/25 .... 15.00 6.75
78 Austin Kearns/25 .... 15.00 6.75
79 R.Johnson D'backs A/100 ..... 10.00 4.50
80 Bernie Williams A/50 .... 15.00 6.75
81 Ichiro Suzuki Btg Base/50 .... 40.00 18.00
82 Kerry Wood A/25 .... 25.00 11.00
83 Kazuhisa Ishii A/50 .... 10.00 4.50
84 R.Johnson Astros/50 .... 15.00 6.75
85 Nick Johnson A/25 .... 15.00 6.75
86 J.Beckett Pinstripe/25 .... 25.00 11.00
87 Curt Schilling Phils/25 .... 25.00 11.00
88 Mike Mussina O's/50 .... 15.00 6.75
89 P.Martinez Dodgers/25 .... 25.00 11.00
90 Barry Zito A/50 .... 15.00 6.75
91 Jim Edmonds/100 .... 8.00 3.60
92 R.Henderson Sox/100 .... 10.00 4.50
93 R.Henderson Padres/50 .... 15.00 6.75
94 R.Henderson M's/50 .... 15.00 6.75
95 R.Henderson Mets/50 .... 15.00 6.75
96 R.Henderson Jays/50 .... 15.00 6.75
97 R.Johnson M's Arm Up/50 ... 15.00 6.75
98 Mark Grace/50 .... 15.00 6.75
99 P.Martinez Expos/25 .... 25.00 11.00
100 Hee Seop Choi/25 .... 15.00 6.75
101 Ivan Rodriguez Rgr/25 .... 25.00 11.00
102 Jeff Kent Giants/25 .... 15.00 6.75
103 Hideo Nomo Sox/5 ....
104 Hideo Nomo Mets/50 .... 20.00 9.00
105 Mike Piazza Dodgers/100 ... 15.00 6.75
106 T.Glavine Braves H/25 .... 25.00 11.00
107 R.Alom Indians Swing/25 ... 25.00 11.00
108 Roger Clemens Sox/100 ...... 15.00 6.75
109 Jason Giambi A's H/25 .... 25.00 11.00
110 Jim Thome Indians A/25 ..... 25.00 11.00
111 Alex Rodriguez M's H/100 .. 15.00 6.75
112 J.Gonz Indians Hands/25 ... 25.00 11.00
113 Torii Hunter Crouch/25 ...... 15.00 6.75
114 Roy Oswalt H/25 .... 15.00 6.75
115 C.Schill D'backs Throw/25 . 25.00 11.00
116 Magglio Ordonez H/25 .... 15.00 6.75
117 R.Palmeiro Rgr H/25 .... 25.00 11.00
118 Andruw Jones A/50 .... 10.00 4.50
119 Manny Ramirez A/50 .... 10.00 4.50
120 Mark Teixeira H/25 .... 25.00 11.00
121 Mark Mulder Stance/25 ...... 15.00 6.75
123 Tim Hudson A/25 .... 15.00 6.75
124 Todd Helton A/50 .... 15.00 6.75
125 Troy Glaus Pinstripe/50 ..... 15.00 6.75
126 Derek Jeter Run Base/50 ... 40.00 18.00
127 Barry Bonds A Base/50 ...... 40.00 18.00
128 Greg Maddux A/100 .... 15.00 6.75
129 R.Clemens Yanks A/100 ..... 15.00 6.75
130 Nomar Garciaparra A/100 .. 15.00 6.75
131 Mike Piazza Mets A/100 ..... 15.00 6.75
132 Alex Rodriguez Rgr H/100 .. 15.00 6.75
133 Ichiro Suzuki Run Base/50 . 40.00 18.00
134 R.Johnson D'backs H/100 .. 10.00 4.50
135 Sammy Sosa A/100 .... 20.00 9.00
136 Alfonso Soriano H/100 .... 10.00 4.50
137 Alfonso Soriano H/100 .... 10.00 4.50
138 J.Giambi Yanks A/100 .... 10.00 4.50
139 Albert Pujols A/100 .... 25.00 11.00
140 Chipper Jones A/25 .... 25.00 11.00
141 Adam Dunn H/50 .... 10.00 4.50
142 P.Martinez Sox A/50 .... 15.00 6.75
143 Vladimir Guerrero A/50 ...... 15.00 6.75
144 Mark Prior A/50 .... 30.00 13.50
145 Barry Zito H/50 .... 15.00 6.75
146 Jeff Bagwell A/50 .... 15.00 6.75
147 Lance Berkman Socks/25 ... 15.00 6.75
148 S.Green Dodgers A/25 .... 15.00 6.75
149 Jason Giambi A's A/25 .... 25.00 11.00
150 R.Johnson M's Arm Out/25 25.00 11.00
151 Alex Rodriguez M's A/100 .. 15.00 6.75
152 Babe Ruth/5 ....
153 Ty Cobb Pants/100 .... 120.00 55.00
154 Jackie Robinson/50 .... 80.00 36.00
155 Lou Gehrig/5 ....
156 Thurman Munson/100 .... 25.00 11.00
157 Roberto Clemente/10 ....
158 Nolan Ryan Rgr/100 .... 50.00 22.00
159 Nolan Ryan Angels/100 ...... 50.00 22.00
160 Nolan Ryan Astros/100 ...... 50.00 22.00
161 Cal Ripken/100 .... 60.00 27.00
162 Don Mattingly/100 .... 40.00 18.00
163 Stan Musial/100 .... 40.00 18.00
164 Tony Gwynn/100 .... 20.00 9.00
165 Yogi Berra/100 .... 20.00 9.00
166 Johnny Bench/100 .... 20.00 9.00
167 Mike Schmidt/100 .... 40.00 18.00
168 George Brett/100 .... 40.00 18.00
169 Ryne Sandberg/100 .... 40.00 18.00
170 Ernie Banks/50 .... 50.00 22.00

2003 Leaf Limited Threads Button

MINT NRMT
RANDOM INSERTS IN PACKS ....

PRINT RUNS B/WN 2-6 COPIES PER..
NO PRICING DUE TO SCARCITY ....

2003 Leaf Limited Threads Double

MINT NRMT
RANDOM INSERTS IN PACKS ....
PRINT RUNS B/WN 5-25 COPIES PER
NO PRICING ON QTY 15 OR LESS ......
3 A.Rod Rgr A Hat-Jsy/25 .... 60.00 27.00
4 M.Tejada Fldg Hat-Jsy/25 .... 25.00 11.00
9 Albert Pujols H Hat-Jsy/15 ....
10 J.Gonz Rgr Btg Hat-Jsy/25 .... 40.00 18.00
12 Craig Biggio H Hat-Jsy/25 .... 40.00 18.00
14 H.Nomo Dgr Jsy-Pants/25 ... 80.00 36.00
15 Vernon Wells Hat-Jsy/25 ...... 25.00 11.00
26 Carlos Beltran Hat-Jsy/25 ..... 25.00 11.00
28 Tim Hudson H Hat-Jsy/25 ..... 25.00 11.00
31 Todd Helton H Hat-Jsy/25 ..... 40.00 18.00
32 L.Berk No Socks Hat-Jsy/25. 25.00 11.00
34 Kazuhisa Ishii H Hat-Jsy/25.. 25.00 11.00
37 J.Gonz Rgr Stand Hat-Jsy/25 40.00 18.00
43 Sammy Sosa H Hat-Jsy/25 .. 80.00 36.00
44 Mark Prior H Hat-Jsy/25 .... 80.00 36.00
47 Mark Teixeira A Hat-Jsy/25 .. 40.00 18.00
51 Andruw Jones H Hat-Jsy/25. 25.00 11.00
54 Barry Bonds H Ball-Base/25. 80.00 36.00
55 R.Palmeiro Rgr A Hat-Jsy/25 40.00 18.00
60 M.Ordonez A Hat-Jsy/25 ...... 25.00 11.00
66 Kerry Wood H Hat-Jsy/5 ....
73 Adam Dunn A Hat-Jsy/25 ..... 25.00 11.00
75 P.Martinez Sox H Hat-Jsy/25 40.00 18.00
78 Austin Kearns Hat-Jsy/25 ..... 25.00 11.00
81 I.Suzuki Btg Ball-Base/25 .... 80.00 36.00
90 Barry Zito A Hat-Jsy/25 .... 40.00 18.00
94 R.Hend M's Hat-Jsy/25 .... 40.00 18.00
101 I.Rodriguez Rgr Hat-Jsy/25 40.00 18.00
109 J.Giambi A's H Hat-Jsy/25 . 40.00 18.00
116 M.Ordonez H Hat-Jsy/25 .... 25.00 11.00
117 R.Palmeiro Rgr H Hat-Jsy/25 40.00 18.00
118 Andruw Jones A Hat-Jsy/25 25.00 11.00
120 Mark Teixeira H Hat-Jsy/25 40.00 18.00
123 Tim Hudson A Hat-Jsy/25 .. 25.00 11.00
124 Todd Helton A Hat-Jsy/25 .. 40.00 18.00
127 Barry Bonds A Ball-Base/25 80.00 36.00
132 A.Rod Rgr H Hat-Jsy/25 ..... 60.00 27.00
133 I.Suzuki Run Ball-Base/25 .. 80.00 36.00
135 Sammy Sosa A Hat-Jsy/25. 80.00 36.00
141 Adam Dunn H Hat-Jsy/25 ... 25.00 11.00
142 P.Martinez Sox A Hat-Jsy/25 40.00 18.00
144 Mark Prior A Hat-Jsy/25 ...... 80.00 36.00
145 Barry Zito H Hat-Jsy/25 ...... 40.00 18.00
146 Jeff Bagwell A Hat-Jsy/25 ... 40.00 18.00
147 L.Berkman Socks Hat-Jsy/25 25.00 11.00
149 J.Giambi A's A Hat-Jsy/25.. 40.00 18.00
152 Babe Ruth Jsy-Pants/5 ....
155 Lou Gehrig Jsy-Pants/5 ....
157 Roberto Clemente Hat-Jsy/5 ....
158 N.Ryan Rgr Jsy-Pants/25 . 120.00 55.00
162 D.Mattingly Btg Glv-Jsy/25 120.00 55.00
164 Tony Gwynn Btg Glv-Jsy/25 60.00 27.00
166 Mike Schmidt Hat-Jsy/25 . 120.00 55.00
168 George Brett Hat-Jsy/25 ... 120.00 55.00
169 Ryne Sandberg Hat-Jsy/25 120.00 55.00

2003 Leaf Limited Threads Double Prime

MINT NRMT
RANDOM INSERTS IN PACKS ....
PRINT RUNS B/WN 1-10 COPIES PER
NO PRICING DUE TO SCARCITY ....

2003 Leaf Limited Threads Number

MINT NRMT
RANDOM INSERTS IN PACKS ....
PRINT RUNS B/WN 1-75 COPIES PER
NO PRICING ON QTY OF 19 OR LESS.
7 Jim Thome Phils A/25 .... 25.00 11.00
18 Josh Beckett White/61 .... 15.00 6.75
24 Jim Thome Indians H/25 ...... 25.00 11.00
25 J.Gonzalez Indians Btg/22 .... 40.00 18.00
29 Deion Sanders/21 .... 40.00 18.00
30 Rafael Palmeiro O's/25 .... 25.00 11.00
33 M.Mussina Yanks H/35 .... 25.00 11.00
40 Luis Gonzalez/20 .... 25.00 11.00
41 Jorge Posada/20 .... 40.00 18.00
42 Mark Mulder Leg/20 .... 25.00 11.00
43 Sammy Sosa H/21 .... 80.00 36.00
44 Mark Prior H/22 .... 80.00 36.00
45 R.Clemens Yanks H/22 .... 60.00 27.00
46 Tom Glavine Mets H/47 .... 15.00 6.75
47 Mark Teixeira A/23 .... 40.00 18.00
48 Manny Ramirez H/24 .... 25.00 11.00
49 Frank Thomas Swing/35 ...... 25.00 11.00
50 Troy Glaus White/25 .... 25.00 11.00
51 Andruw Jones H/25 .... 15.00 6.75
52 J.Giambi Yanks H/25 .... 25.00 11.00
53 Jim Thome Phils H/25 .... 25.00 11.00
55 R.Palmeiro Rgr A/25 .... 25.00 11.00
57 Vladimir Guerrero H/27 .... 25.00 11.00
59 Mike Sweeney/29 .... 15.00 6.75
60 Magglio Ordonez A/30 .... 15.00 6.75
63 Greg Maddux H/31 .... 40.00 18.00
64 Mike Piazza Mets H/31 .... 40.00 18.00
65 T.Glavine Braves A/47 .... 15.00 6.75
66 Kerry Wood H/52 .... 15.00 6.75
67 Frank Thomas Arms/35 .... 25.00 11.00
68 M.Mussina Yanks A/35 .... 25.00 11.00
69 Nick Johnson H/36 .... 10.00 4.50
70 Bernie Williams H/51 .... 15.00 6.75
71 Scott Rolen/27 .... 25.00 11.00
72 C.Schill D'backs Leg/38 .... 15.00 6.75
73 Adam Dunn A/44 .... 10.00 4.50
74 Roy Oswalt A/44 .... 10.00 4.50
75 P.Martinez Sox H/45 .... 15.00 6.75
76 Tom Glavine Mets A/47 .... 15.00 6.75
77 Torii Hunter Swing/48 .... 10.00 4.50
78 Austin Kearns/28 .... 15.00 6.75
79 R.Johnson D'backs A/51 ...... 15.00 6.75
80 Bernie Williams A/51 .... 15.00 6.75
82 Kerry Wood A/34 .... 25.00 11.00
84 R.Johnson Astros/51 .... 15.00 6.75
85 Nick Johnson A/36 .... 10.00 4.50
86 J.Beckett Pinstripe/61 .... 15.00 6.75
87 Curt Schilling Phils/38 .... 15.00 6.75
88 Mike Mussina O's/35 .... 25.00 11.00
89 P.Martinez Dodgers/45 .... 15.00 6.75
90 Barry Zito A/75 .... 15.00 6.75
92 R.Henderson Sox/35 .... 25.00 11.00
93 R.Henderson Padres/24 .... 40.00 18.00
94 R.Henderson M's/35 .... 25.00 11.00
95 R.Henderson Mets/24 .... 40.00 18.00
96 R.Henderson Jays/24 .... 40.00 18.00
97 R.Johnson M's Arm Up/51 ... 15.00 6.75
99 P.Martinez Expos/45 .... 15.00 6.75
102 Jeff Kent Giants/21 .... 25.00 11.00
105 Mike Piazza Dodgers/31 ..... 40.00 18.00
106 T.Glavine Braves H/47 .... 15.00 6.75
108 Roger Clemens Sox/21 .... 60.00 27.00
110 Jim Thome Indians A/25 .... 25.00 11.00
112 J.Gonz Indians Hands/22 ... 40.00 18.00
113 Torii Hunter Crouch/48 ...... 10.00 4.50
114 Roy Oswalt H/44 .... 10.00 4.50
115 C.Schill D'backs Throw/38 . 15.00 6.75
116 Magglio Ordonez H/30 .... 15.00 6.75
117 R.Palmeiro Rgr H/25 .... 25.00 11.00
118 Andruw Jones A/25 .... 15.00 6.75
119 Manny Ramirez A/24 .... 25.00 11.00
120 Mark Teixeira H/23 .... 40.00 18.00
121 Mark Mulder Stance/20 ...... 25.00 11.00
125 Troy Glaus Pinstripe/25 ..... 25.00 11.00
128 Greg Maddux A/31 .... 40.00 18.00
129 R.Clemens Yanks A/22 .... 60.00 27.00
131 Mike Piazza Mets A/31 .... 40.00 18.00
134 R.Johnson D'backs H/51 ..... 15.00 6.75
135 Sammy Sosa A/21 .... 80.00 36.00
138 J.Giambi Yanks A/25 .... 25.00 11.00
141 Adam Dunn H/44 .... 10.00 4.50
142 P.Martinez Sox A/45 .... 15.00 6.75
143 Vladimir Guerrero A/27 ...... 25.00 11.00
145 Barry Zito H/75 .... 15.00 6.75
150 R.Johnson M's Arm Out/51 15.00 6.75
154 Jackie Robinson/42 .... 80.00 36.00
157 Roberto Clemente/21 .... 150.00 70.00
158 Nolan Ryan Rgr/34 .... 80.00 36.00
159 Nolan Ryan Angels/30 .... 80.00 36.00
160 Nolan Ryan Astros/34 .... 80.00 36.00
162 Don Mattingly/23 .... 80.00 36.00
165 Yogi Berra/42 .... 25.00 11.00
167 Mike Schmidt/20 .... 80.00 36.00
169 Ryne Sandberg/23 .... 80.00 36.00

2003 Leaf Limited Threads Position

MINT NRMT
RANDOM INSERTS IN PACKS ....
2-151 PRINT RUNS 25 SERIAL #'d SETS
152-170 PRINTS B/WN 5-25 COPIES PER
NO PRICING ON QTY OF 10 OR LESS.
2 Eric Chavez 15.00 6.75
3 Alex Rodriguez Rgr A 40.00 18.00
4 Miguel Tejada Fldg 15.00 6.75
5 Nomar Garciaparra H 40.00 18.00
6 Jeff Bagwell H 25.00 11.00
7 Jim Thome Phils A 25.00 11.00
8 Pat Burrell w/Bat 15.00 6.75
9 Albert Pujols H 60.00 27.00
10 Juan Gonzalez Rgr Btg 25.00 11.00
11 Shawn Green Jays 15.00 6.75
12 Craig Biggio H 25.00 11.00
13 Chipper Jones H 25.00 11.00
14 Hideo Nomo Dodgers 50.00 22.00
15 Vernon Wells 15.00 6.75
16 Gary Sheffield 15.00 6.75
17 Barry Larkin 25.00 11.00
18 Josh Beckett White 25.00 11.00
19 Edgar Martinez A 25.00 11.00
20 Ivan Rodriguez Marlins 25.00 11.00
21 Jeff Kent Astros 15.00 6.75
22 Roberto Alomar Mets A 25.00 11.00
23 Alfonso Soriano A 25.00 11.00
24 Jim Thome Indians H 25.00 11.00
25 J.Gonzalez Indians Btg 25.00 11.00
26 Carlos Beltran 15.00 6.75
27 S.Green Dodgers H 15.00 6.75
28 Tim Hudson H 15.00 6.75
29 Deion Sanders 25.00 11.00
30 Rafael Palmeiro O's 25.00 11.00
31 Todd Helton H 25.00 11.00
32 L.Berkman No Socks 15.00 6.75
33 Mike Mussina Yanks H 25.00 11.00
34 Kazuhisa Ishii H 15.00 6.75
35 Pat Burrell Run 15.00 6.75
36 Miguel Tejada Btg 15.00 6.75
37 J.Gonzalez Rgr Stand 25.00 11.00
38 Roberto Alomar Mets H 25.00 11.00
39 R.Alomar Indians Bunt 25.00 11.00
40 Luis Gonzalez 15.00 6.75
41 Jorge Posada 25.00 11.00
42 Mark Mulder Leg 15.00 6.75
43 Sammy Sosa H 50.00 22.00
44 Mark Prior H 50.00 22.00
45 R.Clemens Yanks H 40.00 18.00
46 Tom Glavine Mets H 25.00 11.00
47 Mark Teixeira A 25.00 11.00
48 Manny Ramirez H 15.00 6.75
49 Frank Thomas Swing 25.00 11.00
50 Troy Glaus White 25.00 11.00
51 Andruw Jones H 15.00 6.75
52 Jason Giambi Yanks H 25.00 11.00
53 Jim Thome Phils H 25.00 11.00
55 Rafael Palmeiro Rgr A 25.00 11.00
56 Edgar Martinez H 25.00 11.00
57 Vladimir Guerrero H 25.00 11.00
58 Roberto Alomar O's 25.00 11.00
59 Mike Sweeney 15.00 6.75
60 Magglio Ordonez A 15.00 6.75
62 Craig Biggio A 25.00 11.00
63 Greg Maddux H 40.00 18.00
64 Mike Piazza Mets H 40.00 18.00
65 T.Glavine Braves A 25.00 11.00
66 Kerry Wood H 25.00 11.00
67 Frank Thomas Arms 25.00 11.00
68 Mike Mussina Yanks A 25.00 11.00
69 Nick Johnson H 15.00 6.75
70 Bernie Williams H 25.00 11.00
71 Scott Rolen 25.00 11.00
72 C.Schilling D'backs Leg 25.00 11.00
73 Adam Dunn A 15.00 6.75
74 Roy Oswalt A 15.00 6.75
75 Pedro Martinez Sox H 25.00 11.00
76 Tom Glavine Mets A 25.00 11.00
77 Torii Hunter Swing 15.00 6.75
78 Austin Kearns 15.00 6.75
79 R.Johnson D'backs A 25.00 11.00
80 Bernie Williams A 25.00 11.00
82 Kerry Wood A 25.00 11.00
83 Kazuhisa Ishii A 15.00 6.75
84 Randy Johnson Astros 25.00 11.00
85 Nick Johnson A 15.00 6.75
86 J.Beckett Pinstripe 25.00 11.00
87 Curt Schilling Phils 25.00 11.00
88 Mike Mussina O's 25.00 11.00
89 P.Martinez Dodgers 25.00 11.00
90 Barry Zito A 25.00 11.00
91 Jim Edmonds 15.00 6.75
92 R.Henderson Sox 25.00 11.00
93 R.Henderson Padres 25.00 11.00
94 R.Henderson M's 25.00 11.00
95 R.Henderson Mets 25.00 11.00
96 R.Henderson Jays 25.00 11.00
97 R.Johnson M's Arm Up 25.00 11.00
98 Mark Grace 25.00 11.00
99 Pedro Martinez Expos 25.00 11.00
100 Hee Seop Choi 15.00 6.75
101 Ivan Rodriguez Rgr 25.00 11.00
102 Jeff Kent Giants 15.00 6.75
103 Hideo Nomo Sox 50.00 22.00
104 Hideo Nomo Mets 50.00 22.00
105 Mike Piazza Dodgers 40.00 18.00
106 Tom Glavine Braves H 25.00 11.00
107 R.Alomar Indians Swing 25.00 11.00
108 Roger Clemens Sox 40.00 18.00
109 Jason Giambi A's H 25.00 11.00
110 Jim Thome Indians A 25.00 11.00
111 Alex Rodriguez M's H 40.00 18.00
112 J.Gonzalez Indians Hands 25.00 11.00
113 Torii Hunter Crouch 15.00 6.75
114 Roy Oswalt H 15.00 6.75
115 C.Schilling D'backs Throw . 25.00 11.00
116 Magglio Ordonez H 15.00 6.75
117 Rafael Palmeiro Rgr H 25.00 11.00
118 Andruw Jones A 15.00 6.75
119 Manny Ramirez A 15.00 6.75
120 Mark Teixeira H 25.00 11.00
121 Mark Mulder Stance 15.00 6.75
123 Tim Hudson A 15.00 6.75
124 Todd Helton A 25.00 11.00
125 Troy Glaus Pinstripe 25.00 11.00
128 Greg Maddux A 40.00 18.00
129 Roger Clemens Yanks A 40.00 18.00
130 Nomar Garciaparra A 40.00 18.00
131 Mike Piazza Mets A 40.00 18.00
132 Alex Rodriguez Rgr H 40.00 18.00
134 R.Johnson D'backs H 25.00 11.00
135 Sammy Sosa A 50.00 22.00
137 Alfonso Soriano H 25.00 11.00
138 J.Giambi Yanks A 25.00 11.00
139 Albert Pujols A 60.00 27.00
140 Chipper Jones A 25.00 11.00
141 Adam Dunn H 15.00 6.75
142 Pedro Martinez Sox A 25.00 11.00
143 Vladimir Guerrero A 25.00 11.00
144 Mark Prior A 50.00 22.00
145 Barry Zito H 25.00 11.00
146 Jeff Bagwell A 25.00 11.00
147 Lance Berkman Socks 15.00 6.75
148 S.Green Dodgers A 15.00 6.75
149 Jason Giambi A's A 25.00 11.00
150 R.Johnson M's Arm Out 25.00 11.00
151 Alex Rodriguez M's A 40.00 18.00
152 Babe Ruth/5 ....
153 Ty Cobb Pants 150.00 70.00
154 Jackie Robinson/10 ....
155 Lou Gehrig/5 ....
156 Thurman Munson 50.00 22.00
157 Roberto Clemente/5 ....
158 Nolan Ryan Rgr 80.00 36.00
159 Nolan Ryan Angels 80.00 36.00
160 Nolan Ryan Astros 80.00 36.00
161 Cal Ripken 120.00 55.00
162 Don Mattingly 80.00 36.00
163 Stan Musial 80.00 36.00
164 Tony Gwynn 40.00 18.00
165 Yogi Berra 30.00 13.50
166 Johnny Bench 30.00 13.50

167 Mike Schmidt 80.00 36.00
168 George Brett 80.00 36.00
169 Ryne Sandberg 80.00 36.00
170 Ernie Banks/5

2003 Leaf Limited Threads Prime

MINT NRMT
RANDOM INSERTS IN PACKS
2-151 PRINTS 25 #'d PER UNLESS NOTED
152-170 PRINTS B/WN 3-25 COPIES PER
NO PRICING ON QTY OF 10 OR LESS.
2 Eric Chavez 25.00 11.00
3 Alex Rodriguez Rgr A 60.00 27.00
4 Miguel Tejada Fldg 25.00 11.00
5 Nomar Garciaparra H 60.00 27.00
6 Jeff Bagwell H 40.00 18.00
7 Jim Thome Phils A/20 50.00 22.00
8 Pat Burrell w/Bat 25.00 11.00
9 Albert Pujols H 100.00 45.00
10 Juan Gonzalez Rgr Btg 40.00 18.00
11 Shawn Green Jays 25.00 11.00
12 Craig Biggio H 40.00 18.00
13 Chipper Jones H 40.00 18.00
14 Hideo Nomo Dodgers 80.00 36.00
15 Vernon Wells 25.00 11.00
16 Gary Sheffield 25.00 11.00
17 Barry Larkin 40.00 18.00
18 Josh Beckett White 40.00 18.00
19 Edgar Martinez A 40.00 18.00
20 Ivan Rodriguez Marlins 40.00 18.00
21 Jeff Kent Astros 25.00 11.00
22 Roberto Alomar Mets A 40.00 18.00
23 Alfonso Soriano A 40.00 18.00
24 Jim Thome Indians H 40.00 18.00
25 J.Gonzalez Indians Btg 40.00 18.00
26 Carlos Beltran 25.00 11.00
27 S.Green Dodgers H 25.00 11.00
28 Tim Hudson H 25.00 11.00
29 Deion Sanders 40.00 18.00
30 Rafael Palmeiro O's 40.00 18.00
31 Todd Helton H 40.00 18.00
32 L.Berkman No Socks 25.00 11.00
33 Mike Mussina Yanks H 40.00 18.00
34 Kazuhisa Ishii H 25.00 11.00
35 Pat Burrell Run 25.00 11.00
36 Miguel Tejada Btg 25.00 11.00
37 J.Gonzalez Rgr Stand 40.00 18.00
38 Roberto Alomar Mets H 40.00 18.00
39 R.Alomar Indians Bunt 40.00 18.00
40 Luis Gonzalez 25.00 11.00
41 Jorge Posada 40.00 18.00
42 Mark Mulder Leg 25.00 11.00
43 Sammy Sosa H 80.00 36.00
44 Mark Prior H 80.00 36.00
45 Roger Clemens Yanks H 60.00 27.00
46 Tom Glavine Mets H 40.00 18.00
47 Mark Teixeira A 40.00 18.00
48 Manny Ramirez H 25.00 11.00
49 Frank Thomas Swing 40.00 18.00
50 Troy Glaus White 40.00 18.00
51 Andruw Jones H 25.00 11.00
52 Jason Giambi Yanks H 40.00 18.00
53 Jim Thome Phils H 40.00 18.00
55 Rafael Palmeiro Rgr A 40.00 18.00
56 Edgar Martinez H 40.00 18.00
57 Vladimir Guerrero H 40.00 18.00
58 Roberto Alomar O's 40.00 18.00
59 Mike Sweeney 25.00 11.00
60 Magglio Ordonez A 25.00 11.00
62 Craig Biggio A 40.00 18.00
63 Greg Maddux H 60.00 27.00
64 Mike Piazza Mets H 60.00 27.00
65 Tom Glavine Braves A 40.00 18.00
66 Kerry Wood H 40.00 18.00
67 Frank Thomas Arms 40.00 18.00
68 Mike Mussina Yanks A 40.00 18.00
69 Nick Johnson H 25.00 11.00
70 Bernie Williams H 40.00 18.00
71 Scott Rolen 40.00 18.00
72 C.Schilling D'backs Leg 40.00 18.00
73 Adam Dunn A 25.00 11.00
74 Roy Oswalt A 25.00 11.00
75 Pedro Martinez Sox H 40.00 18.00
76 Tom Glavine Mets A 40.00 18.00
77 Torii Hunter Swing 25.00 11.00
78 Austin Kearns 25.00 11.00
79 R.Johnson D'backs A 40.00 18.00
80 Bernie Williams A 40.00 18.00
82 Kerry Wood A 40.00 18.00
83 Kazuhisa Ishii A 25.00 11.00
84 Randy Johnson Astros 40.00 18.00
85 Nick Johnson A 25.00 11.00
86 J.Beckett Pinstripe 40.00 18.00
87 Curt Schilling Phils 40.00 18.00
88 Mike Mussina O's 40.00 18.00
89 P.Martinez Dodgers 40.00 18.00
90 Barry Zito A 40.00 18.00
91 Jim Edmonds 25.00 11.00
92 R.Henderson Sox 40.00 18.00
93 R.Henderson Padres 40.00 18.00
94 R.Henderson M's 40.00 18.00
95 R.Henderson Mets 40.00 18.00
96 R.Henderson Jays 40.00 18.00
97 R.Johnson M's Arm Up 40.00 18.00
98 Mark Grace 40.00 18.00
99 Pedro Martinez Expos 40.00 18.00
100 Hee Seop Choi 25.00 11.00
101 Ivan Rodriguez Rgr 40.00 18.00
102 Jeff Kent Giants 25.00 11.00
104 Hideo Nomo Mets 80.00 36.00
105 Mike Piazza Dodgers 60.00 27.00
106 Tom Glavine Braves H 40.00 18.00
107 R.Alomar Indians Swing 40.00 18.00
108 Roger Clemens Sox 60.00 27.00
109 Jason Giambi A's H 40.00 18.00
110 Jim Thome Indians A 40.00 18.00
111 Alex Rodriguez M's H 60.00 27.00
112 J.Gonz Indians Hands 40.00 18.00
113 Torii Hunter Crouch 25.00 11.00
114 Roy Oswalt H 25.00 11.00
115 C.Schilling D'backs Throw 40.00 18.00
116 Magglio Ordonez H 25.00 11.00
117 Rafael Palmeiro Rgr H 40.00 18.00
118 Andruw Jones A 25.00 11.00
119 Manny Ramirez A 25.00 11.00
120 Mark Teixeira H 40.00 18.00
121 Mark Mulder Stance 25.00 11.00
123 Tim Hudson A 25.00 11.00
124 Todd Helton A 40.00 18.00
125 Troy Glaus Pinstripe 40.00 18.00
128 Greg Maddux A 60.00 27.00
129 Roger Clemens Yanks A 60.00 27.00
130 Nomar Garciaparra A 60.00 27.00
131 Mike Piazza Mets A 60.00 27.00
132 Alex Rodriguez Rgr H 60.00 27.00
134 R.Johnson D'backs H 40.00 18.00
135 Sammy Sosa A 80.00 36.00
137 Alfonso Soriano H 40.00 18.00
138 J.Giambi Yanks A 40.00 18.00
139 Albert Pujols A 100.00 45.00
140 Chipper Jones A 40.00 18.00
141 Adam Dunn H 25.00 11.00
142 P.Martinez Sox A 40.00 18.00
143 Vladimir Guerrero A 40.00 18.00
144 Mark Prior A 80.00 36.00
145 Barry Zito H 40.00 18.00
146 Jeff Bagwell A 40.00 18.00
147 Lance Berkman Socks 25.00 11.00
148 S.Green Dodgers A 25.00 11.00
149 Jason Giambi A's A 40.00 18.00
150 R.Johnson M's Arm Out 40.00 18.00
151 Alex Rodriguez M's A 60.00 27.00
152 Babe Ruth/3
153 Ty Cobb Pants 200.00 90.00
154 Jackie Robinson/10
155 Lou Gehrig/5
156 Thurman Munson 80.00 36.00
157 Roberto Clemente/5
158 Nolan Ryan Rgr 120.00 55.00
159 Nolan Ryan Angels 120.00 55.00
160 Nolan Ryan Astros 120.00 55.00
161 Cal Ripken 150.00 70.00
162 Don Mattingly 120.00 55.00
163 Stan Musial 150.00 70.00
164 Tony Gwynn 60.00 27.00
165 Yogi Berra 50.00 22.00
166 Johnny Bench 50.00 22.00
167 Mike Schmidt 120.00 55.00
168 George Brett 120.00 55.00
169 Ryne Sandberg 120.00 55.00
170 Ernie Banks/10

2003 Leaf Limited Timber

MINT NRMT
RANDOM INSERTS IN PACKS
STATED PRINT RUN 25 SERIAL #'d SETS
CARD 170 PRINT RUN 1 SERIAL #'d CARD
NO 170 PRICING DUE TO SCARCITY
2 Eric Chavez 15.00 6.75
3 Alex Rodriguez Rgr A 40.00 18.00
4 Miguel Tejada Fldg 15.00 6.75
5 Nomar Garciaparra H 40.00 18.00
6 Jeff Bagwell H 25.00 11.00
7 Jim Thome Phils A 25.00 11.00
8 Pat Burrell w/Bat 15.00 6.75
9 Albert Pujols H 60.00 27.00
10 Juan Gonzalez Rgr Btg 25.00 11.00
11 Shawn Green Jays 15.00 6.75
12 Craig Biggio H 25.00 11.00
13 Chipper Jones H 25.00 11.00
14 Hideo Nomo Dodgers 50.00 22.00
15 Vernon Wells 15.00 6.75
16 Gary Sheffield 15.00 6.75
17 Barry Larkin 25.00 11.00
18 Josh Beckett White 25.00 11.00
19 Edgar Martinez A 25.00 11.00
20 Ivan Rodriguez Marlins 25.00 11.00
21 Jeff Kent Astros 15.00 6.75
22 Roberto Alomar Mets A 25.00 11.00
23 Alfonso Soriano A 25.00 11.00
24 Jim Thome Indians H 25.00 11.00
25 J.Gonzalez Indians Btg 25.00 11.00
26 Carlos Beltran 15.00 6.75
27 S.Green Dodgers H 15.00 6.75
28 Tim Hudson H 15.00 6.75
30 Rafael Palmeiro O's 25.00 11.00
31 Todd Helton H 25.00 11.00
32 L.Berkman No Socks 15.00 6.75
33 Mike Mussina Yanks H 25.00 11.00
34 Kazuhisa Ishii H 15.00 6.75
35 Pat Burrell Run 15.00 6.75
36 Miguel Tejada Btg 15.00 6.75
37 J.Gonzalez Rgr Stand 25.00 11.00
38 Roberto Alomar Mets H 25.00 11.00
39 R.Alomar Indians Bunt 25.00 11.00
40 Luis Gonzalez 15.00 6.75
41 Jorge Posada 25.00 11.00
42 Mark Mulder Leg 15.00 6.75
43 Sammy Sosa H 50.00 22.00
44 Mark Prior H 50.00 22.00
45 R.Clemens Yanks H 40.00 18.00
46 Tom Glavine Mets H 25.00 11.00
47 Mark Teixeira A 25.00 11.00
48 Manny Ramirez H 15.00 6.75
49 Frank Thomas Swing 25.00 11.00
50 Troy Glaus White 25.00 11.00
51 Andruw Jones H 15.00 6.75
52 Jason Giambi Yanks H 25.00 11.00
53 Jim Thome Phils H 25.00 11.00
55 Rafael Palmeiro Rgr A 25.00 11.00
56 Edgar Martinez H 25.00 11.00
57 Vladimir Guerrero H 25.00 11.00
58 Roberto Alomar O's 25.00 11.00
59 Mike Sweeney 15.00 6.75
60 Magglio Ordonez A 15.00 6.75
62 Craig Biggio A 25.00 11.00
63 Greg Maddux H 40.00 18.00
64 Mike Piazza Mets H 40.00 18.00
65 T.Glavine Braves A 25.00 11.00
66 Kerry Wood H 25.00 11.00
67 Frank Thomas Arms 25.00 11.00
68 Mike Mussina Yanks A 25.00 11.00
69 Nick Johnson H 15.00 6.75
70 Bernie Williams H 25.00 11.00
71 Scott Rolen 25.00 11.00
72 C.Schilling D'backs Leg 25.00 11.00
73 Adam Dunn A 15.00 6.75
74 Roy Oswalt A 15.00 6.75
75 Pedro Martinez Sox H 25.00 11.00
76 Tom Glavine Mets A 25.00 11.00
77 Torii Hunter Swing 15.00 6.75
78 Austin Kearns 15.00 6.75
79 R.Johnson D'backs A 25.00 11.00
80 Bernie Williams A 25.00 11.00
82 Kerry Wood A 25.00 11.00
83 Kazuhisa Ishii A 15.00 6.75
84 Randy Johnson Astros 25.00 11.00
85 Nick Johnson A 15.00 6.75
86 J.Beckett Pinstripe 25.00 11.00
87 Curt Schilling Phils 25.00 11.00
88 Mike Mussina O's 25.00 11.00
89 P.Martinez Dodgers 25.00 11.00
90 Barry Zito A 25.00 11.00
91 Jim Edmonds 15.00 6.75
92 R.Henderson Sox 25.00 11.00
93 R.Henderson Padres 25.00 11.00
94 R.Henderson M's 25.00 11.00
95 R.Henderson Mets 25.00 11.00
96 R.Henderson Jays 25.00 11.00
97 R.Johnson M's Arm Up 25.00 11.00
98 Mark Grace 25.00 11.00
99 Pedro Martinez Expos 25.00 11.00
101 Ivan Rodriguez Rgr 25.00 11.00
102 Jeff Kent Giants 15.00 6.75
103 Hideo Nomo Sox 50.00 22.00
104 Hideo Nomo Mets 50.00 22.00
105 Mike Piazza Dodgers 40.00 18.00
106 Tom Glavine Braves H 25.00 11.00
107 R.Alomar Indians Swing 25.00 11.00
108 Roger Clemens Sox 40.00 18.00
109 Jason Giambi A's H 25.00 11.00
110 Jim Thome Indians A 25.00 11.00
111 Alex Rodriguez M's H 40.00 18.00
112 J.Gonz Indians Hands 25.00 11.00
113 Torii Hunter Crouch 15.00 6.75
114 Roy Oswalt H 15.00 6.75
115 C.Schilling D'backs Throw 25.00 11.00
116 Magglio Ordonez H 15.00 6.75
117 Rafael Palmeiro Rgr H 25.00 11.00
118 Andruw Jones A 15.00 6.75
119 Manny Ramirez A 15.00 6.75
120 Mark Teixeira H 25.00 11.00
121 Mark Mulder Stance 15.00 6.75
122 Garret Anderson 15.00 6.75
123 Tim Hudson A 15.00 6.75
124 Todd Helton A 25.00 11.00
125 Troy Glaus Pinstripe 25.00 11.00
128 Greg Maddux A 40.00 18.00
129 Roger Clemens Yanks A 40.00 18.00
130 Nomar Garciaparra A 40.00 18.00
131 Mike Piazza Mets A 40.00 18.00
132 Alex Rodriguez Rgr H 40.00 18.00
134 R.Johnson D'backs H 25.00 11.00
135 Sammy Sosa A 50.00 22.00
137 Alfonso Soriano H 25.00 11.00
138 J.Giambi Yanks A 25.00 11.00
139 Albert Pujols A 60.00 27.00
140 Chipper Jones A 25.00 11.00
141 Adam Dunn H 15.00 6.75
142 Pedro Martinez Sox A 25.00 11.00
143 Vladimir Guerrero A 25.00 11.00
144 Mark Prior A 50.00 22.00
145 Barry Zito H 25.00 11.00
146 Jeff Bagwell A 25.00 11.00
147 Lance Berkman Socks 15.00 6.75
148 S.Green Dodgers A 15.00 6.75
149 Jason Giambi A's A 25.00 11.00
150 R.Johnson M's Arm Out 25.00 11.00
151 Alex Rodriguez M's A 40.00 18.00
152 Babe Ruth 300.00 135.00
153 Ty Cobb 150.00 70.00
155 Lou Gehrig 200.00 90.00
156 Thurman Munson 50.00 22.00
157 Roberto Clemente 150.00 70.00
158 Nolan Ryan Rgr 80.00 36.00
159 Nolan Ryan Angels 80.00 36.00
160 Nolan Ryan Astros 80.00 36.00
161 Cal Ripken 120.00 55.00
162 Don Mattingly 80.00 36.00
163 Stan Musial 60.00 27.00
164 Tony Gwynn 40.00 18.00
165 Yogi Berra 30.00 13.50
166 Johnny Bench 30.00 13.50
167 Mike Schmidt 80.00 36.00
168 George Brett 80.00 36.00
169 Ryne Sandberg 80.00 36.00
170 Ernie Banks/1

2003 Leaf Limited TNT

MINT NRMT
RANDOM INSERTS IN PACKS
PRINT RUNS B/WN 1-25 COPIES PER
NO PRICING ON QTY OF 10 OR LESS.
2 Eric Chavez Bat-Jsy 25.00 11.00
3 A.Rod Rgr A Bat-Jsy 50.00 22.00
4 M.Tejada Fldg Bat-Jsy/10
5 N.Garciaparra H Bat-Jsy 50.00 22.00
6 Jeff Bagwell H Bat-Jsy 40.00 18.00
7 J.Thome Phils A Bat-Jsy 40.00 18.00
8 P.Burrell w/Bat Bat-Jsy 25.00 11.00
9 Albert Pujols H Bat-Jsy 60.00 27.00
10 J.Gonz Rgr Btg Bat-Jsy 40.00 18.00
11 S.Green Jays Bat-Jsy 25.00 11.00
12 Craig Biggio H Bat-Jsy 40.00 18.00
13 C.Jones H Bat-Jsy 40.00 18.00
14 H.Nomo Dodgers Bat-Jsy 50.00 22.00
15 Vernon Wells Bat-Jsy 25.00 11.00
16 G.Sheffield Bat-Jsy 25.00 11.00
17 Barry Larkin Bat-Jsy 40.00 18.00
18 J.Beckett White Bat-Jsy 40.00 18.00
19 E.Martinez A Bat-Jsy 40.00 18.00
20 I.Rodriguez Marlins Bat-Jsy 40.00 18.00
21 Jeff Kent Astros Bat-Jsy 25.00 11.00
22 R.Alomar Mets A Bat-Jsy 40.00 18.00
23 A.Soriano A Bat-Jsy 40.00 18.00
24 J.Thome Indians H Bat-Jsy 40.00 18.00
25 J.Gonz Indians Btg Bat-Jsy 40.00 18.00
26 Carlos Beltran Bat-Jsy 25.00 11.00
27 S.Green Dodgers H Bat-Jsy 25.00 11.00
28 Tim Hudson H Bat-Jsy 25.00 11.00
30 R.Palmeiro O's Bat-Jsy 40.00 18.00
31 Todd Helton H Bat-Jsy 40.00 18.00
32 L.Berk No Socks Bat-Jsy 25.00 11.00
33 M.Mussina Yanks H Bat-Jsy 40.00 18.00
34 Kazuhisa Ishii H Bat-Jsy 25.00 11.00
35 Pat Burrell Run Bat-Jsy 25.00 11.00
36 M.Tejada Btg Bat-Jsy/10
37 J.Gonz Rgr Stand Bat-Jsy 40.00 18.00
38 R.Alomar Mets H Bat-Jsy 40.00 18.00
39 R.Alom Indians Bunt Bat-Jsy 40.00 18.00
40 Luis Gonzalez Bat-Jsy 25.00 11.00
41 Jorge Posada Bat-Jsy 40.00 18.00
42 M.Mulder Leg Bat-Jsy 25.00 11.00
43 Sammy Sosa H Bat-Jsy 50.00 22.00
44 Mark Prior H Bat-Jsy 60.00 27.00
45 R.Clemens Yanks H Bat-Jsy 50.00 22.00
46 T.Glavine Mets H Bat-Jsy 40.00 18.00
47 Mark Teixeira A Bat-Jsy 40.00 18.00
48 Manny Ramirez H Bat-Jsy 25.00 11.00
49 F.Thomas Swing Bat-Jsy 40.00 18.00
50 Troy Glaus White Bat-Jsy 40.00 18.00
51 Andruw Jones H Bat-Jsy 25.00 11.00
52 J.Giambi Yanks H Bat-Jsy 40.00 18.00
53 J.Thome Phils H Bat-Jsy 40.00 18.00
55 R.Palmeiro Rgr A Bat-Jsy 40.00 18.00
56 E.Martinez H Bat-Jsy 40.00 18.00
57 V.Guerrero H Bat-Jsy 40.00 18.00
59 Mike Sweeney Bat-Jsy 25.00 11.00
60 M.Ordonez A Bat-Jsy 25.00 11.00
62 Craig Biggio A Bat-Jsy 40.00 18.00
63 Greg Maddux H Bat-Jsy 50.00 22.00
64 M.Piazza Mets H Bat-Jsy 50.00 22.00
65 T.Glavine Braves A Bat-Jsy 40.00 18.00
66 Kerry Wood H Bat-Jsy 40.00 18.00
67 F.Thomas Arms Bat-Jsy 40.00 18.00
68 M.Mussina Yanks A Bat-Jsy 40.00 18.00
69 Nick Johnson H Bat-Jsy 25.00 11.00
70 Bernie Williams H Bat-Jsy 40.00 18.00
71 Scott Rolen Bat-Jsy 40.00 18.00
72 C.Schill D'backs Leg Bat-Jsy 40.00 18.00
73 Adam Dunn A Bat-Jsy 25.00 11.00
74 Roy Oswalt A Bat-Jsy 25.00 11.00
75 P.Martinez Sox H Bat-Jsy 40.00 18.00
76 T.Glavine Mets A Bat-Jsy 40.00 18.00
77 T.Hunter Swing Bat-Jsy 25.00 11.00
78 Austin Kearns Bat-Jsy 25.00 11.00
79 R.John D'backs A Bat-Jsy 40.00 18.00
80 Bernie Williams A Bat-Jsy 40.00 18.00
82 Kerry Wood A Bat-Jsy 40.00 18.00
83 Kazuhisa Ishii A Bat-Jsy 25.00 11.00
84 R.Johnson Astros Bat-Jsy 40.00 18.00
85 Nick Johnson A Bat-Jsy 25.00 11.00
86 J.Beckett Pinstripe Bat-Jsy 40.00 18.00
87 C.Schilling Phils Bat-Jsy 40.00 18.00
88 Mike Mussina O's Bat-Jsy 40.00 18.00
89 P.Martinez Dgr Bat-Jsy 40.00 18.00
90 Barry Zito A Bat-Jsy 40.00 18.00
91 Jim Edmonds Bat-Jsy 25.00 11.00
92 R.Henderson Sox Bat-Jsy 40.00 18.00
93 R.Hend Padres Bat-Jsy 40.00 18.00
94 R.Henderson M's Bat-Jsy 40.00 18.00
95 R.Hend Mets Bat-Jsy 40.00 18.00
96 R.Hend Jays Bat-Jsy 40.00 18.00
97 R.John M's Arm Up Bat-Jsy 40.00 18.00
98 Mark Grace Bat-Jsy 40.00 18.00
99 P.Martinez Expos Bat-Jsy 40.00 18.00
101 I.Rodriguez Rgr Bat-Jsy 40.00 18.00
102 Jeff Kent Giants Bat-Jsy 25.00 11.00
103 Hideo Nomo Sox Bat-Jsy 50.00 22.00
104 Hideo Nomo Mets Bat-Jsy 50.00 22.00
105 M.Piazza Dodgers Bat-Jsy 50.00 22.00
106 T.Glav Braves H Bat-Jsy 40.00 18.00
107 R.Alom Ind Swing Bat-Jsy 40.00 18.00
108 R.Clemens Sox Bat-Jsy 50.00 22.00
109 J.Giambi A's H Bat-Jsy 40.00 18.00
110 J.Thome Indians A Bat-Jsy 40.00 18.00
111 A.Rod M's H Bat-Jsy 50.00 22.00
112 J.Gonz Ind Hands Bat-Jsy 40.00 18.00
113 T.Hunter Crouch Bat-Jsy 25.00 11.00
114 Roy Oswalt H Bat-Jsy 25.00 11.00
115 C.Schill D'b Throw Bat-Jsy 40.00 18.00
116 M.Ordonez H Bat-Jsy 25.00 11.00
117 R.Palmeiro Rgr H Bat-Jsy 40.00 18.00
118 Andruw Jones A Bat-Jsy 25.00 11.00
119 Manny Ramirez A Bat-Jsy 25.00 11.00
120 Mark Teixeira H Bat-Jsy 40.00 18.00
121 M.Mulder Stance Bat-Jsy 25.00 11.00
123 Tim Hudson A Bat-Jsy 25.00 11.00
124 Todd Helton A Bat-Jsy 40.00 18.00
125 T.Glaus Pinstripe Bat-Jsy 40.00 18.00
128 Greg Maddux A Bat-Jsy 50.00 22.00
129 R.Clemens Yanks A Bat-Jsy 50.00 22.00
130 N.Garciaparra A Bat-Jsy 50.00 22.00
131 M.Piazza Mets A Bat-Jsy 50.00 22.00
132 A.Rod Rgr H Bat-Jsy 50.00 22.00
134 R.John D'backs H Bat-Jsy 40.00 18.00
135 Sammy Sosa A Bat-Jsy 50.00 22.00
137 A.Soriano H Bat-Jsy 40.00 18.00
138 J.Giambi Yanks A Bat-Jsy 40.00 18.00
139 Albert Pujols A Bat-Jsy 60.00 27.00
140 Chipper Jones A Bat-Jsy 40.00 18.00
141 Adam Dunn H Bat-Jsy 25.00 11.00
142 P.Martinez Sox A Bat-Jsy 40.00 18.00
143 V.Guerrero A Bat-Jsy 40.00 18.00
144 Mark Prior A Bat-Jsy 60.00 27.00
145 Barry Zito H Bat-Jsy 40.00 18.00
146 Jeff Bagwell A Bat-Jsy 40.00 18.00
147 L.Berkman Socks Bat-Jsy 25.00 11.00
148 S.Green Dgr A Bat-Jsy 25.00 11.00
149 J.Giambi A's A Bat-Jsy 40.00 18.00
150 R.John M's Arm Out Bat-Jsy 40.00 18.00
151 A.Rod M's A Bat-Jsy 50.00 22.00
152 Babe Ruth Bat-Jsy/5
153 Ty Cobb Bat-Pants/10
155 Lou Gehrig Bat-Jsy/5
156 Thurman Munson Bat-Jsy 80.00 36.00
157 Roberto Clemente Bat-Jsy/5
158 Nolan Ryan Rgr Bat-Jsy 100.00 45.00
159 N.Ryan Angels Bat-Jsy 100.00 45.00
160 N.Ryan Astros Bat-Jsy 100.00 45.00
161 Cal Ripken Bat-Jsy 120.00 55.00
162 Don Mattingly Bat-Jsy 100.00 45.00
163 Stan Musial Bat-Jsy 100.00 45.00
164 Tony Gwynn Bat-Jsy 50.00 22.00
165 Yogi Berra Bat-Jsy 60.00 27.00
166 Johnny Bench Bat-Jsy 60.00 27.00
167 Mike Schmidt Bat-Jsy 100.00 45.00
168 George Brett Bat-Jsy 100.00 45.00
169 Ryne Sandberg Bat-Jsy 100.00 45.00
170 Ernie Banks Bat-Jsy/1

2003 Leaf Limited TNT Prime

MINT NRMT
*TNT PRIME: .5X TO 1.2X BASIC TNT
RANDOM INSERTS PACKS
PRINT RUNS B/WN 1-25 COPIES PER
NO PRICING ON QTY OF 10 OR LESS.

2003 Leaf Limited 7th Inning Stretch Jersey

MINT NRMT
RANDOM INSERTS IN PACKS
PRINT RUNS B/WN 40-50 COPIES PER
1 Alex Rodriguez 25.00 11.00
3 Sammy Sosa 30.00 13.50
4 Juan Gonzalez 15.00 6.75
5 Albert Pujols 40.00 18.00
6 Chipper Jones 15.00 6.75
7 Alfonso Soriano/40 15.00 6.75
8 Jim Thome 15.00 6.75
9 Mike Piazza 25.00 11.00
10 Rafael Palmeiro 15.00 6.75

2003 Leaf Limited Jersey Numbers

MINT NRMT
1-54 PRINT RUNS B/WN 5-100 COPIES PER
55-100 PRINT RUNS B/WN 5-25 COPIES PER
NO PRICING ON QTY OF 10 OR LESS.
RANDOM INSERTS IN PACKS
1 Rod Carew Angels/50 25.00 11.00
2 Nolan Ryan Angels/50 60.00 27.00
3 Reggie Jackson Angels/50 25.00 11.00
4 Brooks Robinson/50 40.00 18.00
5 Frank Robinson/25 25.00 11.00
6 Cal Ripken/100 60.00 27.00
7 Carlton Fisk W.Sox/50 25.00 11.00
8 Roger Clemens/100 20.00 9.00
9 Carlton Fisk R.Sox/5
10 Lou Boudreau/50 15.00 6.75
11 Bob Feller/25 40.00 18.00
12 Al Kaline/10
13 Alan Trammell/50 25.00 11.00
14 Harmon Killebrew/50 40.00 18.00
15 Rod Carew Twins/50 25.00 11.00
16 Kirby Puckett/50 40.00 18.00
17 Babe Ruth/5
18 Lou Gehrig/5
19 Yogi Berra/50 40.00 18.00
20 Thurman Munson/50 40.00 18.00
21 Don Mattingly/50 40.00 18.00
22 Roger Maris Pants/10
23 Rickey Henderson/5
24 Reggie Jackson A's/5
25 Alex Rodriguez/100 20.00 9.00
26 Randy Johnson M's/50 15.00 6.75
27 Nolan Ryan Rgr/100 50.00 22.00
28 Dale Murphy/50 40.00 18.00
29 Warren Spahn/50 25.00 11.00
30 Eddie Mathews/50 40.00 18.00
31 Ernie Banks/5
32 Ryne Sandberg/100 40.00 18.00
33 Johnny Bench/50 40.00 18.00
34 Joe Morgan/50 15.00 6.75
35 Randy Johnson Astros/50 15.00 6.75
36 Nolan Ryan Astros/100 50.00 22.00
37 Pee Wee Reese/50 25.00 11.00
38 Duke Snider/50 25.00 11.00
39 Jackie Robinson/25 100.00 45.00
40 Robin Yount/50 50.00 22.00
41 Paul Molitor/50 25.00 11.00
42 Pedro Martinez/50 15.00 6.75
43 Randy Johnson Expos/50 15.00 6.75
44 Tom Seaver/25 40.00 18.00
45 Gary Carter/50 15.00 6.75
46 Mike Schmidt/50 50.00 22.00
47 Steve Carlton/50 15.00 6.75
48 Willie Stargell/50 25.00 11.00
49 Roberto Clemente/5
50 Ozzie Smith/50 50.00 22.00
51 Stan Musial/100 40.00 18.00
52 Enos Slaughter/50 25.00 11.00
53 Orlando Cepeda/50 15.00 6.75
54 Willie McCovey/50 25.00 11.00
55 Brooks Robinson
Frank Robinson/10
56 Lou Boudreau
Bob Feller/10
57 Harmon Killebrew 100.00 45.00
Rod Carew/25
58 Harmon Killebrew 100.00 45.00
Kirby Puckett/25
59 Babe Ruth
Lou Gehrig/5

60 Babe Ruth
Yogi Berra/5
61 Babe Ruth
Thurman Munson/5
62 Babe Ruth
Don Mattingly/5
63 Babe Ruth
Roger Maris Pants/5
64 Lou Gehrig
Yogi Berra/5
65 Lou Gehrig
Thurman Munson/5
66 Lou Gehrig
Don Mattingly/5
67 Lou Gehrig
Roger Maris Pants/5
68 Yogi Berra 80.00 36.00
Thurman Munson/25
69 Yogi Berra 100.00 45.00
Don Mattingly/25
70 Yogi Berra
Roger Maris/5
71 Dale Murphy 80.00 36.00
Warren Spahn/25
72 Dale Murphy 80.00 36.00
Eddie Mathews/25
73 Warren Spahn 80.00 36.00
Eddie Mathews/25
74 Johnny Bench 60.00 27.00
Joe Morgan/25
75 Pee Wee Reese 60.00 27.00
Duke Snider/25
76 Pee Wee Reese
Jackie Robinson/10
77 Duke Snider
Jackie Robinson/10
78 Robin Yount 100.00 45.00
Paul Molitor/25
79 Mike Schmidt
Steve Carlton/25
80 Willie Stargell
Roberto Clemente/5
81 Ozzie Smith 100.00 45.00
Stan Musial/25
82 Stan Musial 100.00 45.00
Enos Slaughter/25
83 Orlando Cepeda 60.00 27.00
Willie McCovey/25
84 Nolan Ryan 100.00 45.00
Reggie Jackson/25
85 Brooks Robinson
Cal Ripken/25
86 Frank Robinson
Cal Ripken/10
87 Carlton Fisk
Roger Clemens/5
88 Al Kaline
Alan Trammell/10
89 Rickey Henderson
Reggie Jackson/5
90 Alex Rodriguez 50.00 22.00
Randy Johnson/25
91 Pedro Martinez 50.00 22.00
Randy Johnson/25
92 Tom Seaver
Gary Carter/10
93 Ernie Banks
Ryne Sandberg/10
94 Reggie Jackson A's 60.00 27.00
Reggie Jackson Angels/25
95 Nolan Ryan Angels 100.00 45.00
Nolan Ryan Rgr/25
96 Nolan Ryan Rgr 100.00 45.00
Nolan Ryan Astros/25
97 Nolan Ryan Astros 100.00 45.00
Nolan Ryan Angels/25
98 Nolan Ryan 100.00 45.00
Randy Johnson/25
99 Cal Ripken 150.00 70.00
Rafael Palmeiro/25
100 Dale Murphy 80.00 36.00
Deion Sanders/25

2003 Leaf Limited Jersey Numbers Retired

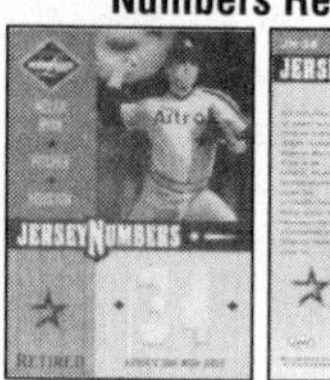

MINT NRMT
RANDOM INSERTS IN PACKS
PRINT RUNS B/WN 1-72 COPIES PER
NO PRICING ON QTY OF 19 OR LESS.
1 Rod Carew Angels/29 .... 40.00 18.00
2 Nolan Ryan Angels/30 .... 80.00 36.00
4 Brooks Robinson/5
5 Frank Robinson/20 .... 30.00 13.50
7 Carlton Fisk R.Sox/27 .... 40.00 18.00
9 Carlton Fisk W.Sox/72 .... 25.00 11.00
10 Lou Boudreau/5
11 Bob Feller/19
12 Al Kaline/6
14 Harmon Killebrew/3
15 Rod Carew Twins/29 .... 40.00 18.00
16 Kirby Puckett/34 .... 50.00 22.00
17 Babe Ruth/3
18 Lou Gehrig/4
19 Yogi Berra/8
20 Thurman Munson/15
21 Don Mattingly/23 .... 80.00 36.00
22 R.Maris Pants/9
27 Nolan Ryan Rgr/34 .... 80.00 36.00
28 Dale Murphy/3
29 Warren Spahn/21 .... 50.00 22.00
30 Eddie Mathews/41 .... 25.00 11.00
31 Ernie Banks/14
33 Johnny Bench/5
34 Joe Morgan/8
36 Nolan Ryan Astros/34 .... 80.00 36.00
37 Pee Wee Reese/1
38 Duke Snider/4
39 Jackie Robinson/42 .... 80.00 36.00
40 Robin Yount/19
41 Paul Molitor/4
44 Tom Seaver/41 .... 25.00 11.00
46 Mike Schmidt/20 .... 80.00 36.00
47 Steve Carlton/32 .... 25.00 11.00
48 Willie Stargell/8
49 Roberto Clemente/21 .... 150.00 70.00
50 Ozzie Smith/1
51 Stan Musial/6
52 Enos Slaughter/9
53 Orlando Cepeda/30 .... 25.00 11.00
54 Willie McCovey/44 .... 25.00 11.00

2003 Leaf Limited Leather

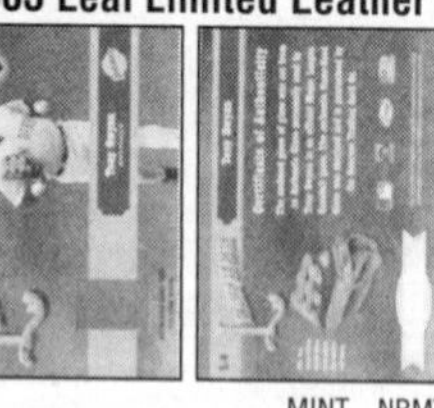

MINT NRMT
RANDOM INSERTS IN PACKS
PRINT RUNS B/WN 10-25 COPIES PER
NO PRICNG ON QTY OF 10 OR LESS
1 Alex Rodriguez/25 .... 60.00 27.00
2 Chipper Jones/25 .... 40.00 18.00
3 Jimmie Foxx/25 .... 100.00 45.00
4 Kirby Puckett/25 .... 40.00 18.00
5 Mike Schmidt/25 .... 120.00 55.00
6 Roger Clemens/25 .... 60.00 27.00
7 Steve Carlton/25 .... 40.00 18.00
8 Tony Gwynn/25 .... 60.00 27.00
9 Nolan Ryan/10
10 Vladimir Guerrero/25 .... 40.00 18.00
11 Adam Dunn/25 .... 40.00 18.00
12 Andruw Jones/25 .... 40.00 18.00
13 Curt Schilling/25 .... 40.00 18.00
14 Randy Johnson/25 .... 40.00 18.00
15 Mark Prior/25 .... 80.00 36.00

2003 Leaf Limited Leather Gold

MINT NRMT
RANDOM INSERTS IN PACKS
PRINT RUNS B/WN 5-10 COPIES PER
NO PRICING DUE TO SCARCITY

2003 Leaf Limited Leather and Lace

MINT NRMT
RANDOM INSERTS IN PACKS
STATED PRINT RUN 10 SERIAL #'d SETS
N.RYAN PRINT RUN 5 SERIAL #'d CARDS
NO PRICING DUE TO SCARCITY

2003 Leaf Limited Leather and Lace Gold

MINT NRMT
RANDOM INSERTS IN PACKS
STATED PRINT RUN 5 SERIAL #'d SETS
NO PRICING DUE TO SCARCITY

2003 Leaf Limited Lineups Bat

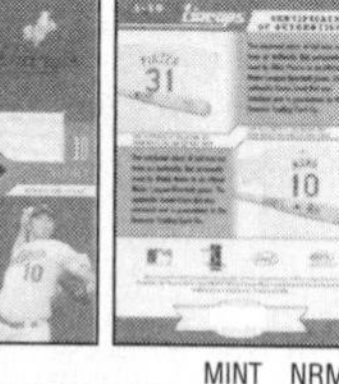

MINT NRMT
RANDOM INSERTS IN PACKS
PRINT RUNS B/WN 25-50 COPIES PER
ALL ARE DUAL BAT CARDS UNLESS NOTED
CARD NUMBER 3 DOES NOT EXIST
1 Paul Molitor 50.00 22.00
Robin Yount/50
2 Don Mattingly 50.00 22.00
Bernie Williams/50
4 Hideki Matsui Ball 100.00 45.00
Derek Jeter Ball/25
5 Ryne Sandberg 50.00 22.00
Andre Dawson/50
6 George Brett 80.00 36.00
Bo Jackson/50
7 Reggie Jackson 40.00 18.00
Jose Canseco/50
8 Mark Grace 50.00 22.00
Ryne Sandberg/50
9 Rickey Henderson 40.00 18.00
Jose Canseco/50
10 Mike Piazza 40.00 18.00
Hideo Nomo/50

2003 Leaf Limited Lineups Button

MINT NRMT
RANDOM INSERTS IN PACKS
STATED PRINT RUN 1 SERIAL #'d SET

NO PRICING DUE TO SCARCITY
2 Don Mattingly
Bernie Williams
3 Sammy Sosa
Hee Seop Choi
6 George Brett
Bo Jackson
10 Mike Piazza
Hideo Nomo

2003 Leaf Limited Lineups Jersey

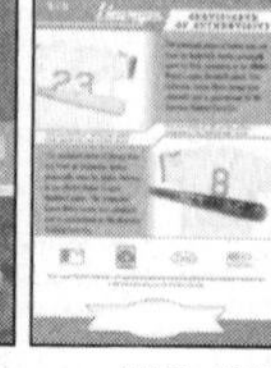

MINT NRMT
RANDOM INSERTS IN PACKS
PRINT RUNS B/WN 25
NO PRICING ON QTY OF 5 OR LESS
ALL ARE DUAL JSY CARDS UNLESS NOTED
1 Paul Molitor 50.00 22.00
Robin Yount/50
2 Don Mattingly 50.00 22.00
Bernie Williams/50
3 Sammy Sosa 40.00 18.00
Hee Seop Choi/50
4 Hideki Matsui Base 50.00 22.00
Derek Jeter Base/50
5 Ryne Sandberg 50.00 22.00
Andre Dawson/50
6 George Brett 80.00 36.00
Bo Jackson/50
7 Reggie Jackson
Jose Canseco/5
8 Mark Grace 50.00 22.00
Ryne Sandberg/50
9 Rickey Henderson
Jose Canseco/5
10 Mike Piazza 40.00 18.00
Hideo Nomo/50

2003 Leaf Limited Lineups Jersey Tag

MINT NRMT
RANDOM INSERTS IN PACKS
PRINT RUNS B/WN 4-5 COPIES PER
NO PRICING DUE TO SCARCITY
1 Paul Molitor
Robin Yount/5
2 Don Mattingly
Bernie Williams/5
3 Sammy Sosa
Hee Seop Choi/5
6 George Brett
Bo Jackson/5
7 Reggie Jackson
Jose Canseco/4
8 Mark Grace
Ryne Sandberg/5
9 Rickey Henderson
Jose Canseco/4
10 Mike Piazza
Hideo Nomo/5

2003 Leaf Limited Lumberjacks Barrel

MINT NRMT
RANDOM INSERTS IN PACKS
PRINT RUNS B/WN 1-2 COPIES PER
NO PRICING DUE TO SCARCITY
1 Babe Ruth/2
2 Lou Gehrig/1
3 Roberto Clemente/1
4 Stan Musial/1
5 Rogers Hornsby/1
6 Don Mattingly/1
7 Rickey Henderson/2
8 Cal Ripken/1
9 Yogi Berra/1
10 Reggie Jackson/1
11 George Brett/1
12 Mel Ott/1
13 Roger Maris/1
14 Ryne Sandberg/1
15 Eddie Mathews/1
16 Richie Ashburn/1
17 Mike Schmidt/1
18 Tony Gwynn/1
19 Ty Cobb/1
20 Thurman Munson/2
21 Jimmie Foxx/1
22 Duke Snider/1
23 Ernie Banks/2
24 Alex Rodriguez/1
25 Nomar Garciaparra/2
29 Mike Piazza/1
30 Alfonso Soriano/2
31 Al Kaline/1
32 Harmon Killebrew/2
33 Dale Murphy/1
34 Orlando Cepeda/1
35 Willie McCovey/1
36 Willie Stargell/1
37 Brooks Robinson/1

2003 Leaf Limited Lumberjacks Bat

MINT NRMT
1-37 PRINT RUNS B/WN 1-25 COPIES PER
38-45 PRINT RUNS B/WN 1-25 COPIES PER
NO PRICING ON QTY OF 15 OR LESS.
RANDOM INSERTS IN PACKS
1 Babe Ruth/25 .... 300.00 135.00
2 Lou Gehrig/25 .... 200.00 90.00
3 Roberto Clemente/25 .... 150.00 70.00
4 Stan Musial/25 .... 60.00 27.00
5 Rogers Hornsby/25 .... 80.00 36.00
6 Don Mattingly/25 .... 80.00 36.00
7 Rickey Henderson/25 .... 25.00 11.00
8 Cal Ripken/25 .... 120.00 55.00
9 Yogi Berra/25 .... 50.00 22.00
10 Reggie Jackson/25 .... 40.00 18.00
11 George Brett/25 .... 80.00 36.00
12 Mel Ott/25 .... 60.00 27.00
13 Roger Maris/25 .... 100.00 45.00
14 Ryne Sandberg/25 .... 80.00 36.00
15 Eddie Mathews/15
16 Richie Ashburn/25 .... 40.00 18.00
17 Mike Schmidt/25 .... 80.00 36.00
18 Tony Gwynn/25 .... 40.00 18.00
19 Ty Cobb/25 .... 150.00 70.00
20 Thurman Munson/25 .... 50.00 22.00
21 Jimmie Foxx/25 .... 80.00 36.00
22 Duke Snider/25 .... 40.00 18.00
23 Ernie Banks/1
24 Alex Rodriguez/25 .... 40.00 18.00
25 Nomar Garciaparra/25 .... 40.00 18.00
26 Hideki Matsui Base/25 .... 100.00 45.00
27 Ichiro Suzuki Base/25 .... 60.00 27.00
28 Barry Bonds Base/25 .... 60.00 27.00
29 Mike Piazza/25 .... 40.00 18.00
30 Alfonso Soriano/25 .... 25.00 11.00
31 Al Kaline/25 .... 50.00 22.00
32 Harmon Killebrew/5
33 Dale Murphy/25 .... 50.00 22.00
34 Orlando Cepeda/5
35 Willie McCovey/25 .... 40.00 18.00
36 Willie Stargell/5
37 Brooks Robinson/25 .... 50.00 22.00
38 Hideki Matsui Base 120.00 55.00
Ichiro Suzuki Base/25
39 Ryne Sandberg
Ernie Banks/1
40 Don Mattingly 250.00 110.00
Lou Gehrig/25
41 Yogi Berra 80.00 36.00
Thurman Munson/25
42 Mike Schmidt 100.00 45.00
Richie Ashburn/25
43 Stan Musial 120.00 55.00
Rogers Hornsby/25
44 Don Mattingly 150.00 70.00
Roger Maris/25
45 Babe Ruth
Lou Gehrig/15

2003 Leaf Limited Lumberjacks Bat Black

MINT NRMT
RANDOM INSERTS IN PACKS
PRINT RUNS B/WN 1-5 COPIES PER
NO PRICING DUE TO SCARCITY

2003 Leaf Limited Lumberjacks Bat Silver

MINT NRMT
RANDOM INSERTS IN PACKS
PRINT RUNS B/WN 1-10 COPIES PER
NO PRICING DUE TO SCARCITY

2003 Leaf Limited Lumberjacks Bat-Jersey

MINT NRMT
1-37 PRINT RUNS B/WN 1-25 COPIES PER
38-45 PRINT RUNS B/WN 1-25 COPIES PER
NO PRICING ON QTY OF 15 OR LESS.
RANDOM INSERTS IN PACKS
ALL ARE BAT-JSY COMBOS UNLESS NOTED
1 Babe Ruth/5
2 Lou Gehrig/10
3 Roberto Clemente/10
4 Stan Musial/25 .... 100.00 45.00

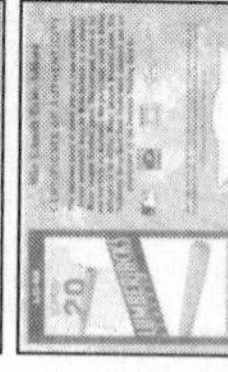

6 Don Mattingly/25 .... 120.00 55.00
7 Rickey Henderson/5
8 Cal Ripken/25 .... 150.00 70.00
9 Yogi Berra/25 .... 60.00 27.00
10 Reggie Jackson/5
11 George Brett/25 .... 120.00 55.00
12 Mel Ott/15
13 Roger Maris Bat-Pants/25 .... 150.00 70.00
14 Ryne Sandberg/25 .... 120.00 55.00
15 Eddie Mathews/25 .... 60.00 27.00
17 Mike Schmidt/25 .... 120.00 55.00
18 Tony Gwynn/25 .... 60.00 27.00
19 Ty Cobb Bat-Pants/15
20 Thurman Munson/25 .... 80.00 36.00
22 Duke Snider/15
23 Ernie Banks/1
24 Alex Rodriguez/25 .... 60.00 27.00
25 Nomar Garciaparra/25 .... 60.00 27.00
26 Hideki Matsui Base-Ball/25 .... 150.00 70.00
27 Ichiro Suzuki Base-Ball/25 .... 80.00 36.00
28 Barry Bonds Base-Ball/25 .... 80.00 36.00
29 Mike Piazza/25 .... 60.00 27.00
30 Alfonso Soriano/25 .... 40.00 18.00
31 Al Kaline/10
32 Harmon Killebrew/10
33 Dale Murphy/25 .... 60.00 27.00
34 Orlando Cepeda/5
35 Willie McCovey/25 .... 50.00 22.00
36 Willie Stargell/25 .... 50.00 22.00
37 Brooks Robinson/25 .... 60.00 27.00
38A Hideki Matsui Base 120.00 55.00
Ichiro Suzuki Ball/25
38B Hideki Matsui Ball 120.00 55.00
Ichiro Suzuki Base/25
39A Ryne Sandberg Bat
Ernie Banks Jsy/5
39B Ryne Sandberg Jsy
Ernie Banks Bat/1
40A Don Mattingly Jsy
Lou Gehrig Bat/10
40B Don Mattingly Bat
Lou Gehrig Jsy/5
41A Yogi Berra Jsy 80.00 36.00
Thurman Munson Bat/25
41B Yogi Berra Bat 80.00 36.00
Thurman Munson Jsy/25
42 Mike Schmidt Jsy 100.00 45.00
Richie Ashburn Bat/25
43 Stan Musial Jsy 120.00 55.00
Rogers Hornsby Bat/25
44 Don Mattingly Bat
Roger Maris Pants/5
45A Babe Ruth Jsy
Lou Gehrig Bat/5
45B Babe Ruth Bat
Lou Gehrig Jsy/5

2003 Leaf Limited Lumberjacks Bat-Jersey Black

MINT NRMT
RANDOM INSERTS IN PACKS
PRINT RUNS B/WN 1-5 COPIES PER
NO PRICING DUE TO SCARCITY

2003 Leaf Limited Lumberjacks Bat-Jersey Silver

MINT NRMT
RANDOM INSERTS IN PACKS
PRINT RUNS B/WN 1-10 COPIES PER
NO PRICING DUE TO SCARCITY

2003 Leaf Limited Lumberjacks Jersey

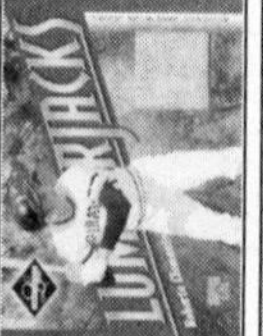

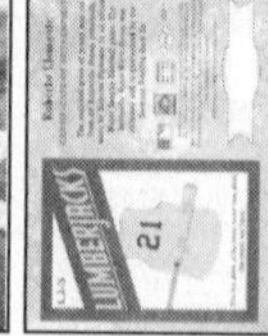

MINT NRMT
1-37 PRINT RUNS B/WN 1-25 COPIES PER
38-45 PRINT RUNS B/WN 1-25 COPIES PER
NO PRICING ON QTY OF 15 OR LESS.
RANDOM INSERTS IN PACKS
1 Babe Ruth/5
2 Lou Gehrig/10
3 Roberto Clemente/10
4 Stan Musial/25 .... 60.00 27.00
6 Don Mattingly/25 .... 80.00 36.00
7 Rickey Henderson/10
8 Cal Ripken/25 .... 120.00 55.00
9 Yogi Berra/25 .... 40.00 18.00
10 Reggie Jackson/10
11 George Brett/25 .... 80.00 36.00
12 Mel Ott/25 .... 60.00 27.00
13 Roger Maris Pants/10
14 Ryne Sandberg/25 .... 80.00 36.00
15 Eddie Mathews/25 .... 40.00 18.00
17 Mike Schmidt/25 .... 80.00 36.00
18 Tony Gwynn/25 .... 40.00 18.00
19 Ty Cobb Pants/5
20 Thurman Munson/25 .... 50.00 22.00
22 Duke Snider/25 .... 30.00 13.50
23 Ernie Banks/5

24 Alex Rodriguez/25 40.00 18.00
25 Nomar Garciaparra/25 40.00 18.00
26 Hideki Matsui Ball/25 100.00 45.00
27 Ichiro Suzuki Ball/25 60.00 27.00
28 Barry Bonds Ball/25 60.00 27.00
29 Mike Piazza/25 40.00 18.00
30 Alfonso Soriano/25 25.00 11.00
31 Al Kaline/10
32 Harmon Killebrew/25 40.00 18.00
33 Dale Murphy/25 40.00 18.00
34 Orlando Cepeda/25 20.00 9.00
35 Willie McCovey/25 30.00 13.50
36 Willie Stargell/25 30.00 13.50
37 Brooks Robinson/25 40.00 18.00
38 Hideki Matsui Ball 120.00 55.00
Ichiro Suzuki Ball/25
39 Ryne Sandberg
Ernie Banks/5
40 Don Mattingly
Lou Gehrig/15
41 Yogi Berra 80.00 36.00
Thurman Munson/25
44 Don Mattingly
Roger Maris Pants/5
45 Babe Ruth
Lou Gehrig/5

2003 Leaf Limited Lumberjacks Jersey Black

MINT NRMT
RANDOM INSERTS IN PACKS
PRINT RUNS B/WN 1-5 COPIES PER
NO PRICING DUE TO SCARCITY

2003 Leaf Limited Lumberjacks Jersey Silver

MINT NRMT
RANDOM INSERTS IN PACKS
PRINT RUNS B/WN 3-10 COPIES PER
NO PRICING DUE TO SCARCITY

2003 Leaf Limited Player Threads

MINT NRMT
RANDOM INSERTS IN PACKS
PRINT RUNS B/WN 5-50 COPIES PER
NO PRICING ON QTY OF 5 OR LESS
1 Roger Clemens/50 25.00 11.00
2 Alex Rodriguez/50 25.00 11.00
3 Pedro Martinez/50 15.00 6.75
4 Randy Johnson/50 15.00 6.75
5 Curt Schilling/50 15.00 6.75
6 Reggie Jackson/5
7 Nolan Ryan/50 60.00 27.00
8 Hideo Nomo/50 40.00 18.00
9 Mike Piazza/50 25.00 11.00
10 Rickey Henderson Padres/5
11 Rickey Henderson Mets/50 15.00 6.75
12 Ivan Rodriguez/50 15.00 6.75
13 Gary Sheffield/50 10.00 4.50
14 Jeff Kent/50 10.00 4.50
15 Roberto Alomar/50 15.00 6.75
16 Rafael Palmeiro/50 15.00 6.75
17 Juan Gonzalez/50 15.00 6.75
18 Shawn Green/50 10.00 4.50
19 Jason Giambi/50 15.00 6.75
20 Jim Thome/50 15.00 6.75
21 Scott Rolen/50 15.00 6.75
22 Mike Mussina/50 15.00 6.75
23 Tom Glavine/50 15.00 6.75
24 Sammy Sosa/50 25.00 11.00

2003 Leaf Limited Player Threads Prime

MINT NRMT
RANDOM INSERTS IN PACKS
PRINT RUNS B/WN 5-10 COPIES PER
NO PRICING DUE TO SCARCITY

2003 Leaf Limited Player Threads Double

MINT NRMT
RANDOM INSERTS IN PACKS
STATED PRINT RUN 50 SERIAL #'d SETS
CARD 6/10 PRINT RUN 5 SERIAL #'d SETS
1 R.Clemens Yanks-Sox 40.00 18.00
2 Alex Rodriguez Rgr-M's 40.00 18.00
3 P.Martinez Sox-Dodgers 25.00 11.00
4 Randy Johnson D'backs-Astros 25.00 11.00
5 C.Schilling D'backs-Phils 25.00 11.00
6 R.Jackson A's-Angels/5
7 Nolan Ryan Rgr-Astros 80.00 36.00
8 H.Nomo Dodgers-Sox 60.00 27.00
9 M.Piazza Mets-Dodgers 40.00 18.00
10 R.Henderson Padres-Sox/5
11 R.Henderson Mets-M's 25.00 11.00
12 I.Rodriguez Marlins-Rgr 25.00 11.00
13 G.Sheffield Braves-Dodgers 15.00 6.75
14 Jeff Kent Astros-Giants 15.00 6.75
15 R.Alomar Mets-Indians 25.00 11.00
16 Rafael Palmeiro Rgr-O's 25.00 11.00
17 J.Gonzalez Rgr-Indians 25.00 11.00
18 S.Green Dodgers-Jays 15.00 6.75
19 Jason Giambi Yanks-A's 25.00 11.00
20 Jim Thome Phils-Indians 25.00 11.00
21 Scott Rolen Cards-Phils 25.00 11.00
22 Mike Mussina Yanks-O's 25.00 11.00
23 Tom Glavine Mets-Braves 25.00 11.00
24 Sammy Sosa Cubs-Sox 40.00 18.00

2003 Leaf Limited Player Threads Double Prime

MINT NRMT
RANDOM INSERTS IN PACKS
PRINT RUNS B/WN 5-10 COPIES PER
NO PRICING DUE TO SCARCITY

2003 Leaf Limited Player Threads Triple

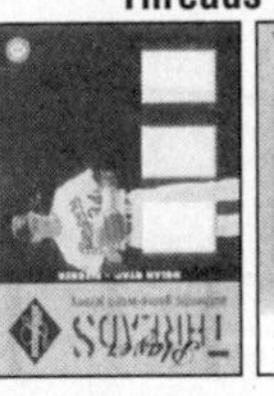
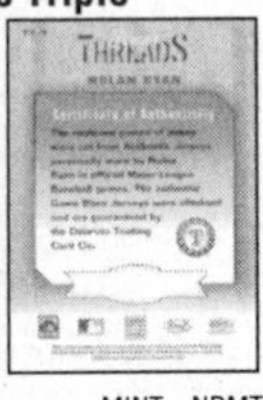

MINT NRMT
RANDOM INSERTS IN PACKS
STATED PRINT RUN 50 SERIAL #'d SETS
HENDERSON PADRES-SOX-A'S 5 #'d CARDS
NO HENDERSON PADRES-SOX-A'S PRICING
4 R.John D'backs-Astros-M's 40.00 18.00
7 N.Ryan Rgr-Astros-Angels 120.00 55.00
8 H.Nomo Dodgers-Sox-Mets 100.00 45.00
10 R.Henderson Padres-Sox-A's/5
11 R.Henderson Mets-M's-Jays 40.00 18.00
13 G.Sheffield Braves-Dgr-Brew 25.00 11.00
14 J.Kent Astros-Giants-Jays 25.00 11.00
15 R.Alomar Mets-Indians-O's 40.00 18.00

2003 Leaf Limited Player Threads Triple Prime

MINT NRMT
RANDOM INSERTS IN PACKS
PRINT RUNS B/WN 5-10 COPIES PER
NO PRICING DUE TO SCARCITY

2003 Leaf Limited Team Threads

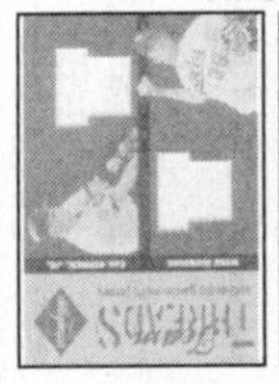

MINT NRMT
RANDOM INSERTS IN PACKS
PRINT RUNS B/WN 10-50 COPIES PER
NO PRICING ON QTY OF 10 OR LESS
25 Jackie Robinson
Duke Snider/10
26 Alex Rodriguez 80.00 36.00
Nolan Ryan/50
27 Mike Piazza 40.00 18.00
Hideo Nomo/50
28 Cal Ripken 100.00 45.00
Mike Mussina/50
29 Hideo Nomo 40.00 18.00
Kazuhisa Ishii/50
30 Nolan Ryan 50.00 22.00
Randy Johnson/50

2003 Leaf Limited Team Threads Prime

MINT NRMT
RANDOM INSERTS IN PACKS
PRINT RUNS B/WN 5-10 COPIES PER
NO PRICING DUE TO SCARCITY

2003 Leaf Limited Team Trademarks Autographs

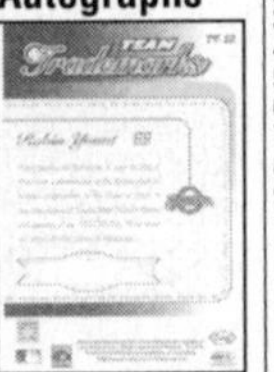

MINT NRMT
RANDOM INSERTS IN PACKS
PRINT RUNS B/WN 5-25 COPIES PER
NO PRICING ON QTY OF 10 OR LESS
1 Alan Trammell/25 60.00 27.00
2 Joe Morgan/5
3 Jim Palmer/25 50.00 22.00
4 Bob Feller/5
5 Gary Carter/25 60.00 27.00
6 Andre Dawson/25 50.00 22.00
7 Duke Snider/5
8 Dale Murphy/25 80.00 36.00
9 Bo Jackson/5
10 Bobby Doerr/25 40.00 18.00
11 Brooks Robinson/25 80.00 36.00
12 Eric Davis/25 50.00 22.00
13 Fred Lynn/25 40.00 18.00
14 Harmon Killebrew/10
15 Jack Morris/25 40.00 18.00
16 Al Kaline/25 80.00 36.00
17 Deion Sanders/25 120.00 55.00
18 Luis Aparicio/25 40.00 18.00
19 Orlando Cepeda/5
20 Phil Rizzuto/25 60.00 27.00
21 Reggie Jackson/5
22 Robin Yount/5
23 Rod Carew Twins/5
24 Will Clark/25 150.00 70.00
25 Willie McCovey/5
26 Tony Gwynn/5
27 Nolan Ryan Astros/5
28 Cal Ripken/5
29 Stan Musial/5
30 Mike Schmidt/5
31 Rod Carew Angels/5
32 Nolan Ryan Rgr/5
33 George Brett/5
34 Nolan Ryan Angels/5
35 Alex Rodriguez/5
36 Roger Clemens/5
37 Greg Maddux/5
38 Albert Pujols/5
39 Alfonso Soriano/5
40 Mark Grace/5

2003 Leaf Limited Team Trademarks Autographs Jersey

MINT NRMT
RANDOM INSERTS IN PACKS
PRINT RUNS B/WN 1-47 COPIES PER
NO PRICING ON QTY OF 24 OR LESS
1 Alan Trammell/3
2 Joe Morgan/8
3 Jim Palmer/22
4 Bob Feller/19
5 Gary Carter/8
6 Andre Dawson/8
7 Duke Snider/4
8 Dale Murphy/3
9 Bo Jackson/16
10 Bobby Doerr/1
11 Brooks Robinson/5
12 Eric Davis/44 50.00 22.00
13 Fred Lynn/19
14 Harmon Killebrew/3
15 Jack Morris/47 40.00 18.00
16 Al Kaline/6
17 Deion Sanders/24
18 Luis Aparicio/11
19 Orlando Cepeda/30 50.00 22.00
20 Phil Rizzuto/10
21 Reggie Jackson/9
22 Robin Yount/19
23 Rod Carew Twins/29 80.00 36.00
24 Will Clark/22
25 Willie McCovey/44 60.00 27.00
26 Tony Gwynn/19
27 Nolan Ryan Astros/34 200.00 90.00
28 Cal Ripken/8
29 Stan Musial/6
30 Mike Schmidt/20
31 Rod Carew Angels/29 80.00 36.00
32 Nolan Ryan Rgr/34 200.00 90.00
33 George Brett/5
34 Nolan Ryan Angels/30 200.00 90.00
35 Alex Rodriguez/3
36 Roger Clemens/22
37 Greg Maddux/31 200.00 90.00
38 Albert Pujols/5
39 Alfonso Soriano/12
40 Mark Grace/17

2003 Leaf Limited Team Trademarks Threads Number

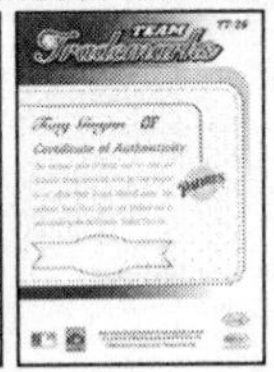

MINT NRMT
RANDOM INSERTS IN PACKS
PRINT RUNS B/WN 1-47 COPIES PER
NO PRICING ON QTY OF 19 OR LESS
1 Alan Trammell/3
2 Joe Morgan/8
3 Jim Palmer/22 30.00 13.50
4 Bob Feller/19
5 Gary Carter/8
6 Andre Dawson/8
7 Duke Snider/4
8 Dale Murphy/3
9 Bo Jackson/16
10 Bobby Doerr/1
11 Brooks Robinson/5
12 Eric Davis/44 15.00 6.75
13 Fred Lynn/19
14 Harmon Killebrew/3
15 Jack Morris/47 15.00 6.75
16 Al Kaline/6
17 Deion Sanders/24 50.00 22.00
18 Luis Aparicio/11
19 Orlando Cepeda/30 25.00 11.00
20 Phil Rizzuto/10
21 Reggie Jackson/9
22 Robin Yount/19
23 Rod Carew Twins/29 40.00 18.00
24 Will Clark/22 100.00 45.00
25 Willie McCovey/44 25.00 11.00
26 Tony Gwynn/19
27 Nolan Ryan Astros/34 80.00 36.00
28 Cal Ripken/8
29 Stan Musial/6
30 Mike Schmidt/20 80.00 36.00
31 Rod Carew Angels/29 40.00 18.00
32 Nolan Ryan Rgr/34 80.00 36.00
33 George Brett/5
34 Nolan Ryan Angels/30 80.00 36.00
35 Alex Rodriguez/3
36 Roger Clemens/22 60.00 27.00
37 Greg Maddux/31 40.00 18.00
38 Albert Pujols/5
39 Alfonso Soriano/12
40 Mark Grace/17

2003 Leaf Limited Team Trademarks Threads Prime

MINT NRMT
RANDOM INSERTS IN PACKS
PRINT RUNS B/WN 5-25 COPIES PER
NO PRICING ON QTY OF 10 OR LESS
1 Alan Trammell/25 60.00 27.00
2 Joe Morgan/25 40.00 18.00
3 Jim Palmer/25 40.00 18.00
4 Bob Feller/10
5 Gary Carter/25 60.00 27.00
6 Andre Dawson/25 40.00 18.00
7 Duke Snider/25 60.00 27.00
8 Dale Murphy/25 60.00 27.00
9 Bo Jackson/25 60.00 27.00
10 Bobby Doerr/20 50.00 22.00
11 Brooks Robinson/25 80.00 36.00
12 Eric Davis/25 40.00 18.00
13 Fred Lynn/25 25.00 11.00
14 Harmon Killebrew/25 80.00 36.00
15 Jack Morris/25 25.00 11.00
16 Al Kaline/5
17 Deion Sanders/25 60.00 27.00
18 Luis Aparicio/25 40.00 18.00
19 Orlando Cepeda/25 40.00 18.00
20 Phil Rizzuto/10
21 Reggie Jackson/5
22 Robin Yount/25 80.00 36.00
23 Rod Carew Twins/25 60.00 27.00
24 Will Clark/25 120.00 55.00
25 Willie McCovey/25 60.00 27.00
26 Tony Gwynn/25 60.00 27.00
27 Nolan Ryan Astros/25 120.00 55.00
28 Cal Ripken/25 150.00 70.00
29 Stan Musial/25 150.00 70.00
30 Mike Schmidt/25 120.00 55.00
31 Rod Carew Angels/25 60.00 27.00
32 Nolan Ryan Rgr/25 120.00 55.00
33 George Brett/25 120.00 55.00
34 Nolan Ryan Angels/25 120.00 55.00
35 Alex Rodriguez/25 60.00 27.00
36 Roger Clemens/20 80.00 36.00
37 Greg Maddux/25 60.00 27.00
38 Albert Pujols/25 100.00 45.00
39 Alfonso Soriano/25 40.00 18.00
40 Mark Grace/25 60.00 27.00

1996 Leaf Preferred

The 1996 Leaf Preferred set was issued by Donruss in one series totalling 150 cards. The six-card packs retailed for $3.49 each. Each card was printed on 20-point card stock for extra thickness and durability. The fronts feature a color action player photo and silver foil printing. The backs carry another player photo, player information and statistics. One in every ten packs contained an insert card.

Nm-Mt Ex-Mt
COMPLETE SET (150) 25.00 7.50
1 Ken Griffey Jr. 1.25 .35
2 Rico Brogna .30 .09
3 Gregg Jefferies .30 .09
4 Reggie Sanders .30 .09
5 Manny Ramirez .30 .09
6 Shawn Green .30 .09
7 Tino Martinez .50 .15
8 Jeff Bagwell .50 .15
9 Marc Newfield .30 .09
10 Ray Lankford .30 .09
11 Jay Bell .30 .09
12 Greg Maddux 1.25 .35
13 Frank Thomas .75 .23
14 Travis Fryman .30 .09
15 Mark McGwire 2.00 .60
16 Chuck Knoblauch .30 .09
17 Sammy Sosa 1.25 .35
18 Matt Williams .30 .09
19 Roger Clemens 1.50 .45
20 Rondell White .30 .09
21 Ivan Rodriguez .75 .23
22 Cal Ripken 2.50 .75
23 Ben McDonald .30 .09
24 Kenny Lofton .30 .09
25 Mike Piazza 1.25 .35
26 David Cone .30 .09
27 Gary Sheffield .30 .09
28 Tim Salmon .50 .15
29 Andres Galarraga .30 .09
30 Johnny Damon .30 .09
31 Ozzie Smith 1.25 .35
32 Carlos Baerga .30 .09
33 Raul Mondesi .30 .09
34 Moises Alou .30 .09
35 Alex Rodriguez 1.50 .45
36 Mike Mussina .75 .23
37 Jason Isringhausen .30 .09
38 Barry Larkin .75 .23
39 Bernie Williams .50 .15
40 Chipper Jones .75 .23
41 Joey Hamilton .30 .09
42 Charles Johnson .30 .09
43 Juan Gonzalez .75 .23
44 Greg Vaughn .30 .09
45 Robin Ventura .30 .09
46 Albert Belle .30 .09
47 Rafael Palmeiro .50 .15
48 Brian L.Hunter .30 .09
49 Mo Vaughn .30 .09
50 Paul O'Neill .50 .15
51 Mark Grace .50 .15
52 Randy Johnson .75 .23
53 Pedro Martinez .75 .23
54 Marty Cordova .30 .09
55 Garret Anderson .30 .09
56 Joe Carter .30 .09
57 Jim Thome .75 .23
58 Edgardo Alfonzo .30 .09
59 Dante Bichette .30 .09
60 Darryl Hamilton .30 .09
61 Roberto Alomar .75 .23
62 Fred McGriff .50 .15
63 Kirby Puckett .75 .23
64 Hideo Nomo .75 .23
65 Alex Fernandez .30 .09
66 Ryan Klesko .30 .09
67 Wade Boggs .50 .15
68 Eddie Murray .75 .23
69 Eric Karros .30 .09
70 Jim Edmonds .30 .09
71 Edgar Martinez .50 .15
72 Andy Pettitte .50 .15
73 Mark Grudzielanek .30 .09
74 Tom Glavine .50 .15
75 Ken Caminiti .30 .09
76 Will Clark .75 .23
77 Craig Biggio .50 .15
78 Brady Anderson .30 .09
79 Tony Gwynn 1.00 .30
80 Larry Walker .50 .15
81 Brian Jordan .30 .09
82 Lenny Dykstra .30 .09
83 Butch Huskey .30 .09
84 Jack McDowell .30 .09
85 Cecil Fielder .30 .09
86 Jose Canseco .75 .23
87 Jason Giambi .75 .23
88 Rickey Henderson .75 .23
89 Kevin Seitzer .30 .09
90 Carlos Delgado .30 .09
91 Ryne Sandberg 1.25 .35
92 Dwight Gooden .50 .15
93 Michael Tucker .30 .09
94 Barry Bonds 2.00 .60
95 Eric Young .30 .09
96 Dean Palmer .30 .09
97 Henry Rodriguez .30 .09
98 John Mabry .30 .09
99 J.T. Snow .30 .09
100 Andre Dawson .30 .09
101 Ismael Valdes .30 .09
102 Charles Nagy .30 .09
103 Jay Buhner .30 .09
104 Derek Bell .30 .09
105 Paul Molitor .50 .15
106 Hal Morris .30 .09
107 Ray Durham .30 .09
108 Bernard Gilkey .30 .09
109 John Valentin .30 .09
110 Melvin Nieves .30 .09
111 John Smoltz .50 .15
112 Terrell Wade .30 .09
113 Chad Mottola .30 .09
114 Tony Clark .30 .09
115 John Wasdin .30 .09
116 Derek Jeter 2.00 .60
117 Rey Ordonez .30 .09
118 Jason Thompson .30 .09
119 Robin Jennings .30 .09
120 Rocky Coppinger RC .30 .09
121 Billy Wagner .30 .09
122 Steve Gibralter .30 .09
123 Jermaine Dye .30 .09
124 Jason Kendall .30 .09
125 Mike Grace RC .30 .09
126 Jason Schmidt .30 .09
127 Paul Wilson .30 .09
128 Alan Benes .30 .09
129 Justin Thompson .30 .09
130 Brooks Kieschnick .30 .09
131 George Arias .30 .09
132 O.Fernandez RC .30 .09
133 Todd Hollandsworth .30 .09
134 Eric Owens .30 .09
135 Chan Ho Park .30 .09
136 Mark Loretta .30 .09
137 Ruben Rivera .30 .09
138 Jeff Suppan .30 .09
139 Ugueth Urbina .30 .09
140 LaTroy Hawkins .30 .09
141 Chris Snopek .30 .09
142 Edgar Renteria .30 .09
143 Raul Casanova .30 .09
144 Jose Herrera .30 .09
145 Matt Lawton RC .30 .09
146 Ralph Milliard RC .30 .09
147 Frank Thomas CL .50 .15
148 Jeff Bagwell CL .30 .09
149 Ken Griffey Jr. CL .75 .23
150 Mike Piazza CL .75 .23

1996 Leaf Preferred Press Proofs

Parallel to the regular set except for gold foil printing on front, these 150 cards are each marked as "I of 500", but not serial-numbered to 500. The cards were seeded at an approximate rate of one in every 48 packs.

Nm-Mt Ex-Mt
*STARS: 12.5X TO 30X BASIC CARDS
*ROOKIES: 8X TO 20X BASIC CARDS

1996 Leaf Preferred Staremaster

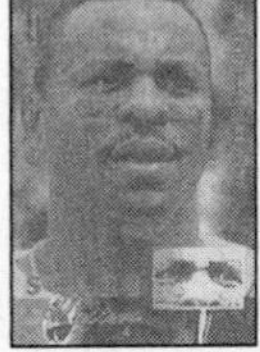

Randomly inserted at an approximate rate of one in every 144 packs, these twelve cards feature mug shots of the games most intense stares. Each card is printed on silver holographic card stock. Only 2,500 of each card was produced and are individually numbered.

	Nm-Mt	Ex-Mt
COMPLETE SET (12)	250.00	75.00
1 Chipper Jones	12.00	3.60
2 Alex Rodriguez	25.00	7.50
3 Derek Jeter	30.00	9.00
4 Tony Gwynn	15.00	4.50
5 Frank Thomas	12.00	3.60
6 Ken Griffey Jr.	20.00	6.00
7 Cal Ripken	40.00	12.00
8 Greg Maddux	20.00	6.00
9 Albert Belle	5.00	1.50
10 Barry Bonds	30.00	9.00
11 Jeff Bagwell	8.00	2.40
12 Mike Piazza	20.00	6.00

1996 Leaf Preferred Steel

Seeded one per pack, this all-steel, metalized set features silver framed color action player photos of the leagues most dominant players on a silver tinted background with a scriptive letter "S". The backs carry another player photo with the card logo as background and player statistics.

	Nm-Mt	Ex-Mt
COMPLETE SET (77)	100.00	30.00
*GOLD: 4X TO 10X BASIC STEEL		
GOLD: RANDOM INSERTS IN PACKS		
1 Frank Thomas	2.50	.75
2 Paul Molitor	1.50	.45
3 Kenny Lofton	1.00	.30
4 Travis Fryman	1.00	.30
5 Jeff Conine	1.00	.30
6 Barry Bonds	6.00	1.80
7 Gregg Jefferies	1.00	.30
8 Alex Rodriguez	5.00	1.50
9 Wade Boggs	1.50	.45
10 David Justice	2.50	.75
11 Hideo Nomo	2.50	.75
12 Roberto Alomar	2.50	.75
13 Todd Hollandsworth	1.00	.30
14 Mark McGwire	6.00	1.80
15 Rafael Palmeiro	1.50	.45
16 Will Clark	2.50	.75
17 Cal Ripken	8.00	2.40
18 Derek Bell	1.00	.30
19 Gary Sheffield	1.00	.30
20 Juan Gonzalez	2.50	.75
21 Garret Anderson	1.00	.30
22 Mo Vaughn	1.00	.30
23 Robin Ventura	1.00	.30
24 Carlos Baerga	1.00	.30
25 Tim Salmon	1.50	.45
26 Matt Williams	1.00	.30
27 Fred McGriff	1.50	.45
28 Rondell White	1.00	.30
29 Ray Lankford	1.00	.30
30 Lenny Dykstra	1.00	.30
31 J.T. Snow	1.00	.30
32 Sammy Sosa	4.00	1.20
33 Chipper Jones	2.50	.75
34 Bobby Bonilla	1.00	.30
35 Paul Wilson	1.00	.30
36 Darren Daulton	1.00	.30
37 Larry Walker	1.50	.45
38 Raul Mondesi	1.00	.30
39 Jeff Bagwell	1.50	.45
40 Derek Jeter	6.00	1.80
41 Kirby Puckett	2.50	.75
42 Jason Isringhausen	1.00	.30
43 Vinny Castilla	1.00	.30
44 Jim Edmonds	1.00	.30
45 Ron Gant	1.00	.30
46 Carlos Delgado	1.00	.30
47 Jose Canseco	2.50	.75
48 Tony Gwynn	3.00	.90
49 Mike Mussina	2.50	.75
50 Charles Johnson	1.00	.30
51 Mike Piazza	4.00	1.20
52 Ken Griffey Jr.	4.00	1.20
53 Greg Maddux	4.00	1.20
54 Mark Grace	1.50	.45
55 Ryan Klesko	1.00	.30
56 Dennis Eckersley	1.50	.45
57 Rickey Henderson	2.50	.75
58 Michael Tucker	1.00	.30
59 Joe Carter	1.00	.30
60 Randy Johnson	2.50	.75
61 Brian Jordan	1.00	.30
62 Shawn Green	1.00	.30
63 Roger Clemens	5.00	1.50
64 Andres Galarraga	1.00	.30
65 Johnny Damon	1.00	.30
66 Ryne Sandberg	4.00	1.20
67 Alan Benes	1.00	.30
68 Albert Belle	1.00	.30
69 Barry Larkin	2.50	.75
70 Marty Cordova	1.00	.30
71 Dante Bichette	1.00	.30
72 Craig Biggio	1.50	.45
73 Reggie Sanders	1.00	.30
74 Moises Alou	1.00	.30
75 Chuck Knoblauch	1.00	.30
76 Cecil Fielder	1.00	.30
77 Manny Ramirez	1.00	.30

1996 Leaf Preferred Steel Gold Promos

One of 77 different Leaf Preferred Steel Gold Promo cards was inserted into 1996 Leaf Preferred dealer order forms and hobby media press releases. The cards parallel the standard Steel Gold inserts except for the text "promotional card" running diagonally across the back of the card.

	Nm-Mt	Ex-Mt
COMPLETE SET (77)	250.00	75.00
1 Frank Thomas	4.00	1.20
2 Paul Molitor	4.00	1.20
3 Kenny Lofton	2.00	.60
4 Travis Fryman	1.50	.45
5 Jeff Conine	1.00	.30
6 Barry Bonds	8.00	2.40
7 Gregg Jefferies	1.00	.30
8 Alex Rodriguez	10.00	3.00
9 Wade Boggs	5.00	1.50
10 David Justice	3.00	.90
11 Hideo Nomo	8.00	2.40
12 Roberto Alomar	3.00	.90
13 Todd Hollandsworth	1.00	.30
14 Mark McGwire	12.00	3.60
15 Rafael Palmeiro	3.00	.90
16 Will Clark	3.00	.90
17 Cal Ripken	15.00	4.50
18 Derek Bell	1.00	.30
19 Gary Sheffield	4.00	1.20
20 Juan Gonzalez	4.00	1.20
21 Garret Anderson	1.50	.45
22 Mo Vaughn	1.50	.45
23 Robin Ventura	3.00	.90
24 Carlos Baerga	1.00	.30
25 Tim Salmon	2.00	.60
26 Matt Williams	2.00	.60
27 Fred McGriff	2.00	.60
28 Rondell White	1.50	.45
29 Ray Lankford	1.00	.30
30 Lenny Dykstra	1.50	.45
31 J.T. Snow	1.50	.45
32 Sammy Sosa	8.00	2.40
33 Chipper Jones	8.00	2.40
34 Bobby Bonilla	1.00	.30
35 Paul Wilson	1.00	.30
36 Darren Daulton	1.50	.45
37 Larry Walker	1.50	.45
38 Raul Mondesi	3.00	.90
39 Jeff Bagwell	5.00	1.50
40 Derek Jeter	15.00	4.50
41 Kirby Puckett	4.00	1.20
42 Jason Isringhausen	1.50	.45
43 Vinny Castilla	1.50	.45
44 Jim Edmonds	3.00	.90
45 Ron Gant	1.00	.30
46 Carlos Delgado	3.00	.90
47 Jose Canseco	3.00	.90
48 Tony Gwynn	8.00	2.40
49 Mike Mussina	3.00	.90
50 Charles Johnson	1.00	.30
51 Mike Piazza	10.00	3.00
52 Ken Griffey Jr.	10.00	3.00
53 Greg Maddux	10.00	3.00
54 Mark Grace	3.00	.90
55 Ryan Klesko	1.50	.45
56 Dennis Eckersley	4.00	1.20
57 Rickey Henderson	6.00	1.80
58 Michael Tucker	1.00	.30
59 Joe Carter	1.50	.45
60 Randy Johnson	6.00	1.80
61 Brian Jordan	1.50	.45
62 Shawn Green	2.00	.60
63 Roger Clemens	8.00	2.40
64 Andres Galarraga	3.00	.90
65 Johnny Damon	2.00	.60
66 Ryne Sandberg	4.00	1.20
67 Alan Benes	1.00	.30
68 Albert Belle	1.50	.45
69 Barry Larkin	3.00	.90
70 Marty Cordova	1.00	.30
71 Dante Bichette	1.50	.45
72 Craig Biggio	3.00	.90
73 Reggie Sanders	1.00	.30
74 Moises Alou	1.50	.45
75 Chuck Knoblauch	1.50	.45
76 Cecil Fielder	1.50	.45
77 Manny Ramirez	5.00	1.50

1996 Leaf Preferred Steel Power

This eight-card set combines a micro-etched foil card with corner interior lightening-symbol diecutting and honors eight of the top power hitters. The fronts carry a color player photo while the backs display a statement explaining why the player is included in the set along with his 1995 season hitting statistics. Only 5,000 sets were produced, and each card carries a serial number.

	Nm-Mt	Ex-Mt
COMPLETE SET (8)	100.00	30.00
1 Albert Belle	4.00	1.20
2 Mo Vaughn	4.00	1.20
3 Ken Griffey Jr.	15.00	4.50
4 Cal Ripken	30.00	9.00
5 Mike Piazza	15.00	4.50
6 Barry Bonds	25.00	7.50
7 Jeff Bagwell	6.00	1.80
8 Frank Thomas	10.00	3.00

1998 Leaf Rookies and Stars

The 1998 Leaf Rookies and Stars set was issued in one series totalling 339 cards. The nine-card packs retailed for $2.99 each. The product was released very late in the year going live in December, 1998. This late release allowed for the inclusion of several rookies added to the 40 man roster at the end of the 1998 season. The set contains the topical

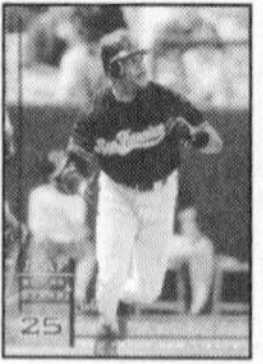
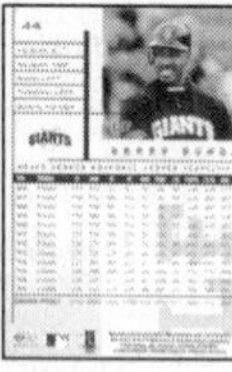

subsets: Power Tools (131-160), Team Line-Up (161-190), and Rookies (191-300). Cards 131-230 were shortprinted, being seeded at a rate of 1:2 packs. In addition, 39 cards were tacked on to the end of the set (301-339) just prior to release. These cards were seeded at noticeably shorter rates (approximately 1:8 packs) than other subsets. Several key Rookie Cards, including J.D. Drew, Troy Glaus, Gabe Kapler and Ruben Mateo appear within this run of "high series" cards. Though not confirmed by the manufacturer, it is believed that card number 317 Ryan Minor was printed in a lesser amount than the other cards in the high series. All card fronts feature full-bleed color action photos. The featured player's name lines the bottom of the card with his jersey number in the lower left corner. This product was originally created by Pinnacle in their final days as a card manufacturer. After Playoff went out of business, Playoff paid for the right to distribute this product and release it late in 1998 as much of the product had already been created. Because of the especially strong selection of Rookie Cards and an large number of shortprints, this set endured to become one of the more popular and notable base brand issues of the late 1990's.

	Nm-Mt	Ex-Mt
COMPLETE SET (339)	300.00	90.00
COMP.SET w/o SP's (200)	25.00	7.50
COMMON (1-130/231-300)	.30	.09
COMMON (131-190)	1.00	.30
COMMON (191-230)	2.00	.60
COMMON RC (191-230)	2.50	.75
COMMON (301-339)	2.50	.75
COMMON RC (301-339)	4.00	1.20
2 Roberto Alomar	.75	.23
3 Randy Johnson	.75	.23
4 Manny Ramirez	.30	.09
5 Paul Molitor	.50	.15
6 Mike Mussina	.75	.23
7 Jim Thome	.75	.23
8 Tino Martinez	.50	.15
9 Gary Sheffield	.30	.09
10 Chuck Knoblauch	.30	.09
11 Bernie Williams	.50	.15
12 Tim Salmon	.50	.15
13 Sammy Sosa	1.25	.35
14 Wade Boggs	.50	.15
15 Andres Galarraga	.30	.09
16 Pedro Martinez	.75	.23
17 David Justice	.30	.09
18 Chan Ho Park	.30	.09
19 Jay Buhner	.30	.09
20 Ryan Klesko	.30	.09
21 Barry Larkin	.75	.23
22 Will Clark	.75	.23
23 Raul Mondesi	.30	.09
24 Rickey Henderson	.75	.23
25 Jim Edmonds	.30	.09
26 Ken Griffey Jr.	1.25	.35
27 Frank Thomas	.75	.23
28 Cal Ripken	2.50	.75
29 Alex Rodriguez	1.25	.35
30 Mike Piazza	1.25	.35
31 Greg Maddux	1.25	.35
32 Chipper Jones	.75	.23
33 Tony Gwynn	1.00	.30
34 Derek Jeter	2.00	.60
35 Jeff Bagwell	.50	.15
36 Juan Gonzalez	.75	.23
37 Nomar Garciaparra	1.25	.35
38 Andruw Jones	.30	.09
39 Hideo Nomo	.75	.23
40 Roger Clemens	1.50	.45
41 Mark McGwire	2.00	.60
42 Scott Rolen	.50	.15
43 Vladimir Guerrero	.75	.23
44 Barry Bonds	2.00	.60
45 Darin Erstad	.30	.09
46 Albert Belle	.30	.09
47 Kenny Lofton	.30	.09
48 Mo Vaughn	.30	.09
49 Ivan Rodriguez	.75	.23
50 Jose Cruz Jr.	.30	.09
51 Tony Clark	.30	.09
52 Larry Walker	.50	.15
53 Mark Grace	.50	.15
54 Edgar Martinez	.50	.15
55 Fred McGriff	.50	.15
56 Rafael Palmeiro	.50	.15
57 Matt Williams	.30	.09
58 Craig Biggio	.50	.15
59 Ken Caminiti	.30	.09
60 Jose Canseco	.75	.23
61 Brady Anderson	.30	.09
62 Moises Alou	.30	.09
63 Justin Thompson	.30	.09
64 John Smoltz	.50	.15
65 Carlos Delgado	.30	.09
66 J.T. Snow	.30	.09
67 Jason Giambi	.75	.23
68 Garret Anderson	.30	.09
69 Rondell White	.30	.09
70 Eric Karros	.30	.09
71 Javier Lopez	.30	.09
72 Pat Hentgen	.30	.09
73 Dante Bichette	.30	.09
74 Charles Johnson	.30	.09
75 Tom Glavine	.50	.15
76 Rusty Greer	.30	.09
77 Travis Fryman	.30	.09
78 Todd Hundley	.30	.09
79 Ray Lankford	.30	.09
80 Denny Neagle	.30	.09
81 Henry Rodriguez	.30	.09
82 Sandy Alomar Jr.	.30	.09
83 Robin Ventura	.30	.09
84 John Olerud	.30	.09
85 Omar Vizquel	.30	.09
86 Darren Dreifort	.30	.09
87 Kevin Brown	.30	.09
88 Curt Schilling	.50	.15
89 Francisco Cordova	.30	.09
90 Brad Radke	.30	.09
91 David Cone	.30	.09
92 Paul O'Neill	.50	.15
93 Vinny Castilla	.30	.09
94 Marquis Grissom	.30	.09
95 Brian L.Hunter	.30	.09
96 Kevin Appier	.30	.09
97 Bobby Bonilla	.30	.09
98 Eric Young	.30	.09
99 Jason Kendall	.30	.09
100 Shawn Green	.30	.09
101 Edgardo Alfonzo	.30	.09
102 Alan Benes	.30	.09
103 Bobby Higginson	.30	.09
104 Todd Greene	.30	.09
105 Jose Guillen	.30	.09
106 Neifi Perez	.30	.09
107 Edgar Renteria	.30	.09
108 Chris Stynes	.30	.09
109 Todd Walker	.30	.09
110 Brian Jordan	.30	.09
111 Joe Carter	.30	.09
112 Ellis Burks	.30	.09
113 Brett Tomko	.30	.09
114 Mike Cameron	.30	.09
115 Shannon Stewart	.30	.09
116 Kevin Orie	.30	.09
117 Brian Giles	.30	.09
118 Hideki Irabu	.30	.09
119 Delino DeShields	.30	.09
120 David Segui	.30	.09
121 Dustin Hermanson	.30	.09
122 Kevin Young	.30	.09
123 Jay Bell	.30	.09
124 Doug Glanville	.30	.09
125 John Roskos RC	.30	.09
126 Damon Hollins	.30	.09
127 Matt Stairs	.30	.09
128 Cliff Floyd	.30	.09
129 Derek Bell	.30	.09
130 Darryl Strawberry	.50	.15
131 Ken Griffey Jr. PT SP	4.00	1.20
132 Tim Salmon PT SP	1.50	.45
133 M.Ramirez PT SP	1.00	.30
134 Paul Konerko PT SP	1.00	.30
135 Frank Thomas PT SP	2.50	.75
136 Todd Helton PT SP	1.50	.45
137 Larry Walker PT SP	1.50	.45
138 Mo Vaughn PT SP	1.00	.30
139 Travis Lee PT SP	1.00	.30
140 Ivan Rodriguez PT SP	2.50	.75
141 Ben Grieve PT SP	1.00	.30
142 Brad Fullmer PT SP	1.00	.30
143 Alex Rodriguez PT SP	4.00	1.20
144 Mike Piazza PT SP	4.00	1.20
145 Greg Maddux PT SP	4.00	1.20
146 Chipper Jones PT SP	2.50	.75
147 Kenny Lofton PT SP	1.00	.30
148 Albert Belle PT SP	1.00	.30
149 Barry Bonds PT SP	6.00	1.80
150 V.Guerrero PT SP	2.50	.75
151 Tony Gwynn PT SP	3.00	.90
152 Derek Jeter PT SP	6.00	1.80
153 Jeff Bagwell PT SP	1.50	.45
154 Juan Gonzalez PT SP	2.50	.75
155 N.Garciaparra PT SP	4.00	1.20
156 Andruw Jones PT SP	1.00	.30
157 Hideo Nomo PT SP	2.50	.75
158 Roger Clemens PT SP	5.00	1.50
159 Mark McGwire PT SP	6.00	1.80
160 Scott Rolen PT SP	1.50	.45
161 Travis Lee TLU SP	1.00	.30
162 Ben Grieve TLU SP	1.00	.30
163 Jose Guillen TLU SP	1.00	.30
164 Mike Piazza TLU SP	4.00	1.20
165 Kevin Appier TLU SP	1.00	.30
166 M.Grissom TLU SP	1.00	.30
167 Rusty Greer TLU SP	1.00	.30
168 Ken Caminiti TLU SP	1.00	.30
169 Craig Biggio TLU SP	1.50	.45
170 K.Griffey Jr. TLU SP	4.00	1.20
171 Larry Walker TLU SP	1.50	.45
172 Barry Larkin TLU SP	2.50	.75
173 A.Galarraga TLU SP	1.00	.30
174 Wade Boggs TLU SP	1.50	.45
175 Sammy Sosa TLU SP	4.00	1.20
176 T.Dunwoody TLU SP	1.00	.30
177 Jim Thome TLU SP	2.50	.75
178 Paul Molitor TLU SP	1.50	.45
179 Tony Clark TLU SP	1.00	.30
180 Jose Cruz Jr. TLU SP	1.00	.30
181 Darin Erstad TLU SP	1.00	.30
182 Barry Bonds TLU SP	6.00	1.80
183 Vlad.Guerrero TLU SP	2.50	.75
184 Scott Rolen TLU SP	1.50	.45
185 M.McGwire TLU SP	6.00	1.80
186 N.Garciaparra TLU SP	4.00	1.20
187 Gary Sheffield TLU SP	1.00	.30
188 Cal Ripken TLU SP	8.00	2.40
189 F.Thomas TLU SP	2.50	.75
190 Andy Pettitte TLU SP	1.50	.45
191 Paul Konerko SP	2.00	.60
192 Todd Helton SP	3.00	.90
193 Mark Kotsay SP	2.00	.60
194 Brad Fullmer SP	2.00	.60
195 K.Millwood SP RC	15.00	4.50
196 David Ortiz SP	2.00	.60
197 Kerry Wood SP	5.00	1.50
198 Miguel Tejada SP	3.00	.90
199 Fernando Tatis SP	2.00	.60
200 Jaret Wright SP	2.00	.60
201 Ben Grieve SP	2.00	.60
202 Travis Lee SP	2.00	.60
203 Wes Helms SP	2.00	.60
204 Geoff Jenkins SP	10.00	3.00
205 Russell Branyan SP	2.00	.60
206 Esteban Yan SP RC	4.00	1.20
207 Ben Ford SP RC	2.50	.75
208 Rich Butler SP RC	2.50	.75
209 Ryan Jackson SP RC	2.50	.75
210 A.J. Hinch SP	2.00	.60
211 M.Ordonez SP RC	40.00	12.00
212 Dave Dellucci SP RC	2.50	.75
213 Billy McMillon SP	2.00	.60
214 Mike Lowell SP RC	15.00	4.50
215 Todd Erdos SP RC	2.50	.75
216 C.Mendoza SP RC	2.50	.75
217 F.Catalanotto SP RC	6.00	1.80
218 Julio Ramirez SP RC	4.00	1.20
219 John Halama SP RC	4.00	1.20
220 Wilson Delgado SP	2.00	.60
221 Mike Judd SP RC	4.00	1.20
222 Rolando Arrojo SP RC	4.00	1.20
223 Jason LaRue SP RC	4.00	1.20
224 Manny Aybar SP RC	4.00	1.20
225 Jorge Velandia SP	2.00	.60
226 Mike Kinkade SP RC	4.00	1.20
227 Carlos Lee SP RC	12.00	3.60
228 Bobby Hughes SP	2.00	.60
229 R.Christenson SP RC	2.50	.75
230 Masato Yoshii SP RC	6.00	1.80
231 Richard Hidalgo	.30	.09
232 Rafael Medina	.30	.09
233 Damian Jackson	.30	.09
234 Derek Lowe	.30	.09
235 Mario Valdez	.30	.09
236 Eli Marrero	.30	.09
237 Juan Encarnacion	.30	.09
238 Livan Hernandez	.30	.09
239 Bruce Chen	.30	.09
240 Eric Milton	.30	.09
241 Jason Varitek	.30	.09
242 Scott Elarton	.30	.09
243 Manuel Barrios RC	.30	.09
244 Mike Caruso	.30	.09
245 Tom Evans	.30	.09
246 Pat Cline	.30	.09
247 Matt Clement	.30	.09
248 Karim Garcia	.30	.09
249 Richie Sexson	.30	.09
250 Sidney Ponson	.30	.09
251 Randall Simon	.30	.09
252 Tony Saunders	.30	.09
253 Javier Valentin	.30	.09
254 Danny Clyburn	.30	.09
255 Michael Coleman	.30	.09
256 Hanley Frias RC	.30	.09
257 Miguel Cairo	.30	.09
258 Rob Stanifer RC	.30	.09
259 Lou Collier	.30	.09
260 Abraham Nunez	.30	.09
261 Ricky Ledee	.50	.15
262 Carl Pavano	.30	.09
263 Derrek Lee	.30	.09
264 Jeff Abbott	.30	.09
265 Bob Abreu	.30	.09
266 Bartolo Colon	.30	.09
267 Mike Drumright	.30	.09
268 Daryle Ward	.30	.09
269 Gabe Alvarez	.30	.09
270 Josh Booty	.30	.09
271 Damian Moss	.30	.09
272 Brian Rose	.30	.09
273 Jarrod Washburn	.30	.09
274 Bobby Estalella	.30	.09
275 Enrique Wilson	.30	.09
276 Derrick Gibson	.30	.09
277 Ken Cloude	.30	.09
278 Kevin Witt	.30	.09
279 Donnie Sadler	.30	.09
280 Sean Casey	.30	.09
281 Jacob Cruz	.30	.09
282 Ron Wright	.30	.09
283 Jeremi Gonzalez	.30	.09
284 Desi Relaford	.30	.09
285 Bobby Smith	.30	.09
286 Javier Vazquez	.30	.09
287 Steve Woodard	.30	.09
288 Greg Norton	.30	.09
289 Cliff Politte	.30	.09
290 Felix Heredia	.30	.09
291 Braden Looper	.30	.09
292 Felix Martinez	.30	.09
293 Brian Meadows	.30	.09
294 Edwin Diaz	.30	.09
295 Pat Watkins	.30	.09
296 Marc Pisciotta RC	.30	.09
297 Rick Gorecki	.30	.09
298 DaRond Stovall	.30	.09
299 Andy Larkin	.30	.09
300 Felix Rodriguez	.30	.09
301 Blake Stein SP	2.50	.75
302 John Rocker SP RC	6.00	1.80
303 J.Baughman SP RC	4.00	1.20
304 Jesus Sanchez SP RC	6.00	1.80
305 Randy Winn SP	2.50	.75
306 Lou Merloni SP	2.50	.75
307 Jim Parque SP RC	6.00	1.80
308 Dennis Reyes SP	2.50	.75
309 O.Hernandez SP RC	15.00	4.50
310 Jason Johnson SP	2.50	.75
311 Torii Hunter SP	2.50	.75
312 M.Piazza Marlins SP	10.00	3.00
313 Mike Frank SP RC	4.00	1.20
314 Troy Glaus SP RC	120.00	36.00
315 Jin Ho Cho SP RC	6.00	1.80
316 Ruben Mateo SP RC	6.00	1.80
317 Ryan Minor SP RC	6.00	1.80
318 Aramis Ramirez SP	2.50	.75
319 Adrian Beltre SP	2.50	.75
320 Matt Anderson SP RC	6.00	1.80
321 Gabe Kapler SP RC	10.00	3.00
322 Jeremy Giambi SP RC	6.00	1.80
323 Carlos Beltran SP	2.50	.75
324 Dermal Brown SP	2.50	.75
325 Ben Davis SP	2.50	.75
326 Eric Chavez SP	4.00	1.20
327 Bobby Howry SP RC	6.00	1.80
328 Roy Halladay SP	2.50	.75
329 George Lombard SP	2.50	.75
330 Michael Barrett SP	2.50	.75
331 F. Seguignol SP RC	4.00	1.20
332 J.D. Drew SP RC	50.00	15.00
333 Odalis Perez SP RC	10.00	3.00
334 Alex Cora SP RC	6.00	1.80
335 P.Polanco SP RC	6.00	1.80
336 Armando Rios SP RC	6.00	1.80
337 Sammy Sosa HR SP	10.00	3.00
338 Mark McGwire HR SP	15.00	4.50
339 Sammy Sosa Mark McGwire CL SP	12.00	3.60

1998 Leaf Rookies and Stars Longevity

Randomly inserted in packs, this 339-card set is a parallel to the Leaf Rookies and Stars base set. The set is serially numbered to 50 (although only 49 sets were actually produced because the first set - cards numbered "1/50" were given a holographic foil coating) and printed on foil board with foil stamping.

Nm-Mt Ex-Mt
*STARS 1-130/231-300: 15X TO 40X BASIC
*ROOKIES 1-130/231-300: 20X TO 50X BASIC
*STARS 131-190: 3X TO 8X BASIC ....
*STARS 191-230: 3X TO 8X BASIC ....
*ROOKIES 191-230: 1.25X TO 3X BASIC
*STARS 301-339: 2.5X TO 6X BASIC .
*ROOKIES 301-339: 1X TO 2.5X BASIC

1998 Leaf Rookies and Stars True Blue

Randomly inserted in packs, this 339-card set is a parallel to the Leaf Rookies and Stars base set. Only 500 sets were printed (though the cards are not serial numbered - instead, they say "1 of 500" on back) and each card features blue foil stamping accents.

Nm-Mt Ex-Mt
*STARS 1-130/231-300: &&6X TO &&15X BASIC
*ROOKIES 1-130/231-300: 3X TO 8X BASIC CARDS
*LO SP STARS 131-190: 1X TO 2.5X BASIC
*LO SP STARS 191-230: 2X TO 5X BASIC
*ROOKIES 191-230: $$.5X TO $$1.2X BASIC
*STARS 301-339: .75X TO 2X BASIC .
*ROOKIES 301-339: .4X TO 1X BASIC

1998 Leaf Rookies and Stars Crosstraining

Randomly inserted in packs, this 10-card set is an insert to the Leaf Rookies and Stars brand. The set is sequentially numbered to 1000. The cards are printed on foil board. Each card front highlights a color action player photo surrounded by a crosstraining shoe sole design. The same player is highlighted on the back with information on his different skills.

	Nm-Mt	Ex-Mt
COMPLETE SET (10)	120.00	36.00
1 Kenny Lofton	4.00	1.20
2 Ken Griffey Jr.	15.00	4.50
3 Alex Rodriguez	15.00	4.50
4 Greg Maddux	15.00	4.50
5 Barry Bonds	25.00	7.50
6 Ivan Rodriguez	10.00	3.00
7 Chipper Jones	10.00	3.00
8 Jeff Bagwell	6.00	1.80
9 Nomar Garciaparra	15.00	4.50
10 Derek Jeter	25.00	7.50

1998 Leaf Rookies and Stars Crusade Update Green

Randomly inserted in packs, this 30-card set is an insert to the Leaf Rookies and Stars brand and was intended as an update to the 100 Crusade insert cards seeded in 1998 Donruss Update, 1998 Leaf and 1998 Donruss packs (thus the numbering 101-130). The set is sequentially numbered to 250. The fronts feature color action photos placed on a background of a Crusade shield design. The set features three parallel versions printed with a "Spectra-tech" holographic technology. First year serial-numbered cards of Kevin Millwood and Magglio Ordonez are featured in this set.

	Nm-Mt	Ex-Mt
COMPLETE SET (30)	300.00	90.00
101 Richard Hidalgo	15.00	4.50
102 Paul Konerko	15.00	4.50
103 Miguel Tejada	25.00	7.50
104 Fernando Tatis	10.00	3.00
105 Travis Lee	10.00	3.00
106 Wes Helms	10.00	3.00
107 Rich Butler	10.00	3.00
108 Mark Kotsay	10.00	3.00
109 Eli Marrero	10.00	3.00
110 David Ortiz	15.00	4.50
111 Juan Encarnacion	10.00	3.00
112 Jaret Wright	10.00	3.00
113 Livan Hernandez	10.00	3.00
114 Ron Wright	10.00	3.00
115 Ryan Christenson	10.00	3.00
116 Eric Milton	10.00	3.00
117 Brad Fullmer	10.00	3.00
118 Karim Garcia	10.00	3.00
119 Abraham Nunez	10.00	3.00
120 Ricky Ledee	10.00	3.00
121 Carl Pavano	10.00	3.00
122 Derrek Lee	15.00	4.50
123 A.J. Hinch	10.00	3.00
124 Brian Rose	10.00	3.00
125 Bobby Estalella	10.00	3.00
126 Kevin Millwood	25.00	7.50
127 Kerry Wood	25.00	7.50
128 Sean Casey	15.00	4.50
129 Russell Branyan	10.00	3.00
130 Magglio Ordonez	40.00	12.00

1998 Leaf Rookies and Stars Crusade Update Purple

Randomly inserted in packs, this 30-card set is a parallel to the Leaf Rookies and Stars Crusade Update set. The set is sequentially numbered to 100.

Nm-Mt Ex-Mt
*PURPLE: .75X TO 2X GREEN ....
*PURPLE: .75X TO 2X GREEN RC'S ...

1998 Leaf Rookies and Stars Extreme Measures

Randomly inserted in packs, this 10-card set is an insert to the Leaf Rookies and Stars brand. The cards are printed on foil board and sequentially numbered to 1000. However, a parallel version was created wherby a specific amount of each card was die cut to a featured statistic. The result, was varying print runs of the non-die cut cards. Specific print runs for each card are provided in our checklist after the player's name. Card fronts feature color action photos and highlights the featured player's extreme statistics.

	Nm-Mt	Ex-Mt
COMPLETE SET (10)	120.00	36.00
1 Ken Griffey Jr./944	15.00	4.50
2 Frank Thomas/653	10.00	3.00
3 Tony Gwynn/628	12.00	3.60
4 Mark McGwire/942	25.00	7.50
5 Larry Walker/280	6.00	1.80
6 Mike Piazza/960	15.00	4.50
7 Roger Clemens/708	20.00	6.00
8 Greg Maddux/980	15.00	4.50
9 Jeff Bagwell/873	6.00	1.80
10 Nomar Garciaparra/989	15.00	4.50

1998 Leaf Rookies and Stars Extreme Measures Die Cuts

Randomly inserted in packs, this 10-card set is a parallel to the Leaf Rookies and Stars Extreme Measures set. The set is sequentially numbered to 1000. The low serial numbered cards are die-cut to showcase a specific statistic for each player. For example, Ken Griffey hit 56 home runs last year, so the 1st 56 of his cards are die-cut and cards serial numbered from 57 through 1000 are not.

	Nm-Mt	Ex-Mt
1 Ken Griffey Jr./56	50.00	15.00
2 Frank Thomas/347	15.00	4.50
3 Tony Gwynn/372	15.00	4.50
4 Mark McGwire/58	80.00	24.00
5 Larry Walker/720	10.00	3.00
6 Mike Piazza/40	50.00	15.00
7 Roger Clemens/292	25.00	7.50
8 Greg Maddux/20		
9 Jeff Bagwell/127	20.00	6.00
10 Nomar Garciaparra/11		

1998 Leaf Rookies and Stars Freshman Orientation Samples

To preview the late-released 1998 Leaf Rookies and Stars product, all dealer wholesale order forms contained one sample card from four different insert sets (Freshman Orientation, Great American Heroes. Major League Hard Drives and Standing Ovations). The samples each feature the large "SAMPLE" text printed diagonally across the card back and a blank area intended for serial numbering on back. Apparently, MLB disallowed Donruss/Leaf the rights to use the word "chase" in a product name, fearing it insinuated aspects of gambling. However, the name was officially changed after Playoff took over Pinnacle's bankruptcy assets.

	Nm-Mt	Ex-Mt
COMPLETE SET (20)	40.00	12.00
1 Todd Helton	5.00	1.50
2 Ben Grieve	2.00	.60
3 Travis Lee	1.00	.30
4 Paul Konerko	3.00	.90
5 Jaret Wright	1.00	.30
6 Livan Hernandez	1.00	.30
7 Brad Fullmer	2.00	.60
8 Carl Pavano	1.00	.30
9 Richard Hidalgo	2.00	.60
10 Miguel Tejada	4.00	1.20
11 Mark Kotsay	1.00	.30
12 David Ortiz	2.00	.60
13 Juan Encarnacion	2.00	.60
14 Fernando Tatis	2.00	.60
15 Kevin Millwood	4.00	1.20
16 Kerry Wood	4.00	1.20
17 Magglio Ordonez	10.00	3.00
18 Derrek Lee	2.00	.60
19 Jose Cruz Jr.	2.50	.75
20 A.J. Hinch	1.00	.30

1998 Leaf Rookies and Stars Freshman Orientation

Randomly inserted in packs, this 20-card set is an insert to the Leaf Rookies and Stars brand. The set is sequentially numbered to 5000 and printed with holographic foil. The fronts feature color photos of the top up and coming stars in the game today surrounded by a background of banners and baseballs. The backs highlight the date of the featured player's Major League debut.

	Nm-Mt	Ex-Mt
COMPLETE SET (20)	25.00	7.50
1 Todd Helton	2.00	.60
2 Ben Grieve	1.00	.30
3 Travis Lee	1.00	.30
4 Paul Konerko	1.50	.45
5 Jaret Wright	1.00	.30
6 Livan Hernandez	1.00	.30
7 Brad Fullmer	1.00	.30
8 Carl Pavano	1.00	.30
9 Richard Hidalgo	1.50	.45
10 Miguel Tejada	2.00	.60
11 Mark Kotsay	1.00	.30
12 David Ortiz	1.50	.45
13 Juan Encarnacion	1.00	.30
14 Fernando Tatis	1.00	.30
15 Kevin Millwood	5.00	1.50
16 Kerry Wood	3.00	.90
17 Magglio Ordonez	5.00	1.50
18 Derrek Lee	1.50	.45
19 Jose Cruz Jr.	1.50	.45
20 A.J. Hinch	1.00	.30

1998 Leaf Rookies and Stars Great American Heroes Samples

To preview the late-released 1998 Leaf Rookies and Stars product, all dealer wholesale order forms contained one sample card from four different insert sets (Freshman Orientation, Great American Heroes. Major League Hard Drives and Standing Ovations). The samples each feature the large "SAMPLE" text printed diagonally across the card back and a blank area intended for serial numbering on back. Apparently, MLB disallowed Donruss/Leaf the rights to use the word "chase" in a product name, fearing it insinuated aspects of gambling. However, the name was officially changed after Playoff took over Pinnacle's bankruptcy assets.

	Nm-Mt	Ex-Mt
COMPLETE SET (20)	80.00	24.00
1 Frank Thomas	3.00	.90
2 Cal Ripken	10.00	3.00
3 Ken Griffey Jr.	6.00	1.80
4 Alex Rodriguez	6.00	1.80
5 Greg Maddux	5.00	1.50
6 Mike Piazza	6.00	1.80
7 Chipper Jones	5.00	1.50
8 Tony Gwynn	4.00	1.20
9 Jeff Bagwell	2.50	.75
10 Juan Gonzalez	2.50	.75
11 Hideo Nomo	5.00	1.50
12 Roger Clemens	5.00	1.50
13 Mark McGwire	8.00	2.40
14 Barry Bonds	5.00	1.50
15 Kenny Lofton	1.50	.45
16 Larry Walker	1.00	.30
17 Paul Molitor	2.50	.75
18 Wade Boggs	2.50	.75
19 Barry Larkin	2.00	.60
20 Andres Galarraga	1.50	.45

1998 Leaf Rookies and Stars Great American Heroes

Randomly inserted in packs, this 20-card set is an insert to the Leaf Rookies and Stars brand. The set is sequentially numbered to 2500 and stamped with holographic foil. The fronts feature color player photos placed in an open star with "Great American Heroes" written in the upper right corner. In remembrance of his turbulent 1998 season, Mike Piazza is featured on three different versions (pictured separately as a Dodger, Marlin and Met).

	Nm-Mt	Ex-Mt
COMPLETE SET (20)	150.00	45.00
1 Frank Thomas	6.00	1.80
2 Cal Ripken	20.00	6.00
3 Ken Griffey Jr.	10.00	3.00
4 Alex Rodriguez	10.00	3.00
5 Greg Maddux	10.00	3.00
6 Mike Piazza Dodgers	10.00	3.00
6B Mike Piazza Marlins	10.00	3.00
6C Mike Piazza Mets	10.00	3.00
7 Chipper Jones	6.00	1.80
8 Tony Gwynn	8.00	2.40
9 Jeff Bagwell	4.00	1.20
10 Juan Gonzalez	6.00	1.80
11 Hideo Nomo	6.00	1.80
12 Roger Clemens	12.00	3.60
13 Mark McGwire	15.00	4.50
14 Barry Bonds	15.00	4.50
15 Kenny Lofton	2.50	.75
16 Larry Walker	4.00	1.20
17 Paul Molitor	4.00	1.20
18 Wade Boggs	4.00	1.20
19 Barry Larkin	6.00	1.80
20 Andres Galarraga	2.50	.75

1998 Leaf Rookies and Stars Greatest Hits

Randomly inserted in packs, this 20-card set features color photos of the season's great rookies as well as stars of the game. The backs carry player information. Only 2500 serially numbered sets were produced.

	Nm-Mt	Ex-Mt
COMPLETE SET (20)	120.00	36.00
1 Ken Griffey Jr.	10.00	3.00
2 Frank Thomas	6.00	1.80
3 Cal Ripken	20.00	6.00
4 Alex Rodriguez	10.00	3.00
5 Ben Grieve	6.00	1.80
6 Mike Piazza	10.00	3.00
7 Chipper Jones	6.00	1.80
8 Tony Gwynn	8.00	2.40
9 Derek Jeter	15.00	4.50
10 Jeff Bagwell	4.00	1.20
11 Tino Martinez	4.00	1.20
12 Juan Gonzalez	6.00	1.80
13 Nomar Garciaparra	10.00	3.00
14 Mark McGwire	15.00	4.50
15 Scott Rolen	4.00	1.20
16 David Justice	2.50	.75
17 Darin Erstad	2.50	.75
18 Mo Vaughn	2.50	.75
19 Ivan Rodriguez	6.00	1.80
20 Travis Lee	4.00	1.20

1998 Leaf Rookies and Stars Home Run Derby

Randomly inserted in packs, this 20-card set is an insert to the Leaf Rookies and Stars brand. The set is sequentially numbered to 2500 and printed on foil board. The card fronts feature color player photos of today's top homerun hitters surrounded by a nostalgic bordered background that takes a look at the TV show from the 50's with the same name.

	Nm-Mt	Ex-Mt
COMPLETE SET (20)	100.00	30.00
1 Tino Martinez	4.00	1.20
2 Jim Thome	6.00	1.80
3 Larry Walker	4.00	1.20
4 Tony Clark	2.50	.75
5 Jose Cruz Jr.	2.50	.75
6 Barry Bonds	15.00	4.50
7 Scott Rolen	4.00	1.20
8 Paul Konerko	2.50	.75
9 Travis Lee	2.50	.75
10 Todd Helton	6.00	1.80
11 Mark McGwire	15.00	4.50
12 Andruw Jones	2.50	.75
13 Nomar Garciaparra	10.00	3.00
14 Juan Gonzalez	6.00	1.80
15 Jeff Bagwell	4.00	1.20
16 Chipper Jones	6.00	1.80
17 Mike Piazza	10.00	3.00
18 Frank Thomas	6.00	1.80
19 Ken Griffey Jr.	10.00	3.00
20 Albert Belle	2.50	.75

1998 Leaf Rookies and Stars Leaf MVP's

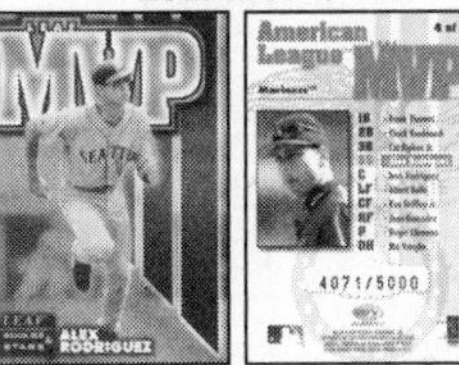

Randomly inserted in packs, this 20-card set is an insert to the Leaf Rookies and Stars brand. Each card is printed on foil board, with a red background and sequentially numbered to 5000 - although the first 500 of each card was die cut for a parallel set. Thus, only cards serial numbered from 501 through 5000 are featured in this set. The fronts feature color action photos on top of an "MVP" logo in the background.

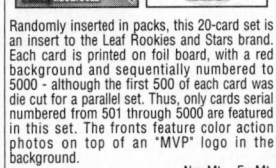

	Nm-Mt	Ex-Mt
COMPLETE SET (20)	80.00	24.00
*PENNANT ED: 1.5X TO 4X BASIC LEAF MVP		
PENNANT ED.1ST 500 SERIAL #'d SETS		
RANDOM INSERTS IN PACKS		
1 Frank Thomas	4.00	1.20
2 Chuck Knoblauch	1.50	.45
3 Cal Ripken	12.00	3.60
4 Alex Rodriguez	6.00	1.80
5 Ivan Rodriguez	4.00	1.20
6 Albert Belle	1.50	.45
7 Ken Griffey Jr.	6.00	1.80
8 Juan Gonzalez	4.00	1.20
9 Roger Clemens	8.00	2.40
10 Mo Vaughn	1.50	.45
11 Jeff Bagwell	2.50	.75
12 Craig Biggio	2.50	.75
13 Chipper Jones	4.00	1.20
14 Barry Larkin	4.00	1.20
15 Mike Piazza	6.00	1.80
16 Barry Bonds	10.00	3.00
17 Andruw Jones	1.50	.45
18 Tony Gwynn	5.00	1.50
19 Greg Maddux	6.00	1.80
20 Mark McGwire	10.00	3.00

1998 Leaf Rookies and Stars Major League Hard Drives Samples

To preview the late-released 1998 Leaf Rookies and Stars product, all dealer wholesale order forms contained one sample card from four different insert sets (Freshman Orientation, Great American Heroes. Major League Hard Drives and Standing Ovations). The samples each feature the large "SAMPLE" text printed diagonally across the card back and a blank area intended for serial numbering on back. Apparently, MLB disallowed Donruss/Leaf the rights to use the word "chase" in a product name, fearing it insinuated aspects of gambling. However, the name was officially changed after Playoff took over Pinnacle's bankruptcy assets.

	Nm-Mt	Ex-Mt
COMPLETE SET (20)	60.00	18.00
1 Jeff Bagwell	2.50	.75
2 Juan Gonzalez	2.50	.75
3 Nomar Garciaparra	6.00	1.80
4 Ken Griffey Jr.	6.00	1.80
5 Frank Thomas	3.00	.90
6 Cal Ripken	10.00	3.00
7 Alex Rodriguez	6.00	1.80
8 Mike Piazza	6.00	1.80
9 Chipper Jones	5.00	1.50
10 Tony Gwynn	4.00	1.20
11 Derek Jeter	10.00	3.00
12 Mo Vaughn	1.00	.30
13 Ben Grieve	1.00	.30
14 Manny Ramirez	2.50	.75
15 Vladimir Guerrero	3.00	.90
16 Scott Rolen	2.00	.60
17 Darin Erstad	2.00	.60
18 Kenny Lofton	1.50	.45
19 Brad Fullmer	1.00	.30
20 David Justice	1.50	.45

1998 Leaf Rookies and Stars Major League Hard Drives

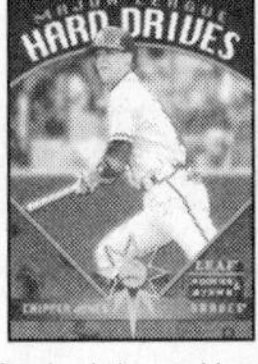
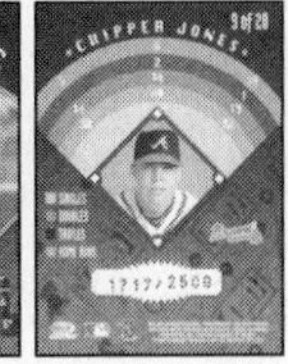

Randomly inserted in packs, this 20-card set is an insert to the Leaf Rookies and Stars brand. The set is printed with holographic foil stamping and sequentially numbered to 2500. The fronts feature color action photos of some of today's hottest hitting machines placed in a baseball diamond background. In remembrance of his turbulent 1998 season, Mike Piazza is featured on three different versions (pictured separately as a Dodger, Marlin and Met). All three versions of the Piazza card had 2500 cards printed.

	Nm-Mt	Ex-Mt
COMPLETE SET (20)	150.00	45.00
1 Jeff Bagwell	4.00	1.20
2 Juan Gonzalez	6.00	1.80
3 Nomar Garciaparra	10.00	3.00
4 Ken Griffey Jr.	10.00	3.00
5 Frank Thomas	6.00	1.80
6 Cal Ripken	20.00	6.00
7 Alex Rodriguez	10.00	3.00
8 Mike Piazza Dodgers	10.00	3.00
8B Mike Piazza Marlins	10.00	3.00
8C Mike Piazza Mets	10.00	3.00
9 Chipper Jones	6.00	1.80
10 Tony Gwynn	8.00	2.40
11 Derek Jeter	15.00	4.50
12 Mo Vaughn	2.50	.75
13 Ben Grieve	6.00	1.80
14 Manny Ramirez	2.50	.75
15 Vladimir Guerrero	6.00	1.80
16 Scott Rolen	4.00	1.20
17 Darin Erstad	2.50	.75
18 Kenny Lofton	2.50	.75
19 Brad Fullmer	2.50	.75
20 David Justice	2.50	.75

1998 Leaf Rookies and Stars Standing Ovations Samples

To preview the late-released 1998 Leaf Rookies and Stars product, all dealer wholesale order forms contained one sample card from four different insert sets (Freshman Orientation, Great American Heroes. Major League Hard Drives and Standing Ovations). The samples each feature the large "SAMPLE" text printed diagonally across the card back and a blank area intended for serial numbering on back. Apparently, MLB disallowed Donruss/Leaf the rights to use the word "chase" in a product name, fearing it insinuated aspects of gambling. However, the name was officially changed after Playoff took over Pinnacle's bankruptcy assets.

	Nm-Mt	Ex-Mt
COMPLETE SET (10)	50.00	15.00
1 Barry Bonds	5.00	1.50
2 Mark McGwire	8.00	2.40
3 Ken Griffey Jr.	6.00	1.80
4 Frank Thomas	2.50	.75
5 Tony Gwynn	4.00	1.20
6 Cal Ripken	10.00	3.00
7 Greg Maddux	6.00	1.80
8 Roger Clemens	5.00	1.50
9 Paul Molitor	2.50	.75
10 Ivan Rodriguez	2.50	.75

1998 Leaf Rookies and Stars Standing Ovations

Randomly inserted in packs, this 10-card set is an insert to the Leaf Rookies and Stars brand set. The set is sequentially numbered to 5000 and printed with holographic foil stamping. The fronts feature full-bleed color photos. The featured player's ovation deserved accomplishments are found lining the bottom of the card along with his name and team.

	Nm-Mt	Ex-Mt
COMPLETE SET (10)	50.00	15.00
1 Barry Bonds	10.00	3.00
2 Mark McGwire	10.00	3.00
3 Ken Griffey Jr.	6.00	1.80
4 Frank Thomas	4.00	1.20
5 Tony Gwynn	5.00	1.50
6 Cal Ripken	12.00	3.60
7 Greg Maddux	6.00	1.80
8 Roger Clemens	8.00	2.40
9 Paul Molitor	2.50	.75
10 Ivan Rodriguez	4.00	1.20

1998 Leaf Rookies and Stars Ticket Masters

Randomly inserted in packs, this 20-card set is an insert to the Leaf Rookies and Stars base set. The set is sequentially numbered to 2500, but the first 250 cards were die cut for a parallel set. This double-sided set is printed on foil-board and features color photos of players from the same team.

	Nm-Mt	Ex-Mt
COMPLETE SET (20)	150.00	45.00
*DIE CUTS: 1.25X TO 3X BASIC TICKET		
DIE CUTS 1ST 250 SERIAL #'d SETS..		
RANDOM INSERTS IN PACKS		
1 Ken Griffey Jr. / Alex Rodriguez	12.00	3.60
2 Frank Thomas / Albert Belle	8.00	2.40
3 Cal Ripken / Roberto Alomar	25.00	7.50
4 Greg Maddux / Chipper Jones	12.00	3.60
5 Tony Gwynn / Ken Caminiti	10.00	3.00
6 Derek Jeter / Andy Pettitte	20.00	6.00
7 Jeff Bagwell / Craig Biggio	5.00	1.50
8 Juan Gonzalez / Ivan Rodriguez	8.00	2.40
9 Nomar Garciaparra / Mo Vaughn	12.00	3.60
10 Vladimir Guerrero / Brad Fullmer	8.00	2.40
11 Andruw Jones / Andres Galarraga	3.00	.90
12 Tino Martinez / Chuck Knoblauch	5.00	1.50
13 Raul Mondesi / Paul Konerko	3.00	.90
14 Roger Clemens / Jose Cruz Jr.	15.00	4.50
15 Mark McGwire / Brian Jordan	20.00	6.00
16 Kenny Lofton / Manny Ramirez	3.00	.90
17 Larry Walker / Todd Helton	5.00	1.50
18 Darin Erstad / Tim Salmon	3.00	.90
19 Travis Lee / Matt Williams	3.00	.90
20 Ben Grieve / Jason Giambi	8.00	2.40

2001 Leaf Rookies and Stars Samples

Inserted one per sealed Beckett Baseball Card Monthly issue number 202, these 100 cards feature veterans from the Leaf Rookies and Stars set. Each card has the word Sample stamped on the back.

	Nm-Mt	Ex-Mt
*SINGLES: 1.5X TO 4X BASIC CARDS		

2001 Leaf Rookies and Stars

This 300 card set was issued in five card packs. All cards numbered over 100 were shortprinted. Cards numbered 101-200 were inserted at a rate of one in four while cards numbered 201-300 were inserted at a rate of one in 24.

	Nm-Mt	Ex-Mt
COMP.SET w/o SP'S (100)	20.00	6.00
COMMON CARD (1-100)	.30	.09
COMMON (101-200)	3.00	.90
COMMON (201-300)	10.00	3.00
1 Alex Rodriguez	1.25	.35
2 Derek Jeter	2.00	.60
3 Aramis Ramirez	.30	.09
4 Cliff Floyd	.30	.09
5 Nomar Garciaparra	1.25	.35
6 Craig Biggio	.50	.15
7 Ivan Rodriguez	.75	.23
8 Cal Ripken	2.50	.75
9 Fred McGriff	.50	.15
10 Chipper Jones	.75	.23
11 Roberto Alomar	.75	.23
12 Moises Alou	.30	.09
13 Freddy Garcia	.30	.09
14 Bobby Abreu	.30	.09
15 Shawn Green	.30	.09
16 Jason Giambi	.75	.23
17 Todd Helton	.50	.15
18 Robert Fick	.30	.09
19 Tony Gwynn	1.00	.30
20 Luis Gonzalez	.30	.09
21 Sean Casey	.30	.09
22 Roger Clemens	1.50	.45
23 Brian Giles	.30	.09
24 Manny Ramirez	.30	.09
25 Barry Bonds	2.00	.60
26 Richard Hidalgo	.30	.09
27 Vladimir Guerrero	.75	.23
28 Kevin Brown UER Batting headers for stats	.30	.09
29 Mike Sweeney	.30	.09
30 Ken Griffey Jr.	1.25	.35
31 Mike Piazza	1.25	.35
32 Richie Sexson	.30	.09
33 Matt Morris	.30	.09
34 Jorge Posada	.50	.15
35 Eric Chavez	.30	.09
36 Mark Buehrle	.30	.09
37 Jeff Bagwell	.50	.15
38 Curt Schilling	.50	.15
39 Bartolo Colon	.30	.09
40 Mark Quinn	.30	.09
41 Tony Clark	.30	.09
42 Brad Radke	.30	.09
43 Gary Sheffield	.30	.09
44 Doug Mientkiewicz	.30	.09
45 Pedro Martinez	.75	.23
46 Carlos Lee	.30	.09
47 Troy Glaus	.50	.15
48 Preston Wilson	.30	.09
49 Phil Nevin	.30	.09
50 Chan Ho Park	.30	.09
51 Randy Johnson	.75	.23
52 Jermaine Dye	.30	.09
53 Terrence Long	.30	.09
54 Joe Mays	.30	.09
55 Scott Rolen	.50	.15
56 Miguel Tejada	.30	.09
57 Jim Thome	.75	.23
58 Jose Vidro	.30	.09
59 Gabe Kapler	.30	.09
60 Darin Erstad	.30	.09
61 Jim Edmonds	.30	.09
62 Jarrod Washburn	.30	.09
63 Tom Glavine	.50	.15
64 Adrian Beltre	.30	.09
65 Sammy Sosa	1.25	.35
66 Juan Gonzalez	.75	.23
67 Rafael Furcal	.30	.09
68 Mike Mussina	.75	.23
69 Mark McGwire	2.00	.60
70 Ryan Klesko	.30	.09
71 Raul Mondesi	.30	.09
72 Trot Nixon	.50	.15
73 Barry Larkin	.75	.23
74 Rafael Palmeiro	.50	.15
75 Mark Mulder	.30	.09
76 Carlos Delgado	.30	.09
77 Mike Hampton	.30	.09
78 Carl Everett	.30	.09
79 Paul Konerko	.30	.09
80 Larry Walker	.50	.15
81 Kerry Wood	.75	.23
82 Frank Thomas	.75	.23
83 Andruw Jones	.30	.09
84 Eric Milton	.30	.09
85 Ben Grieve	.30	.09
86 Carlos Beltran	.30	.09
87 Tim Hudson	.30	.09
88 Hideo Nomo	.75	.23
89 Greg Maddux	1.25	.35
90 Edgar Martinez	.50	.15
91 Lance Berkman	.30	.09
92 Pat Burrell	.30	.09
93 Jeff Kent	.30	.09
94 Magglio Ordonez	.30	.09
95 Cristian Guzman	.30	.09
96 Jose Canseco	.75	.23
97 J.D. Drew	.30	.09
98 Bernie Williams	.50	.15
99 Kazuhiro Sasaki	.30	.09
100 Rickey Henderson	.75	.23
101 Wilson Guzman RC	3.00	.90
102 Nick Neugebauer	3.00	.90
103 Lance Davis RC	3.00	.90
104 Felipe Lopez	3.00	.90
105 Toby Hall	3.00	.90
106 Jack Cust	3.00	.90
107 Jason Karnuth RC	3.00	.90
108 Bart Miadich RC	3.00	.90
109 Brian Roberts RC	3.00	.90
110 Brandon Larson RC	3.00	.90
111 Sean Douglass RC	3.00	.90
112 Joe Crede	3.00	.90
113 Tim Redding	3.00	.90
114 Adam Johnson	3.00	.90
115 Marcus Giles	3.00	.90
116 Jose Ortiz	3.00	.90
117 Jose Mieses RC	3.00	.90
118 Nick Maness RC	3.00	.90
119 Les Walrond RC	3.00	.90
120 Travis Phelps RC	3.00	.90
121 Troy Mattes RC	3.00	.90
122 Carlos Garcia RC	3.00	.90
123 Bill Ortega RC	3.00	.90
124 Gene Altman RC	3.00	.90
125 Nate Frese RC	3.00	.90
126 Alfonso Soriano	5.00	1.50
127 Jose Nunez RC	3.00	.90
128 Bob File RC	3.00	.90
129 Dan Wright	3.00	.90
130 Nick Johnson	3.00	.90
131 Brent Abernathy	3.00	.90
132 Steve Green RC	3.00	.90
133 Billy Sylvester RC	3.00	.90
134 Scott MacRae RC	3.00	.90
135 Kris Keller RC	3.00	.90
136 Scott Stewart RC	3.00	.90
137 Henry Mateo RC	3.00	.90
138 Timo Perez	3.00	.90
139 Nate Teut RC	3.00	.90
140 Jason Michaels RC	3.00	.90
141 Junior Spivey RC	5.00	1.50
142 Carlos Pena	3.00	.90
143 Wilmy Caceres RC	3.00	.90
144 David Lundquist	3.00	.90
145 Jack Wilson RC	3.00	.90
146 Jeremy Fikac RC	3.00	.90
147 Alex Escobar	3.00	.90
148 Abraham Nunez	3.00	.90
149 Xavier Nady	3.00	.90
150 Michael Cuddyer	3.00	.90
151 Greg Miller RC	3.00	.90
152 Eric Munson	3.00	.90
153 Aubrey Huff	3.00	.90
154 Tim Christman RC	3.00	.90
155 Erick Almonte RC	3.00	.90
156 Mike Penney RC	3.00	.90
157 Delvin James RC	3.00	.90
158 Ben Sheets	3.00	.90
159 Jason Hart	3.00	.90
160 Jose Acevedo RC	3.00	.90
161 Will Ohman RC	3.00	.90
162 Erik Hiljus RC	3.00	.90
163 Juan Moreno RC	3.00	.90
164 Mike Koplove RC	3.00	.90
165 Pedro Santana RC	3.00	.90
166 Jimmy Rollins	3.00	.90
167 Matt White RC	3.00	.90
168 Cesar Crespo RC	3.00	.90
169 Carlos Hernandez	3.00	.90
170 Chris George	3.00	.90
171 Brad Voyles RC	3.00	.90
172 Luis Pineda RC	3.00	.90
173 Carlos Zambrano RC	3.00	.90
174 Nate Cornejo	3.00	.90
175 Jason Smith RC	3.00	.90
176 Craig Monroe RC	3.00	.90
177 Cody Ransom RC	3.00	.90
178 John Grabow RC	3.00	.90
179 Pedro Feliz	3.00	.90
180 Jeremy Owens RC	3.00	.90
181 Kurt Ainsworth	3.00	.90
182 Luis Lopez	3.00	.90
183 Stubby Clapp RC	3.00	.90
184 Ryan Freel RC	3.00	.90
185 Duaner Sanchez RC	3.00	.90
186 Jason Jennings	3.00	.90
187 Kyle Lohse RC	5.00	1.50
188 Jerrod Riggan RC	3.00	.90
189 Joe Beimel RC	3.00	.90
190 Nick Punto RC	3.00	.90
191 Willie Harris RC	3.00	.90
192 Ryan Jensen RC	3.00	.90
193 Adam Pettyjohn RC	3.00	.90
194 Donaldo Mendez RC	3.00	.90
195 Bret Prinz RC	3.00	.90
196 Paul Phillips RC	3.00	.90
197 Brian Lawrence RC	3.00	.90
198 Cesar Izturis	3.00	.90
199 Blaine Neal RC	3.00	.90
200 Josh Fogg RC	10.00	3.00
201 Josh Towers RC	10.00	3.00
202 T.Spooneybarger RC	10.00	3.00
203 Michael Rivera RC	10.00	3.00
204 Juan Cruz RC	10.00	3.00
205 Albert Pujols RC	100.00	30.00
206 Josh Beckett	12.00	3.60
207 Roy Oswalt	12.00	3.60
208 Elpidio Guzman RC	10.00	3.00
209 Horacio Ramirez RC	12.00	3.60
210 Corey Patterson	10.00	3.00
211 Geronimo Gil RC	10.00	3.00
212 Jay Gibbons RC	15.00	4.50
213 O.Woodards RC	10.00	3.00
214 David Espinosa	10.00	3.00
215 Angel Berroa RC	20.00	6.00
216 B.Duckworth RC	10.00	3.00
217 Brian Reith RC	10.00	3.00
218 David Brous RC	10.00	3.00
219 Bud Smith RC	10.00	3.00
220 Ramon Vazquez RC	10.00	3.00
221 Mark Teixeira RC	50.00	15.00
222 Justin Atchley RC	10.00	3.00
223 Tony Cogan RC	10.00	3.00
224 Grant Balfour RC	10.00	3.00
225 Ricardo Rodriguez RC	10.00	3.00
226 Brian Rogers RC	10.00	3.00
227 Adam Dunn	10.00	3.00
228 Wilson Betemit RC	10.00	3.00
229 Juan Diaz RC	10.00	3.00
230 Jackson Melian RC	10.00	3.00
231 Claudio Vargas RC	10.00	3.00
232 Wilkin Ruan RC	10.00	3.00
233 J.Duchscherer RC	10.00	3.00
234 Kevin Olsen RC	10.00	3.00
235 Tony Fiore RC	10.00	3.00
236 Jeremy Affeldt RC	12.00	3.60
237 Mike Maroth RC	10.00	3.00
238 C.C. Sabathia	10.00	3.00
239 Cory Aldridge RC	10.00	3.00
240 Zach Day RC	12.00	3.60
241 Brett Jodie RC	10.00	3.00
242 Winston Abreu RC	10.00	3.00
243 Travis Hafner RC	15.00	4.50
244 Joe Kennedy RC	10.00	3.00
245 Rick Bauer RC	10.00	3.00
246 Mike Young	12.00	3.60
247 Ken Vining RC	10.00	3.00
248 Doug Nickle RC	10.00	3.00
249 Pablo Ozuna	10.00	3.00
250 Dustan Mohr RC	10.00	3.00
251 Ichiro Suzuki RC	60.00	18.00
252 Ryan Drese RC	10.00	3.00
253 Morgan Ensberg RC	15.00	4.50
254 George Perez RC	10.00	3.00
255 Roy Smith RC	10.00	3.00
256 Juan Uribe RC	10.00	3.00
257 Dewon Brazelton RC	12.00	3.60
258 Endy Chavez RC	10.00	3.00
259 Kris Foster	10.00	3.00
260 Eric Knott RC	10.00	3.00
261 Corky Miller RC	10.00	3.00
262 Larry Bigbie	10.00	3.00
263 Andres Torres RC	10.00	3.00
264 Adrian Hernandez RC	10.00	3.00
265 Johnny Estrada RC	12.00	3.60
266 David Williams RC	10.00	3.00
267 Steve Lomasney	10.00	3.00
268 Victor Zambrano RC	12.00	3.60
269 Keith Ginter	10.00	3.00
270 Casey Fossum RC	10.00	3.00
271 Josue Perez RC	10.00	3.00
272 Josh Phelps	10.00	3.00
273 Mark Prior RC	100.00	30.00
274 Brandon Berger RC	10.00	3.00
275 Scott Podsednik RC	30.00	9.00
276 Jorge Julio RC	10.00	3.00
277 Esix Snead RC	10.00	3.00
278 Brandon Knight RC	10.00	3.00
279 Saul Rivera RC	10.00	3.00
280 Benito Baez RC	10.00	3.00
281 Rob MacKowiak RC	10.00	3.00
282 Eric Hinske RC	12.00	3.60
283 Juan Rivera	10.00	3.00
284 Kevin Joseph RC	10.00	3.00
285 Juan A. Pena RC	10.00	3.00
286 Brandon Lyon RC	10.00	3.00
287 Adam Everett	10.00	3.00
288 Eric Valent	10.00	3.00
289 Ken Harvey	10.00	3.00
290 Bert Snow RC	10.00	3.00
291 Wily Mo Pena	10.00	3.00
292 Rafael Soriano RC	15.00	4.50
293 Carlos Valderrama RC	10.00	3.00
294 Christian Parker RC	10.00	3.00
295 Tsuyoshi Shinjo RC	15.00	4.50
296 Martin Vargas RC	10.00	3.00
297 Luke Hudson RC	10.00	3.00
298 Dee Brown	10.00	3.00
299 Alexis Gomez RC	10.00	3.00
300 Angel Santos RC	10.00	3.00

2001 Leaf Rookies and Stars Autographs

Randomly inserted in packs, these 76 cards feature signed cards of some of the prospects and rookies included in the Leaf Rookie and Stars set. According to Donruss/Playoff most players signed 250 cards for inclusion in this product. A few signed 100 cards so we have included that information in our checklist next to the player's name.

	Nm-Mt	Ex-Mt
107 Jason Karnuth	10.00	3.00
110 Brandon Larson/100	25.00	7.50
117 Jose Mieses	10.00	3.00
118 Nick Maness	10.00	3.00
119 Les Walrond	10.00	3.00
122 Carlos Garcia	10.00	3.00
123 Bill Ortega	10.00	3.00
124 Gene Altman	10.00	3.00
125 Nate Frese	10.00	3.00
130 Nick Johnson/100	25.00	7.50
133 Billy Sylvester	10.00	3.00
135 Kris Keller	10.00	3.00
139 Nate Teut	10.00	3.00
140 Jason Michaels	10.00	3.00
143 Wilmy Caceres	10.00	3.00
145 Jack Wilson/100	25.00	7.50
151 Greg Miller	10.00	3.00
155 Erick Almonte	10.00	3.00
156 Mike Penney	10.00	3.00
157 Delvin James	10.00	3.00
161 Will Ohman	10.00	3.00
167 Matt White	10.00	3.00
180 Jeremy Owens	10.00	3.00
184 Ryan Freel	10.00	3.00
185 Duaner Sanchez	10.00	3.00
193 Adam Pettyjohn/100	15.00	4.50
194 Donaldo Mendez/100	15.00	4.50
196 Paul Phillips	10.00	3.00
197 Brian Lawrence/100	25.00	7.50
199 Blaine Neal	10.00	3.00
201 Josh Towers/100	15.00	4.50
203 Michael Rivera	10.00	3.00
204 Juan Cruz/100	25.00	7.50
205 Albert Pujols SP		
207 Roy Oswalt SP		
208 Elpidio Guzman/100	15.00	4.50
209 Horacio Ramirez	25.00	7.50
210 Corey Patterson SP		
211 Geronimo Gil	10.00	3.00
212 Jay Gibbons/100	40.00	12.00
213 Orlando Woodards	10.00	3.00
215 Angel Berroa/100	50.00	15.00
216 B. Duckworth/100	25.00	7.50
218 David Brous	10.00	3.00
219 Bud Smith SP		
221 Mark Teixeira/100	200.00	60.00
223 Tony Cogan	10.00	3.00
225 Ricardo Rodriguez	10.00	3.00
226 Brian Rogers	10.00	3.00
227 Adam Dunn SP	50.00	15.00
228 Wilson Betemit/100	25.00	7.50
231 Claudio Vargas	10.00	3.00
232 Wilkin Ruan	10.00	3.00
234 Kevin Olsen	10.00	3.00
236 Jeremy Affeldt	25.00	7.50
237 Mike Maroth	10.00	3.00
238 C.C. Sabathia SP		
239 Cory Aldridge	10.00	3.00
240 Zach Day	15.00	4.50
243 Travis Hafner	40.00	12.00
244 Joe Kennedy/100	25.00	7.50
254 George Perez	10.00	3.00
256 Juan Uribe	10.00	3.00
257 Dewon Brazelton/100	40.00	12.00
261 Corky Miller/100	25.00	7.50
263 Andres Torres/100	15.00	4.50
265 Johnny Estrada/100	40.00	12.00
266 David Williams	10.00	3.00
270 Casey Fossum	10.00	3.00
273 Mark Prior/100	500.00	150.00
274 Brandon Berger	10.00	3.00
277 Esix Snead	10.00	3.00
282 Eric Hinske	25.00	7.50
292 Rafael Soriano	40.00	12.00
293 Carlos Valderrama	10.00	3.00
299 Alexis Gomez	10.00	3.00

2001 Leaf Rookies and Stars Longevity

Randomly inserted into packs, these cards parallel the Leaf Rookie and Stars set. Cards numbered 1-100 are serial numbered to 50 while cards numbered 101-300 are serial numbered to 25.

	Nm-Mt	Ex-Mt
*LONGEVITY: 1-100: 12.5X TO 30X BASIC CARDS		

2001 Leaf Rookies and Stars Dress for Success

Inserted one per 96 packs, these 25 cards feature two swatches of game-used memorabilia on each card.

	Nm-Mt	Ex-Mt
DFS-1 Cal Ripken	50.00	15.00
DFS-2 Mike Piazza	25.00	7.50
DFS-3 Barry Bonds	50.00	15.00
DFS-4 Frank Thomas	20.00	6.00
DFS-5 Nomar Garciaparra	30.00	9.00
DFS-6 Richie Sexson	15.00	4.50
DFS-7 Brian Giles	15.00	4.50
DFS-8 Todd Helton	20.00	6.00
DFS-9 Ivan Rodriguez	20.00	6.00
DFS-10 Andruw Jones	15.00	4.50
DFS-11 Juan Gonzalez	20.00	6.00
DFS-12 Vladimir Guerrero	20.00	6.00
DFS-13 Greg Maddux	25.00	7.50
DFS-14 Tony Gwynn	25.00	7.50
DFS-15 Randy Johnson	20.00	6.00
DFS-16 Jeff Bagwell	20.00	6.00
DFS-17 Kerry Wood SP		
DFS-18 Roberto Alomar	20.00	6.00
DFS-19 Chipper Jones	20.00	6.00
DFS-20 Pedro Martinez	20.00	6.00
DFS-21 Shawn Green	15.00	4.50
DFS-22 Magglio Ordonez	15.00	4.50
DFS-23 Darin Erstad SP		
DFS-24 Rafael Palmeiro SP		
DFS-25 Edgar Martinez	20.00	6.00

2001 Leaf Rookies and Stars Dress for Success Prime Cuts

Randomly inserted into packs, these cards parallel the Dress for Success insert set. Each card had a stated print run of 50 serial numbered sets.

	Nm-Mt	Ex-Mt
*PRIME CUTS: 1.25X TO 3X BASIC DRESS		
DFS-17 Kerry Wood	80.00	24.00
DFS-23 Darin Erstad	40.00	12.00
DFS-24 Rafael Palmeiro	50.00	15.00

2001 Leaf Rookies and Stars Freshman Orientation

Inserted into packs at odds of one in 96, these 25 cards feature leading prospects along with a piece of game-used memorabilia. The Dunn, Pujols and Gibbons cards are shortprinted compared to the rest of the set.

	Nm-Mt	Ex-Mt
FO-1 Adam Dunn Bat SP		
FO-2 Josh Towers Pants	10.00	3.00
FO-3 Vernon Wells Jsy	10.00	3.00
FO-4 Corey Patterson Pants	10.00	3.00
FO-5 Albert Pujols Bat SP		
FO-6 Ben Sheets Jsy	10.00	3.00
FO-7 Pedro Feliz Bat	10.00	3.00
FO-8 Keith Ginter Bat	10.00	3.00
FO-9 Luis Rivas Bat	10.00	3.00
FO-10 Andres Torres Bat	10.00	3.00
FO-11 Carlos Valderrama Jsy	10.00	3.00
FO-12 Brandon Inge Jsy	10.00	3.00
FO-13 Jay Gibbons Cap SP		
FO-14 Cesar Izturis Bat	10.00	3.00
FO-15 Marcus Giles Jsy	10.00	3.00
FO-16 Tsuyoshi Shinjo Jsy	20.00	6.00
FO-17 Eric Valent Bat	10.00	3.00
FO-18 David Espinosa Bat	10.00	3.00
FO-19 Aubrey Huff Jsy	10.00	3.00
FO-20 Wilmy Caceres Jsy	10.00	3.00
FO-21 Bud Smith Jsy	10.00	3.00
FO-22 Ricardo Rodriguez Pants	10.00	3.00
FO-23 Wes Helms Jsy	10.00	3.00
FO-24 Jason Hart Bat	10.00	3.00
FO-25 Dee Brown Jsy	10.00	3.00

2001 Leaf Rookies and Stars Freshman Orientation Autographs

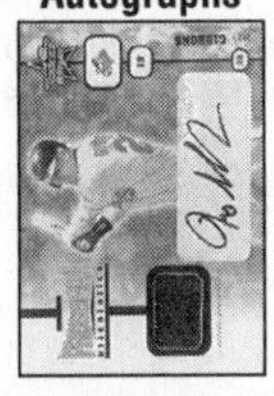

Randomly inserted into packs, these 21 cards parallel the Freshman Orientation insert set. Each of these players signed 100 cards or less for this product. If the player signed less than 100 cards we have notated that with an SP in our checklist.

	Nm-Mt	Ex-Mt
FO-1 Adam Dunn Bat SP		
FO-2 Josh Towers Pants SP		
FO-4 Corey Patterson Pants SP		
FO-5 Albert Pujols Bat SP		
FO-6 Ben Sheets Jsy SP		
FO-7 Pedro Feliz Bat	20.00	6.00
FO-8 Keith Ginter Bat	20.00	6.00
FO-9 Luis Rivas Bat	20.00	6.00
FO-10 Andres Torres Bat	20.00	6.00
FO-11 Carlos Valderrama Jsy	20.00	6.00
FO-13 Jay Gibbons Cap	40.00	12.00
FO-14 Cesar Izturis Bat	20.00	6.00
FO-15 Marcus Giles Jsy	20.00	6.00
FO-17 Eric Valent Bat	20.00	6.00
FO-18 David Espinosa Bat	20.00	6.00
FO-19 Aubrey Huff Jsy	20.00	6.00
FO-20 Wilmy Caceres Jsy	20.00	6.00
FO-21 Bud Smith Jsy SP		
FO-22 Ricardo Rodriguez Pants	20.00	6.00
FO-24 Jason Hart Bat	20.00	6.00
FO-25 Dee Brown Jsy	20.00	6.00

2001 Leaf Rookies and Stars Freshman Orientation Class Officers

Randomly inserted into packs, these cards parallel the Freshman Orientation insert set. Each card had a stated print run of 50 serial numbered sets.

	Nm-Mt	Ex-Mt
*CLASS OFFICER: .75X TO 2X BASIC FRESH		
FO-1 Adam Dunn Bat	15.00	4.50
FO-5 Albert Pujols Bat	150.00	45.00
FO-13 Jay Gibbons Cap	25.00	7.50

2001 Leaf Rookies and Stars Great American Treasures

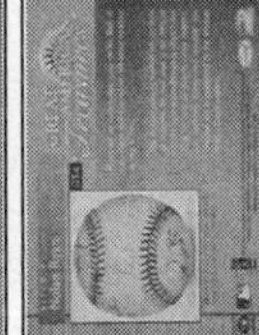

Inserted at a rate of one in 1,120 packs, these 20 cards feature pieces of memorabilia from key moments in a players career.

	Nm-Mt	Ex-Mt
GT1 Barry Bonds HR Jsy		
GT2 Magglio Ordonez HR Bat	40.00	12.00
GT3 Derek Jeter 1st Game Ball		
GT4 Nolan Ryan 7th No-Hit Ball		
GT5 Sammy Sosa June HR Ball		
GT6 Tom Glavine 96 WS Jsy	50.00	15.00
GT7 Ivan Rodriguez 99 MVP Bat	50.00	15.00
GT8 Pedro Martinez 300 K Ball		
GT9 Mark McGwire 60 HR Game Ball		
GT10 Ted Williams 517 HR Ball		
GT11 Ryne Sandberg 91 AS Bat	60.00	18.00
GT12 Barry Bonds 500 HR Game Ball		
GT13 Hideo Nomo No-Hit Ball		
GT14 Roger Maris 61 HR Game Ball		
GT15 Ty Cobb 09 WS Ball		
GT16 Harmon Killebrew 570 HR Bat		
GT17 Magglio Ordonez 00 AS Cap		
GT18 Wade Boggs WS Bat	50.00	15.00
GT19 Hank Aaron 755 HR Cap		
GT20 David Cone Perfect Ball-Ticket		

2001 Leaf Rookies and Stars Great American Treasures Autograph

This four card parallel to the Great American Treasure set features signed cards by these players on cards relating to a key event in their career. Due to scarcity, no pricing information is provided.

	Nm-Mt	Ex-Mt
GT6 Tom Glavine 96 WS Jsy		
GT11 Ryne Sandberg 91 AS Bat		
GT16 Harmon Killebrew 570 HR Bat		
GT18 Wade Boggs WS Bat		

2001 Leaf Rookies and Stars Players Collection

Randomly inserted into packs, these 15 cards feature four different types of memorabilia from three key superstars. Each player also had a quad card with one piece each of the four types of memorabilia featured. Each card is serial numbered to 100 except for the quad cards which are serial numbered to 25.

	Nm-Mt	Ex-Mt
PC-1 Tony Gwynn Bat SP	40.00	12.00
PC-2 Tony Gwynn Jsy	40.00	12.00
PC-3 Tony Gwynn Pants	40.00	12.00
PC-4 Tony Gwynn Shoe	40.00	12.00
PC-5 Tony Gwynn Quad/25		
PC-6 Cal Ripken White Jsy SP	100.00	30.00
PC-7 Cal Ripken Bat SP	100.00	30.00
PC-8 Cal Ripken Glove	100.00	30.00
PC-9 Cal Ripken Gray Jsy	100.00	30.00
PC-10 Cal Ripken Quad		
PC-11 Barry Bonds Jsy	80.00	24.00
PC-12 Barry Bonds Shoe	80.00	24.00
PC-13 Barry Bonds Pants	80.00	24.00
PC-14 Barry Bonds Bat	80.00	24.00
PC-15 Barry Bonds Quad/25		

2001 Leaf Rookies and Stars Players Collection Autographs

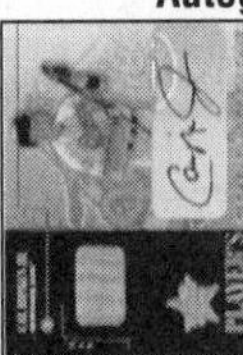

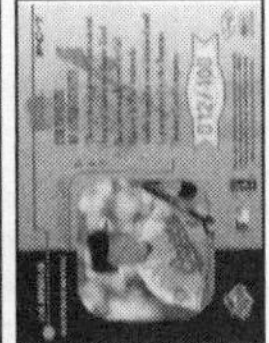

Randomly inserted into packs, these three cards feature signed cards of the players along with a memorabilia piece. Due to market scarcity, no pricing is provided.

	Nm-Mt	Ex-Mt
PC-1 Tony Gwynn Bat		
PC-6 Cal Ripken Jsy		
PC-7 Cal Ripken Bat		

2001 Leaf Rookies and Stars Slideshow

Randomly inserted into packs, each card features a jersey swatch along with a snapshot of major league action. Most players have 100 serial numbered cards but a few have less and we have notated those players with an SP.

	Nm-Mt	Ex-Mt
S-1 Cal Ripken	100.00	30.00
S-2 Chipper Jones SP	40.00	12.00
S-3 Jeff Bagwell	25.00	7.50
S-4 Larry Walker	25.00	7.50
S-5 Greg Maddux SP	60.00	18.00
S-6 Ivan Rodriguez	25.00	7.50
S-7 Andruw Jones SP	15.00	4.50
S-8 Lance Berkman SP	15.00	4.50
S-9 Luis Gonzalez SP	15.00	4.50
S-10 Tony Gwynn	40.00	12.00
S-11 Troy Glaus SP	25.00	7.50
S-12 Todd Helton	25.00	7.50
S-13 Roberto Alomar	25.00	7.50
S-14 Barry Bonds	80.00	24.00
S-15 Vladimir Guerrero SP	25.00	7.50
S-16 Sean Casey SP	15.00	4.50
S-17 Curt Schilling SP	25.00	7.50
S-18 Frank Thomas	25.00	7.50
S-19 Pedro Martinez	25.00	7.50
S-20 Juan Gonzalez	25.00	7.50
S-21 Randy Johnson	25.00	7.50
S-22 Kerry Wood SP	25.00	7.50
S-23 Mike Sweeney	15.00	4.50
S-24 Magglio Ordonez	15.00	4.50
S-25 Kazuhiro Sasaki	15.00	4.50
S-26 Manny Ramirez	15.00	4.50
S-27 Roger Clemens	80.00	24.00
S-28 Albert Pujols SP	100.00	30.00
S-29 Hideo Nomo	50.00	15.00
S-30 Miguel Tejada SP	15.00	4.50

2001 Leaf Rookies and Stars Statistical Standouts

Inserted at packs at a rate of one in 96, these 25 cards feature star players along with a swatch of game-used materials. A few of these cards were printed in shorter quantites than the others and we have notated those with an SP.

	Nm-Mt	Ex-Mt
*SUPER: 1X TO 2.5X BASIC STAT. STANDOUT		
SUPER STATED PRINT RUN 50 SERIAL #'D SETS		
RANDOM INSERTS IN PACKS		
SS-1 Ichiro Suzuki	40.00	12.00
SS-2 Barry Bonds SP		
SS-3 Ivan Rodriguez	15.00	4.50
SS-4 Jeff Bagwell	15.00	4.50
SS-5 Vladimir Guerrero SP		
SS-6 Mike Sweeney	10.00	3.00
SS-7 Miguel Tejada	10.00	3.00
SS-8 Mike Piazza SP		
SS-9 Darin Erstad	10.00	3.00
SS-10 Alex Rodriguez	25.00	7.50
SS-11 Jason Giambi	15.00	4.50
SS-12 Cal Ripken	40.00	12.00
SS-13 Albert Pujols	60.00	18.00
SS-14 Carlos Delgado	10.00	3.00
SS-15 Rafael Palmeiro	15.00	4.50
SS-16 Lance Berkman	10.00	3.00
SS-17 Luis Gonzalez SP		
SS-18 Sammy Sosa SP		
SS-19 Andruw Jones SP		
SS-20 Derek Jeter	40.00	12.00
SS-21 Edgar Martinez	15.00	4.50
SS-22 Troy Glaus	15.00	4.50
SS-23 Magglio Ordonez	10.00	3.00
SS-24 Mark McGwire	40.00	12.00
SS-25 Manny Ramirez	10.00	3.00

2001 Leaf Rookies and Stars Triple Threads

Randomly inserted into packs, each of these cards feature three swatches of game-worn jerseys from players of the same franchise. Each of these cards are serial numbered to 100.

	Nm-Mt	Ex-Mt
TT1 Pedro Martinez, Manny Ramirez, Nomar Garciaparra	100.00	30.00
TT2 Frank Robinson, Cal Ripken, Brooks Robinson	150.00	45.00
TT3 Yogi Berra, Lou Gehrig, Babe Ruth	800.00	240.00
TT4 Andre Dawson, Ryne Sandberg, Ernie Banks	150.00	45.00
TT5 Warren Spahn, Hank Aaron, Eddie Mathews	150.00	45.00
TT6 Greg Maddux, Chipper Jones, Andruw Jones	100.00	30.00
TT7 Nolan Ryan, Ivan Rodriguez, Juan Gonzalez	150.00	45.00
TT8 Lance Berkman, Jeff Bagwell, Craig Biggio	80.00	24.00
TT9 Rod Carew, Harmon Killebrew, Kirby Puckett	80.00	24.00
TT10 Luis Gonzalez, Curt Schilling, Randy Johnson	80.00	24.00

2002 Leaf Rookies and Stars

This 501 card set was issued in November, 2002. This set was issued in six card packs which came 24 packs to a box and 20 boxes to

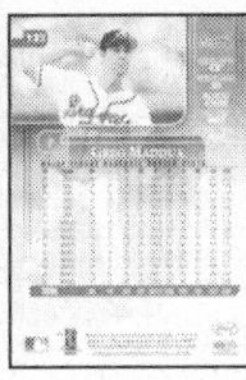

a case with an SRP of $3 per pack. Originally designed as a 400 card set, this set mushroomed to 501 when 101 variations of some of the basic cards were discovered upon release. These cards feature some of the players who have been on more than one team with cards from their time with that earlier team. Those variation cards were inserted at stated odds of one in four. In addition, cards numbered 301 through 400, which featured a mix of rookies and prospects, were issued at stated odds of one in two. Another subset, which was not printed in shorter supply, was an award winner group from cards numbered 251 through 300.

	Nm-Mt	Ex-Mt
COMP.SET w/o SP's (300)	40.00	12.00
COMMON CARD (1-300)	.30	.09
COMMON SP (1-300)	2.00	.60
COMMON CARD (301-400)	1.00	.30
1 Darin Erstad	.30	.09
2 Garret Anderson	.30	.09
3 Troy Glaus	.50	.15
4 David Eckstein	.30	.09
5 Adam Kennedy	.30	.09
6 Kevin Appier Angels	.30	.09
6A Kevin Appier Mets SP	2.00	.60
6B Kevin Appier Royals SP	2.00	.60
7 Jarrod Washburn	.30	.09
8 David Segui	.30	.09
9 Jay Gibbons	.30	.09
10 Tony Batista	.30	.09
11 Scott Erickson	.30	.09
12 Jeff Conine	.30	.09
13 Melvin Mora	.30	.09
14 Shea Hillenbrand	.30	.09
15 Manny Ramirez Red Sox	.30	.09
15A Manny Ramirez Indians SP	2.00	.60
16 Pedro Martinez Red Sox	.75	.23
16A Ped. Martinez Dodgers SP	4.00	1.20
16B Pedro Martinez Expos SP	4.00	1.20
17 Nomar Garciaparra	1.25	.35
18 Rickey Henderson Red Sox	.75	.23
18A Ri. Henderson Angels SP	4.00	1.20
18B Rickey Henderson A's SP	4.00	1.20
18C Ri. Henderson Bl.Jays SP	4.00	1.20
18D Rickey Henderson M's SP	4.00	1.20
18E Rickey Henderson Mets SP	4.00	1.20
18F Ri. Henderson Padres SP	4.00	1.20
18G Ri. Henderson Yanks SP	4.00	1.20
19 Johnny Damon Red Sox	.30	.09
19A Johnny Damon A's SP	2.00	.60
19B Johnny Damon Royals SP	2.00	.60
20 Trot Nixon	.50	.15
21 Derek Lowe	.30	.09
22 Jason Varitek	.30	.09
23 Tim Wakefield	.30	.09
24 Frank Thomas	.75	.23
25 Kenny Lofton White Sox	.30	.09
25A Kenny Lofton Indians SP	2.00	.60
26 Magglio Ordonez	.30	.09
27 Ray Durham	.30	.09
28 Mark Buehrle	.30	.09
29 Paul Konerko White Sox	.30	.09
29A Paul Konerko Dodgers SP	2.00	.60
29B Paul Konerko Reds SP	2.00	.60
30 Jose Valentin	.30	.09
31 C.C. Sabathia	.30	.09
32 Ellis Burks Indians	.30	.09
32A Ellis Burks Giants SP	2.00	.60
32B Ellis Burks Red Sox SP	2.00	.60
32C Ellis Burks Rockies SP	2.00	.60
33 Omar Vizquel Indians	.30	.09
33A Omar Vizquel Mariners SP	2.00	.60
34 Jim Thome	.75	.23
35 Matt Lawton	.30	.09
36 Travis Fryman Indians	.30	.09
36A Travis Fryman Tigers SP	2.00	.60
37 Robert Fick	.30	.09
38 Bobby Higginson	.30	.09
39 Steve Sparks	.30	.09
40 Mike Rivera	.30	.09
41 Wendell Magee	.30	.09
42 Randall Simon	.30	.09
43 Carlos Pena Yankees	.30	.09
43A Carlos Pena A's SP	2.00	.60
43B Carlos Pena Rangers SP	2.00	.60
44 Mike Sweeney	.30	.09
45 Chuck Knoblauch	.30	.09
46 Carlos Beltran	.30	.09
47 Joe Randa	.30	.09
48 Paul Byrd	.30	.09
49 Mac Suzuki	.30	.09
50 Torii Hunter	.30	.09
51 Jacque Jones	.30	.09
52 David Ortiz	.30	.09
53 Corey Koskie	.30	.09
54 Brad Radke	.30	.09
55 Doug Mientkiewicz	.30	.09
56 A.J. Pierzynski	.30	.09
57 Dustan Mohr	.30	.09
58 Derek Jeter	2.00	.60
59 Bernie Williams	.50	.15
60 Roger Clemens Yankees	1.50	.45
60A R.Clemens Blue Jays SP	8.00	2.40
60B R.Clemens Red Sox SP	8.00	2.40
61 Mike Mussina Yankees	.75	.23
61A Mike Mussina Orioles SP	4.00	1.20
62 Jorge Posada	.50	.15
63 Alfonso Soriano	.50	.15
64 Jason Giambi Yankees	.75	.23
64A Jason Giambi A's SP	4.00	1.20
65 Robin Ventura Yankees	.30	.09
65A Robin Ventura Mets SP	2.00	.60
65B Robin Ventura White Sox SP	2.00	.60
66 Andy Pettitte	.50	.15
67 David Wells Yankees	.30	.09
67A David Wells Blue Jays SP	2.00	.60
67B David Wells Tigers SP	2.00	.60
68 Nick Johnson	.30	.09
69 Jeff Weaver Yankees	.30	.09
69A Jeff Weaver Tigers SP	2.00	.60
70 Raul Mondesi Yankees	.30	.09
70A R.Mondesi Blue Jays SP	2.00	.60
70B Raul Mondesi Dodgers SP	2.00	.60
71 Tim Hudson	.30	.09
72 Barry Zito	.50	.15
73 Mark Mulder	.30	.09
74 Miguel Tejada	.30	.09
75 Eric Chavez	.30	.09
76 Billy Koch A's	.30	.09
76A Billy Koch Blue Jays SP	2.00	.60
77 Jermaine Dye A's	.30	.09
77A Jermaine Dye Royals SP	2.00	.60
78 Scott Hatteberg	.30	.09
79 Ichiro Suzuki	1.25	.35
80 Edgar Martinez	.50	.15
81 Mike Cameron Mariners	.30	.09
81A M.Cameron White Sox SP	2.00	.60
82 John Olerud Mariners	.30	.09
82A John Olerud Blue Jays SP	2.00	.60
82B John Olerud Mets SP	2.00	.60
83 Bret Boone	.30	.09
84 Dan Wilson	.30	.09
85 Freddy Garcia	.30	.09
86 Jamie Moyer	.30	.09
87 Carlos Guillen	.30	.09
88 Ruben Sierra	.30	.09
89 Kazuhiro Sasaki	.30	.09
90 Mark McLemore	.30	.09
91 Ben Grieve	.30	.09
92 Aubrey Huff	.30	.09
93 Steve Cox	.30	.09
94 Toby Hall	.30	.09
95 Randy Winn	.30	.09
96 Brent Abernathy	.30	.09
97 Chan Ho Park Rangers	.30	.09
97A Chan Ho Park Dodgers SP	2.00	.60
98 Alex Rodriguez Rangers	1.25	.35
98A A.Rodriguez Mariners SP	6.00	1.80
99 Juan Gonzalez Rangers	.75	.23
99A Juan Gonzalez Indians SP	4.00	1.20
99B Juan Gonzalez Tigers SP	4.00	1.20
100 Rafael Palmeiro Rangers	.50	.15
100A Rafael Palmeiro Cubs SP	2.50	.75
100B Raf. Palmeiro Orioles SP	2.50	.75
101 Ivan Rodriguez	.75	.23
102 Rusty Greer	.30	.09
103 Kenny Rogers Rangers	.30	.09
103A Kenny Rogers A's SP	2.00	.60
103B Ken. Rogers Yankees SP	2.00	.60
104 Hank Blalock	.75	.23
105 Mark Teixeira	.75	.23
106 Carlos Delgado	.30	.09
107 Shannon Stewart	.30	.09
108 Eric Hinske	.30	.09
109 Roy Halladay	.30	.09
110 Felipe Lopez	.30	.09
111 Vernon Wells	.30	.09
112 Curt Schilling D'backs	.50	.15
112A Curt Schilling Phillies SP	2.50	.75
113 Randy Johnson D'backs	.75	.23
113A Randy Johnson Astros SP	4.00	1.20
113B Randy Johnson Expos SP	4.00	1.20
113C R.Johnson Mariners SP	4.00	1.20
114 Luis Gonzalez D'backs	.30	.09
114A Luis Gonzalez Astros SP	2.00	.60
114B Luis Gonzalez Cubs SP	2.00	.60
115 Mark Grace D'backs	.50	.15
115A Mark Grace Cubs SP	2.50	.75
116 Junior Spivey	.30	.09
117 Tony Womack	.30	.09
118 Matt Williams D'backs	.30	.09
118A Matt Williams Giants SP	2.00	.60
118B Matt Williams Indians SP	2.00	.60
119 Danny Bautista	.30	.09
120 Byung-Hyun Kim	.30	.09
121 Craig Counsell	.30	.09
122 Greg Maddux Braves	1.25	.35
122A Greg Maddux Cubs SP	6.00	1.80
123 Tom Glavine	.50	.15
124 John Smoltz Braves	.50	.15
124A John Smoltz Tigers SP	2.50	.75
125 Chipper Jones	.75	.23
126 Gary Sheffield	.30	.09
127 Andruw Jones	.30	.09
128 Vinny Castilla	.30	.09
129 Damian Moss	.30	.09
130 Rafael Furcal	.30	.09
131 Kerry Wood	.75	.23
132 Fred McGriff Cubs	.50	.15
132A F.McGriff Blue Jays SP	2.50	.75
132B Fred McGriff Braves SP	2.50	.75
132C F.McGriff Devil Rays SP	2.50	.75
132D Fred McGriff Padres SP	2.50	.75
133 Sammy Sosa Cubs	1.25	.35
133A Sammy Sosa Rangers SP	6.00	1.80
133B S.Sosa White Sox SP	6.00	1.80
134 Alex Gonzalez	.30	.09
135 Corey Patterson	.30	.09
136 Moises Alou	.30	.09
137 Mark Prior	1.50	.45
138 Jon Lieber	.30	.09
139 Matt Clement	.30	.09
140 Ken Griffey Jr. Reds	1.25	.35
140A K.Griffey Jr. Mariners SP	6.00	1.80
141 Barry Larkin	.75	.23
142 Adam Dunn	.30	.09
143 Sean Casey Reds	.30	.09
143A Sean Casey Indians SP	2.00	.60
144 Jose Rijo	.30	.09
145 Elmer Dessens	.30	.09
146 Austin Kearns	.30	.09
147 Corky Miller	.30	.09
148 Todd Walker Reds	.30	.09
148A Todd Walker Rockies SP	2.00	.60
149 Chris Reitsma	.30	.09
150 Ryan Dempster	.30	.09
151 Larry Walker Rockies	.50	.15
151A Larry Walker Expos SP	2.50	.75
152 Todd Helton	.50	.15
153 Juan Uribe	.30	.09
154 Juan Pierre	.30	.09
155 Mike Hampton	.30	.09
156 Todd Zeile	.30	.09
157 Josh Beckett	.50	.15
158 Mike Lowell Marlins	.30	.09

158A Mike Lowell Yankees SP 2.00 .60
159 Derrek Lee .30 .09
160 A.J. Burnett .30 .09
161 Luis Castillo .30 .09
162 Tim Raines .30 .09
163 Preston Wilson .30 .09
164 Juan Encarnacion .30 .09
165 Jeff Bagwell .50 .15
166 Craig Biggio .50 .15
167 Lance Berkman .30 .09
168 Wade Miller .30 .09
169 Roy Oswalt .30 .09
170 Richard Hidalgo .30 .09
171 Carlos Hernandez .30 .09
172 Daryle Ward .30 .09
173 Shawn Green Dodgers .30 .09
173A S.Green Blue Jays SP 2.00 .60
174 Adrian Beltre .30 .09
175 Paul Lo Duca .30 .09
176 Eric Karros .30 .09
177 Kevin Brown .30 .09
178 Hideo Nomo Dodgers .75 .23
178A Hideo Nomo Brewers SP 4.00 1.20
178B Hideo Nomo Mets SP 4.00 1.20
178C Hideo Nomo Red Sox SP 4.00 1.20
178D Hideo Nomo Tigers SP 4.00 1.20
179 Odalis Perez .30 .09
180 Eric Gagne .50 .15
181 Brian Jordan .30 .09
182 Cesar Izturis .30 .09
183 Geoff Jenkins .30 .09
184 Richie Sexson Brewers .30 .09
184A Richie Sexson Indians SP 2.00 .60
185 Jose Hernandez .30 .09
186 Ben Sheets .30 .09
187 Ruben Quevedo .30 .09
188 Jeffrey Hammonds .30 .09
189 Alex Sanchez .30 .09
190 Vladimir Guerrero .75 .23
191 Jose Vidro .30 .09
192 Orlando Cabrera .30 .09
193 Michael Barrett .30 .09
194 Javier Vazquez .30 .09
195 Tony Armas Jr. .30 .09
196 Andres Galarraga .30 .09
197 Tomo Ohka .30 .09
198 Bartolo Colon Expos .30 .09
198A Bartolo Colon Indians SP 2.00 .60
199 Cliff Floyd Expos .30 .09
199A Cliff Floyd Marlins SP 2.00 .60
200 Mike Piazza Mets 1.25 .35
200A Mike Piazza Dodgers SP 6.00 1.80
200B Mike Piazza Marlins SP 6.00 1.80
201 Jeromy Burnitz .30 .09
202 Roberto Alomar Mets .75 .23
202A Rob. Alomar Bl.Jays SP 4.00 1.20
202B Ro. Alomar Indians SP 4.00 1.20
202C Ro. Alomar Orioles SP 4.00 1.20
202D Ro. Alomar Padres SP 4.00 1.20
203 Mo Vaughn Mets .30 .09
203A Mo Vaughn Angels SP 2.00 .60
203B Mo Vaughn Red Sox SP 2.00 .60
204 Al Leiter Mets .30 .09
204A Al Leiter Blue Jays SP 2.00 .60
205 Pedro Astacio .30 .09
206 Edgardo Alfonzo .30 .09
207 Armando Benitez .30 .09
208 Scott Rolen .50 .15
209 Pat Burrell .30 .09
210 Bobby Abreu Phillies .30 .09
210A Bobby Abreu Astros SP 2.00 .60
211 Mike Lieberthal .30 .09
212 Brandon Duckworth .30 .09
213 Jimmy Rollins .30 .09
214 Jeremy Giambi .30 .09
215 Vicente Padilla .30 .09
216 Travis Lee .30 .09
217 Jason Kendall .30 .09
218 Brian Giles Pirates .30 .09
218A Brian Giles Indians SP 2.00 .60
219 Aramis Ramirez .30 .09
220 Pokey Reese .30 .09
221 Kip Wells .30 .09
222 Josh Fogg Pirates .30 .09
222A Josh Fogg White Sox SP 2.00 .60
223 Mike Williams .30 .09
224 Ryan Klesko Padres .30 .09
224A Ryan Klesko Braves SP 2.00 .60
225 Phil Nevin Padres .30 .09
225A Phil Nevin Tigers SP 2.00 .60
226 Brian Lawrence .30 .09
227 Mark Kotsay .30 .09
228 Brett Tomko .30 .09
229 Trevor Hoffman Padres .30 .09
229A Tr. Hoffman Marlins SP 2.00 .60
230 Barry Bonds Giants 2.00 .60
230A Barry Bonds Pirates SP 10.00 3.00
231 Jeff Kent Giants .30 .09
231A Jeff Kent Blue Jays SP 2.00 .60
232 Rich Aurilia .30 .09
233 Tsuyoshi Shinjo Giants .30 .09
233A Tsuyoshi Shinjo Mets SP 2.00 .60
234 Benito Santiago Giants .30 .09
234A Ben. Santiago Padres SP 2.00 .60
235 Kirk Rueter .30 .09
236 Kurt Ainsworth .30 .09
237 Livan Hernandez .30 .09
238 Russ Ortiz .30 .09
239 David Bell .30 .09
240 Jason Schmidt .30 .09
241 Reggie Sanders .30 .09
242 Jim Edmonds Cardinals .30 .09
242A Jim Edmonds Angels SP 2.00 .60
243 J.D. Drew .30 .09
244 Albert Pujols 1.50 .45
245 Fernando Vina .30 .09
246 Tino Martinez Cardinals .50 .15
246A T.Martinez Mariners SP 2.50 .75
246B T.Martinez Yankees SP 2.50 .75
247 Edgar Renteria .30 .09
248 Matt Morris .30 .09
249 Woody Williams .30 .09
250 Jason Isringhausen Cards .30 .09
250A J.Isringhausen A's SP 2.00 .60
251 Cal Ripken 82 ROY 2.50 .75
252 Cal Ripken 83 MVP 2.50 .75
253 Cal Ripken 91 MVP 2.50 .75
254 Cal Ripken 91 AS 2.50 .75
255 Ryne Sandberg 84 MVP 1.50 .45
256 Don Mattingly 85 MVP 2.00 .60
257 Don Mattingly 85-94 GLV 2.00 .60
258 Roger Clemens 01 CY 1.50 .45
259 Roger Clemens 87 CY 1.50 .45
260 Roger Clemens 91 CY 1.50 .45
261 Roger Clemens 97 CY 1.50 .45
262 Roger Clemens 98 CY 1.50 .45
263 Roger Clemens 86 CY 1.50 .45
264 Roger Clemens 86 MVP 1.50 .45
265 Rickey Henderson 90 MVP .75 .23
266 Rickey Henderson 81 GLV .75 .23
267 Jose Canseco 88 MVP .50 .15
268 Barry Bonds 01 MVP 2.00 .60
269 Barry Bonds 90 MVP 2.00 .60
270 Barry Bonds 92 MVP 2.00 .60
271 Barry Bonds 93 MVP 2.00 .60
272 Jeff Bagwell 94 MVP .30 .09
273 Kirby Puckett 91 ALCS .75 .23
274 Kirby Puckett 93 AS .75 .23
275 Greg Maddux 95 CY 1.25 .35
276 Greg Maddux 92 CY 1.25 .35
277 Greg Maddux 93 CY 1.25 .35
278 Greg Maddux 94 CY 1.25 .35
279 Ken Griffey Jr. 97 MVP 1.25 .35
280 Mike Piazza 93 ROY 1.25 .35
281 Kirby Puckett 86-89 GLV .75 .23
282 Mike Piazza 96 AS 1.25 .35
283 Frank Thomas 93 MVP .50 .15
284 Hideo Nomo 95 ROY .50 .15
285 Randy Johnson 01 CY .50 .15
286 Juan Gonzalez 96 MVP .50 .15
287 Derek Jeter 96 ROY 2.00 .60
288 Derek Jeter 00 WS 2.00 .60
289 Derek Jeter 00 AS 2.00 .60
290 Nomar Garciaparra 97 ROY 1.25 .35
291 Pedro Martinez 00 CY .50 .15
292 Kerry Wood 98 ROY .50 .15
293 Sammy Sosa 98 MVP 1.25 .35
294 Chipper Jones 99 MVP .50 .15
295 Ivan Rodriguez 99 MVP .50 .15
296 Ivan Rodriguez 92-01 GLV .50 .15
297 Albert Pujols 01 ROY 1.50 .45
298 Ichiro Suzuki 01 ROY 1.25 .35
299 Ichiro Suzuki 01 MVP 1.25 .35
300 Ichiro Suzuki 01 GLV 1.25 .35
301 So Taguchi RS RC 1.25 .35
302 Kazuhisa Ishii RS RC 3.00 .90
303 Jeremy Lambert RS RC 1.00 .30
304 Sean Burroughs RS 1.00 .30
305 P.J. Bevis RS RC 1.00 .30
306 Jon Rauch RS 1.00 .30
307 Scotty Layfield RS RC 1.00 .30
308 Miguel Asencio RS RC 1.00 .30
309 Franklyn German RS RC 1.00 .30
310 Luis Ugueto RS RC 1.00 .30
311 Jorge Sosa RS RC 1.00 .30
312 Felix Escalona RS RC 1.00 .30
313 Jose Valverde RS RC 1.25 .35
314 Jeremy Ward RS RC 1.00 .30
315 Kevin Gryboski RS RC 1.00 .30
316 Francis Beltran RS RC 1.00 .30
317 Joe Thurston RS 1.00 .30
318 Cliff Lee RS RC 2.00 .60
319 Takahito Nomura RS RC 1.00 .30
320 Bill Hall RS 1.00 .30
321 Marlon Byrd RS 1.00 .30
322 Andy Shibilo RS RC 1.00 .30
323 Edwin Almonte RS RC 1.00 .30
324 Brandon Backe RS RC 1.00 .30
325 Chone Figgins RS RC 1.00 .30
326 Brian Mallette RS RC 1.00 .30
327 Rodrigo Rosario RS RC 1.00 .30
328 Anderson Machado RS RC 1.00 .30
329 Jorge Padilla RS RC 1.00 .30
330 Allan Simpson RS RC 1.00 .30
331 Doug Devore RS RC 1.00 .30
332 Drew Henson RS 1.00 .30
333 Raul Chavez RS RC 1.00 .30
334 Tom Shearn RS RC 1.00 .30
335 Ben Howard RS RC 1.00 .30
336 Chris Baker RS RC 1.00 .30
337 Travis Hughes RS RC 1.00 .30
338 Kevin Mench RS 1.00 .30
339 Brian Tallet RS RC 1.25 .35
340 Mike Moriarty RS RC 1.00 .30
341 Corey Thurman RS RC 1.00 .30
342 Terry Pearson RS RC 1.00 .30
343 Steve Kent RS RC 1.00 .30
344 Satoru Komiyama RS RC 1.00 .30
345 Jason Lane RS 1.00 .30
346 Freddy Sanchez RS RC 1.00 .30
347 Brandon Puffer RS RC 1.00 .30
348 Clay Condrey RS RC 1.00 .30
349 Rene Reyes RS RC 1.00 .30
350 Hee Seop Choi RS 1.25 .35
351 Rodrigo Lopez RS 1.00 .30
352 Colin Young RS RC 1.00 .30
353 Jason Simontacchi RS RC 1.00 .30
354 Oliver Perez RS RC 1.25 .35
355 Kirk Saarloos RS RC 1.00 .30
356 Marcus Thames RS 1.00 .30
357 Jeff Austin RS RC 1.00 .30
358 Justin Kaye RS 1.00 .30
359 Julio Mateo RS RC 1.00 .30
360 Mike A. Smith RS RC 1.00 .30
361 Chris Snelling RS RC 2.50 .75
362 Dennis Tankersley RS 1.00 .30
363 Runelvys Hernandez RS RC 1.00 .30
364 Aaron Cook RS RC 1.00 .30
365 Joe Borchard RS 1.00 .30
366 Earl Snyder RS RC 1.00 .30
367 Shane Nance RS RC 1.00 .30
368 Aaron Guiel RS RC 1.00 .30
369 Steve Bechler RS RC 1.00 .30
370 Tim Kalita RS RC 1.00 .30
371 Shawn Sedlacek RS RC 1.00 .30
372 Eric Good RS RC 1.00 .30
373 Eric Junge RS RC 1.00 .30
374 Matt Thornton RS RC 1.00 .30
375 Travis Driskill RS RC 1.00 .30
376 Mitch Wylie RS RC 1.00 .30
377 John Ennis RS RC 1.00 .30
378 Reed Johnson RS RC 1.25 .35
379 Juan Brito RS RC 1.00 .30
380 Ron Calloway RS RC 1.00 .30
381 Adrian Burnside RS RC 1.00 .30
382 Josh Bard RS RC 1.00 .30
383 Matt Childers RS RC 1.00 .30
384 Gustavo Chacin RS RC 1.00 .30
385 Luis Martinez RS RC 1.00 .30
386 Trey Hodges RS RC 1.00 .30
387 Hansel Izquierdo RS RC 1.00 .30
388 Jeriome Robertson RS RC 1.00 .30
389 Victor Alvarez RS RC 1.00 .30
390 David Ross RS RC 1.00 .30
391 Ron Chiavacci RS 1.00 .30
392 Adam Walker RS RC 1.00 .30
393 Mike Gonzalez RS RC 1.00 .30
394 John Foster RS RC 1.00 .30
395 Kyle Kane RS RC 1.00 .30
396 Cam Esslinger RS RC 1.00 .30
397 Kevin Frederick RS RC 1.00 .30
398 Franklin Nunez RS RC 1.00 .30
399 Todd Donovan RS RC 1.00 .30
400 Kevin Cash RS RC 1.00 .30

2002 Leaf Rookies and Stars Great American Signings

Randomly inserted into packs, this is a partial parallel to the basic Leaf Rookies and Stars set. These cards feature the basic card along with the attached "sticker" autograph. Since cards were issued to different stated print runs, we have notated that information next to the player's name in our checklist. If a card has a stated print run of 25 or fewer it is not printed due to market scarcity.

Nm-Mt Ex-Mt
9 Jay Gibbons/150 15.00 4.50
18 Rickey Henderson/20
40 Mike Rivera/175 10.00 3.00
49 Mac Suzuki/100 50.00 15.00
59 Bernie Williams/15
60 Roger Clemens/10
63 Alfonso Soriano/25
68 Nick Johnson/175 15.00 4.50
92 Aubrey Huff/175 15.00 4.50
96 Brent Abernathy/175 10.00 3.00
108 Eric Hinske/175 10.00 3.00
131 Kerry Wood/25
141 Barry Larkin/25
142 Adam Dunn/25
146 Austin Kearns/75 15.00 4.50
169 Roy Oswalt/100 15.00 4.50
182 Cesar Izturis/175 10.00 3.00
190 Vladimir Guerrero/15
210 Bobby Abreu/25
221 Kip Wells/175 10.00 3.00
226 Brian Lawrence/175 10.00 3.00
244 Albert Pujols/25
256 Don Mattingly/25
301 So Taguchi/50
302 Kazuhisa Ishii/25
309 Franklyn German/175 10.00 3.00
310 Luis Ugueto/175 10.00 3.00
312 Felix Escalona/100 15.00 4.50
316 Francis Beltran/175 10.00 3.00
320 Bill Hall/175 10.00 3.00
324 Brandon Backe/175 10.00 3.00
327 Rodrigo Rosario/175 10.00 3.00
328 Anderson Machado/175 10.00 3.00
329 Jorge Padilla/175 10.00 3.00
331 Doug Devore/175 10.00 3.00
332 Drew Henson/50 40.00 12.00
333 Raul Chavez/175 10.00 3.00
334 Tom Shearn/175 10.00 3.00
335 Ben Howard/175 10.00 3.00
336 Chris Baker/175 10.00 3.00
337 Travis Hughes/175 10.00 3.00
341 Corey Thurman/175 10.00 3.00
344 Satoru Komiyama/75 15.00 4.50
345 Jason Lane/150 10.00 3.00
349 Rene Reyes/175 10.00 3.00
354 Oliver Perez/175 15.00 4.50
361 Chris Snelling/175 25.00 7.50
362 Dennis Tankersley/175 10.00 3.00

2002 Leaf Rookies and Stars Longevity

Randomly inserted into packs, this is a parallel to the basic Leaf Rookie and Stars set. Cards numbered between 1-300 (and including all of the variations) were printed to a stated print run of 100 serial numbered sets while cards 301 through 400 were printed to a stated print run of 25 serial numbered sets.

Nm-Mt Ex-Mt
*LONGEVITY 1-300: 6X TO 15X BASIC
*LONGEVITY 1-300: 1.25X TO 3X BASIC SP'S
*RETIRED STARS 251-300: 12.5X TO 30X

2002 Leaf Rookies and Stars BLC Homers

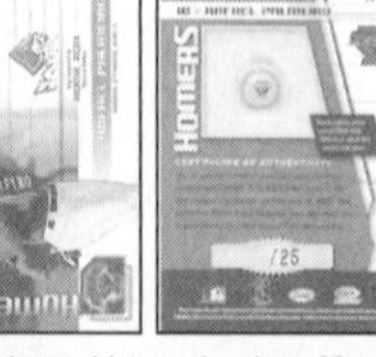

Randomly inserted into packs, these 30 cards feature pieces of baseball's used during the Big League Challenge held in Las Vegas before the 2002 season began. Each card has a stated print run of 25 serial numbered sets.

Nm-Mt Ex-Mt
LUIS GONZALEZ (1-3) 25.00 7.50
TODD HELTON (4-11) 40.00 12.00
JIM THOME (12-14) 40.00 12.00
RAFAEL PALMEIRO (15-19) 40.00 12.00
TROY GLAUS (20-22) 40.00 12.00
GARY SHEFFIELD (23-25) 25.00 7.50
MIKE PIAZZA (26-30) 60.00 18.00

2002 Leaf Rookies and Stars Dress for Success

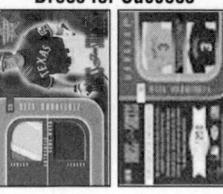

Randomly inserted into packs, these 15 cards feature two game-used memorabilia pieces from the featured players. Each card was also issued to a stated print run of 250 serial numbered sets.

Nm-Mt Ex-Mt
1 Mike Piazza Jsy-Jsy 25.00 7.50
2 Cal Ripken Jsy-Jsy 60.00 18.00
3 Carlos Delgado Jsy-Jsy 20.00 6.00
4 Chipper Jones Jsy-Jsy 25.00 7.50
5 Bernie Williams Jsy-Shoe 25.00 7.50
6 Carlos Beltran Jsy-Shoe 20.00 6.00
7 Curt Schilling Jsy-Jsy 25.00 7.50
8 Greg Maddux Jsy-Jsy 25.00 7.50
9 Ivan Rodriguez Jsy-Jsy 25.00 7.50
10 Alex Rodriguez Jsy-Jsy 40.00 12.00
11 Roger Clemens Jsy-Jsy 40.00 12.00
12 Todd Helton Jsy-Jsy 25.00 7.50
13 Jim Edmonds Shoe-Jsy 20.00 6.00
14 Manny Ramirez Jsy-Fld Glv. 20.00 6.00
15 Mark Buehrle Jsy-Shoe 20.00 6.00

2002 Leaf Rookies and Stars Freshman Orientation

Inserted in packs at a stated rate of one in 142, these 20 cards feature not only players who debuted during the 2002 season but also a game-used memorabilia piece from that player.

Nm-Mt Ex-Mt
*CLASS OFFICERS: .6X TO 1.5X BASIC
CLASS OFFICERS RANDOM IN PACKS
CLASS OFFICERS PRINT RUN 50 #'d SETS
1 Andres Torres Bat 15.00 4.50
2 Mark Ellis Jsy 15.00 4.50
3 Erik Bedard Bat 15.00 4.50
4 Delvin James Jsy 15.00 4.50
5 Austin Kearns Bat 15.00 4.50
6 Josh Pearce Bat 15.00 4.50
7 Rafael Soriano Jsy 15.00 4.50
8 Jason Lane Bat 15.00 4.50
9 Mark Prior Jsy 30.00 9.00
10 Alfredo Amezaga Bat 15.00 4.50
11 Ryan Ludwick Bat 15.00 4.50
12 So Taguchi Bat 25.00 7.50
13 Duaner Sanchez Bat 15.00 4.50
14 Kazuhisa Ishii Jsy 20.00 6.00
15 Zach Day Pants 15.00 4.50
16 Eric Cyr Bat 15.00 4.50
17 Francis Beltran Jsy 15.00 4.50
18 Joe Borchard Jsy 15.00 4.50
19 Jeremy Affeldt Shoe 15.00 4.50
20 Alexis Gomez Shoe 15.00 4.50

2002 Leaf Rookies and Stars Freshman Orientation Class Officers

Randomly inserted into packs, this is a parallel to the Freshman Orientation insert set. Each of these cards was issued to a stated print run of 50 serial numbered sets.

Nm-Mt Ex-Mt
*CLASS OFFICERS: .6X TO 1.5X BASIC FRESH

2002 Leaf Rookies and Stars Statistical Standouts

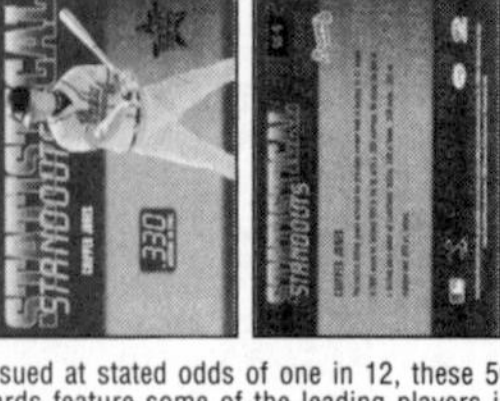

Issued at stated odds of one in 12, these 50 cards feature some of the leading players in baseball.

Nm-Mt Ex-Mt
1 Adam Dunn 2.50 .75
2 Alex Rodriguez 10.00 3.00
3 Andruw Jones 2.50 .75
4 Brian Giles 2.50 .75
5 Chipper Jones 6.00 1.80
6 Cliff Floyd 2.50 .75
7 Craig Biggio 4.00 1.20
8 Frank Thomas 6.00 1.80
9 Fred McGriff 4.00 1.20
10 Garret Anderson 2.50 .75
11 Greg Maddux 10.00 3.00
12 Luis Gonzalez 2.50 .75
13 Magglio Ordonez 2.50 .75
14 Ivan Rodriguez 6.00 1.80
15 Ken Griffey Jr. 10.00 3.00
16 Ichiro Suzuki 10.00 3.00
17 Jason Giambi 6.00 1.80
18 Derek Jeter 15.00 4.50
19 Sammy Sosa 10.00 3.00
20 Albert Pujols 12.00 3.60
21 J.D. Drew 2.50 .75
22 Jeff Bagwell 4.00 1.20
23 Jim Edmonds 2.50 .75
24 Jose Vidro 2.50 .75
25 Juan Encarnacion 2.50 .75
26 Kerry Wood 6.00 1.80
27 Al Leiter 2.50 .75
28 Curt Schilling 4.00 1.20
29 Manny Ramirez 2.50 .75
30 Lance Berkman 2.50 .75
31 Miguel Tejada 2.50 .75
32 Mike Piazza 10.00 3.00
33 Nomar Garciaparra 10.00 3.00
34 Omar Vizquel 2.50 .75
35 Pat Burrell 2.50 .75
36 Paul Konerko 2.50 .75
37 Rafael Palmeiro 4.00 1.20
38 Randy Johnson 6.00 1.80
39 Richie Sexson 2.50 .75
40 Roger Clemens 12.00 3.60
41 Shawn Green 2.50 .75
42 Todd Helton 4.00 1.20
43 Tom Glavine 4.00 1.20
44 Troy Glaus 4.00 1.20
45 Vladimir Guerrero 6.00 1.80
46 Mike Sweeney 2.50 .75
47 Alfonso Soriano 4.00 1.20
48 Barry Zito 4.00 1.20
49 John Smoltz 4.00 1.20
50 Ellis Burks 2.50 .75

2002 Leaf Rookies and Stars Statistical Standouts Materials

Randomly inserted into packs, this is a parallel to the basic Statistical Standouts insert set. These cards feature a game-used memorabilia piece from each player. Please note that some cards were issued in shorter supply and we have notated that information along with the stated print run information next to the player's name in our checklist.

Nm-Mt Ex-Mt
SUPER: RANDOM INSERTS IN PACKS
SUPER PRINT RUN 25 SERIAL #'d SETS
SUPER: NO PRICING DUE TO SCARCITY
1 Adam Dunn Bat/200 15.00 4.50
2 Alex Rodriguez Bat/200 20.00 6.00
3 Andruw Jones Bat/200 15.00 4.50
4 Brian Giles Bat 15.00 4.50
5 Chipper Jones Bat/200 20.00 6.00
6 Cliff Floyd Jsy 15.00 4.50
7 Craig Biggio Pants 20.00 6.00
8 Frank Thomas Jsy/125 20.00 6.00
9 Fred McGriff Bat 20.00 6.00
10 Garret Anderson Bat
11 Greg Maddux Jsy/200 20.00 6.00
12 Luis Gonzalez Jsy 15.00 4.50
13 Magglio Ordonez Bat/150 15.00 4.50
14 Ivan Rodriguez Jsy/100
15 Ken Griffey Jr. Base/100 25.00 7.50
16 Ichiro Suzuki Base/100
17 Jason Giambi Base 20.00 6.00
18 Derek Jeter Base/100
19 Sammy Sosa Base/100 25.00 7.50
20 Albert Pujols Base/100
21 J.D. Drew Bat/150 15.00 4.50
22 Jeff Bagwell Pants/150
23 Jim Edmonds Bat 15.00 4.50
24 Jose Vidro Bat 15.00 4.50
25 Juan Encarnacion Bat 10.00 3.00
26 Kerry Wood Jsy/200 20.00 6.00
27 Al Leiter Jsy 15.00 4.50
28 Curt Schilling Jsy/225
29 Manny Ramirez Bat/100
30 Lance Berkman Bat/150
31 Miguel Tejada Jsy 15.00 4.50
32 Mike Piazza Bat/200 20.00 6.00
33 Nomar Garciaparra Bat/200 25.00 7.50
34 Omar Vizquel Jsy 15.00 4.50
35 Pat Burrell Bat 15.00 4.50
36 Paul Konerko Jsy 15.00 4.50
37 Rafael Palmeiro Bat 20.00 6.00
38 Randy Johnson Jsy/200 20.00 6.00
39 Richie Sexson Jsy 15.00 4.50
40 Roger Clemens Jsy/200 30.00 9.00
41 Shawn Green Jsy 15.00 4.50
42 Todd Helton Jsy/175 20.00 6.00
43 Tom Glavine Jsy/125 20.00 6.00
44 Troy Glaus Jsy 20.00 6.00
45 Vladimir Guerrero Jsy 20.00 6.00
46 Mike Sweeney Bat 15.00 4.50
47 Alfonso Soriano Jsy/200 20.00 6.00
48 Barry Zito Jsy/100 20.00 6.00
49 John Smoltz Jsy
50 Ellis Burks Jsy/50 15.00 4.50

2002 Leaf Rookies and Stars Triple Threads

Randomly inserted into packs, this 10 card set featured three players who have something in common along with a memorabilia piece of each player featured on the card. Each card was also issued to a stated print run of 100 serial numbered sets.

Nm-Mt Ex-Mt
1 Reggie Jackson 100.00 30.00
Alfonso Soriano
Don Mattingly

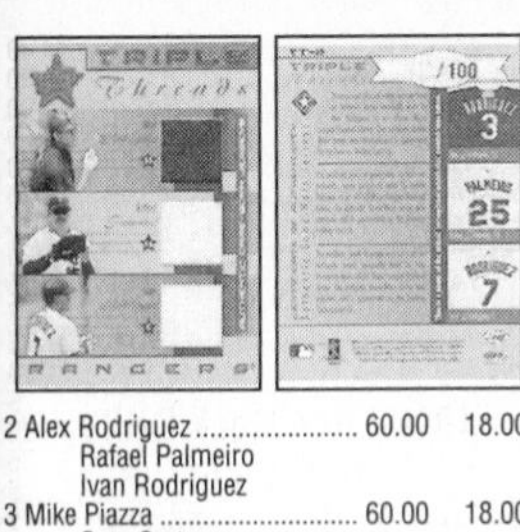

2 Alex Rodriguez 60.00 18.00
Rafael Palmeiro
Ivan Rodriguez
3 Mike Piazza 60.00 18.00
Gary Carter
Rickey Henderson
4 Dale Murphy 50.00 15.00
Andruw Jones
Chipper Jones
5 Mike Schmidt 100.00 30.00
Steve Carlton
Scott Rolen
6 Rickey Henderson 50.00 15.00
Rickey Henderson
Rickey Henderson
7 Johnny Bench 100.00 30.00
Joe Morgan
Tom Seaver
8 Randy Johnson 50.00 15.00
Pedro Martinez
Vladimir Guerrero
9 Nolan Ryan 100.00 30.00
Rod Carew
Troy Glaus
10 Lou Brock 100.00 30.00
J.D Drew
Stan Musial

2002 Leaf Rookies and Stars View Masters

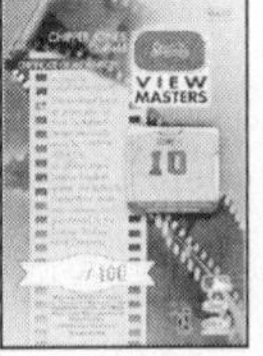

Randomly inserted into packs, these 20 cards feature some of the leading players in the game in a style reminiscent of the old "View Masters" which became popular in the 1950's. Each of these cards were printed to a stated print run of 100 serial numbered sets and have a game used-memorabilia piece attached to them.

Nm-Mt Ex-Mt
SLIDESHOW: RANDOM INSERTS IN PACKS
SLIDESHOW PRINT 25 SERIAL #'d SETS
SLIDESHOW: NO PRICE DUE TO SCARCITY
1 Carlos Delgado 25.00 7.50
2 Todd Helton 25.00 7.50
3 Tony Gwynn 40.00 12.00
4 Bernie Williams 25.00 7.50
5 Luis Gonzalez 25.00 7.50
6 Larry Walker 25.00 7.50
7 Troy Glaus 25.00 7.50
8 Alfonso Soriano 25.00 7.50
9 Curt Schilling 25.00 7.50
10 Chipper Jones 40.00 12.00
11 Vladimir Guerrero 40.00 12.00
12 Adam Dunn 25.00 7.50
13 Rickey Henderson 40.00 12.00
14 Miguel Tejada 25.00 7.50
15 Kazuhisa Ishii 40.00 12.00
16 Greg Maddux 40.00 12.00
17 Pedro Martinez 40.00 12.00
18 Nomar Garciaparra 50.00 15.00
19 Mike Piazza 40.00 12.00
20 Lance Berkman 25.00 7.50

1996 Leaf Signature

The 1996 Leaf Signature Set was issued by Donruss in two series totalling 150 cards. The four-card packs carried a suggested retail price of $9.99 each. It's interesting to note that the Extended Series was the last of the 1996 releases. In fact, it was released in January, 1997 - so late in the year that it's categorization as a 1996 issue was a bit of a stretch at that time. Production for the Extended Series was only 40 percent that of the regular issue. Extended Series packs actually contained a mix of both series cards, thus the Extended Series cards are somewhat scarcer. Card fronts feature borderless color action player photos with the card name printed in a silver foil emblem. The backs carry player information. Rookie Cards include Darin Erstad. This product was a benchmark release in hobby history due to it's inclusion of one or more autograph cards per pack (explaining it's high suggested retail pack price). The product was highly successful upon release and opened the doors for wide incorporation of autograph cards into a wide array of brands from that point forward.

Nm-Mt Ex-Mt
COMPLETE SET (150) 100.00 30.00
COMP. SERIES 1 (100) 60.00 18.00
COMPLETE SERIES 2 (50) 40.00 12.00
COMMON CARD (1-100) .50 .15
COMMON (101-150) .30 .09
1 Mike Piazza 2.00 .60
2 Juan Gonzalez 1.25 .35
3 Greg Maddux 2.00 .60
4 Marc Newfield .50 .15
5 Wade Boggs .75 .23
6 Ray Lankford .50 .15
7 Frank Thomas 1.25 .35
8 Rico Brogna .50 .15
9 Tim Salmon .75 .23
10 Ken Griffey Jr. 2.00 .60
11 Manny Ramirez .50 .15
12 Cecil Fielder .50 .15
13 Gregg Jefferies .50 .15
14 Rondell White .50 .15
15 Cal Ripken 4.00 1.20
16 Alex Rodriguez 2.50 .75
17 Bernie Williams .75 .23
18 Andres Galarraga .50 .15
19 Mike Mussina 1.25 .35
20 Chuck Knoblauch .50 .15
21 Joe Carter .50 .15
22 Jeff Bagwell .75 .23
23 Mark McGwire 3.00 .90
24 Sammy Sosa 2.00 .60
25 Reggie Sanders .50 .15
26 Chipper Jones 1.25 .35
27 Jeff Cirillo .50 .15
28 Roger Clemens 2.50 .75
29 Craig Biggio .75 .23
30 Gary Sheffield .50 .15
31 Paul O'Neill .75 .23
32 Johnny Damon .50 .15
33 Jason Isringhausen .50 .15
34 Jay Bell .50 .15
35 Henry Rodriguez .50 .15
36 Matt Williams .50 .15
37 Randy Johnson 1.25 .35
38 Fred McGriff .75 .23
39 Jason Giambi 1.25 .35
40 Ivan Rodriguez 1.25 .35
41 Raul Mondesi .50 .15
42 Barry Larkin 1.25 .35
43 Ryan Klesko .50 .15
44 Joey Hamilton .50 .15
45 Todd Hundley .50 .15
46 Jim Edmonds .50 .15
47 Dante Bichette .50 .15
48 Roberto Alomar 1.25 .35
49 Mark Grace .75 .23
50 Brady Anderson .50 .15
51 Hideo Nomo 1.25 .35
52 Ozzie Smith 2.00 .60
53 Robin Ventura .50 .15
54 Andy Pettitte .75 .23
55 Kenny Lofton .50 .15
56 John Mabry .50 .15
57 Paul Molitor .75 .23
58 Rey Ordonez .50 .15
59 Albert Belle .50 .15
60 Charles Johnson .50 .15
61 Edgar Martinez .75 .23
62 Derek Bell .50 .15
63 Carlos Delgado .50 .15
64 Raul Casanova .50 .15
65 Ismael Valdes .50 .15
66 J.T. Snow .50 .15
67 Derek Jeter 3.00 .90
68 Jason Kendall .50 .15
69 John Smoltz .75 .23
70 Chad Mottola .50 .15
71 Jim Thome 1.25 .35
72 Will Clark 1.25 .35
73 Mo Vaughn .50 .15
74 John Wasdin .50 .15
75 Rafael Palmeiro .75 .23
76 Mark Grudzielanek .50 .15
77 Larry Walker .75 .23
78 Alan Benes .50 .15
79 Michael Tucker .50 .15
80 Billy Wagner .50 .15
81 Paul Wilson .50 .15
82 Greg Vaughn .50 .15
83 Dean Palmer .50 .15
84 Ryne Sandberg 2.00 .60
85 Eric Young .50 .15
86 Jay Buhner .50 .15
87 Tony Clark .50 .15
88 Jermaine Dye .50 .15
89 Barry Bonds 3.00 .90
90 Ugueth Urbina .50 .15
91 Charles Nagy .50 .15
92 Ruben Rivera .50 .15
93 Todd Hollandsworth .50 .15
94 Darin Erstad RC 6.00 1.80
95 Brooks Kieschnick .50 .15
96 Edgar Renteria .50 .15
97 Lenny Dykstra .50 .15
98 Tony Gwynn 1.50 .45
99 Kirby Puckett 1.25 .35
100 Checklist .50 .15
101 Andruw Jones 2.50 .75
102 Alex Ochoa .30 .09
103 David Cone .50 .15
104 Rusty Greer .50 .15
105 Jose Canseco 1.25 .35
106 Ken Caminiti .50 .15
107 Mariano Rivera .75 .23
108 Ron Gant .50 .15
109 Darryl Strawberry .75 .23
110 Vladimir Guerrero 3.00 .90
111 George Arias .30 .09
112 Jeff Conine .50 .15
113 Bobby Higginson .50 .15
114 Eric Karros .50 .15
115 Brian Hunter .30 .09
116 Eddie Murray 1.25 .35
117 Todd Walker .75 .23
118 Chan Ho Park .50 .15
119 John Jaha .30 .09
120 Dave Justice .50 .15
121 Makoto Suzuki .30 .09
122 Scott Rolen 1.25 .35
123 Tino Martinez .75 .23
124 Kimera Bartee .30 .09
125 Garret Anderson .50 .15
126 Brian Jordan .50 .15
127 Andre Dawson .50 .15
128 Javier Lopez .50 .15
129 Bill Pulsipher .30 .09
130 Dwight Gooden .75 .23
131 Al Martin .30 .09
132 Terrell Wade .30 .09
133 Steve Gibralter .30 .09
134 Tom Glavine .75 .23
135 Kevin Appier .50 .15
136 Tim Raines .50 .15
137 Curtis Pride .30 .09
138 Todd Greene .30 .09
139 Bobby Bonilla .50 .15
140 Trey Beamon .30 .09
141 Marty Cordova .30 .09
142 Rickey Henderson 1.25 .35
143 Ellis Burks .50 .15
144 Dennis Eckersley .50 .15
145 Kevin Brown .50 .15
146 Carlos Baerga .30 .09
147 Brett Butler .50 .15
148 Marquis Grissom .30 .09
149 Karim Garcia .30 .09
150 Frank Thomas CL .75 .23

1996 Leaf Signature Gold Press Proofs

Randomly inserted in first series packs at an approximate rate of one in 12 and second series packs at an approximate rate of one in 8, this 150-card set is parallel to the regular version. The design is similar to the regular card with the exception of the card name being printed in a gold foil emblem and the words "Press Proof" printed in gold foil vertically down the side.

Nm-Mt Ex-Mt
*SER.1 STARS: 4X TO 10X BASIC CARDS
*SER.1 ROOKIES: 1.25X TO 3X BASIC CARDS
*SER.2 STARS: 3X TO 8X BASIC CARDS

1996 Leaf Signature Platinum Press Proofs

Randomly inserted exclusively into Extended Series packs at the rate of one in 24, this 150-card set is parallel to the regular Leaf Signature Set. Only 150 sets were produced. Unlike the multi-series base set and Gold Press Proofs, these scarce Platinum cards were issued in one comprehensive series. The cards are similar in design to the regular set with the exception of holographic platinum foil stamping.

Nm-Mt Ex-Mt
*SER.1 STARS: 10X TO 25X BASIC CARDS
*SER. 1 ROOKIES: 2.5X TO 6X BASIC CARDS
*SER.2 STARS: 8X TO 20X BASIC CARDS

1996 Leaf Signature Autographs

Inserted into 1996 Leaf Signature Series first series packs, these unnumbered cards were one of the first major autograph issues featured in an MLB-licensed trading card set. First series packs contained at least one autograph, with the chance of getting more. Donruss/Leaf reports that all but 10 players in the Leaf Signature Series signed close to 5,000 total autographs (3,500 bronze, 1,000 silver, 500 gold). The 10 players who signed 1,000 (700 bronze, 200 silver, 100 gold) are: Roberto Alomar, Wade Boggs, Derek Jeter, Kenny Lofton, Paul Molitor, Raul Mondesi, Manny Ramirez, Alex Rodriguez, Frank Thomas and Mo Vaughn. It's also important to note that six additional players did not submit their cards in time to be included in first series packs. Thus, their cards were thrown into Extended Series packs. Those six players are as follows: Brian L.Hunter, Carlos Delgado, Phil Plantier, Jim Thome, Terrell Wade and Ernie Young. Thome signed only silver and gold foil cards, thus the Bronze set is considered complete at 251 cards. Prices below refer exclusively to Bronze versions. Blue and black ink variations have been found for Carlos Delgado, Alex Rodriguez and Michael Tucker. No consistent premiums for these variations has been tracked. Finally, an autographed jumbo silver foil version of the Frank Thomas card was distributed to dealers in March, 1997. Dealers received either this first series or the Extended Series jumbo Thomas for every Extended Series case ordered. Each Thomas jumbo is individually serial numbered to 1,500. A standard-size promo card of Frank Thomas with a fascimile signature was also created and released several weeks before this set's release.

Nm-Mt Ex-Mt
1 Kurt Abbott 5.00 1.50
2 Juan Acevedo 5.00 1.50
3 Terry Adams 5.00 1.50
4 Manny Alexander 5.00 1.50
5 Roberto Alomar SP 50.00 15.00
6 Moises Alou 10.00 3.00
7 Wilson Alvarez 5.00 1.50
8 Garret Anderson 15.00 4.50
9 Shane Andrews 5.00 1.50
10 Andy Ashby 5.00 1.50
11 Pedro Astacio 5.00 1.50
12 Brad Ausmus 5.00 1.50
13 Bobby Ayala 5.00 1.50
14 Carlos Baerga 5.00 1.50
15 Harold Baines 15.00 4.50
16 Jason Bates 5.00 1.50
17 Allen Battle 5.00 1.50
18 Rich Becker 5.00 1.50
19 David Bell 5.00 1.50
20 Rafael Belliard 5.00 1.50
21 Andy Benes 5.00 1.50
22 Armando Benitez 10.00 3.00
23 Jason Bere 5.00 1.50
24 Geronimo Berroa 5.00 1.50
25 Willie Blair 5.00 1.50
26 Mike Blowers 5.00 1.50
27 Wade Boggs SP 50.00 15.00
28 Ricky Bones 5.00 1.50
29 Mike Bordick 10.00 3.00
30 Toby Borland 5.00 1.50
31 Ricky Bottalico 5.00 1.50
32 Darren Bragg 5.00 1.50
33 Jeff Branson 5.00 1.50
34 Tilson Brito 5.00 1.50
35 Rico Brogna 5.00 1.50
36 Scott Brosius 10.00 3.00
37 Damon Buford 5.00 1.50
38 Mike Busby 5.00 1.50
39 Tom Candiotti 5.00 1.50
40 Frank Castillo 5.00 1.50
41 Andujar Cedeno 5.00 1.50
42 Domingo Cedeno 5.00 1.50
43 Roger Cedeno 5.00 1.50
44 Norm Charlton 5.00 1.50
45 Jeff Cirillo 5.00 1.50
46 Will Clark 25.00 7.50
47 Jeff Conine 10.00 3.00
48 Steve Cooke 5.00 1.50
49 Joey Cora 5.00 1.50
50 Marty Cordova 5.00 1.50
51 Rheal Cormier 5.00 1.50
52 Felipe Crespo 5.00 1.50
53 Chad Curtis 5.00 1.50
54 Johnny Damon 10.00 3.00
55 Russ Davis 5.00 1.50
56 Andre Dawson 15.00 4.50
57 Carlos Delgado 25.00 7.50
58 Doug Drabek 5.00 1.50
59 Darren Dreifort 5.00 1.50
60 Shawon Dunston 5.00 1.50
61 Ray Durham 10.00 3.00
62 Jim Edmonds 15.00 4.50
63 Joey Eischen 5.00 1.50
64 Jim Eisenreich 5.00 1.50
65 Sal Fasano 5.00 1.50
66 Jeff Fassero 5.00 1.50
67 Alex Fernandez 5.00 1.50
68 Darrin Fletcher 5.00 1.50
69 Chad Fonville 5.00 1.50
70 Kevin Foster 5.00 1.50
71 John Franco 10.00 3.00
72 Julio Franco 10.00 3.00
73 Marvin Freeman 5.00 1.50
74 Travis Fryman 10.00 3.00
75 Gary Gaetti 10.00 3.00
76 Carlos Garcia 5.00 1.50
77 Jason Giambi 25.00 7.50
78 Benji Gil 5.00 1.50
79 Greg Gohr 5.00 1.50
80 Chris Gomez 5.00 1.50
81 Leo Gomez 5.00 1.50
82 Tom Goodwin 5.00 1.50
83 Mike Grace 5.00 1.50
84 Mike Greenwell 5.00 1.50
85 Rusty Greer 10.00 3.00
86 Mark Grudzielanek 5.00 1.50
87 Mark Gubicza 5.00 1.50
88 Juan Guzman 5.00 1.50
89 Darryl Hamilton 5.00 1.50
90 Joey Hamilton 5.00 1.50
91 Chris Hammond 5.00 1.50
92 Mike Hampton 10.00 3.00
93 Chris Haney 5.00 1.50
94 Todd Haney 5.00 1.50
95 Erik Hanson 5.00 1.50
96 Pete Harnisch 5.00 1.50
97 LaTroy Hawkins 5.00 1.50
98 Charlie Hayes 5.00 1.50
99 Jimmy Haynes 5.00 1.50
100 Roberto Hernandez 5.00 1.50
101 Bobby Higginson 10.00 3.00
102 Glenallen Hill 5.00 1.50
103 Ken Hill 5.00 1.50
104 Sterling Hitchcock 5.00 1.50
105 Trevor Hoffman 15.00 4.50
106 Dave Hollins 5.00 1.50
107 Dwayne Hosey 5.00 1.50
108 Thomas Howard 5.00 1.50
109 Steve Howe 5.00 1.50
110 John Hudek 5.00 1.50
111 Rex Hudler 5.00 1.50
112 Brian L.Hunter 5.00 1.50
113 Butch Huskey 5.00 1.50
114 Mark Hutton 5.00 1.50
115 Jason Jacome 5.00 1.50
116 John Jaha 5.00 1.50
117 Reggie Jefferson 5.00 1.50
118 Derek Jeter SP 150.00 45.00
119 Bobby Jones 5.00 1.50
120 Todd Jones 5.00 1.50
121 Brian Jordan 10.00 3.00
122 Kevin Jordan 5.00 1.50
123 Jeff Juden 5.00 1.50
124 Ron Karkovice 5.00 1.50
125 Roberto Kelly 5.00 1.50
126 Mark Kiefer 5.00 1.50
127 Brooks Kieschnick 5.00 1.50
128 Jeff King 5.00 1.50
129 Mike Lansing 5.00 1.50
130 Matt Lawton 10.00 3.00
131 Al Leiter 10.00 3.00
132 Mark Leiter 5.00 1.50
133 Curtis Leskanic 5.00 1.50
134 Darren Lewis 5.00 1.50
135 Mark Lewis 5.00 1.50
136 Felipe Lira 5.00 1.50
137 Pat Listach 5.00 1.50
138 Keith Lockhart 5.00 1.50
139 Kenny Lofton SP 25.00 7.50
140 John Mabry 5.00 1.50
141 Mike Macfarlane 5.00 1.50
142 Kirt Manwaring 5.00 1.50
143 Al Martin 5.00 1.50
144 Norberto Martin 5.00 1.50
145 Dennis Martinez 10.00 3.00
146 Pedro Martinez 50.00 15.00
147 Sandy Martinez 5.00 1.50
148 Mike Matheny 5.00 1.50
149 T.J. Mathews 5.00 1.50
150 David McCarty 5.00 1.50
151 Ben McDonald 5.00 1.50
152 Pat Meares 5.00 1.50
153 Orlando Merced 5.00 1.50
154 Jose Mesa 5.00 1.50
155 Matt Mieske 5.00 1.50
156 Orlando Miller 5.00 1.50
157 Mike Mimbs 5.00 1.50
158 Paul Molitor SP 40.00 12.00
159 Raul Mondesi SP 25.00 7.50
160 Jeff Montgomery 5.00 1.50
161 Mickey Morandini 5.00 1.50
162 Lyle Mouton 5.00 1.50
163 James Mouton 5.00 1.50
164 Jamie Moyer 15.00 4.50
165 Rodney Myers 5.00 1.50
166 Denny Neagle 5.00 1.50
167 Robb Nen 10.00 3.00
168 Marc Newfield 5.00 1.50
169 Dave Nilsson 5.00 1.50
170 Jon Nunnally 5.00 1.50
171 Chad Ogea 5.00 1.50
172 Troy O'Leary 5.00 1.50
173 Rey Ordonez 5.00 1.50
174 Jayhawk Owens 5.00 1.50
175 Tom Pagnozzi 5.00 1.50
176 Dean Palmer 5.00 1.50
177 Roger Pavlik 5.00 1.50
178 Troy Percival 10.00 3.00
179 Carlos Perez 5.00 1.50
180 Robert Perez 5.00 1.50
181 Andy Pettitte 40.00 12.00
182 Phil Plantier 5.00 1.50
183 Mike Potts 5.00 1.50
184 Curtis Pride 10.00 3.00
185 Ariel Prieto 5.00 1.50
186 Bill Pulsipher 5.00 1.50
187 Brad Radke 10.00 3.00
188 Manny Ramirez SP 40.00 12.00
189 Joe Randa 5.00 1.50
190 Pat Rapp 5.00 1.50
191 Bryan Rekar 5.00 1.50
192 Shane Reynolds 5.00 1.50
193 Arthur Rhodes 5.00 1.50
194 Mariano Rivera 50.00 15.00
195 Alex Rodriguez SP 120.00 36.00
196 Frank Rodriguez 5.00 1.50
197 Mel Rojas 5.00 1.50
198 Ken Ryan 5.00 1.50
199 Bret Saberhagen 10.00 3.00
200 Tim Salmon 15.00 4.50
201 Rey Sanchez 5.00 1.50
202 Scott Sanders 5.00 1.50
203 Steve Scarsone 5.00 1.50
204 Curt Schilling 25.00 7.50
205 Jason Schmidt 15.00 4.50
206 David Segui 5.00 1.50
207 Kevin Seitzer 5.00 1.50
208 Scott Servais 5.00 1.50
209 Don Slaught 5.00 1.50
210 Zane Smith 5.00 1.50
211 Paul Sorrento 5.00 1.50
212 Scott Stahoviak 5.00 1.50
213 Mike Stanley 5.00 1.50
214 Terry Steinbach 5.00 1.50
215 Kevin Stocker 5.00 1.50
216 Jeff Suppan 5.00 1.50
217 Bill Swift 5.00 1.50
218 Greg Swindell 5.00 1.50
219 Kevin Tapani 5.00 1.50
220 Danny Tartabull 5.00 1.50
221 Julian Tavarez 5.00 1.50
222 Frank Thomas SP 60.00 18.00
223 Ozzie Timmons 5.00 1.50
224 Michael Tucker 5.00 1.50
225 Ismael Valdes 5.00 1.50
226 Jose Valentin 5.00 1.50
227 Todd Van Poppel 5.00 1.50
228 Mo Vaughn SP 25.00 7.50
229 Quilvio Veras 5.00 1.50
230 Fernando Vina 10.00 3.00
231 Joe Vitiello 5.00 1.50
232 Jose Vizcaino 5.00 1.50
233 Omar Vizquel 15.00 4.50
234 Terrell Wade 5.00 1.50
235 Paul Wagner 5.00 1.50
236 Matt Walbeck 5.00 1.50
237 Jerome Walton 5.00 1.50
238 Turner Ward 5.00 1.50
239 Allen Watson 5.00 1.50
240 David Weathers 5.00 1.50
241 Walt Weiss 5.00 1.50
242 Turk Wendell 5.00 1.50
243 Rondell White 10.00 3.00
244 Brian Williams 5.00 1.50
245 George Williams 5.00 1.50
246 Paul Wilson 5.00 1.50
247 Bobby Witt 5.00 1.50
248 Bob Wolcott 5.00 1.50
249 Eric Young 5.00 1.50
250 Ernie Young 5.00 1.50
251 Greg Zaun 5.00 1.50
NNO F.Thomas Jumbo AU 40.00 12.00
NNO Frank Thomas Sample 2.00 .60
Fascimile Auto

1996 Leaf Signature Autographs Gold

Randomly inserted primarily in first series packs, this 252-card set is parallel to the regular set and is similar in design with the exception of the gold foil printing on each card front. Each player signed 500 cards, except for the SP's of which only 100 of each are signed. Jim Thome erroneously signed 514 Gold cards.

	Nm-Mt	Ex-Mt
*GOLD: .6X TO 1.5X BRONZE CARDS		
223 Jim Thome SP/514	50.00	15.00

1996 Leaf Signature Autographs Silver

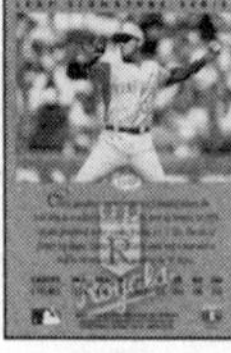

Randomly inserted primarily in first series packs, this 252-card set is parallel to the regular set and is similar in design with the exception of the silver foil printing on each card front. Each player signed 1000 silver cards, except for the SP's of which only 200 are signed. Jim Thome erroneously signed 410 Silver cards.

	Nm-Mt	Ex-Mt
*SILVER: .5X TO 1.2X BRONZE CARDS		
223 Jim Thome SP/410	50.00	15.00

1996 Leaf Signature Extended Autographs

At least two autographed cards from this 217-card set were inserted in every Extended Series pack. Super Packs with four autographed cards were seeded one in every 12 packs. Most players signed 5000 cards, but short prints (500-2500 of each) do exist. On average, one in every nine packs contains a short print. All short print cards are individually noted in our checklist. By mistake, Andruw Jones, Ryan Klesko, Andy Pettitte, Kirby Puckett and Frank Thomas signed a few hundred of each of their cards in blue ink instead of black. No difference in price has been noted. Also, the Juan Gonzalez, Andruw Jones and Alex Rodriguez cards available in packs were not signed. All three cards had information on the back on how to mail them into Donruss/Leaf for an actual signed version. The deadline to exchange these cards was December 31st, 1998. In addition, middle relievers Doug Creek and Steve Parris failed to sign all 5000 of their cards. Creek submitted 1,950 cards and Parris submitted 1,800. Finally, an autographed jumbo version of the Extended Series Frank Thomas card was distributed to dealers in March, 1997. Dealers received either this card or the first series jumbo Thomas for every Extended Series case ordered. Each Extended Thomas jumbo is individually serial numbered to 1,500. A very popular Sammy Sosa card, one of his only certified autographs, is the key card in the set.

	Nm-Mt	Ex-Mt
1 Scott Aldred	5.00	1.50
2 Mike Aldrete	5.00	1.50
3 Rich Amaral	5.00	1.50
4 Alex Arias	5.00	1.50
5 Paul Assenmacher	5.00	1.50
6 Roger Bailey	5.00	1.50
7 Erik Bennett	5.00	1.50
8 Sean Bergman	5.00	1.50
9 Doug Bochtler	5.00	1.50
10 Tim Bogar	5.00	1.50
11 Pat Borders	5.00	1.50
12 Pedro Borbon	5.00	1.50
13 Shawn Boskie	5.00	1.50
14 Rafael Bournigal	5.00	1.50
15 Mark Brandenburg	5.00	1.50
16 John Briscoe	5.00	1.50
17 Jorge Brito	5.00	1.50
18 Doug Brocail	5.00	1.50
19 Jay Buhner SP/1000	25.00	7.50
20 Scott Bullett	5.00	1.50
21 Dave Burba	5.00	1.50
22 Ken Caminiti SP/1000	25.00	7.50
23 John Cangelosi	5.00	1.50
24 Cris Carpenter	5.00	1.50
25 Chuck Carr	5.00	1.50
26 Larry Casian	5.00	1.50
27 Tony Castillo	5.00	1.50
28 Jason Christiansen	5.00	1.50
29 Archi Cianfrocco	5.00	1.50
30 Mark Clark	5.00	1.50
31 Terry Clark	5.00	1.50
32 R. Clemens SP1000	150.00	45.00
33 Jim Converse	5.00	1.50
34 Dennis Cook	5.00	1.50
35 Francisco Cordova	5.00	1.50
36 Jim Corsi	5.00	1.50
37 Tim Crabtree	5.00	1.50
38 Doug Creek SP/1950	15.00	4.50
39 John Cummings	5.00	1.50
40 Omar Daal	5.00	1.50
41 Rich DeLucia	5.00	1.50
42 Mark Dewey	5.00	1.50
43 Alex Diaz	5.00	1.50
44 Jermaine Dye SP/2500	25.00	7.50
45 Ken Edenfield	5.00	1.50
46 Mark Eichhorn	5.00	1.50
47 John Ericks	5.00	1.50
48 Darin Erstad	15.00	4.50
49 Alvaro Espinoza	5.00	1.50
50 Jorge Fabregas	5.00	1.50
51 Mike Fetters	5.00	1.50
52 John Flaherty	5.00	1.50
53 Bryce Florie	5.00	1.50
54 Tony Fossas	5.00	1.50
55 Lou Frazier	5.00	1.50
56 Mike Gallego	5.00	1.50
57 Karim Garcia SP/2500	15.00	4.50
58 Jason Giambi	25.00	7.50
59 Ed Giovanola	5.00	1.50
60 Tom Glavine SP/1250	50.00	15.00
61 Juan Gonzalez SP/1000	50.00	15.00
62 Craig Grebeck	5.00	1.50
63 Buddy Groom	5.00	1.50
64 Kevin Gross	5.00	1.50
65 Eddie Guardado	10.00	3.00
66 Mark Guthrie	5.00	1.50
67 Tony Gwynn SP/1000	60.00	18.00
68 Chip Hale	5.00	1.50
69 Darren Hall	5.00	1.50
70 Lee Hancock	5.00	1.50
71 Dave Hansen	5.00	1.50
72 Bryan Harvey	5.00	1.50
73 Bill Haselman	5.00	1.50
74 Mike Henneman	5.00	1.50
75 Doug Henry	5.00	1.50
76 Gil Heredia	5.00	1.50
77 Carlos Hernandez	5.00	1.50
78 Jose Hernandez	5.00	1.50
79 Darren Holmes	5.00	1.50
80 Mark Holzemer	5.00	1.50
81 Rick Honeycutt	5.00	1.50
82 Chris Hook	5.00	1.50
83 Chris Howard	5.00	1.50
84 Jack Howell	5.00	1.50
85 David Hulse	5.00	1.50
86 Edwin Hurtado	5.00	1.50
87 Jeff Huson	5.00	1.50
88 Mike James	5.00	1.50
89 Derek Jeter SP/1000	150.00	45.00
90 Brian Johnson	5.00	1.50
91 R. Johnson SP1000	120.00	36.00
92 Mark Johnson	5.00	1.50
93 Andruw Jones SP/2000	40.00	12.00
94 Chris Jones	5.00	1.50
95 Ricky Jordan	5.00	1.50
96 Matt Karchner	5.00	1.50
97 Scott Karl	5.00	1.50
98 Jason Kendall SP/2500	25.00	7.50
99 Brian Keyser	5.00	1.50
100 Mike Kingery	5.00	1.50
101 Wayne Kirby	5.00	1.50
102 Ryan Klesko SP/1000	25.00	7.50
103 C. Knoblauch SP1000	25.00	7.50
104 Chad Kreuter	5.00	1.50
105 Tom Lampkin	5.00	1.50
106 Scott Leius	5.00	1.50
107 Jon Lieber	5.00	1.50
108 Nelson Liriano	5.00	1.50
109 Scott Livingstone	5.00	1.50
110 Graeme Lloyd	5.00	1.50
111 Kenny Lofton SP/1000	25.00	7.50
112 Luis Lopez	5.00	1.50
113 Torey Lovullo	5.00	1.50
114 Greg Maddux SP/500	200.00	60.00
115 Mike Maddux	5.00	1.50
116 Dave Magadan	5.00	1.50
117 Mike Magnante	5.00	1.50
118 Joe Magrane	5.00	1.50
119 Pat Mahomes	5.00	1.50
120 Matt Mantei	5.00	1.50
121 John Marzano	5.00	1.50
122 Terry Mathews	5.00	1.50
123 Chuck McElroy	5.00	1.50
124 Fred McGriff SP/1000	60.00	18.00
125 Mark McLemore	5.00	1.50
126 Greg McMichael	5.00	1.50
127 Blas Minor	5.00	1.50
128 Dave Mlicki	5.00	1.50
129 Mike Mohler	5.00	1.50
130 Paul Molitor SP/1000	40.00	12.00
131 Steve Montgomery	5.00	1.50
132 Mike Mordecai	5.00	1.50
133 Mike Morgan	5.00	1.50
134 Mike Munoz	5.00	1.50
135 Greg Myers	5.00	1.50
136 Jimmy Myers	5.00	1.50
137 Mike Myers	5.00	1.50
138 Bob Natal	5.00	1.50
139 Dan Naulty	5.00	1.50
140 Jeff Nelson	10.00	3.00
141 Warren Newson	5.00	1.50
142 Chris Nichting	5.00	1.50
143 Melvin Nieves	5.00	1.50
144 Charlie O'Brien	5.00	1.50
145 Alex Ochoa	5.00	1.50
146 Omar Olivares	5.00	1.50
147 Joe Oliver	5.00	1.50
148 Lance Painter	5.00	1.50
149 R. Palmeiro SP2000	50.00	15.00
150 Mark Parent	5.00	1.50
151 Steve Parris SP/1800	15.00	4.50
152 Bob Patterson	5.00	1.50
153 Tony Pena	5.00	1.50
154 Eddie Perez	5.00	1.50
155 Yorkis Perez	5.00	1.50
156 Robert Person	5.00	1.50
157 Mark Petkovsek	5.00	1.50
158 Andy Pettitte SP/1000	80.00	24.00
159 J.R. Phillips	5.00	1.50
160 Hipolito Pichardo	5.00	1.50
161 Eric Plunk	5.00	1.50
162 Jimmy Poole	5.00	1.50
163 K. Puckett SP/1000	80.00	24.00
164 Paul Quantrill	5.00	1.50
165 Tom Quinlan	5.00	1.50
166 Jeff Reboulet	5.00	1.50
167 Jeff Reed	5.00	1.50
168 Steve Reed	5.00	1.50
169 Carlos Reyes	5.00	1.50
170 Bill Risley	5.00	1.50
171 Kevin Ritz	5.00	1.50
172 Kevin Roberson	5.00	1.50
173 Rich Robertson	5.00	1.50
174 A. Rodriguez SP/500	150.00	45.00
175 I. Rodriguez SP1250	50.00	15.00
176 Bruce Ruffin	5.00	1.50
177 Juan Samuel	5.00	1.50
178 Tim Scott	5.00	1.50
179 Kevin Sefcik	5.00	1.50
180 Jeff Shaw	5.00	1.50
181 Danny Sheaffer	5.00	1.50
182 Craig Shipley	5.00	1.50
183 Dave Silvestri	5.00	1.50
184 Aaron Small	5.00	1.50
185 John Smoltz SP/1000	100.00	30.00
186 Luis Sojo	5.00	1.50
187 S. Sosa SP/1000	300.00	90.00
188 Steve Sparks	5.00	1.50
189 Tim Spehr	5.00	1.50
190 Russ Springer	5.00	1.50
191 Matt Stairs	5.00	1.50
192 Andy Stankiewicz	5.00	1.50
193 Mike Stanton	5.00	1.50
194 Kelly Stinnett	5.00	1.50
195 Doug Strange	5.00	1.50
196 Mark Sweeney	5.00	1.50
197 Jeff Tabaka	5.00	1.50
198 Jesus Tavarez	5.00	1.50
199 F. Thomas SP1000	60.00	18.00
200 Larry Thomas	5.00	1.50
201 Mark Thompson	5.00	1.50
202 Mike Timlin	5.00	1.50
203 Steve Trachsel	5.00	1.50
204 Tom Urbani	5.00	1.50
205 Julio Valera	5.00	1.50
206 Dave Valle	5.00	1.50
207 Wm. VanLandingham	5.00	1.50
208 Mo Vaughn SP/1000	25.00	7.50
209 Dave Veres	5.00	1.50
210 Ed Vosberg	5.00	1.50
211 Don Wengert	5.00	1.50
212 Matt Whiteside	5.00	1.50
213 Bob Wickman	5.00	1.50
214 M.Williams SP/1250	25.00	7.50
215 Mike Williams	5.00	1.50
216 Woody Williams	10.00	3.00
217 Craig Worthington	5.00	1.50
NNO F.Thomas Jumbo AU	40.00	12.00

1996 Leaf Signature Extended Autographs Century Marks

Randomly inserted exclusively into Extended Series packs, cards from this 31-card parallel set feature a selection of star and rising young prospect players taken from the more comprehensive 217-card Extended Autograph set. The cards differ by a special blue holographic foil treatment. Only 100 of each card exists. In addition, Juan Gonzalez, Derek Jeter, Andruw Jones, Rafael Palmeiro and Alex Rodriguez did not sign the cards distributed in packs. All of these players cards had information on the back on how to mail them into Leaf/Donruss to receive a signed version.

	Nm-Mt	Ex-Mt
1 Jay Buhner	60.00	18.00
2 Ken Caminiti	60.00	18.00
3 Roger Clemens	200.00	60.00
4 Jermaine Dye	60.00	18.00
5 Darin Erstad	80.00	24.00
6 Karim Garcia	25.00	7.50
7 Jason Giambi	120.00	36.00
8 Tom Glavine	120.00	36.00
9 Juan Gonzalez	120.00	36.00
10 Tony Gwynn	120.00	36.00
11 Derek Jeter	300.00	90.00
12 Randy Johnson	150.00	45.00
13 Andruw Jones	100.00	30.00
14 Jason Kendall	60.00	18.00
15 Ryan Klesko	60.00	18.00
16 Chuck Knoblauch	60.00	18.00
17 Kenny Lofton	60.00	18.00
18 Greg Maddux	200.00	60.00
19 Fred McGriff	120.00	36.00
20 Paul Molitor	120.00	36.00
21 Alex Ochoa	25.00	7.50
22 Rafael Palmeiro	120.00	36.00
23 Andy Pettitte	120.00	36.00
24 Kirby Puckett	120.00	36.00
25 Alex Rodriguez	250.00	75.00
26 Ivan Rodriguez	120.00	36.00
27 John Smoltz	120.00	36.00
28 Sammy Sosa	500.00	150.00
29 Frank Thomas	120.00	36.00
30 Mo Vaughn	60.00	18.00
31 Matt Williams	120.00	36.00

1923 Lections

These 2 1/2" by 4" blank-backed horizontal cards are on heavy cardboard stock. The player's picture is on the left side and a game diagram is one the right. Any additional findings to this checklist are appreciated.

	Ex-Mt	VG
COMPLETE SET	12000.00	6000.00
1 Frank Chance MG	1000.00	500.00
2 Howard Ehmke	500.00	250.00
3 Frank Frisch	1000.00	500.00
4 Rogers Hornsby	2000.00	1000.00
5 Charlie Jamieson	500.00	250.00
6 Bob Meusel	800.00	400.00
7 Irish Meusel	500.00	250.00
8 Babe Ruth	5000.00	2500.00
9 Charles Schmidt	500.00	250.00
10 Bob Shawkey	600.00	300.00

1993 Legendary Foils Promos

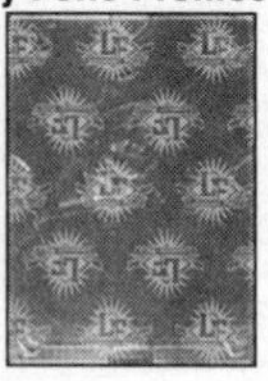

Dubbed the Sports Legends Series, these plaques, which measure approximately 2 5/8" by 3 3/4", feature Hall of Famers from baseball, football, basketball and hockey. They will be released at a rate of one card from each sport per month. Production was limited to 100,000 plaques for any one Hall of Famer and All-Gold Series plaques were limited to 5,000. These cards are all notated with a promo message.

	Nm-Mt	Ex-Mt
COMPLETE SET	4.00	1.20
1 Satchel Paige	2.00	.60
2 Honus Wagner	2.00	.60

1993-94 Legendary Foils

The Legendary Foils Sport Series is a monthly series featuring baseball Hall of Famers. There are two editions. One is the Gold Edition, limited to 5,000 sets, and the Colored Edition, limited to 95,000 cards per player. The cards measure approximately 3 1/2" by 5" and come in a blue and black custom designed folder. The embossed fronts carry the players portrait and a short career summary. The Gold Edition cards are shiny gold on a matte gold background, while the Color Edition cards have a blue background. The serial number also appears on the front. The backs are silver and carry Legendary Foil logos.

	Nm-Mt	Ex-Mt
COMPLETE SET	40.00	12.00
1 Roberto Clemente	6.00	1.80
2 Dizzy Dean	3.00	.90
3 Lou Gehrig	6.00	1.80
4 Rogers Hornsby	3.00	.90
5 Carl Hubbell	3.00	.90
6 Walter Johnson	3.00	.90
7 Tony Lazzeri	2.00	.60
8 Satchel Paige	4.00	1.20
9 Babe Ruth	8.00	2.40
10 Casey Stengel	3.00	.90
11 Pie Traynor	3.00	.90
12 Honus Wagner	3.00	.90

1993-94 Legendary Foils Hawaii IX

This Legendary Foils card of Babe Ruth was given out at the Ninth Hawaiian Show. Just 300 cards were produced. It measures approximately 2 5/8" by 3 3/4". On a matte gold background, the embossed front carries the player's portrait inside a circle and a short career summary in shiny gold lettering underneath it. Two bats on each side frame the text, and a baseball appears above each pair of bats. The top of the card is rounded alongside the two baseballs and the top part of the circle. The words "Hawaii IX" is printed on the bottom of the front. The back is silver, carrying the Legendary Foil logo and a production number. Where the serial number appears on regular series cards, this card reads "Hawaii IX."

	Nm-Mt	Ex-Mt
1 Babe Ruth	5.00	1.50

1996 Liberty Sports

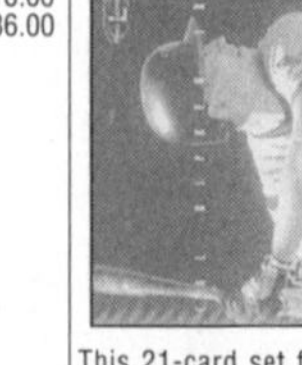

This 21-card set features borderless color action player photos and was produced by Liberty Satellite Sports. The backs carry player information, career statistics, and sponsor logos. It is believed that this set was produced especially for executives and media members at the various Fox satellites around the nation.

	Nm-Mt	Ex-Mt
COMPLETE SET (21)	200.00	60.00
1 Cal Ripken Jr.	50.00	15.00
2 Paul O'Neill	3.00	.90
3 Mo Vaughn	3.00	.90
4 Travis Fryman	3.00	.90
5 Brian Jordan	3.00	.90
6 Ken Griffey Jr.	30.00	9.00
7 Craig Biggio	5.00	1.50
8 Chili Davis	3.00	.90
9 Greg Maddux	30.00	9.00
10 Gary Sheffield	6.00	1.80
11 Frank Thomas	15.00	4.50
12 Barry Larkin	5.00	1.50
13 John Franco	3.00	.90
14 Albert Belle	3.00	.90
15 Mark McGwire	40.00	12.00
16 Barry Bonds	25.00	7.50
17 Lenny Dykstra	2.00	.60
NNO Mickey Lopez	2.00	.60
NNO Title Card	2.00	.60
NNO Tim Salmon	5.00	1.50
NNO Matt Williams	4.00	1.20

1992 Lime Rock Griffey Holograms

This three-card standard-size set was produced by Lime Rock and features baseball's "first family," the Griffeys. Included with each set was a serially numbered coupon that entitled the holder to a free issue of Lime Rock's Inside Trader Club Quarterly News. The sets were sold in a box and included a gold-embossed folder for displaying the cards. According to Lime Rock, 250,000 sets and 5,000 strips were produced. Moreover, 2,500 cards were personally autographed and randomly inserted. Members of Lime Rock's Inside Trader Club had the exclusive right to purchase the same cards as a strip. Also, 750 promo sets were produced and distributed at the National Sports Collectors Convention in Atlanta (the promo cards are blank backed). The cards were also produced in a gold version (reportedly 1,000 sets). Each standard-size, full-bleed hologram captures Ken Sr., Ken Jr. and Craig in game action. At the top of each front appear the words "Griffey Baseball" in the background. Also the player's autograph is inscribed across the holograms. On a pastel green background, the backs carry a color close-up photo, career summary and statistics.

	Nm-Mt	Ex-Mt
COMPLETE SET (3)	5.00	1.50
1 Ken Griffey Sr.	1.00	.30
2 Ken Griffey Jr.	4.00	1.20
3 Craig Griffey	.50	.15

1992 Lime Rock Griffey Holograms Autographs

This three-card standard-size set was produced by Lime Rock and features baseball's "first family," the Griffeys. 2,500 of these cards were personally autographed and randomly inserted.

	Nm-Mt	Ex-Mt
COMPLETE SET (3)	150.00	45.00
1 Ken Griffey Sr.	150.00	45.00
2 Ken Griffey Jr.	25.00	7.50
3 Craig Griffey	5.00	1.50

1991 Line Drive

This 50-card standard-size set features notable retired players and managers. The fronts of card numbers 1-42 have color player photos with blue borders on a white card face. Card Nos. 43-50 are similar in design but have sepia-toned photos. The backs of all cards are horizontally oriented and feature biography, career highlights and lifetime statistics, all inside a red border.

	Nm-Mt	Ex-Mt
COMPLETE SET (50)	7.50	2.20
1 Don Drysdale	.25	.07
2 Joe Torre	.25	.07
3 Bob Gibson	.25	.07
4 Bobby Richardson	.25	.07
5 Ron Santo	.25	.07
6 Eric Soderholm	.05	.02
7 Yogi Berra	.50	.15
8 Steve Garvey	.25	.07
9 Steve Carlton	.25	.07
10 Toby Harrah	.05	.02
11 Luis Tiant	.15	.04
12 Earl Weaver MG	.25	.07
13 Bill Mazeroski	.25	.07
14 Don Baylor	.15	.04
15 Lew Burdette	.10	.03
16 Jim Lonborg	.05	.02
17 Jerry Grote	.05	.02
18 Ernie Banks	.50	.15
19 Doug DeCinces	.10	.03
20 Jimmy Piersall	.10	.03
21 Ken Holtzman	.05	.02
22 Manny Mota	.05	.02
23 Alvin Dark	.10	.03
24 Lou Brock	.25	.07
25 Ralph Houk	.05	.02
26 Graig Nettles	.10	.03
27 Bill White	.15	.04
28 Billy Williams	.25	.07
29 Willie Horton	.10	.03
30 Tommie Agee	.05	.02
31 Rico Petrocelli	.05	.02

32 Julio Cruz	.05	.02
33 Robin Roberts	.25	.07
34 Dave Johnson	.05	.02
35 Wilbur Wood	.05	.02
36 Cesar Cedeno	.05	.02
37 George Foster	.10	.03
38 Thurman Munson	.25	.07
39 Roberto Clemente	1.00	.30
40 Eddie Mathews	.25	.07
41 Harmon Killebrew	.25	.07
42 Monte Irvin	.25	.07
43 Bob Feller	.25	.07
44 Jimmie Foxx	.25	.07
45 Walter Johnson	.25	.07
46 Casey Stengel	.25	.07
47 Satchel Paige	.75	.23
48 Ty Cobb	1.00	.30
49 Mickey Cochrane	.25	.07
50 Dizzy Dean	.25	.07

1991 Line Drive Mattingly

This set was issued to commemorate the career of Yankee star Don Mattingly. These standard-size cards feature a photo of Mattingly on the front from various points of his career with information about that part of his career on the back.

	Nm-Mt	Ex-Mt
COMPLETE SET (6)	6.00	1.80
COMMON CARD (1-6)	1.00	.30

1991 Line Drive Sandberg

This 20-card standard-size set was sold as part of a boxed Ryne Sandberg Baseball Card Kit that included a personalized collector's album, the Ryne Sandberg Story and a free mail-in offer to receive an 8" X 10" color photo of a top baseball star. The cards feature color action photos, with blue borders on the left half of the card and red on the right half, on a white card face. In blue and red lettering, the player's name appears above the picture. In dark blue lettering and red borders, the back presents assorted information on Sandberg.

	Nm-Mt	Ex-Mt
COMPLETE SET (20)	10.00	3.00
COMMON CARD (1-20)	.50	.15

1973-74 Linnett Portraits

Measuring 8 1/2" by 11", these 179 charcoal drawings are facial portraits by noted sports artist Charles Linnett. The player's facsimile autograph is inscribed across the lower right corner. The backs are blank. Three portraits of players from the same team or major stars issued in those groups of three were included in each clear plastic packet. A checklist was also included in each packet, with an offer to order individual player portraits for 50 cents each. Originally, the suggested retail price was 99 cents. In later issues, the price was raised to $1.19. The portraits are unnumbered and listed alphabetically by teams as follows: Atlanta Braves (1-6), Baltimore Orioles (7-13), Boston Red Sox (14-32), California Angels (33-38), Chicago Cubs (39-46), Chicago White Sox (47-53), Cincinnati Reds (54-59), Cleveland Indians (60-67), Detroit Tigers (68-79), Houston Astros (80-86), Kansas City Royals (87-91), Los Angeles Dodgers (92-97), Milwaukee Brewers (98-103), Minnesota Twins (104-109), New York Mets (110-125), New York Yankees (126-136), Oakland A's (137-141), Philadelphia Phillies (142-147), Pittsburgh Pirates (148-153), San Diego Padres (154-156), San Francisco Giants (157-164), St. Louis Cardinals (165-171), and Texas Rangers (172-179). The Mets packages were as follows: Jon Matlack, Felix Millan and Duffy Dyer; Rusty Staub, Jerry Koosman and John Milner; and Wayne Garrett, Cleon Jones and Bud Harrelson.

	NM	Ex
COMPLETE SET	450.00	180.00
1 Hank Aaron	15.00	6.00
2 Darrell Evans	2.50	1.00
3 Ralph Garr	2.00	.80
4 Dave Johnson	2.50	1.00
5 Mike Lum	1.50	.60
6 Carl Morton	1.50	.60
7 Mark Belanger	2.00	.80
8 Paul Blair	1.50	.60
9 Al Bumbry	1.50	.60
10 Bobby Grich	2.50	1.00
11 Lee May	2.00	.80
12 Jim Palmer	8.00	3.20
13 Brooks Robinson	8.00	3.20
14 Luis Aparicio	4.00	1.60
15 Bob Bolin	1.50	.60
16 Danny Cater	1.50	.60
17 Orlando Cepeda	4.00	1.60
18 John Curtis	1.50	.60
19 Dwight Evans	3.00	1.20
20 Carlton Fisk	5.00	2.00
21 Doug Griffin	1.50	.60
22 Mario Guerrero	1.50	.60
23 Tommy Harper	1.50	.60
24 John Kennedy	1.50	.60
25 Bill Lee	2.50	1.00
26 Rick Miller	1.50	.60
27 Bob Montgomery	1.50	.60
28 Marty Pattin	1.50	.60
29 Rico Petrocelli	2.00	.80
30 Luis Tiant	3.00	1.20
31 Bob Veale	1.50	.60
32 Carl Yastrzemski	8.00	3.20
33 Bob Oliver	1.50	.60
34 Frank Robinson	5.00	2.00
35 Nolan Ryan	25.00	10.00
36 Bill Singer	1.50	.60
37 Lee Stanton	1.50	.60
38 Bobby Valentine	2.50	1.00
39 Bill Bonham	1.50	.60
40 Jose Cardenal	1.50	.60
41 Don Kessinger	2.00	.80
42 Bob Locker	1.50	.60
43 Rick Monday	2.00	.80
44 Ron Santo	3.00	1.20
45 Steve Stone	2.00	.80
46 Billy Williams	5.00	2.00
47 Dick Allen	3.00	1.20
48 Ed Herrmann	1.50	.60
49 Eddie Leon	1.50	.60
50 Bill Melton	1.50	.60
51 Jorge Orta	1.50	.60
52 Rick Reichardt	1.50	.60
53 Wilbur Wood	1.50	.60
54 Johnny Bench	8.00	3.20
55 Cesar Geronimo	1.50	.60
56 Don Gullett	1.50	.60
57 Joe Morgan	5.00	2.00
58 Tony Perez	4.00	1.60
59 Pete Rose	15.00	6.00
60 Buddy Bell	2.50	1.00
61 Chris Chambliss	2.00	.80
62 John Ellis	1.50	.60
63 George Hendrick	1.50	.60
64 Steve Kline	1.50	.60
65 Gaylord Perry	5.00	2.00
66 Jim Perry	2.00	.80
67 Charlie Spikes	1.50	.60
68 Norm Cash	3.00	1.20
69 Bill Freehan	2.50	1.00
70 John Hiller	1.50	.60
71 Willie Horton	2.00	.80
72 Al Kaline	8.00	3.20
73 Mickey Lolich	3.00	1.20
74 Dick McAuliffe	2.00	.80
75 Jim Northrup	2.00	.80
76 Ben Oglivie	1.50	.60
77 Aurelio Rodriguez	1.50	.60
78 Fred Scherman	1.50	.60
79 Mickey Stanley	1.50	.60
80 Cesar Cedeno	2.00	.80
81 Greg Gross	1.50	.60
82 Roger Metzger	1.50	.60
83 Jerry Reuss	2.00	.80
84 Dave Roberts (P)	1.50	.60
85 Bob Watson	2.00	.80
86 Don Wilson	1.50	.60
87 John Mayberry	1.50	.60
88 Amos Otis	1.50	.60
89 Fred Patek	1.50	.60
90 Cookie Rojas	1.50	.60
91 Paul Splittorff	1.50	.60
92 Bill Buckner	2.00	.80
93 Willie Crawford	1.50	.60
94 Joe Ferguson	1.50	.60
95 Dave Lopes	2.00	.80
96 Bill Russell	2.00	.80
97 Don Sutton	4.00	1.60
98 John Briggs	1.50	.60
99 Jim Colborn	1.50	.60
100 Pedro Garcia	1.50	.60
101 Dave May	1.50	.60
102 Don Money	1.50	.60
103 George Scott	2.00	.80
104 Bert Blyleven	3.00	1.20
105 Steve Braun	1.50	.60
106 Steve Brye	1.50	.60
107 Rod Carew	8.00	3.20
108 Bobby Darwin	1.50	.60
109 Danny Thompson	1.50	.60
110 Duffy Dyer	1.50	.60
111 Wayne Garrett	1.50	.60
112 Bud Harrelson	1.50	.60
113 Cleon Jones	1.50	.60
114 Jerry Koosman	2.00	.80
115 Teddy Martinez	1.50	.60
116 Jon Matlack	1.50	.60
117 Jim McAndrew	1.50	.60
118 Tug McGraw	2.50	1.00
119 Felix Millan	1.50	.60
120 John Milner	1.50	.60
121 Harry Parker	1.50	.60
122 Tom Seaver	10.00	4.00
123 Rusty Staub	3.00	1.20
124 George Stone	1.50	.60
125 George Theodore	1.50	.60
126 Bernie Allen	1.50	.60
127 Felipe Alou	3.00	1.20
128 Matty Alou	2.50	1.00
129 Ron Blomberg	1.50	.60
130 Sparky Lyle	2.50	1.00
131 Gene Michael	1.50	.60
132 Thurman Munson	5.00	2.00
133 Bobby Murcer	2.50	1.00
134 Graig Nettles	3.00	1.20
135 Lou Piniella	2.50	1.00
136 Mel Stottlemyre	2.00	.80
137 Sal Bando	2.00	.80
138 Bert Campaneris	2.50	1.00
139 Rollie Fingers	5.00	2.00
140 Jim Hunter	5.00	2.00
141 Reggie Jackson	10.00	4.00
142 Bob Boone	2.50	1.00
143 Larry Bowa	2.00	.80
144 Steve Carlton	8.00	3.20
145 Dave Cash	1.50	.60
146 Greg Luzinski	2.50	1.00
147 Willie Montanez	1.50	.60
148 Ken Brett	1.50	.60
149 Dave Giusti	1.50	.60
150 Ed Kirkpatrick	1.50	.60
151 Al Oliver	3.00	1.20
152 Manny Sanguillen	2.00	.80
153 Willie Stargell	8.00	3.20
154 Nate Colbert	1.50	.60
155 John Grubb	1.50	.60
156 Dave Roberts (3B)	1.50	.60
157 Bobby Bonds	3.00	1.20
158 Ron Bryant	1.50	.60
159 Dave Kingman	3.00	1.20
160 Garry Maddox	1.50	.60
161 Gary Matthews	2.00	.80
162 Willie McCovey	5.00	2.00
163 Sam McDowell	2.00	.80
164 Chris Speier	1.50	.60
165 Lou Brock	5.00	2.00
166 Bernie Carbo	1.50	.60
167 Bob Gibson	8.00	3.20
168 Lynn McGlothen	1.50	.60
169 Ted Simmons	3.00	1.20
170 Reggie Smith	2.50	1.00
171 Joe Torre	3.00	1.20
172 Jim Bibby	1.50	.60
173 Jeff Burroughs	2.00	.80
174 David Clyde	1.50	.60
175 Jim Fregosi	2.00	.80
176 Toby Harrah	1.50	.60
177 Vic Harris	1.50	.60
178 Ferguson Jenkins	3.00	1.20
179 Dave Nelson	1.50	.60

1976 Linnett Superstars

The Linnett Superstars set contains 36 oversized cards measuring approximately 4" by 5 5/8". The cards feature black and white facial portraits of the players, with various color borders. In the corners of the portrait appear four different logos: MLB, MLBPA, team and PeeWee's. The backs have a picture and discussion of either great cars of the world or sailing ships. The cards are checklisted below according to teams as follows: Cincinnati Reds, (90-101) Boston Red Sox, (102-113) and Los Angeles Dodgers (114-125).

	NM	Ex
COMPLETE SET	75.00	30.00
90 Don Gullett	1.00	.40
91 Johnny Bench	8.00	3.20
92 Tony Perez	5.00	2.00
93 Mike Lum	1.00	.40
94 Ken Griffey	2.00	.80
95 George Foster	1.50	.60
96 Joe Morgan	5.00	2.00
97 Pete Rose	10.00	4.00
98 Dave Concepcion	2.00	.80
99 Cesar Geronimo	1.00	.40
100 Dan Driessen	1.00	.40
101 Pedro Borbon	1.00	.40
102 Carl Yastrzemski	8.00	3.20
103 Fred Lynn	2.00	.80
104 Dwight Evans	2.00	.80
105 Ferguson Jenkins	5.00	2.00
106 Rico Petrocelli	1.50	.60
107 Denny Doyle	1.00	.40
108 Luis Tiant	2.00	.80
109 Carlton Fisk	5.00	2.00
110 Rick Burleson	1.50	.60
111 Bill Lee	1.50	.60
112 Rick Wise	1.00	.40
113 Jim Rice	2.50	1.00
114 Davey Lopes	1.50	.60
115 Steve Garvey	2.00	.80
116 Bill Russell	1.00	.40
117 Ron Cey	2.00	.80
118 Steve Yeager	1.00	.40
119 Doug Rau	1.00	.40
120 Don Sutton	3.00	1.20
121 Joe Ferguson	1.00	.40
122 Mike Marshall	1.00	.40
123 Bill Buckner	1.00	.40
124 Rick Rhoden	1.00	.40
125 Ted Sizemore	1.00	.40

1988 Little Sun Black Sox

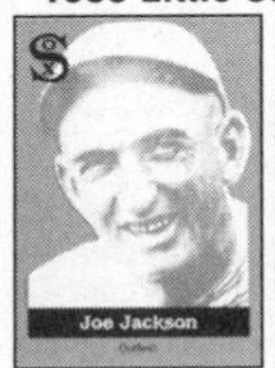

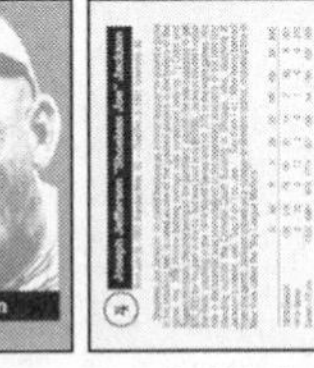

This 15-card set was produced by Little Sun of Monrovia, California, and recounts the history of the Black Sox scandal of 1919. The fronts feature sepia player portraits with player information and statistics on the back. Only 5,000 of the set were produced.

	Nm-Mt	Ex-Mt
COMPLETE SET (15)	8.00	3.20
1 Black Sox Scandal	.25	.10
2 Chick Gandil	1.00	.40
3 Eddie Cicotte	1.00	.40
4 Joe Jackson	2.00	.80
5 Buck Weaver	1.00	.40
6 Swede Risberg	.50	.20
7 Happy Felsch	.25	.10
8 Lefty Williams	.25	.10
9 Fred McMullin	.25	.10
10 Eddie Collins	1.00	.40
11 Kid Gleason MG	.25	.10
12 Charles Comiskey OWN	.50	.20
13 Abe Attell	.75	.30
14 Arnold Rothstein	.25	.10
15 Judge Landis	.50	.20
NNO Title Card	.25	.10

1990 Little Sun Writers

This 24-card standard-size set honors some of the more influential writers in baseball history, i.e., "major league writers." The cards have yellow and green borders surrounding black and white photos of the writers pictured. The writer's name is given in black lettering below the picture. The backs have brief biographies of the writers along with "Did you know" features usually about writers not in the set.

	Nm-Mt	Ex-Mt
COMPLETE SET (24)	5.00	1.50
1 Checklist Card	.25	.07
2 Henry Chadwick	.50	.15
3 Jacob C. Morse	.25	.07
4 Francis C. Richter	.25	.07
5 Grantland Rice	.75	.23
6 Lee Allen	.25	.07
7 Joe Reichler	.25	.07
8 Red Smith	.75	.23
9 Dick Young	.50	.15
10 Jim Brosnan	.50	.15
11 Charles Einstein	.50	.15
12 Lawrence Ritter	.75	.23
13 Roger Kahn	.75	.23
14 Robert Creamer	.50	.15
15 W.P. Kinsella	.50	.15
16 Harold Seymour	.50	.15
17 Ron Shelton	.50	.15
18 Tom Clark	.25	.07
19 Mark Harris	.50	.15
20 John Holway	.50	.15
21 Peter Golenbock	.25	.07
22 Jim Bouton	1.00	.30
23 John Thorn	.50	.15
24 Mike Shannon (Not the ex-Cardinal player)	.25	.07

1993 Lofton Champs SkyBox

This one-card set was createdto promote Champs Manufacturing. The front has a posed photo of Kenny Lofton on a motorcycle while the back has biographical information about Lofton.

	MINT	NRMT
FC2 Kenny Lofton	5.00	2.20

1968 Lolich Macomb Mall

This one card set, which is a photograph which measures 8 1/2" by 11" features Mickey Lolich and was given away to commemorate his appearance at the Macomb Mall in 1968.

	NM	Ex
1 Mickey Lolich	5.00	2.00

1887 Lone Jack N370

There are rulers and celebrities as well as baseball players in this set of sepia photographs issued by the Lone Jack Cigarette Company of Lynchburg, Va. The ballplayers are all members of the 1886 St. Louis Club which won the World Championship, and the pictures are identical to those found in set N172.

	Ex-Mt	VG
COMPLETE SET	40000.00	20000.00
1 Al Bushong	3000.00	1500.00
2 Bob Caruthers	4000.00	2000.00
3 Charles Commiskey(sic)	6000.00	3000.00
4 Dave Foutz	3000.00	1500.00
5 William Gleason	4000.00	2000.00
6 Nat Hudson	3000.00	1500.00
7 Rudy Kimler (sic)	3000.00	1500.00
8 Arlie Latham	5000.00	2500.00
9 Hugh Nicol	3000.00	1500.00
10 James O'Neil (sic)	4000.00	2000.00
11 Bill (Yank) Robinson	3000.00	1500.00
12 Chris Von Der Ahe OWN	5000.00	2500.00
13 Curt Welsh (sic)	4000.00	2000.00

1981 Long Beach Press Telegram

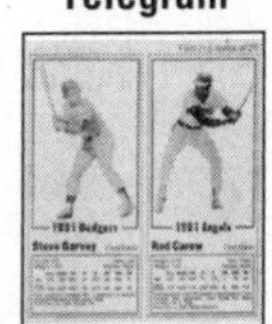

This 26-card set was distributed as a cut-out in the Long Beach Press Telegram and measures approximately 6 1/2" by 7 1/4". Each cut-out is really two cards each displaying a black-and-white player photo with player information and statistics printed below each picture.

	Nm-Mt	Ex-Mt
COMPLETE SET (54)	35.00	14.00
1 Steve Garvey / Rod Carew	4.00	1.60
2 Davey Lopes / Bobby Grich	1.50	.60
3A Bill Russell / Rick Burleson (Russell listed as 2nd Base)	1.50	.60
3B Bill Russell / Rich Burleson (Russell listed as SS)	1.00	.40
4 Ron Cey / Butch Hobson	1.50	.60
5 Dusty Baker / Don Baylor	2.00	.80
6 Ken Landreaux / Fred Lynn	1.00	.40
7 Pedro Guerrero / Dan Ford	1.00	.40
8 Mike Scioscia / Brian Downing	1.00	.40
9 Jerry Reuss / Geoff Zahn	1.50	.60
10 Fernando Valenzuela / Jesse Jefferson	2.50	1.00
11 Burt Hooton / Mike Witt	1.00	.40
12 Rick Sutcliffe / Ken Forsch	1.50	.60
13 Bob Welch / Bill Travers	1.50	.60
14 Bobby Castillo / Andy Hassler	1.00	.40
15 Steve Howe / Don Aase	1.50	.60
16 Terry Forster / Luis Sanchez	1.00	.40
17 Reggie Smith / Juan Beniquez	1.50	.60
18A Derrel Thomas / Ed Ott (Ott has a face shot)	1.00	.40
18B Derrel Thomas / Ed Ott (Ott has an action shot)	1.00	.40
19 Steve Yeager / Tom Brunansky	2.00	.80
20 Rick Monday / Bert Campaneris	1.00	.40
21 Joe Ferguson / Fred Patek	1.00	.40
22 Jay Johnstone / Juan Beniquez	1.00	.40
23 Dave Goltz / John D'Acquisto	1.00	.40
24 Dave Stewart / Steve Renko	2.50	1.00
25 Pepe Frias / Larry Harlow	1.00	.40
26 Tom Lasorda MG / Jim Fregosi MG	2.50	1.00

1886 Lorillard Team Cards

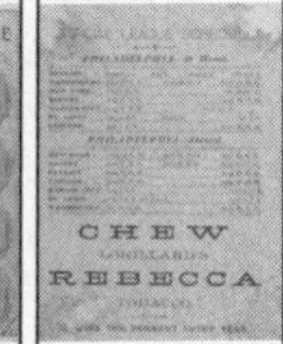

These four cards, which measure approximately 4" by 5" feature composite "head" shots of members of four National League teams. The backs feature schedules for these teams, as well as an advertisement for Lorillard Tobacco.

	Ex-Mt	VG
COMPLETE SET (4)	18000.00	9000.00
1 Chicago NL	4000.00	2000.00
2 Detroit NL	5000.00	2500.00
3 New York NL	6000.00	3000.00
4 Philadelphia NL	3000.00	1500.00

1982-89 Louisville Slugger

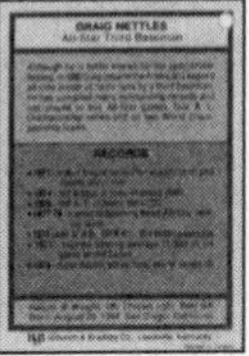

This set consists of standard size tags that were attached to Louisville Slugger products. Each card has a hole in its upper left corner. Each card has white borders surrounding the a color player's photo in the middle, with his name circled in blue on top and the "Louisville Slugger" ID on the bottom. The backs have biographical information as well as year by year highlights. The cards are unnumbered and checklisted below in alphabetical order.

	Nm-Mt	Ex-Mt
COMPLETE SET	10.00	4.00
1 Eric Davis	2.50	1.00
2 Steve Garvey Dodgers	2.00	.80
3 Steve Garvey Padres	2.00	.80
4 Pedro Guerrero	1.00	.40
5 Orel Hershiser	1.50	.60
6 Ray Knight	1.00	.40
7 Fred Lynn	1.00	.40
8 Gary Matthews	1.50	.60
9 Graig Nettles	1.50	.60

Yankees
10 Graig Nettles 1.50 .60
Padres
11 Mike Pagliarulo 1.00 .40
12 Rick Rhoden 1.00 .40
13 Andy Van Slyke 1.50 .60
14 Lou Whitaker 1.50 .60

1987 M and M's Star Lineup

The Mars Candy Company is the sponsor of this 24-card set of cards. The cards were printed in perforated pairs. The pairs measure approximately 5" by 3 1/2" whereas the individual cards measure the standard 2 1/2" by 3 1/2". The players are shown without team logos. The cards were designed and produced by MSA, Mike Schechter Associates. The cards are numbered on the front and back. The backs show statistics for every year since 1980 even if the player was not even playing during those earlier years. The values below are for individual players; panels intact would be valued at 25 percent more than the sum of the two individual players.

Nm-Mt Ex-Mt
COMPLETE PANEL SET 10.00 4.00
COMPLETE IND. SET (24) 6.00 2.40
1 Wally Joyner .40 .16
2 Tony Pena .20 .08
3 Mike Schmidt .60 .24
4 Ryne Sandberg 1.00 .40
5 Wade Boggs .40 .16
6 Jack Morris .20 .08
7 Roger Clemens 1.00 .40
8 Harold Baines .20 .08
9 Dale Murphy .40 .16
10 Jose Canseco .75 .30
11 Don Mattingly 1.00 .40
12 Gary Carter .50 .20
13 Cal Ripken 2.00 .80
14 George Brett 1.00 .40
15 Kirby Puckett .50 .20
16 Joe Carter .40 .16
17 Mike Witt .10 .04
18 Mike Scott .10 .04
19 Fernando Valenzuela .20 .08
20 Steve Garvey .30 .12
21 Steve Sax .10 .04
22 Nolan Ryan 2.00 .80
23 Tony Gwynn 1.00 .40
24 Ozzie Smith 1.00 .40

1953 MacGregor Staff

This set features black-and-white photos of players on the MacGregor Sporting Goods Advisory Staff. The cards measure approximately 8" by 9 1/8" with facsimile autographs on the fronts and blank backs. The cards are unnumbered and checklisted below in alphabetical order. The checklist may be incomplete.

NM Ex
COMPLETE SET 100.00 50.00
1 Ralph Kiner 25.00 12.50
2 Ted Kluszewski 20.00 10.00
3 Robin Roberts 25.00 12.50
4 Al Schoendienst 20.00 10.00
5 Warren Spahn 25.00 12.50

1960 MacGregor Staff

This 25-card set represents members of the MacGregor Sporting Goods Advisory Staff. Since the cards are unnumbered they ordered below in alphabetical order. The cards are blank backed and measure approximately 3 3/4" by 5". The photos are in black and white. The catalog designation for the set is H801-10. Cards have a facsimile autograph in white lettering on the front. These cards were sent out as complete sets as mailing envelopes have been seen.

NM Ex
COMPLETE SET (25) 550.00 220.00
1 Hank Aaron 120.00 47.50
2 Richie Ashburn 20.00 8.00
3 Gus Bell 12.00 4.80
4 Lou Berberet 10.00 4.00
5 Jerry Casale 10.00 4.00
6 Del Crandall 12.00 4.80
7 Art Ditmar 10.00 4.00
8 Gene Freese 10.00 4.00
9 James Gilliam 15.00 6.00
10 Ted Kluszewski 20.00 8.00
11 Jim Landis 10.00 4.00
12 Al Lopez MG 15.00 6.00
13 Willie Mays 150.00 60.00
14 Bill Mazeroski 20.00 8.00
15 Mike McCormick 12.00 4.80
16 Gil McDougald 15.00 6.00
17 Russ Nixon 10.00 4.00
18 Bill Rigney MG 10.00 4.00
19 Robin Roberts 20.00 8.00
20 Frank Robinson 40.00 16.00
21 John Roseboro 12.00 4.80
22 Red Schoendienst 20.00 8.00
23 Bill Skowron 15.00 6.00
24 Daryl Spencer 10.00 4.00
25 Johnny Temple 10.00 4.00

1965 MacGregor Staff

This ten-card set represents members of the MacGregor Sporting Goods Advisory Staff. Since the cards are unnumbered they are ordered below in alphabetical order. The cards are blank backed and measure approximately 3 9/16" by 5 1/8". The photos are in black and white. The catalog designation for the set is H825-2.

NM Ex
COMPLETE SET (10) 350.00 140.00
1 Roberto Clemente 150.00 60.00
2 Al Downing 10.00 4.00
3 Johnny Edwards 10.00 4.00
4 Ron Hansen 10.00 4.00
5 Deron Johnson 10.00 4.00
6 Willie Mays 125.00 50.00
7 Tony Oliva 20.00 8.00
8 Claude Osteen 10.00 4.00
9 Bobby Richardson 20.00 8.00
10 Zoilo Versalles 10.00 4.00

1950 Mack 66 Years in the Big Leagues

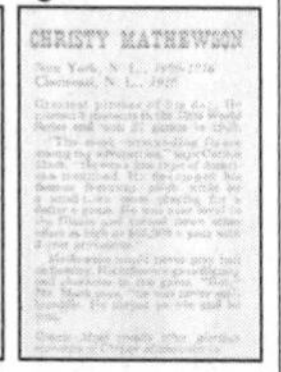

These four black and white (with a seeming sepia tone) cards were issued in conjuction with the release of Connie Mack's Book "My 66 Years in the Big Leagues". The players featured are Mack's most memorable three personalities. The cards were also shipped in a special promotional envelope to inspire more sales of the book. The cards measure 2 1/4" by 3 1/2" and were printed on thin white stock.

NM Ex
COMPLETE SET (4) 1300.00 650.00
1 Connie Mack 250.00 125.00
2 Christy Mathewson 400.00 200.00
3 Babe Ruth 800.00 400.00
4 Rube Waddell 200.00 100.00

1995 Major League Players Alumni Autograph

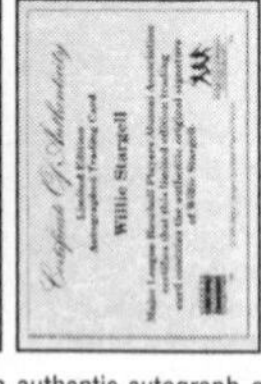

These cards feature an authentic autograph of the player along with an action shot. The "Legends Autograph Collection" logo is on the upper left corner. The back features career history, a brief bio and career statistics. The card also came with a certificate of authenticity from the MLBP Alumni Association.

Nm-Mt Ex-Mt
COMPLETE SET 45.00 13.50
1 Harmon Killebrew AU 15.00 4.50
2 Brooks Robinson AU 15.00 4.50
3 Willie Stargell AU 15.00 4.50

1996 Major League Alumni

This one card standard-size set features Hall of Famer Brooks Robinson. The front of the card features Brooks ready to field while the back has information about Robinson's playing career as well as what he done after his career along with a line of complete career statistics.

Nm-Mt Ex-Mt
1 Brooks Robinson 5.00 1.50

1998-01 Major League Dad

Apparently issued over a period of year, these standard-size full-bleed cards feature popular players posing along with their kids. The fronts have the words "Major League Dad". The backs include various player information along with a plea for dads to support their children, no matter what the circumstances.

Nm-Mt Ex-Mt
COMPLETE SET 8.00 2.40
1 Greg Vaughn 1.50 .45
2 Wally Joyner 1.50 .45
3 Jeff Shaw 1.50 .45
4 Tim Salmon 3.00 .90
5 Chad Kreuter 1.00 .30

1989 Major League Movie

These 11 cards measure approximately 2 3/4" by 3 1/2". They were issued to promote the movie "Major League". The cards have color photos surrounded by blue borders. The actor and the role they play are noted on the bottom of the card. Their position on the imaginary Cleveland Indians is mentioned in the upper right corner. The backs are blank. We have sequenced this set in alphabetical order by actor.

Nm-Mt Ex-Mt
COMPLETE SET (11) 15.00 6.00
1 Tom Berenger 2.00 .80
2 Corbin Bernsen 2.50 1.00
3 James Gammon 1.00 .40
4 Dennis Haysbert 1.00 .40
5 Andy Romano 1.00 .40
6 Chelcie Ross 1.00 .40
7 Charlie Sheen 2.50 1.00
8 Wesley Snipes 4.00 1.60
9 Steve Yeager 1.50 .60
10 Charlie Sheen 2.00 .80
Dennis Haysbert
Tom Berenger
Wesley Snipes
11 Andy Romano 1.00 .40
James Gannon
Steve Yeager

1992 Manning 1919 Black Sox Reprints

Designed by TNTL Studios, (Toms River, NJ) this 26-card set measures approximately 2" by 3" and features reprinted photos of members of the 1919 White Sox team. The photos are black-and-white cut-outs against white backgrounds. Some of the cards have thin black borders but most do not. The "Shoeless Joe" Jackson card has a red border stripe and a color background that shows grass and sky. The backs of the borderless cards are blank. The backs of the other cards contain player information. The cards are unnumbered and checklisted below in alphabetical order.

Nm-Mt Ex-Mt
COMPLETE SET (26) 5.00 1.50
1 Joe Benz .10 .03
2 Eddie Cicotte .30 .09
3 Eddie Collins .50 .15
4 Shano Collins .10 .03
5 Charles Comiskey OWN .30 .09
6 Dave Danforth .10 .03
7 Red Faber .30 .09
8 Happy Felsch .30 .09
9 Chick Gandil .20 .06
10 Kid Gleason MG .20 .06
11 Joe Jackson 1.00 .30
Color background
12 Joe Jackson 1.00 .30
13 Joe Jenkins .10 .03
14 Ted Jourdan .10 .03
15 Nemo Leibold .10 .03
16 Bryd Lynn .10 .03
17 Fred McMullen .20 .06
18 Eddie Murphy .10 .03
19 Swede Risberg .20 .06
20 Pants Rowland GM .10 .03
21 Reb Russell .10 .03
22 Ray Schalk .30 .09
23 James Scott .10 .03
24 Buck Weaver .50 .15
25 Lefty Williams .20 .06
26 Mellie Wolfgang .10 .03

1995 Mantle Donor Card

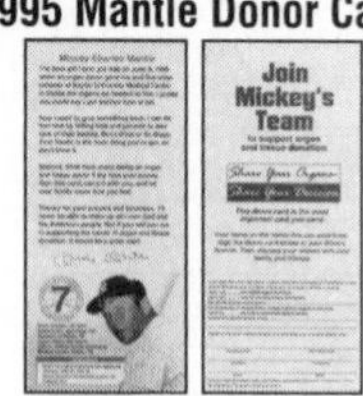

This card was issued almost immediately after Mickey Mantle received a liver tranplant on June 8, 1995. The purpose of this card was to encourage others to donate their organs to donor if it were ever needed. This card was issued by the Mickey Mantle Foundation. This card when in its original state measures 3 1/2" by 7 1/2" but part of the card could be perforated and kept as the organ donor card. That card, which feature a picture of the Mick on the front, measures 3 1/2" by 2 1/2". While we have put a nominal monetary value on this card, we prefer that the card not be traded in the secondary market, rather that it be given to people to fill out and be used if needed.

Nm-Mt Ex-Mt
1 Mickey Mantle 1.00 .30

1980 Mantle Reserve Life

This one-card set features a painting of Mickey Mantle in various baseball playing action with a facsimile autograph printed in the top right. The set commemorates him as the Director of Public Relations for Reserve Life Insurance Company. The back displays player information and career statistics.

NM Ex
1 Mickey Mantle 10.00 4.00

1997 Mantle 23K

This one card metallic set features Mickey Mantle. The front of the card has a Mantle relief with the words "MVP 1956, 1957 and 1962." The back has a portrait and action relief of Mantle along with his career stats and vital stats. This card is serial numbered to 5000.

Nm-Mt Ex-Mt
1 Mickey Mantle 20.00 6.00

1991 Mantle Video

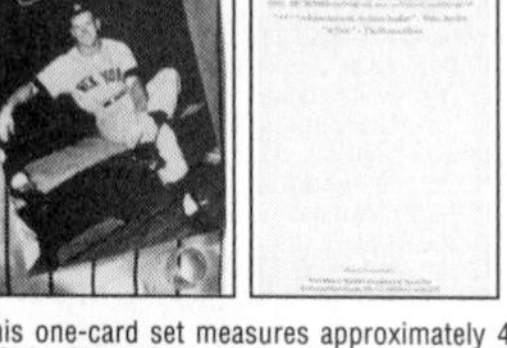

This one-card set measures approximately 4 1/8" by 6" and features a sepia color photo of Mickey Mantle. The set was produced as an advertisement for a video about him. The back displays information about how the video could be purchased and a small advertisement for Mickey Mantle's Restaurant at the bottom.

Nm-Mt Ex-Mt
1 Mickey Mantle 3.00 .90

1923 Maple Crispette V117

This 30-card set was produced by Maple Crispette Co. of Montreal around 1923. The cards are black and white and measure approximately 1 3/8" by 2 1/4". The card backs explain a send-in offer for a ball, bat or glove in return for 30 baseball (or hockey) cards collected. The cards are numbered on the front. The Stengel card was undoubtedly the short-printed card in the set that made the send-in offer a very difficult task to fulfill.

Ex-Mt VG
COMPLETE SET (30) 12000.00 6000.00
1 Jesse Barnes 40.00 20.00
2 Pie Traynor 80.00 40.00
3 Ray Schalk 80.00 40.00
4 Eddie Collins 80.00 40.00
5 Lee Fohl MG 40.00 20.00
6 Howard Summa 40.00 20.00
7 Waite Hoyt 80.00 40.00
8 Babe Ruth 2000.00 1000.00
9 Cozy Dolan CO 40.00 20.00
10 Johnny Bassler 40.00 20.00
11 George Dauss 40.00 20.00
12 Joe Sewell 80.00 40.00
13 Syl Johnson 40.00 20.00
14 Ivy Wingo 40.00 20.00
15 Casey Stengel SP 8000.00 4000.00
16 Arnold Statz 40.00 20.00
17 Emil Meusel 40.00 20.00
18 Bill Jacobson 40.00 20.00
19 Jim Bottomley 80.00 40.00
20 Sam Bohne 40.00 20.00
21 Bucky Harris 80.00 40.00
22 Ty Cobb 1200.00 600.00
23 Roger Peckinpaugh 50.00 25.00
24 Muddy Ruel 40.00 20.00
25 Bill McKechnie 80.00 40.00
26 Riggs Stephenson 50.00 25.00
27 Herb Pennock 80.00 40.00
28 Ed Roush 80.00 40.00
29 Bill Wambsganss 50.00 25.00
30 Walter Johnson 300.00 150.00

1980 Marchant Exhibits

These 32 exhibit cards, which measure the same as the original issue, was relased in 1980 and made by card dealer Paul Marchant who issued this set to honor various popular players. This set, clearly marked as reprints, are unnumbered and are sequenced in alphabetical order. According to the manufacturer only 5,000 of these sets were produced.

NM Ex
COMPLETE SET 6.00 2.40
1 Johnny Antonelli .10 .04
2 Richie Ashburn .30 .12
3 Earl Averill .20 .08
4 Ernie Banks .30 .12
5 Ewell Blackwell .10 .04
6 Lou Brock .30 .12
7 Dean Chance .10 .04
8 Roger Craig .10 .04
9 Lou Gehrig 1.00 .40
10 Gil Hodges .30 .12
11 Jackie Jensen .10 .04
12 Charlie Keller .10 .04
13 George Kell .20 .08
14 Alex Kellner .10 .04
15 Harmon Killebrew .20 .08
16 Dale Long .10 .04
17 Sal Maglie .10 .04
18 Roger Maris .50 .20
19 Willie Mays .75 .30
20 Minnie Minoso .20 .08
21 Stan Musial .50 .20
22 Billy Pierce .10 .04
23 Jim Piersall .10 .04
24 Eddie Plank .20 .08
25 Pete Reiser .10 .04
26 Brooks Robinson .30 .12
27 Pete Runnels .10 .04
28 Herb Score .10 .04
29 Warren Spahn .30 .12
30 Billy Williams .30 .12
31 1948 Indians Team .10 .04
32 1948 Braves Team .10 .04

1980 Marchant Exhibits HOF

Noted long-time dealer Paul Marchant bought out the rights to use the exhibit name in 1980. He then issued this set, which measured the same size as the original exhibits to honor various Hall of Famers. This set was very noticeably marked as a "reprint" so there would be no confusion with the original cards. According to the manufacturer, 10,000 of these sets were produced.

NM Ex
COMPLETE SET 12.00 4.80
1 Grover C. Alexander .20 .08
2 Lou Boudreau .20 .08
3 Roger Bresnahan .10 .04
4 Roy Campanella .30 .12
5 Frank Chance .10 .04
6 Ty Cobb .75 .30
7 Mickey Cochrane .20 .08
8 Dizzy Dean .50 .20
9 Bill Dickey .20 .08
10 Joe DiMaggio 1.00 .40
11 Johnny Evers .20 .08
12 Jimmy Foxx .30 .12
13 Lefty Gomez .20 .08
14 Hank Greenberg .20 .08
15 Lefty Grove .20 .08
16 Rogers Hornsby .30 .12
17 Carl Hubbell .20 .08
18 Hughie Jennings .10 .04
19 Walter Johnson .50 .20
20 Nap Lajoie .30 .12
21 Bob Lemon .20 .08
22 Mickey Mantle 1.00 .40
23 Christy Mathewson .30 .12
24 Mel Ott .20 .08
25 Satchel Paige .50 .20
26 Jackie Robinson 1.00 .40
27 Babe Ruth 1.50 .60
28 Tris Speaker .30 .12
29 Joe Tinker .20 .08
30 Honus Wagner .30 .12
31 Ted Williams .75 .30
32 Cy Young .30 .12

1977-78 Mariners Postcards

This 23-card set features photos of the 1978 Seattle Mariners printed on 3 1/2" by 3 5/8" black and white postcard-size cards. They

either have standard postcard backs or blank backs. The cards are unnumbered and checklisted below in alphabetical order.

	NM	Ex
COMPLETE SET (23)	10.00	4.00
1 Glenn Abbott Long Hair	.50	.20
2 Glenn Abbott Short Hair	.50	.20
3 Jose Baez	.50	.20
4 Bruce Bochte	.50	.20
5 Don Bryant CO	.50	.20
6 Steve Burke	.50	.20
7 Jim Busby CO	.50	.20
8 Julio Cruz	.50	.20
9 John Hale	.50	.20
10 Rick Honeycutt	.50	.20
11 Tom House	.50	.20
12 Darrell Johnson MG	.50	.20
13 Rick Jones	.50	.20
14 Ruppert Jones	.50	.20
15 Bill Laxton	.50	.20
16 Byron McLaughlin	.50	.20
17 Dan Meyer	.50	.20
18 Larry Milbourne	.50	.20
19 Paul Mitchell	.50	.20
20 John Montague	.50	.20
21 Dave Pagan	.50	.20
22 Mike Parrott	.50	.20
23 Vada Pinson CO	.75	.30
24 Dick Pole	.50	.20
25 Shane Rawley	.50	.20
26 Craig Reynolds	.50	.20
27 Leon Roberts	.50	.20
28 Bob Robertson	.50	.20
29 Enrique Romo	.50	.20
30 Tommy Smith	.50	.20
31 Lee Stanton Smiling	.50	.20
32 Lee Stanton Letters on Uniform	.50	.20
33 Bill Stein Mountain Background	.50	.20
34 Bill Stein Fence Background	.50	.20
35 Bob Stinson Fence Background	.50	.20
36 Bob Stinson Hill Background	.50	.20
37 Wes Stock CO	.50	.20
38 Fred Thomas	.50	.20
39 Jim Todd	.50	.20
40 Gary Wheelock	.50	.20

1978 Mariners Fred Meyer

These thirteen portraits were issued by Fred Meyer and featured members of the Seattle Mariners. The fronts feature player portraits against a blue background and the backs are blank. We have sequenced this set in alphabetical order. Interestingly a cover sheet was issued for this set and included photos of Darrell Johnson (who was the Mariners first manager) and Dick Pole. Neither Johnson nor Pole was included in the set.

	NM	Ex
COMPLETE SET (12)	50.00	20.00
1 Glenn Abbott	5.00	2.00
2 Jose Baez	5.00	2.00
3 Bruce Bochte	5.00	2.00
4 Julio Cruz	5.00	2.00
5 John Hale	5.00	2.00
6 Ruppert Jones	5.00	2.00
7 Danny Meyer	5.00	2.00
8 Craig Reynolds	5.00	2.00
9 Enrique Romo	5.00	2.00
10 Lee Stanton	5.00	2.00
11 Bill Stein	5.00	2.00
12 Bob Stinson	5.00	2.00
13 Bill Stein	10.00	4.00
Julio Cruz		
Danny Meyer		
Ruppert Jones		
Darrell Johnson		
Craig Reynolds		
Jose Baez		
Bob Stinson		
Glenn Abbott		
Bruce Bochte		
Lee Stanton		
Enrique Romo		
John Hale		
Dick Pole		

1979 Mariners Postcards

These 29 postcards, which measure 3 34/" by 5 1/2" feature members of the 1979 Seattle Mariners. The fronts have a player photo, a facsimile signature as well as the "Seattle Mariners" team logo on the bottom. The backs are standard postcard backs. Since these cards are unnumbered, we have sequenced this set in alphabetical order.

	NM	Ex
COMPLETE SET (29)	15.00	6.00
1 Glenn Abbott	.50	.20
2 Floyd Bannister	.50	.20
3 Bruce Bochte	.50	.20
4 Don Bryant CO	.50	.20
5 Larry Cox	.50	.20
6 Julio Cruz	.50	.20
7 Joe Decker	.50	.20
8 Rob Dressler	.50	.20
9 John Hale	.50	.20
10 Rick Honeycutt	.50	.20
11 Willie Horton	.75	.30
12 Darrell Johnson MG	.50	.20
13 Odell Jones	.50	.20
14 Ruppert Jones	.50	.20
15 Byron McLaughlin	.50	.20
16 Mario Mendoza	.50	.20
17 Dan Meyer	.50	.20
18 Larry Milbourne	.50	.20
19 John Montague	.50	.20
20 Tom Paciorek	.50	.20
21 Mike Parrott	.50	.20
22 Vada Pinson CO	.75	.30
23 Shane Rawley	.50	.20
24 Leon Roberts	.50	.20
25 Joe Simpson	.50	.20
26 Bill Stein	.50	.20
27 Bob Stinson	.50	.20
28 Wes Stock CO	.50	.20
29 Bobby Valentine	.75	.30

1980 Mariners Postcards

These postcards which measure 3 3/4" by 5 1/2" feature members of the 1980 Seattle Mariners. These are unnumbered so we have sequenced them in alphabetical order. One way to differentiate these postcards from earlier Mariner postcards is that the the words "Baseball Club" were absent from under Mariners on the front. The two late season cards; Wills and Walton, come without a postcard back

	NM	Ex
COMPLETE SET	12.00	4.80
1 Glenn Abbott	.50	.20
2 Jim Anderson	.50	.20
3 Floyd Bannister	.50	.20
4 Jim Beattie	.50	.20
5 Juan Beniquez	.50	.20
6 Bruce Bochte	.50	.20
7 Don Bryant CO	.50	.20
8 Ted Cox	.50	.20
9 Rodney Craig	.50	.20
10 Julo Cruz	.50	.20
11 Rob Dressler	.50	.20
12 Dave Heaverlo	.50	.20
13 Marc Hill	.50	.20
14 Rick Honeycutt	.50	.20
15 Willie Horton	.75	.30
16 Darrell Johnson MG	.50	.20
17 Bill Mazeroski CO	1.00	.40
18 Byron McLaughlin	.50	.20
19 Mario Mendoza	.50	.20
20 Larry Milbourne	.50	.20
21 Dan Meyer	.50	.20
22 Tom Paciorek	.50	.20
23 Mike Parrott	.50	.20
24 Vada Pinson CO	.75	.30
25 Shane Rawley	.50	.20
26 Dave Roberts	.50	.20
27 Leon Roberts	.50	.20
28 Joe Simpson	.50	.20
29 Bill Stein	.50	.20
30 Wes Stock CO	.50	.20
31 Reggie Walton	.50	.20
32 Maury Wills MG	1.00	.40

1981 Mariners Police

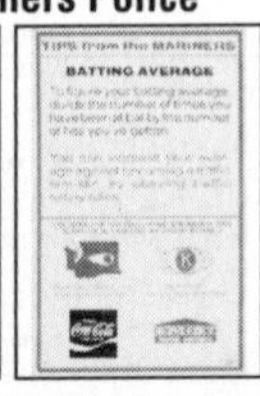

The cards in this 16-card set measure approximately 2 5/8" by 4 1/8". The full color Seattle Mariners Police set of this year was sponsored by the Washington State Crime Prevention Association, the Kiwanis Club, Coca-Cola and Ernst Home Centers. The fronts feature the player's name, his position, and the Seattle Mariners name in addition to the player's photo. The backs, in red and blue, feature Tips from the Mariners and the logos of the four sponsors of the set. The cards are numbered in the lower left corners of the backs. This set was also produced with blank backs and sticker backs. Blank back sets are valued at 2X the price listed. The sticker back sets are available in very limited quantities and no price is established for those cards.

	Nm-Mt	Ex-Mt
COMPLETE SET (16)	8.00	3.20
1 Jeff Burroughs	1.00	.40
2 Floyd Bannister	.50	.20
3 Glenn Abbott	.50	.20
4 Jim Anderson	.50	.20
5 Danny Meyer	.50	.20
6 Julio Cruz	.50	.20
7 Dave Edler	.50	.20
8 Kenny Clay	.50	.20
9 Lenny Randle	.50	.20
10 Mike Parrott	.50	.20
11 Tom Paciorek	.50	.20
12 Jerry Narron	.75	.30
13 Richie Zisk	.75	.30
14 Maury Wills MG	1.50	.60
15 Joe Simpson	.50	.20
16 Shane Rawley	.50	.20

1981 Mariners Postcards

This 31-card set features black and white photos which measure 3 3/4" by 5 1/2" of the 1981 Seattle Mariners printed on postcard-size cards. The cards are unnumbered and checklisted below in alphabetical order. All Mariners postcards from 1981 to 1984 were issued in the 3 3/4" by 5 1/2" and all have postcard backs.

	Nm-Mt	Ex-Mt
COMPLETE SET (31)	15.00	6.00
1 Glenn Abbott	.50	.20
2 Brian Allard	.50	.20
3 Jim Anderson	.50	.20
4 Larry Anderson	.50	.20
5 Rick Auerbach	.50	.20
6 Floyd Bannister	.50	.20
7 Bruce Bochte	.50	.20
8 Terry Bulling	.50	.20
9 Jeff Burroughs	.75	.30
10 Bryan Clark	.50	.20
11 Kenny Clay	.50	.20
12 Julio Cruz	.50	.20
13 Tommy Davis CO	.75	.30
14 Jerry Don Gleaton	.50	.20
15 Dick Drago	.50	.20
16 Dave Edler	.50	.20
17 Frank Funk CO	.50	.20
18 Gary Gray	.50	.20
19 Dave Henderson	1.50	.60
20 Rene Lachemann CO	.50	.20
21 Dan Meyer	.50	.20
22 Jerry Narron	.75	.30
23 Tom Paciorek	.50	.20
24 Mike Parrott	.50	.20
25 Jim Presley	1.50	.60
26 Lenny Randle	.50	.20
27 Shane Rawley	.50	.20
28 Cananea Reyes	.50	.20
29 Joe Simpson	.50	.20
30 Wes Stock CO	.50	.20
31 Richie Zisk	.50	.20

1982 Mariners Postcards

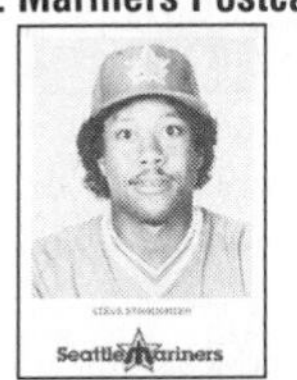

This 34-card set features 3 3/4" bv 5 1/2" black and white photos of the 1982 Seattle Mariners printed on postcard-size cards. The cards are unnumbered and checklisted below in alphabetical order. There is also a report of a 4" by 5" set issued the same year with blank backs. Any confirmation on these cards are appreciated.

	Nm-Mt	Ex-Mt
COMPLETE SET (32)	15.00	6.00
1 Glenn Abbott	.50	.20
2 Brian Allard	.50	.20
3 Larry Anderson	.50	.20
4 Floyd Bannister	.50	.20
5 Jim Beattie	.75	.30
6 Bruce Bochte	.50	.20
7 Thad Bosley	.50	.20
8 Bobby Brown	.50	.20
9 Bud Bulling	.50	.20
10 Manny Castillo	.50	.20
11 Bill Caudill	.50	.20
12 Bryan Clark	.50	.20
13 Chuck Cottier CO	.50	.20
14 Al Cowens	.50	.20
15 Julio Cruz	.50	.20
16 Todd Cruz	.50	.20
17 Dave Duncan CO	.50	.20
18 Jim Essian	.50	.20
19 Gary Gray	.50	.20
20 Dave Henderson	1.50	.60
21 Rene Lachemann MG	.50	.20
22 Jim Maler	.50	.20
23 Mike Moore	.50	.20
24 Gene Nelson	.50	.20
25 Gaylord Perry	2.50	1.00
26 Vada Pinson CO	1.00	.40
27 Bill Plummer CO	.50	.20
28 Lenny Randle	.50	.20
29 Paul Serna	.50	.20
30 Joe Simpson	.50	.20
31 Mike Stanton	.50	.20
32 Steve Stroughter	.50	.20
33 Ed Vandeberg	.50	.20
34 Richie Zisk	.50	.20

1983 Mariners Nalley's

Six members of the 1983 Seattle Mariners are featured in this set. The oversized photos, approximately 8 3/4" by 10 3/4", are in full-color and take up the entire back of potato chip box. Next to the player photo is statistics and a biography. We have arranged the listing of this set in alphabetical order.

	Nm-Mt	Ex-Mt
COMPLETE SET	20.00	8.00
1 Bill Caudill	3.00	1.20
2 Al Cowens	3.00	1.20
3 Todd Cruz	3.00	1.20
4 Gaylord Perry	6.00	2.40
5 Rick Sweet	3.00	1.20
6 Richie Zisk	4.00	1.60

1984 Mariners Mother's

The cards in this 28-card set measure the standard size. In 1984, The Los Angeles-based Mother's Cookies Co. issued five sets of cards featuring players from major league teams. The Seattle Mariners set features current players depicted by photos. Similar to their 1952 and 1953 issues, the cards have rounded corners. The backs of the cards contain the Mother's Cookies logo. The cards were distributed in partial sets to fans at the respective stadiums of the teams involved. Whereas 20 cards were given to each patron, a redemption card, redeemable for eight more cards was included. Unfortunately, the eight cards received by redeeming the coupon were not necessarily the eight needed to complete a set. Hobbyist Barry Colla was involved in the production of these sets. The key card in the set is Mark Langston, one of his earliest cards issued.

	Nm-Mt	Ex-Mt
COMPLETE SET (28)	12.50	5.00
1 Del Crandall MG	.25	.10
2 Barry Bonnell	.25	.10
3 Dave Henderson	.50	.20
4 Bob Kearney	.25	.10
5 Mike Moore	.25	.10
6 Spike Owen	.50	.20
7 Gorman Thomas	.50	.20
8 Ed VandeBerg	.25	.10
9 Matt Young	.25	.10
10 Larry Milbourne	.25	.10
11 Dave Beard	.25	.10
12 Jim Beattie	.50	.20
13 Mark Langston	3.00	1.20
14 Orlando Mercado	.25	.10
15 Jack Perconte	.25	.10
16 Pat Putnam	.25	.10
17 Paul Mirabella	.25	.10
18 Domingo Ramos	.25	.10
19 Al Cowens	.25	.10
20 Mike Stanton	.25	.10
21 Steve Henderson	.25	.10
22 Bob Stoddard	.25	.10
23 Alvin Davis	1.00	.40
24 Phil Bradley	.75	.30
25 Roy Thomas	.25	.10
26 Darnell Coles	.50	.20
27 Rick Sweet CO	.25	.10
Frank Funk CO		
Ben Hines CO		
Chuck Cottier CO		
Phil Roof CO		
28 Seattle Kingdome CL	.25	.10

1984 Mariners Postcards

These postcards, which measure approximately 3 3/4" by 5 1/2" have closeup photos on the front with the players name and team logo on the bottom. The back of the cards have a postcard back. Since the cards are unnumbered, we have sequenced them in alphabetical order. Harold Reynolds, later to become a stalwart on ESPN, had a postcard two years before his Rookie Card in this set.

	Nm-Mt	Ex-Mt
COMPLETE SET	15.00	6.00
1 Jim Beattie	.75	.30
2 Barry Bonnell	.50	.20
3 Phil Bradley	.50	.20
4 Darnell Coles	.50	.20
5 Chuck Cottier CO	.50	.20
6 Al Cowens	.50	.20
7 Del Crandall MG	.50	.20
8 Alvin Davis	.75	.30
9 Steve Henderson	.50	.20
10 Bob Kearney	.50	.20
11 Mark Langston	1.50	.60
12 Larry Milbourne	.50	.20
13 Paul Mirabella	.50	.20
14 Mike Moore	.50	.20
15 Ricky Nelson	.50	.20
16 Spike Owen	.50	.20
17 Jack Perconte	.50	.20
18 Harold Reynolds	1.50	.60
19 Phil Roof CO	.50	.20
20 Mike Stanton	.50	.20
21 Bob Stoddard	.50	.20
22 Rick Sweet	.50	.20
23 Bill Swift	.50	.20
24 Gorman Thomas	.75	.30
25 Roy Thomas	.50	.20
26 Ed Vande Berg	.50	.20
27 Matt Young	.50	.20

1985 Mariners Mother's

The cards in this 28-card set measure the standard size. In 1985, the Los Angeles based Mother's Cookies Co. again issued five sets of cards featuring players from major league teams. The Seattle Mariners set features current players depicted by photos on cards with rounded corners. The backs of the cards contain the Mother's Cookies logo. Cards were passed out at the stadium on August 10.

	Nm-Mt	Ex-Mt
COMPLETE SET (28)	8.00	3.20
1 Chuck Cottier MG	.25	.10
2 Alvin Davis	.75	.30
3 Mark Langston	1.00	.40
4 Dave Henderson	.50	.20
5 Ed VandeBerg	.25	.10
6 Al Cowens	.25	.10
7 Spike Owen	.25	.10
8 Mike Moore	.25	.10
9 Gorman Thomas	.50	.20
10 Barry Bonnell	.25	.10
11 Jack Perconte	.25	.10
12 Domingo Ramos	.25	.10
13 Bob Kearney	.25	.10
14 Matt Young	.25	.10
15 Jim Beattie	.50	.20
16 Mike Stanton	.25	.10
17 David Valle	.25	.10
18 Ken Phelps	.25	.10
19 Salome Barojas	.25	.10
20 Jim Presley	.50	.20
21 Phil Bradley	.50	.20
22 Dave Geisel	.25	.10
23 Harold Reynolds	1.50	.60
24 Ed Nunez	.25	.10
25 Mike Morgan	.25	.10
26 Ivan Calderon	.50	.20
27 Marty Martinez CO	.25	.10
Jim Mahoney CO		
Phil Roof CO		
Phil Regan CO		
Deron Johnson CO		
28 Seattle Kingdome CL	.25	.10

1986 Mariners Greats TCMA

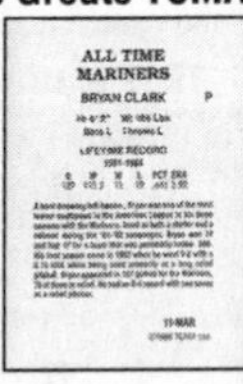

This 12-card standard-size set features some of the best players for the Mariners first decade. The front has a player photo, his name as well as his position. The back has vital statistics, a biography and career totals.

	Nm-Mt	Ex-Mt
COMPLETE SET (12)	2.00	.80
1 Pat Putnam	.25	.10
2 Larry Milbourne	.25	.10
3 Todd Cruz	.25	.10
4 Bill Stein	.25	.10
5 Leon Roberts	.25	.10
6 Leroy Stanton	.25	.10
7 Dan Meyer	.25	.10
8 Bob Stinson	.25	.10
9 Glenn Abbott	.25	.10
10 John Montague	.25	.10
11 Bryan Clark	.25	.10
12 Rene Lachemann MG	.25	.10

1986 Mariners Mother's

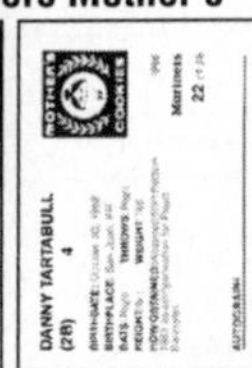

This set consists of 28 full-color, rounded-corner cards each measuring the standard size. Starter sets (only 20 cards but also including a certificate for eight more cards) were given out at the ballpark and collectors were encouraged to trade to fill in the rest of their set. Cards were originally given out on July 27th at the Seattle Kingdome.

	Nm-Mt	Ex-Mt
COMPLETE SET (28)	8.00	3.20
1 Dick Williams MG	.50	.20
2 Alvin Davis	.50	.20
3 Mark Langston	1.00	.40
4 Dave Henderson	.50	.20
5 Steve Yeager	.25	.10
6 Al Cowens	.25	.10
7 Jim Presley	.25	.10
8 Phil Bradley	.25	.10
9 Gorman Thomas	.25	.10
10 Barry Bonnell	.25	.10
11 Milt Wilcox	.25	.10
12 Domingo Ramos	.25	.10
13 Paul Mirabella	.25	.10

	Nm-Mt	Ex-Mt
14 Matt Young	.25	.10
15 Ivan Calderon	.50	.20
16 Bill Swift	.25	.10
17 Pete Ladd	.25	.10
18 Ken Phelps	.25	.10
19 Karl Best	.25	.10
20 Spike Owen	.25	.10
21 Mike Moore	.25	.10
22 Danny Tartabull	1.00	.40
23 Bob Kearney	.25	.10
24 Edwin Nunez	.25	.10
25 Mike Morgan	.25	.10
26 Roy Thomas	.25	.10
27 Jim Beattie	.50	.20
28 Deron Johnson CO	.25	.10
Marty Martinez CO		
Phil Roof CO		
Phil Regan CO		
Ozzie Virgil CO CL		

1986 Mariners Pacific Northwest Bell

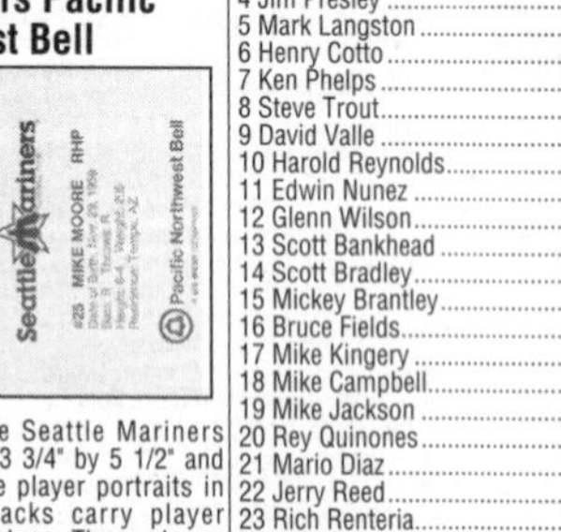

This 16-card set of the Seattle Mariners measures approximately 3 3/4" by 5 1/2" and features black-and-white player portraits in white borders. The backs carry player information and sponsor logo. The cards are unnumbered and checklisted below in alphabetical order.

	Nm-Mt	Ex-Mt
COMPLETE SET (16)	15.00	6.00
1 Jim Beattie	1.25	.50
2 Karl Best	1.00	.40
3 Phil Bradley	1.00	.40
4 Alvin Davis	1.00	.40
5 Lee Guetterman	1.00	.40
6 Mark Huismann	1.00	.40
7 Mark Langston	1.50	.60
8 Mike Moore	1.00	.40
9 Mike Morgan	1.00	.40
10 Ken Phelps	1.00	.40
11 Harold Reynolds	2.00	.80
12 Bill Swift	1.00	.40
13 Danny Tartabull	1.50	.60
14 Dave Valle	1.00	.40
15 Steve Yeager	1.00	.40
16 Matt Young	1.00	.40

1987 Mariners Mother's

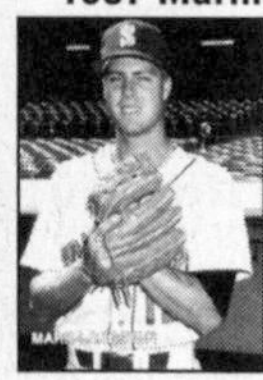

This set consists of 28 full-color, rounded-corner cards each measuring the standard size. Starter sets (only 20 cards but also including a certificate for eight more cards) were given out at the ballpark and collectors were encouraged to trade to fill in the rest of their set. Cards were originally given out on August 9th at the Seattle Kingdome. Photos were taken by Barry Colla. The sets were reportedly given out free to the first 20,000 paid admissions at the game.

	Nm-Mt	Ex-Mt
COMPLETE SET (28)	8.00	3.20
1 Dick Williams MG	.50	.20
2 Alvin Davis	.50	.20
3 Mike Moore	.25	.10
4 Jim Presley	.25	.10
5 Mark Langston	1.00	.40
6 Phil Bradley	.25	.10
7 Ken Phelps	.25	.10
8 Mike Morgan	.25	.10
9 David Valle	.25	.10
10 Harold Reynolds	.75	.30
11 Edwin Nunez	.25	.10
12 Bob Kearney	.25	.10
13 Scott Bankhead	.25	.10
14 Scott Bradley	.25	.10
15 Mickey Brantley	.25	.10
16 Mark Huismann	.25	.10
17 Mike Kingery	.50	.20
18 John Moses	.25	.10
19 Donell Nixon	.25	.10
20 Rey Quinones	.25	.10
21 Domingo Ramos	.25	.10
22 Jerry Reed	.25	.10
23 Rich Renteria	.25	.10
24 Rich Monteleone	.25	.10
25 Mike Trujillo	.25	.10
26 Bill Wilkinson	.25	.10
27 John Christensen	.25	.10
28 Billy Connors CO	.50	.20
Frank Howard CO		
Bobby Tolan CO		
Ozzie Virgil CO		
Phil Roof CO CL		

1988 Mariners Mother's

This set consists of 28 full-color, rounded-corner cards each measuring the standard size. Starter sets (only 20 cards but also including a certificate for eight more cards) were given out at the ballpark and collectors were encouraged to trade to fill in the rest of their set. Cards were originally given out on August 14th at the Seattle Kingdome. Photos were taken by Barry

Colla. The sets were reportedly given out free to the first 20,000 paid admissions at the game.

	Nm-Mt	Ex-Mt
COMPLETE SET (28)	8.00	3.20
1 Dick Williams MG	.50	.20
2 Alvin Davis	.50	.20
3 Mike Moore	.25	.10
4 Jim Presley	.25	.10
5 Mark Langston	1.00	.40
6 Henry Cotto	.25	.10
7 Ken Phelps	.25	.10
8 Steve Trout	.25	.10
9 David Valle	.25	.10
10 Harold Reynolds	.75	.30
11 Edwin Nunez	.25	.10
12 Glenn Wilson	.25	.10
13 Scott Bankhead	.25	.10
14 Scott Bradley	.25	.10
15 Mickey Brantley	.25	.10
16 Bruce Fields	.25	.10
17 Mike Kingery	.25	.10
18 Mike Campbell	.25	.10
19 Mike Jackson	.75	.30
20 Rey Quinones	.25	.10
21 Mario Diaz	.25	.10
22 Jerry Reed	.25	.10
23 Rich Renteria	.25	.10
24 Julio Solano	.25	.10
25 Bill Swift	.25	.10
26 Bill Wilkinson	.25	.10
27 Mariners Coaches	.25	.10
28 Henry Genzale EQMG	.25	.10
Rick Griffin TR CL		

1989 Mariners Mother's

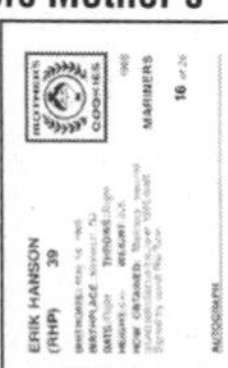

The 1989 Mother's Cookies Seattle Mariners set contains 28 standard-size cards with rounded corners. The fronts have borderless color photos, and the horizontally oriented backs have biographical information. Starter sets containing 20 of these cards were given away at a Mariners home game during the 1989 season. Ken Griffey Jr. has a card in his Rookie Card season in this set.

	Nm-Mt	Ex-Mt
COMPLETE SET (28)	20.00	8.00
1 Jim Lefebvre MG	.25	.10
2 Alvin Davis	.50	.20
3 Ken Griffey Jr.	10.00	4.00
4 Jim Presley	.25	.10
5 Mark Langston	.75	.30
6 Henry Cotto	.25	.10
7 Mickey Brantley	.25	.10
8 Jeffrey Leonard	.25	.10
9 Dave Valle	.25	.10
10 Harold Reynolds	.75	.30
11 Edgar Martinez	2.00	.80
12 Tom Niedenfuer	.25	.10
13 Scott Bankhead	.25	.10
14 Scott Bradley	.25	.10
15 Omar Vizquel	2.50	1.00
16 Erik Hanson	.25	.10
17 Bill Swift	.25	.10
18 Mike Campbell	.25	.10
19 Mike Jackson	.50	.20
20 Rich Renteria	.25	.10
21 Mario Diaz	.25	.10
22 Jerry Reed	.25	.10
23 Darnell Coles	.25	.10
24 Steve Trout	.25	.10
25 Mike Schooler	.25	.10
26 Julio Solano	.25	.10
27 Mike Paul CO	.25	.10
Gene Clines CO		
Bill Plummer CO		
Bob Didier CO		
Rusty Kuntz CO		
28 Henry Genzale EQMG	.25	.10
Rick Griffin TR CL		

1990 Mariners Mother's

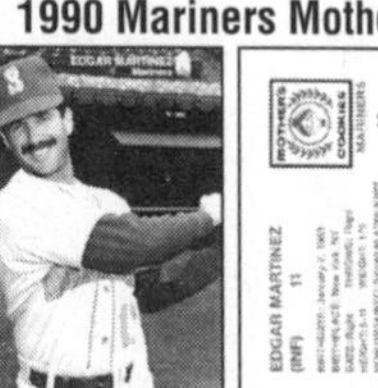

1990 Mother's Cookies Seattle Mariners set contains 28 standard-size cards with the traditional Mother's Cookies rounded corners. The cards have full-color fronts and biographical information with no stats on the back. These Mariners cards were released for the August 5th game and given to the first 25,000 people who passed through the gates. They were distributed in 20-card random packets at the game and eight more at the redemption booths. However, both groups of cards were random and there was no guarantee of getting a complete set in the cards. The promotional idea was that the only way one could finish the set was to trade for them. The redemption for eight more cards were available at the Kingdome Card Show on August 12, 1990.

	Nm-Mt	Ex-Mt
COMPLETE SET (28)	20.00	6.00
1 Jim Lefebvre MG	.25	.07
2 Alvin Davis	.50	.15
3 Ken Griffey Jr.	8.00	2.40
4 Jeffrey Leonard	.25	.07
5 David Valle	.25	.07
6 Harold Reynolds	.75	.23
7 Jay Buhner	2.00	.60
8 Erik Hanson	.25	.07
9 Henry Cotto	.25	.07
10 Edgar Martinez	1.25	.35
11 Bill Swift	.25	.07
12 Omar Vizquel	1.00	.30
13 Randy Johnson	4.00	1.20
14 Greg Briley	.25	.07
15 Gene Harris	.25	.07
16 Matt Young	.25	.07
17 Pete O'Brien	.25	.07
18 Brent Knackert	.25	.07
19 Mike Jackson	.50	.15
20 Brian Holman	.25	.07
21 Mike Schooler	.25	.07
22 Darnell Coles	.25	.07
23 Keith Comstock	.25	.07
24 Scott Bankhead	.25	.07
25 Scott Bradley	.25	.07
26 Mike Brumley	.25	.07
27 Rusty Kuntz CO	.25	.07
Gene Clines CO		
Bill Plummer CO		
Mike Paul CO		
Bob Didier CO		
28 Henry Genzale EQ.MG	.25	.07
Tom Newberg ATR		
Rick Griffin TR CL		

1991 Mariners Country Hearth

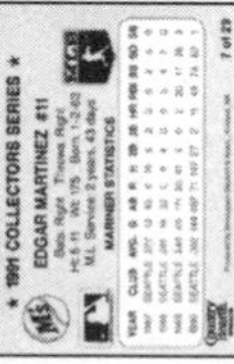

This 30-card standard-size set was sponsored and produced by the Country Hearth Breads and Langendorf Baking Company, and individual cards were inserted unprotected in specially marked loaves of Country Hearth. In addition, the cards (ten at a time) were given away to fans attending the Mariners home game at the Seattle Kingdome on August 17, 1991. According to sources, only 20,000 sets were produced, and all cards were produced in equal quantities. This set is difficult to acquire in near mint or better condition as any card inserted into the bread was not properly protected and have moisture spots on them.

	Nm-Mt	Ex-Mt
COMPLETE SET (30)	25.00	7.50
1 Jim Lefebvre MG	.50	.15
2 Jeff Schaefer	.50	.15
3 Harold Reynolds	1.00	.30
4 Greg Briley	.50	.15
5 Scott Bradley	.50	.15
6 Dave Valle	.50	.15
7 Edgar Martinez	2.50	.75
8 Pete O'Brien	.50	.15
9 Omar Vizquel	1.50	.45
10 Tino Martinez	2.50	.75
11 Scott Bankhead	.50	.15
12 Bill Swift	.50	.15
13 Jay Buhner	2.50	.75
14 Alvin Davis	.75	.23
15 Ken Griffey Jr. (Ready to swing)	5.00	1.50
16 Tracy Jones	.50	.15
17 Brent Knackert	.50	.15
18 Henry Cotto	.50	.15
19 Ken Griffey Sr. (Watching ball after hit)	1.50	.45
20 Keith Comstock	.50	.15
21 Brian Holman	.50	.15
22 Russ Swan	.50	.15
23 Mike Jackson	.75	.23
24 Erik Hanson	.50	.15
25 Mike Schooler	.50	.15
26 Randy Johnson	3.00	.90
27 Rich DeLucia	.50	.15
28 Ken Griffey Jr. / Ken Griffey Sr.	2.50	.75
29 Mariner Moose / Mascot	.75	.23
NNO Title Card	1.50	.45

1992 Mariners Mother's

The 1992 Mother's Cookies Mariners set contains 28 cards with rounded corners measuring the standard size.

	Nm-Mt	Ex-Mt
COMPLETE SET (28)	15.00	4.50
1 Bill Plummer MG	.25	.07
2 Ken Griffey Jr.	4.00	1.20
3 Harold Reynolds	.75	.23
4 Kevin Mitchell	.50	.15
5 David Valle	.25	.07
6 Jay Buhner	1.50	.45
7 Erik Hanson	.25	.07
8 Pete O'Brien	.25	.07
9 Henry Cotto	.25	.07
10 Mike Schooler	.25	.07
11 Tino Martinez	2.50	.75
12 Dennis Powell	.25	.07
13 Randy Johnson	2.50	.75
14 Dave Cochrane	.25	.07
15 Greg Briley	.25	.07
16 Omar Vizquel	1.00	.30
17 Dave Fleming	.25	.07
18 Matt Sinatro	.25	.07
19 Jeff Nelson	.50	.15
20 Edgar Martinez	1.00	.30
21 Calvin Jones	.25	.07
22 Russ Swan	.25	.07
23 Jim Acker	.25	.07
24 Jeff Schaefer	.25	.07
25 Clay Parker	.25	.07
26 Brian Holman	.25	.07
27 Dan Warthen CO	.25	.07
Russ Nixon CO		
Rusty Kuntz CO		
Marty Martinez CO		
Gene Clines CO		
Roger Hansen CO		
28 Checklist	.25	.07

1993 Mariners Dairy Queen

Subtitled "Magic Mariner Moments," the four cards comprising this set were issued with metal pins which came attached to cardboard tabs beneath the perforated card bottoms. The cards measure approximately 2 1/2" by 3 7/8" and feature gray-bordered color action player photos on their fronts. The player's name appears in black lettering within a white bar near the bottom of the picture and the Mariners logo rests in the lower left. The player's accomplishment is displayed in a green banner across the top of the photo. The white back is framed by a thin black line and carries the player's name in black lettering above text describing his accomplishment. At the bottom are drawings of the four pins and the week of issue for each card and pin combination. The white metal pins feature the player's name and number in green lettering upon a white jersey. The set's subtitle and the player's accomplishment are carried in red and green banners, respectively, across the top of the pin.

	Nm-Mt	Ex-Mt
COMPLETE SET (4)	12.00	3.60
1 Randy Johnson	4.00	1.20
2 Edgar Martinez	2.50	.75
3 Chris Bosio	1.00	.30
4 Ken Griffey Jr.	6.00	1.80

1993 Mariners Mother's

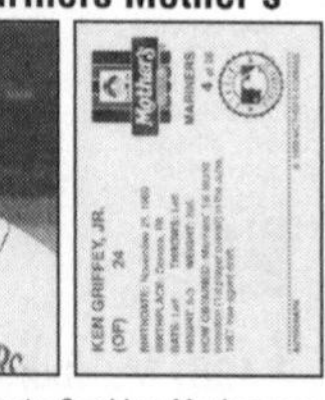

The 1993 Mother's Cookies Mariners set consists of 28 standard-size cards with rounded corners.

	Nm-Mt	Ex-Mt
COMPLETE SET (28)	15.00	4.50
1 Lou Piniella MG	.75	.23
2 Dave Fleming	.25	.07
3 Pete O'Brien	.25	.07
4 Ken Griffey Jr.	4.00	1.20
5 Henry Cotto	.25	.07
6 Jay Buhner	1.50	.45
7 David Valle	.25	.07
8 Dwayne Henry	.25	.07
9 Mike Felder	.25	.07
10 Norm Charlton	.25	.07
11 Edgar Martinez	1.00	.30
12 Erik Hanson	.25	.07
13 Mike Blowers	.25	.07
14 Omar Vizquel	.75	.23
15 Randy Johnson	2.50	.75
16 Russ Swan	.25	.07
17 Tino Martinez	1.50	.45
18 Rich DeLucia	.25	.07
19 Jeff Nelson	.50	.15
20 Chris Bosio	.25	.07
21 Tim Leary	.25	.07
22 Mackey Sasser	.25	.07
23 Dennis Powell	.25	.07
24 Mike Hampton	1.50	.45
25 Fernando Vina	.75	.23
26 John Cummings	.25	.07
27 Rich Amaral	.25	.07
28 Sam Perlozzo CO	.50	.15
Sam Mejias CO		
Lee Elia CO		
Sammy Ellis CO		
John McLaren CO		
Ken Griffey Sr. CO CL		

1993 Mariners Stadium Club

This 30-card standard-size set features the 1993 Seattle Mariners. The set was issued in hobby (plastic box) and retail (blister) form.

	Nm-Mt	Ex-Mt
COMP.FACT SET (30)	8.00	2.40
1 Ken Griffey Jr.	2.50	.75
2 Desi Relaford	.25	.07
3 Dave Wainhouse	.10	.03
4 Rich Amaral	.10	.03
5 Brian Deak	.10	.03
6 Bret Boone	.75	.23
7 Bill Haselman	.10	.03
8 Dave Fleming	.10	.03
9 Fernando Vina	.50	.15
10 Greg Litton	.10	.03
11 Mackey Sasser	.10	.03
12 Lee Tinsley	.10	.03
13 Norm Charlton	.10	.03
14 Russ Swan	.10	.03
15 Brian Holman	.10	.03
16 Randy Johnson	1.50	.45
17 Erik Hanson	.10	.03
18 Tino Martinez	.75	.23
19 Marc Newfield	.10	.03
20 Dave Valle	.10	.03
21 John Cummings	.10	.03
22 Mike Hampton	1.00	.30
23 Jay Buhner	.50	.15
24 Edgar Martinez	.75	.23
25 Omar Vizquel	.50	.15
26 Pete O'Brien	.10	.03
27 Brian Turang	.10	.03
28 Chris Bosio	.10	.03
29 Mike Felder	.10	.03
30 Shawn Estes	.25	.07

1994 Mariners Mother's

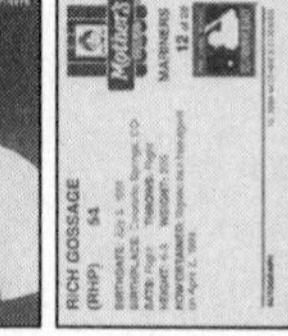

The 1994 Mariners Mother's Cookies set consists of 28 standard-size cards with rounded corners. The set includes a coupon with a mail-in offer to obtain a trading card collectors album for 3.95. The set had limited distribution since the original Mother's promotion day was cancelled due to the Kingdome closure and then the baseball strike.

	Nm-Mt	Ex-Mt
COMPLETE SET (28)	18.00	5.50
1 Lou Piniella MG	.75	.23
2 Randy Johnson	2.50	.75
3 Eric Anthony	.25	.07
4 Ken Griffey Jr.	5.00	1.50
5 Felix Fermin	.25	.07
6 Jay Buhner	1.50	.45
7 Chris Bosio	.25	.07
8 Reggie Jefferson	.25	.07
9 Greg Hibbard	.25	.07
10 Dave Fleming	.25	.07
11 Rich Amaral	.25	.07
12 Rich Gossage	1.00	.30
13 Edgar Martinez	1.00	.30
14 Bobby Ayala	.25	.07
15 Darren Bragg	.25	.07
16 Tino Martinez	1.50	.45
17 Mike Blowers	.25	.07
18 John Cummings	.25	.07
19 Keith Mitchell	.25	.07
20 Bill Haselman	.25	.07
21 Greg Pirkl	.25	.07
22 Mackey Sasser	.25	.07
23 Tim Davis	.25	.07
24 Dan Wilson	.25	.07
25 Jeff Nelson	.50	.15
26 Kevin King	.25	.07
27 Torey Lovullo	.25	.07
28 Sam Perlozzo CO	.25	.07
Lee Elia CO		
Sammy Ellis CO		
John McLaren CO		
Sam Mejias CO CL		

1995 Mariners Mother's

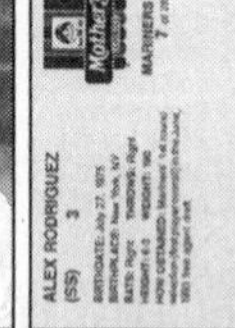

This 1995 Mother's Cookies Seattle Mariners set consists of 28 standard-size cards with rounded corners.

	Nm-Mt	Ex-Mt
COMPLETE SET (28)	20.00	6.00
1 Lou Piniella MG	.75	.23
2 Randy Johnson	2.50	.75
3 Dave Fleming	.25	.07
4 Ken Griffey Jr.	4.00	1.20

	Nm-Mt	Ex-Mt
5 Edgar Martinez	1.00	.30
6 Jay Buhner	1.00	.30
7 Alex Rodriguez	8.00	2.40
8 Joey Cora	.25	.07
9 Tim Davis	.25	.07
10 Mike Blowers	.25	.07
11 Chris Bosio	.25	.07
12 Dan Wilson	.25	.07
13 Rich Amaral	.25	.07
14 Bobby Ayala	.25	.07
15 Darren Bragg	.25	.07
16 Bob Wells	.25	.07
17 Doug Strange	.25	.07
18 Chad Kreuter	.25	.07
19 Rafael Carmona	.25	.07
20 Luis Sojo	.25	.07
21 Tim Belcher	.25	.07
22 Steve Frey	.25	.07
23 Tino Martinez	1.00	.30
24 Felix Fermin	.25	.07
25 Jeff Nelson	.50	.15
26 Alex Diaz	.25	.07
27 Bill Risley	.25	.07
28 Sam Perlozzo CO Matt Sinatro CO Lee Elia CO Sam Mejias CO John McLaren CO Bobby Cuellar CO CL	.25	.07

1995 Mariners Pacific

Produced by Pacific, this 50-card boxed standard-size set highlights the events leading up to the Seattle Mariners clinching the American League Western Division Pennant and their playoff run during the Division Series and the American League Championship Series. The set divides into game action shots (1-17) and player (and manager) cards (18-50).

	Nm-Mt	Ex-Mt
COMPLETE SET (50)	15.00	4.50
1 Ken Griffey Jr. IA	1.00	.30
2 Vince Coleman IA	.10	.03
3 Luis Sojo IA	.10	.03
4 Mariners win the West	.40	.12
5 Randy Johnson IA	.60	.18
6 Ken Griffey Jr. IA	1.00	.30
7 Tino Martinez HL Edgar Martinez	.40	.12
8 Edgar Martinez IA	.25	.07
9 Ken Griffey Jr. IA	1.00	.30
10 Thunder in the Kingdome	.25	.07
11 Win ends years of futility	.25	.07
12 Bob Wolcott IA	.10	.03
13 Jay Buhner IA	.25	.07
14 Randy Johnson IA	.60	.18
15 Lou Piniella IA	.25	.07
16 Joey Cora IA	.10	.03
17 Dave Niehaus ANN	.60	.18
18 Rich Amaral	.10	.03
19 Bobby Ayala	.10	.03
20 Tim Belcher	.10	.03
21 Andy Benes	.10	.03
22 Mike Blowers	.10	.03
23 Chris Bosio	.10	.03
24 Darren Bragg	.10	.03
25 Jay Buhner	.60	.18
26 Rafael Carmona	.10	.03
27 Norm Charlton	.10	.03
28 Vince Coleman	.10	.03
29 Joey Cora	.10	.03
30 Alex Diaz	.10	.03
31 Felix Fermin	.10	.03
32 Ken Griffey Jr.	2.00	.60
33 Lee Guetterman	.10	.03
34 Randy Johnson	1.25	.35
35 Edgar Martinez	.60	.18
36 Tino Martinez	.40	.12
37 Jeff Nelson	.25	.07
38 Warren Newson	.10	.03
39 Greg Pirkl	.10	.03
40 Arquimedez Pozo	.10	.03
41 Bill Risley	.10	.03
42 Alex Rodriguez	3.00	.90
43 Luis Sojo	.10	.03
44 Doug Strange	.10	.03
45 Salomon Torres	.10	.03
46 Bob Wells	.10	.03
47 Chris Widger	.10	.03
48 Dan Wilson	.25	.07
49 Bob Wolcott	.10	.03
50 Lou Piniella MG	.25	.07

1996 Mariners Mother's

This 28-card set consists of borderless posed color player portraits. The player's and team's names appear in one of the top rounded corners. The backs carry biographical information and the sponsor's logo on a white background in red and purple print. A blank slot for the player's autograph rounds out the back.

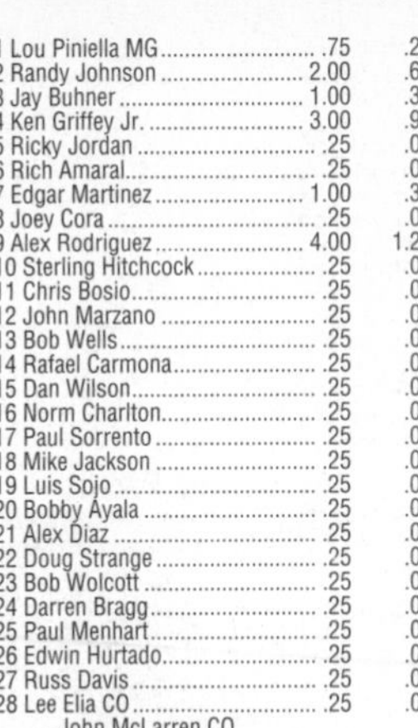

	Nm-Mt	Ex-Mt
COMPLETE SET (28)	15.00	4.50
1 Lou Piniella MG	.75	.23
2 Randy Johnson	2.00	.60
3 Jay Buhner	1.00	.30
4 Ken Griffey Jr.	3.00	.90
5 Ricky Jordan	.25	.07
6 Rich Amaral	.25	.07
7 Edgar Martinez	1.00	.30
8 Joey Cora	.25	.07
9 Alex Rodriguez	4.00	1.20
10 Sterling Hitchcock	.25	.07
11 Chris Bosio	.25	.07
12 John Marzano	.25	.07
13 Bob Wells	.25	.07
14 Rafael Carmona	.25	.07
15 Dan Wilson	.25	.07
16 Norm Charlton	.25	.07
17 Paul Sorrento	.25	.07
18 Mike Jackson	.25	.07
19 Luis Sojo	.25	.07
20 Bobby Ayala	.25	.07
21 Alex Diaz	.25	.07
22 Doug Strange	.25	.07
23 Bob Wolcott	.25	.07
24 Darren Bragg	.25	.07
25 Paul Menhart	.25	.07
26 Edwin Hurtado	.25	.07
27 Russ Davis	.25	.07
28 Lee Elia CO John McLarren CO Steve Smith CO Matt Sinatro CO Sam Mejias CO Bobby Cuellar CO CL	.25	.07

1997 Mariners Score

This 15-card set of the Seattle Mariners was issued in five-card packs with a suggested retail price of $1.30 each. The fronts feature color player photos with special team specific color foil stamping. The backs carry player information. Only 100 cases were made for each team. Platinum parallel cards were inserted at a rate of 1:6, Premier parallel cards at a rate of 1:31.

	Nm-Mt	Ex-Mt
COMPLETE SET (15)	8.00	2.40
*PLATINUM: 4X BASIC CARDS		
*PREMIER: 20X BASIC CARDS		
1 Chris Bosio	.25	.07
2 Edgar Martinez	1.00	.30
3 Alex Rodriguez	4.00	1.20
4 Paul Sorrento	.25	.07
5 Bob Wells	.25	.07
6 Ken Griffey Jr.	3.00	.90
7 Jay Buhner	1.00	.30
8 Dan Wilson	.25	.07
9 Randy Johnson	2.00	.60
10 Joey Cora	.25	.07
11 Mark Whiten	.25	.07
12 Rich Amaral	.25	.07
13 Raul Ibanez	1.00	.30
14 Jamie Moyer	.60	.18
15 Mac Suzuki	.25	.07

1997 Mariners Upper Deck Pepsi Game

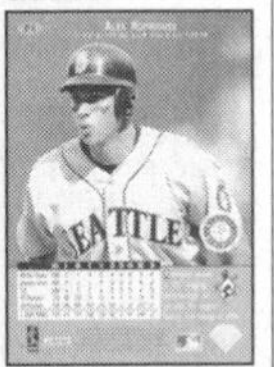

Produced by Upper Deck and sponsored by the Pepsi-Cola Company, this set features borderless color player photos of the Seattle Mariners and was given away at a Mariners game.

	Nm-Mt	Ex-Mt
COMPLETE SET (21)	15.00	4.50
P1 Joey Cora	.25	.07
P2 Ken Griffey Jr.	3.00	.90
P3 Jay Buhner	.75	.23
P4 Alex Rodriguez	4.00	1.20
P5 Norm Charlton	.25	.07
P6 Edgar Martinez	1.00	.30
P7 Paul Sorrento	.25	.07
P8 Randy Johnson	2.00	.60
P9 Rich Amaral	.25	.07
P10 Russ Davis	.25	.07
P11 Greg McCarthy	.25	.07
P12 Jamie Moyer	.75	.23
P13 Jeff Fassero	.25	.07
P14 Scott Sanders	.25	.07
P15 Dan Wilson	.25	.07
P16 Mike Blowers	.25	.07
P17 Bobby Ayala	.25	.07
P18 Brent Gates	.25	.07
P19 John Marzano	.25	.07
P20 Lou Piniella MG	.50	.15
NNO Sponsor Card Pepsi-Cola Co. Coupon	.25	.07

1997 Mariners Upper Deck Pepsi Insert

This 19 card set, issued in 1997 by Upper Deck, was inserted randomly into 12-packs of Pepsi. These cards are differentiated from the

set given away at the ballpark by their having a "M" prefix.

	Nm-Mt	Ex-Mt
COMPLETE SET	50.00	15.00
M1 Joey Cora	2.00	.60
M2 Ken Griffey Jr.	8.00	2.40
M3 Jay Buhner	4.00	1.20
M4 Alex Rodriguez	10.00	3.00
M5 Norm Charlton	2.00	.60
M6 Edgar Martinez	4.00	1.20
M7 Paul Sorrento	2.00	.60
M8 Randy Johnson	5.00	1.50
M9 Rich Amaral	2.00	.60
M10 Russ Davis	2.00	.60
M11 Bob Wolcott	2.00	.60
M12 Jamie Moyer	3.00	.90
M13 Bob Wells	2.00	.60
M14 Mac Suzuki	2.00	.60
M15 Dan Wilson	2.00	.60
M16 Tim Davis	2.00	.60
M17 Bobby Ayala	2.00	.60
M18 Salomon Torres	2.00	.60
M19 Raul Ibanez	3.00	.90

1998 Mariners Score

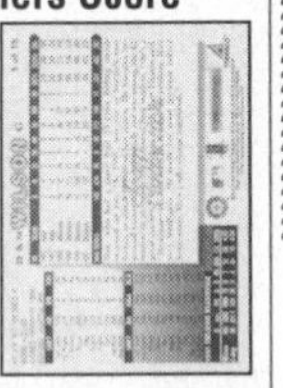

This 15-card set was issued in special retail packs and features color photos of the Seattle Mariners team. The backs carry player information. A special platinum parallel set was also issued and randomly inserted in packs.

	Nm-Mt	Ex-Mt
COMPLETE SET (15)	8.00	2.40
*PLATINUM: 5X BASIC CARDS		
1 Dan Wilson	.25	.07
2 Alex Rodriguez	3.00	.90
3 Jeff Fassero	.25	.07
4 Ken Griffey Jr.	2.50	.75
5 Bobby Ayala	.25	.07
6 Jay Buhner	.50	.15
7 Mike Timlin	.25	.07
8 Edgar Martinez	1.00	.30
9 Randy Johnson	1.50	.45
10 Joey Cora	.25	.07
11 Heathcliff Slocumb	.25	.07
12 Russ Davis	.25	.07
13 Paul Sorrento	.25	.07
14 Rich Amaral	.25	.07
15 Jamie Moyer	.75	.23

2000 Mariners Getwell Tour

These cards feature members of the Seattle Mariners and were sponsored by a local "Blue Cross" organization. The word "Mariners" is on the top with the players photo taking up most of the card and the players name, team logo and "Getwell tour" logo on the bottom. Since these cards are unnumbered, we have sequenced them in alphabetical order.

	Nm-Mt	Ex-Mt
COMPLETE SET	50.00	15.00
1 Paul Abbott	1.00	.30
2 David Bell	2.00	.60
3 Mike Cameron	2.00	.60
4 Norm Charlton	1.00	.30
5 Jeff Cirillo	1.00	.30
6 Ryan Franklin	1.00	.30
7 Charles Gipson	1.00	.30
8 Carlos Guillen	1.00	.30
9 Raul Ibanez	2.00	.60
10 Stan Javier	1.00	.30
11 Tom Lampkin	1.00	.30
12 Edgar Martinez	4.00	1.20
13 Mark McLemore	1.00	.30
14 Jamie Moyer	3.00	.90
15 Dave Myers	1.00	.30
16 John Olerud	3.00	.90
17 Jose Paniagua	1.00	.30
18 Joel Pineiro	6.00	1.80
19 Arthur Lee Rhodes	2.00	.60
20 Rick Rizzs ANN	1.00	.30
21 Kazuhiro Sasaki	4.00	1.20
22 Aaron Sele	1.00	.30
23 Matt Sinatro	1.00	.30
24 Ichiro Suzuki	10.00	3.00
25 Dave Valle ANN	1.00	.30

2000 Mariners Keebler

This 28 card standard-size set features members of the 2000 Seattle Mariners. The cards have rounded corners in the tradition of

the Mother Cookies sets they are patterned after. Please note there is a Kazuhiro Sasaki rookie year card in this set.

	Nm-Mt	Ex-Mt
COMPLETE SET (28)	18.00	5.50
1 Lou Piniella MG	.50	.15
2 Alex Rodriguez	4.00	1.20
3 Jamie Moyer	.75	.23
4 Edgar Martinez	1.00	.30
5 Kazuhiro Sasaki	3.00	.90
6 Jay Buhner	.75	.23
7 Rickey Henderson	1.50	.45
8 John Olerud	1.00	.30
9 Aaron Sele	.25	.07
10 Charles Gipson	.25	.07
11 Arthur Rhodes	.25	.07
12 Dan Wilson	.25	.07
13 Jose Mesa	.25	.07
14 Mike Cameron	.75	.23
15 John Halama	.25	.07
16 Mark McLemore	.25	.07
17 Brett Tomko	.25	.07
18 Tom Lampkin	.25	.07
19 Freddy Garcia	1.00	.30
20 John Mabry	.25	.07
21 Paul Abbott	.25	.07
22 Stan Javier	.25	.07
23 Gil Meche	.25	.07
24 David Bell	.50	.15
25 Frankie Rodriguez	.25	.07
26 Raul Ibanez	.75	.23
27 Jose Paniagua	.25	.07
28 Larry Bowa CO John McLarenCO John Moses CO Gerald Perry CO Bryan Price CO Matt Sinatro CO	.25	.07

2001 Mariners FanFest

These nine cards, commemorating past and present Seattle Mariners, were distributed at the John Hancock All-Star Game Fanfest in Seattle from July 6th-10th, 2001. Attendees of the Fanfest could redeem five wrappers from a variety of 2001 MLB products for one of the nine different cards. Each of the participating companies (Donruss Playoff, Fleer, Topps and Upper Deck) produced cards for two different players. In addition, Krause Publications produced one card. Fans could exchange their wrappers at the aforementioned companies booths at the Fanfest show.

	Nm-Mt	Ex-Mt
COMPLETE SET (9)	50.00	15.00
1 Jay Buhner Fleer	2.00	.60
2 Ken Griffey Jr. UD	10.00	3.00
3 Randy Johnson Donruss	8.00	2.40
4 Edgar Martinez Topps	3.00	.90
5 John Olerud Topps	2.00	.60
6 Lou Piniella UD	1.00	.30
7 Alex Rodriguez Donruss	10.00	3.00
8 Ichiro Suzuki Fleer	20.00	6.00
9 Alvin Davis Harold Reynolds Krause	1.00	.30

2001 Mariners Keebler

This 28 card standard-size (albeit with rounded corners) features members of the 2001 Seattle Mariners. This set features a card of Ichiro Suzuki in his rookie season.

	Nm-Mt	Ex-Mt
COMPLETE SET (28)	30.00	9.00
1 Lou Piniella MG	.75	.23
2 Edgar Martinez	1.00	.30
3 Mike Cameron	.75	.23
4 Jamie Moyer	.75	.23
5 Ichiro Suzuki	20.00	6.00
6 Jay Buhner	1.00	.30
7 Kazuhiro Sasaki	1.50	.45
8 John Olerud	1.00	.30
9 Aaron Sele	.25	.07
10 Bret Boone	.75	.23
11 Arthur Rhodes	.50	.15
12 Al Martin	.25	.07
13 Jeff Nelson	.50	.15
14 Dan Wilson	.25	.07
15 John Halama	.25	.07
16 Stan Javier	.25	.07
17 Brett Tomko	.25	.07
18 Carlos Guillen	.25	.07
19 Freddy Garcia	1.00	.30
20 David Bell	.50	.15
21 Paul Abbott	.25	.07
22 Mark McLemore	.50	.15
23 Tom Lampkin	.25	.07
24 Charles Gipson	.25	.07
25 Ryan Franklin	.50	.15
26 Anthony Sanders	.25	.07
27 Jose Paniagua	.25	.07
28 Lee Elia CO John McLaren CO John Moses CO Dave Myers CO Gerald Perry CO Bryan Price CO Matt Sinatro Co	.25	.07

2001 Mariners Seattle Post-Intelligencer

These items, featuring members of the 2001, Seattle Mariners were issued by the Seattle Post-Intelligencer Newspaper. Since these are unnumbered, we have sequenced them in alphabetical order.

	Nm-Mt	Ex-Mt
COMPLETE SET (8)	25.00	7.50
1 Bret Boone	4.00	1.20
2 Mike Cameron	3.00	.90
3 Freddy Garcia	4.00	1.20
4 Edgar Martinez	4.00	1.20
5 Jeff Nelson	2.50	.75
6 John Olerud	2.50	.75
7 Kazuhiro Sasaki	2.50	.75
8 Ichiro Suzuki	6.00	1.80

2002 Mariners Franz Upper Deck

Issued one per special loaf of Franz bread, this 16 card set features the 2002 mariners. The cards used the basic Upper Deck design except that the Franz logo is on the bottom and a Mariners 25th anniversary is on the upper right. The backs have a photo, a brief blurb as well as 2001 statistics.

	Nm-Mt	Ex-Mt
COMPLETE SET	8.00	2.40
1 John Olerud	1.00	.30
2 Edgar Martinez	1.00	.30
3 Ichiro Suzuki	2.00	.60
4 Carlos Guillen	.25	.07
5 Jeff Cirillo	.25	.07
6 Bret Boone	.75	.23
7 Ben Davis	.25	.07
8 Ruben Sierra	.50	.15
9 Mike Cameron	.75	.23
10 Freddy Garcia	1.00	.30
11 Kazuhiro Sasaki	1.00	.30
12 Jamie Moyer	.75	.23
13 Dan Wilson	.25	.07
14 Jeff Nelson	.50	.15
15 James Baldwin	.25	.07
16 Mark McLemore	.25	.07

2002 Mariners Knothole

This 27-card standard-size set was issued as a premium to youngsters who signed up for the Mariners Knothole gang. These cards have the 2002 Knothole gang logo in the upper left corner. The player's name and position in on the bottom. The back has biographical information and career information about the player.

	Nm-Mt	Ex-Mt
COMPLETE SET	8.00	2.40
1 Paul Abbott	.25	.07
2 Alex Arias	.25	.07
3 James Baldwin	.25	.07
4 Bret Boone	1.00	.30
5 Mike Cameron	.75	.23
6 Jeff Cirillo	.25	.07
7 Ben Davis	.25	.07
8 Ryan Franklin	.50	.15
9 Freddy Garcia	1.00	.30
10 Charles Gipson	.25	.07
11 Carlos Guillen	.25	.07
12 John Halama	.25	.07
13 Shigetoshi Hasegawa	.50	.15
14 Edgar Martinez	1.00	.30
15 Mark McLemore	.50	.15
16 Jamie Moyer	.75	.23
17 Jeff Nelson	.50	.15
18 John Olerud	1.00	.30
19 Joel Pineiro	1.00	.30
20 Desi Relaford	.25	.07
21 Arthur Rhodes	.25	.07
22 Kazuhiro Sasaki	.50	.15
23 Ruben Sierra	.50	.15
24 Ichiro Suzuki	1.50	.45
25 Dan Wilson	.25	.07
26 Lou Piniella MG	.50	.15
27 John McLaren CO	.25	.07

John Moses CO
Dave Myers CO
Gerald Perry CO
Bryan Price CO
Matt Sinatro CO

2003 Mariners Keebler

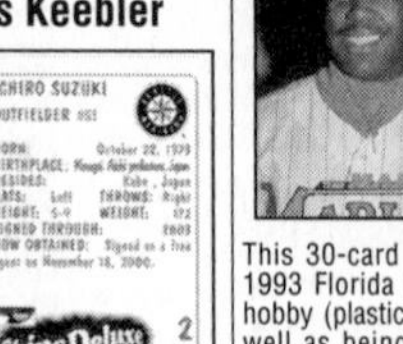

This 28 card standard-size set with rounded corners features members of the 2003 Seattle Mariners. These cards were given away at a Dodgers game with each fan receiving 20 different cards and eight of the same card they could trade to finish their set.

	MINT	NRMT
COMPLETE SET	12.00	5.50
1 Bob Melvin MG	.25	.11
2 Ichiro Suzuki	2.00	.90
3 Edgar Martinez	1.00	.45
4 Jamie Moyer	.75	.35
5 Mike Cameron	.75	.35
6 Bret Boone	1.00	.45
7 Kazuhiro Sasaki	.50	.23
8 John Olerud	.75	.35
9 Mark McLemore	.50	.23
10 Arthur Rhodes	.50	.23
11 Randy Winn	.50	.23
12 Freddy Garcia	1.00	.45
13 Dan Wilson	.25	.11
14 Jeff Nelson	.50	.23
15 Carlos Guillen	.25	.11
16 Ryan Franklin	.50	.23
17 Ben Davis	.25	.11
18 Joel Pineiro	.75	.35
19 Jeff Cirillo	.25	.11
20 Shigetoshi Hasegawa	.50	.23
21 Greg Colbrunn	.25	.11
22 John Mabry	.25	.11
23 Julio Mateo	.25	.11
24 Willie Bloomquist	.50	.23
25 Gil Meche	.25	.11
26 Giovanni Carrara	.25	.11
27 Chris Snelling	.50	.23
28 Orlando Gomez CO Lamar Johnson CO Rene Lachemann CO John Moses CO Dave Myers CO Bryan Price CO	.25	.11

1962 Maris Game

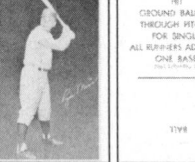

These cards, were issued as part of the Roger Maris board game issued in 1962. Since each of the 88 cards in the set feature the same photo, we are only listing one card from the set. Each card is the same value. These cards came from the "Roger Maris Baseball Game" which was produced by Play-Rite.

	NM	Ex
1 Roger Maris	8.00	3.20

1993 Marlins Florida Agriculture

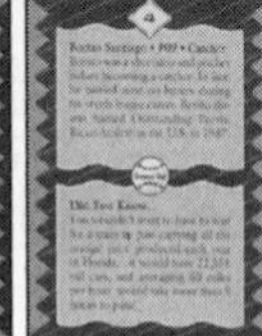

These were given out in eight-card perforated sheets at the Sunshine State Games in Tallahassee in July 1993. The sheet measures approximately 7" by 10" and features two rows of standard-size cards. Also a 8 1/12" by 11" playing-field board was included with the set for use in playing a baseball card game. The fronts feature color photos of the players posing with various fruits and vegetables. The Florida Agriculture Department's Fresh 2-U logo appears in the upper left. The backs carry player information on the upper panel and Florida agricultural statistics on the lower panel.

	Nm-Mt	Ex-Mt
COMPLETE SET (8)	6.00	1.80
1 Title Card	.75	.23
2 Billy the Marlin (Mascot)	1.50	.45
3 Ryan Bowen	.75	.23
4 Benito Santiago	1.00	.30
5 Richie Lewis	.75	.23
6 Bret Barberie	.75	.23
7 Rich Renteria	.75	.23
8 Jeff Conine	2.00	.60

1993 Marlins Stadium Club

This 30-card standard-size set features the 1993 Florida Marlins. The set was issued in hobby (plastic box) and retail (blister) form as well as being distributed in shrinkwrapped cardboard boxes with a manager card pictured on it.

	Nm-Mt	Ex-Mt
COMP. FACT SET (30)	4.00	1.20
1 Nigel Wilson	.10	.03
2 Bryan Harvey	.10	.03
3 Bob McClure	.10	.03
4 Alex Arias	.10	.03
5 Walt Weiss	.10	.03
6 Charlie Hough	.25	.07
7 Scott Chiamparino	.10	.03
8 Junior Felix	.10	.03
9 Jack Armstrong	.10	.03
10 Dave Magadan	.10	.03
11 Cris Carpenter	.10	.03
12 Benito Santiago	.25	.07
13 Jeff Conine	.10	.03
14 Jerry Don Gleaton	.10	.03
15 Steve Decker	.10	.03
16 Ryan Bowen	.10	.03
17 Ramon Martinez	.10	.03
18 Bret Barberie	.10	.03
19 Monty Fariss	.10	.03
20 Trevor Hoffman	.75	.23
21 Scott Pose	.10	.03
22 Mike Myers	.10	.03
23 Geronimo Berroa	.10	.03
24 Darrell Whitmore	.10	.03
25 Chuck Carr	.10	.03
26 Dave Weathers	.10	.03
27 Matt Turner	.10	.03
28 Jose Martinez	.10	.03
29 Orestes Destrade	.10	.03
30 Carl Everett	.25	.07

1993 Marlins Publix

Sponsored by Coca-Cola, this 30-card standard-size inaugural season Marlins set features color player action photos on its fronts. The cards are unnumbered and checklisted below in alphabetical order.

	Nm-Mt	Ex-Mt
COMPLETE SET (30)	12.00	3.60
1 Luis Aquino	.25	.07
2 Alex Arias	.25	.07
3 Jack Armstrong	.25	.07
4 Bret Barberie	.25	.07
5 Ryan Bowen	.25	.07
6 Greg Briley	.25	.07
7 Chuck Carr	.25	.07
8 Jeff Conine	1.00	.30
9 Henry Cotto	.25	.07
10 Orestes Destrade	.25	.07
11 Chris Hammond	.50	.15
12 Bryan Harvey	.50	.15
13 Charlie Hough	.75	.23
14 Joe Klink	.25	.07
15 Rene Lachemann MG	.25	.07
16 Richie Lewis	.25	.07
17 Bob Natal	.25	.07
18 Robb Nen	1.00	.30
19 Pat Rapp	.25	.07
20 Rich Renteria	.25	.07
21 Rich Rodriguez	.25	.07
22 Benito Santiago	.50	.15
23 Gary Sheffield	1.50	.45
24 Matt Turner	.25	.07
25 Walt Weiss	.50	.15
26 Darrell Whitmore	.25	.07
27 Nigel Wilson	.25	.07
28 Marcel Lachemann CO Vada Pinson CO Doug Rader CO Frank Reberger CO Cookie Rojas CO	.50	.15
29 Billy the Marlin (Mascot)	.50	.15
30 Coupon card	.25	.07

1993 Marlins U.S. Playing Cards

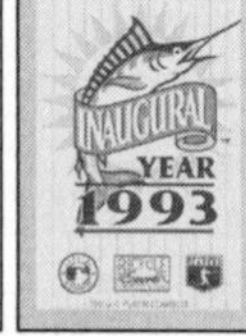

This 56-card standard-size set celebrates the 1993 Inaugural Year of the Florida Marlins. Since this set is similar to a playing card set, the set is checklisted below as if it were a playing card deck. In the checklist C means Clubs, D means Diamonds, H means Hearts, S means Spades, and JK means Joker. The cards are checklisted in playing order by suits and numbers are assigned to Aces, (1) Jacks, (11) Queens, (12) and Kings (13). Included in the set are a Marlins' opening day player roster card and a 1993 home schedule card. The jokers, home schedule card and the opening day player roster card are unnumbered and listed at the end of our checklist.

	Nm-Mt	Ex-Mt
COMP. FACT SET (56)	4.00	1.20
1C Walt Weiss	.05	.02
1D Dave Magadan	.05	.02
1H Benito Santiago	.10	.03
1S Alex Arias	.05	.02
2C Dave Magadan	.05	.02
2D Jack Armstrong	.05	.02
2H Walt Weiss	.05	.02
2S Benito Santiago	.10	.03
3C Cris Carpenter	.05	.02
3D Bryan Harvey	.05	.02
3H Monty Fariss	.05	.02
3S Ryan Bowen	.05	.02
4C Dave Magadan	.05	.02
4D Richie Lewis	.05	.02
4H Chris Hammond	.05	.02
4S Steve Decker	.05	.02
5C Bob McClure	.05	.02
5D Scott Pose	.05	.02
5H Joe Klink	.05	.02
5S Jeff Conine	.30	.09
6C Junior Felix	.05	.02
6D Rich Renteria	.05	.02
6H Chuck Carr	.05	.02
6S Bret Barberie	.05	.02
7C Walt Weiss	.05	.02
7D Trevor Hoffman	.50	.15
7H Alex Arias	.05	.02
7S Orestes Destrade	.05	.02
8C Steve Decker	.05	.02
8D Jim Corsi	.05	.02
8H Charlie Hough	.10	.03
8S Greg Briley	.05	.02
9C Jeff Conine	.30	.09
9D Ryan Bowen	.05	.02
9H Junior Felix	.05	.02
9S Charlie Hough	.10	.03
10C Bryan Harvey	.05	.02
10D Orestes Destrade	.05	.02
10H Jim Corsi	.05	.02
10S Rob Natal	.05	.02
11C Orestes Destrade	.05	.02
11D Bret Barberie	.05	.02
11H Jeff Conine	.30	.09
11S Jack Armstrong	.05	.02
12C Chris Hammond	.10	.03
12D Chuck Carr	.05	.02
12H Trevor Hoffman	.50	.15
12S Junior Felix	.05	.02
13C Monty Farris	.05	.02
13D Cris Carpenter	.05	.02
13H Rich Renteria	.05	.02
13S Richie Lewis	.05	.02
JKO National League Logo	.05	.02
NNO 1993 Home Schedule	.05	.02

1993 Marlins Upper Deck

This 27-card set of the Florida Marlins features the same design as the players' 1993 regular Upper Deck cards. The difference is found in the gold foil stamping. The cards are checklisted below according to their corresponding numbers in the regular Upper Deck set.

	Nm-Mt	Ex-Mt
COMPLETE SET (27)	5.00	1.50
9 Nigel Wilson	.10	.03
435 Charles Johnson	.60	.18
479 Dave Magadan Orestes Destrade Bret Barberie Jeff Conine	.10	.03
506 Jose Martinez	.10	.03
518 Charlie Hough	.25	.07
524 Orestes Destrade	.10	.03
528 Dave Magadan	.10	.03
533 Walt Weiss	.10	.03
552 Bret Barberie	.10	.03
590 Chuck Carr	.10	.03
631 Alex Arias	.10	.03
634 Greg Briley	.10	.03
661 Chris Hammond	.10	.03
684 Bryan Harvey	.25	.07
711 Luis Aquino	.10	.03
715 Joe Klink	.10	.03
717 Monty Fariss	.10	.03
726 Cris Carpenter	.10	.03
744 Steve Decker	.10	.03
754 Jeff Conine	.40	.12
758 Jack Armstrong	.10	.03
762 Scott Pose	.10	.03
771 Junior Felix	.10	.03
773 Trevor Hoffman	.60	.18
776 Benito Santiago	.25	.07
780 Ryan Bowen	.10	.03
825 Nigel Wilson CL	.10	.03

1994 Marlins Team Issue

This 17-card blank-backed set of the Florida Marlins measures approximately 3 1/2" by 5" and features black-and-white player portraits with white borders. The cards are unnumbered and checklisted below in alphabetical order.

	Nm-Mt	Ex-Mt
COMPLETE SET (17)	12.00	3.60
1 Bret Barberie	.50	.15
2 Ryan Bowen	.50	.15
3 Chuck Carr	.50	.15
4 Jeff Conine	1.50	.45
5 Chris Hammond	.75	.23
6 Bryan Harvey	.75	.23
7 Charlie Hough	1.00	.30
8 Charles Johnson	.75	.23
9 Richie Lewis	.50	.15
10 Dave Magadan	.50	.15
11 Bob Natal	.50	.15
12 Robb Nen	1.50	.45
13 Pat Rapp	.50	.15
14 Rich Renteria	.50	.15
15 Benito Santiago	.75	.23
16 Gary Sheffield	2.00	.60
17 Darrell Whitmore	.50	.15

1997 Marlins Pacific

This 33-card set was produced by Pacific for the Florida Marlins and sponsored by NationsBank. The cards were distributed to 16,000 kids twelve years old and under at the Marlins Kids Opening Day game on June 27, 1996. The fronts feature borderless color action player photos. The backs carry a small player portrait, player information and statistics printed in both Spanish and English.

	Nm-Mt	Ex-Mt
COMPLETE SET (33)	8.00	2.40
1 Kurt Abbott	.25	.07
2 Moises Alou	.50	.15
3 Alex Arias	.25	.07
4 Bobby Bonilla	.50	.15
5 Kevin Brown	1.00	.30
6 John Cangelosi	.25	.07
7 Luis Castillo	1.00	.30
8 Jeff Conine	.75	.23
9 Jim Eisenreich	.50	.15
10 Alex Fernandez	.25	.07
11 Cliff Floyd	1.00	.30
12 Rick Helling	.25	.07
13 Felix Heredia	.25	.07
14 Mark Hutton	.25	.07
15 Charles Johnson	.50	.15
16 Al Leiter	1.00	.30
17 Robb Nen	.50	.15
18 Jay Powell	.25	.07
19 Pat Rapp	.25	.07
20 Edgar Renteria	.75	.23
21 Tony Saunders	.25	.07
22 Gary Sheffield	1.50	.45
23 Devon White	.25	.07
24 Gregg Zaun	.25	.07
25 Jim Leyland MG	.25	.07
26 Rich Donnelly CO	.25	.07
27 Bruce Kimm CO	.25	.07
28 Jerry Manuel CO	.25	.07
29 Milt May CO	.25	.07
30 Larry Rothschild CO	.25	.07
31 Tommy Sandt CO	.25	.07
32 Billy the Marlin(Mascot)	.25	.07
NNO Title Card CL	.25	.07

2000 Marlins Kids

These 5" by 7" cards feature members of the Florida Marlins. The fronts have a posed portrait and action shot surrounded by black borders. The players name and uniform number are on the bottom. The back has biographical information along with a piece of advice for kids. The cards also say "Cornerstones for Kids" on the bottom. Since the cards are unnumbered, we have sequenced them in alphabetical order.

	Nm-Mt	Ex-Mt
COMPLETE SET	15.00	4.50
1 Armando Almanza	.50	.15
2 Antonio Alfonseca	.75	.23
3 David Berg	.50	.15
4 John Boles MG	.50	.15
5 Joe Breeden CO	.50	.15
6 A.J. Burnett	.75	.23
7 Luis Castillo	1.50	.45
8 Vic Darensbourg	.50	.15
9 Ryan Dempster	.50	.15
10 Rich Dubee CO	.50	.15
11 Alex Fernandez	.50	.15
12 Cliff Floyd	1.00	.30
13 Alex Gonzalez	.50	.15
14 Fredi Gonzalez CO	.50	.15
15 Mark Kotsay	.50	.15
16 Mike Lowell	1.50	.45
17 Derrek Lee	1.50	.45
18 Braden Looper	.50	.15
19 Jack Maloof CO	.50	.15
20 Dan Miceli	.50	.15
21 Kevin Millar	1.00	.30
22 Vladimir Nunez	.50	.15
23 Brad Penny	.75	.23
24 Mike Redmond	.50	.15
25 Jesus Sanchez	.50	.15
26 Preston Wilson	1.00	.30

2002 Marlins Kids

This set, which measures approximately 5" by 7", features members of the 2002 Marlins. The fronts are designed in two different styles while the backs have the same basic information as to the player's biographical information as well as a safety tip. Since these cards are unnumbered, we have sequenced them in alphabetical order.

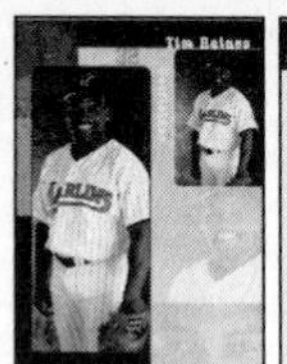
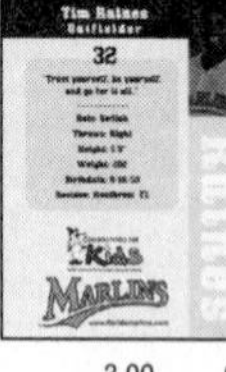

	Nm-Mt	Ex-Mt
COMPLETE SET	8.00	2.40
1 Armando Almanza	.50	.15
2 Josh Beckett	3.00	.90
3 A.J. Burnett	.75	.23
4 Luis Castillo	1.50	.45
5 Ryan Dempster	.50	.15
6 Cliff Floyd	1.50	.45
7 Andy Fox	.50	.15
8 Charles Johnson	.75	.23
9 Derrek Lee	1.50	.45
10 Braden Looper	.50	.15
11 Mike Lowell	1.50	.45
12 Kevin Millar	1.00	.30
13 Vladimir Nunez	.50	.15
14 Eric Owens	.50	.15
15 Tim Raines	1.50	.45
16 Mike Redmond	.50	.15
17 Michael Tejera	.50	.15

2003 Marlins Team Issue

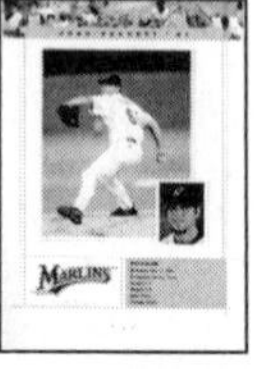

These blank-backed cards, which measured 5" by 7" featured members of the 2003 Florida Marlins. The cards, which have white borders on three sides, feature both an action and portrait of the featured player as well as biographical information. Since these cards are unnumbered, we have sequenced them in alphabetical order.

	MINT	NRMT
COMPLETE SET	15.00	6.75
1 Armando Almanza	.50	.23
2 Josh Beckett	2.50	1.10
3 A.J. Burnett	.75	.35
4 Luis Castillo	1.50	.70
5 Juan Encarnacion	.75	.35
6 Andy Fox	.50	.23
7 Alex Gonzalez	.75	.35
8 Todd Hollandsworth	.50	.23
9 Derrek Lee	1.50	.70
10 Braden Looper	.75	.35
11 Mike Lowell	1.50	.70
12 Jack McKeon MG	.75	.35
13 Carl Pavano	1.00	.45
14 Brad Penny	.75	.35
15 Juan Pierre	1.50	.70
16 Mark Redman	.50	.23
17 Mike Redmond	.50	.23
18 Ivan Rodriguez	2.00	.90
19 Tim Spooneybarger	.50	.23
20 Michael Tejera	.50	.23

1994 Mascot Mania

Given out in Pittsburgh during July 9 through 12, 1994, this 16-card set measures the standard size and features 16 MLB mascots. The cards are unnumbered and checklisted below in alphabetical order.

	Nm-Mt	Ex-Mt
COMPLETE SET (16)	8.00	2.40
1 Bernie Brewer Milwaukee Brewers	.50	.15
2 Billy the Marlin Florida Marlins	.50	.15
3 BJ Birdy Toronto Blue Jays	.50	.15
4 Bluepper San Diego Padres	.50	.15
5 Dinger Colorado Rockies	.50	.15
6 Fredbird St. Louis Cardinals	.50	.15
7 Homer the Brave Atlanta Braves	.50	.15
8 Mariner Moose Seattle Mariners	.50	.15
9 Orbit Houston Astros	.50	.15
10 Oriole Bird Baltimore Orioles	.50	.15
11 Phillie Phanatic Philadelphia Phillies	1.00	.30
12 Pirate Parrot Pittsburgh Pirates	.50	.15
13 Rally Atlanta Braves	1.00	.30
14 Slider Cleveland Indians	1.00	.30
15 Trunk Oakland Athletics	.50	.15
16 Youppi Montreal Expos	.50	.15

1989 Master Bread Discs

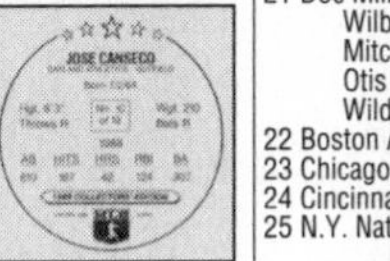

The 1989 Master Bread disc set contains 12 discs each measuring 2 3/4" in diameter. The set was produced by MSA; there are no team logos featured on the disc. The year and lifetime statistics are featured for each player on the back of the disc. The set features only American League players.

	Nm-Mt	Ex-Mt
COMPLETE SET (12)	20.00	8.00
1 Frank Viola	.50	.20
2 Kirby Puckett	2.50	1.00
3 Gary Gaetti	.50	.20
4 Alan Trammell	1.50	.60
5 Wade Boggs	2.50	1.00
6 Don Mattingly	5.00	2.00
7 Wally Joyner	1.00	.40
8 Paul Molitor	2.50	1.00
9 George Brett	5.00	2.00
10 Jose Canseco	2.00	.80
11 Julio Franco	1.00	.40
12 Cal Ripken Jr.	10.00	4.00

1989 Mathewson Bucknell

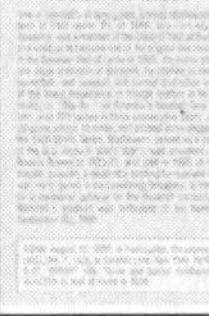

This one card set, which measures approximately 2 5/8" by 3 1/2" was issued by Bucknell to commemorate the dedication of the stadium there in his honor. The front has a drawing by noted sports artist M. Schact and the back has information about Mathewson's time both at Bucknell and as a major league pitcher.

	MINT	NRMT
1 Christy Mathewson	2.00	.90

1992 Mattingly's Restaurant

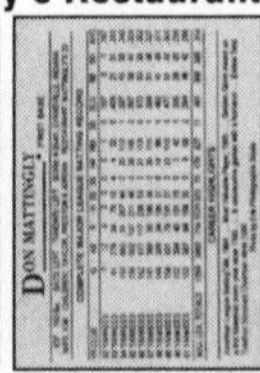

This standard-size card was sold as a fund-raiser at Don Mattingly's restaurant in Evansville, Indiana. The front features Mattingly along with two handicapped youths. The back has vital statistics, career information and some highlights.

	Nm-Mt	Ex-Mt
1 Don Mattingly	3.00	.90

1909-17 Max Stein/United States Publishing House PC758

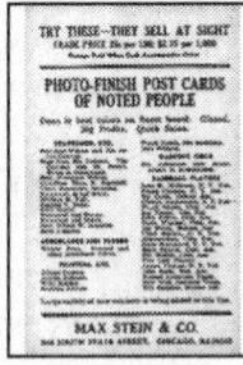

These sepia-colored postcards were issued from the 1909-16 time period. The Marquard and Zimmerman cards have "United States Pub." marked on the back, leading to the theory that perhaps these two cards belong to another postcard set. The backs are quite attractive.

	Ex-Mt	VG
COMPLETE SET (25)	8000.00	4000.00
1 Ping Bodie	150.00	75.00
2 Frank Chance	300.00	150.00
3 Ty Cobb	1200.00	600.00
4 Johnny Evers	250.00	125.00
5 Rube Marquard	250.00	125.00
6 Christy Mathewson	600.00	300.00
7 John McGraw MG	300.00	150.00
8 Chief Meyers	200.00	100.00
9 Marty O'Toole	150.00	75.00
10 Frank Schulte	150.00	75.00
11 Tris Speaker	300.00	150.00
12 Jake Stahl	150.00	75.00
13 Jim Thorpe	800.00	400.00
14 Joe Tinker	300.00	150.00
15 Honus Wagner	600.00	300.00
16 Ed Walsh	300.00	150.00
17 Buck Weaver	300.00	150.00
18 Joe Wood	200.00	100.00
19 Heinie Zimmerman	150.00	75.00
20 Johnny Evers Jimmy Archer Mike Hechinger Roger Bresnahan Tom Needham	250.00	125.00
21 Doc Miller Wilbur Good Mitchell Otis Clymer Wildfire Schulte	150.00	75.00
22 Boston American Team	300.00	150.00
23 Chicago Cubs 1916	300.00	150.00
24 Cincinnati Reds 1916	300.00	150.00
25 N.Y. National Team	300.00	150.00

1895 Mayo N300

The Mayo Tobacco Works of Richmond, Va., issued this set of 48 ballplayers about 1895. Some recent speculation has been made that this set was issued beginning in 1894. The cards contain sepia portraits although some pictures appear to be black and white. There are 40 different individuals known in the set; cards 1 to 28 appear in uniform, while the last twelve (29-40) appear in street clothes. Eight of the former also appear with variations in uniform. The player's name appears within the picture area and a "Mayo's Cut Plug" ad is printed in a panel at the base of the card. Similar to the football set issued around the same time, the cards have black blank backs.

	Ex-Mt	VG
COMPLETE SET (48)	60000.00	30000.00
1 Cap Anson: Chicago	5000.00	2500.00
2 Jimmy Bannon RF: Boston	800.00	400.00
3A Dan Brouthers 1B: Baltimore	2000.00	1000.00
3B Dan Brouthers 1B: Louisville	2500.00	1250.00
4 John Clarkson P: St. Louis	2000.00	1000.00
5 Tommy W. Corcoran SS: Brooklyn	800.00	400.00
6 Lave Cross 2B: Philadelphia	800.00	400.00
7 Hugh Duffy CF: Boston	2000.00	1000.00
8A Buck Ewing RF: Cincinnati	2500.00	1250.00
8B Buck Ewing RF: Cleveland	2500.00	1250.00
9 Dave Foutz 1B: Brooklyn	800.00	400.00
10 Charlie Ganzel C: Boston	800.00	400.00
11A Jack Glasscock SS: Pittsburgh	1000.00	500.00
11B Jack Glasscock SS: Louisville	1000.00	500.00
12 Mike Griffin CF: Brooklyn	800.00	400.00
13A George Haddock P: Philadelphia	800.00	400.00
13B George Haddock P: no team	800.00	400.00
14 Bill Joyce CF: Brooklyn	800.00	400.00
15 Wm.(Brickyard) Kennedy P: Brooklyn	800.00	400.00
16A Tom F. Kinslow C: Pitts.	1200.00	600.00
16B Tom F. Kinslow C: no team	1200.00	600.00
17 Arlie Latham 3B: Cincinnati	1500.00	750.00
18 Herman Long SS: Boston	1200.00	600.00
19 Tom Lovett P: Boston	800.00	400.00
20 Link Lowe 2B: Boston	1500.00	750.00
21 Tommy McCarthy LF: Boston	2500.00	1250.00
22 Yale Murphy SS: New York	800.00	400.00
23 Billy Nash 3B: Boston	800.00	400.00
24 Kid Nicols P: Boston	2500.00	1250.00
25A Fred Pfeffer 2B: Louisville	800.00	400.00
25B Fred Pfeffer (Retired)	800.00	400.00
26A Amos Rusie P: New York	3000.00	1500.00
26B Amos Russie (Sic) P: New York	3000.00	1500.00
27 Tommy Tucker 1B: Boston	800.00	400.00
28A John Ward 2B: New York	2000.00	1000.00
28B John Ward (Retired)	2500.00	1250.00
29 Charlie S. Abbey CF: Washington	800.00	400.00
30 Ed W. Cartwright FB: Washington	800.00	400.00
31 William F. Dahlen SS: Chicago	1500.00	750.00
32 Tom P. Daly 2B: Brooklyn	800.00	400.00
33 Ed J. Delehanty LF: Phila.	3000.00	1500.00
34 Bill W. Hallman 2B: Phila.	800.00	400.00
35 Billy Hamilton CF: Phila.	2000.00	1000.00
36 Wilbert Robinson C: Baltimore	2000.00	1000.00
37 James Ryan RF: Chicago	1500.00	750.00
38 Billy Shindle 3B: Brooklyn	800.00	400.00
39 George J. Smith SS: Cinc.	800.00	400.00
40 Otis H. Stockdale P: Washington	800.00	400.00

1950-69 J.D. McCarthy PC753

One of the most prolific producers of postward postcards was J.D McCarthy on Michigan. During the 1950's and 1960's, thousands of these black and white postcards were issued. Most of the popular players of that era have been featured on the McCarthy postcards and a checklist is not provided. Some McCarthy postcards are much more difficult to obtain. Among the scarcities known are Jehoise Heard (less than 10 have been proven to exist) and Gus Triandos Orioles portrait card. We are interested in any additions to this currently short list of scarcities.

	NM	Ex
COMMON PLAYER (1950'S)	10.00	5.00
COMMON PLAYER (1960'S)	5.00	2.50

1998 McGwire Dental

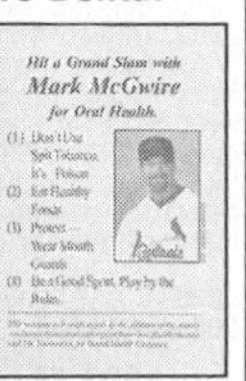

This one card set feature slugger Mark McGwire. The front has a color action shot and the back has advice on how to protect ones teeth.

	Nm-Mt	Ex-Mt
1 Mark McGwire	5.00	1.50

1998 Mark McGwire Little League

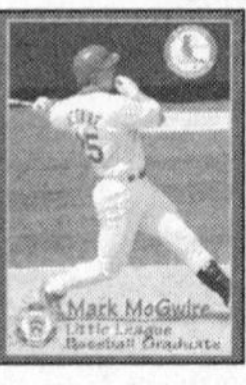

This one-card set features a color action photo of Mark McGwire with a thin yellow and wider green borders. The back displays Safety Tips for Little Leaguers.

	Nm-Mt	Ex-Mt
1 Mark McGwire	5.00	1.50

1998 McGwire St Louis 62

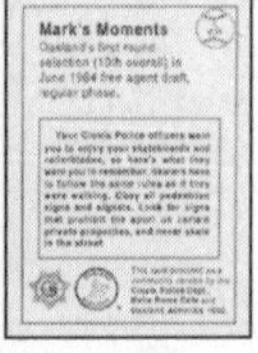

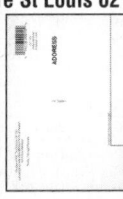

This one card postcard set, which measures approximately 6" by 4" feature three different poses of Mark McGwire during the at-bat in which he hit his 62nd homer.

	Nm-Mt	Ex-Mt
1 Mark McGwire	2.00	.60

1992 McGwire Police

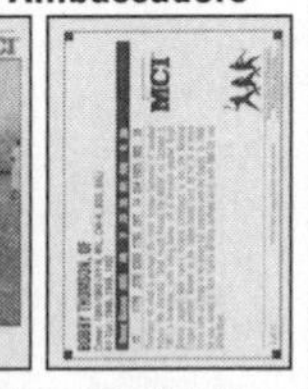

This 24-card standard-size set was sponsored by the Clovis Police Department, The Oakland A's, and 25 Clovis area businesses. The program raised $9,200 in a four-day period. Both businesses and officers gave out 12 1/2" by 18" posters and cards, and graduating DARE students also received cards. The cards were cut from the poster, but some uncut posters (measuring approximately 20" by 25") with the cards still attached were given away to VIPs and sponsors for framing. The fronts feature color action photos of Mark McGwire on a green card face. The pictures have bright yellow borders, and the upper left corner is cut off to display the City of Clovis insignia. The player's name is printed in bright yellow print at the top. The backs features "Mark's Moments-(various facts about McGwire) and public service messages. The cards are numbered on the back.

	Nm-Mt	Ex-Mt
COMPLETE SET (24)	40.00	12.00
COMMON CARD (1-24)	2.00	.60

1992 MCI Ambassadors

Sponsored by MCI, the third annual Ambassadors of Baseball World Tour set consists of 16 cards. The cards were distributed by MCI to military personnel during the world tour of military bases. The standard-size cards feature white-bordered color photos of baseball stars of the past.

	Nm-Mt	Ex-Mt
COMPLETE SET (16)	80.00	24.00
1 Earl Weaver MG	6.00	1.80
2 Steve Garvey	6.00	1.80
3 Doug Flynn	4.00	1.20
4 Bert Campaneris	5.00	1.50
5 Bill Madlock	5.00	1.50
6 Graig Nettles	5.00	1.50
7 Dave Kingman	5.00	1.50
8 Paul Blair	3.00	.90
9 Jeff Burroughs	3.00	.90
10 Rick Waits	3.00	.90
11 Elias Sosa	3.00	.90
12 Tug McGraw	5.00	1.50
13 Ferguson Jenkins	10.00	3.00
14 Bob Feller	10.00	3.00
15 Ferguson Jenkins (Special art card)	6.00	1.80
16 Title card	3.00	.90

1993 MCI Ambassadors

This 14-card, standard-size set was sponsored by MCI for the 1993 Ambassadors of Baseball World Tour. The cards contain a color portrait or action shot of baseball veterans with an irregular white border.

	Nm-Mt	Ex-Mt
COMPLETE SET (14)	50.00	15.00
1 Vida Blue	4.00	1.20
2 Paul Blair	4.00	1.20
3 Mudcat Grant	4.00	1.20
4 Phil Niekro	6.00	1.80
5 Bob Feller	6.00	1.80
6 Joe Charboneau	4.00	1.20
7 Joe Rudi	4.00	1.20
8 Catfish Hunter	6.00	1.80
9 Manny Sanguillen	4.00	1.20
10 Harmon Killebrew	6.00	1.80
11 Al Oliver	6.00	1.80
12 Bob Dernier	3.00	.90
13 Graig Nettles Sparky Lyle	6.00	1.80
NNO Title Card	3.00	.90

1994 MCI Ambassadors

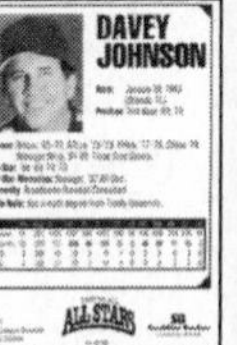

The 1994 Ambassadors of Baseball 15-card standard-size set was sponsored by Major League Baseball Players Alumni and MCI. The sets were released at a few select military bases where the retired players appeared in charity games. The front design is the same as the 1993 issue, with the MCI logo at the upper right and the Ambassadors of Baseball World Tour logo at the lower left. The two tribute cards list the names of players who served during World War II.

	Nm-Mt	Ex-Mt
COMPLETE SET (15)	35.00	10.50
1 Sparky Lyle	4.00	1.20
2 John Stearns	2.00	.60
3 Bobby Thomson	6.00	1.80
4 Jimmy Wynn	2.00	.60
5 Ferguson Jenkins	6.00	1.80
6 Tug McGraw	4.00	1.20
7 Paul Blair	2.00	.60
8 Ron LeFlore	2.00	.60
9 Manny Sanguillen	2.00	.60
10 Doug Flynn	2.00	.60
11 Bill North	2.00	.60
S1 Doug Flynn (Instructing children)	2.00	.60
S2 World War II Tribute Card (AL)	4.00	1.20
S3 World War II Tribute Card (NL)	4.00	1.20
S4 Manny Sanguillen (Signing autographs)	4.00	1.20

1995 MCI Ambassadors

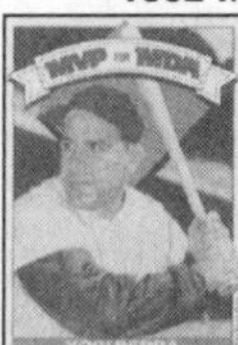

This 16-card standard-size set was sponsored by MCI, MLB, and Major League Baseball Players Alumni. Approximately 2,000 sets were produced and distributed at certain U.S. military bases where the retired players appeared in charity games.

	Nm-Mt	Ex-Mt
COMPLETE SET (16)	35.00	10.50
1 Vida Blue	3.00	.90
2 Bert Campaneris	3.00	.90
3 Tug McGraw	3.00	.90
4 Doug Flynn	2.00	.60
5 Paul Blair	2.00	.60
6 Harmon Killebrew	5.00	1.50
7 Sparky Lyle	3.00	.90
8 Steve Garvey	5.00	1.50
9 Bert Blyleven	3.00	.90
10 Omar Moreno	2.00	.60
11 Bill Lee	2.00	.60
12 Maury Wills	3.00	.90
13 Dave Parker	3.00	.90
14 Luis Aparicio	5.00	1.50
15 Brooks Robinson	5.00	1.50
16 George Foster	3.00	.90

1991 MDA All-Stars

This 20-card standard-size set was produced by Smith-Kline Beecham for the Muscular Dystrophy Association. It includes 18 All-Star Alumni cards that feature retired baseball All-Stars. A vinyl album designed to house the cards was also issued. Since the set was licensed by the Major League Baseball Players Alumni, all team logos have been airbrushed out.

	Nm-Mt	Ex-Mt
COMPLETE SET (20)	12.00	3.60
1 Steve Carlton	1.50	.45
2 Ted Simmons	.50	.15
3 Willie Stargell	1.00	.30
4 Bill Mazeroski	.75	.23
5 Ron Santo	.75	.23
6 Dave Concepcion	.50	.15
7 Bobby Bonds	.75	.23
8 George Foster	.50	.15
9 Billy Williams	1.00	.30
10 Whitey Ford	1.50	.45
11 Yogi Berra	1.50	.45
12 Boog Powell	.75	.23
13 Davey Johnson	.50	.15
14 Brooks Robinson	1.50	.45
15 Jim Fregosi	.50	.15
16 Harmon Killebrew	1.50	.45
17 Ted Williams	4.00	1.20
18 Al Kaline	1.50	.45
NNO MDA Fact Card Brooks Robinson Tommy	1.50	.45
NNO Title Card	.50	.15

1992 MDA MVP

This 20-card limited edition set of alumni MVPs was sponsored by SmithKline Beecham Consumer Brands and was produced for the Muscular Dystrophy Association.

	Nm-Mt	Ex-Mt
COMPLETE SET (20)	15.00	4.50
1 Yogi Berra	2.50	.75
2 Dick Groat	.50	.15
3 Maury Wills	.75	.23
4 Brooks Robinson	1.50	.45
5 Orlando Cepeda	1.00	.30
6 Harmon Killebrew	1.50	.45
7 Boog Powell	1.00	.30
8 Vida Blue	.75	.23
9 Jeff Burroughs	.50	.15
10 George Foster	.50	.15
11 Rod Carew	1.50	.45
12 Jim Rice	.75	.23
13 Don Baylor	.75	.23
14 Willie Stargell	1.50	.45
15 Rollie Fingers	1.00	.30
16 Ray Knight	.50	.15
17 History Card	.50	.15

18 Trivia Card .50 .15
19 Fact Sheet .50 .15
(Players Alumni)
20 Harmon Killebrew 1.00 .30
Drew
Fact Sheet

1986 Meadow Gold Blank Back

This unnumbered set of 16 full-color cards is blank backed. The cards were found (one card per package) on the flap of 1/2 gallon cartons of Meadow Gold "Double Play" ice cream. The cards are attractive but the team logos have been airbrushed away. The cards measure approximately 2 3/8" by 3 1/2." The accent colors used on the front of the cards are light blue and red. The Ripken card is supposedly a little more difficult to find.

Nm-Mt Ex-Mt
COMPLETE SET (16) 45.00 18.00
1 Wade Boggs 3.00 1.20
2 George Brett 5.00 2.00
3 Carlton Fisk 3.00 1.20
4 Steve Garvey 2.00 .80
5 Dwight Gooden 2.00 .80
6 Pedro Guerrero 1.50 .60
7 Reggie Jackson 3.00 1.20
8 Don Mattingly 5.00 2.00
9 Willie McGee 2.00 .80
10 Dale Murphy 2.50 1.00
11 Cal Ripken 8.00 3.20
12 Pete Rose 3.00 1.20
13 Ryne Sandberg 4.00 1.60
14 Mike Schmidt 3.00 1.20
15 Fernando Valenzuela 2.00 .80
16 Dave Winfield 3.00 1.20

1986 Meadow Gold Milk

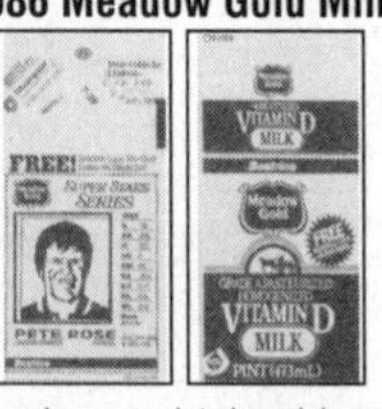

These cards were printed crudely on milk cartons of various sizes of Meadow Gold milk. The cards are approximately 2 1/2" by 3 3/16" and are very similar to the Keller's Butter cards. The same art was used on the Schmidt card which is in both sets. Both Keller's and Meadow Gold are subsidiaries of Beatrice Foods. The set was licensed by Mike Schechter Associates and the Major League Baseball Players' Association. The cards are blank backed and are printed in red and brown on white waxed cardboard. Complete boxes would bring double the values listed below. Since the cards are unnumbered, they are listed below in alphabetical order.

Nm-Mt Ex-Mt
COMPLETE SET (12) 50.00 20.00
1 Wade Boggs 4.00 1.60
2 George Brett 6.00 2.40
3 Steve Carlton 4.00 1.60
4 Dwight Gooden 2.50 1.00
5 Don Mattingly 6.00 2.40
6 Willie McGee 2.00 .80
7 Dale Murphy 4.00 1.60
8 Cal Ripken 12.00 4.80
9 Pete Rose 4.00 1.60
10 Ryne Sandberg 6.00 2.40
11 Mike Schmidt 4.00 1.60
12 Fernando Valenzuela 2.50 1.00

1986 Meadow Gold Stat Back

Meadow Gold produced three sets in 1986, but this was the only one with printing on the back. This full-color set contains 20 star players. The cards were distributed as two-card panels with Meadow Gold popsicles, fudgesicles and bubblegum coolers. As with the other sets, this one was only licensed by the Major League Players Association and hence the team logos have been artistically removed. The back printing is in red on white card stock. The cards measure approximately 2 9/16" by 3 1/2" and are numbered on the back. Two of the cards were misspelled by Meadow Gold as noted in the checklist below. Intact panels are valued at 50 percent more than the sum of the individual players making up the panel.

Nm-Mt Ex-Mt
COMPLETE SET (20) 35.00 14.00
1 George Brett 5.00 2.00
2 Fernando Valenzuela 1.25 .50
3 Dwight Gooden 1.25 .50
4 Dale Murphy 1.50 .60
5 Don Mattingly 5.00 2.00
6 Reggie Jackson 2.00 .80
7 Dave Winfield 2.00 .80
8 Pete Rose 2.00 .80
9 Wade Boggs 2.00 .80
10 Willie McGee 1.25 .50
11 Cal Ripken ERR 6.00 2.40
sic, Ripkin
12 Ryne Sandberg 4.00 1.60
13 Carlton Fisk 2.00 .80
14 Jim Rice 1.25 .50
15 Steve Garvey 1.25 .50
16 Mike Schmidt 4.00 1.60
17 Bruce Sutter 1.00 .40
18 Pedro Guerrero 1.00 .40
19 Rick Sutcliffe ERR 1.00 .40
sic, Sutcliffe
20 Rich Gossage 1.00 .40

1911 Mecca Double Folders T201

The cards in this 50-card set measure approximately 2 1/4" by 4 11/16". The 1911 Mecca Double Folder issue contains unnumbered cards. This issue was one of the first to list statistics of players portrayed on the cards. Each card portrays two players, one when the card is folded, another when the card is unfolded. The card of Dougherty and Lord is considered scarce.

Ex-Mt VG
COMPLETE SET (50) 5500.00 2800.00
1 Frank Baker 200.00 100.00
Eddie Collins
2 Jack Barry 60.00 30.00
Jack Lapp
3 Bill Bergen 150.00 75.00
Zach Wheat
4 Walter Blair 60.00 30.00
Roy Hartzell
5 Roger Bresnahan 200.00 100.00
Miller Huggins
6 Al Bridwell 500.00 250.00
Christy Matthewson UER
Mathewson
7 Johnny Butler 60.00 30.00
Bill Abstein
8 Bobby Byrne 125.00 60.00
Fred Clarke
9 Frank Chance 300.00 150.00
Johnny Evers
10 Tommy Clarke 60.00 30.00
Harry Gaspar
11 Ty Cobb 1200.00 600.00
Sam Crawford
12 Leonard Cole 60.00 30.00
Johnny Kling
13 Jack Coombs 60.00 30.00
Ira Thomas
14 Jake Daubert 60.00 30.00
Nap Rucker
15 Patsy Dougherty 300.00 150.00
Harry Lord
16 Red Dooin 60.00 30.00
John Titus
17 Tom Downey 60.00 30.00
H Baker
No Player named Baker played for KC in 1910
18 Jimmy Dygert 60.00 30.00
Cy Seymour
19 Kid Elberfeld 60.00 30.00
George McBride UER
20 Cy Falkenberg 200.00 100.00
Nap Lajoie
21 E.Fitzpatrick 60.00 30.00
Ed Killian
22 Larry Gardner 200.00 100.00
Tris Speaker
23 George Gibson 60.00 30.00
Tommy Leach
24 Peaches Graham 60.00 30.00
Al Mattern
25 Arnold Hauser 60.00 30.00
Johnny Lush
26 Buck Herzog 60.00 30.00
Dots Miller
27 Harry Hinchman 60.00 30.00
Charles Hickman
28 Solly Hofman 150.00 75.00
Mordecai Brown
29 Hugh Jennings 125.00 60.00
Ed Summers
30 Otis Johnson 60.00 30.00
Russ Ford
31 Tom McCarty 100.00 50.00
Joe McGinnity
32 Ulysses McGlyn 60.00 30.00
Jimmy Barrett
33 Larry McLean 60.00 30.00
Eddie Grant
34 Fred Merkle 60.00 30.00
Hooks Wiltse
35 Chief Meyers 60.00 30.00
Larry Doyle
36 Earl Moore 60.00 30.00
Hans Lobert
37 Fred Odwell 60.00 30.00
Red Downs
38 Rube Oldring 125.00 60.00
Chief Bender
39 Fred Payne 125.00 60.00
Ed Walsh
40 Michael Simon 60.00 30.00
Lefty Leifield
41 Charles Starr 60.00 30.00
James McCabe
42 James Stephens 60.00 30.00
Frank LaPorte
43 George Stovall 60.00 30.00
Terry Turner
44 Gabby Street 500.00 250.00
Walter Johnson
45 Ralph Stroud 60.00 30.00
Bill Donovan
46 Ed Sweeney 100.00 50.00
Hal Chase
47 Johny Thoney 100.00 50.00
Eddie Cicotte
48 Bobby Wallace 100.00 50.00
Joe Lake
49 Joseph Ward 60.00 30.00
Edward Foster
50 O.Williams 60.00 30.00
Sam Woodruff

1992 Megacards Ruth Prototypes

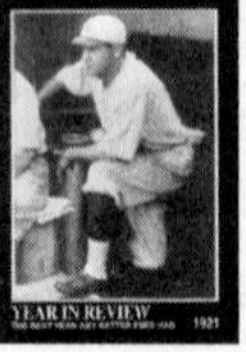

Nine prototypes were produced to preview Megacards 1992 Babe Ruth Collection. The cards are very similar to the Conlon sets produced in conjunction with The Sporting News. The cards are standard size. These cards were clearly marked as prototypes, and the bulk of the 12,000 cards produced were included in mailings to hobby dealers. In general, some subtle differences in photos are found with some of the prototype cards.

Nm-Mt Ex-Mt
COMPLETE SET (9) 25.00 7.50
COMMON CARD 3.00 .90

1992 Megacards Ruth

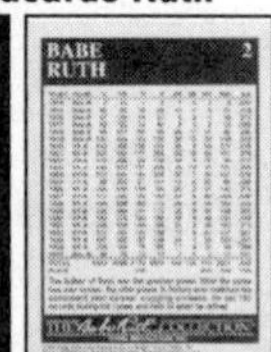

Released by Megacards, the 1992 Babe Ruth Collection consists of 165 standard-size cards, including a card for every year of his career. The cards are very similar to the Conlon sets produced in conjunction with The Sporting News. The cards were sold in both ten-card packs and 22-card blister packs. Complete sets were also available in a commemorative tin. The set is arranged as follows: Babe Ruth (1-4), Year in Review (5-29), World Series (30-39), Place in History (40-70), Career Highlights (71-97), Trivia (98-104), Sultan of SWAT (105-115), The Bambino-The Man (116-142), and Being Remembered (143-163). The set concludes with checklist cards (164-165). The set could also be purchased in a special commemorative tin.

Nm-Mt Ex-Mt
COMPLETE SET (165) 18.00 5.50
COMP.FACT SET (165)
COMMON CARD (1-165) .10 .03
1 Babe Ruth .40 .12
Lifetime Pitching
Statistics 1916
7 Babe Ruth .10 .03
Ernie Shore
Dutch Leonard
Rube Foster
Won 17 of His Last
21 Decisions 1915
9 Babe Ruth .25 .07
Defeats Walter Johnson for 6th Time
1917
19 Babe Ruth .60 .18
Lou Gehrig
Earle Combs
Tony Lazzeri
The Best Baseball
Team in History 1927
31 Babe Ruth .25 .07
Rube Foster
John Wycoff
Ernie Shore
Dutch Leonard
Vean Gregg
Carl Mays
Herb Pennock
Hurls 14 Inning
Complete Game Gem 1916
36 Babe Ruth .25 .07
Rogers Hornsby
Belts 4 Home Runs in
Losing Cause 1926
37 Babe Ruth
Lloyd Waner
Yanks Destroy Bucs in
Four Games 1927
39 Babe Ruth .60 .18
Lou Gehrig
Joe McCarthy MG
Yanks Sweep Cubs
1932
42 Babe Ruth .60 .18
Eddie Collins
Ty Cobb
Lifetime-2,174 Runs Scored
1928
43 Babe Ruth .60 .18
Ty Cobb
Tris Speaker
Lifetime-5,793 Total Bases
1942
47 Babe Ruth .40 .12
Jimmie Foxx
Lifetime 8.5 Home Run Percentage
1934
50 Babe Ruth .40 .12
Honus Wagner
Lifetime-2,211 RBIs
51 Babe Ruth .60 .18
Lou Gehrig
Tris Speaker
Ty Cobb
Lifetime-.342 BA 1928
52 Babe Ruth .40 .12
Jimmie Foxx
Lifetime-.690 SA 1934
55 Babe Ruth .60 .18
Lou Gehrig
Season-177 Runs Scored 1939
57 Babe Ruth .25 .07
Rogers Hornsby
Season-457 Total Bases 1926
58 Babe Ruth .25 .07
Hank Greenberg
Season-119 Extra Base Hits 1947
59 Babe Ruth .60 .18
Lou Gehrig
Season 171 RBI's 1934
60 Babe Ruth .60 .18
Lou Gehrig
Season-60 Home Runs 1927
62 Babe Ruth .25 .07
Rogers Hornsby
Season-.847 SA 1920
70 Babe Ruth .60 .18
Lou Gehrig
World Series- .744SA 1927
73 Babe Ruth .40 .12
Walter Johnson
Babe Derails Big Train 1942
76 Babe Ruth .25 .07
Jacob Ruppert OWN
Becomes a Yankee 1920
79 Babe Ruth .60 .18
George Sisler
Ty Cobb
Wins Only Batting Title 1924
80 Babe Ruth .10 .03
Hits 3 Home Runs
in Series Game
October 6, 1926
81 Babe Ruth .75 .23
Lou Gehrig
Smack 107 Home Runs
1927
82 Babe Ruth .25 .07
60th Home Run: September 30, 1927
86 Babe Ruth .60 .18
Lou Gehrig
The Called Shot
The Believers 1932
87 Babe Ruth .25 .07
Bob Meusel
Mark Koenig
The Called Shot
The Doubters 1948
89 Babe Ruth .60 .18
Lou Gehrig
Jimmie Foxx
Slams First HR in
First AS Game 1933
91 Babe Ruth .25 .07
Lennie Bielski
Hits 700th Home Run 1934
92 Babe Ruth .25 .07
Banzai Beibu Russu-
In Japan 1934
94 Babe Ruth .40 .12
Honus Wagner
Grover Alexander
Tris Speaker
Nap Lajoie
George Sisler
Walter Johnson
Eddie Collins
Connie Mack
Ty Cobb
Inaugurated Into HOF 1939
95 Babe Ruth .25 .07
Faces Walter Johnson Again
August 23, 1942
96 Babe Ruth Day .25 .07
Ford Frick
Mel Allen
April 27, 1947
97 Babe Ruth .25 .07
Farewell 1948
100 Hub Pruett .25 .07
Babe Buster 1929
102 Babe Ruth .25 .07
Miller Huggins MG
Never Won a Triple Crown 1926
118 Brother Matthias .10 .03
120 Babe Ruth .25 .07
Helen Ruth
121 Babe's Ruth .25 .07
Claire Ruth
122 Babe Ruth .40 .12
Lou Gehrig
Appreciation Day
July 4, 1939
123 Babe Ruth .25 .07
Herb Pennock
124 Babe Ruth .25 .07
Miller Huggins MG
125 Babe Ruth .60 .18
Ty Cobb
126 Babe Ruth .40 .12
Walter Johnson 1942
128 Babe Ruth .60 .18
Lou Gehrig
Barnstorming
131 Babe Ruth .25 .07
Jacob Ruppert OWN
Big Bucks 1927
134 Babe Ruth .25 .07
Gary Cooper as Lou Gehrig
in the Movies
140 Babe Ruth .25 .07
Johnny Sylvester
141 Babe Ruth .25 .07
Warren G. Harding PRES
Moving with the Great 1923
143 Babe Ruth .25 .07
Remembered by Bill James 1928
144 Babe Ruth .25 .07
Remembered by Bill James 1929
145 Babe Ruth .25 .07
Remembered by Bill James 1920
146 Babe Ruth .40 .12
Remembered by Mel Allen 1923
147 Babe Ruth .40 .12
Remembered by Mel Allen 1928
148 Babe Ruth .25 .07
Remembered by Wes Ferrell 1930
149 Babe Ruth .60 .18
George Bush
Remembered by George Bush 1948
150 Babe Ruth .60 .18
George Bush
Ethan Allen
Remembered by Ethan Allen 1948
151 Babe Ruth .25 .07
Dorothy Ruth
Remembered by Daughter Dorothy 1926
152 Babe Ruth .25 .07
Julia Ruth
Remembered by Daughter Julia 1947
153 Babe Ruth .25 .07
Julia Ruth
Remembered by Daughter Julia 1938
154 Babe Ruth .25 .07
Mark Koenig
Remembered by Mark Koenig 1927
155 Babe Ruth .25 .07
Remembered by Donald Honig 1927
156 Babe Ruth .25 .07
Remembered by Lloyd Waner and
Waite Hoyt 1948
157 Babe Ruth .25 .07
Remembered by Waite Hoyt 1938
158 Babe Ruth .25 .07
Kiki Cuyler
Remembered by Bill Dickey 1938
159 Babe Ruth .25 .07
Kenesaw M. Landis COMM
Bob Meusel
Remembered by Bob Meusel 1922
160 Babe Ruth .25 .07
Ty Cobb
Spanky Joslin
Remembered by Jim Chapman 1941
161 Babe Ruth .25 .07
Christy Walsh AGENT#-Remembered by
Christy Walsh 1926
163 Babe Ruth .25 .07
Remembered by Grantland Rice 1923

1994 Megacards Ruthian Shots

Produced by Megacards and titled "Ruthian Shots," this five-card standard-size set was given away at card shows when the collector purchased a 1994 Conlon Collection wax box.

Nm-Mt Ex-Mt
COMPLETE SET (5) 10.00 3.00
COMMON CARD (1-5) 2.00 .60
1 Babe Ruth 3.00 .90
Pitcher for the
Boston Red Sox
3 Babe Ruth 4.00 1.20
Lou Gehrig
Fishing
5 Babe Ruth 2.50 .75
Miller Huggins MG
Together in car

1995 Megacards Griffey Jr. Wish List

In this 25-card standard-size set, Ken Griffey Jr. shares his personal thoughts about the game, his dreams for the future and his commitment to terminally ill and underprivileged children. The suggested retail price for each set was $9.99. Just 100,000 sets were produced, with a percentage of all proceeds to benefit the Make-A-Wish Foundation. A sweepstakes card inside each pack entitled the collector to be entered in a chance drawing of 500 autographed collectibles (including 5 jerseys, 10 bats, 60 balls and 425 cards from this set). Also included in each set was one of three Ken Griffey Jr. MegaCaps.

Nm-Mt Ex-Mt
COMPLETE SET (25) 10.00 3.00
COMMON CARD (1-25) .50 .15
XX Ken Griffey AU 200.00 60.00

1995 Megacards Ruth

This 25-card standard-size set offers classic glimpses and new insights into Babe Ruth. Twenty-one cards are in black-and-white, while four cards feature computer-enhanced color (11-12, 21, 24). The suggested retail price for each set was 9.99. All card fronts carry the Babe Ruth 100th Anniversary logo in gold foil. One hundred thousand sets were produced. Each set included an official entry blank to a sweepstakes featuring the following prizes: 1 Babe Ruth autographed ball, 200 Don Mattingly autographed cards, 200 Ken Griffey Jr. autographed cards and 100 Babe Ruth 165-card sets. Also included in each set was one of three limited edition (34,000) Babe Ruth Megacaps.

Nm-Mt Ex-Mt
COMPLETE SET (25) 10.00 3.00
COMMON CARD (1-25) .25 .07
3 Jimmie Foxx .75 .23
Babe Ruth
Lou Gehrig
Al Simmons
No Slugger Comes Close
5 Babe Ruth .50 .15
Bill Dickey
Ray Hayworth
He Knew the Way Home
6 Babe Ruth 1.00 .30
Lou Gehrig
He Didn't Leave Them Stranded
9 Lloyd Waner .75 .23
Babe Ruth
Paul Waner
Lou Gehrig
.342 Plus Power
12 Babe Ruth 1.50 .45
Lou Gehrig
Career Year
Color
13 Babe Ruth 1.00 .30
Don Mattingly
Lou Gehrig
Mr. Yankee
14 Babe and "The Kid" 1.50 .45
Babe Ruth
Ken Griffey Jr.
18 Babe Ruth .50 .15
Miller Huggins MG
The Rewards of Greatness
21 Babe Ruth 1.50 .45
Ken Griffey Jr.
Babe and Today's Best
Color
24 Dizzy Dean .50 .15
Frankie Frisch
Babe Ruth
Mickey Cochrane
Schoolboy Rowe
How He Changed the Game
Color

1910 Mello Mints E105

The cards in this 50-card set measure 1 1/2" by 2 3/4". The cards were manufactured by the Texas Gum Company. The cards themselves are unnumbered and the fronts are identical to these found in E92. Printed on paper, the backs are horizontally aligned and carry advertising for "Smith's Mello-Mint". The set was issued about 1910. The cards have been alphabetized and numbered in the checklist below. The complete set price includes all variation cards listed in the checklist below.

Ex-Mt VG
COMPLETE SET (50) 20000.00 10000.00
1 Jack Barry 150.00 75.00
2 Harry Bemis 150.00 75.00
3A Chief Bender 300.00 150.00
(blue background)
3B Chief Bender 300.00 150.00
(green background)
4 Bill Bergen 150.00 75.00
5 Bob Bescher 150.00 75.00
6 Al Bridwell 150.00 75.00
7 Doc Casey 150.00 75.00
8 Frank Chance 400.00 200.00
9 Hal Chase 250.00 125.00
10 Ty Cobb 4000.00 2000.00
11 Eddie Collins 600.00 300.00
12 Sam Crawford 300.00 150.00
13 Harry Davis 150.00 75.00
14 Art Devlin 200.00 100.00
15 Bill Donovan 150.00 75.00
16 Red Dooin 150.00 75.00
17 Mickey Doolan 150.00 75.00
18 Patsy Dougherty 150.00 75.00
19A Larry Doyle 200.00 100.00
batting
19B Larry Doyle 200.00 100.00
throwing
20 Johnny Evers 500.00 250.00
21 George Gibson 150.00 75.00
22 Topsy Hartsel 150.00 75.00
23 Fred Jacklitsch 150.00 75.00
24 Hugh Jennings 300.00 150.00
25 Red Kleinow 150.00 75.00
26 Otto Knabe 150.00 75.00
27 John Knight 150.00 75.00
28 Nap Lajoie 1000.00 500.00
29 Hans Lobert 150.00 75.00
30 Sherry Magee 200.00 100.00
31 Christy Mathewson 1500.00 750.00
32 John McGraw MG 600.00 300.00
33 Larry McLean 150.00 75.00
34A Dots Miller 150.00 75.00
batting
34B Dots Miller 150.00 75.00
fielding
35 Danny Murphy 150.00 75.00
36 William O'Hara 150.00 75.00
37 Germany Schaefer 200.00 100.00
38 George Schlei 150.00 75.00
39 Charles Schmidt 150.00 75.00
40 Johnny Seigle 150.00 75.00
41 David Shean 150.00 75.00
42 Frank Smith 150.00 75.00
43 Joe Tinker 500.00 250.00
44A Honus Wagner 2000.00 1000.00
batting
44B Honus Wagner 2000.00 1000.00
throwing
45 Cy Young 1200.00 600.00
46 Heinie Zimmerman 150.00 75.00

1996 Metal Universe Promo Sheet

This set consists of one sheet picturing samples of nine cards. The front features color action player photos of nine different players each on a different metallic background. The back carries color portraits of the same players with biographical and statistical information. The words, "Promotional Sample," are stamped diagonally on both the front and back of each player's card.

Nm-Mt Ex-Mt
XX Complete Sheet 5.00 1.50
Todd Greene
Jon Nunnally
Brad Radke
Don Mattingly
Alex Rodriguez
Ivan Rodriguez
Chipper Jones
Eric Karros
Jeff King

1996 Metal Universe

The Metal Universe set (created by Fleer) was issued in one series totalling 250 standard-size cards. The cards were issued in foil-wrapped packs. The theme for the set was based on intermingling fantasy comic book elements with baseball, thus each card features a player set against a wide variety of bizarre backgrounds. The cards are grouped alphabetically within teams below.

Nm-Mt Ex-Mt
COMPLETE SET (250) 40.00 12.00
1 Roberto Alomar .75 .23
2 Brady Anderson .30 .09
3 Bobby Bonilla .30 .09
4 Chris Hoiles .30 .09
5 Ben McDonald .30 .09
6 Mike Mussina .75 .23
7 Randy Myers .30 .09
8 Rafael Palmeiro .50 .15
9 Cal Ripken 2.50 .75
10 B.J. Surhoff .30 .09
11 Luis Alicea .30 .09
12 Jose Canseco .75 .23
13 Roger Clemens 1.50 .45
14 Wil Cordero .30 .09
15 Tom Gordon .30 .09
16 Mike Greenwall .30 .09
17 Tim Naehring .30 .09
18 Troy O'Leary .30 .09
19 Mike Stanley .30 .09
20 John Valentin .30 .09
21 Mo Vaughn .30 .09
22 Tim Wakefield .30 .09
23 Garret Anderson .30 .09
24 Chili Davis .30 .09
25 Gary DiSarcina .30 .09
26 Jim Edmonds .30 .09
27 Chuck Finley .30 .09
28 Todd Greene .30 .09
29 Mark Langston .30 .09
30 Troy Percival .30 .09
31 Tony Phillips .30 .09
32 Tim Salmon .50 .15
33 Lee Smith .30 .09
34 J.T. Snow .30 .09
35 Ray Durham .30 .09
36 Alex Fernandez .30 .09
37 Ozzie Guillen .30 .09
38 Roberto Hernandez .30 .09
39 Lyle Mouton .30 .09
40 Frank Thomas .75 .23
41 Robin Ventura .30 .09
42 Sandy Alomar Jr. .30 .09
43 Carlos Baerga .30 .09
44 Albert Belle .30 .09
45 Orel Hershiser .30 .09
46 Kenny Lofton .30 .09
47 Dennis Martinez .30 .09
48 Jack McDowell .30 .09
49 Jose Mesa .30 .09
50 Eddie Murray .75 .23
51 Charles Nagy .30 .09
52 Manny Ramirez .30 .09
53 Julian Tavarez .30 .09
54 Jim Thome .75 .23
55 Omar Vizquel .30 .09
56 Chad Curtis .30 .09
57 Cecil Fielder .30 .09
58 John Flaherty .30 .09
59 Travis Fryman .30 .09
60 Chris Gomez .30 .09
61 Felipe Lira .30 .09
62 Kevin Appier .30 .09
63 Johnny Damon .30 .09
64 Tom Goodwin .30 .09
65 Mark Gubicza .30 .09
66 Jeff Montgomery .30 .09
67 Jon Nunnally .30 .09
68 Ricky Bones .30 .09
69 Jeff Cirillo .30 .09
70 John Jaha .30 .09
71 Dave Nilsson .30 .09
72 Joe Oliver .30 .09
73 Kevin Seitzer .30 .09
74 Greg Vaughn .30 .09
75 Marty Cordova .30 .09
76 Chuck Knoblauch .30 .09
77 Pat Meares .30 .09
78 Paul Molitor .50 .15
79 Pedro Munoz .30 .09
80 Kirby Puckett .75 .23
81 Brad Radke .30 .09
82 Scott Stahoviak .30 .09
83 Matt Walbeck .30 .09
84 Wade Boggs .50 .15
85 David Cone .30 .09
86 Joe Girardi .30 .09
87 Derek Jeter 2.00 .60
88 Jim Leyritz .30 .09
89 Tino Martinez .50 .15
90 Don Mattingly 2.00 .60
91 Paul O'Neill .50 .15
92 Andy Pettitte .50 .15
93 Tim Raines .30 .09
94 Kenny Rogers .30 .09
95 Ruben Sierra .30 .09
96 John Wetteland .30 .09
97 Bernie Williams .50 .15
98 Geronimo Berroa .30 .09
99 Dennis Eckersley .30 .09
100 Brent Gates .30 .09
101 Mark McGwire 2.00 .60
102 Steve Ontiveros .30 .09
103 Terry Steinbach .30 .09
104 Jay Buhner .30 .09
105 Vince Coleman .30 .09
106 Joey Cora .30 .09
107 Ken Griffey, Jr. 1.25 .35
108 Randy Johnson .75 .23
109 Edgar Martinez .50 .15
110 Alex Rodriguez 1.50 .45
111 Paul Sorrento .30 .09
112 Will Clark .75 .23
113 Juan Gonzalez .75 .23
114 Rusty Greer .30 .09
115 Dean Palmer .30 .09
116 Ivan Rodriguez .75 .23
117 Mickey Tettleton .30 .09
118 Joe Carter .30 .09
119 Alex Gonzalez .30 .09
120 Shawn Green .30 .09
121 Erik Hanson .30 .09
122 Pat Hentgen .30 .09
123 Sandy Martinez .30 .09
124 Otis Nixon .30 .09
125 John Olerud .30 .09
126 Steve Avery .30 .09
127 Tom Glavine .50 .15
128 Marquis Grissom .30 .09
129 Chipper Jones .75 .23
130 David Justice .30 .09
131 Ryan Klesko .30 .09
132 Mark Lemke .30 .09
133 Javier Lopez .30 .09
134 Greg Maddux 1.25 .35
135 Fred McGriff .50 .15
136 John Smoltz .50 .15
137 Mark Wohlers .30 .09
138 Frank Castillo .30 .09
139 Shawon Dunston .30 .09
140 Luis Gonzalez .30 .09
141 Mark Grace .50 .15
142 Brian McRae .30 .09
143 Jaime Navarro .30 .09
144 Rey Sanchez .30 .09
145 Ryne Sandberg 1.25 .35
146 Sammy Sosa 1.25 .35
147 Bret Boone .30 .09
148 Curtis Goodwin .30 .09
149 Barry Larkin .75 .23
150 Hal Morris .30 .09
151 Reggie Sanders .30 .09
152 Pete Schourek .30 .09
153 John Smiley .30 .09
154 Dante Bichette .30 .09
155 Vinny Castilla .30 .09
156 Andres Galarraga .30 .09
157 Bret Saberhagen .30 .09
158 Bill Swift .30 .09
159 Larry Walker .50 .15
160 Walt Weiss .30 .09
161 Kurt Abbott .30 .09
162 John Burkett .30 .09
163 Greg Colbrunn .30 .09
164 Jeff Conine .30 .09
165 Chris Hammond .30 .09
166 Charles Johnson .30 .09
167 Al Leiter .30 .09
168 Pat Rapp .30 .09
169 Gary Sheffield .30 .09
170 Quilvio Veras .30 .09
171 Devon White .30 .09
172 Jeff Bagwell .50 .15
173 Derek Bell .30 .09
174 Sean Berry .30 .09
175 Craig Biggio .50 .15
176 Doug Drabek .30 .09
177 Tony Eusebio .30 .09
178 Brian L.Hunter .30 .09
179 Orlando Miller .30 .09
180 Shane Reynolds .30 .09
181 Mike Blowers .30 .09
182 Roger Cedeno .30 .09
183 Eric Karros .30 .09
184 Ramon Martinez .30 .09
185 Raul Mondesi .30 .09
186 Hideo Nomo .75 .23
187 Mike Piazza 1.25 .35
188 Moises Alou .30 .09
189 Yamil Benitez .30 .09
190 Darrin Fletcher .30 .09
191 Cliff Floyd .30 .09
192 Pedro Martinez .75 .23
193 Carlos Perez .30 .09
194 David Segui .30 .09
195 Tony Tarasco .30 .09
196 Rondell White .30 .09
197 Edgardo Alfonzo .30 .09
198 Rico Brogna .30 .09
199 Carl Everett .30 .09
200 Todd Hundley .30 .09
201 Jason Isringhausen .30 .09
202 Lance Johnson .30 .09
203 Bobby Jones .30 .09
204 Jeff Kent .30 .09
205 Bill Pulsipher .30 .09
206 Jose Vizcaino .30 .09
207 Ricky Bottalico .30 .09
208 Darren Daulton .30 .09
209 Lenny Dykstra .30 .09
210 Jim Eisenreich .30 .09
211 Gregg Jefferies .30 .09
212 Mickey Morandini .30 .09
213 Heathcliff Slocumb .30 .09
214 Jay Bell .30 .09
215 Carlos Garcia .30 .09
216 Jeff King .30 .09
217 Al Martin .30 .09
218 Orlando Merced .30 .09
219 Dan Miceli .30 .09
220 Denny Neagle .30 .09
221 Andy Benes .30 .09
222 Royce Clayton .30 .09
223 Gary Gaetti .30 .09
224 Ron Gant .30 .09
225 Bernard Gilkey .30 .09
226 Brian Jordan .30 .09
227 Ray Lankford .30 .09
228 John Mabry .30 .09
229 Ozzie Smith 1.25 .35
230 Todd Stottlemyre .30 .09
231 Andy Ashby .30 .09
232 Brad Ausmus .30 .09
233 Ken Caminiti .30 .09
234 Steve Finley .30 .09
235 Tony Gwynn 1.00 .30
236 Joey Hamilton .30 .09
237 Rickey Henderson .75 .23
238 Trevor Hoffman .30 .09
239 Wally Joyner .30 .09
240 Rod Beck .30 .09
241 Barry Bonds 2.00 .60
242 Glenallen Hill .30 .09
243 Stan Javier .30 .09
244 Mark Leiter .30 .09
245 Deion Sanders .50 .15
246 Wm. Van Landingham .30 .09
247 Matt Williams .30 .09
248 Checklist .30 .09
249 Checklist .30 .09
250 Checklist .30 .09

1996 Metal Universe Platinum

The 1996 Fleer Metal Universe Platinum is a 250-card parallel version of the regular series and were inserted one per pack. The silver foil backgrounds differentiate these from the regular cards.

Nm-Mt Ex-Mt
COMPLETE SET (250) 120.00 36.00
*STARS: 1.25X TO 3X BASIC CARDS.
*ROOKIES: 1.25X TO 3X BASIC CARDS

1996 Metal Universe Heavy Metal

Randomly inserted in packs at a rate of one in eight this 10-card set features the Power Hitters of Baseball. The fronts feature a color action player cut-out over a silver foil background. The backs carry a player portrait and information about the player.

Nm-Mt Ex-Mt
COMPLETE SET (10) 25.00 7.50
1 Albert Belle 1.00 .30
2 Barry Bonds 6.00 1.80
3 Juan Gonzalez 2.50 .75
4 Ken Griffey Jr. 4.00 1.20
5 Mark McGwire 6.00 1.80
6 Mike Piazza 4.00 1.20
7 Sammy Sosa 4.00 1.20
8 Frank Thomas 2.50 .75
9 Mo Vaughn 1.00 .30
10 Matt Williams 1.00 .30

1996 Metal Universe Mining For Gold

Randomly inserted in retail packs only at a rate of one in 12, this 12-card set highlights major prospects and rookies. The fronts feature a player photo on the top half with the words "Mining for Gold" on the bottom. The backs

feature another player photo along with a brief blurb.

Nm-Mt Ex-Mt
COMPLETE SET (12) 60.00 18.00
1 Yamil Benitez 3.00 .90
2 Marty Cordova 3.00 .90
3 Shawn Green 3.00 .90
4 Todd Greene 3.00 .90
5 Brian Hunter 3.00 .90
6 Derek Jeter 20.00 6.00
7 Charles Johnson 3.00 .90
8 Chipper Jones 8.00 2.40
9 Hideo Nomo 8.00 2.40
10 Alex Ochoa 3.00 .90
11 Andy Pettitte 5.00 1.50
12 Quilvio Veras 3.00 .90

1996 Metal Universe Mother Lode

Randomly inserted in hobby packs only at a rate of one in 12, this 12-card set features multi-tool players. The fronts carry a color action player cut-out over a silver-foil, scroll-design background. The backs display another player photo and information about the player.

Nm-Mt Ex-Mt
COMPLETE SET (12) 50.00 15.00
1 Barry Bonds 10.00 3.00
2 Jim Edmonds 1.50 .45
3 Ken Griffey Jr. 6.00 1.80
4 Kenny Lofton 1.50 .45
5 Raul Mondesi 1.50 .45
6 Rafael Palmeiro 2.50 .17
7 Manny Ramirez 1.50 .45
8 Cal Ripken 12.00 3.60
9 Tim Salmon 2.50 .75
10 Ryne Sandberg 6.00 1.80
11 Frank Thomas 4.00 1.20
12 Matt Williams 1.50 .45

1996 Metal Universe Platinum Portraits

Randomly inserted in packs at a rate of one in four, this 10-card set features ten of the hottest young stars. The fronts display a player portrait on a platinum foil background. The backs carry a color action player photo and why the player is hot.

Nm-Mt Ex-Mt
COMPLETE SET (10) 10.00 3.00
1 Garret Anderson .75 .23
2 Marty Cordova .75 .23
3 Jim Edmonds .75 .23
4 Jason Isringhausen .75 .23
5 Chipper Jones 2.00 .60
6 Ryan Klesko .75 .23
7 Hideo Nomo 2.00 .60
8 Carlos Perez .75 .23
9 Manny Ramirez .75 .23
10 Rondell White .75 .23

1996 Metal Universe Titanium

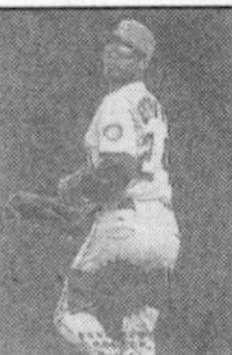

Randomly inserted in packs at a rate of one in 24, this 10-card set features ten of the fans' favorite players. The fronts feature an action color player cut-out on a foil baseball background. The backs display a player portrait and why the player is liked by the fans.

Nm-Mt Ex-Mt
COMPLETE SET (10) 80.00 24.00
1 Albert Belle 2.50 .75
2 Barry Bonds 15.00 4.50
3 Ken Griffey Jr. 10.00 3.00
4 Tony Gwynn 8.00 2.40
5 Greg Maddux 10.00 3.00

6 Mike Piazza 10.00 3.00
7 Cal Ripken 20.00 6.00
8 Frank Thomas 6.00 1.80
9 Mo Vaughn 2.50 .75
10 Matt Williams 2.50 .75

1997 Metal Universe

The 1997 Metal Universe set, (produced by Fleer), was issued in one series totalling 250 cards and distributed in eight-card foil packs with a suggested retail price of $2.49. Printed in 100 percent etched foil with UV-coating, the fronts features color photos of star players on full-bleed backgrounds of comic book art with the player's name, team, position and card logo printed near the bottom of the card. The backs carry another player photo and statistics. An Alex Rodriguez promo card was distributed to dealers and hobby media several weekd prior to the product's release.

Nm-Mt Ex-Mt
COMPLETE SET (250) 30.00 9.00
1 Roberto Alomar .75 .23
2 Brady Anderson .30 .09
3 Rocky Coppinger .30 .09
4 Chris Hoiles .30 .09
5 Eddie Murray .75 .23
6 Mike Mussina .75 .23
7 Rafael Palmeiro .50 .15
8 Cal Ripken 2.50 .75
9 B.J. Surhoff .30 .09
10 Brant Brown .30 .09
11 Mark Grace .50 .15
12 Brian McRae .30 .09
13 Jaime Navarro .30 .09
14 Ryne Sandberg 1.25 .35
15 Sammy Sosa 1.25 .35
16 Amaury Telemaco .30 .09
17 Steve Trachsel .30 .09
18 Darren Bragg .30 .09
19 Jose Canseco .75 .23
20 Roger Clemens 1.50 .45
21 Nomar Garciaparra 1.25 .35
22 Tom Gordon .30 .09
23 Tim Naehring .30 .09
24 Mike Stanley .30 .09
25 John Valentin .30 .09
26 Mo Vaughn .30 .09
27 Jermaine Dye .30 .09
28 Tom Glavine .50 .15
29 Marquis Grissom .30 .09
30 Andruw Jones .30 .09
31 Chipper Jones .75 .23
32 Ryan Klesko .30 .09
33 Greg Maddux 1.25 .35
34 Fred McGriff .50 .15
35 John Smoltz .50 .15
36 Garret Anderson .30 .09
37 George Arias .30 .09
38 Gary DiSarcina .30 .09
39 Jim Edmonds .30 .09
40 Darin Erstad .30 .09
41 Chuck Finley .30 .09
42 Troy Percival .30 .09
43 Tim Salmon .50 .15
44 Bret Boone .30 .09
45 Jeff Brantley .30 .09
46 Eric Davis .30 .09
47 Barry Larkin .75 .23
48 Hal Morris .30 .09
49 Mark Portugal .30 .09
50 Reggie Sanders .30 .09
51 John Smiley .30 .09
52 Wilson Alvarez .30 .09
53 Harold Baines .30 .09
54 James Baldwin .30 .09
55 Albert Belle .30 .09
56 Mike Cameron .30 .09
57 Ray Durham .30 .09
58 Alex Fernandez .30 .09
59 Roberto Hernandez .30 .09
60 Tony Phillips .30 .09
61 Frank Thomas .75 .23
62 Robin Ventura .30 .09
63 Jeff Cirillo .30 .09
64 Jeff D'Amico .30 .09
65 John Jaha .30 .09
66 Scott Karl .30 .09
67 Ben McDonald .30 .09
68 Marc Newfield .30 .09
69 Dave Nilsson .30 .09
70 Jose Valentin .30 .09
71 Dante Bichette .30 .09
72 Ellis Burks .30 .09
73 Vinny Castilla .30 .09
74 Andres Galarraga .30 .09
75 Kevin Ritz .30 .09
76 Larry Walker .50 .15
77 Walt Weiss .30 .09
78 Jamey Wright .30 .09
79 Eric Young .30 .09
80 Julio Franco .30 .09
81 Orel Hershiser .30 .09
82 Kenny Lofton .30 .09
83 Jack McDowell .30 .09
84 Jose Mesa .30 .09
85 Charles Nagy .30 .09
86 Manny Ramirez .30 .09
87 Jim Thome .75 .23
88 Omar Vizquel .30 .09
89 Matt Williams .30 .09
90 Kevin Appier .30 .09
91 Johnny Damon .30 .09
92 Chili Davis .30 .09
93 Tom Goodwin .30 .09
94 Keith Lockhart .30 .09
95 Jeff Montgomery .30 .09
96 Craig Paquette .30 .09
97 Jose Rosado .30 .09
98 Michael Tucker .30 .09
99 Wilton Guerrero .30 .09
100 Todd Hollandsworth .30 .09
101 Eric Karros .30 .09
102 Ramon Martinez .30 .09
103 Raul Mondesi .30 .09
104 Hideo Nomo .75 .23
105 Mike Piazza 1.25 .35
106 Ismael Valdes .30 .09
107 Todd Worrell .30 .09
108 Tony Clark .30 .09
109 Travis Fryman .30 .09
110 Bob Higginson .30 .09
111 Mark Lewis .30 .09
112 Melvin Nieves .30 .09
113 Justin Thompson .30 .09
114 Wade Boggs .50 .15
115 David Cone .30 .09
116 Cecil Fielder .30 .09
117 Dwight Gooden .50 .15
118 Derek Jeter 2.00 .60
119 Tino Martinez .50 .15
120 Paul O'Neill .50 .15
121 Andy Pettitte .50 .15
122 Mariano Rivera .50 .15
123 Darryl Strawberry .50 .15
124 John Wetteland .30 .09
125 Bernie Williams .50 .15
126 Tony Batista .30 .09
127 Geronimo Berroa .30 .09
128 Scott Brosius .30 .09
129 Jason Giambi .75 .23
130 Jose Herrera .30 .09
131 Mark McGwire 2.00 .60
132 John Wasdin .30 .09
133 Bob Abreu .30 .09
134 Jeff Bagwell .50 .15
135 Derek Bell .30 .09
136 Craig Biggio .50 .15
137 Brian Hunter .30 .09
138 Darryl Kile .30 .09
139 Orlando Miller .30 .09
140 Shane Reynolds .30 .09
141 Billy Wagner .30 .09
142 Donne Wall .30 .09
143 Jay Buhner .30 .09
144 Jeff Fassero .30 .09
145 Ken Griffey Jr. 1.25 .35
146 Sterling Hitchcock .30 .09
147 Randy Johnson .75 .23
148 Edgar Martinez .50 .15
149 Alex Rodriguez 1.25 .35
150 Paul Sorrento .30 .09
151 Dan Wilson .30 .09
152 Moises Alou .30 .09
153 Darrin Fletcher .30 .09
154 Cliff Floyd .30 .09
155 Mark Grudzielanek .30 .09
156 Vladimir Guerrero .75 .23
157 Mike Lansing .30 .09
158 Pedro Martinez .75 .23
159 Henry Rodriguez .30 .09
160 Rondell White .30 .09
161 Will Clark .75 .23
162 Juan Gonzalez .75 .23
163 Rusty Greer .30 .09
164 Ken Hill .30 .09
165 Mark McLemore .30 .09
166 Dean Palmer .30 .09
167 Roger Pavlik .30 .09
168 Ivan Rodriguez .75 .23
169 Mickey Tettleton .30 .09
170 Bobby Bonilla .30 .09
171 Kevin Brown .30 .09
172 Greg Colbrunn .30 .09
173 Jeff Conine .30 .09
174 Jim Eisenreich .30 .09
175 Charles Johnson .30 .09
176 Al Leiter .30 .09
177 Robb Nen .30 .09
178 Edgar Renteria .30 .09
179 Gary Sheffield .30 .09
180 Devon White .30 .09
181 Joe Carter .30 .09
182 Carlos Delgado .30 .09
183 Alex Gonzalez .30 .09
184 Shawn Green .30 .09
185 Juan Guzman .30 .09
186 Pat Hentgen .30 .09
187 Orlando Merced .30 .09
188 John Olerud .30 .09
189 Robert Perez .30 .09
190 Ed Sprague .30 .09
191 Mark Clark .30 .09
192 John Franco .30 .09
193 Bernard Gilkey .30 .09
194 Todd Hundley .30 .09
195 Lance Johnson .30 .09
196 Bobby Jones .30 .09
197 Alex Ochoa .30 .09
198 Rey Ordonez .30 .09
199 Paul Wilson .30 .09
200 Ricky Bottalico .30 .09
201 Gregg Jefferies .30 .09
202 Wendell Magee .30 .09
203 Mickey Morandini .30 .09
204 Ricky Otero .30 .09
205 Scott Rolen .50 .15
206 Benito Santiago .30 .09
207 Curt Schilling .50 .15
208 Rich Becker .30 .09
209 Marty Cordova .30 .09
210 Chuck Knoblauch .30 .09
211 Pat Meares .30 .09
212 Paul Molitor .50 .15
213 Frank Rodriguez .30 .09
214 Terry Steinbach .30 .09
215 Todd Walker .30 .09
216 Andy Ashby .30 .09
217 Ken Caminiti .30 .09
218 Steve Finley .30 .09
219 Tony Gwynn 1.00 .30
220 Joey Hamilton .30 .09
221 Rickey Henderson .75 .23
222 Trevor Hoffman .30 .09
223 Wally Joyner .30 .09
224 Scott Sanders .30 .09
225 Fernando Valenzuela .30 .09
226 Greg Vaughn .30 .09
227 Alan Benes .30 .09
228 Andy Benes .30 .09
229 Dennis Eckersley .30 .09
230 Ron Gant .30 .09
231 Brian Jordan .30 .09
232 Ray Lankford .30 .09
233 John Mabry .30 .09
234 Tom Pagnozzi .30 .09
235 Todd Stottlemyre .30 .09
236 Jermaine Allensworth .30 .09
237 Francisco Cordova .30 .09
238 Jason Kendall .30 .09
239 Jeff King .30 .09
240 Al Martin .30 .09
241 Rod Beck .30 .09
242 Barry Bonds 2.00 .60
243 Shawn Estes .30 .09
244 Mark Gardner .30 .09
245 Glenallen Hill .30 .09
246 Bill Mueller RC 2.00 .60
247 J.T. Snow .30 .09
248 Checklist 1-107 .30 .09
249 Checklist 108-207 .30 .09
250 CL 208-250/inserts .30 .09
P149 A. Rodriguez Promo 1.50 .45

1997 Metal Universe Blast Furnace

Randomly inserted in hobby packs only at a rate of one in 48, this 12-card set features color photos of some of baseball's biggest sluggers.

Nm-Mt Ex-Mt
COMPLETE SET (12) 100.00 30.00
1 Jeff Bagwell 5.00 1.50
2 Albert Belle 3.00 .90
3 Barry Bonds 20.00 6.00
4 Andres Galarraga 3.00 .90
5 Juan Gonzalez 8.00 2.40
6 Ken Griffey Jr. 12.00 3.60
7 Todd Hundley 3.00 .90
8 Mark McGwire 20.00 6.00
9 Mike Piazza 12.00 3.60
10 Alex Rodriguez 12.00 3.60
11 Frank Thomas 8.00 2.40
12 Mo Vaughn 3.00 .90

1997 Metal Universe Emerald Autographs

These autographed cards were distributed via mail to lucky collectors that sent in an Emerald Autograph Exchange card seeded at a rate of one in 20 boxes. The autographed cards parallel the corresponding basic cards except of course for the signature on front, coupled with special emerald foil and an embossed Fleer/SkyBox stamp. In addition, the area used for the card number on back of the regular issue card is replaced by a logo stating "certified emerald autograph". These autographed cards are unnumbered and have been assigned numbers based upon alphabetical order of each player's last name.

Nm-Mt Ex-Mt
*EXCH.CARDS: .1X TO .25X BASIC CARDS
AU1 Darin Erstad 15.00 4.50
AU2 Todd Hollandsworth 10.00 3.00
AU3 Alex Ochoa 10.00 3.00
AU4 Alex Rodriguez 120.00 36.00
AU5 Scott Rolen 25.00 7.50
AU6 Todd Walker 15.00 4.50

1997 Metal Universe Magnetic Field

Randomly inserted in packs at a rate of one in 12, this ten-card set honors "Gold Glovers" who appear to have a special attraction to the ball. The fronts feature color player photos on refractive foil backgrounds.

Nm-Mt Ex-Mt
COMPLETE SET (10) 25.00 7.50
1 Roberto Alomar 2.50 .75
2 Jeff Bagwell 1.50 .45
3 Barry Bonds 6.00 1.80
4 Ken Griffey Jr. 4.00 1.20
5 Derek Jeter 6.00 1.80
6 Kenny Lofton 1.00 .30
7 Edgar Renteria 1.00 .30
8 Cal Ripken 8.00 2.40
9 Alex Rodriguez 4.00 1.20
10 Matt Williams 1.00 .30

1997 Metal Universe Mining for Gold

Randomly inserted in packs at a rate of one in nine, this 10-card set features some of baseball's brightest young stars on die-cut "ingot" cards with pearlized gold coating.

Nm-Mt Ex-Mt
COMPLETE SET (10) 15.00 4.50
1 Bob Abreu 1.00 .30
2 Kevin Brown C 1.00 .30
3 Nomar Garciaparra 4.00 1.20
4 Vladimir Guerrero 2.50 .75
5 Wilton Guerrero 1.00 .30
6 Andruw Jones 1.00 .30
7 Curt Lyons 1.00 .30
8 Neifi Perez 1.00 .30
9 Scott Rolen 1.50 .45
10 Todd Walker 1.00 .30

1997 Metal Universe Mother Lode

Randomly inserted in packs at a rate of one in 288, this 12-card set features color player photos on die-cut cards in 100 percent etched foil.

Nm-Mt Ex-Mt
COMPLETE SET (12) 300.00 90.00
1 Roberto Alomar 20.00 6.00
2 Jeff Bagwell 12.00 3.60
3 Barry Bonds 50.00 15.00
4 Ken Griffey Jr. 30.00 9.00
5 Andruw Jones 8.00 2.40
6 Chipper Jones 20.00 6.00
7 Kenny Lofton 8.00 2.40
8 Mike Piazza 30.00 9.00
9 Cal Ripken 60.00 18.00
10 Alex Rodriguez 30.00 9.00
11 Frank Thomas 20.00 6.00
12 Matt Williams 8.00 2.40

1997 Metal Universe Platinum Portraits

Randomly inserted in packs at a rate of one in 36, this 10-card set features color photos of some of Baseball's rising stars with backgrounds of platinum-colored etched foil.

Nm-Mt Ex-Mt
COMPLETE SET (10) 50.00 15.00
1 James Baldwin 3.00 .90
2 Jermaine Dye 3.00 .90
3 Todd Hollandsworth 3.00 .90
4 Derek Jeter 20.00 6.00
5 Chipper Jones 8.00 2.40
6 Jason Kendall 3.00 .90
7 Rey Ordonez 3.00 .90
8 Andy Pettitte 5.00 1.50
9 Edgar Renteria 3.00 .90
10 Alex Rodriguez 12.00 3.60

1997 Metal Universe Titanium

Randomly inserted in packs at a rate of one in 24, this 10-card set honors some of baseball's favorite superstars. The fronts feature color player photos printed on die-cut embossed cards and sculpted on 100 percent etched foil.

Nm-Mt Ex-Mt
COMPLETE SET (10) 80.00 24.00
1 Jeff Bagwell 3.00 .90
2 Albert Belle 2.00 .60
3 Ken Griffey Jr. 8.00 2.40
4 Chipper Jones 5.00 1.50
5 Greg Maddux 8.00 2.40
6 Mark McGwire 12.00 3.60
7 Mike Piazza 8.00 2.40
8 Cal Ripken 15.00 4.50
9 Alex Rodriguez 8.00 2.40
10 Frank Thomas 5.00 1.50

1998 Metal Universe

The 1998 Metal Universe set, produced by Fleer, was issued in one series totalling 220 cards. The fronts feature color player photos with metal etching. The backs carry player information. The set contains the topical subset: Hardball Galaxy (203-217). An Alex Rodriguez promo card was distributed along with all dealer order forms. The card is identical to the regular issue Rodriguez card except for the text "PROMOTIONAL SAMPLE" written diagonally along the card back.

Nm-Mt Ex-Mt
COMPLETE SET (220) 40.00 12.00
1 Jose Cruz Jr. .30 .09
2 Jeff Abbott .30 .09
3 Rafael Palmeiro .50 .15
4 Ivan Rodriguez .75 .23
5 Jaret Wright .30 .09
6 Derek Bell .30 .09
7 Chuck Finley .30 .09
8 Travis Fryman .30 .09
9 Randy Johnson .75 .23
10 Derrek Lee .30 .09
11 Bernie Williams .50 .15
12 Carlos Baerga .30 .09
13 Ricky Bottalico .30 .09
14 Ellis Burks .30 .09
15 Russ Davis .30 .09
16 Nomar Garciaparra 1.25 .35
17 Joey Hamilton .30 .09
18 Jason Kendall .30 .09
19 Darryl Kile .30 .09
20 Edgardo Alfonzo .30 .09
21 Moises Alou .30 .09
22 Bobby Bonilla .30 .09
23 Jim Edmonds .30 .09
24 Jose Guillen .30 .09
25 Chuck Knoblauch .30 .09
26 Javy Lopez .30 .09
27 Billy Wagner .30 .09
28 Kevin Appier .30 .09
29 Joe Carter .30 .09
30 Todd Dunwoody .30 .09
31 Gary Gaetti .30 .09
32 Juan Gonzalez .75 .23
33 Jeffrey Hammonds .30 .09
34 Roberto Hernandez .30 .09
35 Dave Nilsson .30 .09
36 Manny Ramirez .30 .09
37 Robin Ventura .30 .09
38 Rondell White .30 .09
39 Vinny Castilla .30 .09
40 Will Clark .75 .23
41 Scott Hatteberg .30 .09
42 Russ Johnson .30 .09
43 Ricky Ledee .30 .09
44 Kenny Lofton .30 .09
45 Paul Molitor .50 .15
46 Justin Thompson .30 .09
47 Craig Biggio .50 .15
48 Damion Easley .30 .09
49 Brad Radke .30 .09
50 Ben Grieve .30 .09
51 Mark Bellhorn .30 .09
52 Henry Blanco .30 .09
53 Mariano Rivera .50 .15
54 Reggie Sanders .30 .09
55 Paul Sorrento .30 .09
56 Terry Steinbach .30 .09
57 Mo Vaughn .30 .09
58 Brady Anderson .30 .09
59 Tom Glavine .50 .15
60 Sammy Sosa 1.25 .35
61 Larry Walker .50 .15
62 Rod Beck .30 .09
63 Jose Canseco .75 .23
64 Steve Finley .30 .09
65 Pedro Martinez .75 .23
66 John Olerud .30 .09
67 Scott Rolen .50 .15
68 Ismael Valdes .30 .09
69 Andrew Vessel .30 .09
70 Mark Grudzielanek .30 .09
71 Eric Karros .30 .09
72 Jeff Shaw .30 .09
73 Lou Collier .30 .09
74 Edgar Martinez .50 .15
75 Vladimir Guerrero .75 .23
76 Paul Konerko .30 .09
77 Kevin Orie .30 .09
78 Kevin Polcovich .30 .09
79 Brett Tomko .30 .09
80 Jeff Bagwell .50 .15
81 Barry Bonds 2.00 .60
82 David Justice .30 .09
83 Hideo Nomo .75 .23
84 Ryne Sandberg 1.25 .35
85 Shannon Stewart .30 .09
86 Derek Wallace .30 .09
87 Tony Womack .30 .09
88 Jason Giambi .75 .23
89 Mark Grace .50 .15
90 Pat Hentgen .30 .09
91 Raul Mondesi .30 .09
92 Matt Morris .30 .09
93 Matt Perisho .30 .09
94 Tim Salmon .50 .15
95 Jeremi Gonzalez .30 .09
96 Shawn Green .30 .09
97 Todd Greene .30 .09
98 Ruben Rivera .30 .09
99 Deion Sanders .50 .15

1997 Metal Universe

100 Alex Rodriguez 1.25 .35
101 Will Cunnane .30 .09
102 Ray Lankford .30 .09
103 Ryan McGuire .30 .09
104 Charles Nagy .30 .09
105 Rey Ordonez .30 .09
106 Mike Piazza 1.25 .35
107 Tony Saunders .30 .09
108 Curt Schilling .50 .15
109 Fernando Tatis .30 .09
110 Mark McGwire 2.00 .60
111 Dave Dellucci RC .30 .09
112 Garret Anderson .30 .09
113 Shane Bowers RC .30 .09
114 David Cone .30 .09
115 Jeff King .30 .09
116 Matt Williams .30 .09
117 Aaron Boone .30 .09
118 Dennis Eckersley .30 .09
119 Livan Hernandez .30 .09
120 Richard Hidalgo .30 .09
121 Bobby Higginson .30 .09
122 Tino Martinez .50 .15
123 Tim Naehring .30 .09
124 Jose Vidro .30 .09
125 John Wetteland .30 .09
126 Jay Bell .30 .09
127 Albert Belle .30 .09
128 Marty Cordova .30 .09
129 Chili Davis .30 .09
130 Jason Dickson .30 .09
131 Rusty Greer .30 .09
132 Hideki Irabu .30 .09
133 Greg Maddux 1.25 .35
134 Billy Taylor .30 .09
135 Jim Thome .75 .23
136 Gerald Williams .30 .09
137 Jeff Cirillo .30 .09
138 Delino DeShields .30 .09
139 Andres Galarraga .30 .09
140 Willie Greene .30 .09
141 John Jaha .30 .09
142 Charles Johnson .30 .09
143 Ryan Klesko .30 .09
144 Paul O'Neill .50 .15
145 Robinson Checo .30 .09
146 Roberto Alomar .75 .23
147 Wilson Alvarez .30 .09
148 Bobby Jones .30 .09
149 Raul Casanova .30 .09
150 Andruw Jones .30 .09
151 Mike Lansing .30 .09
152 Mickey Morandini .30 .09
153 Neifi Perez .30 .09
154 Pokey Reese .30 .09
155 Edgar Renteria .30 .09
156 Eric Young .30 .09
157 Darin Erstad .30 .09
158 Kelvim Escobar .30 .09
159 Carl Everett .30 .09
160 Tom Gordon .30 .09
161 Ken Griffey Jr. 1.25 .35
162 Al Martin .30 .09
163 Bubba Trammell .30 .09
164 Carlos Delgado .30 .09
165 Kevin Brown .50 .15
166 Ken Caminiti .30 .09
167 Roger Clemens 1.50 .45
168 Ron Gant .30 .09
169 Jeff Kent .30 .09
170 Mike Mussina .75 .23
171 Dean Palmer .30 .09
172 Henry Rodriguez .30 .09
173 Matt Stairs .30 .09
174 Jay Buhner .30 .09
175 Frank Thomas .75 .23
176 Mike Cameron .30 .09
177 Johnny Damon .30 .09
178 Tony Gwynn 1.00 .30
179 John Smoltz .50 .15
180 B.J. Surhoff .30 .09
181 Antone Williamson .30 .09
182 Alan Benes .30 .09
183 Jeromy Burnitz .30 .09
184 Tony Clark .30 .09
185 Shawn Estes .30 .09
186 Todd Helton .50 .15
187 Todd Hundley .30 .09
188 Chipper Jones .75 .23
189 Mark Kotsay .30 .09
190 Barry Larkin .75 .23
191 Mike Lieberthal .30 .09
192 Andy Pettitte .50 .15
193 Gary Sheffield .30 .09
194 Jeff Suppan .30 .09
195 Mark Wohlers .30 .09
196 Dante Bichette .30 .09
197 Trevor Hoffman .30 .09
198 J.T. Snow .30 .09
199 Derek Jeter 2.00 .60
200 Cal Ripken 2.50 .75
201 Steve Woodard .30 .09
202 Ray Durham .30 .09
203 Barry Bonds HG .75 .23
204 Tony Clark HG .30 .09
205 Roger Clemens HG .75 .23
206 Ken Griffey Jr. HG .75 .23
207 Deion Sanders HG .30 .09
208 Derek Jeter HG 1.00 .30
209 Randy Johnson HG .50 .15
210 Brady Anderson HG .30 .09
211 Hideo Nomo HG .50 .15
212 Mike Piazza HG .75 .23
213 Cal Ripken HG 1.25 .35
214 Alex Rodriguez HG .75 .23
215 Frank Thomas HG .50 .15
216 Mo Vaughn HG .30 .09
217 Larry Walker HG .30 .09
218 Ken Griffey Jr. CL .75 .23
219 Alex Rodriguez CL .75 .23
220 Frank Thomas CL .50 .15
P100 A. Rodriguez Promo 1.50 .45

1998 Metal Universe Precious Metal Gems

Randomly inserted only in hobby packs, cards from this 217-card set parallel the base set (except for the last three checklists cards in the set). Only 50 of these sets were produced and each card is serial numbered on back. In addition, five "Ultimate Gems" exchange cards (good for one complete Precious Gems set) were randomly seeded into packs. Due to this promotion, cards from only the first 45 serial numbered sets were seeded into packs. Sets serial numbered between 46-50 were held back for the Ultimate Gems exchange program.

Nm-Mt Ex-Mt
*STARS: 12.5X TO 30X BASIC CARDS
*ROOKIES: 12.5X TO 30X BASIC CARDS

1998 Metal Universe All-Galactic Team

Randomly inserted in packs at the rate of one in 192, this 18-card set features color player photos on backgrounds of planets. The backs carry player information.

Nm-Mt Ex-Mt
COMPLETE SET (18) 300.00 90.00
1 Ken Griffey Jr. 20.00 6.00
2 Frank Thomas 12.00 3.60
3 Chipper Jones 12.00 3.60
4 Albert Belle 5.00 1.50
5 Juan Gonzalez 12.00 3.60
6 Jeff Bagwell 8.00 2.40
7 Andruw Jones 5.00 1.50
8 Cal Ripken 40.00 12.00
9 Derek Jeter 30.00 9.00
10 Nomar Garciaparra 20.00 6.00
11 Darin Erstad 5.00 1.50
12 Greg Maddux 20.00 6.00
13 Alex Rodriguez 20.00 6.00
14 Mike Piazza 20.00 6.00
15 Vladimir Guerrero 12.00 3.60
16 Jose Cruz Jr. 5.00 1.50
17 Mark McGwire 30.00 9.00
18 Scott Rolen 8.00 2.40

1998 Metal Universe Diamond Heroes

Randomly inserted in packs at the rate of one in 18, this six-card set features color photos of five top players in a mini-comic book form.

Nm-Mt Ex-Mt
COMPLETE SET (6) 12.00 3.60
1 Ken Griffey Jr. 2.50 .75
2 Frank Thomas 1.50 .45
3 Andruw Jones .60 .18
4 Alex Rodriguez 2.50 .75
5 Jose Cruz Jr. .60 .18
6 Cal Ripken 5.00 1.50

1998 Metal Universe Platinum Portraits

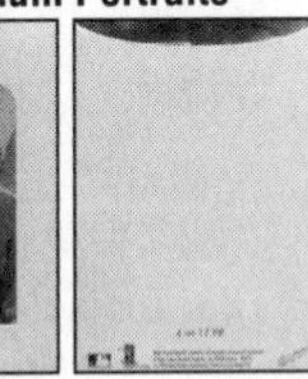

Randomly inserted in packs at the rate of one in 360, this 12-card set features color portraits of top players highlighted with platinum-colored etched foil.

Nm-Mt Ex-Mt
COMPLETE SET (12) 200.00 60.00
1 Ken Griffey Jr. 25.00 7.50
2 Frank Thomas 15.00 4.50
3 Chipper Jones 15.00 4.50
4 Jose Cruz Jr. 6.00 1.80
5 Andruw Jones 6.00 1.80
6 Cal Ripken 50.00 15.00
7 Derek Jeter 40.00 12.00
8 Darin Erstad 6.00 1.80
9 Greg Maddux 25.00 7.50
10 Alex Rodriguez 25.00 7.50
11 Mike Piazza 25.00 7.50
12 Vladimir Guerrero 15.00 4.50

1998 Metal Universe Titanium

Randomly inserted in packs at the rate of one in 96, this 15-card set features color photos of top stars printed on die-cut embossed cards and sculpted on etched foil.

Nm-Mt Ex-Mt
COMPLETE SET (15) 150.00 45.00
1 Ken Griffey Jr. 15.00 4.50
2 Frank Thomas 10.00 3.00
3 Chipper Jones 10.00 3.00
4 Jose Cruz Jr. 4.00 1.20
5 Juan Gonzalez 10.00 3.00
6 Scott Rolen 6.00 1.80
7 Andruw Jones 4.00 1.20
8 Cal Ripken 30.00 9.00
9 Derek Jeter 25.00 7.50
10 Nomar Garciaparra 15.00 4.50
11 Darin Erstad 4.00 1.20
12 Greg Maddux 15.00 4.50
13 Alex Rodriguez 15.00 4.50
14 Mike Piazza 15.00 4.50
15 Vladimir Guerrero 10.00 3.00

1998 Metal Universe Universal Language

Randomly inserted in packs at the rate of one in six, this 20-card set features color photos of players whose culture provides illustration and copy is done in the player's native language.

Nm-Mt Ex-Mt
COMPLETE SET (20) 50.00 15.00
1 Ken Griffey Jr. 3.00 .90
2 Frank Thomas 2.00 .60
3 Chipper Jones 2.00 .60
4 Albert Belle .75 .23
5 Juan Gonzalez 2.00 .60
6 Jeff Bagwell 1.25 .35
7 Andruw Jones .75 .23
8 Cal Ripken 6.00 1.80
9 Derek Jeter 5.00 1.50
10 Nomar Garciaparra 3.00 .90
11 Darin Erstad .75 .23
12 Greg Maddux 3.00 .90
13 Alex Rodriguez 3.00 .90
14 Mike Piazza 3.00 .90
15 Vladimir Guerrero 2.00 .60
16 Jose Cruz Jr. .75 .23
17 Hideo Nomo 2.00 .60
18 Kenny Lofton .75 .23
19 Tony Gwynn 2.50 .75
20 Scott Rolen 1.25 .35

1999 Metal Universe Sample Sheet

This non-perforated six card sheet was distributed to wholesale dealer and retail accounts several weeks prior to the national release of 1999 Metal Universe in an effort to preview the cards. The sheet measures 5" by 10.5". The cards are identical to their standard issue counterpart releases except on the back where the word "SAMPLE" replaces the card number. Since the sheet is non-perforated, it's consistently traded (and therefore priced below) as one unit. In addition, a special version of this sheet - signed by J.D. Drew - was distributed to attendees at the 15th Annual Hawaii Trade Conference in February, 1999. Only 325 autographed sheets were printed, each of which is adorned with a circular gold foil SkyBox seal in the middle of the sheet. Drew signed the sheet in black ink over his own card. Each autographed sheet is serial numbered by hand in black ink.

Nm-Mt Ex-Mt
NNOA Albert Belle 25.00 7.50
J.D.Drew AUTO
Derek Jeter
Mike Piazza
Alex Rodriguez
Sammy Sosa
NNO Albert Belle 5.00 1.50
J.D. Drew
Derek Jeter
Mike Piazza
Alex Rodriguez
Sammy Sosa

1999 Metal Universe

This 300-card set, produced by Fleer, was distributed in eight-card hobby and retail packs carrying a suggested retail price of $2.69. The product was released in January, 1999. Card fronts feature color action player photos with brushed metal backgrounds in 100 percent etched silver foil and an embossed nameplate with the look of forged steel. The backs carry player information. The set includes the following subsets: Caught on the Fly (233-247), Building Blocks (248-272), and M.L.P.D. (273-300) which features prominent and dominant stars. In an unannounced promotion, thirty-five hand-numbered J.D. Drew Building Blocks subset sample cards were signed by the athlete and randomly seeded into packs. Each of these cards has an embossed authentication seal and the word SAMPLE replaces the card number on back.

Nm-Mt Ex-Mt
COMPLETE SET (300) 50.00 15.00
1 Mark McGwire 2.00 .60
2 Jim Edmonds .30 .09
3 Travis Fryman .30 .09
4 Tom Gordon .30 .09
5 Jeff Bagwell .50 .15
6 Rico Brogna .30 .09
7 Tom Evans .30 .09
8 John Franco .30 .09
9 Juan Gonzalez .75 .23
10 Paul Molitor .50 .15
11 Roberto Alomar .75 .23
12 Mike Hampton .30 .09
13 Orel Hershiser .30 .09
14 Todd Stottlemyre .30 .09
15 Robin Ventura .30 .09
16 Todd Walker .30 .09
17 Bernie Williams .50 .15
18 Shawn Estes .30 .09
19 Richie Sexson .30 .09
20 Kevin Millwood .30 .09
21 David Ortiz .30 .09
22 Mariano Rivera .50 .15
23 Ivan Rodriguez .75 .23
24 Mike Sirotka .30 .09
25 David Justice .30 .09
26 Carl Pavano .30 .09
27 Albert Belle .30 .09
28 Will Clark .75 .23
29 Jose Cruz Jr. .30 .09
30 Trevor Hoffman .30 .09
31 Dean Palmer .30 .09
32 Edgar Renteria .30 .09
33 David Segui .30 .09
34 B.J. Surhoff .30 .09
35 Miguel Tejada .30 .09
36 Bob Wickman .30 .09
37 Charles Johnson .30 .09
38 Andruw Jones .30 .09
39 Mike Lieberthal .30 .09
40 Eli Marrero .30 .09
41 Neifi Perez .30 .09
42 Jim Thome .75 .23
43 Barry Bonds 2.00 .60
44 Carlos Delgado .30 .09
45 Chuck Finley .30 .09
46 Brian Meadows .30 .09
47 Tony Gwynn 1.00 .30
48 Jose Offerman .30 .09
49 Cal Ripken 2.50 .75
50 Alex Rodriguez 1.25 .35
51 Esteban Yan .30 .09
52 Matt Stairs .30 .09
53 Fernando Vina .30 .09
54 Rondell White .30 .09
55 Kerry Wood .75 .23
56 Dmitri Young .30 .09
57 Ken Caminiti .30 .09
58 Alex Gonzalez .30 .09
59 Matt Mantei .30 .09
60 Tino Martinez .50 .15
61 Hal Morris .30 .09
62 Rafael Palmeiro .50 .15
63 Troy Percival .30 .09
64 Bobby Smith .30 .09
65 Ed Sprague .30 .09
66 Brett Tomko .30 .09
67 Steve Trachsel .30 .09
68 Ugueth Urbina .30 .09
69 Jose Valentin .30 .09
70 Kevin Brown .50 .15
71 Shawn Green .30 .09
72 Dustin Hermanson .30 .09
73 Livan Hernandez .30 .09
74 Geoff Jenkins .30 .09
75 Jeff King .30 .09
76 Chuck Knoblauch .50 .15
77 Edgar Martinez .50 .15
78 Fred McGriff .50 .15
79 Mike Mussina .75 .23
80 Dave Nilsson .30 .09
81 Kenny Rogers .30 .09
82 Tim Salmon .50 .15
83 Reggie Sanders .30 .09
84 Wilson Alvarez .30 .09
85 Rod Beck .30 .09
86 Jose Guillen .30 .09
87 Bob Higginson .30 .09
88 Gregg Olson .30 .09
89 Jeff Shaw .30 .09
90 Masato Yoshii .30 .09
91 Todd Helton .50 .15
92 David Dellucci .30 .09
93 Johnny Damon .30 .09
94 Cliff Floyd .30 .09
95 Ken Griffey Jr. 1.25 .35
96 Juan Guzman .30 .09
97 Derek Jeter 2.00 .60
98 Barry Larkin .75 .23
99 Quinton McCracken .30 .09
100 Sammy Sosa 1.25 .35
101 Kevin Young .30 .09
102 Jay Bell .30 .09
103 Jay Buhner .30 .09
104 Jeff Conine .30 .09
105 Ryan Jackson .30 .09
106 Sidney Ponson .30 .09
107 Jeromy Burnitz .30 .09
108 Roberto Hernandez .30 .09
109 A.J. Hinch .30 .09
110 Hideki Irabu .30 .09
111 Paul Konerko .30 .09
112 Henry Rodriguez .30 .09
113 Shannon Stewart .30 .09
114 Tony Womack .30 .09
115 Wilton Guerrero .30 .09
116 Andy Benes .30 .09
117 Jeff Cirillo .30 .09
118 Chili Davis .30 .09
119 Eric Davis .30 .09
120 Vladimir Guerrero .75 .23
121 Dennis Reyes .30 .09
122 Rickey Henderson .75 .23
123 Mickey Morandini .30 .09
124 Jason Schmidt .30 .09
125 J.T. Snow .30 .09
126 Justin Thompson .30 .09
127 Billy Wagner .30 .09
128 Armando Benitez .30 .09
129 Sean Casey .30 .09
130 Brad Fullmer .30 .09
131 Ben Grieve .30 .09
132 Robb Nen .30 .09
133 Shane Reynolds .30 .09
134 Todd Zeile .30 .09
135 Brady Anderson .30 .09
136 Aaron Boone .30 .09
137 Orlando Cabrera .30 .09
138 Jason Giambi .75 .23
139 Randy Johnson .75 .23
140 Jeff Kent .30 .09
141 John Wetteland .30 .09
142 Rolando Arrojo .30 .09
143 Scott Brosius .30 .09
144 Mark Grace .50 .15
145 Jason Kendall .30 .09
146 Travis Lee .30 .09
147 Gary Sheffield .30 .09
148 David Cone .30 .09
149 Jose Hernandez .30 .09
150 Todd Jones .30 .09
151 Al Martin .30 .09
152 Ismael Valdes .30 .09
153 Wade Boggs .50 .15
154 Garret Anderson .30 .09
155 Bobby Bonilla .30 .09
156 Darryl Kile .30 .09
157 Ryan Klesko .30 .09
158 Tim Wakefield .30 .09
159 Kenny Lofton .30 .09
160 Jose Canseco .75 .23
161 Doug Glanville .30 .09
162 Todd Hundley .30 .09
163 Brian Jordan .30 .09
164 Steve Finley .30 .09
165 Tom Glavine .50 .15
166 Al Leiter .30 .09
167 Raul Mondesi .30 .09
168 Desi Relaford .30 .09
169 Bret Saberhagen .30 .09
170 Omar Vizquel .30 .09
171 Larry Walker .50 .15
172 Bobby Abreu .30 .09
173 Moises Alou .30 .09
174 Mike Caruso .30 .09
175 Royce Clayton .30 .09
176 Bartolo Colon .30 .09
177 Marty Cordova .30 .09
178 Darin Erstad .30 .09
179 Nomar Garciaparra 1.25 .35
180 Andy Ashby .30 .09
181 Dan Wilson .30 .09
182 Larry Sutton .30 .09
183 Tony Clark .30 .09
184 Andres Galarraga .30 .09
185 Ray Durham .30 .09
186 Hideo Nomo .75 .23
187 Steve Woodard .30 .09
188 Scott Rolen .50 .15
189 Mike Stanley .30 .09
190 Jaret Wright .30 .09
191 Vinny Castilla .30 .09
192 Jason Christiansen .30 .09
193 Paul Bako .30 .09
194 Carlos Perez .30 .09
195 Mike Piazza 1.25 .35
196 Fernando Tatis .30 .09
197 Mo Vaughn .30 .09
198 Devon White .30 .09
199 Ricky Gutierrez .30 .09
200 Charlie Hayes .30 .09
201 Brad Radke .30 .09
202 Rick Helling .30 .09
203 John Smoltz .50 .15
204 Frank Thomas .75 .23
205 David Wells .30 .09
206 Roger Clemens 1.50 .45
207 Mark Grudzielanek .30 .09
208 Chipper Jones .75 .23
209 Ray Lankford .30 .09
210 Pedro Martinez .75 .23
211 Manny Ramirez .30 .09
212 Greg Vaughn .30 .09
213 Craig Biggio .50 .15
214 Rusty Greer .30 .09
215 Greg Maddux 1.25 .35
216 Rick Aguilera .30 .09
217 Andy Pettitte .50 .15
218 Dante Bichette .30 .09
219 Damion Easley .30 .09
220 Matt Morris .30 .09
221 John Olerud .30 .09
222 Chan Ho Park .30 .09
223 Curt Schilling .50 .15
224 John Valentin .30 .09
225 Matt Williams .30 .09
226 Ellis Burks .30 .09
227 Tom Goodwin .30 .09
228 Javy Lopez .30 .09
229 Eric Milton .30 .09
230 Paul O'Neill .50 .15
231 Magglio Ordonez .30 .09
232 Derrek Lee .30 .09
233 Ken Griffey Jr. FLY .75 .23
234 Randy Johnson FLY .50 .15
235 Alex Rodriguez FLY .75 .23
236 Darin Erstad FLY .30 .09
237 Juan Gonzalez FLY .50 .15
238 Derek Jeter FLY 1.00 .30
239 Tony Gwynn FLY .50 .15
240 Kerry Wood FLY .50 .15
241 Cal Ripken FLY 1.25 .35
242 Sammy Sosa FLY .75 .23
243 Greg Maddux FLY .75 .23
244 Mark McGwire FLY 1.00 .30
245 Chipper Jones FLY .50 .15
246 Barry Bonds FLY .75 .23
247 Ben Grieve FLY .30 .09
248 Ben Davis BB .30 .09
249 Robert Fick BB .30 .09
250 Carlos Guillen BB .30 .09
251 Mike Frank BB .30 .09
252 Ryan Minor BB .30 .09

253 Troy Glaus BB .50 .15
254 Matt Anderson BB .30 .09
255 Josh Booty BB .30 .09
256 Gabe Alvarez BB .30 .09
257 Gabe Kapler BB .30 .09
258 Enrique Wilson BB .30 .09
259 Alex Gonzalez BB .30 .09
260 Preston Wilson BB .30 .09
261 Eric Chavez BB .30 .09
262 Adrian Beltre BB .30 .09
263 Corey Koskie BB .30 .09
264 Robert Machado BB .30 .09
265 Orl. Hernandez BB .30 .09
266 Matt Clement BB .30 .09
267 Luis Ordaz BB .30 .09
268 Jeremy Giambi BB .30 .09
269 J.D. Drew BB .30 .09
270 Cliff Politte BB .30 .09
271 Carlton Loewer BB .30 .09
272 Aramis Ramirez BB .30 .09
273 Ken Griffey Jr. MLPD .75 .23
274 Ra. Johnson MLPD .50 .15
275 Alex Rodriguez MLPD .75 .23
276 Darin Erstad MLPD .30 .09
277 Scott Rolen MLPD .30 .09
278 Juan Gonzalez MLPD .50 .15
279 Jeff Bagwell MLPD .30 .09
280 Mike Piazza MLPD .75 .23
281 Derek Jeter MLPD 1.00 .30
282 Travis Lee MLPD .30 .09
283 Tony Gwynn MLPD .50 .15
284 Kerry Wood MLPD .50 .15
285 Albert Belle MLPD .30 .09
286 Sammy Sosa MLPD .75 .23
287 Mo Vaughn MLPD .30 .09
288 N. Garciaparra MLPD .75 .23
289 FrankThomas MLPD .50 .15
290 Cal Ripken MLPD 1.25 .35
291 Greg Maddux MLPD .75 .23
292 Chipper Jones MLPD .50 .15
293 Ben Grieve MLPD .30 .09
294 Andruw Jones MLPD .30 .09
295 Mark McGwire MLPD 1.00 .30
296 Roger Clemens MLPD .75 .23
297 Barry Bonds MLPD .75 .23
298 Ken Griffey Jr. CL .75 .23
299 Kerry Wood CL .50 .15
300 Alex Rodriguez CL .75 .23
SAMP J.D. Drew AU/35 40.00 12.00

1999 Metal Universe Precious Metal Gems

Randomly inserted in hobby packs only, this 300-card set is a parallel version of the base set printed on etched gold holographic foil cards. Only 50 serially numbered sets were produced.

Nm-Mt Ex-Mt
*STARS: 20X TO 50X BASIC CARDS ..

1999 Metal Universe Boyz With The Wood

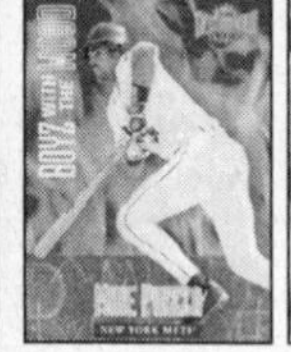
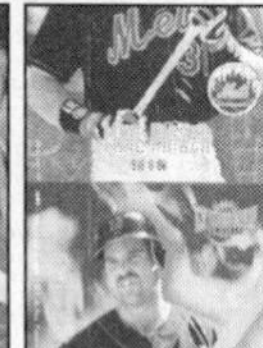

Randomly inserted in packs at the rate of one in 18, this 15-card set features color action photos of the game's most prolific hitters printed on special four-sided cards with a copyrighted design by Intervisual.

Nm-Mt Ex-Mt
COMPLETE SET (15) 60.00 18.00
1 Ken Griffey Jr. 5.00 1.50
2 Frank Thomas 3.00 .90
3 Jeff Bagwell 2.00 .60
4 Juan Gonzalez 3.00 .90
5 Mark McGwire 8.00 2.40
6 Scott Rolen 2.00 .60
7 Travis Lee 1.25 .35
8 Tony Gwynn 4.00 1.20
9 Mike Piazza 5.00 1.50
10 Chipper Jones 3.00 .90
11 Nomar Garciaparra 5.00 1.50
12 Derek Jeter 8.00 2.40
13 Cal Ripken 10.00 3.00
14 Andruw Jones 1.25 .35
15 Alex Rodriguez 5.00 1.50

1999 Metal Universe Diamond Soul

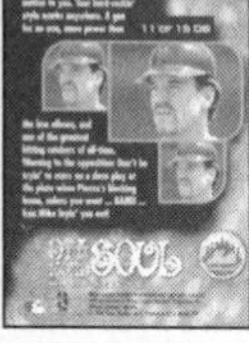

Randomly inserted in packs at the rate of one in 72, this 15-card set features color action player images printed on sturdy "Galactic" patterned Lenticular card stock with gold foil stamping.

Nm-Mt Ex-Mt
COMPLETE SET (15) 250.00 75.00
1 Cal Ripken 30.00 9.00
2 Alex Rodriguez 15.00 4.50
3 Chipper Jones 10.00 3.00
4 Derek Jeter 25.00 7.50
5 Frank Thomas 10.00 3.00
6 Greg Maddux 15.00 4.50
7 Juan Gonzalez 10.00 3.00
8 Ken Griffey Jr. 15.00 4.50
9 Kerry Wood 10.00 3.00
10 Mark McGwire 25.00 7.50
11 Mike Piazza 15.00 4.50
12 Nomar Garciaparra 15.00 4.50
13 Scott Rolen 6.00 1.80
14 Tony Gwynn 12.00 3.60
15 Travis Lee 4.00 1.20

1999 Metal Universe Linchpins

Randomly inserted in packs at the rate of one in 360, this 10-card set features color action images of clubhouse and field leaders silhouetted on a card with a multitude of laser die-cut pins in the background.

Nm-Mt Ex-Mt
COMPLETE SET (10) 300.00 90.00
1 Mike Piazza 25.00 7.50
2 Mark McGwire 40.00 12.00
3 Kerry Wood 15.00 4.50
4 Ken Griffey Jr. 25.00 7.50
5 Greg Maddux 25.00 7.50
6 Frank Thomas 15.00 4.50
7 Derek Jeter 40.00 12.00
8 Chipper Jones 15.00 4.50
9 Cal Ripken 50.00 15.00
10 Alex Rodriguez 25.00 7.50

1999 Metal Universe Neophytes

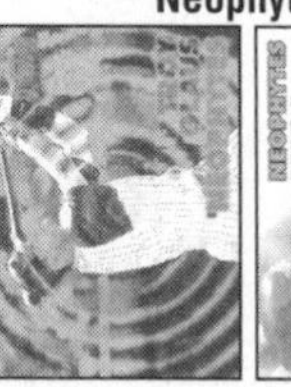

Randomly inserted in packs at the rate of one in six, this 15-card set features color photos of top young stars printed on horizontal, silver-foil stamped cards.

Nm-Mt Ex-Mt
COMPLETE SET (15) 10.00 3.00
1 Troy Glaus 1.25 .35
2 Travis Lee .75 .23
3 Scott Elarton .75 .23
4 Ricky Ledee .75 .23
5 Richard Hidalgo .75 .23
6 J.D. Drew .75 .23
7 Paul Konerko .75 .23
8 Orlando Hernandez .75 .23
9 Mike Caruso .75 .23
10 Mike Frank .75 .23
11 Miguel Tejada .75 .23
12 Matt Anderson .75 .23
13 Kerry Wood 2.00 .60
14 Gabe Alvarez .75 .23
15 Adrian Beltre .75 .23

1999 Metal Universe Planet Metal

Randomly inserted in packs at the rate of one in 36, this 15-card set features color images of some of the best players of the game printed on die-cut cards that feature a metallic view of Earth in the background.

Nm-Mt Ex-Mt
COMPLETE SET (15) 120.00 36.00
1 Alex Rodriguez 10.00 3.00
2 Andruw Jones 2.50 .75
3 Cal Ripken 20.00 6.00
4 Chipper Jones 6.00 1.80
5 Darin Erstad 2.50 .75
6 Derek Jeter 15.00 4.50
7 Frank Thomas 6.00 1.80
8 Travis Lee 2.50 .75
9 Scott Rolen 4.00 1.20
10 Nomar Garciaparra 10.00 3.00
11 Mike Piazza 10.00 3.00
12 Mark McGwire 15.00 4.50
13 Ken Griffey Jr. 10.00 3.00
14 Juan Gonzalez 6.00 1.80
15 Jeff Bagwell 4.00 1.20

2000 Metal

The 2000 Metal set, produced by Fleer, was released in late March, 2000 as a 250-card set. The set features 200 player cards and 50 prospect cards (numbers 201 through 250) that are short printed at one in two packs. Each pack contained 10-cards and carried a suggested retail price of 1.99. A promotional sample card featuring Alex Rodriguez was distributed to dealers and hobby media several weeks before the product went live.

Nm-Mt Ex-Mt
COMPLETE SET (250) 60.00 18.00
COMP.SET w/o SP's (200) 20.00 6.00
COMMON CARD (1-200) .25 .07
COMMON (201-250) .50 .15
1 Tony Gwynn .75 .23
2 Derek Jeter 1.50 .45
3 Johnny Damon .25 .07
4 Javy Lopez .25 .07
5 Preston Wilson .25 .07
6 Derek Bell .25 .07
7 Richie Sexson .25 .07
8 Vinny Castilla .25 .07
9 Billy Wagner .25 .07
10 Carlos Beltran .25 .07
11 Chris Singleton .25 .07
12 Nomar Garciaparra 1.00 .30
13 Carlos Febles .25 .07
14 Jason Varitek .25 .07
15 Luis Gonzalez .25 .07
16 Jon Lieber .25 .07
17 Mo Vaughn .25 .07
18 Dave Burba .25 .07
19 Brady Anderson .25 .07
20 Carlos Lee .25 .07
21 Chuck Finley .25 .07
22 Alex Gonzalez .25 .07
23 Matt Williams .25 .07
24 Chipper Jones .60 .18
25 Pokey Reese .25 .07
26 Todd Helton .40 .12
27 Mike Mussina .60 .18
28 Butch Huskey .25 .07
29 Jeff Bagwell .40 .12
30 Juan Encarnacion .25 .07
31 A.J. Burnett .25 .07
32 Micah Bowie .25 .07
33 Brian Jordan .25 .07
34 Scott Erickson .25 .07
35 Sean Casey .25 .07
36 John Smoltz .40 .12
37 Edgard Clemente .25 .07
38 Mike Hampton .25 .07
39 Tom Glavine .40 .12
40 Albert Belle .25 .07
41 Jim Thome .60 .18
42 Jermaine Dye .25 .07
43 Sammy Sosa 1.00 .30
44 Pedro Martinez .60 .18
45 Paul Konerko .25 .07
46 Damion Easley .25 .07
47 Cal Ripken 2.00 .60
48 Jose Lima .25 .07
49 Mike Lowell .25 .07
50 Randy Johnson .60 .18
51 Dean Palmer .25 .07
52 Tim Salmon .40 .12
53 Kevin Millwood .25 .07
54 Mark Grace .40 .12
55 Aaron Boone .25 .07
56 Omar Vizquel .25 .07
57 Moises Alou .25 .07
58 Travis Fryman .25 .07
59 Erubiel Durazo .25 .07
60 Carl Everett .25 .07
61 Charles Johnson .25 .07
62 Trot Nixon .40 .12
63 Andres Galarraga .25 .07
64 Magglio Ordonez .25 .07
65 Pedro Astacio .25 .07
66 Roberto Alomar .60 .18
67 Pete Harnisch .25 .07
68 Scott Williamson .25 .07
69 Alex Fernandez .25 .07
70 Robin Ventura .40 .12
71 Chad Allen .25 .07
72 Darin Erstad .25 .07
73 Ron Coomer .25 .07
74 Ellis Burks .25 .07
75 Kent Bottenfield .25 .07
76 Ken Griffey Jr. 1.00 .30
77 Mike Piazza 1.00 .30
78 Jorge Posada .40 .12
79 Dante Bichette .25 .07
80 Adrian Beltre .25 .07
81 Andruw Jones .25 .07
82 Wilson Alvarez .25 .07
83 Edgardo Alfonzo .25 .07
84 Brian Giles .25 .07
85 Gary Sheffield .25 .07
86 Matt Stairs .25 .07
87 Bret Boone .25 .07
88 Kenny Rogers .25 .07
89 Barry Bonds 1.50 .45
90 Scott Rolen .40 .12
91 Edgar Renteria .25 .07
92 Larry Walker .40 .12
93 Roger Cedeno .25 .07
94 Kevin Brown .40 .12
95 Lee Stevens .25 .07
96 Brad Radke .25 .07
97 Andy Pettitte .40 .12
98 Bobby Higginson .25 .07
99 Eric Chavez .25 .07
100 Alex Rodriguez 1.00 .30
101 Shannon Stewart .25 .07
102 Ryan Rupe .25 .07
103 Freddy Garcia .25 .07
104 John Jaha .25 .07
105 Greg Maddux 1.00 .30
106 Hideki Irabu .25 .07
107 Rey Ordonez .25 .07
108 Troy O'Leary .25 .07
109 Frank Thomas .60 .18
110 Corey Koskie .25 .07
111 Bernie Williams .40 .12
112 Barry Larkin .60 .18
113 Kevin Appier .25 .07
114 Curt Schilling .40 .12
115 Bartolo Colon .25 .07
116 Edgar Martinez .40 .12
117 Ray Lankford .25 .07
118 Todd Walker .25 .07
119 John Wetteland .25 .07
120 David Nilsson .25 .07
121 Tino Martinez .40 .12
122 Phil Nevin .25 .07
123 Ben Grieve .25 .07
124 Ron Gant .25 .07
125 Jeff Kent .25 .07
126 Rick Helling .25 .07
127 Russ Ortiz .25 .07
128 Troy Glaus .40 .12
129 Chan Ho Park .25 .07
130 Jeromy Burnitz .25 .07
131 Aaron Sele .25 .07
132 Mike Sirotka .25 .07
133 Brad Ausmus .25 .07
134 Jose Rosado .25 .07
135 Mariano Rivera .40 .12
136 Jason Giambi .60 .18
137 Mike Lieberthal .25 .07
138 Chris Carpenter .25 .07
139 Henry Rodriguez .25 .07
140 Mike Sweeney .25 .07
141 Vladimir Guerrero .60 .18
142 Charles Nagy .25 .07
143 Jason Kendall .25 .07
144 Matt Lawton .25 .07
145 Michael Barrett .25 .07
146 David Cone .25 .07
147 Bobby Abreu .25 .07
148 Fernando Tatis .25 .07
149 Jose Canseco .60 .18
150 Craig Biggio .40 .12
151 Matt Mantei .25 .07
152 Jacque Jones .25 .07
153 John Halama .25 .07
154 Trevor Hoffman .25 .07
155 Rondell White .25 .07
156 Reggie Sanders .25 .07
157 Steve Finley .25 .07
158 Roberto Hernandez .25 .07
159 Geoff Jenkins .25 .07
160 Chris Widger .25 .07
161 Orel Hershiser .25 .07
162 Tim Hudson .40 .12
163 Kris Benson .25 .07
164 Kevin Young .25 .07
165 Rafael Palmeiro .40 .12
166 David Wells .25 .07
167 Ben Davis .25 .07
168 Jamie Moyer .25 .07
169 Randy Wolf .25 .07
170 Jeff Cirillo .25 .07
171 Warren Morris .25 .07
172 Billy Koch .25 .07
173 Marquis Grissom .25 .07
174 Geoff Blum .25 .07
175 Octavio Dotel .25 .07
176 Orlando Hernandez .25 .07
177 J.D. Drew .25 .07
178 Carlos Delgado .25 .07
179 Sterling Hitchcock .25 .07
180 Shawn Green .25 .07
181 Tony Clark .25 .07
182 Joe McEwing .25 .07
183 Fred McGriff .40 .12
184 Tony Batista .25 .07
185 Al Leiter .25 .07
186 Roger Clemens 1.25 .35
187 Al Martin .25 .07
188 Eric Milton .25 .07
189 Bobby Smith .25 .07
190 Rusty Greer .25 .07
191 Shawn Estes .25 .07
192 Ken Caminiti .25 .07
193 Eric Karros .25 .07
194 Manny Ramirez .25 .07
195 Jim Edmonds .25 .07
196 Paul O'Neill .40 .12
197 Rico Brogna .25 .07
198 Ivan Rodriguez .60 .18
199 Doug Glanville .25 .07
200 Mark McGwire 1.50 .45
201 Mark Quinn PROS .50 .15
202 Norm Hutchins PROS .50 .15
203 Ramon Ortiz PROS .50 .15
204 Brett Laxton PROS .50 .15
205 J.Anderson PROS .50 .15
206 Calvin Murray PROS .50 .15
207 Wilton Veras PROS .50 .15
208 C.Hermansen PROS .50 .15
209 Nick Johnson PROS .50 .15
210 Kevin Barker PROS .50 .15
211 Casey Blake PROS .50 .15
212 Chad Meyers PROS .50 .15
213 Kip Wells PROS .50 .15
214 Eric Munson PROS .50 .15
215 Lance Berkman PROS .50 .15
216 Wily Pena PROS .50 .15
217 G.Matthews Jr. PROS .50 .15
218 Travis Dawkins PROS .50 .15
219 Josh Beckett PROS 1.50 .45
220 Tony Armas Jr. PROS .50 .15
221 A.Soriano PROS 1.25 .35
222 Pat Burrell PROS .75 .23
223 Danys Baez PROS RC .75 .23
224 Adam Kennedy PROS .50 .15
225 Ruben Mateo PROS .50 .15
226 Vernon Wells PROS .50 .15
227 Brian Cooper PROS .50 .15
228 Jeff DaVanon PROS RC .50 .15
229 Glen Barker PROS .50 .15
230 R.Cancel PROS .50 .15
231 D.Jimenez PROS .50 .15
232 Adam Piatt PROS .50 .15
233 Buddy Carlyle PROS .50 .15
234 C.Hutchinson PROS .50 .15
235 Matt Riley PROS .50 .15
236 Cole Liniak PROS .50 .15
237 Ben Petrick PROS .50 .15
238 Peter Bergeron PROS .50 .15
239 Cesar King PROS .50 .15
240 Aaron Myette PROS .50 .15
241 Eric Gagne PROS 1.25 .35
242 Joe Nathan PROS .50 .15
243 Bruce Chen PROS .50 .15
244 Rob Bell PROS .50 .15
245 Juan Sosa PROS RC .50 .15
246 Julio Ramirez PROS .50 .15
247 Wade Miller PROS .50 .15
248 T.Coquillette RC .50 .15
249 Rob Ramsay PROS .50 .15
250 Rick Ankiel PROS .50 .15
P100 A.Rodriguez Promo 2.00 .60

2000 Metal Emerald

Randomly inserted in packs, this insert is a complete parallel of the 2000 Metal base set. The cards feature an emerald green foil background. Cards 1-200 are inserted at a rate of one in four, while cards 201-250 are inserted at a rate of one in eight.

Nm-Mt Ex-Mt
COMPLETE SET (250) 300.00 90.00
*STARS 1-200: 6X TO 15X BASIC ......
*PROSPECTS 201-250: .75X TO 2X BASIC

2000 Metal Base Shredders

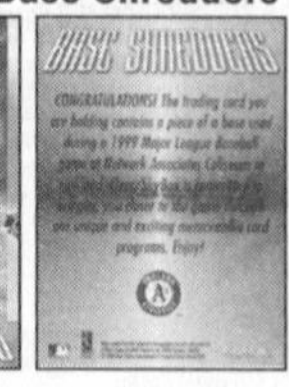

Randomly inserted in packs at one in 288, this 18-card insert set features a swatch from an actual game-used base.

Nm-Mt Ex-Mt
1 Roberto Alomar 10.00 3.00
2 Manny Ramirez 8.00 2.40
3 Tony Gwynn 15.00 4.50
4 Ben Davis 8.00 2.40
5 Vladimir Guerrero 10.00 3.00
6 Michael Barrett 8.00 2.40
7 Eric Munson 8.00 2.40
8 Tony Clark 8.00 2.40
9 Ben Grieve 8.00 2.40
10 Miguel Tejada 8.00 2.40
11 Rafael Palmeiro 10.00 3.00
12 Ivan Rodriguez 10.00 3.00
13 Matt Williams 8.00 2.40
14 Erubiel Durazo 8.00 2.40
15 Mo Vaughn 8.00 2.40
16 Troy Glaus 10.00 3.00
17 Larry Walker 10.00 3.00
18 Todd Helton 10.00 3.00

2000 Metal Fusion

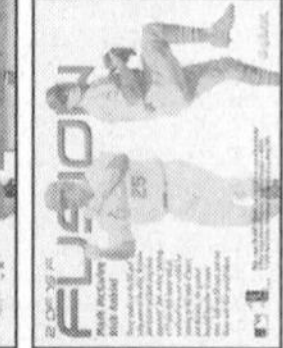

Randomly inserted in packs at one in four, this 15-card insert set features dual-player cards of some of the greatest teammates in the game. Card backs carry a "F" prefix.

Nm-Mt Ex-Mt
COMPLETE SET (15) 25.00 7.50
F1 Ken Griffey Jr. 1.50 .45
Alex Rodriguez
F2 Mark McGwire 2.50 .75
Rick Ankiel
F3 Scott Rolen .60 .18
Curt Schilling
F4 Pedro Martinez 1.50 .45
Nomar Garciaparra
F5 Carlos Beltran .40 .12
Carlos Febles
F6 Sammy Sosa 1.50 .45
Mark Grace
F7 Vladimir Guerrero 1.00 .30
Ugueth Urbina
F8 Roger Clemens 2.50 .75
Derek Jeter
F9 Jeff Bagwell .60 .18
Craig Biggio
F10 Chipper Jones 1.00 .30
Andruw Jones
F11 Cal Ripken 3.00 .90
Mike Mussina
F12 Manny Ramirez .40 .12
Roberto Alomar
F13 Sean Casey 1.00 .30
Barry Larkin
F14 Ivan Rodriguez 1.00 .30
Rafael Palmeiro
F15 Mike Piazza 1.50 .45
Robin Ventura

2000 Metal Heavy Metal

Randomly inserted in packs at one in 20, this insert set features 10 of the leagues most powerful players. Card backs carry a "GS" prefix.

Nm-Mt Ex-Mt
COMPLETE SET (10) 40.00 12.00
GS1 Sammy Sosa 3.00 .90
GS2 Mark McGwire 5.00 1.50
GS3 Ken Griffey Jr. 3.00 .90
GS4 Mike Piazza 3.00 .90

GS5 Nomar Garciaparra	3.00	.90
GS6 Alex Rodriguez	3.00	.90
GS7 Manny Ramirez	.75	.23
GS8 Jeff Bagwell	1.25	.35
GS9 Chipper Jones	2.00	.60
GS10 Vladimir Guerrero	2.00	.60

2000 Metal Hitting Machines

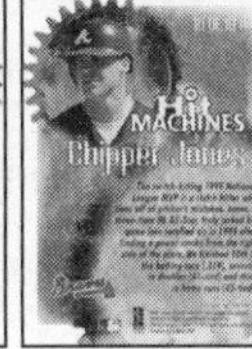

Randomly inserted in packs at one in 20, this insert set features 10 of the greatest hitters in the league. Card backs carry a "H" prefix.

	Nm-Mt	Ex-Mt
COMPLETE SET (10)	30.00	9.00
H1 Ken Griffey Jr.	3.00	.90
H2 Mark McGwire	5.00	1.50
H3 Frank Thomas	2.00	.60
H4 Tony Gwynn	2.50	.75
H5 Rafael Palmeiro	1.25	.35
H6 Bernie Williams	1.25	.35
H7 Derek Jeter	5.00	1.50
H8 Sammy Sosa	3.00	.90
H9 Mike Piazza	3.00	.90
H10 Chipper Jones	2.00	.60

2000 Metal Platinum Portraits

Randomly inserted in packs at one in eight, this insert set features 10 portrait shots of players on silver foiled cards. Card backs carry a "PP" prefix.

	Nm-Mt	Ex-Mt
COMPLETE SET (10)	20.00	6.00
PP1 Carlos Beltran	.60	.18
PP2 Vladimir Guerrero	1.50	.45
PP3 Manny Ramirez	.60	.18
PP4 Ivan Rodriguez	1.50	.45
PP5 Sean Casey	.60	.18
PP6 Alex Rodriguez	2.50	.75
PP7 Derek Jeter	4.00	1.20
PP8 Nomar Garciaparra	2.50	.75
PP9 Vernon Wells	.60	.18
PP10 Shawn Green	.60	.18

2000 Metal Talent Show

Randomly inserted in packs at one in four, this insert set features 15 of the major leagues top prospects. Card backs carry a "TS" prefix.

	Nm-Mt	Ex-Mt
COMPLETE SET (15)	8.00	2.40
TS1 Rick Ankiel	.50	.15
TS2 Matt Riley	.50	.15
TS3 Chad Hermansen	.50	.15
TS4 Ruben Mateo	.50	.15
TS5 Eric Munson	.50	.15
TS6 Alfonso Soriano	1.00	.30
TS7 Wilton Veras	.50	.15
TS8 Vernon Wells	.50	.15
TS9 Erubiel Durazo	.50	.15
TS10 Pat Burrell	.60	.18
TS11 Ben Davis	.50	.15
TS12 A.J. Burnett	.50	.15
TS13 Peter Bergeron	.50	.15
TS14 Mark Quinn	.50	.15
TS15 Ben Petrick	.50	.15

1979 Metallic Creations

These 3" by 5" portrait cards were issued with a 3 1/2" statuette. The cards were drawn by P. Herek and feature a full drawing of the player as well as two action shots In the background. Each player also has a fascimile autograph on the front. The back has career statistics on them. The cards are unnumbered and we have sequenced them in alphabetical order. While the Cedeno, Koufax and Ryan cards are known, there have been extremely few statues spotted of these players, therefore we are callinlg these cards SP's.

	NM	Ex
COMPLETE SET	400.00	160.00
COMMON CARD	10.00	4.00
COMMON SP	20.00	10.00
1 Hank Aaron	20.00	8.00
2 Rod Carew	12.00	4.80
3 Cesar Cedeno SP	20.00	10.00
4 Ty Cobb	20.00	8.00
5 Steve Garvey	10.00	4.00
6 Lou Gehrig	20.00	8.00
7 Ron Guidry	10.00	4.00
8 Rogers Hornsby	15.00	6.00
9 Walter Johnson	15.00	6.00
10 Ralph Kiner	12.00	4.80
11 Sandy Koufax SP	60.00	24.00
12 Dave Lopes	10.00	4.00
13 Christy Mathewson	12.00	4.80
14 Willie Mays	20.00	8.00
15 Willie McCovey	12.00	4.80
16 Mel Ott	15.00	6.00
17 Babe Ruth	30.00	12.00
18 Nolan Ryan SP	80.00	32.00
19 Tris Speaker	12.00	4.80
20 Honus Wagner	15.00	6.00

1993 Metallic Images

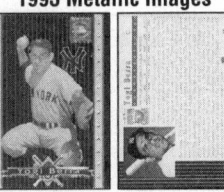

As part of the Cooperstown Collection, this 20-card set came within a special collector tin and had its own individually numbered certificate of authenticity. Production was reportedly limited to 49,900 sets. The metallic cards have rounded corners and edges, measure approximately the standard size, and feature player photos, some action, others posed, reproduced on pinstriped fronts, with the player's team name above the photo. The cards are numbered on the back in alphabetical order except for Blue and Berra. A promo card featuring Willie Mays was issued to dealers.

	Nm-Mt	Ex-Mt
COMPLETE SET (20)	45.00	13.50
1 Hank Aaron	8.00	2.40
2 Vida Blue	1.00	.30
3 Yogi Berra	4.00	1.20
4 Bobby Bonds	2.00	.60
5 Lou Brock	3.00	.90
6 Lew Burdette	1.00	.30
7 Rod Carew	3.00	.90
8 Rocky Colavito	2.00	.60
9 George Foster	1.00	.30
10 Bob Gibson	3.00	.90
11 Mickey Lolich	1.00	.30
12 Willie Mays	8.00	2.40
13 Johnny Mize	3.00	.90
14 Don Newcombe	1.00	.30
15 Gaylord Perry	3.00	.90
16 Boog Powell	2.00	.60
17 Bill Skowron	1.00	.30
18 Warren Spahn	3.00	.90
19 Willie Stargell	3.00	.90
20 Luis Tiant	1.00	.30
P1 Willie Mays Promo	3.00	.90

1994 Metallic Impressions Mantle

Produced by Metallic Impressions, this 10-card standard-size set reproduces in metal the Baseball Heroes cards randomly inserted into 1994 Upper Deck second series packs. The ten cards were issued in an embossed collector's tin with an individually numbered certificate of authenticity. The fronts show photos commemorating key milestones in Mantle's career. The inserted paper backs contain career highlights and a small scrapbook-like photo. 19,950 of these sets were produced.

	Nm-Mt	Ex-Mt
COMP. FACT SET (10)	30.00	9.00
COMMON CARD (1-10)	3.00	.90

1995 Metallic Impressions Ripken

This 10-card metal-on-metal set traces Cal Ripken's career as he was just coming up from the minors to the nights he tied and broke Lou Gehrig's record. The cards are packaged in a collectors tin. Just 29,950 sets were produced and each included a Certificate of Authenticity. The fronts display color photos while the backs present commentary.

	Nm-Mt	Ex-Mt
COMP. FACT SET (10)	30.00	9.00
COMMON CARD (1-10)	3.00	.90

1995 Metallic Impressions Ryan

Produced by Metallic Impressions, this 10-card metal set is a retrospect of Nolan Ryan's Hall of Fame career. The cards have embossed fronts and smooth rolled edges. Each set is packaged in a collector's tin and accompanied by an individually numbered certificate of authenticity. The production run was limited to 14,950 sets.

	Nm-Mt	Ex-Mt
COMP. FACT SET (10)	30.00	9.00
COMMON CARD (1-10)	3.00	.90

1996 Metallic Impressions Gehrig

Produced by Metallic Impressions, this five-card metal set features sepia photos of Lou Gehrig printed on metal card stock with a commentary on different phases of his career on the backs. The cards have embossed front highlights and smooth rolled edges. Each set is packaged in a collector's tin.

	Nm-Mt	Ex-Mt
COMP. FACT SET (5)	10.00	3.00
COMMON CARD (1-5)	2.50	.75

1996 Metallic Impressions Griffey 5

Produced by Metallic Impressions, this five-card metal set is a recap Ken Griffey, Jr. career. The cards have color action player photos on front and smooth rolled edges. Each set is packaged in a collector's tin.

	Nm-Mt	Ex-Mt
COMP. FACT SET (5)	15.00	4.50
COMMON CARD (1-5)	3.00	.90

1996 Metallic Impressions Griffey 10

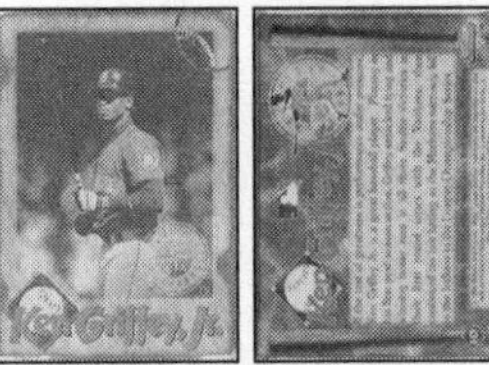

Produced by Metallic Impressions, this 10-card metal set is a retrospect of Ken Griffey, Jr. career. The cards have color action player photos on front and smooth rolled edges. Each set is packaged in a collector's tin and accompanied by an individually numbered certificate of authenticity. The production run was limited to 24,000 sets.

	Nm-Mt	Ex-Mt
COMP. FACT SET (10)	30.00	9.00
COMMON CARD (1-10)	3.00	.90

1996 Metallic Impressions Ruth

Produced by Metallic Impressions, this five-card metal set features black-and-white photos of Babe Ruth printed on metal card stock with a commentary on different phases of his career on the backs. The cards have embossed front highlights and smooth rolled edges. Each set is packaged in a collector's tin.

	Nm-Mt	Ex-Mt
COMP. FACT SET (5)	10.00	3.00
COMMON CARD (1-5)	2.50	.75

1970 Metropolitan Museum of Art Burdick

This eight-card set consists of West German-made cards from Jefferson Burdick's collection at the Metropolitan Museum of Art. The cards feature black-and-white player photos measuring approximately 2 3/4" by 3 3/4". The cards are unnumbered and checklisted below in alphabetical order.

	NM	Ex
COMPLETE SET (8)	50.00	20.00
1 Max Bishop R315	5.00	2.00
2 Lou Gehrig R315	25.00	10.00
3 Carl Hubbell R315	15.00	6.00
4 Kores Portland	5.00	2.00
5 Leard Venice	5.00	2.00
6 Babe Ruth R315	30.00	12.00
7 Dazzy Vance R315	10.00	4.00
8 Zacher Oaks	5.00	2.00

1962 Mets Jay Publishing

This 12-card set of the original New York Mets measures approximately 5" X 7". The fronts feature black-and-white posed player photos with the player's and team name printed below in the white border. These cards were packaged 12 to a packet. The backs are blank. The cards are unnumbered and checklisted below in alphabetical order. A complete set in the original envelope is valued at fifty percent higher.

	NM	Ex
COMPLETE SET (12)	60.00	24.00
1 Gus Bell	4.00	1.60
2 Elio Chacon	3.00	1.20
3 Roger Craig	5.00	2.00
4 Gil Hodges	15.00	6.00
5 Jay Hook	3.00	1.20
6 Al Jackson	4.00	1.60
7 Hobie Landrith	3.00	1.20
8 Bob Miller	3.00	1.20
9 Charlie Neal	4.00	1.60
10 Casey Stengel MG	15.00	6.00
11 Frank Thomas	5.00	2.00
12 Don Zimmer	6.00	2.40

1962-65 Mets Requena Photo

These 8" by 10" color photographs feature members of the New York Mets and were taken by known sports photographer Louis Requenna. These photos were taken throughout the early seasons of the Mets. Since these photos are unnumbered, we have sequenced them in alphabetical order.

	NM	Ex
COMPLETE SET	500.00	200.00
1 George Altman	15.00	6.00
2 Ed Bauta	15.00	6.00
3 Larry Bearnarth	15.00	6.00
4 Yogi Berra CO	40.00	16.00
5 Chris Cannizzaro Portrait	15.00	6.00
6 Chris Cannizzaro Batting	15.00	6.00
7 Chris Cannizzaro Kneeling	15.00	6.00
8 Chris Cannizzaro Squatting	15.00	6.00
9 Duke Carmel	15.00	6.00
10 Joe Christopher Kneeling	15.00	6.00
11 Joe Christopher Standing	15.00	6.00
12 Roger Craig	20.00	8.00
13 Ray Daviault	15.00	6.00
14 John DeMerit	15.00	6.00
15 Don Heffner CO	15.00	6.00
16 Jay Hook	15.00	6.00
17 Ron Hunt Ralph Kiner ANN	25.00	10.00
18 Ed Kranepool	20.00	8.00
19 Felix Mantilla	15.00	6.00
20 Jim Marshall	15.00	6.00
21 Danny Napoleon	15.00	6.00
22 Charlie Neal	15.00	6.00
23 Jimmy Piersall	20.00	8.00
24 Joe Pignatano	15.00	6.00
25 Duke Snider Full Length Photo	30.00	12.00
26 Duke Snider Portrait	30.00	12.00
27 Casey Stengel MG	40.00	16.00
28 Ron Swoboda	20.00	8.00

1963 Mets Jay Publishing

This 12-card set of the New York Mets measures approximately 5" by 7". The fronts feature black-and-white posed player photos with the player's and team name printed below in the white border. These cards were packaged 12 to a packet.The backs are blank. The cards are unnumbered and checklisted below in alphabetical order.

	NM	Ex
COMPLETE SET (12)	50.00	20.00
1 Larry Burright	2.50	1.00
2 Roger Craig	4.00	1.60
3 Jim Hickman	3.00	1.20
4 Gil Hodges	12.00	4.80
5 Jay Hook	3.00	1.20
6 Al Jackson	3.00	1.20
7 Rod Kanehl	3.00	1.20
8 Charlie Neal	3.00	1.20
9 Duke Snider	12.00	4.80
10 Casey Stengel MG	12.00	4.80
11 Frank Thomas	3.00	1.20
12 Marv Throneberry	4.00	1.60

1964 Mets Jay Publishing

This 12-card set of the New York Mets measures approximately 5" by 7". The fronts feature black and white posed player photos with the player's and team name printed below in the white border. These cards were packaged 12 to an oversized envelope. The backs are blank. The cards are unnumbered and sequenced below in alphabetical order.

	NM	Ex
COMPLETE SET (12)	40.00	16.00
1 Larry Bearnarth	2.50	1.00
2 Duke Carmel	2.50	1.00
3 Choo Choo Coleman	3.00	1.20
4 Jesse Gonder	2.50	1.00
5 Tim Harkness	2.50	1.00
6 Jim Hickman	3.00	1.20
7 Ron Hunt	4.00	1.60
8 Al Jackson	3.00	1.20
9 Rod Kanehl	3.00	1.20
10 Duke Snider	10.00	4.00
11 Casey Stengel MG	10.00	4.00
12 Carlton Willey	2.50	1.00

1964 Mets Team Issue

This 12-card set of the New York Mets measures approximately 5" by 7". The fronts feature black and white posed player photos. The set was sold at the ballpark or could be obtained through mail order. The backs are blank. The cards are unnumbered and sequenced below in alphabetical order.

	NM	Ex
COMPLETE SET (12)	30.00	12.00
1 George Altman	2.00	.80
2 Larry Bearnarth	2.00	.80
3 Jesse Gonder	2.00	.80
4 Tim Harkness	2.00	.80
5 Jim Hickman	2.00	.80
6 Jay Hook	2.00	.80
7 Ron Hunt	3.00	1.20
8 Al Jackson	2.00	.80
9 Tracy Stallard	2.00	.80
10 Casey Stengel MG	8.00	3.20
11 Frank Thomas	3.00	1.20
12 Carl Willey	2.00	.80

1965 Mets Jay Publishing

This 12-card set of the New York Mets measures approximately 5" by 5". The fronts feature black and white posed player photos with the player's and team name printed below in the white border. The cards were packaged 12 to an envelope. The backs are blank and are sequenced in alphabetical order.

	NM	Ex
COMPLETE SET (12)	35.00	14.00
1 Larry Bearnarth	2.00	.80
2 Yogi Berra	10.00	4.00
3 Chris Cannizzaro	2.00	.80
4 Galen Cisco	2.00	.80
5 Jack Fisher	2.00	.80
6 Jim Hickman	2.00	.80
7 Ron Hunt	2.00	.80
8 Al Jackson	2.00	.80
9 Ed Kranepool	2.50	1.00
10 Roy McMillan	2.00	.80
11 Warren Spahn	8.00	3.20
12 Casey Stengel MG	8.00	3.20

1965 Mets Postcards

This 10-card set were issued by B and E, feature color player photos and measures approximately 3" by 5". The backs display the player's statistical record and the Mets insignia in green. The cards are unnumbered and checklisted below in alphabetical order.

	NM	Ex
COMPLETE SET (10)	100.00	40.00
1 Yogi Berra	25.00	10.00
2 Joe Christopher	5.00	2.00
3 Jack Fisher	5.00	2.00
4 Ron Hunt	5.00	2.00
5 Al Jackson	5.00	2.00
6 Ed Kranepool	6.00	2.40
7 Roy McMillan	5.00	2.00
8 Warren Spahn	25.00	10.00
9 Casey Stengel MG	25.00	10.00
10 Carl Willey	5.00	2.00

1966 Mets Postcards

This six-card set features color player photos in the same style as the 1965 Mets Postcards set and measures approximately 3" by 5". The backs carry the player's name, Mets insignia, and B and E Advertising in Haledon, NJ as the publisher. There is no reference to the player's statistical record.

	NM	Ex
COMPLETE SET (6)	30.00	12.00
1 Al Jackson	5.00	2.00
2 Ron Hunt	6.00	2.40
3 Ed Kranepool	5.00	2.00
4 Wes Westrum MG	5.00	2.00
5 Cleon Jones	6.00	2.40
6 Tug McGraw	10.00	4.00

1966 Mets Team Issue

This 12-card set of the New York Mets measures approximately 5" by 7". The fronts feature black and white posed player photos. The set was sold at the ballpark or could be obtained through mail order. The backs are blank. The cards are unnumbered and sequenced below in alphabetical order.

	NM	Ex
COMPLETE SET (12)	30.00	12.00
1 Yogi Berra CO	8.00	3.20
2 Ken Boyer	5.00	2.00
3 Don Cardwell	2.00	.80
4 Tommy Davis	3.00	1.20
5 Jack Fisher	2.00	.80
6 Jerry Grote	3.00	1.20
7 Chuck Hiller	2.00	.80
8 Cleon Jones	3.00	1.20
9 Ed Kranepool	3.00	1.20
10 Don Shaw	2.00	.80
11 Ron Swoboda	3.00	1.20
12 Wes Westrum MG	2.00	.80

1967 Mets Postcards

This five-card set features color player photos and measure approximately 3" by 5". The backs carry the player's name printed in black. The cards are unnumbered and checklisted below in alphabetical order. Tom Seaver has a card in his Rookie Card year.

	NM	Ex
COMPLETE SET (5)	50.00	20.00
1 Tommy Davis	8.00	3.20
2 Jack Fisher	5.00	2.00
3 Jerry Grote	8.00	3.20
4 Ed Kranepool	8.00	3.20
5 Tom Seaver	30.00	12.00

1967 Mets Team Issue

This 12-card set of the New York Mets measures approximately 4 13/16" by 7" and features black-and-white player photos in a white border with blank backs. These cards were originally packaged 12 to a packet. The cards are unnumbered and checklisted below in alphabetical order.

	NM	Ex
COMPLETE SET (12)	25.00	10.00
1 Yogi Berra CO	8.00	3.20
2 Ken Boyer	5.00	2.00
3 Don Cardwell	2.00	.80
4 Tommy Davis	3.00	1.20
5 Jack Fisher	2.00	.80
6 Jerry Grote	3.00	1.20
7 Chuck Hiller	2.00	.80
8 Cleon Jones	2.00	.80
9 Ed Kranepool	3.00	1.20
10 Bob Shaw	2.00	.80
11 Ron Swoboda	3.00	1.20
12 Wes Westrum MG	2.00	.80

1969 Mets Boy Scouts

This set of the New York Mets, which measures 2 1/2" by 3 1/2" is believed to be a regional Long Island Boy Scout release and features black-and-white player photos with facsimile autographs. The backs carry the words, "Boy power-Manpower" and "Go Team for 1969." The following checklist may be incomplete and known additions are welcomed. Since these cards are unnumbered, we have sequenced them in alphabetical order.

	NM	Ex
COMPLETE SET	250.00	100.00
1 Tommie Agee	30.00	12.00
2 Bud Harrelson	30.00	12.00
3 Cleon Jones	30.00	12.00
4 Tom Seaver	120.00	47.50
5 Art Shamsky	25.00	10.00
6 Ron Swoboda	30.00	12.00

1969 Mets Citgo

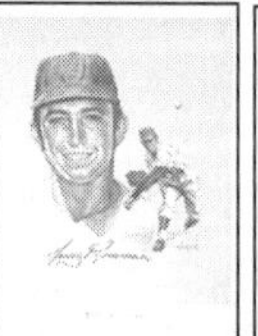

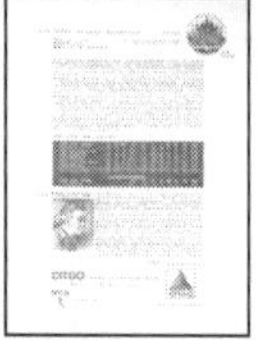

These eight 8" by 10" prints were drawn by John Wheeldon. These prints were available at Citgo for a nominal fee after a gasoline fill-up. The fronts feature a large portait pose and a smaller action pose on a colorful background. The backs have the CITGO, MLB and Mets skyline logos, the player's biography and lifetime records. There is also a picture and bio of the artist on the back. The prints are unnumbered and listed in alphabetical order.

	NM	Ex
COMPLETE SET (8)	60.00	24.00
1 Tommie Agee	6.00	2.40
2 Ken Boswell	5.00	2.00
3 Gary Gentry	5.00	2.00
4 Jerry Grote	6.00	2.40
5 Ed Kranepool	6.00	2.40
6 Jerry Koosman	8.00	3.20
7 Cleon Jones	5.00	2.00
8 Tom Seaver	20.00	8.00

1969 Mets New York Daily News

These 9" by 12" blank-backed charcoal drawings were issued by the Daily News to celebrate the Miracle Mets. An artist named Bruce Stark drew the pictures which were put on white textured paper. Each drawing has a fascimile autograph on the lower left. The blank-backed items are unnumbered and are sequenced in alphabetical order and came in a special folder which featured additional artwork.

	NM	Ex
COMPLETE SET (20)	125.00	50.00
1 Tommie Agee	5.00	2.00
2 Ken Boswell	4.00	1.60
3 Don Cardwell	4.00	1.60
4 Donn Clendenon	5.00	2.00
5 Wayne Garrett	4.00	1.60
6 Gary Gentry	4.00	1.60
7 Jerry Grote	5.00	2.00
8 Derrel(Bud) Harrelson	8.00	3.20
9 Gil Hodges MG	15.00	6.00
10 Cleon Jones	8.00	3.20
11 Jerry Koosman	8.00	3.20
12 Ed Kranepool	5.00	2.00
13 Jim McAndrew	4.00	1.60
14 Frank(Tug) McGraw	8.00	3.20
15 Nolan Ryan	40.00	16.00
16 Tom Seaver	30.00	12.00
17 Art Shamsky	4.00	1.60
18 Ron Swoboda	5.00	2.00
19 Ron Taylor	4.00	1.60
20 Al Weis	4.00	1.60

1969 Mets Team Issue

This 16-card set of the New York Mets features black and white posed player photos with a facsimile player autograph. The set was sold at the ballpark or could be obtained through mail order. The backs are blank. The cards are unnumbered and sequenced below in alphabetical order.

	NM	Ex
COMPLETE SET (16)	80.00	32.00
1 Tommie Agee	4.00	1.60
2 Yogi Berra CO	8.00	3.20
3 Ken Boswell	4.00	1.60
4 Ed Charles	3.00	1.20
5 Kevin Collins	3.00	1.20
6 Bud Harrelson	4.00	1.60
7 Gil Hodges MG	6.00	2.40
8 Al Jackson	3.00	1.20
9 Cleon Jones	4.00	1.60
10 Jerry Koosman	6.00	2.40
11 Ed Kranepool	4.00	1.60
12 Nolan Ryan	15.00	6.00
13 Tom Seaver	20.00	8.00
14 Art Shamsky	3.00	1.20
15 Ron Swoboda	4.00	1.60
16 Ron Taylor	3.00	1.20

1969 Mets Team Issue Color

This five-card set of the New York Mets features color player photos measuring approximately 7" by 8 3/4". The backs are blank. The cards are unnumbered and checklisted below in alphabetical order.

	NM	Ex
COMPLETE SET (5)	40.00	16.00
1 Bud Harrelson	5.00	2.00
2 Jerry Koosman	8.00	3.20
3 Ed Kranepool	5.00	2.00
4 Tom Seaver	20.00	8.00
5 Ron Swoboda	5.00	2.00

1970 Mets Nestle's Quik

These cards, which measure approximately 3" by 5" when cut from the back of Nestle Quik containers feature members of the 1969 Mets in highlights from different games of the 1969 World Series. This list is incomplete and all additions are appreciated to this checklist.

	NM	Ex
COMPLETE SET	30.00	12.00
2 Jerry Koosman	12.00	4.80
3 Tommie Agee	10.00	4.00
4 Ron Swoboda	10.00	4.00

1970 Mets Team Issue

This 12-card set of the New York Mets features black-and-white player photos measuring approximately 4 3/4" by 7 1/2". The player's name and team name is printed above the photo. The backs are blank. The set was originally sold at the ballpark or through mail order. The cards are unnumbered and checklisted below in alphabetical order.

	NM	Ex
COMPLETE SET (12)	30.00	12.00
1 Tommie Agee	2.50	1.00
2 Ken Boswell	2.00	.80
3 Donn Clendenon	2.00	.80
4 Joe Foy	2.00	.80
5 Jerry Grote	2.50	1.00
6 Bud Harrelson	2.00	.80
7 Gil Hodges MG	4.00	1.60
8 Cleon Jones	2.50	1.00
9 Jerry Koosman	3.00	1.20
10 Tom Seaver	6.00	2.40
11 Art Shamsky	2.00	.80
12 Ron Swoboda	2.50	1.00

1970 Mets Team Issue Color

This five-card set of the New York Mets features color player photos measuring approximately 7" by 8 3/4". The backs are blank. The cards are unnumbered and checklisted below in alphabetical order.

	NM	Ex
COMPLETE SET (5)	15.00	6.00
1 Bud Harrelson	2.00	.80
2 Jerry Koosman	3.00	1.20
3 Ed Kranepool	2.00	.80
4 Tom Seaver	6.00	2.40
5 Ron Swoboda	2.00	.80

1971 Mets Team Issue Autographs

This seven-card set of the New York Mets features black-and-white player photos measuring approximately 5 1/4" by 6 1/2" with a blue facsimile autograph printed across the front of the player's jersey. The cards are unnumbered and checklisted below in alphabetical order.

	NM	Ex
COMPLETE SET (7)	15.00	6.00
1 Tommie Agee	3.00	1.20
2 Danny Frisella	2.00	.80
3 Gary Gentry	2.00	.80
4 Jim McAndrew	2.00	.80
5 Art Shamsky	2.00	.80
6 Ken Singleton	3.00	1.20
7 Ron Taylor	2.00	.80

1971 Mets Team Issue Color

This set of the New York Mets features color player photos measuring approximately 7" by 8 3/4". Only six players are listed below, all these players are from the "A" set. Since most teams from this period also had a "B" set, it is presumed that there are six other players in this set as well. Cards have blank backs.The cards are unnumbered and checklisted below in alphabetical order.

	NM	Ex
COMPLETE SET	12.00	4.80
1 Tommie Agee	3.00	1.20
2 Bob Aspromonte	2.00	.80
3 Ken Boswell	2.00	.80
4 Donn Clendenon	2.00	.80
5 Jerry Grote	3.00	1.20
6 Jerry Koosman	4.00	1.60

1972 Mets Team Issue

The 1972 New York Mets Team Issue set was distributed in two different six-photo packs as Set A and Set B. The sets feature color player photos measuring approximately 7" by 8 3/4". The cards are unnumbered and checklisted below alphabetically within each set. Set A consists

of cards 1-6, and Set B contains cards 7-12.

	NM	Ex
COMPLETE SET (12)	35.00	14.00
1 Tommie Agee	3.00	1.20
2 Ken Boswell	2.00	.80
3 Jerry Grote	2.00	.80
4 Cleon Jones	2.00	.80
5 Tom Seaver	10.00	4.00
6 Rusty Staub	5.00	2.00
7 Jim Fregosi	2.00	.80
8 Wayne Garrett	2.00	.80
9 Gary Gentry	2.00	.80
10 Bud Harrelson	3.00	1.20
11 Jerry Koosman	4.00	1.60
12 Ed Kranepool	3.00	1.20

1973 Mets Team Issue

This 1973 New York Mets Team set was distributed in two different six-photo packs. The set features color player photos measuring approximately 7" by 8 3/4". The cards are unnumbered and checklisted below alphabetically. No distinction is made in the checklist as to which pack contains each player's photo as there is in the 1972 set.

	NM	Ex
COMPLETE SET (12)	35.00	14.00
1 Ken Boswell	2.00	.80
2 Jim Fregosi	2.50	1.00
3 Jerry Grote	2.50	1.00
4 Bud Harrelson	2.50	1.00
5 Cleon Jones	2.50	1.00
6 Jerry Koosman	3.00	1.20
7 Ed Kranepool	2.50	1.00
8 Willie Mays	8.00	3.20
9 Tug McGraw	2.50	1.00
10 Felix Millan	2.00	.80
11 Tom Seaver	5.00	2.00
12 Rusty Staub	4.00	1.60

1974 Mets Dairylea Photo Album

This set was issued in two fold-out strip booklets, each of which measures 8" by 8" in size. The inside front cover contains several small photos; the rest of the bookley contains white bordered portraits. The complete set comes in a white folder. Both the folder and booklets have the Mets logo on the front and the Dairylea trademark on the back. The books and photos are unnumbered and are sequenced the way they came in the booklet. Card numbers 1-13 are from the first book while numbers 14-20 are from the second book. The complete set in booklet form is valued at $45. Individual photos are valued below. Players from George Theodore to Bob Apodaca are all on the inside front cover in the first album. All people listed from Yogi Berra to the end of the set were in the inside front cover of the second booklet.

	NM	Ex
COMPLETE SET (20)	35.00	14.00
1 George Theodore	1.50	.60
2 Ron Hodges	1.50	.60
3 George Stone	1.50	.60
4 Duffy Dyer	1.50	.60
5 Jack Aker	1.50	.60
6 Jim Gosger	1.50	.60
7 Bob Apodaca	1.50	.60
8 Tom Seaver	12.00	4.80
9 Bud Harrelson	2.00	.80
10 Ed Kranepool	2.00	.80
11 Rusty Staub	3.00	1.20
12 Ray Sadecki	1.50	.60
13 Yogi Berra MG Willie Mays CO	10.00	4.00
14 Ken Boswell	1.50	.60
15 Cleon Jones	2.00	.80
16 Jerry Grote	3.00	1.20
17 Jerry Koosman	3.00	1.20
18 Wayne Garrett	1.50	.60

1974 Mets Japan Ed Broder

This 11-card set of the New York Mets features black-and-white player photos measuring approximately 1 7/8" by 3" and commemorates the 1974 New York Mets Tour of Japan. The backs carry the player's name, team name, tour, and the Mets logo. The cards are unnumbered and checklisted below alphabetically. This set was originally available from Broder for $1.50.

	NM	Ex
COMPLETE SET (11)	20.00	8.00
1 Yogi Berra MG	2.50	1.00
2 Wayne Garrett	1.00	.40
3 Gil Hodges	2.50	1.00
4 Jerry Koosman	2.00	.80
5 Ed Kranepool John Milner Joe Torre	1.00	.40
6 Jon Matlack	1.00	.40
7 Felix Millan	1.00	.40
8 John Milner	1.00	.40
9 Tom Seaver	5.00	2.00
10 George Theodore	1.00	.40
11 Joe Torre	2.50	1.00

1975 Mets 1963 Morey

These 3 1/2" by 5 1/2" photos feature members of the 1963 Mets and were issued in color. This set was produced by long time hobbyist Jeffrey Morey.

	NM	Ex
COMPLETE SET	15.00	6.00
1 Craig Anderson	.50	.20
2 Ed Bauta	.50	.20
3 Larry Bearnarth	.50	.20
4 Chris Cannizzaro	.50	.20
5 Duke Carmel	.50	.20
6 Chico Fernandez	.50	.20
7 Jesse Gonder	.50	.20
8 Pumpsie Green	.50	.20
9 Tim Harkness	.50	.20
10 Solly Hemus CO	.50	.20
11 Jim Hickman	.50	.20
12 Joe Hicks	.50	.20
13 Will Huckle	.50	.20
14 Rod Kanehl	.50	.20
15 Ed Kranepool	.75	.30
16 Joe Christopher	.50	.20
17 Marty Kutyna	.50	.20
18 Cookie Lavagetto CO	.50	.20
19 Al Moran	.50	.20
20 Choo Choo Coleman	.50	.20
21 Roger Craig	.75	.30
22 Steve Dillon	.50	.20
23 Grover Powell	.50	.20
24 Ted Schreiber	.50	.20
25 Norm Sherry	.50	.20
26 Dick Smith	.50	.20
27 Tracy Stallard	.50	.20
28 Casey Stengel MG	3.00	1.20
29 Ernie White CO	.50	.20
30 Polo Grounds	1.00	.40

1975 Mets SSPC

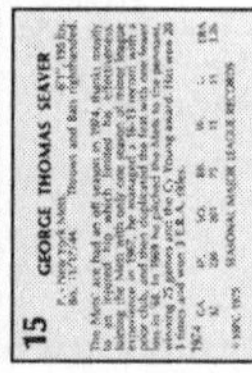

This 22-card standard-size set of New York Mets features white-bordered posed color player photos on their fronts, which are free of any other markings. The white back carries the player's name in red lettering above his blue-lettered biography and career highlights. The cards are numbered on the back within a circle formed by the player's team name. A similar set of New York Yankees was produced at the same time. The set is dated to 1975 because that year was Dave Kingman's first year as a Met and George Stone's last year.

	NM	Ex
COMPLETE SET (22)	15.00	6.00
1 John Milner	.50	.20
2 Henry Webb	.50	.20
3 Tom Hall	.50	.20
4 Del Unser	.50	.20
5 Wayne Garrett	.50	.20
6 Jesus Alou	.75	.30
7 Rusty Staub	1.50	.60
8 John Stearns	.75	.30
9 Dave Kingman	1.00	.40
10 Ed Kranepool	.75	.30
11 Cleon Jones	.75	.30
12 Tom Seaver	8.00	3.20
13 George Stone	.50	.20
14 Jerry Koosman	1.00	.40
15 Bob Apodaca	.50	.20
16 Felix Millan	.75	.30
17 Gene Clines	.50	.20
18 Mike Phillips	.50	.20
19 Yogi Berra MG	4.00	1.60
20 Joe Torre	1.50	.60
21 Jon Matlack	1.00	.40
22 Ricky Baldwin	.50	.20

1976 Mets '63 SSPC

These 18 standard-size cards honored members of the 1963 New York Mets. These cards have color photos covering almost all of the front except for a small white border. The horizontal backs have vital statistics; a biography written as it would have been after the '63 season and career information up to that point. The cards are unnumbered and we have sequenced them in alphabetical order. These cards were inserted in the 1976 Summer edition of Collectors Quarterly.

	NM	Ex
COMPLETE SET (18)	30.00	12.00
1 Ed Bauta	1.00	.40
2 Duke Carmel	1.00	.40
3 Joe Christopher	1.00	.40
4 Choo Choo Coleman	2.00	.80
5 Steve Dillon	1.00	.40
6 Jesse Gonder	1.00	.40
7 Pumpsie Green	1.00	.40
8 Jim Hickman	1.50	.60
9 Rod Kanehl	1.00	.40
10 Al Moran	1.00	.40
11 Grover Powell	1.00	.40
12 Ted Schreiber	1.00	.40
13 Norm Sherry	1.00	.40
14 Dick Smith	1.00	.40
15 Duke Snider	5.00	2.00
16 Tracy Stallard	1.00	.40
17 Casey Stengel MG	5.00	2.00
18 Ernie White CO	1.00	.40

1976 Mets MSA Placemats

This set of four placemats was produced by Creative Dimensions, liscensed by Major League Baseball, and issued by MSA. Each placemat measures 14 1/4" by 11 1/4", has a clear matte finish, and pictures three players, each appearing in a 3" diameter circle. Player statistics and additional artwork complete the placemat. Logos have been airbrushed from the caps as is typical of all MSA products. Placemats are unnumbered and listed below in first player uniform number.

	NM	Ex
COMPLETE SET (4)	20.00	8.00
1 Bud Harrelson	15.00	6.00
Tom Seaver		
Jerry Grote		
2 Ed Kranepool	6.00	2.40
Dave Kingman		
Joe Torre		
3 Bob Apodaca	3.00	1.20
Felix Millan		
Del Unser		
4 Jerry Koosman	5.00	2.00
Mickey Lolich		
Jon Matlack		

1977 Mets Dairylea Photo Album

This 27-card set features 8" by 8" player photos and was issued in an album that was given away at the Mets game of April 17th in Shea Stadium. The cards are unnumbered and checklisted below in alphabetical order.

	NM	Ex
COMPLETE SET (27)	25.00	10.00
1 Luis Alvarado	.75	.30
Leo Foster		
2 Bob Apodaca	.75	.30
3 Billy Baldwin	.75	.30
4 Bruce Boisclair	.75	.30
5 Nino Espinosa	.75	.30
6 Jerry Grote	1.00	.40
7 Bud Harrelson	1.00	.40
8 Ron Hodges	.75	.30
9 Dave Kingman	2.00	.80
10 Jerry Koosman	1.50	.60
11 Ed Kranepool	.75	.30
12 Skip Lockwood	.75	.30
13 Joe Frazier MG	.75	.30
Joe Pignatano CO		
Tom Burgess CO		
Willie Mays CO		
Rube Walker CO		
Denny Sommers CO		
14 Jon Matlack	.75	.30
15 Lee Mazzilli	2.00	.80
16 Felix Millan	.75	.30
17 John Milner	.75	.30
18 Bob Myrick	.75	.30
19 Mike Phillips	.75	.30
20 Ray Sadecki	.75	.30
21 Tom Seaver	4.00	1.60
22 Roy Staiger	.75	.30
23 John Stearns	.75	.30
24 Craig Swan	.75	.30
25 Jackson Todd	.75	.30
26 Joe Torre	2.00	.80
27 Mike Vail	.75	.30

1978 Mets Dairylea Photo Album

This photo album was distributed at the Mets home game of May 30, 1978. This edition consists of a single booklet, 8" by 8" in size, bound on the left side. Each page contains a white-bordered, unnumbered portrait. They are listed below in the order they appear in the album.

	NM	Ex
COMPLETE SET (27)	25.00	10.00
1 Joe Torre MG	2.50	1.00
With Coaches		
2 Bruce Boisclair	1.00	.40
3 Mike Bruhert	1.00	.40

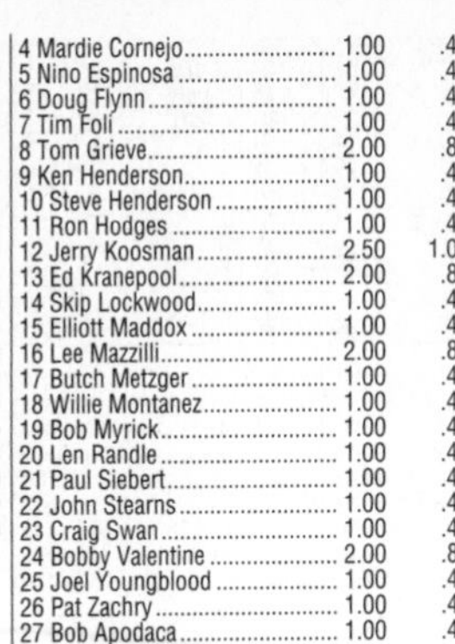

4 Mardie Cornejo	1.00	.40
5 Nino Espinosa	1.00	.40
6 Doug Flynn	1.00	.40
7 Tim Foli	1.00	.40
8 Tom Grieve	2.00	.80
9 Ken Henderson	1.00	.40
10 Steve Henderson	1.00	.40
11 Ron Hodges	1.00	.40
12 Jerry Koosman	2.50	1.00
13 Ed Kranepool	2.00	.80
14 Skip Lockwood	1.00	.40
15 Elliott Maddox	1.00	.40
16 Lee Mazzilli	2.00	.80
17 Butch Metzger	1.00	.40
18 Willie Montanez	1.00	.40
19 Bob Myrick	1.00	.40
20 Len Randle	1.00	.40
21 Paul Siebert	1.00	.40
22 John Stearns	1.00	.40
23 Craig Swan	1.00	.40
24 Bobby Valentine	2.00	.80
25 Joel Youngblood	1.00	.40
26 Pat Zachry	1.00	.40
27 Bob Apodaca	1.00	.40
Sergio Ferrer		

1981 Mets Magic Memory

This four card set, which measures 6 7/*' by 4 7/8" features memorable Mets teams and managers. The relevant pictures are on the card front with the backs being brown with white printing, and show statistics. Each card was individually wrapped in cellophane and distributed as a promotion at Mets home games in 1981. The cards are most commonly found with the cellophane intact and are priced accordingly below. The scheduled dates for these giveaways were July 2, July 16, July 23 and August 6. Unfortunately, due to the baseball strike of 1981 the cards were all distributed at later dates in the season. According to information released in 1981, approximately 20,000 of these sets were issued.

	Nm-Mt	Ex-Mt
COMPLETE SET (4)	30.00	12.00
1 1962 Mets Team Photo	8.00	3.20
2 1969 Mets Team Photo	8.00	3.20
3 1973 Mets Team Photo	8.00	3.20
4 Casey Stengel MG	10.00	4.00
Gil Hodges MG		
Yogi Berra MG		
Joe Torre MG		

1982 Mets Galasso '62

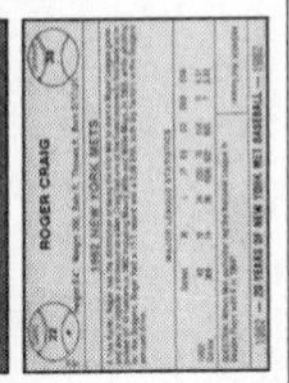

This 32-card standard-size set features posed black-and-white portraits of the 1962 New York Mets. The fronts are bordered in royal blue with the player's name and position printed in orange on the lower edge. The horizontal backs are printed in blue and orange with player biography, career highlights and statistics. A trivia question appears on the bottom, with the answer printed upside down next to it. These sets were issued with signed Marv Throneberry cards. The original issue price from Renata Galasso was $4.50.

	Nm-Mt	Ex-Mt
COMPLETE SET (32)	10.00	4.00
1 Marv Throneberry AU	10.00	4.00
2 Richie Ashburn	1.00	.40
3 Charlie Neal	.25	.10
4 Cliff Cook	.25	.10
5 Elio Chacon	.25	.10
6 Chris Cannizzaro	.25	.10
7 Jim Hickman	.25	.10
8 Rod Kanehl	.25	.10
9 Gene Woodling	.50	.20
10 Gil Hodges	1.00	.40
11 Al Jackson	.25	.10
12 Sammy Taylor	.25	.10
13 Felix Mantilla	.25	.10
14 Ken MacKenzie	.25	.10
15 Craig Anderson	.25	.10
16 Bob Moorhead	.25	.10
17 Joe Christopher	.25	.10
18 Bob Miller	.25	.10
19 Frank Thomas	.75	.30
20 Wilmer Mizell	.25	.10
21 Bill Hunter	.25	.10
22 Roger Craig	.75	.30
23 Jay Hook	.25	.10
24 Team Photo	.75	.30
25 Choo-Choo Coleman	.50	.20
26 Casey Stengel MG	1.00	.40
27 Cookie Lavagetto CO	.25	.10
28 Solly Hemus CO	.25	.10
29 Rogers Hornsby CO	1.00	.40
30 Red Kress CO	.25	.10
31 Red Ruffing CO	1.00	.40
32 George Weiss GM	1.00	.40

1982 Mets Photo Album

These photos were perforated on bound edge. Each blank-backed color photo would measure 7 3/4" by 8" if detached. These is a Facsmile autograph in red at lower left; the uniform number in red at upper right. The back album cover carries an ad for Sportschannel. These photos are unnumbered and we have checklisted them below in alphabetical order.

	Nm-Mt	Ex-Mt
COMPLETE SET (28)	7.50	3.00
1 Neil Allen	.25	.10
2 Wally Backman	.25	.10
3 Bob Bailor	.25	.10
4 George Bamberger MG	.25	.10
5 Hubie Brooks	.50	.20
6 Pete Falcone	.25	.10
7 George Foster	.75	.30
8 Ron Gardenhire	1.00	.40
9 Tom Hausman	.25	.10
10 Ron Hodges	.25	.10
11 Mike Howard	.25	.10
12 Randy Jones	.25	.10
13 Mike Jorgensen	.25	.10
14 Dave Kingman	1.00	.40
15 Ed Lynch	.25	.10
16 Jesse Orosco	.50	.20
17 Charlie Puleo	.25	.10
18 Gary Rajsich	.25	.10
19 Mike Scott	.50	.20
20 Rusty Staub	1.00	.40
21 John Stearns	.25	.10
22 Craig Swan	.25	.10
23 Ellis Valentine	.25	.10
24 Tom Veryzer	.25	.10
25 Mookie Wilson	.75	.30
26 Pat Zachry	.25	.10
27 Brian J. Giles	.25	.10
Rick Ownbey		
28 Jim Frey CO	.50	.20
Bud Harrelson CO		
Frank Howard CO		
Bill Monbouquette CO		

1984 Mets Fan Club

The cards in this eight-player set measure 2 1/2" by 3 1/2". The sheets were produced by Topps for the New York Mets and feature only Mets. The full sheet measures 7 1/2" by 10 1/2". Cards are together on the sheet but are perforated for those collectors who want to separate the individual player cards. The middle (ninth) card is a Mets Fan club membership card which details various promotional days at Shea Stadium on the back. The cards are numbered on the back and printed in orange and blue.

	Nm-Mt	Ex-Mt
COMPLETE SET (8)	7.50	3.00
1 Dave Johnson MG	.75	.30
2 Ron Darling	1.00	.40
3 George Foster	1.00	.40
4 Keith Hernandez	.75	.30
5 Jesse Orosco	.75	.30
6 Rusty Staub	1.50	.60
7 Darryl Strawberry	2.00	.80
8 Mookie Wilson	1.00	.40
NNO Membership Card	.50	.20

1985 Mets Colla Postcards

This 31-card set features color photos on a postcard format and was mailed in response to fan letters. The backs carry a pre-printed thank you note from the players. Because of legal problems with Barry Colla's licensing agreement, he can no longer sell his postcards making singles difficult to find and these cards are usually found as a set.

	Nm-Mt	Ex-Mt
COMPLETE SET (31)	12.00	4.80
1 Dave Johnson MG	.50	.20
2 Ruben Santana	.25	.10
3 Ed Lynch	.50	.20
4 Howard Johnson	.75	.30
5 Doug Sisk	.25	.10
6 Sid Fernandez	.75	.30
7 Bruce Berenyi	.25	.10
8 Ron Gardenhire	.50	.20
9 Brent Gaff	.25	.10
10 Roger McDowell	.50	.20
11 Ray Knight	.25	.10
12 John Christensen	.25	.10
13 Danny Heep	.25	.10
14 Clint Hurdle	.50	.20
15 Mets Coaches	.25	.10
16 Bill Latham	.25	.10
17 Terry Blocker	.25	.10
18 Wally Backman	.25	.10
19 Dwight Gooden	2.00	.80
20 Ron Darling	.75	.30
21 Jesse Orosco	.50	.20
22 Darryl Strawberry	.75	.30
23 Gary Carter	1.50	.60
24 Kevin Chapman	.25	.10
25 Keith Hernandez	.75	.30
26 George Foster	.50	.20
27 Rusty Staub	.75	.30
28 Mookie Wilson	.75	.30
29 Team Photo	.25	.10
30 Ronn Reynolds	.25	.10
31 Tom Gorman	.25	.10

1985 Mets Fan Club

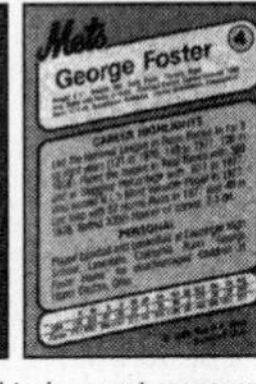

The cards in this eight-player set measure 2 1/2" by 3 1/2". The sheets were produced by Topps for the New York Mets and feature only Mets players. The full sheet measures approximately 7 1/2" by 10 1/2". Cards are together on the sheet but are perforated for those collectors who want to separate the individual player cards. The middle (ninth) card is a Mets Fan club membership card. The set was available as a membership premium for joining the Junior Mets Fan Club for 4.00. The cards are listed below in alphabetical order for convenience.

	Nm-Mt	Ex-Mt
COMPLETE SET (8)	8.00	3.20
1 Wally Backman	.50	.20
2 Bruce Berenyi	.50	.20
3 Gary Carter	2.00	.80
4 George Foster	.75	.30
5 Dwight Gooden	2.50	1.00
6 Keith Hernandez	1.00	.40
7 Doug Sisk	.50	.20
8 Darryl Strawberry	1.00	.40
NNO Membership Card	.50	.20

1985 Mets TCMA

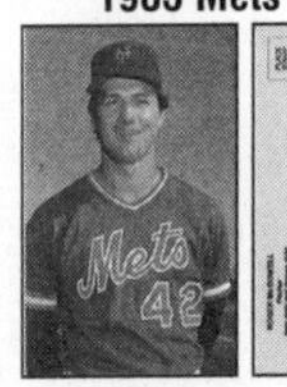

These cards measure 3 1/2" by 5 1/2". The borderless fronts consist of nothing but the photos. The postcard format backs give player identification, vital statistics and previous season stats. The cards are numbered with "NYM85-XX" in the upper right.

	Nm-Mt	Ex-Mt
COMPLETE SET (40)	15.00	6.00
1 Davey Johnson MG	.50	.20
2 Vern Hoscheit CO	.25	.10
3 Bill Robinson CO	.25	.10
4 Mel Stottlemyre CO	.25	.10
5 Bobby Valentine CO	.25	.10
6 Bruce Berenyi	.25	.10
7 Jeff Bettendorf	.25	.10
8 Ron Darling	.50	.20
9 Sid Fernandez	.50	.20
10 Brent Gaff	.25	.10
11 Wes Gardner	.25	.10
12 Dwight Gooden	2.00	.80
13 Tom Gorman	.25	.10
14 Ed Lynch	.25	.10
15 Jesse Orosco	.50	.20
16 Calvin Schiraldi	.25	.10
17 Doug Sisk	.25	.10
18 Gary Carter	1.50	.60
19 John Gibbons	.25	.10
20 Ronn Reynolds	.25	.10
21 Wally Backman	.25	.10
22 Kelvin Chapman	.25	.10
23 Ron Gardenhire	.50	.20
24 Keith Hernandez	1.00	.40
25 Howard Johnson	.75	.30
26 Ray Knight	.25	.10
27 Kevin Mitchell	1.00	.40
28 Terry Blocker	.25	.10
29 Rafael Santana	.25	.10
30 Billy Beane	.75	.30
31 John Christensen	.25	.10
32 Len Dykstra	2.00	.80
33 George Foster	.75	.30
34 Danny Heep	.25	.10
35 Darryl Strawberry	.75	.30
36 Mookie Wilson	.75	.30
37 Jeff Bittiger	.25	.10
38 Clint Hurdle	.50	.20
39 LaSchelle Tarver	.25	.10
40 Roger McDowell	.50	.20

1986 Mets Colla Postcards

This 26-card set features color photos on a postcard format and was mailed in response to fan letters. The backs carry a pre-printed thank you note from the players.

	Nm-Mt	Ex-Mt
COMPLETE SET (26)	20.00	8.00
1 Team Photo	1.00	.40
2 Dwight Gooden	1.50	.60
3 Gary Carter	2.00	.80
4 Darryl Strawberry	1.00	.40
5 Dave Johnson MG	.75	.30
6 Keith Hernandez	1.50	.60
7 Mookie Wilson	.75	.30
8 Jesse Orosco	.75	.30
9 Roger McDowell	.75	.30
10 Ray Knight	.50	.20
11 Howard Johnson	.75	.30
12 George Foster	.75	.30
13 Ron Darling	.75	.30
14 Rick Aguilera	.75	.30
15 Len Dykstra	1.00	.40
16 Wally Backman	.50	.20
17 Bud Harrelson CO	.50	.20
18 Danny Heep	.50	.20
19 Bruce Berenyi	.50	.20
20 Sid Fernandez	.50	.20
21 Tim Corcoran	.50	.20
22 Randy Myers	1.00	.40
23 Stan Jefferson	.50	.20
24 Barry Lyons	.50	.20
25 Bob Ojeda	.50	.20
26 Tim Teufel	.50	.20

1986 Mets Fan Club

The cards in this eight-player set measure 2 1/2" by 3 1/2". The sheets were produced by Topps for the New York Mets and feature only Mets. The full sheet measures approximately 7 1/2" by 10 1/2". Cards are together on the sheet but are perforated for those collectors who want to separate the individual player cards. The middle (ninth) card is a Mets Fan club membership card. The set was available as a membership premium for joining the Junior Mets Fan Club for 5.00. The cards are listed below in alphabetical order for convenience.

	Nm-Mt	Ex-Mt
COMPLETE SET (8)	8.00	3.20
1 Wally Backman	.50	.20
2 Gary Carter	2.00	.80
3 Ron Darling	.75	.30
4 Dwight Gooden	1.50	.60
5 Keith Hernandez	1.00	.40
6 Howard Johnson	.75	.30
7 Roger McDowell	.75	.30
8 Darryl Strawberry	1.00	.40
NNO Membership Card	.50	.20

1986 Mets Greats TCMA

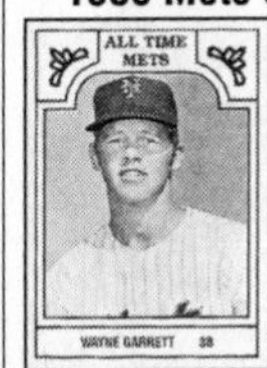

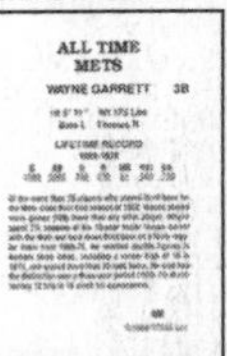

These 12 standard-size cards feature some of the best Mets from their first 25 seasons. The cards feature black-and-white player photos, his name, and position on the front. The backs have career totals, vital statistics and a biography.

	Nm-Mt	Ex-Mt
COMPLETE SET (12)	5.00	2.00
1 Ed Kranepool	.25	.10
2 Ron Hunt	.25	.10
3 Bud Harrelson	.25	.10
4 Wayne Garrett	.25	.10
5 Cleon Jones	.50	.20
6 Tommie Agee	.25	.10
7 Rusty Staub	.75	.30
8 Jerry Grote	.50	.20
9 Gary Gentry	.25	.10
10 Jerry Koosman	.75	.30
11 Tug McGraw	.75	.30
12 Gil Hodges MG	1.00	.40

1986 Mets TCMA

These cards measure 3 1/2" by 5 1/2". The borderless fronts consist of nothing but the photos. The postcard format backs give player identification, vital statistics and previous season stats. The cards are numbered with "NYM86-XX" in the upper right.

	Nm-Mt	Ex-Mt
COMPLETE SET (40)	15.00	6.00
1 Rick Aguilera	1.00	.40
2 Bruce Berenyi	.25	.10
3 Ron Darling	.50	.20
4 Sid Fernandez	.50	.20
5 Dwight Gooden	1.00	.40
6 Tom Gorman	.25	.10
7 Ed Lynch	.25	.10
8 Roger McDowell	.50	.20
9 Randy Myers	1.00	.40
10 Bob Ojeda	.25	.10

11 Jesse Orosco .50 .20
12 Doug Sisk .25 .10
13 Gary Carter 1.50 .60
14 John Gibbons .25 .10
15 Barry Lyons .25 .10
16 Wally Backman .25 .10
17 Ron Gardenhire .50 .20
18 Keith Hernandez 1.00 .40
19 Howard Johnson .50 .20
20 Ray Knight .25 .10
21 Kevin Mitchell 1.00 .40
22 Rafael Santana .25 .10
23 Tim Teufel .25 .10
24 Lenny Dykstra 1.00 .40
25 George Foster .50 .20
26 Danny Heep .25 .10
27 Mel Stottlemyre CO .25 .10
28 Darryl Strawberry .75 .30
29 Mookie Wilson .75 .30
31 Randy Niemann .25 .10
32 Ed Hearn .25 .10
33 Stan Jefferson .25 .10
34 Bill Robinson CO .25 .10
35 Shawn Abner .25 .10
36 Terry Blocker .25 .10
37 Davey Johnson MG .75 .30
38 Bud Harrelson CO .25 .10
39 Vern Hoscheit CO .25 .10
40 Greg Pavlick CO .25 .10
43 Tim Corcoran .25 .10

1986 Mets World Series Champs

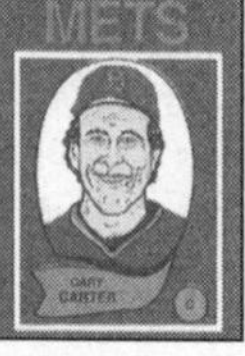
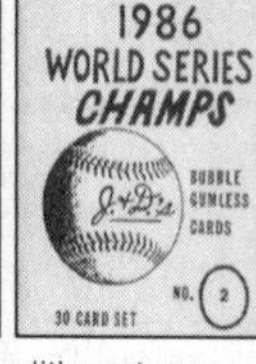

This 30-card limited edition set measures approximately 2 1/2" by 3 5/16" and was distributed by Jim and Dave's Sportcards. The cards were poorly cut and therefore not uniform in size. The set features the 1986 World Series champion Mets team and claims to be bubble gumless cards. This unattractive blue card front displays a head shot drawing of the player with an oval matte effect and an inner white border. There has been some debate about the legitimacy of these cards, as many dealers believe that they should be classified the same as broder cards.

Nm-Mt Ex-Mt
COMPLETE SET (30) 10.00 4.00
1 Keith Hernandez 1.00 .40
2 Gary Carter 1.50 .60
3 Wally Backman .25 .10
4 Len Dykstra 1.00 .40
5 Roger McDowell .75 .30
6 Rick Aguilera 1.00 .40
7 Rafael Santana .25 .10
8 Ed Hearn .25 .10
9 Doug Sisk .25 .10
10 Bruce Berenyi .25 .10
11 Darryl Strawberry .75 .30
12 Dwight Gooden 1.00 .40
13 Lee Mazzilli .50 .20
14 Danny Heep .25 .10
15 Howard Johnson .50 .20
16 Bob Ojeda .50 .20
17 Rick Anderson .25 .10
18 Kevin Elster 1.00 .40
19 Dave Magadan 1.00 .40
20 Randy Myers 1.00 .40
21 Mookie Wilson .75 .30
22 Ron Darling .50 .20
23 Davey Johnson MG .50 .20
24 Sid Fernandez .50 .20
25 Tim Teufel .25 .10
26 Randy Niemann .25 .10
27 Jesse Orosco .50 .20
28 Kevin Mitchell 1.00 .40
29 Ray Knight .25 .10
30 Checklist .25 .10

1987 Mets 1969 TCMA

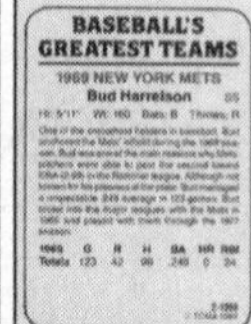

The Miracle Mets of 1969 are remembered in this standard-size set. Some of the leading players are featured with a photo, identification and position. The backs have a biography and stats from that amazing season.

Nm-Mt Ex-Mt
COMPLETE SET (9) 3.00 1.20
1 Ed Kranepool .50 .20
2 Bud Harrelson .50 .20
3 Cleon Jones .50 .20
Tommie Agee
Ron Swoboda
4 Jerry Koosman .75 .30
5 Gary Gentry .25 .10
6 Tug McGraw .75 .30
7 Ron Taylor .25 .10
8 Jerry Grote .50 .20
9 Ken Boswell .25 .10

1987 Mets Colla Postcards

This 54-card set features color photos on a postcard format and was mailed in response to fan letters. The backs carry a pre-printed thank

you note from the players.

Nm-Mt Ex-Mt
COMPLETE SET (54) 30.00 12.00
1 Team Photo 1.00 .40
2 Gary Carter 2.00 .80
3 Len Dykstra .75 .30
4 Dwight Gooden 1.00 .40
5 Howard Johnson .75 .30
6 Lee Mazzilli .75 .30
7 Roger McDowell .50 .20
8 Darryl Strawberry 1.00 .40
9 Mookie Wilson .75 .30
10 Wally Backman .50 .20
11 Ron Darling .75 .30
12 Sid Fernandez .75 .30
13 Keith Hernandez 1.00 .40
14 Bob Ojeda .50 .20
15 Dave Johnson MG .75 .30
16 Dave Magadan .75 .30
17 Kevin McReynolds .50 .20
18 Randy Myers 1.00 .40
19 Jesse Orosco .75 .30
20 Ruben Santana .50 .20
21 Tim Teufel .50 .20
22 Rick Aguilera .75 .30
23 Rick Anderson .50 .20
24 Jose Bautista .50 .20
25 Terry Blocker .50 .20
26 Bob Buchanan .50 .20
27 Tom Burns .50 .20
28 Mark Carreon .50 .20
29 Charlie Corbell .50 .20
30 Reggie Dobie .50 .20
31 Kevin Elster .75 .30
32 John Gibbons .50 .20
33 Brian Givens .50 .20
34 Bud Harrelson CO .50 .20
35 Vein Hoscheit CO .50 .20
36 Clint Hurdle .75 .30
37 Marcus Lawton .50 .20
38 Terry Leach .50 .20
39 Tom McCarthy .50 .20
40 Keith Miller .50 .20
41 Kevin Mitchell .75 .30
42 Greg Olson .50 .20
43 Al Pedrique .50 .20
44 Sam Perlozzo CO .50 .20
45 Bill Robinson CO .50 .20
46 Zolio Sanchez .50 .20
47 Doug Sisk .50 .20
48 Mel Stottlemyre CO .50 .20
49 Gary Walter .50 .20
50 Dave West .50 .20
51 Ralph Kiner ANN 1.50 .60
52 Bob Murphy ANN 1.00 .40
53 Gary Thorne ANN .50 .20
55 Barry Lyons .50 .20

1987 Mets Fan Club

The cards in this eight-player set measure 2 1/2" by 3 1/2". The sheets were produced by Topps for the New York Mets and feature only Mets. The full sheet measures approximately 7 1/2" by 10 1/2". Cards are together on the sheet but are perforated for those collectors who want to separate the individual player cards. The cards have an outer orange border. The set was available as a membership premium for joining the Junior Mets Fan Club for 6.00. The set and club were also sponsored by Farmland Dairies Milk. The cards are unnumbered on the back although they do contain the player's uniform number on the front.

Nm-Mt Ex-Mt
COMPLETE SET (9) 8.00 3.20
1 Gary Carter 2.00 .80
2 Ron Darling .75 .30
3 Len Dykstra 1.50 .60
4 Roger McDowell .50 .20
5 Kevin McReynolds .75 .30
6 Bob Ojeda .50 .20
7 Darryl Strawberry 1.00 .40
8 Mookie Wilson 1.00 .40
9 Mets Team Card .50 .20
(1986 World Champs)

1988 Mets Colla Postcards

This 55-card set features color photos on a postcard format and was mailed in response to fan letters. The backs carry a pre-printed thank you note from the players

Nm-Mt Ex-Mt
COMPLETE SET (55) 30.00 12.00
1 Gary Carter 2.00 .80
2 Ron Darling .75 .30
3 Len Dykstra .75 .30
4 Dwight Gooden 1.50 .60
5 Keith Hernandez 1.00 .40
6 Howard Johnson .75 .30
7 Roger McDowell .50 .20
8 Randy Myers .75 .30
9 Darryl Strawberry 1.00 .40
10 Tim Teufel .50 .20
11 Mookie Wilson .75 .30
12 Team Photo 1.00 .40
13 Rick Aguilera .75 .30
14 Wally Backman .50 .20
15 Mark Carreon .50 .20
16 David Cone 1.50 .60
17 Joacquin Contreras .50 .20
18 Andre David .50 .20
19 Reggie Dobie .50 .20
20 Ken Dowell .50 .20
21 Rob Dromerhauser .50 .20
22 Kevin Elster .75 .30
23 Sid Fernandez .75 .30
24 Steve Frey .50 .20
25 Bud Harrelson CO .50 .20
26 Vern Hoscheit CO .50 .20
27 Gregg Jefferies 1.00 .40
28 Steve Jelic .50 .20
29 Dave Johnson MG .75 .30
30 Marcus Lawton .50 .20
31 Terry Leach .50 .20
32 Phil Lombardi .50 .20
33 Barry Lyons .50 .20
34 Dave Magadan .50 .20
35 Lee Mazzilli .75 .30
36 Tom McCarthy .50 .20
37 Kevin McReynolds .50 .20
38 Keith Miller .50 .20
39 Randy Milligan .50 .20
40 John Mitchell .50 .20
41 Bob Ojeda .50 .20
42 Greg Pavlick CO .50 .20
43 Sam Perlozzo CO .50 .20
44 Darren Reed .50 .20
45 Bill Robinson CO .50 .20
46 Rich Rodriguez .50 .20
47 Jose Roman .50 .20
48 Jack Savage .50 .20
49 Mel Stottlemyre CO .50 .20
50 Gary Walter .50 .20
51 Todd Welborn .50 .20
52 Dave West .50 .20
53 Bob Murphy ANN 1.00 .40
54 Arthur Richman FO .50 .20
55 Gary Thorne ANN .50 .20

1988 Mets Donruss Team Book

The 1988 Donruss Mets Team Book set features 27 cards (three pages with nine cards on each page) plus a large full-page puzzle of Stan Musial. Cards are in full color and are standard size. The set was distributed as a four-page book; although the puzzle page was perforated, the card pages were not. The cover of the "Team Collection" book is primarily bright red. Card fronts are very similar in design to the 1988 Donruss regular issue. The card numbers on the backs are the same for those players that are the same as in the regular Donruss set; the new players pictured are numbered on the back as "NEW." The book is usually sold intact. When cut from the book into individual cards, these cards are distinguishable from the regular 1988 Donruss cards since these have a 1988 copyright on the back whereas the regular issue has a 1987 copyright on the back.

Nm-Mt Ex-Mt
COMPLETE SET (27) 3.00 1.20
37 Kevin Elster RR .25 .10
69 Dwight Gooden .25 .10
76 Ron Darling .10 .04
118 Sid Fernandez .10 .04
199 Gary Carter 1.00 .40
241 Wally Backman .10 .04
316 Keith Hernandez .25 .10
323 Dave Magadan .10 .04
364 Len Dykstra .25 .10
439 Darryl Strawberry .50 .20
446 Rick Aguilera .25 .10
562 Keith Miller .10 .04
569 Howard Johnson .25 .10
603 Terry Leach .10 .04
614 Lee Mazzilli .10 .04
617 Kevin McReynolds .10 .04
619 Barry Lyons .10 .04
620 Randy Myers .50 .20
632 Bob Ojeda .10 .04
648 Tim Teufel .10 .04
651 Roger McDowell .10 .04
652 Mookie Wilson .25 .10
653 David Cone .75 .30
657 Gregg Jefferies .25 .10
NEW Jeff Innis .10 .04
NEW Mackey Sasser .10 .04
NEW Gene Walter .10 .04

1988 Mets Fan Club

The cards in this nine-player set measure 2 1/2" by 3 1/2". The sheets were produced by Topps for the New York Mets and feature only Mets. The full sheet measures 7 1/2" by 10 1/2". Cards are together on the sheet but are

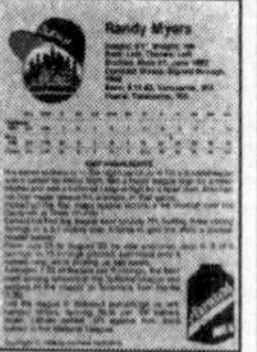

perforated for those collectors who want to separate the individual player cards. The cards have an outer orange border and an inner dark blue border. The set was available as a membership premium for joining the Junior Mets Fan Club for 6.00. The set and club were also sponsored by Farmland Dairies Milk. The cards are unnumbered on the back although they do contain the player's uniform number on the front.

Nm-Mt Ex-Mt
COMPLETE SET (9) 6.00 2.40
8 Gary Carter 2.00 .80
16 Dwight Gooden 1.00 .40
17 Keith Hernandez 1.00 .40
18 Darryl Strawberry 1.00 .40
20 Howard Johnson .75 .30
21 Kevin Elster .50 .20
42 Roger McDowell .50 .20
48 Randy Myers 1.50 .60
50 Sid Fernandez .75 .30

1988 Mets Kahn's

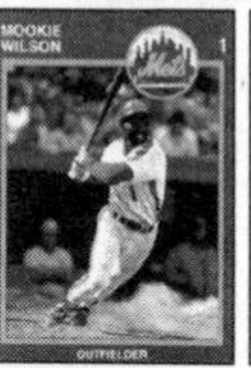

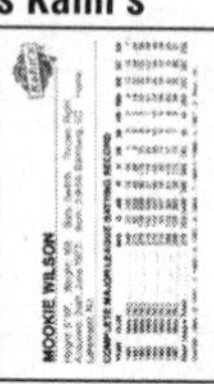

These 32-card standard-size sets were issued to the first 48,000 fans at the June 30th game between the New York Mets and the Houston Astros at Shea Stadium. The set includes 30 players, a team card, and a discount coupon card (to be redeemed at the grocery store). The cards are unnumbered except for uniform number and feature full-color photos bordered in blue and orange on the front. The Kahn's logo is printed in red in the corner of the reverse.

Nm-Mt Ex-Mt
COMPLETE SET (32) 12.00 4.80
1 Mookie Wilson .50 .20
2 Mackey Sasser .25 .10
3 Bud Harrelson CO .50 .20
4 Len Dykstra .75 .30
5 Davey Johnson MG .50 .20
6 Wally Backman .25 .10
8 Gary Carter 1.25 .50
11 Tim Teufel .25 .10
12 Ron Darling .50 .20
13 Lee Mazzilli .50 .20
15 Rick Aguilera .75 .30
16 Dwight Gooden 1.00 .40
17 Keith Hernandez 1.00 .40
18 Darryl Strawberry .75 .30
19 Bob Ojeda .25 .10
20 Howard Johnson .75 .30
21 Kevin Elster .50 .20
22 Kevin McReynolds .50 .20
26 Terry Leach .25 .10
28 Bill Robinson CO .25 .10
29 Dave Magadan .50 .20
30 Mel Stottlemyre CO .50 .20
31 Gene Walter .25 .10
33 Barry Lyons .25 .10
34 Sam Perlozzo CO .25 .10
42 Roger McDowell .25 .10
44 David Cone 2.00 .80
48 Randy Myers 1.00 .40
50 Sid Fernandez .75 .30
52 Greg Pavlick CO .25 .10
NNO Team Photo Card .50 .20
NNO Discount Coupon .25 .10

1989 Mets 1969 Calendar

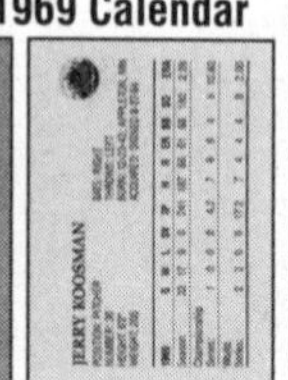

This 12-card standard size set was issued as an insert in the 1989 Met Calendar. This set features some of the most important people involved in the 1969 Miracle Met season. The cards photos are framed. The sets feature a good mix of portrait and game action photos and the backs have only the stats from 1969 on the back. The set is checklisted alphabetically below.

Nm-Mt Ex-Mt
COMPLETE SET (12) 5.00 2.00
1 Tommie Agee .50 .20
2 Donn Clendenon .50 .20
3 Wayne Garrett .25 .10
4 Jerry Grote .50 .20
5 Bud Harrelson .50 .20
6 Gil Hodges MG 1.00 .40
7 Cleon Jones .50 .20
8 Jerry Koosman 1.00 .40
9 Ed Kranepool .50 .20
10 Tug McGraw 1.00 .40
11 Tom Seaver 2.00 .80
12 Ron Swoboda .50 .20

1989 Mets Colla Postcards

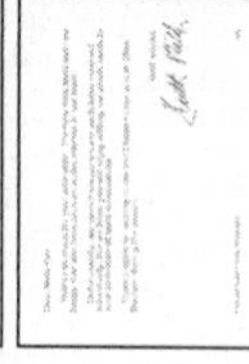

This 58-card set features color photos on a postcard format and was mailed in response to fan letters. The backs carry a pre-printed thank you note from the players.

Nm-Mt Ex-Mt
COMPLETE SET (58) 30.00 12.00
1 Mets Team 1.00 .40
2 Darryl Strawberry 1.00 .40
3 Gary Carter 2.00 .80
4 Dave Cone 1.50 .60
5 Ron Darling .75 .30
6 Len Dykstra .75 .30
7 Kevin Elster .50 .20
8 Dwight Gooden 1.50 .60
9 Keith Hernandez .75 .30
10 Gregg Jefferies .50 .20
11 Howard Johnson .50 .20
12 Lee Mazzilli .75 .30
13 Kevin McReynolds .50 .20
14 Kevin Miller .50 .20
15 Randy Myers .75 .30
16 Bob Ojeda .50 .20
17 Mackey Sasser .50 .20
18 Tim Teufel .50 .20
19 Mookie Wilson .75 .30
20 Don Aase .50 .20
21 Rick Aguilera .75 .30
22 Blaine Beatty .50 .20
23 Terry Bross .50 .20
24 Kevin Brown .50 .20
25 Mark Carreon .50 .20
26 Rob Dromerhouser .50 .20
27 Tim Drummond .50 .20
28 Sid Fernandez .75 .30
29 Steve Frey .50 .20
30 Wayne Garland CO .50 .20
31 Brian Givens .50 .20
32 Bud Harrelson CO .50 .20
33 Vern Horscheit CO .50 .20
34 Clint Hurdle .75 .30
35 Jeff Innis .50 .20
36 Steve Jelic .50 .20
37 Dave Johnson MG .50 .20
38 Terry Leach .50 .20
39 Dave Liddell .50 .20
40 Phil Lombardi .50 .20
41 Barry Lyons .50 .20
42 Dave Magadan .50 .20
43 Roger McDowell .50 .20
44 John Mitchell .50 .20
45 Bob Murphy ANN 1.00 .40
46 Ed Nunez .50 .20
47 Greg Pavlick CO .50 .20
48 Sam Perlozzo .50 .20
49 Darren Reed .50 .20
50 Bill Robinson CO .50 .20
51 Jack Savage .50 .20
52 Craig Shipley .50 .20
53 Bob Sykes .50 .20
54 Mel Stottlemyre CO .75 .30
55 Jeff Tamargo .50 .20
56 Kevin Tapani 1.50 .60
57 Dave West .50 .20
58 Wally Whitehurst .50 .20

1989 Mets Fan Club

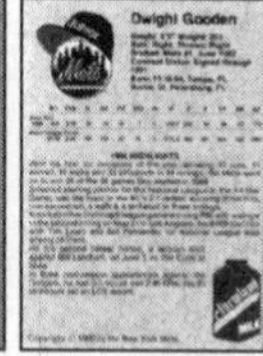

This set was produced by Topps for the Mets Fan Club as a sheet of nine cards each featuring a member of the New York Mets. The individual cards are standard size; however the set is typically traded as a sheet rather than as individual cards.

Nm-Mt Ex-Mt
COMPLETE SET (9) 6.00 2.40
8 Gary Carter 2.00 .80
9 Gregg Jefferies .50 .20
16 Dwight Gooden 1.00 .40
18 Darryl Strawberry 1.00 .40
22 Kevin McReynolds .75 .30
25 Keith Miller .50 .20
42 Roger McDowell .50 .20
44 David Cone 1.50 .60
NNO Mets Team Card .50 .20
(Eastern Div. Champs)

1989 Mets Kahn's

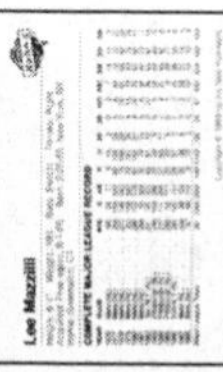

The 1989 Kahn's Mets set contains 36 (32 original and four update) standard-size cards. The fronts have color photos with Mets' colored borders (blue, orange and white). The horizontally oriented backs have career stats. The cards were available from Kahn's by sending three UPC symbols from Kahn's products and a coupon appearing in certain local newspapers. There was also a small late-season update set of Kahn's Mets showing new players who joined the Mets during the season, Jeff Innis, Keith Miller, Jeff Musselman, and Frank Viola. This "Update" subset was distributed at a different Mets Baseball Card Night game than the main set. The main set is referenced alphabetically by subject's name. The update cards are given the prefix "U" in the checklist below.

	Nm-Mt	Ex-Mt
COMPLETE SET (36)	8.00	3.20
1 Don Aase	.10	.04
2 Rick Aguilera	.75	.30
3 Mark Carreon	.10	.04
4 Gary Carter	1.00	.40
5 David Cone	.75	.30
6 Ron Darling	.25	.10
7 Kevin Elster	.10	.04
8 Sid Fernandez	.50	.20
9 Dwight Gooden	.75	.30
10 Bud Harrelson CO	.75	.30
11 Keith Hernandez	.75	.30
12 Gregg Jefferies	.10	.04
13 Davey Johnson MG	.25	.10
14 Howard Johnson	.50	.20
15 Barry Lyons	.10	.04
16 Dave Magadan	.10	.04
17 Lee Mazzilli	.25	.10
18 Kevin McReynolds	.25	.10
19 Randy Myers	.75	.30
20 Bob Ojeda	.10	.04
21 Greg Pavlick CO	.10	.04
22 Sam Perlozzo CO	.10	.04
23 Bill Robinson CO	.10	.04
24 Juan Samuel	.10	.04
25 Mackey Sasser	.10	.04
26 Mel Stottlemyre CO	.25	.10
27 Darryl Strawberry	.25	.10
28 Tim Teufel	.10	.04
29 Dave West	.10	.04
30 Mookie Wilson	.25	.10
31 Mets Team Photo	.25	.10
32 Sponsors Card	.10	.04
U1 Jeff Innis	.75	.30
U2 Keith Miller	.75	.30
U3 Jeff Musselman	.75	.30
U4 Frank Viola	1.00	.40

1989 Mets Rini Postcards 1969

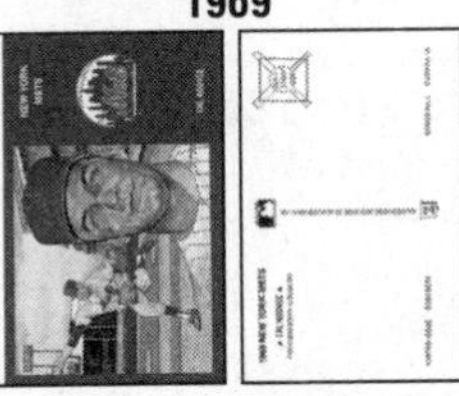

This set of 36 postcards measures 3 1/2" by 5 1/2", were limited to 5,000 produced, and showcases the 1969 New York Mets. On a blue background, the horizontal fronts feature color drawings by Susan Rini. The player cards are sequenced in alphabetical order.

	Nm-Mt	Ex-Mt
COMPLETE SET (36)	15.00	6.00
1 Championship Trophy	.25	.10
2 Shea Stadium	.25	.10
3 Tommie Agee	.75	.30
4 Ken Boswell	.25	.10
5 Ed Charles	.25	.10
6 Don Cardwell	.25	.10
7 Donn Clendenon	.25	.10
8 Jack DiLauro	.25	.10
9 Duffy Dyer	.25	.10
10 Wayne Garrett	.25	.10
11 Jerry Grote	1.00	.40
12 Rod Gaspar	.25	.10
13 Gary Gentry	.25	.10
14 Bud Harrelson	1.00	.40
15 Gil Hodges MG	2.00	.80
16 Cleon Jones	.75	.30
17 Ed Kranepool	1.00	.40
18 Cal Koonce	.25	.10
19 Jerry Koosman	1.00	.40
20 Jim McAndrew	.25	.10
21 Tug McGraw	1.00	.40
22 J.C. Martin	.25	.10
23 Bob Pfeil	.25	.10
24 Nolan Ryan	5.00	2.00
25 Ron Swoboda	.75	.30
26 Tom Seaver	3.00	1.20
27 Art Shamsky	.25	.10
28 Ron Taylor	.25	.10
29 Al Weis	.25	.10
30 Joe Pignatano CO	.25	.10
31 Eddie Yost CO	.25	.10
32 Ralph Kiner ANN	1.00	.40
33 Bob Murphy ANN	.75	.30
34 Lindsey Nelson ANN	.50	.20
35 Yogi Berra CO	1.00	.40
36 Rube Walker CO	.25	.10

1990 Mets Colla Postcards

This 53-card set features color photos on a postcard format and was mailed in response to fan letters. The backs carry a pre-printed thank you note from the players.

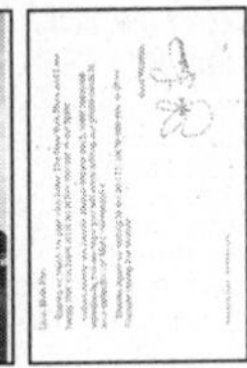

	Nm-Mt	Ex-Mt
COMPLETE SET (53)	30.00	9.00
1 Mets Team	1.00	.30
2 John Franco	1.00	.30
3 Dwight Gooden	1.50	.45
4 Howard Johnson	.75	.23
5 Gregg Jefferies	.50	.15
6 Darryl Strawberry	1.00	.30
7 Kevin Elster	.50	.15
8 Bud Harrelson CO	.50	.15
9 Dave Johnson MG	.75	.23
10 Tim Teufel	.50	.15
11 Frank Viola	.75	.23
12 Dave Cone	1.50	.45
13 Ron Darling	.75	.23
14 Sid Fernandez	.75	.23
15 Clint Hurdle	.75	.23
16 Barry Lyons	.50	.15
17 Kevin McReynolds	.50	.15
18 Dave Magadan	.50	.15
19 Mike Marshall	.50	.15
20 Keith Miller	.50	.15
21 Jeff Musselman	.50	.15
22 Bob Ojeda	.50	.15
23 Alejandro Pena	.50	.15
24 Mackey Sasser	.50	.15
25 Blaine Beatty	.50	.15
26 Terry Bross	.50	.15
27 Kevin Brown	.50	.15
28 Mark Carreon	.50	.15
29 Mike Cubbage CO	.50	.15
30 Chris Donnells	.50	.15
31 Rob Dromerhouser	.50	.15
32 Doc Edwards CO	.50	.15
33 Vern Hoscheit CO	.50	.15
34 Keith Hughes	.50	.15
35 Todd Hundley	1.50	.45
36 Jeff Innis	.50	.15
37 Brent Knackert	.50	.15
38 Phil Lombardi	.50	.15
39 Julio Machado	.50	.15
40 Terry McDaniel	.50	.15
41 Orlando Mercado	.50	.15
42 Keith Miller	.50	.15
43 Tom O'Malley	.50	.15
44 Greg Pavlick CO	.50	.15
45 Darren Reed	.50	.15
46 John Roseboro	.50	.15
47 Pete Schourek	.75	.23
48 Bob Sikes	.50	.15
49 Mel Stottlemyre CO	.75	.23
50 Lou Thornton	.50	.15
51 Dave Trautwein	.50	.15
52 Julio Valera	.50	.15
53 Wally Whitehurst	.50	.15

1990 Mets Fan Club

The 1990 Mets Fan Club Tropicana set was issued by the New York Mets fan club in association with the Tropicana Juice Company. For the seventh year, the Mets issued a perforated card sheet in conjunction with their fan clubs. This nine-card, standard-size set is skip-numbered and arranged by uniform numbers.

	Nm-Mt	Ex-Mt
COMPLETE SET (9)	6.00	1.80
9 Gregg Jefferies	.50	.15
16 Dwight Gooden	1.00	.30
18 Darryl Strawberry	1.00	.30
20 Howard Johnson	.75	.23
21 Kevin Elster	.50	.15
25 Keith Miller	.50	.15
29 Frank Viola	1.00	.30
44 David Cone	1.50	.45
50 Sid Fernandez	.75	.23

1990 Mets Hall of Fame

This six-card set was issued by the New York Mets in conjunction with AIWA and the Wiz Home Entertainment Centers. The cards measure approximately 5" by 7" and are in the postcard type format. One set was given away to each fan attending the Mets' home game on September 9, 1990. The fronts feature borderless player photos, while the backs have brief statistics and a sponsor advertisement. The cards are unnumbered and checklisted below by year of induction.

	Nm-Mt	Ex-Mt
COMPLETE SET	10.00	3.00
1 Casey Stengel MG 1981 and Gil Hodges MG 1982	4.00	1.20
2 Bud Harrelson 1986	1.00	.30
3 Rusty Staub 1986	2.50	.75
4 Tom Seaver 1988	6.00	1.80
5 Jerry Koosman 1989	2.00	.60
6 Ed Kranepool 1990	1.00	.30

1990 Mets Kahn's

The 1990 Kahn's Mets set was given away as a New York Mets stadium promotion. This standard-size set is skip-numbered by uniform number within the set and features 34 cards and two Kahn's coupon cards. Three players,

Thornton, Magadan, and Mercado are wearing different uniform numbers than listed on the front of their cards. In addition to the Shea Stadium promotion, the complete set was also available in specially marked three-packs of Kahn's Wieners.

	Nm-Mt	Ex-Mt
COMPLETE SET (34)	8.00	2.40
1 Lou Thornton	.25	.07
2 Mackey Sasser	.25	.07
3 Bud Harrelson CO	.50	.15
4 Mike Cubbage CO	.25	.07
5 Davey Johnson MG	.50	.15
6 Mike Marshall	.25	.07
9 Gregg Jefferies	.25	.07
10 Dave Magadan	.25	.07
11 Tim Teufel	.25	.07
13 Jeff Musselman	.25	.07
15 Ron Darling	.50	.15
16 Dwight Gooden	.75	.23
18 Darryl Strawberry	.75	.23
19 Bob Ojeda	.25	.07
20 Howard Johnson	.75	.23
21 Kevin Elster	.25	.07
22 Kevin McReynolds	.25	.07
25 Keith Miller	.25	.07
26 Alejandro Pena	.25	.07
27 Tom O'Malley	.25	.07
29 Frank Viola	.50	.15
30 Mel Stottlemyre CO	.50	.15
31 John Franco	1.00	.30
32 Doc Edwards CO	.25	.07
33 Barry Lyons	.25	.07
35 Orlando Mercado	.25	.07
40 Jeff Innis	.25	.07
44 David Cone	1.00	.30
45 Mark Carreon	.25	.07
47 Wally Whitehurst	.25	.07
48 Julio Machado	.25	.07
50 Sid Fernandez	.75	.23
52 Greg Pavlick CO	.25	.07
NNO Team Photo	.50	.15

1990 Mets Topps TV

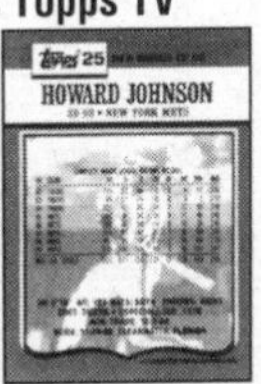

This Mets team set contains 66 cards measuring the standard size. Cards numbered 1-34 were with the parent club, while cards 35-66 were in the farm system.

	Nm-Mt	Ex-Mt
COMPLETE FACT. SET (66)	20.00	6.00
1 Dave Johnson MG	.50	.15
2 Mike Cubbage CO	.25	.07
3 Doc Edwards CO	.25	.07
4 Bud Harrelson CO	.25	.07
5 Greg Pavlick CO	.25	.07
6 Mel Stottlemyre CO	.50	.15
7 Blaine Beatty	.25	.07
8 David Cone	5.00	1.50
9 Ron Darling	.25	.07
10 Sid Fernandez	.25	.07
11 John Franco	1.50	.45
12 Dwight Gooden	4.00	1.20
13 Jeff Innis	.25	.07
14 Julio Machado	.25	.07
15 Jeff Musselman	.25	.07
16 Bob Ojeda	.25	.07
17 Alejandro Pena	.25	.07
18 Frank Viola	.50	.15
19 Wally Whitehurst	.25	.07
20 Barry Lyons	.25	.07
21 Orlando Mercado	.25	.07
22 Mackey Sasser	.25	.07
23 Kevin Elster	.25	.07
24 Gregg Jefferies	.25	.07
25 Howard Johnson	.50	.15
26 Dave Magadan	.25	.07
27 Mike Marshall	.25	.07
28 Tom O'Malley	.25	.07
29 Tim Teufel	.25	.07
30 Mark Carreon	.25	.07
31 Kevin McReynolds	.25	.07
32 Keith Miller	.25	.07
33 Darryl Strawberry	2.00	.60
34 Lou Thornton	.25	.07
35 Shawn Barton	.25	.07
36 Tim Bogar	.25	.07
37 Terry Bross	.25	.07
38 Kevin Brown	.25	.07
39 Mike DeButch	.25	.07
40 Alex Diaz	.25	.07
41 Chris Donnels	.25	.07
42 Jeff Gardner	.25	.07
43 Denny Gonzalez	.25	.07
44 Kenny Graves	.25	.07
45 Manny Hernandez	.25	.07
46 Keith Hughes	.25	.07
47 Todd Hundley	6.00	1.80
48 Chris Jelic	.25	.07
49 Dave Liddell	.25	.07
50 Terry McDaniel	.25	.07
51 Cesar Mejia	.25	.07
52 Scott Nielsen	.25	.07
53 Dale Plummer	.25	.07
54 Darren Reed	.25	.07
55 Gil Roca	.25	.07
56 Jaime Roseboro	.25	.07
57 Roger Samuels	.25	.07
58 Zoilo Sanchez	.25	.07
59 Pete Schourek	1.50	.45
60 Craig Shipley	.25	.07
61 Ray Soff	.25	.07
62 Steve Swisher MG	.25	.07
63 Kelvin Torve	.25	.07
64 Dave Trautwein	.25	.07
65 Julio Valera	.25	.07
66 Alan Zinter	.50	.15

1991 Mets Colla Postcards

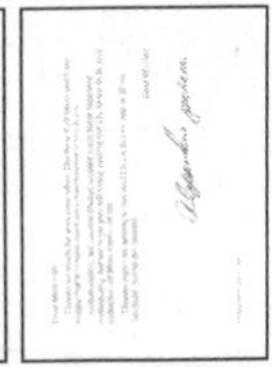

This 52-card set features color photos on a postcard format and was mailed in response to fan letters. The backs carry a pre-printed thank you note from the players.

	Nm-Mt	Ex-Mt
COMPLETE SET (52)	25.00	7.50
2 Mets Team	1.00	.30
3 John Franco	1.00	.30
4 Dwight Gooden	1.00	.30
5 Gregg Jefferies	.50	.15
6 Dave Magadan	.50	.15
7 Daryl Boston	.50	.15
8 Vince Coleman	.50	.15
9 Bud Harrelson MG	.50	.15
10 Tim Teufel	.50	.15
11 Frank Viola	.75	.23
12 Hubie Brooks	.75	.23
13 Mark Carreon	.50	.15
14 Dave Cone	1.50	.45
15 Kevin Elster	.50	.15
16 Sid Fernandez	.75	.23
17 Tommy Herr	.50	.15
18 Howard Johnson	.75	.23
19 Kevin McReynolds	.50	.15
20 Darren Reed	.50	.15
21 Mackey Sasser	.50	.15
22 Kevin Baez	.50	.15
23 Blaine Beatty	.50	.15
24 Terry Bross	.50	.15
25 Chuck Carr	.50	.15
26 Rick Cerone	.50	.15
27 Mike Cubbage CO	.50	.15
28 Ron Darling	.50	.15
29 Chris Donnells	.50	.15
30 D.J. Dozier	.50	.15
31 Rob Dromerhouser	.50	.15
32 Doc Edwards CO	.50	.15
33 Eric Hillman	.50	.15
34 Todd Hundley	1.50	.45
35 Clint Hurdle CO	.50	.15
36 Jeff Innis	.50	.15
37 John Johnstone	.50	.15
38 Terry McDaniel	.50	.15
39 Orlando Mercado	.50	.15
40 Keith Miller	.50	.15
41 Charlie O'Brien	.50	.15
42 Greg Pavlick CO	.50	.15
43 Alejandro Pena	.50	.15
44 Terry Puhl	.50	.15
45 Pete Schourek	1.00	.30
46 Doug Simons	.50	.15
47 Tom Spencer CO	.50	.15
48 Mel Stottlemyre CO	.50	.15
49 Kelvin Torve	.50	.15
50 Julio Valera	.50	.15
51 Wally Whitehurst	.50	.15
52 Anthony Young	.50	.15
53 Alan Zinter	.50	.15

1991 Mets Kahn's

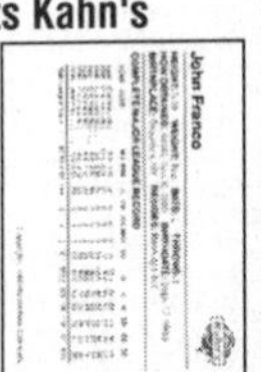

The 1991 Kahn's Mets set contains 33 cards measuring the standard size. The set is skip-numbered on the card fronts by uniform number and includes two Kahn's coupon cards. The front features color action player photos, on a white and blue pinstripe pattern. The player's name is given in an orange stripe below the picture. In a horizontal format the back presents biographical information, major league statistics, and minor league statistics where appropriate. A complete set was given away to each fan attending the New York Mets game at Shea Stadium on June 17, 1991.

	Nm-Mt	Ex-Mt
COMPLETE SET (33)	8.00	2.40
1 Vince Coleman	.50	.15
2 Mackey Sasser	.25	.07
3 Bud Harrelson MG	.50	.15
4 Mike Cubbage CO	.25	.07
5 Charlie O'Brien	.25	.07
7 Hubie Brooks	.50	.15
8 Daryl Boston	.25	.07
9 Gregg Jefferies	.25	.07
10 Dave Magadan	.25	.07
11 Tim Teufel	.25	.07
13 Rick Cerone	.25	.07
15 Ron Darling	.50	.15
16 Dwight Gooden	1.00	.30
17 David Cone	1.00	.30
20 Howard Johnson	.75	.23
21 Kevin Elster	.25	.07
22 Kevin McReynolds	.25	.07
25 Keith Miller	.25	.07
26 Alejandro Pena	.25	.07
28 Tom Herr	.25	.07
29 Frank Viola	.50	.15
30 Mel Stottlemyre CO	.50	.15
31 John Franco	1.00	.30
32 Doc Edwards CO	.25	.07
40 Jeff Innis	.25	.07
43 Doug Simons	.25	.07
45 Mark Carreon	.25	.07
47 Wally Whitehurst	.25	.07
48 Pete Schourek	.75	.23
50 Sid Fernandez	.50	.15
51 Tom Spencer CO	.25	.07
52 Greg Pavlick CO	.25	.07
NNO 1991 New York Mets Team photo	.50	.15

1991 Mets Photo Album Pergament

These 30 blank back photos were issued to honor the 1991 New York Mets. Each color photo has an picture of the player along with their position in the upper right corner. The bottom is devoted to the players name. The backs are blank and the photos are ordered in the way the appear in the perfect bound (the photos are not perforated) album. The back of the album and an multi-page advertisment in the middle is sponsored by Pergament Home Centers.

	Nm-Mt	Ex-Mt
COMPLETE SET (30)	15.00	4.50
1 Bud Harrelson MG	.50	.15
2 Mike Cubbage CO	.50	.15
3 Doc Edwards CO	.50	.15
4 Greg Pavlick CO	.50	.15
5 Tom Spencer CO	.50	.15
6 Mel Stottlemyre CO	.75	.23
7 Daryl Boston	.50	.15
8 Hubie Brooks	.50	.15
9 Tim Burke	.50	.15
10 Mark Carreon	.50	.15
11 Rick Cerone	.50	.15
12 Vince Coleman	.50	.15
13 David Cone	1.50	.45
14 Kevin Elster	.50	.15
15 Sid Fernandez	.75	.23
16 John Franco	1.00	.30
17 Dwight Gooden	.75	.23
18 Jeff Innis	.50	.15
19 Gregg Jefferies	.50	.15
20 Howard Johnson	.75	.23
21 Dave Magadan	.50	.15
22 Kevin McReynolds	.50	.15
23 Keith Miller	.50	.15
24 Charlie O'Brien	.50	.15
25 Mackey Sasser	.50	.15
26 Pete Schourek	.75	.23
27 Doug Simons	.50	.15
28 Garry Templeton	.50	.15
29 Frank Viola	.75	.23
30 Wally Whitehurst	.50	.15

1991 Mets WIZ

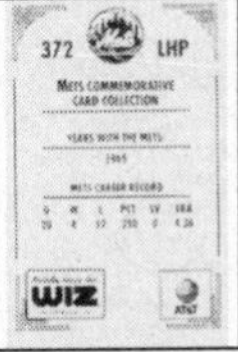

This 450-card commemorative New York Mets set was sponsored by WIZ Home Entertainment Centers and ATT. The set was issued on 30 (approximately) 10" by 9" perforated sheets (15 cards per sheet); after perforation, the cards measure approximately 2" by 3". the cards are numbered on the back and listed in alphabetical order. The set purports to show every player who ever played for the New York Mets. The set was issued in three series to be distributed at three home games during the year, e.g., the first series was issued to all fans attending the Mets home game on May 25, 1991.

	Nm-Mt	Ex-Mt
COMPLETE SET (450)	50.00	15.00
1 Don Aase	.10	.03
2 Tommie Agee	.25	.07
3 Rick Aguilera	.50	.15
4 Jack Aker	.10	.03
5 Neil Allen	.10	.03
6 Bill Almon	.10	.03
7 Sandy Alomar Sr.	.25	.07
8 Jesus Alou	.25	.07
9 George Altman	.10	.03
10 Luis Alvarado	.10	.03
11 Craig Anderson	.10	.03
12 Rick Anderson	.10	.03
13 Bob Apodaca	.10	.03
14 Gerry Arrigo	.10	.03
15 Richie Ashburn	3.00	.90
16 Tucker Ashford	.10	.03
17 Bob Aspromonte	.10	.03
18 Benny Ayala	.10	.03
19 Wally Backman	.25	.07
20 Kevin Baez	.10	.03
21 Bob Bailor	.10	.03

1991 Mets WIZ

22 Rick Baldwin	.10	.03
23 Billy Baldwin	.10	.03
24 Lute Barnes	.10	.03
25 Ed Bauta	.10	.03
26 Billy Beane	.10	.03
27 Larry Bearnarth	.10	.03
28 Blaine Beatty	.10	.03
29 Jim Beauchamp	.10	.03
30 Gus Bell	.25	.07
31 Dennis Bennett	.10	.03
32 Butch Benton	.10	.03
33 Juan Berenguer	.10	.03
34 Bruce Berenyi	.10	.03
35 Dwight Bernard	.10	.03
36 Yogi Berra	3.00	.90
37 Jim Bethke	.10	.03
38 Mike Bishop	.10	.03
39 Terry Blocker	.10	.03
40 Bruce Bochy	.10	.03
41 Bruce Boisclair	.10	.03
42 Dan Boitano	.10	.03
43 Mark Bomback	.10	.03
44 Don Bosch	.10	.03
45 Daryl Boston	.10	.03
46 Ken Boswell	.10	.03
47 Ed Bouchee	.10	.03
48 Larry Bowa	.25	.07
49 Ken Boyer	.50	.15
50 Mark Bradley	.10	.03
51 Eddie Bressoud	.10	.03
52 Hubie Brooks	.25	.07
53 Kevin D. Brown	.10	.03
54 Leon Brown	.10	.03
55 Mike Bruhert	.10	.03
56 Jerry Buchek	.10	.03
57 Larry Burright	.10	.03
58 Ray Burris	.10	.03
59 John Candelaria	.25	.07
60 Chris Cannizzaro	.10	.03
61 Buzz Capra	.10	.03
62 Jose Cardenal	.25	.07
63 Don Cardwell	.10	.03
64 Duke Carmel	.10	.03
65 Chuck Carr	.10	.03
66 Mark Carreon	.10	.03
67 Gary Carter	2.00	.60
68 Elio Chacon	.10	.03
69 Dean Chance	.25	.07
70 Kelvin Chapman	.10	.03
71 Ed Charles	.10	.03
72 Rich Chiles	.10	.03
73 Harry Chiti	.10	.03
74 John Christensen	.10	.03
75 Joe Christopher	.10	.03
76 Galen Cisco	.10	.03
77 Donn Clendenon	.25	.07
78 Gene Clines	.10	.03
79 Choo Choo Coleman	.25	.07
80 Kevin Collins	.10	.03
81 David Cone	2.00	.60
82 Bill Connors	.10	.03
83 Cliff Cook	.10	.03
84 Tim Corcoran	.10	.03
85 Mardie Cornejo	.10	.03
86 Billy Cowan	.10	.03
87 Roger Craig	.25	.07
88 Jerry Cram	.10	.03
89 Mike Cubbage	.10	.03
90 Ron Darling	.25	.07
91 Ray Daviault	.10	.03
92 Tommy Davis	.50	.15
93 John DeMerit	.10	.03
94 Bill Denehy	.10	.03
95 Jack DiLauro	.10	.03
96 Carlos Diaz	.10	.03
97 Mario Diaz	.10	.03
98 Steve Dillon	.10	.03
99 Sammy Drake	.10	.03
100 Jim Dwyer	.10	.03
101 Duffy Dyer	.10	.03
102 Len Dykstra	.75	.23
103 Tom Edens	.10	.03
104 Dave Eilers	.10	.03
105 Larry Elliot	.10	.03
106 Dock Ellis	.25	.07
107 Kevin Elster	.50	.15
108 Nino Espinosa	.10	.03
109 Chuck Estrada	.10	.03
110 Francisco Estrada	.10	.03
111 Pete Falcone	.10	.03
112 Sid Fernandez	.50	.15
113 Chico Fernandez	.10	.03
114 Sergio Ferrer	.10	.03
115 Jack Fisher	.10	.03
116 Mike Fitzgerald	.10	.03
117 Shaun Fitzmaurice	.10	.03
118 Gil Flores	.10	.03
119 Doug Flynn	.10	.03
120 Tim Foli	.10	.03
121 Rich Folkers	.10	.03
122 Larry Foss	.10	.03
123 George Foster	.50	.15
124 Leo Foster	.10	.03
125 Joe Foy	.10	.03
126 John Franco	.75	.23
127 Jim Fregosi	.25	.07
128 Bob Friend	.25	.07
129 Danny Frisella	.10	.03
130 Brent Gaff	.10	.03
131 Bob Gallagher	.10	.03
132 Ron Gardenhire	.25	.07
133 Rob Gardner	.10	.03
134 Wes Gardner	.10	.03
135 Wayne Garrett	.10	.03
136 Rod Gaspar	.10	.03
137 Gary Gentry	.25	.07
138 John Gibbons	.10	.03
139 Bob Gibson	.10	.03
140 Brian Giles	.10	.03
141 Joe Ginsberg	.10	.03
142 Ed Glynn	.10	.03
143 Jesse Gonder	.10	.03
144 Dwight Gooden	1.50	.45
145 Greg Goossen	.25	.07
146 Tom Gorman	.10	.03
147 Jim Gosger	.10	.03
148 Bill Graham	.10	.03
149 Wayne Graham	.10	.03
150 Dallas Green	.25	.07
151 Pumpsie Green	.10	.03
152 Tom Grieve	.25	.07
153 Jerry Grote	.25	.07
154 Joe Grzenda	.10	.03
155 Don Hahn	.10	.03
156 Tom Hall	.10	.03
157 Jack Hamilton	.10	.03
158 Ike Hampton	.10	.03
159 Tim Harkness	.10	.03
160 Bud Harrelson	.25	.07
161 Greg A. Harris	.25	.07
162 Greg Harts	.10	.03
163 Andy Hassler	.10	.03
164 Tom Hausman	.10	.03
165 Ed Hearn	.10	.03
166 Richie Hebner	.25	.07
167 Danny Heep	.10	.03
168 Jack Heidemann	.10	.03
169 Bob Heise	.10	.03
170 Ken Henderson	.10	.03
171 Steve Henderson	.10	.03
172 Bob Hendley	.10	.03
173 Phil Hennigan	.10	.03
174 Bill Hepler	.10	.03
175 Ron Herbel	.10	.03
176 Manny Hernandez	.10	.03
177 Keith Hernandez	.75	.23
178 Tommy Herr	.25	.07
179 Rick Herrscher	.10	.03
180 Jim Hickman	.10	.03
181 Joe Hicks	.10	.03
182 Chuck Hiller	.10	.03
183 Dave Hillman	.10	.03
184 Jerry Hinsley	.10	.03
185 Gil Hodges	2.50	.75
186 Ron Hodges	.10	.03
187 Scott Holman	.10	.03
188 Jay Hook	.10	.03
189 Mike Howard	.10	.03
190 Jesse Hudson	.10	.03
191 Keith Hughes	.10	.03
192 Todd Hundley	2.00	.60
193 Ron Hunt	.25	.07
194 Willard Hunter	.10	.03
195 Clint Hurdle	.25	.07
196 Jeff Innis	.10	.03
197 Al Jackson	.10	.03
198 Roy Lee Jackson	.10	.03
199 Gregg Jefferies	.25	.07
200 Stan Jefferson	.10	.03
201 Chris Jelic	.10	.03
202 Bob D. Johnson	.10	.03
203 Howard Johnson	.50	.15
204 Bob W. Johnson	.10	.03
205 Randy Jones	.25	.07
206 Sherman Jones	.10	.03
207 Cleon Jones	.25	.07
208 Ross Jones	.10	.03
209 Mike Jorgensen	.10	.03
210 Rod Kanehl	.25	.07
211 Dave Kingman	.75	.23
212 Bobby Klaus	.10	.03
213 Jay Kleven	.10	.03
214 Lou Klimchock	.10	.03
215 Ray Knight	.50	.15
216 Kevin Kobel	.10	.03
217 Gary Kolb	.10	.03
218 Cal Koonce	.10	.03
219 Jerry Koosman	.50	.15
220 Ed Kranepool	.50	.15
221 Gary Kroll	.10	.03
222 Clem Labine	.50	.15
223 Jack Lamabe	.10	.03
224 Hobie Landrith	.10	.03
225 Frank Lary	.25	.07
226 Bill Latham	.10	.03
227 Terry Leach	.10	.03
228 Tim Leary	.10	.03
229 John Lewis	.10	.03
230 David Liddell	.10	.03
231 Phil Linz	.25	.07
232 Ron Locke	.10	.03
233 Skip Lockwood	.10	.03
234 Mickey Lolich	.50	.15
235 Phil Lombardi	.10	.03
236 Al Luplow	.10	.03
237 Ed Lynch	.10	.03
238 Barry Lyons	.10	.03
239 Ken MacKenzie	.10	.03
240 Julio Machado	.10	.03
241 Elliott Maddox	.10	.03
242 Dave Magadan	.25	.07
243 Pepe Mangual	.10	.03
244 Phil Mankowski	.10	.03
245 Felix Mantilla	.10	.03
246 Mike G. Marshall	.25	.07
247 Dave Marshall	.10	.03
248 Jim Marshall	.10	.03
249 Mike A. Marshall	.25	.07
250 J.C. Martin	.10	.03
251 Jerry Martin	.10	.03
252 Teddy Martinez	.10	.03
253 Jon Matlack	.25	.07
254 Jerry May	.10	.03
255 Willie Mays	10.00	3.00
256 Lee Mazzilli	.25	.07
257 Jim McAndrew	.10	.03
258 Bob McClure	.10	.03
259 Roger McDowell	.25	.07
260 Tug McGraw	.50	.15
261 Jeff McKnight	.10	.03
262 Roy McMillan	.25	.07
263 Kevin McReynolds	.25	.07
264 George Medich	.10	.03
265 Orlando Mercado	.10	.03
266 Butch Metzger	.10	.03
267 Felix Millan	.25	.07
268 Bob G. Miller	.10	.03
269 Bob L. Miller	.10	.03
270 Dyar Miller	.10	.03
271 Larry Miller	.10	.03
272 Keith Miller	.10	.03
273 Randy Milligan	.10	.03
274 John Milner	.10	.03
275 John Mitchell	.10	.03
276 Kevin Mitchell	.50	.15
277 Wilmer Mizell	.25	.07
278 Herb Moford	.10	.03
279 Willie Montanez	.25	.07
280 Joe Moock	.10	.03
281 Tommy Moore	.10	.03
282 Bob Moorhead	.10	.03
283 Jerry Morales	.10	.03
284 Al Moran	.10	.03
285 Jose Moreno	.10	.03
286 Bill Murphy	.10	.03
287 Dale Murray	.10	.03
288 Dennis Musgraves	.10	.03
289 Jeff Musselman	.10	.03
290 Randy Myers	.75	.23
291 Bob Myrick	.10	.03
292 Danny Napoleon	.10	.03
293 Charlie Neal	.25	.07
294 Randy Niemann	.10	.03
295 Joe Nolan	.10	.03
296 Dan Norman	.10	.03
297 Ed Nunez	.10	.03
298 Charlie O'Brien	.10	.03
299 Tom O'Malley	.10	.03
300 Bob Ojeda	.25	.07
301 Jose Oquendo	.10	.03
302 Jesse Orosco	.50	.15
303 Junior Ortiz	.10	.03
304 Brian Ostrosser	.10	.03
305 Amos Otis	.25	.07
306 Rick Ownbey	.10	.03
307 John Pacella	.10	.03
308 Tom Paciorek	.10	.03
309 Harry Parker	.10	.03
310 Tom Parsons	.10	.03
311 Al Pedrique	.10	.03
312 Brock Pemberton	.10	.03
313 Alejandro Pena	.10	.03
314 Bobby Pfeil	.10	.03
315 Mike Phillips	.10	.03
316 Jim Piersall	.50	.15
317 Joe Pignatano	.10	.03
318 Grover Powell	.10	.03
319 Rich Puig	.10	.03
320 Charlie Puleo	.10	.03
321 Gary Rajsich	.10	.03
322 Mario Ramirez	.10	.03
323 Lenny Randle	.10	.03
324 Bob Rauch	.10	.03
325 Jeff Reardon	.75	.23
326 Darren Reed	.10	.03
327 Hal Reniff	.10	.03
328 Ronn Reynolds	.10	.03
329 Tom Reynolds	.10	.03
330 Dennis Ribant	.10	.03
331 Gordie Richardson	.10	.03
332 Dave Roberts	.10	.03
333 Les Rohr	.10	.03
334 Luis Rosado	.10	.03
335 Don Rose	.10	.03
336 Don Rowe	.10	.03
337 Dick Rusteck	.10	.03
338 Nolan Ryan	15.00	4.50
339 Ray Sadecki	.10	.03
340 Joe Sambito	.10	.03
341 Amado Samuel	.10	.03
342 Juan Samuel	.10	.03
343 Ken Sanders	.10	.03
344 Rafael Santana	.10	.03
345 Mackey Sasser	.10	.03
346 Mac Scarce	.10	.03
347 Jim Schaffer	.10	.03
348 Dan Schatzeder	.10	.03
349 Calvin Schiraldi	.10	.03
350 Al Schmelz	.10	.03
351 Dave Schneck	.10	.03
352 Ted Schreiber	.10	.03
353 Don Schulze	.10	.03
354 Mike Scott	.25	.07
355 Ray Searage	.10	.03
356 Tom Seaver	5.00	1.50
357 Dick Selma	.10	.03
358 Art Shamsky	.25	.07
359 Bob Shaw	.25	.07
360 Don Shaw	.10	.03
361 Norm Sherry	.25	.07
362 Craig Shipley	.10	.03
363 Bart Shirley	.10	.03
364 Bill Short	.10	.03
365 Paul Siebert	.10	.03
366 Ken Singleton	.50	.15
367 Doug Sisk	.10	.03
368 Bobby Gene Smith	.10	.03
369 Charley Smith	.10	.03
370 Dick Smith	.10	.03
371 Duke Snider	3.00	.90
372 Warren Spahn	3.00	.90
373 Larry Stahl	.10	.03
374 Roy Staiger	.10	.03
375 Tracy Stallard	.10	.03
376 Leroy Stanton	.10	.03
377 Rusty Staub	.50	.15
378 John Stearns	.25	.07
379 John Stephenson	.10	.03
380 Randy Sterling	.10	.03
381 George Stone	.10	.03
382 Darryl Strawberry	.75	.23
383 John Strohmayer	.10	.03
384 Brent Strom	.10	.03
385 Dick Stuart	.25	.07
386 Tom Sturdivant	.10	.03
387 Bill Sudakis	.10	.03
388 John Sullivan	.10	.03
389 Darrell Sutherland	.10	.03
390 Ron Swoboda	.25	.07
391 Craig Swan	.10	.03
392 Rick Sweet	.10	.03
393 Pat Tabler	.10	.03
394 Kevin Tapani	.50	.15
395 Randy Tate	.10	.03
396 Frank Taveras	.10	.03
397 Chuck Taylor	.10	.03
398 Ron Taylor	.10	.03
399 Bob Taylor	.10	.03
400 Sammy Taylor	.10	.03
401 Walt Terrell	.10	.03
402 Ralph Terry	.25	.07
403 Tim Teufel	.10	.03
404 George Theodore	.10	.03
405 Frank J. Thomas	.50	.15
406 Lou Thornton	.10	.03
407 Marv Throneberry	.50	.15
408 Dick Tidrow	.10	.03
409 Rusty Tillman	.10	.03
410 Jackson Todd	.10	.03
411 Joe Torre	.75	.23
412 Mike Torrez	.25	.07
413 Kelvin Torve	.10	.03
414 Alex Trevino	.10	.03
415 Wayne Twitchell	.10	.03
416 Del Unser	.10	.03
417 Mike Vail	.10	.03
418 Bobby Valentine	.50	.15
419 Ellis Valentine	.10	.03
420 Julio Valera	.10	.03
421 Tom Veryzer	.10	.03
422 Frank Viola	.50	.15
423 Bill Wakefield	.10	.03
424 Gene Walter	.10	.03
425 Claudell Washington	.25	.07
426 Hank Webb	.10	.03
427 Al Weis	.10	.03
428 Dave West	.10	.03
429 Wally Whitehurst	.10	.03
430 Carl Willey	.10	.03
431 Nick Willhite	.10	.03
432 Charlie Williams	.10	.03
433 Mookie Wilson	.50	.15
434 Herm Winningham	.10	.03
435 Gene Woodling	.25	.07
436 Billy Wynne	.10	.03
437 Joel Youngblood	.10	.03
438 Pat Zachry	.10	.03
439 Don Zimmer	.25	.07
NNO Checklist 1-20	.10	.03
NNO Checklist 41-60	.10	.03
NNO Checklist 81-100	.10	.03
NNO Checklist 121-140	.10	.03
NNO Checklist 161-180	.10	.03
NNO Checklist 201-220	.10	.03
NNO Checklist 241-260	.10	.03
NNO Checklist 281-300	.10	.03
NNO Checklist 321-340	.10	.03
NNO Checklist 361-380	.10	.03
NNO Checklist 401-420	.10	.03

1992 Mets Colla Postcards

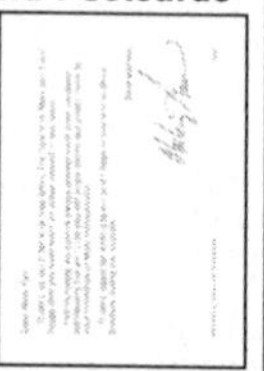

This 39-card set features color photos on a postcard format and was mailed in response to fan letters. The backs carry a pre-printed thank you note from the players.

	Nm-Mt	Ex-Mt
COMPLETE SET (39)	25.00	7.50
1 Team Picture	1.00	.30
2 Bobby Bonilla	.50	.15
3 Dwight Gooden	1.50	.45
4 Howard Johnson	.75	.23
5 Bret Saberhagen	.75	.23
6 David Cone	1.50	.45
7 Dave Magadan	.75	.23
8 Eddie Murray	2.00	.60
9 Willie Randolph	.75	.23
10 Tim Burke	.50	.15
11 Daryl Boston	.50	.15
12 Vince Coleman	.50	.15
13 Kevin Elster	.50	.15
14 Sid Fernandez	.75	.23
15 John Franco	1.00	.30
16 Todd Hundley	1.50	.45
17 Charlie O'Brien	.50	.15
18 Mackey Sasser	.50	.15
19 Jeff Torborg MG	.50	.15
20 Wally Whitehurst	.50	.15
21 Chris Donnels	.50	.15
22 D.J. Dozier	.50	.15
23 Dave Gallagher	.50	.15
24 Paul Gibson	.50	.15
25 Junior Noboa	.50	.15
26 Bill Pecota	.50	.15
27 Pete Schourek	.50	.15
28 Doug Simons	.50	.15
29 Mel Stottlemyre CO	.75	.23
30 Julio Valera	.50	.15
31 Julian Vasquez	.50	.15
32 Anthony Young	.50	.15
33 Mike Cubbage CO	.50	.15
34 Barry Foote CO	.50	.15
35 Clint Hurdle CO	.50	.15
36 Dave LaRoche CO	.50	.15
37 Tom McCraw CO	.50	.15
38 Jerry Stephenson CO	.50	.15
40 Jeff Innis	.50	.15

1992 Mets Kahn's

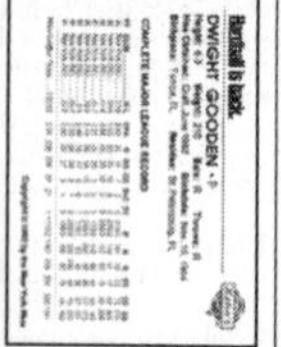

The 1992 Kahn's New York Mets set consists of 35 standard-size cards. The set included two manufacturer's coupons (one for 50 cents off Kahn's Beef Franks and another for the same amount off Kahn's Corn Dogs). The cards are skip-numbered by uniform number on the front and checklisted below accordingly.

	Nm-Mt	Ex-Mt
COMPLETE SET (35)	8.00	2.40
1 Vince Coleman	.50	.15
2 Mackey Sasser	.25	.07
3 Junior Noboa	.25	.07
4 Mike Cubbage CO	.25	.07
6 Daryl Boston	.25	.07
8 Dave Gallagher	.25	.07
9 Todd Hundley	1.00	.30
10 Jeff Torborg MG	.25	.07
11 Dick Schofield	.25	.07
12 Willie Randolph	.75	.23
15 Kevin Elster	.25	.07
16 Dwight Gooden	1.00	.30
17 David Cone	1.00	.30
18 Bret Saberhagen	.50	.15
19 Anthony Young	.25	.07
20 Howard Johnson	.75	.23
22 Charlie O'Brien	.25	.07
25 Bobby Bonilla	.50	.15
26 Barry Foote CO	.25	.07
27 Tom McCraw CO	.25	.07
28 Dave LaRoche CO	.25	.07
29 Dave Magadan	.25	.07
30 Mel Stottlemyre CO	.50	.15
31 John Franco	1.00	.30
32 Bill Pecota	.25	.07
33 Eddie Murray	1.25	.35
40 Jeff Innis	.25	.07
44 Tim Burke	.25	.07
45 Paul Gibson	.25	.07
47 Wally Whitehurst	.25	.07
50 Sid Fernandez	.50	.15
51 John Stephenson CO	.25	.07
NNO Team Photo	.50	.15
NNO Manufacturer's Coupon Kahn's Beef Franks	.25	.07
NNO Manufacturer's Coupon Kahn's Corn Dogs	.25	.07

1992 Mets Modell

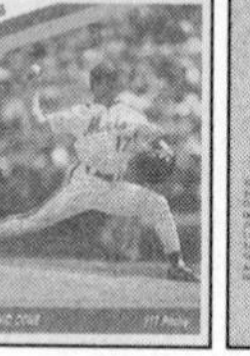
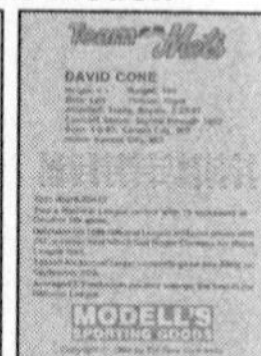

Measuring 7 1/2" by 10 1/2", this 9-card perforated sheet was sponsored by Modell's Sporting Goods and distributed as a membership benefit to Team Mets, the junior fan club. If the cards were separated, they would measure the standard size. The cards are unnumbered and checklisted below in alphabetical order.

	Nm-Mt	Ex-Mt
COMPLETE SET (9)	5.00	1.50
1 Bobby Bonilla	.50	.15
2 Vince Coleman	.50	.15
3 David Cone	1.50	.45
4 Dwight Gooden	1.00	.30
5 Todd Hundley	.75	.23
6 Howard Johnson	.75	.23
7 Eddie Murray	2.00	.60
8 Willie Randolph	.75	.23
9 Bret Saberhagen	.75	.23

1993 Mets Colla Postcards

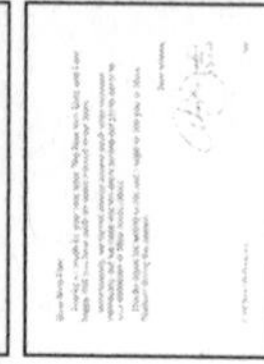

This 31-card set features color photos on a postcard format and was mailed in response to fan letters. The backs carry a pre-printed thank you note from the players. Because of legal problems with Barry Colla's licensing agreement, he can no longer sell his postcards making singles difficult to find and usually must be purchased as a set.

	Nm-Mt	Ex-Mt
COMPLETE SET (31)	15.00	4.50
21 Team Photo	1.00	.30
22 Bobby Bonilla	.75	.23
23 Dwight Gooden	1.50	.45
24 Howard Johnson	.75	.23
25 Bret Saberhagen	.75	.23
26 Tim Bogar	.50	.15
27 Vince Coleman	.50	.15
28 Mark Dewey	.50	.15
29 Mike Draper	.50	.15
30 Sid Fernandez	.75	.23
31 Tony Fernandez	.75	.23
32 John Franco	.75	.23
33 Dave Gallagher	.50	.15
34 Paul Gibson	.50	.15
35 Eric Hillman	.50	.15
36 Todd Hundley	.75	.23
37 Jeff Innis	.50	.15
38 Jeff Kent	1.50	.45
39 Mike Maddux	.50	.15
40 Jeff McKnight	.50	.15
41 Eddie Murray	2.00	.60
42 Charlie O'Brien	.50	.15
43 Joe Orsulak	.50	.15
44 Darren Reed	.50	.15
45 Pete Schourek	.50	.15
46 Frank Tanana	.75	.23
47 Ryan Thompson	.50	.15
48 Jeff Torborg CO	.50	.15
49 Chico Walker	.50	.15
50 Anthony Young	.50	.15
110 Dallas Green MG	.50	.15

1993 Mets Kahn's

This 29-card set measures the standard size and features white-bordered color player photos on their fronts. The cards are skip-numbered by uniform number on the front and checklisted below accordingly.

	Nm-Mt	Ex-Mt
COMPLETE SET (29)	8.00	2.40
1 Tony Fernandez	.50	.15
6 Joe Orsulak	.25	.07
7 Jeff McKnight	.25	.07

Card	Nm-Mt	Ex-Mt
8 Dave Gallagher	.25	.07
9 Todd Hundley	.75	.23
11 Vince Coleman	.50	.15
12 Jeff Kent	1.50	.45
16 Dwight Gooden	1.00	.30
18 Bret Saberhagen	.50	.15
19 Anthony Young	.25	.07
20 Howard Johnson	.75	.23
21 Darren Reed	.25	.07
22 Charlie O'Brien	.25	.07
23 Tim Bogar	.25	.07
25 Bobby Bonilla	.25	.07
29 Frank Tanana	.50	.15
31 John Franco	1.00	.30
33 Eddie Murray	1.50	.45
34 Chico Walker	.25	.07
40 Jeff Innis	.25	.07
44 Ryan Thompson	.25	.07
47 Mike Draper	.25	.07
48 Pete Schourek	.50	.15
50 Sid Fernandez	.50	.15
51 Mike Maddux	.25	.07
NNO Team Photo	.50	.15
NNO Title Card	.25	.07
NNO Manufacturer's Coupon	.25	.07
Kahn's Corn Dogs		
NNO Manufacturer's Coupon	.25	.07
Kahn's Hot Dogs		

1994 Mets '69 Capital Cards Postcard Promos

Licensed by Miracle of 1969 Enterprises, Inc., this boxed set of 32 postcards commemorates the 25th Anniversary of the World Championship season of the 1969 Mets. Capital Cards commissioned renowned sports artist Ron Lewis to create from oil paintings these postcards, which measure 3 1/2" by 5 1/2". Just 25,000 postcard sets were produced, with each having a unique serial number. Also 5,000 individually-numbered uncut sheets were produced. The cards are numbered on the back and the word "PROMO" is stamped across each back.

Card	Nm-Mt	Ex-Mt
COMPLETE SET (32)	20.00	6.00
1 Title Card	.50	.15
2 Gil Hodges MG	1.50	.45
3 Rube Walker CO	.50	.15
4 Yogi Berra CO	2.50	.75
5 Joe Pignatano CO	.50	.15
6 Ed Yost CO	.50	.15
7 Tommie Agee	.75	.23
8 Ken Boswell	.50	.15
9 Don Cardwell	.50	.15
10 Ed Charles	.50	.15
11 Donn Clendenon	.75	.23
12 Jack DiLauro	.50	.15
13 Duffy Dyer	.50	.15
14 Wayne Garrett	.50	.15
15 Rod Gasper	.50	.15
16 Gary Gentry	.50	.15
17 Jerry Grote	.75	.23
18 Bud Harrelson	.75	.23
19 Cleon Jones	.75	.23
20 Cal Koonce	.50	.15
21 Jerry Koosman	1.00	.30
22 Ed Kranepool	.75	.23
23 J.C. Martin	.50	.15
24 Jim McAndrew	.50	.15
25 Tug McGraw	1.50	.45
26 Bob Pfeil	.50	.15
27 Nolan Ryan	10.00	3.00
28 Tom Seaver	5.00	1.50
29 Art Shamsky	.50	.15
30 Ron Swoboda	.75	.23
31 Ron Taylor	.50	.15
32 Al Weis	.50	.15

1994 Mets '69 Commemorative Sheet

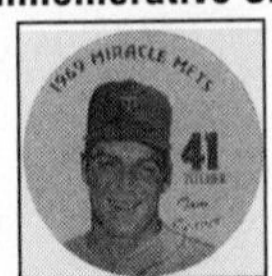

Issued in a 14 1/2" by 11 1/4" blue padded gold-stamped certificate holder, this commemorative sheet featuring 31 perforated caps was released on the 25th anniversary of the 1969 World Champion Mets. Each cap measures 1 5/8" in diameter, and the color player cutouts displayed are the same as those in the Ron Lewis postcard set. The words "1969 Miracle Mets" is gold foil-stamped at the top following the curve; likewise, the player's name is similarly impressed on the front. The backs are blank. The 31 caps are arranged on a sheet that has at its center a special 25th anniversary Mets logo. The enclosed certificate of authenticity carries the sheet serial number and total production figures (25,000). The caps are unnumbered and listed below just as they are in the postcard set, with nonplayers listed first.

Card	Nm-Mt	Ex-Mt
COMPLETE SET (31)	15.00	4.50
1 Gil Hodges MG	1.00	.30
2 Rube Walker CO	.25	.07
3 Yogi Berra CO	1.00	.30
4 Joe Pignatano CO	.25	.07
5 Ed Yost CO	.25	.07
6 Tommie Agee	.50	.15
7 Ken Boswell	.25	.07
8 Don Cardwell	.25	.07
9 Ed Charles	.25	.07
10 Donn Clendenon	.50	.15
11 Jack DiLauro	.25	.07
12 Duffy Dyer	.25	.07
13 Wayne Garrett	.25	.07
14 Rod Gaspar UER	.25	.07
(Name misspelled Gasper on front)		
15 Gary Gentry	.25	.07
16 Jerry Grote	.50	.15
17 Bud Harrelson	.50	.15
18 Cleon Jones	.50	.15
19 Cal Koonce	.25	.07
20 Jerry Koosman	.75	.23
21 Ed Kranepool	.50	.15
22 J.C. Martin	.25	.07
23 Jim McAndrew	.25	.07
24 Tug McGraw	1.00	.30
25 Bobby Pfeil	.25	.07
26 Nolan Ryan	5.00	1.50
27 Tom Seaver	2.50	.75
28 Art Shamsky	.25	.07
29 Ron Swoboda	.50	.15
30- Ron Taylor	.25	.07
31 Al Weis	.25	.07
NNO Uncut Sheet		

1994 Mets '69 Spectrum Promos

Issued to herald the commemorative 25th anniversary 1969 Miracle Mets 70-card set, these standard-size promos feature on their fronts white-bordered color photos framed by red lines. The 25th anniversary logo appears in one corner. The blue backs carry player or team season highlights. The "For Promotional Use Only" disclaimer appears within a white ellipse on the back. The cards are numbered on the back with a "P" prefix.

Card	Nm-Mt	Ex-Mt
COMPLETE SET (3)	3.00	.90
P1 Tom Seaver	2.00	.60
P2 Jerry Koosman	1.00	.30
P3 Met Mania	1.00	.30
Oct. 20, 1969 (Parade showing Seaver and Koosman)		

1994 Mets '69 Tribute

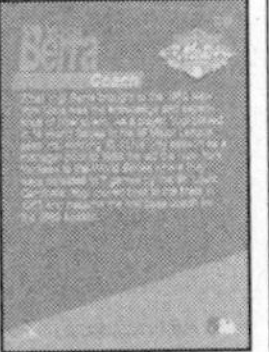

This 70-card standard-size boxed set commemorates the 1969 New York Mets championship team. Only 25,000 of these sets were produced and each box contains a Certificate of Authenticity indicating the set number.The fronts feature color and black-and-white posed and action player photos on a white background with a thin red border. In gold foil across the top is printed "The Miracle of '69," "The '69 Countdown," or "World Champions" with the player's name at the bottom in red and blue print. The backs carry the player's name, position, career highlights, and 1969 season statistics.

Card	Nm-Mt	Ex-Mt
COMPLETE SET (70)	10.00	3.00
1 Commemorative Card	.10	.03
2 Team Photo	.25	.07
3 Tom Seaver	1.50	.45
4 Jerry Koosman	.50	.15
5 Tommie Agee	.25	.07
6 Bud Harrelson	.25	.07
7 Nolan Ryan	3.00	.90
8 Jerry Grote	.25	.07
9 Ron Swoboda	.25	.07
10 Donn Clendenon	.25	.07
11 Art Shamsky	.25	.07
12 Tug McGraw	.75	.23
13 Ed Kranepool	.25	.07
14 Cleon Jones	.25	.07
15 Ron Taylor	.10	.03
16 Gary Gentry	.10	.03
17 Ken Boswell	.10	.03
18 Ed Charles	.10	.03
19 J.C. Martin	.10	.03
20 Al Weis	.10	.03
21 Jack DiLauro	.10	.03
22 Duffy Dyer	.10	.03
23 Wayne Garrett	.10	.03
24 Jim McAndrew	.10	.03
25 Rod Gaspar	.10	.03
26 Don Cardwell	.10	.03
27 Bob Pfeil	.10	.03
28 Cal Koonce	.10	.03
29 Gil Hodges MG	.75	.23
30 Yogi Berra CO	.75	.23
31 Joe Pignatano CO	.10	.03
32 Rube Walker CO	.10	.03
33 Eddie Yost CO	.10	.03
34 First Ever Met Game	.10	.03
35 Opening Day 1969	.10	.03
36 Ed Kranepool	.10	.03
Breaks Homerun Record		
37 Jerry Koosman	.25	.07
Sets Club Strikeout Record		
38 Donn Clendenon	.10	.03
Mets Trade for		
39 Jerry Koosman	.25	.07
23 Scoreless Innings		
40 Begin 7 Game Winning Streak	.10	.03
41 Vs Division Leading Cubs	.10	.03
42 Tom Seaver	.75	.23
Near Perfect Game		
43 Mets Trail by 3 1/2 Games	.10	.03
44 All-Star Break	.10	.03
45 All-Star Game	.10	.03
46 Mets Sweep Atlanta	.10	.03
47 Mets Sweep Padres	.10	.03
48 Jerry Koosman	.25	.07
Mets Defeat Cubs		
Strikes Out 13		
49 Defeat Cubs, 1/2 Game Back	.10	.03
50 1st Place!	.10	.03
51 9 Game Winning Streak	.10	.03
52 Tom Seaver	.75	.23
Earns 22nd Victory		
53 Steve Carlton	.75	.23
Strikes out 19		
Mets Win		
54 Jerry Koosman	.25	.07
Pitches 15th Complete Game		
55 Eastern Division Champs!	.10	.03
56 100th Victory	.10	.03
57 Mets Prepare for Braves	.10	.03
58 N.L.C.S. Game 1	.10	.03
59 N.L.C.S. Game 2	.10	.03
60 N.L.C.S. Game 3	.10	.03
61 1969 World Series, Game 1	.10	.03
62 1969 World Series, Game 2	.10	.03
63 1969 World Series, Game 3	.10	.03
64 1969 World Series, Game 4	.10	.03
65 1969 World Series, Game 5	.10	.03
66 World Champions	.10	.03
67 World Champions	.10	.03
68 World Champions	.10	.03
69 World Champions	.10	.03
NNO Checklist	.10	.03

1994 Mets '69 Year Book

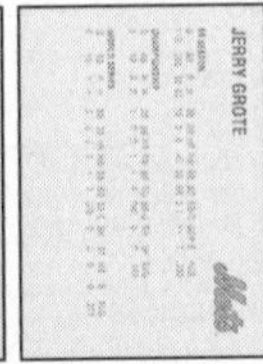

Measuring 8 1/4" by 10 7/8", this perforated sheet of nine player cards was inserted inside a reprint of the 1969 Official Year Book issued to celebrate the 25th anniversary of the World Champion Mets. If the cards were separated, they would measure 2 3/4" by 3 1/2". Inside white outer borders, the fronts feature a mix of posed and action color photos framed by an orange-and-purple inner border design. The player's name is printed in the top border, while the team logo and the uniform number are superposed over the picture. On a white background, the backs present statistics for the 1969 season, National League championship series, and the World Series. The cards are unnumbered and are checklisted below in alphabetical order.

Card	Nm-Mt	Ex-Mt
COMPLETE SET (9)	2.50	.75
1 Ed Charles	.25	.07
2 Donn Clendenon	.50	.15
3 Jerry Grote	.50	.15
4 Bud Harrelson	.50	.15
5 Cleon Jones	.50	.15
6 Jerry Koosman	.75	.23
7 Art Shamsky UER	.25	.07
(Listed as infield; should be outfield)		
8 Ron Swoboda	.50	.15
9 Team Photo	.25	.07

1994 Mets Community Relations

This two-card black and white set measures approximately 2 3/4" by 4". These cards were used by these former Mets when visiting hospitals or making other personal experiences.

Card	Nm-Mt	Ex-Mt
COMPLETE SET (2)	3.00	.90
1 Bud Harrelson	1.00	.30
2 Mookie Wilson	2.00	.60

1994 Mets Team Issue

Consisting of nine cards, this 7 1/2" by 10 1/2" perforated sheet features some past and current Mets. The cards are unnumbered and are checklisted below starting with the upper left and proceeding across and down to the lower right. The cards are also found with PruCare sponsoring on the back. There is no price differential for that set.

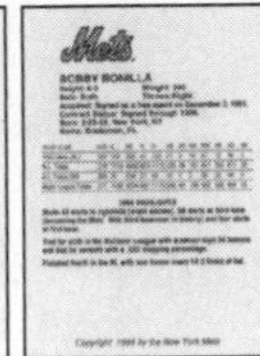

Card	Nm-Mt	Ex-Mt
COMPLETE SET (9)	6.00	1.80
1 Bobby Bonilla	.75	.23
2 Dwight Gooden	1.00	.30
3 John Franco	1.00	.30
4 Jeff Kent	1.50	.45
5 Kevin McReynolds	.50	.15
6 Ryan Thompson	.50	.15
7 Jeromy Burnitz	1.00	.30
8 Bud Harrelson	1.00	.30
9 Mookie Wilson	1.00	.30

1994 Mets Tribute Sheet '69 Spectrum

This UV-coated sheet measures 8 1/2" by 11" and pays tribute to the 1969 Miracle Mets on their 25th anniversary. Production was limited to 10,000 sheets. The blue front is a photo montage. A large photo in the middle of the sheet depicts the Mets on-field celebration upon winning the 1969 World Series. It is flanked on the right by a team photo and on the left by a shot of the Mets running onto the field to celebrate. A player photo appears in each corner: Jerry Koosman at the upper left, Tom Seaver at the upper right, Ron Swoboda at the lower left and Don Clendenon at the lower right. The 1969 Miracle Mets 25th Anniversary logo lies just below the large middle photo. The back carries a synopsis of the team's accomplishments. There were also an unspecified number of "Promo" versions produced of this sheet.

Card	Nm-Mt	Ex-Mt
1 '69 Mets 25th Ann.Sheet	5.00	1.50

1995 Mets Colla Postcards

These cards measure the standard postcard size -- feature a full color glossy borderless photo on the front and a printed message thanking the fan for his/her support on the back

Card	Nm-Mt	Ex-Mt
COMPLETE SET (32)	20.00	6.00
1 Mets Team	1.00	.30
2 Bobby Bonilla	.75	.23
3 John Franco	.75	.23
4 Jeff Kent	1.50	.45
5 Bret Saberhagen	.75	.23
6 Edgardo Alfonzo	1.50	.45
7 Tim Bogar	.50	.15
8 Rico Brogna	.50	.15
9 Brett Butler	.75	.23
10 Jerry DiPoto	.50	.15
11 Carl Everett	.75	.23
12 Brook Fordyce	.50	.15
13 Eric Gunderson	.50	.15
14 Pete Harnisch	.50	.15
15 Doug Henry	.50	.15
16 Todd Hundley	.75	.23
17 Jason Jacome	.50	.15
18 Bobby Jones	.50	.15
19 Kevin Lomon	.50	.15
20 Josias Manzanillo	.50	.15
21 Blas Minor	.50	.15
22 Dave Mlicki	.50	.15
23 Kevin Northrup	.50	.15
24 Joe Orsulak	.50	.15
25 Ricky Otero	.50	.15
26 Mike Remlinger	.50	.15
27 David Segui	.75	.23
28 Bill Spiers	.50	.15
29 Kelly Stinnett	.50	.15
30 Ryan Thompson	.50	.15
31 Jose Vizcaino	.50	.15
32 Dallas Green MG	.50	.15

1995 Mets Kahn's

This 34-card set was sponsored by Kahn's and was issued with two manufacturer's coupons. The cards are unnumbered and checklisted below in alphabetical order.

Card	Nm-Mt	Ex-Mt
COMPLETE SET (34)	6.00	1.80
1 Edgardo Alfonzo	.75	.23
2 Jeff Barry	.10	.03
3 Tim Bogar	.10	.03
4 Bobby Bonilla	.25	.07
5 Rico Brogna	.10	.03
6 Brett Butler	.75	.23
7 Mike Cubbage CO	.10	.03
8 Jerry DiPoto	.10	.03
9 John Franco	.75	.23
10 Dallas Green MG	.10	.03
11 Eric Gunderson	.10	.03
12 Pete Harnisch	.10	.03
13 Doug Henry	.10	.03
14 Frank Howard CO	.50	.15
15 Todd Hundley	.75	.23
16 Jason Isringhausen	.75	.23
17 Bobby Jones	.10	.03
18 Chris Jones	.10	.03
19 Jeff Kent	.75	.23
20 Aaron Ledesma	.10	.03
21 Tom McCraw CO	.10	.03
22 Dave Mlicki	.10	.03
23 Blas Minor	.10	.03
24 Joe Orsulak	.10	.03
25 Ricky Otero	.10	.03
26 Greg Pavlick CO	.10	.03
27 Bill Pulsipher	.10	.03
28 Bret Saberhagen	.25	.07
29 Bill Spiers	.10	.03
30 Kelly Stinnett	.10	.03
31 Steve Swisher CO	.10	.03
32 Ryan Thompson	.10	.03
33 Jose Vizcaino	.10	.03
34 Bobby Wine CO	.10	.03

1996 Mets Kahn's

This 34-card set was sponsored by Kahn's and issued with two manufacturer's coupons. The fronts display color player photos set on a black background with the team logo at the bottom and red and gray bars across the top. The backs carry player information and career statistics. The cards are unnumbered and checklisted below in alphabetical order.

Card	Nm-Mt	Ex-Mt
COMPLETE SET (34)	12.00	3.60
1 Edgardo Alfonzo	1.00	.30
2 Tim Bogar	.25	.07
3 Rico Brogna	.25	.07
4 Paul Byrd	.25	.07
5 Mark Clark	.25	.07
6 Mike Cubbage CO	.25	.07
7 Jerry DiPoto	.25	.07
8 Carl Everett	.75	.23
9 John Franco	1.00	.30
10 Bernard Gilkey	.25	.07
11 Dallas Green MG	.25	.07
12 Pete Harnisch	.25	.07
13 Doug Henry	.25	.07
14 Frank Howard CO	.50	.15
15 Todd Hundley	1.00	.30
16 Butch Huskey	.25	.07
17 Jason Isringhausen	1.00	.30
18 Lance Johnson	.25	.07
19 Bobby Jones	.25	.07
20 Chris Jones	.25	.07
21 Brent Mayne	.25	.07
22 Tom McCraw CO	.25	.07
23 Dave Mlicki	.25	.07
24 Alex Ochoa	.25	.07
25 Rey Ordonez	.25	.07
26 Greg Pavlick CO	.25	.07
27 Robert Person	.25	.07
28 Bill Pulsipher	.25	.07
29 Steve Swisher CO	.25	.07
30 Andy Tomberlin	.25	.07
31 Paul Wilson	.25	.07
32 Bobby Wine CO	.25	.07
NNO Manufacturer's Coupon	.25	.07
Kahn's Corn Dogs		
NNO Manufacturer's Coupon	.25	.07
Kahn's Hot Dogs		

1998 Mets Postcards

These 35 color cards measure 3 3/4" by 5 1/4" and feature members of the 1998 Mets. The backs have stats and also the player's uniform number. We have sequenced this set alphabetically.

Card	Nm-Mt	Ex-Mt
COMPLETE SET (36)	20.00	6.00
1 Edgardo Alfonzo	1.50	.45
2 Bob Apodaca CO	.50	.15
3 Carlos Baerga	.75	.23
4 Bruce Benedict CO	.50	.15
5 Brian Bohanon	.50	.15
6 Alberto Castillo	.50	.15
7 Dennis Cook	.50	.15
8 John Franco	1.00	.30
9 Matt Franco	.50	.15
10 Bernard Gilkey	.50	.15
11 John Hudek	.50	.15
12 Todd Hundley	.75	.23
13 Butch Huskey	.50	.15
14 Bobby Jones	.50	.15
15 Al Leiter	1.00	.30
16 Luis Lopez	.50	.15
17 Greg McMichael	.50	.15
18 Brian McRae	.50	.15
19 Randy Niemann CO	.50	.15
20 Hideo Nomo	1.50	.45
21 John Olerud	1.00	.30
22 Rey Ordonez	.50	.15
23 Mike Piazza	3.00	.90
24 Rick Reed	.75	.23
25 Armando Reynoso	.50	.15
26 Tom Robson CO	.50	.15
27 Cookie Rojas CO	.50	.15
28 Mel Rojas	.50	.15
29 Tim Spehr	.50	.15
30 Jim Tatum	.50	.15
31 Bobby Valentine MG	.50	.15
32 Turk Wendell	.50	.15
33 Mookie Wilson CO	.75	.23
34 Masato Yoshii	1.00	.30
35 Mr. Met	.50	.15
Mascot		

1999 Mets Postcards

These postcards featured members of the 1999 New York Mets. The only numbering on these cards are by uniform numbers so we have sequenced them alphabetically. The photos are all credited to Marc S. Levine. The cards measure 3 3/4" by 5 1/2" and have biographical backs.

Nm-Mt Ex-Mt

COMPLETE SET 15.00 4.50
1 Edgardo Alfonzo 1.50 .45
2 Armando Benitez 1.50 .45
3 Bobby Bonilla .75 .23
4 Roger Cedeno .75 .23
5 Dennis Cook .50 .15
6 John Franco .75 .23
7 Matt Franco .50 .15
8 Rickey Henderson 2.50 .75
9 Orel Hershiser .75 .23
10 Bobby Jones .50 .15
11 Al Leiter 1.00 .30
12 Luis Lopez .50 .15
13 Greg McMichael .50 .15
14 Brian McRae .50 .15
15 John Olerud 1.00 .30
16 Rey Ordonez .50 .15
17 Mike Piazza 3.00 .90
18 Todd Pratt .50 .15
19 Rick Reed .75 .23
20 Bobby Valentine MG .75 .23
21 Robin Ventura .75 .23
22 Turk Wendell .50 .15
23 Masato Yoshii .75 .23
24 New York Mets .75 .23

2000 Mets Postcards

Similar in size to previous Mets issues, these cards feature the players surrounded by black borders. The players name, uniform number and position are at the top with the words "Amazing again" and "2000 Mets" are at the bottom. The backs have names, numbers, position and some vital stats. A few Rickey Henderson's have surfaced in the secondary market, but as they were pulled very quickly after his leaving the Mets, we have noted that as a short print. As the cards were unnumbered, we have sequenced them in alphabetical order.

Nm-Mt Ex-Mt
COMPLETE SET 30.00 9.00
1 Kurt Abbott .50 .15
2 Benny Agbayani
3 Edgardo Alfonzo 2.00 .60
4 Derek Bell .50 .15
5 Armando Benitez 2.00 .60
6 Dennis Cook .50 .15
7 John Franco 2.00 .60
8 Matt Franco .50 .15
9 Darryl Hamilton .50 .15
10 Mike Hampton 1.50 .45
11 Rickey Henderson SP 12.00 3.60
12 Bobby Jones .50 .15
13 Al Jackson CO .50 .15
14 Al Leiter 1.50 .45
15 Pat Mahomes .50 .15
16 Melvin Mora 1.50 .45
17 Jon Nunnally .50 .15
18 Rey Ordonez .50 .15
19 Jay Payton 1.00 .30
20 Mike Piazza 5.00 1.50
21 Todd Pratt .50 .15
22 Rick Reed .50 .15
23 Tom Robson CO .50 .15
24 Rich Rodriguez .50 .15
25 Cookie Rojas CO .50 .15
26 Glendon Rusch .50 .15
27 John Stearns CO .50 .15
28 Bobby Valentine MG 1.00 .30
29 Robin Ventura 1.00 .30
30 Turk Wendell .50 .15
31 Mookie Wilson CO 1.00 .30
32 Todd Zeile 1.00 .30

2000 Mets Star Ledger

These small cards were sent as part of perforated sheets to only people who sold the Newark Star Ledger. The fronts have a color photo of the player with his name and position on the bottom. The backs have some biographical information, stats from 2000 and some personal information. Since these cards are unnumbered, we have sequenced them in alphabetical order. The Star Ledger did a sheet for both the Yankees and for the Mets.

Nm-Mt Ex-Mt
COMPLETE SET 50.00 15.00
1 Kurt Abbott 1.00 .30
2 Benny Agbayani 2.00 .60
3 Edgardo Alfonzo 4.00 1.20
4 Derek Bell 1.00 .30
5 Armando Benitez 4.00 1.20
6 Mike Bordick 1.00 .30
7 Dennis Cook 1.00 .30
8 John Franco 4.00 1.20
9 Matt Franco 1.00 .30
10 Darryl Hamilton 1.00 .30
11 Mike Hampton 3.00 .90
12 Lenny Harris 1.00 .30
13 Bobby J. Jones 1.00 .30
14 Al Leiter 3.00 .90
15 Pat Mahomes 1.00 .30
16 Joe McEwing 1.00 .30
17 Jay Payton 2.00 .60
18 Timo Perez 3.00 .90
19 Mike Piazza 10.00 3.00
20 Todd Pratt 1.00 .30
21 Rick Reed 1.00 .30
22 Glendon Rusch 1.00 .30
23 Bubba Trammell 1.00 .30
24 Bobby Valentine MG 2.00 .60
25 Robin Ventura 2.00 .60
26 Turk Wendell 1.00 .30
27 Rick White 1.00 .30
28 Todd Zeile 2.00 .60

2001 Mets Team Issue

The 28-card set is measured 3 1/4" x 5 1/2". It has black narrow borders with a photo album-type format. The fronts have the player's name, number and position at the bottom. The Mets' logo is in the upper left-hand corner. The backs have the player's name and number in the top white. Personal info is superimposed on the back over a Mets logo with a facsimile autograph at the bottom. The Mets' address is also at the bottom.

Nm-Mt Ex-Mt
COMPLETE SET (28) 20.00 6.00
1 Benny Agbayani .75 .23
2 Edgardo Alfonzo 1.50 .45
3 Kevin Appier .50 .15
4 Armando Benitez 1.50 .45
5 Dave Engle .50 .15
6 Bob Floyd CO .50 .15
7 John Franco 1.50 .45
8 Lenny Harris .50 .15
9 Charlie Hough CO .50 .15
10 Al Leiter 1.00 .30
11 Joe McEwing .50 .15
12 Randy Niemann CO .50 .15
13 Rey Ordonez .50 .15
14 Jay Payton .75 .23
15 Timo Perez .50 .15
16 Mike Piazza 3.00 .90
17 Desi Relaford .50 .15
18 Glendon Rusch .50 .15
19 Tsuyoshi Shinjo 1.50 .45
20 John Stearns CO .50 .15
21 Jorge Luis Toca .50 .15
22 Steve Trachsel .50 .15
23 Bobby Valentine MG .75 .23
24 Robin Ventura 1.00 .30
25 Donne Wall .50 .15
26 Rick White .50 .15
27 Mookie Wilson CO .75 .23
28 Todd Zeile .75 .23

2002 Mets 40th Anniversary Fleer

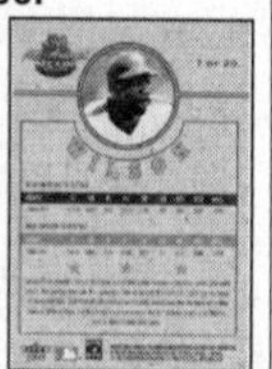

This 20 card standard-size set was given away at a Mets game during the 2002 season. These were the players voted on by fans as their all-time Mets to celebrate the Mets 40th anniversary in the National League. The fronts have the players photo on the top with their name, position and uniform number on the bottom. The backs have Met and total career statistics along with some interesting player facts.

Nm-Mt Ex-Mt
COMPLETE SET (20) 10.00 3.00
1 Gil Hodges MG 1.50 .45
2 Keith Hernandez 1.00 .30
3 Edgardo Alfonzo 1.00 .30
4 Howard Johnson .50 .15
5 Bud Harrelson .25 .07
6 Mike Piazza 2.00 .60
7 Mookie Wilson .50 .15
8 Darryl Strawberry .50 .15
9 Lenny Dykstra .50 .15
10 Tom Seaver 3.00 .90
11 Jerry Koosman .50 .15
12 Roger McDowell .25 .07
13 John Franco .50 .15
14 Ed Kranepool .25 .07
15 Rusty Staub .75 .23
16 Bob Murphy ANN .50 .15
17 Ralph Kiner ANN 1.00 .30
18 New York Mets 1962 Team Photo .50 .15
19 New York Mets 1969 Team Photo .50 .15
20 New York Mets 1986 Team Photo .50 .15

2002 Mets Fleer 9/11

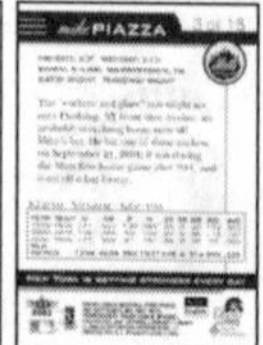

This 15-card set, which was designed to be given away at a Mets game on 9/11, was released only im limited circulation. The cards feature UV Coating along with the player's photo as well as the "Statue of Liberty" in the background. The back of the card features information about how to continue dealing with the horrific events of 9/11/2001 as well as information about the player.

Nm-Mt Ex-Mt
COMPLETE SET 15.00 4.50
1 New York Mets .75 .23
Team Photo
2 Al Leiter 1.00 .30
3 Mike Piazza 3.00 .90
4 Al Leiter 1.00 .30
Wearing Police Cap
5 Mo Vaughn .75 .23
6 Roberto Alomar 1.50 .45
7 Edgardo Alfonzo 1.50 .45
8 Uniform Patch .50 .15
9/11/01
9 Rey Ordonez .50 .15
10 Roger Cedeno .50 .15
11 Timo Perez .50 .15
12 Mike Piazza 5.00 1.50
NYPD Helmet
13 Jeromy Burnitz .75 .23
14 Bobby Valentine MG .50 .15
15 United States Flag .50 .15

2002 Mets Palm Beach Post

This 10 card standard-size set was issued as inserts by the Palm Beach Post where the New York Mets went to spring training. The front has a posed action shot while the back has basic biographical information. Since these cards are unnumbered, except for uniform number, we have sequenced them in alphabetical order.

Nm-Mt Ex-Mt
COMPLETE SET 10.00 3.00
1 Edgardo Alfonzo 1.50 .45
2 Armando Benitez 1.50 .45
3 John Franco 1.50 .45
4 Al Leiter 1.00 .30
5 Joe McEwing .50 .15
6 Rey Ordonez .50 .15
7 Jay Payton .75 .23
8 Timo Perez .50 .15
9 Mike Piazza 3.00 .90
10 Bobby Valentine MG .75 .23

2003 Mets Team Issue

This 36-card set, which measures approximately 3 3/4" by 5 1/2" was issued as a complete set from the Mets. The cards are mainly action shots with the player's name, position and uniform number on the bottom. The backs have player information as well as a fascimile autograph. Since these cards are unnumbered, we have sequenced them in alphabetical order.

MINT NRMT
COMPLETE SET 20.00 9.00
1 Roberto Alomar 1.50 .70
2 Pedro Astacio .50 .23
3 Don Baylor CO .75 .35
4 Jay Bell .50 .23
5 Armando Benitez 1.50 .70
6 Jeromy Burnitz .75 .35
7 Jaime Cerda .50 .23
8 Roger Cedeno .50 .23
9 Tony Clark .50 .23
10 David Cone 1.50 .70
11 Cliff Floyd 1.00 .45
12 John Franco 1.50 .70
13 Matt Galante CO .50 .23
14 Tom Glavine 1.50 .70
15 Art Howe MG .50 .23
16 Al Leiter .50 .23
17 Graeme Lloyd .50 .23
18 Juan Lopez .50 .23
19 Joe McEwing .50 .23
20 Timo Perez .50 .23
21 Gary Pettis CO .50 .23
22 Mike Piazza 2.50 1.10
23 Grant Roberts .75 .35
24 Vern Ruhle CO .50 .23
25 Rey Sanchez .50 .23
26 Jae Seo 1.50 .70
27 Tsuyoshi Shinjo .75 .35
28 Mike Stanton .50 .23
29 Scott Strickland .50 .23
30 Steve Trachsel .75 .35
31 Mo Vaughn .75 .35
32 Rick Waits CO .50 .23
33 Denny Walling CO .50 .23
34 David Weathers
35 Ty Wigginton 1.50 .70
36 Vance Wilson .75 .35

1993 Metz Baking

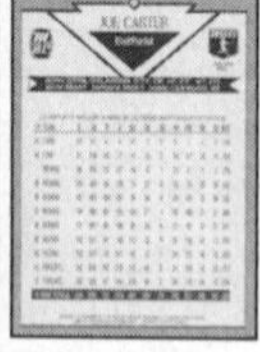

This 40-card standard-size set was produced by MSA (Michael Schechter Associates) for Metz Baking Co. The cards were issued in two series and feature on their fronts oval color drawings of the players with team names or logos airbrushed from their caps and uniforms. One card was inserted into packages of Metz products distributed in the Midwest. The cards are unnumbered and checklisted below in alphabetical order within each 20-card series.

Nm-Mt Ex-Mt
COMPLETE SET (40) 8.00 2.40
1 Wade Boggs .50 .15
2 Barry Bonds 1.50 .45
3 Bobby Bonilla .05 .02
4 Joe Carter .10 .03
5 Roger Clemens 1.50 .45
6 Doug Drabek .05 .02
7 Cecil Fielder .10 .03
8 Dwight Gooden .10 .03
9 Ken Griffey Jr. 2.50 .75
10 Tony Gwynn 1.50 .45
11 Howard Johnson .05 .02
12 Wally Joyner .10 .03
13 Dave Justice .20 .06
14 Don Mattingly 1.50 .45
15 Jack McDowell .05 .02
16 Kirby Puckett .50 .15
17 Cal Ripken 3.00 .90
18 Ryne Sandberg 1.25 .35
19 Darryl Strawberry .10 .03
20 Danny Tartabull .05 .02
21 Dante Bichette .10 .03
22 Jose Canseco .40 .12
23 Will Clark .50 .15
24 Shawon Dunston .05 .02
25 Dennis Eckersley .40 .12
26 Carlton Fisk .50 .15
27 Andres Galarraga .20 .06
28 Kirk Gibson .10 .03
29 Mark Grace .20 .06
30 Rickey Henderson .75 .23
31 Kent Hrbek .10 .03
32 Barry Larkin .20 .06
33 Paul Molitor .40 .12
34 Terry Pendleton .05 .02
35 Nolan Ryan 3.00 .90
36 Ozzie Smith 1.00 .30
37 Mickey Tettleton .05 .02
38 Alan Trammell .15 .04
39 Andy Van Slyke .05 .02
40 Dave Winfield .50 .15

1927 Middy Bread

These 44 cards blank-backed, which measure approximately 2 1/4" by 4" were issued in the St Louis area and feature members of the Browns and Cardinals. It seems as if 22 cards for each of the teams were issued. Since the cards are unnumbered, we have sequenced them alphabetically by team with the Cardinals from card 1 through 22 and the Browns from 23 through 44. A Ross Youngs card was recently discovered and looks as if it fits in this set. More information about that card is certainly appreciated.

Ex-Mt VG
COMPLETE SET (44) 5000.00 2500.00
1 Grover Alexander 400.00 200.00
2 Herman Bell 100.00 50.00
3 Lester Bell 100.00 50.00
4 Ray Blades 100.00 50.00
5 Jim Bottomley 200.00 100.00
6 Danny Clark 100.00 50.00
7 Taylor Douthit 100.00 50.00
8 Frank Frisch 250.00 125.00
9 Chick Hafey 200.00 100.00
10 Jesse Haines 200.00 100.00
11 Vic Keen 100.00 50.00
12 Bob McGraw 100.00 50.00
13 Bob O'Farrell 100.00 50.00
14 Art Reinhardt 100.00 50.00
15 Jimmy Ring 100.00 50.00
16 Walter Roettger 100.00 50.00
17 Robert Schang 100.00 50.00
18 Willie Sherdel 100.00 50.00
19 Billy Southworth 120.00 60.00
20 Tommy Thevenow 100.00 50.00
21 George Toporcer 100.00 50.00
22 Spencer Adams 100.00 50.00
23 Win Ballou 100.00 50.00
24 Walter Beck 100.00 50.00
25 Herschel Bennett 100.00 50.00
26 Stewart Bolen 100.00 50.00
27 Leo Dixon 100.00 50.00
28 Chester Falk 100.00 50.00
29 Milt Gaston 100.00 50.00
30 Walter Gerber 100.00 50.00
31 Sam Jones 120.00 60.00
32 Carlisle Littlejohn 100.00 50.00
33 Oscar Melillo 100.00 50.00
34 Bing Miller 120.00 60.00
35 Otis Miller 100.00 50.00
36 Billie Mullen 100.00 50.00
37 Ernie Nevers 200.00 100.00
38 Steve O'Neil 120.00 60.00
39 Harry Rice 100.00 50.00
40 George Sisler 250.00 125.00
41 Walter Stewart 100.00 50.00
42 Elom Van Gilder 100.00 50.00
43 Ken Williams 150.00 75.00
44 Ernie Wingard 100.00 50.00
45 Ross Youngs 200.00 100.00

1993 Milk Bone Super Stars

This 20-card standard-size set was featured in specially marked packages of Milk Bone Flavor Snacks and Dog Treats. Two cards were inserted in each package. Also the complete set could be obtained by sending in a mail-in form along with three Super Star Seals plus 2.50.

Nm-Mt Ex-Mt
COMPLETE SET (20) 15.00 4.50
1 Paul Molitor 1.50 .45
2 Tom Glavine 1.50 .45
3 Barry Larkin 1.00 .30
4 Mark McGwire 6.00 1.80
5 Bill Swift .25 .07
6 Ken Caminiti .75 .23
7 Will Clark 1.50 .45
8 Rafael Palmeiro 1.00 .30
9 Matt Young .25 .07
10 Todd Zeile .50 .15
11 Wally Joyner .50 .15
12 Cal Ripken 8.00 2.40
13 Tom Foley .25 .07
14 Ben McDonald .25 .07
15 Larry Walker 1.00 .30
16 Rob Dibble .25 .07
17 Brett Butler .50 .15
18 Joe Girardi .25 .07
19 Brady Anderson .50 .15
20 Craig Biggio .75 .23

1971 Milk Duds

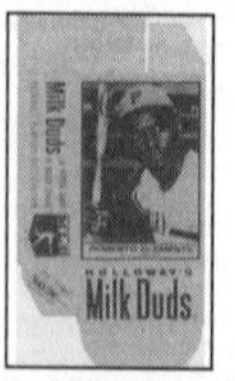

The cards in this 69-card set measure 1 13/16" by 2 5/8". The 1971 Milk Duds set contains 32 American League cards and 37 National League cards. The cards are actually numbered, but the very small number appears only on the flap of the box; nevertheless the numbers below are ordered alphabetically by player's name within league. American Leaguers are numbered 1-32 and National Leaguers 33-69. The cards are sepia toned on a tan background and were issued on the backs of five-cent boxes of Milk Duds candy. The prices listed in the checklist are for complete boxes. Cards cut from boxes are approximately one-half of the listed price. The names of three of the players in the set were misspelled and are noted in the checklist below as errors. Three of the boxes were double printed, i.e., twice as many were produced or printed compared to the other players. These double-printed players are indicated below by DP in the checklist after the player's name. According to published reports around the time of issue, Dick Bosman was supposedly going to be in this set but a bad photo negated his card being printed.

NM Ex
COMPLETE SET (69) 1000.00 400.00
COMMON DP 15.00 6.00
1 Luis Aparicio 20.00 8.00
2 Stan Bahnsen 8.00 3.20
3 Danny Cater 8.00 3.20
4 Ray Culp 8.00 3.20
5 Ray Fosse 8.00 3.20
6 Bill Freehan 12.00 4.80
7 Jim Fregosi 10.00 4.00
8 Tommy Harper 8.00 3.20
9 Frank Howard 12.00 4.80
10 Jim Hunter 25.00 10.00
11 Tommy John 12.00 4.80
12 Alex Johnson 8.00 3.20
13 Dave Johnson 10.00 4.00
14 Harmon Killebrew DP 15.00 6.00
15 Sam McDowell 10.00 4.00
16 Dave McNally 8.00 3.20
17 Bill Melton 8.00 3.20
18 Andy Messersmith 8.00 3.20
19 Thurman Munson 20.00 8.00
20 Tony Oliva 15.00 6.00
21 Jim Palmer 20.00 8.00
22 Jim Perry 10.00 4.00
23 Fritz Peterson 8.00 3.20
24 Rico Petrocelli 8.00 3.20
25 Boog Powell 12.00 4.80
26 Brooks Robinson DP 15.00 6.00
27 Frank Robinson 30.00 12.00
28 George Scott 8.00 3.20
29 Reggie Smith 10.00 4.00
30 Mel Stottlemyer ERR 10.00 4.00
(sic, Stottlemyre)
31 Cesar Tovar 8.00 3.20
32 Roy White 8.00 3.20
33 Hank Aaron 60.00 24.00
34 Ernie Banks 40.00 16.00
35 Glen Beckert ERR 8.00 3.20
(sic, Glenn)
36 Johnny Bench 50.00 20.00
37 Lou Brock 30.00 12.00
38 Rico Carty 10.00 4.00
39 Orlando Cepeda 20.00 8.00
40 Roberto Clemente 100.00 40.00
41 Willie Davis 8.00 3.20
42 Dick Dietz 8.00 3.20
43 Bob Gibson 20.00 8.00
44 Bill Grabarkewitz 8.00 3.20
45 Bud Harrelson 8.00 3.20
46 Jim Hickman 8.00 3.20
47 Ken Holtzman 8.00 3.20
48 Randy Hundley 8.00 3.20
49 Fergie Jenkins 20.00 8.00
50 Don Kessinger 10.00 4.00
51 Willie Mays 60.00 24.00
52 Willie McCovey 20.00 8.00
53 Dennis Menke 8.00 3.20
54 Jim Merritt 8.00 3.20
55 Felix Millan 8.00 3.20
56 Claud Osteen ERR 8.00 3.20
(sic, Claude)
57 Milt Pappas 10.00 4.00
(pictured in
Oriole uniform)
58 Tony Perez 20.00 8.00
59 Gaylord Perry 20.00 8.00
60 Pete Rose DP 30.00 12.00
61 Manny Sanguillen 10.00 4.00
62 Ron Santo 15.00 6.00
63 Tom Seaver 30.00 12.00
64 Wayne Simpson 8.00 3.20
65 Rusty Staub 12.00 4.80
66 Bobby Tolan 8.00 3.20
67 Joe Torre 15.00 6.00

Card	NM	Ex
68 Luke Walker	8.00	3.20
69 Billy Williams	20.00	8.00

1969 Milton Bradley

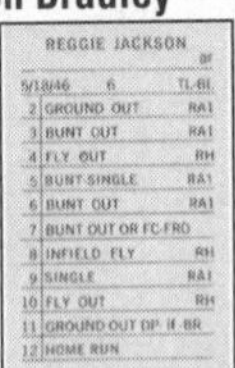

These cards were distributed as part of a baseball game produced by Milton Bradley in 1969. The cards each measure approximately 2" by 3" and have square corners. The card fronts show a black and white photo of the player with his name above the photo in a white border. The game outcomes are printed on the card backs. The game was played by rolling two dice. The outcomes (two through twelve) on the back of the player's card related to the sum of the two dice. The card backs are printed in red and black on white card stock; the player's name on back and successful outcomes for the batter such as hits are printed in red. Team logos have been airbrushed from the photos in this set. The cards are typically found with perforation notches visible. Since the cards are unnumbered, they are listed below in alphabetical order. One way to tell the 1969 and 1972 Milton Bradley sets apart is that the 1969 cards all the red digits 1 do not have a base while the 1972 red digit cards all have a base.

	NM	Ex
COMPLETE SET (296)	225.00	90.00
1 Hank Aaron	15.00	6.00
2 Ted Abernathy	.25	.10
3 Jerry Adair	.25	.10
4 Tommy Agee	.25	.10
5 Bernie Allen	.25	.10
6 Hank Allen	.25	.10
7 Richie Allen	1.00	.40
8 Gene Alley	.25	.10
9 Bob Allison	.50	.20
10 Felipe Alou	1.00	.40
11 Jesus Alou	.25	.10
12 Matty Alou	.50	.20
13 Max Alvis	.25	.10
14 Mike Andrews	.25	.10
15 Luis Aparicio	4.00	1.60
16 Jose Arcia	.25	.10
17 Bob Aspromonte	.25	.10
18 Joe Azcue	.25	.10
19 Ernie Banks	8.00	3.20
20 Steve Barber	.25	.10
21 John Bateman	.25	.10
22 Glenn Beckert	.25	.10
23 Gary Bell	.25	.10
24 Johnny Bench	20.00	8.00
25 Ken Berry	.25	.10
26 Frank Bertaina	.25	.10
27 Paul Blair	.25	.10
28 Wade Blasingame	.25	.10
29 Curt Blefary	.25	.10
30 John Boccabella	.25	.10
31 Bobby Bonds	4.00	1.60
32 Sam Bowens	.25	.10
33 Ken Boyer	1.00	.40
34 Charles Bradford	.25	.10
35 Darrell Brandon	.25	.10
36 Jim Brewer	.25	.10
37 John Briggs	.25	.10
38 Nelson Briles	.25	.10
39 Ed Brinkman	.25	.10
40 Lou Brock	6.00	2.40
41 Gates Brown	.25	.10
42 Larry Brown	.25	.10
43 George Brunet	.25	.10
44 Jerry Buchek	.25	.10
45 Don Buford	.25	.10
46 Jim Bunning	4.00	1.60
47 Johnny Callison	.75	.30
48 Bert Campaneris	.75	.30
49 Jose Cardenal	.25	.10
50 Leo Cardenas	.25	.10
51 Don Cardwell	.25	.10
52 Rod Carew	8.00	3.20
53 Paul Casanova	.25	.10
54 Norm Cash	1.00	.40
55 Danny Cater	.25	.10
56 Orlando Cepeda	3.00	1.20
57 Dean Chance	.50	.20
58 Ed Charles	.25	.10
59 Horace Clarke	.25	.10
60 Roberto Clemente	25.00	10.00
61 Donn Clendenon	.25	.10
62 Ty Cline	.25	.10
63 Nate Colbert	.25	.10
64 Joe Coleman	.25	.10
65 Bob Cox	3.00	1.20
66 Mike Cuellar	1.00	.40
67 Ray Culp	.25	.10
68 Clay Dalrymple	.25	.10
69 Jim Davenport	.25	.10
70 Vic Davalillo	.25	.10
71 Ron Davis	.25	.10
72 Tommy Davis	.75	.30
73 Willie Davis	.50	.20
74 Chuck Dobson	.25	.10
75 John Donaldson	.25	.10
76 Al Downing	.25	.10
77 Moe Drabowsky	.25	.10
78 Dick Ellsworth	.25	.10
79 Mike Epstein	.25	.10
80 Andy Etchebarren	.25	.10
81 Ron Fairly	.50	.20
82 Dick Farrell	.25	.10
83 Curt Flood	1.00	.40
84 Joe Foy	.25	.10
85 Tito Francona	.25	.10
86 Bill Freehan	1.00	.40
87 Jim Fregosi	.75	.30
88 Woodie Fryman	.25	.10
89 Len Gabrielson	.25	.10
90 Clarence Gaston	.75	.30
91 Jake Gibbs	.25	.10
92 Russ Gibson	.25	.10
93 Dave Giusti	.25	.10
94 Tony Gonzalez	.25	.10
95 Jim Gosger	.25	.10
96 Julio Gotay	.25	.10
97 Dick Green	.25	.10
98 Jerry Grote	.50	.20
99 Jimmie Hall	.25	.10
100 Tom Haller	.25	.10
101 Steve Hamilton	.25	.10
102 Ron Hansen	.25	.10
103 Jim Hardin	.25	.10
104 Tommy Harper	.50	.20
105 Bud Harrelson	.50	.20
106 Ken Harrelson	1.00	.40
107 Jim Ray Hart	.25	.10
108 Woodie Held	.25	.10
109 Tommy Helms	.25	.10
110 Elrod Hendricks	.25	.10
111 Mike Hershberger	.25	.10
112 Jack Hiatt	.25	.10
113 Jim Hickman	.25	.10
114 John Hiller	.25	.10
115 Chuck Hinton	.25	.10
116 Ken Holtzman	.50	.20
117 Joel Horlen	.25	.10
118 Tony Horton	.50	.20
119 Willie Horton	.75	.30
120 Frank Howard	1.00	.40
121 Dick Howser	.25	.10
122 Randy Hundley	.25	.10
123 Ron Hunt	.25	.10
124 Jim Hunter	4.00	1.60
125 Al Jackson	.25	.10
126 Larry Jackson	.25	.10
127 Reggie Jackson	20.00	8.00
128 Sonny Jackson	.25	.10
129 Pat Jarvis	.25	.10
130 Julian Javier	.25	.10
131 Ferguson Jenkins	4.00	1.60
132 Manny Jimenez	.25	.10
133 Tommy John	2.00	.80
134 Bob Johnson	.25	.10
135 Dave Johnson	1.00	.40
136 Deron Johnson	.25	.10
137 Lou Johnson	.25	.10
138 Jay Johnstone	1.00	.40
139 Cleon Jones	.50	.20
140 Dalton Jones	.25	.10
141 Duane Josephson	.25	.10
142 Jim Kaat	2.00	.80
143 Al Kaline	8.00	3.20
144 Don Kessinger	.50	.20
145 Harmon Killebrew	5.00	2.00
146 Hal King	.25	.10
147 Ed Kirkpatrick	.25	.10
148 Fred Klages	.25	.10
149 Ron Kline	.25	.10
150 Bobby Knoop	.25	.10
151 Gary Kolb	.25	.10
152 Andy Kosco	.25	.10
153 Ed Kranepool	.50	.20
154 Lew Krausse	.25	.10
155 Hal Lanier	.25	.10
156 Jim LeFebvre	.25	.10
157 Denny Lemaster	.25	.10
158 Dave Leonhard	.25	.10
159 Don Lock	.25	.10
160 Mickey Lolich	1.00	.40
161 Jim Lonborg	.75	.30
162 Mike Lum	.25	.10
163 Sparky Lyle	2.50	1.00
164 Jim Maloney	.50	.20
165 Juan Marichal	4.00	1.60
166 J.C. Martin	.25	.10
167 Marty Martinez	.25	.10
168 Tom Matchick	.25	.10
169 Ed Mathews	5.00	2.00
170 Jerry May	.25	.10
171 Lee May	.50	.20
172 Lee Maye	.25	.10
173 Willie Mays	15.00	6.00
174 Dal Maxvill	.25	.10
175 Bill Mazeroski	2.00	.80
176 Dick McAuliffe	.25	.10
177 Al McBean	.25	.10
178 Tim McCarver	1.00	.40
179 Bill McCool	.25	.10
180 Mike McCormick	.50	.20
181 Willie McCovey	5.00	2.00
182 Tom McCraw	.25	.10
183 Lindy McDaniel	.25	.10
184 Sam McDowell	.75	.30
185 Orlando McFarlane	.25	.10
186 Jim McGlothlin	.25	.10
187 Denny McLain	1.00	.40
188 Ken McMullen	.25	.10
189 Dave McNally	.75	.30
190 Gerry McNertney	.25	.10
191 Denis Menke	.25	.10
192 Felix Millan	.25	.10
193 Don Mincher	.25	.10
194 Rick Monday	.50	.20
195 Joe Morgan	5.00	2.00
196 Bubba Morton	.25	.10
197 Manny Mota	.50	.20
198 Jim Nash	.25	.10
199 Dave Nelson	.25	.10
200 Dick Nen	.25	.10
201 Phil Niekro	4.00	1.60
202 Jim Northrup	.50	.20
203 Rich Nye	.25	.10
204 Johnny Odom	.25	.10
205 Tony Oliva	2.00	.80
206 Gene Oliver	.25	.10
207 Phil Ortega	.25	.10
208 Claude Osteen	.50	.20
209 Ray Oyler	.25	.10
210 Jose Pagan	.25	.10
211 Jim Pagliaroni	.25	.10
212 Milt Pappas	.50	.20
213 Wes Parker	.50	.20
214 Camilo Pascual	.25	.10
215 Don Pavletich	.25	.10
216 Joe Pepitone	.75	.30
217 Tony Perez	3.00	1.20
218 Gaylord Perry	4.00	1.60
219 Jim Perry	1.00	.40
220 Gary Peters	.25	.10
221 Rico Petrocelli	.50	.20
222 Adolpho Phillips	.25	.10
223 Tom Phoebus	.25	.10
224 Vada Pinson	1.00	.40
225 Boog Powell	2.00	.80
226 Frank Quilici	.25	.10
227 Doug Rader	.25	.10
228 Rich Reese	.25	.10
229 Phil Regan	.25	.10
230 Rick Reichardt	.25	.10
231 Rick Renick	.25	.10
232 Roger Repoz	.25	.10
233 Dave Ricketts	.25	.10
234 Bill Robinson	.25	.10
235 Brooks Robinson	8.00	3.20
236 Frank Robinson	8.00	3.20
237 Bob Rodgers	.25	.10
238 Cookie Rojas	.25	.10
239 Rich Rollins	.25	.10
240 Phil Roof	.25	.10
241 Pete Rose	12.00	4.80
242 John Roseboro	.50	.20
243 Chico Ruiz	.25	.10
244 Ray Sadecki	.25	.10
245 Chico Salmon	.25	.10
246 Jose Santiago	.25	.10
247 Ron Santo	1.00	.40
248 Tom Satriano	.25	.10
249 Paul Schaal	.25	.10
250 Tom Seaver	12.00	4.80
251 Art Shamsky	.25	.10
252 Mike Shannon	.75	.30
253 Chris Short	.25	.10
254 Dick Simpson	.25	.10
255 Duke Sims	.25	.10
256 Reggie Smith	1.00	.40
257 Willie Smith	.25	.10
258 Russ Snyder	.25	.10
259 Al Spangler	.25	.10
260 Larry Stahl	.25	.10
261 Lee Stange	.25	.10
262 Mickey Stanley	.25	.10
263 Willie Stargell	5.00	2.00
264 Rusty Staub	1.00	.40
265 Mel Stottlemyre	1.00	.40
266 Ed Stroud	.25	.10
267 Don Sutton	4.00	1.60
268 Ron Swoboda	.50	.20
269 Jose Tartabull	.25	.10
270 Tony Taylor	.50	.20
271 Luis Tiant	1.00	.40
272 Bill Tillman	.25	.10
273 Bobby Tolan	.25	.10
274 Jeff Torborg	.25	.10
275 Joe Torre	2.50	1.00
276 Cesar Tovar	.25	.10
277 Dick Tracewski	.25	.10
278 Tom Tresh	1.00	.40
279 Ted Uhlaender	.25	.10
280 Del Unser	.25	.10
281 Sandy Valdespino	.25	.10
282 Fred Valentine	.25	.10
283 Bob Veale	.25	.10
284 Zoilo Versalles	.50	.20
285 Pete Ward	.25	.10
286 Al Weis	.25	.10
287 Don Wert	.25	.10
288 Bill White	1.00	.40
289 Roy White	.50	.20
290 Fred Whitfield	.25	.10
291 Hoyt Wilhelm	4.00	1.60
292 Billy Williams	4.00	1.60
293 Maury Wills	2.00	.80
294 Earl Wilson	.25	.10
295 Wilbur Wood	.25	.10
296 Jerry Zimmerman	.25	.10

1970 Milton Bradley

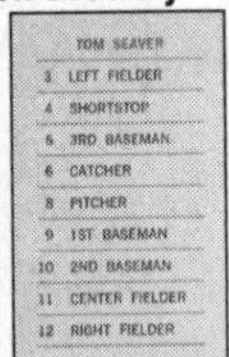

These cards were distributed as part of a baseball game produced by Milton Bradley in 1970. The cards each measure approximately 2 3/16" by 3 1/2" and have rounded corners. The card fronts show a black and white photo of the player with his name and vital statistics below the photo in a white border. The game outcomes are printed on the card backs. The card backs are printed in red and black on white card stock; the player's name is printed in red at the top of the card. Team logos have been airbrushed from the photos in this set. Since the cards are unnumbered, they are listed below in alphabetical order. Thirty two game cards were also included in the original box, those cards are not priced here. This set is sometimes found in the original box and unwrapped. If the cards are in that condition, there is a 25 percent premium for the set.

	NM	Ex
COMPLETE SET (28)	150.00	60.00
1 Hank Aaron	20.00	8.00
2 Lou Brock	8.00	3.20
3 Ernie Banks	8.00	3.20
4 Rod Carew	10.00	4.00
5 Roberto Clemente	25.00	10.00
6 Tommy Davis	.75	.30
7 Bill Freehan	.75	.30
8 Jim Fregosi	.75	.30
9 Tom Haller	.50	.20
10 Frank Howard	1.00	.40
11 Reggie Jackson	15.00	6.00
12 Harmon Killebrew	5.00	2.00
13 Mickey Lolich	1.00	.40
14 Juan Marichal	5.00	2.00
15 Willie Mays	20.00	8.00
16 Willie McCovey	6.00	2.40
17 Sam McDowell	.75	.30
18 Denis Menke	.50	.20
19 Don Mincher	.50	.20
20 Phil Niekro	5.00	2.00
21 Rico Petrocelli	.75	.30
22 Boog Powell	1.50	.60
23 Frank Robinson	8.00	3.20
24 Pete Rose	12.00	4.80
25 Ron Santo	1.50	.60
26 Tom Seaver	12.00	4.80
27 Mel Stottlemyre	.75	.30
28 Tony Taylor	.50	.20

1972 Milton Bradley

These cards were distributed as part of a baseball game produced by Milton Bradley in 1972. The cards each measure approximately 2" by 3" and have square corners. The card fronts show a black and white photo of the player with his name above the photo in a white border. The game outcomes are printed on the card backs. The game was played by rolling two dice. The outcomes (two through twelve) on the back of the player's card related to the sum of the two dice. The card backs are printed in red and black on white card stock; successful outcomes for the batter such as hits are printed in red. Team logos have been airbrushed from the photos in this set. The cards are typically found with perforation notches visible. Since the cards are unnumbered, they are listed below in alphabetical order.

	NM	Ex
COMPLETE SET (372)	250.00	100.00
1 Hank Aaron	30.00	12.00
2 Tommie Aaron	.25	.10
3 Ted Abernathy	.25	.10
4 Jerry Adair	.25	.10
5 Tommy Agee	.50	.20
6 Bernie Allen	.25	.10
7 Hank Allen	.25	.10
8 Richie Allen	2.50	1.00
9 Gene Alley	.25	.10
10 Bob Allison	.25	.10
11 Sandy Alomar	.25	.10
12 Felipe Alou	1.00	.40
13 Jesus Alou	.50	.20
14 Matty Alou	.75	.30
15 Max Alvis	.25	.10
16 Brant Alyea	.25	.10
17 Mike Andrews	.25	.10
18 Luis Aparicio	5.00	2.00
19 Jose Arcia	.25	.10
20 Jerry Arrigo	.25	.10
21 Bob Aspromonte	.25	.10
22 Joe Azcue	.25	.10
23 Bob Bailey	.25	.10
24 Sal Bando	1.00	.40
25 Ernie Banks	12.00	4.80
26 Steve Barber	.25	.10
27 Bob Barton	.25	.10
28 John Bateman	.25	.10
29 Glenn Beckert	.50	.20
30 Johnny Bench	15.00	6.00
31 Ken Berry	.25	.10
32 Frank Bertaina	.25	.10
33 Paul Blair	.50	.20
34 Steve Blass	.25	.10
35 Curt Blefary	.25	.10
36 Bobby Bolin	.25	.10
37 Bobby Bonds	2.50	1.00
38 Don Bosch	.25	.10
39 Dick Bosman	.25	.10
40 Dave Boswell	.25	.10
41 Ken Boswell	.25	.10
42 Cletis Boyer	.75	.30
43 Charles Bradford	.25	.10
44 Ron Brand	.25	.10
45 Ken Brett	.25	.10
46 Jim Brewer	.25	.10
47 John Briggs	.25	.10
48 Nelson Briles	.25	.10
49 Ed Brinkman	.25	.10
50 Jim Britton	.25	.10
51 Lou Brock	10.00	4.00
52 Gates Brown	.25	.10
53 Larry Brown	.25	.10
54 Ollie Brown	.25	.10
55 George Brunet	.25	.10
56 Don Buford	.25	.10
57 Wally Bunker	.25	.10
58 Jim Bunning	5.00	2.00
59 Bill Butler	.25	.10
60 Johnny Callison	.75	.30
61 Bert Campaneris	.75	.30
62 Jose Cardenal	.25	.10
63 Leo Cardenas	.25	.10
64 Don Cardwell	.25	.10
65 Rod Carew	10.00	4.00
66 Cisco Carlos	.25	.10
67 Steve Carlton	12.00	4.80
68 Clay Carroll	.25	.10
69 Paul Casanova	.25	.10
70 Norm Cash	2.50	1.00
71 Danny Cater	.25	.10
72 Orlando Cepeda	4.00	1.60
73 Dean Chance	.50	.20
74 Horace Clarke	.25	.10
75 Roberto Clemente	40.00	16.00
76 Donn Clendenon	.25	.10
77 Ty Cline	.25	.10
78 Nate Colbert	.25	.10
79 Joe Coleman	.25	.10
80 Billy Conigliaro	.25	.10
81 Casey Cox	.25	.10
82 Mike Cuellar	.75	.30
83 Ray Culp	.25	.10
84 George Culver	.25	.10
85 Jim Davenport	.25	.10
86 Vic Davalillo	.25	.10
87 Tommy Davis	.75	.30
88 Willie Davis	.50	.20
89 Larry Dierker	.50	.20
90 Dick Dietz	.25	.10
91 Chuck Dobson	.25	.10
92 Pat Dobson	.25	.10
93 John Donaldson	.25	.10
94 Al Downing	.25	.10
95 Moe Drabowsky	.25	.10
96 John Edwards	.25	.10
97 Thomas Egan	.25	.10
98 Dick Ellsworth	.25	.10
99 Mike Epstein	.25	.10
100 Andy Etchebarren	.25	.10
101 Ron Fairly	.75	.30
102 Frank Fernandez	.25	.10
103 Al Ferrara	.25	.10
104 Mike Fiore	.25	.10
105 Curt Flood	1.00	.40
106 Joe Foy	.25	.10
107 Tito Francona	.25	.10
108 Bill Freehan	1.00	.40
109 Jim Fregosi	.75	.30
110 Woodie Fryman	.25	.10
111 Vern Fuller	.25	.10
112 Phil Gagliano	.25	.10
113 Clarence Gaston	.25	.10
114 Jake Gibbs	.25	.10
115 Russ Gibson	.25	.10
116 Dave Giusti	.25	.10
117 Fred Gladding	.25	.10
118 Tony Gonzalez	.25	.10
119 Jim Gosger	.25	.10
120 Jim Grant	.25	.10
121 Dick Green	.25	.10
122 Tom Griffin	.25	.10
123 Jerry Grote	.25	.10
124 Tom Hall	.25	.10
125 Tom Haller	.25	.10
126 Steve Hamilton	.25	.10
127 Bill Hands	.25	.10
128 Jim Hannan	.25	.10
129 Ron Hansen	.25	.10
130 Jim Hardin	.25	.10
131 Steve Hargan	.25	.10
132 Tommy Harper	.50	.20
133 Bud Harrelson	.50	.20
134 Ken Harrelson	1.00	.40
135 Jim Ray Hart	.25	.10
136 Richie Hebner	.50	.20
137 Mike Hedlund	.25	.10
138 Tommy Helms	.25	.10
139 Elrod Hendricks	.25	.10
140 Ron Herbel	.25	.10
141 Jackie Hernandez	.25	.10
142 Mike Hershberger	.25	.10
143 Jack Hiatt	.25	.10
144 Dennis Higgins	.25	.10
146 John Hiller	.25	.10
147 Chuck Hinton	.25	.10
148 Larry Hisle	.25	.10
149 Ken Holtzman	.50	.20
150 Joel Horlen	.25	.10
151 Tony Horton	.25	.10
152 Willie Horton	.75	.30
153 Frank Howard	1.00	.40
154 Bob Humphreys	.25	.10
155 Randy Hundley	.25	.10
156 Ron Hunt	.25	.10
157 Jim Hunter	5.00	2.00
158 Grant Jackson	.25	.10
159 Reggie Jackson	20.00	8.00
160 Sonny Jackson	.25	.10
161 Pat Jarvis	.25	.10
162 Larry Jaster	.25	.10
163 Julian Javier	.25	.10
164 Ferguson Jenkins	5.00	2.00
165 Tommy John	2.50	1.00
166 Alex Johnson	.50	.20
167 Bob Johnson	.25	.10
168 Dave Johnson	1.00	.40
169 Deron Johnson	.25	.10
170 Jay Johnstone	.50	.20
171 Cleon Jones	.50	.20
172 Dalton Jones	.25	.10
173 Mack Jones	.25	.10
174 Rick Joseph	.25	.10
175 Duane Josephson	.25	.10
176 Jim Kaat	2.50	1.00
177 Al Kaline	10.00	4.00
178 Dick Kelley	.25	.10
179 Pat Kelly	.25	.10
180 Jerry Kenney	.25	.10
181 Don Kessinger	.50	.20
182 Harmon Killebrew	8.00	3.20
183 Ed Kirkpatrick	.25	.10
184 Bobby Knoop	.25	.10
185 Cal Koonce	.25	.10
186 Jerry Koosman	1.00	.40
187 Andy Kosco	.25	.10
188 Ed Kranepool	.50	.20
189 Ted Kubiak	.25	.10
190 Jose Laboy	.25	.10
191 Joe Lahoud	.25	.10
192 Bill Landis	.25	.10
193 Hal Lanier	.25	.10
194 Fred Lasher	.25	.10
195 John Lazar	.25	.10
196 Jim LeFebvre	.25	.10
197 Denny Lemaster	.25	.10
198 Dave Leonhard	.25	.10
199 Frank Linzy	.25	.10
200 Mickey Lolich	1.00	.40
201 Jim Lonborg	.50	.20
202 Sparky Lyle	1.00	.40
203 Jim Maloney	.50	.20
204 Juan Marichal	6.00	2.40
205 David Marshall	.25	.10
206 J.C. Martin	.25	.10
207 Marty Martinez	.25	.10
208 Tom Matchick	.25	.10
209 Carlos May	.25	.10
210 Jerry May	.25	.10
211 Lee May	.50	.20
212 Lee Maye	.25	.10
213 Willie Mays	25.00	10.00
214 Dal Maxvill	.25	.10
215 Bill Mazeroski	1.00	.40
216 Dick McAuliffe	.50	.20
217 Al McBean	.25	.10
218 Tim McCarver	1.00	.40
219 Bill McCool	.25	.10
220 Mike McCormick	.50	.20
221 Willie McCovey	8.00	3.20
222 Tom McCraw	.25	.10
223 Lindy McDaniel	.25	.10
224 Sam McDowell	.75	.30
225 Leon McFadden	.25	.10

226 Dan McGinn .25 .10
227 Jim McGlothlin .25 .10
228 Tug McGraw 1.00 .40
229 Denny McLain 1.00 .40
230 Ken McMullen .25 .10
231 Dave McNally .75 .30
232 Gerry McNertney .25 .10
233 Bill Melton .25 .10
234 Denis Menke .25 .10
235 Andy Messersmith .50 .20
236 Felix Millan .25 .10
237 Norm Miller .25 .10
238 Don Mincher .25 .10
239 Rick Monday .50 .20
240 Don Money .25 .10
241 Barry Moore .25 .10
242 Bob Moose .25 .10
243 Dave Morehead .25 .10
244 Joe Morgan 8.00 3.20
245 Manny Mota .50 .20
246 Curt Motton .25 .10
247 Bob Murcer 1.00 .40
248 Tom Murphy .25 .10
249 Ivan Murrell .25 .10
250 Jim Nash .25 .10
251 Joe Niekro 1.00 .40
252 Phil Niekro 6.00 2.40
253 Gary Nolan .25 .10
254 Jim Northrup .50 .20
255 Rich Nye .25 .10
256 Johnny Odom .25 .10
257 John O'Donoghue .25 .10
258 Tony Oliva 1.00 .40
259 Bob Oliver .25 .10
260 Claude Osteen .50 .20
261 Ray Oyler .25 .10
262 Jose Pagan .25 .10
263 Jim Palmer 6.00 2.40
264 Milt Pappas .50 .20
265 Wes Parker .50 .20
266 Freddie Patek .25 .10
267 Mike Paul .25 .10
268 Joe Pepitone .75 .30
269 Tony Perez 4.00 1.60
270 Gaylord Perry 6.00 2.40
271 Jim Perry .75 .30
272 Gary Peters .25 .10
273 Rico Petrocelli .75 .30
274 Tom Phoebus .25 .10
275 Lou Piniella 1.00 .40
276 Vada Pinson 1.00 .40
277 Boog Powell 1.00 .40
278 Jimmie Price .25 .10
279 Frank Quilici .25 .10
280 Doug Rader .25 .10
281 Ron Reed .25 .10
282 Rich Reese .25 .10
283 Phil Regan .25 .10
284 Rick Reichardt .25 .10
285 Rick Renick .25 .10
286 Roger Repoz .25 .10
287 Merv Rettenmund .25 .10
288 Dave Ricketts .25 .10
289 Juan Rios .25 .10
290 Bill Robinson .25 .10
291 Brooks Robinson 10.00 4.00
292 Frank Robinson 10.00 4.00
293 Aurelio Rodriguez .25 .10
294 Ellie Rodriguez .25 .10
295 Cookie Rojas .25 .10
296 Rich Rollins .25 .10
297 Vincente Romo .25 .10
298 Phil Roof .25 .10
299 Pete Rose 12.00 4.80
300 John Roseboro .50 .20
301 Chico Ruiz .25 .10
302 Mike Ryan .25 .10
303 Ray Sadecki .25 .10
304 Chico Salmon .25 .10
305 Manny Sanguillen .50 .20
306 Ron Santo 1.00 .40
307 Tom Satriano .25 .10
308 Ted Savage .25 .10
309 Paul Schaal .25 .10
310 Dick Schofield .25 .10
311 George Scott .50 .20
312 Tom Seaver 20.00 8.00
313 Art Shamsky .25 .10
314 Mike Shannon .75 .30
315 Chris Short .25 .10
316 Duke Sims .25 .10
317 Bill Singer .25 .10
318 Reggie Smith 1.00 .40
319 Willie Smith .25 .10
320 Russ Snyder .25 .10
321 Al Spangler .25 .10
322 Jim Spencer .25 .10
323 Ed Spiezio .25 .10
324 Larry Stahl .25 .10
325 Lee Stange .25 .10
326 Mickey Stanley .50 .20
327 Willie Stargell 10.00 4.00
328 Rusty Staub 1.00 .40
329 Jim Stewart .25 .10
330 George Stone .25 .10
331 Bill Stoneman .50 .20
332 Mel Stottlemyre 1.00 .40
333 Ed Stroud .25 .10
334 Ken Suarez .25 .10
335 Gary Sutherland .25 .10
336 Don Sutton 5.00 2.00
337 Ron Swoboda .50 .20
338 Fred Talbot .25 .10
339 Jose Tartabull .25 .10
340 Ken Tatum .25 .10
341 Tony Taylor .50 .20
342 Luis Tiant 1.00 .40
343 Bob Tillman .25 .10
344 Bobby Tolan .25 .10
345 Jeff Torborg .25 .10
346 Joe Torre 1.00 .40
347 Cesar Tovar .25 .10
348 Tom Tresh 1.00 .40
349 Ted Uhlaender .25 .10
350 Del Unser .25 .10
351 Bob Veale .25 .10
352 Zoilo Versalles .50 .20
353 Luke Walker .25 .10
354 Pete Ward .25 .10
355 Eddie Watt .25 .10
356 Ramon Webster .25 .10
357 Al Weis .25 .10
358 Don Wert .25 .10
359 Bill White 1.00 .40
360 Roy White .75 .30
361 Hoyt Wilhelm 4.00 1.60
362 Billy Williams 8.00 3.20
363 Walt Williams .25 .10
364 Maury Wills 1.00 .40
365 Don Wilson .25 .10
366 Earl Wilson .25 .10
367 Bobby Wine .25 .10
368 Rick Wise .50 .20
369 Wilbur Wood .25 .10
370 Woody Woodward .25 .10
371 Clyde Wright .25 .10
372 Jim Wynn 1.00 .40

1984 Milton Bradley

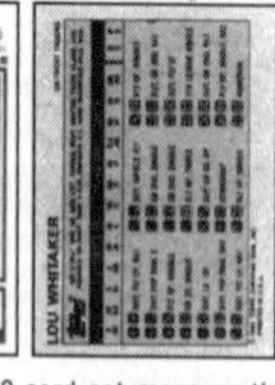

The cards in this 30-card set measure the standard size. This set of full color cards was produced by Topps for the Milton Bradley Co. The set was included in a board game entitled Championship Baseball. The fronts feature portraits of the players and the name, Championship Baseball, by Milton Bradley. The backs feature the Topps logo, statistics for the past year (pitchers' cards have career statistics), and dice rolls which are part of the board game. Pitcher cards have no dice roll charts. There are 15 players from each league. These unnumbered cards are listed below in alphabetical order. The cap logos and uniforms have been air-brushed to remove all team references. Many of these cards have been seen with bad centering.

Nm-Mt Ex-Mt
COMPLETE SET (30) 15.00 6.00
1 Wade Boggs 3.00 1.20
2 George Brett 4.00 1.60
3 Rod Carew .75 .30
4 Steve Carlton .75 .30
5 Gary Carter .75 .30
6 Dave Concepcion .25 .10
7 Cecil Cooper .25 .10
8 Andre Dawson .60 .24
9 Carlton Fisk 1.00 .40
10 Steve Garvey .25 .10
11 Pedro Guerrero .10 .04
12 Ron Guidry .25 .10
13 Rickey Henderson 2.00 .80
14 Reggie Jackson 1.00 .40
15 Ron Kittle .10 .04
16 Bill Madlock .10 .04
17 Dale Murphy 1.00 .40
18 Al Oliver .10 .04
19 Darrell Porter .10 .04
20 Cal Ripken 6.00 2.40
21 Pete Rose 1.50 .60
22 Steve Sax .10 .04
23 Mike Schmidt 1.50 .60
24 Ted Simmons .25 .10
25 Ozzie Smith 2.50 1.00
26 Dave Stieb .10 .04
27 Fernando Valenzuela .25 .10
28 Lou Whitaker .60 .24
29 Dave Winfield 1.00 .40
30 Robin Yount 1.00 .40

1977 Johnny Mize

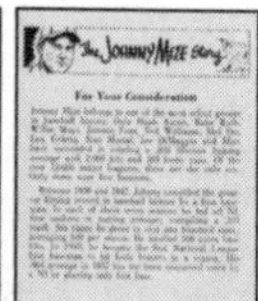

This 20-card set measures 3 1/8" by 3 3/4" and features both vertical and horizontal black-and-white photos of Johnny Mize at various stages of his life. The photos are bordered in gold and gray by a design similar to picture frame. The card title is printed below the photo in script. The backs are white and carry a variety of information. Some contain statistics, while others have quotes from other ball players or career information. The cards are unnumbered and checklisted below in alphabetical order according to either the card's title or the last name of an individual pictured with Johnny Mize. Two postage paid postcards were also included for buyers of the set to send to HOF Veteran Committee voters to support Mize's case for the HOF.

NM Ex
COMPLETE SET 15.00 6.00
COMMON CARD .75 .30
1 Johnny Mize 1.50 .60
Buddy Blattner
Sid Gordon
Ernie Lombardi
Willard Marshall
5 Johnny Mize 1.50 .60
Happy Chandler COMM
Bucky Harris MG
11 Johnny Mize 1.00 .40
Terry Moore
13 Johnny Mize 1.00 .40
Allie Reynolds
Billy Johnson
14 Johnny Mize 2.00 .80
Roy Rogers
16 Johnny Mize 2.00 .80
Enos Slaughter
1939
20 Johnny Mize 1.00 .40
Gene Woodling
Vic Raschi
1952

1992 MJB Holographics Prototypes

The premier edition of Holoprism 1991 Rookies of the Year presented Chuck Knoblauch, the American League Rookie of the Year, and Jeff Bagwell, the National League Rookie of the Year. MJB Holographics issued a prototype card which corresponded to the first card of each set. The cards are marked "Prototype."

Nm-Mt Ex-Mt
COMPLETE SET (2) 3.00 .90
R1 Jeff Bagwell 2.00 .60
R1 Chuck Knoblauch 1.00 .30

1992 MJB Holographics Bagwell

The premier edition of Holoprism 1991 Rookies of the Year presented Chuck Knoblauch, the American League Rookie of the Year, and Jeff Bagwell, the National League Rookie of the Year. Each four-card holographic set was issued in a plastic "jewel box," similar to that used for storing and protecting audio compact disks. The top has a window through which the consumer can view the top card, while the back of the case displays a certificate of authenticity with the serial number of the set and the production run (250,000 sets). Also Bagwell and Knoblauch each autographed 500 cards that were randomly inserted throughout the sets. These autograph cards are rarely seen in the secondary market.

Nm-Mt Ex-Mt
COMPLETE SET (4) 1.50 .45
COMMON CARD (1-4) .50 .15
AU Jeff Bagwell AU/500 60.00 18.00

1992 MJB Holographics Knoblauch

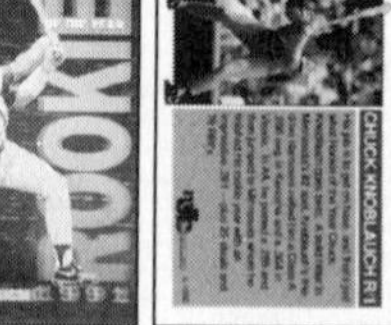

The premier edition of Holoprism 1991 Rookies of the Year presented Chuck Knoblauch, the American League Rookie of the Year, and Jeff Bagwell, the National League Rookie of the Year. Each four-card holographic set was issued in a plastic "jewel box," similar to that used for storing and protecting audio compact disks. The top has a window through which the consumer can view the top card, while the back of the case displays a certificate of authenticity with the serial number of the set and the production run (250,000 sets). Also Bagwell and Knoblauch each autographed 500 cards that were randomly inserted throughout the sets. These autograph cards are rarely seen in the secondary market.

Nm-Mt Ex-Mt
COMPLETE SET (4) 1.50 .45
COMMON CARD (1-4) .50 .15
AU Chuck Knoblauch AU/500 30.00 9.00

1969 MLB Official Stamps

Each team is represented by nine players; hence the set consists of 216 player stamps each measuring approximately 1 3/4" by 2 7/8". There are two large albums available, one for each league. Also there are four smaller divisional albums each measuring approximately 4" by 7" and holding all the player stamps for a particular division. Stamps are unnumbered but are presented here in alphabetical order by team, Baltimore Orioles (1-9), Boston Red Sox (10-18), California Angels (19-27), Chicago White Sox (28-36), Cleveland Indians (37-45), Detroit Tigers (46-54), Kansas City Royals (55-63), Minnesota Twins (64-72), New York Yankees (73-81), Oakland A's (82-90), Seattle Pilots (91-99), Washington Senators (100-108), Atlanta Braves (109-117), Chicago Cubs (118-126), Cincinnati Reds (127-135), Houston Astros (136-144), Los Angeles Dodgers (145-153), Montreal Expos (154-162), New York Mets (163-171), Philadelphia Phillies (172-180), Pittsburgh Pirates (181-189), San Diego Padres (190-198), San Francisco Giants (199-207), and St. Louis Cardinals (208-216).

NM Ex
COMPLETE SET (216) 80.00 32.00
1 Paul Blair .30 .12
2 Don Buford .20 .08
3 Andy Etchebarren .20 .08
4 Dave Johnson .40 .16
5 Dave McNally .30 .12
6 Tom Phoebus .20 .08
7 Boog Powell .50 .20
8 Brooks Robinson 1.50 .60
9 Frank Robinson 1.50 .60
10 Mike Andrews .20 .08
11 Ray Culp .20 .08
12 Dick Ellsworth .20 .08
13 Ken Harrelson .40 .16
14 Jim Lonborg .30 .12
15 Rico Petrocelli .30 .12
16 Jose Santiago .20 .08
17 George Scott .30 .12
18 Reggie Smith .40 .16
19 George Brunet .20 .08
20 Vic Davalillo .20 .08
21 Jim Fregosi .40 .16
22 Chuck Hinton .20 .08
23 Bobby Knoop .20 .08
24 Jim McGlothlin .20 .08
25 Rick Reichardt .20 .08
26 Roger Repoz .20 .08
27 Bob Rodgers .40 .16
28 Luis Aparicio 1.00 .40
29 Ken Berry .20 .08
30 Joe Horlen .20 .08
31 Tommy John .50 .20
32 Duane Josephson .20 .08
33 Tom McCraw .20 .08
34 Gary Peters .20 .08
35 Pete Ward .20 .08
36 Wilbur Wood .30 .12
37 Max Alvis .20 .08
38 Joe Azcue .20 .08
39 Larry Brown .20 .08
40 Jose Cardenal .20 .08
41 Tony Horton .30 .12
42 Sam McDowell .30 .12
43 Sonny Siebert .20 .08
44 Luis Tiant .40 .16
45 Zoilo Versalles .20 .08
46 Norm Cash .40 .16
47 Bill Freehan .40 .16
48 Willie Horton .40 .16
49 Al Kaline 1.50 .60
50 Mickey Lolich .40 .16
51 Dick McAuliffe .20 .08
52 Denny McLain .50 .20
53 Jim Northrup .20 .08
54 Mickey Stanley .20 .08
55 Jerry Adair .20 .08
56 Wally Bunker .20 .08
57 Moe Drabowsky .20 .08
58 Joe Foy .20 .08
59 Ed Kirkpatrick .20 .08
60 Dave Morehead .20 .08
61 Roger Nelson .20 .08
62 Paul Schaal .20 .08
63 Steve Whitaker .20 .08
64 Bob Allison .30 .12
65 Rod Carew 1.50 .60
66 Dean Chance .30 .12
67 Jim Kaat .50 .20
68 Harmon Killebrew 1.00 .40
69 Tony Oliva .50 .20
70 John Roseboro .20 .08
71 Cesar Tovar .20 .08
72 Ted Uhlaender .20 .08
73 Horace Clarke .20 .08
74 Jake Gibbs .20 .08
75 Steve Hamilton .20 .08
76 Joe Pepitone .30 .12
77 Fritz Peterson .20 .08
78 Bill Robinson .30 .12
79 Mel Stottlemyre .30 .12
80 Tom Tresh .40 .16
81 Roy White .30 .12
82 Sal Bando .30 .12
83 Bert Campaneris .40 .16
84 Danny Cater .20 .08
85 John Donaldson .20 .08
86 Mike Hershberger .20 .08
87 Jim Hunter 1.00 .40
88 Rick Monday .30 .12
89 Jim Nash .20 .08
90 John Odom .20 .08
91 Jack Aker .20 .08
92 Steve Barber .20 .08
93 Gary Bell .20 .08
94 Tommy Davis .30 .12
95 Tommy Harper .20 .08
96 Don Mincher .20 .08
97 Ray Oyler .20 .08
98 Rich Rollins .20 .08
99 Chico Salmon .20 .08
100 Bernie Allen .20 .08
101 Ed Brinkman .20 .08
102 Paul Casanova .20 .08
103 Joe Coleman Jr. .20 .08
104 Mike Epstein .20 .08
105 Frank Howard .50 .20
106 Ken McMullen .20 .08
107 Camilo Pascual .20 .08
108 Ed Stroud .20 .08
109 Hank Aaron 2.50 1.00
110 Felipe Alou .40 .16
111 Bob Aspromonte .20 .08
112 Rico Carty .30 .12
113 Orlando Cepeda .75 .30
114 Pat Jarvis .20 .08
115 Felix Millan .20 .08
116 Phil Niekro .75 .30
117 Milt Pappas .20 .08
118 Ernie Banks 1.50 .60
119 Glenn Beckert .20 .08
120 Bill Hands .20 .08
121 Randy Hundley .20 .08
122 Fergie Jenkins .75 .30
123 Don Kessinger .30 .12
124 Phil Regan .20 .08
125 Ron Santo .50 .20
126 Billy Williams 1.00 .40
127 Johnny Bench 1.50 .60
128 Tony Cloninger .20 .08
129 Tommy Helms .20 .08
130 Jim Maloney .30 .12
131 Lee May .30 .12
132 Jim Merritt .20 .08
133 Gary Nolan .20 .08
134 Tony Perez .75 .30
135 Pete Rose 2.00 .80
136 Jesus Alou .20 .08
137 Curt Blefary .20 .08
138 Larry Dierker .30 .12
139 Johnny Edwards .20 .08
140 Denis Menke .20 .08
141 Joe Morgan 1.00 .40
142 Doug Rader .30 .12
143 Don Wilson .20 .08
144 Jim Wynn .30 .12
145 Willie Davis .30 .12
146 Ron Fairly .30 .12
147 Len Gabrielson .20 .08
148 Tom Haller .20 .08
149 Jim LeFebvre .20 .08
150 Claude Osteen .20 .08
151 Wes Parker .30 .12
152 Bill Singer .20 .08
153 Don Sutton .75 .30
154 Bob Bailey .20 .08
155 John Bateman .20 .08
156 Ty Cline .20 .08
157 Jim Fairey .20 .08
158 Jim Grant .20 .08
159 Mack Jones .20 .08
160 Manny Mota .30 .12
161 Rusty Staub .50 .20
162 Maury Wills .50 .20
163 Tommy Agee .20 .08
164 Ed Charles .20 .08
165 Jerry Grote .30 .12
166 Bud Harrelson .40 .16
167 Cleon Jones .30 .12
168 Jerry Koosman .40 .16
169 Ed Kranepool .20 .08
170 Tom Seaver 2.00 .80
171 Ron Swoboda .20 .08
172 Richie Allen .50 .20
173 Johnny Briggs .20 .08
174 Johnny Callison .30 .12
175 Woody Fryman .20 .08
176 Cookie Rojas .20 .08
177 Mike Ryan .20 .08
178 Chris Short .20 .08
179 Tony Taylor .20 .08
180 Rick Wise .30 .12
181 Gene Alley .20 .08
182 Matty Alou .30 .12
183 Jim Bunning .75 .30
184 Roberto Clemente 4.00 1.60
185 Ron Davis .20 .08
186 Jerry May .20 .08
187 Bill Mazeroski .50 .20
188 Willie Stargell 1.00 .40
189 Bob Veale .20 .08
190 Ollie Brown .20 .08
191 Al Ferrara .20 .08
192 Tony Gonzales .20 .08
193 Dick Kelley .20 .08
194 Bill McCool .20 .08
195 Dick Selma .20 .08
196 Tommy Sisk .20 .08
197 Ed Spiezio .20 .08
198 Larry Stahl .20 .08
199 Jim Ray Hart .30 .12
200 Ron Hunt .20 .08
201 Hal Lanier .40 .16
202 Frank Linzy .20 .08
203 Juan Marichal 1.00 .40
204 Willie Mays 2.50 1.00
205 Mike McCormick .30 .12
206 Willie McCovey 1.00 .40
207 Gaylord Perry .75 .30
208 Nelson Briles .20 .08
209 Lou Brock 1.25 .50
210 Curt Flood .50 .20
211 Bob Gibson 1.25 .50
212 Julian Javier .20 .08
213 Dal Maxvill .20 .08
214 Tim McCarver .50 .20
215 Mike Shannon .30 .12
216 Joe Torre .30 .12

1970 MLB Official Stamps

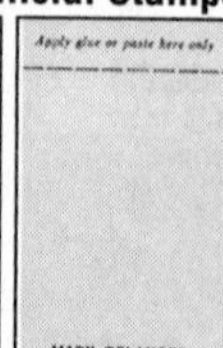

These unnumbered stamps are organized below alphabetically within teams; there are 24 teams each featuring 12 player stamps. This set is much tougher to find than the set produced the year before. They are essentially the same size at 1 7/8" by 2 15/16" and as with the prior set they are not gummed on the back. Stamps are unnumbered but are presented here in alphabetical order by team, Atlanta Braves (1-12), Chicago Cubs (13-24), Cincinnati Reds (25-36), Houston Astros (37-48), Los Angeles Dodgers (49-60), Montreal Expos (61-72), New York Mets (73-84), Philadelphia Phillies (85-96), Pittsburgh Pirates (97-108), San Diego Padres (109-120), San Francisco Giants (121-132), St. Louis Cardinals (133-144), Baltimore Orioles (145-156), Boston Red Sox (157-168), California Angels (169-180), Chicago White Sox (181-192), Cleveland Indians (193-204), Detroit Tigers (205-216), Kansas City Royals (217-228), Minnesota Twins (229-240), New York Yankees (241-252), Oakland A's (253-264), Seattle Pilots (265-276) and Washington Senators (277-288).

	NM	Ex
COMPLETE SET (288)	150.00	60.00
1 Hank Aaron	5.00	2.00
2 Bob Aspromonte	.20	.08
3 Rico Carty	.30	.12
4 Orlando Cepeda	.50	.20
5 Bob Didier	.20	.08
6 Tony Gonzales	.20	.08
7 Pat Jarvis	.20	.08
8 Felix Millan	.20	.08
9 Jim Nash	.20	.08
10 Phil Niekro	1.50	.60
11 Milt Pappas	.30	.12
12 Ron Reed	.20	.08
13 Ernie Banks	2.50	1.00
14 Glenn Beckert	.30	.12
15 Johnny Callison	.30	.12
16 Bill Hands	.20	.08
17 Randy Hundley	.20	.08
18 Ken Holtzman	.30	.12
19 Fergie Jenkins	1.50	.60
20 Don Kessinger	.30	.12
21 Phil Regan	.20	.08
22 Ron Santo	.50	.20
23 Dick Selma	.20	.08
24 Billy Williams	1.50	.60
25 Johnny Bench	2.50	1.00
26 Tony Cloninger	.20	.08
27 Wayne Granger	.20	.08
28 Tommy Helms	.20	.08
29 Jim Maloney	.30	.12
30 Lee May	.30	.12
31 Jim McGlothlin	.20	.08
32 Jim Merritt	.20	.08
33 Gary Nolan	.20	.08
34 Tony Perez	1.50	.60
35 Pete Rose	4.00	1.60
36 Bobby Tolan	.20	.08
37 Jesus Alou	.20	.08
38 Tommy Davis	.30	.12
39 Larry Dierker	.30	.12
40 Johnny Edwards	.20	.08
41 Fred Gladding	.20	.08
42 Denver Lemaster	.20	.08
43 Denis Menke	.20	.08
44 Joe Morgan	1.50	.60
45 Joe Pepitone	.30	.12
46 Doug Rader	.20	.08
47 Don Wilson	.20	.08
48 Jim Wynn	.30	.12
49 Willie Davis	.30	.12
50 Len Gabrielson	.20	.08
51 Tom Haller	.20	.08
52 Jim LeFebvre	.20	.08
53 Manny Mota	.30	.12
54 Claude Osteen	.30	.12
55 Wes Parker	.30	.12
56 Bill Russell	.50	.20
57 Bill Singer	.20	.08
58 Ted Sizemore	.20	.08
59 Don Sutton	1.50	.60
60 Maury Wills	.50	.20
61 Johnny Bateman	.20	.08
62 Bob Bailey	.20	.08
63 Ron Brand	.20	.08
64 Ty Cline	.20	.08
65 Ron Fairly	.30	.12
66 Mack Jones	.20	.08
67 Jose Laboy	.20	.08
68 Claude Raymond	.20	.08
69 Joe Sparma	.20	.08
70 Rusty Staub	.50	.20
71 Bill Stoneman	.20	.08
72 Bobby Wine	.20	.08
73 Tommy Agee	.30	.12
74 Donn Clendenon	.20	.08
75 Joe Foy	.20	.08
76 Jerry Grote	.30	.12
77 Bud Harrelson	.30	.12
78 Cleon Jones	.30	.12
79 Jerry Koosman	.40	.16
80 Ed Kranepool	.30	.12
81 Nolan Ryan	15.00	6.00
82 Tom Seaver	3.00	1.20
83 Ron Swoboda	.30	.12
84 Al Weis	.20	.08
85 Johnny Briggs	.20	.08
86 Jim Bunning	1.50	.60
87 Curt Flood	.50	.20
88 Woody Fryman	.20	.08
89 Larry Hisle	.30	.12
90 Joe Hoerner	.20	.08
91 Grant Jackson	.20	.08
92 Tim McCarver	.50	.20
93 Mike Ryan	.20	.08
94 Chris Short	.20	.08
95 Tony Taylor	.20	.08
96 Rick Wise	.30	.12
97 Gene Alley	.20	.08
98 Matty Alou	.30	.12
99 Roberto Clemente	10.00	4.00
100 Ron Davis	.20	.08
101 Richie Hebner	.20	.08
102 Jerry May	.20	.08
103 Bill Mazeroski	.75	.30
104 Bob Moose	.20	.08
105 Al Oliver	.50	.20
106 Manny Sanguillen	.30	.12
107 Willie Stargell	2.00	.80
108 Bob Veale	.20	.08
109 Ollie Brown	.20	.08
110 Dave Campbell	.40	.16
111 Nate Colbert	.20	.08
112 Pat Dobson	.30	.12
113 Al Ferrara	.20	.08
114 Dick Kelley	.20	.08
115 Clay Kirby	.20	.08
116 Bill McCool	.20	.08
117 Frank Reberger	.20	.08
118 Tommie Sisk	.20	.08
119 Ed Spiezio	.20	.08
120 Larry Stahl	.20	.08
121 Bobby Bonds	.50	.20
122 Jim Davenport	.30	.12
123 Dick Dietz	.20	.08
124 Jim Ray Hart	.30	.12
125 Ron Hunt	.20	.08
126 Hal Lanier	.40	.16
127 Frank Linzy	.20	.08
128 Juan Marichal	1.50	.60
129 Willie Mays	8.00	3.20
130 Mike McCormick	.30	.12
131 Willie McCovey	1.50	.60
132 Gaylord Perry	1.50	.60
133 Richie Allen	.50	.20
134 Nelson Briles	.20	.08
135 Lou Brock	2.00	.80
136 Jose Cardenal	.20	.08
137 Steve Carlton	2.50	1.00
138 Vic Davalillo	.20	.08
139 Bob Gibson	2.00	.80
140 Julian Javier	.20	.08
141 Dal Maxvill	.20	.08
142 Cookie Rojas	.30	.12
143 Mike Shannon	.40	.16
144 Joe Torre	.50	.20
145 Mark Belanger	.30	.12
146 Paul Blair	.30	.12
147 Don Buford	.20	.08
148 Mike Cuellar	.30	.12
149 Andy Etchebarren	.20	.08
150 Dave Johnson	.40	.16
151 Dave McNally	.30	.12
152 Tom Phoebus	.20	.08
153 Boog Powell	.50	.20
154 Brooks Robinson	2.50	1.00
155 Frank Robinson	2.50	1.00
156 Chico Salmon	.20	.08
157 Mike Andrews	.20	.08
158 Ray Culp	.20	.08
159 Jim Lonborg	.30	.12
160 Sparky Lyle	.50	.20
161 Gary Peters	.20	.08
162 Rico Petrocelli	.40	.16
163 Vicente Romo	.20	.08
164 Tom Satriano	.20	.08
165 George Scott	.30	.12
166 Sonny Siebert	.20	.08
167 Reggie Smith	.40	.16
168 Carl Yastrzemski	2.50	1.00
169 Sandy Alomar	.30	.12
170 Jose Azcue	.20	.08
171 Tom Egan	.20	.08
172 Jim Fregosi	.40	.16
173 Alex Johnson	.30	.12
174 Jay Johnstone	.30	.12
175 Rudy May	.20	.08
176 Andy Messersmith	.30	.12
177 Rick Reichardt	.20	.08
178 Roger Repoz	.20	.08
179 Aurelio Rodriguez	.20	.08
180 Ken Tatum	.20	.08
181 Luis Aparicio	1.50	.60
182 Ken Berry	.20	.08
183 Buddy Bradford	.20	.08
184 Ron Hansen	.20	.08
185 Joe Horlen	.20	.08
186 Tommy John	1.00	.40
187 Duane Josephson	.20	.08
188 Bobby Knoop	.20	.08
189 Tom McCraw	.20	.08
190 Bill Melton	.20	.08
191 Walt Williams	.20	.08
192 Wilbur Wood	.30	.12
193 Max Alvis	.20	.08
194 Larry Brown	.20	.08
195 Dean Chance	.20	.08
196 Dick Ellsworth	.30	.12
197 Vern Fuller	.20	.08
198 Ken Harrelson	.50	.20
199 Chuck Hinton	.20	.08
200 Tony Horton	.30	.12
201 Sam McDowell	.40	.16
202 Vada Pinson	.50	.20
203 Duke Sims	.20	.08
204 Ted Uhlaender	.20	.08
205 Norm Cash	.40	.16
206 Bill Freehan	.40	.16
207 Willie Horton	.40	.16
208 Al Kaline	2.00	.80
209 Mike Kilkenny	.20	.08
210 Mickey Lolich	.50	.20
211 Dick McAuliffe	.30	.12
212 Denny McLain	.50	.20
213 Jim Northrup	.30	.12
214 Mickey Stanley	.30	.12
215 Tom Tresh	.30	.12
216 Earl Wilson	.20	.08
217 Jerry Adair	.20	.08
218 Wally Bunker	.20	.08
219 Bill Butler	.20	.08
220 Moe Drabowsky	.20	.08
221 Jackie Hernandez	.20	.08
222 Pat Kelly	.20	.08
223 Ed Kirkpatrick	.20	.08
224 Dave Morehead	.20	.08
225 Roger Nelson	.20	.08
226 Bob Oliver	.20	.08
227 Lou Piniella	.50	.20
228 Paul Schaal	.20	.08
229 Bob Allison	.30	.12
230 Dave Boswell	.20	.08
231 Leo Cardenas	.20	.08
232 Rod Carew	2.50	1.00
233 Jim Kaat	1.00	.40
234 Harmon Killebrew	2.00	.80
235 Tony Oliva	.50	.20
236 Jim Perry	.30	.12
237 Ron Perranoski	.30	.12
238 Rich Reese	.20	.08
239 Luis Tiant	.50	.20
240 Cesar Tovar	.30	.12
241 Jack Aker	.20	.08
242 Curt Blefary	.20	.08
243 Danny Cater	.20	.08
244 Horace Clarke	.20	.08
245 Jake Gibbs	.20	.08
246 Steve Hamilton	.20	.08
247 Bobby Murcer	.50	.20
248 Fritz Peterson	.20	.08
249 Bill Robinson	.20	.08
250 Mel Stottlemyre	.40	.16
251 Pete Ward	.20	.08
252 Roy White	.30	.12
253 Felipe Alou	.40	.16
254 Sal Bando	.40	.16
255 Bert Campaneris	.30	.12
256 Chuck Dobson	.20	.08
257 Tito Francona	.20	.08
258 Dick Green	.20	.08
259 Jim Hunter	1.50	.60
260 Reggie Jackson	5.00	2.00
261 Don Mincher	.20	.08
262 Rick Monday	.30	.12
263 John Odom	.20	.08
264 Ray Oyler	.20	.08
265 Steve Barber	.20	.08
266 Bobby Bolin	.20	.08
267 George Brunet	.20	.08
268 Wayne Comer	.20	.08
269 John Donaldson	.20	.08
270 Tommy Harper	.30	.12
271 Mike Hegan	.20	.08
272 Mike Hershberger	.20	.08
273 Steve Hovley	.20	.08
274 Bob Locker	.20	.08
275 Gerry McNertney	.20	.08
276 Rich Rollins	.20	.08
277 Bernie Allen	.20	.08
278 Dick Bosman	.20	.08
279 Ed Brinkman	.20	.08
280 Paul Casanova	.20	.08
281 Joe Coleman	.20	.08
282 Mike Epstein	.20	.08
283 Frank Howard	.50	.20
284 Ken McMullen	.20	.08
285 John Roseboro	.30	.12
286 Ed Stroud	.20	.08
287 Del Unser	.20	.08
288 Zoilo Versalles	.30	.12

1971 MLB Official Stamps

This set of stamps consists of 600 stamps contained in 25 stamp books (each containing 24 stamps) labeled Today's 1971 Team. The stamps are usually found still in the team albums. The value of each album intact with all its stamps would be the sum of the prices of all the individual player stamps inside the album. Stamps are unnumbered but are presented here in alphabetical order by team, Atlanta Braves (1-24), Chicago Cubs (25-48), Cincinnati Reds (49-72), Houston Astros (73-96), Los Angeles Dodgers (97-120), Montreal Expos (121-144), New York Mets (145-168), Philadelphia Phillies (169-192), Pittsburgh Pirates (193-216), San Diego Padres (217-240), San Francisco Giants (241-264), St. Louis Cardinals (265-288), Baltimore Orioles AL (289-312), Boston Red Sox (313-336), California Angels (337-360), Chicago White Sox (361-384), Cleveland Indians (385-408), Detroit Tigers (409-432), Kansas City Royals (433-456), Milwaukee Brewers (457-480), Minnesota Twins (481-504), New York Yankees (505-528), Oakland A's (529-552), Washington Senators (553-576) and All-Stars (577-600).

	NM	Ex
COMPLETE SET (576)	150.00	60.00
1 Hank Aaron	4.00	1.60
2 Tommy Aaron	.10	.04
3 Hank Allen	.10	.04
4 Clete Boyer	.30	.12
5 Oscar Brown	.10	.04
6 Rico Carty	.20	.08
7 Orlando Cepeda	1.00	.40
8 Bob Didier	.10	.04
9 Ralph Garr	.20	.08
10 Gil Garrido	.10	.04
11 Ron Herbel	.10	.04
12 Sonny Jackson	.10	.04
13 Pat Jarvis	.10	.04
14 Larry Jaster	.10	.04
15 Hal King	.10	.04
16 Mike Lum	.10	.04
17 Felix Millan	.10	.04
18 Jim Nash	.10	.04
19 Phil Niekro	1.25	.50
20 Bob Priddy	.10	.04
21 Ron Reed	.10	.04
22 George Stone	.10	.04
23 Cecil Upshaw	.10	.04
24 Hoyt Wilhelm	1.00	.40
25 Ernie Banks	2.00	.80
26 Glenn Beckert	.10	.04
27 Danny Breeden	.10	.04
28 Johnny Callison	.20	.08
29 Jim Colborn	.10	.04
30 Joe Decker	.10	.04
31 Bill Hands	.10	.04
32 Jim Hickman	.10	.04
33 Ken Holtzman	.20	.08
34 Randy Hundley	.10	.04
35 Fergie Jenkins	1.00	.40
36 Don Kessinger	.20	.08
37 J.C. Martin	.10	.04
38 Bob Miller	.10	.04
39 Milt Pappas	.10	.04
40 Joe Pepitone	.20	.08
41 Juan Pizarro	.10	.04
42 Paul Popovich	.10	.04
43 Phil Regan	.10	.04
44 Roberto Rodriguez	.10	.04
45 Ken Rudolph	.10	.04
46 Ron Santo	.40	.16
47 Hector Torres	.10	.04
48 Billy Williams	1.25	.50
49 Johnny Bench	2.00	.80
50 Angel Bravo	.10	.04
51 Bernie Carbo	.10	.04
52 Clay Carroll	.10	.04
53 Darrel Chaney	.10	.04
54 Ty Cline	.10	.04
55 Tony Cloninger	.10	.04
56 Dave Concepcion	.40	.16
57 Pat Corrales	.10	.04
58 Greg Garrett	.10	.04
59 Wayne Granger	.10	.04
60 Don Gullett	.10	.04
61 Tommy Helms	.10	.04
62 Lee May	.20	.08
63 Jim McGlothlin	.10	.04
64 Hal McRae	.20	.08
65 Jim Merritt	.10	.04
66 Gary Nolan	.10	.04
67 Tony Perez	1.00	.40
68 Pete Rose	3.00	1.20
69 Wayne Simpson	.10	.04
70 Jimmy Stewart	.10	.04
71 Bobby Tolan	.10	.04
72 Woody Woodward	.10	.04
73 Jesus Alou	.20	.08
74 Jack Billingham	.10	.04
75 Ron Cook	.10	.04
76 George Culver	.10	.04
77 Larry Dierker	.20	.08
78 Jack DiLauro	.10	.04
79 Johnny Edwards	.10	.04
80 Fred Gladding	.10	.04
81 Tom Griffin	.10	.04
82 Skip Guinn	.10	.04
83 Jack Hiatt	.10	.04
84 Denver Lemaster	.10	.04
85 Marty Martinez	.10	.04
86 John Mayberry	.20	.08
87 Denis Menke	.10	.04
88 Norm Miller	.10	.04
89 Joe Morgan	1.00	.40
90 Doug Rader	.10	.04
91 Jim Ray	.10	.04
92 Scipio Spinks	.10	.04
93 Bob Watkins	.10	.04
94 Bob Watson	.30	.12
95 Don Wilson	.10	.04
96 Jim Wynn	.30	.12
97 Rich Allen	.40	.16
98 Jim Brewer	.10	.04
99 Bill Buckner	.40	.16
100 Willie Crawford	.10	.04
101 Willie Davis	.30	.12
102 Al Downing	.10	.04
103 Steve Garvey	1.25	.50
104 Billy Grabarkewitz	.10	.04
105 Tom Haller	.10	.04
106 Jim LeFebvre	.10	.04
107 Pete Mikkelsen	.10	.04
108 Joe Moeller	.10	.04
109 Manny Mota	.20	.08
110 Claude Osteen	.10	.04
111 Wes Parker	.20	.08
112 Jose Pena	.10	.04
113 Bill Russell	.20	.08
114 Duke Sims	.10	.04
115 Bill Singer	.10	.04
116 Mike Strahler	.10	.04
117 Bill Sudakis	.10	.04
118 Don Sutton	1.25	.50
119 Jeff Torborg	.10	.04
120 Maury Wills	1.00	.40
121 Bob Bailey	.10	.04
122 John Bateman	.10	.04
123 John Boccabella	.10	.04
124 Ron Brand	.10	.04
125 Boots Day	.10	.04
126 Jim Fairey	.10	.04
127 Ron Fairly	.20	.08
128 Jim Gosger	.10	.04
129 Don Hahn	.10	.04
130 Ron Hunt	.10	.04
131 Mack Jones	.10	.04
132 Jose Laboy	.10	.04
133 Mike Marshall	.20	.08
134 Dan McGinn	.10	.04
135 Carl Morton	.10	.04
136 John O'Donoghue	.10	.04
137 Adolpho Phillips	.10	.04
138 Claude Raymond	.10	.04
139 Steve Renko	.10	.04
140 Marv Staehle	.10	.04
141 Rusty Staub	.40	.16
142 Bill Stoneman	.10	.04
143 Gary Sutherland	.10	.04
144 Bobby Wine	.10	.04
145 Tommy Agee	.20	.08
146 Bob Aspromonte	.10	.04
147 Ken Boswell	.10	.04
148 Dean Chance	.20	.08
149 Donn Clendenon	.20	.08
150 Duffy Dyer	.10	.04
151 Dan Frisella	.10	.04
152 Wayne Garrett	.10	.04
153 Gary Gentry	.10	.04
154 Jerry Grote	.10	.04
155 Bud Harrelson	.30	.12
156 Cleon Jones	.20	.08
157 Jerry Koosman	.40	.16
158 Ed Kranepool	.20	.08
159 Dave Marshall	.10	.04
160 Jim McAndrew	.10	.04
161 Tug McGraw	.40	.16
162 Nolan Ryan	10.00	4.00
163 Ray Sadecki	.10	.04
164 Tom Seaver	2.00	.80
165 Art Shamsky	.10	.04
166 Ron Swoboda	.20	.08
167 Ron Taylor	.10	.04
168 Al Weis	.10	.04
169 Larry Bowa	.40	.16
170 Johnny Briggs	.10	.04
171 Byron Browne	.10	.04
172 Jim Bunning	1.00	.40
173 Billy Champion	.10	.04
174 Mike Compton	.10	.04
175 Denny Doyle	.10	.04
176 Roger Freed	.10	.04
177 Woody Fryman	.10	.04
178 Oscar Gamble	.20	.08
179 Terry Harmon	.10	.04
180 Larry Hisle	.20	.08
181 Joe Hoerner	.10	.04
182 Deron Johnson	.10	.04
183 Barry Lersch	.10	.04
184 Tim McCarver	.40	.16
185 Don Money	.10	.04
186 Mike Ryan	.10	.04
187 Dick Selma	.10	.04
188 Chris Short	.10	.04
189 Ron Stone	.10	.04
190 Tony Taylor	.20	.08
191 Rick Wise	.10	.04
192 Billy Wilson	.10	.04
193 Gene Alley	.10	.04
194 Steve Blass	.10	.04
195 Nelson Briles	.10	.04
196 Jim Campanis	.10	.04
197 Dave Cash	.10	.04
198 Roberto Clemente	6.00	2.40
199 Vic Davalillo	.10	.04
200 Dock Ellis	.10	.04
201 Jim Grant	.10	.04
202 Dave Giusti	.10	.04
203 Richie Hebner	.20	.08
204 Jackie Hernandez	.10	.04
205 Johnny Jeter	.10	.04
206 Lou Marone	.10	.04
207 Jose Martinez	.10	.04
208 Bill Mazeroski	.75	.30
209 Bob Moose	.10	.04
210 Al Oliver	.40	.16
211 Jose Pagan	.10	.04
212 Bob Robertson	.10	.04
213 Manny Sanguillen	.20	.08
214 Willie Stargell	1.00	.40
215 Bob Veale	.10	.04
216 Luke Walker	.10	.04
217 Jose Arcia	.10	.04
218 Bob Barton	.10	.04
219 Fred Beene	.10	.04
220 Ollie Brown	.10	.04
221 Dave Campbell	.30	.12
222 Chris Cannizzaro	.10	.04
223 Nate Colbert	.10	.04
224 Mike Corkins	.10	.04
225 Tommy Dean	.10	.04
226 Al Ferrara	.10	.04
227 Rod Gaspar	.10	.04
228 Clarence Gaston	.20	.08
229 Enzo Hernandez	.10	.04
230 Clay Kirby	.10	.04
231 Don Mason	.10	.04
232 Ivan Murrell	.10	.04
233 Gerry Nyman	.10	.04
234 Tom Phoebus	.10	.04
235 Dave Roberts	.10	.04
236 Gary Ross	.10	.04
237 Al Santorini	.10	.04
238 Al Severinsen	.10	.04
239 Ron Slocum	.10	.04
240 Ed Spiezio	.10	.04
241 Bobby Bonds	.40	.16
242 Ron Bryant	.10	.04
243 Don Carrithers	.10	.04
244 John Cumberland	.10	.04
245 Mike Davison	.10	.04
246 Dick Dietz	.10	.04
247 Tito Fuentes	.10	.04
248 Russ Gibson	.10	.04
249 Jim Ray Hart	.10	.04
250 Bob Heise	.10	.04
251 Ken Henderson	.10	.04
252 Steve Huntz	.10	.04
253 Frank Johnson	.10	.04
254 Jerry Johnson	.10	.04
255 Hal Lanier	.10	.04
256 Juan Marichal	1.00	.40
257 Willie Mays	4.00	1.60
258 Willie McCovey	1.50	.60
259 Don McMahon	.10	.04
260 Jackie Moyer	.10	.04
261 Gaylord Perry	1.25	.50
262 Frank Reberger	.10	.04
263 Rich Robertson	.10	.04
264 Bernie Williams	.10	.04
265 Matty Alou	.30	.12
266 Jim Beauchamp	.10	.04
267 Frank Bertaina	.10	.04
268 Lou Brock	1.50	.60
269 George Brunet	.10	.04
270 Jose Cardenal	.20	.08
271 Steve Carlton	1.50	.60
272 Moe Drabowsky	.10	.04
273 Bob Gibson	1.50	.60
274 Joe Hague	.10	.04
275 Julian Javier	.20	.08
276 Leron Lee	.10	.04
277 Frank Linzy	.10	.04
278 Dal Maxvill	.10	.04
279 Gerry McNertney	.10	.04
280 Fred Norman	.10	.04
281 Milt Ramirez	.10	.04
282 Dick Schofield	.10	.04
283 Mike Shannon	.10	.04
284 Ted Sizemore	.10	.04
285 Bob Stinson	.10	.04
286 Carl Taylor	.10	.04
287 Joe Torre	.75	.30
288 Mike Torrez	.20	.08
289 Mark Belanger	.20	.08
290 Paul Blair	.20	.08
291 Don Buford	.10	.04
292 Terry Crowley	.10	.04
293 Mike Cuellar	.20	.08
294 Clay Dalrymple	.10	.04
295 Pat Dobson	.10	.04
296 Andy Etchebarren	.10	.04
297 Dick Hall	.10	.04
298 Jim Hardin	.10	.04
299 Elrod Hendricks	.10	.04
300 Grant Jackson	.10	.04
301 Dave Johnson	.40	.16
302 Dave Leonhard	.10	.04
303 Marcelino Lopez	.10	.04
304 Dave McNally	.20	.08
305 Curt Motton	.10	.04
306 Jim Palmer	1.50	.60
307 Boog Powell	.30	.12
308 Merv Rettenmund	.10	.04
309 Brooks Robinson	1.50	.60
310 Frank Robinson	1.50	.60
311 Pete Richert	.10	.04
312 Chico Salmon	.10	.04
313 Luis Aparicio	1.00	.40
314 Bobby Bolin	.10	.04
315 Ken Brett	.10	.04
316 Billy Conigliaro	.20	.08
317 Ray Culp	.10	.04
318 Mike Fiore	.10	.04

319 John Kennedy .10 .04
320 Cal Koonce .10 .04
321 Joe Lahoud .10 .04
322 Bill Lee .20 .08
323 Jim Lonborg .20 .08
324 Sparky Lyle .40 .16
325 Mike Nagy .10 .04
326 Don Pavletich .10 .04
327 Gary Peters .10 .04
328 Rico Petrocelli .30 .12
329 Vicente Romo .10 .04
330 Tom Satriano .10 .04
331 George Scott .30 .12
332 Sonny Siebert .10 .04
333 Reggie Smith .40 .16
334 Jarvis Tatum .10 .04
335 Ken Tatum .10 .04
336 Carl Yastrzemski 2.00 .80
337 Sandy Alomar .20 .08
338 Jose Azcue .10 .04
339 Ken Berry .10 .04
340 Gene Brabender .10 .04
341 Billy Cowan .10 .04
342 Tony Conigliaro .40 .16
343 Eddie Fisher .10 .04
344 Jim Fregosi .30 .12
345 Tony Gonzalez .10 .04
346 Alex Johnson .10 .04
347 Fred Lasher .10 .04
348 Jim Maloney .10 .04
349 Rudy May .10 .04
350 Ken McMullen .10 .04
351 Andy Messersmith .20 .08
352 Gerry Moses .10 .04
353 Syd O'Brien .10 .04
354 Mel Queen .10 .04
355 Roger Repoz .10 .04
356 Archie Reynolds .10 .04
357 Chico Ruiz .10 .04
358 Jim Spencer .10 .04
359 Clyde Wright .10 .04
360 Billy Wynne .10 .04
361 Mike Andrews .10 .04
362 Luis Alvarado .10 .04
363 Tom Egan .10 .04
364 Steve Hamilton .10 .04
365 Ed Herrmann .10 .04
366 Joel Horlen .10 .04
367 Tommy John .40 .16
368 Bart Johnson .10 .04
369 Jay Johnstone .10 .04
370 Duane Josephson .10 .04
371 Pat Kelly .10 .04
372 Bobby Knoop .10 .04
373 Carlos May .10 .04
374 Lee Maye .10 .04
375 Tom McCraw .10 .04
376 Bill Melton .10 .04
377 Rich Morales .10 .04
378 Tom Murphy .10 .04
379 Don O'Riley .10 .04
380 Rick Reichardt .10 .04
381 Bill Robinson .10 .04
382 Bob Spence .10 .04
383 Walt Williams .10 .04
384 Wilbur Wood .20 .08
385 Rick Austin .10 .04
386 Buddy Bradford .10 .04
387 Larry Brown .10 .04
388 Lou Camilli .10 .04
389 Vince Colbert .10 .04
390 Ray Fosse .10 .04
391 Alan Foster .10 .04
392 Roy Foster .10 .04
393 Rich Hand .10 .04
394 Steve Hargan .10 .04
395 Ken Harrelson .40 .16
396 Jack Heidemann .10 .04
397 Phil Hennigan .10 .04
398 Dennis Higgins .10 .04
399 Chuck Hinton .10 .04
400 Tony Horton .20 .08
401 Ray Lamb .10 .04
402 Eddie Leon .10 .04
403 Sam McDowell .30 .12
404 Graig Nettles .40 .16
405 Mike Paul .10 .04
406 Vada Pinson .40 .16
407 Ken Suarez .10 .04
408 Ted Uhlaender .10 .04
409 Eddie Brinkman .10 .04
410 Gates Brown .10 .04
411 Ike Brown .10 .04
412 Les Cain .10 .04
413 Norm Cash .40 .16
414 Joe Coleman .10 .04
415 Bill Freehan .30 .12
416 Cesar Gutierrez .10 .04
417 John Hiller .20 .08
418 Willie Horton .30 .12
419 Dalton Jones .10 .04
420 Al Kaline 1.50 .60
421 Mike Kilkenny .10 .04
422 Mickey Lolich .40 .16
423 Dick McAuliffe .20 .08
424 Joe Niekro .40 .16
425 Jim Northrup .20 .08
426 Daryl Patterson .10 .04
427 Jimmie Price .10 .04
428 Bob Reed .10 .04
429 Aurelio Rodriguez .10 .04
430 Fred Scherman .10 .04
431 Mickey Stanley .10 .04
432 Tom Timmerman .10 .04
433 Ted Abernathy .10 .04
434 Wally Bunker .10 .04
435 Tom Burgmeier .10 .04
436 Bill Butler .10 .04
437 Bruce Dal Canton .10 .04
438 Dick Drago .10 .04
439 Bobby Floyd .10 .04
440 Gail Hopkins .10 .04
441 Joe Keough .10 .04
442 Ed Kirkpatrick .10 .04
443 Tom Matchick .10 .04
444 Jerry May .10 .04
445 Aurelio Monteagudo .10 .04
446 Dave Morehead .10 .04
447 Bob Oliver .10 .04
448 Amos Otis .20 .08
449 Fred Patek .20 .08
450 Lou Piniella .40 .16
451 Cookie Rojas .10 .04
452 Jim Rooker .10 .04
453 Paul Schaal .10 .04
454 Rich Severson .10 .04
455 George Spriggs .10 .04
456 Carl Taylor .10 .04
457 Dave Baldwin .10 .04
458 Ted Savage .10 .04
459 Dick Ellsworth .10 .04
460 John Gelnar .10 .04
461 Tommy Harper .20 .08
462 Mike Hegan .10 .04
463 Bob Humphreys .10 .04
464 Andy Kosco .10 .04
465 Lew Krausse .10 .04
466 Ted Kubiak .10 .04
467 Skip Lockwood .10 .04
468 Dave May .10 .04
469 Bob Meyer .10 .04
470 John Morris .10 .04
471 Marty Pattin .10 .04
472 Roberto Pena .10 .04
473 Ellie Rodriguez .10 .04
474 Phil Roof .10 .04
475 Ken Sanders .10 .04
476 Russ Snyder .10 .04
477 Bill Tillman .10 .04
478 Bill Voss .10 .04
479 Danny Walton .10 .04
480 Floyd Wicker .10 .04
481 Brant Alyea .10 .04
482 Bert Blyleven .40 .16
483 Dave Boswell .10 .04
484 Leo Cardenas .10 .04
485 Rod Carew 2.00 .80
486 Tom Hall .10 .04
487 Jim Holt .10 .04
488 Jim Kaat .40 .16
489 Harmon Killebrew 1.00 .40
490 Charlie Manuel .20 .08
491 George Mitterwald .10 .04
492 Tony Oliva .40 .16
493 Ron Perranoski .10 .04
494 Jim Perry .20 .08
495 Frank Quilici .10 .04
496 Rich Reese .10 .04
497 Rick Renick .10 .04
498 Danny Thompson .20 .08
499 Luis Tiant .30 .12
500 Tom Tischinski .10 .04
501 Cesar Tovar .20 .08
502 Stan Williams .10 .04
503 Dick Woodson .10 .04
504 Bill Zepp .10 .04
505 Jack Aker .10 .04
506 Stan Bahnsen .10 .04
507 Curt Blefary .10 .04
508 Bill Burbach .10 .04
509 Danny Cater .10 .04
510 Horace Clarke .10 .04
511 John Ellis .10 .04
512 Jake Gibbs .10 .04
513 Ron Hansen .10 .04
514 Mike Kekich .10 .04
515 Jerry Kenney .10 .04
516 Ron Klimkowski .10 .04
517 Steve Kline .10 .04
518 Mike McCormick .10 .04
519 Lindy McDaniel .10 .04
520 Gene Michael .20 .08
521 Thurman Munson 2.00 .80
522 Bobby Murcer .40 .16
523 Fritz Peterson .10 .04
524 Mel Stottlemyre .40 .16
525 Pete Ward .10 .04
526 Gary Waslewski .10 .04
527 Roy White .30 .12
528 Ron Woods .10 .04
529 Felipe Alou .40 .16
530 Sal Bando .30 .12
531 Vida Blue .40 .16
532 Bert Campaneris .30 .12
533 Ron Clark .10 .04
534 Chuck Dobson .10 .04
535 Dave Duncan .10 .04
536 Frank Fernandez .10 .04
537 Rollie Fingers 1.00 .40
538 Dick Green .10 .04
539 Steve Hovley .10 .04
540 Jim Hunter 1.50 .60
541 Reggie Jackson 3.00 1.20
542 Marcel Lachemann .10 .04
543 Paul Lindblad .10 .04
544 Bob Locker .10 .04
545 Don Mincher .10 .04
546 Rick Monday .30 .12
547 John Odom .10 .04
548 Jim Roland .10 .04
549 Joe Rudi .30 .12
550 Diego Segui .10 .04
551 Bob Stickels .10 .04
552 Gene Tenace .20 .08
553 Bernie Allen .10 .04
554 Dick Bosman .10 .04
555 Jackie Brown .10 .04
556 Paul Casanova .10 .04
557 Casey Cox .10 .04
558 Tim Cullen .10 .04
559 Mike Epstein .10 .04
560 Curt Flood .40 .16
561 Joe Foy .10 .04
562 Jim French .10 .04
563 Bill Gogolewski .10 .04
564 Tom Grieve .30 .12
565 Joe Grzenda .10 .04
566 Frank Howard .40 .16
567 Gerry Janeski .10 .04
568 Darold Knowles .10 .04
569 Elliott Maddox .10 .04
570 Denny McLain .40 .16
571 Dave Nelson .10 .04
572 Horacio Pina .10 .04
573 Jim Shellenback .10 .04
574 Ed Stroud .10 .04
575 Del Unser .10 .04
576 Don Wert .10 .04
577 Hank Aaron 4.00 1.60
578 Luis Aparicio 1.00 .40
579 Ernie Banks 2.00 .80
580 Johnny Bench 2.00 .80
581 Rico Carty .20 .08
582 Roberto Clemente 6.00 2.40
583 Bob Gibson 1.25 .50
584 Willie Horton .30 .12
585 Frank Howard .40 .16
586 Reggie Jackson 3.00 1.20
587 Fergie Jenkins 1.00 .40
588 Alex Johnson .10 .04
589 Al Kaline 1.50 .60
590 Harmon Killebrew 1.00 .40
591 Willie Mays 4.00 1.60
592 Sam McDowell .20 .08
593 Denny McLain .40 .16
594 Boog Powell .40 .16
595 Brooks Robinson 1.50 .60
596 Frank Robinson 1.50 .60
597 Pete Rose 3.00 1.20
598 Tom Seaver 2.00 .80
599 Rusty Staub .40 .16
600 Carl Yastrzemski 2.00 .80

2000 MLB Showdown Promos

This 35-card promo set was released to fans and hobby dealers during spring-training in early 2000. The set features promotional cards of some of major league's top players. Please note that the cards are unnumbered, and are listed below in alphabetical order.

Nm-Mt Ex-Mt
COMPLETE SET (35) 50.00 15.00
1 Bob Abreu 1.00 .30
2 Sandy Alomar Jr. .50 .15
3 Jeff Bagwell 2.50 .75
4 Michael Barrett .50 .15
5 Ron Belliard .50 .15
6 Craig Biggio 1.50 .45
7 Sean Casey 1.00 .30
8 Luis Castillo 1.00 .30
9 Carlos Delgado 2.50 .75
10 J.D. Drew 1.00 .30
11 Erubiel Durazo 1.50 .45
12 Ray Durham 1.00 .30
13 Damion Easley .50 .15
14 Carlos Febles .50 .15
15 Troy Glaus 2.00 .60
16 Mark Grace 2.00 .60
17 Rusty Greer 1.00 .30
18 Ben Grieve .50 .15
19 Tony Gwynn 5.00 1.50
20 Todd Helton 2.50 .75
21 Andruw Jones 2.50 .75
22 Andrew Jones OB8 2.50 .75
23 Andruw Jones OB10 2.50 .75
24 Chipper Jones 4.00 1.20
25 Jeff Kent 1.50 .45
26 Corey Koskie 1.00 .30
27 Edgar Martinez 1.50 .45
28 Fred McGriff 1.50 .45
29 Warren Morris .50 .15
30 Rafael Palmeiro 2.00 .60
31 Gary Sheffield 2.50 .75
32 B.J. Surhoff 1.00 .30
33 Jason Varitek 1.00 .30
34 Robin Ventura 1.50 .45
35 Bernie Williams 2.00 .60

2000 MLB Showdown Diamond Star Promos

This 19-card promo set was released to fans during spring-training in early 2000. The set features promotional cards of some of major leagues top hitters. Please note that the cards are unnumbered, and are listed below in alphabetical order.

Nm-Mt Ex-Mt
COMPLETE SET (19) 30.00 9.00
1 Sandy Alomar 1.00 .30
2 Jeff Bagwell 2.50 .75
3 Craig Biggio 1.50 .45
4 Carlos Delgado 2.50 .75
5 Ray Durham 1.00 .30
6 Damion Easley .50 .15
7 Mark Grace 2.00 .60
8 Rusty Greer 1.00 .30
9 Tony Gwynn 5.00 1.50
10 Chipper Jones 4.00 1.20
11 Jeff Kent 2.00 .60
12 Edgar Martinez 1.50 .45
13 Fred McGriff 1.50 .45
14 Rafael Palmeiro 2.50 .75
15 Gary Sheffield 2.50 .75
16 B.J. Surhoff 1.00 .30
17 Jason Varitek 1.00 .30
18 Robin Ventura 1.50 .45
19 Bernie Williams 2.00 .60

2000 MLB Showdown Future Star Promos

This 13-card promo set was released to fans during spring-training in early 2000. The set features promotional cards of some of major league's top prospects. Please note that the cards are unnumbered, and are listed below in alphabetical order.

Nm-Mt Ex-Mt
COMPLETE SET (13) 15.00 4.50
1 Bob Abreu 2.50 .75
2 Michael Barrett 1.00 .30
3 Ron Belliard .50 .15
4 Sean Casey 1.00 .30
5 Luis Castillo 1.50 .45
6 J.D. Drew 1.00 .30
7 Erubiel Durazo 1.50 .45
8 Carlos Febles .50 .15
9 Troy Glaus 2.00 .60
10 Ben Grieve 1.00 .30
11 Todd Helton 3.00 .90
12 Corey Koskie 1.00 .30
13 Warren Morris .50 .15

2000 MLB Showdown Home Run Hitter Promos

This 14-card promo set was released to fans during spring-training in early 2000. The set features promotional cards of some of major league's top power hitters. Please note that the cards are unnumbered, and are listed below in alphabetical order.

Nm-Mt Ex-Mt
COMPLETE SET (14) 50.00 15.00
1 Barry Bonds 5.00 1.50
2 Jose Canseco 2.00 .60
3 Nomar Garciaparra 4.00 1.20
4 Jason Giambi 2.50 .75
5 Shawn Green 2.00 .60
6 Ken Griffey Jr. 6.00 1.80
7 Andruw Jones 2.50 .75
8 Chipper Jones 4.00 1.20
9 Mark McGwire 8.00 2.40
10 Rafael Palmeiro 2.00 .60
11 Mike Piazza 6.00 1.80
12 Manny Ramirez 2.50 .75
13 Alex Rodriguez 6.00 1.80
14 Sammy Sosa 5.00 1.50

2000 MLB Showdown 1st Edition

The 2000 MLB Showdown product was released in late April, 2000 as a 462-card baseball game. The 1st Edition cards were released with a silver stamp on front of the card indicating the first print run. The set features 400-player cards and 62 foil superstar cards that were short printed at one in three packs. The 1st Edition packs were released as nine-card packs and carried a suggested retail price of 2.99. Please note that the 1st Edition Greg Maddux and David Cone foil cards were released in starter sets, as well as in packs. Also note that Dennis Cook, Al Leiter, and Kenny Rogers were printed as RHP, but are actually LHP in real life.

Nm-Mt Ex-Mt
COMPLETE SET (462) 200.00 60.00
COMP.SET w/o FOIL (400) 80.00 24.00
COMMON CARD (1-462) .25 .07
COMMON FOIL 3.00 .90
1 Garret Anderson .75 .23
2 Tim Belcher .25 .07
3 Gary DiSarcina UER .25 .07
Tim Salmon incorrectly pictured
4 Darin Erstad .75 .23
5 Chuck Finley FOIL 5.00 1.50
6 Troy Glaus 1.25 .35
7 Todd Greene .25 .07
8 Jeff Huson .25 .07
9 Orlando Palmeiro .25 .07
10 Troy Percival .75 .23
11 Mark Petkovsek .25 .07
12 Tim Salmon 1.25 .35
13 Steve Sparks .25 .07
14 Mo Vaughn .75 .23
15 Matt Walbeck .25 .07
16 Jay Bell FOIL 5.00 1.50
17 Andy Benes .25 .07
18 Omar Daal .25 .07
19 Steve Finley .75 .23
20 Andy Fox .25 .07
21 Hanley Frias .25 .07
22 Bernard Gilkey .25 .07
23 Luis Gonzalez FOIL 5.00 1.50
24 Randy Johnson FOIL 8.00 2.40
25 Travis Lee .25 .07
26 Matt Mantei .25 .07
27 Dan Plesac .25 .07
28 Kelly Stinnett .25 .07
29 Greg Swindell .25 .07
30 Matt Williams FOIL 5.00 1.50
31 Tony Womack .25 .07
32 Bret Boone .75 .23
33 Tom Glavine 1.25 .35
34 Jose Hernandez .25 .07
35 Brian Hunter .25 .07
36 Andruw Jones .75 .23
37 Chipper Jones FOIL 8.00 2.40
38 Brian Jordan .25 .07
39 Ryan Klesko .75 .23
40 Keith Lockhart .25 .07
41 Greg Maddux FOIL * 3.00 .90
42 Kevin Millwood FOIL 5.00 1.50
43 Eddie Perez .25 .07
44 Mike Remlinger .25 .07
45 John Rocker .25 .07
46 John Smoltz 1.25 .35
47 Walt Weiss .25 .07
48 Gerald Williams .25 .07
49 Rich Amaral .25 .07
50 Brady Anderson .75 .23
51 Albert Belle .75 .23
52 Mike Bordick .25 .07
53 Jeff Conine .75 .23
54 Delino DeShields .75 .23
55 Scott Erickson .25 .07
56 Charles Johnson .75 .23
57 Mike Mussina 2.00 .60
58 Jesse Orosco .25 .07
59 Sidney Ponson .25 .07
60 Jeff Reboulet .25 .07
61 Cal Ripken FOIL 20.00 6.00
62 B.J. Surhoff .75 .23
63 Mike Timlin .25 .07
64 Rod Beck .25 .07
65 Damon Buford .25 .07
66 Rheal Cormier .25 .07
67 N.Garciaparra FOIL 12.00 3.60
68 Butch Huskey .25 .07
69 Darren Lewis .25 .07
70 Derek Lowe .75 .23
71 Pedro Martinez FOIL 8.00 2.40
72 Trot Nixon 1.25 .35
73 Jose Offerman .25 .07
74 Troy O'Leary .25 .07
75 Mark Portugal .25 .07
76 Pat Rapp .25 .07
77 Mike Stanley .25 .07
78 John Valentin .25 .07
79 Jason Varitek .75 .23
80 Tim Wakefield .75 .23
81 Rick Aguilera .75 .23
82 Jeff Blauser .25 .07
83 Kyle Farnsworth .25 .07
84 Gary Gaetti .75 .23
85 Mark Grace 1.25 .35
86 Lance Johnson .25 .07
87 Jon Lieber .25 .07
88 Mickey Morandini .25 .07
89 Jose Nieves .25 .07
90 Jeff Reed .25 .07
91 Henry Rodriguez .25 .07
92 Scott Sanders .25 .07
93 Benito Santiago .75 .23
94 Sammy Sosa FOIL 20.00 6.00
95 Steve Trachsel .25 .07
96 James Baldwin .25 .07
97 Mike Caruso .25 .07
98 Ray Durham .75 .23
99 Brook Fordyce .25 .07
100 Bob Howry .25 .07
101 Paul Konerko .75 .23
102 Carlos Lee .75 .23
103 Greg Norton .25 .07
104 Magglio Ordonez .75 .23
105 Jim Parque .25 .07
106 Bill Simas .25 .07
107 Chris Singleton .25 .07
108 Mike Sirotka .25 .07
109 Frank Thomas FOIL 8.00 2.40
110 Craig Wilson .25 .07
111 Aaron Boone .75 .23
112 Mike Cameron .75 .23
113 Sean Casey FOIL 5.00 1.50
114 Danny Graves .25 .07
115 Pete Harnisch .25 .07
116 Barry Larkin FOIL 8.00 2.40
117 Pokey Reese .25 .07
118 Scott Sullivan .25 .07
119 Eddie Taubensee .25 .07
120 Brett Tomko .25 .07
121 Michael Tucker .25 .07
122 Greg Vaughn .75 .23
123 Ron Villone .25 .07
124 Scott Williamson FOIL 3.00 .90
125 Dmitri Young .75 .23
126 Roberto Alomar FOIL 8.00 2.40
127 Harold Baines .75 .23
128 Dave Burba .25 .07
129 Bartolo Colon .25 .07
130 Einar Diaz .25 .07
131 Travis Fryman .75 .23
132 Mike Jackson .25 .07
133 David Justice .75 .23
134 Kenny Lofton FOIL 5.00 1.50
135 Charles Nagy .25 .07
136 Manny Ramirez FOIL 5.00 1.50
137 Richie Sexson .75 .23
138 Paul Shuey .25 .07
139 Jim Thome FOIL 8.00 2.40
140 Omar Vizquel .75 .23
141 Enrique Wilson .25 .07
142 Kurt Abbott .25 .07
143 Pedro Astacio .25 .07
144 Jeff Barry .25 .07
145 Dante Bichette .75 .23
146 Henry Blanco .25 .07
147 Brian Bohanon .25 .07
148 Vinny Castilla .75 .23
149 Jerry Dipoto .25 .07
150 Todd Helton 1.25 .35
151 Darryl Kile .75 .23
152 Curtis Leskanic .25 .07
153 Neifi Perez .25 .07
154 Terry Shumpert .25 .07
155 Dave Veres .25 .07
156 Larry Walker FOIL 5.00 1.50
157 Brad Ausmus .25 .07
158 Frank Catalanotto .25 .07
159 Tony Clark .25 .07
160 Deivi Cruz .25 .07
161 Damion Easley .25 .07
162 Juan Encarnacion .25 .07
163 Karim Garcia .25 .07
164 Bobby Higginson .25 .07
165 Todd Jones .25 .07
166 Gabe Kapler .25 .07
167 Dave Mlicki .25 .07
168 Brian Moehler .25 .07
169 C.J. Nitkowski .25 .07
170 Dean Palmer FOIL 5.00 1.50
171 Jeff Weaver .25 .07
172 Antonio Alfonseca .25 .07
173 Bruce Aven .25 .07
174 Dave Berg .25 .07
175 Luis Castillo FOIL 5.00 1.50
176 Ryan Dempster .25 .07
177 Brian Edmondson .25 .07
178 Alex Gonzalez .25 .07
179 Mark Kotsay .25 .07
180 Derrek Lee .75 .23
181 Braden Looper .25 .07
182 Mike Lowell .75 .23
183 Brian Meadows .25 .07
184 Mike Redmond .25 .07
185 Dennis Springer .25 .07
186 Preston Wilson .75 .23
187 Jeff Bagwell FOIL 5.00 1.50
188 Derek Bell .25 .07
189 Craig Biggio 1.25 .35
190 Tim Bogar .25 .07
191 Ken Caminiti .75 .23
192 Scott Elarton .25 .07
193 Tony Eusebio .25 .07
194 Carl Everett FOIL 5.00 1.50

195 Mike Hampton FOIL 5.00 1.50
196 Richard Hidalgo .75 .23
197 Stan Javier .25 .07
198 Jose Lima .25 .07
199 Jay Powell .25 .07
200 Shane Reynolds .25 .07
201 Bill Spiers .25 .07
202 Billy Wagner FOIL 5.00 1.50
203 Carlos Beltran FOIL 5.00 1.50
204 Johnny Damon .75 .23
205 Jermaine Dye .25 .07
206 Carlos Febles .25 .07
207 Jeremy Giambi .25 .07
208 Chad Kreuter .25 .07
209 Jeff Montgomery .25 .07
210 Joe Randa .75 .23
211 Jose Rosado .25 .07
212 Rey Sanchez .25 .07
213 Scott Service .25 .07
214 Tim Spehr .25 .07
215 Jeff Suppan .25 .07
216 Mike Sweeney .75 .23
217 Jay Witasick .25 .07
218 Adrian Beltre .75 .23
219 Pedro Borbon .25 .07
220 Kevin Brown FOIL 5.00 1.50
221 Mark Grudzielanek .25 .07
222 Dave Hansen .25 .07
223 Todd Hundley .25 .07
224 Eric Karros .75 .23
225 Raul Mondesi .75 .23
226 Chan Ho Park .75 .23
227 Jeff Shaw .25 .07
228 Gary Sheffield FOIL 5.00 1.50
229 Ismael Valdes .25 .07
230 Jose Vizcaino .25 .07
231 Devon White .25 .07
232 Eric Young .25 .07
233 Ron Belliard .25 .07
234 Sean Berry .25 .07
235 Jeromy Burnitz FOIL 5.00 1.50
236 Jeff Cirillo .25 .07
237 Marquis Grissom .25 .07
238 Geoff Jenkins .75 .23
239 Scott Karl .25 .07
240 Mark Loretta .25 .07
241 Mike Myers .25 .07
242 David Nilsson FOIL 3.00 .90
243 Hideo Nomo 2.00 .60
244 Alex Ochoa .25 .07
245 Jose Valentin .25 .07
246 Bob Wickman .25 .07
247 Steve Woodard .25 .07
248 Chad Allen .25 .07
249 Ron Coomer .25 .07
250 Cristian Guzman .75 .23
251 Denny Hocking .25 .07
252 Torii Hunter .75 .23
253 Corey Koskie .75 .23
254 Matt Lawton .25 .07
255 Joe Mays .25 .07
256 Doug Mientkiewicz .75 .23
257 Eric Milton .25 .07
258 Brad Radke FOIL 5.00 1.50
259 Terry Steinbach .25 .07
260 Mike Trombley .25 .07
261 Todd Walker .75 .23
262 Bob Wells .25 .07
263 Shane Andrews .25 .07
264 Michael Barrett .25 .07
265 Orlando Cabrera .25 .07
266 Brad Fullmer .25 .07
267 Vlad. Guerrero FOIL 8.00 2.40
268 Wilton Guerrero .25 .07
269 Dustin Hermanson .25 .07
270 Steve Kline .25 .07
271 Manny Martinez .25 .07
272 Mike Thurman .25 .07
273 Ugueth Urbina .25 .07
274 Javier Vazquez .75 .23
275 Jose Vidro .75 .23
276 Rondell White .75 .23
277 Chris Widger .25 .07
278 Edgardo Alfonzo FOIL 5.00 1.50
279 Armando Benitez .75 .23
280 Roger Cedeno .25 .07
281 Dennis Cook UER .25 .07
Mistakenly printed as a RHP
282 Shawon Dunston .25 .07
283 Matt Franco .25 .07
284 Darryl Hamilton .25 .07
285 R. Henderson FOIL 8.00 2.40
286 Orel Hershiser .75 .23
287 Al Leiter UER .75 .23
Mistakenly printed as a RHP
288 John Olerud .75 .23
289 Rey Ordonez .25 .07
290 Mike Piazza FOIL 10.00 3.00
291 Kenny Rogers UER .75 .23
Mistakenly printed as a RHP
292 Robin Ventura 1.25 .35
293 Turk Wendell .25 .07
294 Masato Yoshii .25 .07
295 Scott Brosius .25 .07
296 Roger Clemens FOIL 12.00 3.60
297 David Cone FOIL * 2.00 .60
298 Chad Curtis .25 .07
299 Chili Davis .75 .23
300 Orlando Hernandez .75 .23
301 Derek Jeter FOIL 12.00 3.60
302 Chuck Knoblauch .75 .23
303 Ricky Ledee .25 .07
304 Tino Martinez 1.25 .35
305 Ramiro Mendoza .25 .07
306 Paul O'Neill 1.25 .35
307 Andy Pettitte 1.25 .35
308 Jorge Posada 1.25 .35
309 Mariano Rivera FOIL 5.00 1.50
310 Mike Stanton .25 .07
311 Bernie Williams FOIL 5.00 1.50
312 Kevin Appier .75 .23
313 Eric Chavez .75 .23
314 Ryan Christenson .25 .07
315 Jason Giambi FOIL 8.00 2.40
316 Ben Grieve .25 .07
317 Buddy Groom .25 .07
318 Gil Heredia .25 .07
319 A.J. Hinch .25 .07
320 John Jaha .25 .07
321 Doug Jones .25 .07
322 Omar Olivares .25 .07
323 Tony Phillips .25 .07
324 Matt Stairs .25 .07
325 Miguel Tejada .75 .23
326 Randy Velarde FOIL 3.00 .90
327 Bobby Abreu FOIL 5.00 1.50
328 Marlon Anderson .25 .07
329 Alex Arias .25 .07
330 Rico Brogna .25 .07
331 Paul Byrd .25 .07
332 Ron Gant .75 .23
333 Doug Glanville .25 .07
334 Wayne Gomes .25 .07
335 Kevin Jordan .25 .07
336 Mike Lieberthal .75 .23
337 Steve Montgomery .25 .07
338 Chad Ogea .25 .07
339 Scott Rolen 1.25 .35
340 Curt Schilling FOIL 5.00 1.50
341 Kevin Sefcik .25 .07
342 Mike Benjamin .25 .07
343 Kris Benson .25 .07
344 Adrian Brown .25 .07
345 Brant Brown .25 .07
346 Brad Clontz .25 .07
347 Brian Giles FOIL 5.00 1.50
348 Jason Kendall FOIL 5.00 1.50
349 Al Martin .25 .07
350 Warren Morris .25 .07
351 Todd Ritchie .25 .07
352 Scott Sauerbeck .25 .07
353 Jason Schmidt .75 .23
354 Ed Sprague .25 .07
355 Mike Williams .25 .07
356 Kevin Young .25 .07
357 Andy Ashby .25 .07
358 Ben Davis .25 .07
359 Tony Gwynn FOIL 8.00 2.40
360 Sterling Hitchcock .25 .07
361 Trevor Hoffman FOIL 5.00 1.50
362 Damian Jackson .25 .07
363 Wally Joyner .75 .23
364 Phil Nevin .75 .23
365 Eric Owens .25 .07
366 Ruben Rivera .25 .07
367 Reggie Sanders .75 .23
368 John Vander Wal .25 .07
369 Quilvio Veras .25 .07
370 Matt Whisenant .25 .07
371 Woody Williams .25 .07
372 Rich Aurilia .75 .23
373 Marvin Benard .25 .07
374 Barry Bonds FOIL 20.00 6.00
375 Ellis Burks .25 .07
376 Alan Embree .25 .07
377 Shawn Estes .25 .07
378 John Johnstone .25 .07
379 Jeff Kent .25 .07
380 Brent Mayne .25 .07
381 Bill Mueller .75 .23
382 Robb Nen .75 .23
383 Russ Ortiz .75 .23
384 Kirk Rueter .25 .07
385 F.P. Santangelo .25 .07
386 J.T. Snow .75 .23
387 David Bell .25 .07
388 Jay Buhner .75 .23
389 Russ Davis .25 .07
390 Freddy Garcia .75 .23
391 Ken Griffey Jr. FOIL 12.00 3.60
392 John Halama .25 .07
393 Brian Hunter .25 .07
394 Raul Ibanez .25 .07
395 Tom Lampkin .25 .07
396 Edgar Martinez FOIL 5.00 1.50
397 Jose Mesa .25 .07
398 Jamie Moyer .75 .23
399 Jose Paniagua .25 .07
400 Alex Rodriguez FOIL 10.00 3.00
401 Dan Wilson .25 .07
402 Manny Aybar .25 .07
403 Ricky Bottalico .25 .07
404 Kent Bottenfield .25 .07
405 Darren Bragg .25 .07
406 Alberto Castillo .25 .07
407 J.D. Drew .75 .23
408 Jose Jimenez .25 .07
409 Ray Lankford .25 .07
410 Joe McEwing .25 .07
411 Willie McGee .75 .23
412 Mark McGwire FOIL 25.00 7.50
413 Darren Oliver .25 .07
414 Lance Painter .25 .07
415 Edgar Renteria .75 .23
416 Fernando Tatis FOIL 3.00 .90
417 Wilson Alvarez .25 .07
418 Rolando Arrojo .25 .07
419 Wade Boggs 1.25 .35
420 Miguel Cairo .25 .07
421 Jose Canseco FOIL 8.00 2.40
422 John Flaherty .25 .07
423 Roberto Hernandez .25 .07
424 Dave Martinez .25 .07
425 Fred McGriff 1.25 .35
426 Paul Sorrento .25 .07
427 Kevin Stocker .25 .07
428 Bubba Trammell .25 .07
429 Rick White .25 .07
430 Randy Winn .25 .07
431 Bobby Witt .25 .07
432 Royce Clayton .25 .07
433 Tim Crabtree .25 .07
434 Juan Gonzalez 2.00 .60
435 Rusty Greer .25 .07
437 Rick Helling .25 .07
438 Mark McLemore .25 .07
439 Mike Morgan .25 .07
440 Rafael Palmeiro FOIL 5.00 1.50
441 Ivan Rodriguez FOIL 8.00 2.40
442 Aaron Sele .25 .07
443 Lee Stevens .75 .23
444 Mike Venafro .25 .07
445 John Wetteland .25 .07
446 Todd Zeile .75 .23
447 Jeff Zimmerman FOIL 3.00 .90
448 Tony Batista .75 .23
449 Homer Bush .25 .07
450 Jose Cruz Jr. .25 .07
451 Carlos Delgado .75 .23
452 Kelvim Escobar .25 .07
453 Tony Fernandez FOIL 3.00 .90
454 Darrin Fletcher .25 .07
455 Shawn Green FOIL 5.00 1.50
456 Pat Hentgen .25 .07
457 Billy Koch .25 .07
458 Graeme Lloyd .25 .07
459 Brian McRae .25 .07
460 David Segui .25 .07
461 Shannon Stewart .75 .23
462 David Wells .25 .07

2000 MLB Showdown Unlimited

Randomly inserted into starter sets, this 462-card set is a partial parallel of the MLB Showdown 1st Edition set. This set does not have the silver 1st edition stamp. The starter sets carried a suggested retail price of $9.99.

Nm-Mt Ex-Mt
COMPLETE SET (462) 200.00 60.00
COMP.SET w/o FOIL (400) 50.00 15.00
*UNLIMITED: .2X TO .5X 1ST EDITION
*UNL.FOIL: .2X TO .5X BASIC FOIL

2000 MLB Showdown Strategy

Inserted into packs at a rate of two per pack, and starter sets at 40 per starter set, this 55-card insert set features the strategy cards necessary for playing the MLB Showdown game. Cards carry an "S" prefix.

Nm-Mt Ex-Mt
COMPLETE SET (55) 20.00 6.00
S1 Umpire .25 .07
Bad Call
S2 Mike Stanley .25 .07
Big Inning
S3 Tony Phillips .25 .07
Bobbled in Outfield
S4 Manny Ramirez .25 .07
Clutch Hitting
S5 Chuck Knoblauch .25 .07
Do or Die
S6 Dodgers Outfielder .25 .07
Down the Middle
S7 Carl Everett .25 .07
Ducks on Pond
S8 Barry Bonds 1.25 .35
Favorable Matchup
S9 Deivi Cruz .25 .07
Free Steal
S10 Jose Offerman .25 .07
Get Under It
S11 Rickey Henderson .50 .15
Great Lead
S12 Damian Jackson .25 .07
Hard Slide
S13 Derek Jeter 1.25 .35
High Fives
S14 Paul O' Neill .30 .09
Last Chance
S15 Derek Jeter 1.25 .35
Long Single
S16 Rangers Pitcher .25 .07
Out of Gas
S17 Rickey Henderson .50 .15
Out of Position
S18 Chipper Jones .50 .15
Play the Percentages
S19 Omar Vizquel .25 .07
Rally Cap
S20 Mike Henneman .25 .07
Rattled
S21 Miguel Tejada .25 .07
Runner Not Held
S22 Rockies Pitcher .25 .07
Slow Roller
S23 Braves Pitcher .25 .07
Stick a Fork in Him
S24 Sammy Sosa .75 .23
Swing for Fences
S25 Bernie Williams .30 .09
To the Warning Track
S26 Mark McGwire 1.25 .35
Whiplash
S27 Will Clark .50 .15
Wide Throw
S28 Eddie Taubensee .25 .07
Wild Pitch
S29 Walt Weiss .25 .07
By the Book
S30 Billy Wagner .25 .07
Dominating
S31 Orlando Hernandez .25 .07
Full Windup
S32 Rey Ordonez .25 .07
Ryan Klesko
Good Fielding
S33 Jason Kendall .25 .07
Gun 'Em Down!
S34 Sammy Sosa .75 .23
He's Got a Gun
S35 David Cone .25 .07
In the Groove
S36 Pedro Martinez .50 .15
In the Zone
S37 S.F. Giants .25 .07
Infield In
S38 Randy Johnson .50 .15
Intimidation
S39 Ken Griffey Jr. .75 .23
Just Over Wall
S40 Padres Pitcher .25 .07
Knock Down
S41 Jesse Orosco .25 .07
Lefty Specialist
S42 Mariano Rivera .30 .09
Nerves of Steel
S43 Randy Johnson .50 .15
Nothing but Heat
S44 Bobby Hughes .25 .07
Pitchout
S45 John Rocker .25 .07
Pumped Up
S46 Greg Maddux .75 .23
Quick Pitch
S47 Carlos Baerga .25 .07
Ryan Klesko
Rally Killer
S48 Chuck Knoblauch .25 .07
Short Fly
S49 Pedro Martinez .50 .15
Three Up, Three Down
S50 Derek Jeter 1.25 .35
Trick Pitch
S51 Sammy Sosa .75 .23
Belt-High
S52 Joe Torre .25 .07
Change in Strategy
S53 Pokey Reese .25 .07
Grounder to Second
S54 Mark Grace .30 .09
Stealing Signals
S55 Cal Ripken 1.50 .45
Swing at Anything

2000 MLB Showdown Pennant Run 1st Edition

The 2000 MLB Showdown Pennant Run product was released in late August, 2000 as a 150-card set. The 1st Edition cards were released with a silver stamp on front of the card indicating the first print run. The set features 130-player cards and 20 foil superstar cards that were short printed at one in three packs. The 1st Edition packs were released as nine-card packs and carried a suggested retail price of 2.99. Please note that these cards were only released in pack form, there were no starters sets produced of Pennant Run.

Nm-Mt Ex-Mt
COMPLETE SET (150) 100.00 30.00
COMP.SET w/o FOIL (130) 25.00 7.50
COMMON CARD (1-150) .25 .07
COMMON FOIL 3.00 .90
1 Kent Bottenfield .25 .07
2 Ken Hill .25 .07
3 Adam Kennedy .25 .07
4 Ben Molina .25 .07
5 Scott Spiezio .25 .07
6 Brian Anderson .25 .07
7 Erubiel Durazo FOIL 3.00 .90
8 Armando Reynoso .25 .07
9 Russ Springer .25 .07
10 Todd Stottlemyre .25 .07
11 Tony Womack .25 .07
12 Andres Galarraga FOIL 3.00 .90
13 Javy Lopez FOIL 3.00 .90
14 Kevin McGlinchy .25 .07
15 Terry Mulholland .25 .07
16 Reggie Sanders .75 .23
17 Harold Baines .75 .23
18 Will Clark 2.00 .60
19 Mike Trombley .25 .07
20 Manny Alexander .25 .07
21 Carl Everett FOIL 3.00 .90
22 Ramon Martinez FOIL 3.00 .90
23 Bret Saberhagen .75 .23
24 John Wasdin .25 .07
25 Joe Girardi .25 .07
26 Ricky Gutierrez .25 .07
27 Glenallen Hill .25 .07
28 Kevin Tapani .25 .07
29 Kerry Wood FOIL 8.00 2.40
30 Eric Young .25 .07
31 Keith Foulke FOIL 3.00 .90
32 Mark Johnson .25 .07
33 Sean Lowe .25 .07
34 Jose Valentin .25 .07
35 Dante Bichette .75 .23
36 Ken Griffey Jr. FOIL 12.00 3.60
37 Denny Neagle .25 .07
38 Steve Parris .25 .07
39 Dennys Reyes .25 .07
40 Sandy Alomar Jr. .25 .07
41 Chuck Finley FOIL 3.00 .90
42 Steve Karsay .25 .07
43 Steve Reed .25 .07
44 Jaret Wright .25 .07
45 Jeff Cirillo .25 .07
46 Tom Goodwin .25 .07
47 Jeffrey Hammonds .25 .07
48 Mike Lansing .25 .07
49 Aaron Ledesma .25 .07
50 Brent Mayne .25 .07
51 Doug Brocail .25 .07
52 Robert Fick .75 .23
53 Juan Gonzalez 2.00 .60
54 Hideo Nomo 2.00 .60
55 Luis Polonia .25 .07
56 Brant Brown .25 .07
57 Alex Fernandez .25 .07
58 Cliff Floyd .75 .23
59 Dan Miceli .25 .07
60 Vladimir Nunez .25 .07
61 Moises Alou FOIL 3.00 .90
62 Roger Cedeno FOIL 3.00 .90
63 Octavio Dotel .25 .07
64 Mitch Meluskey .25 .07
65 Daryle Ward .25 .07
66 Mark Quinn FOIL 3.00 .90
67 Brad Rigby .25 .07
68 Blake Stein .25 .07
69 Mac Suzuki .25 .07
70 Terry Adams .25 .07
71 Darren Dreifort .25 .07
72 Kevin Elster .25 .07
73 Shawn Green FOIL 3.00 .90
74 Todd Hollandsworth .25 .07
75 Gregg Olson .25 .07
76 Kevin Barker .25 .07
77 Jose Hernandez .25 .07
78 Dave Weathers .25 .07
79 Hector Carrasco .25 .07
80 Eddie Guardado .75 .23
81 Jacque Jones .75 .23
82 David Ortiz .75 .23
83 Peter Bergeron .25 .07
84 Hideki Irabu .25 .07
85 Lee Stevens .25 .07
86 Anthony Telford .25 .07
87 Derek Bell .25 .07
88 John Franco .75 .23
89 Mike Hampton FOIL 3.00 .90
90 Bobby Jones .25 .07
91 Todd Pratt .25 .07
92 Todd Zeile .75 .23
93 Jason Grimsley .25 .07
94 Roberto Kelly .25 .07
95 Jim Leyritz .25 .07
96 Ramiro Mendoza .25 .07
97 Rich Becker .25 .07
98 Ramon Hernandez .25 .07
99 Tim Hudson FOIL 5.00 1.50
100 Jason Isringhausen .25 .07
101 Mike Magnante .25 .07
102 Olmedo Saenz .25 .07
103 Mickey Morandini .25 .07
104 Robert Person .25 .07
105 Desi Relaford .25 .07
106 Jason Christiansen .25 .07
107 Wil Cordero .25 .07
108 Francisco Cordova .25 .07
109 Chad Hermansen .25 .07
110 Pat Meares .25 .07
111 Aramis Ramirez .75 .23
112 Bret Boone .75 .23
113 Matt Clement .75 .23
114 Carlos Hernandez .25 .07
115 Ryan Klesko .75 .23
116 Dave Magadan .25 .07
117 Al Martin .25 .07
118 Bobby Estalella .25 .07
119 Livan Hernandez .25 .07
120 Doug Mirabelli .25 .07
121 Joe Nathan .25 .07
122 Mike Cameron .75 .23
123 Mark McLemore .25 .07
124 Gil Meche .75 .23
125 John Olerud .75 .23
126 Arthur Rhodes .25 .07
127 Aaron Sele FOIL 3.00 .90
128 Jim Edmonds FOIL 3.00 .90
129 Pat Hentgen .25 .07
130 Darryl Kile .75 .23
131 Eli Marrero .25 .07
132 Dave Veres .25 .07
133 Fernando Vina .75 .23
134 Vinny Castilla .75 .23
135 Juan Guzman .25 .07
136 Ryan Rupe .25 .07
137 Greg Vaughn FOIL 3.00 .90
138 Gerald Williams .25 .07
139 Esteban Yan .25 .07
140 Tom Evans .25 .07
141 Gabe Kapler .25 .07
142 Ruben Mateo FOIL 3.00 .90
143 Kenny Rogers .75 .23
144 David Segui .25 .07
145 Tony Batista .75 .23
146 Chris Carpenter .25 .07
147 Brad Fullmer .25 .07
148 Alex Gonzalez .25 .07
149 Roy Halladay .75 .23
150 Raul Mondesi FOIL 3.00 .90

2000 MLB Showdown Pennant Run Strategy

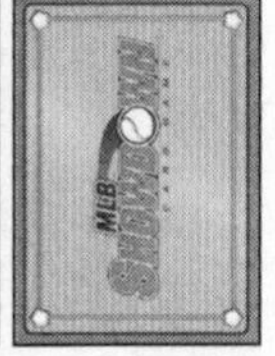

Inserted into packs at a rate of two per pack, this 25-card insert set features the strategy cards necessary for playing the MLB Showdown game. Cards carry an "S" prefix.

Nm-Mt Ex-Mt
COMPLETE SET (25) 10.00 3.00
S1 Aaron Boone .25 .07
S2 Chipper Jones .50 .15
S3 Bob Abreu .25 .07
S4 Fernando Tatis .25 .07
S5 Rod Carew .30 .09
S6 J.D. Drew .25 .07
S7 John Vander Wal .25 .07
S8 Pokey Reese .25 .07
S9 Greg Maddux .75 .23
S10 Cincinnati Reds .25 .07
S11 Larry Walker .30 .09
S12 Alex Rodriguez .75 .23
S13 Alex Rodriguez .75 .23
S14 New York Mets .25 .07
S15 Kevin Brown .30 .09
S16 Paul O'Neill .30 .09
S17 Scott Williamson .25 .07
S18 Jamie Moyer .25 .07
S19 Bernie Williams .30 .09
S20 John Franco .25 .07
S21 Pittsburgh Pirates .25 .07
S22 John Rocker .25 .07

S23 Mike Lansing .25 .07
S24 Roger Clemens .75 .23
Joe Torre
S25 Derek Jeter 1.25 .35

2001 MLB Showdown Ace Pitcher Promos

This 20-card promo set was released to fans and to members of the hobby media during spring-training in early 2001. The set features promotional cards of some of major leagues top pitchers. Please note that the cards are unnumbered, and are listed below in alphabetical order.

Nm-Mt Ex-Mt
COMPLETE SET (20) 20.00 6.00
1 Kris Benson .50 .15
2 Kevin Brown 1.00 .30
3 Roger Clemens 5.00 1.50
4 Bartolo Colon 1.00 .30
5 Jeff D'Amico .50 .15
6 Ryan Dempster .75 .23
7 Adam Eaton .50 .15
8 Scott Elarton .50 .15
9 Livan Hernandez .50 .15
10 Tim Hudson 1.50 .45
11 Randy Johnson 2.00 .60
12 Darryl Kile .50 .15
13 Al Leiter 1.00 .30
14 Jon Lieber .75 .23
15 Greg Maddux 5.00 1.50
16 Pedro Martinez 3.00 .90
17 Brad Radke .75 .23
18 Javier Vazquez 1.00 .30
19 Jeff Weaver .50 .15
20 David Wells 1.00 .30

2001 MLB Showdown Diamond Star Promos

This 20-card promo set was released to fans and to members of the hobby media during spring-training in early 2001. The set features promotional cards of some of major leagues top hitters. Please note that the cards are unnumbered, and are listed below in alphabetical order.

Nm-Mt Ex-Mt
COMPLETE SET (20) 30.00 9.00
1 Roberto Alomar 1.50 .45
2 Carlos Delgado 2.00 .60
3 Jason Giambi 2.00 .60
4 Troy Glaus 2.50 .75
5 Luis Gonzalez 1.50 .45
6 Tony Gwynn 5.00 1.50
7 Todd Helton 2.50 .75
8 Richard Hidalgo .75 .23
9 Bobby Higginson .50 .15
10 Andruw Jones 2.00 .60
11 David Justice 1.00 .30
12 Jeff Kent 1.50 .45
13 Ivan Rodriguez 2.50 .75
14 Gary Sheffield 2.00 .60
15 Mike Sweeney 1.50 .45
16 Miguel Tejada 2.50 .75
17 Frank Thomas 2.50 .75
18 Greg Vaughn .75 .23
19 Robin Ventura .75 .23
20 Rondell White .75 .23

2001 MLB Showdown Future Star Promos

This 13-card promo set was released to fans and to members of the hobby media during spring-training in early 2001. The set features promotional cards of some of major league's top prospects. Please note that the cards are unnumbered, and are listed below in alphabetical order.

Nm-Mt Ex-Mt
COMPLETE SET (13) 10.00 3.00
1 Peter Bergeron .50 .15
2 Pat Burrell 1.50 .45
3 Mike Cameron 1.00 .30
4 Sean Casey .75 .23
5 J.D. Drew .75 .23
6 Corey Koskie .75 .23
7 Melvin Mora .75 .23
8 Trot Nixon 1.50 .45
9 Eric Owens .50 .15
10 Jay Payton .75 .23
11 Aramis Ramirez 1.00 .30
12 Richie Sexson 1.00 .30
13 Preston Wilson .75 .23

2001 MLB Showdown 1st Edition

The 2001 MLB Showdown product was released in mid-April, 2001 as a 462-card baseball game. The 1st Edition cards were released with a silver stamp on front of the card indicating the first print run. The set features 400-player cards and 62 foil superstar cards that were short printed at one in three packs. The 1st Edition packs were released as nine-card packs and carried a suggested retail price of 2.99.

Nm-Mt Ex-Mt
COMPLETE SET (462) 400.00 120.00
COMP.SET w/o FOIL (400) 100.00 30.00
COMMON CARD (1-462) .25 .07
COMMON FOIL 3.00 .90
ERSTAD/VLADDIE IN EVERY STARTER DECK
1 Garret Anderson .75 .23
2 Darin Erstad FOIL * 3.00 .90
3 Ron Gant .75 .23
4 Troy Glaus FOIL 5.00 1.50
5 Shigetoshi Hasegawa .75 .23
6 Adam Kennedy .25 .07
7 Al Levine RC .25 .07
8 Ben Molina .25 .07
9 Troy Percival .75 .23
10 Mark Petkovsek .25 .07
11 Tim Salmon 1.50 .45
12 Scott Schoeneweis .25 .07
13 Scott Spiezio .25 .07
14 Mo Vaughn .75 .23
15 Jarrod Washburn .75 .23
16 Brian Anderson .25 .07
17 Danny Bautista .25 .07
18 Jay Bell .75 .23
19 Greg Colbrunn .25 .07
20 Steve Finley .75 .23
21 Luis Gonzalez 3.00 .90
22 Randy Johnson FOIL 8.00 2.40
23 Byung-Hyun Kim .75 .23
24 Matt Mantei .25 .07
25 Mike Morgan .25 .07
26 Curt Schilling 1.50 .45
27 Kelly Stinnett .25 .07
28 Greg Swindell .25 .07
29 Matt Williams .75 .23
30 Tony Womack .25 .07
31 Andy Ashby .25 .07
32 Bobby Bonilla .75 .23
33 Rafael Furcal FOIL 3.00 .90
34 Andres Galarraga .75 .23
35 Tom Glavine FOIL 5.00 1.50
36 Andruw Jones .75 .23
37 Chipper Jones FOIL 8.00 2.40
38 Brian Jordan .75 .23
39 Wally Joyner .75 .23
40 Keith Lockhart .25 .07
41 Javy Lopez .75 .23
42 Greg Maddux FOIL 10.00 3.00
43 Kevin Millwood .75 .23
44 Mike Remlinger .25 .07
45 John Rocker .25 .07
46 B.J. Surhoff .75 .23
47 Quilvio Veras .25 .07
48 Brady Anderson .75 .23
49 Albert Belle .75 .23
50 Jeff Conine .75 .23
51 Delino DeShields .25 .07
52 Buddy Groom .25 .07
53 Trenidad Hubbard .25 .07
54 Luis Matos .75 .23
55 Jose Mercedes .25 .07
56 Melvin Mora .25 .07
57 Mike Mussina FOIL 8.00 2.40
58 Sidney Ponson .75 .23
59 Pat Rapp .25 .07
60 Chris Richard .25 .07
61 Cal Ripken FOIL 15.00 4.50
62 Mike Trombley .25 .07
63 Rolando Arrojo .25 .07
64 Dante Bichette .75 .23
65 Rheal Cormier .25 .07
66 Carl Everett .75 .23
67 Rich Garces .25 .07
68 N. Garciaparra FOIL 12.00 3.60
69 Mike Lansing .25 .07
70 Darren Lewis .25 .07
71 Derek Lowe .75 .23
72 Pedro Martinez FOIL 8.00 2.40
73 Ramon Martinez .75 .23
74 Trot Nixon 1.50 .45
75 Jose Offerman .25 .07
76 Troy O'Leary .25 .07
77 Jason Varitek .75 .23
78 Rick Aguilera .25 .07
79 Damon Buford .25 .07
80 Joe Girardi .25 .07
81 Mark Grace 1.50 .45
82 Willie Greene .25 .07
83 Ricky Gutierrez .25 .07
84 Felix Heredia .25 .07
85 Jon Lieber .25 .07
86 Jeff Reed .25 .07
87 Sammy Sosa FOIL 15.00 4.50
88 Kevin Tapani .25 .07
89 Todd Van Poppel .25 .07
90 Rondell White .75 .23
91 Kerry Wood 2.50 .75
92 Eric Young .25 .07
93 James Baldwin .25 .07
94 Ray Durham .75 .23
95 Keith Foulke FOIL 3.00 .90
96 Bob Howry .25 .07
97 Charles Johnson FOIL 3.00 .90
98 Mark Johnson .25 .07
99 Paul Konerko .75 .23
100 Carlos Lee .75 .23
101 Magglio Ordonez .75 .23
102 Jim Parque .25 .07
103 Herbert Perry .25 .07
104 Bill Simas .25 .07
105 Chris Singleton .25 .07
106 Mike Sirotka .25 .07
107 Frank Thomas FOIL 8.00 2.40
108 Jose Valentin .25 .07
109 Kelly Wunsch .25 .07
110 Aaron Boone .75 .23
111 Sean Casey .75 .23
112 Danny Graves .75 .23
113 Ken Griffey Jr. FOIL 12.00 3.60
114 Pete Harnisch .25 .07
115 Barry Larkin FOIL 8.00 2.40
116 Alex Ochoa .25 .07
117 Steve Parris .25 .07
118 Pokey Reese .25 .07
119 Chris Stynes .25 .07
120 Scott Sullivan .25 .07
121 Eddie Taubensee .25 .07
122 Michael Tucker .25 .07
123 Ron Villone .25 .07
124 Dmitri Young .75 .23
125 Roberto Alomar FOIL 8.00 2.40
126 Sandy Alomar Jr. .25 .07
127 Jason Bere .25 .07
128 Dave Burba .25 .07
129 Bartolo Colon .75 .23
130 Wil Cordero .25 .07
131 Chuck Finley .75 .23
132 Travis Fryman .75 .23
133 Steve Karsay .25 .07
134 Kenny Lofton .75 .23
135 Manny Ramirez FOIL .75 .23
136 David Segui .25 .07
137 Jim Thome 2.50 .75
138 Omar Vizquel .75 .23
139 Bob Wickman .25 .07
140 Pedro Astacio .25 .07
141 Brian Bohanon .25 .07
142 Jeff Cirillo .25 .07
143 Jeff Frye .25 .07
144 Jeffrey Hammonds .25 .07
145 Todd Helton FOIL 5.00 1.50
146 Todd Hollandsworth .25 .07
147 Butch Huskey .25 .07
148 Jose Jimenez .25 .07
149 Brent Mayne .25 .07
150 Neifi Perez .25 .07
151 Terry Shumpert .25 .07
152 Larry Walker 1.50 .45
153 Gabe White FOIL 3.00 .90
154 Masato Yoshii .25 .07
155 Matt Anderson .25 .07
156 Brad Ausmus .25 .07
157 Rich Becker .25 .07
158 Tony Clark .25 .07
159 Deivi Cruz .25 .07
160 Damion Easley .25 .07
161 Juan Encarnacion .25 .07
162 Juan Gonzalez 2.50 .75
163 Shane Halter .25 .07
164 Bobby Higginson .75 .23
165 Todd Jones FOIL 3.00 .90
166 Brian Moehler .25 .07
167 Hideo Nomo 2.50 .75
168 Dean Palmer .75 .23
169 Jeff Weaver .25 .07
170 Antonio Alfonseca .25 .07
171 Luis Castillo FOIL 3.00 .90
172 Ryan Dempster FOIL 3.00 .90
173 Cliff Floyd .75 .23
174 Alex Gonzalez .25 .07
175 Mark Kotsay .25 .07
176 Derrek Lee .75 .23
177 Braden Looper .25 .07
178 Mike Lowell .75 .23
179 Brad Penny .25 .07
180 Mike Redmond .25 .07
181 Henry Rodriguez .25 .07
182 Jesus Sanchez .25 .07
183 Mark Smith .25 .07
184 Preston Wilson .75 .23
185 Moises Alou .75 .23
186 Jeff Bagwell FOIL 5.00 1.50
187 Lance Berkman .75 .23
188 Craig Biggio 1.50 .45
189 Tim Bogar .25 .07
190 Jose Cabrera .25 .07
191 Octavio Dotel .25 .07
192 Scott Elarton FOIL 3.00 .90
193 Richard Hidalgo .75 .23
194 Chris Holt .25 .07
195 Jose Lima .25 .07
196 Julio Lugo .25 .07
197 Mitch Meluskey .25 .07
198 Bill Spiers .25 .07
199 Daryle Ward .25 .07
200 Carlos Beltran .75 .23
201 Ricky Bottalico .25 .07
202 Johnny Damon FOIL 3.00 .90
203 Jermaine Dye .75 .23
204 Carlos Febles .25 .07
205 Dave McCarty .25 .07
206 Mark Quinn .25 .07
207 Joe Randa .25 .07
208 Dan Reichert .25 .07
209 Rey Sanchez .25 .07
210 Jose Santiago .25 .07
211 Jeff Suppan .25 .07
212 Mac Suzuki .75 .23
213 Mike Sweeney .75 .23
214 Gregg Zaun .25 .07
215 Terry Adams .25 .07
216 Adrian Beltre .75 .23
217 Kevin Brown FOIL 3.00 .90
218 Alex Cora .25 .07
219 Darren Dreifort .25 .07
220 Tom Goodwin .25 .07
221 Shawn Green .75 .23
222 Mark Grudzielanek .25 .07
223 Dave Hansen .25 .07
224 Todd Hundley .25 .07
225 Eric Karros .75 .23
226 Chad Kreuter .25 .07
227 Chan Ho Park .75 .23
228 Jeff Shaw .25 .07
229 Gary Sheffield FOIL 3.00 .90
230 Juan Acevedo .25 .07
231 Ron Belliard .25 .07
232 Henry Blanco .25 .07
233 Jeromy Burnitz .75 .23
234 Jeff D'Amico FOIL 3.00 .90
235 Valerio De Los Santos .25 .07
236 Marquis Grissom .25 .07
237 Charlie Hayes .25 .07
238 Jimmy Haynes .25 .07
239 Jose Hernandez .25 .07
240 Geoff Jenkins .75 .23
241 Curtis Leskanic .25 .07
242 Mark Loretta .25 .07
243 Richie Sexson .75 .23
244 Dave Weathers .25 .07
245 Jay Canizaro .25 .07
246 Ron Coomer .25 .07
247 Cristian Guzman .75 .23
248 LaTroy Hawkins .25 .07
249 Denny Hocking .25 .07
250 Torii Hunter .75 .23
251 Jacque Jones .75 .23
252 Corey Koskie .75 .23
253 Matt Lawton .25 .07
254 Matt LeCroy .25 .07
255 Eric Milton .25 .07
256 David Ortiz .75 .23
257 Brad Radke FOIL 3.00 .90
258 Mark Redman .25 .07
259 Bob Wells .25 .07
260 Michael Barrett .25 .07
261 Peter Bergeron .25 .07
262 Milton Bradley .75 .23
263 Orlando Cabrera .25 .07
264 Vladimir Guerrero FOIL * 8.00 2.40
265 Wilton Guerrero .25 .07
266 Dustin Hermanson .25 .07
267 Terry Jones .25 .07
268 Steve Kline .25 .07
269 Felipe Lira .25 .07
270 Mike Mordecai .25 .07
271 Lee Stevens .25 .07
272 Anthony Telford .25 .07
273 Javier Vazquez .75 .23
274 Jose Vidro FOIL 3.00 .90
275 Edgardo Alfonzo FOIL 3.00 .90
276 Derek Bell .25 .07
277 Armando Benitez .75 .23
278 Mike Bordick .25 .07
279 Mike Hampton FOIL 3.00 .90
280 Lenny Harris .25 .07
281 Al Leiter .75 .23
282 Jay Payton .25 .07
283 Mike Piazza FOIL 10.00 3.00
284 Todd Pratt .25 .07
285 Glendon Rusch .25 .07
286 Bubba Trammell .25 .07
287 Robin Ventura .75 .23
288 Turk Wendell .25 .07
289 Rick White .25 .07
290 Todd Zeile .75 .23
291 Scott Brosius .75 .23
292 Roger Clemens FOIL 12.00 3.60
293 Jason Grimsley .25 .07
294 Orlando Hernandez .75 .23
295 Derek Jeter FOIL 12.00 3.60
296 Dave Justice .75 .23
297 Chuck Knoblauch .75 .23
298 Tino Martinez 1.50 .45
299 Denny Neagle .25 .07
300 Jeff Nelson .25 .07
301 Paul O'Neill 1.50 .45
302 Andy Pettitte 1.50 .45
303 Jorge Posada 1.50 .45
304 Mariano Rivera FOIL 5.00 1.50
305 Jose Vizcaino .25 .07
306 Bernie Williams FOIL 5.00 1.50
307 Kevin Appier .75 .23
308 Eric Chavez .75 .23
309 Ryan Christenson .25 .07
310 Jason Giambi FOIL 8.00 2.40
311 Jeremy Giambi .25 .07
312 Ben Grieve .25 .07
313 Gil Heredia .25 .07
314 Ramon Hernandez .25 .07
315 Tim Hudson FOIL 3.00 .90
316 Jason Isringhausen .25 .07
317 Terrence Long FOIL 3.00 .90
318 Jim Mecir .25 .07
319 Mark Mulder .75 .23
320 Matt Stairs .25 .07
321 Miguel Tejada .75 .23
322 Randy Velarde .75 .23
323 Bobby Abreu .75 .23
324 Jeff Brantley .25 .07
325 Pat Burrell .75 .23
326 Omar Daal .25 .07
327 Rob Ducey .25 .07
328 Doug Glanville .25 .07
329 Wayne Gomes .25 .07
330 Kevin Jordan .25 .07
331 Travis Lee .25 .07
332 Mike Lieberthal .75 .23
333 Vicente Padilla .25 .07
334 Robert Person .25 .07
335 Scott Rolen FOIL 5.00 1.50
336 Kevin Sefcik .25 .07
337 Randy Wolf .75 .23
338 Jimmy Anderson .25 .07
339 Mike Benjamin .25 .07
340 Kris Benson .25 .07
341 Adrian Brown .25 .07
342 Brian Giles FOIL 3.00 .90
343 Jason Kendall FOIL 3.00 .90
344 Pat Meares .25 .07
345 Warren Morris .25 .07
346 Aramis Ramirez .75 .23
347 Todd Ritchie .25 .07
348 Scott Sauerbeck .25 .07
349 Jose Silva .25 .07
350 John VanderWal .25 .07
351 Mike Williams .25 .07
352 Kevin Young .75 .23
353 Carlos Almanzar .25 .07
354 Bret Boone .75 .23
355 Matt Clement .75 .23
356 Adam Eaton .25 .07
357 Wiki Gonzalez .25 .07
358 Trevor Hoffman FOIL 3.00 .90
359 Damian Jackson .25 .07
360 Ryan Klesko .75 .23
361 Phil Nevin FOIL 3.00 .90
362 Eric Owens .25 .07
363 Desi Relaford .25 .07
364 Ruben Rivera .25 .07
365 Kevin Walker .25 .07
366 Woody Williams .25 .07
367 Jay Witasick .25 .07
368 Rich Aurilia .75 .23
369 Marvin Benard .25 .07
370 Barry Bonds FOIL 20.00 6.00
371 Ellis Burks .75 .23
372 Bobby Estalella .25 .07
373 Doug Henry .25 .07
374 Livan Hernandez .25 .07
375 Jeff Kent FOIL 3.00 .90
376 Doug Mirabelli .25 .07
377 Bill Mueller .75 .23
378 Calvin Murray .25 .07
379 Robb Nen FOIL 3.00 .90
380 Russ Ortiz .75 .23
381 Armando Rios .25 .07
382 Felix Rodriguez .25 .07
383 Kirk Rueter .25 .07
384 J.T. Snow .75 .23
385 Paul Abbott .25 .07
386 David Bell .25 .07
387 Jay Buhner .75 .23
388 Mike Cameron .75 .23
389 John Halama .25 .07
390 Rickey Henderson 2.50 .75
391 Al Martin .25 .07
392 Edgar Martinez FOIL 5.00 1.50
393 Mark McLemore .25 .07
394 John Olerud .75 .23
395 Jose Paniagua .25 .07
396 Arthur Rhodes .25 .07
397 Alex Rodriguez FOIL 10.00 3.00
398 Kazuhiro Sasaki FOIL 3.00 .90
399 Aaron Sele .25 .07
400 Dan Wilson .25 .07
401 Rick Ankiel FOIL 3.00 .90
402 Will Clark 2.50 .75
403 J.D. Drew .75 .23
404 Jim Edmonds FOIL 3.00 .90
405 Pat Hentgen .25 .07
406 Darryl Kile .75 .23
407 Ray Lankford .25 .07
408 Mike Matheny .25 .07
409 Mark McGwire FOIL 20.00 6.00
410 Craig Paquette .25 .07
411 Placido Polanco .25 .07
412 Edgar Renteria .75 .23
413 Garrett Stephenson .25 .07
414 Fernando Tatis .25 .07
415 Mike Timlin .25 .07
416 Dave Veres .25 .07
417 Fernando Vina .75 .23
418 Miguel Cairo .25 .07
419 Vinny Castilla .75 .23
420 Steve Cox .25 .07
421 Doug Creek .25 .07
422 John Flaherty .25 .07
423 Jose Guillen .25 .07
424 Roberto Hernandez FOIL 3.00 .90
425 Russ Johnson .25 .07
426 Albie Lopez .25 .07
427 Felix Martinez .25 .07
428 Fred McGriff 1.50 .45
429 Bryan Rekar .25 .07
430 Greg Vaughn .75 .23
431 Gerald Williams .25 .07
432 Esteban Yan .25 .07
433 Luis Alicea .25 .07
434 Frank Catalanotto .25 .07
435 Royce Clayton .25 .07
436 Tim Crabtree .25 .07
437 Chad Curtis .25 .07
438 Rusty Greer .75 .23
439 Rick Helling .25 .07
440 Gabe Kapler .25 .07
441 Mike Lamb .25 .07
442 Ricky Ledee .25 .07
443 Rafael Palmeiro 1.50 .45
444 Ivan Rodriguez FOIL 8.00 2.40
445 Kenny Rogers .75 .23
446 Mike Venafro .25 .07
447 John Wetteland .75 .23
448 Tony Batista FOIL 3.00 .90
449 Jose Cruz Jr. .75 .23
450 Carlos Delgado FOIL 3.00 .90
451 Kelvim Escobar .25 .07
452 Darrin Fletcher .25 .07
453 Brad Fullmer .25 .07
454 Alex Gonzalez .25 .07
455 Mark Guthrie .25 .07
456 Billy Koch .25 .07
457 Esteban Loaiza .75 .23
458 Raul Mondesi .75 .23
459 Mickey Morandini .25 .07
460 Paul Quantrill .25 .07
461 Shannon Stewart .75 .23
462 David Wells FOIL 3.00 .90

2001 MLB Showdown Unlimited

Randomly inserted into starter sets, this 462-card set is a partial parallel of the MLB Showdown 1st Edition set. This set does not have the silver 1st edition stamp.

Nm-Mt Ex-Mt
COMPLETE SET (462) 200.00 60.00
COMP.SET w/o FOIL (400) 50.00 15.00
*UNLIMITED: .2X TO .5X 1ST EDITION
*UNL.FOIL: .2X TO .5X IST ED.FOIL....

2001 MLB Showdown Strategy

Inserted into packs at a rate of two per pack, and starter sets at 40 per starter set, this 75-card insert set features the strategy cards necessary for playing the MLB Showdown game. Card numbers carry an "S" prefix.

Nm-Mt Ex-Mt
COMPLETE SET (75) 20.00 6.00

S1 Jorge Posada .30 .09
Change Sides
S2 Nomar Garciaparra .75 .23
Clutch Hitter
S3 Manny Ramirez .25 .07
Clutch Hitting
S4 Bernie Williams .60 .18
Derek Jeter
Contact Hitter
S5 Sammy Sosa .75 .23
Deep in the Gap
S6 Brian Buchanon .25 .07
Dog Meat
S7 Jay Canizaro .25 .07
Double Steal
S8 Michael Tucker .25 .07
Down the Middle
S9 Drag Bunt .25 .07
Phillies Player
S10 Luis Castillo .25 .07
Drained
S11 Carl Everett .25 .07
Ducks on the Pond
S12 Carlos Delgado .25 .07
Favorable Matchup
S13 Fight it Off .25 .07
S14 Benji Molina .25 .07
Free Swinger
S15 Eric Young .25 .07
Fuel on the Fire
S16 Hiding an Injury .25 .07
S17 Nomar Garciaparra .75 .23
In Motion
S18 Alex Ochoa .25 .07
Last Chance
S19 Reds Player .25 .07
Lean Into It
S20 Rickey Henderson .50 .15
Nuisance
S21 Alex Gonzalez .25 .07
Off Balance
S22 Hideo Nomo .50 .15
Out of Gas
S23 Sean Casey .25 .07
Overthrow
S24 Angels Player .25 .07
Play the Percentages
S25 Power Hitter .25 .07
S26 Chuch Knoblauch .25 .07
Protect the Runner
S27 Todd Helton .30 .09
Pull The Ball
S28 Tim Salmon .30 .09
Rally Cap
S29 Randy Johnson .50 .15
Rough Outing
S30 Johnny Damon .25 .07
Runner not Held
S31 Cincinnati Reds .25 .07
Running On Fumes
S32 Alex Rodriguez .75 .23
Ruptured Duck
S33 Pokey Reese .25 .07
Sail Into Center
S34 Mark McGwire 1.25 .35
Say The Magic Word
S35 Pirates Pitcher .25 .07
Shell Shocked
S36 Homer Bush .25 .07
Singles Hitter
S37 Smash Up the Middle .25 .07
Cubs Player
S38 Twins Pitcher .25 .07
Stick a Fork in Him
S39 Take What's Given .25 .07
S40 Brian Giles .25 .07
To The Warning Track
S41 Shawn Dunston .25 .07
Turn On It
S42 Curtis Leskanic .25 .07
Anointed Closer
S43 By the Book .25 .07
S44 Bobby Higginson .25 .07
Cannon
S45 Orioles Player .25 .07
Choke
S46 Greg Maddux .75 .23
Fast Worker
S47 Fans .25 .07
Flamethrower
S48 Kevin Brown .25 .07
Full Windup
S49 Omar Vizquel .25 .07
Goose Egg
S50 Tom Glavine .30 .09
Great Start
S51 Neifi Perez .25 .07
Great Throw
S52 Mike Lamb .25 .07
Gutsy Play
S53 Pokey Reese .25 .07
Highlight Reel
S54 Insult to Injury .25 .07
S55 Randy Johnson .50 .15
In the Groove
S56 Job Well Done .25 .07
S57 Fans .25 .07
Just Foul
S58 Bernie Williams .30 .09
Just Over the Wall
S59 Barry Bonds 1.25 .35
Leaping Catch
S60 Jason Christiansen .25 .07
Lefty Specialist
S61 Eddie Taubensee .25 .07
Low and Away
S62 Chicago White Sox .25 .07
Mound Conference
S63 Todd Jones .25 .07
Nerves of Steel
S64 Pitchout .25 .07
S65 Brian Moehler .25 .07
Scuff the Ball
S66 Livan Hernandez .25 .07
Sloppy Bunt
S67 Omar Vizquel .25 .07
Soft Hands
S68 Byung-Hyun Kim .25 .07
Submarine Pitch
S69 Visibly Upset .25 .07
S70 Benito Santiago .25 .07
What Were You Thinking
S71 Kevin Brown .25 .07
Air it Out
S72 Pedro Martinez .50 .15
Bear Down
S73 Bobby Cox .25 .07
Brainstorm
S74 Dmitri Young .25 .07
Game of Inches
S75 Moises Alou .25 .07
Second Look

2001 MLB Showdown Pennant Run

The 2001 MLB Showdown Pennant Run product was released in mid-July, 2001 as a 175-card baseball game. The 1st Edition cards were released with a silver stamp on front of the card indicating the first print run. The set features 148-player cards and 27 foil superstar cards that were short printed at one in three packs. The 1st Edition packs were released as nine-card packs and carried a suggested retail price of 2.99.

Nm-Mt Ex-Mt
COMPLETE SET (175) 200.00 60.00
COMP.SET w/o FOIL (150) 40.00 12.00
COMMON CARD (1-175) .25 .07
COMMON FOIL 5.00 1.50
1 Randy Velarde .25 .07
2 Dustin Hermanson .25 .07
3 Jamie Moyer .75 .23
4 Aaron Fultz .25 .07
5 Barry Zito FOIL 10.00 3.00
6 Adam Piatt .25 .07
7 Ben Grieve .25 .07
8 C.C. Sabathia FOIL 5.00 1.50
9 Eddie Guardado .75 .23
10 Matt Kinney .25 .07
11 Blake Stein .25 .07
12 Billy Wagner FOIL 5.00 1.50
13 Chris Holt .25 .07
14 Homer Bush .25 .07
15 Vladimir Nunez .25 .07
16 C.J. Nitkowski .25 .07
17 Juan Pierre .75 .23
18 Jose Valentin .25 .07
19 Juan Gonzalez 2.50 .75
20 Derek Bell .25 .07
21 Wade Miller .75 .23
22 Shawn Estes .25 .07
23 Enrique Wilson .25 .07
24 Dave Magadan .25 .07
25 Jason Christiansen .25 .07
26 Paul Shuey .25 .07
27 Mark Wohlers .25 .07
28 John Riedling .25 .07
29 Francisco Cordova .25 .07
30 Craig House .25 .07
31 Scott Strickland .25 .07
32 Octavio Dotel .25 .07
33 Jimmy Rollins FOIL 5.00 1.50
34 Carl Pavano .25 .07
35 Sandy Alomar Jr. .25 .07
36 Hideki Irabu .25 .07
37 Tom Gordon .25 .07
38 Roosevelt Brown .25 .07
39 Alex Rodriguez FOIL 15.00 4.50
40 Andres Galarraga .75 .23
41 Rob Bell .25 .07
42 Jason Schmidt .75 .23
43 Rod Beck .25 .07
44 Paul Rigdon .25 .07
45 Dan Miceli .25 .07
46 Ricky Bones .25 .07
47 Mike Hampton FOIL 8.00 2.40
48 Cliff Politte .25 .07
49 Chris Stynes .25 .07
50 Ramiro Mendoza .25 .07
51 Todd Walker .75 .23
52 Fernando Seguignol .25 .07
53 Mark Guthrie .25 .07
54 Tony Armas Jr. .25 .07
55 Billy McMillon .25 .07
56 Gary Bennett .25 .07
57 Corey Patterson FOIL 5.00 1.50
58 Juan Guzman .25 .07
59 Joe Crede .25 .07
60 A.J. Pierzynski .75 .23
61 Ben Davis .25 .07
62 Alan Embree .25 .07
63 Jon Garland FOIL 5.00 1.50
64 Ryan Kohlmeier .25 .07
65 Andy Benes .25 .07
66 Ron Gant .75 .23
67 Jerry Hairston Jr. .25 .07
68 Odalis Perez .25 .07
69 Lance Painter .25 .07
70 David Segui .25 .07
71 Russ Davis .25 .07
72 Jeff Zimmerman .25 .07
73 Dennys Reyes .25 .07
74 Jamey Wright .25 .07
75 Rico Brogna .25 .07
76 Geraldo Guzman .25 .07
77 Eric Gagne 1.50 .45
78 Bruce Chen .25 .07
79 Justin Speier .25 .07
80 Randy Keisler .25 .07
81 Ellis Burks FOIL 8.00 2.40
82 Alfonso Soriano 1.50 .45
83 Jeff Nelson .25 .07
84 Wes Helms .25 .07
85 Freddy Garcia FOIL 5.00 1.50
86 Erubiel Durazo .25 .07
87 Ben Sheets FOIL 5.00 1.50
88 Jose Ortiz FOIL 5.00 1.50
89 Paul Wilson .25 .07
90 Onan Masaoka .25 .07
91 Jose Rosado .25 .07
92 A.J. Burnett .25 .07
93 Bubba Trammell .25 .07
94 Mike Fetters .25 .07
95 Jacob Cruz .25 .07
96 John Franco .75 .23
97 Armando Reynoso .75 .23
98 Lou Pote .25 .07
99 D'Angelo Jimenez FOIL 5.00 1.50
100 Julio Zuleta .25 .07
101 Charles Johnson FOIL 8.00 2.40
102 Tsuyoshi Shinjo RC 2.50 .75
103 Brett Tomko .25 .07
104 Marcus Giles .75 .23
105 Craig Counsell .25 .07
106 Ruben Mateo .25 .07
107 Andy Ashby .25 .07
108 Marlon Anderson .25 .07
109 Mark Grace 1.50 .45
110 Russ Branyan .25 .07
111 Julian Tavarez .25 .07
112 Joey Hamilton .25 .07
113 Jason LaRue .25 .07
114 Benji Gil .25 .07
115 Bill Mueller .75 .23
116 Mike Stanton .25 .07
117 Ray King .25 .07
118 Timo Perez .25 .07
119 Johnny Damon FOIL 5.00 1.50
120 Matt Morris .75 .23
121 Kevin Appier .75 .23
122 Frank Castillo .25 .07
123 Mike Darr .25 .07
124 Felipe Crespo .25 .07
125 John Smoltz FOIL 8.00 2.40
126 Ben Weber .25 .07
127 Luis Rivas .25 .07
128 Travis Harper .25 .07
129 Aubrey Huff .75 .23
130 Paul LoDuca .75 .23
131 Eric Davis .75 .23
132 Fernando Tatis .25 .07
133 Ugueth Urbina .25 .07
134 Steve Kline .25 .07
135 Tanyon Sturtze .25 .07
136 Scott Hatteberg .25 .07
137 Tomokazu Ohka FOIL 5.00 1.50
138 Melvin Mora .25 .07
139 Kip Wells .75 .23
140 Ken Caminiti .75 .23
141 Dave Martinez .25 .07
142 Robert Fick .75 .23
143 Mike Bordick .75 .23
144 Doug Mientkiewicz .75 .23
145 Darryl Hamilton .25 .07
146 Shane Reynolds .25 .07
147 Vernon Wells FOIL 5.00 1.50
148 Rey Ordonez .25 .07
149 Brad Ausmus .25 .07
150 Jay Powell .25 .07
151 Todd Hundley .25 .07
152 Travis Miller .25 .07
153 Tyler Houston .25 .07
154 Nelson Cruz .25 .07
155 Manny Ramirez FOIL 5.00 1.50
156 Luis Lopez .25 .07
157 Luis Sojo .25 .07
158 Tony Gwynn FOIL 8.00 2.40
159 Roger Cedeno .25 .07
160 Royce Clayton .25 .07
161 Olmedo Saenz .25 .07
162 Brook Fordyce .25 .07
163 Dee Brown .25 .07
164 David Wells FOIL 5.00 1.50
165 Jack Wilson RC .75 .23
166 Pedro Feliz .25 .07
167 Hideo Nomo 2.50 .75
168 Albert Pujols FOIL RC 25.00 7.50
169 Ichiro Suzuki FOIL RC 20.00 6.00
170 Ramon Ortiz .75 .23
171 Mike Holtz .25 .07
172 Chris Woodward .25 .07
173 Mike Mussina FOIL 10.00 3.00
174 Carlos Guillen .25 .07
175 Ben Petrick FOIL 5.00 1.50

2001 MLB Showdown Pennant Run Strategy

Inserted into packs at a rate of two per pack, this 75-card insert set features the strategy cards necessary for playing the MLB Showdown Pennant Run game. Card numbers carry an "S" prefix.

Nm-Mt Ex-Mt
COMPLETE SET (25) 15.00 4.50
S1 Johnny Damon .25 .07
Advance on Throw
S2 Ruben Mateo .25 .07
Ball in the Dirt
S3 Mark McGwire 1.25 .35
Sammy Sosa
Constant Pressure
S4 Jeff Liefer .25 .07
Emergency Bunt
S5 Cal Ripken 1.50 .45
1st-Pitch Swinging
S6 Mike Piazza .75 .23
Go Up Hacking
S7 Derek Jeter 1.25 .35
Speedster
S8 Jose Valentin .25 .07
Sprint to Second
S9 Benito Santiago .25 .07
Wild Thing
S10 Pokey Reese .25 .07
Wipeout
S11 Tony Gwynn .60 .18
Caught Napping
S12 Greg Maddux .75 .23
Comebacker
S13 Julio Zuleta .25 .07
Confusion
S14 Ray Durham .25 .07
Double-Play
S15 Abraham Nunez .25 .07
Fired Up
S16 Rey Ordonez .25 .07
Focused
S17 Roger Clemens 1.00 .30
Going the Distance
S18 Rick Ankiel .25 .07
Great Pickoff Move
S19 Greg Maddux .75 .23
Groundball Pitcher
S20 Danny Graves .25 .07
Hung It
S21 Mark McGwire 1.25 .35
Pitch Around
S22 Al Leiter .25 .07
Pour It On
S23 Barry Bonds 1.25 .35
Clutch Performance
S24 Mascot .25 .07
Dot Racing
S25 Dennys Reyes .25 .07
It's Crunch Time

2002 MLB Showdown

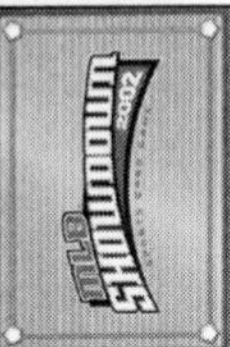

The 2002 MLB Showdown product was released in mid-April, 2002 as a 356-card baseball game. The set features 300-player cards and 56 foil superstar cards that were short printed at one in three booster packs.

Nm-Mt Ex-Mt
COMP.SET w/o FOIL (300) 60.00 18.00
COMMON CARD (1-356) .50 .15
COMMON FOIL 3.00 .90
1 Garret Anderson 1.00 .30
2 David Eckstein .50 .15
3 Darin Erstad 1.00 .30
4 Troy Glaus FOIL 8.00 2.40
5 Adam Kennedy .50 .15
6 Ben Molina .50 .15
7 Ramon Ortiz .50 .15
8 Troy Percival 1.00 .30
9 Tim Salmon 1.50 .45
10 Scott Schoeneweis .50 .15
11 Scott Spiezio .50 .15
12 Jarrod Washburn 1.00 .30
13 Miguel Batista .50 .15
14 Jay Bell 1.00 .30
15 Craig Counsell .50 .15
16 David Dellucci .50 .15
17 Erubiel Durazo .50 .15
18 Steve Finley 1.00 .30
19 Luis Gonzalez FOIL 5.00 1.50
20 Mark Grace 1.50 .45
21 Randy Johnson FOIL 10.00 3.00
22 Byung-Hyun Kim 1.00 .30
23 Albie Lopez .50 .15
24 Curt Schilling FOIL 8.00 2.40
25 Matt Williams 1.00 .30
26 Tony Womack .50 .15
27 Marcus Giles FOIL 5.00 1.50
28 Tom Glavine 1.50 .45
29 Andruw Jones 1.00 .30
30 Chipper Jones FOIL 10.00 3.00
31 Brian Jordan 1.00 .30
32 Steve Karsay .50 .15
33 Javy Lopez 1.00 .30
34 Greg Maddux FOIL 10.00 3.00
35 Jason Marquis .50 .15
36 Mike Remlinger .50 .15
37 Rey Sanchez .50 .15
38 B. J. Surhoff 1.00 .30
39 Brady Anderson 1.00 .30
40 Tony Batista FOIL 5.00 1.50
41 Mike Bordick 1.00 .30
42 Jeff Conine 1.00 .30
43 Buddy Groom .50 .15
44 Jerry Hairston Jr. .50 .15
45 Jason Johnson .50 .15
46 Melvin Mora .50 .15
47 Chris Richard .50 .15
48 B. J. Ryan .50 .15
49 Josh Towers .50 .15
50 Rolando Arrojo .50 .15
51 Rod Beck .50 .15
52 Dante Bichette 1.00 .30
53 David Cone 1.00 .30
54 Carl Everett 1.00 .30
55 Rich Garces .50 .15
56 Derek Lowe 1.00 .30
57 Trot Nixon 1.50 .45
58 Hideo Nomo 2.50 .75
59 Jose Offerman .50 .15
60 Troy O'Leary .50 .15
61 Manny Ramirez FOIL 5.00 1.50
62 Delino DeShields .50 .15
63 Kyle Farnsworth .50 .15
64 Jeff Fassero .50 .15
65 Ricky Gutierrez .50 .15
66 Todd Hundley .50 .15
67 Jon Lieber .50 .15
68 Fred McGriff 1.50 .45
69 Bill Mueller 1.00 .30
70 Corey Patterson 1.00 .30
71 Sammy Sosa FOIL 15.00 4.50
72 Julian Tavarez .50 .15
73 Kerry Wood 2.50 .75
74 Eric Young .50 .15
75 Mark Buehrle FOIL 5.00 1.50
76 Royce Clayton .50 .15
77 Joe Crede .50 .15
78 Ray Durham 1.00 .30
79 Keith Foulke .50 .15
80 Bob Howry .50 .15
81 Mark Johnson .50 .15
82 Paul Konerko 1.00 .30
83 Carlos Lee 1.00 .30
84 Sean Lowe .50 .15
85 Magglio Ordonez 1.00 .30
86 Jose Valentin .50 .15
87 Aaron Boone 1.00 .30
88 Jim Brower .50 .15
89 Sean Casey 1.00 .30
90 Brady Clark .50 .15
91 Adam Dunn FOIL 5.00 1.50
92 Danny Graves .50 .15
93 Ken Griffey Jr. FOIL 10.00 3.00
94 Pokey Reese .50 .15
95 Chris Reitsma .50 .15
96 Kelly Stinnett .50 .15
97 Dmitri Young 1.00 .30
98 Roberto Alomar FOIL 10.00 3.00
99 Danys Baez .50 .15
100 Russell Branyan .50 .15
101 Ellis Burks 1.00 .30
102 Bartolo Colon 1.00 .30
103 Marty Cordova .50 .15
104 Einar Diaz .50 .15
105 Juan Gonzalez 2.50 .75
106 Ricardo Rincon .50 .15
107 C. C. Sabathia FOIL 5.00 1.50
108 Paul Shuey .50 .15
109 Jim Thome FOIL 10.00 3.00
110 Omar Vizquel 1.00 .30
111 Bob Wickman .50 .15
112 Shawn Chacon .50 .15
113 Jeff Cirillo .50 .15
114 Mike Hampton 1.00 .30
115 Todd Helton FOIL 8.00 2.40
116 Greg Norton .50 .15
117 Ben Petrick .50 .15
118 Juan Pierre 1.00 .30
119 Terry Shumpert .50 .15
120 Larry Walker FOIL 8.00 2.40
121 Matt Anderson .50 .15
122 Roger Cedeno .50 .15
123 Tony Clark .50 .15
124 Deivi Cruz .50 .15
125 Damion Easley .50 .15
126 Shane Halter .50 .15
127 Bobby Higginson FOIL 5.00 1.50
128 Jose Macias .50 .15
129 Steve Sparks .50 .15
130 Jeff Weaver .50 .15
131 Antonio Alfonseca .50 .15
132 Josh Beckett FOIL 8.00 2.40
133 A. J. Burnett .50 .15
134 Luis Castillo 1.00 .30
135 Ryan Dempster .50 .15
136 Cliff Floyd 1.00 .30
137 Alex Gonzalez .50 .15
138 Braden Looper .50 .15
139 Mike Lowell 1.00 .30
140 Eric Owens .50 .15
141 Brad Penny .50 .15
142 Preston Wilson 1.00 .30
143 Moises Alou 1.00 .30
144 Brad Ausmus .50 .15
145 Jeff Bagwell FOIL 8.00 2.40
146 Lance Berkman FOIL 5.00 1.50
147 Craig Biggio 1.50 .45
148 Octavio Dotel .50 .15
149 Richard Hidalgo 1.00 .30
150 Julio Lugo .50 .15
151 Wade Miller 1.00 .30
152 Roy Oswalt FOIL 5.00 1.50
153 Shane Reynolds .50 .15
154 Jose Vizcaino .50 .15
155 Daryle Ward .50 .15
156 Carlos Beltran FOIL 5.00 1.50
157 Dee Brown .50 .15
158 Roberto Hernandez .50 .15
159 Mark Quinn .50 .15
160 Joe Randa .50 .15
161 Dan Reichert .50 .15
162 Jeff Suppan .50 .15
163 Mike Sweeney 1.00 .30
164 Kris Wilson .50 .15
165 Terry Adams .50 .15
166 Adrian Beltre 1.00 .30
167 Alex Cora .50 .15
168 Tom Goodwin .50 .15
169 Shawn Green 1.00 .30
170 Marquis Grissom .50 .15
171 Mark Grudzielanek .50 .15
172 Eric Karros 1.00 .30
173 Paul LoDuca FOIL 5.00 1.50
174 Chan Ho Park 1.00 .30
175 Luke Prokopec .50 .15
176 Gary Sheffield 1.00 .30
177 Ronnie Belliard .50 .15
178 Henry Blanco .50 .15
179 Jeromy Burnitz 1.00 .30
180 Mike DeJean .50 .15
181 Chad Fox .50 .15
182 Jose Hernandez .50 .15
183 Geoff Jenkins 1.00 .30
184 Mark Loretta .50 .15
185 Nick Neugebauer .50 .15
186 Richie Sexson 1.00 .30
187 Ben Sheets FOIL 5.00 1.50
188 Devon White .50 .15
189 Cristian Guzman FOIL 5.00 1.50

190 Torii Hunter 1.00 .30
191 Jacque Jones 1.00 .30
192 Corey Koskie 1.00 .30
193 Joe Mays .50 .15
194 Doug Mientkiewicz 1.00 .30
195 Eric Milton .50 .15
196 David Ortiz 1.00 .30
197 A. J. Pierzynski 1.00 .30
198 Brad Radke 1.00 .30
199 Luis Rivas .50 .15
200 Tony Armas Jr. .50 .15
201 Michael Barrett .50 .15
202 Peter Bergeron .50 .15
203 Orlando Cabrera .50 .15
204 Vladimir Guerrero FOIL 10.00 3.00
205 Graeme Lloyd .50 .15
206 Scott Strickland .50 .15
207 Fernando Tatis .50 .15
208 Mike Thurman .50 .15
209 Javier Vazquez 1.00 .30
210 Jose Vidro 1.00 .30
211 Brad Wilkerson .50 .15
212 Edgardo Alfonzo 1.00 .30
213 Kevin Appier 1.00 .30
214 Armando Benitez 1.00 .30
215 Alex Escobar .50 .15
216 John Franco 1.00 .30
217 Al Leiter 1.00 .30
218 Rey Ordonez .50 .15
219 Mike Piazza FOIL 10.00 3.00
220 Glendon Rusch .50 .15
221 Tsuyoshi Shinjo 1.00 .30
222 Steve Trachsel .50 .15
223 Todd Zeile 1.00 .30
224 Roger Clemens FOIL 15.00 4.50
225 Derek Jeter FOIL 15.00 4.50
226 Nick Johnson 1.00 .30
227 David Justice 1.00 .30
228 Tino Martinez 1.50 .45
229 Ramiro Mendoza .50 .15
230 Mike Mussina FOIL 10.00 3.00
231 Andy Pettitte 1.50 .45
232 Jorge Posada 1.50 .45
233 Mariano Rivera FOIL 8.00 2.40
234 Alfonso Soriano 1.50 .45
235 Mike Stanton .50 .15
236 Bernie Williams FOIL 8.00 2.40
237 Eric Chavez 1.00 .30
238 Johnny Damon 1.00 .30
239 Jermaine Dye 1.00 .30
240 Jason Giambi FOIL 10.00 3.00
241 Jeremy Giambi .50 .15
242 Ramon Hernandez .50 .15
243 Tim Hudson FOIL 5.00 1.50
244 Jason Isringhausen .50 .15
245 Terrence Long 1.00 .30
246 Mark Mulder FOIL 5.00 1.50
247 Olmedo Saenz .50 .15
248 Miguel Tejada 1.00 .30
249 Barry Zito 1.50 .45
250 Bobby Abreu 1.00 .30
251 Marlon Anderson .50 .15
252 Ricky Bottalico .50 .15
253 Pat Burrell 1.00 .30
254 Omar Daal .50 .15
255 Johnny Estrada .50 .15
256 Nelson Figueroa .50 .15
257 Travis Lee .50 .15
258 Robert Person .50 .15
259 Scott Rolen FOIL 8.00 2.40
260 Jimmy Rollins FOIL 5.00 1.50
261 Randy Wolf 1.00 .30
262 Brian Giles FOIL 5.00 1.50
263 Jason Kendall 1.00 .30
264 Josias Manzanillo .50 .15
265 Warren Morris .50 .15
266 Aramis Ramirez 1.00 .30
267 Todd Ritchie .50 .15
268 Craig Wilson .50 .15
269 Jack Wilson .50 .15
270 Kevin Young .50 .15
271 Ben Davis .50 .15
272 Wiki Gonzalez .50 .15
273 Rickey Henderson 2.50 .75
274 Junior Herndon .50 .15
275 Trevor Hoffman 1.00 .30
276 Damian Jackson .50 .15
277 D'Angelo Jimenez .50 .15
278 Mark Kotsay .50 .15
279 Phil Nevin FOIL 5.00 1.50
280 Bubba Trammell .50 .15
281 Rich Aurilia FOIL 5.00 1.50
282 Marvin Benard .50 .15
283 Barry Bonds FOIL 40.00 12.00
284 Shawn Estes .50 .15
285 Pedro Feliz .50 .15
286 Jeff Kent FOIL 5.00 1.50
287 Robb Nen 1.00 .30
288 Russ Ortiz 1.00 .30
289 Felix Rodriguez .50 .15
290 Kirk Rueter .50 .15
291 Benito Santiago 1.00 .30
292 J.T. Snow 1.00 .30
293 John Vander Wal .50 .15
294 Bret Boone FOIL 5.00 1.50
295 Mike Cameron 1.00 .30
296 Freddy Garcia FOIL 5.00 1.50
297 Carlos Guillen .50 .15
298 Edgar Martinez FOIL 8.00 2.40
299 Mark McLemore .50 .15
300 Jamie Moyer 1.00 .30
301 Jeff Nelson .50 .15
302 John Olerud 1.00 .30
303 Arthur Rhodes .50 .15
304 Kazuhiro Sasaki FOIL 5.00 1.50
305 Aaron Sele .50 .15
306 Ichiro Suzuki FOIL 10.00 3.00
307 Dan Wilson .50 .15
308 J.D. Drew FOIL 5.00 1.50
309 Jim Edmonds FOIL 5.00 1.50
310 Dustin Hermanson .50 .15
311 Darryl Kile 1.00 .30
312 Steve Kline .50 .15
313 Mike Matheny .50 .15
314 Matt Morris 1.00 .30
315 Craig Paquette .50 .15
316 Placido Polanco .50 .15
317 Albert Pujols FOIL 12.00 3.60
318 Edgar Renteria 1.00 .30
319 Bud Smith .50 .15
320 Dave Veres .50 .15
321 Fernando Vina 1.00 .30
322 Brent Abernathy .50 .15
323 Steve Cox .50 .15
324 Ben Grieve .50 .15
325 Aubrey Huff 1.00 .30
326 Joe Kennedy FOIL 3.00 .90
327 Tanyon Sturtze .50 .15
328 Jason Tyner .50 .15
329 Greg Vaughn 1.00 .30
330 Paul Wilson .50 .15
331 Esteban Yan .50 .15
332 Frank Catalanotto .50 .15
333 Chad Curtis .50 .15
334 Doug Davis .50 .15
335 Gabe Kapler .50 .15
336 Mike Lamb .50 .15
337 Darren Oliver .50 .15
338 Rafael Palmeiro 1.50 .45
339 Alex Rodriguez FOIL 15.00 4.50
340 Ivan Rodriguez FOIL 10.00 3.00
341 Mike Venafro .50 .15
342 Michael Young 1.00 .30
343 Jeff Zimmerman .50 .15
344 Chris Carpenter .50 .15
345 Jose Cruz Jr. 1.00 .30
346 Carlos Delgado FOIL 5.00 1.50
347 Kelvim Escobar .50 .15
348 Darrin Fletcher .50 .15
349 Brad Fullmer .50 .15
350 Alex S.Gonzalez .50 .15
351 Billy Koch .50 .15
352 Esteban Loaiza 1.00 .30
353 Raul Mondesi 1.00 .30
354 Paul Quantrill .50 .15
355 Shannon Stewart 1.00 .30
356 Vernon Wells 1.00 .30

2002 MLB Showdown Strategy

Inserted into packs at a rate of two per pack, this 50-card insert set features the strategy cards necessary for playing the MLB Showdown game. Card numbers carry an "S" prefix.

Nm-Mt Ex-Mt
COMPLETE SET (50) 15.00 4.50
S1 Bernie Williams .40 .12
Bad Call
S2 Mike Piazza .75 .23
Clutch Hitting
S3 Troy Glaus .40 .12
Crowd the Plate
S4 Down the Middle SP .50 .15
S5 Corey Patterson .50 .15
Drag Bunt SP
S6 Ducks on the Pond .25 .07
S7 Barry Bonds 1.25 .35
Fuel on the Fire
S8 Craig Biggio .40 .12
Last Chance
S9 Nuisance/Mets SP .50 .15
S10 Out of Gas/Cubs .25 .07
S11 Manny Ramirez .50 .15
Payoff Pitch SP
S12 Pro Baserunner/Phillies SP .50 .15
S13 Protect the Runner SP .50 .15
S14 Rafael Palmeiro .40 .12
Pull the Ball
S15 Tom Goodwin .25 .07
Rally Cap
S16 Rough Outing .25 .07
S17 Runner Not Held/Cardinals .25 .07
S18 Run on Fumes/Giants SP .50 .15
S19 Ruptured Duck SP .50 .15
S20 Jose Cruz Jr. .25 .07
Sit on the Fastball
S21 Kevin Appier .25 .07
Stick a Fork in Him
S22 Barry Bonds 1.25 .35
Sweet Swing
S23 Johnny Damon .50 .15
Take Given SP
S24 Warning Track/Pirates .25 .07
S25 Lance Berkman .25 .07
Turn On It
S26 Brad Radke .25 .07
By the Book
S27 Cut Off in the Gap SP .50 .15
S28 Andy Pettitte .40 .12
Full Windup
S29 Barry Zito .40 .12
Great Start
S30 Ichiro Suzuki .75 .23
Great Throw
S31 Brent Abernathy .50 .15
HL Reel SP
S32 Curt Schilling .40 .12
Insult to Injury
S33 Mark Mulder .25 .07
In the Groove
S34 Mariano Rivera .40 .12
Intimidation
S35 Arthur Rhodes .50 .15
Job Well Done SP
S36 Just Over the Wall SP .50 .15
S37 Abraham Nunez .25 .07
Knock Ball Down
S38 Billy Wagner .25 .07
Lefty Specialist
S39 Randy Johnson .50 .15
Low and Away
S40 Trevor Hoffman .25 .07
Nerves of Steel
S41 Pitchout SP .50 .15
S42 Pumped Up .25 .07
S43 Kazuhiro Sasaki .25 .07
Put Out the Fire
S44 Rally Killer SP .50 .15
S45 Sloppy Bunt/Indians SP .50 .15
S46 Byung-Hyun Kim .50 .15
Submarine Pitch SP
S47 Change in Strategy .25 .07
S48 Grounder to 2nd/Reds SP .50 .15
S49 Crunch Time/Dodgers SP .50 .15
S50 Sean Casey .25 .07
Second Look

2002 MLB Showdown All-Star Game

This set was distributed exclusively in an attractive sealed All-Star Game box of which carried a suggested retail price of $29.99. Each box contained the 50 All-Star Game cards plus an additional 50 Strategy cards (all of which were reissued from the basic Strategy card set initially distributed in the basic 2002 MLB Showdown product earlier that year. Interestingly, the 50 Strategy cards are NOT a full run of cards 1-50. Rather, each box contains two separate stacks of 25 Strategy cards (one for each game player) of which include a skip-numbered selection of cards (including several duplicates) designed especially for game play. The box also contains 30 team tab checklists, a rulebook, an All-Star theme playmat and one 20-sided die. The fifty new All-Star cards feature a similar design that runs throughout all of the 2002 MLB Showdown brands - attractive full bleed images on cards shaped like playing cards (with rounded edges). The All-Star Game logo is prominently placed on the lower left front corner (along with the checklist number in a tiny black box) with various statistics to play the game on the lower right corner. The card backs simply feature the brand logo.

Nm-Mt Ex-Mt
COMP.FACT.SET (100) 40.00 12.00
COMPLETE SET (50) 30.00 9.00
1 Garret Anderson 1.00 .30
2 Tony Batista 1.00 .30
3 Mark Buehrle 1.00 .30
4 Johnny Damon 1.00 .30
5 Robert Fick 1.00 .30
6 Freddy Garcia 1.00 .30
7 Nomar Garciaparra 4.00 1.20
8 Jason Giambi 2.50 .75
9 Roy Halladay 1.00 .30
10 Shea Hillenbrand 1.00 .30
11 Torii Hunter 1.00 .30
12 Ichiro Suzuki 4.00 1.20
13 Derek Jeter 6.00 1.80
14 Paul Konerko 1.00 .30
15 Derek Lowe 1.00 .30
16 Jorge Posada 1.50 .45
17 Manny Ramirez 1.00 .30
18 Mariano Rivera 1.50 .45
19 Alex Rodriguez 4.00 1.20
20 Kazuhiro Sasaki 1.00 .30
21 Alfonso Soriano 1.50 .45
22 Mike Sweeney 1.00 .30
23 Robin Ventura 1.00 .30
24 Omar Vizquel 1.00 .30
25 Barry Zito 1.50 .45
26 Lance Berkman 1.00 .30
27 Barry Bonds 6.00 1.80
28 Luis Castillo 1.00 .30
29 Adam Dunn 1.00 .30
30 Eric Gagne 1.50 .45
31 Luis Gonzalez 1.00 .30
32 Shawn Green 1.00 .30
33 Vladimir Guerrero 2.50 .75
34 Todd Helton 2.50 .75
35 Jose Hernandez 1.00 .30
36 Andruw Jones 1.00 .30
37 Mike Lowell 1.00 .30
38 Robb Nen 1.00 .30
39 Vicente Padilla 1.00 .30
40 Odalis Perez 1.00 .30
41 Mike Piazza 4.00 1.20
42 Scott Rolen 1.50 .45
43 Jimmy Rollins 1.00 .30
44 Benito Santiago 1.00 .30
45 Curt Schilling 2.50 .75
46 John Smoltz 1.50 .45
47 Sammy Sosa 4.00 1.20
48 Junior Spivey 1.00 .30
49 Jose Vidro 1.00 .30
50 Mike Williams 1.00 .30

2003 MLB Showdown

This 304 card set was issued in April, 2003. Fifty two cards in this set are foil cards and those cards were issued at a stated rate of one in three. A promo card featuring Pee Wee Reese was issued to dealers to preview the product. The promo card can be differentiated from Reese's basic card by the fact that it's numbered on back as "P51".

Nm-Mt Ex-Mt
COMP.SET w/o FOIL (252) 60.00 18.00
COMMON CARD (1-304) .50 .15
COMMON FOIL 3.00 .90
1 Garret Anderson FOIL 5.00 1.50
2 David Eckstein FOIL 3.00 .90
3 Darin Erstad 1.00 .30
4 Brad Fullmer .50 .15
5 Troy Glaus 1.50 .45
6 Adam Kennedy .50 .15
7 Bengie Molina .50 .15
8 Ramon Ortiz .50 .15
9 Orlando Palmeiro .50 .15
10 Troy Percival 1.00 .30
11 Tim Salmon 1.50 .45
12 Jarrod Washburn FOIL 5.00 1.50
13 Miguel Batista .50 .15
14 Danny Bautista .50 .15
15 Craig Counsell .50 .15
16 Steve Finley 1.00 .30
17 Luis Gonzalez FOIL 5.00 1.50
18 Mark Grace 1.50 .45
19 Randy Johnson FOIL 10.00 3.00
20 Byung-Hyun Kim 1.00 .30
21 Quinton McCracken .50 .15
22 Curt Schilling FOIL 20.00 6.00
23 Junior Spivey FOIL 3.00 .90
24 Tony Womack .50 .15
25 Vinny Castilla 1.00 .30
26 Julio Franco .50 .15
27 Rafael Furcal FOIL 5.00 1.50
28 Marcus Giles 1.00 .30
29 Tom Glavine FOIL 8.00 2.40
30 Andruw Jones FOIL 5.00 1.50
31 Keith Lockhart .50 .15
32 Javy Lopez 1.00 .30
33 Greg Maddux FOIL 10.00 3.00
34 Kevin Millwood 1.00 .30
35 Gary Sheffield 1.00 .30
36 John Smoltz FOIL 8.00 2.40
37 Tony Batista 1.00 .30
38 Mike Bordick 1.00 .30
39 Jeff Conine 1.00 .30
40 Marty Cordova .50 .15
41 Jay Gibbons 1.00 .30
42 Geronimo Gil .50 .15
43 Jerry Hairston .50 .15
44 Jorge Julio .50 .15
45 Rodrigo Lopez .50 .15
46 Gary Matthews Jr. .50 .15
47 Melvin Mora .50 .15
48 Sidney Ponson 1.00 .30
49 Chris Singleton .50 .15
50 John Burkett .50 .15
51 Tony Clark .50 .15
52 Johnny Damon 1.00 .30
53 Alan Embree .50 .15
54 Nomar Garciaparra FOIL 10.00 3.00
55 Shea Hillenbrand 1.00 .30
56 Derek Lowe FOIL 5.00 1.50
57 Pedro Martinez FOIL 10.00 3.00
58 Trot Nixon 1.50 .45
59 Manny Ramirez 1.00 .30
60 Rey Sanchez .50 .15
61 Ugueth Urbina .50 .15
62 Jason Varitek 1.00 .30
63 Moises Alou 1.00 .30
64 Mark Bellhorn .50 .15
65 Roosevelt Brown .50 .15
66 Matt Clement 1.00 .30
67 Joe Girardi .50 .15
68 Alex Gonzalez .50 .15
69 Todd Hundley .50 .15
70 Jon Lieber .50 .15
71 Fred McGriff 1.50 .45
72 Bill Mueller 1.00 .30
73 Corey Patterson 1.00 .30
74 Mark Prior FOIL 10.00 3.00
75 Sammy Sosa FOIL 15.00 4.50
76 Mark Buehrle FOIL 5.00 1.50
77 Jon Garland .50 .15
78 Tony Graffanino .50 .15
79 Paul Konerko FOIL 5.00 1.50
80 Carlos Lee 1.00 .30
81 Magglio Ordonez FOIL 5.00 1.50
82 Frank Thomas 2.50 .75
83 Dan Wright .50 .15
84 Aaron Boone 1.00 .30
85 Sean Casey 1.00 .30
86 Elmer Dessens .50 .15
87 Adam Dunn 1.00 .30
88 Danny Graves .50 .15
89 Joey Hamilton .50 .15
90 Jimmy Haynes .50 .15
91 Austin Kearns FOIL 5.00 1.50
92 Barry Larkin 2.50 .75
93 Jason LaRue .50 .15
94 Reggie Taylor .50 .15
95 Todd Walker 1.00 .30
96 Danys Baez .50 .15
97 Milton Bradley 1.00 .30
98 Ellis Burks 1.00 .30
99 Einar Diaz .50 .15
100 Ricky Gutierrez .50 .15
101 Matt Lawton .50 .15
102 Chris Magruder .50 .15
103 C. C. Sabathia 1.00 .30
104 Lee Stevens .50 .15
105 Jim Thome FOIL 10.00 3.00
106 Omar Vizquel 1.00 .30
107 Bob Wickman .50 .15
108 Gary Bennett .50 .15
109 Mike Hampton 1.00 .30
110 Todd Helton 1.50 .45
111 Jose Jimenez .50 .15
112 Denny Neagle .50 .15
113 Jose Ortiz .50 .15
114 Juan Pierre 1.00 .30
115 Juan Uribe .50 .15
116 Larry Walker FOIL 1.50 .45
117 Todd Zeile 1.00 .30
118 Juan Acevedo .50 .15
119 Robert Fick 1.00 .30
120 Bobby Higginson 1.00 .30
121 Damian Jackson .50 .15
122 Craig Paquette .50 .15
123 Carlos Pena .50 .15
124 Mark Redman .50 .15
125 Randall Simon .50 .15
126 Steve Sparks .50 .15
127 Dmitri Young 1.00 .30
128 A. J. Burnett .50 .15
129 Luis Castillo 1.00 .30
130 Juan Encarnacion .50 .15
131 Alex Gonzalez .50 .15
132 Charles Johnson 1.00 .30
133 Derrek Lee 1.00 .30
134 Mike Lowell 1.00 .30
135 Vladimir Nunez .50 .15
136 Eric Owens .50 .15
137 Preston Wilson 1.00 .30
138 Brad Ausmus .50 .15
139 Lance Berkman FOIL 5.00 1.50
140 Craig Biggio 1.50 .45
141 Geoff Blum .50 .15
142 Richard Hidalgo 1.00 .30
143 Julio Lugo .50 .15
144 Orlando Merced .50 .15
145 Billy Wagner 1.00 .30
146 Carlos Beltran 1.00 .30
147 Paul Byrd .50 .15
148 Raul Ibanez .50 .15
149 Chuck Knoblauch 1.00 .30
150 Brent Mayne .50 .15
151 Neifi Perez .50 .15
152 Joe Randa .50 .15
153 Mike Sweeney 1.00 .30
154 Adrian Beltre 1.00 .30
155 Eric Gagne FOIL 5.00 1.50
156 Shawn Green 1.00 .30
157 Marquis Grissom .50 .15
158 Mark Grudzielanek .50 .15
159 Kazuhisa Ishii FOIL 5.00 1.50
160 Cesar Izturis .50 .15
161 Brian Jordan 1.00 .30
162 Eric Karros 1.00 .30
163 Paul Lo Duca FOIL 5.00 1.50
164 Hideo Nomo 2.50 .75
165 Jesse Orosco .50 .15
166 Odalis Perez .50 .15
167 Mike DeJean .50 .15
168 Jose Hernandez .50 .15
169 Geoff Jenkins 1.00 .30
170 Alex Sanchez .50 .15
171 Richie Sexson 1.00 .30
172 Ben Sheets 1.00 .30
173 Eric Young .50 .15
174 Eddie Guardado 1.00 .30
175 Cristian Guzman 1.00 .30
176 Torii Hunter FOIL 5.00 1.50
177 Jacque Jones 1.00 .30
178 Corey Koskie 1.00 .30
179 Doug Mientkiewicz 1.00 .30
180 Eric Milton .50 .15
181 A. J. Pierzynski 1.00 .30
182 Michael Barrett .50 .15
183 Orlando Cabrera .50 .15
184 Cliff Floyd .50 .15
185 Vladimir Guerrero FOIL 15.00 4.50
186 Tomo Ohka .50 .15
187 Fernando Tatis .50 .15
188 Javier Vazquez 1.00 .30
189 Jose Vidro FOIL 5.00 1.50
190 Brad Wilkerson .50 .15
191 Edgardo Alfonzo 1.00 .30
192 Roberto Alomar 2.50 .75
193 Pedro Astacio .50 .15
194 Armando Benitez 1.00 .30
195 Jeromy Burnitz 1.00 .30
196 Al Leiter 1.00 .30
197 Rey Ordonez .50 .15
198 Timo Perez .50 .15
199 Mike Piazza FOIL 12.00 3.60
200 Steve Trachsel .50 .15
201 Mo Vaughn 1.00 .30
202 Roger Clemens 5.00 1.50
203 Jason Giambi FOIL 10.00 3.00
204 Derek Jeter 6.00 1.80
205 Nick Johnson 1.00 .30
206 Steve Karsay .50 .15
207 Mike Mussina FOIL 10.00 3.00
208 Jorge Posada 1.50 .45
209 Mariano Rivera FOIL 8.00 2.40
210 Alfonso Soriano FOIL 8.00 2.40
211 Mike Stanton .50 .15
212 Robin Ventura 1.00 .30
213 Jeff Weaver .50 .15
214 Rondell White 1.00 .30
215 Bernie Williams FOIL 8.00 2.40
216 Eric Chavez 1.00 .30
217 Jermaine Dye 1.00 .30
218 Scott Hatteberg .50 .15
219 Tim Hudson 1.00 .30
220 Billy Koch 1.00 .30
221 Terrence Long 1.00 .30
222 Mark Mulder 1.00 .30
223 Miguel Tejada FOIL 5.00 1.50
224 Barry Zito FOIL 8.00 2.40
225 Bobby Abreu 1.00 .30
226 Marlon Anderson .50 .15
227 Pat Burrell 1.00 .30
228 Brandon Duckworth .50 .15
229 Jeremy Giambi .50 .15
230 Doug Glanville .50 .15
231 Mike Lieberthal 1.00 .30
232 Jose Mesa .50 .15
233 Vicente Padilla .50 .15
234 Jimmy Rollins 1.00 .30
235 Adrian Brown .50 .15
236 Josh Fogg .50 .15
237 Brian Giles 1.00 .30
238 Jason Kendall 1.00 .30
239 Pokey Reese .50 .15
240 Kip Wells .50 .15
241 Mike Williams FOIL 3.00 .90
242 Craig Wilson .50 .15
243 Jack Wilson .50 .15
244 Kevin Young .50 .15
245 Trevor Hoffman FOIL 5.00 1.50
246 Mark Kotsay .50 .15
247 Ray Lankford .50 .15
248 Brian Lawrence .50 .15
249 Phil Nevin .50 .15
250 Kurt Ainsworth .50 .15
251 David Bell .50 .15
252 Barry Bonds FOIL 30.00 9.00
253 Ryan Jensen .50 .15
254 Jeff Kent FOIL 5.00 1.50
255 Robb Nen .50 .15
256 Reggie Sanders .50 .15
257 Benito Santiago 1.00 .30
258 Tsuyoshi Shinjo 1.00 .30
259 J. T. Snow 1.00 .30
260 Bret Boone 1.00 .30

261 Mike Cameron 1.00 .30
262 Jeff Cirillo .50 .15
263 Freddy Garcia 1.00 .30
264 Carlos Guillen .50 .15
265 Mark McLemore .50 .15
266 Jamie Moyer 1.00 .30
267 John Olerud 1.00 .30
268 Joel Pineiro FOIL 5.00 1.50
269 Kazuhiro Sasaki FOIL 5.00 1.50
270 Ruben Sierra .50 .15
271 Dan Wilson .50 .15
272 Ichiro Suzuki FOIL 10.00 3.00
273 J.D. Drew 1.00 .30
274 Jim Edmonds FOIL 5.00 1.50
275 Jason Isringhausen 1.00 .30
276 Matt Morris FOIL 5.00 1.50
277 Albert Pujols FOIL 12.00 3.60
278 Edgar Renteria 1.00 .30
279 Scott Rolen FOIL 8.00 2.40
280 Jason Simontacchi .50 .15
281 Fernando Vina 1.00 .30
282 Brent Abernathy .50 .15
283 Steve Cox .50 .15
284 Chris Gomez .50 .15
285 Ben Grieve .50 .15
286 Joe Kennedy .50 .15
287 Tanyon Sturtze .50 .15
288 Paul Wilson .50 .15
289 Randy Winn FOIL 3.00 .90
290 Juan Gonzalez 2.50 .75
291 Hideki Irabu .50 .15
292 Rafael Palmeiro FOIL 8.00 2.40
293 Herbert Perry .50 .15
294 Alex Rodriguez FOIL 15.00 4.50
295 Ivan Rodriguez 2.50 .75
296 Kenny Rogers 1.00 .30
297 Ismael Valdes .50 .15
298 Mike Young 1.00 .30
299 Dave Berg .50 .15
300 Carlos Delgado 1.00 .30
301 Kelvim Escobar .50 .15
302 Roy Halladay FOIL 5.00 1.50
303 Eric Hinske FOIL 3.00 .90
304 Shannon Stewart 1.00 .30
P51 Pee Wee Reese Promo

2003 MLB Showdown Strategy

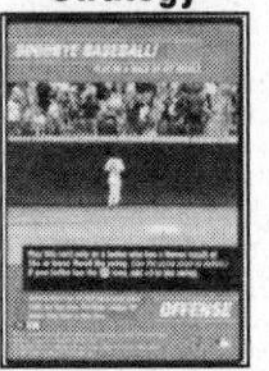

Issued at a stated rate of two per pack, these 50 cards feature various known terms as well as a photo to go with the caption. Whenever possible, we have notated who the player is before the caption in our data base.

Nm-Mt Ex-Mt
COMPLETE SET (50) 15.00 4.50
S1 Sean Casey .25 .07
Bad Call
S2 Ellis Burks .25 .07
Clutch Hitting
S3 Danny Graves .25 .07
Down Middle
S4 Mark Mulder .25 .07
Drag Bunt
S5 Ducks on the Pond .25 .07
S6 Benito Santiago .25 .07
Fuel on Fire
S7 Ichiro Suzuki .75 .23
Goodbye BB
S8 Ichiro Suzuki .75 .23
Great Addition
S9 Ichiro Suzuki .75 .23
Last Chance
S10 Barry Larkin .50 .15
Nuisance
S11 Jacque Jones .25 .07
Protect Runner
S12 Jim Thome .50 .15
Pull the Ball
S13 Tino Martinez .40 .12
Rally Cap
S14 Eric Hinske .25 .07
Rookie's Chance
S15 Runner Not Held .25 .07
S16 Vladimir Guerrero .50 .15
See Clearly
S17 Deivi Cruz .25 .07
Serious Wheels
S18 Carlos Guillen .25 .07
Sit on Fastball
S19 David Eckstein .25 .07
Take Given
S20 Derek Jeter 1.25 .35
Turn On It
S21 Barry Bonds 1.25 .35
Valuable Asset
S22 Mark Mulder .25 .07
Aces Up
S23 Dan Reichert .25 .07
By the Book
S24 Denny Neagle .25 .07
Change It Up
S25 Juan Encarnacion .25 .07
Cut Off Gap
S26 Chris Reitsma .25 .07
Full Windup
S27 Juan Encarnacion .25 .07
Good Leather
S28 Mark Mulder .25 .07
Great Start
S29 Danny Bautista .25 .07
Great Throw
S30 Jose Hernandez .25 .07
Highlight Reel
S31 In the Groove .25 .07
S32 David Eckstein .25 .07
Insult to Injury
S33 Job Well Done .25 .07
S34 David Justice .25 .07
Just Over Wall
S35 Luis Gonzalez .25 .07
Knock Ball Down
S36 Ricardo Rincon .25 .07
Lefty Specialist
S37 Eric Gagne .40 .12
Nerves of Steel
S38 Carlos Febles .25 .07
Paint Corner
S39 Raul Ibanez .25 .07
Pumped Up
S40 Mark Wohlers .25 .07
Put Out Fire
S41 Abraham Nunez .25 .07
Rally Killer
S42 Byung-Hyun Kim .25 .07
Submarine Pitch
S43 Dave Roberts .25 .07
Throwing Heat
S44 What a Relief! .25 .07
S45 Change in Strategy .25 .07
S46 Giovanni Carrara .25 .07
Feast or Famine
S47 Barry Larkin .50 .15
Grounder to 2nd
S48 It's Crunch Time .25 .07
S49 Shane Halter .25 .07
Just Over Rail
S50 Art Howe .25 .07
Ray Knight
Outmanaged

2004 MLB Showdown

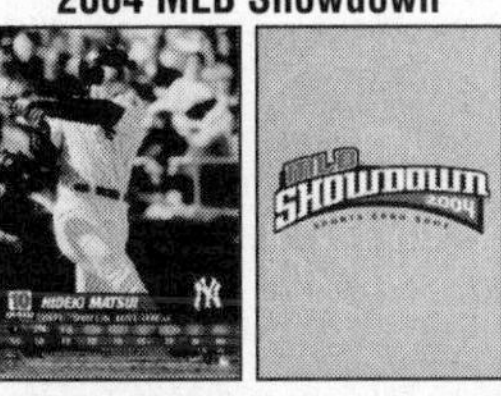

This 348 card set was released in March 2004. The set featured a wide assortment of stars and common players and was issued both in "Starter decks" as well as in booster packs. Many cards were issued with "foil" and those cards are notated in our checklist.

Nm-Mt Ex-Mt
COMP.SET w/o FOIL (298) 60.00 18.00
COMMON CARD .50 .15
COMMON FOIL 3.00 .90
FOIL STATED ODDS 1:3
1 Garret Anderson FOIL UER 5.00 1.50
Name Spelled Garrett
2 David Eckstein .50 .15
3 Darin Erstad 1.00 .30
4 Troy Glaus 1.50 .45
5 Bengie Molina .50 .15
6 Ramon Ortiz .50 .15
7 Eric Owens .50 .15
8 Tim Salmon 1.50 .45
9 Scot Shields .50 .15
10 Scott Spiezio .50 .15
11 Jarrod Washburn 1.00 .30
12 Rod Barajas .50 .15
13 Alex Cintron 1.00 .30
14 Elmer Dessens .50 .15
15 Steve Finley 1.00 .30
16 Luis Gonzalez FOIL 5.00 1.50
17 Mark Grace 1.50 .45
18 Shea Hillenbrand 1.00 .30
19 Matt Kata 1.00 .30
20 Quinton McCracken .50 .15
21 Curt Schilling FOIL 8.00 2.40
22 Vinny Castilla 1.00 .30
23 Robert Fick .50 .15
24 Rafael Furcal 1.00 .30
25 Marcus Giles 1.00 .30
26 Andruw Jones 1.00 .30
27 Chipper Jones FOIL 10.00 3.00
28 Ray King .50 .15
29 Javy Lopez FOIL 5.00 1.50
30 Greg Maddux 4.00 1.20
31 Russ Ortiz 1.00 .30
32 Gary Sheffield FOIL 8.00 2.40
33 Tony Batista 1.00 .30
34 Deivi Cruz .50 .15
35 Travis Driskill .50 .15
36 Brook Fordyce .50 .15
37 Jay Gibbons 1.00 .30
38 Pat Hentgen .50 .15
39 Jorge Julio .50 .15
40 Rodrigo Lopez .50 .15
41 Luis Matos FOIL 5.00 1.50
42 Melvin Mora .50 .15
43 Brian Roberts .50 .15
44 B.J. Surhoff 1.00 .30
45 Johnny Damon 1.00 .30
46 Alan Embree .50 .15
47 Nomar Garciaparra FOIL 10.00 3.00
48 Byung-Hyun Kim 1.00 .30
49 Derek Lowe 1.00 .30
50 Pedro Martinez FOIL 15.00 4.50
51 Bill Mueller FOIL 8.00 2.40
52 Trot Nixon 1.50 .45
53 David Ortiz 1.00 .30
54 Manny Ramirez 1.00 .30
55 Jason Varitek 1.00 .30
56 Tim Wakefield 1.00 .30
57 Todd Walker 1.00 .30
58 Antonio Alfonseca .50 .15
59 Moises Alou 1.00 .30
60 Paul Bako .50 .15
61 Alex Gonzalez .50 .15
62 Tom Goodwin .50 .15
63 Mark Grudzielanek .50 .15
64 Eric Karros 1.00 .30
65 Kenny Lofton 1.00 .30
66 Ramon E. Martinez .50 .15
67 Corey Patterson 1.00 .30
68 Mark Prior FOIL 20.00 6.00
69 Aramis Ramirez 1.00 .30
70 Mike Remlinger .50 .15
71 Sammy Sosa FOIL 10.00 3.00
72 Kerry Wood FOIL 10.00 3.00
73 Carlos Zambrano 1.00 .30
74 Mark Buehrle 1.00 .30
75 Bartolo Colon 1.00 .30
76 Joe Crede 1.00 .30
77 Tom Gordon .50 .15
78 Paul Konerko 1.00 .30
79 Carlos Lee 1.00 .30
80 Damaso Marte .50 .15
81 Miguel Olivo .50 .15
82 Magglio Ordonez FOIL 5.00 1.50
83 Frank Thomas 2.50 .75
84 Jose Valentin .50 .15
85 Sean Casey 1.00 .30
86 Juan Castro .50 .15
87 Adam Dunn 1.00 .30
88 Danny Graves .50 .15
89 Ken Griffey Jr. 4.00 1.20
90 D'Angelo Jimenez .50 .15
91 Austin Kearns 1.00 .30
92 Barry Larkin 2.50 .75
93 Jason LaRue .50 .15
94 Chris Reitsma .50 .15
95 Reggie Taylor .50 .15
96 Paul Wilson .50 .15
97 Danys Baez .50 .15
98 Josh Bard .50 .15
99 Casey Blake .50 .15
100 Jason Boyd .50 .15
101 Milton Bradley FOIL 5.00 1.50
102 Ellis Burks 1.00 .30
103 Coco Crisp .50 .15
104 Jody Gerut 1.00 .30
105 Travis Hafner 1.00 .30
106 Matt Lawton .50 .15
107 John McDonald .50 .15
108 Terry Mulholland .50 .15
109 C.C. Sabathia 1.00 .30
110 Omar Vizquel 1.00 .30
111 Ronnie Belliard .50 .15
112 Shawn Chacon .50 .15
113 Todd Helton FOIL 10.00 3.00
114 Charles Johnson 1.00 .30
115 Darren Oliver .50 .15
116 Jay Payton 1.00 .30
117 Justin Speier .50 .15
118 Chris Stynes .50 .15
119 Larry Walker 1.50 .45
120 Preston Wilson 1.00 .30
121 Jeremy Bonderman 1.00 .30
122 Shane Halter .50 .15
123 Bobby Higginson 1.00 .30
124 Brandon Inge .50 .15
125 Wilfredo Ledezma .50 .15
126 Chris Mears .50 .15
127 Warren Morris .50 .15
128 Carlos Pena .50 .15
129 Ramon Santiago .50 .15
130 Andres Torres .50 .15
131 Dmitri Young 1.00 .30
132 Josh Beckett 1.50 .45
133 Miguel Cabrera 2.50 .75
134 Luis Castillo 1.00 .30
135 Juan Encarnacion 1.00 .30
136 Alex Gonzalez .50 .15
137 Derrek Lee 1.00 .30
138 Braden Looper .50 .15
139 Mike Lowell 1.00 .30
140 Juan Pierre 1.00 .30
141 Mark Redman .50 .15
142 Ivan Rodriguez FOIL 10.00 3.00
143 Tim Spooneybarger .50 .15
144 Dontrelle Willis FOIL 5.00 1.50
145 Brad Ausmus .50 .15
146 Jeff Bagwell 1.50 .45
147 Lance Berkman 1.50 .45
148 Craig Biggio 1.50 .45
149 Geoff Blum .50 .15
150 Octavio Dotel FOIL 8.00 2.40
151 Morgan Ensberg .50 .15
152 Adam Everett .50 .15
153 Richard Hidalgo FOIL 5.00 1.50
154 Jeff Kent 1.00 .30
155 Brad Lidge .50 .15
156 Roy Oswalt 1.00 .30
157 Jeriome Robertson .50 .15
158 Billy Wagner FOIL 8.00 2.40
159 Carlos Beltran FOIL 10.00 3.00
160 Angel Berroa 1.00 .30
161 Jason Grimsley .50 .15
162 Aaron Guiel .50 .15
163 Runelvys Hernandez .50 .15
164 Raul Ibanez .50 .15
165 Curtis Leskanic .50 .15
166 Jose Lima .50 .15
167 Mike MacDougal .50 .15
168 Brent Mayne .50 .15
169 Joe Randa .50 .15
170 Desi Relaford .50 .15
171 Mike Sweeney 1.00 .30
172 Michael Tucker .50 .15
173 Adrian Beltre 1.00 .30
174 Kevin Brown FOIL 5.00 1.50
175 Ron Coomer .50 .15
176 Alex Cora .50 .15
177 Eric Gagne FOIL 20.00 6.00
178 Shawn Green 1.00 .30
179 Cesar Izturis 1.00 .30
180 Brian Jordan 1.00 .30
181 Paul Lo Duca 1.00 .30
182 Fred McGriff 1.50 .45
183 Hideo Nomo 2.50 .75
184 Paul Quantrill .50 .15
185 Dave Roberts .50 .15
186 Royce Clayton .50 .15
187 Keith Ginter .50 .15
188 Wes Helms .50 .15
189 Geoff Jenkins 1.00 .30
190 Brooks Kieschnick .50 .15
191 Eddie Perez .50 .15
192 Scott Podsednik FOIL 10.00 3.00
193 Richie Sexson FOIL 5.00 1.50
194 Ben Sheets 1.00 .30
195 John Vander Wal .50 .15
196 Chris Gomez .50 .15
197 Cristian Guzman 1.00 .30
198 LaTroy Hawkins 1.00 .30
199 Torii Hunter 1.00 .30
200 Jacque Jones 1.00 .30
201 Corey Koskie 1.00 .30
202 Doug Mientkiewicz 1.00 .30
203 A.J. Pierzynski 1.00 .30
204 Brad Radke 1.00 .30
205 Shannon Stewart FOIL 5.00 1.50
206 Michael Barrett .50 .15
207 Orlando Cabrera FOIL 3.00 .90
208 Endy Chavez .50 .15
209 Zach Day .50 .15
210 Vladimir Guerrero FOIL 10.00 3.00
211 Fernando Tatis .50 .15
212 Javier Vazquez 1.00 .30
213 Jose Vidro 1.00 .30
214 Brad Wilkerson .50 .15
215 Tony Clark .50 .15
216 Cliff Floyd 1.00 .30
217 John Franco 1.00 .30
218 Joe McEwing .50 .15
219 Timo Perez .50 .15
220 Jason Phillips .50 .15
221 Mike Piazza 4.00 1.20
222 Jose Reyes FOIL 8.00 2.40
223 Steve Trachsel .50 .15
224 Dave Weathers .50 .15
225 Ty Wigginton .50 .15
226 Roger Clemens FOIL 15.00 4.50
227 Chris Hammond .50 .15
228 Derek Jeter FOIL 15.00 4.50
229 Nick Johnson 1.00 .30
230 Hideki Matsui 4.00 1.20
231 Mike Mussina FOIL 10.00 3.00
232 Andy Pettitte 1.50 .45
233 Jorge Posada 1.50 .45
234 Mariano Rivera 1.50 .45
235 Alfonso Soriano 1.50 .45
236 Jeff Weaver .50 .15
237 Bernie Williams 1.50 .45
238 Enrique Wilson .50 .15
239 Chad Bradford .50 .15
240 Eric Byrnes .50 .15
241 Mark Ellis .50 .15
242 Keith Foulke FOIL 8.00 2.40
243 Scott Hatteberg .50 .15
244 Ramon Hernandez .50 .15
245 Tim Hudson FOIL 8.00 2.40
246 Terrence Long 1.00 .30
247 Mark Mulder FOIL 5.00 1.50
248 Ricardo Rincon .50 .15
249 Chris Singleton .50 .15
250 Miguel Tejada 1.00 .30
251 Barry Zito 1.50 .45
252 Bobby Abreu 1.00 .30
253 David Bell .50 .15
254 Pat Burrell 1.00 .30
255 Marlon Byrd .50 .15
256 Rheal Cormier .50 .15
257 Vicente Padilla .50 .15
258 Tomas Perez .50 .15
259 Placido Polanco .50 .15
260 Jimmy Rollins 1.00 .30
261 Carlos Silva .50 .15
262 Jim Thome FOIL 10.00 3.00
263 Randy Wolf FOIL 5.00 1.50
264 Kris Benson .50 .15
265 Jeff D'Amico .50 .15
266 Adam Hyzdu .50 .15
267 Jason Kendall FOIL 5.00 1.50
268 Brian Meadows .50 .15
269 Abraham Nunez .50 .15
270 Reggie Sanders .50 .15
271 Matt Stairs .50 .15
272 Jack Wilson .50 .15
273 Gary Bennett .50 .15
274 Sean Burroughs 1.00 .30
275 Adam Eaton .50 .15
276 Luther Hackman .50 .15
277 Ryan Klesko 1.00 .30
278 Brian Lawrence .50 .15
279 Mark Loretta .50 .15
280 Phil Nevin 1.00 .30
281 Ramon Vazquez .50 .15
282 Edgardo Alfonzo 1.00 .30
283 Rich Aurilia 1.00 .30
284 Jim Brower .50 .15
285 Jose Cruz Jr. 1.00 .30
286 Ray Durham 1.00 .30
287 Andres Galarraga 1.00 .30
288 Marquis Grissom .50 .15
289 Neifi Perez .50 .15
290 Felix Rodriguez .50 .15
291 Benito Santiago 1.00 .30
292 Jason Schmidt FOIL 5.00 1.50
293 J.T. Snow 1.00 .30
294 Tim Worrell .50 .15
295 Bret Boone FOIL 8.00 2.40
296 Mike Cameron 1.00 .30
297 Ryan Franklin .50 .15
298 Carlos Guillen .50 .15
299 Shigetoshi Hasegawa 1.00 .30
300 Edgar Martinez 1.50 .45
301 Mark McLemore .50 .15
302 Jamie Moyer FOIL 5.00 1.50
303 John Olerud .50 .15
304 Ichiro Suzuki FOIL 10.00 3.00
305 Dan Wilson .50 .15
306 Randy Winn .50 .15
307 J.D. Drew 1.00 .30
308 Jeff Fassero .50 .15
309 Bo Hart 1.00 .30
310 Jason Isringhausen .50 .15
311 Tino Martinez 1.50 .45
312 Mike Matheny .50 .15
313 Orlando Palmeiro .50 .15
314 Albert Pujols FOIL 20.00 6.00
315 Edgar Renteria FOIL 8.00 2.40
316 Garrett Stephenson .50 .15
317 Woody Williams FOIL 5.00 1.50
318 Rocco Baldelli 2.50 .75
319 Lance Carter .50 .15
320 Carl Crawford 1.00 .30
321 Toby Hall .50 .15
322 Travis Harper .50 .15
323 Aubrey Huff FOIL 5.00 1.50
324 Travis Lee .50 .15
325 Julio Lugo .50 .15
326 Damian Rolls .50 .15
327 Jorge Sosa .50 .15
328 Hank Blalock 1.00 .30
329 Francisco Cordero .50 .15
330 Aaron Fultz .50 .15
331 Juan Gonzalez 2.50 .75
332 Rafael Palmeiro 1.50 .45
333 Alex Rodriguez FOIL 30.00 9.00
334 Mark Teixeira 1.00 .30
335 John Thomson .50 .15
336 Ismael Valdes .50 .15
337 Michael Young 1.00 .30
338 Frank Catalanotto .50 .15
339 Carlos Delgado 1.00 .30
340 Kelvim Escobar .50 .15
341 Roy Halladay FOIL 15.00 4.50
342 Eric Hinske .50 .15
343 Orlando Hudson .50 .15
344 Greg Myers .50 .15
345 Josh Phelps .50 .15
346 Cliff Politte .50 .15
347 Vernon Wells FOIL 5.00 1.50
348 Chris Woodward .50 .15

2004 MLB Showdown Strategy

Nm-Mt Ex-Mt
COMPLETE SET (50) 8.00 2.40
TWO PER BOOSTER PACK
S1 Lenny Harris .25 .07
Bad Call
S2 Adam Dunn .25 .07
Burned
S3 Alex Rodriguez .75 .23
Check Swing
S4 Manny Ramirez .25 .07
Deep in Gap
S5 Pokey Reese .25 .07
Drained
S6 Ducks on Pond/Wrigley Field .25 .07
S7 Ichiro Suzuki .75 .23
Great Addition
S8 Alex Gonzalez .25 .07
Hard Slide
S9 Juan Pierre .25 .07
Inside Park HR
S10 Sean Casey .25 .07
Options
S11 Steve Trachsel .25 .07
Frying Pan
S12 Dontrelle Willis .25 .07
Play the Percentages
S13 Albert Pujols 1.00 .30
Pointers
S14 Jeff Cirillo .25 .07
Poor Positioning
S15 Carlos Delgado .25 .07
Pull the Ball
S16 Tony LaRussa MG .25 .07
Rough Outing
S17 Nomar Garciaparra .75 .23
Slow Roller
S18 Bob Cluck CO .25 .07
Stick a Fork
S19 Bernie Williams .40 .12
Sweet Swing
S20 Adam Dunn .25 .07
Take What's Given
S21 Larry Bowa MG .25 .07
Think Again
S22 Jeff Bagwell .40 .12
Turn on It
S23 Russ Ortiz .25 .07
Aces Up
S24 Ben Broussard .25 .07
Caught Leaning
S25 Mark Prior 1.00 .30
Caught Corner
S26 Michael Cuddyer .25 .07
Choke
S27 Jack Wilson .25 .07
Cover Second
S28 Roy Halladay .25 .07
Dominating
S29 Frank Thomas .50 .15
Foul Ball
S30 Rafael Furcal .25 .07
Good Leather
S31 Jason Giambi .50 .15
Hooking Foul
S32 A.J.Burnett .25 .07
In the Zone
S33 Omar Vizquel .25 .07
Infield In
S34 Lined Out Play/Foul Pole .25 .07
S35 Curt Schilling .40 .12
Locate
S36 Locked In/Padres Catcher .25 .07
S37 Nerves Steel/Marlins Pitcher .25 .07
S38 Curt Schilling .40 .12
Paint Corner
S39 Kerry Wood .50 .15
Power Pitching
S40 Alex Cora .25 .07
Short Fly
S41 Nomar Garciaparra .75 .23
Sloppy Bunt
S42 Kazuhiro Sasaki .25 .07
Split-Finger
S43 Mike Scioscia MG .25 .07
Top-Level
S44 Chris Hammond .25 .07
Tough Nails
S45 Jamie Moyer .25 .07
Change Strategy
S46 Orlando Cabrera .25 .07
Close Call
S47 Art Howe MG .25 .07
New Strategies
S48 Rob Mackowiak .25 .07
Second Look

S49 Michael Cuddyer .25 .07
Swing Anything
S50 Jason Schmidt .25 .07
Think Twice

2002 MLB Showdown Pennant Run

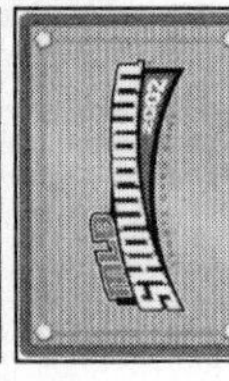

This 125 card set was issued in October, 2002 and feauted many players who would be important to their teams during the late part of the 2002 season. The 25 foil cards were issued at a stated rate of one in three.

Nm-Mt Ex-Mt
COMP.SET w/o SP's (100) 40.00 12.00
COMMON CARD (1-125) .40 .12
COMMON FOIL 3.00 .90
1 J.C. Romero .40 .12
2 Robb Nen .60 .18
3 Raul Mondesi .60 .18
4 Mike Piazza 2.50 .75
5 Scott Rolen 1.00 .30
6 Shigetoshi Hasegawa .60 .18
7 Shannon Stewart .60 .18
8 David Eckstein FOIL 3.00 .90
9 Melvin Mora .40 .12
10 Jose Rijo .40 .12
11 Einar Diaz .40 .12
12 A.J. Burnett .40 .12
13 Mike Sweeney .60 .18
14 Jorge Posada FOIL 8.00 2.40
15 Mark Kotsay .40 .12
16 Doug Davis .40 .12
17 Steve Woodard .40 .12
18 Sun Woo Kim .40 .12
19 Sean Casey .60 .18
20 Juan Acevedo .40 .12
21 Dustan Mohr .40 .12
22 Mariano Rivera 1.00 .30
23 Kip Wells .40 .12
24 Kenny Lofton FOIL 5.00 1.50
25 Steve Cox .40 .12
26 Josh Fogg FOIL 3.00 .90
27 Ruben Sierra .40 .12
28 Sandy Alomar Jr. .40 .12
29 Vicente Padilla FOIL 3.00 .90
30 Carlos Beltran .60 .18
31 Mike Lowell .60 .18
32 Omar Vizquel .60 .18
33 Ricky Stone RC .60 .18
34 Geoff Jenkins .60 .18
35 Eric Karros .60 .18
36 Ryan Drese .40 .12
37 Adam Dunn .60 .18
38 Hank Blalock 1.50 .45
39 Marcus Giles .60 .18
40 Joe Randa .40 .12
41 Bob Wickman .40 .12
42 Roy Halladay .60 .18
43 Craig Counsell .40 .12
44 Derek Lowe .60 .18
45 Ray Durham .60 .18
46 Paul Shuey .40 .12
47 Cliff Floyd .60 .18
48 Shawn Green .60 .18
49 Torii Hunter FOIL 5.00 1.50
50 Edgardo Alfonzo .60 .18
51 Carlos Pena .40 .12
52 Sean Burroughs .60 .18
53 Placido Polanco .40 .12
54 Rafael Palmeiro 1.00 .30
55 Nate Cornejo .40 .12
56 Tim Salmon 1.00 .30
57 Craig Biggio 1.00 .30
58 Eric Hinske FOIL 3.00 .90
59 Rickey Henderson 1.50 .45
60 Nick Johnson .60 .18
61 Rey Ordonez .40 .12
62 Jose Hernandez .40 .12
63 Antonio Alfonseca .40 .12
64 Alfonso Soriano FOIL 8.00 2.40
65 Eric Chavez .60 .18
66 B.J. Surhoff FOIL 5.00 1.50
67 Austin Kearns FOIL 5.00 1.50
68 Jacob Cruz .40 .12
69 Armando Benitez .60 .18
70 Derek Jeter 4.00 1.20
71 Ryan Jensen .40 .12
72 Kevin Mench .40 .12
73 Mike Remlinger .40 .12
74 Luis Castillo .60 .18
75 Kazuhisa Ishii FOIL RC 8.00 2.40
76 Bobby Abreu .60 .18
77 Dave Veres .40 .12
78 Tony Batista .60 .18
79 Rey Sanchez .40 .12
80 Jason Grimsley .40 .12
81 Al Leiter FOIL 5.00 1.50
82 Kerry Wood FOIL 10.00 3.00
83 Ellis Burks .60 .18
84 Corey Patterson .60 .18
85 Adrian Beltre .60 .18
86 Barry Zito 1.00 .30
87 Doug Mientkiewicz .60 .18
88 Jeffrey Hammonds .40 .12
89 Jeremy Giambi .40 .12
90 Tsuyoshi Shinjo .60 .18
91 Roger Clemens SS FOIL 12.00 3.60
92 John Franco SS .60 .18
93 Alex Rodriguez SS FOIL 15.00 4.50
94 Barry Bonds SS FOIL 30.00 9.00
95 Fred McGriff SS 1.00 .30
96 Chuck Finley SS .60 .18
97 Jose Rijo SS .40 .12
98 Jeff Bagwell SS FOIL 8.00 2.40
99 Ron Gant SS .60 .18
100 Tom Glavine SS 1.00 .30
101 Mike Mussina SS 1.50 .45
102 Gary Sheffield SS .60 .18
103 Barry Larkin SS 1.50 .45
104 Jim Thome SS 1.50 .45
105 Chipper Jones SS FOIL 10.00 3.00
106 Rickey Henderson SS 1.50 .45
107 Randy Johnson SS FOIL 10.00 3.00
108 Mike Piazza SS FOIL 10.00 3.00
109 John Smoltz SS 1.00 .30
110 Edgar Martinez SS 1.00 .30
111 Larry Walker SS 1.00 .30
112 Pedro Martinez SS FOIL 10.00 3.00
113 Sammy Sosa SS FOIL 20.00 6.00
114 Roberto Alomar SS FOIL 10.00 3.00
115 Curt Schilling SS FOIL 8.00 2.40
116 Chuck Knoblauch SS .60 .18
117 Frank Thomas SS 1.50 .45
118 Jeff Kent SS .60 .18
119 Kenny Lofton SS .60 .18
120 Ken Griffey Jr. SS 2.50 .75
121 Trevor Hoffman SS FOIL 5.00 1.50
122 Mo Vaughn SS .60 .18
123 Robin Ventura SS .60 .18
124 Ellis Burks SS .60 .18
125 Tim Raines SS .60 .18

2002 MLB Showdown Pennant Run Strategy

Issued at a stated rate of two per pack, these 23 cards feature "strategy" insert cards. Cards numbered 19 and 24 were actually issued in the trade deadline packs.

Nm-Mt Ex-Mt
COMPLETE SET (23) 8.00 2.40
S1 Bernie Williams .40 .12
Bad Call
S2 Mike Piazza .75 .23
Clutch Hitting
S3 Troy Glaus .40 .12
Crowd Plate
S4 Down the Middle .25 .07
S5 Ducks on the Pond .25 .07
S6 Alex Rodriguez .75 .23
Free Steal
S7 Overthrow .25 .07
S8 Payoff Pitch .25 .07
S9 Tom Goodwin .25 .07
Rally Cap
S10 Nate Cornejo .25 .07
Rattled
S11 Rick Ankiel .25 .07
Shell-Shocked
S12 Scott Sullivan .25 .07
Shelled
S13 Dave Williams .25 .07
Comebacker
S14 Fast Worker .25 .07
S15 Andy Pettitte .40 .12
Full Windup
S16 Ichiro Suzuki .75 .23
Great Throw
S17 Hung It .25 .07
S18 Mark Mulder .25 .07
In Groove
S20 Curt Schilling .40 .12
Insult Injury
S21 Trevor Hoffman .25 .07
Nerves Steel
S22 Pitchout .25 .07
S23 Brian Moehler .25 .07
Scuff Ball
S25 Change in Strategy .25 .07

2003 MLB Showdown Pennant Run

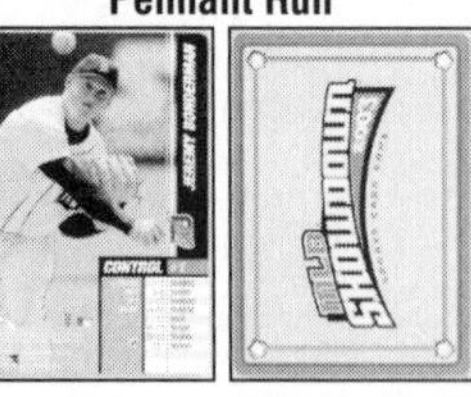

This 125 card set was released in August, 2003 season. Interspersed throughout the set is 25 foil cards. Those foil cards were inserted at a stated rate of one per three. Cards numbered 106 through 115 feature players from early in their career while cards numbered 116 through 125 feature Hall of Famers.

MINT NRMT
COMP.SET w/o SP's (100) 40.00 18.00
COMMON CARD (1-125) .50 .23
COMMON FOIL 3.00 1.35
1 Jeremy Bonderman RC 3.00 1.35
2 Tom Goodwin .50 .23
3 Terry Mulholland .50 .23
4 Jake Westbrook .50 .23
5 Jake Peavy 1.00 .45
6 Felix Rodriguez .50 .23
7 Marlon Byrd 1.00 .45
8 Toby Hall .50 .23
9 Roberto Hernandez .50 .23
10 Carlos Silva .50 .23
11 Chris Hammond .50 .23
12 David Dellucci .50 .23
13 R.A. Dickey .50 .23
14 Cliff Politte .50 .23
15 Russ Springer .50 .23
16 Vance Wilson .50 .23
17 Scott Williamson .50 .23
18 Ryan Franklin .50 .23
19 Juan Castro .50 .23
20 Craig Monroe .50 .23
21 Joe Beimel .50 .23
22 John Halama .50 .23
23 Eli Marrero .50 .23
24 Felipe Lopez .50 .23
25 Mike MacDougal .50 .23
26 Kris Benson .50 .23
27 Josh Beckett 1.50 .70
28 Carlos Febles .50 .23
29 Luis Rivas .50 .23
30 Scott Sullivan .50 .23
31 John Thomson .50 .23
32 Lance Carter .50 .23
33 Chris George .50 .23
34 Rocky Biddle .50 .23
35 Brandon Lyon .50 .23
36 Eric Munson .50 .23
37 Kirk Rueter .50 .23
38 Scott Schoeneweis .50 .23
39 Casey Blake .50 .23
40 Francisco Cordero .50 .23
41 Tom Gordon .50 .23
42 Neifi Perez .50 .23
43 Chad Bradford .50 .23
44 Miguel Cairo .50 .23
45 Mike Matheny .50 .23
46 Mike Timlin .50 .23
47 D.J. Carrasco RC .50 .23
48 Eddie Perez .50 .23
49 Gregg Zaun .50 .23
50 Ronnie Belliard .50 .23
51 Ricardo Rodriguez .50 .23
52 B.J. Ryan .50 .23
53 Michael Tucker .50 .23
54 Rheal Cormier .50 .23
55 Felix Heredia .50 .23
56 Alex Cora .50 .23
57 Travis Lee .50 .23
58 Ted Lilly .50 .23
59 Tom Wilson .50 .23
60 Jeff D'Amico .50 .23
61 Adam Eaton .50 .23
62 Travis Harper .50 .23
63 Mark Loretta .50 .23
64 Ricky Stone .50 .23
65 Wil Cordero .50 .23
66 Cliff Floyd 1.00 .45
67 Livan Hernandez .50 .23
68 Paul Quantrill .50 .23
69 Ben Davis .50 .23
70 Shawn Estes .50 .23
71 Chris Stynes .50 .23
72 Jay Payton .50 .23
73 Ramon Hernandez .50 .23
74 Jason Johnson .50 .23
75 John Vander Wal .50 .23
76 Shawn Chacon FOIL 3.00 1.35
77 D'Angelo Jimenez .50 .23
78 Desi Relaford .50 .23
79 Rich Aurilia 1.00 .45
80 Rod Barajas .50 .23
81 Jose Cruz FOIL 5.00 2.20
82 Kyle Lohse .50 .23
83 Rondell White 1.00 .45
84 Gil Meche FOIL 5.00 2.20
85 Jose Guillen .50 .23
86 Kenny Lofton 1.00 .45
87 Zach Day FOIL 3.00 1.35
88 Mark Redman .50 .23
89 Melvin Mora FOIL 5.00 2.20
90 Todd Walker 1.00 .45
91 Torii Hunter 1.00 .45
92 Frank Catalanotto .50 .23
93 Andres Galarraga 1.00 .45
94 Jason Schmidt 1.00 .45
95 Eric Byrnes .50 .23
96 Hank Blalock FOIL 8.00 3.60
97 Jacque Jones FOIL 5.00 2.20
98 Michael Young 1.00 .45
99 Carl Everett 1.00 .45
100 Preston Wilson 1.00 .45
101 Esteban Loaiza 1.00 .45
102 Raul Mondesi FOIL 5.00 2.20
103 Carlos Delgado FOIL 5.00 2.20
104 Gary Sheffield FOIL 5.00 2.20
105 Kevin Appier 1.00 .45
106 Jesse Orosco SS .50 .23
107 Pat Hentgen SS .50 .23
108 Matt Williams SS 1.00 .45
109 David Cone SS FOIL 5.00 2.20
110 Mark Grace SS FOIL 8.00 3.60
111 Carlos Baerga SS FOIL 3.00 1.35
112 Greg Maddux SS FOIL 10.00 4.50
113 Kevin Brown SS FOIL 8.00 3.60
114 Ivan Rodriguez SS FOIL 15.00 6.75
115 John Olerud SS FOIL 5.00 2.20
116 Larry Doby CC 1.00 .45
117 Yogi Berra CC FOIL 10.00 4.50
118 Hoyt Wilhelm CC FOIL 15.00 6.75
119 Pee Wee Reese CC 1.50 .70
120 Br. Robinson CC FOIL 10.00 4.50
121 Robin Yount CC FOIL 12.00 5.50
122 Reggie Jackson CC FOIL 15.00 6.75
123 Har. Killebrew CC FOIL 15.00 6.75
124 Rod Carew CC FOIL 15.00 6.75
125 Nolan Ryan CC FOIL 15.00 6.75

2003 MLB Showdown Pennant Run Strategy

Issued at a stated rate of two per pack, these 25 cards feature various known terms as well as a photo to go with the caption. Whenever possible, we have notated who the player is before the caption in our data base.

MINT NRMT
COMPLETE SET (25) 8.00 3.60
1 Omar Vizquel .25 .11
Change Sides
2 Jerry Hairston Jr. .25 .11
Emergency Bunt
3 Bret Boone .25 .11
Get Under It
4 Dave Hansen .25 .11
In Motion
5 Out of Position .25 .11
6 Einar Diaz .25 .11
Passed Ball
7 Jack McKeon .25 .11
Say the Magic Word
8 Suicide Squeeze .25 .11
9 Brian Giles .25 .11
To the Warning Track
10 Keith Osik .25 .11
Block the Plate
11 Curt Schilling .40 .18
Brent Butler
Comebacker
12 Kazuhisa Ishii .25 .11
Good Matchup
13 Austin Kearns .25 .11
Ground Rule Double
14 Pedro Martinez .50 .23
In the Zone
15 Infield In .25 .11
16 Wilkin Ruan .25 .11
Pickoff Attempt
17 Roger Clemens 1.00 .45
Play the Odds
18 Austin Kearns .25 .11
Playing Shallow
19 Quick Pitch .25 .11
20 Jason Jennings .25 .11
Sinker
21 Jay Bell .25 .11
Up and In
22 Dee Brown .25 .11
Good Scouting
23 Buck Showalter .25 .11
Looking Ahead
24 Old Tricks .25 .11
25 Buck Showalter MG .75 .35
Alex Rodriguez
Think Twice

2002 MLB Showdown Trading Deadline

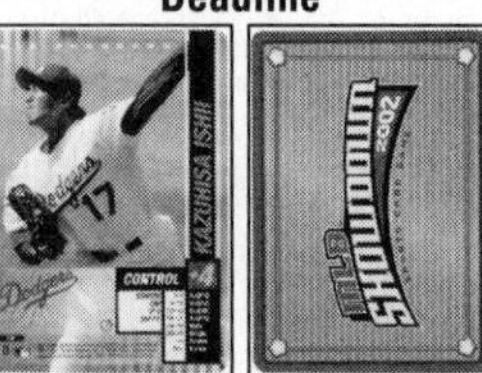

The 2002 MLB Showdown product was released in mid summer, 2002 as a 150-card baseball game which updated the regular MLB Showdown set. The set features 125-player cards and 25 foil superstar cards that were short printed at one in three booster packs.

Nm-Mt Ex-Mt
COMP.SET w/o SP'S (125) 40.00 12.00
COMMON CARD (1-150) .50 .15
COMMON FOIL 3.00 .90
1 Jason Giambi FOIL 10.00 3.00
2 Chris Singleton .50 .15
3 Ben Davis .50 .15
4 Tsuyoshi Shinjo 1.00 .30
5 Brian Jordan 1.00 .30
6 Tony Clark .50 .15
7 Moises Alou FOIL 5.00 1.50
8 Todd Walker 1.00 .30
9 Ricky Gutierrez .50 .15
10 Brad Fullmer .50 .15
11 Jeromy Burnitz 1.00 .30
12 Gary Sheffield FOIL 8.00 2.40
13 Marty Cordova FOIL 3.00 .90
14 Todd Zeile 1.00 .30
15 Alex Gonzalez .50 .15
16 Kenny Lofton 1.00 .30
17 Vinny Castilla 1.00 .30
18 Craig Paquette .50 .15
19 Michael Tucker .50 .15
20 Cesar Izturis .50 .15
21 Eric Young .50 .15
22 Chuck Knoblauch 1.00 .30
23 Roberto Alomar FOIL 10.00 3.00
24 David Bell .50 .15
25 Johnny Damon 1.00 .30
26 Roger Cedeno .50 .15
27 Robin Ventura 1.00 .30
28 David Justice FOIL 5.00 1.50
29 Brady Anderson 1.00 .30
30 Pokey Reese .50 .15
31 Reggie Sanders FOIL 5.00 1.50
32 Jeff Cirillo FOIL 3.00 .90
33 Juan Encarnacion .50 .15
34 Tino Martinez FOIL 8.00 2.40
35 Carl Everett FOIL 5.00 1.50
36 Danny Bautista .50 .15
37 Rafael Furcal 1.00 .30
38 Dmitri Young FOIL 5.00 1.50
39 Jay Gibbons 1.00 .30
40 Brian Buchanan .50 .15
41 David Segui .50 .15
42 Barry Larkin FOIL 10.00 3.00
43 John Vander Wal .50 .15
44 Brent Mayne .50 .15
45 Neifi Perez .50 .15
46 Lenny Harris .50 .15
47 Jason LaRue .50 .15
48 Travis Fryman 1.00 .30
49 Juan Uribe .50 .15
50 Shea Hillenbrand 1.00 .30
51 Aaron Rowand .50 .15
52 Jose Ortiz .50 .15
53 Robert Fick 1.00 .30
54 Doug Glanville .50 .15
55 Charles Johnson FOIL 5.00 1.50
56 Derrek Lee 1.00 .30
57 Carlos Febles .50 .15
58 Luis Rivas .50 .15
59 Lee Stevens .50 .15
60 Mike Lieberthal 1.00 .30
61 Ryan Klesko FOIL 8.00 2.40
62 Chris Gomez .50 .15
63 Randy Winn .50 .15
64 Rusty Greer 1.00 .30
65 Felipe Lopez .50 .15
66 Carlos Pena .50 .15
67 Toby Hall .50 .15
68 Milton Bradley 1.00 .30
69 Matt Lawton .50 .15
70 Gregg Zaun .50 .15
71 Eric Hinske .50 .15
72 Alex Ochoa .50 .15
73 Rondell White 1.00 .30
74 Armando Rios .50 .15
75 Desi Relaford .50 .15
76 Nomar Garciaparra FOIL 10.00 3.00
77 Frank Thomas FOIL 10.00 3.00
78 Mitch Meluskey .50 .15
79 Morgan Ensberg 1.00 .30
80 Mo Vaughn FOIL 5.00 1.50
81 Adrian Brown .50 .15
82 Juan Gonzalez FOIL 10.00 3.00
83 Tom Wilson RC 1.00 .30
84 Matt Stairs .50 .15
85 Andres Galarraga 1.00 .30
86 Sidney Ponson 1.00 .30
87 Jesus Colome .50 .15
88 Juan Cruz .50 .15
89 Eddie Guardado 1.00 .30
90 Jon Garland .50 .15
91 Denny Neagle .50 .15
92 Chad Durbin .50 .15
93 Kevin Brown FOIL 5.00 1.50
94 Elmer Dessens .50 .15
95 Eric Gagne 1.50 .45
96 Jamey Wright .50 .15
97 Pedro Martinez FOIL 2.50 .75
98 Jason Bere .50 .15
99 Ugueth Urbina .50 .15
100 Carl Pavano .50 .15
101 Kip Wells .50 .15
102 Paul Abbott .50 .15
103 Billy Wagner FOIL 5.00 1.50
104 Erik Hiljus .50 .15
105 Brandon Duckworth .50 .15
106 Ruben Quevedo .50 .15
107 Jimmy Anderson .50 .15
108 Bobby Jones .50 .15
109 Livan Hernandez .50 .15
110 Curtis Leskanic .50 .15
111 Tom Gordon .50 .15
112 Jeff Austin RC 1.00 .30
113 Joel Pineiro 1.00 .30
114 Chad Bradford .50 .15
115 Woody Williams .50 .15
116 Victor Zambrano FOIL 3.00 .90
117 Jose Mesa .50 .15
118 Roy Halladay 1.00 .30
119 Steve Karsay .50 .15
120 Hideo Nomo 2.50 .75
121 Jeff Farnsworth .50 .15
122 Dave Weathers .50 .15
123 Sean Lowe .50 .15
124 Mike Myers .50 .15
125 Jason Schmidt 1.00 .30
126 Mike Williams .50 .15
127 Terry Adams .50 .15
128 Chan Ho Park FOIL 5.00 1.50
129 Jeff D'Amico .50 .15
130 Kevin Appier FOIL 5.00 1.50
131 Glendon Rusch .50 .15
132 Jason Isringhausen .50 .15
133 Todd Ritchie .50 .15
134 Shawn Estes .50 .15
135 Kevin Millwood 1.00 .30
136 Aaron Sele .50 .15
137 Rick Helling .50 .15
138 Billy Koch .50 .15
139 Paul Quantrill .50 .15
140 Tim Spooneybarger .50 .15
141 Jorge Julio .50 .15
142 Carlos Hernandez .50 .15
143 Rick Ankiel .50 .15
144 Scott Erickson .50 .15
145 Denny Hocking .50 .15
146 Kazuhisa Ishii RC 5.00 1.50
147 Pedro Astacio .50 .15
148 Satoru Komiyama RC 1.00 .30
149 Kurt Ainsworth .50 .15
150 John Smoltz FOIL 8.00 2.40

2002 MLB Showdown Trading Deadline Strategy

Inserted into packs at a rate of two per pack, this 25-card insert set features the strategy cards necessary for playing the MLB Showdown game. Card numbers carry an "S" prefix.

Nm-Mt Ex-Mt
COMPLETE SET (25) 6.00 1.80
S1 Luis Gonzalez .25 .07
Big Inning
S2 Jeff Cirillo .25 .07
Do or Die
S3 Alex Rodriguez .75 .23
Free Steal
S4 Tsuyoshi Shinjo .25 .07
Lean Into It
S5 Overthrow/Cubs-Mets .25 .07
S6 Corey Patterson .25 .07
Pointers
S7 David Justice .25 .07
Pro Hitter
S8 Nate Cornejo .25 .07

Rattled
S9 Scott Sullivan .25 .07
Shelled
S10 Rick Ankiel .25 .07
Shell-Shocked
S11 Swing Fences/Cubs .25 .07
S12 Marlon Anderson .25 .07
Tricky Hop
S13 Whiplash .25 .07
S14 Aaron Boone .25 .07
Choke
S15 Dave Williams .25 .07
Comebacker
S16 Takahito Nomura .25 .07
Fast Worker
S17 Paul Abbott .25 .07
Focused
S18 Hung It .25 .07
S19 Rick Helling .25 .07
In the Zone
S20 Brian Moehler .25 .07
Scuff Ball
S21 Joel Pineiro .25 .07
Swiss Army
S22 What Were You Thinking? .25 .07
S23 Alex Gonzalez .25 .07
Whoops
S24 Brian Giles .25 .07
Bear Down
S25 Rich Aurilia .25 .07
Game Inches

2003 MLB Showdown Trading Deadline

This 145 card set was released during the 2003 season. Interspersed throughout the set is 25 foil cards. Those foil cards were inserted at a stated rate of one per three. Please note there is no card number 140. Kerry Wood's foil card was mistakenly numbered as number 60 and thus we have created a 60A and a 60B listing.

MINT NRMT
COMP.SET w/o SP's (120) 40.00 18.00
COMMON CARD (1-145) .50 .23
COMMON FOIL 3.00 1.35
1 So Taguchi 1.00 .45
2 Ryan Drese .50 .23
3 Mike Hampton 1.00 .45
4 Sandy Alomar Jr. .50 .23
5 Steve Sparks .50 .23
6 Chan Ho Park 1.00 .45
7 Roger Cedeno .50 .23
8 Antonio Osuna .50 .23
9 Ryan Dempster .50 .23
10 Jesse Orosco .50 .23
11 Angel Berroa 1.00 .45
12 Sean Burroughs 1.00 .45
13 Matt Mantei .50 .23
14 Einar Diaz .50 .23
15 Ken Griffey Jr. 4.00 1.80
16 Rey Sanchez .50 .23
17 Antonio Alfonseca .50 .23
18 Carl Crawford 1.00 .45
19 Rey Ordonez .50 .23
20 Brandon Inge .50 .23
21 Hank Blalock 1.50 .70
22 Albie Lopez .50 .23
23 Aaron Sele .50 .23
24 Willie Bloomquist 1.00 .45
25 Shigetoshi Hasegawa 1.00 .45
26 Steve Kline .50 .23
27 Ramiro Mendoza .50 .23
28 Mike Stanton .50 .23
29 Carlos Zambrano 1.00 .45
30 Dean Palmer .50 .23
31 Mark Grudzielanek .50 .23
32 Matt Williams 1.00 .45
33 Michael Cuddyer .50 .23
34 Glendon Rusch .50 .23
35 Hee Seop Choi 1.00 .45
36 Mike Bordick 1.00 .45
37 Ray King .50 .23
38 Bill Mueller 1.00 .45
39 John McDonald .50 .23
40 Brent Butler .50 .23
41 Josh Bard .50 .23
42 Xavier Nady .50 .23
43 J.C. Romero .50 .23
44 Paul Shuey .50 .23
45 Eric Karros 1.00 .45
46 Runelvys Hernandez .50 .23
47 Braden Looper .50 .23
48 Dave Roberts .50 .23
49 Deivi Cruz .50 .23
50 Todd Hollandsworth .50 .23
51 Billy Koch .50 .23
52 Brandon Villafuerte .50 .23
53 Ricardo Rincon .50 .23
54 Joe Crede .50 .23
55 Juan Pierre 1.00 .45
56 Tsuyoshi Shinjo 1.00 .45
57 Ugueth Urbina .50 .23
58 Luis Vizcaino FOIL 3.00 1.35
59 Ben Weber .50 .23
60A Kerry Wood 2.50 1.10
60B Kerry Wood FOIL 10.00 4.50
61 Tim Worrell .50 .23
62 Royce Clayton .50 .23
63 Chone Figgins .50 .23
64 Ken Huckaby .50 .23
65 Brian Anderson .50 .23
66 Aramis Ramirez 1.00 .45
67 Edgar Martinez 1.50 .70
68 Keith Foulke .50 .23
69 LaTroy Hawkins .50 .23
70 Mike Remlinger .50 .23
71 Lyle Overbay .50 .23
72 Buddy Groom .50 .23
73 Orlando Hudson .50 .23
74 Francisco Rodriguez FOIL 5.00 2.20
75 Craig Biggio 1.50 .70
76 Todd Zeile 1.00 .45
77 Vernon Wells 1.00 .45
78 Casey Fossum .50 .23
79 Wes Helms .50 .23
80 Robert Fick 1.00 .45
81 Scott Spiezio .50 .23
82 Ty Wigginton 1.00 .45
83 Elmer Dessens .50 .23
84 Arthur Rhodes .50 .23
85 Matt Stairs .50 .23
86 Miguel Olivo .50 .23
87 Tino Martinez 1.50 .70
88 Travis Hafner 1.00 .45
89 Octavio Dotel .50 .23
90 Jimmy Rollins 1.00 .45
91 Placido Polanco .50 .23
92 Kevin Brown 1.00 .45
93 John Patterson .50 .23
94 Andy Pettitte 1.50 .70
95 Bobby Kielty .50 .23
96 Jeremy Giambi .50 .23
97 Brandon Phillips .50 .23
98 Fred McGriff 1.50 .70
99 Damian Moss .50 .23
100 Russ Ortiz 1.00 .45
101 Mark Teixeira 1.50 .70
102 Tom Glavine FOIL 8.00 3.60
103 Chris Woodward .50 .23
104 Brad Radke 1.00 .45
105 Edgardo Alfonzo 1.00 .45
106 Jose Contreras FOIL RC 8.00 3.60
107 Josh Beckett 1.50 .70
108 Johan Santana 1.00 .45
109 Brandon Larson .50 .23
110 Randall Simon .50 .23
111 Randy Winn FOIL 3.00 1.35
112 Ray Durham 1.00 .45
113 Omar Daal FOIL 3.00 1.35
114 David Wells FOIL 5.00 2.20
115 Wade Miller 1.00 .45
116 Bartolo Colon FOIL 5.00 2.20
117 Ryan Klesko FOIL 5.00 2.20
118 Jeff Bagwell 1.50 .70
119 Roy Oswalt FOIL 5.00 2.20
120 Orlando Hernandez FOIL 5.00 2.20
121 Ivan Rodriguez FOIL 10.00 4.50
122 Tim Wakefield 1.00 .45
123 Josh Phelps .50 .23
124 Woody Williams .50 .23
125 Chipper Jones FOIL 10.00 4.50
126 Randy Wolf 1.00 .45
127 Kevin Millwood FOIL 5.00 2.20
128 Jeff Kent FOIL 5.00 2.20
129 Rocco Baldelli FOIL 8.00 3.60
130 Hideki Matsui FOIL RC 15.00 6.75
131 Jim Thome FOIL 10.00 4.50
132 Kazuhiro Sasaki RS 1.00 .45
133 Jason Jennings RS FOIL 3.00 1.35
134 Rafael Furcal RS 1.00 .45
135 Derek Jeter RS FOIL 15.00 6.75
136 Benito Santiago RS 1.00 .45
137 Jeff Bagwell RS 1.50 .70
138 Carlos Beltran RS 1.00 .45
139 Scott Rolen RS FOIL 8.00 3.60
141 Tim Salmon RS 1.00 .45
142 Ichiro Suzuki RS FOIL 10.00 4.50
143 Mike Piazza RS FOIL 10.00 4.50
144 Albert Pujols RS 5.00 2.20
145 Nomar Garciaparra RS FOIL 10.00 4.50

2003 MLB Showdown Trading Deadline Strategy

Issued at a stated rate of two per pack, these 25 cards feature various known terms as well as a photo to go with the caption. Whenever possible, we have notated who the player is before the caption in our data base.

MINT NRMT
COMPLETE SET (25) 8.00 3.60
S1 Sammy Sosa .75 .35
Clutch Hitting
S2 Brad Wilkerson .25 .11
Clutch Rookie
S3 Hideki Matsui 2.00 .90
Great Addition
S4 Brent Mayne .25 .11
Headed Home
S5 Jose Vizcaino .40 .18
Jeff Bagwell
High Fives
S6 Barry Bonds 1.25 .55
Long Gone!
S7 On the Move .25 .11
S8 Edgar Martinez .40 .18
Take What's Given
S9 Eric Hinske .25 .11
Who Is This Guy
S10 Jason Jennings .25 .11
Add by Subtrac
S11 Orlando Hudson .25 .11
De-nied!
S12 Roger Clemens 1.00 .45
Digging Deep
S13 Randy Johnson .50 .23
Lock It Down
S14 Matt Herges .25 .11
New Arrival
S15 Einar Diaz .25 .11
Not So Fast
S16 Ichiro Suzuki .75 .35
Pitch Around
S17 Francisco Rodriguez .25 .11
Rookie Fireballer
S18 John Smoltz .25 .11
Split-Finger Fastball
S19 Brian Buchanan .25 .11
Still Learning
S20 Barry Zito .40 .18
3 up 3 Down
S21 Brent Butler .25 .11
Triple Dip
S22 Brainstorm .25 .11
S23 Gary Varsho .25 .11
Outmanaged
S24 Mark McLemore .25 .11
Stealing Signals
S25 Mike Cameron .25 .11
Swing at Anything

1977 Montefusco/D'Acquisto Restaurant

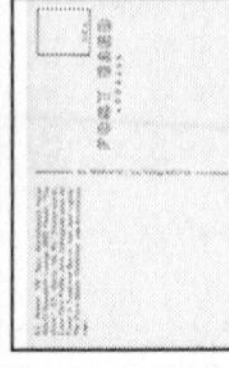

This postcard which features action shots of 1970's pitchers John "The Count" Montefusco as well as John D'Acquisto. In addition, there is a photo of the two Giant pitchers sitting at a table in their eatery. The back has information about this place.

NM Ex
1 John Montefusco 3.00 1.20
John D'Acquisto

1993-99 Moonlight Graham

These five standard-size cards honor Archibald Graham, who was immortalized in the movie "Field of Dreams". These cards were sold to benefit the Doc Graham scholarship funds. Each card has a different design. These cards are all currently available from the Moonlight Graham web site at three dollars per card.

Nm-Mt Ex-Mt
COMPLETE SET (5) 10.00 3.00
COMMON CARD (1-5) 3.00 .90
5 Archibald Graham 5.00 1.50
Joe Jackson
Play Ball
1999

1991 MooTown Snackers

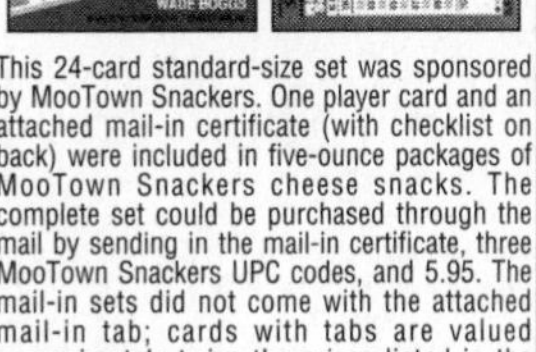

This 24-card standard-size set was sponsored by MooTown Snackers. One player card and an attached mail-in certificate (with checklist on back) were included in five-ounce packages of MooTown Snackers cheese snacks. The complete set could be purchased through the mail by sending in the mail-in certificate, three MooTown Snackers UPC codes, and 5.95. The mail-in sets did not come with the attached mail-in tab; cards with tabs are valued approximately twice the prices listed in the checklist below.

Nm-Mt Ex-Mt
COMPLETE SET (24) 30.00 9.00
1 Jose Canseco 1.00 .30
2 Kirby Puckett 2.00 .60
3 Barry Bonds 4.00 1.20
4 Ken Griffey Jr. 5.00 1.50
5 Ryne Sandberg 4.00 1.20
6 Tony Gwynn 4.00 1.20
7 Kal Daniels .25 .07
8 Ozzie Smith 4.00 1.20
9 Dave Justice 1.00 .30
10 Sandy Alomar Jr. .50 .15
11 Wade Boggs 2.00 .60
12 Ozzie Guillen .50 .15
13 Dave Magadan .25 .07
14 Cal Ripken 8.00 2.40
15 Don Mattingly 4.00 1.20
16 Ruben Sierra .50 .15
17 Robin Yount 1.50 .45
18 Len Dykstra .50 .15
19 George Brett 4.00 1.20
20 Lance Parrish .25 .07
21 Chris Sabo .25 .07
22 Craig Biggio 1.00 .30
23 Kevin Mitchell .25 .07
24 Cecil Fielder .50 .15

1992 MooTown Snackers

This 24-card standard-size set was produced by MSA (Michael Schechter Associates) for

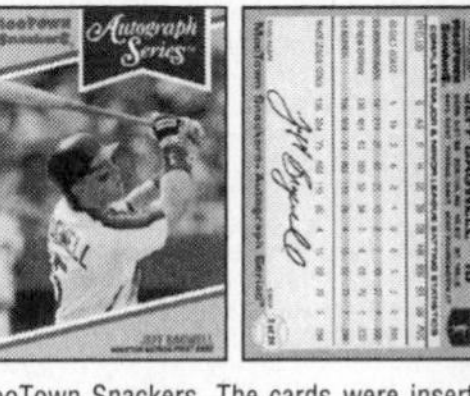

MooTown Snackers. The cards were inserted inside 5 ounce and 10 ounce cheese snack packages. It is reported that more than two million cards were produced. Collectors could also obtain the complete set through a mail-in offer. The cards obtained via mail did not come with the mali-in offer tabs. Cards with tabs have twice the value of the prices below. .

Nm-Mt Ex-Mt
COMPLETE SET (24) 30.00 9.00
1 Albert Belle .50 .15
2 Jeff Bagwell 2.00 .60
3 Jose Rijo .25 .07
4 Roger Clemens 4.00 1.20
5 Kevin Maas .25 .07
6 Kirby Puckett 2.00 .60
7 Ken Griffey Jr. 5.00 1.50
8 Will Clark 1.50 .45
9 Felix Jose .25 .07
10 Cecil Fielder .50 .15
11 Darryl Strawberry .50 .15
12 John Smiley .25 .07
13 Roberto Alomar 1.00 .30
14 Paul Molitor 1.50 .45
15 Andre Dawson .75 .23
16 Terry Mulholland .25 .07
17 Fred McGriff .75 .23
18 Dwight Gooden .50 .15
19 Rickey Henderson 2.00 .60
20 Nolan Ryan 8.00 2.40
21 George Brett 4.00 1.20
22 Tom Glavine 1.00 .30
23 Cal Ripken 8.00 2.40
24 Frank Thomas 2.00 .60

1987 Mother's McGwire

This set consists of four, full-color, rounded-corner cards each showing a different pose of A's slugging rookie Mark McGwire. Cards were originally given out at the national Card Collectors Convention in San Francisco. Later they were available through a mail-in offer involving collectors sending in two proofs-of-purchase from any Mother's Cookies products to get one free card. Photos were taken by Doug McWilliams.

Nm-Mt Ex-Mt
COMPLETE SET (4) 35.00 14.00
COMMON CARD (1-4) 10.00 4.00

1988 Mother's Will Clark

This regional set consists of four full-color, rounded-corner cards each showing a different pose of Giants' slugging first baseman Will Clark. Cards were originally found in 18 oz. packages of "Big Bags" of Mother's Cookies at stores in the Northern California area in February and March of 1988. Card backs are done in red and purple on white card stock.

Nm-Mt Ex-Mt
COMPLETE SET (4) 15.00 6.00
COMMON CARD (1-4) 4.00 1.60

1988 Mother's McGwire

This regional set consists of four full-color, rounded-corner cards each showing a different pose of The Athletics' slugging first baseman Mark McGwire. Cards were originally found in 18 oz. packages of "Big Bags" of Mother's Cookies at stores in the Northern California area in February and March, 1988. Card backs are done in red and purple on white card stock.

Nm-Mt Ex-Mt
COMPLETE SET (4) 35.00 14.00
COMMON CARD (1-4) 10.00 4.00

1989 Mother's Canseco

The 1989 Mother's Jose Canseco set contains four standard-size cards with rounded corners. The fronts have borderless color photos, and the horizontally oriented backs have biographical information. One card was included in each specially marked box of Mother's Cookies.

Nm-Mt Ex-Mt
COMPLETE SET (4) 10.00 4.00
COMMON CARD (1-4) 3.00 1.20

1989 Mother's Will Clark

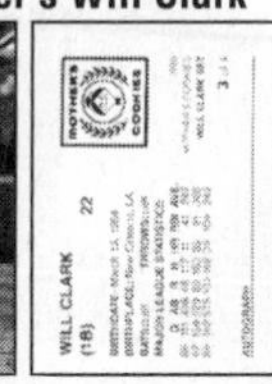

The 1989 Mother's Cookies Will Clark set contains four standard-size cards with rounded corners. The fronts have borderless color photos, and the horizontally oriented backs have biographical information. One card was included in each specially marked box of Mother's Cookies.

Nm-Mt Ex-Mt
COMPLETE SET (4) 10.00 4.00
COMMON CARD (1-4) 3.00 1.20

1989 Mother's Griffey Jr.

The 1989 Mother's Cookies Ken Griffey Jr. set contains four standard-size cards with rounded corners. The fronts have borderless color photos, and the horizontal backs have biographical information. One card was included in each specially marked box of Mother's Cookies. The photos were shot by noted sports photographer Barry Colla. It has been reported that card No. 2 is a little more difficult to find than the other cards in the set.

Nm-Mt Ex-Mt
COMPLETE SET (4) 50.00 20.00
COMMON CARD (1-4) 12.00 4.80
2 Ken Griffey Jr. 15.00 6.00
(Baseball in hand)

1989 Mother's McGwire

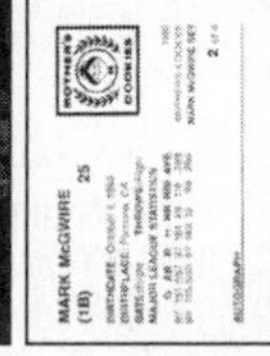

The 1989 Mother's Cookies Mark McGwire set contains four standard-size cards with rounded corners. The fronts have borderless color photos, and the horizontal backs have biographical information. One card was included in each specially marked box of Mother's Cookies.

Nm-Mt Ex-Mt
COMPLETE SET (4) 20.00 8.00
COMMON CARD (1-4) 5.00 2.00

1990 Mother's Canseco

This is a standard Mother's Cookies set with four cards each measuring the standard size with rounded corners issued to capitalize on Jose Canseco's popularity. This four-card set features Canseco in various batting poses.

Nm-Mt Ex-Mt
COMPLETE SET (4) 10.00 3.00
COMMON CARD (1-4) 3.00 .90

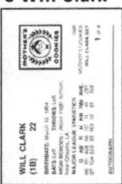

1990 Mother's Will Clark

This is a standard Mother's Cookies set with four cards each measuring the standard size with rounded corners issued to capitalize on Will Clark's popularity. This four-card set features Clark in various poses as indicated in the checklist below.

	Nm-Mt	Ex-Mt
COMPLETE SET (4)	10.00	3.00
COMMON CARD (1-4)	3.00	.90

1990 Mother's McGwire

This is a standard Mother's Cookies set with four cards each measuring the standard size with rounded corners issued to capitalize on Mark McGwire's popularity. This four-card set features McGwire in various poses as indicated in the checklist below.

	Nm-Mt	Ex-Mt
COMPLETE SET (4)	20.00	6.00
COMMON CARD (1-4)	5.00	1.50

1990 Mother's Ryan

This is a typical Mother's Cookies set with four cards each measuring the standard size with rounded corners honoring Ryan's more than 5,000 strikeouts over his career. This four-card set features Ryan in various pitching poses. The second card in the set is considered tougher to find than the other three in the set. This four-card set was also issued as an unperforated strip.

	Nm-Mt	Ex-Mt
COMPLETE SET (4)	15.00	4.50
COMMON CARD (1-4)	4.00	1.20
2 Nolan Ryan (Dugout pose)	5.00	1.50

1990 Mother's Matt Williams

This is a standard Mother's Cookies set with four cards each measuring the standard size with rounded corners issued to capitalize on Matt Williams' popularity. This four-card set features Williams in various poses as indicated in the checklist below.

	Nm-Mt	Ex-Mt
COMPLETE SET (4)	8.00	2.40
COMMON CARD (1-4)	2.00	.60

1991 Mother's Griffeys

The 1991 Mother's Cookies Father and Son set featuring both major-league playing members of the Griffey family contains four cards with rounded corners measuring the standard size.

	Nm-Mt	Ex-Mt
COMPLETE SET (4)	6.00	1.80
1 Ken Griffey Jr.	3.00	.90
2 Ken Griffey Sr.	.75	.23
3 Ken Griffey Sr. / Ken Griffey Jr.	2.00	.60
4 Ken Griffey Sr. / Ken Griffey Jr.	2.00	.60

1991 Mother's Ryan

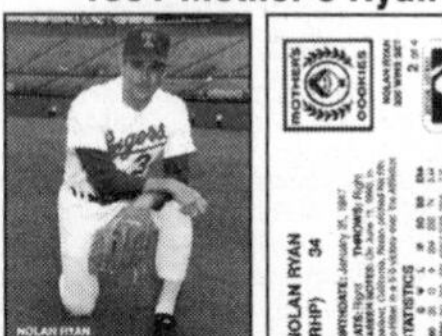

This four-card standard-size rounded-corner set was sponsored by Mother's Cookies in honor of Nolan Ryan, baseball's latest 300-game winner. One card was packaged in each box of Mother's Cookies 18-ounce family size bags of five different flavored cookies (Chocolate Chip, Cookie Parade, Oatmeal Raisin, Fudge'N Chips, and Costadas). Also collectors could purchase an uncut strip of the four cards for 7.95 with four proof-of-purchase seals, and a protective sleeve for $1. This four-card set was also issued as an unperforated strip.

	Nm-Mt	Ex-Mt
COMPLETE SET (4)	10.00	3.00
COMMON CARD (1-4)	2.50	.75

1992 Mother's Bagwell

This four-card, standard-size set was sponsored by Mother's Cookies. The fronts have rounded corners and feature posed color full-bleed photos of Jeff Bagwell, the 1991 National League Rookie of the Year.

	Nm-Mt	Ex-Mt
COMPLETE SET (4)	8.00	2.40
COMMON CARD (1-4)	2.00	.60

1992 Mother's Knoblauch

This four-card set measures the standard size and was sponsored by Mother's Cookies in honor of the 1991 American League Rookie of the Year, Chuck Knoblauch.

	Nm-Mt	Ex-Mt
COMPLETE SET (4)	8.00	2.40
COMMON CARD (1-4)	2.00	.60

1992 Mother's Ryan Advertisement

These six ad sheets feature some of the actual card photos used in the 1992 Mothers Ryan set. The left side of the panel is used for the card while the right side tells you what type of cookies the cards are available in.

	Nm-Mt	Ex-Mt
COMPLETE SET (6)	15.00	4.50
COMMON CARD (1-6)	3.00	.90

1992 Mother's Ryan 7 No-Hitters

The 1992 Mother's Nolan Ryan Seven No-Hitters set contains eight standard-size cards with rounded corners and glossy full-bleed color photos. Card Nos. 1-4 were included in 18-ounce Mother's Cookies family size "Big Bag" cookies. Card Nos. 5-8 were in 16-ounce packages of "sandwich~ cookies. The set was also available as an uncut sheet through a mail-in offer on specially marked packages for $7.95 plus four proofs of purchase. The horizontally oriented backs are printed in red and purple and feature biographical information, career notes, highlights, and statistics for each of his no-hitters (except card No. 8).

	Nm-Mt	Ex-Mt
COMPLETE SET (8)	12.00	3.60
COMMON CARD (1-8)	1.50	.45

1993 Mother's Ryan Farewell

This ten-card standard-size set has rounded corners and was issued by Mother's Cookies to bid farewell to Nolan Ryan. This set was also issued as a 7 5/8" by 14" sheet consisting of two rows with five cards in each row. This set was rereleased in 1994 with a 1994 date. The cards are valued the same for either year. The 1993 set is much more difficult to acquire as

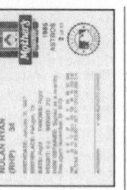

no extra quantities entered the secondary market.

	Nm-Mt	Ex-Mt
COMPLETE SET (10)	10.00	3.00
COMMON CARD (1-10)	1.25	.35

1994 Mother's Piazza

Issued to showcase the '93 NL ROY, these four standard-size cards have rounded corners and feature borderless posed color photos of Mike Piazza on their fronts. One card was included in each package of six varieties of Mother's Big Bag Cookies. The set was also issued as an uncut strip of four cards. The cards are numbered on the back as "X of 4."

	Nm-Mt	Ex-Mt
COMPLETE SET (4)	8.00	2.40
COMMON CARD (1-4)	2.00	.60

1994 Mother's Piazza/Salmon

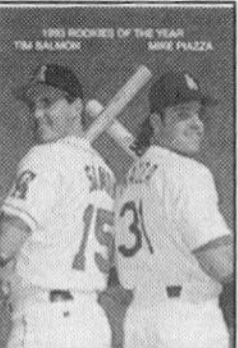
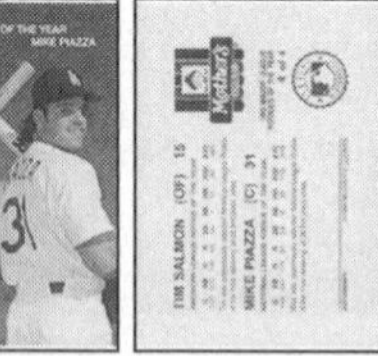

This four-card standard-size rounded-corner set was issued to honor Mike Piazza and Tim Salmon as the 1993 Rookies of the Year. Featuring both players on each card, these cards were packaged one per bag of Mother's Major League Double Headers. The set was also issued as an uncut strip of four cards. The cards are numbered on the back as "X of 4." Mother's Cookies also produced two chase cards, which were issued in either red or blue foil versions, and were reportedly inserted at a rate of one card per 1,000 packages of Mother's Big Bag Cookies. Less than 10,000 of the foil cards were reportedly produced. The blue card is numbered on the back "1 in a 1000 Blue", the red card "1 in 1000 Red."

	Nm-Mt	Ex-Mt
COMPLETE SET (4)	6.00	1.80
COMMON CARD (1-4)	1.50	.45

1994 Mother's Salmon

This four-card standard size set sponsored by Mother's Cookies features Tim Salmon, the 1993 AL Rookie of the Year. One card was included in each package of six varieties of Mother's Big Bag Cookies. The cards are numbered on the back as "X of 4."

	Nm-Mt	Ex-Mt
COMPLETE SET (4)	6.00	1.80
COMMON CARD (1-4)	1.50	.45

1976 Motorola Old Timers

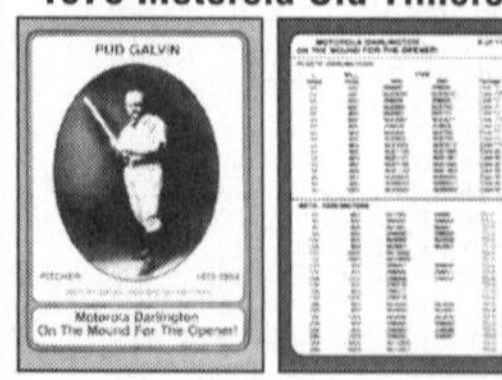

This 11-card standard-size set, issued by Motorola for their stockholders meeting in 1976, honored some of Baseball's all-time greats. The front of the cards were about the player while the backs of the cards talked in technical terms about Motorola products. The cards are also made on a thin (paper-like) card stock and are very flimsy. Certain dealers have reported that there was also an edible version made of organic substances of these cards issued. There are reports that this set was privately produced for Motorola by long time hobbyist Mike Cramer.

	NM	Ex
COMPLETE SET (11)	30.00	12.00
1 Honus Wagner	5.00	2.00
2 Nap Lajoie	2.50	1.00
3 Ty Cobb	8.00	3.20
4 William Wambsganss	1.00	.40
5 Mordecai Brown	1.50	.60
6 Ray Schalk	1.50	.60
7 Frank Frisch	2.00	.80
8 Pud Galvin	1.50	.60
9 Babe Ruth	10.00	4.00
10 Grover C. Alexander	2.50	1.00
11 Frank L. Chance	2.00	.80

1999 Mountain Dew Scratch-off

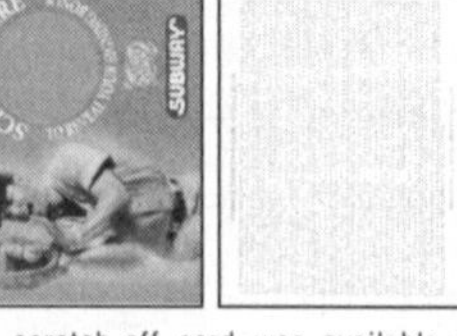

This scratch-off card was available at participating Subway Sandwich shops in 1999. Sponsored by Pepsi Cola, winning cards revealed one of three prizes: A Brady Anderson T-Shirt (1000 total), Brady Anderson autographed baseball glove (40 total), or a Brady Anderson autographed baseball bat (10 total).

	Nm-Mt	Ex-Mt
1 Brady Anderson	3.00	.90

1943 MP and Co. R302-1

The 1943 MP and Co. baseball card set consists of 24 player drawings each measuring 2 11/16" by 2 1/4". This company specialized in producing strips of cards to be sold in candy stores and provided a low quality but persistent challenge to other current sets. These unnumbered cards have been alphabetized and numbered in the checklist below. There is a variation on Foxx due to his acquisition by the Cubs from the Red Sox on June 1, 1942.

	Ex-Mt	VG
COMPLETE SET (24)	400.00	200.00
1 Ernie Bonham	12.00	6.00
2 Lou Boudreau	25.00	12.50
3 Dolph Camilli	15.00	7.50
4 Mort Cooper	12.00	6.00
5 Walker Cooper	12.00	6.00
6 Joe Cronin	25.00	12.50
7 Hank Danning	12.00	6.00
8 Bill Dickey	30.00	15.00
9 Joe DiMaggio	100.00	50.00
10 Bob Feller	30.00	15.00
11 Jimmy Foxx (Chicago Cubs)	50.00	25.00
12 Hank Greenberg	50.00	25.00
13 Stan Hack	12.00	6.00
14 Tommy Henrich	20.00	10.00
15 Carl Hubbell	25.00	12.50
16 Joe Medwick	25.00	12.50
17 John Mize	25.00	12.50
18 Lou Novikoff	12.00	6.00
19 Mel Ott	30.00	15.00
20 Pee Wee Reese	30.00	15.00
21 Pete Reiser	20.00	10.00
22 Red Ruffing	25.00	12.50
23 Johnny Vander Meer	20.00	10.00
24 Ted Williams	100.00	50.00

1949 MP and Co. R302-2

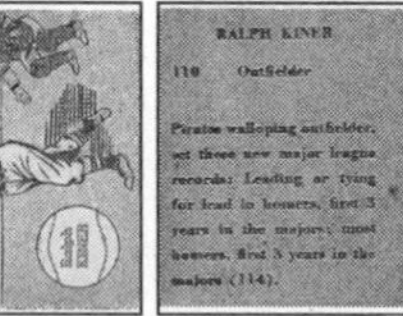
RALPH KINER
110 Outfielder
Pirates walloping outfielder, set three new major league records: Leading or tying for lead in homers, first 3 years in the majors; most homers, first 3 years in the majors (114).

The 1949 rendition of MP and Co. was basically a re-issue of the 1943 set with different players and numbers on the back. Cards again measure approximately 2 11/16" by 2 1/4". The card fronts are even more washed out than the previous set. Card numbers 104, 118, and 120 are unknown and may be related to the two unnumbered cards found in the set. The catalog also lists this set as W523.

	NM	Ex
COMPLETE SET	350.00	180.00
100 Lou Boudreau	20.00	10.00
101 Ted Williams	80.00	40.00
102 Buddy Kerr	10.00	5.00
103 Bob Feller	25.00	12.50
104 Unknown		
105 Joe DiMaggio	80.00	40.00
106 Pee Wee Reese	25.00	12.50
107 Ferris Fain	10.00	5.00
108 Andy Pafko	10.00	5.00
109 Del Ennis	15.00	7.50
110 Ralph Kiner	25.00	12.50
111 Nippy Jones	10.00	5.00
112 Del Rice	10.00	5.00
113 Hank Sauer	12.00	6.00
114 Gil Coan	10.00	5.00
115 Eddie Joost	10.00	5.00
116 Alvin Dark	15.00	7.50
117 Larry Berra	30.00	15.00
118 Unknown		
119 Bob Lemon	20.00	10.00
120 Unknown		
121 Johnny Pesky	15.00	7.50
122 Johnny Sain	15.00	7.50
123 Hoot Evers	10.00	5.00
124 Larry Doby	25.00	12.50
xx Tom Henrich (unnumbered)	15.00	7.50
xx Al Kozar (unnumbered)	10.00	5.00

1992 Mr. Turkey Superstars

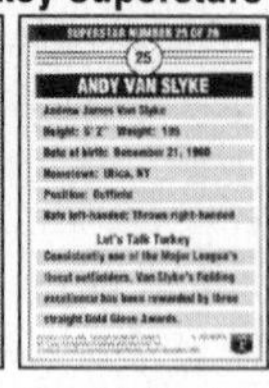

This 26-card set was sponsored by Mr. Turkey. One card was found on the back panel of Mr. Turkey products, such as Hardwood Smoked Turkey Pastrami. The standard-size player card is not perforated. The cards are numbered on the back; the card numbering is actually alphabetical by player's name.

	Nm-Mt	Ex-Mt
COMPLETE SET (26)	25.00	7.50
1 Jim Abbott	.50	.15
2 Roberto Alomar	1.00	.30
3 Sandy Alomar Jr.	.50	.15
4 Craig Biggio	.75	.23
5 George Brett	2.50	.75
6 Will Clark	1.25	.35
7 Roger Clemens	2.50	.75
8 Cecil Fielder	.50	.15
9 Carlton Fisk	1.25	.35
10 Andres Galarraga	1.00	.30
11 Dwight Gooden	.50	.15
12 Ken Griffey Jr.	4.00	1.20
13 Tony Gwynn	2.50	.75
14 Rickey Henderson	1.25	.35
15 Dave Justice	1.00	.30
16 Don Mattingly	2.50	.75
17 Dale Murphy	1.00	.30
18 Kirby Puckett	2.50	.75
19 Cal Ripken	5.00	1.50
20 Nolan Ryan	5.00	1.50
21 Chris Sabo	.25	.07
22 Ryne Sandberg	2.50	.75
23 Ozzie Smith	1.50	.45
24 Darryl Strawberry	.50	.15
25 Andy Van Slyke	.50	.15
26 Robin Yount	1.25	.35

1995 Mr. Turkey Baseball Greats

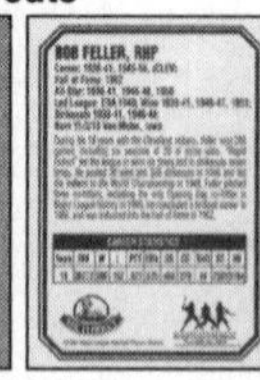

These five standard-size cards were sponsored by Mr. Turkey. The cards are unnumbered and checklisted below in alphabetical order.

	Nm-Mt	Ex-Mt
COMPLETE SET (5)	8.00	2.40
1 Bob Feller	2.50	.75
2 Al Kaline	2.50	.75
3 Tug McGraw	1.00	.30
4 Boog Powell	1.50	.45
5 Warren Spahn	2.50	.75

1981 MSA Mini Discs

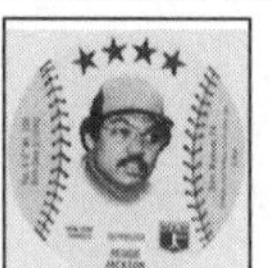

This set of 32 discs, each measuring approximately 2 3/4" in diameter was apparently approved by the Major League Players Associations under the auspices of Mike Schecter Associates These discs are also known as the Peter Pan discs. These blank backed discs and were distributed a couple of different ways. The discs are unnumbered and are listed alphabetically. One way to tell that these were issued in 1981 is that Reggie Jackson is listed as a New York Yankee. 1981 would prove to be Reggie's final year in New York.

	Nm-Mt	Ex-Mt
COMPLETE SET (32)	25.00	10.00
1 Buddy Bell	.25	.10
2 Johnny Bench	1.00	.40
3 Bruce Bochte	.10	.04
4 George Brett	8.00	3.20
5 Bill Buckner	.10	.04
6 Rod Carew	1.00	.40
7 Steve Carlton	1.00	.40
8 Cesar Cedeno	.25	.10
9 Jack Clark	.10	.04
10 Cecil Cooper	.10	.04
11 Bucky Dent	.25	.10
12 Carlton Fisk	5.00	2.00
13 Steve Garvey	.50	.20
14 Rich Gossage	.25	.10
15 Mike Hargrove	.25	.10
16 Keith Hernandez	.25	.10
17 Bob Horner	.10	.04
18 Reggie Jackson	5.00	2.00
19 Steve Kemp	.10	.04
20 Ron LeFlore	.10	.04
21 Fred Lynn	.25	.10
22 Lee Mazzilli	.10	.04
23 Eddie Murray	6.00	2.40
24 Mike Norris	.10	.04

	Nm-Mt	Ex-Mt
25 Dave Parker	.25	.10
26 J.R. Richard	.10	.04
27 Pete Rose	4.00	1.60
28 Mike Schmidt	4.00	1.60
29 Tom Seaver	1.00	.40
30 Roy Smalley	.10	.04
31 Willie Stargell	1.00	.40
32 Garry Templeton	.10	.04

1986 MSA Jay's Potato Chip Discs

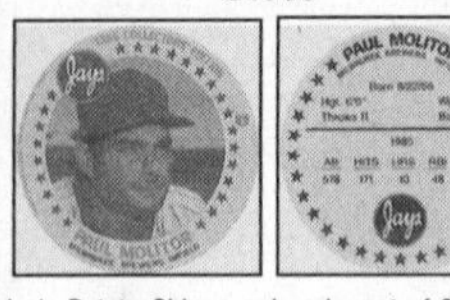

Jay's Potato Chips produced a set of 20 discs in conjunction with Mike Schechter Associates and the Major League Baseball Players Association. The discs have a bright yellow border with red and blue trim. Each disc is approximately 2 3/4" in diameter. The discs are not numbered and hence are assigned numbers below alphabetically. The disc backs contain very sparse personal or statistical information about the player. The players featured are from the Chicago Cubs, Chicago White Sox and Milwaukee Brewers.

	Nm-Mt	Ex-Mt
COMPLETE SET (20)	25.00	10.00
1 Harold Baines	1.00	.40
2 Cecil Cooper	.50	.20
3 Jody Davis	.50	.20
4 Bob Dernier	.50	.20
5 Richard Dotson	.50	.20
6 Shawon Dunston	1.00	.40
7 Carlton Fisk	6.00	2.40
8 Jim Gantner	.50	.20
9 Ozzie Guillen	2.00	.80
10 Teddy Higuera	.50	.20
11 Ron Kittle	.50	.20
12 Paul Molitor	6.00	2.40
13 Keith Moreland	.50	.20
14 Earnest Riles	.50	.20
15 Ryne Sandberg	10.00	4.00
16 Tom Seaver	6.00	2.40
17 Lee Smith	1.50	.60
18 Rick Sutcliffe	.50	.20
19 Greg Walker	.50	.20
20 Robin Yount	6.00	2.40

1986 MSA Jiffy Pop Discs

Jiffy Pop Popcorn introduced a set of 20 discs produced in conjunction with the Major League Baseball Players Association and Mike Schechter Associates. A single disc was inserted inside each specially marked package. The discs are numbered on the back and have a yellow border on the front. Discs are approximately 2 3/4" in diameter. The disc backs contain very sparse personal or statistical information about the player.

	Nm-Mt	Ex-Mt
COMPLETE SET (20)	40.00	16.00
1 Jim Rice	1.50	.60
2 Wade Boggs	4.00	1.60
3 Lance Parrish	1.00	.40
4 George Brett	6.00	2.40
5 Robin Yount	2.50	1.00
6 Don Mattingly	8.00	3.20
7 Dave Winfield	5.00	2.00
8 Reggie Jackson	6.00	2.40
9 Cal Ripken	10.00	4.00
10 Eddie Murray	8.00	3.20
11 Pete Rose	6.00	2.40
12 Ryne Sandberg	8.00	3.20
13 Nolan Ryan	10.00	4.00
14 Fernando Valenzuela	1.50	.60
15 Willie McGee	1.50	.60
16 Dale Murphy	2.00	.80
17 Mike Schmidt	6.00	2.40
18 Steve Garvey	1.50	.60
19 Gary Carter	4.00	1.60
20 Dwight Gooden	1.50	.60

1987 MSA Iced Tea Discs

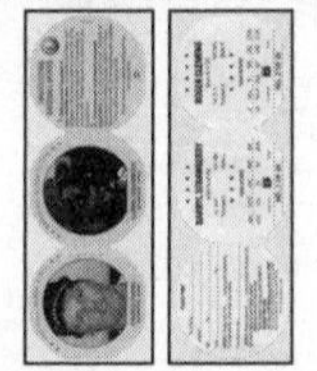

A set of 20 "Baseball Super Star" discs was produced in conjunction with the Major League Baseball Players Association and Mike Schechter Associates for various grocery chains. Sets were issued for Weis Markets, Key Foods, Our Own Tea and many others. The discs were issued as panels of three featuring two players and an offer disc. The discs have a bright yellow border on the front. Discs measure approximately 2 3/4" in diameter. Some dealers have speculated that noted hobby dealer John Broggi made the player selection for this set as well as the other iced tea disc sets. The disc backs contain very sparse personal or statistical information about the player. The base set is listed here but also complete player and price information can be found for each set listed in this description.

	Nm-Mt	Ex-Mt
COMPLETE SET (20)	10.00	4.00
1 Darryl Strawberry	.25	.10
2 Roger Clemens	1.50	.60
3 Ron Darling	.10	.04
4 Keith Hernandez	.25	.10
5 Tony Pena	.25	.10
6 Don Mattingly	1.50	.60
7 Eric Davis	.25	.10
8 Gary Carter	1.00	.40
9 Dave Winfield	1.00	.40
10 Wally Joyner	.75	.30
11 Mike Schmidt	1.00	.40
12 Robby Thompson	.10	.04
13 Wade Boggs	1.00	.40
14 Cal Ripken	3.00	1.20
15 Dale Murphy	.50	.20
16 Tony Gwynn	2.00	.80
17 Jose Canseco	.25	.10
18 Rickey Henderson	1.00	.40
19 Lance Parrish	.10	.04
20 Dave Righetti	.10	.04

1987 MSA Jiffy Pop Discs

Jiffy Pop Popcorn introduced a set of 20 discs produced in conjunction with the Major League Baseball Players Association and Mike Schechter Associates. A single disc was inserted inside each specially marked package. The discs are numbered on the back and have a white border (with red stitching to resemble a baseball) on the front. Discs are approximately 2 3/4" in diameter. The disc backs contain very sparse personal or statistical information about the player.

	Nm-Mt	Ex-Mt
COMPLETE SET (20)	30.00	12.00
1 Ryne Sandberg	8.00	3.20
2 Dale Murphy	2.00	.80
3 Jack Morris	1.50	.60
4 Keith Hernandez	1.50	.60
5 George Brett	10.00	4.00
6 Don Mattingly	10.00	4.00
7 Ozzie Smith	8.00	3.20
8 Cal Ripken	15.00	6.00
9 Dwight Gooden	1.50	.60
10 Pedro Guerrero	1.00	.40
11 Lou Whitaker	1.50	.60
12 Roger Clemens	12.00	4.80
13 Lance Parrish	1.00	.40
14 Rickey Henderson	6.00	2.40
15 Fernando Valenzuela	1.50	.60
16 Mike Schmidt	8.00	3.20
17 Darryl Strawberry	1.50	.60
18 Mike Scott	1.00	.40
19 Jim Rice	1.50	.60
20 Wade Boggs	6.00	2.40

1988 MSA Fantastic Sam's Discs

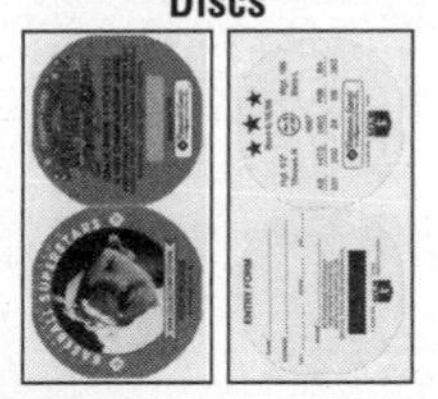

Fantastic Sam's is a national chain of family haircutters with more than 1200 locations. There are 20 numbered discs in the set each with an orange border. The set was produced in conjunction with Mike Schechter Associates. One disc was given away free each time a customer visited a participating Fantastic Sam's. Each disc is connected by a perforation to a contest disc with a scratch-off for a potential (baseball related) prize. Each disc is approximately 2 3/4" in diameter. No team logos are shown in this set.

	Nm-Mt	Ex-Mt
COMPLETE SET (20)	6.00	2.40
1 Kirby Puckett	1.50	.60
2 George Brett	2.00	.80
3 Mark McGwire	2.50	1.00
4 Wally Joyner	.50	.20
5 Paul Molitor	1.50	.60
6 Alan Trammell	.75	.30
7 George Bell	.25	.10
8 Wade Boggs	1.50	.60
9 Don Mattingly	2.00	.80
10 Julio Franco	.50	.20
11 Ozzie Smith	1.50	.60
12 Will Clark	1.00	.40
13 Dale Murphy	.75	.30
14 Eric Davis	.25	.10
15 Andre Dawson	1.00	.40
16 Tim Raines	.50	.20
17 Darryl Strawberry	.50	.20
18 Tony Gwynn	1.50	.60
19 Mike Schmidt	1.00	.40
20 Pedro Guerrero	.25	.10

1988 MSA Hostess Discs

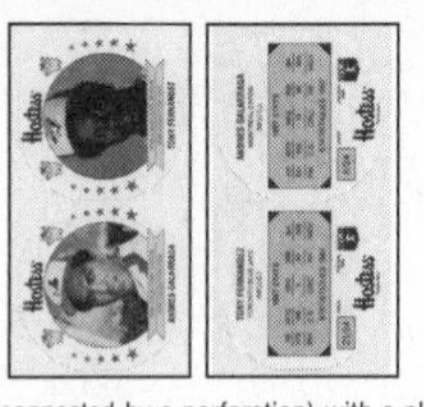

This set of 24 discs was produced by Hostess Potato Chips in conjunction with Mike Schechter Associates and the Major League Baseball Players Association. This set is one of the few disc sets to actually show the team logos. The set is subtitled Hostess Summer Doubleheaders and actually features a double disc (connected by a perforation) with a player from the Montreal Expos and a player from the Toronto Blue Jays. Each disc is approximately 2 5/8" in diameter. The discs are numbered; Montreal Expos are numbered 1-12 and Toronto Blue Jays are 13-24.

	Nm-Mt	Ex-Mt
COMPLETE SET (24)	4.00	1.60
1 Mitch Webster	.10	.04
2 Tim Burke	.10	.04
3 Tom Foley	.10	.04
4 Herm Winningham	.10	.04
5 Hubie Brooks	.10	.04
6 Mike Fitzgerald	.10	.04
7 Tim Wallach	.25	.10
8 Andres Galarraga	.75	.30
9 Floyd Youmans	.10	.04
10 Neal Heaton	.10	.04
11 Tim Raines	.50	.20
12 Casey Candaele	.10	.04
13 Jim Clancy	.10	.04
14 Rance Mulliniks	.10	.04
15 Fred McGriff	.75	.30
16 Ernie Whitt	.10	.04
17 Dave Stieb	.25	.10
18 Mark Eichhorn	.10	.04
19 Jesse Barfield	.25	.10
20 Lloyd Moseby	.10	.04
21 Tony Fernandez	.50	.20
22 George Bell	.25	.10
23 Tom Henke	.25	.10
24 Jimmy Key	.75	.30

1988 MSA Iced Tea Discs

A set of 20 "Baseball Super Star" discs was produced in conjunction with the Major League Baseball Players Association and Mike Schechter Associates for various grocery chains. Sets were issued for Tetley Tea, Weis Markets, Key Foods, Our Own Tea and many others. The discs were issued as panels of three featuring two players and an offer disc. The discs have a blue border on the front. Discs are approximately 2 3/4" in diameter. The disc backs contain very sparse personal or statistical information about the player.

	Nm-Mt	Ex-Mt
COMPLETE SET (20)	10.00	4.00
1 Wade Boggs	1.50	.60
2 Ellis Burks	.75	.30
3 Don Mattingly	2.00	.80
4 Mark McGwire	3.00	1.20
5 Matt Nokes	.10	.04
6 Kirby Puckett	2.00	.80
7 Billy Ripken	.10	.04
8 Kevin Seitzer	.10	.04
9 Roger Clemens	2.50	1.00
10 Will Clark	.75	.30
11 Vince Coleman	.10	.04
12 Eric Davis	.25	.10
13 Dave Magadan	.10	.04
14 Dale Murphy	.50	.20
15 Benito Santiago	.25	.10
16 Mike Schmidt	1.00	.40
17 Darryl Strawberry	.25	.10
18 Dwight Gooden	.25	.10
19 Steve Bedrosian	.10	.04
20 Fernando Valenzuela	.25	.10

1988 MSA Jiffy Pop Discs

Jiffy Pop Popcorn introduced a set of 20 discs produced in conjunction with the Major League Baseball Players Association and Mike Schechter Associates. A single disc was inserted inside each specially marked package. The discs are numbered (alphabetically) on the back and have a light blue border on the front. Discs are approximately 2 3/4" in diameter. The disc backs contain very sparse personal or statistical information about the player.

	Nm-Mt	Ex-Mt
COMPLETE SET (20)	15.00	6.00
1 Buddy Bell	.50	.20
2 Wade Boggs	4.00	1.60
3 Gary Carter	2.50	1.00
4 Jack Clark	.50	.20
5 Will Clark	4.00	1.60
6 Roger Clemens	6.00	2.40
7 Vince Coleman	.50	.20
8 Andre Dawson	2.00	.80
9 Keith Hernandez	.50	.20
10 Kent Hrbek	.50	.20
11 Wally Joyner	1.00	.40
12 Paul Molitor	2.50	1.00
13 Eddie Murray	2.50	1.00
14 Tim Raines	1.00	.40
15 Bret Saberhagen	.50	.20
16 Alan Trammell	1.50	.60
17 Ozzie Virgil	.50	.20
18 Tim Wallach	.50	.20
19 Dave Winfield	4.00	1.60
20 Robin Yount	2.50	1.00

1989 MSA Holsum Discs

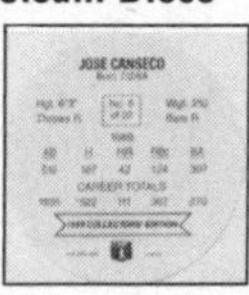

1989 Holsum Discs set is actually several sets of 20 discs issued for the following regional bakeries: Foxes Holsum (North Carolina and South Carolina), Butter Krust Bakeries (most of Pennsylvania), Phoenix Holsum (Arizona), Schafer's (Michigan) and Rainer Farms Homestyle. In Canada, Ben's Limited of Halifax distributed the discs under the Holsum/Schafer's imprint. The discs measure approximately 2 3/4" in diameter. This set was produced by MSA (Michael Schechter Associates) and like most of the MSA sets, there are no team logos on the discs. There is also an uncorrected error with Mark Grace's disc which pictures Vance Law on it.

	Nm-Mt	Ex-Mt
COMPLETE SET (20)	12.50	5.00
1 Wally Joyner	.50	.20
2 Wade Boggs	1.50	.60
3 Ozzie Smith	2.00	.80
4 Don Mattingly	2.00	.80
5 Jose Canseco	1.50	.60
6 Tony Gwynn	3.00	1.20
7 Eric Davis	.50	.20
8 Kirby Puckett	1.50	.60
9 Kevin Seitzer	.25	.10
10 Darryl Strawberry	.50	.20
11 Gregg Jefferies	.25	.10
12 Mark Grace UER (Photo actually Vance Law)	3.00	1.20
13 Matt Nokes	.25	.10
14 Mark McGwire	4.00	1.60
15 Bobby Bonilla	.50	.20
16 Roger Clemens	3.00	1.20
17 Frank Viola	.25	.10
18 Orel Hershiser	.50	.20
19 Dave Cone	.50	.20
20 Kirk Gibson	.50	.20

1989 MSA Iced Tea Discs

These 20 discs of MSA's Third Annual Collectors' Edition measure approximately 2 5/8" in diameter and feature on their fronts posed color player head shots within red stars on yellow backgrounds. The player's name and team appear in black lettering near the bottom. There are no team logos featured on the discs. The backs carry player biography and 1988 statistics in blue lettering. The cards are numbered on the back as "X of 20." The sets were also produced under the Tetley Teas label and inserted into their tea bag boxes.

	Nm-Mt	Ex-Mt
COMPLETE SET (20)	30.00	12.00
1 Don Mattingly	6.00	2.40
2 Dave Cone	3.00	1.20
3 Mark McGwire	8.00	3.20
4 Will Clark	4.00	1.60
5 Darryl Strawberry	2.00	.80
6 Dwight Gooden	2.00	.80
7 Wade Boggs	5.00	2.00
8 Roger Clemens	6.00	2.40
9 Benito Santiago	2.00	.80
10 Orel Hershiser	2.00	.80
11 Eric Davis	2.00	.80
12 Kirby Puckett	5.00	2.00
13 Dave Winfield	5.00	2.00
14 Andre Dawson	4.00	1.60
15 Steve Bedrosian	1.00	.40
16 Cal Ripken	12.00	4.80
17 Andy Van Slyke	1.00	.40
18 Jose Canseco	2.00	.80
19 Jose Oquendo	1.00	.40
20 Dale Murphy	4.00	1.60

1990 MSA Holsum Discs

The 1990 Holsum Discs set, subtitled "Superstars," is a 20-disc set with each disc measuring approximately 2 3/4" in diameter. The front of each disc features a full color player photo with a red border. The player's name, team and position appear below the photo. The white back carries the player's name and biography at the top, followed below by 1989 and career statistics. Typical of many of the sets produced by MSA (Michael Schechter Associates), the teams' logos are airbrushed out. The discs are numbered on the back. In Canada, Ben's Limited of Halifax distributed the discs under the Holsum imprint.

	Nm-Mt	Ex-Mt
COMPLETE SET (20)	5.00	1.50
1 George Bell	.10	.03
2 Tim Raines	.25	.07
3 Tom Henke	.10	.03
4 Andres Galarraga	.75	.23
5 Bret Saberhagen	.10	.03
6 Mark Davis	.10	.03
7 Robin Yount	.75	.23
8 Rickey Henderson	1.00	.30
9 Kevin Mitchell	.10	.03
10 Howard Johnson	.10	.03
11 Will Clark	.75	.23
12 Orel Hershiser	.25	.07
13 Fred McGriff	.50	.15
14 Dave Stewart	.10	.03
15 Vince Coleman	.10	.03
16 Steve Sax	.10	.03
17 Kirby Puckett	.75	.23
18 Tony Gwynn	1.25	.35
19 Jerome Walton	.10	.03
20 Gregg Olson	.10	.03

1990 MSA Iced Tea Discs

Issued in three-disc perforated strips, these 20 discs measure approximately 2 5/8" in diameter. Some of the discs have Tetley's Third Annual Collector's Edition on their fronts, while others read "Fourth Annual Collectors' Edition" and "Super Stars" on their fronts. Each strip contains two player discs and one disc for ordering a Tetley Press Sheet Calendar. Each red-bordered player disc features a color player head shot framed by a yellow line. The player's name and team name appear below the photo. The white back carries the player's name and team name at the bottom; above are the player's biography and 1989 stats. The discs are numbered on the back as "X of 20." Each disc is a tri-fold, consisting of two color player photos and a mail-in offer to receive a 15" by 25" press sheet calendar of the complete set of 20 players for only $3.50 plus four discs.

	Nm-Mt	Ex-Mt
COMPLETE SET (20)	30.00	9.00
1 Will Clark	2.50	.75
2 Howard Johnson	1.00	.30
3 Chris Sabo	1.00	.30
4 Jose Canseco	2.00	.60
5 Bo Jackson	1.50	.45
6 Kevin Mitchell	1.00	.30
7 Wade Boggs	3.00	.90
8 Ken Griffey Jr.	6.00	1.80
9 George Bell	1.00	.30
10 Dwight Gooden	1.50	.45
11 Bobby Bonilla	1.00	.30
12 Ryne Sandberg	5.00	1.50
13 Kirby Puckett	3.00	.90
14 Don Mattingly	5.00	1.50
15 Mark McGwire	8.00	2.40
16 Frank Viola	1.00	.30
17 Bret Saberhagen	1.00	.30
18 Mike Greenwell	1.00	.30
19 Steve Sax	1.00	.30
20 Nolan Ryan	10.00	3.00

1991 MSA Holsum Discs

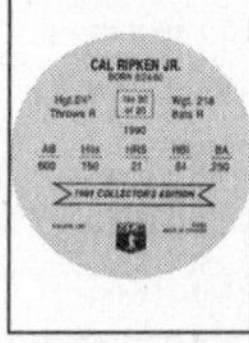

The 1991 Holsum Discs set, subtitled "Superstars" is a 20-disc set with each disc measuring approximately 2 3/4" in diameter. The discs feature on their fronts white-bordered color player head shots. The player's name, team and position appear below the photo. The white back carries the player's name and biography at the top, followed below by 1990 statistics. Typical of many of the sets produced by MSA, (Michael Schechter Associates) the teams' logos are airbrushed out. In Canada, Ben's Limited of Halifax distributed the discs under the Holsum imprint.

	Nm-Mt	Ex-Mt
COMPLETE SET (20)	250.00	75.00
1 Darryl Strawberry	3.00	.90
2 Eric Davis	3.00	.90
3 Tim Wallach	2.00	.60
4 Kevin Mitchell	2.00	.60
5 Tony Gwynn	25.00	7.50
6 Ryne Sandberg	20.00	6.00
7 Doug Drabek	2.00	.60
8 Randy Myers	2.00	.60
9 Ken Griffey Jr.	30.00	9.00
10 Alan Trammell	4.00	1.20
11 Ken Griffey Sr.	2.00	.60
12 Rickey Henderson	20.00	6.00
13 Roger Clemens	25.00	7.50
14 Bob Welch	2.00	.60
15 Kelly Gruber	2.00	.60
16 Mark McGwire	40.00	12.00
17 Cecil Fielder	3.00	.90
18 Dave Stieb	2.00	.60
19 Nolan Ryan	50.00	15.00
20 Cal Ripken	50.00	15.00

1992 MSA Ben's Super Hitters Discs

The 1992 Ben's Disc set is a 20-disc set, with each disc measuring approximately 2 3/4" in diameter. The set is subtitled "Super Hitters". The discs feature on their fronts white-bordered color player head shots. The player's name, team and position appear below the photo. The white back carries the player's name and biography at the top, followed below by 1991 statistics. As is typical of many of the sets produced by MSA (Michael Schechter Associates), the teams' logos are airbrushed out.

	Nm-Mt	Ex-Mt
COMPLETE SET (20)	30.00	9.00
1 Cecil Fielder	1.50	.45
2 Joe Carter	1.50	.45
3 Roberto Alomar	2.50	.75
4 Devon White	1.00	.30
5 Kelly Gruber	1.00	.30
6 Cal Ripken Jr.	10.00	3.00
7 Kirby Puckett	5.00	1.50
8 Paul Molitor	3.00	.90
9 Julio Franco	1.50	.45
10 Ken Griffey Jr.	6.00	1.80
11 Frank Thomas	3.00	.90
12 Jose Canseco	3.00	.90
13 Danny Tartabull	1.00	.30
14 Terry Pendleton	1.00	.30
15 Tony Gwynn	5.00	1.50
16 Howard Johnson	1.00	.30
17 Will Clark	2.00	.60
18 Barry Bonds	5.00	1.50
19 Ryne Sandberg	5.00	1.50
20 Bobby Bonilla	1.00	.30

1993 MSA Ben's Super Pitchers Discs

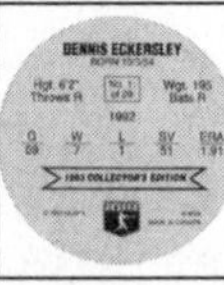

The 1993 Ben's Disc set is a 20-disc set, with each disc measuring approximately 2 3/4" in diameter. The set is subtitled "Super Pitchers". As is typical of many of the sets produced by MSA (Michael Schechter Associates), the teams' logos are airbrushed out. The discs feature white-bordered color player head shots on their fronts with the player's name, team and position appearing near the bottom. The white backs carry the player's name, biography and 1992 stats.

	Nm-Mt	Ex-Mt
COMPLETE SET (20)	10.00	3.00
1 Dennis Eckersley	1.50	.45
2 Chris Bosio	.25	.07
3 Jack Morris	.50	.15
4 Greg Maddux	3.00	.90
5 Dennis Martinez	.50	.15
6 Tom Glavine	1.25	.35
7 Doug Drabek	.25	.07
8 John Smoltz	.75	.23
9 Randy Myers	.50	.15
10 Jack McDowell	.25	.07
11 John Wetteland	.75	.23
12 Roger Clemens	2.00	.60
13 Mike Mussina	1.00	.30
14 Juan Guzman	.25	.07
15 Jose Rijo	.25	.07
16 Tom Henke	.50	.15
17 Gregg Olson	.50	.15
18 Jim Abbott	.50	.15
19 Jimmy Key	.50	.15
20 Rheal Cormier	.25	.07

1992 MTV Rock n' Jock

This three-card standard-size set was sponsored by MTV to promote the Third Annual Rock n' Jock Softball Challenge held January 11, 1992, in Los Angeles. According to the card backs, 20,000 sets were produced. The fronts feature color player photos, and each card has a different color inner border (1-brick red; 2-kelly green; 3-blue). The outer border of all cards consists of yellow, orange, and purple stars on a white background. The backs have a black and white version of the outer border of the fronts and present an advertisement for the softball challenge. There has been some debate over the years about whether or not this is a legitimate set; however an MTV PR person at the time acknowledged that the set was produced for the event by MTV.

	Nm-Mt	Ex-Mt
COMPLETE SET (3)	5.00	1.50
1 Hammer	.25	.07
2 Frank Thomas	2.00	.60
3 Ken Griffey Jr.	3.00	.90

1988 Willard Mullin Postcards

These 24 postcards feature the drawings of Willard Mullin, among the most known sports cartoonists. These cards were issued by Holmes Publishing in 1988. The cards measure 3 1/2" by 5" and feature reprints of Mullin's best works.

	Nm-Mt	Ex-Mt
COMPLETE SET (24)	12.50	5.00
1 Williard Mullin	.10	.04
2 Casey Stengel	.75	.30
3 Dizzy Dean	.50	.20
Paul Dean		
4 Joe DiMaggio	2.00	.80
5 Babe Ruth	2.00	.80
Hank Greenberg		
6 Brooklyn Bum #1	.10	.04
7 Pete Reiser	.25	.10
8 Dixie Walker	.25	.10
9 Branch Rickey	.25	.10
Bum #2 Flatbush Willie		
10 Jackie Robinson	3.00	1.20
Abraham Lincoln		
11 George Weiss	.50	.20
Casey Stengel		
12 Flatbush Willie	.10	.04
13 Flatbush Willie	.10	.04
14 Jim Gilliam	.25	.10
15 Duke Snider	.75	.30
16 Flatbush Willie	.25	.10
Walt Alston		
17 Flatbush Willie	.10	.04
18 Stan Musial	1.50	.60
19 Giants leave NY	.10	.04
20 Flatbush Willie	.10	.04
21 Unknown	.10	.04
22 Willie Mays	2.00	.80
23 Mickey Mantle	3.00	1.20
24 Amazing Mets	.25	.10

1985 Feg Murray's Cartoon Greats

This postcard set features the work of cartoonist Feg Murray. These cards feature reproductions of some of Murray's best works.

	Nm-Mt	Ex-Mt
COMPLETE SET (20)	8.00	3.20
1 Feg Murray	.25	.10
2 Ty Cobb	1.00	.40
3 Dizzy Dean	.75	.30
4 Bill Dickey	.50	.20
5 Jimmy Foxx	.75	.30
6 Frank Frisch	.50	.20
7 Lou Gehrig	1.00	.40
8 Charles Gehringer	.75	.30
9 Lefty Grove	.75	.30
10 Gabby Hartnett	.50	.20
11 Waite Hoyt	.50	.20
12 Carl Hubbell	.75	.30
13 John McGraw	.75	.30
14 Mel Ott	.75	.30
15 Babe Ruth	1.50	.60
The Million-Dollar Baby		
16 Babe Ruth	1.50	.60
Ain't It the Ruth		
17 Al Simmons	.75	.30
18 Casey Stengel	.75	.30
19 Bill Terry	.50	.20
20 Paul Waner	.75	.30

1992 Musial AFUD

This five-card set, presented by the American Foundation for Urologic Disease, measures approximately 3 1/2" by 5 1/2". The fronts feature black-and-white photos of Stan Musial, spokesperson for the Prostate Cancer Education Campaign, during his career and now. Small pictures of Stan Musial are on all but one card. The set is packaged in a folder that includes information for obtaining materials to promote awareness of prostate cancer. The cards are unnumbered and checklisted.

	Nm-Mt	Ex-Mt
COMPLETE SET (5)	15.00	4.50
COMMON CARD (1-5)	3.00	.90

1963 Musial Colt 45 Tribute

This 5" by 7" one-card blank-backed set was issued to commemorate Stan Musial's last series in Houston during the 1963 season. The front has a posed photo of Stan along with the words "Farewell Houston Appearance August 23-24-25, 1963.

	NM	Ex
1 Stan Musial	15.00	6.00

1985 Musial TTC

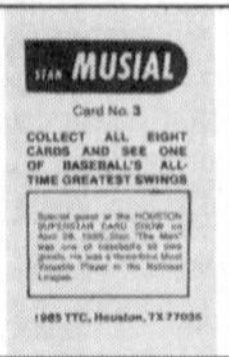

This eight-card set of Stan Musial produced by TTC of Houston, Texas, in the 1952 Bowman style, measures approximately 2 1/8" by 3 3/8". The fronts feature black-and-white photos of Stan Musial in the various stages of swinging the bat. The backs carry his name, card number, and a different career fact on each card as checklisted below.

	Nm-Mt	Ex-Mt
COMPLETE SET (8)	8.00	3.20
COMMON CARD (1-8)	1.00	.40

1992 MVP 2 Highlights

Produced by MVP Sports, this 20-card set presents an outstanding baseball player from each league for the nine positions as well as one designated hitter from each league. The cards have rounded corners and measure 2 1/2" by 3 1/2."

	Nm-Mt	Ex-Mt
COMPLETE SET (20)	10.00	3.00
1 Willie Mays	2.00	.60
2 Hank Aaron	2.00	.60
3 Ted Williams	2.50	.75
4 Yogi Berra	1.00	.30
5 Ernie Banks	1.00	.30
6 Lou Brock	.75	.23
7 Steve Carlton	1.00	.30
8 Harmon Killebrew	.75	.23
9 Gaylord Perry	.75	.23
10 Rusty Staub	.50	.15
11 Lou Boudreau	.75	.23
12 Larry Doby	.50	.15
13 Orlando Cepeda	.50	.15
14 Bill Mazeroski	.50	.15
15 Don Baylor	.50	.15
16 Bill Madlock	.25	.07
17 Joe Torre	.75	.23
18 Boog Powell	.50	.15
19 Graig Nettles	.50	.15
20 Dave Johnson	.50	.15

1992 MVP Game

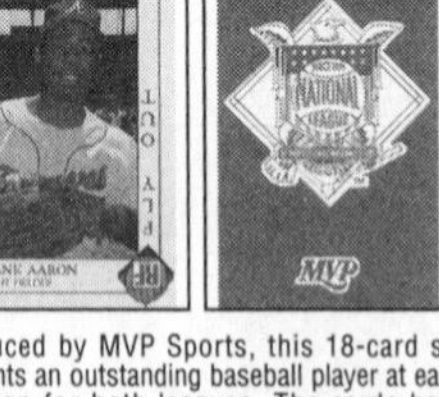

Produced by MVP Sports, this 18-card set presents an outstanding baseball player at each position for both leagues. The cards have rounded corners and measure 2 1/4" by 3 1/2." The design but not the size is similar to that of playing cards. The backs of the American League (cards 1-9) cards are predominantly red and have the AL emblem, while the backs of the National League (cards 10-18) cards are predominantly purple and carry the NL emblem. Since the cards are unnumbered, we have checklisted them below alphabetically within leagues.

	Nm-Mt	Ex-Mt
COMPLETE SET (18)	10.00	3.00
1 Don Baylor	.50	.15
2 Yogi Berra	1.00	.30
3 Lou Boudreau	.75	.23
4 Larry Doby	.75	.23
5 Dave Johnson	.50	.15
6 Harmon Killebrew	.75	.23
7 Graig Nettles	.50	.15
8 Gaylord Perry	.75	.23
9 Ted Williams	2.50	.75
10 Hank Aaron	2.00	.60
11 Ernie Banks	1.00	.30
12 Lou Brock	.75	.23
13 Steve Carlton	1.00	.30
14 Orlando Cepeda	.75	.23
15 Bill Madlock	.25	.07
16 Willie Mays	2.00	.60
17 Bill Mazeroski	.50	.15
18 Joe Torre	.75	.23

1889 N526 No. 7 Cigars

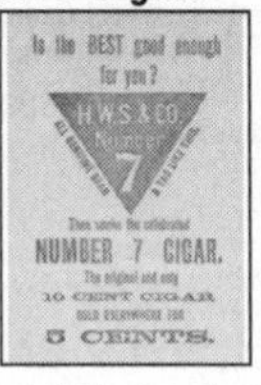

This set is comprised exclusively of members of the Boston Baseball Club, who are portrayed in black and white line drawings. The tobacco brand No. 7 Cigars has not yet been linked to a specific manufacturer. These cards were issued in 1889 and are similar to another series bearing Diamond S brand advertising.

	Ex-Mt	VG
COMPLETE SET (15)	6000.00	3000.00
1 Charles W. Bennett	400.00	200.00
2 Dennis (Dan) Brouthers	600.00	300.00
3 Tom T. Brown	400.00	200.00
4 John G. Clarkson	600.00	300.00
5 Charles W. Ganzell	400.00	200.00
6 James A. Hart	400.00	200.00
7 Richard F. Johnston	400.00	200.00
8 Mike J. (King) Kelly	1000.00	500.00
Captain		
9 M.J. (Kid) Madden	400.00	200.00
10 William Nash	400.00	200.00
11 Jos. Quinn	400.00	200.00
12 Charles Radbourne	600.00	300.00
13 J.B. Ray (sic)	400.00	200.00
14 Hardie Richardson	400.00	200.00
15 William Sowders	400.00	200.00

1969 Nabisco Team Flakes

The cards in this 24-card set measure either 1 15/16" by 3" or 1 3/4" by 2 15/16" depending on the amount of yellow border area provided between the "cut lines." The 1969 Nabisco Team Flakes set of full color, blank-backed and unnumbered cards was issued on the backs of Team Flakes cereal boxes. The cards are numbered in the checklist below in alphabetical order. There were three different panels or box backs containing eight cards each. The cards have yellow borders and are devoid of team insignias. The wider cards are tougher and should be valued at approximately 1.5X to 2X the narrower cards. The catalog designation is F275-34. Based on the alphabetical order of the player on the top left corner, we have identified the sheet that each player was on. The Aaron sheet is labelled S1, Pete Rose is labelled S2 and Ron Santo is labelled S3. These cards are actually called Mini Posters by Nabisco and all of these photos were also available in 2 feet by 3 feet posters that a kid could mail away for.

	NM	Ex
COMPLETE SET (24)	600.00	240.00
1 Hank Aaron S1	80.00	32.00
2 Richie Allen S1	15.00	6.00
3 Lou Brock S2	40.00	16.00
4 Paul Casanova S1	6.00	2.40
5 Roberto Clemente S3	100.00	40.00
6 Al Ferrara S3	6.00	2.40
7 Bill Freehan S2	10.00	4.00
8 Jim Fregosi S1	10.00	4.00
9 Bob Gibson S3	40.00	16.00
10 Tony Horton S2	10.00	4.00
11 Tommy John S3	15.00	6.00
12 Al Kaline S3	40.00	16.00
13 Jim Lonborg S2	6.00	2.40
14 Juan Marichal S1	40.00	16.00
15 Willie Mays S2	80.00	32.00
16 Rick Monday S2	6.00	2.40
17 Tony Oliva S1	15.00	6.00
18 Brooks Robinson S1	40.00	16.00
19 Frank Robinson S3	40.00	16.00
20 Pete Rose S2	60.00	24.00
21 Ron Santo S3	20.00	8.00
22 Tom Seaver S2	60.00	24.00
23 Rusty Staub S1	10.00	4.00
24 Mel Stottlemyre S3	6.00	2.40

1992 Nabisco

This 36-card standard-size set was sponsored by Nabisco and inserted in Shreddies cereal boxes and other Nabisco products in Canada. Three collector cards were protected by a cardboard sleeve that included two Bingo game symbols and a checklist on its back. The inside of each cereal box featured a Baseball Bingo Game Board. The collector became eligible to win prizes when he completed one vertical row, which consists of two required symbols and two correctly answered trivia questions. The odd number cards are Montreal Expos, while the even number cards are Toronto Blue Jays. Each card commemorates an outstanding achievement in the history of these two baseball franchises.

	Nm-Mt	Ex-Mt
COMPLETE SET (36)	15.00	4.50
1 Bill Lee	.75	.23
2 Cliff Johnson	.50	.15
3 Ken Singleton	1.00	.30
4 Al Woods	.50	.15
5 Ron Hunt	.75	.23
6 Barry Bonnell	.50	.15
7 Tony Perez	1.50	.45
8 Willie Upshaw	.50	.15
9 Coco Laboy	.50	.15
10 Famous Moments 1	.50	.15
October 5, 1985		
Blue Jays win AL East		
11 Bob Bailey	.50	.15
12 Dave McKay	.50	.15
13 Rodney Scott	.50	.15
14 Jerry Garvin	.50	.15
15 Famous Moments 2	.50	.15
October 11, 1981		
Expos win NL East		
16 Rick Bosetti	.50	.15
17 Larry Parrish	.75	.23
18 Bill Singer	.50	.15
19 Ron Fairly	.75	.23
20 Damaso Garcia	.50	.15
21 Al Oliver	1.00	.30
22 Famous Moments 3	.50	.15
September 30, 1989		
Blue Jays capture		
Divisional Championship		
23 Claude Raymond	.50	.15
24 Buck Martinez	.75	.23
25 Rusty Staub	1.50	.45
26 Otto Velez	.50	.15
27 Mack Jones	.50	.15
28 Garth Iorg	.50	.15
29 Bill Stoneman	.75	.23
30 Doug Ault	.50	.15
31 Famous Moments 4	.50	.15
July 6, 1982		
Expos hosts 1st AS		
Game played outside US		
32 Jesse Jefferson	.50	.15
33 Steve Rogers	.75	.23
34 Ernie Whitt	.50	.15
35 John Boccabella	.50	.15
36 Bob Bailor	.50	.15
xx Album	1.50	.45

1993 Nabisco All-Star Autographs

Available by sending two proofs of purchase from specially marked Nabisco packages and 5.00, each card features an autographed color action photo of a former star on its front and comes in a special card holder along with a certificate of authenticity. Don Drysdale tragically passed away between his signing the cards and the beginning of the promotion. Nabisco honored all requests until they ran out of cards on Drysdale. The cards are unnumbered and are checklisted in alphabetical order.

	Nm-Mt	Ex-Mt
COMPLETE SET (6)	125.00	38.00
1 Ernie Banks	15.00	4.50
2 Don Drysdale	60.00	18.00
3 Catfish Hunter	30.00	9.00
4 Phil Niekro	10.00	3.00
5 Brooks Robinson	15.00	4.50
6 Willie Stargell	20.00	6.00

1994 Nabisco All-Star Autographs

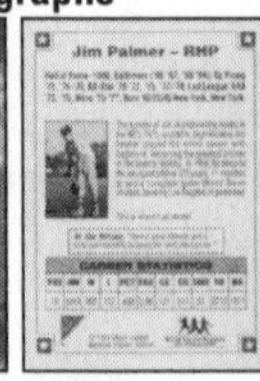

The Nabisco Biscuit Company and the Major League Baseball Players Alumni Association cosponsored the "Nabisco All-Star Legends" program, which featured these four autographed baseball cards as well as All-Star appearances nationwide and free tickets to minor league baseball games. Measuring the standard size, one card could be obtained by mailing 5.00 and two proofs of purchase from Oreo, Oreo Double Stuff, Chips Ahoy, Ritz, Wheat Thins, Better Cheddars, Nabisco Grahams, and Honey Maid Grahams crackers. Each autographed card was accompanied by an MLBPAA certificate of authenticity. The cards are unnumbered and checklisted below in alphabetical order.

	Nm-Mt	Ex-Mt
COMPLETE SET (4)	60.00	18.00
1 Bob Gibson	20.00	6.00
2 Jim Palmer	15.00	4.50
3 Frank Robinson	20.00	6.00
4 Duke Snider	20.00	6.00

2000 Nabisco All Stars

This 11-card standard-size set features retired players. The cards were issued as part of a Nestle promotion and are not numbered. A player photo is set against a background of a ball and a flag. The Nestle logo is in the upper left hand corner. Therefore, the cards are sequenced in alphabetical order.

	Nm-Mt	Ex-Mt
COMPLETE SET (11)	20.00	6.00
1 Yogi Berra	2.50	.75
2 Gary Carter	1.50	.45
3 Orlando Cepeda	2.00	.60
4 George Foster	.50	.15
5 Steve Garvey	1.50	.45
6 John Kruk	.50	.15
7 Joe Morgan	2.50	.75
8 Dot Richardson	5.00	1.50
9 Brooks Robinson	2.50	.75
10 Mike Schmidt	2.00	.60
11 Ozzie Smith	2.50	.75

1910 Nadja Caramel E92

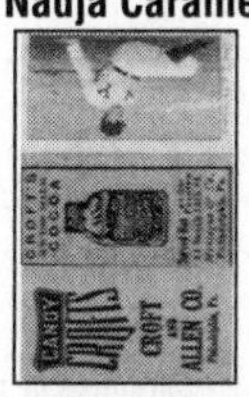

The cards in this 62-card set measure 1 1/2" by 2 3/4". This set was issued about 1910 by Dockman, Nadja, and Croft and Allen. There are four known reverses, with the "Base Ball Gum" (Dockman) back the most common, and the "Nadja" back the most difficult (Nadja backs with blue printing on the obverse belong to E104). The set contains poses identical to those in E101, E102, and E105. The ten cards marked with an asterisk are not found with Dockman back and are somewhat more difficult to find. The eight cards which are coded NADJA are available only with a Nadja back; these cards are quite scarce. Of the 40 cards which are available in all the back variations, the Croft back carries a slight premium while the Nadja back would carry double the value listed.

	Ex-Mt	VG
COMPLETE SET (62)	15000.00	7500.00
1 Bill Bailey NADJA	120.00	60.00
2 Jack Barry	200.00	100.00
3 Harry Bemis	100.00	50.00
4A Chief Bender (striped cap)	350.00	180.00
4B Chief Bender (white cap)	200.00	100.00
5 Bill Bergen	100.00	50.00
6 Bob Bescher	100.00	50.00
7 Roger Breshnahan	200.00	100.00
8 Al Bridwell	100.00	50.00
9 Joe Casey	100.00	50.00
10 Frank Chance	200.00	100.00
11 Hal Chase	150.00	75.00
12 Ty Cobb	6000.00	3000.00
13 Eddie Collins	600.00	300.00
14 Sam Crawford	200.00	100.00
15 Harry Davis	100.00	50.00
16 Art Devlin	100.00	50.00
17 Bill Donovan	100.00	50.00
18 Red Dooin	200.00	100.00
19 Mickey Doolan	100.00	50.00
20 Patsy Dougherty	100.00	50.00
21A Larry Doyle (batting)	120.00	60.00
21B Larry Doyle (throwing)	120.00	60.00
22 Rube Ellis	100.00	50.00
23 Johnny Evers	600.00	300.00
24 George Gibson	100.00	50.00
25 Topsy Hartsel	100.00	50.00
26A Fred Hartzell NADJA (batting)	120.00	60.00
26B Fred Hartzell NADJA (fielding)	120.00	60.00
27A Harry Howell NADJA (ready to pitch)	120.00	60.00
27B Harry Howell NADJA (follow through)	120.00	60.00
28 Fred Jacklitsch	200.00	100.00
29 Hugh Jennings	200.00	100.00
30 Red Kleinow	100.00	50.00
31 Otto Knabe	200.00	100.00
32 John Knight	200.00	100.00
33 Nap Lajoie	350.00	180.00
34 Hans Lobert	100.00	50.00
35 Sherry Magee	120.00	60.00
36 Christy Mathewson	600.00	300.00
37 John McGraw	200.00	100.00
38 Larry McLean	100.00	50.00
39A J.B. Miller (batting)	100.00	50.00
39B J.B. Miller (fielding)	200.00	100.00
40 Danny Murphy	100.00	50.00
41 Rebel Oakes	100.00	50.00
42 Bill O'Hara	100.00	50.00
43 Ed Phelps NADJA	120.00	60.00
44 Germany Schaefer	120.00	60.00
45 Admiral Schlei	100.00	50.00
46 Boss Schmidt	100.00	50.00
47 John Siegle	100.00	50.00
48 Dave Shean	100.00	50.00
49 Frank Smith	100.00	50.00
50A George Stone NADJA L.F., St. Louis AM. on bottom	120.00	60.00
50B George Stone NAJDA St. Louis Amer. On bottom	100.00	50.00
51 Joe Tinker	200.00	100.00
52A Honus Wagner (batting)	600.00	300.00
52B Honus Wagner (throwing)	600.00	300.00
53 Bobby Wallace NADJA	300.00	150.00
54 Cy Young	300.00	150.00
54 Rebel Oakes NADJA	100.00	50.00
55 Heinie Zimmerman	100.00	50.00

1910 Nadja E104

The cards in this 59-card set measure 1 1/2" by 2 3/4". The title of this set comes from the distinctive "Play Ball and eat Nadja Caramels" advertisement found on the reverse of some of the cards. The great majority of the known cards, however, are blank backed. They are grouped together because they have similar obverses and captions in blue print ("Nadja" cards with brown print captions belong to set E92). The cards are unnumbered and were issued in 1910. They have been alphabetized and numbered in the checklist below. The asterisked cards are more difficult and are referenced as Type 3. Nadja reverses are valued at three times the prices below.

	Ex-Mt	VG
COMPLETE SET (59)	8000.00	4000.00
1 Bill Abstein	120.00	60.00
2 Babe Adams	150.00	75.00
3 Red Ames	120.00	60.00
4 Frank Baker	200.00	100.00
5 Jack Barry	100.00	50.00
6 Johnny Bates	120.00	60.00
7 Chief Bender	200.00	100.00
8 Kitty Bransfield	120.00	60.00
9 Al Bridwell	120.00	60.00
10 Fred Clarke	200.00	100.00
11 Eddie Collins	200.00	100.00
12 Doc Crandall	120.00	60.00
13 Sam Crawford	400.00	200.00
14 Harry Davis	100.00	50.00
15 Jim Delahanty	120.00	60.00
16 Larry Doyle	120.00	60.00
17 Jimmy Dygert	100.00	50.00
18 George Gibson	100.00	50.00
19 Eddie Grant	120.00	60.00
20 Topsy Hartsel	100.00	50.00
21 Ham Hyatt	100.00	50.00
22 Fred Jacklitsch	120.00	60.00
23 Hugh Jennings	400.00	200.00
24 Davy Jones	120.00	60.00
25 Tom Jones	120.00	60.00
26 Otto Knabe	120.00	60.00
27 Harry Krause	100.00	50.00
28 John Lapp	100.00	50.00
29 Tommy Leach	100.00	50.00
30 Sam Leever	100.00	50.00
31 Paddy Livingston	100.00	50.00
32 Bris Lord	100.00	50.00
33 Connie Mack MG	400.00	200.00
34 Nicholas Maddox	100.00	50.00
35 John McGraw	400.00	200.00
36 Matthew McIntyre	120.00	60.00
37 Dots Miller	100.00	50.00
38 Earl Moore	120.00	60.00
39 Lew Moren	120.00	60.00
40 Cy Morgan	100.00	50.00
41 George Moriarty	120.00	60.00
42 George Mullin	120.00	60.00
43 Danny Murphy	100.00	50.00
44 Red Murray	120.00	60.00
45 Simon Nicholls	120.00	60.00
46 Charlie O'Leary	120.00	60.00
47 Rube Oldring	100.00	50.00
48 Deacon Phillippe	120.00	60.00
49 Eddie Plank	300.00	150.00
50 George Schlei	120.00	60.00
51 Cy Seymour	120.00	60.00
52 Tully Sparks	120.00	60.00
53 Amos Strunk	100.00	50.00
54 Ed Summers	120.00	60.00
55 Ira Thomas	100.00	50.00
56 Honus Wagner	500.00	250.00
57 Ed Willett	120.00	60.00
58 Vic Willis	200.00	100.00
59 Chief Wilson	100.00	50.00

1967 Nassau Health Ford

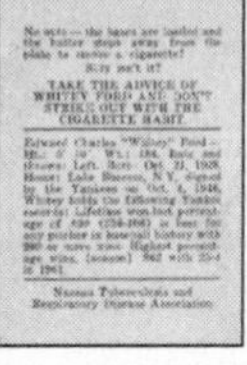

This one-card set was issued by Nassau Tuberculosis and Respiratory Disease Association and features a black-and-white photo of Whitey Ford. The back carries player information and a message about the dangers of cigarette smoking.

	NM	Ex
1 Whitey Ford	25.00	10.00

1921-23 National Caramel E220

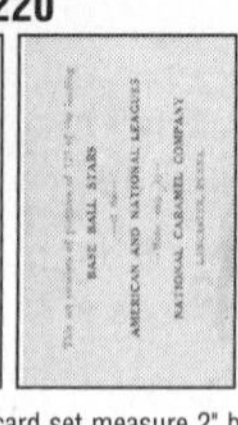

The cards in this 120-card set measure 2" by 3 1/4". There are 114 different players and six variations known for the "Baseball Stars" set marketed by the National Caramel Company. The cards are unnumbered and contain black and white photos; they are similar to set E122 but the coarse screening effect of the latter is missing. Some players appear in two poses, Burns is found with two teams, and three names are misspelled on the cards. The set was probably issued in 1922, the same year as was E122. The cards have been alphabetized and numbered in the checklist below. The complete set price includes all variation cards listed in the checklist below.

	Ex-Mt	VG
COMPLETE SET (120)	9000.00	4500.00
1 Babe Adams	60.00	30.00
2 Grover C. Alexander	100.00	50.00
3 James Austin	50.00	25.00
4 Jim Bagbyk sic, Bagby	50.00	25.00
5 Frank Baker	100.00	50.00
6 Dave Bancroft	100.00	50.00
7 Turner Barber	50.00	25.00
8 Geo.H. Burns Cleveland	50.00	25.00
9 Geo.J. Burns Cincinnati	50.00	25.00
10 Joe Bush	60.00	30.00
11 Leon Cadore	50.00	25.00
12 Max Carey	80.00	40.00
13 Ty Cobb	1000.00	500.00
14 Eddie Collins	100.00	50.00
15 John Collins	50.00	25.00
16 Wilbur Cooper	50.00	25.00
17 Stan Coveleskie	100.00	50.00
18 Walton Cruise	50.00	25.00
19 William Cunningham	50.00	25.00
20 George Cutshaw	50.00	25.00
21 Jake Daubert	60.00	30.00
22 Chas.A. Deal	50.00	25.00
23 Bill Doak	50.00	25.00
24 Joe Dugan	60.00	30.00
25A Jimmy Dykes batting	60.00	30.00
25B Jimmy Dykes fielding	60.00	30.00
26 Red Faber	100.00	50.00
27A Chick Fewster	60.00	30.00
27B Wilson Fewster	60.00	30.00
28 Ira Flagstead	50.00	25.00
29 Art Fletcher	50.00	25.00
30 Frankie Frisch	100.00	50.00
31 Larry Gardner	50.00	25.00
32 Walter Gerber	50.00	25.00
33 Charles Glazner	50.00	25.00
34 Hank Gowdy	60.00	30.00
35 J.C. Graney	50.00	25.00
36 Tommy Griffith	50.00	25.00
37 Charlie Grimm	80.00	40.00
38 Heine Groh	60.00	30.00
39 Byron Harris	50.00	25.00
40 Sam Harris	50.00	25.00
41 Harry Heilmann	100.00	50.00
42 Claude Hendrix	50.00	25.00
43 Walter Henline	50.00	25.00
44 Chas. Hollocher	50.00	25.00
45 Harry Hooper	100.00	50.00
46 Rogers Hornsby	300.00	150.00
47 Waite Hoyt	100.00	50.00
48 Wilbert Hubbell	60.00	30.00
49 Bill Jacobson	50.00	25.00
50 Walter Johnson	400.00	200.00
51 Jimmy Johnston	50.00	25.00
52 Joe Judge	50.00	25.00
53 George Kelly N.Y. Giants	100.00	50.00
54 Dick Kerr	60.00	30.00
55A Pete Kilduff bending	50.00	25.00
55B Pete Kilduff leaping	50.00	25.00
56 Larry Kopf	50.00	25.00
57 Dutch Leonard	60.00	30.00
58 Nemo Leibold	50.00	25.00
59 Walter Mails	60.00	30.00
60 Walter Maranville	100.00	50.00
61 Carl Mays	60.00	30.00
62 Lee Meadows	50.00	25.00
63 Bob Meusel	80.00	40.00
64 Emil Meusel	50.00	25.00
65 Clyde Milan	60.00	30.00
66 Earl Neale	80.00	40.00
67 Robert Nehf (picture actually Arthur Nehf)	60.00	30.00
68 Bernie Neis	50.00	25.00
69 Joe Oeschger	50.00	25.00
70 Robert O'Farrell	60.00	30.00
71 Ivan Olson	60.00	30.00
72 Steve O'Neill	60.00	30.00
73 Geo. Paskert	50.00	25.00
74 Roger Peckinpaugh	60.00	30.00
75 Herb Pennock	100.00	50.00
76 Cy Perkins	50.00	25.00
77 Scott Perry	50.00	25.00
78 Jeff Pfeffer	50.00	25.00
79 Val Picinich	50.00	25.00
80 Wally Pipp	60.00	30.00
81 Derrill Pratt	50.00	25.00
82 Goldie Rapp	50.00	25.00
83 Edgar Rice	100.00	50.00
84 Jimmy Ring	50.00	25.00
85 Ed Roush	100.00	50.00
86 Babe Ruth	1200.00	600.00
87 Wally Schang	50.00	25.00
88 Raymond Schmandt	50.00	25.00
89 Everett Scott	60.00	30.00
90 Joe Sewell	100.00	50.00
91 Maurice Shannon	50.00	25.00
92 Bob Shawkey	80.00	40.00
93 Urban Shocker	60.00	30.00
94 George Sisler	100.00	50.00
95 Earl Smith	50.00	25.00
96 John Smith	50.00	25.00
97 Sherrod Smith	50.00	25.00
98A Frank Snyder crouching	50.00	25.00
98B Frank Snyder standing	50.00	25.00
99 Tris Speaker	150.00	75.00
100 Vernon Spencer	50.00	25.00
101 Casey Stengel	250.00	125.00
102A Milton Stock fielding	50.00	25.00
102B Milton Stock batting	50.00	25.00
103 James Vaughn	50.00	25.00
104 Robert Veach	50.00	25.00
105 Bill Wambsganss	50.00	25.00
106 Aaron Ward	50.00	25.00
107 Zach Wheat	100.00	50.00
108A George Whitted batting	50.00	25.00
108B George Whitted fielding	50.00	25.00
109 Fred C. Williams	60.00	30.00
110 Art Wilson	50.00	25.00
111 Ivy Wingo	50.00	25.00
112 Lawton Witt	50.00	25.00
113 Pep Young	50.00	25.00
114 Ross Young	100.00	50.00

1936 National Chicle Fine Pen Premiums R313

The 1936 Fine Pen Premiums were issued anonymously by the National Chicle Company. The set is complete at 120 cards. Each card measures approximately 3 1/4" by 5 3/8". The cards are blank backed, unnumbered and could be obtained directly from a retail outlet rather than through the mail only. Three types of cards exist. The catalog designation for this set is R313.

	Ex-Mt	VG
COMPLETE SET (120)	2100.00	1050.00
1 Melo Almada	15.00	7.50
2 Paul Andrews	15.00	7.50
3 Elden Auker	15.00	7.50
4 Earl Averill	30.00	15.00
5 Jim Bucher	15.00	7.50
6 Moe Berg	75.00	38.00
7 Wally Berger	25.00	12.50
8 Charles Berry	15.00	7.50
9 Ralph Birkhofer (sic& Birkofer)	15.00	7.50
10 Cy Blanton	15.00	7.50
11 Ossie Bluege	20.00	10.00
12 Cliff Bolton	15.00	7.50
13 Zeke Bonura	15.00	7.50
14 Thos. Bridges	20.00	10.00
15 Sam Byrd	15.00	7.50
16 Dolph Camilli	25.00	12.50
17 Bruce Campbell	15.00	7.50
18 Walter "Kit" Carson	15.00	7.50
19 Ben Chapman	20.00	10.00
20 Rip Collins	20.00	10.00
21 Joe Cronin	30.00	15.00
22 Frank Crosetti	25.00	12.50
23 Paul Derringer	20.00	10.00
24 Bill Dietrich	15.00	7.50
25 Carl Doyle	15.00	7.50
26 Pete Fox	15.00	7.50
27 Frankie Frisch	30.00	15.00
28 Milton Galatzer	15.00	7.50
29 Charley Gehringer	30.00	15.00
30 Charley Gelbert	15.00	7.50
31 Jose Gomez	15.00	7.50
32 Lefty Gomez	30.00	15.00
33 Goose Goslin	30.00	15.00
34 Hank Gowdy	20.00	10.00
35 Hank Greenberg	30.00	15.00
36 Lefty Grove	30.00	15.00
37 Stan Hack	20.00	10.00
38 Odell Hale	15.00	7.50
39 Wild Bill Hallahan	15.00	7.50
40 Mel Harder	20.00	10.00
41 Bucky Harris	30.00	15.00
42 Frank Higgins	15.00	7.50
43 Oral C. Hildebrand	15.00	7.50
44 Myril Hoag	15.00	7.50
45 Rogers Hornsby	50.00	25.00
46 Waite Hoyt	30.00	15.00
47 Willis G. Hudlin(2)	15.00	7.50
48 Woody Jensen (2)	15.00	7.50
49 Wm. Knickerbocker	15.00	7.50
50 Joseph Kuhel	15.00	7.50
51 Cookie Lavagetto	20.00	10.00
52 Thornton Lee	15.00	7.50
53 Red Lucas	15.00	7.50
54 Pepper Martin	25.00	12.50
55 Joe Medwick	30.00	15.00
56 Oscar Melillo	15.00	7.50
57 Buddy Myer	15.00	7.50
58 Wally Moses	15.00	7.50
59 Van L. Mungo	15.00	7.50
60 Lamar Newsom	15.00	7.50
61 Buck Newsom	25.00	12.50
62 Steve O'Neill	20.00	10.00
63 Tommie Padden	15.00	7.50
64 Babe Phillips (sic, Phelps)	15.00	7.50
65 Bill Rogel (sic, Rogell)	15.00	7.50
66 Schoolboy Rowe	20.00	10.00
67 Al Simmons	30.00	15.00
68 Casey Stengel MG	60.00	30.00
69 Bill Swift	15.00	7.50
70 Cecil Travis	15.00	7.50
71 Pie Traynor	30.00	15.00
72 Wm. Urbansky (sic, Urbanski)	15.00	7.50
73 Arky Vaughan	30.00	15.00
74 Joe Vosmik	15.00	7.50
75 Honus Wagner	60.00	30.00
76 Rube Walberg	20.00	10.00
77 Bill Walker	15.00	7.50
78 Gerald Walker	15.00	7.50
79 Bill Werber	15.00	7.50
80 Sam West	15.00	7.50
81 Pinkey Whitney	15.00	7.50
82 Vernon Wiltshere (sic, Wilshere)	15.00	7.50
83 Pep Young	15.00	7.50
84 Babe and his babes	15.00	7.50
85 Stan Bordagaray Geo. Earnshaw	15.00	7.50
86 James Bucher John Babich	15.00	7.50
87 Ben Chapman Bill Werber	15.00	7.50
88 Chicago White Sox 1936	15.00	7.50
89 Fence Busters	15.00	7.50
90 Jimmy Fox Al Simmons Mickey Cochrane	30.00	15.00
91 Gabby Hartnett KiKi Cuyler	30.00	15.00
92 Lefty Gomez and Red Ruffing	50.00	25.00
93 Gabby Hartnett and Lon Warneke	30.00	15.00
94 Diamond Daddies: Connie Mack John McGraw	60.00	30.00
95 Capt. Bill Myer and Chas. Dressen MG	15.00	7.50
96 Paul Waner Lloyd Waner Big Jim Weaver	30.00	15.00
97 Wes Ferrell Rick Ferrell	30.00	15.00
98 Nick Altrock and Al Schacht	20.00	10.00
99 Big Bosses Clash Dykes safe	15.00	7.50
100 Bottomley tagging Gelbert	20.00	10.00
101 Camilli catches Jurges off first	20.00	10.00
102 CCS: Radcliffe safe Harnett catching	20.00	10.00
103 CCS: L.Sewell blocks runner at plate	15.00	7.50
104 CCS: Washington safe	15.00	7.50
105 Joe DiMaggio slams it, Erickson catching	250.00	125.00
106 Double Play-McQuinn to Stine	15.00	7.50
107 Dykes catches Crosetti between 2nd and 3rd	20.00	10.00
108 Glenn uses football play at plate	15.00	7.50
109 Greenberg doubles Dickey catching	30.00	15.00
110 Hasset makes the out (sic, Hassett)	15.00	7.50
111 Lombardi says "Ugh"	30.00	15.00
112 McQuinn gets his man	15.00	7.50
113 Randy Moore hurt stealing second	15.00	7.50
114 T. Moore out at plate, Wilson catching	20.00	10.00
115 Sewell waits for ball while Clift scores	15.00	7.50
116 Talking it over	15.00	7.50
117 There she goes, CCS	15.00	7.50
118 Ump says No Cleveland vs. Detroit	15.00	7.50
119 Lloyd Waner at bat Gabby Hartnett behind plate	30.00	15.00
120 World Series 1935 Goslin out at first	30.00	15.00

1936 National Chicle Maranville Secrets R344

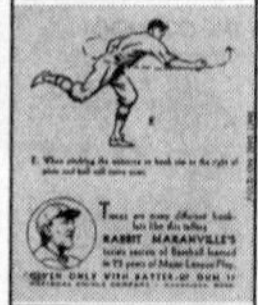

This paper set of 20 was issued in 1936 by the National Chicle Company. Each "card" measures 3 5/8" by 6". It carries the printing "Given only With Batter-Up Gum" on the back page. While the illustration shows the issue to be elongated, the papers were meant to be folded to create a four-page booklet. As the title implies, the set features instructional tips by Rabbit Maranville.

	Ex-Mt	VG
COMPLETE SET (20)	450.00	220.00
COMMON CARD (1-20)	25.00	12.50

1898 National Copper Plate

Measuring 9" by 12", these photos feature star players from the turn of the century. These photos were issued by National Copper Plate Co of Michigan. Since these are unnumbered, we have sequenced them in alphabetical order. There might be more photos known so any additions to this checklist is appreciated.

	Ex-Mt	VG
COMPLETE SET	2000.00	1000.00
1 Cap Anson	1000.00	500.00
2 Clark Griffith	600.00	300.00
3 Kid Nichols	600.00	300.00

1913 National Game WG5

These cards were distributed as part of a baseball game produced in 1913 as indicated by the patent date on the backs of the cards. The cards each measure approximately 2 7/16" by 3 7/16" and have rounded corners. The card fronts show a sepia photo of the player, his name, his team, and the game outcome associated with that particular card. The card backs are all the same, each showing an ornate red and white design with "The National Game" and "Baseball" right in the middle all surrounded by a thick white outer border. Since the cards are unnumbered, they are listed below in alphabetical order. Some of the card photos are oriented horizontally (HOR). There are a number of cards without player identification. These action scenes are not explicitly listed in the checklist below and are valued as a "common" card unless a positive identification can be made of a major Hall of Famer in the action scene on the card.

	Ex-Mt	VG
COMPLETE SET (45)	3000.00	1500.00
COMMON ACTION CARD	15.00	7.50
1 Grover Alexander	100.00	50.00
2 Frank Baker	60.00	30.00
3 Chief Bender	60.00	30.00
4 Bob Bescher	30.00	15.00
5 Joe Birmingham	30.00	15.00
6 Roger Bresnahan	60.00	30.00
7 Nixey Callahan	30.00	15.00
8 Frank Chance	100.00	50.00
9 Hal Chase	50.00	25.00
10 Fred Clarke	60.00	30.00
11 Ty Cobb	300.00	150.00
12 Sam Crawford	60.00	30.00
13 Bill Dahlen	40.00	20.00
14 Jake Daubert	40.00	20.00
15 Red Dooin	30.00	15.00
16 Johnny Evers	100.00	50.00
17 Vean Gregg	30.00	15.00
18 Clark Griffith MG	60.00	30.00
19 Dick Hoblitzel	30.00	15.00
20 Miller Huggins HOR	100.00	50.00
21 Joe Jackson	500.00	250.00
22 Hugh Jennings MG	60.00	30.00
23 Walter Johnson	150.00	75.00
24 Ed Konetchy	30.00	15.00
25 Nap Lajoie	120.00	60.00
26 Connie Mack MG	120.00	60.00
27 Rube Marquard	60.00	30.00
28 Christy Mathewson	150.00	75.00
29 John McGraw MG	120.00	60.00
30 Larry McLean HOR	30.00	15.00
31 Chief Meyers	40.00	20.00
32 Clyde Milan	40.00	20.00
33 Marty O'Toole	30.00	15.00
34 Nap Rucker	40.00	20.00
35 Tris Speaker	120.00	60.00
36 Jake Stahl	40.00	20.00
37 George Stallings MG	30.00	15.00
38 George Stovall	30.00	15.00
39 Bill Sweeney	30.00	15.00
40 Joe Tinker	100.00	50.00
41 Honus Wagner	150.00	75.00
42 Ed Walsh	60.00	30.00
43 Zack Wheat	60.00	30.00
44 Joe Wood	60.00	30.00
45 Cy Young	120.00	60.00
The Grand Old Man		

1952 National Tea Labels

The bread labels in this set are often called "Red Borders" because of their distinctive trim. Each label measures 2 3/4" by 2 11/16". Issued with the bakery products of the National Tea Company, there are thought to be 48 different labels in the set. The six missing labels are thought to consist of two Yankees, two Indians and two Red Sox -- so that there would be exactly three representatives from each of the 16 teams. The labels are also known as the "Bread For Health" set and may have included an album. This set is the toughest of the bread label sets listed. These labels are unnumbered so we have sequenced them in alphabetical order. The catalog designation is D290-2.

	NM	Ex
COMPLETE SET (42)	3500.00	1800.00
1 Gene Bearden	100.00	50.00
2 Yogi Berra	400.00	200.00
3 Lou Brissie	100.00	50.00
4 Sam Chapman	100.00	50.00
5 Chuck Diering	100.00	50.00
6 Dom DiMaggio	200.00	100.00
7 Hank Edwards	100.00	50.00
8 Del Ennis	120.00	60.00
9 Ferris Fain	100.00	50.00
10 Howie Fox	100.00	50.00
11 Sid Gordon	120.00	60.00
12 Johhny Groth	100.00	50.00
13 Granny Hamner	100.00	50.00
14 Sam Jones	100.00	50.00
15 Howie Judson	100.00	50.00
16 Sherm Lollar	100.00	50.00
17 Clarence Marshall	100.00	50.00
18 Don Mueller	100.00	50.00
19 Danny Murtaugh	120.00	60.00
20 Dave Philley	100.00	50.00
21 Jerry Priddy	100.00	50.00
22 Bill Rigney	120.00	60.00
23 Robin Roberts	200.00	100.00
24 Eddie Robinson	100.00	50.00
25 Preacher Roe	150.00	75.00
26 Stan Rojek	100.00	50.00
27 Al Rosen	150.00	75.00
28 Bob Rush	100.00	50.00
29 Hank Sauer	120.00	60.00
30 Johnny Schmitz	100.00	50.00
31 Enos Slaughter	200.00	100.00
32 Duke Snider	400.00	200.00
33 Warren Spahn	300.00	150.00
34 Gerry Staley	100.00	50.00
35 Virgil Stallcup	100.00	50.00
36 George Stirnweiss	100.00	50.00
37 Earl Torgeson	100.00	50.00
38 Dizzy Trout	120.00	60.00
39 Mickey Vernon	150.00	75.00
40 Wally Westlake	100.00	50.00
41 Johnny Wyrostek	100.00	50.00
42 Eddie Yost	120.00	60.00

1995 National Packtime

This 18-card standard-size set was sponsored by MLB, MLBPA, and the six licensed card companies from 1995 (Donruss, Fleer, Pacific, Pinnacle, Topps, and Upper Deck). Each of the six companies produced three cards for the set, which was available only through a mail-in offer for 28 wrappers from any of the six companies listed above plus $2.00 for shipping and handling. All orders had to be postmarked by June 30, 1995; any card sets not purchased by that date were destroyed. Except for the Topps card (which has a ragged white border), all the fronts display full-bleed color action photos. The backs carry a second color photo as well as biography and statistics. The cards are numbered on the back "X of 18." An unnumbered offer card, with a checklist on its back, was found in various 1995 baseball products.

	Nm-Mt	Ex-Mt
COMPLETE SET (18)	8.00	2.40
1 Frank Thomas	.75	.23
2 Matt Williams	.40	.12
3 Juan Gonzalez	.50	.15
4 Bob Hamelin	.10	.03
5 Mike Piazza	1.50	.45
6 Ken Griffey Jr.	1.50	.45
7 Barry Bonds	1.25	.35
8 Tim Salmon	.40	.12
9 Jose Canseco	.60	.18
10 Cal Ripken	2.50	.75
11 Raul Mondesi	.20	.06
12 Alex Rodriguez	1.50	.45
13 Will Clark	.50	.15
14 Fred McGriff	.40	.12
15 Tony Gwynn	1.25	.35
16 Kenny Lofton	.20	.06
17 Deion Sanders	.20	.06
18 Jeff Bagwell	.75	.23

1995 National Packtime 2

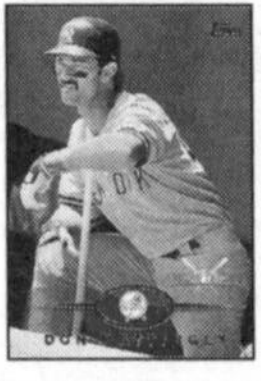

This six-card set was sponsored by MLB, MLBPA and the six licensed card companies (Donruss, Fleer, Pacific, Pinnacle, Topps, and Upper Deck) who each produced one card for the set. The fronts feature borderless color action player photos, while the backs carry player information. The cards are checklisted below in alphabetical order.

	Nm-Mt	Ex-Mt
COMPLETE SET (6)	4.00	1.20
1 Albert Belle	.20	.06
2 Darren Daulton	.10	.03
3 Randy Johnson	1.00	.30
4 Greg Maddux	1.50	.45
5 Don Mattingly	1.25	.35
6 Hideo Nomo	1.00	.30

1986 Negro League Fritsch Samples

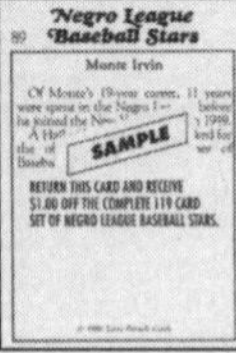

These 1986 Negro League Fritsch Samples were issued to announce the introduction of the 1986 Negro League Fritsch 119-card set. The cards measure the standard-size. The white fronts display a black-and-white player portrait with the set title appearing in red lettering above. The player's name appears below the photo also in red lettering with a red star to the left and right. The backs have blue print framed by a narrow blue line and carry a portion of the narrative to appear on the regular issue card. Stamped across the information is the word "Sample". An offer is made to return the Sample card and receive $1.50 off the complete set of 119 Negro League Baseball Stars.

	Nm-Mt	Ex-Mt
COMPLETE SET (3)	20.00	8.00
1 Buck Leonard	2.50	1.00
7 Ray Dandridge	2.50	1.00
10 Satchel Paige	4.00	1.60
11 Jackie Robinson	4.00	1.60
20 Lou Dials	1.00	.40
Sample in big bold letters		
20A Lou Dials	1.00	.40
Sample enclosed in a box		
30 Josh Gibson	3.00	1.20
89 Monte Irvin	2.50	1.00
90 Cool Papa Bell	2.50	1.00

1986 Negro League Fritsch

This is a 119-card standard-size set of Negro League stars. The set features black and white photos framed by the title "Negro League Baseball Stars" in red above the player's name and the player's name in red below the photo. Each card back features a brief biography of the player pictured on the front of the card. The set was produced by long time Wisconsin card hobbyist Larry Fritsch and featured most of the great players of the old Negro Leagues. An earlier version of the set was produced in 1984 by Decathlon Corporation. Each Decathlon set has a serial number; Decathlon sets are valued at double the prices listed below.

	Nm-Mt	Ex-Mt
COMPLETE SET (119)	10.00	4.00
1 Buck Leonard	.50	.20
2 Ted Page	.25	.10
3 Cool Papa Bell	.50	.20
4 Oscar Charleston	.40	.16
Josh Gibson		
Ted Page		
Judy Johnson		
5 Judy Johnson	.40	.16
6 Monte Irvin	.40	.16
7 Ray Dandridge	.25	.10
8 Oscar Charleston	.50	.20
9 Josh Gibson	1.00	.40
10 Satchel Paige	1.00	.40
11 Jackie Robinson	1.00	.40
12 Lorenzo(Piper) Davis	.15	.06
13 Josh Johnson	.05	.02
14 Lou Dials	.25	.10
15 Andy Porter	.05	.02
16 John Henry Lloyd	.25	.10
17 Andy Watts	.05	.02
18 Rube Foster	.25	.10
19 Martin DiHigo	.50	.20
20 Lou Dials	.25	.10
21 Satchel Paige	1.00	.40
22 Crush Holloway	.05	.02
23 Josh Gibson	1.00	.40
24 Oscar Charleston	.50	.20
25 Jackie Robinson	1.00	.40
26 Larry Brown	.05	.02
27 Hilton Smith	.40	.16
28 Moses F. Walker	.40	.16
29 Jimmie Crutchfield	.25	.10
30 Josh Gibson	1.00	.40
31 Josh Gibson	1.00	.40
32 Bullet Rogan	.25	.10
33 Clint Thomas	.05	.02
34 Rats Henderson	.05	.02
35 Pat Scantlebury	.05	.02
36 Sydney Sy Morton	.05	.02
37 Larry Kimbrough	.05	.02
38 Sam Jethroe	.25	.10
39 Normal(Tweed) Webb	.05	.02
40 Mahlon Duckett	.05	.02
41 Andy Anderson	.05	.02
42 Buster Haywood	.05	.02
43 Bob Trice	.25	.10
44 Buster Clarkson	.05	.02
45 Buck O'Neil	.50	.20
46 Jim Zapp	.05	.02
47 Lorenzo(Piper) Davis	.25	.10
48 Ed Steel	.05	.02
49 Bob Boyd	.25	.10
50 Marlin Carter	.05	.02
51 George Giles	.05	.02
52 Bill Byrd	.05	.02
53 Art Pennington	.05	.02
54 Max Manning	.05	.02
55 Ronald Teasley	.05	.02
56 Ziggy Marcell	.05	.02
57 Bill Cash	.05	.02
58 Joe Scott	.05	.02
59 Joe Fillmore	.05	.02
60 Bob Thurman	.25	.10
61 Larry Kimbrough	.05	.02
62 Verdell Mathis	.05	.02
63 Josh Johnson	.25	.10
64 Ted Radcliffe	.25	.10
65 William Bobby Robinson	.15	.06
66 Bingo DeMoss	.25	.10
67 John Beckwith	.05	.02
68 Bill Jackman	.05	.02
69 Bill Drake	.05	.02
70 Charlie Grant	.25	.10
71 Willie Wells	.50	.20
72 Jose Fernandez	.05	.02
73 Isidro Fabri	.05	.02
74 Frank Austin	.05	.02
75 Dick Lundy	.05	.02
76 Junior Gilliam	.25	.10
77 John Donaldson	.05	.02
78 Rap Dixon	.05	.02
79 Slim Jones	.05	.02
80 Sam Jones	.25	.10
81 Dave Hoskins	.25	.10
82 Jerry Benjamin	.05	.02
83 Luke Easter	.25	.10
84 Ramon Herrera	.05	.02
85 Matthew Carlisle	.05	.02
86 Smokey Joe Williams	.25	.10
87 Marvin Williams	.05	.02
88 William Yancey	.25	.10
89 Monte Irvin	.50	.20
90 Cool Papa Bell	.60	.24
91 Biz Mackey	.40	.16
92 Harry Simpson	.25	.10
93 Lazerio Salazar	.05	.02
94 Bill Perkins	.05	.02
95 Johnny Davis	.05	.02
96 Jelly Jackson	.25	.10
97 Sam Bankhead	.25	.10
98 Hank Thompson	.25	.10
99 William Bell	.05	.02
100 Cliff Bell	.05	.02
101 Dave Barnhill	.05	.02
102 Dan Bankhead	.25	.10
103 Pepper Bassett	.05	.02
104 Newt Allen	.25	.10
105 George Jefferson	.05	.02
106 Pat Paterson	.05	.02
107 Goose Tatum	1.00	.40
108 Dave Malarcher	.25	.10
109 Home Run Johnson	.25	.10
110 Bill Monroe	.05	.02
111 Sammy Hughes	.05	.02
112 Dick Redding	.25	.10
113 Fats Jenkins	.05	.02
114 Jimmie Lyons	.05	.02
115 Mule Suttles	.25	.10
116 Ted Trent	.05	.02
117 George Sweatt	.05	.02
118 Frank Duncan	.05	.02
119 Checklist Card	.05	.02

1987 Negro League Phil Dixon

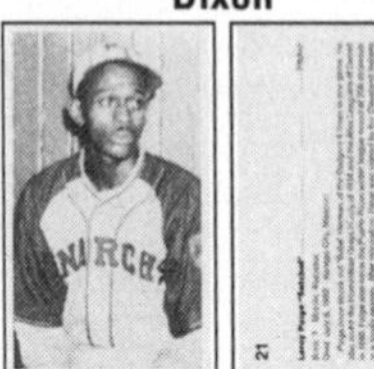

Produced by Phil Dixon, this 45-card set measures approximately 2 15/16" by 5". The fronts feature a mix of posed and action black-and-white player photos bordered in white. The horizontal backs carry the player's name, position, birth and death dates, and a brief career summary.

	Nm-Mt	Ex-Mt
COMPLETE SET (45)	30.00	12.00
1 Samuel Hairston	.75	.30
2 Elander Victor Harris	.50	.20
(Vic)		
3 Theodore(Ted) Trent	.50	.20
4 Edward Joseph Dwight	.75	.30
(Pee Wee)		
5 Jessie Williams	.50	.20
6 Josh Gibson	3.00	1.20
7 Jose De La C. Mendez	.50	.20
8 Joe Green	.50	.20
9 Robert Boyd	.75	.30
(The Rope)		
10 William(Plunk) Drake	.50	.20
11 Alfred(Army) Cooper	.50	.20
12 Charles Isam Taylor	.50	.20
(C.I.)		
13 Dick Whitworth	.50	.20
14 Tobe Smith	.50	.20
15 William(Dizzy)	.50	.20
Dismukes		
16 Richard Thomas Bayas	.50	.20
(Subby)		
17 Hurley Allen McNair	.50	.20
(Mack)		
18 Roy Partlow	.50	.20
19 Carroll Ray Mothell	.50	.20
(Dink)		
20 John(Buck) O'Neil	1.50	.60
21 Leroy(Satchel) Paige	3.00	1.20
22 Moses Fleetwood Walker	1.50	.60
23 Quincy Jordan Gilmore	.50	.20
24 James(Cool Papa) Bell	1.50	.60
25 Andrew(Rube) Foster	1.50	.60
26 George Alexander	.50	.20
Sweatt		
27 Hilton Lee Smith	1.50	.60
28 Thomas Jefferson Young	.50	.20
(T.J.)		
29 Chet Brewer	.75	.30
30 Buck Leonard	1.50	.60
31 Walter Lee Joseph	.75	.30
(Newt)		
32 Eugene Walter Baker	.75	.30
(Gene)		
33 Jackie Robinson	3.00	1.20
34 Wilbur(Bullet) Rogan	.75	.30
35 Norman(Turkey) Stearns	.50	.20
36 Albert(Buster) Haywood	.50	.20
37 Lorenzo(Piper) Davis	.75	.30
38 Francisco Comimbre	.50	.20
(Pancho)		
39 Bob Thurman	.75	.30
40 Booker T. McDaniel	.50	.20
(Cannonball)		
41 Newton Henry Allen	.75	.30
(Colt)		
42 Willie Wells	1.50	.60
43 Connie Johnson	1.00	.40
44 George Franklin Giles	.50	.20
45 Frank(Dunk) Duncan	.50	.20

1988 Negro League Duquesne

This 20-card set was sponsored by the Pittsburgh Pirates with the assistance of Rob Ruck of Chatham College and Duquesne Light Company. The set celebrates Negro League Baseball by depicting major black stars who played or were involved in the negro leagues in the Pittsburgh area. The set was given away at the Pittsburgh Pirates' home game on September 10, 1988. The set was issued in a sheet with five rows of four cards each; after perforation, the cards measure the standard size.

	Nm-Mt	Ex-Mt
COMPLETE SET (20)	25.00	10.00
1 Andrew(Rube) Foster	2.50	1.00
2 1913 Homestead Grays	1.00	.40
3 Cum Posey	1.00	.40
4 1926 Pittsburgh	1.00	.40
Crawfords		
5 Gus Greenlee OWN	1.00	.40
6 John Henry(Pop) Lloyd	2.50	1.00
7 Oscar Charleston	2.50	1.00
8 Smokey Joe Williams	2.50	1.00
9 William(Judy) Johnson	2.50	1.00
10 Martin Dihigo	2.50	1.00
11 LeRoy(Satchel) Paige	4.00	1.60
12 Josh Gibson	4.00	1.60
13 Sam Streeter	1.00	.40
14 James(Cool Papa) Bell	2.50	1.00
15 Ted Page	2.00	.80
16 Walter(Buck) Leonard	2.50	1.00
17 Ray(Hooks) Dandridge	2.50	1.00
18 Willis Moody and	1.00	.40
Ralph(Lefty) Mellix		
19 Harold Tinker	1.00	.40
20 Monte Irvin	2.50	1.00

1989 Negro League Rini Postcards

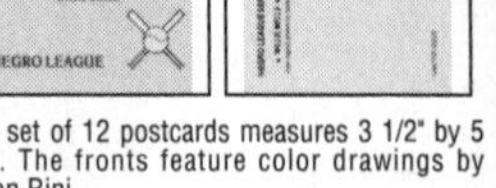

This set of 12 postcards measures 3 1/2" by 5 1/2". The fronts feature color drawings by Susan Rini.

	Nm-Mt	Ex-Mt
COMPLETE SET (12)	5.00	2.00
1 Monte Irvin	1.00	.40
2 Martin Dihigo	.75	.30
3 Clint Thomas	.25	.10
4 Buster Haywood	.25	.10
5 George Giles	.25	.10
6 Isidro Fabri	.25	.10
7 James(Cool Papa) Bell	1.00	.40
8 Josh Gibson	1.00	.40
9 Lou Dials	.50	.20
10 Willie Wells	.75	.30
11 Walter(Buck) Leonard	1.00	.40
12 Jose Fernandez	.25	.10

1990 Negro League Stars

The exclusion of black and Latino players from Major League Baseball from 1889 to 1947 resulted in these same players forming their own teams and leagues, and this 36-card set pays tribute to these men. These standard size cards feature beautiful water color portraits of the players, painted by Mark Chiarello.

	Nm-Mt	Ex-Mt
COMPLETE SET (36)	12.00	3.60
1 Title Card	.50	.15
2 Josh Gibson	2.00	.60
3 Cannonball Redding	.50	.15
4 Biz Mackey	.75	.23
5 Pop Lloyd	1.00	.30
6 Bingo Demoss	.50	.15
7 Willard Brown	.25	.07
8 John Donaldson	.25	.07
9 Monte Irvin	1.00	.30
10 Ben Taylor	.25	.07
11 Willie Wells	.75	.23
12 Dave Brown	.25	.07
13 Leon Day	1.00	.30
14 Ray Dandridge	1.00	.30
15 Turkey Stearnes	.25	.07
16 Rube Foster	1.00	.30
17 Oliver Marcelle	.25	.07
18 Judy Johnson	1.00	.30
19 Christobel Torrienti	.50	.15
20 Satchel Paige	2.00	.60
21 Mule Suttles	.50	.15
22 John Beckwith	.25	.07
23 Martin Dihigo	1.00	.30
24 Willie Foster	.25	.07
25 Dick Lundy	.25	.07
26 Buck Leonard	1.00	.30
27 Smokey Joe Williams	1.00	.30
28 Cool Papa Bell	1.00	.30
29 Bullet Rogan	.50	.15
30 Newt Allen	.50	.15
31 Bruce Petway	.50	.15
32 Jose Mendez	.25	.07
33 Louis Santop	.25	.07
34 Jud Wilson	.25	.07
35 Sammy T. Hughes	.25	.07
36 Oscar Charleston	1.00	.30

1991 Negro League Ron Lewis

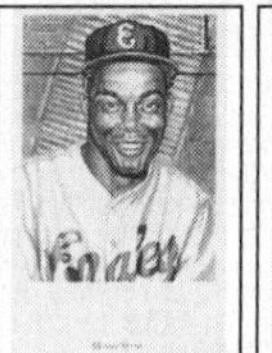

This 30-card boxed set was produced by the Negro League Baseball Players Association and noted sports artist Ron Lewis and was subtitled Living Legends. Production quantities were limited to 10,000 sets, and each card of the set bears a unique serial number on the back. Also 200 uncut sheets were printed. The cards were issued in the postcard format and measure approximately 3 1/2" by 5 1/4". The front design features a full color painting of the player by Ron Lewis. These cards were also issued in 1995 as part of a two series Negro League set. The values are about the same for either set.

	Nm-Mt	Ex-Mt
COMPLETE SET (30)	30.00	9.00
1 George Giles	1.00	.30
2 Bill Cash	1.00	.30
3 Bob Harvey	1.00	.30
4 Lyman Bostock Sr.	1.50	.45
5 Ray Dandridge	2.50	.75
6 Leon Day	2.50	.75
7 Lefty Mathis	1.00	.30
8 Jimmie Crutchfield	1.50	.45
9 Clyde McNeal	1.00	.30
10 Bill Wright	1.00	.30
11 Mahlon Duckett	1.00	.30
12 Bobby Robinson	1.50	.45
13 Max Manning	1.00	.30
14 Armando Vazquez	1.00	.30
15 Jehosie Heard	1.50	.45
16 Quincy Trouppe	1.00	.30
17 Wilmer Fields	1.00	.30
18 Lonnie Blair	1.00	.30
19 Garnett Blair	1.00	.30
20 Monte Irvin	2.50	.75
21 Willie Mays	6.00	1.80
22 Buck Leonard	2.50	.75
23 Frank Evans	1.00	.30
24 Josh Gibson Jr.	2.00	.60
25 Ted Radcliffe	1.50	.45
26 Josh Johnson	1.50	.45
27 Gene Benson	1.00	.30
28 Lester Lockett	1.50	.45
29 Bubba Hyde	1.00	.30
30 Rufus Lewis	1.00	.30

1992 Negro League Kraft

On August 9, 1992, at Lackawanna County Stadium, in Scranton, Pennsylvania, Eclipse Enterprises Inc. sponsored the Negro League Baseball Players Association Night. This 18-card set was created especially for this event by Eclipse artist John Clapp and given out to fans in attendance. Reportedly only 11,000 of the 15,000 sets were distributed; the remainder were kept by Kraft General Foods of Glenville, Illinois.

	Nm-Mt	Ex-Mt
COMPLETE SET (18)	15.00	4.50
1 Leon Day	1.50	.45
2 Clinton(Casey) Jones	.50	.15
3 Lester Lockett	.75	.23
4 Monte Irvin	2.50	.75
5 Armando Vazquez	.50	.15
6 Jimmie Crutchfield	1.00	.30
7 Ted Radcliffe	1.00	.30
8 Albert Haywood	.50	.15
9 Artie Wilson	.75	.23
10 Sam Jethroe	.75	.23
11 Edsall Walker	.50	.15
12 Bill Wright	.50	.15
13 Jim Cohen	.50	.15
14 Andy Porter	.50	.15
15 Tommy Sampson	.50	.15
16 Buck Leonard	3.00	.90
17 Josh Gibson	4.00	1.20
18 Martinez Jackson (Reggie Jackson's father)	1.50	.45

1992 Negro League Paul Lee

On June 2, 1992 at Shea Stadium, Eclipse Enterprises Inc. sponsored the Negro League Baseball Players Association Night. This four-card set was created especially for this event by Eclipse artist Paul Lee, and they were given out to the first 50,000 fans in attendance. Each set included an insert outlining the goals of the association.

	Nm-Mt	Ex-Mt
COMPLETE SET (4)	6.00	1.80
1 Monte Irvin	1.50	.45
2 Walter(Buck) Leonard	1.50	.45
3 Josh Gibson	3.00	.90
4 Ray Dandridge	1.50	.45

1992 Negro League Retort Legends I

This 100-card set was produced by R.D. Retort Enterprises of New Castle, Pennsylvania. The cards were issued in a brown box with the set name and logo stamped in gold. The production run was reported to be 10,000 individually numbered sets. Collectors who purchased the set received The Pictorial Negro League Legends Album, an 8 1/2" by 11" book containing more than 260 vintage Negro League photos, and an address list to facilitate the obtaining of autographs. The cards are "postcard" size, measuring approximately 3 1/2" by 5 1/2". The sepia-toned player photos have white borders, and player's name appears in the bottom white border. The backs carry a player profile and the serial number.

	Nm-Mt	Ex-Mt
COMPLETE SET (100)	75.00	22.00
COMMON PLAYER (1-65)	1.00	.30
COMMON CARD (66-100)	.50	.15
1 Otha Bailey	1.50	.45
2 Harry Barnes	1.00	.30
3 Gene Benson	1.00	.30
4 Bill Beverly	1.00	.30
5 Charlie Biot	1.00	.30
6 Bob Boyd	1.50	.45
7 Allen Bryant	1.00	.30
8 Marlin Carter	1.00	.30
9 Bill Cash	1.00	.30
10 Jim Cohen	1.00	.30
11 Elliot Coleman	1.00	.30
12 Johnnie Cowan	1.00	.30
13 Jimmie Crutchfield	1.50	.45
14 Saul Davis	1.00	.30
15 Piper Davis	1.50	.45
16 Leon Day	2.50	.75
17 Lou Dials	2.00	.60
18 Mahlon Duckett	1.50	.45
19 Felix Evans	1.00	.30
20 Rudy Fernandez	1.00	.30
21 Joe Fillmore	1.00	.30
22 George Giles	1.00	.30
23 Louis Gillis	1.00	.30
24 Stanley Glenn	1.00	.30
25 Willie Grace	1.00	.30
26 Wiley Griggs	1.00	.30
27 Albert Haywood	1.00	.30
28 Jimmy Hill	1.00	.30
29 Cowan Hyde	1.00	.30
30 Monte Irvin	3.00	.90
31 Sam Jethroe	1.50	.45
32 Connie Johnson	1.50	.45
33 Josh Johnson	1.50	.45
34 Clinton Jones	1.00	.30
35 Larry Kimbrough	1.00	.30
36 Clarence King	1.00	.30
37 Jim LaMarque	1.00	.30
38 Buck Leonard	3.00	.90
39 Max Manning	1.00	.30
40 Verdell Mathis	1.00	.30
41 Nath McClinic	1.00	.30
42 Clinton McCord	1.00	.30
43 Clyde McNeal	1.00	.30
44 John Miles	1.00	.30
45 Buck O'Neil	3.00	.90
46 Frank Pearson	1.00	.30
47 Art Pennington	1.00	.30
48 Nathaniel Peoples	1.00	.30
49 Andy Porter	1.00	.30
50 Ted(Double Duty) Radcliffe	1.50	.45
51 Chico Renfroe	1.00	.30
52 Bobby Robinson	1.50	.45
53 Tommy Sampson	1.50	.45
54 Joe Scott	1.00	.30
55 Joe Burt Scott	1.00	.30
56 Herb Simpson	1.00	.30
57 Lonnie Summers	1.00	.30
58 Alfred Surratt	1.50	.45
59 Bob Thurman	1.50	.45
60 Harold Tinker	1.00	.30
61 Quincy Trouppe	1.50	.45
62 Edsall Walker	1.00	.30
63 Al Wilmore	1.00	.30
64 Artie Wilson	1.50	.45
65 Jim Zapp	1.00	.30
66 Grays vs. Stars 1937	.50	.15
67 Grays vs. Eagles 1943	.50	.15
68 Homestead Grays 1944	.50	.15
69 Grays vs. Cuban Stars 1944	.50	.15
70 Grays vs. Cubans 1944	.50	.15
71 Grays vs. Eagles 1945	.50	.15
72 Eagles pitching staff 1941	.50	.15
73 Buckeyes infield 1945	.50	.15
74 Homestead Grays 1948	.50	.15
75 Chicago Murderers Row 1943	.50	.15
76 Indianapolis Clowns 1945	.50	.15
77 East All-Stars 1937	.50	.15
78 East All-Stars 1938	.50	.15
79 East All-Stars 1939	.50	.15
80 East All-Stars 1948	.50	.15
81 West All-Stars 1948	.50	.15
82 Homestead Grays 1931	.50	.15
83 Homestead Grays 1938	.50	.15
84 Pittsburgh Crawfords 1936	.50	.15
85 K.C. Monarchs 1934	.50	.15
86 K.C. Monarchs 1949	.50	.15
87 Chicago American Giants 1941	.50	.15
88 Chicago American Giants 1947	.50	.15
89 Memphis Red Sox 1940	.50	.15
90 Memphis Red Sox 1946	.50	.15
91 Birmingham B.B. 1946	.50	.15
92 Birmingham B.B. 1948	.50	.15
93 Birmingham B.B. 1950	.50	.15
94 Harlem Globetrotters 1948	.50	.15
95 Cleveland Buckeyes 1947	.50	.15
96 Philadelphia Stars 1944	.50	.15
97 Newark Eagles 1939	.50	.15
98 Baltimore Elite Giants 1949	.50	.15
99 Indianapolis Clowns 1943	.50	.15
100 Cincinnati Tigers 1937	.50	.15

1993 Negro League Retort Legends II

This 100-card second series of R.D. Retort Enterprises' Negro League Legends was issued in a brown box that has the set logo on the top stamped in gold foil. The cards have a postcard design, measuring approximately 3 1/2" by 5 1/2", and feature white-bordered sepia-tone player photos on their fronts. The player's (or team's) name appears in the lower margin. The back carries the player's (or team's) name on the left side, which is highlighted by a baseball bat icon. The set's logo appears at the lower right, next to the set's production number (out of 10,000).

	Nm-Mt	Ex-Mt
COMPLETE SET (100)	75.00	22.00
COMMON CARD (1-41)	1.00	.30
COMMON CARD (42-100)	.75	.23
1 Frank Barnes	1.00	.30
2 John L. Bissant	1.00	.30
3 Garnett E. Blair	1.00	.30
4 Jim(Fire Ball) Bolden	1.00	.30
5 Luther H. Branham	1.00	.30
6 Sherwood(Woody) Brewer	1.00	.30
7 Jimmy Dean	1.00	.30
8 Frank Duncan Jr.	1.50	.45
9 Wilmer(Red) Fields	1.00	.30
10 Harold(Beebop) Gordon	1.00	.30
11 Bill Greason	1.00	.30
12 Acie(Skeet) Griggs	1.00	.30
13 Napolean Gulley	1.00	.30
14 Ray Haggins	1.00	.30
15 Wilmer Harris	1.00	.30
16 Bob Harvey	1.00	.30
17 Jehosie Heard	1.50	.45
18 Gordon(Hoppy) Hopkins	1.00	.30
19 Herman(Doc) Horn	1.00	.30
20 James(Sap) Ivory	1.00	.30
21 Henry Kimbro	1.00	.30
22 Milfred(Rick) Laurent	1.00	.30
23 Ernest(The Kid) Long	1.00	.30
24 Frank Marsh	1.00	.30
25 Francis(Fran) Matthews	1.00	.30
26 Jim McCurine	1.00	.30
27 John Mitchell	1.00	.30
28 Lee Moody	1.50	.45
29 Rogers(Shape) Pierre	1.00	.30
30 Nathaniel(Nat) Pollard	1.00	.30
31 Merle Porter	1.00	.30
32 William Powell	1.00	.30
33 Ulysses A. Redd	1.00	.30
34 Harry(Lefty) Rhodes	1.00	.30
35 DeWitt Smallwood (Woody)	1.00	.30
36 Joseph B. Spencer	1.00	.30
37 Riley A. Stewart	1.00	.30
38 Earl Taborn	1.00	.30
39 Ron Teasley	1.00	.30
40 Joe Wiley	1.00	.30
41 Walter(Buck) Leonard	3.00	.90
42 Grays vs. B.E. Giants 1945	.75	.23
43 Grays vs. Monarchs 1945	.75	.23
44 Homestead Grays 1948	.75	.23
45 Pittsburgh Crawfords 1928	.75	.23
46 Pittsburgh Crawfords 1935	.75	.23
47 Kansas City Monarchs 1942	.75	.23
48 John(Buck) O'Neil MG William(Dizzy) Dismukes	.75	.23
49 Chicago American Giants 1942	.75	.23
50 Nashville Elite Giants 1935	.75	.23
51 Baltimore Elite Giants 1941	.75	.23
52 Birmingham Black Barons 1948	.75	.23
53 Birmingham Black Barons 1959	.75	.23
54 Memphis Red Sox 1954	.75	.23
55 Indianapolis ABC's 1923	.75	.23
56 Harlem Globetrotters 1948	.75	.23
57 Harlem Globetrotters 1948	.75	.23
58 Bismarck Barons 1955	.75	.23
59 Culiacan 1952	.75	.23
60 Santurce 1947	.75	.23
61 Pittsburgh Crawfords 1928	.75	.23
62 Pittsburgh Crawfords 1932	.75	.23
63 Pittsburgh Crawfords 1935	.75	.23
64 Homestead Grays 1937	.75	.23
65 Homestead Grays 1938	.75	.23
66 Homestead Grays 1940	.75	.23
67 Homestead Grays 1945	.75	.23
68 Homestead Grays 1948	.75	.23
69 Kansas City Monarchs 1932	.75	.23
70 Kansas City Monarchs 1934	.75	.23
71 Kansas City Monarchs 1941	.75	.23
72 Kansas City Monarchs 1946	.75	.23
73 Chicago American Giants 1950	.75	.23
74 Memphis Red Sox 1949	.75	.23
75 Birmingham Black Barons 1946	.75	.23
76 Birmingham Black Barons 1948	.75	.23
77 Birmingham Black Barons 1951	.75	.23
78 Birmingham Black Barons 1954	.75	.23
79 St. Louis Stars 1931	.75	.23
80 Newark Dodgers 1935	.75	.23
81 Brooklyn Eagles 1935	.75	.23
82 Newark Eagles 1946	.75	.23
83 Philadelphia Stars 1939	.75	.23
84 Philadelphia Stars 1946	.75	.23
85 Philadelphia Stars 1949	.75	.23
86 Nashville Elite Giants 1935	.75	.23
87 Baltimore Elite Giants 1939	.75	.23
88 Baltimore Elite Giants 1949	.75	.23
89 Cleveland Buckeyes 1947	.75	.23
90 Cincinnati Tigers 1936	.75	.23
91 Miami Ethiopian Clowns 1940	.75	.23
92 Indianapolis Clowns 1944	.75	.23
93 Indianapolis Clowns 1948	.75	.23
94 New York Cubans 1943	.75	.23
95 Harlem Globetrotters 1948	.75	.23
96 House of David 1938	1.50	.45
97 E.T. Community 1926	.75	.23
98 Bismarck Giants 1935	.75	.23
99 American All-Stars 1945	.75	.23
100 New York Stars 1949	.75	.23

1995 Negro League Legends I

This boxed set measures the standard size and was produced by the Negro League Baseball Players Association and noted sports artist Ron Lewis. Series I and II were both issued in one box. Just 25,000 sets were produced. The white-bordered fronts feature full color player paintings by Ron Lewis. The backs carry the player's name in white letters inside a pink bar and summarize the player's career.

	Nm-Mt	Ex-Mt
COMPLETE SET (31)	30.00	9.00
1 George Giles	1.00	.30
2 Bill Cash	1.00	.30
3 Bob Harvey	1.00	.30
4 Lyman Bostock Sr.	1.50	.45
5 Ray Dandridge	2.50	.75
6 Leon Day	2.50	.75
7 Verdell Mathis	1.00	.30
8 Jimmie Crutchfield	1.50	.45
9 Clyde McNeal	1.00	.30
10 Bill Wright	1.00	.30
11 Mahlon Duckett	1.00	.30
12 William (Bobby) Robinson	1.50	.45
13 Max Manning	1.00	.30
14 Armando Vasquez	1.00	.30
15 Jehosie Heard	1.50	.45
16 Quincy Trouppe	1.50	.45
17 Wilmer Fields	1.00	.30
18 Lonnie Blair	1.00	.30
19 Garnett Blair	1.00	.30
20 Monte Irvin	3.00	.90
21 Willie Mays	6.00	1.80
22 Walter (Buck) Leonard	3.50	1.05
23 Frank Evans	1.00	.30
24 Josh Gibson Jr.	2.00	.60
25 Ted Radcliffe (Double Duty)	1.50	.45
26 Josh Johnson	1.50	.45
27 Gene Benson	1.00	.30
28 Lester Lockett	1.50	.45
29 Cowan Hyde	1.00	.30
30 Rufus Lewis	1.00	.30
NNO Checklist	1.00	.30

1995 Negro League Legends II

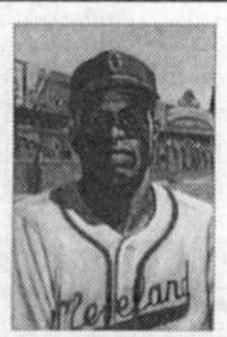
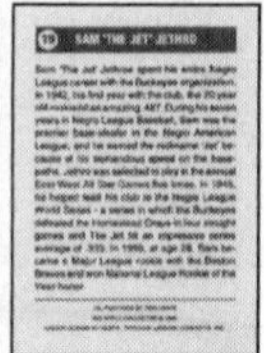

This boxed set measures the standard size and was produced by the Negro League Baseball Players Association and noted sports artist Ron Lewis. Series I and II were both issued in one box. Just 25,000 sets were produced. The white-bordered fronts feature full color player paintings by Ron Lewis. The backs carry the player's name in white letters inside a pink bar and summarize the player's career.

	Nm-Mt	Ex-Mt
COMPLETE SET (33)	30.00	9.00
1 Willie Mays / Ernie Banks / Hank Aaron	5.00	1.50
2 Lester Lockett / Lyman Bostock Sr. / Bill Wright	1.00	.30
3 Josh Gibson / Josh Gibson Jr. / Walter (Buck) Leonard	2.50	.75
4 Max Manning / Monte Irvin / Leon Day	2.00	.60
5 Armando Vazquez / Minnie Minoso / Martin Dihigo	1.50	.45
6 Ted Radcliffe (Double Duty)	1.50	.45
7 William (Bobby) Robinson / Bill Owens / Norman(Turkey) Stearnes	1.00	.30
8 Wilmer Fields / Edsall Walker / Josh Johnson	1.00	.30
9 Artie Wilson / Lionel Hampton	1.50	.45
10 Earl Taborn	1.00	.30
11 Barney Serrell (Bonnie)	1.00	.30
12 Rodolfo Fernandez (Rudy)	1.00	.30
13 Willie Pope	1.00	.30
14 Ray Noble	1.50	.45
15 Jim Cohen	1.00	.30
16 Henry Kimbro	1.00	.30
17 Charlie Biot	1.00	.30
18 Al Wilmore	1.00	.30
19 Sam Jethroe	2.00	.60
20 Tommy Sampson	1.00	.30
21 Charlie Rivera	1.00	.30
22 Claro Duany	1.00	.30
23 Russell Awkard	1.00	.30
24 Art Pennington	1.00	.30
25 Wilmer Harris	1.00	.30
26 Napoleon Gulley	1.00	.30
27 Emilio Navarro	1.00	.30
28 Andy Porter	1.00	.30
29 Willie Grace	1.00	.30
30 Red Moore	1.00	.30
31 Buck O'Neill UER (Card back says Walter "Buck" O'Niel)	2.50	.75
32 Stanley Glenn	1.00	.30
NNO Checklist UER (Says last name of #31 is Leonard should be O'Neill)	1.00	.30

1995 Negro League S.F. Examiner Tribute

This 12-card set was issued as a tribute by the San Francisco Examiner in honor of the Negro League's 75th Anniversary. The set was distributed in an uncut sepia and maroon sheet measuring approximately 14 1/4" by 11 1/4". The cards are unnumbered and checklisted below as they appear on the sheet from the top left to the bottom right.

	Nm-Mt	Ex-Mt
COMPLETE SET (12)	10.00	3.00
1 Walter"Buck" Leonard	1.50	.45
2 James"Cool Papa" Bell	2.00	.60
3 Josh Gibson	3.00	.90
4 William"Judy" Johnson	1.00	.30
5 John Henry"Pop" Lloyd	1.00	.30
6 Leon Day	1.50	.45
7 Martin Dihigo	1.50	.45
8 Monte Irvin	2.00	.60
9 Oscar Charleston	1.00	.30
10 Ray Dandridge	1.50	.45
11 Andrew"Rube" Foster	1.00	.30
12 Leroy"Satchel" Paige	3.00	.90

1996 Negro League Baseball Museum

This nine-card set measures approximately 3 1/2" by 5 1/2" and features black-and-white player photos. The backs carry career information. The cards are unnumbered and

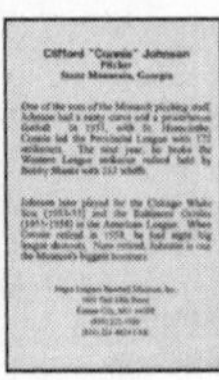

checklisted below in alphabetical order.

	Nm-Mt	Ex-Mt
COMPLETE SET (9)	10.00	3.00
1 Ulysses Hollimon	1.00	.30
2 Herman"Doc" Horn Jr.	1.00	.30
3 Clifford"Connie" Johnson	2.00	.60
4 James"Lefty" LaMarque	1.00	.30
5 Henry"Pistol" Mason	1.50	.45
6 Bob Motley UMP	1.00	.30
7 John"Buck" O'Neil	2.50	.75
8 Jesse Rogers	1.00	.30
9 Alfred"Slick" Surratt	1.50	.45

1997 Negro League Playing Cards

This 56-card set honors the legendary players of the Negro Leagues and was distributed by the International Society of Athletes. The set could be obtained by sending in at least a $45 donation. The fronts of these rounded-corner cards feature black-and-white player photos in white borders. The player's name, position and team name are printed in black in the bottom border. The black backs carry the name of the set and the sponsor printed in gold. Since this set is similar to a playing card set, the set is checklisted below as if it were a playing card deck. In the checklist C means Clubs, D means Diamonds, H means Hearts and S means Spades. The cards are checklisted in playing order by suits and numbers are assigned to Aces (1), Jacks (11), Queens (12) and Kings (13).

	Nm-Mt	Ex-Mt
COMPLETE SET (56)	150.00	45.00
1C Josh Gibson	10.00	3.00
1D Jackie Robinson	15.00	4.50
1H James(Cool Papa) Bell	4.00	1.20
1S Satchel Paige	10.00	3.00
2C Bill Cash	1.50	.45
2D Sam Haynes	1.50	.45
2H Samuel(Harriston) Hairston	2.00	.60
2S Joe Greene	1.50	.45
3C Fran Matthews	1.50	.45
3D Bob(The Rope) Boyd	2.00	.60
3H John(Buck) O'Neil	4.00	1.20
3S James(Red) Moore	1.50	.45
4C Fred(Leap) Bankhead	1.50	.45
4D William(Bonnie) Serrell	1.50	.45
4H Lorenzo(Piper) Davis	2.00	.60
4S Othello(Chico) Renfroe	1.50	.45
5C Alex Radcliffe	1.50	.45
5D Minnie Minoso	4.00	1.20
5H Parnell Woods	1.50	.45
5S William(Judy) Johnson	4.00	1.20
6C Artie Wilson	2.00	.60
6D John Henry(Pop) Lloyd	4.00	1.20
6H Thomas(Pee Wee) Butts	1.50	.45
6S Willie(The Devil) Wells	4.00	1.20
7C Jim Zapp	1.50	.45
7D Art(Superman) Pennington	1.50	.45
7H Oscar Charleston	4.00	1.20
7S Gene Benson	2.00	.60
8C Henry(Kimmie) Kimbro	1.50	.45
8D Francisco(Pancho) Coimbre	1.50	.45
8H Larry Doby	4.00	1.20
8S Willard(Sunnie) Brown	1.50	.45
9C Chet Brewer	1.50	.45
9D Sam(Jet) Jethroe	3.00	.90
9H Hilton Smith	4.00	1.20
9S Martin Dihigo	4.00	1.20
10C Verdell(Lefty) Mathis	1.50	.45
10D Joe Black	4.00	1.20
10H Leon Day	2.00	.60
10S Don Newcombe	4.00	1.20
11C Junior Gilliam	4.00	1.20
11D Monte Irvin	4.00	1.20
11H Walter(Buck) Leonard	4.00	1.20
11S Ray(Hooks) Dandridge	3.00	.90
12C Marcenia(Toni) Stone	4.00	1.20
12D Effie Manley OWN Newark Eagles	2.00	.60
12H Pamela Pryer-Fuller Legends Reunion Organizer	1.50	.45
12S Billie Harden OWN Atlanta Black Crackers	1.50	.45
13C Willie Mays	10.00	3.00
13D Hank Aaron	10.00	3.00
13H Ernie Banks	4.00	1.20
13S Roy(Campy) Campanella	4.00	1.20
JKO Ted(Double Duty) Radcliffe	2.00	.60
SJKO Andrew(Rube) Foster	2.00	.60
NNO Wilmer(Red) Fields	1.50	.45
NNO Clifford(Connie) Johnson	2.00	.60

1921 Neilson's V61

The 1921 Neilson's Chocolate set, titled "Big League Baseball Stars", contains 120 cards and is essentially a reproduction of the E120 set. The cards measure approximately 2" by 3 1/4". The fronts feature oval-shaped black-and-white player photos with ornamented borders. The player's name, position and team also appear on the front. The backs give information about this set and carry an ad for Neilson's chocolate. There are two versions of this set: a numbered paper issue and an unnumbered cardboard issue. Cards of the unnumbered cardboard issue are worth approximately 50 percent more than the values listed in the checklist below.

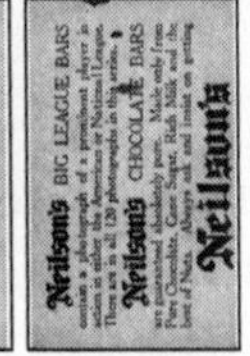

	Ex-Mt	VG
COMPLETE SET (120)	8500.00	4200.00
1 George Burns	50.00	25.00
2 John Tobin	40.00	20.00
3 Tom Zachary	50.00	25.00
4 Joe Bush	50.00	25.00
5 Lu Blue	40.00	20.00
6 Tillie Walker	40.00	20.00
7 Carl Mays	50.00	25.00
8 Goose Goslin	80.00	40.00
9 Ed Rommel	50.00	25.00
10 Charles Robertson	40.00	20.00
11 Ralph Perkins	40.00	20.00
12 Joe Sewell	80.00	40.00
13 Harry Hooper	80.00	40.00
14 Red Faber	80.00	40.00
15 Bibb Falk	40.00	20.00
16 George Uhle	50.00	25.00
17 Emory Rigney	40.00	20.00
18 George Dauss	40.00	20.00
19 Herman Pillette	40.00	20.00
20 Wally Schang	50.00	25.00
21 Lawrence Woodall	40.00	20.00
22 Steve O'Neill	50.00	25.00
23 Bing Miller	40.00	20.00
24 Sylvester Johnson	40.00	20.00
25 Henry Severeid	40.00	20.00
26 Dave Danforth	40.00	20.00
27 Harry Heilmann	80.00	40.00
28 Bert Cole	40.00	20.00
29 Eddie Collins	80.00	40.00
30 Ty Cobb	1200.00	600.00
31 Bill Wambsganss	50.00	25.00
32 George Sisler	80.00	40.00
33 Bob Veach	40.00	20.00
34 Earl Sheely	40.00	20.00
35 Pat Collins	40.00	20.00
36 Frank Davis	40.00	20.00
37 Babe Ruth	2000.00	1000.00
38 Bryan Harris	40.00	20.00
39 Bob Shawkey	60.00	30.00
40 Urban Shocker	50.00	25.00
41 Martin McManus	40.00	20.00
42 Clark Pittenger	40.00	20.00
43 Sam Jones	50.00	25.00
44 Waite Hoyt	80.00	40.00
45 Johnny Mostil	40.00	20.00
46 Mike Menosky	40.00	20.00
47 Walter Johnson	400.00	200.00
48 Wally Pipp	50.00	25.00
49 Walter Gerber	40.00	20.00
50 Ed Gharrity	40.00	20.00
51 Frank Ellerbe	40.00	20.00
52 Kenneth Williams	60.00	30.00
53 Joe Hauser	50.00	25.00
54 Carson Bigbee	40.00	20.00
55 Irish Meusel	40.00	20.00
56 Milton Stock	40.00	20.00
57 Wilbur Cooper	50.00	25.00
58 Tom Griffith	40.00	20.00
59 Butch Henline	40.00	20.00
60 Bubbles Hargrave	40.00	20.00
61 Russel Wrightstone	40.00	20.00
62 Frankie Frisch	80.00	40.00
63 Jack Peters	40.00	20.00
64 Walter Ruether	50.00	25.00
65 Bill Doak	40.00	20.00
66 Marty Callaghan	40.00	20.00
67 Sammy Bohne	40.00	20.00
68 Earl Hamilton	40.00	20.00
69 Grover Alexander	150.00	75.00
70 George Burns	40.00	20.00
71 Max Carey	80.00	40.00
72 Adolph Luque	60.00	30.00
73 Dave Bancroft	80.00	40.00
74 Vic Aldridge	40.00	20.00
75 Jack Smith	40.00	20.00
76 Bob O'Farrell	50.00	25.00
77 Pete Donohue	40.00	20.00
78 Babe Pinelli	50.00	25.00
79 Ed Roush	80.00	40.00
80 Norman Boeckel	40.00	20.00
81 Rogers Hornsby	250.00	125.00
82 George Toporcer	40.00	20.00
83 Ivy Wingo	40.00	20.00
84 Virgil Cheeves	40.00	20.00
85 Vern Clemons	40.00	20.00
86 Lawrence Miller	40.00	20.00
87 Johnny Kelleher	40.00	20.00
88 Heinie Groh	50.00	25.00
89 Burleigh Grimes	80.00	40.00
90 Rabbit Maranville	80.00	40.00
91 Babe Adams	50.00	25.00
92 Lee King	40.00	20.00
93 Art Nehf	50.00	25.00
94 Frank Snyder	40.00	20.00
95 Raymond Powell	40.00	20.00
96 Wilbur Hubbell	40.00	20.00
97 Leon Cadore	40.00	20.00
98 Joe Oeschger	40.00	20.00
99 Jake Daubert	40.00	20.00
100 Will Sherdel	40.00	20.00
101 Hank DeBerry	40.00	20.00
102 Johnny Lavan	40.00	20.00
103 Jesse Haines	80.00	40.00
104 Joe Rapp	40.00	20.00
105 Oscar Ray Grimes	40.00	20.00
106 Ross Youngs	80.00	40.00
107 Art Fletcher	40.00	20.00
108 Clyde Barnhart	40.00	20.00
109 Pat Duncan	40.00	20.00
110 Charlie Hollocher	40.00	20.00
111 Horace Ford	40.00	20.00
112 Bill Cunningham	40.00	20.00
113 Walter Schmidt	40.00	20.00
114 Joe Schultz	40.00	20.00
115 John Morrison	40.00	20.00
116 Jimmy Caveney	40.00	20.00
117 Zach Wheat	80.00	40.00
118 Cy Williams	50.00	25.00
119 George Kelly	80.00	40.00
120 Jimmy Ring	40.00	20.00

1984 Nestle 792

The cards in this 792-card standard-size set are extremely similar to the 1984 Topps regular issue (except for the Nestle logo instead of Topps logo on the front). In conjunction with Topps, the Nestle Company issued this set as six sheets available as a premium. The set was (as detailed on the back of the checklist card for the Nestle Dream Team cards) originally available from the Nestle Company in full sheets of 132 cards, 24" by 48", for 4.95 plus five Nestle candy wrappers per sheet. The backs are virtually identical to the Topps cards of this year, i.e., same player-number correspondence. These sheets have been cut up into individual cards and are available from a few dealers around the country. This is one of the few instances in this hobby where the complete uncut sheet is worth considerably less than the sum of the individual cards due to the expense required in having the sheet cut professionally (and precisely) into individual cards. Supposedly less than 5000 sets were printed. Since the checklist is exactly the same as that of the 1984 Topps, these Nestle cards are generally priced as a multiple of the corresponding Topps card. Individual Nestle cards are priced at up to eight times the corresponding 1984 Topps price. Please see multiplication tables below. Beware also on this set to look for fakes and forgeries. Cards billed as Nestle proofs in black and white are fakes; there are even a few counterfeits in color.

	Nm-Mt	Ex-Mt
COMP. CUT SET (792)	350.00	140.00
*STARS:4X to 8X BASIC CARDS		
*ROOKIES: 3X to 6X BASIC CARDS		

1984 Nestle Dream Team

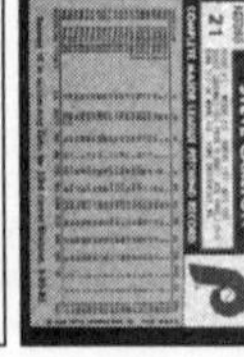

The cards in this 22-card set measure the standard size. In conjunction with Topps, the Nestle Company issued this set entitled the Dream Team. The fronts have the Nestle trademark in the upper frameline, and the backs are identical to the Topps cards of this year except for the number and the Nestle's logo. Cards 1-11 feature stars of the American League while cards 12-22 show National League stars. Each league's "Dream Team" consists of eight position players and three pitchers. The cards were included with the Nestle chocolate bars as a pack of four (three player cards and a checklist header card. This set should not be confused with the Nestle 792-card (same player-number correspondence as 1984 Topps 792) set.

	Nm-Mt	Ex-Mt
COMPLETE SET (22)	25.00	10.00
1 Eddie Murray	2.00	.80
2 Lou Whitaker	1.00	.40
3 George Brett	4.00	1.60
4 Cal Ripken	8.00	3.20
5 Jim Rice	.75	.30
6 Dave Winfield	1.00	.40
7 Lloyd Moseby	.25	.10
8 Lance Parrish	.75	.30
9 LaMarr Hoyt	.25	.10
10 Ron Guidry	.50	.20
11 Dan Quisenberry	.25	.10
12 Steve Garvey	1.00	.40
13 Johnny Ray	.25	.10
14 Mike Schmidt	3.00	1.20
15 Ozzie Smith	3.00	1.20
16 Andre Dawson	1.00	.40
17 Tim Raines	.75	.30
18 Dale Murphy	1.00	.40
19 Tony Pena	.50	.20
20 John Denny	.25	.10
21 Steve Carlton	1.00	.40
22 Al Holland	.25	.10
NNO Checklist	.25	.10

1987 Nestle Dream Team

This 33-card standard-size set is, in a sense, three sets: Golden Era (1-11 gold), AL Modern Era (12-22 red), and NL Modern Era (23-33 blue). Cards have color coded borders by era. The first 11 card photos are in black and white. The Nestle set was apparently not licensed by Major League Baseball and hence the team logos are not shown in the photos. Six-packs of certain Nestle candy bars contained three cards; cards were also available through a send-in offer.

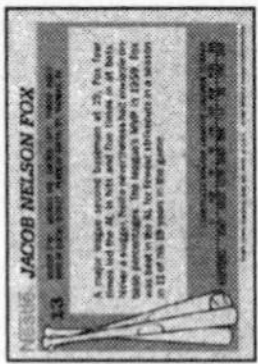

	Nm-Mt	Ex-Mt
COMPLETE SET (33)	15.00	6.00
1 Lou Gehrig	1.50	.60
2 Rogers Hornsby	.25	.10
3 Pie Traynor	.25	.10
4 Honus Wagner	.75	.30
5 Babe Ruth	3.00	1.20
6 Tris Speaker	.25	.10
7 Ty Cobb	2.00	.80
8 Mickey Cochrane	.25	.10
9 Walter Johnson	.75	.30
10 Carl Hubbell	.25	.10
11 Jimmy Foxx	.75	.30
12 Rod Carew	.75	.30
13 Nellie Fox	.25	.10
14 Brooks Robinson	.50	.20
15 Luis Aparicio	.25	.10
16 Frank Robinson	.25	.10
17 Mickey Mantle	3.00	1.20
18 Ted Williams	2.00	.80
19 Yogi Berra	.75	.30
20 Bob Feller	.50	.20
21 Whitey Ford	.50	.20
22 Harmon Killebrew	.25	.10
23 Stan Musial	1.50	.60
24 Jackie Robinson	2.00	.80
25 Eddie Mathews	.25	.10
26 Ernie Banks	.50	.20
27 Roberto Clemente	2.00	.80
28 Willie Mays	2.00	.80
29 Hank Aaron	2.00	.80
30 Johnny Bench	.50	.20
31 Bob Gibson	.50	.20
32 Warren Spahn	.25	.10
33 Duke Snider	.75	.30
NNO Checklist	.15	.06

1988 Nestle

This 44-card standard-size set has yellow borders. This set was produced for Nestle by Mike Schechter Associates and was printed in Canada. The Nestle set was apparently not licensed by Major League Baseball and hence the team logos are not shown in the photos. The backs are printed in red and blue on white card stock.

	Nm-Mt	Ex-Mt
COMPLETE SET (44)	35.00	14.00
1 Roger Clemens	4.00	1.60
2 Dale Murphy	1.00	.40
3 Eric Davis	.50	.20
4 Gary Gaetti	.50	.20
5 Ozzie Smith	2.50	1.00
6 Mike Schmidt	2.00	.80
7 Ozzie Guillen	.50	.20
8 John Franco	.50	.20
9 Andre Dawson	1.00	.40
10 Mark McGwire	6.00	2.40
11 Bret Saberhagen	.50	.20
12 Benito Santiago	.25	.10
13 Jose Uribe	.25	.10
14 Will Clark	1.50	.60
15 Don Mattingly	4.00	1.60
16 Juan Samuel	.25	.10
17 Jack Clark	.25	.10
18 Darryl Strawberry	.50	.20
19 Bill Doran	.25	.10
20 Pete Incaviglia	.25	.10
21 Dwight Gooden	.50	.20
22 Willie Randolph	.50	.20
23 Tim Wallach	.25	.10
24 Pedro Guerrero	.25	.10
25 Steve Bedrosian	.25	.10
26 Gary Carter	1.50	.60
27 Jeff Reardon	.50	.20
28 Dave Righetti	.25	.10
29 Frank White	.50	.20
30 Buddy Bell	.50	.20
31 Tim Raines	.50	.20
32 Wade Boggs	1.50	.60
33 Dave Winfield	1.50	.60
34 George Bell	.50	.20
35 Alan Trammell	.75	.30
36 Joe Carter	.75	.30
37 Jose Canseco	1.50	.60
38 Carlton Fisk	1.50	.60
39 Kirby Puckett	1.50	.60
40 Tony Gwynn	4.00	1.60
41 Matt Nokes	.25	.10
42 Keith Hernandez	.50	.20
43 Nolan Ryan	8.00	3.20
44 Wally Joyner	.50	.20

2002 Nestle

This six-card set was inserted into various Nestle's Ice Cream products as a bonus for buying that companies product. These cards were produced for Nestle by Topps and feature both the Topps and the Nestle logo on the front. These cards were wrapped in cellophane to help protect them from the food.

	Nm-Mt	Ex-Mt
COMPLETE SET	10.00	3.00
1 Barry Bonds	1.50	.45
2 Chipper Jones	1.50	.45
3 Mike Piazza	2.00	.60
4 Alex Rodriguez	1.50	.45
5 Sammy Sosa	1.50	.45
6 Ichiro Suzuki	3.00	.90

1993 Nestle Quik Bunnies

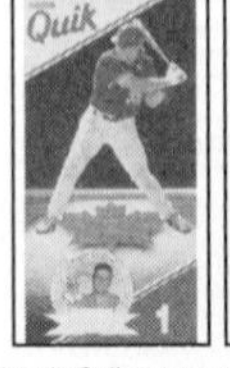

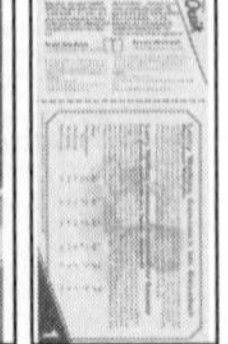

This Nestle Quik set consists of one player card and 23 bunny cards in which the bunny is portrayed in cartoons participating in various sports activities. The card measures approximately 3 13/16" by 7 5/8" and have rounded corners. The Walker card has a color player action cutout superposed over a starry sky with Walker standing over the red maple leaf of the Canadian flag. The Nestle Quik logo appears at the upper left on a yellow diagonal section. A circular headshot of Walker and the bunny at the lower left overlays a brown diagonal section showing the card number. The horizontal back has bilingual major league highlights followed by stats. The left side carries bilingual instructions on how to order a Collector Cards Binder. The cards are numbered on the front and back.

	Nm-Mt	Ex-Mt
COMPLETE SET (24)	6.00	1.80
COMMON BUNNY (2-24)	.25	.07
1 Larry Walker	.25	.07

1895 Newsboy N566

Newsboy Cut Plug was a tobacco brand by the National Tobacco Works of New York. The cabinet cards associated with this brand were offered as premiums in exchange for coupons or tags found in or on the packages. They were believed to have been issued around 1895. Although a number 841 has been seen, this series-which also contains actresses-has never been completely checklisted, and its exact length is not known. At this time, only 12 baseball players have been discovered. We have checklisted only the baseball players and priced them.

	Ex-Mt	VG
COMPLETE SET (13)	15000.00	7500.00
174 W.H. Murphy	1000.00	500.00
175 Amos Rusie	2500.00	1250.00
176 Michael Tiernan	1000.00	500.00
177 Eddie Burke	1000.00	500.00
178 Jack Doyle	1000.00	500.00
179 Shorty Fuller	1000.00	500.00
180 George van Haltren	1000.00	500.00
181 Dave Foutz	1000.00	500.00
182 Jouett Meekin	1000.00	500.00
201 W.H. (Dad) Clark (street clothes)	1000.00	500.00
202 Parke Wilson (street clothes)	1000.00	500.00
586 John M. Ward portrait arms folded	1800.00	900.00
587 John M. Ward standing full length	1800.00	900.00

1992 NewSport

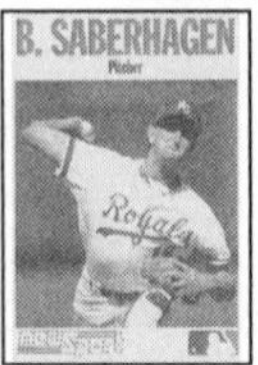

This set of 30 glossy player photos was sponsored by NewSport and issued in France. The month when each card was issued is printed as a tagline on the card back. The set was also available in uncut strips. The cards measure approximately 4" by 6" and display glossy color player photos with white borders. The player's name and position appear in the top border, while the NewSport and MLB logos adorn the bottom of the card face. In French, the backs present biography, complete statistics, and career summary. The cards are unnumbered and checklisted below in alphabetical order.

	Nm-Mt	Ex-Mt
COMPLETE SET (30)	300.00	90.00
1 Roberto Alomar	8.00	2.40
2 Wade Boggs	12.00	3.60
3 George Brett	25.00	7.50
4 Will Clark	10.00	3.00
5 Eric Davis	4.00	1.20
6 Rob Dibble	4.00	1.20
7 Doug Drabek	2.00	.60
8 Julio Franco	4.00	1.20
9 Ken Griffey Jr.	30.00	9.00
10 Rickey Henderson	15.00	4.50
11 Kent Hrbek	2.00	.60
12 Bo Jackson	8.00	2.40
13 Howard Johnson	2.00	.60
14 Barry Larkin	8.00	2.40
15 Don Mattingly	25.00	7.50
16 Fred McGriff	6.00	1.80
17 Mark McGwire	40.00	12.00
18 Jack Morris	2.00	.60
19 Lloyd Moseby	2.00	.60
20 Terry Pendleton	2.00	.60
21 Cal Ripken	50.00	15.00
22 Nolan Ryan	50.00	15.00
23 Bret Saberhagen	2.00	.60
24 Ryne Sandberg	15.00	4.50
25 Benito Santiago	4.00	1.20
26 Mike Scioscia	4.00	1.20
27 Ozzie Smith	20.00	6.00
28 Darryl Strawberry	4.00	1.20
29 Andy Van Slyke	2.00	.60
30 Frank Viola	2.00	.60

1997 New Pinnacle

The 1997 New Pinnacle set was issued in one series totalling 200 cards and distributed in 10-card packs with a suggested retail price of $2.99. The fronts feature borderless color action player photos with gold printing. The backs carry another smaller player photo and biographical and statistical information. An Alex Rodriguez Sample card was distributed to dealers and hobby media several weeks prior to the product's release. Subsets include East meets West (178-187), Aura (188-197) and Checklists (198-200). Notable Rookie Cards include Brian Giles.

	Nm-Mt	Ex-Mt
COMPLETE SET (200)	25.00	7.50
1 Ken Griffey Jr.	1.25	.35
2 Sammy Sosa	1.25	.35
3 Greg Maddux	1.25	.35
4 Matt Williams	.30	.09
5 Jason Isringhausen	.30	.09
6 Gregg Jefferies	.30	.09
7 Chili Davis	.30	.09
8 Paul O'Neill	.50	.15
9 Larry Walker	.50	.15
10 Ellis Burks	.30	.09
11 Cliff Floyd	.30	.09
12 Albert Belle	.30	.09
13 Javier Lopez	.30	.09
14 David Cone	.30	.09
15 Jose Canseco	.75	.23
16 Todd Zeile	.30	.09
17 Bernard Gilkey	.30	.09
18 Andres Galarraga	.30	.09
19 Chris Snopek	.30	.09
20 Tim Salmon	.50	.15
21 Roger Clemens	1.50	.45
22 Reggie Sanders	.30	.09
23 John Jaha	.30	.09
24 Andy Pettitte	.50	.15
25 Kenny Lofton	.30	.09
26 Robb Nen	.30	.09
27 John Wetteland	.30	.09
28 Bobby Bonilla	.30	.09
29 Hideo Nomo	.75	.23
30 Cecil Fielder	.30	.09
31 Garret Anderson	.30	.09
32 Pat Hentgen	.30	.09
33 Dave Justice	.30	.09
34 Billy Wagner	.30	.09
35 Al Leiter	.30	.09
36 Mark Wohlers	.30	.09
37 Rondell White	.30	.09
38 Charles Johnson	.30	.09
39 Mark Grace	.50	.15
40 Pedro Martinez	.75	.23
41 Tom Goodwin	.30	.09
42 Manny Ramirez	.30	.09
43 Greg Vaughn	.30	.09
44 Brian Jordan	.30	.09
45 Mike Piazza	1.25	.35
46 Roberto Hernandez	.30	.09
47 Wade Boggs	.50	.15
48 Scott Sanders	.30	.09
49 Alex Gonzalez	.30	.09
50 Kevin Brown	.30	.09
51 Bob Higginson	.30	.09
52 Ken Caminiti	.30	.09
53 Derek Jeter	2.00	.60
54 Carlos Baerga	.30	.09
55 Jay Buhner	.30	.09
56 Tim Naehring	.30	.09
57 Jeff Bagwell	.50	.15
58 Steve Finley	.30	.09
59 Kevin Appier	.30	.09
60 Jay Bell	.30	.09
61 Ivan Rodriguez	.75	.23
62 Terrell Wade	.30	.09
63 Rusty Greer	.30	.09
64 Juan Guzman	.30	.09
65 Fred McGriff	.50	.15
66 Tino Martinez	.50	.15
67 Ray Lankford	.30	.09
68 Juan Gonzalez	.75	.23
69 Ron Gant	.30	.09
70 Jack McDowell	.30	.09
71 Tony Gwynn	1.00	.30
72 Joe Carter	.30	.09
73 Wilson Alvarez	.30	.09
74 Jason Giambi	.75	.23
75 Brian Hunter	.30	.09
76 Michael Tucker	.30	.09
77 Andy Benes	.30	.09
78 Brady Anderson	.30	.09
79 Ramon Martinez	.30	.09
80 Troy Percival	.30	.09
81 Alex Rodriguez	1.25	.35
82 Jim Thome	.75	.23
83 Denny Neagle	.30	.09
84 Rafael Palmeiro	.50	.15
85 Jose Valentin	.30	.09
86 Marc Newfield	.30	.09
87 Mariano Rivera	.50	.15
88 Alan Benes	.30	.09
89 Jimmy Key	.30	.09
90 Joe Randa	.30	.09
91 Cal Ripken	2.50	.75
92 Craig Biggio	.50	.15
93 Dean Palmer	.30	.09
94 Gary Sheffield	.30	.09
95 Ismael Valdes	.30	.09
96 John Valentin	.30	.09
97 Johnny Damon	.30	.09
98 Mo Vaughn	.30	.09
99 Paul Sorrento	.30	.09
100 Randy Johnson	.75	.23
101 Raul Mondesi	.30	.09
102 Roberto Alomar	.75	.23
103 Royce Clayton	.30	.09
104 Mark Grudzielanek	.30	.09
105 Wally Joyner	.30	.09
106 Wil Cordero	.30	.09
107 Will Clark	.75	.23
108 Chuck Knoblauch	.30	.09
109 Derek Bell	.30	.09
110 Henry Rodriguez	.30	.09
111 Edgar Renteria	.30	.09
112 Travis Fryman	.30	.09
113 Eric Young	.30	.09
114 Sandy Alomar Jr.	.30	.09
115 Darin Erstad	.30	.09
116 Barry Larkin	.75	.23
117 Barry Bonds	2.00	.60
118 Frank Thomas	.75	.23
119 Carlos Delgado	.30	.09
120 Jason Kendall	.30	.09
121 Todd Hollandsworth	.30	.09
122 Jim Edmonds	.30	.09
123 Chipper Jones	.75	.23
124 Jeff Fassero	.30	.09
125 Deion Sanders	.50	.15
126 Matt Lawton	.30	.09
127 Ryan Klesko	.30	.09
128 Mike Mussina	.75	.23
129 Paul Molitor	.50	.15
130 Dante Bichette	.30	.09
131 Bill Pulsipher	.30	.09
132 Todd Hundley	.30	.09
133 J.T. Snow	.30	.09
134 Chuck Finley	.30	.09
135 Shawn Green	.30	.09
136 Charles Nagy	.30	.09
137 Willie Greene	.30	.09
138 Marty Cordova	.30	.09
139 Eddie Murray	.75	.23
140 Ryne Sandberg	1.25	.35
141 Alex Fernandez	.30	.09
142 Mark McGwire	2.00	.60
143 Eric Davis	.30	.09
144 Jermaine Dye	.30	.09
145 Ruben Sierra	.30	.09
146 Damon Buford	.30	.09
147 John Smoltz	.50	.15
148 Alex Ochoa	.30	.09
149 Moises Alou	.30	.09
150 Rico Brogna	.30	.09
151 Terry Steinbach	.30	.09
152 Jeff King	.30	.09
153 Carlos Garcia	.30	.09
154 Tom Glavine	.50	.15
155 Edgar Martinez	.50	.15
156 Kevin Elster	.30	.09
157 Darryl Hamilton	.30	.09
158 Jason Dickson	.30	.09
159 Kevin Orie	.30	.09
160 Bubba Trammell RC	.30	.09
161 Jose Guillen	.30	.09
162 Brant Brown	.30	.09
163 Wendell Magee	.30	.09
164 Scott Spiezio	.30	.09
165 Todd Walker	.30	.09
166 Rod Myers	.30	.09
167 Damon Mashore	.30	.09
168 Wilton Guerrero	.30	.09
169 Vladimir Guerrero	.75	.23
170 Nomar Garciaparra	1.25	.35
171 Shannon Stewart	.30	.09
172 Scott Rolen	.50	.15
173 Bob Abreu	.30	.09
174 Danny Patterson	.30	.09
175 Andruw Jones	.30	.09
176 Brian Giles RC	1.50	.45
177 Dmitri Young	.30	.09
178 Cal Ripken EMW	1.25	.35
179 C. Knoblauch EMW	.30	.09
180 A.Rodriguez EMW	.75	.23
181 A.Galarraga EMW	.30	.09
182 Pedro Martinez EMW	.50	.15
183 B.Anderson EMW	.30	.09
184 Barry Bonds EMW	.75	.23
185 Ivan Rodriguez EMW	.50	.15
186 Gary Sheffield EMW	.30	.09
187 Denny Neagle EMW	.30	.09
188 Mark McGwire AURA	1.00	.30
189 Ellis Burks AURA	.30	.09
190 Alex Rodriguez AURA	.75	.23
191 Mike Piazza AURA	.75	.23
192 Barry Bonds AURA	.75	.23
193 Albert Belle AURA	.30	.09
194 Chipper Jones AURA	.50	.15
195 Juan Gonzalez AURA	.50	.15
196 B.Anderson AURA	.30	.09
197 Frank Thomas AURA	.50	.15
198 Vladimir Guerrero CL	.50	.15
199 Todd Walker CL	.30	.09
200 Scott Rolen CL	.30	.09
S81 A.Rodriguez Sample	2.00	.60

1997 New Pinnacle Artist's Proofs

Randomly inserted in packs at a rate of one in 39, this 200-card set is a fractured parallel version of the regular set and features exclusive Dufex all-foil print technology in varying levels of scarcity utilizing finishes of Red, Blue and Green foil. The 125 Reds are scarce, 50 Blues are scarcer, and the 25 Greens represent the top stars with the scarcest printing. Each card is stamped with the "Artist's Proof" seal.

	Nm-Mt	Ex-Mt
COMMON RED	3.00	.90
COMMON BLUE	6.00	1.80
COMMON GREEN	20.00	6.00
1 Ken Griffey Jr. G	40.00	12.00
2 Sammy Sosa B	30.00	9.00
3 Greg Maddux G	40.00	12.00
4 Matt Williams B	8.00	2.40
5 Jason Isringhausen R	3.00	.90
6 Gregg Jefferies R	3.00	.90
7 Chili Davis R	3.00	.90
8 Paul O'Neill R	5.00	1.50
9 Larry Walker R	5.00	1.50
10 Ellis Burks B	8.00	2.40
11 Cliff Floyd R	3.00	.90
12 Albert Belle G	10.00	3.00
13 Javier Lopez R	3.00	.90
14 David Cone R	3.00	.90
15 Jose Canseco B	20.00	6.00
16 Todd Zeile R	8.00	2.40
17 Bernard Gilkey B	8.00	2.40
18 Andres Galarraga B	8.00	2.40
19 Chris Snopek R	3.00	.90
20 Tim Salmon B	12.00	3.60
21 Roger Clemens B	40.00	12.00
22 Reggie Sanders R	3.00	.90
23 John Jaha R	3.00	.90
24 Andy Pettitte B	12.00	3.60
25 Kenny Lofton G	10.00	3.00
26 Robb Nen R	3.00	.90
27 John Wetteland B	8.00	2.40
28 Bobby Bonilla R	3.00	.90
29 Hideo Nomo G	25.00	7.50
30 Cecil Fielder R	3.00	.90
31 Garret Anderson R	3.00	.90
32 Pat Hentgen R	3.00	.90
33 Dave Justice R	3.00	.90
34 Billy Wagner R	3.00	.90
35 Al Leiter R	3.00	.90
36 Mark Wohlers R	3.00	.90
37 Rondell White R	3.00	.90
38 Charles Johnson R	3.00	.90
39 Mark Grace R	5.00	1.50
40 Pedro Martinez R	8.00	2.40
41 Tom Goodwin R	3.00	.90
42 Manny Ramirez B	8.00	2.40
43 Greg Vaughn R	3.00	.90
44 Brian Jordan B	8.00	2.40
45 Mike Piazza G	40.00	12.00
46 Roberto Hernandez R	3.00	.90
47 Wade Boggs B	12.00	3.60
48 Scott Sanders R	3.00	.90
49 Alex Gonzalez R	3.00	.90
50 Kevin Brown R	3.00	.90
51 Bob Higginson B	8.00	2.40
52 Ken Caminiti B	8.00	2.40
53 Derek Jeter G	60.00	18.00
54 Carlos Baerga R	3.00	.90
55 Jay Buhner B	8.00	2.40
56 Tim Naehring R	3.00	.90
57 Jeff Bagwell G	15.00	4.50
58 Steve Finley R	3.00	.90
59 Kevin Appier R	3.00	.90
60 Jay Bell R	3.00	.90
61 Ivan Rodriguez B	20.00	6.00
62 Terrell Wade R	3.00	.90
63 Rusty Greer R	3.00	.90
64 Juan Guzman R	3.00	.90
65 Fred McGriff R	5.00	1.50
66 Tino Martinez R	5.00	1.50
67 Ray Lankford R	3.00	.90
68 Juan Gonzalez G	25.00	7.50
69 Ron Gant R	3.00	.90
70 Jack McDowell R	3.00	.90
71 Tony Gwynn B	25.00	7.50
72 Joe Carter B	8.00	2.40
73 Wilson Alvarez R	3.00	.90
74 Jason Giambi R	8.00	2.40
75 Brian Hunter R	3.00	.90
76 Michael Tucker R	3.00	.90
77 Andy Benes R	3.00	.90
78 Brady Anderson B	8.00	2.40
79 Ramon Martinez R	3.00	.90
80 Troy Percival B	8.00	2.40
81 Alex Rodriguez G	40.00	12.00
82 Jim Thome B	20.00	6.00
83 Denny Neagle R	3.00	.90
84 Rafael Palmeiro B	12.00	3.60
85 Jose Valentin R	3.00	.90
86 Marc Newfield R	3.00	.90
87 Mariano Rivera B	12.00	3.60
88 Alan Benes R	3.00	.90
89 Jimmy Key R	3.00	.90
90 Joe Randa R	3.00	.90
91 Cal Ripken G	80.00	24.00
92 Craig Biggio R	5.00	1.50
93 Dean Palmer R	3.00	.90
94 Gary Sheffield B	8.00	2.40
95 Ismael Valdes R	3.00	.90
96 John Valentin R	3.00	.90
97 Johnny Damon R	3.00	.90
98 Mo Vaughn G	10.00	3.00
99 Paul Sorrento R	3.00	.90
100 Randy Johnson B	20.00	6.00
101 Raul Mondesi B	8.00	2.40
102 Roberto Alomar B	20.00	6.00
103 Royce Clayton R	3.00	.90
104 Mark Grudzielanek R	3.00	.90
105 Wally Joyner R	3.00	.90
106 Wil Cordero R	3.00	.90
107 Will Clark B	25.00	7.50
108 Chuck Knoblauch B	10.00	3.00
109 Derek Bell R	3.00	.90
110 Henry Rodriguez R	3.00	.90
111 Edgar Renteria R	3.00	.90
112 Travis Fryman R	3.00	.90
113 Eric Young R	3.00	.90
114 Sandy Alomar Jr. R	3.00	.90
115 Darin Erstad B	8.00	2.40
116 Barry Larkin B	20.00	6.00
117 Barry Bonds B	50.00	15.00
118 Frank Thomas G	25.00	7.50
119 Carlos Delgado R	3.00	.90
120 Jason Kendall R	3.00	.90
121 T.Hollandsworth R	3.00	.90
122 Jim Edmonds R	3.00	.90
123 Chipper Jones G	25.00	7.50
124 Jeff Fassero R	3.00	.90
125 Deion Sanders B	12.00	3.60
126 Matt Lawton R	3.00	.90
127 Ryan Klesko R	3.00	.90
128 Mike Mussina R	8.00	2.40
129 Paul Molitor B	12.00	3.60
130 Dante Bichette R	3.00	.90
131 Bill Pulsipher R	3.00	.90
132 Todd Hundley B	8.00	2.40
133 J.T. Snow R	3.00	.90
134 Chuck Finley R	3.00	.90
135 Shawn Green R	3.00	.90
136 Charles Nagy R	3.00	.90
137 Willie Greene R	3.00	.90
138 Marty Cordova R	3.00	.90
139 Eddie Murray R	8.00	2.40
140 Ryne Sandberg R	12.00	3.60
141 Alex Fernandez R	3.00	.90
142 Mark McGwire G	60.00	18.00
143 Eric Davis R	3.00	.90
144 Jermaine Dye R	3.00	.90
145 Ruben Sierra R	3.00	.90
146 Damon Buford R	3.00	.90
147 John Smoltz B	12.00	3.60
148 Alex Ochoa R	3.00	.90
149 Moises Alou R	3.00	.90
150 Rico Brogna R	3.00	.90
151 Terry Steinbach R	3.00	.90
152 Jeff King R	3.00	.90
153 Carlos Garcia R	3.00	.90
154 Tom Glavine R	5.00	1.50
155 Edgar Martinez B	12.00	3.60
156 Kevin Elster R	3.00	.90
157 Darryl Hamilton R	3.00	.90
158 Jason Dickson R	3.00	.90
159 Kevin Orie R	3.00	.90
160 Bubba Trammell R	1.25	.35
161 Jose Guillen B	8.00	2.40
162 Brant Brown R	3.00	.90
163 Wendell Magee R	3.00	.90
164 Scott Spiezio R	3.00	.90
165 Todd Walker B	8.00	2.40
166 Rod Myers R	3.00	.90
167 Damon Mashore R	3.00	.90
168 Wilton Guerrero B	8.00	2.40
169 Vladimir Guerrero G	25.00	7.50
170 Nomar Garciaparra B	30.00	9.00
171 Shannon Stewart R	3.00	.90
172 Scott Rolen R	5.00	1.50
173 Bob Abreu R	3.00	.90
174 Danny Patterson R	3.00	.90
175 Andruw Jones G	10.00	3.00
176 Brian Giles R	12.00	3.60
177 Dmitri Young R	3.00	.90
178 Cal Ripken EMW G	40.00	12.00
179 C.Knoblauch EMW B	8.00	2.40
180 A.Rodriguez EMW G	25.00	7.50
181 A. Galarraga EMW R	3.00	.90
182 P.Martinez EMW R	5.00	1.50
183 B.Anderson EMW R	3.00	.90
184 Barry Bonds EMW B	20.00	6.00
185 I.Rodriguez EMW B	12.00	3.60
186 Gary Sheffield EMW B	8.00	2.40
187 Denny Neagle EMW B	8.00	2.40
188 M.McGwire AURA B	25.00	7.50
189 Ellis Burks AURA R	3.00	.90
190 A.Rodriguez AURA G	25.00	7.50
191 Mike Piazza AURA G	25.00	7.50
192 Barry Bonds AURA B	20.00	6.00
193 Albert Belle AURA G	10.00	3.00
194 C.Jones AURA G	15.00	4.50
195 J.Gonzalez AURA G	15.00	4.50
196 B.Anderson AURA B	8.00	2.40
197 F.Thomas AURA G	15.00	4.50
198 V.Guerrero CL R	5.00	1.50
199 Todd Walker CL R	3.00	.90
200 Scott Rolen CL R	3.00	.90

1997 New Pinnacle Museum Collection

Randomly inserted in packs at a rate of one in nine, this 200-card set is a dufex parallel version of the regular set printed on full gold foil.

	Nm-Mt	Ex-Mt
*STARS: 5X TO 12X BASIC CARDS		
*ROOKIES: 2X TO 5X BASIC CARDS		

1997 New Pinnacle Press Plates

Randomly inserted in packs at the rate of one in 1,250, this all-aluminum set consists of the Authentic Press Plate that transfers the ink to the cardboard for each individual card back and front. Each plate displays an authentication seal on the back along with the personal signature of Pinnacle Chairman and CEO, Jerry Meyer. Each card has eight press plates for each of the four colors used in printing the front and the back. All cards from both the regular sets as well as the insert sets were inserted into packs. A collector who put together any combination of the four press plates from the same card front or back could return the plates to Pinnacle by August 22, 1997 for a bounty of $35,000. A sliding reward scale was imposed with a $30,000 bounty for plates received by August 29, 1997, $25,000 for those received by September 5, 1997, and $20,000 for those received after September 5 but before December 31, 1997. Since supply is so limited, only common card pricing is provided.

	Nm-Mt	Ex-Mt
COMMON FRONT	50.00	15.00
COMMON BACK	25.00	7.50

1997 New Pinnacle Interleague Encounter

Randomly inserted in packs at a rate of one in 240, this 10-card set features a double-front card design printed on mirror blue mylar foil with red foil treatments. A top AL star player is carried on one side with a top NL mega-star on the filpside and the date of the first match-up of the two teams.

	Nm-Mt	Ex-Mt
COMPLETE SET (10)	250.00	75.00
1 Albert Belle / Brian Jordan	6.00	1.80
2 Andruw Jones / Brady Anderson	6.00	1.80
3 Ken Griffey Jr. / Tony Gwynn	25.00	7.50
4 Cal Ripken / Chipper Jones	50.00	15.00
5 Mike Piazza / Ivan Rodriguez	25.00	7.50
6 Derek Jeter / Vladimir Guerrero	40.00	12.00
7 Greg Maddux / Mo Vaughn	25.00	7.50
8 Alex Rodriguez / Hideo Nomo	25.00	7.50
9 Juan Gonzalez / Barry Bonds	40.00	12.00
10 Frank Thomas / Jeff Bagwell	15.00	4.50

1997 New Pinnacle Keeping the Pace

Randomly inserted in packs at a rate of one in 89, this 18-card set features dot matrix holograms of eighteen leading baseball stars.

	Nm-Mt	Ex-Mt
COMPLETE SET (18)	400.00	120.00
1 Juan Gonzalez	15.00	4.50
2 Greg Maddux	25.00	7.50
3 Ivan Rodriguez	15.00	4.50
4 Ken Griffey Jr.	25.00	7.50
5 Alex Rodriguez	25.00	7.50
6 Barry Bonds	40.00	12.00
7 Frank Thomas	15.00	4.50
8 Chuck Knoblauch	6.00	1.80
9 Derek Jeter	40.00	12.00
10 Roger Clemens	30.00	9.00
11 Kenny Lofton	6.00	1.80
12 Tony Gwynn	20.00	6.00
13 Troy Percival	6.00	1.80
14 Cal Ripken	50.00	15.00
15 Andy Pettitte	10.00	3.00
16 Hideo Nomo	15.00	4.50
17 Randy Johnson	15.00	4.50
18 Mike Piazza	25.00	7.50

1997 New Pinnacle Spellbound

Randomly inserted in both hobby and retail packs at a rate of one in 19, this 50-card set features color action player photos superimposed over one of the letters of the player's name and printed on a full-foil, micro-etched card. The completed set for each star player spells both the player's name and the word "Spellbound." The Players names are all spelled out individually per card. After each card number the letter signified on the card is noted.

	Nm-Mt	Ex-Mt
COMMON A.BELLE CARD	2.00	.60
COMMON A.JONES CARD	3.00	.90
COMMON A.RODRIGUEZ	10.00	3.00
COMMON C.JONES CARD	5.00	1.50
COMMON RIPKEN	15.00	4.50
COMMON THOMAS	5.00	1.50
COMMON I.RODRIGUEZ	5.00	1.50
COMMON GRIFFEY	8.00	2.40
COMMON PIAZZA	8.00	2.40

1954 New York Journal American

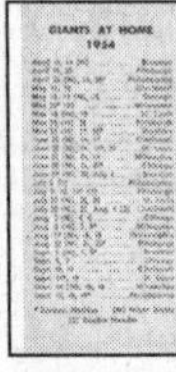

The cards in this 59-card set measure approximately 2" by 4". The 1954 New York Journal American set contains black and white, unnumbered cards issued in conjunction with the newspaper. News stands were given boxes of cards to be distributed with purchases and each card had a serial number for redemption in the contest. The set spotlights New York teams only and carries game schedules on the reverse. The cards have been assigned numbers in the listing below alphabetically within team so that Brooklyn Dodgers are 1-19, New York Giants are 20-39, and New York Yankees are 40-59. There is speculation that a 20th Dodger card may exist. The catalog designation for this set is M127.

	NM	Ex
COMPLETE SET (59)	2000.00	1000.00
1 Joe Black	12.00	6.00
2 Roy Campanella	120.00	60.00
3 Billy Cox	12.00	6.00
4 Carl Erskine	20.00	10.00
5 Carl Furillo	20.00	10.00
6 Jim Gilliam	20.00	10.00
7 Gil Hodges	60.00	30.00
8 Jim Hughes	12.00	6.00
9 Clem Labine	15.00	7.50
10 Billy Loes	12.00	6.00
11 Russ Meyer	12.00	6.00
12 Don Newcombe	20.00	10.00
13 Ervin Palica	12.00	6.00
14 Pee Wee Reese	100.00	50.00
15 Jackie Robinson	200.00	100.00
16 Preacher Roe	20.00	10.00
17 George Shuba	12.00	6.00
18 Duke Snider	120.00	60.00
19 Dick Williams	15.00	7.50
20 John Antonelli	12.00	6.00
21 Alvin Dark	15.00	7.50
22 Marv Grissom	12.00	6.00
23 Ruben Gomez	12.00	6.00
24 Jim Hearn	12.00	6.00
25 Bobby Hofman	12.00	6.00
26 Monte Irvin	40.00	20.00
27 Larry Jansen	12.00	6.00
28 Ray Katt	12.00	6.00
29 Don Liddle	12.00	6.00
30 Whitey Lockman	15.00	7.50
31 Sal Maglie	20.00	10.00
32 Willie Mays	250.00	125.00
33 Don Mueller	12.00	6.00
34 Dusty Rhodes	12.00	6.00
35 Hank Thompson	12.00	6.00
36 Wes Westrum	12.00	6.00
37 Hoyt Wilhelm	40.00	20.00
38 Davey Williams	12.00	6.00
39 Al Worthington	12.00	6.00
40 Hank Bauer	20.00	10.00
41 Yogi Berra	120.00	60.00
42 Harry Byrd	12.00	6.00
43 Andy Carey	12.00	6.00
44 Jerry Coleman	15.00	7.50
45 Joe Collins	12.00	6.00
46 Whitey Ford	80.00	40.00
47 Steve Kraly	12.00	6.00
48 Bob Kuzava	12.00	6.00
49 Frank Leja	12.00	6.00
50 Ed Lopat	20.00	10.00
51 Mickey Mantle	500.00	250.00
52 Gil McDougald	20.00	10.00
53 Bill Miller	12.00	6.00
54 Tom Morgan	12.00	6.00
55 Irv Noren	12.00	6.00
56 Allie Reynolds	20.00	10.00
57 Phil Rizzuto	60.00	30.00
58 Eddie Robinson	12.00	6.00
59 Gene Woodling	15.00	7.50

1973 New York Sunday News M138

These 22 newspaper cutouts feature color caricatures that measure 11 1/4" X 14 3/4". The complete page featuring both players measures 22.5" by 29.5". These are printed on newsprint and are unnumbered. Cards feature Mets and Yankees players. Two cards (One Yankee and one Met) were issued every Sunday from 6/17/73 through 8/26/73 in Cartoon section centerfold. Each pair of players played the same position.

	NM	Ex
COMPLETE SET (22)	150.00	60.00
1 Yogi Berra MG	12.00	4.80
2 Ralph Houk MG	6.00	2.40
3 Tom Seaver	15.00	6.00
4 Mel Stottlemyre	6.00	2.40
5 Ron Blomberg	5.00	2.00
6 John Milner	5.00	2.00
7 Horace Clarke	5.00	2.00
8 Felix Millan	5.00	2.00
9 Bud Harrelson	5.00	2.00
10 Gene Michael	5.00	2.00
11 Jim Fregosi	6.00	2.40
12 Graig Nettles	8.00	3.20
13 Jerry Grote	6.00	2.40
14 Thurman Munson	12.00	4.80
15 Cleon Jones	5.00	2.00
16 Roy White	6.00	2.40
17 Willie Mays	20.00	8.00
18 Bobby Murcer	8.00	3.20
19 Matty Alou	6.00	2.40
20 Rusty Staub	8.00	3.20
21 Sparky Lyle	6.00	2.40
22 Tug McGraw	10.00	4.00

1997 New York Lottery

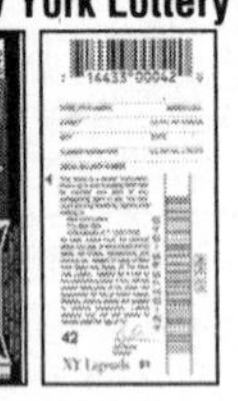

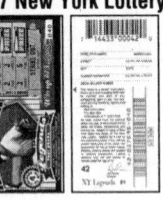

This five-card set features color photos of legendary baseball players printed on a baseball diamond-shaped background. The set measures approximately 4" by 2" and was actually real New York scratch-off lottery ticket stubs that could be obtained for $1 a piece. The backs carry the lottery rules and prize information. The cards are unnumbered and checklisted below in alphabetical order.

	Nm-Mt	Ex-Mt
COMPLETE SET (5)	8.00	2.40
1 Yogi Berra	2.50	.75
2 Keith Hernandez	1.50	.45
3 Gil Hodges	2.50	.75
4 Monte Irvin	2.00	.60
5 Don Larsen	1.00	.30

1916 New York World Advertisements

These 9" by 4" card features four New York Area players. The cards have a player portrait and the rest of the card is devoted to advertising information about the New York World newspaper. Since the cards are unnumbered we have sequenced them in alphabetical order.

	Ex-Mt	VG
COMPLETE SET	800.00	400.00
1 Frank Baker	200.00	100.00
2 Dave Bancroft	200.00	100.00
3 Jake Daubert	200.00	100.00
4 Buck Herzog	125.00	60.00
5 Dave Robertson	100.00	50.00

1990 Nike Mini-Posters

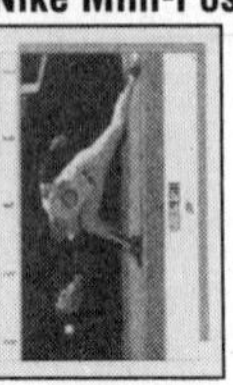

This two-card set features color action player photos and measures approximately 5" by 7". The cards are replicas of large 24" by 36" posters. The backs are blank. The cards are unnumbered and checklisted below in alphabetical order.

	Nm-Mt	Ex-Mt
COMPLETE SET (2)	6.00	1.80
1 Mark Grace	3.00	.90
2 Kirby Puckett	3.00	.90

2003 Nike

This three-card set was issued at the 2003 All-Star Fanfest. The fronts feature athletes used to promote Nike products while the back promoted an appearance of Cubs great Ryne Sandberg at NikeTown during the All-Star Game week activities. Since these cards are unnumbered we have sequenced them in alphabetical order.

	MINT	NRMT
COMPLETE SET	5.00	2.20
1 Torii Hunter	1.00	.45
2 Magglio Ordonez	1.50	.70
3 Alfonso Soriano	2.50	1.10

1989 Nissen

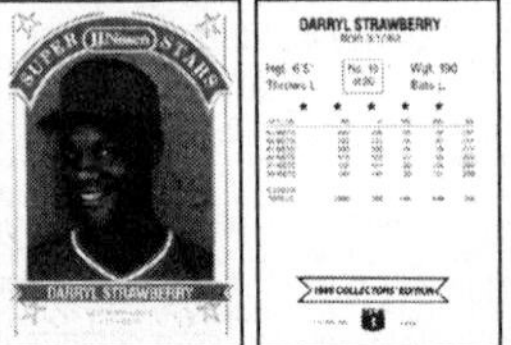

The 1989 J.J. Nissen set contains 20 standard-size cards. The fronts have airbrushed facial photos with white and yellow borders and orange trim. The backs are white and feature career stats. The complete set price below does not include the error version of Mark Grace.

	Nm-Mt	Ex-Mt
COMPLETE SET (20)	8.00	3.20
1 Wally Joyner	.20	.08
2 Wade Boggs	1.00	.40
3 Ellis Burks	.30	.12
4 Don Mattingly	2.00	.80
5 Jose Canseco	.50	.20
6 Mike Greenwell	.10	.04
7 Eric Davis	.20	.08
8 Kirby Puckett	.75	.30
9 Kevin Seitzer	.10	.04
10 Darryl Strawberry	.20	.08
11 Gregg Jefferies	.10	.04
12A Mark Grace ERR (Photo actually Vance Law)	5.00	2.00
12B Mark Grace COR	1.00	.40
13 Matt Nokes	.10	.04
14 Mark McGwire	3.00	1.20
15 Bobby Bonilla	.10	.04
16 Roger Clemens	2.00	.80
17 Frank Viola	.10	.04
18 Orel Hershiser	.20	.08
19 David Cone	.40	.16
20 Ted Williams	2.00	.80

1953 Northland Bread Labels

This 32-label set features two players from each major league team and is one of the popular "Bread For Energy" sets. Each bread label measures 2 11/16" by 2 11/16". Although the labels are printed in black and white, the 1953 Northland Bread set includes a "Baseball Stars" album which provides additional information concerning "Baseball Immortals" and "Baseball Tips." These labels are unnumbered so we have checklisted them in alphabetical order. The amended catalog designation is D290-3A.

	NM	Ex
COMPLETE SET (32)	2000.00	1000.00
1 Cal Abrams	50.00	25.00
2 Richie Ashburn	100.00	50.00
3 Gus Bell	60.00	30.00
4 Jim Busby	50.00	25.00
5 Clint Courtney	50.00	25.00
6 Billy Cox	50.00	25.00
7 Jim Dyck	50.00	25.00
8 Nellie Fox	100.00	50.00
9 Sid Gordon	50.00	25.00
10 Warren Hacker	50.00	25.00
11 Jim Hearn	50.00	25.00
12 Fred Hutchinson	60.00	30.00
13 Monte Irvin	100.00	50.00
14 Jackie Jensen	80.00	40.00
15 Ted Kluszewski	80.00	40.00
16 Bob Lemon	100.00	50.00
17 Mickey McDermott	50.00	25.00
18 Minnie Minoso	80.00	40.00
19 Johnny Mize	100.00	50.00
20 Mel Parnell	50.00	25.00
21 Howie Pollet	50.00	25.00
22 Jerry Priddy	50.00	25.00
23 Allie Reynolds	80.00	40.00
24 Preacher Roe	80.00	40.00
25 Al Rosen	80.00	40.00
26 Connie Ryan	50.00	25.00
27 Hank Sauer	60.00	30.00
28 Red Schoendienst	100.00	50.00
29 Bobby Shantz	60.00	30.00
30 Enos Slaughter	100.00	50.00
31 Warren Spahn	100.00	50.00
32 Gus Zernial	60.00	30.00

1910 Notebook Covers

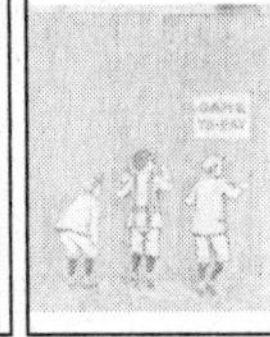

These eight cards are similar in size and appearance to the T-3 set. These cards measure 5" by 7 1/2". The cards are in full colors with red borders. We have checklisted the set in alphabetical order.

	Ex-Mt	VG
COMPLETE SET	4000.00	2000.00
1 Roger Bresnahan	300.00	150.00
2 Ty Cobb	1000.00	500.00
3 Eddie Collins	500.00	250.00
4 Johnny Evers	400.00	200.00
5 Clark Griffith	300.00	150.00
6 Nap Lajoie	500.00	250.00
7 Christy Mathewson	600.00	300.00
8 Honus Wagner	600.00	300.00

1960 Nu-Card Hi-Lites

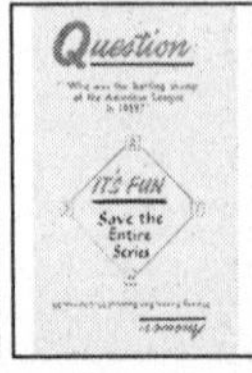

The cards in this 72-card set measure approximately 3 1/4" by 5 3/8". In 1960, the Nu-Card Company introduced its Baseball Hi-Lites set of newspaper style cards. Each card singled out an individual baseball achievement with a picture and story. The reverses contain a baseball quiz. Cards 1-18 are more valuable if found printed totally in black on the front; these are copy-righted CVC as opposed to the NCI designation found on the red and black printed fronts.

	NM	Ex
COMPLETE SET (72)	800.00	325.00
1 Babe Ruth Hits 3 Homers In A Series Game	50.00	20.00
2 Johnny Podres Pitching Wins Series	3.00	1.20
3 Bill Bevans Pitches No-Hitter, Almost	3.00	1.20
4 Box Score Devised By Reporter	3.00	1.20
5 Johnny VanderMeer Pitches Two No Hitters	3.00	1.20
6 Indians Take Bums	3.00	1.20
7 Joe DiMaggio Comes Thru	50.00	20.00
8 Christy Mathewson Pitches Three WS Shutouts	8.00	3.20
9 Harvey Haddix Pitches 12 Perfect Innings	3.00	1.20
10 Bobby Thomson Homer Sinks Dodgers	12.00	4.80
11 Carl Hubbell Strikes Out 5 A.L. Stars	8.00	3.20
12 Pickoff Ends Series	3.00	1.20
13 Cards Take Series From Yanks	3.00	1.20
14 Dizzy Dean Daffy Dean Win Series	8.00	3.20
15 Mickey Owen Drops Third Strike	3.00	1.20
16 Babe Ruth Calls Shot	50.00	20.00
17 Fred Merkle Pulls Boner	5.00	2.00
18 Don Larsen Hurls Perfect W.S. Game	8.00	3.20
19 Mickey Cochrane Bean Ball Ends Career	5.00	2.00
20 Ernie Banks Belts 47 Homers Earns MVP	15.00	6.00
21 Stan Musial Hits 5 Homers in One Day	20.00	8.00
22 Mickey Mantle Hits Longest Homer	50.00	20.00
23 Roy Sievers Captures Home Run Title	3.00	1.20
24 Lou Gehrig 2130 Consecutive Game Record Ends	50.00	20.00
25 Red Schoendienst Key Player Braves Pennant	5.00	2.00
26 Eddie Gaedel Midget Pinch-Hits For St. Louis	5.00	2.00
27 Willie Mays Makes Greatest Catch	25.00	10.00
28 Yogi Berra Homer Puts Yanks In 1st	15.00	6.00
29 Roy Campanella NL MVP	15.00	6.00
30 Bob Turley Hurls Yankees To WS Champions	3.00	1.20
31 Dodgers Take Series From Sox in Six	3.00	1.20
32 Carl Furillo Hero as Dodgers Beat Chicago in 3rd WS Game	3.00	1.20
33 Joe Adcock Gets 4 Homers And A Double	3.00	1.20
34 Bill Dickey Chosen All-Star Catcher	5.00	2.00
35 Lew Burdette Beats Yanks In Three World Series Games	3.00	1.20
36 Umpires Clear White Sox Bench	3.00	1.20
37 Pee Wee Reese Honored As Greatest Dodger SS	12.00	4.80
38 Joe DiMaggio Hits In 56 Straight	50.00	20.00
39 Ted Williams Hits .406 For Season	50.00	20.00
40 Walter Johnson Pitches 56 Straight	10.00	4.00
41 Gil Hodges Hits 4 Home Runs In Nite Game	5.00	2.00
42 Hank Greenberg Returns to Tigers From Army	8.00	3.20
43 Ty Cobb Named Best Player Of All Time	25.00	10.00
44 Robin Roberts Wins 28 Games	5.00	2.00
45 Phil Rizzuto Two Runs Save 1st Place	10.00	4.00
46 Tigers Beat Out Senators For Pennant	3.00	1.20
47 Babe Ruth Hits 60th Home Run	50.00	20.00
48 Cy Young Honored	5.00	2.00
49 Harmon Killebrew Starts Spring Training	12.00	4.80
50 Mickey Mantle Hits Longest Homer at Stadium	50.00	20.00
51 Braves Take Pennant	3.00	1.20
52 Ted Williams Hero Of All-Star Game	40.00	16.00
53 Jackie Robinson Saves Dodgers For Play-off Series	40.00	16.00
54 Fred Snodgrass Muffs Fly	3.00	1.20
55 Duke Snider Belts 2 Homers, Ties Record	15.00	6.00
56 Giants Win 26 Straight	3.00	1.20
57 Ted Kluszewski Stars In 1st Series Win	5.00	2.00
58 Mel Ott Walks 5 Times In Single Game	5.00	2.00
59 Harvey Kuenn Takes A.L. Batting Title	3.00	1.20
60 Bob Feller Hurls 3rd No-Hitter of Career	10.00	4.00
61 Yankees Champs Again	3.00	1.20
62 Hank Aaron Bat Beats Yankees In Series	20.00	8.00
63 Warren Spahn Beats Yanks in W.S.	10.00	4.00
64 Ump's Wrong Call Helps Dodgers Beat Yanks	3.00	1.20
65 Al Kaline Hits 3 Homers Two In Same Inning	12.00	4.80
66 Bob Allison Named AL ROY	3.00	1.20
67 Willie McCovey Blasts Way Into Giant Lineup	10.00	4.00
68 Rocky Colavito Hits 4 Homers in One Game	15.00	6.00
69 Carl Erskine Sets Strike Out Record in World Series	3.00	1.20
70 Sal Maglie Pitches No-Hit Game	3.00	1.20
71 Early Wynn Victory Crushes Yanks	5.00	2.00
72 Nellie Fox AL MVP	15.00	6.00

1961 Nu-Card Scoops

The cards in this 80-card set measure 2 1/2" by 3 1/2". This series depicts great moments in the history of individual ballplayers. Each card is designed as a miniature newspaper front-page, complete with data and picture. Both the number (401-480) and title are printed in red on the obverse, and the story is found on the back. An album was issued to hold the set. The set has been illegally reprinted, which has served to suppress the demand for the originals as well as the reprints.

	NM	Ex
COMPLETE SET (80)	300.00	120.00
401 Jim Gentile	1.00	.40
402 Warren Spahn (No-hitter)	3.00	1.20
403 Bill Mazeroski	1.50	.60
404 Willie Mays: (Three triples)	12.00	4.80
405 Woodie Held	1.00	.40
406 Vern Law	1.00	.40
407 Pete Runnels	.50	.20
408 Lew Burdette (No-hitter)	1.00	.40
409 Dick Stuart	.50	.20
410 Don Cardwell	1.00	.40
411 Camilo Pascual	.50	.20
412 Eddie Mathews	3.00	1.20
413 Dick Groat	1.00	.40
414 Gene Autry OWN	5.00	2.00
415 Bobby Richardson	2.00	.80
416 Roger Maris	8.00	3.20
417 Fred Merkle	.50	.20
418 Don Larsen	1.00	.40
419 Mickey Cochrane	1.50	.60
420 Ernie Banks	4.00	1.60
421 Stan Musial	10.00	4.00
422 Mickey Mantle (Longest homer)	25.00	10.00
423 Roy Sievers	1.00	.40
424 Lou Gehrig	15.00	6.00
425 Red Schoendienst	2.00	.80
426 Eddie Gaedel	3.00	1.20
427 Willie Mays (Greatest catch)	15.00	6.00
428 Jackie Robinson	15.00	6.00
429 Roy Campanella	8.00	3.20
430 Bob Turley	.50	.20
431 Larry Sherry	1.00	.40
432 Carl Furillo	1.50	.60
433 Joe Adcock	.50	.20
434 Bill Dickey	1.50	.60
435 Lew Burdette 3 wins	.50	.20
436 Umpire Clears Bench	1.00	.40
437 Pee Wee Reese	3.00	1.20
438 Joe DiMaggio (56 Game Hit Streak)	15.00	6.00
439 Ted Williams (Hits .406)	15.00	6.00
440 Walter Johnson	3.00	1.20
441 Gil Hodges	2.00	.80
442 Hank Greenberg	3.00	1.20
443 Ty Cobb	12.00	4.80
444 Robin Roberts	3.00	1.20
445 Phil Rizzuto	3.00	1.20
446 Hal Newhouser	3.00	1.20
447 Babe Ruth 60th Homer	30.00	12.00
448 Cy Young	3.00	1.20
449 Harmon Killebrew	3.00	1.20
450 Mickey Mantle Longest homer	30.00	12.00
451 Braves Take Pennant	1.00	.40
452 Ted Williams (All-Star Hero)	15.00	6.00
453 Yogi Berra	8.00	3.20
454 Fred Snodgrass	.50	.20
455 Babe Ruth 3 Homers	25.00	10.00
456 New York Giants 26 Game Streak	.50	.20
457 Ted Kluszewski	1.00	.40
458 Mel Ott	2.00	.80
459 Harvey Kuenn	1.00	.40
460 Bob Feller	4.00	1.60
461 Casey Stengel	3.00	1.20

462 Hank Aaron 15.00 6.00
463 Spahn Beats Yanks 2.00 .80
464 Ump's Wrong Call .50 .20
465 Al Kaline 4.00 1.60
466 Bob Allison 1.00 .40
467 Joe DiMaggio 15.00 6.00
(Four Homers)
468 Rocky Colavito 3.00 1.20
469 Carl Erskine 1.00 .40
470 Sal Maglie 1.00 .40
471 Early Wynn 2.00 .80
472 Nellie Fox 2.50 1.00
473 Marty Marion 1.00 .40
474 Johnny Podres 1.00 .40
475 Mickey Owen 1.00 .40
476 Dean Brothers 2.50 1.00
(Dizzy and Daffy)
477 Christy Mathewson 3.00 1.20
478 Harvey Haddix .50 .20
479 Carl Hubbell 2.00 .80
480 Bobby Thomson 2.00 .80

1983 O'Connell and Son Baseball Greats

This 20-card set features drawings of major league players in circles on color backgrounds and measures approximately 4 3/4" by 6 1/4". The player's name is printed on the front as is the player's team logo. The backs are blank. The cards are unnumbered and checklisted below in alphabetical order.

Nm-Mt Ex-Mt
COMPLETE SET (20) 25.00 10.00
1 Hank Aaron 3.00 1.20
2 Johnny Bench 1.00 .40
3 Yogi Berra 1.00 .40
4 George Brett 2.50 1.00
5 Roy Campanella 1.00 .40
6 Rod Carew 1.00 .40
7 Roberto Clemente 4.00 1.60
8 Bob Gibson 1.00 .40
9 Al Kaline 1.00 .40
10 Mickey Mantle 5.00 2.00
11 Joe Morgan .50 .20
12 Stan Musial 2.00 .80
13 Jim Rice .50 .20
14 Frank Robinson 1.00 .40
15 Pete Rose 2.00 .80
16 Tom Seaver 1.00 .40
17 Duke Snider 1.00 .40
18 Honus Wagner 1.00 .40
19 Carl Yastrzemski 1.00 .40
20 Robin Yount 1.00 .40

1984-89 O'Connell and Son Ink

This comprises the O'Connell and Son Ink Mini-Prints. The first series set (1-36) was released at the 1984 National Convention. With the inception of The Infield Dirt in 1991, an underground hobby publication, the cards have been included free with each issue. The December 1992 issue of The Infield Dirt, issued by the producers of this set, offered the entire set for $34.95. The cards feature pen and ink or pencil drawings of major league players on color backgrounds. The player's name is printed on the front as is the card number.

Nm-Mt Ex-Mt
COMPLETE SET (250) 50.00 20.00
1 Ted Williams 2.00 .80
2 Minnie Minoso .40 .16
3 Sandy Koufax 1.00 .40
4 Al Kaline .40 .16
5 Whitey Ford .40 .16
6 Wade Boggs .40 .16
7 Nolan Ryan 2.00 .80
8 Greg Luzinski .10 .04
9 Cal Ripken 2.00 .80
10 Carl Yastrzemski .40 .16
11 Dale Murphy .30 .12
12 Rocky Colavito .40 .16
13 George Brett 1.50 .60
14 Willie McCovey .40 .16
15 Rod Carew .40 .16
16 Bob Gibson .40 .16
17 Robin Yount .40 .16
18 Steve Carlton .40 .16
19 Harmon Killebrew .40 .16
20 Willie Mays 2.00 .80
21 Reggie Jackson 1.00 .40
22 Eddie Mathews .40 .16
23 Eddie Murray 1.00 .40
24 Johnny Bench .75 .30
25 Mickey Mantle 2.50 1.00
26 Willie Stargell .40 .16
27 Rickey Henderson .40 .16
28 Roger Maris 1.00 .40
29 Darryl Strawberry .20 .08
30 Pete Rose 1.00 .40
31 Jim Rice .20 .08
32 Thurman Munson .30 .12
33 Brooks Robinson .40 .16
34 Fernando Valenzuela .20 .08
35 Tony Oliva .30 .12
36 Henry Aaron 2.00 .80
37 Joe Morgan .40 .16
38 Kent Hrbek .20 .08
39 Yogi Berra .40 .16
40 Stan Musial 1.50 .60
41 Gary Matthews .10 .04
42 Larry Doby .40 .16
43 Steve Garvey .30 .12
44 Bob Horner .10 .04
45 Ron Guidry .20 .08
46 Ernie Banks .40 .16
47 Carlton Fisk .40 .16
48 Pee Wee Reese .40 .16
49 Bobby Shantz .10 .04
50 Joe DiMaggio 2.00 .80
51 Enos Slaughter .40 .16
52 Gary Carter .40 .16
53 Bob Feller .40 .16
54 Phil Rizzuto .40 .16
55 Dave Concepcion .20 .08
56 Ron Kittle .10 .04
57 Dwight Evans .20 .08
58 Johnny Mize .40 .16
59 Richie Ashburn .40 .16
60 Roberto Clemente 2.00 .80
61 Fred Lynn .20 .08
62 Billy Williams .40 .16
63 Dave Winfield .40 .16
64 Robin Roberts .40 .16
65 Billy Martin .30 .12
66 Duke Snider .40 .16
67 Luis Aparicio .40 .16
68 Mickey Vernon .20 .08
69 Mike Schmidt 1.00 .40
70 Frank Robinson .40 .16
71 Bill Madlock .10 .04
72 Rollie Fingers .40 .16
73 Rod Carew .40 .16
74 Carl Erskine .10 .04
75 Lou Brock .40 .16
76 Brooks Robinson .40 .16
77 Roberto Clemente 2.00 .80
78 Nellie Fox .40 .16
79 Bud Harrelson .10 .04
80 Ted Williams 2.00 .80
81 Walter Johnson 1.00 .40
82 Cal Ripken 2.00 .80
83 Lefty Grove .40 .16
84 Lou Whitaker .20 .08
85 Johnny Bench .75 .30
86 Ty Cobb 2.00 .80
87 Mike Schmidt 1.00 .40
88 George Brett 1.50 .60
89 Jim Bunning .40 .16
90 Babe Ruth 2.50 1.00
91 Satchel Paige .75 .30
92 Warren Spahn .40 .16
93 Dale Murphy .30 .12
94 Early Wynn .40 .16
95 Reggie Jackson 1.00 .40
96 Charlie Gehringer .40 .16
97 Jackie Robinson 2.00 .80
98 Lou Gehrig 2.00 .80
99 Hank Aaron 2.00 .80
100 Mickey Mantle 2.50 1.00
101 Sandy Koufax 1.00 .40
102 Ryne Sandberg .75 .30
103 Don Mattingly 1.00 .40
104 Darryl Strawberry .20 .08
105 Tom Seaver .40 .16
106 Bil Klem .20 .08
107 Dwight Gooden .20 .08
108 Pete Rose 1.00 .40
109 Elston Howard .20 .08
110 Honus Wagner .40 .16
111 Waite Hoyt .30 .12
112 Billy Bruton .10 .04
113 Gil Hodges .40 .16
114 Vic Power .10 .04
115 Al Kaline .40 .16
116 Al Lopez .20 .08
117 Rocky Bridges .10 .04
118 Junior Gilliam .20 .08
119 Christy Mathewson .40 .16
120 Hank Greenberg .40 .16
121 Eddie Mathews .40 .16
122 Van Lingle Mungo .10 .04
123 Harry "Suitcase" Simpson .10 .04
124 Carl Yastrzemski .40 .16
125 Pete Rose 1.00 .40
126 Dizzy Dean .40 .16
127 Chi Chi Olivo .10 .04
128 Johnny Vander Meer .10 .04
129 Roberto Clemente 2.00 .80
130 Carl Hubbell .40 .16
131 Willie Mays 2.00 .80
132 Willie Stargell .40 .16
133 Sam Jethroe .10 .04
134 Pete Rose 1.00 .40
135 Jackie Robinson 2.00 .80
136 Yogi Berra .40 .16
137 Grover Alexander .40 .16
138 Joe Morgan .40 .16
139 Rube Foster .30 .12
140 Mickey Mantle 2.50 1.00
141 Ted Williams 2.00 .80
142 Jimmy Foxx .40 .16
143 Pepper Martin .20 .08
144 Henry Aaron 2.00 .80
145 Vida Blue .10 .04
146 Carl Furillo .20 .08
147 Lloyd Waner .30 .12
148 Eddie Dyer .10 .04
149 Casey Stengel .40 .16
150 Mickey Mantle 2.50 1.00
151 Gil Hodges .40 .16
152 Don Mossi .10 .04
153 Ron Swoboda .10 .04
154 Hoyt Wilhelm .30 .12
155 Ed Roush .30 .12
156 Mickey Lolich .20 .08
157 Jim Palmer .40 .16
158 Thurman Munson .30 .12
159 Don Zimmer .10 .04
160 Henry Aaron 2.00 .80
161 Johnny Bench .75 .30
162 Orlando Cepeda .40 .16
163 Honus Wagner .40 .16
164 Tom Seaver .40 .16
165 Willie Mays 2.00 .80
166 Elmer Riddle .10 .04
167 Tony Oliva .30 .12
168 Elmer Flick .20 .08
169 Curt Flood .20 .08
170 Carl Yastrzemski .40 .16
171 Charlie Keller .20 .08
172 Christy Mathewson .40 .16
173 Eddie Plank .40 .16
174 Lou Gehrig 2.00 .80
175 John McGraw .40 .16
176 Mule Haas .10 .04
177 Paul Waner .40 .16
178 Steve Blass .10 .04
179 Honus Wagner .40 .16
180 Jack Barry .10 .04
181 Rocky Colavito .40 .16
182 Danny Murtaugh .10 .04
183 John Edwards .10 .04
184 Pete Rose 1.00 .40
185 Roy Campanella .40 .16
186 Jerry Grote .10 .04
187 Leo Durocher .40 .16
188 Rollie Fingers .40 .16
189 Wes Parker .10 .04
190 Joe Rudi .10 .04
191 Bill Veeck .20 .08
192 Mark Fidrych .30 .12
193 George Foster .20 .08
194 Early Wynn .40 .16
195 Frank Howard .20 .08
196 Graig Nettles .20 .08
197 Juan Pizarro .10 .04
198 Jose Cruz .20 .08
199 Joe Jackson 2.00 .80
200 Stan Musial 1.50 .60
201 Chuck Klein .40 .16
202 Ryne Sandberg .75 .30
203 Richie Allen .30 .12
204 Bo Jackson .10 .04
205 Kevin Mitchell .10 .04
206 Al Smith .20 .08
Early Wynn
Larry Doby
207 Mickey Mantle 2.50 1.00
208 Will Clark .30 .12
209 Cecil Fielder .20 .08
210 Bobby Richardson .20 .08
211 Nolan Ryan 2.00 .80
212 Casey Stengel .40 .16
213 Ted Kluszewski .40 .16
214 Gaylord Perry .40 .16
215 Johnny Vander Meer .20 .08
216 Willie Mays 2.00 .80
217 Goose Goslin .30 .12
218 Bobby Shantz .10 .04
219 Terry Pendleton .10 .04
220 Richie Ashburn .40 .16
221 Robin Yount .40 .16
222 Cal Ripken 2.00 .80
223 Danny Ainge .30 .12
224 Bob Friend .10 .04
225 Orel Hershiser .20 .08
226 Wade Boggs .40 .16
227 Ballpark scene .10 .04
228 Stan Musial 1.50 .60
229 Chris Short .10 .04
230 Johnny Bench .75 .30
231 Nellie Fox .40 .16
232 Ron Santo .40 .16
233 Tony Gwynn 1.25 .50
234 Phil Niekro .40 .16
235 Frank Thomas 2.00 .80
236 Greg Gross .10 .04
237 Ken Griffey Jr. 3.00 1.20
238 Benito Santiago .10 .04
239 Dwight Gooden .20 .08
240 Darryl Strawberry .10 .04
241 Roy Campanella .40 .16
242 Roger Clemens .75 .30
243 Kirby Puckett 1.25 .50
244 Nolan Ryan 2.00 .80
NNO Checklist 6 .10 .04
NNO Checklist 2 .10 .04
NNO Checklist 4 .10 .04
NNO Checklist 3 .10 .04
NNO Checklist 1 .10 .04
NNO Checklist 5 .10 .04

1937 O-Pee-Chee Batter Ups V300

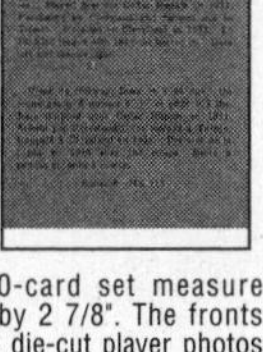

The cards in this 40-card set measure approximately 2 3/8" by 2 7/8". The fronts feature black-and-white die-cut player photos against a ballpark background with small players. The backs carry a short biography and career summary in English and French. The set is peculiar in that card numbering begins with 101. Cards without tops have greatly reduced value. The small ballplayer designs on the obverses are similar to those used on the 1934 American Goudey cards.

Ex-Mt VG
COMPLETE SET (40) 10000.00 5000.00
101 John Lewis 60.00 30.00
102 Jack Hayes 60.00 30.00
103 Earl Averill 150.00 75.00
104 Harland Clift 60.00 30.00
105 Beau Bell 60.00 30.00
106 Jimmie Foxx 400.00 200.00
107 Hank Greenberg 400.00 200.00
108 George Selkirk 80.00 40.00
109 Wally Moses 80.00 40.00
110 Gerry Walker 60.00 30.00
111 Goose Goslin 150.00 75.00
112 Charlie Gehringer 250.00 125.00
113 Hal Trosky 60.00 30.00
114 Buddy Myer 60.00 30.00
115 Luke Appling 150.00 75.00
116 Zeke Bonura 60.00 30.00
117 Tony Lazzeri 150.00 75.00
118 Joe DiMaggio 5000.00 2500.00
119 Bill Dickey 300.00 150.00
120 Bob Feller 800.00 400.00
121 Harry Kelley 60.00 30.00
122 Johnny Allen 80.00 40.00
123 Bob Johnson 80.00 40.00
124 Joe Cronin 150.00 75.00
125 Rip Radcliff 60.00 30.00
126 Cecil Travis 80.00 40.00
127 Joe Kuhel 60.00 30.00
128 Odell Hale 60.00 30.00
129 Sam West 60.00 30.00
130 Ben Chapman 80.00 40.00
131 Monte Pearson 60.00 30.00
132 Rick Ferrell 150.00 75.00
133 Tommy Bridges 80.00 40.00
134 Schoolboy Rowe 80.00 40.00
135 Vernon Kennedy 60.00 30.00
136 Red Ruffing 150.00 75.00
137 Lefty Grove 300.00 150.00
138 Wes Ferrell 100.00 50.00
139 Buck Newsom 100.00 50.00
140 Rogers Hornsby 500.00 250.00

1965 O-Pee-Chee

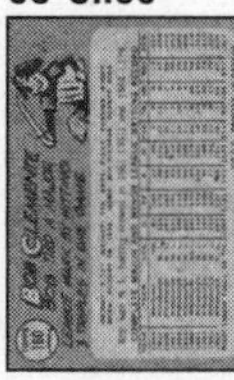

The cards in this 283-card set measure the standard size. This set is essentially the same as the regular 1965 Topps set, except that the words "Printed in Canada" appear on the bottom of the back. On a white border, the fronts feature color player photos with rounded corners. The team name appears within a pennant design below the photo. The player's name and position are also printed on the front. On a blue background, the horizontal backs carry player biography and statistics on a gray card stock. Remember the prices below apply only to the O-Pee- Chee cards -- NOT to the 1965 Topps cards which are much more plentiful. Notable Rookie Cards include Bert Campaneris, Denny McLain, Joe Morgan and Luis Tiant.

NM Ex
COMPLETE SET (283) 2500.00 1000.00
COMMON CARD (1-198) 4.00 1.60
COMMON (199-283) 6.00 2.40
1 Tony Oliva 25.00 10.00
Elston Howard
Brooks Robinson LL
2 Bob Clemente 30.00 12.00
Hank Aaron
Rico Carty LL
3 Harmon Killebrew 60.00 24.00
Mickey Mantle
Boog Powell LL
4 Willie Mays 20.00 8.00
Billy Williams
Jim Ray Hart
Orlando Cepeda
Johnny Callison LL
5 Brooks Robinson 50.00 20.00
Harmon Killebrew
Mickey Mantle
Dick Stuart LL
6 Ken Boyer 15.00 6.00
Willie Mays
Ron Santo LL
7 Dean Chance 10.00 4.00
Joel Horlen LL
8 Sandy Koufax 25.00 10.00
Don Drysdale LL
9 Dean Chance 10.00 4.00
Gary Peters
Dave Wickersham
Juan Pizarro
Wally Bunker LL
10 Larry Jackson 10.00 4.00
Ray Sadecki
Juan Marichal LL
11 Al Downing 10.00 4.00
Dean Chance
Camilo Pascual
12 Bob Veale 10.00 4.00
Don Drysdale
Bob Gibson LL
13 Pedro Ramos 6.00 2.40
14 Len Gabrielson 4.00 1.60
15 Robin Roberts 15.00 6.00
16 Joe Morgan RC 80.00 32.00
Sonny Jackson
17 John Romano 4.00 1.60
18 Bill McCool 4.00 1.60
19 Gates Brown 6.00 2.40
20 Jim Bunning 15.00 6.00
21 Don Blasingame 4.00 1.60
22 Charlie Smith 4.00 1.60
23 Bob Tiefenauer 4.00 1.60
24 Twins Team 10.00 4.00
25 Al McBean 4.00 1.60
26 Bob Knoop 4.00 1.60
27 Dick Bertell 4.00 1.60
28 Barney Schultz 4.00 1.60
29 Felix Mantilla 4.00 1.60
30 Jim Bouton 10.00 4.00
31 Mike White 4.00 1.60
32 Herman Franks MG 4.00 1.60
33 Jackie Brandt 4.00 1.60
34 Cal Koonce 4.00 1.60
35 Ed Charles 4.00 1.60
36 Bob Wine 4.00 1.60
37 Fred Gladding 4.00 1.60
38 Jim King 4.00 1.60
39 Gerry Arrigo 4.00 1.60
40 Frank Howard 8.00 3.20
41 Bruce Howard 4.00 1.60
Marv Staehle
42 Earl Wilson 6.00 2.40
43 Mike Shannon 6.00 2.40
44 Wade Blasingame 4.00 1.60
45 Roy McMillan 6.00 2.40
46 Bob Lee 4.00 1.60
47 Tommy Harper 6.00 2.40
48 Claude Raymond 6.00 2.40
49 Curt Blefary RC 6.00 2.40
John Miller
50 Juan Marichal 15.00 6.00
51 Bill Bryan 4.00 1.60
52 Ed Roebuck 4.00 1.60
53 Dick McAuliffe 6.00 2.40
54 Joe Gibbon 4.00 1.60
55 Tony Conigliaro 20.00 8.00
56 Ron Kline 4.00 1.60
57 Cardinals Team 10.00 4.00
58 Fred Talbot 4.00 1.60
59 Nate Oliver 4.00 1.60
60 Jim O'Toole 6.00 2.40
61 Chris Cannizzaro 4.00 1.60
62 Jim Kaat UER 8.00 3.20
(Misspelled Katt)
63 Ty Cline 4.00 1.60
64 Lou Burdette 6.00 2.40
65 Tony Kubek 15.00 6.00
66 Bill Rigney MG 4.00 1.60
67 Harvey Haddix 6.00 2.40
68 Del Crandall 6.00 2.40
69 Bill Virdon 6.00 2.40
70 Bill Skowron 8.00 3.20
71 John O'Donoghue 4.00 1.60
72 Tony Gonzalez 4.00 1.60
73 Dennis Ribant 4.00 1.60
74 Rico Petrocelli RC 15.00 6.00
Jerry Stephenson
75 Deron Johnson 6.00 2.40
76 Sam McDowell 8.00 3.20
77 Doug Camilli 4.00 1.60
78 Dal Maxvill 6.00 2.40
79 Checklist 1-88 10.00 2.50
80 Turk Farrell 4.00 1.60
81 Don Buford 6.00 2.40
82 Santos Alomar RC 8.00 3.20
John Braun
83 George Thomas 4.00 1.60
84 Ron Herbel 4.00 1.60
85 Willie Smith 4.00 1.60
86 Buster Narum 4.00 1.60
87 Nelson Mathews 4.00 1.60
88 Jack Lamabe 4.00 1.60
89 Mike Hershberger 4.00 1.60
90 Rich Rollins 6.00 2.40
91 Cubs Team 10.00 4.00
92 Dick Howser 6.00 2.40
93 Jack Fisher 4.00 1.60
94 Charlie Lau 6.00 2.40
95 Bill Mazeroski 15.00 6.00
96 Sonny Siebert 6.00 2.40
97 Pedro Gonzalez 4.00 1.60
98 Bob Miller 4.00 1.60
99 Gil Hodges MG 10.00 4.00
100 Ken Boyer 10.00 4.00
101 Fred Newman 4.00 1.60
102 Steve Boros 4.00 1.60
103 Harvey Kuenn 6.00 2.40
104 Checklist 89-176 10.00 2.50
105 Chico Salmon 4.00 1.60
106 Gene Oliver 4.00 1.60
107 Pat Corrales RC 6.00 2.40
Costen Shockley
108 Don Mincher 4.00 1.60
109 Walt Bond 4.00 1.60
110 Ron Santo 8.00 3.20
111 Lee Thomas 6.00 2.40
112 Derrell Griffith 4.00 1.60
113 Steve Barber 4.00 1.60
114 Jim Hickman 6.00 2.40
115 Bobby Richardson 10.00 4.00
116 Dave Dowling 6.00 2.40
Bob Tolan RC
117 Wes Stock 4.00 1.60
118 Hal Lanier 6.00 2.40
119 John Kennedy 4.00 1.60
120 Frank Robinson 40.00 16.00
121 Gene Alley 6.00 2.40
122 Bill Pleis 4.00 1.60
123 Frank Thomas 6.00 2.40
124 Tom Satriano 4.00 1.60
125 Juan Pizarro 4.00 1.60
126 Dodgers Team 10.00 4.00
127 Frank Lary 4.00 1.60
128 Vic Davalillo 4.00 1.60
129 Bennie Daniels 4.00 1.60
130 Al Kaline 40.00 16.00
131 Johnny Keane MG 4.00 1.60
132 Mike Shannon WS 10.00 4.00
133 Mel Stottlemyre WS 10.00 4.00
134 Mickey Mantle WS 100.00 40.00
135 Ken Boyer WS 10.00 4.00
136 Tim McCarver WS 10.00 4.00
137 Jim Bouton WS 10.00 4.00
138 Bob Gibson WS 15.00 6.00
139 WS Summary 10.00 4.00
Cards celebrate
140 Dean Chance 6.00 2.40
141 Charlie James 4.00 1.60
142 Bill Monbouquette 4.00 1.60
143 John Gelnar 4.00 1.60
Jerry May
144 Ed Kranepool 6.00 2.40
145 Luis Tiant RC 20.00 8.00
146 Ron Hansen 4.00 1.60
147 Dennis Bennett 4.00 1.60
148 Willie Kirkland 4.00 1.60
149 Wayne Schurr 4.00 1.60
150 Brooks Robinson 50.00 20.00
151 Athletics Team 10.00 4.00
152 Phil Ortega 4.00 1.60
153 Norm Cash 10.00 4.00
154 Bob Humphreys 4.00 1.60
155 Roger Maris 60.00 24.00
156 Bob Sadowski 4.00 1.60
157 Zoilo Versalles 6.00 2.40
158 Dick Sisler MG 4.00 1.60

159 Jim Duffalo 4.00 1.60
160 Roberto Clemente 200.00 80.00
161 Frank Baumann 4.00 1.60
162 Russ Nixon 4.00 1.60
163 John Briggs 4.00 1.60
164 Al Spangler 4.00 1.60
165 Dick Ellsworth 4.00 1.60
166 George Culver 8.00 3.20
Tommie Agee RC
167 Bill Wakefield 4.00 1.60
168 Dick Green 6.00 2.40
169 Dave Vineyard 4.00 1.60
170 Hank Aaron 120.00 47.50
171 Jim Roland 4.00 1.60
172 Jim Piersall 8.00 3.20
173 Tigers Team 10.00 4.00
174 Joe Jay 4.00 1.60
175 Bob Aspromonte 4.00 1.60
176 Willie McCovey 25.00 10.00
177 Pete Mikkelsen 4.00 1.60
178 Dalton Jones 4.00 1.60
179 Hal Woodeschick 4.00 1.60
180 Bob Allison 6.00 2.40
181 Don Loun 4.00 1.60
Joe McCabe
182 Mike de la Hoz 4.00 1.60
183 Dave Nicholson 4.00 1.60
184 John Boozer 4.00 1.60
185 Max Alvis 4.00 1.60
186 Bill Cowan 4.00 1.60
187 Casey Stengel MG 25.00 10.00
188 Sam Bowens 4.00 1.60
189 Checklist 177-264 10.00 2.50
190 Bill White 8.00 3.20
191 Phil Regan 6.00 2.40
192 Jim Coker 4.00 1.60
193 Gaylord Perry 25.00 10.00
194 Bill Kelso 6.00 2.40
Rick Reichardt
195 Bob Veale 6.00 2.40
196 Ron Fairly 6.00 2.40
197 Diego Segui 4.00 1.60
198 Smoky Burgess 6.00 2.40
199 Bob Heffner 6.00 2.40
200 Joe Torre 10.00 4.00
201 Sandy Valdespino 6.00 2.40
Cesar Tovar RC
202 Leo Burke 6.00 2.40
203 Dallas Green 6.00 2.40
204 Russ Snyder 6.00 2.40
205 Warren Spahn 40.00 16.00
206 Willie Horton 10.00 4.00
207 Pete Rose 150.00 60.00
208 Tommy John 10.00 4.00
209 Pirates Team 10.00 4.00
210 Jim Fregosi 8.00 3.20
211 Steve Ridzik 6.00 2.40
212 Ron Brand 6.00 2.40
213 Jim Davenport 6.00 2.40
214 Bob Purkey 6.00 2.40
215 Pete Ward 6.00 2.40
216 Al Worthington 6.00 2.40
217 Walt Alston MG 10.00 4.00
218 Dick Schofield 6.00 2.40
219 Bob Meyer 6.00 2.40
220 Billy Williams 15.00 6.00
221 John Tsitouris 6.00 2.40
222 Bob Tillman 6.00 2.40
223 Dan Osinski 6.00 2.40
224 Bob Chance 6.00 2.40
225 Bo Belinsky 8.00 3.20
226 Elvio Jimenez 8.00 3.20
Jake Gibbs
227 Bobby Klaus 6.00 2.40
228 Jack Sanford 6.00 2.40
229 Lou Clinton 6.00 2.40
230 Ray Sadecki 6.00 2.40
231 Jerry Adair 6.00 2.40
232 Steve Blass 6.00 2.40
233 Don Zimmer 8.00 3.20
234 White Sox Team 10.00 4.00
235 Chuck Hinton 6.00 2.40
236 Dennis McLain RC 30.00 12.00
237 Bernie Allen 6.00 2.40
238 Joe Moeller 6.00 2.40
239 Doc Edwards 6.00 2.40
240 Bob Bruce 6.00 2.40
241 Mack Jones 6.00 2.40
242 George Brunet 6.00 2.40
243 Ted Davidson 8.00 3.20
Tommy Helms RC
244 Lindy McDaniel 8.00 3.20
245 Joe Pepitone 8.00 3.20
246 Tom Butters 8.00 3.20
247 Wally Moon 8.00 3.20
248 Gus Triandos 6.00 2.40
249 Dave McNally 8.00 3.20
250 Willie Mays 120.00 47.50
251 Billy Herman MG 8.00 3.20
252 Pete Richert 6.00 2.40
253 Danny Cater 6.00 2.40
254 Roland Sheldon 6.00 2.40
255 Camilo Pascual 8.00 3.20
256 Tito Francona 6.00 2.40
257 Jim Wynn 8.00 3.20
258 Larry Bearnarth 6.00 2.40
259 Jim Northrup RC 10.00 4.00
Ray Oyler RC
260 Don Drysdale 30.00 12.00
261 Duke Carmel 6.00 2.40
262 Bud Daley 6.00 2.40
263 Marty Keough 6.00 2.40
264 Bob Buhl 6.00 2.40
265 Jim Pagliaroni 6.00 2.40
266 Bert Campaneris RC 12.00 4.80
267 Senators Team 10.00 4.00
268 Ken McBride 6.00 2.40
269 Frank Bolling 6.00 2.40
270 Milt Pappas 6.00 2.40
271 Don Wert 6.00 2.40
272 Chuck Schilling 6.00 2.40
273 4th Series Checklist 12.00 4.80
274 Lum Harris MG 6.00 2.40
275 Dick Groat 10.00 4.00
276 Hoyt Wilhelm 15.00 6.00
277 Johnny Lewis 6.00 2.40
278 Ken Retzer 6.00 2.40
279 Dick Tracewski 6.00 2.40
280 Dick Stuart 8.00 3.20
281 Bill Stafford 6.00 2.40
282 Dick Estelle 50.00 20.00
Masanori Murakami RC
283 Fred Whitfield 8.00 3.20

1966 O-Pee-Chee

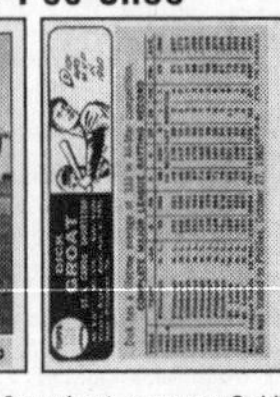

The cards in this 196-card set measure 2 1/2" by 3 1/2". This set is essentially the same as the regular 1966 Topps set, except that the words "Printed in Canada" appear on the bottom of the back, and the background colors are slightly different. On a white border, the fronts feature color player photos. The team name appears within a tilted bar in the top right corner, while the player's name and position are printed inside a bar under the photo. The horizontal backs carry player biography and statistics. Remember the prices below apply only to the O-Pee- Chee cards -- NOT to the 1966 Topps cards which are much more plentiful. Notable Rookie Cards include Jim Palmer.

	NM	Ex
COMPLETE SET (196)	1500.00	600.00

1 Willie Mays 200.00 80.00
2 Ted Abernathy 3.00 1.20
3 Sam Mele MG 3.00 1.20
4 Ray Culp 3.00 1.20
5 Jim Fregosi 4.00 1.60
6 Chuck Schilling 3.00 1.20
7 Tracy Stallard 3.00 1.20
8 Floyd Robinson 3.00 1.20
9 Clete Boyer 4.00 1.60
10 Tony Cloninger 3.00 1.20
11 Brant Alyea 4.00 1.60
Pete Craig
12 John Tsitouris 3.00 1.20
13 Lou Johnson 4.00 1.60
14 Norm Siebern 3.00 1.20
15 Vern Law 4.00 1.60
16 Larry Brown 3.00 1.20
17 John Stephenson 3.00 1.20
18 Roland Sheldon 3.00 1.20
19 Giants Team 6.00 2.40
20 Willie Horton 4.00 1.60
21 Don Nottebart 3.00 1.20
22 Joe Nossek 3.00 1.20
23 Jack Sanford 3.00 1.20
24 Don Kessinger RC 6.00 2.40
25 Pete Ward 4.00 1.60
26 Ray Sadecki 3.00 1.20
27 Darold Knowles 3.00 1.20
Andy Etchebarren
28 Phil Niekro 30.00 12.00
29 Mike Brumley 3.00 1.20
30 Pete Rose 60.00 24.00
31 Jack Cullen 4.00 1.60
32 Adolfo Phillips 3.00 1.20
33 Jim Pagliaroni 3.00 1.20
34 Checklist 1-88 12.00 3.00
35 Ron Swoboda 6.00 2.40
36 Jim Hunter 25.00 10.00
37 Billy Herman MG 4.00 1.60
38 Ron Nischwitz 3.00 1.20
39 Ken Henderson 3.00 1.20
40 Jim Grant 3.00 1.20
41 Don LeJohn 3.00 1.20
42 Aubrey Gatewood 3.00 1.20
43 Don Landrum 3.00 1.20
44 Bill Davis 3.00 1.20
Tom Kelley
45 Jim Gentile 4.00 1.60
46 Howie Koplitz 3.00 1.20
47 J.C. Martin 3.00 1.20
48 Paul Blair 4.00 1.60
49 Woody Woodward 3.00 1.20
50 Mickey Mantle 300.00 120.00
51 Gordon Richardson 3.00 1.20
52 Wes Covington 6.00 2.40
Johnny Callison
53 Bob Duliba 3.00 1.20
54 Jose Pagan 3.00 1.20
55 Ken Harrelson 4.00 1.60
56 Sandy Valdespino 3.00 1.20
57 Jim Lefebvre 4.00 1.60
58 Dave Wickersham 3.00 1.20
59 Reds Team 6.00 2.40
60 Curt Flood 8.00 3.20
61 Bob Bolin 3.00 1.20
62 Merritt Ranew 3.00 1.20
(with sold line)
63 Jim Stewart 3.00 1.20
64 Bob Bruce 3.00 1.20
65 Leon Wagner 3.00 1.20
66 Al Weis 3.00 1.20
67 Cleon Jones 6.00 2.40
Dick Selma
68 Hal Reniff 3.00 1.20
69 Ken Hamlin 3.00 1.20
70 Carl Yastrzemski 40.00 16.00
71 Frank Carpin 3.00 1.20
72 Tony Perez 30.00 12.00
73 Jerry Zimmerman 3.00 1.20
74 Don Mossi 4.00 1.60
75 Tommy Davis 4.00 1.60
76 Red Schoendienst MG 6.00 2.40
77 Johnny Orsino 3.00 1.20
78 Frank Linzy 3.00 1.20
79 Joe Pepitone 6.00 2.40
80 Richie Allen 8.00 3.20
81 Ray Oyler 3.00 1.20
82 Bob Hendley 3.00 1.20
83 Albie Pearson 4.00 1.60
84 Jim Beauchamp 3.00 1.20
Dick Kelley
85 Eddie Fisher 3.00 1.20
86 John Bateman 3.00 1.20
87 Dan Napoleon 3.00 1.20
88 Fred Whitfield 3.00 1.20
89 Ted Davidson 3.00 1.20
90 Luis Aparicio 10.00 4.00
91 Bob Uecker 20.00 8.00
(with traded line)
92 Yankees Team 15.00 6.00
93 Jim Lonborg 4.00 1.60
94 Matty Alou 4.00 1.60
95 Pete Richert 3.00 1.20
96 Felipe Alou 6.00 2.40
97 Jim Merritt 3.00 1.20
98 Don Demeter 3.00 1.20
99 Willie Stargell 8.00 3.20
Donn Clendenon
100 Sandy Koufax 100.00 40.00
101 Checklist 89-176 12.00 3.00
102 Ed Kirkpatrick 3.00 1.20
103 Dick Groat 4.00 1.60
(with traded line)
104 Alex Johnson 4.00 1.60
(with traded line)
105 Milt Pappas 4.00 1.60
106 Rusty Staub 6.00 2.40
107 Larry Stahl 3.00 1.20
Ron Tompkins
108 Bobby Klaus 3.00 1.20
109 Ralph Terry 4.00 1.60
110 Ernie Banks 40.00 16.00
111 Gary Peters 3.00 1.20
112 Manny Mota 4.00 1.60
113 Hank Aguirre 3.00 1.20
114 Jim Gosger 3.00 1.20
115 Bill Henry 3.00 1.20
116 Walt Alston MG 6.00 2.40
117 Jake Gibbs 3.00 1.20
118 Mike McCormick 3.00 1.20
119 Art Shamsky 3.00 1.20
120 Harmon Killebrew 20.00 8.00
121 Ray Herbert 3.00 1.20
122 Joe Gaines 3.00 1.20
123 Frank Bork 3.00 1.20
Jerry May
124 Tug McGraw 6.00 2.40
125 Lou Brock 25.00 10.00
126 Jim Palmer RC 125.00 50.00
127 Ken Berry 3.00 1.20
128 Jim Landis 3.00 1.20
129 Jack Kralick 3.00 1.20
130 Joe Torre 8.00 3.20
131 Angels Team 8.00 3.20
132 Orlando Cepeda 10.00 4.00
133 Don McMahon 3.00 1.20
134 Wes Parker 4.00 1.60
135 Dave Morehead 3.00 1.20
136 Woody Held 3.00 1.20
137 Pat Corrales 3.00 1.20
138 Roger Repoz 3.00 1.20
139 Byron Browne 3.00 1.20
Don Young
140 Jim Maloney 4.00 1.60
141 Tom McCraw 3.00 1.20
142 Don Dennis 3.00 1.20
143 Jose Tartabull 4.00 1.60
144 Don Schwall 3.00 1.20
145 Bill Freehan 4.00 1.60
146 George Altman 3.00 1.20
147 Lum Harris MG 3.00 1.20
148 Bob Johnson 3.00 1.20
149 Dick Nen 3.00 1.20
150 Rocky Colavito 10.00 4.00
151 Gary Wagner 3.00 1.20
152 Frank Malzone 4.00 1.60
153 Rico Carty 4.00 1.60
154 Chuck Hiller 3.00 1.20
155 Marcelino Lopez 3.00 1.20
156 Dick Schofield 3.00 1.20
Hal Lanier
157 Rene Lachemann 4.00 1.60
158 Jim Brewer 3.00 1.20
159 Chico Ruiz 3.00 1.20
160 Whitey Ford 30.00 12.00
161 Jerry Lumpe 3.00 1.20
162 Lee Maye 3.00 1.20
163 Tito Francona 3.00 1.20
164 Tommie Agee 4.00 1.60
Marv Staehle
165 Don Lock 3.00 1.20
166 Chris Krug 3.00 1.20
167 Boog Powell 8.00 3.20
168 Dan Osinski 3.00 1.20
169 Duke Sims 3.00 1.20
170 Cookie Rojas 4.00 1.60
171 Nick Willhite 3.00 1.20
172 Mets Team 8.00 3.20
173 Al Spangler 3.00 1.20
174 Ron Taylor 4.00 1.60
175 Bert Campaneris 6.00 2.40
176 Jim Davenport 3.00 1.20
177 Hector Lopez 3.00 1.20
178 Bob Tillman 3.00 1.20
179 Dennis Aust 4.00 1.60
Bob Tolan
180 Vada Pinson 6.00 2.40
181 Al Worthington 3.00 1.20
182 Jerry Lynch 3.00 1.20
183 Checklist 177-264 12.00 3.00
184 Denis Menke 3.00 1.20
185 Bob Buhl 4.00 1.60
186 Ruben Amaro 3.00 1.20
187 Chuck Dressen MG 4.00 1.60
188 Al Luplow 3.00 1.20
189 John Roseboro 4.00 1.60
190 Jimmie Hall 3.00 1.20
191 Darrell Sutherland 3.00 1.20
192 Vic Power 4.00 1.60
193 Dave McNally 4.00 1.60
194 Senators Team 8.00 3.20
195 Joe Morgan 20.00 8.00
196 Don Pavletich 4.00 1.60

1967 O-Pee-Chee

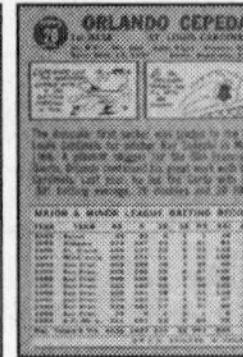

The cards in this 196-card set measure 2 1/2" by 3 1/2". This set is essentially the same as the regular 1967 Topps set, except that the words "Printed in Canada" appear on the bottom right corner of the back. On a white border, fronts feature color player photos with a thin black border. The player's name and position appear in the top part, while the team name is printed in big letters in the bottom part of the photo. On a green background, the backs carry player biography and statistics and two cartoon-like facts. Each checklist card features a small circular picture of a popular player included in that series. Remember the prices below apply only to the O-Pee-Chee cards -- NOT to the 1967 Topps cards which are much more plentiful.

	NM	Ex
COMPLETE SET (196)	1200.00	475.00

1 Frank Robinson 30.00 12.00
Hank Bauer MG
Brooks Robinson
2 Jack Hamilton 3.00 1.20
3 Duke Sims 3.00 1.20
4 Hal Lanier 3.00 1.20
5 Whitey Ford 25.00 10.00
6 Dick Simpson 3.00 1.20
7 Don McMahon 3.00 1.20
8 Chuck Harrison 3.00 1.20
9 Ron Hansen 3.00 1.20
10 Matty Alou 4.00 1.60
11 Barry Moore 3.00 1.20
12 Jim Campanis 4.00 1.60
Bill Singer
13 Joe Sparma 3.00 1.20
14 Phil Linz 4.00 1.60
15 Earl Battey 3.00 1.20
16 Bill Hands 3.00 1.20
17 Jim Gosger 3.00 1.20
18 Gene Oliver 3.00 1.20
19 Jim McGlothlin 3.00 1.20
20 Orlando Cepeda 10.00 4.00
21 Dave Bristol MG 3.00 1.20
22 Gene Brabender 3.00 1.20
23 Larry Elliot 3.00 1.20
24 Bob Allen 3.00 1.20
25 Elston Howard 6.00 2.40
26 Bob Priddy 3.00 1.20
(with traded line)
27 Bob Saverine 3.00 1.20
28 Barry Latman 3.00 1.20
29 Tommy McCraw 3.00 1.20
30 Al Kaline 25.00 10.00
31 Jim Brewer 3.00 1.20
32 Bob Bailey 4.00 1.60
33 Sal Bando RC 8.00 3.20
Randy Schwartz
34 Pete Cimino 3.00 1.20
35 Rico Carty 4.00 1.60
36 Bob Tillman 3.00 1.20
37 Rick Wise 4.00 1.60
38 Bob Johnson 3.00 1.20
39 Curt Simmons 4.00 1.60
40 Rick Reichardt 3.00 1.20
41 Joe Hoerner 3.00 1.20
42 Mets Team 12.00 4.80
43 Chico Salmon 3.00 1.20
44 Joe Nuxhall 4.00 1.60
45 Roger Maris 60.00 24.00
46 Lindy McDaniel 4.00 1.60
47 Ken McMullen 3.00 1.20
48 Bill Freehan 4.00 1.60
49 Roy Face 4.00 1.60
50 Tony Oliva 8.00 3.20
51 Dave Adlesh 3.00 1.20
Wes Bales
52 Dennis Higgins 3.00 1.20
53 Clay Dalrymple 3.00 1.20
54 Dick Green 3.00 1.20
55 Don Drysdale 20.00 8.00
56 Jose Tartabull 4.00 1.60
57 Pat Jarvis 4.00 1.60
58 Paul Schaal 3.00 1.20
59 Ralph Terry 4.00 1.60
60 Luis Aparicio 10.00 4.00
61 Gordy Coleman 3.00 1.20
62 Frank Robinson CL 12.00 3.00
63 Lou Brock 8.00 3.20
Curt Flood
64 Fred Valentine 3.00 1.20
65 Tom Haller 4.00 1.60
66 Manny Mota 4.00 1.60
67 Ken Berry 3.00 1.20
68 Bob Buhl 4.00 1.60
69 Vic Davalillo 3.00 1.20
70 Ron Santo 8.00 3.20
71 Camilo Pascual 4.00 1.60
72 George Korince 4.00 1.60
(photo actually
John Brown)
John (Tom) Matchick
73 Rusty Staub 8.00 3.20
74 Wes Stock 3.00 1.20
75 George Scott 4.00 1.60
76 Jim Barbieri 3.00 1.20
77 Dooley Womack 3.00 1.20
78 Pat Corrales 3.00 1.20
79 Bubba Morton 3.00 1.20
80 Jim Maloney 4.00 1.60
81 Eddie Stanky MG 4.00 1.60
82 Steve Barber 3.00 1.20
83 Ollie Brown 3.00 1.20
84 Tommie Sisk 3.00 1.20
85 Johnny Callison 4.00 1.60
86 Mike McCormick 4.00 1.60
(with traded line)
87 George Altman 3.00 1.20
88 Mickey Lolich 6.00 2.40
89 Felix Millan 4.00 1.60
90 Jim Nash 3.00 1.20
91 Johnny Lewis 3.00 1.20
92 Ray Washburn 3.00 1.20
93 Stan Bahnsen RC 6.00 2.40
Bobby Murcer
94 Ron Fairly 4.00 1.60
95 Sonny Siebert 3.00 1.20
96 Art Shamsky 3.00 1.20
97 Mike Cuellar 6.00 2.40
98 Rich Rollins 3.00 1.20
99 Lee Stange 3.00 1.20
100 Frank Robinson 15.00 6.00
101 Ken Johnson 3.00 1.20
102 Phillies Team 6.00 2.40
103 Mickey Mantle CL 25.00 6.25
104 Minnie Rojas 3.00 1.20
105 Ken Boyer 8.00 3.20
106 Randy Hundley 4.00 1.60
107 Joel Horlen 3.00 1.20
108 Alex Johnson 4.00 1.60
109 Rocky Colavito 8.00 3.20
Leon Wagner
110 Jack Aker 3.00 1.20
111 John Kennedy 3.00 1.20
112 Dave Wickersham 3.00 1.20
113 Dave Nicholson 3.00 1.20
114 Jack Baldschun 3.00 1.20
115 Paul Casanova 3.00 1.20
116 Herman Franks MG 3.00 1.20
117 Darrell Brandon 3.00 1.20
118 Bernie Allen 3.00 1.20
119 Wade Blasingame 3.00 1.20
120 Floyd Robinson 3.00 1.20
121 Ed Bressoud 3.00 1.20
122 George Brunet 3.00 1.20
123 Jim Price 4.00 1.60
Luke Walker
124 Jim Stewart 3.00 1.20
125 Moe Drabowsky 4.00 1.60
126 Tony Taylor 3.00 1.20
127 John O'Donoghue 3.00 1.20
128 Ed Spiezio 3.00 1.20
129 Phil Roof 3.00 1.20
130 Phil Regan 4.00 1.60
131 Yankees Team 12.00 4.80
132 Ozzie Virgil 3.00 1.20
133 Ron Kline 3.00 1.20
134 Gates Brown 3.00 1.20
135 Deron Johnson 4.00 1.60
136 Carroll Sembera 3.00 1.20
137 Ron Clark 3.00 1.20
Jim Ollom
138 Dick Kelley 3.00 1.20
139 Dalton Jones 3.00 1.20
140 Willie Stargell 25.00 10.00
141 John Miller 3.00 1.20
142 Jackie Brandt 3.00 1.20
143 Pete Ward 6.00 2.40
Don Buford
144 Bill Hepler 3.00 1.20
145 Larry Brown 3.00 1.20
146 Steve Carlton 60.00 24.00
147 Tom Egan 3.00 1.20
148 Adolfo Phillips 3.00 1.20
149 Joe Moeller 3.00 1.20
150 Mickey Mantle 300.00 120.00
151 Moe Drabowsky WS 6.00 2.40
152 Jim Palmer WS 10.00 4.00
153 Paul Blair WS 6.00 2.40
154 Brooks Robinson WS 6.00 2.40
Dave McNally
155 W.S. Summary 6.00 2.40
Winners celebrate
156 Ron Herbel 3.00 1.20
157 Danny Cater 3.00 1.20
158 Jimmie Coker 3.00 1.20
159 Bruce Howard 3.00 1.20
160 Willie Davis 4.00 1.60
161 Dick Williams MG 4.00 1.60
162 Billy O'Dell 3.00 1.20
163 Vic Roznovsky 3.00 1.20
164 Dwight Siebler 3.00 1.20
165 Cleon Jones 4.00 1.60
166 Eddie Mathews 20.00 8.00
167 Joe Coleman 3.00 1.20
Tim Cullen
168 Ray Culp 3.00 1.20
169 Horace Clarke 3.00 1.20
170 Dick McAuliffe 4.00 1.60
171 Calvin Koonce 3.00 1.20
172 Bill Heath 3.00 1.20
173 Cardinals Team 6.00 2.40
174 Dick Radatz 4.00 1.60
175 Bobby Knoop 3.00 1.20
176 Sammy Ellis 3.00 1.20
177 Tito Fuentes 3.00 1.20
178 John Buzhardt 3.00 1.20
179 Charles Vaughan 4.00 1.60
Cecil Upshaw
180 Curt Blefary 3.00 1.20
181 Terry Fox 3.00 1.20
182 Ed Charles 3.00 1.20
183 Jim Pagliaroni 3.00 1.20
184 George Thomas 3.00 1.20
185 Ken Holtzman RC 6.00 2.40
186 Ed Kranepool 6.00 2.40
Ron Swoboda
187 Pedro Ramos 3.00 1.20
188 Ken Harrelson 4.00 1.60
189 Chuck Hinton 3.00 1.20
190 Turk Farrell 3.00 1.20
191 Willie Mays CL 15.00 6.00
192 Fred Gladding 3.00 1.20
193 Jose Cardenal 4.00 1.60
194 Bob Allison 4.00 1.60
195 Al Jackson 3.00 1.20
196 Johnny Romano 4.00 1.60

1967 O-Pee-Chee Paper Inserts

These posters measure approximately 5" by 7" and are very similar to the American Topps poster (paper insert) issue, except that they say "Ptd. in Canada" on the bottom. The fronts feature color player photos with thin borders. The player's name and position, team name, and the card number appear inside a circle in the lower right. A facsimile player autograph rounds out the front. The backs are blank. This Canadian version is much more difficult to find than the American version. These numbered "All-Star" inserts have fold lines which are generally not very noticeable when stored carefully. There is some confusion as to whether these posters were issued in 1967 or 1968.

NM Ex
COMPLETE SET (32) 250.00 100.00
1 Boog Powell 5.00 2.00
2 Bert Campaneris 3.00 1.20
3 Brooks Robinson 12.00 4.80
4 Tommie Agee 2.00 .80
5 Carl Yastrzemski 20.00 8.00
6 Mickey Mantle 100.00 40.00
7 Frank Howard 4.00 1.60
8 Sam McDowell 3.00 1.20
9 Orlando Cepeda 8.00 3.20
10 Chico Cardenas 2.00 .80
11 Bob Clemente 60.00 24.00
12 Willie Mays 40.00 16.00
13 Cleon Jones 2.00 .80
14 John Callison 2.00 .80
15 Hank Aaron 40.00 16.00
16 Don Drysdale 12.00 4.80
17 Bobby Knoop 2.00 .80
18 Tony Oliva 5.00 2.00
19 Frank Robinson 12.00 4.80
20 Denny McLain 5.00 2.00
21 Al Kaline 12.00 4.80
22 Joe Pepitone 3.00 1.20
23 Harmon Killebrew 12.00 4.80
24 Leon Wagner 2.00 .80
25 Joe Morgan 12.00 4.80
26 Ron Santo 5.00 2.00
27 Joe Torre 5.00 2.00
28 Juan Marichal 12.00 4.80
29 Matty Alou 3.00 1.20
30 Felipe Alou 4.00 1.60
31 Ron Hunt 2.00 .80
32 Willie McCovey 12.00 4.80

1968 O-Pee-Chee

The cards in this 196-card set measure 2 1/2" by 3 1/2". This set is essentially the same as the regular 1968 Topps set, except that the words "Printed in Canada" appear on the bottom of the back and the backgrounds have a different color. The fronts feature color player photos with rounded corners. The player's name is printed under the photo, while his position and team name appear in a circle in the lower right. On a light brown background, the backs carry player biography and statistics and a cartoon-like trivia question. Each checklist card features a small circular picture of a popular player included in that series. Remember the prices below apply only to the O-Pee-Chee cards -- NOT to the 1968 Topps cards which are much more plentiful. The key card in the set is Nolan Ryan in his Rookie Card year. The first OPC cards of Hall of Famers Rod Carew and Tom Seaver also appear in this set.

NM Ex
COMPLETE SET (196) 2000.00 800.00
1 Bob Clemente 35.00 14.00
Tony Gonzalez
Matty Alou LL
2 Carl Yastrzemski 15.00 6.00
Frank Robinson
Al Kaline LL
3 Orlando Cepeda 25.00 10.00
Bob Clemente
Hank Aaron LL
4 Carl Yastrzemski 15.00 6.00
Harmon Killebrew
Frank Robinson LL
5 Hank Aaron 10.00 4.00
Jim Wynn
Ron Santo
Willie McCovey LL
6 Carl Yastrzemski 10.00 4.00
Harmon Killebrew
Frank Howard LL
7 Phil Niekro 6.00 2.40
Jim Bunning
Chris Short LL
8 Joel Horlen 6.00 2.40
Gary Peters
Sonny Siebert LL
9 Mike McCormick 6.00 2.40
Ferguson Jenkins
Jim Bunning
Claude Osteen LL
10 Jim Lonborg 6.00 2.40
Earl Wilson
Dean Chance LL
11 Jim Bunning 8.00 3.20
Ferguson Jenkins
Gaylord Perry LL
12 Jim Lonborg 6.00 2.40
Sam McDowell
Dean Chance LL
13 Chuck Hartenstein 3.00 1.20
14 Jerry McNertney 3.00 1.20
15 Ron Hunt 3.00 1.20
16 Lou Piniella 8.00 3.20
Richie Scheinblum
17 Dick Hall 3.00 1.20
18 Mike Hershberger 3.00 1.20
19 Juan Pizarro 3.00 1.20
20 Brooks Robinson 30.00 12.00
21 Ron Davis 3.00 1.20
22 Pat Dobson 4.00 1.60
23 Chico Cardenas 4.00 1.60
24 Bobby Locke 3.00 1.20
25 Julian Javier 4.00 1.60
26 Darrell Brandon 3.00 1.20
27 Gil Hodges MG 8.00 3.20
28 Ted Uhlaender 3.00 1.20
29 Joe Verbanic 3.00 1.20
30 Joe Torre 8.00 3.20
31 Ed Stroud 3.00 1.20
32 Joe Gibbon 3.00 1.20
33 Pete Ward 4.00 1.60
34 Al Ferrara 3.00 1.20
35 Steve Hargan 3.00 1.20
36 Bob Moose 4.00 1.60
Bob Robertson
37 Billy Williams 10.00 4.00
38 Tony Pierce 3.00 1.20
39 Cookie Rojas 3.00 1.20
40 Denny McLain 10.00 4.00
41 Julio Gotay 3.00 1.20
42 Larry Haney 3.00 1.20
43 Gary Bell 3.00 1.20
44 Frank Kostro 3.00 1.20
45 Tom Seaver 60.00 24.00
46 Dave Ricketts 3.00 1.20
47 Ralph Houk MG 4.00 1.60
48 Ted Davidson 3.00 1.20
49 Ed Brinkman 3.00 1.20
50 Willie Mays 80.00 32.00
51 Bob Locker 3.00 1.20
52 Hawk Taylor 3.00 1.20
53 Gene Alley 4.00 1.60
54 Stan Williams 3.00 1.20
55 Felipe Alou 6.00 2.40
56 Dave Leonhard 3.00 1.20
Dave May RC
57 Dan Schneider 3.00 1.20
58 Ed Mathews 20.00 8.00
59 Don Lock 3.00 1.20
60 Ken Holtzman 4.00 1.60
61 Reggie Smith 6.00 2.40
62 Chuck Dobson 3.00 1.20
63 Dick Kenworthy 3.00 1.20
64 Jim Merritt 3.00 1.20
65 John Roseboro 4.00 1.60
66 Casey Cox 3.00 1.20
67 Jim Kaat CL 8.00 2.00
68 Ron Willis 3.00 1.20
69 Tom Tresh 4.00 1.60
70 Bob Veale 4.00 1.60
71 Vern Fuller 3.00 1.20
72 Tommy John 8.00 3.20
73 Jim Ray Hart 4.00 1.60
74 Milt Pappas 4.00 1.60
75 Don Mincher 3.00 1.20
76 Jim Britton 4.00 1.60
Ron Reed
77 Don Wilson 4.00 1.60
78 Jim Northrup 8.00 3.20
79 Ted Kubiak 3.00 1.20
80 Rod Carew 60.00 24.00
81 Larry Jackson 3.00 1.20
82 Sam Bowens 3.00 1.20
83 John Stephenson 3.00 1.20
84 Bob Tolan 3.00 1.20
85 Gaylord Perry 10.00 4.00
86 Willie Stargell 10.00 4.00
87 Dick Williams MG 4.00 1.60
88 Phil Regan 4.00 1.60
89 Jake Gibbs 4.00 1.60
90 Vada Pinson 6.00 2.40
91 Jim Ollom 3.00 1.20
92 Ed Kranepool 4.00 1.60
93 Tony Cloninger 3.00 1.20
94 Lee Maye 3.00 1.20
95 Bob Aspromonte 3.00 1.20
96 Frank Coggins 3.00 1.20
Dick Nold
97 Tom Phoebus 3.00 1.20
98 Gary Sutherland 3.00 1.20
99 Rocky Colavito 10.00 4.00
100 Bob Gibson 30.00 12.00
101 Glenn Beckert 4.00 1.60
102 Jose Cardenal 4.00 1.60
103 Don Sutton 10.00 4.00
104 Dick Dietz 3.00 1.20
105 Al Downing 4.00 1.60
106 Dalton Jones 3.00 1.20
107 Juan Marichal CL 8.00 2.00
108 Don Pavletich 3.00 1.20
109 Bert Campaneris 4.00 1.60
110 Hank Aaron 80.00 32.00
111 Rich Reese 3.00 1.20
112 Woody Fryman 3.00 1.20
113 Tom Matchick 4.00 1.60
Daryl Patterson
114 Ron Swoboda 4.00 1.60
115 Sam McDowell 4.00 1.60
116 Ken McMullen 3.00 1.20
117 Larry Jaster 3.00 1.20
118 Mark Belanger 4.00 1.60
119 Ted Savage 3.00 1.20
120 Mel Stottlemyre 6.00 2.40
121 Jimmie Hall 3.00 1.20
122 Gene Mauch MG 4.00 1.60
123 Jose Santiago 3.00 1.20
124 Nate Oliver 3.00 1.20
125 Joel Horlen 3.00 1.20
126 Bobby Etheridge 3.00 1.20
127 Paul Lindblad 3.00 1.20
128 Tom Dukes 3.00 1.20
Alonzo Harris
129 Mickey Stanley 8.00 3.20
130 Tony Perez 10.00 4.00
131 Frank Bertaina 3.00 1.20
132 Bud Harrelson 4.00 1.60
133 Fred Whitfield 3.00 1.20
134 Pat Jarvis 3.00 1.20
135 Paul Blair 4.00 1.60
136 Randy Hundley 4.00 1.60
137 Twins Team 6.00 2.40
138 Ruben Amaro 3.00 1.20
139 Chris Short 3.00 1.20
140 Tony Conigliaro 10.00 4.00
141 Dal Maxvill 3.00 1.20
142 Buddy Bradford 3.00 1.20
Bill Voss
143 Pete Cimino 3.00 1.20
144 Joe Morgan 15.00 6.00
145 Don Drysdale 15.00 6.00
146 Sal Bando 4.00 1.60
147 Frank Linzy 3.00 1.20
148 Dave Bristol MG 3.00 1.20
149 Bob Saverine 3.00 1.20
150 Bob Clemente 80.00 32.00
151 Lou Brock WS 12.00 4.80
152 Carl Yastrzemski WS 12.00 4.80
153 Nellie Briles WS 6.00 2.40
154 Bob Gibson WS 12.00 4.80
155 Jim Lonborg WS 6.00 2.40
156 Rico Petrocelli WS 6.00 2.40
157 World Series Game 7 6.00 2.40
St. Louis wins it
158 WS Summary 6.00 2.40
Cardinals celebrate
159 Don Kessinger 4.00 1.60
160 Earl Wilson 4.00 1.60
161 Norm Miller 3.00 1.20
162 Hal Gilson 4.00 1.60
Mike Torrez
163 Gene Brabender 3.00 1.20
164 Ramon Webster 3.00 1.20
165 Tony Oliva 8.00 3.20
166 Claude Raymond 4.00 1.60
167 Elston Howard 8.00 3.20
168 Dodgers Team 6.00 2.40
169 Bob Bolin 3.00 1.20
170 Jim Fregosi 4.00 1.60
171 Don Nottebart 3.00 1.20
172 Walt Williams 3.00 1.20
173 John Boozer 3.00 1.20
174 Bob Tillman 3.00 1.20
175 Maury Wills 8.00 3.20
176 Bob Allen 3.00 1.20
177 Jerry Koosman RC 1000.00 400.00
Nolan Ryan RC
178 Don Wert 4.00 1.60
179 Bill Stoneman 3.00 1.20
180 Curt Flood 6.00 2.40
181 Jerry Zimmerman 3.00 1.20
182 Dave Giusti 3.00 1.20
183 Bob Kennedy MG 4.00 1.60
184 Lou Johnson 3.00 1.20
185 Tom Haller 3.00 1.20
186 Eddie Watt 3.00 1.20
187 Sonny Jackson 3.00 1.20
188 Cap Peterson 3.00 1.20
189 Bill Landis 3.00 1.20
190 Bill White 4.00 1.60
191 Dan Frisella 3.00 1.20
192 Carl Yastrzemski CL 10.00 2.50
193 Jack Hamilton 3.00 1.20
194 Don Buford 3.00 1.20
195 Joe Pepitone 4.00 1.60
196 Gary Nolan 4.00 1.60

1969 O-Pee-Chee

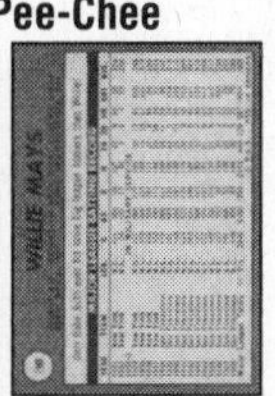

The cards in this 218-card set measure 2 1/2" by 3 1/2". This set is essentially the same as the regular 1969 Topps set, except that the words "Printed in Canada" appear on the bottom of the back and the backgrounds have a purple color. The fronts feature color player photos with rounded corners and thin black borders. The player's name and position are printed inside a circle in the top right corner, while the team name appears in the lower part of the photo. On a magenta background, the backs carry player biography and statistics. Each checklist card features a small circular picture of a popular player included in that series. Remember the prices below apply only to the O-Pee-Chee cards -- NOT to the 1969 Topps cards which are much more plentiful. Notable Rookie Cards include Graig Nettles.

NM Ex
COMPLETE SET (218) 1000.00 400.00
1 Carl Yastrzemski 20.00 8.00
Danny Cater
Tony Oliva LL
2 Pete Rose 8.00 3.20
Matty Alou
Felipe Alou LL
3 Ken Harrelson 6.00 2.40
Frank Howard
Jim Northrup LL
4 Willie McCovey 8.00 3.20
Ron Santo
Billy Williams LL
5 Frank Howard 6.00 2.40
Willie Horton
Ken Harrelson LL
6 Willie McCovey 8.00 3.20
Richie Allen
Ernie Banks LL
7 Luis Tiant 6.00 2.40
Sam McDowell
Dave McNally LL
8 Bob Gibson 8.00 3.20
Bobby Bolin
Bob Veale LL
9 Denny McLain 6.00 2.40
Dave McNally
Luis Tiant
Mel Stottlemyre LL
10 Juan Marichal 8.00 3.20
Bob Gibson
Fergie Jenkins LL
11 Sam McDowell 8.00 3.20
Denny McLain
Luis Tiant LL
12 Bob Gibson 8.00 3.20
Fergie Jenkins
Bill Singer LL
13 Mickey Stanley 4.00 1.60
14 Al McBean 2.00 .80
15 Boog Powell 6.00 2.40
16 Cesar Gutierrez 2.00 .80
Rich Robertson
17 Mike Marshall 4.00 1.60
18 Dick Schofield 2.00 .80
19 Ken Suarez 2.00 .80
20 Ernie Banks 25.00 10.00
21 Jose Santiago 2.00 .80
22 Jesus Alou 4.00 1.60
23 Lew Krausse 2.00 .80
24 Walt Alston MG 6.00 2.40
25 Roy White 4.00 1.60
26 Clay Carroll 4.00 1.60
27 Bernie Allen 2.00 .80
28 Mike Ryan 2.00 .80
29 Dave Morehead 2.00 .80
30 Bob Allison 4.00 1.60
31 Gary Gentry RC 6.00 2.40
Amos Otis RC
32 Sammy Ellis 2.00 .80
33 Wayne Causey 2.00 .80
34 Gary Peters 2.00 .80
35 Joe Morgan 12.00 4.80
36 Luke Walker 2.00 .80
37 Curt Motton 2.00 .80
38 Zoilo Versalles 4.00 1.60
39 Dick Hughes 2.00 .80
40 Mayo Smith MG 2.00 .80
41 Bob Barton 2.00 .80
42 Tommy Harper 4.00 1.60
43 Joe Niekro 4.00 1.60
44 Danny Cater 2.00 .80
45 Maury Wills 6.00 2.40
46 Fritz Peterson 4.00 1.60
47 Paul Popovich 2.00 .80
48 Brant Alyea 2.00 .80
49 Steve Jones 2.00 .80
Ellie Rodriguez
50 Roberto Clemente 80.00 32.00
(Bob on card)
51 Woody Fryman 4.00 1.60
52 Mike Andrews 2.00 .80
53 Sonny Jackson 2.00 .80
54 Cisco Carlos 2.00 .80
55 Jerry Grote 4.00 1.60
56 Rich Reese 2.00 .80
57 Denny McLain CL 8.00 2.00
58 Fred Gladding 2.00 .80
59 Jay Johnstone 4.00 1.60
60 Nelson Briles 4.00 1.60
61 Jimmie Hall 2.00 .80
62 Chico Salmon 2.00 .80
63 Jim Hickman 2.00 .80
64 Bill Monbouquette 2.00 .80
65 Willie Davis 4.00 1.60
66 Mike Adamson 2.00 .80
Merv Rettenmund
67 Bill Stoneman 4.00 1.60
68 Dave Duncan 4.00 1.60
69 Steve Hamilton 4.00 1.60
70 Tommy Helms 4.00 1.60
71 Steve Whitaker 4.00 1.60
72 Ron Taylor 4.00 1.60
73 Johnny Briggs 2.00 .80
74 Preston Gomez MG 2.00 .80
75 Luis Aparicio 8.00 3.20
76 Norm Miller 2.00 .80
77 Ron Perranoski 4.00 1.60
78 Tom Satriano 2.00 .80
79 Milt Pappas 4.00 1.60
80 Norm Cash 4.00 1.60
81 Mel Queen 2.00 .80
82 Rich Hebner RC 10.00 4.00
Al Oliver RC
83 Mike Ferraro 4.00 1.60
84 Bob Humphreys 2.00 .80
85 Lou Brock 25.00 10.00
86 Pete Richert 2.00 .80
87 Horace Clarke 4.00 1.60
88 Rich Nye 2.00 .80
89 Russ Gibson 2.00 .80
90 Jerry Koosman 6.00 2.40
91 Al Dark MG 4.00 1.60
92 Jack Billingham 4.00 1.60
93 Joe Foy 2.00 .80
94 Hank Aguirre 2.00 .80
95 Johnny Bench 60.00 24.00
96 Denver LeMaster 2.00 .80
97 Buddy Bradford 2.00 .80
98 Dave Giusti 2.00 .80
99 Danny Morris 20.00 8.00
Graig Nettles RC
100 Hank Aaron 50.00 20.00
101 Daryl Patterson 2.00 .80
102 Jim Davenport 2.00 .80
103 Roger Repoz 2.00 .80
104 Steve Blass 2.00 .80
105 Rick Monday 4.00 1.60
106 Jim Hannan 2.00 .80
107 Bob Gibson CL 8.00 2.00
108 Tony Taylor 4.00 1.60
109 Jim Lonborg 4.00 1.60
110 Mike Shannon 4.00 1.60
111 John Morris 2.00 .80
112 J.C. Martin 4.00 1.60
113 Dave May 2.00 .80
114 Alan Closter 4.00 1.60
John Cumberland
115 Bill Hands 2.00 .80
116 Chuck Harrison 2.00 .80
117 Jim Fairey 4.00 1.60
118 Stan Williams 2.00 .80
119 Doug Rader 4.00 1.60
120 Pete Rose 25.00 10.00
121 Joe Grzenda 2.00 .80
122 Ron Fairly 4.00 1.60
123 Wilbur Wood 4.00 1.60
124 Hank Bauer MG 4.00 1.60
125 Ray Sadecki 2.00 .80
126 Dick Tracewski 2.00 .80
127 Kevin Collins 4.00 1.60
128 Tommie Aaron 4.00 1.60
129 Bill McCool 2.00 .80
130 Carl Yastrzemski 25.00 10.00
131 Chris Cannizzaro 2.00 .80
132 Dave Baldwin 2.00 .80
133 Johnny Callison 4.00 1.60
134 Jim Weaver 2.00 .80
135 Tommy Davis 4.00 1.60
136 Steve Huntz 2.00 .80
Mike Torrez
137 Wally Bunker 2.00 .80
138 John Bateman 2.00 .80
139 Andy Kosco 2.00 .80
140 Jim Lefebvre 4.00 1.60
141 Bill Dillman 2.00 .80
142 Woody Woodward 2.00 .80
143 Joe Nossek 2.00 .80
144 Bob Hendley 2.00 .80
145 Max Alvis 2.00 .80
146 Jim Perry 4.00 1.60
147 Leo Durocher MG 6.00 2.40
148 Lee Stange 2.00 .80
149 Ollie Brown 2.00 .80
150 Denny McLain 6.00 2.40
151 Clay Dalrymple 4.00 1.60
(Catching, Phillies)
152 Tommie Sisk 2.00 .80
153 Ed Brinkman 2.00 .80
154 Jim Britton 2.00 .80
155 Pete Ward 4.00 1.60
156 Hal Gilson 2.00 .80
Leon McFadden
157 Bob Rodgers 4.00 1.60
158 Joe Gibbon 2.00 .80
159 Jerry Adair 2.00 .80
160 Vada Pinson 6.00 2.40
161 John Purdin 2.00 .80
162 Bob Gibson WS 10.00 4.00
fans 17
163 Willie Horton WS 8.00 3.20
164 Tim McCarver WS 15.00 6.00
with Roger Maris
165 Lou Brock WS 10.00 4.00
166 Al Kaline WS 8.00 3.20
167 Jim Northrup WS 8.00 3.20
168 Mickey Lolich WS 8.00 3.20
Bob Gibson
169 Tigers celebrate 8.00 3.20
Dick McAuliffe
Denny McLain
Willie Horton
170 Frank Howard 4.00 1.60
171 Glenn Beckert 4.00 1.60
172 Jerry Stephenson 2.00 .80
173 Bob Christian 2.00 .80
Gerry Nyman
174 Grant Jackson 2.00 .80
175 Jim Bunning 8.00 3.20
176 Joe Azcue 2.00 .80
177 Ron Reed 2.00 .80
178 Ray Oyler 4.00 1.60
179 Don Pavletich 2.00 .80
180 Willie Horton 4.00 1.60
181 Mel Nelson 2.00 .80
182 Bill Rigney MG 2.00 .80
183 Don Shaw 4.00 1.60
184 Roberto Pena 2.00 .80
185 Tom Phoebus 2.00 .80
186 John Edwards 2.00 .80
187 Leon Wagner 2.00 .80
188 Rick Wise 4.00 1.60
189 Joe Lahoud 2.00 .80
John Thibodeau
190 Willie Mays 80.00 32.00
191 Lindy McDaniel 4.00 1.60
192 Jose Pagan 2.00 .80
193 Don Cardwell 4.00 1.60
194 Ted Uhlaender 2.00 .80
195 John Odom 2.00 .80
196 Lum Harris MG 2.00 .80
197 Dick Selma 2.00 .80
198 Willie Smith 2.00 .80
199 Jim French 2.00 .80
200 Bob Gibson 15.00 6.00
201 Russ Snyder 2.00 .80
202 Don Wilson 4.00 1.60
203 Dave Johnson 4.00 1.60
204 Jack Hiatt 2.00 .80
205 Rick Reichardt 2.00 .80
206 Larry Hisle 4.00 1.60
Barry Lersch
207 Roy Face 4.00 1.60
208 Donn Clendenon 4.00 1.60
(Montreal Expos)
209 Larry Haney UER 2.00 .80
(Reversed negative)
210 Felix Millan 2.00 .80
211 Galen Cisco 2.00 .80
212 Tom Tresh 4.00 1.60
213 Gerry Arrigo 2.00 .80
214 Checklist 3 8.00 2.00
With 69T deckle CL
on back (no player)
215 Rico Petrocelli 4.00 1.60
216 Don Sutton 8.00 3.20
217 John Donaldson 2.00 .80
218 John Roseboro 4.00 1.60

1969 O-Pee-Chee Deckle

This set is very similar to the U.S. deckle version produced by Topps. The cards measure approximately 2 1/8" by 3 1/8" (slightly smaller than the American issue) and are cut with deckle edges. The fronts feature black-and-white player photos with white borders and facsimile autographs in black ink (instead of blue ink like the Topps issue). The backs are blank. The cards are unnumbered and checklisted below in alphabetical order. Remember the prices below apply only to the O-Pee-Chee Deckle cards -- NOT to the 1969 Topps Deckle cards which are much more plentiful.

NM Ex
COMPLETE SET (24) 200.00 80.00
1 Richie Allen 8.00 3.20
2 Luis Aparicio 10.00 4.00
3 Rod Carew 15.00 6.00

4 Roberto Clemente 40.00 16.00
5 Curt Flood 5.00 2.00
6 Bill Freehan 5.00 2.00
7 Bob Gibson 15.00 6.00
8 Ken Harrelson 5.00 2.00
9 Tommy Helms 3.00 1.20
10 Tom Haller 3.00 1.20
11 Willie Horton 5.00 2.00
12 Frank Howard 8.00 3.20
13 Willie McCovey 15.00 6.00
14 Denny McLain 8.00 3.20
15 Juan Marichal 10.00 4.00
16 Willie Mays 30.00 12.00
17 Boog Powell 8.00 3.20
18 Brooks Robinson 15.00 6.00
19 Ron Santo 8.00 3.20
20 Rusty Staub 5.00 2.00
21 Mel Stottlemyre 3.00 1.20
22 Luis Tiant 3.00 1.20
23 Maury Wills 5.00 2.00
24 Carl Yastrzemski 15.00 6.00

1970 O-Pee-Chee

The cards in this 546-card set measure 2 1/2" by 3 1/2". This set is essentially the same as the regular 1970 Topps set, except that the words "Printed in Canada" appear on the backs and the backs are bilingual. On a gray border, the fronts feature color player photos with thin white borders. The player's name and position are printed under the photo, while the team name appears in the upper part of the picture. The horizontal backs carry player biography and statistics in French and English. The card stock is a deeper shade of yellow on the reverse for the O-Pee-Chee cards. Remember the prices below apply only to the O-Pee-Chee cards -- NOT to the 1970 Topps cards which are much more plentiful. Notable Rookie Cards include Thurman Munson.

NM Ex
COMPLETE SET (546) 1500.00 600.00
COMMON CARD (1-459) 1.50 .60
COMMON (460-546) 2.50 1.00
1 New York Mets 30.00 12.00
Team Card
2 Diego Segui 2.00 .80
3 Darrel Chaney 1.50 .60
4 Tom Egan 1.50 .60
5 Wes Parker 2.00 .80
6 Grant Jackson 1.50 .60
7 Gary Boyd 1.50 .60
Russ Nagelson
8 Jose Martinez 1.50 .60
9 Checklist 1-132 15.00 3.70
10 Carl Yastrzemski 20.00 8.00
11 Nate Colbert 1.50 .60
12 John Hiller 2.00 .80
13 Jack Hiatt 1.50 .60
14 Hank Allen 1.50 .60
15 Larry Dierker 1.50 .60
16 Charlie Metro MG 1.50 .60
17 Hoyt Wilhelm 6.00 2.40
18 Carlos May 2.00 .80
19 John Boccabella 1.50 .60
20 Dave McNally 2.00 .80
21 Vida Blue RC 6.00 2.40
Gene Tenace RC
22 Ray Washburn 1.50 .60
23 Bill Robinson 2.00 .80
24 Dick Selma 1.50 .60
25 Cesar Tovar 1.50 .60
26 Tug McGraw 4.00 1.60
27 Chuck Hinton 1.50 .60
28 Billy Wilson 1.50 .60
29 Sandy Alomar 2.00 .80
30 Matty Alou 2.00 .80
31 Marty Pattin 2.00 .80
32 Harry Walker MG 1.50 .60
33 Don Wert 1.50 .60
34 Willie Crawford 1.50 .60
35 Joel Horlen 1.50 .60
36 Danny Breeden 2.00 .80
Bernie Carbo
37 Dick Drago 1.50 .60
38 Mack Jones 1.50 .60
39 Mike Nagy 1.50 .60
40 Rich Allen 4.00 1.60
41 George Lauzerique 1.50 .60
42 Tito Fuentes 1.50 .60
43 Jack Aker 1.50 .60
44 Roberto Pena 1.50 .60
45 Dave Johnson 2.00 .80
46 Ken Rudolph 1.50 .60
47 Bob Miller 1.50 .60
48 Gil Garrido 1.50 .60
49 Tim Cullen 1.50 .60
50 Tommie Agee 2.00 .80
51 Bob Christian 1.50 .60
52 Bruce Dal Canton 1.50 .60
53 John Kennedy 1.50 .60
54 Jeff Torborg 2.00 .80
55 John Odom 1.50 .60
56 Joe Lis 1.50 .60
Scott Reid
57 Pat Kelly 1.50 .60
58 Dave Marshall 1.50 .60
59 Dick Ellsworth 1.50 .60
60 Jim Wynn 2.00 .80
61 Pete Rose 12.00 4.80
Bob Clemente
Cleon Jones LL
62 Rod Carew 3.00 1.20
Reggie Smith
Tony Oliva LL
63 Willie McCovey 3.00 1.20
Ron Santo
Tony Perez LL
64 Harmon Killebrew 6.00 2.40
Boog Powell
Reggie Jackson LL
65 Willie McCovey 6.00 2.40
Hank Aaron
Lee May LL
66 Harmon Killebrew 6.00 2.40
Frank Howard
Reggie Jackson LL
67 Juan Marichal 8.00 3.20
Steve Carlton
Bob Gibson LL
68 Dick Bosman 2.00 .80
Jim Palmer
Mike Cuellar LL
69 Tom Seaver 8.00 3.20
Phil Niekro
Fergie Jenkins
Juan Marichal LL
70 Dennis McLain 2.00 .80
Mike Cuellar
Dave Boswell
Dave McNally
Jim Perry
Mel Stottlemyre LL
71 Fergie Jenkins 3.00 1.20
Bob Gibson
Bill Singer LL
72 Sam McDowell 2.00 .80
Mickey Lolich
Andy Messersmith LL
73 Wayne Granger 1.50 .60
74 Greg Washburn 1.50 .60
Wally Wolf
75 Jim Kaat 2.00 .80
76 Carl Taylor 1.50 .60
77 Frank Linzy 1.50 .60
78 Joe Lahoud 1.50 .60
79 Clay Kirby 1.50 .60
80 Don Kessinger 2.00 .80
81 Dave May 1.50 .60
82 Frank Fernandez 1.50 .60
83 Don Cardwell 1.50 .60
84 Paul Casanova 1.50 .60
85 Max Alvis 1.50 .60
86 Lum Harris MG 1.50 .60
87 Steve Renko 2.00 .80
88 Miguel Fuentes 2.00 .80
Dick Baney
89 Juan Rios 1.50 .60
90 Tim McCarver 3.00 1.20
91 Rich Morales 1.50 .60
92 George Culver 1.50 .60
93 Rick Renick 1.50 .60
94 Fred Patek 2.00 .80
95 Earl Wilson 2.00 .80
96 Leron Lee 3.00 1.20
Jerry Reuss RC
97 Joe Moeller 1.50 .60
98 Gates Brown 2.00 .80
99 Bobby Pfeil 1.50 .60
100 Mel Stottlemyre 2.00 .80
101 Bobby Floyd 1.50 .60
102 Joe Rudi 2.00 .80
103 Frank Reberger 1.50 .60
104 Gerry Moses 1.50 .60
105 Tony Gonzalez 1.50 .60
106 Darold Knowles 1.50 .60
107 Bobby Etheridge 1.50 .60
108 Tom Burgmeier 1.50 .60
109 Garry Jestadt 2.00 .80
Carl Morton
110 Bob Moose 1.50 .60
111 Mike Hegan 2.00 .80
112 Dave Nelson 1.50 .60
113 Jim Ray 1.50 .60
114 Gene Michael 2.00 .80
115 Alex Johnson 2.00 .80
116 Sparky Lyle 3.00 1.20
117 Don Young 1.50 .60
118 George Mitterwald 1.50 .60
119 Chuck Taylor 1.50 .60
120 Sal Bando 2.00 .80
121 Fred Beene 1.50 .60
Terry Crowley
122 George Stone 1.50 .60
123 Don Gutteridge MG 1.50 .60
124 Larry Jaster 1.50 .60
125 Deron Johnson 1.50 .60
126 Marty Martinez 1.50 .60
127 Joe Coleman 1.50 .60
128 Checklist 133-263 8.00 2.00
129 Jimmie Price 1.50 .60
130 Ollie Brown 1.50 .60
131 Ray Lamb 1.50 .60
Bob Stinson
132 Jim McGlothlin 1.50 .60
133 Clay Carroll 1.50 .60
134 Danny Walton 1.50 .60
135 Dick Dietz 1.50 .60
136 Steve Hargan 1.50 .60
137 Art Shamsky 1.50 .60
138 Joe Foy 1.50 .60
139 Rich Nye 1.50 .60
140 Reggie Jackson 60.00 24.00
141 Dave Cash RC 2.00 .80
Johnny Jeter
142 Fritz Peterson 1.50 .60
143 Phil Gagliano 1.50 .60
144 Ray Culp 1.50 .60
145 Rico Carty 2.00 .80
146 Danny Murphy 1.50 .60
147 Angel Hermoso 1.50 .60
148 Earl Weaver MG 5.00 2.00
149 Billy Champion 1.50 .60
150 Harmon Killebrew 10.00 4.00
151 Dave Roberts 1.50 .60
152 Ike Brown 1.50 .60
153 Gary Gentry 1.50 .60
154 Jim Miles 1.50 .60
Jan Dukes
155 Denis Menke 1.50 .60
156 Eddie Fisher 1.50 .60
157 Manny Mota 3.00 1.20
158 Jerry McNertney 2.00 .80
159 Tommy Helms 2.00 .80
160 Phil Niekro 6.00 2.40
161 Richie Scheinblum 1.50 .60
162 Jerry Johnson 1.50 .60
163 Syd O'Brien 1.50 .60
164 Ty Cline 1.50 .60
165 Ed Kirkpatrick 1.50 .60
166 Al Oliver 4.00 1.60
167 Bill Burbach 1.50 .60
168 Dave Watkins 1.50 .60
169 Tom Hall 1.50 .60
170 Billy Williams 8.00 3.20
171 Jim Nash 1.50 .60
172 Garry Hill 3.00 1.20
Ralph Garr RC
173 Jim Hicks 1.50 .60
174 Ted Sizemore 2.00 .80
175 Dick Bosman 1.50 .60
176 Jim Ray Hart 2.00 .80
177 Jim Northrup 2.00 .80
178 Denny LeMaster 1.50 .60
179 Ivan Murrell 1.50 .60
180 Tommy John 3.00 1.20
181 Sparky Anderson MG 8.00 3.20
182 Dick Hall 1.50 .60
183 Jerry Grote 2.00 .80
184 Ray Fosse 1.50 .60
185 Don Mincher 2.00 .80
186 Rick Joseph 2.00 .80
187 Mike Hedlund 1.50 .60
188 Manny Sanguillen 2.00 .80
189 Thurman Munson RC 80.00 32.00
Dave McDonald
190 Joe Torre 4.00 1.60
191 Vicente Romo 1.50 .60
192 Jim Qualls 1.50 .60
193 Mike Wegener 1.50 .60
194 Chuck Manuel 1.50 .60
195 Tom Seaver NLCS 20.00 8.00
196 Ken Boswell NLCS 4.00 1.60
197 Nolan Ryan NLCS 40.00 16.00
198 Mets Celebrate 20.00 8.00
Includes Nolan Ryan
Tommie Agee
Wayne Garrett
199 Mike Cuellar ALCS 4.00 1.60
200 Boog Powell ALCS 4.00 1.60
201 Boog Powell ALCS 4.00 1.60
Andy Etchebarren
202 AL Playoff Summary 4.00 1.60
Orioles celebrate
203 Rudy May 1.50 .60
204 Len Gabrielson 1.50 .60
205 Bert Campaneris 2.00 .80
206 Clete Boyer 2.00 .80
207 Norman McRae 1.50 .60
Bob Reed
208 Fred Gladding 1.50 .60
209 Ken Suarez 1.50 .60
210 Juan Marichal 8.00 3.20
211 Ted Williams MG 20.00 8.00
212 Al Santorini 1.50 .60
213 Andy Etchebarren 1.50 .60
214 Ken Boswell 1.50 .60
215 Reggie Smith 3.00 1.20
216 Chuck Hartenstein 1.50 .60
217 Ron Hansen 1.50 .60
218 Ron Stone 1.50 .60
219 Jerry Kenney 1.50 .60
220 Steve Carlton 20.00 8.00
221 Ron Brand 1.50 .60
222 Jim Rooker 1.50 .60
223 Nate Oliver 1.50 .60
224 Steve Barber 2.00 .80
225 Lee May 2.00 .80
226 Ron Perranoski 1.50 .60
227 John Mayberry RC 2.00 .80
Bob Watkins
228 Aurelio Rodriguez 1.50 .60
229 Rich Robertson 1.50 .60
230 Brooks Robinson 20.00 8.00
231 Luis Tiant 3.00 1.20
232 Bob Didier 1.50 .60
233 Lew Krausse 1.50 .60
234 Tommy Dean 1.50 .60
235 Mike Epstein 1.50 .60
236 Bob Veale 1.50 .60
237 Russ Gibson 1.50 .60
238 Jose Laboy 2.00 .80
239 Ken Berry 1.50 .60
240 Fergie Jenkins 8.00 3.20
241 Al Fitzmorris 1.50 .60
Scott Northey
242 Walter Alston MG 4.00 1.60
243 Joe Sparma 2.00 .80
244 Checklist 264-372 8.00 2.00
245 Leo Cardenas 1.50 .60
246 Jim McAndrew 1.50 .60
247 Lou Klimchock 1.50 .60
248 Jesus Alou 1.50 .60
249 Bob Locker 1.50 .60
250 Willie McCovey 12.00 4.80
251 Dick Schofield 1.50 .60
252 Lowell Palmer 1.50 .60
253 Ron Woods 1.50 .60
254 Camilo Pascual 1.50 .60
255 Jim Spencer 1.50 .60
256 Vic Davalillo 1.50 .60
257 Dennis Higgins 1.50 .60
258 Paul Popovich 1.50 .60
259 Tommie Reynolds 1.50 .60
260 Claude Osteen 2.00 .80
261 Curt Motton 1.50 .60
262 Jerry Morales 1.50 .60
Jim Williams
263 Duane Josephson 1.50 .60
264 Rich Hebner 1.50 .60
265 Randy Hundley 1.50 .60
266 Wally Bunker 1.50 .60
267 Herman Hill 1.50 .60
Paul Ratliff
268 Claude Raymond 2.00 .80
269 Cesar Gutierrez 1.50 .60
270 Chris Short 1.50 .60
271 Greg Goossen 2.00 .80
272 Hector Torres 1.50 .60
273 Ralph Houk MG 2.00 .80
274 Gerry Arrigo 1.50 .60
275 Duke Sims 1.50 .60
276 Ron Hunt 1.50 .60
277 Paul Doyle 1.50 .60
278 Tommie Aaron 1.50 .60
279 Bill Lee 3.00 1.20
280 Donn Clendenon 2.00 .80
281 Casey Cox 1.50 .60
282 Steve Huntz 1.50 .60
283 Angel Bravo 1.50 .60
284 Jack Baldschun 1.50 .60
285 Paul Blair 2.00 .80
286 Jack Jenkins 8.00 3.20
Bill Buckner RC
287 Fred Talbot 1.50 .60
288 Larry Hisle 2.00 .80
289 Gene Brabender 1.50 .60
290 Rod Carew 25.00 10.00
291 Leo Durocher MG 4.00 1.60
292 Eddie Leon 1.50 .60
293 Bob Bailey 2.00 .80
294 Jose Azcue 1.50 .60
295 Cecil Upshaw 1.50 .60
296 Woody Woodward 1.50 .60
297 Curt Blefary 1.50 .60
298 Ken Henderson 1.50 .60
299 Buddy Bradford 1.50 .60
300 Tom Seaver 40.00 16.00
301 Chico Salmon 1.50 .60
302 Jeff James 1.50 .60
303 Brant Alyea 1.50 .60
304 Bill Russell RC 8.00 3.20
305 Don Buford WS 4.00 1.60
306 Donn Clendenon WS 4.00 1.60
307 Tommie Agee WS 4.00 1.60
308 J.C. Martin WS 4.00 1.60
309 Jerry Koosman WS 4.00 1.60
310 WS Celebration 8.00 3.20
Includes Ed Kranepool
Tug McGraw
Ed Charles
311 Dick Green 1.50 .60
312 Mike Torrez 1.50 .60
313 Mayo Smith MG 1.50 .60
314 Bill McCool 1.50 .60
315 Luis Aparicio 8.00 3.20
316 Skip Guinn 1.50 .60
317 Billy Conigliaro 2.00 .80
Luis Alvarado
318 Willie Smith 1.50 .60
319 Clay Dalrymple 1.50 .60
320 Jim Maloney 2.00 .80
321 Lou Piniella 3.00 1.20
322 Luke Walker 1.50 .60
323 Wayne Comer 1.50 .60
324 Tony Taylor 2.00 .80
325 Dave Boswell 1.50 .60
326 Bill Voss 1.50 .60
327 Hal King 1.50 .60
328 George Brunet 1.50 .60
329 Chris Cannizzaro 1.50 .60
330 Lou Brock 12.00 4.80
331 Chuck Dobson 1.50 .60
332 Bobby Wine 2.00 .80
333 Bobby Murcer 3.00 1.20
334 Phil Regan 1.50 .60
335 Bill Freehan 2.00 .80
336 Del Unser 1.50 .60
337 Mike McCormick 2.00 .80
338 Paul Schaal 1.50 .60
339 Johnny Edwards 1.50 .60
340 Tony Conigliaro 4.00 1.60
341 Bill Sudakis 1.50 .60
342 Wilbur Wood 2.00 .80
343 Checklist 373-459 8.00 2.00
344 Marcelino Lopez 1.50 .60
345 Al Ferrara 1.50 .60
346 Red Schoendienst MG 2.00 .80
347 Russ Snyder 2.00 .80
348 Mike Jorgensen 2.00 .80
Jesse Hudson
349 Steve Hamilton 1.50 .60
350 Roberto Clemente 80.00 32.00
351 Tom Murphy 1.50 .60
352 Bob Barton 1.50 .60
353 Stan Williams 1.50 .60
354 Amos Otis 2.00 .80
355 Doug Rader 1.50 .60
356 Fred Lasher 1.50 .60
357 Bob Burda 1.50 .60
358 Pedro Borbon RC 2.00 .80
359 Phil Roof 1.50 .60
360 Curt Flood 3.00 1.20
361 Ray Jarvis 1.50 .60
362 Joe Hague 1.50 .60
363 Tom Shopay 1.50 .60
364 Dan McGinn 2.00 .80
365 Zoilo Versalles 1.50 .60
366 Barry Moore 1.50 .60
367 Mike Lum 1.50 .60
368 Ed Herrmann 1.50 .60
369 Alan Foster 1.50 .60
370 Tommy Harper 2.00 .80
371 Rod Gaspar 1.50 .60
372 Dave Giusti 2.00 .80
373 Roy White 2.00 .80
374 Tommie Sisk 1.50 .60
375 Johnny Callison 3.00 1.20
376 Lefty Phillips MG 1.50 .60
377 Bill Butler 1.50 .60
378 Jim Davenport 1.50 .60
379 Tom Tischinski 1.50 .60
380 Tony Perez 8.00 3.20
381 Bobby Brooks 1.50 .60
Mike Olivo
382 Jack DiLauro 1.50 .60
383 Mickey Stanley 2.00 .80
384 Gary Neibauer 1.50 .60
385 George Scott 2.00 .80
386 Bill Dillman 1.50 .60
387 Orioles Team 4.00 1.60
388 Byron Browne 1.50 .60
389 Jim Shellenback 1.50 .60
390 Willie Davis 3.00 1.20
391 Larry Brown 1.50 .60
392 Walt Hriniak 2.00 .80
393 John Gelnar 1.50 .60
394 Gil Hodges MG 4.00 1.60
395 Walt Williams 1.50 .60
396 Steve Blass 2.00 .80
397 Roger Repoz 1.50 .60
398 Bill Stoneman 1.50 .60
399 Yankees Team 4.00 1.60
400 Denny McLain 4.00 1.60
401 John Harrell 1.50 .60
Bernie Williams
402 Ellie Rodriguez 1.50 .60
403 Jim Bunning 8.00 3.20
404 Rich Reese 1.50 .60
405 Bill Hands 1.50 .60
406 Mike Andrews 1.50 .60
407 Bob Watson 2.00 .80
408 Paul Lindblad 1.50 .60
409 Bob Tolan 1.50 .60
410 Boog Powell 4.00 1.60
411 Dodgers Team 4.00 1.60
412 Larry Burchart 1.50 .60
413 Sonny Jackson 1.50 .60
414 Paul Edmondson 1.50 .60
415 Julian Javier 2.00 .80
416 Joe Verbanic 1.50 .60
417 John Bateman 1.50 .60
418 John Donaldson 1.50 .60
419 Ron Taylor 2.00 .80
420 Ken McMullen 2.00 .80
421 Pat Dobson 2.00 .80
422 Royals Team 4.00 1.60
423 Jerry May 1.50 .60
424 Mike Kilkenny 2.00 .80
425 Bobby Bonds 8.00 3.20
426 Bill Rigney MG 1.50 .60
427 Fred Norman 1.50 .60
428 Don Buford 1.50 .60
429 Randy Bobb 1.50 .60
Jim Cosman
430 Andy Messersmith 2.00 .80
431 Ron Swoboda 2.00 .80
432 Checklist 460-546 8.00 2.00
433 Ron Bryant 1.50 .60
434 Felipe Alou 3.00 1.20
435 Nelson Briles 2.00 .80
436 Phillies Team 4.00 1.60
437 Danny Cater 1.50 .60
438 Pat Jarvis 1.50 .60
439 Lee Maye 1.50 .60
440 Bill Mazeroski 8.00 3.20
441 John O'Donoghue 1.50 .60
442 Gene Mauch MG 2.00 .80
443 Al Jackson 1.50 .60
444 Billy Farmer 1.50 .60
John Matias
445 Vada Pinson 3.00 1.20
446 Billy Grabarkewitz 1.50 .60
447 Lee Stange 1.50 .60
448 Astros Team 4.00 1.60
449 Jim Palmer 15.00 6.00
450 Willie McCovey AS 8.00 3.20
451 Boog Powell AS 4.00 1.60
452 Felix Millan AS 3.00 1.20
453 Rod Carew AS 8.00 3.20
454 Ron Santo AS 4.00 1.60
455 Brooks Robinson AS 8.00 3.20
456 Don Kessinger AS 3.00 1.20
457 Rico Petrocelli AS 4.00 1.60
458 Pete Rose AS 15.00 6.00
459 Reggie Jackson AS 15.00 6.00
460 Matty Alou AS 4.00 1.60
461 Carl Yastrzemski AS 12.00 4.80
462 Hank Aaron AS 20.00 8.00
463 Frank Robinson AS 8.00 3.20
464 Johnny Bench AS 20.00 8.00
465 Bill Freehan AS 4.00 1.60
466 Juan Marichal AS 6.00 2.40
467 Denny McLain AS 6.00 2.40
468 Jerry Koosman AS 4.00 1.60
469 Sam McDowell AS 4.00 1.60
470 Willie Stargell 12.00 4.80
471 Chris Zachary 2.50 1.00
472 Braves Team 4.00 1.60
473 Don Bryant 2.50 1.00
474 Dick Kelley 2.50 1.00
475 Dick McAuliffe 4.00 1.60
476 Don Shaw 2.50 1.00
477 Al Severinsen 2.50 1.00
Roger Freed
478 Bob Heise 2.50 1.00
479 Dick Woodson 2.50 1.00
480 Glenn Beckert 4.00 1.60
481 Jose Tartabull 2.50 1.00
482 Tom Hilgendorf 2.50 1.00
483 Gail Hopkins 2.50 1.00
484 Gary Nolan 4.00 1.60
485 Jay Johnstone 4.00 1.60
486 Terry Harmon 2.50 1.00
487 Cisco Carlos 2.50 1.00
488 J.C. Martin 2.50 1.00
489 Eddie Kasko MG 2.50 1.00
490 Bill Singer 4.00 1.60
491 Graig Nettles 6.00 2.40
492 Keith Lampard 2.50 1.00
Scipio Spinks
493 Lindy McDaniel 4.00 1.60
494 Larry Stahl 2.50 1.00
495 Dave Morehead 2.50 1.00
496 Steve Whitaker 2.50 1.00
497 Eddie Watt 2.50 1.00
498 Al Weis 2.50 1.00
499 Skip Lockwood 2.50 1.00
500 Hank Aaron 60.00 24.00
501 White Sox Team 4.00 1.60
502 Rollie Fingers 12.00 4.80
503 Dal Maxvill 2.50 1.00
504 Don Pavletich 2.50 1.00
505 Ken Holtzman 4.00 1.60
506 Ed Stroud 2.50 1.00
507 Pat Corrales 2.50 1.00
508 Joe Niekro 4.00 1.60
509 Expos Team 6.00 2.40
510 Tony Oliva 6.00 2.40
511 Joe Hoerner 2.50 1.00
512 Billy Harris 2.50 1.00
513 Preston Gomez MG 2.50 1.00
514 Steve Hovley 2.50 1.00
515 Don Wilson 4.00 1.60
516 John Ellis 2.50 1.00
Jim Lyttle
517 Joe Gibbon 2.50 1.00
518 Bill Melton 2.50 1.00
519 Don McMahon 2.50 1.00
520 Willie Horton 4.00 1.60
521 Cal Koonce 2.50 1.00
522 Angels Team 4.00 1.60
523 Jose Pena 2.50 1.00
524 Alvin Dark MG 4.00 1.60
525 Jerry Adair 2.50 1.00
526 Ron Herbel 2.50 1.00
527 Don Bosch 4.00 1.60
528 Elrod Hendricks 2.50 1.00
529 Bob Aspromonte 2.50 1.00
530 Bob Gibson 15.00 6.00
531 Ron Clark 2.50 1.00

532 Danny Murtaugh MG 4.00 1.60
533 Buzz Stephen 2.50 1.00
534 Twins Team 4.00 1.60
535 Andy Kosco 2.50 1.00
536 Mike Kekich 2.50 1.00
537 Joe Morgan 12.00 4.80
538 Bob Humphreys 2.50 1.00
539 Denny Doyle RC 8.00 3.20
Larry Bowa RC
540 Gary Peters 2.50 1.00
541 Bill Heath 2.50 1.00
542 Checklist 547-633 8.00 2.00
543 Clyde Wright 2.50 1.00
544 Reds Team 6.00 2.40
545 Ken Harrelson 4.00 1.60
546 Ron Reed 4.00 1.60

1971 O-Pee-Chee

The cards in this 752-card set measure 2 1/2" by 3 1/2". The 1971 O-Pee-Chee set is a challenge to complete in "Mint" condition because the black borders are easily scratched and damaged. The O-Pee-Chee cards seem to have been cut (into individual cards) not as sharply as the Topps cards; the borders frequently appear slightly frayed. The players are also pictured in black and white on the back of the card. The next-to-last series (524-643) and the last series (644-752) are somewhat scarce. The O-Pee-Chee cards can be distinguished from Topps cards by the "Printed in Canada" on the bottom of the reverse. The reverse color is yellow instead of the green found on the backs of the 1971 Topps cards. The card backs are written in both French and English, except for cards 524-752 which were printed in English only. There are several cards which are different from the corresponding Topps card with a different pose or different team noted in bold type, i.e. "Recently Traded to ..." These changed cards are numbers 31, 32, 73, 144, 151, 161, 172, 182, 191, 202, 207, 248, 289 and 578. Remember, the prices below apply only to the 1971 O-Pee-Chee cards -- NOT Topps cards which are much more plentiful. Notable Rookie Cards include Dusty Baker and Don Baylor (Sharing the same card), Bert Blyleven, Dave Concepcion and Steve Garvey.

NM Ex
COMPLETE SET (752) 2500.00 1000.00
COMMON CARD (1-393) 1.50 .60
COMMON (394-523) 3.00 1.20
COMMON (524-643) 4.00 1.60
COMMON (644-752) 10.00 4.00
1 Orioles Team 20.00 5.00
2 Dock Ellis 1.50 .60
3 Dick McAuliffe 2.00 .80
4 Vic Davalillo 1.50 .60
5 Thurman Munson UER 30.00 12.00
American League is misspelled
6 Ed Spiezio 1.50 .60
7 Jim Holt 1.50 .60
8 Mike McQueen 1.50 .60
9 George Scott 2.00 .80
10 Claude Osteen 2.00 .80
11 Elliott Maddox 1.50 .60
12 Johnny Callison 2.00 .80
13 Charlie Brinkman 1.50 .60
Dick Moloney
14 Dave Concepcion RC 25.00 10.00
15 Andy Messersmith 2.00 .80
16 Ken Singleton RC 3.00 1.20
17 Billy Sorrell 1.50 .60
18 Norm Miller 1.50 .60
19 Skip Pitlock 1.50 .60
20 Reggie Jackson 35.00 14.00
21 Dan McGinn 2.00 .80
22 Phil Roof 1.50 .60
23 Oscar Gamble 1.50 .60
24 Rich Hand 1.50 .60
25 Clarence Gaston 2.00 .80
26 Bert Blyleven RC 10.00 4.00
27 Fred Cambria 1.50 .60
Gene Clines
28 Ron Klimkowski 1.50 .60
29 Don Buford 1.50 .60
30 Phil Niekro 8.00 3.20
31 John Bateman 3.00 1.20
(different pose)
32 Jerry DeVanon 2.00 .80
Recently Traded To Orioles
33 Del Unser 1.50 .60
34 Sandy Vance 1.50 .60
35 Lou Piniella 3.00 1.20
36 Dean Chance 2.00 .80
37 Rich McKinney 1.50 .60
38 Jim Colborn 1.50 .60
39 Lerrin LaGrow 2.00 .80
Gene Lamont RC
40 Lee May 2.00 .80
41 Rick Austin 1.50 .60
42 Boots Day 2.00 .80
43 Steve Kealey 1.50 .60
44 Johnny Edwards 1.50 .60
45 Jim Hunter 8.00 3.20
46 Dave Campbell 2.00 .80
47 Johnny Jeter 1.50 .60
48 Dave Baldwin 1.50 .60
49 Don Money 1.50 .60
50 Willie McCovey 10.00 4.00
51 Steve Kline 1.50 .60
52 Oscar Brown 1.50 .60
Earl Williams RC
53 Paul Blair 2.00 .80
54 Checklist 1-132 11.00 2.70
55 Steve Carlton 18.00 7.25
56 Duane Josephson 1.50 .60
57 Von Joshua 1.50 .60
58 Bill Lee 2.00 .80
59 Gene Mauch MG 2.00 .80
60 Dick Bosman 1.50 .60
61 Alex Johnson 3.00 1.20
Carl Yastrzemski
Tony Oliva LL
62 Rico Carty 2.00 .80
Joe Torre
Manny Sanguillen LL
63 Frank Robinson 3.00 1.20
Tony Conigliaro
Boog Powell LL
64 Johnny Bench 6.00 2.40
Tony Perez
Billy Williams LL
65 Frank Howard 3.00 1.20
Harmon Killebrew
Carl Yastrzemski LL
66 Johnny Bench 6.00 2.40
Billy Williams
Tony Perez LL
67 Diego Segui 3.00 1.20
Jim Palmer
Clyde Wright LL
68 Tom Seaver 3.00 1.20
Wayne Simpson
Luke Walker LL
69 Mike Cuellar 2.00 .80
Dave McNally
Jim Perry LL
70 Bob Gibson 6.00 2.40
Gaylord Perry
Fergie Jenkins LL
71 Sam McDowell 2.00 .80
Mickey Lolich
Bob Johnson LL
72 Tom Seaver 6.00 2.40
Bob Gibson
Fergie Jenkins LL
73 George Brunet 1.50 .60
(St. Louis Cardinals)
74 Pete Hamm 1.50 .60
Jim Nettles
75 Gary Nolan 2.00 .80
76 Ted Savage 1.50 .60
77 Mike Compton 1.50 .60
78 Jim Spencer 1.50 .60
79 Wade Blasingame 1.50 .60
80 Bill Melton 1.50 .60
81 Felix Millan 1.50 .60
82 Casey Cox 1.50 .60
83 Tim Foli RC 2.00 .80
Randy Bobb
84 Marcel Lachemann RC 1.50 .60
85 Bill Grabarkewitz 1.50 .60
86 Mike Kilkenny 2.00 .80
87 Jack Heidemann 1.50 .60
88 Hal King 1.50 .60
89 Ken Brett 1.50 .60
90 Joe Pepitone 2.00 .80
91 Bob Lemon MG 2.00 .80
92 Fred Wenz 1.50 .60
93 Norm McRae 1.50 .60
Denny Riddleberger
94 Don Hahn 2.00 .80
95 Luis Tiant 2.00 .80
96 Joe Hague 1.50 .60
97 Floyd Wicker 1.50 .60
98 Joe Decker 1.50 .60
99 Mark Belanger 2.00 .80
100 Pete Rose 40.00 16.00
101 Les Cain 1.50 .60
102 Ken Forsch 2.00 .80
Larry Howard
103 Rich Severson 1.50 .60
104 Dan Frisella 1.50 .60
105 Tony Conigliaro 2.00 .80
106 Tom Dukes 1.50 .60
107 Roy Foster 1.50 .60
108 John Cumberland 1.50 .60
109 Steve Hovley 1.50 .60
110 Bill Mazeroski 8.00 3.20
111 Loyd Colson 1.50 .60
Bobby Mitchell
112 Manny Mota 2.00 .80
113 Jerry Crider 1.50 .60
114 Billy Conigliaro 2.00 .80
115 Donn Clendenon 2.00 .80
116 Ken Sanders 1.50 .60
117 Ted Simmons RC 10.00 4.00
118 Cookie Rojas 2.00 .80
119 Frank Lucchesi MG 1.50 .60
120 Willie Horton 2.00 .80
121 Jim Dunegan 1.50 .60
Roe Skidmore
122 Eddie Watt 1.50 .60
123 Checklist 133-263 11.00 2.70
124 Don Gullett RC 2.00 .80
125 Ray Fosse 1.50 .60
126 Danny Coombs 1.50 .60
127 Danny Thompson 2.00 .80
128 Frank Johnson 1.50 .60
129 Aurelio Monteagudo 1.50 .60
130 Denis Menke 1.50 .60
131 Curt Blefary 1.50 .60
132 Jose Laboy 2.00 .80
133 Mickey Lolich 2.00 .80
134 Jose Arcia 1.50 .60
135 Rick Monday 2.00 .80
136 Duffy Dyer 1.50 .60
137 Marcelino Lopez 1.50 .60
138 Joe Lis 2.00 .80
Willie Montanez
139 Paul Casanova 1.50 .60
140 Gaylord Perry 6.00 2.40
141 Frank Quilici MG 1.50 .60
142 Mack Jones 2.00 .80
143 Steve Blass 2.00 .80
144 Jackie Hernandez 2.00 .80
(Pittsburgh Pirates)
145 Bill Singer 2.00 .80
146 Ralph Houk MG 2.00 .80
147 Bob Priddy 2.00 .80
148 John Mayberry 2.00 .80
149 Mike Hershberger 1.50 .60
150 Sam McDowell 2.00 .80
151 Tommy Davis 3.00 1.20
(Oakland A's)
152 Lloyd Allen 1.50 .60
Winston Llenas
153 Gary Ross 1.50 .60
154 Cesar Gutierrez 1.50 .60
155 Ken Henderson 1.50 .60
156 Bart Johnson 1.50 .60
157 Bob Bailey 3.00 1.20
158 Jerry Reuss 2.00 .80
159 Jarvis Tatum 1.50 .60
160 Tom Seaver 30.00 12.00
161 Ron Hunt 6.00 2.40
(different pose)
162 Jack Billingham 1.50 .60
163 Buck Martinez 2.00 .80
164 Frank Duffy 2.00 .80
Milt Wilcox
165 Cesar Tovar 1.50 .60
166 Joe Hoerner 1.50 .60
167 Tom Grieve RC 2.00 .80
168 Bruce Dal Canton 1.50 .60
169 Ed Herrmann 1.50 .60
170 Mike Cuellar 2.00 .80
171 Bobby Wine 2.00 .80
172 Duke Sims 2.00 .80
(Los Angeles Dodgers)
173 Gil Garrido 1.50 .60
174 Dave LaRoche 1.50 .60
175 Jim Hickman 1.50 .60
176 Bob Montgomery RC 2.00 .80
Doug Griffin
177 Hal McRae 2.00 .80
178 Dave Duncan 2.00 .80
179 Mike Corkins 1.50 .60
180 Al Kaline 25.00 10.00
181 Hal Lanier 1.50 .60
182 Al Downing 2.00 .80
(Los Angeles Dodgers)
183 Gil Hodges MG 3.00 1.20
184 Stan Bahnsen 1.50 .60
185 Julian Javier 1.50 .60
186 Bob Spence 1.50 .60
187 Ted Abernathy 1.50 .60
188 Bob Valentine RC 6.00 2.40
Mike Strahler
189 George Mitterwald 1.50 .60
190 Bob Tolan 1.50 .60
191 Mike Andrews 2.00 .80
(Chicago White Sox)
192 Billy Wilson 1.50 .60
193 Bob Grich RC 3.00 1.20
194 Mike Lum 1.50 .60
195 Boog Powell ALCS 2.00 .80
196 Dave McNally ALCS 2.00 .80
197 Jim Palmer ALCS 3.00 1.20
198 AL Playoff Summary 2.00 .80
Orioles Celebrate
199 Ty Cline NLCS 2.00 .80
200 Bobby Tolan NLCS 2.00 .80
201 Ty Cline NLCS 2.00 .80
202 Claude Raymond 6.00 2.40
(different pose)
203 Larry Gura 2.00 .80
204 Bernie Smith 1.50 .60
George Kopacz
205 Gerry Moses 1.50 .60
206 Checklist 264-393 11.00 2.70
207 Alan Foster 2.00 .80
(Cleveland Indians)
208 Billy Martin MG 3.00 1.20
209 Steve Renko 2.00 .80
210 Rod Carew 20.00 8.00
211 Phil Hennigan 1.50 .60
212 Rich Hebner 2.00 .80
213 Frank Baker 1.50 .60
214 Al Ferrara 1.50 .60
215 Diego Segui 1.50 .60
216 Reggie Cleveland 2.00 .80
Luis Melendez
217 Ed Stroud 1.50 .60
218 Tony Cloninger 1.50 .60
219 Elrod Hendricks 1.50 .60
220 Ron Santo 3.00 1.20
221 Dave Morehead 1.50 .60
222 Bob Watson 2.00 .80
223 Cecil Upshaw 1.50 .60
224 Alan Gallagher 1.50 .60
225 Gary Peters 1.50 .60
226 Bill Russell 2.00 .80
227 Floyd Weaver 1.50 .60
228 Wayne Garrett 1.50 .60
229 Jim Hannan 1.50 .60
230 Willie Stargell 10.00 4.00
231 Vince Colbert 2.00 .80
John Lowenstein RC
232 John Strohmayer 2.00 .80
233 Larry Bowa 2.00 .80
234 Jim Lyttle 2.00 .80
235 Nate Colbert 1.50 .60
236 Bob Humphreys 1.50 .60
237 Cesar Cedeno RC 2.00 .80
238 Chuck Dobson 1.50 .60
239 Red Schoendienst MG 2.00 .80
240 Clyde Wright 1.50 .60
241 Dave Nelson 1.50 .60
242 Jim Ray 1.50 .60
243 Carlos May 1.50 .60
244 Bob Tillman 1.50 .60
245 Jim Kaat 2.00 .80
246 Tony Taylor 1.50 .60
247 Jerry Cram 2.00 .80
Paul Splittorff
248 Hoyt Wilhelm 10.00 4.00
(Atlanta Braves)
249 Chico Salmon 1.50 .60
250 Johnny Bench 30.00 12.00
251 Frank Reberger 1.50 .60
252 Eddie Leon 1.50 .60
253 Bill Sudakis 1.50 .60
254 Cal Koonce 1.50 .60
255 Bob Robertson 2.00 .80
256 Tony Gonzalez 1.50 .60
257 Nelson Briles 2.00 .80
258 Dick Green 1.50 .60
259 Dave Marshall 1.50 .60
260 Tommy Harper 2.00 .80
261 Darold Knowles 1.50 .60
262 Jim Williams 1.50 .60
Dave Robinson
263 John Ellis 1.50 .60
264 Joe Morgan 10.00 4.00
265 Jim Northrup 2.00 .80
266 Bill Stoneman 2.00 .80
267 Rich Morales 1.50 .60
268 Phillies Team 3.00 1.20
269 Gail Hopkins 1.50 .60
270 Rico Carty 2.00 .80
271 Bill Zepp 1.50 .60
272 Tommy Helms 2.00 .80
273 Pete Richert 1.50 .60
274 Ron Slocum 1.50 .60
275 Vada Pinson 2.00 .80
276 Mike Davison 10.00 4.00
George Foster RC
277 Gary Waslewski 1.50 .60
278 Jerry Grote 2.00 .80
279 Lefty Phillips MG 1.50 .60
280 Fergie Jenkins 8.00 3.20
281 Danny Walton 1.50 .60
282 Jose Pagan 1.50 .60
283 Dick Such 1.50 .60
284 Jim Gosger 2.00 .80
285 Sal Bando 2.00 .80
286 Jerry McNertney 1.50 .60
287 Mike Fiore 1.50 .60
288 Joe Moeller 1.50 .60
289 Rusty Staub 10.00 4.00
(Different pose)
290 Tony Oliva 3.00 1.20
291 George Culver 1.50 .60
292 Jay Johnstone 2.00 .80
293 Pat Corrales 2.00 .80
294 Steve Dunning 1.50 .60
295 Bobby Bonds 6.00 2.40
296 Tom Timmermann 1.50 .60
297 Johnny Briggs 1.50 .60
298 Jim Nelson 1.50 .60
299 Ed Kirkpatrick 1.50 .60
300 Brooks Robinson 25.00 10.00
301 Earl Wilson 1.50 .60
302 Phil Gagliano 1.50 .60
303 Lindy McDaniel 2.00 .80
304 Ron Brand 2.00 .80
305 Reggie Smith 2.00 .80
306 Jim Nash 1.50 .60
307 Don Wert 1.50 .60
308 Cardinals Team 3.00 1.20
309 Dick Ellsworth 1.50 .60
310 Tommie Agee 2.00 .80
311 Lee Stange 1.50 .60
312 Harry Walker MG 1.50 .60
313 Tom Hall 1.50 .60
314 Jeff Torborg 2.00 .80
315 Ron Fairly 3.00 1.20
316 Fred Scherman 1.50 .60
317 Jim Driscoll 1.50 .60
Angel Mangual
318 Rudy May 1.50 .60
319 Ty Cline 1.50 .60
320 Dave McNally 2.00 .80
321 Tom Matchick 1.50 .60
322 Jim Beauchamp 1.50 .60
323 Billy Champion 1.50 .60
324 Graig Nettles 3.00 1.20
325 Juan Marichal 8.00 3.20
326 Richie Scheinblum 1.50 .60
327 Boog Powell WS 2.00 .80
328 Don Buford WS 2.00 .80
329 Frank Robinson WS 3.00 1.20
330 World Series Game 4 2.00 .80
Reds stay alive
331 Brooks Robinson WS 6.00 2.40
332 WS Summary 2.00 .80
Orioles Celebrate
333 Clay Kirby 1.50 .60
334 Roberto Pena 1.50 .60
335 Jerry Koosman 2.00 .80
336 Tigers Team 3.00 1.20
337 Jesus Alou 1.50 .60
338 Gene Tenace 2.00 .80
339 Wayne Simpson 1.50 .60
340 Rico Petrocelli 2.00 .80
341 Steve Garvey RC 35.00 14.00
342 Frank Tepedino 2.00 .80
343 Ed Acosta 2.00 .80
Milt May RC
344 Ellie Rodriguez 1.50 .60
345 Joel Horlen 1.50 .60
346 Lum Harris MG 1.50 .60
347 Ted Uhlaender 1.50 .60
348 Fred Norman 1.50 .60
349 Rich Reese 1.50 .60
350 Billy Williams 6.00 2.40
351 Jim Shellenback 1.50 .60
352 Denny Doyle 1.50 .60
353 Carl Taylor 1.50 .60
354 Don McMahon 1.50 .60
355 Bud Harrelson 3.00 1.20
356 Bob Locker 1.50 .60
357 Reds Team 3.00 1.20
358 Danny Cater 1.50 .60
359 Ron Reed 1.50 .60
360 Jim Fregosi 2.00 .80
361 Don Sutton 8.00 3.20
362 Mike Adamson 1.50 .60
Roger Freed
363 Mike Nagy 1.50 .60
364 Tommy Dean 1.50 .60
365 Bob Johnson 1.50 .60
366 Ron Stone 1.50 .60
367 Dalton Jones 1.50 .60
368 Bob Veale 2.00 .80
369 Checklist 394-523 11.00 4.40
370 Joe Torre 6.00 2.40
371 Jack Hiatt 1.50 .60
372 Lew Krausse 1.50 .60
373 Tom McCraw 1.50 .60
374 Clete Boyer 2.00 .80
375 Steve Hargan 1.50 .60
376 Clyde Mashore 2.00 .80
Ernie McAnally
377 Greg Garrett 1.50 .60
378 Tito Fuentes 1.50 .60
379 Wayne Granger 1.50 .60
380 Ted Williams MG 15.00 6.00
381 Fred Gladding 1.50 .60
382 Jake Gibbs 1.50 .60
383 Rod Gaspar 1.50 .60
384 Rollie Fingers 8.00 3.20
385 Maury Wills 6.00 2.40
386 Red Sox Team 3.00 1.20
387 Ron Herbel 1.50 .60
388 Al Oliver 3.00 1.20
389 Ed Brinkman 1.50 .60
390 Glenn Beckert 2.00 .80
391 Steve Brye 2.00 .80
Cotton Nash
392 Grant Jackson 1.50 .60
393 Merv Rettenmund 2.00 .80
394 Clay Carroll 3.00 1.20
395 Roy White 4.00 1.60
396 Dick Schofield 3.00 1.20
397 Alvin Dark MG 4.00 1.60
398 Howie Reed 4.00 1.60
399 Jim French 3.00 1.20
400 Hank Aaron 70.00 28.00
401 Tom Murphy 3.00 1.20
402 Dodgers Team 6.00 2.40
403 Joe Coleman 3.00 1.20
404 Buddy Harris 3.00 1.20
Roger Metzger
405 Leo Cardenas 3.00 1.20
406 Ray Sadecki 3.00 1.20
407 Joe Rudi 4.00 1.60
408 Rafael Robles 3.00 1.20
409 Don Pavletich 3.00 1.20
410 Ken Holtzman 4.00 1.60
411 George Spriggs 3.00 1.20
412 Jerry Johnson 3.00 1.20
413 Pat Kelly 3.00 1.20
414 Woodie Fryman 3.00 1.20
415 Mike Hegan 3.00 1.20
416 Gene Alley 3.00 1.20
417 Dick Hall 3.00 1.20
418 Adolfo Phillips 4.00 1.60
419 Ron Hansen 3.00 1.20
420 Jim Merritt 3.00 1.20
421 John Stephenson 3.00 1.20
422 Frank Bertaina 3.00 1.20
423 Dennis Saunders 3.00 1.20
Tim Marting
424 Roberto Rodriquez 3.00 1.20
425 Doug Rader 4.00 1.60
426 Chris Cannizzaro 3.00 1.20
427 Bernie Allen 3.00 1.20
428 Jim McAndrew 3.00 1.20
429 Chuck Hinton 3.00 1.20
430 Wes Parker 4.00 1.60
431 Tom Burgmeier 3.00 1.20
432 Bob Didier 3.00 1.20
433 Skip Lockwood 3.00 1.20
434 Gary Sutherland 4.00 1.60
435 Jose Cardenal 4.00 1.60
436 Wilbur Wood 4.00 1.60
437 Danny Murtaugh MG 4.00 1.60
438 Mike McCormick 4.00 1.60
439 Greg Luzinski RC 6.00 2.40
Scott Reid
440 Bert Campaneris 4.00 1.60
441 Milt Pappas 4.00 1.60
442 Angels Team 6.00 2.40
443 Rich Robertson 3.00 1.20
444 Jimmie Price 3.00 1.20
445 Art Shamsky 3.00 1.20
446 Bobby Bolin 3.00 1.20
447 Cesar Geronimo 4.00 1.60
448 Dave Roberts 3.00 1.20
449 Brant Alyea 3.00 1.20
450 Bob Gibson 20.00 8.00
451 Joe Keough 3.00 1.20
452 John Boccabella 4.00 1.60
453 Terry Crowley 3.00 1.20
454 Mike Paul 3.00 1.20
455 Don Kessinger 4.00 1.60
456 Bob Meyer 3.00 1.20
457 Willie Smith 3.00 1.20
458 Ron Lolich 3.00 1.20
Dave Lemonds
459 Jim Lefebvre 3.00 1.20
460 Fritz Peterson 3.00 1.20
461 Jim Ray Hart 3.00 1.20
462 Senators Team 6.00 2.40
463 Tom Kelley 3.00 1.20
464 Aurelio Rodriguez 3.00 1.20
465 Tim McCarver 6.00 2.40
466 Ken Berry 3.00 1.20
467 Al Santorini 3.00 1.20
468 Frank Fernandez 3.00 1.20
469 Bob Aspromonte 3.00 1.20
470 Bob Oliver 3.00 1.20
471 Tom Griffin 3.00 1.20
472 Ken Rudolph 3.00 1.20
473 Gary Wagner 3.00 1.20
474 Jim Fairey 4.00 1.60
475 Ron Perranoski 3.00 1.20
476 Dal Maxvill 3.00 1.20
477 Earl Weaver MG 8.00 3.20
478 Bernie Carbo 3.00 1.20
479 Dennis Higgins 3.00 1.20
480 Manny Sanguillen 4.00 1.60
481 Daryl Patterson 3.00 1.20
482 Padres Team 6.00 2.40
483 Gene Michael 3.00 1.20
484 Don Wilson 3.00 1.20
485 Ken McMullen 3.00 1.20
486 Steve Huntz 3.00 1.20
487 Paul Schaal 3.00 1.20
488 Jerry Stephenson 3.00 1.20
489 Luis Alvarado 3.00 1.20
490 Deron Johnson 3.00 1.20
491 Jim Hardin 3.00 1.20
492 Ken Boswell 3.00 1.20
493 Dave May 3.00 1.20
494 Ralph Garr 4.00 1.60
Rick Kester
495 Felipe Alou 4.00 1.60
496 Woody Woodward 3.00 1.20
497 Horacio Pina 3.00 1.20
498 John Kennedy 3.00 1.20
499 Checklist 524-643 8.00 2.00
500 Jim Perry 4.00 1.60
501 Andy Etchebarren 3.00 1.20
502 Cubs Team 6.00 2.40
503 Gates Brown 4.00 1.60
504 Ken Wright 3.00 1.20
505 Ollie Brown 3.00 1.20
506 Bobby Knoop 3.00 1.20
507 George Stone 3.00 1.20
508 Roger Repoz 3.00 1.20
509 Jim Grant 3.00 1.20
510 Ken Harrelson 4.00 1.60
511 Chris Short 4.00 1.60
512 Dick Mills 3.00 1.20
Mike Garman
513 Nolan Ryan 200.00 80.00
514 Ron Woods 3.00 1.20
515 Carl Morton 4.00 1.60
516 Ted Kubiak 3.00 1.20
517 Charlie Fox MG 3.00 1.20
518 Joe Grzenda 3.00 1.20
519 Willie Crawford 3.00 1.20
520 Tommy John 6.00 2.40
521 Leron Lee 3.00 1.20

522 Twins Team 6.00 2.40
523 John Odom 3.00 1.20
524 Mickey Stanley 6.00 2.40
525 Ernie Banks 75.00 30.00
526 Ray Jarvis 4.00 1.60
527 Cleon Jones 6.00 2.40
528 Wally Bunker 4.00 1.60
529 Enzo Hernandez 6.00 2.40
Bill Buckner
Marty Perez
530 Carl Yastrzemski 50.00 20.00
531 Mike Torrez 4.00 1.60
532 Bill Rigney MG 4.00 1.60
533 Mike Ryan 4.00 1.60
534 Luke Walker 4.00 1.60
535 Curt Flood 6.00 2.40
536 Claude Raymond 6.00 2.40
537 Tom Egan 4.00 1.60
538 Angel Bravo 4.00 1.60
539 Larry Brown 4.00 1.60
540 Larry Dierker 6.00 2.40
541 Bob Burda 4.00 1.60
542 Bob Miller 4.00 1.60
543 Yankees Team 10.00 4.00
544 Vida Blue 6.00 2.40
545 Dick Dietz 4.00 1.60
546 John Matias 4.00 1.60
547 Pat Dobson 4.00 1.60
548 Don Mason 4.00 1.60
549 Jim Brewer 4.00 1.60
550 Harmon Killebrew 30.00 12.00
551 Frank Linzy 4.00 1.60
552 Buddy Bradford 4.00 1.60
553 Kevin Collins 4.00 1.60
554 Lowell Palmer 4.00 1.60
555 Walt Williams 4.00 1.60
556 Jim McGlothlin 4.00 1.60
557 Tom Satriano 4.00 1.60
558 Hector Torres 4.00 1.60
559 Terry Cox 4.00 1.60
Bill Gogolewski
Gary Jones
560 Rusty Staub 8.00 3.20
561 Syd O'Brien 4.00 1.60
562 Dave Giusti 4.00 1.60
563 Giants Team 8.00 3.20
564 Al Fitzmorris 4.00 1.60
565 Jim Wynn 6.00 2.40
566 Tim Cullen 4.00 1.60
567 Walt Alston MG 10.00 4.00
568 Sal Campisi 4.00 1.60
569 Ivan Murrell 4.00 1.60
570 Jim Palmer 40.00 16.00
571 Ted Sizemore 4.00 1.60
572 Jerry Kenney 4.00 1.60
573 Ed Kranepool 6.00 2.40
574 Jim Bunning 10.00 4.00
575 Bill Freehan 6.00 2.40
576 Adrian Garrett 4.00 1.60
Brock Davis
Garry Jestadt
577 Jim Lonborg 6.00 2.40
578 Eddie Kasko 6.00 2.40
(Topps 578 is
Ron Hunt)
579 Marty Pattin 4.00 1.60
580 Tony Perez 25.00 10.00
581 Roger Nelson 4.00 1.60
582 Dave Cash 6.00 2.40
583 Ron Cook 4.00 1.60
584 Indians Team 8.00 3.20
585 Willie Davis 6.00 2.40
586 Dick Woodson 4.00 1.60
587 Sonny Jackson 4.00 1.60
588 Tom Bradley 4.00 1.60
589 Bob Barton 4.00 1.60
590 Alex Johnson 6.00 2.40
591 Jackie Brown 4.00 1.60
592 Randy Hundley 6.00 2.40
593 Jack Aker 4.00 1.60
594 Bob Chlupsa 6.00 2.40
Bob Stinson
Al Hrabosky RC
595 Dave Johnson 6.00 2.40
596 Mike Jorgensen 4.00 1.60
597 Ken Suarez 4.00 1.60
598 Rick Wise 6.00 2.40
599 Norm Cash 6.00 2.40
600 Willie Mays 120.00 47.50
601 Ken Tatum 4.00 1.60
602 Marty Martinez 4.00 1.60
603 Pirates Team 8.00 3.20
604 John Gelnar 4.00 1.60
605 Orlando Cepeda 10.00 4.00
606 Chuck Taylor 4.00 1.60
607 Paul Ratliff 4.00 1.60
608 Mike Wegener 6.00 2.40
609 Leo Durocher MG 8.00 3.20
610 Amos Otis 6.00 2.40
611 Tom Phoebus 4.00 1.60
612 Lou Camilli 4.00 1.60
Ted Ford
Steve Mingori
613 Pedro Borbon 4.00 1.60
614 Billy Cowan 4.00 1.60
615 Mel Stottlemyre 6.00 2.40
616 Larry Hisle 6.00 2.40
617 Clay Dalrymple 4.00 1.60
618 Tug McGraw 6.00 2.40
619 Checklist 644-752 10.00 2.50
620 Frank Howard 6.00 2.40
621 Ron Bryant 4.00 1.60
622 Joe Lahoud 4.00 1.60
623 Pat Jarvis 4.00 1.60
624 Athletics Team 8.00 3.20
625 Lou Brock 40.00 16.00
626 Freddie Patek 6.00 2.40
627 Steve Hamilton 4.00 1.60
628 John Bateman 6.00 2.40
629 John Hiller 8.00 3.20
630 Roberto Clemente 150.00 60.00
631 Eddie Fisher 4.00 1.60
632 Darrel Chaney 4.00 1.60
633 Bobby Brooks 4.00 1.60
Pete Koegel
Scott Northey
634 Phil Regan 4.00 1.60
635 Bobby Murcer 6.00 2.40
636 Denny LeMaster 4.00 1.60
637 Dave Bristol MG 4.00 1.60
638 Stan Williams 4.00 1.60
639 Tom Haller 4.00 1.60
640 Frank Robinson 50.00 20.00
641 Mets Team 20.00 8.00
642 Jim Roland 4.00 1.60
643 Rick Reichardt 4.00 1.60
644 Jim Stewart 10.00 4.00
645 Jim Maloney 12.00 4.80
646 Bobby Floyd 10.00 4.00
647 Juan Pizarro 10.00 4.00
648 Rich Folkers 20.00 8.00
Ted Martinez
Jon Matlack RC
649 Sparky Lyle 15.00 6.00
650 Rich Allen 40.00 16.00
651 Jerry Robertson 10.00 4.00
652 Braves Team 15.00 6.00
653 Russ Snyder 10.00 4.00
654 Don Shaw 10.00 4.00
655 Mike Epstein 10.00 4.00
656 Gerry Nyman 10.00 4.00
657 Jose Azcue 10.00 4.00
658 Paul Lindblad 10.00 4.00
659 Byron Browne 10.00 4.00
660 Ray Culp 10.00 4.00
661 Chuck Tanner MG 15.00 6.00
662 Mike Hedlund 10.00 4.00
663 Marv Staehle 10.00 4.00
664 Archie Reynolds 15.00 6.00
Bob Reynolds
Ken Reynolds
665 Ron Swoboda 15.00 6.00
666 Gene Brabender 10.00 4.00
667 Pete Ward 12.00 4.80
668 Gary Neibauer 10.00 4.00
669 Ike Brown 10.00 4.00
670 Bill Hands 10.00 4.00
671 Bill Voss 10.00 4.00
672 Ed Crosby 10.00 4.00
673 Gerry Janeski 10.00 4.00
674 Expos Team 15.00 6.00
675 Dave Boswell 10.00 4.00
676 Tommie Reynolds 10.00 4.00
677 Jack DiLauro 10.00 4.00
678 George Thomas 10.00 4.00
679 Don O'Riley 10.00 4.00
680 Don Mincher 10.00 4.00
681 Bill Butler 10.00 4.00
682 Terry Harmon 10.00 4.00
683 Bill Burbach 10.00 4.00
684 Curt Motton 10.00 4.00
685 Moe Drabowsky 10.00 4.00
686 Chico Ruiz 10.00 4.00
687 Ron Taylor 12.00 4.80
688 Sparky Anderson MG 50.00 20.00
689 Frank Baker 10.00 4.00
690 Bob Moose 10.00 4.00
691 Bob Heise 10.00 4.00
692 Hal Haydel 10.00 4.00
Rogelio Moret
Wayne Twitchell
693 Jose Pena 10.00 4.00
694 Rick Renick 10.00 4.00
695 Joe Niekro 12.00 4.80
696 Jerry Morales 10.00 4.00
697 Rickey Clark 10.00 4.00
698 Brewers Team 20.00 8.00
699 Jim Britton 12.00 4.80
700 Boog Powell 30.00 12.00
701 Bob Garibaldi 10.00 4.00
702 Milt Ramirez 10.00 4.00
703 Mike Kekich 10.00 4.00
704 J.C. Martin 10.00 4.00
705 Dick Selma 10.00 4.00
706 Joe Foy 10.00 4.00
707 Fred Lasher 10.00 4.00
708 Russ Nagelson 10.00 4.00
709 Dusty Baker RC 120.00 47.50
Don Baylor RC
Tom Paciorek RC
710 Sonny Siebert 10.00 4.00
711 Larry Stahl 10.00 4.00
712 Jose Martinez 10.00 4.00
713 Mike Marshall 20.00 8.00
714 Dick Williams MG 15.00 6.00
715 Horace Clarke 10.00 4.00
716 Dave Leonhard 10.00 4.00
717 Tommie Aaron 12.00 4.80
718 Billy Wynne 10.00 4.00
719 Jerry May 10.00 4.00
720 Matty Alou 12.00 4.80
721 John Morris 10.00 4.00
722 Astros Team 20.00 8.00
723 Vicente Romo 10.00 4.00
724 Tom Tischinski 10.00 4.00
725 Gary Gentry 10.00 4.00
726 Paul Popovich 10.00 4.00
727 Ray Lamb 10.00 4.00
728 Wayne Redmond 10.00 4.00
Keith Lampard
Bernie Williams
729 Dick Billings 10.00 4.00
730 Jim Rooker 10.00 4.00
731 Jim Qualls 10.00 4.00
732 Bob Reed 10.00 4.00
733 Lee Maye 10.00 4.00
734 Rob Gardner 10.00 4.00
735 Mike Shannon 15.00 6.00
736 Mel Queen 10.00 4.00
737 Preston Gomez MG 10.00 4.00
738 Russ Gibson 10.00 4.00
739 Barry Lersch 10.00 4.00
740 Luis Aparicio 40.00 16.00
741 Skip Guinn 10.00 4.00
742 Royals Team 15.00 6.00
743 John O'Donoghue 12.00 4.80
744 Chuck Manuel 10.00 4.00
745 Sandy Alomar 12.00 4.80
746 Andy Kosco 10.00 4.00
747 Al Severinsen 10.00 4.00
Scipio Spinks
Balor Moore
748 John Purdin 10.00 4.00
749 Ken Szotkiewicz 10.00 4.00
750 Denny McLain 20.00 8.00
751 Al Weis 15.00 6.00
752 Dick Drago 12.00 4.80

1972 O-Pee-Chee

The cards in this 525-card set measure 2 1/2" by 3 1/2". The 1972 O-Pee-Chee set is very similar to the 1972 Topps set. On a white background, the fronts feature color player photos with multicolored frames, rounded bottom corners and the top part of the photo also rounded. The player's name and team name appear on the front. The horizontal backs carry player biography and statistics in French and English and have a different color than the 1972 Topps cards. Features appearing for the first time were "Boyhood Photos" (KP: 341-348 and 491-498) and "In Action" cards. The O-Pee-Chee cards can be distinguished from Topps cards by the "Printed in Canada" on the bottom of the back. This was the first year the cards denoted O.P.C. in the copyright line rather than T.C.G. There is one card in the set which is notably different from the corresponding Topps number on the back, No. 465 Gil Hodges, which notes his death in April of 1972. Remember, the prices below apply only to the O-Pee-Chee cards -- NOT Topps cards which are much more plentiful. The cards were packaged in 36 count boxes with eight cards per pack which cost ten cents each. Notable Rookie Cards include Carlton Fisk.

	NM	Ex
COMPLETE SET (525)	1500.00	600.00
COMMON CARD (1-132)	1.00	.40
COMMON PLAYER (133-263)	1.50	.60
COMMON (264-394)	2.00	.80
COMMON (395-525)	2.50	1.00

1 Pirates Team 10.00 2.50
2 Ray Culp 1.00 .40
3 Bob Tolan 1.00 .40
4 Checklist 1-132 6.00 1.50
5 John Bateman 2.00 .80
6 Fred Scherman 1.00 .40
7 Enzo Hernandez 1.00 .40
8 Ron Swoboda 2.00 .80
9 Stan Williams 1.00 .40
10 Amos Otis 2.00 .80
11 Bobby Valentine 2.00 .80
12 Jose Cardenal 1.00 .40
13 Joe Grzenda 1.00 .40
14 Pete Koegel 1.00 .40
Mike Anderson
Wayne Twitchell
15 Walt Williams 1.00 .40
16 Mike Jorgensen 1.00 .40
17 Dave Duncan 2.00 .80
18 Juan Pizarro 1.00 .40
19 Billy Cowan 1.00 .40
20 Don Wilson 1.00 .40
21 Braves Team 2.00 .80
22 Rob Gardner 1.00 .40
23 Ted Kubiak 1.00 .40
24 Ted Ford 1.00 .40
25 Bill Singer 1.00 .40
26 Andy Etchebarren 1.00 .40
27 Bob Johnson 1.00 .40
28 Bob Gebhard 1.00 .40
Steve Brye
Hal Haydel
29 Bill Bonham 1.00 .40
30 Rico Petrocelli 2.00 .80
31 Cleon Jones 2.00 .80
32 Cleon Jones IA 1.00 .40
33 Billy Martin MG 6.00 2.40
34 Billy Martin IA 4.00 1.60
35 Jerry Johnson 1.00 .40
36 Jerry Johnson IA 1.00 .40
37 Carl Yastrzemski 15.00 6.00
38 Carl Yastrzemski IA 8.00 3.20
39 Bob Barton 1.00 .40
40 Bob Barton IA 1.00 .40
41 Tommy Davis 2.00 .80
42 Tommy Davis IA 1.00 .40
43 Rick Wise 2.00 .80
44 Rick Wise IA 1.00 .40
45 Glenn Beckert 2.00 .80
46 Glenn Beckert IA 1.00 .40
47 John Ellis 1.00 .40
48 John Ellis IA 1.00 .40
49 Willie Mays 30.00 12.00
50 Willie Mays IA 15.00 6.00
51 Harmon Killebrew 8.00 3.20
52 Harmon Killebrew IA 6.00 2.40
53 Bud Harrelson 2.00 .80
54 Bud Harrelson IA 1.00 .40
55 Clyde Wright 1.00 .40
56 Rich Chiles 1.00 .40
57 Bob Oliver 1.00 .40
58 Ernie McAnally 2.00 .80
59 Fred Stanley 1.00 .40
60 Manny Sanguillen 2.00 .80
61 Burt Hooton RC 2.00 .80
Gene Hiser
Earl Stephenson
62 Angel Mangual 1.00 .40
63 Duke Sims 1.00 .40
64 Pete Broberg 1.00 .40
65 Cesar Cedeno 2.00 .80
66 Ray Corbin 1.00 .40
67 Red Schoendienst MG 4.00 1.60
68 Jim York 1.00 .40
69 Roger Freed 1.00 .40
70 Mike Cuellar 2.00 .80
71 Angels Team 2.00 .80
72 Bruce Kison 1.00 .40
73 Steve Huntz 1.00 .40
74 Cecil Upshaw 1.00 .40
75 Bert Campaneris 2.00 .80
76 Don Carrithers 1.00 .40
77 Ron Theobald 1.00 .40
78 Steve Arlin 1.00 .40
79 Mike Garman 60.00 24.00
Cecil Cooper RC
Carlton Fisk RC
80 Tony Perez 8.00 3.20
81 Mike Hedlund 1.00 .40
82 Ron Woods 2.00 .80
83 Dalton Jones 1.00 .40
84 Vince Colbert 1.00 .40
85 Joe Torre 4.00 1.60
Ralph Garr
Glenn Beckert LL
86 Tony Oliva 4.00 1.60
Bobby Murcer
Merv Rettenmund LL
87 Joe Torre 6.00 2.40
Willie Stargell
Hank Aaron LL
88 Harmon Killebrew 6.00 2.40
Frank Robinson
Reggie Smith LL
89 Willie Stargell 4.00 1.60
Hank Aaron
Lee May LL
90 Bill Melton 4.00 1.60
Norm Cash
Reggie Jackson LL
91 Tom Seaver 4.00 1.60
Dave Roberts
photo actually
Danny Coombs
Don Wilson LL
92 Vida Blue 4.00 1.60
Wilbur Wood
Jim Palmer LL
93 Fergie Jenkins 6.00 2.40
Steve Carlton
Al Downing
Tom Seaver LL
94 Mickey Lolich 4.00 1.60
Vida Blue
Wilbur Wood LL
95 Tom Seaver 6.00 2.40
Fergie Jenkins
Bill Stoneman LL
96 Mickey Lolich 4.00 1.60
Vida Blue
Joe Coleman LL
97 Tom Kelley 1.00 .40
98 Chuck Tanner MG 2.00 .80
99 Ross Grimsley 1.00 .40
100 Frank Robinson 10.00 4.00
101 Bill Greif 4.00 1.60
J.R. Richard RC
Ray Busse
102 Lloyd Allen 1.00 .40
103 Checklist 133-263 6.00 2.40
104 Toby Harrah RC 2.00 .80
105 Gary Gentry 1.00 .40
106 Brewers Team 2.00 .80
107 Jose Cruz RC 2.00 .80
108 Gary Waslewski 1.00 .40
109 Jerry May 1.00 .40
110 Ron Hunt 2.00 .80
111 Jim Grant 1.00 .40
112 Greg Luzinski 2.00 .80
113 Rogelio Moret 1.00 .40
114 Bill Buckner 2.00 .80
115 Jim Fregosi 2.00 .80
116 Ed Farmer 1.00 .40
117 Cleo James 1.00 .40
118 Skip Lockwood 1.00 .40
119 Marty Perez 1.00 .40
120 Bill Freehan 2.00 .80
121 Ed Sprague 1.00 .40
122 Larry Biittner 1.00 .40
123 Ed Acosta 1.00 .40
124 Alan Closter 1.00 .40
Rusty Torres
Roger Hambright
125 Dave Cash 2.00 .80
126 Bart Johnson 1.00 .40
127 Duffy Dyer 1.00 .40
128 Eddie Watt 1.00 .40
129 Charlie Fox MG 1.00 .40
130 Bob Gibson 10.00 4.00
131 Jim Nettles 1.00 .40
132 Joe Morgan 8.00 3.20
133 Joe Keough 1.50 .60
134 Carl Morton 2.50 1.00
135 Vada Pinson 2.50 1.00
136 Darrel Chaney 1.50 .60
137 Dick Williams MG 2.50 1.00
138 Mike Kekich 1.50 .60
139 Tim McCarver 2.50 1.00
140 Pat Dobson 2.50 1.00
141 Buzz Capra 2.50 1.00
Leroy Stanton
Jon Matlack
142 Chris Chambliss RC 5.00 2.00
143 Garry Jestadt 1.50 .60
144 Marty Pattin 1.50 .60
145 Don Kessinger 2.50 1.00
146 Steve Kealey 1.50 .60
147 Dave Kingman RC 6.00 2.40
148 Dick Billings 1.50 .60
149 Gary Neibauer 1.50 .60
150 Norm Cash 2.50 1.00
151 Jim Brewer 1.50 .60
152 Gene Clines 1.50 .60
153 Rick Auerbach 1.50 .60
154 Ted Simmons 5.00 2.00
155 Larry Dierker 2.50 1.00
156 Twins Team 2.50 1.00
157 Don Gullett 1.50 .60
158 Jerry Kenney 1.50 .60
159 John Boccabella 2.50 1.00
160 Andy Messersmith 2.50 1.00
161 Brock Davis 1.50 .60
162 Jerry Bell 2.50 1.00
Darrell Porter RC UER
Bob Reynolds
(Porter and Bell
photos switched)
163 Tug McGraw 5.00 2.00
164 Tug McGraw IA 2.50 1.00
165 Chris Speier RC 2.50 1.00
166 Chris Speier IA 1.50 .60
167 Deron Johnson 1.50 .60
168 Deron Johnson IA 1.50 .60
169 Vida Blue 5.00 2.00
170 Vida Blue IA 2.50 1.00
171 Darrell Evans 5.00 2.00
172 Darrell Evans IA 2.50 1.00
173 Clay Kirby 1.50 .60
174 Clay Kirby IA 1.50 .60
175 Tom Haller 1.50 .60
176 Tom Haller IA 1.50 .60
177 Paul Schaal 1.50 .60
178 Paul Schaal IA 1.50 .60
179 Dock Ellis 1.50 .60
180 Dock Ellis IA 1.50 .60
181 Ed Kranepool 2.50 1.00
182 Ed Kranepool IA 1.50 .60
183 Bill Melton 1.50 .60
184 Bill Melton IA 1.50 .60
185 Ron Bryant 1.50 .60
186 Ron Bryant IA 1.50 .60
187 Gates Brown 1.50 .60
188 Frank Lucchesi MG 1.50 .60
189 Gene Tenace 2.50 1.00
190 Dave Giusti 1.50 .60
191 Jeff Burroughs RC 5.00 2.00
192 Cubs Team 2.50 1.00
193 Kurt Bevacqua 1.50 .60
194 Fred Norman 1.50 .60
195 Orlando Cepeda 8.00 3.20
196 Mel Queen 1.50 .60
197 Johnny Briggs 1.50 .60
198 Charlie Hough RC 6.00 2.40
Bob O'Brien
Mike Strahler
199 Mike Fiore 1.50 .60
200 Lou Brock 8.00 3.20
201 Phil Roof 1.50 .60
202 Scipio Spinks 1.50 .60
203 Ron Blomberg 1.50 .60
204 Tommy Helms 1.50 .60
205 Dick Drago 1.50 .60
206 Dal Maxvill 1.50 .60
207 Tom Egan 1.50 .60
208 Milt Pappas 2.50 1.00
209 Joe Rudi 2.50 1.00
210 Denny McLain 2.50 1.00
211 Gary Sutherland 2.50 1.00
212 Grant Jackson 1.50 .60
213 Billy Parker 1.50 .60
Art Kusnyer
Tom Silverio
214 Mike McQueen 1.50 .60
215 Alex Johnson 2.50 1.00
216 Joe Niekro 2.50 1.00
217 Roger Metzger 1.50 .60
218 Eddie Kasko MG 1.50 .60
219 Rennie Stennett 2.50 1.00
220 Jim Perry 2.50 1.00
221 NL Playoffs 2.50 1.00
Bucs champs
222 B.Robinson ALCS 5.00 2.00
223 Dave McNally WS 2.50 1.00
224 Dave Johnson WS 2.50 1.00
Mark Belanger
225 Manny Sanguillen WS 2.50 1.00
226 Roberto Clemente WS 8.00 3.20
227 Nellie Briles WS 2.50 1.00
228 Frank Robinson WS 5.00 2.00
Manny Sanguillen
229 Steve Blass WS 2.50 1.00
230 WS Summary 2.50 1.00
Pirates celebrate
231 Casey Cox 1.50 .60
232 Chris Arnold 1.50 .60
Jim Barr
Dave Rader
233 Jay Johnstone 2.50 1.00
234 Ron Taylor 5.00 2.00
235 Merv Rettenmund 1.50 .60
236 Jim McGlothlin 1.50 .60
237 Yankees Team 2.50 1.00
238 Leron Lee 1.50 .60
239 Tom Timmermann 1.50 .60
240 Rich Allen 2.50 1.00
241 Rollie Fingers 8.00 3.20
242 Don Mincher 1.50 .60
243 Frank Linzy 1.50 .60
244 Steve Braun 1.50 .60
245 Tommie Agee 2.50 1.00
246 Tom Burgmeier 1.50 .60
247 Milt May 1.50 .60
248 Tom Bradley 1.50 .60
249 Harry Walker MG 1.50 .60
250 Boog Powell 2.50 1.00
251 Checklist 264-394 6.00 1.50
252 Ken Reynolds 1.50 .60
253 Sandy Alomar 2.50 1.00
254 Boots Day 2.50 1.00
255 Jim Lonborg 2.50 1.00
256 George Foster 2.50 1.00
257 Jim Foor 1.50 .60
Tim Hosley
Paul Jata
258 Randy Hundley 1.50 .60
259 Sparky Lyle 2.50 1.00
260 Ralph Garr 2.50 1.00
261 Steve Mingori 1.50 .60
262 Padres Team 2.50 1.00
263 Felipe Alou 2.50 1.00
264 Tommy John 3.00 1.20
265 Wes Parker 3.00 1.20
266 Bobby Bolin 2.00 .80
267 Dave Concepcion 6.00 2.40
268 Dwain Anderson 2.00 .80
Chris Floethe
269 Don Hahn 2.00 .80
270 Jim Palmer 10.00 4.00
271 Ken Rudolph 2.00 .80
272 Mickey Rivers RC 3.00 1.20
273 Bobby Floyd 2.00 .80
274 Al Severinsen 2.00 .80
275 Cesar Tovar 2.00 .80
276 Gene Mauch MG 3.00 1.20
277 Elliott Maddox 2.00 .80
278 Dennis Higgins 2.00 .80
279 Larry Brown 2.00 .80
280 Willie McCovey 8.00 3.20
281 Bill Parsons 2.00 .80
282 Astros Team 3.00 1.20
283 Darrell Brandon 2.00 .80
284 Ike Brown 2.00 .80
285 Gaylord Perry 10.00 4.00
286 Gene Alley 2.00 .80
287 Jim Hardin 2.00 .80
288 Johnny Jeter 2.00 .80
289 Syd O'Brien 2.00 .80
290 Sonny Siebert 2.00 .80
291 Hal McRae 3.00 1.20

292 Hal McRae IA 2.00 .80
293 Danny Frisella 2.00 .80
294 Danny Frisella IA 2.00 .80
295 Dick Dietz 2.00 .80
296 Dick Dietz IA 2.00 .80
297 Claude Osteen 3.00 1.20
298 Claude Osteen IA 2.00 .80
299 Hank Aaron 50.00 20.00
300 Hank Aaron IA 25.00 10.00
301 George Mitterwald 2.00 .80
302 George Mitterwald IA 2.00 .80
303 Joe Pepitone 3.00 1.20
304 Joe Pepitone IA 2.00 .80
305 Ken Boswell 2.00 .80
306 Ken Boswell IA 2.00 .80
307 Steve Renko 3.00 1.20
308 Steve Renko IA 2.00 .80
309 Roberto Clemente 60.00 24.00
310 Roberto Clemente IA 30.00 12.00
311 Clay Carroll 2.00 .80
312 Clay Carroll IA 2.00 .80
313 Luis Aparicio 10.00 4.00
314 Luis Aparicio IA 6.00 2.40
315 Paul Splittorff 2.00 .80
316 Jim Bibby 3.00 1.20
Jorge Roque
Santiago Guzman
317 Rich Hand 2.00 .80
318 Sonny Jackson 2.00 .80
319 Aurelio Rodriguez 2.00 .80
320 Steve Blass 3.00 1.20
321 Joe Lahoud 2.00 .80
322 Jose Pena 2.00 .80
323 Earl Weaver MG 8.00 3.20
324 Mike Ryan 2.00 .80
325 Mel Stottlemyre 3.00 1.20
326 Pat Kelly 2.00 .80
327 Steve Stone RC 3.00 1.20
328 Red Sox Team 3.00 1.20
329 Roy Foster 2.00 .80
330 Jim Hunter 10.00 4.00
331 Stan Swanson 3.00 1.20
332 Buck Martinez 2.00 .80
333 Steve Barber 2.00 .80
334 Bill Fahey 2.00 .80
Jim Mason
Tom Ragland
335 Bill Hands 2.00 .80
336 Marty Martinez 2.00 .80
337 Mike Kilkenny 3.00 1.20
338 Bob Grich 3.00 1.20
339 Ron Cook 2.00 .80
340 Roy White 3.00 1.20
341 Joe Torre KP 3.00 1.20
342 Wilbur Wood KP 2.00 .80
343 Willie Stargell KP 3.00 1.20
344 Dave McNally KP 2.00 .80
345 Rick Wise KP 2.00 .80
346 Jim Fregosi KP 2.00 .80
347 Tom Seaver KP 8.00 3.20
348 Sal Bando KP 2.00 .80
349 Al Fitzmorris 2.00 .80
350 Frank Howard 3.00 1.20
351 Tom House 3.00 1.20
Rick Kester
Jimmy Britton
352 Dave LaRoche 2.00 .80
353 Art Shamsky 2.00 .80
354 Tom Murphy 2.00 .80
355 Bob Watson 3.00 1.20
356 Gerry Moses 2.00 .80
357 Woodie Fryman 2.00 .80
358 Sparky Anderson MG 8.00 3.20
359 Don Pavletich 2.00 .80
360 Dave Roberts 2.00 .80
361 Mike Andrews 2.00 .80
362 Mets Team 6.00 2.40
363 Ron Klimkowski 2.00 .80
364 Johnny Callison 3.00 1.20
365 Dick Bosman 3.00 1.20
366 Jimmy Rosario 2.00 .80
367 Ron Perranoski 2.00 .80
368 Danny Thompson 2.00 .80
369 Jim LeFebvre 3.00 1.20
370 Don Buford 2.00 .80
371 Denny LeMaster 2.00 .80
372 Lance Clemons 2.00 .80
Monty Montgomery
373 John Mayberry 3.00 1.20
374 Jack Heidemann 2.00 .80
375 Reggie Cleveland 3.00 1.20
376 Andy Kosco 2.00 .80
377 Terry Harmon 2.00 .80
378 Checklist 395-525 8.00 2.00
379 Ken Berry 2.00 .80
380 Earl Williams 2.00 .80
381 White Sox Team 3.00 1.20
382 Joe Gibbon 2.00 .80
383 Brant Alyea 2.00 .80
384 Dave Campbell 3.00 1.20
385 Mickey Stanley 3.00 1.20
386 Jim Colborn 2.00 .80
387 Horace Clarke 3.00 1.20
388 Charlie Williams 2.00 .80
389 Bill Rigney MG 2.00 .80
390 Willie Davis 3.00 1.20
391 Ken Sanders 2.00 .80
392 Fred Cambria 3.00 1.20
Richie Zisk RC
393 Curt Motton 2.00 .80
394 Ken Forsch 3.00 1.20
395 Matty Alou 3.00 1.20
396 Paul Lindblad 2.50 1.00
397 Phillies Team 6.00 2.40
398 Larry Hisle 3.00 1.20
399 Milt Wilcox 3.00 1.20
400 Tony Oliva 6.00 2.40
401 Jim Nash 2.50 1.00
402 Bobby Heise 2.50 1.00
403 John Cumberland 2.50 1.00
404 Jeff Torborg 3.00 1.20
405 Ron Fairly 3.00 1.20
406 George Hendrick RC 3.00 1.20
407 Chuck Taylor 2.50 1.00
408 Jim Northrup 3.00 1.20
409 Frank Baker 2.50 1.00
410 Fergie Jenkins 10.00 4.00
411 Bob Montgomery 2.50 1.00
412 Dick Kelley 2.50 1.00
413 Don Eddy 2.50 1.00
Dave Lemonds
414 Bob Miller 2.50 1.00
415 Cookie Rojas 2.50 1.00
416 Johnny Edwards 2.50 1.00
417 Tom Hall 2.50 1.00
418 Tom Shopay 2.50 1.00
419 Jim Spencer 2.50 1.00
420 Steve Carlton 20.00 8.00
421 Ellie Rodriguez 2.50 1.00
422 Ray Lamb 2.50 1.00
423 Oscar Gamble 3.00 1.20
424 Bill Gogolewski 2.50 1.00
425 Ken Singleton 3.00 1.20
426 Ken Singleton IA 2.50 1.00
427 Tito Fuentes 2.50 1.00
428 Tito Fuentes IA 2.50 1.00
429 Bob Robertson 2.50 1.00
430 Bob Robertson IA 2.50 1.00
431 Clarence Gaston 3.00 1.20
432 Clarence Gaston IA 2.50 1.00
433 Johnny Bench 30.00 12.00
434 Johnny Bench IA 15.00 6.00
435 Reggie Jackson 40.00 16.00
436 Reggie Jackson IA 20.00 8.00
437 Maury Wills 6.00 2.40
438 Maury Wills IA 3.00 1.20
439 Billy Williams 8.00 3.20
440 Billy Williams IA 6.00 2.40
441 Thurman Munson 20.00 8.00
442 Thurman Munson IA 10.00 4.00
443 Ken Henderson 2.50 1.00
444 Ken Henderson IA 2.50 1.00
445 Tom Seaver 40.00 16.00
446 Tom Seaver IA 20.00 8.00
447 Willie Stargell 10.00 4.00
448 Willie Stargell IA 6.00 2.40
449 Bob Lemon MG 3.00 1.20
450 Mickey Lolich 3.00 1.20
451 Tony LaRussa 8.00 3.20
452 Ed Herrmann 2.50 1.00
453 Barry Lersch 2.50 1.00
454 A's Team 6.00 2.40
455 Tommy Harper 3.00 1.20
456 Mark Belanger 3.00 1.20
457 Darcy Fast 2.50 1.00
Derrel Thomas
Mike Ivie
458 Aurelio Monteagudo 2.50 1.00
459 Rick Renick 2.50 1.00
460 Al Downing 2.50 1.00
461 Tim Cullen 2.50 1.00
462 Rickey Clark 2.50 1.00
463 Bernie Carbo 2.50 1.00
464 Jim Roland 2.50 1.00
465 Gil Hodges MG 30.00 12.00
(Mentions his
death on 4/2/72)
466 Norm Miller 2.50 1.00
467 Steve Kline 2.50 1.00
468 Richie Scheinblum 2.50 1.00
469 Ron Herbel 2.50 1.00
470 Ray Fosse 2.50 1.00
471 Luke Walker 2.50 1.00
472 Phil Gagliano 2.50 1.00
473 Dan McGinn 2.50 1.00
474 Don Baylor 18.00 7.25
Roric Harrison
Johnny Oates RC
475 Gary Nolan 2.50 1.00
476 Lee Richard 2.50 1.00
477 Tom Phoebus 2.50 1.00
478 Checklist 5th Series 8.00 2.00
479 Don Shaw 2.50 1.00
480 Lee May 3.00 1.20
481 Billy Conigliaro 2.50 1.00
482 Joe Hoerner 2.50 1.00
483 Ken Suarez 2.50 1.00
484 Lum Harris MG 2.50 1.00
485 Phil Regan 2.50 1.00
486 John Lowenstein 2.50 1.00
487 Tigers Team 6.00 2.40
488 Mike Nagy 2.50 1.00
489 Terry Humphrey 2.50 1.00
Keith Lampard
490 Dave McNally 3.00 1.20
491 Lou Piniella KP 3.00 1.20
492 Mel Stottlemyre KP 3.00 1.20
493 Bob Bailey KP 3.00 1.20
494 Willie Horton KP 3.00 1.20
495 Bill Melton KP 2.50 1.00
496 Bud Harrelson KP 3.00 1.20
497 Jim Perry KP 3.00 1.20
498 Brooks Robinson KP 6.00 2.40
499 Vicente Romo 2.50 1.00
500 Joe Torre 8.00 3.20
501 Pete Hamm 2.50 1.00
502 Jackie Hernandez 2.50 1.00
503 Gary Peters 2.50 1.00
504 Ed Spiezio 2.50 1.00
505 Mike Marshall 3.00 1.20
506 Terry Ley 3.00 1.20
Jim Moyer
Dick Tidrow
507 Fred Gladding 2.50 1.00
508 Ellie Hendricks 2.50 1.00
509 Don McMahon 2.50 1.00
510 Ted Williams MG 15.00 6.00
511 Tony Taylor 2.50 1.00
512 Paul Popovich 2.50 1.00
513 Lindy McDaniel 3.00 1.20
514 Ted Sizemore 3.00 1.20
515 Bert Blyleven 6.00 2.40
516 Oscar Brown 2.50 1.00
517 Ken Brett 2.50 1.00
518 Wayne Garrett 2.50 1.00
519 Ted Abernathy 2.50 1.00
520 Larry Bowa 3.00 1.20
521 Alan Foster 2.50 1.00
522 Dodgers Team 6.00 2.40
523 Chuck Dobson 2.50 1.00
524 Ed Armbrister 2.50 1.00
Mel Behney
525 Carlos May 3.00 1.20

1973 O-Pee-Chee

The cards in this 660-card set measure 2 1/2" by 3 1/2". This set is essentially the same as the regular 1973 Topps set, except that the words "Printed in Canada" appear on the backs and the

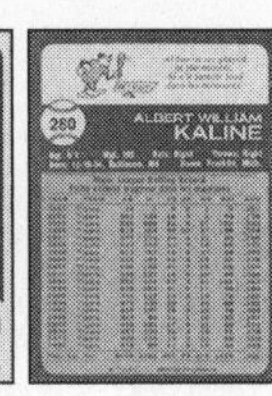

backs are bilingual. On a white border, the fronts feature color player photos with rounded corners and thin black borders. The player's name and position and the team name are also printed on the front. An "All-Time Leaders" series (471-478) appears in this set. Kid pictures appeared again for the second year in a row (341-346). The backs carry player biography and statistics in French and English. The cards are numbered on the back. The backs appear to be more "yellow" than the Topps backs. Remember, the prices below apply only to the O-Pee-Chee cards -- NOT Topps cards which are more plentiful. Unlike the 1973 Topps set, all cards in this set were issued equally and at the same time, i.e., there were no scarce series with the O-Pee-Chee cards. Although there are no scarce series, cards 529-660 attract a slight premium. Because of the premium that high series Topps cards attract, there is a perception that O-Pee-Chee cards of the same number sequence are less available. The key card in this set is the Mike Schmidt Rookie Card. The cards were packaged in 10 count packs with 36 cards in a box. Other Rookie Cards of note in this set include Bob Boone and Dwight Evans.

	NM	Ex
COMPLETE SET (660)	1000.00	400.00
COMMON CARD (1-528)	.75	.30
COMMON (529-660)	3.00	1.20

1 Babe Ruth 40.00 16.00
Hank Aaron
Willie Mays ATL
2 Rich Hebner 1.50 .60
3 Jim Lonborg 1.50 .60
4 John Milner .75 .30
5 Ed Brinkman .75 .30
6 Mac Scarce .75 .30
7 Texas Rangers Team 1.50 .60
8 Tom Hall .75 .30
9 Johnny Oates .75 .30
10 Don Sutton 6.00 2.40
11 Chris Chambliss 1.50 .60
12 Don Zimmer MG 1.50 .60
Dave Garcia CO
Johnny Podres CO
Bob Skinner CO
Whitey Wietelmann CO
13 George Hendrick 1.50 .60
14 Sonny Siebert .75 .30
15 Ralph Garr 1.50 .60
16 Steve Braun .75 .30
17 Fred Gladding .75 .30
18 Leroy Stanton .75 .30
19 Tim Foli .75 .30
20 Stan Bahnsen .75 .30
21 Randy Hundley 1.50 .60
22 Ted Abernathy .75 .30
23 Dave Kingman 1.50 .60
24 Al Santorini .75 .30
25 Roy White 1.50 .60
26 Pirates Team 1.50 .60
27 Bill Gogolewski .75 .30
28 Hal McRae 1.50 .60
29 Tony Taylor 1.50 .60
30 Tug McGraw 1.50 .60
31 Buddy Bell RC 2.50 1.00
32 Fred Norman .75 .30
33 Jim Breazeale .75 .30
34 Pat Dobson .75 .30
35 Willie Davis 1.50 .60
36 Steve Barber .75 .30
37 Bill Robinson 1.50 .60
38 Mike Epstein .75 .30
39 Dave Roberts .75 .30
40 Reggie Smith 1.50 .60
41 Tom Walker .75 .30
42 Mike Andrews .75 .30
43 Randy Moffitt .75 .30
44 Rick Monday 1.50 .60
45 Ellie Rodriguez .75 .30
(photo actually
John Felske)
46 Lindy McDaniel 1.50 .60
47 Luis Melendez .75 .30
48 Paul Splittorff .75 .30
49 Frank Quilici MG 1.50 .60
Vern Morgan CO
Bob Rodgers CO
Ralph Rowe CO
Al Worthington CO
50 Roberto Clemente 50.00 20.00
51 Chuck Seelbach .75 .30
52 Denis Menke .75 .30
53 Steve Dunning .75 .30
54 Checklist 1-132 3.00 .75
55 Jon Matlack 1.50 .60
56 Merv Rettenmund .75 .30
57 Derrel Thomas .75 .30
58 Mike Paul .75 .30
59 Steve Yeager RC 1.50 .60
60 Ken Holtzman 1.50 .60
61 Billy Williams 4.00 1.60
Rod Carew LL
62 Johnny Bench 2.50 1.00
Dick Allen LL
Home Run Leaders
63 Johnny Bench 2.50 1.00
Dick Allen
RBI Leaders
64 Lou Brock 1.50 .60
Bert Campaneris LL
65 Steve Carlton 1.50 .60
Luis Tiant LL
66 Steve Carlton 1.50 .60
Gaylord Perry
Wilbur Wood LL
67 Steve Carlton 40.00 16.00
Nolan Ryan LL
68 Clay Carroll 1.50 .60
Sparky Lyle LL
69 Phil Gagliano .75 .30
70 Milt Pappas 1.50 .60
71 Johnny Briggs .75 .30
72 Ron Reed .75 .30
73 Ed Herrmann .75 .30
74 Billy Champion .75 .30
75 Vada Pinson 1.50 .60
76 Doug Rader .75 .30
77 Mike Torrez 1.50 .60
78 Richie Scheinblum .75 .30
79 Jim Willoughby .75 .30
80 Tony Oliva 4.00 1.60
81 Whitey Lockman MG 1.50 .60
Hank Aguirre CO
Ernie Banks CO
Larry Jansen CO
Pete Reiser CO
82 Fritz Peterson .75 .30
83 Leron Lee .75 .30
84 Rollie Fingers 6.00 2.40
85 Ted Simmons 1.50 .60
86 Tom McCraw .75 .30
87 Ken Boswell .75 .30
88 Mickey Stanley 1.50 .60
89 Jack Billingham .75 .30
90 Brooks Robinson 8.00 3.20
91 Dodgers Team 1.50 .60
92 Jerry Bell .75 .30
93 Jesus Alou .75 .30
94 Dick Billings .75 .30
95 Steve Blass 1.50 .60
96 Doug Griffin .75 .30
97 Willie Montanez 1.50 .60
98 Dick Woodson .75 .30
99 Carl Taylor .75 .30
100 Hank Aaron 30.00 12.00
101 Ken Henderson .75 .30
102 Rudy May .75 .30
103 Celerino Sanchez .75 .30
104 Reggie Cleveland 1.50 .60
105 Carlos May .75 .30
106 Terry Humphrey .75 .30
107 Phil Hennigan .75 .30
108 Bill Russell 1.50 .60
109 Doyle Alexander 1.50 .60
110 Bob Watson 1.50 .60
111 Dave Nelson .75 .30
112 Gary Ross .75 .30
113 Jerry Grote 1.50 .60
114 Lynn McGlothen .75 .30
115 Ron Santo 4.00 1.60
116 Ralph Houk MG 1.50 .60
Jim Hegan CO
Elston Howard CO
Dick Howser CO
Jim Turner CO
117 Ramon Hernandez .75 .30
118 John Mayberry 1.50 .60
119 Larry Bowa 1.50 .60
120 Joe Coleman .75 .30
121 Dave Rader .75 .30
122 Jim Strickland .75 .30
123 Sandy Alomar 1.50 .60
124 Jim Hardin .75 .30
125 Ron Fairly 1.50 .60
126 Jim Brewer .75 .30
127 Brewers Team 1.50 .60
128 Ted Sizemore .75 .30
129 Terry Forster 1.50 .60
130 Pete Rose 25.00 10.00
131 Eddie Kasko MG 1.50 .60
Doug Camilli CO
Don Lenhardt CO
Eddie Popowski CO
Lee Stange CO
132 Matty Alou 1.50 .60
133 Dave Roberts .75 .30
134 Milt Wilcox .75 .30
135 Lee May 1.50 .60
136 Earl Weaver MG 4.00 1.60
George Bamberger CO
Jim Frey CO
Billy Hunter CO
George Staller CO
137 Jim Beauchamp .75 .30
138 Horacio Pina .75 .30
139 Carmen Fanzone .75 .30
140 Lou Piniella 2.50 1.00
141 Bruce Kison .75 .30
142 Thurman Munson 6.00 2.40
143 John Curtis .75 .30
144 Marty Perez .75 .30
145 Bobby Bonds 4.00 1.60
146 Woodie Fryman .75 .30
147 Mike Anderson .75 .30
148 Dave Goltz .75 .30
149 Ron Hunt .75 .30
150 Wilbur Wood 1.50 .60
151 Wes Parker 1.50 .60
152 Dave May .75 .30
153 Al Hrabosky 1.50 .60
154 Jeff Torborg 1.50 .60
155 Sal Bando 1.50 .60
156 Cesar Geronimo .75 .30
157 Denny Riddleberger .75 .30
158 Astros Team 1.50 .60
159 Clarence Gaston 1.50 .60
160 Jim Palmer 8.00 3.20
161 Ted Martinez .75 .30
162 Pete Broberg .75 .30
163 Vic Davalillo .75 .30
164 Monty Montgomery .75 .30
165 Luis Aparicio 6.00 2.40
166 Terry Harmon .75 .30
167 Steve Stone 1.50 .60
168 Jim Northrup 1.50 .60
169 Ron Schueler RC 1.50 .60
170 Harmon Killebrew 6.00 2.40
171 Bernie Carbo .75 .30
172 Steve Kline .75 .30
173 Hal Breeden 1.50 .60
174 Goose Gossage RC 8.00 3.20
175 Frank Robinson 8.00 3.20
176 Chuck Taylor .75 .30
177 Bill Plummer .75 .30
178 Don Rose .75 .30
179 Dick Williams MG 1.50 .60
Jerry Adair CO
Vern Hoscheit CO
Irv Noren CO
Wes Stock CO
180 Fergie Jenkins 4.00 1.60
181 Jack Brohamer .75 .30
182 Mike Caldwell RC 1.50 .60
183 Don Buford .75 .30
184 Jerry Koosman 1.50 .60
185 Jim Wynn 1.50 .60
186 Bill Fahey .75 .30
187 Luke Walker .75 .30
188 Cookie Rojas 1.50 .60
189 Greg Luzinski 2.50 1.00
190 Bob Gibson 8.00 3.20
191 Tigers Team 1.50 .60
192 Pat Jarvis .75 .30
193 Carlton Fisk 10.00 4.00
194 Jorge Orta .75 .30
195 Clay Carroll .75 .30
196 Ken McMullen .75 .30
197 Ed Goodson .75 .30
198 Horace Clarke .75 .30
199 Bert Blyleven 4.00 1.60
200 Billy Williams 6.00 2.40
201 G.Hendrick ALCS 1.50 .60
202 George Foster NLCS 1.50 .60
203 Gene Tenace WS 1.50 .60
204 World Series Game 2 1.50 .60
A's two straight
205 Tony Perez WS 2.50 1.00
206 Gene Tenace WS 1.50 .60
207 Blue Moon Odom WS 1.50 .60
208 Johnny Bench WS 4.00 1.60
209 Bert Campaneris WS 1.50 .60
210 W.S. Summary 1.50 .60
World champions:
A's Win
211 Balor Moore .75 .30
212 Joe Lahoud .75 .30
213 Steve Garvey 4.00 1.60
214 Dave Hamilton .75 .30
215 Dusty Baker 4.00 1.60
216 Toby Harrah 1.50 .60
217 Don Wilson .75 .30
218 Aurelio Rodriguez .75 .30
219 Cardinals Team 1.50 .60
220 Nolan Ryan 100.00 40.00
221 Fred Kendall .75 .30
222 Rob Gardner .75 .30
223 Bud Harrelson 1.50 .60
224 Bill Lee 1.50 .60
225 Al Oliver 1.50 .60
226 Ray Fosse .75 .30
227 Wayne Twitchell .75 .30
228 Bobby Darwin .75 .30
229 Roric Harrison .75 .30
230 Joe Morgan 6.00 2.40
231 Bill Parsons .75 .30
232 Ken Singleton 1.50 .60
233 Ed Kirkpatrick .75 .30
234 Bill North .75 .30
235 Jim Hunter 6.00 2.40
236 Tito Fuentes .75 .30
237 Eddie Mathews MG 4.00 1.60
Lew Burdette CO
Jim Busby CO
Roy Hartsfield CO
Ken Silvestri CO
238 Tony Muser .75 .30
239 Pete Richert .75 .30
240 Bobby Murcer 2.50 1.00
241 Dwain Anderson .75 .30
242 George Culver .75 .30
243 Angels Team 1.50 .60
244 Ed Acosta .75 .30
245 Carl Yastrzemski 12.00 4.80
246 Ken Sanders .75 .30
247 Del Unser .75 .30
248 Jerry Johnson .75 .30
249 Larry Biittner .75 .30
250 Manny Sanguillen 1.50 .60
251 Roger Nelson .75 .30
252 Charlie Fox MG 1.50 .60
Joe Amalfitano CO
Andy Gilbert CO
Don McMahon CO
John McNamara CO
253 Mark Belanger 1.50 .60
254 Bill Stoneman 1.50 .60
255 Reggie Jackson 20.00 8.00
256 Chris Zachary .75 .30
257 Yogi Berra MG 4.00 1.60
Roy McMillan CO
Joe Pignatano CO
Rube Walker CO
Eddie Yost CO
258 Tommy John 2.50 1.00
259 Jim Holt .75 .30
260 Gary Nolan 1.50 .60
261 Pat Kelly .75 .30
262 Jack Aker .75 .30
263 George Scott 1.50 .60
264 Checklist 133-264 2.50 .60
265 Gene Michael 1.50 .60
266 Mike Lum .75 .30
267 Lloyd Allen .75 .30
268 Jerry Morales .75 .30
269 Tim McCarver 2.50 1.00
270 Luis Tiant 2.50 1.00
271 Tom Hutton .75 .30
272 Ed Farmer .75 .30
273 Chris Speier .75 .30
274 Darold Knowles .75 .30
275 Tony Perez 6.00 2.40
276 Joe Lovitto .75 .30
277 Bob Miller .75 .30
278 Orioles Team 1.50 .60
279 Mike Strahler .75 .30
280 Al Kaline 8.00 3.20
281 Mike Jorgensen .75 .30
282 Steve Hovley .75 .30
283 Ray Sadecki .75 .30
284 Glenn Borgmann .75 .30
285 Don Kessinger 1.50 .60
286 Frank Linzy .75 .30
287 Eddie Leon .75 .30
288 Gary Gentry .75 .30

289 Bob Oliver .75 .30
290 Cesar Cedeno 1.50 .60
291 Rogelio Moret .75 .30
292 Jose Cruz 1.50 .60
293 Bernie Allen .75 .30
294 Steve Arlin .75 .30
295 Bert Campaneris 1.50 .60
296 Sparky Anderson MG 4.00 1.60
Alex Grammas CO
Ted Kluszewski CO
George Scherger CO
Larry Shepard CO
297 Walt Williams .75 .30
298 Ron Bryant .75 .30
299 Ted Ford .75 .30
300 Steve Carlton 12.00 4.80
301 Billy Grabarkewitz .75 .30
302 Terry Crowley .75 .30
303 Nelson Briles .75 .30
304 Duke Sims .75 .30
305 Willie Mays 40.00 16.00
306 Tom Burgmeier .75 .30
307 Boots Day .75 .30
308 Skip Lockwood .75 .30
309 Paul Popovich .75 .30
310 Dick Allen 2.50 1.00
311 Joe Decker .75 .30
312 Oscar Brown .75 .30
313 Jim Ray .75 .30
314 Ron Swoboda 1.50 .60
315 John Odom .75 .30
316 Padres Team 1.50 .60
317 Danny Cater .75 .30
318 Jim McGlothlin .75 .30
319 Jim Spencer .75 .30
320 Lou Brock 8.00 3.20
321 Rich Hinton .75 .30
322 Garry Maddox RC 1.50 .60
323 Billy Martin MG 2.50 1.00
Art Fowler CO
Charlie Silvera CO
Dick Tracewski CO
Joe Schultz CO ERR
Schultz name not printed on card
324 Al Downing .75 .30
325 Boog Powell 1.50 .60
326 Darrell Brandon .75 .30
327 John Lowenstein .75 .30
328 Bill Bonham .75 .30
329 Ed Kranepool 1.50 .60
330 Rod Carew 8.00 3.20
331 Carl Morton .75 .30
332 John Felske .75 .30
333 Gene Clines .75 .30
334 Freddie Patek .75 .30
335 Bob Tolan .75 .30
336 Tom Bradley .75 .30
337 Dave Duncan 1.50 .60
338 Checklist 265-396 2.50 .60
339 Dick Tidrow .75 .30
340 Nate Colbert .75 .30
341 Jim Palmer KP 2.50 1.00
342 Sam McDowell KP 1.50 .60
343 Bobby Murcer KP 1.50 .60
344 Jim Hunter KP 2.50 1.00
345 Chris Speier KP .75 .30
346 Gaylord Perry KP 1.50 .60
347 Royals Team 1.50 .60
348 Rennie Stennett .75 .30
349 Dick McAuliffe .75 .30
350 Tom Seaver 15.00 6.00
351 Jimmy Stewart .75 .30
352 Don Stanhouse .75 .30
353 Steve Brye .75 .30
354 Billy Parker .75 .30
355 Mike Marshall 1.50 .60
356 Chuck Tanner MG 1.50 .60
Joe Lonnett CO
Jim Mahoney CO
Al Monchak CO
Johnny Sain CO
357 Ross Grimsley .75 .30
358 Jim Nettles .75 .30
359 Cecil Upshaw .75 .30
360 Joe Rudi 1.50 .60
(photo actually
Gene Tenace)
361 Fran Healy .75 .30
362 Eddie Watt .75 .30
363 Jackie Hernandez .75 .30
364 Rick Wise .75 .30
365 Rico Petrocelli 1.50 .60
366 Brock Davis .75 .30
367 Burt Hooton 1.50 .60
368 Bill Buckner 1.50 .60
369 Lerrin LaGrow .75 .30
370 Willie Stargell 6.00 2.40
371 Mike Kekich .75 .30
372 Oscar Gamble .75 .30
373 Clyde Wright .75 .30
374 Darrell Evans 2.50 1.00
375 Larry Dierker 1.50 .60
376 Frank Duffy .75 .30
377 Gene Mauch MG 2.50 1.00
Dave Bristol CO
Larry Doby CO
Cal McLish CO
Jerry Zimmerman CO
378 Lenny Randle .75 .30
379 Cy Acosta .75 .30
380 Johnny Bench 15.00 6.00
381 Vicente Romo .75 .30
382 Mike Hegan .75 .30
383 Diego Segui .75 .30
384 Don Baylor 4.00 1.60
385 Jim Perry 1.50 .60
386 Don Money .75 .30
387 Jim Barr .75 .30
388 Ben Oglivie 1.50 .60
389 Mets Team 4.00 1.60
390 Mickey Lolich 1.50 .60
391 Lee Lacy RC 1.50 .60
392 Dick Drago .75 .30
393 Jose Cardenal .75 .30
394 Sparky Lyle 1.50 .60
395 Roger Metzger .75 .30
396 Grant Jackson .75 .30
397 Dave Cash 1.50 .60
398 Rich Hand .75 .30
399 George Foster 1.50 .60
400 Gaylord Perry 6.00 2.40
401 Clyde Mashore .75 .30
402 Jack Hiatt .75 .30
403 Sonny Jackson .75 .30
404 Chuck Brinkman .75 .30
405 Cesar Tovar .75 .30
406 Paul Lindblad .75 .30
407 Felix Millan .75 .30
408 Jim Colborn .75 .30
409 Ivan Murrell .75 .30
410 Willie McCovey 6.00 2.40
411 Ray Corbin .75 .30
412 Manny Mota 1.50 .60
413 Tom Timmerman .75 .30
414 Ken Rudolph .75 .30
415 Marty Pattin .75 .30
416 Paul Schaal .75 .30
417 Scipio Spinks .75 .30
418 Bobby Grich 1.50 .60
419 Casey Cox .75 .30
420 Tommie Agee .75 .30
421 Bobby Winkles MG 1.50 .60
Tom Morgan CO
Salty Parker CO
Jimmie Reese CO
John Roseboro CO
422 Bob Robertson .75 .30
423 Johnny Jeter .75 .30
424 Denny Doyle .75 .30
425 Alex Johnson .75 .30
426 Dave LaRoche .75 .30
427 Rick Auerbach .75 .30
428 Wayne Simpson .75 .30
429 Jim Fairey .75 .30
430 Vida Blue 1.50 .60
431 Gerry Moses .75 .30
432 Dan Frisella .75 .30
433 Willie Horton 1.50 .60
434 Giants Team 2.50 1.00
435 Rico Carty 1.50 .60
436 Jim McAndrew .75 .30
437 John Kennedy .75 .30
438 Enzo Hernandez .75 .30
439 Eddie Fisher .75 .30
440 Glenn Beckert .75 .30
441 Gail Hopkins .75 .30
442 Dick Dietz .75 .30
443 Danny Thompson .75 .30
444 Ken Brett .75 .30
445 Ken Berry .75 .30
446 Jerry Reuss 1.50 .60
447 Joe Hague .75 .30
448 John Hiller 1.50 .60
449 Ken Aspromonte MG 2.50 1.00
Rocky Colavito CO
Joe Lutz CO
Warren Spahn CO
450 Joe Torre 2.50 1.00
451 John Vuckovich .75 .30
452 Paul Casanova .75 .30
453 Checklist 397-528 2.50 .60
454 Tom Haller .75 .30
455 Bill Melton .75 .30
456 Dick Green .75 .30
457 John Strohmayer .75 .30
458 Jim Mason .75 .30
459 Jimmy Howarth .75 .30
460 Bill Freehan 1.50 .60
461 Mike Corkins .75 .30
462 Ron Blomberg .75 .30
463 Ken Tatum .75 .30
464 Chicago Cubs Team 2.50 1.00
465 Dave Giusti .75 .30
466 Jose Arcia .75 .30
467 Mike Ryan .75 .30
468 Tom Griffin .75 .30
469 Dan Monzon .75 .30
470 Mike Cuellar 1.50 .60
471 Ty Cobb ATL 10.00 4.00
4191 Hits
472 Lou Gehrig ATL 15.00 6.00
23 Grand Slams
473 Hank Aaron ATL 10.00 4.00
6172 Total Bases
474 Babe Ruth ATL 20.00 8.00
2209 RBI's
475 Ty Cobb ATL 8.00 3.20
.367 Batting Average
476 Walter Johnson ATL 2.50 1.00
113 Shutouts
477 Cy Young ATL 2.50 1.00
511 Wins
478 Walter Johnson ATL 2.50 1.00
3508 Strikeouts
479 Hal Lanier .75 .30
480 Juan Marichal 6.00 2.40
481 White Sox Team Card 2.50 1.00
482 Rick Reuschel RC 2.50 1.00
483 Dal Maxvill .75 .30
484 Ernie McAnally .75 .30
485 Norm Cash 1.50 .60
486 Danny Ozark MG 1.50 .60
Carroll Beringer CO
Billy DeMars CO
Ray Rippelmeyer CO
Bobby Wine CO
487 Bruce Dal Canton .75 .30
488 Dave Campbell 1.50 .60
489 Jeff Burroughs 1.50 .60
490 Claude Osteen 1.50 .60
491 Bob Montgomery .75 .30
492 Pedro Borbon .75 .30
493 Duffy Dyer .75 .30
494 Rich Morales .75 .30
495 Tommy Helms .75 .30
496 Ray Lamb .75 .30
497 Red Schoendienst MG 2.50 1.00
Vern Benson CO
George Kissell CO
Barney Schultz CO
498 Graig Nettles 4.00 1.60
499 Bob Moose .75 .30
500 Oakland A's Team 2.50 1.00
501 Larry Gura .75 .30
502 Bobby Valentine 2.50 1.00
503 Phil Niekro 6.00 2.40
504 Earl Williams .75 .30
505 Bob Bailey .75 .30
506 Bart Johnson .75 .30
507 Darrel Chaney .75 .30
508 Gates Brown .75 .30
509 Jim Nash .75 .30
510 Amos Otis 1.50 .60
511 Sam McDowell 1.50 .60
512 Dalton Jones .75 .30
513 Dave Marshall .75 .30
514 Jerry Kenney .75 .30
515 Andy Messersmith 1.50 .60
516 Danny Walton .75 .30
517 Bill Virdon MG 2.50 1.00
Don Leppert CO
Bill Mazeroski CO
Dave Ricketts CO
Mel Wright CO
518 Bob Veale .75 .30
519 John Edwards .75 .30
520 Mel Stottlemyre 1.50 .60
521 Atlanta Braves Team 2.50 1.00
522 Leo Cardenas .75 .30
523 Wayne Granger .75 .30
524 Gene Tenace 1.50 .60
525 Jim Fregosi 1.50 .60
526 Ollie Brown .75 .30
527 Dan McGinn .75 .30
528 Paul Blair 1.50 .60
529 Milt May 3.00 1.20
530 Jim Kaat 4.00 1.60
531 Ron Woods 3.00 1.20
532 Steve Mingori 3.00 1.20
533 Larry Stahl 3.00 1.20
534 Dave Lemonds 3.00 1.20
535 John Callison 4.00 1.60
536 Phillies Team 6.00 2.40
537 Bill Slayback 3.00 1.20
538 Jim Ray Hart 4.00 1.60
539 Tom Murphy 3.00 1.20
540 Cleon Jones 4.00 1.60
541 Bob Bolin 3.00 1.20
542 Pat Corrales 4.00 1.60
543 Alan Foster 3.00 1.20
544 Von Joshua 3.00 1.20
545 Orlando Cepeda 10.00 4.00
546 Jim York 3.00 1.20
547 Bobby Heise 3.00 1.20
548 Don Durham 3.00 1.20
549 hitey Herzog MG 4.00 1.60
Chuck Estrada CO
Chuck Hiller CO
Jackie Moore CO
550 Dave Johnson 4.00 1.60
551 Mike Kilkenny 4.00 1.60
552 J.C. Martin 3.00 1.20
553 Mickey Scott 3.00 1.20
554 Dave Concepcion 6.00 2.40
555 Bill Hands 3.00 1.20
556 Yankees Team 6.00 2.40
557 Bernie Williams 3.00 1.20
558 Jerry May 3.00 1.20
559 Barry Lersch 3.00 1.20
560 Frank Howard 4.00 1.60
561 Jim Geddes 3.00 1.20
562 Wayne Garrett 3.00 1.20
563 Larry Haney 3.00 1.20
564 Mike Thompson 3.00 1.20
565 Jim Hickman 3.00 1.20
566 Lew Krausse 3.00 1.20
567 Bob Fenwick 3.00 1.20
568 Ray Newman 3.00 1.20
569 Walt Alston MG 8.00 3.20
Red Adams CO
Monty Basgall CO
Jim Gilliam CO
Tom Lasorda CO
570 Bill Singer 4.00 1.60
571 Rusty Torres 3.00 1.20
572 Gary Sutherland 3.00 1.20
573 Fred Beene 3.00 1.20
574 Bob Didier 3.00 1.20
575 Dock Ellis 3.00 1.20
576 Expos Team 8.00 3.20
577 Eric Soderholm 3.00 1.20
578 Ken Wright 3.00 1.20
579 Tom Grieve 4.00 1.60
580 Joe Pepitone 4.00 1.60
581 Steve Kealey 3.00 1.20
582 Darrell Porter 4.00 1.60
583 Bill Greif 3.00 1.20
584 Chris Arnold 3.00 1.20
585 Joe Niekro 4.00 1.60
586 Bill Sudakis 3.00 1.20
587 Rich McKinney 3.00 1.20
588 Checklist 529-660 20.00 5.00
589 Ken Forsch 3.00 1.20
590 Deron Johnson 3.00 1.20
591 Mike Hedlund 3.00 1.20
592 John Boccabella 3.00 1.20
593 Jack McKeon MG 3.00 1.20
Galen Cisco CO
Harry Dunlop CO
Charlie Lau CO
594 Vic Harris 3.00 1.20
595 Don Gullett 4.00 1.60
596 Red Sox Team 6.00 2.40
597 Mickey Rivers 4.00 1.60
598 Phil Roof 3.00 1.20
599 Ed Crosby 3.00 1.20
600 Dave McNally 4.00 1.60
601 Sergio Robles 4.00 1.60
George Pena
Rick Stelmaszek
602 Mel Behney 4.00 1.60
Ralph Garcia
Doug Rau
603 Terry Hughes 4.00 1.60
Bill McNulty
Ken Reitz
604 Jesse Jefferson 4.00 1.60
Dennis O'Toole
Bob Strampe
605 Enos Cabell RC 4.00 1.60
Pat Bourque
Gonzalo Marquez
606 Gary Matthews RC 6.00 2.40
Tom Paciorek
Jorge Roque
607 Pepe Frias 4.00 1.60
Ray Busse
Mario Guerrero
608 Steve Busby RC 6.00 2.40
Dick Colpaert
George Medich
609 Larvell Blanks 6.00 2.40
Pedro Garcia
Dave Lopes RC
610 Jimmy Freeman 4.00 1.60
Charlie Hough
Hank Webb
611 Rich Coggins 4.00 1.60
Jim Wohlford
Richie Zisk
612 Steve Lawson 4.00 1.60
Bob Reynolds
Brent Strom
613 Bob Boone RC 20.00 8.00
Skip Jutze
Mike Ivie
614 Al Bumbry 18.00 7.25
Dwight Evans RC
Charlie Spikes
615 Ron Cey 250.00 100.00
John Hilton
Mike Schmidt RC
616 Norm Angelini 4.00 1.60
Steve Blateric
Mike Garman
617 Rich Chiles 3.00 1.20
618 Andy Etchebarren 3.00 1.20
619 Billy Wilson 3.00 1.20
620 Tommy Harper 4.00 1.60
621 Joe Ferguson 4.00 1.60
622 Larry Hisle 4.00 1.60
623 Steve Renko 3.00 1.20
624 Leo Durocher MG 8.00 3.20
Preston Gomez CO
Grady Hatton CO
Hub Kittle CO
Jim Owens CO
625 Angel Mangual 3.00 1.20
626 Bob Barton 3.00 1.20
627 Luis Alvarado 3.00 1.20
628 Jim Slaton 3.00 1.20
629 Indians Team 6.00 2.40
630 Denny McLain 6.00 2.40
631 Tom Matchick 3.00 1.20
632 Dick Selma 3.00 1.20
633 Ike Brown 3.00 1.20
634 Alan Closter 3.00 1.20
635 Gene Alley 4.00 1.60
636 Rickey Clark 3.00 1.20
637 Norm Miller 3.00 1.20
638 Ken Reynolds 3.00 1.20
639 Willie Crawford 3.00 1.20
640 Dick Bosman 3.00 1.20
641 Reds Team 6.00 2.40
642 Jose Laboy 3.00 1.20
643 Al Fitzmorris 3.00 1.20
644 Jack Heidemann 3.00 1.20
645 Bob Locker 3.00 1.20
646 Del Crandall MG 4.00 1.60
Harvey Kuenn CO
Joe Nossek CO
Bob Shaw CO
Jim Walton CO
647 George Stone 3.00 1.20
648 Tom Egan 3.00 1.20
649 Rich Folkers 3.00 1.20
650 Felipe Alou 6.00 2.40
651 Don Carrithers 3.00 1.20
652 Ted Kubiak 3.00 1.20
653 Joe Hoerner 3.00 1.20
654 Twins Team 6.00 2.40
655 Clay Kirby 3.00 1.20
656 John Ellis 3.00 1.20
657 Bob Johnson 3.00 1.20
658 Elliott Maddox 3.00 1.20
659 Jose Pagan 3.00 1.20
660 Fred Scherman 6.00 2.40

1973 O-Pee-Chee Blue Team Checklists

This 24-card standard-size set is somewhat difficult to find. These blue-bordered team checklist cards are very similar in design to the mass produced red trim team checklist cards issued by O-Pee-Chee the next year and obviously very similar to the Topps issue. The primary difference compared to the Topps issue is the existence of a little French language on the reverse of the O-Pee-Chee. The fronts feature facsimile autographs on a white background. On an orange background, the backs carry the team checklists. The words "Team Checklist" are printed in French and English. The cards are unnumbered and checklisted below in alphabetical order.

NM Ex
COMPLETE SET (24) 125.00 50.00
COMMON TEAM (1-24) 6.00 2.40

1974 O-Pee-Chee

The cards in this 660-card set measure 2 1/2" by 3 1/2". The 1974 O-Pee-Chee cards are very similar to the 1974 Topps cards. Since the O-Pee-Chee cards were printed substantially later than the Topps cards, there was no "San Diego rumored moving to Washington" problem in the O-Pee-Chee set. On a white background, the fronts feature color player photos with rounded corners and blue borders. The player's name and position and the team name also appear on the front. The horizontal backs are golden yellow instead of green like the 1974 Topps and carry player biography and statistics in French and English. There are a number of obverse differences between the two sets as well; they are numbers 3, 4, 5, 6, 7, 8, 9, 99, 166 and 196. The Aaron Specials generally feature two past cards per card instead of four as in the Topps. Remember, the prices below apply only to O-Pee-Chee cards -- they are NOT prices for Topps cards as the Topps cards are generally much more available. The cards were issued in eight card packs with 36 packs to a box. Notable Rookie Cards include Dave Parker and Dave Winfield.

NM Ex
COMPLETE SET (660) 1000.00 400.00
1 Hank Aaron 60.00 24.00
Complete ML record
2 Aaron Special 54-57 12.00 4.80
Records on back
3 Aaron Special 58-59 12.00 4.80
4 Aaron Special 60-61 12.00 4.80
5 Aaron Special 62-63 12.00 4.80
6 Aaron Special 64-65 12.00 4.80
7 Aaron Special 66-67 12.00 4.80
8 Aaron Special 68-69 12.00 4.80
9 Aaron Special 70-73 12.00 4.80
Milestone homers
10 Johnny Bench 25.00 10.00
11 Jim Bibby 1.00 .40
12 Dave May 1.00 .40
13 Tom Hilgendorf 1.00 .40
14 Paul Popovich 1.00 .40
15 Joe Torre 4.00 1.60
16 Orioles Team 2.00 .80
17 Doug Bird 1.00 .40
18 Gary Thomasson 1.00 .40
19 Gerry Moses 1.00 .40
20 Nolan Ryan 80.00 32.00
21 Bob Gallagher 1.00 .40
22 Cy Acosta 1.00 .40
23 Craig Robinson 1.00 .40
24 John Hiller 2.00 .80
25 Ken Singleton 2.00 .80
26 Bill Campbell 1.00 .40
27 George Scott 2.00 .80
28 Manny Sanguillen 2.00 .80
29 Phil Niekro 6.00 2.40
30 Bobby Bonds 4.00 1.60
31 Preston Gomez MG 2.00 .80
Roger Craig CO
Hub Kittle CO
Grady Hatton CO
Bob Lillis CO
32 Johnny Grubb 1.00 .40
33 Don Newhauser 1.00 .40
34 Andy Kosco 1.00 .40
35 Gaylord Perry 6.00 2.40
36 Cardinals Team 2.00 .80
37 Dave Sells 1.00 .40
38 Don Kessinger 2.00 .80
39 Ken Suarez 1.00 .40
40 Jim Palmer 10.00 4.00
41 Bobby Floyd 1.00 .40
42 Claude Osteen 2.00 .80
43 Jim Wynn 2.00 .80
44 Mel Stottlemyre 2.00 .80
45 Dave Johnson 2.00 .80
46 Pat Kelly 1.00 .40
47 Dick Ruthven 1.00 .40
48 Dick Sharon 1.00 .40
49 Steve Renko 2.00 .80
50 Rod Carew 10.00 4.00
51 Bob Heise 1.00 .40
52 Al Oliver 2.00 .80
53 Fred Kendall 1.00 .40
54 Elias Sosa 1.00 .40
55 Frank Robinson 10.00 4.00
56 New York Mets Team 2.00 .80
57 Darold Knowles 1.00 .40
58 Charlie Spikes 1.00 .40
59 Ross Grimsley 1.00 .40
60 Lou Brock 10.00 4.00
61 Luis Aparicio 6.00 2.40
62 Bob Locker 1.00 .40
63 Bill Sudakis 1.00 .40
64 Doug Rau 1.00 .40
65 Amos Otis 2.00 .80
66 Sparky Lyle 2.00 .80
67 Tommy Helms 1.00 .40
68 Grant Jackson 1.00 .40
69 Del Unser 1.00 .40
70 Dick Allen 3.00 1.20
71 Dan Frisella 1.00 .40
72 Aurelio Rodriguez 1.00 .40
73 Mike Marshall 3.00 1.20
74 Twins Team 2.00 .80
75 Jim Colborn 1.00 .40
76 Mickey Rivers 2.00 .80
77 Rich Troedson 1.00 .40
78 Charlie Fox MG 2.00 .80
John McNamara CO
Joe Amalfitano CO
Andy Gilbert CO
Don McMahon CO
79 Gene Tenace 2.00 .80
80 Tom Seaver 20.00 8.00
81 Frank Duffy 1.00 .40
82 Dave Giusti 1.00 .40
83 Orlando Cepeda 6.00 2.40
84 Rick Wise 1.00 .40
85 Joe Morgan 10.00 4.00
86 Joe Ferguson 2.00 .80
87 Fergie Jenkins 6.00 2.40
88 Fred Patek 2.00 .80
89 Jackie Brown 1.00 .40
90 Bobby Murcer 2.00 .80
91 Ken Forsch 1.00 .40
92 Paul Blair 2.00 .80
93 Rod Gilbreath 1.00 .40
94 Tigers Team 2.00 .80
95 Steve Carlton 12.00 4.80
96 Jerry Hairston 1.00 .40
97 Bob Bailey 2.00 .80
98 Bert Blyleven 4.00 1.60
99 George Theodore 3.00 1.20
(Topps 99 is

Brewers Leaders)
100 Willie Stargell 6.00 2.40
101 Bobby Valentine 2.00 .80
102 Bill Greif 1.00 .40
103 Sal Bando 2.00 .80
104 Ron Bryant 1.00 .40
105 Carlton Fisk 15.00 6.00
106 Harry Parker 1.00 .40
107 Alex Johnson 1.00 .40
108 Al Hrabosky 2.00 .80
109 Bobby Grich 2.00 .80
110 Billy Williams 6.00 2.40
111 Clay Carroll 1.00 .40
112 Dave Lopes 3.00 1.20
113 Dick Drago 1.00 .40
114 Angels Team 2.00 .80
115 Willie Horton 2.00 .80
116 Jerry Reuss 2.00 .80
117 Ron Blomberg 1.00 .40
118 Bill Lee 2.00 .80
119 Danny Ozark MG 2.00 .80
Ray Rippelmeyer CO
Bobby Wine CO
Carroll Beringer CO
Billy DeMars CO
120 Wilbur Wood 1.00 .40
121 Larry Lintz 1.00 .40
122 Jim Holt 1.00 .40
123 Nellie Briles 2.00 .80
124 Bobby Coluccio 1.00 .40
125 Nate Colbert 1.00 .40
126 Checklist 1-132 5.00 1.25
127 Tom Paciorek 2.00 .80
128 John Ellis 1.00 .40
129 Chris Speier 1.00 .40
130 Reggie Jackson 25.00 10.00
131 Bob Boone 3.00 1.20
132 Felix Millan 1.00 .40
133 David Clyde 1.00 .40
134 Denis Menke 1.00 .40
135 Roy White 2.00 .80
136 Rick Reuschel 2.00 .80
137 Al Bumbry 2.00 .80
138 Eddie Brinkman 1.00 .40
139 Aurelio Monteagudo 1.00 .40
140 Darrell Evans 3.00 1.20
141 Pat Bourque 1.00 .40
142 Pedro Garcia 1.00 .40
143 Dick Woodson 1.00 .40
144 Walter Alston MG 4.00 1.60
Tom Lasorda CO
Jim Gilliam CO
Red Adams CO
Monty Basgall CO
145 Dock Ellis 1.00 .40
146 Ron Fairly 2.00 .80
147 Bart Johnson 1.00 .40
148 Dave Hilton 1.00 .40
149 Mac Scarce 1.00 .40
150 John Mayberry 2.00 .80
151 Diego Segui 1.00 .40
152 Oscar Gamble 2.00 .80
153 Jon Matlack 2.00 .80
154 Astros Team 2.00 .80
155 Bert Campaneris 2.00 .80
156 Randy Moffitt 1.00 .40
157 Vic Harris 1.00 .40
158 Jack Billingham 1.00 .40
159 Jim Ray Hart 1.00 .40
160 Brooks Robinson 12.00 4.80
161 Ray Burris 2.00 .80
162 Bill Freehan 2.00 .80
163 Ken Berry 1.00 .40
164 Tom House 1.00 .40
165 Willie Davis 2.00 .80
166 Mickey Lolich 4.00 1.60
(Topps 166 is
Royals Leaders)
167 Luis Tiant 3.00 1.20
168 Danny Thompson 1.00 .40
169 Steve Rogers RC 3.00 1.20
170 Bill Melton 1.00 .40
171 Eduardo Rodriguez 1.00 .40
172 Gene Clines 1.00 .40
173 Randy Jones RC 3.00 1.20
174 Bill Robinson 2.00 .80
175 Reggie Cleveland 2.00 .80
176 John Lowenstein 1.00 .40
177 Dave Roberts 1.00 .40
178 Garry Maddox 2.00 .80
179 Yogi Berra MG 8.00 3.20
Rube Walker CO
Eddie Yost CO
Roy McMillan CO
Joe Pignatano CO
180 Ken Holtzman 2.00 .80
181 Cesar Geronimo 1.00 .40
182 Lindy McDaniel 2.00 .80
183 Johnny Oates 1.00 .40
184 Rangers Team 2.00 .80
185 Jose Cardenal 1.00 .40
186 Fred Scherman 1.00 .40
187 Don Baylor 3.00 1.20
188 Rudy Meoli 1.00 .40
189 Jim Brewer 1.00 .40
190 Tony Oliva 3.00 1.20
191 Al Fitzmorris 1.00 .40
192 Mario Guerrero 1.00 .40
193 Tom Walker 1.00 .40
194 Darrell Porter 2.00 .80
195 Carlos May 1.00 .40
196 Jim Hunter 6.00 2.40
(Topps 196 is
Jim Fregosi)
197 Vicente Romo 1.00 .40
198 Dave Cash 1.00 .40
199 Mike Kekich 1.00 .40
200 Cesar Cedeno 2.00 .80
201 Rod Carew 8.00 3.20
Pete Rose LL
202 Reggie Jackson 8.00 3.20
Willie Stargell LL
203 Reggie Jackson 8.00 3.20
Willie Stargell LL
204 Tommy Harper 3.00 1.20
Lou Brock LL
205 Wilbur Wood 2.00 .80
Ron Bryant LL
206 Jim Palmer 6.00 2.40
Tom Seaver LL
207 Nolan Ryan 20.00 8.00
Tom Seaver LL
208 John Hiller 2.00 .80
Mike Marshall LL
209 Ted Sizemore 1.00 .40
210 Bill Singer 1.00 .40
211 Chicago Cubs Team 2.00 .80
212 Rollie Fingers 6.00 2.40
213 Dave Rader 1.00 .40
214 Bill Grabarkewitz 1.00 .40
215 Al Kaline 15.00 6.00
216 Ray Sadecki 1.00 .40
217 Tim Foli 1.00 .40
218 John Briggs 1.00 .40
219 Doug Griffin 1.00 .40
220 Don Sutton 6.00 2.40
221 Chuck Tanner MG 2.00 .80
Jim Mahoney CO
Alex Monchak CO
Johnny Sain CO
Joe Lonnett CO
222 Ramon Hernandez 1.00 .40
223 Jeff Burroughs 3.00 1.20
224 Roger Metzger 1.00 .40
225 Paul Splittorff 1.00 .40
226 Padres Team Card 3.00 1.20
227 Mike Lum 1.00 .40
228 Ted Kubiak 1.00 .40
229 Fritz Peterson 1.00 .40
230 Tony Perez 6.00 2.40
231 Dick Tidrow 1.00 .40
232 Steve Brye 1.00 .40
233 Jim Barr 1.00 .40
234 John Milner 1.00 .40
235 Dave McNally 2.00 .80
236 Red Schoendienst MG 4.00 1.60
Barney Schultz CO
George Kissell CO
Johnny Lewis CO
Vern Benson CO
237 Ken Brett 1.00 .40
238 Fran Healy 1.00 .40
239 Bill Russell 2.00 .80
240 Joe Coleman 1.00 .40
241 Glenn Beckert 1.00 .40
242 Bill Gogolewski 1.00 .40
243 Bob Oliver 1.00 .40
244 Carl Morton 1.00 .40
245 Cleon Jones 1.00 .40
246 Athletics Team 3.00 1.20
247 Rick Miller 1.00 .40
248 Tom Hall 1.00 .40
249 George Mitterwald 1.00 .40
250 Willie McCovey 8.00 3.20
251 Graig Nettles 3.00 1.20
252 Dave Parker RC 15.00 6.00
253 John Boccabella 1.00 .40
254 Stan Bahnsen 1.00 .40
255 Larry Bowa 2.00 .80
256 Tom Griffin 1.00 .40
257 Buddy Bell 3.00 1.20
258 Jerry Morales 1.00 .40
259 Bob Reynolds 2.00 .80
260 Ted Simmons 4.00 1.60
261 Jerry Bell 1.00 .40
262 Ed Kirkpatrick 1.00 .40
263 Checklist 133-264 4.00 1.00
264 Joe Rudi 2.00 .80
265 Tug McGraw 4.00 1.60
266 Jim Northrup 2.00 .80
267 Andy Messersmith 2.00 .80
268 Tom Grieve 2.00 .80
269 Bob Johnson 1.00 .40
270 Ron Santo 4.00 1.60
271 Bill Hands 1.00 .40
272 Paul Casanova 1.00 .40
273 Checklist 265-396 4.00 1.00
274 Fred Beene 1.00 .40
275 Ron Hunt 1.00 .40
276 Bobby Winkles MG 2.00 .80
John Roseboro CO
Tom Morgan CO
Jimmie Reese CO
Salty Parker CO
277 Gary Nolan 2.00 .80
278 Cookie Rojas 2.00 .80
279 Jim Crawford 1.00 .40
280 Carl Yastrzemski 20.00 8.00
281 Giants Team 2.00 .80
282 Doyle Alexander 2.00 .80
283 Mike Schmidt 40.00 16.00
284 Dave Duncan 2.00 .80
285 Reggie Smith 2.00 .80
286 Tony Muser 1.00 .40
287 Clay Kirby 1.00 .40
288 Gorman Thomas 3.00 1.20
289 Rick Auerbach 1.00 .40
290 Vida Blue 2.00 .80
291 Don Hahn 1.00 .40
292 Chuck Seelbach 1.00 .40
293 Milt May 1.00 .40
294 Steve Foucault 1.00 .40
295 Rick Monday 2.00 .80
296 Ray Corbin 1.00 .40
297 Hal Breeden 1.00 .40
298 Roric Harrison 1.00 .40
299 Gene Michael 1.00 .40
300 Pete Rose 30.00 12.00
301 Bob Montgomery 1.00 .40
302 Rudy May 1.00 .40
303 George Hendrick 2.00 .80
304 Don Wilson 1.00 .40
305 Tito Fuentes 1.00 .40
306 Earl Weaver MG 4.00 1.60
Jim Frey CO
George Bamberger CO
Billy Hunter CO
George Staller CO
307 Luis Melendez 1.00 .40
308 Bruce Dal Canton 1.00 .40
309 Dave Roberts 1.00 .40
310 Terry Forster 2.00 .80
311 Jerry Grote 2.00 .80
312 Deron Johnson 1.00 .40
313 Barry Lersch 1.00 .40
314 Brewers Team 2.00 .80
315 Ron Cey 3.00 1.20
316 Jim Perry 2.00 .80
317 Richie Zisk 2.00 .80
318 Jim Merritt 1.00 .40
319 Randy Hundley 1.00 .40
320 Dusty Baker 3.00 1.20
321 Steve Braun 1.00 .40
322 Ernie McAnally 1.00 .40
323 Richie Scheinblum 1.00 .40
324 Steve Kline 1.00 .40
325 Tommy Harper 2.00 .80
326 Sparky Anderson MG 4.00 1.60
Larry Shepard CO
George Scherger CO
Alex Grammas CO
Ted Kluszewski CO
327 Tom Timmermann 1.00 .40
328 Skip Jutze 1.00 .40
329 Mark Belanger 2.00 .80
330 Juan Marichal 6.00 2.40
331 Carlton Fisk 8.00 3.20
Johnny Bench AS
332 Dick Allen 8.00 3.20
Hank Aaron AS
333 Rod Carew 4.00 1.60
Joe Morgan AS
334 Brooks Robinson 4.00 1.60
Ron Santo AS
335 Bert Campaneris 2.00 .80
Chris Speier AS
336 Bobby Murcer 4.00 1.60
Pete Rose AS
337 Amos Otis 2.00 .80
Cesar Cedeno AS
338 Reggie Jackson 8.00 3.20
Billy Williams AS
339 Jim Hunter 4.00 1.60
Rick Wise AS
340 Thurman Munson 12.00 4.80
341 Dan Driessen RC 2.00 .80
342 Jim Lonborg 2.00 .80
343 Royals Team 2.00 .80
344 Mike Caldwell 1.00 .40
345 Bill North 1.00 .40
346 Ron Reed 1.00 .40
347 Sandy Alomar 2.00 .80
348 Pete Richert 1.00 .40
349 John Vukovich 1.00 .40
350 Bob Gibson 10.00 4.00
351 Dwight Evans 4.00 1.60
352 Bill Stoneman 1.00 .40
353 Rich Coggins 1.00 .40
354 Whitey Lockman MG 2.00 .80
J.C. Martin CO
Hank Aguirre CO
Al Spangler CO
Jim Marshall CO
355 Dave Nelson 1.00 .40
356 Jerry Koosman 2.00 .80
357 Buddy Bradford 1.00 .40
358 Dal Maxvill 1.00 .40
359 Brent Strom 1.00 .40
360 Greg Luzinski 3.00 1.20
361 Don Carrithers 1.00 .40
362 Hal King 1.00 .40
363 Yankees Team 3.00 1.20
364 Cito Gaston 2.00 .80
365 Steve Busby 2.00 .80
366 Larry Hisle 2.00 .80
367 Norm Cash 3.00 1.20
368 Manny Mota 2.00 .80
369 Paul Lindblad 2.00 .80
370 Bob Watson 2.00 .80
371 Jim Slaton 1.00 .40
372 Ken Reitz 1.00 .40
373 John Curtis 1.00 .40
374 Marty Perez 1.00 .40
375 Earl Williams 1.00 .40
376 Jorge Orta 1.00 .40
377 Ron Woods 1.00 .40
378 Burt Hooton 2.00 .80
379 Billy Martin MG 3.00 1.20
Frank Lucchesi CO
Art Fowler CO
Charlie Silvera CO
Jackie Moore CO
380 Bud Harrelson 2.00 .80
381 Charlie Sands 1.00 .40
382 Bob Moose 1.00 .40
383 Phillies Team 2.00 .80
384 Chris Chambliss 2.00 .80
385 Don Gullett 2.00 .80
386 Gary Matthews 3.00 1.20
387 Rich Morales 1.00 .40
388 Phil Roof 1.00 .40
389 Gates Brown 1.00 .40
390 Lou Piniella 3.00 1.20
391 Billy Champion 1.00 .40
392 Dick Green 1.00 .40
393 Orlando Pena 1.00 .40
394 Ken Henderson 1.00 .40
395 Doug Rader 1.00 .40
396 Tommy Davis 2.00 .80
397 George Stone 1.00 .40
398 Duke Sims 1.00 .40
399 Mike Paul 1.00 .40
400 Harmon Killebrew 10.00 4.00
401 Elliott Maddox 1.00 .40
402 Jim Rooker 1.00 .40
403 Darrell Johnson MG 2.00 .80
Eddie Popowski CO
Lee Stange CO
Don Zimmer CO
Don Bryant CO
404 Jim Howarth 1.00 .40
405 Ellie Rodriguez 1.00 .40
406 Steve Arlin 1.00 .40
407 Jim Wohlford 1.00 .40
408 Charlie Hough 2.00 .80
409 Ike Brown 1.00 .40
410 Pedro Borbon 1.00 .40
411 Frank Baker 1.00 .40
412 Chuck Taylor 1.00 .40
413 Don Money 2.00 .80
414 Checklist 397-528 4.00 1.00
415 Gary Gentry 1.00 .40
416 White Sox Team 2.00 .80
417 Rich Folkers 1.00 .40
418 Walt Williams 1.00 .40
419 Wayne Twitchell 1.00 .40
420 Ray Fosse 1.00 .40
421 Dan Fife 1.00 .40
422 Gonzalo Marquez 1.00 .40
423 Fred Stanley 1.00 .40
424 Jim Beauchamp 1.00 .40
425 Pete Broberg 1.00 .40
426 Rennie Stennett 1.00 .40
427 Bobby Bolin 1.00 .40
428 Gary Sutherland 1.00 .40
429 Dick Lange 1.00 .40
430 Matty Alou 2.00 .80
431 Gene Garber RC 2.00 .80
432 Chris Arnold 1.00 .40
433 Lerrin LaGrow 1.00 .40
434 Ken McMullen 1.00 .40
435 Dave Concepcion 3.00 1.20
436 Don Hood 1.00 .40
437 Jim Lyttle 1.00 .40
438 Ed Herrmann 1.00 .40
439 Norm Miller 1.00 .40
440 Jim Kaat 4.00 1.60
441 Tom Ragland 1.00 .40
442 Alan Foster 1.00 .40
443 Tom Hutton 1.00 .40
444 Vic Davalillo 1.00 .40
445 George Medich 1.00 .40
446 Len Randle 1.00 .40
447 Frank Quilici MG 2.00 .80
Ralph Rowe CO
Bob Rodgers CO
Vern Morgan CO
448 Ron Hodges 1.00 .40
449 Tom McCraw 1.00 .40
450 Rich Hebner 2.00 .80
451 Tommy John 4.00 1.60
452 Gene Hiser 1.00 .40
453 Balor Moore 1.00 .40
454 Kurt Bevacqua 1.00 .40
455 Tom Bradley 1.00 .40
456 Dave Winfield RC 80.00 32.00
457 Chuck Goggin 1.00 .40
458 Jim Ray 1.00 .40
459 Reds Team 3.00 1.20
460 Boog Powell 3.00 1.20
461 John Odom 1.00 .40
462 Luis Alvarado 1.00 .40
463 Pat Dobson 1.00 .40
464 Jose Cruz 3.00 1.20
465 Dick Bosman 1.00 .40
466 Dick Billings 1.00 .40
467 Winston Llenas 1.00 .40
468 Pepe Frias 1.00 .40
469 Joe Decker 1.00 .40
470 Reggie Jackson ALCS 8.00 3.20
471 Jon Matlack NLCS 2.00 .80
472 Darold Knowles WS 2.00 .80
473 Willie Mays WS 12.00 4.80
474 Bert Campaneris WS 2.00 .80
475 Rusty Staub WS 2.00 .80
476 Cleon Jones WS 2.00 .80
477 Reggie Jackson WS 8.00 3.20
478 Bert Campaneris WS 2.00 .80
479 WS Summary 2.00 .80
A's Celebrate; Win
2nd cons. Championship
480 Willie Crawford 1.00 .40
481 Jerry Terrell 1.00 .40
482 Bob Didier 1.00 .40
483 Braves Team 2.00 .80
484 Carmen Fanzone 1.00 .40
485 Felipe Alou 3.00 1.20
486 Steve Stone 2.00 .80
487 Ted Martinez 1.00 .40
488 Andy Etchebarren 1.00 .40
489 Danny Murtaugh MG 2.00 .80
Don Osborn CO
Don Leppert CO
Bill Mazeroski CO
Bob Skinner CO
490 Vada Pinson 3.00 1.20
491 Roger Nelson 1.00 .40
492 Mike Rogodzinski 1.00 .40
493 Joe Hoerner 1.00 .40
494 Ed Goodson 1.00 .40
495 Dick McAuliffe 2.00 .80
496 Tom Murphy 1.00 .40
497 Bobby Mitchell 1.00 .40
498 Pat Corrales 1.00 .40
499 Rusty Torres 1.00 .40
500 Lee May 2.00 .80
501 Eddie Leon 1.00 .40
502 Dave LaRoche 1.00 .40
503 Eric Soderholm 1.00 .40
504 Joe Niekro 2.00 .80
505 Bill Buckner 2.00 .80
506 Ed Farmer 1.00 .40
507 Larry Stahl 1.00 .40
508 Expos Team 3.00 1.20
509 Jesse Jefferson 1.00 .40
510 Wayne Garrett 1.00 .40
511 Toby Harrah 2.00 .80
512 Joe Lahoud 1.00 .40
513 Jim Campanis 1.00 .40
514 Paul Schaal 1.00 .40
515 Willie Montanez 1.00 .40
516 Horacio Pina 1.00 .40
517 Mike Hegan 1.00 .40
518 Derrel Thomas 1.00 .40
519 Bill Sharp 1.00 .40
520 Tim McCarver 3.00 1.20
521 Ken Aspromonte MG 2.00 .80
Clay Bryant CO
Tony Pacheco CO
522 J.R. Richard 3.00 1.20
523 Cecil Cooper 3.00 1.20
524 Bill Plummer 1.00 .40
525 Clyde Wright 1.00 .40
526 Frank Tepedino 2.00 .80
527 Bobby Darwin 1.00 .40
528 Bill Bonham 1.00 .40
529 Horace Clarke 2.00 .80
530 Mickey Stanley 2.00 .80
531 Gene Mauch MG 3.00 1.20
Dave Bristol CO
Cal McLish CO
Larry Doby CO
Jerry Zimmerman CO
532 Skip Lockwood 1.00 .40
533 Mike Phillips 1.00 .40
534 Eddie Watt 1.00 .40
535 Bob Tolan 1.00 .40
536 Duffy Dyer 1.00 .40
537 Steve Mingori 1.00 .40
538 Cesar Tovar 1.00 .40
539 Lloyd Allen 1.00 .40
540 Bob Robertson 1.00 .40
541 Indians Team 2.00 .80
542 Goose Gossage 3.00 1.20
543 Danny Cater 1.00 .40
544 Ron Schueler 1.00 .40
545 Billy Conigliaro 2.00 .80
546 Mike Corkins 1.00 .40
547 Glenn Borgmann 1.00 .40
548 Sonny Siebert 1.00 .40
549 Mike Jorgensen 1.00 .40
550 Sam McDowell 2.00 .80
551 Von Joshua 1.00 .40
552 Denny Doyle 1.00 .40
553 Jim Willoughby 1.00 .40
554 Tim Johnson 1.00 .40
555 Woody Fryman 1.00 .40
556 Dave Campbell 2.00 .80
557 Jim McGlothlin 1.00 .40
558 Bill Fahey 1.00 .40
559 Darrell Chaney 1.00 .40
560 Mike Cuellar 2.00 .80
561 Ed Kranepool 2.00 .80
562 Jack Aker 1.00 .40
563 Hal McRae 2.00 .80
564 Mike Ryan 1.00 .40
565 Milt Wilcox 1.00 .40
566 Jackie Hernandez 1.00 .40
567 Red Sox Team 2.00 .80
568 Mike Torrez 2.00 .80
569 Rick Dempsey 2.00 .80
570 Ralph Garr 2.00 .80
571 Rich Hand 1.00 .40
572 Enzo Hernandez 1.00 .40
573 Mike Adams 1.00 .40
574 Bill Parsons 1.00 .40
575 Steve Garvey 4.00 1.60
576 Scipio Spinks 1.00 .40
577 Mike Sadek 1.00 .40
578 Ralph Houk MG 2.00 .80
579 Cecil Upshaw 1.00 .40
580 Jim Spencer 1.00 .40
581 Fred Norman 1.00 .40
582 Bucky Dent RC 4.00 1.60
583 Marty Pattin 1.00 .40
584 Ken Rudolph 1.00 .40
585 Merv Rettenmund 1.00 .40
586 Jack Brohamer 1.00 .40
587 Larry Christenson 1.00 .40
588 Hal Lanier 1.00 .40
589 Boots Day 2.00 .80
590 Rogelio Moret 2.00 .80
591 Sonny Jackson 1.00 .40
592 Ed Bane 1.00 .40
593 Steve Yeager 2.00 .80
594 Leroy Stanton 2.00 .80
595 Steve Blass 2.00 .80
596 Wayne Garland 1.00 .40
Fred Holdsworth
Mark Littell
Dick Pole
597 Dave Chalk 2.00 .80
John Gamble
Pete MacKanin
Manny Trillo
598 Dave Augustine 15.00 6.00
Ken Griffey RC
Steve Ontiveros
Jim Tyrone
599 Ron Diorio 3.00 1.20
Dave Freisleben
Frank Riccelli
Greg Shanahan
600 Ron Cash 8.00 3.20
Jim Cox
Bill Madlock RC
Reggie Sanders
601 Ed Armbrister 4.00 1.60
Rich Bladt
Brian Downing RC
Bake McBride RC
602 Glenn Abbott 2.00 .80
Rick Henninger
Craig Swan RC
Dan Vossler
603 Barry Foote 2.00 .80
Tom Lundstedt
Charlie Moore
Sergio Robles
604 Terry Hughes 8.00 3.20
John Knox
Andy Thornton RC
Frank White RC
605 Vic Albury 4.00 1.60
Ken Frailing
Kevin Kobel
Frank Tanana RC
606 Jim Fuller 2.00 .80
Wilbur Howard
Tommy Smith
Otto Velez
607 Leo Foster 2.00 .80
Tom Heintzelman
Dave Rosello
Frank Taveras
608 Bob Apodaca UER 3.00 1.20
Dick Baney
John D'Acquisto
Mike Wallace
Apodaca is spellled Apodaco
609 Rico Petrocelli 2.00 .80
610 Dave Kingman 4.00 1.60
611 Rich Stelmaszek 1.00 .40
612 Luke Walker 1.00 .40
613 Dan Monzon 1.00 .40
614 Adrian Devine 1.00 .40
615 John Jeter 1.00 .40
616 Larry Gura 1.00 .40
617 Ted Ford 1.00 .40
618 Jim Mason 1.00 .40
619 Mike Anderson 1.00 .40
620 Al Downing 1.00 .40
621 Bernie Carbo 1.00 .40
622 Phil Gagliano 1.00 .40
623 Celerino Sanchez 1.00 .40
624 Bob Miller 1.00 .40
625 Ollie Brown 1.00 .40
626 Pirates Team 2.00 .80
627 Carl Taylor 1.00 .40
628 Ivan Murrell 1.00 .40

629 Rusty Staub 3.00 1.20
630 Tommy Agee 2.00 .80
631 Steve Barber 1.00 .40
632 George Culver 1.00 .40
633 Dave Hamilton 1.00 .40
634 Eddie Mathews MG 4.00 1.60
Herm Starrette CO
Connie Ryan CO
Jim Busby CO
Ken Silvestri CO
635 John Edwards 1.00 .40
636 Dave Goltz 1.00 .40
637 Checklist 529-660 4.00 1.60
638 Ken Sanders 1.00 .40
639 Joe Lovitto 1.00 .40
640 Milt Pappas 2.00 .80
641 Chuck Brinkman 1.00 .40
642 Terry Harmon 1.00 .40
643 Dodgers Team 2.00 .80
644 Wayne Granger 1.00 .40
645 Ken Boswell 1.00 .40
646 George Foster 3.00 1.20
647 Juan Beniquez 1.00 .40
648 Terry Crowley 1.00 .40
649 Fernando Gonzalez 1.00 .40
650 Mike Epstein 1.00 .40
651 Leron Lee 1.00 .40
652 Gail Hopkins 1.00 .40
653 Bob Stinson 2.00 .80
654 Jesus Alou 2.00 .80
655 Mike Tyson 1.00 .40
656 Adrian Garrett 1.00 .40
657 Jim Shellenback 1.00 .40
658 Lee Lacy 1.00 .40
659 Joe Lis 1.00 .40
660 Larry Dierker 3.00 1.20

1974 O-Pee-Chee Team Checklists

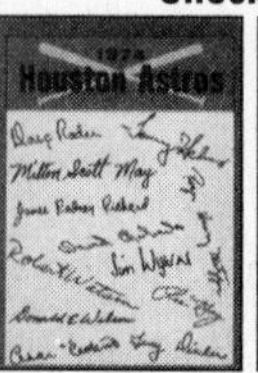

The cards in this 24-card set measure 2 1/2" by 3 1/2". The fronts have red borders and feature the year and team name in a green panel decorated by a crossed bats design, below which is a white area containing facsimile autographs of various players. On a light yellow background, the backs list team members alphabetically, along with their card number, uniform number and position. The words "Team Checklist" appear in French and English. The cards are unnumbered and checklisted below in alphabetical order.

	NM	Ex
COMPLETE SET (24)	50.00	20.00
COMMON TEAM (1-24)	2.50	1.00

1975 O-Pee-Chee

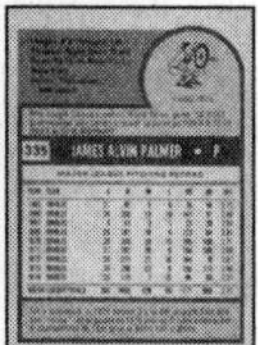

The cards in this 660-card set measure 2 1/2" by 3 1/2". The 1975 O-Pee-Chee cards are very similar to the 1975 Topps cards, yet rather different from previous years' issues. The most prominent change for the fronts is the use of a two-color fram colors surrounding the picture area rather than a single, subdued color. The fronts feature color player photos with rounded corners. The player's name and position, the team name and a facsimile autograph round out the front. The backs are printed in red and green on a yellow-vanilla card stock and carry player biography and statistics in French and English. Cards 189-212 depict the MVPs of both leagues from 1951 through 1974. The first six cards (1-6) feature players breaking records or achieving milestones during the previous season. Cards 306-313 picture league leaders in various statistical categories. Cards 459-466 depict the results of post-season action. Team cards feature a checklist back for players on that team. Remember, the prices below apply only to O-Pee-Chee cards -- they are NOT prices for Topps cards as the Topps cards are generally much more available. The cards were issued in eight card packs. Notable Rookie Cards include George Brett, Fred Lynn, Keith Hernandez, Jim Rice and Robin Yount.

	NM	Ex
COMPLETE SET (660)	1000.00	400.00

1 Hank Aaron HL ! 40.00 16.00
2 Lou Brock HL 4.00 1.60
3 Bob Gibson HL 4.00 1.60
4 Al Kaline HL 8.00 3.20
5 Nolan Ryan HL 30.00 12.00
6 Mike Marshall HL 1.50 .60
7 Steve Busby 12.00 4.80
Dick Bosman
Nolan Ryan HL
8 Rogelio Moret .75 .30
9 Frank Tepedino 1.50 .60
10 Willie Davis 1.50 .60
11 Bill Melton .75 .30
12 David Clyde .75 .30
13 Gene Locklear 1.50 .60
14 Milt Wilcox .75 .30
15 Jose Cardenal 1.50 .60
16 Frank Tanana 2.50 1.00
17 Dave Concepcion 2.50 1.00
18 Ralph Houk MG CL 2.50 1.00
19 Jerry Koosman 1.50 .60
20 Thurman Munson 10.00 4.00
21 Rollie Fingers 5.00 2.00
22 Dave Cash .75 .30
23 Bill Russell 1.50 .60
24 Al Fitzmorris .75 .30
25 Lee May 1.50 .60
26 Dave McNally 1.50 .60
27 Ken Reitz .75 .30
28 Tom Murphy .75 .30
29 Dave Parker 4.00 1.60
30 Bert Blyleven 2.50 1.00
31 Dave Rader .75 .30
32 Reggie Cleveland 1.50 .60
33 Dusty Baker 2.50 1.00
34 Steve Renko .75 .30
35 Ron Santo 1.50 .60
36 Joe Lovitto .75 .30
37 Dave Freisleben .75 .30
38 Buddy Bell 2.50 1.00
39 Andre Thornton 1.50 .60
40 Bill Singer .75 .30
41 Cesar Geronimo 1.50 .60
42 Joe Coleman .75 .30
43 Cleon Jones 1.50 .60
44 Pat Dobson .75 .30
45 Joe Rudi 1.50 .60
46 Danny Ozark MG CL 2.50 1.00
47 Tommy John 2.50 1.00
48 Freddie Patek 1.50 .60
49 Larry Dierker 1.50 .60
50 Brooks Robinson 10.00 4.00
51 Bob Forsch 1.50 .60
52 Darrell Porter 1.50 .60
53 Dave Giusti .75 .30
54 Eric Soderholm .75 .30
55 Bobby Bonds 4.00 1.60
56 Rick Wise 1.50 .60
57 Dave Johnson 1.50 .60
58 Chuck Taylor .75 .30
59 Ken Henderson .75 .30
60 Fergie Jenkins 5.00 2.00
61 Dave Winfield 25.00 10.00
62 Fritz Peterson .75 .30
63 Steve Swisher .75 .30
64 Dave Chalk .75 .30
65 Don Gullett 1.50 .60
66 Willie Horton 1.50 .60
67 Tug McGraw 2.50 1.00
68 Ron Blomberg .75 .30
69 John Odom .75 .30
70 Mike Schmidt 30.00 12.00
71 Charlie Hough 1.50 .60
72 Jack McKeon MG CL 2.50 1.00
73 J.R. Richard 1.50 .60
74 Mark Belanger 1.50 .60
75 Ted Simmons 2.50 1.00
76 Ed Sprague .75 .30
77 Richie Zisk 1.50 .60
78 Ray Corbin .75 .30
79 Gary Matthews 1.50 .60
80 Carlton Fisk 10.00 4.00
81 Ron Reed .75 .30
82 Pat Kelly .75 .30
83 Jim Merritt .75 .30
84 Enzo Hernandez .75 .30
85 Bill Bonham .75 .30
86 Joe Lis .75 .30
87 George Foster 2.50 1.00
88 Tom Egan .75 .30
89 Jim Ray .75 .30
90 Rusty Staub 2.50 1.00
91 Dick Green .75 .30
92 Cecil Upshaw .75 .30
93 Dave Lopes 2.50 1.00
94 Jim Lonborg 1.50 .60
95 John Mayberry 1.50 .60
96 Mike Cosgrove .75 .30
97 Earl Williams .75 .30
98 Rich Folkers .75 .30
99 Mike Hegan .75 .30
100 Willie Stargell 6.00 2.40
101 Gene Mauch MG CL 2.50 1.00
102 Joe Decker .75 .30
103 Rick Miller .75 .30
104 Bill Madlock 2.50 1.00
105 Buzz Capra .75 .30
106 Mike Hargrove RC 4.00 1.60
107 Jim Barr .75 .30
108 Tom Hall .75 .30
109 George Hendrick 1.50 .60
110 Wilbur Wood .75 .30
111 Wayne Garrett .75 .30
112 Larry Hardy .75 .30
113 Elliott Maddox .75 .30
114 Dick Lange .75 .30
115 Joe Ferguson .75 .30
116 Lerrin LaGrow .75 .30
117 Earl Weaver MG CL 4.00 1.60
118 Mike Anderson .75 .30
119 Tommy Helms .75 .30
120 Steve Busby 1.50 .60
(photo actually
Fran Healy)
121 Bill North .75 .30
122 Al Hrabosky 1.50 .60
123 Johnny Briggs .75 .30
124 Jerry Reuss 1.50 .60
125 Ken Singleton 1.50 .60
126 Checklist 1-132 4.00 1.60
127 Glenn Borgmann .75 .30
128 Bill Lee 1.50 .60
129 Rick Monday 1.50 .60
130 Phil Niekro 4.00 1.60
131 Toby Harrah 1.50 .60
132 Randy Moffitt .75 .30
133 Dan Driessen 1.50 .60
134 Ron Hodges .75 .30
135 Charlie Spikes .75 .30
136 Jim Mason .75 .30
137 Terry Forster 1.50 .60
138 Del Unser .75 .30
139 Horacio Pina .75 .30
140 Steve Garvey 4.00 1.60
141 Mickey Stanley 1.50 .60
142 Bob Reynolds .75 .30
143 Cliff Johnson RC 1.50 .60
144 Jim Wohlford .75 .30
145 Ken Holtzman 1.50 .60
146 John McNamara MG CL 2.50 1.00
147 Pedro Garcia .75 .30
148 Jim Rooker .75 .30
149 Tim Foli .75 .30
150 Bob Gibson 8.00 3.20
151 Steve Brye .75 .30
152 Mario Guerrero .75 .30
153 Rick Reuschel 1.50 .60
154 Mike Lum .75 .30
155 Jim Bibby .75 .30
156 Dave Kingman 2.50 1.00
157 Pedro Borbon 1.50 .60
158 Jerry Grote .75 .30
159 Steve Arlin .75 .30
160 Graig Nettles 2.50 1.00
161 Stan Bahnsen .75 .30
162 Willie Montanez .75 .30
163 Jim Brewer .75 .30
164 Mickey Rivers 1.50 .60
165 Doug Rader 1.50 .60
166 Woodie Fryman .75 .30
167 Rich Coggins .75 .30
168 Bill Greif .75 .30
169 Cookie Rojas .75 .30
170 Bert Campaneris 1.50 .60
171 Ed Kirkpatrick .75 .30
172 Darrell Johnson MG CL 4.00 1.60
173 Steve Rogers 1.50 .60
174 Bake McBride 1.50 .60
175 Don Money 1.50 .60
176 Burt Hooton 1.50 .60
177 Vic Correll .75 .30
178 Cesar Tovar .75 .30
179 Tom Bradley .75 .30
180 Joe Morgan 8.00 3.20
181 Fred Beene .75 .30
182 Don Hahn .75 .30
183 Mel Stottlemyre 1.50 .60
184 Jorge Orta .75 .30
185 Steve Carlton 10.00 4.00
186 Willie Crawford .75 .30
187 Denny Doyle .75 .30
188 Tom Griffin .75 .30
189 Larry (Yogi) Berra 6.00 2.40
Roy Campanella MVP
Campanella card never issued
190 Bobby Shantz 2.50 1.00
Hank Sauer MVP
191 Al Rosen 2.50 1.00
Roy Campanella MVP
192 Yogi Berra 6.00 2.40
Willie Mays MVP
193 Yogi Berra 4.00 1.60
Roy Campanella MVP
(Campanella card never issued
194 Mickey Mantle 15.00 6.00
Don Newcombe MVP
195 Mickey Mantle 20.00 8.00
Hank Aaron MVP
196 Jackie Jensen 2.50 1.00
Ernie Banks MVP
197 Nellie Fox 4.00 1.60
Ernie Banks MVP
198 Roger Maris 2.50 1.00
Dick Groat MVP
199 Roger Maris 4.00 1.60
Frank Robinson MVP
200 Mickey Mantle 15.00 6.00
Maury Wills MVP
Wills card never issued
201 Elston Howard 2.50 1.00
Sandy Koufax MVP
202 Brooks Robinson 2.50 1.00
Ken Boyer MVP
203 Zoilo Versalles 2.50 1.00
Willie Mays MVP
204 Frank Robinson 8.00 3.20
Bob Clemente MVP
205 Carl Yastrzemski 2.50 1.00
Orlando Cepeda MVP
206 Denny McLain 2.50 1.00
Bob Gibson MVP
207 Harmon Killebrew 2.50 1.00
Willie McCovey MVP
208 Boog Powell 2.50 1.00
Johnny Bench MVP
209 Vida Blue 2.50 1.00
Joe Torre MVP
210 Rich Allen 2.50 1.00
Johnny Bench MVP
211 Reggie Jackson 8.00 3.20
Pete Rose MVP
212 Jeff Burroughs 2.50 1.00
Steve Garvey MVP
213 Oscar Gamble 1.50 .60
214 Harry Parker .75 .30
215 Bobby Valentine 1.50 .60
216 Wes Westrum MG CL 2.50 1.00
217 Lou Piniella 2.50 1.00
218 Jerry Johnson .75 .30
219 Ed Herrmann .75 .30
220 Don Sutton 4.00 1.60
221 Aurelio Rodriguez .75 .30
222 Dan Spillner .75 .30
223 Robin Yount RC 80.00 32.00
224 Ramon Hernandez .75 .30
225 Bob Grich 1.50 .60
226 Bill Campbell .75 .30
227 Bob Watson 1.50 .60
228 George Brett RC 125.00 50.00
229 Barry Foote 1.50 .60
230 Jim Hunter 4.00 1.60
231 Mike Tyson .75 .30
232 Diego Segui .75 .30
233 Billy Grabarkewitz .75 .30
234 Tom Grieve 1.50 .60
235 Jack Billingham 1.50 .60
236 Dick Williams MG CL 2.50 1.00
237 Carl Morton .75 .30
238 Dave Duncan 1.50 .60
239 George Stone .75 .30
240 Garry Maddox 1.50 .60
241 Dick Tidrow .75 .30
242 Jay Johnstone 1.50 .60
243 Jim Kaat 2.50 1.00
244 Bill Buckner 1.50 .60
245 Mickey Lolich 2.50 1.00
246 Red Schoendienst MG CL 2.50 1.00
247 Enos Cabell .75 .30
248 Randy Jones 2.50 1.00
249 Danny Thompson .75 .30
250 Ken Brett .75 .30
251 Fran Healy .75 .30
252 Fred Scherman .75 .30
253 Jesus Alou .75 .30
254 Mike Torrez 1.50 .60
255 Dwight Evans 2.50 1.00
256 Billy Champion .75 .30
257 Checklist 133-264 4.00 1.00
258 Dave LaRoche .75 .30
259 Len Randle .75 .30
260 Johnny Bench 20.00 8.00
261 Andy Hassler .75 .30
262 Rowland Office .75 .30
263 Jim Perry 1.50 .60
264 John Milner .75 .30
265 Ron Bryant .75 .30
266 Sandy Alomar 1.50 .60
267 Dick Ruthven .75 .30
268 Hal McRae 1.50 .60
269 Doug Rau .75 .30
270 Ron Fairly 1.50 .60
271 Jerry Moses .75 .30
272 Lynn McGlothen .75 .30
273 Steve Braun .75 .30
274 Vicente Romo .75 .30
275 Paul Blair 1.50 .60
276 Chuck Tanner MG CL 2.50 1.00
277 Frank Taveras .75 .30
278 Paul Lindblad .75 .30
279 Milt May .75 .30
280 Carl Yastrzemski 15.00 6.00
281 Jim Slaton .75 .30
282 Jerry Morales .75 .30
283 Steve Foucault .75 .30
284 Ken Griffey Sr. 4.00 1.60
285 Ellie Rodriguez .75 .30
286 Mike Jorgensen .75 .30
287 Roric Harrison .75 .30
288 Bruce Ellingsen .75 .30
289 Ken Rudolph .75 .30
290 Jon Matlack .75 .30
291 Bill Sudakis .75 .30
292 Ron Schueler .75 .30
293 Dick Sharon .75 .30
294 Geoff Zahn .75 .30
295 Vada Pinson 2.50 1.00
296 Alan Foster .75 .30
297 Craig Kusick .75 .30
298 Johnny Grubb .75 .30
299 Bucky Dent 2.50 1.00
300 Reggie Jackson 20.00 8.00
301 Dave Roberts .75 .30
302 Rick Burleson 1.50 .60
303 Grant Jackson .75 .30
304 Danny Murtaugh MG CL 2.50 1.00
305 Jim Colborn .75 .30
306 Rod Carew 2.50 1.00
Ralph Garr LL
307 Dick Allen 4.00 1.60
Mike Schmidt LL
308 Jeff Burroughs 2.50 1.00
Johnny Bench LL
309 Bill North 2.50 1.00
Lou Brock LL
310 Jim Hunter 2.50 1.00
Fergie Jenkins
Andy Messersmith
Phil Niekro LL
311 Jim Hunter 2.50 1.00
Buzz Capra LL
312 Nolan Ryan 20.00 8.00
Steve Carlton LL
313 Terry Forster 1.50 .60
Mike Marshall LL
314 Buck Martinez .75 .30
315 Don Kessinger 1.50 .60
316 Jackie Brown .75 .30
317 Joe Lahoud .75 .30
318 Ernie McAnally .75 .30
319 Johnny Oates .75 .30
320 Pete Rose 40.00 16.00
321 Rudy May .75 .30
322 Ed Goodson .75 .30
323 Fred Holdsworth .75 .30
324 Ed Kranepool 1.50 .60
325 Tony Oliva 2.50 1.00
326 Wayne Twitchell .75 .30
327 Jerry Hairston .75 .30
328 Sonny Siebert .75 .30
329 Ted Kubiak .75 .30
330 Mike Marshall 1.50 .60
331 Frank Robinson MG CL 2.50 1.00
332 Fred Kendall .75 .30
333 Dick Drago .75 .30
334 Greg Gross .75 .30
335 Jim Palmer 8.00 3.20
336 Rennie Stennett .75 .30
337 Kevin Kobel .75 .30
338 Rick Stelmaszek .75 .30
339 Jim Fregosi 1.50 .60
340 Paul Splittorff .75 .30
341 Hal Breeden .75 .30
342 Leroy Stanton .75 .30
343 Danny Frisella .75 .30
344 Ben Oglivie 1.50 .60
345 Clay Carroll 1.50 .60
346 Bobby Darwin .75 .30
347 Mike Caldwell .75 .30
348 Tony Muser .75 .30
349 Ray Sadecki .75 .30
350 Bobby Murcer 1.50 .60
351 Bob Boone 2.50 1.00
352 Darold Knowles .75 .30
353 Luis Melendez .75 .30
354 Dick Bosman .75 .30
355 Chris Cannizzaro .75 .30
356 Rico Petrocelli 1.50 .60
357 Ken Forsch .75 .30
358 Al Bumbry 1.50 .60
359 Paul Popovich .75 .30
360 George Scott 1.50 .60
361 Walter Alston MG CL 2.50 1.00
362 Steve Hargan .75 .30
363 Carmen Fanzone .75 .30
364 Doug Bird .75 .30
365 Bob Bailey .75 .30
366 Ken Sanders .75 .30
367 Craig Robinson .75 .30
368 Vic Albury .75 .30
369 Merv Rettenmund .75 .30
370 Tom Seaver 15.00 6.00
371 Gates Brown .75 .30
372 John D'Acquisto .75 .30
373 Bill Sharp .75 .30
374 Eddie Watt .75 .30
375 Roy White 1.50 .60
376 Steve Yeager 1.50 .60
377 Tom Hilgendorf .75 .30
378 Derrel Thomas .75 .30
379 Bernie Carbo .75 .30
380 Sal Bando 1.50 .60
381 John Curtis .75 .30
382 Don Baylor 2.50 1.00
383 Jim York .75 .30
384 Brewers Team CL 2.50 1.00
Del Crandall MG
385 Dock Ellis .75 .30
386 Checklist 265-396 4.00 1.60
387 Jim Spencer .75 .30
388 Steve Stone 1.50 .60
389 Tony Solaita .75 .30
390 Ron Cey 2.50 1.00
391 Don DeMola .75 .30
392 Bruce Bochte RC 1.50 .60
393 Gary Gentry .75 .30
394 Larvell Blanks .75 .30
395 Bud Harrelson 1.50 .60
396 Fred Norman 1.50 .60
397 Bill Freehan 1.50 .60
398 Elias Sosa .75 .30
399 Terry Harmon .75 .30
400 Dick Allen 2.50 1.00
401 Mike Wallace .75 .30
402 Bob Tolan .75 .30
403 Tom Buskey .75 .30
404 Ted Sizemore .75 .30
405 John Montague .75 .30
406 Bob Gallagher .75 .30
407 Herb Washington RC 2.50 1.00
408 Clyde Wright .75 .30
409 Bob Robertson .75 .30
410 Mike Cueller 1.50 .60
sic, Cuellar
411 George Mitterwald .75 .30
412 Bill Hands .75 .30
413 Marty Pattin .75 .30
414 Manny Mota 1.50 .60
415 John Hiller 1.50 .60
416 Larry Lintz .75 .30
417 Skip Lockwood .75 .30
418 Leo Foster .75 .30
419 Dave Goltz .75 .30
420 Larry Bowa 2.50 1.00
421 Yogi Berra MG CL 4.00 1.60
422 Brian Downing 1.50 .60
423 Clay Kirby .75 .30
424 John Lowenstein .75 .30
425 Tito Fuentes .75 .30
426 George Medich .75 .30
427 Clarence Gaston 1.50 .60
428 Dave Hamilton .75 .30
429 Jim Dwyer .75 .30
430 Luis Tiant 2.50 1.00
431 Rod Gilbreath .75 .30
432 Ken Berry .75 .30
433 Larry Demery .75 .30
434 Bob Locker .75 .30
435 Dave Nelson .75 .30
436 Ken Frailing .75 .30
437 Al Cowens 1.50 .60
438 Don Carrithers .75 .30
439 Ed Brinkman .75 .30
440 Andy Messersmith 1.50 .60
441 Bobby Heise .75 .30
442 Maximino Leon .75 .30
443 Frank Quilici MG CL 2.50 1.00
444 Gene Garber 1.50 .60
445 Felix Millan .75 .30
446 Bart Johnson .75 .30
447 Terry Crowley .75 .30
448 Frank Duffy .75 .30
449 Charlie Williams .75 .30
450 Willie McCovey 8.00 3.20
451 Rick Dempsey 1.50 .60
452 Angel Mangual .75 .30
453 Claude Osteen 1.50 .60
454 Doug Griffin .75 .30
455 Don Wilson .75 .30
456 Bob Coluccio .75 .30
457 Mario Mendoza .75 .30
458 Ross Grimsley .75 .30
459 1974 AL Champs 1.50 .60
A's over Orioles
(Second base action pictured)
460 Frank Taveras NCLS 2.50 1.00
Steve Garvey
461 Reggie Jackson WS 6.00 2.40
462 World Series Game 2 1.50 .60
(Dodger dugout)
463 Rollie Fingers WS 2.50 1.00
464 World Series Game 4 1.50 .60
(A's batter)
465 Joe Rudi WS 1.50 .60
466 WS Summary: 2.50 1.00
A's do it again
Win 3rd straight
(A's group)
467 Ed Halicki .75 .30
468 Bobby Mitchell .75 .30
469 Tom Dettore .75 .30
470 Jeff Burroughs 1.50 .60
471 Bob Stinson .75 .30
472 Bruce Dal Canton .75 .30
473 Ken McMullen .75 .30
474 Luke Walker .75 .30
475 Darrell Evans 1.50 .60
476 Ed Figueroa .75 .30
477 Tom Hutton .75 .30
478 Tom Burgmeier .75 .30
479 Ken Boswell .75 .30
480 Carlos May .75 .30
481 Will McEnaney 1.50 .60
482 Tom McCraw .75 .30
483 Steve Ontiveros .75 .30
484 Glenn Beckert 1.50 .60
485 Sparky Lyle 1.50 .60
486 Ray Fosse .75 .30
487 Preston Gomez MG CL 2.50 1.00
488 Bill Travers .75 .30
489 Cecil Cooper 2.50 1.00
490 Reggie Smith 1.50 .60
491 Doyle Alexander 1.50 .60

492 Rich Hebner 1.50 .60
493 Don Stanhouse .75 .30
494 Pete LaCock .75 .30
495 Nelson Briles 1.50 .60
496 Pepe Frias .75 .30
497 Jim Nettles .75 .30
498 Al Downing .75 .30
499 Marty Perez .75 .30
500 Nolan Ryan 80.00 32.00
501 Bill Robinson 1.50 .60
502 Pat Bourque .75 .30
503 Fred Stanley .75 .30
504 Buddy Bradford .75 .30
505 Chris Speier .75 .30
506 Leron Lee .75 .30
507 Tom Carroll .75 .30
508 Bob Hansen .75 .30
509 Dave Hilton .75 .30
510 Vida Blue 1.50 .60
511 Billy Martin MG CL 2.50 1.00
512 Larry Milbourne .75 .30
513 Dick Pole .75 .30
514 Jose Cruz 2.50 1.00
515 Manny Sanguillen 1.50 .60
516 Don Hood .75 .30
517 Checklist 397-528 4.00 1.60
518 Leo Cardenas .75 .30
519 Jim Todd .75 .30
520 Amos Otis 1.50 .60
521 Dennis Blair .75 .30
522 Gary Sutherland .75 .30
523 Tom Paciorek 1.50 .60
524 John Doherty .75 .30
525 Tom House .75 .30
526 Larry Hisle 1.50 .60
527 Mac Scarce .75 .30
528 Eddie Leon .75 .30
529 Gary Thomasson .75 .30
530 Gaylord Perry 4.00 1.60
531 Sparky Anderson MG CL 6.00 2.40
532 Gorman Thomas 1.50 .60
533 Rudy Meoli .75 .30
534 Alex Johnson .75 .30
535 Gene Tenace 1.50 .60
536 Bob Moose .75 .30
537 Tommy Harper 1.50 .60
538 Duffy Dyer .75 .30
539 Jesse Jefferson .75 .30
540 Lou Brock 8.00 3.20
541 Roger Metzger .75 .30
542 Pete Broberg .75 .30
543 Larry Biittner .75 .30
544 Steve Mingori .75 .30
545 Billy Williams 4.00 1.60
546 John Knox .75 .30
547 Von Joshua .75 .30
548 Charlie Sands .75 .30
549 Bill Butler .75 .30
550 Ralph Garr 1.50 .60
551 Larry Christenson .75 .30
552 Jack Brohamer .75 .30
553 John Boccabella .75 .30
554 Goose Gossage 2.50 1.00
555 Al Oliver 2.50 1.00
556 Tim Johnson .75 .30
557 Larry Gura .75 .30
558 Dave Roberts .75 .30
559 Bob Montgomery .75 .30
560 Tony Perez 4.00 1.60
561 Alvin Dark MG CL 2.50 1.00
562 Gary Nolan 1.50 .60
563 Wilbur Howard .75 .30
564 Tommy Davis 1.50 .60
565 Joe Torre 2.50 1.00
566 Ray Burris .75 .30
567 Jim Sundberg RC 2.50 1.00
568 Dale Murray .75 .30
569 Frank White 1.50 .60
570 Jim Wynn 1.50 .60
571 Dave Lemanczyk .75 .30
572 Roger Nelson .75 .30
573 Orlando Pena .75 .30
574 Tony Taylor .75 .30
575 Gene Clines .75 .30
576 Phil Roof .75 .30
577 John Morris .75 .30
578 Dave Tomlin .75 .30
579 Skip Pitlock .75 .30
580 Frank Robinson 8.00 3.20
581 Darrel Chaney .75 .30
582 Eduardo Rodriguez .75 .30
583 Andy Etchebarren .75 .30
584 Mike Garman .75 .30
585 Chris Chambliss 1.50 .60
586 Tim McCarver 2.50 1.00
587 Chris Ward .75 .30
588 Rick Auerbach .75 .30
589 Clyde King MG CL 2.50 1.00
590 Cesar Cedeno 1.50 .60
591 Glenn Abbott .75 .30
592 Balor Moore .75 .30
593 Gene Lamont .75 .30
594 Jim Fuller .75 .30
595 Joe Niekro 1.50 .60
596 Ollie Brown .75 .30
597 Winston Llenas .75 .30
598 Bruce Kison .75 .30
599 Nate Colbert .75 .30
600 Rod Carew 10.00 4.00
601 Juan Beniquez .75 .30
602 John Vukovich .75 .30
603 Lew Krausse .75 .30
604 Oscar Zamora .75 .30
605 John Ellis .75 .30
606 Bruce Miller .75 .30
607 Jim Holt .75 .30
608 Gene Michael .75 .30
609 Elrod Hendricks .75 .30
610 Ron Hunt .75 .30
611 Bill Virdon MG CL 2.50 1.00
612 Terry Hughes .75 .30
613 Bill Parsons .75 .30
614 Jack Kucek 1.50 .60
Dyar Miller
Vern Ruhle
Paul Siebert
615 Pat Darcy 2.50 1.00
Dennis Leonard RC
Tom Underwood
Hank Webb
616 Dave Augustine 20.00 8.00
Pepe Mangual
Jim Rice RC
John Scott
617 Mike Cubbage 2.50 1.00
Doug DeCinces RC
Reggie Sanders
Manny Trillo
618 Jamie Easterly 1.50 .60
Tom Johnson
Scott McGregor RC
Rick Rhoden
619 Benny Ayala 1.50 .60
Nyls Nyman
Tommy Smith
Jerry Turner
620 Gary Carter RC 25.00 10.00
Marc Hill
Danny Meyer
Leon Roberts
621 John Denny RC 2.50 1.00
Rawly Eastwick
Jim Kern
Juan Veintidos
622 Ed Armbrister 10.00 4.00
Fred Lynn RC
Tom Poquette
Terry Whitfield
623 Phil Garner RC 10.00 4.00
Keith Hernandez
Bob Sheldon
Tom Veryzer
624 Doug Konieczny 1.50 .60
Gary Lavelle
Jim Otten
Eddie Solomon
625 Boog Powell 2.50 1.00
626 Larry Haney .75 .30
(photo actually
Dave Duncan)
627 Tom Walker .75 .30
628 Ron LeFlore RC 1.50 .60
629 Joe Hoerner .75 .30
630 Greg Luzinski 2.50 1.00
631 Lee Lacy .75 .30
632 Morris Nettles .75 .30
633 Paul Casanova .75 .30
634 Cy Acosta .75 .30
635 Chuck Dobson .75 .30
636 Charlie Moore .75 .30
637 Ted Martinez .75 .30
638 Jim Marshall MG CL 2.50 1.00
639 Steve Kline .75 .30
640 Harmon Killebrew 8.00 3.20
641 Jim Northrup 1.50 .60
642 Mike Phillips .75 .30
643 Brent Strom .75 .30
644 Bill Fahey .75 .30
645 Danny Cater .75 .30
646 Checklist 529-660 4.00 1.60
647 C.Washington RC 2.50 1.00
648 Dave Pagan 1.50 .60
649 Jack Heidemann .75 .30
650 Dave May .75 .30
651 John Morlan .75 .30
652 Lindy McDaniel 1.50 .60
653 Lee Richard .75 .30
654 Jerry Terrell .75 .30
655 Rico Carty 1.50 .60
656 Bill Plummer .75 .30
657 Bob Oliver .75 .30
658 Vic Harris .75 .30
659 Bob Apodaca .75 .30
660 Hank Aaron 40.00 16.00

1976 O-Pee-Chee

This is a 660-card standard-size set. The 1976 O-Pee-Chee cards are very similar to the 1976 Topps cards, yet rather different from previous years' issues. The most prominent change is that the backs are much brighter than their American counterparts. The cards parallel the American issue and it is a challenge to find well centered examples of these cards. Notable Rookie Cards include Dennis Eckersley and Ron Guidry.

	NM	Ex
COMPLETE SET (660)	800.00	325.00

1 Hank Aaron RB 20.00 8.00
2 Bobby Bonds RB 3.00 1.20
3 Mickey Lolich RB 1.50 .60
4 Dave Lopes RB 1.50 .60
5 Tom Seaver RB 8.00 3.20
6 Rennie Stennett RB 1.50 .60
7 Jim Umbarger .75 .30
8 Tito Fuentes .75 .30
9 Paul Lindblad .75 .30
10 Lou Brock 8.00 3.20
11 Jim Hughes .75 .30
12 Richie Zisk 1.50 .60
13 John Wockenfuss .75 .30
14 Gene Garber 1.50 .60
15 George Scott 1.50 .60
16 Bob Apodaca .75 .30
17 Billy Martin MG CL 3.00 1.20
18 Dale Murray .75 .30
19 George Brett 60.00 24.00
20 Bob Watson 1.50 .60
21 Dave LaRoche .75 .30
22 Bill Russell 1.50 .60
23 Brian Downing 1.50 .60
24 Cesar Geronimo 1.50 .60
25 Mike Torrez 1.50 .60
26 Andre Thornton 1.50 .60
27 Ed Figueroa .75 .30
28 Dusty Baker 3.00 1.20
29 Rick Burleson 1.50 .60
30 John Montefusco RC 1.50 .60
31 Len Randle .75 .30
32 Danny Frisella .75 .30
33 Bill North .75 .30
34 Mike Garman .75 .30
35 Tony Oliva 3.00 1.20
36 Frank Taveras .75 .30
37 John Hiller 1.50 .60
38 Garry Maddox 1.50 .60
39 Pete Broberg .75 .30
40 Dave Kingman 3.00 1.20
41 Tippy Martinez 1.50 .60
42 Barry Foote 1.50 .60
43 Paul Splittorff .75 .30
44 Doug Rader 1.50 .60
45 Boog Powell 3.00 1.20
46 Walt Alston MG CL 3.00 1.20
47 Jesse Jefferson .75 .30
48 Dave Concepcion 3.00 1.20
49 Dave Duncan 1.50 .60
50 Fred Lynn 3.00 1.20
51 Ray Burris .75 .30
52 Dave Chalk .75 .30
53 Mike Beard .75 .30
54 Dave Rader .75 .30
55 Gaylord Perry 5.00 2.00
56 Bob Tolan .75 .30
57 Phil Garner 1.50 .60
58 Ron Reed .75 .30
59 Larry Hisle 1.50 .60
60 Jerry Reuss 1.50 .60
61 Ron LeFlore 1.50 .60
62 Johnny Oates 1.50 .60
63 Bobby Darwin .75 .30
64 Jerry Koosman 1.50 .60
65 Chris Chambliss 1.50 .60
66 Gus Bell FS 1.50 .60
Buddy Bell
67 Ray Boone FS 1.50 .60
Bob Boone
68 Joe Coleman FS .75 .30
Joe Coleman Jr.
69 Jim Hegan FS .75 .30
Mike Hegan
70 Roy Smalley FS 1.50 .60
Roy Smalley Jr.
71 Steve Rogers 3.00 1.20
72 Hal McRae 1.50 .60
73 Earl Weaver MG CL 3.00 1.20
74 Oscar Gamble 1.50 .60
75 Larry Dierker 1.50 .60
76 Willie Crawford .75 .30
77 Pedro Borbon 1.50 .60
78 Cecil Cooper 1.50 .60
79 Jerry Morales .75 .30
80 Jim Kaat 4.00 1.60
81 Darrell Evans 1.50 .60
82 Von Joshua .75 .30
83 Jim Spencer .75 .30
84 Brent Strom .75 .30
85 Mickey Rivers 1.50 .60
86 Mike Tyson .75 .30
87 Tom Burgmeier .75 .30
88 Duffy Dyer .75 .30
89 Vern Ruhle .75 .30
90 Sal Bando 1.50 .60
91 Tom Hutton .75 .30
92 Eduardo Rodriguez .75 .30
93 Mike Phillips .75 .30
94 Jim Dwyer .75 .30
95 Brooks Robinson 10.00 4.00
96 Doug Bird .75 .30
97 Wilbur Howard .75 .30
98 Dennis Eckersley RC 50.00 20.00
99 Lee Lacy .75 .30
100 Jim Hunter 5.00 2.00
101 Pete LaCock .75 .30
102 Jim Willoughby .75 .30
103 Biff Pocoroba .75 .30
104 Cincinnati Reds 4.00 1.60
Team Card CL
Sparky Anderson MG
105 Gary Lavelle .75 .30
106 Tom Grieve 1.50 .60
107 Dave Roberts .75 .30
108 Don Kirkwood .75 .30
109 Larry Lintz .75 .30
110 Carlos May .75 .30
111 Danny Thompson .75 .30
112 Kent Tekulve RC 3.00 1.20
113 Gary Sutherland .75 .30
114 Jay Johnstone 1.50 .60
115 Ken Holtzman 1.50 .60
116 Charlie Moore .75 .30
117 Mike Jorgensen .75 .30
118 Darrell Johnson MG CL 3.00 1.20
119 Checklist 1-132 3.00 .75
120 Rusty Staub 1.50 .60
121 Tony Solaita .75 .30
122 Mike Cosgrove .75 .30
123 Walt Williams .75 .30
124 Doug Rau .75 .30
125 Don Baylor 4.00 1.60
126 Tom Dettore .75 .30
127 Larvell Blanks .75 .30
128 Ken Griffey Sr. 4.00 1.60
129 Andy Etchebarren .75 .30
130 Luis Tiant 3.00 1.20
131 Bill Stein .75 .30
132 Don Hood .75 .30
133 Gary Matthews 1.50 .60
134 Mike Ivie .75 .30
135 Bake McBride 1.50 .60
136 Dave Goltz .75 .30
137 Bill Robinson 1.50 .60
138 Lerrin LaGrow .75 .30
139 Gorman Thomas 1.50 .60
140 Vida Blue 1.50 .60
141 Larry Parrish RC 3.00 1.20
142 Dick Drago .75 .30
143 Jerry Grote .75 .30
144 Al Fitzmorris .75 .30
145 Larry Bowa 1.50 .60
146 George Medich .75 .30
147 Bill Virdon MG CL 3.00 1.20
148 Stan Thomas .75 .30
149 Tommy Davis 1.50 .60
150 Steve Garvey 4.00 1.60
151 Bill Bonham .75 .30
152 Leroy Stanton .75 .30
153 Buzz Capra .75 .30
154 Bucky Dent 1.50 .60
155 Jack Billingham 1.50 .60
156 Rico Carty 1.50 .60
157 Mike Caldwell .75 .30
158 Ken Reitz .75 .30
159 Jerry Terrell .75 .30
160 Dave Winfield 20.00 8.00
161 Bruce Kison .75 .30
162 Jack Pierce .75 .30
163 Jim Slaton .75 .30
164 Pepe Mangual .75 .30
165 Gene Tenace 1.50 .60
166 Skip Lockwood .75 .30
167 Freddie Patek 1.50 .60
168 Tom Hilgendorf .75 .30
169 Graig Nettles 3.00 1.20
170 Rick Wise .75 .30
171 Greg Gross .75 .30
172 Frank Lucchesi MG CL 3.00 1.20
173 Steve Swisher .75 .30
174 Charlie Hough 1.50 .60
175 Ken Singleton 1.50 .60
176 Dick Lange .75 .30
177 Marty Perez .75 .30
178 Tom Buskey .75 .30
179 George Foster 3.00 1.20
180 Goose Gossage 4.00 1.60
181 Willie Montanez .75 .30
182 Harry Rasmussen .75 .30
183 Steve Braun .75 .30
184 Bill Greif .75 .30
185 Dave Parker 4.00 1.60
186 Tom Walker .75 .30
187 Pedro Garcia .75 .30
188 Fred Scherman .75 .30
189 Claudell Washington 1.50 .60
190 Jon Matlack .75 .30
191 Bill Madlock 1.50 .60
Ted Simmons
Manny Sanguillen LL
192 Rod Carew 4.00 1.60
Fred Lynn
Thurman Munson LL
193 Mike Schmidt 5.00 2.00
Dave Kingman
Greg Luzinski LL
194 Reggie Jackson 5.00 2.00
George Scott
John Mayberry LL
195 Greg Luzinski 3.00 1.20
Johnny Bench
Tony Perez LL
196 George Scott 1.50 .60
John Mayberry
Fred Lynn LL
197 Dave Lopes 3.00 1.20
Joe Morgan
Lou Brock LL
198 Mickey Rivers 1.50 .60
Claudell Washington
Amos Otis LL
199 Tom Seaver 4.00 1.60
Randy Jones
Andy Messersmith LL
200 Jim Hunter 3.00 1.20
Jim Palmer
Vida Blue LL
201 Randy Jones 3.00 1.20
Andy Messersmith
Tom Seaver LL
202 Jim Palmer 5.00 2.00
Jim Hunter
Dennis Eckersley LL
203 Tom Seaver 4.00 1.60
John Montefusco
Andy Messersmith LL
204 Frank Tanana 1.50 .60
Bert Blyleven
Gaylord Perry LL
205 Al Hrabosky 1.50 .60
Rich Gossage LL
206 Manny Trillo .75 .30
207 Andy Hassler .75 .30
208 Mike Lum .75 .30
209 Alan Ashby 1.50 .60
210 Lee May 1.50 .60
211 Clay Carroll 1.50 .60
212 Pat Kelly .75 .30
213 Dave Heaverlo .75 .30
214 Eric Soderholm .75 .30
215 Reggie Smith 1.50 .60
216 Karl Kuehl MG CL 3.00 1.20
217 Dave Freisleben .75 .30
218 John Knox .75 .30
219 Tom Murphy .75 .30
220 Manny Sanguillen 1.50 .60
221 Jim Todd .75 .30
222 Wayne Garrett .75 .30
223 Ollie Brown .75 .30
224 Jim York .75 .30
225 Roy White 1.50 .60
226 Jim Sundberg 1.50 .60
227 Oscar Zamora .75 .30
228 John Hale .75 .30
229 Jerry Remy .75 .30
230 Carl Yastrzemski 15.00 6.00
231 Tom House .75 .30
232 Frank Duffy .75 .30
233 Grant Jackson .75 .30
234 Mike Sadek .75 .30
235 Bert Blyleven 4.00 1.60
236 Whitey Herzog MG CL 3.00 1.20
237 Dave Hamilton .75 .30
238 Larry Biittner .75 .30
239 John Curtis .75 .30
240 Pete Rose 30.00 12.00
241 Hector Torres .75 .30
242 Dan Meyer .75 .30
243 Jim Rooker .75 .30
244 Bill Sharp .75 .30
245 Felix Millan .75 .30
246 Cesar Tovar .75 .30
247 Terry Harmon .75 .30
248 Dick Tidrow .75 .30
249 Cliff Johnson 1.50 .60
250 Fergie Jenkins 5.00 2.00
251 Rick Monday 1.50 .60
252 Tim Nordbrook .75 .30
253 Bill Buckner 1.50 .60
254 Rudy Meoli .75 .30
255 Fritz Peterson .75 .30
256 Rowland Office .75 .30
257 Ross Grimsley .75 .30
258 Nyls Nyman .75 .30
259 Darrel Chaney .75 .30
260 Steve Busby .75 .30
261 Gary Thomasson .75 .30
262 Checklist 133-264 3.00 .75
263 Lyman Bostock RC 3.00 1.20
264 Steve Renko .75 .30
265 Willie Davis 1.50 .60
266 Alan Foster .75 .30
267 Aurelio Rodriguez .75 .30
268 Del Unser .75 .30
269 Rick Austin .75 .30
270 Willie Stargell 5.00 2.00
271 Jim Lonborg 1.50 .60
272 Rick Dempsey 1.50 .60
273 Joe Niekro 1.50 .60
274 Tommy Harper 1.50 .60
275 Rick Manning .75 .30
276 Mickey Scott .75 .30
277 Jim Marshall MG CL 3.00 1.20
278 Bernie Carbo .75 .30
279 Roy Howell .75 .30
280 Burt Hooton 1.50 .60
281 Dave May .75 .30
282 Dan Osborn .75 .30
283 Merv Rettenmund .75 .30
284 Steve Ontiveros .75 .30
285 Mike Cuellar 1.50 .60
286 Jim Wohlford .75 .30
287 Pete Mackanin .75 .30
288 Bill Campbell .75 .30
289 Enzo Hernandez .75 .30
290 Ted Simmons 1.50 .60
291 Ken Sanders .75 .30
292 Leon Roberts .75 .30
293 Bill Castro .75 .30
294 Ed Kirkpatrick .75 .30
295 Dave Cash .75 .30
296 Pat Dobson .75 .30
297 Roger Metzger .75 .30
298 Dick Bosman .75 .30
299 Champ Summers .75 .30
300 Johnny Bench 20.00 8.00
301 Jackie Brown .75 .30
302 Rick Miller .75 .30
303 Steve Foucault .75 .30
304 Dick Williams MG CL 3.00 1.20
305 Andy Messersmith 1.50 .60
306 Rod Gilbreath .75 .30
307 Al Bumbry 1.50 .60
308 Jim Barr .75 .30
309 Bill Melton .75 .30
310 Randy Jones 1.50 .60
311 Cookie Rojas .75 .30
312 Don Carrithers .75 .30
313 Dan Ford .75 .30
314 Ed Kranepool .75 .30
315 Al Hrabosky 1.50 .60
316 Robin Yount 25.00 10.00
317 John Candelaria RC 3.00 1.20
318 Bob Boone 3.00 1.20
319 Larry Gura .75 .30
320 Willie Horton 1.50 .60
321 Jose Cruz 3.00 1.20
322 Glenn Abbott .75 .30
323 Rob Sperring .75 .30
324 Jim Bibby .75 .30
325 Tony Perez 5.00 2.00
326 Dick Pole .75 .30
327 Dave Moates .75 .30
328 Carl Morton .75 .30
329 Joe Ferguson .75 .30
330 Nolan Ryan 50.00 20.00
331 John McNamara MG CL 3.00 1.20
332 Charlie Williams .75 .30
333 Bob Coluccio .75 .30
334 Dennis Leonard 1.50 .60
335 Bob Grich 1.50 .60
336 Vic Albury .75 .30
337 Bud Harrelson 1.50 .60
338 Bob Bailey .75 .30
339 John Denny 1.50 .60
340 Jim Rice 6.00 2.40
341 Lou Gehrig ATG 20.00 8.00
342 Rogers Hornsby ATG 4.00 1.60
343 Pie Traynor ATG 3.00 1.20
344 Honus Wagner ATG 8.00 3.20
345 Babe Ruth ATG 20.00 8.00
346 Ty Cobb ATG 15.00 6.00
347 Ted Williams ATG 18.00 7.25
348 Mickey Cochrane ATG 3.00 1.20
349 Walter Johnson ATG 8.00 3.20
350 Lefty Grove ATG 3.00 1.20
351 Randy Hundley 1.50 .60
352 Dave Giusti .75 .30
353 Sixto Lezcano 1.50 .60
354 Ron Blomberg .75 .30
355 Steve Carlton 10.00 4.00
356 Ted Martinez .75 .30
357 Ken Forsch .75 .30
358 Buddy Bell 1.50 .60
359 Rick Reuschel 1.50 .60
360 Jeff Burroughs 1.50 .60
361 Ralph Houk MG CL 3.00 1.20
362 Will McEnaney 1.50 .60
363 Dave Collins RC 1.50 .60
364 Elias Sosa .75 .30
365 Carlton Fisk 8.00 3.20
366 Bobby Valentine 1.50 .60
367 Bruce Miller .75 .30
368 Wilbur Wood .75 .30
369 Frank White 1.50 .60
370 Ron Cey 1.50 .60
371 Ellie Hendricks .75 .30
372 Rick Baldwin .75 .30
373 Johnny Briggs .75 .30
374 Dan Warthen .75 .30
375 Ron Fairly 1.50 .60
376 Rich Hebner 1.50 .60
377 Mike Hegan .75 .30
378 Steve Stone 1.50 .60
379 Ken Boswell .75 .30
380 Bobby Bonds 4.00 1.60
381 Denny Doyle .75 .30
382 Matt Alexander .75 .30
383 John Ellis .75 .30

384 Danny Ozark MG CL 3.00 1.20
385 Mickey Lolich 1.50 .60
386 Ed Goodson .75 .30
387 Mike Miley .75 .30
388 Stan Perzanowski .75 .30
389 Glenn Adams .75 .30
390 Don Gullett 1.50 .60
391 Jerry Hairston .75 .30
392 Checklist 265-396 3.00 .75
393 Paul Mitchell .75 .30
394 Fran Healy .75 .30
395 Jim Wynn 1.50 .60
396 Bill Lee .75 .30
397 Tim Foli .75 .30
398 Dave Tomlin .75 .30
399 Luis Melendez .75 .30
400 Rod Carew 8.00 3.20
401 Ken Brett .75 .30
402 Don Money 1.50 .60
403 Geoff Zahn .75 .30
404 Enos Cabell .75 .30
405 Rollie Fingers 5.00 2.00
406 Ed Herrmann .75 .30
407 Tom Underwood .75 .30
408 Charlie Spikes .75 .30
409 Dave Lemanczyk .75 .30
410 Ralph Garr 1.50 .60
411 Bill Singer .75 .30
412 Toby Harrah 1.50 .60
413 Pete Varney .75 .30
414 Wayne Garland .75 .30
415 Vada Pinson 4.00 1.60
416 Tommy John 4.00 1.60
417 Gene Clines .75 .30
418 Jose Morales RC 1.50 .60
419 Reggie Cleveland .75 .30
420 Joe Morgan 8.00 3.20
421 Oakland A's CL 3.00 1.20
422 Johnny Grubb .75 .30
423 Ed Halicki .75 .30
424 Phil Roof .75 .30
425 Rennie Stennett .75 .30
426 Bob Forsch .75 .30
427 Kurt Bevacqua .75 .30
428 Jim Crawford .75 .30
429 Fred Stanley .75 .30
430 Jose Cardenal 1.50 .60
431 Dick Ruthven .75 .30
432 Tom Veryzer .75 .30
433 Rick Waits .75 .30
434 Morris Nettles .75 .30
435 Phil Niekro 5.00 2.00
436 Bill Fahey .75 .30
437 Terry Forster .75 .30
438 Doug DeCinces 1.50 .60
439 Rick Rhoden 1.50 .60
440 John Mayberry 1.50 .60
441 Gary Carter 8.00 3.20
442 Hank Webb .75 .30
443 San Francisco Giants CL 3.00 1.20
444 Gary Nolan 1.50 .60
445 Rico Petrocelli 1.50 .60
446 Larry Haney .75 .30
447 Gene Locklear 1.50 .60
448 Tom Johnson .75 .30
449 Bob Robertson .75 .30
450 Jim Palmer 8.00 3.20
451 Buddy Bradford .75 .30
452 Tom Hausman .75 .30
453 Lou Piniella 3.00 1.20
454 Tom Griffin .75 .30
455 Dick Allen 3.00 1.20
456 Joe Coleman .75 .30
457 Ed Crosby .75 .30
458 Earl Williams .75 .30
459 Jim Brewer .75 .30
460 Cesar Cedeno 1.50 .60
461 NL and AL Champs 1.50 .60
Reds sweep Bucs;
Bosox surprise A's
462 World Series 1.50 .60
Reds Champs
463 Steve Hargan .75 .30
464 Ken Henderson .75 .30
465 Mike Marshall 1.50 .60
466 Bob Stinson .75 .30
467 Woodie Fryman .75 .30
468 Jesus Alou .75 .30
469 Rawly Eastwick 1.50 .60
470 Bobby Murcer 1.50 .60
471 Jim Burton .75 .30
472 Bob Davis .75 .30
473 Paul Blair 1.50 .60
474 Ray Corbin .75 .30
475 Joe Rudi 1.50 .60
476 Bob Moose .75 .30
477 Frank Robinson MG CL 3.00 1.20
478 Lynn McGlothen .75 .30
479 Bobby Mitchell .75 .30
480 Mike Schmidt 25.00 10.00
481 Rudy May .75 .30
482 Tim Hosley .75 .30
483 Mickey Stanley .75 .30
484 Eric Raich .75 .30
485 Mike Hargrove 1.50 .60
486 Bruce Dal Canton .75 .30
487 Leron Lee .75 .30
488 Claude Osteen 1.50 .60
489 Skip Jutze .75 .30
490 Frank Tanana 1.50 .60
491 Terry Crowley .75 .30
492 Martin Pattin .75 .30
493 Derrel Thomas .75 .30
494 Craig Swan 1.50 .60
495 Nate Colbert .75 .30
496 Juan Beniquez .75 .30
497 Joe McIntosh .75 .30
498 Glenn Borgmann .75 .30
499 Mario Guerrero .75 .30
500 Reggie Jackson 20.00 8.00
501 Billy Champion .75 .30
502 Tim McCarver 3.00 1.20
503 Elliott Maddox .75 .30
504 Danny Murtaugh MG CL 3.00 1.20
505 Mark Belanger 1.50 .60
506 George Mitterwald .75 .30
507 Ray Bare .75 .30
508 Duane Kuiper .75 .30
509 Bill Hands .75 .30
510 Amos Otis 1.50 .60
511 Jamie Easterley .75 .30
512 Ellie Rodriguez .75 .30
513 Bart Johnson .75 .30
514 Dan Driessen 1.50 .60
515 Steve Yeager 1.50 .60
516 Wayne Granger .75 .30
517 John Milner .75 .30
518 Doug Flynn .75 .30
519 Steve Brye .75 .30
520 Willie McCovey 8.00 3.20
521 Jim Colborn .75 .30
522 Ted Sizemore .75 .30
523 Bob Montgomery .75 .30
524 Pete Falcone .75 .30
525 Billy Williams 5.00 2.00
526 Checklist 397-528 3.00 .75
527 Mike Anderson .75 .30
528 Dock Ellis .75 .30
529 Deron Johnson .75 .30
530 Don Sutton 5.00 2.00
531 Joe Frazier MG CL 3.00 1.20
532 Milt May .75 .30
533 Lee Richard .75 .30
534 Stan Bahnsen .75 .30
535 Dave Nelson .75 .30
536 Mike Thompson .75 .30
537 Tony Muser .75 .30
538 Pat Darcy .75 .30
539 John Balaz .75 .30
540 Bill Freehan 1.50 .60
541 Steve Mingori .75 .30
542 Keith Hernandez 3.00 1.20
543 Wayne Twitchell .75 .30
544 Pepe Frias .75 .30
545 Sparky Lyle 1.50 .60
546 Dave Rosello .75 .30
547 Roric Harrison .75 .30
548 Manny Mota 1.50 .60
549 Randy Tate .75 .30
550 Hank Aaron 40.00 16.00
551 Jerry DaVanon .75 .30
552 Terry Humphrey .75 .30
553 Randy Moffitt .75 .30
554 Ray Fosse .75 .30
555 Dyar Miller .75 .30
556 Gene Mauch MG CL 3.00 1.20
557 Dan Spillner .75 .30
558 Clarence Gaston 1.50 .60
559 Clyde Wright .75 .30
560 Jorge Orta .75 .30
561 Tom Carroll .75 .30
562 Adrian Garrett .75 .30
563 Larry Demery .75 .30
564 Bubble Gum Champ: 3.00 1.20
Kurt Bevacqua
565 Tug McGraw 3.00 1.20
566 Ken McMullen .75 .30
567 George Stone .75 .30
568 Rob Andrews .75 .30
569 Nelson Briles 1.50 .60
570 George Hendrick 1.50 .60
571 Don DeMola .75 .30
572 Rich Coggins .75 .30
573 Bill Travers .75 .30
574 Don Kessinger 1.50 .60
575 Dwight Evans 3.00 1.20
576 Maximino Leon .75 .30
577 Marc Hill .75 .30
578 Ted Kubiak .75 .30
579 Clay Kirby .75 .30
580 Bert Campaneris 1.50 .60
581 Red Schoendienst MG CL 3.00 1.20
582 Mike Kekich .75 .30
583 Tommy Helms .75 .30
584 Stan Wall .75 .30
585 Joe Torre 4.00 1.60
586 Ron Schueler .75 .30
587 Leo Cardenas .75 .30
588 Kevin Kobel .75 .30
589 Santo Alcala 3.00 1.20
Mike Flanagan RC
Joe Pactwa
Pablo Torrealba
590 Henry Cruz 1.50 .60
Chet Lemon RC
Ellis Valentine
Terry Whitfield
591 Steve Grilli 1.50 .60
Craig Mitchell
Jose Sosa
George Throop
592 Willie Randolph RC 10.00 4.00
Dave McKay
Jerry Royster
Roy Staiger
593 Larry Anderson 1.50 .60
Ken Crosby
Mark Littell
Butch Metzger
594 Andy Merchant 1.50 .60
Ed Ott
Royle Stillman
Jerry White
595 Art DeFillipis 1.50 .60
Randy Lerch
Sid Monge
Steve Barr
596 Craig Reynolds 1.50 .60
Lamar Johnson
Johnnie LeMaster
Jerry Manuel
597 Don Aase 1.50 .60
Jack Kucek
Frank LaCorte
Mike Pazik
598 Hector Cruz 1.50 .60
Jamie Quirk
Jerry Turner
Joe Wallis
599 Rob Dressler 10.00 4.00
Ron Guidry RC
Bob McClure
Pat Zachry
600 Tom Seaver 15.00 6.00
601 Ken Rudolph .75 .30
602 Doug Konieczny .75 .30
603 Jim Holt .75 .30
604 Joe Lovitto .75 .30
605 Al Downing .75 .30
606 Alex Grammas MG CL 3.00 1.20
607 Rich Hinton .75 .30
608 Vic Correll .75 .30
609 Fred Norman .75 .30
610 Greg Luzinski 3.00 1.20
611 Rich Folkers .75 .30
612 Joe Lahoud .75 .30
613 Tim Johnson .75 .30
614 Fernando Arroyo .75 .30
615 Mike Cubbage .75 .30
616 Buck Martinez 1.50 .60
617 Darold Knowles .75 .30
618 Jack Brohamer .75 .30
619 Bill Butler .75 .30
620 Al Oliver 1.50 .60
621 Tom Hall .75 .30
622 Rick Auerbach .75 .30
623 Bob Allietta .75 .30
624 Tony Taylor .75 .30
625 J.R. Richard 1.50 .60
626 Bob Sheldon .75 .30
627 Bill Plummer .75 .30
628 John D'Acquisto .75 .30
629 Sandy Alomar 1.50 .60
630 Chris Speier .75 .30
631 Dave Bristol MG CL 3.00 1.20
632 Rogelio Moret .75 .30
633 John Stearns RC 1.50 .60
634 Larry Christenson .75 .30
635 Jim Fregosi 1.50 .60
636 Joe Decker .75 .30
637 Bruce Bochte .75 .30
638 Doyle Alexander 1.50 .60
639 Fred Kendall .75 .30
640 Bill Madlock 3.00 1.20
641 Tom Paciorek 1.50 .60
642 Dennis Blair .75 .30
643 Checklist 529-660 3.00 .75
644 Tom Bradley .75 .30
645 Darrell Porter 1.50 .60
646 John Lowenstein .75 .30
647 Ramon Hernandez .75 .30
648 Al Cowens .75 .30
649 Dave Roberts .75 .30
650 Thurman Munson 10.00 4.00
651 John Odom .75 .30
652 Ed Armbrister .75 .30
653 Mike Norris RC 1.50 .60
654 Doug Griffin .75 .30
655 Mike Vail .75 .30
656 Chuck Tanner MG CL 3.00 1.20
657 Roy Smalley RC 1.50 .60
658 Jerry Johnson .75 .30
659 Ben Oglivie 1.50 .60
660 Dave Lopes 3.00 1.20

1977 O-Pee-Chee

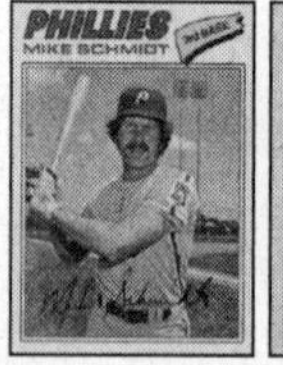

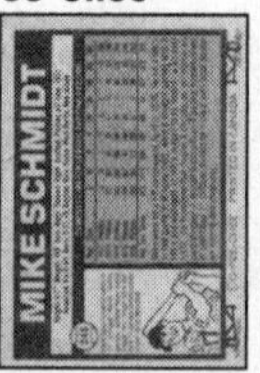

The 1977 O-Pee-Chee set of 264 standard-size cards is not only much smaller numerically than its American counterpart, but also contains many different poses and is loaded with players from the two Canadian teams, including many players from the inaugural year of the Blue Jays and many single cards of players who were on multiplayer rookie cards. On a white background, the fronts feature color player photos with thin black borders. The player's name and position, a facsimile autograph, and the team name also appear on the front. The horizontal backs carry player biography and statistics in French and English. The numbering of this set is different than the U.S. issue, the backs have different colors and the words "O-Pee-Chee Printed in Canada" are printed on the back.

NM Ex
COMPLETE SET (264) 275.00 110.00
1 George Brett 8.00 3.20
Bill Madlock LL
2 Graig Nettles 2.00 .80
Mike Schmidt LL
3 Lee May 1.50 .60
George Foster LL
4 Bill North .75 .30
Dave Lopes LL
5 Jim Palmer 1.50 .60
Randy Jones LL
6 Nolan Ryan 15.00 6.00
Tom Seaver LL
7 Mark Fidrych .75 .30
John Denny LL
8 Bill Campbell .75 .30
Rawly Eastwick LL
9 Mike Jorgensen .75 .30
10 Jim Hunter 2.50 1.00
11 Ken Griffey Sr. 1.50 .60
12 Bill Campbell .30 .12
13 Otto Velez .75 .30
14 Milt May .30 .12
15 Dennis Eckersley 5.00 2.00
16 John Mayberry .75 .30
17 Larry Bowa .75 .30
18 Don Carrithers .75 .30
19 Ken Singleton .75 .30
20 Bill Stein .30 .12
21 Ken Brett .30 .12
22 Gary Woods .75 .30
23 Steve Swisher .30 .12
24 Don Sutton 2.50 1.00
25 Willie Stargell 2.50 1.00
26 Jerry Koosman .75 .30
27 Del Unser .75 .30
28 Bob Grich .75 .30
29 Jim Slaton .30 .12
30 Thurman Munson 5.00 2.00
31 Dan Driessen .30 .12
32 Tom Bruno .75 .30
33 Larry Hisle .75 .30
34 Phil Garner .30 .12
35 Mike Hargrove .75 .30
36 Jackie Brown .75 .30
37 Carl Yastrzemski 8.00 3.20
38 Dave Roberts .30 .12
39 Ray Fosse .30 .12
40 Dave McKay .75 .30
41 Paul Splittorff .30 .12
42 Garry Maddox .30 .12
43 Phil Niekro 2.50 1.00
44 Roger Metzger .30 .12
45 Gary Carter 2.50 1.00
46 Jim Spencer .30 .12
47 Ross Grimsley .30 .12
48 Bob Bailor .75 .30
49 Chris Chambliss .75 .30
50 Will McEnaney .75 .30
51 Lou Brock 4.00 1.60
52 Rollie Fingers 2.50 1.00
53 Chris Speier .30 .12
54 Bombo Rivera .75 .30
55 Pete Broberg .30 .12
56 Bill Madlock 2.00 .80
57 Rick Rhoden .75 .30
58 Don Leppert CO .75 .30
Bob Miller CO
Jackie Moore CO
Harry Warner CO
59 John Candelaria .30 .12
60 Ed Kranepool .30 .12
61 Dave LaRoche .30 .12
62 Jim Rice 2.00 .80
63 Don Stanhouse .75 .30
64 Jason Thompson RC .75 .30
65 Nolan Ryan 40.00 16.00
66 Tom Poquette .30 .12
67 Leon Hooten .75 .30
68 Bob Boone .75 .30
69 Mickey Rivers .75 .30
70 Gary Nolan .30 .12
71 Sixto Lezcano .30 .12
72 Larry Parrish .75 .30
73 Dave Goltz .30 .12
74 Bert Campaneris .75 .30
75 Vida Blue .75 .30
76 Rick Cerone .75 .30
77 Ralph Garr .75 .30
78 Ken Forsch .30 .12
79 Willie Montanez .30 .12
80 Jim Palmer 4.00 1.60
81 Jerry White .75 .30
82 Gene Tenace .75 .30
83 Bobby Murcer .75 .30
84 Garry Templeton 1.50 .60
85 Bill Singer .75 .30
86 Buddy Bell .75 .30
87 Luis Tiant .75 .30
88 Rusty Staub 1.50 .60
89 Sparky Lyle .75 .30
90 Jose Morales .75 .30
91 Dennis Leonard .75 .30
92 Tommy Smith .30 .12
93 Steve Carlton 5.00 2.00
94 John Scott .75 .30
95 Bill Bonham .30 .12
96 Dave Lopes .75 .30
97 Jerry Reuss .75 .30
98 Dave Kingman 1.50 .60
99 Dan Warthen .75 .30
100 Johnny Bench 10.00 4.00
101 Bert Blyleven 1.50 .60
102 Cecil Cooper .75 .30
103 Mike Willis .75 .30
104 Dan Ford .30 .12
105 Frank Tanana .75 .30
106 Bill North .30 .12
107 Joe Ferguson .30 .12
108 Dick Williams MG .75 .30
109 John Denny .75 .30
110 Willie Randolph 1.50 .60
111 Reggie Cleveland .75 .30
112 Doug Howard .75 .30
113 Randy Jones .30 .12
114 Rico Carty .75 .30
115 Mark Fidrych RC 5.00 2.00
116 Darrell Porter .75 .30
117 Wayne Garrett .75 .30
118 Greg Luzinski 1.50 .60
119 Jim Barr .30 .12
120 George Foster 1.50 .60
121 Phil Roof .75 .30
122 Bucky Dent .75 .30
123 Steve Braun .30 .12
124 Checklist 1-132 1.50 .35
125 Lee May .75 .30
126 Woodie Fryman .75 .30
127 Jose Cardenal .75 .30
128 Doug Rau .30 .12
129 Rennie Stennett .30 .12
130 Pete Vuckovich RC .75 .30
131 Cesar Cedeno .75 .30
132 Jon Matlack .30 .12
133 Don Baylor 1.50 .60
134 Darrel Chaney .30 .12
135 Tony Perez 2.50 1.00
136 Aurelio Rodriguez .30 .12
137 Carlton Fisk 6.00 2.40
138 Wayne Garland .30 .12
139 Dave Hilton .75 .30
140 Rawly Eastwick .30 .12
141 Amos Otis .75 .30
142 Tug McGraw .75 .30
143 Rod Carew 6.00 2.40
144 Mike Torrez .75 .30
145 Sal Bando .75 .30
146 Dock Ellis .30 .12
147 Jose Cruz .75 .30
148 Alan Ashby .75 .30
149 Gaylord Perry 2.50 1.00
150 Keith Hernandez .75 .30
151 Dave Pagan .30 .12
152 Richie Zisk .30 .12
153 Steve Rogers .75 .30
154 Mark Belanger .75 .30
155 Andy Messersmith .75 .30
156 Dave Winfield 15.00 6.00
157 Chuck Hartenstein .75 .30
158 Manny Trillo .30 .12
159 Steve Yeager .75 .30
160 Cesar Geronimo .30 .12
161 Jim Rooker .30 .12
162 Tim Foli .75 .30
163 Fred Lynn .75 .30
164 Ed Figueroa .30 .12
165 Johnny Grubb .30 .12
166 Pedro Garcia .75 .30
167 Ron LeFlore .75 .30
168 Rich Hebner .75 .30
169 Larry Herndon RC .75 .30
170 George Brett 30.00 12.00
171 Joe Kerrigan .75 .30
172 Bud Harrelson .75 .30
173 Bobby Bonds 2.00 .80
174 Bill Travers .30 .12
175 John Lowenstein .75 .30
176 Butch Wynegar RC .75 .30
177 Pete Falcone .30 .12
178 Claudell Washington .75 .30
179 Checklist 133-264 1.50 .35
180 Dave Cash .75 .30
181 Fred Norman .30 .12
182 Roy White .75 .30
183 Marty Perez .30 .12
184 Jesse Jefferson .75 .30
185 Jim Sundberg .75 .30
186 Dan Meyer .75 .30
187 Fergie Jenkins 2.50 1.00
188 Tom Veryzer .30 .12
189 Dennis Blair .75 .30
190 Rick Manning .30 .12
191 Doug Bird .30 .12
192 Al Bumbry .75 .30
193 Dave Roberts .30 .12
194 Larry Christenson .30 .12
195 Chet Lemon .75 .30
196 Ted Simmons .75 .30
197 Ray Burris .30 .12
198 Jim Brewer CO .75 .30
Billy Gardner CO
Mickey Vernon CO
Ozzie Virgil CO
199 Ron Cey .75 .30
200 Reggie Jackson 10.00 4.00
201 Pat Zachry .30 .12
202 Doug Ault .75 .30
203 Al Oliver .75 .30
204 Robin Yount 10.00 4.00
205 Tom Seaver 8.00 3.20
206 Joe Rudi .75 .30
207 Barry Foote .75 .30
208 Toby Harrah .75 .30
209 Jeff Burroughs .75 .30
210 George Scott .75 .30
211 Jim Mason .75 .30
212 Vern Ruhle .30 .12
213 Fred Kendall .30 .12
214 Rick Reuschel .75 .30
215 Hal McRae .75 .30
216 Chip Lang .75 .30
217 Graig Nettles 1.50 .60
218 George Hendrick .75 .30
219 Glenn Abbott .30 .12
220 Joe Morgan 5.00 2.00
221 Sam Ewing .75 .30
222 George Medich .30 .12
223 Reggie Smith .75 .30
224 Dave Hamilton .30 .12
225 Pepe Frias .75 .30
226 Jay Johnstone .75 .30
227 J.R. Richard .75 .30
228 Doug DeCinces .75 .30
229 Dave Lemanczyk .75 .30
230 Rick Monday .75 .30
231 Manny Sanguillen .75 .30
232 John Montefusco .30 .12
233 Duane Kuiper .30 .12
234 Ellis Valentine .30 .12
235 Dick Tidrow .30 .12
236 Ben Oglivie .75 .30
237 Rick Burleson .75 .30
238 Roy Hartsfield MG .75 .30
239 Lyman Bostock .75 .30
240 Pete Rose 20.00 8.00
241 Mike Ivie .30 .12
242 Dave Parker 1.50 .60
243 Bill Greif .75 .30
244 Freddie Patek .75 .30
245 Mike Schmidt 15.00 6.00
246 Brian Downing .75 .30
247 Steve Hargan .30 .12
248 Dave Collins .75 .30
249 Felix Millan .30 .12
250 Don Gullett .75 .30
251 Jerry Royster .30 .12
252 Earl Williams .75 .30
253 Frank Duffy .30 .12
254 Tippy Martinez .30 .12
255 Steve Garvey 2.00 .80
256 Alvis Woods .75 .30
257 John Hiller .75 .30
258 Dave Concepcion 1.50 .60
259 Dwight Evans 1.50 .60
260 Pete MacKanin .75 .30
261 George Brett RB 12.00 4.80
262 Minnie Minoso RB .75 .30
263 Jose Morales RB .75 .30
264 Nolan Ryan RB 15.00 6.00

1978 O-Pee-Chee

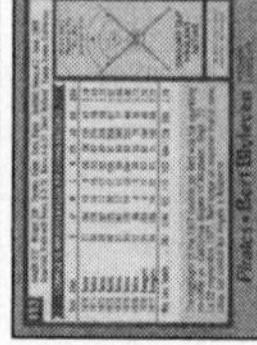

The 242 standard-size cards comprising the 1978 O-Pee-Chee set differ from the cards of the 1978 Topps set by having a higher ratio of cards of players from the two Canadian teams, a practice begun by O-Pee-Chee in 1977 and continued to 1988. The fronts feature white-bordered color player photos, each framed by a colored line. The player's name appears in black lettering at the right of lower white margin. His team name appears in colored cursive lettering, interrupting the framing line at the bottom left of the photo; his position appears within a white baseball icon in an upper corner. The tan and brown horizontal backs carry the player's name, team and position in the brown border at the bottom. Biography, major league statistics, career highlights in both French and English and a bilingual result of an "at bat" in the "Play Ball" game also appear. The asterisked cards have an extra line on the front indicating team change. Double-printed (DP) cards are also noted below. The key card in this set is the Eddie Murray Rookie Card.

NM Ex
COMPLETE SET (242) 200.00 80.00
COMMON CARD (1-242) .25 .10
COMMON DP (1-242) .15 .06
1 Dave Parker 1.50 .60
Rod Carew LL
2 George Foster .60 .24
Jim Rice LL DP
3 George Foster .60 .24
Larry Hisle LL
4 Frank Taveras .25 .10
Freddie Patek LL DP
5 Steve Carlton 2.50 1.00
Dave Goltz
Dennis Leonard
Jim Palmer LL
6 Phil Niekro 6.00 2.40
Nolan Ryan LL DP
7 John Candelaria .60 .24
Frank Tanana LL DP
8 Rollie Fingers 1.25 .50
Bill Campbell LL
9 Steve Rogers DP .30 .12
10 Graig Nettles DP .75 .30
11 Doug Capilla .25 .10
12 George Scott .60 .24
13 Gary Woods .60 .24
14 Tom Veryzer .60 .24
Now with Cleveland as of 12-9-77
15 Wayne Garland .25 .10
16 Amos Otis .60 .24
17 Larry Christenson .25 .10
18 Dave Cash .60 .24
19 Jim Barr .25 .10
20 Ruppert Jones .25 .10
21 Eric Soderholm .25 .10
22 Jesse Jefferson .60 .24
23 Jerry Morales .25 .10
24 Doug Rau .25 .10
25 Rennie Stennett .25 .10
26 Lee Mazzilli .25 .10
27 Dick Williams MG .60 .24
28 Joe Rudi .60 .24
29 Robin Yount 10.00 4.00
30 Don Gullett DP .25 .10
31 Roy Howell DP .15 .06
32 Cesar Geronimo .25 .10
33 Rick Langford DP .15 .06
34 Dan Ford .25 .10
35 Gene Tenace .60 .24
36 Santo Alcala .60 .24
37 Rick Burleson .60 .24
38 Dave Rozema .25 .10
39 Duane Kuiper .25 .10
40 Ron Fairly .60 .24
Now with California as of 12-8-77
41 Dennis Leonard .60 .24
42 Greg Luzinski 1.25 .50
43 Willie Montanez .60 .24
Now with N.Y. Mets as of 12-8-77
44 Enos Cabell .25 .10
45 Ellis Valentine .60 .24
46 Steve Stone .60 .24
47 Lee May DP .30 .12
48 Roy White .60 .24
49 Jerry Garvin .25 .10
50 Johnny Bench 8.00 3.20
51 Garry Templeton .60 .24
52 Doyle Alexander .60 .24
53 Steve Henderson .25 .10
54 Stan Bahnsen .25 .10
55 Dan Meyer .25 .10
56 Rick Reuschel .60 .24
57 Reggie Smith .60 .24
58 Blue Jays Team DP CL .75 .30
59 John Montefusco .25 .10
60 Dave Parker 1.25 .50
61 Jim Bibby .25 .10
62 Fred Lynn .60 .24
63 Jose Morales .60 .24
64 Aurelio Rodriguez .25 .10
65 Frank Tanana .60 .24
66 Darrell Porter .60 .24
67 Otto Velez .25 .10
68 Larry Bowa 1.25 .50
69 Jim Hunter 2.50 1.00
70 George Foster 1.25 .50
71 Cecil Cooper DP .30 .12
72 Gary Alexander DP .15 .06
73 Paul Thormodsgard .25 .10
74 Toby Harrah .60 .24
75 Mitchell Page .25 .10
76 Alan Ashby .25 .10
77 Jorge Orta .25 .10
78 Dave Winfield 10.00 4.00
79 Andy Messersmith .60 .24
Now with N.Y. Yankees as of 12-8-77
80 Ken Singleton .60 .24
81 Will McEnaney .60 .24
82 Lou Piniella .60 .24
83 Bob Forsch .25 .10
84 Dan Driessen .25 .10
85 Dave Lemanczyk .25 .10
86 Paul Dade .25 .10
87 Bill Campbell .25 .10
88 Ron LeFlore .60 .24
89 Bill Madlock .60 .24
90 Tony Perez DP 1.25 .50
91 Freddie Patek .60 .24
92 Glenn Abbott .25 .10
93 Garry Maddox .60 .24
94 Steve Staggs .25 .10
95 Bobby Murcer .60 .24
96 Don Sutton 2.50 1.00
97 Al Oliver 2.50 1.00
Now with Texas Rangers as of 12-8-77
98 Jon Matlack .60 .24
Now with Texas Rangers as of 12-8-77
99 Sam Mejias .60 .24
100 Pete Rose DP 12.00 4.80
101 Randy Jones .25 .10
102 Sixto Lezcano .25 .10
103 Jim Clancy DP .30 .12
104 Butch Wynegar .25 .10
105 Nolan Ryan 40.00 16.00
106 Wayne Gross .25 .10
107 Bob Watson .60 .24
108 Joe Kerrigan .60 .24
Now with Baltimore as of 12-8-77
109 Keith Hernandez .60 .24
110 Reggie Jackson 8.00 3.20
111 Denny Doyle .25 .10
112 Sam Ewing .60 .24
113 Bert Blyleven 2.50 1.00
Now with Pittsburgh as of 12-8-77
114 Andre Thornton .60 .24
115 Milt May .25 .10
116 Jim Colborn .25 .10
117 Warren Cromartie RC 1.25 .50
118 Ted Sizemore .25 .10
119 Checklist 1-121 1.25 .30
120 Tom Seaver 6.00 2.40
121 Luis Gomez .60 .24
122 Jim Spencer .60 .24
Now with N.Y. Yankees as of 12-12-77
123 Leroy Stanton .25 .10
124 Luis Tiant .60 .24
125 Mark Belanger .60 .24
126 Jackie Brown .25 .10
127 Bill Buckner .60 .24
128 Bill Robinson .60 .24
129 Rick Cerone .60 .24
130 Ron Cey 1.25 .50
131 Jose Cruz .60 .24
132 Len Randle DP .15 .06
133 Bob Grich .60 .24
134 Jeff Burroughs .60 .24
135 Gary Carter 2.50 1.00
136 Milt Wilcox .25 .10
137 Carl Yastrzemski 6.00 2.40
138 Dennis Eckersley 3.00 1.20
139 Tim Nordbrook .25 .10
140 Ken Griffey Sr. 1.25 .50
141 Bob Boone 1.25 .50
142 Dave Goltz DP .15 .06
143 Al Cowens .25 .10
144 Bill Atkinson .25 .10
145 Chris Chambliss .60 .24
146 Jim Slaton .60 .24
Now with Detroit Tigers as of 12-9-77
147 Bill Stein .25 .10
148 Bob Bailor .60 .24
149 J.R. Richard .60 .24
150 Ted Simmons .60 .24
151 Rick Manning .25 .10
152 Lerrin LaGrow .25 .10
153 Larry Parrish 1.25 .50
154 Eddie Murray RC 80.00 32.00
155 Phil Niekro 2.50 1.00
156 Bake McBride .60 .24
157 Pete Vuckovich .60 .24
158 Ivan DeJesus .25 .10
159 Rick Rhoden .60 .24
160 Joe Morgan 3.00 1.20
161 Ed Ott .25 .10
162 Don Stanhouse .60 .24
163 Jim Rice 1.25 .50
164 Bucky Dent .60 .24
165 Jim Kern .25 .10
166 Doug Rader .25 .10
167 Steve Kemp .25 .10
168 John Mayberry .60 .24
169 Tim Foli .60 .24
Now with N.Y. Mets as of 12-7-77
170 Steve Carlton 4.00 1.60
171 Pepe Frias .60 .24
172 Pat Zachry .25 .10
173 Don Baylor 1.25 .50
174 Sal Bando DP .30 .12
175 Alvis Woods .60 .24
176 Mike Hargrove .60 .24
177 Vida Blue .60 .24
178 George Hendrick .60 .24
179 Jim Palmer 3.00 1.20
180 Andre Dawson 12.00 4.80
181 Paul Moskau .25 .10
182 Mickey Rivers .60 .24
183 Checklist 122-242 1.25 .30
184 Jerry Johnson .60 .24
185 Willie McCovey 3.00 1.20
186 Enrique Romo .25 .10
187 Butch Hobson .25 .10
188 Rusty Staub 1.25 .50
189 Wayne Twitchell .60 .24
190 Steve Garvey 2.50 1.00
191 Rick Waits .25 .10
192 Doug DeCinces .60 .24
193 Tom Murphy .25 .10
194 Rich Hebner .60 .24
195 Ralph Garr .60 .24
196 Bruce Sutter 1.25 .50
197 Tom Poquette .25 .10
198 Wayne Garrett .25 .10
199 Pedro Borbon .25 .10
200 Thurman Munson 4.00 1.60
201 Rollie Fingers 2.50 1.00
202 Doug Ault .60 .24
203 Phil Garner DP .15 .06
204 Lou Brock 3.00 1.20
205 Ed Kranepool .60 .24
206 Bobby Bonds 1.25 .50
Now with White Sox as of 12-15-77
207 Expos Team DP CL 1.25 .50
208 Bump Wills .25 .10
209 Gary Matthews .60 .24
210 Carlton Fisk 4.00 1.60
211 Jeff Byrd .60 .24
212 Jason Thompson .60 .24
213 Larvell Blanks .25 .10
214 Sparky Lyle .60 .24
215 George Brett 20.00 8.00
216 Del Unser .25 .10
217 Manny Trillo .25 .10
218 Roy Hartsfield MG .60 .24
219 Carlos Lopez .60 .24
Now with Baltimore as of 12-7-77
220 Dave Concepcion 1.25 .50
221 John Candelaria .60 .24
222 Dave Lopes .60 .24
223 Tim Blackwell DP .30 .12
Now with Chicago Cubs as of 2-1-78
224 Chet Lemon .60 .24
225 Mike Schmidt 12.00 4.80
226 Cesar Cedeno .60 .24
227 Mike Willis .60 .24
228 Willie Randolph 1.25 .50
229 Doug Bair .25 .10
230 Rod Carew 4.00 1.60
231 Mike Flanagan .60 .24
232 Chris Speier .25 .10
233 Don Aase .60 .24
Now with California as of 12-8-77
234 Buddy Bell .60 .24
235 Mark Fidrych 2.50 1.00
236 Lou Brock RB 3.00 1.20
237 Sparky Lyle RB .60 .24
238 Willie McCovey RB 2.50 1.00
239 Brooks Robinson RB 2.50 1.00
240 Pete Rose RB 8.00 3.20
241 Nolan Ryan RB 15.00 6.00
242 Reggie Jackson RB 4.00 1.60

1979 O-Pee-Chee

This set is an abridgement of the 1979 Topps set. The 374 standard-size cards comprising the 1979 O-Pee-Chee set differ from the cards of the 1979 Topps set by having a higher ratio of cards of players from the two Canadian teams, a practice begun by O-Pee-Chee in 1977 and continued to 1988. The 1979 O-Pee-Chee set was the largest (374) original baseball card set issued (up to that time) by O-Pee-Chee. The fronts feature white-bordered color player photos. The player's name, position, and team appear in colored lettering within the lower white margin. The green and white horizontal backs carry the player's name, team and position at the top. Biography, major league statistics, career highlights in both French and English and a bilingual trivia question and answer also appear. The asterisked cards have an extra line on the front indicating team change. Double-printed (DP) cards are also noted below. The fronts have an O-Pee-Chee logo in the lower left corner comparable to the Topps logo on the 1979 American Set. The cards are sequenced in the same order as the Topps cards; the O-Pee-Chee cards are in effect a compressed version of the Topps set. The key card in this set is the Ozzie Smith Rookie Card.

NM Ex
COMPLETE SET (374) 175.00 70.00
COMMON CARD (1-374) .25 .10
COMMON DP (1-374) .10 .04
1 Lee May 1.00 .40
2 Dick Drago .25 .10
3 Paul Dade .25 .10
4 Ross Grimsley .25 .10
5 Joe Morgan DP 2.00 .80
6 Kevin Kobel .25 .10
7 Terry Forster .25 .10
8 Paul Molitor 15.00 6.00
9 Steve Carlton 3.00 1.20
10 Dave Goltz .25 .10
11 Dave Winfield 6.00 2.40
12 Dave Rozema .25 .10
13 Ed Figueroa .25 .10
14 Alan Ashby .50 .20
Trade with Blue Jays 11-28-78
15 Dale Murphy 4.00 1.60
16 Dennis Eckersley 2.00 .80
17 Ron Blomberg .25 .10
18 Wayne Twitchell .50 .20
Free Agent as of 3-1-79
19 Al Hrabosky .25 .10
20 Fred Norman .25 .10
21 Steve Garvey DP 1.00 .40
22 Willie Stargell 2.00 .80
23 John Hale .25 .10
24 Mickey Rivers .50 .20
25 Jack Brohamer .25 .10
26 Tom Underwood .25 .10
27 Mark Belanger .50 .20
28 Elliott Maddox .25 .10
29 John Candelaria .50 .20
30 Shane Rawley .25 .10
31 Steve Yeager .50 .20
32 Warren Cromartie 1.00 .40
33 Jason Thompson .50 .20
34 Roger Erickson .25 .10
35 Gary Matthews .50 .20
36 Pete Falcone .50 .20
Traded 12-5-78
37 Dick Tidrow .25 .10
38 Bob Boone 1.00 .40
39 Jim Bibby .25 .10
40 Len Barker .50 .20
Trade with Rangers 10-3-78
41 Robin Yount 6.00 2.40
42 Sam Mejias .50 .20
Traded 12-14-78
43 Ray Burris .25 .10
44 Tom Seaver DP 4.00 1.60
45 Roy Howell .25 .10
46 Jim Todd .50 .20
Free Agent 3-1-79
47 Frank Duffy .25 .10
48 Joel Youngblood .25 .10
49 Vida Blue .50 .20
50 Cliff Johnson .25 .10
51 Nolan Ryan 30.00 12.00
52 Ozzie Smith RC 80.00 32.00
53 Jim Sundberg .50 .20
54 Mike Paxton .25 .10
55 Lou Whitaker 6.00 2.40
56 Dan Schatzeder .25 .10
57 Rick Burleson .25 .10
58 Doug Bair .25 .10
59 Ted Martinez .25 .10
60 Bob Watson .50 .20
61 Jim Clancy .50 .20
62 Rowland Office .25 .10
63 Bobby Murcer .50 .20
64 Don Gullett .50 .20
65 Tom Paciorek .25 .10
66 Rick Rhoden .25 .10
67 Duane Kuiper .25 .10
68 Bruce Boisclair .25 .10
69 Manny Sarmiento .25 .10
70 Wayne Cage .25 .10
71 John Hiller .50 .20
72 Rick Cerone .25 .10
73 Dwight Evans 1.00 .40
74 Buddy Solomon .25 .10
75 Roy White .50 .20
76 Mike Flanagan 1.00 .40
77 Tom Johnson .25 .10
78 Glenn Burke .25 .10
79 Frank Taveras .25 .10
80 Don Sutton 2.00 .80
81 Leon Roberts .25 .10
82 George Hendrick 1.00 .40
83 Aurelio Rodriguez .25 .10
84 Ron Reed .25 .10
85 Alvis Woods .25 .10
86 Jim Beattie DP .10 .04
87 Larry Hisle .25 .10
88 Mike Garman .25 .10
89 Tim Johnson .25 .10
90 Paul Splittorff .25 .10
91 Darrel Chaney .25 .10
92 Mike Torrez .50 .20
93 Eric Soderholm .25 .10
94 Ron Cey .50 .20
95 Randy Jones .50 .20
96 Bill Madlock .50 .20
97 Steve Kemp DP .10 .04
98 Bob Apodaca .25 .10
99 Johnny Grubb .25 .10
100 Larry Milbourne .25 .10
101 Johnny Bench DP 5.00 2.00
102 Dave Lemanczyk .25 .10
103 Reggie Cleveland .25 .10
104 Larry Bowa .50 .20
105 Denny Martinez 2.00 .80
106 Bill Travers .25 .10
107 Willie McCovey 2.50 1.00
108 Wilbur Wood .25 .10
109 Dennis Leonard .50 .20
110 Roy Smalley .50 .20
111 Cesar Geronimo .25 .10
112 Jesse Jefferson .50 .20
113 Dave Revering .25 .10
114 Goose Gossage 1.00 .40
115 Steve Stone .50 .20
Free Agent 11-25-78
116 Doug Flynn .25 .10
117 Bob Forsch .25 .10
118 Paul Mitchell .25 .10
119 Toby Harrah .50 .20
Traded 12-8-78
120 Steve Rogers .50 .20
121 Checklist 1-125 DP .20 .05
122 Balor Moore .25 .10
123 Rick Reuschel .50 .20
124 Jeff Burroughs .50 .20
125 Willie Randolph .50 .20
126 Bob Stinson .25 .10
127 Rick Wise .25 .10
128 Luis Gomez .50 .20
129 Tommy John 2.00 .80
Signed as Free Agent 11-22-78
130 Richie Zisk .25 .10
131 Mario Guerrero .25 .10
132 Oscar Gamble .50 .20
Trade with Padres 10-25-78
133 Don Money .25 .10
134 Joe Rudi .50 .20
135 Woodie Fryman .25 .10
136 Butch Hobson .50 .20
137 Jim Colborn .25 .10
138 Tom Grieve .50 .20
Traded 12-5-78
139 Andy Messersmith .50 .20
Free Agent 2-7-79
140 Andre Thornton .50 .20
141 Ken Kravec .25 .10
142 Bobby Bonds 2.00 .80
Trade with Rangers 10-3-78
143 Jose Cruz 1.00 .40
144 Dave Lopes .50 .20
145 Jerry Garvin .25 .10
146 Pepe Frias .25 .10
147 Mitchell Page .25 .10
148 Ted Sizemore .50 .20
Traded 2-23-79
149 Rich Gale .25 .10
150 Steve Ontiveros .25 .10
151 Rod Carew 3.00 1.20
Traded 2-5-79
152 Lary Sorensen DP .10 .04
153 Willie Montanez .25 .10
154 Floyd Bannister .50 .20
Traded 12-8-78
155 Bert Blyleven 1.00 .40
156 Ralph Garr .50 .20
157 Thurman Munson 3.00 1.20
158 Bob Robertson .50 .20
Free Agent 3-1-79
159 Jon Matlack .25 .10
160 Carl Yastrzemski 5.00 2.00
161 Gaylord Perry 2.00 .80
162 Mike Tyson .25 .10
163 Cecil Cooper .50 .20
164 Pedro Borbon .25 .10
165 Art Howe DP .30 .12
166 Joe Coleman .50 .20
Free Agent 3-1-79
167 George Brett 20.00 8.00
168 Gary Alexander .25 .10
169 Chet Lemon .50 .20
170 Craig Swan .25 .10
171 Chris Chambliss .50 .20
172 John Montague .25 .10
173 Ron Jackson .50 .20
Traded 12-4-78
174 Jim Palmer 2.50 1.00
175 Willie Upshaw 1.00 .40
176 Tug McGraw .50 .20
177 Bill Buckner .50 .20
178 Doug Rau .25 .10
179 Andre Dawson 6.00 2.40
180 Jim Wright .25 .10
181 Garry Templeton .50 .20
182 Bill Bonham .25 .10
183 Lee Mazzilli .25 .10
184 Alan Trammell 8.00 3.20
185 Amos Otis .50 .20
186 Tom Dixon .25 .10
187 Mike Cubbage .25 .10
188 Sparky Lyle 1.00 .40
Traded 11-10-78
189 Juan Bernhardt .25 .10
190 Bump Wills 1.00 .40
(Texas Rangers)
191 Dave Kingman 1.00 .40
192 Lamar Johnson .25 .10
193 Lance Rautzhan .25 .10
194 Ed Herrmann .25 .10
195 Bill Campbell .25 .10
196 Gorman Thomas .50 .20
197 Paul Moskau .25 .10
198 Dale Murray .25 .10
199 John Mayberry .50 .20
200 Phil Garner .25 .10
201 Dan Ford .50 .20
Traded 12-4-78
202 Gary Thomasson .50 .20
Traded 2-15-79
203 Rollie Fingers 2.00 .80
204 Al Oliver .50 .20
205 Doug Ault .50 .20
206 Scott McGregor .50 .20
207 Dave Cash .25 .10
208 Bill Plummer .25 .10
209 Ivan DeJesus .25 .10
210 Jim Rice 1.00 .40
211 Ray Knight .50 .20
212 Paul Hartzell .50 .20
Traded 2-5-79
213 Tim Foli .25 .10
214 Butch Wynegar DP .10 .04
215 Darrell Evans 1.00 .40
216 Ken Griffey Sr. .50 .20
217 Doug DeCinces .50 .20
218 Ruppert Jones .25 .10
219 Bob Montgomery .25 .10
220 Rick Manning .25 .10
221 Chris Speier .25 .10
222 Bobby Valentine .50 .20
223 Dave Parker .50 .20
224 Larry Biittner .25 .10
225 Ken Clay .25 .10
226 Gene Tenace .50 .20
227 Frank White .50 .20
228 Rusty Staub 1.00 .40
229 Lee Lacy .25 .10
230 Doyle Alexander .25 .10
231 Bruce Bochte .25 .10
232 Steve Henderson .25 .10
233 Jim Lonborg .50 .20
234 Dave Concepcion 1.00 .40
235 Jerry Morales .50 .20
Traded 12-4-78
236 Len Randle .25 .10
237 Bill Lee DP .30 .12
Traded 12-7-78
238 Bruce Sutter .50 .20
239 Jim Essian .25 .10
240 Graig Nettles 1.00 .40
241 Otto Velez .25 .10
242 Checklist 126-250 DP .20 .05
243 Reggie Smith .50 .20
244 Stan Bahnsen DP .10 .04
245 Garry Maddox DP .20 .08
246 Joaquin Andujar .50 .20
247 Dan Driessen .25 .10
248 Bob Grich .50 .20
249 Fred Lynn .50 .20
250 Skip Lockwood .25 .10
251 Craig Reynolds .50 .20
Traded 12-5-78
252 Willie Horton .50 .20
253 Rick Waits .25 .10
254 Bucky Dent .50 .20
255 Bob Knepper .25 .10
256 Miguel Dilone .25 .10
257 Bob Owchinko .25 .10
258 Al Cowens .25 .10
259 Bob Bailor .25 .10
260 Larry Christenson .25 .10
261 Tony Perez 2.00 .80
262 Roy Hartsfield MG CL 2.00 .80
263 Glenn Abbott .25 .10
264 Ron Guidry .50 .20
265 Ed Kranepool .25 .10
266 Charlie Hough .50 .20
267 Ted Simmons 1.00 .40
268 Jack Clark .50 .20
269 Enos Cabell .25 .10
270 Gary Carter 2.00 .80
271 Sam Ewing .25 .10
272 Tom Burgmeier .25 .10
273 Freddie Patek .25 .10
274 Frank Tanana .50 .20
275 Leroy Stanton .25 .10
276 Ken Forsch .25 .10
277 Ellis Valentine .25 .10
278 Greg Luzinski .50 .20
279 Rick Bosetti .25 .10
280 John Stearns .25 .10
281 Enrique Romo .50 .20
Traded 12-5-78
282 Bob Bailey .25 .10
283 Sal Bando .50 .20
284 Matt Keough .25 .10
285 Biff Pocoroba .25 .10
286 Mike Lum .50 .20
Free Agent 3-1-79
287 Jay Johnstone .50 .20
288 John Montefusco .25 .10
289 Ed Ott .25 .10
290 Dusty Baker 1.00 .40
291 Rico Carty 1.00 .40

Waivers from A's 10-2-78
292 Nino Espinosa .25 .10
293 Rich Hebner .50 .20
294 Cesar Cedeno .50 .20
295 Darrell Porter .50 .20
296 Rod Gilbreath .25 .10
297 Jim Kern .50 .20
Trade with Indians 10-3-78
298 Claudell Washington .50 .20
299 Luis Tiant 1.00 .40
Signed as Free Agent 11-14-78
300 Mike Parrott .25 .10
301 Pete Broberg .50 .20
Free Agent 3-1-79
302 Greg Gross .50 .20
Traded 2-23-79
303 Darold Knowles .50 .20
Free Agent 2-12-79
304 Paul Blair .50 .20
305 Julio Cruz .25 .10
306 Hal McRae 1.00 .40
307 Ken Reitz .25 .10
308 Tom Murphy .25 .10
309 Terry Whitfield .25 .10
310 J.R. Richard .50 .20
311 Mike Hargrove 1.00 .40
Trade with Rangers 10-25-78
312 Rick Dempsey .50 .20
313 Phil Niekro 2.00 .80
314 Bob Stanley .25 .10
315 Jim Spencer .25 .10
316 George Foster .50 .20
317 Dave LaRoche .25 .10
318 Rudy May .25 .10
319 Jeff Newman .25 .10
320 Rick Monday DP .20 .08
321 Omar Moreno .25 .10
322 Dave McKay .50 .20
323 Mike Schmidt 8.00 3.20
324 Ken Singleton .50 .20
325 Jerry Remy .25 .10
326 Bert Campaneris .50 .20
327 Pat Zachry .25 .10
328 Larry Herndon .25 .10
329 Mark Fidrych 2.00 .80
330 Del Unser .25 .10
331 Gene Garber .50 .20
332 Bake McBride .50 .20
333 Jorge Orta .25 .10
334 Don Kirkwood .25 .10
335 Don Baylor 1.00 .40
336 Bill Robinson .50 .20
337 Manny Trillo .50 .20
Traded 2-23-79
338 Eddie Murray 25.00 10.00
339 Tom Hausman .25 .10
340 George Scott DP .20 .08
341 Rick Sweet .25 .10
342 Lou Piniella .50 .20
343 Pete Rose 12.00 4.80
Free Agent 12-5-79
344 Stan Papi .50 .20
Traded 12-7-78
345 Jerry Koosman 1.00 .40
Traded 12-8-78
346 Hosken Powell .25 .10
347 George Medich .25 .10
348 Ron LeFlore DP .20 .08
349 Dick Williams MG CL 2.00 .80
350 Lou Brock 2.50 1.00
351 Bill North .25 .10
352 Jim Hunter DP 1.00 .40
353 Checklist 251-374 DP .30 .07
354 Ed Halicki .25 .10
355 Tom Hutton .25 .10
356 Mike Caldwell .25 .10
357 Larry Parrish 1.00 .40
358 Geoff Zahn .25 .10
359 Derrel Thomas .50 .20
Signed as Free Agent 11-14-78
360 Carlton Fisk 3.00 1.20
361 John Henry Johnson .25 .10
362 Dave Chalk .25 .10
363 Dan Meyer DP .20 .08
364 Sixto Lezcano .25 .10
365 Rennie Stennett .25 .10
366 Mike Willis .50 .20
367 Buddy Bell DP .20 .08
Traded 12-8-78
368 Mickey Stanley .25 .10
369 Dave Rader .50 .20
Traded 2-23-79
370 Burt Hooton .50 .20
371 Keith Hernandez 1.00 .40
372 Bill Stein .25 .10
373 Hal Dues .25 .10
374 Reggie Jackson DP 5.00 2.00

1980 O-Pee-Chee

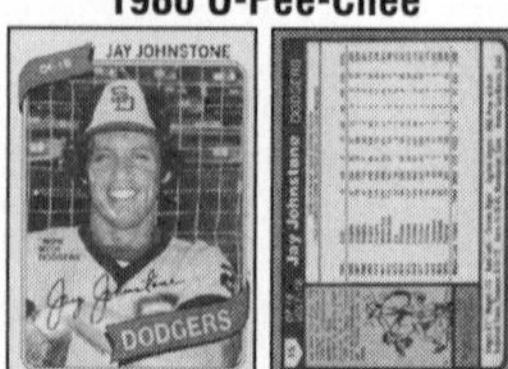

This set is an abridgement of the 1980 Topps set. The cards are printed on white stock rather than the gray stock used by Topps. The 374 standard-size cards also differ from their Topps counterparts by having a higher ratio of cards of players from the two Canadian teams, a practice begun by O-Pee-Chee in 1977 and continued to 1988. The fronts feature white-bordered color player photos framed by a colored line. The player's name appears in the white border at the top and also as a simulated autograph across the photo. The player's position appears within a colored banner at the upper left; his team name appears within a colored banner at the lower right. The blue and white horizontal backs carry the player's name, team and position at the top. Biography, major league statistics and career highlights in both French and English also appear. The cards are numbered on the back. The asterisked cards have an extra line, "Now with (new team name)" on the front indicating team change. Color changes, to correspond to the new team, are apparent on the pennant name and frame on the front. Double-printed (DP) cards are also noted below. The cards in this set were produced in lower quantities than other O-Pee-Chee sets of this era reportedly due to the company being on strike. The cards are sequenced in the same order as the Topps cards.

NM Ex
COMPLETE SET (374) 150.00 60.00
COMMON CARD (1-374) .25 .10
COMMON DP (1-374) .10 .04
1 Craig Swan .25 .10
2 Dennis Martinez 1.25 .50
3 Dave Cash .40 .16
Now With Padres
4 Bruce Sutter .75 .30
5 Ron Jackson .25 .10
6 Balor Moore .40 .16
7 Dan Ford .25 .10
8 Pat Putnam .25 .10
9 Derrel Thomas .25 .10
10 Jim Slaton .25 .10
11 Lee Mazzilli .40 .16
12 Del Unser .25 .10
13 Mark Wagner .25 .10
14 Vida Blue .75 .30
15 Jay Johnstone .40 .16
16 Julio Cruz DP .10 .04
17 Tony Scott .25 .10
18 Jeff Newman DP .10 .04
19 Luis Tiant .40 .16
20 Carlton Fisk 3.00 1.20
21 Dave Palmer .25 .10
22 Bombo Rivera .25 .10
23 Bill Fahey .25 .10
24 Frank White .75 .30
25 Rico Carty .40 .16
26 Bill Bonham DP .10 .04
27 Rick Miller .25 .10
28 J.R. Richard .40 .16
29 Joe Ferguson DP .10 .04
30 Bill Madlock .40 .16
31 Pete Vuckovich .25 .10
32 Doug Flynn .25 .10
33 Bucky Dent .40 .16
34 Mike Ivie .25 .10
35 Bob Stanley .25 .10
36 Al Bumbry .40 .16
37 Gary Carter 2.00 .80
38 John Milner DP .10 .04
39 Sid Monge .25 .10
40 Bill Russell .40 .16
41 John Stearns .25 .10
42 Dave Stieb 1.25 .50
43 Ruppert Jones .40 .16
Now with Yankees
44 Bob Owchinko .25 .10
45 Ron LeFlore .75 .30
Now with Expos
46 Ted Sizemore .25 .10
47 Ted Simmons .40 .16
48 Pepe Frias .40 .16
Now with Rangers
49 Ken Landreaux .25 .10
50 Manny Trillo .40 .16
51 Rick Dempsey .40 .16
52 Cecil Cooper .40 .16
53 Bill Lee .40 .16
54 Victor Cruz .25 .10
55 Johnny Bench 5.00 2.00
56 Rich Dauer .25 .10
57 Frank Tanana .40 .16
58 Francisco Barrios .25 .10
59 Bob Horner .40 .16
60 Fred Lynn DP .20 .08
61 Bob Knepper .25 .10
62 Sparky Lyle .40 .16
63 Larry Cox .25 .10
64 Dock Ellis .40 .16
Now with Pirates
65 Phil Garner .40 .16
66 Greg Luzinski .40 .16
67 Checklist 1-125 .75 .30
68 Dave Lemanczyk .25 .10
69 Tony Perez 1.25 .50
Now with Red Sox
70 Gary Thomasson .25 .10
71 Craig Reynolds .25 .10
72 Amos Otis .40 .16
73 Biff Pocoroba .25 .10
74 Matt Keough .25 .10
75 Bill Buckner .40 .16
76 John Castino .25 .10
77 Goose Gossage 1.25 .50
78 Gary Alexander .25 .10
79 Phil Huffman .25 .10
80 Bruce Bochte .25 .10
81 Darrell Evans .40 .16
82 Terry Puhl .40 .16
83 Jason Thompson .25 .10
84 Lary Sorensen .25 .10
85 Jerry Remy .25 .10
86 Tony Brizzolara .25 .10
87 Willie Wilson DP .20 .08
88 Eddie Murray 12.00 4.80
89 Larry Christenson .25 .10
90 Bob Randall .25 .10
91 Greg Pryor .25 .10
92 Glenn Abbott .25 .10
93 Jack Clark .40 .16
94 Rick Waits .25 .10
95 Luis Gomez .40 .16
Now with Braves
96 Burt Hooton .40 .16
97 John Henry Johnson .25 .10
98 Ray Knight .40 .16
99 Rick Reuschel .40 .16
100 Champ Summers .25 .10
101 Ron Davis .25 .10
102 Warren Cromartie .40 .16
103 Ken Reitz .25 .10
104 Hal McRae .40 .16
105 Alan Ashby .25 .10
106 Kevin Kobel .25 .10
107 Buddy Bell .40 .16
108 Dave Goltz .40 .16
Now with Dodgers
109 John Montefusco .25 .10
110 Lance Parrish .40 .16
111 Mike LaCoss .25 .10
112 Jim Rice .40 .16
113 Steve Carlton 3.00 1.20
114 Sixto Lezcano .25 .10
115 Ed Halicki .25 .10
116 Jose Morales .25 .10
117 Dave Concepcion .75 .30
118 Joe Cannon .25 .10
119 Willie Montanez .40 .16
Now with Padres
120 Lou Piniella .75 .30
121 Bill Stein .25 .10
122 Dave Winfield 5.00 2.00
123 Alan Trammell 2.00 .80
124 Andre Dawson 3.00 1.20
125 Marc Hill .25 .10
126 Don Aase .25 .10
127 Dave Kingman .75 .30
128 Checklist 126-250 .75 .30
129 Dennis Lamp .25 .10
130 Phil Niekro 2.00 .80
131 Tim Foli DP .10 .04
132 Jim Clancy .40 .16
133 Bill Atkinson .40 .16
Now with White Sox
134 Paul Dade DP .10 .04
135 Dusty Baker .40 .16
136 Al Oliver .75 .30
137 Dave Chalk .25 .10
138 Bill Robinson .25 .10
139 Robin Yount 6.00 2.40
140 Dan Schatzeder .40 .16
Now with Tigers
141 Mike Schmidt DP 5.00 2.00
142 Ralph Garr .40 .16
Now with Angels
143 Dale Murphy 2.00 .80
144 Jerry Koosman .40 .16
145 Tom Veryzer .25 .10
146 Rick Bosetti .25 .10
147 Jim Spencer .25 .10
148 Gaylord Perry 2.00 .80
Now with Rangers
149 Paul Blair .40 .16
150 Don Baylor .75 .30
151 Dave Rozema .25 .10
152 Steve Garvey 1.25 .50
153 Elias Sosa .25 .10
154 Larry Gura .25 .10
155 Tim Johnson .25 .10
156 Steve Henderson .25 .10
157 Ron Guidry .40 .16
158 Mike Edwards .25 .10
159 Butch Wynegar .25 .10
160 Randy Jones .25 .10
161 Denny Walling .25 .10
162 Mike Hargrove .40 .16
163 Dave Parker 1.25 .50
164 Roger Metzger .25 .10
165 Johnny Grubb .25 .10
166 Steve Kemp .25 .10
167 Bob Lacey .25 .10
168 Chris Speier .25 .10
169 Dennis Eckersley 1.25 .50
170 Keith Hernandez .40 .16
171 Claudell Washington .40 .16
172 Tom Underwood .40 .16
Now with Yankees
173 Dan Driessen .25 .10
174 Al Cowens .40 .16
Now with Angels
175 Rich Hebner .40 .16
Now with Tigers
176 Willie McCovey 2.00 .80
177 Carney Lansford .40 .16
178 Ken Singleton .40 .16
179 Jim Essian .40 .16
180 Mike Vail .25 .10
181 Randy Lerch .25 .10
182 Larry Parrish .75 .30
183 Checklist 251-374 .75 .30
184 George Hendrick .40 .16
185 Bob Davis .25 .10
186 Gary Matthews .40 .16
187 Lou Whitaker 2.00 .80
188 Darrell Porter DP .20 .08
189 Wayne Gross .25 .10
190 Bobby Murcer .40 .16
191 Willie Aikens .40 .16
Now with Royals
192 Jim Kern .25 .10
193 Cesar Cedeno .40 .16
194 Joel Youngblood .25 .10
195 Ross Grimsley .25 .10
196 Jerry Mumphrey .40 .16
Now with Padres
197 Kevin Bell .25 .10
198 Garry Maddox .40 .16
199 Dave Freisleben .25 .10
200 Ed Ott .25 .10
201 Enos Cabell .25 .10
202 Pete LaCock .25 .10
203 Fergie Jenkins 2.00 .80
204 Milt Wilcox .25 .10
205 Ozzie Smith 15.00 6.00
206 Ellis Valentine .40 .16
207 Dan Meyer .25 .10
208 Barry Foote .25 .10
209 George Foster .40 .16
210 Dwight Evans .40 .16
211 Paul Molitor 10.00 4.00
212 Tony Solaita .25 .10
213 Bill North .25 .10
214 Paul Splittorff .25 .10
215 Bobby Bonds 1.25 .50
Now with Cardinals
216 Butch Hobson .25 .10
217 Mark Belanger .40 .16
218 Grant Jackson .25 .10
219 Tom Hutton DP .10 .04
220 Pat Zachry .25 .10
221 Duane Kuiper .25 .10
222 Larry Hisle DP .10 .04
223 Mike Krukow .25 .10
224 Johnnie LeMaster .25 .10
225 Billy Almon .40 .16
Now with Expos
226 Joe Niekro .40 .16
227 Dave Revering .25 .10
228 Don Sutton 1.25 .50
229 John Hiller .40 .16
230 Alvis Woods .25 .10
231 Mark Fidrych 1.25 .50
232 Duffy Dyer .25 .10
233 Nino Espinosa .25 .10
234 Doug Bair .25 .10
235 George Brett 16.00 6.50
236 Mike Torrez .25 .10
237 Frank Taveras .25 .10
238 Bert Blyleven 1.25 .50
239 Willie Randolph .40 .16
240 Mike Sadek DP .10 .04
241 Jerry Royster .25 .10
242 John Denny .40 .16
Now with Indians
243 Rick Monday .25 .10
244 Jesse Jefferson .40 .16
245 Aurelio Rodriguez .40 .16
Now with Padres
246 Bob Boone .75 .30
247 Cesar Geronimo .25 .10
248 Bob Shirley .25 .10
249 Expos Checklist 1.25 .50
250 Bob Watson .75 .30
Now with Yankees
251 Mickey Rivers .40 .16
252 Mike Tyson DP .20 .08
Now with Cubs
253 Wayne Nordhagen .25 .10
254 Roy Howell .25 .10
255 Lee May .40 .16
256 Jerry Martin .25 .10
257 Bake McBride .25 .10
258 Silvio Martinez .25 .10
259 Jim Mason .25 .10
260 Tom Seaver 5.00 2.00
261 Rich Wortham DP .10 .04
262 Mike Cubbage .25 .10
263 Gene Garber .40 .16
264 Bert Campaneris .40 .16
265 Tom Buskey .25 .10
266 Leon Roberts .25 .10
267 Ron Cey .75 .30
268 Steve Ontiveros .25 .10
269 Mike Caldwell .25 .10
270 Nelson Norman .25 .10
271 Steve Rogers .40 .16
272 Jim Morrison .25 .10
273 Clint Hurdle .40 .16
274 Dale Murray .25 .10
275 Jim Barr .25 .10
276 Jim Sundberg DP .20 .08
277 Willie Horton .40 .16
278 Andre Thornton .40 .16
279 Bob Forsch .25 .10
280 Joe Strain .25 .10
281 Rudy May .40 .16
Now with Yankees
282 Pete Rose 12.00 4.80
283 Jeff Burroughs .40 .16
284 Rick Langford .25 .10
285 Ken Griffey Sr. .75 .30
286 Bill Nahorodny .40 .16
Now with Braves
287 Art Howe .40 .16
288 Ed Figueroa .25 .10
289 Joe Rudi .40 .16
290 Alfredo Griffin .40 .16
291 Dave Lopes .40 .16
292 Rick Manning .40 .16
293 Dennis Leonard .40 .16
294 Bud Harrelson .40 .16
295 Skip Lockwood .40 .16
Now with Red Sox
296 Roy Smalley .25 .10
297 Kent Tekulve .40 .16
298 Scot Thompson .40 .16
299 Ken Kravec .25 .10
300 Blue Jays Checklist 1.25 .50
301 Scott Sanderson .40 .16
302 Charlie Moore .25 .10
303 Nolan Ryan 25.00 10.00
Now with Astros
304 Bob Bailor .40 .16
305 Bob Stinson .25 .10
306 Al Hrabosky .40 .16
Now with Braves
307 Mitchell Page .25 .10
308 Garry Templeton .25 .10
309 Chet Lemon .40 .16
310 Jim Palmer 2.00 .80
311 Rick Cerone .40 .16
Now with Yankees
312 Jon Matlack .25 .10
313 Don Money .25 .10
314 Reggie Jackson 6.00 2.40
315 Brian Downing .25 .10
316 Woodie Fryman .25 .10
317 Alan Bannister .25 .10
318 Ron Reed .25 .10
319 Willie Stargell 2.00 .80
320 Jerry Garvin DP .10 .04
321 Cliff Johnson .40 .16
322 Doug DeCinces .40 .16
323 Gene Richards .25 .10
324 Joaquin Andujar .40 .16
325 Richie Zisk .25 .10
326 Bob Grich .40 .16
327 Gorman Thomas .40 .16
328 Chris Chambliss .75 .30
Now with Braves
329 Butch Edge .75 .30
Pat Kelly
Ted Wilborn
330 Larry Bowa .40 .16
331 Barry Bonnell .40 .16
Now with Blue Jays
332 John Candelaria .40 .16
333 Toby Harrah .40 .16
334 Larry Biittner .40 .16
335 Mike Flanagan .40 .16
336 Ed Kranepool .25 .10
337 Ken Forsch DP .10 .04
338 John Mayberry .40 .16
339 Rick Burleson .40 .16
340 Milt May .40 .16
Now with Giants
341 Roy White .40 .16
342 Joe Morgan 2.00 .80
343 Rollie Fingers 2.00 .80
344 Mario Mendoza .25 .10
345 Stan Bahnsen .25 .10
346 Tug McGraw .40 .16
347 Rusty Staub .40 .16
348 Tommy John .75 .30
349 Ivan DeJesus .25 .10
350 Reggie Smith .40 .16
351 Tony Bernazard RC 1.25 .50
Randy Miller
John Tamargo
352 Floyd Bannister .25 .10
353 Rod Carew DP 1.50 .60
354 Otto Velez .25 .10
355 Gene Tenace .40 .16
356 Freddie Patek .40 .16
Now with Angels
357 Elliott Maddox .25 .10
358 Pat Underwood .25 .10
359 Graig Nettles .75 .30
360 Rodney Scott .25 .10
361 Terry Whitfield .25 .10
362 Fred Norman .40 .16
Now with Expos
363 Sal Bando .40 .16
364 Greg Gross .25 .10
365 Carl Yastrzemski DP 2.00 .80
366 Paul Hartzell .25 .10
367 Jose Cruz .40 .16
368 Shane Rawley .25 .10
369 Jerry White .25 .10
370 Rick Wise .40 .16
Now with Padres
371 Steve Yeager .75 .30
372 Omar Moreno .25 .10
373 Bump Wills .25 .10
374 Craig Kusick .40 .16
Now with Padres

1981 O-Pee-Chee

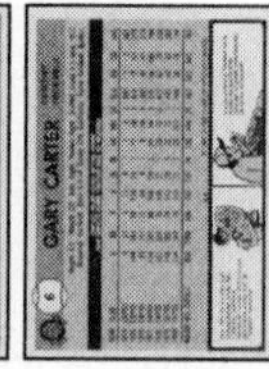

This set is an abridgement of the 1981 Topps set. The 374 standard-size cards comprising the 1981 O-Pee-Chee set differ from the cards of the 1981 Topps set by having a higher ratio of cards of players from the two Canadian teams, a practice begun by O-Pee-Chee in 1977 and continued to 1988. The fronts feature white-bordered color player photos framed by a colored line that is wider at the bottom. The player's name appears in that wider colored area. The player's position and team appear within a colored baseball cap icon at the lower left. The red and white horizontal backs carry the player's name and position at the top. Biography, major league statistics, and career highlights in both French and English also appear. In cases where a player changed teams or was traded before press time, a small line of print on the obverse makes note of the change. Double-printed (DP) cards are also noted below. The card backs are typically found printed on white card stock. There is, however, a "variation" set printed on gray card stock; gray backs are worth 50 percent more than corresponding white backs listed below. Notable Rookie Cards include Harold Baines, Kirk Gibson and Tim Raines.

Nm-Mt Ex-Mt
COMPLETE SET (374) 50.00 20.00
COMMON CARD (1-374) .10 .04
COMMON DP (1-374) .05 .02
1 Frank Pastore .10 .04
2 Phil Huffman .10 .04
3 Len Barker .10 .04
4 Robin Yount 2.00 .80
5 Dave Stieb .25 .10
6 Gary Carter .75 .30
7 Butch Hobson .10 .04
Now with Angels
8 Lance Parrish .25 .10
9 Bruce Sutter .25 .10
Now with Cardinals
10 Mike Flanagan .25 .10
11 Paul Mirabella .10 .04
12 Craig Reynolds .10 .04
13 Joe Charboneau .50 .20
14 Dan Driessen .10 .04
15 Larry Parrish .10 .04
16 Ron Davis .10 .04
17 Cliff Johnson .10 .04
Now with Athletics
18 Bruce Bochte .10 .04
19 Jim Clancy .10 .04
20 Bill Russell .10 .04
21 Ron Oester .10 .04
22 Danny Darwin .10 .04
23 Willie Aikens .10 .04
24 Don Stanhouse .10 .04
25 Sixto Lezcano .10 .04
Now with Cardinals
26 U.L. Washington .10 .04
27 Champ Summers DP .05 .02
28 Enrique Romo .10 .04
29 Gene Tenace .25 .10
30 Jack Clark .25 .10
31 Checklist 1-125 DP .05 .02
32 Ken Oberkfell .10 .04
33 Rick Honeycutt .10 .04
Now with Rangers
34 Al Bumbry .10 .04
35 John Tamargo DP .05 .02
36 Ed Farmer .10 .04
37 Gary Roenicke .10 .04
38 Tim Foli DP .10 .04
39 Eddie Murray 6.00 2.40
40 Roy Howell .10 .04

Now with Brewers
41 Bill Gullickson .50 .20
42 Jerry White DP .05 .02
43 Tim Blackwell .10 .04
44 Steve Henderson .10 .04
45 Enos Cabell .10 .04
Now with Giants
46 Rick Bosetti .10 .04
47 Bill North .10 .04
48 Rich Gossage .50 .20
49 Bob Shirley .10 .04
Now with Cardinals
50 Dave Lopes .25 .10
51 Shane Rawley .10 .04
52 Lloyd Moseby .25 .10
53 Burt Hooton .10 .04
54 Ivan DeJesus .10 .04
55 Mike Norris .10 .04
56 Del Unser .10 .04
57 Dave Revering .10 .04
58 Joel Youngblood .10 .04
59 Steve McCatty .10 .04
60 Willie Randolph .25 .10
61 Butch Wynegar .10 .04
62 Gary Lavelle .10 .04
63 Willie Montanez .10 .04
64 Terry Puhl .10 .04
65 Scott McGregor .10 .04
66 Buddy Bell .25 .10
67 Toby Harrah .25 .10
68 Jim Rice .25 .10
69 Darrell Evans .25 .10
70 Al Oliver DP .20 .08
71 Hal Dues .10 .04
72 Barry Evans DP .05 .02
73 Doug Bair .10 .04
74 Mike Hargrove .25 .10
75 Reggie Smith .25 .10
76 Mario Mendoza .10 .04
Now with Rangers
77 Mike Barlow .10 .04
78 Garth Iorg .10 .04
79 Jeff Reardon RC 1.50 .60
80 Roger Erickson .10 .04
81 Dave Stapleton .10 .04
82 Barry Bonnell .10 .04
83 Dave Concepcion .25 .10
84 Johnnie LeMaster .10 .04
85 Mike Caldwell .10 .04
86 Wayne Gross .10 .04
87 Rick Camp .10 .04
88 Joe Lefebvre .10 .04
89 Darrell Jackson .10 .04
90 Bake McBride .10 .04
91 Tim Stoddard DP .05 .02
92 Mike Easler .10 .04
93 Jim Bibby .10 .04
94 Kent Tekulve .25 .10
95 Jim Sundberg .25 .10
96 Tommy John .50 .20
97 Chris Speier .10 .04
98 Clint Hurdle .25 .10
99 Phil Garner .10 .04
100 Rod Carew 1.50 .60
101 Steve Stone .10 .04
102 Joe Niekro .10 .04
103 Jerry Martin .10 .04
Now with Giants
104 Ron LeFlore DP .10 .04
Now with White Sox
105 Jose Cruz .25 .10
106 Don Money .10 .04
107 Bobby Brown .10 .04
108 Larry Herndon .10 .04
109 Dennis Eckersley .75 .30
110 Carl Yastrzemski 1.50 .60
111 Greg Minton .10 .04
112 Dan Schatzeder .10 .04
113 George Brett 8.00 3.20
114 Tom Underwood .10 .04
115 Roy Smalley .10 .04
116 Carlton Fisk 2.00 .80
Now with White Sox
117 Pete Falcone .10 .04
118 Dale Murphy 1.50 .60
119 Tippy Martinez .10 .04
120 Larry Bowa .25 .10
121 Julio Cruz .10 .04
122 Jim Gantner .25 .10
123 Al Cowens .10 .04
124 Jerry Garvin .10 .04
125 Andre Dawson 2.00 .80
126 Charlie Leibrandt RC .50 .20
127 Willie Stargell .75 .30
128 Andre Thornton .25 .10
129 Art Howe .25 .10
130 Larry Gura .10 .04
131 Jerry Remy .10 .04
132 Rick Dempsey .25 .10
133 Alan Trammell DP .75 .30
134 Mike LaCoss .10 .04
135 Gorman Thomas .10 .04
136 Tim Raines RC 6.00 2.40
Roberto Ramos
Bobby Pate
137 Bill Madlock .25 .10
138 Rich Dotson DP .10 .04
139 Oscar Gamble .10 .04
140 Bob Forsch .10 .04
141 Miguel Dilone .10 .04
142 Jackson Todd .10 .04
143 Dan Meyer .10 .04
144 Garry Templeton .10 .04
145 Mickey Rivers .25 .10
146 Alan Ashby .10 .04
147 Dale Berra .10 .04
148 Randy Jones .10 .04
Now with Mets
149 Joe Nolan .10 .04
150 Mark Fidrych .50 .20
151 Tony Armas .10 .04
152 Steve Kemp .10 .04
153 Jerry Reuss .25 .10
154 Rick Langford .10 .04
155 Chris Chambliss .25 .10
156 Bob McClure .10 .04
157 John Wathan .10 .04
158 John Curtis .10 .04
159 Steve Howe .25 .10
160 Garry Maddox .10 .04
161 Dan Graham .10 .04
162 Doug Corbett .10 .04
163 Rob Dressler .10 .04
164 Bucky Dent .25 .10
165 Alvis Woods .10 .04
166 Floyd Bannister .10 .04
167 Lee Mazzilli .10 .04
168 Don Robinson DP .05 .02
169 John Mayberry .10 .04
170 Woodie Fryman .10 .04
171 Gene Richards .10 .04
172 Rick Burleson .10 .04
Now with Angels
173 Bump Wills .10 .04
174 Glenn Abbott .10 .04
175 Dave Collins .10 .04
176 Mike Krukow .10 .04
177 Rick Monday .25 .10
178 Dave Parker .50 .20
179 Rudy May .10 .04
180 Pete Rose 3.00 1.20
181 Elias Sosa .10 .04
182 Bob Grich .25 .10
183 Fred Norman .10 .04
184 Jim Dwyer .10 .04
Now with Orioles
185 Dennis Leonard .10 .04
186 Gary Matthews .10 .04
187 Ron Hassey DP .05 .02
188 Doug DeCinces .25 .10
189 Craig Swan .10 .04
190 Cesar Cedeno .25 .10
191 Rick Sutcliffe .25 .10
192 Kiko Garcia .10 .04
193 Pete Vuckovich .10 .04
Now with Brewers
194 Tony Bernazard .10 .04
Now with White Sox
195 Keith Hernandez .25 .10
196 Jerry Mumphrey .10 .04
197 Jim Kern .10 .04
198 Jerry Dybzinski .10 .04
199 John Lowenstein .10 .04
200 George Foster .25 .10
201 Phil Niekro .75 .30
202 Bill Buckner .25 .10
203 Steve Carlton 1.50 .60
204 John D'Acquisto .10 .04
Now with Angels
205 Rick Reuschel .25 .10
206 Dan Quisenberry .25 .10
207 Mike Schmidt DP 2.00 .80
208 Bob Watson .25 .10
209 Jim Spencer .10 .04
210 Jim Palmer .75 .30
211 Derrel Thomas .10 .04
212 Steve Nicosia .10 .04
213 Omar Moreno .10 .04
214 Richie Zisk .10 .04
Now with Mariners
215 Larry Hisle .10 .04
216 Mike Torrez .10 .04
217 Rich Hebner .10 .04
218 Britt Burns RC .25 .10
219 Ken Landreaux .10 .04
220 Tom Seaver 2.00 .80
221 Bob Davis .10 .04
Now with Angels
222 Jorge Orta .10 .04
223 Bobby Bonds .25 .10
224 Pat Zachry .10 .04
225 Ruppert Jones .10 .04
226 Duane Kuiper .10 .04
227 Rodney Scott .10 .04
228 Tom Paciorek .25 .10
229 Rollie Fingers .75 .30
Now with Brewers
230 George Hendrick .10 .04
231 Tony Perez .75 .30
232 Grant Jackson .10 .04
233 Damaso Garcia .10 .04
234 Lou Whitaker 1.25 .50
235 Scott Sanderson .10 .04
236 Mike Ivie .10 .04
237 Charlie Moore .10 .04
238 Luis Leal .10 .04
Brian Milner
Ken Schrom
239 Rick Miller DP .05 .02
Now with Red Sox
240 Nolan Ryan 10.00 4.00
241 Checklist 126-250 DP .05 .02
242 Chet Lemon .10 .04
243 Dave Palmer .10 .04
244 Ellis Valentine .10 .04
245 Carney Lansford .25 .10
Now with Red Sox
246 Ed Ott DP .05 .02
247 Glenn Hubbard DP .05 .02
248 Joey McLaughlin .10 .04
249 Jerry Narron .10 .04
250 Ron Guidry .25 .10
251 Steve Garvey .50 .20
252 Victor Cruz .10 .04
253 Bobby Murcer .25 .10
254 Ozzie Smith 8.00 3.20
255 John Stearns .10 .04
256 Bill Campbell .10 .04
257 Rennie Stennett .10 .04
258 Rick Waits .10 .04
259 Gary Lucas .10 .04
260 Ron Cey .25 .10
261 Rickey Henderson 12.00 4.80
262 Sammy Stewart .10 .04
263 Brian Downing .10 .04
264 Mark Bomback .10 .04
265 John Candelaria .25 .10
266 Renie Martin .10 .04
267 Stan Bahnsen .10 .04
268 Montreal Expos CL .50 .20
269 Ken Forsch .10 .04
270 Greg Luzinski .25 .10
271 Ron Jackson .10 .04
272 Wayne Garland .10 .04
273 Milt May .10 .04
274 Rick Wise .10 .04
275 Dwight Evans .50 .20
276 Sal Bando .25 .10
277 Alfredo Griffin .25 .10
278 Rick Sofield .10 .04
279 Bob Knepper .10 .04
Now with Astros
280 Ken Griffey .25 .10
281 Ken Singleton .25 .10
282 Ernie Whitt .25 .10
283 Billy Sample .10 .04
284 Jack Morris .75 .30
285 Dick Ruthven .10 .04
286 Johnny Bench 2.00 .80
287 Dave Smith .25 .10
288 Amos Otis .25 .10
289 Dave Goltz .10 .04
290 Bob Boone DP .20 .08
291 Aurelio Lopez .10 .04
292 Tom Hume .10 .04
293 Charlie Lea .10 .04
294 Bert Blyleven .50 .20
Now with Indians
295 Hal McRae .25 .10
296 Bob Stanley .10 .04
297 Bob Bailor .10 .04
Now with Mets
298 Jerry Koosman .25 .10
299 Elliott Maddox .10 .04
Now with Yankees
300 Paul Molitor 5.00 2.00
301 Matt Keough .10 .04
302 Pat Putnam .10 .04
303 Dan Ford .10 .04
304 John Castino .10 .04
305 Barry Foote .10 .04
306 Lou Piniella .25 .10
307 Gene Garber .10 .04
308 Rick Manning .10 .04
309 Don Baylor .50 .20
310 Vida Blue DP .20 .08
311 Doug Flynn .10 .04
312 Rick Rhoden .10 .04
313 Fred Lynn .25 .10
Now with Angels
314 Rich Dauer .10 .04
315 Kirk Gibson RC 5.00 2.00
316 Ken Reitz .10 .04
Now with Cubs
317 Lonnie Smith .25 .10
318 Steve Yeager .10 .04
319 Rowland Office .10 .04
320 Tom Burgmeier .10 .04
321 Leon Durham RC .25 .10
Now with Cubs
322 Neil Allen .10 .04
323 Ray Burris .10 .04
Now with Expos
324 Mike Willis .10 .04
325 Ray Knight .25 .10
326 Rafael Landestoy .10 .04
327 Moose Haas .10 .04
328 Ross Baumgarten .10 .04
329 Joaquin Andujar .25 .10
330 Frank White .25 .10
331 Toronto Blue Jays CL .25 .10
332 Dick Drago .10 .04
333 Sid Monge .10 .04
334 Joe Sambito .10 .04
335 Rick Cerone .10 .04
336 Eddie Whitson .10 .04
337 Sparky Lyle .25 .10
338 Checklist 251-374 .25 .10
339 Jon Matlack .10 .04
340 Ben Oglivie .10 .04
341 Dwayne Murphy .10 .04
342 Terry Crowley .10 .04
343 Frank Taveras .10 .04
344 Steve Rogers .10 .04
345 Warren Cromartie .10 .04
346 Bill Caudill .10 .04
347 Harold Baines RC 10.00 4.00
348 Frank LaCorte .10 .04
349 Glenn Hoffman .10 .04
350 J.R. Richard .10 .04
351 Otto Velez .10 .04
352 Ted Simmons .25 .10
Now with Brewers
353 Terry Kennedy .10 .04
Now with Padres
354 Al Hrabosky .10 .04
355 Bob Horner .25 .10
356 Cecil Cooper .25 .10
357 Bob Welch .25 .10
358 Paul Moskau .10 .04
359 Dave Rader .10 .04
Now with Angels
360 Willie Wilson .25 .10
361 Dave Kingman DP .25 .10
362 Joe Rudi .10 .04
Now with Red Sox
363 Rich Gale .10 .04
364 Steve Trout .10 .04
365 Graig Nettles DP .30 .12
366 Lamar Johnson .25 .10
367 Denny Martinez .75 .30
368 Manny Trillo .10 .04
369 Frank Tanana .25 .10
Now with White Sox
370 Reggie Jackson 2.00 .80
371 Bill Lee .25 .10
372 Jay Johnstone .25 .10
373 Jason Thompson .10 .04
374 Tom Hutton .10 .04

1981 O-Pee-Chee Posters

The 24 full-color posters comprising the 1981 O-Pee-Chee poster insert set were inserted one per regular wax pack and feature players of the Montreal Expos (numbered 1-12) and the Toronto Blue Jays (numbered 13-24). These posters are typically found with two folds and measure approximately 4 7/8" by 6 7/8". The posters are blank-backed and are numbered at the bottom in French and English. A distinctive red (Expos) or blue (Blue Jays) border surrounds the player photo.

Nm-Mt Ex-Mt
COMPLETE SET (24) 8.00 3.20
1 Willie Montanez .25 .10
2 Rodney Scott .25 .10
3 Chris Speier .25 .10
4 Larry Parrish .50 .20
5 Warren Cromartie .50 .20
6 Andre Dawson 2.00 .80
7 Ellis Valentine .25 .10
8 Gary Carter 1.50 .60
9 Steve Rogers .25 .10
10 Woodie Fryman .25 .10
11 Jerry White .25 .10
12 Scott Sanderson .25 .10
13 John Mayberry .50 .20
14 Damaso Garcia UER .25 .10
(Misspelled Damasa)
15 Alfredo Griffin .25 .10
16 Garth Iorg .25 .10
17 Alvis Woods .25 .10
18 Rick Bosetti .25 .10
19 Barry Bonnell .25 .10
20 Ernie Whitt .25 .10
21 Jim Clancy .25 .10
22 Dave Stieb .75 .30
23 Otto Velez .25 .10
24 Lloyd Moseby .50 .20

1982 O-Pee-Chee

This set is an abridgement of the 1982 Topps set. The 396 standard-size cards comprising the 1982 O-Pee-Chee set differ from the cards of the 1982 Topps set by having a higher ratio of cards of players from the two Canadian teams, a practice begun by O-Pee-Chee in 1977 and continued to 1988. The set contains virtually the same pictures for the players also featured in the 1982 Topps issue, but the O-Pee-Chee photos appear brighter. The fronts feature white-bordered color player photos with colored lines within the wide white margin on the left. The player's name, team and bilingual position appear in colored lettering within the wide bottom margin. The player's name also appears as a simulated autograph across the photo. The blue print on green horizontal backs carry the player's name, bilingual position and biography at the top. The player's major league statistics follow below. The cards are numbered on the back. The asterisked cards have an extra line on the front inside the picture area indicating team change. In Action (IA) and All-Star (AS) cards are indicated in the checklist below; these are included in the set in addition to the player's regular card. The 396 cards in the set were the largest "original" or distinct set total printed up to that time by O-Pee-Chee; the previous high had been 374 in 1979, 1980 and 1981.

Nm-Mt Ex-Mt
COMPLETE SET (396) 45.00 18.00
1 Dan Spillner .10 .04
2 Ken Singleton AS .10 .04
3 John Candelaria .10 .04
4 Frank Tanana .25 .10
Traded to Royals Jan. 15/82
5 Reggie Smith .25 .10
6 Rick Monday .10 .04
7 Scott Sanderson .10 .04
8 Rich Dauer .10 .04
9 Ron Guidry .25 .10
10 Ron Guidry IA .10 .04
11 Tom Brookens .10 .04
12 Moose Haas .10 .04
13 Chet Lemon .25 .10
Traded to Tigers Nov. 27/81
14 Steve Howe .10 .04
15 Ellis Valentine .10 .04
16 Toby Harrah .25 .10
17 Darrell Evans .25 .10
18 Johnny Bench 2.00 .80
19 Ernie Whitt .25 .10
20 Garry Maddox .10 .04
21 Graig Nettles IA .25 .10
22 Al Oliver IA .25 .10
23 Bob Boone .25 .10
Traded to Angels Dec. 9/81
24 Pete Rose IA 1.50 .60
25 Jerry Remy .10 .04
26 Jorge Orta .25 .10
Traded to Dodgers Dec 9/81
27 Bobby Bonds .25 .10
28 Jim Clancy .10 .04
29 Dwayne Murphy .10 .04
30 Tom Seaver 2.00 .80
31 Tom Seaver IA 1.00 .40
32 Claudell Washington .10 .04
33 Bob Shirley .10 .04
34 Bob Forsch .10 .04
35 Willie Aikens .10 .04
36 Rod Carew AS .75 .30
37 Willie Randolph .25 .10
38 Charlie Lea .10 .04
39 Lou Whitaker .75 .30
40 Dave Parker .25 .10
41 Dave Parker IA .25 .10
42 Mark Belanger .25 .10
Traded to Dodgers Dec. 24/81
43 Rick Langford .10 .04
44 Rollie Fingers IA .50 .20
45 Rick Cerone .10 .04
46 Johnny Wockenfuss .10 .04
47 Jack Morris AS .25 .10
48 Cesar Cedeno .10 .04
Traded to Reds Dec. 18/81
49 Alvis Woods .10 .04
50 Buddy Bell .25 .10
51 Mickey Rivers IA .10 .04
52 Steve Rogers .10 .04
53 John Mayberry .25 .10
Dave Stieb TL CL
54 Ron Hassey .10 .04
55 Rick Burleson .10 .04
56 Harold Baines .50 .20
57 Craig Reynolds .10 .04
58 Carlton Fisk AS .75 .30
59 Jim Kern .10 .04
Traded to Reds Feb. 10/82
60 Tony Armas .10 .04
61 Warren Cromartie .10 .04
62 Graig Nettles .25 .10
63 Jerry Koosman .25 .10
64 Pat Zachry .10 .04
65 Terry Kennedy .10 .04
66 Richie Zisk .10 .04
67 Rich Gale .25 .10
Traded to Giants Dec. 10/81
68 Steve Carlton 1.50 .60
69 Greg Luzinski IA .25 .10
70 Tim Raines 2.00 .80
71 Roy Lee Jackson .10 .04
72 Carl Yastrzemski 1.50 .60
73 John Castino .10 .04
74 Joe Niekro .25 .10
75 Tommy John .50 .20
76 Dave Winfield AS .75 .30
77 Miguel Dilone .10 .04
78 Gary Gray .10 .04
79 Tom Hume .10 .04
80 Jim Palmer 1.25 .50
81 Jim Palmer IA .75 .30
82 Vida Blue IA .25 .10
83 Garth Iorg .10 .04
84 Rennie Stennett .10 .04
85 Dave Lopes IA .25 .10
Traded to A's Feb. 8/82
86 Dave Concepcion .25 .10
87 Matt Keough .10 .04
88 Jim Spencer .10 .04
89 Steve Henderson .10 .04
90 Nolan Ryan 10.00 4.00
91 Carney Lansford .25 .10
92 Bake McBride .10 .04
93 Dave Stapleton .10 .04
94 Warren Cromartie .25 .10
Bill Gullickson TL CL
95 Ozzie Smith 10.00 4.00
Traded to Cardinals Feb. 11/82
96 Rich Hebner .10 .04
97 Tim Foli .10 .04
Traded to Angels Dec. 11/82
98 Darrell Porter .10 .04
99 Barry Bonnell .10 .04
100 Mike Schmidt 3.00 1.20
101 Mike Schmidt IA 1.50 .60
102 Dan Briggs .10 .04
103 Al Cowens .10 .04
104 Grant Jackson .25 .10
Traded to Royals Jan. 19/82
105 Kirk Gibson .75 .30
106 Dan Schatzeder .25 .10
Traded to Giants Dec. 9/81
107 Juan Berenguer .10 .04
108 Jack Morris .50 .20
109 Dave Revering .10 .04
110 Carlton Fisk 1.50 .60
111 Carlton Fisk IA .75 .30
112 Billy Sample .10 .04
113 Steve McCatty .10 .04
114 Ken Landreaux .10 .04
115 Gaylord Perry .75 .30
116 Elias Sosa .10 .04
117 Rich Gossage IA .25 .10
118 Terry Francona RC .75 .30
Brad Mills
Bryn Smith
119 Billy Almon .10 .04
120 Gary Lucas .10 .04
121 Ken Oberkfell .10 .04
122 Steve Carlton IA .75 .30
123 Jeff Reardon .50 .20
124 Bill Buckner .25 .10
125 Danny Ainge 1.50 .60
Voluntarily Retired Nov. 30/81
126 Paul Splittorff .10 .04
127 Lonnie Smith .10 .04
Traded to Cardinals Nov. 19/81
128 Rudy May .10 .04
129 Checklist 1-132 .10 .04
130 Julio Cruz .10 .04
131 Stan Bahnsen .10 .04
132 Pete Vuckovich .10 .04
133 Luis Salazar .10 .04
134 Dan Ford .25 .10
Traded to Orioles Jan. 28/82
135 Denny Martinez .75 .30
136 Lary Sorensen .10 .04
137 Fergie Jenkins .75 .30
Traded to Cubs Dec. 15/81
138 Rick Camp .10 .04
139 Wayne Nordhagen .10 .04
140 Ron LeFlore .25 .10
141 Rick Sutcliffe .25 .10
142 Rick Waits .10 .04
143 Mookie Wilson .75 .30
144 Greg Minton .10 .04
145 Bob Horner .25 .10
146 Joe Morgan IA .75 .30
147 Larry Gura .10 .04
148 Alfredo Griffin .10 .04
149 Pat Putnam .10 .04
150 Ted Simmons .25 .10
151 Gary Matthews .25 .10
152 Greg Luzinski .25 .10
153 Mike Flanagan .25 .10
154 Jim Morrison .10 .04
155 Otto Velez .10 .04
156 Frank White .25 .10
157 Doug Corbett .10 .04
158 Brian Downing .10 .04
159 Willie Randolph IA .25 .10
160 Luis Tiant .25 .10

161 Andre Thornton .10 .04
162 Amos Otis .25 .10
163 Paul Mirabella .10 .04
164 Bert Blyleven .50 .20
165 Rowland Office .10 .04
166 Gene Tenace .25 .10
167 Cecil Cooper .25 .10
168 Bruce Benedict .10 .04
169 Mark Clear .10 .04
170 Jim Bibby .10 .04
171 Ken Griffey IA .25 .10
Traded to Yankees Nov 4/81
172 Bill Gullickson .10 .04
173 Mike Scioscia .10 .04
174 Doug DeCinces .25 .10
Traded to Angels Jan 28/82
175 Jerry Mumphrey .10 .04
176 Rollie Fingers .75 .30
177 George Foster IA .25 .10
Traded to Mets Feb 10/82
178 Mitchell Page .10 .04
179 Steve Garvey .75 .30
180 Steve Garvey IA .25 .10
181 Woodie Fryman .10 .04
182 Larry Herndon .10 .04
Traded to Tigers Dec. 9/81
183 Frank White IA .25 .10
184 Alan Ashby .10 .04
185 Phil Niekro .75 .30
186 Leon Roberts .10 .04
187 Rod Carew 1.50 .60
188 Willie Stargell IA .75 .30
189 Joel Youngblood .10 .04
190 J.R. Richard .10 .04
191 Tim Wallach .75 .30
192 Broderick Perkins .10 .04
193 Johnny Grubb .10 .04
194 Larry Bowa .25 .10
Traded to Cubs Jan. 27/82
195 Paul Molitor 3.00 1.20
196 Willie Upshaw .10 .04
197 Roy Smalley .10 .04
198 Chris Speier .10 .04
199 Don Aase .10 .04
200 George Brett 6.00 2.40
201 George Brett IA 3.00 1.20
202 Rick Manning .10 .04
203 Jesse Barfield RC .75 .30
Brian Milner
Boomer Wells
204 Rick Reuschel .25 .10
205 Neil Allen .10 .04
206 Leon Durham .10 .04
207 Jim Gantner .25 .10
208 Joe Morgan .75 .30
209 Gary Lavelle .10 .04
210 Keith Hernandez .25 .10
211 Joe Charboneau .10 .04
212 Mario Mendoza .10 .04
213 Willie Randolph AS .25 .10
214 Lance Parrish .50 .20
215 Mike Krukow .10 .04
Traded to Phillies Dec. 8/81
216 Ron Cey .25 .10
217 Ruppert Jones .10 .04
218 Dave Lopes .25 .10
Traded to A's Feb. 8/82
219 Steve Yeager .10 .04
220 Manny Trillo .10 .04
221 Dave Concepcion IA .25 .10
222 Butch Wynegar .10 .04
223 Lloyd Moseby .10 .04
224 Bruce Bochte .10 .04
225 Ed Ott .10 .04
226 Checklist 133-264 .10 .04
227 Ray Burris .10 .04
228 Reggie Smith IA .25 .10
229 Oscar Gamble .10 .04
230 Willie Wilson .10 .04
231 Brian Kingman .10 .04
232 John Stearns .10 .04
233 Duane Kuiper .10 .04
Traded to Giants Nov. 16/81
234 Don Baylor .25 .10
235 Mike Easler .10 .04
236 Lou Piniella .25 .10
237 Robin Yount 1.50 .60
238 Kevin Saucier .10 .04
239 Jon Matlack .10 .04
240 Bucky Dent .25 .10
241 Bucky Dent IA .10 .04
242 Milt May .10 .04
243 Lee Mazzilli .25 .10
244 Gary Carter .75 .30
245 Ken Reitz .10 .04
246 Scott McGregor AS .10 .04
247 Pedro Guerrero .25 .10
248 Art Howe .25 .10
249 Dick Tidrow .10 .04
250 Tug McGraw .25 .10
251 Fred Lynn .25 .10
252 Fred Lynn IA .10 .04
253 Gene Richards .10 .04
254 George Bell RC .10 .04
255 Tony Perez .75 .30
256 Tony Perez IA .50 .20
257 Rich Dotson .10 .04
258 Bo Diaz .10 .04
Traded to Phillies Nov. 19/81
259 Rodney Scott .10 .04
260 Bruce Sutter .25 .10
261 George Brett AS 3.00 1.20
262 Rick Dempsey .25 .10
263 Mike Phillips .10 .04
264 Jerry Garvin .10 .04
265 Al Bumbry .10 .04
266 Hubie Brooks .10 .04
267 Vida Blue .25 .10
268 Rickey Henderson 5.00 2.00
269 Rick Peters .10 .04
270 Rusty Staub .25 .10
271 Sixto Lezcano .10 .04
Traded to Padres Dec. 10/81
272 Bump Wills .10 .04
273 Gary Allenson .10 .04
274 Randy Jones .10 .04
275 Bob Watson .25 .10
276 Dave Kingman .25 .10
277 Terry Puhl .10 .04
278 Jerry Reuss .25 .10
279 Sammy Stewart .10 .04
280 Ben Oglivie .10 .04
281 Kent Tekulve .25 .10
282 Ken Macha .25 .10
283 Ron Davis .10 .04
284 Bob Grich .25 .10
285 Sparky Lyle .25 .10
286 Rich Gossage AS .25 .10
287 Dennis Eckersley .75 .30
288 Garry Templeton .10 .04
Traded to Padres Dec. 10/81
289 Bob Stanley .10 .04
290 Ken Singleton .10 .04
291 Mickey Hatcher .10 .04
292 Dave Palmer .10 .04
293 Damaso Garcia .10 .04
294 Don Money .10 .04
295 George Hendrick .10 .04
296 Steve Kemp .10 .04
Traded to White Sox Nov. 27/81
297 Dave Smith .10 .04
298 Bucky Dent AS .10 .04
299 Steve Trout .10 .04
300 Reggie Jackson 3.00 1.20
Traded to Angels Jan. 26/82
301 Reggie Jackson IA 1.50 .60
Traded to Angels Jan. 26/82
302 Doug Flynn .25 .10
Traded to Rangers Dec. 14/81
303 Wayne Gross .10 .04
304 Johnny Bench IA .75 .30
305 Don Sutton .75 .30
306 Don Sutton IA .75 .30
307 Mark Bomback .10 .04
308 Charlie Moore .10 .04
309 Jeff Burroughs .10 .04
310 Mike Hargrove .25 .10
311 Enos Cabell .10 .04
312 Lenny Randle .10 .04
313 Ivan DeJesus .10 .04
Traded to Phillies Jan. 27/82
314 Buck Martinez .10 .04
315 Burt Hooton .10 .04
316 Scott McGregor .10 .04
317 Dick Ruthven .10 .04
318 Mike Heath .10 .04
319 Ray Knight .25 .10
Traded to Astros Dec. 18/81
320 Chris Chambliss .10 .04
321 Chris Chambliss IA .10 .04
322 Ross Baumgarten .10 .04
323 Bill Lee .25 .10
324 Gorman Thomas .10 .04
325 Jose Cruz .25 .10
326 Al Oliver .25 .10
327 Jackson Todd .10 .04
328 Ed Farmer .10 .04
Traded to Phillies Jan. 28/82
329 U.L. Washington .10 .04
330 Ken Griffey .25 .10
Traded to Yankees Nov. 4/81
331 John Milner .10 .04
332 Don Robinson .10 .04
333 Cliff Johnson .10 .04
334 Fernando Valenzuela .75 .30
335 Jim Sundberg .25 .10
336 George Foster .25 .10
Traded to Mets Feb. 10/82
337 Pete Rose AS 1.50 .60
338 Dave Lopes AS .25 .10
Traded to A's Feb. 8/82
339 Mike Schmidt AS 1.50 .60
340 Dave Concepcion AS .10 .04
341 Andre Dawson AS .75 .30
342 George Foster AS .25 .10
Traded to Mets Feb. 10/82
343 Dave Parker AS .25 .10
344 Gary Carter AS .25 .10
345 Fernando Valenzuela AS .50 .20
346 Tom Seaver AS .75 .30
347 Bruce Sutter AS .25 .10
348 Darrell Porter IA .10 .04
349 Dave Collins .10 .04
Traded to Yankees Dec. 23/81
350 Amos Otis IA .10 .04
351 Frank Taveras .10 .04
Traded to Expos Dec. 14/81
352 Dave Winfield 1.50 .60
353 Larry Parrish .10 .04
354 Roberto Ramos .10 .04
355 Dwight Evans .25 .10
356 Mickey Rivers .10 .04
357 Butch Hobson .10 .04
358 Carl Yastrzemski IA .75 .30
359 Ron Jackson .10 .04
360 Len Barker .10 .04
361 Pete Rose 3.00 1.20
362 Kevin Hickey RC .10 .04
363 Rod Carew IA .75 .30
364 Hector Cruz .10 .04
365 Bill Madlock .25 .10
366 Jim Rice .25 .10
367 Ron Cey IA .25 .10
368 Luis Leal .10 .04
369 Dennis Leonard .10 .04
370 Mike Norris .10 .04
371 Tom Paciorek .10 .04
Traded to White Sox Dec. 11/81
372 Willie Stargell .75 .30
373 Dan Driessen .10 .04
374 Larry Bowa IA .25 .10
Traded to Cubs Jan. 27/82
375 Dusty Baker .25 .10
376 Joey McLaughlin .10 .04
377 Reggie Jackson AS 1.50 .60
Traded to Angels Jan. 26/82
378 Mike Caldwell .10 .04
379 Andre Dawson 1.50 .60
380 Dave Stieb .25 .10
381 Alan Trammell .75 .30
382 John Mayberry .10 .04
383 John Wathan .10 .04
384 Hal McRae .25 .10
385 Ken Forsch .10 .04
386 Jerry White .10 .04
387 Tom Veryzer .10 .04
Traded to Mets Jan. 8/82
388 Joe Rudi .10 .04
Traded to A's Dec. 4/81
389 Bob Knepper .10 .04
390 Eddie Murray 4.00 1.60
391 Dale Murphy .75 .30
392 Bob Boone IA .25 .10
Traded to Angels Dec. 6/81
393 Al Hrabosky .10 .04
394 Checklist 265-396 .10 .04
395 Omar Moreno .10 .04
396 Rich Gossage .75 .30

1982 O-Pee-Chee Posters

These 24 full-color posters comprising the 1982 O-Pee-Chee poster insert set were inserted one per regular wax pack and feature players of the Montreal Expos (numbered 13-24) and the Toronto Blue Jays (numbered 1-12). These posters are typically found with two folds and measure approximately 4 7/8" by 6 7/8". The posters are blank-backed and are numbered at the bottom in French and English. A distinctive red (Blue Jays) or blue (Expos) border surrounds the player photo.

Nm-Mt Ex-Mt
COMPLETE SET (24) 8.00 3.20
1 John Mayberry .50 .20
2 Damaso Garcia .25 .10
3 Ernie Whitt .25 .10
4 Lloyd Moseby .25 .10
5 Alvis Woods .25 .10
6 Dave Stieb .75 .30
7 Roy Lee Jackson .25 .10
8 Joey McLaughlin .25 .10
9 Luis Leal .25 .10
10 Aurelio Rodriguez .25 .10
11 Otto Velez .25 .10
12 Juan Berenguer UER .25 .10
(Misspelled Berenger)
13 Warren Cromartie .25 .10
14 Rodney Scott .25 .10
15 Larry Parrish .50 .20
16 Gary Carter 1.50 .60
17 Tim Raines 1.00 .40
18 Andre Dawson 2.00 .80
19 Terry Francona .75 .30
20 Steve Rogers .25 .10
21 Bill Gullickson .25 .10
22 Scott Sanderson .25 .10
23 Jeff Reardon 1.00 .40
24 Jerry White .25 .10

1983 O-Pee-Chee

This set is an abridgement of the 1983 Topps set. The 396 standard-size cards comprising the 1983 O-Pee-Chee set differ from the cards of the 1983 Topps set by having a higher ratio of cards of players from the two Canadian teams, a practice begun by O-Pee-Chee in 1977 and continued to 1988. The set contains virtually the same pictures for the players also featured in the 1983 Topps issue. The fronts feature white-bordered color player action photos framed by a colored line. A circular color player head shot also appears on the front at the lower right. The player's name, team and bilingual position appear at the lower left. The pink and white horizontal backs carry the player's name and biography at the top. The player's major league statistics and bilingual career highlights follow below. The asterisked cards have an extra line on the front inside the picture area indicating team change. The O-Pee-Chee logo appears on the front of every card. Super Veteran (SV) and All-Star (AS) cards are indicated in the checklist below; these are included in the set in addition to the player's regular card. The set features Rookie Cards of Tony Gwynn and Ryne Sandberg.

Nm-Mt Ex-Mt
COMPLETE SET (396) 60.00 24.00
1 Rusty Staub .20 .08
2 Larry Parrish .10 .04
3 George Brett 4.00 1.60
4 Carl Yastrzemski 1.25 .50
5 Al Oliver SV .20 .08
6 Bill Virdon MG .10 .04
7 Gene Richards .10 .04
8 Steve Balboni .10 .04
9 Joey McLaughlin .10 .04
10 Gorman Thomas .10 .04
11 Chris Chambliss .20 .08
12 Ray Burris .10 .04
13 Larry Herndon .10 .04
14 Ozzie Smith 2.50 1.00
15 Ron Cey .20 .08
Now with Cubs
16 Willie Wilson .20 .08
17 Kent Tekulve .10 .04
18 Kent Tekulve SV .10 .04
19 Oscar Gamble .10 .04
20 Carlton Fisk 1.00 .40
21 Dale Murphy AS .50 .20
22 Randy Lerch .10 .04
23 Dale Murphy .50 .20
24 Steve Mura .20 .08
Now with White Sox
25 Hal McRae .20 .08
26 Dennis Lamp .10 .04
27 Ron Washington .10 .04
28 Bruce Bochte .10 .04
29 Randy Jones .20 .08
Now with Pirates
30 Jim Rice .20 .08
31 Bill Gullickson .20 .08
32 Dave Concepcion AS .20 .08
33 Ted Simmons SV .20 .08
34 Bobby Cox MG .10 .04
35 Rollie Fingers .50 .20
36 Rollie Fingers SV .30 .12
37 Mike Hargrove .20 .08
38 Roy Smalley .10 .04
39 Terry Puhl .10 .04
40 Fernando Valenzuela .50 .20
41 Garry Maddox .10 .04
42 Dale Murray .20 .08
Now with Yankees
43 Bob Dernier .10 .04
44 Don Robinson .10 .04
45 John Mayberry .10 .04
46 Richard Dotson .10 .04
47 Wayne Nordhagen .10 .04
Now with Cubs
48 Lary Sorensen .10 .04
49 Willie McGee RC 3.00 1.20
50 Bob Horner .10 .04
51 Rusty Staub SV .20 .08
52 Tom Seaver 2.50 1.00
Now with Mets
53 Chet Lemon .10 .04
54 Scott Sanderson .10 .04
55 Mookie Wilson .20 .08
56 Reggie Jackson 1.50 .60
57 Tim Blackwell .10 .04
58 Keith Moreland .10 .04
59 Alvis Woods .20 .08
Now with Athletics
60 Johnny Bench 1.50 .60
61 Johnny Bench SV .75 .30
62 Jim Gott .10 .04
63 Rick Monday .10 .04
64 Gary Matthews .20 .08
65 Jack Morris .20 .08
66 Lou Whitaker .50 .20
67 U.L. Washington .10 .04
68 Eric Show .10 .04
69 Lee Lacy .10 .04
70 Steve Carlton 1.00 .40
71 Steve Carlton SV .75 .30
72 Tom Paciorek .10 .04
73 Manny Trillo .20 .08
Now with Indians
74 Tony Perez SV .30 .12
75 Amos Otis .20 .08
76 Rick Mahler .10 .04
77 Hosken Powell .10 .04
78 Bill Caudill .10 .04
79 Dan Petry .10 .04
80 George Foster .20 .08
81 Joe Morgan .50 .20
Now with Phillies
82 Burt Hooton .10 .04
83 Ryne Sandberg RC 12.00 4.80
84 Alan Ashby .10 .04
85 Ken Singleton .20 .08
86 Tom Hume .10 .04
87 Dennis Leonard .10 .04
88 Jim Gantner .20 .08
89 Leon Roberts .20 .08
Now with Royals
90 Jerry Reuss .20 .08
91 Ben Oglivie .10 .04
92 Sparky Lyle SV .20 .08
93 John Castino .10 .04
94 Phil Niekro .50 .20
95 Alan Trammell .50 .20
96 Gaylord Perry .50 .20
97 Tom Herr .10 .04
98 Vance Law .10 .04
99 Dickie Noles .10 .04
100 Pete Rose 2.50 1.00
101 Pete Rose SV 1.25 .50
102 Dave Concepcion .20 .08
103 Darrell Porter .10 .04
104 Ron Guidry .20 .08
105 Don Baylor .20 .08
Now with Yankees
106 Steve Rogers AS .10 .04
107 Greg Minton .10 .04
108 Glenn Hoffman .10 .04
109 Luis Leal .10 .04
110 Ken Griffey .20 .08
111 Al Oliver .20 .08
Steve Rogers TL CL
112 Luis Pujols .10 .04
113 Julio Cruz .10 .04
114 Jim Slaton .10 .04
115 Chili Davis .50 .20
116 Pedro Guerrero .20 .08
117 Mike Ivie .10 .04
118 Chris Welsh .10 .04
119 Frank Pastore .10 .04
120 Len Barker .10 .04
121 Chris Speier .10 .04
122 Bobby Murcer .20 .08
123 Bill Russell .10 .04
124 Lloyd Moseby .10 .04
125 Leon Durham .10 .04
126 Carl Yastrzemski SV .50 .20
127 John Candelaria .10 .04
128 Phil Garner .10 .04
129 Checklist 1-132 .10 .04
130 Dave Stieb .10 .04
131 Geoff Zahn .10 .04
132 Todd Cruz .10 .04
133 Tony Pena .20 .08
134 Hubie Brooks .10 .04
135 Dwight Evans .20 .08
136 Willie Aikens .10 .04
137 Woodie Fryman .10 .04
138 Rick Dempsey .20 .08
139 Bruce Berenyi .10 .04
140 Willie Randolph .20 .08
141 Eddie Murray 2.50 1.00
142 Mike Caldwell .10 .04
143 Tony Gwynn RC 30.00 12.00
144 Tommy John SV .50 .20
145 Don Sutton .50 .20
146 Don Sutton SV .30 .12
147 Rick Manning .10 .04
148 George Hendrick .10 .04
149 Johnny Ray .10 .04
150 Bruce Sutter .20 .08
151 Bruce Sutter SV .20 .08
152 Jay Johnstone .20 .08
153 Jerry Koosman .20 .08
154 Johnnie LeMaster .10 .04
155 Dan Quisenberry .20 .08
156 Luis Salazar .10 .04
157 Steve Bedrosian .20 .08
158 Jim Sundberg .10 .04
159 Gaylord Perry SV .30 .12
160 Dave Kingman .30 .12
161 Dave Kingman SV .10 .04
162 Mark Clear .10 .04
163 Cal Ripken 10.00 4.00
164 Dave Palmer .10 .04
165 Dan Driessen .10 .04
166 Tug McGraw .30 .12
167 Dennis Martinez .20 .08
168 Juan Eichelberger .20 .08
Now with Indians
169 Doug Flynn .10 .04
170 Steve Howe .10 .04
171 Frank White .20 .08
172 Mike Flanagan .20 .08
173 Andre Dawson AS .30 .12
174 Manny Trillo AS .20 .08
Now with Indians
175 Bo Diaz .10 .04
176 Dave Righetti .20 .08
177 Harold Baines .50 .20
178 Vida Blue .20 .08
179 Luis Tiant SV .20 .08
180 Rickey Henderson 2.50 1.00
181 Rick Rhoden .10 .04
182 Fred Lynn .20 .08
183 Ed VandeBerg .10 .04
184 Dwayne Murphy .10 .04
185 Tim Lollar .10 .04
186 Dave Tobik .10 .04
187 Tug McGraw SV .20 .08
188 Rick Miller .10 .04
189 Dan Schatzeder .10 .04
190 Cecil Cooper .20 .08
191 Jim Beattie .10 .04
192 Rich Dauer .10 .04
193 Al Cowens .10 .04
194 Roy Lee Jackson .10 .04
195 Mike Gates .10 .04
196 Tommy John .50 .20
197 Bob Forsch .10 .04
198 Steve Garvey .50 .20
Now with Padres
199 Brad Mills .10 .04
200 Rod Carew 1.00 .40
201 Rod Carew SV .50 .20
202 Dave Stieb .20 .08
Damaso Garcia TL CL
203 Floyd Bannister .20 .08
Now with White Sox
204 Bruce Benedict .10 .04
205 Dave Parker .20 .08
206 Ken Oberkfell .10 .04
207 Graig Nettles SV .20 .08
208 Sparky Lyle .20 .08
209 Jason Thompson .10 .04
210 Jack Clark .20 .08
211 Jim Kaat .20 .08
212 John Stearns .10 .04
213 Tom Burgmeier .10 .04
214 Jerry White .10 .04
215 Mario Soto .10 .04
216 Scott McGregor .10 .04
217 Tim Stoddard .10 .04
218 Bill Laskey .10 .04
219 Reggie Jackson SV .50 .20
220 Dusty Baker .20 .08
221 Joe Niekro .20 .08
222 Damaso Garcia .10 .04
223 John Montefusco .10 .04
224 Mickey Rivers .10 .04
225 Enos Cabell .10 .04
226 LaMarr Hoyt .10 .04
227 Tim Raines .50 .20
228 Joaquin Andujar .10 .04
229 Tim Wallach .20 .08
230 Fergie Jenkins .50 .20
231 Fergie Jenkins SV .30 .12
232 Tom Brunansky .20 .08
233 Ivan DeJesus .10 .04
234 Bryn Smith .10 .04
235 Claudell Washington .10 .04
236 Steve Renko .10 .04
237 Dan Norman .10 .04
238 Cesar Cedeno .20 .08
239 Dave Stapleton .10 .04
240 Rich Gossage .50 .20
241 Rich Gossage SV .30 .12
242 Bob Stanley .10 .04
243 Rich Gale .20 .08
Now with Reds
244 Sixto Lezcano .10 .04
245 Steve Sax .20 .08
246 Jerry Mumphrey .10 .04
247 Dave Smith .10 .04
248 Bake McBride .10 .04
249 Checklist 133-264 .10 .04
250 Bill Buckner .20 .08
251 Kent Hrbek .50 .20
252 Gene Tenace .10 .04
Now with Pirates
253 Charlie Lea .10 .04
254 Rick Cerone .10 .04
255 Gene Garber .10 .04
256 Gene Garber SV .10 .04
257 Jesse Barfield .20 .08
258 Dave Winfield 1.00 .40
259 Don Money .10 .04
260 Steve Kemp .10 .04
Now with Yankees
261 Steve Yeager .10 .04
262 Keith Hernandez .20 .08
263 Tippy Martinez .10 .04
264 Joe Morgan SV .50 .20
Now with Phillies
265 Joel Youngblood .10 .04
Now with Giants
266 Bruce Sutter AS .20 .08
267 Terry Francona .20 .08
268 Neil Allen .10 .04

269 Ron Oester .10 .04
270 Dennis Eckersley .50 .20
271 Dale Berra .10 .04
272 Al Bumbry .10 .04
273 Lonnie Smith .10 .04
274 Terry Kennedy .10 .04
275 Ray Knight .10 .04
276 Mike Norris .10 .04
277 Rance Mulliniks .10 .04
278 Dan Spillner .10 .04
279 Bucky Dent .20 .08
280 Bert Blyleven .50 .20
281 Barry Bonnell .10 .04
282 Reggie Smith .20 .08
283 Reggie Smith SV .20 .08
284 Ted Simmons .20 .08
285 Lance Parrish .20 .08
286 Larry Christenson .10 .04
287 Ruppert Jones .10 .04
288 Bob Welch .20 .08
289 John Wathan .10 .04
290 Jeff Reardon .20 .08
291 Dave Revering .10 .04
292 Craig Swan .10 .04
293 Graig Nettles .20 .08
294 Alfredo Griffin .10 .04
295 Jerry Remy .10 .04
296 Joe Sambito .10 .04
297 Ron LeFlore .10 .04
298 Brian Downing .10 .04
299 Jim Palmer .50 .20
300 Mike Schmidt 2.00 .80
301 Mike Schmidt SV 1.00 .40
302 Ernie Whitt .10 .04
303 Andre Dawson .50 .20
304 Bobby Murcer SV .20 .08
305 Larry Bowa .20 .08
306 Lee Mazzilli .10 .04
Now with Pirates
307 Lou Piniella .20 .08
308 Buck Martinez .20 .08
309 Jerry Martin .10 .04
310 Greg Luzinski .20 .08
311 Al Oliver .20 .08
312 Mike Torrez .10 .04
Now with Mets
313 Dick Ruthven .10 .04
314 Gary Carter AS .20 .08
315 Rick Burleson .10 .04
316 Phil Niekro SV .30 .12
317 Moose Haas .10 .04
318 Carney Lansford .20 .08
Now with Athletics
319 Tim Foli .10 .04
320 Steve Rogers .10 .04
321 Kirk Gibson .50 .20
322 Glenn Hubbard .10 .04
323 Luis DeLeon .10 .04
324 Mike Marshall .10 .04
325 Von Hayes .10 .04
Now with Phillies
326 Garth Iorg .10 .04
327 Jose Cruz .20 .08
328 Jim Palmer SV .30 .12
329 Darrell Evans .20 .08
330 Buddy Bell .20 .08
331 Mike Krukow .10 .04
Now with Giants
332 Omar Moreno .10 .04
Now with Astros
333 Dave LaRoche .10 .04
334 Dave LaRoche SV .10 .04
335 Bill Madlock .20 .08
336 Garry Templeton .10 .04
337 John Lowenstein .10 .04
338 Willie Upshaw .10 .04
339 Dave Hostetler RC .10 .04
340 Larry Gura .10 .04
341 Doug DeCinces .20 .08
342 Mike Schmidt AS 1.00 .40
343 Charlie Hough .20 .08
344 Andre Thornton .10 .04
345 Jim Clancy .10 .04
346 Ken Forsch .10 .04
347 Sammy Stewart .10 .04
348 Alan Bannister .10 .04
349 Checklist 265-396 .10 .04
350 Robin Yount 1.00 .40
351 Warren Cromartie .10 .04
352 Tim Raines AS .50 .20
353 Tony Armas .10 .04
Now with Red Sox
354 Tom Seaver SV 1.25 .50
Now with Mets
355 Tony Perez .50 .20
Now with Phillies
356 Toby Harrah .10 .04
357 Dan Ford .10 .04
358 Charlie Puleo .10 .04
Now with Reds
359 Dave Collins .10 .04
Now with Blue Jays
360 Nolan Ryan 8.00 3.20
361 Nolan Ryan SV 4.00 1.60
362 Bill Almon .10 .04
Now with Athletics
363 Eddie Milner .10 .04
364 Gary Lucas .10 .04
365 Dave Lopes .20 .08
366 Bob Boone .20 .08
367 Biff Pocoroba .10 .04
368 Richie Zisk .10 .04
369 Tony Bernazard .10 .04
370 Gary Carter .50 .20
371 Paul Molitor 1.25 .50
372 Art Howe .20 .08
373 Pete Rose AS 1.25 .50
374 Glenn Adams .10 .04
375 Pete Vuckovich .10 .04
376 Gary Lavelle .10 .04
377 Lee May .20 .08
378 Lee May SV .20 .08
379 Butch Wynegar .10 .04
380 Ron Davis .10 .04
381 Bob Grich .20 .08
382 Gary Roenicke .10 .04
383 Jim Kaat SV .20 .08
384 Steve Carlton AS .50 .20
385 Mike Easler .10 .04
386 Rod Carew AS .50 .20
387 Bob Grich AS .20 .08
388 George Brett AS 2.00 .80
389 Robin Yount AS .50 .20
390 Reggie Jackson AS .50 .20
391 Rickey Henderson AS .50 .20
392 Fred Lynn AS .20 .08
393 Carlton Fisk AS .50 .20
394 Pete Vuckovich AS .10 .04
395 Larry Gura AS .10 .04
396 Dan Quisenberry AS .10 .04

1984 O-Pee-Chee

This set is an abridgement of the 1984 Topps set. The 396 standard-size cards comprising the 1984 O-Pee-Chee set differ from the cards of the 1984 Topps set by having a higher ratio of cards of players from the two Canadian teams, a practice begun by O-Pee-Chee in 1977 and continued to 1988. The set contains virtually the same pictures for the players also featured in the 1984 Topps issue. The fronts feature white-bordered color player action photos. A color player head shot also appears on the front at the lower left. The player's name and position appear in colored lettering within the white margin at the lower right. His team name appears in vertical colored lettering within the white margin on the left. The red, white and blue horizontal backs carry the player's name and biography at the top. The player's major league statistics and bilingual career highlights follow below. The asterisked cards have an extra line on the front inside the picture area indicating team change. The O-Pee-Chee logo appears on the front of every card. All-Star (AS) cards are indicated in the checklist below; they are included in the set in addition to the player's regular card. Notable Rookie Cards include Don Mattingly and Darryl Strawberry.

Nm-Mt Ex-Mt
COMPLETE SET (396) 35.00 14.00
1 Pascual Perez .05 .02
2 Cal Ripken AS 3.00 1.20
3 Lloyd Moseby AS .05 .02
4 Mel Hall .05 .02
5 Willie Wilson .05 .02
6 Mike Morgan .05 .02
7 Gary Lucas .10 .04
Now with Expos
8 Don Mattingly RC 10.00 4.00
9 Jim Gott .05 .02
10 Robin Yount .50 .20
11 Joey McLaughlin .05 .02
12 Billy Sample .05 .02
13 Oscar Gamble .05 .02
14 Bill Russell .05 .02
15 Burt Hooton .05 .02
16 Omar Moreno .05 .02
17 Dave Lopes .10 .04
18 Dale Berra .05 .02
19 Rance Mulliniks .05 .02
20 Greg Luzinski .10 .04
21 Doug Sisk .05 .02
22 Don Robinson .05 .02
23 Keith Moreland .05 .02
24 Richard Dotson .05 .02
25 Glenn Hubbard .05 .02
26 Rod Carew 1.00 .40
27 Alan Wiggins .05 .02
28 Frank Viola .50 .20
29 Phil Niekro 1.00 .40
Now with Yankees
30 Wade Boggs 3.00 1.20
31 Dave Parker .25 .10
Now with Reds
32 Bobby Ramos .05 .02
33 Tom Burgmeier .05 .02
34 Eddie Milner .05 .02
35 Don Sutton .50 .20
36 Glenn Wilson .05 .02
37 Mike Krukow .05 .02
38 Dave Collins .05 .02
39 Garth Iorg .05 .02
40 Dusty Baker .25 .10
41 Tony Bernazard .10 .04
Now with Indians
42 Claudell Washington .05 .02
43 Cecil Cooper .10 .04
44 Dan Driessen .05 .02
45 Jerry Mumphrey .05 .02
46 Rick Rhoden .05 .02
47 Rudy Law .05 .02
48 Julio Franco .50 .20
49 Mike Norris .05 .02
50 Chris Chambliss .05 .02
51 Pete Falcone .05 .02
52 Mike Marshall .05 .02
53 Amos Otis .10 .04
Now with Pirates
54 Jesse Orosco .10 .04
55 Dave Concepcion .10 .04
56 Gary Allenson .05 .02
57 Dan Schatzeder .05 .02
58 Jerry Remy .05 .02
59 Carney Lansford .10 .04
60 Paul Molitor 1.00 .40
61 Chris Codiroli .05 .02
62 Dave Hostetler .05 .02
63 Ed VandeBerg .05 .02
64 Ryne Sandberg 4.00 1.60
65 Kirk Gibson .50 .20
66 Nolan Ryan 6.00 2.40
67 Gary Ward .05 .02
Now with Rangers
68 Luis Salazar .05 .02
69 Dan Quisenberry AS .05 .02
70 Gary Matthews .05 .02
71 Pete O'Brien .10 .04
72 John Wathan .05 .02
73 Jody Davis .05 .02
74 Kent Tekulve .05 .02
75 Bob Forsch .05 .02
76 Alfredo Griffin .05 .02
77 Bryn Smith .05 .02
78 Mike Torrez .05 .02
79 Mike Hargrove .10 .04
80 Steve Rogers .05 .02
81 Bake McBride .05 .02
82 Doug DeCinces .05 .02
83 Richie Zisk .05 .02
84 Randy Bush .05 .02
85 Atlee Hammaker .05 .02
86 Chet Lemon .05 .02
87 Frank Pastore .05 .02
88 Alan Trammell .50 .20
89 Terry Francona .10 .04
90 Pedro Guerrero .10 .04
91 Dan Spillner .05 .02
92 Lloyd Moseby .05 .02
93 Bob Knepper .05 .02
94 Ted Simmons AS .10 .04
95 Aurelio Lopez .05 .02
96 Bill Buckner .10 .04
97 LaMarr Hoyt .05 .02
98 Tom Brunansky .10 .04
99 Ron Oester .05 .02
100 Reggie Jackson 1.25 .50
101 Ron Davis .05 .02
102 Ken Oberkfell .05 .02
103 Dwayne Murphy .05 .02
104 Jim Slaton .05 .02
Now with Angels
105 Tony Armas .05 .02
106 Ernie Whitt .10 .04
107 Johnnie LeMaster .05 .02
108 Randy Moffitt .05 .02
109 Terry Forster .05 .02
110 Ron Guidry .10 .04
111 Bill Virdon MG .05 .02
112 Doyle Alexander .05 .02
113 Lonnie Smith .05 .02
114 Checklist 1-132 .05 .02
115 Andre Thornton .05 .02
116 Jeff Reardon .10 .04
117 Tom Herr .10 .04
118 Charlie Hough .10 .04
119 Phil Garner .05 .02
120 Keith Hernandez .25 .10
121 Rich Gossage .50 .20
Now with Padres
122 Ted Simmons .10 .04
123 Butch Wynegar .05 .02
124 Damaso Garcia .05 .02
125 Britt Burns .05 .02
126 Bert Blyleven .10 .04
127 Carlton Fisk .50 .20
128 Rick Manning .05 .02
129 Bill Laskey .05 .02
130 Ozzie Smith 2.00 .80
131 Bo Diaz .05 .02
132 Tom Paciorek .05 .02
133 Dave Rozema .05 .02
134 Dave Stieb .05 .02
135 Brian Downing .05 .02
136 Rick Camp .05 .02
137 Willie Aikens .10 .04
Now with Blue Jays
138 Charlie Moore .05 .02
139 George Frazier .10 .04
Now with Indians
140 Storm Davis .05 .02
141 Glenn Hoffman .05 .02
142 Charlie Lea .05 .02
143 Mike Vail .05 .02
144 Steve Sax .10 .04
145 Gary Lavelle .05 .02
146 Gorman Thomas .10 .04
Now with Mariners
147 Dan Petry .05 .02
148 Mark Clear .05 .02
149 Dave Beard .10 .04
Now with Mariners
150 Dale Murphy .50 .20
151 Steve Trout .05 .02
152 Tony Pena .10 .04
153 Geoff Zahn .05 .02
154 Dave Henderson .05 .02
155 Frank White .10 .04
156 Dick Ruthven .05 .02
157 Gary Gaetti .25 .10
158 Lance Parrish .10 .04
159 Joe Price .05 .02
160 Mario Soto .05 .02
161 Tug McGraw .25 .10
162 Bob Ojeda .05 .02
163 George Hendrick .05 .02
164 Scott Sanderson .05 .02
Now with Cubs
165 Ken Singleton .05 .02
166 Terry Kennedy .05 .02
167 Gene Garber .05 .02
168 Juan Bonilla .05 .02
169 Larry Parrish .10 .04
170 Jerry Reuss .10 .04
171 John Tudor .10 .04
Now with Pirates
172 Dave Kingman .10 .04
173 Garry Templeton .05 .02
174 Bob Boone .10 .04
175 Graig Nettles .10 .04
176 Lee Smith .50 .20
177 LaMarr Hoyt AS .05 .02
178 Bill Krueger .05 .02
179 Buck Martinez .05 .02
180 Manny Trillo .10 .04
Now with Giants
181 Lou Whitaker AS .10 .04
182 Darryl Strawberry RC 3.00 1.20
183 Neil Allen .05 .02
184 Jim Rice AS .10 .04
185 Sixto Lezcano .05 .02
186 Tom Hume .05 .02
187 Garry Maddox .05 .02
188 Bryan Little .05 .02
189 Jose Cruz .10 .04
190 Ben Oglivie .05 .02
191 Cesar Cedeno .10 .04
192 Nick Esasky .05 .02
193 Ken Forsch .05 .02
194 Jim Palmer .50 .20
195 Jack Morris .10 .04
196 Steve Howe .05 .02
197 Harold Baines .10 .04
198 Bill Doran .10 .04
199 Willie Hernandez .10 .04
200 Andre Dawson .50 .20
201 Bruce Kison .05 .02
202 Bobby Cox MG .10 .04
203 Matt Keough .05 .02
204 Ron Guidry AS .10 .04
205 Greg Minton .05 .02
206 Al Holland .05 .02
207 Luis Leal .05 .02
208 Jose Oquendo RC .05 .02
209 Leon Durham .05 .02
210 Joe Morgan .75 .30
Now with Athletics
211 Lou Whitaker .10 .04
212 George Brett 3.00 1.20
213 Bruce Hurst .05 .02
214 Steve Carlton 1.00 .40
215 Tippy Martinez .05 .02
216 Ken Landreaux .05 .02
217 Alan Ashby .05 .02
218 Dennis Eckersley .50 .20
219 Craig McMurtry .05 .02
220 Fernando Valenzuela .10 .04
221 Cliff Johnson .05 .02
222 Rick Honeycutt .05 .02
223 George Brett AS 1.50 .60
224 Rusty Staub .10 .04
225 Lee Mazzilli .05 .02
226 Pat Putnam .05 .02
227 Bob Welch .10 .04
228 Rick Cerone .05 .02
229 Lee Lacy .05 .02
230 Rickey Henderson 2.00 .80
231 Gary Redus .05 .02
232 Tim Wallach .10 .04
233 Checklist 133-264 .05 .02
234 Rafael Ramirez .05 .02
235 Matt Young RC .05 .02
236 Ellis Valentine .05 .02
237 John Castino .05 .02
238 Eric Show .05 .02
239 Bob Horner .05 .02
240 Eddie Murray 1.25 .50
241 Billy Almon .05 .02
242 Greg Brock .05 .02
243 Bruce Sutter .10 .04
244 Dwight Evans .10 .04
245 Rick Sutcliffe .10 .04
246 Terry Crowley .05 .02
247 Fred Lynn .10 .04
248 Bill Dawley .05 .02
249 Dave Stapleton .05 .02
250 Bill Madlock .05 .02
251 Jim Sundberg .10 .04
Now with Brewers
252 Steve Yeager .05 .02
253 Jim Wohlford .05 .02
254 Shane Rawley .05 .02
255 Bruce Benedict .05 .02
256 Dave Geisel .05 .02
Now with Mariners
257 Julio Cruz .05 .02
258 Luis Sanchez .05 .02
259 Von Hayes .05 .02
260 Scott McGregor .05 .02
261 Tom Seaver 2.00 .80
Now with White Sox
262 Doug Flynn .05 .02
263 Wayne Gross .05 .02
Now with Orioles
264 Larry Gura .05 .02
265 John Montefusco .05 .02
266 Dave Winfield AS .50 .20
267 Tim Lollar .05 .02
268 Ron Washington .05 .02
269 Mickey Rivers .05 .02
270 Mookie Wilson .10 .04
271 Moose Haas .05 .02
272 Rick Dempsey .10 .04
273 Dan Quisenberry .05 .02
274 Steve Henderson .05 .02
275 Len Matuszek .05 .02
276 Frank Tanana .10 .04
277 Dave Righetti .10 .04
278 Jorge Bell .25 .10
279 Ivan DeJesus .05 .02
280 Floyd Bannister .05 .02
281 Dale Murray .05 .02
282 Andre Robertson .05 .02
283 Rollie Fingers .50 .20
284 Tommy John .25 .10
285 Darrell Porter .05 .02
286 Lary Sorensen .10 .04
Now with Athletics
287 Warren Cromartie .10 .04
Now playing in Japan
288 Jim Beattie .05 .02
289 Blue Jays Leaders .10 .04
Lloyd Moseby
Dave Stieb
(Team checklist back)
290 Dave Dravecky .10 .04
291 Eddie Murray AS .50 .20
292 Greg Bargar .05 .02
293 Tom Underwood .10 .04
Now with Orioles
294 U.L. Washington .05 .02
295 Mike Flanagan .05 .02
296 Rich Gedman .05 .02
297 Bruce Berenyi .05 .02
298 Jim Gantner .10 .04
299 Bill Caudill .10 .04
Now with Athletics
300 Pete Rose 2.50 1.00
Now with Expos
301 Steve Kemp .05 .02
302 Barry Bonnell .10 .04
Now with Mariners
303 Joel Youngblood .05 .02
304 Rick Langford .05 .02
305 Roy Smalley .05 .02
306 Ken Griffey .10 .04
307 Al Oliver .10 .04
308 Ron Hassey .05 .02
309 Len Barker .05 .02
310 Willie McGee .25 .10
311 Jerry Koosman .10 .04
Now with Phillies
312 Jorge Orta .10 .04
Now with Royals
313 Pete Vuckovich .05 .02
314 George Wright .05 .02
315 Bob Grich .10 .04
316 Jesse Barfield .10 .04
317 Willie Upshaw .05 .02
318 Bill Gullickson .05 .02
319 Ray Burris .10 .04
Now with Athletics
320 Bob Stanley .05 .02
321 Ray Knight .05 .02
322 Ken Schrom .05 .02
323 Johnny Ray .05 .02
324 Brian Giles .05 .02
325 Darrell Evans .10 .04
Now with Tigers
326 Mike Caldwell .05 .02
327 Ruppert Jones .05 .02
328 Chris Speier .05 .02
329 Bobby Castillo .05 .02
330 John Candelaria .05 .02
331 Bucky Dent .10 .04
332 Expos Leaders .10 .04
Al Oliver
Charlie Lea
(Team checklist back)
333 Larry Herndon .05 .02
334 Chuck Rainey .05 .02
335 Don Baylor .10 .04
336 Bob James .05 .02
337 Jim Clancy .05 .02
338 Duane Kuiper .05 .02
339 Roy Lee Jackson .05 .02
340 Hal McRae .10 .04
341 Larry McWilliams .05 .02
342 Tim Foli .10 .04
Now with Yankees
343 Fergie Jenkins .50 .20
344 Dickie Thon .05 .02
345 Kent Hrbek .25 .10
346 Larry Bowa .10 .04
347 Buddy Bell .10 .04
348 Toby Harrah .10 .04
Now with Yankees
349 Dan Ford .05 .02
350 George Foster .10 .04
351 Lou Piniella .10 .04
352 Dave Stewart .50 .20
353 Mike Easler .10 .04
Now with Red Sox
354 Jeff Burroughs .05 .02
355 Jason Thompson .05 .02
356 Glenn Abbott .05 .02
357 Ron Cey .10 .04
358 Bob Dernier .05 .02
359 Jim Acker .05 .02
360 Willie Randolph .10 .04
361 Mike Schmidt 1.50 .60
362 David Green .05 .02
363 Cal Ripken 6.00 2.40
364 Jim Rice .10 .04
365 Steve Bedrosian .05 .02
366 Gary Carter .50 .20
367 Chili Davis .10 .04
368 Hubie Brooks .05 .02
369 Steve McCatty .05 .02
370 Tim Raines .50 .20
371 Joaquin Andujar .05 .02
372 Gary Roenicke .05 .02
373 Ron Kittle .05 .02
374 Rich Dauer .05 .02
375 Dennis Leonard .05 .02
376 Rick Burleson .05 .02
377 Eric Rasmussen .05 .02
378 Dave Winfield .50 .20
379 Checklist 265-396 .05 .02
380 Steve Garvey .25 .10
381 Jack Clark .10 .04
382 Odell Jones .05 .02
383 Terry Puhl .05 .02
384 Joe Niekro .10 .04
385 Tony Perez .75 .30
Now with Reds
386 George Hendrick AS .05 .02
387 Johnny Ray AS .05 .02
388 Mike Schmidt AS .50 .20
389 Ozzie Smith AS 1.00 .40
390 Tim Raines AS .25 .10
391 Dale Murphy AS .25 .10
392 Andre Dawson AS .25 .10
393 Gary Carter AS .10 .04
394 Steve Rogers AS .05 .02
395 Steve Carlton AS .50 .20
396 Jesse Orosco AS .05 .02

1985 O-Pee-Chee

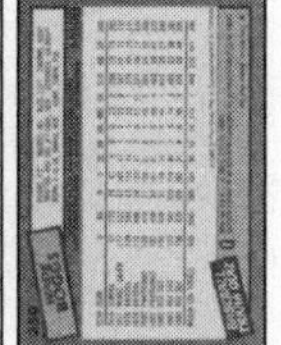

This set is an abridgement of the 1985 Topps set. The 396 standard-size cards comprising the 1985 O-Pee-Chee set differ from the cards of the 1985 Topps set by having a higher ratio of cards of players from the two Canadian teams, a practice begun by O-Pee-Chee in 1977 and continued to 1988. The set contains virtually the same pictures for the players also featured in the 1985 Topps issue. The fronts feature white-bordered color player photos. The player's name, position and team name and logo appear at the bottom of the photo. The green and white horizontal backs carry the player's name and biography at the top. The player's major league statistics and bilingual profile follow below. A bilingual trivia question and answer round out the back. The O-Pee-Chee logo appears on the front of every card. Notable Rookie Cards include Dwight Gooden and Kirby Puckett.

Nm-Mt Ex-Mt
COMPLETE SET (396) 25.00 10.00
1 Tom Seaver .50 .20
2 Gary Lavelle .10 .04
Traded to Blue Jays 1-26-85
3 Tim Wallach .10 .04
4 Jim Wohlford .05 .02
5 Jeff Robinson .05 .02
6 Willie Wilson .05 .02
7 Cliff Johnson .10 .04
Free Agent with Rangers 12-20-84
8 Willie Randolph .10 .04
9 Larry Herndon .05 .02
10 Kirby Puckett RC 4.00 1.60
11 Mookie Wilson .10 .04
12 Dave Lopes .10 .04
Traded to Cubs 8-81-84
13 Tim Lollar .10 .04
Traded to White Sox 12-6-84
14 Chris Bando .05 .02
15 Jerry Koosman .10 .04
16 Bobby Meacham .05 .02
17 Mike Scott .05 .02
18 Rich Gedman .05 .02
19 George Frazier .05 .02
20 Chet Lemon .05 .02
21 Dave Concepcion .10 .04
22 Jason Thompson .05 .02
23 Bret Saberhagen RC* .50 .20
24 Jesse Barfield .05 .02
25 Steve Bedrosian .05 .02
26 Roy Smalley .10 .04
Traded to Twins 2-19-85
27 Bruce Berenyi .05 .02
28 Butch Wynegar .05 .02
29 Alan Ashby .05 .02
30 Cal Ripken 4.00 1.60
31 Luis Leal .05 .02
32 Dave Dravecky .10 .04
33 Tito Landrum .05 .02
34 Pedro Guerrero .10 .04
35 Graig Nettles .10 .04
36 Fred Breining .05 .02
37 Roy Lee Jackson .05 .02
38 Steve Henderson .05 .02
39 Gary Pettis UER .10 .04
Photo actually
Lynn Pettis
40 Phil Niekro .50 .20
41 Dwight Gooden RC 1.50 .60
42 Luis Sanchez .05 .02
43 Lee Smith .50 .20
44 Dickie Thon .05 .02
45 Greg Minton .05 .02
46 Mike Flanagan .05 .02
47 Bud Black .05 .02
48 Tony Fernandez .50 .20
49 Carlton Fisk .50 .20
50 John Candelaria .05 .02
51 Bob Watson .10 .04
Announced his Retirement
52 Rick Leach .05 .02
53 Rick Rhoden .05 .02
54 Cesar Cedeno .10 .04
55 Frank Tanana .10 .04
56 Larry Bowa .10 .04
57 Willie McGee .10 .04
58 Rich Dauer .05 .02
59 Jorge Bell .10 .04
60 George Hendrick .10 .04
Traded to Pirates 12-12-84
61 Donnie Moore .10 .04
Drafted by Angels 1-24-85
62 Mike Ramsey .05 .02
63 Nolan Ryan 3.00 1.20
64 Mark Bailey .05 .02
65 Bill Buckner .10 .04
66 Jerry Reuss .05 .02
67 Mike Schmidt 1.00 .40
68 Von Hayes .05 .02
69 Phil Bradley .10 .04
70 Don Baylor .10 .04
71 Julio Cruz .05 .02
72 Rick Sutcliffe .05 .02
73 Storm Davis .05 .02
74 Mike Krukow .05 .02
75 Willie Upshaw .05 .02
76 Craig Lefferts .05 .02
77 Lloyd Moseby .05 .02
78 Ron Davis .05 .02
79 Rick Mahler .05 .02
80 Keith Hernandez .10 .04
81 Vance Law .10 .04
Traded to Expos 12-7-84
82 Joe Price .05 .02
83 Dennis Lamp .05 .02
84 Gary Ward .05 .02
85 Mike Marshall .05 .02
86 Marvell Wynne .05 .02
87 David Green .05 .02
88 Bryn Smith .05 .02
89 Sixto Lezcano .10 .04
Free Agent with Pirates 1-26-85
90 Rich Gossage .10 .04
91 Jeff Burroughs .10 .04
Purchased by Blue Jays 12-22-84
92 Bobby Brown .05 .02
93 Oscar Gamble .05 .02
94 Rick Dempsey .10 .04
95 Jose Cruz .10 .04
96 Johnny Ray .05 .02
97 Joel Youngblood .05 .02
98 Eddie Whitson .10 .04
Free Agent with 12-28-84
99 Milt Wilcox .05 .02
100 George Brett 3.00 1.20
101 Jim Acker .05 .02
102 Jim Sundberg .10 .04
Traded to Royals 1-18-85
103 Ozzie Virgil .05 .02
104 Mike Fitzgerald .10 .04
Traded to Expos 12-10-84
105 Ron Kittle .05 .02
106 Pascual Perez .05 .02
107 Barry Bonnell .05 .02
108 Lou Whitaker .25 .10
109 Gary Roenicke .05 .02
110 Alejandro Pena .05 .02
111 Doug DeCinces .05 .02
112 Doug Flynn .05 .02
113 Tom Herr .10 .04
114 Bob James .10 .04
Traded to White Sox 12-7-84
115 Rickey Henderson 3.00 1.20
Traded to Yankees 12-8-84
116 Pete Rose .50 .20
117 Greg Gross .05 .02
118 Eric Show .05 .02
119 Buck Martinez .10 .04
120 Steve Kemp .05 .02
Traded to Pirates 12-20-84
121 Checklist 1-132 .05 .02
122 Tom Brunansky .10 .04
123 Dave Kingman .10 .04
124 Gary Templeton .05 .02
125 Kent Tekulve .05 .02
126 Darryl Strawberry .50 .20
127 Mark Gubicza RC .10 .04
128 Ernie Whitt .05 .02
129 Don Robinson .05 .02
130 Al Oliver .10 .04
Traded to Dodgers 2-4-85
131 Mario Soto .05 .02
132 Jeff Leonard .05 .02
133 Andre Dawson .50 .20
134 Bruce Hurst .05 .02
135 Bobby Cox MG CL .10 .04
136 Matt Young .05 .02
137 Bob Forsch .05 .02
138 Ron Darling .10 .04
139 Steve Trout .05 .02
140 Geoff Zahn .05 .02
141 Ken Forsch .05 .02
142 Jerry Willard .05 .02
143 Bill Gullickson .05 .02
144 Mike Mason .05 .02
145 Alvin Davis .10 .04
146 Gary Redus .05 .02
147 Willie Aikens .05 .02
148 Steve Yeager .05 .02
149 Dickie Noles .05 .02
150 Jim Rice .10 .04
151 Moose Haas .05 .02
152 Steve Balboni .05 .02
153 Frank LaCorte .05 .02
154 Angel Salazar .10 .04
Drafted by Cardinals 1-24-85
155 Bob Grich .10 .04
156 Craig Reynolds .05 .02
157 Bill Madlock .05 .02
158 Pat Tabler .05 .02
159 Don Slaught .10 .04
Traded to Rangers 1-18-85
160 Lance Parrish .10 .04
161 Ken Schrom .05 .02
162 Wally Backman .05 .02
163 Dennis Eckersley .50 .20
164 Dave Collins .10 .04
Traded to A's 12-8-84
165 Dusty Baker .25 .10
166 Claudell Washington .05 .02
167 Rick Camp .05 .02
168 Garth Iorg .05 .02
169 Shane Rawley .05 .02
170 George Foster .10 .04
171 Tony Bernazard .05 .02
172 Don Sutton .75 .30
Traded to A's 12-8-84
173 Jerry Remy .05 .02
174 Rick Honeycutt .05 .02
175 Dave Parker .10 .04
176 Buddy Bell .05 .02
177 Steve Garvey .25 .10
178 Miguel Dilone .05 .02
179 Tommy John .25 .10
180 Dave Winfield .50 .20
181 Alan Trammell .25 .10
182 Rollie Fingers .50 .20
183 Larry McWilliams .05 .02
184 Carmen Castillo .05 .02
185 Al Holland .05 .02
186 Jerry Mumphrey .05 .02
187 Chris Chambliss .10 .04
188 Jim Clancy .05 .02
189 Glenn Wilson .05 .02
190 Rusty Staub .10 .04
191 Ozzie Smith 2.00 .80
192 Howard Johnson .25 .10
Traded to Mets 12-7-84
193 Jimmy Key RC .50 .20
194 Terry Kennedy .05 .02
195 Glenn Hubbard .05 .02
196 Pete O'Brien .05 .02
197 Keith Moreland .05 .02
198 Eddie Milner .05 .02
199 Dave Engle .05 .02
200 Reggie Jackson .50 .20
201 Burt Hooton .10 .04
Free Agent with Rangers 1-3-85
202 Gorman Thomas .05 .02
203 Larry Parrish .05 .02
204 Bob Stanley .05 .02
205 Steve Rogers .05 .02
206 Phil Garner .05 .02
207 Ed VandeBerg .05 .02
208 Jack Clark .25 .10
Traded to Cardinals 2-1-85
209 Bill Campbell .05 .02
210 Gary Matthews .05 .02
211 Dave Palmer .05 .02
212 Tony Perez .50 .20
213 Sammy Stewart .05 .02
214 John Tudor .10 .04
Traded to Cardinals 12-12-84
215 Bob Brenly .10 .04
216 Jim Gantner .05 .02
217 Bryan Clark .05 .02
218 Doyle Alexander .05 .02
219 Bo Diaz .05 .02
220 Fred Lynn .10 .04
Free Agent with Orioles 12-11-84
221 Eddie Murray .50 .20
222 Hubie Brooks .05 .02
Traded to Expos 12-10-84
223 Tom Hume .05 .02
224 Al Cowens .05 .02
225 Mike Boddicker .05 .02
226 Len Matuszek .05 .02
227 Danny Darwin .10 .04
Traded to Brewers 1-18-85
228 Scott McGregor .05 .02
229 Dave LaPoint .10 .04
Traded to Giants 2-1-85
230 Gary Carter .75 .30
Traded to Mets 12-10-84
231 Joaquin Andujar .05 .02
232 Rafael Ramirez .05 .02
233 Wayne Gross .05 .02
234 Neil Allen .05 .02
235 Garry Maddox .05 .02
236 Mark Thurmond .05 .02
237 Julio Franco .25 .10
238 Ray Burris .10 .04
Traded to Brewers 12-8-84
239 Tim Teufel .05 .02
240 Dave Stieb .05 .02
241 Brett Butler .10 .04
242 Greg Brock .05 .02
243 Barbaro Garbey .05 .02
244 Greg Walker .05 .02
245 Chili Davis .10 .04
246 Darrell Porter .05 .02
247 Tippy Martinez .05 .02
248 Terry Forster .10 .04
249 Harold Baines .25 .10
250 Jesse Orosco .10 .04
251 Brad Gulden .05 .02
252 Mike Hargrove .10 .04
253 Nick Esasky .05 .02
254 Frank Williams .05 .02
255 Lonnie Smith .05 .02
256 Daryl Sconiers .05 .02
257 Bryan Little .10 .04
Traded to White Sox 12-7-84
258 Terry Francona .10 .04
259 Mark Langston RC .50 .20
260 Dave Righetti .10 .04
261 Checklist 133-264 .05 .02
262 Bob Horner .05 .02
263 Mel Hall .05 .02
264 John Shelby .05 .02
265 Juan Samuel .05 .02
266 Frank Viola .10 .04
267 Jim Fanning MG .05 .02
Now Vice President
Player Development and Scouting
268 Dick Ruthven .05 .02
269 Bobby Ramos .05 .02
270 Dan Quisenberry .05 .02
271 Dwight Evans .10 .04
272 Andre Thornton .05 .02
273 Orel Hershiser 2.00 .80
274 Ray Knight .05 .02
275 Bill Caudill .10 .04
Traded to Blue Jays 12-8-84
276 Charlie Hough .10 .04
277 Tim Raines .25 .10
278 Mike Squires .05 .02
279 Alex Trevino .05 .02
280 Ron Romanick .05 .02
281 Tom Niedenfuer .05 .02
282 Mike Stenhouse .10 .04
Traded to Twins 1-9-85
283 Terry Puhl .05 .02
284 Hal McRae .05 .02
285 Dan Driessen .05 .02
286 Rudy Law .05 .02
287 Walt Terrell .10 .04
Traded to Tigers 12-7-84
288 Jeff Kunkel .05 .02
289 Bob Knepper .05 .02
290 Cecil Cooper .10 .04
291 Bob Welch .05 .02
292 Frank Pastore .05 .02
293 Dan Schatzeder .05 .02
294 Tom Nieto .05 .02
295 Joe Niekro .10 .04
296 Ryne Sandberg 2.00 .80
297 Gary Lucas .05 .02
298 John Castino .05 .02
299 Bill Doran .05 .02
300 Rod Carew .50 .20
301 John Montefusco .05 .02
302 Johnnie LeMaster .05 .02
303 Jim Beattie .05 .02
304 Gary Gaetti .05 .02
305 Dale Berra .10 .04
Traded to Yankees 12-20-84
306 Rick Reuschel .10 .04
307 Ken Oberkfell .05 .02
308 Kent Hrbek .10 .04
309 Mike Witt .05 .02
310 Manny Trillo .05 .02
311 Jim Gott .10 .04
Traded to Giants 1-26-85
312 LaMarr Hoyt .10 .04
Traded to Padres 12-6-84
313 Dave Schmidt .05 .02
314 Ron Oester .05 .02
315 Doug Sisk .05 .02
316 John Lowenstein .05 .02
317 Derrel Thomas .10 .04
Traded to Angels 9-6-84
318 Ted Simmons .10 .04
319 Darrell Evans .10 .04
320 Dale Murphy .25 .10
321 Ricky Horton .05 .02
322 Ken Phelps .05 .02
323 Lee Mazzilli .10 .04
324 Don Mattingly 4.00 1.60
325 John Denny .05 .02
326 Ken Singleton .05 .02
327 Brook Jacoby .05 .02
328 Greg Luzinski .10 .04
Announced his Retirement
329 Bob Ojeda .05 .02
330 Leon Durham .05 .02
331 Bill Laskey .05 .02
332 Ben Oglivie .05 .02
333 Willie Hernandez .05 .02
334 Bob Dernier .05 .02
335 Bruce Benedict .05 .02
336 Rance Mulliniks .05 .02
337 Rick Cerone .10 .04
Traded to Braves 12-6-84
338 Britt Burns .05 .02
339 Danny Heep .05 .02
340 Robin Yount .50 .20
341 Andy Van Slyke .25 .10
342 Curt Wilkerson .05 .02
343 Bill Russell .05 .02
344 Dave Henderson .05 .02
345 Charlie Lea .05 .02
346 Terry Pendleton RC .50 .20
347 Carney Lansford .05 .02
348 Bob Boone .10 .04
349 Mike Easler .05 .02
350 Wade Boggs 1.00 .40
351 Atlee Hammaker .05 .02
352 Joe Morgan .50 .20
353 Damaso Garcia .05 .02
354 Floyd Bannister .05 .02
355 Bert Blyleven .10 .04
356 John Butcher .05 .02
357 Fernando Valenzuela .10 .04
358 Tony Pena .10 .04
359 Mike Smithson .05 .02
360 Steve Carlton .50 .20
361 Alfredo Griffin .10 .04
Traded to A's 12-8-84
362 Craig McMurtry .05 .02
363 Bill Dawley .05 .02
364 Richard Dotson .05 .02
365 Carmelo Martinez .05 .02
366 Ron Cey .10 .04
367 Tony Scott .05 .02
368 Dave Bergman .05 .02
369 Steve Sax .05 .02
370 Bruce Sutter .10 .04
371 Mickey Rivers .05 .02
372 Kirk Gibson .10 .04
373 Scott Sanderson .05 .02
374 Brian Downing .05 .02
375 Jeff Reardon .10 .04
376 Frank DiPino .05 .02
377 Checklist 265-396 .05 .02
378 Alan Wiggins .05 .02
379 Charles Hudson .05 .02
380 Ken Griffey .10 .04
381 Tom Paciorek .05 .02
382 Jack Morris .10 .04
383 Tony Gwynn 3.00 1.20
384 Jody Davis .05 .02
385 Jose DeLeon .05 .02
386 Bob Kearney .05 .02
387 George Wright .05 .02
388 Ron Guidry .10 .04
389 Rick Manning .05 .02
390 Sid Fernandez .10 .04
391 Bruce Bochte .05 .02
392 Dan Petry .05 .02
393 Tim Stoddard .10 .04
Free Agent with Padres 1-2-85
394 Tony Armas .05 .02
395 Paul Molitor .50 .20
396 Mike Heath .05 .02

1985 O-Pee-Chee Posters

The 24 full-color posters in the 1985 O-Pee-Chee poster insert set were inserted one per regular wax pack and feature players of the Montreal Expos (numbered 1-12) and the Toronto Blue Jays (numbered 13-24). These posters are typically found with two folds and measure approximately 4 7/8" by 6 7/8". The posters are blank-backed and are numbered at the bottom in French and English. A distinctive blue (Blue Jays) or red (Expos) border surrounds the player photo.

Nm-Mt Ex-Mt
COMPLETE SET (24) 6.00 2.40
1 Mike Fitzgerald .25 .10
2 Dan Driessen .25 .10
3 Dave Palmer .25 .10
4 U.L. Washington .25 .10
5 Hubie Brooks .25 .10
6 Tim Wallach .50 .20
7 Tim Raines .75 .30
8 Herm Winningham .25 .10
9 Andre Dawson 1.00 .40
10 Charlie Lea .25 .10
11 Steve Rogers .25 .10
12 Jeff Reardon .50 .20
13 Buck Martinez .25 .10
14 Willie Upshaw .25 .10
15 Damaso Garcia UER .25 .10
(Misspelled Domaso)
16 Tony Fernandez .75 .30
17 Rance Mulliniks .25 .10
18 George Bell .50 .20
19 Lloyd Moseby .25 .10
20 Jesse Barfield .50 .20
21 Doyle Alexander .25 .10
22 Dave Stieb .50 .20
23 Bill Caudill .25 .10
24 Gary Lavelle .25 .10

1986 O-Pee-Chee

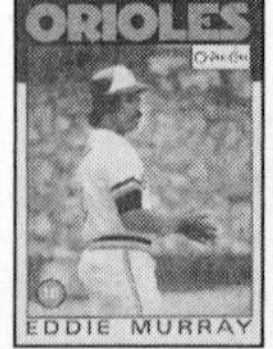

This set is an abridgement of the 1986 Topps set. The 396 standard-size cards comprising the 1986 O-Pee-Chee set differ from the cards of the 1986 Topps set by having a higher ratio of cards of players from the two Canadian teams, a practice begun by O-Pee-Chee in 1977 and continued to 1988. The fronts feature black-and white-bordered color player photos. The player's name appears within the white margin at the bottom. His team name appears within the black margin at the top and his position appears within a colored circle at the photo's lower left. The red horizontal backs carry the player's name and biography at the top. The player's major league statistics follow below. Some backs also have bilingual career highlights, some have bilingual baseball facts and still others have neither. The asterisked cards have an extra line on the front inside the picture area indicating team change. The O-Pee-Chee logo appears on the front of every card.

Nm-Mt Ex-Mt
COMPLETE SET (396) 12.00 4.80
1 Pete Rose 1.00 .40
2 Ken Landreaux .05 .02
3 Rob Picciolo .05 .02
4 Steve Garvey .15 .06
5 Andy Hawkins .05 .02
6 Rudy Law .05 .02
7 Lonnie Smith .05 .02
8 Dwayne Murphy .05 .02
9 Moose Haas .05 .02
10 Tony Gwynn 1.50 .60
11 Bob Ojeda .10 .04
Now with Mets
12 Jose Uribe .05 .02
13 Bob Kearney .05 .02
14 Julio Cruz .05 .02
15 Eddie Whitson .05 .02
16 Rick Schu .05 .02
17 Mike Stenhouse .10 .04
Now with Red Sox
18 Lou Thornton .05 .02
19 Ryne Sandberg .75 .30
20 Lou Whitaker .10 .04
21 Mark Brouhard .05 .02
22 Gary Lavelle .05 .02
23 Manny Lee .05 .02
24 Don Slaught .05 .02
25 Willie Wilson .05 .02
26 Mike Marshall .05 .02
27 Ray Knight .05 .02
28 Mario Soto .05 .02
29 Dave Anderson .05 .02
30 Eddie Murray .75 .30
31 Dusty Baker .10 .04
32 Steve Yeager .10 .04
Now with Mariners
33 Andy Van Slyke .10 .04
34 Dave Righetti .05 .02
35 Jeff Reardon .10 .04
36 Burt Hooton .05 .02
37 Johnny Ray .05 .02
38 Glenn Hoffman .05 .02
39 Rick Mahler .05 .02
40 Ken Griffey .10 .04
41 Brad Wellman .05 .02
42 Joe Hesketh .05 .02
43 Mark Salas .05 .02
44 Jorge Orta .05 .02
45 Damaso Garcia .05 .02
46 Jim Acker .05 .02
47 Bill Madlock .05 .02
48 Bill Almon .05 .02
49 Rick Manning .05 .02
50 Dan Quisenberry .05 .02
51 Jim Gantner .05 .02
52 Kevin Bass .05 .02
53 Len Dykstra RC 1.00 .40
54 John Franco .15 .06
55 Fred Lynn .10 .04
56 Jim Morrison .05 .02
57 Bill Doran .05 .02
58 Leon Durham .05 .02
59 Andre Thornton .05 .02
60 Dwight Evans .10 .04
61 Larry Herndon .05 .02
62 Bob Boone .10 .04
63 Kent Hrbek .15 .06
64 Floyd Bannister .05 .02
65 Harold Baines .15 .06
66 Pat Tabler .05 .02
67 Carmelo Martinez .05 .02
68 Ed Lynch .05 .02
69 George Foster .10 .04
70 Dave Winfield .25 .10
71 Ken Schrom .05 .02
Now with Indians
72 Toby Harrah .05 .02
73 Jackie Gutierrez .05 .02
Now with Orioles
74 Rance Mulliniks .05 .02
75 Jose DeLeon .05 .02
76 Ron Romanick .05 .02
77 Charlie Leibrandt .05 .02
78 Bruce Benedict .05 .02
79 Dave Schmidt .05 .02
Now with White Sox
80 Darryl Strawberry .15 .06
81 Wayne Krenchicki .05 .02
82 Tippy Martinez .05 .02
83 Phil Garner .05 .02
84 Darrell Porter .10 .04
Now with Rangers
85 Tony Perez .25 .10
Eric Davis also
shown in photo
86 Tom Waddell .05 .02
87 Tim Hulett .05 .02
88 Barbaro Garbey .05 .02
Now with A's
89 Randy St. Claire .05 .02
90 Garry Templeton .05 .02
91 Tim Teufel .10 .04
Now with Mets
92 Al Cowens .05 .02
93 Scot Thompson .05 .02
94 Tom Herr .05 .02
95 Ozzie Virgil .10 .04
Now with Braves
96 Jose Cruz .05 .02
97 Gary Gaetti .10 .04
98 Roger Clemens 5.00 2.00

99 Vance Law .05 .02
100 Nolan Ryan 1.50 .60
101 Mike Smithson .05 .02
102 Rafael Santana .05 .02
103 Darrell Evans .10 .04
104 Rich Gossage .10 .04
105 Gary Ward .05 .02
106 Jim Gott .05 .02
107 Rafael Ramirez .05 .02
108 Ted Power .05 .02
109 Ron Guidry .10 .04
110 Scott McGregor .05 .02
111 Mike Scioscia .10 .04
112 Glenn Hubbard .05 .02
113 U.L. Washington .05 .02
114 Al Oliver .10 .04
115 Jay Howell .05 .02
116 Brook Jacoby .05 .02
117 Willie McGee .10 .04
118 Jerry Royster .05 .02
119 Barry Bonnell .05 .02
120 Steve Carlton .25 .10
121 Alfredo Griffin .05 .02
122 David Green .10 .04
Now with Brewers
123 Greg Walker .05 .02
124 Frank Tanana .05 .02
125 Dave Lopes .10 .04
126 Mike Krukow .05 .02
127 Jack Howell .05 .02
128 Greg Harris .05 .02
129 Herm Winningham .05 .02
130 Alan Trammell .15 .06
131 Checklist 1-132 .05 .02
132 Razor Shines .05 .02
133 Bruce Sutter .10 .04
134 Carney Lansford .05 .02
135 Joe Niekro .10 .04
136 Ernie Whitt .05 .02
137 Charlie Moore .05 .02
138 Mel Hall .05 .02
139 Roger McDowell .05 .02
140 John Candelaria .05 .02
141 Bob Rodgers MG CL .05 .02
142 Manny Trillo .10 .04
Now with Cubs
143 Dave Palmer .10 .04
Now with Braves
144 Robin Yount .25 .10
145 Pedro Guerrero .10 .04
146 Von Hayes .05 .02
147 Lance Parrish .10 .04
148 Mike Heath .10 .04
Now with Cardinals
149 Brett Butler .10 .04
150 Joaquin Andujar .10 .04
Now with A's
151 Graig Nettles .10 .04
152 Pete Vuckovich .05 .02
153 Jason Thompson .05 .02
154 Bert Roberge .05 .02
155 Bob Grich .10 .04
156 Roy Smalley .05 .02
157 Ron Hassey .05 .02
158 Bob Stanley .05 .02
159 Orel Hershiser .40 .16
160 Chet Lemon .05 .02
161 Terry Puhl .05 .02
162 Dave LaPoint .10 .04
Now with Tigers
163 Onix Concepcion .05 .02
164 Steve Balboni .05 .02
165 Mike Davis .05 .02
166 Dickie Thon .05 .02
167 Zane Smith .05 .02
168 Jeff Burroughs .05 .02
169 Alex Trevino .10 .04
Now with Dodgers
170 Gary Carter .25 .10
171 Tito Landrum .05 .02
172 Sammy Stewart .10 .04
Now with Red Sox
173 Wayne Gross .05 .02
174 Britt Burns .10 .04
Now with Yankees
175 Steve Sax .05 .02
176 Jody Davis .05 .02
177 Joel Youngblood .05 .02
178 Fernando Valenzuela .10 .04
179 Storm Davis .05 .02
180 Don Mattingly 1.25 .50
181 Steve Bedrosian .10 .04
Now with Phillies
182 Jesse Orosco .10 .04
183 Gary Roenicke .10 .04
Now with Yankees
184 Don Baylor .10 .04
185 Rollie Fingers .25 .10
186 Ruppert Jones .05 .02
187 Scott Fletcher .10 .04
Now with Rangers
188 Bob Dernier .05 .02
189 Mike Mason .05 .02
190 George Hendrick .05 .02
191 Wally Backman .05 .02
192 Oddibe McDowell .05 .02
193 Bruce Hurst .05 .02
194 Ron Cey .10 .04
195 Dave Concepcion .10 .04
196 Doyle Alexander .05 .02
197 Dale Murray .05 .02
198 Mark Langston .10 .04
199 Dennis Eckersley .25 .10
200 Mike Schmidt .25 .10
201 Nick Esasky .05 .02
202 Ken Dayley .05 .02
203 Rick Cerone .05 .02
204 Larry McWilliams .05 .02
205 Brian Downing .05 .02
206 Danny Darwin .05 .02
207 Bill Caudill .05 .02
208 Dave Rozema .05 .02
209 Eric Show .05 .02
210 Brad Komminsk .05 .02
211 Chris Bando .05 .02
212 Chris Speier .05 .02
213 Jim Clancy .05 .02
214 Randy Bush .05 .02
215 Frank White .10 .04
216 Dan Petry .05 .02
217 Tim Wallach .05 .02
218 Mitch Webster .05 .02
219 Dennis Lamp .05 .02
220 Bob Horner .05 .02
221 Dave Henderson .05 .02
222 Dave Smith .05 .02
223 Willie Upshaw .05 .02
224 Cesar Cedeno .10 .04
225 Ron Darling .05 .02
226 Lee Lacy .05 .02
227 John Tudor .05 .02
228 Jim Presley .05 .02
229 Bill Gullickson .10 .04
Now with Reds
230 Terry Kennedy .05 .02
231 Bob Knepper .05 .02
232 Rick Rhoden .05 .02
233 Richard Dotson .05 .02
234 Jesse Barfield .10 .04
235 Butch Wynegar .05 .02
236 Jerry Reuss .10 .04
237 Juan Samuel .05 .02
238 Larry Parrish .05 .02
239 Bill Buckner .10 .04
240 Pat Sheridan .05 .02
241 Tony Fernandez .15 .06
242 Rich Thompson .05 .02
Now with Brewers
243 Rickey Henderson .50 .20
244 Craig Lefferts .05 .02
245 Jim Sundberg .05 .02
246 Phil Niekro .25 .10
247 Terry Harper .05 .02
248 Spike Owen .05 .02
249 Bret Saberhagen .25 .10
250 Dwight Gooden .25 .10
251 Rich Dauer .05 .02
252 Keith Hernandez .10 .04
253 Bo Diaz .05 .02
254 Ozzie Guillen RC .25 .10
255 Tony Armas .05 .02
256 Andre Dawson .25 .10
257 Doug DeCinces .05 .02
258 Tim Burke .05 .02
259 Dennis Boyd .05 .02
260 Tony Pena .10 .04
261 Sal Butera .10 .04
Now with Reds
262 Wade Boggs .75 .30
263 Checklist 133-264 .05 .02
264 Ron Oester .05 .02
265 Ron Davis .05 .02
266 Keith Moreland .05 .02
267 Paul Molitor .50 .20
268 John Denny .10 .04
Now with Reds
269 Frank Viola .10 .04
270 Jack Morris .10 .04
271 Dave Collins .10 .04
Now with Tigers
272 Bert Blyleven .10 .04
273 Jerry Willard .05 .02
274 Matt Young .05 .02
275 Charlie Hough .10 .04
276 Dave Dravecky .10 .04
277 Garth Iorg .05 .02
278 Hal McRae .05 .02
279 Curt Wilkerson .05 .02
280 Tim Raines .10 .04
281 Bill Laskey .10 .04
Now with Giants
282 Jerry Mumphrey .10 .04
Now with Cubs
283 Pat Clements .05 .02
284 Bob James .05 .02
285 Buddy Bell .10 .04
286 Tom Brookens .05 .02
287 Dave Parker .10 .04
288 Ron Kittle .05 .02
289 Johnnie LeMaster .05 .02
290 Carlton Fisk .25 .10
291 Jimmy Key .15 .06
292 Gary Matthews .05 .02
293 Marvell Wynne .05 .02
294 Danny Cox .05 .02
295 Kirk Gibson .10 .04
296 Mariano Duncan RC .15 .06
297 Ozzie Smith 1.00 .40
298 Craig Reynolds .05 .02
299 Bryn Smith .05 .02
300 George Brett 1.00 .40
301 Walt Terrell .05 .02
302 Greg Gross .05 .02
303 Claudell Washington .05 .02
304 Howard Johnson .10 .04
305 Phil Bradley .05 .02
306 R.J. Reynolds .05 .02
307 Bob Brenly .10 .04
308 Hubie Brooks .05 .02
309 Alvin Davis .05 .02
310 Donnie Hill .05 .02
311 Dick Schofield .05 .02
312 Tom Filer .05 .02
313 Mike Fitzgerald .05 .02
314 Marty Barrett .05 .02
315 Mookie Wilson .10 .04
316 Alan Knicely .05 .02
317 Ed Romero .05 .02
Now with Red Sox
318 Glenn Wilson .05 .02
319 Bud Black .05 .02
320 Jim Rice .10 .04
321 Terry Pendleton .15 .06
322 Dave Kingman .10 .04
323 Gary Pettis .05 .02
324 Dan Schatzeder .05 .02
325 Juan Beniquez .10 .04
Now with Orioles
326 Kent Tekulve .05 .02
327 Mike Pagliarulo .05 .02
328 Pete O'Brien .05 .02
329 Kirby Puckett 2.00 .80
330 Rick Sutcliffe .05 .02
331 Alan Ashby .05 .02
332 Willie Randolph .10 .04
333 Tom Henke .10 .04
334 Ken Oberkfell .05 .02
335 Don Sutton .25 .10
336 Dan Gladden .10 .04
337 George Vukovich .05 .02
338 Jorge Bell .10 .04
339 Jim Dwyer .05 .02
340 Cal Ripken 1.50 .60
341 Willie Hernandez .05 .02
342 Gary Redus .10 .04
Now with Phillies
343 Jerry Koosman .10 .04
344 Jim Wohlford .05 .02
345 Donnie Moore .05 .02
346 Floyd Youmans .05 .02
347 Gorman Thomas .05 .02
348 Cliff Johnson .05 .02
349 Ken Howell .05 .02
350 Jack Clark .10 .04
351 Gary Lucas .10 .04
Now with Angels
352 Bob Clark .05 .02
353 Dave Stieb .05 .02
354 Tony Bernazard .05 .02
355 Lee Smith .25 .10
356 Mickey Hatcher .05 .02
357 Ed VandeBerg .10 .04
Now with Dodgers
358 Rick Dempsey .05 .02
359 Bobby Cox MG CL .10 .04
Now General Manager of Atlanta Braves
360 Lloyd Moseby .05 .02
361 Shane Rawley .05 .02
362 Garry Maddox .05 .02
363 Buck Martinez .10 .04
364 Ed Nunez .05 .02
365 Luis Leal .05 .02
366 Dale Berra .05 .02
367 Mike Boddicker .05 .02
368 Greg Brock .05 .02
369 Al Holland .05 .02
370 Vince Coleman RC .15 .06
371 Rod Carew .25 .10
372 Ben Oglivie .05 .02
373 Lee Mazzilli .10 .04
374 Terry Francona .10 .04
375 Rich Gedman .05 .02
376 Charlie Lea .05 .02
377 Joe Carter 1.00 .40
378 Bruce Bochte .05 .02
379 Bobby Meacham .05 .02
380 LaMarr Hoyt .05 .02
381 Jeff Leonard .05 .02
382 Ivan Calderon RC .10 .04
383 Chris Brown RC .05 .02
384 Steve Trout .05 .02
385 Cecil Cooper .10 .04
386 Cecil Fielder 1.50 .60
387 Tim Flannery .05 .02
388 Chris Codiroli .05 .02
389 Glenn Davis .05 .02
390 Tom Seaver .25 .10
391 Julio Franco .15 .06
392 Tom Brunansky .05 .02
393 Rob Wilfong .05 .02
394 Reggie Jackson .25 .10
395 Scott Garrelts .05 .02
396 Checklist 265-396 .05 .02

1986 O-Pee-Chee Box Bottoms

O-Pee-Chee printed four different four-card panels on the bottoms of its 1986 wax pack boxes. If cut, each card would measure approximately the standard size. These 16 cards, in alphabetical order and designated A through P, are considered a separate set from the regular issue, but are styled almost exactly the same, differing only in the player photo and colors for the team name, borders and position on the front. The backs are identical, except for the letter designations instead of numbers.

	Nm-Mt	Ex-Mt
COMPLETE SET (16)	10.00	4.00
A George Bell	.25	.10
B Wade Boggs	1.00	.40
C George Brett	3.00	1.20
D Vince Coleman	.25	.10
E Carlton Fisk	1.00	.40
F Dwight Gooden	.75	.30
G Pedro Guerrero	.25	.10
H Ron Guidry	.50	.20
I Reggie Jackson	1.00	.40
J Don Mattingly	3.00	1.20
K Oddibe McDowell	.25	.10
L Willie McGee	.50	.20
M Dale Murphy	1.00	.40
N Pete Rose	1.00	.40
O Bret Saberhagen	.50	.20
P Fernando Valenzuela	.50	.20

1987 O-Pee-Chee

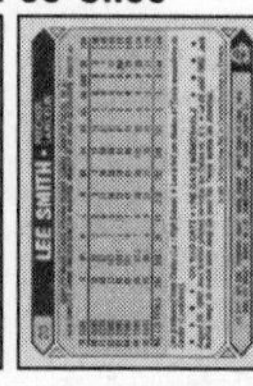

This set is an abridgement of the 1987 Topps set. The 396 standard-size cards comprising the 1987 O-Pee-Chee set differ from the cards of the 1987 Topps set by having a higher ratio of cards of players from the two Canadian teams, a practice begun by O-Pee-Chee in 1977 and continued to 1988. The fronts feature wood grain bordered color player photos. The player's name appears in the colored rectangle at the lower right. His team logo appears at the upper left. The yellow, white and blue horizontal backs carry the player's name and bilingual position at the top. The player's major league statistics follow below. Some backs also have bilingual career highlights, some have bilingual baseball facts and still others have both or neither. The asterisked cards have an extra line on the front inside the picture area indicating team change. The O-Pee-Chee logo appears on the front of every card. Notable Rookie Cards include Barry Bonds.

	Nm-Mt	Ex-Mt
COMPLETE SET (396)	15.00	6.00

1 Ken Oberkfell .05 .02
2 Jack Howell .05 .02
3 Hubie Brooks .05 .02
4 Bob Grich .10 .04
5 Rick Leach .05 .02
6 Phil Niekro .25 .10
7 Rickey Henderson .50 .20
8 Terry Pendleton .10 .04
9 Jay Tibbs .05 .02
10 Cecil Cooper .10 .04
11 Mario Soto .05 .02
12 George Bell .05 .02
13 Nick Esasky .05 .02
14 Larry McWilliams .05 .02
15 Dan Quisenberry .05 .02
16 Ed Lynch .05 .02
17 Pete O'Brien .05 .02
18 Luis Aguayo .05 .02
19 Matt Young .10 .04
Now with Dodgers
20 Gary Carter .25 .10
21 Tom Paciorek .05 .02
22 Doug DeCinces .05 .02
23 Lee Smith .15 .06
24 Jesse Barfield .05 .02
25 Bert Blyleven .10 .04
26 Greg Brock .10 .04
Now with Brewers
27 Dan Petry .05 .02
28 Rick Dempsey .10 .04
Now with Indians
29 Jimmy Key .15 .06
30 Tim Raines .10 .04
31 Bruce Hurst .05 .02
32 Manny Trillo .05 .02
33 Andy Van Slyke .10 .04
34 Ed VandeBerg .10 .04
Now with Indians
35 Sid Bream .05 .02
36 Dave Winfield .25 .10
37 Scott Garrelts .05 .02
38 Dennis Leonard .05 .02
39 Marty Barrett .05 .02
40 Dave Righetti .05 .02
41 Bo Diaz .05 .02
42 Gary Redus .05 .02
43 Tom Niedenfuer .05 .02
44 Greg Harris .05 .02
45 Jim Presley .05 .02
46 Danny Gladden .05 .02
47 Roy Smalley .05 .02
48 Wally Backman .05 .02
49 Tom Seaver .25 .10
50 Dave Smith .05 .02
51 Mel Hall .05 .02
52 Tim Flannery .05 .02
53 Julio Cruz .05 .02
54 Dick Schofield .05 .02
55 Tim Wallach .05 .02
56 Glenn Davis .05 .02
57 Darren Daulton .15 .06
58 Chico Walker .05 .02
59 Garth Iorg .05 .02
60 Tony Pena .10 .04
61 Ron Hassey .05 .02
62 Dave Dravecky .05 .02
63 Jorge Orta .05 .02
64 Al Nipper .05 .02
65 Tom Browning .05 .02
66 Marc Sullivan .05 .02
67 Todd Worrell .10 .04
68 Glenn Hubbard .05 .02
69 Carney Lansford .10 .04
70 Charlie Hough .05 .02
71 Lance McCullers .05 .02
72 Walt Terrell .05 .02
73 Bob Kearney .05 .02
74 Dan Pasqua .05 .02
75 Ron Darling .05 .02
76 Robin Yount .25 .10
77 Pat Tabler .05 .02
78 Tom Foley .05 .02
79 Juan Nieves .05 .02
80 Wally Joyner RC .50 .20
81 Wayne Krenchicki .05 .02
82 Kirby Puckett .60 .24
83 Bob Ojeda .05 .02
84 Mookie Wilson .10 .04
85 Kevin Bass .05 .02
86 Kent Tekulve .05 .02
87 Mark Salas .05 .02
88 Brian Downing .05 .02
89 Ozzie Guillen .10 .04
90 Dave Stieb .10 .04
91 Rance Mulliniks .05 .02
92 Mike Witt .05 .02
93 Charlie Moore .05 .02
94 Jose Uribe .05 .02
95 Oddibe McDowell .05 .02
96 Ray Soff .05 .02
97 Glenn Wilson .05 .02
98 Brook Jacoby .05 .02
99 Darryl Motley .10 .04
Now with Braves
100 Steve Garvey .15 .06
101 Frank White .10 .04
102 Mike Moore .05 .02
103 Rick Aguilera .10 .04
104 Buddy Bell .10 .04
105 Floyd Youmans .05 .02
106 Lou Whitaker .10 .04
107 Ozzie Smith .75 .30
108 Jim Gantner .05 .02
109 R.J. Reynolds .05 .02
110 John Tudor .05 .02
111 Alfredo Griffin .05 .02
112 Mike Flanagan .05 .02
113 Neil Allen .05 .02
114 Ken Griffey .10 .04
115 Donnie Moore .05 .02
116 Bob Horner .05 .02
117 Ron Shepherd .05 .02
118 Cliff Johnson .05 .02
119 Vince Coleman .05 .02
120 Eddie Murray .25 .10
121 Dwayne Murphy .05 .02
122 Jim Clancy .05 .02
123 Ken Landreaux .05 .02
124 Tom Nieto .10 .04
Now with Twins
125 Bob Brenly .10 .04
126 George Brett .75 .30
127 Vance Law .05 .02
128 Checklist 1-132 .05 .02
129 Bob Knepper .05 .02
130 Dwight Gooden .15 .06
131 Juan Bonilla .05 .02
132 Tim Burke .05 .02
133 Bob McClure .05 .02
134 Scott Bailes .05 .02
135 Mike Easler .10 .04
Now with Phillies
136 Ron Romanick .10 .04
Now with Yankees
137 Rich Gedman .05 .02
138 Bob Dernier .05 .02
139 John Denny .05 .02
140 Bret Saberhagen .10 .04
141 Herm Winningham .05 .02
142 Rick Sutcliffe .05 .02
143 Ryne Sandberg .40 .16
144 Mike Scioscia .10 .04
145 Charlie Kerfeld .05 .02
146 Jim Rice .10 .04
147 Steve Trout .05 .02
148 Jesse Orosco .10 .04
149 Mike Boddicker .05 .02
150 Wade Boggs .40 .16
151 Dane Iorg .05 .02
152 Rick Burleson .10 .04
Now with Orioles
153 Duane Ward RC .10 .04
154 Rick Reuschel .05 .02
155 Nolan Ryan .75 .30
156 Bill Caudill .05 .02
157 Danny Darwin .05 .02
158 Ed Romero .05 .02
159 Bill Almon .05 .02
160 Julio Franco .10 .04
161 Kent Hrbek .10 .04
162 Chili Davis .15 .06
163 Kevin Gross .05 .02
164 Carlton Fisk .25 .10
165 Jeff Reardon .15 .06
Now with Twins
166 Bob Boone .10 .04
167 Rick Honeycutt .05 .02
168 Dan Schatzeder .05 .02
169 Jim Wohlford .05 .02
170 Phil Bradley .05 .02
171 Ken Schrom .05 .02
172 Ron Oester .05 .02
173 Juan Beniquez .10 .04
Now with Royals
174 Tony Armas .05 .02
175 Bob Stanley .05 .02
176 Steve Buechele .05 .02
177 Keith Moreland .05 .02
178 Cecil Fielder .15 .06
179 Gary Gaetti .10 .04
180 Chris Brown .05 .02
181 Tom Herr .05 .02
182 Lee Lacy .05 .02
183 Ozzie Virgil .05 .02
184 Paul Molitor .25 .10
185 Roger McDowell .05 .02
186 Mike Marshall .05 .02
187 Ken Howell .05 .02
188 Rob Deer .05 .02
189 Joe Hesketh .05 .02
190 Jim Sundberg .05 .02
191 Kelly Gruber .05 .02
192 Cory Snyder .05 .02
193 Dave Concepcion .10 .04
194 Kirk McCaskill .05 .02
195 Mike Pagliarulo .05 .02
196 Rick Manning .05 .02
197 Brett Butler .10 .04
198 Tony Gwynn 1.25 .50
199 Mariano Duncan .05 .02
200 Pete Rose .25 .10
201 John Cangelosi .05 .02
202 Danny Cox .05 .02
203 Butch Wynegar .10 .04
Now with Angels
204 Chris Chambliss .10 .04
205 Graig Nettles .10 .04
206 Chet Lemon .05 .02
207 Don Aase .05 .02
208 Mike Mason .05 .02
209 Alan Trammell .15 .06
210 Lloyd Moseby .05 .02
211 Richard Dotson .05 .02
212 Mike Fitzgerald .05 .02
213 Darrell Porter .05 .02
214 Checklist 265-396 .05 .02
215 Mark Langston .05 .02
216 Steve Farr .05 .02
217 Dann Bilardello .05 .02
218 Gary Ward .10 .04
Now with Yankees
219 Cecilio Guante .10 .04
Now with Yankees
220 Joe Carter .25 .10
221 Ernie Whitt .05 .02
222 Denny Walling .05 .02
223 Charlie Leibrandt .05 .02
224 Wayne Tolleson .05 .02
225 Mike Smithson .05 .02
226 Zane Smith .05 .02
227 Terry Puhl .05 .02
228 Eric Davis .15 .06
229 Don Mattingly .75 .30
230 Don Baylor .10 .04
231 Frank Tanana .05 .02
232 Tom Brookens .05 .02
233 Steve Bedrosian .05 .02
234 Wallace Johnson .05 .02
235 Alvin Davis .05 .02
236 Tommy John .10 .04
237 Jim Morrison .05 .02
238 Ricky Horton .05 .02
239 Shane Rawley .05 .02
240 Steve Balboni .05 .02
241 Mike Krukow .05 .02
242 Rick Mahler .05 .02

243 Bill Doran .05 .02
244 Mark Clear .05 .02
245 Willie Upshaw .05 .02
246 Hal McRae .05 .02
247 Jose Canseco 1.50 .60
248 George Hendrick .05 .02
249 Doyle Alexander .05 .02
250 Teddy Higuera .05 .02
251 Tom Hume .05 .02
252 Denny Martinez .10 .04
253 Eddie Milner .10 .04
Now with Giants
254 Steve Sax .05 .02
255 Juan Samuel .05 .02
256 Dave Bergman .05 .02
257 Bob Forsch .05 .02
258 Steve Yeager .05 .02
259 Don Sutton .25 .10
260 Vida Blue .15 .06
Now with A's
261 Tom Brunansky .05 .02
262 Joe Sambito .05 .02
263 Mitch Webster .05 .02
264 Checklist 133-264 .05 .02
265 Darrell Evans .10 .04
266 Dave Kingman .10 .04
267 Howard Johnson .05 .02
268 Greg Pryor .05 .02
269 Tippy Martinez .05 .02
270 Jody Davis .05 .02
271 Steve Carlton .25 .10
272 Andres Galarraga .50 .20
273 Fernando Valenzuela .10 .04
274 Jeff Hearron .05 .02
275 Ray Knight .10 .04
Now with Orioles
276 Bill Madlock .10 .04
277 Tom Henke .05 .02
278 Gary Pettis .05 .02
279 Jimy Williams MG CL .05 .02
280 Jeffrey Leonard .05 .02
281 Bryn Smith .05 .02
282 John Cerutti .05 .02
283 Gary Roenicke .10 .04
Now with Braves
284 Joaquin Andujar .05 .02
285 Dennis Boyd .05 .02
286 Tim Hulett .05 .02
287 Craig Lefferts .05 .02
288 Tito Landrum .05 .02
289 Manny Lee .05 .02
290 Leon Durham .05 .02
291 Johnny Ray .05 .02
292 Franklin Stubbs .05 .02
293 Bob Rodgers MG CL .05 .02
294 Terry Francona .10 .04
295 Len Dykstra .15 .06
296 Tom Candiotti .05 .02
297 Frank DiPino .05 .02
298 Craig Reynolds .05 .02
299 Jerry Hairston .05 .02
300 Reggie Jackson .50 .20
Now with A's
301 Luis Aquino .05 .02
302 Greg Walker .05 .02
303 Terry Kennedy .10 .04
Now with Orioles
304 Phil Garner .05 .02
305 John Franco .10 .04
306 Bill Buckner .10 .04
307 Kevin Mitchell RC .25 .10
Now with Padres
308 Don Slaught .05 .02
309 Harold Baines .10 .04
310 Frank Viola .05 .02
311 Dave Lopes .10 .04
312 Cal Ripken .75 .30
313 John Candelaria .05 .02
314 Bob Sebra .05 .02
315 Bud Black .05 .02
316 Brian Fisher .10 .04
Now with Pirates
317 Clint Hurdle .10 .04
318 Earnest Riles .05 .02
319 Dave LaPoint .10 .04
Now with Cardinals
320 Barry Bonds RC 8.00 3.20
321 Tim Stoddard .05 .02
322 Ron Cey .15 .06
Now with A's
323 Al Newman .05 .02
324 Jerry Royster .10 .04
Now with White Sox
325 Garry Templeton .05 .02
326 Mark Gubicza .05 .02
327 Andre Thornton .05 .02
328 Bob Welch .10 .04
329 Tony Fernandez .10 .04
330 Mike Scott .05 .02
331 Jack Clark .10 .04
332 Danny Tartabull .10 .04
Now with Royals
333 Greg Minton .05 .02
334 Ed Correa .05 .02
335 Candy Maldonado .05 .02
336 Dennis Lamp .10 .04
Now with Indians
337 Sid Fernandez .05 .02
338 Greg Gross .05 .02
339 Willie Hernandez .05 .02
340 Roger Clemens 1.25 .50
341 Mickey Hatcher .05 .02
342 Bob James .05 .02
343 Jose Cruz .10 .04
344 Bruce Sutter .05 .02
345 Andre Dawson .25 .10
346 Shawon Dunston .05 .02
347 Scott McGregor .05 .02
348 Carmelo Martinez .05 .02
349 Storm Davis .10 .04
Now with Padres
350 Keith Hernandez .10 .04
351 Andy McGaffigan .05 .02
352 Dave Parker .10 .04
353 Ernie Camacho .05 .02
354 Eric Show .05 .02
355 Don Carman .05 .02
356 Floyd Bannister .05 .02
357 Willie McGee .10 .04
358 Atlee Hammaker .05 .02
359 Dale Murphy .25 .10
360 Pedro Guerrero .05 .02
361 Will Clark RC .75 .30
362 Bill Campbell .05 .02
363 Alejandro Pena .05 .02
364 Dennis Rasmussen .05 .02
365 Rick Rhoden .10 .04
Now with Yankees
366 Randy St. Claire .05 .02
367 Willie Wilson .10 .04
368 Dwight Evans .10 .04
369 Moose Haas .10 .04
370 Fred Lynn .10 .04
371 Mark Eichhorn .05 .02
372 Dave Schmidt .10 .04
Now with Orioles
373 Jerry Reuss .05 .02
374 Lance Parrish .10 .04
375 Ron Guidry .10 .04
376 Jack Morris .10 .04
377 Willie Randolph .10 .04
378 Joel Youngblood .05 .02
379 Darryl Strawberry .15 .06
380 Rich Gossage .10 .04
381 Dennis Eckersley .25 .10
382 Gary Lucas .05 .02
383 Ron Davis .05 .02
384 Pete Incaviglia .10 .04
385 Orel Hershiser .10 .04
386 Kirk Gibson .10 .04
387 Don Robinson .05 .02
388 Darnell Coles .05 .02
389 Von Hayes .05 .02
390 Gary Matthews .05 .02
391 Jay Howell .05 .02
392 Tim Laudner .05 .02
393 Rod Scurry .05 .02
394 Tony Bernazard .05 .02
395 Damaso Garcia .10 .04
Now with Braves
396 Mike Schmidt .25 .10

1987 O-Pee-Chee Box Bottoms

O-Pee-Chee printed two different four-card panels on the bottoms of its 1987 wax pack boxes. If cut, each card would measure approximately 2 1/8" by 3". These eight cards, in alphabetical order and designated A through H, are considered a separate set from the regular issue, but are styled almost exactly the same, differing only in the player photo and colors for the team name, borders and position on the front. On the horizontal backs, purple borders frame a yellow panel that presents bilingual text describing an outstanding achievement or milestone in the player's career.

	Nm-Mt	Ex-Mt
COMPLETE SET (8)	6.00	2.40
A Don Baylor	.50	.20
B Steve Carlton	1.50	.60
C Ron Cey	.50	.20
D Cecil Cooper	.50	.20
E Rickey Henderson	1.50	.60
F Jim Rice	.50	.20
G Don Sutton	1.50	.60
H Dave Winfield	1.50	.60

1988 O-Pee-Chee

This set is an abridgement of the 1988 Topps set. The 396 standard-size cards comprising the 1988 O-Pee-Chee set differ from the cards of the 1988 Topps set by having a higher ratio of cards of players from the two Canadian teams, a practice begun by O-Pee-Chee in 1977 and continued to 1988. The fronts feature white-bordered color player photos framed by a colored line. The player's name appears in the colored diagonal stripe at the lower right. His team name appears at the top. The orange horizontal backs carry the player's name, position and biography printed across the row of baseball icons at the top. The player's major league statistics follow below. Some backs also have bilingual career highlights, some have bilingual baseball facts and still others have both or neither. The asterisked cards have an extra line on the front inside the picture area indicating team change. They are styled like the 1988 Topps regular issue cards. The O-Pee-Chee logo appears on the front of every card. This set includes the first two 1987 draft picks of both the Montreal Expos and the Toronto Blue Jays.

	Nm-Mt	Ex-Mt
COMPLETE SET (396)	10.00	4.00

1 Chris James .05 .02
2 Steve Buechele .05 .02
3 Mike Henneman .10 .04
4 Eddie Murray .25 .10
5 Bret Saberhagen .10 .04
6 Nathan Minchey .10 .04
7 Harold Reynolds .10 .04
8 Bo Jackson .25 .10
9 Mike Easler .05 .02
10 Ryne Sandberg .25 .10
11 Mike Young .05 .02
12 Tony Phillips .05 .02
13 Andres Thomas .05 .02
14 Tim Burke .05 .02
15 Chili Davis .15 .06
Now with Angels
16 Jim Lindeman .05 .02
17 Ron Oester .05 .02
18 Craig Reynolds .05 .02
19 Juan Samuel .05 .02
20 Kevin Gross .05 .02
21 Cecil Fielder .10 .04
22 Greg Swindell .05 .02
23 Jose DeLeon .05 .02
24 Jim Deshaies .05 .02
25 Andres Galarraga .25 .10
26 Mitch Williams .05 .02
27 R.J. Reynolds .05 .02
28 Jose Nunez .05 .02
29 Angel Salazar .05 .02
30 Sid Fernandez .05 .02
31 Keith Moreland .05 .02
32 John Kruk .10 .04
33 Rob Deer .05 .02
34 Ricky Horton .05 .02
35 Harold Baines .15 .06
36 Jamie Moyer .10 .04
37 Kevin McReynolds .05 .02
38 Ron Darling .05 .02
39 Ozzie Smith .50 .20
40 Orel Hershiser .10 .04
41 Bob Melvin .10 .04
42 Alfredo Griffin .10 .04
Now with Dodgers
43 Dick Schofield .05 .02
44 Terry Steinbach .05 .02
45 Kent Hrbek .10 .04
46 Darnell Coles .05 .02
47 Jimmy Key .10 .04
48 Alan Ashby .05 .02
49 Julio Franco .10 .04
50 Hubie Brooks .05 .02
51 Chris Bando .05 .02
52 Fernando Valenzuela .10 .04
53 Kal Daniels .05 .02
54 Jim Clancy .05 .02
55 Phil Bradley .10 .04
Now with Phillies
56 Andy McGaffigan .05 .02
57 Mike LaValliere .05 .02
58 Dave Magadan .05 .02
59 Danny Cox .05 .02
60 Rickey Henderson .25 .10
61 Jim Rice .10 .04
62 Calvin Schiraldi .10 .04
Now with Cubs
63 Jerry Mumphrey .05 .02
64 Ken Caminiti RC .50 .20
65 Leon Durham .05 .02
66 Shane Rawley .05 .02
67 Ken Oberkfell .05 .02
68 Keith Hernandez .10 .04
69 Bob Brenly .10 .04
70 Roger Clemens 1.00 .40
71 Gary Pettis .10 .04
Now with Tigers
72 Dennis Eckersley .10 .04
73 Dave Smith .05 .02
74 Cal Ripken 1.50 .60
75 Joe Carter .25 .10
76 Denny Martinez .10 .04
77 Juan Beniquez .05 .02
78 Tim Laudner .05 .02
79 Ernie Whitt .05 .02
80 Mark Langston .05 .02
81 Dale Sveum .05 .02
82 Dion James .05 .02
83 Dave Valle .05 .02
84 Bill Wegman .05 .02
85 Howard Johnson .05 .02
86 Benito Santiago .05 .02
87 Casey Candaele .05 .02
88 Delino DeShields XRC .50 .20
89 Dave Winfield .25 .10
90 Dale Murphy .25 .10
91 Jay Howell .10 .04
Now with Dodgers
92 Ken Williams RC .10 .04
93 Bob Sebra .05 .02
94 Tim Wallach .05 .02
95 Lance Parrish .05 .02
96 Todd Benzinger .05 .02
97 Scott Garrelts .05 .02
98 Jose Guzman .05 .02
99 Jeff Reardon .10 .04
100 Jack Clark .10 .04
101 Tracy Jones .05 .02
102 Barry Larkin .75 .30
103 Curt Young .05 .02
104 Juan Nieves .05 .02
105 Terry Pendleton .10 .04
106 Rob Ducey .05 .02
107 Scott Bailes .05 .02
108 Eric King .05 .02
109 Mike Pagliarulo .05 .02
110 Teddy Higuera .05 .02
111 Pedro Guerrero .05 .02
112 Chris Brown .05 .02
113 Kelly Gruber .05 .02
114 Jack Howell .05 .02
115 Johnny Ray .05 .02
116 Mark Eichhorn .05 .02
117 Tony Pena .10 .04
118 Bob Welch .10 .04
Now with Athletics
119 Mike Kingery .05 .02
120 Kirby Puckett .60 .24
121 Charlie Hough .10 .04
122 Tony Bernazard .05 .02
123 Tom Candiotti .05 .02
124 Ray Knight .05 .02
125 Bruce Hurst .05 .02
126 Steve Jeltz .05 .02
127 Ron Guidry .10 .04
128 Duane Ward .05 .02
129 Greg Minton .05 .02
130 Buddy Bell .10 .04
131 Denny Walling .05 .02
132 Donnie Hill .05 .02
133 Wayne Tolleson .05 .02
134 Bob Rodgers MG CL .05 .02
135 Todd Worrell .10 .04
136 Brian Dayett .05 .02
137 Chris Bosio .05 .02
138 Mitch Webster .05 .02
139 Jerry Browne .05 .02
140 Jesse Barfield .05 .02
141 Doug DeCinces .10 .04
Now with Cardinals
142 Andy Van Slyke .10 .04
143 Doug Drabek .10 .04
144 Jeff Parrett .05 .02
145 Bill Madlock .10 .04
146 Larry Herndon .05 .02
147 Bill Buckner .10 .04
148 Carmelo Martinez .05 .02
149 Ken Howell .05 .02
150 Eric Davis .10 .04
151 Randy Ready .05 .02
152 Jeffrey Leonard .05 .02
153 Dave Stieb .10 .04
154 Jeff Stone .05 .02
155 Dave Righetti .05 .02
156 Gary Matthews .10 .04
157 Gary Carter .25 .10
158 Bob Boone .10 .04
159 Glenn Davis .05 .02
160 Willie McGee .10 .04
161 Bryn Smith .05 .02
162 Mark McLemore RC .05 .02
163 Dale Mohorcic .05 .02
164 Mike Flanagan .05 .02
165 Robin Yount .25 .10
166 Bill Doran .05 .02
167 Rance Mulliniks .05 .02
168 Wally Joyner .15 .06
169 Cory Snyder .05 .02
170 Rich Gossage .10 .04
171 Rick Mahler .05 .02
172 Henry Cotto .05 .02
173 George Bell .05 .02
174 B.J. Surhoff .10 .04
175 Kevin Bass .05 .02
176 Jeff Reed .05 .02
177 Frank Tanana .05 .02
178 Darryl Strawberry .10 .04
179 Lou Whitaker .10 .04
180 Terry Kennedy .05 .02
181 Mariano Duncan .05 .02
182 Ken Phelps .05 .02
183 Bob Dernier .10 .04
Now with Phillies
184 Ivan Calderon .05 .02
185 Rick Rhoden .05 .02
186 Rafael Palmeiro .75 .30
187 Kelly Downs .05 .02
188 Spike Owen .05 .02
189 Bobby Bonilla .10 .04
190 Candy Maldonado .05 .02
191 John Cerutti .05 .02
192 Devon White .10 .04
193 Brian Fisher .05 .02
194 Alex Sanchez .05 .02
195 Dan Quisenberry .05 .02
196 Dave Engle .05 .02
197 Lance McCullers .05 .02
198 Franklin Stubbs .05 .02
199 Scott Bradley .05 .02
200 Wade Boggs .25 .10
201 Kirk Gibson .10 .04
202 Brett Butler .10 .04
Now with Giants
203 Dave Anderson .05 .02
204 Donnie Moore .05 .02
205 Nelson Liriano .05 .02
206 Danny Gladden .05 .02
207 Dan Pasqua .10 .04
Now with White Sox
208 Robby Thompson .05 .02
209 Richard Dotson .10 .04
Now with Yankees
210 Willie Randolph .10 .04
211 Danny Tartabull .05 .02
212 Greg Brock .05 .02
213 Albert Hall .05 .02
214 Dave Schmidt .05 .02
215 Von Hayes .05 .02
216 Herm Winningham .05 .02
217 Mike Davis .10 .04
Now with Dodgers
218 Charlie Leibrandt .05 .02
219 Mike Stanley .10 .04
220 Tom Henke .05 .02
221 Dwight Evans .10 .04
222 Willie Wilson .05 .02
223 Stan Jefferson .05 .02
224 Mike Dunne .05 .02
225 Mike Scioscia .10 .04
226 Larry Parrish .05 .02
227 Mike Scott .05 .02
228 Wallace Johnson .05 .02
229 Jeff Musselman .05 .02
230 Pat Tabler .05 .02
231 Paul Molitor .25 .10
232 Bob James .05 .02
233 Joe Niekro .05 .02
234 Oddibe McDowell .05 .02
235 Gary Ward .05 .02
236 Ted Power .10 .04
Now with Royals
237 Pascual Perez .05 .02
238 Luis Polonia .05 .02
239 Mike Diaz .05 .02
240 Lee Smith .10 .04
Now with Red Sox
241 Willie Upshaw .05 .02
242 Tom Niedenfuer .05 .02
243 Tim Raines .10 .04
244 Jeff D. Robinson .05 .02
245 Rich Gedman .05 .02
246 Scott Bankhead .05 .02
247 Andre Dawson .25 .10
248 Brook Jacoby .05 .02
249 Mike Marshall .05 .02
250 Nolan Ryan 1.50 .60
251 Tom Foley .05 .02
252 Bob Brower .05 .02
253 Checklist .05 .02
254 Scott McGregor .05 .02
255 Ken Griffey .10 .04
256 Ken Schrom .05 .02
257 Gary Gaetti .10 .04
258 Ed Nunez .05 .02
259 Frank Viola .05 .02
260 Vince Coleman .05 .02
261 Reid Nichols .05 .02
262 Tim Flannery .05 .02
263 Glenn Braggs .05 .02
264 Garry Templeton .05 .02
265 Bo Diaz .05 .02
266 Matt Nokes .05 .02
267 Barry Bonds 2.00 .80
268 Bruce Ruffin .05 .02
269 Ellis Burks RC .50 .20
270 Mike Witt .05 .02
271 Ken Gerhart .05 .02
272 Lloyd Moseby .05 .02
273 Garth Iorg .05 .02
274 Mike Greenwell .05 .02
275 Kevin Seitzer .10 .04
276 Luis Salazar .05 .02
277 Shawon Dunston .05 .02
278 Rick Reuschel .05 .02
279 Randy St.Claire .05 .02
280 Pete Incaviglia .05 .02
281 Mike Boddicker .05 .02
282 Jay Tibbs .05 .02
283 Shane Mack .05 .02
284 Walt Terrell .05 .02
285 Jim Presley .05 .02
286 Greg Walker .05 .02
287 Dwight Gooden .10 .04
288 Jim Morrison .05 .02
289 Gene Garber .05 .02
290 Tony Fernandez .15 .06
291 Ozzie Virgil .05 .02
292 Carney Lansford .10 .04
293 Jim Acker .05 .02
294 Tommy Hinzo .05 .02
295 Bert Blyleven .10 .04
296 Ozzie Guillen .10 .04
297 Zane Smith .05 .02
298 Milt Thompson .05 .02
299 Len Dykstra .10 .04
300 Don Mattingly .75 .30
301 Bud Black .05 .02
302 Jose Uribe .05 .02
303 Manny Lee .05 .02
304 Sid Bream .05 .02
305 Steve Sax .05 .02
306 Billy Hatcher .05 .02
307 John Shelby .05 .02
308 Lee Mazzilli .10 .04
309 Bill Long .05 .02
310 Tom Herr .05 .02
311 Derek Bell XRC .50 .20
312 George Brett .60 .24
313 Bob McClure .05 .02
314 Jimy Williams MG CL .05 .02
315 Dave Parker .10 .04
Now with Athletics
316 Doyle Alexander .05 .02
317 Dan Plesac .05 .02
318 Mel Hall .05 .02
319 Ruben Sierra .05 .02
320 Alan Trammell .15 .06
321 Mike Schmidt .25 .10
322 Wally Ritchie .05 .02
323 Rick Leach .05 .02
324 Danny Jackson .05 .02
Now with Reds
325 Glenn Hubbard .05 .02
326 Frank White .10 .04
327 Larry Sheets .05 .02
328 John Cangelosi .05 .02
329 Bill Gullickson .05 .02
330 Eddie Whitson .05 .02
331 Brian Downing .05 .02
332 Gary Redus .05 .02
333 Wally Backman .05 .02
334 Dwayne Murphy .05 .02
335 Claudell Washington .05 .02
336 Dave Concepcion .10 .04
337 Jim Gantner .05 .02
338 Marty Barrett .05 .02
339 Mickey Hatcher .05 .02
340 Jack Morris .10 .04
341 John Franco .05 .02
342 Ron Robinson .05 .02
343 Greg Gagne .05 .02
344 Steve Bedrosian .05 .02
345 Scott Fletcher .05 .02
346 Vance Law .10 .04
Now with Cubs
347 Joe Johnson .10 .04
Now with Angels
348 Jim Eisenreich .25 .10
349 Alvin Davis .05 .02
350 Will Clark .50 .20
351 Mike Aldrete .05 .02
352 Billy Ripken .05 .02
353 Dave Stewart .10 .04
354 Neal Heaton .05 .02
355 Roger McDowell .05 .02
356 John Tudor .05 .02
357 Floyd Bannister .10 .04
Now with Royals
358 Rey Quinones .05 .02
359 Glenn Wilson .10 .04
Now with Mariners
360 Tony Gwynn .75 .30
361 Greg Maddux 3.00 1.20
362 Juan Castillo .05 .02
363 Willie Fraser .05 .02
364 Nick Esasky .05 .02
365 Floyd Youmans .05 .02
366 Chet Lemon .05 .02
367 Matt Young .10 .04
Now with A's
368 Gerald Young .05 .02
369 Bob Stanley .05 .02
370 Jose Canseco .25 .10
371 Joe Hesketh .05 .02
372 Rick Sutcliffe .05 .02
373 Checklist 133-264 .05 .02
374 Checklist 265-396 .05 .02
375 Tom Brunansky .05 .02
376 Jody Davis .05 .02
377 Sam Horn .05 .02
378 Mark Gubicza .05 .02
379 Rafael Ramirez .10 .04
Now with Astros
380 Joe Magrane .05 .02
381 Pete O'Brien .05 .02
382 Lee Guetterman .05 .02
383 Eric Bell .05 .02
384 Gene Larkin .10 .04
385 Carlton Fisk .25 .10
386 Mike Fitzgerald .05 .02
387 Kevin Mitchell .10 .04
388 Jim Winn .05 .02
389 Mike Smithson .05 .02
390 Darrell Evans .10 .04

391 Terry Leach .05 .02
392 Charlie Kerfeld .05 .02
393 Mike Krukow .05 .02
394 Mark McGwire 5.00 2.00
395 Fred McGriff .50 .20
396 DeWayne Buice .05 .02

1988 O-Pee-Chee Box Bottoms

O-Pee-Chee printed four different four-card panels on the bottoms of its 1988 wax pack boxes. If cut, each card would measure approximately the standard size. These 16 cards, in alphabetical order and designated A through P, are considered a separate set from the regular issue but are styled almost exactly the same, differing only in the player photo and colors for the team name, borders and position on the front. The backs are identical, except for the letter designations instead of numbers.

Nm-Mt Ex-Mt
COMPLETE SET (16) 15.00 6.00
A Don Baylor .25 .10
B Steve Bedrosian .10 .04
C Juan Beniquez .10 .04
D Bob Boone .25 .10
E Darrell Evans .25 .10
F Tony Gwynn 5.00 2.00
G John Kruk .25 .10
H Marvell Wynne .10 .04
I Joe Carter .75 .30
J Eric Davis .25 .10
K Howard Johnson .10 .04
L Darryl Strawberry .25 .10
M Rickey Henderson 1.50 .60
N Nolan Ryan 8.00 3.20
O Mike Schmidt 1.25 .50
P Kent Tekulve .10 .04

1989 O-Pee-Chee

The 1989 O-Pee-Chee baseball set contains 396 standard-size cards that feature white bordered color player photos framed by colored lines. The player's name and team appear at the lower right. The bilingual pinkish horizontal backs are bordered in black and carry the player's biography and statistics.

Nm-Mt Ex-Mt
COMPLETE SET (396) 15.00 6.00
COMP. FACT. SET (396) 15.00 6.00
1 Brook Jacoby .05 .02
2 Atlee Hammaker .05 .02
3 Jack Clark .05 .02
4 Dave Stieb .10 .04
5 Bud Black .05 .02
6 Damon Berryhill .05 .02
7 Mike Scioscia .10 .04
8 Jose Uribe .05 .02
9 Mike Aldrete .05 .02
10 Andre Dawson .25 .10
11 Bruce Sutter .10 .04
12 Dale Sveum .05 .02
13 Dan Quisenberry .10 .04
14 Tom Niedenfuer .05 .02
15 Robby Thompson .05 .02
16 Ron Robinson .05 .02
17 Brian Downing .05 .02
18 Rick Rhoden .05 .02
19 Greg Gagne .05 .02
20 Allan Anderson .05 .02
21 Eddie Whitson .05 .02
22 Billy Ripken .05 .02
23 Mike Fitzgerald .05 .02
24 Shane Rawley .05 .02
25 Frank White .10 .04
26 Don Mattingly 1.00 .40
27 Fred Lynn .05 .02
28 Mike Moore .05 .02
29 Kelly Gruber .05 .02
30 Dwight Gooden .10 .04
31 Dan Pasqua .05 .02
32 Dennis Rasmussen .05 .02
33 B.J. Surhoff .10 .04
34 Sid Fernandez .05 .02
35 John Tudor .05 .02
36 Mitch Webster .05 .02
37 Doug Drabek .05 .02
38 Bobby Witt .05 .02
39 Mike Maddux .05 .02
40 Steve Sax .05 .02
41 Orel Hershiser .10 .04
42 Pete Incaviglia .05 .02
43 Guillermo Hernandez .05 .02
44 Kevin Coffman .05 .02
45 Kal Daniels .05 .02
46 Carlton Fisk .25 .10
47 Carney Lansford .05 .02
48 Tim Burke .05 .02
49 Alan Trammell .15 .06
50 George Bell .05 .02
51 Tony Gwynn 1.25 .50
52 Bob Brenly .10 .04
53 Ruben Sierra .10 .04
54 Otis Nixon .05 .02
55 Julio Franco .10 .04
56 Pat Tabler .05 .02
57 Alvin Davis .05 .02
58 Kevin Seitzer .05 .02
59 Mark Davis .05 .02
60 Tom Brunansky .05 .02
61 Jeff Treadway .05 .02
62 Alfredo Griffin .05 .02
63 Keith Hernandez .10 .04
64 Alex Trevino .05 .02
65 Rick Reuschel .05 .02
66 Bob Walk .05 .02
67 Dave Palmer .05 .02
68 Pedro Guerrero .05 .02
69 Jose Oquendo .05 .02
70 Mark McGwire 2.00 .80
71 Mike Boddicker .05 .02
72 Wally Backman .05 .02
73 Pascual Perez .05 .02
74 Joe Hesketh .05 .02
75 Tom Henke .05 .02
76 Nelson Liriano .05 .02
77 Doyle Alexander .05 .02
78 Tim Wallach .05 .02
79 Scott Bankhead .05 .02
80 Cory Snyder .05 .02
81 Dave Magadan .05 .02
82 Randy Ready .05 .02
83 Steve Buechele .05 .02
84 Bo Jackson .25 .10
85 Kevin McReynolds .05 .02
86 Jeff Reardon .10 .04
87 Tim "Rock" Raines .10 .04
88 Melido Perez .05 .02
89 Dave LaPoint .05 .02
90 Vince Coleman .05 .02
91 Floyd Youmans .05 .02
92 Buddy Bell .10 .04
93 Andres Galarraga .25 .10
94 Tony Pena .10 .04
95 Gerald Young .05 .02
96 Rick Cerone .05 .02
97 Ken Oberkfell .05 .02
98 Larry Sheets .05 .02
99 Chuck Crim .05 .02
100 Mike Schmidt .25 .10
101 Ivan Calderon .05 .02
102 Kevin Bass .05 .02
103 Chili Davis .10 .04
104 Randy Myers .10 .04
105 Ron Darling .05 .02
106 Willie Upshaw .05 .02
107 Jose DeLeon .05 .02
108 Fred Manrique .05 .02
109 Johnny Ray .05 .02
110 Paul Molitor .25 .10
111 Rance Mulliniks .05 .02
112 Jim Presley .05 .02
113 Lloyd Moseby .05 .02
114 Lance Parrish .05 .02
115 Jody Davis .05 .02
116 Matt Nokes .05 .02
117 Dave Anderson .05 .02
118 Checklist 1-132 .05 .02
119 Rafael Belliard .05 .02
120 Frank Viola .05 .02
121 Roger Clemens 1.00 .40
122 Luis Salazar .05 .02
123 Mike Stanley .05 .02
124 Jim Traber .05 .02
125 Mike Krukow .05 .02
126 Sid Bream .05 .02
127 Joel Skinner .05 .02
128 Milt Thompson .05 .02
129 Terry Clark .05 .02
130 Gerald Perry .05 .02
131 Bryn Smith .05 .02
132 Kirby Puckett .75 .30
133 Bill Long .05 .02
134 Jim Gantner .05 .02
135 Jose Rijo .05 .02
136 Joey Meyer .05 .02
137 Geno Petralli .05 .02
138 Wallace Johnson .05 .02
139 Mike Flanagan .05 .02
140 Shawon Dunston .05 .02
141 Eric Plunk .05 .02
142 Bobby Bonilla .05 .02
143 Jack McDowell .40 .16
144 Mookie Wilson .05 .02
145 Dave Stewart .10 .04
146 Gary Pettis .05 .02
147 Eric Show .05 .02
148 Eddie Murray .40 .16
149 Lee Smith .10 .04
150 Fernando Valenzuela .10 .04
151 Bob Walk .05 .02
152 Harold Baines .15 .06
153 Albert Hall .05 .02
154 Don Carman .05 .02
155 Marty Barrett .05 .02
156 Chris Sabo .05 .02
157 Bret Saberhagen .25 .10
158 Danny Cox .05 .02
159 Tom Foley .05 .02
160 Jeffrey Leonard .05 .02
161 Brady Anderson RC .75 .30
162 Rich Gossage .10 .04
163 Greg Brock .05 .02
164 Joe Carter .15 .06
165 Mike Dunne .05 .02
166 Jeff Russell .05 .02
167 Dan Plesac .05 .02
168 Willie Wilson .05 .02
169 Mike Jackson .10 .04
170 Tony Fernandez .15 .06
171 Jamie Moyer .15 .06
172 Jim Gott .05 .02
173 Mel Hall .05 .02
174 Mark McGwire 2.00 .80
175 John Shelby .05 .02
176 Jeff Parrett .05 .02
177 Tim Belcher .05 .02
178 Rich Gedman .05 .02
179 Ozzie Virgil .05 .02
180 Mike Scott .05 .02
181 Dickie Thon .05 .02
182 Rob Murphy .05 .02
183 Oddibe McDowell .05 .02
184 Wade Boggs .25 .10
185 Claudell Washington .05 .02
186 Randy Johnson RC 3.00 1.20
187 Paul O'Neill .10 .04
188 Todd Benzinger .05 .02
189 Kevin Mitchell .10 .04
190 Mike Witt .05 .02
191 Sil Campusano .05 .02
192 Ken Gerhart .05 .02
193 Bob Rodgers MG .05 .02
194 Floyd Bannister .05 .02
195 Ozzie Guillen .05 .02
196 Ron Gant .10 .04
197 Neal Heaton .05 .02
198 Bill Swift .05 .02
199 Dave Parker .10 .04
200 George Brett .75 .30
201 Bo Diaz .05 .02
202 Brad Moore .05 .02
203 Rob Ducey .05 .02
204 Bert Blyleven .10 .04
205 Dwight Evans .10 .04
206 Roberto Alomar .75 .30
207 Henry Cotto .05 .02
208 Harold Reynolds .10 .04
209 Jose Guzman .05 .02
210 Dale Murphy .25 .10
211 Mike Pagliarulo .05 .02
212 Jay Howell .05 .02
213 Rene Gonzales .05 .02
214 Scott Garrelts .05 .02
215 Kevin Gross .05 .02
216 Jack Howell .05 .02
217 Kurt Stillwell .05 .02
218 Mike LaValliere .05 .02
219 Jim Clancy .05 .02
220 Gary Gaetti .10 .04
221 Hubie Brooks .05 .02
222 Bruce Ruffin .05 .02
223 Jay Buhner .25 .10
224 Cecil Fielder .10 .04
225 Willie McGee .10 .04
226 Bill Doran .05 .02
227 John Farrell .05 .02
228 Nelson Santovenia .05 .02
229 Jimmy Key .10 .04
230 Ozzie Smith .75 .30
231 Dave Schmidt .10 .04
232 Jody Reed .05 .02
233 Gregg Jefferies .05 .02
234 Tom Browning .05 .02
235 John Kruk .10 .04
236 Charles Hudson .05 .02
237 Todd Stottlemyre .10 .04
238 Don Slaught .05 .02
239 Tim Laudner .05 .02
240 Greg Maddux 1.25 .50
241 Brett Butler .10 .04
242 Checklist 133-264 .05 .02
243 Bob Boone .10 .04
244 Willie Randolph .10 .04
245 Jim Rice .10 .04
246 Rey Quinones .05 .02
247 Checklist 265-396 .05 .02
248 Stan Javier .05 .02
249 Tim Leary .05 .02
250 Cal Ripken 1.50 .60
251 John Dopson .05 .02
252 Billy Hatcher .05 .02
253 Robin Yount .25 .10
254 Mickey Hatcher .05 .02
255 Bob Horner .05 .02
256 Benny Santiago .10 .04
257 Luis Rivera .05 .02
258 Fred McGriff .25 .10
259 Dave Wells .05 .02
260 Dave Winfield .25 .10
261 Rafael Ramirez .05 .02
262 Nick Esasky .05 .02
263 Barry Bonds 1.00 .40
264 Joe Magrane .15 .06
265 Kent Hrbek .10 .04
266 Jack Morris .10 .04
267 Jeff M. Robinson .05 .02
268 Ron Kittle .05 .02
269 Candy Maldonado .05 .02
270 Wally Joyner .10 .04
271 Glenn Braggs .05 .02
272 Ron Hassey .05 .02
273 Jose Lind .05 .02
274 Mark Eichhorn .05 .02
275 Danny Tartabull .05 .02
276 Paul Kilgus .05 .02
277 Mike Davis .05 .02
278 Andy McGaffigan .05 .02
279 Scott Bradley .05 .02
280 Bob Knepper .05 .02
281 Gary Redus .05 .02
282 Rickey Henderson .10 .04
283 Andy Allanson .05 .02
284 Rick Leach .05 .02
285 John Candelaria .05 .02
286 Dick Schofield .05 .02
287 Bryan Harvey .05 .02
288 Randy Bush .05 .02
289 Ernie Whitt .10 .04
290 John Franco .10 .04
291 Todd Worrell .05 .02
292 Teddy Higuera .10 .04
293 Keith Moreland .05 .02
294 Juan Berenguer .05 .02
295 Scott Fletcher .05 .02
296 Roger McDowell .05 .02
Now with Indians 12-6-88
297 Mark Grace .75 .30
298 Chris James .05 .02
299 Frank Tanana .05 .02
300 Darryl Strawberry .10 .04
301 Charlie Leibrandt .05 .02
302 Gary Ward .05 .02
303 Brian Fisher .05 .02
304 Terry Steinbach .05 .02
305 Dave Smith .05 .02
306 Greg Minton .05 .02
307 Lance McCullers .05 .02
308 Phil Bradley .05 .02
309 Terry Kennedy .05 .02
310 Rafael Palmeiro .25 .10
311 Ellis Burks .15 .06
312 Doug Jones .05 .02
313 Denny Martinez .10 .04
314 Pete O'Brien .05 .02
315 Greg Swindell .05 .02
316 Walt Weiss .05 .02
317 Pete Stanicek .05 .02
318 Gene Nelson .05 .02
319 Danny Jackson .05 .02
320 Lou Whitaker .10 .04
321 Will Clark .25 .10
322 John Smiley .05 .02
323 Mike Marshall .05 .02
324 Gary Carter .25 .10
325 Jesse Barfield .05 .02
326 Dennis Boyd .05 .02
327 Dave Henderson .05 .02
328 Chet Lemon .05 .02
329 Bob Melvin .10 .04
330 Eric Davis .10 .04
331 Ted Power .05 .02
332 Carmelo Martinez .05 .02
333 Bob Ojeda .05 .02
334 Steve Lyons .10 .04
335 Dave Righetti .10 .04
336 Steve Balboni .05 .02
337 Calvin Schiraldi .05 .02
338 Vance Law .05 .02
339 Zane Smith .05 .02
340 Kirk Gibson .10 .04
341 Jim Deshaies .05 .02
342 Tom Brookens .05 .02
343 Pat Borders 1.50 .60
344 Devon White .10 .04
345 Charlie Hough .10 .04
346 Rex Hudler .05 .02
347 John Cerutti .05 .02
348 Kirk McCaskill .05 .02
349 Len Dykstra .10 .04
350 Andy Van Slyke .10 .04
351 Jeff D. Robinson .05 .02
352 Rick Schu .05 .02
353 Bruce Benedict .05 .02
354 Bill Wegman .05 .02
355 Mark Langston .05 .02
356 Steve Farr .05 .02
357 Richard Dotson .05 .02
358 Andres Thomas .05 .02
359 Alan Ashby .05 .02
360 Ryne Sandberg .75 .30
361 Kelly Downs .05 .02
362 Jeff Musselman .05 .02
363 Barry Larkin .25 .10
364 Rob Deer .05 .02
365 Mike Henneman .05 .02
366 Nolan Ryan 1.50 .60
367 Johnny Paredes .05 .02
368 Bobby Thigpen .05 .02
369 Mickey Brantley .05 .02
370 Dennis Eckersley .25 .10
371 Manny Lee .05 .02
372 Juan Samuel .05 .02
373 Tracy Jones .05 .02
374 Mike Greenwell .05 .02
375 Terry Pendleton .10 .04
376 Steve Lombardozzi .05 .02
377 Mitch Williams .05 .02
378 Glenn Davis .05 .02
379 Mark Gubicza .05 .02
380 Orel Hershiser WS .50 .20
381 Jimy Williams MG .05 .02
382 Kirk Gibson WS .25 .10
383 Howard Johnson .05 .02
384 David Cone .25 .10
385 Von Hayes .05 .02
386 Luis Polonia .05 .02
387 Danny Gladden .05 .02
388 Pete Smith .05 .02
389 Jose Canseco .50 .20
390 Mickey Hatcher .05 .02
391 Wil Tejada .05 .02
392 Duane Ward .05 .02
393 Rick Mahler .05 .02
394 Rick Sutcliffe .05 .02
395 Dave Martinez .05 .02
396 Ken Dayley .05 .02

1989 O-Pee-Chee Box Bottoms

These standard-size box bottom cards feature on their fronts blue-bordered color player photos. The player's name and team appear at the bottom right. The horizontal black back carries bilingual career highlights within a purple panel. The value of the panels uncut is slightly greater, perhaps by 25 percent greater, than the value of the individual cards cut up carefully. The sixteen cards in this set honor players (and one manager) who reached career milestones during the 1988 season.The cards are lettered on the back.

Nm-Mt Ex-Mt
COMPLETE SET (16) 12.00 4.80
A George Brett 2.00 .80
B Bill Buckner .25 .10
C Darrell Evans .25 .10
D Rich Gossage .25 .10
E Greg Gross .10 .04
F Rickey Henderson 1.00 .40
G Keith Hernandez .25 .10
H Tom Lasorda MG .25 .10
I Jim Rice .25 .10
J Cal Ripken 3.00 1.20
K Nolan Ryan 3.00 1.20
L Mike Schmidt .75 .30
M Bruce Sutter .25 .10
N Don Sutton .75 .30
O Kent Tekulve .10 .04
P Dave Winfield .75 .30

1990 O-Pee-Chee

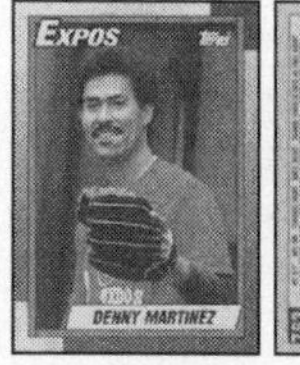
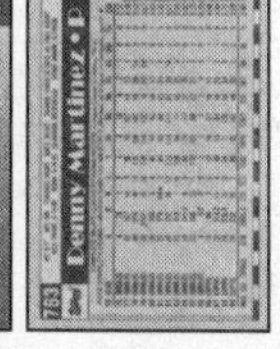

The 1990 O-Pee-Chee baseball set was a 792-card standard-size set. For the first time since 1976, O-Pee-Chee issued the exact same set as Topps. The only distinctions are the bilingual text and the O-Pee-Chee copyright on the backs. The fronts feature color player photos bordered in various colors. The player's name appears at the bottom and his team name is printed at the top. The yellow horizontal backs carry the player's name, biography and position at the top, followed below by major league statistics. Cards 385-407 feature All-Stars, while cards 661-665 are Turn Back the Clock cards. Notable Rookie Cards include Juan Gonzalez, Sammy Sosa, Frank Thomas and Bernie Williams.

Nm-Mt Ex-Mt
COMPLETE SET (792) 20.00 6.00
COMP.FACT.SET (792) 25.00 7.50
1 Nolan Ryan 2.00 .60
2 Nolan Ryan Salute 1.00 .30
3 Nolan Ryan Salute 1.00 .30
4 Nolan Ryan Salute 1.00 .30
5 Nolan Ryan Salute UER 1.00 .30
(Says Texas Stadium rather than Arlington Stadium)
6 Vince Coleman RB .05 .02
7 Rickey Henderson RB .10 .03
8 Cal Ripken RB .75 .23
9 Eric Plunk .05 .02
10 Barry Larkin .25 .07
11 Paul Gibson .05 .02
12 Joe Girardi .05 .02
13 Mark Williamson .05 .02
14 Mike Fetters .05 .02
15 Teddy Higuera .05 .02
16 Kent Anderson .05 .02
17 Kelly Downs .05 .02
18 Carlos Quintana .05 .02
19 Al Newman .05 .02
20 Mark Gubicza .05 .02
21 Jeff Torborg MG .05 .02
22 Bruce Ruffin .05 .02
23 Randy Velarde .05 .02
24 Joe Hesketh .05 .02
25 Willie Randolph .10 .03
26 Don Slaught .10 .03
Now with Pirates 12/4/89
27 Rick Leach .05 .02
28 Duane Ward .05 .02
29 John Cangelosi .05 .02
30 David Cone .25 .07
31 Henry Cotto .05 .02
32 John Farrell .05 .02
33 Greg Walker .05 .02
34 Tony Fossas .05 .02
35 Benito Santiago .10 .03
36 John Costello .05 .02
37 Domingo Ramos .05 .02
38 Wes Gardner .05 .02
39 Curt Ford .05 .02
40 Jay Howell .05 .02
41 Matt Williams .15 .04
42 Jeff M. Robinson .05 .02
43 Dante Bichette .25 .07
44 Roger Salkeld FDP RC .05 .02
45 Dave Parker UER .15 .04
Born in Jackson not Calhoun
46 Rob Dibble .05 .02
47 Brian Harper .05 .02
48 Zane Smith .05 .02
49 Tom Lawless .05 .02
50 Glenn Davis .05 .02
51 Doug Rader MG .05 .02
52 Jack Daugherty .05 .02
53 Mike LaCoss .05 .02
54 Joel Skinner .05 .02
55 Darrell Evans UER .10 .03
HR total should be 414, not 424
56 Franklin Stubbs .05 .02
57 Greg Vaughn .25 .07
58 Keith Miller .05 .02
59 Ted Power .10 .03
Now with Pirates 11/21/89
60 George Brett .75 .23
61 Deion Sanders .25 .07
62 Ramon Martinez .15 .04
63 Mike Pagliarulo .05 .02
64 Danny Darwin .05 .02
65 Devon White .05 .02
66 Greg Litton .05 .02
67 Scott Sanderson .10 .03
Now with Athletics 12/13/89
68 Dave Henderson .05 .02
69 Todd Frohwirth .05 .02
70 Mike Greenwell .05 .02
71 Allan Anderson .05 .02
72 Jeff Huson .05 .02
73 Bob Milacki .05 .02
74 Jeff Jackson FDP RC .05 .02
75 Doug Jones .05 .02
76 Dave Valle .05 .02
77 Dave Bergman .05 .02
78 Mike Flanagan .05 .02
79 Ron Kittle .05 .02
80 Jeff Russell .05 .02
81 Bob Rodgers MG .05 .02
82 Scott Terry .05 .02
83 Hensley Meulens .05 .02
84 Ray Searage .05 .02
85 Juan Samuel .10 .03
Now with Dodgers 12/20/89
86 Paul Kilgus .10 .03
Now with Blue Jays 12/7/89
87 Rick Luecken .10 .03
Now with Braves 12/17/89
88 Glenn Braggs .05 .02
89 Clint Zavaras .05 .02
90 Jack Clark .10 .03
91 Steve Frey .05 .02
92 Mike Stanley .05 .02
93 Shawn Hillegas .05 .02
94 Herm Winningham .05 .02
95 Todd Worrell .05 .02
96 Jody Reed .05 .02
97 Curt Schilling 2.00 .60
98 Jose Gonzalez .05 .02
99 Rich Monteleone .05 .02
100 Will Clark .25 .07
101 Shane Rawley .05 .02
Now with Red Sox

1/9/90
102 Stan Javier .05 .02
103 Marvin Freeman .05 .02
104 Bob Knepper .05 .02
105 Randy Myers .10 .03
Now with Reds
12/8/89
106 Charlie O'Brien .05 .02
107 Fred Lynn .10 .03
Now with Padres
12/7/89
108 Rod Nichols .05 .02
109 Roberto Kelly .05 .02
110 Tommy Helms MG .05 .02
111 Ed Whited .05 .02
112 Glenn Wilson .05 .02
113 Manny Lee .05 .02
114 Mike Bielecki .05 .02
115 Tony Pena .15 .04
Now with Red Sox
11/28/89
116 Floyd Bannister .05 .02
117 Mike Sharperson .05 .02
118 Erik Hanson .05 .02
119 Billy Hatcher .05 .02
120 John Franco .15 .04
Now with Mets
12/8/89
121 Robin Ventura .25 .07
122 Shawn Abner .05 .02
123 Rich Gedman .05 .02
124 Dave Dravecky .05 .02
125 Kent Hrbek .10 .03
126 Randy Kramer .05 .02
127 Mike Devereaux .05 .02
128 Checklist 1 .05 .02
129 Ron Jones .05 .02
130 Bert Blyleven .10 .03
131 Matt Nokes .05 .02
132 Lance Blankenship .05 .02
133 Ricky Horton .05 .02
134 E.Cunningham FDP RC .05 .02
135 Dave Magadan .05 .02
136 Kevin Brown .25 .07
137 Marty Pevey .05 .02
138 Al Leiter .25 .07
139 Greg Brock .05 .02
140 Andre Dawson .25 .07
141 John Hart MG .05 .02
142 Jeff Wetherby .05 .02
143 Rafael Belliard .05 .02
144 Bud Black .05 .02
145 Terry Steinbach .05 .02
146 Rob Richie .05 .02
147 Chuck Finley .10 .03
148 Edgar Martinez .15 .04
149 Steve Farr .05 .02
150 Kirk Gibson .10 .03
151 Rick Mahler .05 .02
152 Lonnie Smith .05 .02
153 Randy Milligan .05 .02
154 Mike Maddux .10 .03
Now with Dodgers
12/21/89
155 Ellis Burks .15 .04
156 Ken Patterson .05 .02
157 Craig Biggio .25 .07
158 Craig Lefferts .10 .03
Now with Padres
12/7/89
159 Mike Felder .05 .02
160 Dave Righetti .05 .02
161 Harold Reynolds .10 .03
162 Todd Zeile .15 .04
163 Phil Bradley .05 .02
164 Jeff Juden FDP RC .05 .02
165 Walt Weiss .05 .02
166 Bobby Witt .05 .02
167 Kevin Appier .15 .04
168 Jose Lind .05 .02
169 Richard Dotson .10 .03
Now with Royals
12/6/89
170 George Bell .05 .02
171 Russ Nixon MG .05 .02
172 Tom Lampkin .05 .02
173 Tim Belcher .05 .02
174 Jeff Kunkel .05 .02
175 Mike Moore .05 .02
176 Luis Quinones .05 .02
177 Mike Henneman .05 .02
178 Chris James .05 .02
Now with Indians
12/6/89
179 Brian Holton .05 .02
180 Tim Raines .10 .03
181 Juan Agosto .05 .02
182 Mookie Wilson .10 .03
183 Steve Lake .05 .02
184 Danny Cox .05 .02
185 Ruben Sierra .10 .03
186 Dave LaPoint .05 .02
187 Rick Wrona .05 .02
188 Mike Smithson .10 .03
Now with Angels
12/19/89
189 Dick Schofield .05 .02
190 Rick Reuschel .05 .02
191 Pat Borders .05 .02
192 Don August .05 .02
193 Andy Benes .10 .03
194 Glenallen Hill .05 .02
195 Tim Burke .05 .02
196 Gerald Young .05 .02
197 Doug Drabek .05 .02
198 Mike Marshall .10 .03
Now with Mets
12/20/89
199 Sergio Valdez .05 .02
200 Don Mattingly 1.00 .30
201 Cito Gaston MG .05 .02
202 Mike Macfarlane .05 .02
203 Mike Roesler .05 .02
204 Bob Dernier .05 .02
205 Mark Davis .10 .03
Now with Royals
12/11/89
206 Nick Esasky .10 .03
Now with Braves
11/17/89
207 Bob Ojeda .05 .02
208 Brook Jacoby .05 .02
209 Greg Mathews .05 .02
210 Ryne Sandberg .50 .15
211 John Cerutti .05 .02
212 Joe Orsulak .05 .02
213 Scott Bankhead .05 .02
214 Terry Francona .10 .03
215 Kirk McCaskill .05 .02
216 Ricky Jordan .05 .02
217 Don Robinson .05 .02
218 Wally Backman .05 .02
219 Donn Pall .05 .02
220 Barry Bonds 1.00 .30
221 Gary Mielke .05 .02
222 Kurt Stillwell UER .05 .02
Graduate misspelled
as gradute
223 Tommy Gregg .05 .02
224 Delino DeShields RC .25 .07
225 Jim Deshaies .05 .02
226 Mickey Hatcher .05 .02
227 Kevin Tapani RC .25 .07
228 Dave Martinez .05 .02
229 David Wells .25 .07
230 Keith Hernandez .15 .04
Now with Indians
12/7/89
231 Jack McKeon MG .10 .03
232 Darnell Coles .05 .02
233 Ken Hill .10 .03
234 Mariano Duncan .05 .02
235 Jeff Reardon .10 .03
Now with Red Sox
12/6/89
236 Hal Morris .05 .02
Now with Reds
12/12/89
237 Kevin Ritz .05 .02
238 Felix Jose .05 .02
239 Eric Show .05 .02
240 Mark Grace .25 .07
241 Mike Krukow .05 .02
242 Fred Manrique .05 .02
243 Barry Jones .05 .02
244 Bill Schroeder .05 .02
245 Roger Clemens 1.00 .30
246 Jim Eisenreich .05 .02
247 Jerry Reed .05 .02
248 Dave Anderson .10 .03
Now with Giants&(11/29/89
249 Mike(Texas) Smith .05 .02
250 Jose Canseco .25 .07
251 Jeff Blauser .05 .02
252 Otis Nixon .05 .02
253 Mark Portugal .05 .02
254 Francisco Cabrera .05 .02
255 Bobby Thigpen .05 .02
256 Marvell Wynne .05 .02
257 Jose DeLeon .05 .02
258 Barry Lyons .05 .02
259 Lance McCullers .05 .02
260 Eric Davis .10 .03
261 Whitey Herzog MG .10 .03
262 Checklist 2 .05 .02
263 Mel Stottlemyre Jr. .05 .02
264 Bryan Clutterbuck .05 .02
265 Pete O'Brien .10 .03
Now with Mariners
12/7/89
266 German Gonzalez .05 .02
267 Mark Davidson .05 .02
268 Rob Murphy .05 .02
269 Dickie Thon .05 .02
270 Dave Stewart .10 .03
271 Chet Lemon .05 .02
272 Bryan Harvey .05 .02
273 Bobby Bonilla .05 .02
274 Mauro Gozzo .05 .02
275 Mickey Tettleton .10 .03
276 Gary Thurman .05 .02
277 Lenny Harris .05 .02
278 Pascual Perez .10 .03
Now with Yankees
11/27/89
279 Steve Buechele .05 .02
280 Lou Whitaker .10 .03
281 Kevin Bass .10 .03
Now with Giants
11/20/89
282 Derek Lilliquist .05 .02
283 Joey Belle .25 .07
284 Mark Gardner .05 .02
285 Willie McGee .10 .03
286 Lee Guetterman .05 .02
287 Vance Law .05 .02
288 Greg Briley .05 .02
289 Norm Charlton .05 .02
290 Robin Yount .25 .07
291 Dave Johnson MG .10 .03
292 Jim Gott .10 .03
Now with Dodgers
12/7/89
293 Mike Gallego .05 .02
294 Craig McMurtry .05 .02
295 Fred McGriff .25 .07
296 Jeff Ballard .05 .02
297 Tom Herr .05 .02
298 Dan Gladden .05 .02
299 Adam Peterson .05 .02
300 Bo Jackson .10 .03
301 Don Aase .05 .02
302 Marcus Lawton .05 .02
303 Rick Cerone .10 .03
Now with Yankees
12/19/89
304 Marty Clary .05 .02
305 Eddie Murray .25 .07
306 Tom Niedenfuer .05 .02
307 Bip Roberts .05 .02
308 Jose Guzman .05 .02
309 Eric Yelding .05 .02
310 Steve Bedrosian .05 .02
311 Dwight Smith .05 .02
312 Dan Quisenberry .05 .02
313 Gus Polidor .05 .02
314 Donald Harris FDP .05 .02
315 Bruce Hurst .05 .02
316 Carney Lansford .10 .03
317 Mark Guthrie .05 .02
318 Wallace Johnson .05 .02
319 Dion James .05 .02
320 Dave Stieb .10 .03
321 Joe Morgan MG .05 .02
322 Junior Ortiz .05 .02
323 Willie Wilson .05 .02
324 Pete Harnisch .05 .02
325 Robby Thompson .05 .02
326 Tom McCarthy .05 .02
327 Ken Williams .10 .03
328 Curt Young .05 .02
329 Oddibe McDowell .05 .02
330 Ron Darling .05 .02
331 Juan Gonzalez RC 4.00 1.20
332 Paul O'Neill .25 .07
333 Bill Wegman .05 .02
334 Johnny Ray .05 .02
335 Andy Hawkins .05 .02
336 Ken Griffey Jr. 3.00 .90
337 Lloyd McClendon .10 .03
338 Dennis Lamp .05 .02
339 Dave Clark .10 .03
Now with Cubs
11/20/89
340 Fernando Valenzuela .10 .03
341 Tom Foley .05 .02
342 Alex Trevino .05 .02
343 Frank Tanana .05 .02
344 George Canale .05 .02
345 Harold Baines .15 .04
346 Jim Presley .05 .02
347 Junior Felix .05 .02
348 Gary Wayne .05 .02
349 Steve Finley .25 .07
350 Bret Saberhagen .10 .03
351 Roger Craig MG .05 .02
352 Bryn Smith .10 .03
Now with Cardinals
11/29/89
353 Sandy Alomar Jr. .15 .04
Now with Indians
12/6/89
354 Stan Belinda .05 .02
355 Marty Barrett .05 .02
356 Randy Ready .05 .02
357 Dave West .05 .02
358 Andres Thomas .05 .02
359 Jimmy Jones .05 .02
360 Paul Molitor .25 .07
361 Randy McCament .05 .02
362 Damon Berryhill .05 .02
363 Dan Petry .05 .02
364 Rolando Roomes .05 .02
365 Ozzie Guillen .10 .03
366 Mike Heath .05 .02
367 Mike Morgan .05 .02
368 Bill Doran .05 .02
369 Todd Burns .05 .02
370 Tim Wallach .05 .02
371 Jimmy Key .10 .03
372 Terry Kennedy .05 .02
373 Alvin Davis .05 .02
374 Steve Cummings RC .05 .02
375 Dwight Evans .10 .03
376 Checklist 3 UER .05 .02
Higuera misalphabet-
ized in Brewer list
377 Mickey Weston .05 .02
378 Luis Salazar .10 .03
379 Steve Rosenberg .05 .02
380 Dave Winfield .25 .07
381 Frank Robinson MG .15 .04
382 Jeff Musselman .05 .02
383 John Morris .05 .02
384 Pat Combs .05 .02
385 Fred McGriff AS .10 .03
386 Julio Franco AS .05 .02
387 Wade Boggs AS .10 .03
388 Cal Ripken AS .75 .23
389 Robin Yount AS .10 .03
390 Ruben Sierra AS .05 .02
391 Kirby Puckett AS .25 .07
392 Carlton Fisk AS .10 .03
393 Bret Saberhagen AS .05 .02
394 Jeff Ballard AS .05 .02
395 Jeff Russell AS .05 .02
396 A.Bartlett Giamatti RC .25 .07
COMM MEM
397 Will Clark AS .10 .03
398 Ryne Sandberg AS .25 .07
399 Howard Johnson AS .05 .02
400 Ozzie Smith AS .25 .07
401 Kevin Mitchell AS .05 .02
402 Eric Davis AS .05 .02
403 Tony Gwynn AS .25 .07
404 Craig Biggio AS .15 .04
405 Mike Scott AS .05 .02
406 Joe Magrane AS .05 .02
407 Mark Davis AS .05 .02
Now with Royals
12/11/89
408 Trevor Wilson .05 .02
409 Tom Brunansky .05 .02
410 Joe Boever .05 .02
411 Ken Phelps .05 .02
412 Jamie Moyer .05 .02
413 Brian DuBois .05 .02
414 F.Thomas FDP RC 4.00 1.20
415 Shawon Dunston .05 .02
416 Dave Johnson (P) .05 .02
417 Jim Gantner .05 .02
418 Tom Browning .05 .02
419 Beau Allred RC .05 .02
420 Carlton Fisk .25 .07
421 Greg Minton .05 .02
422 Pat Sheridan .05 .02
423 Fred Toliver .10 .03
Now with Yankees
9/27/89
424 Jerry Reuss .05 .02
425 Bill Landrum .05 .02
426 Jeff Hamilton UER .05 .02
Stats say he fanned
197 times in 1987
but he only had 147 at bats
427 Carmen Castillo .05 .02
428 Steve Davis .10 .03
Now with Dodgers
12/12/89
429 Tom Kelly MG .05 .02
430 Pete Incaviglia .05 .02
431 Randy Johnson .75 .23
432 Damaso Garcia .10 .03
Now with Yankees
12/22/89
433 Steve Olin .10 .03
434 Mark Carreon .05 .02
435 Kevin Seitzer .05 .02
436 Mel Hall .05 .02
437 Les Lancaster .05 .02
438 Greg Myers .05 .02
439 Jeff Parrett .05 .02
440 Alan Trammell .15 .04
441 Bob Kipper .05 .02
442 Jerry Browne .05 .02
443 Cris Carpenter .05 .02
444 Kyle Abbott FDP .05 .02
445 Danny Jackson .05 .02
446 Dan Pasqua .05 .02
447 Atlee Hammaker .05 .02
448 Greg Gagne .05 .02
449 Dennis Rasmussen .05 .02
450 Rickey Henderson .75 .23
451 Mark Lemke .05 .02
452 Luis DeLosSantos .05 .02
453 Jody Davis .05 .02
454 Jeff King .05 .02
455 Jeffrey Leonard .05 .02
456 Chris Gwynn .05 .02
457 Gregg Jefferies .05 .02
458 Bob McClure .05 .02
459 Jim Lefebvre MG .05 .02
460 Mike Scott .05 .02
461 Carlos Martinez .05 .02
462 Denny Walling .05 .02
463 Drew Hall .05 .02
464 Jerome Walton .05 .02
465 Kevin Gross .05 .02
466 Rance Mulliniks .05 .02
467 Juan Nieves .05 .02
468 Bill Ripken .05 .02
469 John Kruk .10 .03
470 Frank Viola .05 .02
471 Mike Brumley .10 .03
Now with Orioles
1/10/90
472 Jose Uribe .05 .02
473 Joe Price .05 .02
474 Rich Thompson .05 .02
475 Bob Welch .05 .02
476 Brad Komminsk .05 .02
477 Willie Fraser .05 .02
478 Mike LaValliere .05 .02
479 Frank White .10 .03
480 Sid Fernandez .05 .02
481 Garry Templeton .05 .02
482 Steve Carter .05 .02
483 Alejandro Pena .10 .03
Now with Mets
12/20/89
484 Mike Fitzgerald .05 .02
485 John Candelaria .05 .02
486 Jeff Treadway .05 .02
487 Steve Searcy .05 .02
488 Ken Oberkfell .10 .03
Now with Astros
12/6/89
489 Nick Leyva MG .05 .02
490 Dan Plesac .05 .02
491 Dave Cochrane RC .05 .02
492 Ron Oester .05 .02
493 Jason Grimsley .05 .02
494 Terry Puhl .05 .02
495 Lee Smith .10 .03
496 Cecil Espy UER .05 .02
'88 stats have 3 SB's
should be 33
497 Dave Schmidt .10 .03
Now with Expos
12/13/89
498 Rick Schu .05 .02
499 Bill Long .05 .02
500 Kevin Mitchell .05 .02
501 Matt Young .10 .03
Now with Mariners
12/8/89
502 Mitch Webster .10 .03
Now with Indians
11/20/89
503 Randy St.Claire .05 .02
504 Tom O'Malley .05 .02
505 Kelly Gruber .05 .02
506 Tom Glavine .25 .07
507 Gary Redus .05 .02
508 Terry Leach .05 .02
509 Tom Pagnozzi .05 .02
510 Dwight Gooden .10 .03
511 Clay Parker .05 .02
512 Gary Pettis .10 .03
Now with Rangers
11/24/89
513 Mark Eichhorn .10 .03
Now with Angels
12/13/89
514 Andy Allanson .05 .02
515 Len Dykstra .10 .03
516 Tim Leary .05 .02
517 Roberto Alomar .25 .07
518 Bill Krueger .05 .02
519 Bucky Dent MG .05 .02
520 Mitch Williams .05 .02
521 Craig Worthington .05 .02
522 Mike Dunne .10 .03
Now with Padres
12/4/89
523 Jay Bell .05 .02
524 Daryl Boston .05 .02
525 Wally Joyner .10 .03
526 Checklist 4 .05 .02
527 Ron Hassey .05 .02
528 Kevin Wickander UER .10 .03
Monthly scoreboard
strikeout total was 2.2
that was his innings
pitched total
529 Greg A. Harris .05 .02
530 Mark Langston .10 .03
Now with Angels
12/4/89
531 Ken Caminiti .25 .07
532 Cecilio Guante .10 .03
Now with Indians
11/21/89
533 Tim Jones .05 .02
534 Louie Meadows .05 .02
535 John Smoltz .25 .07
536 Bob Geren .05 .02
537 Mark Grant .05 .02
538 Bill Spiers UER .05 .02
Photo actually George Canale
539 Neal Heaton .05 .02
540 Danny Tartabull .05 .02
541 Pat Perry .05 .02
542 Darren Daulton .10 .03
543 Nelson Liriano .05 .02
544 Dennis Boyd .10 .03
Now with Expos
12/7/89
545 Kevin McReynolds .05 .02
546 Kevin Hickey .05 .02
547 Jack Howell .05 .02
548 Pat Clements .05 .02
549 Don Zimmer MG .05 .02
550 Julio Franco .10 .03
551 Tim Crews .05 .02
552 Mike(Miss.) Smith .05 .02
553 Scott Scudder UER .05 .02
Cedar Rapids
554 Jay Buhner .25 .07
555 Jack Morris .10 .03
556 Gene Larkin .05 .02
557 Jeff Innis .05 .02
558 Rafael Ramirez .05 .02
559 Andy McGaffigan .05 .02
560 Steve Sax .05 .02
561 Ken Dayley .05 .02
562 Chad Kreuter .05 .02
563 Alex Sanchez .05 .02
564 Tyler Houston FDP RC .05 .02
565 Scott Fletcher .05 .02
566 Mark Knudson .05 .02
567 Ron Gant .10 .03
568 John Smiley .05 .02
569 Ivan Calderon .05 .02
570 Cal Ripken 1.50 .45
571 Brett Butler .10 .03
572 Greg W. Harris .05 .02
573 Danny Heep .05 .02
574 Bill Swift .05 .02
575 Lance Parrish .05 .02
576 Mike Dyer RC .05 .02
577 Charlie Hayes .05 .02
578 Joe Magrane .05 .02
579 Art Howe MG .05 .02
580 Joe Carter .10 .03
581 Ken Griffey Sr. .10 .03
582 Rick Honeycutt .05 .02
583 Bruce Benedict .05 .02
584 Phil Stephenson .05 .02
585 Kal Daniels .05 .02
586 Edwin Nunez .05 .02
587 Lance Johnson .05 .02
588 Rick Rhoden .05 .02
589 Mike Aldrete .05 .02
590 Ozzie Smith .50 .15
591 Todd Stottlemyre .10 .03
592 R.J. Reynolds .05 .02
593 Scott Bradley .05 .02
594 Luis Sojo .05 .02
595 Greg Swindell .05 .02
596 Jose DeJesus .05 .02
597 Chris Bosio .05 .02
598 Brady Anderson .25 .07
599 Frank Williams .05 .02
600 Darryl Strawberry .10 .03
601 Luis Rivera .05 .02
602 Scott Garrelts .05 .02
603 Tony Armas .05 .02
604 Ron Robinson .05 .02
605 Mike Scioscia .10 .03
606 Storm Davis .10 .03
Now with Royals
12/7/89
607 Steve Jeltz .05 .02
608 Eric Anthony .05 .02
609 Sparky Anderson MG .10 .03
610 Pedro Guerrero .05 .02
611 Walt Terrell .10 .03
Now with Pirates
11/29/89
612 Dave Gallagher .05 .02
613 Jeff Pico .05 .02
614 Nelson Santovenia .05 .02
615 Rob Deer .05 .02
616 Brian Holman .05 .02
617 Geronimo Berroa .05 .02
618 Ed Whitson .05 .02
619 Rob Ducey .05 .02
620 Tony Castillo .05 .02
621 Melido Perez .05 .02
622 Sid Bream .05 .02
623 Jim Corsi .05 .02
624 Darrin Jackson .05 .02
625 Roger McDowell .05 .02
626 Bob Melvin .10 .03
627 Jose Rijo .05 .02
628 Candy Maldonado .10 .03
Now with Indians
11/28/89
629 Eric Hetzel .05 .02
630 Gary Gaetti .10 .03
631 John Wetteland .25 .07
632 Scott Lusader .05 .02
633 Dennis Cook .05 .02
634 Luis Polonia .05 .02
635 Brian Downing .05 .02
636 Jesse Orosco .10 .03
637 Craig Reynolds .05 .02
638 Jeff Montgomery .10 .03
639 Tony LaRussa MG .10 .03
640 Rick Sutcliffe .10 .03
641 Doug Strange .05 .02
642 Jack Armstrong .05 .02
643 Alfredo Griffin .05 .02
644 Paul Assenmacher .05 .02
645 Jose Oquendo .05 .02
646 Checklist 5 .05 .02
647 Rex Hudler .10 .03
648 Jim Clancy .10 .03
649 Dan Murphy .05 .02
650 Mike Witt .05 .02
651 Rafael Santana .10 .03
Now with Indians
1/10/90
652 Mike Boddicker .05 .02

653 John Moses .05 .02
654 Paul Coleman FDP RC .05 .02
655 Gregg Olson .05 .02
656 Mackey Sasser .05 .02
657 Terry Mulholland .05 .02
658 Donell Nixon .05 .02
659 Greg Cadaret .05 .02
660 Vince Coleman .05 .02
661 Dick Howser TBC'85 UER .05 .02
Seaver's 300th on 7/11/85 should be 8/4/85
662 Mike Schmidt TBC'80 .25 .07
663 Fred Lynn TBC'75 .05 .02
664 Johnny Bench TBC'70 .25 .07
665 Sandy Koufax TBC'65 .50 .15
666 Brian Fisher .05 .02
667 Curt Wilkerson .05 .02
668 Joe Oliver .05 .02
669 Tom Lasorda MG .15 .04
670 Dennis Eckersley .25 .07
671 Bob Boone .10 .03
672 Roy Smith .05 .02
673 Joey Meyer .05 .02
674 Spike Owen .05 .02
675 Jim Abbott .15 .04
676 Randy Kutcher .05 .02
677 Jay Tibbs .05 .02
678 Kirt Manwaring UER .05 .02
'88 Phoenix stats repeated
679 Gary Ward .05 .02
680 Howard Johnson .05 .02
681 Mike Schooler .05 .02
682 Dann Bilardello .05 .02
683 Kenny Rogers .10 .03
684 Julio Machado .05 .02
685 Tony Fernandez .05 .02
686 Carmelo Martinez .10 .03
Now with Phillies
12/4/89
687 Tim Birtsas .05 .02
688 Milt Thompson .05 .02
689 Rich Yett .10 .03
Now with Twins
12/26/89
690 Mark McGwire 1.50 .45
691 Chuck Cary .05 .02
692 Sammy Sosa RC 8.00 2.40
693 Calvin Schiraldi .05 .02
694 Mike Stanton .05 .02
695 Tom Henke .05 .02
696 B.J. Surhoff .10 .03
697 Mike Davis .05 .02
698 Omar Vizquel .25 .07
699 Jim Leyland MG .05 .02
700 Kirby Puckett 1.00 .30
701 Bernie Williams RC 2.00 .60
702 Tony Phillips .05 .02
Now with Tigers
12/5/89
703 Jeff Brantley .05 .02
704 Chip Hale .05 .02
705 Claudell Washington .05 .02
706 Geno Petralli .05 .02
707 Luis Aquino .05 .02
708 Larry Sheets .10 .03
Now with Tigers
1/10/90
709 Juan Berenguer .05 .02
710 Von Hayes .05 .02
711 Rick Aguilera .10 .03
712 Todd Benzinger .05 .02
713 Tim Drummond .05 .02
714 Marquis Grissom RC .50 .15
715 Greg Maddux 1.00 .30
716 Steve Balboni .05 .02
717 Ron Karkovice .05 .02
718 Gary Sheffield .50 .15
719 Wally Whitehurst .05 .02
720 Andres Galarraga .25 .07
721 Lee Mazzilli .10 .03
722 Felix Fermin .05 .02
723 Jeff D. Robinson .05 .02
Now with Yankees
12/4/89
724 Juan Bell .05 .02
725 Terry Pendleton .10 .03
726 Gene Nelson .05 .02
727 Pat Tabler .05 .02
728 Jim Acker .05 .02
729 Bobby Valentine MG .05 .02
730 Tony Gwynn .75 .23
731 Don Carman .05 .02
732 Ernest Riles .05 .02
733 John Dopson .05 .02
734 Kevin Elster .05 .02
735 Charlie Hough .10 .03
736 Rick Dempsey .05 .02
737 Chris Sabo .05 .02
738 Gene Harris .05 .02
739 Dale Sveum .05 .02
740 Jesse Barfield .05 .02
741 Steve Wilson .05 .02
742 Ernie Whitt .05 .02
743 Tom Candiotti .05 .02
744 Kelly Mann .05 .02
745 Hubie Brooks .05 .02
746 Dave Smith .05 .02
747 Randy Bush .05 .02
748 Doyle Alexander .05 .02
749 Mark Parent UER .05 .02
'87 BA .80, should be .080
750 Dale Murphy .25 .07
751 Steve Lyons .10 .03
752 Tom Gordon .15 .04
753 Chris Speier .05 .02
754 Bob Walk .05 .02
755 Rafael Palmeiro .25 .07
756 Ken Howell .05 .02
757 Larry Walker RC 1.25 .35
758 Mark Thurmond .05 .02
759 Tom Trebelhorn MG .05 .02
760 Wade Boggs .25 .07
761 Mike Jackson .10 .03
762 Doug Dascenzo .05 .02
763 Dennis Martinez .10 .03
764 Tim Teufel .05 .02
765 Chili Davis .10 .03
766 Brian Meyer .05 .02
767 Tracy Jones .05 .02
768 Chuck Crim .05 .02
769 Greg Hibbard .05 .02
770 Cory Snyder .05 .02
771 Pete Smith .05 .02
772 Jeff Reed .05 .02
773 Dave Leiper .05 .02
774 Ben McDonald .05 .02
775 Andy Van Slyke .10 .03
776 Charlie Leibrandt .10 .03
Now with Braves
12/17/89
777 Tim Laudner .05 .02
778 Mike Jeffcoat .05 .02
779 Lloyd Moseby .10 .03
Now with Tigers
12/7/89
780 Orel Hershiser .10 .03
781 Mario Diaz .05 .02
782 Jose Alvarez .10 .03
Now with Giants
12/4/89
783 Checklist 6 .05 .02
784 Scott Bailes .10 .03
Now with Angels
1/9/90
785 Jim Rice .10 .03
786 Eric King .05 .02
787 Rene Gonzales .05 .02
788 Frank DiPino .05 .02
789 John Wathan MG .05 .02
790 Gary Carter .25 .07
791 Alvaro Espinoza .05 .02
792 Gerald Perry .05 .02

1990 O-Pee-Chee Box Bottoms

The 1990 O-Pee-Chee box bottom cards comprise four different box bottoms from the bottoms of wax pack boxes, with four cards each, for a total of 16 standard-size cards. The cards are nearly identical to the 1990 Topps Box Bottom cards. The fronts feature green-bordered color player action shots. The player's name appears at the bottom and his team name appears at the upper left. The yellow-green horizontal backs carry player career highlights in both English and French. The cards are lettered (A-P) rather than numbered on the back.

	Nm-Mt	Ex-Mt
COMPLETE SET (16)	10.00	3.00
A Wade Boggs	.75	.23
B George Brett	1.50	.45
C Andre Dawson	.50	.15
D Darrell Evans	.20	.06
E Dwight Gooden	.20	.06
F Rickey Henderson	1.00	.30
G Tom Lasorda MG	.50	.15
H Fred Lynn	.10	.03
I Mark McGwire	2.50	.75
J Dave Parker	.20	.06
K Jeff Reardon	.20	.06
L Rick Reuschel	.10	.03
M Jim Rice	.20	.06
N Cal Ripken	3.00	.90
O Nolan Ryan	3.00	.90
P Ryne Sandberg	1.50	.45

1991 O-Pee-Chee

The 1991 O-Pee-Chee baseball set contains 792 standard-size cards. For the second time since 1976, O-Pee-Chee issued the exact same set as Topps. The only distinctions are the bilingual text and the O-Pee-Chee copyright on the backs. The fronts feature white-bordered color action player photos framed by two different colored lines. The player's name and position appear at the bottom of the photo, with his team name appearing just above. The Topps 40th anniversary logo appears in the upper left corner. The traded players have their new teams and dates of trade printed on the photo. The pinkish horizontal backs present player biography, statistics and bilingual career highlights. Cards 386-407 are an All-Star subset. Notable Rookie Cards include Carl Everett and Chipper Jones.

	Nm-Mt	Ex-Mt
COMPLETE SET (792)	15.00	4.50
COMP. FACT.SET (792)	20.00	6.00

1 Nolan Ryan 2.00 .60
2 George Brett RB .40 .12
3 Carlton Fisk RB .10 .03
4 Kevin Maas RB .05 .02
5 Cal Ripken RB .75 .23
6 Nolan Ryan RB 1.00 .30
7 Ryne Sandberg RB .15 .04
8 Bobby Thigpen RB .05 .02
9 Darrin Fletcher .05 .02
10 Gregg Olson .05 .02
11 Roberto Kelly .05 .02
12 Paul Assenmacher .05 .02
13 Mariano Duncan .05 .02
14 Dennis Lamp .05 .02
15 Von Hayes .05 .02
16 Mike Heath .05 .02
17 Jeff Brantley .05 .02
18 Nelson Liriano .05 .02
19 Jeff D. Robinson .05 .02
20 Pedro Guerrero .05 .02
21 Joe Morgan MG .05 .02
22 Storm Davis .05 .02
23 Jim Gantner .05 .02
24 Dave Martinez .05 .02
25 Tim Belcher .05 .02
26 Luis Sojo UER .05 .02
Born in Barquisimeto not Caracas
Now with Angels
12/2/90
27 Bobby Witt .05 .02
28 Alvaro Espinoza .05 .02
29 Bob Walk .05 .02
30 Gregg Jefferies .05 .02
31 Colby Ward .05 .02
32 Mike Simms .05 .02
33 Barry Jones .05 .02
34 Atlee Hammaker .05 .02
35 Greg Maddux 1.00 .30
36 Donnie Hill .05 .02
37 Tom Bolton .05 .02
38 Scott Bradley .05 .02
39 Jim Neidlinger .05 .02
40 Kevin Mitchell .05 .02
41 Ken Dayley .10 .03
Now with Blue Jays
11/26/90
42 Chris Hoiles .05 .02
43 Roger McDowell .05 .02
44 Mike Felder .05 .02
45 Chris Sabo .05 .02
46 Tim Drummond .05 .02
47 Brook Jacoby .05 .02
48 Dennis Boyd .05 .02
49 Pat Borders .05 .02
50 Bob Welch .05 .02
51 Art Howe MG .05 .02
52 Francisco Oliveras .05 .02
53 Mike Sharperson UER .05 .02
Born in 1961, not 1960
54 Gary Mielke .05 .02
55 Jeffrey Leonard .05 .02
56 Jeff Parrett .05 .02
57 Jack Howell .05 .02
58 Mel Stottlemyre Jr. .05 .02
59 Eric Yelding .05 .02
60 Frank Viola .05 .02
61 Stan Javier .05 .02
62 Lee Guetterman .05 .02
63 Milt Thompson .05 .02
64 Tom Herr .05 .02
65 Bruce Hurst .05 .02
66 Terry Kennedy .05 .02
67 Rick Honeycutt .05 .02
68 Gary Sheffield .50 .15
69 Steve Wilson .05 .02
70 Ellis Burks .10 .03
71 Jim Acker .05 .02
72 Junior Ortiz .05 .02
73 Craig Worthington .05 .02
74 Shane Andrews RC .05 .02
75 Jack Morris .10 .03
76 Jerry Browne .05 .02
77 Drew Hall .05 .02
78 Geno Petralli .05 .02
79 Frank Thomas .75 .23
80 Fernando Valenzuela .10 .03
81 Cito Gaston MG .05 .02
82 Tom Glavine .40 .12
83 Daryl Boston .05 .02
84 Bob McClure .05 .02
85 Jesse Barfield .05 .02
86 Les Lancaster .05 .02
87 Tracy Jones .05 .02
88 Bob Tewksbury .05 .02
89 Darren Daulton .10 .03
90 Danny Tartabull .05 .02
91 Greg Colbrunn .05 .02
92 Danny Jackson .10 .03
Now with Cubs
11/21/90
93 Ivan Calderon .05 .02
94 John Dopson .05 .02
95 Paul Molitor .40 .12
96 Trevor Wilson .05 .02
97 Brady Anderson .25 .07
98 Sergio Valdez .05 .02
99 Chris Gwynn .05 .02
100 Don Mattingly 1.00 .30
101 Rob Ducey .05 .02
102 Gene Larkin .05 .02
103 Tim Costo .05 .02
104 Don Robinson .05 .02
105 Kevin McReynolds .05 .02
106 Ed Nunez .10 .03
Now with Brewers
12/4/90
107 Luis Polonia .05 .02
108 Matt Young .10 .03
Now with Red Sox
12/4/90
109 Greg Riddoch MG .05 .02
110 Tom Henke .05 .02
111 Andres Thomas .05 .02
112 Frank DiPino .05 .02
113 Carl Everett RC 1.00 .30
114 Lance Dickson .05 .02
115 Hubie Brooks .10 .03
Now with Mets
12/15/90
116 Mark Davis .05 .02
117 Dion James .05 .02
118 Tom Edens .05 .02
119 Carl Nichols .05 .02
120 Joe Carter .15 .04
Now with Blue Jays
12/5/90
121 Eric King .10 .03
Now with Indians
12/4/90
122 Paul O'Neill .40 .12
123 Greg A. Harris .05 .02
124 Randy Bush .05 .02
125 Steve Bedrosian .10 .03
Now with Twins
12/5/90
126 Bernard Gilkey .10 .03
127 Joe Price .05 .02
128 Travis Fryman .25 .07
Front has SS, back has SS-3B
129 Mark Eichhorn .05 .02
130 Ozzie Smith .50 .15
131 Checklist 1 .05 .02
132 Jamie Quirk .05 .02
133 Greg Briley .05 .02
134 Kevin Elster .05 .02
135 Jerome Walton .05 .02
136 Dave Schmidt .05 .02
137 Randy Ready .05 .02
138 Jamie Moyer .15 .04
Now with Cardinals
1/10/91
139 Jeff Treadway .05 .02
140 Fred McGriff .25 .07
Now with Padres
12/5/90
141 Nick Leyva MG .05 .02
142 Curt Wilkerson .10 .03
Now with Pirates
1/9/91
143 John Smiley .05 .02
144 Dave Henderson .05 .02
145 Lou Whitaker .10 .03
146 Dan Plesac .05 .02
147 Carlos Baerga .05 .02
148 Rey Palacios .05 .02
149 Al Osuna RC UER .05 .02
Shown with glove on right hand
bio says throws right
150 Cal Ripken 1.50 .45
151 Tom Browning .05 .02
152 Mickey Hatcher .05 .02
153 Bryan Harvey .05 .02
154 Jay Buhner .10 .03
155 Dwight Evans .15 .04
Now with Orioles
12/6/90
156 Carlos Martinez .05 .02
157 John Smoltz .25 .07
158 Jose Uribe .05 .02
159 Joe Boever .05 .02
160 Vince Coleman .05 .02
161 Tim Leary .05 .02
162 Ozzie Canseco .05 .02
163 Dave Johnson .05 .02
164 Edgar Diaz .05 .02
165 Sandy Alomar Jr. .10 .03
166 Harold Baines .15 .04
167 Randy Tomlin .05 .02
168 John Olerud .25 .07
169 Luis Aquino .05 .02
170 Carlton Fisk .40 .12
171 Tony LaRussa MG .10 .03
172 Pete Incaviglia .05 .02
173 Jason Grimsley .05 .02
174 Ken Caminiti .25 .07
175 Jack Armstrong .05 .02
176 John Orton .05 .02
177 Reggie Harris .05 .02
178 Dave Valle .05 .02
179 Pete Harnisch .05 .02
Now with Astros
1/10/91
180 Tony Gwynn .75 .23
181 Duane Ward .05 .02
182 Junior Noboa .05 .02
183 Clay Parker .05 .02
184 Gary Green .05 .02
185 Joe Magrane .05 .02
186 Rod Booker .05 .02
187 Greg Cadaret .05 .02
188 Damon Berryhill .05 .02
189 Daryl Irvine .05 .02
190 Matt Williams .15 .04
191 Willie Blair .10 .03
Now with Indians
11/6/90
192 Rob Deer .10 .03
Now with Tigers
11/21/90
193 Felix Fermin .05 .02
194 Xavier Hernandez .05 .02
195 Wally Joyner .10 .03
196 Jim Vatcher .05 .02
197 Chris Nabholz .05 .02
198 R.J. Reynolds .05 .02
199 Mike Hartley .05 .02
200 Darryl Strawberry .15 .04
Now with Dodgers
11/8/90
201 Tom Kelly MG .05 .02
202 Jim Leyritz .05 .02
203 Gene Harris .05 .02
204 Herm Winningham .05 .02
205 Mike Perez .05 .02
206 Carlos Quintana .05 .02
207 Gary Wayne .05 .02
208 Willie Wilson .05 .02
209 Ken Howell .05 .02
210 Lance Parrish .05 .02
211 Brian Barnes .05 .02
212 Steve Finley .25 .07
Now with Astros
1/10/91
213 Frank Wills .05 .02
214 Joe Girardi .05 .02
215 Dave Smith .10 .03
Now with Cubs
12/17/90
216 Greg Gagne .05 .02
217 Chris Bosio .05 .02
218 Rick Parker .05 .02
219 Jack McDowell .05 .02
220 Tim Wallach .05 .02
221 Don Slaught .05 .02
222 Brian McRae RC .25 .07
223 Allan Anderson .05 .02
224 Juan Gonzalez .50 .15
225 Randy Johnson .60 .18
226 Alfredo Griffin .05 .02
227 Steve Avery UER .05 .02
Pitched 13 games for Durham in 1989, not 2
228 Rex Hudler .05 .02
229 Rance Mulliniks .05 .02
230 Sid Fernandez .05 .02
231 Doug Rader MG .05 .02
232 Jose DeJesus .05 .02
233 Al Leiter .10 .03
234 Scott Erickson .10 .03
235 Dave Parker .10 .03
236 Frank Tanana .05 .02
237 Rick Cerone .05 .02
238 Mike Dunne .05 .02
239 Darren Lewis .10 .03
Now with Giants
12/4/90
240 Mike Scott .05 .02
241 Dave Clark UER .05 .02
Career totals 19 HR and 5 3B should be 22 and 3
242 Mike LaCoss .05 .02
243 Lance Johnson .05 .02
244 Mike Jeffcoat .05 .02
245 Kal Daniels .05 .02
246 Kevin Wickander .05 .02
247 Jody Reed .05 .02
248 Tom Gordon .10 .03
249 Bob Melvin .10 .03
250 Dennis Eckersley .10 .03
251 Mark Lemke .05 .02
252 Mel Rojas .10 .03
253 Garry Templeton .05 .02
254 Shawn Boskie .05 .02
255 Brian Downing .05 .02
256 Greg Hibbard .05 .02
257 Tom O'Malley .05 .02
258 Chris Hammond .05 .02
259 Hensley Meulens .05 .02
260 Harold Reynolds .10 .03
261 Bud Harrelson MG .05 .02
262 Tim Jones .05 .02
263 Checklist 2 .05 .02
264 Dave Hollins .05 .02
265 Mark Gubicza .05 .02
266 Carmelo Castillo .05 .02
267 Mark Knudson .05 .02
268 Tom Brookens .05 .02
269 Joe Hesketh .05 .02
270 Mark McGwire 1.50 .45
271 Omar Olivares .05 .02
272 Jeff King .05 .02
273 Johnny Ray .05 .02
274 Ken Williams .10 .03
275 Alan Trammell .15 .04
276 Bill Swift .05 .02
277 Scott Coolbaugh .10 .03
Now with Padres
12/12/90
278 Alex Fernandez UER .05 .02
No '90 White Sox stats
279 Jose Gonzalez .05 .02
280 Bret Saberhagen .10 .03
281 Larry Sheets .05 .02
282 Don Carman .05 .02
283 Marquis Grissom .10 .03
284 Billy Spiers .05 .02
285 Jim Abbott .10 .03
286 Ken Oberkfell .05 .02
287 Mark Grant .05 .02
288 Derrick May .05 .02
289 Tim Birtsas .05 .02
290 Steve Sax .05 .02
291 John Wathan MG .05 .02
292 Bud Black .05 .02
293 Jay Bell .05 .02
294 Mike Moore .05 .02
295 Rafael Palmeiro .40 .12
296 Mark Williamson .05 .02
297 Manny Lee .05 .02
298 Omar Vizquel .25 .07
299 Scott Radinsky .05 .02
300 Kirby Puckett 1.00 .30
301 Steve Farr .10 .03
Now with Yankees
11/26/90
302 Tim Teufel .05 .02
303 Mike Boddicker .10 .03
Now with Royals
11/21/90
304 Kevin Reimer .05 .02
305 Mike Scioscia .10 .03
306 Lonnie Smith .05 .02
307 Andy Benes .05 .02
308 Tom Pagnozzi .05 .02
309 Norm Charlton .05 .02
310 Gary Carter .25 .07
311 Jeff Pico .05 .02
312 Charlie Hayes .05 .02
313 Ron Robinson .05 .02
314 Gary Pettis .05 .02
315 Roberto Alomar .40 .12
316 Gene Nelson .05 .02
317 Mike Fitzgerald .05 .02
318 Rick Aguilera .10 .03
319 Jeff McKnight .05 .02
320 Tony Fernandez .10 .03
Now with Padres
12/5/90
321 Bob Rodgers MG .05 .02
322 Terry Shumpert .05 .02
323 Cory Snyder .05 .02
324 Ron Kittle .05 .02
325 Brett Butler .10 .03
Now with Dodgers
12/15/90
326 Ken Patterson .05 .02
327 Ron Hassey .05 .02
328 Walt Terrell .05 .02
329 Dave Justice UER .40 .12
Drafted third round on card should say fourth pick
330 Dwight Gooden .10 .03
331 Eric Anthony .05 .02
332 Kenny Rogers .15 .04
Now with White Sox
12/4/90
333 C.Jones FDP RC 6.00 1.80
334 Todd Benzinger .05 .02
335 Mitch Williams .05 .02
336 Matt Nokes .05 .02
337 Keith Comstock .05 .02

338 Luis Rivera .05 .02
339 Larry Walker .25 .07
340 Ramon Martinez .05 .02
341 John Moses .05 .02
342 Mickey Morandini .05 .02
343 Jose Oquendo .05 .02
344 Jeff Russell .05 .02
345 Len Dykstra .10 .03
346 Jesse Orosco .10 .03
347 Greg Vaughn .25 .07
348 Todd Stottlemyre .10 .03
349 Dave Gallagher .10 .03
Now with Angels
12/4/90
350 Glenn Davis .05 .02
351 Joe Torre MG .10 .03
352 Frank White .10 .03
353 Tony Castillo .05 .02
354 Sid Bream .10 .03
Now with Braves
12/5/90
355 Chili Davis .10 .03
356 Mike Marshall .05 .02
357 Jack Savage .05 .02
358 Mark Parent .10 .03
Now with Rangers
12/12/90
359 Chuck Cary .05 .02
360 Tim Raines .15 .04
Now with White Sox
12/23/90
361 Scott Garrelts .05 .02
362 Hector Villanueva .05 .02
363 Rick Mahler .05 .02
364 Dan Pasqua .05 .02
365 Mike Schooler .05 .02
366 Checklist 3 .05 .02
367 Dave Walsh RC .05 .02
368 Felix Jose .05 .02
369 Steve Searcy .05 .02
370 Kelly Gruber .05 .02
371 Jeff Montgomery .05 .02
372 Spike Owen .05 .02
373 Darrin Jackson .05 .02
374 Larry Casian .05 .02
375 Tony Pena .10 .03
376 Mike Harkey .05 .02
377 Rene Gonzales .05 .02
378 Wilson Alvarez .25 .07
379 Randy Velarde .05 .02
380 Willie McGee .15 .04
Now with Giants
12/3/90
381 Jim Leyland MG .05 .02
382 Mackey Sasser .05 .02
383 Pete Smith .05 .02
384 Gerald Perry .10 .03
Now with Cardinals
12/13/90
385 Mickey Tettleton .10 .03
Now with Tigers
1/12/90
386 Cecil Fielder AS .10 .03
387 Julio Franco AS .05 .02
388 Kelly Gruber AS .05 .02
389 Alan Trammell AS .10 .03
390 Jose Canseco AS .25 .07
391 Rickey Henderson AS .40 .12
392 Ken Griffey Jr. AS .75 .23
393 Carlton Fisk AS .10 .03
394 Bob Welch AS .05 .02
395 Chuck Finley AS .05 .02
396 Bobby Thigpen AS .05 .02
397 Eddie Murray AS .10 .03
398 Ryne Sandberg AS .15 .04
399 Matt Williams AS .15 .04
400 Barry Larkin AS .10 .03
401 Barry Bonds AS .50 .15
402 Darryl Strawbery AS .10 .03
403 Bobby Bonilla AS .05 .02
404 Mike Scioscia AS .05 .02
405 Doug Drabek AS .05 .02
406 Frank Viola AS .05 .02
407 John Franco AS .05 .02
408 Earnie Riles .10 .03
Now with Athletics
12/4/90
409 Mike Stanley .05 .02
410 Dave Righetti .10 .03
Now with Giants
12/4/90
411 Lance Blankenship .05 .02
412 Dave Bergman .05 .02
413 Terry Mulholland .05 .02
414 Sammy Sosa .60 .18
415 Rick Sutcliffe .10 .03
416 Randy Milligan .05 .02
417 Bill Krueger .05 .02
418 Nick Esasky .05 .02
419 Jeff Reed .05 .02
420 Bobby Thigpen .05 .02
421 Alex Cole .05 .02
422 Rick Reuschel .05 .02
423 Rafael Ramirez UER .05 .02
Born 1959, not 1958
424 Calvin Schiraldi .05 .02
425 Andy Van Slyke .05 .02
426 Joe Grahe .05 .02
427 Rick Dempsey .05 .02
428 John Barfield .05 .02
429 Stump Merrill MG .05 .02
430 Gary Gaetti .10 .03
431 Paul Gibson .05 .02
432 Delino DeShields .10 .03
433 Pat Tabler .05 .02
Now with Blue Jays
12/5/90
434 Julio Machado .05 .02
435 Kevin Maas .05 .02
436 Scott Bankhead .05 .02
437 Doug Dascenzo .05 .02
438 Vicente Palacios .05 .02
439 Dickie Thon .05 .02
440 George Bell .05 .02
Now with Cubs
12/6/90
441 Zane Smith .05 .02
442 Charlie O'Brien .05 .02
443 Jeff Innis .05 .02
444 Glenn Braggs .05 .02
445 Greg Swindell .05 .02
446 Craig Grebeck .05 .02
447 John Burkett .05 .02
448 Craig Lefferts .05 .02
449 Juan Berenguer .05 .02
450 Wade Boggs .40 .12
451 Neal Heaton .05 .02
452 Bill Schroeder .05 .02
453 Lenny Harris .05 .02
454 Kevin Appier .10 .03
455 Walt Weiss .05 .02
456 Charlie Leibrandt .05 .02
457 Todd Hundley .25 .07
458 Brian Holman .05 .02
459 Tom Trebelhorn MG .05 .02
460 Dave Stieb .10 .03
461 Robin Ventura .25 .07
462 Steve Frey .05 .02
463 Dwight Smith .05 .02
464 Steve Buechele .05 .02
465 Ken Griffey Sr. .10 .03
466 Charles Nagy .10 .03
467 Dennis Cook .05 .02
468 Tim Hulett .05 .02
469 Chet Lemon .05 .02
470 Howard Johnson .05 .02
471 Mike Lieberthal RC 1.00 .30
472 Kirt Manwaring .05 .02
473 Curt Young .05 .02
474 Phil Plantier .05 .02
475 Teddy Higuera .05 .02
476 Glenn Wilson .05 .02
477 Mike Fetters .05 .02
478 Kurt Stillwell .05 .02
479 Bob Patterson .05 .02
480 Dave Magadan .05 .02
481 Eddie Whitson .05 .02
482 Tino Martinez .25 .07
483 Mike Aldrete .05 .02
484 Dave LaPoint .05 .02
485 Terry Pendleton .15 .04
Now with Braves
12/3/90
486 Tommy Greene .05 .02
487 Rafael Belliard .10 .03
Now with Braves
12/18/90
488 Jeff Manto .05 .02
489 Bobby Valentine MG .05 .02
490 Kirk Gibson .15 .04
Now with Royals
12/1/90
491 Kurt Miller .05 .02
492 Ernie Whitt .05 .02
493 Jose Rijo .05 .02
494 Chris James .05 .02
495 Charlie Hough .15 .04
Now with White Sox
12/20/90
496 Marty Barrett .05 .02
497 Ben McDonald .05 .02
498 Mark Salas .05 .02
499 Melido Perez .05 .02
500 Will Clark .40 .12
501 Mike Bielecki .05 .02
502 Carney Lansford .10 .03
503 Roy Smith .05 .02
504 Julio Valera .05 .02
505 Chuck Finley .10 .03
506 Darnell Coles .05 .02
507 Steve Jeltz .05 .02
508 Mike York .05 .02
509 Glenallen Hill .05 .02
510 John Franco .10 .03
511 Steve Balboni .05 .02
512 Jose Mesa .05 .02
513 Jerald Clark .05 .02
514 Mike Stanton .05 .02
515 Alvin Davis .05 .02
516 Karl Rhodes .05 .02
517 Joe Oliver .05 .02
518 Cris Carpenter .05 .02
519 Sparky Anderson MG .10 .03
520 Mark Grace .40 .12
521 Joe Orsulak .05 .02
522 Stan Belinda .05 .02
523 Rodney McCray .05 .02
524 Darrel Akerfelds .05 .02
525 Willie Randolph .10 .03
526 Moises Alou .10 .03
527 Checklist 4 .05 .02
528 Denny Martinez .10 .03
529 Marc Newfield .05 .02
530 Roger Clemens 1.00 .30
531 Dave Rohde .05 .02
532 Kirk McCaskill .05 .02
533 Oddibe McDowell .05 .02
534 Mike Jackson .10 .03
535 Ruben Sierra .10 .03
536 Mike Witt .05 .02
537 Jose Lind .05 .02
538 Bip Roberts .05 .02
539 Scott Terry .05 .02
540 George Brett .75 .23
541 Domingo Ramos .05 .02
542 Rob Murphy .05 .02
543 Junior Felix .05 .02
544 Alejandro Pena .05 .02
545 Dale Murphy .40 .12
546 Jeff Ballard .05 .02
547 Mike Pagliarulo .05 .02
548 Jaime Navarro .05 .02
549 John McNamara MG .05 .02
550 Eric Davis .10 .03
551 Bob Kipper .05 .02
552 Jeff Hamilton .05 .02
553 Joe Klink .05 .02
554 Brian Harper .05 .02
555 Turner Ward .05 .02
556 Gary Ward .05 .02
557 Wally Whitehurst .05 .02
558 Otis Nixon .10 .03
559 Adam Peterson .05 .02
560 Greg Smith .10 .03
Now with Dodgers
12/14/90
561 Tim McIntosh .05 .02
562 Jeff Kunkel .05 .02
563 Brent Knackert .05 .02
564 Dante Bichette .10 .03
565 Craig Biggio .15 .04
566 Craig Wilson .05 .02
567 Dwayne Henry .05 .02
568 Ron Karkovice .05 .02
569 Curt Schilling .75 .23
Now with Astros
1/10/91
570 Barry Bonds 1.00 .30
571 Pat Combs .05 .02
572 Dave Anderson .05 .02
573 Rich Rodriguez UER .05 .02
Stats say drafted 4th
but bio says 9th round
574 John Marzano .05 .02
575 Robin Yount .40 .12
576 Jeff Kaiser .05 .02
577 Bill Doran .05 .02
578 Dave West .05 .02
579 Roger Craig MG .05 .02
580 Dave Stewart .10 .03
581 Luis Quinones .05 .02
582 Marty Clary .05 .02
583 Tony Phillips .05 .02
584 Kevin Brown .15 .04
585 Pete O'Brien .05 .02
586 Fred Lynn .05 .02
587 Jose Offerman UER .05 .02
Text says signed 7/24/88
but bio says 1986
588 Mark Whiten .05 .02
589 Scott Ruskin .05 .02
590 Eddie Murray .40 .12
591 Ken Hill .05 .02
592 B.J. Surhoff .10 .03
593 Mike Walker .05 .02
594 Rich Garces .05 .02
595 Bill Landrum .05 .02
596 Ronnie Walden .05 .02
597 Jerry Don Gleaton .05 .02
598 Sam Horn .05 .02
599 Greg Myers .05 .02
600 Bo Jackson .10 .03
601 Bob Ojeda .10 .03
Now with Dodgers
12/15/90
602 Casey Candaele .05 .02
603 Wes Chamberlain .05 .02
604 Billy Hatcher .05 .02
605 Jeff Reardon .10 .03
606 Jim Gott .05 .02
607 Edgar Martinez .15 .04
608 Todd Burns .05 .02
609 Jeff Torborg MG .05 .02
610 Andres Galarraga .25 .07
611 Dave Eiland .05 .02
612 Steve Lyons .10 .03
613 Eric Show .05 .02
Now with Athletics
12/10/90
614 Luis Salazar .05 .02
615 Bert Blyleven .10 .03
616 Todd Zeile .10 .03
617 Bill Wegman .05 .02
618 Sil Campusano .05 .02
619 David Wells .15 .04
620 Ozzie Guillen .10 .03
621 Ted Power .10 .03
Now with Reds
12/14/90
622 Jack Daugherty .05 .02
623 Jeff Blauser .05 .02
624 Tom Candiotti .05 .02
625 Terry Steinbach .05 .02
626 Gerald Young .05 .02
627 Tim Layana .05 .02
628 Greg Litton .05 .02
629 Wes Gardner .10 .03
Now with Padres
12/15/90
630 Dave Winfield .40 .12
631 Mike Morgan .05 .02
632 Lloyd Moseby .05 .02
633 Kevin Tapani .05 .02
634 Henry Cotto .05 .02
635 Andy Hawkins .05 .02
636 Geronimo Pena .05 .02
637 Bruce Ruffin .05 .02
638 Mike Macfarlane .05 .02
639 Frank Robinson MG .10 .03
640 Andre Dawson .25 .07
641 Mike Henneman .05 .02
642 Hal Morris .05 .02
643 Jim Presley .05 .02
644 Chuck Crim .05 .02
645 Juan Samuel .05 .02
646 Andujar Cedeno .05 .02
647 Mark Portugal .05 .02
648 Lee Stevens .05 .02
649 Bill Sampen .05 .02
650 Jack Clark .10 .03
Now with Red Sox
12/15/90
651 Alan Mills .05 .02
652 Kevin Romine .05 .02
653 Anthony Telford .05 .02
654 Paul Sorrento .10 .03
655 Erik Hanson .05 .02
656 Checklist 5 .05 .02
657 Mike Kingery .05 .02
658 Scott Aldred .05 .02
659 Oscar Azocar .05 .02
660 Lee Smith .10 .03
661 Steve Lake .05 .02
662 Rob Dibble .05 .02
663 Greg Brock .05 .02
664 John Farrell .05 .02
665 Mike LaValliere .05 .02
666 Danny Darwin .05 .02
Now with Red Sox
12/19/90
667 Kent Anderson .05 .02
668 Bill Long .05 .02
669 Lou Piniella MG .10 .03
670 Rickey Henderson .75 .23
671 Andy McGaffigan .05 .02
672 Shane Mack .05 .02
673 Greg Olson UER .05 .02
6 RBI in '88 at Tidewater
and 2 RBI in '87
should be 48 and 15
674 Kevin Gross .10 .03
Now with Dodgers
12/3/90
675 Tom Brunansky .05 .02
676 Scott Chiamparino .05 .02
677 Billy Ripken .05 .02
678 Mark Davidson .05 .02
679 Bill Bathe .05 .02
680 David Cone .25 .07
681 Jeff Schaefer .05 .02
682 Ray Lankford .25 .07
683 Derek Lilliquist .05 .02
684 Milt Cuyler .05 .02
685 Doug Drabek .05 .02
686 Mike Gallego .05 .02
687 John Cerutti .05 .02
688 Rosario Rodriguez .10 .03
Now with Pirates
12/20/90
689 John Kruk .10 .03
690 Orel Hershiser .10 .03
691 Mike Blowers .10 .03
692 Efrain Valdez .05 .02
693 Francisco Cabrera .05 .02
694 Randy Veres .05 .02
695 Kevin Seitzer .05 .02
696 Steve Olin .05 .02
697 Shawn Abner .05 .02
698 Mark Guthrie .05 .02
699 Jim Lefebvre MG .05 .02
700 Jose Canseco .40 .12
701 Pascual Perez .05 .02
702 Tim Naehring .05 .02
703 Juan Agosto .10 .03
Now with Cardinals
12/14/90
704 Devon White .15 .04
Now with Blue Jays
12/2/90
705 Robby Thompson .05 .02
706 Brad Arnsberg .05 .02
707 Jim Eisenreich .05 .02
708 John Mitchell .05 .02
709 Matt Sinatro .05 .02
710 Kent Hrbek .10 .03
711 Jose DeLeon .05 .02
712 Ricky Jordan .05 .02
713 Scott Scudder .05 .02
714 Marvell Wynne .05 .02
715 Tim Burke .05 .02
716 Bob Geren .05 .02
717 Phil Bradley .05 .02
718 Steve Crawford .05 .02
719 Keith Miller .05 .02
720 Cecil Fielder .10 .03
721 Mark Lee .05 .02
722 Wally Backman .05 .02
723 Candy Maldonado .05 .02
724 David Segui .05 .02
725 Ron Gant .10 .03
726 Phil Stephenson .05 .02
727 Mookie Wilson .10 .03
728 Scott Sanderson .10 .03
Now with Yankees
12/31/90
729 Don Zimmer MG .05 .02
730 Barry Larkin .40 .12
731 Jeff Gray .05 .02
732 Franklin Stubbs .10 .03
Now with Brewers
12/5/90
733 Kelly Downs .05 .02
734 John Russell .05 .02
735 Ron Darling .05 .02
736 Dick Schofield .05 .02
737 Tim Crews .05 .02
738 Mel Hall .05 .02
739 Russ Swan .05 .02
740 Ryne Sandberg .50 .15
741 Jimmy Key .10 .03
742 Tommy Gregg .05 .02
743 Bryn Smith .05 .02
744 Nelson Santovenia .05 .02
745 Doug Jones .05 .02
746 John Shelby .05 .02
747 Tony Fossas .05 .02
748 Al Newman .05 .02
749 Greg W. Harris .05 .02
750 Bobby Bonilla .05 .02
751 Wayne Edwards .05 .02
752 Kevin Bass .05 .02
753 Paul Marak UER .05 .02
Stats say drafted in May
but bio says Jan.
754 Bill Pecota .05 .02
755 Mark Langston .05 .02
756 Jeff Huson .05 .02
757 Mark Gardner .05 .02
758 Mike Devereaux .05 .02
759 Bobby Cox MG .05 .02
760 Benny Santiago .10 .03
761 Larry Andersen .10 .03
Now with Padres
12/21/90
762 Mitch Webster .05 .02
763 Dana Kiecker .05 .02
764 Mark Carreon .05 .02
765 Shawon Dunston .05 .02
766 Jeff M. Robinson .10 .03
Now with Orioles
1/12/91
767 Dan Wilson RC .25 .07
768 Donn Pall .05 .02
769 Tim Sherrill .05 .02
770 Jay Howell .05 .02
771 Gary Redus UER .05 .02
Born in Tanner, should say Athens
772 Kent Mercker UER .05 .02
Born in Indianapolis
should say Dublin, Ohio
773 Tom Foley .05 .02
774 Dennis Rasmussen .05 .02
775 Julio Franco .10 .03
776 Brent Mayne .05 .02
777 John Candelaria .05 .02
778 Dan Gladden .05 .02
779 Carmelo Martinez .05 .02
780 Randy Myers .10 .03
781 Darryl Hamilton .05 .02
782 Jim Deshaies .05 .02
783 Joel Skinner .05 .02
784 Willie Fraser .10 .03
Now with Blue Jays
12/2/90
785 Scott Fletcher .05 .02
786 Eric Plunk .05 .02
787 Checklist 6 .05 .02
788 Bob Milacki .05 .02
789 Tom Lasorda MG .40 .12
790 Ken Griffey Jr. 1.50 .45
791 Mike Benjamin .05 .02
792 Mike Greenwell .05 .02

1991 O-Pee-Chee Box Bottoms

The 1991 O-Pee-Chee Box Bottom cards comprise four different box bottoms from the bottoms of wax pack boxes, with four cards each, for a total of 16 standard-size cards. The cards are nearly identical to the 1991 Topps Box Bottom cards. The fronts feature yellow-bordered color player action shots. The player's name and position appear at the bottom and his team name appears just above. The traded players have their new teams and dates of trade printed on the photo. The pink and blue horizontal backs carry player career highlights in both English and French. The cards are lettered (A-P) rather than numbered on the back.

Nm-Mt Ex-Mt
COMPLETE SET (16) 10.00 3.00
A Bert Blyleven .50 .15
B George Brett 1.50 .45
C Brett Butler .25 .07
D Andre Dawson .75 .23
E Dwight Evans .25 .07
F Carlton Fisk 1.00 .30
G Alfredo Griffin .10 .03
H Rickey Henderson 1.00 .30
I Willie McGee .25 .07
J Dale Murphy .75 .23
K Eddie Murray 1.00 .30
L Dave Parker .25 .07
M Jeff Reardon .25 .07
N Nolan Ryan 3.00 .90
O Juan Samuel .10 .03
P Robin Yount 1.00 .30

1992 O-Pee-Chee

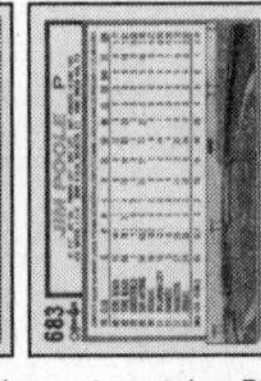

The 1992 O-Pee-Chee set contains 792 standard-size cards. These cards were sold in ten-card wax packs with a stick of bubble gum. The fronts have either posed or action color player photos on a white card face. Different color stripes frame the pictures, and the player's name and team name appear in two short color stripes respectively at the bottom. In English and French, the horizontally oriented backs have biography and complete career batting or pitching record. In addition, some of the cards have a picture of a baseball field and stadium on the back. Special subsets included are Record Breakers (2-5), Prospects (58, 126, 179, 473, 551, 591, 618, 656, 676) and a five-card tribute to Gary Carter (45, 387, 389, 399, 402). Each wax pack wrapper served as an entry blank offering each collector the chance to win one of 1,000 complete factory sets of 1992 O-Pee-Chee Premier baseball cards.

Nm-Mt Ex-Mt
COMPLETE SET (792) 25.00 7.50
COMP. FACT.SET (792) 30.00 9.00
1 Nolan Ryan 2.00 .60
2 Rickey Henderson RB .40 .12
(Some cards have print
marks that show 1.991
on the front)
3 Jeff Reardon RB .05 .02
4 Nolan Ryan RB 1.00 .30
5 Dave Winfield RB .15 .04
6 Brien Taylor RC .05 .02
7 Jim Olander .05 .02
8 Bryan Hickerson .05 .02
9 Jon Farrell .05 .02
10 Wade Boggs .40 .12
11 Jack McDowell .05 .02
12 Luis Gonzalez .40 .12
13 Mike Scioscia .10 .03
14 Wes Chamberlain .05 .02
15 Dennis Martinez .10 .03
16 Jeff Montgomery .10 .03
17 Randy Milligan .05 .02
18 Greg Cadaret .05 .02
19 Jamie Quirk .05 .02
20 Bip Roberts .05 .02
21 Buck Rodgers MG .05 .02
22 Bill Wegman .05 .02
23 Chuck Knoblauch .25 .07
24 Randy Myers .10 .03
25 Ron Gant .10 .03
26 Mike Bielecki .05 .02
27 Juan Gonzalez .40 .12
28 Mike Schooler .05 .02
29 Mickey Tettleton .05 .02
30 John Kruk .10 .03
31 Bryn Smith .05 .02
32 Chris Nabholz .05 .02
33 Carlos Baerga .05 .02
34 Jeff Juden .05 .02
35 Dave Righetti .05 .02
36 Scott Ruffcorn .05 .02
37 Luis Polonia .05 .02
38 Tom Candiotti .10 .03
Now with Dodgers
12-3-91
39 Greg Olson .05 .02
40 Cal Ripken 4.00 1.20
Lou Gehrig
41 Craig Lefferts .05 .02

42 Mike Macfarlane .05 .02
43 Jose Lind .05 .02
44 Rick Aguilera .10 .03
45 Gary Carter .25 .07
46 Steve Farr .05 .02
47 Rex Hudler .10 .03
48 Scott Scudder .05 .02
49 Damon Berryhill .05 .02
50 Ken Griffey Jr. 1.25 .35
51 Tom Runnells MG .05 .02
52 Juan Bell .05 .02
53 Tommy Gregg .05 .02
54 David Wells .15 .04
55 Rafael Palmeiro .40 .12
56 Charlie O'Brien .05 .02
57 Donn Pall .05 .02
58 Brad Ausmus .40 .12
Jim Campanis Jr.
Dave Nilsson
Doug Robbins
59 Mo Vaughn .25 .07
60 Tony Fernandez .05 .02
61 Paul O'Neill .40 .12
62 Gene Nelson .05 .02
63 Randy Ready .05 .02
64 Bob Kipper .10 .03
Now with Twins
12-17-91
65 Willie McGee .10 .03
66 Scott Stahoviak .05 .02
67 Luis Salazar .05 .02
68 Marvin Freeman .05 .02
69 Kenny Lofton .40 .12
Now with Indians
12-10-91
70 Gary Gaetti .10 .03
71 Erik Hanson .05 .02
72 Eddie Zosky .05 .02
73 Brian Barnes .05 .02
74 Scott Leius .05 .02
75 Bret Saberhagen .10 .03
76 Mike Gallego .05 .02
77 Jack Armstrong .10 .03
Now with Indians
11-15-91
78 Ivan Rodriguez .50 .15
79 Jesse Orosco .10 .03
80 David Justice .15 .04
81 Ced Landrum .05 .02
82 Doug Simons .05 .02
83 Tommy Greene .05 .02
84 Leo Gomez .05 .02
85 Jose DeLeon .05 .02
86 Steve Finley .10 .03
87 Bob McDonald .05 .02
88 Darrin Jackson .05 .02
89 Neal Heaton .05 .02
90 Robin Yount .25 .07
91 Jeff Reed .05 .02
92 Lenny Harris .05 .02
93 Reggie Jefferson .05 .02
94 Sammy Sosa .75 .23
95 Scott Bailes .05 .02
96 Tom McKinnon .05 .02
97 Luis Rivera .05 .02
98 Mike Harkey .05 .02
99 Jeff Treadway .05 .02
100 Jose Canseco .40 .12
101 Omar Vizquel .10 .03
102 Scott Kamieniecki .05 .02
103 Ricky Jordan .05 .02
104 Jeff Ballard .05 .02
105 Felix Jose .05 .02
106 Mike Boddicker .05 .02
107 Dan Pasqua .05 .02
108 Mike Timlin .05 .02
109 Roger Craig MG .05 .02
110 Ryne Sandberg .50 .15
111 Mark Carreon .05 .02
112 Oscar Azocar .05 .02
113 Mike Greenwell .05 .02
114 Mark Portugal .05 .02
115 Terry Pendleton .05 .02
116 Willie Randolph .10 .03
Now with Mets
12-20-91
117 Scott Terry .05 .02
118 Chili Davis .10 .03
119 Mark Gardner .05 .02
120 Alan Trammell .15 .04
121 Derek Bell .10 .03
122 Gary Varsho .05 .02
123 Bob Ojeda .05 .02
124 Shawn Livsey .05 .02
125 Chris Hoiles .05 .02
126 Ryan Klesko .25 .07
John Jaha
Rico Brogna
Dave Staton
127 Carlos Quintana .05 .02
128 Kurt Stillwell .05 .02
129 Melido Perez .05 .02
130 Alvin Davis .05 .02
131 Checklist 1-132 .05 .02
132 Eric Show .05 .02
133 Rance Mulliniks .05 .02
134 Darryl Kile .05 .02
135 Von Hayes .10 .03
Now with Angels
12-8-91
136 Bill Doran .05 .02
137 Jeff D. Robinson .05 .02
138 Monty Fariss .05 .02
139 Jeff Innis .05 .02
140 Mark Grace UER .40 .12
Home Calie., should be Calif.
141 Jim Leyland MG UER .05 .02
(No closed parenthesis
after East in 1991)
142 Todd Van Poppel .05 .02
143 Paul Gibson .05 .02
144 Bill Swift .05 .02
145 Danny Tartabull .10 .03
Now with Yankees
1-6-92
146 Al Newman .05 .02
147 Cris Carpenter .05 .02
148 Anthony Young .05 .02
149 Brian Bohanon .05 .02
150 Roger Clemens UER 1.00 .30
(League leading ERA in
1990 not italicized)
151 Jeff Hamilton .05 .02
152 Charlie Leibrandt .05 .02
153 Ron Karkovice .05 .02
154 Hensley Meulens .05 .02
155 Scott Bankhead .05 .02
156 Manny Ramirez RC 5.00 1.50
157 Keith Miller .10 .03
Now with Royals
12-11-91
158 Todd Frohwirth .05 .02
159 Darrin Fletcher .10 .03
Now with Expos
12-9-91
160 Bobby Bonilla .05 .02
161 Casey Candaele .05 .02
162 Paul Faries .05 .02
163 Dana Kiecker .05 .02
164 Shane Mack .05 .02
165 Mark Langston .05 .02
166 Geronimo Pena .05 .02
167 Andy Allanson .05 .02
168 Dwight Smith .05 .02
169 Chuck Crim .10 .03
Now with Angels
12-10-91
170 Alex Cole .05 .02
171 Bill Plummer MG .05 .02
172 Juan Berenguer .05 .02
173 Brian Downing .05 .02
174 Steve Frey .05 .02
175 Orel Hershiser .10 .03
176 Ramon Garcia .05 .02
177 Dan Gladden .10 .03
Now with Tigers
12-19-91
178 Jim Acker .05 .02
179 Bobby DeJardin .05 .02
Cesar Bernhardt
Armando Moreno
Andy Stankiewicz
180 Kevin Mitchell .10 .03
181 Hector Villanueva .05 .02
182 Jeff Reardon .10 .03
183 Brent Mayne .05 .02
184 Jimmy Jones .05 .02
185 Benito Santiago .10 .03
186 Cliff Floyd 2.00 .60
187 Ernie Riles .05 .02
188 Jose Guzman .05 .02
189 Junior Felix .05 .02
190 Glenn Davis .05 .02
191 Charlie Hough .10 .03
192 Dave Fleming .05 .02
193 Omar Olivares .05 .02
194 Eric Karros .25 .07
195 David Cone .25 .07
196 Frank Castillo .05 .02
197 Glenn Braggs .05 .02
198 Scott Aldred .05 .02
199 Jeff Blauser .05 .02
200 Len Dykstra .10 .03
201 Buck Showalter MG RC .25 .07
202 Rick Honeycutt .05 .02
203 Greg Myers .05 .02
204 Trevor Wilson .05 .02
205 Jay Howell .05 .02
206 Luis Sojo .05 .02
207 Jack Clark .10 .03
208 Julio Machado .05 .02
209 Lloyd McClendon .10 .03
210 Ozzie Guillen .10 .03
211 Jeremy Hernandez .05 .02
212 Randy Velarde .05 .02
213 Les Lancaster .05 .02
214 Andy Mota .05 .02
215 Rich Gossage .10 .03
216 Brent Gates .05 .02
217 Brian Harper .05 .02
218 Mike Flanagan .05 .02
219 Jerry Browne .05 .02
220 Jose Rijo .05 .02
221 Skeeter Barnes .05 .02
222 Jaime Navarro .05 .02
223 Mel Hall .05 .02
224 Bret Barberie .05 .02
225 Roberto Alomar .40 .12
226 Pete Smith .05 .02
227 Daryl Boston .05 .02
228 Eddie Whitson .05 .02
229 Shawn Boskie .05 .02
230 Dick Schofield .05 .02
231 Brian Drahman .05 .02
232 John Smiley .05 .02
233 Mitch Webster .05 .02
234 Terry Steinbach .05 .02
235 Jack Morris .15 .04
Now with Blue Jays
12-18-91
236 Bill Pecota .10 .03
Now with Mets
12-11-91
237 Jose Hernandez .05 .02
238 Greg Litton .05 .02
239 Brian Holman .05 .02
240 Andres Galarraga .25 .07
241 Gerald Young .05 .02
242 Mike Mussina .60 .18
243 Alvaro Espinoza .05 .02
244 Darren Daulton .10 .03
245 John Smoltz .25 .07
246 Jason Pruitt .05 .02
247 Chuck Finley .10 .03
248 Jim Gantner .05 .02
249 Tony Fossas .05 .02
250 Ken Griffey Sr. .10 .03
251 Kevin Elster .05 .02
252 Dennis Rasmussen .05 .02
253 Terry Kennedy .05 .02
254 Ryan Bowen .05 .02
255 Robin Ventura .10 .03
256 Mike Aldrete .05 .02
257 Jeff Russell .05 .02
258 Jim Lindeman .05 .02
259 Ron Darling .05 .02
260 Devon White .10 .03
261 Tom Lasorda MG .25 .07
262 Terry Lee .05 .02
263 Bob Patterson .05 .02
264 Checklist 133-264 .05 .02
265 Teddy Higuera .05 .02
266 Roberto Kelly .05 .02
267 Steve Bedrosian .05 .02
268 Brady Anderson .15 .04
269 Ruben Amaro Jr. .05 .02
270 Tony Gwynn .75 .23
271 Tracy Jones .05 .02
272 Jerry Don Gleaton .05 .02
273 Craig Grebeck .05 .02
274 Bob Scanlan .05 .02
275 Todd Zeile .10 .03
276 Shawn Green RC 4.00 1.20
277 Scott Chiamparino .05 .02
278 Darryl Hamilton .05 .02
279 Jim Clancy .05 .02
280 Carlos Martinez .05 .02
281 Kevin Appier .10 .03
282 John Wehner .05 .02
283 Reggie Sanders .10 .03
284 Gene Larkin .05 .02
285 Bob Welch .05 .02
286 Gilberto Reyes .05 .02
287 Pete Schourek .05 .02
288 Andujar Cedeno .05 .02
289 Mike Morgan .10 .03
Now with Cubs
12-3-91
290 Bo Jackson .10 .03
291 Phil Garner MG .05 .02
292 Ray Lankford .25 .07
293 Mike Henneman .05 .02
294 Dave Valle .05 .02
295 Alonzo Powell .05 .02
296 Tom Brunansky .05 .02
297 Kevin Brown .15 .04
298 Kelly Gruber .05 .02
299 Charles Nagy .05 .02
300 Don Mattingly 1.00 .30
301 Kirk McCaskill .10 .03
Now with White Sox
12-28-91
302 Joey Cora .05 .02
303 Dan Plesac .05 .02
304 Joe Oliver .05 .02
305 Tom Glavine .40 .12
306 Al Shirley .05 .02
307 Bruce Ruffin .05 .02
308 Craig Shipley .05 .02
309 Dave Martinez .10 .03
Now with Reds
12-11-91
310 Jose Mesa .05 .02
311 Henry Cotto .05 .02
312 Mike LaValliere .05 .02
313 Kevin Tapani .05 .02
314 Jeff Huson .05 .02
315 Juan Samuel .05 .02
316 Curt Schilling .40 .12
317 Mike Bordick .10 .03
318 Steve Howe .05 .02
319 Tony Phillips .05 .02
320 George Bell .05 .02
321 Lou Piniella MG .10 .03
322 Tim Burke .05 .02
323 Milt Thompson .05 .02
324 Danny Darwin .05 .02
325 Joe Orsulak .05 .02
326 Eric King .05 .02
327 Jay Buhner .15 .04
328 Joel Johnston .05 .02
329 Franklin Stubbs .05 .02
330 Will Clark .40 .12
331 Steve Lake .05 .02
332 Chris Jones .10 .03
Now with Astros
12-19-91
333 Pat Tabler .05 .02
334 Kevin Gross .05 .02
335 Dave Henderson .05 .02
336 Greg Anthony .05 .02
337 Alejandro Pena .05 .02
338 Shawn Abner .05 .02
339 Tom Browning .05 .02
340 Otis Nixon .05 .02
341 Bob Geren .10 .03
Now with Reds
12-2-91
342 Tim Spehr .05 .02
343 John Vander Wal .05 .02
344 Jack Daugherty .05 .02
345 Zane Smith .05 .02
346 Rheal Cormier .05 .02
347 Kent Hrbek .10 .03
348 Rick Wilkins .05 .02
349 Steve Lyons .10 .03
350 Gregg Olson .05 .02
351 Greg Riddoch MG .05 .02
352 Ed Nunez .05 .02
353 Braulio Castillo .05 .02
354 Dave Bergman .05 .02
355 Warren Newson .05 .02
356 Luis Quinones .05 .02
Now with Twins
1-9-92
357 Mike Witt .05 .02
358 Ted Wood .05 .02
359 Mike Moore .05 .02
360 Lance Parrish .05 .02
361 Barry Jones .05 .02
362 Javier Ortiz .05 .02
363 John Candelaria .05 .02
364 Glenallen Hill .05 .02
365 Duane Ward .05 .02
366 Checklist 265-396 .05 .02
367 Rafael Belliard .05 .02
368 Bill Krueger .05 .02
369 Steve Whitaker .05 .02
370 Shawon Dunston .05 .02
371 Dante Bichette .15 .04
372 Kip Gross .10 .03
Now with Dodgers
11-27-91
373 Don Robinson .05 .02
374 Bernie Williams .40 .12
375 Bert Blyleven .10 .03
376 Chris Donnels .05 .02
377 Bob Zupcic .25 .07
378 Joel Skinner .05 .02
379 Steve Chitren .05 .02
380 Barry Bonds 1.00 .30
381 Sparky Anderson MG .10 .03
382 Sid Fernandez .05 .02
383 Dave Hollins .05 .02
384 Mark Lee .05 .02
385 Tim Wallach .05 .02
386 Lance Blankenship .05 .02
387 Gary Carter TRIB .25 .07
388 Ron Tingley .05 .02
389 Gary Carter TRIB .25 .07
390 Gene Harris .05 .02
391 Jeff Schaefer .05 .02
392 Mark Grant .05 .02
393 Carl Willis .05 .02
394 Al Leiter .10 .03
395 Ron Robinson .05 .02
396 Tim Hulett .05 .02
397 Craig Worthington .05 .02
398 John Orton .05 .02
399 Gary Carter TRIB .25 .07
400 John Dopson .05 .02
401 Moises Alou .25 .07
402 Gary Carter TRIB .25 .07
403 Matt Young .05 .02
404 Wayne Edwards .05 .02
405 Nick Esasky .05 .02
406 Dave Eiland .05 .02
407 Mike Brumley .05 .02
408 Bob Milacki .05 .02
409 Geno Petralli .05 .02
410 Dave Stewart .10 .03
411 Mike Jackson .10 .03
412 Luis Aquino .05 .02
413 Tim Teufel .05 .02
414 Jeff Ware .05 .02
415 Jim Deshaies .05 .02
416 Ellis Burks .10 .03
417 Allan Anderson .05 .02
418 Alfredo Griffin .05 .02
419 Wally Whitehurst .05 .02
420 Sandy Alomar Jr. .10 .03
421 Juan Agosto .05 .02
422 Sam Horn .05 .02
423 Jeff Fassero .05 .02
424 Paul McClellan .05 .02
425 Cecil Fielder .10 .03
426 Tim Raines .10 .03
427 Eddie Taubensee .10 .03
428 Dennis Boyd .05 .02
429 Tony LaRussa MG .10 .03
430 Steve Sax .05 .02
431 Tom Gordon .10 .03
432 Billy Hatcher .05 .02
433 Cal Eldred .05 .02
434 Wally Backman .05 .02
435 Mark Eichhorn .05 .02
436 Mookie Wilson .10 .03
437 Scott Servais .05 .02
438 Mike Maddux .05 .02
439 Chico Walker .05 .02
440 Doug Drabek .05 .02
441 Rob Deer .05 .02
442 Dave West .05 .02
443 Spike Owen .05 .02
444 Tyrone Hill .05 .02
445 Matt Williams .15 .04
446 Mark Lewis .05 .02
447 David Segui .05 .02
448 Tom Pagnozzi .05 .02
449 Jeff Johnson .05 .02
450 Mark McGwire 1.50 .45
451 Tom Henke .05 .02
452 Wilson Alvarez .10 .03
453 Gary Redus .05 .02
454 Darren Holmes .05 .02
455 Pete O'Brien .05 .02
456 Pat Combs .05 .02
457 Hubie Brooks .05 .02
Now with Angels
12-10-91
458 Frank Tanana .05 .02
459 Tom Kelly MG .05 .02
460 Andre Dawson .15 .04
461 Doug Jones .05 .02
462 Rich Rodriguez .05 .02
463 Mike Simms .05 .02
464 Mike Jeffcoat .05 .02
465 Barry Larkin .40 .12
466 Stan Belinda .05 .02
467 Lonnie Smith .05 .02
468 Greg A. Harris .05 .02
469 Jim Eisenreich .05 .02
470 Pedro Guerrero .05 .02
471 Jose DeJesus .05 .02
472 Rich Rowland .05 .02
473 Frank Bolick .40 .12
Craig Paquette
Tom Redington
Paul Russo UER
Line around top border
474 Mike Rossiter .05 .02
475 Robby Thompson .05 .02
476 Randy Bush .05 .02
477 Greg Hibbard .05 .02
478 Dale Sveum .10 .03
Now with Phillies
12-11-91
479 Chito Martinez .05 .02
480 Scott Sanderson .05 .02
481 Tino Martinez .25 .07
482 Jimmy Key .10 .03
483 Terry Shumpert .05 .02
484 Mike Hartley .05 .02
485 Chris Sabo .05 .02
486 Bob Walk .05 .02
487 John Cerutti .05 .02
488 Scott Cooper .05 .02
489 Bobby Cox MG .10 .03
490 Julio Franco .10 .03
491 Jeff Brantley .10 .03
492 Mike Devereaux .10 .03
493 Jose Offerman .05 .02
494 Gary Thurman .05 .02
495 Carney Lansford .10 .03
496 Joe Grahe .05 .02
497 Andy Ashby .10 .03
498 Gerald Perry .05 .02
499 Dave Otto .05 .02
500 Vince Coleman .05 .02
501 Rob Mallicoat .05 .02
502 Greg Briley .05 .02
503 Pascual Perez .05 .02
504 Aaron Sele RC 1.00 .30
505 Bobby Thigpen .05 .02
506 Todd Benzinger .05 .02
507 Candy Maldonado .05 .02
508 Bill Gullickson .05 .02
509 Doug Dascenzo .05 .02
510 Frank Viola .05 .02
511 Kenny Rogers .05 .02
512 Mike Heath .05 .02
513 Kevin Bass .05 .02
514 Kim Batiste .05 .02
515 Delino DeShields .10 .03
516 Ed Sprague .05 .02
517 Jim Gott .05 .02
518 Jose Melendez .05 .02
519 Hal McRae MG .05 .02
520 Jeff Bagwell .75 .23
521 Joe Hesketh .05 .02
522 Milt Cuyler .05 .02
523 Shawn Hillegas .05 .02
524 Don Slaught .05 .02
525 Randy Johnson .50 .15
526 Doug Piatt .05 .02
527 Checklist 397-528 .05 .02
528 Steve Foster .05 .02
529 Joe Girardi .10 .03
530 Jim Abbott .10 .03
531 Larry Walker .15 .04
532 Mike Huff .05 .02
533 Mackey Sasser .05 .02
534 Benji Gil .05 .02
535 Dave Stieb .05 .02
536 Willie Wilson .05 .02
537 Mark Leiter .05 .02
538 Jose Uribe .05 .02
539 Thomas Howard .05 .02
540 Ben McDonald .05 .02
541 Jose Tolentino .05 .02
542 Keith Mitchell .05 .02
543 Jerome Walton .05 .02
544 Cliff Brantley .05 .02
545 Andy Van Slyke .10 .03
546 Paul Sorrento .05 .02
547 Herm Winningham .05 .02
548 Mark Guthrie .05 .02
549 Joe Torre MG .10 .03
550 Darryl Strawberry .10 .03
551 Wilfredo Cordero 2.00 .60
Chipper Jones
Manny Alexander
Alex Arias UER
No line around top border
552 Dave Gallagher .05 .02
553 Edgar Martinez .15 .04
554 Donald Harris .05 .02
555 Frank Thomas .50 .15
556 Storm Davis .05 .02
557 Dickie Thon .05 .02
558 Scott Garrelts .05 .02
559 Steve Olin .05 .02
560 Rickey Henderson .75 .23
561 Jose Vizcaino .05 .02
562 Wade Taylor .05 .02
563 Pat Borders .05 .02
564 Jimmy Gonzalez .05 .02
565 Lee Smith .10 .03
566 Bill Sampen .05 .02
567 Dean Palmer .10 .03
568 Bryan Harvey .05 .02
569 Tony Pena .10 .03
570 Lou Whitaker .10 .03
571 Randy Tomlin .05 .02
572 Greg Vaughn .10 .03
573 Kelly Downs .05 .02
574 Steve Avery UER .05 .02
(Should be 13 games
for Durham in 1989)
575 Kirby Puckett 1.00 .30
576 Heathcliff Slocumb .05 .02
577 Kevin Seitzer .05 .02
578 Lee Guetterman .05 .02
579 Johnny Oates MG .05 .02
580 Greg Maddux 1.00 .30
581 Stan Javier .05 .02
582 Vicente Palacios .05 .02
583 Mel Rojas .05 .02
584 Wayne Rosenthal .05 .02
585 Lenny Webster .05 .02
586 Rod Nichols .05 .02
587 Mickey Morandini .05 .02
588 Russ Swan .05 .02
589 Mariano Duncan .05 .02
Now with Phillies
12-10-91
590 Howard Johnson .05 .02
591 Jeromy Burnitz .25 .07
Jacob Brumfield
Alan Cockrell
D.J. Dozier
592 Denny Neagle .10 .03
593 Steve Decker .05 .02
594 Brian Barber .05 .02
595 Bruce Hurst .05 .02
596 Kent Mercker .05 .02
597 Mike Magnante .05 .02
598 Jody Reed .05 .02
599 Steve Searcy .05 .02
600 Paul Molitor .40 .12
601 Dave Smith .05 .02
602 Mike Fetters .05 .02
603 Luis Mercedes .05 .02
604 Chris Gwynn .10 .03
Now with Royals
12-11-91
605 Scott Erickson .10 .03
606 Brook Jacoby .05 .02
607 Todd Stottlemyre .10 .03
608 Scott Bradley .05 .02
609 Mike Hargrove MG .10 .03
610 Eric Davis .10 .03
611 Brian Hunter .05 .02
612 Pat Kelly .05 .02
613 Pedro Munoz .05 .02
614 Al Osuna .05 .02
615 Matt Merullo .05 .02
616 Larry Andersen .05 .02
617 Junior Ortiz .05 .02
618 Cesar Hernandez .05 .02

Steve Hosey
Jeff McNeely
Dan Peltier
619 Danny Jackson .05 .02
620 George Brett .75 .23
621 Dan Gakeler .05 .02
622 Steve Buechele .05 .02
623 Bob Tewksbury .05 .02
624 Shawn Estes RC 1.00 .30
625 Kevin McReynolds .05 .02
626 Chris Haney .05 .02
627 Mike Sharperson .05 .02
628 Mark Williamson .05 .02
629 Wally Joyner .10 .03
630 Carlton Fisk .40 .12
631 Armando Reynoso .05 .02
632 Felix Fermin .05 .02
633 Mitch Williams .05 .02
634 Manuel Lee .05 .02
635 Harold Baines .15 .04
636 Greg W. Harris .05 .02
637 Orlando Merced .05 .02
638 Chris Bosio .05 .02
639 Wayne Housie .05 .02
640 Xavier Hernandez .05 .02
641 David Howard .05 .02
642 Tim Crews .05 .02
643 Rick Cerone .05 .02
644 Terry Leach .05 .02
645 Deion Sanders .25 .07
646 Craig Wilson .05 .02
647 Marquis Grissom .10 .03
648 Scott Fletcher .05 .02
649 Norm Charlton .05 .02
650 Jesse Barfield .05 .02
651 Joe Slusarski .05 .02
652 Bobby Rose .05 .02
653 Dennis Lamp .05 .02
654 Allen Watson .05 .02
655 Brett Butler .10 .03
656 (Rudy Pemberton .15 .04
Henry Rodriguez
Lee Tinsley
Gerald Williams
657 Dave Johnson .05 .02
658 Checklist 529-660 .05 .02
659 Brian McRae .05 .02
660 Fred McGriff .15 .04
661 Bill Landrum .05 .02
662 Juan Guzman .05 .02
663 Greg Gagne .05 .02
664 Ken Hill .10 .03
Now with Expos
11-25-91
665 Dave Haas .05 .02
666 Tom Foley .05 .02
667 Roberto Hernandez .10 .03
668 Dwayne Henry .05 .02
669 Jim Fregosi MG .05 .02
670 Harold Reynolds .10 .03
671 Mark Whiten .05 .02
672 Eric Plunk .05 .02
673 Todd Hundley .10 .03
674 Mo Sanford .05 .02
675 Bobby Witt .05 .02
676 Sam Militello .05 .02
Pat Mahomes
Turk Wendell
Roger Salkeld
677 John Marzano .05 .02
678 Joe Klink .05 .02
679 Pete Incaviglia .05 .02
680 Dale Murphy .40 .12
681 Rene Gonzales .05 .02
682 Andy Benes .05 .02
683 Jim Poole .05 .02
684 Trever Miller .05 .02
685 Scott Livingstone .05 .02
686 Rich DeLucia .05 .02
687 Harvey Pulliam .05 .02
688 Tim Belcher .05 .02
689 Mark Lemke .05 .02
690 John Franco .10 .03
691 Walt Weiss .05 .02
692 Scott Ruskin .10 .03
Now with Reds
12-11-91
693 Jeff King .05 .02
694 Mike Gardiner .05 .02
695 Gary Sheffield .50 .15
696 Joe Boever .05 .02
697 Mike Felder .05 .02
698 John Habyan .05 .02
699 Cito Gaston MG .05 .02
700 Ruben Sierra .10 .03
701 Scott Radinsky .05 .02
702 Lee Stevens .05 .02
703 Mark Wohlers .05 .02
704 Curt Young .05 .02
705 Dwight Evans .10 .03
706 Rob Murphy .05 .02
707 Gregg Jefferies .10 .03
Now with Royals
12-11-91
708 Tom Bolton .05 .02
709 Chris James .05 .02
710 Kevin Maas .05 .02
711 Ricky Bones .05 .02
712 Curt Wilkerson .05 .02
713 Roger McDowell .05 .02
714 Pokey Reese RC .50 .15
715 Craig Biggio .15 .04
716 Kirk Dressendorfer .05 .02
717 Ken Dayley .05 .02
718 B.J. Surhoff .10 .03
719 Terry Mulholland .05 .02
720 Kirk Gibson .10 .03
721 Mike Pagliarulo .05 .02
722 Walt Terrell .05 .02
723 Jose Oquendo .05 .02
724 Kevin Morton .05 .02
725 Dwight Gooden .10 .03
726 Kirt Manwaring .05 .02
727 Chuck McElroy .05 .02
728 Dave Burba .05 .02
729 Art Howe MG .05 .02
730 Ramon Martinez .05 .02
731 Donnie Hill .05 .02
732 Nelson Santovenia .05 .02
733 Bob Melvin .10 .03
734 Scott Hatteberg .05 .02
735 Greg Swindell .10 .03
Now with Reds
11-15-91
736 Lance Johnson .05 .02
737 Kevin Reimer .05 .02
738 Dennis Eckersley .25 .07
739 Rob Ducey .05 .02
740 Ken Caminiti .15 .04
741 Mark Gubicza .05 .02
742 Billy Spiers .05 .02
743 Darren Lewis .05 .02
744 Chris Hammond .05 .02
745 Dave Magadan .05 .02
746 Bernard Gilkey .10 .03
747 Willie Banks .05 .02
748 Matt Nokes .05 .02
749 Jerald Clark .05 .02
750 Travis Fryman .10 .03
751 Steve Wilson .05 .02
752 Billy Ripken .05 .02
753 Paul Assenmacher .05 .02
754 Charlie Hayes .05 .02
755 Alex Fernandez .05 .02
756 Gary Pettis .05 .02
757 Rob Dibble .05 .02
758 Tim Naehring .05 .02
759 Jeff Torborg MG .05 .02
760 Ozzie Smith .50 .15
761 Mike Fitzgerald .05 .02
762 John Burkett .05 .02
763 Kyle Abbott .05 .02
764 Tyler Green .05 .02
765 Pete Harnisch .05 .02
766 Mark Davis .05 .02
767 Kal Daniels .05 .02
768 Jim Thome .40 .12
769 Jack Howell .05 .02
770 Sid Bream .05 .02
771 Arthur Rhodes .05 .02
772 Garry Templeton .05 .02
773 Hal Morris .05 .02
774 Bud Black .05 .02
775 Ivan Calderon .05 .02
776 Doug Henry .05 .02
777 John Olerud .15 .04
778 Tim Leary .05 .02
779 Jay Bell .10 .03
780 Eddie Murray .50 .15
Now with Mets
11-27-91
781 Paul Abbott .05 .02
782 Phil Plantier .05 .02
783 Joe Magrane .05 .02
784 Ken Patterson .05 .02
785 Albert Belle .15 .04
786 Royce Clayton .05 .02
787 Checklist 661-792 .05 .02
788 Mike Stanton .05 .02
789 Bobby Valentine MG .05 .02
790 Joe Carter .10 .03
791 Danny Cox .05 .02
792 Dave Winfield .50 .15
Now with Blue Jays
12-19-91

1992 O-Pee-Chee Box Bottoms

This set consists of four display box bottoms, each featuring one of four team photos of the divisional champions from the 1991 season. The oversized cards measure approximately 5" by 7" and the card's title appears within a ghosted rectangle near the bottom of the white-bordered color photo. The unnumbered horizontal plain-cardboard backs carry the team's season highlights in both English and French in blue lettering.

Nm-Mt Ex-Mt
COMPLETE SET (4) 3.00 .90
1 Pirates Prevail .50 .15
2 Braves Beat Bucs .75 .23
3 Blue Jays Claim Crown 1.00 .30
4 Kirby Puckett 1.50 .45
Twins Tally in Tenth

1993 O-Pee-Chee

The 1993 O-Pee-Chee baseball set consists of 396 standard-size cards. This is the first year that the regular series does not parallel in design the series that Topps issued. The set was sold in wax packs with eight cards plus a random insert card from either a four-card World Series Heroes subset or an 18-card World Series Champions subset. The fronts features color action player photos with white borders. The player's name appears in a silver stripe across the bottom that overlaps the O-Pee-Chee logo. The backs display color close-ups next to a panel containing biographical data. The panel and a stripe at the bottom reflect the team colors. A white box in the center of the card contains statistics and bilingual (English and French) career highlights.

Nm-Mt Ex-Mt
COMPLETE SET (396) 50.00 15.00
1 Jim Abbott .50 .15
Now with Yankees
12/6/92
2 Eric Anthony .10 .03
3 Harold Baines .25 .07
4 Roberto Alomar .75 .23
5 Steve Avery .10 .03
6 Jim Austin .10 .03
7 Mark Wohlers .10 .03
8 Steve Buechele .10 .03
9 Pedro Astacio .10 .03
10 Moises Alou .25 .07
11 Rod Beck .10 .03
12 Sandy Alomar .25 .07
13 Bret Boone .75 .23
14 Bryan Harvey .10 .03
15 Bobby Bonilla .10 .03
16 Brady Anderson .25 .07
17 Andy Benes .10 .03
18 Ruben Amaro Jr. .10 .03
19 Jay Bell .10 .03
20 Kevin Brown .50 .15
21 Scott Bankhead .25 .07
Now with Red Sox
12/8/92
22 Denis Boucher .10 .03
23 Kevin Appier .25 .07
24 Pat Kelly .10 .03
25 Rick Aguilera .10 .03
26 George Bell .10 .03
27 Steve Farr .10 .03
28 Chad Curtis .10 .03
29 Jeff Bagwell 1.50 .45
30 Lance Blankenship .10 .03
31 Derek Bell .10 .03
32 Damon Berryhill .10 .03
33 Ricky Bones .10 .03
34 Rheal Cormier .10 .03
35 Andre Dawson .75 .23
Now with Red Sox
12/2/92
36 Brett Butler .25 .07
37 Sean Berry .10 .03
38 Bud Black .10 .03
39 Carlos Baerga .25 .07
40 Jay Buhner .50 .15
41 Charlie Hough .25 .07
42 Sid Fernandez .10 .03
43 Luis Mercedes .10 .03
44 Jerald Clark .25 .07
Now with Rockies
11/17/92
45 Wes Chamberlain .10 .03
46 Barry Bonds 2.50 .75
Now with Giants
12/8/92
47 Jose Canseco .75 .23
48 Tim Belcher .10 .03
49 David Nied .10 .03
50 George Brett 1.50 .45
51 Cecil Fielder .25 .07
52 Chili Davis .25 .07
Now with Angels
12/11/92
53 Alex Fernandez .10 .03
54 Charlie Hayes .25 .07
Now with Rockies
11/17/92
55 Rob Ducey .10 .03
56 Craig Biggio .50 .15
57 Mike Bordick .10 .03
58 Pat Borders .10 .03
59 Jeff Blauser .10 .03
60 Chris Bosio .25 .07
Now with Mariners
12/3/92
61 Bernard Gilkey .10 .03
62 Shawon Dunston .10 .03
63 Tom Candiotti .10 .03
64 Darrin Fletcher .10 .03
65 Jeff Brantley .25 .07
66 Albert Belle .25 .07
67 Dave Fleming .10 .03
68 John Franco .25 .07
69 Glenn Davis .10 .03
70 Tony Fernandez .25 .07
Now with Mets
10/26/92
71 Darren Daulton .25 .07
72 Doug Drabek .25 .07
Now with Astros
12/1/92
73 Julio Franco .25 .07
74 Tom Browning .10 .03
75 Tom Gordon .25 .07
76 Travis Fryman .25 .07
77 Scott Erickson .10 .03
78 Carlton Fisk .75 .23
79 Roberto Kelly .25 .07
Now with Reds
11/3/92
80 Gary DiSarcina .10 .03
81 Ken Caminiti .50 .15
82 Ron Darling .10 .03
83 Joe Carter .25 .07
84 Sid Bream .10 .03
85 Cal Eldred .10 .03
86 Mark Grace .50 .15
87 Eric Davis .25 .07
88 Ivan Calderon .25 .07
Now with Red Sox
12/8/92
89 John Burkett .10 .03
90 Felix Fermin .10 .03
91 Ken Griffey Jr. 2.50 .75
92 Dwight Gooden .25 .07
93 Mike Devereaux .10 .03
94 Tony Gwynn 2.00 .60
95 Mariano Duncan .10 .03
96 Jeff King .10 .03
97 Juan Gonzalez .75 .23
98 Norm Charlton .25 .07
Now with Mariners
11/17/92
99 Mark Gubicza .10 .03
100 Danny Gladden .10 .03
101 Greg Gagne .25 .07
Now with Royals
12/8/92
102 Ozzie Guillen .25 .07
103 Don Mattingly 2.00 .60
104 Damion Easley .10 .03
105 Casey Candaele .10 .03
106 Dennis Eckersley .75 .23
107 David Cone .50 .15
Now with Royals
12/8/92
108 Ron Gant .10 .03
109 Mike Fetters .10 .03
110 Mike Harkey .10 .03
111 Kevin Gross .10 .03
112 Archi Cianfrocco .10 .03
113 Will Clark .75 .23
114 Glenallen Hill .10 .03
115 Erik Hanson .10 .03
116 Todd Hundley .25 .07
117 Leo Gomez .10 .03
118 Bruce Hurst .10 .03
119 Len Dykstra .25 .07
120 Jose Lind .25 .07
Now with Royals
11/19/92
121 Jose Guzman .25 .07
Now with Cubs
12/1/92
122 Rob Dibble .10 .03
123 Gregg Jefferies .10 .03
124 Bill Gullickson .10 .03
125 Brian Harper .10 .03
126 Roberto Hernandez .25 .07
127 Sam Militello .10 .03
128 Junior Felix .25 .07
Now with Marlins
11/17/92
129 Andujar Cedeno .10 .03
130 Rickey Henderson 1.00 .30
131 Bob MacDonald .10 .03
132 Tom Glavine .75 .23
133 Scott Fletcher .25 .07
Now with Red Sox
11/30/92
134 Brian Jordan .25 .07
135 Greg Maddux 2.50 .75
Now with Braves
12/9/92
136 Orel Hershiser .25 .07
137 Greg Colbrunn .10 .03
138 Royce Clayton .10 .03
139 Thomas Howard .10 .03
140 Randy Johnson 1.00 .30
141 Jeff Innis .10 .03
142 Chris Hoiles .10 .03
143 Darrin Jackson .10 .03
144 Tommy Greene .10 .03
145 Mike LaValliere .10 .03
146 David Hulse .10 .03
147 Barry Larkin .50 .15
148 Wally Joyner .25 .07
149 Mike Henneman .10 .03
150 Kent Hrbek .25 .07
151 Bo Jackson .75 .23
152 Rich Monteleone .10 .03
153 Chuck Finley .25 .07
154 Steve Finley .25 .07
155 Dave Henderson .10 .03
156 Kelly Gruber .25 .07
Now with Angels
12/8/92
157 Brian Hunter .10 .03
158 Darryl Hamilton .10 .03
159 Derrick May .10 .03
160 Jay Howell .10 .03
161 Wil Cordero .10 .03
162 Bryan Hickerson .10 .03
163 Reggie Jefferson .10 .03
164 Edgar Martinez .50 .15
165 Nigel Wilson .10 .03
166 Howard Johnson .10 .03
167 Tim Hulett .10 .03
168 Mike Maddux .25 .07
Now with Mets
12/17/92
169 Dave Hollins .10 .03
170 Zane Smith .10 .03
171 Rafael Palmeiro .75 .23
172 Dave Martinez .25 .07
Now with Giants
12/9/92
173 Rusty Meacham .10 .03
174 Mark Leiter .10 .03
175 Chuck Knoblauch .75 .23
176 Lance Johnson .10 .03
177 Matt Nokes .10 .03
178 Luis Gonzalez .75 .23
179 Jack Morris .25 .07
180 David Justice .75 .23
181 Doug Henry .10 .03
182 Felix Jose .10 .03
183 Delino DeShields .75 .23
184 Rene Gonzales .25 .07
185 Pete Harnisch .10 .03
186 Mike Moore .25 .07
Now with Tigers
12/9/92
187 Juan Guzman .10 .03
188 John Olerud .50 .15
189 Ryan Klesko .25 .07
190 John Jaha .10 .03
191 Ray Lankford .25 .07
192 Jeff Fassero .10 .03
193 Darren Lewis .10 .03
194 Mark Lewis .10 .03
195 Alan Mills .10 .03
196 Wade Boggs 1.00 .30
Now with Yankees
12/15/92
197 Hal Morris .10 .03
198 Ron Karkovice .10 .03
199 Joe Grahe .10 .03
200 Butch Henry .25 .07
Now with Rockies
11/17/92
201 Mark McGwire 3.00 .90
202 Tom Henke .25 .07
Now with Rangers
12/15/92
203 Ed Sprague .10 .03
204 Charlie Leibrandt .25 .07
Now with Rangers
12/9/92
205 Pat Listach .10 .03
206 Omar Olivares .10 .03
207 Mike Morgan .10 .03
208 Eric Karros .50 .15
209 Marquis Grissom .25 .07
210 Willie McGee .25 .07
211 Derek Lilliquist .10 .03
212 Tino Martinez .75 .23
213 Jeff Kent .50 .15
214 Mike Mussina .75 .23
215 Randy Myers .25 .07
Now with Cubs
12/9/92
216 John Kruk .25 .07
217 Tom Brunansky .10 .03
218 Paul O'Neill .50 .15
Now with Yankees
11/3/92
219 Scott Livingstone .10 .03
220 John Valentin .10 .03
221 Eddie Zosky .10 .03
222 Pete Smith .10 .03
223 Bill Wegman .10 .03
224 Todd Zeile .25 .07
225 Tim Wallach .25 .07
Now with Dodgers
12/24/92
226 Mitch Williams .10 .03
227 Tim Wakefield .50 .15
228 Frank Viola .10 .03
229 Nolan Ryan 3.00 .90
230 Kirk McCaskill .10 .03
231 Melido Perez .10 .03
232 Mark Langston .10 .03
233 Xavier Hernandez .10 .03
234 Jerry Browne .10 .03
235 Dave Stieb .25 .07
Now with White Sox
12/8/92
236 Mark Lemke .10 .03
237 Paul Molitor .75 .23
Now with Blue Jays
12/7/92
238 Geronimo Pena .10 .03
239 Ken Hill .10 .03
240 Jack Clark .10 .03
241 Greg Myers .10 .03
242 Pete Incaviglia .25 .07
Now with Phillies
12/8/92
243 Ruben Sierra .25 .07
244 Todd Stottlemyre .10 .03
245 Pat Hentgen .25 .07
246 Melvin Nieves .10 .03
247 Jaime Navarro .10 .03
248 Donovan Osborne .10 .03
249 Brian Barnes .10 .03
250 Cory Snyder .25 .07
Now with Dodgers
12/5/92
251 Kenny Lofton .50 .15
252 Kevin Mitchell .25 .07
Now with Reds
11/17/92
253 Dave Magadan .25 .07
Now with Marlins
12/8/92
254 Ben McDonald .10 .03
255 Fred McGriff .50 .15
256 Mickey Morandini .10 .03
257 Randy Tomlin .10 .03
258 Dean Palmer .25 .07
259 Roger Clemens 2.00 .60
260 Joe Oliver .10 .03
261 Jeff Montgomery .25 .07
262 Tony Phillips .10 .03
263 Shane Mack .10 .03
264 Jack McDowell .10 .03
265 Mike Macfarlane .10 .03
266 Luis Polonia .10 .03
267 Doug Jones .10 .03
268 Terry Steinbach .10 .03
269 Jimmy Key .25 .07
Now with Yankees
12/10/92
270 Pat Tabler .10 .03
271 Otis Nixon .10 .03
272 Dave Nilsson .10 .03
273 Tom Pagnozzi .10 .03
274 Ryne Sandberg 1.50 .45
275 Ramon Martinez .10 .03
276 Tim Laker .10 .03
277 Bill Swift .10 .03
278 Charles Nagy .10 .03
279 Harold Reynolds .50 .15
Now with Orioles
12/11/92
280 Eddie Murray .75 .23
281 Gregg Olson .10 .03
282 Frank Seminara .10 .03
283 Terry Mulholland .10 .03
284 Kevin Reimer .25 .07
Now with Brewers
11/17/92
285 Mike Greenwell .10 .03
286 Jose Rijo .10 .03
287 Brian McRae .10 .03
288 Frank Tanana .25 .07
Now with Mets
12/10/92
289 Pedro Munoz .10 .03
290 Tim Raines .25 .07
291 Andy Stankiewicz .10 .03
292 Tim Salmon .75 .23
293 Jimmy Jones .10 .03
294 Dave Stewart .25 .07
Now with Blue Jays
12/8/92
295 Mike Timlin .10 .03
296 Greg Olson .10 .03
297 Dan Plesac .25 .07
Now with Cubs
12/8/92
298 Mike Perez .10 .03
299 Jose Offerman .10 .03
300 Denny Martinez .25 .07
301 Robby Thompson .10 .03
302 Bret Saberhagen .25 .07
303 Joe Orsulak .25 .07
Now with Mets
12/18/92

304 Tim Naehring	.10	.03
305 Bip Roberts	.10	.03
306 Kirby Puckett	1.50	.45
307 Steve Sax	.10	.03
308 Danny Tartabull	.10	.03
309 Jeff Juden	.10	.03
310 Duane Ward	.10	.03
311 Alejandro Pena	.25	.07
Now with Pirates 12/10/92		
312 Kevin Seitzer	.10	.03
313 Ozzie Smith	1.00	.30
314 Mike Piazza	3.00	.90
315 Chris Nabholz	.10	.03
316 Tony Pena	.25	.07
317 Gary Sheffield	1.00	.30
318 Mark Portugal	.10	.03
319 Walt Weiss	.25	.07
Now with Marlins 11/17/92		
320 Manuel Lee	.25	.07
Now with Rangers 12/19/92		
321 David Wells	.50	.15
322 Terry Pendleton	.10	.03
323 Billy Spiers	.10	.03
324 Lee Smith	.25	.07
325 Bob Scanlan	.10	.03
326 Mike Scioscia	.25	.07
327 Spike Owen	.25	.07
Now with Yankees 12/4/92		
328 Mackey Sasser	.25	.07
Now with Mariners 12/23/92		
329 Arthur Rhodes	.10	.03
330 Ben Rivera	.10	.03
331 Ivan Rodriguez	1.00	.30
332 Phil Plantier	.25	.07
Now with Padres 12/10/92		
333 Chris Sabo	.10	.03
334 Mickey Tettleton	.10	.03
335 John Smiley	.25	.07
Now with Reds 11/30/92		
336 Bobby Thigpen	.10	.03
337 Randy Velarde	.10	.03
338 Luis Sojo	.25	.07
Now with Blue Jays 12/8/92		
339 Scott Servais	.10	.03
340 Bob Welch	.10	.03
341 Devon White	.10	.03
342 Jeff Reardon	.25	.07
343 B.J. Surhoff	.25	.07
344 Bob Tewksbury	.10	.03
345 Jose Vizcaino	.10	.03
346 Mike Sharperson	.10	.03
347 Mel Rojas	.10	.03
348 Matt Williams	.50	.15
349 Steve Olin	.10	.03
350 Mike Schooler	.10	.03
351 Ryan Thompson	.10	.03
352 Cal Ripken	3.00	.90
353 Benito Santiago	.50	.15
Now with Marlins 12/16/92		
354 Curt Schilling	.75	.23
355 Andy Van Slyke	.10	.03
356 Kenny Rogers	.10	.03
357 Jody Reed	.25	.07
Now with Dodgers 11/17/92		
358 Reggie Sanders	.25	.07
359 Kevin McReynolds	.10	.03
360 Alan Trammell	.50	.15
361 Kevin Tapani	.10	.03
362 Frank Thomas	1.00	.30
363 Bernie Williams	.75	.23
364 John Smoltz	.25	.07
365 Robin Yount	1.00	.30
366 John Wetteland	.25	.07
367 Bob Zupcic	.10	.03
368 Julio Valera	.10	.03
369 Brian Williams	.10	.03
370 Willie Wilson	.10	.03
Now with Cubs 12/18/92		
371 Dave Winfield	1.00	.30
Now with Twins 12/17/92		
372 Deion Sanders	.50	.15
373 Greg Vaughn	.25	.07
374 Todd Worrell	.25	.07
Now with Dodgers 12/9/92		
375 Darryl Strawberry	.25	.07
376 John Vander Wal	.10	.03
377 Mike Benjamin	.10	.03
378 Mark Whiten	.10	.03
379 Omar Vizquel	.25	.07
380 Anthony Young	.10	.03
381 Rick Sutcliffe	.10	.03
382 Candy Maldonado	.25	.07
Now with Cubs 12/11/92		
383 Francisco Cabrera	.10	.03
384 Larry Walker	.50	.15
385 Scott Cooper	.10	.03
386 Gerald Williams	.10	.03
387 Robin Ventura	.50	.15
388 Carl Willis	.10	.03
389 Lou Whitaker	.25	.07
390 Hipolito Pichardo	.10	.03
391 Rudy Seanez	.10	.03
392 Greg Swindell	.25	.07
Now with Astros 12/4/92		
393 Mo Vaughn	.75	.23
394 Checklist 1-132	.10	.03
395 Checklist 133-264	.10	.03
396 Checklist 265-396	.10	.03

1993 O-Pee-Chee World Champions

This 18-card standard-size set was randomly inserted in 1993 O-Pee-Chee wax packs and features the Toronto Blue Jays, the 1992 World

Series Champions. The standard-size cards are similar to the regular issue, with glossy color action player photos with white borders on the fronts. They differ in having a gold (rather than silver) stripe across the bottom, which intersects a 1992 World Champions logo. The backs carry statistics on a burnt orange box against a light blue panel with bilingual (English and French) career highlights.

	Nm-Mt	Ex-Mt
COMPLETE SET (18)	4.00	1.20
1 Roberto Alomar	1.00	.30
2 Pat Borders	.10	.03
3 Joe Carter	.25	.07
4 David Cone	.75	.23
5 Kelly Gruber	.10	.03
6 Juan Guzman	.10	.03
7 Tom Henke	.10	.03
8 Jimmy Key	.25	.07
9 Manuel Lee	.10	.03
10 Candy Maldonado	.10	.03
11 Jack Morris	.25	.07
12 John Olerud	.50	.15
13 Ed Sprague	.25	.07
14 Todd Stottlemyre	.25	.07
15 Duane Ward	.10	.03
16 Devon White	.10	.03
17 Dave Winfield	.50	.15
18 Cito Gaston MG	.10	.03

1993 O-Pee-Chee World Series Heroes

This four-card standard-size set was randomly inserted in 1993 O-Pee-Chee wax packs. These cards were more difficult to find than the 18-card World Series Champions insert set. The fronts feature color action player photos with white borders. The words "World Series Heroes" appear in a dark blue stripe above the picture, while the player's name is printed in the bottom white border. A 1992 World Series logo overlays the picture at the lower right corner. Over a ghosted version of the 1992 World Series logo, the backs summarize, in English and French, the player's outstanding performance in the 1992 World Series. The cards are numbered on the back in alphabetical order by player's name.

	Nm-Mt	Ex-Mt
COMPLETE SET (4)	1.50	.45
1 Pat Borders	.25	.07
2 Jimmy Key	.50	.15
3 Ed Sprague	.25	.07
4 Dave Winfield	1.00	.30

1994 O-Pee-Chee

The 1994 O-Pee-Chee baseball set consists of 270 standard-size cards. Production was limited to 2,500 individually numbered cases. Each display box contained 36 packs and one 5" by 7" All-Star Jumbo card. Each foil pack contained 14 regular cards plus either one chase card or one redemption card.

	Nm-Mt	Ex-Mt
COMPLETE SET (270)	15.00	4.50
1 Paul Molitor	.25	.07
2 Kirt Manwaring	.05	.02
3 Brady Anderson	.10	.03
4 Scott Cooper	.05	.02
5 Kevin Stocker	.05	.02
6 Alex Fernandez	.05	.02
7 Jeff Montgomery	.05	.02
8 Danny Tartabull	.05	.02
9 Damion Easley	.05	.02
10 Andujar Cedeno	.05	.02
11 Steve Karsay	.05	.02
12 Dave Stewart	.10	.03
13 Fred McGriff	.15	.04
14 Jaime Navarro	.05	.02
15 Allen Watson	.05	.02
16 Ryne Sandberg	.60	.18
17 Arthur Rhodes	.05	.02
18 Marquis Grissom	.10	.03
19 John Burkett	.05	.02
20 Robby Thompson	.05	.02
21 Denny Martinez	.10	.03
22 Ken Griffey Jr.	1.50	.45
23 Orestes Destrade	.05	.02
24 Dwight Gooden	.10	.03
25 Rafael Palmeiro	.25	.07
26 Pedro A.Martinez	.05	.02
27 Wes Chamberlain	.05	.02
28 Juan Gonzalez	.25	.07
29 Kevin Mitchell	.05	.02
30 Dante Bichette	.10	.03
31 Howard Johnson	.05	.02
32 Mickey Tettleton	.05	.02
33 Robin Ventura	.15	.04
34 Terry Mulholland	.05	.02
35 Bernie Williams	.25	.07
36 Eduardo Perez	.05	.02
37 Rickey Henderson	.50	.15
38 Terry Pendleton	.05	.02
39 John Smoltz	.25	.07
40 Derrick May	.05	.02
41 Pedro Martinez	.50	.15
42 Mark Portugal	.05	.02
43 Albert Belle	.10	.03
44 Edgar Martinez	.15	.04
45 Gary Sheffield	.50	.15
46 Bret Saberhagen	.10	.03
47 Ricky Gutierrez	.05	.02
48 Orlando Merced	.05	.02
49 Mike Greenwell	.05	.02
50 Jose Rijo	.05	.02
51 Jeff Granger	.05	.02
52 Mike Henneman	.05	.02
53 Dave Winfield	.25	.07
54 Don Mattingly	1.00	.30
55 J.T. Snow	.10	.03
56 Todd Van Poppel	.05	.02
57 Chipper Jones	.75	.23
58 Darryl Hamilton	.05	.02
59 Delino DeShields	.05	.02
60 Rondell White	.10	.03
61 Eric Anthony	.05	.02
62 Charlie Hough	.05	.02
63 Sid Fernandez	.05	.02
64 Derek Bell	.05	.02
65 Phil Plantier	.05	.02
66 Curt Schilling	.40	.12
67 Roger Clemens	1.00	.30
68 Jose Lind	.05	.02
69 Andres Galarraga	.25	.07
70 Tim Belcher	.05	.02
71 Ron Karkovice	.05	.02
72 Alan Trammell	.15	.04
73 Pete Harnisch	.05	.02
74 Mark McGwire	1.50	.45
75 Ryan Klesko	.10	.03
76 Ramon Martinez	.05	.02
77 Gregg Jefferies	.05	.02
78 Steve Buechele	.05	.02
79 Bill Swift	.05	.02
80 Matt Williams	.15	.04
81 Randy Johnson	.50	.15
82 Mike Mussina	.25	.07
83 Andy Benes	.05	.02
84 Dave Staton	.05	.02
85 Steve Cooke	.05	.02
86 Andy Van Slyke	.05	.02
87 Ivan Rodriguez	.50	.15
88 Frank Viola	.05	.02
89 Aaron Sele	.10	.03
90 Ellis Burks	.10	.03
91 Wally Joyner	.10	.03
92 Rick Aguilera	.05	.02
93 Kirby Puckett	.75	.23
94 Roberto Hernandez	.05	.02
95 Mike Stanley	.05	.02
96 Roberto Alomar	.25	.07
97 James Mouton	.05	.02
98 Chad Curtis	.05	.02
99 Mitch Williams	.05	.02
100 Carlos Delgado	.50	.15
101 Greg Maddux	1.00	.30
102 Brian Harper	.05	.02
103 Tom Pagnozzi	.05	.02
104 Jose Offerman	.05	.02
105 John Wetteland	.10	.03
106 Carlos Baerga	.10	.03
107 Dave Magadan	.05	.02
108 Bobby Jones	.05	.02
109 Tony Gwynn	1.00	.30
110 Jeromy Burnitz	.15	.04
111 Bip Roberts	.05	.02
112 Carlos Garcia	.05	.02
113 Jeff Russell	.05	.02
114 Armando Reynoso	.05	.02
115 Ozzie Guillen	.10	.03
116 Bo Jackson	.15	.04
117 Terry Steinbach	.05	.02
118 Deion Sanders	.25	.07
119 Randy Myers	.05	.02
120 Mark Whiten	.05	.02
121 Manny Ramirez	.50	.15
122 Ben McDonald	.05	.02
123 Darren Daulton	.10	.03
124 Kevin Young	.05	.02
125 Barry Larkin	.25	.07
126 Cecil Fielder	.10	.03
127 Frank Thomas	.50	.15
128 Luis Polonia	.05	.02
129 Steve Finley	.10	.03
130 John Olerud	.10	.03
131 John Jaha	.05	.02
132 Darren Lewis	.05	.02
133 Orel Hershiser	.10	.03
134 Chris Bosio	.05	.02
135 Ryan Thompson	.05	.02
136 Chris Sabo	.05	.02
137 Tommy Greene	.05	.02
138 Andre Dawson	.15	.04
139 Roberto Kelly	.05	.02
140 Ken Hill	.05	.02
141 Greg Gagne	.05	.02
142 Julio Franco	.10	.03
143 Chili Davis	.10	.03
144 Dennis Eckersley	.25	.07
145 Joe Carter	.10	.03
146 Mark Grace	.15	.04
147 Mike Piazza	1.00	.30
148 J.R. Phillips	.05	.02
149 Rich Amaral	.05	.02
150 Benny Santiago	.10	.03
151 Jeff King	.05	.02
152 Dean Palmer	.10	.03
153 Hal Morris	.05	.02
154 Mike Macfarlane	.05	.02
155 Chuck Knoblauch	.10	.03
156 Pat Kelly	.05	.02
157 Greg Swindell	.05	.02
158 Chuck Finley	.10	.03
159 Devon White	.10	.03
160 Duane Ward	.05	.02
161 Sammy Sosa	.75	.23
162 Javy Lopez	.15	.04
163 Eric Karros	.10	.03
164 Royce Clayton	.05	.02
165 Salomon Torres	.05	.02
166 Jeff Kent	.10	.03
167 Chris Hoiles	.05	.02
168 Len Dykstra	.10	.03
169 Jose Canseco	.25	.07
170 Bret Boone	.15	.04
171 Charlie Hayes	.05	.02
172 Lou Whitaker	.10	.03
173 Jack McDowell	.05	.02
174 Jimmy Key	.10	.03
175 Mark Langston	.05	.02
176 Darryl Kile	.05	.02
177 Juan Guzman	.05	.02
178 Pat Borders	.05	.02
179 Cal Eldred	.05	.02
180 Jose Guzman	.05	.02
181 Ozzie Smith	.60	.18
182 Rod Beck	.05	.02
183 Dave Fleming	.05	.02
184 Eddie Murray	.40	.12
185 Cal Ripken	1.50	.45
186 Dave Hollins	.05	.02
187 Will Clark	.25	.07
188 Otis Nixon	.05	.02
189 Joe Oliver	.05	.02
190 Roberto Mejia	.05	.02
191 Felix Jose	.05	.02
192 Tony Phillips	.05	.02
193 Wade Boggs	.50	.15
194 Tim Salmon	.15	.04
195 Ruben Sierra	.10	.03
196 Steve Avery	.05	.02
197 B.J. Surhoff	.10	.03
198 Todd Zeile	.10	.03
199 Raul Mondesi	.25	.07
200 Barry Bonds	1.00	.30
201 Sandy Alomar	.10	.03
202 Bobby Bonilla	.05	.02
203 Mike Devereaux	.05	.02
204 Ricky Bottalico RC	.05	.02
205 Kevin Brown	.15	.04
206 Jason Bere	.05	.02
207 Reggie Sanders	.10	.03
208 David Nied	.05	.02
209 Travis Fryman	.10	.03
210 James Baldwin	.10	.03
211 Jim Abbott	.10	.03
212 Jeff Bagwell	.75	.23
213 Bob Welch	.05	.02
214 Jeff Blauser	.05	.02
215 Brett Butler	.10	.03
216 Pat Listach	.05	.02
217 Bob Tewksbury	.05	.02
218 Mike Lansing	.05	.02
219 Wayne Kirby	.05	.02
220 Chuck Carr	.05	.02
221 Harold Baines	.10	.03
222 Jay Bell	.05	.02
223 Cliff Floyd	.15	.04
224 Rob Dibble	.05	.02
225 Kevin Appier	.10	.03
226 Eric Davis	.10	.03
227 Matt Walbeck	.05	.02
228 Tim Raines	.10	.03
229 Paul O'Neill	.10	.03
230 Craig Biggio	.15	.04
231 Brent Gates	.05	.02
232 Rob Butler	.05	.02
233 David Justice	.15	.04
234 Rene Arocha	.05	.02
235 Mike Morgan	.05	.02
236 Denis Boucher	.05	.02
237 Kenny Lofton	.10	.03
238 Jeff Conine	.10	.03
239 Bryan Harvey	.05	.02
240 Danny Jackson	.05	.02
241 Al Martin	.05	.02
242 Tom Henke	.05	.02
243 Erik Hanson	.05	.02
244 Walt Weiss	.05	.02
245 Brian McRae	.05	.02
246 Kevin Tapani	.05	.02
247 David McCarty	.05	.02
248 Doug Drabek	.05	.02
249 Troy Neel	.05	.02
250 Tom Glavine	.25	.07
251 Ray Lankford	.10	.03
252 Wil Cordero	.05	.02
253 Larry Walker	.10	.03
254 Charles Nagy	.05	.02
255 Kirk Rueter	.05	.02
256 John Franco	.10	.03
257 John Kruk	.10	.03
258 Alex Gonzalez	.05	.02
259 Mo Vaughn	.25	.07
260 David Cone	.15	.04
261 Kent Hrbek	.10	.03
262 Lance Johnson	.05	.02
263 Luis Gonzalez	.25	.07
264 Mike Bordick	.05	.02
265 Ed Sprague	.05	.02
266 Moises Alou	.15	.04
267 Omar Vizquel	.10	.03
268 Jay Buhner	.10	.03
269 Checklist	.05	.02
270 Checklist	.05	.02

1994 O-Pee-Chee All-Star Redemptions

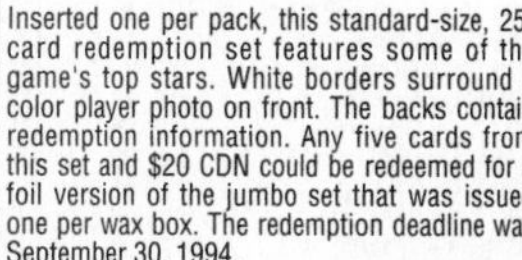

Inserted one per pack, this standard-size, 25-card redemption set features some of the game's top stars. White borders surround a color player photo on front. The backs contain redemption information. Any five cards from this set and $20 CDN could be redeemed for a foil version of the jumbo set that was issued one per wax box. The redemption deadline was September 30, 1994.

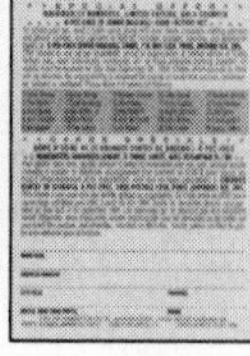

	Nm-Mt	Ex-Mt
COMPLETE SET (25)	12.00	3.60
1 Frank Thomas	1.00	.30
2 Paul Molitor	1.00	.30
3 Barry Bonds	1.50	.45
4 Juan Gonzalez	.75	.23
5 Jeff Bagwell	1.25	.35
6 Carlos Baerga	.40	.12
7 Ryne Sandberg	1.00	.30
8 Ken Griffey Jr.	2.00	.60
9 Mike Piazza	2.00	.60
10 Tim Salmon	.40	.12
11 Marquis Grissom	.40	.12
12 Albert Belle	.40	.12
13 Fred McGriff	.60	.18
14 Jack McDowell	.20	.06
15 Cal Ripken	3.00	.90
16 John Olerud	.40	.12
17 Kirby Puckett	1.00	.30
18 Roger Clemens	2.00	.60
19 Larry Walker	.40	.12
20 Cecil Fielder	.40	.12
21 Roberto Alomar	.75	.23
22 Greg Maddux	2.50	.75
23 Joe Carter	.40	.12
24 David Justice	.40	.12
25 Kenny Lofton	.60	.18

1994 O-Pee-Chee Jumbo All-Stars

These 5" by 7" parallel cards were included as a bonus at the bottom of every 1994 OPC box. According to published reports, approximately 2,400 of each card was produced. A foil version exists for these cards. They are currently valued the same as the regular cards.

	Nm-Mt	Ex-Mt
COMPLETE SET (25)	35.00	10.50
FOIL: SAME VALUE AS BASIC JUMBOS		
1 Frank Thomas	2.00	.60
2 Paul Molitor	1.50	.45
3 Barry Bonds	4.00	1.20
4 Juan Gonzalez	1.00	.30
5 Jeff Bagwell	2.00	.60
6 Carlos Baerga	.50	.15
7 Ryne Sandberg	3.00	.90
8 Ken Griffey Jr.	5.00	1.50
9 Mike Piazza	5.00	1.50
10 Tim Salmon	1.00	.30
11 Marquis Grissom	.50	.15
12 Albert Belle	.50	.15
13 Fred McGriff	.75	.23
14 Jack McDowell	.25	.07
15 Cal Ripken	8.00	2.40
16 John Olerud	.50	.15
17 Kirby Puckett	2.00	.60
18 Roger Clemens	4.00	1.20
19 Larry Walker	.50	.15
20 Cecil Fielder	.50	.15
21 Roberto Alomar	1.00	.30
22 Greg Maddux	5.00	1.50
23 Joe Carter	.50	.15
24 David Justice	.50	.15
25 Kenny Lofton	.75	.23

1994 O-Pee-Chee Jumbo All-Stars Foil

These cards, parallel to the Jumbo All-Stars a collector received when buying a 1994 O-Pee-Chee Box were given a foil treatment. These cards were available by a collector accumulating five cards from the All-Star redemption set and sending in $20 Canadian. These cards were to be available to collectors by early October, 1994.

	Nm-Mt	Ex-Mt
COMPLETE SET (25)	20.00	6.00
*SAME PRICE AS REGULAR JUMBO ALL-STAR		

1994 O-Pee-Chee Diamond Dynamos

This 18-card standard-size set was randomly inserted into 1994 OPC packs. According to the company approximately 5,000 sets were produced. The fronts feature player photos as well as red foil lettering while the backs have gold foil stamping. Between one or two cards from this set was included in each box.

	Nm-Mt	Ex-Mt
COMPLETE SET (18)	25.00	7.50

1 Mike Piazza 20.00 6.00
2 Robert Mejia 1.00 .30
3 Wayne Kirby 1.00 .30
4 Kevin Stocker 1.00 .30
5 Chris Gomez 1.00 .30
6 Bobby Jones 1.00 .30
7 David McCarty 1.00 .30
8 Kirk Rueter 1.00 .30
9 J.T. Snow 1.50 .45
10 Wil Cordero 1.00 .30
11 Tim Salmon 6.00 1.80
12 Jeff Conine 2.00 .60
13 Jason Bere 1.00 .30
14 Greg McMichael 1.00 .30
15 Brent Gates 1.00 .30
16 Allen Watson 1.00 .30
17 Aaron Sele 1.50 .45
18 Carlos Garcia 1.00 .30

1994 O-Pee-Chee Hot Prospects

This nine-card standard-size insert set features some of 1994's leading prospects. According to the manufacturer, approximately 6,666 sets were produced. The cards features gold and red foil stamping, player photos on both sides and complete minor league stats. An average of one card was included in each display box.

Nm-Mt Ex-Mt
COMPLETE SET (9) 20.00 6.00
1 Cliff Floyd 2.00 .60
2 James Mouton .50 .15
3 Salomon Torres .50 .15
4 Raul Mondesi 2.50 .75
5 Carlos Delgado 5.00 1.50
6 Manny Ramirez 6.00 1.80
7 Javy Lopez 2.50 .75
8 Alex Gonzalez .50 .15
9 Ryan Klesko 4.00 1.20

1994 O-Pee-Chee World Champions

This nine card insert set features members of the 1993 World Series champion Toronto Blue Jays. Randomly inserted in packs at a rate of one in 36, the player is superimposed over a background containing the phrase, "1993 World Series Champions". The backs contain World Series statistics from 1992 and 1993 and highlights.

Nm-Mt Ex-Mt
COMPLETE SET (9) 15.00 4.50
1 Rickey Henderson 8.00 2.40
2 Devon White 1.50 .45
3 Paul Molitor 3.00 .90
4 Joe Carter 1.50 .45
5 John Olerud 2.00 .60
6 Roberto Alomar 2.50 .75
7 Ed Sprague 1.00 .30
8 Pat Borders 1.00 .30
9 Tony Fernandez 2.00 .60

1991 O-Pee-Chee Premier

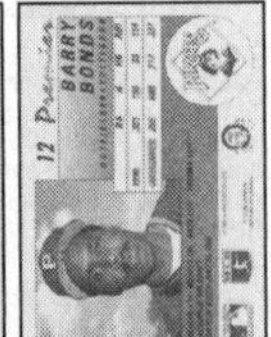

The 1991 OPC Premier set contains 132 standard-size cards. The fronts feature color action player photos on a white card face. All the pictures are bordered in gold above, while the color of the border stripes on the other three sides varies from card to card. The player's name, team name, and position (the last item in English and French) appear below the picture. In a horizontal format, the backs have a color head shot and the team logo in a circular format. Biography and statistics (1990 and career) are presented on an orange and yellow striped background. The cards are arranged in alphabetical order and numbered on the back. Small packs of these cards were given out at the Fan Fest to commemorate the 1991 All-Star Game in Canada.

Nm-Mt Ex-Mt
COMPLETE SET (132) 10.00 3.00
COMP. FACT.SET (132) 15.00 4.50
1 Roberto Alomar .25 .07
2 Sandy Alomar Jr. .10 .03
3 Moises Alou .10 .03
4 Brian Barnes .05 .02
5 Steve Bedrosian .05 .02
6 George Bell .05 .02
7 Juan Bell .05 .02
8 Albert Belle .10 .03
9 Bud Black .05 .02
10 Mike Boddicker .05 .02
11 Wade Boggs .40 .12
12 Barry Bonds .75 .23
13 Denis Boucher RC .05 .02
14 George Brett .75 .23
15 Hubie Brooks .05 .02
16 Brett Butler .10 .03
17 Ivan Calderon .05 .02
18 Jose Canseco .25 .07
19 Gary Carter .40 .12
20 Joe Carter .10 .03
21 Jack Clark .10 .03
22 Will Clark .25 .07
23 Roger Clemens .75 .23
24 Alex Cole .05 .02
25 Vince Coleman .05 .02
26 Jeff Conine RC .15 .04
27 Milt Cuyler .05 .02
28 Danny Darwin .05 .02
29 Eric Davis .10 .03
30 Glenn Davis .05 .02
31 Andre Dawson .25 .07
32 Ken Dayley .05 .02
33 Steve Decker .05 .02
34 Delino DeShields .10 .03
35 Lance Dickson RC .05 .02
36 Kirk Dressendorfer RC .05 .02
37 Shawon Dunston .05 .02
38 Dennis Eckersley .40 .12
39 Dwight Evans .10 .03
40 Howard Farmer .05 .02
41 Junior Felix .05 .02
42 Alex Fernandez .05 .02
43 Tony Fernandez .10 .03
44 Cecil Fielder .10 .03
45 Carlton Fisk .40 .12
46 Willie Fraser .05 .02
47 Gary Gaetti .10 .03
48 Andres Galarraga .25 .07
49 Ron Gant .10 .03
50 Kirk Gibson .10 .03
51 Bernard Gilkey .05 .02
52 Leo Gomez .05 .02
53 Rene Gonzales .05 .02
54 Juan Gonzalez .40 .12
55 Dwight Gooden .10 .03
56 Ken Griffey Jr. 1.25 .35
57 Kelly Gruber .05 .02
58 Pedro Guerrero .05 .02
59 Tony Gwynn .75 .23
60 Chris Hammond .05 .02
61 Ron Hassey .05 .02
62 Rickey Henderson .50 .15
939 Stolen Bases
63 Tom Henke .05 .02
64 Orel Hershiser .10 .03
65 Chris Hoiles .05 .02
66 Todd Hundley .10 .03
67 Pete Incaviglia .05 .02
68 Danny Jackson .05 .02
69 Barry Jones .05 .02
70 Dave Justice .25 .07
71 Jimmy Key .10 .03
72 Ray Lankford .25 .07
73 Darren Lewis .05 .02
74 Kevin Maas .05 .02
75 Denny Martinez .10 .03
76 Tino Martinez .25 .07
77 Don Mattingly .75 .23
78 Willie McGee .10 .03
79 Fred McGriff .15 .04
80 Hensley Meulens .05 .02
81 Kevin Mitchell .05 .02
82 Paul Molitor .40 .12
83 Mickey Morandini .05 .02
84 Jack Morris .10 .03
85 Dale Murphy .25 .07
86 Eddie Murray .40 .12
87 Chris Nabholz .05 .02
88 Tim Naehring .05 .02
89 Otis Nixon .05 .02
90 Jose Offerman .05 .02
91 Bob Ojeda .05 .02
92 John Olerud .15 .04
93 Gregg Olson .05 .02
94 Dave Parker .10 .03
95 Terry Pendleton .10 .03
96 Kirby Puckett .50 .15
97 Tim Raines .10 .03
98 Jeff Reardon .10 .03
99 Dave Righetti .10 .03
100 Cal Ripken 1.50 .45
101 Mel Rojas .05 .02
102 Nolan Ryan 1.50 .45
7th No-Hitter
103 Ryne Sandberg .50 .15
104 Scott Sanderson .05 .02
105 Benny Santiago .10 .03
106 Pete Schourek RC .05 .02
107 Gary Scott .05 .02
108 Terry Shumpert .05 .02
109 Ruben Sierra .10 .03
110 Doug Simons .05 .02
111 Dave Smith .05 .02
112 Ozzie Smith .75 .23
113 Cory Snyder .05 .02
114 Luis Sojo .05 .02
115 Dave Stewart .10 .03
116 Dave Stieb .05 .02
117 Darryl Strawberry .10 .03
118 Pat Tabler .05 .02
119 Wade Taylor .05 .02
120 Bobby Thigpen .05 .02
121 Frank Thomas .50 .15
122 Mike Timlin RC .05 .02
123 Alan Trammell .15 .04
124 Mo Vaughn .10 .03
125 Tim Wallach .05 .02
126 Devon White .10 .03
127 Mark Whiten .05 .02
128 Bernie Williams .50 .15
129 Willie Wilson .05 .02
130 Dave Winfield .40 .12
131 Robin Yount .40 .12
132 Checklist 1-132 .05 .02

1992 O-Pee-Chee Premier

The 1992 OPC Premier baseball set consists of 198 standard-size cards. The fronts feature a mix of color action and posed player photos bordered in white. Gold stripes edge the picture on top and below, while colored stripes edge the pictures on the left and right sides. The player's name, position, and team appear in the bottom white border. In addition to a color head shot, the backs carry biography and the team logo on a panel that shades from green to blue as well as statistics on a black panel.

Nm-Mt Ex-Mt
COMPLETE SET (198) 8.00 2.40
COMP. FACT.SET (198) 12.00 3.60
1 Wade Boggs .40 .12
2 John Smiley .05 .02
3 Checklist 1-99 .05 .02
4 Ron Gant .10 .03
5 Mike Bordick .05 .02
6 Charlie Hayes .05 .02
7 Kevin Morton .05 .02
8 Checklist 100-198 .05 .02
9 Chris Gwynn .05 .02
10 Melido Perez .05 .02
11 Dan Gladden .05 .02
12 Brian McRae .05 .02
13 Dennis Martinez .10 .03
14 Bob Scanlan .05 .02
15 Julio Franco .10 .03
16 Ruben Amaro Jr. .05 .02
17 Mo Sanford .05 .02
18 Scott Bankhead .05 .02
19 Dickie Thon .05 .02
20 Chris James .05 .02
21 Mike Huff .05 .02
22 Orlando Merced .05 .02
23 Chris Sabo .05 .02
24 Jose Canseco .25 .07
25 Reggie Sanders .10 .03
26 Chris Nabholz .05 .02
27 Kevin Seitzer .05 .02
28 Ryan Bowen .05 .02
29 Gary Carter .40 .12
30 Wayne Rosenthal .05 .02
31 Alan Trammell .15 .04
32 Doug Drabek .05 .02
33 Craig Shipley .05 .02
34 Ryne Sandberg .25 .07
35 Chuck Knoblauch .10 .03
36 Bret Barberie .05 .02
37 Tim Naehring .05 .02
38 Omar Olivares .05 .02
39 Royce Clayton .05 .02
40 Brent Mayne .05 .02
41 Darrin Fletcher .05 .02
42 Howard Johnson .05 .02
43 Steve Sax .05 .02
44 Greg Swindell .05 .02
45 Andre Dawson .25 .07
46 Kent Hrbek .10 .03
47 Dwight Gooden .10 .03
48 Mark Leiter .05 .02
49 Tom Glavine .25 .07
50 Mo Vaughn .25 .07
51 Doug Jones .05 .02
52 Brian Barnes .05 .02
53 Rob Dibble .10 .03
54 Kevin McReynolds .05 .02
55 Ivan Rodriguez .50 .15
56 Scott Livingstone UER .05 .02
(Photo actually
Travis Fryman)
57 Mike Magnante .05 .02
58 Pete Schourek .05 .02
59 Frank Thomas .50 .15
60 Kirk McCaskill .05 .02
61 Wally Joyner .10 .03
62 Rick Aguilera .10 .03
63 Eric Karros .25 .07
64 Tino Martinez .25 .07
65 Bryan Hickerson .05 .02
66 Ruben Sierra .10 .03
67 Willie Randolph .10 .03
68 Bill Landrum .05 .02
69 Bip Roberts .05 .02
70 Cecil Fielder .10 .03
71 Pat Kelly .05 .02
72 Kenny Lofton .40 .12
73 John Franco .10 .03
74 Phil Plantier .05 .02
75 Dave Martinez .05 .02
76 Warren Newson .05 .02
77 Chito Martinez .05 .02
78 Brian Hunter .05 .02
79 Jack Morris .10 .03
80 Eric King .05 .02
81 Nolan Ryan 1.50 .45
82 Bret Saberhagen .10 .03
83 Roberto Kelly .05 .02
84 Ozzie Smith .75 .23
85 Chuck McElroy .05 .02
86 Carlton Fisk .25 .07
87 Mike Mussina .50 .15
88 Mark Carreon .05 .02
89 Ken Hill .05 .02
90 Rick Cerone .05 .02
91 Deion Sanders .25 .07
92 Don Mattingly .75 .23
93 Danny Tartabull .05 .02
94 Keith Miller .05 .02
95 Gregg Jefferies .05 .02
96 Barry Larkin .25 .07
97 Kevin Mitchell .10 .03
98 Rick Sutcliffe .10 .03
99 Mark McGwire 1.00 .30
100 Albert Belle .10 .03
101 Gregg Olson .05 .02
102 Kirby Puckett .50 .15
103 Luis Gonzalez .25 .07
104 Randy Myers .10 .03
105 Roger Clemens .75 .23
106 Tony Gwynn .75 .23
107 Jeff Bagwell .50 .15
108 John Wetteland .10 .03
109 Bernie Williams .25 .07
110 Scott Kamieniecki .05 .02
111 Robin Yount .40 .12
112 Dean Palmer .10 .03
113 Tim Belcher .05 .02
114 George Brett .75 .23
115 Frank Viola .05 .02
116 Kelly Gruber .05 .02
117 David Justice .25 .07
118 Scott Leius .05 .02
119 Jeff Fassero .10 .03
120 Sammy Sosa .75 .23
121 Al Osuna .05 .02
122 Wilson Alvarez .10 .03
123 Jose Offerman .05 .02
124 Mel Rojas .05 .02
125 Shawon Dunston .05 .02
126 Pete Incaviglia .05 .02
127 Von Hayes .05 .02
128 Dave Gallagher .05 .02
129 Eric Davis .10 .03
130 Roberto Alomar .25 .07
131 Mike Gallego .05 .02
132 Robin Ventura .10 .03
133 Bill Swift .05 .02
134 John Kruk .10 .03
135 Craig Biggio .15 .04
136 Eddie Taubensee .10 .03
137 Cal Ripken 1.50 .45
138 Charles Nagy .05 .02
139 Jose Melendez .05 .02
140 Jim Abbott .10 .03
141 Paul Molitor .40 .12
142 Tom Candiotti .05 .02
143 Bobby Bonilla .05 .02
144 Matt Williams .15 .04
145 Brett Butler .10 .03
146 Will Clark .25 .07
147 Rickey Henderson .50 .15
148 Ray Lankford .10 .03
149 Bill Pecota .05 .02
150 Dave Winfield .40 .12
151 Darren Lewis .05 .02
152 Bob MacDonald .05 .02
153 David Segui .10 .03
154 Benny Santiago .10 .03
155 Chuck Finley .10 .03
156 Andujar Cedeno .05 .02
157 Barry Bonds .75 .23
158 Joe Grahe .05 .02
159 Frank Castillo .05 .02
160 Dave Burba .05 .02
161 Leo Gomez .05 .02
162 Orel Hershiser .10 .03
163 Delino DeShields .10 .03
164 Sandy Alomar Jr. .10 .03
165 Denny Neagle .05 .02
166 Fred McGriff .15 .04
167 Ken Griffey Jr. 1.50 .45
168 Juan Guzman .05 .02
169 Bobby Rose .05 .02
170 Steve Avery .05 .02
171 Rich DeLucia .05 .02
172 Mike Timlin .05 .02
173 Randy Johnson .50 .15
174 Paul Gibson .05 .02
175 David Cone .25 .07
176 Marquis Grissom .10 .03
177 Kurt Stillwell .05 .02
178 Mark Whiten .05 .02
179 Darryl Strawberry .05 .02
180 Mike Morgan .05 .02
181 Scott Scudder .05 .02
182 George Bell .05 .02
183 Alvin Davis .05 .02
184 Len Dykstra .10 .03
185 Kyle Abbott .05 .02
186 Chris Haney .05 .02
187 Junior Noboa .05 .02
188 Dennis Eckersley .40 .12
189 Derek Bell .05 .02
190 Lee Smith .10 .03
191 Andres Galarraga .25 .07
192 Jack Armstrong .05 .02
193 Eddie Murray .40 .12
194 Joe Carter .10 .03
195 Terry Pendleton .05 .02
196 Darryl Kile .10 .03
197 Rod Beck RC .25 .07
198 Hubie Brooks .05 .02

1993 O-Pee-Chee Premier

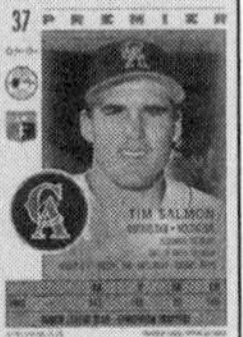

The 1993 OPC Premier set consists of 132 standard-size cards. The foil packs contain eight regular cards and one Star Performer insert card. The white-bordered fronts feature a mix of color action and posed player photos. The player's name and position are printed in the lower left border. The backs carry a color head shot, biography, 1992 statistics, and the team logo. According to O-Pee-Chee, only 4,000 cases were produced.

Nm-Mt Ex-Mt
COMPLETE SET (132) 5.00 1.50
1 Barry Bonds .50 .15
2 Chad Curtis .05 .02
3 Chris Bosio .05 .02
4 Cal Eldred .05 .02
5 Dan Walters .05 .02
6 Rene Arocha RC .05 .02
7 Delino DeShields .05 .02
8 Spike Owen .05 .02
9 Jeff Russell .05 .02
10 Phil Plantier .05 .02
11 Mike Christopher .05 .02
12 Darren Daulton .10 .03
13 Scott Cooper .05 .02
14 Paul O'Neill .10 .03
15 Jimmy Key .10 .03
16 Dickie Thon .05 .02
17 Greg Gohr .05 .02
18 Andre Dawson .15 .04
19 Steve Cooke .05 .02
20 Tony Fernandez .15 .04
21 Mark Gardner .05 .02
22 Dave Martinez .05 .02
23 Jose Guzman .05 .02
24 Chili Davis .10 .03
25 Randy Knorr .05 .02
26 Mike Piazza 1.00 .30
27 Benji Gil .05 .02
28 Dave Winfield .25 .07
29 Wil Cordero .05 .02
30 Butch Henry .05 .02
31 Eric Young .05 .02
32 Orestes Destrade .05 .02
33 Randy Myers .10 .03
34 Tom Brunansky .05 .02
35 Dan Wilson .10 .03
36 Juan Guzman .05 .02
37 Tim Salmon .20 .06
38 Bill Krueger .05 .02
39 Larry Walker .10 .03
40 David Hulse RC .05 .02
41 Ken Ryan RC .05 .02
42 Jose Lind .05 .02
43 Benny Santiago .10 .03
44 Ray Lankford .10 .03
45 Dave Stewart .10 .03
46 Don Mattingly .50 .15
47 Fernando Valenzuela .10 .03
48 Scott Fletcher .05 .02
49 Wade Boggs .25 .07
50 Norm Charlton .05 .02
51 Carlos Baerga .10 .03
52 John Olerud .15 .04
53 Willie Wilson .05 .02
54 Dennis Moeller .05 .02
55 Joe Orsulak .05 .02
56 John Smiley .05 .02
57 Al Martin .05 .02
58 Andres Galarraga .20 .06
59 Billy Ripken .05 .02
60 Dave Stieb .10 .03
61 Dave Magadan .05 .02
62 Todd Worrell .10 .03
63 Sherman Obando RC .05 .02
64 Kent Bottenfield .05 .02
65 Vinny Castilla .40 .12
66 Charlie Hayes .05 .02
67 Mike Hartley .05 .02
68 Harold Baines .15 .04
69 John Cummings RC .05 .02
70 J.T. Snow RC .20 .06
71 Graeme Lloyd RC .05 .02
72 Frank Bolick .05 .02
73 Doug Drabek .05 .02
74 Milt Thompson .05 .02
75 Tim Pugh RC .05 .02
76 John Kruk .10 .03
77 Tom Henke .05 .02
78 Kevin Young .05 .02
79 Ryan Thompson .05 .02
80 Mike Hampton .20 .06
81 Jose Canseco .20 .06
82 Mike Lansing RC .10 .03
83 Candy Maldonado .05 .02
84 Alex Arias .05 .02
85 Troy Neel .05 .02
86 Greg Swindell .05 .02
87 Tim Wallach .05 .02
88 Andy Van Slyke .05 .02
89 Harold Reynolds .10 .03
90 Bryan Harvey .05 .02
91 Jerald Clark .05 .02
92 David Cone .15 .04
93 Ellis Burks .05 .02
94 Scott Bankhead .05 .02
95 Pete Incaviglia .05 .02
96 Cecil Fielder .10 .03
97 Sean Berry .05 .02
98 Gregg Jefferies .05 .02
99 Billy Brewer .05 .02
100 Scott Sanderson .05 .02
101 Walt Weiss .05 .02
102 Travis Fryman .10 .03
103 Barry Larkin .20 .06
104 Darren Holmes .05 .02
105 Ivan Calderon .05 .02
106 Terry Jorgensen .05 .02
107 David Nied .05 .02
108 Tim Bogar RC .05 .02
109 Roberto Kelly .05 .02
110 Mike Moore .05 .02
111 Carlos Garcia .05 .02
112 Mike Bielecki .05 .02
113 Trevor Hoffman .20 .06
114 Rich Amaral .05 .02
115 Jody Reed .05 .02
116 Charlie Liebrandt .05 .02
117 Greg Gagne .05 .02
118 Darrell Sherman RC .05 .02
119 Jeff Conine .05 .02
120 Tim Laker RC .05 .02
121 Kevin Seitzer .05 .02
122 Jeff Mutis .05 .02
123 Rico Rossy .05 .02
124 Paul Molitor .25 .07
125 Cal Ripken 1.00 .30
126 Greg Maddux .75 .23
127 Greg McMichael RC .05 .02
128 Felix Jose .05 .02
129 Dick Schofield .05 .02
130 Jim Abbott .10 .03
131 Kevin Reimer .05 .02
132 Checklist 1-132 .05 .02

1993 O-Pee-Chee Premier Star Performers

The 1993 OPC Premier Star Performers 22-card standard-size set was inserted one per 1993 OPC Premier foil packs. The fronts display a gold outer border with a narrow white inner border that frames a color action player photo. The subset title is printed on a green stripe across the top of the photo and the player's name and position are printed below the photo on the lower border. The backs contain a kelly-green border surrounding a white box that carries a player head shot, biography and career summary in both French and English. A ghosted team logo appears beneath the career summary. A parallel set of Foil Star Performers was randomly inserted in foil packs. The gold foil-stamped set logo rests in a lower corner. The Foil Star Performers are valued at a multiple of the regular Star Performers cards.

	Nm-Mt	Ex-Mt
*FOIL STARS: 12.5X TO 25X BASIC CARDS		
FOIL STARS RANDOM INSERTS IN PACKS		
1 Frank Thomas	.50	.15
2 Fred McGriff	.20	.06
3 Roberto Alomar	.25	.07
4 Ryne Sandberg	.60	.18
5 Edgar Martinez	.20	.06
6 Gary Sheffield	.40	.12
7 Juan Gonzalez	.50	.15
8 Eric Karros	.20	.06
9 Ken Griffey Jr.	1.25	.35
10 Deion Sanders	.20	.06
11 Kirby Puckett	.50	.15
12 Will Clark	.25	.07
13 Joe Carter	.15	.04
14 Barry Bonds	1.00	.30
15 Pat Listach	.10	.03
16 Mark McGwire	1.25	.35
17 Kenny Lofton	.25	.07
18 Roger Clemens	1.00	.30
19 Greg Maddux	1.25	.35
20 Nolan Ryan	2.00	.60
21 Tom Glavine	.40	.12
22 Dennis Eckersley	.40	.12

1993 O-Pee-Chee Premier Top Draft Picks

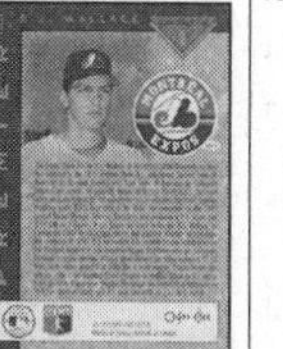

Randomly inserted in foil packs, this four-card standard-size set features the top two draft picks of the Toronto Blue Jays and Montreal Expos. Each borderless front carries a posed color player photo, with the player's name and team appearing vertically in gold foil within a team color-coded stripe. The set's gold foil-highlighted logo rests in a lower corner. The back carries a posed player color headshot in the upper left of a mottled, light blue panel. The player's team's logo appears alongside and his career highlights follow below.

	Nm-Mt	Ex-Mt
COMPLETE SET (4)	6.00	1.80
1 B.J. Wallace	1.00	.30
2 Shannon Stewart	2.50	.75
3 Rod Henderson	1.00	.30
4 Todd Steverson	1.00	.30

1982-90 Ohio Hall of Fame

This set of tri-colored cards measures 3" x 6" and contains biographies and statistics on the backs. Cards are numbered and checklisted below. This set was continued for many years thereafter and our list is incomplete and all help is appreciated.

	Nm-Mt	Ex-Mt
COMPLETE SET (65)	80.00	32.00
1 Ohio Hall of Fame	.75	.30
2 Checklist	.75	.30
3 Nick Cullop	.75	.30
4 Dean Chance	.75	.30
5 Bob Feller	4.00	1.60
6 Jesse Haines	1.50	.60
7 Waite Hoyt	1.50	.60
8 Ernie Lombardi	1.50	.60
9 Mike Powers	.75	.30
10 Edd Roush	1.50	.60
11 Red Ruffing	1.50	.60
12 Luke Sewell	.75	.30
13 Tris Speaker	3.00	1.20
14 Cy Young	3.00	1.20
15 Walter Alston	1.00	.40
16 Lou Boudreau	1.50	.60
17 Warren Giles	1.00	.40
18 Ted Kluszewski	1.50	.60
19 William McKinley	1.50	.60
20 Roger Peckinpaugh	.75	.30
21 Johnny VanderMeer	1.00	.40
22 Early Wynn	1.50	.60
23 Earl Averill	1.50	.60
24 Stan Coveleskie	1.50	.60
25 Lefty Grove	2.00	.80
26 Nap Lajoie	2.00	.80
27 Al Lopez	1.00	.40
28 Eddie Onslow	.75	.30
29 Branch Rickey	1.00	.40
30 Frank Robinson	2.00	.80
31 George Sisler	1.50	.60
32 Bob Lemon	1.50	.60
33 Satchel Paige	5.00	2.00
34 Bucky Walters	1.00	.40
35 Gus Bell	.75	.30
36 Rocky Colavito	1.50	.60
37 Mel Harder	1.00	.40
38 Tom Henrich	1.00	.40
39 Miller Huggins	1.00	.40
40 Fred Hutchinson	.75	.30
41 Eppa Rixey	1.50	.60
42 Joe Sewell	1.50	.60
43 George Uhle	.75	.30
44 Bill Veeck	1.00	.40
45 Estel Crabtree	.75	.30
46 Harvey Haddix	.75	.30
47 Noodles Hahn	.75	.30
48 Joe Jackson	6.00	2.40
49 Kenesaw Landis	1.00	.40
50 Thurman Munson	1.50	.60
51 Gabe Paul	.75	.30
52 Vada Pinson	1.00	.40
53 Wally Post	.75	.30
54 Vic Wertz	.75	.30
55 Paul Derringer	.75	.30
56 John Galbreath	.75	.30
57 Rube Marquard	1.50	.60
58 Bill McKechnie	1.00	.40
59 Rocky Nelson	.75	.30
60 Al Rosen	1.00	.40
61 Lew Fonseca	.75	.30
62 Larry MacPhail	1.00	.40
63 Joe Nuxhall	.75	.30
64 Birdie Tebbetts	.75	.30
65 Gene Woodling	.75	.30
66 Ethan Allen	.75	.30
70 Tot Pressnell	.75	.30
76 George Sisler Jr	.75	.30
79 Woody English	.75	.30
81 Frank Baumholz	.75	.30
83 Sam McDowell	1.00	.40
91 Denny Galehouse	.75	.30
92 Brooks Lawrence	.75	.30
99 Bob Wren CO	.75	.30
102 Willis Hudlin	.75	.30
103 Gene Michael	.75	.30

1997 Ohio Lottery

This five-card set features color head photos of legendary baseball players printed on a diamond and baseball background. The set measures approximately 4" by 2 1/4" and was actually real Ohio scratch-off lottery ticket stubs that could be obtained for $1 a piece. The backs carry the lottery rules and prize information. The cards are unnumbered and checklisted below in alphabetical order.

	Nm-Mt	Ex-Mt
COMPLETE SET (5)	8.00	2.40
1 Rocky Colavito	2.00	.60
2 Larry Doby	2.50	.75
3 George Foster	1.00	.30
4 Tony Perez	2.50	.75
5 Gaylord Perry	2.50	.75

1959 Oklahoma Today Major Leaguers

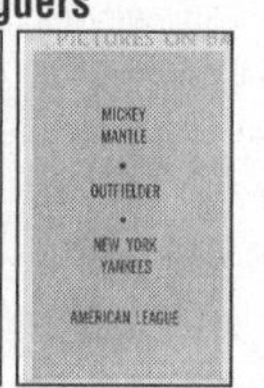

These 20 cards which measure 1 11/16" by 2 3/4" were featured on the back cover of the Summer 1959 Issue of Oklahoma Today. The card fronts feature Black and White photos on color backgrounds (8 green, 8 gold and 4 light blue). The bottom 1/4" of the front has a white panel with the players name in red. The backs are grey with the player's name, position team and league. The checklist below is as the players appear on the uncut covers in 4 rows of 5 cards starting on the top left. In the complete book form -- this set is valued at two to three times the values listed below.

	NM	Ex
COMPLETE SET (20)	150.00	75.00
1 Paul Waner	5.00	2.50
2 Lloyd Waner	5.00	2.50
3 Jerry Walker	2.00	1.00
4 Tom Sturdivant	2.00	1.00
5 Warren Spahn	8.00	4.00
6 Allie Reynolds	3.00	1.50
7 Dale Mitchell	2.00	1.00
8 Cal McLish	2.00	1.00
9 Von McDaniel	2.00	1.00
10 Lindy McDaniel	2.00	1.00
11 Pepper Martin	4.00	2.00
12 Mickey Mantle	100.00	50.00
13 Carl Hubbell	5.00	2.50
14 Paul Dean	2.00	1.00
15 Dizzy Dean	5.00	2.50
16 Don Demeter	2.00	1.00
17 Alvin Dark	3.00	1.50
18 Johnny Callison	3.00	1.50
19 Harry Brecheen	2.00	1.00
20 Jerry Adair	2.00	1.00

1886 Old Judge N167

These cards measure approximately 1 1/2" by 2 1/2". All the players portrayed are members of the New York National team which became the Giants. We have sequenced this set in alphabetical order.

	Ex-Mt	VG
COMPLETE SET (14)	120000.00	60000.00
1 Roger Connor	12000.00	6000.00
2 Larry Corcoran	6000.00	3000.00
3 Tom Deasley	6000.00	3000.00
4 Mike Dorgan	6000.00	3000.00
5 Dude Esterbrook	6000.00	3000.00
6 Buck Ewing	12000.00	6000.00
7 Joe Gerhardt	6000.00	3000.00
8 Pete Gillespie	6000.00	3000.00
9 Tim Keefe	12000.00	6000.00
10 Jim Mutrie MG	10000.00	5000.00
11 James O'Rourke	12000.00	6000.00
12 Danny Richardson	6000.00	3000.00
13 John M. Ward	12000.00	6000.00
14 Mickey Welsh (sic)	12000.00	6000.00

1887-90 Old Judge N172

The Goodwin Company's baseball series depicts hundreds of ballplayers from more than 40 major and minor league teams as well as boxers and wrestlers. The cards (approximately 1 1/2" by 2 1/2") are actually photographs from the Hall studio in New York which were pasted onto thick cardboard. The pictures are sepia in color with either a white or pink cast, and the cards are blank backed. They are found either numbered or unnumbered, with or without a copyright date, and with hand printed or machine printed names. All known cards have the name "Goodwin Co., New York" at the base. The cards were marketed during the period 1887-1890 in packs of "Old Judge" and "Gypsy Queen" cigarettes (cards marked with the latter brand are worth double the values listed below). They have been listed alphabetically and assigned numbers in the checklist below for simplicity's sake; the various poses known for some players also have not been listed for the same reason. Some of the players are pictured in horizontal (HOR) poses. In all, more than 2300 different Goodwin cards are known to collectors, with more being discovered every year. Cards from the "Spotted Tie" sub-series are denoted in the checklist below by SPOT. The Lee Gibson, Egyptian Healey, Bid McPhee and Amos Rusie cards are currently considered unique and are not priced due to market scarcity.

	Ex-Mt	VG
COMP.SET	300000.00	150000.00
COMMON CARD	250.00	125.00
COMMON (DOUBLE)	300.00	150.00
COM.BROWNS CHAMP	400.00	200.00
COMMON CARD (PCL)	5000.00	2500.00
COMMON SPOTTED TIE	800.00	400.00
1 Gus Albert	250.00	125.00
2 Charles Alcott	250.00	125.00
3 Alexander	250.00	125.00
4 Myron Allen	250.00	125.00
5 Bob Allen	250.00	125.00
6 Uncle Bill Alvord	250.00	125.00
7 Varney Anderson	2500.00	1250.00
8 Ed Andrews: Phila.	250.00	125.00
9 Ed Andrews and	300.00	150.00
Buster Hoover		
10 Wally Andrews	250.00	125.00
11 Bill Annis	250.00	125.00
12A Cap Anson: Chicago	30000.00	15000.00
(In uniform)		
12B Cap Anson: Chicago	3000.00	1500.00
(Not in uniform)		
13 Old Hoss Ardner	250.00	125.00
14 Tug Arundel:	250.00	125.00
Indianapolis-Whites		
15 Jersey Bakley: Cleve.	250.00	125.00
16 Clarence Baldwin:	250.00	125.00
Cincinnati		
17 Mark(Fido) Baldwin:	250.00	125.00
Chicago-Columbus		
18 Lady Baldwin:	300.00	150.00
Detroit		
19 James Banning: Wash.	250.00	125.00
20 Samuel Barkley:	250.00	125.00
Pittsburgh-K.C.		
21 Bald Billy Barnie:	300.00	150.00
Mgr. Baltimore		
22 Charles Bassett:	250.00	125.00
Indianapolis-N.Y.		
23 Charles Bastian:	250.00	125.00
Phila.-Chicago		
24 Charles Bastian and	300.00	150.00
Schriver:		
Philadelphia		
25 Ebenezer Beatin:	250.00	125.00
Cleve.		
26 Jake Beckley:	1000.00	500.00
Eagle Eye		
Whites-Pittsburgh		
27 Stephen Behel SPOT	6000.00	3000.00
28 Charles Bennett:	250.00	125.00
Detroit-Boston		
29 Louis Bierbauer: A's	250.00	125.00
30 Louis Bierbauer and	300.00	150.00
Robert Gamble:		
Athletics		
31 Bill Bishop:	250.00	125.00
Pittsburgh-Syracuse		
32 William Blair:	250.00	125.00
A's-Hamiltons		
33 Ned Bligh: Columbus	250.00	125.00
34 Bogart: Indianapolis	250.00	125.00
35 Boyce: Washington	250.00	125.00
36 Jake Boyd: Maroons	300.00	150.00
37 Honest John Boyle:	250.00	125.00
St. Louis-Chicago		
38 Handsome Henry Boyle	250.00	125.00
Indianapolis-N.Y.		
39 Nick Bradley:	250.00	125.00
K.C.- Worchester		
40 George(Grin) Bradley	250.00	125.00
Sioux City		
41 Stephen Brady SPOT	1000.00	500.00
42 E.L. Breckinridge:	5000.00	2500.00
Sacramento PCL		
43 Timothy Brosnan:	250.00	125.00
Minneapolis		
44 Timothy Brosnan	250.00	125.00
Sioux City		
45 Cal Broughton:	250.00	125.00
St. Paul		
46 Big Dan Brouthers:	800.00	400.00
Detroit-Boston		
47 Thomas Brown:	250.00	125.00
Pittsburgh-Boston		
48 California Brown:	250.00	125.00
New York		
49 Pete Browning:	800.00	400.00
Gladiator		
Louisville		
50 Charles Brynan:	250.00	125.00
Chicago-Des Moines		
51 Al Buckenberger MG:	250.00	125.00
Columbus		
52 Dick Buckley:	250.00	125.00
Indianapolis-N.Y.		
53 Charles Buffington:	250.00	125.00
Philadelphia		
54 Ernest Burch:	250.00	125.00
Brooklyn-Whites		
55 Bill Burdick:	250.00	125.00
Omaha-Indianapolis		
56 Black Jack Burdock:	250.00	125.00
Boston-Brooklyn		
57 Robert Burks:	250.00	125.00
Sioux City		
58 George Burnham	300.00	150.00
Watch		
Mgr. Indianapolis		
59 Burns: Omaha	250.00	125.00
60 Jimmy Burns: K.C.	250.00	125.00
61 Tommy(Oyster) Burns	300.00	150.00
Baltimore-Brooklyn		
62 Thomas E. Burns:	250.00	125.00
Chicago		
63 Doc Bushong: Brook.	250.00	125.00
64 Doc Bushong:	500.00	250.00
Browns Champs		
65 Patsy Cahill: Ind.	250.00	125.00
66 Count Campau:	250.00	125.00
Kansas City-Detroit		
67 Jimmy Canavan:	250.00	125.00
Omaha		
68 Bart Cantz:	250.00	125.00
Whites-Baltimore		
69 Handsome Jack Carney	250.00	125.00
Washington		
70 Hick Carpenter	250.00	125.00
Cincinnati		
71 Cliff Carroll: Wash.	250.00	125.00
72 Scrappy Carroll:	250.00	125.00
St.Paul-Chicago		
73 Frederick Carroll:	250.00	125.00
Pitts.		
74 Jumbo Cartwright:	250.00	125.00
Kansas City-St. Joe		
75 Bob Caruthers:	500.00	250.00
Parisian		
Brooklyn		
76 Bob Caruthers:	500.00	250.00
Parisian		
Browns Champs		
77 Daniel Casey: Phila.	250.00	125.00
78 Icebox Chamberlain:	250.00	125.00
St. Louis		
79 Cupid Childs:	250.00	125.00
Phila.-Syracuse		
80 Bob Clark:	250.00	125.00
Washington		
81 Owen Clark:	250.00	125.00
Washington		
82 William H. Clarke and	300.00	150.00
Mickey Hughes:		
Brooklyn HOR		
83 William(Dad) Clarke:	250.00	125.00
Chicago-Omaha		
84 Pete Connell:	250.00	125.00
Des Moines		
85 John Clarkson:	800.00	400.00
Chicago-Boston		
86 Jack Clements:	250.00	125.00
Philadelphia		
87 Elmer Cleveland:	250.00	125.00
Omaha-New York		
88 Monk Cline:	250.00	125.00
K.C.-Sioux City		
89 Cody: Des Moines	250.00	125.00
90 John Coleman:	250.00	125.00
Pittsburgh - A's		
91 Bill Collins:	250.00	125.00
New York-Newark		
92 Hub Collins:	250.00	125.00
Louisville-Brooklyn		
93 Charles Comiskey:	1200.00	600.00
Browns Champs		
94 Commy Comiskey:	1000.00	500.00
St. Louis-Chicago		
95 Roger Connor:	1000.00	500.00
Script		
96 Roger Connor:	1000.00	500.00
New York		
97 Richard Conway:	250.00	125.00
Boston-Worchester		
98 Peter Conway:	250.00	125.00
Det.-Pitts.-Ind.		
99 James Conway: K.C.	250.00	125.00
100 Paul Cook:	250.00	125.00
Louisville		
101 Jimmy Cooney:	250.00	125.00
Omaha-Chicago		
102 Larry Corcoran:	500.00	250.00
Indianapolis-London		
103 Pop Corkhill:	250.00	125.00
Cincinnati-Brooklyn		
104 Cannon Ball Crane:	250.00	125.00
New York		
105 Samuel Crane: Wash.	250.00	125.00
106 Jack Crogan	300.00	150.00
Maroons		
107 John Crooks:	250.00	125.00
Whites-Omaha		
108 Lave Cross:	250.00	125.00
Louisville-A's-		
Phila.		
109 Bill Crossley: Milw.	250.00	125.00
110 Joe Crotty SPOT	800.00	400.00
111 Joe Crotty:	250.00	125.00
Sioux City		
112 Billy Crowell:	250.00	125.00
Cleveland-St. Joe		
113 Jim Cudworth:	250.00	125.00
St. Louis-Worchester		
114 Bert Cunningham:	250.00	125.00
Baltimore-Phila.		
115 Tacks Curtis:	250.00	125.00
St. Joe		
116 Ed Cushman SPOT	1000.00	500.00
117 Ed Cushman:	2000.00	1000.00
Toledo		
118 Tony Cusick: Mil.	2500.00	1250.00
119 Vincent Dailey	5000.00	2500.00
Oakland PCL		
120 Edward Dailey:	250.00	125.00
Phil.-Wash.-		
Columbus		
121 Edward Dailey:	500.00	250.00
Columbus		
122 Bill Daley: Boston	250.00	125.00
123 Con Daley:	250.00	125.00
Boston-Indianapolis		
124 Abner Dalrymple:	250.00	125.00
Pittsburgh-Denver		
125 Tom Daly:	300.00	150.00
Chicago-Wash.-Cleve.		
126 James Daly: Minn.	250.00	125.00
127 Law Daniels: K.C.	250.00	125.00
128 Dell Darling:	250.00	125.00
Chicago		
129 Wm. Darnbrough:	250.00	125.00
Denver		
130 D. Davin: Milwaukee	800.00	400.00
131 Jumbo Davis: K.C.	250.00	125.00
132 Pat Dealey: Wash	250.00	125.00
133 Thomas Deasley:	250.00	125.00
New York-Washington		
Throwing		
134 Thomas Deasley	250.00	125.00
Fielding		
135 Edward Decker: Phil.	250.00	125.00
136 Big Ed Delahanty:	2000.00	1000.00
Philadelphia		
137 Jeremiah Denny:	250.00	125.00
Indianapolis-		
New York		
138 James Devlin: St.L.	250.00	125.00
139 Thomas Dolan:	250.00	125.00
Whites-		
St. Louis-Denver		
140 Jack Donahue:	5000.00	2500.00
San Francisco PCL		
141 James Donahue SPOT	800.00	400.00
142 James Donahue: K.C.	250.00	125.00
143 James Donnelly:	250.00	125.00
Washington		
144 Charles Dooley	5000.00	2500.00
Oakland PCL		
145 J. Doran: Omaha	1200.00	600.00
146 Michael Dorgan: N.Y.	250.00	125.00
147 Cornelius Doyle	5000.00	2500.00
San Fran. PCL		
148 Homerun Duffe: St.L.	250.00	125.00
149 Hugh Duffy: Chicago	1000.00	500.00
150 Dan Dugdale:	300.00	150.00
Maroons-Minneapolis		
151 Duck Duke: Minn.	250.00	125.00
152 Sure Shot Dunlap:	250.00	125.00
Pittsburgh		
153 J. Dunn: Maroons	300.00	150.00
154 Jesse(Cyclone)Duryea	250.00	125.00
St. Paul-Cinc.		
155 John Dwyer:	300.00	150.00
Chicago-Maroons		
156 Billy Earle:	250.00	125.00
Cincinnati-St.Paul		
157 Buck Ebright: Wash.	250.00	125.00
158 Red Ehret:	250.00	125.00
Louisville		

159 R. Emmerke: 250.00 125.00 Des Moines
160 Dude Esterbrook: 250.00 125.00 Louisville-Ind.- New York-All Star
161 Henry Esterday: 250.00 125.00 K.C.-Columbus
162 Long John Ewing: 250.00 125.00 Louisville-N.Y.
163 Buck Ewing 800.00 400.00 New York
164 Buck Ewing 800.00 400.00 and Mascot: New York
165 Jay Faatz: Cleveland 250.00 125.00
166 Clinkgers Fagan: 250.00 125.00 Kansas City-Denver
167 William Farmer: 250.00 125.00 Pittsburgh-St. Paul
168 Sidney Farrar: 300.00 150.00 Philadelphia
169 John(Moose) Farrell: 250.00 125.00 Wash.-Baltimore
170 Charles(Duke)Farrell 250.00 125.00 Chicago
171 Frank Fennelly: 250.00 125.00 Cincinnati-A's
172 Chas. Ferguson: 250.00 125.00 Phila.
173 Colonel Ferson: 250.00 125.00 Washington
174 Wallace Fessenden: 300.00 150.00 Umpire National
175 Jocko Fields: Pitts. 250.00 125.00
176 Fischer: Maroons 300.00 150.00
177 Thomas Flanigan: 250.00 125.00 Cleve.-Sioux City
178 Silver Flint: 250.00 125.00 Chicago
179 Thomas Flood: 250.00 125.00 St. Joe
180 Flynn: Omaha 2000.00 1000.00
181 James Fogarty: 250.00 125.00 Philadelphia
182 Frank(Monkey)Foreman 250.00 125.00 Baltimore-Cinc.
183 Thomas Forster: 250.00 125.00 Milwaukee-Hartford
184 Elmer E. Foster 800.00 400.00 SPOT
185 Elmer Foster: 250.00 125.00 New York-Chicago
186 F.W. Foster SPOT 1000.00 500.00 T.W. Forster (Sic)
187 Scissors Foutz: 400.00 200.00 Browns Champ
188 Scissors Foutz: 250.00 125.00 Brooklyn
189 Julie Freeman: 250.00 125.00 St.L.-Milwaukee
190 Will Fry: St. Joe 250.00 125.00
191 Fred Fudger 5000.00 2500.00 Oakland PCL
192 William Fuller: 250.00 125.00 Milwaukee
193 Shorty Fuller: 250.00 125.00 St.Louis
194 Christopher Fullmer: 250.00 125.00 Baltimore
195 Christopher Fullmer 300.00 150.00 and Tom Tucker: Baltimore HOR
196 Honest John Gaffney: 400.00 200.00 Mgr. Washington
197 Pud Galvin: Pitts. 1000.00 500.00
198 Robert Gamble: A's 250.00 125.00
199 Charles Ganzel: 250.00 125.00 Detroit-Boston
200 Frank(Gid) Gardner: 250.00 125.00 Phila.-Washington
201 Gid Gardner and 300.00 150.00 Miah Murray: Washington HOR
202 Hank Gastreich: 250.00 125.00 Columbus
203 Emil Geiss: Chicago 250.00 125.00
204 Frenchy Genins: 250.00 125.00 Sioux City
205 William George: N.Y. 250.00 125.00
206 Move Up Joe Gerhardt 250.00 125.00 All Star-Jersey City
207 Pretzels Getzein: 250.00 125.00 Detroit-Ind.
208 Lee Gibson: A's 250.00 125.00
209 Robert Gilks: Cleve. 250.00 125.00
210 Pete Gillespie: N.Y. 250.00 125.00
211 Barney Gilligan 250.00 125.00 Washington-Detroit
212 Frank Gilmore: Wash. 250.00 125.00
213 Pebbly Jack Glasscock 400.00 200.00 Indianapolis-N.Y.
214 Kid Gleason: Phila. 400.00 200.00
215 Brother Bill Gleason 250.00 125.00 A's-Louisville
216 William Bill Gleason 400.00 200.00 Browns Champs
217 Mouse Glenn: 250.00 125.00 Sioux City
218 Michael Goodfellow: 250.00 125.00 Cleveland-Detroit
219 George Gore 250.00 125.00 (Pianolegs) New York
220 Frank Graves: Minn. 250.00 125.00
221 William Greenwood: 250.00 125.00 Baltimore-Columbus
222 Michael Greer: 250.00 125.00 Cleveland-Brooklyn
223 Mike Griffin: 250.00 125.00 Baltimore-Phila NL
224 Clark Griffith: 1000.00 500.00 Milwaukee
225 Henry Gruber: Cleve. 250.00 125.00
226 Addison Gumbert: 250.00 125.00 Chicago-Boston
227 Thomas Gunning: 250.00 125.00 Philadelphia-A's
228 Joseph Gunson: K.C. 250.00 125.00
229 George Haddock: 250.00 125.00 Washington
230 William Hafner: K.C. 250.00 125.00
231 Willie Hahm: 250.00 125.00 Chicago Mascot
232 William Hallman: 250.00 125.00 Philadelphia
233 Billy Hamilton: 1200.00 600.00 Kansas City-Phila.
234 Willie Hamm and 400.00 200.00 Ned Williamson: Chicago
235 Frank Hankinson: 800.00 400.00 SPOT
236 Frank Hankinson: 250.00 125.00 Kansas City
237 Ned Hanlon: 800.00 400.00 Det.-Boston-Pitts.
238 William Hanrahan: 300.00 150.00 Maroons-Minn.
239 A.G. Hapeman: 5000.00 2500.00 Sacramento PCL
240 Pa Harkins: 250.00 125.00 Brooklyn-Baltimore
241 William Hart: 250.00 125.00 Cinc.-Des Moines
242 Wm. Hasamdear: K.C. 250.00 125.00
243 Colonel Hatfield: 250.00 125.00 New York
244 Egyptian Healey: 250.00 125.00 Wash.-Indianapolis
245 Egyptian Healey 250.00 125.00 Washington
246 J.C. Healy: 250.00 125.00 Omaha-Denver
247 Guy Hecker: 250.00 125.00 Louisville
248 Tony Hellman: 250.00 125.00 Sioux City
249 Hardie Henderson: 250.00 125.00 Brook.-Pitts.-Balt.
250 Hardie Henderson 300.00 150.00 and Michael Greer: Brooklyn
251 Moxie Hengle: 300.00 150.00 Maroons-Minneapolis
252 John Henry: Phila. 250.00 125.00
253 Edward Herr: 250.00 125.00 Whites-Milwaukee
254 Hunkey Hines: Whites 250.00 125.00
255 Paul Hines: 250.00 125.00 Wash.-Indianapolis
256 Texas Wonder Hoffman: 250.00 125.00 Denver
257 Eddie Hogan: Cleve. 250.00 125.00
258 William Holbert 800.00 400.00 SPOT
259 William Holbert: 250.00 125.00 Brooklyn-Mets- Jersey City
260 James(Bugs) Holliday: 250.00 125.00 Des Moines-Cinc.
261 Charles Hoover: 300.00 150.00 Maroons-Chi.-K.C.
262 Buster Hoover: 250.00 125.00 Phila.-Toronto
263 Jack Horner: 250.00 125.00 Milwaukee-New Haven
264 Jack Horner and 300.00 150.00 E.H. Warner: Milwaukee
265 Michael Horning: 250.00 125.00 Boston-Balt.-N.Y.
266 Pete Hotaling: 250.00 125.00 Cleveland
267 William Howes: 250.00 125.00 Minn..-St. Paul
268 Dummy Hoy: 800.00 400.00 Washington
269 Nat Hudson: 400.00 200.00 Browns Champ
270 Nat Hudson: 250.00 125.00 St. Paul
271 Mickey Hughes: Brk. 250.00 125.00
272 Hungler: Sioux City 250.00 125.00
273 Wild Bill Hutchinson: 250.00 125.00 Chicago
274 John Irwin: 250.00 125.00 Wash.-Wilkes Barre
275 Cutrate Irwin: 250.00 125.00 Phila.-Boston-Wash.
276 A.C. Jantzen: Minn. 250.00 125.00
277 Frederick Jevne: 250.00 125.00 Minn.-St. Paul
278 John Johnson: 250.00 125.00 K.C.-Columbus
279 Richard Johnston: 250.00 125.00 Boston
280 Jordan 250.00 125.00 Minneapolis
281 Heinie Kappell: 250.00 125.00 Columbus-Cincinnati
282 Sir Timothy Keefe: 800.00 400.00 New York
283 Tim Keefe and 600.00 300.00 Danny Richardson: Stealing 2nd Base New York HOR
284 George Keefe: Wash. 250.00 125.00
285 James Keenan: Cinc. 250.00 125.00
286 Mike(King) Kelly 2000.00 1000.00 10,000 Chic-Boston
287 Honest John Kelly: 400.00 200.00 Mgr. Louisville
288 Kelly: (Umpire) 300.00 150.00 Western Association
289 Charles Kelly: 600.00 300.00 Philadelphia
290 Kelly and Powell: 300.00 150.00 Umpire and Manager Sioux City
291 Rudolph Kemmler: 400.00 200.00 Browns Champ
292 Rudolph Kemmler: 250.00 125.00 St. Paul
293 Theodore Kennedy: 300.00 150.00 Des Moines-Omaha
294 J.J. Kenyon: 250.00 125.00 Whites-Des Moines
295 John Kerins: 250.00 125.00 Louisville
296 Matthew Kilroy: 250.00 125.00 Baltimore-Boston
297 Charles King: 250.00 125.00 St.L.-Chi.
298 Aug. Kloff: 250.00 125.00 Minn.-St.Joe
299 William Klusman: 250.00 125.00 Milwaukee-Denver
300 Phillip Knell: 250.00 125.00 St. Joe-Phila.
301 Fred Knouf: 250.00 125.00 St. Louis
302 Charles Kremmeyer: 5000.00 2500.00 Sacramento PCL
303 William Krieg: 250.00 125.00 Wash.-St. Joe-Minn.
304 William Krieg and 300.00 150.00 Aug. Kloff: Minneapolis
305 Gus Krock: Chicago 250.00 125.00
306 Willie Kuehne: 250.00 125.00 Pittsburgh
307 Frederick Lange: 300.00 150.00 Maroons
308 Ted Larkin: A's 250.00 125.00
309 Arlie Latham: 600.00 300.00 Browns Champ
310 Arlie Latham: 400.00 200.00 St. Louis-Chicago
311 John Lauer: 250.00 125.00 Pittsburgh
312 John Leighton 250.00 125.00 Omaha
313 Rube Levy 5000.00 2500.00 San Fran. PCL
314 Tom Loftus MG: 250.00 125.00 Whites-Cleveland
315 Herman(Germany)Long 400.00 200.00 Maroons-K.C.
316 Danny Long 5000.00 2500.00 Oak. PCL
317 Tom Lovett: 250.00 125.00 Omaha-Brooklyn
318 Bobby(Link) Lowe: 400.00 200.00 Milwaukee
319 Jack Lynch SPOT 1000.00 500.00
320 John Lynch: 250.00 125.00 All Stars
321 Dennis Lyons: A's 250.00 125.00
322 Harry Lyons: St. L. 250.00 125.00
323 Connie Mack: Wash. 2500.00 1250.00
324 Joe(Reddie) Mack: 250.00 125.00 Louisville
325 James(Little Mack) 250.00 125.00 Macullar: Des Moines- Milwaukee
326 Kid Madden: Boston 250.00 125.00
327 Daniel Mahoney: 250.00 125.00 St. Joe
328 Willard(Grasshopper) 250.00 125.00 Maines: St. Paul
329 Fred Mann: 250.00 125.00 St.Louis-Hartford
330 Jimmy Manning: K.C. 250.00 125.00
331 Charles(Lefty) Marr: 250.00 125.00 Col.-Cinc.
332 Mascot(Willie 300.00 150.00 Breslin): New York
333 Samuel Maskery: 250.00 125.00 Milwaukee- Des Moines
334 Bobby Mathews: A's 250.00 125.00
335 Michael Mattimore: 250.00 125.00 New York-A's
336 Albert Maul: Pitts. 250.00 125.00
337 Albert Mays SPOT 800.00 400.00
338 Albert Mays: 250.00 125.00 Columbus
339 James McAleer: 250.00 125.00 Cleveland
340 Thomas McCarthy: 800.00 400.00 Phila.-St. Louis
341 John McCarthy: K.C. 250.00 125.00
342 James McCauley: 300.00 150.00 Maroons-Phila.
343 William McClellan: 250.00 125.00 Brooklyn-Denver
344 John McCormack: 250.00 125.00 Whites
345 Big Jim McCormick: 250.00 125.00 Chicago-Pittsburgh
346 McCreachery: 800.00 400.00 Mgr. Indianapolis
347 James(Chippy)McGarr: 250.00 125.00 St. Louis-K.C.
348 Jack McGeachy: Ind. 250.00 125.00
349 John McGlone: 250.00 125.00 Cleveland-Detroit
350 James(Deacon)McGuire 250.00 125.00 Phila.-Toronto
351 Bill McGunnigle: 400.00 200.00 Mgr. Brooklyn
352 Ed McKean: Cleveland 250.00 125.00
353 Alex McKinnon: 250.00 125.00 Pittsburgh
354 Thomas McLaughlin 800.00 400.00 SPOT
355 John(Bid) McPhee: 500.00 250.00 Cincinnati
356 James McQuaid: 250.00 125.00 Denver
357 John McQuaid: 300.00 150.00 Umpire Amer. Assoc.
358 Jame McTamany: 250.00 125.00 Brook.-Col.-K.C.
359 George McVey: 250.00 125.00 Mil.-Denver-St. Joe
360 Peter Meegan 5000.00 2500.00 San Fran. PCL
361 John Messitt: Omaha 250.00 125.00
362 George(Doggie)Miller 250.00 125.00 Pittsburgh
363 Joseph Miller: 250.00 125.00 Omaha-Minneapolis
364 Jocko Milligan: 250.00 125.00 St. Louis-Phila.
365 E.L. Mills: 250.00 125.00 Milwaukee
366 Minnehan: 250.00 125.00 Minneapolis
367 Samuel Moffet: Ind 250.00 125.00
368 Honest Morrell: 250.00 125.00 Boston-Washington
369 Ed Morris 250.00 125.00 (Cannonball): Pittsburgh
370 Morrisey: St. Paul 250.00 125.00
371 Tony(Count) Mullane: 400.00 200.00 Cincinnati
372 Joseph Mulvey: 250.00 125.00 Philadelphia
373 P.L. Murphy: 250.00 125.00 St. Paul
374 Pat J. Murphy: 250.00 125.00 New York
375 Miah Murray: Wash. 250.00 125.00
376 James(Truthful) 300.00 150.00 Mutrie: Mgr. N.Y.
377 George Myers: 250.00 125.00 Indianapolis-Phila.
378 Al(Cod) Myers: 250.00 125.00 Washington
379 Thomas Nagle: 250.00 125.00 Omaha-Chi.
380 Billy Nash: Boston 250.00 125.00
381 Jack(Candy) Nelson: 800.00 400.00 SPOT
382 Kid Nichols: Omaha 1200.00 600.00
383 Samuel Nichols: 250.00 125.00 Pittsburgh
384 J.W. Nicholson 300.00 150.00 Maroons-Minn.
385 Tom Nicholson 250.00 125.00 (Parson) Whites-Cleveland
386 Nicholls Nicol 400.00 200.00 Browns Champ
387 Hugh Nicol: Cinc. 250.00 125.00
388 Hugh Nicol and 300.00 150.00 Long John Reilly: Cincinnati
389 Frederick Nyce 250.00 125.00 Whites-Burlington
390 Doc Oberlander 250.00 125.00 Cleveland-Syracuse
391 Jack O'Brien 250.00 125.00 Brooklyn-Baltimore
392 William O'Brien: 250.00 125.00 Washington
393 William O'Brien and 300.00 150.00 John Irwin: Washington
394 Darby O'Brien: 250.00 125.00 Brooklyn
395 John O'Brien: Cleve. 250.00 125.00
396 P.J. O'Connell: 250.00 125.00 Omaha-Des Moines
397 John O'Connor: 250.00 125.00 Cincinnati-Columbus
398 Hank O'Day: 400.00 200.00 Washington-New York
399 O'Day 250.00 125.00 Sacramento
400 James O'Neil: 250.00 125.00 St. Louis-Chicago
401 James O'Neil: 400.00 200.00 Browns Champs
402 Norris "Tip" O'Neill 5000.00 2500.00 Oakland PCL
403 Orator O'Rourke: 1000.00 500.00 New York
404 Thomas O'Rourke: 250.00 125.00 Boston-Jersey City
405 David Orr SPOT 800.00 400.00
406 David Orr: 250.00 125.00 All Star- Brooklyn-Columbus
407 Parsons: Minneapolis 250.00 125.00
408 Owen Patton: 250.00 125.00 Minn.-Des Moines
409 James Peeples: 250.00 125.00 Brooklyn-Columbus
410 James Peeples and 300.00 150.00 Hardie Henderson: Brooklyn
411 Hip Perrier: 5000.00 2500.00 San Francisco PCL
412 Patrick Pettee: 250.00 125.00 Milwaukee-London
413 Patrick Pettee and 300.00 150.00 Bobby Lowe: Milwaukee
414 Dandelion Pfeffer: 250.00 125.00 Chi.
415 Dick Phelan: 250.00 125.00 Des Moines
416 William Phillips: 250.00 125.00 Brooklyn-Kansas City
417 John Pickett: 250.00 125.00 St. Paul-K.C.-Phila.
418 George Pinkney: 250.00 125.00 Brooklyn
419 Thomas Poorman: 250.00 125.00 A's-Milwaukee
420 Henry Porter: 250.00 125.00 Brooklyn-Kansas City
421 James Powell: 250.00 125.00 Sioux City
422 Tom Powers: 5000.00 2500.00 San Francisco PCL
423 Bill Purcell: 250.00 125.00 (Blondie) Baltimore-A's
424 Thomas Quinn: 250.00 125.00 Baltimore
425 Joseph Quinn: 250.00 125.00 Des Moines-Boston
426 Old Hoss Radbourne: 1200.00 600.00 Boston (Portrait)
427 Old Hoss Radbourne: 1000.00 500.00 Boston (Non- portrait)
428 Shorty Radford: 250.00 125.00 Brooklyn-Cleveland
429 Tom Ramsey: 250.00 125.00 Louisville
430 Rehse: Minneapolis 250.00 125.00
431 Long John Reilly: 250.00 125.00 Cincinnati
432 Charles Reilly: 250.00 125.00 (Princeton) St.Paul
433 Charles Reynolds: 250.00 125.00 Kansas City
434 Hardie Richardson 250.00 125.00 Detroit-Boston
435 Danny Richardson: 250.00 125.00 New York
436 Charles Ripslager 800.00 400.00 SPOT
437 John Roach 250.00 125.00 New York
438 Wilbert Robinson 1200.00 600.00 Uncle Robbie: A's
439 M.C. Robinson: Minn. 250.00 125.00
440 Yank Robinson: 250.00 125.00 St. Louis
441 Wm.(Yank) Robinson: 400.00 200.00 Browns Champs
442 George Rooks: 300.00 150.00 Maroons-Detroit
443 James(Chief) Roseman 1500.00 750.00 SPOT
444 Davis Rowe: 250.00 125.00 Mgr. K.C.-Denver
445 Jack Rowe: Detroit- 250.00 125.00 Pittsburgh
446 Amos (Hoosier 3000.00 1500.00 Thunderbolt) Rusie: Indianapolis
447 Amos Rusie New York
448 James Ryan: Chicago 400.00 200.00
449 Henry Sage: 250.00 125.00 Des Moines-Toledo
450 Henry Sage and 300.00 150.00 William Van Dyke: Des Moines-Toledo
451 Sanders: Omaha 250.00 125.00
452 Al(Ben) Sanders: 250.00 125.00 Philadelphia
453 Frank Scheibeck: 250.00 125.00 Detroit
454 Albert Schellhase: 250.00 125.00 St. Joseph
455 William Schenkle: 250.00 125.00 Milwaukee
456 Bill Schildknecht: 250.00 125.00 Des Moines-Milwaukee
457 Gus(Pink Whiskers) 250.00 125.00 Schmelz Mgr. Cincinnati
458 Lewis Schoeneck 300.00 150.00 (Jumbo): Maroons-Indianapolis
459 Pop Schriver: Phila 250.00 125.00
460 John Seery: Ind. 250.00 125.00
461 William Serad 250.00 125.00 Cincinnnati-Toronto
462 Edward Seward: A's 250.00 125.00
463 George(Orator)Shafer 250.00 125.00 Des Moines
464 Frank Shafer: 250.00 125.00 St. Paul
465 Daniel Shannon: 250.00 125.00 Omaha-L'ville-Phila.
466 William Sharsig: 300.00 150.00 Mgr. Athletics
467 Samuel Shaw: 250.00 125.00 Baltimore-Newark
468 John Shaw: 250.00 125.00 Minneapolis
469 William Shindle: 250.00 125.00 Baltimore-Phila.
470 George Shock: Wash. 250.00 125.00
471 Otto Shomberg: Ind. 250.00 125.00
472 Lev Shreve: Ind. 250.00 125.00
473 Ed(Baldy) Silch: 250.00 125.00 Brooklyn-Denver
474 Michael Slattery: 250.00 125.00 New York
475 Sam(Skyrocket)Smith: 250.00 125.00 Louisville
476 John(Phenomenal) 1500.00 750.00 Smith (Portrait)
477 John(Phenomenal) 250.00 125.00 Smith: Balt.-A's (Non-portrait)
478 Elmer Smith: 250.00 125.00 Cincinnati
479 Fred(Sam) Smith: 250.00 125.00 Des Moines
480 George Smith 250.00 125.00 (Germany) Brooklyn
481 Pop Smith: 250.00 125.00 Pitt.-Bos.-Phila.
482 Nick Smith: St. Joe 250.00 125.00
483 P.T. Somers: 250.00 125.00 St. Louis
484 Joe Sommer: Balt 250.00 125.00
485 Pete Sommers: 250.00 125.00 Chicago-New York
486 William Sowders: 250.00 125.00 Boston-Pittsburgh
487 John Sowders: 250.00 125.00 St. Paul-Kansas City
488 Charles Sprague: 300.00 150.00 Maroons-Chi.-Cleve.
489 Edward Sproat: 250.00 125.00 Whites
490 Harry Staley: 250.00 125.00 Whites-Pittsburgh
491 Daniel Stearns: 250.00 125.00 Des Moines-K.C.
492 Billy(Cannonball) 250.00 125.00 Stemmyer: Boston-Cleveland
493 B.F. Stephens: Milw 250.00 125.00
494 John C. Sterling: 250.00 125.00 Minneapolis
495 Leonard Stockwell 5000.00 2500.00 S.F. PCL
496 Harry Stovey: 500.00 250.00 A's-Boston
497 C. Scott Stratton: 250.00 125.00 Louisville
498 Joseph Straus: 250.00 125.00 Omaha-Milwaukee
499 John(Cub) Stricker: 250.00 125.00 Cleveland
500 Marty Sullivan: 250.00 125.00 Chicago-Ind.
501 Michael Sullivan: 250.00 125.00 A's
502 Billy Sunday: 1200.00 600.00 Chicago-Pittsburgh

503 Sy Sutcliffe: Cleve.	250.00	125.00
504 Ezra Sutton: Boston-Milwaukee	250.00	125.00
505 Ed Cyrus Swartwood: Brook.-D.Moines-Ham.	250.00	125.00
506 Parke Swartzel: K.C.	250.00	125.00
507 Peter Sweeney: Wash.	250.00	125.00
508 Louis Sylvester: Sacramento PCL	5000.00	2500.00
509 Ed(Dimples) Tate: Boston-Baltimore	250.00	125.00
510 Patsy Tebeau: Chi.-Cleve.-Minn.	400.00	200.00
511 John Tener: Chicago	300.00	150.00
512 Bill(Adonis) Terry: Brooklyn	250.00	125.00
513 Big Sam Thompson: Detroit-Philadelphia	800.00	400.00
514 Silent Mike Tiernan: New York	300.00	150.00
515 Ledell Titcomb: N.Y.	250.00	125.00
516 Phillip Tomney: Louisville	250.00	125.00
517 Stephen Toole: Brooklyn-K.C.-Rochester	250.00	125.00
518 George Townsend A's	250.00	125.00
519 William Traffley: Des Moines	250.00	125.00
520 George Treadway: St. Paul-Denver	250.00	125.00
521 Samuel Trott: Baltimore-Newark	250.00	125.00
522 Sam Trott and Tommy(Oyster) Burns: Baltimore HOR	300.00	150.00
523 Tom(Foghorn) Tucker: Baltimore	250.00	125.00
524 William Tuckerman: St. Paul	250.00	125.00
525 Turner: Minneapolis	250.00	125.00
526 Lawrence Twitchell: Detroit-Cleveland	250.00	125.00
527 James Tyng: Phila.	250.00	125.00
528 William Van Dyke: Des Moines-Toledo	250.00	125.00
529 George(Rip) VanHaltren Chicago	250.00	125.00
530 Harry Vaughn: (Farmer) Louisville-New York	250.00	125.00
531 Peek-a-Boo Veach: St. Paul	500.00	250.00
532 Veach: Sacra. PCL	5000.00	2500.00
533 Leon Viau: Cincinnati	250.00	125.00
534 William Vinton: Minneapolis	250.00	125.00
535 Joseph Visner: Brooklyn	250.00	125.00
536 Christian VonDer Ahe Owner Browns Champ	500.00	250.00
537 Joseph Walsh Omaha	250.00	125.00
538 John(Monte) Ward: New York	1000.00	500.00
539 E.H. Warner: Milwaukee	500.00	250.00
540 William Watkins: Mgr. Detroit-Kansas City	300.00	150.00
541 Bill Weaver: (Farmer) Louisville	250.00	125.00
542 Charles Weber: Sioux City	250.00	125.00
543 George Weidman (Stump): Detroit-New York	250.00	125.00
544 William Weidner: Columbus	250.00	125.00
545 Curtis Welch: Browns Champ	400.00	200.00
546 Curtis Welch: A's	300.00	150.00
547 Curtis Welch and Bill Gleason: Athletics	400.00	200.00
548 Smilin'Mickey Welch: All Star-New York	1000.00	500.00
549 Jake Wells: K.C.	250.00	125.00
550 Frank Wells: Des Moines-Mil.	300.00	150.00
551 Joseph Werrick: Louisville-St. Paul	250.00	125.00
552 Milton(Buck) West: Minneapolis	250.00	125.00
553 Gus(Cannonball) Weyhing: A's	250.00	125.00
554 John Weyhing: Athletics-Columbus	250.00	125.00
555 Bobby Wheelock: Boston-Detroit	250.00	125.00
556 Whitacre: A's	250.00	125.00
557 Pat Whitaker: Balt.	250.00	125.00
558 Deacon White: Detroit-Pittsburgh	400.00	200.00
559 William White: Louisville	250.00	125.00
560 Jim(Grasshopper) Whitney: Wash.-Indianapolis	250.00	125.00
561 Arthur Whitney: Pittsburgh-New York	250.00	125.00
562 G. Whitney: St. Joseph	250.00	125.00
563 James Williams: Mgr. Cleveland	300.00	150.00
564 Ned Williamson: Chi.	400.00	200.00
565 Williamson and Mascot	300.00	150.00
566 C.H. Willis: Omaha	250.00	125.00
567 Walt Wilmot: Washington-Chicago	250.00	125.00
568 George Winkleman: Minneapolis-Hartford Issued only in 1889	600.00	300.00
569 Samuel Wise: Boston-Washington	250.00	125.00
570 William Wolf (Chicken) Louisville	250.00	125.00
571 George(Dandy) Wood: Philadelphia	250.00	125.00
572 Peter Wood: Phila.	250.00	125.00
573 Harry Wright: Mgr. Philadelphia	3000.00	1500.00
574 Charles Zimmer (Chief) Cleveland	250.00	125.00
575 Frank Zinn: Athletics	250.00	125.00

1949 Olmes Studios

This set measures 3 1/2" by 5 1/2" and features Philadelphia players only. Two poses of Ferris Fain exist. The Olmes Studio identification is printed on the back of the postcard

	NM	Ex
COMPLETE SET (8)	80.00	40.00
1 Sam Chapman	10.00	5.00
2 Ferris Fain	15.00	7.50
3 Dick Fowler	10.00	5.00
4 Bob Hooper	10.00	5.00
5 Barney McCoskey	10.00	5.00
6 Robin Roberts	20.00	10.00
7 Carl Scheib	10.00	5.00
8 Joe Tipton	10.00	5.00

1982 On Deck Discs

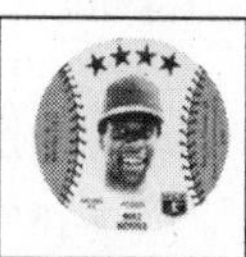

These discs, which were distributed in On Deck Cookie packaging features the same players as the 1981 MSA Discs. This set, however -- unlike the 1981 MSA Discs clearly state on the back that they are from a 1982 Collector series set.

	Nm-Mt	Ex-Mt
COMPLETE SET (32)	25.00	10.00
1 Buddy Bell	.25	.10
2 Johnny Bench	1.00	.40
3 Bruce Bochte	.25	.10
4 George Brett	8.00	3.20
5 Bill Buckner	.25	.10
6 Rod Carew	1.00	.40
7 Steve Carlton	1.00	.40
8 Cesar Cedeno	.25	.10
9 Jack Clark	.25	.10
10 Cecil Cooper	.25	.10
11 Bucky Dent	.25	.10
12 Carlton Fisk	5.00	2.00
13 Steve Garvey	.50	.20
14 Rich Gossage	.50	.20
15 Mike Hargrove	.25	.10
16 Keith Hernandez	.25	.10
17 Bob Horner	.25	.10
18 Reggie Jackson	5.00	2.00
19 Steve Kemp	.25	.10
20 Ron LeFlore	.25	.10
21 Fred Lynn	.25	.10
22 Lee Mazzilli	.25	.10
23 Eddie Murray	4.00	1.60
24 Mike Norris	.25	.10
25 Dave Parker	.25	.10
26 J.R. Richard	.25	.10
27 Pete Rose	4.00	1.60
28 Mike Schmidt	4.00	1.60
29 Tom Seaver	1.00	.40
30 Roy Smalley	.25	.10
31 Willie Stargell	1.00	.40
32 Garry Templeton	.25	.10

2000 Opening Day 2K

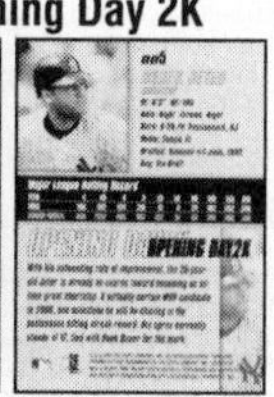

All four MLB licensed card manufacturers (Fleer, Pacific, Topps and Upper Deck) participated in this cross-company retail-only promotion to honor Opening Day 2000. The cards were distributed at K-Mart in March and April of 2000. Each manufacturer selected eight players of their choice. Cards 1-8 were issued in Topps Opening Day, 9-16 were issued in Fleer Tradition, cards 17-24 were issued in Upper Deck Victory and Upper Deck Hitter's Club, and 25-32 were issued in Pacific. Each card shares similar design elements to the base brand they're sourced from, but all have been given a bold unifying, gold foil strip stating "Opening Day 2K" on the right side of the card front. These cards were seeded at a rate of one in five packs across all participating brands.

	Nm-Mt	Ex-Mt
COMPLETE SET (32)	40.00	12.00
OD1 Mark McGwire T	3.00	.90
OD2 Barry Bonds T	3.00	.90
OD3 Ivan Rodriguez T	1.00	.30
OD4 Sean Casey T	.50	.15
OD5 Derek Jeter T	3.00	.90
OD6 Vladimir Guerrero T	1.00	.30
OD7 Preston Wilson T	.50	.15
OD8 Ben Grieve T	.50	.15
OD9 Cal Ripken F	4.00	1.20
OD10 Alex Rodriguez F	2.00	.60
OD11 Mike Piazza F	2.00	.60
OD12 Jeff Bagwell F	.60	.18
OD14 Jason Kendall F	.50	.15
OD15 Magglio Ordonez F	.50	.15
OD16 Carlos Delgado F	.50	.15
OD17 Ken Griffey Jr. UD	2.00	.60
OD18 Sammy Sosa UD	2.00	.60
OD19 Pedro Martinez UD	1.00	.30
OD20 Manny Ramirez UD	.50	.15
OD21 Shawn Green UD	.50	.15
OD22 Carlos Beltran UD	.50	.15
OD23 Juan Gonzalez UD	1.00	.30
OD24 Jeromy Burnitz UD	.50	.15
OD25 Mo Vaughn P	.50	.15
OD26 Chipper Jones P	1.00	.30
OD27 N. Garciaparra P	2.00	.60
OD28 Larry Walker P	.60	.18
OD29 Corey Koskie P	.50	.15
OD30 Scott Rolen P	.60	.18
OD31 Tony Gwynn P	1.50	.45
OD32 Jose Canseco P	1.00	.30

1976 Orbakers Discs

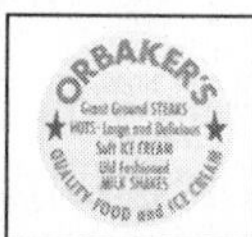

This is yet another variety of the 1976 Discs. These have Orbaker backs and are valued as a multiple of the Crane Discs

	NM	Ex
COMPLETE SET (70)	25.00	10.00
1 Hank Aaron	3.00	1.20
2 Johnny Bench	2.00	.80
3 Vida Blue	.30	.12
4 Larry Bowa	.30	.12
5 Lou Brock	2.00	.80
6 Jeff Burroughs	.15	.06
7 John Candelaria	.15	.06
8 Jose Cardenal	.15	.06
9 Rod Carew	2.00	.80
10 Steve Carlton	2.00	.80
11 Dave Cash	.15	.06
12 Cesar Cedeno	.30	.12
13 Ron Cey	.30	.12
14 Carlton Fisk	2.50	1.00
15 Tito Fuentes	.15	.06
16 Steve Garvey	1.00	.40
17 Ken Griffey	.30	.12
18 Don Gullett	.15	.06
19 Willie Horton	.15	.06
20 Al Hrabosky	.15	.06
21 Catfish Hunter	2.00	.80
22A Reggie Jackson Oakland Athletics	6.00	2.40
22B Reggie Jackson Baltimore Orioles	2.00	.80
23 Randy Jones	.15	.06
24 Jim Kaat	.60	.24
25 Don Kessinger	.15	.06
26 Dave Kingman	.60	.24
27 Jerry Koosman	.30	.12
28 Mickey Lolich	.30	.12
29 Greg Luzinski	.60	.24
30 Fred Lynn	.60	.24
31 Bill Madlock	.30	.12
32A Carlos May Chicago White Sox	1.00	.40
32B Carlos May New York Yankees	.15	.06
33 John Mayberry	.15	.06
34 Bake McBride	.15	.06
35 Doc Medich	.15	.06
36A Andy Messersmith Los Angeles Dodgers	1.00	.40
36B Andy Messersmith Atlanta Braves	.15	.06
37 Rick Monday	.15	.06
38 John Montefusco	.15	.06
39 Jerry Morales	.15	.06
40 Joe Morgan	2.00	.80
41 Thurman Munson	1.00	.40
42 Bobby Murcer	.60	.24
43 Al Oliver	.60	.24
44 Jim Palmer	2.00	.80
45 Dave Parker	1.00	.40
46 Tony Perez	1.00	.40
47 Jerry Reuss	.15	.06
48 Brooks Robinson	2.00	.80
49 Frank Robinson	2.00	.80
50 Steve Rogers	.15	.06
51 Pete Rose	2.50	1.00
52 Nolan Ryan	5.00	2.00
53 Manny Sanguillen	.15	.06
54 Mike Schmidt	3.00	1.20
55 Tom Seaver	2.50	1.00
56 Ted Simmons	.60	.24
57 Reggie Smith	.30	.12
58 Willie Stargell	2.00	.80
59 Rusty Staub	.60	.24
60 Rennie Stennett	.15	.06
61 Don Sutton	2.00	.80
62A Andre Thornton Chicago Cubs	1.00	.40
62B Andre Thornton Montreal Expos	.15	.06
63 Luis Tiant	.60	.24
64 Joe Torre	1.00	.40
65 Mike Tyson	.15	.06
66 Bob Watson	.30	.12
67 Wilbur Wood	.15	.06
68 Jimmy Wynn	.15	.06
69 Carl Yastrzemski	2.00	.80
70 Richie Zisk	.15	.06

1939 Orcajo Photo Art PC786

The postcards in this set measures 3 1/2" by 5 1/2" and comes in three styles. The first contains an Orcajo Photo Art back. Type 2 is marked "Courtesy of Val Decker Packing Co., Piquality Brand Meats" on the front. Type 3 is marked "Metropolitan Clothing Co" on the front. The cards are listed in the checklist below by type. The set is broken down this way: Type 1 are cards 1-26; Type 2 are 27-31 and Type 3 are cards 32-33. The set was issued in 1939 and features a card of Joe DiMaggio, the only apparent non-Cincinnati player. The cards are sepia in color and feature white borders.

	Ex-Mt	VG
COMPLETE SET (33)	3500.00	1800.00
1 Wally Berger	100.00	50.00
2 Nino Bongiovanni	80.00	40.00
3 Frenchy Bordagray	80.00	40.00
4 Harry Craft	100.00	50.00
5 Ray Davis	80.00	40.00
6 Paul Derringer	100.00	50.00
7 Joe DiMaggio	800.00	400.00
8 Linus Frey	80.00	40.00
9 Lee Gamble	80.00	40.00
10 Ival Goodman	80.00	40.00
11 Hank Gowdy CO	80.00	40.00
12 Lee Grissom	80.00	40.00
13 Williard Herschberger Name in White	100.00	50.00
14 Eddie Joost	100.00	50.00
15 Frank McCormick	100.00	50.00
16 Bill McKecknie MG	150.00	75.00
17 Billy Meyers	80.00	40.00
18 Whitey Moore	80.00	40.00
19 Lew Riggs	80.00	40.00
20 Les Scarsella	80.00	40.00
21 Milburn Shoffner	80.00	40.00
22 Junior Thompson	80.00	40.00
23 Bucky Walters	120.00	60.00
24 Bill Werber	100.00	50.00
25 Dick West	80.00	40.00
26 Jimmie Wilson	80.00	40.00
27 Alan Cooke	80.00	40.00
28 Linus Frey small projection	80.00	40.00
29 Williard Herschberger Name in black	80.00	40.00
30 Ernie Lombardi Name plain	150.00	75.00
31 Johnny Vander Meer	120.00	60.00
32 Ernie Lombardi name fancy	150.00	75.00
33 Johnny Vander Meer	120.00	60.00

2001 Oreo/Ritz

These four standard-size cards feature two cards each of baseball superstars Ken Griffey Jr. and Derek Jeter. The Griffey cards were produced by Upper Deck while Fleer produced the Derek Jeter cards. Since the cards are unnumbered, we have sequenced them by player.

	Nm-Mt	Ex-Mt
COMPLETE SET (4)	5.00	1.50
DJ1 Derek Jeter	2.00	.60
DJ2 Derek Jeter	2.00	.60
KG1 Ken Griffey Jr.	1.00	.30
KG2 Ken Griffey Jr.	1.00	.30

1994 Origins of Baseball

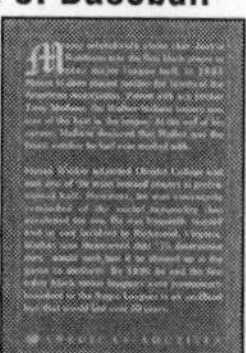

Published by the American Archives Publishing Co. (Beverly Hills, CA), this boxed set of 100 standard-size cards recounts the historic origins of baseball from 1744 to 1899. According to the title card, limited edition uncut sheets of the set as well as 8" by 10" reproductions of certain cards were also produced.

	Nm-Mt	Ex-Mt
COMP. FACT SET (104)	10.00	3.00
1 Abner Doubleday	.25	.07
2 Doubleday Field	.05	.02
3 Rounders 1744	.05	.02
4 Early Baseball 700 AD	.05	.02
5 The Knickerbockers	.05	.02
6 Alexander Cartwright	.25	.07
7 Baseball in the 1850's	.05	.02
8 Social Clubs	.05	.02
9 Brooklyn Eckfords	.05	.02
10 New England Baseball	.05	.02
11 Henry Chadwick	.25	.07
12 Brooklyn Excelsiors	.05	.02
13 Abraham Lincoln	.75	.23
14 Andrew Johnson	.15	.04
15 First Enclosed Park	.05	.02
16 Brooklyn Atlantics	.05	.02
17 James Creighton	.15	.04
18 Baseball in the 1860's	.05	.02
19 1869 Red Stockings	.05	.02
20 Cincinnati Celebration	.05	.02
21 Harry Wright	.25	.07
22 Boston Ball Club 1872	.25	.07
23 Arthur Cummings	.25	.07
24 William Hulbert	.15	.04
25 George Wright	.25	.07
26 Albert Spalding	.25	.07
27 Albert Bushong	.15	.04
28 Bid McPhee	.15	.04
29 James O'Rourke	.15	.04
30 Pud Galvin	.25	.07
31 Edwin Bligh	.15	.04
32 William Purcell	.15	.04
33 Roger Connor	.25	.07
34 Cincinnati Ball Club	.05	.02
35 Peter Browning	.15	.04
36 William Gleason	.15	.04
37 Paul Hines	.15	.04
38 Baseball in the 1880's	.05	.02
39 Robert Carruthers	.15	.04
40 New York Metropolitans	.05	.02
41 Saint George's Field	.05	.02
42 Charles Radbourne	.25	.07
43 George Andrews	.15	.04
44 William Hoy	.25	.07
45 Chicago Ball Club	.05	.02
46 Cap Anson	.75	.23
47 John Clarkson	.25	.07
48 Mike Kelly	.75	.23
49 Buffalo Bisons 1887	.05	.02
50 Moses Walker	.75	.23
51 Detroit Ball Club	.05	.02
52 Little League	.05	.02
53 Louisville Ball Club	.05	.02
54 John Farrell	.15	.04
55 Walter Latham	.15	.04
56 Fred Dunlap	.15	.04
57 Tim Keefe	.25	.07
58 Cincinnati Ball Club	.05	.02
59 1889 World Tour	.05	.02
60 Dan Brouthers	.25	.07
61 John M. Ward	.25	.07
62 Albert Spalding	.25	.07
63 The Baseball Cap	.05	.02
64 Tom Esterbrook	.15	.04
65 Mark Baldwin	.15	.04
66 Tony Mullane	.25	.07
67 John Glasscock	.15	.04
68 Amos Rusie	.25	.07
69 Jake Beckley	.25	.07
70 Jimmy Collins	.25	.07
71 Charles Comiskey	.25	.07
72 Tom Connolly	.25	.07
73 Mickey Welch	.25	.07
74 Ed Delahanty	.25	.07
75 Hugh Duffy	.25	.07
76 Buck Ewing	.25	.07
77 Clark Griffith	.25	.07
78 Kid Nichols	.25	.07
79 Billy Hamilton	.25	.07
80 Ban Johnson	.15	.04
81 Willie Keeler	.25	.07
82 Bobby Wallace	.25	.07
83 Nap Lajoie	.75	.23
84 Connie Mack	.75	.23
85 Fred Clarke	.25	.07
86 Tommy McCarthy	.25	.07
87 John McGraw	.75	.23
88 Jesse Burkett	.25	.07
89 Frank Chance	.25	.07
90 Mordecai Brown	.25	.07
91 New York Nationals	.05	.02
92 Jack Chesbro	.15	.04
93 Sam Thompson	.25	.07
94 Boston vs. New York	.05	.02
95 Rube Waddell	.25	.07
96 Joe Kelley	.25	.07
97 Addie Joss	.25	.07
98 Boston Beaneaters	.05	.02
99 Baltimore Baseball Club	.05	.02
100 The Game in 1899	.05	.02
z3 Acknowledgments	.05	.02
zNNO0 Title card (Proof of ownership)	.05	.02
zNNO0 Bibliography card	.05	.02
NNO0 Certificate of Authenticity	.05	.02

1894 Orioles Team Issue

These cards which measure 3 7/8" by 2 3/8" featured players from the great Baltimore Oriole teams of the 1890's. This set has the players photographed in black tie regalia. The back of each card credits the Alpha Photo Engraving Company of Baltimore, Maryland.

	Ex-Mt	VG
COMPLETE SET (14)	7000.00	3500.00
1 Frank Bonner	400.00	200.00
2 Walter Brodie	400.00	200.00
3 Dan Brouthers	800.00	400.00
4 Charles Esper	400.00	200.00
5 Kid Gleason	500.00	250.00
6 Ned Hanlon MG	600.00	300.00
7 William Hawke	400.00	200.00
8 George Hemmings	400.00	200.00
9 Hugh Jennings	800.00	400.00

10 Joe Kelley	800.00	400.00
11 John McGraw	1000.00	500.00
12 John McMahon	400.00	200.00
13 Henry Reitz	400.00	200.00
14 Wilbert Robinson	800.00	400.00

1954 Orioles Esskay

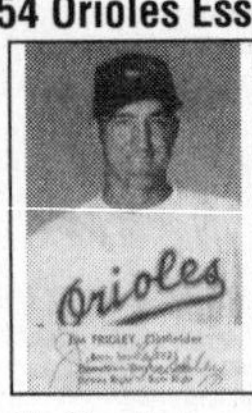

The cards in this 36-card set measure 2 1/4" by 3 1/2". The 1954 Esskay Meats set contains color, unnumbered cards featuring Baltimore Orioles only. The cards were issued in panels of two on boxes of Esskay hot dogs; consequently, many have grease stains on the cards and are quite difficult to obtain in mint condition. The 1954 Esskay set can be distinguished from the 1955 Esskay set supposedly by the white or off-white (the 1955 set) backs of the cards. The backs of the 1954 cards are also supposedly "waxed" to a greater degree than the 1955 cards. The catalog designation is F181-1. Since the cards are unnumbered, they are ordered below in alphabetical order for convenience. These cards were issued in conjunction with the "Bobo Newsome" TV Show.

	NM	Ex
COMPLETE SET (36)	3250.00	1600.00
1 Cal Abrams	100.00	50.00
2 Neil Berry	100.00	50.00
3 Michael Blyzka	100.00	50.00
4 Harry Brecheen	125.00	60.00
5 Gil Coan	100.00	50.00
6 Joe Coleman	100.00	50.00
7 Clint Courtney	125.00	60.00
8 Charles E. Diering	100.00	50.00
9 Jimmie Dykes MG	125.00	60.00
10 Frank Fanovich	100.00	50.00
11 Howard Fox	100.00	50.00
12 Jim Fridley	100.00	50.00
13 Chico Garcia	100.00	50.00
14 Jehosie Heard	100.00	50.00
15 Darrell Johnson	125.00	60.00
16 Robert D. Kennedy	125.00	60.00
17 Dick Kokos	100.00	50.00
18 Dave Koslo	100.00	50.00
19 Lou Kretlow	100.00	50.00
20 Dick Kryhoski	100.00	50.00
21 Bob Kuzava	100.00	50.00
22 Don Larsen	200.00	100.00
23 Don Lenhardt	100.00	50.00
24 Dick Littlefield	100.00	50.00
25 Sam Mele	100.00	50.00
26 Les Moss	100.00	50.00
27 Ray L. Murray	100.00	50.00
28 Bobo Newsom	125.00	60.00
29 Tom Oliver CO	100.00	50.00
30 Duane Pillette	100.00	50.00
31 Francis M. Skaff CO	100.00	50.00
32 Marlin Stuart	100.00	50.00
33 Bob Turley	200.00	100.00
34 Eddie Waitkus	100.00	50.00
35 Vic Wertz	125.00	60.00
36 Robert G. Young	100.00	50.00

1954-55 Orioles Postcards

This set features glossy black-and-white portraits of the Baltimore Orioles with white borders. The backs carry a postcard format. The cards are unnumbered and checklisted below in alphabetical order.

	NM	Ex
COMPLETE SET	2400.00	1200.00
1 Cal Abrams	40.00	20.00
2 Bob Alexander	40.00	20.00
3 Mike Blyzka	40.00	20.00
4 Jim Brideweser	40.00	20.00
5 Hal Brown	40.00	20.00
6 Harry Byrd	40.00	20.00
7 Bob Chakales	40.00	20.00
8 Wayne Causey	40.00	20.00
9 Gil Coan	40.00	20.00
10 Joe Coleman	40.00	20.00
11 Clint Courtney	40.00	20.00
12 Billy Cox	60.00	30.00
13 Chuck Diering	40.00	20.00
14 Harry Dorish	40.00	20.00
15 Jim Dyck	40.00	20.00
16 Jimmy Dykes MG	60.00	30.00
17 Howie Fox	40.00	20.00
18 Jim Fridley	40.00	20.00
19 Chico Garcia	40.00	20.00
20 Ted Gray	40.00	20.00
21 Bob Hale	40.00	20.00
22 Bill Hunter	60.00	30.00
23 Don Johnson	40.00	20.00
24 Bob Kennedy	40.00	20.00
25 Lou Kretlow	40.00	20.00
26 Dick Kryhoski	40.00	20.00
27 Bob Kuzava	40.00	20.00
28 Don Larsen	80.00	40.00
29 Don Leppert	40.00	20.00
30 Ed Lopat	60.00	30.00
31 Fred Marsh	40.00	20.00
32 Jim McDonald	40.00	20.00
33 Sam Mele	40.00	20.00
34 Willie Miranda	40.00	20.00
35 Les Moss	40.00	20.00
36 Ray Murray	40.00	20.00
37 Bob Nelson	40.00	20.00
38 Billy O'Dell	40.00	20.00
39 Dave Philley	40.00	20.00
40 Erv Palica	40.00	20.00
41 Duane Pillette	40.00	20.00
42 Dave Pope	40.00	20.00
43 Paul Richards	60.00	30.00
44 Saul Rogovin	40.00	20.00
45 Art Schallock	40.00	20.00
46 Frank Skaff	40.00	20.00
47 Hal Smith	40.00	20.00
48 Vern Stephens	60.00	30.00
49 Marlin Stuart	40.00	20.00
50 Gus Triandos	60.00	30.00
51 Bob Turley (Portrait)	60.00	30.00
52 Bob Turley (Throwing)	60.00	30.00
53 Eddie Waitkus	50.00	25.00
54 Wally Westlake	40.00	20.00
55 Bill Wright	40.00	20.00
56 Gene Woodling	60.00	30.00
57 Bobby Young	40.00	20.00
58 George Zuverink	40.00	20.00

1955 Orioles Esskay

The cards in this 27-card set measure 2 1/4" by 3 1/2". The 1955 Esskay Meats set was issued in panels of two on boxes of Esskay hot dogs. This set of full color, blank back, unnumbered cards features Baltimore Orioles only. Many of the players in the 1954 Esskay set were also issued in this set. The catalog designation is F181-2. Since the cards are unnumbered, they are ordered below in alphabetical order for convenience. The 1955 set is supposedly somewhat more difficult to find than the 1954 set.

	NM	Ex
COMPLETE SET (27)	2500.00	1250.00
1 Cal Abrams	100.00	50.00
2 Robert Alexander	100.00	50.00
3 Harry Brecheen CO	120.00	60.00
4 Harry Byrd	100.00	50.00
5 Gil Coan	100.00	50.00
6 Joe Coleman	100.00	50.00
7 William Cox	120.00	60.00
8 Chuck Diering	100.00	50.00
9 Walter Evers	120.00	60.00
10 Don Johnson	100.00	50.00
11 Bob Kennedy	120.00	60.00
12 Lou Kretlow	100.00	50.00
13 Bob Kuzava	100.00	50.00
14 Fred Marsh	100.00	50.00
15 Charles Maxwell	120.00	60.00
16 Jim McDonald	100.00	50.00
17 Bill Miller	100.00	50.00
18 Willie Miranda	120.00	60.00
19 Ray Moore	100.00	50.00
20 Les Moss	100.00	50.00
21 Bobo Newsom	120.00	60.00
22 Duane Pillette	100.00	50.00
23 Harold W. Smith	100.00	50.00
24 Gus Triandos	120.00	60.00
25 Eddie Waitkus	100.00	50.00
26 Gene Woodling	150.00	75.00
27 Robert G. Young	100.00	50.00

1956 Orioles Postcards

This 38-card set features glossy black-and-white portraits of the Baltimore Orioles in white borders and printed on a postcard format. Cards 1-28 were blank in the bottom margins for autographs. Card 29-37 had the player's name and nickname printed on the front. There were two cards of different players numbered 20. Please note that there is some duplications in the Orioles Postcards lists and years. We will continue to work on further clarifying each set and year.

	NM	Ex
COMPLETE SET (38)	1500.00	750.00
1 George Zuverink	40.00	20.00
2 Wayne Causey	40.00	20.00
3 Bob Nelson	40.00	20.00
4 Jim Pyburn	40.00	20.00
5 Willie Miranda	40.00	20.00
6 Jim Dyck	40.00	20.00
7 Dave Philley	40.00	20.00
8 Erv Palica	40.00	20.00
9 Gus Triandos	50.00	25.00
10 Hal Smith	40.00	20.00
11 Dave Pope	40.00	20.00
12 Tom Gastall	40.00	20.00
13 Jim Wilson	40.00	20.00
14 Hal Brown	40.00	20.00
15 Harry Dorish	40.00	20.00
16 Ray Moore	40.00	20.00
17 Bob Hale	40.00	20.00
18 Tito Francona	40.00	20.00
19 Don Ferrarese	40.00	20.00
20 Bob Boyd	40.00	20.00
20 George Kell	80.00	40.00
21 Babe Birrer	40.00	20.00
22 Bill Wright	40.00	20.00
23 Billy Gardner	50.00	25.00
24 Paul Richards MG	50.00	25.00
25 Mel Held	40.00	20.00
26 Chuck Diering	40.00	20.00
27 Fred Marsh	40.00	20.00
28 Bobby Adams	40.00	20.00
29 Walter Evers	40.00	20.00
30 Robert Nieman	40.00	20.00
31 George Kell	80.00	40.00
32 Jose Fornieles	40.00	20.00
33 William Loes	50.00	25.00
34 John Schmitz	40.00	20.00
35 Clifford Johnson	40.00	20.00
36 Joseph Frazier	40.00	20.00
37 Richard Williams	50.00	25.00

1958 Orioles Jay Publishing

This 12-card set of the Baltimore Orioles measures approximately 5" by 7" and features black-and-white player photos in a white border. These cards were packaged 12 to a packet. The backs are blank. The cards are unnumbered and checklisted below in alphabetical order.

	NM	Ex
COMPLETE SET (12)	35.00	17.50
1 Bob Boyd	3.00	1.50
2 Jim Busby	3.00	1.50
3 Billy Gardner	3.00	1.50
4 Connie Johnson	3.00	1.50
5 Billy Loes	4.00	2.00
6 Willy Miranda	3.00	1.50
7 Bob Nieman	3.00	1.50
8 Bill O'Dell	3.00	1.50
9 Al Pilarcik	3.00	1.50
10 Paul Richards MG	5.00	2.50
11 Gus Triandos	5.00	2.50
12 George Zuverink	3.00	1.50

1959 Orioles Jay Publishing

This 12-card set of the Baltimore Orioles measures approximately 5" by 7" and features black-and-white player photos in a white border. These cards were packaged 12 to a packet. The backs are blank. The cards are unnumbered and checklisted below in alphabetical order.

	NM	Ex
COMPLETE SET (12)	50.00	25.00
1 Bob Boyd	3.00	1.50
2 Chico Carrasquel	3.00	1.50
3 Billy Gardner	3.00	1.50
4 Bob Nieman	3.00	1.50
5 Billy O'Dell	3.00	1.50
6 Milt Pappas	5.00	2.50
7 Brooks Robinson	15.00	7.50
8 Willie Tasby	3.00	1.50
9 Gus Triandos	3.00	1.50
10 Jerry Walker	3.00	1.50
11 James(Hoyt) Wilhelm	10.00	5.00
12 Gene Woodling	3.00	1.50

1960 Orioles Jay Publishing

This 12-card set of the Baltimore Orioles measures approximately 5" by 7" and features black-and-white player photos in a white border. These cards were packaged 12 to a packet and originally sold for 25 cents. The backs are blank. The cards are unnumbered and checklisted below in alphabetical order.

	NM	Ex
COMPLETE SET (12)	40.00	16.00
1 Jackie Brandt	2.50	1.00
2 Marv Breeding	2.50	1.00
3 Jack Fisher	2.50	1.00
4 Ron Hansen	2.50	1.00
5 Milt Pappas	3.00	1.20
6 Paul Richards MG	3.00	1.20
7 Brooks Robinson	12.00	4.80
8 Willie Tasby	2.50	1.00
9 Gus Triandos	2.50	1.00
10 Jerry Walker	2.50	1.00
11 Hoyt Wilhelm	8.00	3.20
12 Gene Woodling	3.00	1.20

1960 Orioles Postcards

This 12-card set of the Baltimore Orioles features black-and-white player portraits in white borders. The backs are blank. The cards are unnumbered and checklisted below in alphabetical order.

	NM	Ex
COMPLETE SET (12)	100.00	40.00
1 Jackie Brandt	10.00	4.00
2 Harry Brecheen CO	10.00	4.00
3 Marv Breeding	10.00	4.00
4 Chuck Estrada	10.00	4.00
5 Jack Fisher	10.00	4.00
6 Jim Gentile (After Swing)	12.00	4.80
7 Gordon Jones (Pitching)	10.00	4.00
8 Dave Philley	10.00	4.00
9 Willie Tasby	10.00	4.00
10 Gus Triandos	10.00	4.00
11 Jerry Walker	10.00	4.00
12 Gene Woodling	12.00	4.80

1961 Orioles Postcards

This 22-card set features black-and-white portraits of the Baltimore Orioles with white borders and printed on a cream colored paper. The backs are blank. The cards are unnumbered and checklisted below in alphabetical order.

	NM	Ex
COMPLETE SET (22)	225.00	90.00
1 Jerry Adair	10.00	4.00
2 Jackie Brandt	10.00	4.00
3 Marv Breeding	10.00	4.00
4 Hal Brown	10.00	4.00
5 Jim Busby	10.00	4.00
6 Walt Dropo	10.00	4.00
7 Chuck Estrada	10.00	4.00
8 Jack Fisher	10.00	4.00
9 Hank Foiles	10.00	4.00
10 Jim Gentile	15.00	6.00
11 Ron Hansen	10.00	4.00
12 Whitey Herzog	15.00	6.00
13 Billy Hoeft	10.00	4.00
14 Milt Pappas	15.00	6.00
15 Dave Philley	10.00	4.00
16 Brooks Robinson	25.00	10.00
17 Russ Snyder	10.00	4.00
18 Gene Stephens	10.00	4.00
19 Wes Stock	10.00	4.00
20 Gus Triandos	10.00	4.00
21 Jerry Walker	10.00	4.00
22 Hoyt Wilhelm	20.00	8.00

1962 Orioles Jay Publishing

This 12-card set of the Baltimore Orioles measures approximately 5" by 7". The fronts feature black-and-white posed player photos with the player's and team name printed below in the white border. These cards were packaged 12 to a packet. The backs are blank. The cards are unnumbered and checklisted below in alphabetical order.

	NM	Ex
COMPLETE SET (12)	25.00	10.00
1 Jerry Adair	2.00	.80
2 Steve Barber	2.00	.80
3 Jackie Brandt	2.00	.80
4 Marv Breeding	2.00	.80
5 Hector Brown	2.00	.80
6 Chuck Estrada	2.00	.80
7 Jim Gentile	3.00	1.20
8 Ron Hansen	2.00	.80
9 Milt Pappas	2.50	1.00
10 Brooks Robinson	8.00	3.20
11 Earl Robinson	2.00	.80
12 Gus Triandos	2.00	.80

1962 Orioles Postcards

This 33-card set features black-and-white player portraits with white borders. The backs are blank. The cards are unnumbered and checklisted below in alphabetical order. Boog Powell appears in his Rookie Card season.

	NM	Ex
COMPLETE SET (33)	350.00	140.00
1 Jerry Adair	10.00	4.00
2 Steve Barber (Portrait)	10.00	4.00
3 Steve Barber (Ready to throw)	10.00	4.00
4 Jackie Brandt	10.00	4.00
5 Marv Breeding	10.00	4.00
6 Hal Brown	10.00	4.00
7 Chuck Estrada	10.00	4.00
8 Jack Fisher	10.00	4.00
9 Jim Gentile	15.00	6.00
10 Dick Hall	10.00	4.00
11 Ron Hansen	10.00	4.00
12 Whitey Herzog	15.00	6.00
13 Billy Hitchcock MG	15.00	6.00
14 Billy Hoeft	10.00	4.00
15 Hobie Landrith	10.00	4.00
16 Charlie Lau	10.00	4.00
17 Jim Lehew	10.00	4.00
18 Dave Nicholson	10.00	4.00
19 Milt Pappas	15.00	6.00
20 Boog Powell	25.00	10.00
21 Art Quirk	10.00	4.00
22 Robin Roberts	20.00	8.00
23 Brooks Robinson	25.00	10.00
24 Earl Robinson	10.00	4.00
25 Billy Short	10.00	4.00
26 Russ Snyder	10.00	4.00
27 Wes Stock	10.00	4.00
28 Johnny Temple	10.00	4.00
29 Marv Throneberry	12.00	4.80
30 Gus Triandos	10.00	4.00
31 Ozzie Virgil	10.00	4.00
32 Hoyt Wilhelm	20.00	8.00
33 Dick Williams	12.00	4.80

1963 Orioles Jay Publishing

This 12-card set of the Baltimore Orioles measures approximately 5" by 7". The fronts feature black-and-white posed player photos with the player's and team name printed below in the white border. These cards were packaged 12 to a packet. The backs are blank. The cards are unnumbered and checklisted below in alphabetical order.

	NM	Ex
COMPLETE SET (12)	35.00	14.00
1 Jerry Adair	2.00	.80
2 Luis Aparicio	6.00	2.40
3 Steve Barber	2.00	.80
4 Jackie Brandt	2.00	.80
5 Chuck Estrada	2.00	.80
6 Jim Gentile	3.00	1.20
7 Billy Hitchcock MG	2.00	.80
8 John Orsino	2.00	.80
9 Milt Pappas	3.00	1.20
10 Robin Roberts	6.00	2.40
11 Brooks Robinson	8.00	3.20
12 Wes Stock	2.00	.80

1963 Orioles Postcards

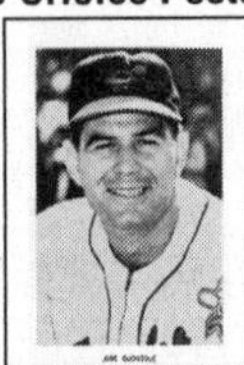

This 34-card set features black-and-white portraits of the Baltimore Orioles with white borders. The backs are blank. The cards are unnumbered and checklisted below in alphabetical order.

	NM	Ex
COMPLETE SET (34)	350.00	140.00
1 Jerry Adair	10.00	4.00
2 Luis Aparicio	20.00	8.00
3 Luke Appling CO	20.00	8.00
4 Steve Barber	15.00	6.00
5 Hank Bauer CO	15.00	6.00
6 Jack Brandt	10.00	4.00
7 Harry Brecheen CO	15.00	6.00
8 Dick Brown	10.00	4.00
9 Pete Burnside	10.00	4.00
10 Chuck Estrada	10.00	4.00
11 Joe Gaines	10.00	4.00
12 Jim Gentile	15.00	6.00
13 Dick Hall	10.00	4.00
14 Billy Hitchcock MG	15.00	6.00
15 Bob Johnson	10.00	4.00
16 Hobie Landrith	10.00	4.00
17 Charlie Lau	12.00	4.80
18 Mike McCormick	10.00	4.00
19 Dave McNally	20.00	8.00
20 John Miller	10.00	4.00
21 Stu Miller	10.00	4.00
22 Buster Narum	10.00	4.00
23 John Orsino (Catching)	10.00	4.00
24 John Orsino	10.00	4.00
25 Milt Pappas	15.00	6.00
26 Boog Powell	20.00	8.00
27 Robin Roberts	20.00	8.00
28 Brooks Robinson	25.00	10.00
29 Bob Saverine	10.00	4.00
30 Al Smith	10.00	4.00
31 Russ Snyder	10.00	4.00
32 Wes Stock	10.00	4.00
33 Dean Stone	10.00	4.00
34 Fred Valentine	10.00	4.00

1964 Orioles Jay Publishing

This 12-card set of the Baltimore Orioles measures approximately 5" by 7". The fronts feature black-and-white posed player photos with the player's and team name printed below in the white border. These cards were packaged 12 to a packet. The backs are blank. The cards are unnumbered and checklisted below in alphabetical order.

	NM	Ex
COMPLETE SET (12)	35.00	14.00
1 Luis Aparicio	5.00	2.00
2 Steve Barber	3.00	1.20
3 Hank Bauer MG	4.00	1.60
4 Jackie Brandt	2.50	1.00
5 Chuck Estrada	2.50	1.00
6 Willie Kirkland	2.50	1.00
7 John Orsino	2.50	1.00
8 Milt Pappas	3.00	1.20
9 Boog Powell	5.00	2.00
10 Robin Roberts	5.00	2.00
11 Brooks Robinson	10.00	4.00
12 Norm Siebern	2.50	1.00

1964 Orioles Postcards

This 36-card set features black-and-white portraits of the Baltimore Orioles with white borders. The backs are blank. The cards are unnumbered and checklisted below in alphabetical order.

	NM	Ex
COMPLETE SET (36)	300.00	120.00
1 Jerry Adair	8.00	3.20
2 Luis Aparicio	15.00	6.00
3 Steve Barber (Light ink autograph)	12.00	4.80
4 Steve Barber (Dark ink autograph)	12.00	4.80
5 Hank Bauer MG	12.00	4.80
6 Frank Bertaina	8.00	3.20
7 Sam Bowens (Closer head shot)	8.00	3.20
8 Sam Bowens	8.00	3.20
9 Jack Brandt	8.00	3.20
10 Harry Brecheen CO	12.00	4.80
11 Dick Brown	8.00	3.20
12 Wally Bunker	8.00	3.20
13 Chuck Estrada	8.00	3.20
14 Joe Gaines	8.00	3.20
15 Harvey Haddix	8.00	3.20
16 Dick Hall	8.00	3.20
17 Larry Haney	8.00	3.20
18 Billy Hunter CO	8.00	3.20
19 Lou Jackson	8.00	3.20
20 Bob Johnson	8.00	3.20
21 Willie Kirkland	8.00	3.20
22 Charley Lau	8.00	3.20
23 Mike McCormick	8.00	3.20
24 Dave McNally	12.00	4.80
25 Stu Miller	8.00	3.20
26 John Orsino	8.00	3.20
27 Milt Pappas	12.00	4.80
28 Boog Powell	15.00	6.00
29 Robin Roberts	15.00	6.00
30 Brooks Robinson	20.00	8.00
31 Earl Robinson	8.00	3.20

32 Bob Saverine 8.00 3.20
33 Norm Siebern 8.00 3.20
34 Russ Snyder 8.00 3.20
35 Wes Stock 8.00 3.20
36 Dave Vinyard 8.00 3.20

1965 Orioles Jay Publishing

This 12-card set of the Pittsburgh Pirates measures approximately 5" by 7". The fronts feature black-and-white posed player photos with the player's and team name printed below in the white border. These cards were packaged 12 to a packet. The backs are blank. The cards are unnumbered and checklisted below in alphabetical order.

	NM	Ex
COMPLETE SET (12)	30.00	12.00
1 Jerry Adair	2.00	.80
2 Luis Aparicio	4.00	1.60
3 Steve Barber	2.50	1.00
4 Hank Bauer MG	3.00	1.20
5 Sam Bowens	2.00	.80
6 Wally Bunker	2.00	.80
7 John Orsino	2.00	.80
8 Milt Pappas	2.50	1.00
9 Boog Powell	4.00	1.60
10 Brooks Robinson	6.00	2.40
11 Norm Siebern	2.00	.80
12 Dave Vineyard	2.00	.80

1965 Orioles Postcards

This 34-card set features black-and-white portraits of the Baltimore Orioles with white borders. The backs are blank. The cards are unnumbered and checklisted below in alphabetical order. Jim Palmer's postcard predates his Rookie Card.

	NM	Ex
COMPLETE SET (34)	300.00	120.00
1 Jerry Adair	8.00	3.20
2 Luis Aparicio	15.00	6.00
3 Steve Barber	12.00	4.80
4 Hank Bauer MG	12.00	4.80
5 Paul Blair	12.00	4.80
6 Curt Blefary	8.00	3.20
7 Sam Bowens	8.00	3.20
8 Jack Brandt	8.00	3.20
9 Harry Brecheen CO	10.00	4.00
10 Dick Brown	8.00	3.20
11 Wally Bunker	8.00	3.20
12 Sam Bowens	8.00	3.20
13 Dick Hall	8.00	3.20
14 Billy Hunter CO	10.00	4.00
15 Bob Johnson	8.00	3.20
16 Davey Johnson	15.00	6.00
17 Darold Knowles	8.00	3.20
18 Don Larsen	15.00	6.00
19 Charley Lau	8.00	3.20
20 Sherm Lollar CO	8.00	3.20
21 Dave McNally	15.00	6.00
22 John Miller	8.00	3.20
23 Stu Miller	8.00	3.20
24 John Orsino	8.00	3.20
25 Jim Palmer	30.00	12.00
26 Milt Pappas	12.00	4.80
27 Boog Powell	15.00	6.00
28 Robin Roberts	15.00	6.00
29 Brooks Robinson	25.00	10.00
30 Norm Siebern	8.00	3.20
31 Russ Snyder	8.00	3.20
32 Dave Vineyard	8.00	3.20
33 Carl Warwick	8.00	3.20
34 Gene Woodling CO	10.00	4.00

1966 Orioles Postcards

This 34-card set features black-and-white portraits of the Baltimore Orioles with white borders. The backs are blank. The cards are unnumbered and checklisted below in alphabetical order. Jim Palmer has a postcard in his Rookie Card year.

	NM	Ex
COMPLETE SET (34)	200.00	80.00
1 Luis Aparicio	15.00	6.00
2 Steve Barber	10.00	4.00
3 Frank Bertaina	8.00	3.20
4 Paul Blair	10.00	4.00
5 Curt Blefary	8.00	3.20
6 Sam Bowens	8.00	3.20
7 Gene Brabender	8.00	3.20
8 Harry Brecheen CO	8.00	3.20
9 Wally Bunker (Looking forward)	8.00	3.20
10 Wally Bunker (Looking to the side)	8.00	3.20
11 Camilo Carreon	8.00	3.20
12 Moe Drabowsky	8.00	3.20
13 Andy Etchebarren	8.00	3.20
14 Eddie Fisher	8.00	3.20
15 Dick Hall	8.00	3.20
16 Woodie Held	8.00	3.20
17 Billy Hunter CO	8.00	3.20
18 Bob Johnson	8.00	3.20
19 Davey Johnson	12.00	4.80
20 Charley Lau	8.00	3.20
21 Sherm Lollar CO (Closer head photo)	8.00	3.20
22 Sherm Lollar CO	8.00	3.20
23 Dave McNally	10.00	4.00
24 John Miller	8.00	3.20
25 Stu Miller	8.00	3.20
26 Jim Palmer	15.00	6.00
27 Boog Powell	15.00	6.00
28 Brooks Robinson	20.00	8.00
29 Frank Robinson	20.00	8.00
30 Vic Roznovsky	8.00	3.20
31 Billy Short	8.00	3.20
32 Russ Snyder	8.00	3.20
33 Eddie Watt	8.00	3.20
34 Gene Woodling CO	8.00	3.20

1967-69 Orioles Postcards

This 107-card set features black-and-white portraits of the Baltimore Orioles with white borders. The backs are blank. Some of the cards carry facsimile autographs. The cards are unnumbered and checklisted below in alphabetical order.

	NM	Ex
COMPLETE SET (107)	500.00	200.00
1 Mike Adamson	5.00	2.00
2 Luis Aparicio	10.00	4.00
3 George Bamberger CO (Larger head shot)	5.00	2.00
4 George Bamberger CO	5.00	2.00
5 Steve Barber	5.00	2.00
6 Hank Bauer MG	8.00	3.20
7 Fred Beene	5.00	2.00
8 Mark Belanger	6.00	2.40
9 Mark Belanger (Closer head shot)	6.00	2.40
10 Mark Belanger (Artist's rendition)	6.00	2.40
11 Frank Bertaina	5.00	2.00
12 Frank Bertaina (Lighter portrait)	5.00	2.00
13 Paul Blair (Lighter looking to left)	6.00	2.40
14 Paul Blair (Darker looking to left)	6.00	2.40
15 Paul Blair (Looking straight ahead)	6.00	2.40
16 Curt Blefary	5.00	2.00
17 Sam Bowens	5.00	2.00
18 Gene Brabender	5.00	2.00
19 Harry Brecheen CO	5.00	2.00
20 Don Buford (Looking straight ahead)	5.00	2.00
21 Don Buford (Dark closer head shot)	5.00	2.00
22 Don Buford (Lighter closer head shot)	5.00	2.00
23 Don Buford (Name in bold print)	5.00	2.00
24 Wally Bunker (Dark portrait)	5.00	2.00
25 Wally Bunker (Lighter protrait)	5.00	2.00
26 Terry Crowley	5.00	2.00
27 Mike Cuellar (Light portrait)	8.00	3.20
28 Mike Cuellar (Dark portrait)	8.00	3.20
29 Clay Dalrymple	5.00	2.00
30 Bill Dillman	5.00	2.00
31 Moe Drabowsky (Looking to the left)	5.00	2.00
32 Moe Drabowsky (Looking straight ahead)	5.00	2.00
33 Mike Epstein	5.00	2.00
34 Andy Etchebarren (Looking to the left)	5.00	2.00
35 Andy Etchebarren (Cream colored paper)	5.00	2.00
36 Andy Etchebarren (Clearer looking to left)	5.00	2.00
37 Andy Etchebarren (Looking straight ahead)	5.00	2.00
38 Chico Fernandez	5.00	2.00
39 Eddie Fisher	5.00	2.00
40 Bobby Floyd	5.00	2.00
41 Jim Frey CO	5.00	2.00
42 Dick Hall	5.00	2.00
43 Larry Haney	5.00	2.00
44 Larry Haney (Larger portrait)	5.00	2.00
45 Jim Hardin	5.00	2.00
46 Elrod Hendricks (Looking straight ahead)	5.00	2.00
47 Elrod Hendricks (Looking slightly to the left)	5.00	2.00
48 Elrod Hendricks (Closer looking to the left photo)	5.00	2.00
49 Vern Hoscheit CO	5.00	2.00
50 Bruce Howard	5.00	2.00
51 Billy Hunter CO (Looking to the left)	5.00	2.00
52 Bill Hunter CO (Darker looking to left)	5.00	2.00
53 Billy Hunter CO (Autographed and looking straight ahead)	5.00	2.00
54 Bob Johnson	5.00	2.00
55 Dave Johnson (Autographed artist's version)	8.00	3.20
56 Davey Johnson	8.00	3.20
57 Dave Johnson Darker portrait)	8.00	3.20
58 Charlie Lau	5.00	2.00
59 Dave Leonhard (Autographed)	5.00	2.00
60 Dave Leonhard (Name is spelled as Leonard)	5.00	2.00
61 Dave Leonhard (Closer head view)	5.00	2.00
62 Dave Leonhard (Different cap)	5.00	2.00
63 Sherm Lollar CO	5.00	2.00
64 Marcelino Lopez	5.00	2.00
65 Dave May	5.00	2.00
66 Dave May (Closer head shot)	5.00	2.00
67 Dave McNally (Looking to left)	8.00	3.20
68 Dave McNally (Looking straight ahead)	8.00	3.20
69 Stu Miller	5.00	2.00
70 John Morris	5.00	2.00
71 Curt Motton (Light portrait)	5.00	2.00
72 Curt Motton (Darker portrait)	5.00	2.00
73 Roger Nelson	5.00	2.00
74 John O'Donoghue	5.00	2.00
75 Jim Palmer (Looking to the right)	15.00	6.00
76 Jim Palmer (Head turned straight)	15.00	6.00
77 Jim Palmer (Looking to the left)	15.00	6.00
78 Tom Phoebus	5.00	2.00
79 Tom Phoebus (Darker portrait)	5.00	2.00
80 Tom Phoebus (Lighter portrait)	5.00	2.00
81 Boog Powell (Light portrait)	10.00	4.00
82 Boog Powell (Larger head shot)	10.00	4.00
83 Boog Powell (Lighter portrait	10.00	4.00
84 Merv Rettenmund	5.00	2.00
85 Merv Rettenmund (Darker portrait)	5.00	2.00
86 Merv Rettenmund (Lighter portrait)	5.00	2.00
87 Pete Richert (Not smiling)	5.00	2.00
88 Pete Richert (Smiling)	5.00	2.00
89 Brooks Robinson	15.00	6.00
90 Brooks Robinson (Darker autographed version)	15.00	6.00
91 Brooks Robinson (Lighter portrait)	15.00	6.00
92 Brooks Robinson (Shows mail cancellation)	15.00	6.00
93 Brooks Robinson (Farther away head shot)	15.00	6.00
94 Frank Robinson	15.00	6.00
95 Vic Roznovsky	5.00	2.00
96 Chico Salmon	5.00	2.00
97 Ray Scarborough CO	5.00	2.00
98 Al Severinsen	5.00	2.00
99 Russ Snyder	5.00	2.00
100 George Staller CO	5.00	2.00
101 Fred Valentine	5.00	2.00
102 Eddie Watt	5.00	2.00
103 Ed Watt (Autographed)	5.00	2.00
104 Earl Weaver MG	10.00	4.00
105 Gene Woodling CO (Looking straight ahead)	5.00	2.00
106 Gene Woodling CO (Autographed and darker)	5.00	2.00
107 Gene Woodling CO (Autographed and lighter	5.00	2.00

1968 Orioles Dexter Press/Coca Cola Postcards

This 12-card set features posed borderless color photos of the Baltimore Orioles printed on postcard-size cards. The backs carry the player's biography and a facsimile autograph with a Dexter press serial number.

	NM	Ex
COMPLETE SET (12)	75.00	30.00
1 Mark Belanger	6.00	2.40
2 Paul Blair	6.00	2.40
3 Curt Blefary	5.00	2.00
4 Don Buford	5.00	2.00
5 Moe Drabowsky	5.00	2.00
6 Andy Etchebarren	5.00	2.00
7 Dave Johnson	10.00	4.00
8 Dave McNally	8.00	3.20
9 Tom Phoebus	5.00	2.00
10 Boog Powell	10.00	4.00
11 Brooks Robinson	15.00	6.00
12 Frank Robinson	15.00	6.00

1969 Orioles Postcards Color

This three-card set features borderless color portraits of the Baltimore Orioles printed on postcard size cards. The backs are blank. The cards are unnumbered and checklisted below in alphabetical order.

	NM	Ex
COMPLETE SET (3)	25.00	10.00
1 Bob Grich	8.00	3.20
2 Dave Johnson	8.00	3.20
3 Brooks Robinson	15.00	6.00

1970 Orioles Black and White

This 15-piece set features blank-backed, white-bordered, 8" X 10" black-and-white photos. The player's name appears in black within the bottom border. A facsimile autograph is printed across the photo. The word "Tadder" is pasted into photos at lower right. Photos are unnumbered and checklisted below in alphabetical order.

	NM	Ex
COMPLETE SET (15)	50.00	20.00
1 Mark Belanger	5.00	2.00
2 Don Buford	3.00	1.20
3 Mike Cuellar	5.00	2.00
4 Clay Dalrymple	3.00	1.20
5 Andy Etchebarren	3.00	1.20
6 Dave Johnson	6.00	2.40
7 Dave McNally	5.00	2.00
8 Curt Motton	3.00	1.20
9 Jim Palmer	10.00	4.00
10 Boog Powell	6.00	2.40
11 Merv Rettenmund	3.00	1.20
12 Frank Robinson	10.00	4.00
13 Chico Salmon	3.00	1.20
14 Eddie Watt	3.00	1.20
15 Earl Weaver MG	6.00	2.40

1970 Orioles Postcards

This 32-card set features color portraits of the Baltimore Orioles with white borders and printed on postcard size cards. The backs are blank. The cards are unnumbered and checklisted below in alphabetical order. According to information published at the time, these cards could be ordered from the Orioles at 10 cents each, 12 cards for a dollar or $2.50 for the whole set.

	NM	Ex
COMPLETE SET (32)	125.00	50.00
1 George Bamberger CO	4.00	1.60
2 Mark Belanger	5.00	2.00
3 Paul Blair	6.00	2.40
4 Don Buford	4.00	1.60
5 Terry Crowley	4.00	1.60
6 Mike Cuellar	6.00	2.40
7 Clay Dalrymple	4.00	1.60
8 Moe Drabowsky	4.00	1.60
9 Andy Etchebarren	4.00	1.60
10 Jim Frey CO	4.00	1.60
11 Dick Hall	4.00	1.60
12 Jim Hardin	4.00	1.60
13 Elrod Hendricks (No buttons showing)	4.00	1.60
14 Elrod Hendricks (One button showing)	4.00	1.60
15 Billy Hunter CO	4.00	1.60
16 Dave Johnson	6.00	2.40
17 Dave Leonhard	4.00	1.60
18 Marcelino Lopez	4.00	1.60
19 Dave McNally	6.00	2.40
20 Dave McNally (Darker portrait)	6.00	2.40
21 Curt Motton	4.00	1.60
22 Jim Palmer	12.00	4.80
23 Tom Phoebus	4.00	1.60
24 Boog Powell	8.00	3.20
25 Merv Rettenmund	4.00	1.60
26 Pete Richert	4.00	1.60
27 Brooks Robinson	12.00	4.80
28 Frank Robinson	12.00	4.80
29 Chico Salmon	4.00	1.60
30 George Staller CO	4.00	1.60
31 Eddie Watt	4.00	1.60
32 Earl Weaver MG	8.00	3.20

1971 Orioles Aldama

This crude 12 card blank backed cards are credited to artist Carl Aldama. A drawing of the player along with his last name is on the front. There are two different Brooks Robinson cards in this set.

	NM	Ex
COMPLETE SET (12)	80.00	32.00
1 Mark Belanger	2.50	1.00
2 Paul Blair	2.00	.80
3 Mike Cuellar	3.00	1.20
4 Ellie Hendricks	2.00	.80
5 Dave Johnson	5.00	2.00
6 Dave McNally	3.00	1.20
7 Jim Palmer	15.00	6.00
8 Boog Powell	5.00	2.00
9 Brooks Robinson (Uniform number visible on back)	15.00	6.00
10 Brooks Robinson (Facing front)	15.00	6.00
11 Frank Robinson	15.00	6.00
12 Earl Weaver MG	8.00	3.20

1971 Orioles Champions

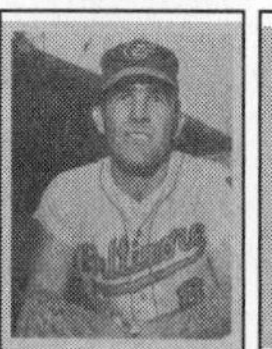

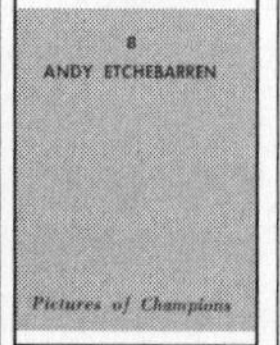

Subtitled "Pictures of Champions," this 16-card set measures 2 1/8" by 2 3/4". Since the card stock is orange, the close-up photos on the fronts are orange-tinted and have orange borders. The orange backs have the jersey number, player's name and the set subtitle. The cards are unnumbered and checklisted below in alphabetical order.

	NM	Ex
COMPLETE SET (16)	80.00	32.00
1 Mark Belanger	6.00	2.40
2 Don Buford	4.00	1.60
3 Mike Cuellar	6.00	2.40
4 Andy Etchebarren	4.00	1.60
5 Dick Hall	4.00	1.60
6 Ellie Hendricks	4.00	1.60
7 Dave Johnson	8.00	3.20
8 Dave Leonhard	4.00	1.60
9 Dave May	4.00	1.60
10 Dave McNally	6.00	2.40
11 Jim Palmer	12.00	4.80
12 Pete Richert	4.00	1.60
13 Brooks Robinson	12.00	4.80
14 Frank Robinson	12.00	4.80
15 Eddie Watt	4.00	1.60
16 Earl Weaver MG	8.00	3.20

1971 Orioles Postcards

This 30-card set features color portraits of the Baltimore Orioles with white borders and printed on postcard size cards. The backs are blank. The cards are unnumbered and checklisted below in alphabetical order.

	NM	Ex
COMPLETE SET (30)	120.00	47.50
1 George Bamberger CO	4.00	1.60
2 Mark Belanger	5.00	2.00
3 Paul Blair	6.00	2.40
4 Don Buford	4.00	1.60
5 Mike Cuellar	6.00	2.40
6 Clay Dalrymple	4.00	1.60
7 Jerry DaVanon	4.00	1.60
8 Pat Dobson	5.00	2.00
9 Tom Dukes	4.00	1.60
10 Andy Etchebarren	4.00	1.60
11 Jim Frey CO	4.00	1.60
12 Dick Hall	4.00	1.60
13 Jim Hardin	4.00	1.60
14 Elrod Hendricks	4.00	1.60
15 Billy Hunter CO	4.00	1.60
16 Grant Jackson	4.00	1.60
17 Dave Johnson	6.00	2.40
18 Dave McNally	6.00	2.40
19 Curt Motton	4.00	1.60
20 Jim Palmer	10.00	4.00
21 Boog Powell	8.00	3.20
22 Merv Rettenmund	4.00	1.60
23 Pete Richert	4.00	1.60
24 Brooks Robinson	10.00	4.00
25 Frank Robinson	10.00	4.00
26 Chico Salmon	4.00	1.60
27 Tom Shopay	4.00	1.60
28 George Staller CO	4.00	1.60
29 Ed Watt	4.00	1.60
30 Earl Weaver MG	8.00	3.20

1972 Orioles DMV

The 1972 Baltimore Orioles Police/Safety set was issued on a thin unperforated cardboard sheet measuring 12 1/2" by 8". When the players are cut into individual cards, they measure approximately 2 1/2" by 4". The color of the sheet is pale yellow, and consequently the black and white borderless player photos have a similar cast. The player's name, position, and team name appear below the pictures. The backs have different safety messages sponsored by the Office of Traffic Safety, D.C. Department of Motor Vehicles. The cards are unnumbered and checklisted below in alphabetical order.

	NM	Ex
COMPLETE SET (10)	30.00	12.00
1 Mark Belanger	4.00	1.60
2 Paul Blair	3.00	1.20
3 Don Buford	3.00	1.20
4 Mike Cuellar	3.00	1.20
5 Dave Johnson	4.00	1.60
6 Dave McNally	4.00	1.60
7 Boog Powell	5.00	2.00
8 Brooks Robinson	10.00	4.00
9 Merv Rettenmund	2.00	.80
10 Earl Weaver MG	5.00	2.00

1972 Orioles Postcards

This 33-card set features color portraits of the Baltimore Orioles with white borders and printed on postcard size cards. The backs are blank. The cards are unnumbered and checklisted below in alphabetical order.

	NM	Ex
COMPLETE SET (33)	125.00	50.00
1 Doyle Alexander	4.00	1.60
2 George Bamberger CO	4.00	1.60
3 Don Baylor	6.00	2.40
4 Mark Belanger	5.00	2.00
5 Paul Blair	6.00	2.40
6 Dave Boswell	4.00	1.60
7 Don Buford	4.00	1.60
8 Richie Coggins	4.00	1.60
9 Terry Crowley	4.00	1.60
10 Mike Cuellar	6.00	2.40
11 Pat Dobson	4.00	1.60
12 Andy Etchebarren	4.00	1.60
13 Jim Frey CO	4.00	1.60
14 Bobby Grich	6.00	2.40
15 Roric Harrison	4.00	1.60
16 Elrod Hendricks	4.00	1.60
17 Billy Hunter CO	4.00	1.60
18 Grant Jackson	4.00	1.60
19 Dave Johnson	6.00	2.40
20 Dave Leonhard	4.00	1.60
21 Dave McNally	6.00	2.40
22 Johnny Oates	5.00	2.00
23 Jim Palmer	12.00	4.80
24 Boog Powell	8.00	3.20
25 John"Boog" Powell	8.00	3.20
26 Merv Rettenmund	4.00	1.60
27 Brooks Robinson	12.00	4.80
28 Chico Salmon	4.00	1.60
29 Mickey Scott	4.00	1.60
30 Tom Shopay	4.00	1.60
31 George Staller CO	4.00	1.60
32 Eddie Watt	4.00	1.60
33 Earl Weaver MG	8.00	3.20

1973 Orioles Johnny Pro

This 25-card set measures approximately 4 1/4" by 7 1/4" and features members of the 1973 Baltimore Orioles. The cards were designed to be pushed-out in a style similar to the 1964 Topps Stand Ups. The sides of the cards have a small advertisement for Johnny Pro Enterprises and even gives a phone number where they could have been reached. Oddly, the Orlando Pena card was not available in a die-cut version. The cards have the player's photo against a distinctive solid green background.

The cards are blank backed. There are several variations within the set; the complete set price below includes all of the variation cards. The set is checklisted in order by uniform number. According to informed sources, there were 15,000 sets produced.

	NM	Ex
COMPLETE SET (25)	200.00	80.00
1 Al Bumbry	4.00	1.60
2 Rich Coggins	4.00	1.60
3A Bobby Grich	8.00	3.20
(Fielding)		
3B Bobby Grich	20.00	8.00
(Batting)		
4 Earl Weaver MG	10.00	4.00
5A Brooks Robinson	25.00	10.00
(Fielding)		
5B Brooks Robinson	50.00	20.00
(Batting)		
6 Paul Blair	6.00	2.40
7 Mark Belanger	6.00	2.40
8 Andy Etchebarren	4.00	1.60
10 Elrod Hendricks	4.00	1.60
11 Terry Crowley	4.00	1.60
12 Tommy Davis	6.00	2.40
13 Doyle Alexander	6.00	2.40
14 Merv Rettenmund	4.00	1.60
15 Frank Baker	4.00	1.60
19 Dave McNally	6.00	2.40
21 Larry Brown	4.00	1.60
22A Jim Palmer	20.00	8.00
22B Jim Palmer	40.00	16.00
(Pitching)		
23 Grant Jackson	4.00	1.60
25 Don Baylor	8.00	3.20
26 John(Boog) Powell	15.00	6.00
27 Orlando Pena	15.00	6.00
(NOT die-cut)		
32 Earl Williams	4.00	1.60
34 Bob Reynolds	4.00	1.60
35 Mike Cuellar	6.00	2.40
39 Eddie Watt	4.00	1.60

1973-74 Orioles Postcards

These 43 cards feature color portraits of the Baltimore Orioles with white borders and printed on postcard size cards. The backs are blank. The cards are unnumbered and checklisted below in alphabetical order.

	NM	Ex
COMPLETE SET (43)	60.00	24.00
1 Doyle Alexander	1.00	.40
(Dark)		
2 Doyle Alexander	1.00	.40
(Light)		
3 Frank Baker	1.00	.40
4 George Bamberger CO	1.00	.40
5 Don Baylor	2.50	1.00
6 Mark Belanger	2.00	.80
7 Paul Blair	1.50	.60
8 Larry Brown	1.00	.40
9 Al Bumbry	1.00	.40
10 Al Bumbry	1.00	.40
11 Enos Cabell	1.00	.40
12 Rich Coggins	1.00	.40
13 Terry Crowley	1.00	.40
14 Jim Fuller	1.00	.40
15 Wayne Garland	1.00	.40
16 Mike Cuellar	1.50	.60
17 Tommy Davis	1.50	.60
18 Andy Etchebarren	1.00	.40
19 Jim Frey CO	1.00	.40
20 Bob Grich	2.50	1.00
21 Ross Grimsley	1.00	.40
22 Roric Harrison	1.00	.40
23 Ellie Hendricks	1.00	.40
24 Don Hood	1.00	.40
25 Billy Hunter CO	1.00	.40
26 Grant Jackson	1.00	.40
27 Jesse Jefferson	1.00	.40
28 Dave McNally	2.00	.80
(Looking right)		
29 Dave McNally	2.00	.80
(Looking left)		
30 Johnny Oates	1.00	.40
31 Jim Palmer	5.00	2.00
(Autographed)		
32 Jim Palmer	5.00	2.00
(Eyes looking left)		
33 Orlando Pena	1.00	.40
34 Boog Powell	3.00	1.20
35 Merv Rettenmund	1.00	.40
36 Bob Reynolds	1.00	.40
37 Brooks Robinson	5.00	2.00
38 Mickey Scott	1.00	.40
39 George Staller CO	1.00	.40
40 Eddie Watt	1.00	.40
41 Earl Weaver MG	2.50	1.00
42 Earl Williams	1.00	.40
(Smiling)		
43 Earl Williams	1.00	.40
(Non-smiling)		

1975 Orioles Postcards

This 30-card set of the Baltimore Orioles features player photos on postcard-size cards. The cards are unnumbered and checklisted below in alphabetical order.

	NM	Ex
COMPLETE SET (30)	30.00	12.00
1 Doyle Alexander	.75	.30
2 George Bamberger CO	.75	.30
3 Don Baylor	2.00	.80
4 Mark Belanger	.75	.30
5 Paul Blair	1.00	.40
6 Al Bumbry	.75	.30
7 Mike Cuellar	1.00	.40
8 Tommy Davis	1.00	.40
9 Doug DeCinces	1.50	.60
10 Dave Duncan	.75	.30
11 Jim Frey CO	.75	.30
12 Wayne Garland	.75	.30
13 Bob Grich	.75	.30
14 Ross Grimsley	.75	.30
15 Elrod Hendricks	.75	.30
16 Billy Hunter CO	.75	.30
17 Grant Jackson	.75	.30
18 Jesse Jefferson	.75	.30
19 Dave Johnson	.75	.30
20 Lee May	1.00	.40
21 Tim Nordbrook	.75	.30
22 Jim Northrup	.75	.30
23 Jim Palmer	4.00	1.60
24 Bob Reynolds	.75	.30
25 Brooks Robinson	5.00	2.00
26 Tom Shopay	.75	.30
27 Ken Singleton	1.50	.60
28 George Staller CO	.75	.30
29 Mike Torrez	.75	.30
30 Earl Weaver MG	2.00	.80

1976 Orioles English's Chicken Lids

This set features round black-and-white player photos and measures approximately 8 1/4" in diameter. The backs are blank. The cards are unnumbered and checklisted below in alphabetical order; however, the checklist is incomplete. Cuellar, Holtzman and Palmer are all the large size cards. Ten other cards were issued and those lids measure 7" in diameter.

	NM	Ex
COMPLETE SET	75.00	30.00
1 Mark Belanger	6.00	2.40
2 Paul Blair	5.00	2.00
3 Al Bumbry	5.00	2.00
4 Mike Cuellar	5.00	2.00
5 Dave Duncan	6.00	2.40
6 Bobby Grich	5.00	2.00
7 Ross Grimsley	5.00	2.00
8 Ellie Hendricks	5.00	2.00
9 Ken Holtzman	5.00	2.00
10 Lee May	6.00	2.40
11 Jim Palmer	12.00	4.80
12 Brooks Robinson	12.00	4.80
13 Ken Singleton	6.00	2.40

1976 Orioles Postcards

This 38-card set of the Baltimore Orioles features glossy player photos with white borders on postcard-size cards. The cards are unnumbered and checklisted below in alphabetical order. An important card in this set is of Reggie Jackson, during his only season as an Oriole and one of the few Jackson Oriole cards available.

	NM	Ex
COMPLETE SET (38)	40.00	16.00
1 Doyle Alexander	.75	.30
2 Bob Bailor	.75	.30
3 George Bamberger CO	.75	.30
4 Mark Belanger	1.50	.60
5 Paul Blair	.75	.30
6 Al Bumbry	.75	.30
7 Terry Crowley	.75	.30
8 Mike Cuellar	1.00	.40
9 Doug DeCinces	1.00	.40
10 Rick Dempsey	1.00	.40
11 Dave Duncan	.75	.30
12 Mike Flanagan	.75	.30
13 Jim Frey CO	.75	.30
14 Wayne Garland	.75	.30
15 Bobby Grich	1.00	.40
16 Ross Grimsley	.75	.30
17 Tommy Harper	.75	.30
18 Elrod Hendricks	.75	.30
19 Fred Holdsworth	.75	.30
20 Bill Hunter CO	.75	.30
21 Grant Jackson	.75	.30
22 Reggie Jackson	10.00	4.00
23 Tippy Martinez	.75	.30
24 Lee May	1.00	.40
25 Rudy May	.75	.30
26 Dyar Miller	.75	.30
27 Andres Mora	.75	.30
28 Tony Muser	.75	.30
29 Tim Nordbrook	.75	.30
30 Dave Pagan	.75	.30
31 Jim Palmer	4.00	1.60
32 Cal Ripken Sr. CO	.75	.30
33 Brooks Robinson	4.00	1.60
34 Brooks Robinson	4.00	1.60
Triangle in lower right corner		
35 Tom Shopay	.75	.30
36 Ken Singleton	1.00	.40
37 Royle Stillman	.75	.30
38 Earl Weaver MG	2.00	.80

1977 Orioles Postcards

This 22-card set features glossy color portraits of the Baltimore Orioles with white borders and measures approximately 3 3/8" by 5 1/4". The backs are blank. The cards are unnumbered and checklisted below in alphabetical order. The Eddie Murray postcard predates his Rookie Card.

	NM	Ex
COMPLETE SET (22)	25.00	10.00
1 Mark Belanger	1.00	.40
2 Al Bumbry	.75	.30
3 Rich Dauer	.75	.30
4 Doug DeCinces	1.00	.40
5 Rick Dempsey	1.00	.40
6 Kiko Garcia	.75	.30
7 Ross Grimsley	.75	.30
8 Larry Harlow	.75	.30
9 Fred Holdsworth	.75	.30
10 Bill Hunter CO	.75	.30
11 Pat Kelly	.75	.30
12 Dennis Martinez	2.00	.80
13 Tippy Martinez	.75	.30
14 Scott McGregor	.75	.30
15 Eddie Murray	8.00	3.20
16 Brooks Robinson	4.00	1.60
(Light background)		
17 Brooks Robinson	4.00	1.60
(Dark background)		
18 Tom Shopay	.75	.30
19 Ken Singleton	1.00	.40
20 Dave Skaggs	.75	.30
21 Billy Smith	.75	.30
22 Earl Weaver MG	2.00	.80

1978 Orioles Postcards

This 34-card set features glossy color portraits of the Baltimore Orioles with white borders and measures approximately 3 3/8" by 5 1/4". The backs are blank. The cards are unnumbered and checklisted below in alphabetical order.

	NM	Ex
COMPLETE SET (34)	30.00	12.00
1 Mark Belanger	1.00	.40
2 Nelson Briles	.75	.30
3 Al Bumbry	1.00	.40
4 Terry Crowley	.75	.30
5 Rich Dauer	.75	.30
6 Doug DeCinces	1.00	.40
7 Rick Dempsey	1.00	.40
8 Mike Flanagan	1.50	.60
9 Jim Frey CO	.75	.30
10 Kiko Garcia	.75	.30
11 Larry Harlow	.75	.30
12 Ellie Hendricks	.75	.30
13 Pat Kelly	.75	.30
14 Joe Kerrigan	.75	.30
15 Carlos Lopez	.75	.30
16 Dennis Martinez	2.00	.80
17 Tippy Martinez	.75	.30
18 Lee May	1.00	.40
19 Scott McGregor	.75	.30
20 Ray Miller CO	.75	.30
21 Andres Mora	.75	.30
22 Eddie Murray	3.00	1.20
23 Tony Muser	.75	.30
24 Jim Palmer	3.00	1.20
25 Cal Ripken Sr. CO	.75	.30
26 Frank Robinson CO	2.00	.80
27 Gary Roenicke	.75	.30
28 Ken Singleton	1.00	.40
29 Dave Skaggs	.75	.30
30 Billy Smith	.75	.30
31 Don Stanhouse	.75	.30
32 Earl Stephenson	.75	.30
33 Tim Stoddard	1.00	.40
34 Earl Weaver MG	2.00	.80

1979 Orioles Postcards

This 18-card set features glossy color portraits of the Baltimore Orioles with white borders and measures approximately 3 3/8" by 5 1/4". The backs are blank. The cards are unnumbered and checklisted below in alphabetical order.

	NM	Ex
COMPLETE SET (18)	15.00	6.00
1 Benny Ayala	.75	.30
2 Al Bumbry	.75	.30
3 Rich Dauer	.75	.30
4 Doug DeCinces	1.00	.40
5 Rick Dempsey	1.00	.40
6 Mike Flanagan	1.00	.40
7 Jim Frey CO	.75	.30
8 Joe Kerrigan	.75	.30
9 John Lowenstein	.75	.30
10 Scott McGregor	.75	.30
11 Ray Miller CO	.75	.30
12 Eddie Murray	3.00	1.20
13 Jim Palmer	3.00	1.20
14 Sammy Stewart	.75	.30
(Red trim)		
15 Sammy Stewart	.75	.30
(Orange trim)		
16 Steve Stone	1.50	.60
17 Earl Weaver MG	2.00	.80
18 The Bird(Mascot)	.75	.30

1980 Orioles Postcards

This 24-card blank-backed set features glossy color portraits of the Baltimore Orioles with white borders and measures approximately 3 3/8" by 5 1/4". The cards are unnumbered and checklisted below in alphabetical order. Any of these cards were available from the team for 10 cents each.

	NM	Ex
COMPLETE SET (24)	18.00	7.25
1 Benny Ayala	.50	.20
2 Mark Belanger	.50	.20
3 Terry Crowley	.50	.20
4 Doug DeCinces	.75	.30
5 Mike Flanagan	.75	.30
6 Dave Ford	.50	.20
7 Kiko Garcia	.50	.20
8 Dan Graham	.50	.20
9 Ellie Hendricks CO	.50	.20
10 Pat Kelly	.50	.20
11 Joe Kerrigan	.50	.20
12 John Lowenstein	.50	.20
13 Scott McGregor	.50	.20
14 Ray Miller CO	.50	.20
15 Eddie Murray	4.00	1.60
16 Jim Palmer	3.00	1.20
17 Gary Roenicke	.50	.20
18 Lenn Sakata	.50	.20
19 Ken Singleton	.75	.30
20 Tim Stoddard	.50	.20
21 Steve Stone	.75	.30
22 Earl Weaver MG	1.50	.60
23 The Bird(Mascot)	.50	.20
24 Memorial Stadium	.50	.20

1981 Orioles 1966 Franchise

This 32 card standard-size set was issued by the Franchise of Bel Air, Maryland. This set commemorated the 15th anniversary of the first Orioles World Championship.

	Nm-Mt	Ex-Mt
COMPLETE SET (32)	60.00	24.00
1 Title Card	2.00	.80
2 Team Card	2.00	.80
3 Luis Aparicio	4.00	1.60
4 Steve Barber	2.50	1.00
5 Hank Bauer MG	2.50	1.00
6 Paul Blair	3.00	1.20
7 Curt Blefary	2.00	.80
8 Sam Bowens	2.00	.80
9 Gene Brabender	2.00	.80
10 Harry Brecheen CO	2.00	.80
11 Wally Bunker	2.00	.80
12 Moe Drabowsky	2.00	.80
13 Andy Etchebarren	2.00	.80
14 Eddie Fisher	2.00	.80
15 Dick Hall	2.00	.80
16 Larry Haney	2.00	.80
17 Woodie Held	2.00	.80
18 Billy Hunter CO	2.00	.80
19 Bob Johnson	2.00	.80
20 Dave Johnson	3.00	1.20
21 Sherm Lollar CO	2.00	.80
22 Dave McNally	2.50	1.00
23 John Miller	2.00	.80
24 Stu Miller	2.00	.80
25 Jim Palmer	6.00	2.40
26 John (Boog) Powell	4.00	1.60
27 Brooks Robinson	6.00	2.40
28 Frank Robinson	6.00	2.40
29 Vic Roznovsky	2.00	.80
30 Russ Snyder	2.00	.80
31 Eddie Watt	2.00	.80
32 Gene Woodling CO	2.00	.80

1981 Orioles Postcards

This 25-card set features glossy color portraits of the Baltimore Orioles with white borders and measures approximately 3 1/2" by 5 1/4". The backs carry a postcard format with Memorial Stadium address. The cards are unnumbered and checklisted below in alphabetical order. An early major league Cal Ripken Jr. card is in this set.

	Nm-Mt	Ex-Mt
COMPLETE SET (25)	30.00	12.00
1 Benny Ayala	.50	.20
2 Al Bumbry	.50	.20
3 Terry Crowley	.50	.20
4 Rich Dauer	.50	.20
5 Rick Dempsey	.75	.30
6 Jim Dwyer	.50	.20
7 Elrod Hendricks CO	.50	.20
8 Wayne Krenchicki	.50	.20
9 Dennis Martinez	1.00	.40
10 Tippy Martinez	.50	.20
11 Ray Miller CO	.50	.20
12 Jose Morales	.50	.20
13 Eddie Murray	3.00	1.20
14 Jim Palmer	2.50	1.00
15 Cal Ripken Jr.	15.00	6.00
16 Ralph Rowe CO	.50	.20
17 Lenn Sakata	.50	.20
18 Jeff Schneider	.50	.20
19 John Shelby	.50	.20
20 Ken Singleton	.50	.20
21 Sammy Stewart	.50	.20
22 Steve Stone	.50	.20
23 Jimmy Williams CO	.50	.20
24 The Bird(Mascot)	.50	.20
25 Memorial Stadium	.50	.20

1982 Orioles Postcards

This six-card set features glossy color portraits of the Baltimore Orioles with white borders and measures approximately 3 1/2" by 5 1/4". The backs carry a postcard format and Memorial Stadium address. The cards are unnumbered and checklisted below in alphabetical order. Cal Ripken Jr. has a card in his Rookie Card season.

	Nm-Mt	Ex-Mt
COMPLETE SET (6)	8.00	3.20
1 Rich Dauer	.50	.20
2 Mike Flanagan	1.00	.40
3 Ross Grimsley	.50	.20
4 Cal Ripken Jr.	5.00	2.00
5 Ken Singleton	1.00	.40
6 Sammy Stewart	.50	.20

1983 Orioles Postcards

This 33-card set of the Baltimore Orioles measures 3 1/2" by 5 1/8" and features white-bordered, color player portraits with the player's name in the bottom margin. The backs carry a postcard format. The cards are unnumbered and checklisted below in alphabetical order.

	Nm-Mt	Ex-Mt
COMPLETE SET (33)	15.00	6.00
1 Joe Altobelli MG	.50	.20
2 Benny Ayala	.50	.20
3 Mike Boddicker	1.00	.40
4 Bob Bonner	.50	.20
5 Al Bumbry	.50	.20
6 Todd Cruz	.50	.20
7 Rich Dauer	.50	.20
8 Storm Davis	.75	.30
9 Rick Dempsey	.75	.30
10 Jim Dwyer	.50	.20
11 Mike Flanagan	.75	.30
12 Dan Ford	.50	.20
13 Ellie Hendricks CO	.50	.20
14 John Lowenstein	.50	.20
15 Dennis Martinez	1.00	.40
16 Tippy Martinez	.50	.20
17 Scott McGregor	.50	.20
18 Ray Miller CO	.50	.20
19 Eddie Murray	3.00	1.20
20 Joe Nolan	.50	.20
21 Jim Palmer	1.50	.60
22 Allan Ramirez	.50	.20
23 Cal Ripken Jr.	6.00	2.40
24 Cal Ripken Sr. CO	.50	.20
25 Gary Roenicke	.50	.20
26 Ralph Rowe CO	.50	.20
27 Lenn Sakata	.50	.20
28 Ken Singleton	.75	.30
29 Sammy Stewart	.50	.20
30 Tim Stoddard	.75	.30
31 Earl Weaver MG	1.50	.60
32 Jimmy Williams CO	.50	.20
33 Memorial Stadium	.50	.20

1984 Orioles English's Discs

This disc set salutes the 1983 Baltimore Orioles Champion team; the discs come into two sizes, measuring either 7 1/4" or 8 3/8" in diameter. The fronts feature a black-and-white head shot on a white background encircled by orange. His name, position, team name biographical information and brief statistics are printed on the white circle. The phrase "English's Salutes" and "1983 Champions" are printed in black print in the orange border. The discs are unnumbered and checklisted below in alphabetical order. The backs are blank so we have sequenced this set in alphabetical order.

	Nm-Mt	Ex-Mt
COMPLETE SET (13)	50.00	20.00
1 Mike Boddicker	.50	.20
2 Rich Dauer	.50	.20
3 Storm Davis	.50	.20
4 Rick Dempsey	1.00	.40
5 Mike Flanagan	1.00	.40
6 John Lowenstein	.50	.20
7 Tippy Martinez	.50	.20
8 Scott McGregor	.50	.20
9 Eddie Murray	10.00	4.00
10 Jim Palmer	6.00	2.40
11 Cal Ripken	40.00	16.00
12 Gary Roenicke	.50	.20
13 Ken Singleton	1.00	.40

1984 Orioles Postcards

This 43-card set features glossy color portraits of the Baltimore Orioles with white borders and measures approximately 3 1/2" by 5 1/4". The backs carry a postcard format and Memorial Stadium address. The cards are unnumbered and checklisted below in alphabetical order.

	Nm-Mt	Ex-Mt
COMPLETE SET (43)	25.00	10.00
1 Joe Altobelli MG	.50	.20
2 Bennie Ayala	.50	.20
3 Mike Boddicker	.75	.30
(Autographed)		
4 Mike Boddicker	.75	.30
5 Mark Brown	.50	.20
6 Al Bumbry	.50	.20
7 Todd Cruz	.50	.20
8 Rich Dauer	.50	.20
9 Storm Davis	.50	.20
10 Rick Dempsey	.75	.30
11 Ken Dixon	.50	.20
12 Jim Dwyer	.50	.20
13 Mike Flanagan	.75	.30
14 Dan Ford	.50	.20
15 Wayne Gross	.50	.20
16 Ellie Hendricks CO	.50	.20
17 John Lowenstein	.50	.20
18 Dennis Martinez	1.00	.40
19 Tippy Martinez	.50	.20
20 Scott McGregor	.50	.20
21 Ray Miller CO	.50	.20
(Higher name)		
22 Ray Miller CO	.50	.20
(Lower name)		
23 Eddie Murray	2.50	1.00
24 Joe Nolan	.50	.20
25 Jim Palmer	1.50	.60
26 Floyd Rayford	.50	.20
27 Cal Ripken Jr.	5.00	2.00
28 Cal Ripken Sr. CO	.50	.20
29 Vic Rodriguez	.50	.20
30 Gary Roenicke	.50	.20
31 Ralph Rowe CO	.50	.20
32 Lenn Sakata	.50	.20
33 Larry Sheets	.50	.20
34 John Shelby		
35 Ken Singleton	.75	.30
36 Nate Snell	.50	.20
37 Sammy Stewart	.50	.20
38 Bill Swaggerty	.50	.20
39 Jim Traber	.50	.20
40 Tom Underwood	.50	.20
41 Jimmy Williams CO	.50	.20
42 Mike Young	.50	.20
43 The Bird(Mascot)	.50	.20
44 Memorial Stadium	.50	.20

1985 Orioles Health

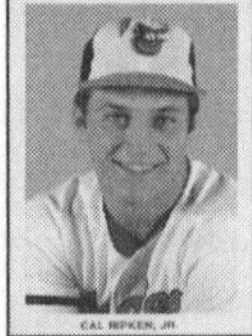

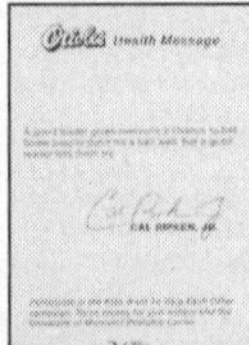

This 20-card set features color player portraits that measure approximately 3 1/2" by 5 1/4" in a white border. The backs carry a "Health Message" and the player's signature above his name. Some of the players have two cards with the same picture but a different health message on the back. Cal Ripken Jr. has three cards with three different health messages. The cards are unnumbered and checklisted below in alphabetical order. A set in considered complete with any one card of the players for whom more than one card was issued.

	Nm-Mt	Ex-Mt
COMPLETE SET (20)	10.00	4.00
1 Don Aase	.25	.10
2 Mike Boddicker (2)	.50	.20
3 Storm Davis	.25	.10
4 Rick Dempsey (2)	.50	.20
5 Ken Dixon	.25	.10
6 Jim Dwyer	.25	.10
7 Mike Flanagan (2)	.50	.20
8 Lee Lacy	.25	.10
9 Fred Lynn (2)	.50	.20
10 Dennis Martinez	.75	.30
11 Tippy Martinez	.25	.10
12 Scott McGregor	.25	.10
13 Eddie Murray (2)	2.50	1.00
14 Floyd Rayford (2)	.25	.10
15 Cal Ripken Jr. (3)	5.00	2.00
16 Larry Sheets (2)	.25	.10
17 John Shelby	.25	.10
18 Earl Weaver MG	1.00	.40
19 Alan Wiggins	.25	.10
20 Mike Young	.25	.10

1985 Orioles Postcards

This 38-card set features glossy color portraits of the Baltimore Orioles with white borders and measures approximately 3 1/2" by 5 1/4". The backs carry a postcard format and Memorial Stadium address. The cards are unnumbered and checklisted below in alphabetical order.

	Nm-Mt	Ex-Mt
COMPLETE SET (38)	25.00	10.00
1 Don Aase	.50	.20
2 Mike Boddicker	.75	.30
3 Al Bumbry	.50	.20
4 Fritz Connally	.50	.20
5 Terry Crowley	.50	.20
6 Rich Dauer	.50	.20
7 Rick Dempsey	.75	.30
8 Ken Dixon	.50	.20
9 Mike Flanagan	.75	.30
10 Ellie Hendricks CO (Darker portrait)	.50	.20
11 Ellie Hendricks CO	.50	.20
12 Lee Lacy	.50	.20
13 Fred Lynn	.75	.30
14 Fred Lynn	.75	.30
15 Dennis Martinez	1.00	.40
16 Tippy Martinez	.50	.20
17 Scott McGregor	.50	.20
18 Ray Miller CO	.50	.20
19 Eddie Murray	2.50	1.00
20 Joe Nolan	.50	.20
21 Al Pardo	.50	.20
22 Floyd Rayford	.50	.20
23 Floyd Rayford (Darker portrait)	.50	.20
24 Cal Ripken Jr.	5.00	2.00
25 Cal Ripken Sr. CO	.50	.20
26 Frank Robinson CO	1.50	.60
27 Gary Roenicke	.50	.20
28 Ken Rowe	.50	.20
29 Lenn Sakata	.50	.20
30 Larry Sheets	.50	.20
31 John Shelby	.50	.20
32 Nate Snell	.50	.20
33 Sammy Stewart	.50	.20
34 Bill Swaggerty	.50	.20
35 Alan Wiggins	.50	.20
36 Jimmy Williams CO	.50	.20
37 Mike Young	.50	.20
38 Memorial Stadium	.50	.20

1986 Orioles Greats TCMA

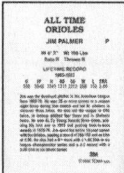

This 12-card standard-size set features some of the best Baltimore Orioles since 1954. The fronts display player photos, his name as well as a position identification. The back has vital statistics, career totals and a biography.

	Nm-Mt	Ex-Mt
COMPLETE SET (12)	6.00	2.40
1 Hoyt Wilhelm	1.00	.40
2 Hank Bauer MG	.50	.20
3 Jim Palmer	1.50	.60
4 Dave McNally	.50	.20
5 Paul Blair	.25	.10
6 Gus Triandos	.25	.10
7 Frank Robinson	1.50	.60
8 Ken Singleton	.25	.10
9 Luis Aparicio	1.00	.40
10 Brooks Robinson	1.50	.60
11 John "Boog" Powell	1.00	.40
12 Dave Johnson	.50	.20

1986 Orioles Health

This 21-card set features color player portraits that measure approximately 3 1/2" by 5 1/4" in a white border. The backs carry a "Health Message" and the player's signature above his name. Some of the players have two or three cards with the same picture but a different health message on the back. One of Mike Flanagan's cards displays a "Safety Message." The cards are unnumbered and checklisted below in alphabetical order. The complete set price includes only one card for each player who have mulitple cards issued.

	Nm-Mt	Ex-Mt
COMPLETE SET (21)	18.00	7.25
1 Don Aase (2)	.50	.20
2 Mike Boddicker (2)	.50	.20
3 Storm Davis (2)	.50	.20
4 Rick Dempsey (2)	.75	.30
5 Ken Dixon	.50	.20
6 Jim Dwyer	.50	.20
7 Mike Flanagan (3)	.75	.30
8 Lee Lacy	.50	.20
9 Fred Lynn (2)	.75	.30
10 Dennis Martinez	1.00	.40
11 Tippy Martinez	.50	.20
12 Scott McGregor	.50	.20
13 Eddie Murray (3)	2.50	1.00
14 Floyd Rayford (2)	.50	.20
15 Cal Ripken Jr. (3)	5.00	2.00
16 Larry Sheets (2)	.50	.20
17 John Shelby	.50	.20
18 Nate Snell	.50	.20
19 Earl Weaver MG	1.50	.60
20 Alan Wiggins	.50	.20
21 Mike Young (2)	.50	.20

1986 Orioles Postcards

This 27-card set features glossy color portraits of the Baltimore Orioles with white borders and measures approximately 3 1/2" by 5 1/4". The backs carry a postcard format and Memorial Stadium address. The cards are unnumbered and checklisted below in alphabetical order.

	Nm-Mt	Ex-Mt
COMPLETE SET (27)	20.00	8.00
1 Juan Beniquez	.50	.20
2 Mike Boddicker	.50	.20
3 Juan Bonilla	.50	.20
4 Rich Bordi	.50	.20
5 Storm Davis	.50	.20
6 Rick Dempsey	.75	.30
7 Ken Dixon	.50	.20
8 Jim Dwyer	.50	.20
9 Brad Havens	.50	.20
10 Elrod Hendricks CO	.50	.20
11 Scott McGregor	.50	.20
12 Eddie Murray	2.50	1.00
13 Tom O'Malley	.50	.20
14 Floyd Rayford	.50	.20
15 Cal Ripken Jr.	5.00	2.00
16 Cal Ripken Sr. CO	.50	.20
17 Frank Robinson CO	1.50	.60
18 Ken Rowe CO	.50	.20
19 Larry Sheets	.50	.20
20 John Shelby	.50	.20
21 Nate Snell	.50	.20
22 Jim Traber	.50	.20
23 Earl Weaver MG	1.50	.60
24 Alan Wiggins	.50	.20
25 Jimmy Williams CO	.50	.20
26 Mike Young	.50	.20
27 The Bird(Mascot)	.50	.20

1987 Orioles French Bray

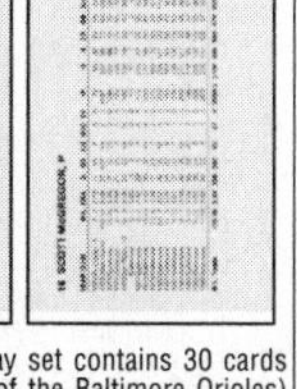

The 1987 French Bray set contains 30 cards (featuring members of the Baltimore Orioles) measuring approximately 2 1/4" by 3". The fronts have facial photos with white and orange borders; the horizontally oriented backs are white and feature career stats. The cards were given away in perforated sheet form on Photo Card Day at the Orioles home game on July 26, 1987. A large team photo was also included as one of the three panels in this perforated card set. The cards are unnumbered except for uniform number.

	Nm-Mt	Ex-Mt
COMPLETE SET (30)	20.00	8.00
2 Alan Wiggins	.25	.10
3 Bill Ripken	.50	.20
6 Floyd Rayford	.25	.10
7 Cal Ripken Sr. MG	.25	.10
8 Cal Ripken Jr.	10.00	4.00
9 Jim Dwyer	.25	.10
10 Terry Crowley CO	.25	.10
15 Terry Kennedy	.25	.10
16 Scott McGregor	.25	.10
18 Larry Sheets	.25	.10
19 Fred Lynn	.50	.20
20 Frank Robinson CO	2.00	.80
24 Dave Schmidt	.25	.10
25 Ray Knight	.25	.10
27 Lee Lacy	.25	.10
31 Mark Wiley CO	.25	.10
32 Mark Williamson	.25	.10
33 Eddie Murray	3.00	1.20
38 Ken Gerhart	.25	.10
39 Ken Dixon	.25	.10
40 Jimmy Williams CO	.25	.10
42 Mike Griffin	.25	.10
43 Mike Young	.25	.10
44 Elrod Hendricks CO	.25	.10
45 Eric Bell	.25	.10
46 Mike Flanagan	.50	.20
49 Tom Niedenfuer	.25	.10
52 Mike Boddicker	.50	.20
54 John Habyan	.25	.10
57 Tony Arnold	.25	.10

1987 Orioles Postcards

This 45-card set features glossy color portraits of the Baltimore Orioles with white borders and measures approximately 3 1/2" by 5 1/4". The backs carry a postcard format and Memorial Stadium address. The Mike Griffin, Mike Hart, Bill Ripken and Ron Washington cards display black-and-white player photos and have blank backs. There is another Bill Ripken card with a glossy front but it also has a blank back. All the aforementioned blank backed cards were issued late in 1987 and are in shorter supply. Hence, they are labeled with a SP designation below. The cards are unnumbered and checklisted below in alphabetical order.

	Nm-Mt	Ex-Mt
COMPLETE SET (45)	40.00	16.00
COMMON CARD (1-45)	.50	.20
COMMON SP	4.00	1.60
1 Don Aase	.50	.20
2 Tony Arnold	.50	.20
3 Jeff Ballard	.50	.20
4 Eric Bell	.50	.20
5 Mike Boddicker	.75	.30
6 Rick Burleson	.50	.20
7 Terry Crowley CO	.50	.20
8 Luis De Leon	.50	.20
9 Ken Dixon	.50	.20
10 Jim Dwyer	.50	.20
11 Mike Flanagan	.75	.30
12 Ken Gerhart	.50	.20
13 Rene Gonzales	.50	.20
14 Mike Griffin SP	4.00	1.60
15 John Habyan	.50	.20
16 Mike Hart SP	4.00	1.60
17 Elrod Hendricks CO	.50	.20
18 Elrod Hendricks (Larger bottom margin)	.50	.20
19 Terry Kennedy	.50	.20
20 Ray Knight	.50	.20
21 Lee Lacy	.50	.20
22 Fred Lynn	.75	.30
23 Scott McGregor	.50	.20
24 Eddie Murray	3.00	1.20
25 Tom Niedenfuer	.50	.20
26 Jack O'Connor	.50	.20
27 Floyd Rayford	.50	.20
28 Bill Ripken (2) SP	5.00	2.00
29 Cal Ripken Jr.	5.00	2.00
30 Cal Ripken Sr. MG	.50	.20
31 Brooks Robinson	1.50	.60
32 Frank Robinson CO	1.50	.60
33 Dave Schmidt	.50	.20
34 Larry Sheets	.50	.20
35 John Shelby	.50	.20
36 Dave Van Gorder	.50	.20
37 Ron Washington SP	4.00	1.60
38 Alan Wiggins	.50	.20
39 Mark Wiley CO	.50	.20
40 Jimmy Williams CO	.50	.20
41 Mark Williamson	.50	.20
42 Mike Young	.50	.20
43 The Bird(Mascot)	.50	.20
44 Memorial Stadium	.50	.20

1988 Orioles French Bray

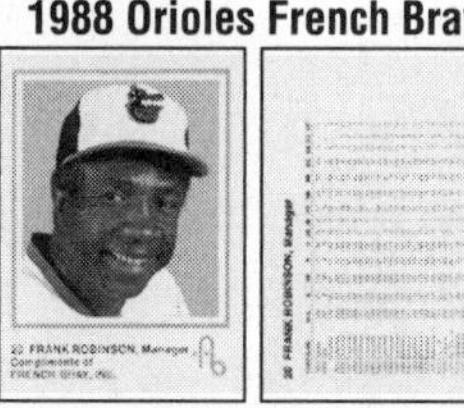

This set was distributed as a perforated set of 30 full-color cards attached to a large team photo on July 31, 1988, the Baltimore Orioles' Photo Card Day. The cards measure approximately 2 1/4" by 3 1/16". Card backs are simply done in black and white with statistics but no narrative or any personal information. Cards are unnumbered except for uniform number. Card front have a thin orange inner border and have the French Bray (Printing and Graphic Communication) logo in the lower right corner.

	Nm-Mt	Ex-Mt
COMPLETE SET (30)	15.00	6.00
2 Don Buford CO	.25	.10
6 Joe Orsulak	.25	.10
7 Bill Ripken	.50	.20
8 Cal Ripken	8.00	3.20
9 Jim Dwyer	.25	.10
10 Terry Crowley CO	.25	.10
12 Mike Morgan	.25	.10
14 Mickey Tettleton	1.00	.40
15 Terry Kennedy	.25	.10
17 Pete Stanicek	.25	.10
18 Larry Sheets	.25	.10
19 Fred Lynn	.75	.30
20 Frank Robinson MG	1.00	.40
23 Oswald Peraza	.25	.10
24 Dave Schmidt	.25	.10
25 Rick Schu	.25	.10
28 Jim Traber	.25	.10
31 Herm Starrette CO	.25	.10
33 Eddie Murray	2.50	1.00
34 Jeff Ballard	.25	.10
38 Ken Gerhart	.25	.10
40 Minnie Mendoza CO	.25	.10
41 Don Aase	.25	.10
44 Elrod Hendricks CO	.25	.10
47 John Hart CO	.25	.10
48 Jose Bautista	.25	.10
49 Tom Niedenfuer	.25	.10
52 Mike Boddicker	.50	.20
53 Jay Tibbs	.25	.10
88 Rene Gonzales	.25	.10

1988 Orioles Postcards

This 42-card set features glossy color portraits of the Baltimore Orioles with white borders and measures approximately 3 1/2" by 5 1/4". The backs carry a postcard format and Memorial Stadium address. The cards are unnumbered and checklisted below in alphabetical order. Similar to 1987; a couple of players were issued later in the year in Black and White with Blank Backs. In 1988, it was Brady Anderson and Joe Durham.

	Nm-Mt	Ex-Mt
COMPLETE SET (42)	35.00	14.00
COMMON CARD (1-42)	.50	.20
COMMON SP	4.00	1.60
1 Don Aase	.50	.20
2 Brady Anderson SP	8.00	3.20
3 Jeff Ballard	.50	.20
4 Jose Bautista	.50	.20
5 Eric Bell	.50	.20
6 Mike Boddicker	.50	.20
7 Don Buford CO	.50	.20
8 Terry Crowley CO	.50	.20
9 Joe Durham CO SP	4.00	1.60
10 Jim Dwyer	.50	.20
11 Ken Gerhart	.50	.20
12 Rene Gonzales	.50	.20
13 John Habyan	.50	.20
14 John Hart CO	.50	.20
15 Ellie Hendricks CO	.50	.20
16 Keith Hughes	.50	.20
17 Terry Kennedy	.50	.20
18 Fred Lynn	.75	.30
19 Scott McGregor	.50	.20
20 Minnie Mendoza CO	.50	.20
21 Mike Morgan	.50	.20
21 Tom Niedenfuer	.50	.20
22 Eddie Murray	2.50	1.00
23 John Oates CO	.50	.20
24 Joe Orsulak	.50	.20
25 Oswald Peraza	.50	.20
26 Bill Ripken	.50	.20
27 Cal Ripken Jr.	5.00	2.00
28 Cal Ripken Sr. MG	.50	.20
29 Frank Robinson CO	1.50	.60
30 Wade Rowdon	.50	.20
31 Dave Schmidt	.50	.20
32 Rick Schu	.50	.20
33 Larry Sheets	.50	.20
34 Doug Sisk	.50	.20
35 Pete Stanicek	.50	.20
36 Herm Starrette CO	.50	.20
37 Mickey Tettleton	1.50	.60
38 Mark Thurmond	.50	.20
39 Jay Tibbs	.50	.20
40 Jim Traber	.50	.20
41 Mark Williamson	.50	.20
42 The Bird(Mascot)	.50	.20
43 Memorial Stadium	.50	.20

1989 Orioles French Bray

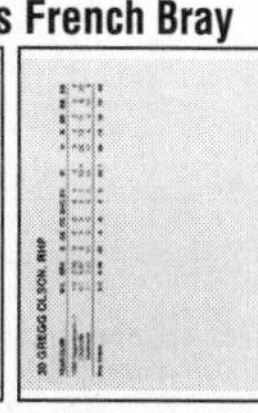

The 1989 French Bray/WWF Orioles set contains 31 cards measuring approximately 2 1/4" by 3". The fronts have facial photos with orange and white borders; the backs are white and feature career stats. The set was given away at a Baltimore home game on May 12, 1989. The cards are numbered by the players' uniform numbers.

	Nm-Mt	Ex-Mt
COMPLETE SET (32)	12.00	4.80
3 Bill Ripken	.25	.10
6 Joe Orsulak	.25	.10
7 Cal Ripken Sr. CO	.25	.10
8 Cal Ripken Jr.	5.00	2.00
9 Brady Anderson	2.50	1.00
10 Steve Finley	2.50	1.00
11 Craig Worthington	.25	.10
12 Mike Devereaux	.25	.10
14 Mickey Tettleton	.75	.30
15 Randy Milligan	.25	.10
16 Phil Bradley	.25	.10
18 Bob Milacki	.25	.10
19 Larry Sheets	.25	.10
20 Frank Robinson MG	1.00	.40
21 Mark Thurmond	.25	.10
23 Kevin Hickey	.25	.10
24 Dave Schmidt	.25	.10
28 Jim Traber	.25	.10
29 Jeff Ballard	.25	.10
30 Gregg Olson	1.00	.40
31 Al Jackson CO	.25	.10
32 Mark Williamson	.25	.10
36 Bob Melvin	.50	.20
37 Brian Holton	.25	.10
40 Tom McCraw CO	.25	.10
42 Pete Harnisch	.50	.20
43 Francisco Melendez	.25	.10
44 Elrod Hendricks CO	.25	.10
46 Johnny Oates CO	.25	.10
48 Jose Bautista	.25	.10
88 Rene Gonzales	.25	.10
NNO Sponsor ad	.25	.10

1989 Orioles Postcards

This 41-card set features glossy color portraits of the Baltimore Orioles with white borders and measures approximately 3 1/2" by 5 1/4". The backs carry a postcard format and Memorial Stadium address. The Dave Johnson, Ben McDonald, and Curt Schilling cards display black-and-white player photos with blank backs. Similar to the previous two years, these cards were printed later in the year and are shorter supply. Therefore, they are marked as SP's below. The cards are unnumbered and checklisted below in alphabetical order.

	Nm-Mt	Ex-Mt
COMPLETE SET (41)	40.00	16.00
COMMON CARD (1-41)	.50	.20
COMMON SP	4.00	1.60
1 Brady Anderson	1.50	.60
2 Jeff Ballard	.50	.20
3 Jose Bautista	.50	.20
4 Phil Bradley	.50	.20
5 Mike Devereaux	.50	.20
6 Joe Durham CO	.50	.20
7 Steve Finley	1.50	.60
8 Rene Gonzales	.50	.20
9 John Habyan	.50	.20
10 Pete Harnisch	.50	.20
11 Elrod Hendricks CO	.50	.20
12 Kevin Hickey	.50	.20
13 Brian Holton	.50	.20
14 Al Jackson CO	.50	.20
15 Dave Johnson SP	4.00	1.60
16 Tom McCraw CO	.50	.20
17 Ben McDonald SP	5.00	2.00
18 Bob Melvin	.50	.20
19 Bob Milacki	.50	.20
20 Randy Milligan	.50	.20
21 Curt Motton CO	.50	.20
22 John Oates CO	.50	.20
23 Gregg Olson	1.50	.60
24 Joe Orsulak	.50	.20
25 Bill Ripken	.50	.20
26 Cal Ripken Jr.	6.00	2.40
27 Cal Ripken Sr. CO	.50	.20
28 Frank Robinson MG	1.50	.60
29 Curt Schilling SP	15.00	6.00
30 Dave Schmidt	.50	.20
31 Rick Schu	.50	.20
32 Larry Sheets	.50	.20
33 Pete Stanicek	.50	.20
34 Mickey Tettleton	1.00	.40
35 Mark Thurmond	.50	.20
36 Jay Tibbs	.50	.20
37 Jim Traber	.50	.20
38 Mark Williamson	.50	.20
39 Craig Worthington	.50	.20
40 The Bird(Mascot)	.50	.20
41 Memorial Stadium	.50	.20

1990 Orioles Postcards

This 19-card set features glossy color portraits of the Baltimore Orioles with white borders and measures approximately 3 1/2" by 5 1/4". The backs display a postcard format and Memorial Stadium address. Many of the cards in this set were issued in Black and White with blank backs. They are notated below with BW. The cards are unnumbered and checklisted below in alphabetical order.

	Nm-Mt	Ex-Mt
COMPLETE SET (19)	50.00	15.00
COMMON CARD (1-19)	.50	.15
COMMON BW	3.00	.90
1 Jeff Ballard BW	3.00	.90
2 Rex Barney ANN BW	4.00	1.20
3 Marty Brown	.50	.15
4 Joe Durham BW	3.00	.90
5 Steve Finley	1.50	.45
6 Dave Gallagher BW	3.00	.90
7 Rene Gonzales	.50	.15
8 Dick Hall BW	3.00	.90
9 Kevin Hickey BW	3.00	.90
10 Sam Horn	.50	.15
11 Tim Hulett	.50	.15
12 Dave Johnson	.50	.15
13 Dave Johnson BW	3.00	.90
14 Ron Kittle BW	3.00	.90
15 Brad Komminsk	.50	.15
16 Ben McDonald BW	4.00	1.20
17 Jose Mesa BW	4.00	1.20
18 Jon Miller ANN BW	4.00	1.20
19 Randy Milligan	.50	.15
20 Randy Milligan BW	3.00	.90
21 John Mitchell	.50	.15
22 Joe Price	.50	.15
23 Bill Ripken BW	3.00	.90
24 Frank Robinson	1.50	.45
25 Dave Segui UER (Spelled Sequi on front)	1.50	.45
26 Anthony Telford BW	3.00	.90
27 Jay Tibbs	.50	.15
28 Mickey Weston	.50	.15
29 Orioles Ball Girls BW	4.00	1.20
30 The Bird(Mascot)	.50	.15
31 Memorial Stadium	.50	.15

1991 Orioles Crown

This 501-card set was produced by the Baltimore Orioles in conjunction with Crown Gasoline Stations and Coca-Cola. The cards measure approximately 2 1/2" by 3 1/8" and feature every Oriole player in the team's modern history (1954-1991). The cards were issued in four series, with ten twelve-card sheets per set. The first set was given away at the Orioles May 17th game against the California Angels, and the following day the set went on sale at Baltimore area Crown gasoline stations for 1.99 with an eight gallon fill-up. The second set was given away at the Orioles June 28th game against the Boston Red Sox, and again it went on sale the following day at Crown gasoline stations. The third set was given away at the Orioles August 11th game against the Chicago White Sox and went on sale on the same day. The fourth set went on sale at Crown gasoline stations on September 16. The cards are arranged alphabetically by player and checklisted below accordingly.

	Nm-Mt	Ex-Mt
COMPLETE SET (501)	60.00	18.00
1 Don Aase	.10	.03
2 Cal Abrams	.10	.03
3 Jerry Adair	.10	.03
4 Bobby Adams	.10	.03
5 Mike Adamson	.10	.03
6 Jay Aldrich	.10	.03
7 Bob Alexander	.10	.03
8 Doyle Alexander	.25	.07
9 Brady Anderson	1.00	.30
10 John Anderson	.10	.03
11 Mike Anderson	.10	.03
12 Luis Aparicio	1.50	.45
13 Tony Arnold	.10	.03
14 Bobby Avila	.25	.07
15 Benny Ayala	.10	.03

16 Bob Bailor .10 .03
17 Frank Baker .10 .03
18 Jeff Ballard .10 .03
19 George Bamberger .25 .07
20 Steve Barber .25 .07
21 Ray(Buddy) Barker .10 .03
22 Ed Barnowski .10 .03
23 Jose Bautista .10 .03
24 Don Baylor .75 .23
25 Charlie Beamon .10 .03
26 Fred Beene .10 .03
27 Mark Belanger .50 .15
28 Eric Bell .10 .03
29 Juan Bell .10 .03
30 Juan Beniquez .10 .03
31 Neil Berry .10 .03
32 Frank Bertaina .10 .03
33 Fred Besana .10 .03
34 Vern Bickford .10 .03
35 Babe Birrer .10 .03
36 Paul Blair .50 .15
37 Curt Blefary .25 .07
38 Mike Blyzka .10 .03
39 Mike Boddicker .25 .07
40 Juan Bonilla .10 .03
41 Bob Bonner .10 .03
42 Dan Boone .10 .03
43 Rich Bordi .10 .03
44 Dave Boswell .10 .03
45 Sam Bowens .10 .03
46 Bob Boyd .10 .03
47 Gene Brabender .10 .03
48 Phil Bradley .10 .03
49 Jackie Brandt .10 .03
50 Marv Breeding .10 .03
51 Jim Bridewester .10 .03
52 Nelson Briles .25 .07
53 Dick Brown .10 .03
54 Hal Brown .10 .03
55 Larry Brown .10 .03
56 Mark Brown .10 .03
57 Marty Brown .10 .03
58 George Brunet .10 .03
59 Don Buford .25 .07
60 Al Bumbry .25 .07
61 Wally Bunker .25 .07
62 Leo Burke .10 .03
63 Rick Burleson .25 .07
64 Pete Burnside .10 .03
65 Jim Busby .10 .03
66 John Buzhardt .10 .03
67 Harry Byrd .10 .03
68 Enos Cabell .10 .03
69 Chico Carrasquel .25 .07
70 Camilo Carreon .10 .03
71 Foster Castleman .10 .03
72 Wayne Causey .10 .03
73 Art Ceccarelli .10 .03
74 Bob Chakales .10 .03
75 Tony Chevez .10 .03
76 Tom Chism .10 .03
77 Gino Cimoli .10 .03
78 Gil Coan .10 .03
79 Rich Coggins .10 .03
80 Joe Coleman .10 .03
81 Rip Coleman .10 .03
82 Fritz Connally .10 .03
83 Sandy Consuegra .10 .03
84 Doug Corbett .10 .03
85 Mark Corey .10 .03
86 Clint Courtney .10 .03
87 Billy Cox .25 .07
88 Dave Criscione .10 .03
89 Terry Crowley .10 .03
90 Todd Cruz .10 .03
91 Mike Cuellar .50 .15
92 Angie Dagres .10 .03
93 Clay Dalrymple .10 .03
94 Rich Dauer .10 .03
95 Jerry DaVanon .10 .03
96 Butch Davis .10 .03
97 Storm Davis .25 .07
98 Tommy Davis .50 .15
99 Doug DeCinces .25 .07
100 Luis DeLeon .10 .03
101 Ike Delock .10 .03
102 Rick Dempsey .25 .07
103 Mike Devereaux .50 .15
104 Chuck Diering .10 .03
105 Gordon Dillard .10 .03
106 Bill Dillman .10 .03
107 Mike Dimmel .10 .03
108 Ken Dixon .10 .03
109 Pat Dobson .25 .07
110 Tom Dodd .10 .03
111 Harry Dorish .10 .03
112 Moe Drabowsky .25 .07
113 Dick Drago .10 .03
114 Walt Dropo .25 .07
115 Tom Dukes .10 .03
116 Dave Duncan .25 .07
117 Ryne Duren .50 .15
118 Joe Durham .10 .03
119 Jim Dwyer .10 .03
120 Jim Dyck .10 .03
121 Mike Epstein .25 .07
122 Chuck Essegian .10 .03
123 Chuck Estrada .10 .03
124 Andy Etchebarren .10 .03
125 Hoot Evers .10 .03
126 Ed Farmer .10 .03
127 Chico Fernandez .10 .03
128 Don Ferrarese .10 .03
129 Jim Finigan .10 .03
130 Steve Finley .75 .23
131 Mike Fiore .10 .03
132 Eddie Fisher .10 .03
133 Jack Fisher .10 .03
134 Tom Fisher .10 .03
135 Mike Flanagan .50 .15
136 John Flinn .10 .03
137 Bobby Floyd .10 .03
138 Hank Foiles .10 .03
139 Dan Ford .10 .03
140 Dave Ford .10 .03
141 Mike Fornieles .10 .03
142 Howie Fox .10 .03
143 Tito Francona .25 .07
144 Joe Frazier .10 .03
145 Roger Freed .10 .03
146 Jim Fridley .10 .03
147 Jim Fuller .10 .03
148 Joe Gaines .10 .03
149 Vinicio(Chico) Garcia .10 .03
150 Kiko Garcia .10 .03
151 Billy Gardner .10 .03
152 Wayne Garland .10 .03
153 Tommy Gastall .10 .03
154 Jim Gentile .50 .15
155 Ken Gerhart .10 .03
156 Paul Gilliford .10 .03
157 Joe Ginsberg .10 .03
158 Leo Gomez .10 .03
159 Rene Gonzales .10 .03
160 Billy Goodman .25 .07
161 Dan Graham .10 .03
162 Ted Gray .10 .03
163 Gene Green .10 .03
164 Lenny Green .10 .03
165 Bobby Grich .50 .15
166 Nuje Griffin .10 .03
167 Ross Grimsley .10 .03
168 Wayne Gross .10 .03
169 Glenn Gulliver .10 .03
170 Jackie Gutierrez .10 .03
171 John Habyan .10 .03
172 Harvey Haddix .25 .07
173 Bob Hale .10 .03
174 Dick Hall .10 .03
175 Bert Hamric .10 .03
176 Larry Haney .10 .03
177 Ron Hansen .25 .07
178 Jim Hardin .10 .03
179 Larry Harlow .10 .03
180 Pete Harnisch .25 .07
181 Tommy Harper .25 .07
182 Bob Harrison .10 .03
183 Roric Harrison .10 .03
184 Jack Harshman .10 .03
185 Mike Hart .10 .03
186 Pete Hartzell .10 .03
187 Grady Hatton .10 .03
188 Brad Havens .10 .03
189 Drungo Hazewood .10 .03
190 Jehosie Heard .10 .03
191 Mel Held .10 .03
192 Woodie Held .10 .03
193 Ellie Hendricks .25 .07
194 Leo Hernandez .10 .03
195 Whitey Herzog .75 .23
196 Kevin Hickey .10 .03
197 Billy Hoeft .10 .03
198 Chris Hoiles .50 .15
199 Fred Holdsworth .10 .03
200 Brian Holton .10 .03
201 Ken Holtzman .25 .07
202 Don Hood .10 .03
203 Sam Horn .10 .03
204 Art Houtteman .25 .07
205 Bruce Howard .10 .03
206 Rex Hudler .25 .07
207 Phil Huffman .10 .03
208 Keith Hughes .10 .03
209 Mark Huismann .10 .03
210 Tim Hulett .10 .03
211 Billy Hunter .10 .03
212 Dave Huppert .10 .03
213 Jim Hutto .10 .03
214 Dick Hyde .10 .03
215 Grant Jackson .25 .07
216 Lou Jackson .10 .03
217 Reggie Jackson 5.00 1.50
218 Ron Jackson UER .10 .03
Wrong player pictured
219 Jesse Jefferson .10 .03
220 Stan Jefferson .10 .03
221 Bob Johnson .10 .03
222 Connie Johnson .10 .03
223 Darrell Johnson .10 .03
224 Dave Johnson .10 .03
225 Davey Johnson .75 .23
226 David Johnson .10 .03
227 Don Johnson .10 .03
228 Ernie Johnson .25 .07
229 Gordon Jones .10 .03
230 Ricky Jones .10 .03
231 O'Dell Jones .10 .03
232 Sam Jones .25 .07
233 George Kell 1.50 .45
234 Frank Kellert .10 .03
235 Pat Kelly .25 .07
236 Bob Kennedy .25 .07
237 Terry Kennedy .25 .07
238 Joe Kerrigan .10 .03
239 Mike Kinnunen .10 .03
240 Willie Kirkland .10 .03
241 Ron Kittle .25 .07
242 Billy Klaus .10 .03
243 Ray Knight .50 .15
244 Darold Knowles .10 .03
245 Dick Kokos .10 .03
246 Brad Komminsk .10 .03
247 Dave Koslo .10 .03
248 Wayne Krenchicki .10 .03
249 Lou Kretlow .10 .03
250 Dick Kryhoski .10 .03
251 Bob Kuzava .10 .03
252 Lee Lacy .10 .03
253 Hobie Landrith .10 .03
254 Tito Landrum .10 .03
255 Don Larsen .50 .15
256 Charlie Lau .10 .03
257 Jim Lehew .10 .03
258 Ken Lehman .10 .03
259 Don Lenhardt .10 .03
260 Dave Leonhard .10 .03
261 Don Leppert .10 .03
262 Dick Littlefield .10 .03
263 Charlie Locke .10 .03
264 Whitey Lockman .25 .07
265 Billy Loes .25 .07
266 Ed Lopat .50 .15
267 Carlos Lopez .10 .03
268 Marcelino Lopez .10 .03
269 John Lowenstein .10 .03
270 Steve Luebber .10 .03
271 Dick Luebke .10 .03
272 Fred Lynn .50 .15
273 Bobby Mabe .10 .03
274 Elliott Maddox .10 .03
275 Hank Majeski .10 .03
276 Roger Marquis .10 .03
277 Freddie Marsh .10 .03
278 Jim Marshall .10 .03
279 Morrie Martin .10 .03
280 Dennis Martinez .75 .23
281 Tippy Martinez .25 .07
282 Tom Matchick .10 .03
283 Charlie Maxwell .25 .07
284 Dave May .10 .03
285 Lee May .50 .15
286 Rudy May .25 .07
287 Mike McCormick .25 .07
288 Ben McDonald .25 .07
289 Jim McDonald .10 .03
290 Scott McGregor .25 .07
291 Mickey McGuire .10 .03
292 Jeff McKnight .10 .03
293 Dave McNally .75 .23
294 Sam Mele .10 .03
295 Francisco Melendez .10 .03
296 Bob Melvin .25 .07
297 Jose Mesa .75 .23
298 Eddie Miksis .10 .03
299 Bob Milacki .10 .03
300 Bill Miller .10 .03
301 Dyar Miller .10 .03
302 John Miller .10 .03
303 Randy Miller .10 .03
304 Stu Miller .25 .07
305 Randy Milligan .10 .03
306 Paul Mirabella .10 .03
307 Willie Miranda .10 .03
308 John Mitchell .10 .03
309 Paul Mitchell .10 .03
310 Ron Moeller .10 .03
311 Bob Molinaro .10 .03
312 Ray Moore .10 .03
313 Andres Mora .10 .03
314 Jose Morales .10 .03
315 Keith Moreland .10 .03
316 Mike Morgan .10 .03
317 Dan Morogiello .10 .03
318 John Morris .10 .03
319 Les Moss .10 .03
320 Curt Motton .10 .03
321 Eddie Murray 5.00 1.50
322 Ray Murray .10 .03
323 Tony Muser .10 .03
324 Buster Narum .10 .03
325 Bob Nelson .10 .03
326 Roger Nelson .10 .03
327 Carl Nichols .10 .03
328 Dave Nicholson .10 .03
329 Tim Niedenfuer .10 .03
330 Bob Nieman .10 .03
331 Donell Nixon .10 .03
332 Joe Nolan .10 .03
333 Dickie Noles .10 .03
334 Tim Nordbrook .10 .03
335 Jim Northrup .25 .07
336 Jack O'Connor .10 .03
337 Billy O'Dell .25 .07
338 John O'Donoghue .10 .03
339 Tom O'Malley .10 .03
340 Johnny Oates .10 .03
341 Chuck Oertel .10 .03
342 Bob Oliver .10 .03
343 Gregg Olson .50 .15
344 John Orsino .10 .03
345 Joe Orsulak .10 .03
346 John Pacella .10 .03
347 Dave Pagan .10 .03
348 Erv Palica .10 .03
349 Jim Palmer 5.00 1.50
350 John Papa .10 .03
351 Milt Pappas .50 .15
352 Al Pardo .10 .03
353 Kelly Paris .10 .03
354 Mike Parrott .10 .03
355 Tom Patton .10 .03
356 Albie Pearson .25 .07
357 Orlando Pena .10 .03
358 Oswald Peraza .10 .03
359 Buddy Peterson .10 .03
360 Dave Philley .10 .03
361 Tom Phoebus .10 .03
362 Al Pilarcik .10 .03
363 Duane Pillette .10 .03
364 Lou Piniella .75 .23
(Pictured wearing a KC Royals cap)
365 Dave Pope .10 .03
366 Arnie Portocarrero .10 .03
367 Boog Powell .75 .23
368 Johnny Powers .10 .03
369 Carl Powis .10 .03
370 Joe Price .10 .03
371 Jim Pyburn .10 .03
372 Art Quirk .10 .03
373 Jamie Quirk .10 .03
374 Allan Ramirez .10 .03
375 Floyd Rayford .10 .03
376 Mike Reinbach .10 .03
377 Merv Rettenmund .10 .03
378 Bob Reynolds .10 .03
379 Del Rice .10 .03
(Wearing St. Louis Cardinals cap)
380 Pete Richert .10 .03
381 Jeff Rineer .10 .03
382 Bill Ripken .25 .07
383 Cal Ripken 10.00 3.00
384 Robin Roberts 1.50 .45
385 Brooks Robinson 5.00 1.50
386 Earl Robinson .10 .03
387 Eddie Robinson .10 .03
388 Frank Robinson 5.00 1.50
389 Sergio Robles .10 .03
390 Aurelio Rodriguez .10 .03
391 Vic Rodriguez .10 .03
392 Gary Roenicke .10 .03
393 Saul Rogovin .10 .03
(Wearing Philadelphia Phillies cap)
394 Wade Rowdon .10 .03
395 Ken Rowe .10 .03
396 Willie Royster .10 .03
397 Vic Roznovsky .10 .03
398 Ken Rudolph .10 .03
399 Lenn Sakata .10 .03
400 Chico Salmon .10 .03
401 Orlando Sanchez .10 .03
(Pictured wearing St. Louis Cardinals cap)
402 Bob Saverine .10 .03
403 Art Schallock .10 .03
404 Bill Scherrer .10 .03
(Wearing Detroit Tigers cap)
405 Curt Schilling 1.50 .45
406 Dave Schmidt .10 .03
407 Johnny Schmitz .10 .03
408 Jeff Schneider .10 .03
409 Rick Schu .10 .03
410 Mickey Scott .10 .03
411 Kal Segrist .10 .03
412 David Segui .50 .15
413 Al Severinsen .10 .03
414 Larry Sheets .25 .07
415 John Shelby .10 .03
416 Barry Shetrone .10 .03
417 Tom Shopay .10 .03
418 Bill Short .10 .03
419 Norm Siebern .25 .07
420 Nelson Simmons .10 .03
421 Ken Singleton .50 .15
422 Doug Sisk .10 .03
423 Dave Skaggs .10 .03
424 Lou Sleater .10 .03
425 Al Smith .25 .07
426 Billy Smith .10 .03
427 Hal Smith .10 .03
428 Mike(Texas) Smith .10 .03
429 Nate Smith .10 .03
430 Nate Snell .10 .03
431 Russ Snyder .10 .03
432 Don Stanhouse .10 .03
433 Pete Stanicek .10 .03
434 Herm Starrette .10 .03
435 John Stefaro .10 .03
436 Gene Stephens .10 .03
437 Vern Stephens .25 .07
438 Earl Stephenson .10 .03
439 Sammy Stewart .10 .03
440 Royle Stillman .10 .03
441 Wes Stock .10 .03
442 Tim Stoddard .25 .07
443 Dean Stone .10 .03
444 Jeff Stone .10 .03
445 Steve Stone .25 .07
446 Marlin Stuart .10 .03
447 Gordie Sundin .10 .03
448 Bill Swaggerty .10 .03
449 Willie Tasby .10 .03
450 Joe Taylor .10 .03
451 Dorn Taylor .10 .03
452 Anthony Telford .10 .03
453 Johnny Temple .25 .07
454 Mickey Tettleton .50 .15
455 Valmy Thomas .10 .03
(Wearing Philadelphia Phillies cap)
456 Bobby Thomson .75 .23
(Wearing Boston Red Sox cap)
457 Marv Throneberry .50 .15
458 Mark Thurmond .10 .03
459 Jay Tibbs .10 .03
460 Mike Torrez .25 .07
461 Jim Traber .10 .03
462 Gus Triandos .50 .15
463 Paul(Dizzy) Trout .25 .07
(Wearing Detroit Tigers cap)
464 Bob Turley .50 .15
465 Tom Underwood .10 .03
466 Fred Valentine .10 .03
467 Dave Van Gorder .10 .03
468 Dave Vineyard .10 .03
469 Ozzie Virgil .25 .07
470 Eddie Waitkus .25 .07
471 Greg Walker .10 .03
472 Jerry Walker .10 .03
473 Pete Ward .10 .03
474 Carl Warwick .10 .03
475 Ron Washington .10 .03
476 Eddie Watt .10 .03
477 Don Welchel .10 .03
478 George Werley .10 .03
479 Vic Wertz .25 .07
480 Wally Westlake .10 .03
(Wearing a Pittsburgh Pirates cap)
481 Mickey Weston .10 .03
482 Alan Wiggins .10 .03
483 Bill Wight .10 .03
484 Hoyt Wilhelm 1.50 .45
485 Dallas Williams .10 .03
486 Dick Williams .50 .15
487 Earl Williams .10 .03
488 Mark Williamson .10 .03
489 Jim Wilson .10 .03
490 Gene Woodling .25 .07
491 Craig Worthington .10 .03
492 Bobby Young .10 .03
493 Mike Young .10 .03
494 Frank Zupo .10 .03
495 George Zuverink .10 .03
496 Glenn Davis .25 .07
497 Dwight Evans .75 .23
498 Dave Gallagher .10 .03
499 Paul Kilgus .10 .03
500 Jeff Robinson .10 .03
501 Ernie Whitt .10 .03

1991 Orioles Postcards

This 36-card set features glossy color portraits of the Baltimore Orioles with white borders and measures approximately 3 1/2" by 5 1/4". The backs display a postcard format and Memorial Stadium address. The cards of Kevin Hickey, Chito Martinez, Jim Poole, and Anthony Telford carry black-and-white player photos and blank backs. The cards of Glenn Davis, Dwight Evans, and Bob Milacki are also available with blank backs. The cards are unnumbered and checklisted below in alphabetical order.

	Nm-Mt	Ex-Mt
COMPLETE SET (36)	30.00	9.00
COMMON CARD (1-36)	.50	.15
COMMON BW	3.00	.90
1 Brady Anderson	1.50	.45
2 Jeff Ballard	.50	.15
3 Juan Bell	.50	.15
4 Glenn Davis	.75	.23
5 Mike Devereaux	.50	.15
6 Dwight Evans	1.00	.30
7 Mike Flanagan	.75	.23
8 Todd Frohwirth	.50	.15
9 Leo Gomez	.50	.15
10 Elrod Hendricks CO	.50	.15
11 Kevin Hickey BW	3.00	.90
12 Chris Hoiles	.50	.15
13 Sam Horn	.50	.15
14 Dave Johnson	.50	.15
15 Paul Kilgus	.50	.15
16 Chito Martinez BW	3.00	.90
17 Ben McDonald	.50	.15
18 Jeff McKnight	.50	.15
19 Jose Mesa	.75	.23
20 Bob Milacki	.50	.15
21 Randy Milligan	.50	.15
22 Gregg Olson	.75	.23
23 Joe Orsulak	.50	.15
24 Mark Williamson	.50	.15
24 Jim Poole BW	3.00	.90
25 Bill Ripken	.50	.15
26 Cal Ripken Jr.	5.00	1.50
27 Brooks Robinson	1.50	.45
28 Frank Robinson	1.50	.45
29 Jeff Robinson	.50	.15
30 Dave Segui	.75	.23
31 Roy Smith	.50	.15
32 Anthony Telford BW	3.00	.90
33 Ernie Whitt	.50	.15
35 The Bird(Mascot)	.50	.15
36 Memorial Stadium	.50	.15

1992 Orioles Postcards

This 40-card set features borderless color photos of the Baltimore Orioles. The backs carry a message to the Orioles fans with a facsimile player signature. The backs of the cards of John Oates and Arthur Rhodes display a postcard format. The photo of Arthur Rhodes is black-and-white. The cards are unnumbered and checklisted below in alphabetical order.

	Nm-Mt	Ex-Mt
COMPLETE SET (40)	30.00	9.00
1 Brady Anderson (Running)	1.50	.45
2 Brady Anderson (With bat)	1.50	.45
3 Greg Biagini CO	.50	.15
4 Dick Bosman CO	.50	.15
5 Glenn Davis	.75	.23
6 Storm Davis	.50	.15
7 Rick Dempsey	.75	.23
8 Mike Devereaux	.50	.15
9 Mike Flanagan	.75	.23
10 Todd Frohwirth	.50	.15
11 Leo Gomez	.50	.15
12 Elrod Hendricks CO	.50	.15
13 Chris Hoiles	.50	.15
14 Sam Horn	.50	.15
15 Tim Hulett	.50	.15
16 Davey Lopes CO	.75	.23
17 Chito Martinez	.50	.15
18 Ben McDonald	.50	.15
19 Mark McLemore	.75	.23
20 Jose Mesa	.75	.23
21 Bob Milacki	.50	.15
22 Randy Milligan	.50	.15
23 Alan Mills	.50	.15
24 Mike Mussina (Arms extended)	3.00	.90
25 Mike Mussina (Beginning of pitch)	3.00	.90
26 John Oates MG	.50	.15
27 Gregg Olson	.75	.23
28 Joe Orsulak	.50	.15
29 Jim Poole	.50	.15
30 Arthur Rhodes	.50	.15
31 Bill Ripken	.50	.15
32 Cal Ripken Jr.	5.00	1.50
33 David Segui	.75	.23
34 Rick Sutcliffe	.75	.23
35 Jeff Tackett (End of batting swing)	.50	.15
36 Jeff Tackett (Batting)	.50	.15
37 Mark Williamson	.50	.15
38 Oriole Bird(Mascot)	.50	.15
39 Postcard Back	.50	.15
40 Camden Yards	.50	.15

1993 Orioles Crown Action Stand Ups

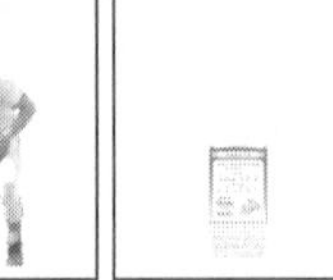

This set was issued in three distict series through Crown Petroleum service stations. These cards featured mainly retired Orioles players. Even though this set was issued in three distinct series, we have numbered them and priced them as one complete set. However, within each series, we have grouped the cards in alphabetical order.

	Nm-Mt	Ex-Mt
COMPLETE SET (12)	20.00	6.00
1 Rick Dempsey	1.50	.45
2 Jim Palmer	4.00	1.20
3 Brooks Robinson	4.00	1.20
4 Frank Robinson	4.00	1.20
5 Bobby Grich	1.50	.45
6 Tippy Martinez	1.00	.30
7 Cal Ripken Jr.	8.00	2.40
8 Earl Weaver MG	2.50	.75
9 Paul Blair	1.00	.30
10 Terry Crowley	1.00	.30
11 Boog Powell	2.50	.75
12 Ken Singleton	1.50	.45

1993 Orioles Postcards

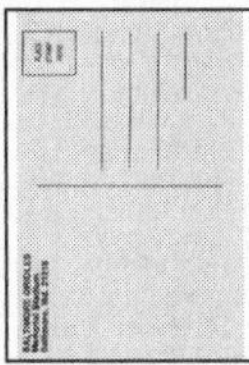

This 38-card set features borderless glossy color portraits and action photos of the Baltimore Orioles and measures approximately 3 1/2" by 5 1/4". The backs display a message to the Orioles fan with a facsimile signature. The photos of Paul Carey and Dick Hall are black-and-white. The cards of Dick Hall, Dave Johnson, Jim Palmer, and Harold Reynolds carry postcard format backs. The cards are unnumbered and checklisted below in alphabetical order.

	Nm-Mt	Ex-Mt
COMPLETE SET (38)	30.00	9.00
COMMON CARD (1-38)	.50	.15
COMMON BW	2.00	.60
1 Brady Anderson	1.50	.45
2 Harold Baines	1.00	.30
3 Greg Biagini CO	.50	.15
4 Dick Bosman CO	.50	.15
5 Damon Buford	.50	.15
6 Paul Carey BW	2.00	.60
7 Mike Devereaux (Hatless)	.50	.15
8 Mike Devereaux (Wearing batting helmet)	.50	.15
9 Mike Ferraro CO	.50	.15
10 Leo Gomez	.50	.15
11 Dick Hall BW	2.00	.60
12 Jeffrey Hammonds	.50	.15
13 Elrod Hendricks CO	.50	.15
14 Chris Hoiles	.50	.15
15 Dave Johnson	1.50	.45
16 Ben McDonald	.50	.15
17 Mark McLemore	.75	.23
18 Alan Mills	.50	.15
19 Jamie Moyer	1.00	.30
20 Mike Mussina	3.00	.90
21 Jerry Narron CO	.50	.15
22 Johnny Oates MG	.50	.15
23 Sherman Obando	.50	.15
24 Gregg Olson	.75	.23
25 Jim Palmer	2.50	.75
26 Brad Pennington	.50	.15
27 Jim Poole	.50	.15
28 Harold Reynolds (Portrait)	3.00	.90
29 Harold Reynolds (Batting)	.75	.23
30 Arthur Rhodes	.50	.15
31 Cal Ripken Jr.	5.00	1.50
32 David Segui	.75	.23
33 Rick Sutcliffe	.75	.23
34 Jeff Tackett	.50	.15
35 Fernando Valenzuela Wind-Up	1.00	.30
36 Fernando Valenzuela Follow-Thru	1.00	.30
37 Jack Voigt	.50	.15
38 Mark Williamson	.50	.15
39 Camden Yards	.50	.15

1994 Orioles Postcards

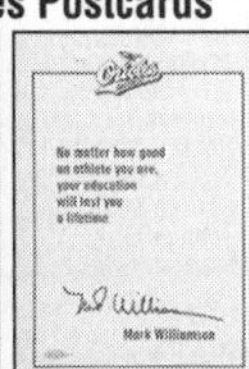

This 37-card set features borderless color photos of the Baltimore Orioles with a matte finish and measures approximately 3 1/2" by 5". The backs display one of 13 different messages with a facsimile signature printed below. The Paul Blair and Boog Powell cards carry black-and-white player photos with blank backs. The cards are unnumbered and checklisted below in alphabetical order.

	Nm-Mt	Ex-Mt
COMPLETE SET (37)	30.00	9.00
COMMON CARD (1-37)	.50	.15
COMMON BW	1.50	.45
1 Brady Anderson	1.50	.45
2 Harold Baines	1.00	.30
3 Greg Biagini CO	.50	.15
4 Paul Blair BW	1.50	.45
5 Tom Bolton	.50	.15
6 Dick Bosman CO	.50	.15
7 Don Buford CO	.50	.15
8 Mike Devereaux	.50	.15
9 Mark Eichhorn	.50	.15
10 Sid Fernandez	.50	.15
11 Leo Gomez	.50	.15
12 Jeffrey Hammonds	.75	.23
13 Elrod Hendricks CO	.50	.15
14 Chris Hoiles	.50	.15
15 Tim Hulett	.50	.15
16 Davey Lopes CO	.75	.23
17 Ben McDonald	.50	.15
18 Mark McLemore	.75	.23
19 Alan Mills	.50	.15
20 Jamie Moyer	1.00	.30
21 Mike Mussina	2.50	.75
22 Jerry Narron CO	.50	.15
23 Johnny Oates MG	.50	.15
24 Mike Oquist	.50	.15
25 Rafael Palmeiro	1.50	.45
26 Jim Poole	.50	.15
27 Boog Powell BW	3.00	.90
28 Arthur Rhodes	.50	.15
29 Cal Ripken Jr.	5.00	1.50
30 Chris Sabo	.50	.15
31 Lee Smith	.75	.23
32 Lonnie Smith	.50	.15
33 Jeff Tackett	.50	.15
34 Jack Voigt	.50	.15
35 Mark Williamson	.50	.15
36 The Oriole Bird Mascot	.50	.15
37 Camden Yards	.50	.15

1994 Orioles Program

This 108-card set includes all current and minor league players in the Baltimore Orioles' organization. The set was issued in twelve nine-card perforated sheets, with each sheet issued in game day programs which sold for 3.00. Reportedly only 21,000 of each unperforated sheet were produced. Each 7 1/2" by 10 1/2" sheet consists of nine standard-size cards. The cards are unnumbered and checklisted below in alphabetical order.

	Nm-Mt	Ex-Mt
COMPLETE SET (108)	30.00	9.00
1 Manny Alexander	.25	.07
2 Brady Anderson	1.00	.30
3 Matt Anderson	.25	.07
4 Harold Baines	1.00	.30
5 Miles Barnden	.25	.07
6 Kimera Bartee	.25	.07
7 Juan Bautista	.25	.07
8 Armando Benitez	1.00	.30
9 Joe Borowski	.25	.07
10 Brian Brewer	.25	.07
11 Brandon Bridgers	.25	.07
12 Cory Brown	.25	.07
13 Damon Buford	.25	.07
14 Clayton Byrne	.25	.07
15 Rocco Cafaro	.25	.07
16 Paul Carey	.25	.07
17 Carlos Chavez	.25	.07
18 Eric Chavez	.25	.07
19 Steve Chitren	.25	.07
20 Mike Cook	.25	.07
21 Shawn Curran	.25	.07
22 Kevin Curtis	.25	.07
23 Joey Dawley	.25	.07
24 Jim Dedrick	.25	.07
25 Cesar Devarez	.25	.07
26 Mike Devereaux	.25	.07
27 Brian DuBois	.25	.07
28 Keith Eaddy	.25	.07
29 Mark Eichhorn	.25	.07
30 Scott Emerson	.25	.07
31 Vaughn Eshelman	.25	.07
32 Craig Faulkner	.25	.07
33 Sid Fernandez	.50	.15
34 Rick Forney	.25	.07
35 Jim Foster	.25	.07
36 Jesse Garcia	.25	.07
37 Mike Garguilo	.25	.07
38 Rich Gedman	.25	.07
39 Leo Gomez	.25	.07
40 Rene Gonzales	.25	.07
41 Curtis Goodwin	.25	.07
42 Kris Gresham	.25	.07
43 Shane Hale	.25	.07
44 Jeffrey Hammonds	.50	.15
45 Jimmy Haynes	.25	.07
46 Chris Hoiles	.25	.07
47 Tim Hulett	.25	.07
48 Matt Jarvis	.25	.07
49 Scott Klingenbeck	.25	.07
50 Rick Krivda	.25	.07
51 David Lamb	.25	.07
52 Chris Lemp	.25	.07
53 T.R. Lewis	.25	.07
54 Bryan Link	.25	.07
55 John Lombardi	.25	.07
56 Rob Lukachyk	.25	.07
57 Calvin Maduro	.25	.07
58 Barry Manuel	.25	.07
59 Lincoln Martin	.25	.07
60 Scott McClain	.25	.07
61 Ben McDonald	.25	.07
62 Kevin McGehee	.25	.07
63 Mark McLemore	.50	.15
64 Miguel Mejia	.25	.07
65 Feliciano Mercedes	.25	.07
66 Jose Millares	.25	.07
67 Brent Miller	.25	.07
68 Alan Mills	.25	.07
69 Jamie Moyer	.75	.23
70 Mike Mussina	2.50	.75
71 Sherman Obando	.25	.07
72 Alex Ochoa	.25	.07
73 John O'Donoghue	.25	.07
74 Mike Oquist	.25	.07
75 Bo Ortiz	.25	.07
76 Billy Owens	.25	.07
77 Rafael Palmeiro	2.00	.60
78 Dave Paveloff	.25	.07
79 Brad Pennington	.25	.07
80 Bill Percibal	.25	.07
81 Jim Poole	.25	.07
82 Jay Powell	.50	.15
83 Arthur Rhodes	.25	.07
84 Matt Riemer	.25	.07
85 Cal Ripken	5.00	1.50
86 Kevin Ryan	.25	.07
87 Chris Sabo	.25	.07
88 Brian Sackinsky	.25	.07
89 Francisco Saneaux	.25	.07
90 Jason Satre	.25	.07
91 David Segui	.50	.15
92 Jose Serra	.25	.07
93 Larry Shenk	.25	.07
94 Lee Smith	.75	.23
95 Lonnie Smith	.50	.15
96 Mark Smith	.25	.07
97 Garrett Stephenson	.50	.15
98 Jeff Tackett	.25	.07
99 Brad Tyler	.25	.07
100 Pedro Ulises	.25	.07
101 Jack Voigt	.25	.07
102 Jim Walker	.25	.07
103 B.J. Waszgis	.25	.07
104 Jim Wawruck	.25	.07
105 Mel Wearing	.25	.07
106 Mark Williamson	.25	.07
107 Brian Wood	.25	.07
108 Greg Zaun	.25	.07

1994 Orioles U.S. Playing Cards

These 56 playing standard-size cards have rounded corners, and feature color posed and action player photos on their white-bordered fronts. The player's name and position appear near the bottom. The white and black backs carry the logos for the Orioles, baseball's 125th Anniversary, MLBPA, and Bicycle Sports Collection. The set is checklisted below in playing card order by suits and assigned numbers to aces (1), jacks (11), queens (12), and kings (13).

	Nm-Mt	Ex-Mt
COMP. FACT SET (56)	5.00	1.50
1C Chris Hoiles	.05	.02
1D Mike Mussina	.75	.23
1H Cal Ripken Jr.	1.50	.45
1S Mark McLemore	.10	.03
2C Mike Cook	.05	.02
2D Mike Oquist	.05	.02
2H Harold Baines	.15	.04
2S Manny Alexander	.05	.02
3C Paul Carey	.05	.02
3D Brad Pennington	.05	.02
3H John O'Donoghue	.05	.02
3S Kevin McGehee	.05	.02
4C Jeff Tackett	.05	.02
4D Jeffrey Hammonds	.10	.03
4H Sid Fernandez	.05	.02
4S Jim Poole	.05	.02
5C Arthur Rhodes	.05	.02
5D Jack Voigt	.05	.02
5H Alan Mills	.05	.02
5S Leo Gomez	.05	.02
6C Damon Buford	.05	.02
6D Chris Sabo	.05	.02
6H Jamie Moyer	.15	.04
6S Tim Hulett	.05	.02
7C David Segui	.10	.03
7D Rafael Palmeiro	.75	.23
7H Harold Baines	.15	.04
7S Mike Devereaux	.05	.02
8C Ben McDonald	.05	.02
8D Chris Hoiles	.05	.02
8H Mark McLemore	.10	.03
8S Brady Anderson	.50	.15
9C Cal Ripken Jr.	1.50	.45
9D Jim Poole	.05	.02
9H Jeff Tackett	.05	.02
9S Mike Mussina	.75	.23
10C Brad Pennington	.05	.02
10D Leo Gomez	.05	.02
10H Arthur Rhodes	.05	.02
10S Sherman Obando	.05	.02
11C Jack Voigt	.05	.02
11D Tim Hulett	.05	.02
11H Damon Buford	.05	.02
11S Alan Mills	.05	.02
12C Jeffrey Hammonds	.10	.03
12D Mike Devereaux	.05	.02
12H David Segui	.10	.03
12S Jamie Moyer	.15	.04
13C Rafael Palmeiro	.75	.23
13D Brady Anderson	.50	.15
13H Ben McDonald	.05	.02
13S Harold Baines	.15	.04
NNO Featured Players	.05	.02

1995 Orioles Postcards

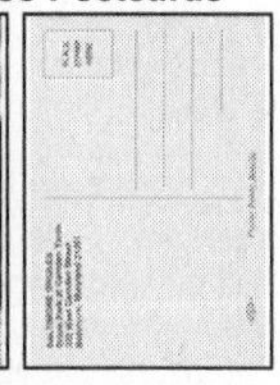

This set features borderless color photos of the Baltimore Orioles with a matte finish and measures approximately 3 1/2" by 5". The backs carry one of 10 different messages with a facsimile signature printed below. The cards of Bobby Bonilla, Al Bumbry, Jim Dedrick, Jeff Huson, Rick Krivda, and Mike Smith display a postcard format on the backs with a Camden Yards return address. The cards are unnumbered and checklisted below in alphabetical order. Some cards were issued for the Orioles Winter Caravan. The are also interspersed with the regular cards. The players featured on the Winter Carnival Cards were usually retired players. They are notated with a WC after their names.

	Nm-Mt	Ex-Mt
COMPLETE SET (52)	30.00	9.00
1 Manny Alexander	.50	.15
2 Brady Anderson	1.50	.45
3 Harold Baines	1.00	.30
4 Bret Barberie	.50	.15
5 Rex Barney ANN WC	1.00	.30
6 Kevin Bass	.50	.15
7 Armando Benitez	1.50	.45
8 Paul Blair	.75	.23
9 Bobby Bonilla	.75	.23
10 Steve Boros CO	.50	.15
11 Kevin Brown	1.50	.45
12 Al Bumbry CO Also in the WC set	.50	.15
13 Terry Clark	.50	.15
14 Chuck Cottier CO	.50	.15
15 Jim Dedrick	.50	.15
16 Mark Eichhorn	.50	.15
17 Scott Erickson	.50	.15
18 Sid Fernandez	.75	.23
19 Mike Flanagan CO	.75	.23
20 Leo Gomez	.50	.15
21 Curtis Goodwin	.50	.15
22 Dick Hall WC	.50	.15
23 Jeffrey Hammonds	.75	.23
24 Gene Harris	.50	.15
25 Chris Hoiles	.50	.15
26 Jeff Huson	.50	.15
27 Doug Jones	.75	.23
28 Rick Krivda	.50	.15
29 Mark Lee	.50	.15
30 Jeff Manto	.50	.15
31 Tippy Martinez WC	.50	.15
32 Lee May CO	.75	.23
33 Jon Miller ANN WC	.75	.23
34 Alan Mills	.50	.15
35 Jamie Moyer	1.00	.30
36 Mike Mussina	2.50	.75
37 Mike Oquist	.50	.15
38 Jesse Orosco	.75	.23
39 Jim Palmer WC	2.50	.75
40 Rafael Palmeiro	1.50	.45
41 Boog Powell WC	1.50	.45
42 Phil Regan MG	.50	.15
43 Arthur Rhodes	.50	.15
44 Cal Ripken Jr.	5.00	1.50
45 Brooks Robinson WC	2.50	.75
46 Larry Sheets WC	.50	.15
47 Mark Smith	.50	.15
48 Bill Swaggerty WC	.50	.15
49 Chuck Thompson ANN WC	.75	.23
50 Gregg Zaun	.50	.15
51 The Oriole Bird(Mascot)	.50	.15
52 Camden Yards	.50	.15

1996 Orioles Fleer

These 20 standard-size cards feature the same design as the regular Fleer issue, except they are UV coated, use silver foil and are numbered "x of 20". The team set packs were available at retail locations and hobby shops in 10-card packs for a suggested retail price of $1.99.

	Nm-Mt	Ex-Mt
COMPLETE SET (20)	6.00	1.80
1 Roberto Alomar	1.00	.30
2 Brady Anderson	.40	.12
3 Armando Benitez	.40	.12
4 Bobby Bonilla	.20	.06
5 Scott Erickson	.20	.06
6 Jeffrey Hammonds	.10	.03
7 Jimmy Haynes	.10	.03
8 Chris Hoiles	.10	.03
9 Rick Krivda	.10	.03
10 Kent Mercker	.10	.03
11 Mike Mussina	1.00	.30
12 Randy Myers	.20	.06
13 Jesse Orosco	.20	.06
14 Rafael Palmeiro	.75	.23
15 Cal Ripken	3.00	.90
16 B.J. Surhoff	.20	.06
17 Tony Tarasco	.10	.03
18 David Wells	.40	.12
19 Logo card	.10	.03
20 Checklist	.10	.03

1996 Orioles Postcards

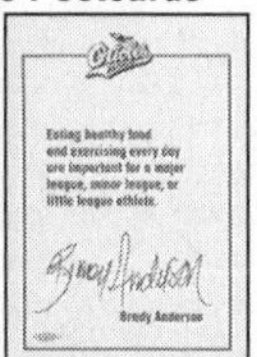

This 39-card set features borderless color photos of the Baltimore Orioles with a matte finish and measures approximately 3 1/2" by 5". The backs display one of seven different messages or a postcard format. The cards are unnumbered and checklisted below in alphabetical order.

	Nm-Mt	Ex-Mt
COMPLETE SET (39)	20.00	6.00
1 Manny Alexander	.50	.15
2 Roberto Alomar	1.50	.45
3 Brady Anderson	1.50	.45
4 Armando Benitez	1.50	.45
5 Bobby Bonilla	.75	.23
6 Jim Dedrick	.50	.15
7 Mike Devereaux	.50	.15
8 Pat Dobson CO	.50	.15
9 Rick Down CO	.50	.15
10 Scott Erickson	.75	.23
11 Andy Etchebarren CO	.50	.15
12 Jeffrey Hammonds	.75	.23
13 Jimmy Haynes	.50	.15
14 Ellie Hendricks CO	.50	.15
15 Chris Hoiles	.50	.15
16 Jeff Huson	.50	.15
17 Davey Johnson MG	.75	.23
18 Rick Krivda	.50	.15
19 Roger McDowell	.50	.15
20 Roger McDowell (Black-and-white)	.50	.15
21 Kent Mercker	.50	.15
22 Alan Mills	.50	.15
23 Mike Mussina	2.50	.75
24 Randy Myers	.75	.23
25 Jesse Orosco	.75	.23
26 Rafael Palmeiro	1.50	.45
27 Sam Perlozzo CO	.50	.15
28 Luis Polonia	.50	.15
29 Arthur Rhodes	.50	.15
30 Bill Ripken	.50	.15
31 Cal Ripken Jr.	5.00	1.50
32 Mark Smith	.50	.15
33 John Steams CO	.50	.15
34 B.J. Surhoff	1.00	.30
35 Earl Weaver MG	1.50	.45
36 David Wells	1.50	.45
37 Gregg Zaun	.50	.15
38 The Bird	.50	.15
39 Camden Yards	.50	.15

1997 Orioles Postcards

This 35-card set features borderless color postcards of the Baltimore Orioles. Each photo has a matte finish and measures approximately 3 1/2" by 5". The backs display either a blank autograph back, a "Profile" back, or one of two different postcard format backs. The cards are unnumbered and checklisted below in alphabetical order.

	Nm-Mt	Ex-Mt
COMPLETE SET (35)	15.00	4.50
1 Roberto Alomar	1.50	.45
2 Brady Anderson	1.50	.45
3 Armando Benitez	1.50	.45
4 Mike Bordick (Portrait)	.50	.15
5 Mike Bordick (Leaning back)	.50	.15
6 Shawn Boskie	.50	.15
7 Rocky Coppinger	.50	.15
8 Rocky Coppinger (Closer view)	.50	.15
9 Eric Davis (Portrait)	.75	.23
10 Eric Davis (Batting)	.75	.23
11 David Dellucci	.50	.15
12 Scott Erickson	.75	.23
13 Jeffrey Hammonds	.50	.15
14 Chris Hoiles	.50	.15
15 Pete Incaviglia (Lighter photo)	.50	.15
16 Pete Incaviglia (Darker photo)	.50	.15
17 Mike Johnson	.50	.15
18 Scott Kamieniecki	.50	.15
19 Jimmy Key	.50	.15
20 Terry Mathews	.50	.15
21 Ray Miller CO	.50	.15
22 Alan Mills	.50	.15
23 Mike Mussina	2.50	.75
24 Randy Myers	.75	.23
25 Jesse Orosco	.75	.23
26 Rafael Palmeiro	1.50	.45
27 Jeff Reboulet	.50	.15
28 Arthur Rhodes	.50	.15
29 Cal Ripken Jr.	5.00	1.50
30 Nerio Rodriguez	.50	.15
31 B.J. Surhoff	.75	.23
32 Tony Tarasco	.50	.15
33 Lenny Webster	.50	.15
34 Brian Williams	.50	.15
35 The Bird(Mascot)	.50	.15

1997 Orioles Score

This 15-card set of the Baltimore Orioles was issued in five-card packs with a suggested retail price of $1.30 each. The fronts feature color player photos with special team specific color foil stamping. The backs carry player information. Only 100 cases were made for each team. Platinum parallel cards were inserted at a rate of 1:6, Premier parallel cards at a rate of 1:31.

	Nm-Mt	Ex-Mt
COMPLETE SET (15)	8.00	2.40
*PLATINUM: 5X BASIC CARDS		
*PREMIER: 20X BASIC CARDS		
1 Rafael Palmeiro	.75	.23
2 Eddie Murray	1.00	.30
3 Roberto Alomar	.75	.23
4 Rocky Coppinger	.25	.07
5 Brady Anderson	.60	.18
6 Bobby Bonilla	.40	.12
7 Cal Ripken	4.00	1.20
8 Mike Mussina	.75	.23
9 Nerio Rodriguez	.25	.07
10 Randy Myers	.40	.12
11 B.J. Surhoff	.40	.12
12 Jeffrey Hammonds	.25	.07

Card	Nm-Mt	Ex-Mt
13 Chris Hoiles	.25	.07
14 Jimmy Haynes	.25	.07
15 David Wells	.60	.18

1997 Orioles Sun

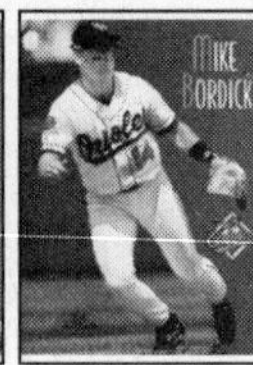

This seven-card set distributed by the Baltimore Sun measures approximately 9 3/4" by 13" and features color player photos of the Baltimore Orioles. Most of the cards are two-sided with pictures on both sides. The cards are unnumbered and checklisted below in alphabetical order.

	Nm-Mt	Ex-Mt
COMPLETE SET (7)	10.00	3.00
1 Jimmy Key	2.00	.60
All Stars		
2 Roberto Alomar	1.50	.45
Todd Zeile		
Chris Hoiles		
Cal Ripken Jr.		
Eddie Murray		
Bobby Bonilla		
B.J. Surhoff		
Brady Anderson		
Rafael Palmeiro		
3 Roberto Alomar	1.00	.30
Rafael Palmeiro		
4 Brady Anderson	1.00	.30
Randy Myers		
5 Mike Bordick	2.50	.75
Cal Ripken Jr.		
6 Mike Mussina	1.00	.30
Scott Erickson		
7 1997 All-Stars	1.50	.45
Brady Anderson		
Roberto Alomar		
Cal Ripken Jr.		
Randy Myers		
Mike Mussina		

1998 Orioles Score

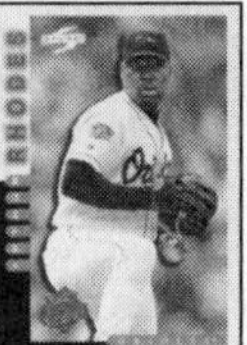
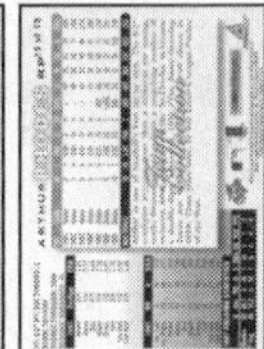

This 15-card set was issued in special retail packs and features color photos of the Baltimore Orioles team. The backs carry player information. A special platinum parallel set was also issued and randomly inserted in packs.

	Nm-Mt	Ex-Mt
COMPLETE SET (15)	8.00	2.40
*PLATINUM: 5X BASIC CARDS		
1 Roberto Alomar	1.00	.30
2 Jimmy Key	.50	.15
3 Cal Ripken	4.00	1.20
4 Brady Anderson	.50	.15
5 Geronimo Berroa	.25	.07
6 Chris Hoiles	.25	.07
7 Rafael Palmeiro	1.00	.30
8 Mike Mussina	1.00	.30
9 Randy Myers	.50	.15
10 Mike Bordick	.25	.07
11 Scott Erickson	.50	.15
12 Armando Benitez	1.00	.30
13 B.J. Surhoff	.50	.15
14 Jeffrey Hammonds	.25	.07
15 Arthur Rhodes	.25	.07

1999 Orioles Postcards

These postcards were issued by the Baltimore Orioles and feature members of the 1999 Orioles. Some of the poses were repeats of the postcards released in previous years and a few of the early releases have postcards backs. The players with postcards backs who were acquired by the Orioles before the season began are: Chip Alley, Albert Belle, Will Clark, Terry Crowley CO, Delino DeShields, Charles Johnson, Ryan Minor, Calvin Pickering and Alvie Shepard. We have sequenced these postcards in alphabetical order.

	Nm-Mt	Ex-Mt
COMPLETE SET (45)	30.00	9.00
1 Brady Anderson	.75	.23
2 Chip Alley	.50	.15
3 Rich Amaral	.50	.15
4 Harold Baines	.75	.23
5 Albert Belle	.75	.23
Player Profile Back		
6 Albert Belle	.75	.23
PC Back		
7 Ricky Bones	.50	.15
8 Mike Bordick	.50	.15
9 Will Clark	1.50	.45
Player Profile Back		
10 Will Clark	1.50	.45
PC Back		
11 Jeff Conine	.50	.15
12 Rocky Coppinger	.50	.15
13 Terry Crowley CO	.50	.15
PC Back		
14 Terry Crowley CO	.50	.15
Player Profile Back		
15 Delino DeShields	.50	.15
Early Release		
16 Delino DeShields	.50	.15
PC Back		
17 Scott Erickson	.75	.23
18 Mike Fetters	.50	.15
19 Mike Figga	.50	.15
20 Marv Foley CO	.50	.15
21 Juan Guzman	.50	.15
22 Ellie Hendricks CO	.50	.15
Message Back		
23 Doug Johns	.50	.15
24 Charles Johnson	.50	.15
PC Back		
25 Charles Johnson	.50	.15
Player Profile Back		
26 Jason Johnson	.50	.15
27 Scott Kamienicki	.50	.15
28 Bruce Kison CO	.50	.15
29 Ray Miller MG	.50	.15
30 Ryan Minor	.50	.15
31 Eddie Murray CO	1.50	.45
32 Mike Mussina	1.50	.45
33 Jesse Orosco	.75	.23
34 Sam Perlozzo CO	.50	.15
35 Calvin Pickering	.50	.15
36 Sidney Ponson	.50	.15
37 Jeff Reboulet	.50	.15
38 Arthur Rhodes	.50	.15
39 Cal Ripken Jr.	4.00	1.20
40 Alvie Shepard	.50	.15
41 B.J. Surhoff	.75	.23
42 Mike Timlin	.50	.15
43 Lenny Webster	.50	.15
44 Bird	.50	.15
Mascot		
45 Camden Yards	.50	.15

1999 Orioles Sheet Coke

This commemorative sheet was issued at the end of the 1999 Orioles season to honor individual highlights attained by various Orioles during the 1999 season. Six players are featured and the sheets are individually numbered.

	Nm-Mt	Ex-Mt
1 Cal Ripken	5.00	1.50
Will Clark		
Jesse Orosco		
Harold Baines		
Brady Anderson		
Mike Bordick		

2001 Orioles Postcards

These 36 oversize borderless postcards feature members of the 2001 Baltimore Orioles. While the fronts are all similar, the backs have either biographical and personal information; just the players name or a standard postcard back. Since these postcards are unnumbered; we have sequenced them in alphabetical order.

	Nm-Mt	Ex-Mt
COMPLETE SET (36)	20.00	6.00
1 Brady Anderson	1.00	.30
2 Mike Bordick	.50	.15
3 Jeff Conine	.75	.23
4 Terry Crowley CO	.50	.15
5 Delino DeShields	.50	.15
6 Scott Erickson	.75	.23
7 Brook Fordyce	.50	.15
8 Jay Gibbons	1.50	.45
9 Buddy Groom	.50	.15
10 Jerry Hairston Jr.	1.00	.30
11 Mike Hargrove MG	.50	.15
12 Elrod Hendricks CO	.50	.15
13 Pat Hentgen	.75	.23
14 Jason Johnson	.50	.15
15 Mike Kinkade	.50	.15
16 Ryan Kohlmeier	.50	.15
17 Fernando Lunar	.50	.15
18 Luis Matos	.50	.15
19 Chuck McElroy	.50	.15
20 Jose Mercedes	.50	.15
21 Alan Mills	.50	.15
22 Melvin Mora	.50	.15
23 Eddie Murray CO	1.50	.45
24 Greg Myers	.50	.15
25 Chad Paronto	.50	.15
26 Sam Perlozzo CO	.50	.15
27 Sidney Ponson	.50	.15
28 Chris Richard	.50	.15
29 Cal Ripken Jr	3.00	.90
30 B.J. Ryan	.50	.15
31 David Segui	.75	.23
32 Willis Roberts	.50	.15
33 Josh Towers	.75	.23
34 Mike Trombley	.50	.15
35 Tom Trebelhorn CO	.50	.15
36 Mark Wiley CO	.50	.15

2002 Orioles Postcards

These full color postcards measure approximately 3 1/2" by 5" and feature members of the 2002 Baltimore Orioles. The borderless fronts feature full color photos while the backs have basic player information. This set is unnumbered and we have catalogued them in alphabetical order.

	Nm-Mt	Ex-Mt
COMPLETE SET (41)	20.00	6.00
1 Tony Batista	.75	.23
2 Rick Bauer	.50	.15
3 Erik Bedard	.50	.15
4 Larry Bigbie	.50	.15
5 Mike Bordick	.50	.15
6 Jeff Conine	.75	.23
7 Marty Cordova	.50	.15
8 Terry Crowley CO	.50	.15
9 Rick Dempsey CO	.75	.23
10 Sean Douglass	.50	.15
11 Travis Driskill	.50	.15
12 Scott Erickson	.75	.23
13 Brook Fordyce	.50	.15
14 Luis Garcia	.50	.15
15 Jay Gibbons	1.00	.30
16 Geronimo Gil	.50	.15
17 Buddy Groom	.50	.15
18 Jerry Hairston	1.00	.30
19 Mike Hargrove MG	.50	.15
20 Elrod Hendricks CO	.50	.15
21 Pat Hentgen	.50	.15
22 Jason Johnson	.50	.15
23 Jorge Julio	1.50	.45
24 Rodrigo Lopez	.75	.23
25 Calvin Maduro	.50	.15
26 Luis Matos	.50	.15
27 Gary Matthews Jr.	.75	.23
28 Melvin Mora	1.00	.30
29 Mike Moriarty	.50	.15
30 John Parrish	.50	.15
31 Sam Perlozzo CO	.50	.15
32 Sidney Ponson	1.50	.45
33 Chris Richard	.75	.23
34 Brian Roberts	.50	.15
35 Willis Roberts	.50	.15
36 B.J. Ryan	.50	.15
37 David Segui	.75	.23
38 Chris Singleton	.75	.23
39 Josh Towers	.50	.15
40 Tom Trebelhorn CO	.50	.15
41 Mark Wiley CO	.50	.15

2002 Orioles Program

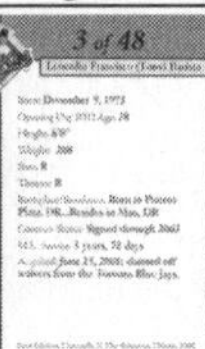

Inserted into the 2002 Orioles Programs were these little cards which feature the players photo on the front and some brief information about them on the back.

	Nm-Mt	Ex-Mt
COMPLETE SET (48)	10.00	3.00
1 Checklist	.25	.07
2 John Bale	.25	.07
3 Tony Batista	.50	.15
4 Rick Bauer	.25	.07
5 Erik Bedard	.25	.07
6 Larry Bigbie	.25	.07
7 Mike Bordick	.25	.07
8 Jeff Conine	.50	.15
9 Marty Cordova	.25	.07
10 Sean Douglass	.25	.07
11 Scott Erickson	.50	.15
12 Brook Fordyce	.25	.07
13 Kris Foster	.25	.07
14 Jay Gibbons	.75	.23
15 Geronimo Gil	.25	.07
16 Buddy Groom	.25	.07
17 Jerry Hairston	.75	.23
18 Pat Hentgen	.25	.07
19 Jason Johnson	.25	.07
20 Jorge Julio	1.00	.30
21 Fernando Lunar	.25	.07
22 Calvin Maduro	.25	.07
23 Luis Matos	.25	.07
24 Melvin Mora	.75	.23
25 John Parrish	.25	.07
26 Sydney Ponson	1.00	.30
27 Chris Richard	.50	.15
28 Luis Rivera	.25	.07
29 Brian Roberts	.25	.07
30 Willis Roberts	.25	.07
31 Eddie Rogers	.50	.15
32 B.J. Ryan	.25	.07
33 David Segui	.50	.15
34 Chris Singleton	.25	.07
35 John Stephens	.25	.07
36 Josh Towers	.25	.07
37 Mike Hargrove MG	.50	.15
38 Terry Crowley CO	.25	.07
39 Rick Dempsey CO	.25	.07
40 Elrod Hendricks CO	.50	.15
41 Sam Perlozzo CO	.25	.07
42 Tom Trebelhorn CO	.25	.07
43 Mark Wiley CO	.25	.07
44 The Bird	.25	.07
Mascot		
45 OPCY Birds Eye	.25	.07
46 OPCY Interior	.25	.07
47 OPCY Façade	.25	.07
48 Eutaw Street	.25	.07

1994 Oscar Mayer Round-Ups

The 1994 Oscar Mayer Superstar Round-Up set consists of 30 circular pop-up cards measuring about 2 1/2" in diameter and features 15 players from the American (1-15) and National (16-30) Leagues. One card was inserted in each specially marked 16-oz. package of Oscar Mayer bologna available in April and May. On-pack and in-store point-of-purchase mail-in offers enabled consumers to order a boxed American and/or National League 15-card set for 1.95 plus proof-of-purchase for each set. The black-bordered fronts feature color action player shots that are perforated and cut out in such a way so that when the tab at the top is pulled, the photo becomes three-dimensional. Also revealed is a trivia question and answer, and the player's statistics. The set's title appears at the top within the black border in blue lettering on American League cards and green lettering on National League cards. The player's name, position, and team appear below the photo. The back displays the player's name, position, team, and career highlights. A color player action cutout appears alongside. The cards are numbered on the front toward the lower right, following alphabetical order by league.

	Nm-Mt	Ex-Mt
COMPLETE SET (30)	12.00	3.60
1 Jim Abbott	.40	.12
2 Kevin Appier	.20	.06
3 Roger Clemens	1.50	.45
4 Cecil Fielder	.40	.12
5 Juan Gonzalez	.75	.23
6 Ken Griffey Jr.	2.00	.60
7 Kenny Lofton	.60	.18
8 Jack McDowell	.20	.06
9 Paul Molitor	1.00	.30
10 Kirby Puckett	1.00	.30
11 Cal Ripken Jr.	3.00	.90
12 Tim Salmon	.60	.18
13 Ruben Sierra	.40	.12
14 Frank Thomas	1.00	.30
15 Greg Vaughn	.40	.12
16 Jeff Bagwell	1.00	.30
17 Barry Bonds	1.50	.45
18 Bobby Bonilla	.40	.12
19 Jeff Conine	.20	.06
20 Lenny Dykstra	.40	.12
21 Andres Galarraga	.75	.23
22 Marquis Grissom	.20	.06
23 Tony Gwynn	1.50	.45
24 Gregg Jefferies	.20	.06
25 John Kruk	.40	.12
26 Greg Maddux	2.00	.60
27 Mike Piazza	2.00	.60
28 Jose Rijo	.20	.06
29 Ryne Sandberg	1.00	.30
30 Andy Van Slyke	.40	.12

1987 Our Own Tea Discs

These Discs, which feature the Our Own Tea name on the front, are a parallel issue to the 1987 MSA Iced Tea Discs. They are valued the same as the regular Discs.

	Nm-Mt	Ex-Mt
COMPLETE SET (20)	8.00	3.20
1 Darryl Strawberry	.10	.04
2 Roger Clemens	1.50	.60
3 Ron Darling	.10	.04
4 Keith Hernandez	.20	.08
5 Tony Pena	.20	.08
6 Don Mattingly	1.50	.60
7 Eric Davis	.20	.08
8 Gary Carter	.75	.30
9 Dave Winfield	.75	.30
10 Wally Joyner	.60	.24
11 Mike Schmidt	.75	.30
12 Robby Thompson	.10	.04
13 Wade Boggs	.75	.30
14 Cal Ripken	3.00	1.20
15 Dale Murphy	.40	.16
16 Tony Gwynn	2.00	.80
17 Jose Canseco	.60	.24
18 Rickey Henderson	1.25	.50
19 Lance Parrish	.10	.04
20 Dave Righetti	.10	.04

1988 Our Own Tea Discs

For the second year, MSA issued iced tea discs with the Our Own Tea label on the front. These discs are parallel to the regular Iced Tea discs and are valued the same

	Nm-Mt	Ex-Mt
COMPLETE SET (20)	10.00	4.00
1 Wade Boggs	.75	.30
2 Ellis Burks	.60	.24
3 Don Mattingly	1.50	.60
4 Mark McGwire	2.50	1.00
5 Matt Nokes	.10	.04
6 Kirby Puckett	.75	.30
7 Billy Ripken	.10	.04
8 Kevin Seitzer	.10	.04
9 Roger Clemens	1.50	.60
10 Will Clark	.60	.24
11 Vince Coleman	.10	.04
12 Eric Davis	.20	.08
13 Dave Magadan	.10	.04
14 Dale Murphy	.40	.16
15 Benito Santiago	.20	.08
16 Mike Schmidt	.75	.30
17 Darryl Strawberry	.20	.08
18 Steve Bedrosian	.10	.04
19 Dwight Gooden	.20	.08
20 Fernando Valenzuela	.20	.08

1989 Our Own Tea Discs

For the third season, Our Own Tea was one of the companies which distributed the MSA Iced Tea Discs. These discs say Our Own on the front and are valued the same as the MSA Iced Tea discs.

	Nm-Mt	Ex-Mt
COMPLETE SET (20)	30.00	12.00
1 Don Mattingly	6.00	2.40
2 Dave Cone	2.00	.80
3 Mark McGwire	10.00	4.00
4 Will Clark	2.50	1.00
5 Darryl Strawberry	1.50	.60
6 Dwight Gooden	1.50	.60
7 Wade Boggs	3.00	1.20
8 Roger Clemens	6.00	2.40
9 Benito Santiago	1.50	.60
10 Orel Hershiser	1.50	.60
11 Eric Davis	1.50	.60
12 Kirby Puckett	4.00	1.60
13 Dave Winfield	3.00	1.20
14 Andre Dawson	2.50	1.00
15 Steve Bedrosian	1.00	.40
16 Cal Ripken	12.00	4.80
17 Andy Van Slyke	1.00	.40
18 Jose Canseco	2.50	1.00
19 Jose Oquendo	1.00	.40
20 Dale Murphy	2.00	.80

1936-41 Overland Candy R301

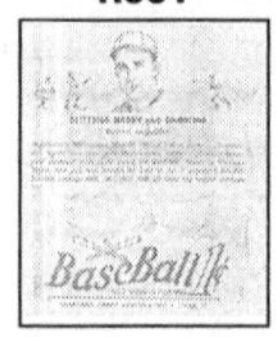

These unnumbered cards (which are actually wrappers) measure 5" by 5 1/4" and were issued over a period of time in the 1930's. A drawing of the player is on the top of the wrapper with his name and biography underneath him. The Overland Candy Co logo is noted on the bottom. Wrappers are known with or without the ingredient list. No extra value is given for either variation.

	Ex-Mt	VG
COMPLETE SET	15000.00	7500.00
1 Mel Almada	200.00	100.00
2 Luke Appling	400.00	200.00
3 Earl Averill	400.00	200.00
4 Wally Berger	250.00	125.00
5 Zeke Bonura	250.00	125.00
6 Phil Cavaretta	250.00	125.00
7 Ben Chapman	200.00	100.00
8 Harland Clift	200.00	100.00
9 Johnny Cooney	200.00	100.00
Boston		
10 Johnny Cooney	200.00	100.00
Brooklyn		
11 Bill Dietrich	200.00	100.00
Chicago		
12 Bill Dietrich	200.00	100.00
Philadelphia		
13 Joe DiMaggio	2000.00	1000.00
14 Jimmie Foxx	400.00	200.00
15 Lou Gehrig	1500.00	750.00
16 Charley Gehringer	400.00	200.00
17 Jose Luis Gomez	200.00	100.00
18 Lefty Gomez	400.00	200.00
19 Joe Gordon	300.00	150.00
20 Hank Greenberg	400.00	200.00
21 Lefty Grove	400.00	200.00
22 Mule Haas	200.00	100.00
23 Rollie Hemsley	200.00	100.00
24 Pinky Higgins	200.00	100.00
25 Oral Hildebrand	200.00	100.00
26 Bob Johnson	250.00	125.00
27 Buck Jordan	200.00	100.00
28 Fabian Kowalik	200.00	100.00
28 Ken Keltner	250.00	125.00
29 Cookie Lavagetto	200.00	100.00
30 Tony Lazzeri	400.00	200.00
31 Samuel A. Leslie	200.00	100.00
32 Danny Litwhiler	200.00	100.00
33 Ted Lyons	400.00	200.00
34 George McQuinn	200.00	100.00
35 Johnny Mize	400.00	200.00
36 Frankie Pytlak	200.00	100.00
37 Rip Radcliff	200.00	100.00
38 Pete Reiser	300.00	150.00
39 Red Rolfe	250.00	125.00
40 Schoolboy Rowe	250.00	125.00
41 Al Simmons	400.00	200.00
42 Cecil Travis	250.00	125.00
43 Hal Trosky	250.00	125.00
44 Joe Vosmik	200.00	100.00
45 Bill Werber	200.00	100.00
46 Max West	200.00	100.00
47 Sam West	200.00	100.00
48 Whit Wyatt	200.00	100.00

1921 Oxford Confectionery E253

This 20 card set measures 1 5/8" by 2 3/4" and almost the whole front is a player photo. The player's name and team is on the bottom. The backs note that these cards are produced solely for the Oxford Confectionery Company and lists a player checklist.

	Ex-Mt	VG
COMPLETE SET (20)	6000.00	3000.00
1 Grover C. Alexander	300.00	150.00
2 Dave Bancroft	200.00	100.00
3 Max Carey	200.00	100.00
4 Ty Cobb	1200.00	600.00
5 Eddie Collins	300.00	150.00
6 Frankie Frisch	250.00	125.00
7 Burleigh Grimes	200.00	100.00
8 Bill Holke	100.00	50.00
9 Rogers Hornsby	400.00	200.00
10 Walter Johnson	600.00	300.00
11 Lee Meadows	100.00	50.00
12 Cy Perkins	100.00	50.00
13 Del Pratt	100.00	50.00
14 Ed Roush	200.00	100.00
15 Babe Ruth	2000.00	1000.00
16 Ray Schalk	200.00	100.00
17 George Sisler	250.00	125.00
18 Tris Speaker	300.00	150.00
19 Cy Williams	100.00	50.00
20 Whitey Witt	100.00	50.00

1980-83 Pacific Legends

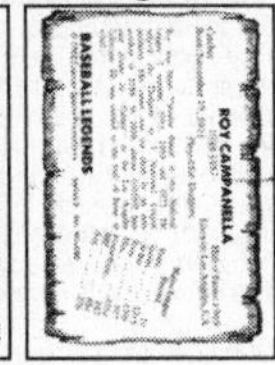

This 120-card standard-size set is actually four 30-card subsets plus a four-card wax box bottom panel (cards 121-124). The golden-toned set was distributed by series over several years beginning in 1980 with the first 30 cards. The set was produced by Pacific Trading Cards and is frequently referred to as Cramer Legends, for the founder of Pacific Trading cards, Mike Cramer. Even though the wax box cards are numbered from 121-124 and called "Series 5," the set is considered complete without them. Each series was originally available from Pacific Trading card for $2.95 each.

	NRMT	VG-E
COMPLETE SET (120)	30.00	13.50
COMMON CARD (1-120)	.10	.05
COMMON CARD (121-124)	.50	.23
1 Babe Ruth	3.00	1.35
2 Heinie Manush	.20	.09
3 Rabbit Maranville	.20	.09
4 Earl Averill	.20	.09
5 Joe DiMaggio	2.50	1.10
6 Mickey Mantle	3.00	1.35
7 Hank Aaron	1.50	.70
8 Stan Musial	.75	.35
9 Bill Terry	.20	.09
10 Sandy Koufax	.50	.23
11 Ernie Lombardi	.20	.09
12 Dizzy Dean	.50	.23
13 Lou Gehrig	2.50	1.10
14 Walter Alston	.20	.09
15 Jackie Robinson	1.50	.70
16 Jimmie Foxx	.30	.14
17 Billy Southworth	.10	.05
18 Honus Wagner	.75	.35
19 Duke Snider	.50	.23
20 Rogers Hornsby UER	.50	.23
(At bat total of		
1873 is incorrect)		
21 Paul Waner	.20	.09
22 Luke Appling	.20	.09
23 Billy Herman	.20	.09
24 Lloyd Waner	.20	.09
25 Fred Hutchinson	.10	.05
26 Eddie Collins	.20	.09
27 Lefty Grove	.30	.14
28 Chuck Connors	.30	.14
29 Lefty O'Doul	.10	.05
30 Hank Greenberg	.50	.23
31 Ty Cobb	2.00	.90
32 Enos Slaughter	.20	.09
33 Ernie Banks	.50	.23
34 Christy Mathewson	.50	.23
35 Mel Ott	.30	.14
36 Pie Traynor	.20	.09
37 Clark Griffith	.20	.09
38 Mickey Cochrane	.20	.09
39 Joe Cronin	.20	.09
40 Leo Durocher	.20	.09
41 Home Run Baker	.20	.09
42 Joe Tinker	.20	.09
43 John McGraw	.20	.09
44 Bill Dickey	.20	.09
45 Walter Johnson	.50	.23
46 Frankie Frisch	.20	.09
47 Casey Stengel	.30	.14
48 Willie Mays	1.50	.70
49 Johnny Mize	.20	.09
50 Roberto Clemente	2.00	.90
51 Burleigh Grimes	.20	.09
52 Pee Wee Reese	.50	.23
53 Bob Feller	.50	.23
54 Brooks Robinson	.50	.23
55 Sam Crawford	.20	.09
56 Robin Roberts	.30	.14
57 Warren Spahn	.30	.14
58 Joe McCarthy	.20	.09
59 Jocko Conlan	.20	.09
60 Satchel Paige	1.00	.45
61 Ted Williams	2.00	.90
62 George Kelly	.20	.09
63 Gil Hodges	.30	.14
64 Jim Bottomley	.20	.09
65 Al Kaline	.50	.23
66 Harvey Kuenn	.10	.05
67 Yogi Berra	.50	.23
68 Nellie Fox	.10	.05
69 Harmon Killebrew	.30	.14
70 Edd Roush	.20	.09
71 Mordecai Brown	.20	.09
72 Gabby Hartnett	.20	.09
73 Early Wynn	.20	.09
74 Nap Lajoie	.20	.09
75 Charlie Grimm	.10	.05
76 Joe Garagiola	.20	.09
77 Ted Lyons	.20	.09
78 Mickey Vernon	.10	.05
79 Lou Boudreau	.20	.09
80 Al Dark	.10	.05
81 Ralph Kiner	.30	.14
82 Phil Rizzuto	.30	.14
83 Stan Hack	.10	.05
84 Frank Chance	.20	.09
85 Ray Schalk	.20	.09
86 Bill McKechnie	.20	.09
87 Travis Jackson	.20	.09
88 Pete Reiser	.10	.05
89 Carl Hubbell	.20	.09
90 Roy Campanella	.50	.23
91 Cy Young	.30	.14
92 Kiki Cuyler	.20	.09
93 Chief Bender	.20	.09
94 Richie Ashburn	.30	.14
95 Riggs Stephenson	.10	.05
96 Minnie Minoso	.10	.05
97 Hack Wilson	.20	.09
98 Al Lopez	.20	.09
99 Willie Keeler	.20	.09
100 Fred Lindstrom	.20	.09
101 Roger Maris	.30	.14
102 Roger Bresnahan	.20	.09
103 Monty Stratton	.20	.09
104 Goose Goslin	.20	.09
105 Earle Combs	.20	.09
106 Pepper Martin	.10	.05
107 Joe Jackson	1.50	.70
108 George Sisler	.20	.09
109 Red Ruffing	.20	.09
110 Johnny Vander Meer	.10	.05
111 Herb Pennock	.20	.09
112 Chuck Klein	.20	.09
113 Paul Derringer	.10	.05
114 Addie Joss	.20	.09
115 Bobby Thomson	.10	.05
116 Chick Hafey	.20	.09
117 Lefty Gomez	.20	.09
118 George Kell	.20	.09
119 Al Simmons	.20	.09
120 Bob Lemon	.20	.09
121 Hoyt Wilhelm	.50	.23
122 Arky Vaughan	.50	.23
123 Frank Robinson	1.50	.70
124 Grover Alexander	1.00	.45

1984 Pacific Trading Cards Postcards

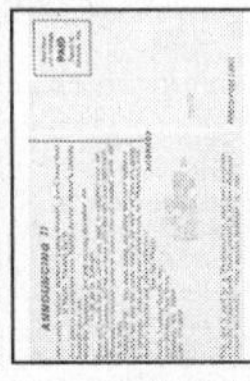

These postcards were sent from Pacific Trading Cards to members of their mailing list to announce events in what was then their flagship store. The fronts feature famous major leaguers while the backs feature information about upcoming events at Pacific's store

	Nm-Mt	Ex-Mt
COMPLETE SET	10.00	4.00
1 Bob Feller	3.00	1.20
2 Babe Ruth	10.00	4.00

1988 Pacific Eight Men Out

This 110-card standard-size set, produced by Mike Cramer's Pacific Trading Cards of Edmonds, Washington, was released in conjunction with the popular movie of the same name, which told the story of the "fix" of the 1919 World Series between the Cincinnati Reds and the Chicago "Black- Sox. The cards have a raspberry-colored border on the card fronts as well as raspberry-colored print on the white card stock backs. The cards were available either as wax packs or as collated sets. Generally the cards relating to the movie (showing actors) are in full-color whereas the vintage photography showing the actual players involved is in a sepia tone.

	Nm-Mt	Ex-Mt
COMPLETE SET (110)	8.00	3.20
1 We're Going To See	.15	.06
The Sox		
2 White Sox Win	.05	.02
The Pennant		
3 The Series	.05	.02
4 1919 Chicago White	.05	.02
Sox		
5 The Black Sox Scandal	.05	.02
6 Eddie Cicotte 29-7	.15	.06
in 1919		
7 Buck's Their	.15	.06
Favorite		
8 Eddie Collins	.25	.10
9 Michael Rooker as	.05	.02
Chick Gandil		
10 Charlie Sheen as	.50	.20
Hap Felsch		
11 James Read as	.05	.02
Lefty Williams		
12 John Cusack as	.25	.10
Buck Weaver		
13 D.B. Sweeney as	.25	.10
Joe Jackson		
14 David Strathairn as	.05	.02
Eddie Cicotte		
15 Perry Lang as	.15	.06
Fred McMullin		
16 Don Harvey as	.05	.02
Swede Risberg		
17 The Gambler Burns	.05	.02
And Maharg		
18 Sleepy Bill Burns	.05	.02
19 The Key is Cicotte	.05	.02
20 C'mon Betsy	.05	.02
21 The Fix	.05	.02
22 Chick Approaches	.05	.02
Cicotte		
23 Kid Gleason MG	.05	.02
24 Charles Comiskey OWN	.05	.02
25 Chick Gandil	.15	.06
1st Baseman		
26 Swede Risberg	.05	.02
27 Sport Sullivan	.05	.02
28 Abe Attell And	.05	.02
Arnold Rothstein		
29 Hugh Fullerton	.05	.02
Sportswriter		
30 Ring Lardner	.05	.02
Sportswriter		
31 Shoeless Joe	.25	.10
His Batting Eye		
32 Shoeless Joe	.50	.20
33 Buck Can't Sleep	.05	.02
34 George "Buck" Weaver	.15	.06
35 Hugh and Ring	.05	.02
Confront Kid		
36 Joe Doesn't Want	.15	.06
To Play		
37 Shoeless Joe	.50	.20
Jackson		
38 Sore Arm, Cicotte	.05	.02
Old Man Cicotte		
39 The Fix Is On	.05	.02
40 Buck Plays To Win	.05	.02
41 Hap Makes A	.05	.02
Great Catch		
42 Hugh and Ring Suspect	.05	.02
43 Ray Gets Things Going	.05	.02
44 Lefty Loses Game Two	.05	.02
45 Lefty Crosses Up	.05	.02
Catcher Ray Schalk		
46 Chick's RBI Wins	.05	.02
Game Three		
47 Dickie Kerr Wins	.05	.02
Game Three		
48 Chick Leaves Buck	.05	.02
At Third		
49 Williams Loses	.05	.02
Game Five		
50 Ray Schalk	.05	.02
51 Schalk Blocks	.05	.02
The Plate		
52 Schalk Is Thrown Out	.05	.02
53 Chicago Stickball	.05	.02
Game		
54 I'm Forever Blowing	.05	.02
Ball Games		
55 Felsch Scores Jackson	.25	.10
56 Kerr Wins Game Six	.05	.02
57 Where's The Money	.05	.02
58 Cicotte Wins Game	.05	.02
Seven		
59 Kid Watches Eddie	.05	.02
60 Lefty Is Threatened	.05	.02
61 James	.05	.02
Get Your Arm Ready		
Fast		
62 Shoeless Joe's	.50	.20
Home Run		
63 Buck Played His Best	.15	.06
64 Hugh Exposes The Fix	.05	.02
65 Sign The Petition	.05	.02
66 Baseball Owners Hire	.05	.02
A Commissioner		
67 Judge Kenesaw	.15	.06
Mountain Landis		
68 Grand Jury Summoned	.05	.02
69 Say It Ain't So,	.25	.10
Joe		
70 The Swede's A Hard	.05	.02
Guy		
71 Buck Loves The Game	.05	.02
72 The Trial	.05	.02
73 Kid Gleason Takes	.05	.02
The Stand		
74 The Verdict	.05	.02
75 Eight Men Out	.05	.02
76 Oscar(Happy) Felsch	.15	.06
77 Who's Joe Jackson	.25	.10
78 Ban Johnson PRES	.15	.06
79 Judge Landis COMM	.15	.06
80 Charles Comiskey OWN	.15	.06
81 Heinie Groh	.05	.02
82 Slim Sallee	.05	.02
83 Dutch Ruether	.05	.02
84 Edd Roush	.25	.10
85 Morrie Rath	.05	.02
86 Bill Rariden	.05	.02
87 Jimmy Ring	.05	.02
88 Greasy Neale	.15	.06
89 Pat Moran MG	.05	.02
90 Adolfo Luque	.05	.02
91 Larry Kopf	.05	.02
92 Ray Fisher	.05	.02
93 Hod Eller	.05	.02
94 Pat Duncan	.05	.02
95 Jake Daubert	.05	.02
96 Red Faber	.25	.10
97 Dickie Kerr	.05	.02
98 Shano Collins	.05	.02
99 Eddie Collins	.25	.10
100 Ray Schalk	.25	.10
101 Nemo Leibold	.05	.02
102 Kid Gleason MG	.15	.06
103 Swede Risberg	.15	.06
104 Eddie Cicotte	.15	.06
105 Fred McMullin	.15	.06
106 Chick Gandil	.25	.10
107 Buck Weaver	.25	.10
108 Lefty Williams	.15	.06
109 Happy Felsch	.15	.06
110 Joe Jackson	1.00	.40

1988 Pacific Legends I

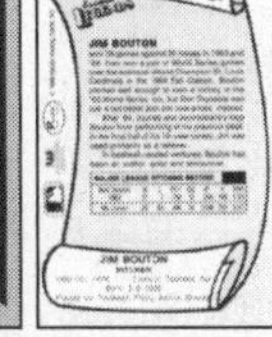

This attractive set of 110 full-color standard-size silver-bordered cards was produced by Mike Cramer's Pacific Trading Cards of Edmonds, Washington. Card backs are printed in yellow, black, and gray on white card stock. The cards were available either as wax packs or as collated sets. The players pictured in the set had retired many years before, but most are still well remembered. The statistics on the card backs give the player's career and "best season" statistics. The set was licensed by Major League Baseball Players Alumni.

	Nm-Mt	Ex-Mt
COMPLETE SET (110)	10.00	4.00
COMP. FACT SET (110)	10.00	4.00
1 Hank Aaron	1.50	.60
2 Red Schoendienst	.15	.06
3 Brooks Robinson	.25	.10
4 Luke Appling	.15	.06
5 Gene Woodling	.05	.02
6 Stan Musial	.75	.30
7 Mickey Mantle	3.00	1.20
8 Richie Ashburn	.25	.10
9 Ralph Kiner	.25	.10
10 Phil Rizzuto	.25	.10
11 Harvey Haddix	.05	.02
12 Ken Boyer	.10	.04
13 Clete Boyer	.05	.02
14 Ken Harrelson	.10	.04
15 Robin Roberts	.25	.10
16 Catfish Hunter	.25	.10
17 Frank Howard	.10	.04
18 Jim Perry	.05	.02
19A Elston Howard ERR	.25	.10
(Reversed negative)		
19B Elston Howard COR	.25	.10
20 Jim Bouton	.10	.04
21 Pee Wee Reese	.25	.10
22A Mel Stottlemyre ERR	.15	.06
(Spelled Stottlemyer		
on card front)		
22B Mel Stottlemyre COR	.15	.06
23 Hank Sauer	.05	.02
24 Willie Mays	1.50	.60
25 Tom Tresh	.05	.02
26 Roy Sievers	.05	.02
27 Leo Durocher	.25	.10
28 Al Dark	.05	.02
29 Tony Kubek	.10	.04
30 Johnny VanderMeer	.10	.04
31 Joe Adcock	.05	.02
32 Bob Lemon	.25	.10
33 Don Newcombe	.10	.04
34 Thurman Munson	.50	.20
35 Earl Battey	.05	.02
36 Ernie Banks	.50	.20
37 Matty Alou	.05	.02
38 Dave McNally	.05	.02
39 Mickey Lolich	.10	.04
40 Jackie Robinson	2.00	.80
41 Allie Reynolds	.10	.04
42A Don Larsen ERR	.15	.06
(Misspelled Larson		
on card front)		
42B Don Larsen COR	.15	.06
43 Fergie Jenkins	.25	.10
44 Jim Gilliam	.10	.04
45 Bobby Thomson	.10	.04
46 Sparky Anderson	.10	.04
47 Roy Campanella	.50	.20
48 Marv Throneberry	.05	.02
49 Bill Virdon	.05	.02
50 Ted Williams UER	1.50	.60
Birthdate is wrong		
51 Minnie Minoso	.10	.04
52 Bob Turley	.05	.02
53 Yogi Berra	.50	.20
54 Juan Marichal	.25	.10
55 Duke Snider	.50	.20
56 Harvey Kuenn	.05	.02
57 Nellie Fox	.25	.10
58 Felipe Alou	.10	.04
59 Tony Oliva	.10	.04
60 Bill Mazeroski	.25	.10
61 Bobby Shantz	.05	.02
62 Mark Fidrych	.15	.06
63 Johnny Mize	.25	.10
64 Ralph Terry	.05	.02
65 Gus Bell	.05	.02
66 Jerry Koosman	.05	.02
67 Mike McCormick	.05	.02
68 Lou Burdette	.05	.02
69 George Kell	.25	.10
70 Vic Raschi	.05	.02
71 Chuck Connors	.25	.10
72 Ted Kluszewski	.25	.10
73 Bobby Doerr	.25	.10
74 Bobby Richardson	.10	.04
75 Carl Erskine	.10	.04
76 Hoyt Wilhelm	.25	.10
77 Bob Purkey	.05	.02
78 Bob Friend	.05	.02
79 Monte Irvin	.25	.10
80A Jim Lonborg ERR	.15	.06
(Misspelled Longborg		
on card front)		
80B Jim Lonborg COR	.15	.06
81 Wally Moon	.05	.02
82 Moose Skowron	.05	.02
83 Tommy Davis	.05	.02
84 Enos Slaughter	.25	.10
85 Sal Maglie UER	.05	.02
(1945-1917 on back)		
86 Harmon Killebrew	.25	.10
87 Gil Hodges	.15	.06
88 Jim Kaat	.10	.04
89 Roger Maris	.50	.20
90 Billy Williams	.25	.10
91 Luis Aparicio	.25	.10
92 Jim Bunning	.25	.10
93 Bill Freehan	.10	.04
94 Orlando Cepeda	.15	.06
95 Early Wynn	.25	.10
96 Tug McGraw	.10	.04
97 Ron Santo	.25	.10
98 Del Crandall	.05	.02
99 Sal Bando	.05	.02
100 Joe DiMaggio	2.50	1.00
101 Bob Feller	.50	.20
102 Larry Doby	.15	.06
103 Rollie Fingers	.25	.10
104 Al Kaline	.25	.10
105 Johnny Podres	.05	.02
106 Lou Boudreau	.25	.10
107 Zoilo Versalles	.05	.02
108 Dick Groat	.05	.02
109 Warren Spahn	.25	.10
110 Johnny Bench	.50	.20

1989 Pacific Griffey Candy Bar

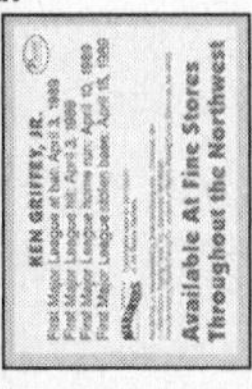

Produced by the Pacific Candy Co., this set features a color batting image of Ken Griffey, Jr. of the Seattle Mariners on a blue, white, or yellow background with silver borders and advertises the milk chocolate Ken Griffey, Jr. Candy Bar available at stores throughout the Northwest. The back displays player information. Griffey is allergic to chocolate so he could not eat the candy bar named for him.

	Nm-Mt	Ex-Mt
COMPLETE SET (3)	15.00	6.00
COMMON CARD (1A-1C)	5.00	2.00

1989 Pacific Legends II

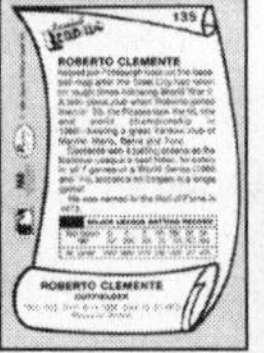

The 1989 Pacific Legends Series II set contains 110 standard-size cards. The fronts have vintage color photos with silver borders. The backs are gray and feature career highlights and lifetime statistics. The cards were distributed as factory sets as well as in ten-card wax packs.

	Nm-Mt	Ex-Mt
COMPLETE SET (110)	10.00	4.00
COMP.FACT SET (110)	10.00	4.00
111 Reggie Jackson	.50	.20
112 Rich Reese	.05	.02
113 Frankie Frisch	.15	.06
114 Ed Kranepool	.05	.02
115 Al Hrabosky	.05	.02
116 Eddie Mathews	.25	.10
117 Ty Cobb	1.50	.60
118 Jim Davenport	.05	.02
119 Buddy Lewis	.05	.02
120 Virgil Trucks	.05	.02
121 Del Ennis	.05	.02
122 Dick Radatz	.05	.02
123 Andy Pafko	.05	.02
124 Wilbur Wood	.05	.02
125 Joe Sewell	.15	.06
126 Herb Score	.10	.04
127 Paul Waner	.15	.06
128 Lloyd Waner	.15	.06
129 Brooks Robinson	.50	.20
130 Bo Belinsky	.10	.04
131 Phil Cavarretta	.05	.02
132 Claude Osteen	.05	.02
133 Tito Francona	.05	.02
134 Billy Pierce	.10	.04
135 Roberto Clemente	1.50	.60
136 Spud Chandler	.05	.02
137 Enos Slaughter	.15	.06
138 Ken Holtzman	.05	.02
139 John Hopp	.05	.02
140 Tony LaRussa	.10	.04
141 Ryne Duren	.05	.02
142 Glenn Beckert UER	.05	.02
(Misspelled Glen on		
card front)		
143 Ken Keltner	.05	.02
144 Hank Bauer	.10	.04
145 Roger Craig	.10	.04
146 Frank Baker	.15	.06
147 Jim O'Toole	.05	.02
148 Rogers Hornsby	.40	.16
149 Jose Cardenal	.05	.02
150 Bobby Doerr	.15	.06
151 Mickey Cochrane	.15	.06
152 Gaylord Perry	.15	.06
153 Frank Thomas	.05	.02
154 Ted Williams	1.50	.60
155 Sam McDowell	.05	.02
156 Bob Feller	.50	.20
157 Bert Campaneris	.05	.02
158 Thornton Lee UER	.05	.02
(Misspelled Thorton		
on card front)		
159 Gary Peters	.05	.02
160 Joe Medwick	.15	.06
161 Joe Nuxhall	.05	.02
162 Joe Schultz	.05	.02
163 Harmon Killebrew	.25	.10
164 Bucky Walters	.05	.02
165 Bob Allison	.05	.02
166 Lou Boudreau	.15	.06
167 Joe Cronin	.15	.06
168 Mike Torrez	.05	.02
169 Rich Rollins	.05	.02
170 Tony Cuccinello	.05	.02
171 Hoyt Wilhelm	.15	.06
172 Ernie Harwell ANN	.10	.04
173 George Foster	.05	.02
174 Lou Gehrig	1.50	.60
175 Dave Kingman	.10	.04
176 Babe Ruth	2.00	.80
177 Joe Black	.05	.02
178 Roy Face	.05	.02
179 Earl Weaver MG	.15	.06
180 Johnny Mize	.15	.06

181 Roger Cramer .05 .02
182 Jim Piersall .10 .04
183 Ned Garver .05 .02
184 Billy Williams .15 .06
185 Lefty Grove .15 .06
186 Jim Grant .05 .02
187 Elmer Valo .05 .02
188 Ewell Blackwell .05 .02
189 Mel Ott .15 .06
190 Harry Walker .05 .02
191 Bill Campbell .05 .02
192 Walter Johnson .25 .10
193 Catfish Hunter .15 .06
194 Charlie Keller .05 .02
195 Hank Greenberg .15 .06
196 Bobby Murcer .10 .04
197 Al Lopez .10 .04
198 Vida Blue .10 .04
199 Shag Crawford UMP .05 .02
200 Arky Vaughan .15 .06
201 Smoky Burgess .05 .02
202 Rip Sewell .05 .02
203 Earl Averill .15 .06
204 Milt Pappas .05 .02
205 Mel Harder .05 .02
206 Sam Jethroe .05 .02
207 Randy Hundley .05 .02
208 Jesse Haines .05 .02
209 Jack Brickhouse ANN .05 .02
210 Whitey Ford .25 .10
211 Honus Wagner .50 .20
212 Phil Niekro .15 .06
213 Gary Bell .05 .02
214 Jon Matlack .05 .02
215 Moe Drabowsky .05 .02
216 Edd Roush .15 .06
217 Joel Horlen .05 .02
218 Casey Stengel .25 .10
219 Burt Hooton .05 .02
220 Joe Jackson 1.50 .60

1989-90 Pacific Senior League

The 1989-90 Pacific Trading Cards Senior League set contains 220 standard-size cards. The fronts feature color photos with silver borders and player names and positions at the bottom. The horizontally oriented backs are red, white, and blue, and show vital statistics and career highlights. The cards were distributed as a boxed set with 15 card-sized logo stickers/puzzle pieces as well as in wax packs. There are several In Action cards in the set, designated by IA in the checklist below. The Nettles card was corrected very late according to the set's producer.

NRMT-MT NM
COMPLETE SET (220) 10.00 4.50
COMP. FACT SET (220) 10.00 4.50
1 Bobby Tolan MG .10 .05
2 Sergio Ferrer .05 .02
3 David Rajsich .05 .02
4 Ron LeFlore .10 .05
5 Steve Henderson .05 .02
6 Jerry Martin .05 .02
7 Gary Rajsich .05 .02
8 Elias Sosa .05 .02
9 Jon Matlack .10 .05
10 Steve Kemp .10 .05
11 Lenny Randle .05 .02
12 Roy Howell .05 .02
13 Milt Wilcox .05 .02
14 Alan Bannister .05 .02
15 Dock Ellis .10 .05
16 Mike Williams .05 .02
17 Luis Gomez .05 .02
18 Joe Sambito .05 .02
19 Bake McBride .05 .02
20 Pat Zachry UER .05 .02
(Photo actually Dick Bosman)
21 Dwight Lowry .05 .02
22 Ozzie Virgil Sr. CO .05 .02
23 Randy Lerch .05 .02
24 Butch Benton .05 .02
25 Tom Zimmer CO UER .05 .02
(No bio information)
26 Al Holland UER .05 .02
(Photo actually Nardi Contreras)
27 Sammy Stewart .05 .02
28 Bill Lee .10 .05
29 Ferguson Jenkins .50 .23
30 Leon Roberts .05 .02
31 Rick Wise .10 .05
32 Butch Hobson .05 .02
33 Pete LaCock .05 .02
34 Bill Campbell .05 .02
35 Doug Simunic .05 .02
36 Mario Guerrero .05 .02
37 Jim Willoughby .05 .02
38 Joe Pittman .05 .02
39 Mark Bomback .05 .02
40 Tommy McMillan .05 .02
41 Gary Allenson .05 .02
42 Cecil Cooper .15 .07
43 John LaRosa .05 .02
44 Darrell Brandon .05 .02
45 Bernie Carbo .05 .02
46 Mike Cuellar .15 .07
47 Al Bumbry .05 .02
48 Gene Richards .05 .02
49 Pedro Borbon .05 .02
50 Julio Solo .05 .02
51 Ed Nottle MG .05 .02
52 Jim Bibby .05 .02
53 Doug Griffin CO .05 .02
54 Ed Clements .05 .02
55 Dalton Jones .05 .02
56 Earl Weaver MG .50 .23
57 Jesus De La Rosa .05 .02
58 Paul Casanova .05 .02
59 Frank Riccelli .05 .02
60 Rafael Landestoy UER .05 .02
(Misspelled Raphael on card back)
61 George Hendrick .10 .05
62 Cesar Cedeno .15 .07
63 Bert Campaneris .15 .07
64 Derrel Thomas .05 .02
65 Bobby Ramos .05 .02
66 Grant Jackson .05 .02
67 Steve Whitaker .05 .02
68 Pedro Ramos .05 .02
69 Joe Hicks UER .05 .02
(No height or weight information)
70 Taylor Duncan .05 .02
71 Tom Shopay .05 .02
72 Ken Clay .05 .02
73 Mike Kekich .05 .02
74 Ed Halicki .05 .02
75 Ed Figueroa .05 .02
76 Paul Blair .05 .02
77 Luis Tiant .15 .07
78 Stan Bahnsen .05 .02
79 Rennie Stennett .05 .02
80 Bobby Molinaro .05 .02
81 Jim Gideon .05 .02
82 Orlando Gonzalez .05 .02
83 Amos Otis .10 .05
84 Dennis Leonard .05 .02
85 Pat Putnam .05 .02
86 Rick Manning .05 .02
87 Pat Dobson MG .05 .02
88 Marty Castillo .05 .02
89 Steve McCatty .05 .02
90 Doug Bird .05 .02
91 Rick Waits .05 .02
92 Ron Jackson .05 .02
93 Tim Hosley .05 .02
94 Steve Luebber .05 .02
95 Rich Gale .05 .02
96 Champ Summers .05 .02
97 Dave LaRoche .05 .02
98 Bobby Jones .05 .02
99 Kim Allen .05 .02
100 Wayne Garland .05 .02
101 Tom Spencer .05 .02
102 Dan Driessen .10 .05
103 Ron Pruitt .05 .02
104 Tim Ireland .05 .02
105 Dan Driessen IA .05 .02
106 Pepe Frias UER .05 .02
(Misspelled Pepi on card front)
107 Eric Rasmussen .05 .02
108 Don Hood .05 .02
109 Joe Coleman CO UER .05 .02
(Photo actually Tony Torchia)
110 Jim Slaton .05 .02
111 Clint Hurdle .10 .05
112 Larry Milbourne .05 .02
113 Al Holland .05 .02
114 George Foster .15 .07
115 Graig Nettles MG .15 .07
116 Oscar Gamble .10 .05
117 Ross Grimsley .05 .02
118 Bill Travers .05 .02
119 Jose Beniquez .05 .02
120 Jerry Grote IA .05 .02
121 John D'Acquisto .05 .02
122 Tom Murphy .05 .02
123 Walt Williams UER .05 .02
(Listed as pitcher)
124 Roy Thomas .05 .02
125 Jerry Grote .10 .05
126A Jim Nettles ERR .25 .11
(Writing on bat knob)
126B Jim Nettles COR 2.50 1.10
127 Randy Niemann .05 .02
128 Bobby Bonds .50 .23
129 Ed Glynn .05 .02
130 Ed Hicks .05 .02
131 Ivan Murrell .05 .02
132 Graig Nettles MG .25 .11
133 Hal McRae .25 .11
134 Pat Kelly .05 .02
135 Sammy Stewart .05 .02
136 Bruce Kison .05 .02
137 Jim Morrison .05 .02
138 Omar Moreno .05 .02
139 Tom Brown .05 .02
140 Steve Dillard .05 .02
141 Gary Alexander .05 .02
142 Al Oliver .25 .11
143 Rick Lysander .05 .02
144 Tippy Martinez .05 .02
145 Al Cowens .05 .02
146 Gene Clines .05 .02
147 Willie Aikens .05 .02
148 Tommy Moore .05 .02
149 Clete Boyer MG .10 .05
150 Stan Cliburn .05 .02
151 Ken Kravec .05 .02
152 Garth Iorg .05 .02
153 Rick Peterson .05 .02
154 Wayne Nordhagen UER .05 .02
(Misspelled Nordgahen on card back)
155 Danny Meyer .05 .02
156 Wayne Garrett .05 .02
157 Wayne Krenchicki .05 .02
158 Graig Nettles .25 .11
159 Earl Stephenson .05 .02
160 Carl Taylor .05 .02
161 Rollie Fingers .50 .23
162 Toby Harrah .10 .05
163 Mickey Rivers .10 .05
164 Dave Kingman .15 .07
165 Paul Mirabella .05 .02
166 Dick Williams MG .10 .05
167 Luis Pujols .05 .02
168 Tito Landrum .05 .02
169 Tom Underwood .05 .02
170 Mark Wagner .05 .02
171 Odell Jones .05 .02
172 Doug Capilla .05 .02
173 Alfie Rondon .05 .02
174 Lowell Palmer .05 .02
175 Juan Eichelberger .05 .02
176 Wes Clements .05 .02
177 Rodney Scott .05 .02
178 Ron Washington .05 .02
179 Al Hrabosky .10 .05
180 Sid Monge .05 .02
181 Randy Johnson .05 .02
182 Tim Stoddard .10 .05
183 Dick Williams MG .10 .05
184 Lee Lacy .05 .02
185 Jerry White .05 .02
186 Dave Kingman .15 .07
187 Checklist 1-110 .05 .02
188 Jose Cruz .10 .05
189 Jamie Easterly .05 .02
190 Ike Blessit .05 .02
191 Johnny Grubb .05 .02
192 Dave Cash .05 .02
193 Doug Corbett .05 .02
194 Bruce Bochy .05 .02
195 Mark Corey .05 .02
196 Gil Rondon .05 .02
197 Jerry Martin .05 .02
198 Gerry Pirtle .05 .02
199 Gates Brown MG .05 .02
200 Bob Galasso .05 .02
201 Bake McBride .05 .02
202 Wayne Granger .05 .02
203 Larry Milbourne .05 .02
204 Tom Paciorek .05 .02
205 U.L. Washington .05 .02
206 Larvell Blanks .05 .02
207 Bob Shirley .05 .02
208 Pete Falcone .05 .02
209 Sal Butera .05 .02
210 Roy Branch .05 .02
211 Dyar Miller .05 .02
212 Paul Siebert .05 .02
213 Ken Reitz .05 .02
214 Bill Madlock .15 .07
215 Vida Blue .15 .07
216 Dave Hilton .05 .02
217 Pedro Ramos CO and .05 .02
Charlie Bree CO
218 Checklist 111-220 .05 .02
219 Pat Dobson MG and .15 .07
Earl Weaver MG
220 Curt Flood COMM .15 .07

1990 Pacific Gwynn Candy Bar

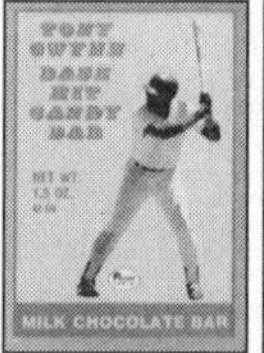

Produced by the Pacific Candy Co., this card features a color action player photo of Tony Gwynn of the San Diego Padres on a tan background in a silver frame and advertises the milk chocolate Tony Gwynn Base Hit Candy Bar. The back displays player information.

Nm-Mt Ex-Mt
1 Tony Gwynn 3.00 .90

1990 Pacific Legends

The 1990 Pacific Legends issue was a 110-card standard-size set issued by Pacific Trading Cards. The set numbering is basically arranged in two alphabetical sequences. This set was available in both factory set and wax packs form. The set does include some active players, Willie Wilson and Jesse Barfield, the last two players in the set.

Nm-Mt Ex-Mt
COMPLETE SET (110) 10.00 3.00
COMP. FACT SET (110) 10.00 3.00
1 Hank Aaron .75 .23
2 Tommie Agee .05 .02
3 Luke Appling .15 .04
4 Sal Bando .05 .02
5 Ernie Banks .50 .15
6 Don Baylor .10 .03
7 Yogi Berra .50 .15
8 Vida Blue .05 .02
9 Lou Boudreau .15 .04
10 Clete Boyer .05 .02
11 George Bamberger .05 .02
12 Lou Brock .25 .07
13 Ralph Branca .05 .02
14 Carl Erskine .05 .02
15 Bert Campaneris .05 .02
16 Steve Carlton .25 .07
17 Rod Carew .25 .07
18 Rocky Colavito .25 .07
19 Frankie Crosetti .10 .03
20 Larry Doby .15 .04
21 Bobby Doerr .15 .04
22 Walt Dropo .05 .02
23 Rick Ferrell .15 .04
24 Joe Garagiola .10 .03
25 Ralph Garr .05 .02
26 Dick Groat .05 .02
27 Steve Garvey .10 .03
28 Bob Gibson .25 .07
29 Don Drysdale .25 .07
30 Billy Herman .15 .04
31 Bobby Grich .05 .02
32 Monte Irvin .15 .04
33 Dave Johnson .05 .02
34 Don Kessinger .05 .02
35 Harmon Killebrew .15 .04
36 Ralph Kiner .15 .04
37 Vern Law .05 .02
38 Ed Lopat .05 .02
39 Bill Mazeroski .15 .04
40 Rick Monday .05 .02
41 Manny Mota .05 .02
42 Don Newcombe .10 .03
43 Gaylord Perry .15 .04
44 Jim Piersall .10 .03
45 Johnny Podres .10 .03
46 Boog Powell .15 .04
47 Robin Roberts .15 .04
48 Ron Santo .15 .04
49 Herb Score .10 .03
50 Enos Slaughter .15 .04
51 Warren Spahn .25 .07
52 Rusty Staub .10 .03
53 Frank Torre .05 .02
54 Bob Horner .05 .02
55 Lee May .05 .02
56 Bill White .10 .03
57 Hoyt Wilhelm .15 .04
58 Billy Williams .15 .04
59 Ted Williams UER .75 .23
Card credits him with an extra batting title
60 Tom Seaver .50 .15
61 Carl Yastrzemski .25 .07
62 Marv Throneberry .05 .02
63 Steve Stone .05 .02
64 Rico Petrocelli .05 .02
65 Orlando Cepeda .15 .04
66 Eddie Mathews .15 .04
67 Joe Sewell .15 .04
68 Catfish Hunter .15 .04
69 Alvin Dark .10 .03
70 Richie Ashburn .15 .04
71 Dusty Baker .10 .03
72 George Foster .05 .02
73 Eddie Yost .05 .02
74 Buddy Bell .05 .02
75 Manny Sanguillen .05 .02
76 Jim Bunning .15 .04
77 Smoky Burgess .05 .02
78 Al Rosen .05 .02
79 Gene Conley .05 .02
80 Dave Dravecky .05 .02
81 Charlie Gehringer .15 .04
82 Billy Pierce .05 .02
83 Willie Horton .05 .02
84 Ron Hunt .05 .02
85 Bob Feller .25 .07
86 George Kell .15 .04
87 Dave Kingman .15 .04
88 Jerry Koosman .10 .03
89 Clem Labine .05 .02
90 Tony LaRussa .10 .03
91 Dennis Leonard .05 .02
92 Dale Long .05 .02
93 Sparky Lyle .05 .02
94 Gil McDougald .05 .02
95 Don Mossi .05 .02
96 Phil Niekro .15 .04
97 Tom Paciorek .05 .02
98 Mel Parnell .05 .02
99 Lou Piniella .10 .03
100 Bobby Richardson .10 .03
101 Phil Rizzuto .25 .07
102 Brooks Robinson .25 .07
103 Pete Runnels .05 .02
104 Diego Segui .05 .02
105 Bobby Shantz .05 .02
106 Bobby Thomson .10 .03
107 Joe Torre .10 .03
108 Earl Weaver MG .15 .04
109 Willie Wilson .05 .02
110 Jesse Barfield .05 .02

1991 Pacific Prototype

This standard-size card was produced by Pacific Trading Cards in order to help them secure a liscense with Major League Baseball. The front has a photo of Ryne Sandberg along with the necessary identification. The back is basically blank. The card has room for vital statistics, a brief biography and some statistics and each section is framed in red. A very limited number of these cards were produced. Almost all of these cards were destroyed. A prototype card of Leon Durham was produced in 1988. As far as is known, no copies of the Durham card have ever surfaced in the secondary market.

Nm-Mt Ex-Mt
1 Ryne Sandberg 1200.00 350.00

1991 Pacific Ryan Texas Express I

This 110-card standard-size set, Texas Express, traces the career of Nolan Ryan from the start of his career into the 1991 season as well as his personal life with his family on his ranch in Alvin, Texas. This set was issued by Pacific Trading cards and was the first set featuring an individual baseball player to be sold in wax packs since the 1959 Fleer Ted Williams issue. The cards were available in 12-card foil packs and factory sets. Moreover, eight unnumbered bonus cards (1-6 No Hitters, 1991 25th Season, and Rookie year with the Mets) were produced in quantities of 1,000 of each card in gold foil and 10,000 of each card in silver foil; these bonus cards were randomly inserted in foil packs only. After the first and second series of Pacific Nolan Ryan Texas Express had sold out, Pacific reissued card numbers 1-220 in 1993, and the cards produced in this reissue may be distinguished by the 27th season logo, which was introduced to collectors in the 30-card 27th Season series. Currently there is no value differential between the two types.

Nm-Mt Ex-Mt
COMPLETE SET (110) 12.00 3.60
COMP. FACT (110) 12.00 3.60
COMMON CARD (1-110) .10 .03
1 Nolan Ryan .40 .12
Future Hall of Famer
11 Nolan Ryan .25 .07
Gil Hodges MG
Keep the Ball Down
29 Nolan Ryan .15 .04
Fastest Pitch Ever Thrown
Clocked at 100.9 MPH
30 Nolan Ryan .15 .04
No-Hitter Number 3
31 Nolan Ryan .15 .04
No-Hitter Number 4
32 Nolan Ryan .15 .04
Frank Tanana
36 Nolan Ryan .15 .04
Starting Pitcher
40 Nolan Ryan .15 .04
Home Run
42 Nolan Ryan .15 .04
Record 5th No-Hitter
43 Nolan Ryan .15 .04
No-Hitter Number 5
45 Nolan Ryan .25 .07
Passes Walter Johnson
46 Nolan Ryan .15 .04
Strikeout 4000
61 Nolan Ryan .15 .04
Dan Smith
63 Nolan Ryan .15 .04
Last Pitch No-Hitter Number 6
64 Nolan Ryan .15 .04
Sweet Number 6
68 Nolan Ryan .25 .07
Brad Arnsberg
Geno Petralli
300 Game Win Battery
75 Nolan Ryan .15 .04
Pitcher Texas Rangers
77 Nolan Ryan .25 .07
Throwing Spirals
92 Nolan Ryan 1.00 .30
A Real Gamer
Bloody lip
and blood all over jersey
93 Nolan Ryan .25 .07
Jim Sundberg
Ranger Battery Mates
107 Nolan Ryan .15 .04
The Ryan Family
110 Nolan Ryan .40 .12
Lynn Nolan Ryan

1991 Pacific Ryan Inserts 8

These eight standard-size cards were inserts in 1991 Pacific Nolan Ryan Texas Express foil packs. As with the regular issue, the fronts display glossy color photos that are bordered in silver foil and either purple/red or red/orange border stripes. The cards are unnumbered and checklisted in chronological order. Besides the silver cards, they were also issued on a much more limited basis in gold. The gold versions are valued at quadruple the prices listed below.

Nm-Mt Ex-Mt
COMPLETE SET (8) 100.00 30.00
COMMON CARD (1-8) 15.00 4.50

1991 Pacific Ryan 7th No-Hitter

This seven-card standard-size set was produced by Pacific Trading Cards Inc. to capture various moments of Nolan Ryan's 7th no-hitter. These cards were produced in the following numbers: 1,000 of each card in gold foil and 10,000 of each card in silver foil. These cards were randomly inserted in foil packs only. Supposedly as many as half of the cards were destroyed and never released. The prices below refer to the silver versions; the gold versions would be valued at quadruple the prices below. In addition to silver and gold, two other border versions have surfaced. One type has silver prism borders, the other has gold hologram-like borders. It is not known how these cards were distributed, but they are scarcer than the gold border cards and are valued at six times the prices below.

Nm-Mt Ex-Mt

COMPLETE SET (7) 100.00 30.00
COMMON CARD (1-7) 15.00 4.50

1991 Pacific Senior League

Pacific Trading Cards released this 160-card set just after the Senior League suspended operations. The standard size cards were sold in wax packs and as complete sets. Apparently there are two different versions of cards for the following players: Jim Rice, Rollie Fingers, Vida Blue, Dave Cash, Dan Norman, Ron LeFlore, Cesar Cedeno, Rafael Landestoy, and Dan Driessen.

Nm-Mt Ex-Mt
COMPLETE SET (160) 8.00 2.40
COMP.FACT SET (160) 8.00 2.40
1 Dan Driessen .10 .03
2 Marty Castillo .05 .02
3 Jerry White .05 .02
4 Bud Anderson .05 .02
5 Ron Jackson .05 .02
6 Fred Stanley CO .05 .02
7 Steve Luebber .05 .02
8 Jerry Terrell CO .05 .02
9 Pat Dobson .10 .03
10 Ken Kravec .05 .02
11 Gil Rondon .05 .02
12 Dyar Miller CO .05 .02
13 Bobby Molinaro .05 .02
14 Jerry Martin .05 .02
15 Rick Waits .05 .02
16 Steve McCatty .05 .02
17 Roger Slagle .05 .02
18 Mike Ramsey .05 .02
19 Rich Gale .05 .02
20 Larry Harlow .05 .02
21 Dan Rohn .05 .02
22 Don Cooper .05 .02
23 Marv Foley .05 .02
24 Rafael Landestoy .05 .02
25 Eddie Milner .05 .02
26 Amos Otis .10 .03
27 Odell Jones .05 .02
28 Tippy Martinez .05 .02
29 Stu Cliburn .05 .02
30 Stan Cliburn .05 .02
31 Tony Cloninger CO .05 .02
32 Jeff Jones .05 .02
33 Ken Reitz .05 .02
34 Dave Sax .05 .02
35 Orlando Gonzalez .05 .02
36 Jose Cruz .10 .03
37 Mickey Mahler .05 .02
38 Derek Botelho .05 .02
39 Rick Lysander .05 .02
40 Cesar Cedeno .10 .03
41 Garth Iorg .05 .02
42 Wayne Krenchicki .05 .02
43 Clete Boyer CO .10 .03
44 Dan Boone .05 .02
45 George Vukovich .05 .02
46 Omar Moreno .05 .02
47 Ron Washington .05 .02
48 Ron Washington MVP .05 .02
49 Rick Peterson .05 .02
50 Tack Wilson .05 .02
51 Stan Cliburn .05 .02
Stu Cliburn
52 Rick Lysander POY .05 .02
53 Cesar Cedeno and .10 .03
Pete LaCock
54 Jim Marshall MG and .05 .02
Clete Boyer MG
55 Doug Simunic .05 .02
56 Pat Kelly .05 .02
57 Roy Branch .05 .02
58 Dave Cash .10 .03
59 Bobby Jones .05 .02
60 Hector Cruz .05 .02
61 Reggie Cleveland .05 .02
62 Gary Lance .05 .02
63 Ron LeFlore .10 .03
64 Dan Norman .05 .02
65 Renie Martin .05 .02
66 Pete Mackanin MG .05 .02
67 Frank Riccelli .05 .02
68 Alfie Rondon .05 .02
69 Rodney Scott .05 .02
70 Jim Tracy .05 .02
71 Ed Dennis .05 .02
72 Rick Lindell .05 .02
73 Stu Pepper .05 .02
74 Jeff Youngbauer .05 .02
75 Russ Foster .05 .02
76 Jeff Capriati .05 .02
77 Art DeFreites .05 .02
78 Alfie Rondon .05 .02
79 Reggie Cleveland IA .05 .02
80 Dave Cash .05 .02
81 Vida Blue .15 .04
82 Ed Glynn .05 .02
83 Bob Owchinko .05 .02
84 Bill Fleming .05 .02
85 Ron Roenicke .05 .02
Gary Roenicke
86 Tom Thompson CO .05 .02
87 Derrel Thomas UER .05 .02
(Name misspelled
Derrell)
88 Jim Willoughby .05 .02
89 Jim Pankovits .05 .02
90 Jack Cooley CO .05 .02
91 Lenn Sakata .05 .02
92 Mike Brocki .05 .02
93 Chuck Fick .05 .02
94 Tom Benedict .05 .02
95 Anthony Davis .25 .07
96 Cardell Camper .05 .02
97 Leon Roberts .05 .02
98 Roger Erickson .05 .02
99 Kim Allen .05 .02
100 Dave Skaggs .05 .02
101 Joe Decker .05 .02
102 U.L. Washington .05 .02
103 Don Fletcher .05 .02
104 Gary Roenicke .05 .02
105 Rich Dauer MG .05 .02
106 Ron Roenicke .05 .02
107 Mike Norris .05 .02
108 Ferguson Jenkins .50 .15
109 Ronn Reynolds .05 .02
110 Pete Falcone .05 .02
111 Gary Allenson .05 .02
112 Mark Wagner .05 .02
113 Jack Lazorko .05 .02
114 Bob Galasso .05 .02
115 Ron Davis .05 .02
116 Lenny Randle .05 .02
117 Ricky Peters .05 .02
118 Jim Dwyer .05 .02
119 Juan Eichelberger .05 .02
120 Pete LaCock .10 .03
121 Tony Scott .05 .02
122 Rick Lancellotti .05 .02
123 Barry Bonnell .05 .02
124 Dave Hilton .05 .02
125 Bill Campbell .05 .02
126 Rollie Fingers .50 .15
127 Jim Marshall MG .05 .02
128 Razor Shines .10 .03
129 Guy Sularz .05 .02
130 Roy Thomas .05 .02
131 Joel Youngblood .05 .02
132 Ernie Camacho .05 .02
133 Dave Hilton CO .05 .02
Jim Marshall MG
and Fred Stanley CO
134 Ken Landreaux .05 .02
135 Dave Rozema .05 .02
136 Tom Zimmer CO .05 .02
137 Elias Sosa .05 .02
138 Ossie Virgil Sr. CO .05 .02
139 Al Holland .05 .02
140 Milt Wilcox .05 .02
141 Jerry Reed .05 .02
142 Chris Welsh .05 .02
143 Luis Gomez .05 .02
144 Steve Henderson .05 .02
145 Butch Benton .05 .02
146 Bill Lee .10 .03
147 Todd Cruz .05 .02
148 Jim Rice .25 .07
149 Tito Landrum .05 .02
150 Ozzie Virgil Jr. .05 .02
151 Joe Pittman .05 .02
152 Bobby Tolan MG .05 .02
153 Len Barker .05 .02
154 Dave Rajsich .05 .02
155 Glenn Gulliver .05 .02
156 Gary Rajsich .05 .02
157 Joe Sambito .05 .02
158 Frank Vito .05 .02
159 Ozzie Virgil Jr. .05 .02
Ozzie Virgil Sr.
160 Dave Rajsich .05 .02
Gary Rajsich

1992 Pacific Ryan Magazine 6

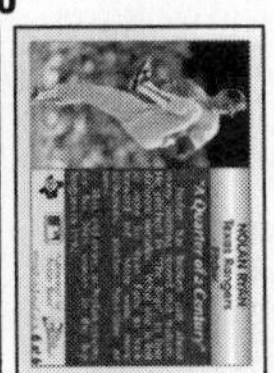

These six standard size cards were inserted (bound) into the July 1992 Volume 2, Issue 2 of Trading Cards magazine as a pair of two-card strips. These are very similar to the hard-to-find inserts that Pacific inserted into the Ryan Texas Express second series foil packs. These "magazine cards" are only differentiable by the fact that they lack the words "Limited Edition" on the copyright line on their backs.

Nm-Mt Ex-Mt
COMPLETE SET (6) 8.00 2.40
COMMON CARD (1-6) 1.50 .45

1992 Pacific Ryan Texas Express II

For the second year, Pacific issued a 110-card standard-size set titled Texas Express. A six-card insert set was randomly inserted in foil packs, with 1,000 autographed and numbered of card number 1. This set was also issued in a factory set form with no inserts. This set is essentially an extension or second series of the 1991 Pacific Nolan Ryan set and is numbered that way. After the first and second series of Pacific Nolan Ryan Texas Express had sold out, Pacific reissued card numbers 1-220 in 1993, and the cards produced in this reissue may be distinguished by the 27th season logo, which was introduced to collectors in the 30-card 27th Season series. Currently there is no value differential between the two types.

Nm-Mt Ex-Mt
COMPLETE SET (110) 10.00 3.00
COMP.FACT (110) 10.00 3.00
COMMON CARD (111-220) .10 .03
111 Nolan Ryan .25 .07
The Golden Arm
118 Nolan Ryan .15 .04
The Cowboy
122 Nolan Ryan .15 .04
New York Strikeout Record
124 Nolan Ryan .25 .07
Hall of Fame Victims
129 Nolan Ryan .15 .04
Strikeout Record
130 Nolan Ryan .15 .04
Number One
132 Nolan Ryan .15 .04
Number Two
134 Nolan Ryan .15 .04
Number Three
135 Nolan Ryan .25 .07
Bob Feller
Pure Speed
138 Nolan Ryan .15 .04
Number Four
142 Nolan Ryan .15 .04
Strong Houston Staff
143 Nolan Ryan .15 .04
Number Five
148 Nolan Ryan .25 .07
Breaks Walter Johnson's Record
149 Nolan Ryan .25 .07
Reese Ryan
156 Nolan Ryan .15 .04
Like Father Like Son
170 Nolan Ryan .15 .04
Number Six
171 Nolan Ryan .15 .04
300th Win
173 Nolan Ryan .25 .07
Man of the Year
177 Nolan Ryan .15 .04
Mike Stanley
Stanley's Delight
178 Nolan Ryan .15 .04
After Nolan's 7th No-Hitter
187 Nolan Ryan .15 .04
Number Seven
188 Nolan Ryan .15 .04
Passes Phil Niekro
189 Nolan Ryan .15 .04
Trails Don Sutton
198 Nolan Ryan .25 .07
Goose Gossage
200 Nolan Ryan .35 .10
Roger Clemens
Don't Mess With Texas
204 Nolan Ryan .15 .04
Bobby Valentine MG
Manager's Delight
206 Nolan Ryan .25 .07
The Quarterback
208 Nolan Ryan .15 .04
Tom House CO
Passing Along Wisdom
211 Nolan Ryan .15 .04
Seven No-Hitters
219 Nolan Ryan .15 .04
Receives The Victor Award
220 Nolan Ryan .25 .07
1992: Nolan's 26th Season

1992 Pacific Ryan Gold

These eight standard size cards were one of two insert subsets randomly packed in 1992 Pacific Nolan Ryan Texas Express II 12-card and 24-card foil packs. Supposedly 10,000 of each card were produced. The cards feature high gloss color action photos of Ryan pitching his seven no-hitters. The pictures are bordered in gold foil and either red/orange (1-4) or purple/red border (5-8) stripes. Inside a flaming baseball design, the backs of cards 1-7 display statistics for that no-hitter while card No. 8 summarizes all seven no-hitters. The cards are unnumbered and checklisted in chronological order of the events.

Nm-Mt Ex-Mt
COMPLETE SET (8) 175.00 52.50
COMMON CARD (1-8) 25.00 7.50

1992 Pacific Ryan Limited

These six standard size cards were one of two insert subsets randomly packed in 1992 Pacific Nolan Ryan Texas Express II 12-card and 24-card foil packs. Only 3,000 of each card were produced and, as an added bonus, 1,000 of card number 1 were autographed by Ryan. A similar-looking pair of two-card strips was inserted (bound) into all issues of the July 1992 Volume 2, Issue 2 of Trading Cards magazine. However these "magazine cards" lack the words "Limited Edition" on the copyright line on their backs. Nolan's name appears in a red, white, and blue bar above a red box containing either career highlights (2, 3, 6), statistics (4) or a poem (5).

Nm-Mt Ex-Mt
COMPLETE SET (6) 125.00 38.00
COMMON CARD (1-6) 25.00 7.50
AU Nolan Ryan 150.00 45.00
Card #1, 1000 signed

1992 Pacific Seaver

This 110-card standard-size set traces the career of Tom Seaver. The set was sold in 12-card foil packs or as a factory set for $12.95 through a mail-in offer. Autograph cards of Tom Seaver were randomly inserted into packs.

Nm-Mt Ex-Mt
COMPLETE SET (110) 8.00 2.40
COMP.FACT SET (110) 8.00 2.40
COMMON CARD (1-110) .10 .03
1 Tom Seaver .40 .12
Stand-out High School
Basketball Player
8 Tom Seaver .15 .04
1967 Rookie of the Year
15 Tom Seaver .15 .04
1969 Cy Young Winner
16 Tom Seaver .15 .04
Pitcher of the Year
22 Tom Seaver .15 .04
Second Cy Young Award
57 Tom Seaver .25 .07
Luke Appling
Ozzie Guillen
Blast From the Past
59 Tom Seaver .15 .04
LaMarr Hoyt
Cy Young Winners
60 Tom Seaver .25 .07
Carlton Fisk
Two Legends of the Game
61 Tom Seaver .15 .04
Placido Domingo
Singing Praise
63 Tom Seaver .15 .04
Sarah Seaver
Anne Seaver
Nancy Seaver
The Seaver Family
65 Tom Seaver .15 .04
Traded to the Red Sox
67 Tom Seaver .15 .04
Red Sox Man
68 Tom Seaver .15 .04
Boston Red Sox Pitcher
82 Tom Seaver .40 .12
Nolan Ryan
85 Tom Seaver .40 .12
Nolan Ryan
300 Win Club
91 Tom Seaver .15 .04
Tom Terrific
104 Tom Seaver .15 .04
George Thomas Seaver
106 Tom Seaver .15 .04
Receives the
Judge Emil Fuchs Award
110 Tom Seaver .15 .04
Breaking Walter Johnson's
Strikeout Record

1992 Pacific Seaver Inserts 6

These six standard-size cards were one of two insert subsets (depicting career highlights of Tom Seaver) randomly packed in 1992 Pacific Tom Seaver 12-card foil packs. The two insert sets are numbered the same, the primary physical difference being a white border or a gold foil border on the card front. Only 3,000 of each non-gold card were produced and, as an added bonus, 1,000 of each card number 1 were autographed by Seaver. According to Pacific, 10,000 of each gold card were produced. However, it seems like the numbers reported by Pacific were actually transposed when the cards were issued. There seem to be more non-gold (White) card issued than Gold cards. The six career highlight cards feature high gloss color action player photos on their fronts edged by a color stripe on the left and framed by a white (or gold) outer border. The "Tom Terrific" logo overlays the stripe at the lower left corner. The backs of the gold foil insert cards are identical to those of the regular inserts and are distinguished only by their non-glossy finish. The values for the gold and white versions are the same at this time.

Nm-Mt Ex-Mt
COMPLETE SET (6) 125.00 38.00
COMMON CARD (1-6) 25.00 7.50
AU1 Tom Seaver AU 75.00 22.00

1993 Pacific Ryan 27th Season

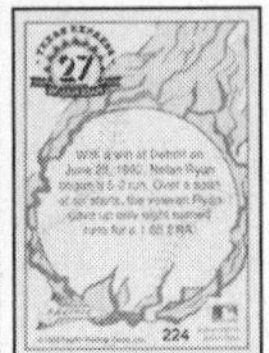

Pacific issued this 30-card standard-size set to honor Nolan Ryan being the first player in Major League Baseball history to appear in 27 seasons. The series was available in collector sets inside an attractive complete set box as well as in 25-cent five-card foil packs; the foil packs contained series I, series II, 27th Season series, and randomly inserted bonus cards. The cards are numbered on the back in continuation of the Texas Express first and second series. Beginning in mid-June, displays of Advil featuring Ryan and two-card packs appeared in stores nationwide. The two-card foil packs were available with the purchase of a bottle of 24 or more Advil Tablets or Caplets. On June 20, 1993, an offer to purchase the entire set was featured in Sunday newspapers. By mailing the Advil proof of purchase and $3.49 plus $1.50 for shipping to Pacific, the complete 30-card set could be obtained; the offer expired Dec. 31, 1993.

Nm-Mt Ex-Mt
COMPLETE SET (30) 12.00 3.60
COMMON CARD (221-250) .25 .07
241 Nolan Ryan .75 .23
Tom Seaver
242 Nolan Ryan .75 .23
Rod Carew
Angels' Number 30 Retired
245 Nolan Ryan .50 .15
Jimmie Reese CO
Great Friends
246 Nolan Ryan .50 .15
Gene Autry
Cowboys
250 Nolan Ryan .50 .15
Tom Seaver
Pacific Pride
NNO Pacific Trading Cards .15 .04
(Advertisement;
Cover card)

1993 Pacific Ryan Farewell McCormick

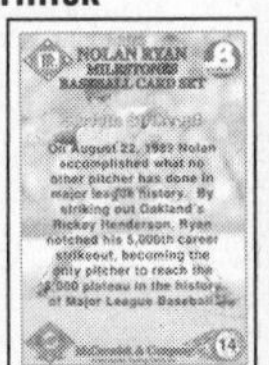

Given away to fans attending a Texas Rangers game at Arlington Stadium during Nolan Ryan Appreciation Week, this 21-card, standard-size set was produced by Pacific Trading Cards, Inc. for McCormick and Company.

Nm-Mt Ex-Mt
COMPLETE SET (21) 10.00 3.00
COMMON CARD (1-20) .50 .15

1993 Pacific Ryan Limited

Six more standard-size cards (7-12), numbered in continuation of the 1992 set, were issued in 1993 and have a 1993 copyright notice on the card back. The card design was not significantly altered, and the backs contain the words "Limited Edition", as do the first six cards. Card numbers 7-12 were issued with gold foil borders, and the production run was 3,000 of each card. Gold foil versions of card Nos. 7-9 were given away only at the Bellevue (WA) Sports Collectors Classic IV each day of the show; card numbers 10-12 were randomly inserted in the 25-cent Changemaker packs. Although the cards are most commonly found with gold borders, white border cards have also been reported.

Nm-Mt Ex-Mt
COMPLETE SET (6) 125.00 38.00
COMMON CARD (7-12) 25.00 7.50

1993 Pacific Ryan Prism Inserts

This 20-card prism standard-size set was issued by Pacific to honor the career of Nolan Ryan. The cards were randomly inserted into 1993 Nolan Ryan 25-cent Changemaker five-card packs. The production figures were reportedly 10,000 of each card. Gold versions of these sets are known as well. The Gold versions are currently valued at 2X the prices listed below.

Nm-Mt Ex-Mt
COMPLETE SET (20) 150.00 45.00
COMMON CARD (1-20) 8.00 2.40
*GOLD: 2X PRISM

1993 Pacific Spanish

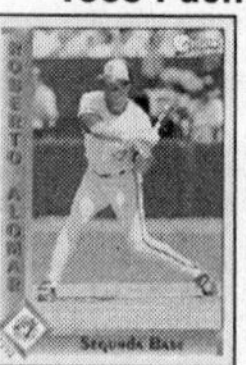

Issued in two 330-card series, these 660 standard-size cards represent Pacific's first effort at a nationally distributed, MLB-licensed card set. All text on both sides is in Spanish. The cards are numbered on the back, grouped alphabetically within teams, and checklisted below alphabetically according to teams in both series. Each series card numbering is alphabetical by players within teams with the teams themselves in order by team nickname. Very early in the printing, Rob Maurer (number 313) was printed with, very obviously, someone else's photo on the card. This very tough card is rarely seen in the hobby and since it is so thinly traded there is no established market value. On the Third Annual Latin Night at Yankee Stadium (July 22, 1993; New York Yankees versus California Angels), four-card foil packs, featuring a title card and three player cards, were given away.

Nm-Mt Ex-Mt
COMPLETE SET (660) 40.00 12.00
COMP. SERIES 1 (330) 25.00 7.50
COMP. SERIES 2 (330) 15.00 4.50
COMMON CARD (1-330) .05 .02
COMMON (331-660) .10 .03
1 Rafael Belliard .05 .02
2 Sid Bream .05 .02
3 Francisco Cabrera .05 .02
4 Marvin Freeman .05 .02
5 Ron Gant .10 .03
6 Tom Glavine .50 .15
7 Brian Hunter .05 .02
8 David Justice .30 .09
9 Ryan Klesko .10 .03
10 Melvin Nieves .05 .02
11 Deion Sanders .30 .09
12 John Smoltz .30 .09
13 Mark Wohlers .05 .02
14 Brady Anderson .10 .03
15 Glenn Davis .05 .02
16 Mike Devereaux .05 .02
17 Leo Gomez .05 .02
18 Chris Hoiles .05 .02
19 Chito Martinez .05 .02
20 Ben McDonald .05 .02
21 Mike Mussina .30 .09
22 Gregg Olson .05 .02
23 Joe Orsulak .05 .02
24 Cal Ripken 3.00 .90
25 David Segui .05 .02
26 Rick Sutcliffe .05 .02
27 Wade Boggs .75 .23
28 Tom Brunansky .05 .02
29 Ellis Burks .10 .03
30 Roger Clemens 1.50 .45
31 John Dopson .05 .02
32 John Flaherty .05 .02
33 Mike Greenwell .05 .02
34 Tony Pena .10 .03
35 Carlos Quintana .05 .02
36 Luis Rivera .05 .02
37 Mo Vaughn .30 .09
38 Frank Viola .05 .02
39 Matt Young .05 .02
40 Scott Bailes .05 .02
41 Bert Blyleven .20 .06
42 Chad Curtis .05 .02
43 Gary DiSarcina .05 .02
44 Chuck Finley .10 .03
45 Mike Fitzgerald .05 .02
46 Gary Gaetti .10 .03
47 Rene Gonzales .05 .02
48 Mark Langston .05 .02
49 Scott Lewis .05 .02
50 Luis Polonia .05 .02
51 Tim Salmon .30 .09
52 Lee Stevens .05 .02
53 Steve Buechele .05 .02
54 Frank Castillo .05 .02
55 Doug Dascenzo .05 .02
56 Andre Dawson .30 .09
57 Shawon Dunston .05 .02
58 Mark Grace .20 .06
59 Mike Morgan .05 .02
60 Luis Salazar .05 .02
61 Rey Sanchez .05 .02
62 Ryne Sandberg 1.00 .30
63 Dwight Smith .05 .02
64 Jerome Walton .05 .02
65 Rick Wilkins .05 .02
66 Wilson Alvarez .10 .03
67 George Bell .05 .02
68 Joey Cora .05 .02
69 Alex Fernandez .05 .02
70 Carlton Fisk .50 .15
71 Craig Grebeck .05 .02
72 Ozzie Guillen .10 .03
73 Jack McDowell .05 .02
74 Scott Radinsky .05 .02
75 Tim Raines .10 .03
76 Bobby Thigpen .05 .02
77 Frank Thomas .75 .23
78 Robin Ventura .30 .09
79 Tom Browning .05 .02
80 Jacob Brumfield .05 .02
81 Rob Dibble .05 .02
82 Bill Doran .05 .02
83 Billy Hatcher .05 .02
84 Barry Larkin .30 .09
85 Hal Morris .05 .02
86 Joe Oliver .05 .02
87 Jeff Reed .05 .02
88 Jose Rijo .05 .02
89 Bip Roberts .05 .02
90 Chris Sabo .05 .02
91 Sandy Alomar Jr. .10 .03
92 Brad Arnsberg .05 .02
93 Carlos Baerga .10 .03
94 Albert Belle .10 .03
95 Felix Fermin .05 .02
96 Mark Lewis .05 .02
97 Kenny Lofton .20 .06
98 Carlos Martinez .05 .02
99 Rod Nichols .05 .02
100 Dave Rohde .05 .02
101 Scott Scudder .05 .02
102 Paul Sorrento .05 .02
103 Mark Whiten .05 .02
104 Mark Carreon .05 .02
105 Milt Cuyler .05 .02
106 Rob Deer .05 .02
107 Cecil Fielder .10 .03
108 Travis Fryman .10 .03
109 Dan Gladden .05 .02
110 Bill Gullickson .05 .02
111 Les Lancaster .05 .02
112 Mark Leiter .05 .02
113 Tony Phillips .05 .02
114 Mickey Tettleton .05 .02
115 Alan Trammell .20 .06
116 Lou Whitaker .10 .03
117 Jeff Bagwell 1.00 .30
118 Craig Biggio .30 .09
119 Joe Boever .05 .02
120 Casey Candaele .05 .02
121 Andujar Cedeno .05 .02
122 Steve Finley .20 .06
123 Luis Gonzalez .30 .09
124 Pete Harnisch .05 .02
125 Jimmy Jones .05 .02
126 Mark Portugal .05 .02
127 Rafael Ramirez .05 .02
128 Mike Simms .05 .02
129 Eric Yelding .05 .02
130 Luis Aquino .05 .02
131 Kevin Appier .10 .03
132 Mike Boddicker .05 .02
133 George Brett 1.50 .45
134 Tom Gordon .05 .02
135 Mark Gubicza .05 .02
136 David Howard .05 .02
137 Gregg Jefferies .05 .02
138 Wally Joyner .10 .03
139 Brian McRae .05 .02
140 Jeff Montgomery .05 .02
141 Terry Shumpert .05 .02
142 Curtis Wilkerson .05 .02
143 Brett Butler .10 .03
144 Eric Davis .10 .03
145 Kevin Gross .05 .02
146 Dave Hansen .05 .02
147 Lenny Harris .05 .02
148 Carlos Hernandez .05 .02
149 Orel Hershiser .10 .03
150 Jay Howell .05 .02
151 Eric Karros .20 .06
152 Ramon Martinez .05 .02
153 Jose Offerman .05 .02
154 Mike Sharperson .05 .02
155 Darryl Strawberry .10 .03
156 Jim Gantner .05 .02
157 Darryl Hamilton .05 .02
158 Doug Henry .05 .02
159 John Jaha .05 .02
160 Pat Listach .05 .02
161 Jaime Navarro .05 .02
162 Dave Nilsson .05 .02
163 Jesse Orosco .10 .03
164 Kevin Seitzer .05 .02
165 B.J. Surhoff .10 .03
166 Greg Vaughn .10 .03
167 Robin Yount .50 .15
168 Rick Aguilera .10 .03
169 Scott Erickson .05 .02
170 Mark Guthrie .05 .02
171 Kent Hrbek .10 .03
172 Chuck Knoblauch .30 .09
173 Gene Larkin .05 .02
174 Shane Mack .05 .02
175 Pedro Munoz .05 .02
176 Mike Pagliarulo .05 .02
177 Kirby Puckett .60 .18
178 Kevin Tapani .05 .02
179 Gary Wayne .05 .02
180 Moises Alou .10 .03
181 Brian Barnes .05 .02
182 Archi Cianfrocco .05 .02
183 Delino DeShields .10 .03
184 Darrin Fletcher .05 .02
185 Marquis Grissom .10 .03
186 Ken Hill .05 .02
187 Dennis Martinez .10 .03
188 Bill Sampen .05 .02
189 John Vander Wal .05 .02
190 Larry Walker .20 .06
191 Tim Wallach .05 .02
192 Bobby Bonilla .10 .03
193 Daryl Boston .05 .02
194 Vince Coleman .05 .02
195 Kevin Elster .05 .02
196 Sid Fernandez .05 .02
197 John Franco .10 .03
198 Dwight Gooden .10 .03
199 Howard Johnson .05 .02
200 Willie Randolph .10 .03
201 Bret Saberhagen .10 .03
202 Dick Schofield .05 .02
203 Pete Schourek .05 .02
204 Greg Cadaret .05 .02
205 John Habyan .05 .02
206 Pat Kelly .05 .02
207 Kevin Maas .05 .02
208 Don Mattingly 1.50 .45
209 Matt Nokes .05 .02
210 Melido Perez .05 .02
211 Scott Sanderson .05 .02
212 Andy Stankiewicz .05 .02
213 Danny Tartabull .05 .02
214 Randy Velarde .10 .03
215 Bernie Williams .30 .09
216 Harold Baines .10 .03
217 Mike Bordick .05 .02
218 Scott Brosius .10 .03
219 Jerry Browne .05 .02
220 Ron Darling .05 .02
221 Dennis Eckersley .40 .12
222 Rickey Henderson .75 .23
223 Rick Honeycutt .05 .02
224 Mark McGwire 2.50 .75
225 Ruben Sierra .10 .03
226 Terry Steinbach .05 .02
227 Bob Welch .05 .02
228 Willie Wilson .05 .02
229 Ruben Amaro .05 .02
230 Kim Batiste .05 .02
231 Juan Bell .05 .02
232 Wes Chamberlain .05 .02
233 Darren Daulton .10 .03
234 Mariano Duncan .05 .02
235 Lenny Dykstra .10 .03
236 Dave Hollins .05 .02
237 Stan Javier .05 .02
238 John Kruk .10 .03
239 Mickey Morandini .05 .02
240 Terry Mulholland .05 .02
241 Mitch Williams .05 .02
242 Stan Belinda .05 .02
243 Jay Bell .05 .02
244 Carlos Garcia .05 .02
245 Jeff King .05 .02
246 Mike LaValliere .05 .02
247 Lloyd McClendon .05 .02
248 Orlando Merced .05 .02
249 Paul Miller .05 .02
250 Gary Redus .05 .02
251 Don Slaught .05 .02
252 Zane Smith .05 .02
253 Andy Van Slyke .10 .03
254 Tim Wakefield .20 .06
255 Andy Benes .05 .02
256 Dann Bilardello .05 .02
257 Tony Gwynn 1.50 .45
258 Greg W. Harris .05 .02
259 Darrin Jackson .05 .02
260 Mike Maddux .05 .02
261 Fred McGriff .20 .06
262 Rich Rodriguez .05 .02
263 Benito Santiago .10 .03
264 Gary Sheffield .40 .12
265 Kurt Stillwell .05 .02
266 Tim Teufel .05 .02
267 Bud Black .05 .02
268 John Burkett .05 .02
269 Will Clark .30 .09
270 Royce Clayton .05 .02
271 Bryan Hickerson .05 .02
272 Chris James .05 .02
273 Darren Lewis .05 .02
274 Willie McGee .10 .03
275 Jim McNamara .05 .02
276 Francisco Oliveras .05 .02
277 Robby Thompson .05 .02
278 Matt Williams .20 .06
279 Trevor Wilson .05 .02
280 Bret Boone .20 .06
281 Greg Briley .05 .02
282 Jay Buhner .10 .03
283 Henry Cotto .05 .02
284 Rich DeLucia .05 .02
285 Dave Fleming .05 .02
286 Ken Griffey Jr. 2.00 .60
287 Erik Hanson .05 .02
288 Randy Johnson .75 .23
289 Tino Martinez .20 .06
290 Edgar Martinez .20 .06
291 Dave Valle .05 .02
292 Omar Vizquel .10 .03
293 Luis Alicea .05 .02
294 Bernard Gilkey .05 .02
295 Felix Jose .05 .02
296 Ray Lankford .10 .03
297 Omar Olivares .05 .02
298 Jose Oquendo .05 .02
299 Tom Pagnozzi .05 .02
300 Geronimo Pena .05 .02
301 Gerald Perry .05 .02
302 Ozzie Smith 1.00 .30
303 Lee Smith .10 .03
304 Bob Tewksbury .05 .02
305 Todd Zeile .20 .06
306 Kevin Brown .20 .06
307 Todd Burns .05 .02
308 Jose Canseco .40 .12
309 Hector Fajardo .05 .02
310 Julio Franco .10 .03
311A Juan Gonzalez 1.50 .45
White uniform on back
311B Juan Gonzalez 1.50 .45
Blue uniform on back
312 Jeff Huson .05 .02
313A Rob Maurer ERR
Believed to be Donald Harris pictured
313B Rob Maurer .05 .02
314 Rafael Palmeiro .30 .09
315 Dean Palmer .10 .03
316 Ivan Rodriguez .75 .23
317 Nolan Ryan 3.00 .90
318 Dickie Thon .05 .02
319 Roberto Alomar .30 .09
320 Derek Bell .05 .02
321 Pat Borders .05 .02
322 Joe Carter .10 .03
323 Kelly Gruber .05 .02
324 Juan Guzman .05 .02
325 Manny Lee .05 .02
326 Jack Morris .10 .03
327 John Olerud .20 .06
328 Ed Sprague .05 .02
329 Todd Stottlemyre .05 .02
330 Duane Ward .05 .02
331 Steve Avery .10 .03
332 Damon Berryhill .10 .03
333 Jeff Blauser .10 .03
334 Mark Lemke .10 .03
335 Greg Maddux 3.00 .90
336 Kent Mercker .10 .03
337 Otis Nixon .10 .03
338 Greg Olson .10 .03
339 Bill Pecota .10 .03
340 Terry Pendleton .20 .06
341 Mike Stanton .10 .03
342 Todd Frohwirth .10 .03
343 Tim Hulett .10 .03
344 Mark McLemore .20 .06
345 Luis Mercedes .10 .03
346 Alan Mills .10 .03
347 Sherman Obando .10 .03
348 Jim Poole .10 .03
349 Harold Reynolds .20 .06
350 Arthur Rhodes .10 .03
351 Jeff Tackett .10 .03
352 Fernando Valenzuela .20 .06
353 Scott Bankhead .10 .03
354 Ivan Calderon .10 .03
355 Scott Cooper .10 .03
356 Danny Darwin .10 .03
357 Scott Fletcher .10 .03
358 Tony Fossas .10 .03
359 Greg A. Harris .10 .03
360 Joe Hesketh .10 .03
361 Jose Melendez .10 .03
362 Paul Quantrill .10 .03
363 John Valentin .10 .03
364 Mike Butcher .10 .03
365 Chuck Crim .10 .03
366 Chili Davis .20 .06
367 Damion Easley .10 .03
368 Steve Frey .10 .03
369 Joe Grahe .10 .03
370 Greg Myers .10 .03
371 John Orton .10 .03
372 J.T. Snow RC .75 .23
373 Ron Tingley .10 .03
374 Julio Valera .10 .03
375 Paul Assenmacher .10 .03
376 Jose Bautista .10 .03
377 Jose Guzman .10 .03
378 Greg Hibbard .10 .03
379 Candy Maldonado .10 .03
380 Derrick May .10 .03
381 Dan Plesac .10 .03
382 Tommy Shields .10 .03
383 Sammy Sosa 2.50 .75
384 Jose Vizcaino .10 .03
385 Matt Walbeck .10 .03
386 Ellis Burks .20 .06
387 Roberto Hernandez .20 .06
388 Mike Huff .10 .03
389 Bo Jackson .50 .15
390 Lance Johnson .10 .03
391 Ron Karkovice .10 .03
392 Kirk McCaskill .10 .03
393 Donn Pall .10 .03
394 Dan Pasqua .10 .03
395 Steve Sax .10 .03
396 Dave Stieb .10 .03
397 Bobby Ayala .10 .03
398 Tim Belcher .10 .03
399 Jeff Branson .10 .03
400 Cesar Hernandez .10 .03
401 Roberto Kelly .10 .03
402 Randy Milligan .10 .03
403 Kevin Mitchell .10 .03
404 Juan Samuel .10 .03
405 Reggie Sanders .10 .03
406 John Smiley .10 .03
407 Dan Wilson .10 .03
408 Mike Christopher .10 .03
409 Dennis Cook .10 .03
410 Alvaro Espinoza .10 .03
411 Glenallen Hill .10 .03
412 Reggie Jefferson .10 .03
413 Derek Lilliquist .10 .03
414 Jose Mesa .20 .06
415 Charles Nagy .10 .03
416 Junior Ortiz .10 .03
417 Eric Plunk .10 .03
418 Ted Power .10 .03
419 Scott Aldred .10 .03
420 Andy Ashby .10 .03
421 Freddie Benavides .10 .03
422 Dante Bichette .20 .06
423 Willie Blair .10 .03
424 Vinny Castilla .30 .09
425 Jerald Clark .10 .03
426 Alex Cole .10 .03
427 Andres Galarraga .50 .15
428 Joe Girardi .10 .03
429 Charlie Hayes .10 .03
430 Butch Henry .10 .03
431 Darren Holmes .10 .03
432 Dale Murphy .50 .15
433 David Nied .10 .03
434 Jeff Parrett .10 .03
435 Steve Reed .10 .03
436 Armando Reynoso .10 .03
437 Bruce Ruffin .10 .03
438 Bryn Smith .10 .03
439 Jim Tatum .10 .03
440 Eric Young .20 .06
441 Skeeter Barnes .10 .03
442 Tom Bolton .10 .03
443 Kirk Gibson .20 .06
444 Chad Kreuter .10 .03
445 Bill Krueger .10 .03
446 Scott Livingstone .10 .03
447 Bob MacDonald .10 .03
448 Mike Moore .10 .03
449 Mike Munoz .10 .03
450 Gary Thurman .10 .03
451 David Wells .30 .09
452 Alex Arias .10 .03
453 Jack Armstrong .10 .03
454 Bret Barberie .10 .03
455 Ryan Bowen .10 .03
456 Cris Carpenter .10 .03
457 Chuck Carr .10 .03
458 Jeff Conine .20 .06
459 Steve Decker .10 .03
460 Orestes Destrade .10 .03
461 Monty Fariss .10 .03
462 Junior Felix .10 .03
463 Bryan Harvey .10 .03
464 Trevor Hoffman .50 .15
465 Charlie Hough .20 .06
466 Dave Magadan .10 .03
467 Bob McClure .10 .03
468 Rob Natal .10 .03
469 Scott Pose .10 .03
470 Rich Renteria .10 .03
471 Benito Santiago .20 .06
472 Matt Turner .10 .03
473 Walt Weiss .10 .03
474 Eric Anthony .10 .03
475 Chris Donnels .10 .03
476 Doug Drabek .10 .03
477 Xavier Hernandez .10 .03
478 Doug Jones .10 .03
479 Darryl Kile .10 .03
480 Scott Servais .10 .03
481 Greg Swindell .10 .03
482 Eddie Taubensee .10 .03
483 Jose Uribe .10 .03
484 Brian Williams .10 .03
485 Billy Brewer .10 .03
486 David Cone .30 .09
487 Greg Gagne .10 .03
488 Phil Hiatt .10 .03
489 Jose Lind .10 .03
490 Brent Mayne .10 .03
491 Kevin McReynolds .10 .03
492 Keith Miller .10 .03
493 Hipolito Pichardo .10 .03
494 Harvey Pulliam .10 .03
495 Rico Rossy .10 .03
496 Pedro Astacio .10 .03
497 Tom Candiotti .10 .03
498 Tom Goodwin .10 .03
499 Jim Gott .10 .03
500 Pedro Martinez 1.50 .45
501 Roger McDowell .10 .03
502 Mike Piazza 4.00 1.20
503 Jody Reed .10 .03
504 Rick Trlicek .10 .03
505 Mitch Webster .10 .03
506 Steve Wilson .10 .03
507 Jim Austin .10 .03
508 Ricky Bones .10 .03
509 Alex Diaz .10 .03
510 Mike Fetters .10 .03
511 Teddy Higuera .10 .03
512 Graeme Lloyd .10 .03
513 Carlos Maldonado .10 .03
514 Josias Manzanillo .10 .03
515 Kevin Reimer .10 .03
516 Bill Spiers .10 .03
517 Bill Wegman .10 .03
518 Willie Banks .10 .03
519 J.T. Bruett .10 .03
520 Brian Harper .10 .03
521 Terry Jorgensen .10 .03
522 Scott Leius .10 .03
523 Pat Mahomes .10 .03
524 Dave McCarty .10 .03
525 Jeff Reboulet .10 .03
526 Mike Trombley .10 .03
527 Carl Willis .10 .03
528 Dave Winfield 1.25 .35
529 Sean Berry .10 .03
530 Frank Bolick .10 .03
531 Kent Bottenfield .10 .03
532 Wilfredo Cordero .10 .03
533 Jeff Fassero .10 .03
534 Tim Laker .10 .03
535 Mike Lansing .10 .03
536 Chris Nabholz .10 .03
537 Mel Rojas .10 .03
538 John Wetteland .20 .06
539 Ted Wood .10 .03
540 Mike Draper .10 .03
541 Tony Fernandez .20 .06
542 Todd Hundley .20 .06
543 Jeff Innis .10 .03
544 Jeff McKnight .10 .03
545 Eddie Murray 1.00 .30
546 Charlie O'Brien .10 .03
547 Frank Tanana .20 .06
548 Ryan Thompson .10 .03
549 Chico Walker .10 .03
550 Anthony Young .10 .03
551 Jim Abbott .20 .06
552 Wade Boggs 1.25 .35
553 Steve Farr .10 .03
554 Neal Heaton .10 .03
555 Steve Howe .10 .03
556 Dion James .10 .03
557 Scott Kamieniecki .10 .03
558 Jimmy Key .20 .06
559 Jim Leyritz .10 .03
560 Paul O'Neill .20 .06
561 Spike Owen .10 .03
562 Lance Blankenship .10 .03
563 Joe Boever .10 .03
564 Storm Davis .10 .03
565 Kelly Downs .10 .03
566 Eric Fox .10 .03
567 Rich Gossage .20 .06
568 Dave Henderson .10 .03
569 Shawn Hillegas .10 .03
570 Mike Mohler .10 .03
571 Troy Neel .10 .03
572 Dale Sveum .10 .03
573 Larry Andersen .10 .03
574 Bob Ayrault .10 .03
575 Jose DeLeon .10 .03
576 Jim Eisenreich .20 .06
577 Pete Incaviglia .10 .03
578 Danny Jackson .10 .03
579 Ricky Jordan .10 .03
580 Ben Rivera .10 .03
581 Curt Schilling .75 .23
582 Milt Thompson .10 .03
583 David West .10 .03
584 John Candelaria .10 .03
585 Steve Cooke .10 .03
586 Tom Foley .10 .03
587 Al Martin .10 .03
588 Blas Minor .10 .03
589 Dennis Moeller .10 .03
590 Denny Neagle .20 .06
591 Tom Prince .10 .03

592 Randy Tomlin .10 .03
593 Bob Walk .10 .03
594 Kevin Young .20 .06
595 Pat Gomez .10 .03
596 Ricky Gutierrez .10 .03
597 Gene Harris .10 .03
598 Jeremy Hernandez .10 .03
599 Phil Plantier .10 .03
600 Tim Scott .10 .03
601 Frank Seminara .10 .03
602 Darrell Sherman .10 .03
603 Craig Shipley .10 .03
604 Guillermo Velasquez .10 .03
605 Dan Walters .10 .03
606 Mike Benjamin .10 .03
607 Barry Bonds 2.50 .75
608 Jeff Brantley .20 .06
609 Dave Burba .10 .03
610 Craig Colbert .10 .03
611 Mike Jackson .10 .03
612 Kirt Manwaring .10 .03
613 Dave Martinez .10 .03
614 Dave Righetti .20 .06
615 Kevin Rogers .10 .03
616 Bill Swift .10 .03
617 Rich Amaral .10 .03
618 Mike Blowers .10 .03
619 Chris Bosio .10 .03
620 Norm Charlton .10 .03
621 John Cummings .10 .03
622 Mike Felder .10 .03
623 Bill Haselman .10 .03
624 Tim Leary .10 .03
625 Pete O'Brien .10 .03
626 Russ Swan .10 .03
627 Fernando Vina .50 .15
628 Rene Arocha .10 .03
629 Rod Brewer .10 .03
630 Ozzie Canseco .10 .03
631 Rheal Cormier .10 .03
632 Brian Jordan .20 .06
633 Joe Magrane .10 .03
634 Donovan Osborne .10 .03
635 Mike Perez .10 .03
636 Stan Royer .10 .03
637 Hector Villanueva .10 .03
638 Tracy Woodson .10 .03
639 Benji Gil .10 .03
640 Tom Henke .20 .06
641 David Hulse .10 .03
642 Charlie Leibrandt .10 .03
643 Robb Nen .20 .06
644 Dan Peltier .10 .03
645 Billy Ripken .10 .03
646 Kenny Rogers .20 .06
647 John Russell .10 .03
648 Dan Smith .10 .03
649 Matt Whiteside .10 .03
650 William Canate .10 .03
651 Darnell Coles .10 .03
652 Al Leiter .20 .06
653 Domingo Martinez .10 .03
654 Paul Molitor 1.00 .30
655 Luis Sojo .10 .03
656 Dave Stewart .20 .06
657 Mike Timlin .10 .03
658 Turner Ward .10 .03
659 Devon White .20 .06
660 Eddie Zosky .10 .03

1993 Pacific Beisbol Amigos

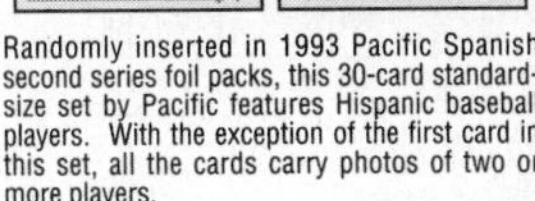

Randomly inserted in 1993 Pacific Spanish second series foil packs, this 30-card standard-size set by Pacific features Hispanic baseball players. With the exception of the first card in this set, all the cards carry photos of two or more players.

	Nm-Mt	Ex-Mt
COMPLETE SET (30)	80.00	24.00
1 Edgar Martinez	2.00	.60
2 Luis Polonia Stan Javier	1.00	.30
3 George Bell Julio Franco	1.00	.30
4 Ozzie Guillen Ivan Rodriguez	4.00	1.20
5 Carlos Baerga Sandy Alomar Jr.	1.50	.45
6 Sandy Alomar Jr. Alvaro Espinoza Paul Sorrento Carlos Baerga Felix Fermin Junior Ortiz Jose Mesa Carlos Martinez	1.50	.45
7 Sandy Alomar Jr. Roberto Alomar	4.00	1.20
8 Jose Lind Felix Jose	1.00	.30
9 Ricky Bones Jaime Navarro	1.00	.30
10 Jamie Navarro Jesse Orosco	1.00	.30
11 Tino Martinez Edgar Martinez	2.00	.60
12 Juan Gonzalez Ivan Rodriguez	12.00	3.60
13 Juan Gonzalez Julio Franco	6.00	1.80
14 Julio Franco Jose Canseco Rafael Palmeiro	10.00	3.00
15 Juan Gonzalez Jose Canseco	15.00	4.50
16 Ivan Rodriguez Benji Gil	2.50	.75
17 Jose Guzman Frank Castillo	1.00	.30
18 Rey Sanchez Jose Vizcaino	1.00	.30
19 Derrick May Sammy Sosa	10.00	3.00
20 Sammy Sosa UER Candy Maldonado Sammy is from Dominican Republic not Puerto Rico	10.00	3.00
21 Jose Rijo Juan Samuel	1.00	.30
22 Freddie Benavides Andres Galarraga	2.00	.60
23 Guillermo Velasquez Benito Santiago	1.00	.30
24 Luis Gonzalez Andujar Cedeno	2.00	.60
25 Wilfredo Cordero Dennis Martinez	1.50	.45
26 Moises Alou Wilfredo Cordero	1.50	.45
27 Ozzie Canseco Jose Canseco	2.50	.75
28 Jose Oquendo Luis Alicea	1.00	.30
29 Luis Alicea Rene Arocha	1.00	.30
30 Geronimo Pena Luis Alicea	1.00	.30

1993 Pacific Spanish Gold Estrellas

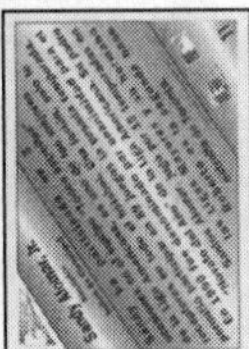

Randomly inserted Spanish first series foil packs, this 20-card standard-size set features the top Latin players at each position. Just 10,000 complete sets were produced for insertion. All the text on this set is in Spanish.

	Nm-Mt	Ex-Mt
COMPLETE SET (20)	15.00	4.50
1 Moises Alou	1.00	.30
2 Bobby Bonilla	.50	.15
3 Tony Fernandez	.50	.15
4 Felix Jose	.50	.15
5 Dennis Martinez	1.00	.30
6 Orlando Merced	.50	.15
7 Jose Oquendo	.50	.15
8 Geronimo Pena	.50	.15
9 Jose Rijo	.50	.15
10 Benito Santiago	1.00	.30
11 Sandy Alomar Jr.	1.00	.30
12 Carlos Baerga	1.00	.30
13 Jose Canseco	3.00	.90
14 Juan Gonzalez	2.50	.75
15 Juan Guzman	.50	.15
16 Edgar Martinez	1.50	.45
17 Rafael Palmeiro	2.00	.60
18 Ruben Sierra	1.00	.30
19 Danny Tartabull	.50	.15
20 Omar Vizquel	1.00	.30

1993 Pacific Jugadores Calientes

Randomly inserted in 1993 Pacific Spanish second series foil packs, this 36-card standard-size set by Pacific is titled "Jugadores Calientes" and features cut-out action photos of the players over a borderless, prismatic background. The cards are arranged alphabetically according to the American (1-18) and National (19-36) Leagues.

	Nm-Mt	Ex-Mt
COMPLETE SET (36)	200.00	60.00
1 Rich Amaral	1.00	.30
2 George Brett	15.00	4.50
3 Jay Buhner	3.00	.90
4 Roger Clemens	15.00	4.50
5 Kirk Gibson	2.00	.60
6 Juan Gonzalez	6.00	1.80
7 Ken Griffey Jr.	20.00	6.00
8 Bo Jackson	4.00	1.20
9 Kenny Lofton	3.00	.90
10 Mark McGwire	25.00	7.50
11 Sherman Obando	1.00	.30
12 John Olerud	3.00	.90
13 Carlos Quintana	1.00	.30
14 Ivan Rodriguez	8.00	2.40
15 Nolan Ryan	30.00	9.00
16 J.T. Snow	5.00	1.50
17 Fernando Valenzuela	2.00	.60
18 Dave Winfield	8.00	2.40
19 Moises Alou	2.00	.60
20 Jeff Bagwell	12.00	3.60
21 Barry Bonds	15.00	4.50
22 Bobby Bonilla	1.00	.30
23 Vinny Castilla	4.00	1.20
24 Andujar Cedeno	1.00	.30
25 Orestes Destrade	1.00	.30
26 Andres Galarraga	4.00	1.20
27 Mark Grace	4.00	1.20
28 Tony Gwynn	15.00	4.50
29 Roberto Kelly	1.00	.30
30 John Kruk	2.00	.60
31 Dave Magadan	1.00	.30
32 Derrick May	1.00	.30
33 Orlando Merced	1.00	.30
34 Mike Piazza	25.00	7.50
35 Armando Reynoso	1.00	.30
36 Jose Vizcaino	1.00	.30

1993 Pacific Spanish Prism Inserts

Randomly inserted into Spanish series I foil packs, this 20-card standard-size set highlights top Latin players in Major League Baseball. Ten thousand of these sets were produced for insertion.

	Nm-Mt	Ex-Mt
COMPLETE SET (20)	60.00	18.00
1 Francisco Cabrera	3.00	.90
2 Jose Lind	3.00	.90
3 Dennis Martinez	4.00	1.20
4 Ramon Martinez	3.00	.90
5 Jose Rijo	3.00	.90
6 Benito Santiago	4.00	1.20
7 Roberto Alomar	6.00	1.80
8 Sandy Alomar Jr.	4.00	1.20
9 Carlos Baerga	4.00	1.20
10 George Bell	3.00	.90
11 Jose Canseco	6.00	1.80
12 Alex Fernandez	3.00	.90
13 Julio Franco	4.00	1.20
14 Juan Gonzalez	8.00	2.40
15 Ozzie Guillen	4.00	1.20
16 Teddy Higuera	3.00	.90
17 Edgar Martinez	5.00	1.50
18 Hipolito Pichardo	3.00	.90
19 Luis Polonia	3.00	.90
20 Ivan Rodriguez	10.00	3.00

1994 Pacific Promos

Measuring the standard size, these eight promo cards were issued to show the design of the forthcoming 1994 Pacific Crown Collection set. The cards were given away at the Super Bowl Card Show in Atlanta, to Pacific's master hobby lists of dealers and writers, and used as sales samples. The production run was reportedly approximately 10,000 sets. The fronts feature full-bleed color action player photos, except at the bottom where a gold foil stripe separates the picture from a marbleized team color-coded stripe. The disclaimer "For Promotional Use Only" is stamped diagonally in black lettering across both sides of the card. The cards are arranged alphabetically and numbered on the back with a "P" prefix.

	Nm-Mt	Ex-Mt
COMPLETE SET (8)	10.00	3.00
P1 Carlos Baerga	.50	.15
P2 Joe Carter	.50	.15
P3 Juan Gonzalez	1.00	.30
P4 Ken Griffey Jr.	2.50	.75
P5 Greg Maddux	2.00	.60
P6 Mike Piazza	2.50	.75
P7 Tim Salmon	.75	.23
P8 Frank Thomas	1.00	.30

1994 Pacific

The 660 standard-size cards comprising this set feature color player action shots on their fronts that are borderless, except at the bottom, where a team color-coded marbleized border set off by a gold-foil line carries the team color-coded player's name. The cards are grouped alphabetically within teams. The set closes with an Award Winners subset (655-660). There are no key Rookie Cards in this set.

	Nm-Mt	Ex-Mt
COMPLETE SET (660)	50.00	15.00
1 Steve Avery	.10	.03
2 Steve Bedrosian	.10	.03
3 Damon Berryhill	.10	.03
4 Jeff Blauser	.10	.03
5 Sid Bream	.10	.03
6 Francisco Cabrera	.10	.03
7 Ramon Caraballo	.10	.03
8 Ron Gant	.20	.06
9 Tom Glavine	.30	.09
10 Chipper Jones	.50	.15
11 Dave Justice	.20	.06
12 Ryan Klesko	.20	.06
13 Mark Lemke	.10	.03
14 Javier Lopez	.20	.06
15 Greg Maddux	.75	.23
16 Fred McGriff	.30	.09
17 Greg McMichael	.10	.03
18 Kent Mercker	.10	.03
19 Otis Nixon	.10	.03
20 Terry Pendleton	.20	.06
21 Deion Sanders	.30	.09
22 John Smoltz	.30	.09
23 Tony Tarasco	.10	.03
24 Manny Alexander	.10	.03
25 Brady Anderson	.20	.06
26 Harold Baines	.20	.06
27 Damon Buford	.10	.03
28 Paul Carey	.10	.03
29 Mike Devereaux	.10	.03
30 Todd Frohwirth	.10	.03
31 Leo Gomez	.10	.03
32 Jeffrey Hammonds	.10	.03
33 Chris Hoiles	.10	.03
34 Tim Hulett	.10	.03
35 Ben McDonald	.10	.03
36 Mark McLemore	.10	.03
37 Alan Mills	.10	.03
38 Mike Mussina	.50	.15
39 Sherman Obando	.10	.03
40 Gregg Olson	.10	.03
41 Mike Pagliarulo	.10	.03
42 Jim Poole	.10	.03
43 Harold Reynolds	.20	.06
44 Cal Ripken	1.50	.45
45 David Segui	.10	.03
46 Fernando Valenzuela	.20	.06
47 Jack Voigt	.10	.03
48 Scott Bankhead	.10	.03
49 Roger Clemens	1.00	.30
50 Scott Cooper	.10	.03
51 Danny Darwin	.10	.03
52 Andre Dawson	.20	.06
53 John Dopson	.10	.03
54 Scott Fletcher	.10	.03
55 Tony Fossas	.10	.03
56 Mike Greenwell	.10	.03
57 Billy Hatcher	.10	.03
58 Jeff McNeely	.10	.03
59 Jose Melendez	.10	.03
60 Tim Naehring	.10	.03
61 Tony Pena	.10	.03
62 Paul Quantrill	.10	.03
63 Carlos Quintana	.10	.03
64 Luis Rivera	.10	.03
65 Jeff Russell	.10	.03
66 Aaron Sele	.10	.03
67 John Valentin	.10	.03
68 Mo Vaughn	.20	.06
69 Frank Viola	.20	.06
70 Bob Zupcic	.10	.03
71 Mike Butcher	.10	.03
72 Rod Correia	.10	.03
73 Chad Curtis	.10	.03
74 Chili Davis	.20	.06
75 Gary DiSarcina	.10	.03
76 Damion Easley	.10	.03
77 John Farrell	.10	.03
78 Chuck Finley	.20	.06
79 Joe Grahe	.10	.03
80 Stan Javier	.10	.03
81 Mark Langston	.10	.03
82 Phil Leftwich RC	.10	.03
83 Torey Lovullo	.10	.03
84 Joe Magrane	.10	.03
85 Greg Myers	.10	.03
86 Eduardo Perez	.10	.03
87 Luis Polonia	.10	.03
88 Tim Salmon	.30	.09
89 J.T. Snow	.20	.06
90 Kurt Stillwell	.10	.03
91 Ron Tingley	.10	.03
92 Chris Turner	.10	.03
93 Julio Valera	.10	.03
94 Jose Bautista	.10	.03
95 Shawn Boskie	.10	.03
96 Steve Buechele	.10	.03
97 Frank Castillo	.10	.03
98 Mark Grace UER (stats have 98 home runs in 1993; should be 14)	.30	.09
99 Jose Guzman	.10	.03
100 Mike Harkey	.10	.03
101 Greg Hibbard	.10	.03
102 Doug Jennings	.10	.03
103 Derrick May	.10	.03
104 Mike Morgan	.10	.03
105 Randy Myers	.10	.03
106 Karl Rhodes	.10	.03
107 Kevin Roberson	.10	.03
108 Rey Sanchez	.10	.03
109 Ryne Sandberg	.75	.23
110 Tommy Shields	.10	.03
111 Dwight Smith	.10	.03
112 Sammy Sosa	.75	.23
113 Jose Vizcaino	.10	.03
114 Turk Wendell	.10	.03
115 Rick Wilkins	.10	.03
116 Willie Wilson	.10	.03
117 Ed. Zambrano RC	.10	.03
118 Wilson Alvarez	.10	.03
119 Tim Belcher	.10	.03
120 Jason Bere	.10	.03
121 Rodney Bolton	.10	.03
122 Ellis Burks	.20	.06
123 Joey Cora	.10	.03
124 Alex Fernandez	.10	.03
125 Ozzie Guillen	.10	.03
126 Craig Grebeck	.10	.03
127 Roberto Hernandez	.10	.03
128 Bo Jackson	.50	.15
129 Lance Johnson	.10	.03
130 Ron Karkovice	.10	.03
131 Mike LaValliere	.10	.03
132 Norberto Martin	.10	.03
133 Kirk McCaskill	.10	.03
134 Jack McDowell	.10	.03
135 Scott Radinsky	.10	.03
136 Tim Raines	.20	.06
137 Steve Sax	.10	.03
138 Frank Thomas	.50	.15
139 Dan Pasqua	.10	.03
140 Robin Ventura	.20	.06
141 Jeff Branson	.10	.03
142 Tom Browning	.10	.03
143 Jacob Brumfield	.10	.03
144 Tim Costo	.10	.03
145 Rob Dibble	.20	.06
146 Brian Dorsett	.10	.03
147 Steve Foster	.10	.03
148 Cesar Hernandez	.10	.03
149 Roberto Kelly	.10	.03
150 Barry Larkin	.50	.15
151 Larry Luebbers	.10	.03
152 Kevin Mitchell	.10	.03
153 Joe Oliver	.10	.03
154 Tim Pugh	.10	.03
155 Jeff Reardon	.20	.06
156 Jose Rijo	.10	.03
157 Bip Roberts	.10	.03
158 Chris Sabo	.10	.03
159 Juan Samuel	.10	.03
160 Reggie Sanders	.20	.06
161 John Smiley	.10	.03
162 Jerry Spradlin	.10	.03
163 Gary Varsho	.10	.03
164 Sandy Alomar Jr.	.10	.03
165 Albert Belle	.20	.06
166 Carlos Baerga	.10	.03
167 Mark Clark	.10	.03
168 Alvaro Espinoza	.10	.03
169 Felix Fermin	.10	.03
170 Reggie Jefferson	.10	.03
171 Wayne Kirby	.10	.03
172 Tom Kramer	.10	.03
173 Kenny Lofton	.20	.06
174 Jesse Levis	.10	.03
175 Candy Maldonado	.10	.03
176 Carlos Martinez	.10	.03
177 Jose Mesa	.10	.03
178 Jeff Mutis	.10	.03
179 Charles Nagy	.10	.03
180 Bob Ojeda	.10	.03
181 Junior Ortiz	.10	.03
182 Eric Plunk	.10	.03
183 Manny Ramirez	.30	.09
184 Jeff Treadway	.10	.03
185 Bill Wertz	.10	.03
186 Paul Sorrento	.10	.03
187 Freddie Benavides	.10	.03
188 Dante Bichette	.20	.06
189 Willie Blair	.10	.03
190 Daryl Boston	.10	.03
191 Pedro Castellano	.10	.03
192 Vinny Castilla	.20	.06
193 Jerald Clark	.10	.03
194 Alex Cole	.10	.03
195 Andres Galarraga	.20	.06
196 Joe Girardi	.10	.03
197 Charlie Hayes	.10	.03
198 Darren Holmes	.10	.03
199 Chris Jones	.10	.03
200 Curt Leskanic	.10	.03
201 Roberto Mejia	.10	.03
202 David Nied	.10	.03
203 Jayhawk Owens	.10	.03
204 Steve Reed	.10	.03
205 Armando Reynoso	.10	.03
206 Bruce Ruffin	.10	.03
207 Keith Shepherd	.10	.03
208 Jim Tatum	.10	.03
209 Eric Young	.10	.03
210 Skeeter Barnes	.10	.03
211 Danny Bautista	.10	.03
212 Tom Bolton	.10	.03
213 Eric Davis	.20	.06
214 Storm Davis	.10	.03
215 Cecil Fielder	.20	.06
216 Travis Fryman	.20	.06
217 Kirk Gibson	.20	.06
218 Dan Gladden	.10	.03
219 John Doherty	.10	.03
220 Chris Gomez	.10	.03
221 David Haas	.10	.03
222 Bill Krueger	.10	.03
223 Chad Kreuter	.10	.03
224 Mark Leiter	.10	.03
225 Bob MacDonald	.10	.03
226 Mike Moore	.10	.03
227 Tony Phillips	.10	.03
228 Rich Rowland	.10	.03
229 Mickey Tettleton	.10	.03
230 Alan Trammell	.30	.09
231 Lou Whitaker	.20	.06
232 David Wells	.20	.06
233 Luis Aquino	.10	.03
234 Alex Arias	.10	.03
235 Jack Armstrong	.10	.03
236 Ryan Bowen	.10	.03
237 Chuck Carr	.10	.03
238 Matias Carrillo	.10	.03
239 Jeff Conine	.20	.06
240 Henry Cotto	.10	.03
241 Orestes Destrade	.10	.03
242 Chris Hammond	.10	.03
243 Bryan Harvey	.10	.03
244 Charlie Hough	.20	.06
245 Richie Lewis	.10	.03
246 Mitch Lyden	.10	.03
247 Dave Magadan	.10	.03
248 Bob Natal	.10	.03
249 Benito Santiago	.20	.06
250 Gary Sheffield	.20	.06
251 Matt Turner	.10	.03
252 David Weathers	.10	.03
253 Walt Weiss	.10	.03
254 Darrell Whitmore	.10	.03
255 Nigel Wilson	.10	.03
256 Eric Anthony	.10	.03
257 Jeff Bagwell	.30	.09
258 Kevin Bass	.10	.03
259 Craig Biggio	.30	.09
260 Ken Caminiti	.20	.06
261 Andujar Cedeno	.10	.03
262 Chris Donnels	.10	.03
263 Doug Drabek	.10	.03
264 Tom Edens	.10	.03
265 Steve Finley	.20	.06
266 Luis Gonzalez	.20	.06
267 Pete Harnisch	.10	.03
268 Xavier Hernandez	.10	.03
269 Todd Jones	.10	.03
270 Darryl Kile	.20	.06
271 Al Osuna	.10	.03
272 Rick Parker	.10	.03
273 Mark Portugal	.10	.03
274 Scott Servais	.10	.03
275 Greg Swindell	.10	.03
276 Eddie Taubensee	.10	.03
277 Jose Uribe	.10	.03
278 Brian Williams	.10	.03
279 Kevin Appier	.20	.06
280 Billy Brewer	.10	.03
281 David Cone	.20	.06
282 Greg Gagne	.10	.03
283 Tom Gordon	.10	.03

284 Chris Gwynn .10 .03
285 John Habyan .10 .03
286 Chris Haney .10 .03
287 Phil Hiatt .10 .03
288 David Howard .10 .03
289 Felix Jose .10 .03
290 Wally Joyner .20 .06
291 Kevin Koslofski .10 .03
292 Jose Lind .10 .03
293 Brent Mayne .10 .03
294 Mike Macfarlane .10 .03
295 Brian McRae .10 .03
296 Kevin McReynolds .10 .03
297 Keith Miller .10 .03
298 Jeff Montgomery .10 .03
299 Hipolito Pichardo .10 .03
300 Rico Rossy .10 .03
301 Curtis Wilkerson .10 .03
302 Pedro Astacio .10 .03
303 Rafael Bournigal .10 .03
304 Brett Butler .20 .06
305 Tom Candiotti .10 .03
306 Omar Daal .10 .03
307 Jim Gott .10 .03
308 Kevin Gross .10 .03
309 Dave Hansen .10 .03
310 Carlos Hernandez .10 .03
311 Orel Hershiser .20 .06
312 Eric Karros .20 .06
313 Pedro Martinez .50 .15
314 Ramon Martinez .10 .03
315 Roger McDowell .10 .03
316 Raul Mondesi .20 .06
317 Jose Offerman .10 .03
318 Mike Piazza 1.00 .30
319 Jody Reed .10 .03
320 Henry Rodriguez .10 .03
321 Cory Snyder .10 .03
322 Darryl Strawberry .30 .09
323 Tim Wallach .10 .03
324 Steve Wilson .10 .03
325 Juan Bell .10 .03
326 Ricky Bones .10 .03
327 Alex Diaz RC .10 .03
328 Cal Eldred .10 .03
329 Darryl Hamilton .10 .03
330 Doug Henry .10 .03
331 John Jaha .10 .03
332 Pat Listach .10 .03
333 Graeme Lloyd .10 .03
334 Carlos Maldonado .10 .03
335 Angel Miranda .10 .03
336 Jaime Navarro .10 .03
337 Dave Nilsson .10 .03
338 Rafael Novoa .10 .03
339 Troy O'Leary .10 .03
340 Jesse Orosco .10 .03
341 Kevin Seitzer .10 .03
342 Bill Spiers .10 .03
343 William Suero .10 .03
344 B.J. Surhoff .20 .06
345 Dickie Thon .10 .03
346 Jose Valentin .10 .03
347 Greg Vaughn .20 .06
348 Robin Yount .75 .23
349 Willie Banks .10 .03
350 Bernardo Brito .10 .03
351 Scott Erickson .10 .03
352 Mark Guthrie .10 .03
353 Chip Hale .10 .03
354 Brian Harper .10 .03
355 Kent Hrbek .20 .06
356 Terry Jorgensen .10 .03
357 Chuck Knoblauch .20 .06
358 Gene Larkin .10 .03
359 Scott Leius .10 .03
360 Shane Mack .10 .03
361 David McCarty .10 .03
362 Pat Meares .10 .03
363 Pedro Munoz .10 .03
364 Derek Parks .10 .03
365 Kirby Puckett .50 .15
366 Jeff Reboulet .10 .03
367 Kevin Tapani .10 .03
368 Mike Trombley .10 .03
369 George Tsamis .10 .03
370 Carl Willis .10 .03
371 Dave Winfield .20 .06
372 Moises Alou .20 .06
373 Brian Barnes .10 .03
374 Sean Berry .10 .03
375 Frank Bolick .10 .03
376 Wil Cordero .10 .03
377 Delino DeShields .10 .03
378 Jeff Fassero .10 .03
379 Darrin Fletcher .10 .03
380 Cliff Floyd .20 .06
381 Lou Frazier .10 .03
382 Marquis Grissom .10 .03
383 Gil Heredia .10 .03
384 Mike Lansing .10 .03
385 Oreste Marrero RC .10 .03
386 Dennis Martinez .20 .06
387 Curtis Pride RC .20 .06
388 Mel Rojas .10 .03
389 Kirk Rueter .20 .06
390 Joe Siddall .10 .03
391 John Vander Wal .10 .03
392 Larry Walker .30 .09
393 John Wetteland .20 .06
394 Rondell White .20 .06
395 Tim Bogar .10 .03
396 Bobby Bonilla .20 .06
397 Jeromy Burnitz .20 .06
398 Mike Draper .10 .03
399 Sid Fernandez .10 .03
400 John Franco .20 .06
401 Dave Gallagher .10 .03
402 Dwight Gooden .30 .09
403 Eric Hillman .10 .03
404 Todd Hundley .10 .03
405 Butch Huskey .10 .03
406 Jeff Innis .10 .03
407 Howard Johnson .10 .03
408 Jeff Kent .20 .06
409 Ced Landrum .10 .03
410 Mike Maddux .10 .03
411 Josias Manzanillo .10 .03
412 Jeff McKnight .10 .03
413 Eddie Murray .50 .15
414 Tito Navarro .10 .03
415 Joe Orsulak .10 .03
416 Bret Saberhagen .20 .06
417 Dave Telgheder .10 .03
418 Ryan Thompson .10 .03
419 Chico Walker .10 .03
420 Jim Abbott .30 .09
421 Wade Boggs .30 .09
422 Mike Gallego .10 .03
423 Mark Hutton .10 .03
424 Dion James .10 .03
425 Domingo Jean .10 .03
426 Pat Kelly .10 .03
427 Jimmy Key .20 .06
428 Jim Leyritz .10 .03
429 Kevin Maas .10 .03
430 Don Mattingly 1.25 .35
431 Bobby Munoz .10 .03
432 Matt Nokes .10 .03
433 Paul O'Neill .30 .09
434 Spike Owen .10 .03
435 Melido Perez .10 .03
436 Lee Smith .20 .06
437 Andy Stankiewicz .10 .03
438 Mike Stanley .10 .03
439 Danny Tartabull .10 .03
440 Randy Velarde .10 .03
441 Bernie Williams .30 .09
442 Gerald Williams .10 .03
443 Mike Witt .10 .03
444 Marcos Armas .10 .03
445 Lance Blankenship .10 .03
446 Mike Bordick .10 .03
447 Ron Darling UER .10 .03
Reversed negative on front
448 Dennis Eckersley .20 .06
449 Brent Gates .10 .03
450 Rich Gossage .20 .06
451 Scott Hemond .10 .03
452 Dave Henderson .10 .03
453 Shawn Hillegas .10 .03
454 Rick Honeycutt .10 .03
455 Scott Lydy .10 .03
456 Mark McGwire 1.25 .35
457 Henry Mercedes .10 .03
458 Mike Mohler .10 .03
459 Troy Neel .10 .03
460 Edwin Nunez .10 .03
461 Craig Paquette .10 .03
462 Ruben Sierra .10 .03
463 Terry Steinbach .10 .03
464 Todd Van Poppel .10 .03
465 Bob Welch .10 .03
466 Bobby Witt .10 .03
467 Ruben Amaro .10 .03
468 Larry Andersen .10 .03
469 Kim Batiste .10 .03
470 Wes Chamberlain .10 .03
471 Darren Daulton .20 .06
472 Mariano Duncan .10 .03
473 Len Dykstra .20 .06
474 Jim Eisenreich .10 .03
475 Tommy Greene .10 .03
476 Dave Hollins .10 .03
477 Pete Incaviglia .10 .03
478 Danny Jackson .10 .03
479 John Kruk .20 .06
480 Tony Longmire .10 .03
481 Jeff Manto .10 .03
482 Mickey Morandini .10 .03
483 Terry Mulholland .10 .03
484 Todd Pratt .10 .03
485 Ben Rivera .10 .03
486 Curt Schilling .30 .09
487 Kevin Stocker .10 .03
488 Milt Thompson .10 .03
489 David West .10 .03
490 Mitch Williams .10 .03
491 Jeff Ballard .10 .03
492 Jay Bell .20 .06
493 Scott Bullett .10 .03
494 Dave Clark .10 .03
495 Steve Cooke .10 .03
496 Midre Cummings .10 .03
497 Mark Dewey .10 .03
498 Carlos Garcia .10 .03
499 Jeff King .10 .03
500 Al Martin .10 .03
501 Lloyd McClendon .10 .03
502 Orlando Merced .10 .03
503 Blas Minor .10 .03
504 Denny Neagle .20 .06
505 Tom Prince .10 .03
506 Don Slaught .10 .03
507 Zane Smith .10 .03
508 Randy Tomlin .10 .03
509 Andy Van Slyke .20 .06
510 Paul Wagner .10 .03
511 Tim Wakefield .20 .06
512 Bob Walk .10 .03
513 John Wehner .10 .03
514 Kevin Young .10 .03
515 Billy Bean .10 .03
516 Andy Benes .10 .03
517 Derek Bell .10 .03
518 Doug Brocail .10 .03
519 Jarvis Brown .10 .03
520 Phil Clark .10 .03
521 Mark Davis .10 .03
522 Jeff Gardner .10 .03
523 Pat Gomez .10 .03
524 Ricky Gutierrez .10 .03
525 Tony Gwynn .60 .18
526 Gene Harris .10 .03
527 Kevin Higgins .10 .03
528 Trevor Hoffman .20 .06
529 Luis Lopez .10 .03
530 Pedro A.Martinez RC .10 .03
531 Melvin Nieves .10 .03
532 Phil Plantier .10 .03
533 Frank Seminara .10 .03
534 Craig Shipley .10 .03
535 Tim Teufel .10 .03
536 Guillermo Velasquez .10 .03
537 Wally Whitehurst .10 .03
538 Rod Beck .10 .03
539 Todd Benzinger .10 .03
540 Barry Bonds 1.25 .35
541 Jeff Brantley .10 .03
542 Dave Burba .10 .03
543 John Burkett .10 .03
544 Will Clark .50 .15
545 Royce Clayton .10 .03
546 Bryan Hickerson .10 .03
547 Mike Jackson .10 .03
548 Darren Lewis .10 .03
549 Kirt Manwaring .10 .03
550 Dave Martinez .10 .03
551 Willie McGee .20 .06
552 Jeff Reed .10 .03
553 Dave Righetti .20 .06
554 Kevin Rogers .10 .03
555 Steve Scarsone .10 .03
556 Bill Swift .10 .03
557 Robby Thompson .10 .03
558 Salomon Torres .10 .03
559 Matt Williams .20 .06
560 Trevor Wilson .10 .03
561 Rich Amaral .10 .03
562 Mike Blowers .10 .03
563 Chris Bosio .10 .03
564 Jay Buhner .20 .06
565 Norm Charlton .10 .03
566 Jim Converse .10 .03
567 Rich DeLucia .10 .03
568 Mike Felder .10 .03
569 Dave Fleming .10 .03
570 Ken Griffey Jr. .75 .23
571 Bill Haselman .10 .03
572 Dwayne Henry .10 .03
573 Brad Holman .10 .03
574 Randy Johnson .50 .15
575 Greg Litton .10 .03
576 Edgar Martinez .30 .09
577 Tino Martinez .30 .09
578 Jeff Nelson .10 .03
579 Marc Newfield .10 .03
580 Roger Salkeld .10 .03
581 Mackey Sasser .10 .03
582 Brian Turang RC .10 .03
583 Omar Vizquel .20 .06
584 Dave Valle .10 .03
585 Luis Alicea .10 .03
586 Rene Arocha .10 .03
587 Rheal Cormier .10 .03
588 Tripp Cromer .10 .03
589 Bernard Gilkey .10 .03
590 Lee Guetterman .10 .03
591 Gregg Jefferies .10 .03
592 Tim Jones .10 .03
593 Paul Kilgus .10 .03
594 Les Lancaster .10 .03
595 Omar Olivares .10 .03
596 Jose Oquendo .10 .03
597 Donovan Osborne .10 .03
598 Tom Pagnozzi .10 .03
599 Erik Pappas .10 .03
600 Geronimo Pena .10 .03
601 Mike Perez .10 .03
602 Gerald Perry .10 .03
603 Stan Royer .10 .03
604 Ozzie Smith .75 .23
605 Bob Tewksbury .10 .03
606 Allen Watson .10 .03
607 Mark Whiten .10 .03
608 Todd Zeile .10 .03
609 Jeff Bronkey .10 .03
610 Kevin Brown .20 .06
611 Jose Canseco .50 .15
612 Doug Dascenzo .10 .03
613 Butch Davis .10 .03
614 Mario Diaz .10 .03
615 Julio Franco .20 .06
616 Benji Gil .10 .03
617 Juan Gonzalez .50 .15
618 Tom Henke .10 .03
619 Jeff Huson .10 .03
620 David Hulse .10 .03
621 Craig Lefferts .10 .03
622 Rafael Palmeiro .30 .09
623 Dean Palmer .20 .06
624 Bob Patterson .10 .03
625 Roger Pavlik .10 .03
626 Gary Redus .10 .03
627 Ivan Rodriguez .50 .15
628 Kenny Rogers .20 .06
629 Jon Shave .10 .03
630 Doug Strange .10 .03
631 Matt Whiteside .10 .03
632 Roberto Alomar .50 .15
633 Pat Borders .10 .03
634 Scott Brow .10 .03
635 Rob Butler .10 .03
636 Joe Carter .20 .06
637 Tony Castillo .10 .03
638 Mark Eichhorn .10 .03
639 Tony Fernandez .10 .03
640 Huck Flener RC .10 .03
641 Alfredo Griffin .10 .03
642 Juan Guzman .10 .03
643 Rickey Henderson .50 .15
644 Pat Hentgen .10 .03
645 Randy Knorr .10 .03
646 Al Leiter .20 .06
647 Domingo Martinez .10 .03
648 Paul Molitor .30 .09
649 Jack Morris .20 .06
650 John Olerud .20 .06
651 Ed Sprague .10 .03
652 Dave Stewart .20 .06
653 Devon White .10 .03
654 Woody Williams .20 .06
655 Barry Bonds MVP .60 .18
656 Greg Maddux CY .50 .15
657 Jack McDowell CY .10 .03
658 Mike Piazza ROY .50 .15
659 Tim Salmon ROY .20 .06
660 Frank Thomas MVP .30 .09

1994 Pacific All-Latino

Randomly inserted in Pacific purple foil packs at a rate of one in 25, this 20-card standard-size set spotlights the greatest Latin players chosen by the Pacific staff. Print run was limited to 8,000 sets. The set subdivides into National League (1-10) and American League (11-20) players.

Nm-Mt Ex-Mt
COMPLETE SET (20) 25.00 7.50
1 Benito Santiago 2.50 .75
2 Dave Magadan 1.25 .35
3 Andres Galarraga 2.50 .75
4 Luis Gonzalez 2.50 .75
5 Jose Offerman 1.25 .35
6 Bobby Bonilla 2.50 .75
7 Dennis Martinez 2.50 .75
8 Mariano Duncan 1.25 .35
9 Orlando Merced 1.25 .35
10 Jose Rijo 1.25 .35
11 Danny Tartabull 1.25 .35
12 Ruben Sierra 1.25 .35
13 Ivan Rodriguez 6.00 1.80
14 Juan Gonzalez 6.00 1.80
15 Jose Canseco 6.00 1.80
16 Rafael Palmeiro 4.00 1.20
17 Roberto Alomar 6.00 1.80
18 Eduardo Perez 1.25 .35
19 Alex Fernandez 1.25 .35
20 Omar Vizquel 2.50 .75

1994 Pacific Checklists

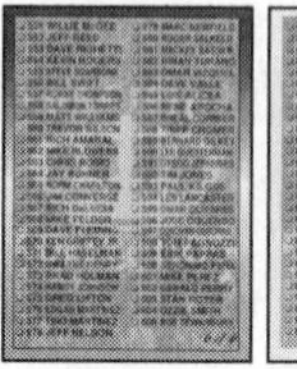

These six standard-size checklists were randomly inserted into 1994 Pacific packs. They are simple lists of cards with boxes to mark off your collection next to the number. The cards are numbered on the front as "x" of 6.

Nm-Mt Ex-Mt
COMPLETE SET (6) 2.00 .60
COMMON CARD (1-6) .40 .12

1994 Pacific Gold Prisms

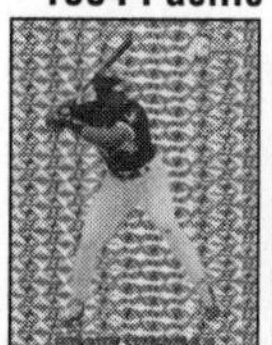
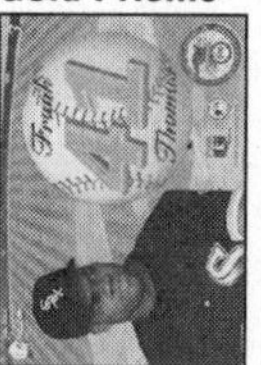

Randomly inserted in Pacific purple foil packs at a rate of one in 25, this 20-card standard-size prismatic "Home Run Leaders" set honors the top 1993 home run leaders. Print run was reportedly limited to 8,000 sets. The set subdivides into American League (1-10) and National League (11-20) players.

Nm-Mt Ex-Mt
COMPLETE SET (20) 80.00 24.00
1 Juan Gonzalez 6.00 1.80
2 Ken Griffey Jr. 10.00 3.00
3 Frank Thomas 6.00 1.80
4 Albert Belle 2.50 .75
5 Rafael Palmeiro 4.00 1.20
6 Joe Carter 2.50 .75
7 Dean Palmer 2.50 .75
8 Mickey Tettleton 1.25 .35
9 Tim Salmon 4.00 1.20
10 Danny Tartabull 1.25 .35
11 Barry Bonds 15.00 4.50
12 Dave Justice 2.50 .75
13 Matt Williams 2.50 .75
14 Fred McGriff 4.00 1.20
15 Ron Gant 2.50 .75
16 Mike Piazza 12.00 3.60
17 Bobby Bonilla 2.50 .75
18 Phil Plantier 1.25 .35
19 Sammy Sosa 10.00 3.00
20 Rick Wilkins 1.25 .35

1994 Pacific Silver Prisms

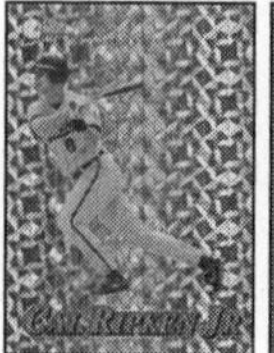

Randomly inserted in Pacific foil packs, this 36-card standard-size set is also known as "Jewels of the Crown". The triangular versions were randomly inserted in purple packs and the more common circular one per black retail pack. The print run was reportedly limited to 8,000 sets. The set divides into American League (1-18) and National League (19-36) players.

Nm-Mt Ex-Mt
COMPLETE SET (36) 120.00 36.00
*CIRCULAR: .2X TO .5X SILVER PRISM
ONE CIRCULAR PER BLACK RETAIL PACK
1 Robin Yount 8.00 2.40
2 Juan Gonzalez 5.00 1.50
3 Rafael Palmeiro 3.00 .90
4 Paul Molitor 3.00 .90
5 Roberto Alomar 5.00 1.50
6 John Olerud 2.00 .60
7 Randy Johnson 5.00 1.50
8 Ken Griffey Jr. 8.00 2.40
9 Wade Boggs 3.00 .90
10 Don Mattingly 12.00 3.60
11 Kirby Puckett 5.00 1.50
12 Tim Salmon 3.00 .90
13 Frank Thomas 5.00 1.50
14 Fernando Valenzuela 2.00 .60
15 Cal Ripken 15.00 4.50
16 Carlos Baerga 1.00 .30
17 Kenny Lofton 2.00 .60
18 Cecil Fielder 2.00 .60
19 John Burkett 1.00 .30
20 Andres Galarraga 2.00 .60
21 Charlie Hayes 1.00 .30
22 Orestes Destrade 1.00 .30
23 Jeff Conine 2.00 .60
24 Jeff Bagwell 3.00 .90
25 Mark Grace 3.00 .90
26 Ryne Sandberg 8.00 2.40
27 Gregg Jefferies 1.00 .30
28 Barry Bonds 12.00 3.60
29 Mike Piazza 10.00 3.00
30 Greg Maddux 8.00 2.40
31 Darren Daulton 2.00 .60
32 John Kruk 2.00 .60
33 Lenny Dykstra 2.00 .60
34 Orlando Merced 1.00 .30
35 Tony Gwynn 6.00 1.80
36 Robby Thompson 1.00 .30

1995 Pacific

This 450-card standard-size set was issued in one series. The full-bleed fronts have action photos; the "Pacific Collection" logo is on the upper left and the player's name is at the bottom. The horizontal backs have a player photo on the left with 1994 stats and some career highlights on the right. The career highlights are in both English and Spanish. The cards are numbered in the lower right corner. The cards are grouped alphabetically within teams and checklisted below alphabetically according to teams for each league. There are no key Rookie Cards in this set.

Nm-Mt Ex-Mt
COMPLETE SET (450) 50.00 15.00
1 Steve Avery .10 .03
2 Rafael Belliard .10 .03
3 Jeff Blauser .10 .03
4 Tom Glavine .30 .09
5 David Justice .20 .06
6 Mike Kelly .10 .03
7 Roberto Kelly .10 .03
8 Ryan Klesko .20 .06
9 Mark Lemke .10 .03
10 Javier Lopez .20 .06
11 Greg Maddux .75 .23
12 Fred McGriff .30 .09
13 Greg McMichael .10 .03
14 Jose Oliva .10 .03
15 John Smoltz .30 .09
16 Tony Tarasco .10 .03
17 Brady Anderson .20 .06
18 Harold Baines .20 .06
19 Armando Benitez .20 .06
20 Mike Devereaux .10 .03
21 Leo Gomez .10 .03
22 Jeffrey Hammonds .10 .03
23 Chris Hoiles .10 .03
24 Ben McDonald .10 .03
25 Mark McLemore .10 .03
26 Jamie Moyer .20 .06
27 Mike Mussina .50 .15
28 Rafael Palmeiro .30 .09
29 Jim Poole .10 .03
30 Cal Ripken Jr. 1.50 .45
31 Lee Smith .20 .06
32 Mark Smith .10 .03
33 Jose Canseco .50 .15
34 Roger Clemens 1.00 .30
35 Scott Cooper .10 .03
36 Andre Dawson .20 .06
37 Tony Fossas .10 .03
38 Mike Greenwell .10 .03
39 Chris Howard .10 .03
40 Jose Melendez .10 .03
41 Nate Minchey .10 .03
42 Tim Naehring .10 .03
43 Otis Nixon .10 .03
44 Carlos Rodriguez .10 .03
45 Aaron Sele .10 .03
46 Lee Tinsley .10 .03
47 Sergio Valdez .10 .03
48 John Valentin .10 .03
49 Mo Vaughn .20 .06
50 Brian Anderson .10 .03
51 Garret Anderson .20 .06
52 Rod Correia .10 .03
53 Chad Curtis .10 .03
54 Mark Dalesandro .10 .03
55 Chili Davis .20 .06
56 Gary DiSarcina .10 .03
57 Damion Easley .10 .03
58 Jim Edmonds .20 .06
59 Jorge Fabregas .10 .03
60 Chuck Finley .20 .06
61 Bo Jackson .50 .15
62 Mark Langston .10 .03
63 Eduardo Perez .10 .03
64 Tim Salmon .30 .09
65 J.T. Snow .20 .06
66 Willie Banks .10 .03
67 Jose Bautista .10 .03
68 Shawon Dunston .10 .03
69 Kevin Foster .10 .03
70 Mark Grace .30 .09

71 Jose Guzman .10 .03
72 Jose Hernandez .10 .03
73 Blaise Ilsley .10 .03
74 Derrick May .10 .03
75 Randy Myers .10 .03
76 Karl Rhodes .10 .03
77 Kevin Roberson .10 .03
78 Rey Sanchez .10 .03
79 Sammy Sosa .75 .23
80 Steve Trachsel .10 .03
81 Eddie Zambrano .10 .03
82 Wilson Alvarez .10 .03
83 Jason Bere .10 .03
84 Joey Cora .10 .03
85 Jose DeLeon .10 .03
86 Alex Fernandez .10 .03
87 Julio Franco .20 .06
88 Ozzie Guillen .10 .03
89 Joe Hall .10 .03
90 Roberto Hernandez .10 .03
91 Darrin Jackson .10 .03
92 Lance Johnson .10 .03
93 Norberto Martin .10 .03
94 Jack McDowell .10 .03
95 Tim Raines .20 .06
96 Olmedo Saenz .10 .03
97 Frank Thomas .50 .15
98 Robin Ventura .20 .06
99 Bret Boone .20 .06
100 Jeff Brantley .10 .03
101 Jacob Brumfield .10 .03
102 Hector Carrasco .10 .03
103 Brian Dorsett .10 .03
104 Tony Fernandez .10 .03
105 Willie Greene .10 .03
106 Erik Hanson .10 .03
107 Kevin Jarvis .10 .03
108 Barry Larkin .50 .15
109 Kevin Mitchell .10 .03
110 Hal Morris .10 .03
111 Jose Rijo .10 .03
112 Johnny Ruffin .10 .03
113 Deion Sanders .30 .09
114 Reggie Sanders .20 .06
115 Sandy Alomar Jr. .10 .03
116 Ruben Amaro .10 .03
117 Carlos Baerga .10 .03
118 Albert Belle .20 .06
119 Alvaro Espinoza .10 .03
120 Rene Gonzales .10 .03
121 Wayne Kirby .10 .03
122 Kenny Lofton .20 .06
123 Candy Maldonado .10 .03
124 Dennis Martinez .20 .06
125 Eddie Murray .50 .15
126 Charles Nagy .10 .03
127 Tony Pena .10 .03
128 Manny Ramirez .20 .06
129 Paul Sorrento .10 .03
130 Jim Thome .50 .15
131 Omar Vizquel .20 .06
132 Dante Bichette .20 .06
133 Ellis Burks .20 .06
134 Vinny Castilla .20 .06
135 Marvin Freeman .10 .03
136 Andres Galarraga .20 .06
137 Joe Girardi .10 .03
138 Charlie Hayes .10 .03
139 Mike Kingery .10 .03
140 Nelson Liriano .10 .03
141 Roberto Mejia .10 .03
142 David Nied .10 .03
143 Steve Reed .10 .03
144 Armando Reynoso .10 .03
145 Bruce Ruffin .10 .03
146 John Vander Wal .10 .03
147 Walt Weiss .10 .03
148 Skeeter Barnes .10 .03
149 Tim Belcher .10 .03
150 Junior Felix .10 .03
151 Cecil Fielder .20 .06
152 Travis Fryman .20 .06
153 Kirk Gibson .20 .06
154 Chris Gomez .10 .03
155 Buddy Groom .10 .03
156 Chad Kreuter .10 .03
157 Mike Moore .10 .03
158 Tony Phillips .10 .03
159 Juan Samuel .10 .03
160 Mickey Tettleton .10 .03
161 Alan Trammell .30 .09
162 David Wells .20 .06
163 Lou Whitaker .20 .06
164 Kurt Abbott .10 .03
165 Luis Aquino .10 .03
166 Alex Arias .10 .03
167 Bret Barberie .10 .03
168 Jerry Browne .10 .03
169 Chuck Carr .10 .03
170 Matias Carrillo .10 .03
171 Greg Colbrunn .10 .03
172 Jeff Conine .20 .06
173 Carl Everett .20 .06
174 Robb Nen .20 .06
175 Yorkis Perez .10 .03
176 Pat Rapp .10 .03
177 Benito Santiago .20 .06
178 Gary Sheffield .20 .06
179 Darrell Whitmore .10 .03
180 Jeff Bagwell .30 .09
181 Kevin Bass .10 .03
182 Craig Biggio .30 .09
183 Andujar Cedeno .10 .03
184 Doug Drabek .10 .03
185 Tony Eusebio .10 .03
186 Steve Finley .20 .06
187 Luis Gonzalez .20 .06
188 Pete Harnisch .10 .03
189 John Hudek .10 .03
190 Orlando Miller .10 .03
191 James Mouton .10 .03
192 Roberto Petagine .10 .03
193 Shane Reynolds .10 .03
194 Greg Swindell .10 .03
195 Dave Veres .10 .03
196 Kevin Appier .20 .06
197 Stan Belinda .10 .03
198 Vince Coleman .10 .03
199 David Cone .20 .06
200 Gary Gaetti .20 .06
201 Greg Gagne .10 .03
202 Mark Gubicza .10 .03
203 Bob Hamelin .10 .03
204 Dave Henderson .10 .03
205 Felix Jose .10 .03
206 Wally Joyner .20 .06
207 Jose Lind .10 .03
208 Mike Macfarlane .10 .03
209 Brian McRae .10 .03
210 Jeff Montgomery .10 .03
211 Hipolito Pichardo .10 .03
212 Pedro Astacio .10 .03
213 Brett Butler .20 .06
214 Omar Daal .10 .03
215 Delino DeShields .10 .03
216 Darren Dreifort .10 .03
217 Carlos Hernandez .10 .03
218 Orel Hershiser .20 .06
219 Garey Ingram .10 .03
220 Eric Karros .20 .06
221 Ramon Martinez .10 .03
222 Raul Mondesi .20 .06
223 Jose Offerman .10 .03
224 Mike Piazza .75 .23
225 Henry Rodriguez .10 .03
226 Ismael Valdes .10 .03
227 Tim Wallach .10 .03
228 Jeff Cirillo .10 .03
229 Alex Diaz .10 .03
230 Cal Eldred .10 .03
231 Mike Fetters .10 .03
232 Brian Harper .10 .03
233 Ted Higuera .10 .03
234 John Jaha .10 .03
235 Graeme Lloyd .10 .03
236 Jose Mercedes .10 .03
237 Jaime Navarro .10 .03
238 Dave Nilsson .10 .03
239 Jesse Orosco .10 .03
240 Jody Reed .10 .03
241 Jose Valentin .10 .03
242 Greg Vaughn .20 .06
243 Turner Ward .10 .03
244 Rick Aguilera .10 .03
245 Rich Becker .10 .03
246 Jim Deshaies .10 .03
247 Steve Dunn .10 .03
248 Scott Erickson .10 .03
249 Kent Hrbek .20 .06
250 Chuck Knoblauch .20 .06
251 Scott Leius .10 .03
252 David McCarty .10 .03
253 Pat Meares .10 .03
254 Pedro Munoz .10 .03
255 Kirby Puckett .50 .15
256 Carlos Pulido .10 .03
257 Kevin Tapani .10 .03
258 Matt Walbeck .10 .03
259 Dave Winfield .20 .06
260 Moises Alou .20 .06
261 Juan Bell .10 .03
262 Freddie Benavides .10 .03
263 Sean Berry .10 .03
264 Wil Cordero .10 .03
265 Jeff Fassero .10 .03
266 Darrin Fletcher .10 .03
267 Cliff Floyd .20 .06
268 Marquis Grissom .10 .03
269 Gil Heredia .10 .03
270 Ken Hill .10 .03
271 Pedro Martinez .50 .15
272 Mel Rojas .10 .03
273 Larry Walker .30 .09
274 John Wetteland .20 .06
275 Rondell White .20 .06
276 Tim Bogar .10 .03
277 Bobby Bonilla .20 .06
278 Rico Brogna .10 .03
279 Jeromy Burnitz .20 .06
280 John Franco .20 .06
281 Eric Hillman .10 .03
282 Todd Hundley .10 .03
283 Jeff Kent .20 .06
284 Mike Maddux .10 .03
285 Joe Orsulak .10 .03
286 Luis Rivera .10 .03
287 Bret Saberhagen .20 .06
288 David Segui .10 .03
289 Ryan Thompson .10 .03
290 Fernando Vina .20 .06
291 Jose Vizcaino .10 .03
292 Jim Abbott .30 .09
293 Wade Boggs .30 .09
294 Russ Davis .10 .03
295 Mike Gallego .10 .03
296 Xavier Hernandez .10 .03
297 Steve Howe .10 .03
298 Jimmy Key .20 .06
299 Don Mattingly 1.25 .35
300 Terry Mulholland .10 .03
301 Paul O'Neill .30 .09
302 Luis Polonia .10 .03
303 Mike Stanley .10 .03
304 Danny Tartabull .10 .03
305 Randy Velarde .10 .03
306 Bob Wickman .10 .03
307 Bernie Williams .30 .09
308 Mark Acre .10 .03
309 Geronimo Berroa .10 .03
310 Mike Bordick .10 .03
311 Dennis Eckersley .20 .06
312 Rickey Henderson .50 .15
313 Stan Javier .10 .03
314 Miguel Jimenez .10 .03
315 Francisco Matos RC .10 .03
316 Mark McGwire 1.25 .35
317 Troy Neel .10 .03
318 Steve Ontiveros .10 .03
319 Carlos Reyes .10 .03
320 Ruben Sierra .10 .03
321 Terry Steinbach .10 .03
322 Bob Welch .10 .03
323 Bobby Witt .10 .03
324 Larry Andersen .10 .03
325 Kim Batiste .10 .03
326 Darren Daulton .20 .06
327 Mariano Duncan .10 .03
328 Lenny Dykstra .20 .06
329 Jim Eisenreich .10 .03
330 Danny Jackson .10 .03
331 John Kruk .20 .06
332 Tony Longmire .10 .03
333 Tom Marsh .10 .03
334 Mickey Morandini .10 .03
335 Bobby Munoz .10 .03
336 Todd Pratt .10 .03
337 Tom Quinlan .10 .03
338 Kevin Stocker .10 .03
339 Fernando Valenzuela .20 .06
340 Jay Bell .20 .06
341 Dave Clark .10 .03
342 Steve Cooke .10 .03
343 Carlos Garcia .10 .03
344 Jeff King .10 .03
345 Jon Lieber .10 .03
346 Ravelo Manzanillo .10 .03
347 Al Martin .10 .03
348 Orlando Merced .10 .03
349 Denny Neagle .20 .06
350 Alejandro Pena .10 .03
351 Don Slaught .10 .03
352 Zane Smith .10 .03
353 Andy Van Slyke .20 .06
354 Rick White .10 .03
355 Kevin Young .10 .03
356 Andy Ashby .10 .03
357 Derek Bell .10 .03
358 Andy Benes .10 .03
359 Phil Clark .10 .03
360 Donnie Elliott .10 .03
361 Ricky Gutierrez .10 .03
362 Tony Gwynn .60 .18
363 Trevor Hoffman .20 .06
364 Tim Hyers .10 .03
365 Luis Lopez .10 .03
366 Jose Martinez .10 .03
367 Pedro A. Martinez .10 .03
368 Phil Plantier .10 .03
369 Bip Roberts .10 .03
370 A.J. Sager .10 .03
371 Jeff Tabaka .10 .03
372 Todd Benzinger .10 .03
373 Barry Bonds .75 .23
374 John Burkett .10 .03
375 Mark Carreon .10 .03
376 Royce Clayton .10 .03
377 Pat Gomez .10 .03
378 Erik Johnson .10 .03
379 Darren Lewis .10 .03
380 Kirt Manwaring .10 .03
381 Dave Martinez .10 .03
382 John Patterson .10 .03
383 Mark Portugal .10 .03
384 Darryl Strawberry .30 .09
385 Salomon Torres .10 .03
386 W. VanLandingham .10 .03
387 Matt Williams .20 .06
388 Rich Amaral .10 .03
389 Bobby Ayala .10 .03
390 Mike Blowers .10 .03
391 Chris Bosio .10 .03
392 Jay Buhner .20 .06
393 Jim Converse .10 .03
394 Tim Davis .10 .03
395 Felix Fermin .10 .03
396 Dave Fleming .10 .03
397 Goose Gossage .20 .06
398 Ken Griffey Jr. .75 .23
399 Randy Johnson .50 .15
400 Edgar Martinez .30 .09
401 Tino Martinez .30 .09
402 Alex Rodriguez 1.25 .35
403 Dan Wilson .10 .03
404 Luis Alicea .10 .03
405 Rene Arocha .10 .03
406 Bernard Gilkey .10 .03
407 Gregg Jefferies .10 .03
408 Ray Lankford .10 .03
409 Terry McGriff .10 .03
410 Omar Olivares .10 .03
411 Jose Oquendo .10 .03
412 Vicente Palacios .10 .03
413 Geronimo Pena .10 .03
414 Mike Perez .10 .03
415 Gerald Perry .10 .03
416 Ozzie Smith .75 .23
417 Bob Tewksbury .10 .03
418 Mark Whiten .10 .03
419 Todd Zeile .10 .03
420 Esteban Beltre .10 .03
421 Kevin Brown .20 .06
422 Cris Carpenter .10 .03
423 Will Clark .50 .15
424 Hector Fajardo .10 .03
425 Jeff Frye .10 .03
426 Juan Gonzalez .50 .15
427 Rusty Greer .20 .06
428 Rick Honeycutt .10 .03
429 David Hulse .10 .03
430 Manny Lee .10 .03
431 Junior Ortiz .10 .03
432 Dean Palmer .20 .06
433 Ivan Rodriguez .50 .15
434 Dan Smith .10 .03
435 Roberto Alomar .50 .15
436 Pat Borders .10 .03
437 Scott Brow .10 .03
438 Rob Butler .10 .03
439 Joe Carter .20 .06
440 Tony Castillo .10 .03
441 Domingo Cedeno .10 .03
442 Brad Cornett .10 .03
443 Carlos Delgado .20 .06
444 Alex Gonzalez .10 .03
445 Juan Guzman .10 .03
446 Darren Hall .10 .03
447 Paul Molitor .30 .09
448 John Olerud .20 .06
449 Robert Perez .10 .03
450 Devon White .20 .06

1995 Pacific Gold Crown Die Cuts

Inserted approximately one in every 18 packs, these cards are in a diecut design. The cards are sequenced in alphabetical order according to team name.

Nm-Mt Ex-Mt
COMPLETE SET (20) 150.00 45.00

1 Greg Maddux 12.00 3.60
2 Fred McGriff 5.00 1.50
3 Rafael Palmeiro 5.00 1.50
4 Cal Ripken Jr. 25.00 7.50
5 Jose Canseco 8.00 2.40
6 Frank Thomas 8.00 2.40
7 Albert Belle 3.00 .90
8 Manny Ramirez 3.00 .90
9 Andres Galarraga 3.00 .90
10 Jeff Bagwell 5.00 1.50
11 Chan Ho Park 1.50 .45
12 Raul Mondesi 3.00 .90
13 Mike Piazza 12.00 3.60
14 Kirby Puckett 8.00 2.40
15 Barry Bonds 12.00 3.60
16 Ken Griffey Jr. 12.00 3.60
17 Alex Rodriguez 20.00 6.00
18 Juan Gonzalez 8.00 2.40
19 Roberto Alomar 8.00 2.40
20 Carlos Delgado 3.00 .90

1995 Pacific Gold Prisms

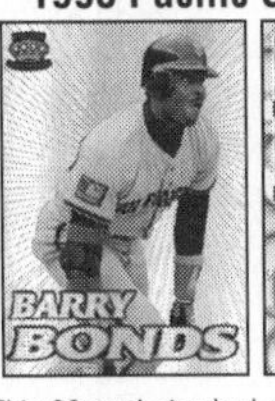

This 36-card standard-size set was inserted approximately one in every 12 packs.

Nm-Mt Ex-Mt
COMPLETE SET (36) 120.00 36.00
1 Jose Canseco 6.00 1.80
2 Gregg Jefferies 1.25 .35
3 Fred McGriff 4.00 1.20
4 Joe Carter 2.50 .75
5 Tim Salmon 4.00 1.20
6 Wade Boggs 4.00 1.20
7 Dave Winfield 2.50 .75
8 Bob Hamelin 1.25 .35
9 Cal Ripken Jr. 20.00 6.00
10 Don Mattingly 15.00 4.50
11 Juan Gonzalez 6.00 1.80
12 Carlos Delgado 2.50 .75
13 Barry Bonds 10.00 3.00
14 Albert Belle 2.50 .75
15 Raul Mondesi 2.50 .75
16 Jeff Bagwell 4.00 1.20
17 Mike Piazza 10.00 3.00
18 Rafael Palmeiro 4.00 1.20
19 Frank Thomas 6.00 1.80
20 Matt Williams 2.50 .75
21 Ken Griffey Jr. 10.00 3.00
22 Will Clark 6.00 1.80
23 Bobby Bonilla 2.50 .75
24 Kenny Lofton 2.50 .75
25 Paul Molitor 4.00 1.20
26 Kirby Puckett 6.00 1.80
27 David Justice 2.50 .75
28 Jeff Conine 2.50 .75
29 Bret Boone 2.50 .75
30 Larry Walker 4.00 1.20
31 Cecil Fielder 2.50 .75
32 Manny Ramirez 2.50 .75
33 Javier Lopez 2.50 .75
34 Jimmy Key 2.50 .75
35 Andres Galarraga 2.50 .75
36 Tony Gwynn 8.00 2.40

1995 Pacific Latinos Destacados

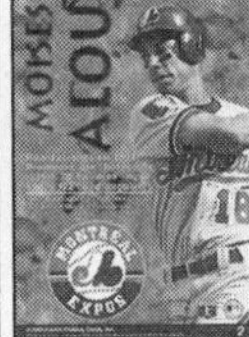

This 36-card standard size set was inserted approximately one in every nine packs. A literal translation for this set is Hot Hispanics and features only Spanish players. The cards are numbered and arranged in alphabetical order.

Nm-Mt Ex-Mt
COMPLETE SET (36) 50.00 15.00
1 Roberto Alomar 5.00 1.50
2 Moises Alou 2.00 .60
3 Wilson Alvarez 1.00 .30
4 Carlos Baerga 1.00 .30
5 Geronimo Berroa 1.00 .30
6 Jose Canseco 5.00 1.50
7 Hector Carrasco 1.00 .30
8 Wil Cordero 1.00 .30
9 Carlos Delgado 2.00 .60
10 Damion Easley 1.00 .30
11 Tony Eusebio 1.00 .30
12 Hector Fajardo 1.00 .30
13 Andres Galarraga 2.00 .60
14 Carlos Garcia 1.00 .30
15 Chris Gomez 1.00 .30
16 Alex Gonzalez 1.00 .30
17 Juan Gonzalez 5.00 1.50
18 Luis Gonzalez 2.00 .60
19 Felix Jose 1.00 .30
20 Javier Lopez 2.00 .60
21 Luis Lopez 1.00 .30
22 Dennis Martinez 2.00 .60
23 Orlando Miller 1.00 .30
24 Raul Mondesi 2.00 .60
25 Jose Oliva 1.00 .30
26 Rafael Palmeiro 3.00 .90
27 Yorkis Perez 1.00 .30
28 Manny Ramirez 2.00 .60
29 Jose Rijo 1.00 .30
30 Alex Rodriguez 12.00 3.60
31 Ivan Rodriguez 5.00 1.50
32 Carlos Rodriguez 1.00 .30
33 Sammy Sosa 8.00 2.40
34 Tony Tarasco 1.00 .30
35 Ismael Valdes 1.00 .30
36 Bernie Williams 3.00 .90

1995 Pacific Harvey Riebe

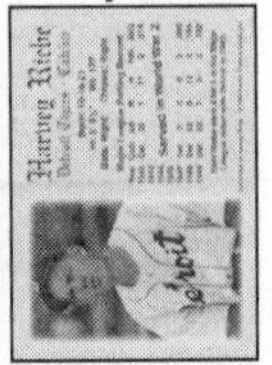

Produced by Pacific, this standard-size card celebrates the baseball career of Harvey Riebe. The card is unnumbered. Riebe had never before been featured on any card.

Nm-Mt Ex-Mt
1 Harvey Riebe 1.00 .30

1996 Pacific

This 450-card set was issued in 12-card packs. The fronts feature borderless color action player photos with double-etched gold foil printing. The horizontal backs carry a color player portrait with player information in both English and Spanish and 1995 season player statistics.

Nm-Mt Ex-Mt
COMPLETE SET (450) 40.00 12.00
1 Steve Avery .20 .06
2 Ryan Klesko .20 .06
3 Pedro Borbon .20 .06
4 Chipper Jones .50 .15
5 Kent Mercker .20 .06
6 Greg Maddux .75 .23
7 Greg McMichael .20 .06
8 Mark Wohlers .20 .06
9 Fred McGriff .30 .09
10 John Smoltz .30 .09
11 Rafael Belliard .20 .06
12 Mark Lemke .20 .06
13 Tom Glavine .30 .09
14 Javier Lopez .20 .06
15 Jeff Blauser .20 .06
16 David Justice .20 .06
17 Marquis Grissom .20 .06
18 Greg Maddux CY .50 .15
19 Randy Myers .20 .06
20 Scott Servais .20 .06
21 Sammy Sosa .75 .23
22 Kevin Foster .20 .06
23 Jose Hernandez .20 .06
24 Jim Bullinger .20 .06
25 Mike Perez .20 .06
26 Shawon Dunston .20 .06
27 Rey Sanchez .20 .06
28 Frank Castillo .20 .06
29 Jaime Navarro .20 .06
30 Brian McRae .20 .06
31 Mark Grace .30 .09
32 Roberto Rivera .20 .06
33 Luis Gonzalez .20 .06
34 Hector Carrasco .20 .06
35 Bret Boone .20 .06
36 Thomas Howard .20 .06
37 Hal Morris .20 .06
38 John Smiley .20 .06
39 Jeff Brantley .20 .06
40 Barry Larkin .50 .15
41 Mariano Duncan .20 .06
42 Xavier Hernandez .20 .06
43 Pete Schourek .20 .06
44 Reggie Sanders .20 .06
45 Dave Burba .20 .06
46 Jeff Branson .20 .06
47 Mark Portugal .20 .06
48 Ron Gant .20 .06
49 Benito Santiago .20 .06
50 Barry Larkin MVP .20 .06
51 Steve Reed .20 .06
52 Kevin Ritz .20 .06
53 Dante Bichette .20 .06
54 Darren Holmes .20 .06
55 Ellis Burks .20 .06
56 Walt Weiss .20 .06
57 Armando Reynoso .20 .06
58 Vinny Castilla .20 .06
59 Jason Bates .20 .06
60 Mike Kingery .20 .06
61 Bryan Rekar .20 .06
62 Curtis Leskanic .20 .06
63 Bret Saberhagen .20 .06
64 Andres Galarraga .20 .06
65 Larry Walker .30 .09
66 Joe Girardi .20 .06
67 Quilvio Veras .20 .06

68 Robb Nen .20 .06
69 Mario Diaz .20 .06
70 Chuck Carr .20 .06
71 Alex Arias .20 .06
72 Pat Rapp .20 .06
73 Rich Garces .20 .06
74 Kurt Abbott .20 .06
75 Andre Dawson .20 .06
76 Greg Colbrunn .20 .06
77 John Burkett .20 .06
78 Terry Pendleton .20 .06
79 Jesus Tavarez .20 .06
80 Charles Johnson .20 .06
81 Yorkis Perez .20 .06
82 Jeff Conine .20 .06
83 Gary Sheffield .20 .06
84 Brian L. Hunter .20 .06
85 Derrick May .20 .06
86 Greg Swindell .20 .06
87 Derek Bell .20 .06
88 Dave Veres .20 .06
89 Jeff Bagwell .30 .09
90 Todd Jones .20 .06
91 Orlando Miller .20 .06
92 Pedro A. Martinez .20 .06
93 Tony Eusebio .20 .06
94 Craig Biggio .30 .09
95 Shane Reynolds .20 .06
96 James Mouton .20 .06
97 Doug Drabek .20 .06
98 Dave Magadan .20 .06
99 Ricky Gutierrez .20 .06
100 Hideo Nomo .50 .15
101 Delino DeShields .20 .06
102 Tom Candiotti .20 .06
103 Mike Piazza .75 .23
104 Ramon Martinez .20 .06
105 Pedro Astacio .20 .06
106 Chad Fonville .20 .06
107 Raul Mondesi .20 .06
108 Ismael Valdes .20 .06
109 Jose Offerman .20 .06
110 Todd Worrell .20 .06
111 Eric Karros .20 .06
112 Brett Butler .20 .06
113 Juan Castro .20 .06
114 Roberto Kelly .20 .06
115 Omar Daal .20 .06
116 Antonio Osuna .20 .06
117 Hideo Nomo ROY .30 .09
118 Mike Lansing .20 .06
119 Mel Rojas .20 .06
120 Sean Berry .20 .06
121 David Segui .20 .06
122 Tavo Alvarez .20 .06
123 Pedro J.Martinez .50 .15
124 F.P. Santangelo .20 .06
125 Rondell White .20 .06
126 Cliff Floyd .20 .06
127 Henry Rodriguez .20 .06
128 Tony Tarasco .20 .06
129 Yamil Benitez .20 .06
130 Carlos Perez .20 .06
131 Wil Cordero .20 .06
132 Jeff Fassero .20 .06
133 Moises Alou .20 .06
134 John Franco .20 .06
135 Rico Brogna .20 .06
136 Dave Mlicki .20 .06
137 Bill Pulsipher .20 .06
138 Jose Vizcaino .20 .06
139 Carl Everett .20 .06
140 Edgardo Alfonzo .20 .06
141 Bobby Jones .20 .06
142 Alberto Castillo .20 .06
143 Joe Orsulak .20 .06
144 Jeff Kent .20 .06
145 Ryan Thompson .20 .06
146 Jason Isringhausen .20 .06
147 Todd Hundley .20 .06
148 Alex Ochoa .20 .06
149 Charlie Hayes .20 .06
150 Michael Mimbs .20 .06
151 Darren Daulton .20 .06
152 Toby Borland .20 .06
153 Andy Van Slyke .20 .06
154 Mickey Morandini .20 .06
155 Sid Fernandez .20 .06
156 Tom Marsh .20 .06
157 Kevin Stocker .20 .06
158 Paul Quantrill .20 .06
159 Gregg Jefferies .20 .06
160 Ricky Bottalico .20 .06
161 Lenny Dykstra .20 .06
162 Mark Whiten .20 .06
163 Tyler Green .20 .06
164 Jim Eisenreich .20 .06
165 Heathcliff Slocumb .20 .06
166 Esteban Loaiza .20 .06
167 Rich Aude .20 .06
168 Jason Christiansen .20 .06
169 Ramon Morel .20 .06
170 Orlando Merced .20 .06
171 Paul Wagner .20 .06
172 Jeff King .20 .06
173 Jay Bell .20 .06
174 Jacob Brumfield .20 .06
175 Nelson Liriano .20 .06
176 Dan Miceli .20 .06
177 Carlos Garcia .20 .06
178 Denny Neagle .20 .06
179 Angelo Encarnacion .20 .06
180 Al Martin .20 .06
181 Midre Cummings .20 .06
182 Eddie Williams .20 .06
183 Roberto Petagine .20 .06
184 Tony Gwynn .60 .18
185 Andy Ashby .20 .06
186 Melvin Nieves .20 .06
187 Phil Clark .20 .06
188 Brad Ausmus .20 .06
189 Bip Roberts .20 .06
190 Fernando Valenzuela .20 .06
191 Marc Newfield .20 .06
192 Steve Finley .20 .06
193 Trevor Hoffman .20 .06
194 Andujar Cedeno .20 .06
195 Jody Reed .20 .06
196 Ken Caminiti .20 .06
197 Joey Hamilton .20 .06
198 Tony Gwynn BAC .30 .09
199 Shawn Barton .20 .06
200 Deion Sanders .30 .09
201 Rikkert Faneyte .20 .06
202 Barry Bonds 1.25 .35
203 Matt Williams .20 .06
204 Jose Bautista .20 .06
205 Mark Leiter .20 .06
206 Mark Carreon .20 .06
207 Robby Thompson .20 .06
208 Terry Mulholland .20 .06
209 Rod Beck .20 .06
210 Royce Clayton .20 .06
211 J.R. Phillips .20 .06
212 Kirt Manwaring .20 .06
213 Glenallen Hill .20 .06
214 W.VanLandingham .20 .06
215 Scott Cooper .20 .06
216 Bernard Gilkey .20 .06
217 Allen Watson .20 .06
218 Donovan Osborne .20 .06
219 Ray Lankford .20 .06
220 Tony Fossas .20 .06
221 Tom Pagnozzi .20 .06
222 John Mabry .20 .06
223 Tripp Cromer .20 .06
224 Mark Petkovsek .20 .06
225 Mike Morgan .20 .06
226 Ozzie Smith .75 .23
227 Tom Henke .20 .06
228 Jose Oquendo .20 .06
229 Brian Jordan .20 .06
230 Cal Ripken 1.50 .45
231 Scott Erickson .20 .06
232 Harold Baines .20 .06
233 Jeff Manto .20 .06
234 Jesse Orosco .20 .06
235 Jeffrey Hammonds .20 .06
236 Brady Anderson .20 .06
237 Manny Alexander .20 .06
238 Chris Hoiles .20 .06
239 Rafael Palmeiro .30 .09
240 Ben McDonald .20 .06
241 Curtis Goodwin .20 .06
242 Bobby Bonilla .20 .06
243 Mike Mussina .50 .15
244 Kevin Brown .20 .06
245 Armando Benitez .20 .06
246 Jose Canseco .50 .15
247 Erik Hanson .20 .06
248 Mo Vaughn .30 .09
249 Tim Naehring .20 .06
250 Vaughn Eshelman .20 .06
251 Mike Greenwell .20 .06
252 Troy O'Leary .20 .06
253 Tim Wakefield .20 .06
254 Dwayne Hosey .20 .06
255 John Valentin .20 .06
256 Rick Aguilera .20 .06
257 Mike Macfarlane .20 .06
258 Roger Clemens 1.00 .30
259 Luis Alicea .20 .06
260 Mo Vaughn MVP .20 .06
261 Mark Langston .20 .06
262 Jim Edmonds .20 .06
263 Rod Correia .20 .06
264 Tim Salmon .30 .09
265 J.T. Snow .20 .06
266 Orlando Palmeiro .20 .06
267 Jorge Fabregas .20 .06
268 Jim Abbott .30 .09
269 Eduardo Perez .20 .06
270 Lee Smith .20 .06
271 Gary DiSarcina .20 .06
272 Damion Easley .20 .06
273 Tony Phillips .20 .06
274 Garret Anderson .20 .06
275 Chuck Finley .20 .06
276 Chili Davis .20 .06
277 Lance Johnson .20 .06
278 Alex Fernandez .20 .06
279 Robin Ventura .20 .06
280 Chris Snopek .20 .06
281 Brian Keyser .20 .06
282 Lyle Mouton .20 .06
283 Luis Andujar .20 .06
284 Tim Raines .20 .06
285 Larry Thomas .20 .06
286 Ozzie Guillen .20 .06
287 Frank Thomas .50 .15
288 Roberto Hernandez .20 .06
289 Dave Martinez .20 .06
290 Ray Durham .20 .06
291 Ron Karkovice .20 .06
292 Wilson Alvarez .20 .06
293 Omar Vizquel .20 .06
294 Eddie Murray .50 .15
295 Sandy Alomar Jr. .20 .06
296 Orel Hershiser .20 .06
297 Jose Mesa .20 .06
298 Julian Tavarez .20 .06
299 Dennis Martinez .20 .06
300 Carlos Baerga .20 .06
301 Manny Ramirez .20 .06
302 Jim Thome .50 .15
303 Kenny Lofton .20 .06
304 Tony Pena .20 .06
305 Alvaro Espinoza .20 .06
306 Paul Sorrento .20 .06
307 Albert Belle .20 .06
308 Danny Bautista .20 .06
309 Chris Gomez .20 .06
310 Jose Lima .20 .06
311 Phil Nevin .20 .06
312 Alan Trammell .30 .09
313 Chad Curtis .20 .06
314 John Flaherty .20 .06
315 Travis Fryman .20 .06
316 Todd Steverson .20 .06
317 Brian Bohanon .20 .06
318 Lou Whitaker .20 .06
319 Bobby Higginson .20 .06
320 Steve Rodriguez .20 .06
321 Cecil Fielder .20 .06
322 Felipe Lira .20 .06
323 Juan Samuel .20 .06
324 Bob Hamelin .20 .06
325 Tom Goodwin .20 .06
326 Johnny Damon .20 .06
327 Hipolito Pichardo .20 .06
328 Dilson Torres .20 .06
329 Kevin Appier .20 .06
330 Mark Gubicza .20 .06
331 Jon Nunnally .20 .06
332 Gary Gaetti .20 .06
333 Brent Mayne .20 .06
334 Brent Cookson .20 .06
335 Tom Gordon .20 .06
336 Wally Joyner .20 .06
337 Greg Gagne .20 .06
338 Fernando Vina .20 .06
339 Joe Oliver .20 .06
340 John Jaha .20 .06
341 Jeff Cirillo .20 .06
342 Pat Listach .20 .06
343 Dave Nilsson .20 .06
344 Steve Sparks .20 .06
345 Ricky Bones .20 .06
346 David Hulse .20 .06
347 Scott Karl .20 .06
348 Darryl Hamilton .20 .06
349 B.J. Surhoff .20 .06
350 Angel Miranda .20 .06
351 Sid Roberson .20 .06
352 Matt Mieske .20 .06
353 Jose Valentin .20 .06
354 Matt Lawton RC .40 .12
355 Eddie Guardado .20 .06
356 Brad Radke .20 .06
357 Pedro Munoz .20 .06
358 Scott Stahoviak .20 .06
359 Erik Schullstrom .20 .06
360 Pat Meares .20 .06
361 Marty Cordova .20 .06
362 Scott Leius .20 .06
363 Matt Walbeck .20 .06
364 Rich Becker .20 .06
365 Kirby Puckett .50 .15
366 Oscar Munoz .20 .06
367 Chuck Knoblauch .20 .06
368 Marty Cordova ROY .20 .06
369 Bernie Williams .30 .09
370 Mike Stanley .20 .06
371 Andy Pettitte .30 .09
372 Jack McDowell .20 .06
373 Sterling Hitchcock .20 .06
374 David Cone .20 .06
375 Randy Velarde .20 .06
376 Don Mattingly 1.25 .35
377 Melido Perez .20 .06
378 Wade Boggs .30 .09
379 Ruben Sierra .20 .06
380 Tony Fernandez .20 .06
381 John Wetteland .20 .06
382 Mariano Rivera .30 .09
383 Derek Jeter 1.25 .35
384 Paul O'Neill .30 .09
385 Mark McGwire 1.25 .35
386 Scott Brosius .20 .06
387 Don Wengert .20 .06
388 Terry Steinbach .20 .06
389 Brent Gates .20 .06
390 Craig Paquette .20 .06
391 Mike Bordick .20 .06
392 Ariel Prieto .20 .06
393 Dennis Eckersley .20 .06
394 Carlos Reyes .20 .06
395 Todd Stottlemyre .20 .06
396 Rickey Henderson .50 .15
397 Geronimo Berroa .20 .06
398 Steve Ontiveros .20 .06
399 Mike Gallego .20 .06
400 Stan Javier .20 .06
401 Randy Johnson .50 .15
402 Norm Charlton .20 .06
403 Mike Blowers .20 .06
404 Tino Martinez .30 .09
405 Dan Wilson .20 .06
406 Andy Benes .20 .06
407 Alex Diaz .20 .06
408 Edgar Martinez .30 .09
409 Chris Bosio .20 .06
410 Ken Griffey Jr. .75 .23
411 Luis Sojo .20 .06
412 Bob Wolcott .20 .06
413 Vince Coleman .20 .06
414 Rich Amaral .20 .06
415 Jay Buhner .20 .06
416 Alex Rodriguez 1.00 .30
417 Joey Cora .20 .06
418 Randy Johnson CY .30 .09
419 Edgar Martinez BAC .20 .06
420 Ivan Rodriguez .50 .15
421 Mark McLemore .20 .06
422 Mickey Tettleton .20 .06
423 Juan Gonzalez .50 .15
424 Will Clark .50 .15
425 Kevin Gross .20 .06
426 Dean Palmer .20 .06
427 Kenny Rogers .20 .06
428 Bob Tewksbury .20 .06
429 Benji Gil .20 .06
430 Jeff Russell .20 .06
431 Rusty Greer .20 .06
432 Roger Pavlik .20 .06
433 Esteban Beltre .20 .06
434 Otis Nixon .20 .06
435 Paul Molitor .30 .09
436 Carlos Delgado .20 .06
437 Ed Sprague .20 .06
438 Juan Guzman .20 .06
439 Domingo Cedeno .20 .06
440 Pat Hentgen .20 .06
441 Tomas Perez .20 .06
442 John Olerud .20 .06
443 Shawn Green .30 .09
444 Al Leiter .20 .06
445 Joe Carter .20 .06
446 Robert Perez .20 .06
447 Devon White .20 .06
448 Tony Castillo .20 .06
449 Alex Gonzalez .20 .06
450 Roberto Alomar .50 .15

1996 Pacific Cramer's Choice

Randomly inserted in packs at a rate of one in 721, this 10-card set features the top Major League Baseball players as chosen by Pacific President and CEO, Michael Cramer. The fronts display a color player cut-out on a pyramid diecut shaped background. The backs carry

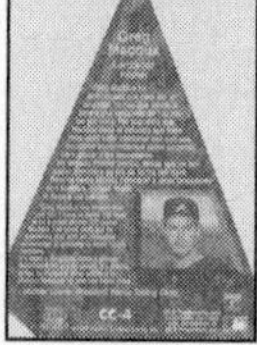

information about why the player was selected for this set in both English and Spanish.

	Nm-Mt	Ex-Mt
COMPLETE SET (10)	300.00	90.00
CC1 Roberto Alomar	30.00	9.00
CC2 Wade Boggs	20.00	6.00
CC3 Cal Ripken	100.00	30.00
CC4 Greg Maddux	50.00	15.00
CC5 Frank Thomas	30.00	9.00
CC6 Tony Gwynn	40.00	12.00
CC7 Mike Piazza	50.00	15.00
CC8 Ken Griffey Jr.	50.00	15.00
CC9 Manny Ramirez	20.00	6.00
CC10 Edgar Martinez	20.00	6.00

1996 Pacific Estrellas Latinas

Randomly inserted in packs at a rate of four in 37, this 36-card set salutes the great Latino players in the major leagues today. The fronts feature color player action cut-outs on a black and gold foil background. The horizontal backs carry a player portrait with information about the player in both English and Spanish.

	Nm-Mt	Ex-Mt
COMPLETE SET (36)	40.00	12.00
EL1 Roberto Alomar	3.00	.90
EL2 Moises Alou	1.25	.35
EL3 Carlos Baerga	1.25	.35
EL4 Geronimo Berroa	1.25	.35
EL5 Ricky Bones	1.25	.35
EL6 Bobby Bonilla	1.25	.35
EL7 Jose Canseco	3.00	.90
EL8 Vinny Castilla	1.25	.35
EL9 Pedro Martinez	3.00	.90
EL10 John Valentin	1.25	.35
EL11 Andres Galarraga	1.25	.35
EL12 Juan Gonzalez	3.00	.90
EL13 Ozzie Guillen	1.25	.35
EL14 Esteban Loaiza	1.25	.35
EL15 Javier Lopez	1.25	.35
EL16 Dennis Martinez	1.25	.35
EL17 Edgar Martinez	2.00	.60
EL18 Tino Martinez	2.00	.60
EL19 Orlando Merced	1.25	.35
EL20 Jose Mesa	1.25	.35
EL21 Raul Mondesi	1.25	.35
EL22 Jaime Navarro	1.25	.35
EL23 Rafael Palmeiro	2.00	.60
EL24 Carlos Perez	1.25	.35
EL25 Manny Ramirez	1.25	.35
EL26 Alex Rodriguez	6.00	1.80
EL27 Ivan Rodriguez	3.00	.90
EL28 David Segui	1.25	.35
EL29 Ruben Sierra	1.25	.35
EL30 Sammy Sosa	5.00	1.50
EL31 Julian Tavarez	1.25	.35
EL32 Ismael Valdes	1.25	.35
EL33 Fernando Valenzuela	1.25	.35
EL34 Quilvio Veras	1.25	.35
EL35 Omar Vizquel	1.25	.35
EL36 Bernie Williams	2.00	.60

1996 Pacific Gold Crown Die Cuts

Randomly inserted in packs at a rate of one in 37, this 36-card set features 1996 Major League Baseball Super Stars. The fronts display color action player photos with a diecut gold crown at the top and gold foil printing. The backs carry a color player portrait and information about the player in English and Spanish.

	Nm-Mt	Ex-Mt
COMPLETE SET (36)	150.00	45.00
DC1 Roberto Alomar	8.00	2.40
DC2 Will Clark	8.00	2.40
DC3 Johnny Damon	3.00	.90
DC4 Don Mattingly	20.00	6.00
DC5 Edgar Martinez	5.00	1.50
DC6 Manny Ramirez	3.00	.90
DC7 Mike Piazza	12.00	3.60
DC8 Quilvio Veras	3.00	.90
DC9 Rickey Henderson	8.00	2.40
DC10 Jeff Bagwell	5.00	1.50
DC11 Andres Galarraga	3.00	.90
DC12 Tim Salmon	5.00	1.50
DC13 Ken Griffey Jr.	12.00	3.60
DC14 Sammy Sosa	12.00	3.60
DC15 Cal Ripken	25.00	7.50
DC16 Raul Mondesi	3.00	.90
DC17 Jose Canseco	8.00	2.40
DC18 Frank Thomas	8.00	2.40
DC19 Hideo Nomo	8.00	2.40
DC20 Wade Boggs	5.00	1.50
DC21 Reggie Sanders	3.00	.90
DC22 Carlos Baerga	3.00	.90
DC23 Mo Vaughn	3.00	.90
DC24 Ivan Rodriguez	8.00	2.40
DC25 Kirby Puckett	8.00	2.40
DC26 Albert Belle	3.00	.90
DC27 Vinny Castilla	3.00	.90
DC28 Greg Maddux	12.00	3.60
DC29 Dante Bichette	3.00	.90
DC30 Deion Sanders	5.00	1.50
DC31 Chipper Jones	8.00	2.40
DC32 Cecil Fielder	3.00	.90
DC33 Randy Johnson	8.00	2.40
DC34 Mark McGwire	20.00	6.00
DC35 Tony Gwynn	10.00	3.00
DC36 Barry Bonds	20.00	6.00

1996 Pacific Hometowns

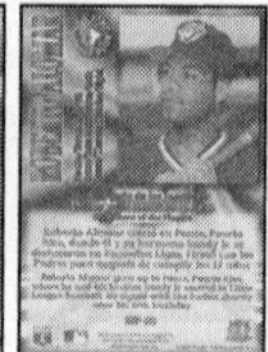

Randomly inserted in packs at a rate of two in 37, this 20-card set features color action player photos with a gold foil border on the left and gold foil printing. The backs carry a player portrait with the player's hometown or city and country and player information printed in both English and Spanish.

	Nm-Mt	Ex-Mt
COMPLETE SET (20)	60.00	18.00
HP1 Mike Piazza	6.00	1.80
HP2 Greg Maddux	6.00	1.80
HP3 Tony Gwynn	5.00	1.50
HP4 Carlos Baerga	1.50	.45
HP5 Don Mattingly	10.00	3.00
HP6 Cal Ripken	12.00	3.60
HP7 Chipper Jones	4.00	1.20
HP8 Andres Galarraga	1.50	.45
HP9 Manny Ramirez	1.50	.45
HP10 Roberto Alomar	4.00	1.20
HP11 Ken Griffey Jr.	6.00	1.80
HP12 Jose Canseco	4.00	1.20
HP13 Frank Thomas	4.00	1.20
HP14 Vinny Castilla	1.50	.45
HP15 Roberto Kelly	1.50	.45
HP16 Dennis Martinez	1.50	.45
HP17 Kirby Puckett	4.00	1.20
HP18 Raul Mondesi	1.50	.45
HP19 Hideo Nomo	4.00	1.20
HP20 Edgar Martinez	2.50	.75

1996 Pacific Milestones

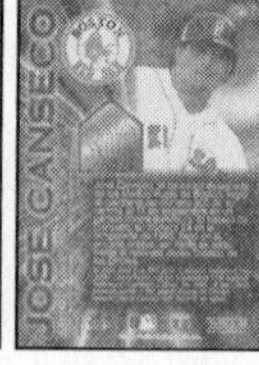

Randomly inserted in packs at a rate of one in 37, this 10-card set denotes the outstanding milestone and record-breaking achievements of baseball's superstars in 1995. The fronts feature a color action player cut-out on a blue foil background with embossed symbols represting the team logo, baseball, and the milestone or achievement. The backs carry a player portrait with the milestone or achievement printed in both English and Spanish.

	Nm-Mt	Ex-Mt
COMPLETE SET (10)	50.00	15.00
M1 Albert Belle	1.50	.45
M2 Don Mattingly	10.00	3.00
M3 Tony Gwynn	5.00	1.50
M4 Jose Canseco	4.00	1.20
M5 Marty Cordova	1.50	.45
M6 Wade Boggs	2.50	.75
M7 Greg Maddux	6.00	1.80
M8 Eddie Murray	4.00	1.20
M9 Ken Griffey Jr.	6.00	1.80
M10 Cal Ripken	12.00	3.60

1996 Pacific October Moments

Randomly inserted in packs at a rate of one in 37, this 20-card set highlights 1995 postseason heroics and the players involved. The fronts feature borderless color player action photos with a bronze foil background and printing. The backs carry a player portrait with the heroic action printed in both English and Spanish.

	Nm-Mt	Ex-Mt
COMPLETE SET (20)	80.00	24.00
OM1 Carlos Baerga	2.50	.75
OM2 Albert Belle	2.50	.75

OM3 Dante Bichette 2.50 .75
OM4 Jose Canseco 6.00 1.80
OM5 Tom Glavine 4.00 1.20
OM6 Ken Griffey Jr. 10.00 3.00
OM7 Randy Johnson 6.00 1.80
OM8 Chipper Jones 6.00 1.80
OM9 David Justice 2.50 .75
OM10 Ryan Klesko 2.50 .75
OM11 Kenny Lofton 2.50 .75
OM12 Javier Lopez 2.50 .75
OM13 Greg Maddux 10.00 3.00
OM14 Edgar Martinez 4.00 1.20
OM15 Don Mattingly 15.00 4.50
OM16 Hideo Nomo 6.00 1.80
OM17 Mike Piazza 10.00 3.00
OM18 Manny Ramirez 2.50 .75
OM19 Reggie Sanders 2.50 .75
OM20 Jim Thome 6.00 1.80

1996 Pacific/Advil Nolan Ryan

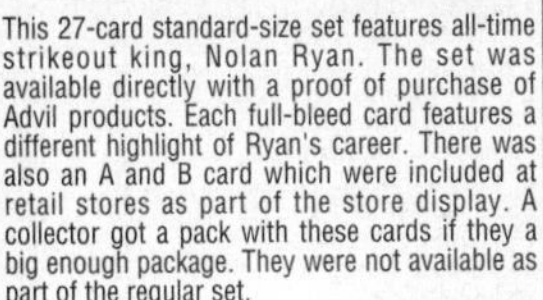

This 27-card standard-size set features all-time strikeout king, Nolan Ryan. The set was available directly with a proof of purchase of Advil products. Each full-bleed card features a different highlight of Ryan's career. There was also an A and B card which were included at retail stores as part of the store display. A collector got a pack with these cards if they a big enough package. They were not available as part of the regular set.

Nm-Mt Ex-Mt
COMPLETE SET (27) 15.00 4.50
COMMON CARD (1-27) .60 .18
A Nolan Ryan 2.50 .75
B Nolan Ryan 2.50 .75

1996 Pacific Baerga Softball

This eight card set features major league baseball players who donated their time to participate in the Second Annual Carlos Baerga Celebrities Softball Game, played Dec. 8 in Bayamon, Puerto Rico. Two cards from the set were distributed to each attendee of the game. The fronts carry colored action player photos from the softball game. The backs display color player portraits with player information in both Spanish and English.

Nm-Mt Ex-Mt
COMPLETE SET (8) 6.00 1.80
1 Carlos Baerga .50 .15
2 Mike Piazza 2.50 .75
3 Bernie Williams 1.00 .30
4 Frank Thomas 1.25 .35
5 Roberto Alomar 1.00 .30
6 Edgar Martinez .75 .23
7 Kenny Lofton .75 .23
8 Sammy Sosa 2.00 .60

1997 Pacific

This 450-card set was issued in one series and distributed in 12-card packs. The fronts feature color action player photos foiled in gold. The backs carry player information in both English and Spanish with player statistics. No subsets are featured as the manufacturer focused on providing collectors with the most comprehensive selection of major league players as possible. Rookie Cards include Brian Giles.

Nm-Mt Ex-Mt
COMPLETE SET (450) 50.00 15.00
1 Garret Anderson .30 .09
2 George Arias .30 .09
3 Chili Davis .30 .09
4 Gary DiSarcina .30 .09
5 Jim Edmonds .30 .09
6 Darin Erstad .30 .09
7 Jorge Fabregas .30 .09
8 Chuck Finley .30 .09
9 Rex Hudler .30 .09
10 Mark Langston .30 .09
11 Orlando Palmeiro .30 .09
12 Troy Percival .30 .09
13 Tim Salmon .50 .15
14 J.T. Snow .30 .09
15 Randy Velarde .30 .09
16 Manny Alexander .30 .09
17 Roberto Alomar .75 .23
18 Brady Anderson .30 .09
19 Armando Benitez .30 .09
20 Bobby Bonilla .30 .09
21 Rocky Coppinger .30 .09
22 Scott Erickson .30 .09
23 Jeffrey Hammonds .30 .09
24 Chris Hoiles .30 .09
25 Eddie Murray .75 .23
26 Mike Mussina .75 .23
27 Randy Myers .30 .09
28 Rafael Palmeiro .50 .15
29 Cal Ripken 2.50 .75
30 B.J. Surhoff .30 .09
31 Tony Tarasco .30 .09
32 Esteban Beltre .30 .09
33 Darren Bragg .30 .09
34 Jose Canseco .75 .23
35 Roger Clemens 1.50 .45
36 Wil Cordero .30 .09
37 Alex Delgado .30 .09
38 Jeff Frye .30 .09
39 Nomar Garciaparra 1.25 .35
40 Tom Gordon .30 .09
41 Mike Greenwell .30 .09
42 Reggie Jefferson .30 .09
43 Tim Naehring .30 .09
44 Troy O'Leary .30 .09
45 Heathcliff Slocumb .30 .09
46 Lee Tinsley .30 .09
47 John Valentin .30 .09
48 Mo Vaughn .30 .09
49 Wilson Alvarez .30 .09
50 Harold Baines .30 .09
51 Ray Durham .30 .09
52 Alex Fernandez .30 .09
53 Ozzie Guillen .30 .09
54 Roberto Hernandez .30 .09
55 Ron Karkovice .30 .09
56 Darren Lewis .30 .09
57 Norberto Martin .30 .09
58 Dave Martinez .30 .09
59 Lyle Mouton .30 .09
60 Jose Munoz .30 .09
61 Tony Phillips .30 .09
62 Kevin Tapani .30 .09
63 Danny Tartabull .30 .09
64 Frank Thomas .75 .23
65 Robin Ventura .30 .09
66 Sandy Alomar Jr. .30 .09
67 Albert Belle .30 .09
68 Julio Franco .30 .09
69 Brian Giles RC 1.50 .45
70 Danny Graves .30 .09
71 Orel Hershiser .30 .09
72 Jeff Kent .30 .09
73 Kenny Lofton .30 .09
74 Dennis Martinez .30 .09
75 Jack McDowell .30 .09
76 Jose Mesa .30 .09
77 Charles Nagy .30 .09
78 Manny Ramirez .30 .09
79 Julian Tavarez .30 .09
80 Jim Thome .75 .23
81 Jose Vizcaino .30 .09
82 Omar Vizquel .30 .09
83 Brad Ausmus .30 .09
84 Kimera Bartee .30 .09
85 Raul Casanova .30 .09
86 Tony Clark .30 .09
87 Travis Fryman .30 .09
88 Bobby Higginson .30 .09
89 Mark Lewis .30 .09
90 Jose Lima .30 .09
91 Felipe Lira .30 .09
92 Phil Nevin .30 .09
93 Melvin Nieves .30 .09
94 Curtis Pride .30 .09
95 Ruben Sierra .30 .09
96 Alan Trammell .50 .15
97 Kevin Appier .30 .09
98 Tim Belcher .30 .09
99 Johnny Damon .30 .09
100 Tom Goodwin .30 .09
101 Bob Hamelin .30 .09
102 David Howard .30 .09
103 Jason Jacome .30 .09
104 Keith Lockhart .30 .09
105 Mike Macfarlane .30 .09
106 Jeff Montgomery .30 .09
107 Jose Offerman .30 .09
108 Hipolito Pichardo .30 .09
109 Joe Randa .30 .09
110 Bip Roberts .30 .09
111 Chris Stynes .30 .09
112 Mike Sweeney .30 .09
113 Joe Vitiello .30 .09
114 Jeromy Burnitz .30 .09
115 Chuck Carr .30 .09
116 Jeff Cirillo .30 .09
117 Mike Fetters .30 .09
118 David Hulse .30 .09
119 John Jaha .30 .09
120 Scott Karl .30 .09
121 Jesse Levis .30 .09
122 Mark Loretta .30 .09
123 Mike Matheny .30 .09
124 Ben McDonald .30 .09
125 Matt Mieske .30 .09
126 Angel Miranda .30 .09
127 Dave Nilsson .30 .09
128 Jose Valentin .30 .09
129 Fernando Vina .30 .09
130 Ron Villone .30 .09
131 Gerald Williams .30 .09
132 Rick Aguilera .30 .09
133 Rich Becker .30 .09
134 Ron Coomer .30 .09
135 Marty Cordova .30 .09
136 Eddie Guardado .30 .09
137 Denny Hocking .30 .09
138 Roberto Kelly .30 .09
139 Chuck Knoblauch .30 .09
140 Matt Lawton .30 .09
141 Pat Meares .30 .09
142 Paul Molitor .50 .15
143 Greg Myers .30 .09
144 Jeff Reboulet .30 .09
145 Scott Stahoviak .30 .09
146 Todd Walker .30 .09
147 Wade Boggs .50 .15
148 David Cone .30 .09
149 Mariano Duncan .30 .09
150 Cecil Fielder .30 .09
151 Dwight Gooden .50 .15
152 Derek Jeter 2.00 .60
153 Jim Leyritz .30 .09
154 Tino Martinez .50 .15
155 Paul O'Neill .50 .15
156 Andy Pettitte .50 .15
157 Tim Raines .30 .09
158 Mariano Rivera .50 .15
159 Ruben Rivera .30 .09
160 Kenny Rogers .30 .09
161 Darryl Strawberry .50 .15
162 John Wetteland .30 .09
163 Bernie Williams .50 .15
164 Tony Batista .30 .09
165 Geronimo Berroa .30 .09
166 Mike Bordick .30 .09
167 Scott Brosius .30 .09
168 Brent Gates .30 .09
169 Jason Giambi .75 .23
170 Jose Herrera .30 .09
171 Brian Lesher RC .30 .09
172 Damon Mashore .30 .09
173 Mark McGwire 2.00 .60
174 Ariel Prieto .30 .09
175 Carlos Reyes .30 .09
176 Matt Stairs .30 .09
177 Terry Steinbach .30 .09
178 John Wasdin .30 .09
179 Ernie Young .30 .09
180 Rich Amaral .30 .09
181 Bobby Ayala .30 .09
182 Jay Buhner .30 .09
183 Rafael Carmona .30 .09
184 Norm Charlton .30 .09
185 Joey Cora .30 .09
186 Ken Griffey Jr. 1.25 .35
187 Sterling Hitchcock .30 .09
188 Dave Hollins .30 .09
189 Randy Johnson .75 .23
190 Edgar Martinez .50 .15
191 Jamie Moyer .30 .09
192 Alex Rodriguez 1.25 .35
193 Paul Sorrento .30 .09
194 Salomon Torres .30 .09
195 Bob Wells .30 .09
196 Dan Wilson .30 .09
197 Will Clark .75 .23
198 Kevin Elster .30 .09
199 Rene Gonzales .30 .09
200 Juan Gonzalez .75 .23
201 Rusty Greer .30 .09
202 Darryl Hamilton .30 .09
203 Mike Henneman .30 .09
204 Ken Hill .30 .09
205 Mark McLemore .30 .09
206 Darren Oliver .30 .09
207 Dean Palmer .30 .09
208 Roger Pavlik .30 .09
209 Ivan Rodriguez .75 .23
210 Kurt Stillwell .30 .09
211 Mickey Tettleton .30 .09
212 Bobby Witt .30 .09
213 Tilson Brito .30 .09
214 Jacob Brumfield .30 .09
215 Miguel Cairo .30 .09
216 Joe Carter .30 .09
217 Felipe Crespo .30 .09
218 Carlos Delgado .30 .09
219 Alex Gonzalez .30 .09
220 Shawn Green .30 .09
221 Juan Guzman .30 .09
222 Pat Hentgen .30 .09
223 Charlie O'Brien .30 .09
224 John Olerud .30 .09
225 Robert Perez .30 .09
226 Tomas Perez .30 .09
227 Juan Samuel .30 .09
228 Ed Sprague .30 .09
229 Mike Timlin .30 .09
230 Rafael Belliard .30 .09
231 Jermaine Dye .30 .09
232 Tom Glavine .50 .15
233 Marquis Grissom .30 .09
234 Andruw Jones .30 .09
235 Chipper Jones .75 .23
236 David Justice .30 .09
237 Ryan Klesko .30 .09
238 Mark Lemke .30 .09
239 Javier Lopez .30 .09
240 Greg Maddux 1.25 .35
241 Fred McGriff .50 .15
242 Denny Neagle .30 .09
243 Eddie Perez .30 .09
244 John Smoltz .50 .15
245 Mark Wohlers .30 .09
246 Brant Brown .30 .09
247 Scott Bullett .30 .09
248 Leo Gomez .30 .09
249 Luis Gonzalez .30 .09
250 Mark Grace .50 .15
251 Jose Hernandez .30 .09
252 Brooks Kieschnick .30 .09
253 Brian McRae .30 .09
254 Jaime Navarro .30 .09
255 Mike Perez .30 .09
256 Rey Sanchez .30 .09
257 Ryne Sandberg 1.25 .35
258 Scott Servais .30 .09
259 Sammy Sosa 1.25 .35
260 Pedro Valdes .30 .09
261 Turk Wendell .30 .09
262 Bret Boone .30 .09
263 Jeff Branson .30 .09
264 Jeff Brantley .30 .09
265 Dave Burba .30 .09
266 Hector Carrasco .30 .09
267 Eric Davis .30 .09
268 Willie Greene .30 .09
269 Lenny Harris .30 .09
270 Thomas Howard .30 .09
271 Barry Larkin .75 .23
272 Hal Morris .30 .09
273 Joe Oliver .30 .09
274 Eric Owens .30 .09
275 Jose Rijo .30 .09
276 Reggie Sanders .30 .09
277 Eddie Taubensee .30 .09
278 Jason Bates .30 .09
279 Dante Bichette .30 .09
280 Ellis Burks .30 .09
281 Vinny Castilla .30 .09
282 Andres Galarraga .30 .09
283 Quinton McCracken .30 .09
284 Jayhawk Owens .30 .09
285 Jeff Reed .30 .09
286 Bryan Rekar .30 .09
287 Armando Reynoso .30 .09
288 Kevin Ritz .30 .09
289 Bruce Ruffin .30 .09
290 John Vander Wal .30 .09
291 Larry Walker .50 .15
292 Walt Weiss .30 .09
293 Eric Young .30 .09
294 Kurt Abbott .30 .09
295 Alex Arias .30 .09
296 Miguel Batista .30 .09
297 Kevin Brown .30 .09
298 Luis Castillo .30 .09
299 Greg Colbrunn .30 .09
300 Jeff Conine .30 .09
301 Charles Johnson .30 .09
302 Al Leiter .30 .09
303 Robb Nen .30 .09
304 Joe Orsulak .30 .09
305 Yorkis Perez .30 .09
306 Edgar Renteria .30 .09
307 Gary Sheffield .30 .09
308 Jesus Tavarez .30 .09
309 Quilvio Veras .30 .09
310 Devon White .30 .09
311 Jeff Bagwell .50 .15
312 Derek Bell .30 .09
313 Sean Berry .30 .09
314 Craig Biggio .50 .15
315 Doug Drabek .30 .09
316 Tony Eusebio .30 .09
317 Ricky Gutierrez .30 .09
318 Xavier Hernandez .30 .09
319 Brian L. Hunter .30 .09
320 Darryl Kile .30 .09
321 Derrick May .30 .09
322 Orlando Miller .30 .09
323 James Mouton .30 .09
324 Bill Spiers .30 .09
325 Pedro Astacio .30 .09
326 Brett Butler .30 .09
327 Juan Castro .30 .09
328 Roger Cedeno .30 .09
329 Delino DeShields .30 .09
330 Karim Garcia .30 .09
331 Todd Hollandsworth .30 .09
332 Eric Karros .30 .09
333 Oreste Marrero .30 .09
334 Ramon Martinez .30 .09
335 Raul Mondesi .30 .09
336 Hideo Nomo .75 .23
337 Antonio Osuna .30 .09
338 Chan Ho Park .30 .09
339 Mike Piazza 1.25 .35
340 Ismael Valdes .30 .09
341 Moises Alou .30 .09
342 Omar Daal .30 .09
343 Jeff Fassero .30 .09
344 Cliff Floyd .30 .09
345 Mark Grudzielanek .30 .09
346 Mike Lansing .30 .09
347 Pedro Martinez .75 .23
348 Sherman Obando .30 .09
349 Jose Paniagua .30 .09
350 Henry Rodriguez .30 .09
351 Mel Rojas .30 .09
352 F.P. Santangelo .30 .09
353 David Segui .30 .09
354 Dave Silvestri .30 .09
355 Ugueth Urbina .30 .09
356 Rondell White .30 .09
357 Edgardo Alfonzo .30 .09
358 Carlos Baerga .30 .09
359 Tim Bogar .30 .09
360 Rico Brogna .30 .09
361 Alvaro Espinoza .30 .09
362 Carl Everett .30 .09
363 John Franco .30 .09
364 Bernard Gilkey .30 .09
365 Todd Hundley .30 .09
366 Butch Huskey .30 .09
367 Jason Isringhausen .30 .09
368 Bobby Jones .30 .09
369 Lance Johnson .30 .09
370 Brent Mayne .30 .09
371 Alex Ochoa .30 .09
372 Rey Ordonez .30 .09
373 Ron Blazier .30 .09
374 Ricky Bottalico .30 .09
375 David Doster .30 .09
376 Lenny Dykstra .30 .09
377 Jim Eisenreich .30 .09
378 Bobby Estalella .30 .09
379 Gregg Jefferies .30 .09
380 Kevin Jordan .30 .09
381 Ricardo Jordan .30 .09
382 Mickey Morandini .30 .09
383 Ricky Otero .30 .09
384 Benito Santiago .30 .09
385 Gene Schall .30 .09
386 Curt Schilling .50 .15
387 Kevin Sefcik .30 .09
388 Kevin Stocker .30 .09
389 Jermaine Allensworth .30 .09
390 Jay Bell .30 .09
391 Jason Christiansen .30 .09
392 Francisco Cordova .30 .09
393 Mark Johnson .30 .09
394 Jason Kendall .30 .09
395 Jeff King .30 .09
396 Jon Lieber .30 .09
397 Nelson Liriano .30 .09
398 Esteban Loaiza .30 .09
399 Al Martin .30 .09
400 Orlando Merced .30 .09
401 Ramon Morel .30 .09
402 Luis Alicea .30 .09
403 Alan Benes .30 .09
404 Andy Benes .30 .09
405 Terry Bradshaw .30 .09
406 Royce Clayton .30 .09
407 Dennis Eckersley .30 .09
408 Gary Gaetti .30 .09
409 Mike Gallego .30 .09
410 Ron Gant .30 .09
411 Brian Jordan .30 .09
412 Ray Lankford .30 .09
413 John Mabry .30 .09
414 Willie McGee .30 .09
415 Tom Pagnozzi .30 .09
416 Ozzie Smith 1.25 .35
417 Todd Stottlemyre .30 .09
418 Mark Sweeney .30 .09
419 Andy Ashby .30 .09
420 Ken Caminiti .30 .09
421 Archi Cianfrocco .30 .09
422 Steve Finley .30 .09
423 Chris Gomez .30 .09
424 Tony Gwynn 1.00 .30
425 Joey Hamilton .30 .09
426 Rickey Henderson .75 .23
427 Trevor Hoffman .30 .09
428 Brian Johnson .30 .09
429 Wally Joyner .30 .09
430 Scott Livingstone .30 .09
431 Jody Reed .30 .09
432 Craig Shipley .30 .09
433 Fernando Valenzuela .30 .09
434 Greg Vaughn .30 .09
435 Rich Aurilia .30 .09
436 Kim Batiste .30 .09
437 Jose Bautista .30 .09
438 Rod Beck .30 .09
439 Marvin Benard .30 .09
440 Barry Bonds 2.00 .60
441 Shawon Dunston .30 .09
442 Shawn Estes .30 .09
443 Osvaldo Fernandez .30 .09
444 Stan Javier .30 .09
445 David McCarty .30 .09
446 Bill Mueller RC 2.00 .60
447 Steve Scarsone .30 .09
448 Robby Thompson .30 .09
449 Rick Wilkins .30 .09
450 Matt Williams .30 .09

1997 Pacific Light Blue

These Light Blue parallel foil cards were found one per pack exclusively in Wal-Mart and Sam's 14-card retail packs. The cards are very similar in design to the scarce Silver parallels randomly seeded in basic packs resulting in a source of confusion for dealers and collectors alike. The Light Blue parallels are not as reflective as the Silvers. Collectors should take extreme caution when purchasing Silver or Light Blue cards.

Nm-Mt Ex-Mt
*STARS: 2.5X TO 6X BASIC CARDS ...
*ROOKIES: 1.25X TO 3X BASIC CARDS

1997 Pacific Silver

Randomly inserted in packs at a rate of one in 73, this 450-card set is a silver foil parallel version of the regular set and is similar in design. Only 67 of these sets were produced.

Nm-Mt Ex-Mt
*STARS: 20X TO 50X BASIC CARDS ..
*ROOKIES: 6X TO 15X BASIC CARDS

1997 Pacific Card-Supials

Randomly inserted in packs at a rate of one in 37, this 36-paired-card insert set features color action player photos of some of the greatest players in the Major Leagues. A smaller card was made to pair with the regular size card of the same player. The backs carry a slot for insertion of the small card.

Nm-Mt Ex-Mt
COMP.LARGE SET (36) 100.00 30.00
*MINIS: .25X TO .6X LARGE SUPIALS
1 Roberto Alomar 6.00 1.80
2 Brady Anderson 2.50 .75
3 Eddie Murray 6.00 1.80
4 Cal Ripken 20.00 6.00
5 Jose Canseco 6.00 1.80
6 Mo Vaughn 2.50 .75
7 Frank Thomas 6.00 1.80
8 Albert Belle 2.50 .75
9 Omar Vizquel 2.50 .75
10 Chuck Knoblauch 2.50 .75
11 Paul Molitor 4.00 1.20
12 Wade Boggs 4.00 1.20
13 Derek Jeter 15.00 4.50
14 Andy Pettitte 4.00 1.20
15 Mark McGwire 15.00 4.50
16 Jay Buhner 2.50 .75
17 Ken Griffey Jr. 10.00 3.00
18 Alex Rodriguez 10.00 3.00
19 Juan Gonzalez 6.00 1.80
20 Ivan Rodriguez 6.00 1.80
21 Andruw Jones 2.50 .75
22 Chipper Jones 6.00 1.80
23 Ryan Klesko 2.50 .75
24 Greg Maddux 10.00 3.00
25 Ryne Sandberg 10.00 3.00
26 Andres Galarraga 2.50 .75
27 Gary Sheffield 2.50 .75
28 Jeff Bagwell 4.00 1.20
29 Todd Hollandsworth 2.50 .75
30 Hideo Nomo 6.00 1.80
31 Mike Piazza 10.00 3.00
32 Todd Hundley 2.50 .75
33 Dennis Eckersley 2.50 .75
34 Ken Caminiti 2.50 .75
35 Tony Gwynn 8.00 2.40
36 Barry Bonds 15.00 4.50

1997 Pacific Cramer's Choice

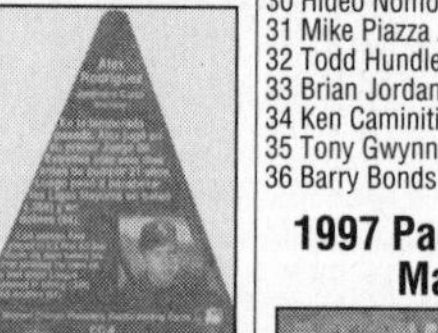

Randomly inserted in packs at a rate of one in 721, this 10-card set features the top Major League Baseball players as chosen by Pacific President and CEO, Michael Cramer. The fronts display a color player cut-out on a pyramid die-cut shaped background. The backs carry information about why the player was selected for this set in both English and Spanish.

	Nm-Mt	Ex-Mt
1 Roberto Alomar	25.00	7.50
2 Frank Thomas	25.00	7.50
3 Albert Belle	10.00	3.00
4 Andy Pettitte	15.00	4.50
5 Ken Griffey Jr.	40.00	12.00
6 Alex Rodriguez	40.00	12.00
7 Chipper Jones	25.00	7.50
8 John Smoltz	15.00	4.50
9 Mike Piazza	40.00	12.00
10 Tony Gwynn	30.00	9.00

1997 Pacific Fireworks Die Cuts

Randomly inserted in packs at a rate of one in 73, this 20-card set features color action player photos on a fireworks die-cut background. The backs carry player information in both English and Spanish.

	Nm-Mt	Ex-Mt
COMPLETE SET (20)	150.00	45.00
1 Roberto Alomar	8.00	2.40
2 Brady Anderson	3.00	.90
3 Eddie Murray	8.00	2.40
4 Cal Ripken	25.00	7.50
5 Frank Thomas	8.00	2.40
6 Albert Belle	3.00	.90
7 Derek Jeter	20.00	6.00
8 Andy Pettitte	5.00	1.50
9 Bernie Williams	5.00	1.50
10 Mark McGwire	20.00	6.00
11 Ken Griffey Jr.	12.00	3.60
12 Alex Rodriguez	12.00	3.60
13 Juan Gonzalez	8.00	2.40
14 Andruw Jones	3.00	.90
15 Chipper Jones	8.00	2.40
16 Hideo Nomo	8.00	2.40
17 Mike Piazza	12.00	3.60
18 Henry Rodriguez	3.00	.90
19 Tony Gwynn	10.00	3.00
20 Barry Bonds	20.00	6.00

1997 Pacific Gold Crown Die Cuts

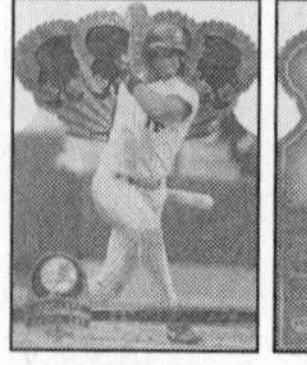
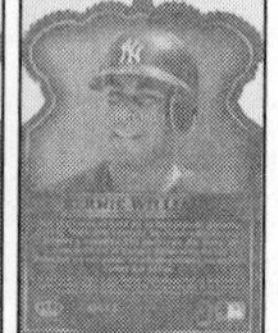

Randomly inserted in packs at a rate of one in 37, this 36-card set honors some of Major League Baseball's Super Stars of today. The fronts feature color action player photos with a die-cut gold crown at the top and gold foil printing. The backs carry player information in both English and Spanish.

	Nm-Mt	Ex-Mt
COMPLETE SET (36)	200.00	60.00
1 Roberto Alomar	8.00	2.40
2 Brady Anderson	3.00	.90
3 Mike Mussina	8.00	2.40
4 Eddie Murray	8.00	2.40
5 Cal Ripken	25.00	7.50
6 Jose Canseco	8.00	2.40
7 Frank Thomas	8.00	2.40
8 Albert Belle	3.00	.90
9 Omar Vizquel	3.00	.90
10 Wade Boggs	5.00	1.50
11 Derek Jeter	20.00	6.00
12 Andy Pettitte	5.00	1.50
13 Mariano Rivera	5.00	1.50
14 Bernie Williams	5.00	1.50
15 Mark McGwire	20.00	6.00
16 Ken Griffey Jr.	12.00	3.60
17 Edgar Martinez	5.00	1.50
18 Alex Rodriguez	12.00	3.60
19 Juan Gonzalez	8.00	2.40
20 Ivan Rodriguez	8.00	2.40
21 Andruw Jones	3.00	.90
22 Chipper Jones	8.00	2.40
23 Ryan Klesko	3.00	.90
24 John Smoltz	5.00	1.50
25 Ryne Sandberg	12.00	3.60
26 Andres Galarraga	3.00	.90
27 Edgar Renteria	3.00	.90
28 Jeff Bagwell	5.00	1.50
29 Todd Hollandsworth	3.00	.90
30 Hideo Nomo	8.00	2.40
31 Mike Piazza	12.00	3.60
32 Todd Hundley	3.00	.90
33 Brian Jordan	3.00	.90
34 Ken Caminiti	3.00	.90
35 Tony Gwynn	10.00	3.00
36 Barry Bonds	20.00	6.00

1997 Pacific Latinos of the Major Leagues

Randomly inserted in packs at a rate of two in 37, this 36-card set salutes the great Latino players in the Major Leagues today. The fronts feature color player action images on a gold foil background of their name. The backs carry player information in both English and Spanish.

	Nm-Mt	Ex-Mt
COMPLETE SET (36)	50.00	15.00
1 George Arias	1.50	.45
2 Roberto Alomar	4.00	1.20
3 Rafael Palmeiro	2.50	.75
4 Bobby Bonilla	1.50	.45
5 Jose Canseco	4.00	1.20
6 Wilson Alvarez	1.50	.45
7 Dave Martinez	1.50	.45
8 Julio Franco	1.50	.45
9 Manny Ramirez	1.50	.45
10 Omar Vizquel	1.50	.45
11 Marty Cordova	1.50	.45
12 Roberto Kelly	1.50	.45
13 Tino Martinez	2.50	.75
14 Mariano Rivera	2.50	.75
15 Ruben Rivera	1.50	.45
16 Bernie Williams	2.50	.75
17 Geronimo Berroa	1.50	.45
18 Joey Cora	1.50	.45
19 Edgar Martinez	2.50	.75
20 Alex Rodriguez	6.00	1.80
21 Juan Gonzalez	4.00	1.20
22 Ivan Rodriguez	4.00	1.20
23 Andruw Jones	1.50	.45
24 Javier Lopez	1.50	.45
25 Sammy Sosa	6.00	1.80
26 Vinny Castilla	1.50	.45
27 Andres Galarraga	1.50	.45
28 Ramon Martinez	1.50	.45
29 Raul Mondesi	1.50	.45
30 Ismael Valdes	1.50	.45
31 Pedro Martinez	4.00	1.20
32 Henry Rodriguez	1.50	.45
33 Carlos Baerga	1.50	.45
34 Rey Ordonez	1.50	.45
35 Fernando Valenzuela	1.50	.45
36 Osvaldo Fernandez	1.50	.45

1997 Pacific Triple Crown Die Cuts

Randomly inserted in packs at a rate of one in 145, this 20-card set features color player images over a gold foil diamond-shaped background with a die-cut gold crown at the top. The backs carry player information in both English and Spanish.

	Nm-Mt	Ex-Mt
COMPLETE SET (20)	200.00	60.00
1 Brady Anderson	6.00	1.80
2 Rafael Palmeiro	10.00	3.00
3 Mo Vaughn	6.00	1.80
4 Frank Thomas	15.00	4.50
5 Albert Belle	6.00	1.80
6 Jim Thome	15.00	4.50
7 Cecil Fielder	6.00	1.80
8 Mark McGwire	40.00	12.00
9 Ken Griffey Jr.	25.00	7.50
10 Alex Rodriguez	25.00	7.50
11 Juan Gonzalez	15.00	4.50
12 Andruw Jones	6.00	1.80
13 Chipper Jones	15.00	4.50
14 Dante Bichette	6.00	1.80
15 Ellis Burks	6.00	1.80
16 Andres Galarraga	6.00	1.80
17 Jeff Bagwell	10.00	3.00
18 Mike Piazza	25.00	7.50
19 Ken Caminiti	6.00	1.80
20 Barry Bonds	40.00	12.00

1997 Pacific Baerga Softball

This 10-card set features major league baseball players who donated their time to participate in the Fourth Annual Carlos Baerga Celebrities Softball Game, played December 14 in Hayto Rey, Puerto Rico, with proceeds from the game going to various Children's foundations throughout Puerto Rico. Two cards from the set were distributed in promo packs to the first 12,000 people at the game. The fronts carry color action player photos from the previous year's softball game, gold-foil stamping, and the game's official logo. The backs display color player portraits with player information in both Spanish and English.

	Nm-Mt	Ex-Mt
COMPLETE SET (10)	8.00	2.40
1 Carlos Baerga	.50	.15
2 Bernie Williams	1.00	.30
3 Ivan Rodriguez	1.25	.35
4 Sandy Alomar Jr.	.50	.15
5 Joey Cora	.25	.07
6 Roberto Alomar	1.00	.30
7 Moises Alou	.50	.15
8 Rey Ordonez	.25	.07
9 Derek Jeter	5.00	1.50
10 David Justice	.50	.15

1998 Pacific

The 1998 Pacific set was issued in one series totalling 450 cards and distributed in 12-card packs with a suggested retail price of $2.49. The fronts features borderless color player photos with gold foil highlights. The backs carry player information in both Spanish and English. As is standard with base-brand Pacific, the entire set is devoid of subset cards, instead focusing on a comprehensive selection of major league players.

	Nm-Mt	Ex-Mt
COMPLETE SET (450)	60.00	18.00
1 Luis Alicea	.30	.09
2 Garret Anderson	.30	.09
3 Jason Dickson	.30	.09
4 Gary DiSarcina	.30	.09
5 Jim Edmonds	.30	.09
6 Darin Erstad	.30	.09
7 Chuck Finley	.30	.09
8 Shigetoshi Hasegawa	.30	.09
9 Rickey Henderson	.75	.23
10 Dave Hollins	.30	.09
11 Mark Langston	.30	.09
12 Orlando Palmeiro	.30	.09
13 Troy Percival	.30	.09
14 Tony Phillips	.30	.09
15 Tim Salmon	.50	.15
16 Allen Watson	.30	.09
17 Roberto Alomar	.75	.23
18 Brady Anderson	.30	.09
19 Harold Baines	.30	.09
20 Armando Benitez	.30	.09
21 Geronimo Berroa	.30	.09
22 Mike Bordick	.30	.09
23 Eric Davis	.30	.09
24 Scott Erickson	.30	.09
25 Chris Hoiles	.30	.09
26 Jimmy Key	.30	.09
27 Aaron Ledesma	.30	.09
28 Mike Mussina	.75	.23
29 Randy Myers	.30	.09
30 Jesse Orosco	.30	.09
31 Rafael Palmeiro	.50	.15
32 Jeff Reboulet	.30	.09
33 Cal Ripken	2.50	.75
34 B.J. Surhoff	.30	.09
35 Steve Avery	.30	.09
36 Darren Bragg	.30	.09
37 Wil Cordero	.30	.09
38 Jeff Frye	.30	.09
39 Nomar Garciaparra	1.25	.35
40 Tom Gordon	.30	.09
41 Bill Haselman	.30	.09
42 Scott Hatteberg	.30	.09
43 Butch Henry	.30	.09
44 Reggie Jefferson	.30	.09
45 Tim Naehring	.30	.09
46 Troy O'Leary	.30	.09
47 Jeff Suppan	.30	.09
48 John Valentin	.30	.09
49 Mo Vaughn	.30	.09
50 Tim Wakefield	.30	.09
51 James Baldwin	.30	.09
52 Albert Belle	.30	.09
53 Tony Castillo	.30	.09
54 Doug Drabek	.30	.09
55 Ray Durham	.30	.09
56 Jorge Fabregas	.30	.09
57 Ozzie Guillen	.30	.09
58 Matt Karchner	.30	.09
59 Norberto Martin	.30	.09
60 Dave Martinez	.30	.09
61 Lyle Mouton	.30	.09
62 Jaime Navarro	.30	.09
63 Frank Thomas	.75	.23
64 Mario Valdez	.30	.09
65 Robin Ventura	.30	.09
66 Sandy Alomar Jr.	.30	.09
67 Paul Assenmacher	.30	.09
68 Tony Fernandez	.30	.09
69 Brian Giles	.30	.09
70 Marquis Grissom	.30	.09
71 Orel Hershiser	.30	.09
72 Mike Jackson	.30	.09
73 David Justice	.30	.09
74 Albie Lopez	.30	.09
75 Jose Mesa	.30	.09
76 Charles Nagy	.30	.09
77 Chad Ogea	.30	.09
78 Manny Ramirez	.30	.09
79 Jim Thome	.75	.23
80 Omar Vizquel	.30	.09
81 Matt Williams	.30	.09
82 Jaret Wright	.30	.09
83 Willie Blair	.30	.09
84 Raul Casanova	.30	.09
85 Tony Clark	.30	.09
86 Deivi Cruz	.30	.09
87 Damion Easley	.30	.09
88 Travis Fryman	.30	.09
89 Bobby Higginson	.30	.09
90 Brian L. Hunter	.30	.09
91 Todd Jones	.30	.09
92 Dan Miceli	.30	.09
93 Brian Moehler	.30	.09
94 Mel Nieves	.30	.09
95 Jody Reed	.30	.09
96 Justin Thompson	.30	.09
97 Bubba Trammell	.30	.09
98 Kevin Appier	.30	.09
99 Jay Bell	.30	.09
100 Yamil Benitez	.30	.09
101 Johnny Damon	.30	.09
102 Chili Davis	.30	.09
103 Jermaine Dye	.30	.09
104 Jed Hansen	.30	.09
105 Jeff King	.30	.09
106 Mike Macfarlane	.30	.09
107 Felix Martinez	.30	.09
108 Jeff Montgomery	.30	.09
109 Jose Offerman	.30	.09
110 Dean Palmer	.30	.09
111 Hipolito Pichardo	.30	.09
112 Jose Rosado	.30	.09
113 Jeromy Burnitz	.30	.09
114 Jeff Cirillo	.30	.09
115 Cal Eldred	.30	.09
116 John Jaha	.30	.09
117 Doug Jones	.30	.09
118 Scott Karl	.30	.09
119 Jesse Levis	.30	.09
120 Mark Loretta	.30	.09
121 Ben McDonald	.30	.09
122 Jose Mercedes	.30	.09
123 Matt Mieske	.30	.09
124 Dave Nilsson	.30	.09
125 Jose Valentin	.30	.09
126 Fernando Vina	.30	.09
127 Gerald Williams	.30	.09
128 Rick Aguilera	.30	.09
129 Rich Becker	.30	.09
130 Ron Coomer	.30	.09
131 Marty Cordova	.30	.09
132 Eddie Guardado	.30	.09
133 LaTroy Hawkins	.30	.09
134 Denny Hocking	.30	.09
135 Chuck Knoblauch	.30	.09
136 Matt Lawton	.30	.09
137 Pat Meares	.30	.09
138 Paul Molitor	.50	.15
139 David Ortiz	.30	.09
140 Brad Radke	.30	.09
141 Terry Steinbach	.30	.09
142 Bob Tewksbury	.30	.09
143 Javier Valentin	.30	.09
144 Wade Boggs	.50	.15
145 David Cone	.30	.09
146 Chad Curtis	.30	.09
147 Cecil Fielder	.30	.09
148 Joe Girardi	.30	.09
149 Dwight Gooden	.30	.09
150 Hideki Irabu	.30	.09
151 Derek Jeter	2.00	.60
152 Tino Martinez	.50	.15
153 Ramiro Mendoza	.30	.09
154 Paul O'Neill	.50	.15
155 Andy Pettitte	.50	.15
156 Jorge Posada	.50	.15
157 Mariano Rivera	.50	.15
158 Rey Sanchez	.30	.09
159 Luis Sojo	.30	.09
160 David Wells	.30	.09
161 Bernie Williams	.50	.15
162 Rafael Bournigal	.30	.09
163 Scott Brosius	.30	.09
164 Jose Canseco	.75	.23
165 Jason Giambi	.75	.23
166 Ben Grieve	.30	.09
167 Dave Magadan	.30	.09
168 Brent Mayne	.30	.09
169 Jason McDonald	.30	.09
170 Izzy Molina	.30	.09
171 Ariel Prieto	.30	.09
172 Carlos Reyes	.30	.09
173 Scott Spiezio	.30	.09
174 Matt Stairs	.30	.09
175 Bill Taylor	.30	.09
176 Dave Telgheder	.30	.09
177 Steve Wojciechowski	.30	.09
178 Rich Amaral	.30	.09
179 Bobby Ayala	.30	.09
180 Jay Buhner	.30	.09
181 Rafael Carmona	.30	.09
182 Ken Cloude	.30	.09
183 Joey Cora	.30	.09
184 Russ Davis	.30	.09
185 Jeff Fassero	.30	.09
186 Ken Griffey Jr.	1.25	.35
187 Raul Ibanez	.30	.09
188 Randy Johnson	.75	.23
189 Roberto Kelly	.30	.09
190 Edgar Martinez	.50	.15
191 Jamie Moyer	.30	.09
192 Omar Olivares	.30	.09
193 Alex Rodriguez	1.25	.35
194 Heathcliff Slocumb	.30	.09
195 Paul Sorrento	.30	.09
196 Dan Wilson	.30	.09
197 Scott Bailes	.30	.09
198 John Burkett	.30	.09
199 Domingo Cedeno	.30	.09
200 Will Clark	.75	.23
201 Hanley Frias RC	.30	.09
202 Juan Gonzalez	.75	.23
203 Tom Goodwin	.30	.09
204 Rusty Greer	.30	.09
205 Wilson Heredia	.30	.09
206 Darren Oliver	.30	.09
207 Bill Ripken	.30	.09
208 Ivan Rodriguez	.75	.23
209 Lee Stevens	.30	.09
210 Fernando Tatis	.30	.09
211 John Wetteland	.30	.09
212 Bobby Witt	.30	.09
213 Jacob Brumfield	.30	.09
214 Joe Carter	.30	.09
215 Roger Clemens	1.50	.45
216 Felipe Crespo	.30	.09
217 Jose Cruz Jr.	.30	.09
218 Carlos Delgado	.30	.09
219 Mariano Duncan	.30	.09
220 Carlos Garcia	.30	.09
221 Alex Gonzalez	.30	.09
222 Juan Guzman	.30	.09
223 Pat Hentgen	.30	.09
224 Orlando Merced	.30	.09
225 Tomas Perez	.30	.09
226 Paul Quantrill	.30	.09
227 Benito Santiago	.30	.09
228 Woody Williams	.30	.09
229 Rafael Belliard	.30	.09
230 Jeff Blauser	.30	.09
231 Pedro Borbon	.30	.09
232 Tom Glavine	.50	.15
233 Tony Graffanino	.30	.09
234 Andruw Jones	.30	.09
235 Chipper Jones	.75	.23
236 Ryan Klesko	.30	.09
237 Mark Lemke	.30	.09
238 Kenny Lofton	.30	.09
239 Javier Lopez	.30	.09
240 Fred McGriff	.50	.15
241 Greg Maddux	1.25	.35
242 Denny Neagle	.30	.09
243 John Smoltz	.50	.15
244 Michael Tucker	.30	.09
245 Mark Wohlers	.30	.09
246 Manny Alexander	.30	.09
247 Miguel Batista	.30	.09
248 Mark Clark	.30	.09
249 Doug Glanville	.30	.09
250 Jeremi Gonzalez	.30	.09
251 Mark Grace	.50	.15
252 Jose Hernandez	.30	.09
253 Lance Johnson	.30	.09
254 Brooks Kieschnick	.30	.09
255 Kevin Orie	.30	.09
256 Ryne Sandberg	1.25	.35
257 Scott Servais	.30	.09
258 Sammy Sosa	1.25	.35
259 Kevin Tapani	.30	.09
260 Ramon Tatis	.30	.09
261 Bret Boone	.30	.09
262 Dave Burba	.30	.09
263 Brook Fordyce	.30	.09
264 Willie Greene	.30	.09
265 Barry Larkin	.75	.23
266 Pedro A. Martinez	.30	.09
267 Hal Morris	.30	.09
268 Joe Oliver	.30	.09
269 Eduardo Perez	.30	.09
270 Pokey Reese	.30	.09
271 Felix Rodriguez	.30	.09
272 Deion Sanders	.50	.15
273 Reggie Sanders	.30	.09
274 Jeff Shaw	.30	.09
275 Scott Sullivan	.30	.09
276 Brett Tomko	.30	.09
277 Roger Bailey	.30	.09
278 Dante Bichette	.30	.09
279 Ellis Burks	.30	.09
280 Vinny Castilla	.30	.09
281 Frank Castillo	.30	.09
282 Mike DeJean RC	.30	.09
283 Andres Galarraga	.30	.09
284 Darren Holmes	.30	.09
285 Kirt Manwaring	.30	.09
286 Quinton McCracken	.30	.09
287 Neifi Perez	.30	.09
288 Steve Reed	.30	.09
289 John Thomson	.30	.09
290 Larry Walker	.50	.15
291 Walt Weiss	.30	.09
292 Kurt Abbott	.30	.09
293 Antonio Alfonseca	.30	.09
294 Moises Alou	.30	.09
295 Alex Arias	.30	.09
296 Bobby Bonilla	.30	.09
297 Kevin Brown	.50	.15
298 Craig Counsell	.30	.09
299 Darren Daulton	.30	.09
300 Jim Eisenreich	.30	.09
301 Alex Fernandez	.30	.09
302 Felix Heredia	.30	.09
303 Livan Hernandez	.30	.09
304 Charles Johnson	.30	.09
305 Al Leiter	.30	.09
306 Robb Nen	.30	.09
307 Edgar Renteria	.30	.09
308 Gary Sheffield	.30	.09
309 Devon White	.30	.09
310 Bob Abreu	.30	.09
311 Brad Ausmus	.30	.09
312 Jeff Bagwell	.50	.15
313 Derek Bell	.30	.09
314 Sean Berry	.30	.09
315 Craig Biggio	.50	.15
316 Ramon Garcia	.30	.09
317 Luis Gonzalez	.30	.09
318 Ricky Gutierrez	.30	.09
319 Mike Hampton	.30	.09
320 Richard Hidalgo	.30	.09
321 Thomas Howard	.30	.09
322 Darryl Kile	.30	.09
323 Jose Lima	.30	.09
324 Shane Reynolds	.30	.09
325 Bill Spiers	.30	.09
326 Tom Candiotti	.30	.09
327 Roger Cedeno	.30	.09
328 Greg Gagne	.30	.09
329 Karim Garcia	.30	.09
330 Wilton Guerrero	.30	.09
331 Todd Hollandsworth	.30	.09
332 Eric Karros	.30	.09
333 Ramon Martinez	.30	.09
334 Raul Mondesi	.30	.09
335 Otis Nixon	.30	.09
336 Hideo Nomo	.75	.23
337 Antonio Osuna	.30	.09
338 Chan Ho Park	.30	.09
339 Mike Piazza	1.25	.35
340 Dennis Reyes	.30	.09
341 Ismael Valdes	.30	.09

342 Todd Worrell .30 .09
343 Todd Zeile .30 .09
344 Darrin Fletcher .30 .09
345 Mark Grudzielanek .30 .09
346 Vladimir Guerrero .75 .23
347 Dustin Hermanson .30 .09
348 Mike Lansing .30 .09
349 Pedro Martinez .75 .23
350 Ryan McGuire .30 .09
351 Jose Paniagua .30 .09
352 Carlos Perez .30 .09
353 Henry Rodriguez .30 .09
354 F.P. Santangelo .30 .09
355 David Segui .30 .09
356 Ugueth Urbina .30 .09
357 Marc Valdes .30 .09
358 Jose Vidro .30 .09
359 Rondell White .30 .09
360 Juan Acevedo .30 .09
361 Edgardo Alfonzo .30 .09
362 Carlos Baerga .30 .09
363 Carl Everett .30 .09
364 John Franco .30 .09
365 Bernard Gilkey .30 .09
366 Todd Hundley .30 .09
367 Butch Huskey .30 .09
368 Bobby Jones .30 .09
369 T.Kashiwada RC .30 .09
370 Greg McMichael .30 .09
371 Brian McRae .30 .09
372 Alex Ochoa .30 .09
373 John Olerud .30 .09
374 Rey Ordonez .30 .09
375 Turk Wendell .30 .09
376 Ricky Bottalico .30 .09
377 Rico Brogna .30 .09
378 Len Dykstra .30 .09
379 Bobby Estalella .30 .09
380 Wayne Gomes .30 .09
381 Tyler Green .30 .09
382 Gregg Jefferies .30 .09
383 Mark Leiter .30 .09
384 Mike Lieberthal .30 .09
385 Mickey Morandini .30 .09
386 Scott Rolen .50 .15
387 Curt Schilling .50 .15
388 Kevin Stocker .30 .09
389 Danny Tartabull .30 .09
390 Jermaine Allensworth .30 .09
391 Adrian Brown .30 .09
392 Jason Christiansen .30 .09
393 Steve Cooke .30 .09
394 Francisco Cordova .30 .09
395 Jose Guillen .30 .09
396 Jason Kendall .30 .09
397 Jon Lieber .30 .09
398 Esteban Loaiza .30 .09
399 Al Martin .30 .09
400 Kevin Polcovich .30 .09
401 Joe Randa .30 .09
402 Ricardo Rincon .30 .09
403 Tony Womack .30 .09
404 Kevin Young .30 .09
405 Andy Benes .30 .09
406 Royce Clayton .30 .09
407 Delino DeShields .30 .09
408 Mike Difelice RC .30 .09
409 Dennis Eckersley .30 .09
410 John Frascatore .30 .09
411 Gary Gaetti .30 .09
412 Ron Gant .30 .09
413 Brian Jordan .30 .09
414 Ray Lankford .30 .09
415 Willie McGee .30 .09
416 Mark McGwire 2.00 .60
417 Matt Morris .30 .09
418 Luis Ordaz .30 .09
419 Todd Stottlemyre .30 .09
420 Andy Ashby .30 .09
421 Jim Bruske .30 .09
422 Ken Caminiti .30 .09
423 Will Cunnane .30 .09
424 Steve Finley .30 .09
425 John Flaherty .30 .09
426 Chris Gomez .30 .09
427 Tony Gwynn 1.00 .30
428 Joey Hamilton .30 .09
429 Carlos Hernandez .30 .09
430 Sterling Hitchcock .30 .09
431 Trevor Hoffman .30 .09
432 Wally Joyner .30 .09
433 Greg Vaughn .30 .09
434 Quilvio Veras .30 .09
435 Wilson Alvarez .30 .09
436 Rod Beck .30 .09
437 Barry Bonds 2.00 .60
438 Jacob Cruz .30 .09
439 Shawn Estes .30 .09
440 Darryl Hamilton .30 .09
441 Roberto Hernandez .30 .09
442 Glenallen Hill .30 .09
443 Stan Javier .30 .09
444 Brian Johnson .30 .09
445 Jeff Kent .30 .09
446 Bill Mueller .30 .09
447 Kirk Rueter .30 .09
448 J.T. Snow .30 .09
449 Julian Tavarez .30 .09
450 Jose Vizcaino .30 .09

1998 Pacific Platinum Blue

Randomly inserted in packs at the rate of one in 73, this 450 card set is parallel to the base set and is similar in design. The difference is found in the platinum blue foil highlights. According to the manufacturer, only 67 sets were produced.

Nm-Mt Ex-Mt
*STARS: 12.5X TO 30X BASIC CARDS

1998 Pacific Red Threatt

Inserted one per Wal-Mart pack, this 450-card set is parallel to the base set and is similar in design. The difference is found in the red foil highlights.

Nm-Mt Ex-Mt
*STARS: 2.5X TO 6X BASIC CARDS ...

1998 Pacific Silver

Inserted one per pack, this 450-card set is parallel to the base set and is similar in design. The difference is found in the silver foil highlights.

Nm-Mt Ex-Mt
*STARS: 2X TO 5X BASIC CARDS

1998 Pacific Cramer's Choice

Randomly inserted in packs at the rate of one in 721, this 10-card set features top Major League players as chosen by Michael Cramer. The fronts display a color player cut-out on a pyramid die-cut shaped background. The backs carry information about why the player was selected for this set in both Spanish and English.

Nm-Mt Ex-Mt
1 Greg Maddux 50.00 15.00
2 Roberto Alomar 30.00 9.00
3 Cal Ripken 100.00 30.00
4 Nomar Garciaparra 50.00 15.00
5 Larry Walker 20.00 6.00
6 Mike Piazza 50.00 15.00
7 Mark McGwire 80.00 24.00
8 Tony Gwynn 40.00 12.00
9 Ken Griffey Jr. 50.00 15.00
10 Roger Clemens 60.00 18.00

1998 Pacific Gold Crown Die Cuts

Randomly inserted in packs at the rate of one in 37, this 36-card set features color action player photos with a die-cut crown at the top printed on a holographic silver foil background and gold etching on the trim. The backs carry player information in both Spanish and English.

Nm-Mt Ex-Mt
COMPLETE SET (36) 250.00 75.00
1 Chipper Jones 10.00 3.00
2 Greg Maddux 15.00 4.50
3 Denny Neagle 4.00 1.20
4 Roberto Alomar 10.00 3.00
5 Rafael Palmeiro 6.00 1.80
6 Cal Ripken 30.00 9.00
7 Nomar Garciaparra 15.00 4.50
8 Mo Vaughn 4.00 1.20
9 Frank Thomas 10.00 3.00
10 Sandy Alomar Jr. 4.00 1.20
11 David Justice 4.00 1.20
12 Manny Ramirez 4.00 1.20
13 Andres Galarraga 4.00 1.20
14 Larry Walker 6.00 1.80
15 Moises Alou 4.00 1.20
16 Livan Hernandez 4.00 1.20
17 Gary Sheffield 4.00 1.20
18 Jeff Bagwell 6.00 1.80
19 Raul Mondesi 4.00 1.20
20 Hideo Nomo 10.00 3.00
21 Mike Piazza 15.00 4.50
22 Derek Jeter 25.00 7.50
23 Tino Martinez 6.00 1.80
24 Bernie Williams 6.00 1.80
25 Ben Grieve 4.00 1.20
26 Mark McGwire 25.00 7.50
27 Tony Gwynn 12.00 3.60
28 Barry Bonds 25.00 7.50
29 Ken Griffey Jr. 15.00 4.50
30 Randy Johnson 10.00 3.00
31 Edgar Martinez 6.00 1.80
32 Alex Rodriguez 15.00 4.50
33 Juan Gonzalez 10.00 3.00
34 Ivan Rodriguez 10.00 3.00
35 Roger Clemens 20.00 6.00
36 Jose Cruz Jr. 4.00 1.20

1998 Pacific Home Run Hitters

Randomly inserted in packs at the rate of one in 73, this 20-card set features color player cut-outs of top home run hitters printed on full-foil cards with the number of home runs they hit in 1997 embossed in the background. The backs carry player information in both Spanish and English.

Nm-Mt Ex-Mt
COMPLETE SET (20) 150.00 45.00
1 Rafael Palmeiro 8.00 2.40
2 Mo Vaughn 5.00 1.50
3 Sammy Sosa 20.00 6.00
4 Albert Belle 5.00 1.50
5 Frank Thomas 12.00 3.60
6 David Justice 5.00 1.50
7 Jim Thome 12.00 3.60
8 Matt Williams 5.00 1.50
9 Vinny Castilla 5.00 1.50
10 Andres Galarraga 5.00 1.50
11 Larry Walker 8.00 2.40
12 Jeff Bagwell 8.00 2.40
13 Mike Piazza 20.00 6.00
14 Tino Martinez 8.00 2.40
15 Mark McGwire 30.00 9.00
16 Barry Bonds 30.00 9.00
17 Jay Buhner 5.00 1.50
18 Ken Griffey Jr. 20.00 6.00
19 Alex Rodriguez 20.00 6.00
20 Juan Gonzalez 12.00 3.60

1998 Pacific In The Cage

Randomly inserted in packs at the rate of one in 145, this 20-card set features color player cut-outs of the league's best hitters printed on a die-cut card with a laser-cut batting cage as the background. The backs carry player information in both Spanish and English.

Nm-Mt Ex-Mt
COMPLETE SET (20) 250.00 75.00
1 Chipper Jones 12.00 3.60
2 Roberto Alomar 12.00 3.60
3 Cal Ripken 40.00 12.00
4 Nomar Garciaparra 20.00 6.00
5 Frank Thomas 12.00 3.60
6 Sandy Alomar Jr. 5.00 1.50
7 David Justice 5.00 1.50
8 Larry Walker 8.00 2.40
9 Bobby Bonilla 5.00 1.50
10 Mike Piazza 20.00 6.00
11 Tino Martinez 8.00 2.40
12 Bernie Williams 8.00 2.40
13 Mark McGwire 30.00 9.00
14 Tony Gwynn 15.00 4.50
15 Barry Bonds 30.00 9.00
16 Ken Griffey Jr. 20.00 6.00
17 Edgar Martinez 8.00 2.40
18 Alex Rodriguez 20.00 6.00
19 Juan Gonzalez 12.00 3.60
20 Ivan Rodriguez 12.00 3.60

1998 Pacific Latinos of the Major Leagues

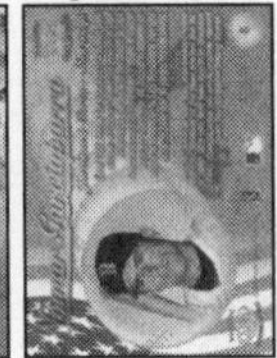

Randomly inserted in packs at the rate of two in 37, this 36-card set features color action photos of top players of Hispanic decent printed on foil cards with images of South and North America, the player's team logo, and the United States Flag in the background. The backs carry player information in both Spanish and English.

Nm-Mt Ex-Mt
COMPLETE SET (36) 80.00 24.00
1 Andruw Jones 2.00 .60
2 Javier Lopez 2.00 .60
3 Roberto Alomar 5.00 1.50
4 Geronimo Berroa 2.00 .60
5 Rafael Palmeiro 3.00 .90
6 Nomar Garciaparra 8.00 2.40
7 Sammy Sosa 8.00 2.40
8 Ozzie Guillen 2.00 .60
9 Sandy Alomar Jr. 2.00 .60
10 Manny Ramirez 2.00 .60
11 Omar Vizquel 2.00 .60
12 Vinny Castilla 2.00 .60
13 Andres Galarraga 2.00 .60
14 Moises Alou 2.00 .60
15 Bobby Bonilla 2.00 .60
16 Livan Hernandez 2.00 .60
17 Edgar Renteria 2.00 .60
18 Wilton Guerrero 2.00 .60
19 Raul Mondesi 2.00 .60
20 Ismael Valdes 2.00 .60
21 Fernando Vina 2.00 .60
22 Pedro Martinez 5.00 1.50
23 Edgardo Alfonzo 2.00 .60
24 Carlos Baerga 2.00 .60
25 Rey Ordonez 2.00 .60
26 Tino Martinez 3.00 .90
27 Mariano Rivera 3.00 .90
28 Bernie Williams 3.00 .90
29 Jose Canseco 5.00 1.50
30 Joey Cora 2.00 .60
31 Roberto Kelly 2.00 .60
32 Edgar Martinez 3.00 .90
33 Alex Rodriguez 8.00 2.40
34 Juan Gonzalez 5.00 1.50
35 Ivan Rodriguez 5.00 1.50
36 Jose Cruz Jr. 2.00 .60

1998 Pacific Team Checklists

Randomly inserted in packs at the rate of one in 37, this 30-card set features color player photos printed on a die-cut card in the shape of the end of a baseball bat with a laser cut team

logo. The two 1998 expansion teams, the Arizona Diamondbacks and the Tampa Bay Devil Rays, are included in these checklists.

Nm-Mt Ex-Mt
COMPLETE SET (30) 150.00 45.00
1 Tim Salmon 3.00 .90
Jim Edmonds
2 Cal Ripken 25.00 7.50
Roberto Alomar
3 Nomar Garciaparra 12.00 3.60
Mo Vaughn
4 Frank Thomas 8.00 2.40
Albert Belle
5 Sandy Alomar Jr. 3.00 .90
Manny Ramirez
6 Justin Thompson 3.00 .90
Tony Clark
7 Johnny Damon 3.00 .90
Jermaine Dye
8 Dave Nilsson 3.00 .90
Jeff Cirillo
9 Paul Molitor 5.00 1.50
Chuck Knoblauch
10 Tino Martinez 20.00 6.00
Derek Jeter
11 Ben Grieve 8.00 2.40
Jose Canseco
12 Ken Griffey Jr. 12.00 3.60
Alex Rodriguez
13 Juan Gonzalez 8.00 2.40
Ivan Rodriguez
14 Jose Cruz Jr. 15.00 4.50
Roger Clemens
15 Greg Maddux 12.00 3.60
Chipper Jones
16 Sammy Sosa 12.00 3.60
Mark Grace
17 Barry Larkin 8.00 2.40
Deion Sanders
18 Larry Walker 3.00 .90
Andres Galarraga
19 Moises Alou 3.00 .90
Bobby Bonilla
20 Jeff Bagwell 5.00 1.50
Craig Biggio
21 Mike Piazza 12.00 3.60
Hideo Nomo
22 Pedro Martinez 8.00 2.40
Henry Rodriguez
23 Rey Ordonez 3.00 .90
Carlos Baerga
24 Curt Schilling 5.00 1.50
Scott Rolen
25 Al Martin 3.00 .90
Tony Womack
26 Mark McGwire 20.00 6.00
Dennis Eckersley
27 Tony Gwynn 10.00 3.00
Wally Joyner
28 Barry Bonds 20.00 6.00
J.T.Snow
29 Matt Williams 3.00 .90
Jay Bell
30 Fred McGriff 5.00 1.50
Roberto Hernandez

1998 Pacific Home Run Heroes

This six-card standard-size set was issued exclusively through Wal-Mart. The set was issued in a special can and retailed for $4.95 when issued.

Nm-Mt Ex-Mt
COMP. FACT SET (6) 5.00 1.50
1 Mark McGwire 2.50 .75
2 Sammy Sosa 1.50 .45
3 Ken Griffey Jr. 2.00 .60
4 Greg Vaughn .20 .06
5 Albert Belle .30 .09
6 Jose Canseco .75 .23

1998 Pacific Home Run History

This 72-card set honors Mark McGwire's and Sammy Sosa's record-breaking home run race during the 1998 season. The set was created exclusively for QVC and was available during a 24-hour period on the cable television shopping channel on September 28, 1998. The cards feature color action player photos and the home run number or some other important fact about the player. Two bonus cards were included in the set: Mark McGwire as the Home Run Champion and Cal Ripken Jr. as the Consecutive Games Champion. Only 142,500 sets were produced.

Nm-Mt Ex-Mt
COMPLETE SET (72) 30.00 9.00
COMMON SOSA (1-70) .50 .15
COMMON MCGWIRE 1.00 .30
43 Mark McGwire 2.00 .60
70!!!
67 Mark McGwire 1.00 .30
Sammy Sosa
68 Mark McGwire 1.00 .30
Sammy Sosa
69 Mark McGwire 1.00 .30
Sammy Sosa
70 Mark McGwire 1.00 .30
Sammy Sosa
HRC1 Mark McGwire 3.00 .90
Home Run Champion
HRC2 Cal Ripken 3.00 .90
All-Time Consecutive Games King

1998 Pacific Nestle

This 20-card set features color action player photos in a red border. The backs carry a player portrait with career statistics and information about the player in Spanish in a blue border. The first five numbers have two cards with different players and card design. The harder to obtain cards have the letter "B" after their number in the checklist below.

Nm-Mt Ex-Mt
COMPLETE SET (20) 15.00 4.50
1A Bernie Williams 1.00 .30
1B Ismael Valdes .25 .07
2A Tino Martinez .40 .12
2B Juan Gonzalez 1.50 .45
3A Alex Rodriguez 3.00 .90
3B Ivan Rodriguez 1.25 .35
4A Edgar Martinez .60 .18
4B Joey Cora .25 .07
5A Andres Galarraga .60 .18
5B Livan Hernandez .25 .07
6 Manny Ramirez 1.25 .35
7 Carlos Baerga .40 .12
8 Pedro Martinez 1.25 .35
9 Vinny Castilla .40 .12
10 Sammy Sosa 3.00 .90
11 Nomar Garciaparra 3.00 .90
12 Javy Lopez .40 .12
13 Sandy Alomar Jr. .40 .12
14 Roberto Alomar 1.00 .30
15 Jose Canseco 1.25 .35

1999 Pacific

This 500 card standard-size set was issued in 10 card packs that had a SRP of $2.19 per pack. Each Box containted 36 packs and each case had 20 boxes. Continuing the trend begun in 1998 with Pacific On-Line, Pacific issued two versions of 50 of the star or leading prospect players in the set with both an action version as well as a head shot. Thus the cards are actually numbered from 1 through 450, but the 50 additional headshot cards (carrying identical numbering to the action cards) bring the total number of cards in the set to 500. The complete set includes both versions of each player. The head shots were inserted one per pack. An unnumbered Tony Gwynn sample card was distributed to dealers and hobby media prior to the product's release. The card is easy to recognize by the bold, diagonal "SAMPLE" text running across the back.

Nm-Mt Ex-Mt
COMPLETE SET (500) 80.00 24.0
1 Garret Anderson .30
2 Jason Dickson .30
3 Gary DiSarcina .30
4 Jim Edmonds .30
5 Darin Erstad .30
6 Chuck Finley .30
7 Shigetoshi Hasegawa .30
8 Ken Hill .30
9 Dave Hollins .30
10 Phil Nevin .30
11 Troy Percival .30
12 Tim Salmon * .50
12A Tim Salmon Headshot .50
13 Brian Anderson .30
14 Tony Batista .30
15 Jay Bell .30
16 Andy Benes .30
17 Yamil Benitez .30
18 Omar Daal .30
19 David Dellucci .30
20 Karim Garcia .30
21 Bernard Gilkey .30
22 Travis Lee * .30
22A Travis Lee Headshot .30
23 Aaron Small .30
24 Kelly Stinnett .30
25 Devon White .30
26 Matt Williams .30
27 Bruce Chen * .30
27A Bruce Chen Headshot .30
28 Andres Galarraga * .30
28A A.Galarraga Headshot .30
29 Tom Glavine .50
30 Ozzie Guillen .30
31 Andruw Jones .30
32 Chipper Jones * .75
32A C.Jones Headshot .75

33 Ryan Klesko .30 .09
34 George Lombard .30 .09
35 Javy Lopez .30 .09
36 Greg Maddux * 1.25 .35
36A G.Maddux Headshot 1.25 .35
37 Marty Malloy * .30 .09
37A M.Malloy Headshot .30 .09
38 Dennis Martinez .30 .09
39 Kevin Millwood .30 .09
40 Alex Rodriguez * 1.25 .35
40A Alex Rodriguez Headshot 1.25 .35
41 Denny Neagle .30 .09
42 John Smoltz .50 .15
43 Michael Tucker .30 .09
44 Walt Weiss .30 .09
45 Roberto Alomar * .75 .23
45A R.Alomar Headshot .75 .23
46 Brady Anderson .30 .09
47 Harold Baines .30 .09
48 Mike Bordick .30 .09
49 Danny Clyburn * .30 .09
49A D.Clyburn Headshot .30 .09
50 Eric Davis .30 .09
51 Scott Erickson .30 .09
52 Chris Hoiles .30 .09
53 Jimmy Key .30 .09
54 Ryan Minor * .30 .09
54A Ryan Minor Headshot .30 .09
55 Mike Mussina .75 .23
56 Jesse Orosco .30 .09
57 Rafael Palmeiro * .50 .15
57A R.Palmeiro Headshot .50 .15
58 Sidney Ponson .30 .09
59 Arthur Rhodes .30 .09
60 Cal Ripken * 2.50 .75
60A Cal Ripken Headshot 2.50 .75
61 B.J. Surhoff .30 .09
62 Steve Avery .30 .09
63 Darren Bragg .30 .09
64 Dennis Eckersley .30 .09
65 Nomar Garciaparra * 1.25 .35
65A Nomar Garciaparra Headshot 1.25 .35
66 Sammy Sosa * 1.25 .35
66A S.Sosa Headshot 1.25 .35
67 Tom Gordon .30 .09
68 Reggie Jefferson .30 .09
69 Darren Lewis .30 .09
70 Mark McGwire * 2.00 .60
70A M.McGwire Headshot 2.00 .60
71 Pedro Martinez .75 .23
72 Troy O'Leary .30 .09
73 Bret Saberhagen .30 .09
74 Mike Stanley .30 .09
75 John Valentin .30 .09
76 Jason Varitek .30 .09
77 Mo Vaughn .30 .09
8 Tim Wakefield .30 .09
9 Manny Alexander .30 .09
0 Rod Beck .30 .09
1 Brant Brown .30 .09
Mark Clark .30 .09
Gary Gaetti .30 .09
Mark Grace .50 .15
Jose Hernandez .30 .09
ance Johnson .30 .09
ason Maxwell * .30 .09
J.Maxwell Headshot .30 .09
ickey Morandini .30 .09
rry Mulholland .30 .09
nry Rodriguez .30 .09
ott Servais .30 .09
in Tapani .30 .09
ro Valdes .30 .09
y Wood .75 .23
Abbott .30 .09
s Baldwin .30 .09
t Belle .30 .09
Cameron .30 .09
Caruso .30 .09
ordero .30 .09
Durham .30 .09
Navarro .30 .09
Norton .30 .09
io Ordonez .30 .09
irotka .30 .09
Thomas * .75 .23
mas Headshot .75 .23
Ventura .30 .09
ilson .30 .09
oone .30 .09
ne .30 .09
ey .30 .09
isch .30 .09
ek .30 .09
in .75 .23
erez .30 .09
nger .30 .09
ders .30 .09
s .30 .09
nsee .30 .09
.30 .09
.30 .09
.30 .09
Jr .30 .09
.30 .09
.30 .09
.30 .09
.30 .09
.50 .15
.30 .09
.30 .09
.30 .09
.30 .09
.30 .09
.30 .09
shot .30 .09
.30 .09
.75 .23
t .75 .23
.30 .09
.30 .09
.30 .09
.30 .09
.30 .09
.30 .09
.30 .09
.30 .09
.30 .09

143A Edgard Clemente Headshot .30 .09
144 Derrick Gibson * .30 .09
144A D. Gibson Headshot .30 .09
145 Curtis Goodwin .30 .09
146 Todd Helton * .50 .15
146A T.Helton Headshot .50 .15
147 Bobby Jones .30 .09
148 Darryl Kile .30 .09
149 Mike Lansing .30 .09
150 Chuck McElroy .30 .09
151 Neifi Perez .30 .09
152 Jeff Reed .30 .09
153 John Thomson .30 .09
154 Larry Walker * .50 .15
154A L.Walker Headshot .50 .15
155 Jamey Wright .30 .09
156 Kimera Bartee .30 .09
157 Geronimo Berroa .30 .09
158 Raul Casanova .30 .09
159 Frank Catalanotto .30 .09
160 Tony Clark .30 .09
161 Deivi Cruz .30 .09
162 Damion Easley .30 .09
163 Juan Encarnacion .30 .09
164 Luis Gonzalez .30 .09
165 Seth Greisinger .30 .09
166 Bob Higginson .30 .09
167 Brian L.Hunter .30 .09
168 Todd Jones .30 .09
169 Justin Thompson .30 .09
170 Antonio Alfonseca .30 .09
171 Dave Berg .30 .09
172 John Cangelosi .30 .09
173 Craig Counsell .30 .09
174 Todd Dunwoody .30 .09
175 Cliff Floyd .30 .09
176 Alex Gonzalez .30 .09
177 Livan Hernandez .30 .09
178 Ryan Jackson .30 .09
179 Mark Kotsay .30 .09
180 Derrek Lee .30 .09
181 Matt Mantei .30 .09
182 Brian Meadows .30 .09
183 Edgar Renteria .30 .09
184 Moises Alou * .30 .09
184A M.Alou Headshot .30 .09
185 Brad Ausmus .30 .09
186 Jeff Bagwell * .50 .15
186A J.Bagwell Headshot .50 .15
187 Derek Bell .30 .09
188 Sean Berry .30 .09
189 Craig Biggio .50 .15
190 Carl Everett .30 .09
191 Ricky Gutierrez .30 .09
192 Mike Hampton .30 .09
193 Doug Henry .30 .09
194 Richard Hidalgo .30 .09
195 Randy Johnson .75 .23
196 Russ Johnson * .30 .09
196A R.Johnson Headshot .30 .09
197 Shane Reynolds .30 .09
198 Bill Spiers .30 .09
199 Kevin Appier .30 .09
200 Tim Belcher .30 .09
201 Jeff Conine .30 .09
202 Johnny Damon .30 .09
203 Jermaine Dye .30 .09
204 Jeremy Giambi * .30 .09
204A Je. Giambi Headshot .30 .09
205 Jeff King .30 .09
206 Shane Mack .30 .09
207 Jeff Montgomery .30 .09
208 Hal Morris .30 .09
209 Jose Offerman .30 .09
210 Dean Palmer .30 .09
211 Jose Rosado .30 .09
212 Glendon Rusch .30 .09
213 Larry Sutton .30 .09
214 Mike Sweeney .30 .09
215 Bobby Bonilla .30 .09
216 Alex Cora .30 .09
217 Darren Dreifort .30 .09
218 Mark Grudzielanek .30 .09
219 Todd Hollandsworth .30 .09
220 Trenidad Hubbard .30 .09
221 Charles Johnson .30 .09
222 Eric Karros .30 .09
223 Matt Luke .30 .09
224 Ramon Martinez .30 .09
225 Raul Mondesi .30 .09
226 Chan Ho Park .30 .09
227 Jeff Shaw .30 .09
228 Gary Sheffield .30 .09
229 Eric Young .30 .09
230 Jeromy Burnitz .30 .09
231 Jeff Cirillo .30 .09
232 Marquis Grissom .30 .09
233 Bobby Hughes .30 .09
234 John Jaha .30 .09
235 Geoff Jenkins .30 .09
236 Scott Karl .30 .09
237 Mark Loretta .30 .09
238 Mike Matheny .30 .09
239 Mike Myers .30 .09
240 Dave Nilsson .30 .09
241 Bob Wickman .30 .09
242 Jose Valentin .30 .09
243 Fernando Vina .30 .09
244 Rick Aguilera .30 .09
245 Ron Coomer .30 .09
246 Marty Cordova .30 .09
247 Denny Hocking .30 .09
248 Matt Lawton .30 .09
249 Pat Meares .30 .09
250 Paul Molitor * .50 .15
250A P.Molitor Headshot .50 .15
251 Otis Nixon .30 .09
252 Alex Ochoa .30 .09
253 David Ortiz .30 .09
254 A.J. Pierzynski .30 .09
255 Brad Radke .30 .09
256 Terry Steinbach .30 .09
257 Bob Tewksbury .30 .09
258 Todd Walker .30 .09
259 Shane Andrews .30 .09
260 Shayne Bennett .30 .09
261 Orlando Cabrera .30 .09
262 Brad Fullmer .30 .09
263 Vladimir Guerrero .75 .23
264 Wilton Guerrero .30 .09

265 Dustin Hermanson .30 .09
266 Terry Jones RC .30 .09
267 Steve Kline .30 .09
268 Carl Pavano .30 .09
269 F.P. Santangelo .30 .09
270 Fernando Seguignol * .30 .09
270A Fernando Seguignol Headshot .30 .09
271 Ugueth Urbina .30 .09
272 Jose Vidro .30 .09
273 Chris Widger .30 .09
274 Edgardo Alfonzo .30 .09
275 Carlos Baerga .30 .09
276 John Franco .30 .09
277 Todd Hundley .30 .09
278 Butch Huskey .30 .09
279 Bobby Jones .30 .09
280 Al Leiter .30 .09
281 Greg McMichael .30 .09
282 Brian McRae .30 .09
283 Hideo Nomo .75 .23
284 John Olerud .30 .09
285 Rey Ordonez .30 .09
286 Mike Piazza * 1.25 .35
286A M.Piazza Headshot 1.25 .35
287 Turk Wendell .30 .09
288 Masato Yoshii .30 .09
289 David Cone .30 .09
290 Chad Curtis .30 .09
291 Joe Girardi .30 .09
292 Orlando Hernandez .30 .09
293 Hideki Irabu * .30 .09
293A H.Irabu Headshot .30 .09
294 Derek Jeter * 2.00 .60
294A D.Jeter Headshot 2.00 .60
295 Chuck Knoblauch .30 .09
296 Mike Lowell * .30 .09
296A M.Lowell Headshot .30 .09
297 Tino Martinez .50 .15
298 Ramiro Mendoza .30 .09
299 Paul O'Neill .50 .15
300 Andy Pettitte .50 .15
301 Jorge Posada .50 .15
302 Tim Raines .30 .09
303 Mariano Rivera .50 .15
304 David Wells .30 .09
305 Bernie Williams * .50 .15
305A Bernie Williams Headshot .50 .15
306 Mike Blowers .30 .09
307 Tom Candiotti .30 .09
308 Eric Chavez * .30 .09
308A E.Chavez Headshot .30 .09
309 Ryan Christenson .30 .09
310 Jason Giambi .75 .23
311 Ben Grieve * .30 .09
311A Ben Grieve Headshot .30 .09
312 Rickey Henderson .75 .23
313 A.J. Hinch .30 .09
314 Jason McDonald .30 .09
315 Bip Roberts .30 .09
316 Kenny Rogers .30 .09
317 Scott Spiezio .30 .09
318 Matt Stairs .30 .09
319 Miguel Tejada .30 .09
320 Bob Abreu .30 .09
321 Alex Arias .30 .09
322 Gary Bennett RC .30 .09
322A Gary Bennett RC Headshot .30 .09
323 Ricky Bottalico .30 .09
324 Rico Brogna .30 .09
325 Bobby Estalella .30 .09
326 Doug Glanville .30 .09
327 Kevin Jordan .30 .09
328 Mark Leiter .30 .09
329 Wendell Magee .30 .09
330 Mark Portugal .30 .09
331 Desi Relaford .30 .09
332 Scott Rolen .50 .15
333 Curt Schilling .50 .15
334 Kevin Sefcik .30 .09
335 Adrian Brown .30 .09
336 Emil Brown .30 .09
337 Lou Collier .30 .09
338 Francisco Cordova .30 .09
339 Freddy Garcia .30 .09
340 Jose Guillen .30 .09
341 Jason Kendall .30 .09
342 Al Martin .30 .09
343 Abraham Nunez .30 .09
344 Aramis Ramirez .30 .09
345 Ricardo Rincon .30 .09
346 Jason Schmidt .30 .09
347 Turner Ward .30 .09
348 Tony Womack .30 .09
349 Kevin Young .30 .09
350 Juan Acevedo .30 .09
351 Delino DeShields .30 .09
352 J.D. Drew * .30 .09
352A J.D. Drew Headshot .30 .09
353 Ron Gant .30 .09
354 Brian Jordan .30 .09
355 Ray Lankford .30 .09
356 Eli Marrero .30 .09
357 Kent Mercker .30 .09
358 Matt Morris .30 .09
359 Luis Ordaz .30 .09
360 Donovan Osborne .30 .09
361 Placido Polanco .30 .09
362 Fernando Tatis .30 .09
363 Andy Ashby .30 .09
364 Kevin Brown .50 .15
365 Ken Caminiti .30 .09
366 Steve Finley .30 .09
367 Chris Gomez .30 .09
368 Tony Gwynn * 1.00 .30
368A T.Gwynn Headshot 1.00 .30
369 Joey Hamilton .30 .09
370 Carlos Hernandez .30 .09
371 Trevor Hoffman .30 .09
372 Wally Joyner .30 .09
373 Jim Leyritz .30 .09
374 Ruben Rivera .30 .09
375 Greg Vaughn .30 .09
376 Quilvio Veras .30 .09
377 Rich Aurilia .30 .09
378 Barry Bonds * 2.00 .60
378A B.Bonds Headshot 1.50 .45
379 Ellis Burks .30 .09
380 Joe Carter .30 .09

381 Stan Javier .30 .09
382 Brian Johnson .30 .09
383 Jeff Kent .30 .09
384 Jose Mesa .30 .09
385 Bill Mueller .30 .09
386 Robb Nen .30 .09
387 Armando Rios * .30 .09
387A A.Rios Headshot .30 .09
388 Kirk Rueter .30 .09
389 Rey Sanchez .30 .09
390 J.T. Snow .30 .09
391 David Bell .30 .09
392 Jay Buhner .30 .09
393 Ken Cloude .30 .09
394 Russ Davis .30 .09
395 Jeff Fassero .30 .09
396 Ken Griffey Jr. * 1.25 .35
396A Ken Griffey Jr. Headshot 1.25 .35
397 Giomar Guevara RC .30 .09
398 Carlos Guillen .30 .09
399 Edgar Martinez .50 .15
400 Shane Monahan .30 .09
401 Jamie Moyer .30 .09
402 David Segui .30 .09
403 Makoto Suzuki .30 .09
404 Mike Timlin .30 .09
405 Dan Wilson .30 .09
406 Wilson Alvarez .30 .09
407 Rolando Arrojo .30 .09
408 Wade Boggs .50 .15
409 Miguel Cairo .30 .09
410 Roberto Hernandez .30 .09
411 Mike Kelly .30 .09
412 Aaron Ledesma .30 .09
413 Albie Lopez .30 .09
414 Dave Martinez .30 .09
415 Quinton McCracken .30 .09
416 Fred McGriff .50 .15
417 Bryan Rekar .30 .09
418 Paul Sorrento .30 .09
419 Randy Winn .30 .09
420 John Burkett .30 .09
421 Will Clark .75 .23
422 Royce Clayton .30 .09
423 Juan Gonzalez * .75 .23
423A Juan Gonzalez Headshot .75 .23
424 Tom Goodwin .30 .09
425 Rusty Greer .30 .09
426 Rick Helling .30 .09
427 Roberto Kelly .30 .09
428 Mark McLemore .30 .09
429 Ivan Rodriguez * .75 .23
429A Ivan Rodriguez Headshot .75 .23
430 Aaron Sele .30 .09
431 Lee Stevens .30 .09
432 Todd Stottlemyre .30 .09
433 John Wetteland .30 .09
434 Todd Zeile .30 .09
435 Jose Canseco * .75 .23
435A J.Canseco Headshot .75 .23
436 Roger Clemens * 1.50 .45
436A R.Clemens Headshot 1.50 .45
437 Felipe Crespo .30 .09
438 Jose Cruz Jr. .30 .09
439 Carlos Delgado .30 .09
440 Tom Evans * .30 .09
440A T.Evans Headshot .30 .09
441 Tony Fernandez .30 .09
442 Darrin Fletcher .30 .09
443 Alex Gonzalez .30 .09
444 Shawn Green .30 .09
445 Roy Halladay .30 .09
446 Pat Hentgen .30 .09
447 Juan Samuel .30 .09
448 Benito Santiago .30 .09
449 Shannon Stewart .30 .09
450 Woody Williams .30 .09
NNO Tony Gwynn Sample 1.00 .30

1999 Pacific Platinum Blue

This 500 card set is a parallel version to the basic 1999 Pacific set. Each card front features platinum-blue foil accents. These cards were issued one every 73 packs.

Nm-Mt Ex-Mt
*STARS: 10X TO 25X BASIC CARDS..

1999 Pacific Red

This parallel to the regular Pacific set was issued one per retail pack. Each card front features red foil accents.

Nm-Mt Ex-Mt
*STARS: 2X TO 5X BASIC CARDS ......

1999 Pacific Cramer's Choice

This 10 card set continues the Pacific tradition of having their President/CEO/Founder Mike Cramer select 10 players for the honor of being included in this set to honor the leading players in baseball. The die-cut design features the players photo on the front to go with back commentary on why they deserve the honor. 299 serial numbered sets were produced (of which card is stamped in black ink on back).

	Nm-Mt	Ex-Mt
COMPLETE SET (10)	400.00	120.00
1 Cal Ripken	80.00	24.00
2 Nomar Garciaparra	40.00	12.00
3 Frank Thomas	25.00	7.50
4 Ken Griffey Jr.	40.00	12.00
5 Alex Rodriguez	40.00	12.00
6 Greg Maddux	40.00	12.00
7 Sammy Sosa	40.00	12.00
8 Kerry Wood	25.00	7.50
9 Mark McGwire	60.00	18.00
10 Tony Gwynn	30.00	9.00

1999 Pacific Dynagon Diamond

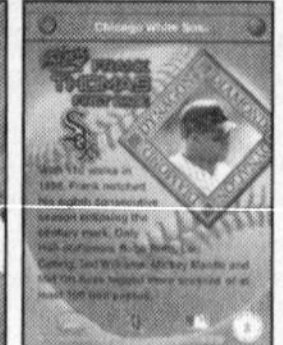

This 20 card set, seeded at a rate of four in 37 packs, contains some of baseball biggest stars in action against a mirror patterned full-foil background. The fronts feature a little baseball diamond design in the lower left corner.

	Nm-Mt	Ex-Mt
COMPLETE SET (20)	80.00	24.00
*TITANIUM: 4X TO 10X BASIC DYN.DIAM.		
TITANIUM: RANDOM INS.IN HOBBY PACKS		
TITANIUM PRINT RUN 99 SERIAL #'d SETS		
1 Cal Ripken	10.00	3.00
2 Nomar Garciaparra	5.00	1.50
3 Frank Thomas	3.00	.90
4 Derek Jeter	8.00	2.40
5 Ben Grieve	1.25	.35
6 Ken Griffey Jr.	5.00	1.50
7 Alex Rodriguez	5.00	1.50
8 Juan Gonzalez	3.00	.90
9 Travis Lee	1.25	.35
10 Chipper Jones	3.00	.90
11 Greg Maddux	5.00	1.50
12 Sammy Sosa	5.00	1.50
13 Kerry Wood	3.00	.90
14 Jeff Bagwell	2.00	.60
15 Hideo Nomo	3.00	.90
16 Mike Piazza	5.00	1.50
17 J.D. Drew	1.25	.35
18 Mark McGwire	8.00	2.40
19 Tony Gwynn	4.00	1.20
20 Barry Bonds	8.00	2.40

1999 Pacific Gold Crown Die Cuts

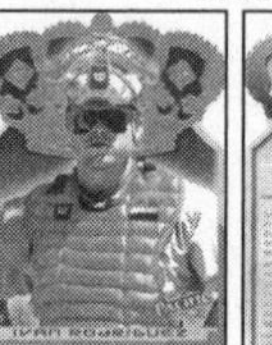

This die-cut set featuring Pacific's popular Gold Crown design were inserted one every 37 packs. Thirty-six of baseball's leading players are featured in this set which contains dual foiling and were printed on 24 point stock.

	Nm-Mt	Ex-Mt
COMPLETE SET (36)	400.00	120.00
1 Darin Erstad	4.00	1.20
2 Cal Ripken	30.00	9.00
3 Nomar Garciaparra	15.00	4.50
4 Pedro Martinez	10.00	3.00
5 Mo Vaughn	4.00	1.20
6 Frank Thomas	10.00	3.00
7 Kenny Lofton	4.00	1.20
8 Manny Ramirez	4.00	1.20
9 Paul Molitor	6.00	1.80
10 Derek Jeter	25.00	7.50
11 Bernie Williams	6.00	1.80
12 Ben Grieve	4.00	1.20
13 Ken Griffey Jr.	15.00	4.50
14 Alex Rodriguez	15.00	4.50
15 Wade Boggs	6.00	1.80
16 Juan Gonzalez	10.00	3.00
17 Ivan Rodriguez	10.00	3.00
18 Jose Canseco	10.00	3.00
19 Roger Clemens	20.00	6.00
20 Travis Lee	4.00	1.20
21 Chipper Jones	10.00	3.00
22 Greg Maddux	15.00	4.50
23 Sammy Sosa	15.00	4.50
24 Kerry Wood	10.00	3.00
25 Todd Helton	6.00	1.80
26 Larry Walker	6.00	1.80
27 Jeff Bagwell	6.00	1.80
28 Craig Biggio	6.00	1.80
29 Raul Mondesi	4.00	1.20
30 Vladimir Guerrero	10.00	3.00
31 Mike Piazza	15.00	4.50
32 Scott Rolen	6.00	1.80
33 J.D. Drew	4.00	1.20
34 Mark McGwire	25.00	7.50
35 Tony Gwynn	12.00	3.60
36 Barry Bonds	25.00	7.50

1999 Pacific Hot Cards

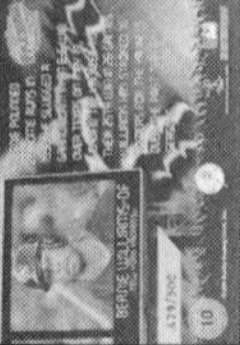

This ten card set features a selection of top stars. Only 500 serial numbered sets were produced. Hot Cards were distributed at year's end to dealers that applied for the Hot Card registry program. Each pacific product issued in 1999 had an insert set designated as a Hot

Card registry set. Shop owners that had customers pull a card from the designated Hot Card registry set could then report the find to Pacific and register the card online. For their efforts, the dealers were rewarded with these special exchange cards. These were the products which were noted as eligible for the "Hot Card Registry": 1999 Private Stock Exclusive, 1999 Prism Holographic Blue, 1999 Aurora signed cards of Tony Gwynn, 1999 Paramount Cooperstown Bound Pacific Proofs, 1999 Invincible Giants of the Game, 1999 Crown Royale Cramer's Choice Red, 1999 Revolution Tier 1, 1999 Omega 5-Tool Talents Tier 1, 2000 Pacific Premire Date, 2000 Private Stock PS-2000 Rookies, 2000 Paramount Fielder's Choice Gold Glove and 2000 Crown Collection Platinum Blue. No dealer was eligible for more than five sets per product.

	Nm-Mt	Ex-Mt
COMPLETE SET (10)	120.00	36.00
1 Alex Rodriguez	12.00	3.60
2 Tony Gwynn	10.00	3.00
3 Ken Griffey Jr.	12.00	3.60
4 Sammy Sosa	12.00	3.60
5 Ivan Rodriguez	8.00	2.40
6 Derek Jeter	20.00	6.00
7 Cal Ripken	25.00	7.50
8 Mark McGwire	20.00	6.00
9 J.D. Drew	3.00	.90
10 Bernie Williams	5.00	1.50

1999 Pacific Team Checklists

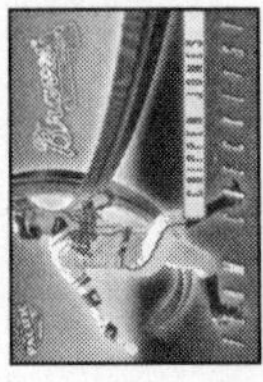

The old tradtion of knowing which players one needs to collect for all the cards of their favorite team is resurrected on these cards. Each card, which was inserted two per 37 packs has a photo of a star player for that team on the front and the complete team checklist on the back. Another photo of the featured player is included on the back as well.

	Nm-Mt	Ex-Mt
COMPLETE SET (30)	150.00	45.00
1 Darin Erstad	2.00	.60
2 Cal Ripken	15.00	4.50
3 Nomar Garciaparra	8.00	2.40
4 Frank Thomas	5.00	1.50
5 Manny Ramirez	2.00	.60
6 Damion Easley	2.00	.60
7 Jeff King	2.00	.60
8 Paul Molitor	3.00	.90
9 Derek Jeter	12.00	3.60
10 Ben Grieve	2.00	.60
11 Ken Griffey Jr.	8.00	2.40
12 Wade Boggs	3.00	.90
13 Juan Gonzalez	5.00	1.50
14 Roger Clemens	10.00	3.00
15 Travis Lee	2.00	.60
16 Chipper Jones	5.00	1.50
17 Sammy Sosa	8.00	2.40
18 Barry Larkin	5.00	1.50
19 Todd Helton	3.00	.90
20 Mark Kotsay	2.00	.60
21 Jeff Bagwell	3.00	.90
22 Raul Mondesi	2.00	.60
23 Jeff Cirillo	2.00	.60
24 Vladimir Guerrero	5.00	1.50
25 Mike Piazza	8.00	2.40
26 Scott Rolen	3.00	.90
27 Jason Kendall	2.00	.60
28 Mark McGwire	12.00	3.60
29 Tony Gwynn	6.00	1.80
30 Barry Bonds	12.00	3.60

1999 Pacific Timelines

This hobby only set features 20 leading players. Three photos of each player are featured on the front, including many with these players original teams. These cards give a chronological history of each players career. This inserted was limited to 199 serial numbered sets.

	Nm-Mt	Ex-Mt
COMPLETE SET (20)	600.00	180.00
1 Cal Ripken	80.00	24.00
2 Frank Thomas	25.00	7.50
3 Jim Thome	25.00	7.50
4 Paul Molitor	15.00	4.50
5 Bernie Williams	15.00	4.50
6 Derek Jeter	60.00	18.00
7 Ken Griffey Jr.	40.00	12.00
8 Alex Rodriguez	40.00	12.00
9 Wade Boggs	15.00	4.50
10 Jose Canseco	25.00	7.50
11 Roger Clemens	50.00	15.00
12 Andres Galarraga	10.00	3.00
13 Chipper Jones	25.00	7.50
14 Greg Maddux	40.00	12.00
15 Sammy Sosa	40.00	12.00
16 Larry Walker	15.00	4.50
17 Randy Johnson	25.00	7.50
18 Mike Piazza	40.00	12.00
19 Mark McGwire	60.00	18.00
20 Tony Gwynn	30.00	9.00

1999 Pacific Players Choice

These cards, which are 1999 Pacific cards but were specially stamped for the Players Choice ceremony are parallels of the regular 1999 Pacific Cards. They are printed in different amounts so we have put the number of each card printed next to the players name.

	Nm-Mt	Ex-Mt
COMPLETE SET	200.00	60.00
32 Chipper Jones/70	30.00	9.00
36 Greg Maddux/71	30.00	9.00
60 Cal Ripken/71	50.00	15.00
66 Sammy Sosa/70	25.00	7.50
71 Pedro Martinez/36	15.00	4.50
134 Manny Ramirez/71	15.00	4.50
186 Jeff Bagwell/71	15.00	4.50
234 John Jaha/33	6.00	1.80
378 Barry Bonds/70	25.00	7.50
396 Ken Griffey Jr./100	30.00	9.00

2000 Pacific

Though numbered 1-450, fifty supertsars were featured in both action and portrait variations on the card front photos. Therefore the set is considered complete at 500 cards. The product was issued in 12 card packs with 24 packs in each box and 20 boxes per case. The packs carried a suggested retail price of $2.49 each. Special Jewel Collection packs were issued for the 7/11 convenience store chain and they contained 12 cards with an SRP of $2.99. A Tony Gwynn Sample card was distributed to dealers and hobby media several weeks prior to the release of the product. The Gwynn card is readily identifiable by the bold "SAMPLE" text running diagonally across the card back.

	Nm-Mt	Ex-Mt
COMPLETE SET (500)	50.00	15.00
1 Garret Anderson	.30	.09
2 Tim Belcher	.30	.09
3 Gary DiSarcina	.30	.09
4 Trent Durrington	.30	.09
5 Jim Edmonds	.30	.09
6 Darin Erstad ACTION	.30	.09
6A Darin Erstad POR	.30	.09
7 Chuck Finley	.30	.09
8 Troy Glaus	.50	.15
9 Todd Greene	.30	.09
10 Bret Hemphill	.30	.09
11 Ken Hill	.30	.09
12 Ramon Ortiz	.30	.09
13 Troy Percival	.30	.09
14 Mark Petkovsek	.30	.09
15 Tim Salmon	.50	.15
16 Mo Vaughn ACTION	.30	.09
16A Mo Vaughn POR	.30	.09
17 Jay Bell	.30	.09
18 Omar Daal	.30	.09
19 Erubiel Durazo	.30	.09
20 Steve Finley	.30	.09
21 Bernard Gilkey	.30	.09
22 Luis Gonzalez	.30	.09
23 Randy Johnson	.75	.23
24 Byung-Hyun Kim	.30	.09
25 Travis Lee	.30	.09
26 Matt Mantei	.30	.09
27 Armando Reynoso	.30	.09
28 Rob Ryan	.30	.09
29 Kelly Stinnett	.30	.09
30 Todd Stottlemyre	.30	.09
31 Matt Williams ACTION	.30	.09
31A Matt Williams POR	.30	.09
32 Tony Womack	.30	.09
33 Bret Boone	.30	.09
34 Andres Galarraga	.30	.09
35 Tom Glavine	.50	.15
36 Ozzie Guillen	.30	.09
37 Andruw Jones ACTION	.30	.09
37A Andruw Jones POR	.30	.09
38 Chipper Jones ACTION	.75	.23
38A Chipper Jones POR	.75	.23
39 Brian Jordan	.30	.09
40 Ryan Klesko	.30	.09
41 Javy Lopez	.30	.09
42 Greg Maddux ACTION	1.25	.35
42A Greg Maddux POR	1.25	.35
43 Kevin Millwood	.30	.09
44 John Rocker	.30	.09
45 Randall Simon	.30	.09
46 John Smoltz	.50	.15
47 Gerald Williams	.30	.09
48 Brady Anderson	.30	.09
49 Albert Belle ACTION	.30	.09
49A Albert Belle POR	.30	.09
50 Mike Bordick	.30	.09
51 Will Clark	.75	.23
52 Jeff Conine	.30	.09
53 Delino DeShields	.30	.09
54 Jerry Hairston Jr.	.30	.09
55 Charles Johnson	.30	.09
56 Eugene Kingsale	.30	.09
57 Ryan Minor	.30	.09
58 Mike Mussina	.75	.23
59 Sidney Ponson	.30	.09
60 Cal Ripken ACTION	2.50	.75
60A Cal Ripken POR	2.50	.75
61 B.J. Surhoff	.30	.09
62 Mike Timlin	.30	.09
63 Rod Beck	.30	.09
64 N.Garciaparra ACTION	1.25	.35
64A N.Garciaparra POR	1.25	.35
65 Tom Gordon	.30	.09
66 Butch Huskey	.30	.09
67 Derek Lowe	.30	.09
68 P.Martinez ACTION	.75	.23
68A Pedro Martinez POR	.75	.23
69 Trot Nixon	.50	.15
70 Jose Offerman	.30	.09
71 Troy O'Leary	.30	.09
72 Pat Rapp	.30	.09
73 Donnie Sadler	.30	.09
74 Mike Stanley	.30	.09
75 John Valentin	.30	.09
76 Jason Varitek	.30	.09
77 Wilton Veras	.30	.09
78 Tim Wakefield	.30	.09
79 Rick Aguilera	.30	.09
80 Manny Alexander	.30	.09
81 Roosevelt Brown	.30	.09
82 Mark Grace	.50	.15
83 Glenallen Hill	.30	.09
84 Lance Johnson	.30	.09
85 Jon Lieber	.30	.09
86 Cole Liniak	.30	.09
87 Chad Meyers	.30	.09
88 Mickey Morandini	.30	.09
89 Jose Nieves	.30	.09
90 Henry Rodriguez	.30	.09
91 Sammy Sosa ACTION	1.25	.35
91A Sammy Sosa POR	1.25	.35
92 Kevin Tapani	.30	.09
93 Kerry Wood	.75	.23
94 Mike Caruso	.30	.09
95 Ray Durham	.30	.09
96 Brook Fordyce	.30	.09
97 Bobby Howry	.30	.09
98 Paul Konerko	.30	.09
99 Carlos Lee	.30	.09
100 Aaron Myette	.30	.09
101 Greg Norton	.30	.09
102 Magglio Ordonez	.30	.09
103 Jim Parque	.30	.09
104 Liu Rodriguez	.30	.09
105 Chris Singleton	.30	.09
106 Mike Sirotka	.30	.09
107 F.Thomas ACTION	.75	.23
107A Frank Thomas POR	.75	.23
108 Kip Wells	.30	.09
109 Aaron Boone	.30	.09
110 Mike Cameron	.30	.09
111 Sean Casey ACTION	.30	.09
111A Sean Casey POR	.30	.09
112 Jeffrey Hammonds	.30	.09
113 Pete Harnisch	.30	.09
114 Barry Larkin ACTION	.75	.23
114A Barry Larkin POR	.75	.23
115 Jason LaRue	.30	.09
116 Denny Neagle	.30	.09
117 Pokey Reese	.30	.09
118 Scott Sullivan	.30	.09
119 Eddie Taubensee	.30	.09
120 Greg Vaughn	.30	.09
121 Scott Williamson	.30	.09
122 Dmitri Young	.30	.09
123 R.Alomar ACTION	.75	.23
123A R.Alomar POR	.75	.23
124 Sandy Alomar Jr.	.30	.09
125 Harold Baines	.30	.09
126 Russell Branyan	.30	.09
127 Dave Burba	.30	.09
128 Bartolo Colon	.30	.09
129 Travis Fryman	.30	.09
130 Mike Jackson	.30	.09
131 David Justice	.30	.09
132 Kenny Lofton ACTION	.30	.09
132A Kenny Lofton POR	.30	.09
133 Charles Nagy	.30	.09
134 M.Ramirez ACTION	.30	.09
134A Manny Ramirez POR	.30	.09
135 Dave Roberts	.30	.09
136 Richie Sexson	.30	.09
137 Jim Thome	.75	.23
138 Omar Vizquel	.30	.09
139 Jaret Wright	.30	.09
140 Pedro Astacio	.30	.09
141 Dante Bichette	.30	.09
142 Brian Bohanon	.30	.09
143 Vinny Castilla ACTION	.30	.09
143A Vinny Castilla POR	.30	.09
144 Edgard Clemente	.30	.09
145 Derrick Gibson	.30	.09
146 Todd Helton	.50	.15
147 Darryl Kile	.30	.09
148 Mike Lansing	.30	.09
149 Kirt Manwaring	.30	.09
150 Neifi Perez	.30	.09
151 Ben Petrick	.30	.09
152 Juan Sosa RC	.30	.09
153 Dave Veres	.30	.09
154 Larry Walker ACTION	.50	.15
154A Larry Walker POR	.50	.15
155 Brad Ausmus	.30	.09
156 Dave Borkowski	.30	.09
157 Tony Clark	.30	.09
158 Francisco Cordero	.30	.09
159 Deivi Cruz	.30	.09
160 Damion Easley	.30	.09
161 Juan Encarnacion	.30	.09
162 Robert Fick	.30	.09
163 Bobby Higginson	.30	.09
164 Gabe Kapler	.30	.09
165 Brian Moehler	.30	.09
166 Dean Palmer	.30	.09
167 Luis Polonia	.30	.09
168 Justin Thompson	.30	.09
169 Jeff Weaver	.30	.09
170 Antonio Alfonseca	.30	.09
171 Bruce Aven	.30	.09
172 A.J. Burnett	.30	.09
173 Luis Castillo	.30	.09
174 Ramon Castro	.30	.09
175 Ryan Dempster	.30	.09
176 Alex Fernandez	.30	.09
177 Cliff Floyd	.30	.09
178 Amaury Garcia	.30	.09
179 Alex Gonzalez	.30	.09
180 Mark Kotsay	.30	.09
181 Mike Lowell	.30	.09
182 Brian Meadows	.30	.09
183 Kevin Orie	.30	.09
184 Julio Ramirez	.30	.09
185 Preston Wilson	.30	.09
186 Moises Alou	.30	.09
187 Jeff Bagwell ACTION	.50	.15
187A Jeff Bagwell POR	.50	.15
188 Glen Barker	.30	.09
189 Derek Bell	.30	.09
190 Craig Biggio ACTION	.50	.15
190A Craig Biggio POR	.50	.15
191 Ken Caminiti	.30	.09
192 Scott Elarton	.30	.09
193 Carl Everett	.30	.09
194 Mike Hampton	.30	.09
195 Carlos E. Hernandez	.30	.09
196 Richard Hidalgo	.30	.09
197 Jose Lima	.30	.09
198 Shane Reynolds	.30	.09
199 Bill Spiers	.30	.09
200 Billy Wagner	.30	.09
201 C. Beltran ACTION	.30	.09
201A Carlos Beltran POR	.30	.09
202 Dermal Brown	.30	.09
203 Johnny Damon	.30	.09
204 Jermaine Dye	.30	.09
205 Carlos Febles	.30	.09
206 Jeremy Giambi	.30	.09
207 Mark Quinn	.30	.09
208 Joe Randa	.30	.09
209 Dan Reichert	.30	.09
210 Jose Rosado	.30	.09
211 Rey Sanchez	.30	.09
212 Jeff Suppan	.30	.09
213 Mike Sweeney	.30	.09
214 Kevin Brown ACTION	.30	.09
214A Kevin Brown POR	.30	.09
215 Darren Dreifort	.30	.09
216 Eric Gagne	.75	.23
217 Mark Grudzielanek	.30	.09
218 Todd Hollandsworth	.30	.09
219 Todd Hundley	.30	.09
220 Eric Karros	.30	.09
221 Raul Mondesi	.30	.09
222 Chan Ho Park	.30	.09
223 Jeff Shaw	.30	.09
224 G.Sheffield ACTION	.30	.09
224A Gary Sheffield POR	.30	.09
225 Ismael Valdes	.30	.09
226 Devon White	.30	.09
227 Eric Young	.30	.09
228 Kevin Barker	.30	.09
229 Ron Belliard	.30	.09
230 J.Burnitz ACTION	.30	.09
230A Jeromy Burnitz POR	.30	.09
231 Jeff Cirillo	.30	.09
232 Marquis Grissom	.30	.09
233 Geoff Jenkins	.30	.09
234 Mark Loretta	.30	.09
235 David Nilsson	.30	.09
236 Hideo Nomo	.75	.23
237 Alex Ochoa	.30	.09
238 Kyle Peterson	.30	.09
239 Fernando Vina	.30	.09
240 Bob Wickman	.30	.09
241 Steve Woodard	.30	.09
242 Chad Allen	.30	.09
243 Ron Coomer	.30	.09
244 Marty Cordova	.30	.09
245 Cristian Guzman	.30	.09
246 Denny Hocking	.30	.09
247 Jacque Jones	.30	.09
248 Corey Koskie	.30	.09
249 Matt Lawton	.30	.09
250 Joe Mays	.30	.09
251 Eric Milton	.30	.09
252 Brad Radke	.30	.09
253 Mark Redman	.30	.09
254 Terry Steinbach	.30	.09
255 Todd Walker	.30	.09
256 Tony Armas Jr.	.30	.09
257 Michael Barrett	.30	.09
258 Peter Bergeron	.30	.09
259 Geoff Blum	.30	.09
260 Orlando Cabrera	.30	.09
261 Trace Coquillette RC	.30	.09
262 Brad Fullmer	.30	.09
263 V.Guerrero ACTION	.75	.23
263A V.Guerrero POR	.75	.23
264 Wilton Guerrero	.30	.09
265 Dustin Hermanson	.30	.09
266 Manny Martinez RC	.30	.09
267 Ryan McGuire	.30	.09
268 Ugueth Urbina	.30	.09
269 Jose Vidro	.30	.09
270 Rondell White	.30	.09
271 Chris Widger	.30	.09
272 Edgardo Alfonzo	.30	.09
273 Armando Benitez	.30	.09
274 Roger Cedeno	.30	.09
275 Dennis Cook	.30	.09
276 Octavio Dotel	.30	.09
277 John Franco	.30	.09
278 Darryl Hamilton	.30	.09
279 Rickey Henderson	.75	.23
280 Orel Hershiser	.30	.09
281 Al Leiter	.30	.09
282 John Olerud ACTION	.30	.09
282A John Olerud POR	.30	.09
283 Rey Ordonez	.30	.09
284 Mike Piazza ACTION	1.25	.35
284A Mike Piazza POR	1.25	.35
285 Kenny Rogers	.30	.09
286 Jorge Toca	.30	.09
287 Robin Ventura	.50	.15
288 Scott Brosius	.30	.09
289 R.Clemens ACTION	1.50	.45
289A Roger Clemens POR	1.50	.45
290 David Cone	.30	.09
291 Chili Davis	.30	.09
292 Orlando Hernandez	.30	.09
293 Hideki Irabu	.30	.09
294 Derek Jeter ACTION	2.00	.60
294A Derek Jeter POR	2.00	.60
295 Chuck Knoblauch	.30	.09
296 Ricky Ledee	.30	.09
297 Jim Leyritz	.30	.09
298 Tino Martinez	.50	.15
299 Paul O'Neill	.50	.15
300 Andy Pettitte	.50	.15
301 Jorge Posada	.50	.15
302 Mariano Rivera	.50	.15
303 Alfonso Soriano	.75	.23
304 B.Williams ACTION	.50	.15
304A Bernie Williams POR	.50	.15
305 Ed Yarnall	.30	.09
306 Kevin Appier	.30	.09
307 Rich Becker	.30	.09
308 Eric Chavez	.30	.09
309 Jason Giambi	.75	.23
310 Ben Grieve	.30	.09
311 Ramon Hernandez	.30	.09
312 Tim Hudson	.50	.15
313 John Jaha	.30	.09
314 Doug Jones	.30	.09
315 Omar Olivares	.30	.09
316 Mike Oquist	.30	.09
317 Matt Stairs	.30	.09
318 Miguel Tejada	.30	.09
319 Randy Velarde	.30	.09
320 Bob Abreu	.30	.09
321 Marlon Anderson	.30	.09
322 Alex Arias	.30	.09
323 Rico Brogna	.30	.09
324 Paul Byrd	.30	.09
325 Ron Gant	.30	.09
326 Doug Glanville	.30	.09
327 Wayne Gomes	.30	.09
328 Mike Lieberthal	.30	.09
329 Robert Person	.30	.09
330 Desi Relaford	.30	.09
331 Scott Rolen ACTION	.50	.15
331A Scott Rolen POR	.50	.15
332 Curt Schilling ACTION	.50	.15
332A Curt Schilling POR	.50	.15
333 Kris Benson	.30	.09
334 Adrian Brown	.30	.09
335 Brant Brown	.30	.09
336 Brian Giles	.30	.09
337 Chad Hermansen	.30	.09
338 Jason Kendall	.30	.09
339 Al Martin	.30	.09
340 Pat Meares	.30	.09
341 W.Morris ACTION	.30	.09
341A Warren Morris POR	.30	.09
342 Todd Ritchie	.30	.09
343 Jason Schmidt	.30	.09
344 Ed Sprague	.30	.09
345 Mike Williams	.30	.09
346 Kevin Young	.30	.09
347 Rick Ankiel	.30	.09
348 Ricky Bottalico	.30	.09
349 Kent Bottenfield	.30	.09
350 Darren Bragg	.30	.09
351 Eric Davis	.30	.09
352 J.D. Drew ACTION	.30	.09
352A J.D. Drew POR	.30	.09
353 Adam Kennedy	.30	.09
354 Ray Lankford	.30	.09
355 Joe McEwing	.30	.09
356 M.McGwire ACTION	2.00	.60
356A Mark McGwire POR	2.00	.60
357 Matt Morris	.30	.09
358 Darren Oliver	.30	.09
359 Edgar Renteria	.30	.09
360 Fernando Tatis	.30	.09
361 Andy Ashby	.30	.09
362 Ben Davis	.30	.09
363 Tony Gwynn ACTION	1.00	.30
363A Tony Gwynn POR	1.00	.30
364 Sterling Hitchcock	.30	.09
365 Trevor Hoffman	.30	.09
366 Damian Jackson	.30	.09
367 Wally Joyner	.30	.09
368 Dave Magadan	.30	.09
369 Gary Matthews Jr.	.30	.09
370 Phil Nevin	.30	.09
371 Eric Owens	.30	.09
372 Ruben Rivera	.30	.09
373 R.Sanders ACTION	.30	.09
373A Reggie Sanders POR	.30	.09
374 Quilvio Veras	.30	.09
375 Rich Aurilia	.30	.09
376 Marvin Benard	.30	.09
377 Barry Bonds ACTION	2.00	.60
377A Barry Bonds POR	2.00	.60
378 Ellis Burks	.30	.09
379 Shawn Estes	.30	.09
380 Livan Hernandez	.30	.09
381 Jeff Kent ACTION	.30	.09
381A Jeff Kent POR	.30	.09
382 Brent Mayne	.30	.09
383 Bill Mueller	.30	.09
384 Calvin Murray	.30	.09
385 Robb Nen	.30	.09
386 Russ Ortiz	.30	.09
387 Kirk Rueter	.30	.09
388 J.T. Snow	.30	.09
389 David Bell	.30	.09
390 Jay Buhner	.30	[illegible]
391 Russ Davis	.30	[illegible]
392 Freddy Garcia ACTION	.30	[illegible]
392A Freddy Garcia POR	.30	[illegible]
393 K.Griffey Jr. ACTION	1.25	[illegible]
393A Ken Griffey Jr. POR	1.25	[illegible]
394 Carlos Guillen	.30	[illegible]
395 John Halama	.30	[illegible]
396 Brian L.Hunter	.30	[illegible]
397 Ryan Jackson	.30	[illegible]
398 Edgar Martinez	.50	[illegible]
399 Gil Meche	.30	[illegible]
400 Jose Mesa	.30	[illegible]
401 Jamie Moyer	.30	[illegible]
402 A.Rodriguez ACTION	1.25	[illegible]
402A Alex Rodriguez POR	1.25	[illegible]
403 Dan Wilson	.30	[illegible]
404 Wilson Alvarez	.30	[illegible]
405 Rolando Arrojo	.30	[illegible]
406 Wade Boggs ACTION	.50	[illegible]
406A Wade Boggs POR	.50	[illegible]
407 Miguel Cairo	.30	[illegible]
408 Jose Canseco ACTION	.75	[illegible]
408A Jose Canseco POR	.75	[illegible]
409 John Flaherty	.30	[illegible]
410 Jose Guillen	.30	[illegible]
411 Roberto Hernandez	.30	[illegible]
412 Terrell Lowery	.30	[illegible]
413 Dave Martinez	.30	[illegible]
414 Quinton McCracken	.30	[illegible]
415 Fred McGriff ACTION	.50	[illegible]
415A Fred McGriff POR	.50	[illegible]
416 Ryan Rupe	.30	[illegible]
417 Kevin Stocker	.30	[illegible]
418 Bubba Trammell	.30	[illegible]
419 Royce Clayton	.30	[illegible]
420 J.Gonzalez ACTION	.75	[illegible]
420A Juan Gonzalez POR	.75	[illegible]
421 Tom Goodwin	.30	[illegible]

422 Rusty Greer .30 .09
423 Rick Helling .30 .09
424 Roberto Kelly .30 .09
425 Ruben Mateo .30 .09
426 Mark McLemore .30 .09
427 Mike Morgan .30 .09
428 Rafael Palmeiro .50 .15
429 I.Rodriguez ACTION .75 .23
429A Ivan Rodriguez POR .75 .23
430 Aaron Sele .30 .09
431 Lee Stevens .30 .09
432 John Wetteland .30 .09
433 Todd Zeile .30 .09
434 Jeff Zimmerman .30 .09
435 Tony Batista .30 .09
436 Casey Blake .30 .09
437 Homer Bush .30 .09
438 Chris Carpenter .30 .09
439 Jose Cruz Jr. .30 .09
440 C.Delgado ACTION .30 .09
440A Carlos Delgado POR .30 .09
441 Tony Fernandez .30 .09
442 Darrin Fletcher .30 .09
443 Alex Gonzalez .30 .09
444 Shawn Green ACTION .30 .09
444A Shawn Green POR .30 .09
445 Roy Halladay .30 .09
446 Billy Koch .30 .09
447 David Segui .30 .09
448 Shannon Stewart .30 .09
449 David Wells .30 .09
450 Vernon Wells .30 .09
SAMP T.Gwynn Sample 1.00 .30

2000 Pacific Copper

Randomly inserted in hobby packs, these parallel cards feature copper foil and are serial numbered to 99 cards.

Nm-Mt Ex-Mt
*STARS: 8X TO 20X BASIC CARDS ....
*ROOKIES: 5X TO 12X BASIC CARDS

2000 Pacific Emerald Green

Randomly inserted exclusively into Jewel Collection retail packs, this set parallels the regular Pacific set and is serial numbered to 99 cards. This set is printed in green foil which is how it can be differentiated from the regular cards.

Nm-Mt Ex-Mt
*STARS: 8X TO 20X BASIC CARDS ....
*ROOKIES: 5X TO 12X BASIC CARDS

2000 Pacific Gold

Randomly inserted in retail packs, this is a parallel of the regular Pacific Set. These cards are printed in gold foil and are serial numbered o 199 which are two ways of differentiating hem from the regular Pacific cards.

Nm-Mt Ex-Mt
STARS: 5X TO 12X BASIC CARDS ....
ROOKIES: 3X TO 8X BASIC CARDS ..

2000 Pacific Platinum Blue

ndomly inserted in all Pacific packs, these s parallel the basic Pacific set. The cards blue foil accents on them and are serial bered to 75.

Nm-Mt Ex-Mt
RS: 10X TO 25X BASIC CARDS ..
KIES: 6X TO 15X BASIC CARDS

00 Pacific Premiere Date

one per 24 pack hobby box, this set s the regular Pacific set. These cards are umbered to 37 and feature a large e Date" logo on front.

Nm-Mt Ex-Mt
20X TO 50X BASIC CARDS ..
S: 12.5X TO 30X BASIC CARDS

2000 Pacific Ruby

cards per Jewel Collection retail set parallels the regular 2000 Pacific by-colored foil on the player's name ake it easy to differentiate from the ndard cards.

Nm-Mt Ex-Mt
ET (500) 250.00 75.00
5X TO 3X BASIC CARDS .
5X TO 2X BASIC CARDS

Pacific Command Performers

inserted one in every 24 cial retail (7/11) packs. The es some of the leading

Nm-Mt Ex-Mt
150.00 45.00
JEWEL RETAIL PACKS
0 SERIAL #'d SETS
DUE TO SCARCITY
5.00 1.50
8.00 2.40
15.00 4.50
8.00 2.40
8.00 2.40
2.00 .60
2.00 .60
3.00 .90
3.00 .90
5.00 1.50

11 Mike Piazza 8.00 2.40
12 Roger Clemens 10.00 3.00
13 Derek Jeter 12.00 3.60
14 Mark McGwire 12.00 3.60
15 Tony Gwynn 6.00 1.80
16 Barry Bonds 12.00 3.60
17 Ken Griffey Jr. 8.00 2.40
18 Alex Rodriguez 8.00 2.40
19 Ivan Rodriguez 5.00 1.50
20 Shawn Green 2.00 .60

2000 Pacific Cramer's Choice

Inserted at a rate of one in every 721 packs, these die-cut cards feature 10 players Pacific founder Mike Cramer considers to be among the very best players in baseball.

	Nm-Mt	Ex-Mt
COMPLETE SET (10)	500.00	150.00
1 Chipper Jones	25.00	7.50
2 Cal Ripken	80.00	24.00
3 Nomar Garciaparra	40.00	12.00
4 Sammy Sosa	40.00	12.00
5 Mike Piazza	40.00	12.00
6 Derek Jeter	60.00	18.00
7 Mark McGwire	60.00	18.00
8 Tony Gwynn	30.00	9.00
9 Ken Griffey Jr.	40.00	12.00
10 Alex Rodriguez	40.00	12.00

2000 Pacific Diamond Leaders

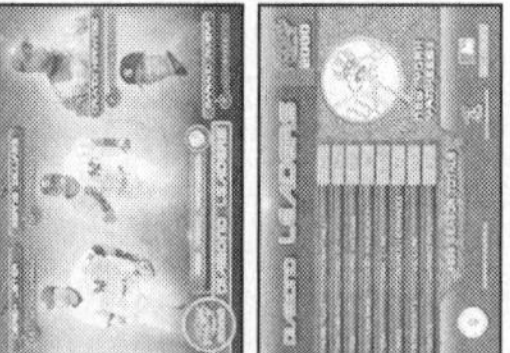

Inserted two every 25 packs, this 30 card set features three or more leaders from each team in various statistical categories. The cards are printed in holographic silver foil and are sequenced in alphabetical order by league.

	Nm-Mt	Ex-Mt
COMPLETE SET (30)	80.00	24.00
1 Garret Anderson Chuck Finley Troy Percival Mo Vaughn	1.25	.35
2 Albert Belle Mike Mussina B.J. Surhoff	3.00	.90
3 Nomar Garciaparra Pedro Martinez Troy O'Leary	5.00	1.50
4 Ray Durham Magglio Ordonez Frank Thomas	3.00	.90
5 Bartolo Colon Manny Ramirez Omar Vizquel	1.25	.35
6 Deivi Cruz Dave Mlicki Dean Palmer	1.25	.35
7 Johnny Damon Jermaine Dye Jose Rosado Mike Sweeney	1.25	.35
8 Corey Koskie Eric Milton Brad Radke	1.25	.35
9 Orlando Hernandez Derek Jeter Mariano Rivera Bernie Williams	8.00	2.40
10 Jason Giambi Tim Hudson Matt Stairs	3.00	.90
11 Freddy Garcia Ken Griffey Jr. Edgar Martinez	5.00	1.50
12 Jose Canseco Roberto Hernandez Fred McGriff	3.00	.90
13 Rafael Palmeiro Ivan Rodriguez John Wetteland	3.00	.90
14 Carlos Delgado Shannon Stewart David Wells	1.25	.35
15 Luis Gonzalez Randy Johnson Matt Williams	3.00	.90
16 Chipper Jones Brian Jordan Greg Maddux	5.00	1.50
17 Mark Grace Jon Lieber Sammy Sosa	5.00	1.50
18 Sean Casey Pete Harnisch Greg Vaughn	1.25	.35
19 Pedro Astacio Dante Bichette Larry Walker	2.00	.60
20 Luis Castillo Alex Fernandez Preston Wilson	1.25	.35
21 Jeff Bagwell Mike Hampton Billy Wagner	2.00	.60
22 Kevin Brown Mark Grudzielanek Eric Karros	1.25	.35
23 Jeromy Burnitz Jeff Cirillo Marquis Grissom Hideo Nomo	3.00	.90
24 Vladimir Guerrero Dustin Hermanson Ugueth Urbina	3.00	.90
25 Roger Cedeno Rickey Henderson Mike Piazza	5.00	1.50
26 Bob Abreu Mike Lieberthal Curt Schilling	2.00	.60
27 Brian Giles Jason Kendall Kevin Young	1.25	.35
28 Kent Bottenfield Ray Lankford Mark McGwire	8.00	2.40
29 Tony Gwynn Trevor Hoffman Reggie Sanders	4.00	1.20
30 Barry Bonds Jeff Kent Russ Ortiz	8.00	2.40

2000 Pacific Gold Crown Die Cuts

Inserted one every 25 packs, this 36 card set features a selection of baseball's top stars. This set uses the Gold Crown Die Cut style used on many Pacific products and has a dual foil design utilizing both holographic gold and holographic silver. In addition the cards are printed on extra sturdy 24 point stock.

	Nm-Mt	Ex-Mt
1 Mo Vaughn	3.00	.90
2 Matt Williams	3.00	.90
3 Andruw Jones	3.00	.90
4 Chipper Jones	8.00	2.40
5 Greg Maddux	12.00	3.60
6 Cal Ripken	25.00	7.50
7 Nomar Garciaparra	12.00	3.60
8 Pedro Martinez	8.00	2.40
9 Sammy Sosa	12.00	3.60
10 Magglio Ordonez	3.00	.90
11 Frank Thomas	8.00	2.40
12 Sean Casey	3.00	.90
13 Roberto Alomar	8.00	2.40
14 Manny Ramirez	3.00	.90
15 Larry Walker	5.00	1.50
16 Jeff Bagwell	5.00	1.50
17 Craig Biggio	5.00	1.50
18 Carlos Beltran	3.00	.90
19 Vladimir Guerrero	8.00	2.40
20 Mike Piazza	12.00	3.60
21 Roger Clemens	15.00	4.50
22 Derek Jeter	20.00	6.00
23 Bernie Williams	5.00	1.50
24 Scott Rolen	5.00	1.50
25 Warren Morris	3.00	.90
26 J.D. Drew	3.00	.90
27 Mark McGwire	20.00	6.00
28 Tony Gwynn	10.00	3.00
29 Barry Bonds	20.00	6.00
30 Ken Griffey Jr.	12.00	3.60
31 Alex Rodriguez	12.00	3.60
32 Jose Canseco	8.00	2.40
33 Juan Gonzalez	8.00	2.40
34 Rafael Palmeiro	5.00	1.50
35 Ivan Rodriguez	8.00	2.40
36 Shawn Green	3.00	.90

2000 Pacific Ornaments

Inserted two every 25 packs, these 20 cards are designed in the shape of Christmas ornaments. The cards have full custom holographic patterned silver foil and a string loop on top so they can be hung on a tree. Five different holiday shapes were featured.

	Nm-Mt	Ex-Mt
COMPLETE SET (20)	120.00	36.00
1 Mo Vaughn	2.00	.60
2 Chipper Jones	5.00	1.50
3 Greg Maddux	8.00	2.40
4 Cal Ripken	15.00	4.50
5 Nomar Garciaparra	8.00	2.40
6 Sammy Sosa	8.00	2.40
7 Frank Thomas	5.00	1.50
8 Manny Ramirez	2.00	.60
9 Larry Walker	3.00	.90
10 Jeff Bagwell	3.00	.90
11 Mike Piazza	8.00	2.40
12 Roger Clemens	10.00	3.00
13 Derek Jeter	12.00	3.60
14 Scott Rolen	3.00	.90
15 J.D. Drew	2.00	.60
16 Mark McGwire	12.00	3.60
17 Tony Gwynn	6.00	1.80
18 Ken Griffey Jr.	8.00	2.40
19 Alex Rodriguez	8.00	2.40
20 Ivan Rodriguez	5.00	1.50

2000 Pacific Past and Present

These 20 stars were inserted at a rate of one every 24 packs. The cards have a laminated full foil front featuring a current photo and a photoengraved-style back featuring a photo early in the player's career.

	Nm-Mt	Ex-Mt
COMPLETE SET (20)	250.00	75.00
PROOFS RANDOM INSERTS IN PACKS		
PROOFS PRINT RUN 1 SERIAL #'d SET		
PROOFS NOT PRICED DUE TO SCARCITY		
1 Chipper Jones	8.00	2.40
2 Greg Maddux	12.00	3.60
3 Cal Ripken	25.00	7.50
4 Nomar Garciaparra	12.00	3.60
5 Pedro Martinez	8.00	2.40
6 Sammy Sosa	12.00	3.60
7 Frank Thomas	8.00	2.40
8 Manny Ramirez	3.00	.90
9 Larry Walker	5.00	1.50
10 Jeff Bagwell	5.00	1.50
11 Mike Piazza	12.00	3.60
12 Roger Clemens	15.00	4.50
13 Derek Jeter	20.00	6.00
14 Mark McGwire	20.00	6.00
15 Tony Gwynn	10.00	3.00
16 Barry Bonds	20.00	6.00
17 Ken Griffey Jr.	12.00	3.60
18 Alex Rodriguez	12.00	3.60
19 Wade Boggs	5.00	1.50
20 Ivan Rodriguez	8.00	2.40

2000 Pacific Reflections

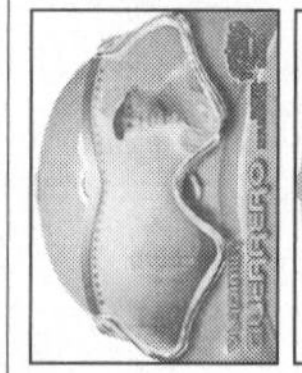

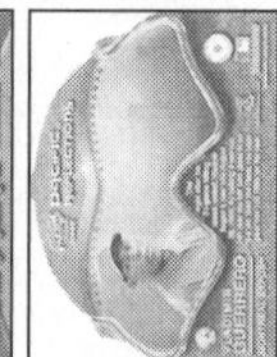

Inserted one every 97 packs, these 20 cards feature some of the leading baseball stars. The cards mere produced using a special cel sunglasses on cap design. The player's headshot photo is seen on one side of the sunglasses.

	Nm-Mt	Ex-Mt
COMPLETE SET (20)	400.00	120.00
1 Andruw Jones	6.00	1.80
2 Chipper Jones	15.00	4.50
3 Cal Ripken	50.00	15.00
4 Nomar Garciaparra	25.00	7.50
5 Sammy Sosa	25.00	7.50
6 Frank Thomas	15.00	4.50
7 Manny Ramirez	6.00	1.80
8 Jeff Bagwell	10.00	3.00
9 Vladimir Guerrero	15.00	4.50
10 Mike Piazza	25.00	7.50
11 Derek Jeter	40.00	12.00
12 Bernie Williams	10.00	3.00
13 Scott Rolen	10.00	3.00
14 J.D. Drew	6.00	1.80
15 Mark McGwire	40.00	12.00
16 Tony Gwynn	20.00	6.00
17 Ken Griffey Jr.	25.00	7.50
18 Alex Rodriguez	25.00	7.50
19 Juan Gonzalez	15.00	4.50
20 Ivan Rodriguez	15.00	4.50

2000 Pacific Backyard Baseball

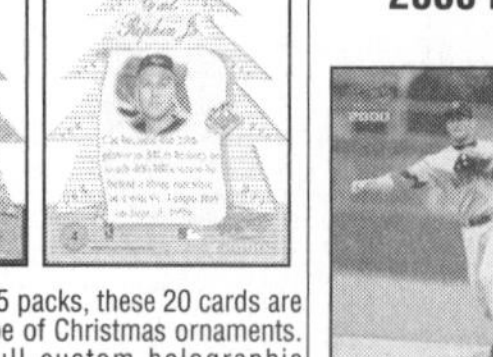

This 10 card standard-size set features leading superstars of baseball along with a couple of other "kid" cards. Since these cards are unnumbered, we have sequenced them in alphabetical order.

	Nm-Mt	Ex-Mt
COMPLETE SET (10)	15.00	4.50
1 Nomar Garciaparra	2.00	.60
2 Juan Gonzalez	1.00	.30
3 Ken Griffey Jr	2.50	.75
4 Tony Gwynn	2.00	.60
5 Chipper Jones	2.00	.60
6 Mark McGwire	3.00	.90
7 Cal Ripken Jr	4.00	1.20
8 Ivan Rodriguez	1.00	.30
9 Annie Frazier Cartoon	.25	.07
10 Pablo Sanchez Cartoon	.25	.07

2001 Pacific

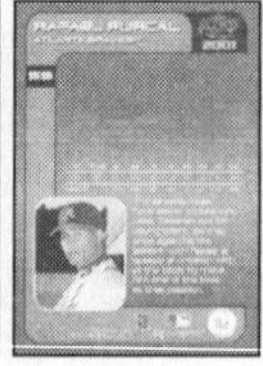

The 2001 Pacific product was released in December, 2000 and features a 500-card base set. Each pack contained 12 cards, and carried a suggested retail price of 2.99.

	Nm-Mt	Ex-Mt
COMPLETE SET (500)	100.00	30.00
1 Garret Anderson	.30	.09
2 Gary DiSarcina	.30	.09
3 Darin Erstad	.30	.09
4 Seth Etherton	.30	.09
5 Ron Gant	.30	.09
6 Troy Glaus	.50	.15
7 Shigetoshi Hasegawa	.30	.09
8 Adam Kennedy	.30	.09
9 Ben Molina	.30	.09
10 Ramon Ortiz	.30	.09
11 Troy Percival	.30	.09
12 Tim Salmon	.50	.15
13 Scott Schoeneweis	.30	.09
14 Mo Vaughn	.30	.09
15 Jarrod Washburn	.30	.09
16 Brian Anderson	.30	.09
17 Danny Bautista	.30	.09
18 Jay Bell	.30	.09
19 Greg Colbrunn	.30	.09
20 Erubiel Durazo	.30	.09
21 Steve Finley	.30	.09
22 Luis Gonzalez	.30	.09
23 Randy Johnson	.75	.23
24 Byung-Hyun Kim	.30	.09
25 Matt Mantei	.30	.09
26 Armando Reynoso	.30	.09
27 Todd Stottlemyre	.30	.09
28 Matt Williams	.30	.09
29 Tony Womack	.30	.09
30 Andy Ashby	.30	.09
31 Bobby Bonilla	.30	.09
32 Rafael Furcal	.30	.09
33 Andres Galarraga	.30	.09
34 Tom Glavine	.50	.15
35 Andruw Jones	.30	.09
36 Chipper Jones	.75	.23
37 Brian Jordan	.30	.09
38 Wally Joyner	.30	.09
39 Keith Lockhart	.30	.09
40 Javy Lopez	.30	.09
41 Greg Maddux	1.25	.35
42 Kevin Millwood	.30	.09
43 John Rocker	.30	.09
44 Reggie Sanders	.30	.09
45 John Smoltz	.50	.15
46 B.J. Surhoff	.30	.09
47 Quilvio Veras	.30	.09
48 Walt Weiss	.30	.09
49 Brady Anderson	.30	.09
50 Albert Belle	.30	.09
51 Jeff Conine	.30	.09
52 Delino DeShields	.30	.09
53 Brook Fordyce	.30	.09
54 Jerry Hairston Jr.	.30	.09
55 Mark Lewis	.30	.09
56 Luis Matos	.30	.09
57 Melvin Mora	.30	.09
58 Mike Mussina	.75	.23
59 Chris Richard	.30	.09
60 Cal Ripken	2.50	.75
61 Manny Alexander	.30	.09
62 Rolando Arrojo	.30	.09
63 Midre Cummings	.30	.09
64 Carl Everett	.30	.09
65 Nomar Garciaparra	1.25	.35
66 Mike Lansing	.30	.09
67 Darren Lewis	.30	.09
68 Derek Lowe	.30	.09
69 Pedro Martinez	.75	.23
70 Ramon Martinez	.30	.09
71 Trot Nixon	.50	.15
72 Troy O'Leary	.30	.09
73 Jose Offerman	.30	.09
74 Tomo Ohka	.30	.09
75 Jason Varitek	.30	.09
76 Rick Aguilera	.30	.09
77 Shane Andrews	.30	.09
78 Brant Brown	.30	.09
79 Damon Buford	.30	.09
80 Joe Girardi	.30	.09
81 Mark Grace	.50	.15
82 Willie Greene	.30	.09
83 Ricky Gutierrez	.30	.09
84 Jon Lieber	.30	.09
85 Sammy Sosa	1.25	.35
86 Kevin Tapani	.30	.09
87 Rondell White	.30	.09
88 Kerry Wood	.75	.23
89 Eric Young	.30	.09
90 Harold Baines	.30	.09
91 James Baldwin	.30	.09
92 Ray Durham	.30	.09
93 Cal Eldred	.30	.09
94 Keith Foulke	.30	.09
95 Charles Johnson	.30	.09
96 Paul Konerko	.30	.09
97 Carlos Lee	.30	.09
98 Magglio Ordonez	.30	.09
99 Jim Parque	.30	.09
100 Herbert Perry	.30	.09
101 Chris Singleton	.30	.09
102 Mike Sirotka	.30	.09
103 Frank Thomas	.75	.23
104 Jose Valentin	.30	.09
105 Rob Bell	.30	.09
106 Aaron Boone	.30	.09
107 Sean Casey	.30	.09
108 Danny Graves	.30	.09
109 Ken Griffey Jr.	1.25	.35

110 Pete Harnisch .30 .09
111 Brian Hunter .30 .09
112 Barry Larkin .75 .23
113 Pokey Reese .30 .09
114 Benito Santiago .30 .09
115 Chris Stynes .30 .09
116 Michael Tucker .30 .09
117 Ron Villone .30 .09
118 Scott Williamson .30 .09
119 Dmitri Young .30 .09
120 Roberto Alomar .75 .23
121 Sandy Alomar Jr. .30 .09
122 Russell Branyan .30 .09
123 Dave Burba .30 .09
124 Bartolo Colon .30 .09
125 Wil Cordero .30 .09
126 Einar Diaz .30 .09
127 Chuck Finley .30 .09
128 Travis Fryman .30 .09
129 Kenny Lofton .30 .09
130 Charles Nagy .30 .09
131 Manny Ramirez .30 .09
132 David Segui .30 .09
133 Jim Thome .75 .23
134 Omar Vizquel .30 .09
135 Brian Bohanon .30 .09
136 Jeff Cirillo .30 .09
137 Jeff Frye .30 .09
138 Jeffrey Hammonds .30 .09
139 Todd Helton .50 .15
140 Todd Hollandsworth .30 .09
141 Jose Jimenez .30 .09
142 Brent Mayne .30 .09
143 Neifi Perez .30 .09
144 Ben Petrick .30 .09
145 Juan Pierre .30 .09
146 Larry Walker .50 .15
147 Todd Walker .30 .09
148 Masato Yoshii .30 .09
149 Brad Ausmus .30 .09
150 Rich Becker .30 .09
151 Tony Clark .30 .09
152 Deivi Cruz .30 .09
153 Damion Easley .30 .09
154 Juan Encarnacion .30 .09
155 Robert Fick .30 .09
156 Juan Gonzalez .75 .23
157 Bobby Higginson .30 .09
158 Todd Jones .30 .09
159 Wendell Magee Jr. .30 .09
160 Brian Moehler .30 .09
161 Hideo Nomo .75 .23
162 Dean Palmer .30 .09
163 Jeff Weaver .30 .09
164 Antonio Alfonseca .30 .09
165 Dave Berg .30 .09
166 A.J. Burnett .30 .09
167 Luis Castillo .30 .09
168 Ryan Dempster .30 .09
169 Cliff Floyd .30 .09
170 Alex Gonzalez .30 .09
171 Mark Kotsay .30 .09
172 Derrek Lee .30 .09
173 Mike Lowell .30 .09
174 Mike Redmond .30 .09
175 Henry Rodriguez .30 .09
176 Jesus Sanchez .30 .09
177 Preston Wilson .30 .09
178 Moises Alou .30 .09
179 Jeff Bagwell .50 .15
180 Glen Barker .30 .09
181 Lance Berkman .30 .09
182 Craig Biggio .50 .15
183 Tim Bogar .30 .09
184 Ken Caminiti .30 .09
185 Roger Cedeno .30 .09
186 Scott Elarton .30 .09
187 Tony Eusebio .30 .09
188 Richard Hidalgo .30 .09
189 Jose Lima .30 .09
190 Mitch Meluskey .30 .09
191 Shane Reynolds .30 .09
192 Bill Spiers .30 .09
193 Billy Wagner .30 .09
194 Daryle Ward .30 .09
195 Carlos Beltran .30 .09
196 Ricky Bottalico .30 .09
197 Johnny Damon .30 .09
198 Jermaine Dye .30 .09
199 Jorge Fabregas .30 .09
200 David McCarty .30 .09
201 Mark Quinn .30 .09
202 Joe Randa .30 .09
203 Jeff Reboulet .30 .09
204 Rey Sanchez .30 .09
205 Blake Stein .30 .09
206 Jeff Suppan .30 .09
207 Mac Suzuki .30 .09
208 Mike Sweeney .30 .09
209 Greg Zaun .30 .09
210 Adrian Beltre .30 .09
211 Kevin Brown .30 .09
212 Alex Cora .30 .09
213 Darren Dreifort .30 .09
214 Tom Goodwin .30 .09
215 Shawn Green .30 .09
216 Mark Grudzielanek .30 .09
217 Todd Hundley .30 .09
218 Eric Karros .30 .09
219 Chad Kreuter .30 .09
220 Jim Leyritz .30 .09
221 Chan Ho Park .30 .09
222 Jeff Shaw .30 .09
223 Gary Sheffield .30 .09
224 Devon White .30 .09
225 Ron Belliard .30 .09
226 Henry Blanco .30 .09
227 Jeromy Burnitz .30 .09
228 Jeff D'Amico .30 .09
229 Marquis Grissom .30 .09
230 Charlie Hayes .30 .09
231 Jimmy Haynes .30 .09
232 Tyler Houston .30 .09
233 Geoff Jenkins .30 .09
234 Mark Loretta .30 .09
235 James Mouton .30 .09
236 Richie Sexson .30 .09
237 Jamey Wright .30 .09
238 Jay Canizaro .30 .09
239 Ron Coomer .30 .09
240 Cristian Guzman .30 .09
241 Denny Hocking .30 .09
242 Torii Hunter .30 .09
243 Jacque Jones .30 .09
244 Corey Koskie .30 .09
245 Matt Lawton .30 .09
246 Matt LeCroy .30 .09
247 Eric Milton .30 .09
248 David Ortiz .30 .09
249 Brad Radke .30 .09
250 Mark Redman .30 .09
251 Michael Barrett .30 .09
252 Peter Bergeron .30 .09
253 Milton Bradley .30 .09
254 Orlando Cabrera .30 .09
255 Vladimir Guerrero .75 .23
256 Wilton Guerrero .30 .09
257 Dustin Hermanson .30 .09
258 Hideki Irabu .30 .09
259 Fernando Seguignol .30 .09
260 Lee Stevens .30 .09
261 Andy Tracy .30 .09
262 Javier Vazquez .30 .09
263 Jose Vidro .30 .09
264 Edgardo Alfonzo .30 .09
265 Derek Bell .30 .09
266 Armando Benitez .30 .09
267 Mike Bordick .30 .09
268 John Franco .30 .09
269 Darryl Hamilton .30 .09
270 Mike Hampton .30 .09
271 Lenny Harris .30 .09
272 Al Leiter .30 .09
273 Joe McEwing .30 .09
274 Rey Ordonez .30 .09
275 Jay Payton .30 .09
276 Mike Piazza 1.25 .35
277 Glendon Rusch .30 .09
278 Bubba Trammell .30 .09
279 Robin Ventura .30 .09
280 Todd Zeile .30 .09
281 Scott Brosius .30 .09
282 Jose Canseco .75 .23
283 Roger Clemens 1.50 .45
284 David Cone .30 .09
285 Dwight Gooden .50 .15
286 Orlando Hernandez .30 .09
287 Glenallen Hill .30 .09
288 Derek Jeter 2.00 .60
289 David Justice .30 .09
290 Chuck Knoblauch .30 .09
291 Tino Martinez .50 .15
292 Denny Neagle .30 .09
293 Paul O'Neill .50 .15
294 Andy Pettitte .50 .15
295 Jorge Posada .50 .15
296 Mariano Rivera .50 .15
297 Luis Sojo .30 .09
298 Jose Vizcaino .30 .09
299 Bernie Williams .50 .15
300 Kevin Appier .30 .09
301 Eric Chavez .30 .09
302 Ryan Christenson .30 .09
303 Jason Giambi .75 .23
304 Jeremy Giambi .30 .09
305 Ben Grieve .30 .09
306 Gil Heredia .30 .09
307 Ramon Hernandez .30 .09
308 Tim Hudson .30 .09
309 Jason Isringhausen .30 .09
310 Terrence Long .30 .09
311 Mark Mulder .30 .09
312 Adam Piatt .30 .09
313 Matt Stairs .30 .09
314 Miguel Tejada .30 .09
315 Randy Velarde .30 .09
316 Alex Arias .30 .09
317 Pat Burrell .30 .09
318 Omar Daal .30 .09
319 Travis Lee .30 .09
320 Mike Lieberthal .30 .09
321 Randy Wolf .30 .09
322 Bobby Abreu .30 .09
323 Jeff Brantley .30 .09
324 Bruce Chen .30 .09
325 Doug Glanville .30 .09
326 Kevin Jordan .30 .09
327 Robert Person .30 .09
328 Scott Rolen .50 .15
329 Jimmy Anderson .30 .09
330 Mike Benjamin .30 .09
331 Kris Benson .30 .09
332 Adrian Brown .30 .09
333 Brian Giles .30 .09
334 Jason Kendall .30 .09
335 Pat Meares .30 .09
336 Warren Morris .30 .09
337 Aramis Ramirez .30 .09
338 Todd Ritchie .30 .09
339 Jason Schmidt .30 .09
340 John VanderWal .30 .09
341 Mike Williams .30 .09
342 Enrique Wilson .30 .09
343 Kevin Young .30 .09
344 Rick Ankiel .30 .09
345 Andy Benes .30 .09
346 Will Clark .75 .23
347 Eric Davis .30 .09
348 J.D. Drew .30 .09
349 Shawon Dunston .30 .09
350 Jim Edmonds .30 .09
351 Pat Hentgen .30 .09
352 Darryl Kile .30 .09
353 Ray Lankford .30 .09
354 Mike Matheny .30 .09
355 Mark McGwire 2.00 .60
356 Craig Paquette .30 .09
357 Edgar Renteria .30 .09
358 Garrett Stephenson .30 .09
359 Fernando Tatis .30 .09
360 Dave Veres .30 .09
361 Fernando Vina .30 .09
362 Bret Boone .30 .09
363 Matt Clement .30 .09
364 Ben Davis .30 .09
365 Adam Eaton .30 .09
366 Wiki Gonzalez .30 .09
367 Tony Gwynn 1.00 .30
368 Damian Jackson .30 .09
369 Ryan Klesko .30 .09
370 John Mabry .30 .09
371 Dave Magadan .30 .09
372 Phil Nevin .30 .09
373 Eric Owens .30 .09
374 Desi Relaford .30 .09
375 Ruben Rivera .30 .09
376 Woody Williams .30 .09
377 Rich Aurilia .30 .09
378 Marvin Benard .30 .09
379 Barry Bonds 2.00 .60
380 Ellis Burks .30 .09
381 Bobby Estalella .30 .09
382 Shawn Estes .30 .09
383 Mark Gardner .30 .09
384 Livan Hernandez .30 .09
385 Jeff Kent .30 .09
386 Bill Mueller .30 .09
387 Robb Nen .30 .09
388 Russ Ortiz .30 .09
389 Armando Rios .30 .09
390 Kirk Rueter .30 .09
391 J.T. Snow .30 .09
392 David Bell .30 .09
393 Jay Buhner .30 .09
394 Mike Cameron .30 .09
395 Freddy Garcia .30 .09
396 Carlos Guillen .30 .09
397 John Halama .30 .09
398 Rickey Henderson .75 .23
399 Al Martin .30 .09
400 Edgar Martinez .50 .15
401 Mark McLemore .30 .09
402 Jamie Moyer .30 .09
403 John Olerud .30 .09
404 Joe Oliver .30 .09
405 Alex Rodriguez 1.25 .35
406 Kazuhiro Sasaki .30 .09
407 Aaron Sele .30 .09
408 Dan Wilson .30 .09
409 Miguel Cairo .30 .09
410 Vinny Castilla .30 .09
411 Steve Cox .30 .09
412 John Flaherty .30 .09
413 Jose Guillen .30 .09
414 Roberto Hernandez .30 .09
415 Russ Johnson .30 .09
416 Felix Martinez .30 .09
417 Fred McGriff .50 .15
418 Greg Vaughn .30 .09
419 Gerald Williams .30 .09
420 Luis Alicea .30 .09
421 Frank Catalanotto .30 .09
422 Royce Clayton .30 .09
423 Chad Curtis .30 .09
424 Rusty Greer .30 .09
425 Bill Haselman .30 .09
426 Rick Helling .30 .09
427 Gabe Kapler .30 .09
428 Mike Lamb .30 .09
429 Ricky Ledee .30 .09
430 Ruben Mateo .30 .09
431 Rafael Palmeiro .50 .15
432 Ivan Rodriguez .75 .23
433 Kenny Rogers .30 .09
434 John Wetteland .30 .09
435 Jeff Zimmerman .30 .09
436 Tony Batista .30 .09
437 Homer Bush .30 .09
438 Chris Carpenter .30 .09
439 Marty Cordova .30 .09
440 Jose Cruz Jr. .30 .09
441 Carlos Delgado .30 .09
442 Darrin Fletcher .30 .09
443 Brad Fullmer .30 .09
444 Alex Gonzalez .30 .09
445 Billy Koch .30 .09
446 Raul Mondesi .30 .09
447 Mickey Morandini .30 .09
448 Shannon Stewart .30 .09
449 Steve Trachsel .30 .09
450 David Wells .30 .09
451 Juan Alvarez .30 .09
452 Shawn Wooten .30 .09
453 Ismael Villegas .30 .09
454 Carlos Casimiro .30 .09
455 Morgan Burkhart .30 .09
456 Paxton Crawford .30 .09
457 Dernell Stenson .30 .09
458 Ross Gload .30 .09
459 Raul Gonzalez .30 .09
460 Corey Patterson .30 .09
461 Julio Zuleta .30 .09
462 Rocky Biddle .30 .09
463 Joe Crede .30 .09
464 Matt Ginter .30 .09
465 Aaron Myette .30 .09
466 Mike Bell .30 .09
467 Travis Dawkins .30 .09
468 Mark Watson .30 .09
469 Elvis Pena .30 .09
470 Eric Munson .30 .09
471 Pablo Ozuna .30 .09
472 Frank Charles .30 .09
473 Mike Judd .30 .09
474 Hector Ramirez .30 .09
475 Jack Cressend .30 .09
476 Talmadge Nunnari .75 .23
477 Jorge Toca .30 .09
478 Alfonso Soriano .50 .15
479 Jay Tessmer .30 .09
480 Jake Westbrook .30 .09
481 Eric Byrnes .30 .09
482 Jose Ortiz .30 .09
483 Tike Redman .30 .09
484 Domingo Guzman .30 .09
485 Rodrigo Lopez .30 .09
486 Xavier Nady .30 .09
487 Pedro Feliz .30 .09
488 Damon Minor .30 .09
489 Ryan Vogelsong .30 .09
490 Joel Pineiro .75 .23
491 Justin Brunette .30 .09
492 Keith McDonald .30 .09
493 Aubrey Huff .30 .09
494 Kenny Kelly .30 .09
495 Damian Rolls .30 .09
496 John Bale UER .30 .09
1999 ERA is in save column
497 Pasqual Coco .30 .09
498 Matt DeWitt .30 .09
499 Leo Estrella .30 .09
500 Josh Phelps .30 .09

2001 Pacific Extreme LTD

Randomly inserted into packs, this 500-card set is a complete parallel of the 2001 Pacific base set. Each card in this set features the words "Extreme LTD" printed diagonally across front of each card. Every card in this set is individually serial numbered to 45.

Nm-Mt Ex-Mt
*STARS: 20X TO 50X BASIC CARDS..

2001 Pacific Hobby LTD

Randomly inserted into hobby packs, this 500-card set is a complete parallel of the 2001 Pacific base set. Each card in this set features the words "Hobby LTD" printed diagonally across front of each card. Every card in this set is individually serial numbered to 70.

Nm-Mt Ex-Mt
*STARS: 12.5X TO 30X BASIC CARDS

2001 Pacific Premiere Date

Randomly inserted into hobby packs (approx. one per box), this 500-card set is a complete parallel of the 2001 Pacific base set. Each card in this set features the words "Premiere Date" printed diagonally across front of each card. Every card in this set is individually serial numbered to 36.

Nm-Mt Ex-Mt
*STARS: 25X TO 60X BASIC CARDS..

2001 Pacific Retail LTD

Randomly inserted into retail packs, this 500-card set is a complete parallel of the 2001 Pacific base set. Each card in this set features the words "Retail LTD" printed diagonally across front of each card. Every card in this set is individually serial numbered to 85.

Nm-Mt Ex-Mt
*STARS: 10X TO 25X BASIC CARDS..

2001 Pacific Cramer's Choice

Inserted at a rate of one in every 721 packs, these die-cut cards feature 10 players Pacific founder Mike Cramer considers to be among the very best players in baseball.

Nm-Mt Ex-Mt
COMPLETE SET (10) 500.00 150.00
*CANVAS: .75X TO 2X BASIC CRAMER
CANVAS RANDOM INSERTS IN PACKS
*STYRENE: .6X TO 1.5X BASIC CRAMER
STYRENE RANDOM INSERTS IN PACKS
1 Cal Ripken 80.00 24.00
2 Nomar Garciaparra 40.00 12.00
3 Sammy Sosa 40.00 12.00
4 Frank Thomas 25.00 7.50
5 Ken Griffey Jr. 40.00 12.00
6 Mike Piazza 40.00 12.00
7 Derek Jeter 60.00 18.00
8 Mark McGwire 60.00 18.00
9 Barry Bonds 50.00 15.00
10 Alex Rodriguez 40.00 12.00

2001 Pacific Cramer's Choice Canvas

Randomly inserted into packs, this 10-card insert is a complete parallel of the Cramer's Choice insert. Please note that these cards were printed on canvas paper, and have a rigid texture.

Nm-Mt Ex-Mt
*CANVAS: 1X TO 2X BASIC CRAMER.

2001 Pacific Decade's Best

Randomly inserted into packs at two in 37, this 36-card insert features some of the most productive players in the 90's. Please note that we have included an "A" and "N" prefix below to differentiate the National and American league players.

Nm-Mt Ex-Mt
COMPLETE SET (36) 120.00 36.00
A1 Rickey Henderson 3.00 .90
A2 Rafael Palmeiro 2.00 .60
A3 Cal Ripken 10.00 3.00
A4 Jose Canseco 3.00 .90
A5 Juan Gonzalez 3.00 .90
A6 Frank Thomas 3.00 .90
A7 Albert Belle 1.25 .35
A8 Edgar Martinez 2.00 .60
A9 Mo Vaughn 1.25 .35
A10 Derek Jeter 8.00 2.40
A11 Mark McGwire 8.00 2.40
A12 Alex Rodriguez 5.00 1.50
A13 Ken Griffey Jr. 5.00 1.50
A14 Nomar Garciaparra 5.00 1.50
A15 Roger Clemens 6.00 1.80
A16 Bernie Williams 2.00 .60
A17 Ivan Rodriguez 3.00 .90
A18 Pedro Martinez 3.00 .90
N1 Barry Bonds 8.00 2.40
N2 Jeff Bagwell 2.00 .60
N3 Tom Glavine 2.00 .60
N4 Gary Sheffield 1.25 .35
N5 Fred McGriff 2.00 .60
N6 Greg Maddux 5.00 1.50
N7 Mike Piazza 5.00 1.50
N8 Tony Gwynn 4.00 1.20
N9 Hideo Nomo 3.00 .90
N10 Andres Galarraga 1.25 .35
N11 Larry Walker 2.00 .60
N12 Scott Rolen 2.00 .60
N13 Pedro Martinez 3.00 .90
N14 Sammy Sosa 5.00 1.50
N15 Mark McGwire 8.00 2.40
N16 Kerry Wood 3.00 .90
N17 Chipper Jones 3.00 .90
N18 Mark Grace 2.00 .60

2001 Pacific Game Jersey

Randomly inserted into packs, this five-card insert features game-used jersey cards of players like Tony Gwynn and Alex Rodriguez. Please note that this is a skip-numbered set.

Nm-Mt Ex-Mt
3 Gary Sheffield 10.00 3.00
5 Scott Rolen 15.00 4.50
7 Tony Gwynn 20.00 6.00
8 Alex Rodriguez 25.00 7.50
9 Rafael Palmeiro 15.00 4.50

2001 Pacific Game Jersey Patch

Randomly inserted into packs, this five-card insert is a complete parallel of the Game Jersey insert. These cards feature a swatch from the patch portion of these jerseys. The individual print runs are listed below. Please note that this is a skip-numbered set.

Nm-Mt Ex-Mt
3 Gary Sheffield/226 25.00 7.50
5 Scott Rolen/157 40.00 12.00
7 Tony Gwynn/183 60.00 18.00
8 Alex Rodriguez/221 100.00 30.00
9 Rafael Palmeiro/154 40.00 12.00

2001 Pacific Gold Crown Die Cuts

Inserted one every 73 packs, this 36 card set features a selection of baseball's top stars. This set uses the Gold Crown Die Cut style used on many Pacific products. Please note that there is also a Blue and Purple parallel of this insert. Also note that autographed versions exist of six players.

Nm-Mt Ex-Mt
*BLUE: .6X TO 1.5X BASIC CROWN...
BLUE RANDOM INSERTS IN PACKS...
BLUE PRINT RUN 100 SERIAL #'d SETS
*PURPLE: 1X TO 2.5X BASIC CROWN
PURPLE RANDOM INSERTS IN PACKS
PURPLE PRINT RUN 50 SERIAL #'d SETS
CARD NUMBER 27 DOES NOT EXIST.
ANKIEL/BURRELL BOTH NUMBERED 26
1 Darin Erstad 4.00 1.20
2 Troy Glaus 4.00 1.20
3 Randy Johnson 4.00 1.20
4 Rafael Furcal 4.00 1.20
5 Andruw Jones 4.00 1.20
6 Chipper Jones 4.00 1.20
7 Greg Maddux 6.00 1.80
8 Cal Ripken 12.00 3.60
9 Nomar Garciaparra 6.00 1.80
10 Pedro Martinez 4.00 1.20
11 Corey Patterson 4.00 1.20
12 Sammy Sosa 6.00 1.80
13 Frank Thomas 4.00 1.20
14 Ken Griffey Jr. 6.00 1.80
15 Manny Ramirez 4.00 1.20
16 Todd Helton 4.00 1.20
17 Jeff Bagwell 4.00 1.20
18 Shawn Green 4.00 1.20
19 Gary Sheffield 4.00 1.20
20 Vladimir Guerrero 4.00 1.20
21 Mike Piazza 6.00 1.80
22 Jose Canseco 4.00 1.20

	Nm-Mt	Ex-Mt
23 Roger Clemens	8.00	2.40
24 Derek Jeter	10.00	3.00
25 Jason Giambi	4.00	1.20
26 Rick Ankiel	4.00	1.20
26 Pat Burrell	4.00	1.20
28 Jim Edmonds	4.00	1.20
29 Mark McGwire	10.00	3.00
30 Tony Gwynn	5.00	1.50
31 Barry Bonds	10.00	3.00
32 Rickey Henderson	4.00	1.20
33 Edgar Martinez	4.00	1.20
34 Alex Rodriguez	6.00	1.80
35 Ivan Rodriguez	4.00	1.20
36 Carlos Delgado	4.00	1.20

2001 Pacific Gold Crown Die Cuts Autograph

Randomly inserted into packs, this six-card insert features autographed Gold Crown Die Cuts of players like Barry Bonds and Chipper Jones. Please note that this is a partial parallell of the Gold Crown Die Cuts, and that the crown portion of these cards is stamped with green foil.

	Nm-Mt	Ex-Mt
6 Chipper Jones	80.00	24.00
11 Corey Patterson	25.00	7.50
13 Frank Thomas	80.00	24.00
19 Gary Sheffield	40.00	12.00
28 Jim Edmonds	25.00	7.50
31 Barry Bonds	120.00	36.00

2001 Pacific On the Horizon

Randomly inserted into packs at one in 145, this 10-card insert features players that are on the verge of stardom.

	Nm-Mt	Ex-Mt
COMPLETE SET (10)	100.00	30.00
1 Rafael Furcal	10.00	3.00
2 Corey Patterson	10.00	3.00
3 Russell Branyan	10.00	3.00
4 Juan Pierre	10.00	3.00
5 Mark Quinn	10.00	3.00
6 Alfonso Soriano	15.00	4.50
7 Adam Piatt	10.00	3.00
8 Pat Burrell	10.00	3.00
9 Kazuhiro Sasaki	10.00	3.00
10 Aubrey Huff	10.00	3.00

2001 Pacific Ornaments

Inserted two every 37 packs, these 24 cards are designed in the shape of Christmas ornaments. The cards have full custom holographic patterned silver foil and a string loop on top so they can be hung on a tree. Please note that cards 21-24 were inserted into retail packs only.

	Nm-Mt	Ex-Mt
COMPLETE SET (24)	150.00	45.00
1 Rafael Furcal	4.00	1.20
2 Chipper Jones	5.00	1.50
3 Greg Maddux	8.00	2.40
4 Cal Ripken	15.00	4.50
5 Nomar Garciaparra	8.00	2.40
6 Pedro Martinez	5.00	1.50
7 Sammy Sosa	8.00	2.40
8 Frank Thomas	5.00	1.50
9 Ken Griffey Jr.	8.00	2.40
10 Manny Ramirez	4.00	1.20
11 Todd Helton	4.00	1.20
12 Vladimir Guerrero	5.00	1.50
13 Mike Piazza	8.00	2.40
14 Roger Clemens	10.00	3.00
15 Derek Jeter	12.00	3.60
16 Pat Burrell	4.00	1.20
17 Rick Ankiel	4.00	1.20
18 Mark McGwire	12.00	3.60
19 Barry Bonds	12.00	3.60
20 Alex Rodriguez	8.00	2.40
21 Troy Glaus	4.00	1.20
22 Tom Glavine	4.00	1.20
23 Jim Edmonds	4.00	1.20
24 Ivan Rodriguez	5.00	1.50

1999 Pacific Crown Collection

The 1999 Pacific Crown Collection was issued in one series totalling 300 cards and was distributed in 12-card packs. The cards were

intended for distribution primarily to Latin America and Mexico, thus the text on them is bilingual but predominantly Spanish. The same pattern holds true for Crown Collection insert cards. The fronts feature color action player photos. The backs carry player information and career statistics. An unnumbered Tony Gwynn sample card was distributed to dealers and hobby media prior to the product's release. The card is easy to recognize by the bold, diagonal "SAMPLE" text running across the back.

	Nm-Mt	Ex-Mt
COMPLETE SET (300)	50.00	15.00
1 Garret Anderson	.30	.09
2 Gary DiSarcina	.30	.09
3 Jim Edmonds	.30	.09
4 Darin Erstad	.30	.09
5 Shigetoshi Hasegawa	.30	.09
6 Norberto Martin	.30	.09
7 Omar Olivares	.30	.09
8 Orlando Palmeiro	.30	.09
9 Tim Salmon	.50	.15
10 Randy Velarde	.30	.09
11 Tony Batista	.30	.09
12 Jay Bell	.30	.09
13 Yamil Benitez	.30	.09
14 Omar Daal	.30	.09
15 David Dellucci	.30	.09
16 Karim Garcia	.30	.09
17 Travis Lee	.30	.09
18 Felix Rodriguez	.30	.09
19 Devon White	.30	.09
20 Matt Williams	.30	.09
21 Andres Galarraga	.30	.09
22 Tom Glavine	.50	.15
23 Ozzie Guillen	.30	.09
24 Andruw Jones	.30	.09
25 Chipper Jones	.75	.23
26 Ryan Klesko	.30	.09
27 Javy Lopez	.30	.09
28 Greg Maddux	1.25	.35
29 Dennis Martinez	.30	.09
30 Odalis Perez	.30	.09
31 Rudy Seanez	.30	.09
32 John Smoltz	.50	.15
33 Roberto Alomar	.75	.23
34 Armando Benitez	.30	.09
35 Scott Erickson	.30	.09
36 Juan Guzman	.30	.09
37 Mike Mussina	.75	.23
38 Jesse Orosco	.30	.09
39 Rafael Palmeiro	.50	.15
40 Sidney Ponson	.30	.09
41 Cal Ripken	2.50	.75
42 B.J. Surhoff	.30	.09
43 Lenny Webster	.30	.09
44 Dennis Eckersley	.30	.09
45 Nomar Garciaparra	1.25	.35
46 Darren Lewis	.30	.09
47 Pedro Martinez	.75	.23
48 Troy O'Leary	.30	.09
49 Bret Saberhagen	.30	.09
50 John Valentin	.30	.09
51 Mo Vaughn	.30	.09
52 Tim Wakefield	.30	.09
53 Manny Alexander	.30	.09
54 Rod Beck	.30	.09
55 Gary Gaetti	.30	.09
56 Mark Grace	.50	.15
57 Felix Heredia	.30	.09
58 Jose Hernandez	.30	.09
59 Henry Rodriguez	.30	.09
60 Sammy Sosa	1.25	.35
61 Kevin Tapani	.30	.09
62 Kerry Wood	.75	.23
63 James Baldwin	.30	.09
64 Albert Belle	.30	.09
65 Mike Caruso	.30	.09
66 Carlos Castillo	.30	.09
67 Wil Cordero	.30	.09
68 Jaime Navarro	.30	.09
69 Magglio Ordonez	.30	.09
70 Frank Thomas	.75	.23
71 Robin Ventura	.30	.09
72 Bret Boone	.30	.09
73 Sean Casey	.30	.09
74 Guillermo Garcia RC	.30	.09
75 Barry Larkin	.75	.23
76 Melvin Nieves	.30	.09
77 Eduardo Perez	.30	.09
78 Roberto Petagine	.30	.09
79 Reggie Sanders	.30	.09
80 Eddie Taubensee	.30	.09
81 Brett Tomko	.30	.09
82 Sandy Alomar Jr.	.30	.09
83 Bartolo Colon	.30	.09
84 Joey Cora	.30	.09
85 Einar Diaz	.30	.09
86 David Justice	.30	.09
87 Kenny Lofton	.30	.09
88 Manny Ramirez	.30	.09
89 Jim Thome	.75	.23
90 Omar Vizquel	.30	.09
91 Enrique Wilson	.30	.09
92 Pedro Astacio	.30	.09
93 Dante Bichette	.30	.09
94 Vinny Castilla	.30	.09
95 Edgard Clemente	.30	.09
96 Todd Helton	.50	.15
97 Darryl Kile	.30	.09
98 Mike Munoz	.30	.09
99 Neifi Perez	.30	.09
100 Jeff Reed	.30	.09
101 Larry Walker	.50	.15
102 Gabe Alvarez	.30	.09
103 Kimera Bartee	.30	.09
104 Frank Castillo	.30	.09
105 Tony Clark	.30	.09
106 Deivi Cruz	.30	.09
107 Damion Easley	.30	.09
108 Luis Gonzalez	.30	.09
109 Marino Santana	.30	.09
110 Justin Thompson	.30	.09
111 Antonio Alfonseca	.30	.09
112 Alex Fernandez	.30	.09
113 Cliff Floyd	.30	.09
114 Alex Gonzalez	.30	.09
115 Livan Hernandez	.30	.09
116 Mark Kotsay	.30	.09
117 Derrek Lee	.30	.09
118 Edgar Renteria	.30	.09
119 Jesus Sanchez	.30	.09
120 Moises Alou	.30	.09
121 Jeff Bagwell	.50	.15
122 Derek Bell	.30	.09
123 Craig Biggio	.50	.15
124 Tony Eusebio	.30	.09
125 Ricky Gutierrez	.30	.09
126 Richard Hidalgo	.30	.09
127 Randy Johnson	.75	.23
128 Jose Lima	.30	.09
129 Shane Reynolds	.30	.09
130 Johnny Damon	.30	.09
131 Carlos Febles	.30	.09
132 Jeff King	.30	.09
133 Mendy Lopez	.30	.09
134 Hal Morris	.30	.09
135 Jose Offerman	.30	.09
136 Jose Rosado	.30	.09
137 Jose Santiago RC	.30	.09
138 Bobby Bonilla	.30	.09
139 Roger Cedeno	.30	.09
140 Alex Cora	.30	.09
141 Eric Karros	.30	.09
142 Raul Mondesi	.30	.09
143 Antonio Osuna	.30	.09
144 Chan Ho Park	.30	.09
145 Gary Sheffield	.30	.09
146 Ismael Valdes	.30	.09
147 Jeromy Burnitz	.30	.09
148 Jeff Cirillo	.30	.09
149 Valerio De Los Santos	.30	.09
150 Marquis Grissom	.30	.09
151 Scott Karl	.30	.09
152 Dave Nilsson	.30	.09
153 Al Reyes	.30	.09
154 Rafael Roque RC	.30	.09
155 Jose Valentin	.30	.09
156 Fernando Vina	.30	.09
157 Rick Aguilera	.30	.09
158 Hector Carrasco	.30	.09
159 Marty Cordova	.30	.09
160 Eddie Guardado	.30	.09
161 Paul Molitor	.50	.15
162 Otis Nixon	.30	.09
163 Alex Ochoa	.30	.09
164 David Ortiz	.30	.09
165 Frank Rodriguez	.30	.09
166 Todd Walker	.30	.09
167 Miguel Batista	.30	.09
168 Orlando Cabrera	.30	.09
169 Vladimir Guerrero	.75	.23
170 Wilton Guerrero	.30	.09
171 Carl Pavano	.30	.09
172 Robert Perez	.30	.09
173 F.P. Santangelo	.30	.09
174 Fernando Seguignol	.30	.09
175 Ugueth Urbina	.30	.09
176 Javier Vazquez	.30	.09
177 Edgardo Alfonzo	.30	.09
178 Carlos Baerga	.30	.09
179 John Franco	.30	.09
180 Luis Lopez	.30	.09
181 Hideo Nomo	.75	.23
182 John Olerud	.30	.09
183 Rey Ordonez	.30	.09
184 Mike Piazza	1.25	.35
185 Armando Reynoso	.30	.09
186 Masato Yoshii	.30	.09
187 David Cone	.30	.09
188 Orlando Hernandez	.30	.09
189 Hideki Irabu	.30	.09
190 Derek Jeter	2.00	.60
191 Ricky Ledee	.30	.09
192 Tino Martinez	.50	.15
193 Ramiro Mendoza	.30	.09
194 Paul O'Neill	.50	.15
195 Jorge Posada	.50	.15
196 Mariano Rivera	.50	.15
197 Luis Sojo	.30	.09
198 Bernie Williams	.50	.15
199 Rafael Bournigal	.30	.09
200 Eric Chavez	.30	.09
201 Ryan Christenson	.30	.09
202 Jason Giambi	.75	.23
203 Ben Grieve	.30	.09
204 Rickey Henderson	.75	.23
205 A.J. Hinch	.30	.09
206 Kenny Rogers	.30	.09
207 Miguel Tejada	.30	.09
208 Jorge Velandia	.30	.09
209 Bobby Abreu	.30	.09
210 Marlon Anderson	.30	.09
211 Alex Arias	.30	.09
212 Bobby Estalella	.30	.09
213 Doug Glanville	.30	.09
214 Scott Rolen	.50	.15
215 Curt Schilling	.50	.15
216 Kevin Sefcik	.30	.09
217 Adrian Brown	.30	.09
218 Francisco Cordova	.30	.09
219 Freddy Garcia	.30	.09
220 Jose Guillen	.30	.09
221 Jason Kendall	.30	.09
222 Al Martin	.30	.09
223 Abraham Nunez	.30	.09
224 Aramis Ramirez	.30	.09
225 Ricardo Rincon	.30	.09
226 Kevin Young	.30	.09
227 J.D. Drew	.30	.09
228 Ron Gant	.30	.09
229 Jose Jimenez	.30	.09
230 Brian Jordan	.30	.09
231 Ray Lankford	.30	.09
232 Eli Marrero	.30	.09
233 Mark McGwire	2.00	.60
234 Luis Ordaz	.30	.09
235 Placido Polanco	.30	.09
236 Fernando Tatis	.30	.09
237 Andy Ashby	.30	.09
238 Kevin Brown	.50	.15
239 Ken Caminiti	.30	.09
240 Steve Finley	.30	.09
241 Chris Gomez	.30	.09
242 Tony Gwynn	1.00	.30
243 Carlos Hernandez	.30	.09
244 Trevor Hoffman	.30	.09
245 Wally Joyner	.30	.09
246 Ruben Rivera	.30	.09
247 Greg Vaughn	.30	.09
248 Quilvio Veras	.30	.09
249 Rich Aurilia	.30	.09
250 Barry Bonds	2.00	.60
251 Stan Javier	.30	.09
252 Jeff Kent	.30	.09
253 Ramon E.Martinez RC	.30	.09
254 Jose Mesa	.30	.09
255 Armando Rios	.30	.09
256 Rich Rodriguez	.30	.09
257 Rey Sanchez	.30	.09
258 J.T. Snow	.30	.09
259 Julian Tavarez	.30	.09
260 Jeff Fassero	.30	.09
261 Ken Griffey Jr.	1.25	.35
262 Giomar Guevara RC	.30	.09
263 Carlos Guillen	.30	.09
264 Raul Ibanez	.30	.09
265 Edgar Martinez	.50	.15
266 Jamie Moyer	.30	.09
267 Alex Rodriguez	1.25	.35
268 David Segui	.30	.09
269 Makato Suzuki	.30	.09
270 Wilson Alvarez	.30	.09
271 Rolando Arrojo	.30	.09
272 Wade Boggs	.50	.15
273 Miguel Cairo	.30	.09
274 Roberto Hernandez	.30	.09
275 Aaron Ledesma	.30	.09
276 Albie Lopez	.30	.09
277 Quinton McCracken	.30	.09
278 Fred McGriff	.50	.15
279 Esteban Yan	.30	.09
280 Luis Alicea	.30	.09
281 Will Clark	.75	.23
282 Juan Gonzalez	.75	.23
283 Rusty Greer	.30	.09
284 Rick Helling	.30	.09
285 Xavier Hernandez	.30	.09
286 Roberto Kelly	.30	.09
287 Esteban Loaiza	.30	.09
288 Ivan Rodriguez	.75	.23
289 Aaron Sele	.30	.09
290 John Wetteland	.30	.09
291 Jose Canseco	.75	.23
292 Roger Clemens	1.50	.45
293 Felipe Crespo	.30	.09
294 Jose Cruz Jr.	.30	.09
295 Carlos Delgado	.30	.09
296 Kelvim Escobar	.30	.09
297 Tony Fernandez	.30	.09
298 Alex Gonzalez	.30	.09
299 Tomas Perez	.30	.09
300 Juan Samuel	.30	.09
NNO Tony Gwynn Sample	1.00	.30

1999 Pacific Crown Collection Platinum Blue

Randomly inserted in packs at the rate of one in 73, this 300-card set is a blue foil parallel version of the base set. The easiest way to tell these cards apart from the regular issue is that the "Pacific Collection" logo as well as the player's name is printed in a deep blue foil.

	Nm-Mt	Ex-Mt
*STARS: 10X TO 25X BASIC CARDS		

1999 Pacific Crown Collection Red

Randomly inserted into retail Treat packs at the rate of four in 37, this 300-card set is a red foil parallel version of the the base set.

	Nm-Mt	Ex-Mt
*STARS: 2X TO 5X BASIC CARDS		

1999 Pacific Crown Collection In The Cage

Randomly inserted in packs at the rate of one in 145, this 20-card set features color player photos with a backstop fence as the background printed on laser-cut cards.

	Nm-Mt	Ex-Mt
COMPLETE SET (20)	400.00	120.00
1 Chipper Jones	15.00	4.50
2 Cal Ripken	50.00	15.00
3 Nomar Garciaparra	25.00	7.50
4 Sammy Sosa	25.00	7.50
5 Frank Thomas	15.00	4.50
6 Manny Ramirez	6.00	1.80
7 Todd Helton	10.00	3.00
8 Moises Alou	6.00	1.80
9 Vladimir Guerrero	15.00	4.50
10 Mike Piazza	25.00	7.50
11 Derek Jeter	40.00	12.00
12 Ben Grieve	6.00	1.80
13 J.D. Drew	6.00	1.80
14 Mark McGwire	40.00	12.00
15 Tony Gwynn	20.00	6.00
16 Ken Griffey Jr.	25.00	7.50
17 Edgar Martinez	10.00	3.00
18 Alex Rodriguez	25.00	7.50
19 Juan Gonzalez	15.00	4.50
20 Ivan Rodriguez	15.00	4.50

1999 Pacific Crown Collection Latinos of the Major Leagues

Randomly inserted in packs at the rate of two in 37, this 36-card set features color photos of some of the top Latin players in the Major Leagues printed on a colorful swirl-design background with a faint player head photo in one top corner.

	Nm-Mt	Ex-Mt
COMPLETE SET (36)	80.00	24.00
1 Roberto Alomar	5.00	1.50
2 Rafael Palmeiro	3.00	.90
3 Nomar Garciaparra	8.00	2.40
4 Pedro Martinez	5.00	1.50
5 Magglio Ordonez	2.00	.60
6 Sandy Alomar Jr.	2.00	.60
7 Bartolo Colon	2.00	.60
8 Manny Ramirez	2.00	.60
9 Omar Vizquel	2.00	.60
10 Enrique Wilson	2.00	.60
11 David Ortiz	2.00	.60
12 Orlando Hernandez	2.00	.60
13 Tino Martinez	3.00	.90
14 Mariano Rivera	3.00	.90
15 Bernie Williams	3.00	.90
16 Edgar Martinez	3.00	.90
17 Alex Rodriguez	8.00	2.40
18 David Segui	2.00	.60
19 Rolando Arrojo	2.00	.60
20 Juan Gonzalez	5.00	1.50
21 Ivan Rodriguez	5.00	1.50
22 Jose Canseco	5.00	1.50
23 Jose Cruz Jr.	2.00	.60
24 Andres Galarraga	2.00	.60
25 Andruw Jones	2.00	.60
26 Javy Lopez	2.00	.60
27 Sammy Sosa	8.00	2.40
28 Vinny Castilla	2.00	.60
29 Alex Gonzalez	2.00	.60
30 Moises Alou	2.00	.60
31 Bobby Bonilla	2.00	.60
32 Raul Mondesi	2.00	.60
33 Fernando Vina	2.00	.60
34 Vladimir Guerrero	5.00	1.50
35 Carlos Baerga	2.00	.60
36 Rey Ordonez	2.00	.60

1999 Pacific Crown Collection Pacific Cup

Randomly inserted in packs at the rate of one in 721, this 10-card set features color player photos of some of the League's top players printed on a die-cut card with a winner's trophy cup as the background.

	Nm-Mt	Ex-Mt
COMPLETE SET (10)	250.00	75.00
1 Cal Ripken	50.00	15.00
2 Nomar Garciaparra	25.00	7.50
3 Frank Thomas	15.00	4.50
4 Ken Griffey Jr.	30.00	9.00
5 Alex Rodriguez	25.00	7.50
6 Greg Maddux	25.00	7.50
7 Sammy Sosa	25.00	7.50
8 Kerry Wood	15.00	4.50
9 Mark McGwire	40.00	12.00
10 Tony Gwynn	20.00	6.00

1999 Pacific Crown Collection Tape Measure

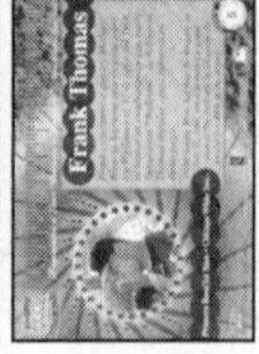

Randomly inserted in packs at the rate of one in 73, this 20-card set features color photos of top players printed on laser cut cards with a colorful background and a facsimile tape measure and team logo.

	Nm-Mt	Ex-Mt
COMPLETE SET (20)	200.00	60.00
1 Andres Galarraga	4.00	1.20
2 Chipper Jones	10.00	3.00
3 Nomar Garciaparra	15.00	4.50
4 Sammy Sosa	15.00	4.50
5 Frank Thomas	10.00	3.00
6 Manny Ramirez	4.00	1.20
7 Vinny Castilla	4.00	1.20
8 Moises Alou	4.00	1.20
9 Jeff Bagwell	6.00	1.80
10 Raul Mondesi	4.00	1.20
11 Vladimir Guerrero	10.00	3.00

12 Mike Piazza 15.00 4.50
13 J.D. Drew 4.00 1.20
14 Mark McGwire 25.00 7.50
15 Greg Vaughn 4.00 1.20
16 Ken Griffey Jr. 15.00 4.50
17 Alex Rodriguez 15.00 4.50
18 Juan Gonzalez 10.00 3.00
19 Ivan Rodriguez 10.00 3.00
20 Jose Canseco 10.00 3.00

1999 Pacific Crown Collection Team Checklists

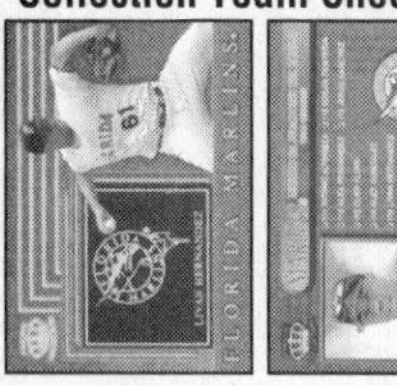
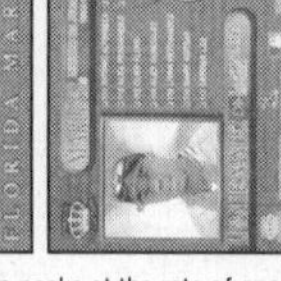

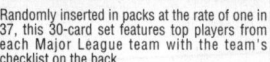

Randomly inserted in packs at the rate of one in 37, this 30-card set features top players from each Major League team with the team's checklist on the back.

Nm-Mt Ex-Mt
COMPLETE SET (30) 250.00 75.00
1 Darin Erstad 3.00 .90
2 Travis Lee 3.00 .90
3 Chipper Jones 8.00 2.40
4 Cal Ripken 25.00 7.50
5 Nomar Garciaparra 12.00 3.60
6 Sammy Sosa 12.00 3.60
7 Frank Thomas 8.00 2.40
8 Barry Larkin 8.00 2.40
9 Manny Ramirez 3.00 .90
10 Larry Walker 5.00 1.50
11 Bob Higginson 3.00 .90
12 Livan Hernandez 3.00 .90
13 Moises Alou 3.00 .90
14 Jeff King 3.00 .90
15 Raul Mondesi 3.00 .90
16 Marquis Grissom 3.00 .90
17 David Ortiz 3.00 .90
18 Vladimir Guerrero 8.00 2.40
19 Mike Piazza 12.00 3.60
20 Derek Jeter 20.00 6.00
21 Ben Grieve 3.00 .90
22 Scott Rolen 5.00 1.50
23 Jason Kendall 3.00 .90
24 Mark McGwire 20.00 6.00
25 Tony Gwynn 10.00 3.00
26 Barry Bonds 20.00 6.00
27 Ken Griffey Jr. 12.00 3.60
28 Wade Boggs 5.00 1.50
29 Juan Gonzalez 8.00 2.40
30 Jose Canseco 8.00 2.40

1999 Pacific Crown Collection Players Choice

These cards, which parallel the regular Crown Collection Cards were issued by Pacific to be given away at the Players Choice award ceremony. The cards have a "Players Choice" stamp on them and are skip numbered to match their number. These cards were produced in varying quantites so we have put the print run next to the players name

Nm-Mt Ex-Mt
COMPLETE SET 200.00 60.00
10 Randy Velarde/35 10.00 3.00
41 Cal Ripken Jr./25
47 Pedro Martinez/38 30.00 9.00
88 Manny Ramirez/39 30.00 9.00
112 Alex Fernandez/39 10.00 3.00
128 Jose Lima/38 10.00 3.00

2000 Pacific Crown Collection

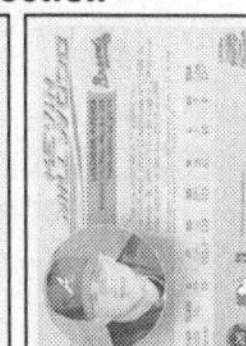

This 300-card single series set was released in February, 2000. Ten card packs carried an SRP of $2.49. The basic cards feature a full-color action shotframed by a white broder with the player's name, team and Crown Collection logo in gold foil. Subset Team Cards are sprinkled throughout the set. In addition, a Tony Gwynn sample card was distributed to dealers and hobby media several weeks prior to the product's release. The card is easy to identify by the "SAMPLE" text running diagonally across the back and lack of a card number.

Nm-Mt Ex-Mt
COMPLETE SET (300) 40.00 12.00
1 Garret Anderson .30 .09
2 Darin Erstad .30 .09
3 Ben Molina .30 .09
4 Ramon Ortiz .30 .09
5 Orlando Palmeiro .30 .09
6 Troy Percival .30 .09
7 Tim Salmon .50 .15
8 Mo Vaughn .30 .09
9 Mo Vaughn TC .30 .09
10 Jay Bell .30 .09
11 Omar Daal .30 .09
12 Erubiel Durazo .30 .09
13 Steve Finley .30 .09
14 Hanley Frias .30 .09
15 Luis Gonzalez .30 .09
16 Randy Johnson .75 .23
17 Matt Williams .30 .09
18 Matt Williams TC .30 .09
19 Andres Galarraga .30 .09
20 Tom Glavine .50 .15
21 Andruw Jones .30 .09
22 Chipper Jones .75 .23
23 Brian Jordan .30 .09
24 Javy Lopez .30 .09
25 Greg Maddux 1.25 .35
26 Kevin Millwood .30 .09
27 Eddie Perez .30 .09
28 John Smoltz .50 .15
29 Chipper Jones TC .50 .15
30 Albert Belle .30 .09
31 Jesse Garcia .30 .09
32 Jerry Hairston Jr. .30 .09
33 Charles Johnson .30 .09
34 Mike Mussina .75 .23
35 Sidney Ponson .30 .09
36 Cal Ripken 2.50 .75
37 B.J. Surhoff .30 .09
38 Cal Ripken TC 1.25 .35
39 Nomar Garciaparra 1.25 .35
40 Pedro Martinez .75 .23
41 Ramon Martinez .30 .09
42 Trot Nixon .50 .15
43 Jose Offerman .30 .09
44 Troy O'Leary .30 .09
45 John Valentin .30 .09
46 Wilton Veras .30 .09
47 Nomar Garciaparra TC .75 .23
48 Mark Grace .50 .15
49 Felix Heredia .30 .09
50 Jose Molina .30 .09
51 Jose Nieves .30 .09
52 Henry Rodriguez .30 .09
53 Sammy Sosa 1.25 .35
54 Kerry Wood .75 .23
55 Sammy Sosa TC .75 .23
56 Mike Caruso .30 .09
57 Carlos Castillo .30 .09
58 Jason Dellaero .30 .09
59 Carlos Lee .30 .09
60 Magglio Ordonez .30 .09
61 Jesus Pena .30 .09
62 Liu Rodriguez .30 .09
63 Frank Thomas .75 .23
64 Magglio Ordonez TC .30 .09
65 Aaron Boone .30 .09
66 Mike Cameron .30 .09
67 Sean Casey .30 .09
68 Juan Guzman .30 .09
69 Barry Larkin .75 .23
70 Pokey Reese .30 .09
71 Eddie Taubensee .30 .09
72 Greg Vaughn .30 .09
73 Sean Casey TC .30 .09
74 Roberto Alomar .75 .23
75 Sandy Alomar Jr. .30 .09
76 Bartolo Colon .30 .09
77 Jacob Cruz .30 .09
78 Einar Diaz .30 .09
79 David Justice .30 .09
80 Kenny Lofton .30 .09
81 Manny Ramirez .30 .09
82 Richie Sexson .30 .09
83 Jim Thome .75 .23
84 Omar Vizquel .30 .09
85 Enrique Wilson .30 .09
86 Manny Ramirez TC .30 .09
87 Pedro Astacio .30 .09
88 Henry Blanco .30 .09
89 Vinny Castilla .30 .09
90 Edgard Clemente .30 .09
91 Todd Helton .50 .15
92 Neifi Perez .30 .09
93 Terry Shumpert .30 .09
94 Juan Sosa RC .30 .09
95 Larry Walker .50 .15
96 Larry Walker TC .50 .15
97 Tony Clark .30 .09
98 Deivi Cruz .30 .09
99 Damion Easley .30 .09
100 Juan Encarnacion .30 .09
101 Karim Garcia .30 .09
102 Luis Garcia RC .30 .09
103 Juan Gonzalez .75 .23
104 Jose Macias .30 .09
105 Dean Palmer .30 .09
106 Juan Encarnacion TC .30 .09
107 Antonio Alfonseca .30 .09
108 Armando Almanza .30 .09
109 Bruce Aven .30 .09
110 Luis Castillo .30 .09
111 Ramon Castro .30 .09
112 Alex Fernandez .30 .09
113 Cliff Floyd .30 .09
114 Alex Gonzalez .30 .09
115 Michael Tejera RC .30 .09
116 Preston Wilson .30 .09
117 Luis Castillo TC .30 .09
118 Jeff Bagwell .50 .15
119 Craig Biggio .50 .15
120 Jose Cabrera .30 .09
121 Tony Eusebio .30 .09
122 Carl Everett .30 .09
123 Ricky Gutierrez .30 .09
124 Mike Hampton .30 .09
125 Richard Hidalgo .30 .09
126 Jose Lima .30 .09
127 Billy Wagner .30 .09
128 Jeff Bagwell TC .30 .09
129 Carlos Beltran .30 .09
130 Johnny Damon .30 .09
131 Jermaine Dye .30 .09
132 Carlos Febles .30 .09
133 Jeremy Giambi .30 .09
134 Jose Rosado .30 .09
135 Rey Sanchez .30 .09
136 Jose Santiago .30 .09
137 Carlos Beltran TC .30 .09
138 Chad Allen .30 .09
139 Craig Counsell .30 .09
140 Shawn Green .30 .09
141 Eric Karros .30 .09
142 Chan Ho Park .30 .09
143 Angel Pena .30 .09
144 Gary Sheffield .30 .09
145 Jose Vizcaino .30 .09
146 Devon White .30 .09
147 Eric Karros TC .30 .09
148 Ron Belliard .30 .09
149 Jason Bere .30 .09
150 Jeromy Burnitz .30 .09
151 Marquis Grissom .30 .09
152 Geoff Jenkins .30 .09
153 Dave Nilsson .30 .09
154 Rafael Roque .30 .09
155 Jose Valentin .30 .09
156 Fernando Vina .30 .09
157 Jeromy Burnitz TC .30 .09
158 Chad Allen .30 .09
159 Ron Coomer .30 .09
160 Eddie Guardado .30 .09
161 Cristian Guzman .30 .09
162 Jacque Jones .30 .09
163 Javier Valentin .30 .09
164 Todd Walker .30 .09
165 Ron Coomer TC .30 .09
166 Michael Barrett .30 .09
167 Miguel Batista .30 .09
168 Vladimir Guerrero .75 .23
169 Wilton Guerrero .30 .09
170 Fernando Seguignol .30 .09
171 Ugueth Urbina .30 .09
172 Javier Vazquez .30 .09
173 Jose Vidro .30 .09
174 Rondell White .30 .09
175 Vladimir Guerrero TC .50 .15
176 Edgardo Alfonzo .30 .09
177 Armando Benitez .30 .09
178 Roger Cedeno .30 .09
179 Octavio Dotel .30 .09
180 Melvin Mora .30 .09
181 Rey Ordonez .30 .09
182 Mike Piazza 1.25 .35
183 Jorge Toca .30 .09
184 Robin Ventura .50 .15
185 Edgardo Alfonzo TC .30 .09
186 Roger Clemens 1.50 .45
187 David Cone .30 .09
188 Orlando Hernandez .30 .09
189 Derek Jeter 2.00 .60
190 Ricky Ledee .30 .09
191 Tino Martinez .50 .15
192 Ramiro Mendoza .30 .09
193 Jorge Posada .50 .15
194 Mariano Rivera .50 .15
195 Alfonso Soriano .75 .23
196 Bernie Williams .50 .15
197 Derek Jeter TC 1.00 .30
198 Eric Chavez .30 .09
199 Jason Giambi .75 .23
200 Ben Grieve .30 .09
201 Ramon Hernandez .30 .09
202 Tim Hudson .50 .15
203 John Jaha .30 .09
204 Omar Olivares .30 .09
205 Olmedo Saenz .30 .09
206 Matt Stairs .30 .09
207 Miguel Tejada .30 .09
208 Tim Hudson TC .30 .09
209 Rico Brogna .30 .09
210 Bob Abreu .30 .09
211 Marlon Anderson .30 .09
212 Alex Arias .30 .09
213 Doug Glanville .30 .09
214 Robert Person .30 .09
215 Scott Rolen .50 .15
216 Curt Schilling .50 .15
217 Scott Rolen TC .50 .15
218 Francisco Cordova .30 .09
219 Brian Giles .30 .09
220 Jason Kendall .30 .09
221 Warren Morris .30 .09
222 Abraham Nunez .30 .09
223 Aramis Ramirez .30 .09
224 Jose Silva .30 .09
225 Kevin Young .30 .09
226 Brian Giles TC .30 .09
227 Rick Ankiel .30 .09
228 Ricky Bottalico .30 .09
229 J.D. Drew .30 .09
230 Ray Lankford .30 .09
231 Mark McGwire 2.00 .60
232 Eduardo Perez .30 .09
233 Placido Polanco .30 .09
234 Edgar Renteria .30 .09
235 Fernando Tatis .30 .09
236 Mark McGwire TC 1.00 .30
237 Carlos Almanzar .30 .09
238 Wiki Gonzalez .30 .09
239 Tony Gwynn 1.00 .30
240 Trevor Hoffman .30 .09
241 Damian Jackson .30 .09
242 Wally Joyner .30 .09
243 Ruben Rivera .30 .09
244 Reggie Sanders .30 .09
245 Quilvio Veras .30 .09
246 Tony Gwynn TC .50 .15
247 Rich Aurilia .30 .09
248 Marvin Benard .30 .09
249 Barry Bonds 2.00 .60
250 Ellis Burks .30 .09
251 Miguel Del Toro .30 .09
252 Edwards Guzman .30 .09
253 Livan Hernandez .30 .09
254 Jeff Kent .30 .09
255 Russ Ortiz .30 .09
256 Armando Rios .30 .09
257 Barry Bonds TC .75 .23
258 Rafael Bournigal .30 .09
259 Freddy Garcia .30 .09
260 Ken Griffey Jr. 1.25 .35
261 Carlos Guillen .30 .09
262 Raul Ibanez .30 .09
263 Edgar Martinez .50 .15
264 Jose Mesa .30 .09
265 Jamie Moyer .30 .09
266 John Olerud .30 .09
267 Jose Paniagua .30 .09
268 Alex Rodriguez 1.25 .35
269 Alex Rodriguez TC .75 .23
270 Wilson Alvarez .30 .09
271 Wade Boggs .50 .15
272 Miguel Cairo .30 .09
273 Jose Canseco .75 .23
274 Jose Guillen .30 .09
275 Roberto Hernandez .30 .09
276 Albie Lopez .30 .09
277 Quinton McCracken .30 .09
278 Fred McGriff .50 .15
279 Esteban Yan .30 .09
280 Jose Canseco TC .30 .09
281 Rusty Greer .30 .09
282 Roberto Kelly .30 .09
283 Esteban Loaiza .30 .09
284 Ruben Mateo .30 .09
285 Rafael Palmeiro .50 .15
286 Ivan Rodriguez .75 .23
287 Aaron Sele .30 .09
288 John Wetteland .30 .09
289 Ivan Rodriguez TC .50 .15
290 Tony Batista .30 .09
291 Jose Cruz Jr. .30 .09
292 Carlos Delgado .30 .09
293 Kelvim Escobar .30 .09
294 Tony Fernandez .30 .09
295 Billy Koch .30 .09
296 Raul Mondesi .30 .09
297 Willis Otanez .30 .09
298 David Segui .30 .09
299 David Wells .30 .09
300 Carlos Delgado TC .30 .09
SAMP T.Gwynn Sample 1.00 .30

2000 Pacific Crown Collection Holographic Purple

Issued randomly in all packs, these cards are serial numbered to 199 and parallel the regular cards. They can be differentiated by the names of the players being printed in Holographic purple.

Nm-Mt Ex-Mt
*STARS: 5X TO 10X BASIC CARDS
*ROOKIES: 3X TO 6X BASIC CARDS

2000 Pacific Crown Collection Platinum Blue

Randomly inserted in packs, these cards with name printed in platinum blue parallel the regular set and are limited to 67 serial numbered sets.

Nm-Mt Ex-Mt
*STARS: 12.5X TO 25X BASIC CARDS
*ROOKIES: 7.5X TO 15X BASIC CARDS

2000 Pacific Crown Collection Premiere Date

Inserted at a rate of one in 36, these cards parallel the regular cards and have the "Premiere Date" logo on the front and are serial numbered to 27.

Nm-Mt Ex-Mt
*STARS: 30X TO 60X BASIC CARDS
*ROOKIES: 20X TO 40X BASIC CARDS

2000 Pacific Crown Collection In the Cage

Inserted at a rate of one in 145 packs, these 20 cards feature some of the leading hitters in the game.

Nm-Mt Ex-Mt
COMPLETE SET (20) 400.00 120.00
1 Mo Vaughn 6.00 1.80
2 Chipper Jones 15.00 4.50
3 Cal Ripken 50.00 15.00
4 Nomar Garciaparra 25.00 7.50
5 Sammy Sosa 25.00 7.50
6 Frank Thomas 15.00 4.50
7 Roberto Alomar 15.00 4.50
8 Manny Ramirez 6.00 1.80
9 Larry Walker 10.00 3.00
10 Jeff Bagwell 10.00 3.00
11 Vladimir Guerrero 15.00 4.50
12 Mike Piazza 25.00 7.50
13 Derek Jeter 40.00 12.00
14 Bernie Williams 10.00 3.00
15 Mark McGwire 40.00 12.00
16 Tony Gwynn 20.00 6.00
17 Ken Griffey Jr. 25.00 7.50
18 Alex Rodriguez 25.00 7.50
19 Rafael Palmeiro 10.00 3.00
20 Ivan Rodriguez 15.00 4.50

2000 Pacific Crown Collection Latinos of the Major Leagues

Issued at a rate of two in 37 packs, these horizontal cards feature 36 of the leading players of Latin descent in the majors.

Nm-Mt Ex-Mt
COMPLETE SET (36) 80.00 24.00
*PARALLELS: 1.25X TO 3X BASIC LATINOS
PARALLELS RANDOM INSERTS IN PACKS
PARALLELS PRINT RUN 99 SERIAL #'d SETS
1 Erubiel Durazo 1.50 .45
2 Luis Gonzalez 1.50 .45
3 Andruw Jones 1.50 .45
4 Nomar Garciaparra 6.00 1.80
5 Pedro Martinez 4.00 1.20
6 Sammy Sosa 6.00 1.80
7 Carlos Lee 1.50 .45
8 Magglio Ordonez 1.50 .45
9 Roberto Alomar 4.00 1.20
10 Manny Ramirez 1.50 .45
11 Omar Vizquel 1.50 .45
12 Vinny Castilla 1.50 .45
13 Juan Gonzalez 4.00 1.20
14 Luis Castillo 1.50 .45
15 Jose Lima 1.50 .45
16 Carlos Beltran 1.50 .45
17 Vladimir Guerrero 4.00 1.20
18 Edgardo Alfonzo 1.50 .45
19 Roger Cedeno 1.50 .45
20 Rey Ordonez 1.50 .45
21 Orlando Hernandez 1.50 .45
22 Tino Martinez 2.50 .75
23 Mariano Rivera 2.50 .75
24 Bernie Williams 2.50 .75
25 Miguel Tejada 1.50 .45
26 Bob Abreu 1.50 .45
27 Fernando Tatis 1.50 .45
28 Freddy Garcia 1.50 .45
29 Edgar Martinez 2.50 .75
30 Alex Rodriguez 6.00 1.80
31 Jose Canseco 4.00 1.20
32 Ruben Mateo 1.50 .45
33 Rafael Palmeiro 2.50 .75
34 Ivan Rodriguez 4.00 1.20
35 Carlos Delgado 1.50 .45
36 Raul Mondesi 1.50 .45

2000 Pacific Crown Collection Moment of Truth

Inserted at a rate of one in 37, these 30 cards feature some of the leading players in baseball.

Nm-Mt Ex-Mt
COMPLETE SET (30) 200.00 60.00
1 Mo Vaughn 2.50 .75
2 Chipper Jones 6.00 1.80
3 Greg Maddux 10.00 3.00
4 Albert Belle 2.50 .75
5 Cal Ripken 20.00 6.00
6 Nomar Garciaparra 10.00 3.00
7 Pedro Martinez 6.00 1.80
8 Sammy Sosa 10.00 3.00
9 Frank Thomas 6.00 1.80
10 Barry Larkin 6.00 1.80
11 Kenny Lofton 2.50 .75
12 Manny Ramirez 2.50 .75
13 Larry Walker 4.00 1.20
14 Juan Gonzalez 6.00 1.80
15 Jeff Bagwell 4.00 1.20
16 Craig Biggio 4.00 1.20
17 Carlos Beltran 2.50 .75
18 Vladimir Guerrero 6.00 1.80
19 Mike Piazza 10.00 3.00
20 Roger Clemens 12.00 3.60
21 Derek Jeter 15.00 4.50
22 Bernie Williams 4.00 1.20
23 Mark McGwire 15.00 4.50
24 Tony Gwynn 8.00 2.40
25 Barry Bonds 15.00 4.50
26 Ken Griffey Jr. 10.00 3.00
27 Alex Rodriguez 10.00 3.00
28 Rafael Palmeiro 4.00 1.20
29 Ivan Rodriguez 6.00 1.80
30 Carlos Delgado 2.50 .75

2000 Pacific Crown Collection Pacific Cup

Issued at a rate in 721 packs, these 10 horizontal cards feature the very best players in the game.

Nm-Mt Ex-Mt
COMPLETE SET (10) 350.00 105.00
1 Cal Ripken 50.00 15.00
2 Nomar Garciaparra 25.00 7.50
3 Pedro Martinez 15.00 4.50
4 Sammy Sosa 25.00 7.50
5 Vladimir Guerrero 15.00 4.50
6 Derek Jeter 40.00 12.00
7 Mark McGwire 40.00 12.00
8 Tony Gwynn 20.00 6.00
9 Ken Griffey Jr. 25.00 7.50
10 Alex Rodriguez 25.00 7.50

2000 Pacific Crown Collection Timber 2000

Inserted at a rate of one in 73, these 20 horizontal cards feature some of the leading batters in the game.

Nm-Mt Ex-Mt
COMPLETE SET (20) 250.00 75.00
1 Chipper Jones 10.00 3.00
2 Nomar Garciaparra 15.00 4.50
3 Sammy Sosa 15.00 4.50
4 Magglio Ordonez 4.00 1.20

5 Manny Ramirez 4.00 1.20
6 Vinny Castilla 4.00 1.20
7 Juan Gonzalez 10.00 3.00
8 Jeff Bagwell 6.00 1.80
9 Shawn Green 4.00 1.20
10 Vladimir Guerrero 10.00 3.00
11 Mike Piazza 15.00 4.50
12 Derek Jeter 25.00 7.50
13 Bernie Williams 6.00 1.80
14 Mark McGwire 25.00 7.50
15 Ken Griffey Jr. 15.00 4.50
16 Alex Rodriguez 15.00 4.50
17 Jose Canseco 10.00 3.00
18 Rafael Palmeiro 6.00 1.80
19 Ivan Rodriguez 10.00 3.00
20 Carlos Delgado 4.00 1.20

1998 Pacific Invincible

The 1998 Pacific Invincible set was issued in one series totalling 150 cards and was distributed in five-card packs with an SRP of $2.99. The fronts feature a color action player photo as well as a head shot printed on an inlaid cel window with gold foil printing. The backs carry another player photo with a paragraph highlighting the player's career accomplishments.

Nm-Mt Ex-Mt
COMPLETE SET (150) 100.00 30.00
1 Garret Anderson 1.50 .45
2 Jim Edmonds 1.50 .45
3 Darin Erstad 1.50 .45
4 Chuck Finley 1.50 .45
5 Tim Salmon 2.50 .75
6 Roberto Alomar 4.00 1.20
7 Brady Anderson 1.50 .45
8 Geronimo Berroa 1.00 .30
9 Eric Davis 1.50 .45
10 Mike Mussina 4.00 1.20
11 Rafael Palmeiro 2.50 .75
12 Cal Ripken 12.00 3.60
13 Steve Avery 1.00 .30
14 Nomar Garciaparra 6.00 1.80
15 John Valentin 1.00 .30
16 Mo Vaughn 1.50 .45
17 Albert Belle 1.50 .45
18 Ozzie Guillen 1.00 .30
19 Norberto Martin 1.00 .30
20 Frank Thomas 4.00 1.20
21 Robin Ventura 1.50 .45
22 Sandy Alomar Jr. 1.50 .45
23 David Justice 1.50 .45
24 Kenny Lofton 1.50 .45
25 Manny Ramirez 1.50 .45
26 Jim Thome 4.00 1.20
27 Omar Vizquel 1.50 .45
28 Matt Williams 1.50 .45
29 Jaret Wright 1.00 .30
30 Raul Casanova 1.00 .30
31 Tony Clark 1.00 .30
32 Deivi Cruz 1.00 .30
33 Bobby Higginson 1.50 .45
34 Justin Thompson 1.00 .30
35 Yamil Benitez 1.00 .30
36 Johnny Damon 1.50 .45
37 Jermaine Dye 1.50 .45
38 Jed Hansen 1.00 .30
39 Larry Sutton 1.00 .30
40 Jeromy Burnitz 1.50 .45
41 Jeff Cirillo 1.00 .30
42 Dave Nilsson 1.00 .30
43 Jose Valentin 1.00 .30
44 Fernando Vina 1.50 .45
45 Marty Cordova 1.00 .30
46 Chuck Knoblauch 1.50 .45
47 Paul Molitor 2.50 .75
48 Brad Radke 1.50 .45
49 Terry Steinbach 1.00 .30
50 Wade Boggs 2.50 .75
51 Hideki Irabu 1.00 .30
52 Derek Jeter 10.00 3.00
53 Tino Martinez 2.50 .75
54 Andy Pettitte 2.50 .75
55 Mariano Rivera 2.50 .75
56 Bernie Williams 2.50 .75
57 Jose Canseco 4.00 1.20
58 Jason Giambi 4.00 1.20
59 Ben Grieve 1.00 .30
60 Aaron Small 1.00 .30
61 Jay Buhner 1.50 .45
62 Ken Cloude 1.00 .30
63 Joey Cora 1.00 .30
64 Ken Griffey Jr. 6.00 1.80
65 Randy Johnson 4.00 1.20
66 Edgar Martinez 2.50 .75
67 Alex Rodriguez 6.00 1.80
68 Will Clark 4.00 1.20
69 Juan Gonzalez 4.00 1.20
70 Rusty Greer 1.50 .45
71 Ivan Rodriguez 4.00 1.20
72 Joe Carter 1.50 .45
73 Roger Clemens 8.00 2.40
74 Jose Cruz Jr. 1.50 .45
75 Carlos Delgado 1.50 .45
76 Andruw Jones 1.50 .45
77 Chipper Jones 4.00 1.20
78 Ryan Klesko 1.50 .45
79 Javier Lopez 1.50 .45
80 Greg Maddux 6.00 1.80
81 Miguel Batista 1.00 .30
82 Jeremi Gonzalez 1.00 .30
83 Mark Grace 2.50 .75
84 Kevin Orie 1.00 .30
85 Sammy Sosa 6.00 1.80
86 Barry Larkin 4.00 1.20
87 Deion Sanders 2.50 .75
88 Reggie Sanders 1.50 .45
89 Chris Stynes 1.00 .30
90 Dante Bichette 1.50 .45
91 Vinny Castilla 1.50 .45
92 Andres Galarraga 1.50 .45
93 Neifi Perez 1.00 .30
94 Larry Walker 2.50 .75
95 Moises Alou 1.50 .45
96 Bobby Bonilla 1.50 .45
97 Kevin Brown 2.50 .75
98 Craig Counsell 1.00 .30
99 Livan Hernandez 1.00 .30
100 Edgar Renteria 1.50 .45
101 Gary Sheffield 1.50 .45
102 Jeff Bagwell 2.50 .75
103 Craig Biggio 2.50 .75
104 Luis Gonzalez 1.50 .45
105 Darryl Kile 1.50 .45
106 Wilton Guerrero 1.00 .30
107 Eric Karros 1.50 .45
108 Ramon Martinez 1.00 .30
109 Raul Mondesi 1.50 .45
110 Hideo Nomo 4.00 1.20
111 Chan Ho Park 1.50 .45
112 Mike Piazza 6.00 1.80
113 Mark Grudzielanek 1.00 .30
114 Vladimir Guerrero 4.00 1.20
115 Pedro Martinez 4.00 1.20
116 Henry Rodriguez 1.00 .30
117 David Segui 1.00 .30
118 Edgardo Alfonzo 1.50 .45
119 Carlos Baerga 1.00 .30
120 John Franco 1.50 .45
121 John Olerud 1.50 .45
122 Rey Ordonez 1.00 .30
123 Ricky Bottalico 1.00 .30
124 Gregg Jefferies 1.00 .30
125 Mickey Morandini 1.00 .30
126 Scott Rolen 2.50 .75
127 Curt Schilling 2.50 .75
128 Jose Guillen 1.50 .45
129 Esteban Loaiza 1.50 .45
130 Al Martin 1.00 .30
131 Tony Womack 1.00 .30
132 Dennis Eckersley 1.50 .45
133 Gary Gaetti 1.50 .45
134 Curtis King 1.00 .30
135 Ray Lankford 1.00 .30
136 Mark McGwire 10.00 3.00
137 Ken Caminiti 1.50 .45
138 Steve Finley 1.50 .45
139 Tony Gwynn 5.00 1.50
140 Carlos Hernandez 1.00 .30
141 Wally Joyner 1.50 .45
142 Barry Bonds 10.00 3.00
143 Jacob Cruz 1.00 .30
144 Shawn Estes 1.00 .30
145 Stan Javier 1.00 .30
146 J.T. Snow 1.50 .45
147 N.Garciaparra ROY 4.00 1.20
148 Scott Rolen ROY 1.50 .45
149 Ken Griffey Jr. MVP 4.00 1.20
150 Larry Walker MVP 1.50 .45

1998 Pacific Invincible Platinum Blue

Randomly inserted in packs at the rate of one in 73, this 150-card set is parallel to the base set with platinum blue foil highlighting.

Nm-Mt Ex-Mt
*STARS: 2X TO 5X BASIC CARDS

1998 Pacific Invincible Silver

Randomly seeded into hobby and retail packs at a rate of 2:37, cards from this 150-card set are parallel to the base set. Silver foil highlighting differentiates them.

Nm-Mt Ex-Mt
*STARS: 1X TO 2.5X BASIC CARDS

1998 Pacific Invincible Cramer's Choice Green

Randomly inserted in packs, this 10-card set features color photos of great players as selected by Michael Cramer printed with green foil highlights. Only 99 serial numbered sets were produced. Each card is die cut into an attractive pyramid shape and features green foil sparkling backgrounds.

Nm-Mt Ex-Mt
COMP.GREEN SET (10) 400.00 120.00
*DARK BLUE: .5X TO 1.2X GREEN
*LIGHT BLUE: .6X TO 1.5X GREEN
*RED: 1X TO 2.5X GREEN
*GOLD: X TO X GREEN
RANDOM INSERTS IN PACKS
GREEN PRINT RUN 99 SERIAL #'d SETS
DARK BLUE PRINT RUN 80 SERIAL #'d SETS
LIGHT BLUE PRINT RUN 50 SERIAL #'d SETS
RED PRINT RUN 25 SERIAL #'d SETS
GOLD PRINT RUN 15 SERIAL #'d SETS
PURPLE PRINT RUN 10 SERIAL #'d SETS
GREEN CARDS LISTED BELOW!

1 Greg Maddux 50.00 15.00
2 Roberto Alomar 30.00 9.00
3 Cal Ripken 100.00 30.00
4 Nomar Garciaparra 50.00 15.00
5 Larry Walker 20.00 6.00
6 Mike Piazza 50.00 15.00
7 Mark McGwire 80.00 24.00
8 Tony Gwynn 40.00 12.00
9 Ken Griffey Jr. 50.00 15.00
10 Roger Clemens 60.00 18.00

1998 Pacific Invincible Gems of the Diamond

Inserted in packs at the rate of four per pack, this 220-card set features color action player photos with gold foil printing.

Nm-Mt Ex-Mt
COMPLETE SET (220) 50.00 15.00
1 Jim Edmonds .30 .09
2 Todd Greene .30 .09
3 Ken Hill .30 .09
4 Mike Holtz .30 .09
5 Mike James .30 .09
6 Chad Kreuter .30 .09
7 Tim Salmon .50 .15
8 Roberto Alomar .75 .23
9 Brady Anderson .30 .09
10 Dave Dellucci .30 .09
11 Jeffrey Hammonds .30 .09
12 Mike Mussina .75 .23
13 Rafael Palmeiro .50 .15
14 Arthur Rhodes .30 .09
15 Cal Ripken 2.50 .75
16 Nerio Rodriguez .30 .09
17 Tony Tarasco .30 .09
18 Lenny Webster .30 .09
19 Mike Benjamin .30 .09
20 Rich Garces .30 .09
21 Nomar Garciaparra 1.25 .35
22 Shane Mack .30 .09
23 Jose Malave .30 .09
24 Jesus Tavarez .30 .09
25 Mo Vaughn .30 .09
26 John Wasdin .30 .09
27 Jeff Abbott .30 .09
28 Albert Belle .30 .09
29 Mike Cameron .30 .09
30 Al Levine .30 .09
31 Robert Machado .30 .09
32 Greg Norton .30 .09
33 Magglio Ordonez 2.00 .60
34 Mike Sirotka .30 .09
35 Frank Thomas .75 .23
36 Mario Valdez .30 .09
37 Sandy Alomar Jr. .30 .09
38 David Justice .30 .09
39 Jack McDowell .30 .09
40 Eric Plunk .30 .09
41 Manny Ramirez .30 .09
42 Kevin Seitzer .30 .09
43 Paul Shuey .30 .09
44 Omar Vizquel .30 .09
45 Kimera Bartee .30 .09
46 Glenn Dishman .30 .09
47 Orlando Miller .30 .09
48 Mike Myers .30 .09
49 Phil Nevin .30 .09
50 A.J. Sager .30 .09
51 Ricky Bones .30 .09
52 Scott Cooper .30 .09
53 Shane Halter .30 .09
54 David Howard .30 .09
55 Glendon Rusch .30 .09
56 Joe Vitiello .30 .09
57 Jeff D'Amico .30 .09
58 Mike Fetters .30 .09
59 Mike Matheny .30 .09
60 Jose Mercedes .30 .09
61 Ron Villone .30 .09
62 Jack Voigt .30 .09
63 Brent Brede .30 .09
64 Chuck Knoblauch .30 .09
65 Paul Molitor .50 .15
66 Todd Ritchie .30 .09
67 Frankie Rodriguez .30 .09
68 Scott Stahoviak .30 .09
69 Greg Swindell .30 .09
70 Todd Walker .30 .09
71 Wade Boggs .50 .15
72 Hideki Irabu .30 .09
73 Derek Jeter 2.00 .60
74 Pat Kelly .30 .09
75 Graeme Lloyd .30 .09
76 Tino Martinez .50 .15
77 Jeff Nelson .30 .09
78 Scott Pose .30 .09
79 Mike Stanton .30 .09
80 Darryl Strawberry .50 .15
81 Bernie Williams .50 .15
82 Tony Batista .30 .09
83 Mark Bellhorn .30 .09
84 Ben Grieve .30 .09
85 Pat Lennon .30 .09
86 Brian Lesher .30 .09
87 Miguel Tejada .50 .15
88 George Williams .30 .09
89 Joey Cora .30 .09
90 Rob Ducey .30 .09
91 Ken Griffey Jr. 1.25 .35
92 Randy Johnson .75 .23
93 Edgar Martinez .50 .15
94 John Marzano .30 .09
95 Greg McCarthy .30 .09
96 Alex Rodriguez 1.25 .35
97 Andy Sheets .30 .09
98 Mike Timlin .30 .09
99 Lee Tinsley .30 .09
100 Damon Buford .30 .09
101 Alex Diaz .30 .09
102 Benji Gil .30 .09
103 Juan Gonzalez .75 .23
104 Eric Gunderson .30 .09
105 Danny Patterson .30 .09
106 Ivan Rodriguez .75 .23
107 Mike Simms .30 .09
108 Luis Andujar .30 .09
109 Joe Carter .30 .09
110 Roger Clemens 1.50 .45
111 Jose Cruz Jr. .30 .09
112 Shawn Green .30 .09
113 Robert Perez .30 .09
114 Juan Samuel .30 .09
115 Ed Sprague .30 .09
116 Shannon Stewart .30 .09
117 Danny Bautista .30 .09
118 Chipper Jones .75 .23
119 Ryan Klesko .30 .09
120 Keith Lockhart .30 .09
121 Javier Lopez .30 .09
122 Greg Maddux 1.25 .35
123 Kevin Millwood 1.50 .45
124 Mike Mordecai .30 .09
125 Eddie Perez .30 .09
126 Randall Simon .30 .09
127 Miguel Cairo .30 .09
128 Dave Clark .30 .09
129 Kevin Foster .30 .09
130 Mark Grace .50 .15
131 Tyler Houston .30 .09
132 Mike Hubbard .30 .09
133 Kevin Orie .30 .09
134 Ryne Sandberg 1.25 .35
135 Sammy Sosa 1.25 .35
136 Lenny Harris .30 .09
137 Kent Mercker .30 .09
138 Mike Morgan .30 .09
139 Deion Sanders .50 .15
140 Chris Stynes .30 .09
141 Gabe White .30 .09
142 Jason Bates .30 .09
143 Vinny Castilla .30 .09
144 Andres Galarraga .30 .09
145 Curtis Leskanic .30 .09
146 Jeff McCurry .30 .09
147 Mike Munoz .30 .09
148 Larry Walker .50 .15
149 Jamey Wright .30 .09
150 Moises Alou .30 .09
151 Bobby Bonilla .30 .09
152 Kevin Brown .50 .15
153 John Cangelosi .30 .09
154 Jeff Conine .30 .09
155 Cliff Floyd .30 .09
156 Jay Powell .30 .09
157 Edgar Renteria .30 .09
158 Tony Saunders .30 .09
159 Gary Sheffield .30 .09
160 Jeff Bagwell .50 .15
161 Tim Bogar .30 .09
162 Tony Eusebio .30 .09
163 Chris Holt .30 .09
164 Ray Montgomery .30 .09
165 Luis Rivera .30 .09
166 Eric Anthony .30 .09
167 Brett Butler .30 .09
168 Juan Castro .30 .09
169 Tripp Cromer .30 .09
170 Raul Mondesi .30 .09
171 Hideo Nomo .75 .23
172 Mike Piazza 1.25 .35
173 Tom Prince .30 .09
174 Adam Riggs .30 .09
175 Shane Andrews .30 .09
176 Shayne Bennett .30 .09
177 Raul Chavez .30 .09
178 Pedro Martinez .75 .23
179 Sherman Obando .30 .09
180 Andy Stankiewicz .30 .09
181 Alberto Castillo .30 .09
182 Shawn Gilbert .30 .09
183 Luis Lopez .30 .09
184 Roberto Petagine .30 .09
185 Armando Reynoso .30 .09
186 Midre Cummings .30 .09
187 Kevin Jordan .30 .09
188 Desi Relaford .30 .09
189 Scott Rolen .50 .15
190 Ken Ryan .30 .09
191 Kevin Sefcik .30 .09
192 Emil Brown .30 .09
193 Lou Collier .30 .09
194 Francisco Cordova .30 .09
195 Kevin Elster .30 .09
196 Mark Smith .30 .09
197 Marc Wilkins .30 .09
198 Manny Aybar .30 .09
199 Jose Bautista .30 .09
200 David Bell .30 .09
201 Rigo Beltran .30 .09
202 Delino DeShields .50 .15
203 Dennis Eckersley .30 .09
204 John Mabry .30 .09
205 Eli Marrero .30 .09
206 Willie McGee .30 .09
207 Mark McGwire 2.00 .60
208 Ken Caminiti .30 .09
209 Tony Gwynn 1.00 .30
210 Chris Jones .30 .09
211 Craig Shipley .30 .09
212 Pete Smith .30 .09
213 Jorge Velandia .30 .09
214 Dario Veras .30 .09
215 Rich Aurilia .30 .09
216 Damon Berryhill .30 .09
217 Barry Bonds 2.00 .60
218 Osvaldo Fernandez .30 .09
219 Dante Powell .30 .09
220 Rich Rodriguez .30 .09

1998 Pacific Invincible Interleague Players

Randomly inserted one in every 73 packs, this 30-card set features color player photos which when placed side by side form the MLB Interleague log in the center. Each card is bordered with white leather-like material.

Nm-Mt Ex-Mt
COMPLETE SET (30) 400.00 120.00
1A Roberto Alomar 15.00 4.50
1N Craig Biggio 10.00 3.00
2A Cal Ripken 50.00 15.00
2N Chipper Jones 15.00 4.50
3A Nomar Garciaparra 25.00 7.50
3N Scott Rolen 10.00 3.00
4A Mo Vaughn 6.00 1.80
4N Andres Galarraga 6.00 1.80
5A Frank Thomas 15.00 4.50
5N Tony Gwynn 20.00 6.00
6A Albert Belle 6.00 1.80
6N Barry Bonds 40.00 12.00
7A Hideki Irabu 4.00 1.20
7N Hideo Nomo 15.00 4.50
8A Derek Jeter 40.00 12.00
8N Rey Ordonez 4.00 1.20
9A Tino Martinez 10.00 3.00
9N Mark McGwire 40.00 12.00
10A Alex Rodriguez 25.00 7.50
10N Edgar Renteria 6.00 1.80
11A Ken Griffey Jr. 25.00 7.50
11N Larry Walker 10.00 3.00
12A Randy Johnson 15.00 4.50
12N Greg Maddux 25.00 7.50
13A Ivan Rodriguez 15.00 4.50
13N Mike Piazza 25.00 7.50
14A Roger Clemens 30.00 9.00
14N Pedro Martinez 15.00 4.50
15A Jose Cruz Jr. 6.00 1.80
15N Wilton Guerrero 4.00 1.20

1998 Pacific Invincible Moments in Time

Randomly inserted in packs at the rate of one in 145, this 20-card set features color player photos with full foil coverage printed on a scoreboard screen with laser-cut stadium scoreboard features defining categories for a specific game in the player's career.

Nm-Mt Ex-Mt
COMPLETE SET (20) 300.00 90.00
1 Chipper Jones 20.00 6.00
2 Cal Ripken 60.00 18.00
3 Frank Thomas 20.00 6.00
4 David Justice 8.00 2.40
5 Andres Galarraga 8.00 2.40
6 Larry Walker 12.00 3.60
7 Livan Hernandez 5.00 1.50
8 Wilton Guerrero 5.00 1.50
9 Hideo Nomo 20.00 6.00
10 Mike Piazza 30.00 9.00
11 Pedro Martinez 20.00 6.00
12 Bernie Williams 12.00 3.60
13 Ben Grieve 5.00 1.50
14 Scott Rolen 12.00 3.60
15 Mark McGwire 50.00 15.00
16 Tony Gwynn 25.00 7.50
17 Ken Griffey Jr. 30.00 9.00
18 Alex Rodriguez 30.00 9.00
19 Juan Gonzalez 20.00 6.00
20 Jose Cruz Jr. 8.00 2.40

1998 Pacific Invincible Photoengravings

Randomly inserted in packs at the rate of one in 37, this 18-card set features filtered photos with clear facial player shots with unique old-style design elements artwork.

Nm-Mt Ex-Mt
COMPLETE SET (18) 100.00 30.00
1 Greg Maddux 10.00 3.00
2 Cal Ripken 20.00 6.00
3 Nomar Garciaparra 10.00 3.00
4 Frank Thomas 6.00 1.80
5 Larry Walker 4.00 1.20
6 Mike Piazza 10.00 3.00
7 Hideo Nomo 6.00 1.80
8 Pedro Martinez 6.00 1.80
9 Derek Jeter 15.00 4.50
10 Tino Martinez 4.00 1.20
11 Mark McGwire 15.00 4.50
12 Tony Gwynn 8.00 2.40
13 Barry Bonds 15.00 4.50
14 Ken Griffey Jr. 10.00 3.00
15 Alex Rodriguez 10.00 3.00
16 Ivan Rodriguez 6.00 1.80
17 Roger Clemens 12.00 3.60
18 Jose Cruz Jr. 2.50 .75

1998 Pacific Invincible Team Checklists

Randomly inserted two in 37 packs, this 30-card set features a collage of action player images printed with full foil coverage with an etching pattern and the team logo in the background. The backs carry player checklists for the entire 1998 Pacific Prisms Invincible product.

	Nm-Mt	Ex-Mt
COMPLETE SET (30)	120.00	36.00
1 Jim Edmonds	6.00	1.80
Tim Salmon		
Darin Erstad		
Garret Anderson		
Rickey Henderson		
2 Greg Maddux	8.00	2.40
Chipper Jones		
Javier Lopez		
Ryan Klesko		
Andruw Jones		
3 Cal Ripken	20.00	6.00
Roberto Alomar		
Brady Anderson		
Mike Mussina		
Rafael Palmeiro		
4 Nomar Garciaparra	10.00	3.00
Mo Vaughn		
Steve Avery		
John Valentin		
5 Sammy Sosa	10.00	3.00
Mark Grace		
Ryne Sandberg		
Jeremi Gonzalez		
6 Frank Thomas	6.00	1.80
Albert Belle		
Robin Ventura		
Ozzie Guillen		
7 Barry Larkin	6.00	1.80
Deion Sanders		
Reggie Sanders		
Brett Tomko		
8 Sandy Alomar	6.00	1.80
Manny Ramirez		
David Justice		
Jim Thome		
Omar Vizquel		
9 Andres Galarraga	4.00	1.20
Larry Walker		
Vinny Castilla		
Dante Bichette		
Ellis Burks		
10 Justin Thompson	2.50	.75
Tony Clark		
Deivi Cruz		
Bobby Higginson		
11 Gary Sheffield	2.50	.75
Edgar Renteria		
Livan Hernandez		
Charles Johnson		
Bobby Bonilla		
12 Jeff Bagwell	4.00	1.20
Craig Biggio		
Richard Hidalgo		
Darryl Kile		
13 Johnny Damon	2.50	.75
Jermaine Dye		
Chili Davis		
Jose Rosado		
14 Mike Piazza	10.00	3.00
Wilton Guerrero		
Raul Mondesi		
Hideo Nomo		
Ramon Martinez		
15 Dave Nilsson	2.50	.75
Fernando Vina		
Jeromy Burnitz		
Julio Franco		
Jeff Cirillo		
16 Paul Molitor	4.00	1.20
Chuck Knoblauch		
Brad Radke		
Terry Steinbach		
Marty Cordova		
17 Henry Rodriguez	6.00	1.80
Vladimir Guerrero		
Pedro Martinez		
David Segui		
Mark Grudzielanek		
18 Carlos Baerga	2.50	.75
Todd Hundley		
Rey Ordonez		
John Olerud		
Edgardo Alfonzo		
19 Derek Jeter	15.00	4.50
Tino Martinez		
Bernie Williams		
Andy Pettitte		
Mariano Rivera		
20 Jose Canseco	6.00	1.80
Ben Grieve		
Jason Giambi		
Matt Stairs		
21 Curt Schilling	4.00	1.20
Scott Rolen		
Gregg Jefferies		
Len Dykstra		
Ricky Bottalico		
22 Al Martin	2.50	.75
Tony Womack		
Jose Guillen		
Esteban Loaiza		
23 Mark McGwire	15.00	4.50
Dennis Eckersley		
Delino DeShields		
Willie McGee		
Ray Lankford		
24 Tony Gwynn	8.00	2.40
Ken Caminiti		
Wally Joyner		
Steve Finley		
25 Barry Bonds	15.00	4.50
J.T. Snow		
Stan Javier		
Rod Beck		
Jose Vizcaino		
26 Ken Griffey Jr.	10.00	3.00
Alex Rodriguez		
Edgar Martinez		
Randy Johnson		
Jay Buhner		
27 Juan Gonzalez	6.00	1.80
Ivan Rodriguez		
Will Clark		
John Wetteland		
Rusty Greer		
28 Jose Cruz Jr.	12.00	3.60
Roger Clemens		
Pat Hentgen		
Joe Carter		
29 Yamil Benitez	2.50	.75
Devon White		
Matt Williams		
Jay Bell		
30 ade Boggs	4.00	1.20
Paul Sorrento		
Fred McGriff		
Roberto Hernandez		

1999 Pacific Invincible

The 1999 Pacific Invincible set was issued in one series totalling 150 cards and was distributed in three-card packs with an SRP of $2.99. The fronts feature a color action player photo as well as a head shot printed on an inlaid cel window with gold foil printing. The backs carry information about the player.

	Nm-Mt	Ex-Mt
COMPLETE SET (150)	180.00	55.00
1 Jim Edmonds	1.25	.35
2 Darin Erstad	1.25	.35
3 Troy Glaus	2.00	.60
4 Tim Salmon	2.00	.60
5 Mo Vaughn	1.25	.35
6 Steve Finley	1.25	.35
7 Randy Johnson	3.00	.90
8 Travis Lee	.75	.23
9 Dante Powell	.75	.23
10 Matt Williams	1.25	.35
11 Bret Boone	1.25	.35
12 Andruw Jones	1.25	.35
13 Chipper Jones	3.00	.90
14 Brian Jordan	1.25	.35
15 Ryan Klesko	1.25	.35
16 Javy Lopez	1.25	.35
17 Greg Maddux	5.00	1.50
18 Brady Anderson	1.25	.35
19 Albert Belle	1.25	.35
20 Will Clark	3.00	.90
21 Mike Mussina	3.00	.90
22 Cal Ripken	10.00	3.00
23 Nomar Garciaparra	5.00	1.50
24 Pedro Martinez	3.00	.90
25 Trot Nixon	2.00	.60
26 Jose Offerman	.75	.23
27 Donnie Sadler	.75	.23
28 John Valentin	.75	.23
29 Mark Grace	2.00	.60
30 Lance Johnson	.75	.23
31 Henry Rodriguez	.75	.23
32 Sammy Sosa	5.00	1.50
33 Kerry Wood	3.00	.90
34 McKay Christensen	.75	.23
35 Ray Durham	1.25	.35
36 Jeff Liefer	.75	.23
37 Frank Thomas	3.00	.90
38 Mike Cameron	1.25	.35
39 Barry Larkin	3.00	.90
40 Greg Vaughn	1.25	.35
41 Dmitri Young	1.25	.35
42 Roberto Alomar	3.00	.90
43 Sandy Alomar Jr.	.75	.23
44 David Justice	1.25	.35
45 Kenny Lofton	1.25	.35
46 Manny Ramirez	1.25	.35
47 Jim Thome	3.00	.90
48 Dante Bichette	1.25	.35
49 Vinny Castilla	1.25	.35
50 Darryl Hamilton	.75	.23
51 Todd Helton	2.00	.60
52 Neifi Perez	.75	.23
53 Larry Walker	2.00	.60
54 Tony Clark	.75	.23
55 Damion Easley	.75	.23
56 Bob Higginson	1.25	.35
57 Brian L.Hunter	.75	.23
58 Gabe Kapler	.75	.23
59 Cliff Floyd	1.25	.35
60 Alex Gonzalez	.75	.23
61 Mark Kotsay	.75	.23
62 Derrek Lee	1.25	.35
63 Braden Looper	.75	.23
64 Moises Alou	1.25	.35
65 Jeff Bagwell	2.00	.60
66 Craig Biggio	2.00	.60
67 Ken Caminiti	1.25	.35
68 Scott Elarton	.75	.23
69 Mitch Meluskey	.75	.23
70 Carlos Beltran	1.25	.35
71 Johnny Damon	1.25	.35
72 Carlos Febles	.75	.23
73 Jeremy Giambi	.75	.23
74 Kevin Brown	2.00	.60
75 Todd Hundley	.75	.23
76 Paul LoDuca	1.25	.35
77 Raul Mondesi	1.25	.35
78 Gary Sheffield	1.25	.35
79 Geoff Jenkins	1.25	.35
80 Jeromy Burnitz	1.25	.35
81 Marquis Grissom	.75	.23
82 Jose Valentin	.75	.23
83 Fernando Vina	1.25	.35
84 Corey Koskie	1.25	.35
85 Matt Lawton	.75	.23
86 Christian Guzman	1.25	.35
87 Torii Hunter	1.25	.35
88 Doug Mientkiewicz RC	2.50	.75
89 Michael Barrett	.75	.23
90 Brad Fullmer	.75	.23
91 Vladimir Guerrero	3.00	.90
92 Fernando Seguignol	.75	.23
93 Ugueth Urbina	.75	.23
94 Bobby Bonilla	1.25	.35
95 Rickey Henderson	3.00	.90
96 Rey Ordonez	.75	.23
97 Mike Piazza	5.00	1.50
98 Robin Ventura	1.25	.35
99 Roger Clemens	6.00	1.80
100 Derek Jeter	8.00	2.40
101 Chuck Knoblauch	1.25	.35
102 Tino Martinez	2.00	.60
103 Paul O'Neill	2.00	.60
104 Bernie Williams	2.00	.60
105 Eric Chavez	1.25	.35
106 Ryan Christenson	.75	.23
107 Jason Giambi	3.00	.90
108 Ben Grieve	.75	.23
109 Miguel Tejada	1.25	.35
110 Marlon Anderson	.75	.23
111 Doug Glanville	.75	.23
112 Scott Rolen	2.00	.60
113 Curt Schilling	2.00	.60
114 Brian Giles	1.25	.35
115 Warren Morris	.75	.23
116 Jason Kendall	1.25	.35
117 Kris Benson	.75	.23
118 J.D. Drew	1.25	.35
119 Ray Lankford	.75	.23
120 Mark McGwire	8.00	2.40
121 Matt Clement	1.25	.35
122 Tony Gwynn	4.00	1.20
123 Trevor Hoffman	1.25	.35
124 Wally Joyner	1.25	.35
125 Reggie Sanders	1.25	.35
126 Barry Bonds	8.00	2.40
127 Ellis Burks	1.25	.35
128 Jeff Kent	1.25	.35
129 Stan Javier	.75	.23
130 J.T. Snow	1.25	.35
131 Jay Buhner	1.25	.35
132 Freddy Garcia RC	3.00	.90
133 Ken Griffey Jr.	5.00	1.50
134 Russ Davis	.75	.23
135 Edgar Martinez	2.00	.60
136 Alex Rodriguez	5.00	1.50
137 David Segui	.75	.23
138 Rolando Arrojo	.75	.23
139 Wade Boggs	2.00	.60
140 Jose Canseco	3.00	.90
141 Quinton McCracken	.75	.23
142 Fred McGriff	2.00	.60
143 Juan Gonzalez	3.00	.90
144 Tom Goodwin	.75	.23
145 Rusty Greer	1.25	.35
146 Ivan Rodriguez	3.00	.90
147 Jose Cruz Jr.	1.25	.35
148 Carlos Delgado	1.25	.35
149 Shawn Green	1.25	.35
150 Roy Halladay	1.25	.35

1999 Pacific Invincible Opening Day

Randomly inserted in hobby packs only at the rate of one in 25 (basically one per box), this 150-card set is parallel to the Pacific Invincible base set. Only 69 serial-numbered sets were produced. Each card carries a large sunburst gold-foil "Opening Day" logo on the front with the serial numbering in the center.

	Nm-Mt	Ex-Mt
*STARS: 4X TO 10X BASIC CARDS		
*ROOKIES: 2.5X TO 6X BASIC CARDS		

1999 Pacific Invincible Platinum Blue

Randomly inserted into packs, this 150-card set is parallel to the base set with platinum blue foil highlighting. Only 67 serial-numbered sets were produced.

	Nm-Mt	Ex-Mt
*STARS: 4X TO 10X BASIC CARDS		
*ROOKIES: 2.5X TO 6X BASIC CARDS		

1999 Pacific Invincible Diamond Magic

Randomly inserted into packs at the rate of one in 49, this 10-card set features color action photos of top players with silver and gold foil highlights.

	Nm-Mt	Ex-Mt
COMPLETE SET (10)	120.00	36.00
1 Cal Ripken	25.00	7.50
2 Nomar Garciaparra	12.00	3.60
3 Sammy Sosa	12.00	3.60
4 Frank Thomas	8.00	2.40
5 Mike Piazza	12.00	3.60
6 J.D. Drew	3.00	.90
7 Mark McGwire	20.00	6.00
8 Tony Gwynn	10.00	3.00
9 Ken Griffey Jr.	12.00	3.60
10 Alex Rodriguez	12.00	3.60

1999 Pacific Invincible Flash Point

Randomly inserted into packs at the rate of one in 25, this 20-card set features color photos of top players with gold foil highlights.

	Nm-Mt	Ex-Mt
COMPLETE SET (20)	150.00	45.00
1 Mo Vaughn	2.50	.75
2 Chipper Jones	6.00	1.80
3 Greg Maddux	10.00	3.00
4 Cal Ripken	20.00	6.00
5 Nomar Garciaparra	10.00	3.00
6 Sammy Sosa	10.00	3.00
7 Frank Thomas	6.00	1.80
8 Manny Ramirez	2.50	.75
9 Vladimir Guerrero	6.00	1.80
10 Mike Piazza	10.00	3.00
11 Roger Clemens	12.00	3.60
12 Derek Jeter	15.00	4.50
13 Ben Grieve	1.50	.45
14 Scott Rolen	4.00	1.20
15 J.D. Drew	2.50	.75
16 Mark McGwire	15.00	4.50
17 Tony Gwynn	8.00	2.40
18 Ken Griffey Jr.	10.00	3.00
19 Alex Rodriguez	10.00	3.00
20 Juan Gonzalez	6.00	1.80

1999 Pacific Invincible Giants of the Game

These jumbo cards, which measure approximately 35" by 51" were available exclusively through obtaining one of the scarce exchange cards randomly seeded into packs. The lucky collector who pulled one of these exchange cards not only got the large card but his exchange card back. The jumbo cards features color cut-outs of top players silhouetted on a background of city buildings. Only 10 serial-numbered sets were produced. No pricing is available due to scarcity, but a checklist is provided.

	Nm-Mt	Ex-Mt
1 Cal Ripken		
2 Nomar Garciaparra		
3 Sammy Sosa		
4 Frank Thomas		
5 Mike Piazza		
6 J.D. Drew		
7 Mark McGwire		
8 Tony Gwynn		
9 Ken Griffey Jr.		
10 Alex Rodriguez		

1999 Pacific Invincible Sandlot Heroes

Inserted one per pack, this 40-card set features color photos of 20 top players. Each player has two versions of his card.

	Nm-Mt	Ex-Mt
COMPLETE SET (40)	30.00	9.00
1 Mo Vaughn	.25	.07
2 Chipper Jones	.60	.18
3 Greg Maddux	1.00	.30
4 Cal Ripken	2.00	.60
5 Nomar Garciaparra	1.00	.30
6 Sammy Sosa	1.00	.30
7 Frank Thomas	.60	.18
8 Manny Ramirez	.25	.07
9 Vladimir Guerrero	.60	.18
10 Mike Piazza	1.00	.30
11 Roger Clemens	1.25	.35
12 Derek Jeter	1.50	.45
13 Eric Chavez	.25	.07
14 Ben Grieve	.15	.04
15 J.D. Drew	.25	.07
16 Mark McGwire	1.50	.45
17 Tony Gwynn	.75	.23
18 Ken Griffey Jr.	1.00	.30
19 Alex Rodriguez	1.00	.30
20 Juan Gonzalez	.60	.18

1999 Pacific Invincible Sandlot Heroes SportsFest

Issued as a wrapper redemption during the Chicago SportsFest in August 1999, these cards parallel the regular Sandlot Heroes cards. These redemption cards have a large SportsFest logo on the front as well as being serial numbered "X" of 10 on the front. Due to market scarcity, no pricing is provided.

	Nm-Mt	Ex-Mt
1 Mo Vaughn		
1B Mo Vaughn		
2 Chipper Jones		
2B Chipper Jones		
3 Greg Maddux		
3B Greg Maddux		
4 Cal Ripken		
4B Cal Ripken		
5 Nomar Garciaparra		
5B Nomar Garciaparra		
6 Sammy Sosa		
6B Sammy Sosa		
7 Frank Thomas		
7B Frank Thomas		
8 Manny Ramirez		
8B Manny Ramirez		
9 Vladimir Guerrero		
9B Vladimir Guerrero		
10 Mike Piazza		
10B Mike Piazza		
11 Roger Clemens		
11B Roger Clemens		
12 Derek Jeter		
12B Derek Jeter		
13 Eric Chavez		
13B Eric Chavez		
14 Ben Grieve		
14B Ben Grieve		
15 J.D. Drew		
15B J.D. Drew		
16 Mark McGwire		
16B Mark McGwire		
17 Tony Gwynn		
17B Tony Gwynn		
18 Ken Griffey Jr.		
18B Ken Griffey Jr.		
19 Alex Rodriguez		
19B Alex Rodriguez		
20 Juan Gonzalez		
20B Juan Gonzalez		

1999 Pacific Invincible Seismic Force

Inserted one per pack, this 40-card set features color portraits of 20 top players. Each player has two versions of his card.

	Nm-Mt	Ex-Mt
COMPLETE SET (40)	40.00	12.00
1 Mo Vaughn	.25	.07
2 Chipper Jones	.60	.18
3 Greg Maddux	1.00	.30
4 Cal Ripken	2.00	.60
5 Nomar Garciaparra	1.00	.30
6 Sammy Sosa	1.00	.30
7 Frank Thomas	.60	.18
8 Manny Ramirez	.25	.07
9 Vladimir Guerrero	.60	.18
10 Mike Piazza	1.00	.30
11 Bernie Williams	.40	.12
12 Derek Jeter	1.50	.45
13 Ben Grieve	.15	.04
14 J.D. Drew	.25	.07
15 Mark McGwire	1.50	.45
16 Tony Gwynn	.75	.23
17 Ken Griffey Jr.	1.00	.30
18 Alex Rodriguez	1.00	.30
19 Juan Gonzalez	.60	.18
20 Ivan Rodriguez	.60	.18

1999 Pacific Invincible Seismic Force SportsFest

This parallel to the Seismic Force set was issued by Pacific at the Philadelphia SportsFest Show in June, 1999 as a box redemption. For dealers and collectors who opened a box of Pacific product at the show, they received one of these cards serial numbered to 20, and the cards have the words "Pacific Trading Cards, SportsFest 1999, Philadelphia June 1999" embossed on them as well. Due to market scarcity, no pricing is provided.

	Nm-Mt	Ex-Mt
1 Mo Vaughn		
2 Chipper Jones		
3 Greg Maddux		
4 Cal Ripken		
5 Nomar Garciaparra		
6 Sammy Sosa		
7 Frank Thomas		
8 Manny Ramirez		
9 Vladimir Guerrero		
10 Mike Piazza		
11 Bernie Williams		
12 Derek Jeter		
13 Ben Grieve		
14 J.D. Drew		
15 Mark McGwire		
16 Tony Gwynn		
17 Ken Griffey Jr.		
18 Alex Rodriguez		
19 Juan Gonzalez		
20 Ivan Rodriguez		

1999 Pacific Invincible Thunder Alley

Randomly inserted in packs at the rate of one in 121, this 20-card set features color images of powerful top players silhouetted on a background of the player's team logo.

	Nm-Mt	Ex-Mt
1 Mo Vaughn	6.00	1.80
2 Chipper Jones	15.00	4.50
3 Cal Ripken	50.00	15.00
4 Nomar Garciaparra	25.00	7.50
5 Sammy Sosa	25.00	7.50
6 Frank Thomas	15.00	4.50
7 Manny Ramirez	6.00	1.80
8 Todd Helton	10.00	3.00
9 Vladimir Guerrero	15.00	4.50
10 Mike Piazza	25.00	7.50
11 Derek Jeter	40.00	12.00
12 Ben Grieve	4.00	1.20
13 Scott Rolen	10.00	3.00
14 J.D. Drew	6.00	1.80
15 Mark McGwire	40.00	12.00
16 Tony Gwynn	20.00	6.00
17 Ken Griffey Jr.	25.00	7.50
18 Alex Rodriguez	25.00	7.50
19 Juan Gonzalez	15.00	4.50
20 Ivan Rodriguez	15.00	4.50

1999 Pacific Invincible Players Choice

These cards, which parallel the regular Pacific Invincible cards were issued by Pacific to be given away at the Players Choice award ceremony. The cards have a "Players Choice" stamp on them and are skip numbered to match their number. These cards were produced in varying quantites so we have put the print run next to the players name

	Nm-Mt	Ex-Mt
7 Randy Johnson/131	15.00	4.50
10 Matt Williams/130	6.00	1.80
13 Chipper Jones/118	20.00	6.00
17 Greg Maddux/133	25.00	7.50
22 Cal Ripken Jr./137	40.00	12.00
24 Pedro Martinez/130	12.00	3.60
32 Sammy Sosa/124	20.00	6.00
42 Roberto Alomar/118	10.00	3.00
65 Jeff Bagwell/118	12.00	3.60
70 Carlos Beltran/142	6.00	1.80
115 Warren Morris/133	5.00	1.50
126 Barry Bonds/137	20.00	6.00
132 Freddy Garcia/100	5.00	1.50
133 Ken Griffey Jr./113	25.00	7.50

2000 Pacific Invincible

The 2000 Pacific Invincible product was originally intended for release in August, 2000 but was delayed to mid-October in an effort to incorporate game-used equipment insert cards into the product. The base set features 150 veteran and prospect cards. Each pack contained three cards and carried a suggested retail price of $2.99. Notable Rookie Cards include Kazuhiro Sasaki.

	Nm-Mt	Ex-Mt
COMPLETE SET (150)	100.00	30.00
1 Darin Erstad	1.25	.35
2 Troy Glaus	2.00	.60
3 Ramon Ortiz	.75	.23
4 Tim Salmon	2.00	.60
5 Mo Vaughn	1.25	.35
6 Erubiel Durazo	.75	.23
7 Luis Gonzalez	1.25	.35
8 Randy Johnson	3.00	.90
9 Matt Williams	.75	.23
10 Rafael Furcal	1.25	.35
11 Andres Galarraga	1.25	.35
12 Tom Glavine	2.00	.60
13 Andruw Jones	1.25	.35
14 Chipper Jones	3.00	.90
15 Greg Maddux	5.00	1.50
16 Kevin Millwood	1.25	.35
17 Albert Belle	1.25	.35
18 Will Clark	3.00	.90
19 Mike Mussina	3.00	.90
20 Matt Riley	.75	.23
21 Cal Ripken	10.00	3.00
22 Carl Everett	1.25	.35
23 Nomar Garciaparra	5.00	1.50
24 Steve Lomasney	.75	.23
25 Pedro Martinez	3.00	.90
26 Tomo Ohka RC	1.25	.35
27 Wilton Veras	.75	.23
28 Mark Grace	2.00	.60
29 Sammy Sosa	5.00	1.50
30 Kerry Wood	3.00	.90
31 Eric Young	.75	.23
32 Julio Zuleta RC	1.25	.35
33 Paul Konerko	1.25	.35
34 Carlos Lee	1.25	.35
35 Magglio Ordonez	1.25	.35
36 Josh Paul	.75	.23
37 Frank Thomas	3.00	.90
38 Rob Bell	.75	.23
39 Dante Bichette	1.25	.35
40 Sean Casey	1.25	.35
41 Ken Griffey Jr.	5.00	1.50
42 Barry Larkin	3.00	.90
43 Pokey Reese	.75	.23
44 Roberto Alomar	3.00	.90
45 Manny Ramirez	1.25	.35
46 Richie Sexson	1.25	.35
47 Jim Thome	3.00	.90
48 Omar Vizquel	1.25	.35
49 Jeff Cirillo	.75	.23
50 Todd Helton	2.00	.60
51 Neifi Perez	.75	.23
52 Larry Walker	2.00	.60
53 Tony Clark	.75	.23
54 Juan Encarnacion	.75	.23
55 Juan Gonzalez	3.00	.90
56 Hideo Nomo	3.00	.90
57 Luis Castillo	1.25	.35
58 Alex Gonzalez	.75	.23
59 Brad Penny	.75	.23
60 Preston Wilson	1.25	.35
61 Moises Alou	1.25	.35
62 Jeff Bagwell	2.00	.60
63 Lance Berkman	1.25	.35
64 Craig Biggio	2.00	.60
65 Roger Cedeno	.75	.23
66 Jose Lima	.75	.23
67 Carlos Beltran	1.25	.35
68 Johnny Damon	1.25	.35
69 Chad Durbin RC	.75	.23
70 Jermaine Dye	1.25	.35
71 Carlos Febles	.75	.23
72 Mark Quinn	.75	.23
73 Kevin Brown	1.25	.35
74 Eric Gagne	3.00	.90
75 Shawn Green	1.25	.35
76 Eric Karros	1.25	.35
77 Gary Sheffield	1.25	.35
78 Kevin Barker	.75	.23
79 Ron Belliard	.75	.23
80 Jeromy Burnitz	1.25	.35
81 Geoff Jenkins	1.25	.35
82 Jacque Jones	1.25	.35
83 Corey Koskie	1.25	.35
84 Matt LeCroy	.75	.23
85 David Ortiz	1.25	.35
86 Johan Santana RC	5.00	1.50
87 Todd Walker	1.25	.35
88 Peter Bergeron	.75	.23
89 Vladimir Guerrero	3.00	.90
90 Jose Vidro	1.25	.35
91 Rondell White	1.25	.35
92 Edgardo Alfonzo	1.25	.35
93 Derek Bell	.75	.23
94 Mike Hampton	1.25	.35
95 Rey Ordonez	.75	.23
96 Mike Piazza	5.00	1.50
97 Robin Ventura	1.25	.35
98 Roger Clemens	6.00	1.80
99 Orlando Hernandez	1.25	.35
100 Derek Jeter	8.00	2.40
101 Alfonso Soriano	3.00	.90
102 Bernie Williams	2.00	.60
103 Eric Chavez	1.25	.35
104 Jason Giambi	3.00	.90
105 Ben Grieve	.75	.23
106 Tim Hudson	2.00	.60
107 Miguel Tejada	1.25	.35
108 Bob Abreu	1.25	.35
109 Doug Glanville	.75	.23
110 Mike Lieberthal	1.25	.35
111 Scott Rolen	2.00	.60
112 Brian Giles	1.25	.35
113 Chad Hermansen	.75	.23
114 Jason Kendall	1.25	.35
115 Warren Morris	.75	.23
116 Aramis Ramirez	1.25	.35
117 Rick Ankiel	.75	.23
118 J.D. Drew	1.25	.35
119 Mark McGwire	8.00	2.40
120 Fernando Tatis	.75	.23
121 Fernando Vina	1.25	.35
122 Bret Boone	1.25	.35
123 Ben Davis	.75	.23
124 Tony Gwynn	4.00	1.20
125 Trevor Hoffman	1.25	.35
126 Ryan Klesko	1.25	.35
127 Rich Aurilia	1.25	.35
128 Barry Bonds	8.00	2.40
129 Ellis Burks	1.25	.35
130 Jeff Kent	1.25	.35
131 Freddy Garcia	1.25	.35
132 Carlos Guillen	.75	.23
133 Edgar Martinez	2.00	.60
134 John Olerud	1.25	.35
135 Rob Ramsay	.75	.23
136 Alex Rodriguez	5.00	1.50
137 Kazuhiro Sasaki RC	4.00	1.20
138 Jose Canseco	3.00	.90
139 Vinny Castilla	1.25	.35
140 Fred McGriff	2.00	.60
141 Greg Vaughn UER Mo Vaughn is pictured	1.25	.35
142 Dan Wheeler	.75	.23
143 Gabe Kapler	.75	.23
144 Ruben Mateo	.75	.23
145 Rafael Palmeiro	2.00	.60
146 Ivan Rodriguez	3.00	.90
147 Tony Batista	1.25	.35
148 Carlos Delgado	1.25	.35
149 Raul Mondesi	1.25	.35
150 Vernon Wells	1.25	.35

2000 Pacific Invincible Holographic Purple

Randomly inserted into packs, this 150-card set is a complete parallel of the Pacific Invincible base set. Each card in the set feature purple foil and are individually serial numbered to 299.

Nm-Mt Ex-Mt

*STARS: 1X TO 2.5X BASIC CARDS ...
*ROOKIES: 1.25X TO 3X BASIC CARDS

2000 Pacific Invincible Platinum Blue

Randomly inserted into packs, this 150-card set is a complete parallel of the Pacific Invincible base set. Each card in the set feature blue foil, and are individually serial numbered to 67.

Nm-Mt Ex-Mt

*STARS: 3X TO 8X BASIC CARDS ......
*ROOKIES: 4X TO 10X BASIC CARDS

2000 Pacific Invincible Diamond Aces

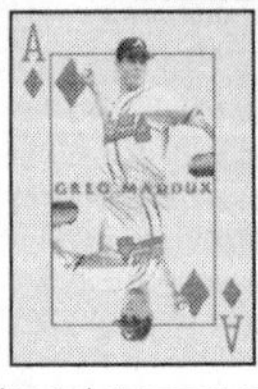

Inserted at one per pack, this 20-card insert features some of the best pitchers in the major leagues.

	Nm-Mt	Ex-Mt
COMPLETE SET (20)	10.00	3.00
*ACES 399: 3X TO 8X BASIC ACES		
ACES 399 RANDOM INSERTS IN PACKS		
ACES 399 PRINT RUN 399 SERIAL #'d SETS		
1 Randy Johnson	.75	.23
2 Greg Maddux	1.25	.35
3 Tom Glavine	.50	.15
4 John Smoltz	.30	.09
5 Mike Mussina	.75	.23
6 Pedro Martinez	.75	.23
7 Kerry Wood	.75	.23
8 Bartolo Colon	.20	.06
9 Brad Penny	.20	.06
10 Billy Wagner	.20	.06
11 Kevin Brown	.30	.09
12 Mike Hampton	.30	.09
13 Roger Clemens	1.50	.45
14 David Cone	.20	.06
15 Orlando Hernandez	.30	.09
16 Mariano Rivera	.30	.09
17 Tim Hudson	.50	.15
18 Trevor Hoffman	.30	.09
19 Rick Ankiel	.20	.06
20 Freddy Garcia	.30	.09

2000 Pacific Invincible Eyes of the World

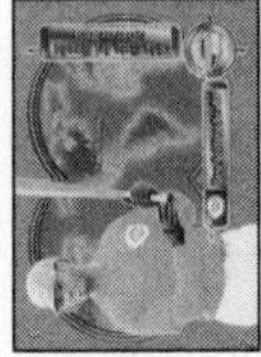
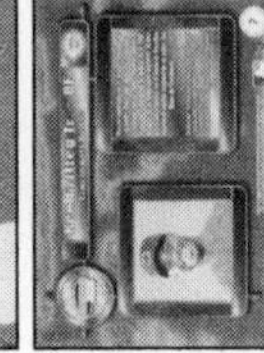

Randomly inserted into packs at one in 37, this 20-card insert features some of the league's top stars and a map showing where they are from.

	Nm-Mt	Ex-Mt
COMPLETE SET (20)	120.00	36.00
1 Erubiel Durazo	1.50	.45
2 Andruw Jones	2.50	.75
3 Cal Ripken	20.00	6.00
4 Nomar Garciaparra	10.00	3.00
5 Pedro Martinez	6.00	1.80
6 Sammy Sosa	10.00	3.00
7 Ken Griffey Jr.	10.00	3.00
8 Manny Ramirez	2.50	.75
9 Larry Walker	4.00	1.20
10 Juan Gonzalez	6.00	1.80
11 Carlos Beltran	2.50	.75
12 Vladimir Guerrero	6.00	1.80
13 Orlando Hernandez	2.50	.75
14 Derek Jeter	15.00	4.50
15 Mark McGwire	15.00	4.50
16 Tony Gwynn	8.00	2.40
17 Freddy Garcia	2.50	.75
18 Alex Rodriguez	10.00	3.00
19 Jose Canseco	6.00	1.80
20 Ivan Rodriguez	6.00	1.80

2000 Pacific Invincible Game Gear

Randomly inserted into packs, this 32-card insert features game-used memorabilia cards from some of the biggest names in MLB. The set features game-used jersey, bat-jersey, and jersey patch cards. Each card is serial numbered on the front in gold foil. Stated print runs are provided in our checklist.

	Nm-Mt	Ex-Mt
1 Jeff Bagwell Jsy/1000	10.00	3.00
2 Tom Glavine Jsy/1000	10.00	3.00
3 Mark Grace Jsy/1000	10.00	3.00
4 Eric Karros Jsy/1000	8.00	2.40
5 Edgar Martinez Jsy/800	10.00	3.00
6 Manny Ramirez Jsy/975	8.00	2.40
7 Cal Ripken Jsy/1000	25.00	7.50
8 Alex Rodriguez Jsy/900	15.00	4.50
9 Ivan Rodriguez Jsy/675	10.00	3.00
10 Mo Vaughn Jsy/1000	8.00	2.40
11 Edgar Martinez Bat-Jsy/200	20.00	6.00
12 Manny Ramirez Bat-Jsy/145	15.00	4.50
13 Alex Rodriguez Bat-Jsy/200	25.00	7.50
14 Ivan Rodriguez Bat-Jsy/200	20.00	6.00
15 Edgar Martinez Bat/200	15.00	4.50
16 Manny Ramirez Bat/200	10.00	3.00
17 Ivan Rodriguez Bat/200	15.00	4.50
18 Alex Rodriguez Bat/200	20.00	6.00
19 Jeff Bagwell Patch/125	25.00	7.50
20 Tom Glavine Patch/110	25.00	7.50
21 Mark Grace Patch/125	25.00	7.50
22 Tony Gwynn Patch/65	50.00	15.00
23 Chipper Jones Patch/	40.00	12.00
24 Eric Karros Patch/125	15.00	4.50
25 Greg Maddux Patch/80	80.00	24.00
26 Edgar Martinez Patch/125	25.00	7.50
27 Manny Ramirez Patch/125	15.00	4.50
28 Cal Ripken Patch/125	100.00	30.00
29 Alex Rodriguez Patch/125	60.00	18.00
30 Ivan Rodriguez Patch/125	40.00	12.00
31 Frank Thomas Patch/125	40.00	12.00
32 Mo Vaughn Patch/125	15.00	4.50

2000 Pacific Invincible Kings of the Diamond

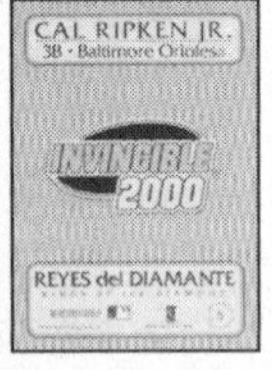

Inserted at one per pack, this 30-card insert features some of the top hitters in the major leagues.

	Nm-Mt	Ex-Mt
COMPLETE SET (30)	20.00	6.00
*KINGS 299: 4X TO 10X BASIC KINGS		
KINGS 299 RANDOM INSERTS IN PACKS		
KINGS 299 PRINT RUN 299 SERIAL #'d SETS		
1 Mo Vaughn	.30	.09
2 Erubiel Durazo	.20	.06
3 Andruw Jones	.30	.09
4 Chipper Jones	.75	.23
5 Cal Ripken	2.50	.75
6 Nomar Garciaparra	1.25	.35
7 Sammy Sosa	1.25	.35
8 Frank Thomas	.75	.23
9 Sean Casey	.30	.09
10 Ken Griffey Jr.	1.25	.35
11 Manny Ramirez	.30	.09
12 Larry Walker	.50	.15
13 Juan Gonzalez	.75	.23
14 Jeff Bagwell	.50	.15
15 Craig Biggio	.50	.15
16 Carlos Beltran	.30	.09
17 Shawn Green	.30	.09
18 Vladimir Guerrero	.75	.23
19 Mike Piazza	1.25	.35
20 Derek Jeter	2.00	.60
21 Bernie Williams	.50	.15
22 Ben Grieve	.20	.06
23 Scott Rolen	.50	.15
24 Mark McGwire	2.00	.60
25 Tony Gwynn	1.00	.30
26 Barry Bonds	2.00	.60
27 Alex Rodriguez	1.25	.35
28 Jose Canseco	.75	.23
29 Rafael Palmeiro	.50	.15
30 Ivan Rodriguez	.75	.23

2000 Pacific Invincible Lighting the Fire

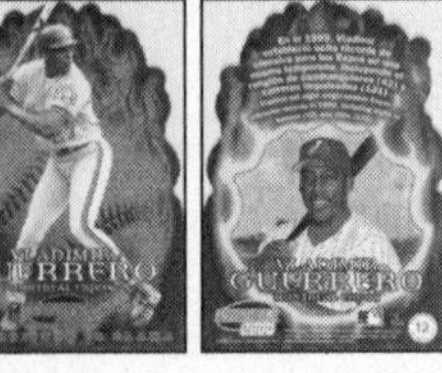

Randomly inserted into packs at one in 73, this 20-card die-cut insert features players that can catch fire at any point during the season.

	Nm-Mt	Ex-Mt
COMPLETE SET (20)	300.00	90.00
1 Chipper Jones	10.00	3.00
2 Greg Maddux	15.00	4.50
3 Cal Ripken	30.00	9.00
4 Nomar Garciaparra	15.00	4.50
5 Pedro Martinez	10.00	3.00
6 Ken Griffey Jr.	15.00	4.50
7 Sammy Sosa	15.00	4.50
8 Manny Ramirez	4.00	1.20
9 Juan Gonzalez	10.00	3.00
10 Jeff Bagwell	6.00	1.80
11 Shawn Green	4.00	1.20
12 Vladimir Guerrero	10.00	3.00
13 Mike Piazza	15.00	4.50
14 Roger Clemens	20.00	6.00
15 Derek Jeter	25.00	7.50
16 Mark McGwire	25.00	7.50
17 Tony Gwynn	12.00	3.60
18 Alex Rodriguez	15.00	4.50
19 Jose Canseco	10.00	3.00
20 Ivan Rodriguez	10.00	3.00

2000 Pacific Invincible Ticket to Stardom

Randomly inserted into packs at one in 181, this 20-card set features some of the major league's best players on cards that resemble ticket stubs.

	Nm-Mt	Ex-Mt
COMPLETE SET (20)	500.00	150.00
1 Andruw Jones	8.00	2.40
2 Chipper Jones	20.00	6.00
3 Cal Ripken	60.00	18.00
4 Nomar Garciaparra	30.00	9.00
5 Pedro Martinez	20.00	6.00
6 Ken Griffey Jr.	30.00	9.00
7 Sammy Sosa	30.00	9.00
8 Manny Ramirez	8.00	2.40
9 Jeff Bagwell	12.00	3.60
10 Shawn Green	8.00	2.40
11 Vladimir Guerrero	20.00	6.00
12 Mike Piazza	30.00	9.00
13 Derek Jeter	50.00	15.00
14 Alfonso Soriano	20.00	6.00
15 Scott Rolen	12.00	3.60
16 Rick Ankiel	5.00	1.50
17 Mark McGwire	50.00	15.00
18 Tony Gwynn	25.00	7.50
19 Alex Rodriguez	30.00	9.00
20 Ivan Rodriguez	20.00	6.00

2000 Pacific Invincible Wild Vinyl

Randomly inserted into packs, this 10-card insert features the league's top hitters on a vinyl based card. Please note that each card is individually serial numbered to 10. Pricing in not available due to scarcity.

	Nm-Mt	Ex-Mt
1 Chipper Jones		
2 Cal Ripken		
3 Nomar Garciaparra		
4 Ken Griffey Jr.		
5 Sammy Sosa		
6 Mike Piazza		
7 Derek Jeter		
8 Mark McGwire		
9 Tony Gwynn		
10 Alex Rodriguez		

1998 Pacific Omega

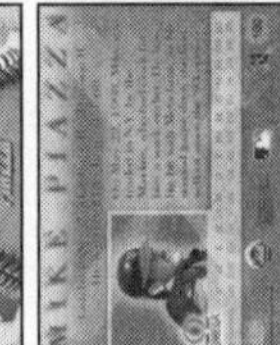

The 1998 Pacific Omega set was issued in one series totalling 250 cards. The cards were issued in eight-card packs with an SRP of $1.99. In addition, a Tony Gwynn sample card was issued prior to the product's release. The card was distributed to dealers and hobby media to preview the product. It's identical in design to a standard Aurora card except for the word "SAMPLE" printed diagonally against the back of the card coupled with a large MLB "Genuine Merchandise" sticker. Notable Rookie Cards include Kevin Millwood and Magglio Ordonez,

	Nm-Mt	Ex-Mt
COMPLETE SET (250)	40.00	12.00
1 Garret Anderson	.30	.09
2 Gary DiSarcina	.30	.09
3 Jim Edmonds	.30	.09
4 Darin Erstad	.30	.09
5 Cecil Fielder	.30	.09
6 Chuck Finley	.30	.09
7 Shigetoshi Hasegawa	.30	.09
8 Tim Salmon	.50	.15
9 Brian Anderson	.30	.09
10 Jay Bell	.30	.09
11 Andy Benes	.30	.09
12 Yamil Benitez	.30	.09
13 Jorge Fabregas	.30	.09
14 Travis Lee	.30	.09
15 Devon White	.30	.09
16 Matt Williams	.30	.09
17 Andres Galarraga	.30	.09
18 Tom Glavine	.50	.15
19 Andruw Jones	.30	.09
20 Chipper Jones	.75	.23
21 Ryan Klesko	.30	.09
22 Javy Lopez	.30	.09
23 Greg Maddux	1.25	.35

24 Kevin Millwood RC 1.50 .45
25 Denny Neagle .30 .09
26 John Smoltz .50 .15
27 Roberto Alomar .75 .23
28 Brady Anderson .30 .09
29 Joe Carter .30 .09
30 Eric Davis .30 .09
31 Jimmy Key .30 .09
32 Mike Mussina .75 .23
33 Rafael Palmeiro .50 .15
34 Cal Ripken 2.50 .75
35 B.J. Surhoff .30 .09
36 Dennis Eckersley .30 .09
37 Nomar Garciaparra 1.25 .35
38 Reggie Jefferson .30 .09
39 Derek Lowe .30 .09
40 Pedro Martinez .75 .23
41 Brian Rose .30 .09
42 John Valentin .30 .09
43 Jason Varitek .30 .09
44 Mo Vaughn .30 .09
45 Jeff Blauser .30 .09
46 Jeremi Gonzalez .30 .09
47 Mark Grace .50 .15
48 Lance Johnson .30 .09
49 Kevin Orie .30 .09
50 Henry Rodriguez .30 .09
51 Sammy Sosa 1.25 .35
52 Kerry Wood .75 .23
53 Albert Belle .30 .09
54 Mike Cameron .30 .09
55 Mike Caruso .30 .09
56 Ray Durham .30 .09
57 Jaime Navarro .30 .09
58 Greg Norton .30 .09
59 Magglio Ordonez RC 2.00 .60
60 Frank Thomas .75 .23
61 Robin Ventura .30 .09
62 Bret Boone .30 .09
63 Willie Greene .30 .09
64 Barry Larkin .75 .23
65 Jon Nunnally .30 .09
66 Eduardo Perez .30 .09
67 Reggie Sanders .30 .09
68 Brett Tomko .30 .09
69 Sandy Alomar Jr. .30 .09
70 Travis Fryman .30 .09
71 David Justice .30 .09
72 Kenny Lofton .30 .09
73 Charles Nagy .30 .09
74 Manny Ramirez .30 .09
75 Jim Thome .75 .23
76 Omar Vizquel .30 .09
77 Enrique Wilson .30 .09
78 Jaret Wright .30 .09
79 Dante Bichette .30 .09
80 Ellis Burks .30 .09
81 Vinny Castilla .30 .09
82 Todd Helton .50 .15
83 Darryl Kile .30 .09
84 Mike Lansing .30 .09
85 Neifi Perez .30 .09
86 Larry Walker .50 .15
87 Raul Casanova .30 .09
88 Tony Clark .30 .09
89 Luis Gonzalez .30 .09
90 Bobby Higginson .30 .09
91 Brian Hunter .30 .09
92 Bip Roberts .30 .09
93 Justin Thompson .30 .09
94 Josh Booty .30 .09
95 Craig Counsell .30 .09
96 Livan Hernandez .30 .09
97 Ryan Jackson RC .30 .09
98 Mark Kotsay .30 .09
99 Derrek Lee .30 .09
100 Mike Piazza 1.25 .35
101 Edgar Renteria .30 .09
102 Cliff Floyd .30 .09
103 Moises Alou .30 .09
104 Jeff Bagwell .50 .15
105 Derek Bell .30 .09
106 Sean Berry .30 .09
107 Craig Biggio .50 .15
108 John Halama RC .30 .09
109 Richard Hidalgo .30 .09
110 Shane Reynolds .30 .09
111 Tim Belcher .30 .09
112 Brian Bevil .30 .09
113 Jeff Conine .30 .09
114 Johnny Damon .30 .09
115 Jeff King .30 .09
116 Jeff Montgomery .30 .09
117 Dean Palmer .30 .09
118 Terry Pendleton .30 .09
119 Bobby Bonilla .30 .09
120 Wilton Guerrero .30 .09
121 Todd Hollandsworth .30 .09
122 Charles Johnson .30 .09
123 Eric Karros .30 .09
124 Paul Konerko .30 .09
125 Ramon Martinez .30 .09
126 Raul Mondesi .30 .09
127 Hideo Nomo .75 .23
128 Gary Sheffield .30 .09
129 Ismael Valdes .30 .09
130 Jeromy Burnitz .30 .09
131 Jeff Cirillo .30 .09
132 Todd Dunn .30 .09
133 Marquis Grissom .30 .09
134 John Jaha .30 .09
135 Scott Karl .30 .09
136 Dave Nilsson .30 .09
137 Jose Valentin .30 .09
138 Fernando Vina .30 .09
139 Rick Aguilera .30 .09
140 Marty Cordova .30 .09
141 Pat Meares .30 .09
142 Paul Molitor .50 .15
143 David Ortiz .30 .09
144 Brad Radke .30 .09
145 Terry Steinbach .30 .09
146 Todd Walker .30 .09
147 Shane Andrews .30 .09
148 Brad Fullmer .30 .09
149 Mark Grudzielanek .30 .09
150 Vladimir Guerrero .75 .23
151 F.P. Santangelo .30 .09
152 Jose Vidro .30 .09
153 Rondell White .30 .09
154 Carlos Baerga .30 .09
155 Bernard Gilkey .30 .09
156 Todd Hundley .30 .09
157 Butch Huskey .30 .09
158 Bobby Jones .30 .09
159 Brian McRae .30 .09
160 John Olerud .30 .09
161 Rey Ordonez .30 .09
162 Masato Yoshii RC .50 .15
163 David Cone .30 .09
164 Hideki Irabu .30 .09
165 Derek Jeter 2.00 .60
166 Chuck Knoblauch .30 .09
167 Tino Martinez .50 .15
168 Paul O'Neill .50 .15
169 Andy Pettitte .50 .15
170 Mariano Rivera .50 .15
171 Darryl Strawberry .50 .15
172 David Wells .30 .09
173 Bernie Williams .50 .15
174 Ryan Christenson RC .30 .09
175 Jason Giambi .75 .23
176 Ben Grieve .30 .09
177 Rickey Henderson .75 .23
178 A.J. Hinch .30 .09
179 Kenny Rogers .30 .09
180 Ricky Bottalico .30 .09
181 Rico Brogna .30 .09
182 Doug Glanville .30 .09
183 Gregg Jefferies .30 .09
184 Mike Lieberthal .30 .09
185 Scott Rolen .50 .15
186 Curt Schilling .50 .15
187 Jermaine Allensworth .30 .09
188 Lou Collier .30 .09
189 Jose Guillen .30 .09
190 Jason Kendall .30 .09
191 Al Martin .30 .09
192 Tony Womack .30 .09
193 Kevin Young .30 .09
194 Royce Clayton .30 .09
195 Delino DeShields .30 .09
196 Gary Gaetti .30 .09
197 Ron Gant .30 .09
198 Brian Jordan .30 .09
199 Ray Lankford .30 .09
200 Mark McGwire 2.00 .60
201 Todd Stottlemyre .30 .09
202 Kevin Brown .50 .15
203 Ken Caminiti .30 .09
204 Steve Finley .30 .09
205 Tony Gwynn 1.00 .30
206 Carlos Hernandez .30 .09
207 Wally Joyner .30 .09
208 Greg Vaughn .30 .09
209 Barry Bonds 2.00 .60
210 Shawn Estes .30 .09
211 Orel Hershiser .30 .09
212 Stan Javier .30 .09
213 Jeff Kent .30 .09
214 Bill Mueller .30 .09
215 Robb Nen .30 .09
216 J.T. Snow .30 .09
217 Jay Buhner .30 .09
218 Ken Cloude .30 .09
219 Joey Cora .30 .09
220 Ken Griffey Jr. 1.25 .35
221 Glenallen Hill .30 .09
222 Randy Johnson .75 .23
223 Edgar Martinez .50 .15
224 Jamie Moyer .30 .09
225 Alex Rodriguez 1.25 .35
226 David Segui .30 .09
227 Dan Wilson .30 .09
228 Rolando Arrojo RC .30 .09
229 Wade Boggs .50 .15
230 Miguel Cairo .30 .09
231 Roberto Hernandez .30 .09
232 Quinton McCracken .30 .09
233 Fred McGriff .50 .15
234 Paul Sorrento .30 .09
235 Kevin Stocker .30 .09
236 Will Clark .75 .23
237 Juan Gonzalez .75 .23
238 Rusty Greer .30 .09
239 Rick Helling .30 .09
240 Roberto Kelly .30 .09
241 Ivan Rodriguez .75 .23
242 Aaron Sele .30 .09
243 John Wetteland .30 .09
244 Jose Canseco .75 .23
245 Roger Clemens 1.50 .45
246 Jose Cruz Jr. .30 .09
247 Carlos Delgado .30 .09
248 Alex Gonzalez .30 .09
249 Ed Sprague .30 .09
250 Shannon Stewart .30 .09
NNO Tony Gwynn Sample 1.00 .30

1998 Pacific Omega Red

These red foil parallel cards were distributed exclusively in retail Treat Entertainment (a.k.a. Wal-Mart) packs at a rate of one in four. The cards parallel the basic 250-card set, except for the red foil player image on the right hand side and the red foil Omega logo in the upper left corner of the card front (basic cards feature silver foil in both areas).

Nm-Mt Ex-Mt
*STARS: 5X TO 12X BASIC CARDS ....
*ROOKIES: 2.5X TO 6X BASIC CARDS

1998 Pacific Omega EO Portraits

Randomly inserted in packs at a rate of one in 73, this 20-card set is an insert to the Pacific Omega base set. The fronts feature 20 exciting player photos on exclusive Electro-Optical technology. The featured player's name and team run across the bottom border. The Omega logo sits in the upper left corner.

Nm-Mt Ex-Mt
COMPLETE SET (20) 250.00 75.00
EO PORTRAIT 1 OF 1 PARALLELS EXIST
EO PORT. 1 OF 1'S TOO SCARCE TO PRICE
1 Cal Ripken 40.00 12.00
2 Nomar Garciaparra 20.00 6.00
3 Mo Vaughn 5.00 1.50
4 Frank Thomas 12.00 3.60
5 Manny Ramirez 5.00 1.50
6 Ben Grieve 5.00 1.50
7 Ken Griffey Jr. 20.00 6.00
8 Alex Rodriguez 20.00 6.00
9 Juan Gonzalez 12.00 3.60
10 Ivan Rodriguez 12.00 3.60
11 Travis Lee 5.00 1.50
12 Greg Maddux 20.00 6.00
13 Chipper Jones 12.00 3.60
14 Kerry Wood 12.00 3.60
15 Larry Walker 8.00 2.40
16 Jeff Bagwell 8.00 2.40
17 Mike Piazza 20.00 6.00
18 Mark McGwire 30.00 9.00
19 Tony Gwynn 15.00 4.50
20 Barry Bonds 30.00 9.00

1998 Pacific Omega Face To Face

Randomly inserted in packs at a rate of one in 145, this 10-card set is an insert to the Pacific Omega base set. Each card front features a background of "brick wall" design and salutes two superstars. The featured player's names run across the bottom border separated by the Omega logo.

Nm-Mt Ex-Mt
COMPLETE SET (10) 150.00 45.00
1 Alex Rodriguez 20.00 6.00
Nomar Garciaparra
2 Mark McGwire 30.00 9.00
Ken Griffey Jr.
3 Mike Piazza 20.00 6.00
Sandy Alomar Jr.
4 Kerry Wood 25.00 7.50
Roger Clemens
5 Cal Ripken 40.00 12.00
Paul Molitor
6 Tony Gwynn 15.00 4.50
Wade Boggs
7 Frank Thomas 12.00 3.60
Chipper Jones
8 Travis Lee 5.00 1.50
Ben Grieve
9 Hideo Nomo 12.00 3.60
Hideki Irabu
10 Juan Gonzalez 5.00 1.50
Manny Ramirez

1998 Pacific Omega Online Inserts

Randomly inserted in packs at a rate of four in 37, this 36-card set is an insert to the Pacific Omega base set. The card fronts feature a color game action photo on a fully foiled hi-tech web designed card. With this card, you can log on to bigleaguers.com and majorleaguebaseball.com and keep track of your favorite players.

Nm-Mt Ex-Mt
COMPLETE SET (36) 120.00 36.00
1 Cal Ripken 15.00 4.50
2 Nomar Garciaparra 8.00 2.40
3 Pedro Martinez 5.00 1.50
4 Mo Vaughn 2.00 .60
5 Frank Thomas 5.00 1.50
6 Sandy Alomar Jr. 2.00 .60
7 Manny Ramirez 2.00 .60
8 Jaret Wright 2.00 .60
9 Paul Molitor 3.00 .90
10 Derek Jeter 12.00 3.60
11 Bernie Williams 3.00 .90
12 Ben Grieve 2.00 .60
13 Ken Griffey Jr. 8.00 2.40
14 Edgar Martinez 3.00 .90
15 Alex Rodriguez 8.00 2.40
16 Wade Boggs 3.00 .90
17 Juan Gonzalez 5.00 1.50
18 Ivan Rodriguez 5.00 1.50
19 Roger Clemens 10.00 3.00
20 Travis Lee 2.00 .60
21 Matt Williams 2.00 .60
22 Andres Galarraga 2.00 .60
23 Chipper Jones 5.00 1.50
24 Greg Maddux 8.00 2.40
25 Sammy Sosa 8.00 2.40
26 Kerry Wood 5.00 1.50
27 Barry Larkin 5.00 1.50
28 Larry Walker 3.00 .90
29 Derrek Lee 2.00 .60
30 Jeff Bagwell 3.00 .90
31 Hideo Nomo 5.00 1.50
32 Mike Piazza 8.00 2.40
33 Scott Rolen 3.00 .90
34 Mark McGwire 12.00 3.60
35 Tony Gwynn 6.00 1.80
36 Barry Bonds 12.00 3.60

1998 Pacific Omega Prisms

Randomly inserted in packs at a rate of one in 37, this 20-card set is an insert to the Pacific Omega base set. The fronts feature a background of Omega's patented prismatic foil to help showcase 20 of the game's top players. The featured player's name is found in the lower right corner with his team logo in the lower left corner.

Nm-Mt Ex-Mt
COMPLETE SET (20) 150.00 45.00
1 Cal Ripken 20.00 6.00
2 Nomar Garciaparra 10.00 3.00
3 Pedro Martinez 6.00 1.80
4 Frank Thomas 6.00 1.80
5 Manny Ramirez 2.50 .75
6 Brian Giles 6.00 1.80
7 Derek Jeter 15.00 4.50
8 Ben Grieve 2.50 .75
9 Ken Griffey Jr. 10.00 3.00
10 Alex Rodriguez 10.00 3.00
11 Juan Gonzalez 6.00 1.80
12 Travis Lee 2.50 .75
13 Chipper Jones 6.00 1.80
14 Greg Maddux 10.00 3.00
15 Kerry Wood 6.00 1.80
16 Larry Walker 4.00 1.20
17 Hideo Nomo 6.00 1.80
18 Mike Piazza 10.00 3.00
19 Mark McGwire 15.00 4.50
20 Tony Gwynn 8.00 2.40

1998 Pacific Omega Rising Stars

Randomly inserted in packs at a rate of four in 37, this 30-card hobby only set is an insert to the Pacific Omega base set. Each card features several prospects from the team featured.

Nm-Mt Ex-Mt
*TIER 1: 4X TO 10X BASIC RISING STARS
TIER 1 PRINT RUN 100 SERIAL #'d SETS
TIER 1 CARDS ARE 2/10/16/19/20/25
*TIER 2: 5X TO 12X BASIC RISING STARS
TIER 2 PRINT RUN 75 SERIAL #'d SETS
TIER 2 CARDS ARE 3/12/18/23/26/27
*TIER 3: 6X TO 15X BASIC RISING STARS
TIER 3 PRINT RUN 50 SERIAL #'d SETS
TIER 3 CARDS ARE 1/7/15/17/22/28 ..
*TIER 4: 12.5X TO 30X BASIC RISING STARS
TIER 4 PRINT RUN 25 SERIAL #'d SETS
TIER 4 CARDS ARE 6/9/11/14/21/29 ..
TIER 5 STATED PRINT RUN 1 SET .....
TIER 5 CARDS ARE 4/5/8/13/24/30 ...
TIER 5 NOT PRICED DUE TO SCARCITY
TIER 1-5: RANDOM INSERTS IN PACKS
1 Nerio Rodriguez 2.00 .60
Sidney Ponson
2 Frank Catalanotto 3.00 .90
Roberto Duran
Sean Runyan
3 Kevin L.Brown 2.00 .60
Carlos Almanzar
4 Aaron Boone 2.00 .60
Pat Watkins
Scott Winchester
5 Brian Meadows 2.00 .60
Andy Larkin
Antonio Alfonseca
6 DaRond Stovall 2.00 .60
Trey Moore
Shayne Bennett
7 Felix Martinez 2.00 .60
Larry Sutton
Brian Bevil
8 Homer Bush 2.00 .60
Mike Buddie
9 Rich Butler 2.00 .60
Esteban Yan
10 Dave Hollins 2.00 .60
Brian Edmondson
11 Lou Collier 2.00 .60
Jose Silva
Javier Martinez
12 Steve Sinclair 2.00 .60
Mark Dalesandro
13 Jason Varitek 2.00 .60
Brian Rose
Brian Shouse
14 Mike Caruso 2.00 .60
Jeff Abbott
Tom Fordham
15 Jason Johnson 2.00 .60
Bobby Smith
16 Dave Berg 2.00 .60
Mark Kotsay
Jesus Sanchez
17 Richard Hidalgo 2.00 .60
John Halama
Trever Miller
18 Geoff Jenkins 2.00 .60
Bobby Hughes
Steve Woodard
19 Eli Marrero 2.00 .60
Cliff Politte
Mike Busby
20 Desi Relaford 2.00 .60
Darrin Winston
21 Todd Helton 3.00 .90
Bobby Jones
22 Rolando Arrojo 5.00 1.50
Miguel Cairo
Dan Carlson
23 David Ortiz 2.00 .60
Jose Valentin
Eric Milton
24 Magglio Ordonez 6.00 1.80
Greg Norton
25 Brad Fullmer 2.00 .60
Javier Vazquez
Rick DeHart
26 Paul Konerko 2.00 .60
Matt Luke
27 Derrek Lee 2.00 .60
Ryan Jackson
John Roskos
28 Ben Grieve 2.00 .60
A.J.Hinch
Ryan Christenson
29 Travis Lee 2.00 .60
Karim Garcia
Dave Dellucci
30 Kerry Wood 5.00 1.50
Marc Pisciotta

1999 Pacific Omega

The 1999 Pacific Omega set was issued in one series for a total of 250 cards and distributed in six-card packs. The set features color player photos printed on silver foiled cards in a three-panel horizontal design. A Tony Gwynn Sample card was distributed to dealers and hobby media several weeks prior to the release of the product. The card can be readily identified by the bold "SAMPLE" text running across the back. An embossed stamped version of this same sample card was distributed exclusively at the 1999 Chicago Sportsfest card at the Pacific booth.

Nm-Mt Ex-Mt
COMPLETE SET (250) 40.00 12.00
COMMON CARD (1-250) .30 .09
COMMON DUAL-PLAYER .40 .12
1 Garret Anderson .30 .09
2 Jim Edmonds .30 .09
3 Darin Erstad .30 .09
4 Chuck Finley .30 .09
5 Troy Glaus .50 .15
6 Troy Percival .30 .09
7 Chris Pritchett .30 .09
8 Tim Salmon .50 .15
9 Mo Vaughn .30 .09
10 Jay Bell .30 .09
11 Steve Finley .30 .09
12 Luis Gonzalez .30 .09
13 Randy Johnson .75 .23
14 Byung-Hyun Kim RC 2.00 .60
15 Travis Lee .30 .09
16 Matt Williams .30 .09
17 Tony Womack .30 .09
18 Bret Boone .30 .09
19 Mark DeRosa .30 .09
20 Tom Glavine .50 .15
21 Andruw Jones .30 .09
22 Chipper Jones .75 .23
23 Brian Jordan .30 .09
24 Ryan Klesko .30 .09
25 Javy Lopez .30 .09
26 Greg Maddux 1.25 .35
27 John Smoltz .50 .15
28 Bruce Chen .40 .12
Odalis Perez
29 Brady Anderson .30 .09
30 Harold Baines .30 .09
31 Albert Belle .30 .09
32 Will Clark .75 .23
33 Delino DeShields .30 .09
34 Jerry Hairston Jr. .30 .09
35 Charles Johnson .30 .09
36 Mike Mussina .75 .23
37 Cal Ripken 2.50 .75
38 B.J. Surhoff .30 .09
39 Jin Ho Cho .30 .09
40 Nomar Garciaparra 1.25 .35
41 Pedro Martinez .75 .23
42 Jose Offerman .30 .09
43 Troy O'Leary .30 .09
44 John Valentin .30 .09
45 Jason Varitek .30 .09
46 Juan Pena RC .40 .12
Brian Rose
47 Mark Grace .50 .15
48 Glenallen Hill .30 .09
49 Tyler Houston .30 .09
50 Mickey Morandini .30 .09
51 Henry Rodriguez .30 .09
52 Sammy Sosa 1.25 .35
53 Kevin Tapani .30 .09
54 Mike Caruso .30 .09
55 Ray Durham .30 .09
56 Paul Konerko .30 .09
57 Carlos Lee .30 .09
58 Magglio Ordonez .30 .09
59 Mike Sirotka .30 .09
60 Frank Thomas .75 .23
61 Mark Johnson .40 .12
Chris Singleton
62 Mike Cameron .30 .09
63 Sean Casey .30 .09
64 Pete Harnisch .30 .09
65 Barry Larkin .75 .23

1999 Pacific Omega

66 Pokey Reese .30 .09
67 Greg Vaughn .30 .09
68 Scott Williamson .30 .09
69 Dmitri Young .30 .09
70 Roberto Alomar .75 .23
71 Sandy Alomar Jr. .30 .09
72 Travis Fryman .30 .09
73 David Justice .30 .09
74 Kenny Lofton .30 .09
75 Manny Ramirez .30 .09
76 Richie Sexson .30 .09
77 Jim Thome .75 .23
78 Omar Vizquel .30 .09
79 Jaret Wright .30 .09
80 Dante Bichette .30 .09
81 Vinny Castilla .30 .09
82 Todd Helton .50 .15
83 Darryl Hamilton .30 .09
84 Darryl Kile .30 .09
85 Neifi Perez .30 .09
86 Larry Walker .50 .15
87 Tony Clark .30 .09
88 Damion Easley .30 .09
89 Juan Encarnacion .30 .09
90 Bobby Higginson .30 .09
91 Gabe Kapler .30 .09
92 Dean Palmer .30 .09
93 Justin Thompson .30 .09
94 Jeff Weaver .60 .18
Masao Kida RC
95 Bruce Aven .30 .09
96 Luis Castillo .30 .09
97 Alex Fernandez .30 .09
98 Cliff Floyd .30 .09
99 Alex Gonzalez .30 .09
100 Mark Kotsay .30 .09
101 Preston Wilson .30 .09
102 Moises Alou .30 .09
103 Jeff Bagwell .50 .15
104 Craig Biggio .50 .15
105 Derek Bell .30 .09
106 Mike Hampton .30 .09
107 Richard Hidalgo .30 .09
108 Jose Lima .30 .09
109 Billy Wagner .30 .09
110 Russ Johnson .40 .12
Daryle Ward
111 Carlos Beltran .30 .09
112 Johnny Damon .30 .09
113 Jermaine Dye .30 .09
114 Carlos Febles .30 .09
115 Jeremy Giambi .30 .09
116 Joe Randa .30 .09
117 Mike Sweeney .30 .09
118 Orber Moreno .40 .12
Jose Santiago RC
119 Kevin Brown .50 .15
120 Todd Hundley .30 .09
121 Eric Karros .30 .09
122 Raul Mondesi .30 .09
123 Chan Ho Park .30 .09
124 Angel Pena .30 .09
125 Gary Sheffield .30 .09
126 Devon White .30 .09
127 Eric Young .30 .09
128 Ron Belliard .30 .09
129 Jeromy Burnitz .30 .09
130 Jeff Cirillo .30 .09
131 Marquis Grissom .30 .09
132 Geoff Jenkins .30 .09
133 David Nilsson .30 .09
134 Hideo Nomo .75 .23
135 Fernando Vina .30 .09
136 Ron Coomer .30 .09
137 Marty Cordova .30 .09
138 Corey Koskie .30 .09
139 Brad Radke .30 .09
140 Todd Walker .30 .09
141 Chad Allen RC .40 .12
Torii Hunter
142 Cristian Guzman .40 .12
Jacque Jones
143 Michael Barrett .30 .09
144 Orlando Cabrera .30 .09
145 Vladimir Guerrero .75 .23
146 Wilton Guerrero .30 .09
147 Ugueth Urbina .30 .09
148 Rondell White .30 .09
149 Chris Widger .30 .09
150 Edgardo Alfonzo .30 .09
151 Roger Cedeno .30 .09
152 Octavio Dotel .30 .09
153 Rickey Henderson .75 .23
154 John Olerud .30 .09
155 Rey Ordonez .30 .09
156 Mike Piazza 1.25 .35
157 Robin Ventura .30 .09
158 Scott Brosius .30 .09
159 Roger Clemens 1.50 .45
160 David Cone .30 .09
161 Chili Davis .30 .09
162 Orlando Hernandez .30 .09
163 Derek Jeter 2.00 .60
164 Chuck Knoblauch .30 .09
165 Tino Martinez .50 .15
166 Paul O'Neill .50 .15
167 Bernie Williams .50 .15
168 Jason Giambi .75 .23
169 Ben Grieve .30 .09
170 Chad Harville RC .30 .09
171 Tim Hudson RC 3.00 .90
172 Tony Phillips .30 .09
173 Kenny Rogers .30 .09
174 Matt Stairs .30 .09
175 Miguel Tejada .30 .09
176 Eric Chavez .40 .12
Olmedo Saenz
177 Bobby Abreu .30 .09
178 Ron Gant .30 .09
179 Doug Glanville .30 .09
180 Mike Lieberthal .30 .09
181 Desi Relaford .30 .09
182 Scott Rolen .50 .15
183 Curt Schilling .50 .15
184 Marlon Anderson .40 .12
Randy Wolf
185 Brant Brown .30 .09
186 Brian Giles .30 .09
187 Jason Kendall .30 .09
188 Al Martin .30 .09
189 Ed Sprague .30 .09
190 Kevin Young .30 .09
191 Kris Benson .40 .12
Warren Morris
192 Kent Bottenfield .30 .09
193 Eric Davis .30 .09
194 J.D. Drew .30 .09
195 Ray Lankford .30 .09
196 Joe McEwing RC .30 .09
197 Mark McGwire 2.00 .60
198 Edgar Renteria .30 .09
199 Fernando Tatis .30 .09
200 Andy Ashby .30 .09
201 Ben Davis .30 .09
202 Tony Gwynn 1.00 .30
203 Trevor Hoffman .30 .09
204 Wally Joyner .30 .09
205 Gary Matthews Jr. .30 .09
206 Ruben Rivera .30 .09
207 Reggie Sanders .30 .09
208 Rich Aurilia .30 .09
209 Marvin Benard .30 .09
210 Barry Bonds 2.00 .60
211 Ellis Burks .30 .09
212 Stan Javier .30 .09
213 Jeff Kent .30 .09
214 Robb Nen .30 .09
215 J.T. Snow .30 .09
216 Gil Meche .30 .09
217 David Bell .30 .09
218 Freddy Garcia RC .75 .23
219 Ken Griffey Jr. 1.25 .35
220 Brian L.Hunter .30 .09
221 John Halama .30 .09
222 Edgar Martinez .50 .15
223 Jamie Moyer .30 .09
224 Alex Rodriguez 1.25 .35
225 Jay Buhner .30 .09
226 Rolando Arrojo .30 .09
227 Wade Boggs .50 .15
228 Miguel Cairo .30 .09
229 Jose Canseco .75 .23
230 Dave Martinez .30 .09
231 Fred McGriff .50 .15
232 Kevin Stocker .30 .09
233 Michael Duvall RC .40 .12
David Lamb
234 Royce Clayton .30 .09
235 Juan Gonzalez .75 .23
236 Rusty Greer .30 .09
237 Ruben Mateo .30 .09
238 Rafael Palmeiro .50 .15
239 Ivan Rodriguez .75 .23
240 John Wetteland .30 .09
241 Todd Zeile .30 .09
242 Jeff Zimmerman RC .30 .09
243 Homer Bush .30 .09
244 Jose Cruz Jr. .30 .09
245 Carlos Delgado .30 .09
246 Tony Fernandez .30 .09
247 Shawn Green .30 .09
248 Shannon Stewart .30 .09
249 David Wells .30 .09
250 Roy Halladay .40 .12
Billy Koch
S1 Tony Gwynn Sample 2.00 .60
S1A T.Gwynn Samp. Stamp 5.00 1.50

1999 Pacific Omega Copper

Randomly inserted in hobby packs only, this 250-card set is a copper foil parallel version of the base set. Only 99 serial-numbered sets were produced.

Nm-Mt Ex-Mt
*STARS: 8X TO 20X BASIC CARDS ...
*RC'S/DUAL: 5X TO 12X BASIC CARDS

1999 Pacific Omega Gold

Randomly inserted in retail packs, this 250-card set is a gold foil parallel version of the base set. Only 299 serial-numbered sets were produced.

Nm-Mt Ex-Mt
*STARS: 4X TO 10X BASIC CARDS ...
*RC'S/DUAL: 2X TO 5X BASIC CARDS

1999 Pacific Omega Platinum Blue

Randomly inserted in all packs, this 250-card set is a platinum blue foil parallel version of the base set. Only 75 serial-numbered sets were produced.

Nm-Mt Ex-Mt
*STARS: 10X TO 25X BASIC CARDS ..
*RC'S/DUAL: 6X TO 15X BASIC CARDS

1999 Pacific Omega Premiere Date

Inserted one per 24-pack hobby box, this 250-card set is parallel to the base set. Only 50 serial-numbered sets were produced.

Nm-Mt Ex-Mt
*STARS: 12.5X TO 30X BASIC CARDS
*RC'S/DUAL: 8X TO 20X BASIC CARDS

1999 Pacific Omega 5-Tool Talents

Randomly inserted in packs only at the rate of four in 37, this 30-card set features color action photos of some of the best players of the League.

Nm-Mt Ex-Mt
COMPLETE SET (30) 120.00 36.00
1 Randy Johnson 3.00 .90
2 Greg Maddux 5.00 1.50
3 Pedro Martinez 3.00 .90
4 Kevin Brown 2.00 .60
5 Roger Clemens 6.00 1.80
6 Carlos Lee 1.25 .35
7 Gabe Kapler 1.25 .35
8 Carlos Beltran 1.25 .35
9 J.D. Drew 1.25 .35
10 Ruben Mateo 1.25 .35
11 Chipper Jones 3.00 .90
12 Sammy Sosa 5.00 1.50
13 Manny Ramirez 1.25 .35
14 Vladimir Guerrero 3.00 .90
15 Mark McGwire 8.00 2.40
16 Ken Griffey Jr. 5.00 1.50
17 Jose Canseco 3.00 .90
18 Nomar Garciaparra 5.00 1.50
19 Frank Thomas 3.00 .90
20 Larry Walker 2.00 .60
21 Jeff Bagwell 2.00 .60
22 Mike Piazza 5.00 1.50
23 Tony Gwynn 4.00 1.20
24 Juan Gonzalez 3.00 .90
25 Cal Ripken 10.00 3.00
26 Derek Jeter 8.00 2.40
27 Scott Rolen 2.00 .60
28 Barry Bonds 8.00 2.40
29 Alex Rodriguez 5.00 1.50
30 Ivan Rodriguez 3.00 .90

1999 Pacific Omega Debut Duos

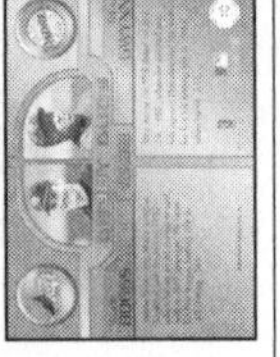

Randomly inserted in packs at the rate of one in 145, this 10-card set features color action photos of two MLB stars from the same debut year. The backs track each player's career development.

Nm-Mt Ex-Mt
COMPLETE SET (10) 200.00 60.00
1 Nomar Garciaparra 20.00 6.00
Vladimir Guerrero
2 Derek Jeter 30.00 9.00
Andy Pettitte
3 Garrett Anderson 20.00 6.00
Alex Rodriguez
4 Chipper Jones 12.00 3.60
Raul Mondesi
5 Pedro Martinez 20.00 6.00
Mike Piazza
6 Mo Vaughn 8.00 2.40
Bernie Williams
7 Juan Gonzalez 20.00 6.00
Ken Griffey Jr.
8 Sammy Sosa 20.00 6.00
Larry Walker
9 Barry Bonds 30.00 9.00
Mark McGwire
10 Wade Boggs 15.00 4.50
Tony Gwynn

1999 Pacific Omega Diamond Masters

Randomly inserted in packs at the rate of four in 37, this 36-card set features color action photos of top players printed on ink-on-foil cards.

Nm-Mt Ex-Mt
COMPLETE SET (36) 150.00 45.00
1 Darin Erstad 1.50 .45
2 Mo Vaughn 1.50 .45
3 Matt Williams 1.50 .45
4 Andruw Jones 1.50 .45
5 Chipper Jones 4.00 1.20
6 Greg Maddux 6.00 1.80
7 Cal Ripken 12.00 3.60
8 Nomar Garciaparra 6.00 1.80
9 Pedro Martinez 4.00 1.20
10 Sammy Sosa 6.00 1.80
11 Frank Thomas 4.00 1.20
12 Kenny Lofton 1.50 .45
13 Manny Ramirez 1.50 .45
14 Larry Walker 2.50 .75
15 Gabe Kapler 1.50 .45
16 Jeff Bagwell 2.50 .75
17 Craig Biggio 2.50 .75
18 Raul Mondesi 1.50 .45
19 Vladimir Guerrero 4.00 1.20
20 Mike Piazza 6.00 1.80
21 Roger Clemens 8.00 2.40
22 Derek Jeter 10.00 3.00
23 Bernie Williams 2.50 .75
24 Scott Rolen 2.50 .75
25 J.D. Drew 1.50 .45
26 Mark McGwire 10.00 3.00
27 Fernando Tatis 1.50 .45
28 Tony Gwynn 5.00 1.50
29 Barry Bonds 10.00 3.00
30 Ken Griffey Jr. 6.00 1.80
31 Alex Rodriguez 6.00 1.80
32 Jose Canseco 4.00 1.20
33 Juan Gonzalez 4.00 1.20
34 Ruben Mateo 1.50 .45
35 Ivan Rodriguez 4.00 1.20
36 Shawn Green 1.50 .45

1999 Pacific Omega EO Portraits

Randomly inserted in packs at the rate of one in 73, this 20-card set features color action photos of top players printed with exclusive Electro-Optical technology. A close-up silhouette of the player appears in the background. A very scare "1 of 1" parallel set was also produced.

Nm-Mt Ex-Mt
COMPLETE SET (20) 400.00 120.00
EO PORTRAIT 1 OF 1 PARALLELS EXIST
EO PORT.1 OF 1'S TOO SCARCE TO PRICE
1 Mo Vaughn 5.00 1.50
2 Chipper Jones 12.00 3.60
3 Greg Maddux 20.00 6.00
4 Cal Ripken 40.00 12.00
5 Nomar Garciaparra 20.00 6.00
6 Sammy Sosa 20.00 6.00
7 Frank Thomas 12.00 3.60
8 Manny Ramirez 5.00 1.50
9 Jeff Bagwell 8.00 2.40
10 Mike Piazza 20.00 6.00
11 Roger Clemens 25.00 7.50
12 Derek Jeter 30.00 9.00
13 Scott Rolen 8.00 2.40
14 Mark McGwire 30.00 9.00
15 Tony Gwynn 15.00 4.50
16 Barry Bonds 30.00 9.00
17 Ken Griffey Jr. 20.00 6.00
18 Alex Rodriguez 20.00 6.00
19 Jose Canseco 12.00 3.60
20 Juan Gonzalez 12.00 3.60

1999 Pacific Omega Hit Machine 3000

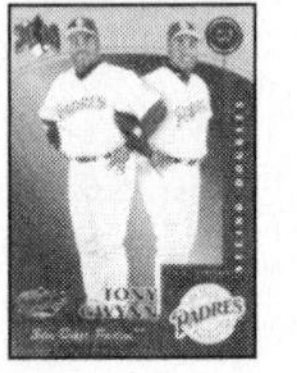

Randomly inserted in packs, this 21-card set features color action photos of Tony Gwynn as he heads towards his 3,000th hit. Only 3,000 serial-numbered sets were produced. Card number 21 was available only at SportsFest collectibles show in Philadelphia.

Nm-Mt Ex-Mt
COMPLETE SET (20) 200.00 60.00
COMMON CARD (1-20) 10.00 3.00
21 Tony Gwynn 15.00 4.50
SportsFest

1999 Pacific Omega HR 99

Randomly inserted in packs at the rate of one in 37, this 20-card set features color action photos of some of baseball's most powerful hitters printed on holographic prism-style foil cards.

Nm-Mt Ex-Mt
COMPLETE SET (20) 150.00 45.00
1 Mo Vaughn 2.50 .75
2 Matt Williams 2.50 .75
3 Chipper Jones 6.00 1.80
4 Albert Belle 2.50 .75
5 Nomar Garciaparra 10.00 3.00
6 Sammy Sosa 10.00 3.00
7 Frank Thomas 6.00 1.80
8 Manny Ramirez 2.50 .75
9 Jeff Bagwell 4.00 1.20
10 Raul Mondesi 2.50 .75
11 Vladimir Guerrero 6.00 1.80
12 Mike Piazza 10.00 3.00
13 Derek Jeter 15.00 4.50
14 Mark McGwire 15.00 4.50
15 Fernando Tatis 2.50 .75
16 Barry Bonds 15.00 4.50
17 Ken Griffey Jr. 10.00 3.00
18 Alex Rodriguez 10.00 3.00
19 Jose Canseco 6.00 1.80
20 Juan Gonzalez 6.00 1.80

1999 Pacific Omega Players Choice

These cards, which parallel the regular Pacific Omega set, were distributed with a special "Players Choice" logo at the Players Choice award ceremony. We have listed these cards in skip number order to match their regular number in the set. And since they were all printed in different numbers we have printed

the print run next to the players name.

Nm-Mt Ex-Mt
68 Scott Williamson/45 8.00 2.40
97 Alex Fernandez/45 8.00 2.40
101 Preston Wilson/45 8.00 2.40
111 Carlos Beltran/40 8.00 2.40
192 Kent Bottenfeld/45 8.00 2.40
218 Freddy Garcia/28 12.00 3.60
238 Rafael Palmeiro/40 12.00 3.60
242 Jeff Zimmerman/45 8.00 2.40

2000 Pacific Omega

The 2000 Pacific Omega product was released in late November, 2000. Each pack contained six cards, and carried a suggested retail price of $2.99. The product features a 255-card base set broken into tiers as follows: 150 Base Veterans (1-150), and 105 Prospects (151-255) that are serial numbered to 999. Notable Rookie Cards include Xavier Nady, Jose Ortiz, Kazuhiro Sasaki and Barry Zito.

Nm-Mt Ex-Mt
COMP.SET w/o SP's (150) 20.00 6.00
COMMON CARD (1-150) .30 .09
COMMON (151-255) 5.00 1.50
1 Garret Anderson .30 .09
2 Darin Erstad .30 .09
3 Troy Glaus .50 .15
4 Tim Salmon .50 .15
5 Mo Vaughn .30 .09
6 Jay Bell .30 .09
7 Steve Finley .30 .09
8 Luis Gonzalez .30 .09
9 Randy Johnson .75 .23
10 Matt Williams .30 .09
11 Andres Galarraga .30 .09
12 Andruw Jones .30 .09
13 Chipper Jones .75 .23
14 Brian Jordan .30 .09
15 Greg Maddux 1.25 .35
16 B.J. Surhoff .30 .09
17 Brady Anderson .30 .09
18 Albert Belle .30 .09
19 Mike Mussina .75 .23
20 Cal Ripken 2.50 .75
21 Carl Everett .30 .09
22 Nomar Garciaparra 1.25 .35
23 Pedro Martinez .75 .23
24 Jason Varitek .30 .09
25 Mark Grace .50 .15
26 Sammy Sosa 1.25 .35
27 Rondell White .30 .09
28 Kerry Wood .75 .23
29 Eric Young .30 .09
30 Ray Durham .30 .09
31 Carlos Lee .30 .09
32 Magglio Ordonez .30 .09
33 Frank Thomas .75 .23
34 Sean Casey .30 .09
35 Ken Griffey Jr. 1.25 .35
36 Barry Larkin .75 .23
37 Pokey Reese .30 .09
38 Roberto Alomar .75 .23
39 Kenny Lofton .30 .09
40 Manny Ramirez .30 .09
41 David Segui .30 .09
42 Jim Thome .75 .23
43 Omar Vizquel .30 .09
44 Jeff Cirillo .30 .09
45 Jeffrey Hammonds .30 .09
46 Todd Helton .50 .15
47 Todd Hollandsworth .30 .09
48 Larry Walker .50 .15
49 Tony Clark .30 .09
50 Juan Encarnacion .30 .09
51 Juan Gonzalez .75 .23
52 Bobby Higginson .30 .09
53 Hideo Nomo .75 .23
54 Dean Palmer .30 .09
55 Luis Castillo .30 .09
56 Cliff Floyd .30 .09
57 Derrek Lee .30 .09
58 Mike Lowell .30 .09
59 Henry Rodriguez .30 .09
60 Preston Wilson .30 .09
61 Moises Alou .30 .09
62 Jeff Bagwell .50 .15
63 Craig Biggio .50 .15
64 Ken Caminiti .30 .09
65 Richard Hidalgo .30 .09
66 Carlos Beltran .30 .09
67 Johnny Damon .30 .09
68 Jermaine Dye .30 .09
69 Joe Randa .30 .09
70 Mike Sweeney .30 .09
71 Adrian Beltre .30 .09
72 Kevin Brown .30 .09
73 Shawn Green .30 .09
74 Eric Karros .30 .09
75 Chan Ho Park .30 .09
76 Gary Sheffield .30 .09
77 Ron Belliard .30 .09
78 Jeromy Burnitz .30 .09
79 Geoff Jenkins .30 .09

Card	Nm-Mt	Ex-Mt
80 Richie Sexson	.30	.09
81 Ron Coomer	.30	.09
82 Jacque Jones	.30	.09
83 Corey Koskie	.30	.09
84 Matt Lawton	.30	.09
85 Vladimir Guerrero	.75	.23
86 Lee Stevens	.30	.09
87 Jose Vidro	.30	.09
88 Edgardo Alfonzo	.30	.09
89 Derek Bell	.30	.09
90 Mike Bordick	.30	.09
91 Mike Piazza	1.25	.35
92 Robin Ventura	.30	.09
93 Jose Canseco	.75	.23
94 Roger Clemens	1.50	.45
95 Orlando Hernandez	.30	.09
96 Derek Jeter	2.00	.60
97 David Justice	.30	.09
98 Tino Martinez	.50	.15
99 Jorge Posada	.50	.15
100 Bernie Williams	.50	.15
101 Eric Chavez	.30	.09
102 Jason Giambi	.75	.23
103 Ben Grieve	.30	.09
104 Miguel Tejada	.30	.09
105 Bobby Abreu	.30	.09
106 Doug Glanville	.30	.09
107 Travis Lee	.30	.09
108 Mike Lieberthal	.30	.09
109 Scott Rolen	.50	.15
110 Brian Giles	.30	.09
111 Jason Kendall	.30	.09
112 Warren Morris	.30	.09
113 Kevin Young	.30	.09
114 Will Clark	.75	.23
115 J.D. Drew	.30	.09
116 Jim Edmonds	.30	.09
117 Mark McGwire	2.00	.60
118 Edgar Renteria	.30	.09
119 Fernando Tatis	.30	.09
120 Fernando Vina	.30	.09
121 Bret Boone	.30	.09
122 Tony Gwynn	1.00	.30
123 Trevor Hoffman	.30	.09
124 Phil Nevin	.30	.09
125 Eric Owens	.30	.09
126 Barry Bonds	2.00	.60
127 Ellis Burks	.30	.09
128 Jeff Kent	.30	.09
129 J.T. Snow	.30	.09
130 Jay Buhner	.30	.09
131 Mike Cameron	.30	.09
132 Rickey Henderson	.75	.23
133 Edgar Martinez	.50	.15
134 John Olerud	.30	.09
135 Alex Rodriguez	1.25	.35
136 Kazuhiro Sasaki RC	1.25	.35
137 Fred McGriff	.50	.15
138 Greg Vaughn	.30	.09
139 Gerald Williams	.30	.09
140 Rusty Greer	.30	.09
141 Gabe Kapler	.30	.09
142 Ricky Ledee	.30	.09
143 Rafael Palmeiro	.50	.15
144 Ivan Rodriguez	.75	.23
145 Tony Batista	.30	.09
146 Jose Cruz Jr.	.30	.09
147 Carlos Delgado	.30	.09
148 Brad Fullmer	.30	.09
149 Shannon Stewart	.30	.09
150 David Wells	.30	.09
151 Juan Alvarez RC	5.00	1.50
Jeff DaVanon RC		
152 Seth Etherton	5.00	1.50
Adam Kennedy		
153 Ramon Ortiz	5.00	1.50
Lou Pote		
154 Derrick Turnbow RC	5.00	1.50
Eric Weaver		
155 Rod Barajas	5.00	1.50
Jason Conti		
156 Byung-Hyun Kim	.30	.09
Rob Ryan		
157 David Cortes RC	5.00	1.50
George Lombard		
158 Ivanon Coffie	5.00	1.50
Melvin Mora		
159 Ryan Kohlmeier RC	10.00	3.00
Luis Matos RC		
160 Willie Morales RC	5.00	1.50
John Parrish RC		
161 Chris Richard RC	5.00	1.50
Jay Spurgeon RC		
162 Israel Alcantara	5.00	1.50
Tomokazu Ohka RC		
163 Paxton Crawford RC	5.00	1.50
Sang-Hoon Lee RC		
164 Mike Mahoney RC	5.00	1.50
Wilton Veras		
165 Daniel Garibay RC	5.00	1.50
Ross Gload RC		
166 Gary Matthews Jr.	5.00	1.50
Phil Norton		
167 Roosevelt Brown	5.00	1.50
Ruben Quevedo		
168 Lorenzo Barcelo RC	5.00	1.50
Rocky Biddle RC		
169 Mark Buehrle	10.00	3.00
John Garland		
170 Aaron Myette	5.00	1.50
Josh Paul		
171 Kip Wells	5.00	1.50
Kelly Wunsch		
172 Rob Bell	5.00	1.50
Travis Dawkins		
173 Hector Mercado RC	5.00	1.50
John Riedling RC		
174 Russell Branyan	5.00	1.50
Sean DePaula RC		
175 Tim Drew	5.00	1.50
Mark Watson RC		
176 Craig House RC	5.00	1.50
Ben Petrick		
177 Robert Fick	5.00	1.50
Jose Macias		
178 Javier Cardona RC	5.00	1.50
Brandon Villafuerte RC		
179 Armando Almanza	5.00	1.50
A.J. Burnett		
180 Ramon Castro	5.00	1.50
Pablo Ozuna		
181 Lance Berkman	5.00	1.50
Jason Green		
182 Julio Lugo	5.00	1.50
Tony McKnight		
183 Mitch Meluskey	5.00	1.50
Wade Miller		
184 Chad Durbin RC	5.00	1.50
Hector Ortiz RC		
185 Dermal Brown	5.00	1.50
Mark Quinn		
186 Eric Gagne	8.00	2.40
Mike Judd		
187 Kane Davis RC	5.00	1.50
Valerio De Los Santos		
188 Santiago Perez RC	5.00	1.50
Paul Rigdon RC		
189 Matt Kinney	5.00	1.50
Matt LeCroy		
190 Jason Maxwell	5.00	1.50
A.J. Pierzynski		
191 J.C. Romero RC	25.00	7.50
Johan Santana RC		
192 Tony Armas Jr.	5.00	1.50
Peter Bergeron		
193 Matt Blank	5.00	1.50
Milton Bradley		
194 T.De La Rosa RC	5.00	1.50
Scott Forster RC		
195 Yovanny Lara RC	5.00	1.50
Talmadge Nunnari RC		
196 Brian Schneider	5.00	1.50
Andy Tracy RC		
197 Scott Strickland	5.00	1.50
T.J. Tucker		
198 Eric Cammack RC	5.00	1.50
Jim Mann RC		
199 Grant Roberts	5.00	1.50
Jorge Toca		
200 Alfonso Soriano	8.00	2.40
Jay Tessmer		
201 Terrence Long	8.00	2.40
Mark Mulder		
202 Pat Burrell	8.00	2.40
Cliff Politte		
203 Jimmy Anderson	5.00	1.50
Bronson Arroyo		
204 Mike Darr	5.00	1.50
Kory DeHaan		
205 Adam Eaton	5.00	1.50
Wiki Gonzalez		
206 Brandon Kolb RC	5.00	1.50
Kevin Walker RC		
207 Damon Minor	5.00	1.50
Calvin Murray		
208 Kevin Hodges RC	200.00	60.00
Joel Pineiro RC		
209 Rob Ramsay	10.00	3.00
Kazuhiro Sasaki		
210 Rick Ankiel	5.00	1.50
Mike Matthews		
211 Steve Cox	5.00	1.50
Travis Harper		
212 Kenny Kelly RC	5.00	1.50
Damian Rolls RC		
213 Doug Davis	5.00	1.50
Scott Sheldon		
214 Brian Sikorski	5.00	1.50
Pedro Valdes		
215 Francisco Cordero	5.00	1.50
B.J. Waszgis RC		
216 Matt DeWitt RC	10.00	3.00
Josh Phelps RC		
217 Vernon Wells	5.00	1.50
Dewayne Wise		
218 Geraldo Guzman RC	5.00	1.50
Jason Marquis		
219 Rafael Furcal	5.00	1.50
Steve Sisco RC		
220 B.J. Ryan	5.00	1.50
Kevin Beirne		
221 Matt Ginter RC	5.00	1.50
Brad Penny		
222 Julio Zuleta RC	5.00	1.50
Eric Munson		
223 Dan Reichert	5.00	1.50
Jeff Williams RC		
224 Jason LaRue	5.00	1.50
Danny Ardoin RC		
225 Ray King	5.00	1.50
Mark Redman		
226 Joe Crede	5.00	1.50
Mike Bell		
227 Juan Pierre RC	10.00	3.00
Jay Payton		
228 Wayne Franklin RC	5.00	1.50
Randy Choate RC		
229 Chris Truby	5.00	1.50
Adam Piatt		
230 Kevin Nicholson	5.00	1.50
Chris Woodward		
231 Barry Zito RC	25.00	7.50
Jason Boyd RC		
232 Brian O'Connor RC	5.00	1.50
Miguel Del Toro		
233 Carlos Guillen	5.00	1.50
Aubrey Huff		
234 Chad Hermansen	5.00	1.50
Jason Tyner		
235 Aaron Fultz RC	5.00	1.50
Ryan Vogelsong RC		
236 Shawn Wooten	5.00	1.50
Vance Wilson		
237 Danny Klassen	5.00	1.50
Mike Lamb RC		
238 Chad Bradford	5.00	1.50
Gene Stechshulte RC		
239 Ismael Villegas RC	5.00	1.50
Hector Ramirez RC		
Matt T.Williams RC		
Luis Vizcaino		
240 Mike Garcia RC	5.00	1.50
Domingo Guzman RC		
Justin Brunette RC		
Pasqual Coco RC		
241 Frank Charles RC	5.00	1.50
Keith McDonald RC		
242 Carlos Casimiro RC	5.00	1.50
Morgan Burkhart RC		
243 Raul Gonzalez RC	5.00	1.50
Shawn Gilbert		
244 Darrell Einertson RC	5.00	1.50
Jeff Sparks RC		
245 Augie Ojeda RC	8.00	2.40
Brady Clark		
Todd Belitz		
Eric Byrnes RC		
246 Leo Estrella RC	5.00	1.50
Charlie Greene		
247 Trace Coquillette RC	5.00	1.50
Pedro Feliz RC		
248 Tike Redman RC	5.00	1.50
David Newhan		
249 Rodrigo Lopez RC	8.00	2.40
John Bale RC		
250 Corey Patterson	8.00	2.40
Jose Ortiz RC		
251 Britt Reames RC	5.00	1.50
Oswaldo Mairena RC		
252 Xavier Nady RC	10.00	3.00
Timo Perez RC		
253 Tom Jacquez RC	8.00	2.40
Vicente Padilla RC		
254 Elvis Pena RC	5.00	1.50
Adam Melhuse RC		
255 Ben Weber RC	5.00	1.50
Alex Cabrera RC		

2000 Pacific Omega Copper

Randomly inserted into hobby packs at one in 73, this 150-card set is a partial parallel of the Omega base set. These cards were produced with copper foil stamping, and each card is individually serial numbered to 45.

	Nm-Mt	Ex-Mt
*STARS: 15X TO 30X BASIC CARDS		
*ROOKIES: 15X TO 40X BASIC		

2000 Pacific Omega Gold

Randomly inserted into retail packs at one in 37, this 150-card set is a partial parallel of the Omega base set. These cards were produced with gold foil stamping, and each card is individually serial numbered to 77.

	Nm-Mt	Ex-Mt
*STARS 1-150: 8X TO 20X BASIC		
*ROOKIES 1-150: 10X TO 25X BASIC.		

2000 Pacific Omega Platinum Blue

Randomly inserted into packs at one in 145, this 150-card set is a partial parallel of the Omega base set. These cards were produced with platinum blue foil stamping, and each card is individually serial numbered to 55.

	Nm-Mt	Ex-Mt
*STARS 1-150: 15X TO 30X BASIC		
*ROOKIES 1-150: 15X TO 40X BASIC.		

2000 Pacific Omega Premiere Date

Randomly inserted into hobby packs at one in 37, this 150-card set is a partial parallel of the Omega base set. These cards were produced with a premiere date stamp, and each card is individually serial numbered to 77.

	Nm-Mt	Ex-Mt
*STARS 1-150: 15X TO 30X BASIC CARDS		
*ROOKIES 1-150: 12.5X TO 30X BASIC		

2000 Pacific Omega AL/NL Contenders

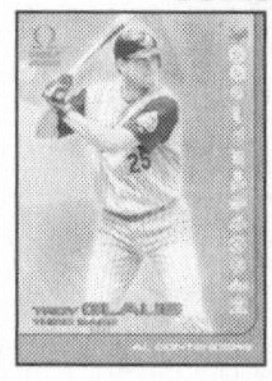

Randomly inserted into packs at 2:37, this 36 card set features superstar caliber players that are on contending teams. Please note that this set is broken into 18 AL contenders, and 18 NL contenders. We have labeled them AL and NL below to help differentiate.

	Nm-Mt	Ex-Mt
COMPLETE AL SET (18)	100.00	30.00
COMPLETE NL SET (18)	100.00	30.00
AL1 Darin Erstad	2.00	.60
AL2 Troy Glaus	3.00	.90
AL3 Mo Vaughn	2.00	.60
AL4 Albert Belle	2.00	.60
AL5 Cal Ripken	15.00	4.50
AL6 Nomar Garciaparra	8.00	2.40
AL7 Pedro Martinez	5.00	1.50
AL8 Frank Thomas	5.00	1.50
AL9 Manny Ramirez	2.00	.60
AL10 Jim Thome	5.00	1.50
AL11 Juan Gonzalez	5.00	1.50
AL12 Roger Clemens	10.00	3.00
AL13 Derek Jeter	12.00	3.60
AL14 Bernie Williams	3.00	.90
AL15 Jason Giambi	5.00	1.50
AL16 Alex Rodriguez	8.00	2.40
AL17 Edgar Martinez	3.00	.90
AL18 Carlos Delgado	2.00	.60
NL1 Randy Johnson	5.00	1.50
NL2 Chipper Jones	5.00	1.50
NL3 Greg Maddux	8.00	2.40
NL4 Sammy Sosa	8.00	2.40
NL5 Sean Casey	2.00	.60
NL6 Ken Griffey Jr.	8.00	2.40
NL7 Todd Helton	3.00	.90
NL8 Jeff Bagwell	3.00	.90
NL9 Shawn Green	2.00	.60
NL10 Gary Sheffield	2.00	.60
NL11 Vladimir Guerrero	5.00	1.50
NL12 Mike Piazza	8.00	2.40
NL13 Scott Rolen	3.00	.90
NL14 Rick Ankiel	2.50	.75
NL15 J.D. Drew	2.00	.60
NL16 Jim Edmonds	2.00	.60
NL17 Mark McGwire	12.00	3.60
NL18 Barry Bonds	12.00	3.60

2000 Pacific Omega EO Portraits

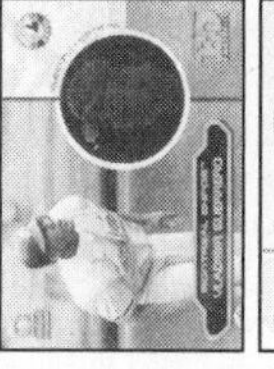

Randomly inserted into packs at one in 73, this 20-card insert features a special die-cut photo of the corresponding player's face.

	Nm-Mt	Ex-Mt
COMPLETE SET (20)	400.00	120.00
ONE OF ONE PARALLELS EXIST		
1 Chipper Jones	12.00	3.60
2 Greg Maddux	20.00	6.00
3 Cal Ripken	40.00	12.00
4 Pedro Martinez	12.00	3.60
5 Nomar Garciaparra	20.00	6.00
6 Sammy Sosa	20.00	6.00
7 Frank Thomas	12.00	3.60
8 Ken Griffey Jr.	20.00	6.00
9 Gary Sheffield	5.00	1.50
10 Vladimir Guerrero	12.00	3.60
11 Mike Piazza	20.00	6.00
12 Roger Clemens	25.00	7.50
13 Derek Jeter	30.00	9.00
14 Pat Burrell	10.00	3.00
15 Rick Ankiel	6.00	1.80
16 Mark McGwire	30.00	9.00
17 Tony Gwynn	15.00	4.50
18 Barry Bonds	30.00	9.00
19 Alex Rodriguez	20.00	6.00
20 Ivan Rodriguez	12.00	3.60

2000 Pacific Omega Full Count

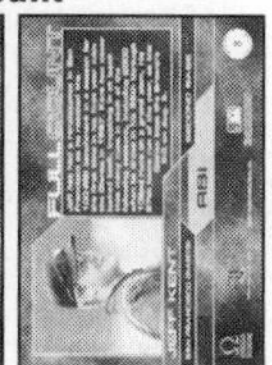

Randomly inserted into hobby packs at 4:37, this 36-card insert features the Major League's RBI, Slugging Percent, Strikeout, and Home Run leaders. Please note that a serial-numbered parallel exists of this insert.

	Nm-Mt	Ex-Mt
COMPLETE SET (36)	120.00	36.00
1 Magglio Ordonez	1.25	.35
2 Manny Ramirez	1.25	.35
4 David Justice	1.25	.35
5 Bernie Williams	2.00	.60
6 Jason Giambi	3.00	.90
7 Scott Rolen	2.00	.60
8 Jeff Kent	1.25	.35
9 Edgar Martinez	2.00	.60
10 Randy Johnson	3.00	.90
11 Greg Maddux	5.00	1.50
12 Mike Mussina	3.00	.90
13 Pedro Martinez	3.00	.90
14 Chuck Finley	1.25	.35
15 Kevin Brown	1.25	.35
16 Roger Clemens	6.00	1.80
17 Tim Hudson	3.00	.90
18 Rick Ankiel	1.50	.45
19 Troy Glaus	2.00	.60
20 Chipper Jones	3.00	.90
21 Nomar Garciaparra	5.00	1.50
22 Jeff Bagwell	2.00	.60
23 Shawn Green	1.25	.35
24 Vladimir Guerrero	3.00	.90
25 Mike Piazza	5.00	1.50
26 Jim Edmonds	1.25	.35
27 Rafael Palmeiro	2.00	.60
28 Cal Ripken	10.00	3.00
29 Sammy Sosa	5.00	1.50
30 Frank Thomas	3.00	.90
31 Ken Griffey Jr.	5.00	1.50
32 Gary Sheffield	1.25	.35
33 Barry Bonds	8.00	2.40
34 Alex Rodriguez	5.00	1.50
35 Mark McGwire	8.00	2.40
36 Carlos Delgado	1.25	.35

2000 Pacific Omega MLB Generations

Randomly inserted into packs at one in 145, this 20-card insert features dual-player cards that picture a modern day superstar with a top prospect.

	Nm-Mt	Ex-Mt
COMPLETE SET (20)	400.00	120.00
1 Mark McGwire	40.00	12.00
Pat Burrell		
2 Cal Ripken	50.00	15.00
Alex Rodriguez		
3 Randy Johnson	15.00	4.50
Rick Ankiel		
4 Tony Gwynn	20.00	6.00
Darin Erstad		
5 Barry Bonds	40.00	12.00
Magglio Ordonez		
6 Frank Thomas	15.00	4.50
Jason Giambi		
7 Roger Clemens	30.00	9.00
Kerry Wood		
8 Mike Piazza	25.00	7.50
Mitch Meluskey		
9 Ken Griffey Jr.	25.00	7.50
Andruw Jones		
10 Bernie Williams	10.00	3.00
J.D. Drew		
11 Chipper Jones	15.00	4.50
Troy Glaus		
12 Andres Galarraga	10.00	3.00
Todd Helton		
13 Juan Gonzalez	15.00	4.50
Vladimir Guerrero		
14 Craig Biggio	10.00	3.00
Rafael Furcal		
15 Sammy Sosa	25.00	7.50
Jermaine Dye		
16 Larry Walker	10.00	3.00
Richard Hidalgo		
17 Greg Maddux	25.00	7.50
Adam Eaton		
18 Barry Larkin	40.00	12.00
Derek Jeter		
19 Roberto Alomar	15.00	4.50
Jose Vidro		
20 Jeff Kent	6.00	1.80
Edgardo Alfonzo		

2000 Pacific Omega Signatures

Randomly inserted into packs, this nine-card insert features autographed cards from players like Nomar Garciaparra and Frank Thomas.

	Nm-Mt	Ex-Mt
1 Darin Erstad	25.00	7.50
2 Nomar Garciaparra	150.00	45.00
4 Magglio Ordonez	25.00	7.50
5 Frank Thomas	60.00	18.00
6 Brady Clark	15.00	4.50
7 Richard Hidalgo	25.00	7.50
8 Gary Sheffield	40.00	12.00
9 Pat Burrell	40.00	12.00
10 Jim Edmonds	25.00	7.50

2000 Pacific Omega Stellar Performers

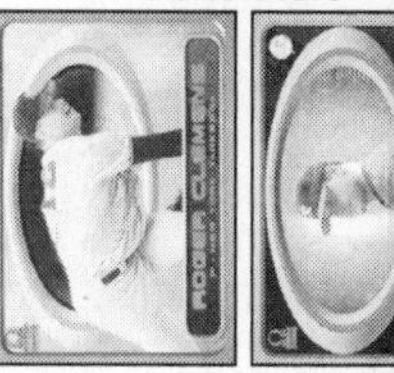

Randomly inserted into packs at one in 37, this 20-card insert features superstar caliber players.

	Nm-Mt	Ex-Mt
COMPLETE SET (20)	200.00	60.00
1 Darin Erstad	2.50	.75
2 Chipper Jones	6.00	1.80
3 Greg Maddux	10.00	3.00
4 Cal Ripken	20.00	6.00
5 Pedro Martinez	6.00	1.80
6 Nomar Garciaparra	10.00	3.00
7 Sammy Sosa	10.00	3.00
8 Frank Thomas	6.00	1.80
9 Ken Griffey Jr.	10.00	3.00
10 Todd Helton	4.00	1.20
11 Jeff Bagwell	4.00	1.20
12 Vladimir Guerrero	6.00	1.80
13 Mike Piazza	10.00	3.00
14 Derek Jeter	15.00	4.50
15 Roger Clemens	12.00	3.60
16 Tony Gwynn	8.00	2.40
17 Barry Bonds	15.00	4.50
18 Alex Rodriguez	10.00	3.00
19 Mark McGwire	15.00	4.50
20 Ivan Rodriguez	6.00	1.80

1998 Pacific Online

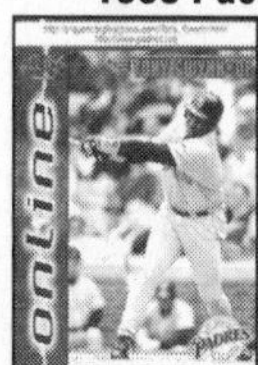

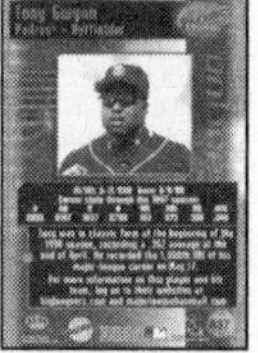

The 1998 Pacific Online set was issued in one series totalling 800 cards, but numbered to only 780. To add some spice to the set, the manufacturer decided to create two versions of twenty top stars. These cards are designed and (unfortunately) numbered identically, but feature totally different photos on both the front and back. For simplification to checklisting, we've added A and B suffixes to these cards, and added descriptions of the photos in an attempt to differentiate them. Cards were initially distributed in nine-card packs with an SRP of $1.49. An unnumbered Tony Gwynn Sample card (featuring entirely different photos and cardback text from the regular issue Gwynn cards) was distributed in dealer order forms several weeks prior to the products shipping date. Notable Rookie Cards include Kevin Millwood and Maggio Ordonez.

Nm-Mt Ex-Mt
COMPLETE SET (800) 180.00 55.00
1 Garret Anderson .40 .12
2 Rich DeLucia .40 .12
3 Jason Dickson .40 .12
4 Gary DiSarcina .40 .12
5 Jim Edmonds .40 .12
6 Darin Erstad .40 .12
7 Cecil Fielder .40 .12
8 Chuck Finley .40 .12
9 Carlos Garcia .40 .12
10 Shigetoshi Hasegawa .40 .12
11 Ken Hill .40 .12
12 Dave Hollins .40 .12
13 Mike Holtz .40 .12
14 Mike James .40 .12
15 Norberto Martin .40 .12
16 Damon Mashore .40 .12
17 Jack McDowell .40 .12
18 Phil Nevin .40 .12
19 Omar Olivares .40 .12
20 Troy Percival .40 .12
21 Rich Robertson .40 .12
22 Tim Salmon .60 .18
23 Craig Shipley .40 .12
24 Matt Walbeck .40 .12
25 Allen Watson .40 .12
26 Jim Edmonds TC .40 .12
27 Brian Anderson .40 .12
28 Tony Batista .40 .12
29 Jay Bell .40 .12
30 Andy Benes .40 .12
31 Yamil Benitez .40 .12
32 Willie Blair .40 .12
33 Brent Brede .40 .12
34 Scott Brow .40 .12
35 Omar Daal .40 .12
36 Dave Dellucci RC .40 .12
37 Edwin Diaz .40 .12
38 Jorge Fabregas .40 .12
39 Andy Fox .40 .12
40 Karim Garcia .40 .12
41 T.Lee Fielding .40 .12
41A T.Lee Hitting .40 .12
42 Barry Manuel .40 .12
43 Gregg Olson .40 .12
44 Felix Rodriguez .40 .12
45 Clint Sodowsky .40 .12
46 Russ Springer .40 .12
47 Andy Stankiewicz .40 .12
48 Kelly Stinnett .40 .12
49 Jeff Suppan .40 .12
50 Devon White .40 .12
51 Matt Williams .40 .12
52 Travis Lee TC .40 .12
53 Danny Bautista .40 .12
54 Rafael Belliard .40 .12
55 Adam Butler RC .40 .12
56 Mike Cather RC .40 .12
57 Brian Edmondson .40 .12
58 Alan Embree .40 .12
59 Andres Galarraga .40 .12
60 Tom Glavine .60 .18
61 Tony Graffanino .40 .12
62 Andruw Jones .40 .12
63 C.Jones Fielding 1.00 .30
63A C.Jones Hitting 1.00 .30
64 Ryan Klesko .40 .12
65 Keith Lockhart .40 .12
66 Javy Lopez .40 .12
67 G.Maddux Hitting 1.50 .45
67A G.Maddux Pitching 1.50 .45
68 Dennis Martinez .40 .12
69 Kevin Millwood RC 2.00 .60
70 Denny Neagle .40 .12
71 Eddie Perez .40 .12
72 Curtis Pride .40 .12
73 John Smoltz .60 .18
74 Michael Tucker .40 .12
75 Walt Weiss .40 .12
76 Gerald Williams .40 .12
77 Mark Wohlers .40 .12
78 Chipper Jones TC .60 .18
79 Roberto Alomar 1.00 .30
80 Brady Anderson .40 .12
81 Harold Baines .40 .12
82 Armando Benitez .40 .12
83 Mike Bordick .40 .12
84 Joe Carter .40 .12
85 Norm Charlton .40 .12
86 Eric Davis .40 .12
87 Doug Drabek .40 .12
88 Scott Erickson .40 .12
89 Jeffrey Hammonds .40 .12
90 Chris Hoiles .40 .12
91 Scott Kamieniecki .40 .12
92 Jimmy Key .40 .12
93 Terry Mathews .40 .12
94 Alan Mills .40 .12
95 Mike Mussina 1.00 .30
96 Jesse Orosco .40 .12
97 Rafael Palmeiro .60 .18
98 Sidney Ponson .40 .12
99 Jeff Reboulet .40 .12
100 Arthur Rhodes .40 .12
101 C.Ripken Hitting 3.00 .90
101A C.Ripken 3.00 .90
Hitting Close-Up
102 Nerio Rodriguez .40 .12
103 B.J. Surhoff .40 .12
104 Lenny Webster .40 .12
105 Cal Ripken TC 1.50 .45
106 Steve Avery .40 .12
107 Mike Benjamin .40 .12
108 Darren Bragg .40 .12
109 Damon Buford .40 .12
110 Jim Corsi .40 .12
111 Dennis Eckersley .40 .12
112 Rich Garces .40 .12
113 N.Garciaparra Fielding 1.50 .45
113A Nomar Garciaparra 1.50 .45
Hitting
114 Tom Gordon .40 .12
115 Scott Hatteberg .40 .12
116 Butch Henry .40 .12
117 Reggie Jefferson .40 .12
118 Mark Lemke .40 .12
119 Darren Lewis .40 .12
120 Jim Leyritz .40 .12
121 Derek Lowe .40 .12
122 Pedro Martinez 1.00 .30
123 Troy O'Leary .40 .12
124 Brian Rose .40 .12
125 Bret Saberhagen .40 .12
126 Donnie Sadler .40 .12
127 Brian Shouse RC .30 .09
128 John Valentin .40 .12
129 Jason Varitek .40 .12
130 Mo Vaughn .40 .12
131 Tim Wakefield .40 .12
132 John Wasdin .40 .12
133 Nomar Garciaparra TC 1.00 .30
134 Terry Adams .40 .12
135 Manny Alexander .40 .12
136 Rod Beck .40 .12
137 Jeff Blauser .40 .12
138 Brant Brown .40 .12
139 Mark Clark .40 .12
140 Jeremi Gonzalez .40 .12
141 Mark Grace .60 .18
142 Jose Hernandez .40 .12
143 Tyler Houston .40 .12
144 Lance Johnson .40 .12
145 Sandy Martinez .40 .12
146 Matt Mieske .40 .12
147 Mickey Morandini .40 .12
148 Terry Mulholland .40 .12
149 Kevin Orie .40 .12
150 Bob Patterson .40 .12
151 Marc Pisciotta RC .40 .12
152 Henry Rodriguez .40 .12
153 Scott Servais .40 .12
154 Sammy Sosa 1.50 .45
155 Kevin Tapani .40 .12
156 Steve Trachsel .40 .12
157 K.Wood Pitching 1.00 .30
157A Kerry Wood 1.00 .30
Pitching Close-Up
158 Kerry Wood TC .60 .18
159 Jeff Abbott .40 .12
160 James Baldwin .40 .12
161 Albert Belle .40 .12
162 Jason Bere .40 .12
163 Mike Cameron .40 .12
164 Mike Caruso .40 .12
165 Carlos Castillo .40 .12
166 Tony Castillo .40 .12
167 Ray Durham .40 .12
168 Scott Eyre .40 .12
169 Tom Fordham .40 .12
170 Keith Foulke .40 .12
171 Lou Frazier .40 .12
172 Matt Karchner .40 .12
173 Chad Kreuter .40 .12
174 Jaime Navarro .40 .12
175 Greg Norton .40 .12
176 Charlie O'Brien .40 .12
177 Magglio Ordonez RC 2.50 .75
178 Ruben Sierra .40 .12
179 Bill Simas .40 .12
180 Mike Sirotka .40 .12
181 Chris Snopek .40 .12
182 F.Thomas Batter's Box 1.00 .30
182A Frank Thomas 1.00 .30
Swing
183 Robin Ventura .40 .12
184 Frank Thomas TC .60 .18
185 Stan Belinda .40 .12
186 Aaron Boone .40 .12
187 Bret Boone .40 .12
188 Brook Fordyce .40 .12
189 Willie Greene .40 .12
190 Pete Harnisch .40 .12
191 Lenny Harris .40 .12
192 Mark Hutton .40 .12
193 Damian Jackson .40 .12
194 Ricardo Jordan .40 .12
195 Barry Larkin 1.00 .30
196 Eduardo Perez .40 .12
197 Pokey Reese .40 .12
198 Mike Remlinger .40 .12
199 Reggie Sanders .40 .12
200 Jeff Shaw .40 .12
201 Chris Stynes .40 .12
202 Scott Sullivan .40 .12
203 Eddie Taubensee .40 .12
204 Brett Tomko .40 .12
205 Pat Watkins .40 .12
206 David Weathers .40 .12
207 Gabe White .40 .12
208 Scott Winchester .40 .12
209 Barry Larkin TC .60 .18
210 Sandy Alomar Jr. .40 .12
211 Paul Assenmacher .40 .12
212 Geronimo Berroa .40 .12
213 Pat Borders .40 .12
214 Jeff Branson .40 .12
215 Dave Burba .40 .12
216 Bartolo Colon .40 .12
217 Shawon Dunston .40 .12
218 Travis Fryman .40 .12
219 Brian Giles .40 .12
220 Dwight Gooden .40 .12
221 Mike Jackson .40 .12
222 David Justice .40 .12
223 Kenny Lofton .40 .12
224 Jose Mesa .40 .12
225 Alvin Morman .40 .12
226 Charles Nagy .40 .12
227 Chad Ogea .40 .12
228 Eric Plunk .40 .12
229 Manny Ramirez .40 .12
230 Paul Shuey .40 .12
231 Jim Thome 1.00 .30
232 Ron Villone .40 .12
233 Omar Vizquel .40 .12
234 Enrique Wilson .40 .12
235 Jaret Wright .40 .12
236 Manny Ramirez TC .40 .12
237 Pedro Astacio .40 .12
238 Jason Bates .40 .12
239 Dante Bichette .40 .12
240 Ellis Burks .40 .12
241 Vinny Castilla .40 .12
242 Greg Colbrunn .40 .12
243 Mike DeJean RC .40 .12
244 Jerry Dipoto .40 .12
245 Curtis Goodwin .40 .12
246 Todd Helton .60 .18
247 Bobby Jones RC .40 .12
248 Darryl Kile .40 .12
249 Mike Lansing .40 .12
250 Curtis Leskanic .40 .12
251 Nelson Liriano .40 .12
252 Kirt Manwaring .40 .12
253 Chuck McElroy .40 .12
254 Mike Munoz .40 .12
255 Neifi Perez .40 .12
256 Jeff Reed .40 .12
257 Mark Thompson .40 .12
258 John Vander Wal .40 .12
259 Dave Veres .40 .12
260 L.Walker Hitting .60 .18
260A Larry Walker .60 .18
Hitting Close Up
261 Jamey Wright .40 .12
262 Larry Walker TC .40 .12
263 Kimera Bartee .40 .12
264 Doug Brocail .40 .12
265 Raul Casanova .40 .12
266 Frank Castillo .40 .12
267 Frank Catalanotto RC .60 .18
268 Tony Clark .40 .12
269 Deivi Cruz .40 .12
270 Roberto Duran RC .40 .12
271 Damion Easley .40 .12
272 Bryce Florie .40 .12
273 Luis Gonzalez .40 .12
274 Bobby Higginson .40 .12
275 Brian Hunter .40 .12
276 Todd Jones .40 .12
277 Greg Keagle .40 .12
278 Jeff Manto .40 .12
279 Brian Moehler .40 .12
280 Joe Oliver .40 .12
281 Joe Randa .40 .12
282 Bill Ripken .40 .12
283 Bip Roberts .40 .12
284 Sean Runyan .40 .12
285 A.J. Sager .40 .12
286 Justin Thompson .40 .12
287 Tony Clark TC .40 .12
288 Antonio Alfonseca .40 .12
289 Dave Berg RC .40 .12
290 Josh Booty .40 .12
291 John Cangelosi .40 .12
292 Craig Counsell .40 .12
293 Vic Darensbourg .40 .12
294 Cliff Floyd .40 .12
295 Oscar Henriquez .40 .12
296 Felix Heredia .40 .12
297 Ryan Jackson RC .40 .12
298 Mark Kotsay .40 .12
299 Andy Larkin .40 .12
300 Derrek Lee .40 .12
301 Brian Meadows .40 .12
302 Rafael Medina .40 .12
303 Jay Powell .40 .12
304 Edgar Renteria .40 .12
305 Jesus Sanchez RC .40 .12
306 Rob Stanifer RC .40 .12
307 Gregg Zaun .40 .12
308 Derrek Lee TC .40 .12
309 Moises Alou .40 .12
310 Brad Ausmus .40 .12
311 J.Bagwell Fielding .60 .18
311A J.Bagwell Hitting .60 .18
312 Derek Bell .40 .12
313 Sean Bergman .40 .12
314 Sean Berry .40 .12
315 Craig Biggio .60 .18
316 Tim Bogar .40 .12
317 Jose Cabrera RC .40 .12
318 Dave Clark .40 .12
319 Tony Eusebio .40 .12
320 Carl Everett .40 .12
321 Ricky Gutierrez .40 .12
322 John Halama RC .40 .12
323 Mike Hampton .40 .12
324 Doug Henry .40 .12
325 Richard Hidalgo .40 .12
326 Jack Howell .40 .12
327 Jose Lima .40 .12
328 Mike Magnante .40 .12
329 Trever Miller .40 .12
330 C.J. Nitkowski .40 .12
331 Shane Reynolds .40 .12
332 Bill Spiers .40 .12
333 Billy Wagner .40 .12
334 Jeff Bagwell TC .40 .12
335 Tim Belcher .40 .12
336 Brian Bevil .40 .12
337 Johnny Damon .40 .12
338 Jermaine Dye .40 .12
339 Sal Fasano .40 .12
340 Shane Halter .40 .12
341 Chris Haney .40 .12
342 Jed Hansen .40 .12
343 Jeff King .40 .12
344 Jeff Montgomery .40 .12
345 Hal Morris .40 .12
346 Jose Offerman .40 .12
347 Dean Palmer .40 .12
348 Terry Pendleton .40 .12
349 Hipolito Pichardo .40 .12
350 Jim Pittsley .40 .12
351 Pat Rapp .40 .12
352 Jose Rosado .40 .12
353 Glendon Rusch .40 .12
354 Scott Service .40 .12
355 Larry Sutton .40 .12
356 Mike Sweeney .40 .12
357 Joe Vitiello .40 .12
358 Matt Whisenant .40 .12
359 Ernie Young .40 .12
360 Jeff King TC .40 .12
361 Bobby Bonilla .40 .12
362 Jim Bruske .40 .12
363 Juan Castro .40 .12
364 Roger Cedeno .40 .12
365 Mike Devereaux .40 .12
366 Darren Dreifort .40 .12
367 Jim Eisenreich .40 .12
368 Wilton Guerrero .40 .12
369 Mark Guthrie .40 .12
370 Darren Hall .40 .12
371 Todd Hollandsworth .40 .12
372 Thomas Howard .40 .12
373 Trenidad Hubbard .40 .12
374 Charles Johnson .40 .12
375 Eric Karros .40 .12
376 Paul Konerko .40 .12
377 Matt Luke .40 .12
378 Ramon Martinez .40 .12
379 Raul Mondesi .40 .12
380 Hideo Nomo 1.00 .30
381 Antonio Osuna .40 .12
382 Chan Ho Park .40 .12
383 Tom Prince .40 .12
384 Scott Radinsky .40 .12
385 Gary Sheffield .40 .12
386 Ismael Valdes .40 .12
387 Jose Vizcaino .40 .12
388 Eric Young .40 .12
389 Gary Sheffield TC .40 .12
390 Jeromy Burnitz .40 .12
391 Jeff Cirillo .40 .12
392 Cal Eldred .40 .12
393 Chad Fox RC .40 .12
394 Marquis Grissom .40 .12
395 Bob Hamelin .40 .12
396 Bobby Hughes .40 .12
397 Darrin Jackson .40 .12
398 John Jaha .40 .12
399 Geoff Jenkins .40 .12
400 Doug Jones .40 .12
401 Jeff Juden .40 .12
402 Scott Karl .40 .12
403 Jesse Levis .40 .12
404 Mark Loretta .40 .12
405 Mike Matheny .40 .12
406 Jose Mercedes .40 .12
407 Mike Myers .40 .12
408 Marc Newfield .40 .12
409 Dave Nilsson .40 .12
410 Al Reyes .40 .12
411 Jose Valentin .40 .12
412 Fernando Vina .40 .12
413 Paul Wagner .40 .12
414 Bob Wickman .40 .12
415 Steve Woodard .40 .12
416 Marquis Grissom TC .40 .12
417 Rick Aguilera .40 .12
418 Ron Coomer .40 .12
419 Marty Cordova .40 .12
420 Brent Gates .40 .12
421 Eddie Guardado .40 .12
422 Denny Hocking .40 .12
423 Matt Lawton .40 .12
424 Pat Meares .40 .12
425 Orlando Merced .40 .12
426 Eric Milton .40 .12
427 Paul Molitor .60 .18
428 Mike Morgan .40 .12
429 Dan Naulty .40 .12
430 Otis Nixon .40 .12
431 Alex Ochoa .40 .12
432 David Ortiz .40 .12
433 Brad Radke .40 .12
434 Todd Ritchie .40 .12
435 Frank Rodriguez .40 .12
436 Terry Steinbach .40 .12
437 Greg Swindell .40 .12
438 Bob Tewksbury .40 .12
439 Mike Trombley .40 .12
440 Javier Valentin .40 .12
441 Todd Walker .40 .12
442 Paul Molitor TC .40 .12
443 Shane Andrews .40 .12
444 Miguel Batista .40 .12
445 Shayne Bennett .40 .12
446 Rick DeHart RC .40 .12
447 Brad Fullmer .40 .12
448 Mark Grudzielanek .40 .12
449 Vladimir Guerrero 1.00 .30
450 Dustin Hermanson .40 .12
451 Steve Kline .40 .12
452 Scott Livingstone .40 .12
453 Mike Maddux .40 .12
454 Derrick May .40 .12
455 Ryan McGuire .40 .12
456 Trey Moore .40 .12
457 Mike Mordecai .40 .12
458 Carl Pavano .40 .12
459 Carlos Perez .40 .12
460 F.P. Santangelo .40 .12
461 DaRond Stovall .40 .12
462 Anthony Telford .40 .12
463 Ugueth Urbina .40 .12
464 Marc Valdes .40 .12
465 Jose Vidro .40 .12
466 Rondell White .40 .12
467 Chris Widger .40 .12
468 Vladimir Guerrero TC .60 .18
469 Edgardo Alfonzo .40 .12
470 Carlos Baerga .40 .12
471 Rich Becker .40 .12
472 Brian Bohanon .40 .12
473 Alberto Castillo .40 .12
474 Dennis Cook .40 .12
475 John Franco .40 .12
476 Matt Franco .40 .12
477 Bernard Gilkey .40 .12
478 John Hudek .40 .12
479 Butch Huskey .40 .12
480 Bobby Jones .40 .12
481 Al Leiter .40 .12
482 Luis Lopez .40 .12
483 Brian McRae .40 .12
484 Dave Mlicki .40 .12
485 John Olerud .40 .12
486 Rey Ordonez .40 .12
487 Craig Paquette .40 .12
488 M.Piazza Hitting 1.50 .45
488A M.Piazza Close-Up 1.50 .45
489 Todd Pratt .40 .12
490 Mel Rojas .40 .12
491 Tim Spehr .40 .12
492 Turk Wendell .40 .12
493 Masato Yoshii RC .60 .18
494 Mike Piazza TC 1.00 .30
495 Willie Banks .40 .12
496 Scott Brosius .40 .12
497 Mike Buddie RC .40 .12
498 Homer Bush .40 .12
499 David Cone .40 .12
500 Chad Curtis .40 .12
501 Chili Davis .40 .12
502 Joe Girardi .40 .12
503 Darren Holmes .40 .12
504 Hideki Irabu .40 .12
505 D.Jeter Fielding 2.50 .75
505A D.Jeter Hitting 2.50 .75
506 Chuck Knoblauch .40 .12
507 Graeme Lloyd .40 .12
508 Tino Martinez .60 .18
509 Ramiro Mendoza .40 .12
510 Jeff Nelson .40 .12
511 Paul O'Neill .60 .18
512 Andy Pettitte .60 .18
513 Jorge Posada .60 .18
514 Tim Raines .40 .12
515 Mariano Rivera .60 .18
516 Luis Sojo .40 .12
517 Mike Stanton .40 .12
518 Darryl Strawberry .60 .18
519 Dale Sveum .40 .12
520 David Wells .40 .12
521 Bernie Williams .60 .18
522 Bernie Williams TC .40 .12
523 Kurt Abbott .40 .12
524 Mike Blowers .40 .12
525 Rafael Bournigal .40 .12
526 Tom Candiotti .40 .12
527 Ryan Christenson RC .40 .12
528 Mike Fetters .40 .12
529 Jason Giambi 1.00 .30
530 B.Grieve Running .40 .12
530A B.Grieve Swinging .40 .12
531 Buddy Groom .40 .12
532 Jimmy Haynes .40 .12
533 Rickey Henderson 1.00 .30
534 A.J. Hinch .40 .12
535 Mike Macfarlane .40 .12
536 Dave Magadan .40 .12
537 T.J. Mathews .40 .12
538 Jason McDonald .40 .12
539 Kevin Mitchell .40 .12
540 Mike Mohler .40 .12
541 Mike Oquist .40 .12
542 Ariel Prieto .40 .12
543 Kenny Rogers .40 .12
544 Aaron Small .40 .12
545 Scott Spiezio .40 .12
546 Matt Stairs .40 .12
547 Bill Taylor .40 .12
548 Dave Telgheder .40 .12
549 Jack Voigt .40 .12
550 Ben Grieve TC .40 .12
551 Bob Abreu .40 .12
552 Ruben Amaro .40 .12
553 Alex Arias .40 .12
554 Matt Beech .40 .12
555 Ricky Bottalico .40 .12
556 Billy Brewer .40 .12
557 Rico Brogna .40 .12
558 Doug Glanville .40 .12
559 Wayne Gomes .40 .12
560 Mike Grace .40 .12
561 Tyler Green .40 .12
562 Rex Hudler .40 .12
563 Gregg Jefferies .40 .12
564 Kevin Jordan .40 .12
565 Mark Leiter .40 .12
566 Mark Lewis .40 .12
567 Mike Lieberthal .40 .12
568 Mark Parent .40 .12
569 Yorkis Perez .40 .12
570 Desi Relaford .40 .12
571 Scott Rolen .60 .18
572 Curt Schilling .60 .18
573 Kevin Sefcik .40 .12
574 Jerry Spradlin .40 .12
575 Garrett Stephenson .40 .12
576 Darrin Winston RC .40 .12
577 Scott Rolen TC .40 .12
578 Jermaine Allensworth .40 .12
579 Jason Christiansen .40 .12
580 Lou Collier .40 .12
581 Francisco Cordova .40 .12
582 Elmer Dessens .40 .12
583 Freddy Garcia .40 .12
584 Jose Guillen .40 .12
585 Jason Kendall .40 .12
586 Jon Lieber .40 .12
587 Esteban Loaiza .40 .12
588 Al Martin .40 .12
589 Javier Martinez RC .40 .12
590 Chris Peters .40 .12
591 Kevin Polcovich .40 .12
592 Ricardo Rincon .40 .12
593 Jason Schmidt .40 .12
594 Jose Silva .40 .12
595 Mark Smith .40 .12
596 Doug Strange .40 .12
597 Turner Ward .40 .12
598 Marc Wilkins .40 .12
599 Mike Williams .40 .12
600 Tony Womack .40 .12
601 Kevin Young .40 .12
602 Tony Womack TC .40 .12
603 Manny Aybar RC .40 .12
604 Kent Bottenfield .40 .12
605 Jeff Brantley .40 .12
606 Mike Busby .40 .12
607 Royce Clayton .40 .12
608 Delino DeShields .40 .12
609 John Frascatore .40 .12
610 Gary Gaetti .40 .12
611 Ron Gant .40 .12
612 David Howard .40 .12
613 Brian Hunter .40 .12
614 Brian Jordan .40 .12
615 Tom Lampkin .40 .12
616 Ray Lankford .40 .12
617 Braden Looper .40 .12
618 John Mabry .40 .12
619 Eli Marrero .40 .12
620 Willie McGee .40 .12
621 M.McGwire Fielding 2.50 .75
621A M.McGwire Hitting 2.50 .75

622 Kent Mercker .40 .12
623 Matt Morris .40 .12
624 Donovan Osborne .40 .12
625 Tom Pagnozzi .40 .12
626 Lance Painter .40 .12
627 Mark Petkovsek .40 .12
628 Todd Stottlemyre .40 .12
629 Mark McGwire TC 1.25 .35
630 Andy Ashby .40 .12
631 Brian Boehringer .40 .12
632 Kevin Brown .60 .18
633 Ken Caminiti .40 .12
634 Steve Finley .40 .12
635 Ed Giovanola .40 .12
636 Chris Gomez .40 .12
637 T.Gwynn Blue Jersey 1.25 .35
637A Tony Gwynn 1.25 .35
White Jersey
638 Joey Hamilton .40 .12
639 Carlos Hernandez .40 .12
640 Sterling Hitchcock .40 .12
641 Trevor Hoffman .40 .12
642 Wally Joyner .40 .12
643 Dan Miceli .40 .12
644 James Mouton .40 .12
645 Greg Myers .40 .12
646 Carlos Reyes .40 .12
647 Andy Sheets .40 .12
648 Pete Smith .40 .12
649 Mark Sweeney .40 .12
650 Greg Vaughn .40 .12
651 Quilvio Veras .40 .12
652 Tony Gwynn TC .60 .18
653 Rich Aurilia .40 .12
654 Marvin Benard .40 .12
655 B.Bonds Hitting 2.50 .75
655A B.Bonds Close-Up 2.50 .75
656 Danny Darwin .40 .12
657 Shawn Estes .40 .12
658 Mark Gardner .40 .12
659 Darryl Hamilton .40 .12
660 Charlie Hayes .40 .12
661 Orel Hershiser .40 .12
662 Stan Javier .40 .12
663 Brian Johnson .40 .12
664 John Johnstone .40 .12
665 Jeff Kent .40 .12
666 Brent Mayne .40 .12
667 Bill Mueller .40 .12
668 Robb Nen .40 .12
669 Jim Poole .40 .12
670 Steve Reed .40 .12
671 Rich Rodriguez .40 .12
672 Kirk Rueter .40 .12
673 Rey Sanchez .40 .12
674 J.T. Snow .40 .12
675 Julian Tavarez .40 .12
676 Barry Bonds TC 1.00 .30
677 Rich Amaral .40 .12
678 Bobby Ayala .40 .12
679 Jay Buhner .40 .12
680 Ken Cloude .40 .12
681 Joey Cora .40 .12
682 Russ Davis .40 .12
683 Rob Ducey .40 .12
684 Jeff Fassero .40 .12
685 Tony Fossas .40 .12
686 K.Griffey Jr. Fielding 1.50 .45
686A K.Griffey Jr. Hitting 1.50 .45
687 Glenallen Hill .40 .12
688 Jeff Huson .40 .12
689 Randy Johnson 1.00 .30
690 Edgar Martinez .60 .18
691 John Marzano .40 .12
692 Jamie Moyer .40 .12
693 A.Rodriguez Fielding 1.50 .45
693A A.Rodriguez Hitting 1.50 .45
694 David Segui .40 .12
695 Heathcliff Slocumb .40 .12
696 Paul Spoljaric .40 .12
697 Bill Swift .40 .12
698 Mike Timlin .40 .12
699 Bob Wells .40 .12
700 Dan Wilson .40 .12
701 Ken Griffey Jr. TC 1.00 .30
702 Wilson Alvarez .40 .12
703 Rolando Arrojo RC .40 .12
704 W.Boggs Fielding .60 .18
704A W.Boggs Hitting .60 .18
705 Rich Butler RC .40 .12
706 Miguel Cairo .40 .12
707 Mike Difelice RC .40 .12
708 John Flaherty .40 .12
709 Roberto Hernandez .40 .12
710 Mike Kelly .40 .12
711 Aaron Ledesma .40 .12
712 Albie Lopez .40 .12
713 Dave Martinez .40 .12
714 Quinton McCracken .40 .12
715 Fred McGriff .60 .18
716 Jim Mecir .40 .12
717 Tony Saunders .40 .12
718 Bobby Smith .40 .12
719 Paul Sorrento .40 .12
720 Dennis Springer .40 .12
721 Kevin Stocker .40 .12
722 Ramon Tatis .40 .12
723 Bubba Trammell .40 .12
724 Esteban Yan RC .40 .12
725 Wade Boggs TC .40 .12
726 Luis Alicea .40 .12
727 Scott Bailes .40 .12
728 John Burkett .40 .12
729 Domingo Cedeno .40 .12
730 Will Clark 1.00 .30
731 Kevin Elster .40 .12
732 J.Gonzalez With Bat 1.00 .30
732A Juan Gonzalez 1.00 .30
Without Bat
733 Tom Goodwin .40 .12
734 Rusty Greer .40 .12
735 Eric Gunderson .40 .12
736 Bill Haselman .40 .12
737 Rick Helling .40 .12
738 Roberto Kelly .40 .12
739 Mark McLemore .40 .12
740 Darren Oliver .40 .12
741 Danny Patterson .40 .12
742 Roger Pavlik .40 .12
743 I.Rodriguez Fielding 1.00 .30
743A I.Rodriguez Hitting 1.00 .30
744 Aaron Sele .40 .12
745 Mike Simms .40 .12
746 Lee Stevens .40 .12
747 Fernando Tatis .40 .12
748 John Wetteland .40 .12
749 Bobby Witt .40 .12
750 Juan Gonzalez TC .60 .18
751 Carlos Almanzar RC .40 .12
752 Kevin Brown .60 .18
753 Jose Canseco 1.00 .30
754 Chris Carpenter .40 .12
755 Roger Clemens 2.00 .60
756 Felipe Crespo .40 .12
757 Jose Cruz Jr. .40 .12
758 Mark Dalesandro .40 .12
759 Carlos Delgado .40 .12
760 Kelvim Escobar .40 .12
761 Tony Fernandez .40 .12
762 Darrin Fletcher .40 .12
763 Alex Gonzalez .40 .12
764 Craig Grebeck .40 .12
765 Shawn Green .40 .12
766 Juan Guzman .40 .12
767 Erik Hanson .40 .12
768 Pat Hentgen .40 .12
769 Randy Myers .40 .12
770 Robert Person .40 .12
771 Dan Plesac .40 .12
772 Paul Quantrill .40 .12
773 Bill Risley .40 .12
774 Juan Samuel .40 .12
775 Steve Sinclair RC .40 .12
776 Ed Sprague .40 .12
777 Mike Stanley .40 .12
778 Shannon Stewart .40 .12
779 Woody Williams .40 .12
780 Roger Clemens TC 1.00 .30
SAMP T.Gwynn Sample 2.00 .60

1998 Pacific Online Red

This parallel to the regular set was issued in special nine-card retail packs. Red foil accents on the player's name and position and the Pacific logo on front make them easy to differentiate. Each retail (aka Wal-Mart) pack contained eight Online Red cards and a Web parallel card.

Nm-Mt Ex-Mt
*STARS: 1.25X TO 3X BASIC CARDS
*ROOKIES: .75X TO 2X BASIC CARDS

1998 Pacific Online Web Cards

Inserted one per pack, this 800-card set is a parallel to the Pacific Online base set. Each cards carried an unique number whereby collectors were supposed to visit Pacific's website and enter the unique number into their search engine to see if they won a special upgraded parallel version of the card. An easy way to differentiate these cards is that the "Pacific" logo, the player's name and the position are all in gold letters.

Nm-Mt Ex-Mt
*STARS: 1.5X TO 4X BASIC CARDS
*ROOKIES: .75X TO 2X BASIC CARDS

1998 Pacific Online Winners

Randomly inserted into packs, this parallel set to the Online set enabled collectors to win various prizes from Pacific Trading Cards.

Nm-Mt Ex-Mt
*WINNER CARDS: 4X TO 10X BASIC CARDS

1995 Pacific Prisms

This 144-card standard-size set was issued for the first time as a stand alone set instead as an insert set. Total production of this product was 2,999 individually numbered cases that contained 20 boxes of 36 packs. The full-bleed fronts feature a player photo against a silver prismatic background with the player's name on the bottom. The backs have a full-color photo with some biographical information. The cards are grouped alphabetically according to teams for each league with AL and NL intermingled. There are no key Rookie Cards in this set. A checklist or team logo card was seeded into every pack.

Nm-Mt Ex-Mt
COMPLETE SET (144) 100.00 30.00
1 David Justice 1.25 .35
2 Ryan Klesko 1.25 .35
3 Javier Lopez 1.25 .35
4 Greg Maddux 5.00 1.50
5 Fred McGriff 2.00 .60
6 Tony Tarasco .75 .23
7 Jeffrey Hammonds .75 .23
8 Mike Mussina 3.00 .90
9 Rafael Palmeiro 2.00 .60
10 Cal Ripken 10.00 3.00
11 Lee Smith 1.25 .35
12 Roger Clemens 6.00 1.80
13 Scott Cooper .75 .23
14 Mike Greenwell .75 .23
15 Carlos Rodriguez .75 .23
16 Mo Vaughn 1.25 .35
17 Chili Davis 1.25 .35
18 Jim Edmonds UER 1.25 .35
Card incorrectly numbered 21
19 Jorge Fabregas .75 .23
20 Bo Jackson 3.00 .90
21 Tim Salmon 2.00 .60
22 Mark Grace 2.00 .60
23 Jose Guzman .75 .23
24 Randy Myers .75 .23
25 Rey Sanchez .75 .23
26 Sammy Sosa 5.00 1.50
27 Wilson Alvarez .75 .23
28 Julio Franco 1.25 .35
29 Ozzie Guillen .75 .23
30 Jack McDowell .75 .23
31 Frank Thomas 3.00 .90
32 Bret Boone 1.25 .35
33 Barry Larkin 3.00 .90
34 Hal Morris .75 .23
35 Jose Rijo .75 .23
36 Deion Sanders 2.00 .60
37 Carlos Baerga .75 .23
38 Albert Belle 1.25 .35
39 Kenny Lofton 1.25 .35
40 Dennis Martinez 1.25 .35
41 Manny Ramirez 1.25 .35
42 Omar Vizquel 1.25 .35
43 Dante Bichette 1.25 .35
44 Marvin Freeman .75 .23
45 Andres Galarraga 1.25 .35
46 Mike Kingery .75 .23
47 Danny Bautista .75 .23
48 Cecil Fielder 1.25 .35
49 Travis Fryman 1.25 .35
50 Tony Phillips .75 .23
51 Alan Trammell 2.00 .60
52 Lou Whitaker 1.25 .35
53 Alex Arias .75 .23
54 Bret Barberie .75 .23
55 Jeff Conine 1.25 .35
56 Charles Johnson 1.25 .35
57 Gary Sheffield 1.25 .35
58 Jeff Bagwell 2.00 .60
59 Craig Biggio 2.00 .60
60 Doug Drabek .75 .23
61 Tony Eusebio .75 .23
62 Luis Gonzalez 1.25 .35
63 David Cone 1.25 .35
64 Bob Hamelin .75 .23
65 Felix Jose .75 .23
66 Wally Joyner 1.25 .35
67 Brian McRae .75 .23
68 Brett Butler 1.25 .35
69 Garey Ingram .75 .23
70 Ramon Martinez .75 .23
71 Raul Mondesi 1.25 .35
72 Mike Piazza 5.00 1.50
73 Henry Rodriguez .75 .23
74 Ricky Bones .75 .23
75 Pat Listach .75 .23
76 Dave Nilsson .75 .23
77 Jose Valentin .75 .23
78 Rick Aguilera .75 .23
79 Denny Hocking .75 .23
80 Shane Mack .75 .23
81 Pedro Munoz .75 .23
82 Kirby Puckett 3.00 .90
83 Dave Winfield 1.25 .35
84 Moises Alou 1.25 .35
85 Wil Cordero .75 .23
86 Cliff Floyd 1.25 .35
87 Marquis Grissom .75 .23
88 Pedro Martinez 3.00 .90
89 Larry Walker 2.00 .60
90 Bobby Bonilla 1.25 .35
91 Jeromy Burnitz 1.25 .35
92 John Franco 1.25 .35
93 Jeff Kent 1.25 .35
94 Jose Vizcaino .75 .23
95 Wade Boggs 2.00 .60
96 Jimmy Key 1.25 .35
97 Don Mattingly 10.00 3.00
98 Paul O'Neill 2.00 .60
99 Luis Polonia .75 .23
100 Danny Tartabull .75 .23
101 Geronimo Berroa .75 .23
102 Rickey Henderson 3.00 .90
103 Ruben Sierra .75 .23
104 Terry Steinbach .75 .23
105 Darren Daulton 1.25 .35
106 Mariano Duncan .75 .23
107 Lenny Dykstra 1.25 .35
108 Mike Lieberthal 1.25 .35
109 Tony Longmire .75 .23
110 Tom Marsh .75 .23
111 Jay Bell 1.25 .35
112 Carlos Garcia .75 .23
113 Orlando Merced .75 .23
114 Andy Van Slyke 1.25 .35
115 Derek Bell .75 .23
116 Tony Gwynn 4.00 1.20
117 Luis Lopez .75 .23
118 Bip Roberts .75 .23
119 Rod Beck .75 .23
120 Barry Bonds 8.00 2.40
121 Darryl Strawberry 2.00 .60
122 W. Van Landingham .75 .23
123 Matt Williams 1.25 .35
124 Jay Buhner 1.25 .35
125 Felix Fermin .75 .23
126 Ken Griffey Jr. 5.00 1.50
127 Randy Johnson 3.00 .90
128 Edgar Martinez 2.00 .60
129 Alex Rodriguez 8.00 2.40
130 Rene Arocha .75 .23
131 Gregg Jefferies .75 .23
132 Mike Perez .75 .23
133 Ozzie Smith 5.00 1.50
134 Jose Canseco 3.00 .90
135 Will Clark 3.00 .90
136 Juan Gonzalez 3.00 .90
137 Ivan Rodriguez 3.00 .90
138 Roberto Alomar 3.00 .90
139 Joe Carter 1.25 .35
140 Carlos Delgado 1.25 .35
141 Alex Gonzalez .75 .23
142 Juan Guzman .75 .23
143 Paul Molitor 2.00 .60
144 John Olerud 1.25 .35

1995 Pacific Prisms Checklist

Either a card from this two-card checklist set or a Pacfific Prisms Team Logo card was inserted in every 1995 Pacific Prism pack. Each side of each card contains the names of 36 players

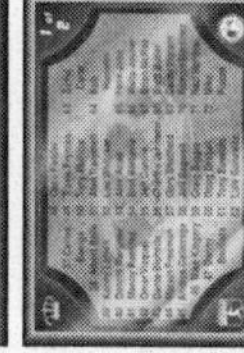

listed in the order in which they appear in the 144-card 1995 Pacific Prisms set.

Nm-Mt Ex-Mt
COMMON CARD (1-2) .25 .07

1995 Pacific Prisms Team Logo

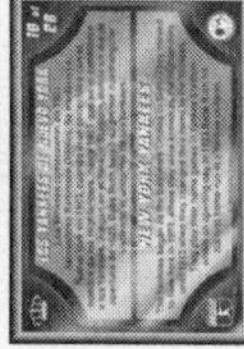

Either a card from this 28-card Pacific Prisms Team Logo set or a Pacific Prisms Checklist card was inserted in every 1995 Pacific Prism pack. The fronts feature colored team logos on a Baseball diamond background. The backs carry information about the team printed in both English and Spanish.

Nm-Mt Ex-Mt
COMPLETE SET (28) 5.00 1.50
COMMON CARD (1-28) .25 .07

1996 Pacific Prisms

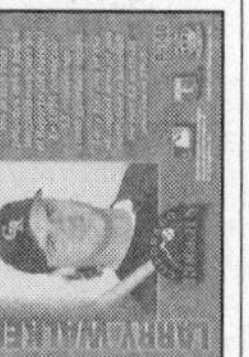

This 144-card set features a color action player cut-out over a double-etched silver foil prismatic background. The backs carry a color player portrait with information about the player in both English and Spanish.

Nm-Mt Ex-Mt
COMPLETE SET (144) 120.00 36.00
P1 Tom Glavine 2.50 .75
P2 Chipper Jones 4.00 1.20
P3 David Justice 1.50 .45
P4 Ryan Klesko 1.50 .45
P5 Javy Lopez 1.50 .45
P6 Greg Maddux 6.00 1.80
P7 Fred McGriff 2.50 .75
P8 Frank Castillo 1.50 .45
P9 Luis Gonzalez 1.50 .45
P10 Mark Grace 2.50 .75
P11 Brian McRae 1.50 .45
P12 Jaime Navarro 1.50 .45
P13 Sammy Sosa 6.00 1.80
P14 Bret Boone 1.50 .45
P15 Ron Gant 1.50 .45
P16 Barry Larkin 4.00 1.20
P17 Reggie Sanders 1.50 .45
P18 Benito Santiago 1.50 .45
P19 Dante Bichette 1.50 .45
P20 Vinny Castilla 1.50 .45
P21 Andres Galarraga 1.50 .45
P22 Bryan Rekar 1.50 .45
P23 Roberto Alomar 4.00 1.20
P24 Jeff Conine 1.50 .45
P25 Andre Dawson 1.50 .45
P26 Charles Johnson 1.50 .45
P27 Gary Sheffield 1.50 .45
P28 Quilvio Veras 1.50 .45
P29 Jeff Bagwell 2.50 .75
P30 Derek Bell 1.50 .45
P31 Craig Biggio 2.50 .75
P32 Tony Eusebio 1.50 .45
P33 Karim Garcia 1.50 .45
P34 Eric Karros 1.50 .45
P35 Ramon Martinez 1.50 .45
P36 Raul Mondesi 1.50 .45
P37 Hideo Nomo 4.00 1.20
P38 Mike Piazza 6.00 1.80
P39 Ismael Valdes 1.50 .45
P40 Moises Alou 1.50 .45
P41 Wil Cordero 1.50 .45
P42 Pedro Martinez 4.00 1.20
P43 Mel Rojas 1.50 .45
P44 David Segui 1.50 .45
P45 Edgardo Alfonzo 1.50 .45
P46 Rico Brogna 1.50 .45
P47 John Franco 1.50 .45
P48 Jason Isringhausen 1.50 .45
P49 Jose Vizcaino 1.50 .45
P50 Ricky Bottalico 1.50 .45
P51 Darren Daulton 1.50 .45
P52 Lenny Dykstra 1.50 .45
P53 Tyler Green 1.50 .45
P54 Gregg Jefferies 1.50 .45
P55 Jay Bell 1.50 .45
P56 Jason Christiansen 1.50 .45
P57 Carlos Garcia 1.50 .45
P58 Esteban Loaiza 1.50 .45
P59 Orlando Merced 1.50 .45
P60 Andujar Cedeno 1.50 .45
P61 Tony Gwynn 5.00 1.50
P62 Melvin Nieves 1.50 .45
P63 Phil Plantier 1.50 .45
P64 Fernando Valenzuela 1.50 .45
P65 Barry Bonds 10.00 3.00
P66 J.R. Phillips 1.50 .45
P67 Deion Sanders 2.50 .75
P68 Matt Williams 1.50 .45
P69 Bernard Gilkey 1.50 .45
P70 Tom Henke 1.50 .45
P71 Brian Jordan 1.50 .45
P72 Ozzie Smith 6.00 1.80
P73 Manny Alexander 1.50 .45
P74 Bobby Bonilla 1.50 .45
P75 Mike Mussina 4.00 1.20
P76 Rafael Palmeiro 2.50 .75
P77 Cal Ripken 12.00 3.60
P78 Jose Canseco 4.00 1.20
P79 Roger Clemens 8.00 2.40
P80 John Valentin 1.50 .45
P81 Mo Vaughn 1.50 .45
P82 Tim Wakefield 1.50 .45
P83 Garret Anderson 1.50 .45
P84 Damion Easley 1.50 .45
P85 Jim Edmonds 1.50 .45
P86 Tim Salmon 2.50 .75
P87 Wilson Alvarez 1.50 .45
P88 Alex Fernandez 1.50 .45
P89 Ozzie Guillen 1.50 .45
P90 Roberto Hernandez 1.50 .45
P91 Frank Thomas 4.00 1.20
P92 Robin Ventura 1.50 .45
P93 Carlos Baerga 1.50 .45
P94 Albert Belle 1.50 .45
P95 Kenny Lofton 1.50 .45
P96 Dennis Martinez 1.50 .45
P97 Eddie Murray 4.00 1.20
P98 Manny Ramirez 1.50 .45
P99 Omar Vizquel 1.50 .45
P100 Chad Curtis 1.50 .45
P101 Cecil Fielder 1.50 .45
P102 Felipe Lira 1.50 .45
P103 Alan Trammell 2.50 .75
P104 Kevin Appier 1.50 .45
P105 Johnny Damon 1.50 .45
P106 Gary Gaetti 1.50 .45
P107 Wally Joyner 1.50 .45
P108 Ricky Bones 1.50 .45
P109 John Jaha 1.50 .45
P110 B.J. Surhoff 1.50 .45
P111 Jose Valentin 1.50 .45
P112 Fernando Vina 1.50 .45
P113 Marty Cordova 1.50 .45
P114 Chuck Knoblauch 1.50 .45
P115 Scott Leius 1.50 .45
P116 Pedro Munoz 1.50 .45
P117 Kirby Puckett 4.00 1.20
P118 Wade Boggs 2.50 .75
P119 Don Mattingly 10.00 3.00
P120 Jack McDowell 1.50 .45
P121 Paul O'Neill 2.50 .75
P122 Ruben Rivera 1.50 .45
P123 Bernie Williams 2.50 .75
P124 Geronimo Berroa 1.50 .45
P125 Rickey Henderson 4.00 1.20
P126 Mark McGwire 10.00 3.00
P127 Terry Steinbach 1.50 .45
P128 Danny Tartabull 1.50 .45
P129 Jay Buhner 1.50 .45
P130 Joey Cora 1.50 .45
P131 Ken Griffey Jr. 6.00 1.80
P132 Randy Johnson 4.00 1.20
P133 Edgar Martinez 2.50 .75
P134 Tino Martinez 2.50 .75
P135 Will Clark 4.00 1.20
P136 Juan Gonzalez 4.00 1.20
P137 Dean Palmer 1.50 .45
P138 Ivan Rodriguez 4.00 1.20
P139 Mickey Tettleton 1.50 .45
P140 Larry Walker 2.50 .75
P141 Joe Carter 1.50 .45
P142 Carlos Delgado 1.50 .45
P143 Alex Gonzalez 1.50 .45
P144 Paul Molitor 2.50 .75

1996 Pacific Prisms Gold

This 144-card parallel set features the same design as the Pacific Prisms set except the prismatic background on the front is printed in double-etched gold foil. Cards were seeded at rate of 1:18 packs. The horizontal backs contain player information in both English and Spanish.

Nm-Mt Ex-Mt
*GOLD: 1.25X TO 3X BASIC CARDS

1996 Pacific Prisms Fence Busters

Randomly inserted in packs at a rate of one in 37, this 20-card set highlights 20 of baseball's hardest hitters. The fronts feature an embossed color player action cut-out with a borderless foil baseball field as background. The backs carry a player photo with information as to why the player was selected for this set in both English and Spanish.

Nm-Mt Ex-Mt
COMPLETE SET (20) 150.00 45.00
FB1 Albert Belle 3.00 .90
FB2 Dante Bichette 3.00 .90
FB3 Barry Bonds 20.00 6.00
FB4 Jay Buhner 3.00 .90
FB5 Jose Canseco 8.00 2.40
FB6 Ken Griffey Jr. 12.00 3.60
FB7 Chipper Jones 8.00 2.40
FB8 Dave Justice 3.00 .90
FB9 Eric Karros 3.00 .90
FB10 Edgar Martinez 5.00 1.50
FB11 Mark McGwire 20.00 6.00
FB12 Eddie Murray 8.00 2.40
FB13 Mike Piazza 12.00 3.60

FB14 Kirby Puckett 8.00 2.40
FB15 Cal Ripken 25.00 7.50
FB16 Tim Salmon 5.00 1.50
FB17 Sammy Sosa 12.00 3.60
FB18 Frank Thomas 8.00 2.40
FB19 Mo Vaughn 3.00 .90
FB20 Larry Walker 5.00 1.50

1996 Pacific Prisms Flame Throwers

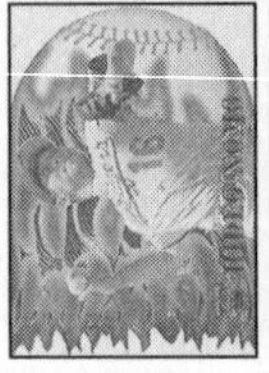

Randomly inserted in packs at a rate of one in 73, this 10-card set features 10 of Major League Baseball's hardest throwing pitchers. The fronts display a color action player photo printed on a diecut baseball-shaped card with gold foil flames indicating the force of the thrown ball. The backs carry another player photo with information of why the player was selected for this set printed in both English and Spanish.

Nm-Mt Ex-Mt
COMPLETE SET (10) 100.00 30.00
FT1 Randy Johnson 15.00 4.50
FT2 Mike Mussina 15.00 4.50
FT3 Roger Clemens 30.00 9.00
FT4 Tom Glavine 10.00 3.00
FT5 Hideo Nomo 15.00 4.50
FT6 Jose Rijo 6.00 1.80
FT7 Greg Maddux 25.00 7.50
FT8 David Cone 6.00 1.80
FT9 Ramon Martinez 6.00 1.80
FT10 Jose Mesa 6.00 1.80

1996 Pacific Prisms Red Hot Stars

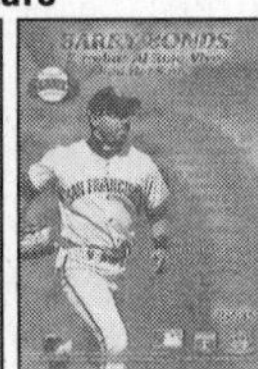

Randomly inserted in packs at a rate of one in 37, this 20-card set features 20 of Major League Baseball's hottest stars. The fronts display a color action player cut-out on a red foil background. The backs carry a color player photo with information about the player printed in both English and Spanish.

Nm-Mt Ex-Mt
COMPLETE SET (20) 200.00 60.00
RH1 Roberto Alomar 8.00 2.40
RH2 Jose Canseco 8.00 2.40
RH3 Chipper Jones 8.00 2.40
RH4 Mike Piazza 12.00 3.60
RH5 Tim Salmon 5.00 1.50
RH6 Jeff Bagwell 5.00 1.50
RH7 Ken Griffey Jr. 12.00 3.60
RH8 Greg Maddux 12.00 3.60
RH9 Kirby Puckett 8.00 2.40
RH10 Frank Thomas 8.00 2.40
RH11 Albert Belle 3.00 .90
RH12 Tony Gwynn 10.00 3.00
RH13 Edgar Martinez 5.00 1.50
RH14 Manny Ramirez 3.00 .90
RH15 Barry Bonds 20.00 6.00
RH16 Wade Boggs 5.00 1.50
RH17 Randy Johnson 8.00 2.40
RH18 Don Mattingly 20.00 6.00
RH19 Cal Ripken 25.00 7.50
RH20 Mo Vaughn 3.00 .90

1997 Pacific Prisms

The 1997 Pacific Prism set was issued in one series totalling 150 cards and displays color action photos of many of the top players from last season. Foiled in gold, the set features a visually stunning inlaid transparent cel on each card. The backs carry player information in both Spanish and English.

Nm-Mt Ex-Mt
COMPLETE SET (150) 100.00 30.00
1 Chili Davis 1.25 .35
2 Jim Edmonds 1.25 .35
3 Darin Erstad 1.25 .35
4 Orlando Palmeiro 1.25 .35
5 Tim Salmon 2.00 .60
6 J.T. Snow 1.25 .35
7 Roberto Alomar 3.00 .90
8 Brady Anderson 1.25 .35
9 Eddie Murray 3.00 .90
10 Mike Mussina 3.00 .90
11 Rafael Palmeiro 2.00 .60
12 Cal Ripken 10.00 3.00
13 Jose Canseco 3.00 .90
14 Roger Clemens 6.00 1.80
15 Nomar Garciaparra 5.00 1.50
16 Reggie Jefferson 1.25 .35
17 Mo Vaughn 1.25 .35
18 Wilson Alvarez 1.25 .35
19 Harold Baines 1.25 .35
20 Alex Fernandez 1.25 .35
21 Danny Tartabull 1.25 .35
22 Frank Thomas 3.00 .90
23 Robin Ventura 1.25 .35
24 Sandy Alomar Jr. 1.25 .35
25 Albert Belle 1.25 .35
26 Kenny Lofton 1.25 .35
27 Jim Thome 3.00 .90
28 Omar Vizquel 1.25 .35
29 Raul Casanova 1.25 .35
30 Tony Clark 1.25 .35
31 Travis Fryman 1.25 .35
32 Bobby Higginson 1.25 .35
33 Melvin Nieves 1.25 .35
34 Justin Thompson 1.25 .35
35 Johnny Damon 1.25 .35
36 Tom Goodwin 1.25 .35
37 Jeff Montgomery 1.25 .35
38 Jose Offerman 1.25 .35
39 John Jaha 1.25 .35
40 Jeff Cirillo 1.25 .35
41 Dave Nilsson 1.25 .35
42 Jose Valentin 1.25 .35
43 Fernando Vina 1.25 .35
44 Marty Cordova 1.25 .35
45 Roberto Kelly 1.25 .35
46 Chuck Knoblauch 1.25 .35
47 Paul Molitor 2.00 .60
48 Todd Walker 1.25 .35
49 Wade Boggs 2.00 .60
50 Cecil Fielder 1.25 .35
51 Derek Jeter 6.00 1.80
52 Tino Martinez 2.00 .60
53 Andy Pettitte 2.00 .60
54 Mariano Rivera 2.00 .60
55 Bernie Williams 2.00 .60
56 Tony Batista 1.25 .35
57 Geronimo Berroa 1.25 .35
58 Jason Giambi 3.00 .90
59 Mark McGwire 8.00 2.40
60 Terry Steinbach 1.25 .35
61 Jay Buhner 1.25 .35
62 Joey Cora 1.25 .35
63 Ken Griffey Jr. 5.00 1.50
64 Edgar Martinez 2.00 .60
65 Alex Rodriguez 5.00 1.50
66 Paul Sorrento 1.25 .35
67 Will Clark 3.00 .90
68 Juan Gonzalez 3.00 .90
69 Rusty Greer 1.25 .35
70 Dean Palmer 1.25 .35
71 Ivan Rodriguez 3.00 .90
72 Joe Carter 1.25 .35
73 Carlos Delgado 1.25 .35
74 Juan Guzman 1.25 .35
75 Pat Hentgen 1.25 .35
76 Ed Sprague 1.25 .35
77 Jermaine Dye 1.25 .35
78 Andruw Jones 1.25 .35
79 Chipper Jones 3.00 .90
80 Ryan Klesko 1.25 .35
81 Javier Lopez 1.25 .35
82 Greg Maddux 6.00 1.80
83 John Smoltz 2.00 .60
84 Mark Grace 2.00 .60
85 Luis Gonzalez 1.25 .35
86 Brooks Kieschnick 1.25 .35
87 Jaime Navarro 1.25 .35
88 Ryne Sandberg 5.00 1.50
89 Sammy Sosa 5.00 1.50
90 Bret Boone 1.25 .35
91 Jeff Brantley 1.25 .35
92 Eric Davis 1.25 .35
93 Barry Larkin 3.00 .90
94 Reggie Sanders 1.25 .35
95 Ellis Burks 1.25 .35
96 Dante Bichette 1.25 .35
97 Vinny Castilla 1.25 .35
98 Andres Galarraga 1.25 .35
99 Eric Young 1.25 .35
100 Kevin Brown 1.25 .35
101 Jeff Conine 1.25 .35
102 Charles Johnson 1.25 .35
103 Edgar Renteria 1.25 .35
104 Gary Sheffield 1.25 .35
105 Jeff Bagwell 2.00 .60
106 Derek Bell 1.25 .35
107 Sean Berry 1.25 .35
108 Craig Biggio 2.00 .60
109 Shane Reynolds 1.25 .35
110 Karim Garcia 1.25 .35
111 Todd Hollandsworth 1.25 .35
112 Ramon Martinez 1.25 .35
113 Raul Mondesi 1.25 .35
114 Hideo Nomo 3.00 .90
115 Mike Piazza 5.00 1.50
116 Ismael Valdes 1.25 .35
117 Moises Alou 1.25 .35
118 Mark Grudzielanek 1.25 .35
119 Pedro Martinez 3.00 .90
120 Henry Rodriguez 1.25 .35
121 F.P. Santangelo 1.25 .35
122 Carlos Baerga 1.25 .35
123 Bernard Gilkey 1.25 .35
124 Todd Hundley 1.25 .35
125 Lance Johnson 1.25 .35
126 Alex Ochoa 1.25 .35
127 Rey Ordonez 1.25 .35
128 Lenny Dykstra 1.25 .35
129 Gregg Jefferies 1.25 .35
130 Ricky Otero 1.25 .35
131 Benito Santiago 1.25 .35
132 Jermaine Allensworth 1.25 .35
133 Francisco Cordova 1.25 .35
134 Carlos Garcia 1.25 .35
135 Jason Kendall 1.25 .35
136 Al Martin 1.25 .35
137 Dennis Eckersley 1.25 .35
138 Ron Gant 1.25 .35
139 Brian Jordan 1.25 .35
140 John Mabry 1.25 .35
141 Ozzie Smith 5.00 1.50
142 Ken Caminiti 1.25 .35
143 Steve Finley 1.25 .35
144 Tony Gwynn 4.00 1.20
145 Wally Joyner 1.25 .35
146 Fernando Valenzuela 1.25 .35
147 Barry Bonds 8.00 2.40
148 Jacob Cruz 1.25 .35
149 Osvaldo Fernandez 1.25 .35
150 Matt Williams 1.25 .35

1997 Pacific Prisms Light Blue

Distributed exclusively in retail outlets at a rate of 1:18 packs, cards from this 150-card set parallel the standard 1997 Pacific Prisms. The light blue foil fronts easily differentiate them from their bronze basic issue counterparts.

Nm-Mt Ex-Mt
*STARS: 1.25X TO 3X BASIC CARDS.

1997 Pacific Prisms Platinum

Randomly inserted in hobby packs at a rate of one in 18, this set is a platinum foiled parallel version of the regular set.

Nm-Mt Ex-Mt
*STARS: 1.25X TO 3X BASIC CARDS.

1997 Pacific Prisms Gate Attractions

Randomly inserted in packs at a rate of one in 73, this 32-card set features some of the league's current most popular players. The fronts display a player image on a baseball with a borderless photo of the inside of a baseball glove as background. The backs contain player information in both Spanish and English.

Nm-Mt Ex-Mt
COMPLETE SET (32) 250.00 75.00
GA1 Roberto Alomar 10.00 3.00
GA2 Brady Anderson 4.00 1.20
GA3 Cal Ripken 30.00 9.00
GA4 Frank Thomas 10.00 3.00
GA5 Kenny Lofton 4.00 1.20
GA6 Omar Vizquel 4.00 1.20
GA7 Paul Molitor 6.00 1.80
GA8 Wade Boggs 6.00 1.80
GA9 Derek Jeter 20.00 6.00
GA10 Andy Pettitte 6.00 1.80
GA11 Bernie Williams 6.00 1.80
GA12 Geronimo Berroa 4.00 1.20
GA13 Mark McGwire 25.00 7.50
GA14 Ken Griffey Jr. 15.00 4.50
GA15 Alex Rodriguez 15.00 4.50
GA16 Juan Gonzalez 10.00 3.00
GA17 Andruw Jones 4.00 1.20
GA18 Chipper Jones 10.00 3.00
GA19 Greg Maddux 20.00 6.00
GA20 Ryne Sandberg 15.00 4.50
GA21 Sammy Sosa 15.00 4.50
GA22 Andres Galarraga 4.00 1.20
GA23 Jeff Bagwell 6.00 1.80
GA24 Todd Hollandsworth 4.00 1.20
GA25 Hideo Nomo 10.00 3.00
GA26 Mike Piazza 15.00 4.50
GA27 Todd Hundley 4.00 1.20
GA28 Lance Johnson 4.00 1.20
GA29 Ozzie Smith 15.00 4.50
GA30 Ken Caminiti 4.00 1.20
GA31 Tony Gwynn 12.00 3.60
GA32 Barry Bonds 25.00 7.50

1997 Pacific Prisms Gems of the Diamond

Randomly inserted at the rate of approximately two per pack, this 220 card bonus set features color action photos with the player's name printed in the bottom gold border. A diamond replica displays the name of the player's team. The backs carry player information in both Spanish and English.

Nm-Mt Ex-Mt
COMPLETE SET (220) 60.00 18.00
GD1 Jim Abbott .60 .18
GD2 Shawn Boskie .25 .07
GD3 Gary Disarcina .25 .07
GD4 Jim Edmonds .40 .12
GD5 Todd Greene .25 .07
GD6 Jack Howell .25 .07
GD7 Jeff Schmidt .25 .07
GD8 Shad Williams .25 .07
GD9 Roberto Alomar 1.00 .30
GD10 Cesar Devarez .25 .07
GD11 Alan Mills .25 .07
GD12 Eddie Murray 1.00 .30
GD13 Jesse Orosco .25 .07
GD14 Arthur Rhodes .25 .07
GD15 Bill Ripken .25 .07
GD16 Cal Ripken 4.00 1.20
GD17 Mark Smith .25 .07
GD18 Roger Clemens 2.50 .75
GD19 Vaughn Eshelman .25 .07
GD20 Rich Garces .25 .07
GD21 Bill Haselman .25 .07
GD22 Dwayne Hosey .25 .07
GD23 Mike Maddux .25 .07
GD24 Jose Malave .25 .07
GD25 Aaron Sele .25 .07
GD26 James Baldwin .25 .07
GD27 Pat Borders .25 .07
GD28 Mike Cameron .40 .12
GD29 Tony Castillo .25 .07
GD30 Domingo Cedeno .25 .07
GD31 Greg Norton .25 .07
GD32 Frank Thomas 1.00 .30
GD33 Albert Belle .40 .12
GD34 Einar Diaz .25 .07
GD35 Alan Embree .25 .07
GD36 Albie Lopez .25 .07
GD37 Chad Ogea .25 .07
GD38 Tony Pena .25 .07
GD39 Joe Roa .25 .07
GD40 Fausto Cruz .25 .07
GD41 Joey Eischen .25 .07
GD42 Travis Fryman .40 .12
GD43 Mike Myers .25 .07
GD44 A.J. Sager .25 .07
GD45 Duane Singleton .25 .07
GD46 Justin Thompson .25 .07
GD47 Jeff Granger .25 .07
GD48 Les Norman .25 .07
GD49 Jon Nunnally .25 .07
GD50 Craig Paquette .25 .07
GD51 Michael Tucker .25 .07
GD52 Julio Valera .25 .07
GD53 Kevin Young .25 .07
GD54 Cal Eldred .25 .07
GD55 Ramon Garcia .25 .07
GD56 Marc Newfield .25 .07
GD57 Al Reyes .25 .07
GD58 Tim Unroe .25 .07
GD59 Tim Vanegmond .25 .07
GD60 Turner Ward .25 .07
GD61 Bob Wickman .25 .07
GD62 Chuck Knoblauch .40 .12
GD63 Paul Molitor .60 .18
GD64 Kirby Puckett 1.00 .30
GD65 Tom Quinlan .25 .07
GD66 Rich Robertson .25 .07
GD67 Dave Stevens .25 .07
GD68 Matt Walbeck .25 .07
GD69 Wade Boggs .60 .18
GD70 Tony Fernandez .25 .07
GD71 Andy Fox .25 .07
GD72 Joe Girardi .25 .07
GD73 Charlie Hayes .25 .07
GD74 Pat Kelly .25 .07
GD75 Jeff Nelson .25 .07
GD76 Melido Perez .25 .07
GD77 Mark Acre .25 .07
GD78 Allen Battle .25 .07
GD79 Rafael Bournigal .25 .07
GD80 Mark McGwire 3.00 .90
GD81 Pedro Munoz .25 .07
GD82 Scott Spiezio .25 .07
GD83 Don Wengert .25 .07
GD84 S.Wojciechowski .25 .07
GD85 Alex Diaz .25 .07
GD86 Ken Griffey Jr. 2.00 .60
GD87 Raul Ibanez .25 .07
GD88 Mike Jackson .25 .07
GD89 John Marzano .25 .07
GD90 Greg McCarthy .25 .07
GD91 Alex Rodriguez 2.00 .60
GD92 Andy Sheets .25 .07
GD93 Mac Suzuki .25 .07
GD94 Benji Gil .25 .07
GD95 Juan Gonzalez 1.00 .30
GD96 Kevin Gross .25 .07
GD97 Gil Heredia .25 .07
GD98 Luis Ortiz .25 .07
GD99 Jeff Russell .25 .07
GD100 Dave Valle .25 .07
GD101 Marty Janzen .25 .07
GD102 Sandy Martinez .25 .07
GD103 Julio Mosquera .25 .07
GD104 Otis Nixon .25 .07
GD105 Paul Spoljaric .25 .07
GD106 Shannon Stewart .40 .12
GD107 Woody Williams .25 .07
GD108 Steve Avery .25 .07
GD109 Mike Bielecki .25 .07
GD110 Pedro Borbon .25 .07
GD111 Ed Giovanola .25 .07
GD112 Chipper Jones 1.00 .30
GD113 Greg Maddux 2.00 .60
GD114 Mike Mordecai .25 .07
GD115 Terrell Wade .25 .07
GD116 Terry Adams .25 .07
GD117 Brian Dorsett .25 .07
GD118 Doug Glanville .25 .07
GD119 Tyler Houston .25 .07
GD120 Robin Jennings .25 .07
GD121 Ryne Sandberg 2.00 .60
GD122 Terry Shumpert .25 .07
GD123 Amaury Telemaco .25 .07
GD124 Steve Trachsel .25 .07
GD125 Curtis Goodwin .25 .07
GD126 Mike Kelly .25 .07
GD127 Chad Mottola .25 .07
GD128 Mark Portugal .25 .07
GD129 Roger Salkeld .25 .07
GD130 John Smiley .25 .07
GD131 Lee Smith .40 .12
GD132 Roger Bailey .25 .07
GD133 Andres Galarraga .40 .12
GD134 Darren Holmes .25 .07
GD135 Curtis Leskanic .25 .07
GD136 Mike Munoz .25 .07
GD137 Jeff Reed .25 .07
GD138 Mark Thompson .25 .07
GD139 Jamey Wright .25 .07
GD140 Andre Dawson .40 .12
GD141 Craig Grebeck .25 .07
GD142 Matt Mantei .25 .07
GD143 Billy McMillon .25 .07
GD144 Kurt Miller .25 .07
GD145 Ralph Milliard .25 .07
GD146 Bob Natal .25 .07
GD147 Joe Siddall .25 .07
GD148 Bob Abreu .40 .12
GD149 Doug Brocail .25 .07
GD150 Danny Darwin .25 .07
GD151 Mike Hampton .40 .12
GD152 Todd Jones .25 .07
GD153 Kirt Manwaring .25 .07
GD154 Alvin Morman .25 .07
GD155 Billy Ashley .25 .07
GD156 Tom Candiotti .25 .07
GD157 Darren Dreifort .25 .07
GD158 Greg Gagne .25 .07
GD159 Wilton Guerrero .25 .07
GD160 Hideo Nomo 1.00 .30
GD161 Mike Piazza 2.00 .60
GD162 Tom Prince .25 .07
GD163 Todd Worrell .25 .07
GD164 Moises Alou .40 .12
GD165 Shane Andrews .25 .07
GD166 Derek Aucoin .25 .07
GD167 Raul Chavez .25 .07
GD168 Darrin Fletcher .25 .07
GD169 Mark Leiter .25 .07
GD170 Henry Rodriguez .25 .07
GD171 Dave Veres .25 .07
GD172 Paul Byrd .25 .07
GD173 Alberto Castillo .25 .07
GD174 Mark Clark .25 .07
GD175 Rey Ordonez .25 .07
GD176 Roberto Petagine .25 .07
GD177 Andy Tomberlin .25 .07
GD178 Derek Wallace .25 .07
GD179 Paul Wilson .25 .07
GD180 Ruben Amaro Jr. .25 .07
GD181 Toby Borland .25 .07
GD182 Rich Hunter .25 .07
GD183 Tony Longmire .25 .07
GD184 Wendell Magee .25 .07
GD185 Bobby Munoz .25 .07
GD186 Scott Rolen .60 .18
GD187 Mike Williams .25 .07
GD188 Trey Beamon .25 .07
GD189 Jason Christiansen .25 .07
GD190 Elmer Dessens .25 .07
GD191 A.Encarnacion .25 .07
GD192 Carlos Garcia .25 .07
GD193 Mike Kingery .25 .07
GD194 Chris Peters .25 .07
GD195 Tony Womack .40 .12
GD196 Brian Barber .25 .07
GD197 David Bell .25 .07
GD198 Tony Fossas .25 .07
GD199 Rick Honeycutt .25 .07
GD200 T.J. Mathews .25 .07
GD201 Miguel Mejia .25 .07
GD202 Donovan Osborne .25 .07
GD203 Ozzie Smith 1.50 .45
GD204 Andres Berumen .25 .07
GD205 Ken Caminiti .40 .12
GD206 Chris Gwynn .25 .07
GD207 Tony Gwynn 1.50 .45
GD208 Rickey Henderson 1.00 .30
GD209 Scott Sanders .25 .07
GD210 Jason Thompson .25 .07
GD211 F.Valenzuela .40 .12
GD212 Tim Worrell .25 .07
GD213 Barry Bonds 3.00 .90
GD214 Jay Canizaro .25 .07
GD215 Doug Creek .25 .07
GD216 Jacob Cruz .25 .07
GD217 Glenallen Hill .25 .07
GD218 Tom Lampkin .25 .07
GD219 Jim Poole .25 .07
GD220 Desi Wilson .25 .07

1997 Pacific Prisms Sizzling Lumber

Randomly inserted in packs at a rate of one in 37, this 36-card set features color photos of three top hitters from each of twelve major league teams. The die-cut cards display red-and-gold foil flames coming from a portion of a baseball bat. The three player cards from the same team form a complete bat on fire when laid top to bottom according to the letters found after the card number. Information is printed in both Spanish and English.

Nm-Mt Ex-Mt
COMPLETE SET (36) 150.00 45.00
SL1A Cal Ripken 20.00 6.00
SL1B Rafael Palmeiro 4.00 1.20
SL1C Roberto Alomar 6.00 1.80
SL2A Frank Thomas 6.00 1.80
SL2B Robin Ventura 2.50 .75
SL2C Harold Baines 2.50 .75
SL3A Albert Belle 2.50 .75
SL3B Manny Ramirez 6.00 1.80
SL3C Kenny Lofton 2.50 .75
SL4A Derek Jeter 12.00 3.60
SL4B Bernie Williams 4.00 1.20
SL4C Wade Boggs 4.00 1.20
SL5A Mark McGwire 15.00 4.50
SL5B Jason Giambi 6.00 1.80
SL5C Geronimo Berroa 2.50 .75
SL6A Ken Griffey Jr. 10.00 3.00
SL6B Alex Rodriguez 10.00 3.00
SL6C Jay Buhner 2.50 .75
SL7A Juan Gonzalez 6.00 1.80
SL7B Dean Palmer 2.50 .75
SL7C Ivan Rodriguez 6.00 1.80
SL8A Ryan Klesko 2.50 .75
SL8B Chipper Jones 6.00 1.80
SL8C Andruw Jones 2.50 .75
SL9A Dante Bichette 2.50 .75
SL9B Andres Galarraga 2.50 .75
SL9C Vinny Castilla 2.50 .75
SL10A Jeff Bagwell 4.00 1.20
SL10B Craig Biggio 4.00 1.20
SL10C Derek Bell 2.50 .75
SL11A Mike Piazza 10.00 3.00
SL11B Raul Mondesi 2.50 .75
SL11C Karim Garcia 2.50 .75
SL12A Tony Gwynn 8.00 2.40
SL12B Ken Caminiti 2.50 .75
SL12C Greg Vaughn 3.00 .90

1997 Pacific Prisms Sluggers and Hurlers

Randomly inserted in packs at a rate of one in 145, cards from this 24-card set feature top hitters and pitchers for a dozen teams printed in a two-card puzzle style matching the hitter and pitcher from the same team to form a complete background picture displaying the team's name.

Nm-Mt Ex-Mt
COMPLETE SET (24) 400.00 120.00
SH1A Cal Ripken 50.00 15.00
SH1B Mike Mussina 15.00 4.50
SH2A Jose Canseco 15.00 4.50
SH2B Roger Clemens 30.00 9.00
SH3A Frank Thomas 15.00 4.50
SH3B Wilson Alvarez 6.00 1.80
SH4A Kenny Lofton 6.00 1.80
SH4B Orel Hershiser 6.00 1.80
SH5A Derek Jeter 30.00 9.00
SH5B Andy Pettitte 10.00 3.00
SH6A Ken Griffey Jr. 25.00 7.50
SH6B Randy Johnson 15.00 4.50
SH7A Alex Rodriguez 25.00 7.50
SH7B Jamie Moyer 6.00 1.80
SH8A Andruw Jones 6.00 1.80
SH8B Greg Maddux 30.00 9.00
SH9A Chipper Jones 15.00 4.50
SH9B John Smoltz 10.00 3.00
SH10A Jeff Bagwell 10.00 3.00
SH10B Shane Reynolds 6.00 1.80
SH11A Mike Piazza 25.00 7.50
SH11B Hideo Nomo 15.00 4.50
SH12A Tony Gwynn 20.00 6.00
SH12B F. Valenzuela 6.00 1.80

1999 Pacific Prism

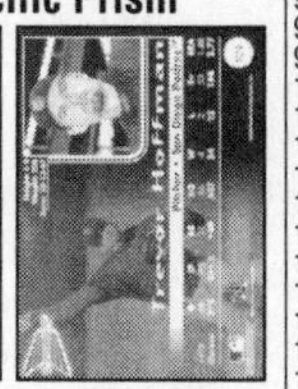

The 1999 Pacific Prism set was issued in one series totalling 150 cards. The fronts feature a color action player cropped photo printed on holographic silver foil cards. The backs carry two more player photos and career statistics. An unnumbered Tony Gwynn sample card was distributed to dealers and hobby media prior to the product's release. The card is easy to recognize by the bold, diagonal "SAMPLE" text running across the back. An additional version of this sample card was distributed to attendees of a private party hosted by Pacific at Hawaii XIV Trade Seminar in February, 1999. This special sample card features a bold gold foil "Pacific Hawaii XIV" logo at the lower right corner of the card front and is also serial numbered to 200 in red ink by hand on the card front.

Nm-Mt Ex-Mt
COMPLETE SET (150) 60.00 18.00
1 Garret Anderson .60 .18
2 Jim Edmonds .60 .18
3 Darin Erstad .60 .18
4 Chuck Finley .60 .18
5 Tim Salmon 1.00 .30
6 Jay Bell .60 .18
7 David Dellucci .40 .12
8 Travis Lee .40 .12
9 Matt Williams .60 .18
10 Andres Galarraga .60 .18
11 Tom Glavine 1.00 .30
12 Andruw Jones .60 .18
13 Chipper Jones 1.50 .45
14 Ryan Klesko .60 .18
15 Javy Lopez .60 .18
16 Greg Maddux 2.50 .75
17 Roberto Alomar 1.50 .45
18 Ryan Minor .40 .12
19 Mike Mussina 1.50 .45
20 Rafael Palmeiro 1.00 .30
21 Cal Ripken 5.00 1.50
22 Nomar Garciaparra 2.50 .75
23 Pedro Martinez 1.50 .45
24 John Valentin .40 .12
25 Mo Vaughn .60 .18
26 Tim Wakefield .60 .18
27 Rod Beck .40 .12
28 Mark Grace 1.00 .30
29 Lance Johnson .40 .12
30 Sammy Sosa 2.50 .75
31 Kerry Wood 1.50 .45
32 Albert Belle .60 .18
33 Mike Caruso .40 .12
34 Magglio Ordonez .60 .18
35 Frank Thomas 1.50 .45
36 Robin Ventura .60 .18
37 Aaron Boone .60 .18
38 Barry Larkin 1.50 .45
39 Reggie Sanders .60 .18
40 Brett Tomko .40 .12
41 Sandy Alomar Jr. .40 .12
42 Bartolo Colon .60 .18
43 David Justice .60 .18
44 Kenny Lofton .60 .18
45 Manny Ramirez .60 .18
46 Richie Sexson .60 .18
47 Jim Thome 1.50 .45
48 Omar Vizquel .60 .18
49 Dante Bichette .60 .18
50 Vinny Castilla .60 .18
51 Edgard Clemente .40 .12
52 Todd Helton 1.00 .30
53 Quinton McCracken .40 .12
54 Larry Walker 1.00 .30
55 Tony Clark .40 .12
56 Damion Easley .40 .12
57 Luis Gonzalez .60 .18
58 Bob Higginson .60 .18
59 Brian Hunter .40 .12
60 Cliff Floyd .60 .18
61 Alex Gonzalez .40 .12
62 Livan Hernandez .40 .12
63 Derrek Lee .60 .18
64 Edgar Renteria .60 .18
65 Moises Alou .60 .18
66 Jeff Bagwell 1.00 .30
67 Derek Bell .40 .12
68 Craig Biggio 1.00 .30
69 Randy Johnson 1.50 .45
70 Johnny Damon .60 .18
71 Jeff King .40 .12
72 Hal Morris .40 .12
73 Dean Palmer .60 .18
74 Eric Karros .60 .18
75 Raul Mondesi .60 .18
76 Chan Ho Park .60 .18
77 Gary Sheffield .60 .18
78 Jeromy Burnitz .60 .18
79 Jeff Cirillo .40 .12
80 Marquis Grissom .40 .12
81 Jose Valentin .40 .12
82 Fernando Vina .60 .18
83 Paul Molitor 1.00 .30
84 Otis Nixon .40 .12
85 David Ortiz .60 .18
86 Todd Walker .60 .18
87 Vladimir Guerrero 1.50 .45
88 Carl Pavano .40 .12
89 Fernando Seguignol .40 .12
90 Ugueth Urbina .40 .12
91 Carlos Baerga .40 .12
92 Bobby Bonilla .60 .18
93 Hideo Nomo 1.50 .45
94 John Olerud .60 .18
95 Rey Ordonez .40 .12
96 Mike Piazza 2.50 .75
97 David Cone .60 .18
98 Orlando Hernandez .60 .18
99 Hideki Irabu .40 .12
100 Derek Jeter 4.00 1.20
101 Tino Martinez 1.00 .30
102 Bernie Williams 1.00 .30
103 Eric Chavez .60 .18
104 Jason Giambi 1.50 .45
105 Ben Grieve .40 .12
106 Rickey Henderson 1.50 .45
107 Bob Abreu .60 .18
108 Doug Glanville .40 .12
109 Scott Rolen 1.00 .30
110 Curt Schilling 1.00 .30
111 Emil Brown .40 .12
112 Jose Guillen .40 .12
113 Jason Kendall .60 .18
114 Al Martin .40 .12
115 Aramis Ramirez .60 .18
116 Kevin Young .60 .18
117 J.D. Drew .60 .18
118 Ron Gant .60 .18
119 Brian Jordan .60 .18
120 Eli Marrero .40 .12
121 Mark McGwire 4.00 1.20
122 Kevin Brown 1.00 .30
123 Tony Gwynn 2.00 .60
124 Trevor Hoffman .60 .18
125 Wally Joyner .60 .18
126 Greg Vaughn .60 .18
127 Barry Bonds 4.00 1.20
128 Ellis Burks .60 .18
129 Jeff Kent .60 .18
130 Robb Nen .60 .18
131 J.T. Snow .60 .18
132 Jay Buhner .60 .18
133 Ken Griffey Jr. 2.50 .75
134 Edgar Martinez 1.00 .30
135 Alex Rodriguez 2.50 .75
136 David Segui .40 .12
137 Rolando Arrojo .40 .12
138 Wade Boggs 1.00 .30
139 Aaron Ledesma .40 .12
140 Fred McGriff 1.00 .30
141 Will Clark 1.50 .45
142 Juan Gonzalez 1.50 .45
143 Rusty Greer .60 .18
144 Ivan Rodriguez 1.50 .45
145 Aaron Sele .40 .12
146 Jose Canseco 1.50 .45
147 Roger Clemens 3.00 .90
148 Jose Cruz Jr. .60 .18
149 Carlos Delgado .60 .18
150 Alex Gonzalez .40 .12
SA Tony Gwynn Sample 1.00 .30
SAH Tony Gwynn Sample 15.00 4.50
Hawaii/200

1999 Pacific Prism Holographic Blue

Randomly inserted in packs, this 150-card set is a holographic blue foil parallel version of the base set. The cards which are serial numbered to 80 serially can be identified as the serial number is on the front.

Nm-Mt Ex-Mt
*STARS: 8X TO 20X BASIC CARDS ....

1999 Pacific Prism Holographic Gold

Randomly inserted in packs, this 150-card set is a holographic gold foil parallel version of the base set. The serial numbering is on the front of the set. 480 sets were produced.

Nm-Mt Ex-Mt
*STARS: 2.5X TO 6X BASIC CARDS ...

1999 Pacific Prism Holographic Mirror

Randomly inserted in packs, this 150-card set is a holographic parallel version of the base set. Only 160 serially numbered sets were produced.

Nm-Mt Ex-Mt
*STARS: 5X TO 12X BASIC CARDS ....

1999 Pacific Prism Holographic Purple

Randomly inserted in hobby packs only, this 150-card set is a holographic purple foil parallel version of the base set. Only 320 serially numbered sets were produced.

Nm-Mt Ex-Mt
*STARS: 3X TO 8X BASIC CARDS ......

1999 Pacific Prism Red

Randomly inserted in retail packs only at the rate of two in 25, this 150-card set is a red foil parallel version of the 1999 Pacific Prism base set.

Nm-Mt Ex-Mt
*STARS: 2X TO 5X BASIC CARDS ......

1999 Pacific Prism Ahead of the Game

Randomly inserted in packs at the rate of one in 49, this 20-card set features color action player photos printed on full gold foil and etched cards. The backs carry a close-up look of the pictured player.

Nm-Mt Ex-Mt
COMPLETE SET (20) 200.00 60.00
1 Darin Erstad 3.00 .90
2 Travis Lee 2.00 .60
3 Chipper Jones 8.00 2.40
4 Cal Ripken 25.00 7.50
5 Nomar Garciaparra 12.00 3.60
6 Sammy Sosa 12.00 3.60
7 Kerry Wood 8.00 2.40
8 Frank Thomas 8.00 2.40
9 Manny Ramirez 3.00 .90
10 Todd Helton 5.00 1.50
11 Jeff Bagwell 5.00 1.50
12 Mike Piazza 12.00 3.60
13 Derek Jeter 20.00 6.00
14 Bernie Williams 5.00 1.50
15 J.D. Drew 3.00 .90
16 Mark McGwire 20.00 6.00
17 Tony Gwynn 10.00 3.00
18 Ken Griffey Jr. 12.00 3.60
19 Alex Rodriguez 12.00 3.60
20 Ivan Rodriguez 8.00 2.40

1999 Pacific Prism Ballpark Legends

Randomly inserted in packs at the rate of one in 193, this 10-card set features color action photos of some of the game's superstars printed on full silver foil cards.

Nm-Mt Ex-Mt
COMPLETE SET (10) 250.00 75.00
1 Cal Ripken 50.00 15.00
2 Nomar Garciaparra 25.00 7.50
3 Frank Thomas 15.00 4.50
4 Ken Griffey Jr. 25.00 7.50
5 Alex Rodriguez 25.00 7.50
6 Greg Maddux 25.00 7.50
7 Sammy Sosa 25.00 7.50
8 Kerry Wood 15.00 4.50
9 Mark McGwire 40.00 12.00
10 Tony Gwynn 20.00 6.00

1999 Pacific Prism Diamond Glory

Randomly inserted in packs at the rate of two in 25, this 20-card set features color action photos of some of baseball's most exciting players on a blue, silver, and copper striped foil background with a large blue star behind the player's image.

Nm-Mt Ex-Mt
COMPLETE SET (20) 80.00 24.00
1 Darin Erstad 1.25 .35
2 Travis Lee .75 .23
3 Chipper Jones 3.00 .90
4 Greg Maddux 5.00 1.50
5 Cal Ripken 10.00 3.00
6 Nomar Garciaparra 5.00 1.50
7 Sammy Sosa 5.00 1.50
8 Kerry Wood 3.00 .90
9 Frank Thomas 3.00 .90
10 Todd Helton 2.00 .60
11 Jeff Bagwell 2.00 .60
12 Mike Piazza 5.00 1.50
13 Derek Jeter 8.00 2.40
14 Bernie Williams 2.00 .60
15 J.D. Drew 1.25 .35
16 Mark McGwire 8.00 2.40
17 Tony Gwynn 4.00 1.20
18 Ken Griffey Jr. 5.00 1.50
19 Alex Rodriguez 5.00 1.50
20 Juan Gonzalez 3.00 .90

1999 Pacific Prism Epic Performers

Randomly inserted in hobby packs only at the rate of one in 97, this 10-card set features color action photos of top players with a swirling sun design behind the player image.

Nm-Mt Ex-Mt
COMPLETE SET (10) 150.00 45.00
1 Cal Ripken 30.00 9.00
2 Nomar Garciaparra 15.00 4.50
3 Frank Thomas 10.00 3.00
4 Ken Griffey Jr. 15.00 4.50
5 Alex Rodriguez 15.00 4.50
6 Greg Maddux 15.00 4.50
7 Sammy Sosa 15.00 4.50
8 Kerry Wood 10.00 3.00
9 Mark McGwire 25.00 7.50
10 Tony Gwynn 12.00 3.60

2000 Pacific Prism

The 2000 Pacific Prism product was released in April, 2000 as a 150-card set. The set features a fine selection of the top stars in major league baseball. Each pack contained five cards and carried a suggested retail price of 2.99.

Nm-Mt Ex-Mt
COMPLETE SET (150) 25.00 7.50
1 Jeff DaVanon RC .50 .15
2 Troy Glaus .60 .18
3 Tim Salmon .60 .18
4 Mo Vaughn .40 .12
5 Jay Bell .40 .12
6 Erubiel Durazo .40 .12
7 Luis Gonzalez .40 .12
8 Randy Johnson 1.00 .30
9 Matt Williams .40 .12
10 Andres Galarraga .40 .12
11 Andruw Jones .40 .12
12 Chipper Jones 1.00 .30
13 Brian Jordan .40 .12
14 Greg Maddux 1.50 .45
15 Kevin Millwood .40 .12
16 John Smoltz .60 .18
17 Albert Belle .40 .12
18 Mike Mussina 1.00 .30
19 Calvin Pickering .40 .12
20 Cal Ripken 3.00 .90
21 B.J. Surhoff .40 .12
22 Nomar Garciaparra 1.50 .45
23 Pedro Martinez 1.00 .30
24 Troy O'Leary .40 .12
25 John Valentin .40 .12
26 Jason Varitek .40 .12
27 Mark Grace .60 .18
28 Henry Rodriguez .40 .12
29 Sammy Sosa 1.50 .45
30 Kerry Wood 1.00 .30
31 Ray Durham .40 .12
32 Carlos Lee .40 .12
33 Magglio Ordonez .40 .12
34 Chris Singleton .40 .12
35 Frank Thomas 1.00 .30
36 Sean Casey .40 .12
37 Travis Dawkins .40 .12
38 Barry Larkin 1.00 .30
39 Pokey Reese .40 .12
40 Scott Williamson .40 .12
41 Roberto Alomar 1.00 .30
42 Bartolo Colon .40 .12
43 David Justice .40 .12
44 Manny Ramirez .40 .12
45 Richie Sexson .40 .12
46 Jim Thome 1.00 .30
47 Omar Vizquel .40 .12
48 Pedro Astacio .40 .12
49 Todd Helton .60 .18
50 Neifi Perez .40 .12
51 Ben Petrick .40 .12
52 Larry Walker .60 .18
53 Tony Clark .40 .12
54 Damion Easley .40 .12
55 Juan Gonzalez 1.00 .30
56 Dean Palmer .40 .12
57 A.J. Burnett .40 .12
58 Luis Castillo .40 .12
59 Cliff Floyd .40 .12
60 Alex Gonzalez .40 .12
61 Preston Wilson .40 .12
62 Jeff Bagwell .60 .18
63 Craig Biggio .60 .18
64 Ken Caminiti .40 .12
65 Jose Lima .40 .12
66 Billy Wagner .40 .12
67 Carlos Beltran .40 .12
68 Johnny Damon .40 .12
69 Jermaine Dye .40 .12
70 Carlos Febles .40 .12
71 Mike Sweeney .40 .12
72 Kevin Brown .60 .18
73 Shawn Green .40 .12
74 Eric Karros .40 .12
75 Chan Ho Park .40 .12
76 Gary Sheffield .40 .12
77 Ron Belliard .40 .12
78 Jeromy Burnitz .40 .12
79 Marquis Grissom .40 .12
80 Geoff Jenkins .40 .12
81 Mark Loretta .40 .12
82 Ron Coomer .40 .12
83 Jacque Jones .40 .12
84 Corey Koskie .40 .12
85 Brad Radke .40 .12
86 Todd Walker .40 .12
87 Michael Barrett .40 .12
88 Peter Bergeron .40 .12
89 Vladimir Guerrero 1.00 .30
90 Jose Vidro .40 .12
91 Rondell White .40 .12
92 Edgardo Alfonzo .40 .12
93 Rickey Henderson 1.00 .30
94 Rey Ordonez .40 .12
95 Mike Piazza 1.50 .45
96 Robin Ventura .60 .18
97 Roger Clemens 2.00 .60
98 Orlando Hernandez .40 .12
99 Derek Jeter 2.50 .75
100 Tino Martinez .60 .18
101 Mariano Rivera .60 .18
102 Alfonso Soriano 1.00 .30
103 Bernie Williams .60 .18
104 Eric Chavez .40 .12
105 Jason Giambi 1.00 .30
106 Ben Grieve .40 .12
107 Tim Hudson .60 .18
108 John Jaha .40 .12
109 Bobby Abreu .40 .12
110 Doug Glanville .40 .12
111 Mike Lieberthal .40 .12
112 Scott Rolen .60 .18
113 Curt Schilling .60 .18
114 Brian Giles .40 .12
115 Jason Kendall .40 .12
116 Warren Morris .40 .12
117 Kevin Young .40 .12
118 Rick Ankiel .40 .12
119 J.D. Drew .40 .12
120 Chad Hutchinson .40 .12
121 Ray Lankford .40 .12
122 Mark McGwire 2.50 .75
123 Fernando Tatis .40 .12
124 Bret Boone .40 .12
125 Ben Davis .40 .12
126 Tony Gwynn 1.25 .35
127 Trevor Hoffman .40 .12
128 Barry Bonds 2.50 .75
129 Ellis Burks .40 .12
130 Jeff Kent .40 .12
131 J.T. Snow .40 .12
132 Freddy Garcia .40 .12
133 Ken Griffey Jr. 1.50 .45
134 Edgar Martinez .60 .18
135 John Olerud .40 .12
136 Alex Rodriguez 1.50 .45
137 Jose Canseco 1.00 .30
138 Vinny Castilla .40 .12
139 Roberto Hernandez .40 .12
140 Fred McGriff .60 .18
141 Rusty Greer .40 .12
142 Ruben Mateo .40 .12
143 Rafael Palmeiro .60 .18
144 Ivan Rodriguez 1.00 .30
145 Lee Stevens .40 .12
146 Tony Batista .40 .12
147 Carlos Delgado .40 .12
148 Shannon Stewart .40 .12
149 David Wells .40 .12
150 Vernon Wells .40 .12

2000 Pacific Prism Drops Silver

Randomly inserted into hobby and retail packs, this 150-card set is a complete parallel of the base set. According to Pacific the print run for this set was 799 non-serial numbered sets. Fifty star players, however, were produced in quantities of 916 of each card. Please refer to the header lines in our checklist for details on these cards.

Nm-Mt Ex-Mt
*STARS: .75X TO 2X BASIC CARDS ...
50 PLAYERS HAVE 916 OF EACH CARD
916 PLAYERS ARE AS FOLLOWS: ......
4/8/9/11/12/14/18/20/22/23/29/30/33/35/36
41/44/46/49/52/55/61/62/63/67/72/7376/78
89/92/95/97/99/103/107/112/114/118/119/122
126/128/132/133/136/137/142/143/144/147

2000 Pacific Prism Holographic Blue

Randomly inserted into hobby and retail packs, this 150-card set is a complete parallel of the base set. Each card is serial numbered to 80, and is backed in blue foil.

Nm-Mt Ex-Mt
*STARS: 6X TO 15X BASIC CARDS ....

2000 Pacific Prism Holographic Gold

Randomly inserted into hobby and retail packs, this 150-card set is a complete parallel of the base set. Each card is serial numbered to 480, and is backed in gold foil.

	Nm-Mt	Ex-Mt
*STARS: 2X TO 5X BASIC CARDS......		

2000 Pacific Prism Holographic Mirror

Randomly inserted into hobby and retail packs, this 150-card set is a complete parallel of the base set. Each card is serial numbered to 160, and is backed by a mirror-like pattern.

	Nm-Mt	Ex-Mt
*STARS: 3X TO 8X BASIC CARDS......		

2000 Pacific Prism Holographic Purple

Randomly inserted into hobby and retail packs, this 150-card set is a complete parallel of the base set. Each card is serial numbered to 99, and is backed in purple foil.

	Nm-Mt	Ex-Mt
*STARS: 5X TO 12X BASIC CARDS....		

2000 Pacific Prism Pebbly Dots

Randomly inserted into hobby and retail packs, this 150-card set is a complete parallel of the base set. According to Pacific there were 691 non-serial numbered sets of this insert produced. Please note that the players with asterisks by their names were produced in lesser quantities.

	Nm-Mt	Ex-Mt
*STARS: 1.25X TO 3X BASIC CARDS .		

2000 Pacific Prism Premiere Date

Randomly inserted into hobby packs, this 150-card set is a complete parallel of the base set. Each card is serial numbered to 61, and is stamped with "Premiere Date" on the front of the card.

	Nm-Mt	Ex-Mt
*STARS: 7.5X TO 15X BASIC CARDS .		

2000 Pacific Prism Proofs

Randomly inserted into hobby and retail packs, this 50-card set is a partial parallel of the base set. There were ten serial numbered sets of this insert produced on white vinyl based stock. No pricing is provided due to the scarcity of these cards.

	Nm-Mt	Ex-Mt
4 Mo Vaughn......................................		
8 Randy Johnson..................................		
9 Matt Williams..................................		
11 Andruw Jones..................................		
12 Chipper Jones.................................		
14 Greg Maddux...................................		
18 Mike Mussina..................................		
20 Cal Ripken....................................		
22 Nomar Garciaparra.............................		
23 Pedro Martinez................................		
29 Sammy Sosa....................................		
30 Kerry Wood....................................		
33 Magglio Ordonez...............................		
35 Frank Thomas..................................		
36 Sean Casey....................................		
41 Roberto Alomar................................		
46 Jim Thome.....................................		
49 Todd Helton...................................		
52 Larry Walker..................................		
55 Juan Gonzalez.................................		
61 Preston Wilson................................		
62 Jeff Bagwell..................................		
63 Craig Biggio..................................		
67 Carlos Beltran................................		
72 Kevin Brown...................................		
73 Shawn Green...................................		
76 Gary Sheffield................................		
78 Jeromy Burnitz................................		
89 Vladimir Guerrero.............................		
92 Edgardo Alfonzo...............................		
95 Mike Piazza...................................		
97 Roger Clemens.................................		
99 Derek Jeter...................................		
103 Bernie Williams..............................		
112 Scott Rolen..................................		
114 Brian Giles..................................		
118 Rick Ankiel..................................		
119 J.D. Drew....................................		
122 Mark McGwire.................................		
126 Tony Gwynn...................................		
128 Barry Bonds..................................		
132 Freddy Garcia................................		
133 Ken Griffey Jr...............................		
134 Edgar Martinez...............................		
136 Alex Rodriguez...............................		
137 Jose Canseco.................................		
142 Ruben Mateo..................................		
143 Rafael Palmeiro..............................		
144 Ivan Rodriguez...............................		
147 Carlos Delgado...............................		

2000 Pacific Prism Rapture Gold

Randomly inserted into retail packs, this 150-card set is a complete parallel of the base set. According to Pacific there were 565 non-serial numbered sets of this insert produced.

	Nm-Mt	Ex-Mt
*STARS: 1.5X TO 4X BASIC CARDS...		

2000 Pacific Prism Rapture Silver

Randomly inserted into hobby packs, this 150-card set is a complete parallel of the base set. According to Pacific there were 916 non-serial numbered sets of this insert produced.

	Nm-Mt	Ex-Mt
*STARS: .75X TO 2X BASIC CARDS...		

2000 Pacific Prism Sheen Silver

Randomly inserted into hobby and retail packs, this 100-card set is a partial parallel of the base set. According to Pacific, the print run for this set was split into two groups whereby 50 cards were produced in quantities 448 non-serial numbered subsets and 50 other cards were produced in quantities of 565 non serial numbered subsets. Subset breakdown can be seen in the header below.

	Nm-Mt	Ex-Mt
1 Jeff DaVanon *	1.50	.45
2 Troy Glaus *	2.00	.60
3 Tim Salmon *	2.00	.60
5 Jay Bell *	1.25	.35
6 Erubiel Durazo *	1.25	.35
7 Luis Gonzalez *	1.25	.35
10 Andres Galarraga *	1.25	.35
13 Brian Jordan *	1.25	.35
15 Kevin Millwood *	1.25	.35
16 John Smoltz *	2.00	.60
17 Albert Belle *	1.25	.35
19 Calvin Pickering *	1.25	.35
21 B.J. Surhoff *	1.25	.35
24 Troy O'Leary *	1.25	.35
25 John Valentin *	1.25	.35
26 Jason Varitek *	1.25	.35
27 Mark Grace *	2.00	.60
28 Henry Rodriguez *	1.25	.35
31 Ray Durham *	1.25	.35
32 Carlos Lee *	1.25	.35
34 Chris Singleton *	1.25	.35
37 Travis Dawkins *	1.25	.35
38 Barry Larkin *	3.00	.90
39 Pokey Reese *	1.25	.35
40 Scott Williamson *	1.25	.35
42 Bartolo Colon	1.25	.35
43 David Justice	1.25	.35
45 Richie Sexson	1.25	.35
47 Omar Vizquel	1.25	.35
48 Pedro Astacio	1.25	.35
50 Neifi Perez	1.25	.35
51 Ben Petrick	1.25	.35
53 Tony Clark	1.25	.35
54 Damion Easley	1.25	.35
56 Dean Palmer	1.25	.35
57 A.J. Burnett	1.25	.35
58 Luis Castillo	1.25	.35
59 Cliff Floyd	1.25	.35
60 Alex Gonzalez	1.25	.35
64 Ken Caminiti	1.25	.35
65 Jose Lima	1.25	.35
66 Billy Wagner	1.25	.35
68 Johnny Damon	1.25	.35
69 Jermaine Dye	1.25	.35
70 Carlos Febles	1.25	.35
71 Mike Sweeney	1.25	.35
74 Eric Karros	1.25	.35
75 Chan Ho Park	1.25	.35
77 Ron Belliard	1.25	.35
79 Marquis Grissom	1.25	.35
80 Geoff Jenkins *	1.25	.35
81 Mark Loretta *	1.25	.35
82 Ron Coomer *	1.25	.35
83 Jacque Jones *	1.25	.35
84 Corey Koskie *	1.25	.35
85 Brad Radke *	1.25	.35
86 Todd Walker *	1.25	.35
87 Michael Barrett *	1.25	.35
88 Peter Bergeron *	1.25	.35
90 Jose Vidro *	1.25	.35
91 Rondell White *	1.25	.35
93 Rickey Henderson *	3.00	.90
94 Rey Ordonez *	1.25	.35
96 Robin Ventura *	2.00	.60
98 Orlando Hernandez *	1.25	.35
100 Tino Martinez *	2.00	.60
101 Mariano Rivera *	2.00	.60
102 Alfonso Soriano *	2.50	.75
104 Eric Chavez *	1.25	.35
105 Jason Giambi *	3.00	.90
106 Ben Grieve *	1.25	.35
107 Tim Hudson *	1.50	.45
108 John Jaha *	1.25	.35
109 Bobby Abreu *	1.25	.35
110 Doug Glanville *	1.25	.35
111 Mike Lieberthal	1.25	.35
113 Curt Schilling	2.00	.60
115 Jason Kendall	1.25	.35
116 Warren Morris	1.25	.35
117 Kevin Young	1.25	.35
120 Chad Hutchinson	1.25	.35
121 Ray Lankford	1.25	.35
123 Fernando Tatis	1.25	.35
124 Bret Boone	1.25	.35
125 Ben Davis	1.25	.35
127 Trevor Hoffman	1.25	.35
129 Ellis Burks	1.25	.35
130 Jeff Kent	1.25	.35
131 J.T. Snow	1.25	.35
134 Edgar Martinez	2.00	.60
135 John Olerud	1.25	.35
138 Vinny Castilla	1.25	.35
139 Roberto Hernandez	1.25	.35
140 Fred McGriff	2.00	.60
141 Rusty Greer	1.25	.35
145 Lee Stevens	1.25	.35
146 Tony Batista	1.25	.35
148 Shannon Stewart	1.25	.35
149 David Wells	1.25	.35
150 Vernon Wells	1.25	.35

2000 Pacific Prism Slider Silver

Randomly inserted into hobby and retail packs, this 150-card set is a complete parallel of the base set. According to Pacific there were three tiers produced of this set. Tier one cards had 334 non-serial numbered sets produced. Tier two cards had 448 non-serial numbered sets produced. Finally, tier three cards had 565 non-serial numbered sets produced.

	Nm-Mt	Ex-Mt
1 Jeff DaVanon T1	1.50	.45
2 Troy Glaus T1	2.00	.60
3 Tim Salmon T1	2.00	.60
4 Mo Vaughn T3	1.25	.35
5 Jay Bell T1	1.25	.35
6 Erubiel Durazo T1	1.25	.35
7 Luis Gonzalez T1	1.25	.35
8 Randy Johnson T3	3.00	.90
9 Matt Williams T3	1.25	.35
10 Andres Galarraga T1	1.25	.35
11 Andruw Jones T3	1.25	.35
12 Chipper Jones T3	3.00	.90
13 Brian Jordan T1	1.25	.35
14 Greg Maddux T3	5.00	1.50
15 Kevin Millwood T1	1.25	.35
16 John Smoltz T1	2.00	.60
17 Albert Belle T1	1.25	.35
18 Mike Mussina T3	3.00	.90
19 Calvin Pickering T1	1.25	.35
20 Cal Ripken T3	10.00	3.00
21 B.J. Surhoff T1	1.25	.35
22 Nomar Garciaparra T3	5.00	1.50
23 Pedro Martinez T3	3.00	.90
24 Troy O'Leary T1	1.25	.35
25 John Valentin T1	1.25	.35
26 Jason Varitek T1	1.25	.35
27 Mark Grace T1	2.00	.60
28 Henry Rodriguez T1	1.25	.35
29 Sammy Sosa T3	5.00	1.50
30 Kerry Wood T3	3.00	.90
31 Ray Durham T1	1.25	.35
32 Carlos Lee T1	1.25	.35
33 Magglio Ordonez T3	1.25	.35
34 Chris Singleton T1	1.25	.35
35 Frank Thomas T3	3.00	.90
36 Sean Casey T3	1.25	.35
37 Travis Dawkins T1	1.25	.35
38 Barry Larkin T1	3.00	.90
39 Pokey Reese T1	1.25	.35
40 Scott Williamson T1	1.25	.35
41 Roberto Alomar T3	3.00	.90
42 Bartolo Colon T2	1.25	.35
43 David Justice T2	1.25	.35
44 Manny Ramirez T3	1.25	.35
45 Richie Sexson T2	1.25	.35
46 Jim Thome T3	3.00	.90
47 Omar Vizquel T2	1.25	.35
48 Pedro Astacio T2	1.25	.35
49 Todd Helton T3	2.00	.60
50 Neifi Perez T2	1.25	.35
51 Ben Petrick T2	1.25	.35
52 Larry Walker T3	2.00	.60
53 Tony Clark T2	1.25	.35
54 Damion Easley T2	1.25	.35
55 Juan Gonzalez T3	3.00	.90
56 Dean Palmer T2	1.25	.35
57 A.J. Burnett T2	1.25	.35
58 Luis Castillo T2	1.25	.35
59 Cliff Floyd T2	1.25	.35
60 Alex Gonzalez T2	1.25	.35
61 Preston Wilson T3	1.25	.35
62 Jeff Bagwell T3	2.00	.60
63 Craig Biggio T3	2.00	.60
64 Ken Caminiti T2	1.25	.35
65 Jose Lima T2	1.25	.35
66 Billy Wagner T2	1.25	.35
67 Carlos Beltran T3	1.25	.35
68 Johnny Damon T2	1.25	.35
69 Jermaine Dye T2	1.25	.35
70 Carlos Febles T2	1.25	.35
71 Mike Sweeney T2	1.25	.35
72 Kevin Brown T3	2.00	.60
73 Shawn Green T3	1.25	.35
74 Eric Karros T2	1.25	.35
75 Chan Ho Park T2	1.25	.35
76 Gary Sheffield T3	1.25	.35
77 Ron Belliard T2	1.25	.35
78 Jeromy Burnitz T3	1.25	.35
79 Marquis Grissom T2	1.25	.35
80 Geoff Jenkins T1	1.25	.35
81 Mark Loretta T1	1.25	.35
82 Ron Coomer T1	1.25	.35
83 Jacque Jones T1	1.25	.35
84 Corey Koskie T1	1.25	.35
85 Brad Radke T1	1.25	.35
86 Todd Walker T1	1.25	.35
87 Michael Barrett T1	1.25	.35
88 Peter Bergeron T1	1.25	.35
89 Vladimir Guerrero T3	3.00	.90
90 Jose Vidro T1	1.25	.35
91 Rondell White T1	1.25	.35
92 Edgardo Alfonzo T3	1.25	.35
93 Rickey Henderson T1	3.00	.90
94 Rey Ordonez T1	1.25	.35
95 Mike Piazza T3	5.00	1.50
96 Robin Ventura T1	2.00	.60
97 Roger Clemens T3	6.00	1.80
98 Orlando Hernandez T1	1.25	.35
99 Derek Jeter T3	8.00	2.40
100 Tino Martinez T1	2.00	.60
101 Mariano Rivera T1	2.00	.60
102 Alfonso Soriano T1	2.50	.75
103 Bernie Williams T3	2.00	.60
104 Eric Chavez T1	1.25	.35
105 Jason Giambi T1	3.00	.90
106 Ben Grieve T1	1.25	.35
107 Tim Hudson T1	1.50	.45
108 John Jaha T1	1.25	.35
109 Bobby Abreu T1	1.25	.35
110 Doug Glanville T1	1.25	.35
111 Mike Lieberthal T2	1.25	.35
112 Scott Rolen T3	2.00	.60
113 Curt Schilling T2	2.00	.60
114 Brian Giles T3	1.25	.35
115 Jason Kendall T2	1.25	.35
116 Warren Morris T2	1.25	.35
117 Kevin Young T2	1.25	.35
118 Rick Ankiel T3	1.00	.30
119 J.D. Drew T3	1.25	.35
120 Chad Hutchinson T2	1.25	.35
121 Ray Lankford T2	1.25	.35
122 Mark McGwire T3	8.00	2.40
123 Fernando Tatis T2	1.25	.35
124 Bret Boone T2	1.25	.35
125 Ben Davis T2	1.25	.35
126 Tony Gwynn T3	4.00	1.20
127 Trevor Hoffman T2	1.25	.35
128 Barry Bonds T3	8.00	2.40
129 Ellis Burks T2	1.25	.35
130 Jeff Kent T2	1.25	.35
131 J.T. Snow T2	1.25	.35
132 Freddy Garcia T3	1.25	.35
133 Ken Griffey Jr. T3	5.00	1.50
134 Edgar Martinez T2	2.00	.60
135 John Olerud T2	1.25	.35
136 Alex Rodriguez T3	5.00	1.50
137 Jose Canseco T3	3.00	.90
138 Vinny Castilla T2	1.25	.35
139 R.Hernandez T2	1.25	.35
140 Fred McGriff T2	2.00	.60
141 Rusty Greer T2	1.25	.35
142 Ruben Mateo T3	1.25	.35
143 Rafael Palmeiro T3	2.00	.60
144 Ivan Rodriguez T3	3.00	.90
145 Lee Stevens T2	1.25	.35
146 Tony Batista T2	1.25	.35
147 Carlos Delgado T3	1.25	.35
148 Shannon Stewart T2	1.25	.35
149 David Wells T2	1.25	.35
150 Vernon Wells T2	1.25	.35

2000 Pacific Prism Texture Silver

Randomly inserted into retail packs, this 150-card set is a complete parallel of the base set. According to Pacific there were 448 non-serial numbered sets of this insert produced.

	Nm-Mt	Ex-Mt
*STARS: 1.25X TO 3X BASIC CARDS .		

2000 Pacific Prism Tinsel Silver

Randomly inserted into hobby packs, this 150-card set is a complete parallel of the base set. According to Pacific there were 331 non-serial numbered sets of this insert produced.

	Nm-Mt	Ex-Mt
*STARS: 2X TO 5X BASIC CARDS......		

2000 Pacific Prism Woodgrain Silver

Randomly inserted into retail packs, this 150-card set is a complete parallel of the base set. According to Pacific there were 331 non-serial numbered sets of this insert produced.

	Nm-Mt	Ex-Mt
*STARS: 2X TO 5X BASIC CARDS......		

2000 Pacific Prism AL/NL Legends

Randomly inserted into packs at one in 25, this 20-card insert set features some of the most legendary American League and National League players. For checklisting purposes, we have assigned an "A'" prefix on all American League cards and an "N" prefix on all National League cards.

	Nm-Mt	Ex-Mt
COMPLETE AL SET (10)	25.00	7.50
COMPLETE NL SET (10)	25.00	7.50
A1 Mo Vaughn	1.00	.30
A2 Cal Ripken	8.00	2.40
A3 Nomar Garciaparra	4.00	1.20
A4 Manny Ramirez	1.00	.30
A5 Roger Clemens	5.00	1.50
A6 Derek Jeter	6.00	1.80
A7 Ken Griffey Jr.	4.00	1.20
A8 Alex Rodriguez	4.00	1.20
A9 Jose Canseco	2.50	.75
A10 Rafael Palmeiro	1.50	.45
N1 Chipper Jones	2.50	.75
N2 Greg Maddux	4.00	1.20
N3 Sammy Sosa	4.00	1.20
N4 Larry Walker	1.50	.45
N5 Jeff Bagwell	1.50	.45
N6 Vladimir Guerrero	2.50	.75
N7 Mike Piazza	4.00	1.20
N8 Mark McGwire	6.00	1.80
N9 Tony Gwynn	3.00	.90
N10 Barry Bonds	6.00	1.80

2000 Pacific Prism Center Stage

Randomly inserted into packs at one in 25, this 20-card die-cut insert set features the best players in major league baseball.

	Nm-Mt	Ex-Mt
COMPLETE SET (20)	50.00	15.00
1 Chipper Jones	3.00	.90
2 Cal Ripken	10.00	3.00
3 Nomar Garciaparra	5.00	1.50
4 Pedro Martinez	3.00	.90
5 Sammy Sosa	5.00	1.50
6 Sean Casey	1.25	.35
7 Manny Ramirez	1.25	.35
8 Jim Thome	3.00	.90
9 Jeff Bagwell	2.00	.60
10 Carlos Beltran	1.25	.35
11 Vladimir Guerrero	3.00	.90
12 Mike Piazza	5.00	1.50
13 Derek Jeter	8.00	2.40
14 Bernie Williams	2.00	.60
15 Scott Rolen	2.00	.60
16 Mark McGwire	8.00	2.40
17 Tony Gwynn	4.00	1.20
18 Ken Griffey Jr.	5.00	1.50
19 Alex Rodriguez	5.00	1.50
20 Ivan Rodriguez	3.00	.90

2000 Pacific Prism Dial-A-Stats

Randomly inserted into packs at one in 193, this 10-card insert set features a dial mechanism that allows you to see a given player's yearly statistics.

	Nm-Mt	Ex-Mt
1 Chipper Jones	10.00	3.00
2 Greg Maddux	15.00	4.50
3 Cal Ripken	30.00	9.00
4 Sammy Sosa	15.00	4.50
5 Mike Piazza	15.00	4.50
6 Roger Clemens	20.00	6.00
7 Mark McGwire	25.00	7.50
8 Tony Gwynn	12.00	3.60
9 Ken Griffey Jr.	15.00	4.50
10 Alex Rodriguez	15.00	4.50

2000 Pacific Prism Prospects Hobby

Randomly inserted into hobby packs at one in 97, this 10-card set features the hottest prospects in major league baseball. Please note that there is a retail only parallel of this set that contains different photos of the listed players.

	Nm-Mt	Ex-Mt
COMPLETE SET (10)	25.00	7.50
*RETAIL PROSPECTS: .4X TO 1X HOBBY		
RETAIL PROSPECTS ODDS 1:97 RETAIL		
RETAIL PROSPECTS HAVE DIF'T PHOTOS		
1 Erubiel Durazo	4.00	1.20
2 Wilton Veras	4.00	1.20
3 Ben Petrick	4.00	1.20
4 Mark Quinn	4.00	1.20
5 Peter Bergeron	4.00	1.20
6 Alfonso Soriano	8.00	2.40
7 Tim Hudson	6.00	1.80
8 Chad Hermansen	4.00	1.20
9 Rick Ankiel	4.00	1.20
10 Ruben Mateo	4.00	1.20

1999 Pacific Private Stock

This 150-card set was distributed in six card packs with a suggested retail price of $4.49. The fronts feature color action player photos printed on super-thick 30 pt. card stock in holographic silver foil. The backs display selected box scores from the 1998 season.

	Nm-Mt	Ex-Mt
COMPLETE SET (150)	80.00	24.00
1 Jeff Bagwell	.75	.23
2 Roger Clemens	2.50	.75
3 J.D. Drew	.50	.15
4 Nomar Garciaparra	2.00	.60
5 Juan Gonzalez	1.25	.35
6 Ken Griffey Jr.	2.00	.60
7 Tony Gwynn	1.50	.45
8 Derek Jeter	3.00	.90
9 Chipper Jones	1.25	.35
10 Travis Lee	.30	.09
11 Greg Maddux	2.00	.60
12 Mark McGwire	3.00	.90
13 Mike Piazza	2.00	.60
14 Manny Ramirez	.50	.15
15 Cal Ripken	4.00	1.20
16 Alex Rodriguez	2.00	.60
17 Ivan Rodriguez	1.25	.35
18 Sammy Sosa	2.00	.60
19 Frank Thomas	1.25	.35
20 Kerry Wood	1.25	.35
21 Roberto Alomar	1.25	.35
22 Moises Alou	.50	.15
23 Albert Belle	.50	.15
24 Craig Biggio	.75	.23
25 Wade Boggs	.75	.23
26 Barry Bonds	3.00	.90
27 Jose Canseco	1.25	.35
28 Jim Edmonds	.50	.15
29 Darin Erstad	.50	.15
30 Andres Galarraga	.50	.15
31 Tom Glavine	.75	.23
32 Ben Grieve	.30	.09
33 Vladimir Guerrero	1.25	.35
34 Wilton Guerrero	.30	.09

35 Todd Helton .75 .23
36 Andruw Jones .50 .15
37 Ryan Klesko .50 .15
38 Kenny Lofton .50 .15
39 Javy Lopez .50 .15
40 Pedro Martinez 1.25 .35
41 Paul Molitor .75 .23
42 Raul Mondesi .50 .15
43 Rafael Palmeiro .75 .23
44 Tim Salmon .75 .23
45 Jim Thome 1.25 .35
46 Mo Vaughn .50 .15
47 Larry Walker .75 .23
48 David Wells .50 .15
49 Bernie Williams .75 .23
50 Jaret Wright .30 .09
51 Bob Abreu .50 .15
52 Garret Anderson .50 .15
53 Rolando Arrojo .30 .09
54 Tony Batista .50 .15
55 Rod Beck .30 .09
56 Derek Bell .30 .09
57 Marvin Benard .30 .09
58 Dave Berg .30 .09
59 Dante Bichette .50 .15
60 Aaron Boone .50 .15
61 Bret Boone .50 .15
62 Scott Brosius .50 .15
63 Brant Brown .30 .09
64 Kevin Brown .75 .23
65 Jeromy Burnitz .50 .15
66 Ken Caminiti .50 .15
67 Mike Caruso .30 .09
68 Sean Casey .50 .15
69 Vinny Castilla .50 .15
70 Eric Chavez .50 .15
71 Ryan Christenson .30 .09
72 Jeff Cirillo .30 .09
73 Tony Clark .30 .09
74 Will Clark 1.25 .35
75 Edgard Clemente .30 .09
76 David Cone .50 .15
77 Marty Cordova .30 .09
78 Jose Cruz Jr. .50 .15
79 Eric Davis .50 .15
80 Carlos Delgado .50 .15
81 David Dellucci .30 .09
82 Delino DeShields .30 .09
83 Gary DiSarcina .30 .09
84 Damion Easley .30 .09
85 Dennis Eckersley .50 .15
86 Cliff Floyd .50 .15
87 Jason Giambi 1.25 .35
88 Doug Glanville .30 .09
89 Alex Gonzalez .30 .09
90 Mark Grace .75 .23
91 Rusty Greer .50 .15
92 Jose Guillen .30 .09
93 Carlos Guillen .30 .09
94 Jeffrey Hammonds .30 .09
95 Rick Helling .30 .09
96 Bob Henley .30 .09
97 Livan Hernandez .30 .09
98 Orlando Hernandez .50 .15
99 Bob Higginson .50 .15
100 Trevor Hoffman .50 .15
101 Randy Johnson 1.25 .35
102 Brian Jordan .50 .15
103 Wally Joyner .50 .15
104 Eric Karros .50 .15
105 Jason Kendall .50 .15
106 Jeff Kent .50 .15
107 Jeff King .30 .09
108 Mark Kotsay .30 .09
109 Ray Lankford .30 .09
110 Barry Larkin 1.25 .35
111 Mark Loretta .30 .09
112 Edgar Martinez .75 .23
113 Tino Martinez .75 .23
114 Quinton McCracken .30 .09
115 Fred McGriff .75 .23
116 Ryan Minor .30 .09
117 Hal Morris .30 .09
118 Bill Mueller .50 .15
119 Mike Mussina 1.25 .35
120 Dave Nilsson .30 .09
121 Otis Nixon .30 .09
122 Hideo Nomo 1.25 .35
123 Paul O'Neill .75 .23
124 Jose Offerman .30 .09
125 John Olerud .50 .15
126 Rey Ordonez .30 .09
127 David Ortiz .50 .15
128 Dean Palmer .50 .15
129 Chan Ho Park .50 .15
130 Aramis Ramirez .50 .15
131 Edgar Renteria .50 .15
132 Armando Rios .30 .09
133 Henry Rodriguez .30 .09
134 Scott Rolen .75 .23
135 Curt Schilling .75 .23
136 David Segui .30 .09
137 Richie Sexson .50 .15
138 Gary Sheffield .50 .15
139 John Smoltz .75 .23
140 Matt Stairs .30 .09
141 Justin Thompson .30 .09
142 Greg Vaughn .50 .15
143 Omar Vizquel .50 .15
144 Tim Wakefield .50 .15
145 Todd Walker .50 .15
146 Devon White .30 .09
147 Rondell White .50 .15
148 Matt Williams .50 .15
149 Enrique Wilson .30 .09
150 Kevin Young .50 .15

1999 Pacific Private Stock Exclusive

Randomly inserted in hobby packs, this 20-card set features action color photos of top players with an alternate photo of the player on the front and back and a special foil logo. The first 20 players in the regular set are featured in this set. Only 299 sets were produced and serially numbered.

Nm-Mt Ex-Mt
COMPLETE SET (20) 500.00 150.00
*STARS: 3X TO 8X BASIC CARDS

1999 Pacific Private Stock Platinum

Randomly inserted in packs, this 50-card set features action color photos of the first 50 players in the same design as the base set only with alternate foil color and a special foil logo. Only 199 sets were produced and serially numbered.

Nm-Mt Ex-Mt
*STARS: 5X TO 12X BASIC CARDS

1999 Pacific Private Stock Preferred

Randomly inserted in packs, this 20-card set features action color photos of the first 20 players with alternate team logo and background and a special foil logo. Only 399 sets were produced and serially numbered.

Nm-Mt Ex-Mt
COMPLETE SET (20) 400.00 120.00
*STARS: 2.5X TO 6X BASIC CARDS

1999 Pacific Private Stock Vintage

Randomly inserted in packs, this 50-card set features action color photos of the first 50 players in the same design as the base set only with a special foil logo. Only 99 sets were produced and serially numbered.

Nm-Mt Ex-Mt
*STARS: 8X TO 20X BASIC CARDS

1999 Pacific Private Stock PS-206

Inserted one per pack, this 150-card set is a smaller parallel version of the base set. The cards measure approximately 1 1/2" by 2 5/8" and feature blue ink backs.

Nm-Mt Ex-Mt
*SINGLES: .75X TO 2X BASIC PRI. STOCK

1999 Pacific Private Stock PS-206 Red

Randomly inserted one in 25 hobby only packs and one in 33 retail packs, this 150-card set is a smaller parallel version of the base set and features red ink backs. The cards measure approximately 1 1/2" by 2. 5/8".

Nm-Mt Ex-Mt
*PS-206 RED: 5X TO 12X BASIC PRI.STOCK

1999 Pacific Private Stock Home Run History

Randomly inserted in hobby packs at the rate of 2:25 and in retail packs at 1:17, this 22-card set features action color photos commemorating the spectacular feats of Mark McGwire and Sammy Sosa with holographic silver foil highlights.

Nm-Mt Ex-Mt
COMMON MCGWIRE 6.00 1.80
COMMON SOSA 4.00 1.20
1 Mark McGwire 61 6.00 1.80
3 Mark McGwire 62 10.00 3.00
15 Mark McGwire 70 15.00 4.50
16 Sammy Sosa 66 12.00 3.60
17 Mark McGwire 10.00 3.00
w/J.D. Drew
18 Sammy Sosa 4.00 1.20
A Season of Celebration
19 Sammy Sosa 8.00 2.40
Mark McGwire
Awesome Power
20 Mark McGwire 8.00 2.40
Sammy Sosa
Transcending Sports
21 Mark McGwire 15.00 4.50
Crown Die Cut
22 Cal Ripken 20.00 6.00
Crown Die Cut

1999 Pacific Private Stock Players Choice

These cards parallel the regular Private Stock set. They have a special "Players Choice" logo stamped on them and were given away at the Players Choice award ceremony in Las Vegas. Each card was printed in different quantities so we have put the quantity next to the players name. Due to market scarcity, no pricing is provided.

Nm-Mt Ex-Mt
14 Manny Ramirez/25
18 Sammy Sosa/15

2000 Pacific Private Stock

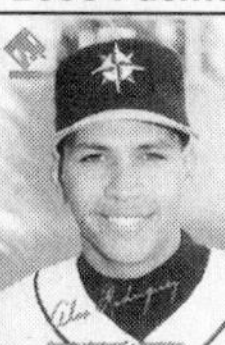

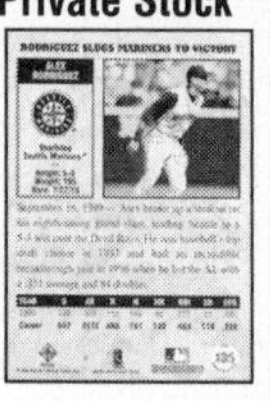

This 150 card set was issued in seven card packs with 24 packs in a box. The SRP on these packs are $4.49 and the set includes 25 short printed cards (notated in our checklist with SP) of 2000 Rookies. The set is sequenced in alphabetical order in team order which is also alphabetical.

Nm-Mt Ex-Mt
COMPLETE SET (150) 100.00 30.00
COMP.SET w/o SP's (125) 40.00 12.00
COMMON CARD (1-150) .50 .15
COMMON SP PROSPECT 5.00 1.50
1 Darin Erstad .50 .15
2 Troy Glaus .75 .23
3 Tim Salmon .75 .23
4 Mo Vaughn .50 .15
5 Jay Bell .50 .15
6 Luis Gonzalez .50 .15
7 Randy Johnson 1.25 .35
8 Matt Williams .50 .15
9 Andruw Jones .50 .15
10 Chipper Jones 1.25 .35
11 Brian Jordan .50 .15
12 Greg Maddux 2.00 .60
13 Kevin Millwood .50 .15
14 Albert Belle .50 .15
15 Mike Mussina 1.25 .35
16 Cal Ripken 4.00 1.20
17 B.J. Surhoff .50 .15
18 Nomar Garciaparra 2.00 .60
19 Butch Huskey .50 .15
20 Pedro Martinez 1.25 .35
21 Troy O'Leary .50 .15
22 Mark Grace .75 .23
23 Bo Porter SP 5.00 1.50
24 Henry Rodriguez .50 .15
25 Sammy Sosa 2.00 .60
26 Kerry Wood 1.25 .35
27 Jason Dellaero SP 5.00 1.50
28 Ray Durham .50 .15
29 Paul Konerko .50 .15
30 Carlos Lee .50 .15
31 Magglio Ordonez .50 .15
32 Frank Thomas 1.25 .35
33 Mike Cameron .50 .15
34 Sean Casey .50 .15
35 Barry Larkin 1.25 .35
36 Greg Vaughn .50 .15
37 Roberto Alomar 1.25 .35
38 Russell Branyan SP 5.00 1.50
39 Kenny Lofton .50 .15
40 Manny Ramirez .50 .15
41 Richie Sexson .50 .15
42 Jim Thome 1.25 .35
43 Omar Vizquel .50 .15
44 Pedro Astacio .50 .15
45 Vinny Castilla .50 .15
46 Todd Helton .75 .23
47 Ben Petrick SP 5.00 1.50
48 Juan Sosa SP RC 5.00 1.50
49 Larry Walker .75 .23
50 Tony Clark .50 .15
51 Damion Easley .50 .15
52 Juan Encarnacion .50 .15
53 Robert Fick SP 5.00 1.50
54 Dean Palmer .50 .15
55 A.J. Burnett SP 5.00 1.50
56 Luis Castillo .50 .15
57 Alex Gonzalez .50 .15
58 Julio Ramirez SP 5.00 1.50
59 Preston Wilson .50 .15
60 Jeff Bagwell .75 .23
61 Craig Biggio .75 .23
62 Ken Caminiti .50 .15
63 Carl Everett .50 .15
64 Mike Hampton .50 .15
65 Billy Wagner .50 .15
66 Carlos Beltran .50 .15
67 Dermal Brown SP 5.00 1.50
68 Jermaine Dye .50 .15
69 Carlos Febles .50 .15
70 Mark Quinn SP 5.00 1.50
71 Mike Sweeney .50 .15
72 Kevin Brown .75 .23
73 Eric Gagne SP 8.00 2.40
74 Eric Karros .50 .15
75 Raul Mondesi .50 .15
76 Gary Sheffield .50 .15
77 Jeromy Burnitz .50 .15
78 Jeff Cirillo .50 .15
79 Geoff Jenkins .50 .15
80 David Nilsson .50 .15
81 Ron Coomer .50 .15
82 Jacque Jones .50 .15
83 Corey Koskie .50 .15
84 Brad Radke .50 .15
85 Tony Armas Jr. SP 5.00 1.50
86 Peter Bergeron SP 5.00 1.50
87 Vladimir Guerrero 1.25 .35
88 Jose Vidro .50 .15
89 Rondell White .50 .15
90 Edgardo Alfonzo .50 .15
91 Roger Cedeno .50 .15
92 Rickey Henderson 1.25 .35
93 Jay Payton SP 5.00 1.50
94 Mike Piazza 2.00 .60
95 Jorge Toca SP 5.00 1.50
96 Robin Ventura .75 .23
97 Roger Clemens 2.50 .75
98 David Cone .50 .15
99 Derek Jeter 3.00 .90
100 D'Angelo Jimenez SP 5.00 1.50
101 Tino Martinez .75 .23
102 Alfonso Soriano SP 8.00 2.40
103 Bernie Williams .75 .23
104 Jason Giambi 1.25 .35
105 Ben Grieve .50 .15
106 Tim Hudson .75 .23
107 Matt Stairs .50 .15
108 Bob Abreu .50 .15
109 Doug Glanville .50 .15
110 Scott Rolen .75 .23
111 Curt Schilling .75 .23
112 Brian Giles .50 .15
113 Chad Hermansen SP 5.00 1.50
114 Jason Kendall .50 .15
115 Warren Morris .50 .15
116 Rick Ankiel SP 5.00 1.50
117 J.D. Drew .50 .15
118 Adam Kennedy SP 5.00 1.50
119 Ray Lankford .50 .15
120 Mark McGwire 3.00 .90
121 Fernando Tatis .50 .15
122 Mike Darr SP 5.00 1.50
123 Ben Davis .50 .15
124 Tony Gwynn 1.50 .45
125 Trevor Hoffman .50 .15
126 Reggie Sanders .50 .15
127 Barry Bonds 3.00 .90
128 Ellis Burks .50 .15
129 Jeff Kent .50 .15
130 J.T. Snow .50 .15
131 Freddy Garcia .50 .15
132 Ken Griffey Jr. 2.00 .60
133 Carlos Guillen SP 5.00 1.50
134 Edgar Martinez .75 .23
135 Alex Rodriguez 2.00 .60
136 Miguel Cairo .50 .15
137 Jose Canseco 1.25 .35
138 Steve Cox SP 5.00 1.50
139 Roberto Hernandez .50 .15
140 Fred McGriff .75 .23
141 Juan Gonzalez 1.25 .35
142 Rusty Greer .50 .15
143 Ruben Mateo SP 5.00 1.50
144 Rafael Palmeiro .75 .23
145 Ivan Rodriguez 1.25 .35
146 Carlos Delgado .50 .15
147 Tony Fernandez .50 .15
148 Shawn Green .50 .15
149 Shannon Stewart .50 .15
150 Vernon Wells SP 5.00 1.50

2000 Pacific Private Stock Gold Portraits

Randomly inserted in hobby packs, this parallel set to the regular Pacific Private Stock set is framed in gold foil. These cards are serial numbered to 99.

Nm-Mt Ex-Mt
*STARS: 6X TO 15X BASIC CARDS
*PROSPECTS: .5X TO 1.2X BASIC CARDS

2000 Pacific Private Stock Premiere Date

Inserted one per hobby box, this parallel set is serial numbered to 34. Each card carries a small Premiere Date foil logo on front with the serial numbering.

Nm-Mt Ex-Mt
*STARS: 10X TO 25X BASIC CARDS
*PROSPECTS: .75X TO 2X BASIC CARDS

2000 Pacific Private Stock Silver Portraits

Randomly inserted into retail packs, this set parallels the regular Private Stock set. The cards have silver foil framing and are serial numbered to 199.

Nm-Mt Ex-Mt
*STARS: 4X TO 10X BASIC CARDS
*PROSPECTS: .3X TO .8X BASIC CARDS

2000 Pacific Private Stock Artist's Canvas

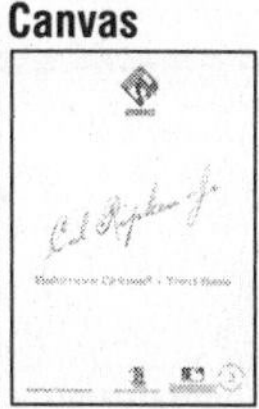

Inserted one every 49 packs, these 20 cards featuring leading baseball stars are printed on real artist's canvas.

Nm-Mt Ex-Mt
COMPLETE SET (20) 500.00 150.00
PROOFS RANDOM INSERTS IN PACKS
PROOFS PRINT RUN 1 SERIAL #'d SET
PROOFS NOT PRICED DUE TO SCARCITY
1 Chipper Jones 10.00 3.00
2 Greg Maddux 15.00 4.50
3 Cal Ripken 30.00 9.00
4 Nomar Garciaparra 15.00 4.50
5 Sammy Sosa 15.00 4.50
6 Frank Thomas 10.00 3.00
7 Manny Ramirez 4.00 1.20
8 Larry Walker 6.00 1.80
9 Jeff Bagwell 6.00 1.80
10 Vladimir Guerrero 10.00 3.00
11 Mike Piazza 15.00 4.50
12 Roger Clemens 20.00 6.00
13 Derek Jeter 25.00 7.50
14 Mark McGwire 25.00 7.50
15 Tony Gwynn 12.00 3.60
16 Barry Bonds 25.00 7.50
17 Ken Griffey Jr. 15.00 4.50
18 Alex Rodriguez 15.00 4.50
19 Juan Gonzalez 10.00 3.00
20 Ivan Rodriguez 10.00 3.00

2000 Pacific Private Stock Extreme Action

Inserted two every 25 packs, this 20 card set features excellent photos of many of baseball top stars.

Nm-Mt Ex-Mt
COMPLETE SET (20) 120.00 36.00
1 Andruw Jones 2.00 .60
2 Chipper Jones 5.00 1.50
3 Cal Ripken 15.00 4.50
4 Nomar Garciaparra 8.00 2.40
5 Sammy Sosa 8.00 2.40
6 Frank Thomas 5.00 1.50
7 Roberto Alomar 5.00 1.50
8 Manny Ramirez 2.00 .60
9 Larry Walker 3.00 .90
10 Jeff Bagwell 3.00 .90
11 Vladimir Guerrero 5.00 1.50
12 Mike Piazza 8.00 2.40
13 Derek Jeter 12.00 3.60
14 Bernie Williams 3.00 .90
15 Scott Rolen 3.00 .90
16 Mark McGwire 12.00 3.60
17 Tony Gwynn 6.00 1.80
18 Ken Griffey Jr. 8.00 2.40
19 Alex Rodriguez 8.00 2.40
20 Ivan Rodriguez 5.00 1.50

2000 Pacific Private Stock Reserve

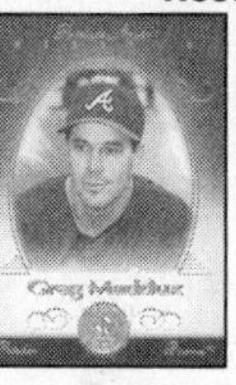

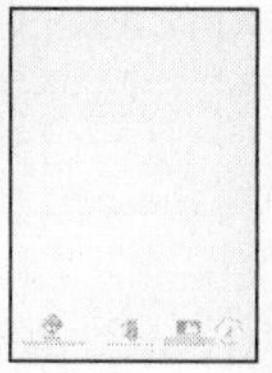

Issued one every 25 hobby packs, these 20 cards feature players on an unusual paper stock with a special foil seal on the front.

Nm-Mt Ex-Mt
COMPLETE SET (20) 250.00 75.00
1 Chipper Jones 8.00 2.40
2 Greg Maddux 12.00 3.60
3 Cal Ripken 25.00 7.50
4 Nomar Garciaparra 12.00 3.60
5 Sammy Sosa 12.00 3.60
6 Frank Thomas 8.00 2.40
7 Manny Ramirez 3.00 .90
8 Larry Walker 5.00 1.50
9 Jeff Bagwell 5.00 1.50
10 Vladimir Guerrero 8.00 2.40
11 Mike Piazza 12.00 3.60
12 Roger Clemens 15.00 4.50
13 Derek Jeter 20.00 6.00
14 Mark McGwire 20.00 6.00
15 Tony Gwynn 10.00 3.00
16 Barry Bonds 20.00 6.00
17 Ken Griffey Jr. 12.00 3.60
18 Alex Rodriguez 12.00 3.60
19 Ivan Rodriguez 8.00 2.40
20 Shawn Green 3.00 .90

2000 Pacific Private Stock PS-2000 Action

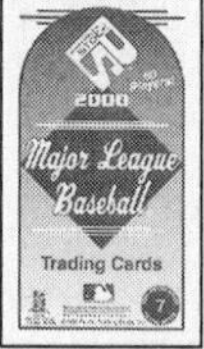

Issued two per pack, these cards features 60 of the best players from the Private Stock set. These cards are printed in a smaller size than the regular cards and features high action photos of these players.

Nm-Mt Ex-Mt
COMPLETE SET (60) 25.00 7.50
1 Mo Vaughn .40 .12
2 Greg Maddux 1.50 .45
3 Andruw Jones .40 .12
4 Chipper Jones 1.00 .30
5 Cal Ripken 3.00 .90
6 Nomar Garciaparra 1.50 .45
7 Pedro Martinez 1.00 .30
8 Sammy Sosa 1.50 .45
9 Jason Dellaero .40 .12
10 Magglio Ordonez .40 .12
11 Frank Thomas 1.00 .30
12 Sean Casey .40 .12
13 Russell Branyan .40 .12
14 Manny Ramirez .40 .12
15 Richie Sexson .40 .12
16 Ben Petrick .40 .12
17 Juan Sosa .40 .12
18 Larry Walker .60 .18
19 Robert Fick .40 .12
20 Craig Biggio .60 .18
21 Jeff Bagwell .60 .18
22 Carlos Beltran .40 .12
23 Dermal Brown 4.00 1.20
24 Mark Quinn 4.00 1.20
25 Eric Gagne 6.00 1.80
26 Jeromy Burnitz .40 .12
27 Tony Armas Jr. 4.00 1.20
28 Peter Bergeron 4.00 1.20
29 Vladimir Guerrero 1.00 .30
30 Edgardo Alfonzo .40 .12

31 Mike Piazza	1.50	.45
32 Jorge Toca	4.00	1.20
33 Roger Clemens	2.00	.60
34 Alfonso Soriano	6.00	1.80
35 Bernie Williams	.60	.18
36 Derek Jeter	2.50	.75
37 Tim Hudson	.60	.18
38 Bob Abreu	.40	.12
39 Scott Rolen	.60	.18
40 Brian Giles	.40	.12
41 Chad Hermansen	4.00	1.20
42 Warren Morris	.40	.12
43 Rick Ankiel	4.00	1.20
44 J.D. Drew	.40	.12
45 Adam Kennedy	4.00	1.20
46 Mark McGwire	2.50	.75
47 Mike Darr	4.00	1.20
48 Tony Gwynn	1.25	.35
49 Barry Bonds	2.50	.75
50 Ken Griffey Jr.	1.50	.45
51 Carlos Guillen	4.00	1.20
52 Alex Rodriguez	1.50	.45
53 Juan Gonzalez	1.00	.30
54 Ruben Mateo	4.00	1.20
55 Ivan Rodriguez	1.00	.30
56 Rafael Palmeiro	.60	.18
57 Jose Canseco	1.00	.30
58 Steve Cox	4.00	1.20
59 Shawn Green	.40	.12
60 Vernon Wells	4.00	1.20

2000 Pacific Private Stock PS-2000 New Wave

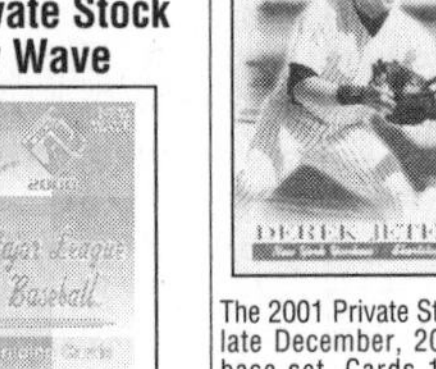

Randomly inserted in packs, this set features 20 of baseball's youngest stars and are serial numbered to 199.

	Nm-Mt	Ex-Mt
COMPLETE SET (20)	200.00	60.00
1 Andruw Jones	5.00	1.50
2 Chipper Jones	12.00	3.60
3 Nomar Garciaparra	20.00	6.00
4 Magglio Ordonez	5.00	1.50
5 Sean Casey	5.00	1.50
6 Manny Ramirez	5.00	1.50
7 Richie Sexson	5.00	1.50
8 Carlos Beltran	5.00	1.50
9 Jeromy Burnitz	5.00	1.50
10 Vladimir Guerrero	12.00	3.60
11 Edgardo Alfonzo	5.00	1.50
12 Derek Jeter	30.00	9.00
13 Tim Hudson	8.00	2.40
14 Bob Abreu	5.00	1.50
15 Scott Rolen	8.00	2.40
16 Brian Giles	5.00	1.50
17 Warren Morris	5.00	1.50
18 J.D. Drew	5.00	1.50
19 Alex Rodriguez	20.00	6.00
20 Shawn Green	5.00	1.50

2000 Pacific Private Stock PS-2000 Rookies

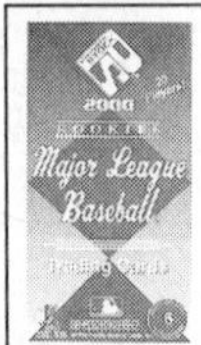

Randomly inserted into packs, these 20 cards feature players assumed to be among the best rookies of 2000 and are serial numbered to 99.

	Nm-Mt	Ex-Mt
COMPLETE SET (20)	120.00	36.00
1 Jason Dellaero	8.00	2.40
2 Russell Branyan	8.00	2.40
3 Ben Petrick	8.00	2.40
4 Juan Sosa	8.00	2.40
5 Robert Fick	8.00	2.40
6 Dermal Brown	8.00	2.40
7 Mark Quinn	8.00	2.40
8 Eric Gagne	10.00	3.00
9 Tony Armas Jr.	8.00	2.40
10 Peter Bergeron	8.00	2.40
11 Jorge Toca	8.00	2.40
12 Alfonso Soriano	10.00	3.00
13 Chad Hermansen	8.00	2.40
14 Rick Ankiel	8.00	2.40
15 Adam Kennedy	8.00	2.40
16 Mike Darr	8.00	2.40
17 Carlos Guillen	8.00	2.40
18 Steve Cox	8.00	2.40
19 Ruben Mateo	8.00	2.40
20 Vernon Wells	8.00	2.40

2000 Pacific Private Stock PS-2000 Stars

Randomly inserted into Private Stock packs, these cards feature classic portrait photos of 20 superstars. This set is sequentially numbered to 299.

	Nm-Mt	Ex-Mt
COMPLETE SET (20)	250.00	75.00
1 Mo Vaughn	4.00	1.20
2 Greg Maddux	15.00	4.50
3 Cal Ripken	30.00	9.00
4 Pedro Martinez	10.00	3.00
5 Sammy Sosa	15.00	4.50
6 Frank Thomas	10.00	3.00
7 Larry Walker	6.00	1.80
8 Craig Biggio	6.00	1.80
9 Jeff Bagwell	6.00	1.80
10 Mike Piazza	15.00	4.50
11 Roger Clemens	20.00	6.00
12 Bernie Williams	6.00	1.80
13 Mark McGwire	25.00	7.50
14 Tony Gwynn	12.00	3.60
15 Barry Bonds	25.00	7.50
16 Ken Griffey Jr.	15.00	4.50
17 Juan Gonzalez	10.00	3.00
18 Ivan Rodriguez	10.00	3.00
19 Rafael Palmeiro	6.00	1.80
20 Jose Canseco	10.00	3.00

2001 Pacific Private Stock

The 2001 Private Stock product was released in late December, 2000 and offers a 150-card base set. Cards 1-125 focused on veteran players and were commonly seeded at a rate of about four per pack. Cards 126-150 focused on prospects and were seeded at a rate of 1:4 hobby packs. Each hobby pack contained seven cards, and carried a suggested retail price of $14.99. Please note that each hobby pack included one memorabilia card. Retail packs contained five cards, carried an SRP of $2.99 and did not include a memorabilia card in every pack. This was Pacific's last MLB licensed baseball product issued as they decided to not renew their baseball license as of January 1st, 2001.

	Nm-Mt	Ex-Mt
COMPLETE SET (150)	150.00	45.00
COMP.SET w/o SP's (125)	50.00	15.00
COMMON CARD (1-125)	.50	.15
COMMON (126-150)	5.00	1.50
1 Darin Erstad	.50	.15
2 Troy Glaus	.75	.23
3 Tim Salmon	.75	.23
4 Mo Vaughn	.50	.15
5 Steve Finley	.50	.15
6 Luis Gonzalez	.50	.15
7 Randy Johnson	1.25	.35
8 Matt Williams	.50	.15
9 Rafael Furcal	.50	.15
10 Andres Galarraga	.50	.15
11 Tom Glavine	.75	.23
12 Andruw Jones	.50	.15
13 Chipper Jones	1.25	.35
14 Greg Maddux	2.00	.60
15 B.J. Surhoff	.50	.15
16 Brady Anderson	.50	.15
17 Albert Belle	.50	.15
18 Mike Mussina	1.25	.35
19 Cal Ripken	4.00	1.20
20 Carl Everett	.50	.15
21 Nomar Garciaparra	2.00	.60
22 Pedro Martinez	1.25	.35
23 Mark Grace	.75	.23
24 Sammy Sosa	2.00	.60
25 Kerry Wood	1.25	.35
26 Carlos Lee	.50	.15
27 Magglio Ordonez	.50	.15
28 Frank Thomas	1.25	.35
29 Sean Casey	.50	.15
30 Ken Griffey Jr.	2.00	.60
31 Barry Larkin	1.25	.35
32 Pokey Reese	.50	.15
33 Roberto Alomar	1.25	.35
34 Kenny Lofton	.50	.15
35 Manny Ramirez	.50	.15
36 Jim Thome	1.25	.35
37 Omar Vizquel	.50	.15
38 Jeff Cirillo	.50	.15
39 Jeffrey Hammonds	.50	.15
40 Todd Helton	.75	.23
41 Larry Walker	.75	.23
42 Tony Clark	.50	.15
43 Juan Encarnacion	.50	.15
44 Juan Gonzalez	1.25	.35
45 Hideo Nomo	1.25	.35
46 Cliff Floyd	.50	.15
47 Derek Lee	.50	.15
48 Henry Rodriguez	.50	.15
49 Preston Wilson	.50	.15
50 Jeff Bagwell	.75	.23
51 Craig Biggio	.75	.23
52 Richard Hidalgo	.50	.15
53 Moises Alou	.50	.15
54 Carlos Beltran	.50	.15
55 Johnny Damon	.50	.15
56 Jermaine Dye	.50	.15
57 Mac Suzuki	.50	.15
58 Mike Sweeney	.50	.15
59 Adrian Beltre	.50	.15
60 Kevin Brown	.50	.15
61 Shawn Green	.50	.15
62 Eric Karros	.50	.15
63 Chan Ho Park	.50	.15
64 Gary Sheffield	.50	.15
65 Jeromy Burnitz	.50	.15
66 Geoff Jenkins	.50	.15
67 Richie Sexson	.50	.15
68 Jacque Jones	.50	.15
69 Matt Lawton	.50	.15
70 Eric Milton	.50	.15
71 Vladimir Guerrero	1.25	.35
72 Jose Vidro	.50	.15
73 Edgardo Alfonzo	.50	.15
74 Mike Hampton	.50	.15
75 Mike Piazza	2.00	.60
76 Robin Ventura	.50	.15
77 Jose Canseco	1.25	.35
78 Roger Clemens	2.50	.75
79 Derek Jeter	3.00	.90
80 David Justice	.50	.15
81 Jorge Posada	.75	.23
82 Bernie Williams	.75	.23
83 Jason Giambi	1.25	.35
84 Ben Grieve	.50	.15
85 Tim Hudson	.50	.15
86 Terrence Long	.50	.15
87 Miguel Tejada	.50	.15
88 Bob Abreu	.50	.15
89 Pat Burrell	.50	.15
90 Mike Lieberthal	.50	.15
91 Scott Rolen	.75	.23
92 Kris Benson	.50	.15
93 Brian Giles	.50	.15
94 Jason Kendall	.50	.15
95 Aramis Ramirez	.50	.15
96 Rick Ankiel	.50	.15
97 Will Clark	1.25	.35
98 J.D. Drew	.50	.15
99 Jim Edmonds	.50	.15
100 Mark McGwire	3.00	.90
101 Fernando Tatis	.50	.15
102 Adam Eaton	.50	.15
103 Tony Gwynn	1.50	.45
104 Phil Nevin	.50	.15
105 Eric Owens	.50	.15
106 Barry Bonds	3.00	.90
107 Jeff Kent	.50	.15
108 J.T. Snow	.50	.15
109 Rickey Henderson	1.25	.35
110 Edgar Martinez	.75	.23
111 John Olerud	.50	.15
112 Alex Rodriguez	2.00	.60
113 Kazuhiro Sasaki	.50	.15
114 Vinny Castilla	.50	.15
115 Fred McGriff	.75	.23
116 Greg Vaughn	.50	.15
117 Gabe Kapler	.50	.15
118 Ruben Mateo	.50	.15
119 Rafael Palmeiro	.75	.23
120 Ivan Rodriguez	1.25	.35
121 Tony Batista	.50	.15
122 Jose Cruz Jr.	.50	.15
123 Carlos Delgado	.50	.15
124 Shannon Stewart	.50	.15
125 David Wells	.50	.15
126 Shawn Wooten SP	5.00	1.50
127 George Lombard SP	5.00	1.50
128 Morgan Burkhart SP	5.00	1.50
129 Ross Gload SP	5.00	1.50
130 Corey Patterson SP	8.00	2.40
131 Julio Zuleta SP	5.00	1.50
132 Joe Crede SP	5.00	1.50
133 Matt Ginter SP	5.00	1.50
134 Travis Dawkins SP	5.00	1.50
135 Eric Munson SP	5.00	1.50
136 Dee Brown SP	5.00	1.50
137 Luke Prokopec SP	5.00	1.50
138 Timo Perez SP	5.00	1.50
139 Alfonso Soriano SP	8.00	2.40
140 Jake Westbrook SP	5.00	1.50
141 Eric Byrnes SP	5.00	1.50
142 Adam Hyzdu SP	5.00	1.50
143 Jimmy Rollins SP	8.00	2.40
144 Xavier Nady SP	8.00	2.40
145 Ryan Vogelsong SP	5.00	1.50
146 Joel Pineiro SP	10.00	3.00
147 Aubrey Huff SP	8.00	2.40
148 Kenny Kelly SP	5.00	1.50
149 Josh Phelps SP	8.00	2.40
150 Vernon Wells SP	8.00	2.40

2001 Pacific Private Stock Gold Portraits

Randomly inserted into hobby packs, this 150-card insert is a complete parallel of the 2001 Pacific Private Stock base set. These cards are individually serial numbered to 75, and feature a gold border.

Nm-Mt Ex-Mt

*STARS 1-125: 8X TO 20X BASIC CARDS
*PROSPECTS 126-150: .75X TO 2X BASIC

2001 Pacific Private Stock Premiere Date

Randomly inserted into packs at two in 21 hobby, this 150-card insert is a complete parallel of the 2001 Pacific Private Stock base set. These cards are individually serial numbered to 90, and feature a "Premiere Date" stamp on the card fronts.

Nm-Mt Ex-Mt

*STARS 1-125: 8X TO 20X BASIC CARDS
*PROSPECTS 126-150: .75X TO 2X BASIC

2001 Pacific Private Stock Silver

Produced as the basic issue cards in retail packs, this 150-card set is a straight parallel of the regular issue gold foil cards distributed in hobby packs. Two to three Silver cards came seeded in each retail pack.

Nm-Mt Ex-Mt

*STARS 1-125: .75X TO 2X BASIC CARDS
*PROSPECTS: 126-150: .4X TO 1X BASIC

2001 Pacific Private Stock Silver Portraits

Randomly inserted into retail packs at three in 25, this 150-card insert is a complete parallel of the 2001 Pacific Private Stock base set. These cards are individually serial numbered to 290, and feature a silver border.

Nm-Mt Ex-Mt

*STARS 1-125: 3X TO 8X BASIC CARDS
*PROSPECTS 126-150: .5X TO 1.2X BASIC

2001 Pacific Private Stock Artist's Canvas

Randomly inserted into packs at one in 21 hobby and one in 49 retail, this 20-card insert features some of baseball's top stars. These cards were printed on actual canvas paper.

	Nm-Mt	Ex-Mt
COMPLETE SET (20)	400.00	120.00
PROOFS PRINT RUN 1 SERIAL #'d SET		
PROOFS NOT PRICED DUE TO SCARCITY		
1 Randy Johnson	12.00	3.60
2 Chipper Jones	12.00	3.60
3 Greg Maddux	20.00	6.00
4 Cal Ripken	40.00	12.00
5 Nomar Garciaparra	20.00	6.00
6 Pedro Martinez	12.00	3.60
7 Sammy Sosa	20.00	6.00
8 Frank Thomas	12.00	3.60
9 Ken Griffey Jr.	20.00	6.00
10 Manny Ramirez	8.00	2.40
11 Vladimir Guerrero	12.00	3.60
12 Mike Piazza	20.00	6.00
13 Roger Clemens	25.00	7.50
14 Derek Jeter	30.00	9.00
15 Jason Giambi	12.00	3.60
16 Rick Ankiel	8.00	2.40
17 Mark McGwire	30.00	9.00
18 Barry Bonds	30.00	9.00
19 Alex Rodriguez	20.00	6.00
20 Ivan Rodriguez	12.00	3.60

2001 Pacific Private Stock Extreme Action

Randomly inserted into packs at two in 21 hobby and 1:25 retail, this 20-card insert features players that are extremely talented.

	Nm-Mt	Ex-Mt
COMPLETE SET (20)	120.00	36.00
1 Darin Erstad	2.00	.60
2 Troy Glaus	3.00	.90
3 Rafael Furcal	2.00	.60
4 Cal Ripken	15.00	4.50
5 Nomar Garciaparra	8.00	2.40
6 Sammy Sosa	8.00	2.40
7 Frank Thomas	5.00	1.50
8 Ken Griffey Jr.	8.00	2.40
9 Roberto Alomar	5.00	1.50
10 Vladimir Guerrero	5.00	1.50
11 Derek Jeter	12.00	3.60
12 Mike Piazza	8.00	2.40
13 Jason Giambi	5.00	1.50
14 Miguel Tejada	2.00	.60
15 Jim Edmonds	2.00	.60
16 Mark McGwire	12.00	3.60
17 Barry Bonds	12.00	3.60
18 Jeff Kent	2.00	.60
19 Alex Rodriguez	8.00	2.40
20 Ivan Rodriguez	5.00	1.50

2001 Pacific Private Stock Game Gear

Inserted into packs at one per pack hobby and one in 49 retail, this 178-card insert features game-used memorabilia cards from some of the Major League's top players. Please note that cards 100, 176, and 177 do not exist. Though originally claimed by Pacific not to exist, a few copies of number 37, Sammy Sosa, later surfaced in the secondary market a few months after the products rlelease. Not much is known about this card but we will continue to monitor this card.

	Nm-Mt	Ex-Mt
1 Garret Anderson Bat	10.00	3.00
2 Darin Erstad Jsy	10.00	3.00
3 Ron Gant Bat	10.00	3.00
4 Troy Glaus Jsy	15.00	4.50
5 Tim Salmon Bat	15.00	4.50
6 Mo Vaughn Jsy Grey Away Uniform	10.00	3.00
7 Mo Vaughn Jsy White Home Uniform	10.00	3.00
8 Mo Vaughn Bat	10.00	3.00
9 Jay Bell Jsy	10.00	3.00
10 Jay Bell Bat	10.00	3.00
11 Erubiel Durazo Jsy Black Away Uniform	10.00	3.00
12 Erubiel Durazo Jsy White Home Uniform	10.00	3.00
13 Erubiel Durazo Bat	10.00	3.00
14 Steve Finley Bat	10.00	3.00
15 Randy Johnson Jsy	15.00	4.50
16 Byung-Hyun Kim Jsy White Home Uniform	10.00	3.00
17 Byung-Hyun Kim Jsy Grey Away Uniform	10.00	3.00
18 Matt Williams Jsy Grey Home Uniform	10.00	3.00
19 Matt Williams Jsy White Home Uniform	10.00	3.00
20 Matt Williams Jsy Purple Away Uniform	10.00	3.00
21 Bobby Bonilla Jsy	10.00	3.00
22 Rafael Furcal Bat	10.00	3.00
23 Andruw Jones Bat	10.00	3.00
24 Chipper Jones Jsy	15.00	4.50
25 Chipper Jones Bat	15.00	4.50
26 Brian Jordan Jsy	10.00	3.00
27 Javier Lopez Bat	10.00	3.00
28 Greg Maddux Jsy	15.00	4.50
29 Greg Maddux Bat	15.00	4.50
30 Brady Anderson Bat	10.00	3.00
31 Albert Belle Bat	10.00	3.00
32 Nomar Garciaparra Bat	20.00	6.00
33 Pedro Martinez Bat	15.00	4.50
34 Jose Offerman Bat	10.00	3.00
35 Damon Buford Jsy	10.00	3.00
36 Jose Nieves Bat	10.00	3.00
37 Sammy Sosa Jsy SP		
38 Kerry Wood Bat	15.00	4.50
39 James Baldwin Jsy	10.00	3.00
40 Ray Durham Jsy	10.00	3.00
41 Ray Durham Bat	10.00	3.00
42 Carlos Lee Bat	10.00	3.00
43 Magglio Ordonez Jsy	10.00	3.00
44 Magglio Ordonez Bat	10.00	3.00
45 Chris Singleton Jsy	10.00	3.00
46 Aaron Boone Bat	10.00	3.00
47 Sean Casey Bat	10.00	3.00
48 Barry Larkin Jsy	15.00	4.50
49 Pokey Reese Jsy	10.00	3.00
50 Pokey Reese Bat	10.00	3.00
51 Dmitri Young Bat	10.00	3.00
52 Roberto Alomar Bat	15.00	4.50
53 Einar Diaz Bat	10.00	3.00
54 Kenny Lofton Jsy	10.00	3.00
55 David Segui Bat	10.00	3.00
56 Omar Vizquel Jsy	10.00	3.00
57 Luis Castillo Jsy	10.00	3.00
58 Jeff Cirillo Jsy	10.00	3.00
59 Jeff Frye Bat	10.00	3.00
60 Todd Helton Jsy	15.00	4.50
61 Todd Helton Bat	15.00	4.50
62 Neifi Perez Bat	10.00	3.00
63 Larry Walker Jsy	15.00	4.50
64 Larry Walker Bat	15.00	4.50
65 Masato Yoshii Jsy	10.00	3.00
66 Brad Ausmus Jsy	10.00	3.00
67 Rich Becker Bat	10.00	3.00
68 Tony Clark Bat	10.00	3.00
69 Deivi Cruz Bat	10.00	3.00
70 Juan Gonzalez Bat	15.00	4.50
71 Dean Palmer Bat	10.00	3.00
72 Cliff Floyd Jsy White Home Uniform	10.00	3.00
73 Cliff Floyd Jsy Teal Away Uniform	10.00	3.00
74 Cliff Floyd Bat	10.00	3.00
75 Alex Gonzalez Jsy	10.00	3.00
76 Alex Gonzalez Marlins Bat	10.00	3.00
77 Mark Kotsay Bat	10.00	3.00
78 Derrek Lee Bat	10.00	3.00
79 Pablo Ozuna Jsy	10.00	3.00
80 Craig Biggio Bat	15.00	4.50
81 Ken Caminiti Bat	10.00	3.00
82 Roger Cedeno Bat	10.00	3.00
83 Ricky Bottalico Bat	10.00	3.00
84 Dee Brown Bat	10.00	3.00
85 Jermaine Dye Bat	10.00	3.00
86 David McCarty Bat	10.00	3.00
87 Hector Ortiz Bat	10.00	3.00
88 Joe Randa Bat	10.00	3.00
89 Adrian Beltre Jsy	10.00	3.00
90 Kevin Brown Jsy	10.00	3.00
91 Alex Cora Bat	10.00	3.00
92 Darren Dreifort Bat	10.00	3.00
93 Shawn Green Jsy White Home Uniform	10.00	3.00
94 Shawn Green Jsy Grey Away Uniform	10.00	3.00
95 Shawn Green Bat	10.00	3.00
96 Todd Hundley Jsy	10.00	3.00
97 Eric Karros Bat	10.00	3.00
98 Chan Ho Park Jsy	10.00	3.00
99 Chan Ho Park Bat	10.00	3.00
101 Gary Sheffield Bat	10.00	3.00
102 Ismael Valdes Bat	10.00	3.00
103 Jeromy Burnitz Bat	10.00	3.00
104 Marquis Grissom Bat	10.00	3.00
105 Matt Lawton Bat	10.00	3.00
106 Fernando Seguignol Bat	10.00	3.00
107 Edgardo Alfonzo Jsy White Home Uniform - Full Swing	10.00	3.00
108 Edgardo Alfonzo Jsy White Home Uniform - Dropping Bat	10.00	3.00
109 Edgardo Alfonzo Jsy Black Home Uniform	10.00	3.00
110 Derek Bell Jsy White Home Uniform	10.00	3.00
111 Derek Bell Jsy Black Away Uniform	10.00	3.00
112 Armando Benitez Bat	10.00	3.00
113 Al Leiter Bat	10.00	3.00
114 Rey Ordonez Jsy Grey Away Uniform - Fielding	10.00	3.00
115 Rey Ordonez Jsy White White Home Uniform	10.00	3.00
116 Rey Ordonez Jsy Grey Away Uniform - Bunting	10.00	3.00
117 Rey Ordonez Bat	10.00	3.00
118 Jay Payton Bat	10.00	3.00
119 Mike Piazza Jsy	20.00	6.00
120 Robin Ventura Jsy	10.00	3.00

Black Away Uniform - Hitting
121 Robin Ventura Jsy 10.00 3.00
Black Away Uniform - Fielding
122 Robin Ventura Jsy 10.00 3.00
White Home Uniform
123 Luis Polonia Bat 10.00 3.00
124 Bernie Williams Bat 15.00 4.50
125 Eric Chavez Jsy 10.00 3.00
126 Jason Giambi Jsy 15.00 4.50
127 Jason Giambi Bat 15.00 4.50
128 Ben Grieve Jsy 10.00 3.00
129 Ben Grieve Bat 10.00 3.00
130 Ramon Hernandez Bat 10.00 3.00
131 Tim Hudson Jsy 10.00 3.00
132 Terrence Long Bat 10.00 3.00
133 Mark Mulder Jsy 10.00 3.00
134 Adam Piatt Jsy 10.00 3.00
135 Olmedo Saenz Bat 10.00 3.00
136 Matt Stairs Bat 10.00 3.00
137 Mike Stanley Bat 10.00 3.00
138 Miguel Tejada Bat 10.00 3.00
139 Travis Lee Bat 10.00 3.00
140 Brian Giles Bat 10.00 3.00
141 Jason Kendall Jsy 10.00 3.00
142 Will Clark Bat 15.00 4.50
143 J.D. Drew Bat 10.00 3.00
144 Jim Edmonds Bat 10.00 3.00
145 Mark McGwire Bat 100.00 30.00
146 Edgar Renteria Bat 10.00 3.00
147 Garrett Stephenson 10.00 3.00
Jsy
148 Tony Gwynn Jsy 15.00 4.50
149 Ruben Rivera Bat 10.00 3.00
150 Barry Bonds Jsy 30.00 9.00
151 Barry Bonds Bat 30.00 9.00
152 Ellis Burks Jsy 10.00 3.00
153 J.T. Snow Bat 10.00 3.00
154 Jay Buhner Jsy 10.00 3.00
155 Jay Buhner Bat 10.00 3.00
156 Carlos Guillen Jsy 10.00 3.00
157 Carlos Guillen Bat 10.00 3.00
158 Rickey Henderson Bat 15.00 4.50
159 Edgar Martinez Bat 15.00 4.50
160 Gil Meche Jsy 10.00 3.00
161 John Olerud Bat 10.00 3.00
162 Joe Oliver Bat 10.00 3.00
163 Alex Rodriguez Jsy SP 100.00 30.00
164 Kazuhiro Sasaki Jsy 10.00 3.00
165 Dan Wilson Jsy 10.00 3.00
166 Dan Wilson Bat 10.00 3.00
167 Vinny Castilla Bat 10.00 3.00
168 Jose Guillen Bat 10.00 3.00
169 Fred McGriff Jsy 15.00 4.50
170 Rusty Greer Bat 10.00 3.00
171 Mike Lamb Bat 10.00 3.00
172 Ruben Mateo Jsy 10.00 3.00
173 Ruben Mateo Bat 10.00 3.00
174 Rafael Palmeiro Jsy 15.00 4.50
175 Rafael Palmeiro Bat 15.00 4.50
178 Tony Batista Bat 10.00 3.00
179 Marty Cordova Bat 10.00 3.00
180 Jose Cruz Jr. Bat 10.00 3.00
181 Alex Gonzalez 10.00 3.00
Blue Jays Bat
182 Raul Mondesi Bat 10.00 3.00

2001 Pacific Private Stock Game Jersey Patch

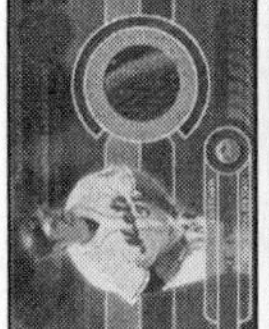

These premium inserts parallel the more common Game Gear jersey cards. Unlike those cards, however, instead of a basic jersey swatch each of these cards features a swatch of fabric that incorporates part of a patch from the featured players jersey. Please note, in addition to the patch itself, that you can distinguish these cards from the jersey cards due to the fact that these cards state "Authentic Game Worn Patch" on the gold rim around the patch swatch on the card front. The set is skip-numbered due to the fact that it's card numbering scheme hails from the Game Gear set which included bats and jerseys.

Nm-Mt Ex-Mt
2 Darin Erstad 25.00 7.50
4 Troy Glaus 40.00 12.00
6 Mo Vaughn Grey 25.00 7.50
7 Mo Vaughn White 25.00 7.50
9 Jay Bell 25.00 7.50
11 Erubiel Durazo Black 15.00 4.50
12 Erubiel Durazo White 15.00 4.50
15 Randy Johnson 60.00 18.00
16 Byung-Hyun Kim White 25.00 7.50
17 Byung-Hyun Kim Grey 25.00 7.50
18 Matt Williams Grey 25.00 7.50
19 Matt Williams White 25.00 7.50
20 Matt Williams Purple 25.00 7.50
21 Bobby Bonilla 25.00 7.50
24 Chipper Jones 60.00 18.00
26 Brian Jordan 25.00 7.50
28 Greg Maddux 120.00 36.00
35 Damon Buford 15.00 4.50
39 James Baldwin 15.00 4.50
40 Ray Durham 25.00 7.50
43 Magglio Ordonez 25.00 7.50
45 Chris Singleton 15.00 4.50
48 Barry Larkin 40.00 12.00
49 Pokey Reese 15.00 4.50
54 Kenny Lofton 25.00 7.50
56 Omar Vizquel 25.00 7.50
57 Luis Castillo 25.00 7.50
58 Jeff Cirillo 15.00 4.50
60 Todd Helton 40.00 12.00
63 Larry Walker 40.00 12.00
65 Masato Yoshii 15.00 4.50
66 Brad Ausmus 15.00 4.50
72 Cliff Floyd White 25.00 7.50
73 Cliff Floyd Teal 25.00 7.50
75 Alex Gonzalez 15.00 4.50
79 Pablo Ozuna 15.00 4.50
89 Adrian Beltre 25.00 7.50
90 Kevin Brown 25.00 7.50
93 Shawn Green White 25.00 7.50
94 Shawn Green Grey 25.00 7.50
96 Todd Hundley 15.00 4.50
98 Chan Ho Park 25.00 7.50
107 Edgardo Alfonzo 25.00 7.50
White Swing
108 Edgardo Alfonzo 25.00 7.50
White Drop
109 Edgardo Alfonzo 25.00 7.50
Black
110 Derek Bell White 15.00 4.50
111 Derek Bell Black 15.00 4.50
114 Rey Ordonez 15.00 4.50
Grey Field
115 Rey Ordonez White 15.00 4.50
116 Rey Ordonez 15.00 4.50
Grey Bunt
119 Mike Piazza 120.00 36.00
120 Robin Ventura 25.00 7.50
Black Hit
121 Robin Ventura 25.00 7.50
Black Field
122 Robin Ventura White 25.00 7.50
125 Eric Chavez 25.00 7.50
126 Jason Giambi 40.00 12.00
128 Ben Grieve 15.00 4.50
131 Tim Hudson 25.00 7.50
133 Mark Mulder 25.00 7.50
134 Adam Piatt 15.00 4.50
141 Jason Kendall 25.00 7.50
147 Garrett Stephenson 15.00 4.50
148 Tony Gwynn 100.00 30.00
150 Barry Bonds 150.00 45.00
152 Ellis Burks 25.00 7.50
154 Jay Buhner 25.00 7.50
156 Carlos Guillen 15.00 4.50
160 Gil Meche 25.00 7.50
163 Alex Rodriguez SP
164 Kazuhiro Sasaki 25.00 7.50
165 Dan Wilson 15.00 4.50
169 Fred McGriff 40.00 12.00
172 Ruben Mateo 15.00 4.50
174 Rafael Palmeiro 40.00 12.00

2001 Pacific Private Stock PS-206 Action

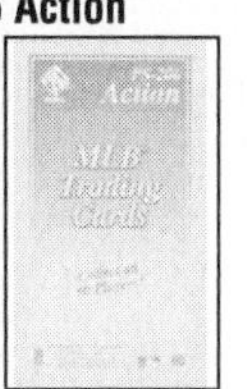

Randomly inserted into packs at two in one, this 60-card insert features a design very similar to the T-206 cards from the past. These cards are much smaller than basic sized cards, and feature top players in action photos.

Nm-Mt Ex-Mt
COMPLETE SET (60) 25.00 7.50
1 Darin Erstad .40 .12
2 Troy Glaus .60 .18
3 Randy Johnson 1.00 .30
4 Rafael Furcal .40 .12
5 Tom Glavine .60 .18
6 Andruw Jones .40 .12
7 Chipper Jones 1.00 .30
8 Greg Maddux 1.50 .45
9 Albert Belle .40 .12
10 Mike Mussina 1.00 .30
11 Cal Ripken 3.00 .90
12 Nomar Garciaparra 1.50 .45
13 Pedro Martinez 1.00 .30
14 Mark Grace .60 .18
15 Sammy Sosa 1.50 .45
16 Kerry Wood 1.00 .30
17 Magglio Ordonez .40 .12
18 Frank Thomas 1.00 .30
19 Ken Griffey Jr. 1.50 .45
20 Barry Larkin 1.00 .30
21 Roberto Alomar 1.00 .30
22 Manny Ramirez .40 .12
23 Jim Thome 1.00 .30
24 Jeff Cirillo .40 .12
25 Todd Helton .60 .18
26 Larry Walker .60 .18
27 Juan Gonzalez 1.00 .30
28 Hideo Nomo 1.00 .30
29 Preston Wilson .40 .12
30 Jeff Bagwell .60 .18
31 Craig Biggio .60 .18
32 Johnny Damon .40 .12
33 Jermaine Dye .40 .12
34 Shawn Green .40 .12
35 Gary Sheffield .40 .12
36 Vladimir Guerrero 1.00 .30
37 Mike Piazza 1.50 .45
38 Jose Canseco 1.00 .30
39 Roger Clemens 2.00 .60
40 Derek Jeter 2.50 .75
41 Bernie Williams .60 .18
42 Jason Giambi 1.00 .30
43 Ben Grieve .40 .12
44 Pat Burrell .40 .12
45 Scott Rolen .60 .18
46 Rick Ankiel .40 .12
47 J.D. Drew .40 .12
48 Jim Edmonds .40 .12
49 Mark McGwire 2.50 .75
50 Tony Gwynn 1.25 .35
51 Barry Bonds 2.50 .75
52 Jeff Kent .40 .12
53 Edgar Martinez .60 .18
54 Alex Rodriguez 1.50 .45
55 Kazuhiro Sasaki .40 .12
56 Fred McGriff .60 .18
57 Rafael Palmeiro .60 .18
58 Ivan Rodriguez 1.00 .30
59 Tony Batista .40 .12
60 Carlos Delgado .40 .12

2001 Pacific Private Stock PS-206 New Wave

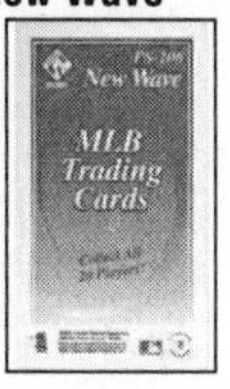

Randomly inserted into packs at one in 60 hobby and one in 480 retail, this 20-card insert features some of today's top young talents on cards that resemble the T-206 design. Each card in this set is individually serial numbered to 199.

Nm-Mt Ex-Mt
COMPLETE SET (20) 120.00 36.00
1 Darin Erstad 5.00 1.50
2 Troy Glaus 8.00 2.40
3 Rafael Furcal 5.00 1.50
4 Andruw Jones 5.00 1.50
5 Magglio Ordonez 5.00 1.50
6 Carlos Lee 5.00 1.50
7 Todd Helton 8.00 2.40
8 Johnny Damon 5.00 1.50
9 Jermaine Dye 5.00 1.50
10 Vladimir Guerrero 12.00 3.60
11 Jason Giambi 12.00 3.60
12 Ben Grieve 5.00 1.50
13 Pat Burrell 5.00 1.50
14 Rick Ankiel 5.00 1.50
15 J.D. Drew 5.00 1.50
16 Adam Eaton 5.00 1.50
17 Kazuhiro Sasaki 5.00 1.50
18 Ruben Mateo 5.00 1.50
19 Tony Batista 5.00 1.50
20 Carlos Delgado 5.00 1.50

2001 Pacific Private Stock PS-206 Rookies

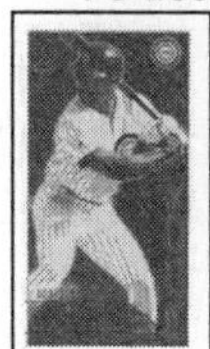
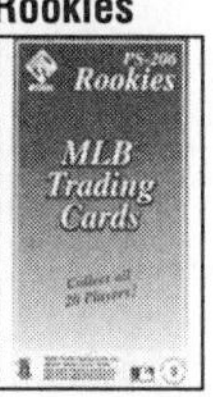

Randomly inserted into packs at one in 120 hobby and one in 480 retail, this 20-card insert features top rookies on cards that resemble the T-206 design. Each card in this set is individually serial numbered to 125.

Nm-Mt Ex-Mt
COMPLETE SET (20) 150.00 45.00
1 George Lombard 10.00 3.00
2 Morgan Burkhart 10.00 3.00
3 Corey Patterson 10.00 3.00
4 Julio Zuleta 10.00 3.00
5 Joe Crede 10.00 3.00
6 Matt Ginter 10.00 3.00
7 Aaron Myette 10.00 3.00
8 Travis Dawkins 10.00 3.00
9 Eric Munson 10.00 3.00
10 Dee Brown 10.00 3.00
11 Luke Prokopec 10.00 3.00
12 Jorge Toca 10.00 3.00
13 Alfonso Soriano 15.00 4.50
14 Eric Byrnes 10.00 3.00
15 Adam Hyzdu 10.00 3.00
16 Jimmy Rollins 10.00 3.00
17 Joel Pineiro 20.00 6.00
18 Aubrey Huff 10.00 3.00
19 Kenny Kelly 10.00 3.00
20 Vernon Wells 10.00 3.00

2001 Pacific Private Stock PS-206 Stars

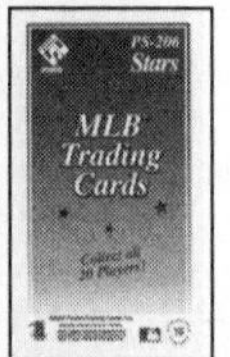

Randomly inserted into packs at one in 40 hobby and one in 240 retail, this 20-card insert features some of today's top superstars on cards that resemble the T-206 design. Each card in this set is individually serial numbered to 315.

Nm-Mt Ex-Mt
COMPLETE SET (20) 250.00 75.00
1 Chipper Jones 10.00 3.00
2 Greg Maddux 15.00 4.50
3 Cal Ripken 30.00 9.00
4 Nomar Garciaparra 15.00 4.50
5 Pedro Martinez 10.00 3.00
6 Sammy Sosa 15.00 4.50
7 Frank Thomas 10.00 3.00
8 Ken Griffey Jr. 15.00 4.50
9 Manny Ramirez 8.00 2.40
10 Jeff Bagwell 8.00 2.40
11 Gary Sheffield 8.00 2.40
12 Mike Piazza 15.00 4.50
13 Roger Clemens 20.00 6.00
14 Derek Jeter 25.00 7.50
15 Rick Ankiel 8.00 2.40
16 Mark McGwire 25.00 7.50
17 Tony Gwynn 12.00 3.60
18 Barry Bonds 25.00 7.50
19 Alex Rodriguez 15.00 4.50
20 Ivan Rodriguez 10.00 3.00

2001 Pacific Private Stock Reserve

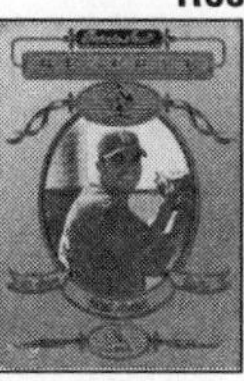
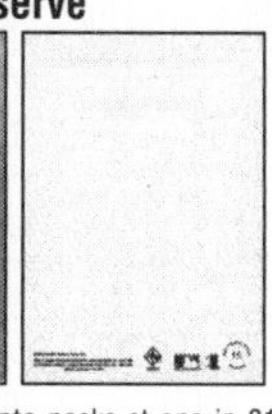

Randomly inserted into packs at one in 21 hobby, this 20-card insert features some of the Major League's finest athletes on canvas type paper with gold foil lettering.

Nm-Mt Ex-Mt
COMPLETE SET (20) 250.00 75.00
1 Randy Johnson 8.00 2.40
2 Chipper Jones 8.00 2.40
3 Greg Maddux 12.00 3.60
4 Cal Ripken 25.00 7.50
5 Nomar Garciaparra 12.00 3.60
6 Pedro Martinez 8.00 2.40
7 Sammy Sosa 12.00 3.60
8 Frank Thomas 8.00 2.40
9 Ken Griffey Jr. 12.00 3.60
10 Todd Helton 5.00 1.50
11 Vladimir Guerrero 8.00 2.40
12 Mike Piazza 12.00 3.60
13 Roger Clemens 15.00 4.50
14 Derek Jeter 20.00 6.00
15 Rick Ankiel 5.00 1.50
16 Mark McGwire 20.00 6.00
17 Tony Gwynn 10.00 3.00
18 Barry Bonds 20.00 6.00
19 Alex Rodriguez 12.00 3.60
20 Ivan Rodriguez 8.00 2.40

2000 Pacific Vanguard

The 2000 Pacific Vanguard product was released in May, 2000 as a 100-card set. The set features a blend of veterans and prospects. Each pack contained four cards and carried a suggested retail price of $3.99.

Nm-Mt Ex-Mt
COMPLETE SET (100) 25.00 7.50
1 Troy Glaus .50 .15
2 Tim Salmon .50 .15
3 Mo Vaughn .30 .09
4 Albert Belle .30 .09
5 Mike Mussina .75 .23
6 Cal Ripken 2.50 .75
7 Nomar Garciaparra 1.25 .35
8 Pedro Martinez .75 .23
9 Troy O'Leary .30 .09
10 Wilton Veras .30 .09
11 Magglio Ordonez .30 .09
12 Chris Singleton .30 .09
13 Frank Thomas .75 .23
14 Roberto Alomar .75 .23
15 Russell Branyan .30 .09
16 Manny Ramirez .30 .09
17 Jim Thome .75 .23
18 Omar Vizquel .30 .09
19 Tony Clark .30 .09
20 Juan Gonzalez .75 .23
21 Dean Palmer .30 .09
22 Carlos Beltran .30 .09
23 Johnny Damon .30 .09
24 Jermaine Dye .30 .09
25 Mark Quinn .30 .09
26 Jacque Jones .30 .09
27 Corey Koskie .30 .09
28 Brad Radke .30 .09
29 Roger Clemens 1.50 .45
30 Derek Jeter 2.00 .60
31 Alfonso Soriano .75 .23
32 Bernie Williams .50 .15
33 Eric Chavez .30 .09
34 Jason Giambi .75 .23
35 Ben Grieve .30 .09
36 Tim Hudson .50 .15
37 Mike Cameron .30 .09
38 Freddy Garcia .30 .09
39 Edgar Martinez .50 .15
40 Alex Rodriguez 1.25 .35
41 Jose Canseco .75 .23
42 Vinny Castilla .30 .09
43 Fred McGriff .50 .15
44 Rusty Greer .30 .09
45 Ruben Mateo .30 .09
46 Rafael Palmeiro .50 .15
47 Ivan Rodriguez .75 .23
48 Carlos Delgado .30 .09
49 Shannon Stewart .30 .09
50 Vernon Wells .30 .09
51 Erubiel Durazo .30 .09
52 Randy Johnson .75 .23
53 Matt Williams .30 .09
54 Andruw Jones .30 .09
55 Chipper Jones .75 .23
56 Greg Maddux 1.25 .35
57 Mark Grace .50 .15
58 Sammy Sosa 1.25 .35
59 Kerry Wood .75 .23
60 Sean Casey .30 .09
61 Ken Griffey Jr. 1.25 .35
62 Barry Larkin .75 .23
63 Todd Helton .50 .15
64 Ben Petrick .30 .09
65 Larry Walker .50 .15
66 Luis Castillo .30 .09
67 Alex Gonzalez .30 .09
68 Preston Wilson .30 .09
69 Jeff Bagwell .50 .15
70 Craig Biggio .50 .15
71 Billy Wagner .30 .09
72 Kevin Brown .50 .15
73 Shawn Green .30 .09
74 Gary Sheffield .30 .09
75 Kevin Barker .30 .09
76 Ron Belliard .30 .09
77 Jeromy Burnitz .30 .09
78 Michael Barrett .30 .09
79 Peter Bergeron .30 .09
80 Vladimir Guerrero .75 .23
81 Edgardo Alfonzo .30 .09
82 Rey Ordonez .30 .09
83 Mike Piazza 1.25 .35
84 Robin Ventura .50 .15
85 Bobby Abreu .30 .09
86 Mike Lieberthal .30 .09
87 Scott Rolen .50 .15
88 Brian Giles .30 .09
89 Chad Hermansen .30 .09
90 Jason Kendall .30 .09
91 Rick Ankiel .30 .09
92 J.D. Drew .30 .09
93 Mark McGwire 2.00 .60
94 Fernando Tatis .30 .09
95 Ben Davis .30 .09
96 Tony Gwynn 1.00 .30
97 Trevor Hoffman .30 .09
98 Barry Bonds 2.00 .60
99 Ellis Burks .30 .09
100 Jeff Kent .30 .09
SAMP Tony Gwynn 1.50 .45

2000 Pacific Vanguard Green

Randomly inserted into packs, this 100-card green-foiled set is a complete parallel of the Vanguard base set. The 50 A.L. players in this set are individually serial numbered to 99, and the 50 N.L. players are individually serial numbered to 199.

Nm-Mt Ex-Mt
*AL STARS 1-50: 4X TO 10X BASIC ...
*NL STARS 51-100: 2.5X TO 6X BASIC

2000 Pacific Vanguard Holographic Gold

Randomly inserted into packs, this 100-card gold-foiled set is a complete parallel of the Vanguard base set. The 50 A.L. players in this set are individually serial numbered to 199, and the N.L. players are individually serial numbered to 99.

Nm-Mt Ex-Mt
*AL STARS 1-50: 4X TO 10X BASIC ...
*NL STARS 51-100: 6X TO 15X BASIC

2000 Pacific Vanguard Premiere Date

Randomly inserted into hobby packs at one in 25, this 100-card set is a complete parallel of the Vanguard base set. There were only 135 serial numbered sets produced of this insert.

Nm-Mt Ex-Mt
*STARS: 4X TO 10X BASIC CARDS ....

2000 Pacific Vanguard Cosmic Force

Randomly inserted into packs at one in 73, this insert features headshots of ten of the major leagues most popular stars.

Nm-Mt Ex-Mt
COMPLETE SET (10) 150.00 45.00
1 Chipper Jones 4.00 1.20
2 Cal Ripken 12.00 3.60
3 Nomar Garciaparra 6.00 1.80
4 Sammy Sosa 6.00 1.80
5 Ken Griffey Jr. 6.00 1.80
6 Mike Piazza 6.00 1.80
7 Derek Jeter 10.00 3.00
8 Mark McGwire 10.00 3.00
9 Tony Gwynn 8.00 2.40
10 Alex Rodriguez 6.00 1.80

2000 Pacific Vanguard Diamond Architects

Randomly inserted into packs at one in 25, this insert set features the blueprints of different ballparks, and the superstars that play there.

Nm-Mt Ex-Mt
COMPLETE SET (20) 150.00 45.00
1 Chipper Jones 2.50 .75

2 Greg Maddux 4.00 1.20
3 Cal Ripken 8.00 2.40
4 Nomar Garciaparra 4.00 1.20
5 Sammy Sosa 4.00 1.20
6 Ken Griffey Jr. 4.00 1.20
7 Manny Ramirez 1.00 .30
8 Larry Walker 1.50 .45
9 Jeff Bagwell 1.50 .45
10 Vladimir Guerrero 2.50 .75
11 Mike Piazza 4.00 1.20
12 Roger Clemens 5.00 1.50
13 Derek Jeter 6.00 1.80
14 Bernie Williams 1.50 .45
15 Scott Rolen 1.50 .45
16 Mark McGwire 6.00 1.80
17 Tony Gwynn 5.00 1.50
18 Alex Rodriguez 4.00 1.20
19 Rafael Palmeiro 1.50 .45
20 Ivan Rodriguez 2.50 .75

2000 Pacific Vanguard Game-Worn Jerseys

Randomly inserted into packs at one in 120, this five card insert set features swatches from actual game-used jerseys.

Nm-Mt Ex-Mt
1 Chipper Jones 15.00 4.50
2 Greg Maddux 25.00 7.50
3 Frank Thomas 15.00 4.50
4 Tony Gwynn 20.00 6.00
5 Alex Rodriguez 25.00 7.50

2000 Pacific Vanguard High Voltage

Inserted into packs at a stated rate of one per pack, this 36-card insert set features some of the most electrifying players in major league baseball. Please note that there are four parallels to this insert (Green, Gold, Holo-Silver, and Red).

Nm-Mt Ex-Mt
COMPLETE SET (36) 25.00 7.50
*GOLD: 5X TO 12X BASIC VOLTAGE
GOLD PRINT RUN 199 SERIAL #'d SETS
*GREEN: 8X TO 20X BASIC VOLTAGE
GREEN PRINT RUN 99 SERIAL #'d SETS
HOLO.SILVER PRINT RUN 10 SERIAL #'d SETS
HOLO.SILVER NOT PRICED DUE TO SCARCITY
*RED: 3X TO 8X BASIC VOLTAGE
RED PRINT RUN 299 SERIAL #'d SETS
PARALLELS RANDOM IN HOB/RET PACKS
1 Mo Vaughn .25 .07
2 Erubiel Durazo .25 .07
3 Randy Johnson .60 .18
4 Andruw Jones .25 .07
5 Chipper Jones .60 .18
6 Greg Maddux 1.00 .30
7 Cal Ripken 2.00 .60
8 Nomar Garciaparra 1.00 .30
9 Pedro Martinez .60 .18
10 Sammy Sosa 1.00 .30
11 Frank Thomas .60 .18
12 Sean Casey .25 .07
13 Ken Griffey Jr. 1.00 .30
14 Barry Larkin .60 .18
15 Manny Ramirez .25 .07
16 Jim Thome .60 .18
17 Larry Walker .40 .12
18 Jeff Bagwell .40 .12
19 Craig Biggio .40 .12
20 Carlos Beltran .25 .07
21 Shawn Green .25 .07
22 Vladimir Guerrero .60 .18
23 Edgardo Alfonzo .25 .07
24 Mike Piazza 1.00 .30
25 Roger Clemens 1.25 .35
26 Derek Jeter 1.50 .45
27 Bernie Williams .40 .12
28 Scott Rolen .40 .12
29 Brian Giles .25 .07
30 Rick Ankiel .25 .07
31 Mark McGwire 1.50 .45
32 Tony Gwynn .75 .23
33 Barry Bonds 1.50 .45
34 Alex Rodriguez 1.00 .30
35 Rafael Palmeiro .40 .12
36 Ivan Rodriguez .60 .18

2000 Pacific Vanguard Press

Randomly inserted into packs at two in 25, this 20-card set features 10 A.L. players and 10 N.L. players.

Nm-Mt Ex-Mt
COMPLETE A.L. SET (10) 30.00 9.00
COMPLETE N.L. SET (10) 40.00 12.00
A1 Cal Ripken 4.00 1.20
A2 Nomar Garciaparra 2.00 .60
A3 Pedro Martinez 1.25 .35
A4 Manny Ramirez .50 .15
A5 Carlos Beltran .50 .15
A6 Roger Clemens 2.50 .75
A7 Derek Jeter 3.00 .90
A8 Alex Rodriguez 2.00 .60
A9 Rafael Palmeiro .75 .23
A10 Ivan Rodriguez 1.25 .35
N1 Chipper Jones 1.25 .35
N2 Greg Maddux 2.00 .60
N3 Sammy Sosa 2.00 .60
N4 Ken Griffey Jr. 2.00 .60
N5 Larry Walker .75 .23
N6 Jeff Bagwell .75 .23
N7 Vladimir Guerrero 1.25 .35
N8 Mike Piazza 2.00 .60
N9 Mark McGwire 3.00 .90
N10 Tony Gwynn 1.50 .45

1958 Packard Bell

This seven-card set includes members of the Los Angeles Dodgers and San Francisco Giants and was issued in both teams' first year on the West Coast. This black and white, unnumbered set features cards measuring approximately 3 3/8" by 5 3/8". The backs are advertisements for Packard Bell (a television and radio manufacturer) along with a schedule for either the Giants or Dodgers. There were four Giants printed and three Dodgers. The catalog designation for this set is H805-5. Since the cards are unnumbered, they are listed below alphabetically.

NM Ex
COMPLETE SET (7) 500.00 250.00
1 Walt Alston MG 80.00 40.00
2 Johnny Antonelli 40.00 20.00
3 Jim Gilliam 50.00 25.00
4 Gil Hodges 80.00 40.00
5 Willie Mays 250.00 125.00
6 Bill Rigney MG 40.00 20.00
7 Hank Sauer 40.00 20.00

1969 Padres Team Issue

Measuring approximately 5" by 7", these cards feature members of the 1969 San Diego Padres during their debut season. Since these cards are unnumbered, we have sequenced them in alphabetical order. This list may be incomplete so any additions are appreciated.

MINT NRMT
COMPLETE SET 60.00 27.00
1 Nate Colbert 8.00 3.60
2 Bill Davis 5.00 2.20
3 Tom Dukes 5.00 2.20
4 Tony Gonzalez 5.00 2.20
5 Walt Hriniak 6.00 2.70
6 Chris Krug 5.00 2.20
7 Billy McCool 5.00 2.20
8 Ivan Murrell 5.00 2.20
9 John Podres 6.00 2.70
10 Frank Reberger 5.00 2.20
11 Rafael Robles 5.00 2.20
12 John Sipin 5.00 2.20
13 Tommie Sisk 5.00 2.20
14 Larry Stahl 5.00 2.20

1969 Padres Volpe

These eight 8 1/2" by 11 cards feature members of the San Diego Padres in their inagural season. These cards feature two drawings (a large portrait shot as well as an smaller action pose) by noted sport artist Nicholas Volpe on the front. The backs have the Padres logo as well as a biography of Volpe. These cards are unnumbered and we have sequenced them in alphabetical order.

NM Ex
COMPLETE SET (8) 25.00 10.00
1 Ollie Brown 3.00 1.20
2 Tommy Dean 2.50 1.00
3 Al Ferrera 2.50 1.00
4 Clarence Gaston 5.00 2.00
5 Preston Gomez MG 3.00 1.20
6 Johnny Podres 4.00 1.60
7 Al Santorini 2.50 1.00
8 Ed Spiezio 2.50 1.00

1971 Padres Team Issue

Measuring approximately 5" by 7", these cards feature members of the 1971 San Diego Padres. Since these cards are unnumbered, we have sequenced them in alphabetical order.

MINT NRMT
COMPLETE SET 12.00 5.50
1 Dave Campbell 2.00 .90
2 Chris Cannizzaro 1.00 .45
3 Tommy Dean 1.00 .45
4 Al Ferrara 1.00 .45
5 Enzo Hernandez 1.00 .45
6 Steve Huntz 1.00 .45
7 Van Kelly 1.00 .45
8 Bill Laxton 1.00 .45
9 Gerry Nyman 1.00 .45
10 Tom Phoebus 1.00 .45
11 Al Santorini 1.00 .45
12 Ron Slocum 1.00 .45
13 Ramon Webster 1.00 .45

1972 Padres Colbert Commemorative

This 8 1/2" by 11" photo features Nate Colbert and honors his spectacular doubleheader feat of August 1, 1972 in which he hit five homers and drove in 13 runs. Colbert is posed with a bat and balls which show what occured that day.

MINT NRMT
1 Nate Colbert 10.00 4.50

1972 Padres Postcards

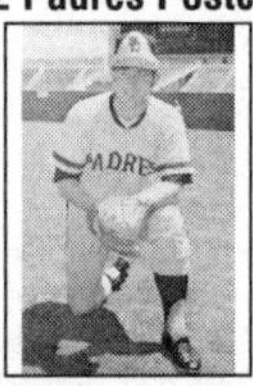

This 28-card set of the San Diego Padres features borderless black-and-white player photos measuring approximately 3 3/8" by 5 3/8". The backs are blank. The cards are unnumbered and checklisted below in alphabetical order.

NM Ex
COMPLETE SET (28) 100.00 40.00
1 Ed Acosta 4.00 1.60
2 Steve Arlin 4.00 1.60
3 Bob Barton 4.00 1.60
4 Ollie Brown 5.00 2.00
5 Mike Caldwell 4.00 1.60
6 Dave Campbell 6.00 2.40
7 Nate Colbert 6.00 2.40
8 Mike Corkins 4.00 1.60
9 Roger Craig CO 6.00 2.40
10 Clarence Gaston 8.00 3.20
11 Bill Grief 4.00 1.60
12 Enzo Hernandez 4.00 1.60
13 Gary Jestadt 4.00 1.60
14 John Jeter 4.00 1.60
15 Fred Kendall 4.00 1.60
16 Clay Kirby 4.00 1.60
17 Leron Lee 4.00 1.60
18 Jerry Morales 4.00 1.60
19 Ivan Murrell 4.00 1.60
20 Fred Norman 4.00 1.60
21 Rafael Robles 4.00 1.60
22 Gary Ross 4.00 1.60
23 Mark Schaeffer 4.00 1.60
24 Ed Spiezio 4.00 1.60
25 Ron Taylor 4.00 1.60
26 Derrel Thomas 4.00 1.60
27 Whitey Wietelemann CO 4.00 1.60
28 Don Zimmer MG 6.00 2.40

1973 Padres Dean's

This 30-card set of the San Diego Padres was issued in five series. The cards measure 5 1/2" by 8 1/2" and are printed on very thin paper. The fronts feature white-bordered black-and-white player portraits with the player's name and position, sponsor and team logos below the photo. The backs are blank. The cards are unnumbered and checklisted below in alphabetical order. Dave Winfield is featured in his rookie season in an item which predates his Rookie Card.

NM Ex
COMPLETE SET (30) 60.00 24.00
1 Steve Arlin 2.00 .80
2 Mike Caldwell 2.00 .80
3 Dave Campbell 4.00 1.60
4 Nate Colbert 3.00 1.20
5 Mike Corkins 2.00 .80
6 Pat Corrales CO 2.00 .80
7 Dave Garcia CO 2.00 .80
8 Clarence Gaston 3.00 1.20
9 Bill Greif 2.00 .80
10 John Grubb 2.00 .80
11 Enzo Hernandez 2.00 .80
12 Randy Jones 5.00 2.00
13 Fred Kendall 2.00 .80
14 Clay Kirby 2.00 .80
15 Leron Lee 2.00 .80
16 Dave Marshall 2.00 .80
17 Don Mason 2.00 .80
18 Jerry Morales 2.00 .80
19 Ivan Murrell 2.00 .80
20 Fred Norman 2.00 .80
21 Johnny Podres CO 3.00 1.20
22 Dave Roberts 2.00 .80
23 Vicente Romo 2.00 .80
24 Gary Ross 2.00 .80
25 Bob Skinner CO 2.00 .80
26 Derrel Thomas 2.00 .80
27 Rich Troedson 2.00 .80
28 Whitey Wietelmann CO 2.00 .80
29 Dave Winfield 25.00 10.00
30 Don Zimmer MG 3.00 1.20

1974 Padres Dean's

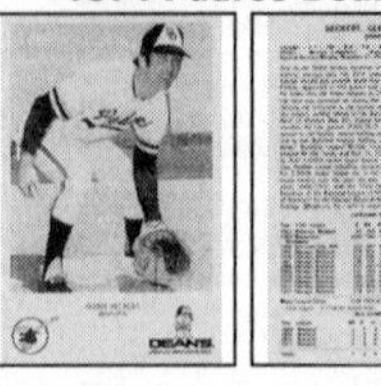

These cards measure 5 1/2" by 8 1/2" and are printed on very thin paper. The fronts feature white-bordered black-and-white player photos with the player's name and position, and sponsor and team logos below the photo. The backs carry the player's career summary, biography and statistics. The cards are unnumbered and checklisted below in alphabetical order. Some of these cards are also known to come with blank backs. Dave Winfield appears in his Rookie Card season.

NM Ex
COMPLETE SET (30) 75.00 30.00
1 Matty Alou 3.00 1.20
2 Bob Barton 2.00 .80
3 Glenn Beckert 2.00 .80
4 Jack Bloomfield CO 2.00 .80
5 Nate Colbert 2.00 .80
6 Mike Corkins 2.00 .80
7 Jim Davenport CO 2.00 .80
8 Dave Freisleben 2.00 .80
9 Cito Gaston 4.00 1.60
10 Bill Greif 2.00 .80
11 John Grubb 2.00 .80
12 Larry Hardy 2.00 .80
13 Enzo Hernandez 2.00 .80
14 Dave Hilton 2.00 .80
15 Randy Jones 4.00 1.60
16 Fred Kendall 2.00 .80
17 Gene Locklear 2.00 .80
18 Willie McCovey 10.00 4.00
19 John McNamara MG 2.00 .80
20 Rich Morales 2.00 .80
21 Bill Poesdel CO 2.00 .80
22 Dave Roberts 2.00 .80
23 Vicente Romo 2.00 .80
24 Dan Spillner 2.00 .80
25 Derrel Thomas 2.00 .80
26 Bob Tolan 2.00 .80
27 Rich Troedson 2.00 .80
28 Whitey Wietelmann CO 3.00 1.20
29 Bernie Williams 2.00 .80
30 Dave Winfield 20.00 8.00

1974 Padres McDonald Discs

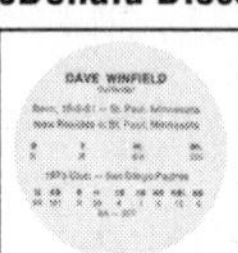

Measuring approximately 2 3/8" in diameter, members of the 1974 Padres are featured in this set. Among the players featured in this set is Dave Winfield during his Rookie Card season. These items were given out at the July 30th Padres game. According to informed sources, 60,000 photo balls were produced for the event. A baseball holder was also produced. These have a value of approximately $25. The set was originally available for $3 from the manufacturer.

NM Ex
COMPLETE SET (15) 50.00 20.00
1 Matty Alou 5.00 2.00
2 Glen Beckert 3.00 1.20
3 Nate Colbert 4.00 1.60
4 Bill Greif 3.00 1.20
5 John Grubb 3.00 1.20
6 Enzo Hernandez 3.00 1.20
7 Randy Jones 4.00 1.60
8 Fred Kendall 3.00 1.20
9 Willie McCovey 10.00 4.00
10 John McNamara MG 3.00 1.20
11 Dave Roberts 3.00 1.20
12 Bobby Tolan 4.00 1.60
13 Dave Winfield 20.00 8.00
14 Ronald McDonald 3.00 1.20
Has giveaway dates
15 Padres Sked 3.00 1.20

1974 Padres Team Issue

This 18-card set features black-and-white photos of the San Diego Padres measuring approximately 3 5/16" by 5 5/16". The cards are unnumbered and checklisted below in alphabetical order.

NM Ex
COMPLETE SET (18) 20.00 8.00
1 Bob Barton .50 .20
2 Glenn Beckert .50 .20
3 Mike Corkins .50 .20
4 Dave Freisleben .50 .20
5 Bill Greif .50 .20
6 Larry Hardy .50 .20
7 Randy Jones .75 .30
8 Willie McCovey 5.00 2.00
(Batting)
9 Willie McCovey 5.00 2.00
(Leaning on bat)
10 Dave Roberts .50 .20
(Catching)
11 Dave Roberts .50 .20
(Leaning on bat)
12 Vicente Romo .50 .20
13 Dan Spillner .50 .20
14 Derrel Thomas .50 .20
15 Bobby Tolan .50 .20
16 Dave Tomlin .50 .20
17 Rich Troedson .50 .20
18 Dave Winfield 10.00 4.00

1975 Padres Dean's

These cards measure 5 1/2" by 8 1/2" and are printed on very thin paper. The fronts feature black-and-white player photos with the player's name and position, and sponsor and team logos below the photo. The backs carry the player's career summary, biography and statistics. The cards are unnumbered and checklisted below in alphabetical order. Randy Hundley and Hector Torres were late season trade and their cards have blank backs.

NM Ex
COMPLETE SET (30) 75.00 30.00
1 Jim Davenport CO 2.00 .80
2 Bob Davis 2.00 .80
3 Rich Folkers 2.00 .80
4 Alan Foster 2.00 .80
5 Dave Freisleben 2.00 .80
6 Tito Fuentes 2.00 .80
7 Danny Frisella 2.00 .80
8 Bill Greif 2.00 .80
9 Johnny Grubb 2.00 .80
10 Enzo Hernandez 2.00 .80
11 Randy Hundley 3.00 1.20
12 Mike Ivie 2.00 .80
13 Jerry Johnson 2.00 .80
14 Randy Jones 4.00 1.60
15 Fred Kendall 2.00 .80
16 Ted Kubiak 2.00 .80
17 Gene Locklear 2.00 .80
18 Willie McCovey 10.00 4.00
19 Joe McIntosh 2.00 .80
20 John McNamara MG 2.00 .80
21 Tom Morgan CO 2.00 .80
22 Dick Sharon 2.00 .80
23 Dick Sisler CO 2.00 .80
24 Dan Spillner 2.00 .80
25 Brent Strom 2.00 .80
26 Bobby Tolan 2.00 .80
27 Dave Tomlin 2.00 .80
28 Hector Torres 2.00 .80
29 Whitey Wietelmann CO 2.00 .80
30 Dave Winfield 15.00 6.00

1977 Padres Family Fun

This set of the San Diego Padres was produced by Huish Family Fun Centers and measures approximately 5 1/2" by 8 1/2". The fronts feature black-and-white player photos with white borders. The backs carry biographical information and career statistics. The set was distributed in eight-card packs with sponsor coupons printed on the pack wrappers. The cards are unnumbered and checklisted below in alphabetical order.

NM Ex
COMPLETE SET (8) 15.00 6.00
1 Joey Amalfitano CO 2.00 .80
2 Alvin Dark MG 3.00 1.20
3 Randy Jones 2.50 1.00
4 Bob Owchinko 2.00 .80
5 Dave Roberts 2.00 .80
6 Rick Sawyer 2.00 .80
7 Pat Scanlon 2.00 .80
8 Jerry Turner 2.00 .80

1977 Padres Schedule Cards

This 89-card set was issued in 1977 and features members of the 1977 San Diego Padres as well as former Padres and others connected with the Padres in some capacity. The cards measure approximately 2 1/4" by 3 3/8" and have brown and white photos on the front of the cards with a schedule of the 1977 Padres special events on the back. A thin line borders the front photo with the team name and player name appearing below in the same sepia tone. The set is checklisted alphabetically in the list below. The complete set price below refers to the set with all variations listed. The blank-backed cards may have been issued in a different year than the other schedule-back cards.

NM Ex
COMPLETE SET (89) 50.00 20.00

1A Bill Almon .50 .20
(Kneeling)
1B Bill Almon .75 .30
(Shown chest up
bat on shoulder)
2 Matty Alou .75 .30
3 Joe Amalfitano CO .25 .10
4A Steve Arlin .50 .20
(Follow through)
4B Steve Arlin .50 .20
(Glove to chest)
5 Bob Barton .75 .30
6 Buzzie Bavasi GM .50 .20
7 Glenn Beckert .75 .30
8 Vic Bernal .25 .10
9 Ollie Brown .75 .30
10A Dave Campbell .75 .30
(Bat on shoulder)
10B Dave Campbell .75 .30
(Kneeling, capless)
11 Mike Champion .25 .10
12 Mike Champion and .25 .10
Bill Almon
13A Nate Colbert .75 .30
(Shown waist up)
13B Nate Colbert 1.00 .40
(Shown full figure;
blank back)
14 Nate Colbert and .75 .30
friend (Kneeling next
to child with bat)
15 Jerry Coleman ANN .75 .30
16 Roger Craig CO .50 .20
17 John D'Acquisto .25 .10
18 Bob Davis .25 .10
19 Willie Davis 1.00 .40
20 Jim Eakle .25 .10
(Tuba Man)
21A Rollie Fingers 2.00 .80
(Shown waist up
both hands in glove
in front of body)
21B Rollie Fingers 2.00 .80
(Head shot)
22A Dave Freisleben 2.50 1.00
(Washington jersey and
cap& blank back)
22B Dave Freisleben .50 .20
(Kneeling)
23A Clarence Gaston 1.00 .40
(Bat on shoulder
adres on jersey)
23B Clarence Gaston 1.00 .40
(Bat on shoulder
dre on jersey)
24 Tom Griffin .25 .10
25 Johnny Grubb .50 .20
26A George Hendrick .75 .30
(Shown chest up
wearing warm-up jacket)
26B George Hendrick .75 .30
(Shown waist up
wearing white jersey)
27 Enzo Hernandez .25 .10
28 Enzo Hernandez and .75 .30
Nate Colbert
29A Mike Ivie .75 .30
(Batting pose, shown
from thighs up)
29B Mike Ivie .75 .30
(Batting pose
shown from shoulders up
blank back)
29C Mike Ivie .75 .30
(Bat on shoulder)
30A Randy Jones .75 .30
(Following Through)
30B Randy Jones 1.00 .40
(Holding Cy Young Award)
31 Randy Jones and 1.00 .40
Bowie Kuhn COMM
(Randy holding trophy)
32A Fred Kendall .75 .30
(Batting pose)
32B Fred Kendall .75 .30
(Ball in right hand)
33 Mike Kilkenny .75 .30
(Blank back)
34A Clay Kirby .75 .30
(Follow through)
34B Clay Kirby .75 .30
(Glove near to chest)
35 Ray Kroc OWN 1.00 .40
(Blank back)
36 Dave Marshall .75 .30
37A Willie McCovey 3.00 1.20
With mustache
bat on shoulder)
37B Willie McCovey 3.00 1.20
Without mustache
blank back)
38A John McNamara MG .75 .30
(Looking to his left
blank back)
38B John McNamara MG .75 .30
(Looking to his right)
38C John McNamara MG .75 .30
(Looking straight
ahead, smiling)
39 Luis Melendez .25 .10
40 Butch Metzger .25 .10
41 Bob Miller CO .25 .10
42A Fred Norman .75 .30
(Short hair, kneeling)
42B Fred Norman .75 .30
(Long hair, arms
over head)
43 Bob Owchinko .25 .10
44 Doug Rader .75 .30
45 Merv Rettenmund .25 .10
46A Gene Richards .75 .30
(Shown chest up
stands in background)
46B Gene Richards .50 .20
(Shown from thighs up)
47 Dave Roberts .25 .10
48 Rick Sawyer .25 .10
49 Bob Shirley .25 .10
50 Bob Skinner CO .50 .20
51 Ballard Smith GM .75 .30
52 Ed Spiezio .75 .30
53 Dan Spillner .25 .10
54 Brent Strom .25 .10
55 Gary Sutherland .25 .10
56 Gene Tenace .75 .30
57A Derrell Thomas .75 .30
(Head shot
wearing glasses)
57B Derrell Thomas .75 .30
(Kneeling, not
wearing glasses)
58A Bobby Tolan .75 .30
(Batting pose)
58B Bobby Tolan .75 .30
(Kneeling, holding
cleats in hand)
59 Dave Tomlin .25 .10
60A Jerry Turner .75 .30
(Batting pose, gloveless
wall in background)
60B Jerry Turner .75 .30
(Batting pose
both hands gloved)
61 Bobby Valentine 1.00 .40
62 Dave Wehrmeister .25 .10
63 Whitey Wietelmann CO .25 .10
64 Don Williams CO .25 .10
65A Dave Winfield 10.00 4.00
(Batting pose, waist
up, field in background)
65B Dave Winfield 10.00 4.00
(Batting, stands in
background, black bat
telescoped)
65C Dave Winfield 10.00 4.00
(Two bats on shoulder)
65D Dave Winfield 10.00 4.00
(Full figure, leaning
on bat, blank back)

1978 Padres Family Fun

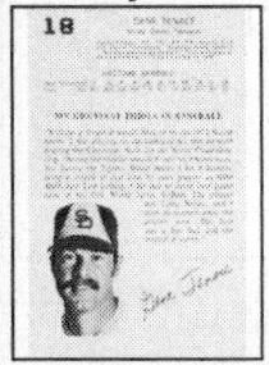

This 39-card set features members of the 1978 San Diego Padres. These large cards measure approximately 3 1/2" by 5 1/2" and are framed in a style similar to the 1962 Topps set with wood-grain borders. The cards have full color photos on the front of the card along with the Padres logo and Family Fun Centers underneath the photo in circles and the name of the player on the bottom of the card. The backs of the card asked each person what their greatest thrill in baseball was. This set is especially noteworthy for having one of the earliest Ozzie Smith cards printed. The set is checklisted alphabetically in the list below. This set was also available in uncut sheet form.

	NM	Ex
COMPLETE SET (39)	50.00	20.00
1 Bill Almon	.50	.20
2 Tucker Ashford	.50	.20
3 Chuck Baker	.50	.20
4 Dave Campbell ANN	.75	.30
5 Mike Champion	.50	.20
6 Jerry Coleman ANN	.75	.30
7 Roger Craig MG	1.00	.40
8 John D'Acquisto	.50	.20
9 Bob Davis	.50	.20
10 Chuck Estrada CO	.50	.20
11 Rollie Fingers	4.00	1.60
12 Dave Freisleben	.50	.20
13 Oscar Gamble	.75	.30
14 Fernando Gonzalez	.50	.20
15 Billy Herman CO	1.50	.60
16 Randy Jones	.75	.30
17 Ray Kroc OWN	1.50	.60
18 Mark Lee	.50	.20
19 Mickey Lolich	1.00	.40
20 Bob Owchinko	.50	.20
21 Broderick Perkins	.50	.20
22 Gaylord Perry	4.00	1.60
23 Eric Rasmussen	.50	.20
24 Don Reynolds	.50	.20
25 Gene Richards	.50	.20
26 Dave Roberts	.50	.20
27 Phil Roof CO	.50	.20
28 Bob Shirley	.50	.20
29 Ozzie Smith	25.00	10.00
30 Dan Spillner	.50	.20
31 Rick Sweet	.50	.20
32 Gene Tenace	.75	.30
33 Derrel Thomas	.50	.20
34 Jerry Turner	.50	.20
35 Dave Wehrmeister	.50	.20
36 Whitey Wietelmann CO	.50	.20
37 Don Williams CO	.50	.20
38 Dave Winfield	10.00	4.00
39 1978 All-Star Game	.75	.30

1979 Padres Family Fun

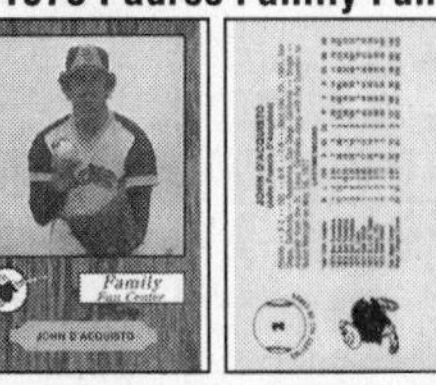

This set features photos of the San Diego Padres and has Family Fun Center printed in a bar on the front. These cards were also produced by Dean's photo processors.

	NM	Ex
COMPLETE SET	30.00	12.00
1 Roger Craig MG	.50	.20
2 John D'Acquisto	.50	.20
3 Ozzie Smith	10.00	4.00
4 KGB Chicken	1.50	.60
5 Gene Richards	.50	.20
6 Jerry Turner	.50	.20
7 Bob Owchinko	.50	.20
8 Gene Tenace	1.00	.40
9 Whitey Wietelmann CO	.50	.20
10 Bill Almon	.50	.20
11 Dave Winfield	5.00	2.00
12 Mike Hargrove	.75	.30
13 Fernando Gonzalez	.50	.20
14 Barry Evans	.50	.20
15 Steve Mura	.50	.20
16 Chuck Estrada CO	.50	.20
17 Bill Fahey	.50	.20
18 Gaylord Perry	3.00	1.20
19 Dan Briggs	.50	.20
20 Billy Herman CO	1.50	.60
21 Mickey Lolich	1.00	.40
22 Broderick Perkins	.50	.20
23 Fred Kendall	.50	.20
24 Rollie Fingers	3.00	1.20
25 Kurt Bevacqua	.50	.20
26 Jerry Coleman ANN	1.00	.40
27 Don Williams	.50	.20
28 Paul Dade	.50	.20
29 Randy Jones	.75	.30
30 Eric Rasmussen	.50	.20
31 Bobby Tolan	.50	.20
32 Doug Rader	.50	.20
33 Dave Campbell ANN	.75	.30
34 Jay Johnstone	1.00	.40
35 Mark Lee	.50	.20
36 Bob Shirley	.50	.20

1980 Padres Family Fun

This 36 card set was issued in six card increments six times during the 1980 season. We have sequenced these cards in the order they were given out during the season.

	NM	Ex
COMPLETE SET	25.00	10.00
1 Randy Jones	.75	.30
2 John D'Acquisto	.50	.20
3 Jerry Coleman CO	1.50	.60
4 Ozzie Smith	5.00	2.00
5 Gene Richards	.50	.20
6 Bill Fahey	.50	.20
7 John Curtis	.50	.20
8 Al Heist CO	.50	.20
9 Gary Lucas	.50	.20
10 Gene Tenace	.50	.20
11 Willie Montanez	.50	.20
12 Aurelio Rodriguez	.50	.20
13 Eric Rasmussen	.50	.20
14 Tim Flannery	.50	.20
15 Chuck Estrada CO	.50	.20
16 Eddie Doucette	.50	.20
17 Bob Shirley	.50	.20
18 The Chicken	1.50	.60
19 Dave Winfield	3.00	1.20
20 Kurt Bevacqua	.50	.20
21 Paul Dade	.50	.20
22 Dave Cash	.50	.20
23 Don Williams CO	.50	.20
24 Rollie Fingers	2.00	.80
25 Jerry Mumphrey	.50	.20
26 Fred Kendall	.50	.20
27 Steve Mura	.50	.20
28 Dennis Kinney	.50	.20
29 Von Joshua	.50	.20
30 Dick Phillips CO	.50	.20
31 Dave Campbell ANN	.75	.30
32 Juan Eichelberger	.50	.20
33 Rick Wise	.50	.20
34 Bobby Tolan	.50	.20
35 Jerry Turner	.50	.20
36 Barry Evans	.50	.20

1981 Padres Family Fun

These cards were issued as part of six-card sheets. Six players as well as a coupon were issued on each sheet. We are pricing all cards indivually as cut off from these sheets. There is a premium of 25 percent for a complete sheet. We have catalogued these cards individually and sequenced them in alphabetical order.

	Nm-Mt	Ex-Mt
COMPLETE SET (24)	15.00	6.00
1 Randy Bass	.50	.20
2 Kurt Bevacqua	.50	.20
3 Daniel Boone	.50	.20
4 Ed Brinkman CO	.50	.20
5 Dave Cash	.50	.20
6 Paul Dade	.50	.20
7 Dave Edwards	.50	.20
8 Chuck Estrada CO	.50	.20
9 Rollie Fingers	1.50	.60
10 Frank Howard MG	1.00	.40
11 Jack Krol CO	.50	.20
12 Joe Lefebvre	.50	.20
13 Tim Lollar	.50	.20
14 Gary Lucas	.50	.20
15 Gene Richards	.50	.20
16 Luis Salazar	.50	.20
17 Ozzie Smith	3.00	1.20
18 Ed Stevens	.50	.20
19 Craig Stimac	.50	.20
20 Steve Swisher	.50	.20
21 Jerry Turner	.50	.20
22 John Urrea	.50	.20
23 Don Williams	.50	.20
24 Dave Winfield	2.00	.80

1983 Padres Team Issue

This 32-card set of the San Diego Padres features color player photos and measures approximately 3 1/2" by 5 1/2". The cards are unnumbered and checklisted below in alphabetical order.

	Nm-Mt	Ex-Mt
COMPLETE SET (32)	25.00	10.00
1 Kurt Bevacqua	.50	.20
2 Juan Bonilla	.50	.20
3 Greg Booker	.50	.20
4 Nate Colbert CO	.50	.20
5 Luis DeLeon	.50	.20
6 Dave Dravecky	.50	.20
7 Tim Flannery	.50	.20
8 Steve Garvey	1.50	.60
9 Tony Gwynn	12.00	4.80
10 Ruppert Jones	.50	.20
11 Terry Kennedy	.50	.20
12 Jack Krol CO	.50	.20
13 Sixto Lezcano	.50	.20
14 Tim Lollar	.50	.20
15 Gary Lucas	.50	.20
16 Jack McKeon GM	.75	.30
17 Kevin McReynolds	1.50	.60
18 Sid Monge	.50	.20
19 John Montefusco	.50	.20
20 Mario Ramirez	.50	.20
21 Gene Richards	.50	.20
22 Luis Salazar	.50	.20
23 Norm Sherry CO	.50	.20
24 Eric Show	.50	.20
25 Elias Sosa	.50	.20
26 Mark Thurmond	.50	.20
27 Bobby Tolan CO	.50	.20
28 Jerry Turner	.50	.20
29 Ossie Virgil CO	.50	.20
30 Ed Whitson	.50	.20
31 Alan Wiggins	.50	.20
32 Dick Williams MG	.75	.30

1984 Padres Mother's

The cards in this 28-card set measure 2 1/2" by 3 1/2". In 1984, the Los Angeles based Mother's Cookies Co. issued five sets of cards featuring players from major league teams. The San Diego Padres set features current players depicted by photos. Similar to their 1952 and 1953 issues, the cards have rounded corners. The backs of the cards contain the Mother's Cookies logo. The cards were distributed in partial sets to fans at the respective stadiums of the teams involved. Whereas 20 cards were given to each patron, a redemption card, redeemable for eight more cards was included. Unfortunately, the eight cards received by redeeming the coupon were not necessarily the eight needed to complete a set. Hobbyist Barry Colla was involved in the production of these sets.

	Nm-Mt	Ex-Mt
COMPLETE SET (28)	20.00	8.00
1 Dick Williams MG	.50	.20
2 Rich Gossage	1.00	.40
3 Tim Lollar	.25	.10
4 Eric Show	.25	.10
5 Terry Kennedy	.25	.10
6 Kurt Bevacqua	.50	.20
7 Steve Garvey	2.00	.80
8 Garry Templeton	.50	.20
9 Tony Gwynn	12.00	4.80
10 Alan Wiggins	.25	.10
11 Dave Dravecky	1.00	.40
12 Tim Flannery	.25	.10
13 Kevin McReynolds	1.00	.40
14 Bobby Brown	.25	.10
15 Ed Whitson	.25	.10
16 Doug Gwosdz	.25	.10
17 Luis DeLeon	.25	.10
18 Andy Hawkins	.50	.20
19 Craig Lefferts	.50	.20
20 Carmelo Martinez	.25	.10
21 Sid Monge	.25	.10
22 Graig Nettles	1.00	.40
23 Mario Ramirez	.25	.10
24 Luis Salazar	.25	.10
25 Champ Summers	.25	.10
26 Mark Thurmond	.25	.10
27 Harry Dunlop CO Jack Krol CO Ozzie Virgil CO Norm Sherry CO Deacon Jones	.25	.10
28 Padres' Checklist	.25	.10

1984 Padres Smokey

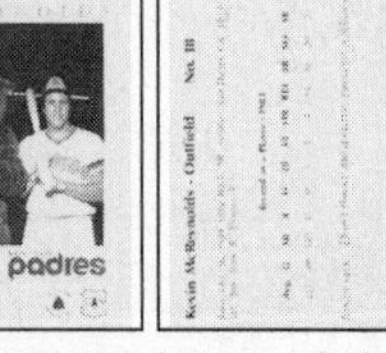

The cards in this 29-card set measure 2 1/2" by 3 3/4". This unnumbered, full color set features the Fire Prevention Bear and a Padres player, coach, manager, or associate on each card. The set was given out at the ballpark at the May 14th game against the Expos. Logos of the California Department of Forestry and the U.S. Forest Service appear in conjunction with a Smokey the Bear logo on the obverse. The set commemorates the 40th birthday of Smokey the Bear. The backs contain short biographical data, statistics and a fire prevention hint from the player pictured on the front.

	Nm-Mt	Ex-Mt
COMPLETE SET (29)	12.00	4.80
1 Kurt Bevacqua	.50	.20
2 Bobby Brown	.25	.10
3 Dave Campbell ANN	.50	.20
4 The Chicken	1.00	.40
5 Jerry Coleman ANN	.50	.20
6 Luis DeLeon	.25	.10
7 Dave Dravecky	1.00	.40
8 Harry Dunlop CO	.25	.10
9 Tim Flannery	.25	.10
10 Steve Garvey	1.00	.40
11 Doug Gwosdz	.25	.10
12 Tony Gwynn	6.00	2.40
13 Doug Harvey UMP	.75	.30
14 Terry Kennedy	.50	.20
15 Jack Krol CO	.25	.10
16 Tim Lollar	.25	.10
17 Jack McKeon VP	.50	.20
18 Kevin McReynolds	.75	.30
19 Sid Monge	.25	.10
20 Luis Salazar	.25	.10
21 Norm Sherry CO	.25	.10
22 Eric Show	.25	.10
23 Smokey the Bear	.25	.10
24 Garry Templeton	.25	.10
25 Mark Thurmond	.25	.10
26 Ozzie Virgil CO	.25	.10
27 Ed Whitson	.25	.10
28 Alan Wiggins	.25	.10
29 Dick Williams MG	.50	.20

1985 Padres Mother's

The cards in this 28-card set measure 2 1/2" by 3 1/2". In 1985, the Los Angeles based Mother's Cookies Co. again issued five sets of cards featuring players from major league teams. The San Diego Padres set features current players depicted by photos on cards with rounded corners. The backs of the cards contain the Mother's Cookies logo. Cards were passed out at the stadium on August 11.

	Nm-Mt	Ex-Mt
COMPLETE SET (28)	10.00	4.00
1 Dick Williams MG	.50	.20
2 Tony Gwynn	5.00	2.00
3 Kevin McReynolds	.50	.20
4 Graig Nettles	1.00	.40
5 Rich Gossage	1.00	.40
6 Steve Garvey	1.00	.40
7 Garry Templeton	.25	.10
8 Dave Dravecky	.75	.30
9 Eric Show	.25	.10
10 Terry Kennedy	.50	.20
11 Luis DeLeon	.25	.10
12 Bruce Bochy	.50	.20
13 Andy Hawkins	.25	.10
14 Kurt Bevacqua	.50	.20
15 Craig Lefferts	.25	.10
16 Mario Ramirez	.25	.10
17 LaMarr Hoyt	.25	.10
18 Jerry Royster	.25	.10
19 Tim Stoddard	.50	.20
20 Tim Flannery	.25	.10
21 Mark Thurmond	.25	.10
22 Greg Booker	.25	.10
23 Bobby Brown	.25	.10
24 Carmelo Martinez	.25	.10
25 Al Bumbry	.25	.10
26 Jerry Davis	.25	.10
27 Jack Krol CO Harry Dunlop CO Deacon Jones CO	.25	.10
28 Padres' Checklist Jack Murphy Stadium	.25	.10

1986 Padres Greats TCMA

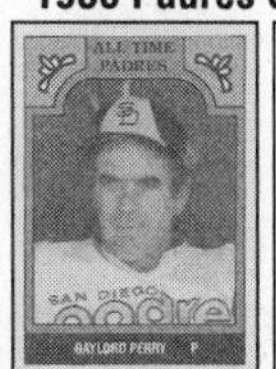

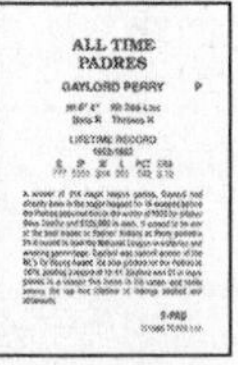

This 12-card standard-size set features some of the leading Padres players from their first two decades. The player's photo and name are on the front. The backs are used to give more player information.

	Nm-Mt	Ex-Mt
COMPLETE SET (12)	4.00	1.60
1 Nate Colbert	.50	.20
2 Tito Fuentes	.25	.10
3 Enzo Hernandez	.25	.10
4 Dave Roberts	.25	.10
5 Gene Richards	.25	.10
6 Ollie Brown	.25	.10
7 Clarence Gaston	.75	.30
8 Fred Kendall	.25	.10
9 Gaylord Perry	1.00	.40
10 Randy Jones	.50	.20
11 Rollie Fingers	1.00	.40
12 Preston Gomez MG	.25	.10

1987 Padres Bohemian Hearth Bread

The Bohemian Hearth Bread Company issued this 22-card set of San Diego Padres. The cards measure 2 1/2" by 3 1/2" and feature a distinctive yellow border on the front of the cards. Card backs provide career year-by-year statistics and are numbered.

	Nm-Mt	Ex-Mt
COMPLETE SET (22)	50.00	20.00
1 Garry Templeton	1.00	.40

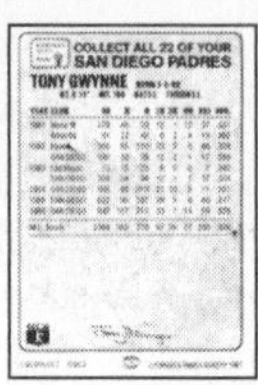

4 Joey Cora 2.50 1.00
5 Randy Ready 1.00 .40
6 Steve Garvey 5.00 2.00
7 Kevin Mitchell 2.50 1.00
8 John Kruk 4.00 1.60
9 Benito Santiago 10.00 4.00
10 Larry Bowa MG 1.50 .60
11 Tim Flannery 1.00 .40
14 Carmelo Martinez 1.00 .40
16 Marvell Wynne 1.00 .40
19 Tony Gwynn UER 25.00 10.00
Spelled Gwynne on the card
21 James Steels 1.00 .40
22 Stan Jefferson 1.00 .40
30 Eric Show 1.00 .40
31 Ed Whitson 1.00 .40
34 Storm Davis 1.00 .40
37 Craig Lefferts 1.00 .40
40 Andy Hawkins 1.00 .40
41 Lance McCullers 1.00 .40
43 Dave Dravecky 4.00 1.60
54 Rich Gossage 5.00 2.00

1986-87 Padres Fire Prevention Tips Booklets

These four Fire Prevention Booklets feature members of the San Diego Padres. The first three booklets issued are somewhat smaller and were issued in 1986. than than the fourth and fitth books issued and were issued in 1987. These booklets are unnumbered and we have sequenced them in alphabetical order

Nm-Mt Ex-Mt
COMPLETE SET (5) 15.00 6.00
1 Dave Dravecky 3.00 1.20
2 Tim Flannery 2.00 .80
3 Tony Gwynn 10.00 4.00
4 Lance McCullers 2.00 .80
5 Benito Santiago 5.00 2.00

1988 Padres Coke

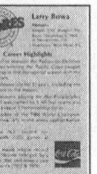

These cards were actually issued as two separate promotions. The first eight cards were issued as a perforated sheet (approximately 7 1/2" by 10 1/2") as a Coca Cola Junior Padres Club promotion. The other 12 cards were issued later on specific game days to members of the Junior Padres Club. All the cards are standard size, 2 1/2" by 3 1/2" and are unnumbered. Cards that were on the perforated panel are indicated by PAN in the checklist below. Since the cards are unnumbered, they are listed below by uniform number, which is featured prominently on the card fronts.

Nm-Mt Ex-Mt
COMPLETE SET (21) 35.00 14.00
COMMON PANEL PLAYER .50 .20
COMMON NON-PANEL PLAYER 1.50 .60
1 Garry Templeton PAN .75 .30
5 Randy Ready PAN .50 .20
7 Keith Moreland 1.50 .60
8 John Kruk 5.00 2.00
9 Benito Santiago 2.00 .80
10 Larry Bowa MG PAN 1.00 .40
11 Tim Flannery PAN .50 .20
14 Carmelo Martinez 1.50 .60
15 Jack McKeon MG 2.00 .80
19 Tony Gwynn 20.00 8.00
22 Stan Jefferson 1.50 .60
27 Mark Parent 1.50 .60
30 Eric Show 1.50 .60
31 Eddie Whitson 1.50 .60
35 Chris Brown PAN .50 .20
41 Lance McCullers 1.50 .60
45 Jimmy Jones PAN .50 .20
48 Mark Davis PAN .75 .30
51 Greg Booker 1.50 .60
55 Mark Grant PAN .50 .20
NNO Padres Logo PAN .50 .20
(Program explanation on reverse)

1988 Padres Smokey

The cards in this 31-card set measure approximately 3 3/4" by 5 3/4". This unnumbered, full color set features the Fire Prevention Bear, Smokey, and a Padres player, coach, manager, or associate on each card. The set was given out at Jack Murphy Stadium to fans under the age of 14 during the Smokey Bear Day game promotion. The logo of the California Department of Forestry appears on the reverse in conjunction with a Smokey the Bear logo on the obverse. The backs contain short biographical data and a fire prevention hint from Smokey. The set is numbered below in alphabetical order. The card backs are actually postcards that can be addressed and mailed. Cards of Larry Bowa and Candy Sierra were printed but were not officially released since they were no longer members of the Padres by the time the cards were to be distributed. Roberto Alomar appears in his Rookie Card year in this set.

Nm-Mt Ex-Mt
COMPLETE SET (31) 30.00 12.00
1 Shawn Abner .50 .20
2 Roberto Alomar 8.00 3.20
3 Sandy Alomar CO 1.00 .40
4 Greg Booker .50 .20
5 Chris Brown .50 .20
6 Mark Davis 1.00 .40
7 Pat Dobson CO .50 .20
8 Tim Flannery .50 .20
9 Mark Grant .50 .20
10 Tony Gwynn 12.00 4.80
11 Andy Hawkins .50 .20
12 Stan Jefferson .50 .20
13 Jimmy Jones .50 .20
14 John Kruk 2.00 .80
15 Dave Leiper .50 .20
16 Shane Mack .50 .20
17 Carmelo Martinez .50 .20
18 Lance McCullers .50 .20
19 Keith Moreland .50 .20
20 Eric Nolte .50 .20
21 Amos Otis CO .50 .20
22 Mark Parent .50 .20
23 Randy Ready .50 .20
24 Greg Riddoch CO .50 .20
25 Benito Santiago 1.50 .60
26 Eric Show .50 .20
27 Denny Sommers CO .50 .20
28 Garry Templeton 1.00 .40
29 Dickie Thon .50 .20
30 Ed Whitson .50 .20
31 Marvell Wynne .50 .20

1989 Padres Coke

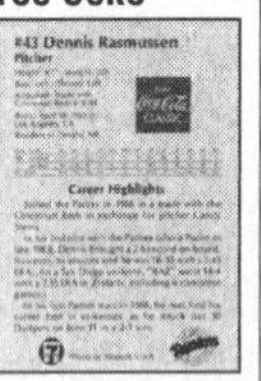

These cards were actually issued as two separate promotions. The first nine cards were issued as a perforated sheet (approximately 7 1/2" by 10 1/2") as a Coca Cola Junior Padres Club promotion. The other 12 cards were issued later on specific game days to members of the Junior Padres Club. All the cards are standard size and are unnumbered. Cards that were on the perforated panel are indicated by PAN in the checklist below. Since the cards are unnumbered, they are listed below in alphabetical order by subject. Marvell Wynne was planned for the set but was not issued since he was traded before the set was released; Walt Terrell also is tougher to find due to his mid-season trade.

Nm-Mt Ex-Mt
COMPLETE SET (21) 35.00 14.00
COMMON PANEL CARD .50 .20
COMMON NON-PAN CARD 1.50 .60
1 Roberto Alomar PAN 6.00 2.40
2 Jack Clark 1.50 .60
3 Mark Davis 1.50 .60
4 Tim Flannery 1.50 .60
5 Mark Grant 1.50 .60
6 Tony Gwynn 15.00 6.00
7 Bruce Hurst 1.50 .60
8 Chris James 1.50 .60
9 Carmelo Martinez PAN .50 .20
10 Jack McKeon MG PAN .50 .20
11 Mark Parent 1.50 .60
12 Dennis Rasmussen PAN .50 .20
13 Randy Ready PAN .50 .20
14 Bip Roberts 1.50 .60
15 Luis Salazar 1.50 .60
16 Benito Santiago 1.50 .60
17 Eric Show PAN .50 .20
18 Garry Templeton PAN .50 .20
19 Walt Terrell SP 8.00 3.20
20 Ed Whitson PAN .50 .20
NNO Padres Logo PAN .50 .20

1989 Padres Magazine

These 2 1/2" by 3 1/2" cards came as an insert in issues of "Padres" magazine sold in San Diego. These cards were sponsored by San Diego Sports Collectibles, a major hobby dealer. The cards feature beautiful full-color photos on the front and interesting did-you-know facts on the back along with one line of career statistics. The cards of retired Padres feature a highlight of their career in San Diego. The suggested retail price of each of the six different Padres magazines was 1.50.

Nm-Mt Ex-Mt
COMPLETE SET (24) 15.00 6.00
1 Jack McKeon MG .25 .10
2 Sandy Alomar Jr. 1.00 .40
3 Tony Gwynn 10.00 4.00
4 Willie McCovey HL 1.00 .40
5 John Kruk .50 .20
6 Jack Clark .50 .20
7 Eric Show .25 .10
8 Rollie Fingers HL 1.00 .40
9 Sandy Alomar Sr. 2.00 .80
Sandy Alomar Jr.
Roberto Alomar
10 Carmelo Martinez .25 .10
11 Benito Santiago .50 .20
12 Nate Colbert HL .25 .10
13 Mark Davis .25 .10
14 Roberto Alomar 6.00 2.40
15 Tim Flannery .25 .10
16 Randy Jones HL .50 .20
17 Dennis Rasmussen .25 .10
18 Greg W. Harris .25 .10
19 Garry Templeton .25 .10
20 Steve Garvey HL .75 .30
21 Bruce Hurst .25 .10
22 Ed Whitson .25 .10
23 Chris James .25 .10
24 Gaylord Perry HL 1.00 .40

1989 Padres Postcards

This 36-card set of the San Diego Padres features color player photos on a postcard format and measures approximately 3 3/4" by 5 3/4". The cards are unnumbered and checklisted below in alphabetical order.

Nm-Mt Ex-Mt
COMPLETE SET (36) 20.00 8.00
1 Shawn Abner .50 .20
2 Roberto Alomar 3.00 1.20
3 Sandy Alomar Jr. 1.50 .60
4 Sandy Alomar Sr. CO .50 .20
5 Jack Clark .75 .30
6 Jerald Clark .50 .20
7 Pat Clements .50 .20
8 Mark Davis .50 .20
9 Pat Dobson CO .50 .20
10 Tim Flannery .50 .20
11 Mark Grant .50 .20
12 Gary Green .50 .20
13 Tony Gwynn 5.00 2.00
14 Greg Harris .50 .20
15 Bruce Hurst .50 .20
16 Chris James .50 .20
17 Dave Leiper .50 .20
18 Carmelo Martinez .50 .20
19 Jack McKeon MG .75 .30
20 Rob Nelson .50 .20
21 Amos Otis CO .50 .20
22 Mike Pagliarulo .50 .20
23 Mark Parent .50 .20
24 Dennis Rasmussen .50 .20
25 Greg Riddoch CO .50 .20
26 Bip Roberts .50 .20
27 Luis Salazar .50 .20
28 Benito Santiago 1.00 .40
29 Eric Show .50 .20
30 Don Schulze .50 .20
31 Tony Siegle VP .50 .20
32 Denny Sommers CO .50 .20
33 Garry Templeton .50 .20
34 Fred Toliver .50 .20
35 Ed Whitson .50 .20
36 Marvell Wynne .50 .20

1989 Padres Show Kay

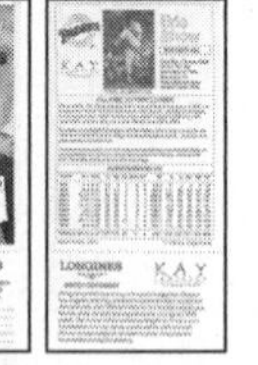

This one-card set measures approximately 2 1/2" by 4 7/8" and featues a color photo of San Diego Padres pitcher, Eric Show, on the top portion of the card with player information and career statistics on the back. The part below the picture held a lapel pin commemorating Eric Show becoming the Padres all-time victory leader with 93 wins. This portion could be torn off and brought to any Kay Jewelers for a chance to win a Longines watch.

Nm-Mt Ex-Mt
1 Eric Show 5.00 2.00

1990 Padres Coke

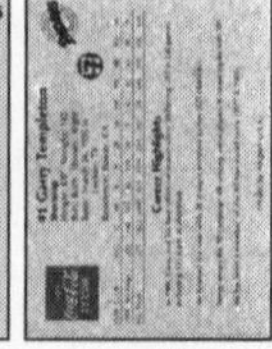

These standard-size cards were issued in two forms: a 7 1/2" by 10 5/8" perforated sheet featuring eight player cards and the Padre logo card (marked by PAN below) as well as 12 individual player cards. The sheet was issued to Coca-Cola Junior Padres Club Members as a starter set, and club members who attended the first six Junior Padres Club games received two additional cards per game. The cards are unnumbered and checklisted below in alphabetical order, with the team logo card listed at the end.

Nm-Mt Ex-Mt
COMPLETE SET (21) 30.00 9.00
COMMON PANEL CARD .50 .15
COMMON NON-PAN CARD 1.00 .30
1 Roberto Alomar 8.00 2.40
2 Andy Benes PAN 1.00 .30
3 Joe Carter 6.00 1.80
4 Jack Clark 1.50 .45
5 Mark Grant PAN .50 .15
6 Tony Gwynn 12.00 3.60
7 Greg W. Harris 1.00 .30
8 Bruce Hurst 1.00 .30
9 Craig Lefferts 1.00 .30
10 Fred Lynn 1.50 .45
11 Jack McKeon MG PAN .50 .15
12 Mike Pagliarulo 1.00 .30
13 Mark Parent PAN .50 .15
14 Dennis Rasmussen PAN .50 .15
15 Bip Roberts PAN .75 .23
16 Benito Santiago 2.00 .60
17 Calvin Schiraldi 1.00 .30
18 Eric Show PAN .50 .15
19 Garry Templeton 1.00 .30
20 Ed Whitson PAN .50 .15
NNO Padres Logo PAN .50 .15

1990 Padres Magazine/Unocal

This 24-card set was sponsored by Unocal 76 and was available in the San Diego Padres' game programs for 17.50. The cards were divided into six series, and each series was issued on a 5" by 9" sheet of four cards with a sponsor's coupon. After perforation, the cards measure the standard size. Some players appear in more than one series. Coupons from the magazine were to be turned into Unocal for 25 Jack McKeon, 26 Bip Roberts, and 27 Joe Carter.

Nm-Mt Ex-Mt
COMPLETE SET (27) 20.00 6.00
COMMON CARD (1-24) .25 .07
COMMON CARD (25-27) .75 .23
1 Tony Gwynn 6.00 1.80
2 Benito Santiago .75 .23
3 Mike Pagliarulo .25 .07
4 Dennis Rasmussen .25 .07
5 Eric Show .25 .07
6 Darrin Jackson .25 .07
7 Mark Parent .25 .07
8 Jerry Coleman ANN .50 .15
Rick Monday ANN
9 Andy Benes 1.00 .30
10 Roberto Alomar 4.00 1.20
11 Craig Lefferts .25 .07
12 Ed Whitson .25 .07
13 Calvin Schiraldi .25 .07
14 Garry Templeton .25 .07
15 Tony Gwynn 8.00 2.40
16 Bob Chandler ANN .25 .07
Ted Leitner ANN
17 Fred Lynn .50 .15
18 Jack Clark .50 .15
19 Mike Dunne .25 .07
20 Mark Grant .25 .07
21 Benito Santiago .75 .23
22 Sandy Alomar Sr. CO .50 .15
Pat Dobson CO
Amos Otis CO
Greg Riddoch CO
Denny Sommers CO
23 Bruce Hurst .25 .07
24 Greg W. Harris .25 .07
25 Jack McKeon MG 1.00 .30
26 Bip Roberts 1.00 .30
27 Joe Carter 3.00 .90

1990 Padres Postcards

These postcards feature the members of the 1990 San Diego Padres. The year can be identified as 1990 was Joe Carter's only year with the Padres. Since these cards are unnumbered, we have sequenced them in alphabetical order.

MINT NRMT
COMPLETE SET 20.00 9.00
1 Shawn Abner .50 .23
2 Roberto Alomar 2.00 .90
3 Sandy Alomar Sr. CO .50 .23
4 Andy Benes .75 .35
5 Joe Carter .75 .35
6 Jerald Clark .50 .23
7 Jack Clark .75 .35
8 Pat Clements .50 .23
9 Joey Cora .50 .23
10 Pat Dobson CO .50 .23
11 Mike Dunne .50 .23
12 Mark Grant .50 .23
13 Tony Gwynn 4.00 1.80
14 Bruce Hurst .50 .23
15 Greg Harris .50 .23
16 Darrin Jackson .50 .23
17 Craig Lefferts .50 .23
18 Fred Lynn .75 .35
19 Jack McKeon MG .75 .35
20 Amos Otis CO .50 .23
21 Mike Pagliarulo .50 .23
22 Mark Parent .50 .23
23 Dennis Rasmussen .50 .23
24 Greg Riddoch CO .50 .23
25 Bip Roberts .50 .23
26 Benito Santiago 1.00 .45
27 Calvin Schiraldi .50 .23
28 Eric Show .50 .23
29 Denny Sommers CO .50 .23
30 Phil Stephenson .50 .23
31 Garry Templeton .50 .23
32 Ed Whitson .50 .23

1991 Padres Coke

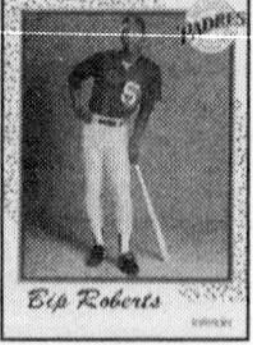

These nine standard-size cards were sponsored by Coca-Cola and issued in perforated sheets that measure approximately 7 3/4" by 10 3/4". They feature on their fronts posed studio shots of players and announcers for the Padres. The cards are unnumbered and checklisted below in alphabetical order.

Nm-Mt Ex-Mt
COMPLETE SET (9) 8.00 2.40
1 Bob Chandler ANN 1.00 .30
2 Jerry Coleman ANN 1.50 .45
3 Paul Faries 1.00 .30
4 Craig Lefferts 1.00 .30
5 Ted Leitner ANN 1.00 .30
6 Rick Monday ANN 1.00 .30
7 Greg Riddoch MG 1.00 .30
8 Bip Roberts 1.00 .30
9 Title card 1.00 .30

1991 Padres Magazine/Rally's

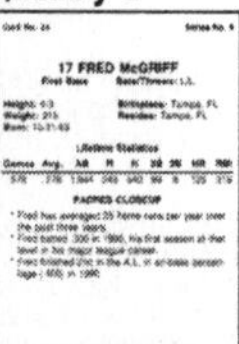

This 30-card set was sponsored by Rally's Hamburgers. The first 27 cards were divided into six series, and each series was issued on a 5" by 9" sheet of four cards with a sponsor's coupon. After perforation, the cards measure the standard size. Some players appear on more than one sheet, and there are variations involving Schiraldi, Gardner, and Presley, who were released during the season. For example, on the fourth sheet (13-16), Clark replaced Schiraldi; likewise Hurst replaced Gardner on the fifth sheet (17-20) and Roberts (who also appears on the third sheet) replaced Presley on the sixth sheet (21-24). The last three cards were available as part of a promotion whereby fans could tear out a coupon from the Padres Magazine and bring the coupon to one of eight Rally's Hamburgers locations in San Diego County in order to redeem one card.

Nm-Mt Ex-Mt
COMPLETE SET (30) 25.00 7.50
COMMON CARD (1-24) .25 .07
COMMON CARD (25-27) 1.00 .30
COMMON SP 3.00 .90
1 Greg Riddoch MG .25 .07
2 Dennis Rasmussen .25 .07
3 Thomas Howard .25 .07
4 Tom Lampkin .25 .07
5 Bruce Hurst .25 .07
6 Darrin Jackson .25 .07
7 Jerald Clark .25 .07
8 Shawn Abner .25 .07
9 Bip Roberts 1.00 .30
10 Marty Barrett .25 .07
11 Jim Vatcher .25 .07
12 Greg Gross .25 .07
13 Greg W. Harris .25 .07
14 Ed Whitson .25 .07
15A Calvin Schiraldi SP 3.00 .90
15B Jerald Clark 1.00 .30
16 Rich Rodriguez .25 .07
17 Larry Andersen .25 .07
18 Andy Benes 1.25 .35
19A Wes Gardner SP 3.00 .90
19B Bruce Hurst 1.00 .30
20 Paul Faries .25 .07
21 Craig Lefferts .25 .07
22 Tony Gwynn 8.00 2.40
23A Jim Presley SP 3.00 .90
23B Bip Roberts 1.00 .30
24 Fred McGriff 4.00 1.20
25 Gaylord Perry 2.00 .60
26 Benito Santiago 1.25 .35
27 Tony Fernandez 1.00 .30

1991 Padres Smokey

This 39-card set of the San Diego Padres measures approximately 3 1/2" by 5" and features color player photos on the fronts.

Nm-Mt Ex-Mt
COMPLETE SET (39) 15.00 4.50
1 Shawn Abner .25 .07
2 Larry Andersen .25 .07
3 Andy Benes .25 .07
4 Jerald Clark .25 .07
5 Pat Clements .25 .07
6 Scott Coolbaugh .25 .07
7 John Costello .25 .07
8 Bruce Dorsett .25 .07

	Nm-Mt	Ex-Mt
9 Paul Faries	.25	.07
10 Tony Fernandez	.75	.23
11 Tony Gwynn	10.00	3.00
12 Atlee Hammaker	.25	.07
13 Greg Harris	.25	.07
14 Thomas Howard	.25	.07
15 Bruce Hurst	.25	.07
16 Darrin Jackson	.25	.07
17 Bruce Kimm CO	.25	.07
18 Tom Lampkin	.25	.07
19 Craig Lefferts	.25	.07
20 Mike Maddux	.25	.07
21 Fred McGriff	2.00	.60
22 Joe McIlvaine GM	.25	.07
23 Jose Melendez	.25	.07
24 Jose Mota	.25	.07
25 Adam Peterson	.25	.07
26 Rob Picciolo CO	.25	.07
27 Dennis Rasmussen	.25	.07
28 Merv Rettenmund CO	.25	.07
29 Greg Riddoch MG	.25	.07
30 Mike Roarke CO	.25	.07
31 Bip Roberts	.25	.07
32 Steve Rosenberg	.25	.07
33 Benito Santiago	.50	.15
34 Jim Snyder CO	.25	.07
35 Phil Stephenson	.25	.07
36 Tim Teufel	.25	.07
37 Jim Vatcher	.25	.07
38 Kevin Ward	.25	.07
39 Ed Whitson	.25	.07

1992 Padres Carl's Jr.

This 25-card set was sponsored by Carl's Jr. restaurants and issued in perforated nine-card sheets or in a precut set. The cards are printed on thick card stock and measure slightly larger than standard size (2 9/16" by 3 9/16"). The cards are unnumbered and checklisted below in alphabetical order.

	Nm-Mt	Ex-Mt
COMPLETE SET (25)	15.00	4.50
1 Larry Andersen	.25	.07
2 Oscar Azocar	.25	.07
3 Andy Benes	.25	.07
4 Dann Bilardello	.25	.07
5 Jerald Clark	.25	.07
6 Tony Fernandez	.50	.15
7 Tony Gwynn	6.00	1.80
8 Greg W. Harris	.25	.07
9 Bruce Hurst	.25	.07
10 Darrin Jackson	.25	.07
11 Craig Lefferts	.25	.07
12 Mike Maddux	.25	.07
13 Fred McGriff	3.00	.90
14 Jose Melendez	.25	.07
15 Randy Myers	.75	.23
16 Greg Riddoch MG	.25	.07
17 Rich Rodriguez	.25	.07
18 Benito Santiago	.75	.23
19 Gary Sheffield	2.00	.60
20 Craig Shipley	.25	.07
21 Kurt Stillwell	.25	.07
22 Tim Teufel	.25	.07
23 Kevin Ward	.25	.07
24 Ed Whitson	.25	.07
25 All-Star Game Logo	.25	.07

1992 Padres Mother's

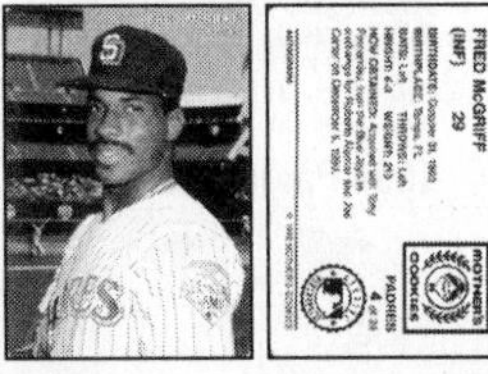

The 1992 Mother's Cookies Padres set contains 28 cards with rounded corners measuring the standard size.

	Nm-Mt	Ex-Mt
COMPLETE SET (28)	12.00	3.60
1 Greg Riddoch MG	.25	.07
2 Greg W. Harris	.25	.07
3 Gary Sheffield	2.00	.60
4 Fred McGriff	2.00	.60
5 Kurt Stillwell	.25	.07
6 Benito Santiago	.75	.23
7 Tony Gwynn	5.00	1.50
8 Tony Fernandez	.50	.15
9 Jerald Clark	.25	.07
10 Dave Eiland	.25	.07
11 Randy Myers	.75	.23
12 Oscar Azocar	.25	.07
13 Dann Bilardello	.25	.07
14 Jose Melendez	.25	.07
15 Darrin Jackson	.25	.07
16 Andy Benes	.25	.07
17 Tim Teufel	.25	.07
18 Jeremy Hernandez	.25	.07
19 Kevin Ward	.25	.07
20 Bruce Hurst	.25	.07
21 Larry Andersen	.25	.07
22 Rich Rodriguez	.25	.07
23 Pat Clements	.25	.07
24 Craig Lefferts	.25	.07
25 Craig Shipley	.25	.07
26 Mike Maddux	.25	.07
27 Jim Snyder CO	.25	.07
Mike Roarke CO		
Rob Picciolo CO		
Merv Rettenmund CO		
Bruce Kimm		
28 Checklist	.25	.07

1992 Padres Police DARE

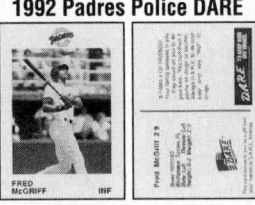

Sponsored by DARE (Drug Abuse Resistance Education) America, this 30-card standard-size set is printed on thin card stock. The cards are unnumbered and checklisted below in alphabetical order, with multi-player cards listed at the end.

	Nm-Mt	Ex-Mt
COMPLETE SET (27)	30.00	9.00
1 Oscar Azocar	.50	.15
2 Bluepper (Mascot)	.50	.15
3 Andy Benes	.50	.15
4 Jerald Clark	.50	.15
5 Jim Deshaies	.50	.15
6 Dave Eiland	.50	.15
7 Tony Fernandez	1.00	.30
8 Tony Gwynn	10.00	3.00
9 Greg W. Harris	.50	.15
10 Bruce Hurst	.50	.15
11 Darrin Jackson	.50	.15
12 Tom Lampkin	.50	.15
13 Craig Lefferts	.50	.15
14 Fred McGriff	5.00	1.50
15 Rob Picciolo	.50	.15
16 Merv Rettenmund CO	.50	.15
17 Greg Riddoch MG	.50	.15
18 Benito Santiago	2.00	.60
19 Frank Seminara	.50	.15
20 Gary Sheffield	4.00	1.20
21 Craig Shipley	.50	.15
22 Phil Stephenson	.50	.15
23 Kurt Stillwell	.50	.15
24 Tim Teufel	.50	.15
25 Dan Walters	.50	.15
26 Kevin Ward	.50	.15
27 Jack Murphy Stadium	.50	.15
28 Bruce Kimm CO	.50	.15
Rob Picciolo CO		
Merv Rettenmund CO		
Mike Roarke CO		
Jim Snyder CO		
29 Larry Andersen	.50	.15
Mike Maddux		
Jose Melendez		
Rich Rodriguez		
Tim Scott		
30 Fred McGriff	2.00	.60
Tony Fernandez		
Gary Sheffield		
Tony Gwynn		

1992 Padres Smokey

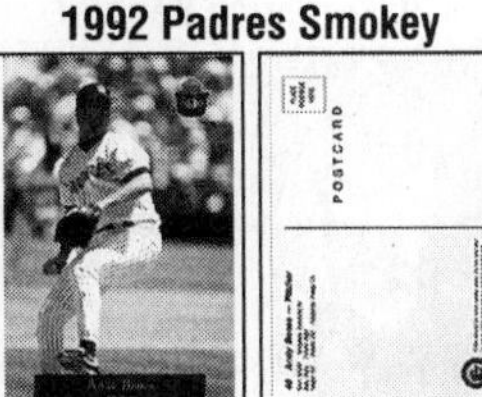

This 36-card set was issued in the postcard format and measures approximately 3 13/16" by 5 11/16". The cards are unnumbered and checklisted below in alphabetical order.

	Nm-Mt	Ex-Mt
COMPLETE SET (36)	20.00	6.00
1 Larry Andersen	.50	.15
2 Oscar Azocar	.50	.15
3 Andy Benes	.75	.23
4 Dann Bilardello	.50	.15
5 Jerald Clark	.50	.15
6 Pat Clements	.50	.15
7 Dave Eiland	.50	.15
8 Tony Fernandez	.75	.23
9 Tony Gwynn	10.00	3.00
10 Gene Harris	.50	.15
11 Greg W. Harris	.50	.15
12 Jeremy Hernandez	.50	.15
13 Bruce Hurst	.50	.15
14 Darrin Jackson	.50	.15
15 Tom Lampkin	.50	.15
16 Bruce Kimm CO	.50	.15
17 Craig Lefferts	.50	.15
18 Mike Maddux	.50	.15
19 Fred McGriff	2.00	.60
20 Jose Melendez	.50	.15
21 Randy Myers	.75	.23
22 Gary Pettis	.50	.15
23 Rob Picciolo CO	.50	.15
24 Merv Rettenmund CO	.50	.15
25 Greg Riddoch MG	.50	.15
26 Mike Roarke CO	.50	.15
27 Rich Rodriguez	.50	.15
28 Benito Santiago	1.00	.30
29 Frank Seminara	.50	.15
30 Gary Sheffield	2.50	.75
31 Craig Shipley	.50	.15
32 Jim Snyder CO	.50	.15
33 Dave Staton	.50	.15
34 Kurt Stillwell	.50	.15
35 Tim Teufel	.50	.15
36 Kevin Ward	.50	.15

1993 Padres Mother's

The 1993 Mother's Cookies Padres set consists of 28 standard-size cards with rounded corners.

	Nm-Mt	Ex-Mt
COMPLETE SET (28)	12.00	3.60
1 Jim Riggleman MG	.25	.07
2 Gary Sheffield	1.00	.30
3 Tony Gwynn	4.00	1.20
4 Fred McGriff	1.00	.30
5 Greg W. Harris	.25	.07
6 Tim Teufel	.25	.07
7 Dave Eiland	.25	.07
8 Phil Plantier	.25	.07
9 Bruce Hurst	.25	.07
10 Ricky Gutierrez	.25	.07
11 Rich Rodriguez	.25	.07
12 Derek Bell	.25	.07
13 Bob Geren	.25	.07
14 Andy Benes	.25	.07
15 Darrell Sherman	.25	.07
16 Frank Seminara	.25	.07
17 Guillermo Velasquez	.25	.07
18 Gene Harris	.25	.07
19 Dan Walters	.25	.07
20 Craig Shipley	.25	.07
21 Phil Clark	.25	.07
22 Jeff Gardner	.25	.07
23 Mike Scioscia	.50	.15
24 Wally Whitehurst	.25	.07
25 Roger Mason	.25	.07
26 Kerry Taylor	.25	.07
27 Tim Scott	.25	.07
28 Bruce Bochy CO	.25	.07
Dan Radison CO		
Mike Roarke CO		
Dave Bialas CO		
Rob Picciolo CO		
Merv Rettenmund CO CL		

1994 Padres Mother's

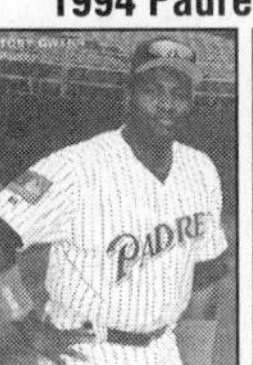

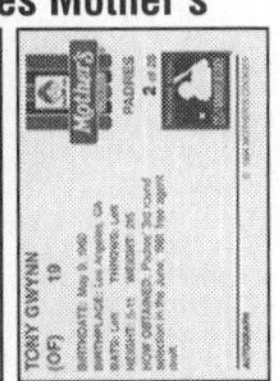

The 1994 Mother's Cookies Padres set consists of 28 standard-size cards with rounded corners.

	Nm-Mt	Ex-Mt
COMPLETE SET (28)	8.00	2.40
1 Jim Riggleman MG	.25	.07
2 Tony Gwynn	3.00	.90
3 Andy Benes	.25	.07
4 Bip Roberts	.25	.07
5 Phil Clark	.25	.07
6 Wally Whitehurst	.25	.07
7 Archi Cianfrocco	.25	.07
8 Derek Bell	.25	.07
9 Ricky Gutierrez	.25	.07
10 Mark Davis	.25	.07
11 Phil Plantier	.25	.07
12 Brian Johnson	.25	.07
13 Billy Bean	.50	.15
14 Craig Shipley	.25	.07
15 Tim Hyers	.25	.07
16 Gene Harris	.25	.07
17 Scott Sanders	.25	.07
18 A.J. Sager	.25	.07
19 Keith Lockhart	.25	.07
20 Tim Mauser	.25	.07
21 Andy Ashby	.50	.15
22 Brad Ausmus	.25	.07
23 Trevor Hoffman	1.00	.30
24 Luis Lopez	.25	.07
25 Doug Brocail	.25	.07
26 Dave Staton	.25	.07
27 Pedro Martinez	.25	.07
28 Sonny Siebert CO	.25	.07
Rob Picciolo CO		
Dave Bialas CO		
Dan Radison CO		
Merv Rettenmund CO		
Bruce Bochy CO CL		

1995 Padres CHP

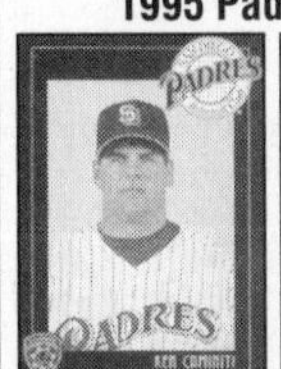

Sponsored by the California Highway Patrol, this 16-card set features color player photos in a blue frame. The backs carry player information and a safety tip.

	Nm-Mt	Ex-Mt
COMPLETE SET (16)	15.00	4.50
1 Tony Gwynn	10.00	3.00
2 Brad Ausmus	.50	.15
3 Andy Ashby	.50	.15
4 Brian Johnson	.50	.15
5 Trevor Hoffman	1.50	.45
6 Scott Sanders	.50	.15
7 Bip Roberts	.50	.15
8 Roberto Petagine	.50	.15
9 Fernando Valenzuela	1.00	.30
10 Ken Caminiti	.75	.23
11 Steve Finley	1.50	.45
12 Andujar Cedeno	.50	.15
13 Jody Reed	.50	.15
14 Eddie Williams	.50	.15
15 Joey Hamilton	.50	.15
16 Bruce Bochy MG	.50	.15
Chief Don Watkins		

1995 Padres Mother's

The 1995 Mother's Cookies San Diego Padres set consists of 28 standard-size cards with rounded corners.

	Nm-Mt	Ex-Mt
COMPLETE SET (28)	10.00	3.00
1 Bruce Bochy MG	.25	.07
2 Tony Gwynn	3.00	.90
3 Ken Caminiti	.50	.15
4 Bip Roberts	.25	.07
5 Andujar Cedeno	.25	.07
6 Andy Benes	.50	.15
7 Phil Clark	.25	.07
8 Fernando Valenzuela	.75	.23
9 Roberto Petagine	.25	.07
10 Brian Johnson	.25	.07
11 Scott Livingstone	.25	.07
12 Brian Williams	.25	.07
13 Jody Reed	.25	.07
14 Steve Finley	1.00	.30
15 Jeff Tabaka	.25	.07
16 Ray Holbert	.25	.07
17 Tim Worrell	.25	.07
18 Eddie Williams	.25	.07
19 Brad Ausmus	.25	.07
20 Willie Blair	.25	.07
21 Trevor Hoffman	1.00	.30
22 Scott Sanders	.25	.07
23 Andy Ashby	.25	.07
24 Joey Hamilton	.25	.07
25 Andres Berumen	.25	.07
26 Melvin Nieves	.25	.07
27 Bryce Florie	.25	.07
28 Merv Rettenmund CO	.50	.15
Graig Nettles CO		
Davey Lopes CO		
Sonny Siebert CO		
Rob Picciolo CO		
Ty Waller CO CL		

1996 Padres Mother's

This 28-card set consists of borderless posed color player portraits in stadium settings.

	Nm-Mt	Ex-Mt
COMPLETE SET (28)	10.00	3.00
1 Bruce Bochy MG	.25	.07
2 Tony Gwynn	3.00	.90
3 Wally Joyner	1.00	.30
4 Rickey Henderson	1.50	.45
5 Ken Caminiti	.50	.15
6 Scott Sanders	.25	.07
7 Steve Finley	1.00	.30
8 Fernando Valenzuela	.75	.23
9 Brian Johnson	.25	.07
10 Jody Reed	.25	.07
11 Bob Tewksbury	.25	.07
12 Andujar Cedeno	.25	.07
13 Sean Bergman	.25	.07
14 Marc Newfield	.25	.07
15 Craig Shipley	.25	.07
16 Scott Livingstone	.25	.07
17 Trevor Hoffman	1.00	.30
18 Doug Bochtler	.25	.07
19 Archi Cianfrocco	.25	.07
20 Joey Hamilton	.25	.07
21 Andy Ashby	.25	.07
22 Chris Gwynn	.25	.07
23 Luis Lopez	.25	.07
24 Tim Worrell	.25	.07
25 Brad Ausmus	.25	.07
26 Willie Blair	.25	.07
27 Bryce Florie	.25	.07
28 Dan Warthen CO	.25	.07
Rob Picciolo CO		
Davey Lopes CP		
Grady Little CO		
Tim Flannery CO		
Merv Rettenmund CO CL		

1997 Padres Mother's

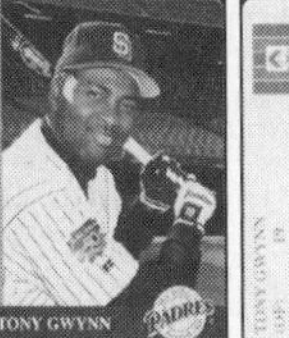

This 28-card set of the San Diego Padres sponsored by Mother's Cookies consists of posed color player photos with rounded corners.

	Nm-Mt	Ex-Mt
COMPLETE SET (28)	12.00	3.60
1 Bruce Bochy MG	.25	.07
2 Tony Gwynn	3.00	.90
3 Ken Caminiti	.50	.15
4 Wally Joyner	.50	.15
5 Rickey Henderson	1.25	.35
6 Greg Vaughn	.50	.15
7 Steve Finley	1.00	.30
8 Fernando Valenzuela	.75	.23
9 John Flaherty	.25	.07
10 Sterling Hitchcock	.25	.07
11 Quilvio Veras	.25	.07
12 Don Slaught	.25	.07
13 Sean Bergman	.25	.07
14 Chris Gomez	.25	.07
15 Craig Shipley	.25	.07
16 Joey Hamilton	.25	.07
17 Scott Livingstone	.25	.07
18 Trevor Hoffman	1.00	.30
19 Doug Bochtler	.25	.07
20 Chris Jones	.25	.07
21 Andy Ashby	.25	.07
22 Archi Cianfrocco	.25	.07
23 Tim Worrell	.25	.07
24 Will Cunnane	.25	.07
25 Carlos Hernandez	.25	.07
26 Tim Scott	.25	.07
27 Dario Veras	.25	.07
28 Greg Booker CO	.25	.07
Tim Flannery CO		
Davey Lopes CO		
Rob Picciolo CO		
Merv Rettenmund CO		
Dan Warthen CO CL		

1998 Padres Junior Hoffman

This 5" by 7" full-bleed blank-backed photo features star reliver Trevor Hoffman. In the upper left is a trademark for the "Junior Padres", with the sponsors, Sparkletts and The Sports Authority noted on the bottom. This was used as a premium for kids joining the "Junior Padres"

	Nm-Mt	Ex-Mt
1 Trevor Hoffman	3.00	.90

1998 Padres Mother's

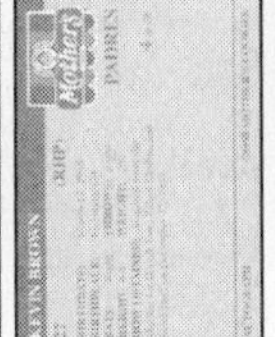

This 28-card set of the San Diego Padres sponsored by Mother's Cookies consists of posed color player photos with rounded corners.

	Nm-Mt	Ex-Mt
COMPLETE SET (28)	10.00	3.00
1 Bruce Bochy MG	.25	.07
2 Tony Gwynn	3.00	.90
3 Ken Caminiti	.50	.15
4 Kevin Brown	1.00	.30
5 Wally Joyner	.50	.15
6 Sterling Hitchcock	.25	.07
7 Greg Vaughn	.50	.15
8 Steve Finley	.75	.23
9 Joey Hamilton	.25	.07
10 Carlos Hernandez	.25	.07
11 Quilvio Veras	.25	.07
12 Trevor Hoffman	1.00	.30
13 Chris Gomez	.25	.07
14 Andy Ashby	.25	.07
15 Greg Myers	.25	.07
16 Mark Langston	.25	.07
17 Andy Sheets	.25	.07
18 Dan Miceli	.25	.07
19 James Mouton	.25	.07
20 Brian Boehringer	.25	.07
21 Archi Cianfrocco	.25	.07
22 Mark Sweeney	.25	.07
23 Pete Smith	.25	.07
24 Eddie Williams	.25	.07
25 Ed Giovanola	.25	.07
26 Carlos Reyes	.25	.07
27 Donne Wall	.25	.07
28 Greg Booker CO	.25	.07
Tim Flannery CO		
Davey Lopes CO		
Rob Picciolo CO		
Merv Rettenmund CO		
Dave Stewart CO CL		

1999 Padres Keebler

This 28 card standard-size set was designed by long time Mother Cookies card creator Wayne Bebb. However, for 1999, Mother's Cookies did not participate in a card promotion so this set was issued by Keebler. Similar to the Mothers promotions, a collector received 20 different cards and 8 same cards that he/she would have to trade to complete their set.

	Nm-Mt	Ex-Mt
COMPLETE SET (28)	10.00	3.00

1 Bruce Bochy MG	.25	.07
2 Tony Gwynn	2.50	.75
3 Wally Joyner	.50	.15
4 Sterling Hitchcock	.25	.07
5 Jim Leyritz	.25	.07
6 Trevor Hoffman	.75	.23
7 Quilvio Veras	.25	.07
8 Dave Magadan	.25	.07
9 Andy Ashby	.25	.07
10 Damian Jackson	.25	.07
11 Dan Miceli	.25	.07
12 Reggie Sanders	.50	.15
13 Chris Gomez	.25	.07
14 Ruben Rivera	.25	.07
15 Greg Myers	.25	.07
16 Ed Vosberg	.25	.07
17 John Vander Wal	.25	.07
18 Donne Wall	.25	.07
19 Eric Owens	.25	.07
20 Brian Boehringer	.25	.07
21 Woody Williams	.50	.15
22 Matt Clement	1.00	.30
23 Carlos Reyes	.25	.07
24 Stan Spencer	.25	.07
25 George Arias	.25	.07
26 Carlos Almanzar	.25	.07
27 Phil Nevin	1.00	.30
28 Greg Booker CO Tim Flannery CO Davey Lopes CO Rob Picciolo CO Merv Rettenmund CO Dave Smith CO CL	.25	.07

1999 Padres MADD

These slightly oversize cards feature both current members of the 1999 San Diego Padres as well as some of the leading players from the first 30 years of the Padres history. Since the cards are unnumbered, we have sequenced them in alphabetical order. Please note that a couple of players have cards in both Spanish and English.

	Nm-Mt	Ex-Mt
COMPLETE SET (23)	20.00	6.00
1 George Arias	1.00	.30
2 Andy Ashby	1.00	.30
3 Ben Davis	2.00	.60
4 Tim Flannery	1.00	.30
5 Steve Garvey	8.00	2.40
6 Chris Gomez	1.00	.30
7 Rich Gossage	3.00	.90
8 Tony Gwynn	8.00	2.40
9 Sterling Hitchcock	1.00	.30
10 Trevor Hoffman	2.00	.60
11 Damian Jackson	1.00	.30
12 Randy Jones	1.50	.45
13 Wally Joyner	1.50	.45
14 Jim Leyritz	1.00	.30
15 Phil Nevin	3.00	.90
16 Eric Owens	1.00	.30
17 Ruben Rivera Outfielder	1.00	.30
18 Ruben Rivera Jardinero	1.00	.30
19 Reggie Sanders	1.50	.45
20 John Vander Wal	1.00	.30
21 Quilvio Veras Second Base	1.00	.30
22 Quilvio Veras Base Segundo	1.00	.30
23 Dave Winfield	6.00	1.80

1999 Padres Postcards

These 4" by 6" postcards feature members of the San Diego Padres. The fronts have a full color player photo while the backs have the players name and position in bold across the top and then some information about him. Since the cards are unnumbered, we have sequenced them in alphabetical order

	Nm-Mt	Ex-Mt
COMPLETE SET	10.00	3.00
1 George Arias	.50	.15
2 Greg Booker CO	.50	.15
3 Matt Clement	1.50	.45
4 Mike Darr	.50	.15
5 Ben Davis	.75	.23
6 Chris Gomez	.50	.15
7 Damian Jackson	.50	.15
8 Jim Leyritz	.50	.15
9 Dave Magadan	.50	.15
10 Gary Matthews Jr.	.50	.15
11 Heath Murray	.50	.15
12 David Newhan	.50	.15
13 Phil Nevin	1.50	.45
14 Eric Owens	.50	.15
15 Ruben Rivera	.50	.15
16 Dave Smith CO	.50	.15
17 John Vander Wal	.50	.15
18 Woody Williams	.75	.23
19 San Diego Padres 1998 NL Champs	.50	.15
20 Logo Card	.50	.15

2000 Padres Keebler

This 28 card set was issued in conjunction with Keebler cookies and features members of the 2000 San Diego Padres. The borderless cards have the players photo over most of the front with the players' name, San Diego Padres team logo and position on the bottom. The back has the player vital statistic information

	Nm-Mt	Ex-Mt
COMPLETE SET (28)	10.00	3.00
1 Bruce Bochy MG	.25	.07
2 Tony Gwynn	2.00	.60
3 Ryan Klesko	.75	.23
4 Sterling Hitchcock	.25	.07
5 Al Martin	.25	.07
6 Trevor Hoffman	.75	.23
7 Bret Boone	.75	.23
8 Dave Magadan	.25	.07
9 Steve Montgomery	.25	.07
10 Damian Jackson	.25	.07
11 Woody Williams	.50	.15
12 Wiki Gonzalez	.25	.07
13 Chris Gomez	.25	.07
14 Ruben Rivera	.25	.07
15 Ed Sprague	.25	.07
16 Carlton Loewer	.25	.07
17 Kory DeHaan	.25	.07
18 Donne Wall	.25	.07
19 Eric Owens	.25	.07
20 Brian Boehringer	.25	.07
21 Phil Nevin	1.00	.30
22 Matt Clement	1.00	.30
23 Brian Meadows	.25	.07
24 Vicente Palacios	.25	.07
25 Carlos Hernandez	.25	.07
26 Carlos Almanzar	.25	.07
27 Kevin Walker	.25	.07
28 Greg Booker CO Tim Flannery CO Ben Oglivie CO Rob Picciolo CO Dave Smith CO Alan Trammell CO	.50	.15

2000 Padres MADD

These 15 oversize cards feature members of the 2000 San Diego Padres and have a player photo on the top along with a coupon for a free soda on the bottom. The backs have player biographical information, some information about MADD (Mothers against Drunk Driving) and information on how you can help fight drunk driving on the road. Since the cards are unnumbered, we have sequenced them in alphabetical order.

	Nm-Mt	Ex-Mt
COMPLETE SET (15)	30.00	9.00
1 Bret Boone	2.00	.60
2 Sean Burroughs	8.00	2.40
3 Buddy Carlyle	1.00	.30
4 Matt Clement	1.00	.30
5 Mike Darr	1.00	.30
6 Ben Davis	1.00	.30
7 Tony Gwynn	10.00	3.00
8 Carlos Hernandez	1.00	.30
9 Trevor Hoffman	2.00	.60
10 Ryan Klesko	3.00	.90
11 Al Martin	1.00	.30
12 Phil Nevin	3.00	.90
13 Eric Owens	1.00	.30
14 Ruben Rivera	1.00	.30
15 Woody Williams	1.50	.45

2000 Padres Postcards

These 4" by 6" postcards feature members of the 2000 San Diego Padres. The full-color fronts feature lots of attractive action shots. The backs feature the "Padres 2000" logo" on top with the players name and some information about that player. It is possible that these cards were a product giveaway "Sycunan". Since these cards are unnumbered, we have sequenced them in alphabetical order.

	Nm-Mt	Ex-Mt
COMPLETE SET	12.00	3.60
1 Carlos Almanzar	.50	.15
2 Bret Boone	1.00	.30
3 Ben Davis	.75	.23
4 Adam Eaton	1.00	.30
5 Todd Erdos	.50	.15
6 Duane Espy	.50	.15
7 Wiki Gonzalez	.50	.15
8 Trevor Hoffman	1.50	.45
9 Damian Jackson	.50	.15
10 Ryan Klesko	1.50	.45
11 Carlton Loewer	.50	.15
12 John Mabry	.50	.15
13 Steve Montgomery	.50	.15
14 Phil Nevin	1.50	.45
15 Kevin Nicholson	.50	.15
16 Eric Owens	.50	.15
17 Desi Relaford	.50	.15
18 Brian Tollberg	.50	.15
19 Joe Vitiello	.50	.15
20 Kevin Walker	.50	.15
21 Jay Witasick	.50	.15

2001 Padres Keebler

This 28 card standard-size set features the rounded corners which had been traditionally associated with Mother's Cookies sets. The packs were distributed at a game with 20 different cards and 8 dupes of the same player which were designed to encourage trading to finish one's sets.

	Nm-Mt	Ex-Mt
COMPLETE SET	10.00	3.00
1 Bruce Bochy MG	.25	.07
2 Tony Gwynn	2.00	.60
3 Trevor Hoffman	1.00	.30
4 Ryan Klesko	1.00	.30
5 Woody Williams	.50	.15
6 Chris Gomez	.25	.07
7 Ben Davis	.50	.15
8 Dave Magadan	.25	.07
9 Rickey Henderson	1.25	.35
10 Wiki Gonzalez	.25	.07
11 Bobby J. Jones	.25	.07
12 Damian Jackson	.25	.07
13 Kevin Jarvis	.25	.07
14 Bubba Trammell	.25	.07
15 Kevin Walker	.25	.07
16 Mark Kotsay	.75	.23
17 Alex Arias	.25	.07
18 Phil Nevin	1.00	.30
19 Jay Witasick	.25	.07
20 Mike Darr	.25	.07
21 Adam Eaton	.75	.23
22 Wascar Serrano	.25	.07
23 Jose Nunez	.25	.07
24 Brian Tolberg	.25	.07
25 Donaldo Mendez	.25	.07
26 Tom Davey	.25	.07
27 Rodney Myers	.25	.07
28 Greg Booker CO Duane Espy CO Tim Flannery CO Rob Picciolo CO Dave Smith CO Alan Trammell CO	.25	.07

2001 Padres MADD

If the coupon on the bottom is removed, these cards measure the standard-size. The front have the player photo along with their uniform number on the left and the player's name on the right. The bottom of the card is a coupon for a free soft-drink. The back has biographical information, drinking safety tips as well as various sponsor logos. Since these cards are unnumbered, we have sequenced them in alphabetical order.

	Nm-Mt	Ex-Mt
COMPLETE SET	25.00	7.50
1 Bruce Bochy MG	1.00	.30
2 Mike Darr	1.00	.30
3 Ben Davis	1.50	.45
4 Adam Eaton	1.50	.45
5 Chris Gomez	1.00	.30
6 Tony Gwynn	6.00	1.80
7 Sterling Hitchcock	1.00	.30
8 Trevor Hoffman	2.50	.75
9 Damian Jackson	1.00	.30
10 Bobby Jones	1.00	.30
11 Ryan Klesko	2.50	.75
12 Dave Magadan	1.00	.30
13 Phil Nevin	2.50	.75
14 Bubba Trammell	1.00	.30
15 Kevin Walker	1.00	.30
16 Woody Williams	1.50	.45
NNO Swinging Friar Mascot	1.00	.30

2001 Padres Postcards

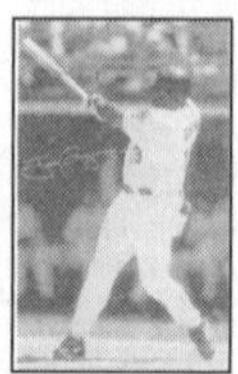

The 33-card set is 4"x6" with colored photos. The Gwynn card and Bochy cards have facsimile autographs. The cards are unnumbered and listed below in alphabetical order. The backs have the player's name, number and position, plus a short bio with the Padres' logo in the corner. Postage box and Krispy Kreme Donut logo in the lower left-hand corner.

	Nm-Mt	Ex-Mt
COMPLET SET (32)	20.00	6.00
1 Alex Arias	.50	.15
2 Bruce Bochy MG	.50	.15
3 Greg Booker CO	.50	.15
4 Mike Colangelo	.50	.15
5 Ben Davis	.50	.15
6 Mike Darr	.50	.15
7 Tom Davey	.50	.15
8 Adam Eaton	1.00	.30
9 Duane Espy CO	.50	.15
10 Tim Flannery CO	.50	.15
11 Wiki Gonzalez	.50	.15
12 Tony Gwynn	4.00	1.20
13 Rickey Henderson	3.00	.90
14 Trevor Hoffman	1.50	.45
15 Damian Jackson	.50	.15
16 Kevin Jarvis	.50	.15
17 Bobby Jones	.50	.15
18 Ryan Klesko	1.50	.45
19 Mark Kotsay	1.00	.30
20 Carlton Loewer	.50	.15
21 Dave Magadan	.50	.15
22 Donaldo Mendez	.50	.15
23 Mark Merila CO	.50	.15
24 Rodney Myers	.50	.15
25 Phil Nevin	1.50	.45
26 Santiago Perez	.50	.15
27 Rob Picciolo CO	.50	.15
28 Brian Tollberg	.50	.15
29 Alan Trammell CO	.75	.23
30 Kevin Walker	.50	.15
31 Woody Williams	.75	.23
32 Jay Witasick	.50	.15

2002 Padres Hall of Fame Upper Deck

This one card set, which measures approximately 7" by 5" features the five people who have played for the San Diego Padres who are in the Hall of Fame. This card was given away to attendees of the June 20, 2002 game. Ozzie Smith is featured in the middle of the card with the other four players surrounding him. This card was produced for the Padres by Upper Deck.

	Nm-Mt	Ex-Mt
1 Ozzie Smith Gaylord Perry Dave Winfield Willie McCovey Rollie Fingers	5.00	1.50

2002 Padres Keebler

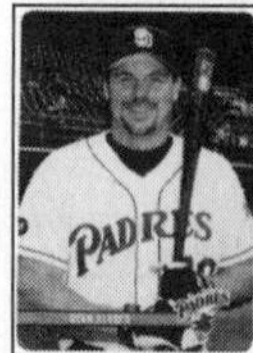
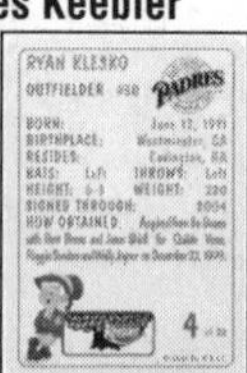

This 28 card standard-size set features members of the 2002 San Diego Padres has rounded corners and was issued in conjuction with Keebler foods. The front of the borderless cards have a player photo with the bottom devoted to the player's name, The Padres logo and the player's position. The back has vital stats.

	Nm-Mt	Ex-Mt
1 Bruce Bochy MG	.25	.07
2 Trevor Hoffman	1.00	.30
3 Sean Burroughs	.75	.23
4 Ryan Klesko	1.00	.30
5 Phil Nevin	.50	.15
6 Kevin Jarvis	.25	.07
7 Ron Gant	.50	.15
8 Ramon Vazquez	.25	.07
9 Alan Embree	.25	.07
10 Wiki Gonzalez	.25	.07
11 Bobby J. Jones	.25	.07
12 Mark Kotsay	.75	.23
13 Brett Tomko	.25	.07
14 Bubba Trammell	.25	.07
15 Tom Lampkin	.25	.07
16 Steve Reed	.25	.07
17 Deivi Cruz	.25	.07
18 Brian Tollberg	.25	.07
19 Trenidad Hubbard	.25	.07
20 Jose Nunez	.25	.07
21 Ray Lankford	.50	.15
22 Kevin Walker	.25	.07
23 Dennis Tankersley	1.00	.30
24 Jeremy Fikac	.25	.07
25 D'Angelo Jimenez	.75	.23
26 Brian Lawrence	.25	.07
27 Adam Eaton	.75	.23
28 Darrel Akerfelds CO Greg Booker CO Duane Espy CO Tim Flannery CO Rob Picciolo CO Alan Trammell CO	.25	.07

2003 Padres Carl's Jr.

This 13 card standard-size set features some of the best players to don a Padres uniform. These cards were issued in various designs depending on when in the team's history the player was in San Diego. The backs feature only

stats from when that player was in San Diego. Since these cards are unnumbered, we have sequenced them in alphabetical order.

	MINT	NRMT
COMPLETE SET	10.00	4.50
1 Roberto Alomar	1.00	.45
2 Bruce Bochy MG	.25	.11
3 Kevin Brown	.75	.35
4 Ken Caminiti	.50	.23
5 Steve Finley	1.00	.45
6 Steve Garvey	1.00	.45
7 Tony Gwynn	2.00	.90
8 Trevor Hoffman	1.00	.45
9 Randy Jones	.25	.11
10 Gaylord Perry	1.00	.45
11 Benito Santiago	.50	.23
12 Ozzie Smith	1.50	.70
13 Dave Winfield	1.50	.70

2003 Padres Keebler

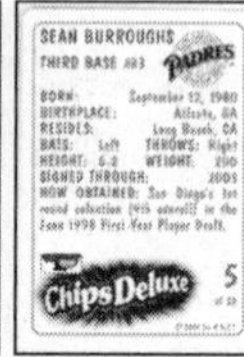

This 28 card standard-size set with rounded corners features members of the 2003 San Diego Padres. These cards were given away at a Dodgers game with each fan receiving 20 different cards and eight of the same card they could trade to finish the set.

	MINT	NRMT
1 Bruce Bochy MG	.25	.11
2 Trevor Hoffman	.75	.35
3 Sean Burroughs	1.00	.45
4 Ryan Klesko	.75	.35
5 Phil Nevin	.75	.35
6 Mark Kotsay	.75	.35
7 Rondell White	.50	.23
8 Brian Lawrence	.25	.11
9 Ramon Vazquez	.25	.11
10 Dave Hansen	.25	.11
11 Kevin Jarvis	.25	.11
12 Jaret Wright	.25	.11
13 Gary Bennett	.25	.11
14 Brandon Villafuerte	.25	.11
15 Lou Merloni	.25	.11
16 Jesse Orosco	.50	.23
17 Kevin Walker	.25	.11
18 Adam Eaton	.50	.23
19 Keith Lockhart	.25	.11
20 Mark Loretta	.25	.11
21 Xavier Nady	.75	.35
22 Jake Peavy	.50	.23
23 Mike Mathews	.25	.11
24 Brian Buchanan	.25	.11
25 Luther Hackman	.25	.11
26 Matt Herges	.25	.11
27 Jay Witasick	.25	.11
28 Darren Balsley CO Dave Lopes CO Dave Magadan CO Rob Picciolo CO Darrell Akerfelds CO Mark Merila CO Tony Muser Co	.25	.11

1996 Paige NoirTech

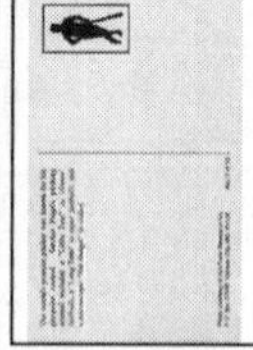

This 12-card set measures approximately 3 1/2" by 5 1/2" and features black-and-white photos of Satchel Paige. The backs carry discriptions of the front pictures in a postcard format.

	Nm-Mt	Ex-Mt
COMPLETE SET (12)	7.50	2.20
COMMON CARD (1-12)	.50	.15
1 Satchel Paige Josh Gibson Cy Perkins	2.00	.60
2 Satchel Paige All-Stars	.75	.23
3 Satchel Paige Dizzy Dean Cecil Travis	1.00	.30
10 Satchel Paige Billie Holiday	1.50	.45
12 Satchel Paige Vernon Gomez	1.00	.30

2003 Palmeiro Donruss 500 Homer

This 5" by 7" one-card set was given away at the June 21st Texas Rangers game as part of the celebrations about Rafael Palmeiro's 500th career homer. The front has a photo of Palmeiro along with the 500 homer logo at the bottom and the Donruss 2003 logo in the upper

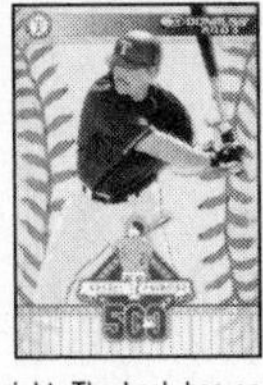

right. The back has another photo of Palmeiro along with biographical inforrmation, a long blurb and a chronological listing of the members of the 500 homer club.

	Nm-Mt	Ex-Mt
1 Rafael Palmeiro	5.00	1.50

2002 Palmeiro Viagra

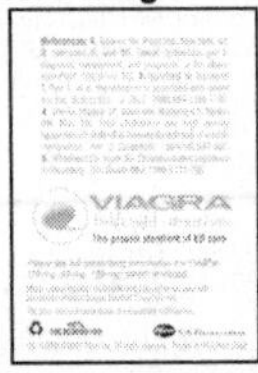

This three-card standard-size set features Rafael Palmeiro who is an official spokesman for Viagra. This set has photos of Palmeiro on the front and information about Viagra on the back.

	Nm-Mt	Ex-Mt
COMPLETE SET	5.00	1.50
1 Rafael Palmeiro Portrait	2.00	.60
2 Rafael Palmeiro Batting Pose	2.00	.60
3 Rafael Palmeiro Shows Palmeiro's Back	1.00	.30

1988 Palmer Healthfest

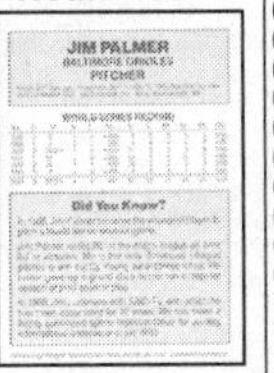

This one card standard-size set feature retired Oriole great Jim Palmer. The front has a full color photo of Palmer surrounded by blue borders. The bottom part of the card mentions the sponsor "Sentars Leigh Hospital" and this card was given out at Healthfest 88. The back has vital stats, World Series stats and some facts about Palmer.

	Nm-Mt	Ex-Mt
1 Jim Palmer	5.00	2.00

1988 Panini Stickers

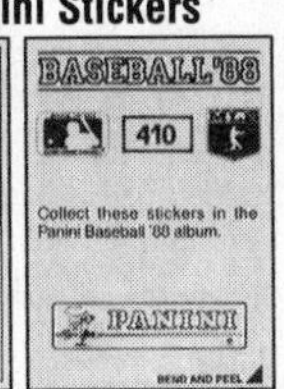

These 480 stickers measure approximately 1 15/16" by 2 11/16" (regular) and 2 1/8" by 2 11/16" (foils). There are 80 foil stickers in the set; these foils are essentially the non-player stickers. A 64-page album onto which the stickers could be affixed was available at retail stores (for 59 cents) and was also given away to Little Leaguers as part of a national promotion. The album features Don Mattingly on the front and a photo of a gold glove on the back. The album and the sticker numbering are organized alphabetically by team with AL teams preceding NL teams. The last 26 stickers in the album are actually lettered rather than numbered but are listed below as numbers 455-480. The stickers were also sold at retail outlets packed with the album as a "Complete Collectors Set." The 1988 Panini Sticker set was heavily promoted as Panini entered the baseball sticker market under its own label after producing Topps' stickers for the previous seven years.

	Nm-Mt	Ex-Mt
COMPLETE SET (480)	40.00	16.00
1 1987 WS Trophy	.05	.02
2 Orioles Emblem	.05	.02
3 Orioles Uniform	.05	.02
4 Eric Bell	.05	.02
5 Mike Boddicker	.05	.02
6 Dave Schmidt	.05	.02
7 Terry Kennedy	.05	.02
8 Eddie Murray	1.00	.40
9 Bill Ripken	.05	.02
10 Orioles TL (Action photo)	.05	.02
11 Orioles W-L Breakdown Cal Ripken IA	1.50	.60
12 Ray Knight	.05	.02
13 Cal Ripken	4.00	1.60
14 Ken Gerhart	.05	.02
15 Fred Lynn	.15	.06
16 Larry Sheets	.05	.02
17 Mike Young	.05	.02
18 Red Sox Emblem	.05	.02
19 Red Sox Uniform	.05	.02
20 Oil Can Boyd	.05	.02
21 Roger Clemens	2.00	.80
22 Bruce Hurst	.05	.02
23 Bob Stanley	.05	.02
24 Rich Gedman	.05	.02
25 Dwight Evans	.15	.06
26 Red Sox TL (Action photo)	.05	.02
27 Red Sox W-L Breakdown (Action photo)	.05	.02
28 Marty Barrett	.05	.02
29 Wade Boggs	1.00	.40
30 Spike Owen	.05	.02
31 Ellis Burks	1.00	.40
32 Mike Greenwell	.05	.02
33 Jim Rice	.15	.06
34 Angels Emblem	.05	.02
35 Angels Uniform	.05	.02
36 Kirk McCaskill	.05	.02
37 Don Sutton	.50	.20
38 Mike Witt	.05	.02
39 Bob Boone	.15	.06
40 Wally Joyner	.15	.06
41 Mark McLemore	.25	.10
42 Angels TL (Action photo)	.05	.02
43 Angels W-L Breakdown Devon White IA	.15	.06
44 Jack Howell	.05	.02
45 Dick Schofield	.05	.02
46 Brian Downing	.15	.06
47 Ruppert Jones	.05	.02
48 Gary Pettis	.05	.02
49 Devon White	.15	.06
50 White Sox Emblem	.05	.02
51 White Sox Uniform	.05	.02
52 Floyd Bannister	.05	.02
53 Richard Dotson	.05	.02
54 Bob James	.05	.02
55 Carlton Fisk	.50	.20
56 Greg Walker	.05	.02
57 Fred Manrique	.05	.02
58 White Sox TL (Action photo)	.05	.02
59 White Sox W-L Breakdown (Action photo)	.05	.02
60 Steve Lyons	.15	.06
61 Ozzie Guillen	.15	.06
62 Harold Baines	.25	.10
63 Ivan Calderon	.05	.02
64 Gary Redus	.05	.02
65 Ken Williams	.25	.10
66 Indians Emblem	.05	.02
67 Indians Uniform	.05	.02
68 Scott Bailes	.05	.02
69 Tom Candiotti	.05	.02
70 Greg Swindell	.05	.02
71 Chris Bando	.05	.02
72 Joe Carter	.40	.16
73 Tommy Hinzo	.05	.02
74 Indians TL (Action photo)	.05	.02
75 Indians W-L Breakdown Juan Bonilla IA	.05	.02
76 Brook Jacoby	.05	.02
77 Julio Franco	.15	.06
78 Brett Butler	.15	.06
79 Mel Hall	.05	.02
80 Cory Snyder	.05	.02
81 Pat Tabler	.05	.02
82 Tigers Emblem	.05	.02
83 Tigers Uniform	.05	.02
84 Willie Hernandez	.05	.02
85 Jack Morris	.15	.06
86 Frank Tanana	.05	.02
87 Walt Terrell	.05	.02
88 Matt Nokes	.05	.02
89 Darrell Evans	.15	.06
90 Tigers TL Darrell Evans IA	.15	.06
91 Tigers W-L Breakdown Carlton Fisk IA	.25	.10
92 Lou Whitaker	.15	.06
93 Tom Brookens	.05	.02
94 Alan Trammell	.25	.10
95 Kirk Gibson	.15	.06
96 Chet Lemon	.05	.02
97 Pat Sheridan	.05	.02
98 Royals Emblem	.05	.02
99 Royals Uniform	.05	.02
100 Charlie Leibrandt	.05	.02
101 Dan Quisenberry	.05	.02
102 Bret Saberhagen	.15	.06
103 Jamie Quirk	.05	.02
104 George Brett	2.00	.80
105 Frank White	.15	.06
106 Royals TL Bret Saberhagen IA	.15	.06
107 Royals W-L Breakdown Bret Saberhagen IA	.15	.06
108 Kevin Seitzer	.15	.06
109 Angel Salazar	.05	.02
110 Bo Jackson	.75	.30
111 Lonnie Smith	.05	.02
112 Danny Tartabull	.05	.02
113 Willie Wilson	.05	.02
114 Brewers Emblem	.05	.02
115 Brewers Uniform	.05	.02
116 Ted Higuera	.05	.02
117 Juan Nieves	.05	.02
118 Dan Plesac	.05	.02
119 Bill Wegman	.05	.02
120 B.J. Surhoff	.25	.10
121 Greg Brock	.05	.02
122 Brewers TL Lou Whitaker IA	.15	.06
123 Brewers W-L Breakdown Jim Gantner IA	.05	.02
124 Jim Gantner	.05	.02
125 Paul Molitor	.60	.24
126 Dale Sveum	.05	.02
127 Glenn Braggs	.05	.02
128 Rob Deer	.05	.02
129 Robin Yount	.50	.20
130 Twins Emblem	.05	.02
131 Twins Uniform	.05	.02
132 Bert Blyleven	.15	.06
133 Jeff Reardon	.15	.06
134 Frank Viola	.15	.06
135 Tim Laudner	.05	.02
136 Kent Hrbek	.15	.06
137 Steve Lombardozzi	.05	.02
138 Twins TL (Action photo)	.05	.02
139 Twins W-L Breakdown (Action photo)	.05	.02
140 Gary Gaetti	.15	.06
141 Greg Gagne	.05	.02
142 Tom Brunansky	.05	.02
143 Dan Gladden	.05	.02
144 Kirby Puckett	.75	.30
145 Gene Larkin	.15	.06
146 Team Emblem New York Yankees	.05	.02
147 Team Uniform New York Yankees	.05	.02
148 Tommy John	.15	.06
149 Rick Rhoden	.05	.02
150 Dave Righetti	.15	.06
151 Rick Cerone	.05	.02
152 Don Mattingly	2.00	.80
153 Willie Randolph	.15	.06
154 1987 Team Leaders Scott Fletcher IA	.05	.02
155 1987 W-L Breakdown Don Mattingly IA	.75	.30
156 Mike Pagliarulo	.05	.02
157 Wayne Tolleson	.05	.02
158 Rickey Henderson	1.00	.40
159 Dan Pasqua	.05	.02
160 Gary Ward	.05	.02
161 Dave Winfield	.50	.20
162 Team Emblem Oakland A's	.05	.02
163 Team Uniform Oakland A's	.05	.02
164 Dave Stewart	.15	.06
165 Curt Young	.05	.02
166 Terry Steinbach	.05	.02
167 Mark McGwire	3.00	1.20
168 Tony Phillips	.05	.02
169 Carney Lansford	.15	.06
170 1987 Team Leaders (Action photo)	.05	.02
171 1987 W-L Breakdown (Action photo)	.05	.02
172 Alfredo Griffin	.05	.02
173 Jose Canseco	.50	.20
174 Mike Davis	.05	.02
175 Reggie Jackson	.75	.30
176 Dwayne Murphy	.05	.02
177 Luis Polonia	.05	.02
178 Team Emblem Seattle Mariners	.05	.02
179 Team Uniform Seattle Mariners	.05	.02
180 Scott Bankhead	.05	.02
181 Mark Langston	.05	.02
182 Edwin Nunez	.05	.02
183 Scott Bradley	.05	.02
184 Dave Valle	.05	.02
185 Alvin Davis	.05	.02
186 1987 Team Leaders Rey Quinones IA	.05	.02
187 1987 W-L Breakdown Jack Howell IA	.05	.02
188 Harold Reynolds	.15	.06
189 Jim Presley	.05	.02
190 Rey Quinones	.05	.02
191 Phil Bradley	.05	.02
192 Mickey Brantley	.05	.02
193 Mike Kingery	.05	.02
194 Team Emblem Texas Rangers	.05	.02
195 Team Uniform Texas Rangers	.05	.02
196 Edwin Correa	.05	.02
197 Charlie Hough	.15	.06
198 Bobby Witt	.05	.02
199 Mike Stanley	.05	.02
200 Pete O'Brien	.05	.02
201 Jerry Browne	.05	.02
202 1987 Team Leaders (Action photo)	.05	.02
203 1987 W-L Breakdown Steve Buechele and Eddie Murray IA	.40	.16
204 Steve Buechele	.05	.02
205 Larry Parrish	.05	.02
206 Scott Fletcher	.05	.02
207 Pete Incaviglia	.05	.02
208 Oddibe McDowell	.05	.02
209 Ruben Sierra	.15	.06
210 Team Emblem Toronto Blue Jays	.05	.02
211 Team Uniform Toronto Blue Jays	.05	.02
212 Mark Eichhorn	.05	.02
213 Tom Henke	.05	.02
214 Jimmy Key	.15	.06
215 Dave Stieb	.05	.02
216 Ernie Whitt	.05	.02
217 Willie Upshaw	.05	.02
218 1987 Team Leaders Willie Upshaw IA	.05	.02
219 1987 W-L Breakdown Harold Reynolds IA	.05	.02
220 Garth Iorg	.05	.02
221 Kelly Gruber	.05	.02
222 Tony Fernandez	.15	.06
223 Jesse Barfield	.05	.02
224 George Bell	.05	.02
225 Lloyd Moseby	.05	.02
226A AL Logo	.05	.02
226B NL Logo	.05	.02
227 Terry Kennedy and Don Mattingly	.75	.30
228 Willie Randolph and Wade Boggs	.40	.16
229 Bret Saberhagen	.15	.06
230 Cal Ripken and George Bell	2.00	.80
231 Rickey Henderson and Dave Winfield	.40	.16
232 Gary Carter and Jack Clark	.15	.06
233 Mike Scott	.05	.02
234 Ryne Sandberg and Mike Schmidt	.75	.30
235 Ozzie Smith and Eric Davis	.40	.16
236 Andre Dawson and Darryl Strawberry	.15	.06
237 Team Emblem Atlanta Braves	.05	.02
238 Team Uniform Atlanta Braves	.05	.02
239 Rick Mahler	.05	.02
240 Zane Smith	.05	.02
241 Ozzie Virgil	.05	.02
242 Gerald Perry	.05	.02
243 Glenn Hubbard	.05	.02
244 Ken Oberkfell	.05	.02
245 1987 Team Leaders (Action photo)	.05	.02
246 1987 W-L Breakdown Jeffrey Leonard IA	.05	.02
247 Rafael Ramirez	.05	.02
248 Ken Griffey	.15	.06
249 Albert Hall	.05	.02
250 Dion James	.05	.02
251 Dale Murphy	.40	.16
252 Gary Roenicke	.05	.02
253 Team Emblem Chicago Cubs	.05	.02
254 Team Uniform Chicago Cubs	.05	.02
255 Jamie Moyer	.40	.16
256 Lee Smith	.15	.06
257 Rick Sutcliffe	.15	.06
258 Jody Davis	.05	.02
259 Leon Durham	.05	.02
260 Ryne Sandberg	1.00	.40
261 1987 Team Leaders (Action photo)	.05	.02
262 1987 W-L Breakdown Jody Davis IA	.05	.02
263 Keith Moreland	.05	.02
264 Shawon Dunston	.05	.02
265 Andre Dawson	.40	.16
266 Dave Martinez	.05	.02
267 Jerry Mumphrey	.05	.02
268 Rafael Palmeiro	1.00	.40
269 Team Emblem Cincinnati Reds	.05	.02
270 Team Uniform Cincinnati Reds	.05	.02
271 John Franco	.15	.06
272 Ted Power	.05	.02
273 Bo Diaz	.05	.02
274 Nick Esasky	.05	.02
275 Dave Concepcion	.15	.06
276 Kurt Stillwell	.05	.02
277 1987 Team Leaders Dave Parker IA	.15	.06
278 1987 W-L Breakdown (Action photo)	.05	.02
279 Buddy Bell	.15	.06
280 Barry Larkin	1.00	.40
281 Kal Daniels	.05	.02
282 Eric Davis	.15	.06
283 Tracy Jones	.05	.02
284 Dave Parker	.15	.06
285 Team Emblem Houston Astros	.05	.02
286 Team Uniform Houston Astros	.05	.02
287 Jim Deshaies	.05	.02
288 Nolan Ryan	4.00	1.60
289 Mike Scott	.05	.02
290 Dave Smith	.05	.02
291 Alan Ashby	.05	.02
292 Glenn Davis	.05	.02
293 1987 Team Leaders (Action photo)	.05	.02
294 1987 W-L Breakdown (Action photo)	.05	.02
295 Bill Doran	.05	.02
296 Denny Walling	.05	.02
297 Craig Reynolds	.05	.02
298 Kevin Bass	.05	.02
299 Jose Cruz	.15	.06
300 Billy Hatcher	.05	.02
301 Team Emblem Los Angeles Dodgers	.05	.02
302 Team Uniform Los Angeles Dodgers	.05	.02
303 Orel Hershiser	.15	.06
304 Fernando Valenzuela	.15	.06
305 Bob Welch	.05	.02
306 Matt Young	.05	.02
307 Mike Scioscia	.15	.06
308 Franklin Stubbs	.05	.02
309 1987 Team Leaders (Action photo)	.05	.02
310 1987 W-L Breakdown (Action photo)	.05	.02
311 Steve Sax	.15	.06
312 Jeff Hamilton	.05	.02
313 Dave Anderson	.05	.02
314 Pedro Guerrero	.15	.06
315 Mike Marshall	.05	.02
316 John Shelby	.05	.02
317 Team Emblem Montreal Expos	.05	.02
318 Team Uniform Montreal Expos	.05	.02
319 Neal Heaton	.05	.02
320 Bryn Smith	.05	.02
321 Floyd Youmans	.05	.02
322 Mike Fitzgerald	.05	.02
323 Andres Galarraga	.40	.16
324 Vance Law	.05	.02
325 1987 Team Leaders Tim Raines IA	.15	.06
326 1987 W-L Breakdown John Kruk IA	.15	.06
327 Tim Wallach	.05	.02
328 Hubie Brooks	.05	.02
329 Casey Candaele	.05	.02
330 Tim Raines	.25	.10
331 Mitch Webster	.05	.02
332 Herm Winningham	.05	.02
333 Team Emblem New York Mets	.05	.02
334 Team Uniform New York Mets	.05	.02
335 Ron Darling	.05	.02
336 Sid Fernandez	.05	.02
337 Dwight Gooden	.15	.06
338 Gary Carter	.50	.20
339 Keith Hernandez	.15	.06
340 Wally Backman	.05	.02
341 1987 Team Leaders Junior Ortiz IA	.05	.02
342 1987 W-L Breakdown Mookie Wilson Darryl Strawberry Tim Teufel IA	.15	.06
343 Howard Johnson	.05	.02
344 Rafael Santana	.05	.02
345 Lenny Dykstra	.15	.06
346 Kevin McReynolds	.05	.02
347 Darryl Strawberry	.15	.06
348 Mookie Wilson	.15	.06
349 Team Emblem Philadelphia Phillies	.05	.02
350 Team Uniform Philadelphia Phillies	.05	.02
351 Steve Bedrosian	.05	.02
352 Shane Rawley	.05	.02
353 Bruce Ruffin	.05	.02
354 Kent Tekulve	.05	.02
355 Lance Parrish	.15	.06
356 Von Hayes	.05	.02
357 1987 Team Leaders (Action photo)	.05	.02
358 1987 W-L Breakdown Glenn Wilson IA	.05	.02
359 Juan Samuel	.05	.02
360 Mike Schmidt	1.00	.40
361 Steve Jeltz	.05	.02
362 Chris James	.05	.02
363 Milt Thompson	.05	.02
364 Glenn Wilson	.05	.02
365 Team Emblem Pittsburgh Pirates	.05	.02
366 Team Uniform Pittsburgh Pirates	.05	.02
367 Mike Dunne	.05	.02
368 Brian Fisher	.05	.02
369 Mike LaValliere	.05	.02
370 Sid Bream	.05	.02
371 Jose Lind	.05	.02
372 Bobby Bonilla	.15	.06
373 1987 Team Leaders Bobby Bonilla IA	.15	.06
374 1987 W-L Breakdown (Action photo)	.05	.02
375 Al Pedrique	.05	.02
376 Barry Bonds	2.00	.80
377 John Cangelosi	.05	.02
378 Mike Diaz	.05	.02
379 R.J. Reynolds	.05	.02
380 Andy Van Slyke	.15	.06
381 Team Emblem St. Louis Cardinals	.05	.02
382 Team Uniform St. Louis Cardinals	.05	.02
383 Danny Cox	.05	.02
384 Bob Forsch	.05	.02
385 Joe Magrane	.05	.02
386 Todd Worrell	.15	.06
387 Tony Pena	.15	.06
388 Jack Clark	.15	.06
389 1987 Team Leaders Tommy Herr IA	.05	.02
390 1987 W-L Breakdown (Action photo)	.05	.02
391 Tom Herr	.05	.02
392 Terry Pendleton	.15	.06
393 Ozzie Smith	1.00	.40
394 Vince Coleman	.05	.02
395 Curt Ford	.05	.02
396 Willie McGee	.15	.06
397 Team Emblem San Diego Padres	.05	.02
398 Team Uniform San Diego Padres	.05	.02
399 Lance McCullers	.05	.02
400 Eric Show	.05	.02
401 Ed Whitson	.05	.02
402 Benito Santiago	.15	.06
403 John Kruk	.15	.06
404 Tim Flannery	.05	.02
405 1987 Team Leaders Benito Santiago IA	.05	.02
406 1987 W-L Breakdown (Action photo)	.05	.02
407 Randy Ready	.05	.02
408 Chris Brown	.05	.02
409 Garry Templeton	.05	.02
410 Tony Gwynn	1.50	.60
411 Stan Jefferson	.05	.02
412 Carmelo Martinez	.05	.02
413 Team Emblem San Francisco Giants	.05	.02
414 Team Uniform San Francisco Giants	.05	.02
415 Kelly Downs	.05	.02
416 Scott Garrelts	.05	.02
417 Mike Krukow	.05	.02
418 Mike LaCoss	.05	.02
419 Bob Brenly	.15	.06
420 Will Clark	1.00	.40
421 1987 Team Leaders Will Clark IA	.25	.10
422 1987 W-L Breakdown (Action photo)	.05	.02
423 Robby Thompson	.15	.06
424 Kevin Mitchell	.15	.06
425 Jose Uribe	.05	.02
426 Mike Aldrete	.05	.02
427 Jeffrey Leonard	.05	.02
428 Candy Maldonado	.05	.02
429 Mike Schmidt	1.00	.40
430 Don Mattingly	2.00	.80
431 Juan Nieves	.05	.02
432 Paul Molitor	.75	.30
433 Benito Santiago	.05	.02
434 Rickey Henderson	.40	.16
435 Nolan Ryan	4.00	1.60
436 Kevin Seitzer	.15	.06
437 Tony Gwynn	1.50	.60
438 Mark McGwire	4.00	1.60
439 Howard Johnson (switch-hitting)	.05	.02

440 Steve Bedrosian .05 .02
441 Darrell Evans .15 .06
442 Eddie Murray 1.00 .40
(switch-hitting)
443 Lou Whitaker IA .15 .06
444 Kirby Puckett and .50 .20
Alan Trammell IA
445 Gary Gaetti .15 .06
446 Jeffrey Leonard .05 .02
447 Tony Pena IA .05 .02
448 Kevin Mitchell IA .15 .06
449 Tony Pena IA .05 .02
450 Randy Bush IA .05 .02
451 Minnesota Twins UL .05 .02
(celebrating)
452 Minnesota Twins UR .05 .02
(celebrating)
453 Minnesota Twins LL .05 .02
(celebrating)
454 Minnesota Twins LR .05 .02
(celebrating)
455 Baltimore Orioles A .05 .02
Pennant and Logo
456 Boston Red Sox B .05 .02
Pennant and Logo
457 California Angels C .05 .02
Pennant and Logo
458 Chicago White Sox D .05 .02
Pennant and Logo
459 Cleveland Indians E .05 .02
Pennant and Logo
460 Detroit Tigers F .05 .02
Pennant and Logo
461 Kansas City Royals G .05 .02
Pennant and Logo
462 Milwaukee Brewers H .05 .02
Pennant and Logo
463 Minnesota Twins I .05 .02
Pennant and Logo
464 New York Yankees J .05 .02
Pennant and Logo
465 Oakland A's K .05 .02
Pennant and Logo
466 Seattle Mariners L .05 .02
Pennant and Logo
467 Texas Rangers M .05 .02
Pennant and Logo
468 Toronto Blue Jays N .05 .02
Pennant and Logo
469 Atlanta Braves O .05 .02
Pennant and Logo
470 Chicago Cubs P .05 .02
Pennant and Logo
471 Cincinnati Reds Q .05 .02
Pennant and Logo
472 Houston Astros R .05 .02
Pennant and Logo
473 Los Angeles Dodgers S .05 .02
Pennant and Logo
474 Montreal Expos T .05 .02
Pennant and Logo
475 New York Mets U .05 .02
Pennant and Logo
476 Phila. Phillies W .05 .02
Pennant and Logo
477 Pittsburgh Pirates W .05 .02
Pennant and Logo
478 St. Louis Cardinals X .05 .02
Pennant and Logo
479 San Diego Padres Y .05 .02
Pennant and Logo
480 San Fran. Giants Z .05 .02
Pennant and Logo
xx Sticker Album 1.00 .40
Don Mattingly on front

1989 Panini Stickers

These 480 stickers measure approximately 1 7/8" by 2 11/16" and feature white-bordered color player action shots. Sticker packets contained six stickers (five paper, one foil) and sold for 30 cents. The set includes 80 foil stickers; the first two stickers are foil, then each of the 26 teams has three foils out of its full complement of 16 stickers. An album onto which the stickers could be affixed was available at retail stores. The album featured Jose Canseco on the front cover and an ad for Oscar Mayer on the back. The stickers are organized alphabetically by city with NL teams preceding AL teams. The following subsets are also included: 1988 World Series Trophy (Foil, 1-2), 1988 Highlights (3-9), 1988 League Championship Series (10-15), 1988 World Series (16-29), 1988 NL Stat Leaders (222-226), 1988 All-Stars (227-244), 1988 AL Stat Leaders (245-249) and 1988 Award Winners (474-480). A rookie year sticker of Randy Johnson is a highlight of this set.

Nm-Mt Ex-Mt
COMPLETE SET (480) 20.00 8.00
1 World Series Trophy .05 .02
2 World Series Trophy .05 .02
3 Mike Schmidt .50 .20
4 Tom Browning .05 .02
5 Doug Jones .05 .02
6 Wrigley Field .05 .02
7 Wade Boggs .50 .20
8 Jose Canseco .50 .20
9 Orel Hershiser .10 .04
10 Oakland wins ALCS .05 .02
11 Oakland wins ALCS .05 .02
12 Dennis Eckersley ALCS .10 .04
13 Orel Hershiser NLCS .10 .04
14 Dodgers win NLCS .05 .02
15 Dodgers win NLCS .05 .02
16 Kirk Gibson .10 .04
17 Kirk Gibson .10 .04
18 Orel Hershiser .10 .04
19 Orel Hershiser .10 .04
20 Mark McGwire 2.50 1.00
21 Tim Belcher .05 .02
22 Jay Howell .05 .02
23 Mickey Hatcher .05 .02
24 Mike Davis .05 .02
25 Orel Hershiser WS MVP .10 .04
26 Dodgers win AS .05 .02
27 Dodgers win AS .05 .02
28 Dodgers win AS .05 .02
29 Dodgers win AS .05 .02
30 Atlanta team logo .05 .02
31 Jose Alvarez .05 .02
32 Tommy Gregg .05 .02
33 Paul Assenmacher .05 .02
34 Tom Glavine .75 .30
35 Rick Mahler .05 .02
36 Pete Smith .05 .02
37 Atlanta-Fulton County .05 .02
Stadium
38 Atlanta team .05 .02
lettering
39 Bruce Sutter .10 .04
40 Gerald Perry .05 .02
41 Jeff Blauser .05 .02
42 Ron Gant .30 .12
43 Andres Thomas .05 .02
44 Dion James .05 .02
45 Dale Murphy .30 .12
46 Cubs team logo .05 .02
47 Doug Dascenzo .05 .02
48 Mike Harkey .05 .02
49 Greg Maddux 2.00 .80
50 Jeff Pico .05 .02
51 Rick Sutcliffe .10 .04
52 Damon Berryhill .05 .02
53 Wrigley Field .05 .02
54 Cubs lettering .05 .02
55 Mark Grace 1.00 .40
56 Ryne Sandberg 1.00 .40
57 Vance Law .05 .02
58 Shawon Dunston .05 .02
59 Andre Dawson .30 .12
60 Rafael Palmeiro .50 .20
61 Mitch Webster .05 .02
62 Reds team logo .05 .02
63 Jack Armstrong .05 .02
64 Chris Sabo .05 .02
65 Tom Browning .05 .02
66 John Franco .10 .04
67 Danny Jackson .05 .02
68 Jose Rijo .05 .02
69 Riverfront Stadium .05 .02
70 Reds team lettering .05 .02
71 Bo Diaz .05 .02
72 Nick Esasky .05 .02
73 Jeff Treadway .05 .02
74 Barry Larkin .50 .20
75 Kal Daniels .05 .02
76 Eric Davis .10 .04
77 Paul O'Neill .20 .08
78 Astros team logo .05 .02
79 Craig Biggio 1.00 .40
80 John Fishel .05 .02
81 Juan Agosto .05 .02
82 Bob Knepper .05 .02
83 Nolan Ryan 3.00 1.20
84 Mike Scott .05 .02
85 The Astrodome .05 .02
86 Astros team lettering .05 .02
87 Dave Smith .05 .02
88 Glenn Davis .05 .02
89 Bill Doran .05 .02
90 Rafael Ramirez .05 .02
91 Kevin Bass .05 .02
92 Billy Hatcher .05 .02
93 Gerald Young .05 .02
94 Dodgers team logo .05 .02
95 Tim Belcher .05 .02
96 Tim Crews .05 .02
97 Orel Hershiser .10 .04
98 Jay Howell .05 .02
99 Tim Leary .05 .02
100 John Tudor .05 .02
101 Dodger Stadium .05 .02
102 Dodgers team .05 .02
lettering
103 Fernando Valenzuela .10 .04
104 Mike Scioscia .10 .04
105 Mickey Hatcher .05 .02
106 Steve Sax .05 .02
107 Kirk Gibson .10 .04
108 Mike Marshall .05 .02
109 John Shelby .05 .02
110 Expos team logo .05 .02
111 Randy Johnson 3.00 1.20
112 Nelson Santovenia .05 .02
113 Tim Burke .05 .02
114 Dennis Martinez .10 .04
115 Pascual Perez .05 .02
116 Bryn Smith .05 .02
117 Olympic Stadium .05 .02
118 Expos team lettering .05 .02
119 Andres Galarraga .30 .12
120 Wallace Johnson .05 .02
121 Tom Foley .05 .02
122 Tim Wallach .05 .02
123 Hubie Brooks .05 .02
124 Tracy Jones .05 .02
125 Tim Raines .10 .04
126 Mets team logo .05 .02
127 Kevin Elster .05 .02
128 Gregg Jefferies .05 .02
129 David Cone .30 .12
130 Ron Darling .05 .02
131 Dwight Gooden .10 .04
132 Roger McDowell .05 .02
133 Shea Stadium .05 .02
134 Mets team lettering .05 .02
135 Randy Myers .10 .04
136 Gary Carter .50 .20
137 Keith Hernandez .10 .04
138 Lenny Dykstra .10 .04
139 Kevin McReynolds .05 .02
140 Darryl Strawberry .10 .04
141 Mookie Wilson .10 .04
142 Phillies team logo .05 .02
143 Ron Jones .05 .02
144 Ricky Jordan .05 .02
145 Steve Bedrosian .05 .02
146 Don Carman .05 .02
147 Kevin Gross .05 .02
148 Bruce Ruffin .05 .02
149 Veterans Stadium .05 .02
150 Phillies team .05 .02
lettering
151 Von Hayes .05 .02
152 Juan Samuel .05 .02
153 Mike Schmidt .75 .30
154 Phil Bradley .05 .02
155 Bob Dernier .05 .02
156 Chris James .05 .02
157 Milt Thompson .05 .02
158 Pirates team logo .05 .02
159 Randy Kramer .05 .02
160 Scott Medvin .05 .02
161 Doug Drabek .05 .02
162 Mike Dunne .05 .02
163 Jim Gott .05 .02
164 Jeff D. Robinson .05 .02
165 Three Rivers Stadium .05 .02
166 Pirates team .05 .02
lettering
167 John Smiley .05 .02
168 Mike LaValliere .05 .02
169 Sid Bream .05 .02
170 Jose Lind .05 .02
171 Bobby Bonilla .10 .04
172 Barry Bonds 1.50 .60
173 Andy Van Slyke .10 .04
174 Cardinals team logo .05 .02
175 Luis Alicea .05 .02
176 John Costello .05 .02
177 Jose DeLeon .05 .02
178 Joe Magrane .05 .02
179 Todd Worrell .05 .02
180 Tony Pena .10 .04
181 Busch Stadium .05 .02
182 Cardinals team .05 .02
lettering
183 Pedro Guerrero .05 .02
184 Jose Oquendo .05 .02
185 Terry Pendleton .10 .04
186 Ozzie Smith .75 .30
187 Tom Brunansky .05 .02
188 Vince Coleman .05 .02
189 Willie McGee .10 .04
190 Padres team logo .05 .02
191 Roberto Alomar 1.00 .40
192 Sandy Alomar Jr. .50 .20
193 Mark Davis .05 .02
194 Andy Hawkins .05 .02
195 Dennis Rasmussen .05 .02
196 Eric Show .05 .02
197 Jack Murphy Stadium .05 .02
198 Padres team lettering .05 .02
199 Benito Santiago .10 .04
200 John Kruk .10 .04
201 Randy Ready .05 .02
202 Garry Templeton .05 .02
203 Tony Gwynn 1.50 .60
204 Carmelo Martinez .05 .02
205 Marvell Wynne .05 .02
206 Giants Team Logo .05 .02
207 Dennis Cook .05 .02
208 Kirt Manwaring .05 .02
209 Kelly Downs .05 .02
210 Rick Reuschel .10 .04
211 Don Robinson .05 .02
212 Will Clark .50 .20
213 Candlestick Park .05 .02
214 Giants team lettering .05 .02
215 Robby Thompson .05 .02
216 Kevin Mitchell .10 .04
217 Jose Uribe .05 .02
218 Matt Williams .75 .30
219 Mike Aldrete .05 .02
220 Brett Butler .10 .04
221 Candy Maldonado .05 .02
222 Tony Gwynn 1.50 .60
223 Darryl Strawberry .05 .02
224 Andres Galarraga .30 .12
225 Orel Hershiser .10 .04
Danny Jackson
226 Nolan Ryan 3.00 1.20
227 Dwight Gooden AS .10 .04
228 Gary Carter AS .10 .04
229 Vince Coleman AS .05 .02
230 Andre Dawson AS .10 .04
231 Darryl Strawberry AS .05 .02
232 Will Clark AS .10 .04
233 Ryne Sandberg AS .30 .12
234 Bobby Bonilla AS .10 .04
235 Ozzie Smith AS .30 .12
236 Terry Steinbach AS .05 .02
237 Frank Viola AS .05 .02
238 Jose Canseco AS .10 .04
239 Rickey Henderson AS .30 .12
240 Dave Winfield AS .30 .12
241 Cal Ripken Jr. AS 1.50 .60
242 Wade Boggs AS .30 .12
243 Paul Molitor AS .30 .12
244 Mark McGwire AS 1.25 .50
245 Wade Boggs AS .30 .12
246 Jose Canseco .50 .20
247 Kirby Puckett .75 .30
248 Frank Viola .05 .02
249 Roger Clemens .75 .30
250 Orioles team logo .05 .02
251 Bob Milacki .05 .02
252 Craig Worthington .05 .02
253 Jeff Ballard .05 .02
254 Tom Niedenfuer .05 .02
255 Dave Schmidt .05 .02
256 Terry Kennedy .05 .02
257 Memorial Stadium .05 .02
258 Orioles team .05 .02
lettering
259 Mickey Tettleton .10 .04
260 Eddie Murray .75 .30
261 Bill Ripken .05 .02
262 Cal Ripken Jr. 3.00 1.20
263 Joe Orsulak .05 .02
264 Larry Sheets .05 .02
265 Pete Stanicek .05 .02
266 Red Sox team logo .05 .02
267 Steve Curry .05 .02
268 Jody Reed .05 .02
269 Oil Can Boyd .05 .02
270 Roger Clemens 1.50 .60
271 Bruce Hurst .05 .02
272 Lee Smith .10 .04
273 Fenway Park .05 .02
274 Red Sox team .05 .02
lettering
275 Todd Benzinger .05 .02
276 Marty Barrett .05 .02
277 Wade Boggs .50 .20
278 Ellis Burks .30 .12
279 Dwight Evans .10 .04
280 Mike Greenwell .05 .02
281 Jim Rice .10 .04
282 Angels team logo .05 .02
283 Dante Bichette 1.00 .40
284 Bryan Harvey .05 .02
285 Kirk McCaskill .05 .02
286 Mike Witt .05 .02
287 Bob Boone .10 .04
288 Brian Downing .10 .04
289 Anaheim Stadium .05 .02
290 Angels team lettering .05 .02
291 Wally Joyner .10 .04
292 Johnny Ray .05 .02
293 Jack Howell .05 .02
294 Dick Schofield .05 .02
295 Tony Armas .05 .02
296 Chili Davis .10 .04
297 Devon White .10 .04
298 White Sox team logo .05 .02
299 Dave Gallagher .05 .02
300 Melido Perez .05 .02
301 Shawn Hillegas .05 .02
302 Jack McDowell .10 .04
303 Bobby Thigpen .05 .02
304 Carlton Fisk .50 .20
305 Comiskey Park .05 .02
306 White Sox team .05 .02
lettering
307 Greg Walker .05 .02
308 Steve Lyons .10 .04
309 Ozzie Guillen .10 .04
310 Harold Baines .20 .08
311 Daryl Boston .05 .02
312 Lance Johnson .05 .02
313 Dan Pasqua .05 .02
314 Indians team logo .05 .02
315 Luis Medina .05 .02
316 Ron Tingley .05 .02
317 Tom Candiotti .05 .02
318 John Farrell .05 .02
319 Doug Jones .05 .02
320 Greg Swindell .05 .02
321 Cleveland Stadium .05 .02
322 Indians team .05 .02
lettering
323 Andy Allanson .05 .02
324 Willie Upshaw .05 .02
325 Julio Franco .10 .04
326 Brook Jacoby .05 .02
327 Joe Carter .20 .08
328 Mel Hall .05 .02
329 Cory Snyder .05 .02
330 Tigers team logo .05 .02
331 Paul Gibson .05 .02
332 Torey Lovullo .05 .02
333 Mike Henneman .05 .02
334 Jack Morris .10 .04
335 Jeff M. Robinson .05 .02
336 Frank Tanana .05 .02
337 Tiger Stadium .05 .02
338 Tigers team lettering .05 .02
339 Matt Nokes .05 .02
340 Tom Brookens .05 .02
341 Lou Whitaker .10 .04
342 Luis Salazar .05 .02
343 Alan Trammell .20 .08
344 Chet Lemon .05 .02
345 Gary Pettis .05 .02
346 Royals team logo .05 .02
347 Luis de los Santos .05 .02
348 Gary Thurman .05 .02
349 Steve Farr .05 .02
350 Mark Gubicza .05 .02
351 Charlie Leibrandt .05 .02
352 Bret Saberhagen .10 .04
353 Royals Stadium .05 .02
354 Royals team lettering .05 .02
355 George Brett 1.25 .50
356 Frank White .10 .04
357 Kevin Seitzer .05 .02
358 Bo Jackson .30 .12
359 Pat Tabler .05 .02
360 Danny Tartabull .05 .02
361 Willie Wilson .05 .02
362 Brewers team logo .05 .02
363 Joey Meyer .05 .02
364 Gary Sheffield 1.50 .60
365 Don August .05 .02
366 Ted Higuera .05 .02
367 Dan Plesac .05 .02
368 B.J. Surhoff .10 .04
369 Milwaukee County .05 .02
Stadium
370 Brewers team .05 .02
lettering
371 Greg Brock .05 .02
372 Jim Gantner .05 .02
373 Paul Molitor .75 .30
374 Dale Sveum .05 .02
375 Glenn Braggs .05 .02
376 Rob Deer .05 .02
377 Robin Yount .50 .20
378 Twins team logo .05 .02
379 German Gonzalez .05 .02
380 Kelvin Torve .05 .02
381 Allan Anderson .05 .02
382 Jeff Reardon .10 .04
383 Frank Viola .05 .02
384 Tim Laudner .05 .02
385 Hubert H. Humphrey .05 .02
Metrodome
386 Twins team lettering .05 .02
387 Kent Hrbek .10 .04
388 Gene Larkin .05 .02
389 Gary Gaetti .10 .04
390 Greg Gagne .05 .02
391 Randy Bush .05 .02
392 Dan Gladden .05 .02
393 Kirby Puckett .60 .24
394 Yankees team logo .05 .02
395 Roberto Kelly .10 .04
396 Al Leiter .30 .12
397 John Candelaria .05 .02
398 Rich Dotson .05 .02
399 Rick Rhoden .05 .02
400 Dave Righetti .05 .02
401 Yankee Stadium .05 .02
402 Yankees team .05 .02
lettering
403 Don Slaught .05 .02
404 Don Mattingly 1.50 .60
405 Willie Randolph .10 .04
406 Mike Pagliarulo .05 .02
407 Rafael Santana .05 .02
408 Rickey Henderson 1.00 .40
409 Dave Winfield .50 .20
410 Athletics team logo .05 .02
411 Todd Burns .05 .02
412 Walt Weiss .10 .04
413 Storm Davis .05 .02
414 Dennis Eckersley .40 .16
415 Dave Stewart .10 .04
416 Bob Welch .05 .02
417 Oakland Alameda .05 .02
County Coliseum
418 Athletics team .05 .02
lettering
419 Terry Steinbach .05 .02
420 Mark McGwire 2.50 1.00
421 Carney Lansford .10 .04
422 Jose Canseco .40 .16
423 Dave Henderson .05 .02
424 Dave Parker .10 .04
425 Luis Polonia .05 .02
426 Mariners team logo .05 .02
427 Mario Diaz .05 .02
428 Edgar Martinez .20 .08
429 Scott Bankhead .05 .02
430 Mark Langston .05 .02
431 Mike Moore .05 .02
432 Scott Bradley .05 .02
433 The Kingdome .05 .02
434 Mariners team .05 .02
lettering
435 Alvin Davis .05 .02
436 Harold Reynolds .10 .04
437 Jim Presley .05 .02
438 Rey Quinones .05 .02
439 Mickey Brantley .05 .02
440 Jay Buhner .50 .20
441 Henry Cotto .05 .02
442 Rangers team logo .05 .02
443 Cecil Espy .05 .02
444 Chad Kreuter .05 .02
445 Jose Guzman .05 .02
446 Charlie Hough .10 .04
447 Jeff Russell .05 .02
448 Bobby Witt .05 .02
449 Arlington Stadium .05 .02
450 Rangers team .05 .02
lettering
451 Geno Petralli .05 .02
452 Pete O'Brien .05 .02
453 Steve Buechele .05 .02
454 Scott Fletcher .05 .02
455 Pete Incaviglia .05 .02
456 Oddibe McDowell .05 .02
457 Ruben Sierra .10 .04
458 Blue Jays team logo .05 .02
459 Rob Ducey .05 .02
460 Todd Stottlemyre .05 .02
461 Tom Henke .05 .02
462 Jimmy Key .05 .02
463 Dave Stieb .10 .04
464 Pat Borders .05 .02
465 Exhibition Stadium .05 .02
466 Blue Jays .05 .02
team lettering
467 Fred McGriff .30 .12
468 Manny Lee .05 .02
469 Kelly Gruber .05 .02
470 Tony Fernandez .10 .04
471 Jesse Barfield .05 .02
472 George Bell .05 .02
473 Lloyd Moseby .05 .02
474 Orel Hershiser .10 .04
475 Frank Viola .05 .02
476 Chris Sabo .05 .02
477 Jose Canseco .50 .20
478 Walt Weiss .05 .02
479 Kirk Gibson .10 .04
480 Jose Canseco .50 .20
xx Sticker Album .75 .30
(Jose Canseco on front)

1990 Panini Stickers

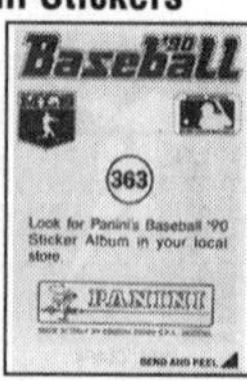

These 388 stickers measure approximately 2 1/8" by 3" and feature on their fronts white-bordered color player action shots. Stickers 186-197 are foils. An album onto which the stickers could be affixed was available at retail stores. The album featured Nolan Ryan on the front and an ad for the Panini 1990 Fan Club Pop Star Sticker Collection on the back. The album also featured a four-page insert without stickers on the 1989 post-season. The album and the sticker numbering are organized by team alphabetically by city with AL teams preceding NL teams. Subsets include 1989 AL Stat Leaders (183-185), 1989 League Championship Series (Foil, 186-187), Excellence in the '80s (Foil, 188-197), 1989 All-Stars (198-213), 1989 NL Stat Leaders (214-216), Tomorrow's Headliners (373-382) and 1989 Highlights (383-388).

Nm-Mt Ex-Mt
COMPLETE SET (388) 15.00 4.50
1 Randy Milligan .05 .02

2 Gregg Olson .10 .03
3 Bill Ripken .05 .02
4 Phil Bradley .05 .02
5 Joe Orsulak .05 .02
6 Bob Milacki .05 .02
7 Cal Ripken 2.50 .75
8 Mickey Tettleton .10 .03
9 Orioles Logo .05 .02
10 Orioles Helmet .05 .02
11 Craig Worthington .05 .02
12 Mike Devereaux .05 .02
13 Jeff Ballard .05 .02
14 Lee Smith .10 .03
15 Marty Barrett .05 .02
16 Mike Greenwell .05 .02
17 Dwight Evans .10 .03
18 John Dopson .05 .02
19 Wade Boggs .50 .15
20 Mike Boddicker .05 .02
21 Ellis Burks .25 .07
22 Red Sox Logo .05 .02
23 Red Sox Helmet .05 .02
24 Roger Clemens 1.25 .35
25 Jody Reed .05 .02
26 Nick Esasky .05 .02
27 Brian Downing .05 .02
28 Bert Blyleven .10 .03
29 Devon White .10 .03
30 Claudell Washington .05 .02
31 Wally Joyner .10 .03
32 Chuck Finley .10 .03
33 Johnny Ray .05 .02
34 Jim Abbott .15 .04
35 Angels Logo .05 .02
36 Angels Helmet .05 .02
37 Kirk McCaskill .05 .02
38 Lance Parrish .05 .02
39 Chili Davis .10 .03
40 Steve Lyons .10 .03
41 Ozzie Guillen .10 .03
42 Melido Perez .05 .02
43 Scott Fletcher .05 .02
44 Carlton Fisk .50 .15
45 Greg Walker .05 .02
46 Dave Gallagher .05 .02
47 Ivan Calderon .05 .02
48 White Sox Logo .05 .02
49 White Sox Helmet .05 .02
50 Bobby Thigpen .05 .02
51 Ron Kittle .05 .02
52 Daryl Boston .05 .02
53 John Farrell .05 .02
54 Jerry Browne .05 .02
55 Pete O'Brien .05 .02
56 Cory Snyder .05 .02
57 Tom Candiotti .05 .02
58 Brook Jacoby .05 .02
59 Greg Swindell .05 .02
60 Felix Fermin .05 .02
61 Indians Logo .05 .02
62 Indians Helmet .05 .02
63 Doug Jones .05 .02
64 Dion James .05 .02
65 Joe Carter .10 .03
66 Mike Heath .05 .02
67 Dave Bergman .05 .02
68 Gary Ward .05 .02
69 Mike Henneman .05 .02
70 Alan Trammell .15 .04
71 Lou Whitaker .10 .03
72 Frank Tanana .05 .02
73 Fred Lynn .05 .02
74 Tigers Logo .05 .02
75 Tigers Helmet .05 .02
76 Jack Morris .10 .03
77 Chet Lemon .05 .02
78 Gary Pettis .05 .02
79 Kurt Stillwell .05 .02
80 Jim Eisenreich .05 .02
81 Bret Saberhagen .10 .03
82 Mark Gubicza .05 .02
83 Frank White .10 .03
84 Bo Jackson .25 .07
85 Jeff Montgomery .10 .03
86 Kevin Seitzer .05 .02
87 Royals Logo .05 .02
88 Royals Helmet .05 .02
89 Tom Gordon .15 .04
90 Danny Tartabull .05 .02
91 George Brett 1.25 .35
92 Robin Yount .50 .15
93 B.J. Surhoff .10 .03
94 Jim Gantner .05 .02
95 Dan Plesac .05 .02
96 Ted Higuera .05 .02
97 Glenn Braggs .05 .02
98 Paul Molitor .75 .23
99 Chris Bosio .05 .02
100 Brewers Logo .05 .02
101 Brewers Helmet .05 .02
102 Rob Deer .05 .02
103 Chuck Crim .05 .02
104 Greg Brock .05 .02
105 Kirby Puckett .60 .18
106 Gary Gaetti .10 .03
107 Roy Smith .05 .02
108 Jeff Reardon .10 .03
109 Randy Bush .05 .02
110 Al Newman .05 .02
111 Dan Gladden .05 .02
112 Kent Hrbek .10 .03
113 Twins Logo .05 .02
114 Twins Helmet .05 .02
115 Greg Gagne .05 .02
116 Brian Harper .05 .02
117 Allan Anderson .05 .02
118 Lee Guetterman .05 .02
119 Roberto Kelly .05 .02
120 Jesse Barfield .05 .02
121 Alvaro Espinoza .05 .02
122 Mel Hall .05 .02
123 Chuck Cary .05 .02
124 Dave Righetti .05 .02
125 Don Mattingly 1.25 .35
126 Yankees Logo .05 .02
127 Yankees Helmet .05 .02
128 Bob Geren .05 .02
129 Steve Sax .05 .02
130 Andy Hawkins .05 .02
131 Bob Welch .05 .02
132 Mark McGwire 2.00 .60
133 Dave Henderson .05 .02
134 Carney Lansford .10 .03
135 Walt Weiss .05 .02
136 Mike Moore .05 .02
137 Dennis Eckersley .40 .12
138 Rickey Henderson .75 .23
139 Athletics Logo .05 .02
140 Athletics Helmet .05 .02
141 Dave Stewart .10 .03
142 Jose Canseco .30 .09
143 Terry Steinbach .05 .02
144 Harold Reynolds .10 .03
145 Darnell Coles .05 .02
146 Brian Holman .05 .02
147 Scott Bankhead .05 .02
148 Greg Briley .05 .02
149 Alvin Davis .05 .02
150 Jeffrey Leonard .05 .02
151 Mike Schooler .05 .02
152 Mariners Logo .05 .02
153 Mariners Helmet .05 .02
154 Randy Johnson 1.00 .30
155 Ken Griffey Jr. 1.50 .45
156 Dave Valle .05 .02
157 Pete Incaviglia .05 .02
158 Fred Manrique .05 .02
159 Jeff Russell .05 .02
160 Nolan Ryan 2.50 .75
161 Geno Petralli .05 .02
162 Ruben Sierra .10 .03
163 Julio Franco .10 .03
164 Rafael Palmeiro .25 .07
165 Rangers Logo .05 .02
166 Rangers Helmet .05 .02
167 Harold Baines .10 .03
168 Kevin Brown .25 .07
169 Steve Buechele .05 .02
170 Fred McGriff .25 .07
171 Kelly Gruber .05 .02
172 Todd Stottlemyre .05 .02
173 Dave Stieb .10 .03
174 Mookie Wilson .10 .03
175 Pat Borders .05 .02
176 Tony Fernandez .10 .03
177 John Cerutti .05 .02
178 Blue Jays Logo .05 .02
179 Blue Jays Helmet .05 .02
180 George Bell .05 .02
181 Jimmy Key .05 .02
182 Nelson Liriano .05 .02
183 Kirby Puckett .50 .15
184 Carney Lansford .10 .03
185 Nolan Ryan 2.50 .75
186 AL Logo .05 .02
187 NL Logo .05 .02
188 World Championship .05 .02
Trophy
189 '88 World Championship .05 .02
LA Dodgers Ring
190 '87 World Championship .05 .02
Minnesota Twins Ring
191 '86 World Championship .05 .02
NY Mets Ring
192 '85 World Championship .05 .02
KC Royals Ring
193 '84 World Championship .05 .02
Detroit Tigers Ring
194 '83 World Championship .05 .02
Baltimore Orioles Ring
195 '82 World Championship .05 .02
St.Louis Cardinals Ring
196 '81 World Championship .05 .02
LA Dodgers Ring
197 '80 World Championship .05 .02
Philadelphia Phillies
Ring
198 Dave Stewart .10 .03
Bo Jackson
199 Wade Boggs .25 .07
Kirby Puckett
200 Harold Baines .10 .03
201 Julio Franco .05 .02
202 Cal Ripken 2.50 .75
203 Ruben Sierra .05 .02
204 Mark McGwire 2.00 .60
205 Terry Steinbach .05 .02
206 Rick Reuschel .25 .07
Ozzie Smith
207 Tony Gwynn .60 .18
Will Clark
208 Kevin Mitchell .05 .02
209 Eric Davis .10 .03
210 Howard Johnson .05 .02
211 Pedro Guerrero .05 .02
212 Ryne Sandberg .75 .23
213 Benito Santiago .05 .02
214 Kevin Mitchell .05 .02
215 Mark Davis .05 .02
216 Vince Coleman .05 .02
217 Jeff Blauser .05 .02
218 Jeff Treadway .05 .02
219 Tom Glavine .50 .15
220 Joe Boever .05 .02
221 Oddibe McDowell .05 .02
222 Dale Murphy .25 .07
223 Derek Lilliquist .05 .02
224 Tommy Gregg .05 .02
225 Braves Logo .05 .02
226 Braves Helmet .05 .02
227 Lonnie Smith .05 .02
228 John Smoltz .75 .23
229 Andres Thomas .05 .02
230 Jerome Walton .05 .02
231 Ryne Sandberg .75 .23
232 Mitch Williams .05 .02
233 Rick Sutcliffe .05 .02
234 Damon Berryhill .05 .02
235 Dwight Smith .05 .02
236 Shawon Dunston .05 .02
237 Greg Maddux 1.50 .45
238 Cubs Logo .05 .02
239 Cubs Helmet .05 .02
240 Andre Dawson .25 .07
241 Mark Grace .40 .12
242 Mike Bielecki .05 .02
243 Jose Rijo .05 .02
244 John Franco .10 .03
245 Paul O'Neill .15 .04
246 Eric Davis .10 .03
247 Tom Browning .05 .02
248 Chris Sabo .05 .02
249 Rob Dibble .05 .02
250 Todd Benzinger .05 .02
251 Reds Logo .05 .02
252 Reds Helmet .05 .02
253 Barry Larkin .25 .07
254 Rolando Roomes .05 .02
255 Danny Jackson .05 .02
256 Terry Puhl .05 .02
257 Dave Smith .05 .02
258 Glenn Davis .05 .02
259 Craig Biggio .50 .15
260 Ken Caminiti .25 .07
261 Kevin Bass .05 .02
262 Mike Scott .10 .03
263 Gerald Young .05 .02
264 Astros Logo .05 .02
265 Astros Helmet .05 .02
266 Rafael Ramirez .05 .02
267 Jim Deshaies .05 .02
268 Bill Doran .05 .02
269 Fernando Valenzuela .10 .03
270 Alfredo Griffin .05 .02
271 Kirk Gibson .10 .03
272 Mike Marshall .05 .02
273 Eddie Murray .60 .18
274 Jay Howell .05 .02
275 Orel Hershiser .10 .03
276 Mike Scioscia .10 .03
277 Dodgers Logo .05 .02
278 Dodgers Helmet .05 .02
279 Willie Randolph .10 .03
280 Kal Daniels .05 .02
281 Tim Belcher .05 .02
282 Pascual Perez .05 .02
283 Tim Raines .15 .04
284 Andres Galarraga .25 .07
285 Spike Owen .05 .02
286 Tim Wallach .05 .02
287 Mark Langston .05 .02
288 Dennis Martinez .10 .03
289 Nelson Santovenia .05 .02
290 Expos Logo .05 .02
291 Expos Helmet .05 .02
292 Tom Foley .05 .02
293 Dave Martinez .05 .02
294 Tim Burke .05 .02
295 Ron Darling .05 .02
296 Kevin Elster .05 .02
297 Dwight Gooden .10 .03
298 Gregg Jefferies .05 .02
299 Sid Fernandez .05 .02
300 Dave Magadan .05 .02
301 David Cone .25 .07
302 Darryl Strawberry .10 .03
303 Mets Logo .05 .02
304 Mets Helmet .05 .02
305 Kevin McReynolds .05 .02
306 Howard Johnson .05 .02
307 Randy Myers .10 .03
308 Roger McDowell .05 .02
309 Tom Herr .05 .02
310 John Kruk .10 .03
311 Randy Ready .05 .02
312 Jeff Parrett .05 .02
313 Lenny Dykstra .10 .03
314 Ken Howell .05 .02
315 Ricky Jordan .05 .02
316 Phillies Logo .05 .02
317 Phillies Helmet .05 .02
318 Dickie Thon .05 .02
319 Von Hayes .05 .02
320 Dennis Cook .05 .02
321 Jay Bell .05 .02
322 Barry Bonds 1.25 .35
323 John Smiley .05 .02
324 Andy Van Slyke .05 .02
325 Bobby Bonilla .10 .03
326 Bill Landrum .05 .02
327 Randy Kramer .05 .02
328 Jose Lind .05 .02
329 Pirates Logo .05 .02
330 Pirates Helmet .05 .02
331 Gary Redus .05 .02
332 Doug Drabek .05 .02
333 Mike LaValliere .05 .02
334 Jose DeLeon .05 .02
335 Pedro Guerrero .05 .02
336 Vince Coleman .05 .02
337 Terry Pendleton .10 .03
338 Ozzie Smith 1.00 .30
339 Willie McGee .10 .03
340 Todd Worrell .05 .02
341 Jose Oquendo .05 .02
342 Cardinals Logo .05 .02
343 Cardinals Helmet .05 .02
344 Tom Brunansky .05 .02
345 Milt Thompson .05 .02
346 Joe Magrane .05 .02
347 Ed Whitson .05 .02
348 Jack Clark .10 .03
349 Roberto Alomar .75 .23
350 Chris James .05 .02
351 Tony Gwynn 1.25 .35
352 Mark Davis .05 .02
353 Greg W. Harris .05 .02
354 Garry Templeton .05 .02
355 Padres Logo .05 .02
356 Padres Helmet .05 .02
357 Bruce Hurst .05 .02
358 Benito Santiago .10 .03
359 Bip Roberts .05 .02
360 Dave Dravecky .10 .03
361 Kevin Mitchell .05 .02
362 Craig Lefferts .05 .02
363 Will Clark .25 .07
364 Steve Bedrosian .05 .02
365 Brett Butler .10 .03
366 Matt Williams .15 .04
367 Scott Garrelts .05 .02
368 Giants Logo .05 .02
369 Giants Helmet .05 .02
370 Rick Reuschel .10 .03
371 Robby Thompson .05 .02
372 Jose Uribe .05 .02
373 Ben McDonald .05 .02
374 Carlos Martinez .10 .03
375 Steve Olin .10 .03
376 Bill Spiers .05 .02
377 Junior Felix .05 .02
378 Joe Oliver .05 .02
379 Eric Anthony .05 .02
380 Ramon Martinez .05 .02
381 Todd Zeile .10 .03
382 Andy Benes .05 .02
383 Vince Coleman .05 .02
384 Bo Jackson .25 .07
385 Howard Johnson .05 .02
386 Dave Dravecky .10 .03
387 Nolan Ryan 2.50 .75
388 Cal Ripken 2.50 .75
xx Sticker Album 1.50 .45
(Nolan Ryan on front)

1991 Panini Stickers

The 1991 Panini baseball set contains 271 stickers measuring 1 1/2" by 2 1/2". The stickers may be pasted in a collectible sticker album that measures 8 1/4" by 10 1/2". After a "Year of the No-Hitter 1990" (1-9) subset, the stickers are checklisted alphabetically according to teams within the NL and then the AL.

Nm-Mt Ex-Mt
COMPLETE SET (271) 15.00 4.50
1 Mark Langston .05 .02
2 Randy Johnson .25 .07
3 Nolan Ryan 2.50 .75
4 Dave Stewart .10 .03
5 Fernando Valenzuela .10 .03
6 Andy Hawkins .05 .02
7 Melido Perez .05 .02
8 Terry Mulholland .05 .02
9 Dave Stieb .10 .03
10 Craig Biggio .50 .15
11 Jim Deshaies .05 .02
12 Dave Smith .05 .02
13 Eric Yelding .05 .02
14 Astros Pennant .05 .02
15 Astros Logo .05 .02
16 Mike Scott .05 .02
17 Ken Caminiti .25 .07
18 Danny Darwin .05 .02
19 Glenn Davis .05 .02
20 Braves Pennant .05 .02
21 Braves Logo .05 .02
22 Lonnie Smith .05 .02
23 Charlie Leibrandt .05 .02
24 Jim Presley .05 .02
25 Greg Olson .05 .02
26 John Smoltz .25 .07
27 Ron Gant .10 .03
28 Jeff Treadway .05 .02
29 Dave Justice .25 .07
30 Jose Oquendo .05 .02
31 Joe Magrane .05 .02
32 Cardinals Pennant .05 .02
33 Cardinals Logo .05 .02
34 Todd Zeile .10 .03
35 Vince Coleman .05 .02
36 Bob Tewksbury .05 .02
37 Pedro Guerrero .05 .02
38 Lee Smith .10 .03
39 Ozzie Smith .75 .23
40 Ryne Sandberg .75 .23
41 Andre Dawson .25 .07
42 Cubs Pennant .05 .02
43 Greg Maddux 1.50 .45
44 Jerome Walton .05 .02
45 Cubs Logo .05 .02
46 Mike Harkey .05 .02
47 Shawon Dunston .05 .02
48 Mark Grace .40 .12
49 Joe Girardi .10 .03
50 Ramon Martinez .05 .02
51 Lenny Harris .05 .02
52 Mike Morgan .05 .02
53 Eddie Murray .60 .18
54 Dodgers Pennant .05 .02
55 Dodgers Logo .05 .02
56 Hubie Brooks .05 .02
57 Mike Scioscia .10 .03
58 Kal Daniels .05 .02
59 Fernando Valenzuela .10 .03
60 Expos Pennant .05 .02
61 Expos Logo .05 .02
62 Spike Owen .05 .02
63 Tim Raines .10 .03
64 Tim Wallach .05 .02
65 Larry Walker .25 .07
66 Dave Martinez .05 .02
67 Mark Gardner .05 .02
68 Dennis Martinez .10 .03
69 Delino DeShields .10 .03
70 Jeff Brantley .10 .03
71 Kevin Mitchell .05 .02
72 Giants Pennant .05 .02
73 Giants Logo .05 .02
74 Don Robinson .05 .02
75 Brett Butler .10 .03
76 Matt Williams .15 .04
77 Robby Thompson .05 .02
78 John Burkett .05 .02
79 Will Clark .25 .07
80 David Cone .10 .03
81 Dave Magadan .05 .02
82 Mets Pennant .05 .02
83 Gregg Jefferies .05 .02
84 Frank Viola .05 .02
85 Mets Logo .05 .02
86 Howard Johnson .05 .02
87 John Franco .10 .03
88 Darryl Strawberry .10 .03
89 Dwight Gooden .10 .03
90 Joe Carter .10 .03
91 Ed Whitson .05 .02
92 Andy Benes .05 .02
93 Benito Santiago .10 .03
94 Padres Pennant .05 .02
95 Padres Logo .05 .02
96 Roberto Alomar .50 .15
97 Bip Roberts .05 .02
98 Jack Clark .10 .03
99 Tony Gwynn 1.50 .45
100 Phillies Pennant .05 .02
101 Phillies Logo .05 .02
102 Charlie Hayes .05 .02
103 Len Dykstra .10 .03
104 Dale Murphy .25 .07
105 Von Hayes .05 .02
106 Dickie Thon .05 .02
107 John Kruk .10 .03
108 Ken Howell .05 .02
109 Darren Daulton .10 .03
110 Jay Bell .05 .02
111 Bobby Bonilla .10 .03
112 Pirates Pennant .05 .02
113 Pirates Logo .05 .02
114 Barry Bonds 1.25 .35
115 Neal Heaton .05 .02
116 Doug Drabek .05 .02
117 Jose Lind .05 .02
118 Andy Van Slyke .05 .02
119 Sid Bream .05 .02
120 Paul O'Neill .10 .03
121 Randy Myers .10 .03
122 Reds Pennant .05 .02
123 Mariano Duncan .05 .02
124 Eric Davis .10 .03
125 Reds Logo .05 .02
126 Jack Armstrong .05 .02
127 Chris Sabo .05 .02
128 Rob Dibble .05 .02
129 Barry Larkin .25 .07
130 National League Logo .05 .02
131 American League Logo .05 .02
132 Dave Winfield .25 .07
133 Lance Parrish .05 .02
134 Chili Davis .10 .03
135 Chuck Finley .10 .03
136 Angels Pennant .05 .02
137 Angels Logo .05 .02
138 Johnny Ray .05 .02
139 Dante Bichette .50 .15
140 Jim Abbott .10 .03
141 Wally Joyner .10 .03
142 Athletics Pennant .05 .02
143 Athletics Logo .05 .02
144 Dave Stewart .10 .03
145 Mark McGwire 2.00 .60
146 Rickey Henderson .75 .23
147 Walt Weiss .05 .02
148 Dennis Eckersley .40 .12
149 Jose Canseco .50 .15
150 Dave Henderson .05 .02
151 Bob Welch .05 .02
152 Tony Fernandez .10 .03
153 David Wells .15 .04
154 Blue Jays Pennant .05 .02
155 Blue Jays Logo .05 .02
156 Pat Borders .05 .02
157 Fred McGriff .25 .07
158 George Bell .05 .02
159 John Olerud .15 .04
160 Dave Stieb .05 .02
161 Kelly Gruber .05 .02
162 Bill Spiers .05 .02
163 Dan Plesac .05 .02
164 Brewers Pennant .05 .02
165 Mark Knudson .05 .02
166 Robin Yount .50 .15
167 Brewers Logo .05 .02
168 Paul Molitor .60 .18
169 B.J. Surhoff .10 .03
170 Gary Sheffield .40 .12
171 Dave Parker .10 .03
172 Sandy Alomar Jr. .10 .03
173 Doug Jones .05 .02
174 Tom Candiotti .05 .02
175 Mitch Webster .05 .02
176 Indians Pennant .05 .02
177 Indians Logo .05 .02
178 Brook Jacoby .05 .02
179 Candy Maldonado .05 .02
180 Carlos Baerga .10 .03
181 Chris James .05 .02
182 Mariners Pennant .05 .02
183 Mariners Logo .05 .02
184 Mike Schooler .05 .02
185 Alvin Davis .05 .02
186 Erik Hanson .05 .02
187 Edgar Martinez .15 .04
188 Randy Johnson .75 .23
189 Ken Griffey Jr. 1.50 .45
190 Jay Buhner .25 .07
191 Harold Reynolds .10 .03
192 Cal Ripken 2.50 .75
193 Gregg Olson .10 .03
194 Orioles Pennant .05 .02
195 Orioles Logo .05 .02
196 Mike Devereaux .05 .02
197 Ben McDonald .05 .02
198 Craig Worthington .05 .02
199 Dave Johnson .05 .02
200 Joe Orsulak .05 .02
201 Randy Milligan .05 .02
202 Ruben Sierra .10 .03
203 Bobby Witt .05 .02
204 Rangers Pennant .05 .02
205 Nolan Ryan 2.50 .75
206 Jeff Huson .05 .02
207 Rangers Logo .05 .02
208 Kevin Brown .15 .04
209 Steve Buechele .05 .02
210 Julio Franco .10 .03
211 Rafael Palmeiro .25 .07
212 Ellis Burks .15 .04
213 Dwight Evans .10 .03
214 Wade Boggs .50 .15
215 Roger Clemens 1.25 .35
216 Red Sox Pennant .05 .02
217 Red Sox Logo .05 .02
218 Jeff Reardon .10 .03
219 Tony Pena .10 .03
220 Jody Reed .05 .02
221 Carlos Quintana .05 .02

222 Royals Pennant .05 .02
223 Royals Logo .05 .02
224 George Brett 1.25 .35
225 Bret Saberhagen .10 .03
226 Bo Jackson .25 .07
227 Kevin Seitzer .05 .02
228 Mark Gubicza .05 .02
229 Jim Eisenreich .05 .02
230 Gerald Perry .05 .02
231 Tom Gordon .10 .03
232 Cecil Fielder .10 .03
233 Lou Whitaker .10 .03
234 Tigers Pennant .05 .02
235 Tigers Logo .05 .02
236 Mike Henneman .05 .02
237 Mike Heath .05 .02
238 Alan Trammell .15 .04
239 Lloyd Moseby .05 .02
240 Dan Petry .05 .02
241 Dave Bergman .05 .02
242 Brian Harper .05 .02
243 Rick Aguilera .10 .03
244 Twins Pennant .05 .02
245 Greg Gagne .05 .02
246 Gene Larkin .05 .02
247 Twins Logo .05 .02
248 Kirby Puckett .60 .18
249 Kevin Tapani .05 .02
250 Gary Gaetti .10 .03
251 Kent Hrbek .10 .03
252 Bobby Thigpen .05 .02
253 Lance Johnson .05 .02
254 Greg Hibbard .05 .02
255 Carlton Fisk .50 .15
256 White Sox Pennant .05 .02
257 White Sox Logo .05 .02
258 Ivan Calderon .05 .02
259 Barry Jones .05 .02
260 Robin Ventura .25 .07
261 Ozzie Guillen .10 .03
262 Yankees Pennant .05 .02
263 Yankees Logo .05 .02
264 Kevin Maas .05 .02
265 Bob Geren .05 .02
266 Dave Righetti .05 .02
267 Don Mattingly 1.25 .35
268 Roberto Kelly .05 .02
269 Alvaro Espinoza .05 .02
270 Oscar Azocar .05 .02
271 Steve Sax .05 .02

1991 Panini Canadian Top 15

The 1991 Panini Top 15 sticker set consists of 136 stickers and features Major League's best players and teams in various statistical categories. An American and a Canadian version were issued. The player's name, team and statistical category (the last item in French and English in the Canadian version) appear below the picture. Moreover, the front also has a number (1-4) indicating the player's finish in that category, the statistic and different color emblems for the National League (blue) and the American League (red). The Gold glove winners have a gold emblem, irrespective of league. The set is subdivided according to the following statistical categories, with National League winners listed first (e.g., 1-4) and then American League winners (e.g., 5-8): batting average (1-8); home runs (9-16); runs batted in (17-24); hits (25-32); slugging average (33-40); stolen bases (41-48); runs (49-56); wins (57-64); earned run average (65-72); strikeouts (73-80); saves (81-88); shutouts (89-96); National League logo (97) and gold glove (98-106); American League logo (107) and gold glove (108-16); and team statistical leaders (117-36). The NL logo (97), AL logo (107) and all the team stickers (117-36) are foil.

Nm-Mt Ex-Mt
COMPLETE SET (136) 30.00 9.00
1 Willie McGee .10 .03
2 Eddie Murray .75 .23
3 Dave Magadan .05 .02
4 Lenny Dykstra .10 .03
5 George Brett 1.50 .45
6 Rickey Henderson .75 .23
7 Rafael Palmeiro .30 .09
8 Alan Trammell .20 .06
9 Ryne Sandberg 1.25 .35
10 Darryl Strawberry .10 .03
11 Kevin Mitchell .05 .02
12 Barry Bonds 1.50 .45
13 Cecil Fielder .10 .03
14 Mark McGwire 2.50 .75
15 Jose Canseco .40 .12
16 Fred McGriff .50 .15
17 Matt Williams .20 .06
18 Bobby Bonilla .05 .02
19 Joe Carter .10 .03
20 Barry Bonds 1.50 .45
21 Cecil Fielder .10 .03
22 Kelly Gruber .05 .02
23 Mark McGwire 2.50 .75
24 Jose Canseco .40 .12
25 Brett Butler .10 .03
26 Lenny Dykstra .10 .03
27 Ryne Sandberg 1.25 .35
28 Barry Larkin .30 .09
29 Rafael Palmeiro .50 .15
30 Wade Boggs .75 .23
31 Roberto Kelly .05 .02
32 Mike Greenwell .05 .02
33 Barry Bonds 1.50 .45
34 Ryne Sandberg 1.25 .35
35 Kevin Mitchell .05 .02
36 Ron Gant .10 .03
37 Cecil Fielder .10 .03
38 Rickey Henderson .75 .23
39 Jose Canseco .40 .12
40 Fred McGriff .50 .15
41 Vince Coleman .05 .02
42 Eric Yelding .05 .02
43 Barry Bonds 1.50 .45
44 Brett Butler .10 .03
45 Rickey Henderson .75 .23
46 Steve Sax .05 .02
47 Roberto Kelly .05 .02
48 Alex Cole .05 .02
49 Ryne Sandberg 1.25 .35
50 Bobby Bonilla .05 .02
51 Brett Butler .10 .03
52 Ron Gant .10 .03
53 Rickey Henderson .75 .23
54 Cecil Fielder .10 .03
55 Harold Reynolds .10 .03
56 Robin Yount .50 .15
57 Doug Drabek .05 .02
58 Ramon Martinez .05 .02
59 Frank Viola .05 .02
60 Dwight Gooden .10 .03
61 Bob Welch .05 .02
62 Dave Stewart .10 .03
63 Roger Clemens 1.50 .45
64 Dave Stieb .10 .03
65 Danny Darwin .05 .02
66 Zane Smith .05 .02
67 Ed Whitson .05 .02
68 Frank Viola .05 .02
69 Roger Clemens 1.50 .45
70 Chuck Finley .10 .03
71 Dave Stewart .10 .03
72 Kevin Appier .10 .03
73 David Cone .10 .03
74 Dwight Gooden .10 .03
75 Ramon Martinez .05 .02
76 Frank Viola .05 .02
77 Nolan Ryan 3.00 .90
78 Bobby Witt .05 .02
79 Erik Hanson .05 .02
80 Roger Clemens 1.50 .45
81 John Franco .10 .03
82 Randy Myers .10 .03
83 Lee Smith .10 .03
84 Craig Lefferts .05 .02
85 Bobby Thigpen .05 .02
86 Dennis Eckersley .40 .12
87 Doug Jones .05 .02
88 Gregg Olson .05 .02
89 Mike Morgan .05 .02
90 Bruce Hurst .05 .02
91 Mark Gardner .05 .02
92 Doug Drabek .05 .02
93 Dave Stewart .10 .03
94 Roger Clemens 1.50 .45
95 Kevin Appier .10 .03
96 Melido Perez .05 .02
97 National League .05 .02
98 Greg Maddux 2.00 .60
99 Benito Santiago .10 .03
100 Andres Galarraga .30 .09
101 Ryne Sandberg 1.25 .35
102 Tim Wallach .05 .02
103 Ozzie Smith 1.25 .35
104 Tony Gwynn 1.50 .45
105 Barry Bonds 1.50 .45
106 Andy Van Slyke .10 .03
107 American League .05 .02
108 Mike Boddicker .05 .02
109 Sandy Alomar Jr. .10 .03
110 Mark McGwire 2.50 .75
111 Harold Reynolds .10 .03
112 Kelly Gruber .05 .02
113 Ozzie Guillen .10 .03
114 Ellis Burks .10 .03
115 Gary Pettis .05 .02
116 Ken Griffey Jr. 2.00 .60
117 Cincinnati Reds .05 .02
Highest Batting Average
118 New York Mets .05 .02
Most Home Runs
119 New York Mets .05 .02
Most Runs Scored
120 Chicago Cubs .05 .02
Most Hits
121 Montreal Expos .05 .02
Most Stolen Bases
122 Boston Red Sox .05 .02
Highest Batting Average
123 Detroit Tigers .05 .02
Most Home Runs
124 Toronto Blue Jays .05 .02
Most Runs Scored
125 Boston Red Sox .05 .02
Most Hits
126 Milwaukee Brewers .05 .02
Most Stolen Bases
127 Philadelphia Phillies .05 .02
Most Double Plays
128 Cincinnati Reds .05 .02
Fewest Errors
129 Montreal Expos .05 .02
Best ERA
130 New York Mets .05 .02
Most Shutouts
131 Cincinnati Reds .05 .02
Most Saves
132 California Angels .05 .02
Most Double Plays
133 Toronto Blue Jays .05 .02
Fewest Errors
134 Oakland Athletics .05 .02
Best ERA
135 Oakland Athletics .05 .02
Most Shutouts
136 Chicago White Sox .05 .02
Most Saves

1991 Panini French Stickers

The French version of the 1991 Panini baseball set contains 360 stickers measuring approximately 2 1/8" by 3". The stickers may be pasted in a collectible sticker album that measures 8 1/4" by 10 1/2". The stickers are checklisted alphabetically according to teams within the NL and then the AL, with the Canadian teams listed after each league. A

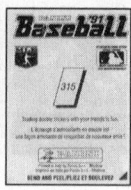

special Year of the No-Hitter (352-360) subset is included at the end of the set.

Nm-Mt Ex-Mt
COMPLETE SET (360) 25.00 7.50
1 MLB Logo .05 .02
2 MLBPA Logo .05 .02
3 Panini Baseball .05 .02
1991 Logo
4 Astros Pennant .05 .02
5 Astros Logo .05 .02
6 Craig Biggio .50 .15
7 Glenn Davis .05 .02
8 Casey Candaele .05 .02
9 Ken Caminiti .10 .03
10 Rafael Ramirez .05 .02
11 Glenn Wilson .05 .02
12 Eric Yelding .05 .02
13 Franklin Stubbs .05 .02
14 Mike Scott .10 .03
15 Danny Darwin .05 .02
16 Braves Pennant .05 .02
17 Braves Logo .05 .02
18 Greg Olson .05 .02
19 Tommy Gregg .05 .02
20 Jeff Treadway .05 .02
21 Jim Presley .05 .02
22 Jeff Blauser .05 .02
23 Ron Gant .10 .03
24 Lonnie Smith .05 .02
25 Dave Justice .50 .15
26 John Smoltz .25 .07
27 Charlie Leibrandt .05 .02
28 Cardinals Pennant .05 .02
29 Cardinals Logo .05 .02
30 Tom Pagnozzi .05 .02
31 Pedro Guerrero .05 .02
32 Jose Oquendo .05 .02
33 Todd Zeile .10 .03
34 Ozzie Smith .75 .23
35 Vince Coleman .05 .02
36 Milt Thompson .05 .02
37 Rex Hudler .10 .03
38 Joe Magrane .05 .02
39 Lee Smith .10 .03
40 Cubs Pennant .05 .02
41 Cubs Logo .05 .02
42 Joe Girardi .10 .03
43 Mark Grace .40 .12
44 Ryne Sandberg .75 .23
45 Luis Salazar .05 .02
46 Shawon Dunston .05 .02
47 Dwight Smith .05 .02
48 Jerome Walton .05 .02
49 Andre Dawson .25 .07
50 Greg Maddux 1.50 .45
51 Mike Harkey .05 .02
52 Dodgers Pennant .05 .02
53 Dodgers Logo .05 .02
54 Mike Scioscia .05 .02
55 Eddie Murray .75 .23
56 Juan Samuel .05 .02
57 Lenny Harris .05 .02
58 Alfredo Griffin .05 .02
59 Hubie Brooks .05 .02
60 Kal Daniels .05 .02
61 Stan Javier .05 .02
62 Ramon Martinez .05 .02
63 Mike Morgan .05 .02
64 Giants Pennant .05 .02
65 Giants Logo .05 .02
66 Terry Kennedy .05 .02
67 Will Clark .25 .07
68 Robby Thompson .05 .02
69 Matt Williams .15 .04
70 Jose Uribe .05 .02
71 Kevin Mitchell .05 .02
72 Brett Butler .10 .03
73 Don Robinson .05 .02
74 John Burkett .05 .02
75 Jeff Brantley .10 .03
76 Mets Pennant .05 .02
77 Mets Logo .05 .02
78 Mackey Sasser .05 .02
79 Dave Magadan .05 .02
80 Gregg Jefferies .05 .02
81 Howard Johnson .05 .02
82 Kevin Elster .05 .02
83 Kevin McReynolds .05 .02
84 Daryl Boston .05 .02
85 Darryl Strawberry .10 .03
86 Dwight Gooden .10 .03
87 Frank Viola .05 .02
88 Padres Pennant .05 .02
89 Padres Logo .05 .02
90 Benito Santiago .15 .04
91 Jack Clark .10 .03
92 Roberto Alomar .60 .18
93 Mike Pagliarulo .05 .02
94 Garry Templeton .05 .02
95 Joe Carter .10 .03
96 Bip Roberts .05 .02
97 Tony Gwynn 1.25 .35
98 Ed Whitson .05 .02
99 Andy Benes .05 .02
100 Phillies Pennant .05 .02
101 Phillies Logo .05 .02
102 Darren Daulton .10 .03
103 Ricky Jordan .05 .02
104 Randy Ready .05 .02
105 Charlie Hayes .05 .02
106 Dickie Thon .05 .02
107 Von Hayes .05 .02
108 Len Dykstra .10 .03
109 Dale Murphy .25 .07
110 Ken Howell .05 .02
111 Roger McDowell .05 .02
112 Pirates Pennant .05 .02
113 Pirates Logo .05 .02
114 Mike LaValliere .05 .02
115 Sid Bream .05 .02
116 Jose Lind .05 .02
117 Jeff King .05 .02
118 Jay Bell .05 .02
119 Barry Bonds 1.25 .35
120 Bobby Bonilla .05 .02
121 Andy Van Slyke .10 .03
122 Doug Drabek .05 .02
123 Neal Heaton .05 .02
124 Reds Pennant .05 .02
125 Reds Logo .05 .02
126 Joe Oliver .05 .02
127 Todd Benzinger .05 .02
128 Mariano Duncan .05 .02
129 Chris Sabo .05 .02
130 Barry Larkin .25 .07
131 Eric Davis .10 .03
132 Billy Hatcher .05 .02
133 Paul O'Neill .10 .03
134 Jose Rijo .05 .02
135 Randy Myers .10 .03
136 Expos Pennant .05 .02
137 Expos Logo .05 .02
138 Mike Fitzgerald .05 .02
139 Andres Galarraga .25 .07
140 Delino DeShields .10 .03
141 Tim Wallach .05 .02
142 Spike Owen .05 .02
143 Tim Raines .10 .03
144 Dave Martinez .05 .02
145 Larry Walker .25 .07
146 Expos Helmet .05 .02
147 Dennis Boyd .05 .02
148 Tim Burke .05 .02
149 Bill Sampen .05 .02
150 Dennis Martinez .10 .03
151 Marquis Grissom .25 .07
152 Otis Nixon .10 .03
153 Jerry Goff .05 .02
154 Steve Frey .05 .02
155 NL Emblem .05 .02
156 AL Emblem .05 .02
157 Benito Santiago .10 .03
158 Will Clark .25 .07
159 Ryne Sandberg .75 .23
160 Chris Sabo .05 .02
161 Ozzie Smith .75 .23
162 Kevin Mitchell .05 .02
163 Len Dykstra .10 .03
164 Darryl Strawberry .10 .03
165 Jack Armstrong .05 .02
166 Sandy Alomar Jr. .10 .03
167 Mark McGwire 2.00 .60
168 Steve Sax .05 .02
169 Wade Boggs .50 .15
170 Cal Ripken 2.50 .75
171 Rickey Henderson .60 .18
172 Ken Griffey Jr. 1.50 .45
173 Jose Canseco .40 .12
174 Bob Welch .05 .02
175 Wrigley Field .05 .02
176 World Series Trophy .05 .02
177 Angels Pennant .05 .02
178 Angels Logo .05 .02
179 Lance Parrish .05 .02
180 Wally Joyner .10 .03
181 Johnny Ray .05 .02
182 Jack Howell .05 .02
183 Dick Schofield .05 .02
184 Dave Winfield .50 .15
185 Devon White .10 .03
186 Dante Bichette .10 .03
187 Chuck Finley .10 .03
188 Jim Abbott .10 .03
189 Athletics Pennant .05 .02
190 Athletics Logo .05 .02
191 Terry Steinbach .05 .02
192 Mark McGwire 2.00 .60
193 Willie Randolph .10 .03
194 Carney Lansford .10 .03
195 Walt Weiss .05 .02
196 Rickey Henderson .60 .18
197 Dave Henderson .05 .02
198 Jose Canseco .40 .12
199 Dave Stewart .10 .03
200 Dennis Eckersley .40 .12
201 Brewers Pennant .05 .02
202 Brewers Logo .05 .02
203 B.J. Surhoff .10 .03
204 Greg Brock .05 .02
205 Paul Molitor .75 .23
206 Gary Sheffield .40 .12
207 Bill Spiers .05 .02
208 Robin Yount .50 .15
209 Rob Deer .05 .02
210 Dave Parker .10 .03
211 Mark Knudson .05 .02
212 Dan Plesac .05 .02
213 Indians Pennant .05 .02
214 Indians Logo .05 .02
215 Sandy Alomar Jr. .10 .03
216 Brook Jacoby .05 .02
217 Jerry Browne .05 .02
218 Carlos Baerga .10 .03
219 Felix Fermin .05 .02
220 Candy Maldonado .05 .02
221 Cory Snyder .05 .02
222 Alex Cole .05 .02
223 Tom Candiotti .10 .03
224 Doug Jones .05 .02
225 Mariners Pennant .05 .02
226 Mariners Logo .05 .02
227 Dave Valle .05 .02
228 Pete O'Brien .05 .02
229 Harold Reynolds .10 .03
230 Edgar Martinez .15 .04
231 Omar Vizquel .25 .07
232 Henry Cotto .05 .02
233 Ken Griffey Jr. 1.50 .45
234 Jay Buhner .25 .07
235 Erik Hanson .05 .02
236 Mike Schooler .05 .02
237 Orioles Pennant .05 .02
238 Orioles Logo .05 .02
239 Mickey Tettleton .10 .03
240 Randy Milligan .05 .02
241 Bill Ripken .05 .02
242 Craig Worthington .05 .02
243 Cal Ripken 2.50 .75
244 Steve Finley .25 .07
245 Mike Devereaux .05 .02
246 Joe Orsulak .05 .02
247 Ben McDonald .05 .02
248 Gregg Olson .10 .03
249 Rangers Pennant .05 .02
250 Rangers Logo .05 .02
251 Geno Petralli .05 .02
252 Rafael Palmeiro .25 .07
253 Julio Franco .10 .03
254 Steve Buechele .05 .02
255 Jeff Huson .05 .02
256 Gary Pettis .05 .02
257 Ruben Sierra .10 .03
258 Pete Incaviglia .05 .02
259 Nolan Ryan 2.50 .75
260 Bobby Witt .05 .02
261 Red Sox Pennant .05 .02
262 Red Sox Logo .05 .02
263 Tony Pena .10 .03
264 Carlos Quintana .05 .02
265 Jody Reed .05 .02
266 Wade Boggs .60 .18
267 Luis Rivera .05 .02
268 Mike Greenwell .05 .02
269 Ellis Burks .15 .04
270 Tom Brunansky .05 .02
271 Roger Clemens 1.25 .35
272 Jeff Reardon .10 .03
273 Royals Pennant .05 .02
274 Royals Logo .05 .02
275 Mike Macfarlane .05 .02
276 George Brett 1.25 .35
277 Bill Pecota .05 .02
278 Kevin Seitzer .05 .02
279 Kurt Stillwell .05 .02
280 Jim Eisenreich .05 .02
281 Bo Jackson .25 .07
282 Danny Tartabull .05 .02
283 Bret Saberhagen .10 .03
284 Tom Gordon .10 .03
285 Tigers Pennant .05 .02
286 Tigers Logo .05 .02
287 Mike Heath .05 .02
288 Cecil Fielder .10 .03
289 Lou Whitaker .10 .03
290 Tony Phillips .05 .02
291 Alan Trammell .15 .04
292 Chet Lemon .05 .02
293 Lloyd Moseby .05 .02
294 Gary Ward .05 .02
295 Dan Petry .05 .02
296 Jack Morris .10 .03
297 Twins Pennant .05 .02
298 Twins Logo .05 .02
299 Brian Harper .05 .02
300 Kent Hrbek .10 .03
301 Al Newman .05 .02
302 Gary Gaetti .10 .03
303 Greg Gagne .05 .02
304 Dan Gladden .05 .02
305 Kirby Puckett .60 .18
306 Gene Larkin .05 .02
307 Kevin Tapani .05 .02
308 Rick Aguilera .10 .03
309 White Sox Pennant .05 .02
310 White Sox Logo .05 .02
311 Carlton Fisk .50 .15
312 Carlos Martinez .05 .02
313 Scott Fletcher .05 .02
314 Robin Ventura .25 .07
315 Ozzie Guillen .10 .03
316 Sammy Sosa 2.00 .60
317 Lance Johnson .05 .02
318 Ivan Calderon .05 .02
319 Greg Hibbard .05 .02
320 Bobby Thigpen .05 .02
321 Yankees Pennant .05 .02
322 Yankees Logo .05 .02
323 Bob Geren .05 .02
324 Don Mattingly 1.25 .35
325 Steve Sax .05 .02
326 Jim Leyritz .10 .03
327 Alvaro Espinoza .05 .02
328 Roberto Kelly .05 .02
329 Oscar Azocar .05 .02
330 Jesse Barfield .05 .02
331 Chuck Cary .05 .02
332 Dave Righetti .05 .02
333 Blue Jays Pennant .05 .02
334 Blue Jays Logo .05 .02
335 Pat Borders .05 .02
336 Fred McGriff .25 .07
337 Manny Lee .05 .02
338 Kelly Gruber .05 .02
339 Tony Fernandez .10 .03
340 George Bell .05 .02
341 Mookie Wilson .10 .03
342 Junior Felix .05 .02
343 Blue Jays Helmet .05 .02
344 Dave Stieb .10 .03
345 Tom Henke .05 .02
346 Greg Myers .05 .02
347 Glenallen Hill .05 .02
348 John Olerud .15 .04
349 Todd Stottlemyre .05 .02
350 David Wells .15 .04
351 Jimmy Key .10 .03
352 Mark Langston .05 .02
353 Randy Johnson .50 .15
354 Nolan Ryan 2.50 .75
355 Dave Stewart .10 .03
356 Fernando Valenzuela .10 .03
357 Andy Hawkins .05 .02
358 Melido Perez .05 .02
359 Terry Mulholland .05 .02
360 Dave Stieb .05 .02

1992 Panini Stickers

These 288 stickers measure approximately 2 1/8" by 3" and feature on their fronts white-bordered color player action shots that are serrated on their left sides and are framed by a colored line on the remaining three sides. The stickers and album used to store them are organized by team. The Best of the Best AL (144-146), The Best of the Best NL (147-149) and 1991 All-Stars (270-288) are the subsets included within the set. A french version of these stickers were made. They are valued at twice the values listed in our checklist.

Nm-Mt Ex-Mt
COMPLETE SET (288) 15.00 4.50
1 Panini Baseball .05 .02
1992 Logo
2 MLB Logo .05 .02
3 MLBPA Logo .05 .02
4 Lance Parrish .05 .02
5 Wally Joyner .10 .03
6 Luis Sojo .05 .02
7 Gary Gaetti .10 .03
8 Dick Schofield .05 .02
9 Junior Felix .05 .02
10 Luis Polonia .05 .02
11 Mark Langston .05 .02
12 Jim Abbott .10 .03
13 Angels Team Logo .05 .02
14 Terry Steinbach .05 .02
15 Mark McGwire 1.50 .45
16 Mike Gallego .05 .02
17 Carney Lansford .10 .03
18 Walt Weiss .05 .02
19 Jose Canseco .40 .12
20 Dave Henderson .05 .02
21 Rickey Henderson .60 .18
22 Dennis Eckersley .40 .12
23 Athletics Team Logo .05 .02
24 Pat Borders .05 .02
25 John Olerud .15 .04
26 Roberto Alomar .25 .07
27 Kelly Gruber .05 .02
28 Manuel Lee .05 .02
29 Joe Carter .10 .03
30 Devon White .05 .02
31 Candy Maldonado .05 .02
32 Dave Stieb .05 .02
33 Blue Jays Team Logo .05 .02
34 B.J. Surhoff .10 .03
35 Franklin Stubbs .05 .02
36 Willie Randolph .10 .03
37 Jim Gantner .05 .02
38 Bill Spiers .05 .02
39 Dante Bichette .10 .03
40 Robin Yount .50 .15
41 Greg Vaughn .15 .04
42 Chris Bosio .05 .02
43 Brewers Team Logo .05 .02
44 Sandy Alomar Jr. .10 .03
45 Mike Aldrete .05 .02
46 Mark Lewis .05 .02
47 Carlos Baerga .10 .03
48 Felix Fermin .05 .02
49 Mark Whiten .05 .02
50 Alex Cole .05 .02
51 Albert Belle .10 .03
52 Greg Swindell .05 .02
53 Indians Team Logo .05 .02
54 Dave Valle .05 .02
55 Pete O'Brien .05 .02
56 Harold Reynolds .10 .03
57 Edgar Martinez .15 .04
58 Omar Vizquel .10 .03
59 Jay Buhner .25 .07
60 Ken Griffey Jr. 1.25 .35
61 Greg Briley .05 .02
62 Randy Johnson .60 .18
63 Mariners Team Logo .05 .02
64 Chris Hoiles .05 .02
65 Randy Milligan .05 .02
66 Bill Ripken .05 .02
67 Leo Gomez .05 .02
68 Cal Ripken 2.00 .60
69 Dwight Evans .10 .03
70 Mike Devereaux .05 .02
71 Joe Orsulak .05 .02
72 Gregg Olson .10 .03
73 Orioles Team Logo .05 .02
74 Ivan Rodriguez .75 .23
75 Rafael Palmeiro .25 .07
76 Julio Franco .05 .02
77 Dean Palmer .10 .03
78 Jeff Huson .05 .02
79 Ruben Sierra .10 .03
80 Gary Pettis .05 .02
81 Juan Gonzalez .75 .23
82 Nolan Ryan 2.00 .60
83 Rangers Team Logo .05 .02
84 Tony Pena .10 .03
85 Carlos Quintana .05 .02
86 Jody Reed .05 .02
87 Wade Boggs .60 .18
88 Luis Rivera .05 .02
89 Tom Brunansky .05 .02
90 Ellis Burks .15 .04
91 Mike Greenwell .05 .02
92 Roger Clemens 1.00 .30
93 Red Sox Team Logo .05 .02
94 Todd Benzinger .05 .02
95 Terry Shumpert .05 .02
96 Bill Pecota .05 .02
97 Kurt Stillwell .05 .02
98 Danny Tartabull .05 .02
99 Brian McRae .05 .02
100 Kirk Gibson .10 .03
101 Bret Saberhagen .10 .03
102 George Brett 1.00 .30
103 Royals Team Logo .05 .02
104 Mickey Tettleton .05 .02
105 Cecil Fielder .10 .03
106 Lou Whitaker .10 .03
107 Travis Fryman .10 .03
108 Alan Trammell .15 .04
109 Rob Deer .05 .02
110 Milt Cuyler .05 .02
111 Lloyd Moseby .05 .02
112 Bill Gullickson .05 .02
113 Tigers Team Logo .05 .02
114 Brian Harper .05 .02
115 Kent Hrbek .10 .03
116 Chuck Knoblauch .25 .07
117 Mike Pagliarulo .05 .02
118 Greg Gagne .05 .02
119 Shane Mack .05 .02
120 Kirby Puckett .50 .15
121 Dan Gladden .05 .02
122 Jack Morris .10 .03
123 Twins Team Logo .05 .02
124 Carlton Fisk .50 .15
125 Frank Thomas .40 .12
126 Joey Cora .05 .02
127 Robin Ventura .15 .04
128 Ozzie Guillen .10 .03
129 Sammy Sosa 1.00 .30
130 Lance Johnson .05 .02
131 Tim Raines .10 .03
132 Bobby Thigpen .05 .02
133 White Sox Team Logo .05 .02
134 Matt Nokes .05 .02
135 Don Mattingly 1.00 .30
136 Steve Sax .05 .02
137 Pat Kelly .05 .02
138 Alvaro Espinoza .05 .02
139 Jesse Barfield .05 .02
140 Roberto Kelly .05 .02
141 Mel Hall .05 .02
142 Scott Sanderson .05 .02
143 Yankees Team Logo .05 .02
144 Cecil Fielder .15 .04
Jose Canseco
145 Julio Franco .10 .03
146 Roger Clemens 1.00 .30
147 Howard Johnson .05 .02
148 Terry Pendleton .05 .02
149 Dennis Martinez .10 .03
150 Astros Team Logo .05 .02
151 Craig Biggio .25 .07
152 Jeff Bagwell .50 .15
153 Casey Candaele .05 .02
154 Ken Caminiti .15 .04
155 Andujar Cedeno .05 .02
156 Mike Simms .05 .02
157 Steve Finley .15 .04
158 Luis Gonzalez .25 .07
159 Pete Harnisch .05 .02
160 Braves Team Logo .05 .02
161 Greg Olson .05 .02
162 Sid Bream .05 .02
163 Mark Lemke .05 .02
164 Terry Pendleton .05 .02
165 Rafael Belliard .05 .02
166 Dave Justice .25 .07
167 Ron Gant .10 .03
168 Lonnie Smith .05 .02
169 Steve Avery .05 .02
170 Cardinals Team Logo .05 .02
171 Tom Pagnozzi .05 .02
172 Pedro Guerrero .10 .03
173 Jose Oquendo .05 .02
174 Todd Zeile .10 .03
175 Ozzie Smith .75 .23
176 Felix Jose .05 .02
177 Ray Lankford .25 .07
178 Jose DeLeon .05 .02
179 Lee Smith .10 .03
180 Cubs Team Logo .05 .02
181 Hector Villanueva .05 .02
182 Mark Grace .25 .07
183 Ryne Sandberg .60 .18
184 Luis Salazar .05 .02
185 Shawon Dunston .05 .02
186 Andre Dawson .25 .07
187 Jerome Walton .05 .02
188 George Bell .05 .02
189 Greg Maddux 1.25 .35
190 Dodgers Team Logo .05 .02
191 Mike Scioscia .10 .03
192 Eddie Murray .60 .18
193 Juan Samuel .05 .02
194 Lenny Harris .05 .02
195 Alfredo Griffin .05 .02
196 Darryl Strawberry .10 .03
197 Brett Butler .10 .03
198 Kal Daniels .05 .02
199 Orel Hershiser .10 .03
200 Expos Team Logo .05 .02
201 Gilberto Reyes .05 .02
202 Andres Galarraga .25 .07
203 Delino DeShields .10 .03
204 Tim Wallach .05 .02
205 Spike Owen .05 .02
206 Larry Walker .25 .07
207 Marquis Grissom .10 .03
208 Ivan Calderon .10 .03
209 Dennis Martinez .10 .03
210 Giants Team Logo .05 .02
211 Steve Decker .05 .02
212 Will Clark .25 .07
213 Robby Thompson .05 .02
214 Matt Williams .15 .04
215 Jose Uribe .05 .02
216 Kevin Bass .05 .02
217 Willie McGee .10 .03
218 Kevin Mitchell .10 .03
219 Dave Righetti .05 .02
220 Mets Team Logo .05 .02
221 Rick Cerone .05 .02
222 Dave Magadan .05 .02
223 Gregg Jefferies .05 .02
224 Howard Johnson .05 .02
225 Kevin Elster .05 .02
226 Hubie Brooks .05 .02
227 Vince Coleman .05 .02
228 Kevin McReynolds .05 .02
229 Frank Viola .05 .02
230 Padres Team Logo .05 .02
231 Benito Santiago .10 .03
232 Fred McGriff .25 .07
233 Bip Roberts .05 .02
234 Jack Howell .05 .02
235 Tony Fernandez .10 .03
236 Tony Gwynn 1.00 .30
237 Darrin Jackson .05 .02
238 Bruce Hurst .05 .02
239 Craig Lefferts .05 .02
240 Phillies Team Logo .05 .02
241 Darren Daulton .10 .03
242 John Kruk .10 .03
243 Mickey Morandini .05 .02
244 Charlie Hayes .05 .02
245 Dickie Thon .05 .02
246 Dale Murphy .25 .07
247 Lenny Dykstra .10 .03
248 Von Hayes .05 .02
249 Terry Mulholland .05 .02
250 Pirates Team Logo .05 .02
251 Mike LaValliere .05 .02
252 Orlando Merced .05 .02
253 Jose Lind .05 .02
254 Steve Buechele .05 .02
255 Jay Bell .05 .02
256 Bobby Bonilla .10 .03
257 Andy Van Slyke .10 .03
258 Barry Bonds 1.00 .30
259 Doug Drabek .05 .02
260 Reds Team Logo .05 .02
261 Joe Oliver .05 .02
262 Hal Morris .05 .02
263 Bill Doran .05 .02
264 Chris Sabo .05 .02
265 Barry Larkin .25 .07
266 Paul O'Neill .15 .04
267 Eric Davis .10 .03
268 Glenn Braggs .05 .02
269 Jose Rijo .05 .02
270 Toronto Skydome .05 .02
271 Sandy Alomar Jr. AS .10 .03
272 Cecil Fielder AS .10 .03
273 Roberto Alomar AS .25 .07
274 Wade Boggs AS .50 .15
275 Cal Ripken AS 1.00 .30
276 Dave Henderson AS .05 .02
277 Ken Griffey Jr. AS .75 .23
278 Rickey Henderson AS .50 .15
279 Jack Morris AS .10 .03
280 Benito Santiago AS .05 .02
281 Will Clark AS .25 .07
282 Ryne Sandberg AS .25 .07
283 Chris Sabo AS .05 .02
284 Ozzie Smith AS .25 .07
285 Andre Dawson AS .15 .04
286 Tony Gwynn AS .50 .15
287 Ivan Calderon AS .05 .02
288 Tom Glavine AS .10 .03

1993 Panini Stickers

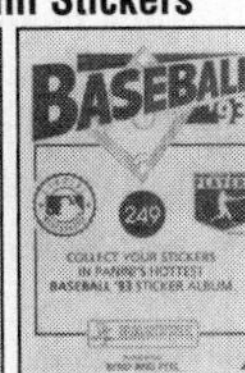

The 300 stickers in this set measure approximately 2 3/8" by 3 3/8" and were to be pasted in a 9" by 11" album. Six stickers were distributed in each 49-cent foil pack. Ten players from each of the American and National League teams are featured, including one glitter sticker of Panini's Future Stars. One card for each team displays the team's logo on the front. The stickers are numbered on the back and checklisted below according to special subsets and teams.

Nm-Mt Ex-Mt
COMPLETE SET (300) 15.00 4.50
1 Angels Logo .05 .02
2 Mark Langston .05 .02
3 Ron Tingley .05 .02
4 Gary Gaetti .10 .03
5 Kelly Gruber .05 .02
6 Gary DiSarcina .05 .02
7 Damion Easley .05 .02
8 Luis Polonia .05 .02
9 Lee Stevens .05 .02
10 Chad Curtis .10 .03
11 Rene Gonzales .05 .02
12 Athletics Logo .05 .02
13 Dennis Eckersley .40 .12
14 Terry Steinbach .05 .02
15 Mark McGwire 2.00 .60
16 Mike Bordick .05 .02
17 Carney Lansford .10 .03
18 Jerry Browne .05 .02
19 Rickey Henderson .75 .23
20 Dave Henderson .05 .02
21 Ruben Sierra .10 .03
22 Ron Darling .05 .02
23 Blue Jays Logo .05 .02
24 Jack Morris .10 .03
25 Pat Borders .05 .02
26 John Olerud .15 .04
27 Roberto Alomar .25 .07
28 Luis Sojo .05 .02
29 Dave Stewart .10 .03
30 Devon White .05 .02
31 Joe Carter .10 .03
32 Derek Bell .05 .02
33 Juan Guzman .05 .02
34 Brewers Logo .05 .02
35 Jaime Navarro .05 .02
36 B.J. Surhoff .10 .03
37 Franklin Stubbs .05 .02
38 Bill Spiers .05 .02
39 Pat Listach .05 .02
40 Kevin Seitzer .05 .02
41 Darryl Hamilton .05 .02
42 Robin Yount .50 .15
43 Kevin Reimer .05 .02
44 Greg Vaughn .10 .03
45 Indians Logo .05 .02
46 Charles Nagy .05 .02
47 Sandy Alomar Jr. .10 .03
48 Reggie Jefferson .05 .02
49 Mark Lewis .05 .02
50 Felix Fermin .05 .02
51 Carlos Baerga .10 .03
52 Albert Belle .10 .03
53 Kenny Lofton .40 .12
54 Mark Whiten .05 .02
55 Paul Sorrento .10 .03
56 Mariners Logo .05 .02
57 Dave Fleming .05 .02
58 Dave Valle .05 .02
59 Pete O'Brien .05 .02
60 Randy Johnson .60 .18
61 Omar Vizquel .15 .04
62 Edgar Martinez .15 .04
63 Ken Griffey Jr. 1.50 .45
64 Henry Cotto .05 .02
65 Jay Buhner .25 .07
66 Tino Martinez .25 .07
67 Orioles Logo .05 .02
68 Ben McDonald .05 .02
69 Mike Mussina .25 .07
70 Chris Hoiles .05 .02
71 Randy Milligan .05 .02
72 Billy Ripken .05 .02
73 Cal Ripken 2.50 .75
74 Leo Gomez .05 .02
75 Mike Devereaux .05 .02
76 Brady Anderson .10 .03
77 Joe Orsulak .05 .02
78 Rangers Logo .05 .02
79 Kevin Brown .15 .04
80 Ivan Rodriguez .60 .18
81 Rafael Palmeiro .25 .07
82 Julio Franco .10 .03
83 Jeff Huson .05 .02
84 Dean Palmer .10 .03
85 Jose Canseco .40 .12
86 Juan Gonzalez .75 .23
87 Nolan Ryan 2.50 .75
88 Brian Downing .05 .02
89 Red Sox Logo .05 .02
90 Roger Clemens 1.25 .35
91 Tony Pena .10 .03
92 Mo Vaughn .10 .03
93 Scott Cooper .05 .02
94 Luis Rivera .05 .02
95 Ellis Burks .10 .03
96 Mike Greenwell .05 .02
97 Andre Dawson .15 .04
98 Ivan Calderon .05 .02
99 Phil Plantier .05 .02
100 Royals Logo .05 .02
101 Kevin Appier .10 .03
102 Mike Macfarlane .05 .02
103 Wally Joyner .10 .03
104 Jim Eisenreich .10 .03
105 Greg Gagne .05 .02
106 Gregg Jefferies .05 .02
107 Kevin McReynolds .05 .02
108 Brian McRae .05 .02
109 Keith Miller .05 .02
110 George Brett 1.00 .30
111 Tigers Logo .05 .02
112 Bill Gullickson .05 .02
113 Mickey Tettleton .05 .02
114 Cecil Fielder .10 .03
115 Tony Phillips .05 .02
116 Scott Livingstone .05 .02
117 Travis Fryman .10 .03
118 Dan Gladden .05 .02
119 Rob Deer .05 .02
120 Frank Tanana .05 .02
121 Skeeter Barnes .05 .02
122 Twins Logo .05 .02
123 Scott Erickson .05 .02
124 Brian Harper .05 .02
125 Kent Hrbek .10 .03
126 Chuck Knoblauch .25 .07
127 Willie Banks .05 .02
128 Scott Leius .05 .02
129 Shane Mack .05 .02
130 Kirby Puckett .50 .15
131 Chili Davis .10 .03
132 Pedro Munoz .05 .02
133 White Sox Logo .05 .02
134 Jack McDowell .05 .02
135 Carlton Fisk .50 .15
136 Frank Thomas .40 .12
137 Steve Sax .05 .02
138 Ozzie Guillen .10 .03
139 Robin Ventura .15 .04
140 Tim Raines .10 .03
141 Lance Johnson .05 .02
142 Ron Karkovice .05 .02
143 George Bell .05 .02
144 Yankees Logo .05 .02
145 Scott Sanderson .05 .02
146 Matt Nokes .05 .02
147 Kevin Maas .05 .02
148 Randy Velarde .05 .02
149 Andy Stankiewicz .05 .02
150 Pat Kelly .05 .02
151 Paul O'Neill .10 .03
152 Wade Boggs .50 .15
153 Danny Tartabull .05 .02
154 Don Mattingly 1.25 .35
155 Edgar Martinez LL .15 .04
156 Kevin Brown LL .15 .04
157 Dennis Eckersley LL .10 .03
158 Gary Sheffield LL .25 .07
159 Tom Glavine LL .60 .18
Greg Maddux
160 Lee Smith LL .10 .03
161 Dennis Eckersley CY .10 .03
162 Dennis Eckersley MVP .10 .03
163 Pat Listach ROY .05 .02
164 Greg Maddux CY .75 .23
165 Barry Bonds MVP .25 .07
166 Eric Karros ROY .15 .04
167 Astros Logo .05 .02
168 Pete Harnisch .05 .02
169 Eddie Taubensee .05 .02
170 Jeff Bagwell 1.00 .30
171 Craig Biggio .40 .12
172 Andujar Cedeno .05 .02
173 Ken Caminiti .10 .03
174 Steve Finley .15 .04
175 Luis Gonzalez .25 .07
176 Eric Anthony .05 .02
177 Casey Candaele .05 .02
178 Braves Logo .05 .02
179 Tom Glavine .40 .12
180 Greg Olson .05 .02
181 Sid Bream .05 .02
182 Mark Lemke .05 .02
183 Jeff Blauser .05 .02
184 Terry Pendleton .05 .02
185 Ron Gant .10 .03
186 Otis Nixon .05 .02
187 Dave Justice .25 .07
188 Deion Sanders .15 .04
189 Cardinals Logo .05 .02
190 Bob Tewksbury .05 .02
191 Tom Pagnozzi .05 .02
192 Lee Smith .10 .03
193 Geronimo Pena .05 .02
194 Ozzie Smith .60 .18
195 Todd Zeile .10 .03
196 Ray Lankford .10 .03
197 Bernard Gilkey .05 .02
198 Felix Jose .05 .02
199 Donovan Osborne .05 .02
200 Cubs Logo .05 .02
201 Mike Morgan .05 .02
202 Rick Wilkins .05 .02
203 Mark Grace .25 .07
204 Ryne Sandberg .60 .18
205 Shawon Dunston .05 .02
206 Steve Buechele .05 .02
207 Kal Daniels .05 .02
208 Sammy Sosa 1.25 .35
209 Derrick May .05 .02
210 Doug Dascenzo .05 .02
211 Dodgers Logo .05 .02
212 Ramon Martinez .05 .02
213 Mike Scioscia .10 .03
214 Eric Karros .15 .04
215 Tim Wallach .05 .02
216 Jose Offerman .05 .02
217 Mike Sharperson .05 .02
218 Brett Butler .10 .03
219 Darryl Strawberry .10 .03
220 Lenny Harris .05 .02
221 Eric Davis .10 .03
222 Expos Logo .05 .02
223 Ken Hill .05 .02
224 Darrin Fletcher .05 .02
225 Greg Colbrunn .05 .02
226 Delino DeShields .05 .02
227 Wil Cordero .05 .02
228 Dennis Martinez .10 .03
229 John Vander Wal .05 .02
230 Marquis Grissom .10 .03
231 Larry Walker .25 .07
232 Moises Alou .10 .03
233 Giants Logo .05 .02
234 Bill Swift .05 .02
235 Kirt Manwaring .05 .02
236 Will Clark .25 .07
237 Robby Thompson .05 .02
238 Royce Clayton .05 .02
239 Matt Williams .15 .04
240 Willie McGee .10 .03
241 Mark Leonard .05 .02
242 Cory Snyder .05 .02
243 Barry Bonds 1.25 .35
244 Mets Logo .05 .02
245 Dwight Gooden .10 .03
246 Todd Hundley .10 .03
247 Eddie Murray .50 .15
248 Sid Fernandez .05 .02
249 Tony Fernandez .10 .03
250 Dave Magadan .05 .02
251 Howard Johnson .05 .02
252 Vince Coleman .05 .02
253 Bobby Bonilla .10 .03
254 Daryl Boston .05 .02
255 Padres Logo .05 .02
256 Bruce Hurst .05 .02
257 Dan Walters .05 .02
258 Fred McGriff .15 .04
259 Kurt Stillwell .05 .02
260 Craig Shipley .05 .02
261 Gary Sheffield .40 .12
262 Tony Gwynn 1.25 .35
263 Oscar Azocar .05 .02
264 Darrin Jackson .05 .02
265 Andy Benes .05 .02
266 Phillies Logo .05 .02
267 Terry Mulholland .05 .02
268 Curt Schilling .40 .12
269 Darren Daulton .10 .03
270 John Kruk .10 .03
271 Mickey Morandini .05 .02
272 Mariano Duncan .05 .02
273 Dave Hollins .05 .02
274 Lenny Dykstra .10 .03
275 Wes Chamberlain .05 .02
276 Stan Javier .05 .02
277 Pirates Logo .05 .02
278 Zane Smith .05 .02
279 Tim Wakefield .15 .04
280 Mike LaValliere .05 .02
281 Orlando Merced .05 .02
282 Stan Belinda .05 .02
283 Jay Bell .05 .02
284 Jeff King .05 .02
285 Andy Van Slyke .10 .03
286 Bob Walk .05 .02
287 Gary Varsho .05 .02
288 Reds Logo .05 .02
289 Jose Rijo .05 .02
290 Joe Oliver .05 .02
291 Hal Morris .05 .02
292 Bip Roberts .05 .02
293 Barry Larkin .25 .07
294 Chris Sabo .05 .02
295 Roberto Kelly .05 .02
296 Kevin Mitchell .05 .02
297 Rob Dibble .05 .02
298 Reggie Sanders .10 .03
299 Marlins Logo .05 .02
300 Rockies Logo .10 .03

1994 Panini Stickers

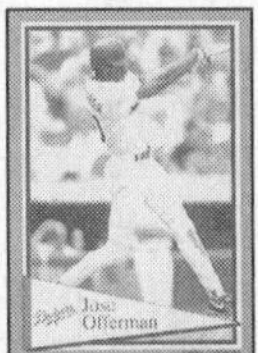

This set of 1994 Panini Baseball consists of 268 stickers measuring approximately 2 3/8" by

3 3/8". The stickers were sold in Panini packets of six, with 50 packets (suggested retail price of 49 cents each) per box. The collectible sticker album measures 9 1/8" by 10 5/8" (suggested retail price of 99 cents) and features eight baseball players on the bright yellow, UV coated cover. The album's inside front cover carries 1993 Team Statistics for the American and National Leagues and also lists the 1993 League Standings. The back inside cover provides information on how to order missing stickers and take advantage of the mail in offer of 30 stickers for $4.00, plus ten '94 Panini wrappers. After presenting the American (5-10) and National League Leaders (11-16), the set is arranged grouped alphabetically within teams and checklisted below alphabetically according to teams for each league.

Nm-Mt Ex-Mt
COMPLETE SET (268) 15.00 4.50
1 WS Opening Ceremony .05 .02
(Upper left)
2 WS Opening Ceremony .05 .02
(Upper right)
3 WS Opening Ceremony .05 .02
(Lower left)
4 WS Opening Ceremony .05 .02
(Lower right)
5 John Olerud .10 .03
Highest Batting Average
6 Juan Gonzalez .10 .03
Most Home Runs
7 Albert Belle .10 .03
Most Runs Batted In
8 Jack McDowell .05 .02
Most Wins
9 Randy Johnson .50 .15
Most Strikeouts
10 Jeff Montgomery .05 .02
Duane Ward
Most Saves (tie)
11 Andres Galarraga .50 .15
Highest Batting Average
12 Barry Bonds .50 .15
Most Home Runs
13 Barry Bonds .50 .15
Most Runs Batted In
14 Tom Glavine .10 .03
John Burkett
Most Wins (tie)
15 Jose Rijo .05 .02
Most Strikeouts
16 Randy Myers .05 .02
Most Saves
17 Brady Anderson .10 .03
18 Harold Baines .10 .03
19 Mike Devereaux .05 .02
20 Chris Hoiles .05 .02
21 Mike Mussina .25 .07
22 Harold Reynolds .05 .02
23 Cal Ripken Jr. 2.00 .60
24 David Segui .05 .02
25 Fernando Valenzuela .10 .03
26 Roger Clemens 1.00 .30
27 Scott Cooper .05 .02
28 Andre Dawson .25 .07
29 Scott Fletcher .05 .02
30 Mike Greenwell .05 .02
31 Billy Hatcher .05 .02
32 Tony Pena .10 .03
33 John Valentin .05 .02
34 Mo Vaughn .10 .03
35 Chad Curtis .05 .02
36 Gary DiSarcina .05 .02
37 Damion Easley .05 .02
38 Mark Langston .05 .02
39 Torey Lovullo .05 .02
40 Greg Myers .05 .02
41 Luis Polonia .05 .02
42 Tim Salmon .25 .07
43 J.T. Snow .10 .03
44 George Bell .05 .02
45 Ellis Burks .10 .03
46 Joey Cora .05 .02
47 Ozzie Guillen .10 .03
48 Roberto Hernandez .05 .02
49 Bo Jackson .25 .07
50 Jack McDowell .05 .02
51 Frank Thomas .50 .15
52 Robin Ventura .10 .03
53 Sandy Alomar Jr. .10 .03
54 Carlos Baerga .10 .03
55 Albert Belle .10 .03
56 Felix Fermin .05 .02
57 Wayne Kirby .05 .02
58 Kenny Lofton .40 .12
59 Charles Nagy .05 .02
60 Paul Sorrento .05 .02
61 Jeff Treadway .05 .02
62 Eric Davis .10 .03
63 Cecil Fielder .10 .03
64 Travis Fryman .10 .03
65 Bill Gullickson .05 .02
66 Mike Moore .05 .02
67 Tony Phillips .05 .02
68 Mickey Tettleton .10 .03
69 Alan Trammell .15 .04
70 Lou Whitaker .10 .03
71 Kevin Appier .10 .03
72 Greg Gagne .05 .02
73 Tom Gordon .10 .03
74 Felix Jose .05 .02
75 Wally Joyner .10 .03
76 Jose Lind .05 .02
77 Mike Macfarlane .05 .02
78 Brian McRae .05 .02
79 Kevin McReynolds .05 .02
80 Darryl Hamilton .05 .02
81 Teddy Higuera .05 .02
82 John Jaha .05 .02
83 Pat Listach .05 .02
84 Dave Nilsson .05 .02
85 Kevin Reimer .05 .02
86 Kevin Seitzer .05 .02
87 B.J. Surhoff .10 .03
88 Greg Vaughn .15 .04
89 Willie Banks .05 .02
90 Brian Harper .05 .02
91 Kent Hrbek .10 .03
92 Chuck Knoblauch .25 .07
93 Shane Mack .05 .02
94 Pat Meares .05 .02
95 Pedro Munoz .05 .02
96 Kirby Puckett .40 .12
97 Dave Winfield .50 .15
98 Jim Abbott .10 .03
99 Wade Boggs .50 .15
100 Mike Gallego .05 .02
101 Pat Kelly .05 .02
102 Don Mattingly 1.00 .30
103 Paul O'Neill .10 .03
104 Mike Stanley .05 .02
105 Danny Tartabull .05 .02
106 Bernie Williams .25 .07
107 Mike Bordick .05 .02
108 Dennis Eckersley .40 .12
109 Dave Henderson .05 .02
110 Mark McGwire 1.50 .45
111 Troy Neel .05 .02
112 Ruben Sierra .10 .03
113 Terry Steinbach .05 .02
114 Todd Van Poppel .05 .02
115 Bob Welch .05 .02
116 Bret Boone .15 .04
117 Jay Buhner .10 .03
118 Ken Griffey Jr. 1.25 .35
119 Randy Johnson .60 .18
120 Rich Amaral .05 .02
121 Edgar Martinez .15 .04
122 Tino Martinez .25 .07
123 Dave Valle .05 .02
124 Omar Vizquel .10 .03
125 Jose Canseco .30 .09
126 Julio Franco .05 .02
127 Juan Gonzalez .75 .23
128 Tom Henke .05 .02
129 Manuel Lee .05 .02
130 Rafael Palmeiro .25 .07
131 Dean Palmer .10 .03
132 Ivan Rodriguez .50 .15
133 Doug Strange .05 .02
134 Roberto Alomar .25 .07
135 Pat Borders .05 .02
136 Joe Carter .10 .03
137 Tony Fernandez .10 .03
138 Juan Guzman .05 .02
139 Rickey Henderson .60 .18
140 Paul Molitor .40 .12
141 John Olerud .10 .03
142 Devon White .10 .03
143 Jeff Blauser .05 .02
144 Ron Gant .10 .03
145 Tom Glavine .40 .12
146 Dave Justice .25 .07
147 Greg Maddux 1.25 .35
148 Fred McGriff .15 .04
149 Terry Pendleton .05 .02
150 Deion Sanders .10 .03
151 John Smoltz .15 .04
152 Shawon Dunston .05 .02
153 Mark Grace .25 .07
154 Derrick May .05 .02
155 Randy Myers .05 .02
156 Ryne Sandberg .50 .15
157 Dwight Smith .05 .02
158 Sammy Sosa 1.00 .30
159 Jose Vizcaino .05 .02
160 Rick Wilkins .05 .02
161 Tom Browning .05 .02
162 Roberto Kelly .05 .02
163 Barry Larkin .15 .04
164 Kevin Mitchell .05 .02
165 Hal Morris .05 .02
166 Joe Oliver .05 .02
167 Jose Rijo .05 .02
168 Chris Sabo .05 .02
169 Reggie Sanders .10 .03
170 Freddie Benavides .05 .02
171 Dante Bichette .10 .03
172 Vinny Castilla .10 .03
173 Jerald Clark .05 .02
174 Andres Galarraga .25 .07
175 Charlie Hayes .05 .02
176 Chris Jones .05 .02
177 Roberto Mejia .05 .02
178 Eric Young .05 .02
179 Bret Barberie .05 .02
180 Chuck Carr .05 .02
181 Jeff Conine .05 .02
182 Orestes Destrade .05 .02
183 Bryan Harvey .05 .02
184 Rich Renteria .05 .02
185 Benito Santiago .10 .03
186 Gary Sheffield .40 .12
187 Walt Weiss .05 .02
188 Eric Anthony .05 .02
189 Jeff Bagwell .75 .23
190 Craig Biggio .40 .12
191 Ken Caminiti .10 .03
192 Andujar Cedeno .05 .02
193 Doug Drabek .05 .02
194 Steve Finley .10 .03
195 Doug Jones .05 .02
196 Darryl Kile .05 .02
197 Brett Butler .10 .03
198 Tom Candiotti .10 .03
199 Dave Hansen .10 .03
200 Orel Hershiser .10 .03
201 Eric Karros .10 .03
202 Jose Offerman .05 .02
203 Mike Piazza 1.50 .45
204 Cory Snyder .05 .02
205 Darryl Strawberry .10 .03
206 Moises Alou .15 .04
207 Sean Berry .05 .02
208 Wil Cordero .05 .02
209 Delino DeShields .05 .02
210 Marquis Grissom .10 .03
211 Ken Hill .05 .02
212 Mike Lansing .05 .02
213 Larry Walker .25 .07
214 John Wetteland .10 .03
215 Bobby Bonilla .10 .03
216 Jeromy Burnitz .15 .04
217 Dwight Gooden .10 .03
218 Todd Hundley .10 .03
219 Howard Johnson .05 .02
220 Jeff Kent .25 .07
221 Eddie Murray .40 .12
222 Bret Saberhagen .10 .03
223 Ryan Thompson .05 .02
224 Darren Daulton .10 .03
225 Mariano Duncan .05 .02
226 Lenny Dykstra .10 .03
227 Jim Eisenreich .10 .03
228 Dave Hollins .05 .02
229 John Kruk .10 .03
230 Curt Schilling .30 .09
231 Kevin Stocker .05 .02
232 Mitch Williams .05 .02
233 Jay Bell .05 .02
234 Steve Cooke .05 .02
235 Carlos Garcia .05 .02
236 Jeff King .05 .02
237 Orlando Merced .05 .02
238 Don Slaught .05 .02
239 Zane Smith .05 .02
240 Andy Van Slyke .05 .02
241 Kevin Young .05 .02
242 Bernard Gilkey .05 .02
243 Gregg Jefferies .05 .02
244 Brian Jordan .10 .03
245 Ray Lankford .10 .03
246 Tom Pagnozzi .05 .02
247 Geronimo Pena .05 .02
248 Ozzie Smith .50 .15
249 Bob Tewksbury .05 .02
250 Mark Whiten .05 .02
251 Brad Ausmus .05 .02
252 Derek Bell .05 .02
253 Andy Benes .05 .02
254 Phil Clark .05 .02
255 Jeff Gardner .05 .02
256 Tony Gwynn 1.00 .30
257 Trevor Hoffman .15 .04
258 Phil Plantier .05 .02
259 Craig Shipley .05 .02
260 Rod Beck .10 .03
261 Barry Bonds 1.00 .30
262 John Burkett .05 .02
263 Will Clark .25 .07
264 Royce Clayton .05 .02
265 Willie McGee .10 .03
266 Bill Swift .05 .02
267 Robby Thompson .05 .02
268 Matt Williams .15 .04

1995 Panini Stickers

FLEER
28
Collect all 156 stickers in the Fleer® Major League Baseball® All-Stars 1995 Edition Album

This 156-sticker set measures approximately 1 15/16" by 3" and was distributed by Fleer. The fronts feature color action player photos framed in different colors on a white background. The player's name and team logo appear in a bar at the bottom. The backs carry the sponsor logos. The set closes with team logos (129-156).

Nm-Mt Ex-Mt
COMPLETE SET (156) 20.00 6.00
1 Tom Glavine .40 .12
2 Doug Drabek .05 .02
3 Rod Beck .10 .03
4 Pedro Martinez .60 .18
5 Danny Jackson .05 .02
6 Greg Maddux 2.00 .60
7 Bret Saberhagen .10 .03
8 Ken Hill .05 .02
9 Marvin Freeman .05 .02
10 Andy Benes .05 .02
11 Wilson Alvarez .05 .02
12 Jimmy Key .10 .03
13 Mike Mussina .25 .07
14 Roger Clemens 1.50 .45
15 Pat Hentgen .10 .03
16 Randy Johnson .75 .23
17 Lee Smith .10 .03
18 David Cone .10 .03
19 Jason Bere .05 .02
20 Dennis Martinez .10 .03
21 Darren Daulton .10 .03
22 Darrin Fletcher .05 .02
23 Tom Pagnozzi .05 .02
24 Mike Piazza 2.00 .60
25 Benito Santiago .10 .03
26 Sandy Alomar Jr. .10 .03
27 Chris Hoiles .05 .02
28 Ivan Rodriguez .75 .23
29 Mike Stanley .05 .02
30 Dave Nilsson .05 .02
31 Jeff Bagwell .75 .23
32 Mark Grace .25 .07
33 Gregg Jefferies .05 .02
34 Andres Galarraga .25 .07
35 Fred McGriff .25 .07
36 Will Clark .25 .07
37 Mo Vaughn .10 .03
38 Don Mattingly 1.50 .45
39 Frank Thomas .50 .15
40 Cecil Fielder .10 .03
41 Robby Thompson .05 .02
42 Delino DeShields .05 .02
43 Carlos Garcia .05 .02
44 Bret Boone .15 .04
45 Craig Biggio .15 .04
46 Roberto Alomar .25 .07
47 Chuck Knoblauch .25 .07
48 Jose Lind .05 .02
49 Carlos Baerga .10 .03
50 Lou Whitaker .10 .03
51 Bobby Bonilla .10 .03
52 Tim Wallach .05 .02
53 Todd Zeile .05 .02
54 Matt Williams .15 .04
55 Ken Caminiti .10 .03
56 Robin Ventura .10 .03
57 Wade Boggs .60 .18
58 Scott Cooper .05 .02
59 Travis Fryman .10 .03
60 Dean Palmer .10 .03
61 Jay Bell .05 .02
62 Barry Larkin .25 .07
63 Ozzie Smith .75 .23
64 Wil Cordero .05 .02
65 Royce Clayton .05 .02
66 Chris Gomez .05 .02
67 Ozzie Guillen .10 .03
68 Cal Ripken Jr. 3.00 .90
69 Omar Vizquel .10 .03
70 Gary DiSarcina .05 .02
71 Dante Bichette .10 .03
72 Lenny Dykstra .10 .03
73 Barry Bonds 1.50 .45
74 Gary Sheffield .40 .12
75 Larry Walker .10 .03
76 Raul Mondesi .15 .04
77 Dave Justice .25 .07
78 Moises Alou .10 .03
79 Tony Gwynn 1.50 .45
80 Deion Sanders .10 .03
81 Kenny Lofton .15 .04
82 Kirby Puckett .50 .15
83 Juan Gonzalez .50 .15
84 Jay Buhner .10 .03
85 Joe Carter .10 .03
86 Ken Griffey Jr. 2.50 .75
87 Ruben Sierra .10 .03
88 Tim Salmon .25 .07
89 Paul O'Neill .10 .03
90 Albert Belle .10 .03
91 Danny Tartabull .05 .02
92 Jose Canseco .40 .12
93 Harold Baines .10 .03
94 Kirk Gibson .10 .03
95 Chili Davis .10 .03
96 Eddie Murray .40 .12
97 Bob Hamelin .05 .02
98 Paul Molitor .40 .12
99 Raul Mondesi .15 .04
100 Ryan Klesko .10 .03
101 Cliff Floyd .10 .03
102 William VanLandingham .05 .02
103 Joey Hamilton .05 .02
104 John Hudek .05 .02
105 Manny Ramirez .50 .15
106 Bob Hamelin .05 .02
107 Rusty Greer .25 .07
108 Chris Gomez .05 .02
109 Greg Maddux 2.00 .60
110 Jeff Bagwell .75 .23
111 Raul Mondesi .15 .04
112 David Cone .15 .04
113 Frank Thomas 1.00 .30
114 Bob Hamelin .05 .02
115 Tony Gwynn 1.50 .45
116 Matt Williams .15 .04
117 Jeff Bagwell .75 .23
118 Craig Biggio .15 .04
119 Andy Benes .05 .02
120 Greg Maddux 2.00 .60
121 John Franco .10 .03
122 Paul O'Neill .10 .03
123 Ken Griffey Jr. 2.00 .60
124 Kirby Puckett .60 .18
125 Kenny Lofton .10 .03
126 Randy Johnson .75 .23
127 Jimmy Key .10 .03
128 Lee Smith .10 .03
129 San Francisco Giants .05 .02
130 Montreal Expos .05 .02
131 Cincinnati Reds .05 .02
132 Los Angeles Dodgers .05 .02
133 New York Mets .05 .02
134 San Diego Padres .05 .02
135 Colorado Rockies .05 .02
136 Pittsburgh Pirates .05 .02
137 Florida Marlins .05 .02
138 Philadelphia Phillies .05 .02
139 Atlanta Braves .05 .02
140 Houston Astros .05 .02
141 St. Louis Cardinals .05 .02
142 Chicago Cubs .05 .02
143 Cleveland Indians .05 .02
144 New York Yankees .05 .02
145 Kansas City Royals .05 .02
146 Chicago White Sox .05 .02
147 Baltimore Orioles .05 .02
148 Seattle Mariners .05 .02
149 Boston Red Sox .05 .02
150 California Angels .05 .02
151 Toronto Blue Jays .05 .02
152 Detroit Tigers .05 .02
153 Texas Rangers .05 .02
154 Oakland Athletics .05 .02
155 Milwaukee Brewers .05 .02
156 Minnesota Twins .05 .02

1996 Panini Stickers

231
Collect all 246 stickers in the Major League Baseball® 1996 Sticker Album

This 246-sticker set was distributed as a complete set in a cellophane wrapper with a suggested retail price of $8. A 60-page album to hold the stickers was included with the set. Stickers to finish ones set were available from the Panini Missing Sticker Club at a cost of $4 for 20 different stickers or $4 for 30 stickers as long as 10 wrappers were sent as well.

Nm-Mt Ex-Mt
COMPLETE SET (246) 12.00 3.60
1 David Justice .25 .07
2 Tom Glavine .40 .12
3 Javier Lopez .10 .03
4 Greg Maddux 1.00 .30
5 Marquis Grissom .05 .02
6 Atlanta Braves Team Logo .05 .02
7 Ryan Klesko .10 .03
8 Chipper Jones 1.00 .30
9 Quilvio Veras .05 .02
10 Chris Hammond .05 .02
11 Charles Johnson .05 .02
12 John Burkett .05 .02
13 Florida Marlins Team Logo .05 .02
14 Jeff Conine .05 .02
15 Gary Sheffield .40 .12
16 Greg Colbrunn .05 .02
17 Moises Alou .15 .04
18 Pedro Martinez .60 .18
19 Rondell White .10 .03
20 Tony Tarasco .05 .02
21 Montreal Expos Team Logo .05 .02
22 Carlos Perez .05 .02
23 David Segui .05 .02
24 Wil Cordero .05 .02
25 Jason Isringhausen .15 .04
26 Rico Brogna .05 .02
27 Edgardo Alfonzo .25 .07
28 Todd Hundley .10 .03
29 New York Mets Team Logo .05 .02
30 Bill Pulsipher .05 .02
31 Carl Everett .10 .03
32 Jose Vizcaino .05 .02
33 Lenny Dykstra .10 .03
34 Charlie Hayes .05 .02
35 Heathcliff Slocumb .05 .02
36 Darren Daulton .10 .03
37 Phil. Phillies Team Logo .05 .02
38 Mickey Morandini .05 .02
39 Gregg Jefferies .05 .02
40 Jim Eisenreich .05 .02
41 Brian McRae .05 .02
42 Luis Gonzalez .25 .07
43 Randy Myers .10 .03
44 Shawon Dunston .05 .02
45 Chicago Cubs Team Logo .05 .02
46 Jaime Navarro .05 .02
47 Mark Grace .25 .07
48 Sammy Sosa 1.00 .30
49 Barry Larkin .25 .07
50 Pete Schourek .05 .02
51 John Smiley .05 .02
52 Reggie Sanders .05 .02
53 Cincinnati Reds Team Logo .05 .02
54 Hal Morris .05 .02
55 Ron Gant .05 .02
56 Bret Boone .15 .04
57 Craig Biggio .15 .04
58 Brian Hunter .05 .02
59 Jeff Bagwell .50 .15
60 Shane Reynolds .05 .02
61 Houston Astros Team Logo .05 .02
62 Derek Bell .05 .02
63 Doug Drabek .05 .02
64 Orlando Miller .05 .02
65 Jay Bell .05 .02
66 Dan Miceli .05 .02
67 Orlando Merced .05 .02
68 Jeff King .05 .02
69 Carlos Garcia .05 .02
70 Pittsburgh Pirates Team Logo .05 .02
71 Al Martin .05 .02
72 Denny Neagle .05 .02
73 Ray Lankford .10 .03
74 Ozzie Smith .75 .23
75 Bernard Gilkey .05 .02
76 John Mabry .05 .02
77 St. Louis Cardinals Team Logo .05 .02
78 Brian Jordan .10 .03
79 Scott Cooper .05 .02
80 Allen Watson .05 .02
81 Dante Bichette .15 .04
82 Bret Saberhagen .10 .03
83 Walt Weiss .05 .02
84 Andres Galarraga .25 .07
85 Colorado Rockies Team Logo .05 .02
86 Larry Walker .10 .03
87 Bill Swift .05 .02
88 Vinny Castilla .15 .04
89 Raul Mondesi .15 .04
90 Roger Cedeno .10 .03
91 Chad Fonville .05 .02
92 Hideo Nomo .50 .15
93 L.A. Dodgers Team Logo .05 .02
94 Ramon Martinez .10 .03
95 Mike Piazza 1.25 .35
96 Eric Karros .10 .03
97 Tony Gwynn 1.00 .30
98 Brad Ausmus .05 .02
99 Trevor Hoffman .10 .03
100 Ken Caminiti .10 .03
101 San Diego Padres Team Logo .05 .02
102 Andy Ashby .05 .02
103 Steve Finley .10 .03
104 Joey Hamilton .10 .03
105 Matt Williams .15 .04
106 Rod Beck .05 .02
107 Barry Bonds 1.00 .30
108 William VanLandingham .05 .02
109 S.F. Giants Team Logo .05 .02
110 Deion Sanders .10 .03
111 Royce Clayton .05 .02
112 Glenallen Hill .05 .02
113 Tony Gwynn 1.00 .30
114 Dante Bichette .15 .04
115 Dante Bichette .15 .04
116 Quilvio Veras .05 .02
117 Hideo Nomo .50 .15
118 Greg Maddux 1.25 .35
119 Randy Myers .05 .02
120 Edgar Martinez .15 .04
121 Albert Belle .10 .03
122 Mo Vaughn .10 .03
123 Kenny Lofton .10 .03
124 Randy Johnson .60 .18
125 Mike Mussina .25 .07
126 Jose Mesa .05 .02
127 Mike Mussina .25 .07
128 Cal Ripken Jr. 2.00 .60
129 Rafael Palmeiro .25 .07
130 Ben McDonald .05 .02
131 Baltimore Orioles Team Logo .05 .02
132 Chris Hoiles .05 .02
133 Bobby Bonilla .05 .02
134 Brady Anderson .10 .03
135 Jose Canseco .40 .12
136 Roger Clemens 1.00 .30
137 Mo Vaughn .10 .03
138 Mike Greenwell .05 .02
139 Boston Red Sox Team Logo .05 .02
140 Tim Wakefield .10 .03

141 John Valentin .05 .02
142 Tim Naehring .05 .02
143 Travis Fryman .10 .03
144 Chad Curtis .05 .02
145 Felipe Lira .05 .02
146 Cecil Fielder .10 .03
147 Detroit Tigers Team Logo .05 .02
148 John Flaherty .05 .02
149 Chris Gomez .05 .02
150 Sean Bergman .05 .02
151 Don Mattingly 1.00 .30
152 Andy Pettitte .10 .03
153 Wade Boggs .60 .18
154 Paul O'Neill .10 .03
155 N.Y. Yankees Team Logo .05 .02
156 Bernie Williams .25 .07
157 Jack McDowell .05 .02
158 David Cone .10 .03
159 Roberto Alomar .25 .07
160 Paul Molitor .40 .12
161 Shawn Green .40 .12
162 Joe Carter .10 .03
163 Toronto Blue Jays Team Logo .05 .02
164 Alex Gonzalez .05 .02
165 Al Leiter .10 .03
166 John Olerud .15 .04
167 Alex Fernandez .05 .02
168 Ray Durham .15 .04
169 Lance Johnson .05 .02
170 Ozzie Guillen .10 .03
171 Chi. White Sox Team Logo .05 .02
172 Robin Ventura .25 .07
173 Frank Thomas .60 .18
174 Tim Raines .10 .03
175 Albert Belle .10 .03
176 Manny Ramirez .50 .15
177 Eddie Murray .40 .12
178 Orel Hershiser .10 .03
179 Cleveland Indians Team Logo .05 .02
180 Kenny Lofton .15 .04
181 Carlos Baerga .10 .03
182 Jose Mesa .10 .03
183 Gary Gaetti .10 .03
184 Tom Goodwin .05 .02
185 Kevin Appier .10 .03
186 Jon Nunnally .05 .02
187 K.C. Royals Team Logo .05 .02
188 Wally Joyner .10 .03
189 Jeff Montgomery .05 .02
190 Johnny Damon .15 .04
191 B.J. Surhoff .10 .03
192 Ricky Bones .05 .02
193 John Jaha .05 .02
194 Dave Nilsson .05 .02
195 Milw. Brewers Team Logo .05 .02
196 Greg Vaughn .10 .03
197 Kevin Seitzer .05 .02
198 Joe Oliver .05 .02
199 Chuck Knoblauch .25 .07
200 Kirby Puckett .30 .09
201 Marty Cordova .05 .02
202 Pat Meares .05 .02
203 Minnesota Twins Team Logo .05 .02
204 Scott Stahoviak .05 .02
205 Matt Walbeck .05 .02
206 Pedro Munoz .05 .02
207 Garret Anderson .10 .03
208 Chili Davis .10 .03
209 Tim Salmon .25 .07
210 J.T. Snow .10 .03
211 California Angels Team Logo .05 .02
212 Jim Edmonds .25 .07
213 Chuck Finley .10 .03
214 Mark Langston .05 .02
215 Dennis Eckersley .40 .12
216 Todd Stottlemyre .05 .02
217 Geronimo Berroa .05 .02
218 Mark McGwire 1.50 .45
219 Oakland A's Team Logo .05 .02
220 Brent Gates .05 .02
221 Terry Steinbach .05 .02
222 Rickey Henderson .60 .18
223 Ken Griffey Jr. 1.25 .35
224 Alex Rodriguez 1.25 .35
225 Tino Martinez .25 .07
226 Randy Johnson .60 .18
227 Seattle Mariners Team Logo .05 .02
228 Jay Buhner .10 .03
229 Vince Coleman .05 .02
230 Edgar Martinez .15 .04
231 Will Clark .25 .07
232 Juan Gonzalez .50 .15
233 Kenny Rogers .05 .02
234 Ivan Rodriguez .40 .12
235 Texas Rangers Team Logo .05 .02
236 Mickey Tettleton .05 .02
237 Dean Palmer .10 .03
238 Otis Nixon .05 .02
239 Hideo Nomo .25 .07
240 Quilvio Veras .05 .02
241 Jason Isringhausen .15 .04
242 Andy Pettitte .10 .03
243 Chipper Jones 1.00 .30
244 Garret Anderson .10 .03
245 Charles Johnson .05 .02
246 Marty Cordova .05 .02

1989 PAO Religious Tracts

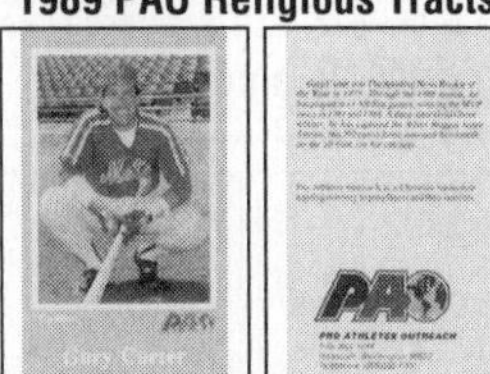

This five-card set features color player photos on a 4 1/8" by 7 5/8" tri-fold card and was distributed by Pro Athletes Outreach, a Christian leadership training ministry to pro players and their families. The cards are unnumbered and checklisted below in alphabetical order.

Nm-Mt Ex-Mt
COMPLETE SET (5) 6.00 2.40
1 Gary Carter 2.50 1.00
2 Alvin Davis 1.50 .60
3 Mike Moore 1.00 .40
4 Frank Pastore 1.00 .40
5 Craig Reynolds 1.00 .40

1978 Papa Gino's Discs

This 40-disc set consists of all American League players with more than half the set being Boston Red Sox players. Papa Gino's was a chain of restaurants located throughout central New England.The discs are 3 3/8" in diameter and have a distinctive thick dark blue border on the front with orange printing. The set was approved by the Major League Baseball Players Association under the auspices of Mike Schechter Associates (MSA) and as such has team logos airbrushed away. The discs are numbered on the back at the bottom; the uniform number is also given at the top of the reverse. The first 25 players in the set are members of the Boston Red Sox. Supposedly eight discs were printed in smaller quantities; these short printed discs are marked SP in the checklist below.

NM Ex
COMPLETE SET (40) 35.00 14.00
COMMON DISC (1-40) .50 .20
COMMON SP 1.00 .40
1 Allen Ripley .50 .20
2 Jerry Remy .50 .20
3 Jack Brohamer .50 .20
4 Butch Hobson .50 .20
5 Dennis Eckersley 3.00 1.20
6 Sam Bowen SP 1.00 .40
7 Rick Burleson .50 .20
8 Carl Yastrzemski 4.00 1.60
9 Bill Lee 1.00 .40
10 Bob Montgomery .50 .20
11 Dick Drago SP 1.00 .40
12 Bob Stanley SP 1.00 .40
13 Fred Kendall SP 1.00 .40
14 Jim Rice SP 2.00 .80
15 George Scott 1.00 .40
16 Tom Burgmeier .50 .20
17 Frank Duffy SP 1.00 .40
18 Jim Wright .50 .20
19 Fred Lynn 1.50 .60
20 Bob Bailey SP 1.00 .40
21 Mike Torrez .50 .20
22 Bill Campbell SP 1.00 .40
23 Luis Tiant 1.50 .60
24 Dwight Evans 2.00 .80
25 Carlton Fisk 4.00 1.60
26 Reggie Jackson 5.00 2.00
27 Thurman Munson 3.00 1.20
28 Ron Guidry 2.00 .80
29 Bruce Bochte .50 .20
30 Richie Zisk .50 .20
31 Jim Palmer 3.00 1.20
32 Mark Fidrych 3.00 1.20
33 Frank Tanana 1.00 .40
34 Buddy Bell 1.50 .60
35 Rod Carew 3.00 1.20
36 George Brett 8.00 3.20
37 Ralph Garr .50 .20
38 Larry Hisle .50 .20
39 Mitchell Page .50 .20
40 John Mayberry .50 .20

1998 Paramount

The 1998 Paramount set (issued by Pacific) consists of 250 standard-size cards issued in six-card packs with an SRP of $1.49. The fronts feature color action photos with silver foil showcasing today's top players and tomorrow's rising stars. The backs offer a second color photo, along with complete year-by-year career stats.

Nm-Mt Ex-Mt
COMPLETE SET (250) 30.00 9.00
1 Garret Anderson .20 .06
2 Gary DiSarcina .20 .06
3 Jim Edmonds .20 .06
4 Darin Erstad .20 .06
5 Cecil Fielder .20 .06
6 Chuck Finley .20 .06
7 Todd Greene .20 .06
8 Shigetoshi Hasegawa .20 .06
9 Tim Salmon .30 .09
10 Roberto Alomar .50 .15
11 Brady Anderson .20 .06
12 Joe Carter .20 .06
13 Eric Davis .20 .06
14 Ozzie Guillen .20 .06
15 Mike Mussina .50 .15
16 Rafael Palmeiro .30 .09
17 Cal Ripken 1.50 .45
18 B.J. Surhoff .20 .06
19 Steve Avery .20 .06
20 Nomar Garciaparra .75 .23
21 Reggie Jefferson .20 .06
22 Pedro Martinez .50 .15
23 Tim Naehring .20 .06
24 John Valentin .20 .06
25 Mo Vaughn .20 .06
26 James Baldwin .20 .06
27 Albert Belle .20 .06
28 Ray Durham .20 .06
29 Benji Gil .20 .06
30 Jaime Navarro .20 .06
31 Magglio Ordonez RC 1.00 .30
32 Frank Thomas .50 .15
33 Robin Ventura .20 .06
34 Sandy Alomar Jr. .20 .06
35 Geronimo Berroa .20 .06
36 Travis Fryman .20 .06
37 David Justice .20 .06
38 Kenny Lofton .20 .06
39 Charles Nagy .20 .06
40 Manny Ramirez .20 .06
41 Jim Thome .50 .15
42 Omar Vizquel .20 .06
43 Jaret Wright .20 .06
44 Raul Casanova .20 .06
45 Frank Catalanotto RC .30 .09
46 Tony Clark .20 .06
47 Bobby Higginson .20 .06
48 Brian Hunter .20 .06
49 Todd Jones .20 .06
50 Bip Roberts .20 .06
51 Justin Thompson .20 .06
52 Kevin Appier .20 .06
53 Johnny Damon .20 .06
54 Jermaine Dye .20 .06
55 Jeff King .20 .06
56 Jeff Montgomery .20 .06
57 Dean Palmer .20 .06
58 Jose Rosado .20 .06
59 Larry Sutton .20 .06
60 Rick Aguilera .20 .06
61 Marty Cordova .20 .06
62 Pat Meares .20 .06
63 Paul Molitor .30 .09
64 Otis Nixon .20 .06
65 Brad Radke .20 .06
66 Terry Steinbach .20 .06
67 Todd Walker .20 .06
68 Hideki Irabu .20 .06
69 Derek Jeter 1.25 .35
70 Chuck Knoblauch .20 .06
71 Tino Martinez .30 .09
72 Paul O'Neill .30 .09
73 Andy Pettitte .30 .09
74 Mariano Rivera .30 .09
75 Bernie Williams .30 .09
76 Mark Bellhorn .20 .06
77 Tom Candiotti .20 .06
78 Jason Giambi .50 .15
79 Ben Grieve .20 .06
80 Rickey Henderson .50 .15
81 Jason McDonald .20 .06
82 Aaron Small .20 .06
83 Miguel Tejada .30 .09
84 Jay Buhner .20 .06
85 Joey Cora .20 .06
86 Jeff Fassero .20 .06
87 Ken Griffey Jr. .75 .23
88 Randy Johnson .50 .15
89 Edgar Martinez .30 .09
90 Alex Rodriguez .75 .23
91 David Segui .20 .06
92 Dan Wilson .20 .06
93 Wilson Alvarez .20 .06
94 Wade Boggs .30 .09
95 Miguel Cairo .20 .06
96 John Flaherty .20 .06
97 Dave Martinez .20 .06
98 Quinton McCracken .20 .06
99 Fred McGriff .30 .09
100 Paul Sorrento .20 .06
101 Kevin Stocker .20 .06
102 John Burkett .20 .06
103 Will Clark .50 .15
104 Juan Gonzalez .50 .15
105 Rusty Greer .20 .06
106 Roberto Kelly .20 .06
107 Ivan Rodriguez .50 .15
108 Fernando Tatis .20 .06
109 John Wetteland .20 .06
110 Jose Canseco .50 .15
111 Roger Clemens 1.00 .30
112 Jose Cruz Jr. .20 .06
113 Carlos Delgado .20 .06
114 Alex Gonzalez .20 .06
115 Pat Hentgen .20 .06
116 Ed Sprague .20 .06
117 Shannon Stewart .20 .06
118 Brian Anderson .20 .06
119 Jay Bell .20 .06
120 Andy Benes .20 .06
121 Yamil Benitez .20 .06
122 Jorge Fabregas .20 .06
123 Travis Lee .20 .06
124 Devon White .20 .06
125 Matt Williams .20 .06
126 Bob Wolcott .20 .06
127 Andres Galarraga .20 .06
128 Tom Glavine .30 .09
129 Andruw Jones .20 .06
130 Chipper Jones .50 .15
131 Ryan Klesko .20 .06
132 Javy Lopez .20 .06
133 Greg Maddux .75 .23
134 Denny Neagle .20 .06
135 John Smoltz .30 .09
136 Rod Beck .20 .06
137 Jeff Blauser .20 .06
138 Mark Grace .30 .09
139 Lance Johnson .20 .06
140 Mickey Morandini .20 .06
141 Kevin Orie .20 .06
142 Sammy Sosa .75 .23
143 Aaron Boone .20 .06
144 Bret Boone .20 .06
145 Dave Burba .20 .06
146 Lenny Harris .20 .06
147 Barry Larkin .50 .15
148 Reggie Sanders .20 .06
149 Brett Tomko .20 .06
150 Pedro Astacio .20 .06
151 Dante Bichette .20 .06
152 Ellis Burks .20 .06
153 Vinny Castilla .20 .06
154 Todd Helton .30 .09
155 Darryl Kile .20 .06
156 Jeff Reed .20 .06
157 Larry Walker .30 .09
158 Bobby Bonilla .20 .06
159 Todd Dunwoody .20 .06
160 Livan Hernandez .20 .06
161 Charles Johnson .20 .06
162 Mark Kotsay .20 .06
163 Derrek Lee .20 .06
164 Edgar Renteria .20 .06
165 Gary Sheffield .20 .06
166 Moises Alou .20 .06
167 Jeff Bagwell .30 .09
168 Derek Bell .20 .06
169 Craig Biggio .30 .09
170 Mike Hampton .20 .06
171 Richard Hidalgo .20 .06
172 Chris Holt .20 .06
173 Shane Reynolds .20 .06
174 Wilton Guerrero .20 .06
175 Eric Karros .20 .06
176 Paul Konerko .20 .06
177 Ramon Martinez .20 .06
178 Raul Mondesi .20 .06
179 Hideo Nomo .50 .15
180 Chan Ho Park .20 .06
181 Mike Piazza .75 .23
182 Ismael Valdes .20 .06
183 Jeromy Burnitz .20 .06
184 Jeff Cirillo .20 .06
185 Todd Dunn .20 .06
186 Marquis Grissom .20 .06
187 John Jaha .20 .06
188 Doug Jones .20 .06
189 Dave Nilsson .20 .06
190 Jose Valentin .20 .06
191 Fernando Vina .20 .06
192 Orlando Cabrera .20 .06
193 Steve Falteisek RC .20 .06
194 Mark Grudzielanek .20 .06
195 Vladimir Guerrero .50 .15
196 Carlos Perez .20 .06
197 F.P. Santangelo .20 .06
198 Jose Vidro .20 .06
199 Rondell White .20 .06
200 Edgardo Alfonzo .20 .06
201 Carlos Baerga .20 .06
202 John Franco .20 .06
203 Bernard Gilkey .20 .06
204 Todd Hundley .20 .06
205 Butch Huskey .20 .06
206 Bobby Jones .20 .06
207 Brian McRae .20 .06
208 John Olerud .20 .06
209 Rey Ordonez .20 .06
210 Ricky Bottalico .20 .06
211 Bobby Estalella .20 .06
212 Doug Glanville .20 .06
213 Gregg Jefferies .20 .06
214 Mike Lieberthal .20 .06
215 Desi Relaford .20 .06
216 Scott Rolen .30 .09
217 Curt Schilling .30 .09
218 Adrian Brown .20 .06
219 Emil Brown .20 .06
220 Francisco Cordova .20 .06
221 Jose Guillen .20 .06
222 Al Martin .20 .06
223 Abraham Nunez .20 .06
224 Tony Womack .20 .06
225 Kevin Young .20 .06
226 Alan Benes .20 .06
227 Royce Clayton .20 .06
228 Gary Gaetti .20 .06
229 Ron Gant .20 .06
230 Brian Jordan .20 .06
231 Ray Lankford .20 .06
232 Mark McGwire 1.25 .35
233 Todd Stottlemyre .20 .06
234 Kevin Brown .30 .09
235 Ken Caminiti .20 .06
236 Steve Finley .20 .06
237 Tony Gwynn .60 .18
238 Wally Joyner .20 .06
239 Ruben Rivera .20 .06
240 Greg Vaughn .20 .06
241 Quilvio Veras .20 .06
242 Barry Bonds 1.25 .35
243 Jacob Cruz .20 .06
244 Shawn Estes .20 .06
245 Orel Hershiser .20 .06
246 Stan Javier .20 .06
247 Brian Johnson .20 .06
248 Jeff Kent .20 .06
249 Robb Nen .20 .06
250 J.T. Snow .20 .06

1998 Paramount Copper

Cards from this 250-card parallel set are inserted in hobby packs one per pack. The fronts feature the same silver foil color action photo shots. The backs offer the same color photos, along with complete year-by-year career stats.

Nm-Mt Ex-Mt
COMPLETE SET (250) 120.00 36.00
*STARS: 1.25X TO 3X BASIC CARDS .
*ROOKIES: 1X TO 2.5X BASIC CARDS

1998 Paramount Gold

Cards from this 250-card parallel set were randomly inserted one per retail pack. The fronts feature the same silver foil color action photo shots. The backs offer the same color photos, along with complete year-by-year career stats.

Nm-Mt Ex-Mt
COMPLETE SET (250) 150.00 45.00
*STARS: 1.5X TO 4X BASIC CARDS ...
*ROOKIES: 1.25X TO 3X BASIC CARDS

1998 Paramount Holographic Silver

Cards from thie 250-card parallel set were randomly inserted in hobby packs and were serially numbered to 99.

Nm-Mt Ex-Mt
*STARS: 15X TO 40X BASIC CARDS ..
*ROOKIES: 10X TO 25X BASIC CARDS

1998 Paramount Inaugural

This 50-card set was issued at SportFest 98 which was held in Philadelphia to debut the 1998 Paramount set. The fronts feature color action player photos with silver foil printing and a gold foil inaugural stamp. The backs carry another color photo with the player's career statistics. Only 1,000 total cards were produced. As a wrapper redemption available only at the show, 20 of each card were serially numbered. Due to market scarcity, no pricing is provided.

Nm-Mt Ex-Mt
COMPLETE SET (50)
1 Albert Belle
2 Barry Bonds
3 Barry Larkin
4 Ben Grieve
5 Bernie Williams
6 Bobby Bonilla
7 Brady Anderson
8 Chipper Jones
9 Craig Biggio
10 Curt Schilling
11 Dante Bichette
12 David Justice
13 Derek Jeter
14 Edgar Renteria
15 Frank Thomas
16 Gary Sheffield
17 Greg Maddux
18 Hideo Nomo
19 Ivan Rodriguez
20 Javy Lopez
21 Jay Buhner
22 Jeff Bagwell
23 Jim Edmonds
24 Jim Thome
25 Jose Cruz Jr.
26 Juan Gonzalez
27 Ken Caminiti
28 Ken Griffey Jr.
29 Larry Walker
30 Manny Ramirez
31 Mark Grace
32 Mark McGwire
33 Mike Piazza
34 Mo Vaughn
35 Nomar Garciaparra
36 Pat Hentgen
37 Paul Molitor
38 Rafael Palmeiro
39 Raul Mondesi
40 Reggie Sanders
41 Roberto Alomar
42 Roger Clemens
43 Ryan Klesko
44 Sammy Sosa
45 Scott Rolen
46 Tim Salmon
47 Tino Martinez
48 Tom Glavine
49 Tony Gwynn
50 Will Clark

1998 Paramount Platinum Blue

This 250-card parallel set was randomly inserted in packs at a rate of 1:73. The fronts feature the same silver foil color action photo shots. The backs offer the same color photos, along with complete year-by-year career stats.

Nm-Mt Ex-Mt
*STARS: 15X TO 40X BASIC CARDS ..
*ROOKIES: 10X TO 25X BASIC CARDS

1998 Paramount Red

Cards from this 250-card parallel set were randomly inserted in ANCO packs at a rate of one per pack. The fronts feature red foil accents. The backs offer the same color photos, along with complete year-by-year career stats.

Nm-Mt Ex-Mt
COMPLETE SET (250) 200.00 60.00
*STARS: 2X TO 5X BASIC CARDS
*ROOKIES: 1.5X TO 4X BASIC CARDS

1998 Paramount Cooperstown Bound

Randomly inserted in packs at a rate of 1:361, this 10-card set salutes 10 of the all-time greats. The fronts feature color action photos on a foiled and etched card.

Nm-Mt Ex-Mt
COMPLETE SET (10) 250.00 75.00
*PROOF: 1.25X TO 3X BASIC COOPERSTOWN
PROOF: RANDOM INSERTS IN HOBBY
PACIFIC PROOFS PRINT RUN 20 SERIAL #'d SETS
1 Greg Maddux 30.00 9.00

2 Cal Ripken 60.00 18.00
3 Frank Thomas 20.00 6.00
4 Mike Piazza 30.00 9.00
5 Paul Molitor 12.00 3.60
6 Mark McGwire 50.00 15.00
7 Tony Gwynn 25.00 7.50
8 Barry Bonds 50.00 15.00
9 Ken Griffey Jr. 30.00 9.00
10 Wade Boggs 12.00 3.60

1998 Paramount Fielder's Choice

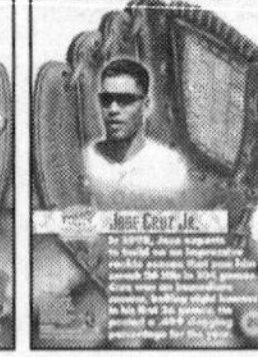

This 20-card set was randomly inserted in packs at a rate of 1:73. The set presents the game's top players with a unique laser-cut baseball mitt design. The fronts feature color action player photos with the player's name and company logo below the photo.

Nm-Mt Ex-Mt
COMPLETE SET (20) 250.00 75.00
1 Chipper Jones 12.00 3.60
2 Greg Maddux 20.00 6.00
3 Cal Ripken 40.00 12.00
4 Nomar Garciaparra 20.00 6.00
5 Frank Thomas 12.00 3.60
6 David Justice 5.00 1.50
7 Larry Walker 8.00 2.40
8 Jeff Bagwell 8.00 2.40
9 Hideo Nomo 12.00 3.60
10 Mike Piazza 20.00 6.00
11 Derek Jeter 30.00 9.00
12 Ben Grieve 5.00 1.50
13 Mark McGwire 30.00 9.00
14 Tony Gwynn 15.00 4.50
15 Barry Bonds 30.00 9.00
16 Ken Griffey Jr. 20.00 6.00
17 Alex Rodriguez 20.00 6.00
18 Wade Boggs 8.00 2.40
19 Ivan Rodriguez 12.00 3.60
20 Jose Cruz Jr. 5.00 1.50

1998 Paramount Special Delivery

Randomly inserted in packs at a rate of 1:37, this 20-card set features three color action photos on the front along with the player's name and "Pacific Paramount" logo.

Nm-Mt Ex-Mt
COMPLETE SET (20) 120.00 36.00
1 Chipper Jones 6.00 1.80
2 Greg Maddux 10.00 3.00
3 Cal Ripken 20.00 6.00
4 Nomar Garciaparra 10.00 3.00
5 Pedro Martinez 6.00 1.80
6 Frank Thomas 6.00 1.80
7 David Justice .... 2.50 .75
8 Larry Walker 4.00 1.20
9 Jeff Bagwell 4.00 1.20
10 Hideo Nomo 6.00 1.80
11 Mike Piazza 10.00 3.00
12 Vladimir Guerrero 6.00 1.80
13 Derek Jeter 15.00 4.50
14 Ben Grieve .... 2.50 .75
15 Mark McGwire 15.00 4.50
16 Tony Gwynn 8.00 2.40
17 Barry Bonds 15.00 4.50
18 Ken Griffey Jr. 10.00 3.00
19 Alex Rodriguez 10.00 3.00
20 Jose Cruz Jr. .... 2.50 .75

1998 Paramount Team Checklists

Randomly inserted in packs at a rate of 2:37, this 30-card set assembled 30 of today's top players to represent their teams. The fronts feature a color photo of the player's head and shoulders with the player's name, team position, and team name. The backs feature that team's checklist for the Paramount main set to help you find all your favorite players.

Nm-Mt Ex-Mt
COMPLETE SET (30) 100.00 30.00
1 Tim Salmon .... 3.00 .90
2 Cal Ripken 15.00 4.50
3 Nomar Garciaparra 8.00 2.40
4 Frank Thomas 5.00 1.50
5 Manny Ramirez .... 2.00 .60
6 Tony Clark .... 2.00 .60
7 Dean Palmer .... 2.00 .60
8 Paul Molitor .... 3.00 .90
9 Derek Jeter 12.00 3.60
10 Ben Grieve .... 2.00 .60
11 Ken Griffey Jr. 8.00 2.40
12 Wade Boggs .... 3.00 .90
13 Ivan Rodriguez 5.00 1.50
14 Roger Clemens 10.00 3.00
15 Matt Williams .... 2.00 .60
16 Chipper Jones 5.00 1.50
17 Sammy Sosa 8.00 2.40
18 Barry Larkin 5.00 1.50
19 Larry Walker .... 3.00 .90
20 Livan Hernandez .... 2.00 .60
21 Jeff Bagwell .... 3.00 .90
22 Mike Piazza 8.00 2.40
23 John Jaha .... 2.00 .60
24 Vladimir Guerrero 5.00 1.50
25 Todd Hundley .... 2.00 .60
26 Scott Rolen .... 3.00 .90
27 Kevin Young .... 2.00 .60
28 Mark McGwire 12.00 3.60
29 Tony Gwynn 6.00 1.80
30 Barry Bonds 12.00 3.60

1999 Paramount

The 1999 Paramount set was issued in one series for a total of 250 cards and distributed in six-card packs with a suggested retail price of $1.49. The set features color action photos of some of today's biggest superstars and tomorrow's up-and-comers in their 1999 uniforms. As was typical with 1999 Pacific products, a Tony Gwynn Sample card was produced and distributed to dealers and hobby media several weeks prior to the product's release. The large "SAMPLE" text running across the back, and lack of a card number make this an easy card to distinguish.

Nm-Mt Ex-Mt
COMPLETE SET (250) 40.00 12.00
1 Garret Anderson .... .20 .06
2 Gary DiSarcina .... .20 .06
3 Jim Edmonds .... .20 .06
4 Darin Erstad .... .20 .06
5 Chuck Finley .... .20 .06
6 Troy Glaus .... .30 .09
7 Troy Percival .... .20 .06
8 Tim Salmon .... .30 .09
9 Mo Vaughn .... .20 .06
10 Tony Batista .... .20 .06
11 Jay Bell .... .20 .06
12 Andy Benes .... .20 .06
13 Steve Finley .... .20 .06
14 Luis Gonzalez .... .20 .06
15 Randy Johnson .... .50 .15
16 Travis Lee .... .20 .06
17 Todd Stottlemyre .... .20 .06
18 Matt Williams .... .20 .06
19 David Dellucci .... .20 .06
20 Bret Boone .... .20 .06
21 Andres Galarraga .... .20 .06
22 Tom Glavine .... .30 .09
23 Andruw Jones .... .20 .06
24 Chipper Jones .... .50 .15
25 Brian Jordan .... .20 .06
26 Ryan Klesko .... .20 .06
27 Javy Lopez .... .20 .06
28 Greg Maddux .... .75 .23
29 John Smoltz .... .30 .09
30 Brady Anderson .... .20 .06
31 Albert Belle .... .20 .06
32 Will Clark .... .50 .15
33 Delino DeShields .... .20 .06
34 Charles Johnson .... .20 .06
35 Mike Mussina .... .50 .15
36 Cal Ripken .... 1.50 .45
37 B.J. Surhoff .... .20 .06
38 Nomar Garciaparra .... .75 .23
39 Reggie Jefferson .... .20 .06
40 Darren Lewis .... .20 .06
41 Pedro Martinez .... .50 .15
42 Troy O'Leary .... .20 .06
43 Jose Offerman .... .20 .06
44 Donnie Sadler .... .20 .06
45 John Valentin .... .20 .06
46 Rod Beck .... .20 .06
47 Gary Gaetti .... .20 .06
48 Mark Grace .... .30 .09
49 Lance Johnson .... .20 .06
50 Mickey Morandini .... .20 .06
51 Henry Rodriguez .... .20 .06
52 Sammy Sosa .... .75 .23
53 Kerry Wood .... .50 .15
54 Mike Caruso .... .20 .06
55 Ray Durham .... .20 .06
56 Paul Konerko .... .20 .06
57 Jaime Navarro .... .20 .06
58 Greg Norton .... .20 .06
59 Magglio Ordonez .... .20 .06
60 Frank Thomas .... .50 .15
61 Aaron Boone .... .20 .06
62 Mike Cameron .... .20 .06
63 Barry Larkin .... .50 .15
64 Hal Morris .... .20 .06
65 Pokey Reese .... .20 .06
66 Brett Tomko .... .20 .06
67 Greg Vaughn .... .20 .06
68 Dmitri Young .... .20 .06
69 Roberto Alomar .... .50 .15
70 Sandy Alomar Jr. .... .20 .06
71 Bartolo Colon .... .20 .06
72 Travis Fryman .... .20 .06
73 David Justice .... .20 .06
74 Kenny Lofton .... .20 .06
75 Manny Ramirez .... .20 .06
76 Richie Sexson .... .20 .06
77 Jim Thome .... .50 .15
78 Omar Vizquel .... .20 .06
79 Dante Bichette .... .20 .06
80 Vinny Castilla .... .20 .06
81 Darryl Hamilton .... .20 .06
82 Todd Helton .... .30 .09
83 Darryl Kile .... .20 .06
84 Mike Lansing .... .20 .06
85 Neifi Perez .... .20 .06
86 Larry Walker .... .30 .09
87 Tony Clark .... .20 .06
88 Damion Easley .... .20 .06
89 Bob Higginson .... .20 .06
90 Brian Hunter .... .20 .06
91 Dean Palmer .... .20 .06
92 Justin Thompson .... .20 .06
93 Todd Dunwoody .... .20 .06
94 Cliff Floyd .... .20 .06
95 Alex Gonzalez .... .20 .06
96 Livan Hernandez .... .20 .06
97 Mark Kotsay .... .20 .06
98 Derrek Lee .... .20 .06
99 Kevin Orie .... .20 .06
100 Moises Alou .... .20 .06
101 Jeff Bagwell .... .30 .09
102 Derek Bell .... .20 .06
103 Craig Biggio .... .30 .09
104 Ken Caminiti .... .20 .06
105 Ricky Gutierrez .... .20 .06
106 Richard Hidalgo .... .20 .06
107 Billy Wagner .... .20 .06
108 Jeff Conine .... .20 .06
109 Johnny Damon .... .20 .06
110 Carlos Febles .... .20 .06
111 Jeremy Giambi .... .20 .06
112 Jeff King .... .20 .06
113 Jeff Montgomery .... .20 .06
114 Joe Randa .... .20 .06
115 Kevin Brown .... .30 .09
116 Mark Grudzielanek .... .20 .06
117 Todd Hundley .... .20 .06
118 Eric Karros .... .20 .06
119 Raul Mondesi .... .20 .06
120 Chan Ho Park .... .20 .06
121 Gary Sheffield .... .20 .06
122 Devon White .... .20 .06
123 Eric Young .... .20 .06
124 Jeromy Burnitz .... .20 .06
125 Jeff Cirillo .... .20 .06
126 Marquis Grissom .... .20 .06
127 Geoff Jenkins .... .20 .06
128 Dave Nilsson .... .20 .06
129 Jose Valentin .... .20 .06
130 Fernando Vina .... .20 .06
131 Rick Aguilera .... .20 .06
132 Ron Coomer .... .20 .06
133 Marty Cordova .... .20 .06
134 Matt Lawton .... .20 .06
135 David Ortiz .... .20 .06
136 Brad Radke .... .20 .06
137 Terry Steinbach .... .20 .06
138 Javier Valentin .... .20 .06
139 Todd Walker .... .20 .06
140 Orlando Cabrera .... .20 .06
141 Brad Fullmer .... .20 .06
142 Vladimir Guerrero .... .50 .15
143 Wilton Guerrero .... .20 .06
144 Carl Pavano .... .20 .06
145 Ugueth Urbina .... .20 .06
146 Rondell White .... .20 .06
147 Chris Widger .... .20 .06
148 Edgardo Alfonzo .... .20 .06
149 Bobby Bonilla .... .20 .06
150 Rickey Henderson .... .50 .15
151 Brian McRae .... .20 .06
152 Hideo Nomo .... .50 .15
153 John Olerud .... .20 .06
154 Rey Ordonez .... .20 .06
155 Mike Piazza .... .75 .23
156 Robin Ventura .... .20 .06
157 Masato Yoshii .... .20 .06
158 Roger Clemens .... 1.00 .30
159 David Cone .... .20 .06
160 Orlando Hernandez .... .20 .06
161 Hideki Irabu .... .20 .06
162 Derek Jeter .... 1.25 .35
163 Chuck Knoblauch .... .20 .06
164 Tino Martinez .... .30 .09
165 Paul O'Neill .... .30 .09
166 Darryl Strawberry .... .30 .09
167 Bernie Williams .... .30 .09
168 Eric Chavez .... .20 .06
169 Ryan Christenson .... .20 .06
170 Jason Giambi .... .50 .15
171 Ben Grieve .... .20 .06
172 Tony Phillips .... .20 .06
173 Tim Raines .... .20 .06
174 Scott Spiezio .... .20 .06
175 Miguel Tejada .... .20 .06
176 Bobby Abreu .... .20 .06
177 Rico Brogna .... .20 .06
178 Ron Gant .... .20 .06
179 Doug Glanville .... .20 .06
180 Desi Relaford .... .20 .06
181 Scott Rolen .... .30 .09
182 Curt Schilling .... .30 .09
183 Brant Brown .... .20 .06
184 Brian Giles .... .20 .06
185 Jose Guillen .... .20 .06
186 Jason Kendall .... .20 .06
187 Al Martin .... .20 .06
188 Ed Sprague .... .20 .06
189 Kevin Young .... .20 .06
190 Eric Davis .... .20 .06
191 J.D. Drew .... .20 .06
192 Ray Lankford .... .20 .06
193 Eli Marrero .... .20 .06
194 Mark McGwire .... 1.25 .35
195 Edgar Renteria .... .20 .06
196 Fernando Tatis .... .20 .06
197 Andy Ashby .... .20 .06
198 Tony Gwynn .... .60 .18
199 Carlos Hernandez .... .20 .06
200 Trevor Hoffman .... .20 .06
201 Wally Joyner .... .20 .06
202 Jim Leyritz .... .20 .06
203 Ruben Rivera .... .20 .06
204 Matt Clement .... .20 .06
205 Quilvio Veras .... .20 .06
206 Rich Aurilia .... .20 .06
207 Marvin Benard .... .20 .06
208 Barry Bonds .... 1.25 .35
209 Ellis Burks .... .20 .06
210 Jeff Kent .... .20 .06
211 Bill Mueller .... .20 .06
212 Robb Nen .... .20 .06
213 J.T. Snow .... .20 .06
214 Jay Buhner .... .20 .06
215 Jeff Fassero .... .20 .06
216 Ken Griffey Jr. .... .75 .23
217 Carlos Guillen .... .20 .06
218 Butch Huskey .... .20 .06
219 Edgar Martinez .... .30 .09
220 Alex Rodriguez .... .75 .23
221 David Segui .... .20 .06
222 Dan Wilson .... .20 .06
223 Rolando Arrojo .... .20 .06
224 Wade Boggs .... .30 .09
225 Jose Canseco .... .50 .15
226 Roberto Hernandez .... .20 .06
227 Dave Martinez .... .20 .06
228 Quinton McCracken .... .20 .06
229 Fred McGriff .... .30 .09
230 Kevin Stocker .... .20 .06
231 Randy Winn .... .20 .06
232 Royce Clayton .... .20 .06
233 Juan Gonzalez .... .50 .15
234 Tom Goodwin .... .20 .06
235 Rusty Greer .... .20 .06
236 Rick Helling .... .20 .06
237 Rafael Palmeiro .... .30 .09
238 Ivan Rodriguez .... .50 .15
239 Aaron Sele .... .20 .06
240 John Wetteland .... .20 .06
241 Todd Zeile .... .20 .06
242 Jose Cruz Jr. .... .20 .06
243 Carlos Delgado .... .20 .06
244 Tony Fernandez .... .20 .06
245 Cecil Fielder .... .20 .06
246 Alex Gonzalez .... .20 .06
247 Shawn Green .... .20 .06
248 Roy Halladay .... .20 .06
249 Shannon Stewart .... .20 .06
250 David Wells .... .20 .06
NNO Tony Gwynn Sample .... 1.00 .30

1999 Paramount Copper

Inserted one per hobby pack only, this 250-card set is a copper foil parallel version of the base set.

Nm-Mt Ex-Mt
COMPLETE SET (250) 100.00 30.00
*STARS: 1.5X TO 4X BASIC CARDS ...

1999 Paramount Gold

Inserted one per retail pack only, this 250-card set is a gold foil parallel version of the base set.

Nm-Mt Ex-Mt
COMPLETE SET (250) 100.00 30.00
*STARS: 1X TO 2.5X BASIC CARDS ...

1999 Paramount Holo-Gold

Randomly inserted in packs, this 250-card set is a holographic gold foil parallel version of the base set. Only 199 serial-numbered sets were produced.

Nm-Mt Ex-Mt
*STARS: 10X TO 25X BASIC CARDS ..

1999 Paramount Holo-Silver

Randomly inserted in hobby packs only, this 250-card set is a holographic silver foil parallel version of the base set. Only 99 serial-numbered sets were produced.

Nm-Mt Ex-Mt
*STARS: 15X TO 40X BASIC CARDS ..

1999 Paramount Opening Day

Randomly inserted in hobby packs only at a rate of one in 36, this 250-card set is parallel to the base set. Only 74 serial-numbered sets were produced.

Nm-Mt Ex-Mt
*STARS: 20X TO 50X BASIC CARDS ..

1999 Paramount Platinum Blue

Randomly inserted in packs at the rate of one in 73, this 250-card set is a platinum blue foil version of the base set.

Nm-Mt Ex-Mt
*STARS: 15X TO 40X BASIC CARDS ..

1999 Paramount Red

Inserted one per retail pack only, this 250-card set is a red foil parallel version of the base set.

Nm-Mt Ex-Mt
COMPLETE SET (250) 100.00 30.00
*STARS: 1.5X TO 4X BASIC CARDS ...

1999 Paramount Cooperstown Bound

Randomly inserted in packs at the rate of one in 361, this 10-card set features color action photos of the all-time great players headed for Cooperstown. A hobby only parallel set was also produced and serially numbered to 20.

Nm-Mt Ex-Mt
COMPLETE SET (10) ....
*PROOFS: 1.5X TO 4X BASIC COOP ...
PROOFS: RANDOM INSERTS IN HOBBY
PAC.PROOFS PRINT RUN 20 SERIAL #'d SETS
1 Greg Maddux 30.00 9.00
2 Cal Ripken 60.00 18.00
3 Nomar Garciaparra 30.00 9.00
4 Sammy Sosa 30.00 9.00
5 Frank Thomas 20.00 6.00
6 Mike Piazza 30.00 9.00
7 Mark McGwire 50.00 15.00
8 Tony Gwynn 25.00 7.50
9 Ken Griffey Jr. 30.00 9.00
10 Alex Rodriguez 30.00 9.00

1999 Paramount Fielder's Choice

Randomly inserted in packs at the rate of one in 73, this 20-card set features some of the League's top players printed on laser-cut cards.

Nm-Mt Ex-Mt
COMPLETE SET (20) 300.00 90.00
1 Chipper Jones 12.00 3.60
2 Greg Maddux 20.00 6.00
3 Cal Ripken 40.00 12.00
4 Nomar Garciaparra 20.00 6.00
5 Sammy Sosa 20.00 6.00
6 Kerry Wood 12.00 3.60
7 Frank Thomas 12.00 3.60
8 Manny Ramirez 5.00 1.50
9 Todd Helton 8.00 2.40
10 Jeff Bagwell 8.00 2.40
11 Mike Piazza 20.00 6.00
12 Derek Jeter 30.00 9.00
13 Bernie Williams 8.00 2.40
14 J.D. Drew 5.00 1.50
15 Mark McGwire 30.00 9.00
16 Tony Gwynn 15.00 4.50
17 Ken Griffey Jr. 20.00 6.00
18 Alex Rodriguez 20.00 6.00
19 Juan Gonzalez 12.00 3.60
20 Ivan Rodriguez 12.00 3.60

1999 Paramount Personal Bests

Randomly inserted in packs at the rate of one in 37, this 36-card set features color action photos of top players who always strive to do their best.

Nm-Mt Ex-Mt
COMPLETE SET (36) 400.00 120.00
1 Darin Erstad 4.00 1.20
2 Mo Vaughn 4.00 1.20
3 Travis Lee 4.00 1.20
4 Chipper Jones 10.00 3.00
5 Greg Maddux 15.00 4.50
6 Albert Belle 4.00 1.20
7 Cal Ripken 30.00 9.00
8 Nomar Garciaparra 15.00 4.50
9 Sammy Sosa 15.00 4.50
10 Andruw Jones 4.00 1.20
11 Frank Thomas 10.00 3.00
12 Roberto Alomar 10.00 3.00
13 Manny Ramirez 4.00 1.20
14 Todd Helton 6.00 1.80
15 Larry Walker 6.00 1.80
16 Jeff Bagwell 6.00 1.80
17 Craig Biggio 6.00 1.80
18 Raul Mondesi 4.00 1.20
19 Vladimir Guerrero 10.00 3.00
20 Hideo Nomo 10.00 3.00
21 Mike Piazza 15.00 4.50
22 Roger Clemens 20.00 6.00
23 Derek Jeter 25.00 7.50
24 Bernie Williams 6.00 1.80
25 Eric Chavez 4.00 1.20
26 Ben Grieve 4.00 1.20
27 Scott Rolen 6.00 1.80
28 J.D. Drew 4.00 1.20
29 Mark McGwire 25.00 7.50
30 Tony Gwynn 12.00 3.60
31 Barry Bonds 25.00 7.50
32 Ken Griffey Jr. 15.00 4.50
33 Alex Rodriguez 15.00 4.50
34 Wade Boggs 6.00 1.80
35 Juan Gonzalez 10.00 3.00
36 Ivan Rodriguez 10.00 3.00

1999 Paramount Team Checklists

Randomly inserted in packs at the rate of two in 37, this 30-card set features top players from each MLB team. The backs carry their team's checklist for the Paramount main set.

	Nm-Mt	Ex-Mt
COMPLETE SET (30)	150.00	45.00
1 Mo Vaughn	2.00	.60
2 Travis Lee	2.00	.60
3 Chipper Jones	5.00	1.50
4 Cal Ripken	15.00	4.50
5 Nomar Garciaparra	8.00	2.40
6 Sammy Sosa	8.00	2.40
7 Frank Thomas	5.00	1.50
8 Barry Larkin	5.00	1.50
9 Manny Ramirez	2.00	.60
10 Larry Walker	3.00	.90
11 Damion Easley	2.00	.60
12 Mark Kotsay	2.00	.60
13 Jeff Bagwell	3.00	.90
14 Jeremy Giambi	2.00	.60
15 Raul Mondesi	2.00	.60
16 Marquis Grissom	2.00	.60
17 Brad Radke	2.00	.60
18 Vladimir Guerrero	5.00	1.50
19 Mike Piazza	8.00	2.40
20 Roger Clemens	10.00	3.00
21 Ben Grieve	2.00	.60
22 Scott Rolen	3.00	.90
23 Jason Kendall	2.00	.60
24 Mark McGwire	12.00	3.60
25 Tony Gwynn	6.00	1.80
26 Barry Bonds	12.00	3.60
27 Ken Griffey Jr.	8.00	2.40
28 Wade Boggs	3.00	.90
29 Juan Gonzalez	5.00	1.50
30 Jose Cruz Jr.	2.00	.60

1999 Paramount Players Choice

These cards, which parallel the regular Paramount cards, were distributed at the 1999 Players Choice award ceremony. The cards, are the same as the regular Paramount cards except they have a "Players Choice" stamped on the front. The cards are skip numbered since they share the same number as the regular cards. Each card was issued in different quantities so we have put the print run next to the players name.

	Nm-Mt	Ex-Mt
COMPLETE SET	300.00	90.00
8 Mike Hampton/75	8.00	2.40
Uses 1998 Paramount card No 1999 Paramount card made for Hampton		
15 Randy Johnson/133	15.00	4.50
18 Matt Williams/108	8.00	2.40
24 Chipper Jones/117	30.00	9.00
28 Greg Maddux/118	30.00	9.00
36 Cal Ripken Jr./60	80.00	24.00
41 Pedro Martinez/118	15.00	4.50
52 Sammy Sosa/98	25.00	7.50
69 Roberto Alomar/133	12.00	3.60
75 Manny Ramirez/139	15.00	4.50
101 Jeff Bagwell/100	15.00	4.50
150 R.Henderson/133	20.00	6.00
208 Barry Bonds/53	40.00	12.00
216 Ken Griffey Jr./97	50.00	15.00
237 Rafael Palmeiro/133	10.00	3.00

2000 Paramount

The 2000 Paramount set was issued in six card packs with 36 packs in a box and 20 boxes in a case. Cases were also available in 12 and six box counts. The packs have an SRP of $1.79 per pack. The set is sequenced in alphabetical order by teams which are also sequenced in alphabetical order. There are no subsets in this set.

	Nm-Mt	Ex-Mt
COMPLETE SET (250)	40.00	12.00
1 Garret Anderson	.20	.06
2 Jim Edmonds	.20	.06
3 Darin Erstad	.20	.06
4 Chuck Finley	.20	.06
5 Troy Glaus	.30	.09
6 Troy Percival	.20	.06
7 Tim Salmon	.30	.09
8 Mo Vaughn	.20	.06
9 Jay Bell	.20	.06
10 Erubiel Durazo	.20	.06
11 Steve Finley	.20	.06
12 Luis Gonzalez	.20	.06
13 Randy Johnson	.50	.15
14 Travis Lee	.20	.06
15 Matt Mantei	.20	.06
16 Matt Williams	.20	.06
17 Tony Womack	.20	.06
18 Bret Boone	.20	.06
19 Tom Glavine	.30	.09
20 Andruw Jones	.20	.06
21 Chipper Jones	.50	.15
22 Brian Jordan	.20	.06
23 Javy Lopez	.20	.06
24 Greg Maddux	.75	.23
25 Kevin Millwood	.20	.06
26 John Rocker	.20	.06
27 John Smoltz	.30	.09
28 Brady Anderson	.20	.06
29 Albert Belle	.20	.06
30 Will Clark	.50	.15
31 Charles Johnson	.20	.06
32 Mike Mussina	.50	.15
33 Cal Ripken	1.50	.45
34 B.J. Surhoff	.20	.06
35 Nomar Garciaparra	.75	.23
36 Derek Lowe	.20	.06
37 Pedro Martinez	.50	.15
38 Trot Nixon	.30	.09
39 Troy O'Leary	.20	.06
40 Jose Offerman	.20	.06
41 John Valentin	.20	.06
42 Jason Varitek	.20	.06
43 Mark Grace	.30	.09
44 Glenallen Hill	.20	.06
45 Jon Lieber	.20	.06
46 Cole Liniak	.20	.06
47 Jose Nieves	.20	.06
48 Henry Rodriguez	.20	.06
49 Sammy Sosa	.75	.23
50 Kerry Wood	.50	.15
51 Jason Dellaero	.20	.06
52 Ray Durham	.20	.06
53 Paul Konerko	.20	.06
54 Carlos Lee	.20	.06
55 Greg Norton	.20	.06
56 Magglio Ordonez	.20	.06
57 Chris Singleton	.20	.06
58 Frank Thomas	.50	.15
59 Aaron Boone	.20	.06
60 Mike Cameron	.20	.06
61 Sean Casey	.20	.06
62 Pete Harnisch	.20	.06
63 Barry Larkin	.50	.15
64 Pokey Reese	.20	.06
65 Greg Vaughn	.20	.06
66 Scott Williamson	.20	.06
67 Roberto Alomar	.50	.15
68 Sean DePaula RC	.25	.07
69 Travis Fryman	.20	.06
70 David Justice	.20	.06
71 Kenny Lofton	.20	.06
72 Manny Ramirez	.20	.06
73 Richie Sexson	.20	.06
74 Jim Thome	.50	.15
75 Omar Vizquel	.20	.06
76 Pedro Astacio	.20	.06
77 Vinny Castilla	.20	.06
78 Derrick Gibson	.20	.06
79 Todd Helton	.30	.09
80 Neifi Perez	.20	.06
81 Ben Petrick	.20	.06
82 Larry Walker	.30	.09
83 Brad Ausmus	.20	.06
84 Tony Clark	.20	.06
85 Deivi Cruz	.20	.06
86 Damion Easley	.20	.06
87 Juan Encarnacion	.20	.06
88 Juan Gonzalez	.50	.15
89 Bobby Higginson	.20	.06
90 Dave Mlicki	.20	.06
91 Dean Palmer	.20	.06
92 Bruce Aven	.20	.06
93 Luis Castillo	.20	.06
94 Ramon Castro	.20	.06
95 Cliff Floyd	.20	.06
96 Alex Gonzalez	.20	.06
97 Mike Lowell	.20	.06
98 Preston Wilson	.20	.06
99 Jeff Bagwell	.30	.09
100 Derek Bell	.20	.06
101 Craig Biggio	.30	.09
102 Ken Caminiti	.20	.06
103 Carl Everett	.20	.06
104 Mike Hampton	.20	.06
105 Jose Lima	.20	.06
106 Billy Wagner	.20	.06
107 Daryle Ward	.20	.06
108 Carlos Beltran	.20	.06
109 Johnny Damon	.20	.06
110 Jermaine Dye	.20	.06
111 Carlos Febles	.20	.06
112 Mark Quinn	.20	.06
113 Joe Randa	.20	.06
114 Jose Rosado	.20	.06
115 Mike Sweeney	.20	.06
116 Kevin Brown	.30	.09
117 Shawn Green	.20	.06
118 Mark Grudzielanek	.20	.06
119 Todd Hollandsworth	.20	.06
120 Eric Karros	.20	.06
121 Chan Ho Park	.20	.06
122 Gary Sheffield	.20	.06
123 Devon White	.20	.06
124 Eric Young	.20	.06
125 Kevin Barker	.20	.06
126 Ron Belliard	.20	.06
127 Jeromy Burnitz	.20	.06
128 Jeff Cirillo	.20	.06
129 Marquis Grissom	.20	.06
130 Geoff Jenkins	.20	.06
131 David Nilsson	.20	.06
132 Chad Allen	.20	.06
133 Ron Coomer	.20	.06
134 Jacque Jones	.20	.06
135 Corey Koskie	.20	.06
136 Matt Lawton	.20	.06
137 Brad Radke	.20	.06
138 Todd Walker	.20	.06
139 Michael Barrett	.20	.06
140 Peter Bergeron	.20	.06
141 Brad Fullmer	.20	.06
142 Vladimir Guerrero	.50	.15
143 Ugueth Urbina	.20	.06
144 Jose Vidro	.20	.06
145 Rondell White	.20	.06
146 Edgardo Alfonzo	.20	.06
147 Armando Benitez	.20	.06
148 Roger Cedeno	.20	.06
149 Rickey Henderson	.50	.15
150 Melvin Mora	.20	.06
151 John Olerud	.20	.06
152 Rey Ordonez	.20	.06
153 Mike Piazza	.75	.23
154 Jorge Toca	.20	.06
155 Robin Ventura	.30	.09
156 Roger Clemens	1.00	.30
157 David Cone	.20	.06
158 Orlando Hernandez	.20	.06
159 Derek Jeter	1.25	.35
160 Chuck Knoblauch	.20	.06
161 Ricky Ledee	.20	.06
162 Tino Martinez	.30	.09
163 Paul O'Neill	.30	.09
164 Mariano Rivera	.30	.09
165 Alfonso Soriano	.50	.15
166 Bernie Williams	.30	.09
167 Eric Chavez	.20	.06
168 Jason Giambi	.50	.15
169 Ben Grieve	.20	.06
170 Tim Hudson	.30	.09
171 John Jaha	.20	.06
172 Matt Stairs	.20	.06
173 Miguel Tejada	.20	.06
174 Randy Velarde	.20	.06
175 Bobby Abreu	.20	.06
176 Marlon Anderson	.20	.06
177 Rico Brogna	.20	.06
178 Ron Gant	.20	.06
179 Doug Glanville	.20	.06
180 Mike Lieberthal	.20	.06
181 Scott Rolen	.30	.09
182 Curt Schilling	.30	.09
183 Brian Giles	.20	.06
184 Chad Hermansen	.20	.06
185 Jason Kendall	.20	.06
186 Al Martin	.20	.06
187 Pat Meares	.20	.06
188 Warren Morris	.20	.06
189 Ed Sprague	.20	.06
190 Kevin Young	.20	.06
191 Rick Ankiel	.20	.06
192 Kent Bottenfield	.20	.06
193 Eric Davis	.20	.06
194 J.D. Drew	.20	.06
195 Adam Kennedy	.20	.06
196 Ray Lankford	.20	.06
197 Joe McEwing	.20	.06
198 Mark McGwire	1.25	.35
199 Edgar Renteria	.20	.06
200 Fernando Tatis	.20	.06
201 Mike Darr	.20	.06
202 Ben Davis	.20	.06
203 Tony Gwynn	.60	.18
204 Trevor Hoffman	.20	.06
205 Damian Jackson	.20	.06
206 Phil Nevin	.20	.06
207 Reggie Sanders	.20	.06
208 Quilvio Veras	.20	.06
209 Rich Aurilia	.20	.06
210 Marvin Benard	.20	.06
211 Barry Bonds	1.25	.35
212 Ellis Burks	.20	.06
213 Livan Hernandez	.20	.06
214 Jeff Kent	.20	.06
215 Russ Ortiz	.20	.06
216 J.T. Snow	.20	.06
217 Paul Abbott	.20	.06
218 David Bell	.20	.06
219 Freddy Garcia	.20	.06
220 Ken Griffey Jr.	.75	.23
221 Carlos Guillen	.20	.06
222 Brian Hunter	.20	.06
223 Edgar Martinez	.30	.09
224 Jamie Moyer	.20	.06
225 Alex Rodriguez	.75	.23
226 Wade Boggs	.30	.09
227 Miguel Cairo	.20	.06
228 Jose Canseco	.50	.15
229 Roberto Hernandez	.20	.06
230 Dave Martinez	.20	.06
231 Quinton McCracken	.20	.06
232 Fred McGriff	.30	.09
233 Kevin Stocker	.20	.06
234 Royce Clayton	.20	.06
235 Rusty Greer	.20	.06
236 Ruben Mateo	.20	.06
237 Rafael Palmeiro	.30	.09
238 Ivan Rodriguez	.50	.15
239 Aaron Sele	.20	.06
240 John Wetteland	.20	.06
241 Todd Zeile	.20	.06
242 Tony Batista	.20	.06
243 Homer Bush	.20	.06
244 Carlos Delgado	.20	.06
245 Tony Fernandez	.20	.06
246 Billy Koch	.20	.06
247 Raul Mondesi	.20	.06
248 Shannon Stewart	.20	.06
249 David Wells	.20	.06
250 Vernon Wells	.20	.06

2000 Paramount Copper

Issued one per hobby pack, these cards parallel the regular Paramount set and have copper foil on them.

	Nm-Mt	Ex-Mt
COMPLETE SET (250)	100.00	30.00
*STARS: 1.5X TO 4X BASIC CARDS ...		
*ROOKIES: 1X TO 2.5X BASIC CARDS		

2000 Paramount Gold

Issued one per retail pack, these cards parallel the regular Paramount set and have gold foil on them.

	Nm-Mt	Ex-Mt
COMPLETE SET (250)	100.00	30.00
*STARS: 1.5X TO 4X BASIC CARDS ...		
*ROOKIES: 1X TO 2.5X BASIC CARDS		

2000 Paramount Green

Seeded at a rate of one per 7-11 pack, these cards parallel the basic Paramount set. Each card carries green foil accents on front instead of the silver foil used on the basic cards.

	Nm-Mt	Ex-Mt
COMPLETE SET (250)	100.00	30.00
*STARS: 2X TO 5X BASIC CARDS		
*ROOKIES: 1.25X TO 3X BASIC CARDS		

2000 Paramount Holographic Gold

Randomly inserted exclusively into retail packs, these cards parallel the regular, have gold holographic foil on the fronts and are serial numbered to 199.

	Nm-Mt	Ex-Mt
*STARS: 8X TO 20X BASIC CARDS		
*ROOKIES: 5X TO 12X BASIC CARDS		

2000 Paramount Holographic Green

Randomly seeded exclusively into 7-11 packs, these cards parallel the basic Paramount set. Each card carries holographic green accents on front and only 99 serial numbered sets were produced.

	Nm-Mt	Ex-Mt
*STARS: 12.5X TO 30X BASIC CARDS		
*ROOKIES: 8X TO 20X BASIC CARDS		

2000 Paramount Holographic Silver

Randomly inserted in hobby packs, these cards parallel the regular Paramount set and have silver holographic foil on them and are serial numbered to 99.

	Nm-Mt	Ex-Mt
*STARS: 12.5X TO 30X BASIC CARDS		
*ROOKIES: 8X TO 20X BASIC CARDS		

2000 Paramount Platinum Blue

Randomly inserted in packs, these cards parallel the regular Paramount set and have platinum foil on them and are serial numbered to 67.

	Nm-Mt	Ex-Mt
*STARS: 15X TO 40X BASIC CARDS ..		
*ROOKIES: 10X TO 25X BASIC CARDS		

2000 Paramount Premiere Date

Inserted one every 36 hobby packs, these cards parallel the regular Paramount set and are serial numbered on the front to 50.

	Nm-Mt	Ex-Mt
*STARS: 20X TO 50X BASIC CARDS ..		
*ROOKIES: 12.5X TO 30X BASIC CARDS		

2000 Paramount Ruby

As a special issue exclusive to 7-11 retail distribution (a nationwide chain of convenience stores), Pacific produced Ruby foil parallel versions of the basic Paramount set (replacing the silver foil fronts used on the standard cards). Each 10-card 7-11 retail pack contained nine Ruby foil parallel cards (essentially replacing the basic Paramount cards).

	Nm-Mt	Ex-Mt
COMPLETE SET (250)	60.00	18.00
*STARS: 1.25X TO 3X BASIC CARDS .		
*ROOKIES: .75X TO 2X BASIC CARDS		

2000 Paramount Cooperstown Bound

Issued approximately one every 361 packs, these 10 cards feature players destined for the Hall of Fame. The cards are printed on a foiled an embossed field using a hand-sculpted die.

	Nm-Mt	Ex-Mt
COMPLETE SET (10)	400.00	120.00
*SINGLES: 10X TO 25X BASIC CARDS		
*PROOF: 1.5X TO 4X BASIC COOPERSTOWN		
PROOF RANDOM INSERTS IN HOBBY PACKS		
PROOF PRINT RUN 20 SERIAL #'d SETS		
CANVAS PROOF RANDOM IN HOBBY PACKS		
CANVAS PROOF PR.RUN 1 SERIAL #'d SET		
CANVAS PROOF TOO SCARCE TO PRICE		
1 Greg Maddux	20.00	6.00
2 Cal Ripken	40.00	12.00
3 Nomar Garciaparra	20.00	6.00
4 Sammy Sosa	20.00	6.00
5 Roger Clemens	25.00	7.50
6 Derek Jeter	30.00	9.00
7 Mark McGwire	30.00	9.00
8 Tony Gwynn	15.00	4.50
9 Ken Griffey Jr.	20.00	6.00
10 Alex Rodriguez	20.00	6.00

2000 Paramount Double Vision

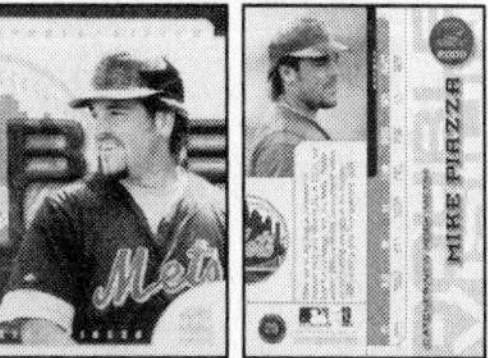

Inserted one every 37 packs, these cards feature two different versions of each of the 18 players featured. Cards numbered from 1 through 18 feature an action photo while cards numbered from 19 through 37 feature a head shot. The two cards for each player are meant to be laid side to side so the complete team logo can be seen in the background.

	Nm-Mt	Ex-Mt
COMPLETE SET (36)	150.00	45.00
1 Chipper Jones	4.00	1.20
2 Cal Ripken	12.00	3.60
3 Nomar Garciaparra	6.00	1.80
4 Pedro Martinez	4.00	1.20
5 Sammy Sosa	6.00	1.80
6 Manny Ramirez	1.50	.45
7 Jeff Bagwell	2.50	.75
8 Craig Biggio	2.50	.75
9 Vladimir Guerrero	4.00	1.20
10 Mike Piazza	6.00	1.80
11 Roger Clemens	8.00	2.40
12 Derek Jeter	10.00	3.00
13 Mark McGwire	10.00	3.00
14 Tony Gwynn	5.00	1.50
15 Ken Griffey Jr.	6.00	1.80
16 Alex Rodriguez	6.00	1.80
17 Rafael Palmeiro	2.50	.75
18 Ivan Rodriguez	4.00	1.20
19 Chipper Jones	4.00	1.20
20 Cal Ripken	12.00	3.60
21 Nomar Garciaparra	6.00	1.80
22 Pedro Martinez	4.00	1.20
23 Sammy Sosa	6.00	1.80
24 Manny Ramirez	1.50	.45
25 Jeff Bagwell	2.50	.75
26 Craig Biggio	2.50	.75
27 Vladimir Guerrero	4.00	1.20
28 Mike Piazza	6.00	1.80
29 Roger Clemens	8.00	2.40
30 Derek Jeter	10.00	3.00
31 Mark McGwire	10.00	3.00
32 Tony Gwynn	5.00	1.50
33 Ken Griffey Jr.	6.00	1.80
34 Alex Rodriguez	6.00	1.80
35 Rafael Palmeiro	2.50	.75
36 Ivan Rodriguez	4.00	1.20

2000 Paramount Fielder's Choice

Inserted one every 73 packs, these 20 cards feature leather like material in the glove's web, creating a design of the player within the glove background.

	Nm-Mt	Ex-Mt
COMPLETE SET (20)		
GOLD GLOVE RANDOM INS.IN HOB/RET		
GOLD GLOVE PRINT RUN 10 SERIAL #'d SETS		
GOLD GLOVE TOO SCARCE TO PRICE		
1 Andruw Jones	1.50	.45
2 Chipper Jones	4.00	1.20
3 Greg Maddux	6.00	1.80
4 Cal Ripken	12.00	3.60
5 Nomar Garciaparra	6.00	1.80
6 Sammy Sosa	6.00	1.80
7 Sean Casey	1.50	.45
8 Manny Ramirez	1.50	.45
9 Larry Walker	2.50	.75
10 Jeff Bagwell	2.50	.75
11 Mike Piazza	6.00	1.80
12 Derek Jeter	10.00	3.00
13 Bernie Williams	2.50	.75
14 Scott Rolen	2.50	.75
15 Mark McGwire	10.00	3.00
16 Tony Gwynn	5.00	1.50
17 Barry Bonds	10.00	3.00
18 Ken Griffey Jr.	6.00	1.80
19 Alex Rodriguez	6.00	1.80
20 Ivan Rodriguez	4.00	1.20

2000 Paramount Maximum Impact

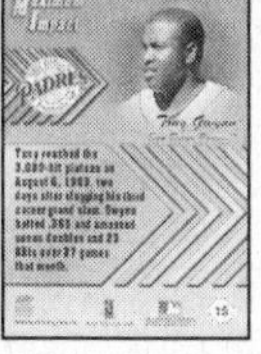

Randomly seeded exclusively into 7-11 retail packs at a rate of 2:25, this 20-card set features a selection of top stars that impact the game in maximum fashion.

	Nm-Mt	Ex-Mt
COMPLETE SET (20)	100.00	30.00
1 Chipper Jones	2.50	.75
2 Cal Ripken	8.00	2.40
3 Nomar Garciaparra	4.00	1.20
4 Pedro Martinez	2.50	.75
5 Sammy Sosa	4.00	1.20
6 Manny Ramirez	1.00	.30
7 Larry Walker	1.50	.45
8 Jeff Bagwell	1.50	.45
9 Carlos Beltran	1.00	.30
10 Vladimir Guerrero	2.50	.75
11 Mike Piazza	4.00	1.20
12 Derek Jeter	6.00	1.80
13 Roger Clemens	5.00	1.50
14 Mark McGwire	6.00	1.80
15 Tony Gwynn	3.00	.90
16 Barry Bonds	6.00	1.80
17 Ken Griffey Jr.	4.00	1.20
18 Alex Rodriguez	4.00	1.20
19 Ivan Rodriguez	2.50	.75
20 Carlos Delgado	1.00	.30

2000 Paramount Season in Review

Inserted two every 37 packs, these 30 cards feature players who either hit a career milestone or had an outstanding highlight during the 1999 season. The cards are printed with a full foil presentation.

	Nm-Mt	Ex-Mt
COMPLETE SET (30)	100.00	30.00
1 Randy Johnson	2.00	.60
2 Matt Williams	.75	.23
3 Chipper Jones	2.00	.60
4 Greg Maddux	3.00	.90
5 Cal Ripken	6.00	1.80
6 Nomar Garciaparra	3.00	.90
7 Pedro Martinez	2.00	.60
8 Sammy Sosa	3.00	.90
9 Manny Ramirez	.75	.23
10 Larry Walker	1.25	.35
11 Jeff Bagwell	1.25	.35
12 Craig Biggio	1.25	.35
13 Carlos Beltran	.75	.23
14 Mark Quinn	.75	.23
15 Vladimir Guerrero	2.00	.60
16 Mike Piazza	3.00	.90
17 Robin Ventura	1.25	.35
18 Roger Clemens	4.00	1.20
19 David Cone	.75	.23
20 Derek Jeter	5.00	1.50
21 Mark McGwire	5.00	1.50
22 Fernando Tatis	.75	.23
23 Tony Gwynn	2.50	.75
24 Barry Bonds	5.00	1.50
25 Ken Griffey Jr.	3.00	.90
26 Alex Rodriguez	3.00	.90
27 Wade Boggs	1.25	.35
28 Jose Canseco	2.00	.60
29 Rafael Palmeiro	1.25	.35
30 Ivan Rodriguez	2.00	.60

2000 Paramount Update

The 2000 Paramount Update set was released in October, 2000 as a 100-card set. The product was sold exclusively in J.C. Penney Christmas catalogs and production was announced at 12,500 sets (though the cards and boxes lack any type of serial numbering). Each set carried a suggested retail price of $29.99. Please note that card backs carry a "U" suffix.

	Nm-Mt	Ex-Mt
COMP.FACT.SET (100)	15.00	4.50
U1 Adam Kennedy	.30	.09
U2 Bengie Molina	.30	.09
U3 Derrick Turnbow RC	.40	.12
U4 Randy Johnson	.75	.23
U5 Danny Klassen	.30	.09
U6 Vicente Padilla RC	1.00	.30
U7 Rafael Furcal	.30	.09
U8 Andres Galarraga	.30	.09
U9 Chipper Jones	.75	.23
U10 Fernando Lunar	.30	.09
U11 Willie Morales RC	.30	.09
U12 Cal Ripken	2.50	.75
U13 B.J. Ryan	.30	.09
U14 Carl Everett	.30	.09
U15 Nomar Garciaparra	1.25	.35
U16 Pedro Martinez	.75	.23
U17 Wilton Veras	.30	.09
U18 Scott Downs RC	.30	.09
U19 Daniel Garibay RC	.30	.09
U20 Sammy Sosa	1.25	.35
U21 Julio Zuleta RC	.40	.12
U22 Josh Paul	.30	.09
U23 Frank Thomas	.75	.23
U24 Rob Bell	.30	.09
U25 Dante Bichette	.30	.09
U26 Travis Dawkins	.30	.09
U27 Ken Griffey Jr.	1.25	.35
U28 Chuck Finley	.30	.09
U29 Manny Ramirez	.30	.09
U30 Paul Rigdon RC	.30	.09
U31 Jeff Cirillo	.30	.09
U32 Larry Walker	.50	.15
U33 Masato Yoshii	.30	.09
U34 Robert Fick	.30	.09
U35 Jose Macias	.30	.09
U36 Juan Gonzalez	.75	.23
U37 Hideo Nomo	.75	.23
U38 Jason Grilli	.30	.09
U39 Pablo Ozuna	.30	.09
U40 Brad Penny	.30	.09
U41 Jeff Bagwell	.50	.15
U42 Lance Berkman	.30	.09
U43 Roger Cedeno	.30	.09
U44 Octavio Dotel	.30	.09
U45 Chad Durbin RC	.30	.09
U46 Eric Gagne	.75	.23
U47 Shawn Green	.30	.09
U48 Jose Hernandez	.30	.09
U49 Matt LeCroy	.30	.09
U50 Johan Santana RC	3.00	.90
U51 Vladimir Guerrero	.75	.23
U52 Hideki Irabu	.30	.09
U53 Andy Tracy RC	.30	.09
U54 Derek Bell	.30	.09
U55 Eric Cammack RC	.30	.09
U56 Mike Hampton	.30	.09
U57 Jay Payton	.30	.09
U58 Mike Piazza	1.25	.35
U59 Todd Zeile	.30	.09
U60 Roger Clemens	1.50	.45
U61 Darrell Einertson RC	.30	.09
U62 Derek Jeter	2.00	.60
U63 Jeremy Giambi	.30	.09
U64 Terrence Long	.30	.09
U65 Mark Mulder	.50	.15
U66 Adam Piatt	.30	.09
U67 Luis Vizcaino	.30	.09
U68 Pat Burrell	.50	.15
U69 Scott Rolen	.50	.15
U70 Chad Hermansen	.30	.09
U71 Rick Ankiel	.30	.09
U72 Jim Edmonds Cards	.30	.09
U73 Mark McGwire	2.00	.60
U74 G. Stechschulte RC	.30	.09
U75 Fernando Vina	.30	.09
U76 Bret Boone	.30	.09
U77 Tony Gwynn	1.00	.30
U78 Ryan Klesko	.30	.09
U79 David Newhan	.30	.09
U80 Kevin Walker RC	.30	.09
U81 Barry Bonds	2.00	.60
U82 Aaron Fultz RC	.30	.09
U83 Ben Weber RC	.40	.12
U84 Rickey Henderson	.75	.23
U85 Kevin Hodges RC	.30	.09
U86 John Olerud	.30	.09
U87 Rob Ramsay	.30	.09
U88 Alex Rodriguez	1.25	.35
U89 Kazuhiro Sasaki RC	1.50	.45
U90 Vinny Castilla	.30	.09
U91 Jeff Sparks RC	.30	.09
U92 Greg Vaughn	.30	.09
U93 Francisco Cordero	.30	.09
U94 Gabe Kapler	.30	.09
U95 Mike Lamb RC	.40	.12
U96 Ivan Rodriguez	.75	.23
U97 Clayton Andrews	.30	.09
U98 Brad Fullmer	.30	.09
U99 Raul Mondesi	.30	.09
U100 Dewayne Wise	.30	.09

1977-81 Bob Parker Hall of Fame

These 103 cards measure 3 1/2" by 5 1/2". The cards are checklisted in alphabetical order. Noted sports artist Bob Parker drew these pictures of Hall of Famers. Between 1977 and 1981 two different continuation series of 23 postcards were issued. They are each entered in order of issue. A couple of other notes. All three series have unnumbered header cards. The first series header does list the cards in numerical order while the other header cards do not. Also the first and third series card are made of similar stock while the middle series consists of a darker tan paper stock.

	NM	Ex
COMPLETE SET (103)	80.00	32.00
1 Grover C. Alexander	1.50	.60
2 Cap Anson	1.50	.60
3 Luke Appling	.75	.30
4 Ernie Banks	1.50	.60
5 Chief Bender	.75	.30
6 Jim Bottomley	.50	.20
7 Dan Brouthers	.50	.20
8 Morgan Bulkeley	.25	.10
9 Roy Campanella	1.00	.40
10 Alex Cartwright	.25	.10
11 Henry Chadwick	.25	.10
12 John Clarkson	.50	.20
13 Ty Cobb	5.00	2.00
14 Eddie Collins	1.00	.40
15 Jimmy Collins	.50	.20
16 Charles Comiskey	1.00	.40
17 Sam Crawford	.75	.30
18 Jerome "Dizzy" Dean	1.00	.40
19 Joe DiMaggio	5.00	2.00
20 Buck Ewing	.75	.30
21 Bob Feller	1.50	.60
22 Lou Gehrig	5.00	2.00
23 Goose Goslin	.75	.30
24 Burleigh Grimes	.75	.30
25 Chick Hafey	.50	.20
26 Rogers Hornsby	1.50	.60
27 Carl Hubbell	1.00	.40
28 Miller Huggins	.50	.20
29 Tim Keefe	.50	.20
30 Mike Kelly	.75	.30
31 Nap Lajoie	1.00	.40
32 Fred Lindstrom	.50	.20
33 Connie Mack	1.00	.40
34 Mickey Mantle	8.00	3.20
35 Heine Manush	.75	.30
36 Joe McGinnity	.50	.20
37 John McGraw	1.00	.40
38 Eddie Plank	.75	.30
39 Eppa Rixey	.50	.20
40 Jackie Robinson	4.00	1.60
41 Eddie Roush	.75	.30
42 Babe Ruth	8.00	3.20
43 Al Simmons	.75	.30
44 Albert Spalding	.75	.30
45 Tris Speaker	1.50	.60
46 Casey Stengel	1.00	.40
47 Bill Terry	.75	.30
48 Rube Waddell	.50	.20
49 Hans Wagner	2.00	.80
50 Paul Waner	.75	.30
51 John M. Ward	.50	.20
52 Ted Williams	5.00	2.00
53 George Wright	.50	.20
54 Harry Wright	.50	.20
55 Mordecai Brown	.50	.20
56 Frank Chance	.75	.30
57 Candy Cummings	.50	.20
58 Frank Frisch	.50	.20
59 Gabby Hartnett	.50	.20
60 Billy Herman	.50	.20
61 Waite Hoyt	.50	.20
62 Walter Johnson	1.50	.60
63 Kenesaw Landis	.25	.10
64 Rube Marquard	.50	.20
65 Christy Mathewson	1.50	.60
66 Eddie Mathews	.75	.30
67 Willie Mays	4.00	1.60
68 Bill McKechnie	.25	.10
69 Stan Musial	3.00	1.20
70 Mel Ott	1.00	.40
71 Satchel Paige	1.00	.40
72 Robin Roberts	.75	.30
73 George Sisler	.50	.20
74 Warren Spahn	.75	.30
75 Joe Tinker	.25	.10
76 Dazzy Vance	.25	.10
77 Cy Young	1.00	.40
78 Home Run Baker	.75	.30
79 Yogi Berra	1.00	.40
80 Max Carey	.25	.10
81 Roberto Clemente	4.00	1.60
82 Mickey Cochrane	.50	.20
83 Roger Connor	.25	.10
84 Joe Cronin	.75	.30
85 Kiki Cuyler	.50	.20
86 Johnny Evers	.75	.30
87 Jimmy Foxx	1.00	.40
88 Charlie Gehringer	.75	.30
89 Lefty Gomez	.75	.30
90 Jesse Haines	.25	.10
91 Will Harridge	.25	.10
92 Monte Irvin	.50	.20
93 Addie Joss	.50	.20
94 Al Kaline	1.00	.40
95 Sandy Koufax	2.50	1.00
96 Rabbit Maranville	.25	.10
97 Jim O'Rourke	.25	.10
98 Wilbert Robinson	.50	.20
99 Pie Traynor	.50	.20
100 Zach Wheat	.25	.10
NNO 3rd series Header	.25	.10
NNO 1st series Header	.25	.10
NNO 2nd series Header	.25	.10

1977 Bob Parker More Baseball Cartoons

These 24 cartoons feature imporant players in Baseball History as drawn by noted sports artist Bob Parker. These cards feature drawings on the front and are blank-backed

	NM	Ex
COMPLETE SET (24)	35.00	14.00
1 Hank Aaron Babe Ruth	5.00	2.00
2 Ernie Banks	1.50	.60
3 Rod Carew	1.00	.40
4 Joe DiMaggio	5.00	2.00
5 Doug Flynn	.25	.10
6 Mike Garcia	.25	.10
7 Steve Garvey Greg Luzinski	.50	.20
8 Lou Gehrig	5.00	2.00
9 Chuck Klein Hack Wilson	.50	.20
10 Don Larsen	.50	.20
11 Fred Lynn	.50	.20
12 Roy Majtyka	.25	.10
13 Pepper Martin	.50	.20
14 Christy Mathewson	1.00	.40
15 Cal McVey	.75	.30
16 Tony Perez	.75	.30
17 Babe Ruth Lou Gehrig	5.00	2.00
18 Everett Scott	.25	.10
19 Bobby Thomson	.50	.20
20 Ted Williams 1939 Version of Williams Drawn in 74	5.00	2.00
21 Ted Williams Last .400 Hitter Drawn in 76	5.00	2.00
22 Bill Madlock	.50	.20
23 Honus Wagner Al Spalding Buck Ewing Henry Chadwick	.75	.30
24 Checklist	.25	.10

1914 Pastime Novelty Postcard

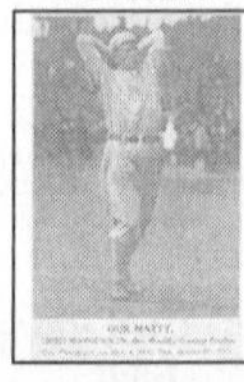

This postcard, issued by the Pastime Novelty company featured Christy Mathewson in a photo taken during the 1913 World Series. Little else is known about ths postcard so all additional information is appreciated.

	Ex-Mt	VG
1 Christy Mathewson	800.00	400.00

1868-71 Peck and Snyder Trade Cards

Issued over a period of years, these cars feature rare photos of some of the earliest professional teams. The Lowells card is currently known as only a photocopy.

	Ex-Mt	VG
COMPLETE SET	40000.00	20000.00
1 Lowells 1868	8000.00	4000.00
2 Atlantics 1868	8000.00	4000.00
3 Chicago White Sox 1870	8000.00	4000.00
4 Mutuals 1870	8000.00	4000.00
5 Philadelphia Athletics 1870	8000.00	4000.00

1910-14 People's T216

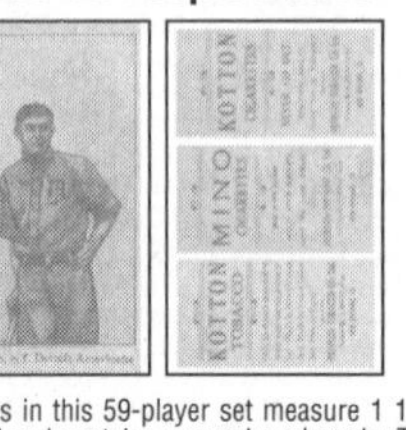

The cards in this 59-player set measure 1 1/2" by 2 5/8" and contains unnumbered cards. The players have been alphabetized and numbered for reference in the checklist below. Back variations within this set include Kotton, Mino and Virginia Cigarettes.

	Ex-Mt	VG
COMPLETE SET	30000.00	15000.00
1A Jack Barry Fielding	120.00	60.00
1B Jack Barry Fielding	120.00	60.00
2 Harry Bemis	120.00	60.00
3A Chief Bender Striped Cap Phila Am.	250.00	125.00
3B Chief Bender Striped Cap Baltimore Fed	250.00	125.00
3C Chief Bender White Cap Phila Am.	250.00	125.00
3D Chief Bender White Cap Baltimore Fed	250.00	125.00
4 Bill Bergen	120.00	60.00
5A Bob Bescher Cincinnati	120.00	60.00
5B Bob Bescher St. Louis Fed	120.00	60.00
6 Roger Bresnahan	250.00	125.00
7A Al Bridwell batting	120.00	60.00
7B Al Bridwell Sliding New York Nat'l	120.00	60.00
7C Al Bridwell Sliding St. Louis Feds	120.00	60.00
8 Donie Bush	150.00	75.00
9 Doc Casey	120.00	60.00
10 Frank Chance	400.00	200.00
11A Hal Chase Portrait	250.00	125.00
11B Hal Chase Fielding New York Am.	250.00	125.00
11C Hal Chase Fielding Buffalo	250.00	125.00
12A Ty Cobb Standing Detroit Am.	2500.00	1250.00
12B Ty Cobb Standing Detroit Americans	2500.00	1250.00
12C Ty Cobb batting	2500.00	1250.00
13 Sam Crawford	250.00	125.00
13A Eddie Collins Philadelphia Amer.	250.00	125.00
13B Eddie Collins Phila Am.	250.00	125.00
13C Eddie Collins Chicago Americans	250.00	125.00
14 Harry Davis	120.00	60.00
15 Ray Demmitt	120.00	60.00
17A Bill Donovan Detroit Amer.	120.00	60.00
17B Bill Donovan N.Y. Americans	120.00	60.00
18A Red Dooin Phila Nat.	120.00	60.00
18B Red Dooin Cincinnati	120.00	60.00
19A Mickey Doolan Phila Nat.	120.00	60.00
19B Mickey Doolan Baltimore Fed.	120.00	60.00
20 Patsy Dougherty	120.00	60.00
21A Larry Doyle N.Y. Nat'l	150.00	75.00
21B Larry Doyle New York Nat'l	150.00	75.00
21C Larry Doyle Throwing	150.00	75.00
22 Clyde Engle	120.00	60.00
23A Johnny Evers Chicago Nat'l	250.00	125.00
23B Johnny Evers Boston National	250.00	125.00
24 Art Fromme	120.00	60.00
25A George Gibson Back Pittsburg Nat'l	120.00	60.00
25B George Gibson Back Pittsburgh Nat'l.	120.00	60.00
25C George Gibson Front Pittsburg Nat'l	120.00	60.00
25D George Gibson Front Pittsburgh Nat'l	120.00	60.00
26A Topsy Hartsel Phila Am.	120.00	60.00
26B Topsy Hartsel Philadelphia Amer.	120.00	60.00
27A Roy Hartzell Catching	120.00	60.00
27B Roy Hartzell Batting	120.00	60.00
28A Fred Jacklitsch Phila Nat.	120.00	60.00
28B Fred Jacklitsch Baltimore Feds	120.00	60.00
29A Hugh Jennings Dance: Red	250.00	125.00
29B Hugh Jennings Dance; Orange	250.00	125.00
30 Red Kleinow	120.00	60.00
31A Otto Knabe Phila Nat.	120.00	60.00
31B Otto Knabe Baltimore Fed.	120.00	60.00
32 John Knight	120.00	60.00
33A Nap Lajoie Portrait	600.00	300.00
33B Nap Lajoie Fielding Cleveland	600.00	300.00
33C Nap Lajoie Fielding Phila Amer.	600.00	300.00
34A Hans Lobert Cincinnati	120.00	60.00
34B Hans Lobert New York Nat'l	120.00	60.00
35 Sherry Magee	150.00	75.00
36 Rube Marquard	250.00	125.00
37A Christy Mathewson Small Print	500.00	250.00
37B Christy Mathewson Large Print	500.00	250.00
38A John McGraw MG Small Print	250.00	125.00
38B John McGraw MG Large Print	250.00	125.00
39 Larry McLean	120.00	60.00
40 George McQuillan	120.00	60.00
41A Dots Miller Batting	120.00	60.00
41B Dots Miller Fielding Pittsburg	120.00	60.00
41C Dots Miller Fielding St. Louis Nat'l	120.00	60.00
42A Danny Murphy Phila Amer.	120.00	60.00
42B Danny Murphy Brooklyn Feds.	120.00	60.00
43 Rebel Oakes	120.00	60.00
44 Bill O'Hara	120.00	60.00
45 Eddie Plank	250.00	125.00
46A Germany Schaefer Washington	150.00	75.00
46B Germany Schaefer Newark Fed.	150.00	75.00
47 Admiral Schlei	120.00	60.00
48 Boss Schmidt	120.00	60.00
49 Dave Shean	120.00	60.00
50 Johnny Siegle	120.00	60.00
51 Tris Speaker	600.00	300.00
52 Oscar Stanage	120.00	60.00
53 George Stovall	120.00	60.00
54 Ed Sweeney	120.00	60.00
55A Joe Tinker Portrait	250.00	125.00
55B Joe Tinker Batting Chicago Nat'l	250.00	125.00
55C Joe Tinker Batting Chicago Feds	250.00	125.00
56A Honus Wagner Batting Pittsburg Nat'l	1200.00	600.00
56B Honus Wagner Batting Pittsburgh Nat'l	1200.00	600.00
56C Honus Wagner Throwing S.S	1200.00	600.00
56D Honus Wagner Throwing #2b	1200.00	600.00
57 Hooks Wiltse	120.00	60.00
58 Cy Young	600.00	300.00
59A Heinie Zimmerman 2B	120.00	60.00
59B Heinie Zimmerman 3B	120.00	60.00

1977 Pepsi Glove Discs

These discs actually form the middle of a glove-shaped tab which was inserted in cartons

of Pepsi-Cola during a baseball related promotion. The disc itself measures 3 3/8" in diameter whereas the glove tab is approximately 9" tall. The backs of the discs and the tab tell how you can get a personalized superstar shirt of Pete Rose, Rico Carty, Joe Morgan, or Rick Manning by sending in Pepsi cap liners. The players are shown in "generic" hats, i.e., the team logos have been airbrushed. This set was sanctioned by the Major League Baseball Players Association. The set is quite heavy in Cleveland Indians and Cincinnati Reds.

NM Ex
COMPLETE SET (72) 60.00 24.00
1 Robin Yount 5.00 2.00
2 Rod Carew 5.00 2.00
3 Butch Wynegar .50 .20
4 Manny Sanguillen .25 .10
5 Mike Hargrove .50 .20
6 Larvell Blanks .25 .10
7 Jim Kern .25 .10
8 Pat Dobson .25 .10
9 Rico Carty .25 .10
10 John Grubb .25 .10
11 Buddy Bell .50 .20
12 Rick Manning .25 .10
13 Dennis Eckersley 5.00 2.00
14 Wayne Garland .25 .10
15 Dave Laroche .25 .10
16 Rick Waits .25 .10
17 Ray Fosse .25 .10
18 Frank Duffy .25 .10
19 Duane Kuiper .25 .10
20 Jim Palmer 5.00 2.00
21 Fred Lynn .50 .20
22 Carlton Fisk 5.00 2.00
23 Carl Yastrzemski 5.00 2.00
24 Nolan Ryan 10.00 4.00
25 Bobby Grich .50 .20
26 Ralph Garr .25 .10
27 Richie Zisk .25 .10
28 Ron LeFlore .25 .10
29 Rusty Staub 1.00 .40
30 Mark Fidrych 4.00 1.60
31 Willie Horton .50 .20
32 George Brett 10.00 4.00
33 Amos Otis .25 .10
34 Reggie Jackson 5.00 2.00
35 Don Gullett .25 .10
36 Thurman Munson 1.50 .60
37 Al Hrabosky .25 .10
38 Mike Tyson .25 .10
39 Gene Tenace .50 .20
40 George Hendrick .25 .10
41 Chris Speier .25 .10
42 John Montefusco .25 .10
43 Pete Rose 5.00 2.00
44 Johnny Bench 5.00 2.00
45 Dan Driessen .25 .10
46 Joe Morgan 3.00 1.20
47 Dave Concepcion 1.00 .40
48 George Foster 1.00 .40
49 Cesar Geronimo .25 .10
50 Ken Griffey 1.00 .40
51 Gary Nolan .25 .10
52 Santo Alcala .25 .10
53 Jack Billingham .25 .10
54 Pedro Borbon .25 .10
55 Rawly Eastwick .25 .10
56 Fred Norman .25 .10
57 Pat Zachry .25 .10
58 Jeff Burroughs .25 .10
59 Manny Trillo .25 .10
60 Bob Watson .50 .20
61 Steve Garvey 1.50 .60
62 Don Sutton 3.00 1.20
63 John Candelaria .25 .10
64 Willie Stargell 3.00 1.20
65 Jerry Reuss .25 .10
66 Dave Cash .25 .10
67 Tom Seaver 5.00 2.00
68 Jon Matlack .25 .10
69 Dave Kingman 1.50 .60
70 Mike Schmidt 5.00 2.00
71 Jay Johnstone .50 .20
72 Greg Luzinski 1.00 .40

1978 Pepsi

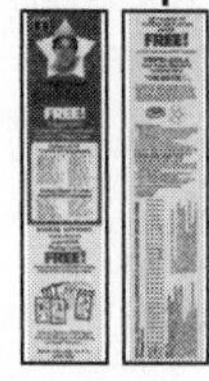

Sponsored by Pepsi-Cola and produced by MSA, this set of 40 collector cards measures approximately 2 1/8" by 9 1/2" and features members of the Cincinnati Reds and 15 national players. A checklist for the Cincinnati Reds (1-25) and for the 15 National players (26-40) is printed. The bottom part of the front has information on how to get a deck of Superstar playing cards free for 250 Pepsi capliners. The backs carry an order form and more detailed information. The cards are unnumbered and checklisted below in alphabetical order by grouping.

NM Ex
COMPLETE SET (40) 75.00 30.00
1 Sparky Anderson MG 2.50 1.00
2 Rick Auerbach 1.00 .40
3 Doug Bair UER 1.00 .40
Name is spelled Blair
4 Johnny Bench 8.00 3.20
5 Bill Bonham 1.00 .40
6 Pedro Borbon 1.00 .40
7 Dave Collins 1.00 .40
8 Dave Concepcion 2.50 1.00
9 Dan Driessen 1.50 .60
10 George Foster 2.00 .80
11 Cesar Geronimo 1.00 .40
12 Ken Griffey 2.50 1.00
13 Ken Henderson 1.00 .40
14 Tom Hume 1.00 .40
15 Junior Kennedy 1.00 .40
16 Ray Knight 2.00 .80
17 Mike Lum 1.00 .40
18 Joe Morgan 5.00 2.00
19 Paul Moskau UER 1.00 .40
Name is spelled Moscau
20 Fred Norman 1.00 .40
21 Pete Rose 8.00 3.20
22 Manny Sarmiento 1.00 .40
23 Tom Seaver 8.00 3.20
24 Dave Tomlin 1.00 .40
25 Don Werner 1.00 .40
26 Buddy Bell 2.00 .80
27 Larry Bowa 1.50 .60
28 George Brett 15.00 6.00
29 Jeff Burroughs 1.00 .40
30 Rod Carew 5.00 2.00
31 Steve Garvey 2.50 1.00
32 Reggie Jackson 8.00 3.20
33 Dave Kingman 2.00 .80
34 Jerry Koosman 1.50 .60
35 Bill Madlock 1.50 .60
36 Jim Palmer 5.00 2.00
37 Nolan Ryan 15.00 6.00
38 Ted Simmons 2.00 .80
39 Carl Yastrzemski 5.00 2.00
40 Richie Zisk 1.00 .40

1989 Pepsi McGwire

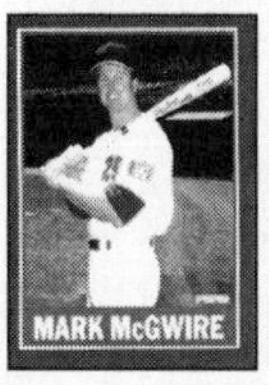

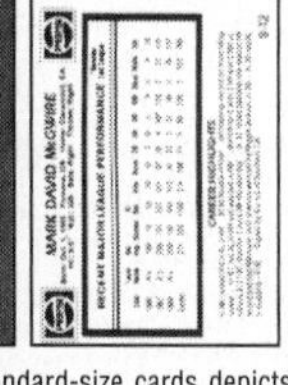

Each of these 12 standard-size cards depicts Mark McGwire. The cards are printed on rather thin card stock. All the pictures used in the set show McGwire in a generic uniform with a Pepsi patch on his upper arm and his number 25 on his chest; in each case his cap or batting helmet is in the Oakland colors but without their logo. The card backs all contain exactly the same statistical and biographical information, only the card number is different. Reportedly cards were distributed inside specially marked 12-packs of Pepsi in the Northern California area.

Nm-Mt Ex-Mt
COMPLETE SET (12) 35.00 14.00
COMMON CARD (1-12) 2.50 1.00

1990 Pepsi Canseco

This ten-card, standard-size set was issued in conjunction with Pepsi-Cola. These blue-bordered cards do not have the team logos. This set is very similar in style to the Pepsi McGwire set issued the year before. All the pictures used in the set are posed showing Canseco in a generic uniform with a Pepsi patch.

Nm-Mt Ex-Mt
COMPLETE SET (10) 10.00 3.00
COMMON CARD (1-10) 1.00 .30

1991 Pepsi Sid Fernandez

A local Hawaii Pepsi bottling company issued a two-card set of El Sid. He is depicted wearing a "Pepsi" uniform. Back has Pepsi logo and El Sid statistics through 1990.

Nm-Mt Ex-Mt
COMPLETE SET (2) 4.00 1.20
COMMON CARD (1-2) 2.00 .60

1991 Pepsi Griffeys

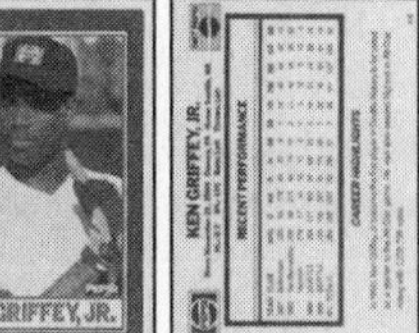

This eight-card standard-size set was sponsored by Pepsi-Cola, and its company logo appears on the front and back of each card. These cards were inserted one per special 12-pack of Pepsi. A ninth card was issued on a very limited basis as only 150 were produced.

Nm-Mt Ex-Mt
COMPLETE SET (8) 10.00 3.00
COMMON CARD (1-6) 1.50 .45
COMMON CARD (7-8) .50 .15
5 Ken Griffey Jr. 1.50 .45
Ken Griffey Sr.
Dad seated)
6 Ken Griffey Jr. 1.50 .45
Ken Griffey Sr.
Dad standing

1991 Pepsi Rickey Henderson

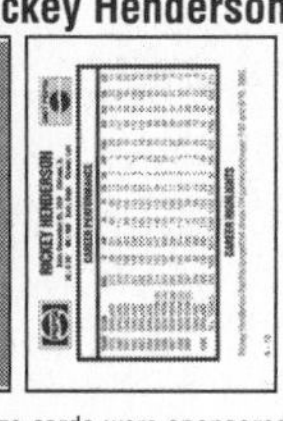

These ten standard-size cards were sponsored by Pepsi and feature Rickey Henderson. In a horizontal format, the backs have the same career performance statistics but differing career highlights.

Nm-Mt Ex-Mt
COMPLETE SET (10) 10.00 3.00
COMMON CARD (1-10) 1.00 .30

1991 Pepsi Rickey Henderson Discs

This four-disc set was issued by Pepsi in honor of Rickey Henderson. The discs measure approximately 2 1/8" in diameter. The fronts feature 3-D color action shots that change to different shots when one holds the discs at a different angle. The discs are unnumbered.

Nm-Mt Ex-Mt
COMPLETE SET (4) 6.00 1.80
COMMON DISC (1-4) 1.50 .45

1991 Pepsi Superstar

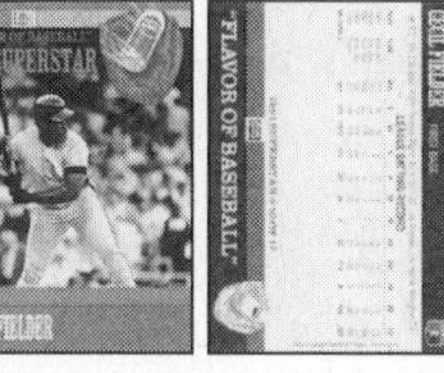

This 17-card set was sponsored by Pepsi-Cola of Florida as part of the "Flavor of Baseball" promotion. The promotion featured a chance to win one of 104 rare, older cards, including one 1952 Mickey Mantle card. The Superstar cards were glued inside specially marked 12 packs of Pepsi-Cola products in Orlando, Tampa, and Miami. It is difficult to remove the cards without creasing them; reportedly area supervisors for Pepsi each received a few sets. The cards measure slightly wider than standard size (2 5/8" by 3 1/2").

Nm-Mt Ex-Mt
COMPLETE SET (17) 80.00 24.00
1 Dwight Gooden 1.50 .45
2 Andre Dawson 2.50 .75
3 Ryne Sandberg 10.00 3.00
4 Dave Stieb 1.50 .45
5 Jose Rijo 1.00 .30
6 Roger Clemens 12.00 3.60
7 Barry Bonds 12.00 3.60
8 Cal Ripken 25.00 7.50
9 Dave Justice 2.50 .75
10 Cecil Fielder 1.50 .45
11 Don Mattingly 12.00 3.60
12 Ozzie Smith 10.00 3.00
13 Kirby Puckett 5.00 1.50
14 Rafael Palmeiro 2.50 .75
15 Bobby Bonilla 1.00 .30
16 Len Dykstra 1.50 .45
17 Jose Canseco 4.00 1.20

1992 Pepsi Diet MSA

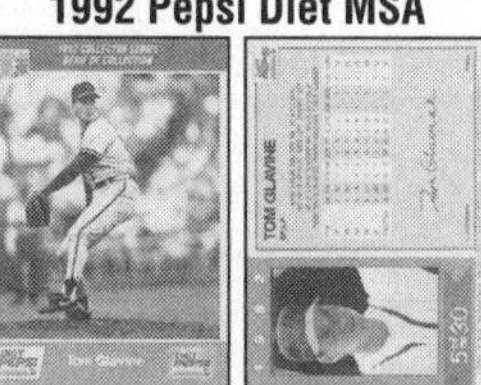

Issued in two different types of three-card packs, (a clear cello and a white cello with bilingual printing) this 30-card standard-size set was issued by MSA (Michael Schechter Associates) for Diet Pepsi in Canada. The packs were given away free with the purchase of Diet Pepsi or Diet Caffeine Free Pepsi. As is typical of MSA sets, the team logos have been airbrushed out. A red and blue trim poster which measures approximately 11" by 14" was also issued. A little mini picture of each player is on the poster.

Nm-Mt Ex-Mt
COMPLETE SET (30) 20.00 6.00
1 Roger Clemens 2.00 .60
2 Dwight Gooden .50 .15
3 Tom Henke .25 .07
4 Dennis Martinez .50 .15
5A Tom Glavine ERR 1.00 .30
Pitching Righthanded
5B Tom Glavine COR 2.00 .60
Pitching lefthanded
6 Jack Morris .50 .15
7 Dennis Eckersley 1.25 .35
8 Jeff Reardon .50 .15
9 Bryan Harvey .25 .07
10 Sandy Alomar Jr. .50 .15
11 Carlton Fisk 1.25 .35
12 Gary Carter 1.25 .35
13 Cecil Fielder .50 .15
14 Will Clark 1.00 .30
15 Roberto Alomar 1.00 .30
16 Ryne Sandberg 2.00 .60
17 Cal Ripken 4.00 1.20
18 Barry Larkin 1.00 .30
19 Ozzie Smith 1.50 .45
20 Kelly Gruber .25 .07
21 Wade Boggs 1.25 .35
22 Tim Wallach .25 .07
23 Howard Johnson .25 .07
24 Jose Canseco 1.00 .30
25 Joe Carter .50 .15
26 Ken Griffey Jr. 3.00 .90
27 Kirby Puckett 1.25 .35
28 Rickey Henderson 1.50 .45
29 Barry Bonds 2.00 .60
30 Dave Winfield 1.25 .35
XX Poster 5.00 1.50
All Players in Set Pictured

2003 Pepsi

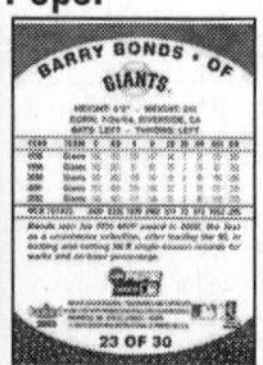

Inserted one per 24-ct cases of Pepsi in a promotion which began in March, 2003, these 30 cards feature a key player from each major league team. Each of these cards measure 2 1/4" by 3". The fronts have the 2003 Fleer design as well as a Pepsi logo while the back has some biographical information, stats for the last five years and a brief blurb.

Nm-Mt Ex-Mt
COMPLETE SET 30.00 9.00
1 Troy Glaus .50 .15
2 Chipper Jones 2.50 .75
3 Randy Johnson 2.50 .75
4 Tony Batista .25 .07
5 Magglio Ordonez .50 .15
6 Ken Griffey Jr. 2.50 .75
7 Omar Vizquel .50 .15
8 Todd Helton 1.00 .30
9 Bobby Higginson .25 .07
10 Luis Castillo .50 .15
11 Jeff Bagwell 1.25 .35
12 Mike Sweeney .75 .23
13 Shawn Green 1.00 .30
14 Richie Sexson .50 .15
15 Torii Hunter .50 .15
16 Vladimir Guerrero 1.25 .35
17 Mike Piazza 3.00 .90
18 Jason Giambi 1.25 .35
19 Barry Zito .75 .23
20 Pat Burrell .50 .15
21 Brian Giles .75 .23
22 Trevor Hoffman .50 .15
23 Barry Bonds 3.00 .90
24 Ichiro Suzuki 2.50 .75
25 Albert Pujols 2.50 .75
26 Ben Grieve .25 .07
27 Alex Rodriguez 3.00 .90
28 Carlos Delgado 1.00 .30
29 Kerry Wood 1.00 .30
30 Pedro Martinez 1.25 .35

1980-02 Perez-Steele Hall of Fame Postcards

President Ronald Reagan was given the first numbered set issued on May 27th, 1981 at the White House.The sets were also issued with continuation rights. These rights have been transferable over the years. These 3 1/2" by 5 1/2" cards feature noted sports artist Dick Perez drawings. The cards were distributed through Perez-Steele galleries. According to the producer, many of these cards are sold to art or postcard collectors. Just 10,000 of these sets were produced.

NRMT VG-E
COMPLETE SET 1500.00 700.00
1 Ty Cobb 40.00 18.00
2 Walter Johnson 10.00 4.50
3 Christy Mathewson 10.00 4.50
4 Babe Ruth 60.00 27.00
5 Honus Wagner 10.00 4.50
6 Morgan Bulkeley 1.00 .45
7 Ban Johnson 1.00 .45
8 Nap Lajoie 5.00 2.20
9 Connie Mack 5.00 2.20
10 John McGraw 5.00 2.20
11 Tris Speaker 5.00 2.20
12 George Wright 1.00 .45
13 Cy Young 5.00 2.20
14 Grover Alexander 5.00 2.20
15 Alex. Cartwright 1.00 .45
16 Henry Chadwick 1.00 .45
17 Cap Anson 2.50 1.10
18 Eddie Collins 5.00 2.20
19 Candy Cummings 1.50 .70
20 Charles Comiskey 1.00 .45
21 Buck Ewing 1.50 .70
22 Lou Gehrig 40.00 18.00
23 Willie Keeler 1.50 .70
24 Hoss Radbourne 1.50 .70
25 George Sisler 15.00 6.75
26 A.G. Spalding 1.50 .70
27 Rogers Hornsby 5.00 2.20
28 Kenesaw Landis 1.00 .45
29 Roger Bresnahan 1.50 .70
30 Dan Brouthers 1.50 .70
31 Fred Clarke 1.50 .70
32 Jimmy Collins 1.50 .70
33 Ed Delahanty 1.50 .70
34 Hugh Duffy 1.50 .70
35 Hughie Jennings 1.50 .70
36 King Kelly 2.50 1.10
37 Jim O'Rourke 1.50 .70
38 Wilbert Robinson 1.50 .70
39 Jesse Burkett 1.50 .70
40 Frank Chance 5.00 2.20
41 Jack Chesbro 1.50 .70
42 Johnny Evers 5.00 2.20
43 Clark Griffith 1.50 .70
44 Thomas McCarthy 1.50 .70
45 Joe McGinnity 1.50 .70
46 Eddie Plank 1.50 .70
47 Joe Tinker 5.00 2.20
48 Rube Waddell 1.50 .70
49 Ed Walsh 1.50 .70
50 Mickey Cochrane 5.00 2.20
51 Frankie Frisch 5.00 2.20
52 Lefty Grove 5.00 2.20
53 Carl Hubbell 10.00 4.50
54 Herb Pennock 1.50 .70
55 Pie Traynor 2.50 1.10
56 Mordecai Brown 1.50 .70
57 Charlie Gehringer 2.50 1.10
58 Kid Nichols 1.50 .70
59 Jimmy Foxx 15.00 6.75
60 Mel Ott 10.00 4.50
61 Harry Heilmann 1.50 .70
62 Paul Waner 5.00 2.20
63 Edward Barrow 1.00 .45
64 Chief Bender 5.00 2.20
65 Tom Connolly 1.00 .45
66 Dizzy Dean 15.00 6.75
67 Bill Klem 1.00 .45
68 Al Simmons 5.00 2.20
69 Bobby Wallace 1.50 .70
70 Harry Wright 1.50 .70
71 Bill Dickey 5.00 2.20
72 Rabbit Maranville 1.50 .70
73 Bill Terry 5.00 2.20
74 Frank Baker 1.50 .70
75 Joe DiMaggio 60.00 27.00
76 Gabby Hartnett 1.50 .70
77 Ted Lyons 1.50 .70
78 Ray Schalk 1.50 .70
79 Dazzy Vance 1.50 .70
80 Joe Cronin 2.50 1.10
81 Hank Greenberg 20.00 9.00
82 Sam Crawford 5.00 2.20
83 Joe McCarthy 1.00 .45
84 Zack Wheat 1.50 .70
85 Max Carey 1.50 .70
86 Billy Hamilton 1.50 .70
87 Bob Feller 15.00 6.75
88 Bill McKechnie 1.00 .45
89 Jackie Robinson 25.00 11.00
90 Edd Roush 2.50 1.10
91 John Clarkson 1.50 .70
92 Elmer Flick 1.50 .70
93 Sam Rice 5.00 2.20
94 Eppa Rixey 1.50 .70
95 Luke Appling 2.50 1.10
96 Red Faber 1.50 .70
97 Burleigh Grimes 1.50 .70
98 Miller Huggins 1.50 .70
99 Tim Keefe 1.50 .70
100 Heinie Manush 1.50 .70
101 John Ward 1.50 .70
102 Pud Galvin 1.50 .70
103 Casey Stengel 10.00 4.50
104 Ted Williams 60.00 27.00
105 Branch Rickey 1.50 .70
106 Red Ruffing 1.50 .70
107 Lloyd Waner 1.50 .70
108 Kiki Cuyler 1.50 .70
109 Goose Goslin 5.00 2.20
110 Joe Medwick 1.50 .70
111 Roy Campanella 10.00 4.50
112 Stan Coveleski 1.50 .70
113 Waite Hoyt 1.50 .70
114 Stan Musial 35.00 16.00
115 Lou Boudreau 12.00 5.50
116 Earle Combs 1.50 .70
117 Ford Frick 1.00 .45
118 Jesse Haines 1.50 .70
119 David Bancroft 1.50 .70
120 Jake Beckley 1.50 .70
121 Chick Hafey 1.00 .45
122 Harry Hooper 1.50 .70
123 Joe Kelley 1.50 .70
124 Rube Marquard 5.00 2.20
125 Satchel Paige 25.00 11.00
126 George Weiss 1.00 .45
127 Yogi Berra 15.00 6.75
128 Josh Gibson 5.00 2.20
129 Lefty Gomez 2.50 1.10
130 William Harridge 1.00 .45
131 Sandy Koufax 20.00 9.00
132 Buck Leonard 15.00 6.75
133 Early Wynn 5.00 2.20
134 Ross Youngs 1.50 .70
135 Roberto Clemente 50.00 22.00
136 Billy Evans 1.00 .45
137 Monte Irvin 8.00 3.60
138 George Kelly 1.50 .70
139 Warren Spahn 10.00 4.50
140 Mickey Welch 1.50 .70
141 Cool Papa Bell 8.00 3.60
142 Jim Bottomley 1.50 .70
143 Jocko Conlan 1.00 .45
144 Whitey Ford 20.00 9.00
145 Mickey Mantle 60.00 27.00
146 Sam Thompson 1.50 .70
147 Earl Averill 2.50 1.10
148 Bucky Harris 1.50 .70
149 Billy Herman 2.50 1.10

150 Judy Johnson 10.00 4.50
151 Ralph Kiner 10.00 4.50
152 Oscar Charleston 2.50 1.10
153 Roger Connor 1.50 .70
154 Cal Hubbard 1.00 .45
155 Bob Lemon 5.00 2.20
156 Fred Lindstrom 1.50 .70
157 Robin Roberts 10.00 4.50
158 Ernie Banks 15.00 6.75
159 Martin Dihigo 5.00 2.20
160 John Lloyd 5.00 2.20
161 Al Lopez 12.00 5.50
162 Amos Rusie 1.50 .70
163 Joe Sewell 1.50 .70
164 Addie Joss 1.50 .70
165 Larry MacPhail 1.00 .45
166 Eddie Mathews 10.00 4.50
167 Warren Giles 1.00 .45
168 Willie Mays 35.00 16.00
169 Hack Wilson 1.50 .70
170 Al Kaline 15.00 6.75
171 Chuck Klein 1.50 .70
172 Duke Snider 20.00 9.00
173 Tom Yawkey 1.00 .45
174 Rube Foster 1.00 .45
175 Bob Gibson 10.00 4.50
176 Johnny Mize 2.50 1.10
177 Hank Aaron 20.00 9.00
178 Happy Chandler 1.00 .45
179 Travis Jackson 1.50 .70
180 Frank Robinson 20.00 9.00
181 Walter Alston 8.00 3.60
182 George Kell 8.00 3.60
183 Juan Marichal 5.00 2.20
184 Brooks Robinson 15.00 6.75
185 Luis Aparicio 10.00 4.50
186 Don Drysdale 5.00 2.20
187 Rick Ferrell 1.50 .70
188 Harmon Killebrew 10.00 4.50
189 Pee Wee Reese 15.00 6.75
190 Lou Brock 15.00 6.75
191 Enos Slaughter 8.00 3.60
192 Arky Vaughan 1.50 .70
193 Hoyt Wilhelm 8.00 3.60
194 Bobby Doerr 8.00 3.60
195 Ernie Lombardi 1.50 .70
196 Willie McCovey 5.00 2.20
197 Ray Dandridge 5.00 2.20
198 Catfish Hunter 5.00 2.20
199 Billy Williams 8.00 3.60
200 Willie Stargell 6.00 2.70
201 Al Barlick 2.50 1.10
202 Johnny Bench 5.00 2.20
203 Red Schoendienst 8.00 3.60
204 Carl Yastrzemski 20.00 9.00
205 Joe Morgan 15.00 6.75
206 Jim Palmer 5.00 2.20
207 Rod Carew 15.00 6.75
208 Ferguson Jenkins 10.00 4.50
209 Tony Lazzeri 1.50 .70
210 Gaylord Perry 8.00 3.60
211 Bill Veeck 1.00 .45
212 Rollie Fingers 8.00 3.60
213 Bill McGowan 1.00 .45
214 Hal Newhouser 10.00 4.50
215 Tom Seaver 20.00 9.00
216 Reggie Jackson 20.00 9.00
217 Steve Carlton 15.00 6.75
218 Leo Durocher 5.00 2.20
219 Phil Rizzuto 20.00 9.00
220 Richie Ashburn 10.00 4.50
221 Leon Day 2.50 1.10
222 William Hulbert 1.00 .45
223 Mike Schmidt 20.00 9.00
224 Vic Willis 5.00 2.20
225 Jim Bunning 10.00 4.50
226 Bill Foster 5.00 2.20
227 Ned Hanlon 5.00 2.20
228 Earl Weaver 10.00 4.50
229 Nellie Fox 1.50 .70
230 Tom Lasorda 10.00 4.50
231 Phil Niekro 8.00 3.60
232 Willie Wells 1.50 .70
233 George Davis 1.50 .70
234 Larry Doby 8.00 3.60
235 Lee MacPhail 1.00 .45
236 Joe Rogan 1.50 .70
237 Don Sutton 8.00 3.60
238 George Brett 20.00 9.00
239 Orlando Cepeda 10.00 4.50
240 Nestor Chylak 1.00 .45
241 Nolan Ryan 25.00 11.00
242 Frank Selee 1.00 .45
243 Joe Williams 1.00 .45
244 Robin Yount 10.00 4.50
245 Sparky Anderson 2.50 1.10
246 Carlton Fisk 10.00 4.50
247 Bid McPhee 1.50 .70
248 Tony Perez 8.00 3.60
249 Turkey Stearnes 5.00 2.20
250 Bill Mazeroski 5.00 2.20
251 Kirby Puckett 15.00 6.75
252 Hilton Smith 1.50 .70
253 Dave Winfield 10.00 4.50
F George H.W. Bush 2.50 1.10
Edward W. Stack
G Franklin A. Steele MEM 1.00 .45
A Abner Doubleday 5.00 2.20
B Stephen C. Clark 1.00 .45
C Paul S. Kerr 1.00 .45
D Edward W. Stack 1.00 .45
E Perez-Steele Galleries 1.00 .45

1989 Perez-Steele Celebration Postcards

This 44-card set celebrates the 50th Anniversary of the National Baseball Hall of Fame and Museum. The cards measure approximately 3 1/2" by 5 1/2" and feature art work by artist Dick Perez. The backs carry a postcard format.

Nm-Mt Ex-Mt
COMPLETE SET (44) 150.00 60.00
1 Hank Aaron 6.00 2.40
2 Luis Aparicio 4.00 1.60
3 Ernie Banks 6.00 2.40
4 Cool Papa Bell 3.00 1.20
5 Johnny Bench 4.00 1.60
6 Yogi Berra 6.00 2.40
7 Lou Boudreau 4.00 1.60
8 Roy Campanella 4.00 1.60
9 Happy Chandler 2.00 .80
10 Jocko Conlan 2.00 .80
11 Ray Dandridge 3.00 1.20
12 Bill Dickey 4.00 1.60
13 Bobby Doerr 4.00 1.60
14 Rick Ferrell 3.00 1.20
15 Charlie Gehringer 4.00 1.60
16 Lefty Gomez 4.00 1.60
17 Billy Herman 2.50 1.00
18 Carfish Hunter 4.00 1.60
19 Monte Irvin 4.00 1.60
20 Judy Johnson 4.00 1.60
21 Al Kaline 6.00 2.40
22 George Kell 4.00 1.60
23 Harmon Killebrew 4.00 1.60
24 Ralph Kiner 4.00 1.60
25 Bob Lemon 3.00 1.20
26 Buck Leonard 4.00 1.60
27 Al Lopez 2.50 1.00
28 Mickey Mantle 10.00 4.00
29 Juan Marichal 4.00 1.60
30 Eddie Mathews 4.00 1.60
31 Willie McCovey 4.00 1.60
32 Johnny Mize 4.00 1.60
33 Stan Musial 6.00 2.40
34 Pee Wee Reese 4.00 1.60
35 Brooks Robinson 4.00 1.60
36 Joe Sewell 3.00 1.20
37 Enos Slaughter 4.00 1.60
38 Duke Snider 4.00 1.60
39 Warren Spahn 4.00 1.60
40 Willie Stargell 4.00 1.60
41 Bill Terry 4.00 1.60
42 Billy Williams 3.00 1.20
43 Ted Williams 10.00 4.00
44 Carl Yastrzemski 4.00 1.60

1990-92 Perez-Steele Master Works

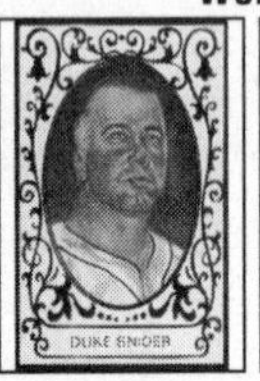

This 50-card set measures 3 1/2" by 5 1/2" and again features the fine artwork of Dick Perez. The set honors living Hall-of Famers at the time of issue and depicts them as if they might have appeared on several vintage card sets. The sets imitated are the Goodwin Champions of 1888, Rose Postcards of 1908, the T205 Gold Borders, 1909 Ramlys and one original design. The sets are numbered and are limited to 10,000 sets. The original issue price for each series was $135.

Nm-Mt Ex-Mt
COMPLETE SET (50) 225.00 70.00
1 Charlie Gehringer 2.00 .60
Ramly
2 Charlie Gehringer 2.00 .60
Goodwin
3 Charlie Gehringer 2.00 .60
Rose
4 Charlie Gehringer 2.00 .60
T205
5 Charlie Gehringer 2.00 .60
Original Drawing
6 Mickey Mantle 15.00 4.50
Ramly
7 Mickey Mantle 15.00 4.50
Goodwin
8 Mickey Mantle 15.00 4.50
Rose
9 Mickey Mantle 15.00 4.50
T205
10 Mickey Mantle 15.00 4.50
Original Drawing
11 Willie Mays 12.00 3.60
Ramly
12 Willie Mays 12.00 3.60
Goodwin
13 Willie Mays 12.00 3.60
Rose
14 Willie Mays 12.00 3.60
T205
15 Willie Mays 12.00 3.60
Original Drawing
16 Duke Snider 6.00 1.80
Ramly
17 Duke Snider 6.00 1.80
Goodwin
18 Duke Snider 6.00 1.80
Rose
19 Duke Snider 6.00 1.80
T205
20 Duke Snider 6.00 1.80
Original Drawing
21 Warren Spahn 3.00 .90
Ramly
22 Warren Spahn 3.00 .90
Goodwin
23 Warren Sphan 3.00 .90
Rose
24 Warren Spahn 3.00 .90
T205
25 Warren Spahn 3.00 .90
Original Drawing
26 Yogi Berra 5.00 1.50
Ramly
27 Yogi Berra 5.00 1.50
Goodwin
28 Yogi Berra 5.00 1.50
Rose
29 Yogi Berra 5.00 1.50
T205
30 Yogi Berra 5.00 1.50
Original Drawing
31 Johnny Mize 2.00 .60
Ramly
32 Johnny Mize 2.00 .60
Goodwin
33 Johnny Mize 2.00 .60
Rose
34 Johnny Mize 2.00 .60
T205
35 Johnny Mize 2.00 .60
Original Drawing
36 Willie Stargell 3.00 .90
Ramly
37 Willie Stargell 3.00 .90
Goodwin
38 Willie Stargell 3.00 .90
Rose
39 Willie Stargell 3.00 .90
T205
40 Willie Stargell 3.00 .90
Original Drawing
41 Ted Williams 12.00 3.60
Ramly
42 Ted Williams 12.00 3.60
Goodwin
43 Ted Williams 12.00 3.60
Rose
44 Ted Williams 12.00 3.60
T205
45 Ted Williams 12.00 3.60
Original Drawing
46 Carl Yastrzemski 5.00 1.50
Ramly
47 Carl Yastrzemski 5.00 1.50
Goodwin
48 Carl Yastrzemski 5.00 1.50
Rose
49 Carl Yastrzemski 5.00 1.50
T205
50 Carl Yastrzemski 5.00 1.50
Original Drawing

1990-97 Perez-Steele Great Moments

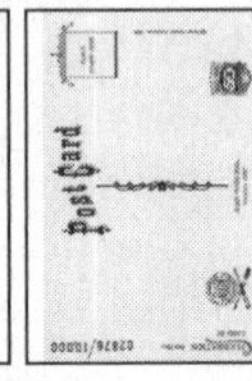

These cards were issued in series of 12 cards each. So far, nine series have been issued. The cards measure 3 1/2" by 5 1/2" and feature leading moments in Hall of Famers careers. These sets are also issued with continuation rights.

Nm-Mt Ex-Mt
COMPLETE SET (108) 250.00 75.00
1 Babe Ruth 20.00 6.00
2 Al Kaline 3.00 .90
3 Jackie Robinson 15.00 4.50
4 Lou Gehrig 15.00 4.50
5 Whitey Ford 5.00 1.50
6 Christy Mathewson 8.00 2.40
7 Roy Campanella 5.00 1.50
8 Walter Johnson 8.00 2.40
9 Hank Aaron 15.00 4.50
10 Cy Young 8.00 2.40
11 Stan Musial 8.00 2.40
12 Ty Cobb 15.00 4.50
13 Ted Williams 15.00 4.50
14 Warren Spahn 3.00 .90
15 Paul Waner 3.00 .90
Lloyd Waner
16 Sandy Koufax 8.00 2.40
17 Robin Roberts 3.00 .90
18 Dizzy Dean 5.00 1.50
19 Mickey Mantle 20.00 6.00
20 Satchel Paige 10.00 3.00
21 Ernie Banks 8.00 2.40
22 Willie McCovey 3.00 .90
23 Johnny Mize 2.00 .60
24 Honus Wagner 5.00 1.50
25 Willie Keeler 2.00 .60
26 Pee Wee Reese 5.00 1.50
27 Monte Irvin 2.00 .60
28 Eddie Mathews 5.00 1.50
29 Enos Slaughter 3.00 .90
30 Rube Marquard 2.00 .60
31 Charlie Gehringer 3.00 .90
32 Roberto Clemente 15.00 4.50
33 Duke Snider 5.00 1.50
34 Ray Dandridge 2.00 .60
35 Carl Hubbell 3.00 .90
36 Bobby Doerr 3.00 .90
37 Bill Dickey 3.00 .90
38 Willie Stargell 3.00 .90
39 Brooks Robinson 5.00 1.50
40 Joe Tinker 5.00 1.50
Johnny Evers
Frank Chance
41 Billy Herman 2.00 .60
42 Grover Alexander 5.00 1.50
43 Luis Aparicio 3.00 .90
44 Lefty Gomez 2.00 .60
45 Eddie Collins 2.00 .60
46 Judy Johnson 3.00 .90
47 Harry Heilmann 2.00 .60
48 Harmon Killebrew 3.00 .90
49 Johnny Bench 8.00 2.40
50 Max Carey 2.00 .60
51 Cool Papa Bell 3.00 .90
52 Rube Waddell 2.00 .60
53 Yogi Berra 8.00 2.40
54 Herb Pennock 2.00 .60
55 Red Schoendienst 3.00 .90
56 Juan Marichal 5.00 1.50
57 Frankie Frisch 2.00 .60
58 Buck Leonard 3.00 .90
59 George Kell 3.00 .90
60 Chuck Klein 2.00 .60
61 King Kelly 2.00 .60
62 Catfish Hunter 5.00 1.50
63 Lou Boudreau 3.00 .90
64 Al Lopez 3.00 .90
65 Willie Mays 15.00 4.50
66 Lou Brock 5.00 1.50
67 Bob Lemon 3.00 .90
68 Joe Sewell 2.00 .60
69 Billy Williams 3.00 .90
70 Rick Ferrell 2.00 .60
71 Arky Vaughan 2.00 .60
72 Carl Yastrzemski 8.00 2.40
73 Tom Seaver 5.00 1.50
74 Rollie Fingers 4.00 1.20
75 Ralph Kiner 4.00 1.20
76 Frank Baker 3.00 .90
77 Rod Carew 4.00 1.20
78 Goose Goslin 3.00 .90
79 Gaylord Perry 4.00 1.20
80 Hack Wilson 4.00 1.20
81 Hal Newhouser 2.00 .60
82 Early Wynn 2.00 .60
83 Bob Feller 5.00 1.50
84 Branch Rickey 2.00 .60
85 Jim Palmer 4.00 1.20
86 Al Barlick 2.00 .60
87 Mickey Mantle 10.00 3.00
Willie Mays
Duke Snider
88 Hank Greenberg 4.00 1.20
89 Joe Morgan 4.00 1.20
90 Chief Bender 3.00 .90
91 Pee Wee Reese 5.00 1.50
Jackie Robinson
92 Jim Bottomley 3.00 .90
93 Ferguson Jenkins 4.00 1.20
94 Frank Robinson 5.00 1.50
95 Hoyt Wilhelm 2.00 .60
96 Cap Anson 3.00 .90
97 Jim Bunning 3.00 .90
98 Richie Ashburn 4.00 1.20
99 Steve Carlton 5.00 1.50
100 Mike Schmidt 5.00 1.50
101 Nellie Fox 3.00 .90
102 Tom Lasorda 3.00 .90
103 Leo Durocher 2.00 .60
104 Reggie Jackson 5.00 1.50
105 Phil Niekro 3.00 .90
106 Phil Rizzuto 4.00 1.20
107 Willie Wells 2.00 .60
108 Earl Weaver 2.00 .60

1995 Perez-Steele Wagner Promotion

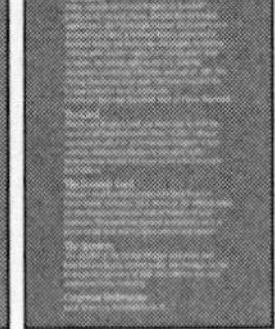

This one card set was issued to go along with the drawing for the T-206 Honus Wagner card run through a promotion at Wal-Mart. The front features a drawing about Honus Wagner while the back has information about the player; the card and the event. This card was given to the first 500 people who visited the exhibit of the famed card at each location.

Nm-Mt Ex-Mt
1 Honus Wagner 5.00 1.50

1981 Perma-Graphic All-Stars

This set commemorates the starters of the 1981 All-Star game. This 18-card set measure 2 1/8" by 3 3/8" and has rounded corners. Because of the players strike of 1981 plenty of time was available to prepare the player's biography with appropriate notes. The set is framed on the front in red for the National League and blue for the American League. This set was originally available from the manufacturer for $21.95

Nm-Mt Ex-Mt
COMPLETE SET (18) 60.00 24.00
1 Gary Carter 6.00 2.40
2 Dave Concepcion 2.50 1.00
3 Andre Dawson 5.00 2.00
4 George Foster 1.00 .40
5 Davey Lopes 2.50 1.00
6 Dave Parker 2.50 1.00
7 Pete Rose 8.00 3.20
8 Mike Schmidt 8.00 3.20
9 Fernando Valenzuela 2.50 1.00
10 George Brett 12.00 4.80
11 Rod Carew 6.00 2.40
12 Bucky Dent 2.50 1.00
13 Carlton Fisk 6.00 2.40
14 Reggie Jackson 6.00 2.40
15 Jack Morris 4.00 1.60
16 Willie Randolph 2.50 1.00
17 Ken Singleton 1.00 .40
18 Dave Winfield 6.00 2.40

1981 Perma-Graphic Credit Cards

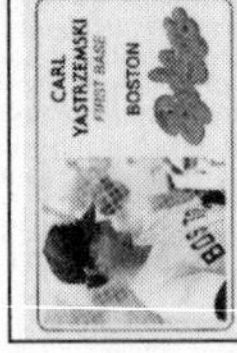

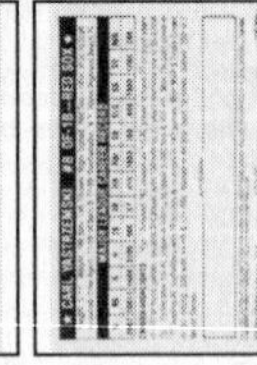

Perma-Graphic began their three-year foray into card manufacturing with this 32-card set of "credit cards~ each measuring approximately 2 1/8" by 3 3/8". The set featured 32 of the leading players of 1981. These sets (made of plastic) were issued with the cooperation of Topps Chewing Gum. This first set of Perma-Graphic cards seems to have been produced in greater quantities than the other five Perma-Graphic sets. These sets were originally available from the manufacturer for $39.95.

Nm-Mt Ex-Mt
COMPLETE SET (32) 60.00 24.00
1 Johnny Bench 4.00 1.60
2 Mike Schmidt 8.00 3.20
3 George Brett 10.00 4.00
4 Carl Yastrzemski 4.00 1.60
5 Pete Rose 4.00 1.60
6 Bob Horner 1.00 .40
7 Reggie Jackson 5.00 2.00
8 Keith Hernandez 2.00 .80
9 George Foster 1.00 .40
10 Garry Templeton 1.00 .40
11 Tom Seaver 5.00 2.00
12 Steve Garvey 2.00 .80
13 Dave Parker 2.00 .80
14 Willie Stargell 3.00 1.20
15 Cecil Cooper 1.00 .40
16 Steve Carlton 4.00 1.60
17 Ted Simmons 1.00 .40
18 Dave Kingman 2.00 .80
19 Rickey Henderson 10.00 4.00
20 Fred Lynn 2.00 .80
21 Dave Winfield 4.00 1.60
22 Rod Carew 4.00 1.60
23 Jim Rice 2.00 .80
24 Bruce Sutter 2.00 .80
25 Cesar Cedeno 1.00 .40
26 Nolan Ryan 12.00 4.80
27 Dusty Baker 1.00 .40
28 Jim Palmer 4.00 1.60
29 Gorman Thomas 1.00 .40
30 Ben Oglivie 1.00 .40
31 Willie Wilson 1.00 .40
32 Gary Carter 4.00 1.60

1982 Perma-Graphic All-Stars

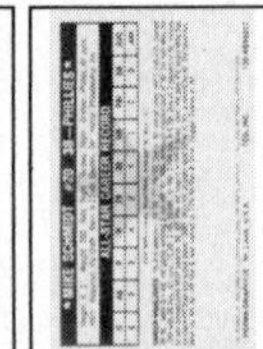

For the second time Perma-Graphic issued a special set commemorating the starters of the 1982 All-Star game. This 18-card set measures 2 1/8" by 3 3/8" and features a colorful design framing the players photo on the front The back again feature one line of complete All-Star game statistics including the 1982 game and career highlites. Perma-Graphic also issued the set in a limited (reportedly 1200 sets produced) "gold" edition, i.e., with a gold tint to the cards. The gold edition cards are valued at a multiplte of the regular set. Please refer to the multiplication table below.

Nm-Mt Ex-Mt
COMPLETE SET (18) 60.00 24.00
*GOLD CARDS:2X BASIC CARDS
1 Dennis Eckersley 6.00 2.40
2 Cecil Cooper 1.50 .60
3 Carlton Fisk 6.00 2.40
4 Robin Yount 6.00 2.40
5 Bobby Grich 1.50 .60
6 Rickey Henderson 8.00 3.20
7 Reggie Jackson 6.00 2.40
8 Fred Lynn 2.50 1.00
9 George Brett 10.00 4.00
10 Gary Carter 6.00 2.40
11 Dave Concepcion 1.50 .60
12 Andre Dawson 4.00 1.60
13 Tim Raines 2.50 1.00
14 Dale Murphy 5.00 2.00
15 Steve Rogers 1.50 .60
16 Pete Rose 6.00 2.40
17 Mike Schmidt 6.00 2.40
18 Manny Trillo 1.50 .60

1982 Perma-Graphic Credit Cards

For the second year Perma-Graphic, in association with Topps produced a high-quality set on plastic honoring the leading players in baseball of 1982. This 24-card set features plastic cards each measuring approximately 2 1/8" by 3 3/8". On the card back there is one line of career statistics along with career highlights. Perma-Graphic also issued the set in a limited (reportedly 900 sets produced) "gold" edition, i.e., with a gold tint to the cards. The gold edition cards are valued at a mulitple of the regular cards. Please see information in our headers for the multiplication value. Again in 1982 Perma-Graphic issued these sets in conjuction and with the approval of Topps Chewing Gum. This set was originally available from the manufacturer for $29.95. Uncut sheets were also available for this set. The SRP on those sheets were $75. The sheets had three copies of each card printed on it.

	Nm-Mt	Ex-Mt
COMPLETE SET (24)	60.00	24.00
*GOLD CARDS: 2X BASIC CARDS		
1 Johnny Bench	5.00	2.00
2 Tom Seaver	5.00	2.00
3 Mike Schmidt	5.00	2.00
4 Gary Carter	5.00	2.00
5 Willie Stargell	3.00	1.20
6 Tim Raines	2.00	.80
7 Bill Madlock	1.00	.40
8 Keith Hernandez	2.00	.80
9 Pete Rose	5.00	2.00
10 Steve Carlton	5.00	2.00
11 Steve Garvey	2.00	.80
12 Fernando Valenzuela	2.00	.80
13 Carl Yastrzemski	5.00	2.00
14 Dave Winfield	5.00	2.00
15 Carney Lansford	1.00	.40
16 Rollie Fingers	2.00	.80
17 Tony Armas	1.00	.40
18 Cecil Cooper	1.00	.40
19 George Brett	10.00	4.00
20 Reggie Jackson	5.00	2.00
21 Rod Carew	5.00	2.00
22 Eddie Murray	8.00	3.20
23 Rickey Henderson	5.00	2.00
24 Kirk Gibson	3.00	1.20

1983 Perma-Graphic All-Stars

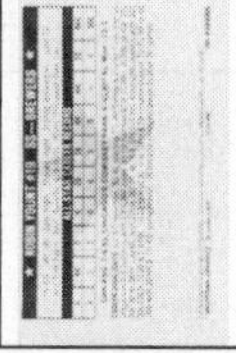

The 1983 All-Star Set was the third set Perma-Graphic issued commemorating the starters of the All-Star game. Again, Perma-Graphic used the Topps photos and issued their sets of plastic cards. This 18-card set features cards each measuring approximately 2 1/8" by 3 3/8". Perma-Graphic also issued the set in a limited "gold" edition, i.e., with a gold tint to the cards. The gold edition cards are valued at a multiple of the regular issue cards. Please see information below for values.

	Nm-Mt	Ex-Mt
COMPLETE SET (18)	60.00	24.00
*GOLD CARDS:2X BASIC CARDS		
1 George Brett	10.00	4.00
2 Rod Carew	6.00	2.40
3 Fred Lynn	2.00	.80
4 Jim Rice	2.00	.80
5 Ted Simmons	2.00	.80
6 Dave Stieb	1.00	.40
7 Manny Trillo	1.00	.40
8 Dave Winfield	6.00	2.40
9 Robin Yount	6.00	2.40
10 Gary Carter	6.00	2.40
11 Andre Dawson	3.00	1.20
12 Dale Murphy	5.00	2.00
13 Al Oliver	1.00	.40
14 Tim Raines	2.00	.80
15 Steve Sax	1.00	.40
16 Mike Schmidt	6.00	2.40
17 Ozzie Smith	8.00	3.20
18 Mario Soto	1.00	.40

1983 Perma-Graphic Credit Cards

This set was the third straight year Perma-Graphic, with approval from Topps issued their high-quality plastic set. This 36-card set which measures 2 1/8" by 3 3/8" have the players photos framed by colorful backgrounds. The backs again feature one line of career statistics and several informative lines of career highlights. Perma-Graphic also issued the set in a limited (reportedly 1000 sets produced) "gold" edition, i.e., with a gold tint to the cards. The gold edition cards are valued at a multiple of the regular issue cards. Please see information below for values.

	Nm-Mt	Ex-Mt
COMPLETE SET (36)	80.00	32.00
*GOLD CARDS:2X BASIC CARDS		
1 Bill Buckner	1.00	.40
2 Steve Carlton	4.00	1.60
3 Gary Carter	4.00	1.60
4 Andre Dawson	3.00	1.20
5 Pedro Guerrero	1.00	.40
6 George Hendrick	1.00	.40
7 Keith Hernandez	2.00	.80
8 Bill Madlock	1.00	.40
9 Dale Murphy	3.00	1.20
10 Al Oliver	1.00	.40
11 Dave Parker	2.00	.80
12 Darrell Porter	1.00	.40
13 Pete Rose	6.00	2.40
14 Mike Schmidt	6.00	2.40
15 Lonnie Smith	1.00	.40
16 Ozzie Smith	8.00	3.20
17 Bruce Sutter	2.00	.80
18 Fernando Valenzuela	3.00	1.20
19 George Brett	10.00	4.00
20 Rod Carew	4.00	1.60
21 Cecil Cooper	1.00	.40
22 Doug DeCinces	1.00	.40
23 Rollie Fingers	4.00	1.60
24 Damaso Garcia	1.00	.40
25 Toby Harrah	1.00	.40
26 Rickey Henderson	6.00	2.40
27 Reggie Jackson	6.00	2.40
28 Hal McRae	1.00	.40
29 Eddie Murray	6.00	2.40
30 Lance Parrish	2.00	.80
31 Jim Rice	2.00	.80
32 Gorman Thomas	1.00	.40
33 Willie Wilson	1.00	.40
34 Dave Winfield	4.00	1.60
35 Carl Yastrzemski	4.00	1.60
36 Robin Yount	4.00	1.60

1991 Petro-Canada Standups

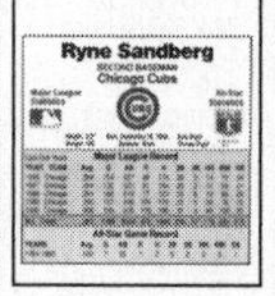

These 3-D action collector cards consist of three cardboard sheets measuring approximately 2 7/8" by 3 13/16" and joined at one end. The front cover has blue and red stripe borders and features either an American or National league logo inside a baseball diamond. The inside cover has a color photo of the crowd at the game. The middle sheet consists of a 3-D standup of the player. The inside of the last sheet has biographical information, career regular season statistics and All-Star game statistics. The back has career highlights in a sky blue box and "Play the All Star Quiz" questions and answers. The set was first released in Toronto at the All-Star Game in conjunction with the All-Star Fanfest. The cards are numbered on the front.

	Nm-Mt	Ex-Mt
COMPLETE SET (26)	10.00	3.00
1 Cal Ripken	2.50	.75
2 Greg Olson	.10	.03
3 Roger Clemens	1.25	.35
4 Ryne Sandberg	.75	.23
5 Dave Winfield	.50	.15
6 Eric Davis	.20	.06
7 Carlton Fisk	.50	.15
8 Mike Scott	.10	.03
9 Sandy Alomar Jr.	.20	.06
10 Tim Wallach	.10	.03
11 Cecil Fielder	.20	.06
12 Dwight Gooden	.20	.06
13 George Brett	1.25	.35
14 Dale Murphy	.30	.09
15 Paul Molitor	.50	.15
16 Barry Bonds	1.25	.35
17 Kirby Puckett	.50	.15
18 Ozzie Smith	1.25	.35
19 Don Mattingly	1.25	.35
20 Will Clark	.40	.12
21 Rickey Henderson	.60	.18
22 Orel Hershiser	.20	.06
23 Ken Griffey Jr.	1.50	.45
24 Tony Gwynn	1.25	.35
25 Nolan Ryan	2.50	.75
26 Kelly Gruber	.10	.03

1909 Philadelphia Caramel E95

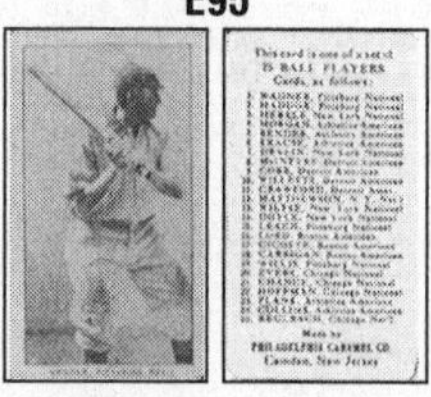

The cards in this 25-card set measure 1 1/2" by 2 3/4". This set of color drawings was issued by the Philadelphia Caramel Company about 1909. The back is checklisted with its own numbering system (begins with "1. Wagner"), but has been alphabetized for convenience in this listing. Blank backs found in this set are probably cut from advertising panels and should not be considered as proof cards.

	Ex-Mt	VG
COMPLETE SET (25)	12000.00	6000.00
1 Chief Bender	400.00	200.00
2 Bill Carrigan	200.00	100.00
3 Frank Chance	600.00	300.00
4 Eddie Cicotte	400.00	200.00
5 Ty Cobb	3000.00	1500.00
6 Eddie Collins	600.00	300.00
7 Sam Crawford	400.00	200.00
8 Art Devlin	200.00	100.00
9 Larry Doyle	250.00	125.00
10 Johnny Evers	400.00	200.00
11 Solly Hoffman	200.00	100.00
12 Harry Krause	200.00	100.00
13 Tommy Leach	200.00	100.00
14 Harry Lord	200.00	100.00
15 Nick Maddox	200.00	100.00
16 Christy Mathewson	1200.00	600.00
17 Matty McIntyre	200.00	100.00
18 Fred Merkle	300.00	150.00
19 Harry (Cy) Morgan	200.00	100.00
20 Eddie Plank	800.00	400.00
21 Ed Reulbach	200.00	100.00
22 Honus Wagner	1500.00	750.00
23 Ed Willett	200.00	100.00
24 Vic Willis	400.00	200.00
25 Hooks Wiltse	200.00	100.00

1912 Philadelphia Caramel E96

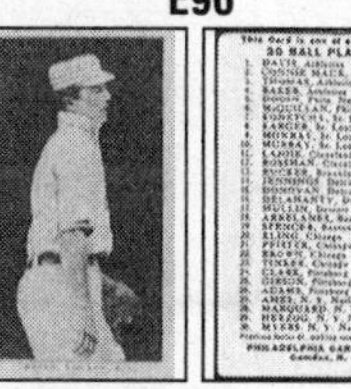

The cards in this 30-card set measure 1 1/2" by 2 3/4". The red printed backs in this set carry the statement "previous Series 25, making total issue 55 cards", and for this reason it is often referred to as the second series of E95. Issued about 1912, the numbering of the original checklist (starts with "1. Davis") has been rearranged alphabetically below. Some blank backs are known.

	Ex-Mt	VG
COMPLETE SET (30)	3600.00	1800.00
1 Babe Adams	120.00	60.00
2 Red Ames	100.00	50.00
3 Frank Arrelanes	100.00	50.00
4 Frank Baker	200.00	100.00
5 Mordecai Brown	200.00	100.00
6 Fred Clark (sic)	200.00	100.00
7 Harry Davis	100.00	50.00
8 Jim Delehanty	100.00	50.00
9 Bill Donovan	100.00	50.00
10 Red Dooin	100.00	50.00
11 George Gibson	100.00	50.00
12 Buck Herzog HOR	100.00	50.00
13 Hugh Jennings MG	200.00	100.00
14 Ed Karger	100.00	50.00
15 Johnny Kling	100.00	50.00
16 Ed Konetchy	100.00	50.00
17 Napoleon Lajoie	500.00	250.00
18 Connie Mack MG	400.00	200.00
19 Rube Marquard	200.00	100.00
20 George McQuillan	100.00	50.00
21 Chief Meyers	120.00	60.00
22 Mike Mowrey	100.00	50.00
23 George Mullin	100.00	50.00
24 Red Murray	100.00	50.00
25 Jack Pfeister	100.00	50.00
26 Claude Rossman	100.00	50.00
27 Nap Rucker	120.00	60.00
28 Tubby Spencer	100.00	50.00
29 Ira Thomas	100.00	50.00
30 Joe Tinker	200.00	100.00

1949 Philadelphia Bulletin

This 59-card set features black-and-white portraits of the Philadelphia A's and Phillies. Six of the portraits were inserted each week in the "Fun Book" section of the "Philadelphia Sunday Bulletin" from May 22 through July 24, 1949. Only five portraits were inserted in the paper the last Sunday. The cards are unnumbered and checklisted below in alphabetical order.

	NM	Ex
COMPLETE SET (59)	250.00	125.00
1 Richie Ashburn	20.00	10.00
2 Joe Astroth	3.00	1.50
3 Bennie Bengough CO	4.00	2.00
4 Hank Biasetti	3.00	1.50
5 Charles Bicknell	3.00	1.50
6 Buddy Blattner	3.00	1.50
7 Hank Borowy	3.00	1.50
8 Lou Brissie	3.00	1.50
9 Earle Brucker CO	3.00	1.50
10 Ralph Caballero	3.00	1.50
11 Sam Chapman	4.00	2.00
12 Joe Coleman	4.00	2.00
13 Dusty Cooke CO	3.00	1.50
14 Thomas Davis	3.00	1.50
15 Blix Donnelly	3.00	1.50
16 Jimmy Dykes CO	5.00	2.50
17 Del Ennis	5.00	2.50
18 Ferris Fain	5.00	2.50
19 Dick Fowler	3.00	1.50
20 Nellie Fox	20.00	10.00
21 Mike Guerra	3.00	1.50
22 Granny Hamner	5.00	2.50
23 Charley Harris	3.00	1.50
24 Ken Heintzleman	3.00	1.50
25 Stan Hollmig	3.00	1.50
26 Willie Jones	3.00	1.50
27 Eddie Joost	4.00	2.00
28 Alex Kellner	3.00	1.50
29 Jim Konstanty	5.00	2.50
30 Stan Lopata	4.00	2.00
31 Connie Mack MG	20.00	10.00
32 Earle Mack CO	4.00	2.00
33 Hank Majeskie	3.00	1.50
34 Phil Marchildon	3.00	1.50
35 Jackie Mayo	3.00	1.50
36 Bill McCahan	3.00	1.50
37 Barney McCoskey	3.00	1.50
38 Russ Meyer	4.00	2.00
39 Eddie Miller	3.00	1.50
40 Wally Moses	3.00	1.50
41 Bill Nicholson	3.00	1.50
42 Cy Perkins CO	3.00	1.50
43 Robin Roberts	15.00	7.50
44 Buddy Rosar	3.00	1.50
45 Schoolboy Rowe	5.00	2.50
46 Eddie Sawyer MG	3.00	1.50
47 Carl Scheib	3.00	1.50
48 Andy Seminick	5.00	2.50
49 Bobby Shantz	6.00	3.00
50 Ken Silvestri	3.00	1.50
51 Al Simmons CO	10.00	5.00
52 Curt Simmons	10.00	5.00
53 Dick Sisler	3.00	1.50
54 Pete Suder	3.00	1.50
55 Ken Trinkle	3.00	1.50
56 Elmer Valo	3.00	1.50
57 Eddie Waitkus	5.00	2.50
58 Don White	3.00	1.50
59 Taft Wright	3.00	1.50

1977 Philadelphia Favorites

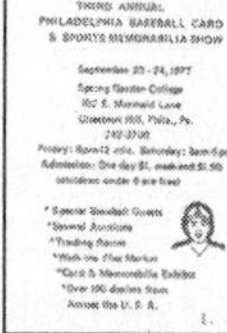

This 25-card set was used as promotional give-aways for the EPSCC in the Delaware Valley area during the summer of 1977 and measures approximately 3 3/4" by 2 1/4". Some complete sets were also available by mail. The fronts feature a sepia photo of a former Phillies or Athletics player with white borders. The player's name, position, team, and years played are printed in the bottom margin.

	NM	Ex
COMPLETE SET (25)	50.00	20.00
1 Connie Mack	5.00	2.00
2 Nap Lajoie	5.00	2.00
3 Eddie Collins	5.00	2.00
4 Lefty Grove	5.00	2.00
5 Al Simmons	2.50	1.00
6 Jimmy Foxx	5.00	2.00
7 Frank Baker	2.50	1.00
8 Ferris Fain	1.00	.40
9 Jimmy Dykes	1.00	.40
10 Willie Jones	1.00	.40
11 Del Ennis	1.00	.40
12 Granny Hamner	1.00	.40
13 Andy Seminick	1.00	.40
14 Robin Roberts	5.00	2.00
15 Ed Delahanty	2.50	1.00
16 Gavvy Cravath	2.00	.80
17 Cy Williams	1.00	.40
18 Chuck Klein	2.50	1.00
19 Richie Ashburn	5.00	2.00
20 Bobby Shantz	1.00	.40
21 Gus Zernial	1.00	.40
22 Eddie Sawyer	1.00	.40
23 G.C. Alexander	2.50	1.00
24 Wally Moses	1.00	.40
25 Connie Mack Stadium (nee Shibe Park)	1.00	.40

1979 Philadelphia Doubleheaders

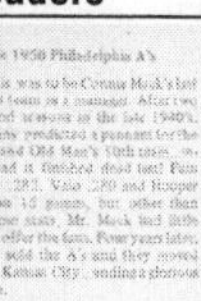

These 27 cards were issued to promote the EPSCC shows that have been put on in the Philadelphia area since the 1970's The set features two 1950 Philadelphia players on each card along with a back that either promoted the March 1979 EPSCC show or the Philadelphia Phillies checklist book. The two managers are the only people who have cards to themselves.

	NM	Ex
COMPLETE SET (30)	30.00	12.00
1 Connie Mack MG	3.00	1.20
2 Joe Astroth / Dick Fowler	1.00	.40
3 Sam Chapman / Lou Brissie	1.00	.40
4 Bob Dillinger / Billy Hitchcock	1.50	.60
5 Ben Guintini / Joe Tipton	1.00	.40
6 Bob Hooper / Barney McCosky	1.00	.40
7 Eddie Joost / Kermit Wahl	1.00	.40
8 Ed Klieman / Mike Guerra	1.00	.40
9 Paul Lehner / Ferris Fain	1.50	.60
10 Earl Mack AMG / Mickey Cochrane CO	2.50	1.00
11 Wally Moses / Carl Scheib	1.00	.40
12 Pete Suder / Alex Kellner	1.00	.40
13 Elmer Valo / Bobby Shantz	1.50	.60
14 Hank Wyse / Gene Markland	1.00	.40
15 Robert Wellman / Joe Coleman	1.00	.40
16 Eddie Sawyer MG	1.50	.60
17 Johnny Blatnik / Ed Wright	1.00	.40
18 Ralph Caballero / Bubba Church	1.00	.40
19 Milo Candini / Hank Bowory	1.00	.40
20 Blix Donnelly / Bill Nicholson	1.50	.60
21 Mike Goliat / Dick Whitman	1.00	.40
22 Granny Hamner / Richie Ashburn	2.50	1.00
23 Ken Heintzelman / Del Ennis	1.00	.40
24 Willie Jones / Russ Meyer	1.00	.40
25 Jim Konstanty / Ken Silvestri	1.00	.40
26 Stan Lopata / Eddie Waitkus	1.00	.40
27 Ed Sanicki / Robin Robers	2.50	1.00
28 Andy Seminick / Ken Trickle	1.00	.40
29 Dick Sisler / Stan Hollmig	1.00	.40
30 Jocko Thompson / Curt Simmons	1.50	.60

1940 Phillies Team Issue

These 31 5 7/8" by 8 1/2" blank backed photos were issued by the Philadelphia Phillies. They are unnumbered and we have sequenced them in alphabetical order.

	Ex-Mt	VG
COMPLETE SET	180.00	90.00
1 Morrie Arnovich	5.00	2.50
2 Bill Atwood	5.00	2.50
3 Walter Beck	5.00	2.50
4 Stan Benjamin	5.00	2.50
5 Wally Berger	8.00	4.00
6 Cy Blanton	5.00	2.50
7 Bob Bragan	10.00	5.00
8 Lloyd Brown	5.00	2.50
9 Roy Bruner	5.00	2.50
10 Kirby Higbe	6.00	3.00
11 Frank Hoerst	5.00	2.50
12 Si Johnson	5.00	2.50
13 Syl Johnson	5.00	2.50
14 Chuck Klein	15.00	7.50
15 Ed Levy	5.00	2.50
16 Dan Litwhiler	6.00	3.00
17 Hans Lobert CO	6.00	3.00
18 Art Mahan	5.00	2.50
19 Hershel Martin	5.00	2.50
20 Joe Marty	5.00	2.50
21 Merrill May	5.00	2.50
22 Mel Mazzera	5.00	2.50
23 Walt Millies	5.00	2.50
24 Alex Monchak	5.00	2.50
25 Ernest Mueller	5.00	2.50
26 Hugh Mulcahy	5.00	2.50
27 Ike Pearson	5.00	2.50
28 Doc Prothro MG	5.00	2.50
29 John Rizzo	5.00	2.50
30 George Scharein	5.00	2.50
31 Ham Schulte	5.00	2.50
32 Clyde Smoll	5.00	2.50
33 Gus Suhr	6.00	3.00
34 Ben Warren	5.00	2.50
35 Del Young	5.00	2.50
36 Philadelphia Phillies	10.00	5.00

1941 Phillies Team Issue

This 26-card set of the Philadelphia Phillies measuring approximately 6" by 8 1/2" features black-and-white player photos with fascimile autographs. The backs are blank. The cards are unnumbered and checklisted below in alphabetical order.

	Ex-Mt	VG
COMPLETE SET (26)	120.00	60.00
1 Morrie Arnovich	5.00	2.50
2 Bill Atwood	5.00	2.50
3 Walter Beck	5.00	2.50
4 Stan Benjamin	5.00	2.50
5 Bob Bragan	8.00	4.00
6 Roy Bruner	5.00	2.50
7 Kirby Higbe	6.00	3.00
8 Frank Hoerst	5.00	2.50
9 Si Johnson	5.00	2.50
10 Syl Johnson	5.00	2.50
11 Chuck Klein	15.00	7.50
12 Ed Levy	5.00	2.50
13 Dan Litwhiler	6.00	3.00
14 Hans Lobert CO	6.00	3.00
15 Hershel Martin	5.00	2.50
16 Joe Marty	5.00	2.50
17 Merrill May	5.00	2.50
18 Walt Millies	5.00	2.50
19 Hugh Mulcahy	5.00	2.50
20 Ike Pearson	5.00	2.50
21 Doc Prothro MG	5.00	2.50
22 George Scharein	5.00	2.50
23 Clyde Smoll	5.00	2.50
24 Gus Suhr	6.00	3.00
25 Ben Warren	5.00	2.50
26 Del Young	5.00	2.50

1943 Phillies Team Issue

This 23-card set of the Philadelphia Phillies measures approximately 6" by 8 1/2" and features black-and-white player photos with

white borders. The backs are blank. The cards are unnumbered and checklisted below in alphabetical order. This set is so large as it presumed that the Phillies kept issuing photos during the year as players were shuttling in and out of the majors during World War II.

	Ex-Mt	VG
COMPLETE SET (23)	180.00	90.00
1 Buster Adams	4.00	2.00
2 Walter Beck	4.00	2.00
3 Stan Benjamin	4.00	2.00
4 Cy Blanton	4.00	2.00
5 Bobby Bragan	5.00	2.50
6 Charlie Brewster	4.00	2.00
7 Paul Busby	4.00	2.00
8 Bennie Culp	4.00	2.00
9 Babe Dahlgren	5.00	2.50
10 Lloyd Dietz	4.00	2.00
11 Nick Etten	5.00	2.50
12 George Eyrich	4.00	2.00
13 Charlie Fuchs	4.00	2.00
14 Al Glossop	4.00	2.00
14 Al Gerheauser	4.00	2.00
15 Frank Hoerst	4.00	2.00
16 Si Johnson	4.00	2.00
17 Bill Killefer	4.00	2.00
18 Newell Kimball	4.00	2.00
19 Chuck Klein	15.00	7.50
20 Ernie Koy	5.00	2.50
22 Danny Litwhiler	5.00	2.50
23 Jack Kraus	4.00	2.00
24 Mickey Livingston	4.00	2.00
25 Hans Lobert CO	4.00	2.00
26 Harry Marnie	4.00	2.00
27 Merrill May	4.00	2.00
28 Rube Melton	4.00	2.00
29 Danny Murtaugh	8.00	4.00
30 Sam Nahem	4.00	2.00
31 Earl Naylor	4.00	2.00
32 Ron Northey	4.00	2.00
33 Tom Padden	4.00	2.00
34 Ike Pearson	4.00	2.00
35 Johnny Podgajny	4.00	2.00
36 Schoolboy Rowe	5.00	2.50
37 Neb Stewart	4.00	2.00
38 Coaker Triplett	4.00	2.00
39 Lloyd Waner	10.00	5.00
40 Ben Warren	4.00	2.00
41 Jimmie Wasdell	4.00	2.00

1949 Phillies Lummis Peanut Butter

The cards in this 12-card set measure 3 1/4" by 4 1/4". The 1949 Lummis set of black and white, unnumbered action poses depicts Philadelphia Phillies only. These "cards" are actually stickers and were distributed locally by Lummis Peanut Butter and Sealtest Dairy Products. The prices listed below are for the Sealtest cards. The harder-to-find Lummis variety are worth double the listed values below. The catalog designation is F343.

	NM	Ex
COMPLETE SET (12)	800.00	400.00
1 Rich Ashburn	200.00	100.00
2 Hank Borowy	50.00	25.00
3 Del Ennis	80.00	40.00
4 Granny Hamner	50.00	25.00
5 Puddinhead Jones	50.00	25.00
6 Russ Meyer	50.00	25.00
7 Bill Nicholson	50.00	25.00
8 Robin Roberts	150.00	75.00
9 Schoolboy Rowe	60.00	30.00
10 Andy Seminick	80.00	40.00
11 Curt Simmons	80.00	40.00
12 Ed Waitkus	60.00	30.00

1950 Phillies Philadelphia Inquirer

This set of cards have posed color photos and measure 4 1/4" X 5 3/4". Cards are printed on newsprint and have facsimile autographs. A brief biography of the player is printed underneath his name. The set is titled on the bottom "Inquirer Fightin" Phillies Album".

	NM	Ex
COMPLETE SET (24)	250.00	125.00
1 Richie Ashburn	25.00	12.50
2 Jimmy Bloodworth	10.00	5.00
3 Putsy Caballero	10.00	5.00
4 Milo Candini	10.00	5.00
5 Bubba Church	10.00	5.00
6 Blix Donnelly	10.00	5.00
7 Del Ennis	15.00	7.50
8 Mike Goliat	10.00	5.00
9 Granny Hamner	12.00	6.00
10 Ken Heintzelman	10.00	5.00
11 Stan Hollmig	10.00	5.00
12 Ken Johnson	10.00	5.00
13 Willie "Puddin-Head" Jones	12.00	6.00
14 Stan Lopata	10.00	5.00
15 Russ Meyer	10.00	5.00
16 Bob Miller	10.00	5.00
17 Bill Nicholson	12.00	6.00
18 Robin Roberts	25.00	12.50
19 Andy Seminick	10.00	5.00
20 Ken Silvestri	10.00	5.00
21 Curt Simmons	15.00	7.50
22 Dick Sisler	12.00	6.00
23 Eddie Waitkus	12.00	6.00
24 Dick Whitman	10.00	5.00

1955 Phillies Felin's Franks

These horizontal 4" by 3 5/8" cards, with rounded corners, features members of the 1955 Philadelphia Phillies.The red bordered cards have the player photo on the left with biographical information underneath. The right side of the card lists a different players information from the 1954 season and asks the collector to identify who the player is. The back has information about the contest these cards are involved with. While 30 cards were printed for this set, this set is scarce enough that not all cards are known so any additional information on missing cards are appreciated.

	NM	Ex
COMPLETE SET	8000.00	4000.00
1 Mayo Smith MG	300.00	150.00
3 Wally Moses CO	300.00	150.00
4 Whit Wyatt CO	300.00	150.00
5 Maje McDonell CO	300.00	150.00
6 Frank Wiechec TR	300.00	150.00
7 Murry Dickson	300.00	150.00
8 Earl Torgeson	300.00	150.00
9 Bobby Morgan	300.00	150.00
10 Jack Meyer	300.00	150.00
11 Bob Miller	300.00	150.00
12 Jim Owens	300.00	150.00
13 Steve Ridzik	300.00	150.00
14 Robin Roberts	1000.00	500.00
16 Herm Wehmeier	300.00	150.00
17 Smoky Burgess	400.00	200.00
18 Stan Lopata	300.00	150.00
19 Gus Niarhos	300.00	150.00
20 Floyd Baker	300.00	150.00
21 Merv Blaylock	300.00	150.00
22 Granny Hamner	400.00	200.00
23 Willie Jones	400.00	200.00
26 Richie Ashburn	800.00	400.00
27 Joe Lonnett	300.00	150.00
28 Mel Clark	300.00	150.00
29 Bob Greenwood	300.00	150.00

1956 Phillies Postcards

These six 3 1/4" by 5 1/2" cards feature white borders, autographs on the picture and were sent by the club in relation to fan requests. These cards are unnumbered and we have sequenced them in alphabetical order.

	NM	Ex
COMPLETE SET (6)	40.00	20.00
1 Richie Ashburn	10.00	5.00
2 Granny Hammer	5.00	2.50
3 Willie Jones	6.00	3.00
4 Stan Lopata	5.00	2.50
5 Robin Roberts	10.00	5.00
6 Curt Simmons	6.00	3.00

1958 Phillies Jay Publishing

This 12-card set of the Philadelphia Phillies measures approximately 5" by 7" and features black-and-white player photos in a white border. These cards were packaged 12 to a packet. The backs are blank. The cards are unnumbered and checklisted below in alphabetical order.

	NM	Ex
COMPLETE SET (12)	50.00	25.00
1 Harry Anderson	3.00	1.50
2 Richie Ashburn	12.00	6.00
3 Bob Bowman	3.00	1.50
4 Dick Farrell	3.00	1.50
5 Chico Fernandez	3.00	1.50
6 Granny Hamner	3.00	1.50
7 Stan Lopata	3.00	1.50
8 Rip Repulski	3.00	1.50
9 Robin Roberts	12.00	6.00
10 Jack Sanford UER Sandford	3.00	1.50
11 Curt Simmons	5.00	2.50
12 Mayo Smith MG	3.00	1.50

1958-60 Phillies Team Issue

This 19-card blank-backed set features black-and-white photos of the Philadelphia Phillies measuring approximately 3 1/4" by 5 1/2". The cards are unnumbered and checklisted below in alphabetical order.

	NM	Ex
COMPLETE SET (19)	75.00	38.00
1 Harry Anderson	3.00	1.50
2 Richie Ashburn	10.00	5.00
3 Ed Bouchee	3.00	1.50
4 John Buzhardt	3.00	1.50
5 Johnny Callison	6.00	3.00
6 Jim Coker	3.00	1.50
7 Clay Dalrymple	3.00	1.50
8 Tony Gonzalez	3.00	1.50
9 Granny Hamner	3.00	1.50
10 Willie Jones	4.00	2.00
11 Stan Lopata	3.00	1.50
12 Art Mahaffey	4.00	2.00
13 Gene Mauch MG	5.00	2.50
14 Wally Post	3.00	1.50
15 Robin Roberts	8.00	4.00
16 Eddie Sawyer MG	3.00	1.50
17 Ray Semproch	3.00	1.50
18 Chris Short	5.00	2.50
19 Curt Simmons	5.00	2.50

1959 Phillies Jay Publishing

This 12-card set of the Philadelphia Phillies measures approximately 5" by 7" and features black-and-white player photos in a white border. These cards were packaged 12 to a packet. The backs are blank. The cards are unnumbered and checklisted below in alphabetical order.

	NM	Ex
COMPLETE SET	40.00	20.00
1 Harry Anderson	3.00	1.50
2 Richie Ashburn	10.00	5.00
3 Ed Bouchee	3.00	1.50
4 Dick Farrell	3.00	1.50
5 Chico Fernandez	3.00	1.50
6 Ruben Gomez	3.00	1.50
7 Harry Hanebrink	3.00	1.50
8 Wally Post	3.00	1.50
9 Robin Roberts	10.00	5.00
10 Eddie Sawyer MG	3.00	1.50
11 Roman Semproch	3.00	1.50
12 Curt Simmons	4.00	2.00

1960 Phillies Jay Publishing

This 12-card set of the Philadelphia Phillies measures approximately 5" X 7". The fronts feature black-and-white posed player photos with the player's and team name printed below in the white border. These cards were packaged 12 to a packet and originally sold for 25 cents. The backs are blank. The cards are unnumbered and checklisted below in alphabetical order.

	NM	Ex
COMPLETE SET (12)	30.00	12.00
1 Ruben Amaro	2.00	.80
2 Harry Anderson	2.00	.80
3 Ed Bouchee	2.00	.80
4 John Callison	3.00	1.20
5 Jim Coker	2.00	.80
6 Al Dark	3.00	1.20
7 Dick Farrell	2.00	.80
8 Pancho Herrera	2.00	.80
9 Jim Owens	2.00	.80
10 Wally Post	3.00	1.20
11 Robin Roberts	10.00	4.00
12 Eddie Sawyer MG	2.00	.80

1962 Phillies Jay Publishing

This 12-card set of the Philadelphia Phillies measures approximately 5" by 7". The fronts feature black-and-white posed player photos with the player's and team name printed below in the white border. These cards were packaged 12 to a packet. The backs are blank. The cards are unnumbered and checklisted below in alphabetical order.

	NM	Ex
COMPLETE SET (12)	20.00	8.00
1 Jack Baldschun	2.00	.80
2 John Callison	3.00	1.20
3 Clay Dalrymple	2.00	.80
4 Don Demeter	2.00	.80
5 Dallas Green	2.50	1.00
6 Art Mahaffey	2.00	.80
7 Gene Mauch MG	2.00	.80
8 Cal McLish	2.00	.80
9 Roy Sievers	2.50	1.00
10 Frank Sullivan	2.00	.80
11 Tony Taylor	2.50	1.00
12 Ken Walters	2.00	.80

1963 Phillies Jay Publishing

This 12-card set of the Philadelphia Phillies measures approximately 5" by 7". The fronts feature black-and-white posed player photos with the player's and team name printed below in the white border. These cards were packaged 12 to a packet. The backs are blank. The cards are unnumbered and checklisted below in alphabetical order.

	NM	Ex
COMPLETE SET (12)	20.00	8.00
1 Ruben Amaro	2.00	.80
2 Jack Baldschun	2.00	.80
3 John Callison	3.00	1.20
4 Clay Dalrymple	2.00	.80
5 Don Demeter	2.00	.80
6 Art Mahaffey	2.00	.80
7 Gene Mauch MG	2.00	.80
8 Cal McLish	2.00	.80
9 Chris Short	2.50	1.00
10 Roy Sievers	2.50	1.00
11 Tony Taylor	2.50	1.00
12 Bobby Wine	2.00	.80

1964 Phillies Jay Publishing

This 12-card set of the Philadelphia Phillies measures approximately 5" by 7". The fronts feature black-and-white posed player photos with the player's and team name printed below in the white border. These cards were packaged 12 to a packet. The backs are blank. The cards are unnumbered and checklisted below in alphabetical order.

	NM	Ex
COMPLETE SET (12)	20.00	8.00
1 Jack Baldschun	2.00	.80
2 John Callison	3.00	1.20
3 Wes Covington	2.00	.80
4 Clay Dalrymple	2.00	.80
5 Tony Gonzalez	2.00	.80
6 Dallas Green	2.50	1.00
7 Don Hoak	2.00	.80
8 Art Mahaffey	2.00	.80
9 Gene Mauch MG	2.00	.80
10 Roy Sievers	2.50	1.00
11 Tony Taylor	2.50	1.00
12 Bob Wine	2.00	.80

1964 Phillies Philadelphia Bulletin

This 27-subject set was produced by the Philadelphia Bulletin newspaper. The catalog designation for this set is M130-5. These large, approximately 8" by 10", photo cards are unnumbered and blank backed. The complete set price below includes both Bunning variation cards.

	NM	Ex
COMPLETE SET (27)	200.00	80.00
1 Richie Allen	25.00	10.00
2 Ruben Amaro	6.00	2.40
3 Jack Baldschun	6.00	2.40
4 Dennis Bennett	6.00	2.40
5 John Boozer	6.00	2.40
6 Johnny Briggs	6.00	2.40
7 Jim Bunning (2)	25.00	10.00
8 Johnny Callison	8.00	3.20
9 Danny Cater	6.00	2.40
10 Wes Covington	6.00	2.40
11 Ray Culp	6.00	2.40
12 Clay Dalrymple	6.00	2.40
13 Tony Gonzalez	6.00	2.40
14 John Herrnstein	6.00	2.40
15 Alex Johnson	6.00	2.40
16 Art Mahaffey	6.00	2.40
17 Gene Mauch MG	8.00	3.20
18 Vic Power	6.00	2.40
19 Ed Roebuck	6.00	2.40
20 Cookie Rojas	8.00	3.20
21 Bobby Shantz	8.00	3.20
22 Chris Short	8.00	3.20
23 Tony Taylor	8.00	3.20
24 Frank Thomas	8.00	3.20
25 Gus Triandos	6.00	2.40
26 Bobby Wine	6.00	2.40
27 Rick Wise	8.00	3.20

1964 Phillies Team Set

This six-card set of the Philadelphia Phillies measures approximately 3 1/4" by 5 1/2" and feature black-and-white player portraits with a facsimile autograph. The backs are blank. The cards are unnumbered and checklisted below in alphabetical order.

	NM	Ex
COMPLETE SET (7)	20.00	8.00
1 Jim Bunning	8.00	3.20
2 Johnny Callison	4.00	1.60
3 Clay Dalrymple	3.00	1.20
4 Tony Gonzalez	3.00	1.20
5 Cookie Rojas	4.00	1.60
6 Chris Short	4.00	1.60
7 Roy Sievers	4.00	1.60

1965 Phillies Ceramic Tiles

These tiles, which measure 6" square, feature members of the Philadelphia Phillies. The players photo and a fascimile autograph are set against a white background. Since these are unnumbered, we have sequenced them in alphabetical order.

	NM	Ex
COMPLETE SET	400.00	160.00
1 Richie Allen	100.00	40.00
2 Bo Belinsky	60.00	24.00
3 Jim Bunning	100.00	40.00
4 John Callison	60.00	24.00
5 Clay Dalrymple	50.00	20.00
6 Gene Mauch MG	50.00	20.00
7 Tony Taylor	50.00	20.00

1965 Phillies Jay Publishing

This 12-card set of the Philadelphia Phillies measures approximately 5" X 7". The fronts feature black-and-white posed player photos with the player's and team's names printed below in the white border. These cards were packaged 12 to a packet and originally sold for 25 cents. The backs are blank. The cards are unnumbered and checklisted below in alphabetical order.

	NM	Ex
COMPLETE SET (12)	25.00	10.00
1 Ruben Amaro	2.00	.80
2 Jack Baldschun	2.00	.80
3 Jim Bunning	6.00	2.40
4 John Callison	3.00	1.20
5 Clay Dalrymple	2.00	.80
6 Dallas Green	2.50	1.00
7 Art Mahaffey	2.00	.80
8 Gene Mauch MG	2.50	1.00
9 Chris Short	2.50	1.00
10 Tony Taylor	2.50	1.00
11 Gus Triandos	2.00	.80
12 Bob Wine	2.00	.80

1966 Phillies Team Issue

This 12-card set features black-and-white photos of the 1966 Philadelphia Phillies. The cards are unnumbered and checklisted below in alphabetical order.

	NM	Ex
COMPLETE SET (12)	30.00	12.00
1 Richie Allen	4.00	1.60
2 Jackie Brandt	2.00	.80
3 Jim Bunning	6.00	2.40
4 John Callison	3.00	1.20
5 Ray Culp	2.00	.80
6 Clay Dalrymple	2.00	.80
7 Tony Gonzalez	2.00	.80
8 Dick Groat	3.00	1.20
9 Phil Linz	2.00	.80
10 Cookie Rojas	2.50	1.00
11 Chris Short	2.00	.80
12 Bill White	3.00	1.20

1967 Phillies Police

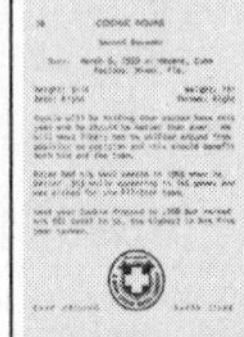

The 1967 Philadelphia Phillies Police/Safety set contains 13 cards measuring approximately 2 13/16" by 4 7/16". The black and white posed player photos on the fronts are bordered in white and have the player's signature inscribed across the picture. In blue print on white, the backs have biography, player profile, and a "Safe Driving" emblem at the bottom. Cards can be found where the players' pictured on the fronts do not match the card backs. For example, the Jim Bunning card has a Dick Ellsworth back, the John Briggs card has a Dick Groat back, the Johnny Callison card has a Bill White back, the Clay Dalrymple card has a Chris Short back, and the Gene Mauch card has a Tony Gonzalez back. The cards are unnumbered and checklisted below in alphabetical order.

	NM	Ex
COMPLETE SET (13)	60.00	24.00
1 Richie Allen	6.00	2.40
2 Jim Bunning	15.00	6.00
3 John Briggs	3.00	1.20
4 Johnny Callison	5.00	2.00
5 Clay Dalrymple	3.00	1.20
6 Dick Ellsworth	3.00	1.20
7 Tony Gonzalez	3.00	1.20
8 Dick Groat	5.00	2.00
9 Larry Jackson	4.00	1.60
10 Gene Mauch MG	4.00	1.60
11 Cookie Rojas	4.00	1.60
12 Chris Short	4.00	1.60
13 Bill White	5.00	2.00

1969 Phillies Team Issue

This 12-card set of the Philadelphia Phillies measures approximately 4 1/4" by 7". The fronts freature black-and-white player portraits in a white border. The player's name and team name are printed above. The backs are blank. The cards are unnumbered and checklisted below in alphabetical order.

	NM	Ex
COMPLETE SET (12)	25.00	10.00
1 Richie Allen	4.00	1.60
2 John Callison	3.00	1.20
3 Woody Fryman	2.00	.80
4 Larry Hisle	2.50	1.00
5 Deron Johnson	2.50	1.00
6 Don Money	2.50	1.00
7 Cookie Rojas	2.50	1.00
8 Mike Ryan	2.00	.80
9 Chris Short	2.50	1.00

10 Bob Skinner MG	2.00	.80
11 Tony Taylor	2.50	1.00
12 Rick Wise	2.50	1.00

1970 Phillies Team Issue

This 12-card set of the Philadelphia Phillies measures approximately 4 1/4" by 7" and features black-and-white player photos in a white border. Packaged 12 to a packet with blank backs, the cards are unnumbered and checklisted below in alphabetical order.

	NM	Ex
COMPLETE SET (12)	25.00	10.00
1 Larry Bowa	4.00	1.60
2 John Briggs	2.00	.80
3 Denny Doyle	2.00	.80
4 Larry Hisle	2.50	1.00
5 Grant Jackson	2.00	.80
6 Deron Johnson	2.50	1.00
7 Rick Joseph	2.00	.80
8 Tim McCarver	4.00	1.60
9 Don Money	2.50	1.00
10 Chris Short	2.50	1.00
11 Tony Taylor	2.50	1.00
12 Rick Wise	2.50	1.00

1971 Phillies Arco Oil

Sponsored by Arco Oil, these 13 pictures of the 1971 Philadelphia Phillies measure approximately 8" by 10" and feature on their fronts white-bordered posed color player photos. The player's name is shown in black lettering within the white margin below the photo. His facsimile autograph appears across the picture. The white back carries the team's and player's names at the top, followed below by position, biography, career highlights, and statistics. An ad at the bottom for picture frames rounds out the back. The cards are unnumbered and checklisted below in alphabetical order.

	NM	Ex
COMPLETE SET (13)	35.00	14.00
1 Larry Bowa	5.00	2.00
2 Jim Bunning	8.00	3.20
3 Roger Freed	2.50	1.00
4 Terry Harmon	2.50	1.00
5 Larry Hisle	3.00	1.20
6 Joe Hoerner	2.50	1.00
7 Deron Johnson	3.00	1.20
8 Tim McCarver	5.00	2.00
9 Don Money	3.00	1.20
10 Dick Selma	2.50	1.00
11 Chris Short	3.00	1.20
12 Tony Taylor	3.00	1.20
13 Rick Wise	3.00	1.20

1972 Phillies Ticketron

These cards, featuring members of the 1972 Phillies, were issued in conjunction with Ticketron. Since these cards are unnumbered, we have sequenced them in alphabetical order.

	NM	Ex
COMPLETE SET	60.00	24.00
1 Mike Anderson	5.00	2.00
2 Larry Bowa	6.00	2.40
3 Steve Carlton	15.00	6.00
4 Deron Johnson	5.00	2.00
5 Frank Lucchesi MG	5.00	2.00
6 Greg Luzinski	10.00	4.00
7 Tim McCarver	10.00	4.00
8 Don Money	5.00	2.00
9 Willie Montanez	5.00	2.00
10 Dick Selma	5.00	2.00

1973 Phillies Team Issue

This 29-card set of the Philadelphia Phillies measures approximately 3 1/4" by 5 1/2" and features black-and-white player photos with white borders. The backs are blank. The cards are unnumbered and checklisted below in alphabetical order. An early card of Mike Schmidt is in this set.

	NM	Ex
COMPLETE SET (29)	40.00	16.00
1 Mike Anderson	1.00	.40
2 Bob Boone	3.00	1.20
3 Larry Bowa	3.00	1.20
4 Darrell Brandon	1.00	.40
5 Ken Brett	1.00	.40
6 Steve Carlton	6.00	2.40
7 Denny Doyle	1.00	.40
8 Terry Harmon	1.00	.40
9 Tommy Hutton	1.00	.40
10 Barry Lersch	1.00	.40
11 Jim Lonborg	2.00	.80
12 Greg Luzinski	3.00	1.20
13 Willie Montanez	1.00	.40
14 Jose Pagan	1.00	.40
15 Bill Robinson	1.00	.40
16 Dick Ruthven	1.00	.40
17 Mike Ryan	1.00	.40
18 Mac Scarce	1.00	.40
19 Mike Schmidt	15.00	6.00
20 Cesar Tovar	1.00	.40
21 Mike Rogodzinski	1.00	.40
22 Wayne Twitchell	1.00	.40
23 Del Unser	1.00	.40
24 Billy Wilson	1.00	.40
25 Danny Ozark MG	1.00	.40
26 Ray Rippelmeyer CO	1.00	.40
27 Carroll Beringer CO	1.00	.40
28 Billy Demars CO	1.00	.40
29 Bobby Wine CO	1.00	.40

1974 Phillies Johnny Pro

This 12-card set measures approximately 3 3/4" by 7 1/8" and features members of the 1974 Philadelphia Phillies. The most significant player in this series is an early card of Mike Schmidt. The cards are designed to be pushed out and have the players photo against a solid white background. The backs are blank and marked the second straight year that Johnny Pro issued cards of a major league team. The set is checklisted by uniform number. According to informed sources, there were less than 15,000 sets produced.

	NM	Ex
COMPLETE SET (12)	300.00	120.00
8 Bob Boone	10.00	4.00
10 Larry Bowa	8.00	3.20
16 Dave Cash	5.00	2.00
19 Greg Luzinski	10.00	4.00
20 Mike Schmidt	200.00	80.00
22 Mike Anderson	5.00	2.00
24 Bill Robinson	6.00	2.40
25 Del Unser	5.00	2.00
27 Willie Montanez	5.00	2.00
32 Steve Carlton	50.00	20.00
37 Ron Schueler	6.00	2.40
41 Jim Lonborg	8.00	3.20

1975 Phillies 1950 TCMA

This 31-card set features black-and-white photos of the 1950 Philadelphia Phillies Baseball team with red lettering. The cards are unnumbered and checklisted below alphabetically.

	NM	Ex
COMPLETE SET (31)	20.00	8.00
1 Richie Ashburn	4.00	1.60
2 Benny Bengough CO	.50	.20
3 Jimmy Bloodworth	.50	.20
4 Hank Borowy	.50	.20
5 Putsy Caballero	.50	.20
6 Emory Church	.50	.20
7 Dusty Cooke CO	.50	.20
8 Blix Donnelly	.50	.20
9 Del Ennis	1.50	.60
10 Mike Goliat	.50	.20
11 Granny Hamner	.75	.30
12 Ken Heintzleman	.50	.20
13 Stan Hollmig	.50	.20
14 Ken Johnson	.50	.20
15 Willie Jones	.75	.30
16 Jim Konstantly	1.00	.40
17 Stan Lopata	.50	.20
18 Eddie Mayo CO	.50	.20
19 Russ Meyer	.50	.20
20 Bob Miller	.50	.20
21 Bill Nicholson	.50	.20
22 Cy Perkins CO	.50	.20
23 Robin Roberts	3.00	1.20
24 Eddie Sawyer MG	.50	.20
25 Andy Seminick	.50	.20
26 Ken Silvestri	.50	.20
27 Curt Simmons	.75	.30
28 Dick Sisler	.75	.30
29 Jocko Thompson	.50	.20
30 Eddie Waitkus	.75	.30
31 Dick Whitman	.50	.20

1975 Phillies Photo Album

These seven 6" by 9" photos were issued by the Philadelphia Phillies and feature some of their leading players in 1975. The player photos are surrounded by red borders and have a fascimile signature. The backs look as they are taken from the Phillies Media Guide. The backs have a small photo, biographical information, a brief blurb and career statistics. Since the photos are unnumbered we have sequenced them in alphabetical order.

	NM	Ex
COMPLETE SET (7)	20.00	8.00
1 Dick Allen	3.00	1.20
2 Larry Bowa	2.50	1.00
3 Dave Cash	1.00	.40
4 Jay Johnstone	1.50	.60
5 Greg Luzinski	2.00	.80
6 Garry Maddox	1.00	.40
7 Mike Schmidt	10.00	4.00

1975 Phillies Postcards

This 31-card set of the Philadelphia Phillies features player photos on postcard-size cards. The cards are unnumbered and checklisted below in alphabetical order.

	NM	Ex
COMPLETE SET (31)	20.00	8.00
1 Dick Allen	1.50	.60
2 Mike Anderson	.50	.20
3 Alan Bannister	.50	.20
4 Carroll Beringer CO	.50	.20
5 Bob Boone	1.50	.60
6 Larry Bowa	.50	.20
7 Ollie Brown	.50	.20
8 Steve Carlton	3.00	1.20
9 Dave Cash	.50	.20
10 Larry Christenson	.50	.20
11 Larry Cox	.50	.20
12 Billy DeMars CO	.50	.20
13 Gene Garber	.75	.30
14 Terry Harmon	.50	.20
15 Tom Hilgendorf	.50	.20
16 Joe Hoerner	.50	.20
17 Tommy Hutton	.50	.20
18 Jay Johnstone	1.00	.40
19 Jim Lonborg	.75	.30
20 Greg Luzinski	1.50	.60
21 Garry Maddox	.75	.30
22 Tim McCarver	1.00	.40
23 Tug McGraw	1.00	.40
24 Danny Ozark MG	.50	.20
25 Ray Ripplemeyer CO	.50	.20
26 Mike Schmidt	6.00	2.40
27 Ron Schueler	.50	.20
28 Tony Taylor	.75	.30
29 Wayne Twitchell	.50	.20
30 Tom Underwood	.50	.20
31 Bobby Wine CO	.50	.20

1976 Phillies Postcards

This 31-card set of the Philadelphia Phillies features player photos on postcard-size cards. The cards are unnumbered and checklisted below in alphabetical order.

	NM	Ex
COMPLETE SET (31)	25.00	10.00
1 Dick Allen	1.50	.60
2 Carroll Beringer CO	.50	.20
3 Bob Boone	1.50	.60
4 Larry Bowa	.50	.20
5 Ollie Brown	.50	.20
6 Steve Carlton	3.00	1.20
7 Dave Cash	.50	.20
8 Larry Christenson	.50	.20
9 Billy DeMars CO	.50	.20
10 Gene Garber	.75	.30
11 Terry Harmon	.50	.20
12 Tommy Hutton	.50	.20
13 Jay Johnstone	1.00	.40
14 Jim Kaat	1.00	.40
15 Jim Lonborg	.75	.30
16 Greg Luzinski	1.00	.40
17 Garry Maddox	.50	.20
18 Jerry Martin	.50	.20
19 Tim McCarver	1.50	.60
20 Tug McGraw	1.00	.40
21 Johnny Oates	.50	.20
22 Danny Ozark CO	.50	.20
23 Ron Reed	.50	.20
24 Ray Ripplemeyer CO	.50	.20
25 Mike Schmidt	5.00	2.00
26 Ron Schueler	.50	.20
27 Tony Taylor	.75	.30
28 Bobby Tolan	.50	.20
29 Wayne Twitchell	.50	.20
30 Tom Underwood	.50	.20
31 Bobby Wine CO	.50	.20

1979 Phillies Burger King

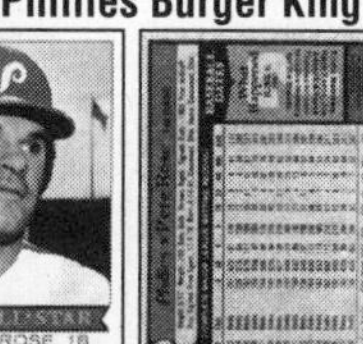

The cards in this 23-card set measure 2 1/2" by 3 1/2". The 1979 Burger King Phillies set follows the regular format of 22 player cards and one unnumbered checklist card. The asterisk indicates where the pose differs from the Topps card of that year. The set features the first card of Pete Rose as a member of the Philadelphia Phillies.

	NM	Ex
COMPLETE SET (23)	10.00	4.00
1 Danny Ozark MG *	.10	.04
2 Bob Boone	.50	.20
3 Tim McCarver	.50	.20
4 Steve Carlton	2.50	1.00
5 Larry Christenson	.10	.04
6 Dick Ruthven	.10	.04
7 Ron Reed	.10	.04
8 Randy Lerch	.10	.04
9 Warren Brusstar	.10	.04
10 Tug McGraw	.30	.12
11 Nino Espinosa *	.10	.04
12 Doug Bird *	.10	.04
13 Pete Rose * (Shown as Reds in 1979 Topps)	4.00	1.60
14 Manny Trillo *	.20	.08
15 Larry Bowa	.30	.12
16 Mike Schmidt	4.00	1.60
17 Pete Mackanin *	.10	.04
18 Jose Cardenal	.10	.04
19 Greg Luzinski	.30	.12
20 Garry Maddox	.20	.08
21 Bake McBride	.10	.04
22 Greg Gross *	.10	.04
NNO Checklist Card TP	.05	.02

1979 Phillies Postcards

These attractive postcards were issued in black and white and many of them featured facsmile autographs. Since the cards are unnumbered, we have sequenced them in alphabetical order.

	NM	Ex
COMPLETE SET	30.00	12.00
1 Ramon Aviles	.50	.20
2 Doug Bird	.50	.20
3 Bob Boone	1.00	.40
4 Larry Bowa	1.50	.60
5 Warren Brusstar	.50	.20
6 Jose Cardenal	.50	.20
7 Steve Carlton	3.00	1.20
8 Larry Christensen	.50	.20
9 Rawly Eastwick	.50	.20
10 Nino Espinosa	.50	.20
11 Greg Gross	.50	.20
12 Bud Harrelson	.50	.20
13 Jim Kaat	1.50	.60
14 Randy Lerch	.50	.20
15 Jim Lonborg	.75	.30
16 Greg Luzinski	1.00	.40
17 Pete Mackanin	.50	.20
18 Garry Maddox	.50	.20
19 Rudy Meoli	.50	.20
20 Bake McBride	.50	.20
21 Tim McCarver	.75	.30
22 Tug McGraw	.75	.30
23 Dickie Noles	.50	.20
24 Danny Ozark MG	.50	.20
25 Dave Rader	.50	.20
26 Ron Reed	.50	.20
27 Pete Rose	5.00	2.00
28 Dick Ruthven	.50	.20
29 Kevin Saucier	.50	.20
30 Mike Schmidt	5.00	2.00
31 Lonnie Smith	.50	.20
32 Tony Taylor CO	.50	.20
33 Bob Tiefenauer CO	.50	.20
34 Manny Trillo Batting	.75	.30
35 Manny Trillo Portrait	.75	.30
36 Del Unser	.50	.20
37 Bobby Wine CO	.50	.20

1979 Phillies Team Issue Drawings

This 10-card set of the Philadelphia Phillies was issued in a clear front envelope and was likely sold at the stadium. The set measures approximately 8 3/4" by 11 5/8" and features art work by Todd Alan Gold. Each card displays two action drawings and a portrait of the same player. The backs are blank. The cards are unnumbered and checklisted below in alphabetical order.

	NM	Ex
COMPLETE SET (10)	20.00	8.00
1 Rich Ashburn	4.00	1.60
2 Bob Boone	3.00	1.20
3 Larry Bowa	2.00	.80
4 Greg Luzinski	2.00	.80
5 Garry Maddox	1.50	.60
6 Bake McBride	1.50	.60
7 Robin Roberts	3.00	1.20
8 Pete Rose	4.00	1.60
9 Mike Schmidt	4.00	1.60
10 Manny Trillo	1.50	.60

1980 Phillies Burger King

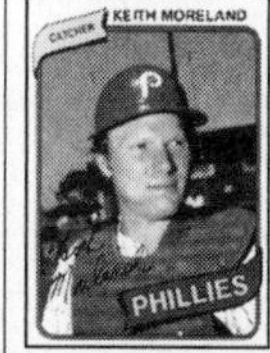

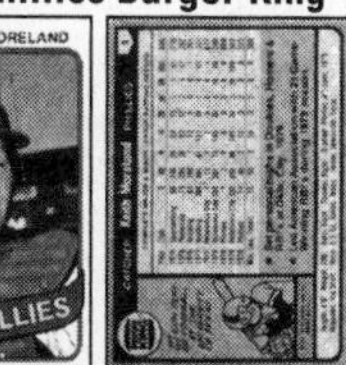

The cards in this 23-card set measure 2 1/2" by 3 1/2". The 1980 edition of Burger King Phillies follows the established pattern of 22 numbered player cards and one unnumbered checklist. Cards marked with asterisks contain poses different from those found in the regular 1980 Topps cards. This was the first Burger King set to carry the Burger King logo and hence does not generate the same confusion that the three previous years do for collectors trying to distinguish Burger King cards from the very similar Topps cards of the same years.

	NM	Ex
COMPLETE SET (23)	8.00	3.20
1 Dallas Green MG *	.20	.08
2 Bob Boone	.30	.12
3 Keith Moreland *	.20	.08
4 Pete Rose	4.00	1.60
5 Manny Trillo	.20	.08
6 Mike Schmidt	4.00	1.60
7 Larry Bowa	.20	.08
8 John Vukovich *	.10	.04
9 Bake McBride	.10	.04
10 Garry Maddox	.20	.08
11 Greg Luzinski	.20	.08
12 Greg Gross	.10	.04
13 Del Unser	.10	.04
14 Lonnie Smith *	.20	.08
15 Steve Carlton	2.50	1.00
16 Larry Christenson	.10	.04
17 Nino Espinosa	.10	.04
18 Randy Lerch	.10	.04
19 Dick Ruthven	.10	.04
20 Tug McGraw	.30	.12
21 Ron Reed	.10	.04
22 Kevin Saucier *	.10	.04
NNO Checklist Card TP	.05	.02

1980 Phillies 1950 TCMA

This 31-card set features black-and-white photos of the 1950 Philadelphia Phillies Baseball team in red borders. The words, "Whiz Kids" are printed in white at the top. The backs carry player information and career statistics. The cards are unnumbered and checklisted below alphabetically.

	NM	Ex
COMPLETE SET (31)	10.00	4.00
1 Richie Ashburn	1.00	.40
2 Benny Bengough CO	.50	.20
3 Jimmy Bloodworth	.25	.10
4 Hank Borowy	.25	.10
5 Putsy Caballero	.25	.10
6 Emory Church	.25	.10
7 Dusty Cooke	.25	.10
8 Blix Donnelly	.25	.10
9 Del Ennis	.75	.30
10 Mike Goliat	.25	.10
11 Granny Hamner	.50	.20
12 Ken Heintzleman	.25	.10
13 Stan Hollmig	.25	.10
14 Ken Johnson	.25	.10
15 Willie Jones	.50	.20
16 Jim Konstantly	.50	.20
17 Stan Lopata	.25	.10
18 Jackie Mayo	.25	.10
19 Russ Meyer	.25	.10
20 Bob Miller	.25	.10
21 Bill Nicholson	.25	.10
22 Cy Perkins CO	.25	.10
23 Robin Roberts	1.00	.40
24 Eddie Sawyer MG	.25	.10
25 Andy Seminick	.50	.20
26 Ken Silvestri	.25	.10
27 Curt Simmons	.50	.20
28 Dick Sisler	.25	.10
29 Jocko Thompson	.25	.10
30 Eddie Waitkus	.50	.20
31 Dick Whitman	.25	.10

1980 Phillies Postcards

These black and white postcards were issued by the Phillies during their World Championship season. Since the cards are unnumbered we have sequenced them in alphabetical order.

	NM	Ex
COMPLETE SET	25.00	10.00
1 Ruben Amaro CO	.50	.20
2 Luis Aguayo	.50	.20
3 Ramon Aviles	.50	.20
4 Bob Boone	1.00	.40
5 Larry Bowa	1.50	.60
6 Warren Brusstar	.50	.20
7 Steve Carlton	3.00	1.20
8 Larry Christenson	.50	.20
9 Billy DeMars CO	.50	.20
10 Lee Elia CO	.50	.20
11 Nino Espinosa	.50	.20
12 Dallas Green MG	.50	.20
13 Greg Gross	.50	.20
14 Lerrin LaGrow	.50	.20
15 Dan Larson	.50	.20
16 Randy Lerch	.50	.20
17 Greg Luzinski	1.00	.40
18 Bake McBride	.75	.30
19 Tug McGraw	1.00	.40
20 Keith Moreland	.50	.20
21 Scott Munninghoff	.50	.20
22 Ron Reed	.50	.20
23 Pete Rose	5.00	2.00
24 Dick Ruthven	.50	.20
25 Mike Ryan CO	.50	.20
26 Kevin Saucier	.50	.20
27 Mike Schmidt	5.00	2.00
28 Lonnie Smith	.75	.30
29 Herm Starette CO	.50	.20
30 Manny Trillo	.75	.30
31 Del Unser	.50	.20
32 George Vukovich	.50	.20
33 Bob Walk	.50	.20
34 Bobby Wine CO	.50	.20

1982 Phillies Tastycake

These blank-back postcards, which measure 3 1/4" by 5 1/2" feature members of the 1982 Philadelphia Phillies. There is a "Tastykake" logo on the bottom of the card. Since these cards are unnumbered, we have sequenced them in alphabetical order.

	Nm-Mt	Ex-Mt
COMPLETE SET (37)	20.00	8.00
1 Luis Aguayo	.50	.20
2 Porfirio Altamirano	.50	.20
3 Dave Bristol CO	.50	.20
4 Warren Brusstar	.50	.20
5 Steve Carlton	3.00	1.20
6 Larry Christenson	.50	.20
7 Pat Corrales MG	.50	.20
8 Dick Davis	.50	.20
9 Mark Davis	.50	.20

10 Ivan DeJesus .50 .20
11 Bob Dernier .50 .20
12 Bo Diaz .50 .20
Action
13 Bo Diaz .50 .20
Portrait
14 Karen Eberhard .75 .30
Ball Girl
15 Ed Farmer .50 .20
16 Greg Gross .50 .20
17 Deron Johnson CO .50 .20
18 Mike Krukow .50 .20
19 Sparky Lyle .75 .30
20 Garry Maddox .75 .30
21 Gary Matthews .75 .30
22 Len Matusek .50 .20
23 Tug McGraw 1.00 .40
24 Sid Monge .50 .20
25 Claude Osteen CO .50 .20
26 Ron Reed .50 .20
27 Dave Roberts .50 .20
28 Pete Rose 4.00 1.60
29 Dick Ruthven .50 .20
30 Mike Ryan .50 .20
31 Mike Schmidt 4.00 1.60
32 Manny Trillo .50 .20
Hat
33 Manny Trillo .50 .20
No Hat
34 Del Unser .50 .20
35 Ossie Virgil Jr. .50 .20
36 George Vukovich .50 .20
37 Bobby Wine CO .50 .20

1983 Phillies Postcards Great Moments

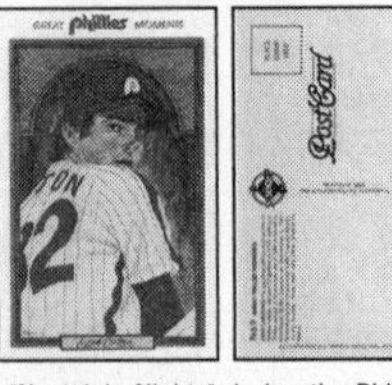

On "Nostalgia Nights" during the Philadelphia Phillies 100th Anniversary season, two collectors' art postcards were presented to fans at every Friday night home game. One card commemorated the great Phillies moments and the players involved in these, and the other card honored great Phillies players and managers that were depicted in the Phillies 1983 calendar. The art work on the card front was reproduced from original watercolors by Dick Perez who is the official artist for the National Baseball Hall of Fame in Cooperstown, New York. The backs carry a postcard format. The 13 cards in the Great Moments set along with the 13 cards in the Great Players and Managers set are combined with a checklist card and a title card to make a 28-card set.

Nm-Mt Ex-Mt
COMPLETE SET (14) 40.00 16.00
1 Richie Ashburn 5.00 2.00
2 Dick Sisler 2.00 .80
Del Ennis
3 Art Mahaffey 2.00 .80
4 Jim Bunning 3.00 1.20
Tony Taylor
5 Mike Schmidt 12.00 4.80
6 Johnny Callison 3.00 1.20
7 Grover Alexander 5.00 2.00
8 Robin Roberts 5.00 2.00
9 Steve Carlton 5.00 2.00
10 Tug McGraw 2.00 .80
Del Unser
11 Rick Wise 2.00 .80
12 Greg Luzinski 2.00 .80
Jim Lonborg
13 Pete Rose 8.00 3.20

1983 Phillies Postcards Great Players and Managers

On "Nostalgia Nights" during the Philadelphia Phillies 100th Anniversary season, two collectors' art postcards were presented to fans at every Friday night home game. One card honored the great Phillies players and managers that were depicted in the Phillies 1983 calendar, and the other card commemorated great Phillies moments and the players involved in these. The art work on the card front is a reproduction fof original watercolors by Dick Perez, the official artist for the National Baseball Hall of Fame in Cooperstown, New York. The backs carry a postcard format. The 13 cards in the Great Players and Managers set along with the 13 cards in the Great Moments set are combined with a checklist card and a title card to make a 28-card set.

Nm-Mt Ex-Mt
COMPLETE SET (14) 40.00 16.00
1 Chuck Klein 3.00 1.20
Johnny Callison
Cy Williams
2 Robin Roberts 10.00 4.00
Steve Carlton
Grover Alexander
3 Bob Boone 2.00 .80
Stan Lopata
Andy Seminick
Bo Diaz
4 Ruben Amaro 2.00 .80
Larry Bowa
Granny Hamner
Bobby Wine
Dave Bancroft
5 Ed Delahanty 4.00 1.60
Gavvy Cravath
Sherry Magee
6 Gary Matthews 3.00 1.20
Greg Luzinski
Del Ennis
7 Eddie Waitkus 5.00 2.00
Pete Rose
Dick Allen
8 Tony Taylor 2.00 .80
Manny Trillo
Cookie Rojas
9 Chris Short 3.00 1.20
Curt Simmons
Jim Bunning
10 Willie Jones 10.00 4.00
Mike Schmidt
Pinky Whitney
11 Eddie Sawyer MG 2.00 .80
Pat Moran MG
Harry Wright MG
Dallas Green MG
12 Tony Gonzalez 4.00 1.60
Richie Ashburn
Garry Maddox
13 Ron Reed 3.00 1.20
Jim Konstanty
Tug McGraw
14 Checklist 2.00 .80

1983 Phillies Tastykake

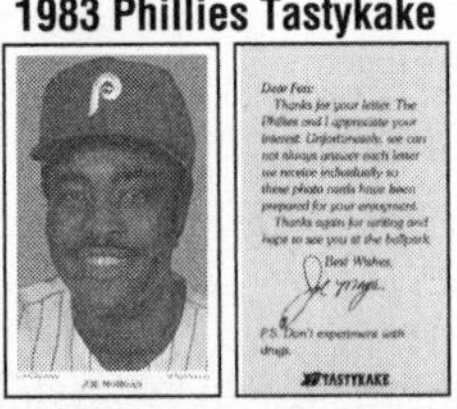

This 31-card set features the Philadelphia Phillies and was sponosred by Tastykake. The cards measure 3 1/2" by 5 1/4" and are printed on thin card stock. Inside white borders, the fronts display posed color headshots with a blue studio background. The backs carry a short letter or slogan from the player and his facsimile autograph. The cards are unnumbered and checklisted below in alphabetical order.

Nm-Mt Ex-Mt
COMPLETE SET (31) 15.00 6.00
1 Luis Aguayo .25 .10
2 Joe Amalfitano CO .25 .10
3 Marty Bystrom .25 .10
4 Steve Carlton 2.50 1.00
5 Larry Christenson .25 .10
6 Pat Corrales MG .25 .10
7 Ivan DeJesus .25 .10
8 John Denny .50 .20
9 Bob Dernier .25 .10
10 Bo Diaz .25 .10
11 Ed Farmer .25 .10
12 Greg Gross .25 .10
13 Von Hayes .25 .10
14 Al Holland .25 .10
15 Garry Maddox .50 .20
16 Gary Matthews .50 .20
17 Tug McGraw .75 .30
18 Larry Milbourne .25 .10
19 Bob Molinaro .25 .10
20 Sid Monge .25 .10
21 Joe Morgan 2.00 .80
22 Tony Perez 1.00 .40
23 Ron Reed .25 .10
24 Bill Robinson .25 .10
25 Pete Rose 4.00 1.60
26 Dick Ruthven .25 .10
27 Mike Schmidt 4.00 1.60
28 Ozzie Virgil .25 .10
29 Coaches .25 .10
30 Philly Phanatic .75 .30
Mascot
31 Veterans Stadium .25 .10

1984 Phillies Tastykake

This set features the Philadelphia Phillies and was sponsored by Tastykake. The card fronts feature a colorful picture of the player or subject inside a white border. The cards measure approximately 3 1/2" by 5 1/4". The set was distributed to fans attending a specific game. There were four additional cards which were put out late in the year updating new players (after the first 40 had been out for some time). The update cards are numbered 41-44 after the first group. The card backs contain a brief message (tip) from the player with his facsimile autograph. The cards are unnumbered but the title card gives a numbering system essentially alphabetically within position; that system is used below for the first 40 cards.

Nm-Mt Ex-Mt
COMPLETE SET (44) 15.00 6.00
COMMON CARD (1-40) .25 .10
COMMON CARD (41-44) .75 .30
1 Logo Card/Checklist .25 .10
2 Team Photo .50 .20
3 Phillie Phanatic .75 .30
(Mascot)
4 Veterans Stadium .25 .10
5 Steve Carlton 2.00 .80
Hall of Fame
6 Mike Schmidt 3.00 1.20
Hall of Fame
7 Phillies Broadcasters .50 .20
8 Paul Owens MG .25 .10
9 Dave Bristol CO .25 .10
10 John Felske CO .25 .10
11 Deron Johnson CO .25 .10
12 Claude Osteen CO .25 .10
13 Mike Ryan CO .25 .10
14 Larry Andersen .25 .10
15 Marty Bystrom .25 .10
16 Bill Campbell .25 .10
17 Steve Carlton 2.00 .80
18 John Denny .50 .20
19 Tony Ghelfi .25 .10
20 Kevin Gross .50 .20
21 Al Holland .25 .10
22 Charles Hudson .25 .10
23 Jerry Koosman .75 .30
24 Tug McGraw 1.00 .40
25 Bo Diaz .25 .10
26 Ozzie Virgil .25 .10
27 John Wockenfuss .25 .10
28 Luis Aguayo .25 .10
29 Ivan DeJesus .25 .10
30 Kiko Garcia .25 .10
31 Len Matuszek .25 .10
32 Juan Samuel 1.00 .40
33 Mike Schmidt 3.00 1.20
34 Tim Corcoran .25 .10
35 Greg Gross .25 .10
36 Von Hayes .50 .20
37 Joe Lefebvre .25 .10
38 Sixto Lezcano .25 .10
39 Garry Maddox .50 .20
40 Glenn Wilson .25 .10
41 Don Carman .75 .30
42 John Russell .75 .30
43 Jeff Stone .75 .30
44 Dave Wehrmeister .75 .30

1985 Phillies CIGNA

This colorful 16-card set (measuring approximately 2 5/8" by 4 1/8") features the Philadelphia Phillies and was also sponsored by CIGNA Corporation. Cards are numbered on the back and contain a safety tip as such the set is frequently categorized and referenced as a safety set. Cards are also numbered by uniform number on the front.

Nm-Mt Ex-Mt
COMPLETE SET (16) 8.00 3.20
1 Juan Samuel .50 .20
2 Von Hayes .50 .20
3 Ozzie Virgil .25 .10
4 Mike Schmidt 4.00 1.60
5 Greg Gross .25 .10
6 Tim Corcoran .25 .10
7 Jerry Koosman .50 .20
8 Jeff Stone .25 .10
9 Glenn Wilson .25 .10
10 Steve Jeltz .25 .10
11 Garry Maddox .50 .20
12 Steve Carlton 2.00 .80
13 John Denny .50 .20
14 Kevin Gross .25 .10
15 Shane Rawley .25 .10
16 Charlie Hudson .25 .10

1985 Phillies Tastykake

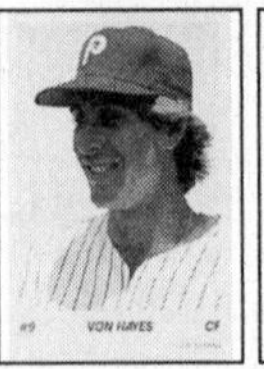
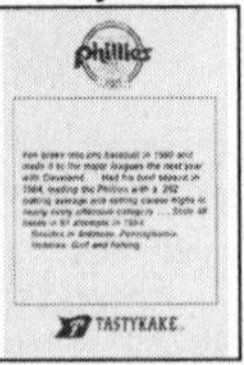

The 1985 Tastykake Philadelphia Phillies set consists of 47 cards, each measuring approximately 3 1/2" by 5 1/4". They feature a color photo of the player framed against white borders. The group shots of the various parts of the teams were posed after the other cards were issued so there are stylistic differences between the group shots and the individual shots. The backs feature brief biographies of the players. The cards are arranged below by position and in alphabetical order within these positions. The set features an early card of Darren Daulton.

Nm-Mt Ex-Mt
COMPLETE SET (47) 15.00 6.00
1 Checklist Card .50 .20
2 John Felske MG .25 .10
3 Dave Bristol CO .25 .10
4 Lee Elia CO .25 .10
5 Claude Osteen CO .25 .10
6 Mike Ryan CO .25 .10
7 Del Unser CO .25 .10
8 John Felske MG .25 .10
Del Unser CO
Dave Bristol CO
Lee Elia CO
Mike Ryan CO
Hank King CO
Claude Osteen CO
9 Pat Zachry .75 .30
Larry Andersen
Charles Hudson
Shane Rawley
John Denny
Steve Carlton
Kevin Gross
Al Holland
Jerry Koosman
Don Carman
Bill Campbell
10 Darren Daulton 1.50 .60
Bo Diaz
Ozzie Virgil
11 Mike Schmidt 1.00 .40
Steve Jeltz
Ivan DeJesus
Juan Samuel
Luis Aguayo
John Russell
12 Tim Corcoran .25 .10
Greg Gross
Von Hayes
Joe Lefebvre
Jeff Stone
Glenn Wilson
13 Larry Andersen .25 .10
14 Steve Carlton 2.00 .80
15 Don Carman .25 .10
16 John Denny .50 .20
17 Tony Ghelfi .25 .10
18 Kevin Gross .25 .10
19 Al Holland .25 .10
20 Charles Hudson .25 .10
21 Jerry Koosman .50 .20
22 Shane Rawley .25 .10
23 Pat Zachry .25 .10
24 Darren Daulton 2.50 1.00
25 Bo Diaz .25 .10
26 Ozzie Virgil .25 .10
27 John Wockenfuss .25 .10
28 Luis Aguayo .25 .10
29 Kiko Garcia .25 .10
30 Steve Jeltz .25 .10
31 John Russell .25 .10
32 Juan Samuel .50 .20
33 Mike Schmidt 3.00 1.20
34 Tim Corcoran .25 .10
35 Greg Gross .25 .10
36 Von Hayes .50 .20
37 Joe Lefebvre .25 .10
38 Garry Maddox .50 .20
39 Jeff Stone .25 .10
40 Glenn Wilson .25 .10
41 Ramon Caraballo .25 .10
and Mike Diaz
42 Mike Maddux .25 .10
and Rodger Cole
43 Rick Schu and .50 .20
Chris James
44 Francisco Melendez .25 .10
and Ken Jackson
45 Randy Salava and .25 .10
Rocky Childress
46 Rich Surhoff and .25 .10
Ralph Citarella
47 Team Photo .50 .20

1986 Phillies CIGNA

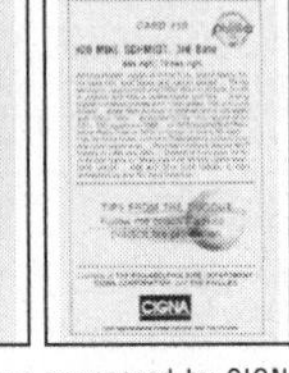

This 16-card set was sponsored by CIGNA Corp. and was given away by the Philadelphia area Fire Departments. Cards measure approximately 2 3/4" by 4 1/8" and feature full color fronts. The card backs are printed in maroon and black on white card stock. Although the uniform numbers are given on the front of the card, the cards are numbered on the back in the order listed below.

Nm-Mt Ex-Mt
COMPLETE SET (16) 8.00 3.20
1 Juan Samuel .50 .20
2 Don Carman .25 .10
3 Von Hayes .50 .20
4 Kent Tekulve .50 .20
5 Greg Gross .25 .10
6 Shane Rawley .25 .10
7 Darren Daulton 2.00 .80
8 Kevin Gross .25 .10
9 Steve Jeltz .25 .10
10 Mike Schmidt 4.00 1.60
11 Steve Bedrosian .50 .20
12 Gary Redus .25 .10
13 Charles Hudson .25 .10
14 John Russell .25 .10
15 Fred Toliver .25 .10
16 Glenn Wilson .25 .10

1986 Phillies Greats TCMA

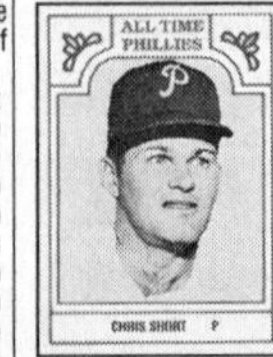

This 12-card standard-size set features some all-time great Phillies. The fronts feature a player photo, his name and position. The backs have vital statistics, a biography and career totals.

Nm-Mt Ex-Mt
COMPLETE SET (12) 4.00 1.60
1 Chuck Klein .75 .30
2 Richie Ashburn 1.00 .40
3 Del Ennis .50 .20
4 Spud Davis .25 .10
5 Grover Alexander 1.00 .40
6 Chris Short .25 .10
7 Jim Konstanty .25 .10
8 Danny Ozark MG .25 .10
9 Larry Bowa .25 .10
10 Richie Allen .50 .20
11 Don Hurst .25 .10
12 Tony Taylor .25 .10

1986 Phillies Keller's

These cards were printed crudely on the boxes of one-pound packages of butter made by Keller's. The cards are approximately 2 1/2" by 2 3/4" and are very similar to the Meadow Gold cards. The same art was used on the Schmidt card which is in both sets. Both Keller's and Meadow Gold are subsidiaries of Beatrice Foods. The set was licensed by Mike Schechter Associates and the Major League Baseball Players' Association. The set contains only Philadelphia Phillies players. The cards are blank backed and are printed in red, dark blue and yellow on white waxed cardboard. Complete boxes would bring double the values listed below. Since the cards are unnumbered they are listed below in alphabetical order.

Nm-Mt Ex-Mt
COMPLETE SET (6) 12.50 5.00
1 Steve Carlton 4.00 1.60
2 Von Hayes .75 .30
3 Gary Redus .75 .30
4 Juan Samuel 1.00 .40
5 Mike Schmidt 6.00 2.40
6 Glenn Wilson .75 .30

1986 Phillies Tastykake

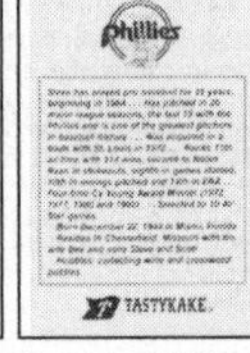

The 1986 Tastykake Philadelphia Phillies set consists of 47 cards, which measure approximately 3 1/2" by 5 1/4". This set features members of the 1986 Philadelphia Phillies. The front of the cards features a full-color photo of the player against white borders while the back has brief biographies. The set has been checklisted for reference below in order by uniform number.

Nm-Mt Ex-Mt
COMPLETE SET (47) 12.00 4.80
2 Jim Davenport CO .25 .10
3 Claude Osteen CO .25 .10
4 Lee Elia CO .25 .10
5 Mike Ryan CO .25 .10
6 John Russell .25 .10
7 John Felske MG .25 .10
8 Juan Samuel .50 .20
9 Von Hayes .25 .10
10 Darren Daulton 2.00 .80
11 Tom Foley .25 .10
12 Glenn Wilson .25 .10
14 Jeff Stone .25 .10
15 Rick Schu .25 .10
16 Luis Aguayo .25 .10
20 Mike Schmidt 3.00 1.20
21 Greg Gross .25 .10
22 Gary Redus .25 .10
23 Joe Lefebvre .25 .10
24 Milt Thompson .25 .10
25 Del Unser CO .25 .10
26 Chris James .25 .10
27 Kent Tekulve .50 .20
28 Shane Rawley .25 .10
29 Ronn Reynolds .25 .10
30 Steve Jeltz .25 .10
31 Garry Maddox .50 .20
32 Steve Carlton 2.00 .80
33 David Shipanoff .25 .10
35 Randy Lerch .25 .10
36 Robin Roberts 1.00 .40
39 Dave Rucker .25 .10
40 Steve Bedrosian .50 .20
41 Tom Hume .25 .10
42 Don Carman .25 .10
43 Fred Toliver .25 .10
46 Kevin Gross .25 .10
47 Larry Andersen .25 .10
48 Dave Stewart .75 .30
49 Charles Hudson .25 .10
50 Rocky Childress .25 .10
NNO Ramon Caraballo .25 .10
Joe Cipolloni
NNO Arturo Gonzalez .25 .10
Mike Maddux
NNO Francisco Melendez .50 .20
Ricky Jordan
NNO Kevin Ward .25 .10
Randy Day
NNO Night to Remember .50 .20
26-7; June 11, 1985
NNO 1915 Phillies .50 .20
NNO 1950 Phillies .50 .20

	Nm-Mt	Ex-Mt
NNO 1980 Phillies	.50	.20
NNO 1983 Phillies	.50	.20

1987 Phillies 1950 TCMA

This nine-card standard-size set honors members of the "Whiz Kids" who won the 1950 National League Pennant. The fronts feature player photos, identification and position. The backs carry some biographical information as well as the 1950 stats.

	Nm-Mt	Ex-Mt
COMPLETE SET (9)	4.00	1.60
1 Eddie Sawyer MG	.25	.10
2 Curt Simmons	.50	.20
3 Jim Konstanty	.50	.20
4 Eddie Waitkus	.25	.10
5 Granny Hamner	.25	.10
6 Del Ennis	.50	.20
7 Richie Ashburn	1.00	.40
8 Dick Sisler	.25	.10
9 Robin Roberts	1.00	.40

1987 Phillies Champion

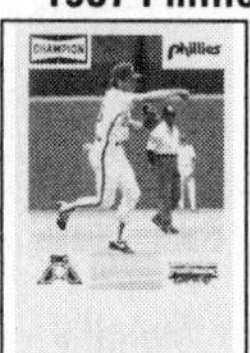

This four-card set which measures approximately 3" by 4 3/4" (with scratch-off tab) is unusual in that there is no way to determine the player's identity other than knowing and recognizing whose photo it is. The top part of the card has a color photo of the player surrounded in the upper left hand corner with a Champion spark plug logo. The Philadelphia Phillies logo is in the upper right hand part of the card. A Pep Boys ad is in the lower left hand corner of the photo and the WIP Philadelphia Sports Radio promo is in the lower right hand corner of the photo. The set is checklisted alphabetically by subject since the cards are unnumbered.

	Nm-Mt	Ex-Mt
COMPLETE SET (4)	18.00	7.25
1 Von Hayes	1.50	.60
2 Steve Jeltz	1.50	.60
3 Juan Samuel	2.00	.80
4 Mike Schmidt	15.00	6.00

1987 Phillies Tastykake

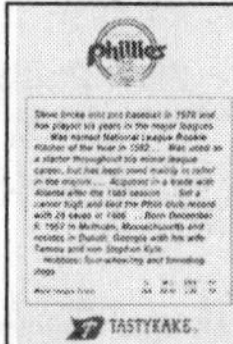

The 1987 Tastykake Philadelphia Phillies set consists of 47 cards which measure approximately 3 1/2" by 5 1/4". The sets again feature full-color photos against a solid white background. There were two number 39s in this set as the Phillies changed personnel during the season, Joe Cowley and Bob Scanlan. For convenience uniform numbers are used below as a basis for numbering and checklisting this set.

	Nm-Mt	Ex-Mt
COMPLETE SET (47)	12.00	4.80
6 John Russell	.25	.10
7 John Felske MG	.25	.10
8 Juan Samuel	.50	.20
9 Von Hayes	.25	.10
10 Darren Daulton	1.00	.40
11 Greg Legg	.25	.10
12 Glenn Wilson	.25	.10
13 Lance Parrish	.75	.30
14 Jeff Stone	.25	.10
15 Rick Schu	.25	.10
16 Luis Aguayo	.25	.10
17 Ron Roenicke	.25	.10
18 Chris James	.25	.10
20 Mike Schmidt	4.00	1.60
21 Greg Gross	.25	.10
23 Joe Cipolloni	.25	.10
24 Milt Thompson	.25	.10
27 Kent Tekulve	.50	.20
28 Shane Rawley	.25	.10
29 Ronn Reynolds	.25	.10
30 Steve Jeltz	.25	.10
33 Mike Jackson	1.00	.40
34 Mike Easler	.25	.10
35 Dan Schatzeder	.25	.10
37 Ken Howell	.25	.10
38 Jim Olander	.25	.10
39A Joe Cowley	.25	.10
39B Bob Scanlan	.25	.10
40 Steve Bedrosian	.50	.20
41 Tom Hume	.25	.10
42 Don Carman	.25	.10
43 Freddie Toliver	.25	.10
44 Mike Maddux	.25	.10
45 Greg Jelks	.25	.10
46 Kevin Gross	.25	.10
47 Bruce Ruffin	.25	.10
48 Marvin Freeman	.25	.10
49 Len Watts	.25	.10
50 Tom Newell	.25	.10
51 Ken Jackson	.25	.10
52 Todd Frohwirth	.25	.10
58 Doug Bair	.25	.10
xx Phillie Phanatic (Mascot)	.75	.30
xx Team Photo	.50	.20
xx Shawn Barton and Rick Lundblade	.25	.10
xx Jeff Kaye and Darren Loy	.25	.10
xx0 Claude Osteen CO Del Unser CO Jim Davenport CO Mike Ryan CO Lee Elia CO	.25	.10

1988 Phillies Tastykake

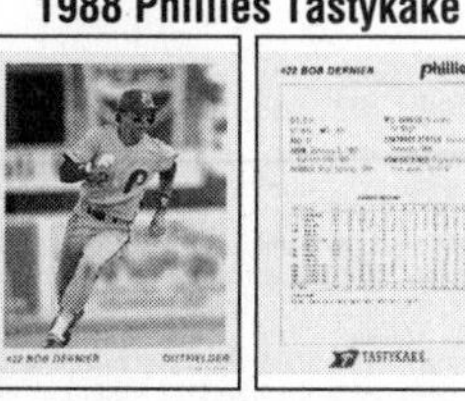

The 1988 Tastykake Philadelphia Phillies set is a 30-card set measuring approximately 4 7/8" by 6 1/4". This set is listed below alphabetically by player. The cards have a full-color photo front and complete player history on the back. There was also a nine-card update set issued later in the year which included a Ricky Jordan card; the update cards are numbered as 31-39 and are blank backed.

	Nm-Mt	Ex-Mt
COMPLETE SET (39)	10.00	4.00
COMMON CARD (1-30)	.25	.10
COMMON CARD (31-39)	.30	.12
1 Luis Aguayo	.25	.10
2 Bill Almon	.25	.10
3 Steve Bedrosian	.50	.20
4 Phil Bradley	.25	.10
5 Jeff Calhoun	.25	.10
6 Don Carman	.25	.10
7 Darren Daulton	1.00	.40
8 Bob Dernier	.25	.10
9A Lee Elia MG (Vertical format)	.50	.20
9B Lee Elia MG (Horizontal format)	.50	.20
10 Todd Frohwirth	.25	.10
11 Greg Gross	.25	.10
12 Kevin Gross	.25	.10
13 Von Hayes	.50	.20
14 Chris James	.25	.10
15 Steve Jeltz	.25	.10
16 Mike Maddux	.25	.10
17 Dave Palmer	.25	.10
18 Lance Parrish	.50	.20
19 Shane Rawley	.25	.10
20 Wally Ritchie	.25	.10
21 Bruce Ruffin	.25	.10
22 Juan Samuel	.50	.20
23 Mike Schmidt	2.00	.80
24 Kent Tekulve	.50	.20
25 Milt Thompson	.25	.10
26 Mike Young	.25	.10
27 Tom Barrett Brad Brink Steve DeAngelis Ron Jones Keith Miller Brad Moore Howard Nichols Shane Turner	.25	.10
28 Team Card	.50	.20
29 Claude Osteen CO Del Unser CO John Vuckovich CO Dave Bristol CO Tony Taylor CO Mike Ryan CO	.25	.10
30 Phillie Phanatic (Mascot)	.50	.20
31 Larry Bowa CO	.40	.16
32 Lee Elia CO	.30	.12
33 Jackie Gutierrez	.30	.12
34 Greg A. Harris	.30	.12
35 Ricky Jordan	.30	.12
36 Keith Miller	.30	.12
37 John Russell	.30	.12
38 John Vukovich CO	.30	.12
39 Garry Maddox ANN Richie Ashburn ANN Chris Wheeler ANN Harry Kalas ANN Andy Musser ANN	.60	.24

1988 Phillies Topps Ashburn Sheet

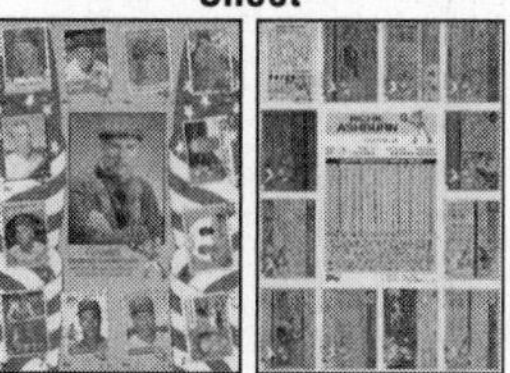

This 13-card set was issued on one perforated sheet measuring approximately 10" by 14" commemorating Richie Ashburn's 40 years in baseball. Sponsored by Campbell's, the sheet features 12 smaller versions of different Topps cards printed on a sky-blue and flag background with a bigger 5" by 7" portrait card in the middle. The back of this card displayed his complete Major League batting record and accomplishments. The cards are listed below according to the year they appeared in the Topps sets.

	Nm-Mt	Ex-Mt
COMPLETE SET (13)	10.00	4.00
COMMON CARD (1-13)	1.00	.40
13 Richie Ashburn 1988 Richie Ashburn	1.50	.60

1989 Phillies Tastykake

This set was a 36-card set of Philadelphia Phillies measuring approximately 4 1/8" by 6" featuring full-color fronts with complete biographical information and career stats on the back. The set is checklisted alphabetically in the list below. The set was a give away to fans attending the Phillies Tastykake Photocard Night on May 13, 1989 and was later available from a mail-away offer. There was also a nine-player extended set issued later during the 1989 season; the extended players are numbered below in alphabetical order, numbers 37-45. Chris James' card lists him as uniform number 26, but his number is 18, while 26 was Ron Jones' number.

	Nm-Mt	Ex-Mt
COMPLETE SET (45)	10.00	4.00
COMMON CARD (1-36)	.25	.10
COMMON CARD (37-45)	.50	.20
1 Steve Bedrosian	.50	.20
2 Larry Bowa CO	.50	.20
3 Don Carman	.25	.10
4 Darren Daulton	1.00	.40
5 Bob Dernier	.25	.10
6 Curt Ford	.25	.10
7 Todd Frohwirth	.25	.10
8 Greg A. Harris	.25	.10
9 Von Hayes	.25	.10
10 Tom Herr	.25	.10
11 Ken Howell	.25	.10
12 Chris James UER (Wrong uniform number on card)	.25	.10
13 Steve Jeltz	.25	.10
14 Ron Jones	.25	.10
15 Ricky Jordan	.25	.10
16 Darold Knowles CO	.25	.10
17 Steve Lake	.25	.10
18 Nick Levya MG	.25	.10
19 Mike Maddux	.25	.10
20 Alex Madrid	.25	.10
21 Larry McWilliams	.25	.10
22 Denis Menke CO	.25	.10
23 Dwayne Murphy	.25	.10
24 Tom Nieto	.25	.10
25 Randy O'Neal	.25	.10
26 Steve Ontiveros	.25	.10
27 Jeff Parrett	.25	.10
28 Bruce Ruffin	.25	.10
29 Mark Ryal	.25	.10
30 Mike Ryan CO	.25	.10
31 Juan Samuel	.50	.20
32 Mike Schmidt	2.50	1.00
33 Tony Taylor CO	.25	.10
34 Dickie Thon	.25	.10
35 John Vukovich CO	.25	.10
36 Floyd Youmans	.25	.10
37 Jim Adduci	.50	.20
38 Eric Bullock	.50	.20
39 Dennis Cook	.50	.20
40 Len Dykstra	1.50	.60
41 Charlie Hayes	.75	.30
42 John Kruk	1.00	.40
43 Roger McDowell	.50	.20
44 Terry Mulholland	.50	.20
45 Randy Ready	.50	.20

1990 Phillies Tastykake

The 1990 Tastykake Philadelphia Phillies set is a 36-card set measuring approximately 4 1/8" by 6" which features players, coaches and manager, four players who have had their uniform numbers retired, broadcasters, and even the Phillies Mascot. The set is checklisted alphabetically, with complete biography and complete stats on the back.

	Nm-Mt	Ex-Mt
COMPLETE SET (36)	10.00	3.00
1 Darrel Akerfelds	.25	.07
2 Rod Booker	.25	.07
3 Sil Campusano	.25	.07
4 Don Carman	.25	.07
5 Pat Combs	.25	.07
6 Dennis Cook	.25	.07
7 Darren Daulton	1.00	.30
8 Len Dykstra	1.00	.30
9 Curt Ford	.25	.07
10 Jason Grimsley	.25	.07
11 Charlie Hayes	.25	.07
12 Von Hayes	.25	.07
13 Tommy Herr	.25	.07
14 Dave Hollins	.50	.15
15 Ken Howell	.25	.07
16 Ron Jones	.25	.07
17 Ricky Jordan	.25	.07
18 John Kruk	.75	.23
19 Steve Lake	.25	.07
20 Nick Levya MG	.25	.07
21 Carmelo Martinez	.25	.07
22 Roger McDowell	.25	.07
23 Chuck McElroy	.25	.07
24 Terry Mulholland	.25	.07
25 Jeff Parrett	.25	.07
26 Randy Ready	.25	.07
27 Bruce Ruffin	.25	.07
28 Dickie Thon	.25	.07
29 Richie Ashburn	1.00	.30
30 Steve Carlton	1.00	.30
31 Robin Roberts	1.00	.30
32 Mike Schmidt	2.00	.60
33 Phillie Phanatic (Mascot)	.75	.23
34 Denis Menke CO Mike Ryan CO John Vukovich CO Hal Lanier CO Darold Knowles CO Larry Bowa CO	.25	.07
35 Chris Wheeler ANN Andy Musser ANN Harry Kalas ANN Richie Ashburn ANN	.50	.15
36 Mike Schmidt ANN Jim Barniak ANN Garry Maddox ANN	.75	.23

1991 Phillies Medford

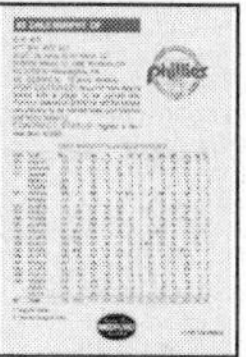

This 35-card set was sponsored by Medford (rather than by Tastykake as in past years), and its company logo is found on the bottom of the reverse. The oversized cards measure approximately 4 1/8" by 6" and feature borderless glossy color action player photos on the obverse. The player's name is given in a red bar at either the top or bottom of the picture. The backs are printed in red and black on white and present biographical as well as statistical information. The cards are unnumbered and checklisted below in alphabetical order.

	Nm-Mt	Ex-Mt
COMPLETE SET (35)	8.00	2.40
1 Darrel Akerfelds	.10	.03
2 Andy Ashby	.25	.07
3 Wally Backman	.10	.03
4 Joe Boever	.10	.03
5 Rod Booker	.10	.03
6 Larry Bowa CO	.25	.07
7 Sil Campusano	.10	.03
8 Wes Chamberlain	.10	.03
9 Pat Combs	.10	.03
10 Danny Cox	.10	.03
11 Darren Daulton	.75	.23
12 Jose DeJesus	.10	.03
13 Len Dykstra	.50	.15
14 Darrin Fletcher	.10	.03
15 Tommy Greene	.10	.03
16 Jason Grimsley	.10	.03
17 Charlie Hayes	.10	.03
18 Von Hayes	.10	.03
19 Dave Hollins	.10	.03
20 Ken Howell	.10	.03
21 Ricky Jordan	.10	.03
22 John Kruk	.50	.15
23 Steve Lake	.10	.03
24 Hal Lanier CO	.10	.03
25 Tim Mauser	.10	.03
26 Roger McDowell	.10	.03
27 Denis Menke CO	.10	.03
28 Mickey Morandini	.25	.07
29 John Morris	.10	.03
30 Terry Mulholland	.10	.03
31 Dale Murphy	.75	.23
32 Johnny Podres CO	.25	.07
33 Randy Ready	.10	.03
34 Dickie Thon	.10	.03
35 John Vukovich CO	.10	.03

1992 Phillies Medford

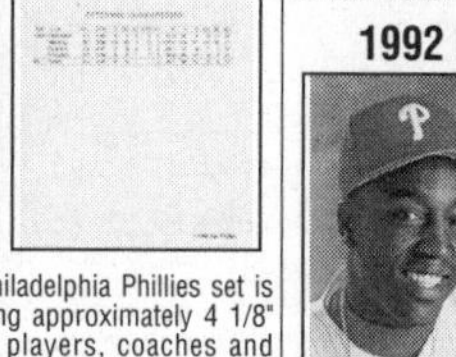

For the second consecutive year, Medford has sponsored a Phillies set, consisting of a first series of 36 cards measuring approximately 4 1/8" by 6" and an extended update series of another ten cards of the same size. The players featured in the update series were mostly mid-season call-ups from the minor leagues. The cards are unnumbered and checklisted below alphabetically within series, with the nonplayer cards listed at the end.

	Nm-Mt	Ex-Mt
COMPLETE SET (46)	12.00	3.60
COMMON CARD (1-36)	.25	.07
COMMON CARD (37-46)	.50	.15
1 Kyle Abbott	.25	.07
2 Ruben Amaro	.25	.07
3 Andy Ashby	.25	.07
4 Wally Backman	.25	.07
5 Kim Batiste	.25	.07
6 Larry Bowa CO	.50	.15
7 Cliff Brantley	.25	.07
8 Wes Chamberlain	.25	.07
9 Danny Cox	.25	.07
10 Darren Daulton	1.00	.30
11 Mariano Duncan	.25	.07
12 Len Dykstra	1.00	.30
13 Jim Fregosi MG	.50	.15
14 Tommy Greene	.25	.07
15 Dave Hollins	.25	.07
16 Barry Jones	.25	.07
17 John Kruk	.75	.23
18 Steve Lake	.25	.07
19 Jim Lindeman	.25	.07
20 Denis Menke CO	.25	.07
21 Mickey Morandini	.50	.15
22 Terry Mulholland	.25	.07
23 Dale Murphy	1.00	.30
24 Johnny Podres CO	.50	.15
25 Wally Ritchie	.25	.07
26 Mel Roberts CO	.25	.07
27 Mike Ryan CO	.25	.07
28 Curt Schilling	2.50	.75
29 Steve Searcy	.25	.07
30 Dale Sveum	.25	.07
31 John Vukovich Dugout Assistant	.25	.07
32 Mitch Williams	.50	.15
33 Phillie Phanatic (Mascot)	.75	.23
34 Team Photo	.50	.15
35 Veterans Stadium	.25	.07
36 Uniforms Through The Years	.50	.15
37 Bob Ayrault	.50	.15
38 Brad Brink	.50	.15
39 Pat Combs	.50	.15
40 Jeff Grotewold	.50	.15
41 Mike Hartley	.50	.15
42 Ricky Jordan	.50	.15
43 Tom Marsh	.50	.15
44 Terry Mulholland	.50	.15
45 Ben Rivera	.50	.15
46 Don Robinson	.50	.15

1993 Phillies Medford

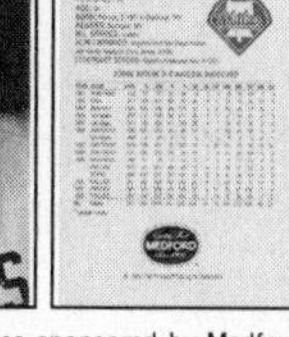

This 35-card set was sponsored by Medford, and its company logo is found on the bottom of the reverse. The oversized cards measure approximately 4 1/8" by 6" and feature borderless glossy color player action photos on their fronts. The cards are unnumbered and checklisted below in alphabetical order.

	Nm-Mt	Ex-Mt
COMPLETE SET (35)	8.00	2.40
1 Kyle Abbott	.25	.07
2 Ruben Amaro	.25	.07
3 Larry Andersen	.25	.07
4 Bob Ayrault	.25	.07
5 Kim Batiste	.25	.07
6 Juan Bell	.25	.07
7 Larry Bowa CO	.50	.15
8 Wes Chamberlain	.25	.07
9 Darren Daulton	1.00	.30
10 Jose DeLeon	.25	.07
11 Mariano Duncan	.25	.07
12 Len Dykstra	1.00	.30
13 Jim Eisenreich	.75	.23
14 Jim Fregosi MG	.50	.15
15 Tyler Green	.25	.07
16 Tommy Greene	.25	.07
17 Dave Hollins	.25	.07
18 Pete Incaviglia	.50	.15
19 Danny Jackson	.25	.07
20 Ricky Jordan	.25	.07
21 John Kruk	.75	.23
22 Denis Menke CO	.25	.07
23 Mickey Morandini	.25	.07
24 Terry Mulholland	.25	.07
25 Phillie Phanatic (Mascot)	.50	.15
26 Johnny Podres CO	.50	.15
27 Todd Pratt	.25	.07
28 Ben Rivera	.25	.07
29 Mel Roberts CO	.25	.07
30 Mike Ryan CO	.25	.07
31 Curt Schilling	2.00	.60
32 Milt Thompson	.25	.07
33 John Vukovich CO	.25	.07
34 David West	.25	.07
35 Mitch Williams	.50	.15

1993 Phillies Stadium Club

This 30-card standard-size set features the 1993 Philadelphia Phillies. The set was issued in hobby (plastic box) and retail (blister) form.

	Nm-Mt	Ex-Mt
COMP. FACT SET (30)	4.00	1.20
1 Darren Daulton	.25	.07
2 Larry Andersen	.10	.03
3 Kyle Abbott	.10	.03

4 Chad McConnell .10 .03
5 Danny Jackson .10 .03
6 Kevin Stocker .10 .03
7 Jim Eisenreich .25 .07
8 Mickey Morandini .10 .03
9 Bob Ayrault .10 .03
10 Doug Lindsey .10 .03
11 Dave Hollins .10 .03
12 Dave West .10 .03
13 Wes Chamberlain .10 .03
14 Curt Schilling 1.25 .35
15 Len Dykstra .25 .07
16 Trevor Humphry .10 .03
17 Terry Mulholland .10 .03
18 Gene Schall .10 .03
19 Mike Lieberthal .50 .15
20 Ben Rivera .10 .03
21 Mariano Duncan .10 .03
22 Pete Incaviglia .10 .03
23 Ron Blazier .10 .03
24 Jeff Jackson .10 .03
25 Jose DeLeon .10 .03
26 Ron Lockett .10 .03
27 Tommy Greene .10 .03
28 Milt Thompson .10 .03
29 Mitch Williams .25 .07
30 John Kruk .25 .07

1994 Phillies Medford

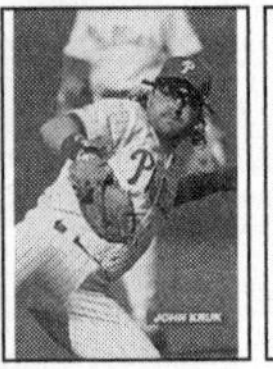

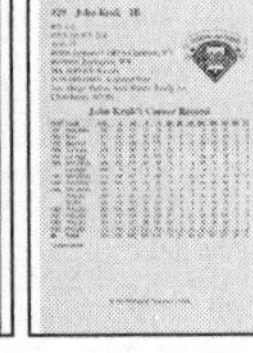

These 36 cards measure approximately 4" by 6" and feature borderless color player photos on their fronts. The player's name appears in white lettering within a red bar on the card face. The white back carries the player's uniform number, name, position, biography, and statistics in red and black lettering. The Phillies logo at the upper right rounds out the card. The cards are unnumbered and checklisted below in alphabetical order.

Nm-Mt Ex-Mt
COMPLETE SET (36) 10.00 3.00
1 Larry Andersen .25 .07
2 Kim Batiste .25 .07
3 Larry Bowa CO .50 .15
4 Wes Chamberlain .25 .07
5 Norm Charlton .25 .07
6 Darren Daulton 1.00 .30
7 Mariano Duncan .25 .07
8 Lenny Dykstra .75 .23
9 Jim Eisenreich .50 .15
10 Jim Fregosi MG .25 .07
11 Tyler Green .25 .07
12 Tommy Greene .25 .07
13 Dave Hollins .50 .15
14 Pete Incaviglia .50 .15
15 Danny Jackson .25 .07
16 Doug Jones .50 .15
17 Ricky Jordan .25 .07
18 Jeff Juden .25 .07
19 John Kruk .75 .23
20 Tony Longmire .25 .07
21 Roger Mason .25 .07
22 Denis Menke CO .25 .07
23 Mickey Morandini .50 .15
24 Bobby Munoz .25 .07
25 Johnny Podres CO .50 .15
26 Todd Pratt .25 .07
27 Ben Rivera .25 .07
28 Mel Roberts CO .25 .07
29 Mike Ryan CO .25 .07
30 Curt Schilling 2.00 .60
31 Heathcliff Slocumb .25 .07
32 Kevin Stocker .25 .07
33 Milt Thompson .25 .07
34 John Vukovich CO .25 .07
35 David West .25 .07
36 Mike Williams .25 .07

1994 Phillies Mellon

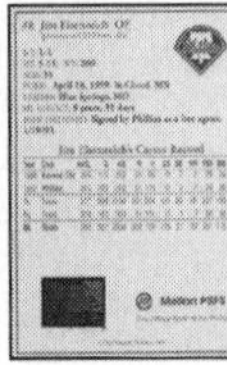

The 1994 Phillies Team Photo/Card Pack was sponsored by Mellon PSFS, "The Official Bank of the Phillies." The set consists of three 12 1/2" by 7" sheets and one 12 1/2" by 3" strip all joined together. The first sheet features a team photo. The second and third sheets consist of two row of five cards each, while the third strip presents one row of five cards. The sheets are perforated and the cards measure the standard-size. The cards are unnumbered and checklisted below in alphabetical order.

Nm-Mt Ex-Mt
COMPLETE SET (26) 8.00 2.40
1 Larry Andersen .25 .07
2 Kim Batiste .25 .07
3 Shawn Boskie .25 .07
4 Darren Daulton 1.00 .30
5 Mariano Duncan .25 .07
6 Lenny Dykstra .75 .23
7 Jim Eisenreich .50 .15
8 Tommy Greene .25 .07
9 Dave Hollins .25 .07
10 Pete Incaviglia .50 .15
11 Danny Jackson .25 .07
12 Doug Jones .50 .15
13 Ricky Jordan .25 .07
14 John Kruk .75 .23
15 Tony Longmire .25 .07
16 Mickey Morandini .50 .15
17 Bobby Munoz .25 .07
18 Todd Pratt .25 .07
19 Paul Quantrill .25 .07
Billy Hatcher
20 Curt Schilling 2.00 .60
21 Heathcliff Slocumb .25 .07
22 Kevin Stocker .25 .07
23 Milt Thompson .25 .07
24 David West .25 .07
25 Mike Williams .25 .07
26 Large Team Photo 2.00 .60
12 1/2" by 7"

1994 Phillies U.S. Playing Cards

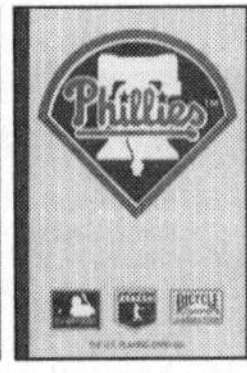

These 56 playing standard-size cards have rounded corners, and feature color posed and action player photos on their white-bordered fronts. The player's name and position appear near the bottom. The blue and gray backs carry the logos for the Phillies, baseball's 125th Anniversary, MLBPA, and Bicycle Sports Collection. The set is checklisted below in playing card order by suits and assigned numbers to aces (1), jacks (11), queens (12), and kings (13).

Nm-Mt Ex-Mt
COMP. FACT SET (56) 3.00 .90
1C Pete Incaviglia .05 .02
1D Terry Mulholland .05 .02
1H Lenny Dykstra .25 .07
1S Dave Hollins .05 .02
2C Lenny Dykstra .25 .07
2D Brad Brink .05 .02
2H Tony Longmire .05 .02
2S Danny Jackson .05 .02
3C Milt Thompson .05 .02
3D Roger Mason .05 .02
3H Kim Batiste .05 .02
3S Todd Pratt .05 .02
4C Mickey Morandini .10 .03
4D Mariano Duncan .05 .02
4H Pete Incaviglia .10 .03
4S David West .05 .02
5C Kevin Stocker .10 .03
5D Danny Jackson .05 .02
5H Ben Rivera .05 .02
5S Lenny Dykstra .25 .07
6C Terry Mulholland .05 .02
6D Jim Eisenreich .10 .03
6H Ricky Jordan .05 .02
6S Wes Chamberlain .05 .02
7C Curt Schilling .75 .23
7D John Kruk .10 .03
7H Dave Hollins .05 .02
7S Tommy Greene .05 .02
8C Darren Daulton .25 .07
8D David West .05 .02
8H Kevin Foster .05 .02
8S Tony Longmire .05 .02
9C Terry Mulholland .05 .02
9D Todd Pratt .05 .02
9H Kevin Stocker .10 .03
9S Brad Brink .05 .02
10C Roger Mason .05 .02
10D Wes Chamberlain .05 .02
10H Mike Williams .05 .02
10S Ricky Jordan .05 .02
11C Mariano Duncan .05 .02
11D Jim Eisenreich .10 .03
11H Milt Thompson .05 .02
11S Kim Batiste .05 .02
12C Ben Rivera .05 .02
12D Mickey Morandini .05 .02
12H Curt Schilling .50 .15
12S Tyler Green .05 .02
13C John Kruk .10 .03
13D Tommy Greene .05 .02
13H Darren Daulton .25 .07
13S Jim Eisenreich .10 .03
NNO Featured Players .05 .02

1995 Phillies

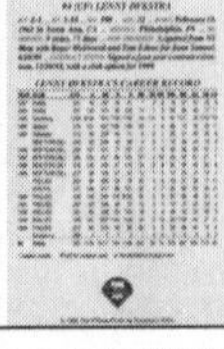

This 36-card set measures approximately 4" by 6". The fronts feature borderless color player photos with the player's name printed in white on a red bar. The white backs carry the player's uniform number, name, position, biography, and statistics in red and black lettering with the team logo below. The cards are unnumbered and checklisted below in alphabetical order.

Nm-Mt Ex-Mt
COMPLETE SET (36) 10.00 3.00
1 Kyle Abbott .25 .07
2 Richie Ashburn HOF 1.00 .30
3 Toby Borland .25 .07
4 Ricky Bottalico .25 .07
5 Larry Bowa CO .50 .15
6 Norm Charlton .25 .07
7 Darren Daulton 1.00 .30
8 Mariano Duncan .25 .07
9 Lenny Dykstra .75 .23
10 Jim Eisenreich .50 .15
11 Jim Fregosi MG .25 .07
12 Dave Gallagher .25 .07
13 Tyler Green .25 .07
14 Gene Harris .25 .07
15 Charlie Hayes .25 .07
16 Dave Hollins .25 .07
17 Gregg Jefferies .25 .07
18 Tony Longmire .25 .07
19 Denis Menke CO .25 .07
20 Michael Mimbs .25 .07
21 Mickey Morandini .25 .07
22 Bobby Munoz .25 .07
23 Johnny Podres CO .50 .15
24 Paul Quantrill .25 .07
25 Randy Ready .25 .07
26 Mel Roberts CO .25 .07
27 Mike Ryan CO .25 .07
28 Curt Schilling 1.50 .45
29 Mike Schmidt HOF 1.00 .30
30 Heathcliff Slocumb .25 .07
31 Kevin Stocker .25 .07
32 Gary Varsho .25 .07
33 John Vukovich CO .25 .07
34 Lenny Webster .25 .07
35 David West .25 .07
36 Team Photo .50 .15

1995 Phillies Mellon

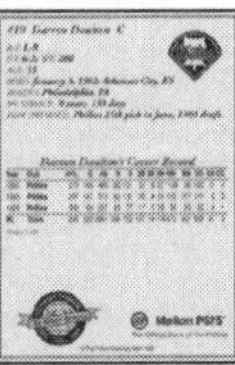

This 25-card set of the Phillies measures the standard size and was issued in perforated sheets. The fronts feature color action player photos on white-and-red pinstripe background. The team name appears in a box above the photo with the player's name printed inside a banner on the bottom. The backs carry a short player biography and career records. The team's Silver Season logo and Mellon Bank's logo at the bottom round out the card. The cards are unnumbered and checklisted below in alphabetical order.

Nm-Mt Ex-Mt
COMPLETE SET (25) 6.00 1.80
1 Kyle Abbott .25 .07
2 Toby Borland .25 .07
3 Ricky Bottalico .25 .07
4 Norm Charlton .25 .07
5 Darren Daulton 1.00 .30
6 Mariano Duncan .25 .07
7 Lenny Dykstra .75 .23
8 Jim Eisenreich .50 .15
9 Dave Gallagher .25 .07
10 Tyler Green .25 .07
11 Gene Harris .25 .07
12 Charlie Hayes .25 .07
13 Dave Hollins .25 .07
14 Gregg Jefferies .25 .07
15 Tony Longmire .25 .07
16 Michael Mimbs .25 .07
17 Mickey Morandini .25 .07
18 Paul Quantrill .25 .07
19 Randy Ready .25 .07
20 Curt Schilling 2.00 .60
21 Heathcliff Slocumb .25 .07
22 Kevin Stocker .25 .07
23 Gary Varsho .25 .07
24 Lenny Webster .25 .07
25 David West .25 .07

1996 Phillies Team Issue

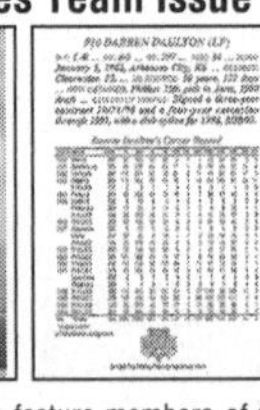

These 4" by 6" cards feature members of the 1996 Philadelphia Phillies. The full-bleed fronts feature color player photos with their names in the upper left corner. The backs have vital statistics and a career record. This set is unnumbered and we have checklisted it in alphabetical order.

Nm-Mt Ex-Mt
COMPLETE SET (36) 8.00 2.40
1 Howard Battle .25 .07
2 Mike Benjamin .25 .07
3 Toby Borland .25 .07
4 Ricky Bottalico .25 .07
5 Larry Bowa CO .50 .15
6 Dave Cash CO .25 .07
7 Carlos Crawford .25 .07
8 Darren Daulton 1.00 .30
9 Lenny Dykstra .75 .23
10 Jim Eisenreich .50 .15
11 Sid Fernandez .50 .15
12 Jim Fregosi MG .25 .07
13 Steve Frey .25 .07
14 Mike Grace .25 .07
15 Tyler Green .25 .07
16 Pete Incaviglia .25 .07
17 Gregg Jefferies .25 .07
18 Kevin Jordan .25 .07
19 Dave Leiper .25 .07
20 Mike Lieberthal .75 .23
21 Denis Menke CO .25 .07
22 Mike Mimbs .25 .07
23 Mickey Morandini .25 .07
24 Terry Mulholland .25 .07
25 Phillie Phanatic .50 .15
26 Johnny Podres CO .50 .15
27 Joe Rigoli CO .25 .07
28 Ken Ryan .25 .07
29 Benito Santiago .50 .15
30 Russ Springer .25 .07
31 Kevin Stocker .25 .07
32 Lee Tinsley .25 .07
33 John Vukovich CO .25 .07
34 Mark Whiten .25 .07
35 Mike Williams .25 .07
36 Todd Zeile .50 .15

1997 Phillies Copi Quik

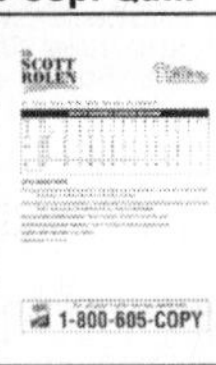

This 28-card set was produced by Copi Quik and features borderless color action player photos measuring approximately 8 1/2" by 11". The backs carry player biographical information and career statistics. The set also includes a 50th Anniversary Jackie Robinson Commemorative Card and several pictures of opposing team members representing the interleague series. These players are indicated with "IL" after their names. A limited number of each card was produced and sequentially numbered. The cards are unnumbered and checklisted below in alphabetical order.

Nm-Mt Ex-Mt
COMPLETE SET (28) 10.00 3.00
1 Ruben Amaro .25 .07
2 Matt Beech .25 .07
3 Ricky Bottalico .25 .07
4 Rico Brogna .25 .07
5 Roger Clemens IL 2.50 .75
6 Darren Daulton .75 .23
7 Terry Francona MG .25 .07
8 Wayne Gomes .25 .07
9 Mike Grace .25 .07
10 Tyler Green .25 .07
11 Rex Hudler .50 .15
12 Gregg Jefferies .25 .07
13 Kevin Jordan .25 .07
14 Mark Leiter .25 .07
15 Mike Lieberthal 1.00 .30
16 Wendell Magee Jr. .25 .07
17 Tino Martinez IL 1.00 .30
18 Mickey Morandini .25 .07
19 Mark Parent .25 .07
20 Ricky Otero .25 .07
21 Phillie Phanatic(Mascot) .50 .15
22 Mark Portugal .25 .07
23 Jackie Robinson 2.00 .60
50th Anniversary
24 Scott Rolen 3.00 .90
25 Curt Schilling 2.00 .60
26 Curt Schilling 2.00 .60
1997 All-Star
27 Garrett Stephenson .25 .07
28 Kevin Stocker .25 .07

1997 Phillies Team Issue

These cards were issued by the Philadelphia Phillies to honor the members of the 1997 Phillies. The cards are unnumbered and we have sequenced them in uniform number order.

Nm-Mt Ex-Mt
COMPLETE SET 15.00 4.50
2 Rico Brogna .50 .15
3 Chuck Cottier CO .50 .15
7 Terry Francona MG .50 .15
8 Mark Parent .50 .15
9 Brad Mills .50 .15
10 Darren Daulton 1.50 .45
12 Mickey Moradini .50 .15
14 Rex Hudler .75 .23
17 Scott Rolen 4.00 1.20
18 John Vuckovich CO .50 .15
19 Kevin Stocker .50 .15
21 Mark Portugal .50 .15
22 Ron Blazier .50 .15
23 Kevin Jordan .50 .15
24 Mike Lieberthal 1.00 .30
25 Gregg Jefferies .50 .15
29 Wendell Magee Jr. .50 .15
31A Kevin Sefcik .75 .23
31B Mark Leiter .75 .23
33 Scott Ruffcorn .50 .15
34 Derrick May .50 .15
35 Bobby Munoz .50 .15
37 Ruben Amaro Jr. .50 .15
38 Curt Schilling 2.50 .75
40 Reggie Harris .50 .15
41 Erik Plantenburg .50 .15
42 Galen Cisco CO .50 .15
45 Danny Tartabull .50 .15
47 Michael Mimbs .50 .15
48 Jerry Spradlin .50 .15
50 Calvin Maduro .50 .15
51 Ken Ryan .50 .15
52 Ricky Bottalico .50 .15
56 Hal McRae CO .50 .15
59 Joe Rigoli .50 .15
NNO Phillie Phanatic .75 .23

1998 Phillies Team Issue

This 36-card set measuring approximately 4" by 6" features borderless color player photos. The backs carry player biographical information and career statistics.The cards are unnumbered and checklisted below in alphabetical order.

Nm-Mt Ex-Mt
COMPLETE SET (36) 10.00 3.00
1 Bobby Abreu 1.00 .30
2 Ruben Amaro .25 .07
3 Alex Arias .25 .07

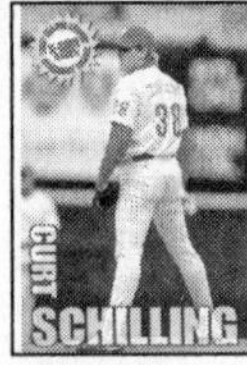

4 Matt Beech .25 .07
5 Ricky Bottalico .25 .07
6 Billy Brewer .25 .07
7 Rico Brogna .25 .07
8 Galen Cisco .25 .07
9 Chuck Cottier CO .25 .07
10 Bobby Estalella .25 .07
11 Terry Francona MG .25 .07
12 Doug Glanville .25 .07
13 Wayne Gomes .25 .07
14 Mike Grace .25 .07
15 Tyler Green .25 .07
16 Ramon Henderson CO .25 .07
17 Rex Hudler .50 .15
18 Gregg Jefferies .25 .07
19 Kevin Jordan .25 .07
20 Mark Leiter .25 .07
21 Mark Lewis .25 .07
22 Mike Lieberthal .75 .23
23 Billy McMillon .25 .07
24 Hal McRae CO .25 .07
25 Brad Mills CO .25 .07
26 Mark Parent .25 .07
27 Mark Portugal .25 .07
28 Desi Relaford .25 .07
29 Scott Rolen 2.00 .60
30 Kevin Sefcik .25 .07
31 Curt Schilling 2.00 .60
32 Jerry Spradlin .25 .07
33 Garrett Stephenson .25 .07
34 John Vukovich CO .25 .07
35 Darrin Winston .25 .07
36 Phillie Phanatic .50 .15

2001 Phillies Modell's

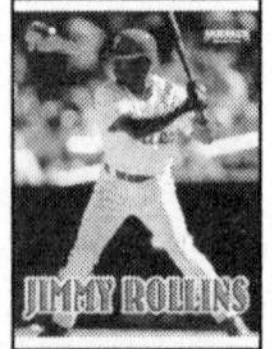

These four 8 1/2" by 11" full-bleed photos were given out at a Philadelphia Phillies game. These were autograph giveaways to the fans coming in. The number of photos the player signed is next to their name and since the photos are unnumbered, we have sequenced them in alphabetical order.

Nm-Mt Ex-Mt
COMPLETE SET (4) 20.00 6.00
1 Marlon Anderson/4000 5.00 1.50
2 Doug Glanville/500 6.00 1.80
3 Jimmy Rollins/3500 6.00 1.80
4 Randy Wolf/4000 5.00 1.50

2002 Phillies Nabisco

This standard-size set was given away during the 2002 season at a Phillies/Brewers game. The card fronts feature the player photo set against a red and blue border which are seperated by some stripes. The horizontal backs have player biographical information along with career statistics. Since these cards are unnumbered, we have sequenced them in alphabetical order.

Nm-Mt Ex-Mt
COMPLETE SET 10.00 3.00
1 Bobby Abreu 1.00 .30
2 Terry Adams .25 .07
3 Marlon Anderson .25 .07
4 Ricky Bottalico .25 .07
5 Larry Bowa MG .50 .15
6 Pat Burrell .25 .07
7 David Coggin .25 .07
8 Rheal Cormier .25 .07
9 Brandon Duckworth .25 .07
10 Jeremy Giambi .25 .07
11 Doug Glanville .25 .07
12 Greg Gross CO .25 .07
13 Ramon Henderson .25 .07
14 Dave Hollins .25 .07
15 Ricky Ledee .25 .07
16 Travis Lee .25 .07
17 Mike Lieberthal .75 .23
18 Jose Mesa .25 .07
19 Jason Michaels .25 .07
20 Doug Nickle .25 .07
21 Vicente Padilla 1.00 .30
22 Tomas Perez .25 .07
23 Robert Person .25 .07
24 Dan Plesac .25 .07
25 Todd Pratt .25 .07
26 Scott Rolen 1.00 .30
27 Jimmy Rollins .50 .15
28 Vern Ruhle CO .25 .07
29 Jose Santiago .25 .07
30 Tony Scott CO .25 .07

31 Carlos Silva	.25	.07
32 Gary Varsho CO	.25	.07
33 John Vukovich CO	.25	.07
34 Turk Wendell	.25	.07
35 Randy Wolf	.75	.23
XX Oreo Coupon	.10	.03

2002 Phillies Team Issue

This set which measures 4" by 6" was issued by the Phillies and sold at the stadium for $6. The fronts have a player photo and the uniform number and player's name. The backs have biographical information along with season and career statistics. Since these cards are not numbered, we have sequenced them in alphabetical order.

	Nm-Mt	Ex-Mt
COMPLETE SET (36)	10.00	3.00
1 Bobby Abreu	1.00	.30
2 Terry Adams	.25	.07
3 Marlon Anderson	.25	.07
4 Ricky Bottalico	.25	.07
5 Larry Bowa MG	.50	.15
6 Pat Burrell	1.50	.45
7 David Coggin	.25	.07
8 Rheal Cormier	.25	.07
9 Brandon Duckworth	.25	.07
10 Doug Glanville	.25	.07
11 Greg Gross CO	.25	.07
12 Ramon Henderson	.25	.07
13 Dave Hollins	.25	.07
14 Ricky Ledee	.25	.07
15 Travis Lee	.50	.15
16 Mike Lieberthal	.75	.23
17 John Mabry	.25	.07
18 Jose Mesa	.50	.15
19 Vicente Padilla	1.00	.30
20 Tomas Perez	.25	.07
21 Robert Person	.25	.07
22 Cliff Politte	.25	.07
23 Todd Pratt	.25	.07
24 Nick Punto	.25	.07
25 Scott Rolen	1.50	.45
26 Jimmy Rollins	.75	.23
27 Vern Ruhle CO	.25	.07
28 Jose Santiago	.25	.07
29 Tony Scott CO	.25	.07
30 Carlos Silva	.25	.07
31 Gary Varsho CO	.25	.07
32 John Vukovich CO	.25	.07
33 Turk Wendell	.25	.07
34 Randy Wolf	.75	.23
35 Scott Graham ANN	.25	.07
Harry Kalas ANN		
Larry Andersen ANN		
Craig Wheeler ANN		
36 Phillie Phanatic MASCOT	.25	.07

2003 Phillies Acme

This 35-card standard-size set was given away as a stadium promotion during the 2002 season. The fronts feature a player photo surrounded by basically brown and blue borders. The player's name in on the bottom while the Acme logo is in the upper right. The horizontal backs feature biographical information as well as career minor and major league statistics.

	Nm-Mt	Ex-Mt
COMPLETE SET	10.00	3.00
1 Bobby Abreu	1.00	.30
2 Terry Adams	.25	.07
3 Marlon Anderson	.25	.07
4 Ricky Bottalico	.25	.07
5 Larry Bowa MG	.50	.15
6 Pat Burrell	.75	.23
7 David Coggin	.25	.07
8 Rheal Cormier	.25	.07
9 Brandon Duckworth	.25	.07
10 Jeremy Giambi	.25	.07
11 Doug Glanville	.25	.07
12 Greg Gross CO	.25	.07
13 Ramon Henderson	.25	.07
14 Dave Hollins	.25	.07
15 Ricky Ledee	.25	.07
16 Travis Lee	.50	.15
17 Mike Lieberthal	.75	.23
18 Jose Mesa	.25	.07
19 Jason Michaels	.25	.07
20 Doug Nickle	.25	.07
21 Vicente Padilla	.50	.15
22 Tomas Perez	.25	.07
23 Robert Person	.25	.07
24 Dan Plesac	.25	.07
25 Todd Pratt	.25	.07
26 Scott Rolen	1.00	.30
27 Jimmy Rollins	.25	.07
28 Vern Ruhle CO	.25	.07
29 Jose Santiago	.25	.07
30 Tony Scott CO	.25	.07
31 Carlos Silva	.25	.07
32 Gary Varsho CO	.25	.07
33 John Vukovich CO	.25	.07
34 Turk Wendell	.25	.07
35 Randy Wolf	.25	.07
XX Oreo Coupon	.10	.03

2003 Phillies Fleer Veteran's Stadium

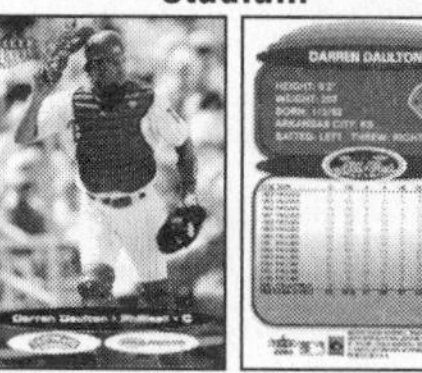

This 12 card standard-size set was issued to commemorate the closing of Veteran's Stadium in Philadelphia. This set was issued by Fleer using their "Ultra" brand and were sponsored by "Tastycake" and "Mab Paints". The players name and position were placed in a gold bar near the bottom. The back features biographical information as well as seasonal and career stats.

	MINT	NRMT
COMPLETE SET (12)	8.00	3.60
1 Steve Carlton	1.00	.45
2 Darren Daulton	.50	.23
3 John Kruk	.50	.23
4 Juan Samuel	.25	.11
5 Mike Schmidt	1.50	.70
6 Larry Bowa	.50	.23
7 Greg Luzinski	.50	.23
8 Garry Maddox	.25	.11
9 Bobby Abreu	1.00	.45
10 Tug McGraw	1.00	.45
11 Curt Schilling	1.00	.45
12 Dallas Green MG	.25	.11

2003 Phillies Team Issue

These color cards, which measure approximately 4" by 6" feature members of the 2003 Philadelphia Phillies. These sets were available from the team for $6. The backs feature biographical information as well as seasonal and career stats. A few cards are also known with a red facsimile autograph. Those players featured are Bobby Abreu, Pat Burrell, Mike Lieberthal, Jimmy Rollins and Jim Thome. In addition, Phillies Caravan cards of Greg Luzinski and Jim Thome were issued in the style of 2002 card. Since these cards are unnumbered, we have sequenced them in alpbetical order.

	MINT	NRMT
COMPLETE SET	10.00	4.50
1 Bobby Abreu	1.00	.45
2 Terry Adams	.25	.11
3 David Bell	.25	.11
4 Larry Bowa MG	.50	.23
5 Pat Burrell	.75	.35
6 Marlon Byrd	.50	.23
7 Rheal Cormier	.25	.11
8 Brandon Duckworth	.25	.11
9 Greg Gross CO	.25	.11
10 Ramon Henderson	.25	.11
11 Tyler Houston	.25	.11
12 Joe Kerrigan CO	.25	.11
13 Ricky Ledee	.25	.11
14 Mike Lieberthal	.75	.35
15 Hector Mercado	.25	.11
16 Jose Mesa	.25	.11
17 Jason Michaels	.25	.11
18 Kevin Millwood	.75	.35
19 Brett Myers	1.00	.45
20 Vicente Padilla	.50	.23
21 Thomas Perez	.25	.11
22 Placido Polanco	.25	.11
23 Dan Plesac	.25	.11
24 Todd Pratt	.25	.11
25 Joe Roa	.25	.11
26 Jimmy Rollins	.50	.23
27 Tony Scott CO	.25	.11
28 Carlos Silva CO	.25	.11
29 Jim Thome	1.50	.70
30 Gary Varsho CO	.25	.11
31 John Vukovich CO	.25	.11
32 Turk Wendell	.25	.11
33 Phillie Phanatic	.25	.11
34 Phillies Annoucers	.25	.11

1987-94 Photo File Hall of Fame

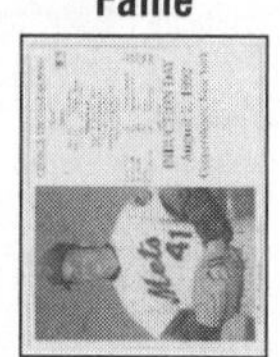

These 8" by 10" cards produced by Photo File displays color photos of various Baseball Hall of Fame inductees. The cards commemorate the induction day ceremonies and include player statistics and biographical information. The cards are checklisted below alphabetically by year.

	Nm-Mt	Ex-Mt
COMPLETE SET	25.00	7.50
1 Ray Dandridge	2.00	.60
2 Bill Veeck	2.00	.60
3 Rollie Fingers	2.50	.75
4 Hal Newhouser	2.00	.60
5 Tom Seaver	4.00	1.20
Pitching		
6 Tom Seaver	4.00	1.20
Still photo		
7 Reggie Jackson	4.00	1.20
Angels Uniform		
8 Reggie Jackson	4.00	1.20
Orioles Uniform		
9 Leo Durocher	2.00	.60
Dodgers Black and White Photo		
10 Steve Carlton	3.00	.90

1993 Photo File Ryan

This eight-card set measures approximately 8" by 10" and commemorates Nolan Ryan's career record seven no-hitters. Each card features a black-and-white or color photo of Ryan as well as the box score from the game. The cards are checklisted below according to the date of the no-hitter.

	Nm-Mt	Ex-Mt
COMPLETE SET (8)	20.00	6.00
COMMON CARD (1-8)	2.50	.75

1914 Piedmont Stamps T330-2

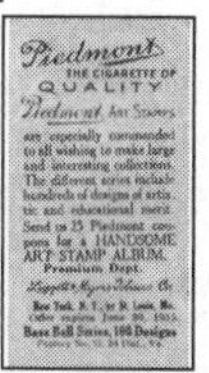

These attractive stamps are approximately 1 7/16" by 2 5/8" and are unnumbered. Unlike most stamps, these have blue printing on the back. On the back there is an offer for an album to house these stamps. This offer expired on June 30, 1915." The front designs are similar to T205.

	Ex-Mt	VG
COMPLETE SET	12000.00	6000.00
1 Leon Ames	80.00	40.00
2 Jimmy Archer	80.00	40.00
3 Jimmy Austin	80.00	40.00
4 Frank Baker	150.00	75.00
5 Cy Barger	80.00	40.00
6 Jack Barry	80.00	40.00
7 Johnny Bates	80.00	40.00
8 Beals Becker	80.00	40.00
9 Chief Bender	150.00	75.00
10 Bob Bescher	80.00	40.00
11 Joe Birmingham	80.00	40.00
12 Walter Blair	80.00	40.00
13 Roger Breshnahan	150.00	75.00
14 Al Bridwell	80.00	40.00
15 Mordecai Brown	150.00	75.00
16 Robert Byrne	80.00	40.00
17 Howie Camnitz	80.00	40.00
18 Bill Carrigan	80.00	40.00
19 Frank Chance	250.00	125.00
20 Hal Chase	150.00	75.00
Identified as Hal Chase		
21 Hal Chase	120.00	60.00
Indentified only as Chase		
22 Eddie Cicotte	150.00	75.00
23 Fred Clarke	150.00	75.00
24 Ty Cobb	800.00	400.00
25 Eddie Collins	150.00	75.00
Mouth Open		
26 Eddie Collins	300.00	150.00
Mouth Closed		
27 Doc Crandall	80.00	40.00
28 Bill Dahlen	100.00	50.00
29 Jake Daubert	120.00	60.00
30 Jim Delahanty	80.00	40.00
31 Josh Devore	80.00	40.00
32 Red Dooin	80.00	40.00
33 Mike Doolan	80.00	40.00
34 Tom Downey	80.00	40.00
35 Larry Doyle	100.00	50.00
36 Joe Egan	80.00	40.00
37 Kid Elberfeld	80.00	40.00
38 Clyde Engle	80.00	40.00
39 Steve Evans	80.00	40.00
40 Johnny Evers	250.00	125.00
41 Ray Fisher	80.00	40.00
42 Art Fletcher	80.00	40.00
43 Russ Ford	80.00	40.00
White Cap		
44 Russ Ford	80.00	40.00
Dark Cap		
45 Arthur Fromme	80.00	40.00
46 George Gibson	80.00	40.00
47 William Goode	80.00	40.00
48 Eddie Grant		
49 Clark Griffith	150.00	75.00
50 Bob Groom	80.00	40.00
51 Bob Harmon	80.00	40.00
52 Arnold Hauser	80.00	40.00
53 Buck Herzog	80.00	40.00
54 Doc Hoblitzell	80.00	40.00
55 Miller Huggins	150.00	75.00
56 John Hummel	80.00	40.00
57 Hugh Jennings MG	250.00	125.00
58 Walter Johnson	400.00	200.00
59 Davy Jones	80.00	40.00
60 William Killifer	120.00	60.00
61 Ed Konetchy	80.00	40.00
62 John Knight	80.00	40.00
63 Frank LaPorte	80.00	40.00
64 Tommy Leach	100.00	50.00
65 Ed Lennox	80.00	40.00
66 Hans Lobert	100.00	50.00
67 Bris Lord	80.00	40.00
68 Sherry Magee	100.00	50.00
69 Rube Marquard	150.00	75.00
70 Christy Mathewson	400.00	200.00
71 George McBride	80.00	40.00
72 John McGraw MG	250.00	125.00
73 Larry McLean	80.00	40.00
74 Chief Meyers	100.00	50.00
75 Fred Merkle	100.00	50.00
76 Clyde Milan	100.00	50.00
77 Dots Miller	80.00	40.00
78 Michael Mitchell	80.00	40.00
79 Pat Moran	80.00	40.00
80 George Moriarty	80.00	40.00
81 George Mullin	100.00	50.00
82 Danny Murphy	80.00	40.00
83 Jack Murray	80.00	40.00
84 Tom Needham	80.00	40.00
85 Rebel Oakes	80.00	40.00
86 Rube Oldring	80.00	40.00
87 Freddy Parent	80.00	40.00
88 Dode Paskert	80.00	40.00
89 Jack Quinn	100.00	50.00
90 Ed Reulbach	120.00	60.00
91 Lewis Ritchie	80.00	40.00
92 John A. Rowan	80.00	40.00
93 Nap Rucker	100.00	50.00
94 Germany Schaefer	100.00	50.00
95 Fred Schulte	100.00	50.00
96 Jim Scott	80.00	40.00
97 Fred Snodgrass	80.00	40.00
98 Tris Speaker	250.00	125.00
99 Oscar Stanage	80.00	40.00
100 George Stovall	80.00	40.00
101 George Suggs	80.00	40.00
102 Jeff Sweeney	80.00	40.00
103 Ira Thomas	80.00	40.00
104 Joe Tinker	150.00	75.00
105 Terry Turner	100.00	50.00
106 Hippo Vaughn	80.00	40.00
107 Heinie Wagner	80.00	40.00
108 Bobby Wallace	150.00	75.00
With Cap		
109 Bobby Wallace	150.00	75.00
No Cap		
110 Ed Walsh	150.00	75.00
111 Zach Wheat	150.00	75.00
112 Kaiser Wilhelm	80.00	40.00
113 Ed Willett	80.00	40.00
114 J. Owen Wilson	80.00	40.00
115 Hooks Wiltse	80.00	40.00
116 Joe Wood	120.00	60.00

1954 Piersall Colonial Meat Products

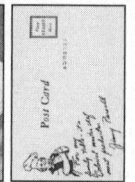

These black and white postcards measure 3 1/2" by 5 3/8" and were issued by Colonial Meat Products. Both of these cards feature Jimmy Piersall; however, the cropping and the color of the facsimile autograph on the front of the card are different. The backs of the cards contain a Colonial Meat advertisement and endorsement by Piersall.

	NM	Ex
COMPLETE SET (2)	30.00	15.00
1 Jimmy Piersall	15.00	7.50
Name in black facsimile autograph pictured on chest		
2 Jimmy Piersall	15.00	7.50
Name in blue facsimilie autograph pictured to hips		

1969 Pilots Post-Intelligencer

This set was originally inserted into copies of the Seattle Post-Intelligencer in 1969. They were drawn by Stu Moldrem, the Post-Intelligencer staff artist. The reprint cards measure approximately 2 1/4" by 5". The fronts feature drawings; and year by year stats. This set is dated 1969 as that was the only year of the Pilots existence. According to reports, the reprint set was issued with the Post-Intelligencer permission. The original cards measure approximately 7" by 3" but there is considerable variation with these numbers. Card number five was printed in the fashion section, rather than the sports section, making this a much harder item to find in 1969 and years later. Therefore, Card number five was never issued in the reprint set. The set was reprinted as a collectors issue in 1977 and is priced seperately. Card number 34 is larger than the other cards in this set.

	NM	Ex
COMPLETE SET (38)	400.00	160.00
COMMON CARD (1-39)	10.00	4.00
COMMON SP	40.00	16.00
1 Don Mincher	10.00	4.00
2 Tommy Harper	12.00	4.80
3 Ray Oyler	10.00	4.00
4 Jerry McNertney	10.00	4.00
5 Joe Schultz MG SP	40.00	16.00
6 Tommy Davis	15.00	6.00
7 Gary Bell	10.00	4.00
8 Chico Salmon	12.00	4.80
9 Jack Aker	10.00	4.00
10 Rich Rollins	10.00	4.00
11 Diego Segui	12.00	4.80
12 Steve Barber	12.00	4.80
13 Wayne Comer	10.00	4.00
14 John Kennedy	10.00	4.00
15 Buzz Stephen	10.00	4.00
16 Jim Gosger	10.00	4.00
17 Mike Ferraro	10.00	4.00
18 Marty Pattin	10.00	4.00
19 Gerry Schoen	10.00	4.00
20 Steve Hovley	10.00	4.00
21 Frank Crosetti CO	20.00	8.00
22 Dick Bates	10.00	4.00
23 Jose Vidal	10.00	4.00
24 Bob Richmond	10.00	4.00
25 Lou Piniella	40.00	16.00
26 John Miklos	10.00	4.00
27 John Morris	10.00	4.00
28 Larry Haney	10.00	4.00
29 Mike Marshall	15.00	6.00
30 Marv Staehle	10.00	4.00
31 Gus Gil	10.00	4.00
32 Sal Maglie CO	15.00	6.00
33 Ron Plaza CO	10.00	4.00
34 Ed O'Brien CO	10.00	4.00
35 Jim Bouton	20.00	8.00
36 Bill Stafford	10.00	4.00
37 Darrell Brandon	10.00	4.00
38 Mike Hegan	10.00	4.00
39 Dick Baney	10.00	4.00

1969 Pilots Wheeldon

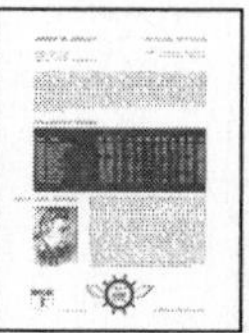

This eight-card set features color player portraits by artist, John Wheeldon, printed on cards measuring approximately 8 1/2" by 11" in white borders. The fronts carry a facsimile autograph with the player's name printed in the wide bottom margin. The backs display player information, career statistics, and a paragraph about the artist. The cards are unnumbered and checklisted below in alphabetical order.

	NM	Ex
COMPLETE SET (8)	30.00	12.00
1 Wayne Comer	4.00	1.60
2 Tommy Harper	4.00	1.60
3 Mike Hegan	4.00	1.60
4 Jerry McNertney	4.00	1.60
5 Don Mincher	4.00	1.60
6 Ray Oyler	4.00	1.60
7 Marty Pattin	4.00	1.60
8 Diego Segui	4.00	1.60

1977 Pilots Post-Intelligencer Reprints

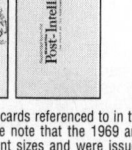

These are the reprint cards referenced to in the 1969 write-up. Please note that the 1969 and 1978 sets are different sizes and were issued almost 10 years apart. They were produced by Frank Caruso, who also produced minor league sets during this period. Please note that card number 5 does not exist in this set.

	NM	Ex
COMPLETE SET (38)	175.00	70.00
1 Don Mincher	4.00	1.60
2 Tommy Harper	5.00	2.00
3 Ray Oyler	4.00	1.60
4 Jerry McNertney	4.00	1.60
6 Tommy Davis	6.00	2.40
7 Gary Bell	4.00	1.60
8 Chico Salmon	4.00	1.60
9 Jack Aker	4.00	1.60
10 Rich Rollins	4.00	1.60
11 Diego Segui	5.00	2.00
12 Steve Barber	5.00	2.00
13 Wayne Comer	4.00	1.60
14 John Kennedy	4.00	1.60
15 Buzz Stephen	4.00	1.60
16 Jim Gosger	4.00	1.60
17 Mike Ferraro	4.00	1.60
18 Marty Pattin	4.00	1.60
19 Gerry Schoen	4.00	1.60
20 Steve Hovley	4.00	1.60
21 Frank Crosetti CO	8.00	3.20
22 Dick Bates	4.00	1.60
23 Jose Vidal	4.00	1.60
24 Bob Richmond	4.00	1.60
25 Lou Piniella	20.00	8.00
26 John Miklos	4.00	1.60
27 John Morris	4.00	1.60
28 Larry Haney	4.00	1.60
29 Mike Marshall	6.00	2.40
30 Marv Staehle	4.00	1.60
31 Gus Gil	4.00	1.60
32 Sal Maglie CO	8.00	3.20
33 Ron Plaza CO	4.00	1.60
34 Ed O'Brien CO	4.00	1.60
35 Jim Bouton	8.00	3.20
36 Bill Stafford	4.00	1.60
37 Darrell Brandon	4.00	1.60
38 Mike Hegan	4.00	1.60
39 Dick Baney	4.00	1.60

1983 Pilots 69 Galasso

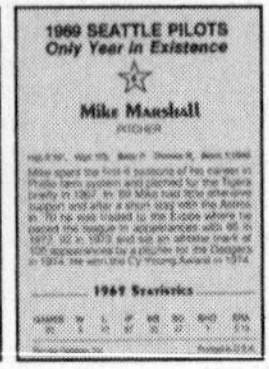

This 43-card standard-size set features members of the Seattle Pilots. The fronts have a player photo with his name and position located under the photo. All of this is surrounded by yellow borders. The backs have a career history along with their stats for the Pilots. Some sets were issued with specially autographed Jim Bouton cards. This set was originally available for $5.50.

	Nm-Mt	Ex-Mt
COMPLETE SET (43)	10.00	4.00
1AU Jim Bouton AU	5.00	2.00
2 Joe Schultz MG	.25	.10
3 Bill Edgerton	.25	.10
4 Gary Timberlake	.25	.10
5 Dick Baney	.25	.10
6 Mike Marshall	.50	.20
7 Jim Gosger	.25	.10
8 Mike Hegan	.25	.10
9 Steve Hovley	.25	.10
10 Don Mincher	.25	.10
11 Miguel Fuentes	.25	.10
12 Dick Bates	.25	.10
13 John O'Donoghue	.25	.10
14 Tommy Davis	.50	.20
15 Jerry McNertney	.25	.10
16 Rich Rollins	.25	.10
17 Fred Talbot	.25	.10
18 John Gelnar	.25	.10
19 Bob Locker	.25	.10
20 Frank Crosetti CO	.75	.30
21 Sal Maglie CO	.50	.20
22 Sibby Sisti CO	.25	.10
23 Ron Plaza CO	.25	.10
24 Federico Velazaquez	.25	.10
25 Diego Segui	.25	.10
26 Steve Barber	.25	.10
27 Jack Aker	.25	.10
28 Marty Pattin	.25	.10
29 Ray Oyler	.25	.10
30 Danny Walton	.25	.10
31 Merritt Ranew	.25	.10
32 John Donaldson	.25	.10
33 Greg Goossen	.50	.20
34 Gary Bell	.25	.10
35 Jim Pagliaroni	.25	.10
36 Mike Ferraro	.25	.10
37 Tommy Harper	.50	.20
38 John Morris	.25	.10
39 Larry Haney	.25	.10
40 Ron Clark	.25	.10
41 Steve Whitaker	.25	.10
42 Wayne Comer	.25	.10
43 Gene Brabender	.25	.10

1911 Pinkerton T5

This 376-card set is called a true Cabinet card set which means a player photograph is affixed to a cardboard backing. The set was produced by the Pinkerton Tobacco Company and could be obtained by sending in a certain number of coupons from Pinkerton tobacco products. Cards numbered 101-875 are Major League player cards. Cards numbered 901-1115 are Minor League players. This is the original checklist as Pinkerton provided in 1911. No individual cards are priced since it is possible that not all exist and some common players may actually be more expensive than major superstars. All pricing information as well as checklist verification is appreciated. A good rule of thumb to use is that commons usually sell for between $400-500 when found and Hall of Famers usually sell for $1000 or more.

Ex-Mt VG

101 Jim Stephens
102 Bobby Wallace
103 Joe Lake
104 George Stone
105 Jack O'Connor
106 Bill Abstein
107 Rube Waddell
108 Roy Hartzell
109 Danny Hoffman
110 Dode Criss
111 Al Schweitzer
112 Art Griggs
113 Bill Bailey
114 Pat Newman
115 Harry Howell
117 Hobe Ferris
118 John McAleese
119 Ray Demmitt
120 Red Fisher
121 Frank Truesdale
122 Barney Pelty
123 Bill Killifer
151 Matty McIntyre
152 Jim Delehanty
153 Hugh Jennings
154 Ralph Works
155 George Moriarity
156 Sam Crawford
157 Charles Schmidt
158 Owen Bush
159 Ty Cobb
160 Wild Bill Donovan
161 Oscar Stanage
162 George Mullin
163 Davy Jones
164 Charles O'Leary
165 Tom Jones
166 Joe Casey
167 Ed Willett
168 Ed Lafitte
169 Ty Cobb
170 Ty Cobb
175 Charles Schmidt
201 John Evers
202 Mordecai Brown
203 King Cole
204 Johnny Cane
205 Heinie Zimmerman
206 Frank Schulte
207 Frank Chance
208 Joe Tinker
209 Orvall Overall
210 Jimmy Archer
211 Johnny Kling
212 James Sheckard
213 Harry McIntyre
214 Lew Richie
215 Ed Ruelbach
216 Artie Hoffman
217 Jack Pfiester
218 Harry Steinfeldt
219 Tom Needham
220 Ginger Beaumont
251 Christy Mathewson
252 Fred Merkle
253 Hooks Wiltse
254 Art Devlin
255 Fred Snodgrass
256 Josh Devore
257 Red Murray
258 Cy Seymour
259 Al Bridwell
260 Larry Doyle
261 Bugs Raymond
262 Doc Crandall
263 Admiral Schlei
264 Hap Myers
265 Bill Dahlen
266 Beals Becker
267 Louis Drucke
301 Fred Luderus
302 John Titus
303 Red Dooin
304 Eddie Stack
305 Kitty Bransfield
306 Sherry Magee
307 Otto Knabe
308 Jimmy Walsh
309 Earl Moore
310 Mickey Doolan
311 Ad Brennan
312 Bob Ewing
313 Lou Schettler
351 Vic Willis
352 Rube Ellis
353 Steve Evans
354 Miller Huggins
355 Arnold Hauser
356 Frank Corridon
357 Roger Bresnahan
358 Slim Sallee
359 Mike Mowrey
360 Ed Konetchy
361 Beckman
362 Rebel Oakes
363 Johnny Lush
364 Ed Phelps
365 Robert Harmon
401 Lew Moren
402 George McQuillian
403 Johnny Bates
404 Eddie Grant
405 Tommy McMillan
406 Tommy Clarke
407 Jack Rowan
408 Beacher
409 Fred Beebe
410 Tom Downey
411 George Suggs
412 Hans Lobert
413 Art Phelan
414 Dode Paskert
415 Ward Miller
416 Dick Egan
417 Art Fromme
418 Bill Burns
419 Clark Griffith
420 Dick Hoblitzell
421 Harry Gasper
422 Dave Altizer
423 Larry McLean
424 Mike Mitchell
451 John Hummel
452 Tony Smith
453 Bill Davidson
454 Ed Lennox
455 Zack Wheat
457 Elmer Knetzer
458 Rube Dessau
459 George Bell
460 Jake Daubert
461 Doc Scanlan
462 Nap Rucker
463 Cy Barger
464 Kaiser Wilhelm
465 Bill Bergen
466 Tex Erwin
501 Charles Bender
502 John Coombs
503 Eddie Plank
504 Amos Strunk
505 Connie Mack MG
506 Ira Thomas
507 Biscoe Lord
508 Snuffy McInnis
509 Jimmy Dygert
510 Rube Oldring
511 Eddie Collins
512 Frank Baker
513 Harry Krause
514 Harry Davis
515 Jack Barry
516 Jack Lapp
517 Cy Morgan
518 Danny Murphy
519 Topsy Hartsell
520 Paddy Livingston
521 Tonny Atkins
522 Eddie Collins
523 Paddy Livingston
551 Doc Gessler
552 Dixie Walker
553 Bill Cunningham
554 John Henry
555 Jack Lelivelt
556 Bobby Groome
557 Doc Ralston
558 Kid Elberfelt
559 Doc Reisling
560 Herman Schaefer
561 Walter Johnson
562 Dolly Gray
562 Joe Wood
563 Wid Conroy
564 Charley Street
565 Bob Unglaub
566 Clyde Milan
567 George Browne
568 George McBride
569 Red Killifer
601 Addie Joss
602 Addie Joss
603 Nap Lajoie
604 Nig Clarke
605 Cy Falkenberg
606 Harry Bemis
607 George Stovall
608 Fred Blanding
609 Elmer Koestner
610 Ted Easterly
611 Willie Mitchell
612 Hornhorst
613 Elmer Flick
614 Speck Harkness
615 Terry Turner
616 Joe Jackson
617 Grover Land
618 Jack Graney
619 Dave Callahan
620 Ben DeMott
621 Neil Ball
622 Dode Birmingham
623 George Kahler
624 Sid Smith
625 Bert Adams
626 Bill Bradley
627 Nap Lajoie
651 Bill Carrigan
653 Heinie Wagner
654 Billy Purtell
655 Frank Smith
656 Harry Lord
658 Duffy Lewis
659 Jack Kleinow
660 Ed Karger
661 Clyde Engle
662 Ben Hunt
663 Charlie Smith
664 Tris Speaker
665 Tom Madden
666 Larry Gardner
667 Harry Hooper
668 Marty McHale
669 Ray Collins
670 Jake Stahl
675 Patsy Donovan
701 Dave Shean
702 Roy Miller
703 Fred Beck
704 Bill Collins
705 Bill Sweeney
706 Buck Herzog
707 Bud Sharpe
708 Cliff Curtis
709 Al Mattern
710 Charles Brown
711 Bill Rariden
712 Grant
713 Ed Abbaticchio
714 George Ferguson
715 Billy Burke
716 Sam Frock
717 Wilbur Good
751 Charlie French
752 Patsy Dougherty
753 Shano Collins
754 Fred Parent
755 Willis Cole
756 Billy Sullivan
757 Rube Suter
758 Chick Gandil
759 Jim Scott
760 Ed Walsh
761 Gavvy Cravath
762 Bobby Messenger
763 Doc White
764 Rollie Zeider
765 Fred Payne
766 Lee Tannehill
767 Eddie Hahn
768 Hugh Duffy
769 Fred Olmstead
770 Lena Blackbourne
771 Cy Young
801 Lew Brockett
802 Frank Laporte
803 Bert Daniels
804 Walter Blair
805 Jack Knight
806 Jimmy Austin
807 Hal Chase
808 Birdie Cree
809 Jack Quinn
810 Walter Manning
811 Jack Warhop
812 Jeff Sweeney
813 Charley Hemphill
814 Harry Wolter
815 Tom Hughes
816 Earl Gardner
851 John Flynn
852 Bill Powell
853 Honus Wagner
854 Bill Powell
855 Fred Clarke
856 Chief Wilson
857 George Gibson
858 Mike Simon
859 Tommy Leach
860 Lefty Leifeld
861 Nick Maddox
862 Dots Miller
863 Howard Camnitz
864 Deacon Phillippe
865 Babe Adams
866 Ed Abbaticchio
867 Paddy O'Connor
868 Bobby Byrne
869 Vin Campbell
870 Robert Ham Hyatt
871 Sam Leever
872 Hans Wagner
873 Hans Wagner
874 Bill McKecknie
875 Kirby White
901 Jimmie Burke MG
902 Charles Carr
903 Larry Cheney
904 Chadbourne
905 Dan Howley
906 Jimmie Burke
907 Mowe
908 Milligan
909 Oberlin
910 Glaze
911 O'Day
912 Kerns
913 Duggan
914 Murch
915 Delehanty
916 Craig
917 Coffee
918 George
919 Williams
920 M. Hayden
951 Joe Cantillion
952 Smith
953 Claude Rossman
1001 Tony James
1002 Jack Powell
1003 William J. Barbeau
1004 Homer Smoot
1051 William Friel
1052 William Friel
1053 Fred Odwell
1054 Alex Reilley
1055 Eugene Packard
1056 Irve Wrattan
1057 Red Nelson
1058 George Perring
1059 Glen Liebhardt
1060 Jimmie O'Rourke
1061 Fred Cook
1062 Charles Arbogast
1063 Jerry Downs
1064 Bunk Congalton
1065 Fred Carish
1066 Red Sitton
1067 George Kaler
1068 Arthur Kruger
1101 Harry Hinchman
Bill Hinchman
Toledo and Columbus
1102 Earl Yingling
1103 Jerry Freeman
1104 Harry Hinchman
1105 Baskette
1106 Denny Sullivan
1107 Carl Robinson
1108 Rodgers
1109 Hi West
1110 Billy Hallman
1111 William Elwert
1112 Charles Hickman
1113 Joe McCarthy
1114 Fred Abbott
1115 Gilligan

1992 Pinnacle

The 1992 Pinnacle set (issued by Score) consists of two series each with 310 standard-size cards. Cards were distributed in first and second series 16-card foil packs and 27-card cello packs. An anti-counterfeit device appears in the bottom border of each card back. A special ribbed plastic lenticular detector card was made available that allowed the user to view the anti-counterfeit device and unscramble the coding with the word "Pinnacle" appearing. Special subsets featured include '92 Rookie Prospects (52, 55, 168, 247-261, 263-280), Idols (281-286/584-591), Sidelines (287-294/592-596), Draft Picks (295-304), Shades (305-310/601-605), Grips (606-612), and Technicians (614-620). Rookie Cards in the set include Brian Jordan, Jeff Kent and Manny Ramirez.

	Nm-Mt	Ex-Mt
COMPLETE SET (620)	40.00	12.00
COMP. SERIES 1 (310)	25.00	7.50
COMP. SERIES 2 (310)	15.00	4.50
1 Frank Thomas	.50	.15
2 Benito Santiago	.20	.06
3 Carlos Baerga	.10	.03
4 Cecil Fielder	.20	.06
5 Barry Larkin	.50	.15
6 Ozzie Smith	.75	.23
7 Willie McGee	.20	.06
8 Paul Molitor	.30	.09
9 Andy Van Slyke	.20	.06
10 Ryne Sandberg	.75	.23
11 Kevin Seitzer	.10	.03
12 Len Dykstra	.20	.06
13 Edgar Martinez	.30	.09
14 Ruben Sierra	.10	.03
15 Howard Johnson	.10	.03
16 Dave Henderson	.10	.03
17 Devon White	.10	.03
18 Terry Pendleton	.20	.06
19 Steve Finley	.20	.06
20 Kirby Puckett	.50	.15
21 Orel Hershiser	.20	.06
22 Hal Morris	.10	.03
23 Don Mattingly	1.25	.35
24 Delino DeShields	.10	.03
25 Dennis Eckersley	.20	.06
26 Ellis Burks	.20	.06
27 Jay Buhner	.20	.06
28 Matt Williams	.20	.06
29 Lou Whitaker	.20	.06
30 Alex Fernandez	.10	.03
31 Albert Belle	.20	.06
32 Todd Zeile	.10	.03
33 Tony Pena	.10	.03
34 Jay Bell	.20	.06
35 Rafael Palmeiro	.30	.09
36 Wes Chamberlain	.10	.03
37 George Bell	.10	.03
38 Robin Yount	.75	.23
39 Vince Coleman	.10	.03
40 Bruce Hurst	.10	.03
41 Harold Baines	.20	.06
42 Chuck Finley	.20	.06
43 Ken Caminiti	.20	.06
44 Ben McDonald	.10	.03
45 Roberto Alomar	.50	.15
46 Chili Davis	.20	.06
47 Bill Doran	.10	.03
48 Jerald Clark	.10	.03
49 Jose Lind	.10	.03
50 Nolan Ryan	2.00	.60
51 Phil Plantier	.10	.03
52 Gary DiSarcina	.10	.03
53 Kevin Bass	.10	.03
54 Pat Kelly	.10	.03
55 Mark Wohlers	.10	.03
56 Walt Weiss	.10	.03
57 Lenny Harris	.10	.03
58 Ivan Calderon	.10	.03
59 Harold Reynolds	.20	.06
60 George Brett	1.25	.35
61 Gregg Olson	.10	.03
62 Orlando Merced	.10	.03
63 Steve Decker	.10	.03
64 John Franco	.20	.06
65 Greg Maddux	.75	.23
66 Alex Cole	.10	.03
67 Dave Hollins	.10	.03
68 Kent Hrbek	.20	.06
69 Tom Pagnozzi	.10	.03
70 Jeff Bagwell	.50	.15
71 Jim Gantner	.10	.03
72 Matt Nokes	.10	.03
73 Brian Harper	.10	.03
74 Andy Benes	.10	.03
75 Tom Glavine	.30	.09
76 Terry Steinbach	.10	.03
77 Dennis Martinez	.20	.06
78 John Olerud	.20	.06
79 Ozzie Guillen	.10	.03
80 Darryl Strawberry	.30	.09
81 Gary Gaetti	.20	.06
82 Dave Righetti	.20	.06
83 Chris Hoiles	.10	.03
84 Andujar Cedeno	.10	.03
85 Jack Clark	.20	.06
86 David Howard	.10	.03
87 Bill Gullickson	.10	.03
88 Bernard Gilkey	.10	.03
89 Kevin Elster	.10	.03
90 Kevin Maas	.10	.03
91 Mark Lewis	.10	.03
92 Greg Vaughn	.20	.06
93 Bret Barberie	.10	.03
94 Dave Smith	.10	.03
95 Roger Clemens	1.00	.30
96 Doug Drabek	.10	.03
97 Omar Vizquel	.20	.06
98 Jose Guzman	.10	.03
99 Juan Samuel	.10	.03
100 Dave Justice	.20	.06
101 Tom Browning	.10	.03
102 Mark Gubicza	.10	.03
103 Mickey Morandini	.10	.03
104 Ed Whitson	.10	.03
105 Lance Parrish	.20	.06
106 Scott Erickson	.10	.03
107 Jack McDowell	.10	.03
108 Dave Stieb	.10	.03
109 Mike Moore	.10	.03
110 Travis Fryman	.20	.06
111 Dwight Gooden	.30	.09
112 Fred McGriff	.30	.09
113 Alan Trammell	.30	.09
114 Roberto Kelly	.10	.03
115 Andre Dawson	.20	.06
116 Bill Landrum	.10	.03
117 Brian McRae	.10	.03
118 B.J. Surhoff	.20	.06
119 Chuck Knoblauch	.20	.06
120 Steve Olin	.10	.03
121 Robin Ventura	.20	.06
122 Will Clark	.50	.15
123 Tino Martinez	.30	.09
124 Dale Murphy	.50	.15
125 Pete O'Brien	.10	.03
126 Ray Lankford	.10	.03
127 Juan Gonzalez	.50	.15
128 Ron Gant	.20	.06
129 Marquis Grissom	.10	.03
130 Jose Canseco	.50	.15
131 Mike Greenwell	.10	.03
132 Mark Langston	.10	.03
133 Brett Butler	.20	.06
134 Kelly Gruber	.10	.03
135 Chris Sabo	.10	.03
136 Mark Grace	.30	.09
137 Tony Fernandez	.10	.03

Card	Nm-Mt	Ex-Mt
138 Glenn Davis	.10	.03
139 Pedro Munoz	.10	.03
140 Craig Biggio	.30	.09
141 Pete Schourek	.10	.03
142 Mike Boddicker	.10	.03
143 Robby Thompson	.10	.03
144 Mel Hall	.10	.03
145 Bryan Harvey	.10	.03
146 Mike LaValliere	.10	.03
147 John Kruk	.20	.06
148 Joe Carter	.20	.06
149 Greg Olson	.10	.03
150 Julio Franco	.20	.06
151 Darryl Hamilton	.10	.03
152 Felix Fermin	.10	.03
153 Jose Offerman	.10	.03
154 Paul O'Neill	.30	.09
155 Tommy Greene	.10	.03
156 Ivan Rodriguez	.50	.15
157 Dave Stewart	.20	.06
158 Jeff Reardon	.20	.06
159 Felix Jose	.10	.03
160 Doug Dascenzo	.10	.03
161 Tim Wallach	.10	.03
162 Dan Plesac	.10	.03
163 Luis Gonzalez	.30	.09
164 Mike Henneman	.10	.03
165 Mike Devereaux	.10	.03
166 Luis Polonia	.10	.03
167 Mike Sharperson	.10	.03
168 Chris Donnels	.10	.03
169 Greg W. Harris	.10	.03
170 Deion Sanders	.30	.09
171 Mike Schooler	.10	.03
172 Jose DeJesus	.10	.03
173 Jeff Montgomery	.10	.03
174 Milt Cuyler	.10	.03
175 Wade Boggs	.30	.09
176 Kevin Tapani	.10	.03
177 Bill Spiers	.10	.03
178 Tim Raines	.20	.06
179 Randy Milligan	.10	.03
180 Rob Dibble	.20	.06
181 Kirt Manwaring	.10	.03
182 Pascual Perez	.10	.03
183 Juan Guzman	.10	.03
184 John Smiley	.10	.03
185 David Segui	.10	.03
186 Omar Olivares	.10	.03
187 Joe Slusarski	.10	.03
188 Erik Hanson	.10	.03
189 Mark Portugal	.10	.03
190 Walt Terrell	.10	.03
191 John Smoltz	.30	.09
192 Wilson Alvarez	.10	.03
193 Jimmy Key	.20	.06
194 Larry Walker	.30	.09
195 Lee Smith	.20	.06
196 Pete Harnisch	.10	.03
197 Mike Harkey	.10	.03
198 Frank Tanana	.10	.03
199 Terry Mulholland	.10	.03
200 Cal Ripken	1.50	.45
201 Dave Magadan	.10	.03
202 Bud Black	.10	.03
203 Terry Shumpert	.10	.03
204 Mike Mussina	.50	.15
205 Mo Vaughn	.20	.06
206 Steve Farr	.10	.03
207 Darrin Jackson	.10	.03
208 Jerry Browne	.10	.03
209 Jeff Russell	.10	.03
210 Mike Scioscia	.10	.03
211 Rick Aguilera	.20	.06
212 Jaime Navarro	.10	.03
213 Randy Tomlin	.10	.03
214 Bobby Thigpen	.10	.03
215 Mark Gardner	.10	.03
216 Norm Charlton	.10	.03
217 Mark McGwire	1.25	.35
218 Skeeter Barnes	.10	.03
219 Bob Tewksbury	.10	.03
220 Junior Felix	.10	.03
221 Sam Horn	.10	.03
222 Jody Reed	.10	.03
223 Luis Sojo	.10	.03
224 Jerome Walton	.10	.03
225 Darryl Kile	.20	.06
226 Mickey Tettleton	.10	.03
227 Dan Pasqua	.10	.03
228 Jim Gott	.10	.03
229 Bernie Williams	.30	.09
230 Shane Mack	.10	.03
231 Steve Avery	.10	.03
232 Dave Valle	.10	.03
233 Mark Leonard	.10	.03
234 Spike Owen	.10	.03
235 Gary Sheffield	.20	.06
236 Steve Chitren	.10	.03
237 Zane Smith	.10	.03
238 Tom Gordon	.10	.03
239 Jose Oquendo	.10	.03
240 Todd Stottlemyre	.10	.03
241 Darren Daulton	.20	.06
242 Tim Naehring	.10	.03
243 Tony Phillips	.10	.03
244 Shawon Dunston	.10	.03
245 Manuel Lee	.10	.03
246 Mike Pagliarulo	.10	.03
247 Jim Thome	.50	.15
248 Luis Mercedes	.10	.03
249 Cal Eldred	.10	.03
250 Derek Bell	.20	.06
251 Arthur Rhodes	.10	.03
252 Scott Cooper	.10	.03
253 Roberto Hernandez	.10	.03
254 Mo Sanford	.10	.03
255 Scott Servais	.10	.03
256 Eric Karros	.20	.06
257 Andy Mota	.10	.03
258 Keith Mitchell	.10	.03
259 Joel Johnston	.10	.03
260 John Wehner	.10	.03
261 Gino Minutelli	.10	.03
262 Greg Gagne	.10	.03
263 Stan Royer	.10	.03
264 Carlos Garcia	.10	.03
265 Andy Ashby	.10	.03
266 Kim Batiste	.10	.03
267 Julio Valera	.10	.03
268 Royce Clayton	.10	.03
269 Gary Scott	.10	.03
270 Kirk Dressendorfer	.10	.03
271 Sean Berry	.10	.03
272 Lance Dickson	.10	.03
273 Rob Maurer	.10	.03
274 Scott Brosius RC	.75	.23
275 Dave Fleming	.10	.03
276 Lenny Webster	.10	.03
277 Mike Humphreys	.10	.03
278 Freddie Benavides	.10	.03
279 Harvey Pulliam	.10	.03
280 Jeff Carter	.10	.03
281 Jim Abbott I Nolan Ryan	.50	.15
282 Wade Boggs I George Brett	.50	.15
283 Ken Griffey Jr. I Rickey Henderson	.50	.15
284 Wally Joyner Dale Murphy	.30	.09
285 Chuck Knoblauch I Ozzie Smith	.30	.09
286 Robin Ventura I Lou Gehrig	.50	.15
287 Robin Yount SIDE	.50	.15
288 Bob Tewksbury SIDE	.10	.03
289 Kirby Puckett SIDE	.30	.09
290 Kenny Lofton SIDE	.20	.06
291 Jack McDowell SIDE	.10	.03
292 John Burkett SIDE	.10	.03
293 Dwight Smith SIDE	.10	.03
294 Nolan Ryan SIDE	1.00	.30
295 M.Ramirez DP RC	2.50	.75
296 Cliff Floyd RC DP UER (Throws right, not left as indicated on back)	1.00	.30
297 Al Shirley DP RC	.15	.04
298 Brian Barber DP RC	.15	.04
299 Jon Farrell DP RC	.15	.04
300 Scott Ruffcorn DP RC	.15	.04
301 Tyrone Hill DP RC	.15	.04
302 Benji Gil DP RC	.25	.07
303 Tyler Green DP RC	.15	.04
304 Allen Watson DP RC	.15	.04
305 Jay Buhner SH	.10	.03
306 Roberto Alomar SH	.20	.06
307 Chuck Knoblauch SH	.10	.03
308 Darryl Strawberry SH	.20	.06
309 Danny Tartabull SH	.10	.03
310 Bobby Bonilla SH	.10	.03
311 Mike Felder	.10	.03
312 Storm Davis	.10	.03
313 Tim Teufel	.10	.03
314 Tom Brunansky	.10	.03
315 Rex Hudler	.10	.03
316 Dave Otto	.10	.03
317 Jeff King	.20	.06
318 Dan Gladden	.10	.03
319 Bill Pecota	.10	.03
320 Franklin Stubbs	.10	.03
321 Gary Carter	.30	.09
322 Melido Perez	.10	.03
323 Eric Davis	.20	.06
324 Greg Myers	.10	.03
325 Pete Incaviglia	.10	.03
326 Von Hayes	.10	.03
327 Greg Swindell	.10	.03
328 Steve Sax	.10	.03
329 Chuck McElroy	.10	.03
330 Gregg Jefferies	.10	.03
331 Joe Oliver	.10	.03
332 Paul Faries	.10	.03
333 David West	.10	.03
334 Craig Grebeck	.10	.03
335 Chris Hammond	.10	.03
336 Billy Ripken	.10	.03
337 Scott Sanderson	.10	.03
338 Dick Schofield	.10	.03
339 Bob Milacki	.10	.03
340 Kevin Reimer	.10	.03
341 Jose DeLeon	.10	.03
342 Henry Cotto	.10	.03
343 Daryl Boston	.10	.03
344 Kevin Gross	.10	.03
345 Milt Thompson	.10	.03
346 Luis Rivera	.10	.03
347 Al Osuna	.10	.03
348 Rob Deer	.10	.03
349 Tim Leary	.10	.03
350 Mike Stanton	.10	.03
351 Dean Palmer	.20	.06
352 Trevor Wilson	.10	.03
353 Mark Eichhorn	.10	.03
354 Scott Aldred	.10	.03
355 Mark Whiten	.10	.03
356 Leo Gomez	.10	.03
357 Rafael Belliard	.10	.03
358 Carlos Quintana	.10	.03
359 Mark Davis	.10	.03
360 Chris Nabholz	.10	.03
361 Carlton Fisk	.30	.09
362 Joe Orsulak	.10	.03
363 Eric Anthony	.10	.03
364 Greg Hibbard	.10	.03
365 Scott Leius	.10	.03
366 Hensley Meulens	.10	.03
367 Chris Bosio	.10	.03
368 Brian Downing	.10	.03
369 Sammy Sosa	.75	.23
370 Stan Belinda	.10	.03
371 Joe Grahe	.10	.03
372 Luis Salazar	.10	.03
373 Lance Johnson	.10	.03
374 Kal Daniels	.10	.03
375 Dave Winfield	.20	.06
376 Brook Jacoby	.10	.03
377 Mariano Duncan	.10	.03
378 Ron Darling	.10	.03
379 Randy Johnson	.50	.15
380 Chito Martinez	.10	.03
381 Andres Galarraga	.20	.06
382 Willie Randolph	.20	.06
383 Charles Nagy	.10	.03
384 Tim Belcher	.10	.03
385 Duane Ward	.10	.03
386 Vicente Palacios	.10	.03
387 Mike Gallego	.10	.03
388 Rich DeLucia	.10	.03
389 Scott Radinsky	.10	.03
390 Damon Berryhill	.10	.03
391 Kirk McCaskill	.10	.03
392 Pedro Guerrero	.20	.06
393 Kevin Mitchell	.10	.03
394 Dickie Thon	.10	.03
395 Bobby Bonilla	.20	.06
396 Bill Wegman	.10	.03
397 Dave Martinez	.10	.03
398 Rick Sutcliffe	.20	.06
399 Larry Andersen	.10	.03
400 Tony Gwynn	.60	.18
401 Rickey Henderson	.50	.15
402 Greg Cadaret	.10	.03
403 Keith Miller	.10	.03
404 Bip Roberts	.10	.03
405 Kevin Brown	.20	.06
406 Mitch Williams	.10	.03
407 Frank Viola	.20	.06
408 Darren Lewis	.10	.03
409 Bob Welch	.10	.03
410 Bob Walk	.10	.03
411 Todd Frohwirth	.10	.03
412 Brian Hunter	.10	.03
413 Ron Karkovice	.10	.03
414 Mike Morgan	.10	.03
415 Joe Hesketh	.10	.03
416 Don Slaught	.10	.03
417 Tom Henke	.10	.03
418 Kurt Stillwell	.10	.03
419 Hector Villaneuva	.10	.03
420 Glenallen Hill	.10	.03
421 Pat Borders	.10	.03
422 Charlie Hough	.20	.06
423 Charlie Leibrandt	.10	.03
424 Eddie Murray	.50	.15
425 Jesse Barfield	.10	.03
426 Mark Lemke	.10	.03
427 Kevin McReynolds	.10	.03
428 Gilberto Reyes	.10	.03
429 Ramon Martinez	.10	.03
430 Steve Buechele	.10	.03
431 David Wells	.20	.06
432 Kyle Abbott	.10	.03
433 John Habyan	.10	.03
434 Kevin Appier	.20	.06
435 Gene Larkin	.10	.03
436 Sandy Alomar Jr.	.10	.03
437 Mike Jackson	.10	.03
438 Todd Benzinger	.10	.03
439 Teddy Higuera	.10	.03
440 Reggie Sanders	.20	.06
441 Mark Carreon	.10	.03
442 Bret Saberhagen	.20	.06
443 Gene Nelson	.10	.03
444 Jay Howell	.10	.03
445 Roger McDowell	.10	.03
446 Sid Bream	.10	.03
447 Mackey Sasser	.10	.03
448 Bill Swift	.10	.03
449 Hubie Brooks	.10	.03
450 David Cone	.20	.06
451 Bobby Witt	.10	.03
452 Brady Anderson	.20	.06
453 Lee Stevens	.10	.03
454 Luis Aquino	.10	.03
455 Carney Lansford	.20	.06
456 Carlos Hernandez	.10	.03
457 Danny Jackson	.10	.03
458 Gerald Young	.10	.03
459 Tom Candiotti	.10	.03
460 Billy Hatcher	.10	.03
461 John Wetteland	.20	.06
462 Mike Bordick	.10	.03
463 Don Robinson	.10	.03
464 Jeff Johnson	.10	.03
465 Lonnie Smith	.10	.03
466 Paul Assenmacher	.10	.03
467 Alvin Davis	.10	.03
468 Jim Eisenreich	.10	.03
469 Brent Mayne	.10	.03
470 Jeff Brantley	.10	.03
471 Tim Burke	.10	.03
472 Pat Mahomes RC	.25	.07
473 Ryan Bowen	.10	.03
474 Bryn Smith	.10	.03
475 Mike Flanagan	.10	.03
476 Reggie Jefferson	.10	.03
477 Jeff Blauser	.10	.03
478 Craig Lefferts	.10	.03
479 Todd Worrell	.10	.03
480 Scott Scudder	.10	.03
481 Kirk Gibson	.20	.06
482 Kenny Rogers	.20	.06
483 Jack Morris	.20	.06
484 Russ Swan	.10	.03
485 Mike Huff	.10	.03
486 Ken Hill	.10	.03
487 Geronimo Pena	.10	.03
488 Charlie O'Brien	.10	.03
489 Mike Maddux	.10	.03
490 Scott Livingstone	.10	.03
491 Carl Willis	.10	.03
492 Kelly Downs	.10	.03
493 Dennis Cook	.10	.03
494 Joe Magrane	.10	.03
495 Bob Kipper	.10	.03
496 Jose Mesa	.10	.03
497 Charlie Hayes	.10	.03
498 Joe Girardi	.10	.03
499 Doug Jones	.10	.03
500 Barry Bonds	1.25	.35
501 Bill Krueger	.10	.03
502 Glenn Braggs	.10	.03
503 Eric King	.10	.03
504 Frank Castillo	.10	.03
505 Mike Gardiner	.10	.03
506 Cory Snyder	.10	.03
507 Steve Howe	.10	.03
508 Jose Rijo	.10	.03
509 Sid Fernandez	.10	.03
510 Archi Cianfrocco RC	.15	.04
511 Mark Guthrie	.10	.03
512 Bob Ojeda	.10	.03
513 John Doherty RC	.15	.04
514 Dante Bichette	.20	.06
515 Juan Berenguer	.10	.03
516 Jeff M. Robinson	.10	.03
517 Mike Macfarlane	.10	.03
518 Matt Young	.10	.03
519 Otis Nixon	.10	.03
520 Brian Holman	.10	.03
521 Chris Haney	.10	.03
522 Jeff Kent RC	1.50	.45
523 Chad Curtis RC	.25	.07
524 Vince Horsman	.10	.03
525 Rod Nichols	.10	.03
526 Peter Hoy	.10	.03
527 Shawn Boskie	.10	.03
528 Alejandro Pena	.10	.03
529 Dave Burba	.10	.03
530 Ricky Jordan	.10	.03
531 Dave Silvestri	.10	.03
532 John Patterson UER RC (Listed as being born in 1960; should be 1967)	.10	.03
533 Jeff Branson	.10	.03
534 Derrick May	.10	.03
535 Esteban Beltre	.10	.03
536 Jose Melendez	.10	.03
537 Wally Joyner	.20	.06
538 Eddie Taubensee RC	.25	.07
539 Jim Abbott	.30	.09
540 Brian Williams RC	.15	.04
541 Donovan Osborne	.10	.03
542 Patrick Lennon	.10	.03
543 Mike Groppuso RC	.15	.04
544 Jarvis Brown	.10	.03
545 Shawn Livsey RC	.15	.04
546 Jeff Ware	.10	.03
547 Danny Tartabull	.10	.03
548 Bobby Jones RC	.25	.07
549 Ken Griffey Jr.	.75	.23
550 Rey Sanchez RC	.25	.07
551 Pedro Astacio RC	.25	.07
552 Juan Guerrero	.10	.03
553 Jacob Brumfield	.10	.03
554 Ben Rivera	.10	.03
555 Brian Jordan RC	.75	.23
556 Denny Neagle	.20	.06
557 Cliff Brantley	.10	.03
558 Anthony Young	.10	.03
559 John Vander Wal	.10	.03
560 Monty Fariss	.10	.03
561 Russ Springer RC	.15	.04
562 Pat Listach RC	.25	.07
563 Pat Hentgen	.10	.03
564 Andy Stankiewicz	.10	.03
565 Mike Perez	.10	.03
566 Mike Bielecki	.10	.03
567 Butch Henry RC	.15	.04
568 Dave Nilsson	.10	.03
569 Scott Hatteberg RC	.25	.07
570 Ruben Amaro	.10	.03
571 Todd Hundley	.10	.03
572 Moises Alou	.20	.06
573 Hector Fajardo RC	.15	.04
574 Todd Van Poppel	.10	.03
575 Willie Banks	.10	.03
576 Bob Zupcic RC	.15	.04
577 J.J. Johnson RC	.15	.04
578 John Burkett	.10	.03
579 Trever Miller RC	.15	.04
580 Scott Bankhead	.10	.03
581 Rich Amaral	.10	.03
582 Kenny Lofton	.50	.15
583 Matt Stairs RC	.25	.07
584 Don Mattingly Rod Carew IDOLS	.50	.15
585 Steve Avery Jack Morris IDOLS	.10	.03
586 Roberto Alomar Sandy Alomar SR. IDOLS	.20	.06
587 Scott Sanderson Catfish Hunter IDOLS	.20	.06
588 Dave Justice Willie Stargell IDOLS	.20	.06
589 Rex Hudler Roger Staubach IDOLS	.50	.15
590 David Cone Jackie Gleason IDOLS	.20	.06
591 Tony Gwynn Willie Davis IDOLS	.30	.09
592 Orel Hershiser SIDE	.10	.03
593 John Wetteland SIDE	.10	.03
594 Tom Glavine SIDE	.20	.06
595 Randy Johnson SIDE	.30	.09
596 Jim Gott SIDE	.10	.03
597 Donald Harris	.10	.03
598 Shawn Hare RC	.15	.04
599 Chris Gardner	.10	.03
600 Rusty Meacham	.10	.03
601 Benito Santiago	.20	.06
602 Eric Davis SHADE	.10	.03
603 Jose Lind SHADE	.10	.03
604 Dave Justice SHADE	.10	.03
605 Tim Raines SHADE	.10	.03
606 Randy Tomlin GRIP	.10	.03
607 Jack McDowell GRIP	.10	.03
608 Greg Maddux GRIP	.50	.15
609 Charles Nagy GRIP	.10	.03
610 Tom Candiotti GRIP	.10	.03
611 David Cone GRIP	.10	.03
612 Steve Avery GRIP	.10	.03
613 Rod Beck GRIP RC	.25	.07
614 R. Henderson TECH	.30	.09
615 Benito Santiago TECH	.10	.03
616 Ruben Sierra TECH	.10	.03
617 Ryne Sandberg TECH	.50	.15
618 Nolan Ryan TECH	1.00	.30
619 Brett Butler TECH	.10	.03
620 Dave Justice TECH	.10	.03

1992 Pinnacle Rookie Idols

This 18-card insert set is a spin-off on the Idols subset featured in the regular series. The cards were randomly inserted in Series II wax packs. The set features full-bleed color photos of 18 rookies along with their pick of sports figures or other individuals who had the greatest impact on their careers. The fronts carry a close-up photo of the rookie superimposed on an action game shot of his idol.

	Nm-Mt	Ex-Mt
COMPLETE SET (18)	120.00	36.00
1 Reggie Sanders and Eric Davis	3.00	.90
2 Hector Fajardo and Jim Abbott	5.00	1.50
3 Gary Cooper and George Brett	20.00	6.00
4 Mark Wohlers and Roger Clemens	15.00	4.50
5 Luis Mercedes and Julio Franco	3.00	.90
6 Willie Banks and Doc Gooden	5.00	1.50
7 Kenny Lofton and Rickey Henderson	8.00	2.40
8 Keith Mitchell and Dave Henderson	1.50	.45
9 Kim Batiste and Barry Larkin	8.00	2.40
10 Todd Hundley and Thurman Munson	8.00	2.40
11 Eddie Zosky and Cal Ripken	25.00	7.50
12 Todd Van Poppel and Nolan Ryan	30.00	9.00
13 Jim Thome and Ryne Sandberg	12.00	3.60
14 Dave Fleming and Bobby Murcer	3.00	.90
15 Royce Clayton and Ozzie Smith	12.00	3.60
16 Donald Harris and Darryl Strawberry	5.00	1.50
17 Chad Curtis and Alan Trammell	5.00	1.50
18 Derek Bell and Dave Winfield	3.00	.90

1992 Pinnacle Slugfest

This 15-card set highlights the games top sluggers.The cards were issued exclusively as an one per pack insert in specially marked cello packs.

	Nm-Mt	Ex-Mt
COMPLETE SET (15)	30.00	9.00
1 Cecil Fielder	.75	.23
2 Mark McGwire	5.00	1.50
3 Jose Canseco	2.00	.60
4 Barry Bonds	5.00	1.50
5 David Justice	.75	.23
6 Bobby Bonilla	.75	.23
7 Ken Griffey Jr.	3.00	.90
8 Ron Gant	.75	.23
9 Ryne Sandberg	3.00	.90
10 Ruben Sierra	.40	.12
11 Frank Thomas	2.00	.60
12 Will Clark	2.00	.60
13 Kirby Puckett	2.00	.60
14 Cal Ripken	6.00	1.80
15 Jeff Bagwell	2.00	.60

1992 Pinnacle Team 2000

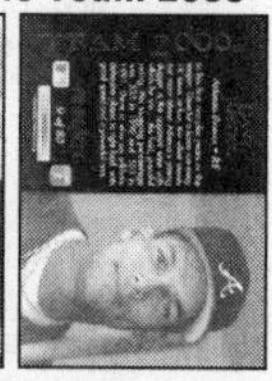

This 80-card standard-size set focuses on young players who were projected to be stars in the year 2000. Cards 1-40 were inserted in Series 1 jumbo packs while cards 41-80 were featured in Series 2 jumbo packs. The insertion rate was three per jumbo pack in either series.

	Nm-Mt	Ex-Mt
COMPLETE SET (80)	30.00	9.00
COMPLETE SERIES 1 (40)	20.00	6.00
COMPLETE SERIES 2 (40)	10.00	3.00
1 Mike Mussina	1.25	.35
2 Phil Plantier	.25	.07
3 Frank Thomas	1.25	.35
4 Travis Fryman	.50	.15
5 Kevin Appier	.50	.15
6 Chuck Knoblauch	.50	.15
7 Pat Kelly	.25	.07
8 Ivan Rodriguez	1.25	.35
9 Dave Justice	.50	.15
10 Jeff Bagwell	1.25	.35
11 Marquis Grissom	.25	.07
12 Andy Benes	.25	.07
13 Gregg Olson	.25	.07
14 Kevin Morton	.25	.07
15 Tim Naehring	.25	.07
16 Dave Hollins	.25	.07
17 Sandy Alomar Jr.	.25	.07
18 Albert Belle	.50	.15
19 Charles Nagy	.25	.07
20 Brian McRae	.25	.07
21 Larry Walker	.75	.23
22 Delino DeShields	.25	.07
23 Jeff Johnson	.25	.07
24 Bernie Williams	.75	.23
25 Jose Offerman	.25	.07
26 Juan Gonzalez	1.25	.35

27A Juan Guzman .25 .07
(Pinnacle logo at top)
27B Juan Guzman .25 .07
(Pinnacle logo at bottom)
28 Eric Anthony .25 .07
29 Brian Hunter .25 .07
30 John Smoltz .75 .23
31 Deion Sanders .75 .23
32 Greg Maddux 2.00 .60
33 Andujar Cedeno .25 .07
34 Royce Clayton .25 .07
35 Kenny Lofton 1.25 .35
36 Cal Eldred .25 .07
37 Jim Thome 1.25 .35
38 Gary DiSarcina .25 .07
39 Brian Jordan 2.00 .60
40 Chad Curtis .60 .18
41 Ben McDonald .25 .07
42 Jim Abbott .75 .23
43 Robin Ventura .50 .15
44 Milt Cuyler .25 .07
45 Gregg Jefferies .25 .07
46 Scott Radinsky .25 .07
47 Ken Griffey Jr. 2.00 .60
48 Roberto Alomar 1.25 .35
49 Ramon Martinez .25 .07
50 Bret Barberie .25 .07
51 Ray Lankford .25 .07
52 Leo Gomez .25 .07
53 Tommy Greene .25 .07
54 Mo Vaughn .50 .15
55 Sammy Sosa 2.00 .60
56 Carlos Baerga .25 .07
57 Mark Lewis .25 .07
58 Tom Gordon .25 .07
59 Gary Sheffield .50 .15
60 Scott Erickson .25 .07
61 Pedro Munoz .25 .07
62 Tino Martinez .75 .23
63 Darren Lewis .25 .07
64 Dean Palmer .50 .15
65 John Olerud .50 .15
66 Steve Avery .25 .07
67 Pete Harnisch .25 .07
68 Luis Gonzalez .75 .23
69 Kim Batiste .25 .07
70 Reggie Sanders .50 .15
71 Luis Mercedes .25 .07
72 Todd Van Poppel .25 .07
73 Gary Scott .25 .07
74 Monty Fariss .25 .07
75 Kyle Abbott .25 .07
76 Eric Karros .50 .15
77 Mo Sanford .25 .07
78 Todd Hundley .25 .07
79 Reggie Jefferson .25 .07
80 Pat Mahomes .60 .18

1992 Pinnacle Team Pinnacle

This 12-card, double-sided insert set features the National League and American League All-Star team as selected by Pinnacle. The standard-size cards were randomly inserted in Series I wax packs. The cards feature illustrations by sports artist Chris Greco with the National League All-Star on one side and the corresponding American League All-Star by position on the other. The words "Team Pinnacle" are printed vertically down the left side of the card in red for American League on one side and blue for National League on the other.

Nm-Mt Ex-Mt
COMPLETE SET (12) 80.00 24.00
1 Roger Clemens 12.00 3.60
and Ramon Martinez
2 Jim Abbott 4.00 1.20
and Steve Avery
3 Ivan Rodriguez 6.00 1.80
and Benito Santiago
4 Frank Thomas 6.00 1.80
and Will Clark
5 Roberto Alomar 10.00 3.00
and Ryne Sandberg
6 Robin Ventura 2.50 .75
and Matt Williams
7 Cal Ripken 20.00 6.00
and Barry Larkin
8 Danny Tartabull 15.00 4.50
and Barry Bonds
9 Ken Griffey Jr. 10.00 3.00
and Brett Butler
10 Ruben Sierra 2.50 .75
and Dave Justice
11 Dennis Eckersley 2.50 .75
and Rob Dibble
12 Scott Radinsky 2.50 .75
and John Franco

1992 Pinnacle Rookies

This 30-card boxed set features top rookies of the 1992 season, with at least one player from each team. A total of 180,000 sets were produced.

Nm-Mt Ex-Mt
COMP.FACT.SET (30) 4.00 1.20
1 Luis Mercedes .20 .06
2 Scott Cooper .20 .06
3 Kenny Lofton .75 .23
4 John Doherty .20 .06
5 Pat Listach .30 .09
6 Andy Stankiewicz .20 .06
7 Derek Bell .30 .09
8 Gary DiSarcina .20 .06
9 Roberto Hernandez .20 .06
10 Joel Johnston .20 .06
11 Pat Mahomes .20 .06
12 Todd Van Poppel .20 .06
13 Dave Fleming .20 .06
14 Monty Fariss .20 .06
15 Gary Scott .20 .06
16 Moises Alou .30 .09
17 Todd Hundley .20 .06
18 Kim Batiste .20 .06
19 Denny Neagle .30 .09
20 Donovan Osborne .20 .06
21 Mark Wohlers .20 .06
22 Reggie Sanders .30 .09
23 Brian Williams .20 .06
24 Eric Karros .30 .09
25 Frank Seminara RC .20 .06
26 Royce Clayton .20 .06
27 Dave Nilsson .20 .06
28 Matt Stairs .30 .09
29 Chad Curtis .30 .09
30 Carlos Hernandez .20 .06

1992 Pinnacle Mantle

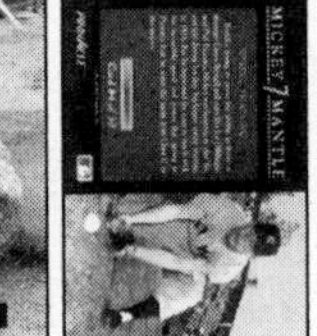

This 30-card standard-size set commemorates the life and career of Mickey Mantle. A total of 180,000 sets were produced. Each set was packaged in a black and blue box that featured a picture of Mantle and a checklist.

Nm-Mt Ex-Mt
COMP. FACT SET (30) 20.00 6.00
COMMON CARD (1-30) .75 .23
1 Mickey Mantle 1.00 .30
Mutt Mantle
Father and Son
24 Mickey Mantle 1.50 .45
Stan Musial
Mick and Stan
25 Whitey Ford 1.00 .30
Yogi Berra
Whitey and Yogi
26 Mickey Mantle 1.00 .30
Billy Martin
Mick and Billy
27 Mickey Mantle 1.00 .30
Casey Stengel MG
Mick and Casey

1993 Pinnacle

The 1993 Pinnacle set (by Score) contains 620 standard-size cards issued in two series of 310 cards each. Cards were distributed in hobby and retail foil packs and 27-card jumbo superpacks. The set includes the following topical subsets: Rookies (238-288, 575-620), Now and Then (289-296, 470-476), Idols (297-303, 477-483), Hometown Heroes (304-310, 484-490), and Draft Picks (455-469). Rookie Cards in this set include Derek Jeter, Jason Kendall and Shannon Stewart.

Nm-Mt Ex-Mt
COMPLETE SET (620) 45.00 13.50
COMP. SERIES 1 (310) 15.00 4.50
COMP. SERIES 2 (310) 30.00 9.00
1 Gary Sheffield .30 .09
2 Cal Eldred .15 .04
3 Larry Walker .50 .15
4 Deion Sanders .50 .15
5 Dave Fleming .15 .04
6 Carlos Baerga .15 .04
7 Bernie Williams .50 .15
8 John Kruk .30 .09
9 Jimmy Key .30 .09
10 Jeff Bagwell .50 .15
11 Jim Abbott .50 .15
12 Terry Steinbach .15 .04
13 Bob Tewksbury .15 .04
14 Eric Karros .30 .09
15 Ryne Sandberg 1.25 .35
16 Will Clark .75 .23
17 Edgar Martinez .50 .15
18 Eddie Murray .75 .23
19 Andy Van Slyke .30 .09
20 Cal Ripken Jr. 2.50 .75
21 Ivan Rodriguez .75 .23
22 Barry Larkin .75 .23
23 Don Mattingly 2.00 .60
24 Gregg Jefferies .15 .04
25 Roger Clemens 1.50 .45
26 Cecil Fielder .30 .09
27 Kent Hrbek .30 .09
28 Robin Ventura .30 .09
29 Rickey Henderson .75 .23
30 Roberto Alomar .75 .23
31 Luis Polonia .15 .04
32 Andujar Cedeno .15 .04
33 Pat Listach .15 .04
34 Mark Grace .50 .15
35 Otis Nixon .15 .04
36 Felix Jose .15 .04
37 Mike Sharperson .15 .04
38 Dennis Martinez .30 .09
39 Willie McGee .30 .09
40 Kenny Lofton .30 .09
41 Randy Johnson .75 .23
42 Andy Benes .15 .04
43 Bobby Bonilla .30 .09
44 Mike Mussina .75 .23
45 Len Dykstra .30 .09
46 Ellis Burks .30 .09
47 Chris Sabo .15 .04
48 Jay Bell .30 .09
49 Jose Canseco .75 .23
50 Craig Biggio .50 .15
51 Wally Joyner .30 .09
52 Mickey Tettleton .15 .04
53 Tim Raines .30 .09
54 Brian Harper .15 .04
55 Rene Gonzales .15 .04
56 Mark Langston .15 .04
57 Jack Morris .30 .09
58 Mark McGwire 2.00 .60
59 Ken Caminiti .30 .09
60 Terry Pendleton .30 .09
61 Dave Nilsson .15 .04
62 Tom Pagnozzi .15 .04
63 Mike Morgan .15 .04
64 Darryl Strawberry .50 .15
65 Charles Nagy .15 .04
66 Ken Hill .15 .04
67 Matt Williams .30 .09
68 Jay Buhner .30 .09
69 Vince Coleman .15 .04
70 Brady Anderson .30 .09
71 Fred McGriff .50 .15
72 Ben McDonald .15 .04
73 Terry Mulholland .15 .04
74 Randy Tomlin .15 .04
75 Nolan Ryan 3.00 .90
76 Frank Viola UER .30 .09
(Card incorrectly states
he has a surgically
repaired elbow)
77 Jose Rijo .15 .04
78 Shane Mack .15 .04
79 Travis Fryman .30 .09
80 Jack McDowell .15 .04
81 Mark Gubicza .15 .04
82 Matt Nokes .15 .04
83 Bert Blyleven .30 .09
84 Eric Anthony .15 .04
85 Mike Bordick .15 .04
86 John Olerud .30 .09
87 B.J. Surhoff .30 .09
88 Bernard Gilkey .15 .04
89 Shawon Dunston .15 .04
90 Tom Glavine .50 .15
91 Brett Butler .30 .09
92 Moises Alou .30 .09
93 Albert Belle .30 .09
94 Darren Lewis .15 .04
95 Omar Vizquel .30 .09
96 Dwight Gooden .50 .15
97 Gregg Olson .15 .04
98 Tony Gwynn 1.00 .30
99 Darren Daulton .30 .09
100 Dennis Eckersley .30 .09
101 Rob Dibble .30 .09
102 Mike Greenwell .15 .04
103 Jose Lind .15 .04
104 Julio Franco .30 .09
105 Tom Gordon .15 .04
106 Scott Livingstone .15 .04
107 Chuck Knoblauch .30 .09
108 Frank Thomas .75 .23
109 Melido Perez .15 .04
110 Ken Griffey Jr. 1.25 .35
111 Harold Baines .30 .09
112 Gary Gaetti .30 .09
113 Pete Harnisch .15 .04
114 David Wells .30 .09
115 Charlie Leibrandt .15 .04
116 Ray Lankford .15 .04
117 Kevin Seitzer .15 .04
118 Robin Yount 1.25 .35
119 Lenny Harris .15 .04
120 Chris James .15 .04
121 Delino DeShields .15 .04
122 Kirt Manwaring .15 .04
123 Glenallen Hill .15 .04
124 Hensley Meulens .15 .04
125 Darrin Jackson .15 .04
126 Todd Hundley .15 .04
127 Dave Hollins .15 .04
128 Sam Horn .15 .04
129 Roberto Hernandez .15 .04
130 Vicente Palacios .15 .04
131 George Brett 2.00 .60
132 Dave Martinez .15 .04
133 Kevin Appier .30 .09
134 Pat Kelly .15 .04
135 Pedro Munoz .15 .04
136 Mark Carreon .15 .04
137 Lance Johnson .15 .04
138 Devon White .15 .04
139 Julio Valera .15 .04
140 Eddie Taubensee .15 .04
141 Willie Wilson .15 .04
142 Stan Belinda .15 .04
143 John Smoltz .50 .15
144 Darryl Hamilton .15 .04
145 Sammy Sosa 1.25 .35
146 Carlos Hernandez .15 .04
147 Tom Candiotti .15 .04
148 Mike Felder .15 .04
149 Rusty Meacham .15 .04
150 Ivan Calderon .15 .04
151 Pete O'Brien .15 .04
152 Erik Hanson .15 .04
153 Billy Ripken .15 .04
154 Kurt Stillwell .15 .04
155 Jeff Kent .75 .23
156 Mickey Morandini .15 .04
157 Randy Milligan .15 .04
158 Reggie Sanders .30 .09
159 Luis Rivera .15 .04
160 Orlando Merced .15 .04
161 Dean Palmer .30 .09
162 Mike Perez .15 .04
163 Scott Erickson .15 .04
164 Kevin McReynolds .15 .04
165 Kevin Maas .15 .04
166 Ozzie Guillen .15 .04
167 Rob Deer .15 .04
168 Danny Tartabull .15 .04
169 Lee Stevens .15 .04
170 Dave Henderson .15 .04
171 Derek Bell .15 .04
172 Steve Finley .30 .09
173 Greg Olson .15 .04
174 Geronimo Pena .15 .04
175 Paul Quantrill .15 .04
176 Steve Buechele .15 .04
177 Kevin Gross .15 .04
178 Tim Wallach .15 .04
179 Dave Valle .15 .04
180 Dave Silvestri .15 .04
181 Bud Black .15 .04
182 Henry Rodriguez .15 .04
183 Tim Teufel .15 .04
184 Mark McLemore .15 .04
185 Bret Saberhagen .30 .09
186 Chris Hoiles .15 .04
187 Ricky Jordan .15 .04
188 Don Slaught .15 .04
189 Mo Vaughn .30 .09
190 Joe Oliver .15 .04
191 Juan Gonzalez .75 .23
192 Scott Leius .15 .04
193 Milt Cuyler .15 .04
194 Chris Haney .15 .04
195 Ron Karkovice .15 .04
196 Steve Farr .15 .04
197 John Orton .15 .04
198 Kelly Gruber .15 .04
199 Ron Darling .15 .04
200 Ruben Sierra .15 .04
201 Chuck Finley .30 .09
202 Mike Moore .15 .04
203 Pat Borders .15 .04
204 Sid Bream .15 .04
205 Todd Zeile .15 .04
206 Rick Wilkins .15 .04
207 Jim Gantner .15 .04
208 Frank Castillo .15 .04
209 Dave Hansen .15 .04
210 Trevor Wilson .15 .04
211 Sandy Alomar Jr. .15 .04
212 Sean Berry .15 .04
213 Tino Martinez .50 .15
214 Chito Martinez .15 .04
215 Dan Walters .15 .04
216 John Franco .30 .09
217 Glenn Davis .15 .04
218 Mariano Duncan .15 .04
219 Mike LaValliere .15 .04
220 Rafael Palmeiro .50 .15
221 Jack Clark .30 .09
222 Hal Morris .15 .04
223 Ed Sprague .15 .04
224 John Valentin .15 .04
225 Sam Militello .15 .04
226 Bob Wickman .15 .04
227 Damion Easley .15 .04
228 John Jaha .15 .04
229 Bob Ayrault .15 .04
230 Mo Sanford .15 .04
231 Walt Weiss .15 .04
232 Dante Bichette .30 .09
233 Steve Decker .15 .04
234 Jerald Clark .15 .04
235 Bryan Harvey .15 .04
236 Joe Girardi .15 .04
237 Dave Magadan .15 .04
238 David Nied .15 .04
239 Eric Wedge RC .15 .04
240 Rico Brogna .15 .04
241 J.T. Bruett .15 .04
242 Jonathan Hurst .15 .04
243 Bret Boone .50 .15
244 Manny Alexander .15 .04
245 Scooter Tucker .15 .04
246 Troy Neel .15 .04
247 Eddie Zosky .15 .04
248 Melvin Nieves .15 .04
249 Ryan Thompson .15 .04
250 Shawn Barton RC .15 .04
251 Ryan Klesko .30 .09
252 Mike Piazza 2.00 .60
253 Steve Hosey .15 .04
254 Shane Reynolds .15 .04
255 Dan Wilson .30 .09
256 Tom Marsh .15 .04
257 Barry Manuel .15 .04
258 Paul Miller .15 .04
259 Pedro Martinez 1.50 .45
260 Steve Cooke .15 .04
261 Johnny Guzman .15 .04
262 Mike Butcher .15 .04
263 Bien Figueroa .15 .04
264 Rich Rowland .15 .04
265 Shawn Jeter .15 .04
266 Gerald Williams .15 .04
267 Derek Parks .15 .04
268 Henry Mercedes .15 .04
269 David Hulse RC .15 .04
270 Tim Pugh RC .15 .04
271 William Suero .15 .04
272 Ozzie Canseco .15 .04
273 Fernando Ramsey RC .15 .04
274 Bernardo Brito .15 .04
275 Dave Mlicki .15 .04
276 Tim Salmon .50 .15
277 Mike Raczka .15 .04
278 Ken Ryan RC .15 .04
279 Rafael Bournigal .15 .04
280 Wil Cordero .15 .04
281 Billy Ashley .15 .04
282 Paul Wagner .15 .04
283 Blas Minor .15 .04
284 Rick Trlicek .15 .04
285 Willie Greene .15 .04
286 Ted Wood .15 .04
287 Phil Clark .15 .04
288 Jesse Levis .15 .04
289 Tony Gwynn NT .50 .15
290 Nolan Ryan NT 1.50 .45
291 Dennis Martinez NT .15 .04
292 Eddie Murray NT .50 .15
293 Robin Yount NT .75 .23
294 George Brett NT 1.00 .30
295 Dave Winfield NT .15 .04
296 Bert Blyleven NT .15 .04
297 Jeff Bagwell .75 .23
Carl Yastrzemski
298 John Smoltz .30 .09
Jack Morris
299 Larry Walker .50 .15
Mike Bossy
300 Gary Sheffield .30 .09
Barry Larkin
301 Ivan Rodriguez .50 .15
Carlton Fisk
302 Delino DeShields .75 .23
Malcolm X
303 Tim Salmon .50 .15
Dwight Evans
304 Bernard Gilkey HH .15 .04
305 Cal Ripken Jr. HH 1.25 .35
306 Barry Larkin HH .30 .09
307 Kent Hrbek HH .15 .04
308 Rickey Henderson HH .50 .15
309 Darryl Strawberry HH .30 .09
310 John Franco HH .15 .04
311 Todd Stottlemyre .15 .04
312 Luis Gonzalez .30 .09
313 Tommy Greene .15 .04
314 Randy Velarde .15 .04
315 Steve Avery .15 .04
316 Jose Oquendo .15 .04
317 Rey Sanchez .15 .04
318 Greg Vaughn .30 .09
319 Orel Hershiser .30 .09
320 Paul Sorrento .15 .04
321 Royce Clayton .15 .04
322 John Vander Wal .15 .04
323 Henry Cotto .15 .04
324 Pete Schourek .15 .04
325 David Segui .15 .04
326 Arthur Rhodes .15 .04
327 Bruce Hurst .15 .04
328 Wes Chamberlain .15 .04
329 Ozzie Smith 1.25 .35
330 Scott Cooper .15 .04
331 Felix Fermin .15 .04
332 Mike Macfarlane .15 .04
333 Dan Gladden .15 .04
334 Kevin Tapani .15 .04
335 Steve Sax .15 .04
336 Jeff Montgomery .15 .04
337 Gary DiSarcina .15 .04
338 Lance Blankenship .15 .04
339 Brian Williams .15 .04
340 Duane Ward .15 .04
341 Chuck McElroy .15 .04
342 Joe Magrane .15 .04
343 Jaime Navarro .15 .04
344 Dave Justice .30 .09
345 Jose Offerman .15 .04
346 Marquis Grissom .15 .04
347 Bill Swift .15 .04
348 Jim Thome .75 .23
349 Archi Cianfrocco .15 .04
350 Anthony Young .15 .04
351 Leo Gomez .15 .04
352 Bill Gullickson .15 .04
353 Alan Trammell .50 .15
354 Dan Pasqua .15 .04
355 Jeff King .15 .04
356 Kevin Brown .30 .09
357 Tim Belcher .15 .04
358 Bip Roberts .15 .04
359 Brent Mayne .15 .04
360 Rheal Cormier .15 .04
361 Mark Guthrie .15 .04
362 Craig Grebeck .15 .04
363 Andy Stankiewicz .15 .04
364 Juan Guzman .15 .04
365 Bobby Witt .15 .04
366 Mark Portugal .15 .04
367 Brian McRae .15 .04
368 Mark Lemke .15 .04
369 Bill Wegman .15 .04
370 Donovan Osborne .15 .04
371 Derrick May .15 .04
372 Carl Willis .15 .04
373 Chris Nabholz .15 .04
374 Mark Lewis .15 .04
375 John Burkett .15 .04
376 Luis Mercedes .15 .04
377 Ramon Martinez .15 .04
378 Kyle Abbott .15 .04
379 Mark Wohlers .15 .04
380 Bob Walk .15 .04
381 Kenny Rogers .30 .09
382 Tim Naehring .15 .04
383 Alex Fernandez .15 .04
384 Keith Miller .15 .04
385 Mike Henneman .15 .04
386 Rick Aguilera .15 .04
387 George Bell .15 .04
388 Mike Gallego .15 .04
389 Howard Johnson .15 .04
390 Kim Batiste .15 .04
391 Jerry Browne .15 .04
392 Damon Berryhill .15 .04
393 Ricky Bones .15 .04
394 Omar Olivares .15 .04
395 Mike Harkey .15 .04
396 Pedro Astacio .15 .04
397 John Wetteland .30 .09
398 Rod Beck .15 .04
399 Thomas Howard .15 .04
400 Mike Devereaux .15 .04
401 Tim Wakefield .30 .09
402 Curt Schilling .50 .15
403 Zane Smith .15 .04
404 Bob Zupcic .15 .04
405 Tom Browning .15 .04
406 Tony Phillips .15 .04
407 John Doherty .15 .04
408 Pat Mahomes .15 .04
409 John Habyan .15 .04
410 Steve Olin .15 .04
411 Chad Curtis .15 .04
412 Joe Grahe .15 .04
413 John Patterson .15 .04

414 Brian Hunter .15 .04
415 Doug Henry .15 .04
416 Lee Smith .30 .09
417 Bob Scanlan .15 .04
418 Kent Mercker .15 .04
419 Mel Rojas .15 .04
420 Mark Whiten .15 .04
421 Carlton Fisk .50 .15
422 Candy Maldonado .15 .04
423 Doug Drabek .15 .04
424 Wade Boggs .50 .15
425 Mark Davis .15 .04
426 Kirby Puckett .75 .23
427 Joe Carter .30 .09
428 Paul Molitor .50 .15
429 Eric Davis .30 .09
430 Darryl Kile .30 .09
431 Jeff Parrett .15 .04
432 Jeff Blauser .15 .04
433 Dan Plesac .15 .04
434 Andres Galarraga .30 .09
435 Jim Gott .15 .04
436 Jose Mesa .15 .04
437 Ben Rivera .15 .04
438 Dave Winfield .30 .09
439 Norm Charlton .15 .04
440 Chris Bosio .15 .04
441 Wilson Alvarez .15 .04
442 Dave Stewart .30 .09
443 Doug Jones .15 .04
444 Jeff Russell .15 .04
445 Ron Gant .30 .09
446 Paul O'Neill .50 .15
447 Charlie Hayes .15 .04
448 Joe Hesketh .15 .04
449 Chris Hammond .15 .04
450 Hipolito Pichardo .15 .04
451 Scott Radinsky .15 .04
452 Bobby Thigpen .15 .04
453 Xavier Hernandez .15 .04
454 Lonnie Smith .15 .04
455 Jamie Arnold DP RC .15 .04
456 B.J. Wallace DP .15 .04
457 Derek Jeter DP RC 15.00 4.50
458 Jason Kendall DP RC 1.00 .30
459 Rick Helling DP .15 .04
460 Derek Wallace DP RC .15 .04
461 Sean Lowe DP RC .15 .04
462 S. Stewart DP RC 1.00 .30
463 Benji Grigsby DP RC .15 .04
464 T. Steverson DP RC .15 .04
465 Dan Serafini DP RC .15 .04
466 Michael Tucker DP .15 .04
467 Chris Roberts DP .15 .04
468 Pete Janicki DP RC .15 .04
469 Jeff Schmidt DP RC .15 .04
470 Don Mattingly NT 1.00 .30
471 Cal Ripken Jr. NT 1.25 .35
472 Jack Morris NT .15 .04
473 Terry Pendleton NT .15 .04
474 Dennis Eckersley NT .30 .09
475 Carlton Fisk NT .30 .09
476 Wade Boggs NT .30 .09
477 Len Dykstra .30 .09
Ken Stabler
478 Danny Tartabull .15 .04
Jose Tartabull
479 Jeff Conine .50 .15
Dale Murphy
480 Gregg Jefferies .15 .04
Ron Cey
481 Paul Molitor .30 .09
Harmon Killebrew
482 John Valentin .15 .04
Dave Concepcion
483 Alex Arias .15 .04
Dave Winfield
484 Barry Bonds HH 1.00 .30
485 Doug Drabek HH .15 .04
486 Dave Winfield HH .15 .04
487 Brett Butler HH .15 .04
488 Harold Baines HH .15 .04
489 David Cone HH .15 .04
490 Willie McGee HH .15 .04
491 Robby Thompson .15 .04
492 Pete Incaviglia .15 .04
493 Manuel Lee .15 .04
494 Rafael Belliard .15 .04
495 Scott Fletcher .15 .04
496 Jeff Frye .15 .04
497 Andre Dawson .30 .09
498 Mike Scioscia .15 .04
499 Spike Owen .15 .04
500 Sid Fernandez .15 .04
501 Joe Orsulak .15 .04
502 Benito Santiago .30 .09
503 Dale Murphy .75 .23
504 Barry Bonds 2.00 .60
505 Jose Guzman .15 .04
506 Tony Pena .15 .04
507 Greg Swindell .15 .04
508 Mike Pagliarulo .15 .04
509 Lou Whitaker .30 .09
510 Greg Gagne .15 .04
511 Butch Henry .15 .04
512 Jeff Brantley .15 .04
513 Jack Armstrong .15 .04
514 Danny Jackson .15 .04
515 Junior Felix .15 .04
516 Milt Thompson .15 .04
517 Greg Maddux 1.25 .35
518 Eric Young .15 .04
519 Jody Reed .15 .04
520 Roberto Kelly .15 .04
521 Darren Holmes .15 .04
522 Craig Lefferts .15 .04
523 Charlie Hough .30 .09
524 Bo Jackson .75 .23
525 Bill Spiers .15 .04
526 Orestes Destrade .15 .04
527 Greg Hibbard .15 .04
528 Roger McDowell .15 .04
529 Cory Snyder .15 .04
530 Harold Reynolds .30 .09
531 Kevin Reimer .15 .04
532 Rick Sutcliffe .30 .09
533 Tony Fernandez .15 .04
534 Tom Brunansky .15 .04
535 Jeff Reardon .30 .09
536 Chili Davis .30 .09
537 Bob Ojeda .15 .04
538 Greg Colbrunn .15 .04
539 Phil Plantier .15 .04
540 Brian Jordan .30 .09
541 Pete Smith .15 .04
542 Frank Tanana .15 .04
543 John Smiley .15 .04
544 David Cone .30 .09
545 Daryl Boston .15 .04
546 Tom Henke .15 .04
547 Bill Krueger .15 .04
548 Freddie Benavides .15 .04
549 Randy Myers .15 .04
550 Reggie Jefferson .15 .04
551 Kevin Mitchell .15 .04
552 Dave Stieb .15 .04
553 Bret Barberie .15 .04
554 Tim Crews .15 .04
555 Doug Dascenzo .15 .04
556 Alex Cole .15 .04
557 Jeff Innis .15 .04
558 Carlos Garcia .15 .04
559 Steve Howe .15 .04
560 Kirk McCaskill .15 .04
561 Frank Seminara .15 .04
562 Cris Carpenter .15 .04
563 Mike Stanley .15 .04
564 Carlos Quintana .15 .04
565 Mitch Williams .15 .04
566 Juan Bell .15 .04
567 Eric Fox .15 .04
568 Al Leiter .30 .09
569 Mike Stanton .15 .04
570 Scott Kamieniecki .15 .04
571 Ryan Bowen .15 .04
572 Andy Ashby .15 .04
573 Bob Welch .15 .04
574 Scott Sanderson .15 .04
575 Joe Kmak .15 .04
576 Scott Pose RC .15 .04
577 Ricky Gutierrez .15 .04
578 Mike Trombley .15 .04
579 Sterling Hitchcock RC .30 .09
580 Rodney Bolton .15 .04
581 Tyler Green .15 .04
582 Tim Costo .15 .04
583 Tim Laker RC .15 .04
584 Steve Reed RC .15 .04
585 Tom Kramer RC .15 .04
586 Robb Nen .30 .09
587 Jim Tatum RC .15 .04
588 Frank Bolick .15 .04
589 Kevin Young .30 .09
590 Matt Whiteside RC .15 .04
591 Cesar Hernandez .15 .04
592 Mike Mohler RC .15 .04
593 Alan Embree .15 .04
594 Terry Jorgensen .15 .04
595 John Cummings RC .15 .04
596 Domingo Martinez RC .15 .04
597 Benji Gil .15 .04
598 Todd Pratt RC .30 .09
599 Rene Arocha RC .30 .09
600 Dennis Moeller .15 .04
601 Jeff Conine .30 .09
602 Trevor Hoffman .30 .09
603 Daniel Smith .15 .04
604 Lee Tinsley .15 .04
605 Dan Peltier .15 .04
606 Billy Brewer .15 .04
607 Matt Walbeck RC .15 .04
608 Richie Lewis RC .15 .04
609 J.T. Snow RC .75 .23
610 Pat Gomez RC .15 .04
611 Phil Hiatt .15 .04
612 Alex Arias .15 .04
613 Kevin Rogers .15 .04
614 Al Martin .15 .04
615 Greg Gohr .15 .04
616 Graeme Lloyd RC .30 .09
617 Kent Bottenfield .15 .04
618 Chuck Carr .15 .04
619 Darrell Sherman RC .15 .04
620 Mike Lansing RC .30 .09

1993 Pinnacle Expansion Opening Day

This nine-card standard-size dual-sided set was issued to commemorate openning day for the two 1993 expansion teams, the Colorado Rockies and the Florida Marlins. The cards were inserted on top of sealed series two hobby boxes. These cards were also available through a mail-in offer. An anti-counterfeit device is printed in the bottom black border. The backs carry the same design as the fronts with a player from the Rockies appearing on one side and a Marlin's player on the flip side. The cards are numbered on both sides.

Nm-Mt Ex-Mt
COMPLETE SET (9) 25.00 7.50
1 Charlie Hough 5.00 1.50
David Nied
2 Benito Santiago 5.00 1.50
Joe Girardi
3 Orestes Destrade 5.00 1.50
Andres Galarraga
4 Bret Barberie 2.50 .75
Eric Young
5 Dave Magadan 2.50 .75
Charlie Hayes
6 Walt Weiss 2.50 .75
Freddie Benavides
7 Jeff Conine 5.00 1.50
Jerald Clark
8 Scott Pose 2.50 .75
Alex Cole
9 Junior Felix 5.00 1.50
Dante Bichette

1993 Pinnacle Rookie Team Pinnacle

Cards from this 10-card standard-size set were randomly inserted into one in every 90 series two foil packs and each features an American League rookie on one side and a National League rookie on the other. Each double-sided card displays paintings by artist Christopher Greco encased by a bold black border. The cards are numbered on the front and back.

Nm-Mt Ex-Mt
COMPLETE SET (10) 100.00 30.00
1 Pedro Martinez 15.00 4.50
Mike Trombley
2 Kevin Rogers 5.00 1.50
Sterling Hitchcock
3 Mike Piazza 25.00 7.50
Jesse Levis
4 Ryan Klesko 8.00 2.40
J.T. Snow
5 John Patterson 10.00 3.00
Bret Boone
6 Kevin Young 5.00 1.50
Domingo Martinez
7 Wil Cordero 5.00 1.50
Manny Alexander
8 Steve Hosey 10.00 3.00
Tim Salmon
9 Ryan Thompson 5.00 1.50
Gerald Williams
10 Melvin Nieves 5.00 1.50
David Hulse

1993 Pinnacle Slugfest

These 30 standard-size cards salute baseball's top hitters and were inserted one per series two jumbo superpacks.

Nm-Mt Ex-Mt
COMPLETE SET (30) 60.00 18.00
1 Juan Gonzalez 4.00 1.20
2 Mark McGwire 10.00 3.00
3 Cecil Fielder 1.50 .45
4 Joe Carter 1.50 .45
5 Fred McGriff 2.50 .75
6 Barry Bonds 10.00 3.00
7 Gary Sheffield 1.50 .45
8 Dave Hollins .75 .23
9 Frank Thomas 4.00 1.20
10 Danny Tartabull .75 .23
11 Albert Belle 1.50 .45
12 Ruben Sierra .75 .23
13 Larry Walker 2.50 .75
14 Jeff Bagwell 2.50 .75
15 David Justice 1.50 .45
16 Kirby Puckett 4.00 1.20
17 John Kruk 1.50 .45
18 Howard Johnson .75 .23
19 Darryl Strawberry 2.50 .75
20 Will Clark 4.00 1.20
21 Kevin Mitchell .75 .23
22 Mickey Tettleton .75 .23
23 Don Mattingly 10.00 3.00
24 Jose Canseco 4.00 1.20
25 George Bell .75 .23
26 Andre Dawson 1.50 .45
27 Ryne Sandberg 6.00 1.80
28 Ken Griffey Jr. 6.00 1.80
29 Carlos Baerga .75 .23
30 Travis Fryman 1.50 .45

1993 Pinnacle Team 2001

This 30-card standard-size set salutes players expected to be stars in the year 2001. The cards were inserted one per pack in first series jumbo superpacks and feature color player action shots on their fronts.

Nm-Mt Ex-Mt
COMPLETE SET (30) 40.00 12.00
1 Wil Cordero .75 .23
2 Cal Eldred .75 .23
3 Mike Mussina 4.00 1.20
4 Chuck Knoblauch 1.50 .45
5 Melvin Nieves .75 .23
6 Tim Wakefield 1.50 .45
7 Carlos Baerga .75 .23
8 Bret Boone 2.50 .75
9 Jeff Bagwell 2.50 .75
10 Travis Fryman 1.50 .45
11 Royce Clayton .75 .23
12 Delino DeShields .75 .23
13 Juan Gonzalez 4.00 1.20
14 Pedro Martinez 8.00 2.40
15 Bernie Williams 2.50 .75
16 Billy Ashley .75 .23
17 Marquis Grissom .75 .23
18 Kenny Lofton 1.50 .45
19 Ray Lankford .75 .23
20 Tim Salmon 2.50 .75
21 Steve Hosey .75 .23
22 Charles Nagy .75 .23
23 Dave Fleming .75 .23
24 Reggie Sanders 1.50 .45
25 Sam Militello .75 .23
26 Eric Karros 1.50 .45
27 Ryan Klesko 1.50 .45
28 Dean Palmer 1.50 .45
29 Ivan Rodriguez 4.00 1.20
30 Sterling Hitchcock 1.50 .45

1993 Pinnacle Team Pinnacle

Cards from this ten-card dual-sided set, featuring a selection of top stars paired of by position, were randomly inserted into one in every 24 first series foil packs. Each double-sided card displays paintings by artist Christopher Greco. A special bonus Team Pinnacle card (11) was available to collectors only through a mail-in offer for ten 1993 Pinnacle baseball wrappers plus 1.50 for shipping and handling. Moreover, hobby dealers who ordered Pinnacle received two bonus cards and an advertisement display promoting the offer.

Nm-Mt Ex-Mt
COMPLETE SET (10) 80.00 24.00
1 Greg Maddux 15.00 4.50
Mike Mussina
2 Tom Glavine 6.00 1.80
John Smiley
3 Darren Daulton 10.00 3.00
Ivan Rodriguez
4 Fred McGriff 10.00 3.00
Frank Thomas
5 Delino DeShields 2.00 .60
Carlos Baerga
6 Gary Sheffield 4.00 1.20
Edgar Martinez
7 Ozzie Smith 15.00 4.50
Pat Listach
8 Barry Bonds 25.00 7.50
Juan Gonzalez
9 Andy Van Slyke 10.00 3.00
Kirby Puckett
10 Larry Walker 6.00 1.80
Joe Carter
B11 Rob Dibble 2.00 .60
Rick Aguilera

1993 Pinnacle Tribute

Inserted in second-series packs at a rate of one in 24, these ten standard-size cards pay tribute to two recent retirees from baseball: George Brett (1-5), and Nolan Ryan (6-10). Score estimates that the chances of finding a tribute chase card are not less than one in 24 count good packs.

Nm-Mt Ex-Mt
COMPLETE SET (10) 60.00 18.00
COMMON BRETT (1-5) 5.00 1.50
COMMON RYAN (6-10) 10.00 3.00

1993 Pinnacle Cooperstown Card Promos

These cards were issued to promote the Cooperstown Card set released by Pinnacle in 1993. These cards are identical to the regular Cooperstown set except for the word "Promo" in big black letter across the back.

Nm-Mt Ex-Mt
COMPLETE SET 10.00 3.00
P11 Andre Dawson Promo 2.00 .60
P27 Eddie Murray Promo 3.00 .90
P30 Mark McGwire Promo 5.00 1.50

1993 Pinnacle Cooperstown

This 30-card standard-size set features full-bleed color player photos of possible future HOF inductees. Promo cards of Andre Dawson, Mark McGwire and Eddie Murray were issued to preview the series.

Nm-Mt Ex-Mt
COMP.FACT SET (30) 10.00 3.00
DUFEX: 40X TO 80X BASIC CARDS ....
1 Nolan Ryan 3.00 .90
2 George Brett 1.50 .45
3 Robin Yount .75 .23
4 Carlton Fisk .75 .23
5 Dale Murphy .30 .09
6 Dennis Eckersley .75 .23
7 Rickey Henderson 1.00 .30
8 Ryne Sandberg .75 .23
9 Ozzie Smith .75 .23
10 Dave Winfield .60 .18
11 Andre Dawson .50 .15
12 Kirby Puckett .50 .15
13 Wade Boggs 1.00 .30
14 Don Mattingly 1.50 .45
15 Barry Bonds 1.50 .45
16 Will Clark .40 .12
17 Cal Ripken 3.00 .90
18 Roger Clemens 1.50 .45
19 Dwight Gooden .20 .06
20 Tony Gwynn 1.50 .45
21 Joe Carter .20 .06
22 Ken Griffey Jr. 2.00 .60
23 Paul Molitor .75 .23
24 Frank Thomas 1.00 .30
25 Juan Gonzalez .50 .15
26 Barry Larkin .40 .12
27 Eddie Murray .50 .15
28 Cecil Fielder .10 .03
29 Roberto Alomar .40 .12
30 Mark McGwire 2.50 .75

1993 Pinnacle DiMaggio

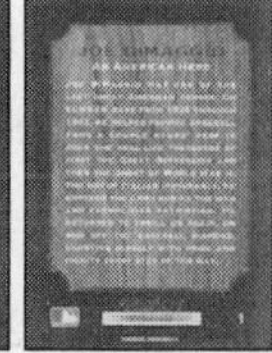

This 30-card standard-size set commemorates the life and career of Joe DiMaggio. Production was limited to 209,000 sets, with each set packaged in a black and gold collector's tin that features a color picture of DiMaggio. A certificate of authenticity card is also included that carries the production number of the set. DiMaggio also signed 9,000 cards for this set. One of 9,000 autographed cards from a special five-card set were randomly inserted into 30-card boxed hobby sets of 1993 Pinnacle Joe DiMaggio.

Nm-Mt Ex-Mt
COMP. FACT SET (30) 20.00 6.00
COMMON CARD (1-30) .75 .23
11 Joe DiMaggio 2.00 .60
Bob Feller
Rapid Robert Feller
vs. Joltin' Joe
21 Joe DiMaggio 1.00 .30
Joe McCarthy MG

1993 Pinnacle DiMaggio Autographs

Joe DiMaggio personally signed a total of 9,000 cards, and one autographed card from this five-card set was randomly inserted in selected 30-card boxed 1993 Pinnacle Joe DiMaggio hobby sets. These five autographed cards are slightly smaller (narrower) than standard size and feature white-bordered black-and-white action shots from DiMaggio's career that place special emphasis on the skills that made him great. DiMaggio's signature appears below the photo within the wide white lower margin.

Nm-Mt Ex-Mt
COMPLETE SET (5) 1000.00 300.00
COMMON CARD (1-5) 200.00 60.00

1993 Pinnacle Home Run Club

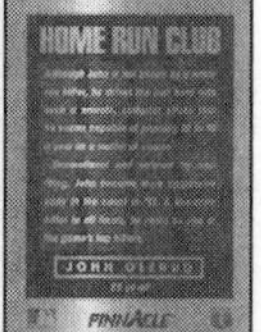

This 48-card boxed standard-size set features players with outstanding home run statistics. Each set contains a certificate of authenticity card that verifies the set is one of 200,000 sets produced and includes the set number printed on a white bar. The checklist is printed on an outer sleeve that encases the black hinged box.

Nm-Mt Ex-Mt
COMP. FACT SET (48) 25.00 7.50
1 Juan Gonzalez 1.25 .35
2 Fred McGriff .75 .23
3 Cecil Fielder .50 .15
4 Barry Bonds 2.50 .75
5 Albert Belle .50 .15
6 Gary Sheffield 1.25 .35
7 Joe Carter .50 .15
8 Mark McGwire 4.00 1.20
9 Darren Daulton .50 .15
10 Jose Canseco 1.25 .35
11 Dave Hollins .25 .07
12 Ryne Sandberg 2.00 .60
13 Ken Griffey Jr. 3.00 .90
14 Larry Walker .50 .15
15 Rob Deer .25 .07
16 Andre Dawson .75 .23
17 Frank Thomas 1.25 .35
18 Mickey Tettleton .25 .07
19 Charlie Hayes .25 .07
20 Ron Gant .25 .07
21 Rickey Henderson 1.50 .45
22 Matt Williams .75 .23
23 Kevin Mitchell .50 .15
24 Robin Ventura 1.00 .30
25 Dean Palmer .50 .15
26 Mike Piazza 3.00 .90
27 J.T. Snow 1.00 .30
28 Jeff Bagwell 1.25 .35
29 John Olerud .75 .23
30 Greg Vaughn .50 .15
31 Dave Justice 1.00 .30
32 Dave Winfield 1.25 .35
33 Danny Tartabull .25 .07
34 Eric Anthony .25 .07
35 Eddie Murray 1.25 .35
36 Jay Buhner .50 .15
37 Derek Bell .25 .07
38 Will Clark 1.00 .30
39 Carlos Baerga .50 .15
40 Mo Vaughn .50 .15
41 Bobby Bonilla .25 .07
42 Tim Salmon .75 .23
43 Bo Jackson 1.00 .30
44 Howard Johnson .25 .07
45 Kent Hrbek .50 .15
46 Ruben Sierra .50 .15
47 Cal Ripken 5.00 1.50
48 Travis Fryman .50 .15

1994 Pinnacle Samples

Sealed in a cello pack, these ten-or 11-card standard-size sample groups were issued to preview the new design of the 1994 Pinnacle baseball set. Both sides of the cards have "SAMPLE" stenciled across them. The ten-card set was the retail version whereas the 11-card set was for the hobby. The hobby and retail versions are only distinguishable after opening by "Hobby Edition" or "Retail Edition" printed on the title card and the inclusion of an eleventh card, Paul Molitor in the hobby samples set. The cards are numbered in a baseball icon at the upper right. Also a two-card sample strip consisting of Olerud and Alou cards was issued.

Nm-Mt Ex-Mt
COMPLETE SET (12) 8.00 2.40
2 Carlos Baerga .50 .15
3 Sammy Sosa 2.50 .75
5 John Olerud .50 .15
7 Moises Alou .50 .15
8 Steve Avery .25 .07
10 Cecil Fielder .50 .15
11 Greg Maddux 3.00 .90
269 Jeff Granger .25 .07
TR1 Paul Molitor 1.50 .45
Tribute
NNO Title card .25 .07
Hobby Edition
(Pinnacle ad)
NNO Title card .25 .07
Retail Edition
(Pinnacle ad)
NNO Jeff Granger .75 .23
1994 Museum Collection

1994 Pinnacle

The 540-card 1994 Pinnacle standard-size set was issued in two series of 270. Cards were issued in hobby and retail foil-wrapped packs. The card fronts feature full-bleed color action player photos with a small foil logo and players name at the base. Subsets include Rookie Prospects (224-261) and Draft Picks (262-270/430-438). Notable Rookie Cards include Trot Nixon, Chan Ho Park and Billy Wagner. A Carlos Delgado Super Rookie one shot insert was put into packs at a rate of one in 360. It is labeled SR1 and is listed at the end of the set.

Nm-Mt Ex-Mt
COMPLETE SET (540) 20.00 6.00
COMP. SERIES 1 (270) 10.00 3.00
COMP. SERIES 2 (270) 10.00 3.00
1 Frank Thomas .50 .15
2 Carlos Baerga .10 .03
3 Sammy Sosa .75 .23
4 Tony Gwynn .60 .18
5 John Olerud .20 .06
6 Ryne Sandberg .75 .23
7 Moises Alou .20 .06
8 Steve Avery .10 .03
9 Tim Salmon .30 .09
10 Cecil Fielder .20 .06
11 Greg Maddux .75 .23
12 Barry Larkin .50 .15
13 Mike Devereaux .10 .03
14 Charlie Hayes .10 .03
15 Albert Belle .20 .06
16 Andy Van Slyke .20 .06
17 Mo Vaughn .20 .06
18 Brian McRae .10 .03
19 Cal Eldred .10 .03
20 Craig Biggio .30 .09
21 Kirby Puckett .50 .15
22 Derek Bell .10 .03
23 Don Mattingly 1.25 .35
24 John Burkett .10 .03
25 Roger Clemens 1.00 .30
26 Barry Bonds 1.25 .35
27 Paul Molitor .30 .09
28 Mike Piazza 1.00 .30
29 Robin Ventura .20 .06
30 Jeff Conine .20 .06
31 Wade Boggs .30 .09
32 Dennis Eckersley .20 .06
33 Bobby Bonilla .20 .06
34 Lenny Dykstra .20 .06
35 Manny Alexander .10 .03
36 Ray Lankford .10 .03
37 Greg Vaughn .20 .06
38 Chuck Finley .20 .06
39 Todd Benzinger .10 .03
40 Dave Justice .20 .06
41 Rob Dibble .20 .06
42 Tom Henke .10 .03
43 David Nied .10 .03
44 Sandy Alomar Jr. .10 .03
45 Pete Harnisch .10 .03
46 Jeff Russell .10 .03
47 Terry Mulholland .10 .03
48 Kevin Appier .20 .06
49 Randy Tomlin .10 .03
50 Cal Ripken Jr. 1.50 .45
51 Andy Benes .10 .03
52 Jimmy Key .20 .06
53 Kirt Manwaring .10 .03
54 Kevin Tapani .10 .03
55 Jose Guzman .10 .03
56 Todd Stottlemyre .10 .03
57 Jack McDowell .10 .03
58 Orel Hershiser .20 .06
59 Chris Hammond .10 .03
60 Chris Nabholz .10 .03
61 Ruben Sierra .10 .03
62 Dwight Gooden .30 .09
63 John Kruk .20 .06
64 Omar Vizquel .20 .06
65 Tim Naehring .10 .03
66 Dwight Smith .10 .03
67 Mickey Tettleton .10 .03
68 J.T. Snow .20 .06
69 Greg McMichael .10 .03
70 Kevin Mitchell .10 .03
71 Kevin Brown .20 .06
72 Scott Cooper .10 .03
73 Jim Thome .50 .15
74 Joe Girardi .10 .03
75 Eric Anthony .10 .03
76 Orlando Merced .10 .03
77 Felix Jose .10 .03
78 Tommy Greene .10 .03
79 Bernard Gilkey .10 .03
80 Phil Plantier .10 .03
81 Danny Tartabull .10 .03
82 Trevor Wilson .10 .03
83 Chuck Knoblauch .20 .06
84 Rick Wilkins .10 .03
85 Devon White .10 .03
86 Lance Johnson .10 .03
87 Eric Karros .20 .06
88 Gary Sheffield .20 .06
89 Wil Cordero .10 .03
90 Ron Darling .10 .03
91 Darren Daulton .20 .06
92 Joe Orsulak .10 .03
93 Steve Cooke .10 .03
94 Darryl Hamilton .10 .03
95 Aaron Sele .10 .03
96 John Doherty .10 .03
97 Gary DiSarcina .10 .03
98 Jeff Blauser .10 .03
99 John Smiley .10 .03
100 Ken Griffey Jr. .75 .23
101 Dean Palmer .20 .06
102 Felix Fermin .10 .03
103 Jerald Clark .10 .03
104 Doug Drabek .10 .03
105 Curt Schilling .30 .09
106 Jeff Montgomery .10 .03
107 Rene Arocha .10 .03
108 Carlos Garcia .10 .03
109 Wally Whitehurst .10 .03
110 Jim Abbott .30 .09
111 Royce Clayton .10 .03
112 Chris Hoiles .10 .03
113 Mike Morgan .10 .03
114 Joe Magrane .10 .03
115 Tom Candiotti .10 .03
116 Ron Karkovice .10 .03
117 Ryan Bowen .10 .03
118 Rod Beck .10 .03
119 John Wetteland .20 .06
120 Terry Steinbach .10 .03
121 Dave Hollins .10 .03
122 Jeff Kent .20 .06
123 Ricky Bones .10 .03
124 Brian Jordan .20 .06
125 Chad Kreuter .10 .03
126 John Valentin .10 .03
127 Hilly Hathaway .10 .03
128 Wilson Alvarez .10 .03
129 Tino Martinez .30 .09
130 Rodney Bolton .10 .03
131 David Segui .10 .03
132 Wayne Kirby .10 .03
133 Eric Young .10 .03
134 Scott Servais .10 .03
135 Scott Radinsky .10 .03
136 Bret Barberie .10 .03
137 John Roper .10 .03
138 Ricky Gutierrez .10 .03
139 Bernie Williams .30 .09
140 Bud Black .10 .03
141 Jose Vizcaino .10 .03
142 Gerald Williams .10 .03
143 Duane Ward .10 .03
144 Danny Jackson .10 .03
145 Allen Watson .10 .03
146 Scott Fletcher .10 .03
147 Delino DeShields .10 .03
148 Shane Mack .10 .03
149 Jim Eisenreich .10 .03
150 Troy Neel .10 .03
151 Jay Bell .20 .06
152 B.J. Surhoff .20 .06
153 Mark Whiten .10 .03
154 Mike Henneman .10 .03
155 Todd Hundley .10 .03
156 Greg Myers .10 .03
157 Ryan Klesko .20 .06
158 Dave Fleming .10 .03
159 Mickey Morandini .10 .03
160 Blas Minor .10 .03
161 Reggie Jefferson .10 .03
162 David Hulse .10 .03
163 Greg Swindell .10 .03
164 Roberto Hernandez .10 .03
165 Brady Anderson .20 .06
166 Jack Armstrong .10 .03
167 Phil Clark .10 .03
168 Melido Perez .10 .03
169 Darren Lewis .10 .03
170 Sam Horn .10 .03
171 Mike Harkey .10 .03
172 Juan Guzman .10 .03
173 Bob Natal .10 .03
174 Deion Sanders .30 .09
175 Carlos Quintana .10 .03
176 Mel Rojas .10 .03
177 Willie Banks .10 .03
178 Ben Rivera .10 .03
179 Kenny Lofton .20 .06
180 Leo Gomez .10 .03
181 Roberto Mejia .10 .03
182 Mike Perez .10 .03
183 Travis Fryman .20 .06
184 Ben McDonald .10 .03
185 Steve Frey .10 .03
186 Kevin Young .10 .03
187 Dave Magadan .10 .03
188 Bobby Munoz .10 .03
189 Pat Rapp .10 .03
190 Jose Offerman .10 .03
191 Vinny Castilla .20 .06
192 Ivan Calderon .10 .03
193 Ken Caminiti .20 .06
194 Benji Gil .10 .03
195 Chuck Carr .10 .03
196 Derrick May .10 .03
197 Pat Kelly .10 .03
198 Jeff Brantley .10 .03
199 Jose Lind .10 .03
200 Steve Buechele .10 .03
201 Wes Chamberlain .10 .03
202 Eduardo Perez .10 .03
203 Bret Saberhagen .20 .06
204 Gregg Jefferies .10 .03
205 Darrin Fletcher .10 .03
206 Kent Hrbek .20 .06
207 Kim Batiste .10 .03
208 Jeff King .10 .03
209 Donovan Osborne .10 .03
210 Dave Nilsson .10 .03
211 Al Martin .10 .03
212 Mike Moore .10 .03
213 Sterling Hitchcock .10 .03
214 Geronimo Pena .10 .03
215 Kevin Higgins .10 .03
216 Norm Charlton .10 .03
217 Don Slaught .10 .03
218 Mitch Williams .10 .03
219 Derek Lilliquist .10 .03
220 Armando Reynoso .10 .03
221 Kenny Rogers .20 .06
222 Doug Jones .10 .03
223 Luis Aquino .10 .03
224 Mike Oquist .10 .03
225 Darryl Scott .10 .03
226 Kurt Abbott RC .25 .07
227 Andy Tomberlin .10 .03
228 Norberto Martin .10 .03
229 Pedro Castellano .10 .03
230 Curtis Pride RC .25 .07
231 Jeff McNeely .10 .03
232 Scott Lydy .10 .03
233 Darren Oliver RC .25 .07
234 Danny Bautista .10 .03
235 Butch Huskey .10 .03
236 Chipper Jones .50 .15
237 Eddie Zambrano RC .10 .03
238 Domingo Jean .10 .03
239 Javier Lopez .20 .06
240 Nigel Wilson .10 .03
241 Drew Denson .10 .03
242 Raul Mondesi .20 .06
243 Luis Ortiz .10 .03
244 Manny Ramirez .30 .09
245 Greg Blosser .10 .03
246 Rondell White .20 .06
247 Steve Karsay .10 .03
248 Scott Stahoviak .10 .03
249 Jose Valentin .10 .03
250 Marc Newfield .10 .03
251 Keith Kessinger .10 .03
252 Carl Everett .20 .06
253 John O'Donoghue .10 .03
254 Turk Wendell .10 .03
255 Scott Ruffcorn .10 .03
256 Tony Tarasco .10 .03
257 Andy Cook .10 .03
258 Matt Mieske .10 .03
259 Luis Lopez .10 .03
260 Ramon Caraballo .10 .03
261 Salomon Torres .10 .03
262 Brooks Kieschnick RC .25 .07
263 Daron Kirkreit .10 .03
264 Bill Wagner RC .50 .15
265 Matt Drews RC .10 .03
266 Scott Christman RC .10 .03
267 Torii Hunter RC 2.00 .60
268 Jamey Wright RC .10 .03
269 Jeff Granger .10 .03
270 Trot Nixon RC .50 .15
271 Randy Myers .10 .03
272 Trevor Hoffman .20 .06
273 Bob Wickman .10 .03
274 Willie McGee .20 .06
275 Hipolito Pichardo .10 .03
276 Bobby Witt .10 .03
277 Gregg Olson .10 .03
278 Randy Johnson .50 .15
279 Robb Nen .20 .06
280 Paul O'Neill .30 .09
281 Lou Whitaker .20 .06
282 Chad Curtis .10 .03
283 Doug Henry .10 .03
284 Tom Glavine .30 .09
285 Mike Greenwell .10 .03
286 Roberto Kelly .10 .03
287 Roberto Alomar .50 .15
288 Charlie Hough .20 .06
289 Alex Fernandez .10 .03
290 Jeff Bagwell .30 .09
291 Wally Joyner .20 .06
292 Andujar Cedeno .10 .03
293 Rick Aguilera .10 .03
294 Darryl Strawberry .30 .09
295 Mike Mussina .50 .15
296 Jeff Gardner .10 .03
297 Chris Gwynn .10 .03
298 Matt Williams .20 .06
299 Brent Gates .10 .03
300 Mark McGwire 1.25 .35
301 Jim Deshaies .10 .03
302 Edgar Martinez .30 .09
303 Danny Darwin .10 .03
304 Pat Meares .10 .03
305 Benito Santiago .20 .06
306 Jose Canseco .50 .15
307 Jim Gott .10 .03
308 Paul Sorrento .10 .03
309 Scott Kamieniecki .10 .03
310 Larry Walker .30 .09
311 Mark Langston .10 .03
312 John Jaha .10 .03
313 Stan Javier .10 .03
314 Hal Morris .10 .03
315 Robby Thompson .10 .03
316 Pat Hentgen .10 .03
317 Tom Gordon .10 .03
318 Joey Cora .10 .03
319 Luis Alicea .10 .03
320 Andre Dawson .20 .06
321 Darryl Kile .20 .06
322 Jose Rijo .10 .03
323 Luis Gonzalez .20 .06
324 Billy Ashley .10 .03
325 David Cone .20 .06
326 Bill Swift .10 .03
327 Phil Hiatt .10 .03
328 Craig Paquette .10 .03
329 Bob Welch .10 .03
330 Tony Phillips .10 .03
331 Archi Cianfrocco .10 .03
332 Dave Winfield .20 .06
333 David McCarty .10 .03
334 Al Leiter .20 .06
335 Tom Browning .10 .03
336 Mark Grace .30 .09
337 Jose Mesa .10 .03
338 Mike Stanley .10 .03
339 Roger McDowell .10 .03
340 Damion Easley .10 .03
341 Angel Miranda .10 .03
342 John Smoltz .30 .09
343 Jay Buhner .20 .06
344 Bryan Harvey .10 .03
345 Joe Carter .20 .06
346 Dante Bichette .20 .06
347 Jason Bere .10 .03
348 Frank Viola .20 .06
349 Ivan Rodriguez .50 .15
350 Juan Gonzalez .50 .15
351 Steve Finley .20 .06
352 Mike Felder .10 .03
353 Ramon Martinez .10 .03
354 Greg Gagne .10 .03
355 Ken Hill .10 .03
356 Pedro Munoz .10 .03
357 Todd Van Poppel .10 .03
358 Marquis Grissom .10 .03
359 Milt Cuyler .10 .03
360 Reggie Sanders .20 .06
361 Scott Erickson .10 .03
362 Billy Hatcher .10 .03
363 Gene Harris .10 .03
364 Rene Gonzales .10 .03
365 Kevin Rogers .10 .03
366 Eric Plunk .10 .03
367 Todd Zeile .10 .03
368 John Franco .20 .06
369 Brett Butler .20 .06
370 Bill Spiers .10 .03
371 Terry Pendleton .20 .06
372 Chris Bosio .10 .03
373 Orestes Destrade .10 .03
374 Dave Stewart .20 .06
375 Darren Holmes .10 .03
376 Doug Strange .10 .03
377 Brian Turang .10 .03
378 Carl Willis .10 .03
379 Mark McLemore .10 .03
380 Bobby Jones .10 .03
381 Scott Sanders .10 .03
382 Kirk Rueter .20 .06
383 Randy Velarde .10 .03
384 Fred McGriff .30 .09
385 Charles Nagy .10 .03
386 Rich Amaral .10 .03
387 Geronimo Berroa .10 .03
388 Eric Davis .20 .06
389 Ozzie Smith .75 .23
390 Alex Arias .10 .03
391 Brad Ausmus .10 .03
392 Cliff Floyd .10 .03
393 Roger Salkeld .10 .03
394 Jim Edmonds .30 .09
395 Jeromy Burnitz .20 .06
396 Dave Staton .10 .03
397 Rob Butler .10 .03
398 Marcos Armas .10 .03
399 Darrell Whitmore .10 .03
400 Ryan Thompson .10 .03
401 Ross Powell RC .10 .03
402 Joe Oliver .10 .03
403 Paul Carey .10 .03
404 Bob Hamelin .10 .03
405 Chris Turner .10 .03
406 Nate Minchey .10 .03
407 Lonnie Maclin RC .10 .03
408 Harold Baines .20 .06
409 Brian Williams .10 .03
410 Johnny Ruffin .10 .03
411 Julian Tavarez RC .10 .03
412 Mark Hutton .10 .03
413 Carlos Delgado .30 .09
414 Chris Gomez .10 .03
415 Mike Hampton .20 .06
416 Alex Diaz RC .10 .03
417 Jeffrey Hammonds .10 .03
418 Jayhawk Owens .10 .03
419 J.R. Phillips .10 .03
420 Cory Bailey RC .10 .03
421 Denny Hocking .10 .03
422 Jon Shave .10 .03
423 Damon Buford .10 .03
424 Troy O'Leary .10 .03
425 Tripp Cromer .10 .03
426 Albie Lopez .10 .03
427 Tony Fernandez .10 .03
428 Ozzie Guillen .10 .03
429 Alan Trammell .30 .09
430 John Wasdin RC .10 .03
431 Marc Valdes .10 .03
432 Brian Anderson RC .25 .07
433 Matt Brunson RC .10 .03
434 Wayne Gomes RC .10 .03
435 Jay Powell RC .10 .03
436 Kirk Presley RC .10 .03
437 Jon Ratliff RC .10 .03
438 Derrek Lee RC .60 .18
439 Tom Pagnozzi .10 .03
440 Kent Mercker .10 .03
441 Phil Leftwich RC .10 .03
442 Jamie Moyer .20 .06
443 John Flaherty .10 .03
444 Mark Wohlers .10 .03
445 Jose Bautista .10 .03
446 Andres Galarraga .20 .06
447 Mark Lemke .10 .03
448 Tim Wakefield .20 .06
449 Pat Listach .10 .03
450 Rickey Henderson .50 .15
451 Mike Gallego .10 .03
452 Bob Tewksbury .10 .03
453 Kirk Gibson .20 .06
454 Pedro Astacio .10 .03
455 Mike Lansing .10 .03
456 Sean Berry .10 .03
457 Bob Walk .10 .03
458 Chili Davis .20 .06
459 Ed Sprague .10 .03
460 Kevin Stocker .10 .03
461 Mike Stanton .10 .03
462 Tim Raines .20 .06
463 Mike Bordick .10 .03
464 David Wells .20 .06
465 Tim Laker .10 .03
466 Cory Snyder .10 .03
467 Alex Cole .10 .03
468 Pete Incaviglia .10 .03
469 Roger Pavlik .10 .03
470 Greg W. Harris .10 .03
471 Xavier Hernandez .10 .03
472 Erik Hanson .10 .03
473 Jesse Orosco .10 .03
474 Greg Colbrunn .10 .03
475 Harold Reynolds .20 .06
476 Greg A. Harris .10 .03
477 Pat Borders .10 .03
478 Melvin Nieves .10 .03
479 Mariano Duncan .10 .03
480 Greg Hibbard .10 .03
481 Tim Pugh .10 .03
482 Bobby Ayala .10 .03
483 Sid Fernandez .10 .03
484 Tim Wallach .10 .03
485 Randy Milligan .10 .03
486 Walt Weiss .10 .03
487 Matt Walbeck .10 .03
488 Mike Macfarlane .10 .03
489 Jerry Browne .10 .03
490 Chris Sabo .10 .03
491 Tim Belcher .10 .03
492 Spike Owen .10 .03
493 Rafael Palmeiro .30 .09
494 Brian Harper .10 .03
495 Eddie Murray .50 .15
496 Ellis Burks .20 .06
497 Karl Rhodes .10 .03
498 Otis Nixon .10 .03
499 Lee Smith .20 .06
500 Bip Roberts .10 .03
501 Pedro Martinez .50 .15
502 Brian Hunter .10 .03
503 Tyler Green .10 .03
504 Bruce Hurst .10 .03
505 Alex Gonzalez .10 .03
506 Mark Portugal .10 .03
507 Bob Ojeda .10 .03
508 Dave Henderson .10 .03
509 Bo Jackson .50 .15
510 Bret Boone .20 .06
511 Mark Eichhorn .10 .03
512 Luis Polonia .10 .03
513 Will Clark .50 .15
514 Dave Valle .10 .03
515 Dan Wilson .10 .03
516 Dennis Martinez .20 .06
517 Jim Leyritz .10 .03
518 Howard Johnson .10 .03
519 Jody Reed .10 .03
520 Julio Franco .20 .06
521 Jeff Reardon .20 .06
522 Willie Greene .10 .03
523 Shawon Dunston .10 .03
524 Keith Mitchell .10 .03
525 Rick Helling .10 .03
526 Mark Kiefer .10 .03
527 Chan Ho Park RC .50 .15
528 Tony Longmire .10 .03
529 Rich Becker .10 .03
530 Tim Hyers RC .10 .03
531 Darrin Jackson .10 .03
532 Jack Morris .20 .06
533 Rick White .10 .03
534 Mike Kelly .10 .03
535 James Mouton .10 .03
536 Steve Trachsel .10 .03

537 Tony Eusebio .10 .03
538 Kelly Stinnett RC .25 .07
539 Paul Spoljaric .10 .03
540 Darren Dreifort .10 .03
SR1 Carlos Delgado 5.00 1.50
Super Rookie

1994 Pinnacle Artist's Proofs

Randomly inserted at a rate of one in 26 hobby and retail packs, cards from this 540-card set parallel that of the basic Pinnacle issue. Each card is embossed with a gold-foil-stamped "Artist's Proof" logo just above the player name. The Pinnacle logo is also done in gold foil. Just 1,000 of each card were printed although none are serial numbered.

Nm-Mt Ex-Mt
*STARS: 10X TO 25X BASIC CARDS..
*ROOKIES: 5X TO 12X BASIC CARDS

1994 Pinnacle Museum Collection

This 540-card set is a parallel dufex to that of the basic Pinnacle issue. They were randomly inserted at a rate of one in four hobby and retail packs. A Museum Collection logo replaces the anti-counterfeit device. Only 6,500 of each card were printed. Five cards (numbers 279, 313, 328, 382 and 387) were available only by mailing in a redemption card randomly seeded into packs. Due to a low response of mailing, these five cards are now by far the toughest cards to find in the set.

Nm-Mt Ex-Mt
*STARS: 2.5X TO 6X BASIC CARDS...
*ROOKIES: 2X TO 5X BASIC CARDS..
279 Robb Nen TRADE 25.00 7.50
313 Stan Javier TRADE 15.00 4.50
328 Craig Paquette TRADE 15.00 4.50
382 Kirk Rueter TRADE 25.00 7.50
387 G.Berroa TRADE 15.00 4.50

1994 Pinnacle Rookie Team Pinnacle

These nine double-front standard-size cards of the "Rookie Team Pinnacle" set feature a top AL and a top NL rookie prospect by position. The insertion rate for these is one per 48 first series packs. These special portrait cards were painted by artists Christopher Greco and Ron DeFelice. The front features the National League player and card number. Both sides contain a gold Rookie Team Pinnacle logo.

Nm-Mt Ex-Mt
COMPLETE SET (9) 60.00 18.00
1 Carlos Delgado 8.00 2.40
Javier Lopez
2 Bob Hamelin 4.00 1.20
J.R. Phillips
3 Jon Shave 4.00 1.20
Keith Kessinger
4 Luis Ortiz 4.00 1.20
Butch Huskey
5 Kurt Abbott 10.00 3.00
Chipper Jones
6 Manny Ramirez 8.00 2.40
Rondell White
7 Jeffrey Hammonds 6.00 1.80
Cliff Floyd
8 Marc Newfield 4.00 1.20
Nigel Wilson
9 Mark Hutton 4.00 1.20
Salomon Torres

1994 Pinnacle Run Creators

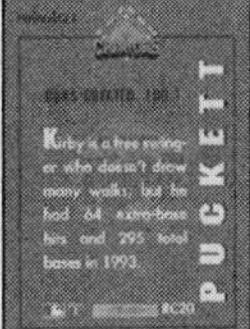

Randomly inserted in either series Pinnacle packs at an approximate rate of one in four jumbo packs, this 44-card standard-size set spotlights top run producers.

Nm-Mt Ex-Mt
COMPLETE SET (44) 80.00 24.00
COMPLETE SERIES 1 (22) 50.00 15.00
COMPLETE SERIES 2 (22) 30.00 9.00
RC1 John Olerud 1.00 .30
RC2 Frank Thomas 2.50 .75
RC3 Ken Griffey Jr. 4.00 1.20
RC4 Paul Molitor 1.50 .45
RC5 Rafael Palmeiro 1.50 .45
RC6 Roberto Alomar 2.50 .75
RC7 Juan Gonzalez 2.50 .75
RC8 Albert Belle 1.00 .30
RC9 Travis Fryman 1.00 .30
RC10 Rickey Henderson 2.50 .75
RC11 Tony Phillips .50 .15
RC12 Mo Vaughn 1.00 .30
RC13 Tim Salmon 1.50 .45
RC14 Kenny Lofton 1.00 .30
RC15 Carlos Baerga .50 .15
RC16 Greg Vaughn 1.00 .30
RC17 Jay Buhner 1.00 .30
RC18 Chris Hoiles .50 .15
RC19 Mickey Tettleton .50 .15
RC20 Kirby Puckett 2.50 .75
RC21 Danny Tartabull .50 .15
RC22 Devon White .50 .15
RC23 Barry Bonds 6.00 1.80
RC24 Lenny Dykstra 1.00 .30
RC25 John Kruk 1.00 .30
RC26 Fred McGriff 1.50 .45
RC27 Gregg Jefferies .50 .15
RC28 Mike Piazza 5.00 1.50
RC29 Jeff Blauser .50 .15
RC30 Andres Galarraga 1.00 .30
RC31 Darren Daulton 1.00 .30
RC32 Dave Justice 1.00 .30
RC33 Craig Biggio 1.50 .45
RC34 Mark Grace 1.50 .45
RC35 Tony Gwynn 3.00 .90
RC36 Jeff Bagwell 1.50 .45
RC37 Jay Bell 1.00 .30
RC38 Marquis Grissom .50 .15
RC39 Matt Williams 1.00 .30
RC40 Charlie Hayes .50 .15
RC41 Dante Bichette 1.00 .30
RC42 Bernard Gilkey .50 .15
RC43 Brett Butler 1.00 .30
RC44 Rick Wilkins .50 .15

1994 Pinnacle Team Pinnacle

Identical in design to the Rookie Team Pinnacle set, these double-front cards feature top players from each of the nine positions. Randomly inserted in second series hobby and retail packs at a rate of one in 48, these special portrait cards were painted by artists Christopher Greco and Ron DeFelice. The front features the National League player and card number. Both sides contain a gold Team Pinnacle logo.

Nm-Mt Ex-Mt
COMPLETE SET (9) 100.00 30.00
1 Jeff Bagwell 6.00 1.80
Frank Thomas
2 Carlos Baerga 1.25 .35
Robby Thompson
3 Matt Williams 2.50 .75
Dean Palmer
4 Cal Ripken Jr. 20.00 6.00
Jay Bell
5 Ivan Rodriguez 12.00 3.60
Mike Piazza
6 Lenny Dykstra 10.00 3.00
Ken Griffey Jr.
7 Juan Gonzalez 15.00 4.50
Barry Bonds
8 Tim Salmon 2.50 .75
Dave Justice
9 Greg Maddux 10.00 3.00
Jack McDowell

1994 Pinnacle Tribute

Randomly inserted in hobby packs at a rate of one in 18, this 18-card set was issued in two series of nine. Showcasing some of the top superstar veterans, the fronts have a color player photo with "Tribute" up the left border in a black stripe.

Nm-Mt Ex-Mt
COMPLETE SET (18) 100.00 30.00
COMPLETE SERIES 1 (9) 30.00 9.00
COMPLETE SERIES 2 (9) 70.00 21.00
TR1 Paul Molitor 2.50 .75
TR2 Jim Abbott 2.50 .75
TR3 Dave Winfield 1.50 .45
TR4 Bo Jackson 4.00 1.20
TR5 David Justice 1.50 .45
TR6 Len Dykstra 1.50 .45
TR7 Mike Piazza 8.00 2.40
TR8 Barry Bonds 10.00 3.00
TR9 Randy Johnson 4.00 1.20
TR10 Ozzie Smith 6.00 1.80
TR11 Mark Whiten .75 .23
TR12 Greg Maddux 6.00 1.80
TR13 Cal Ripken Jr. 12.00 3.60
TR14 Frank Thomas 4.00 1.20
TR15 Juan Gonzalez 4.00 1.20
TR16 Roberto Alomar 4.00 1.20
TR17 Ken Griffey Jr. 6.00 1.80
TR18 Lee Smith 1.50 .45

1994 Pinnacle The Naturals

These 25 standard-size cards were issued as a boxed set and were printed with Pinnacle's Dufex process, which imparts a metallic appearance to the cards. A certificate of authenticity that carries the set's production number out of 100,000 produced was included with every boxed set.

Nm-Mt Ex-Mt
COMP. FACT SET (25) 10.00 3.00
1 Frank Thomas .75 .23
2 Barry Bonds 1.50 .45
3 Ken Griffey Jr. 2.00 .60
4 Juan Gonzalez .40 .12
5 David Justice .40 .12
6 Albert Belle .20 .06
7 Kenny Lofton .30 .09
8 Roberto Alomar .40 .12
9 Tim Salmon .40 .12
10 Randy Johnson .75 .23
11 Kirby Puckett .60 .18
12 Tony Gwynn 1.50 .45
13 Fred McGriff .30 .09
14 Ryne Sandberg 1.25 .35
15 Greg Maddux 2.00 .60
16 Matt Williams .30 .09
17 Lenny Dykstra .20 .06
18 Gary Sheffield .50 .15
19 Mike Piazza 2.50 .75
20 Dean Palmer .20 .06
21 Travis Fryman .20 .06
22 Carlos Baerga .20 .06
23 Cal Ripken 3.00 .90
24 John Olerud .30 .09
25 Roger Clemens 1.50 .45
P18 Gary Sheffield Promo 1.50 .45

1994 Pinnacle New Generation

This 25-card standard-size set spotlights 25 of the most prominent prospects to hit the major leagues. Just 100,000 sets were produced, and a certificate of authenticity carrying the set serial number was printed on the back of the display box. A Cliff Floyd promo card was distributed to dealers and hobby media to preview the set.

Nm-Mt Ex-Mt
COMP. FACT SET (25) 5.00 1.50
NG1 Tim Salmon .20 .06
NG2 Mike Piazza 2.00 .60
NG3 Jason Bere .05 .02
NG4 Jeffrey Hammonds .10 .03
NG5 Aaron Sele .10 .03
NG6 Salomon Torres .05 .02
NG7 Wilfredo Cordero .05 .02
NG8 Allen Watson .05 .02
NG9 J.T. Snow .10 .03
NG10 Cliff Floyd .15 .04
NG11 Jeff McNeely .05 .02
NG12 Butch Huskey .05 .02
NG13 J.R. Phillips .05 .02
NG14 Bobby Jones .05 .02
NG15 Javier Lopez .40 .12
NG16 Scott Ruffcorn .05 .02
NG17 Manny Ramirez .75 .23
NG18 Carlos Delgado .50 .15
NG19 Rondell White .10 .03
NG20 Chipper Jones 1.50 .45
NG21 Billy Ashley .05 .02
NG22 Nigel Wilson .05 .02
NG23 Jeromy Burnitz .10 .03
NG24 Danny Bautista .05 .02
NG25 Darrell Whitmore .05 .02
PNG10 Cliff Floyd 1.50 .45
Promo

1994 Pinnacle Power Surge

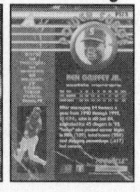

These 25 standard-size cards came in a boxed set from Pinnacle and feature on their fronts borderless color action shots. A Carlos Baerga promo card was distributed to dealers and hobby media to preview the set.

Nm-Mt Ex-Mt
COMP. FACT SET (25) 5.00 1.50
PS1 David Justice .20 .06
PS2 Chris Hoiles .05 .02
PS3 Mo Vaughn .10 .03
PS4 Tim Salmon .20 .06
PS5 J.T. Snow .10 .03
PS6 Frank Thomas .50 .15
PS7 Sammy Sosa 1.00 .30
PS8 Rick Wilkins .05 .02
PS9 Robin Ventura .20 .06
PS10 Reggie Sanders .05 .02
PS11 Albert Belle .10 .03
PS12 Carlos Baerga .10 .03
PS13 Manny Ramirez .50 .15
PS14 Travis Fryman .10 .03
PS15 Gary Sheffield .40 .12
PS16 Jeff Bagwell .50 .15
PS17 Mike Piazza 1.25 .35
PS18 Eric Karros .10 .03
PS19 Cliff Floyd .15 .04
PS20 Mark Whiten .05 .02
PS21 Phil Plantier .05 .02
PS22 Derek Bell .05 .02
PS23 Ken Griffey Jr. 1.25 .35
PS24 Juan Gonzalez .20 .06
PS25 Dean Palmer .10 .03
PS12P C. Baerga Promo .75 .23

1995 Pinnacle Samples

The 1995 Pinnacle Sample set contains nine standard-size cards. The samples are easily distinguished from their regular issue counterparts by zeros in the stat lines. Also the disclaimer "SAMPLE" is diagonally printed across the front and the back.

Nm-Mt Ex-Mt
COMPLETE SET (9) 10.00 3.00
16 Mickey Morandini .50 .15
119 Gary Sheffield 2.00 .60
122 Ivan Rodriguez 2.00 .60
132 Alex Rodriguez 6.00 1.80
208 Bo Jackson 1.50 .45
223 Jose Rijo .50 .15
224 Ryan Klesko .75 .23
US22 Wil Cordero .50 .15
NNO Title Card .50 .15

1995 Pinnacle

This 450-card standard-size set was issued in two series of 225 cards. They were released in 12-card packs, 24 packs to a box and 18 boxes in a case. The full-bleed fronts feature action photos. The player's last name is printed in black ink against a dramatic gold foil background at the base of the card. There are no notable Rookie Cards in this set.

Nm-Mt Ex-Mt
COMPLETE SET (450) 30.00 9.00
COMP. SERIES 1 (225) 15.00 4.50
COMP. SERIES 2 (225) 15.00 4.50
1 Jeff Bagwell .30 .09
2 Roger Clemens 1.00 .30
3 Mark Whiten .10 .03
4 Shawon Dunston .10 .03
5 Bobby Bonilla .20 .06
6 Kevin Tapani .10 .03
7 Eric Karros .20 .06
8 Cliff Floyd .20 .06
9 Pat Kelly .10 .03
10 Jeffrey Hammonds .10 .03
11 Jeff Conine .20 .06
12 Fred McGriff .30 .09
13 Chris Bosio .10 .03
14 Mike Mussina .50 .15
15 Danny Bautista .10 .03
16 Mickey Morandini .10 .03
17 Chuck Finley .20 .06
18 Jim Thome .50 .15
19 Luis Ortiz .10 .03
20 Walt Weiss .10 .03
21 Don Mattingly 1.25 .35
22 Bob Hamelin .10 .03
23 Melido Perez .10 .03
24 Keith Mitchell .10 .03
25 John Smoltz .30 .09
26 Hector Carrasco .10 .03
27 Pat Hentgen .10 .03
28 Derrick May .10 .03
29 Mike Kingery .10 .03
30 Chuck Carr .10 .03
31 Billy Ashley .10 .03
32 Todd Hundley .10 .03
33 Luis Gonzalez .20 .06
34 Marquis Grissom .10 .03
35 Jeff King .10 .03
36 Eddie Williams .10 .03
37 Tom Pagnozzi .10 .03
38 Chris Hoiles .10 .03
39 Sandy Alomar Jr. .10 .03
40 Mike Greenwell .10 .03
41 Lance Johnson .10 .03
42 Junior Felix .10 .03
43 Felix Jose .10 .03
44 Scott Leius .10 .03
45 Ruben Sierra .10 .03
46 Kevin Seitzer .10 .03
47 Wade Boggs .30 .09
48 Reggie Jefferson .10 .03
49 Jose Canseco .50 .15
50 David Justice .20 .06
51 John Smiley .10 .03
52 Joe Carter .20 .06
53 Rick Wilkins .10 .03
54 Ellis Burks .20 .06
55 Dave Weathers .10 .03
56 Pedro Astacio .10 .03
57 Ryan Thompson .10 .03
58 James Mouton .10 .03
59 Mel Rojas .10 .03
60 Orlando Merced .10 .03
61 Matt Williams .20 .06
62 Bernard Gilkey .10 .03
63 J.R. Phillips .10 .03
64 Lee Smith .20 .06
65 Jim Edmonds .20 .06
66 Darrin Jackson .10 .03
67 Scott Cooper .10 .03
68 Ron Karkovice .10 .03
69 Chris Gomez .10 .03
70 Kevin Appier .20 .06
71 Bobby Jones .10 .03
72 Doug Drabek .10 .03
73 Matt Mieske .10 .03
74 Sterling Hitchcock .10 .03
75 John Valentin .10 .03
76 Reggie Sanders .20 .06
77 Wally Joyner .20 .06
78 Turk Wendell .10 .03
79 Charlie Hayes .10 .03
80 Bret Barberie .10 .03
81 Troy Neel .10 .03
82 Ken Caminiti .20 .06
83 Milt Thompson .10 .03
84 Paul Sorrento .10 .03
85 Trevor Hoffman .20 .06
86 Jay Bell .20 .06
87 Mark Portugal .10 .03
88 Sid Fernandez .10 .03
89 Charles Nagy .10 .03
90 Jeff Montgomery .10 .03
91 Chuck Knoblauch .20 .06
92 Jeff Frye .10 .03
93 Tony Gwynn .60 .18
94 John Olerud .20 .06
95 David Nied .10 .03
96 Chris Hammond .10 .03
97 Edgar Martinez .30 .09
98 Kevin Stocker .10 .03
99 Jeff Fassero .10 .03
100 Curt Schilling .30 .09
101 Dave Clark .10 .03
102 Delino DeShields .10 .03
103 Leo Gomez .10 .03
104 Dave Hollins .10 .03
105 Tim Naehring .10 .03
106 Otis Nixon .10 .03
107 Ozzie Guillen .10 .03
108 Jose Lind .10 .03
109 Stan Javier .10 .03
110 Greg Vaughn .20 .06
111 Chipper Jones .50 .15
112 Ed Sprague .10 .03
113 Mike Macfarlane .10 .03
114 Steve Finley .20 .06
115 Ken Hill .10 .03
116 Carlos Garcia .10 .03
117 Lou Whitaker .20 .06
118 Todd Zeile .10 .03
119 Gary Sheffield .20 .06
120 Ben McDonald .10 .03
121 Pete Harnisch .10 .03
122 Ivan Rodriguez .50 .15
123 Wilson Alvarez .10 .03
124 Travis Fryman .20 .06
125 Pedro Munoz .10 .03
126 Mark Lemke .10 .03
127 Jose Valentin .10 .03
128 Ken Griffey Jr. .75 .23
129 Omar Vizquel .20 .06
130 Milt Cuyler .10 .03
131 Steve Trachsel .10 .03
132 Alex Rodriguez 1.25 .35
133 Garret Anderson .20 .06
134 Armando Benitez .20 .06
135 Shawn Green .20 .06
136 Jorge Fabregas .10 .03
137 Orlando Miller .10 .03
138 Rikkert Faneyte .10 .03
139 Ismael Valdes .10 .03
140 Jose Oliva .10 .03
141 Aaron Small .10 .03
142 Tim Davis .10 .03
143 Ricky Bottalico .10 .03
144 Mike Matheny .10 .03
145 Roberto Petagine .10 .03
146 Fausto Cruz .10 .03
147 Bryce Florie .10 .03
148 Jose Lima .10 .03
149 John Hudek .10 .03
150 Duane Singleton .10 .03
151 John Mabry .10 .03
152 Robert Eenhoorn .10 .03
153 Jon Lieber .10 .03
154 Garey Ingram .10 .03
155 Paul Shuey .10 .03
156 Mike Lieberthal .20 .06
157 Steve Dunn .10 .03
158 Charles Johnson .20 .06
159 Ernie Young .10 .03
160 Jose Martinez .10 .03
161 Kurt Miller .10 .03
162 Joey Eischen .10 .03
163 Dave Stevens .10 .03
164 Brian L.Hunter .10 .03
165 Jeff Cirillo .10 .03
166 Mark Smith .10 .03
167 M. Christensen RC .10 .03
168 C.J. Nitkowski .10 .03
169 A. Williamson RC .10 .03
170 Paul Konerko .20 .06
171 Scott Elarton RC .50 .15
172 Jacob Shumate .10 .03
173 Terrence Long .20 .06
174 Mark Johnson RC .20 .06
175 Ben Grieve .20 .06
176 Jayson Peterson RC .10 .03
177 Checklist .10 .03
178 Checklist .10 .03
179 Checklist .10 .03
180 Checklist .10 .03
181 Brian Anderson .10 .03
182 Steve Buechele .10 .03
183 Mark Clark .10 .03
184 Cecil Fielder .20 .06
185 Steve Avery .10 .03
186 Devon White .20 .06
187 Craig Shipley .10 .03
188 Brady Anderson .20 .06
189 Kenny Lofton .20 .06
190 Alex Cole .10 .03
191 Brent Gates .10 .03
192 Dean Palmer .20 .06
193 Alex Gonzalez .10 .03
194 Steve Cooke .10 .03
195 Ray Lankford .10 .03
196 Mark McGwire 1.25 .35
197 Marc Newfield .10 .03
198 Pat Rapp .10 .03
199 Darren Lewis .10 .03
200 Carlos Baerga .10 .03
201 Rickey Henderson .50 .15
202 Kurt Abbott .10 .03
203 Kirt Manwaring .10 .03
204 Cal Ripken 1.50 .45
205 Darren Daulton .20 .06
206 Greg Colbrunn .10 .03

207 Darryl Hamilton .10 .03
208 Bo Jackson .50 .15
209 Tony Phillips .10 .03
210 Geronimo Berroa .10 .03
211 Rich Becker .10 .03
212 Tony Tarasco .10 .03
213 Karl Rhodes .10 .03
214 Phil Plantier .10 .03
215 J.T. Snow .20 .06
216 Mo Vaughn .20 .06
217 Greg Gagne .10 .03
218 Ricky Bones .10 .03
219 Mike Bordick .10 .03
220 Chad Curtis .10 .03
221 Royce Clayton .10 .03
222 Roberto Alomar .50 .15
223 Jose Rijo .10 .03
224 Ryan Klesko .20 .06
225 Mark Langston .10 .03
226 Frank Thomas .50 .15
227 Juan Gonzalez .50 .15
228 Ron Gant .20 .06
229 Javier Lopez .20 .06
230 Sammy Sosa .75 .23
231 Kevin Brown .20 .06
232 Gary DiSarcina .10 .03
233 Albert Belle .20 .06
234 Jay Buhner .20 .06
235 Pedro Martinez .50 .15
236 Bob Tewksbury .10 .03
237 Mike Piazza .75 .23
238 Darryl Kile .20 .06
239 Bryan Harvey .10 .03
240 Andres Galarraga .20 .06
241 Jeff Blauser .10 .03
242 Jeff Kent .20 .06
243 Bobby Munoz .10 .03
244 Greg Maddux .75 .23
245 Paul O'Neill .30 .09
246 Lenny Dykstra .20 .06
247 Todd Van Poppel .10 .03
248 Bernie Williams .30 .09
249 Glenallen Hill .10 .03
250 Duane Ward .10 .03
251 Dennis Eckersley .20 .06
252 Pat Mahomes .10 .03
253 Rusty Greer .20 .06
254 Roberto Kelly .10 .03
255 Randy Myers .10 .03
256 Scott Ruffcorn .10 .03
257 Robin Ventura .20 .06
258 Eduardo Perez .10 .03
259 Aaron Sele .10 .03
260 Paul Molitor .30 .09
261 Juan Guzman .10 .03
262 Darren Oliver .10 .03
263 Mike Stanley .10 .03
264 Tom Glavine .30 .09
265 Rico Brogna .10 .03
266 Craig Biggio .30 .09
267 Darrell Whitmore .10 .03
268 Jimmy Key .20 .06
269 Will Clark .50 .15
270 David Cone .20 .06
271 Brian Jordan .20 .06
272 Barry Bonds 1.25 .35
273 Danny Tartabull .10 .03
274 Ramon J.Martinez .10 .03
275 Al Martin .10 .03
276 Fred McGriff SM .20 .06
277 Carlos Delgado SM .10 .03
278 Juan Gonzalez SM .30 .09
279 Shawn Green SM .10 .03
280 Carlos Baerga SM .10 .03
281 Cliff Floyd SM .10 .03
282 Ozzie Smith SM .50 .15
283 Alex Rodriguez SM .50 .15
284 Kenny Lofton SM .10 .03
285 Dave Justice SM .10 .03
286 Tim Salmon SM .20 .06
287 Manny Ramirez SM .20 .06
288 Will Clark SM .20 .06
289 Garret Anderson SM .10 .03
290 Billy Ashley SM .10 .03
291 Tony Gwynn SM .30 .09
292 Raul Mondesi SM .10 .03
293 Rafael Palmeiro SM .20 .06
294 Matt Williams SM .10 .03
295 Don Mattingly SM .60 .18
296 Kirby Puckett SM .30 .09
297 Paul Molitor SM .20 .06
298 Albert Belle SM .10 .03
299 Barry Bonds SM .60 .18
300 Mike Piazza SM .50 .15
301 Jeff Bagwell SM .20 .06
302 Frank Thomas SM .30 .09
303 Chipper Jones SM .30 .09
304 Ken Griffey Jr. SM .50 .15
305 Cal Ripken Jr. SM .75 .23
306 Eric Anthony .10 .03
307 Todd Benzinger .10 .03
308 Jacob Brumfield .10 .03
309 Wes Chamberlain .10 .03
310 Tino Martinez .30 .09
311 Roberto Mejia .10 .03
312 Jose Offerman .10 .03
313 David Segui .10 .03
314 Eric Young .10 .03
315 Rey Sanchez .10 .03
316 Raul Mondesi .20 .06
317 Bret Boone .20 .06
318 Andre Dawson .20 .06
319 Brian McRae .10 .03
320 Dave Nilsson .10 .03
321 Moises Alou .20 .06
322 Don Slaught .10 .03
323 Dave McCarty .10 .03
324 Mike Huff .10 .03
325 Rick Aguilera .10 .03
326 Rod Beck .10 .03
327 Kenny Rogers .20 .06
328 Andy Benes .10 .03
329 Allen Watson .10 .03
330 Randy Johnson .50 .15
331 Willie Greene .10 .03
332 Hal Morris .10 .03
333 Ozzie Smith .75 .23
334 Jason Bere .10 .03
335 Scott Erickson .10 .03
336 Dante Bichette .20 .06
337 Willie Banks .10 .03
338 Eric Davis .20 .06
339 Rondell White .20 .06
340 Kirby Puckett .50 .15
341 Deion Sanders .30 .09
342 Eddie Murray .50 .15
343 Mike Harkey .10 .03
344 Joey Hamilton .10 .03
345 Roger Salkeld .10 .03
346 Wil Cordero .10 .03
347 John Wetteland .20 .06
348 Geronimo Pena .10 .03
349 Kirk Gibson .20 .06
350 Manny Ramirez .20 .06
351 Wm.VanLandingham .10 .03
352 B.J. Surhoff .20 .06
353 Ken Ryan .10 .03
354 Terry Steinbach .10 .03
355 Bret Saberhagen .20 .06
356 John Jaha .10 .03
357 Joe Girardi .10 .03
358 Steve Karsay .10 .03
359 Alex Fernandez .10 .03
360 Salomon Torres .10 .03
361 John Burkett .10 .03
362 Derek Bell .10 .03
363 Tom Henke .10 .03
364 Gregg Jefferies .10 .03
365 Jack McDowell .10 .03
366 Andujar Cedeno .10 .03
367 Dave Winfield .20 .06
368 Carl Everett .20 .06
369 Danny Jackson .10 .03
370 Jeromy Burnitz .20 .06
371 Mark Grace .30 .09
372 Larry Walker .30 .09
373 Bill Swift .10 .03
374 Dennis Martinez .20 .06
375 Mickey Tettleton .10 .03
376 Mel Nieves .10 .03
377 Cal Eldred .10 .03
378 Orel Hershiser .20 .06
379 David Wells .20 .06
380 Gary Gaetti .20 .06
381 Tim Raines .20 .06
382 Barry Larkin .50 .15
383 Jason Jacome .10 .03
384 Tim Wallach .10 .03
385 Robby Thompson .10 .03
386 Frank Viola .20 .06
387 Dave Stewart .20 .06
388 Bip Roberts .10 .03
389 Ron Darling .10 .03
390 Carlos Delgado .20 .06
391 Tim Salmon .30 .09
392 Alan Trammell .30 .09
393 Kevin Foster .10 .03
394 Jim Abbott .30 .09
395 John Kruk .20 .06
396 Andy Van Slyke .20 .06
397 Dave Magadan .10 .03
398 Rafael Palmeiro .30 .09
399 Mike Devereaux .10 .03
400 Benito Santiago .20 .06
401 Brett Butler .20 .06
402 John Franco .20 .06
403 Matt Walbeck .10 .03
404 Terry Pendleton .20 .06
405 Chris Sabo .10 .03
406 Andrew Lorraine .10 .03
407 Dan Wilson .10 .03
408 Mike Lansing .10 .03
409 Ray McDavid .10 .03
410 Shane Andrews .10 .03
411 Tom Gordon .10 .03
412 Chad Ogea .10 .03
413 James Baldwin .10 .03
414 Russ Davis .10 .03
415 Ray Holbert .10 .03
416 Ray Durham .20 .06
417 Matt Nokes .10 .03
418 Rod Henderson .10 .03
419 Gabe White .10 .03
420 Todd Hollandsworth .10 .03
421 Midre Cummings .10 .03
422 Harold Baines .20 .06
423 Troy Percival .20 .06
424 Joe Vitiello .10 .03
425 Andy Ashby .10 .03
426 Michael Tucker .10 .03
427 Mark Gubicza .10 .03
428 Jim Bullinger .10 .03
429 Jose Malave .10 .03
430 Pete Schourek .10 .03
431 Bobby Ayala .10 .03
432 Marvin Freeman .10 .03
433 Pat Listach .10 .03
434 Eddie Taubensee .10 .03
435 Steve Howe .10 .03
436 Kent Mercker .10 .03
437 Hector Fajardo .10 .03
438 Scott Kamieniecki .10 .03
439 Robb Nen .20 .06
440 Mike Kelly .10 .03
441 Tom Candiotti .10 .03
442 Albie Lopez .10 .03
443 Jeff Granger .10 .03
444 Rich Aude .10 .03
445 Luis Polonia .10 .03
446 Frank Thomas CL .30 .09
447 Ken Griffey Jr. CL .50 .15
448 Mike Piazza CL .50 .15
449 Jeff Bagwell CL .20 .06
450 Jeff Bagwell CL .50 .15
Frank Thomas
Ken Griffey Jr.
Mike Piazza

1995 Pinnacle Artist's Proofs

Inserted one per 36 first series packs and ome per 26 second series packs, this is a parallel set to the regular Pinnacle issue. The words "Artist Proof" are clearly labeled in silver on the card front. The name on the bottom is also set against a silver background.

Nm-Mt Ex-Mt
*STARS: 10X TO 25X BASIC CARDS ..
*ROOKIES: 6X TO 15X BASIC ....

1995 Pinnacle Museum Collection

Inserted one in four packs for hobby and retail and 1:3 for ANCO, this is a parallel to the regular Pinnace issue. These cards use the Dufex technology on front and are clearly labeled on the back as Museum Collection cards. Seven series two cards (numbers 410, 413, 416, 420, 423, 426 and 444) were available only with randomly inserted trade cards. These trade cards expired Dec. 31, 1995. Due to a low response of mailing, these seven cards are by far the toughest to find in this set.

Nm-Mt Ex-Mt
COMMON CARD (1-450) 1.25 .35
*STARS: 4X TO 10X BASIC CARDS ....
*ROOKIES/PROSPECTS: 2.5X to 6X BASIC CARDS ....
410 S. Andrews TRADE 5.00 1.50
413 J. Baldwin TRADE 5.00 1.50
416 Ray Durham TRADE 10.00 3.00
420 T. Hollandsworth TRADE 5.00 1.50
423 Troy Percival TRADE 10.00 3.00
426 M. Tucker TRADE 5.00 1.50
444 Rich Aude TRADE 5.00 1.50

1995 Pinnacle ETA

This six-card standard-sized set was randomly inserted approximately one in every 24 first series hobby packs. This set features players who were among the leading prospects for major league stardom. The fronts feature a player photo as well as a quick information bit. The player's name is located on the top. The busy full-bleed backs feature a player photo and some quick comments.

Nm-Mt Ex-Mt
COMPLETE SET (6) 15.00 4.50
ETA1 Ben Grieve 3.00 .90
ETA2 Alex Ochoa 2.00 .60
ETA3 Joe Vitiello 2.00 .60
ETA4 Johnny Damon 3.00 .90
ETA5 Trey Beamon 2.00 .60
ETA6 Brooks Kieschnick 2.00 .60

1995 Pinnacle Gate Attractions

This 18-card standard-size set was inserted approximately one every 12 second series jumbo packs.

Nm-Mt Ex-Mt
COMPLETE SET (18) 80.00 24.00
GA1 Ken Griffey Jr. 5.00 1.50
GA2 Frank Thomas 3.00 .90
GA3 Cal Ripken 10.00 3.00
GA4 Jeff Bagwell 2.00 .60
GA5 Mike Piazza 5.00 1.50
GA6 Barry Bonds 8.00 2.40
GA7 Kirby Puckett 3.00 .90
GA8 Albert Belle 1.25 .35
GA9 Tony Gwynn 4.00 1.20
GA10 Raul Mondesi 1.25 .35
GA11 Will Clark 3.00 .90
GA12 Don Mattingly 8.00 2.40
GA13 Roger Clemens 6.00 1.80
GA14 Paul Molitor 2.00 .60
GA15 Matt Williams 1.25 .35
GA16 Greg Maddux 5.00 1.50
GA17 Kenny Lofton 1.25 .35
GA18 Cliff Floyd 1.25 .35

1995 Pinnacle New Blood

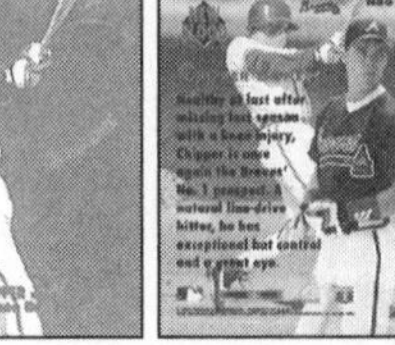

This nine-card standard-size set was inserted approximately one in every 90 second series hobby and retail packs. This set features nine players who were leading prospects entering the 1995 season. The Dufex enhanced fronts feature two player photos.

Nm-Mt Ex-Mt
COMPLETE SET (9) 60.00 18.00
NB1 Alex Rodriguez 20.00 6.00
NB2 Shawn Green 4.00 1.20
NB3 Brian Hunter 2.50 .75
NB4 Garret Anderson 4.00 1.20
NB5 Charles Johnson 4.00 1.20
NB6 Chipper Jones 8.00 2.40
NB7 Carlos Delgado 4.00 1.20
NB8 Billy Ashley 2.50 .75
NB9 J.R. Phillips UER 2.50 .75
Dodgers logo on back
Phillips played for the Giants

1995 Pinnacle Performers

These 18 standard-size cards were randomly inserted approximately one in every 12 first series jumbo packs.

Nm-Mt Ex-Mt
COMPLETE SET (18) 100.00 30.00
PP1 Frank Thomas 6.00 1.80
PP2 Albert Belle 2.50 .75
PP3 Barry Bonds 15.00 4.50
PP4 Juan Gonzalez 6.00 1.80
PP5 Andres Galarraga 2.50 .75
PP6 Raul Mondesi 2.50 .75
PP7 Paul Molitor 4.00 1.20
PP8 Tim Salmon 4.00 1.20
PP9 Mike Piazza 10.00 3.00
PP10 Gregg Jefferies 1.25 .35
PP11 Will Clark 6.00 1.80
PP12 Greg Maddux 10.00 3.00
PP13 Manny Ramirez 2.50 .75
PP14 Kirby Puckett 6.00 1.80
PP15 Shawn Green 2.50 .75
PP16 Rafael Palmeiro 4.00 1.20
PP17 Paul O'Neill 4.00 1.20
PP18 Jason Bere 1.25 .35

1995 Pinnacle Pin Redemption

This 18-card standard-size set was randomly inserted in all second series packs. Printed odds indicate that these cards were inserted approximately one every in 48 hobby and retail packs and one in every 36 jumbo packs. The horizontal full-bleed fronts feature an action photo, a team logo and another small player photo. The backs explain the rules for ordering the "Team Pinnacle" Collector Pin. The offer expired on November 15, 1995.

Nm-Mt Ex-Mt
COMPLETE SET (18) 60.00 18.00
*PINS: .75X TO 1.5X BASIC PIN REDEMPTION
ONE PIN VIA MAIL PER REDEMPTION CARD
1 Greg Maddux 4.00 1.20
2 Mike Mussina 2.50 .75
3 Mike Piazza 4.00 1.20
4 Carlos Delgado 1.00 .30
5 Jeff Bagwell 1.50 .45
6 Frank Thomas 2.50 .75
7 Craig Biggio 1.50 .45
8 Roberto Alomar 2.50 .75
9 Ozzie Smith 4.00 1.20
10 Cal Ripken Jr. 8.00 2.40
11 Matt Williams 1.00 .30
12 Travis Fryman 1.00 .30
13 Barry Bonds 6.00 1.80
14 Ken Griffey Jr. 4.00 1.20
15 Dave Justice 1.00 .30
16 Albert Belle 1.00 .30
17 Tony Gwynn 3.00 .90
18 Kirby Puckett 2.50 .75

1995 Pinnacle Red Hot

Cards from this 25-card standard-size set were randomly inserted into second series hobby and retail packs. The fronts feature a player photo on the right, with his name, an inset portrait and the words "Red Hot" on the left.

Nm-Mt Ex-Mt
COMPLETE SET (25) 80.00 24.00
*WHITE HOT: 1.5X TO 4X RED HOTS .
WHITE HOT SER.2 ODDS 1:36 HOBBY
RH1 Cal Ripken Jr. 8.00 2.40
RH2 Ken Griffey Jr. 4.00 1.20
RH3 Frank Thomas 2.50 .75
RH4 Jeff Bagwell 1.50 .45
RH5 Mike Piazza 4.00 1.20
RH6 Barry Bonds 6.00 1.80
RH7 Albert Belle 1.00 .30
RH8 Tony Gwynn 3.00 .90
RH9 Kirby Puckett 2.50 .75
RH10 Don Mattingly 6.00 1.80
RH11 Matt Williams 1.00 .30
RH12 Greg Maddux 4.00 1.20
RH13 Raul Mondesi 1.00 .30
RH14 Paul Molitor 1.50 .45
RH15 Manny Ramirez 1.00 .30
RH16 Joe Carter 1.00 .30
RH17 Will Clark 2.50 .75
RH18 Roger Clemens 5.00 1.50
RH19 Tim Salmon 1.50 .45
RH20 Dave Justice 1.00 .30
RH21 Kenny Lofton 1.00 .30
RH22 Deion Sanders 1.50 .45
RH23 Roberto Alomar 2.50 .75
RH24 Cliff Floyd 1.00 .30
RH25 Carlos Baerga .50 .15

1995 Pinnacle Team Pinnacle

Randomly inserted in series one hobby and retail packs at a rate of one in 90, this nine-card standard-size set showcases the game's top players in an etched-foil design. Cards are numbered with the prefix "TP". All cards were intentionally issued with two variations, whereby one side of the card or the other had the Dufex effect. Premiums of up to 25 percent may exist for the player with the enhanced side.

Nm-Mt Ex-Mt
COMPLETE SET (9) 150.00 45.00
TP1 Mike Mussina 15.00 4.50
Greg Maddux
TP2 Carlos Delgado 15.00 4.50
Mike Piazza
TP3 Frank Thomas 10.00 3.00
Jeff Bagwell
TP4 Roberto Alomar 10.00 3.00
Craig Biggio
TP5 Cal Ripken 30.00 9.00
Ozzie Smith
TP6 Travis Fryman 4.00 1.20
Matt Williams
TP7 Ken Griffey Jr. 15.00 4.50
Barry Bonds
TP8 Albert Belle 4.00 1.20
David Justice
TP9 Kirby Puckett 10.00 3.00
Tony Gwynn

1995 Pinnacle Upstarts

Top young players are featured in this 30-card standard-size set. The cards were randomly inserted in series one hobby and retail packs at a rate of one in eight. Backs are full-bleed color action photos of the player and are numbered at the top right with the prefix "US".

Nm-Mt Ex-Mt
COMPLETE SET (30) 50.00 15.00
US1 Frank Thomas 3.00 .90
US2 Roberto Alomar 3.00 .90
US3 Mike Piazza 5.00 1.50
US4 Javier Lopez 1.25 .35
US5 Albert Belle 1.25 .35
US6 Carlos Delgado 1.25 .35
US7 Brent Gates .60 .18
US8 Tim Salmon 2.00 .60
US9 Raul Mondesi 1.25 .35
US10 Juan Gonzalez 3.00 .90
US11 Manny Ramirez 1.25 .35
US12 Sammy Sosa 5.00 1.50
US13 Jeff Kent 1.25 .35
US14 Melvin Nieves .60 .18
US15 Rondell White 1.25 .35
US16 Shawn Green 1.25 .35
US17 Bernie Williams 2.00 .60
US18 Aaron Sele .60 .18
US19 Jason Bere .60 .18
US20 Joey Hamilton .60 .18
US21 Mike Kelly .60 .18
US22 Wil Cordero .60 .18
US23 Moises Alou 1.25 .35
US24 Roberto Kelly .60 .18
US25 Deion Sanders 2.00 .60
US26 Steve Karsay .60 .18
US27 Bret Boone 1.25 .35
US28 Willie Greene .60 .18
US29 Billy Ashley .60 .18
US30 Brian Anderson .60 .18

1995 Pinnacle FanFest

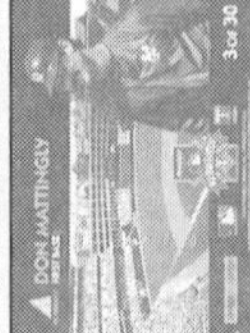

Available in two-card cello packs, this 30-card standard-size set was issued to commemorate the Pinnacle All-Star FanFest July 7-11 in Arlington, Texas.

Nm-Mt Ex-Mt
COMPLETE SET (30) 40.00 12.00
1 Cal Ripken 5.00 1.50
2 Roger Clemens 2.50 .75
3 Don Mattingly 2.50 .75
4 Albert Belle .50 .15

5 Kirby Puckett 1.25 .35
6 Cecil Fielder .50 .15
7 Kevin Appier .50 .15
8 Will Clark 1.00 .30
9 Juan Gonzalez 1.25 .35
10 Ivan Rodriguez 1.25 .35
11 Ken Griffey Jr. 3.00 .90
12 Tim Salmon 1.00 .30
13 Frank Thomas 1.50 .45
14 Roberto Alomar 1.00 .30
15 Rickey Henderson 1.50 .45
16 Raul Mondesi .75 .23
17 Matt Williams .75 .23
18 Ozzie Smith 2.50 .75
19 Deion Sanders .50 .15
20 Tony Gwynn 2.50 .75
21 Greg Maddux 3.00 .90
22 Sammy Sosa 2.50 .75
23 Mike Piazza 3.00 .90
24 Barry Bonds 2.50 .75
25 Jeff Bagwell 1.25 .35
26 Lenny Dykstra .50 .15
27 Rico Brogna .25 .07
28 Larry Walker .75 .23
29 Gary Sheffield 1.25 .35
30 Wil Cordero .25 .07

1996 Pinnacle Samples

This nine-card set was released to preview the first series of the 1996 Pinnacle set. The disclaimer "SAMPLE" is stamped diagonally across both sides of the card.

Nm-Mt Ex-Mt
COMPLETE SET (9) 8.00 2.40
1 Greg Maddux 3.00 .90
2 Bill Pulsipher .25 .07
3 Dante Bichette .40 .12
4 Mike Piazza 3.00 .90
5 Garret Anderson .40 .12
165 Ruben Rivera .25 .07
166 Tony Clark .25 .07
PP2 Mo Vaughn 2.50 .75
Pinnacle Power
NNO Title Card .25 .07

1996 Pinnacle

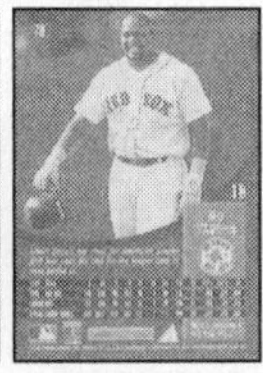

The 1996 Pinnacle set was issued in two separate series of 200 cards each. The 10-card packs retailed for $2.49. On 20-point card stock, the fronts feature full-bleed color action photos, bordered at the bottom by a gold foil triangle. The Series I set features the following topical subsets: The Naturals (134-163), '95 Rookies (164-193) and Checklists (194-200). Series II set features these subsets: Hardball Heroes (30 cards), 300 Series (17 cards), Rookies (25 cards), and Checklists (7 cards). Numbering for the 300 Series subset was based on player's career batting average. At that time, both Paul Molitor and Jeff Bagwell had identical career batting averages of .305, thus Pinnacle numbered both of their 300 Series subset cards as 305. Due to this quirky numbering, the set only runs through card 399, but actually contains 400 cards. A special Cal Ripken Jr. Tribute card was inserted in first series packs at the rate of one in 150.

Nm-Mt Ex-Mt
COMPLETE SET (400) 30.00 9.00
COMP. SERIES 1 (200) 15.00 4.50
COMP. SERIES 2 (200) 15.00 4.50
1 Greg Maddux .75 .23
2 Bill Pulsipher .20 .06
3 Dante Bichette .20 .06
4 Mike Piazza .75 .23
5 Garret Anderson .20 .06
6 Steve Finley .20 .06
7 Andy Benes .20 .06
8 Chuck Knoblauch .20 .06
9 Tom Gordon .20 .06
10 Jeff Bagwell .30 .09
11 Wil Cordero .20 .06
12 John Mabry .20 .06
13 Jeff Frye .20 .06
14 Travis Fryman .20 .06
15 John Wetteland .20 .06
16 Jason Bates .20 .06
17 Danny Tartabull .20 .06
18 Charles Nagy .20 .06
19 Robin Ventura .20 .06
20 Reggie Sanders .20 .06
21 Dave Clark .20 .06
22 Jaime Navarro .20 .06
23 Joey Hamilton .20 .06
24 Al Leiter .20 .06
25 Deion Sanders .30 .09
26 Tim Salmon .30 .09
27 Tino Martinez .30 .09
28 Mike Greenwell .20 .06
29 Phil Plantier .20 .06
30 Bobby Bonilla .20 .06
31 Kenny Rogers .20 .06
32 Chili Davis .20 .06
33 Joe Carter .20 .06
34 Mike Mussina .50 .15
35 Matt Mieske .20 .06
36 Jose Canseco .50 .15
37 Brad Radke .20 .06
38 Juan Gonzalez .50 .15
39 David Segui .20 .06
40 Alex Fernandez .20 .06
41 Jeff Kent .20 .06
42 Todd Zeile .20 .06
43 Darryl Strawberry .30 .09
44 Jose Rijo .20 .06
45 Ramon Martinez .20 .06
46 Manny Ramirez .20 .06
47 Gregg Jefferies .20 .06
48 Bryan Rekar .20 .06
49 Jeff King .20 .06
50 John Olerud .20 .06
51 Marc Newfield .20 .06
52 Charles Johnson .20 .06
53 Robby Thompson .20 .06
54 Brian L. Hunter .20 .06
55 Mike Blowers .20 .06
56 Keith Lockhart .20 .06
57 Ray Lankford .20 .06
58 Tim Wallach .20 .06
59 Ivan Rodriguez .50 .15
60 Ed Sprague .20 .06
61 Paul Molitor .30 .09
62 Eric Karros .20 .06
63 Glenallen Hill .20 .06
64 Jay Bell .20 .06
65 Tom Pagnozzi .20 .06
66 Greg Colbrunn .20 .06
67 Edgar Martinez .30 .09
68 Paul Sorrento .20 .06
69 Kirt Manwaring .20 .06
70 Pete Schourek .20 .06
71 Orlando Merced .20 .06
72 Shawon Dunston .20 .06
73 Ricky Bottalico .20 .06
74 Brady Anderson .20 .06
75 Steve Ontiveros .20 .06
76 Jim Abbott .30 .09
77 Carl Everett .20 .06
78 Mo Vaughn .20 .06
79 Pedro Martinez .50 .15
80 Harold Baines .20 .06
81 Alan Trammell .30 .09
82 Steve Avery .20 .06
83 Jeff Cirillo .20 .06
84 John Valentin .20 .06
85 Bernie Williams .30 .09
86 Andre Dawson .20 .06
87 Dave Winfield .20 .06
88 B.J. Surhoff .20 .06
89 Jeff Blauser .20 .06
90 Barry Larkin .50 .15
91 Cliff Floyd .20 .06
92 Sammy Sosa .75 .23
93 Andres Galarraga .20 .06
94 Dave Nilsson .20 .06
95 James Mouton .20 .06
96 Marquis Grissom .20 .06
97 Matt Williams .20 .06
98 John Jaha .20 .06
99 Don Mattingly 1.25 .35
100 Tim Naehring .20 .06
101 Kevin Appier .20 .06
102 Bobby Higginson .20 .06
103 Andy Pettitte .30 .09
104 Ozzie Smith .75 .23
105 Kenny Lofton .20 .06
106 Ken Caminiti .20 .06
107 Walt Weiss .20 .06
108 Jack McDowell .20 .06
109 Brian McRae .20 .06
110 Gary Gaetti .20 .06
111 Curtis Goodwin .20 .06
112 Dennis Martinez .20 .06
113 Omar Vizquel .20 .06
114 Chipper Jones .50 .15
115 Mark Gubicza .20 .06
116 Ruben Sierra .20 .06
117 Eddie Murray .50 .15
118 Chad Curtis .20 .06
119 Hal Morris .20 .06
120 Ben McDonald .20 .06
121 Marty Cordova .20 .06
122 Ken Griffey Jr. UER .75 .23
Card says Ken homered from both sides
He is only a left hitter
123 Gary Sheffield .20 .06
124 Charlie Hayes .20 .06
125 Shawn Green UER .20 .06
Picture on back is Ed Sprague
126 Jason Giambi .50 .15
127 Mark Langston .20 .06
128 Mark Whiten .20 .06
129 Greg Vaughn .20 .06
130 Mark McGwire 1.25 .35
131 Hideo Nomo .50 .15
132 Eric Karros .50 .15
Mike Piazza
Raul Mondesi
Hideo Nomo
133 Jason Bere .20 .06
134 Ken Griffey Jr. NAT .50 .15
135 Frank Thomas NAT .30 .09
136 Cal Ripken NAT .75 .23
137 Albert Belle NAT .20 .06
138 Mike Piazza NAT .50 .15
139 Dante Bichette NAT .20 .06
140 Sammy Sosa NAT .50 .15
141 Mo Vaughn NAT .20 .06
142 Tim Salmon NAT .20 .06
143 Reggie Sanders NAT .20 .06
144 Cecil Fielder NAT .20 .06
145 Jim Edmonds NAT .20 .06
146 Rafael Palmeiro NAT .20 .06
147 Edgar Martinez NAT .20 .06
148 Barry Bonds NAT .50 .15
149 Manny Ramirez NAT .20 .06
150 Larry Walker NAT .20 .06
151 Jeff Bagwell NAT .30 .09
152 Ron Gant NAT .20 .06
153 Andres Galarraga NAT .20 .06
154 Eddie Murray NAT .30 .09
155 Kirby Puckett NAT .30 .09
156 Will Clark NAT .20 .06
157 Don Mattingly NAT .60 .18
158 Mark McGwire NAT .60 .18
159 Dean Palmer NAT .20 .06
160 Matt Williams NAT .20 .06
161 Fred McGriff NAT .20 .06
162 Joe Carter NAT .20 .06
163 Juan Gonzalez NAT .30 .09
164 Alex Ochoa .20 .06
165 Ruben Rivera .20 .06
166 Tony Clark .20 .06
167 Brian Barber .20 .06
168 Matt Lawton RC .40 .12
169 Terrell Wade .20 .06
170 Johnny Damon .20 .06
171 Derek Jeter 1.25 .35
172 Phil Nevin .20 .06
173 Robert Perez .20 .06
174 C.J. Nitkowski .20 .06
175 Joe Vitiello .20 .06
176 Roger Cedeno .20 .06
177 Ron Coomer .20 .06
178 Chris Widger .20 .06
179 Jimmy Haynes .20 .06
180 Mike Sweeney RC 1.25 .35
181 Howard Battle .20 .06
182 John Wasdin .20 .06
183 Jim Pittsley .20 .06
184 Bob Wolcott .20 .06
185 LaTroy Hawkins .20 .06
186 Nigel Wilson .20 .06
187 Dustin Hermanson .20 .06
188 Chris Snopek .20 .06
189 Mariano Rivera .30 .09
190 Jose Herrera .20 .06
191 Chris Stynes .20 .06
192 Larry Thomas .20 .06
193 David Bell .20 .06
194 Frank Thomas CL .30 .09
195 Ken Griffey Jr. CL .50 .15
196 Cal Ripken CL .75 .23
197 Jeff Bagwell CL .20 .06
198 Mike Piazza CL .50 .15
199 Barry Bonds CL .50 .15
200 Garret Anderson CL .30 .09
Chipper Jones
201 Frank Thomas .50 .15
202 Michael Tucker .20 .06
203 Kirby Puckett .50 .15
204 Alex Gonzalez .20 .06
205 Tony Gwynn .60 .18
206 Moises Alou .20 .06
207 Albert Belle .20 .06
208 Barry Bonds 1.25 .35
209 Fred McGriff .30 .09
210 Dennis Eckersley .20 .06
211 Craig Biggio .30 .09
212 David Cone .20 .06
213 Will Clark .50 .15
214 Cal Ripken 1.50 .45
215 Wade Boggs .30 .09
216 Pete Schourek .20 .06
217 Darren Daulton .20 .06
218 Carlos Baerga .20 .06
219 Larry Walker .30 .09
220 Denny Neagle .20 .06
221 Jim Edmonds .20 .06
222 Lee Smith .20 .06
223 Jason Isringhausen .20 .06
224 Jay Buhner .20 .06
225 John Olerud .20 .06
226 Jeff Conine .20 .06
227 Dean Palmer .20 .06
228 Jim Abbott .30 .09
229 Raul Mondesi .20 .06
230 Tom Glavine .30 .09
231 Kevin Seitzer .20 .06
232 Lenny Dykstra .20 .06
233 Brian Jordan .20 .06
234 Rondell White .20 .06
235 Bret Boone .20 .06
236 Randy Johnson .50 .15
237 Paul O'Neill .30 .09
238 Jim Thome .50 .15
239 Edgardo Alfonzo .20 .06
240 Terry Pendleton .20 .06
241 Harold Baines .20 .06
242 Roberto Alomar .50 .15
243 Mark Grace .30 .09
244 Derek Bell .20 .06
245 Vinny Castilla .20 .06
246 Cecil Fielder .20 .06
247 Roger Clemens 1.00 .30
248 Orel Hershiser .20 .06
249 J.T. Snow .20 .06
250 Rafael Palmeiro .30 .09
251 Bret Saberhagen .20 .06
252 Todd Hollandsworth .20 .06
253 Ryan Klesko .20 .06
254 Greg Maddux HH .50 .15
255 Ken Griffey Jr. HH .50 .15
256 Hideo Nomo HH .30 .09
257 Frank Thomas HH .30 .09
258 Cal Ripken HH .75 .23
259 Jeff Bagwell HH .20 .06
260 Barry Bonds HH .50 .15
261 Mo Vaughn HH .20 .06
262 Albert Belle HH .20 .06
263 Sammy Sosa HH .50 .15
264 Reggie Sanders HH .20 .06
265 Mike Piazza HH .50 .15
266 Chipper Jones HH .30 .09
267 Tony Gwynn HH .30 .09
268 Kirby Puckett HH .30 .09
269 Wade Boggs HH .20 .06
270 Will Clark HH .20 .06
271 Gary Sheffield HH .20 .06
272 Dante Bichette HH .20 .06
273 Randy Johnson HH .30 .09
274 Matt Williams HH .20 .06
275 Alex Rodriguez HH 1.00 .30
276 Tim Salmon HH .20 .06
277 Johnny Damon HH .20 .06
278 Manny Ramirez HH .20 .06
279 Derek Jeter HH .60 .18
280 Eddie Murray HH .30 .09
281 Ozzie Smith HH .50 .15
282 Garret Anderson HH .20 .06
283 Raul Mondesi HH .20 .06
284 Terry Steinbach .20 .06
285 Carlos Garcia .20 .06
286 Dave Justice .20 .06
287 Eric Anthony .20 .06
288 Benji Gil .20 .06
289 Bob Hamelin .20 .06
290 Dwayne Hosey .20 .06
291 Andy Pettitte HH .20 .06
292 Rod Beck .20 .06
293 Shane Andrews .20 .06
294 Julian Tavarez .20 .06
295 Willie Greene .20 .06
296 Ismael Valdes .20 .06
297 Glenallen Hill .20 .06
298 Troy Percival .20 .06
299 Ray Durham .20 .06
300 Jeff Conine 300 .20 .06
301 Ken Griffey Jr. 300 .50 .15
302 Will Clark 300 .20 .06
303 Mike Greenwell 300 .20 .06
304 Carlos Baerga 300 .20 .06
305A Paul Molitor 300 .20 .06
305B Jeff Bagwell 300 .20 .06
306 Mark Grace 300 .20 .06
307 Don Mattingly 300 .60 .18
308 Hal Morris 300 .20 .06
309 Butch Huskey .20 .06
310 Ozzie Guillen .20 .06
311 Erik Hanson .20 .06
312 Kenny Lofton 300 .20 .06
313 Edgar Martinez 300 .20 .06
314 Kurt Abbott .20 .06
315 John Smoltz .30 .09
316 Ariel Prieto .20 .06
317 Mark Carreon .20 .06
318 Kirby Puckett 300 .30 .09
319 Carlos Perez .20 .06
320 Gary DiSarcina .20 .06
321 Trevor Hoffman .20 .06
322 Mike Piazza 300 .50 .15
323 Frank Thomas 300 .30 .09
324 Juan Acevedo .20 .06
325 Bip Roberts .20 .06
326 Javier Lopez .20 .06
327 Benito Santiago .20 .06
328 Mark Lewis .20 .06
329 Royce Clayton .20 .06
330 Tom Gordon .20 .06
331 Ben McDonald .20 .06
332 Dan Wilson .20 .06
333 Ron Gant .20 .06
334 Wade Boggs 300 .20 .06
335 Paul Molitor .30 .09
336 Tony Gwynn 300 .30 .09
337 Sean Berry .20 .06
338 Rickey Henderson .50 .15
339 Wil Cordero .20 .06
340 Kent Mercker .20 .06
341 Kenny Rogers .20 .06
342 Ryne Sandberg .75 .23
343 Charlie Hayes .20 .06
344 Andy Benes .20 .06
345 Sterling Hitchcock .20 .06
346 Bernard Gilkey .20 .06
347 Julio Franco .20 .06
348 Ken Hill .20 .06
349 Russ Davis .20 .06
350 Mike Blowers .20 .06
351 B.J. Surhoff .20 .06
352 Lance Johnson .20 .06
353 Darryl Hamilton .20 .06
354 Shawon Dunston .20 .06
355 Rick Aguilera .20 .06
356 Danny Tartabull .20 .06
357 Todd Stottlemyre .20 .06
358 Mike Bordick .20 .06
359 Jack McDowell .20 .06
360 Todd Zeile .20 .06
361 Tino Martinez .30 .09
362 Greg Gagne .20 .06
363 Mike Kelly .20 .06
364 Tim Raines .20 .06
365 Ernie Young .20 .06
366 Mike Stanley .20 .06
367 Wally Joyner .20 .06
368 Karim Garcia .20 .06
369 Paul Wilson .20 .06
370 Sal Fasano .20 .06
371 Jason Schmidt .20 .06
372 Livan Hernandez RC .50 .15
373 George Arias .20 .06
374 Steve Gibralter .20 .06
375 Jermaine Dye .20 .06
376 Jason Kendall .20 .06
377 Brooks Kieschnick .20 .06
378 Jeff Ware .20 .06
379 Alan Benes .20 .06
380 Rey Ordonez .20 .06
381 Jay Powell .20 .06
382 O. Fernandez RC .25 .07
383 Wilton Guerrero RC .40 .12
384 Eric Owens .20 .06
385 George Williams RC .25 .07
386 Chan Ho Park .20 .06
387 Jeff Suppan .20 .06
388 F.P. Santangelo RC .40 .12
389 Terry Adams .20 .06
390 Bob Abreu .20 .06
391 Quinton McCracken .20 .06
392 Mike Busby RC .25 .07
393 Cal Ripken CL .75 .23
394 Ken Griffey Jr. CL .50 .15
395 Frank Thomas CL .30 .09
396 Chipper Jones CL .30 .09
397 Greg Maddux CL .50 .15
398 Mike Piazza CL .50 .15
399 Ken Griffey Jr CL .50 .15
Cal Ripken Jr.
Chipper Jones
Frank Thomas
Greg Maddux
Mike Piazza
CR1 Cal Ripken Tribute 15.00 4.50

1996 Pinnacle Foil

This 200-card set is a parallel set to the 1996 Pinnacle second series set and was issued in five-card retail super packs which retailed for $2.99. Produced with micro-etched foil fronts, this limited version is similar in design to the regular second series set.

Nm-Mt Ex-Mt
COMPLETE SET (200) 30.00 9.00
*STARS: .75 TO 2X BASIC CARDS ....

1996 Pinnacle Starburst

Randomly inserted in first and second series packs at a rate of one in seven hobby/retail packs, one in six jumbo packs and one in 10 magazine packs, this 200-card quasi-parallel insert set features a select group of major league baseball's hottest superstars derived from the 399-card regular set. Unlike the basic cards, Starburst's are printed on all-foil Dufex card stock. The numbering also differs from the regular issue.

Nm-Mt Ex-Mt
*STARS: 3X TO 8X BASIC CARDS......

1996 Pinnacle Starburst Artist's Proofs

Randomly inserted in hobby and retail packs at a rate of one in 47, jumbo packs at a rate of one in 39 and magazine packs at a rate of one in 67; this 200-card set is a parallel issue to the more common Starburst inserts. The cards are identical to their Starburst counterparts except for the foil "Artist's Proofs" wording on their fronts.

Nm-Mt Ex-Mt
*STARS: 1X TO 2.5X BASIC STARBURST

1996 Pinnacle Christie Brinkley Collection

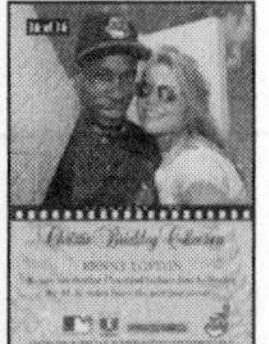

Randomly inserted at the rate of one in 23 packs, this 16-card set features the 1995 World Series participants captured by the lens of supermodel and photographer Christie Brinkley. The fronts feature color player photos in various poses with different backgrounds. The backs carry a color portrait of the player and Ms. Brinkley with an explanation as to why she posed them as she did.

Nm-Mt Ex-Mt
COMPLETE SET (16) 60.00 18.00
1 Greg Maddux 12.00 3.60
2 Ryan Klesko 3.00 .90
3 Dave Justice 3.00 .90
4 Tom Glavine 5.00 1.50
5 Chipper Jones 8.00 2.40
6 Fred McGriff 5.00 1.50
7 Javier Lopez 3.00 .90
8 Marquis Grissom 3.00 .90
9 Jason Schmidt 3.00 .90
10 Albert Belle 3.00 .90
11 Manny Ramirez 3.00 .90
12 Carlos Baerga 3.00 .90
13 Sandy Alomar Jr. 3.00 .90
14 Jim Thome 8.00 2.40
15 Julio Franco 3.00 .90
16 Kenny Lofton 3.00 .90
PCB Christie Brinkley 3.00 .90
Promo, On the Beach

1996 Pinnacle Essence of the Game

Randomly inserted in hobby packs only at a rate of one in 23, this 18-card standard-size set takes a unique perspective, photographically capturing the persona of some of the game's most popular icons. Using a micro-etched print technology, the fronts display a color player cutout on an acetate card studded with stars, with "Essence of the Game" appearing on a holographic design across the top.

Nm-Mt Ex-Mt
COMPLETE SET (18) 120.00 36.00
1 Cal Ripken 20.00 6.00
2 Greg Maddux 10.00 3.00
3 Frank Thomas 6.00 1.80
4 Matt Williams 2.50 .75
5 Chipper Jones 6.00 1.80
6 Reggie Sanders 2.50 .75
7 Ken Griffey Jr. 10.00 3.00
8 Kirby Puckett 6.00 1.80
9 Hideo Nomo 6.00 1.80
10 Mike Piazza 10.00 3.00
11 Jeff Bagwell 4.00 1.20
12 Mo Vaughn 2.50 .75
13 Albert Belle 2.50 .75
14 Tim Salmon 4.00 1.20
15 Don Mattingly 15.00 4.50
16 Will Clark 6.00 1.80
17 Eddie Murray 6.00 1.80
18 Barry Bonds 15.00 4.50

1996 Pinnacle First Rate

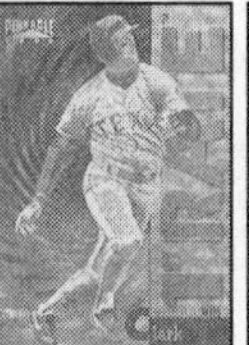
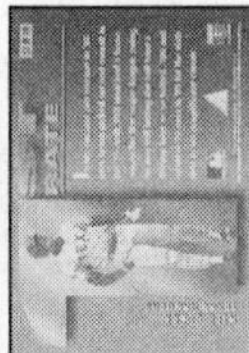

Randomly inserted in retail packs only at a rate of one in 23, this 18-card set features former first-round draft picks who have become major league superstars done in Dufex print.

	Nm-Mt	Ex-Mt
COMPLETE SET (18)	120.00	36.00
1 Ken Griffey Jr.	12.00	3.60
2 Frank Thomas	8.00	2.40
3 Mo Vaughn	3.00	.90
4 Chipper Jones	8.00	2.40
5 Alex Rodriguez	15.00	4.50
6 Kirby Puckett	8.00	
7 Gary Sheffield	3.00	.90
8 Matt Williams	3.00	.90
9 Barry Bonds	20.00	6.00
10 Craig Biggio	5.00	1.50
11 Robin Ventura	3.00	.90
12 Michael Tucker	3.00	.90
13 Derek Jeter	20.00	6.00
14 Manny Ramirez	3.00	.90
15 Barry Larkin	8.00	2.40
16 Shawn Green	3.00	.90
17 Will Clark	8.00	2.40
18 Mark McGwire	20.00	6.00

1996 Pinnacle Power

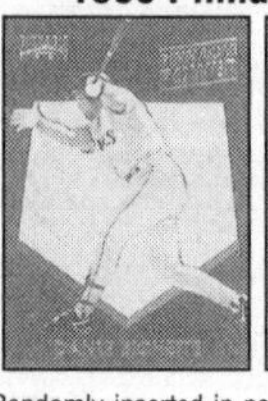

Randomly inserted in packs at a rate of one in 35 retail and hobby packs, or one in 29 jumbo packs, this 20-card set highlights the league's top long-ball hitters in die-cut holographic foil technology.

	Nm-Mt	Ex-Mt
COMPLETE SET (20)	100.00	30.00
1 Frank Thomas	8.00	2.40
2 Mo Vaughn	3.00	.90
3 Ken Griffey Jr.	12.00	3.60
4 Matt Williams	3.00	.90
5 Barry Bonds	20.00	6.00
6 Reggie Sanders	3.00	.90
7 Mike Piazza	12.00	3.60
8 Jim Edmonds	3.00	.90
9 Dante Bichette	3.00	.90
10 Sammy Sosa	12.00	3.60
11 Jeff Bagwell	5.00	1.50
12 Fred McGriff	5.00	1.50
13 Albert Belle	3.00	.90
14 Tim Salmon	5.00	1.50
15 Joe Carter	3.00	.90
16 Manny Ramirez	3.00	.90
17 Eddie Murray	8.00	2.40
18 Cecil Fielder	3.00	.90
19 Larry Walker	5.00	1.50
20 Juan Gonzalez	8.00	2.40

1996 Pinnacle Project Stardom

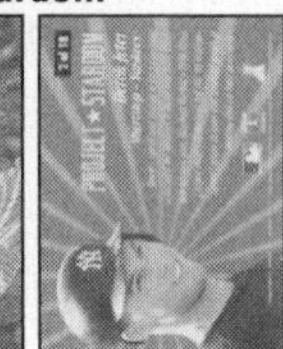

This 18-card set was randomly inserted in hobby packs at the rate of one in 35.

	Nm-Mt	Ex-Mt
COMPLETE SET (18)	120.00	36.00
1 Paul Wilson	4.00	1.20
2 Derek Jeter	25.00	7.50
3 Karim Garcia	4.00	1.20
4 Johnny Damon	4.00	1.20
5 Alex Rodriguez	20.00	6.00
6 Chipper Jones	10.00	3.00
7 Charles Johnson	4.00	1.20
8 Bob Abreu	4.00	1.20
9 Alan Benes	4.00	1.20
10 Richard Hidalgo	4.00	1.20
11 Brooks Kieschnick	4.00	1.20
12 Garret Anderson	4.00	1.20
13 Livan Hernandez	10.00	3.00
14 Manny Ramirez	4.00	1.20
15 Jermaine Dye	4.00	1.20
16 Todd Hollandsworth	4.00	1.20
17 Raul Mondesi	4.00	1.20
18 Ryan Klesko	4.00	1.20

1996 Pinnacle Skylines

Randomly inserted in magazine packs at the rate of one in 29, this 18-card set features baseball's best players pictured against their city's skyline and printed on clear plastic stock. The backs carry the same player portrait with information about the player and the city printed below.

	Nm-Mt	Ex-Mt
COMPLETE SET (18)	300.00	90.00
1 Ken Griffey Jr.	50.00	15.00
2 Frank Thomas	30.00	9.00
3 Greg Maddux	50.00	15.00
4 Cal Ripken	100.00	30.00
5 Albert Belle	12.00	3.60
6 Mo Vaughn	12.00	3.60
7 Mike Piazza	50.00	15.00
8 Wade Boggs	20.00	6.00
9 Will Clark	30.00	9.00
10 Barry Bonds	80.00	24.00
11 Gary Sheffield	12.00	3.60
12 Hideo Nomo	30.00	9.00
13 Tony Gwynn	40.00	12.00
14 Kirby Puckett	30.00	9.00
15 Chipper Jones	30.00	9.00
16 Jeff Bagwell	20.00	6.00
17 Manny Ramirez	12.00	3.60
18 Raul Mondesi	12.00	3.60

1996 Pinnacle Slugfest

Randomly inserted exclusively into one in every 35 series two retail packs, cards from this 18 cards set feature a selection of baseball's top slugging stars.

	Nm-Mt	Ex-Mt
COMPLETE SET (18)	150.00	45.00
1 Frank Thomas	10.00	3.00
2 Ken Griffey Jr.	15.00	4.50
3 Jeff Bagwell	6.00	1.80
4 Barry Bonds	25.00	7.50
5 Mo Vaughn	4.00	1.20
6 Albert Belle	4.00	1.20
7 Mike Piazza	15.00	4.50
8 Matt Williams	4.00	1.20
9 Dante Bichette	4.00	1.20
10 Sammy Sosa	15.00	4.50
11 Gary Sheffield	4.00	1.20
12 Reggie Sanders	4.00	1.20
13 Manny Ramirez	4.00	1.20
14 Eddie Murray	10.00	3.00
15 Juan Gonzalez	10.00	3.00
16 Dean Palmer	4.00	1.20
17 Rafael Palmeiro	6.00	1.80
18 Cecil Fielder	4.00	1.20

1996 Pinnacle Team Pinnacle

Randomly inserted in series one packs at a rate of one in 72, this nine-card set spotlights double-front all-foil Dufex card designs featuring nine top AL and NL players, by position, back-to-back. Only one side of each card is Dufexed.

	Nm-Mt	Ex-Mt
COMPLETE SET (9)	100.00	30.00
1 Frank Thomas Jeff Bagwell	8.00	2.40
2 Chuck Knoblauch Craig Biggio	5.00	1.50
3 Jim Thome Matt Williams	8.00	2.40
4 Barrry Larkin Cal Ripken	25.00	7.50
5 Barry Bonds Tim Salmon	20.00	6.00
6 Ken Griffey Jr. Reggie Sanders	12.00	3.60
7 Albert Belle Sammy Sosa	12.00	3.60
8 Ivan Rodriguez Mike Piazza	12.00	3.60
9 Greg Maddux Randy Johnson	12.00	3.60

1996 Pinnacle Team Spirit

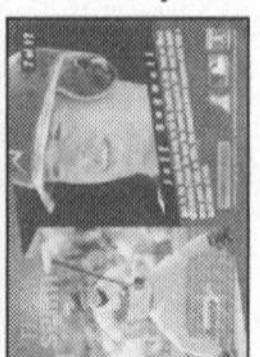

Randomly inserted in series two packs at the rate of one in 72, this 12-card set features color action player images in holographic foil stamping over a silver foil ball outlined in baseball stitching.

	Nm-Mt	Ex-Mt
COMPLETE SET (12)	150.00	45.00
1 Greg Maddux	15.00	4.50
2 Ken Griffey Jr.	15.00	4.50
3 Derek Jeter	25.00	7.50
4 Mike Piazza	15.00	4.50
5 Cal Ripken	30.00	9.00
6 Frank Thomas	10.00	3.00
7 Jeff Bagwell	6.00	1.80
8 Mo Vaughn	4.00	1.20
9 Albert Belle	4.00	1.20
10 Chipper Jones	10.00	3.00
11 Johnny Damon	4.00	1.20
12 Barry Bonds	25.00	7.50

1996 Pinnacle Team Tomorrow

Randomly inserted in series one jumbo packs at a rate of one in 19, this 10-card set is a jumbo exclusive and features the next crop of superstars. The fronts are printed in an all-foil Dufex design with two of the same color player action cutouts--one close up and the other full-length.

	Nm-Mt	Ex-Mt
COMPLETE SET (10)	60.00	18.00
1 Ruben Rivera	4.00	1.20
2 Johnny Damon	4.00	1.20
3 Raul Mondesi	4.00	1.20
4 Manny Ramirez	4.00	1.20
5 Hideo Nomo	10.00	3.00
6 Chipper Jones	10.00	3.00
7 Garret Anderson	4.00	1.20
8 Alex Rodriguez	20.00	6.00
9 Derek Jeter	25.00	7.50
10 Karim Garcia	4.00	1.20

1996 Pinnacle FanFest

This standard-size set was issued by Pinnacle in conjunction with the 1996 Pinnacle All-Star FanFest held in Philadelphia and was distributed in two-card poly packs. The Daulton card (number 30) features Sportflics technology and was inserted at a rate of about 1:60 packs. The Carlton card (number 31) was used for the official FanFest badges; apparently, some loose cards also were given to FanFest volunteers. The Carlton card is not considered part of the complete set. Five other cards (with the same design but no foil stamping or UV coating) were also issued by Pinnacle as part of the celebration. These five cards feature different personalities (most of whom are non-baseball related) involved in the show. The set is considered complete at 30 cards with the Daulton SP.

	Nm-Mt	Ex-Mt
COMPLETE SET (30)	25.00	7.50
COMMON CARD (1-30)	.15	.04
COMMON SP	5.00	1.50
1 Cal Ripken	3.00	.90
2 Greg Maddux	2.00	.60
3 Ken Griffey Jr.	2.00	.60
4 Frank Thomas	.75	.23
5 Jeff Bagwell	.75	.23
6 Hideo Nomo	.60	.18
7 Tony Gwynn	1.50	.45
8 Albert Belle	.25	.07
9 Mo Vaughn	.25	.07
10 Mike Piazza	2.00	.60
11 Dante Bichette	.25	.07
12 Ryne Sandberg	.75	.23
13 Wade Boggs	.75	.23
14 Kirby Puckett	.75	.23
15 Ozzie Smith	1.00	.30
16 Barry Bonds	1.50	.45
17 Gary Sheffield	.75	.23
18 Barry Larkin	.60	.18
19 Kevin Seitzer	.15	.04
20 Jay Bell	.15	.04
21 Chipper Jones	1.50	.45
22 Ivan Rodriguez	.75	.23
23 Cecil Fielder	.25	.07
24 Manny Ramirez	.75	.23
25 Randy Johnson	1.00	.30
26 Moises Alou	.40	.12
27 Mark McGwire	2.50	.75
28 Jason Isringhausen	.25	.07
29 Joe Carter	.25	.07
30 Darren Daulton SP	5.00	1.50
31 Steve Carlton	10.00	3.00
AC1 Amtrak Conductors	3.00	.90
BF1 Ben Franklin	3.00	.90
BS1 Bud Selig COMM	5.00	1.50
ER1 Ed Rendell Mayor of Philadelphia	3.00	.90
JS1 John Street City Councilman	3.00	.90
PP1 Phillie Phanatic	5.00	1.50

1997 Pinnacle

The 1997 Pinnacle set was issued as one series of 200 cards. Cards were distributed in 10-card hobby and retail packs (SRP $2.49) and seven-card magazine packs. This set was released in February, 1997. The set contains the following subsets: Rookies (156-185), Clout (186-197) and Checklists (198-200).

	Nm-Mt	Ex-Mt
COMPLETE SET (200)	20.00	6.00
1 Cecil Fielder	.30	.09
2 Garret Anderson	.30	.09
3 Charles Nagy	.30	.09
4 Darryl Hamilton	.30	.09
5 Greg Myers	.30	.09
6 Eric Davis	.30	.09
7 Jeff Frye	.30	.09
8 Marquis Grissom	.30	.09
9 Curt Schilling	.50	.15
10 Jeff Fassero	.30	.09
11 Alan Benes	.30	.09
12 Orlando Miller	.30	.09
13 Alex Fernandez	.30	.09
14 Andy Pettitte	.50	.15
15 Andre Dawson	.30	.09
16 Mark Grudzielanek	.30	.09
17 Joe Vitiello	.30	.09
18 Juan Gonzalez	.75	.23
19 Mark Whiten	.30	.09
20 Lance Johnson	.30	.09
21 Trevor Hoffman	.30	.09
22 Marc Newfield	.30	.09
23 Jim Eisenreich	.30	.09
24 Joe Carter	.30	.09
25 Jose Canseco	.75	.23
26 Bill Swift	.30	.09
27 Ellis Burks	.30	.09
28 Ben McDonald	.30	.09
29 Edgar Martinez	.50	.15
30 Jamie Moyer	.30	.09
31 Chan Ho Park	.30	.09
32 Carlos Delgado	.30	.09
33 Kevin Mitchell	.30	.09
34 Carlos Garcia	.30	.09
35 Darryl Strawberry	.50	.15
36 Jim Thome	.75	.23
37 Jose Offerman	.30	.09
38 Ryan Klesko	.30	.09
39 Ruben Sierra	.30	.09
40 Devon White	.30	.09
41 Brian Jordan	.30	.09
42 Tony Gwynn	1.00	.30
43 Rafael Palmeiro	.50	.15
44 Dante Bichette	.30	.09
45 Scott Stahoviak	.30	.09
46 Roger Cedeno	.30	.09
47 Ivan Rodriguez	.75	.23
48 Bob Abreu	.30	.09
49 Darryl Kile	.30	.09
50 Darren Dreifort	.30	.09
51 Shawon Dunston	.30	.09
52 Mark McGwire	2.00	.60
53 Tim Salmon	.50	.15
54 Gene Schall	.30	.09
55 Roger Clemens	1.50	.45
56 Rondell White	.30	.09
57 Ed Sprague	.30	.09
58 Craig Paquette	.30	.09
59 David Segui	.30	.09
60 Jaime Navarro	.30	.09
61 Tom Glavine	.50	.15
62 Jeff Brantley	.30	.09
63 Kimera Bartee	.30	.09
64 Fernando Vina	.30	.09
65 Eddie Murray	.75	.23
66 Lenny Dykstra	.30	.09
67 Kevin Elster	.30	.09
68 Vinny Castilla	.30	.09
69 Mike Fetters	.30	.09
70 Brett Butler	.30	.09
71 Robby Thompson	.30	.09
72 Reggie Jefferson	.30	.09
73 Todd Hundley	.30	.09
74 Jeff King	.30	.09
75 Ernie Young	.30	.09
76 Jeff Bagwell	.50	.15
77 Dan Wilson	.30	.09
78 Paul Molitor	.50	.15
79 Kevin Seitzer	.30	.09
80 Kevin Brown	.30	.09
81 Ron Gant	.30	.09
82 Dwight Gooden	.50	.15
83 Todd Stottlemyre	.30	.09
84 Ken Caminiti	.30	.09
85 James Baldwin	.30	.09
86 Jermaine Dye	.30	.09
87 Harold Baines	.30	.09
88 Pat Hentgen	.30	.09
89 Frank Rodriguez	.30	.09
90 Mark Johnson	.30	.09
91 Jason Kendall	.30	.09
92 Alex Rodriguez	1.25	.35
93 Alan Trammell	.50	.15
94 Scott Brosius	.30	.09
95 Delino DeShields	.30	.09
96 Chipper Jones	.75	.23
97 Barry Bonds	2.00	.60
98 Brady Anderson	.30	.09
99 Ryne Sandberg	1.25	.35
100 Albert Belle	.30	.09
101 Jeff Cirillo	.30	.09
102 Frank Thomas	.75	.23
103 Mike Piazza	1.25	.35
104 Rickey Henderson	.75	.23
105 Rey Ordonez	.30	.09
106 Mark Grace	.50	.15
107 Terry Steinbach	.30	.09
108 Ray Durham	.30	.09
109 Barry Larkin	.75	.23
110 Tony Clark	.30	.09
111 Bernie Williams	.50	.15
112 John Smoltz	.50	.15
113 Moises Alou	.30	.09
114 Alex Gonzalez	.30	.09
115 Rico Brogna	.30	.09
116 Eric Karros	.30	.09
117 Jeff Conine	.30	.09
118 Todd Hollandsworth	.30	.09
119 Troy Percival	.30	.09
120 Paul Wilson	.30	.09
121 Orel Hershiser	.30	.09
122 Ozzie Smith	1.25	.35
123 Dave Hollins	.30	.09
124 Ken Hill	.30	.09
125 Rick Wilkins	.30	.09
126 Scott Servais	.30	.09
127 Fernando Valenzuela	.30	.09
128 Mariano Rivera	.50	.15
129 Mark Loretta	.30	.09
130 Shane Reynolds	.30	.09
131 Darren Oliver	.30	.09
132 Steve Trachsel	.30	.09
133 Darren Bragg	.30	.09
134 Jason Dickson	.30	.09
135 Darrin Fletcher	.30	.09
136 Gary Gaetti	.30	.09
137 Joey Cora	.30	.09
138 Terry Pendleton	.30	.09
139 Derek Jeter	2.00	.60
140 Danny Tartabull	.30	.09
141 John Flaherty	.30	.09
142 B.J. Surhoff	.30	.09
143 Mike Sweeney	.30	.09
144 Chad Mottola	.30	.09
145 Andujar Cedeno	.30	.09
146 Tim Belcher	.30	.09
147 Mark Thompson	.30	.09
148 Rafael Bournigal	.30	.09
149 Marty Cordova	.30	.09
150 Osvaldo Fernandez	.30	.09
151 Mike Stanley	.30	.09
152 Ricky Bottalico	.30	.09
153 Donne Wall	.30	.09
154 Omar Vizquel	.30	.09
155 Mike Mussina	.75	.23
156 Brant Brown	.30	.09
157 F.P. Santangelo	.30	.09
158 Ryan Hancock	.30	.09
159 Jeff D'Amico	.30	.09
160 Luis Castillo	.30	.09
161 Darin Erstad	.30	.09
162 Ugueth Urbina	.30	.09
163 Andruw Jones	.30	.09
164 Steve Gibralter	.30	.09
165 Robin Jennings	.30	.09
166 Mike Cameron	.30	.09
167 George Arias	.30	.09
168 Chris Stynes	.30	.09
169 Justin Thompson	.30	.09
170 Jamey Wright	.30	.09
171 Todd Walker	.30	.09
172 Nomar Garciaparra	1.25	.35
173 Jose Paniagua	.30	.09
174 Marvin Benard	.30	.09
175 Rocky Coppinger	.30	.09
176 Quinton McCracken	.30	.09
177 Amaury Telemaco	.30	.09
178 Neifi Perez	.30	.09
179 Todd Greene	.30	.09
180 Jason Thompson	.30	.09
181 Wilton Guerrero	.30	.09
182 Edgar Renteria	.30	.09
183 Billy Wagner	.30	.09
184 Alex Ochoa	.30	.09
185 Dmitri Young	.30	.09
186 Kenny Lofton CT	.30	.09
187 Andres Galarraga CT	.30	.09
188 Chuck Knoblauch CT	.30	.09
189 Greg Maddux CT	1.25	.35
190 Mo Vaughn CT	.30	.09
191 Cal Ripken CT	2.50	.75
192 Hideo Nomo CT	.75	.23
193 Ken Griffey Jr. CT	1.25	.35
194 Sammy Sosa CT	1.25	.35
195 Jay Buhner CT	.30	.09
196 Manny Ramirez CT	.30	.09
197 Matt Williams CT	.30	.09
198 Andruw Jones CL	.30	.09
199 Darin Erstad CL	.30	.09
200 Trey Beamon CL	.30	.09

1997 Pinnacle Artist's Proofs

After three years of producing Artist's Proofs cards, Pinnacle decided to add some changes to their line of scarce parallel cards. Instead of the typical one per box parallel with a little foil logo on front the set was completely redesigned in 1997. Following a similar promotion run in the 1996 Finest brand, the 200-card first series set was broken down into three different groups of cards; 125 bronze, 50 silver and 25 gold. One in every 47 first series packs contained either a bronze, silver or gold Artist's Proofs card. The gold cards are scarcest (only 300 of each were produced), and silver cards are scarcer than bronze cards. Print runs for the bronze and silver cards were never announced. Each group of cards is easy to identify by their bold color-specific backgrounds (i.e. gold cards have gold backgrounds). All three groups share the same Artist's Proof logo on front. These cards were inserted at the following ratios; one in every 47 hobby and retail packs and one in every 55 magazine packs.

	Nm-Mt	Ex-Mt
*BRONZE CARDS: 8X TO 20X BASE CARD HI		
*SILVER CARDS: 10X TO 25X BASE CARD HI		
*GOLD CARDS: 12.5X TO 30X BASE CARD HI		

1997 Pinnacle Museum Collection

Randomly inserted in hobby and retail packs at a rate of one in nine and magazine packs at a rate of one in 13; these cards parallel the regular issue. Etched foil fronts differentiate them from the regular cards.

	Nm-Mt	Ex-Mt
*STARS: 5X TO 12X BASIC CARDS....		

1997 Pinnacle Press Plate Previews

These cards were issued by Pinnacle to preview their Press Plate concept introduced in the 1997 New Pinnacle brand. Cards were actually distributed as chiptoppers within sealed cases of New Pinnacle. The cards are made directly from the printing plates from 1997 Pinnacle baseball. The card backs contain a number, of which dealers were supposed to find a matching number on their actual cases. The one lucky dealer that was shipped a matching case and card combination won a special prize package for their shop.

	Nm-Mt	Ex-Mt
NO PRICING DUE TO SCARCITY		

1997 Pinnacle Cardfrontations

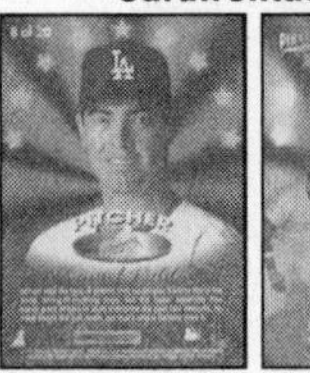

Randomly inserted in hobby packs only at a rate of one in 23, this 20-card set displays color player photos on rainbow holographic foil. The card design features a top pitcher on one side with a top home run hitter on the flip side. Both sides are covered with an opaque peel and reveal protective cover.

	Nm-Mt	Ex-Mt
COMPLETE SET (20)	200.00	60.00
1 Greg Maddux	15.00	4.50
Mike Piazza		
2 Tom Glavine	6.00	1.80
Ken Caminiti		
3 Randy Johnson	30.00	9.00
Cal Ripken		
4 Kevin Appier	25.00	7.50
Mark McGwire		
5 Andy Pettitte	10.00	3.00
Juan Gonzalez		
6 Pat Hentgen	4.00	1.20
Albert Belle		
7 Hideo Nomo	10.00	3.00
Chipper Jones		
8 Ismael Valdes	15.00	4.50
Sammy Sosa		
9 Mike Mussina	4.00	1.20
Manny Ramirez		
10 David Cone	4.00	1.20
Jay Buhner		
11 Mark Wohlers	10.00	3.00
Gary Sheffield		
12 Andy Benes	25.00	7.50
Barry Bonds		
13 Roger Clemens	20.00	6.00
Ivan Rodriguez		
14 Mariano Rivera	15.00	4.50
Ken Griffey Jr.		
15 Dwight Gooden	10.00	3.00
Frank Thomas		
16 John Wetteland	4.00	1.20
Darin Erstad		
17 John Smoltz	6.00	1.80
Brian Jordan		
18 Kevin Brown	6.00	1.80
Jeff Bagwell		
19 Jack McDowell	15.00	4.50
Alex Rodriguez		
20 Charles Nagy	6.00	1.80
Bernie Williams		

1997 Pinnacle Home/Away

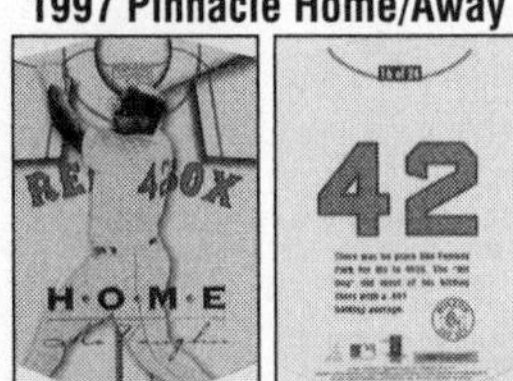

Randomly inserted in only jumbo packs at a rate of one in 33, this 24-card set features color player photos on die-cut cards. The cards were designed and shaped to resemble a player's actual jersey.

	Nm-Mt	Ex-Mt
COMPLETE SET (24)	500.00	150.00
1 Chipper Jones AWAY	12.00	3.60
3 Ken Griffey Jr. AWAY	20.00	6.00
5 Mike Piazza AWAY	20.00	6.00
7 Frank Thomas AWAY	12.00	3.60
9 Jeff Bagwell AWAY	8.00	2.40
11 Alex Rodriguez AWAY	20.00	6.00
13 Barry Bonds AWAY	30.00	9.00
15 Mo Vaughn AWAY	5.00	1.50
17 Derek Jeter AWAY	30.00	9.00
19 Mark McGwire AWAY	30.00	9.00
21 Cal Ripken AWAY	40.00	12.00
23 Albert Belle AWAY	5.00	1.50

1997 Pinnacle Passport to the Majors

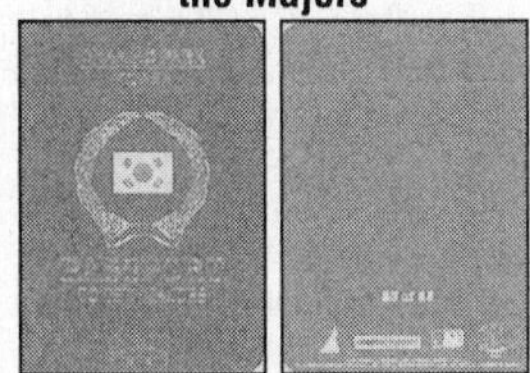

Randomly inserted in all first series packs at a rate of one in 36, this 25-card set features color player photos on a bookfold miniature passport card design and honors the rise to fame of some of the League's most high profile superstars.

	Nm-Mt	Ex-Mt
COMPLETE SET (25)	120.00	36.00
1 Greg Maddux	10.00	3.00
2 Ken Griffey Jr.	10.00	3.00
3 Frank Thomas	6.00	1.80
4 Cal Ripken	20.00	6.00
5 Mike Piazza	10.00	3.00
6 Alex Rodriguez	10.00	3.00
7 Mo Vaughn	2.50	.75
8 Chipper Jones	6.00	1.80
9 Roberto Alomar	6.00	1.80
10 Edgar Martinez	4.00	1.20
11 Javier Lopez	2.50	.75
12 Ivan Rodriguez	6.00	1.80
13 Juan Gonzalez	6.00	1.80
14 Carlos Baerga	2.50	.75
15 Sammy Sosa	10.00	3.00
16 Manny Ramirez	2.50	.75
17 Raul Mondesi	2.50	.75
18 Henry Rodriguez	2.50	.75
19 Rafael Palmeiro	4.00	1.20
20 Rey Ordonez	2.50	.75
21 Hideo Nomo	6.00	1.80
22 Mac Suzuki	2.50	.75
23 Chan Ho Park	2.50	.75
24 Larry Walker	2.50	.75
25 Ruben Rivera	2.50	.75

1997 Pinnacle Shades

Randomly inserted in magazine packs at a rate of one in 23, this 10-card set features color upclose photos of some of the league's best players wearing their favorite pair of sunglasses. The cards have a die-cut design and mirror mylar finish.

	Nm-Mt	Ex-Mt
COMPLETE SET (10)	60.00	18.00
1 Ken Griffey Jr.	4.00	1.20
2 Juan Gonzalez	2.50	.75
3 John Smoltz	1.50	.45
4 Gary Sheffield	1.00	.30
5 Cal Ripken	8.00	2.40
6 Mo Vaughn	1.00	.30
7 Brian Jordan	1.00	.30
8 Mike Piazza	4.00	1.20
9 Frank Thomas	2.50	.75
10 Alex Rodriguez	4.00	1.20

1997 Pinnacle Team Pinnacle

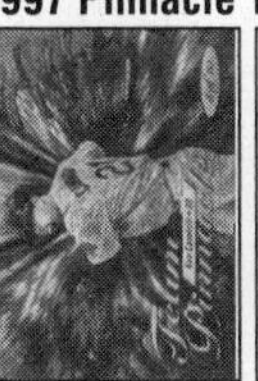
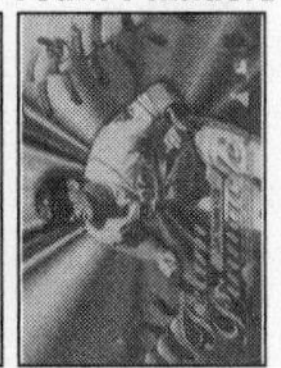

Randomly inserted in packs at a rate of one in 90, this 10-card set matches color player photos of the top American and National League players by position on double-fronted, all-foil Dufex cards. The tenth card is a computer design that makes a full Team Pinnacle picture.

	Nm-Mt	Ex-Mt
COMPLETE SET (10)	120.00	36.00
1 Frank Thomas	12.00	3.60
Jeff Bagwell		
2 Chuck Knoblauch	5.00	1.50
Eric Young		
3 Ken Caminiti	5.00	1.50
Jim Thome		
4 Alex Rodriguez	20.00	6.00
Chipper Jones		
5 Mike Piazza	20.00	6.00
Ivan Rodriguez		
6 Albert Belle	30.00	9.00
Barry Bonds		
7 Ken Griffey Jr.	20.00	6.00
Ellis Burks		
8 Juan Gonzalez	12.00	3.60
Gary Sheffield		
9 John Smoltz	8.00	2.40
Andy Pettitte		
10 Frank Thomas	10.00	3.00
Jeff Bagwell		
Chuck Knoblauch		
Eric Young		
Ken Caminiti		
Jim Thome		
Alex Rodriguez		
Chipper Jones		
Mike Piazza		
Ivan Rodriguez		
Albert Belle		
Barry Bonds		
Ken Griffey Jr.		
Ellis Burks		
Juan Gonzalez		
Gary Sheffield		
John Smoltz		
Andy Pettitte		

1997 Pinnacle All-Star FanFest Promos

This set of seven cards was issued at the Pinnacle all-Star Fanfest held in Cleveland, Ohio, on July 4-8, 1997. The cards feature the same design as the Pinnacle FanFest set. The fronts display color action player photos with gold foil enhancements. The backs carry a schedule of the times for FanFest. Card number 2 differs in that the player photo is in black and white, and the back displays information about

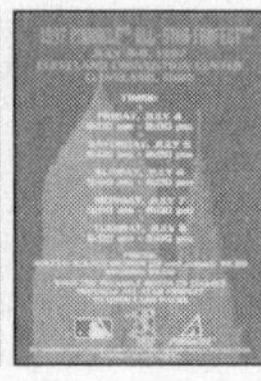

the player. The cards are unnumbered and checklisted below alphabetically.

	Nm-Mt	Ex-Mt
COMPLETE SET (7)	15.00	4.50
1 Roger Clemens	3.00	.90
2 Larry Doby	1.50	.45
3 Greg Maddux	4.00	1.20
4 Hideo Nomo	1.00	.30
5 Andy Pettitte	1.00	.30
6 Mike Piazza	4.00	1.20
7 Ivan Rodriguez	1.25	.35

1997 Pinnacle FanFest

This 21-card set was issued by Pinnacle in conjunction with the 1997 Pinnacle All-Star FanFest held in Cleveland, Ohio, July 4-8, 1997 at the Convention Center. The set was issued in three-card packs and features borderless color action player photos with gold foil stamping. The backs carry a player portrait in a star with player information and statistics printed on a black-and-gray city silhouetted background. Card number 21 could only be obtained with a redemption card at the locations listed on the card's back. The Alomar card is not considered part of the complete set. Twelve other cards with the same design were also issued by Pinnacle as part of the celebration. These twelve cards feature different personalities involved in the show or with the Cleveland Indians. These 12 cards are not considered part of the Fan Fest set and are not included in the complete set price.

	Nm-Mt	Ex-Mt
COMPLETE SET (20)	25.00	7.50
COMMON (FF1-FF20)	.25	.07
COMMON SP	10.00	3.00
COMMON PC CARD	5.00	1.50
FF1 Frank Thomas	1.25	.35
FF2 Jeff Bagwell	1.25	.35
FF3 Chuck Knoblauch	1.00	.30
FF4 Craig Biggio	1.00	.30
FF5 Alex Rodriguez	2.50	.75
FF6 Chipper Jones	2.50	.75
FF7 Cal Ripken	5.00	1.50
FF8 Ken Caminiti	.25	.07
FF9 Juan Gonzalez	1.00	.30
FF10 Barry Bonds	2.50	.75
FF11 Ken Griffey Jr.	3.00	.90
FF12 Andruw Jones	2.00	.60
FF13 Manny Ramirez	1.25	.35
FF14 Tony Gwynn	2.50	.75
FF15 Ivan Rodriguez	1.25	.35
FF16 Mike Piazza	3.00	.90
FF17 Andy Pettitte	.50	.15
FF18 Hideo Nomo	1.00	.30
FF19 Roger Clemens	2.50	.75
FF20 Greg Maddux	3.00	.90
FF21 Sandy Alomar SP	10.00	3.00
PC1 Macie McInnis	5.00	1.50
PC2 Bill Martin	5.00	1.50
PC3 Dick Goddard	5.00	1.50
PC4 Jack Corrigan ANN	5.00	1.50
PC5 Mike Hegan ANN	8.00	2.40
PC6 Rick Manning ANN	10.00	3.00
PC7 John Sanders ANN	5.00	1.50
PC8 Michael R. White	5.00	1.50
Mayor		
PC9 Wilma Smith	5.00	1.50
PC10 Tim Taylor	5.00	1.50
PC11 Robin Swoboda	5.00	1.50
PC12 Slider	8.00	2.40

1998 Pinnacle

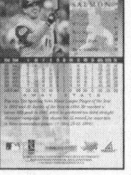

The 1998 Pinnacle set was issued in one series totalling 200 cards and was distributed in 10-card packs with a suggested retail price of $2.99. The fronts feature borderless color player photos with player information on the backs. The set contains the following subsets: Rookies (158-181), Field of Vision (182-187), Goin' Jake (188-197) and Checklists (198-200). Three variations of each card 1-157 were issued. The cards have home, away or seasonal stats on the back and were all produced in equal quantities. This concept of variations on the statistics was met with utter lack of interest and all three versions trade for equal values. In fact, complete sets typically carry a mix of all three stat variations.

	Nm-Mt	Ex-Mt
COMPLETE SET (200)	25.00	7.50
1 Tony Gwynn	1.00	.30
2 Pedro Martinez	.75	.23
3 Kenny Lofton	.30	.09
4 Curt Schilling	.50	.15
5 Shawn Estes	.30	.09
6 Tom Glavine	.50	.15
7 Mike Piazza	1.25	.35
8 Ray Lankford	.30	.09
9 Barry Larkin	.75	.23
10 Tony Womack	.30	.09
11 Jeff Blauser	.30	.09
12 Rod Beck	.30	.09
13 Larry Walker	.50	.15
14 Greg Maddux	1.25	.35
15 Mark Grace	.50	.15
16 Ken Caminiti	.30	.09
17 Bobby Jones	.30	.09
18 Chipper Jones	.75	.23
19 Javier Lopez	.30	.09
20 Moises Alou	.30	.09
21 Royce Clayton	.30	.09
22 Darryl Kile	.30	.09
23 Barry Bonds	2.00	.60
24 Steve Finley	.30	.09
25 Andres Galarraga	.30	.09
26 Denny Neagle	.30	.09
27 Todd Hundley	.30	.09
28 Jeff Bagwell	.50	.15
29 Andy Pettitte	.50	.15
30 Darin Erstad	.30	.09
31 Carlos Delgado	.30	.09
32 Matt Williams	.30	.09
33 Will Clark	.75	.23
34 Vinny Castilla	.30	.09
35 Brad Radke	.30	.09
36 John Olerud	.30	.09
37 Andruw Jones	.30	.09
38 Jason Giambi	.75	.23
39 Scott Rolen	.50	.15
40 Gary Sheffield	.30	.09
41 Jimmy Key	.30	.09
42 Kevin Appier	.30	.09
43 Wade Boggs	.50	.15
44 Hideo Nomo	.75	.23
45 Manny Ramirez	.30	.09
46 Wilton Guerrero	.30	.09
47 Travis Fryman	.30	.09
48 Chili Davis	.30	.09
49 Jeromy Burnitz	.30	.09
50 Craig Biggio	.50	.15
51 Tim Salmon	.50	.15
52 Jose Cruz Jr.	.30	.09
53 Sammy Sosa	1.25	.35
54 Hideki Irabu	.30	.09
55 Chan Ho Park	.30	.09
56 Robin Ventura	.30	.09
57 Jose Guillen	.30	.09
58 Deion Sanders	.50	.15
59 Jose Canseco	.75	.23
60 Jay Buhner	.30	.09
61 Rafael Palmeiro	.50	.15
62 Vladimir Guerrero	.75	.23
63 Mark McGwire	2.00	.60
64 Derek Jeter	2.00	.60
65 Bobby Bonilla	.30	.09
66 Raul Mondesi	.30	.09
67 Paul Molitor	.50	.15
68 Joe Carter	.30	.09
69 Marquis Grissom	.30	.09
70 Juan Gonzalez	.75	.23
71 Kevin Orie	.30	.09
72 Rusty Greer	.30	.09
73 Henry Rodriguez	.30	.09
74 Fernando Tatis	.30	.09
75 John Valentin	.30	.09
76 Matt Morris	.30	.09
77 Ray Durham	.30	.09
78 Geronimo Berroa	.30	.09
79 Scott Brosius	.30	.09
80 Willie Greene	.30	.09
81 Rondell White	.30	.09
82 Doug Drabek	.30	.09
83 Derek Bell	.30	.09
84 Butch Huskey	.30	.09
85 Doug Jones	.30	.09
86 Jeff Kent	.30	.09
87 Jim Edmonds	.30	.09
88 Mark McLemore	.30	.09
89 Todd Zeile	.30	.09
90 Edgardo Alfonzo	.30	.09
91 Carlos Baerga	.30	.09
92 Jorge Fabregas	.30	.09
93 Alan Benes	.30	.09
94 Troy Percival	.30	.09
95 Edgar Renteria	.30	.09
96 Jeff Fassero	.30	.09
97 Reggie Sanders	.30	.09
98 Dean Palmer	.30	.09
99 J.T. Snow	.30	.09
100 Dave Nilsson	.30	.09
101 Dan Wilson	.30	.09
102 Robb Nen	.30	.09
103 Damion Easley	.30	.09
104 Kevin Foster	.30	.09
105 Jose Offerman	.30	.09
106 Steve Cooke	.30	.09
107 Matt Stairs	.30	.09
108 Darryl Hamilton	.30	.09
109 Steve Karsay	.30	.09
110 Gary DiSarcina	.30	.09
111 Dante Bichette	.30	.09
112 Billy Wagner	.30	.09
113 David Segui	.30	.09
114 Bobby Higginson	.30	.09
115 Jeffrey Hammonds	.30	.09
116 Kevin Brown	.30	.09
117 Paul Sorrento	.30	.09
118 Mark Leiter	.30	.09
119 Charles Nagy	.30	.09
120 Danny Patterson	.30	.09
121 Brian McRae	.30	.09
122 Jay Bell	.30	.09
123 Jamie Moyer	.30	.09
124 Carl Everett	.30	.09
125 Greg Colbrunn	.30	.09
126 Jason Kendall	.30	.09
127 Luis Sojo	.30	.09
128 Mike Lieberthal	.30	.09
129 Reggie Jefferson	.30	.09
130 Cal Eldred	.30	.09
131 Orel Hershiser	.30	.09
132 Doug Glanville	.30	.09
133 Willie Blair	.30	.09
134 Neifi Perez	.30	.09
135 Sean Berry	.30	.09
136 Chuck Finley	.30	.09
137 Alex Gonzalez	.30	.09
138 Dennis Eckersley	.30	.09
139 Kenny Rogers	.30	.09
140 Troy O'Leary	.30	.09
141 Roger Bailey	.30	.09
142 Yamil Benitez	.30	.09
143 Wally Joyner	.30	.09
144 Bobby Witt	.30	.09
145 Pete Schourek	.30	.09
146 Terry Steinbach	.30	.09
147 B.J. Surhoff	.30	.09
148 Esteban Loaiza	.30	.09
149 Heathcliff Slocumb	.30	.09
150 Ed Sprague	.30	.09
151 Gregg Jefferies	.30	.09
152 Scott Erickson	.30	.09
153 Jaime Navarro	.30	.09
154 David Wells	.30	.09
155 Alex Fernandez	.30	.09
156 Tim Belcher	.30	.09
157 Mark Grudzielanek	.30	.09
158 Scott Hatteberg	.30	.09
159 Paul Konerko	.30	.09
160 Ben Grieve	.30	.09
161 Abraham Nunez	.30	.09
162 Shannon Stewart	.30	.09
163 Jaret Wright	.30	.09
164 Derrek Lee	.30	.09
165 Todd Dunwoody	.30	.09
166 Steve Woodard	.30	.09
167 Ryan McGuire	.30	.09
168 Jeremi Gonzalez	.30	.09
169 Mark Kotsay	.30	.09
170 Brett Tomko	.30	.09
171 Bobby Estalella	.30	.09
172 Livan Hernandez	.30	.09
173 Todd Helton	.50	.15
174 Garrett Stephenson	.30	.09
175 Pokey Reese	.30	.09
176 Tony Saunders	.30	.09
177 Antone Williamson	.30	.09
178 Bartolo Colon	.30	.09
179 Karim Garcia	.30	.09
180 Juan Encarnacion	.30	.09
181 Jacob Cruz	.30	.09
182 Alex Rodriguez FV	1.25	.35
183 Cal Ripken FV	2.00	.60
Roberto Alomar		
184 Roger Clemens FV	1.50	.45
185 Derek Jeter FV	2.00	.60
186 Frank Thomas FV	.75	.23
187 Ken Griffey Jr. FV	1.25	.35
188 Mark McGwire GJ	2.00	.60
189 Tino Martinez GJ	.50	.15
190 Larry Walker GJ	.50	.15
191 Brady Anderson GJ	.30	.09
192 Jeff Bagwell GJ	.50	.15
193 Ken Griffey Jr. GJ	1.25	.35
194 Chipper Jones GJ	.50	.15
195 Ray Lankford GJ	.30	.09
196 Jim Thome GJ	.75	.23
197 Nomar Garciaparra GJ	1.25	.35
198 Brady Anderson	.50	.15
Jeff Bagwell		
Nomar Garciaparra		
Ken Griffey Jr.		
Chipper Jones		
Ray Lankford		
Tino Martinez		
Mark McGwire		
Jim Thome		
Larry Walker		
199 Tino Martinez CL	.50	.15
200 Jacobs Field CL	.30	.09

1998 Pinnacle Artist's Proofs

Only the top 100 cards from the regular issue of the 1998 Pinnacle set were selected for inclusion in this year's Artist's Proofs gold-foil Dufex partial parallel version. The cards were randomly seeded into packs at a rate of 1:39.

	Nm-Mt	Ex-Mt
*STARS: 1X TO 2.5X MUSEUM COLL.		

1998 Pinnacle Museum Collection

Only the top 100 cards from the regular issue 1998 Pinnacle set were selected for inclusion in this year's Museum Collection all-foil Dufex partial parallel version. The cards were randomly seeded into packs at a rate of 1:9.

	Nm-Mt	Ex-Mt
*STARS: 4X TO 10X BASIC CARDS		
MC NUMBERS DON'T MATCH BASIC CARDS		

1998 Pinnacle Hit It Here Samples

This 10-card set is a sample parallel version of the 1998 Pinnacle Hit It Here insert set. These cards were distributed one per dealer order form.

	Nm-Mt	Ex-Mt
COMPLETE SET (10)	30.00	9.00
1 Larry Walker	1.50	.45
2 Ken Griffey Jr.	6.00	1.80
3 Mike Piazza	6.00	1.80
4 Frank Thomas	3.00	.90
5 Barry Bonds	5.00	1.50
6 Albert Belle	1.50	.45
7 Tino Martinez	1.50	.45
8 Mark McGwire	8.00	2.40
9 Juan Gonzalez	2.00	.60
10 Jeff Bagwell	2.50	.75

1998 Pinnacle Hit It Here

Randomly inserted one in 19 retail and magazine first series packs, and one in 17 first series hobby packs, this 10-card set features color player cut-outs of hot hitters in the league

printed on micro-etched silver foil cards with a target in the background. If one of these hitters hit for the cycle on opening day, one lucky collector holding that specific player's card could win $1million. Each card back featured a special serial number that would be entered into a drawing to determine the winner.

	Nm-Mt	Ex-Mt
COMPLETE SET (10)	30.00	9.00
1 Larry Walker	1.50	.45
2 Ken Griffey Jr.	4.00	1.20
3 Mike Piazza	4.00	1.20
4 Frank Thomas	2.50	.75
5 Barry Bonds	6.00	1.80
6 Albert Belle	1.00	.30
7 Tino Martinez	1.00	.30
8 Mark McGwire	6.00	1.80
9 Juan Gonzalez	2.50	.75
10 Jeff Bagwell	1.50	.45

1998 Pinnacle Power Pack Jumbos Samples

These sample cards were created to promote the then soon-to-be-released Pinnacle Power Packs. One of twenty-four different sample cards was included in wholesale order forms. These over-sized (3.5" by 5") sample cards are identical in design to the regular Power Pack Jumbos except for the large "SAMPLE" text running diagonally across the back of the card.

	Nm-Mt	Ex-Mt
COMPLETE SET (24)	80.00	24.00
1 Alex Rodriguez FV	5.00	1.50
2 Cal Ripken	6.00	1.80
Roberto Alomar FV		
3 Roger Clemens FV	5.00	1.50
4 Derek Jeter FV	10.00	3.00
5 Frank Thomas FV	3.00	.90
6 Ken Griffey Jr. FV	6.00	1.80
7 Mark McGwire GJ	8.00	2.40
8 Tino Martinez GJ	1.00	.30
9 Larry Walker GJ	1.00	.30
10 Brady Anderson GJ	1.00	.30
11 Jeff Bagwell GJ	2.50	.75
12 Ken Griffey Jr. GJ	6.00	1.80
13 Chipper Jones GJ	5.00	1.50
14 Ray Lankford GJ	1.00	.30
15 Jim Thome GJ	2.00	.60
16 Nomar Garciaparra GJ	6.00	1.80
17 Mike Piazza	6.00	1.80
18 Andruw Jones	2.00	.60
19 Greg Maddux	5.00	1.50
20 Tony Gwynn	5.00	1.50
21 Larry Walker	1.00	.30
22 Jeff Bagwell	2.50	.75
23 Chipper Jones	5.00	1.50
24 Scott Rolen	2.00	.60

1998 Pinnacle Power Pack Jumbos

These over-sized (3.5" by 5") cards were distributed at a rate of one per special Pinnacle "Power Pack". In addition to the jumbo card, Power Packs contained 21 regular-issue cards and carried a suggested retail price of $5.99. The twenty-four jumbo cards parallel a selection of regular issue cards including the Field of Vision and Goin' Jake subsets. Besides the obvious disparity in size, the cards also differ in from their base card counterparts with their "x of 24" numbering on back.

	Nm-Mt	Ex-Mt
COMPLETE SET (24)	25.00	7.50
1 Alex Rodriguez FV	1.50	.45
2 Cal Ripken	2.50	.75
Roberto Alomar FV		
3 Roger Clemens FV	2.00	.60
4 Derek Jeter FV	2.50	.75
5 Frank Thomas FV	1.00	.30
6 Ken Griffey Jr. FV	1.50	.45
7 Mark McGwire GJ	2.50	.75
8 Tino Martinez GJ	.60	.18
9 Larry Walker GJ	.60	.18
10 Brady Anderson GJ	.40	.12
11 Jeff Bagwell GJ	.60	.18
12 Ken Griffey Jr. GJ	1.50	.45
13 Chipper Jones GJ	.60	.18
14 Ray Lankford GJ	.40	.12
15 Jim Thome GJ	1.00	.30
16 Nomar Garciaparra GJ	1.50	.45
17 Mike Piazza	1.50	.45
18 Andruw Jones	.40	.12
19 Greg Maddux	1.50	.45
20 Tony Gwynn	1.25	.35
21 Larry Walker	.60	.18
22 Jeff Bagwell	.60	.18
23 Chipper Jones	1.00	.30
24 Scott Rolen	.60	.18

1998 Pinnacle Spellbound

Randomly inserted in hobby packs only at the rate of one in 17, this 50-card set features

game action color photos of nine top players printed on full-foil, micro-etched cards and superimposed over one of the letters of the player's name or nickname. All the cards of the same player needed to be collected in order to spell out the player's name when laid side-by-side.

	Nm-Mt	Ex-Mt
COMMON M.MCGWIRE	10.00	3.00
COMMON R.CLEMENS	8.00	2.40
COMMON F.THOMAS	4.00	1.20
COMMON S.ROLEN	2.50	.75
COMMON K.GRIFFEY	6.00	1.80
COMMON L.WALKER	2.50	.75
COMMON GARCIAPARRA	6.00	1.80
COMMON C.RIPKEN	12.00	3.60
COMMON T.GWYNN	5.00	1.50

1998 Pinnacle Epix Game Orange

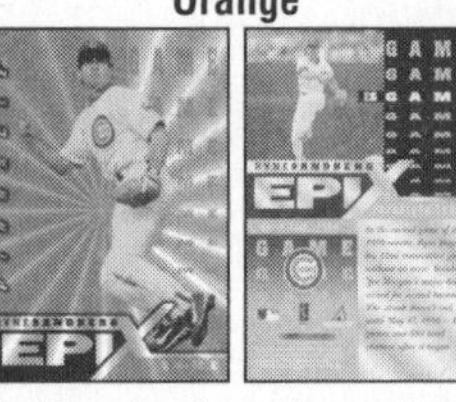

This 18-card partial set is one of twelve different Epix parallel versions. Cards E1-E6 were distributed in basic 1998 Pinnacle packs. Cards E7-E12 were distributed in 1998 Score packs and cards E19-E24 were distributed in 1998 Zenith packs. Missing cards E13-E18 were intended to be seeded within 1998 Pinnacle Certified, but Pinnacle went bankrupt in mid-1998, prior to the intended release of the product. Seeding ratios were only released as a cumulative rate for all versions of Epix cards and they are as follows: Pinnacle 1:21 packs, Score 1:61 packs and Zenith 1:11 packs. Card back text for each GAME card features a highlight of the most memorable game for each player featured. Orange foil fronts and the word "GAME" running down the side furthermore distinguish these cards.

	Nm-Mt	Ex-Mt
*GAME EMERALD: 1.25X TO 3X ORANGE		
*GAME PURPLE: .6X TO 1.5X ORANGE		
E1 Ken Griffey Jr.	5.00	1.50
E2 Juan Gonzalez	3.00	.90
E3 Jeff Bagwell	2.00	.60
E4 Ivan Rodriguez	3.00	.90
E5 Nomar Garciaparra	5.00	1.50
E6 Ryne Sandberg	3.00	.90
E7 Frank Thomas	3.00	.90
E8 Derek Jeter	8.00	2.40
E9 Tony Gwynn	4.00	1.20
E10 Albert Belle	2.00	.60
E11 Scott Rolen	2.00	.60
E12 Barry Larkin	3.00	.90
E19 Mike Piazza	5.00	1.50
E20 Andruw Jones	1.25	.35
E21 Greg Maddux	5.00	1.50
E22 Barry Bonds	8.00	2.40
E23 Paul Molitor	2.00	.60
E24 Eddie Murray	3.00	.90

1998 Pinnacle Epix Moment Orange

This 18-card partial set is one of twelve different Epix parallel versions. Cards E7-E12 were distributed in 1998 Zenith packs. Cards E13-E18 were distributed in basic 1998 Pinnacle packs and cards E19-E24 were distributed in 1998 Score packs. Missing cards E1-E6 were intended to be seeded within 1998 Pinnacle Certified, but Pinnacle went bankrupt in mid-1998, prior to the intended release of the product. Seeding ratios were only released as a cumulative rate for all versions of Epix cards and they are as follows: Pinnacle 1:21 packs, Score 1:61 packs and Zenith 1:11 packs. Card back text for each MOMENT card features a highlight of the most memorable moment for each player featured. Orange foil fronts and the word "MOMENT" running down the side furthermore distinguish these cards.

	Nm-Mt	Ex-Mt
*MOMENT EMERALD: 1.25X TO 3X ORANGE		
*MOMENT PURPLE: .6X TO 1.5X ORANGE		
MOMENT EMERALD PRINT RUN 30 SETS		
E7 Frank Thomas	4.00	1.20
E8 Derek Jeter	10.00	3.00
E9 Tony Gwynn	5.00	1.50
E10 Albert Belle	2.50	.75
E11 Scott Rolen	2.50	.75
E12 Barry Larkin	4.00	1.20
E13 Alex Rodriguez	6.00	1.80
E14 Cal Ripken	10.00	3.00
E15 Chipper Jones	4.00	1.20
E16 Mo Vaughn	1.50	.45
E17 Roger Clemens	8.00	2.40
E18 Mark McGwire	10.00	3.00
E19 Mike Piazza	6.00	1.80
E20 Andruw Jones	1.50	.45
E21 Greg Maddux	6.00	1.80
E22 Barry Bonds	10.00	3.00
E23 Paul Molitor	2.50	.75
E24 Eddie Murray	4.00	1.20

1998 Pinnacle Epix Play Orange

This 24-card set is one of twelve different Epix parallel versions. Cards E1-E6 were distributed in 1998 Score packs. Cards E13-E18 were distributed in 1998 Zenith packs and cards E19-E24 were distributed in basic 1998 Pinnacle packs. Missing cards E7-E12 were intended to be seeded within 1998 Pinnacle Certified, but Pinnacle went bankrupt in mid-1998, prior to the intended release of the product. Seeding ratios were only released as a cumulative rate for all versions of Epix cards and they are as follows: Pinnacle 1:21 packs, Score 1:61 packs and Zenith 1:11 packs. Card back text for each PLAY card features a highlight of the most memorable play for each player featured. Orange foil fronts and the word "PLAY" running down the side furthermore distinguish these cards.

	Nm-Mt	Ex-Mt
*PLAY EMERALD: 1.25X TO 3X ORANGE		
*PLAY PURPLE: .6X TO 1.5X ORANGE		
E1 Ken Griffey Jr.	3.00	.90
E2 Juan Gonzalez	2.00	.60
E3 Jeff Bagwell	1.25	.35
E4 Ivan Rodriguez	2.00	.60
E5 Nomar Garciaparra	3.00	.90
E6 Ryne Sandberg	2.00	.60
E13 Alex Rodriguez	3.00	.90
E14 Cal Ripken	5.00	1.50
E15 Chipper Jones	2.00	.60
E16 Mo Vaughn	.75	.23
E17 Roger Clemens	4.00	1.20
E18 Mark McGwire	5.00	1.50
E19 Mike Piazza	3.00	.90
E20 Andruw Jones	.75	.23
E21 Greg Maddux	3.00	.90
E22 Barry Bonds	5.00	1.50
E23 Paul Molitor	1.25	.35
E24 Eddie Murray	2.00	.60

1998 Pinnacle Epix Season Orange

This 18-card partial set is one of twelve different Epix parallel versions. Cards E1-E6 were distributed in 1998 Zenith packs. Cards E7-E12 were distributed in basic 1998 Pinnacle packs and cards E13-E18 were distributed in 1998 Score packs. Missing cards E19-E24 were intended to be seeded within 1998 Pinnacle Certified, but Pinnacle went bankrupt in mid-1998, prior to the intended release of the product. Seeding ratios were only released as a cumulative rate for all versions of Epix cards and they are as follows: Pinnacle 1:21 packs, Score 1:61 packs and Zenith 1:11 packs. Card back text for each SEASON card features a highlight of the most memorable season for each player featured. Orange foil fronts and the word "SEASON" running down the side furthermore distinguish these cards.

	Nm-Mt	Ex-Mt
*SEASON EMERALD: 1.25X TO 3X ORANGE		
*SEASON PURPLE: .6X TO 1.5X ORANGE		
E1 Ken Griffey Jr.	10.00	3.00
E2 Juan Gonzalez	6.00	1.80
E3 Jeff Bagwell	4.00	1.20
E4 Ivan Rodriguez	6.00	1.80
E5 Nomar Garciaparra	10.00	3.00
E6 Ryne Sandberg	6.00	1.80
E7 Frank Thomas	6.00	1.80
E8 Derek Jeter	15.00	4.50
E9 Tony Gwynn	8.00	2.40
E10 Albert Belle	4.00	1.20
E11 Scott Rolen	4.00	1.20
E12 Barry Larkin	6.00	1.80
E13 Alex Rodriguez	10.00	3.00
E14 Cal Ripken	15.00	4.50
E15 Chipper Jones	6.00	1.80
E16 Mo Vaughn	2.50	.75
E17 Roger Clemens	12.00	3.60
E18 Mark McGwire	15.00	4.50

1998 Pinnacle Uncut

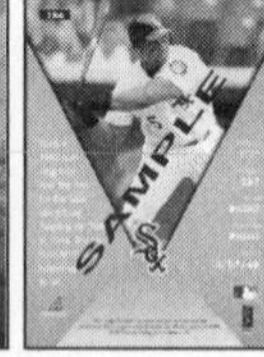

This six-card jumbo-sized set measures approximately 13 5/16" by 18 11/16" and is actually a very large metallic foil treated version of the Pinnacle Field of Vision subset (cards numbered from 182 to 187). Cards were distributed in mass-retail chains in one-card packs with an SRP of $9.99. The cards are listed below with the numbers as they appear in the regular Pinnacle set.

	Nm-Mt	Ex-Mt
COMPLETE SET (6)	80.00	24.00
182 Alex Rodriguez	15.00	4.50
183 Cal Ripken	15.00	4.50
Roberto Alomar		
184 Roger Clemens	10.00	3.00
185 Derek Jeter	15.00	4.50
186 Frank Thomas	10.00	3.00
187 Ken Griffey Jr.	10.00	3.00
S186 F. Thomas Sample	10.00	3.00

1996 Pinnacle Aficionado Promos

This three-card standard-size set was issued to introduce the new Pinnacle Afficionado brand. The set was distributed to hobby dealers along with promotional information concerning the release.

	Nm-Mt	Ex-Mt
COMPLETE SET (3)	5.00	1.50
9 Roger Clemens	3.00	.90
107 Ryan Klesko	1.00	.30
MN7 Albert Belle	1.00	.30
Magic Number		

1996 Pinnacle Aficionado

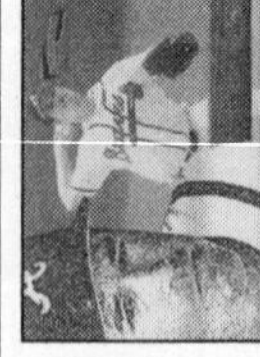
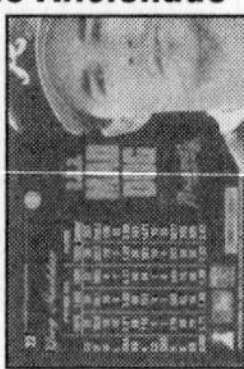

The 1996 Aficionado set was issued in one series totalling 200 cards. The five-card packs retailed for $3.99 and had a special bubble gum scent which was released when the packs were opened. Cards numbered 151-160 are a subset titled "Global Reach" and feature color action player cut-outs of international players on a background of a map, a global baseball, and their country's flag.

	Nm-Mt	Ex-Mt
COMPLETE SET (200)	30.00	9.00
1 Jack McDowell	.40	.12
2 Jay Bell	.40	.12
3 Rafael Palmeiro	.60	.18
4 Wally Joyner	.40	.12
5 Ozzie Smith	1.50	.45
6 Mark McGwire	2.50	.75
7 Kevin Seitzer	.40	.12
8 Fred McGriff	.60	.18
9 Roger Clemens	2.00	.60
10 Randy Johnson	1.00	.30
11 Cecil Fielder	.40	.12
12 David Cone	.40	.12
13 Chili Davis	.40	.12
14 Andres Galarraga	.40	.12
15 Joe Carter	.40	.12
16 Ryne Sandberg	1.50	.45
17 Paul O'Neill	.60	.18
18 Cal Ripken	3.00	.90
19 Wade Boggs	.60	.18
20 Greg Gagne	.40	.12
21 Edgar Martinez	.60	.18
22 Greg Maddux	1.50	.45
23 Ken Caminiti	.40	.12
24 Kirby Puckett	1.00	.30
25 Craig Biggio	.60	.18
26 Will Clark	1.00	.30
27 Ron Gant	.40	.12
28 Eddie Murray	1.00	.30
29 Lance Johnson	.40	.12
30 Tony Gwynn	1.25	.35
31 Dante Bichette	.40	.12
32 Darren Daulton	.40	.12
33 Danny Tartabull	.40	.12
34 Jeff King	.40	.12
35 Tom Glavine	.60	.18
36 Rickey Henderson	1.00	.30
37 Jose Canseco	1.00	.30
38 Barry Larkin	1.00	.30
39 Dennis Martinez	.40	.12
40 Ruben Sierra	.40	.12
41 Bobby Bonilla	.40	.12
42 Jeff Conine	.40	.12
43 Lee Smith	.40	.12
44 Charlie Hayes	.40	.12
45 Walt Weiss	.40	.12
46 Jay Buhner	.40	.12
47 Kenny Rogers	.40	.12
48 Paul Molitor	.60	.18
49 Hal Morris	.40	.12
50 Todd Stottlemyre	.40	.12
51 Mike Stanley	.40	.12
52 Mark Grace	.60	.18
53 Lenny Dykstra	.40	.12
54 Andre Dawson	.40	.12
55 Dennis Eckersley	.40	.12
56 Ben McDonald	.40	.12
57 Ray Lankford	.40	.12
58 Mo Vaughn	.40	.12
59 Frank Thomas	1.00	.30
60 Julio Franco	.40	.12
61 Jim Abbott	.60	.18
62 Greg Vaughn	.40	.12
63 Marquis Grissom	.40	.12
64 Tino Martinez	.60	.18
65 Kevin Appier	.40	.12
66 Matt Williams	.40	.12
67 Sammy Sosa	1.50	.45
68 Larry Walker	.60	.18
69 Ivan Rodriguez	1.00	.30
70 Eric Karros	.40	.12
71 Bernie Williams	.60	.18
72 Carlos Baerga	.40	.12
73 Jeff Bagwell	.60	.18
74 Pete Schourek	.40	.12
75 Ken Griffey Jr.	1.50	.45
76 Bernard Gilkey	.40	.12
77 Albert Belle	.40	.12
78 Chuck Knoblauch	.40	.12
79 John Smoltz	.60	.18
80 Barry Bonds	2.50	.75
81 Vinny Castilla	.40	.12
82 John Olerud	.40	.12
83 Mike Mussina	1.00	.30
84 Alex Fernandez	.40	.12
85 Shawon Dunston	.40	.12
86 Travis Fryman	.40	.12
87 Moises Alou	.40	.12
88 Dean Palmer	.40	.12
89 Gregg Jefferies	.40	.12
90 Jim Thome	1.00	.30
91 Dave Justice	.40	.12
92 B.J. Surhoff	.40	.12
93 Ramon Martinez	.40	.12
94 Gary Sheffield	.40	.12
95 Andy Benes	.40	.12
96 Reggie Sanders	.40	.12
97 Roberto Alomar	1.00	.30
98 Omar Vizquel	.40	.12
99 Juan Gonzalez	1.00	.30
100 Robin Ventura	.40	.12
101 Jason Isringhausen	.40	.12
102 Greg Colbrunn	.40	.12
103 Brian Jordan	.40	.12
104 Shawn Green	.40	.12
105 Brian Hunter	.40	.12
106 Rondell White	.40	.12
107 Ryan Klesko	.40	.12
108 Sterling Hitchcock	.40	.12
109 Manny Ramirez	.40	.12
110 Bret Boone	.40	.12
111 Michael Tucker	.40	.12
112 Julian Tavarez	.40	.12
113 Benji Gil	.40	.12
114 Kenny Lofton	.40	.12
115 Mike Kelly	.40	.12
116 Ray Durham	.40	.12
117 Trevor Hoffman	.40	.12
118 Butch Huskey	.40	.12
119 Phil Nevin	.40	.12
120 Pedro Martinez	1.00	.30
121 Wil Cordero	.40	.12
122 Tim Salmon	.60	.18
123 Jim Edmonds	.40	.12
124 Mike Piazza	1.50	.45
125 Rico Brogna	.40	.12
126 John Mabry	.40	.12
127 Chipper Jones	1.00	.30
128 Johnny Damon	.40	.12
129 Raul Mondesi	.40	.12
130 Denny Neagle	.40	.12
131 Marc Newfield	.40	.12
132 Hideo Nomo	1.00	.30
133 Joe Vitiello	.40	.12
134 Garret Anderson	.40	.12
135 Dave Nilsson	.40	.12
136 Alex Rodriguez	2.00	.60
137 Russ Davis	.40	.12
138 Frank Rodriguez	.40	.12
139 Royce Clayton	.40	.12
140 John Valentin	.40	.12
141 Marty Cordova	.40	.12
142 Alex Gonzalez	.40	.12
143 Carlos Delgado	.40	.12
144 Willie Greene	.40	.12
145 Cliff Floyd	.40	.12
146 Bobby Higginson	.40	.12
147 J.T. Snow	.40	.12
148 Derek Bell	.40	.12
149 Edgardo Alfonzo	.40	.12
150 Charles Johnson	.40	.12
151 Hideo Nomo GR	.60	.18
152 Larry Walker GR	.40	.12
153 Bob Abreu GR	.40	.12
154 Karim Garcia GR	.40	.12
155 Dave Nilsson GR	.40	.12
156 Chan Ho Park GR	.40	.12
157 Dennis Martinez GR	.40	.12
158 Sammy Sosa GR	1.00	.30
159 Rey Ordonez GR	.40	.12
160 Roberto Alomar GR	.40	.12
161 George Arias	.40	.12
162 Jason Schmidt	.40	.12
163 Derek Jeter	2.50	.75
164 Chris Snopek	.40	.12
165 Todd Hollandsworth	.40	.12
166 Sal Fasano	.40	.12
167 Jay Powell	.40	.12
168 Paul Wilson	.40	.12
169 Jim Pittsley	.40	.12
170 LaTroy Hawkins	.40	.12
171 Bob Abreu	.40	.12
172 Mike Grace RC	.40	.12
173 Karim Garcia	.40	.12
174 Richard Hidalgo	.40	.12
175 Felipe Crespo	.40	.12
176 Terrell Wade	.40	.12
177 Steve Gibralter	.40	.12
178 Jermaine Dye	.40	.12
179 Alan Benes	.40	.12
180 Wilton Guerrero RC	.40	.12
181 Brooks Kieschnick	.40	.12
182 Roger Cedeno	.40	.12
183 O. Fernandez RC	.40	.12
184 Matt Lawton RC	.40	.12
185 George Williams	.40	.12
186 Jimmy Haynes	.40	.12
187 Mike Busby RC	.40	.12
188 Chan Ho Park	.40	.12
189 Marc Barcelo	.40	.12
190 Jason Kendall	.40	.12
191 Rey Ordonez	.40	.12
192 Tyler Houston	.40	.12
193 John Wasdin	.40	.12
194 Jeff Suppan	.40	.12
195 Jeff Ware	.40	.12
196 Ken Griffey Jr. CL	1.00	.30
197 Albert Belle CL	.40	.12
198 Mike Piazza CL	1.00	.30
199 Greg Maddux CL	1.00	.30
200 Frank Thomas CL	.60	.18

1996 Pinnacle Aficionado Artist's Proofs

Randomly inserted in packs at a rate of one in 35, this 200-card set is a parallel set to the regular Pinnacle Aficionado set. A gold foil stamp in the shape of an artist's pen with the words, "Artist's Proof," printed above the wood-grain look bar containing the player's name distinguishes it from the regular set.

	Nm-Mt	Ex-Mt
*STARS: 8X TO 20X BASIC CARDS		
*ROOKIES: 5X TO 12X BASIC CARDS		

1996 Pinnacle Aficionado First Pitch Preview

This 100-card set was available through Pinnacle's Web site. Collectors had to answer a series of trivia questions to receive the cards via mail. The set parallels the first 100 cards of the regular issue Aficionado release and thus features only the veteran players that have five or more years of Major League service. The cards are similar in design except for the bronze foil highlights and logo on front designating them as "First Pitch Preview" cards.

Nm-Mt Ex-Mt
*STARS: 6X TO 12X BASIC CARDS ....

1996 Pinnacle Aficionado Magic Numbers

Randomly inserted in packs at a rate of one in 72, this 10-card set is printed on actual maple wood and features ten of today's top superstars. The fronts feature an embossed color action player cut-out on a wood background. The backs carry trivia regarding the player's jersey number and those players from the past and present who share this same jersey number.

	Nm-Mt	Ex-Mt
COMPLETE SET (10)	120.00	36.00
1 Ken Griffey Jr.	15.00	4.50
2 Greg Maddux	15.00	4.50
3 Frank Thomas	10.00	3.00
4 Mo Vaughn	4.00	1.20
5 Jeff Bagwell	6.00	1.80
6 Chipper Jones	10.00	3.00
7 Albert Belle	4.00	1.20
8 Cal Ripken	30.00	9.00
9 Matt Williams	4.00	1.20
10 Sammy Sosa	15.00	4.50

1996 Pinnacle Aficionado Rivals

Randomly inserted in packs at a rate of one in 24, this 24-card set features two spot embossed color player photos of rival players. The backs carry a head photo of each and candid player comments on each other.

	Nm-Mt	Ex-Mt
COMPLETE SET (24)	200.00	60.00
1 Ken Griffey / Frank Thomas	8.00	2.40
2 Frank Thomas / Cal Ripken	15.00	4.50
3 Cal Ripken / Mo Vaughn	15.00	4.50
4 Mo Vaughn / Ken Griffey Jr.	8.00	2.40
5 Ken Griffey Jr. / Cal Ripken	15.00	4.50
6 Frank Thomas / Mo Vaughn	5.00	1.50
7 Cal Ripken / Ken Griffey Jr.	15.00	4.50
8 Mo Vaughn / Frank Thomas	5.00	1.50
9 Ken Griffey Jr. / Mo Vaughn	8.00	2.40
10 Frank Thomas / Ken Griffey Jr.	8.00	2.40
11 Cal Ripken / Frank Thomas	15.00	4.50
12 Mo Vaughn / Cal Ripken	15.00	4.50
13 Mike Piazza / Jeff Bagwell	8.00	2.40
14 Jeff Bagwell / Barry Bonds	12.00	3.60
15 Jeff Bagwell / Mike Piazza	8.00	2.40
16 Tony Gwynn / Mike Piazza	8.00	2.40
17 Mike Piazza / Barry Bonds	8.00	2.40
18 Jeff Bagwell / Tony Gwynn	6.00	1.80
19 Barry Bonds / Mike Piazza	8.00	2.40
20 Tony Gwynn / Jeff Bagwell	6.00	1.80
21 Mike Piazza / Tony Gwynn	8.00	2.40
22 Barry Bonds / Jeff Bagwell	12.00	3.60
23 Tony Gwynn / Barry Bonds	6.00	1.80
24 Barry Bonds / Tony Gwynn	6.00	1.80

1996 Pinnacle Aficionado Slick Picks

Randomly inserted in packs at a rate of one in 10, this 32-card set honors 32 draft picks for their future all-star abilities. Printed using a spectroetch print technology, the fronts feature a color action player photo on a black background on one side with a black-and-white player portrait on the other.

	Nm-Mt	Ex-Mt
COMPLETE SET (32)	150.00	45.00
1 Mike Piazza	8.00	2.40
2 Cal Ripken	15.00	4.50
3 Ken Griffey Jr.	8.00	2.40
4 Paul Wilson	2.00	.60
5 Frank Thomas	5.00	1.50
6 Mo Vaughn	2.00	.60
7 Barry Bonds	12.00	3.60
8 Albert Belle	2.00	.60
9 Jeff Bagwell	3.00	.90
10 Dante Bichette	2.00	.60
11 Hideo Nomo	5.00	1.50
12 Raul Mondesi	2.00	.60
13 Manny Ramirez	2.00	.60
14 Greg Maddux	8.00	2.40
15 Tony Gwynn	6.00	1.80
16 Ryne Sandberg	8.00	2.40
17 Reggie Sanders	2.00	.60
18 Derek Jeter	12.00	3.60
19 Johnny Damon	2.00	.60
20 Alex Rodriguez	10.00	3.00
21 Ryan Klesko	2.00	.60
22 Jim Thome	5.00	1.50
23 Kenny Lofton	2.00	.60
24 Tino Martinez	3.00	.90
25 Randy Johnson	5.00	1.50
26 Wade Boggs	3.00	.90
27 Juan Gonzalez	5.00	1.50
28 Kirby Puckett	5.00	1.50
29 Tim Salmon	3.00	.90
30 Chipper Jones	5.00	1.50
31 Garret Anderson	2.00	.60
32 Eddie Murray	5.00	1.50

1997 Pinnacle Certified

This 150-card set was distributed in six-card hobby only packs with a suggested price of $4.99 and features color action player photos with side triangular silver mylar borders and black-and-white center backgrounds. The backs carry another player photo with player information and statistics. The set is divided into the following subsets: Rookie (106-135) and Certified Stars (136-150) which display a color player image on a background of stars. A Jose Cruz Exchange card was randomly seeded into packs. The deadline to redeem the card was March 31, 1998. Collectors who exchanged this cards received a Cruz card featuring him in a Blue Jay uniform. This number 151 card is not considered part of the complete set.

	Nm-Mt	Ex-Mt
COMPLETE SET (150)	40.00	12.00
1 Barry Bonds	2.50	.75
2 Mo Vaughn	.40	.12
3 Matt Williams	.40	.12
4 Ryne Sandberg	1.50	.45
5 Jeff Bagwell	.60	.18
6 Alan Benes	.40	.12
7 John Wetteland	.40	.12
8 Fred McGriff	.60	.18
9 Craig Biggio	.60	.18
10 Bernie Williams	.60	.18
11 Brian Hunter	.40	.12
12 Sandy Alomar Jr.	.40	.12
13 Ray Lankford	.40	.12
14 Ryan Klesko	.40	.12
15 Jermaine Dye	.40	.12
16 Andy Benes	.40	.12
17 Albert Belle	.40	.12
18 Tony Clark	.40	.12
19 Dean Palmer	.40	.12
20 Bernard Gilkey	.40	.12
21 Ken Caminiti	.40	.12
22 Alex Rodriguez	1.50	.45
23 Tim Salmon	.60	.18
24 Larry Walker	.60	.18
25 Barry Larkin	1.00	.30
26 Mike Piazza	1.50	.45
27 Brady Anderson	.40	.12
28 Cal Ripken	3.00	.90
29 Charles Nagy	.40	.12
30 Paul Molitor	.60	.18
31 Darin Erstad	.40	.12
32 Rey Ordonez	.40	.12
33 Wally Joyner	.40	.12
34 David Cone	.40	.12
35 Sammy Sosa	1.50	.45
36 Dante Bichette	.40	.12
37 Eric Karros	.40	.12
38 Omar Vizquel	.40	.12
39 Roger Clemens	2.00	.60
40 Joe Carter	.40	.12
41 Frank Thomas	1.00	.30
42 Javy Lopez	.40	.12
43 Mike Mussina	1.00	.30
44 Gary Sheffield	.40	.12
45 Tony Gwynn	1.25	.35
46 Jason Kendall	.40	.12
47 Jim Thome	1.00	.30
48 Andres Galarraga	.40	.12
49 Mark McGwire	2.50	.75
50 Troy Percival	.40	.12
51 Derek Jeter	2.50	.75
52 Todd Hollandsworth	.40	.12
53 Ken Griffey Jr.	1.50	.45
54 Randy Johnson	1.00	.30
55 Pat Hentgen	.40	.12
56 Rusty Greer	.40	.12
57 John Jaha	.40	.12
58 Kenny Lofton	.40	.12
59 Chipper Jones	1.00	.30
60 Robb Nen	.40	.12
61 Rafael Palmeiro	.60	.18
62 Mariano Rivera	.60	.18
63 Hideo Nomo	1.00	.30
64 Greg Vaughn	.40	.12
65 Ron Gant	.40	.12
66 Eddie Murray	1.00	.30
67 John Smoltz	.60	.18
68 Manny Ramirez	.40	.12
69 Juan Gonzalez	1.00	.30
70 F.P. Santangelo	.40	.12
71 Moises Alou	.40	.12
72 Alex Ochoa	.40	.12
73 Chuck Knoblauch	.40	.12
74 Raul Mondesi	.40	.12
75 J.T. Snow	.40	.12
76 Rickey Henderson	1.00	.30
77 Bobby Bonilla	.40	.12
78 Wade Boggs	.60	.18
79 Ivan Rodriguez	1.00	.30
80 Brian Jordan	.40	.12
81 Al Leiter	.40	.12
82 Jay Buhner	.40	.12
83 Greg Maddux	1.50	.45
84 Edgar Martinez	.60	.18
85 Kevin Brown	.40	.12
86 Eric Young	.40	.12
87 Todd Hundley	.40	.12
88 Ellis Burks	.40	.12
89 Marquis Grissom	.40	.12
90 Jose Canseco	1.00	.30
91 Henry Rodriguez	.40	.12
92 Andy Pettitte	.60	.18
93 Mark Grudzielanek	.40	.12
94 Dwight Gooden	.60	.18
95 Roberto Alomar	1.00	.30
96 Paul Wilson	.40	.12
97 Will Clark	1.00	.30
98 Rondell White	.40	.12
99 Charles Johnson	.40	.12
100 Jim Edmonds	.40	.12
101 Jason Giambi	1.00	.30
102 Billy Wagner	.40	.12
103 Edgar Renteria	.40	.12
104 Johnny Damon	.40	.12
105 Jason Isringhausen	.40	.12
106 Andruw Jones	.40	.12
107 Jose Guillen	.40	.12
108 Kevin Orie	.40	.12
109 Brian Giles RC	3.00	.90
110 Danny Patterson	.40	.12
111 Vladimir Guerrero	1.00	.30
112 Scott Rolen	.60	.18
113 Damon Mashore	.40	.12
114 Nomar Garciaparra	1.50	.45
115 Todd Walker	.40	.12
116 Wilton Guerrero	.40	.12
117 Bob Abreu	.40	.12
118 Brooks Kieschnick	.40	.12
119 Pokey Reese	.40	.12
120 Todd Greene	.40	.12
121 Dmitri Young	.40	.12
122 Raul Casanova	.40	.12
123 Glendon Rusch	.40	.12
124 Jason Dickson	.40	.12
125 Jorge Posada	.60	.18
126 Rod Myers	.40	.12
127 Bubba Trammell RC	.50	.15
128 Scott Spiezio	.40	.12
129 Hideki Irabu RC	.50	.15
130 Wendell Magee	.40	.12
131 Bartolo Colon	.40	.12
132 Chris Holt	.40	.12
133 Calvin Maduro	.40	.12
134 Ray Montgomery RC	.50	.15
135 Shannon Stewart	.40	.12
136 Ken Griffey Jr. CERT	1.00	.30
137 V. Guerrero CERT	.60	.18
138 Roger Clemens CERT	1.00	.30
139 Mark McGwire CERT	1.25	.35
140 Albert Belle CERT	.40	.12
141 Derek Jeter CERT	1.25	.35
142 Juan Gonzalez CERT	.60	.18
143 Greg Maddux CERT	1.00	.30
144 Alex Rodriguez CERT	1.00	.30
145 Jeff Bagwell CERT	.40	.12
146 Cal Ripken CERT	1.50	.45
147 Tony Gwynn CERT	.60	.18
148 Frank Thomas CERT	.60	.18
149 Hideo Nomo CERT	.40	.12
150 Andruw Jones CERT	.40	.12
151 Jose Cruz Jr.	1.25	.35

1997 Pinnacle Certified Mirror Blue

Randomly inserted in packs at the rate of one in 199, this 150-card set is parallel to the base Pinnacle Certified set. The difference is found in the blue design element. The backs also have mirror blue written on them so the cards can be easily identified.

Nm-Mt Ex-Mt
*STARS: 12.5X TO 30X BASIC CARDS
*ROOKIES: 4X TO 10X BASIC CARDS

1997 Pinnacle Certified Mirror Gold

Randomly inserted in packs at the rate of one in 299, this 150-card set is parallel to the base Pinnacle Certified set. The difference is found in the gold design element.

Nm-Mt Ex-Mt
*STARS: 20X TO 50X BASIC CARDS ..
*ROOKIES: 6X TO 15X BASIC CARDS

1997 Pinnacle Certified Mirror Red

Randomly inserted in packs at the rate of one in 99, this 150-card set is parallel to the base Pinnacle Certified set. The difference is found in the red design element.

Nm-Mt Ex-Mt
*STARS: 6X TO 15X BASIC CARDS ....
*ROOKIES: 2X TO 5X BASIC CARDS ..

1997 Pinnacle Certified Red

Randomly inserted in packs at the rate of one in five, this 150-card set is parallel to the regular set with a solid red tint on the mylar.

Nm-Mt Ex-Mt
*STARS: 1.5X TO 4X BASIC CARDS ...
*ROOKIES: .6X TO 1.5X BASIC CARDS

1997 Pinnacle Certified Certified Team

Randomly inserted in hobby packs at the rate of one in 19, this 20-card set features color player photos on silver-frosted mirror mylar.

	Nm-Mt	Ex-Mt
COMPLETE SET (20)	100.00	30.00
1 Frank Thomas	6.00	1.80
2 Jeff Bagwell	4.00	1.20
3 Derek Jeter	15.00	4.50
4 Chipper Jones	6.00	1.80
5 Alex Rodriguez	10.00	3.00
6 Ken Caminiti	2.50	.75
7 Cal Ripken	20.00	6.00
8 Mo Vaughn	2.50	.75
9 Ivan Rodriguez	6.00	1.80
10 Mike Piazza	10.00	3.00
11 Juan Gonzalez	6.00	1.80
12 Barry Bonds	15.00	4.50
13 Ken Griffey Jr.	10.00	3.00
14 Andruw Jones	2.50	.75
15 Albert Belle	2.50	.75
16 Gary Sheffield	2.50	.75
17 Andy Pettitte	4.00	1.20
18 Hideo Nomo	6.00	1.80
19 Greg Maddux	10.00	3.00
20 John Smoltz	4.00	1.20

1997 Pinnacle Certified Lasting Impressions

Randomly inserted in packs at the rate of one in 19, this 20-card set features color action photos of top veteran stars printed on die-cut Mirror Mylar.

	Nm-Mt	Ex-Mt
COMPLETE SET (20)	80.00	24.00
1 Cal Ripken	12.00	3.60
2 Ken Griffey Jr.	6.00	1.80
3 Mo Vaughn	1.50	.45
4 Brian Jordan	1.50	.45
5 Mark McGwire	10.00	3.00
6 Chuck Knoblauch	1.50	.45
7 Sammy Sosa	6.00	1.80
8 Brady Anderson	1.50	.45
9 Frank Thomas	4.00	1.20
10 Tony Gwynn	5.00	1.50
11 Roger Clemens	8.00	2.40
12 Alex Rodriguez	6.00	1.80
13 Paul Molitor	2.50	.75
14 Kenny Lofton	1.50	.45
15 John Smoltz	2.50	.75
16 Roberto Alomar	4.00	1.20
17 Randy Johnson	4.00	1.20
18 Ryne Sandberg	6.00	1.80
19 Manny Ramirez	1.50	.45
20 Mike Mussina	4.00	1.20

1997 Pinnacle Inside

The 1997 Pinnacle Inside set was issued in one series totalling 150 cards and was distributed inside 24 different collectible player cans with a suggested retail price of $2.99 for a 10-card can. Printed on 14 pt. stock, the fronts feature a color player photo with a thin black-and-white photo as a side border. The set contains a Rookie subset (128-147) and a checklist subset (148-150). The three checklists display black-and-white player photos of American and National League pairings of the 1996 Rookies of the Year, Cy Young winners, and MVPs.

	Nm-Mt	Ex-Mt
COMPLETE SET (150)	40.00	12.00
1 David Cone	.40	.12
2 Sammy Sosa	1.50	.45
3 Joe Carter	.40	.12
4 Juan Gonzalez	1.00	.30
5 Hideo Nomo	1.00	.30
6 Moises Alou	.40	.12
7 Marc Newfield	.40	.12
8 Alex Rodriguez	1.50	.45
9 Kimera Bartee	.40	.12
10 Chuck Knoblauch	.40	.12
11 Jason Isringhausen	.40	.12
12 Jermaine Allensworth	.40	.12
13 Frank Thomas	1.00	.30
14 Paul Molitor	.60	.18
15 John Mabry	.40	.12
16 Greg Maddux	1.50	.45
17 Rafael Palmeiro	.60	.18
18 Brian Jordan	.40	.12
19 Ken Griffey Jr.	1.50	.45
20 Brady Anderson	.40	.12
21 Ruben Sierra	.40	.12
22 Travis Fryman	.40	.12
23 Cal Ripken	3.00	.90
24 Will Clark	1.00	.30
25 Todd Hollandsworth	.40	.12
26 Kevin Brown	.40	.12
27 Mike Piazza	1.50	.45
28 Craig Biggio	.60	.18
29 Paul Wilson	.40	.12
30 Andres Galarraga	.40	.12
31 Chipper Jones	1.00	.30
32 Jason Giambi	1.00	.30
33 Ernie Young	.40	.12
34 Marty Cordova	.40	.12
35 Albert Belle	.40	.12
36 Roger Clemens	2.00	.60
37 Ryne Sandberg	1.50	.45
38 Henry Rodriguez	.40	.12
39 Jay Buhner	.40	.12
40 Raul Mondesi	.40	.12
41 Jeff Fassero	.40	.12
42 Edgar Martinez	.60	.18
43 Trey Beamon	.40	.12
44 Mo Vaughn	.40	.12
45 Gary Sheffield	.40	.12
46 Ray Durham	.40	.12
47 Brett Butler	.40	.12
48 Ivan Rodriguez	1.00	.30
49 Fred McGriff	.60	.18
50 Dean Palmer	.40	.12
51 Rickey Henderson	1.00	.30
52 Andy Pettitte	.60	.18
53 Bobby Bonilla	.40	.12
54 Shawn Green	.40	.12
55 Tino Martinez	.60	.18
56 Tony Gwynn	1.25	.35
57 Tom Glavine	.60	.18
58 Eric Young	.40	.12
59 Kevin Appier	.40	.12
60 Barry Bonds	2.50	.75
61 Wade Boggs	.60	.18
62 Jason Kendall	.40	.12
63 Jeff Bagwell	.60	.18
64 Jeff Conine	.40	.12
65 Greg Vaughn	.40	.12
66 Eric Karros	.40	.12
67 Manny Ramirez	.40	.12
68 John Smoltz	.60	.18
69 Terrell Wade	.40	.12
70 John Wetteland	.40	.12
71 Kenny Lofton	.40	.12
72 Jim Thome	1.00	.30
73 Bill Pulsipher	.40	.12
74 Darryl Strawberry	.60	.18
75 Roberto Alomar	1.00	.30
76 Bobby Higginson	.40	.12
77 James Baldwin	.40	.12
78 Mark McGwire	2.50	.75
79 Jose Canseco	1.00	.30
80 Mark Grudzielanek	.40	.12
81 Ryan Klesko	.40	.12
82 Javy Lopez	.40	.12
83 Ken Caminiti	.40	.12
84 Dave Nilsson	.40	.12
85 Tim Salmon	.60	.18
86 Cecil Fielder	.40	.12
87 Derek Jeter	2.50	.75
88 Garret Anderson	.40	.12
89 Dwight Gooden	.60	.18
90 Carlos Delgado	.40	.12
91 Ugueth Urbina	.40	.12
92 Chan Ho Park	.40	.12
93 Eddie Murray	1.00	.30
94 Alex Ochoa	.40	.12
95 Rusty Greer	.40	.12
96 Mark Grace	.60	.18
97 Pat Hentgen	.40	.12
98 John Jaha	.40	.12
99 Charles Johnson	.40	.12
100 Jermaine Dye	.40	.12
101 Quinton McCracken	.40	.12
102 Troy Percival	.40	.12
103 Shane Reynolds	.40	.12
104 Rondell White	.40	.12
105 Charles Nagy	.40	.12
106 Alan Benes	.40	.12
107 Tom Goodwin	.40	.12
108 Ron Gant	.40	.12
109 Dan Wilson	.40	.12
110 Darin Erstad	.40	.12
111 Matt Williams	.40	.12
112 Barry Larkin	1.00	.30
113 Mariano Rivera	.60	.18
114 Larry Walker	.60	.18
115 Jim Edmonds	.40	.12
116 Michael Tucker	.40	.12
117 Todd Hundley	.40	.12
118 Alex Fernandez	.40	.12
119 J.T. Snow	.40	.12
120 Ellis Burks	.40	.12
121 Steve Finley	.40	.12
122 Mike Mussina	1.00	.30
123 Curtis Pride	.40	.12
124 Derek Bell	.40	.12
125 Dante Bichette	.40	.12
126 Terry Steinbach	.40	.12
127 Randy Johnson	1.00	.30
128 Andruw Jones	.40	.12
129 Vladimir Guerrero	1.00	.30
130 Ruben Rivera	.40	.12
131 Billy Wagner	.40	.12
132 Scott Rolen	.60	.18
133 Rey Ordonez	.40	.12
134 Karim Garcia	.40	.12
135 George Arias	.40	.12
136 Todd Greene	.40	.12
137 Robin Jennings	.40	.12
138 Raul Casanova	.40	.12
139 Steve Gibralter	.40	.12

140 Edgar Renteria .40 .12
141 Chad Mottola .40 .12
142 Dmitri Young .40 .12
143 Tony Clark .40 .12
144 Todd Walker .40 .12
145 Kevin Brown .40 .12
146 Nomar Garciaparra 1.50 .45
147 Neifi Perez .40 .12
148 Derek Jeter CL 1.00 .30
Todd Hollandsworth
149 Pat Hentgen CL .40 .12
John Smoltz
150 Juan Gonzalez CL .40 .12
Ken Caminiti

1997 Pinnacle Inside Club Edition

Randomly inserted in packs at a rate of one in seven, this 150-card set is a parallel rendition of the the regular Pinnacle Inside set and is produced on all silver-foil card stock with gold-foil stamping.

Nm-Mt Ex-Mt
*STARS: 2X TO 5X BASIC CARDS

1997 Pinnacle Inside Diamond Edition

Randomly inserted in packs at a rate of one in 63, this 150-card set is a parallel version of the regular Pinnacle Inside set and is printed on silver foil board with a gold holographic stamp and a die-cut design.

Nm-Mt Ex-Mt
*STARS: 10X TO 25X BASIC CARDS

1997 Pinnacle Inside 40 Something

Randomly inserted in packs at a rate of one in 47, this 16-card set features color player photos of some of the most powerful hitters in the league who have the best chance of pushing past the 40-homer level..

Nm-Mt Ex-Mt
COMPLETE SET (16) 150.00 45.00
1 Juan Gonzalez 12.00 3.60
2 Barry Bonds 30.00 9.00
3 Ken Caminiti 5.00 1.50
4 Mark McGwire 30.00 9.00
5 Todd Hundley 5.00 1.50
6 Albert Belle 5.00 1.50
7 Ellis Burks 5.00 1.50
8 Jay Buhner 5.00 1.50
9 Brady Anderson 5.00 1.50
10 Vinny Castilla 5.00 1.50
11 Mo Vaughn 5.00 1.50
12 Ken Griffey Jr. 20.00 6.00
13 Sammy Sosa 20.00 6.00
14 Andres Galarraga 5.00 1.50
15 Gary Sheffield 5.00 1.50
16 Frank Thomas 12.00 3.60

1997 Pinnacle Inside Cans

This set features replicas of 24 great player cards from the regular Pinnacle Inside set reproduced on the can labels and are painted directly on the metal. Inside each can is information about an opportunity to win a trip to visit a team during their 1998 Spring Training.

Nm-Mt Ex-Mt
COMPLETE SET (24) 25.00 7.50
1 Kenny Lofton .30 .09
2 Frank Thomas .75 .23
3 John Smoltz .50 .15
4 Manny Ramirez .30 .09
5 Alex Rodriguez 1.25 .35
6 Barry Bonds 2.00 .60
7 Mo Vaughn .30 .09
8 Ken Griffey Jr. 1.25 .35
9 Albert Belle .30 .09
10 Greg Maddux 1.25 .35
11 Juan Gonzalez .75 .23
12 Andy Pettitte .50 .15
13 Jeff Bagwell .50 .15
14 Ryan Klesko .30 .09
15 Chipper Jones .75 .23
16 Derek Jeter 2.00 .60
17 Ivan Rodriguez .75 .23
18 Andruw Jones .30 .09
19 Mike Piazza 1.25 .35
20 Hideo Nomo .75 .23
21 Ken Caminiti .30 .09
22 Cal Ripken 2.50 .75
23 Mark McGwire 2.00 .60
24 Tony Gwynn 1.00 .30

1997 Pinnacle Inside Dueling Dugouts

Randomly inserted in packs at a rate of one in 23, this 20-card set features a color photo of a

star player on both sides of the card with a spinning wheel that lines up to reveal comparative statistics.

Nm-Mt Ex-Mt
COMPLETE SET (20) 300.00 90.00
1 Alex Rodriguez 40.00 12.00
Cal Ripken
2 Jeff Bagwell 8.00 2.40
Ken Caminiti
3 Barry Bonds 30.00 9.00
Albert Belle
4 Mike Piazza 20.00 6.00
Ivan Rodriguez
5 Chuck Knoblauch 12.00 3.60
Roberto Alomar
6 Ken Griffey Jr. 20.00 6.00
Andruw Jones
7 Chipper Jones 12.00 3.60
Jim Thome
8 Frank Thomas 12.00 3.60
Mo Vaughn
9 Fred McGriff 30.00 9.00
Mark McGwire
10 Brian Jordan 15.00 4.50
Tony Gwynn
11 Barry Larkin 30.00 9.00
Derek Jeter
12 Kenny Lofton 12.00 3.60
Bernie Williams
13 Juan Gonzalez 5.00 1.50
Manny Ramirez
14 Will Clark 12.00 3.60
Rafael Palmeiro
15 Greg Maddux 20.00 6.00
Roger Clemens
16 John Smoltz 8.00 2.40
Andy Pettitte
17 Mariano Rivera 8.00 2.40
John Wetteland
18 Hideo Nomo 12.00 3.60
Mike Mussina
19 Todd Hollandsworth 5.00 1.50
Darin Erstad
20 Vladimir Guerrero 12.00 3.60
Karim Garcia

1998 Pinnacle Inside

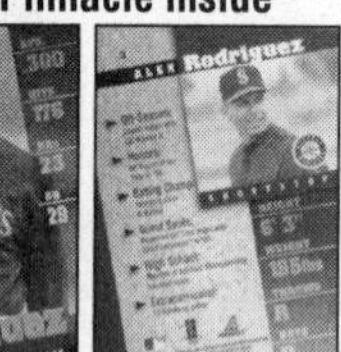

The 1998 Pinnacle Inside set was issued in one series totalling 150 cards and distributed in packs inside 23 different collectible player cans. The fronts feature color player photos while the backs carry player information. The set contains the topical subset: Inside Tips (133-147) and three checklists (148-150).

Nm-Mt Ex-Mt
COMPLETE SET (150) 25.00 7.50
1 Darin Erstad .40 .12
2 Derek Jeter 2.50 .75
3 Alex Rodriguez 1.50 .45
4 Bobby Higginson .40 .12
5 Nomar Garciaparra 1.50 .45
6 Kenny Lofton .40 .12
7 Ivan Rodriguez 1.00 .30
8 Cal Ripken 3.00 .90
9 Todd Hundley .40 .12
10 Chipper Jones 1.00 .30
11 Barry Larkin 1.00 .30
12 Roberto Alomar 1.00 .30
13 Mo Vaughn .40 .12
14 Sammy Sosa 1.50 .45
15 Sandy Alomar Jr. .40 .12
16 Albert Belle .40 .12
17 Scott Rolen .60 .18
18 Pokey Reese .40 .12
19 Ryan Klesko .40 .12
20 Andres Galarraga .40 .12
21 Justin Thompson .40 .12
22 Gary Sheffield .40 .12
23 David Justice .40 .12
24 Ken Griffey Jr. 1.50 .45
25 Andruw Jones .40 .12
26 Jeff Bagwell .60 .18
27 Vladimir Guerrero 1.00 .30
28 Mike Piazza 1.50 .45
29 Chuck Knoblauch .40 .12
30 Rondell White .40 .12
31 Greg Maddux 1.50 .45
32 Andy Pettitte .60 .18
33 Larry Walker .60 .18
34 Bobby Estalella .40 .12
35 Frank Thomas 1.00 .30
36 Tony Womack .40 .12
37 Tony Gwynn 1.25 .35
38 Barry Bonds 2.50 .75
39 Randy Johnson 1.00 .30
40 Mark McGwire 2.50 .75
41 Juan Gonzalez 1.00 .30
42 Tim Salmon .60 .18
43 John Smoltz .60 .18
44 Rafael Palmeiro .60 .18
45 Mark Grace .60 .18
46 Mike Cameron .40 .12
47 Jim Thome 1.00 .30
48 Neifi Perez .40 .12
49 Kevin Brown .60 .18
50 Craig Biggio .60 .18
51 Bernie Williams .60 .18
52 Hideo Nomo 1.00 .30
53 Bob Abreu .40 .12
54 Edgardo Alfonzo .40 .12
55 Wade Boggs .60 .18
56 Jose Guillen .40 .12
57 Ken Caminiti .40 .12
58 Paul Molitor .60 .18
59 Shawn Estes .40 .12
60 Edgar Martinez .60 .18
61 Livan Hernandez .40 .12
62 Ray Lankford .40 .12
63 Rusty Greer .40 .12
64 Jim Edmonds .40 .12
65 Tom Glavine .60 .18
66 Alan Benes .40 .12
67 Will Clark 1.00 .30
68 Garret Anderson .40 .12
69 Javier Lopez .40 .12
70 Mike Mussina 1.00 .30
71 Kevin Orie .40 .12
72 Matt Williams .40 .12
73 Bobby Bonilla .40 .12
74 Ruben Rivera .40 .12
75 Jason Giambi 1.00 .30
76 Todd Walker .40 .12
77 Tino Martinez .60 .18
78 Matt Morris .40 .12
79 Fernando Tatis .40 .12
80 Todd Greene .40 .12
81 Fred McGriff .60 .18
82 Brady Anderson .40 .12
83 Mark Kotsay .40 .12
84 Raul Mondesi .40 .12
85 Moises Alou .40 .12
86 Roger Clemens 2.00 .60
87 Wilton Guerrero .40 .12
88 Shannon Stewart .40 .12
89 Chan Ho Park .40 .12
90 Carlos Delgado .40 .12
91 Jose Cruz Jr. .40 .12
92 Shawn Green .40 .12
93 Robin Ventura .40 .12
94 Reggie Sanders .40 .12
95 Orel Hershiser .40 .12
96 Dante Bichette .40 .12
97 Charles Johnson .40 .12
98 Pedro Martinez 1.00 .30
99 Mariano Rivera .60 .18
100 Joe Randa .40 .12
101 Jeff Kent .40 .12
102 Jay Buhner .40 .12
103 Brian Jordan .40 .12
104 Jason Kendall .40 .12
105 Scott Spiezio .40 .12
106 Desi Relaford .40 .12
107 Bernard Gilkey .40 .12
108 Manny Ramirez .40 .12
109 Tony Clark .40 .12
110 Eric Young .40 .12
111 Johnny Damon .40 .12
112 Glendon Rusch .40 .12
113 Ben Grieve .40 .12
114 Homer Bush .40 .12
115 Miguel Tejada .60 .18
116 Lou Collier .40 .12
117 Derrek Lee .40 .12
118 Jacob Cruz .40 .12
119 Raul Ibanez .40 .12
120 Ryan McGuire .40 .12
121 Antone Williamson .40 .12
122 Abraham Nunez .40 .12
123 Jeff Abbott .40 .12
124 Brett Tomko .40 .12
125 Richie Sexson .40 .12
126 Todd Helton .60 .18
127 Juan Encarnacion .40 .12
128 Richard Hidalgo .40 .12
129 Paul Konerko .40 .12
130 Brad Fullmer .40 .12
131 Jeremi Gonzalez .40 .12
132 Jaret Wright .40 .12
133 Derek Jeter IT 1.25 .35
134 Frank Thomas IT .60 .18
135 Nomar Garciaparra IT 1.00 .30
136 Kenny Lofton IT .40 .12
137 Jeff Bagwell IT .40 .12
138 Todd Hundley IT .40 .12
139 Alex Rodriguez IT 1.00 .30
140 Ken Griffey Jr. IT 1.00 .30
141 Sammy Sosa IT 1.00 .30
142 Greg Maddux IT 1.00 .30
143 Albert Belle IT .40 .12
144 Cal Ripken IT 1.50 .45
145 Mark McGwire IT 1.25 .35
146 Chipper Jones IT .60 .18
147 Charles Johnson IT .40 .12
148 Ken Griffey Jr. CL 1.00 .30
149 Jose Cruz Jr. CL .40 .12
150 Larry Walker CL .40 .12

1998 Pinnacle Inside Club Edition

Randomly inserted in packs at the rate of one in seven, this 150-card set is parallel to the base set and is printed on silver foil card stock with gold foil stamping.

Nm-Mt Ex-Mt
*STARS: 2.5X TO 6X BASIC CARDS

1998 Pinnacle Inside Diamond Edition

Randomly inserted in packs at the rate of one in 67, this 150-card set is parallel to the base set and is printed on silver foil board with a gold holographic stamp and a die-cut design.

Nm-Mt Ex-Mt
*STARS: 8X TO 20X BASIC CARDS

1998 Pinnacle Inside Behind the Numbers

Randomly inserted in packs at the rate of one in 23, this 20-card set features color player photos on the fronts and player information printed on the backs.

Nm-Mt Ex-Mt
COMPLETE SET (20) 200.00 60.00
1 Ken Griffey Jr. 15.00 4.50
2 Cal Ripken 30.00 9.00
3 Alex Rodriguez 15.00 4.50
4 Jose Cruz Jr. 4.00 1.20
5 Mike Piazza 15.00 4.50
6 Nomar Garciaparra 15.00 4.50
7 Scott Rolen 6.00 1.80
8 Andruw Jones 4.00 1.20
9 Frank Thomas 10.00 3.00
10 Mark McGwire 25.00 7.50
11 Ivan Rodriguez 10.00 3.00
12 Greg Maddux 15.00 4.50
13 Roger Clemens 20.00 6.00
14 Derek Jeter 25.00 7.50
15 Tony Gwynn 12.00 3.60
16 Ben Grieve 4.00 1.20
17 Jeff Bagwell 6.00 1.80
18 Chipper Jones 10.00 3.00
19 Hideo Nomo 10.00 3.00
20 Sandy Alomar Jr. 4.00 1.20

1998 Pinnacle Inside Cans

This set features replicas of 23 player cards from the regular Pinnacle Inside set reproduced on the can labels and painted directly on the metal.

Nm-Mt Ex-Mt
COMPLETE SET (23) 25.00 7.50
1 Roger Clemens 2.00 .60
2 Jose Cruz Jr. .40 .12
3 Nomar Garciaparra ROY 1.50 .45
4 Juan Gonzalez 1.00 .30
5 Ben Grieve .40 .12
6 Ken Griffey Jr. 1.50 .45
7 Vladimir Guerrero 1.00 .30
8 Tony Gwynn 1.25 .35
9 Derek Jeter 2.50 .75
10 Andruw Jones .40 .12
11 Chipper Jones 1.00 .30
12 Greg Maddux 1.50 .45
13 Mark McGwire 2.50 .75
14 Hideo Nomo 1.00 .30
15 Mike Piazza 1.50 .45
16 Cal Ripken 3.00 .90
17 Alex Rodriguez 1.50 .45
18 Scott Rolen ROY .60 .18
19 Frank Thomas 1.00 .30
20 Larry Walker MVP .60 .18
21 Arizona Diamondbacks .40 .12
22 Fla. Marlins Champs .40 .12
23 Tamps Bay Devil Rays .40 .12

1998 Pinnacle Inside Cans Gold

Randomly inserted one in every 24 cans, this 23-can set is a gold parallel version of the base can set.

Nm-Mt Ex-Mt
*GOLD CANS: 2.5X TO 6X BASIC CANS

1998 Pinnacle Inside Stand-Up Guys Samples

One of each of these fifty different sample cards was included within wholesale dealer order forms for 1998 Pinnacle Inside baseball. The cards are identical to the Stand-Up Guys cards inserted in packs except for the large "SAMPLE" text on the left hand side of both the front and back of the card.

Nm-Mt Ex-Mt
COMPLETE SET (50) 1500.00 450.00
1AB Mike Piazza 50.00 15.00
Ken Griffey Jr.
Tony Gwynn
Cal Ripken
1CD Ken Griffey Jr. 50.00 15.00
Tony Gwynn
Cal Ripken
Mike Piazza
2AB Nomar Garciaparra 40.00 12.00
Andruw Jones
Scott Rolen
Alex Rodriguez
2CD Andruw Jones 40.00 12.00
Scott Rolen
Alex Rodriguez
Nomar Garciaparra
3AB Chipper Jones 30.00 9.00
Andruw Jones
Javy Lopez
Greg Maddux
3CD Andruw Jones 30.00 9.00
Javy Lopez
Greg Maddux
Chipper Jones
4AB Alex Rodriguez 50.00 15.00
Jay Buhner
Ken Griffey Jr.
Randy Johnson
4CD Jay Buhner 50.00 15.00
Ken Griffey Jr.
Randy Johnson
Alex Rodriguez
5AB Mo Vaughn 50.00 15.00
Frank Thomas
Mark McGwire
Jeff Bagwell
5CD Frank Thomas 50.00 15.00
Mark McGwire
Jeff Bagwell
Mo Vaughn
6AB Barry Larkin 50.00 15.00
Nomar Garciaparra
Alex Rodriguez
Derek Jeter
6CD Nomar Garciaparra 50.00 15.00
Alex Rodriguez
Derek Jeter
Barry Larkin
7AB Javy Lopez 40.00 12.00
Mike Piazza
Charles Johnson
Ivan Rodriguez
7CD Mike Piazza 40.00 12.00
Charles Johnson
Ivan Rodriguez
Javy Lopez
8AB Scott Rolen 50.00 15.00
Cal Ripken
Ken Caminiti
Chipper Jones
8CD Cal Ripken 50.00 15.00
Ken Caminiti
Chipper Jones
Scott Rolen
9AB Jose Guillen 20.00 6.00
Jose Cruz Jr.
Andruw Jones
Vladimir Guerrero
9CD Jose Cruz Jr. 20.00 6.00
Andruw Jones
Vladimir Guerrero
Jose Guillen
10AB Neifi Perez 5.00 1.50
Larry Walker
Ellis Burks
Dante Bichette
10CD Larry Walker 5.00 1.50
Ellis Burks
Dante Bichette
Neifi Perez
11AB Manny Ramirez 25.00 7.50
Juan Gonzalez
Vladimir Guerrero
Sammy Sosa
11CD Juan Gonzalez 25.00 7.50
Vladimir Guerrero
Sammy Sosa
Manny Ramirez
12AB Randy Johnson 30.00 9.00
Greg Maddux
Hideo Nomo
Roger Clemens
12CD Greg Maddux 30.00 9.00
Hideo Nomo
Roger Clemens
Randy Johnson
13AB Fernando Tatis 5.00 1.50
Ben Grieve
Jose Cruz Jr.
Paul Konerko
13CD Ben Grieve 5.00 1.50
Jose Cruz Jr.
Paul Konerko
Fernando Tatis
14AB Craig Biggio 12.00 3.60
Ryne Sandberg
Roberto Alomar
Chuck Knoblauch
14CD Ryne Sandberg 12.00 3.60
Roberto Alomar
Chuck Knoblauch
Craig Biggio
15AB Roberto Alomar 50.00 15.00
Cal Ripken
Rafael Palmeiro
Brady Anderson
15CD Cal Ripken 50.00 15.00
Rafael Palmeiro
Brady Anderson
Roberto Alomar
16AB Garret Anderson 12.00 3.60
Darin Erstad
Tim Salmon
Jim Edmonds
16CD Darin Erstad 12.00 3.60
Tim Salmon
Jim Edmonds
Garret Anderson
17AB Eric Karros 40.00 12.00
Mike Piazza
Raul Mondesi
Hideo Nomo
17CD Mike Piazza 40.00 12.00
Raul Mondesi
Hideo Nomo
Eric Karros
18AB Rusty Greer 15.00 4.50
Ivan Rodriguez
Will Clark
Juan Gonzalez
18CD Ivan Rodriguez 15.00 4.50
Will Clark
Juan Gonzalez
Rusty Greer
19AB Andy Pettitte 50.00 15.00
Derek Jeter
Tino Martinez
Bernie Williams
19CD Derek Jeter 50.00 15.00
Tino Martinez
Bernie Williams
Andy Pettitte
20AB Bernie Williams 50.00 15.00
Kenny Lofton
Brady Anderson
Ken Griffey Jr.
20CD Kenny Lofton 50.00 15.00
Brady Anderson
Ken Griffey Jr.
Bernie Williams

21AB Rickey Henderson 12.00 3.60
Paul Molitor
Ryne Sandberg
Eddie Murray
21CD Paul Molitor 12.00 3.60
Ryne Sandberg
Eddie Murray
Rickey Henderson
22AB Mark McGwire 50.00 15.00
Tony Clark
Jeff Bagwell
Frank Thomas
22CD Tony Clark 50.00 15.00
Jeff Bagwell
Frank Thomas
Mark McGwire
23AB Sandy Alomar 15.00 4.50
Manny Ramirez
David Justice
Jim Thome
23CD Manny Ramirez 15.00 4.50
David Justice
Jim Thome
Sandy Alomar
24AB Dante Bichette 20.00 6.00
Barry Bonds
Jeff Bagwell
Albert Belle
24CD Barry Bonds 20.00 6.00
Jeff Bagwell
Albert Belle
Dante Bichette
25AB Andruw Jones 50.00 15.00
Ken Griffey Jr.
Alex Rodriguez
Frank Thomas
25CD Ken Griffey Jr. 50.00 15.00
Alex Rodriguez
Frank Thomas
Andruw Jones

1998 Pinnacle Inside Stand-Up Guys

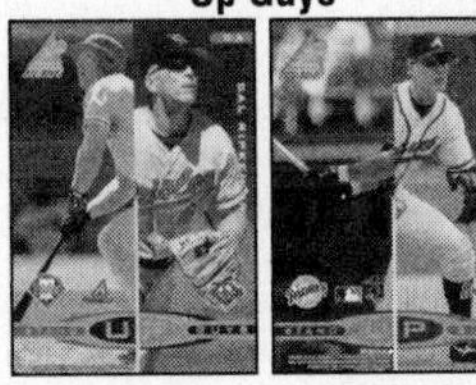

Randomly inserted one per pack, this 50-card set features color images of four players printed on each three dimensional card. Each card is matched to one other card to form 25 stand up cards.

Nm-Mt Ex-Mt
COMPLETE SET (50) 30.00 9.00
1AB Mike Piazza 1.25 .35
Ken Griffey Jr.
Tony Gwynn
Cal Ripken
1CD Ken Griffey Jr. 1.25 .35
Tony Gwynn
Cal Ripken
Mike Piazza
2AB Nomar Garciaparra 1.25 .35
Andruw Jones
Scott Rolen
Alex Rodriguez
2CD Andruw Jones 1.25 .35
Scott Rolen
Alex Rodriguez
Nomar Garciaparra
3AB Chipper Jones 1.25 .35
Andruw Jones
Javy Lopez
Greg Maddux
3CD Andruw Jones 1.25 .35
Javy Lopez
Greg Maddux
Chipper Jones
4AB Alex Rodriguez 1.25 .35
Jay Buhner
Ken Griffey Jr.
Randy Johnson
4CD Jay Buhner 1.25 .35
Ken Griffey Jr.
Randy Johnson
Alex Rodriguez
5AB Mo Vaughn 2.00 .60
Frank Thomas
Mark McGwire
Jeff Bagwell
5CD Frank Thomas 2.00 .60
Mark McGwire
Jeff Bagwell
Mo Vaughn
6AB Barry Larkin 2.00 .60
Nomar Garciaparra
Alex Rodriguez
Derek Jeter
6CD Nomar Garciaparra 2.00 .60
Alex Rodriguez
Derek Jeter
Barry Larkin
7AB Javy Lopez 1.25 .35
Mike Piazza
Charles Johnson
Ivan Rodriguez
7CD Mike Piazza 1.25 .35
Charles Johnson
Ivan Rodriguez
Javy Lopez
8AB Scott Rolen 2.50 .75
Cal Ripken
Ken Caminiti
Chipper Jones
8CD Cal Ripken 2.50 .75
Ken Caminiti
Chipper Jones
Scott Rolen
9AB Jose Guillen .75 .23
Jose Cruz Jr.
Andruw Jones
Vladimir Guerrero
9CD Jose Cruz Jr. .75 .23
Andruw Jones
Vladimir Guerrero
Jose Guillen
10AB Neifi Perez .50 .15
Larry Walker
Ellis Burks
Dante Bichette
10CD Larry Walker .50 .15
Ellis Burks
Dante Bichette
Neifi Perez
11AB Manny Ramirez 1.25 .35
Juan Gonzalez
Vladimir Guerrero
Sammy Sosa
11CD Juan Gonzalez 1.25 .35
Vladimir Guerrero
Sammy Sosa
Manny Ramirez
12AB Randy Johnson 1.25 .35
Greg Maddux
Hideo Nomo
Roger Clemens
12CD Greg Maddux 1.25 .35
Hideo Nomo
Roger Clemens
Randy Johnson
13AB Fernando Tatis .30 .09
Ben Grieve
Jose Cruz Jr.
Paul Konerko
13CD Ben Grieve .30 .09
Jose Cruz Jr.
Paul Konerko
Fernando Tatis
14AB Craig Biggio .75 .23
Ryne Sandberg
Roberto Alomar
Chuck Knoblauch
14CD Ryne Sandberg .75 .23
Roberto Alomar
Chuck Knoblauch
Craig Biggio
15AB Roberto Alomar 2.50 .75
Cal Ripken
Rafael Palmeiro
Brady Anderson
15CD Cal Ripken 2.50 .75
Rafael Palmeiro
Brady Anderson
Roberto Alomar
16AB Garret Anderson .30 .09
Darin Erstad
Tim Salmon
Jim Edmonds
16CD Darin Erstad .30 .09
Tim Salmon
Jim Edmonds
Garret Anderson
17AB Eric Karros 1.25 .35
Mike Piazza
Raul Mondesi
Hideo Nomo
17CD Mike Piazza 1.25 .35
Raul Mondesi
Hideo Nomo
Eric Karros
18AB Rusty Greer .75 .23
Ivan Rodriguez
Will Clark
Juan Gonzalez
18CD Ivan Rodriguez .75 .23
Will Clark
Juan Gonzalez
Rusty Greer
19AB Andy Pettitte 2.00 .60
Derek Jeter
Tino Martinez
Bernie Williams
19CD Derek Jeter 2.00 .60
Tino Martinez
Bernie Williams
Andy Pettitte
20AB Bernie Williams 1.25 .35
Kenny Lofton
Brady Anderson
Ken Griffey Jr.
20CD Kenny Lofton 1.25 .35
Brady Anderson
Ken Griffey Jr.
Bernie Williams
21AB Rickey Henderson .50 .15
Paul Molitor
Ryne Sandberg
Eddie Murray
21CD Paul Molitor .50 .15
Ryne Sandberg
Eddie Murray
Rickey Henderson
22AB Mark McGwire 2.00 .60
Tony Clark
Jeff Bagwell
Frank Thomas
22CD Tony Clark 2.00 .60
Jeff Bagwell
Frank Thomas
Mark McGwire
23AB Sandy Alomar Jr. .30 .09
Manny Ramirez
David Justice
Jim Thome
23CD Manny Ramirez .30 .09
David Justice
Jim Thome
Sandy Alomar
24AB Dante Bichette 2.00 .60
Barry Bonds
Jeff Bagwell
Albert Belle
24CD Barry Bonds 2.00 .60
Jeff Bagwell
Albert Belle
Dante Bichette
25AB Andruw Jones 1.25 .35
Ken Griffey Jr.
Alex Rodriguez
Frank Thomas
25CD Ken Griffey Jr. 1.25 .35
Alex Rodriguez
Frank Thomas
Andruw Jones

1997 Pinnacle Mint

The 1997 Pinnacle Mint set was issued in one series totalling 30 cards and was distributed in packs of three cards and two coins for a suggested retail price of $3.99. The challenge was to fit the coins with the die-cut cards that pictured the same player on the minted coin. Two die-cut cards were inserted in each pack. Either one bronze, silver or gold card was also included in each pack. The fronts featured color action player images on a sepia player portrait background and a cut-out area for the matching coin. Ryan Klesko's die cut card was distributed to dealers as a promo. Die cut cards are listed below.

Nm-Mt Ex-Mt
COMP.DIE CUT SET (30) 10.00 3.00
*BRONZE: .75X TO 2X BASIC CARDS.
*SILVER: 5X TO 12X BASIC CARDS
*GOLD: 10X TO 25X BASIC CARDS
1 Ken Griffey Jr. .75 .23
2 Frank Thomas .50 .15
3 Alex Rodriguez .75 .23
4 Cal Ripken 1.50 .45
5 Mo Vaughn .20 .06
6 Juan Gonzalez .50 .15
7 Mike Piazza .75 .23
8 Albert Belle .20 .06
9 Chipper Jones .50 .15
10 Andruw Jones .20 .06
11 Greg Maddux .75 .23
12 Hideo Nomo .50 .15
13 Jeff Bagwell .30 .09
14 Manny Ramirez .20 .06
15 Mark McGwire 1.25 .35
16 Derek Jeter 1.25 .35
17 Sammy Sosa .75 .23
18 Barry Bonds 1.25 .35
19 Chuck Knoblauch .20 .06
20 Dante Bichette .20 .06
21 Tony Gwynn .60 .18
22 Ken Caminiti .20 .06
23 Gary Sheffield .20 .06
24 Tim Salmon .30 .09
25 Ivan Rodriguez .50 .15
26 Henry Rodriguez .20 .06
27 Barry Larkin .50 .15
28 Ryan Klesko .20 .06
29 Brian Jordan .20 .06
30 Jay Buhner .20 .06
P28 Ryan Klesko Promo 1.00 .30

1997 Pinnacle Mint Coins Brass

Each pack of Pinnacle Mint contained two coins (a mixture of Brass, Nickel and Gold Plated). The Brass coins were the most common. This set features coins minted in brass with embossed player heads and were made to be matched with the die-cut card version of the same player. Two versions of the Manny Ramirez Brass coin were distributed - an erroneous version with the words "fine silver" printed on back, and a corrected version. Judging from market observations, the "fine silver" version appears to be about four times tougher to find than the corrected. In addition to being inserted in packs, Ryan Klesko's Brass coin was distributed to dealers as a promo.

Nm-Mt Ex-Mt
COMPLETE SET (30) 50.00 15.00
*NICKEL: 3X TO 8X BASIC CARDS
*GOLD PLATED: 8X TO 20X BASIC CARDS
GOLD PLATED STATED ODDS 1:48
*SILVER: 40X TO 100X BASIC BRASS
SILVER STATED ODDS 1:2300
1 Ken Griffey Jr. 2.50 .75
2 Frank Thomas 1.50 .45
3 Alex Rodriguez 2.50 .75
4 Cal Ripken 5.00 1.50
5 Mo Vaughn .60 .18
6 Juan Gonzalez 1.50 .45
7 Mike Piazza 2.50 .75
8 Albert Belle .60 .18
9 Chipper Jones 1.50 .45
10 Andruw Jones .60 .18
11 Greg Maddux 2.50 .75
12 Hideo Nomo 1.50 .45
13 Jeff Bagwell 1.00 .30
14A Manny Ramirez COR .60 .18
14B Manny Ramirez ERR .60 .18
says "Fine Silver" on back
15 Mark McGwire 4.00 1.20
16 Derek Jeter 4.00 1.20
17 Sammy Sosa 2.50 .75
18 Barry Bonds 4.00 1.20
19 Chuck Knoblauch .60 .18
20 Dante Bichette .60 .18
21 Tony Gwynn 2.00 .60
22 Ken Caminiti .60 .18
23 Gary Sheffield .60 .18
24 Tim Salmon 1.00 .30
25 Ivan Rodriguez 1.50 .45
26 Henry Rodriguez .60 .18
27 Barry Larkin 1.50 .45
28 Ryan Klesko .60 .18
29 Brian Jordan .60 .18
30 Jay Buhner .60 .18
P28 Ryan Klesko Promo 3.00 .90

1998 Pinnacle Mint Samples

These six promotional cards were distributed exclusively to dealers and hobby media a few months prior to the release of 1998 Pinnacle Mint.

Nm-Mt Ex-Mt
COMPLETE SET (6) 15.00 4.50
12 Greg Maddux 2.50 .75
14 Mark McGwire 3.00 .90
17 Mike Piazza 2.50 .75
18 Cal Ripken 4.00 1.20
22 Frank Thomas 1.50 .45
24 Larry Walker .75 .23

1998 Pinnacle Mint

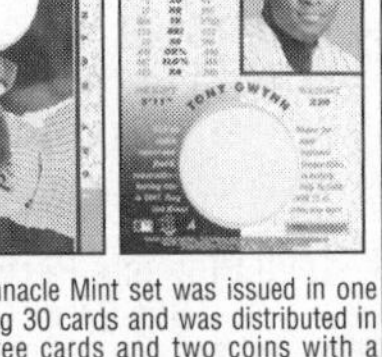

The 1998 Pinnacle Mint set was issued in one series totalling 30 cards and was distributed in packs of three cards and two coins with a suggest retail price of $3.99. The challenge was to fit the coins with the die-cut cards that pictured the same player on the minted coin. Two die-cut cards were inserted one in every hobby pack and one die-cut card in every retail pack. The fronts feature color action player photos with a cut-out area for the matching coin.

Nm-Mt Ex-Mt
COMP.DIE CUT SET (30) 10.00 3.00
*BRONZE: .75X TO 2X DIE CUTS
*SILVER: 4X TO 10X DIE CUTS
*GOLD: 10X TO 25X DIE CUTS
1 Jeff Bagwell .30 .09
2 Albert Belle .20 .06
3 Barry Bonds 1.25 .35
4 Tony Clark .20 .06
5 Roger Clemens 1.00 .30
6 Juan Gonzalez .50 .15
7 Ken Griffey Jr. .75 .23
8 Tony Gwynn .60 .18
9 Derek Jeter 1.25 .35
10 Randy Johnson .50 .15
11 Chipper Jones .50 .15
12 Greg Maddux .75 .23
13 Tino Martinez .30 .09
14 Mark McGwire 1.25 .35
15 Hideo Nomo .50 .15
16 Andy Pettitte .30 .09
17 Mike Piazza .75 .23
18 Cal Ripken 1.50 .45
19 Alex Rodriguez .75 .23
20 Ivan Rodriguez .50 .15
21 Sammy Sosa .75 .23
22 Frank Thomas .50 .15
23 Mo Vaughn .20 .06
24 Larry Walker .30 .09
25 Jose Cruz Jr. .20 .06
26 Nomar Garciaparra .75 .23
27 Vladimir Guerrero .50 .15
28 Livan Hernandez .20 .06
29 Andruw Jones .20 .06
30 Scott Rolen .30 .09

1998 Pinnacle Mint Coins Brass

Randomly inserted two in every hobby pack and one in every retail pack, this 30-coin set features embossed player head images on brass coins and were made to be matched with the die-cut card version of the same player.

Nm-Mt Ex-Mt
COMPLETE SET (30) 60.00 18.00
*BRASS AP's: 5X TO 12X BRASS COINS
*GOLD PLATE: 10X TO 25X BRASS COINS
GOLD PLATED ODDS 1:199 HOBBY/RETAIL
*GOLD PLATED AP's: 15X TO 40X BRASS COINS
GOLD PLATED AP RAND.INS.IN PACKS
GOLD PLATED AP PRINT RUN 100 SETS
*NICKEL: 3X TO 8X BRASS COINS
NICKEL ODDS 1:41 HOBBY/RETAIL
*NICKEL AP: 8X TO 20X BRASS COINS
NICKEL AP ODDS 1:48 HOBBY, 1:97 RETAIL
NICKEL AP PRINT RUN 250 SETS
*SOLID SILVER: 12.5X TO 30X BRASS COINS
SOLID SILVER 1:288 HOBBY, 1:960 RETAIL
1 Jeff Bagwell 1.25 .35
2 Albert Belle .75 .23
3 Barry Bonds 4.00 1.20
4 Tony Clark .75 .23
5 Roger Clemens 4.00 1.20
6 Juan Gonzalez 2.00 .60
7 Ken Griffey Jr. 3.00 .90
8 Tony Gwynn 2.50 .75
9 Derek Jeter 5.00 1.50
10 Randy Johnson 2.00 .60
11 Chipper Jones 2.00 .60
12 Greg Maddux 3.00 .90
13 Tino Martinez 1.25 .35
14 Mark McGwire 5.00 1.50
15 Hideo Nomo 2.00 .60
16 Andy Pettitte 1.25 .35
17 Mike Piazza 3.00 .90
18 Cal Ripken 6.00 1.80
19 Alex Rodriguez 3.00 .90
20 Ivan Rodriguez 2.00 .60
21 Sammy Sosa 3.00 .90
22 Frank Thomas 2.00 .60
23 Mo Vaughn .75 .23
24 Larry Walker 1.25 .35
25 Jose Cruz Jr. .75 .23
26 Nomar Garciaparra 3.00 .90
27 Vladimir Guerrero 2.00 .60
28 Livan Hernandez .75 .23
29 Andruw Jones .75 .23
30 Scott Rolen 1.25 .35

1998 Pinnacle Mint Coins Brass Samples

These three promotional coins were distributed exclusively to dealers and hobby media a few months prior to the release of 1998 Pinnacle Mint.

Nm-Mt Ex-Mt
COMPLETE SET (3) 10.00 3.00
12 Greg Maddux 3.00 .90
14 Mark McGwire 5.00 1.50
22 Frank Thomas 3.00 .90

1998 Pinnacle Mint Gems

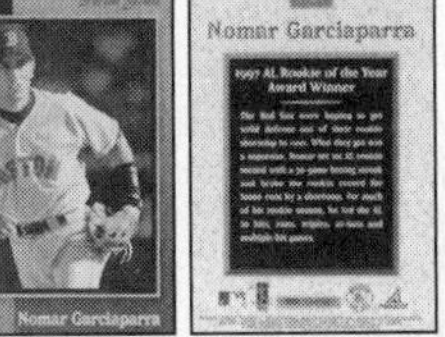

Randomly inserted at the rate of one in 31 hobby packs and one in 47 retail packs, this six-card set features color photos of 1997's top award winners printed on full silver-foil card stock with foil stamped accents.

Nm-Mt Ex-Mt
COMPLETE SET (6) 25.00 7.50
1 Ken Griffey Jr. 6.00 1.80
2 Larry Walker 2.50 .75
3 Roger Clemens 8.00 2.40
4 Pedro Martinez 4.00 1.20
5 Nomar Garciaparra 6.00 1.80
6 Scott Rolen 2.50 .75

1998 Pinnacle Mint Benefactor Mail-Away

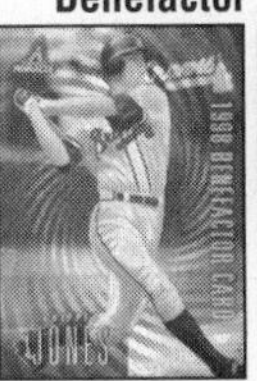

This one card set was available through a mail-order offer on 1998 Pinnacle Mint packs. The card could be ordered for $9.95 plus a $4 shipping and handling charge.

Nm-Mt Ex-Mt
1 Chipper Jones 20.00 6.00

1998 Pinnacle Performers

The 1998 Pinnacle Performers set was issued in one series totalling 150 cards. The eight-card packs retailed for $1.99 each. The set contains the topical subset: Far and Away (138-147) and Checklists (148-150).

Nm-Mt Ex-Mt
COMPLETE SET (150) 20.00 6.00
1 Ken Griffey Jr. .75 .23
2 Frank Thomas .50 .15
3 Cal Ripken 1.50 .45
4 Alex Rodriguez .75 .23
5 Greg Maddux .75 .23
6 Mike Piazza .75 .23
7 Chipper Jones .50 .15
8 Tony Gwynn .60 .18
9 Derek Jeter 1.25 .35
10 Jeff Bagwell .30 .09
11 Juan Gonzalez .50 .15
12 Nomar Garciaparra .75 .23
13 Andruw Jones .20 .06
14 Hideo Nomo .50 .15
15 Roger Clemens 1.00 .30
16 Mark McGwire 1.25 .35
17 Scott Rolen .30 .09
18 Vladimir Guerrero .50 .15
19 Barry Bonds 1.25 .35
20 Darin Erstad .20 .06
21 Albert Belle .20 .06
22 Kenny Lofton .20 .06
23 Mo Vaughn .20 .06
24 Tony Clark .20 .06
25 Ivan Rodriguez .50 .15
26 Jose Cruz Jr. .20 .06
27 Larry Walker .30 .09

28 Jaret Wright .20 .06
29 Andy Pettitte .30 .09
30 Roberto Alomar .50 .15
31 Randy Johnson .50 .15
32 Manny Ramirez .20 .06
33 Paul Molitor .30 .09
34 Mike Mussina .50 .15
35 Jim Thome .50 .15
36 Tino Martinez .30 .09
37 Gary Sheffield .20 .06
38 Chuck Knoblauch .20 .06
39 Bernie Williams .30 .09
40 Tim Salmon .30 .09
41 Sammy Sosa .75 .23
42 Wade Boggs .30 .09
43 Will Clark .50 .15
44 Andres Galarraga .20 .06
45 Raul Mondesi .20 .06
46 Rickey Henderson .50 .15
47 Jose Canseco .50 .15
48 Pedro Martinez .50 .15
49 Jay Buhner .20 .06
50 Ryan Klesko .20 .06
51 Barry Larkin .50 .15
52 Charles Johnson .20 .06
53 Tom Glavine .30 .09
54 Edgar Martinez .30 .09
55 Fred McGriff .30 .09
56 Moises Alou .20 .06
57 Dante Bichette .20 .06
58 Jim Edmonds .20 .06
59 Mark Grace .30 .09
60 Chan Ho Park .20 .06
61 Justin Thompson .20 .06
62 John Smoltz .30 .09
63 Craig Biggio .30 .09
64 Ken Caminiti .20 .06
65 Richard Hidalgo .20 .06
66 Carlos Delgado .20 .06
67 David Justice .20 .06
68 J.T. Snow .20 .06
69 Jason Giambi .50 .15
70 Garret Anderson .20 .06
71 Rondell White .20 .06
72 Matt Williams .20 .06
73 Brady Anderson .20 .06
74 Eric Karros .20 .06
75 Javier Lopez .20 .06
76 Pat Hentgen .20 .06
77 Todd Hundley .20 .06
78 Ray Lankford .20 .06
79 Denny Neagle .20 .06
80 Sandy Alomar Jr. .20 .06
81 Jason Kendall .20 .06
82 Omar Vizquel .20 .06
83 Kevin Brown .30 .09
84 Kevin Appier .20 .06
85 Al Martin .20 .06
86 Rusty Greer .20 .06
87 Bobby Bonilla .20 .06
88 Shawn Estes .20 .06
89 Rafael Palmeiro .30 .09
90 Edgar Renteria .20 .06
91 Alan Benes .20 .06
92 Bobby Higginson .20 .06
93 Mark Grudzielanek .20 .06
94 Jose Guillen .20 .06
95 Neifi Perez .20 .06
96 Jeff Abbott .20 .06
97 Todd Walker .20 .06
98 Eric Young .20 .06
99 Brett Tomko .20 .06
100 Mike Cameron .20 .06
101 Karim Garcia .20 .06
102 Brian Jordan .20 .06
103 Jeff Suppan .20 .06
104 Robin Ventura .30 .09
105 Henry Rodriguez .20 .06
106 Shannon Stewart .20 .06
107 Kevin Orie .20 .06
108 Bartolo Colon .20 .06
109 Bob Abreu .20 .06
110 Vinny Castilla .20 .06
111 Livan Hernandez .20 .06
112 Derrek Lee .20 .06
113 Mark Kotsay .20 .06
114 Todd Greene .20 .06
115 Edgardo Alfonzo .20 .06
116 A.J. Hinch .20 .06
117 Paul Konerko .20 .06
118 Todd Helton .30 .09
119 Miguel Tejada .30 .09
120 Fernando Tatis .20 .06
121 Ben Grieve .20 .06
122 Travis Lee .20 .06
123 Kerry Wood .50 .15
124 Eli Marrero .20 .06
125 David Ortiz .20 .06
126 Juan Encarnacion .20 .06
127 Brad Fullmer .20 .06
128 Richie Sexson .20 .06
129 Aaron Boone .20 .06
130 Enrique Wilson .20 .06
131 Javier Valentin .20 .06
132 Abraham Nunez .20 .06
133 Ricky Ledee .20 .06
134 Carl Pavano .20 .06
135 Bobby Estalella .20 .06
136 Homer Bush .20 .06
137 Brian Rose .20 .06
138 Ken Griffey Jr. FA .50 .15
139 Frank Thomas FA .30 .09
140 Cal Ripken FA .75 .23
141 Alex Rodriguez FA .50 .15
142 Greg Maddux FA .50 .15
143 Chipper Jones FA .30 .09
144 Mike Piazza FA .50 .15
145 Tony Gwynn FA .30 .09
146 Derek Jeter FA .60 .18
147 Jeff Bagwell FA .20 .06
148 Checklist .20 .06
149 Checklist .20 .06
150 Checklist .20 .06

1998 Pinnacle Performers Peak Performers

Randomly inserted in packs at a rate of one in seven, this 150-card set is a parallel to the Pinnacle Performers base set.

Nm-Mt Ex-Mt
*STARS: 3X TO 8X BASIC CARDS......

1998 Pinnacle Performers Big Bang Samples

One of each of these twenty different sample cards was included within wholesale dealer order forms for 1998 Pinnacle Performers baseball. The cards are identical to the Big Bang cards inserted in packs except for the large "SAMPLE" text running diagonally against the back of the card.

Nm-Mt Ex-Mt
COMPLETE SET (20) 150.00 45.00
1 Ken Griffey Jr. 20.00 6.00
2 Frank Thomas 8.00 2.40
3 Mike Piazza 15.00 4.50
4 Chipper Jones 12.00 3.60
5 Alex Rodriguez 15.00 4.50
6 Nomar Garciaparra 15.00 4.50
7 Jeff Bagwell 6.00 1.80
8 Cal Ripken 25.00 7.50
9 Albert Belle 3.00 .90
10 Mark McGwire 20.00 6.00
11 Juan Gonzalez 5.00 1.50
12 Larry Walker 3.00 .90
13 Tino Martinez 3.00 .90
14 Jim Thome 5.00 1.50
15 Manny Ramirez 6.00 1.80
16 Barry Bonds 12.00 3.60
17 Mo Vaughn 3.00 .90
18 Jose Cruz Jr. 3.00 .90
19 Tony Clark 3.00 .90
20 Andruw Jones 5.00 1.50

1998 Pinnacle Performers Big Bang

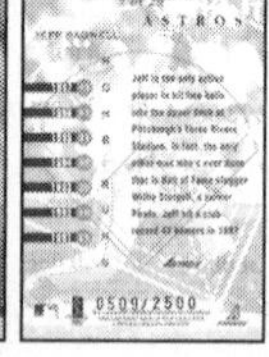

Randomly inserted in packs at a rate of one in 45, this 20-card set is an insert to the Pinnacle Performers base set. The set is sequentially numbered to 2500. The fronts feature a color action photo printed on a baseball diamond background.

Nm-Mt Ex-Mt
COMPLETE SET (20) 150.00 45.00
1 Ken Griffey Jr. 12.00 3.60
2 Frank Thomas 8.00 2.40
3 Mike Piazza 12.00 3.60
4 Chipper Jones 8.00 2.40
5 Alex Rodriguez 12.00 3.60
6 Nomar Garciaparra 12.00 3.60
7 Jeff Bagwell 5.00 1.50
8 Cal Ripken 25.00 7.50
9 Albert Belle 3.00 .90
10 Mark McGwire 20.00 6.00
11 Juan Gonzalez 8.00 2.40
12 Larry Walker 5.00 1.50
13 Tino Martinez 5.00 1.50
14 Jim Thome 8.00 2.40
15 Manny Ramirez 3.00 .90
16 Barry Bonds 20.00 6.00
17 Mo Vaughn 3.00 .90
18 Jose Cruz Jr. 3.00 .90
19 Tony Clark 3.00 .90
20 Andruw Jones 3.00 .90

1998 Pinnacle Performers Big Bang Seasonal Outburst

Randomly inserted in packs, this 20-card set is a parallel insert to the Pinnacle Performers Big Bang set. The striking red foil background (as averse to the silver foil background on basic Big Bang inserts) makes them very easy to differentiate. Print runs for each card were based upon the featured player's home run total for the 1997 season. Those figures are detailed individually in the listings below after each player's name. Unfortunately, more non-serial numbered cards are currently circulating than real serial numbered cards. This is due to quality control return copies, of which were never intended for public release and are typically destroyed one year after the product is released, getting out during Pinnacle's bankruptcy liquidation.

Nm-Mt Ex-Mt
*NON-SERIAL #'d: .2X TO .5X OUTBURST
NNO CARDS NOT INTENDED FOR PUBLIC
1 Ken Griffey Jr./56 30.00 9.00
2 Frank Thomas/35 20.00 6.00
3 Mike Piazza/40 30.00 9.00
4 Chipper Jones/21
5 Alex Rodriguez/23
6 Nomar Garciaparra/30 30.00 9.00
7 Jeff Bagwell/43 12.00 3.60
8 Cal Ripken/17
9 Albert Belle/30 10.00 3.00
10 Mark McGwire/58 50.00 15.00
11 Juan Gonzalez/42 20.00 6.00
12 Larry Walker/49 12.00 3.60
13 Tino Martinez/44 12.00 3.60
14 Jim Thome/40 20.00 6.00
15 Manny Ramirez/26 10.00 3.00
16 Barry Bonds/40 50.00 15.00
17 Mo Vaughn/35 10.00 3.00
18 Jose Cruz Jr./26 10.00 3.00
19 Tony Clark/32 10.00 3.00
20 Andruw Jones/18

1998 Pinnacle Performers Launching Pad

Randomly inserted in packs at a rate of one in nine, this 20-card set is an insert to the

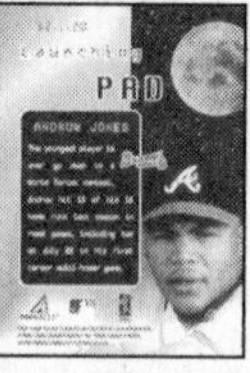

Pinnacle Performers base set. The fronts feature color action photos of 20 of today's greatest hitters surrounded by a background of stars and a moon.

Nm-Mt Ex-Mt
COMPLETE SET (20) 60.00 18.00
1 Ben Grieve 1.00 .30
2 Ken Griffey Jr. 4.00 1.20
3 Derek Jeter 6.00 1.80
4 Frank Thomas 2.50 .75
5 Travis Lee 1.00 .30
6 Vladimir Guerrero 2.50 .75
7 Tony Gwynn 3.00 .90
8 Jose Cruz Jr. 1.00 .30
9 Cal Ripken 8.00 2.40
10 Chipper Jones 2.50 .75
11 Scott Rolen 1.50 .45
12 Andruw Jones 1.00 .30
13 Ivan Rodriguez 2.50 .75
14 Todd Helton 1.50 .45
15 Nomar Garciaparra 4.00 1.20
16 Mark McGwire 6.00 1.80
17 Gary Sheffield 1.00 .30
18 Bernie Williams 1.50 .45
19 Alex Rodriguez 4.00 1.20
20 Mike Piazza 4.00 1.20

1998 Pinnacle Performers Power Trip

Randomly inserted in packs at a rate of one in 21, this 10-card set is an insert to the Pinnacle Performers base set. The set is sequentially numbered to 10,000. The fronts feature a black and white background that shimmers with silver. The 10 color action photos showcase players who are today's power hitters.

Nm-Mt Ex-Mt
COMPLETE SET (10) 40.00 12.00
1 Frank Thomas 3.00 .90
2 Alex Rodriguez 5.00 1.50
3 Nomar Garciaparra 5.00 1.50
4 Jeff Bagwell 2.00 .60
5 Cal Ripken 10.00 3.00
6 Mike Piazza 5.00 1.50
7 Chipper Jones 3.00 .90
8 Ken Griffey Jr. 5.00 1.50
9 Mark McGwire 8.00 2.40
10 Juan Gonzalez 3.00 .90

1998 Pinnacle Performers Swing for the Fences

Randomly inserted in packs at a rate of one in two, this 50-card set is an insert to the Pinnacle Performers base set. Each card is printed on thin stock and features a player action photo set against a royal blue background. The cards were intended as exchange items for a home run game (based upon the NL and AL home run leaders in 1998). Pinnacle's bankruptcy in the Fall of 1998, however, wiped away the Upgrade redemption program. In addition, a scarce exchange card - originally intended as a redemption for a baseball signed Juan Gonzalez - was randomly seeded into packs. None of these cards were ever exchanged due to Pinnacle's bankruptcy.

Nm-Mt Ex-Mt
COMPLETE SET (50) 40.00 12.00
1 Brady Anderson .50 .15
2 Albert Belle .50 .15
3 Jay Buhner .50 .15
4 Jose Canseco 1.25 .35
5 Tony Clark .50 .15
6 Jose Cruz Jr. .50 .15
7 Jim Edmonds .50 .15
8 Cecil Fielder .50 .15
9 Travis Fryman .50 .15
10 Nomar Garciaparra 2.00 .60
11 Juan Gonzalez 1.25 .35
12 Ken Griffey Jr. 2.00 .60
13 David Justice .50 .15
14 Travis Lee .50 .15
15 Edgar Martinez .75 .23
16 Tino Martinez .75 .23
17 Rafael Palmeiro .75 .23
18 Manny Ramirez .50 .15
19 Cal Ripken 4.00 1.20
20 Alex Rodriguez 2.00 .60
21 Tim Salmon .75 .23
22 Frank Thomas 1.25 .35
23 Jim Thome 1.25 .35
24 Mo Vaughn .50 .15
25 Bernie Williams .75 .23
26 Fred McGriff .75 .23
27 Jeff Bagwell .75 .23
28 Dante Bichette .50 .15
29 Barry Bonds 3.00 .90
30 Ellis Burks .50 .15
31 Ken Caminiti .50 .15
32 Vinny Castilla .50 .15
33 Andres Galarraga .50 .15
34 Vladimir Guerrero 1.25 .35
35 Todd Helton .75 .23
36 Todd Hundley .50 .15
37 Andruw Jones .50 .15
38 Chipper Jones 1.25 .35
39 Eric Karros .50 .15
40 Ryan Klesko .50 .15
41 Ray Lankford .50 .15
42 Mark McGwire 3.00 .90
43 Raul Mondesi .50 .15
44 Mike Piazza 2.00 .60
45 Scott Rolen .75 .23
46 Gary Sheffield .50 .15
47 Sammy Sosa 2.00 .60
48 Larry Walker .75 .23
49 Matt Williams .50 .15
50 Wild Card .50 .15

1998 Pinnacle Performers Swing for the Fences Shop Exchange

This 12-card set was created as a promotional tie-in for hobby shop owners, but actually made it's debut in limited fashion at the 1998 All-Star game on July 8th. Cards were subsequently distributed to shop owners in 10-card packets. Collectors could then exchange three 1998 Pinnacle Performers wrappers for one of the twelve different cards or purchase an entire box and receive a 10-card cello pack. The cards parallel the standard Swing for the Fences inserts found in packs, except for the upgraded 20 pt.stock, silver foil-board background and lack of numbering on the card back.

Nm-Mt Ex-Mt
COMPLETE SET (12) 8.00 2.40
1 Jeff Bagwell .50 .15
2 Barry Bonds 1.00 .30
3 Nomar Garciaparra 1.00 .30
4 Juan Gonzalez .75 .23
5 Ken Griffey Jr. 1.25 .35
6 Chipper Jones .75 .23
7 Mark McGwire 1.50 .45
8 Mike Piazza 1.00 .30
9 Cal Ripken 2.00 .60
10 Alex Rodriguez 1.00 .30
11 Scott Rolen .40 .12
12 Frank Thomas .60 .18

1998 Pinnacle Performers Swing for the Fences Point Cards

Randomly inserted into packs at the rate of 1:2, these 50 cards feature different home run totals. Matching the A.L. or N.L. home run champion's card with the correct point card of the player's home run total entitled the collector to mail the two cards (prior to March 1, 1999) in exchange for an assortment of possible prizes. The first 1000 contestants that sent in winning cards received an autographed Juan Gonzalez Swing for the Fences card. Remaining winners received 10-card packs of upgraded Swing for the Fences player cards. All winners were entered into a drawing to win a trip to the 1999 All-Star game in Boston.

Nm-Mt Ex-Mt
COMMON CARD (1-50) .25 .07

1998 Pinnacle Plus Samples

These six sample cards were distributed in 2-card sealed cello packs within dealer order forms and hobby media releases about four to six weeks prior to the release of 1998 Pinnacle Plus baseball. The samples are similar in design to the regular issue Pinnacle Plus cards in that they share the same photography but the cards are printed with basic four-color UV coated photos whereas the real Pinnacle Plus cards were printed on silver foil board. In addition, each card has the text "SAMPLE" running diagonally across the card back.

Nm-Mt Ex-Mt
COMPLETE SET (6) 12.00 3.60
8 Nomar Garciaparra 3.00 .90
9 Ken Griffey Jr. 3.00 .90
24 Frank Thomas 2.00 .60
33 Mike Piazza 3.00 .90
56 Chipper Jones 2.50 .75
72 Larry Walker 1.00 .30

1998 Pinnacle Plus

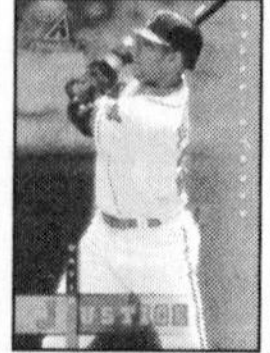

The 1998 Pinnacle Plus set was issued in one series totalling 200 standard size cards. The 10-card packs retailed for $2.99 each. The set contains the subsets: The Naturals (183-194) and Field of Vision (195-200). The Nolan Ryan AU Ball is supposed to not have been redeemed.

Nm-Mt Ex-Mt
COMPLETE SET (200) 25.00 7.50
1 Roberto Alomar .60 .18
2 Sandy Alomar Jr. .25 .07
3 Brady Anderson .25 .07
4 Albert Belle .25 .07
5 Jeff Cirillo .25 .07
6 Roger Clemens 1.25 .35
7 David Cone .25 .07
8 Nomar Garciaparra 1.00 .30
9 Ken Griffey Jr. 1.00 .30
10 Jason Dickson .25 .07
11 Edgar Martinez .40 .12
12 Tino Martinez .40 .12
13 Randy Johnson .60 .18
14 Mark McGwire 1.50 .45
15 David Justice .25 .07
16 Mike Mussina .60 .18
17 Chuck Knoblauch .25 .07
18 Joey Cora .25 .07
19 Pat Hentgen .25 .07
20 Randy Myers .25 .07
21 Cal Ripken 2.00 .60
22 Mariano Rivera .40 .12
23 Jose Rosado .25 .07
24 Frank Thomas .60 .18
25 Alex Rodriguez 1.00 .30
26 Justin Thompson .25 .07
27 Ivan Rodriguez .60 .18
28 Bernie Williams .40 .12
29 Pedro Martinez .60 .18
30 Tony Clark .25 .07
31 Garret Anderson .25 .07
32 Travis Fryman .25 .07
33 Mike Piazza 1.00 .30
34 Carl Pavano .25 .07
35 Kevin Millwood RC 1.25 .35
36 Miguel Tejada .40 .12
37 Willie Blair .25 .07
38 Devon White .25 .07
39 Andres Galarraga .25 .07
40 Barry Larkin .60 .18
41 Al Leiter .25 .07
42 Moises Alou .25 .07
43 Eric Young .25 .07
44 John Jaha .25 .07
45 Bernard Gilkey .25 .07
46 Freddy Garcia .25 .07
47 Ruben Rivera .25 .07
48 Robb Nen .25 .07
49 Ray Lankford .25 .07
50 Kenny Lofton .25 .07
51 Joe Carter .25 .07
52 Jason McDonald .25 .07
53 Quinton McCracken .25 .07
54 Kerry Wood .60 .18
55 Mike Lansing .25 .07
56 Chipper Jones .60 .18
57 Barry Bonds 1.50 .45
58 Brad Fullmer .25 .07
59 Jeff Bagwell .40 .12
60 Rondell White .25 .07
61 Geronimo Berroa .25 .07
62 Magglio Ordonez RC 1.50 .45
63 Dwight Gooden .25 .07
64 Brian Hunter .25 .07
65 Todd Walker .25 .07
66 Frank Catalanotto RC .40 .12
67 Tony Saunders .25 .07
68 Travis Lee .25 .07
69 Michael Tucker .25 .07
70 Reggie Sanders .25 .07
71 Derrek Lee .25 .07
72 Larry Walker .40 .12
73 Marquis Grissom .25 .07
74 Craig Biggio .40 .12
75 Kevin Brown .40 .12
76 J.T. Snow .25 .07
77 Eric Davis .25 .07
78 Jeff Abbott .25 .07
79 Jermaine Dye .25 .07
80 Otis Nixon .25 .07
81 Curt Schilling .40 .12
82 Enrique Wilson .25 .07
83 Tony Gwynn .75 .23
84 Orlando Cabrera .25 .07
85 Ramon Martinez .25 .07
86 Greg Vaughn .25 .07
87 Alan Benes .25 .07
88 Dennis Eckersley .25 .07
89 Jim Thome .60 .18
90 Juan Encarnacion .25 .07
91 Jeff King .25 .07
92 Shannon Stewart .25 .07
93 Roberto Hernandez .25 .07
94 Raul Ibanez .25 .07
95 Darryl Kile .25 .07
96 Charles Johnson .25 .07
97 Rich Becker .25 .07
98 Hal Morris .25 .07
99 Ismael Valdes .25 .07
100 Orel Hershiser .25 .07
101 Mo Vaughn .25 .07
102 Aaron Boone .25 .07
103 Jeff Conine .25 .07
104 Paul O'Neill .40 .12
105 Tom Candiotti .25 .07
106 Wilson Alvarez .25 .07
107 Mike Stanley .25 .07
108 Carlos Delgado .25 .07
109 Tony Batista .25 .07
110 Dante Bichette .25 .07
111 Henry Rodriguez .25 .07
112 Karim Garcia .25 .07
113 Shane Reynolds .25 .07
114 Ken Caminiti .25 .07
115 Jose Silva .25 .07
116 Juan Gonzalez .60 .18
117 Brian Jordan .25 .07
118 Jim Leyritz .25 .07
119 Manny Ramirez .25 .07
120 Fred McGriff .40 .12
121 Brooks Kieschnick .25 .07
122 Sean Casey .25 .07
123 John Smoltz .40 .12
124 Rusty Greer .25 .07
125 Cecil Fielder .25 .07
126 Mike Cameron .25 .07
127 Reggie Jefferson .25 .07
128 Bobby Higginson .25 .07
129 Kevin Appier .25 .07
130 Robin Ventura .25 .07
131 Ben Grieve .25 .07

132 Wade Boggs .40 .12
133 Jose Cruz Jr. .25 .07
134 Jeff Suppan .25 .07
135 Vinny Castilla .25 .07
136 Sammy Sosa 1.00 .30
137 Mark Wohlers .25 .07
138 Jay Bell .25 .07
139 Brett Tomko .25 .07
140 Gary Sheffield .25 .07
141 Tim Salmon .40 .12
142 Jaret Wright .25 .07
143 Kenny Rogers .25 .07
144 Brian Anderson .25 .07
145 Darrin Fletcher .25 .07
146 John Flaherty .25 .07
147 Dmitri Young .25 .07
148 Andruw Jones .25 .07
149 Matt Williams .25 .07
150 Bobby Bonilla .25 .07
151 Mike Hampton .25 .07
152 Al Martin .25 .07
153 Mark Grudzielanek .25 .07
154 Dave Nilsson .25 .07
155 Roger Cedeno .25 .07
156 Greg Maddux 1.00 .30
157 Mark Kotsay .25 .07
158 Steve Finley .25 .07
159 Wilson Delgado .25 .07
160 Ron Gant .25 .07
161 Jim Edmonds .25 .07
162 Jeff Blauser .25 .07
163 Dave Burba .25 .07
164 Pedro Astacio .25 .07
165 Livan Hernandez .25 .07
166 Neifi Perez .25 .07
167 Ryan Klesko .25 .07
168 Fernando Tatis .25 .07
169 Richard Hidalgo .25 .07
170 Carlos Perez .25 .07
171 Bob Abreu .25 .07
172 Francisco Cordova .25 .07
173 Todd Helton .40 .12
174 Doug Glanville .25 .07
175 Brian Rose .25 .07
176 Yamil Benitez .25 .07
177 Darin Erstad .25 .07
178 Scott Rolen .40 .12
179 John Wetteland .25 .07
180 Paul Sorrento .25 .07
181 Walt Weiss .25 .07
182 Vladimir Guerrero .60 .18
183 Ken Griffey Jr. NAT .60 .18
184 Alex Rodriguez NAT .60 .18
185 Cal Ripken NAT 1.00 .30
186 Frank Thomas NAT .40 .12
187 Chipper Jones NAT .40 .12
188 Hideo Nomo NAT .40 .12
189 N.Garciaparra NAT .60 .18
190 Mike Piazza NAT .60 .18
191 Greg Maddux NAT .60 .18
192 Tony Gwynn NAT .40 .12
193 Mark McGwire NAT .75 .23
194 Roger Clemens NAT .60 .18
195 Mike Piazza FV .60 .18
196 Mark McGwire FV .75 .23
197 Chipper Jones FV .40 .12
198 Larry Walker FV .25 .07
199 Hideo Nomo FV .40 .12
200 Barry Bonds FV .60 .18

1998 Pinnacle Plus Artist's Proofs

Randomly inserted in packs at a rate of one in 35, this 60-card set is a partial parallel to the Pinnacle Plus base set offering the same players as the base set, but printed on dot-matrix hologram. These Artist's Proofs carrry different numbers to the basic issue Pinnacle Plus cards.

Nm-Mt Ex-Mt
PP1 Roberto Alomar 12.00 3.60
PP2 Albert Belle 5.00 1.50
PP3 Roger Clemens 25.00 7.50
PP4 Nomar Garciaparra 20.00 6.00
PP5 Ken Griffey Jr. 20.00 6.00
PP6 Tino Martinez 8.00 2.40
PP7 Randy Johnson 12.00 3.60
PP8 Mark McGwire 30.00 9.00
PP9 David Justice 5.00 1.50
PP10 Chuck Knoblauch 5.00 1.50
PP11 Cal Ripken 40.00 12.00
PP12 Frank Thomas 12.00 3.60
PP13 Alex Rodriguez 20.00 6.00
PP14 Ivan Rodriguez 12.00 3.60
PP15 Bernie Williams 8.00 2.40
PP16 Pedro Martinez 12.00 3.60
PP17 Tony Clark 5.00 1.50
PP18 Mike Piazza 20.00 6.00
PP19 Miguel Tejada 6.00 1.80
PP20 Andres Galarraga 5.00 1.50
PP21 Barry Larkin 12.00 3.60
PP22 Kenny Lofton 5.00 1.50
PP23 Chipper Jones 12.00 3.60
PP24 Barry Bonds 30.00 9.00
PP25 Brad Fullmer 5.00 1.50
PP26 Jeff Bagwell 8.00 2.40
PP27 Todd Walker 5.00 1.50
PP28 Travis Lee 4.00 1.20
PP29 Larry Walker 8.00 2.40
PP30 Craig Biggio 8.00 2.40
PP31 Tony Gwynn 15.00 4.50
PP32 Jim Thome 12.00 3.60
PP33 Juan Encarnacion 5.00 1.50
PP34 Mo Vaughn 5.00 1.50
PP35 Karim Garcia 5.00 1.50
PP36 Ken Caminiti 5.00 1.50
PP37 Juan Gonzalez 12.00 3.60
PP38 Manny Ramirez 5.00 1.50
PP39 Fred McGriff 8.00 2.40
PP40 Rusty Greer 5.00 1.50
PP41 Bobby Higginson 5.00 1.50
PP42 Ben Grieve 5.00 1.50
PP43 Wade Boggs 8.00 2.40
PP44 Jose Cruz Jr. 4.00 1.20
PP45 Sammy Sosa 20.00 6.00
PP46 Gary Sheffield 5.00 1.50
PP47 Tim Salmon 8.00 2.40
PP48 Jaret Wright 5.00 1.50
PP49 Andruw Jones 5.00 1.50
PP50 Matt Williams 5.00 1.50
PP51 Greg Maddux 20.00 6.00
PP52 Jim Edmonds 5.00 1.50
PP53 Livan Hernandez 5.00 1.50
PP54 Neifi Perez 5.00 1.50
PP55 Fernando Tatis 4.00 1.20
PP56 Richard Hidalgo 5.00 1.50
PP57 Todd Helton 8.00 2.40
PP58 Darin Erstad 5.00 1.50
PP59 Scott Rolen 8.00 2.40
PP60 Vladimir Guerrero 12.00 3.60

1998 Pinnacle Plus Gold Artist's Proofs

Sequentially numbered to 100, this 60-card set is also a partial parallel to the Pinnacle Plus base set offering the same players, but in a rare gold version.

Nm-Mt Ex-Mt
*STARS: .6X TO 1.5X BASIC AP

1998 Pinnacle Plus All-Star Epix

Randomly inserted in packs at a rate of one in 21, this 24-card insert showcases the All-Star game highlights from baseball's top stars in color action photography with stars and stripes in the background. The first twelve cards were seeded in Score Rookie and Traded packs while the final 12 cards were inserted in Pinnacle Plus packs.

Nm-Mt Ex-Mt
COMPLETE SET (24) 80.00 24.00
1 Ken Griffey Jr. MOM 5.00 1.50
2 Juan Gonzalez MOM 3.00 .90
3 Jeff Bagwell MOM 2.00 .60
4 Ivan Rodriguez MOM 3.00 .90
5 N.Garciaparra MOM 5.00 1.50
6 Ryne Sandberg MOM 6.00 1.80
7 Frank Thomas MOM 3.00 .90
8 Derek Jeter MOM 10.00 3.00
9 Tony Gwynn MOM 4.00 1.20
10 Albert Belle MOM 1.25 .35
11 Scott Rolen MOM 2.00 .60
12 Barry Larkin MOM 3.00 .90
13 Alex Rodriguez MOM 5.00 1.50
14 Cal Ripken MOM 10.00 3.00
15 Chipper Jones MOM 3.00 .90
16 Roger Clemens MOM 6.00 1.80
17 Mo Vaughn MOM 1.25 .35
18 Mark McGwire MOM 8.00 2.40
19 Mike Piazza MOM 5.00 1.50
20 Andruw Jones MOM 1.25 .35
21 Greg Maddux MOM 5.00 1.50
22 Barry Bonds MOM 8.00 2.40
23 Paul Molitor MOM 3.00 .90
24 Hideo Nomo MOM 3.00 .90

1998 Pinnacle Plus Lasting Memories

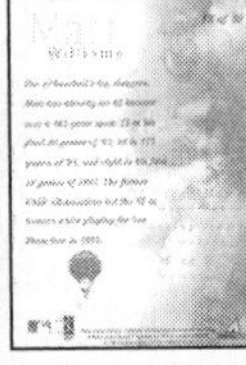

Randomly inserted in packs at a rate of one in five, this 30-card insert features the game's top stars in color action photography on foil board and surrounded by a blue and white cloud-like design.

Nm-Mt Ex-Mt
COMPLETE SET (30) 50.00 15.00
1 Nomar Garciaparra 2.50 .75
2 Ken Griffey Jr. 2.50 .75
3 Livan Hernandez .60 .18
4 Hideo Nomo 1.50 .45
5 Ben Grieve .60 .18
6 Scott Rolen 1.00 .30
7 Roger Clemens 3.00 .90
8 Cal Ripken 5.00 1.50
9 Mo Vaughn .60 .18
10 Frank Thomas 1.50 .45
11 Mark McGwire 4.00 1.20
12 Barry Larkin 1.50 .45
13 Matt Williams .60 .18
14 Jose Cruz Jr. .60 .18
15 Andruw Jones .60 .18
16 Mike Piazza 2.50 .75
17 Jeff Bagwell 1.00 .30
18 Chipper Jones 1.50 .45
19 Juan Gonzalez 1.50 .45
20 Kenny Lofton .60 .18
21 Greg Maddux 2.50 .75
22 Ivan Rodriguez 1.50 .45
23 Alex Rodriguez 2.50 .75
24 Derek Jeter 5.00 1.50
25 Albert Belle .60 .18
26 Barry Bonds 4.00 1.20
27 Larry Walker 1.00 .30
28 Sammy Sosa 2.50 .75
29 Tony Gwynn 2.00 .60
30 Randy Johnson 1.50 .45

1998 Pinnacle Plus Piece of the Game

These cards, randomly inserted at a rate of one in 19; feature 10 of the leading players in baseball.

Nm-Mt Ex-Mt
COMPLETE SET (10) 60.00 18.00
1 Ken Griffey Jr. 8.00 2.40
2 Frank Thomas 5.00 1.50
3 Alex Rodriguez 8.00 2.40
4 Chipper Jones 5.00 1.50
5 Cal Ripken 15.00 4.50
6 Mike Piazza 8.00 2.40
7 Greg Maddux 8.00 2.40
8 Juan Gonzalez 5.00 1.50
9 Nomar Garciaparra 8.00 2.40
10 Larry Walker 3.00 .90

1998 Pinnacle Plus Team Pinnacle

Randomly inserted in packs at a rate of one in 71, this double-sided insert printed on mirror mylar features color action photography of top stars in the American and National Leagues together on the same card.

Nm-Mt Ex-Mt
COMPLETE SET (15) 250.00 75.00
*GOLD: .75X TO 2X BASIC TEAM PINNACLE
GOLD STATED ODDS 1:199 HOBBY ...
MIRROR: RANDOM INSERTS IN PACKS
MIRROR STATED PRINT RUN 25 SETS
1 Mike Piazza 15.00 4.50
Ivan Rodriguez
2 Mark McGwire 25.00 7.50
Mo Vaughn
3 Roberto Alomar 10.00 3.00
Craig Biggio
4 Alex Rodriguez 15.00 4.50
Barry Larkin
5 Cal Ripken 30.00 9.00
Chipper Jones
6 Ken Griffey Jr. 15.00 4.50
Larry Walker
7 Juan Gonzalez 12.00 3.60
Tony Gwynn
8 Albert Belle 25.00 7.50
Barry Bonds
9 Kenny Lofton 4.00 1.20
Andruw Jones
10 Tino Martinez 6.00 1.80
Jeff Bagwell
11 Frank Thomas 10.00 3.00
Andres Galarraga
12 Roger Clemens 15.00 4.50
Greg Maddux
13 Pedro Martinez 10.00 3.00
Hideo Nomo
14 Nomar Garciaparra 15.00 4.50
Scott Rolen
15 Ben Grieve 4.00 1.20
Paul Konerko

1998 Pinnacle Plus Yardwork

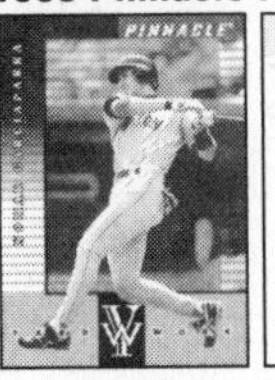

Randomly inserted in packs at a rate of one in nine, this 15-card insert features color action photography printed on foil board with micro-etched foil stamping.

Nm-Mt Ex-Mt
COMPLETE SET (15) 25.00 7.50
1 Mo Vaughn .75 .23
2 Frank Thomas 2.00 .60
3 Albert Belle .75 .23
4 Nomar Garciaparra 3.00 .90
5 Tony Clark .75 .23
6 Tino Martinez 1.25 .35
7 Ken Griffey Jr. 3.00 .90
8 Juan Gonzalez 2.00 .60
9 Sammy Sosa 3.00 .90
10 Jose Cruz Jr. .75 .23
11 Jeff Bagwell 1.25 .35
12 Mike Piazza 3.00 .90
13 Larry Walker 1.25 .35
14 Mark McGwire 5.00 1.50
15 Barry Bonds 5.00 1.50

1998 Pinnacle Snapshots Samples

One of these nine different photo-cards was included in each dealer order form for 1998 Pinnacle Snapshots baseball to preview the upcoming product. The order forms were distributed around April, 1998. These sample photo-cards are identical to the regular issue photo-cards except for the light grey shaded "SAMPLE" text running diagonally against the back of the card.

Nm-Mt Ex-Mt
COMPLETE SET (9) 25.00 7.50
1 Greg Maddux 5.00 1.50
2 Cal Ripken 8.00 2.40
3 Travis Lee 1.25 .35
4 Brian Jordan 1.00 .30
5 Mike Piazza 5.00 1.50
6 Alex Rodriguez 5.00 1.50
7 Edgar Martinez 1.25 .35
8 Joey Cora 1.00 .30
9 Alvaro Espinoza 1.00 .30

1998 Pinnacle Snapshots

These 4" by 6" cards were issued by Pinnacle in eight-card packs which retailed for $1.99. These cards feature a mix of pre-season and early regular season photos and were designed to be sold like "photos" rather than cards. These cards are entered below the way they appear on the original checklist. Please note there are duplications on the various teams. The cards are sequenced by teams using their initials (I.e. Atlanta Braves are AB,)

Nm-Mt Ex-Mt
COMP.ANGELS (18) 6.00 1.80
COMP.BRAVES (18) 15.00 4.50
COMP.DBACKS (18) 10.00 3.00
COMP.ORIOLES (18) 10.00 3.00
COMP.CUBS (18) 6.00 1.80
COMP.INDIANS (18) 10.00 3.00
COMP.ROCKIES (18) 8.00 2.40
COMP.MARINERS (18) 12.00 3.60
COMP.RANGERS (18) 8.00 2.40
COMP.RED SOX (18) 10.00 3.00
COMP.DODGERS (18) 10.00 3.00
COMP.METS (18) 5.00 1.50
COMP.YANKEES (18) 10.00 3.00
COMP.CARDINALS (18) 10.00 3.00
COMP.DEVIL RAYS (18) 6.00 1.80
AA1 Jason Dickson .25 .07
AA2 Gary DiSarcina .25 .07
AA3 Garret Anderson .75 .23
AA4 Shigetoshi Hasegawa .25 .07
AA5 Ken Hill .25 .07
AA6 Todd Greene .25 .07
AA7 Tim Salmon .75 .23
AA8 Jim Edmonds 1.00 .30
AA9 Garret Anderson .50 .15
AA10 Dave Hollins .25 .07
AA11 Todd Greene .25 .07
AA12 Troy Percival .50 .15
AA13 Gary DiSarcina .25 .07
AA14 Cecil Fielder .50 .15
AA15 Darin Erstad 1.00 .30
AA16 Chuck Finley .50 .15
AA17 Jim Edmonds 1.00 .30
AA18 Jason Dickson .25 .07
AB1 Ryan Klesko .50 .15
AB2 Walt Weiss .25 .07
AB3 Tom Glavine 1.00 .30
AB4 Randall Simon .25 .07
AB5 John Smoltz .50 .15
AB6 Chipper Jones 2.50 .75
AB7 Javier Lopez .50 .15
AB8 Greg Maddux 3.00 .90
AB9 Andruw Jones 1.00 .30
AB10 Michael Tucker .25 .07
AB11 Andres Galarraga 1.00 .30
AB12 Andres Galarraga 1.00 .30
AB13 Greg Maddux 3.00 .90
AB14 Wes Helms .25 .07
AB15 Bruce Chen .25 .07
AB16 Denny Neagle .25 .07
AB17 Mark Wohlers .25 .07
AB18 Kevin Millwood 1.50 .45
AD1 Travis Lee .50 .15
AD2 Matt Williams .75 .23
AD3 Jay Bell .25 .07
AD4 Devon White .50 .15
AD5 Andy Benes .25 .07
AD6 Tony Batista 1.00 .30
AD7 Jay Bell .25 .07
AD8 Edwin Diaz .25 .07
AD9 Devon White .25 .07
AD10 Bob Wolcott .25 .07
AD11 Karim Garcia .50 .15
AD12 Yamil Benitez .25 .07
AD13 Jorge Fabregas .25 .07
AD14 Jeff Suppan .25 .07
AD15 Ben Ford .25 .07
AD16 Brian Anderson .25 .07
AD17 Travis Lee .50 .15
AD18 Matt Williams .75 .23
BO1 Cal Ripken 5.00 1.50
BO2 Rocky Coppinger .25 .07
BO3 Eric Davis .50 .15
BO4 Chris Hoiles .25 .07
BO5 Mike Mussina 1.00 .30
BO6 Joe Carter .50 .15
BO7 Rafael Palmeiro 1.00 .30
BO8 B.J. Surhoff .50 .15
BO9 Jimmy Key .50 .15
BO10 Scott Erickson .25 .07
BO11 Armando Benitez .50 .15
BO12 Roberto Alomar 1.00 .30
BO13 Cal Ripken 5.00 1.50
BO14 Mike Bordick .25 .07
BO15 Roberto Alomar 1.00 .30
BO16 Jeffrey Hammonds .25 .07
BO17 Rafael Palmeiro 1.00 .30
BO18 Brady Anderson .50 .15
CC1 Mark Grace .75 .23
CC2 Manny Alexander .25 .07
CC3 Jeremi Gonzalez .25 .07
CC4 Brant Brown .25 .07
CC5 Mark Grace .75 .23
CC6 Lance Johnson .25 .07
CC7 Mark Clark .25 .07
CC8 Kevin Foster .25 .07
CC9 Brant Brown .25 .07
CC10 Kevin Foster .25 .07
CC11 Kevin Tapani .25 .07
CC12 Sammy Sosa 2.50 .75
CC13 Sammy Sosa 2.50 .75
CC14 Pat Cline .25 .07
CC15 Kevin Orie .25 .07
CC16 Steve Trachsel .25 .07
CC17 Lance Johnson .25 .07
CC18 Robin Jennings .25 .07
CI1 Manny Ramirez 1.25 .35
CI2 Travis Fryman .50 .15
CI3 Jaret Wright .25 .07
CI4 Brian Giles 1.00 .30
CI5 Bartolo Colon .75 .23
CI6 Kenny Lofton .75 .23
CI7 David Justice .50 .15
CI8 Brian Giles 1.00 .30
CI9 Sandy Alomar Jr. .50 .15
CI10 Jose Mesa .25 .07
CI11 Jim Thome 1.00 .30
CI12 Sandy Alomar Jr. .50 .15
CI13 Omar Vizquel .50 .15
CI14 Geronimo Berroa .25 .07
CI15 John Smiley .25 .07
CI16 Chad Ogea .25 .07
CI17 Charles Nagy .25 .07
CI18 Enrique Wilson .25 .07
CR1 Larry Walker .50 .15
CR2 Pedro Astacio .25 .07
CR3 Jamey Wright .25 .07
CR4 Darryl Kile .50 .15
CR5 Kirt Manwaring .25 .07
CR6 Todd Helton 1.50 .45
CR7 Mike Lansing .25 .07
CR8 Neifi Perez .25 .07
CR9 Dante Bichette .50 .15
CR10 Derrick Gibson .25 .07
CR11 Neifi Perez .25 .07
CR12 Darryl Kile .50 .15
CR13 Larry Walker .50 .15
CR14 Roger Bailey .25 .07
CR15 Ellis Burks .50 .15
CR16 Dante Bichette .50 .15
CR17 Derrick Gibson .25 .07
CR18 Ellis Burks .50 .15
SM1 Alex Rodriguez 2.50 .75
SM2 Jay Buhner .50 .15
SM3 Russ Davis .25 .07
SM4 Joey Cora .25 .07
SM5 Joey Cora .25 .07
SM6 Jay Buhner .50 .15
SM7 Ken Griffey Jr. 4.00 1.20
SM8 Raul Ibanez .50 .15
SM9 Rich Amaral .25 .07
SM10 Shane Monahan .25 .07
SM11 Alex Rodriguez 3.00 .90
SM12 Dan Wilson .25 .07
SM13 Bob Wells .25 .07
SM14 Randy Johnson 1.25 .35
SM15 Randy Johnson 1.25 .35
SM16 Jeff Fassero .25 .07
SM17 Ken Cloude .25 .07
SM18 Edgar Martinez .75 .23
TR1 Ivan Rodriguez 1.25 .35
TR2 Fernando Tatis .25 .07
TR3 Danny Patterson .25 .07
TR4 Will Clark 1.00 .30
TR5 Kevin Elster .25 .07
TR6 Rusty Greer .50 .15
TR7 Darren Oliver .25 .07
TR8 John Burkett .25 .07
TR9 Tom Goodwin .25 .07
TR10 Roberto Kelly .25 .07
TR11 Aaron Sele .50 .15
TR12 Rick Helling .25 .07
TR13 Mark McLemore .25 .07
TR14 Lee Stevens .25 .07
TR15 John Wetteland .50 .15
TR16 Will Clark 1.00 .30
TR17 Juan Gonzalez 1.25 .35
TR18 Roger Pavlik .25 .07
BRS1 Tim Naehring .25 .07
BRS2 Brian Rose .25 .07
BRS3 Darren Bragg .25 .07
BRS4 Pedro Martinez 1.25 .35
BRS5 Mo Vaughn .50 .15
BRS6 Jim Leyritz .25 .07
BRS7 Troy O'Leary .25 .07
BRS8 Mo Vaughn .50 .15
BRS9 Nomar Garciaparra 2.50 .75
BRS10 Michael Coleman .25 .07
BRS11 Tom Gordon .25 .07
BRS12 Tim Naehring .25 .07
BRS13 Nomar Garciaparra 3.00 .90
BRS14 John Valentin .25 .07
BRS15 Steve Avery .25 .07
BRS16 Damon Buford .25 .07
BRS17 Troy O'Leary .25 .07
BRS18 Bret Saberhagen .50 .15
LAD1 Mike Piazza 3.00 .90
LAD2 Eric Karros .50 .15
LAD3 Raul Mondesi .50 .15
LAD4 Wilton Guerrero .25 .07
LAD5 Darren Dreifort .25 .07
LAD6 Roger Cedeno .50 .15
LAD7 Todd Zeile .50 .15
LAD8 Paul Konerko .75 .23
LAD9 Todd Hollandsworth .25 .07
LAD10 Ismael Valdes .25 .07
LAD11 Hideo Nomo 1.00 .30
LAD12 Ramon Martinez .25 .07
LAD13 Chan Ho Park .25 .07
LAD14 Eric Young .50 .15
LAD15 Dennis Reyes .25 .07
LAD16 Eric Karros .50 .15
LAD17 Mike Piazza 3.00 .90
LAD18 Raul Mondesi .50 .15
NYM1 Rey Ordonez .25 .07
NYM2 Todd Hundley .50 .15
NYM3 Preston Wilson .50 .15

NYM4 Rich Becker .25 .07
NYM5 Bernard Gilkey .25 .07
NYM6 Rey Ordonez .25 .07
NYM7 Butch Huskey .25 .07
NYM8 Carlos Baerga .50 .15
NYM9 Edgardo Alfonzo 1.00 .30
NYM10 Bill Pulsipher .25 .07
NYM11 John Franco .50 .15
NYM12 Todd Pratt .25 .07
NYM13 Brian McRae .25 .07
NYM14 Bobby Jones .25 .07
NYM15 John Olerud .50 .15
NYM16 Todd Hundley .50 .15
NYM17 Jay Payton .50 .15
NYM18 Paul Wilson .25 .07
NYY1 Andy Pettitte .50 .15
NYY2 Darryl Strawberry .50 .15
NYY3 Joe Girardi .25 .07
NYY4 Derek Jeter 5.00 1.50
NYY5 Andy Pettitte .50 .15
NYY6 Tim Raines .50 .15
NYY7 Mariano Rivera .50 .15
NYY8 Tino Martinez .50 .15
NYY9 Derek Jeter 5.00 1.50
NYY10 Hideki Irabu .25 .07
NYY11 Tino Martinez .50 .15
NYY12 David Cone 1.00 .30
NYY13 Bernie Williams 1.00 .30
NYY14 David Cone 1.00 .30
NYY15 Bernie Williams 1.00 .30
NYY16 Chuck Knoblauch .50 .15
NYY17 Paul O'Neill .50 .15
NYY18 David Wells .50 .15
SLC1 Alan Benes .25 .07
SLC2 Ron Gant .25 .07
SLC3 Donovan Osborne .25 .07
SLC4 Eli Marrero .25 .07
SLC5 Mark McGwire 4.00 1.20
SLC6 Delino DeShields .25 .07
SLC7 Tom Pagnozzi .25 .07
SLC8 Delino DeShields .25 .07
SLC9 Mark McGwire 4.00 1.20
SLC10 Royce Clayton .25 .07
SLC11 Brian Jordan .50 .15
SLC12 Ray Lankford .50 .15
SLC13 Brian Jordan .50 .15
SLC14 Matt Morris .75 .23
SLC15 John Mabry .25 .07
SLC16 Luis Ordaz .25 .07
SLC17 Ron Gant .25 .07
SLC18 Todd Stottlemyre .25 .07
TBDR1 Kevin Stocker .25 .07
TBDR2 Paul Sorrento .25 .07
TBDR3 John Flaherty .25 .07
TBDR4 Wade Boggs 1.25 .35
TBDR5 Rich Butler .25 .07
TBDR6 Wilson Alvarez .25 .07
TBDR7 Bubba Trammell .25 .07
TBDR8 Dave Martinez .25 .07
TBDR9 Brooks Kieschnick .25 .07
TBDR10 Tony Saunders .25 .07
TBDR11 Esteban Yan .25 .07
TBDR12 Q.McCracken .25 .07
TBDR13 Albie Lopez .25 .07
TBDR14 R.Hernandez .50 .15
TBDR15 Fred McGriff .75 .23
TBDR16 Bubba Trammell .25 .07
TBDR17 B.Kieschnick .25 .07
TBDR18 Fred McGriff .75 .23

1997 Pinnacle Totally Certified Samples

This set was produced to introduce the Pinnacle Totally Certified Platinum Red, Blue, and Gold Sets. One card from each of the three parallel sets was distributed in each version of this preview set.

	Nm-Mt	Ex-Mt
COMPLETE SET (5)	10.00	3.00
5 Jeff Bagwell RED	1.50	.45
18 Tony Clark RED	1.00	.30
24 Larry Walker BLUE	1.00	.30
39 Roger Clemens BLUE	2.00	.60
41 Frank Thomas GOLD	1.50	.45
53 Ken Griffey Jr. GOLD	5.00	1.50

1997 Pinnacle Totally Certified Platinum Blue

This 150-card set is a parallel version of the more-common 1997 Pinnacle Totally Certified Platinum Red set. Platinum Blue cards were seeded at a rate of one per pack. Only 1,999 sets were produced and each card is sequentially numbered on back.

Nm-Mt Ex-Mt
*STARS: .6X TO 1.5X PLAT.RED
*ROOKIES: .4X TO 1X PLAT.RED

1997 Pinnacle Totally Certified Platinum Gold

This 150-card set is a parallel version of the 1997 Pinnacle Totally Certified Platinum Red set. Platinum Gold cards were randomly seeded into one in every 79 packs. Only 30 sets were produced and each card is sequentially numbered on back.

Nm-Mt Ex-Mt
*STARS: 6X TO 15X PLAT. RED
*ROOKIES: 2X TO 5X PLAT.RED

1997 Pinnacle Totally Certified Platinum Red

This 150-card set is a quasi-parallel version of the 1997 Pinnacle Certified set. The product

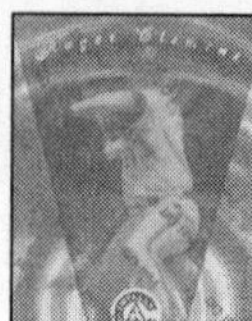

was distributed in three-card packs with a suggested retail price of $6.99. The checklist and player content is identical, but the photos are all different and the cards are designed a little differently. The fronts feature color action player images utilizing full micro-etched, holographic mylar print technology, highlighted with red vignette accent and foil stamping. Platinum Red cards were seeded at a rate of two per pack. Only 3,999 Platinum Red sets were produced and each card is sequentially numbered on back.

	Nm-Mt	Ex-Mt
COMPLETE SET (150)	150.00	45.00
1 Barry Bonds	10.00	3.00
2 Mo Vaughn	1.50	.45
3 Matt Williams	1.50	.45
4 Ryne Sandberg	6.00	1.80
5 Jeff Bagwell	2.50	.75
6 Alan Benes	1.50	.45
7 John Wetteland	1.50	.45
8 Fred McGriff	2.50	.75
9 Craig Biggio	2.50	.75
10 Bernie Williams	2.50	.75
11 Brian Hunter	1.50	.45
12 Sandy Alomar Jr.	1.50	.45
13 Ray Lankford	1.50	.45
14 Ryan Klesko	1.50	.45
15 Jermaine Dye	1.50	.45
16 Andy Benes	1.50	.45
17 Albert Belle	1.50	.45
18 Tony Clark	1.50	.45
19 Dean Palmer	1.50	.45
20 Bernard Gilkey	1.50	.45
21 Ken Caminiti	1.50	.45
22 Alex Rodriguez	6.00	1.80
23 Tim Salmon	2.50	.75
24 Larry Walker	2.50	.75
25 Barry Larkin	4.00	1.20
26 Mike Piazza	6.00	1.80
27 Brady Anderson	1.50	.45
28 Cal Ripken	12.00	3.60
29 Charles Nagy	1.50	.45
30 Paul Molitor	2.50	.75
31 Darin Erstad	1.50	.45
32 Rey Ordonez	1.50	.45
33 Wally Joyner	1.50	.45
34 David Cone	1.50	.45
35 Sammy Sosa	6.00	1.80
36 Dante Bichette	1.50	.45
37 Eric Karros	1.50	.45
38 Omar Vizquel	1.50	.45
39 Roger Clemens	8.00	2.40
40 Joe Carter	1.50	.45
41 Frank Thomas	4.00	1.20
42 Javy Lopez	1.50	.45
43 Mike Mussina	4.00	1.20
44 Gary Sheffield	1.50	.45
45 Tony Gwynn	5.00	1.50
46 Jason Kendall	1.50	.45
47 Jim Thome	4.00	1.20
48 Andres Galarraga	1.50	.45
49 Mark McGwire	10.00	3.00
50 Troy Percival	1.50	.45
51 Derek Jeter	10.00	3.00
52 Todd Hollandsworth	1.50	.45
53 Ken Griffey Jr.	6.00	1.80
54 Randy Johnson	4.00	1.20
55 Pat Hentgen	1.50	.45
56 Rusty Greer	1.50	.45
57 John Jaha	1.50	.45
58 Kenny Lofton	1.50	.45
59 Chipper Jones	4.00	1.20
60 Robb Nen	1.50	.45
61 Rafael Palmeiro	2.50	.75
62 Mariano Rivera	2.50	.75
63 Hideo Nomo	4.00	1.20
64 Greg Vaughn	1.50	.45
65 Ron Gant	1.50	.45
66 Eddie Murray	4.00	1.20
67 John Smoltz	2.50	.75
68 Manny Ramirez	1.50	.45
69 Juan Gonzalez	4.00	1.20
70 F.P. Santangelo	1.50	.45
71 Moises Alou	1.50	.45
72 Alex Ochoa	1.50	.45
73 Chuck Knoblauch	1.50	.45
74 Raul Mondesi	1.50	.45
75 J.T. Snow	1.50	.45
76 Rickey Henderson	4.00	1.20
77 Bobby Bonilla	1.50	.45
78 Wade Boggs	2.50	.75
79 Ivan Rodriguez	4.00	1.20
80 Brian Jordan	1.50	.45
81 Al Leiter	1.50	.45
82 Jay Buhner	1.50	.45
83 Greg Maddux	6.00	1.80
84 Edgar Martinez	2.50	.75
85 Kevin Brown	1.50	.45
86 Eric Young	1.50	.45
87 Todd Hundley	1.50	.45
88 Ellis Burks	1.50	.45
89 Marquis Grissom	1.50	.45
90 Jose Canseco	4.00	1.20
91 Henry Rodriguez	1.50	.45
92 Andy Pettitte	2.50	.75
93 Mark Grudzielanek	1.50	.45
94 Dwight Gooden	2.50	.75
95 Roberto Alomar	4.00	1.20
96 Paul Wilson	1.50	.45
97 Will Clark	4.00	1.20
98 Rondell White	1.50	.45
99 Charles Johnson	1.50	.45
100 Jim Edmonds	1.50	.45
101 Jason Giambi	4.00	1.20
102 Billy Wagner	1.50	.45
103 Edgar Renteria	1.50	.45
104 Johnny Damon	1.50	.45
105 Jason Isringhausen	1.50	.45
106 Andruw Jones	1.50	.45
107 Jose Guillen	1.50	.45
108 Kevin Orie	1.50	.45
109 Brian Giles RC	12.00	3.60
110 Danny Patterson	1.50	.45
111 Vladimir Guerrero	4.00	1.20
112 Scott Rolen	2.50	.75
113 Damon Mashore	1.50	.45
114 Nomar Garciaparra	6.00	1.80
115 Todd Walker	1.50	.45
116 Wilton Guerrero	1.50	.45
117 Bob Abreu	1.50	.45
118 Brooks Kieschnick	1.50	.45
119 Pokey Reese	1.50	.45
120 Todd Greene	1.50	.45
121 Dmitri Young	1.50	.45
122 Raul Casanova	1.50	.45
123 Glendon Rusch	1.50	.45
124 Jason Dickson	1.50	.45
125 Jorge Posada	2.50	.75
126 Rod Myers	1.50	.45
127 Bubba Trammell RC	1.50	.45
128 Scott Spiezio	1.50	.45
129 Hideki Irabu RC	1.50	.45
130 Wendell Magee	1.50	.45
131 Bartolo Colon	1.50	.45
132 Chris Holt	1.50	.45
133 Calvin Maduro	1.50	.45
134 Ray Montgomery	1.50	.45
135 Shannon Stewart	1.50	.45
136 Ken Griffey Jr. CERT	4.00	1.20
137 Vl.Guerrero CERT	2.50	.75
138 Roger Clemens CERT	4.00	1.20
139 Mark McGwire CERT	5.00	1.50
140 Albert Belle CERT	1.50	.45
141 Derek Jeter CERT	5.00	1.50
142 Juan Gonzalez CERT	2.50	.75
143 Greg Maddux CERT	4.00	1.20
144 Alex Rodriguez CERT	4.00	1.20
145 Jeff Bagwell CERT	1.50	.45
146 Cal Ripken CERT	6.00	1.80
147 Tony Gwynn CERT	2.50	.75
148 Frank Thomas CERT	2.50	.75
149 Hideo Nomo CERT	1.50	.45
150 Andruw Jones CERT	1.50	.45

1997 Pinnacle X-Press

The 1997 Pinnacle X-Press set was issued in one series totalling 150 cards and was distributed in two different kinds of packs. The eight-card packs retailed for $1.99. X-Press Metal Works home plate-shaped retail boxes carried a suggested retail price of $14.99 and contained an eight-card regular pack along with a master deck that had eight more cards, plus one Metal Works card. The set contains the topical subsets: Rookies (116-137), Peak Performers (138-147), and Checklists (148-150).

	Nm-Mt	Ex-Mt
COMPLETE SET (150)	15.00	4.50
1 Larry Walker	.30	.09
2 Andy Pettitte	.30	.09
3 Matt Williams	.20	.06
4 Juan Gonzalez	.50	.15
5 Frank Thomas	.50	.15
6 Kenny Lofton	.20	.06
7 Ken Griffey Jr.	.75	.23
8 Andres Galarraga	.20	.06
9 Greg Maddux	.75	.23
10 Hideo Nomo	.50	.15
11 Cecil Fielder	.20	.06
12 Jose Canseco	.50	.15
13 Tony Gwynn	.60	.18
14 Eddie Murray	.50	.15
15 Alex Rodriguez	.75	.23
16 Mike Piazza	.75	.23
17 Ken Hill	.20	.06
18 Chuck Knoblauch	.20	.06
19 Ellis Burks	.20	.06
20 Rafael Palmeiro	.30	.09
21 Vinny Castilla	.20	.06
22 Rusty Greer	.20	.06
23 Chipper Jones	.50	.15
24 Rey Ordonez	.20	.06
25 Mariano Rivera	.30	.09
26 Garret Anderson	.20	.06
27 Edgar Martinez	.30	.09
28 Dante Bichette	.20	.06
29 Todd Hundley	.20	.06
30 Barry Bonds	1.25	.35
31 Barry Larkin	.50	.15
32 Derek Jeter	1.25	.35
33 Marquis Grissom	.20	.06
34 Dave Justice	.20	.06
35 Ivan Rodriguez	.50	.15
36 Jay Buhner	.20	.06
37 Fred McGriff	.30	.09
38 Brady Anderson	.20	.06
39 Tony Clark	.20	.06
40 Eric Young	.20	.06
41 Charles Nagy	.20	.06
42 Mark McGwire	1.25	.35
43 Paul O'Neill	.30	.09
44 Tino Martinez	.30	.09
45 Ryne Sandberg	.75	.23
46 Bernie Williams	.30	.09
47 Albert Belle	.20	.06
48 Jeff Cirillo	.20	.06
49 Tim Salmon	.30	.09
50 Steve Finley	.20	.06
51 Lance Johnson	.20	.06
52 John Smoltz	.30	.09
53 Javier Lopez	.20	.06
54 Roger Clemens	1.00	.30
55 Kevin Appier	.20	.06
56 Ken Caminiti	.20	.06
57 Cal Ripken	1.50	.45
58 Moises Alou	.20	.06
59 Marty Cordova	.20	.06
60 David Cone	.20	.06
61 Manny Ramirez	.20	.06
62 Ray Durham	.20	.06
63 Jermaine Dye	.20	.06
64 Craig Biggio	.30	.09
65 Will Clark	.50	.15
66 Omar Vizquel	.20	.06
67 Bernard Gilkey	.20	.06
68 Greg Vaughn	.20	.06
69 Wade Boggs	.30	.09
70 Dave Nilsson	.20	.06
71 Mark Grace	.30	.09
72 Dean Palmer	.20	.06
73 Sammy Sosa	.75	.23
74 Mike Mussina	.50	.15
75 Alex Fernandez	.20	.06
76 Henry Rodriguez	.20	.06
77 Travis Fryman	.20	.06
78 Jeff Bagwell	.30	.09
79 Pat Hentgen	.20	.06
80 Gary Sheffield	.20	.06
81 Jim Edmonds	.20	.06
82 Darin Erstad	.20	.06
83 Mark Grudzielanek	.20	.06
84 Jim Thome	.50	.15
85 Bobby Higginson	.20	.06
86 Al Martin	.20	.06
87 Jason Giambi	.50	.15
88 Mo Vaughn	.20	.06
89 Jeff Conine	.20	.06
90 Edgar Renteria	.20	.06
91 Andy Ashby	.20	.06
92 Ryan Klesko	.20	.06
93 John Jaha	.20	.06
94 Paul Molitor	.30	.09
95 Brian Hunter	.20	.06
96 Randy Johnson	.50	.15
97 Joey Hamilton	.20	.06
98 Billy Wagner	.20	.06
99 John Wetteland	.20	.06
100 Jeff Fassero	.20	.06
101 Rondell White	.20	.06
102 Kevin Brown	.20	.06
103 Andy Benes	.20	.06
104 Raul Mondesi	.20	.06
105 Todd Hollandsworth	.20	.06
106 Alex Ochoa	.20	.06
107 Bobby Bonilla	.20	.06
108 Brian Jordan	.20	.06
109 Tom Glavine	.30	.09
110 Ron Gant	.20	.06
111 Jason Kendall	.20	.06
112 Roberto Alomar	.50	.15
113 Troy Percival	.20	.06
114 Michael Tucker	.20	.06
115 Joe Carter	.20	.06
116 Andruw Jones	.20	.06
117 Nomar Garciaparra	.75	.23
118 Todd Walker	.20	.06
119 Jose Guillen	.20	.06
120 Bubba Trammell RC	.20	.06
121 Wilton Guerrero	.20	.06
122 Bob Abreu	.20	.06
123 Vladimir Guerrero	.50	.15
124 Dmitri Young	.20	.06
125 Kevin Orie	.20	.06
126 Jose Cruz Jr. RC	.75	.23
127 Brooks Kieschnick	.20	.06
128 Scott Spiezio	.20	.06
129 Brian Giles RC	1.00	.30
130 Jason Dickson	.20	.06
131 Damon Mashore	.20	.06
132 Wendell Magee	.20	.06
133 Matt Morris	.20	.06
134 Scott Rolen	.30	.09
135 Shannon Stewart	.20	.06
136 Deivi Cruz RC	.20	.06
137 Hideki Irabu RC	.20	.06
138 Larry Walker PP	.20	.06
139 Ken Griffey Jr. PP	.50	.15
140 Frank Thomas PP	.30	.09
141 Ivan Rodriguez PP	.30	.09
142 Randy Johnson PP	.30	.09
143 Mark McGwire PP	.60	.18
144 Tino Martinez PP	.20	.06
145 Tony Clark PP	.20	.06
146 Mike Piazza PP	.50	.15
147 Alex Rodriguez PP	.50	.15
148 Roger Clemens CL	.50	.15
149 Greg Maddux CL	.50	.15
150 Hideo Nomo CL	.20	.06

1997 Pinnacle X-Press Men of Summer

Randomly inserted in packs at the rate of one in seven and one in every Master Deck, this 150-card set is parallel to the base set and is printed on full silver foil card stock with foil stamped accents.

Nm-Mt Ex-Mt
*STARS: 4X TO 10X BASIC CARDS
*ROOKIES: 2X TO 5X BASIC CARDS

1997 Pinnacle X-Press Far and Away

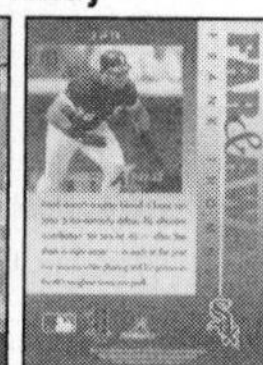

Randomly inserted in regular packs at the rate of one in 19 and one in five in Master Decks, this 18-card set features color photos of the league's top long-ball hitters. The cards are printed with Dufex hand-etched all-foil highlights.

	Nm-Mt	Ex-Mt
COMPLETE SET (18)	80.00	24.00
1 Albert Belle	2.00	.60
2 Mark McGwire	12.00	3.60
3 Frank Thomas	5.00	1.50
4 Mo Vaughn	2.00	.60
5 Jeff Bagwell	3.00	.90
6 Juan Gonzalez	5.00	1.50
7 Mike Piazza	8.00	2.40
8 Andruw Jones	2.00	.60
9 Chipper Jones	5.00	1.50
10 Gary Sheffield	2.00	.60
11 Sammy Sosa	8.00	2.40
12 Darin Erstad	2.00	.60
13 Jay Buhner	2.00	.60
14 Ken Griffey Jr.	8.00	2.40
15 Ken Caminiti	2.00	.60
16 Brady Anderson	2.00	.60
17 Manny Ramirez	2.00	.60
18 Alex Rodriguez	8.00	2.40

1997 Pinnacle X-Press Melting Pot Samples

These cards were sent out to dealers to indicate what the Pinnacle X-Press Melting Pot set would look like. These cards are numbered the same as the regular cards. The differences are that the word "sample" is printed in large black ink on both the front and the back. In addition, all the cards are numbered 000/500.

	Nm-Mt	Ex-Mt
COMPLETE SET (20)	120.00	36.00
1 Jose Guillen	2.00	.60
2 Vladimir Guerrero	6.00	1.80
3 Andruw Jones	4.00	1.20
4 Larry Walker	2.00	.60
5 Manny Ramirez	5.00	1.50
6 Ken Griffey Jr.	10.00	3.00
7 Alex Rodriguez	12.00	3.60
8 Frank Thomas	5.00	1.50
9 Juan Gonzalez	5.00	1.50
10 Ivan Rodriguez	5.00	1.50
11 Hideo Nomo	8.00	2.40
12 Rafael Palmeiro	4.00	1.20
13 Dave Nilsson	2.00	.60
14 Nomar Garciaparra	10.00	3.00
15 Wilton Guerrero	2.00	.60
16 Sammy Sosa	8.00	2.40
17 Edgar Renteria	2.00	.60
18 Cal Ripken	15.00	4.50
19 Derek Jeter	15.00	4.50
20 Rey Ordonez	2.00	.60

1997 Pinnacle X-Press Melting Pot

Randomly inserted in regular packs at the rate of one in 288 and one in 189 in Master Decks, this 20-card set features color photos of top players. The set tracks the players' origins on foil board with heliogram raised ink printing. The fronts carry a portrait of the player with his country's flag as the background. The backs display another player photo, player information, team logo and his native country. Only 500 of this set were produced and are sequentially numbered.

	Nm-Mt	Ex-Mt
COMPLETE SET (20)	300.00	90.00
1 Jose Guillen	6.00	1.80
2 Vladimir Guerrero	15.00	4.50
3 Andruw Jones	6.00	1.80
4 Larry Walker	10.00	3.00
5 Manny Ramirez	6.00	1.80
6 Ken Griffey Jr.	25.00	7.50
7 Alex Rodriguez	25.00	7.50
8 Frank Thomas	15.00	4.50
9 Juan Gonzalez	15.00	4.50
10 Ivan Rodriguez	15.00	4.50
11 Hideo Nomo	15.00	4.50
12 Rafael Palmeiro	10.00	3.00
13 Dave Nilsson	6.00	1.80
14 Nomar Garciaparra	25.00	7.50
15 Wilton Guerrero	6.00	1.80
16 Sammy Sosa	25.00	7.50
17 Edgar Renteria	6.00	1.80
18 Cal Ripken	50.00	15.00
19 Derek Jeter	40.00	12.00
20 Rey Ordonez	6.00	1.80

1997 Pinnacle X-Press Metal Works

Inserted one in every Home Plate Box, this 20-card bronze set features color photos of top players printed on very thick metal stock. The redemption cards below have no expiration date but are no longer valid for exchange due to Pinnacle's bankruptcy in 1998.

	Nm-Mt	Ex-Mt
COMPLETE SET (20)	60.00	18.00

*SILVER: 1.25X TO 3X BRONZE METAL WORKS
SILVER ODDS 1:54 MASTER DECKS.

SILVER REDEMPTION ODDS 1:470 HOBBY
SILVER PRINT RUN 400 SERIAL #'d SETS
*GOLD: 2X TO 5X BRONZE METAL WORKS
GOLD ODDS 1:108 MASTER DECKS...
GOLD REDEMPTION ODDS 1:950 HOBBY
GOLD PRINT RUN 200 SERIAL #'d SETS

1 Ken Griffey Jr.	3.00	.90
2 Frank Thomas	2.00	.60
3 Andruw Jones	.75	.23
4 Alex Rodriguez	3.00	.90
5 Derek Jeter	5.00	1.50
6 Cal Ripken	6.00	1.80
7 Mike Piazza	3.00	.90
8 Chipper Jones	2.00	.60
9 Juan Gonzalez	2.00	.60
10 Greg Maddux	3.00	.90
11 Tony Gwynn	2.50	.75
12 Jeff Bagwell	1.25	.35
13 Albert Belle	.75	.23
14 Mark McGwire	5.00	1.50
15 Nomar Garciaparra	3.00	.90
16 Mo Vaughn	.75	.23
17 Andy Pettitte	1.25	.35
18 Manny Ramirez	.75	.23
19 Kenny Lofton	.75	.23
20 Roger Clemens	4.00	1.20
NNO Gold Red. Card	1.00	.30
NNO Silver Red. Card	1.00	.30

1997 Pinnacle X-Press Swing for the Fences

Randomly inserted in packs at the rate of one in two, cards from this 60-card unnumbered set feature color photos of baseball's top long-distance hitters and are the player cards for the Swing for the Fences Game in which collectors accumulated points in order to win prizes. The object was to find the Home Run Champion from either the National or American League and match it with the exact number of home runs hit during the 1997 season by using a combination of Booster Number Point cards and one Base Number Home Run card. A Booster card was inserted one in every two packs and carried a plus or minus point total that allowed collectors to add or subtract points to get the winning homer total. The Base Number Home Run Card was found in the Home Plate Master Deck packs only and carried a predetermined number of Home Runs (between 20 and 42) assigned to each player. The first 1,000 winners received an autographed card of Andruw Jones of the Atlanta Braves. The next 3,000 winners received random 10-card packs of Upgraded Swing For the Fences cards produced on thicker card stock and printed with a special foil prize-winner stamp. After all redemptions were done, a drawing was held for the grand prize of a trip for two to the 1998 Pinnacle All-Star FanFest with tickets to the All-Star Game in Denver, Colorado. Five runner-up winners received a box of all Pinnacle Trading Cards baseball products for a full year. Since Mark McGwire led the majors in homers, his card was also deemed to be a winner although he did not lead either league in homers.

	Nm-Mt	Ex-Mt
COMPLETE SET (60)	60.00	18.00

*UPG.STARS: 2.5X TO 6X BASE CARD HI
TEN UPGRADES VIA MAIL PER SWING WIN
UPGRADE EXCH.DEADLINE: 3/1/98....
NNO CARDS LISTED IN ALPH.ORDER

1 Sandy Alomar Jr.	.50	.15
2 Moises Alou	.50	.15
3 Brady Anderson	.50	.15
4 Jeff Bagwell	.75	.23
5 Derek Bell	.50	.15
6 Jay Bell	.50	.15
7 Albert Belle	.50	.15
8 Geronimo Berroa	.50	.15
9 Dante Bichette	.50	.15
10 Barry Bonds	3.00	.90
11 Bobby Bonilla	.50	.15
12 Jay Buhner	.50	.15
13 Ellis Burks	.50	.15
14 Ken Caminiti	.50	.15
15 Jose Canseco	1.25	.35
16 Joe Carter	.50	.15
17 Vinny Castilla	.50	.15
18 Tony Clark	.50	.15
19 Carlos Delgado	1.25	.35
20 Jim Edmonds	.50	.15
21 Cecil Fielder	.50	.15
22 Andres Galarraga	.50	.15
23 Ron Gant	.50	.15
24 Bernard Gilkey	.50	.15
25 Juan Gonzalez	1.25	.35
26 Ken Griffey Jr. W	4.00	1.20
27 Vladimir Guerrero	1.25	.35
28 Todd Hundley	.50	.15
29 John Jaha	.50	.15
30 Andruw Jones	.50	.15
31 Chipper Jones	1.25	.35
32 David Justice	.50	.15
33 Jeff Kent	.50	.15
34 Ryan Klesko	.50	.15
35 Barry Larkin	1.25	.35
36 Mike Lieberthal	.50	.15
37 Javier Lopez	.50	.15
38 Edgar Martinez	.75	.23
39 Tino Martinez	.75	.23
40 Fred McGriff	.75	.23
41 Mark McGwire W	6.00	1.80
42 Raul Mondesi	.50	.15
43 Tim Naehring	.50	.15
44 Dave Nilsson	.50	.15
45 Rafael Palmeiro	.75	.23
46 Dean Palmer	.50	.15
47 Mike Piazza	2.00	.60
48 Cal Ripken	4.00	1.20
49 Henry Rodriguez	.50	.15
50 Tim Salmon	.75	.23
51 Gary Sheffield	.50	.15
52 Sammy Sosa	2.00	.60
53 Terry Steinbach	.50	.15
54 Frank Thomas	1.25	.35
55 Jim Thome	1.25	.35
56 Mo Vaughn	.50	.15
57 Larry Walker W	1.50	.45
58 Rondell White	.50	.15
59 Matt Williams	.50	.15
60 Todd Zeile	.50	.15
NNO A.Jones AU EXCH	25.00	7.50

1910 Pirates American Caramels E90-2

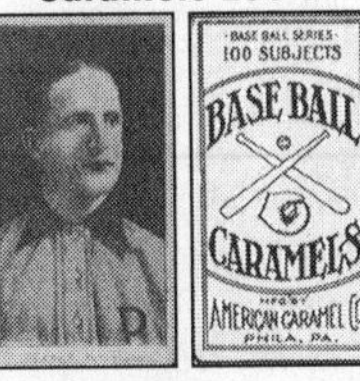

The cards in this 11-card set measure 1 1/2" by 2 3/4". The 1910 E90-2 American Caramels Baseball Star set contains unnumbered cards featuring players from the 1909 Pittsburgh Pirates. The backs of these cards are exactly like the E90-1 cards; however, blue print is used for the names of the players and the teams on the fronts of the cards.

	Ex-Mt	VG
COMPLETE SET (11)	2500.00	1250.00
1 Babe Adams	120.00	60.00
2 Fred Clarke	300.00	150.00
3 George Gibson	100.00	50.00
4 Ham Hyatt	100.00	50.00
5 Tommy Leach	150.00	75.00
6 Sam Leever	100.00	50.00
7 Nick Maddox	100.00	50.00
8 Dots Miller	100.00	50.00
9 Deacon Phillippe	150.00	75.00
10 Honus Wagner	1500.00	750.00
11 Chief Wilson	120.00	60.00

1910 Pirates Tip-Top D322

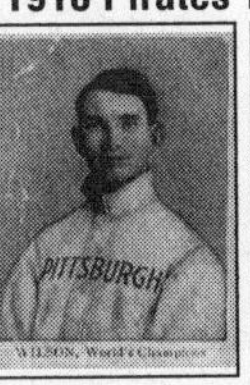

This 25-card set of the Pittsburgh Pirates was distributed by Tip-Top Bread at a rate of one per bread loaf and measures approximately 1 13/15" by 2 3/8". The fronts feature pastel paintings of the World Champion Team. The backs carry a checklist, ad for the bakery, and offer to send the complete set for 50 bread labels.

	Ex-Mt	VG
COMPLETE SET (25)	8000.00	4000.00
1 Barney Dreyfuss PRES	400.00	200.00
2 William Locke	300.00	150.00
3 Fred Clarke MG	600.00	300.00
4 Honus Wagner	2000.00	1000.00
5 Tom Leach	300.00	150.00
6 George Gibson	300.00	150.00
7 Dots Miller	300.00	150.00
8 Howie Camnitz	300.00	150.00
9 Babe Adams	400.00	200.00
10 Lefty Leifield	300.00	150.00
11 Nick Maddox	300.00	150.00
12 Deacon Phillippe	400.00	200.00
13 Bobby Byrne	300.00	150.00
14 Ed Abbaticchio	300.00	150.00
15 Lefty Webb	300.00	150.00
16 Vin Campbell	300.00	150.00
17 Owen Wilson	400.00	200.00
18 Sam Leever	300.00	150.00
19 Mike Simon	300.00	150.00
20 Ham Hyatt	300.00	150.00
21 Paddy O'Connor	300.00	150.00
22 John Flynn	300.00	150.00
23 Kirby White	300.00	150.00
24 Tip Top Boy(Mascot)	300.00	150.00
25 Forbes Field	300.00	150.00

1913 Pirates Voskamps

These cards, which measure approximately 3 5/8" by 2 1/4" feature members of the 1913 Pittsburgh Pirates. Both Hoffman and O'Toole are known to exist in two different versions. Since these cards were unnumbered, we have sequenced them in alphabetical order.

	MINT	NRMT
COMPLETE SET	12000.00	5400.00
1 Babe Adams	600.00	275.00
2 Everitt Booe	500.00	220.00
3 Bobby Byrne	500.00	220.00
4 Howie Camnitz	500.00	220.00
5 Max Carey	1500.00	700.00
6 Joe Conzelman	500.00	220.00
7 Jack Ferry	500.00	220.00
8 George Gibson	500.00	220.00
9 Claude Hendrix	500.00	220.00
10 Solly Hofman	500.00	220.00
11 Ham Hyatt	500.00	220.00
12 Bill Kelly	500.00	220.00
13 Ed Mensor	500.00	220.00
14 Dots Miller	500.00	220.00
15 Marty O'Toole	500.00	220.00
16 Hank Robinson	500.00	220.00
17 Mike Simon	500.00	220.00
18 Jim Viox	500.00	220.00
19 Honus Wagner	3000.00	1350.00
20 Chief Wilson	500.00	220.00

1950 Pirates Team Issue

This set of the Pittsburgh Pirates measures approximately 6 1/2" by 9" and features black-and-white player photos. The backs are blank. The cards are unnumbered and checklisted below in alphabetical order.

	NM	Ex
COMPLETE SET (25)	75.00	38.00
1 Ted Beard	4.00	2.00
2 Gus Bell	6.00	3.00
3 Pete Castiglione	4.00	2.00
4 Cliff Chambers	4.00	2.00
5 Dale Coogan	4.00	2.00
6 Murry Dickson	5.00	2.50
7 Froilan Fernandez	4.00	2.00
8 Johnny Hopp	5.00	2.50
9 Ralph Kiner	15.00	7.50
10 Vernon Law	8.00	4.00
11 Vic Lombardi	4.00	2.00
12 William MacDonald	4.00	2.00
13 Clyde McCullough	4.00	2.00
14 Bill Meyer MG	4.00	2.00
15 Ray Mueller	4.00	2.00
16 Danny Murtaugh	6.00	3.00
17 Jack Phillips	4.00	2.00
18 Mel Queen	4.00	2.00
19 Stan Rojek	4.00	2.00
20 Henry Schenz	4.00	2.00
21 George Strickland	4.00	2.00
22 Earl Turner	4.00	2.00
23 Jim Walsh	4.00	2.00
24 Bill Werle	4.00	2.00
25 Wally Westlake	4.00	2.00

1956 Pirates Team Issue

This 24-card set of the Pittsburgh Pirates features black-and-white player photos with white borders and was sold by the club for 15 cents each. The backs are blank. The cards are unnumbered and checklisted below in alphabetical order. The Bill Mazeroski card in this set predates his Rookie Card.

	NM	Ex
COMPLETE SET (24)	125.00	60.00
1 Luis Arroyo	3.00	1.50
2 Bobby Bragan MG	5.00	2.50
3 Roberto Clemente	50.00	25.00
4 Dick Cole	3.00	1.50
5 Roy Face	5.00	2.50
6 Hank Foiles	3.00	1.50
7 Gene Freese	3.00	1.50
8 Bob Friend	5.00	2.50
9 Dick Groat	5.00	2.50
10 Dick Hall	3.00	1.50
11 Nelson King	3.00	1.50
12 Ronnie Kline	3.00	1.50
13 Danny Kravitz	3.00	1.50
14 Vernon Law	5.00	2.50
15 Dale Long	3.00	1.50
16 Jerry Lynch	3.00	1.50
17 Bill Mazeroski	20.00	10.00
18 Johnny O'Brien	3.00	1.50
19 Curt Roberts	3.00	1.50
20 Jack Shepard	3.00	1.50
21 Bob Skinner	3.00	1.50
22 Frank Thomas	5.00	2.50
23 Bill Virdon	5.00	2.50
24 Lee Walls	3.00	1.50

1957 Pirates Team Issue

This 10-card set of the Pittsburgh Pirates features black-and-white player photos with white borders. The backs are blank. The cards are unnumbered and checklisted below in alphabetical order. The checklist might be incomplete and any confirmed addtions are welcomed.

	NM	Ex
COMPLETE SET (10)	50.00	25.00
1 Roberto Clemente	25.00	12.50
2 Dick Groat	5.00	2.50
3 Danny Kravitz	3.00	1.50
4 Vernon Law	4.00	2.00
5 Dale Long	3.00	1.50
6 Bill Mazeroski	6.00	3.00
7 Johnny O'Brien	3.00	1.50
8 Bob Skinner	3.00	1.50
9 Frank Thomas	4.00	2.00
10 Bill Virdon	5.00	2.50

1958 Pirates Team Issue

This set of the Pittsburgh Pirates measures approximately 5" by 7" and features black-and-white player portraits with white borders. The set was sold by the club through the mail for 50 cents. The cards are unnumbered and checklisted below in alphabetical order. An 8 1/2" by 11" team photo was added to the set along with an 8 1/4" by 10 1/4" glossy photo of Dick Groat (card number 13) with a printed autograph and name in the white border.

	NM	Ex
COMPLETE SET (12)	75.00	38.00
1 Roberto Clemente	25.00	12.50
2 Hank Foiles	3.00	1.50
3 Bob Friend	3.00	1.50
4 Dick Groat	5.00	2.50
5 Ronald Kline	3.00	1.50
6 Bill Mazeroski	10.00	5.00
7 Roman Mejias	3.00	1.50
8 Danny Murtaugh MG	5.00	2.50
9 Bob Skinner	3.00	1.50
10 Dick Stuart	3.00	1.50
11 Frank Thomas	3.00	1.50
12 Bill Virdon	5.00	2.50
13 Dick Groat	6.00	3.00
14 Team Picture	15.00	7.50

1959 Pirates Jay Publishing

This 12-card set of the Pittsburgh Pirates measures approximately 5" by 7" and features black-and-white player photos in a white border. These cards were packaged 12 to a packet. The backs are blank. The cards are unnumbered and checklisted below in alphabetical order.

	NM	Ex
COMPLETE SET	60.00	30.00
1 Roberto Clemente	25.00	12.50
2 Hank Foiles	3.00	1.50
3 Bob Friend	3.00	1.50
4 Dick Groat	5.00	2.50
5 Don Hoak	3.00	1.50
6 Ron Kline	3.00	1.50
7 Ted Kluszewski	6.00	3.00
8 Bill Mazeroski	8.00	4.00
9 Danny Murtaugh MG	3.00	1.50
10 Bob Skinner	3.00	1.50
11 Dick Stuart	3.00	1.50
12 Bill Virdon	4.00	2.00

1960 Pirates Jay Publishing

This 12-card set of the Pittsburgh Pirates measures approximately 5" by 7". The fronts feature black-and-white posed player photos with the player's and team name printed below in the white border. These cards were packaged 12 to a packet and originally sold for 50 cents. The backs are blank. The cards are unnumbered and checklisted below in alphabetical order.

	NM	Ex
COMPLETE SET (12)	60.00	24.00
1 Smoky Burgess	4.00	1.60
2 Gino Cimoli	2.50	1.00
3 Roberto Clemente	25.00	10.00
4 Roy Face	4.00	1.60
5 Bob Friend	3.00	1.20
6 Dick Groat	5.00	2.00
7 Harvey Haddix	3.00	1.20
8 Don Hoak	3.00	1.20
9 Bill Mazeroski	8.00	3.20
10 Danny Murtaugh MG	4.00	1.60
11 Bob Skinner	2.50	1.00
12 Dick Stuart	3.00	1.20

1960 Pirates Tag-Ons

This 10-card set originally sold for $1.98 and features individually die-cut self-sticking figures in full color on one large sheet measuring approximately 10" by 15 1/2". These flexible color-fast Tag-ons are weatherproof and can be applied to any surface. The figures are checklisted below according to the small black numbers printed on their shoulders.

	NM	Ex
COMPLETE SET (10)	60.00	24.00
4 Robert Skinner	5.00	2.00
6 Forrest Burgess	5.00	2.00
7 Dick Stuart	6.00	2.40
9 Bill Mazeroski	10.00	4.00
12 Don Hoak	5.00	2.00
18 Bill Virdon	6.00	2.40
19 Bob Friend	5.00	2.00
21 Roberto Clemente	25.00	10.00
24 Dick Groat	8.00	3.20
26 Roy Face	6.00	2.40
XX Complete Sheet	60.00	24.00

1961 Pirates Riger Ford

This six-card set was distributed by Ford Motor Company and measures approximately 11" by 14". The fronts feature pencil drawings by Robert Riger of six of the 1960 World Champion Pittsburgh Pirates. The cards are unnumbered and checklisted below in alphabetical order.

	NM	Ex
COMPLETE SET (6)	100.00	40.00
1 Roberto Clemente	50.00	20.00
2 Bob Friend	10.00	4.00
3 Dick Groat	20.00	8.00
4 Don Hoak	10.00	4.00
5 Vernon Law	15.00	6.00
6 Bill Mazeroski	25.00	10.00

1962 Pirates Jay Publishing

This 12-card set of the Pittsburgh Pirates measures approximately 5" by 7". The fronts feature black-and-white posed player photos with the player's and team name printed below in the white border. These cards were packaged 12 to a packet. The backs are blank. The cards are unnumbered and checklisted below in alphabetical order.

	NM	Ex
COMPLETE SET (12)	60.00	24.00
1 Smoky Burgess	3.00	1.20
2 Roberto Clemente	25.00	10.00
3 Roy Face	4.00	1.60
4 Bob Friend	3.00	1.20
5 Dick Groat	4.00	1.60
6 Don Hoak	2.50	1.00
7 Vern Law	3.00	1.20
8 Bill Mazeroski	8.00	3.20
9 Danny Murtaugh MG	3.00	1.20
10 Bob Skinner	2.50	1.00
11 Dick Stuart	3.00	1.20
12 Bill Virdon	3.00	1.20

1963 Pirates IDL

This 26-card set measures approximately 4" by 5" and is blank-backed. The fronts have black and white photos on the top of the card along with the IDL Drug Store logo in the lower left corner of the card and the players name printed in block letters underneath the picture. The only card which has any designation as to position is the manager card of Danny Murtaugh. These cards are unnumbered and feature members of the Pittsburgh Pirates. The catalog designation for the set is H801-13 although it is infrequently referenced. The Stargell card is one of his few cards from 1963, his rookie year for cards.

	NM	Ex
COMPLETE SET (26)	150.00	60.00
1 Bob Bailey	5.00	2.00
2 Smoky Burgess	6.00	2.40
3 Don Cardwell	5.00	2.00
4 Roberto Clemente	50.00	20.00
5 Donn Clendenon	6.00	2.40
6 Roy Face	8.00	3.20
7 Earl Francis	5.00	2.00
8 Bob Friend	6.00	2.40
9 Joe Gibbon	5.00	2.00
10 Julio Gotay	5.00	2.00
11 Harvey Haddix	6.00	2.40
12 Johnny Logan	5.00	2.00
13 Bill Mazeroski	15.00	6.00
14 Al McBean	5.00	2.00
15 Danny Murtaugh MG	6.00	2.40
16 Sam Narron CO	5.00	2.00
17 Ron Northey CO	5.00	2.00
18 Frank Oceak CO	5.00	2.00
19 Jim Pagliaroni	5.00	2.00
20 Ted Savage	5.00	2.00
21 Dick Schofield	5.00	2.00
22 Willie Stargell	25.00	10.00
23 Tom Sturdivant	5.00	2.00
24 Virgil Trucks CO	5.00	2.00
25 Bob Veale	5.00	2.00
26 Bill Virdon	6.00	2.40

1963 Pirates Jay Publishing

This 12-card set of the Pittsburgh Pirates measures approximately 5" by 7". The fronts feature black-and-white posed player photos with the player's and team name printed below in the white border. These cards were packaged 12 to a packet. The backs are blank. The cards are unnumbered and checklisted below in alphabetical order.

	NM	Ex
COMPLETE SET (12)	50.00	20.00
1 Bob Bailey	2.50	1.00
2 Smoky Burgess	3.00	1.20
3 Roberto Clemente	25.00	10.00
4 Donn Clendenon	2.50	1.00
5 Roy Face	4.00	1.60
6 Bob Friend	3.00	1.20
7 Harvey Haddix	3.00	1.20
8 Vern Law	3.00	1.20
9 Bill Mazeroski	8.00	3.20
10 Danny Murtaugh MG	3.00	1.20
11 Bob Skinner	2.50	1.00
12 Bill Virdon	3.00	1.20

1964 Pirates Jay Publishing

This 12-card set of the Pittsburgh Pirates measures approximately 5" by 7". The fronts feature black-and-white posed player photos with the player's and team name printed below in the white border. These cards were packaged 12 to a packet. The backs are blank. The cards are unnumbered and checklisted below in alphabetical order.

	NM	Ex
COMPLETE SET (12)	50.00	20.00
1 Bob Bailey	2.00	.80
2 Smoky Burgess	2.50	1.00
3 Roberto Clemente	25.00	10.00
4 Donn Clendenon	2.50	1.00
5 Roy Face	3.00	1.20
6 Bob Friend	2.50	1.00
7 Bill Mazeroski	8.00	3.20
8 Danny Murtaugh MG	2.50	1.00
9 Dick Schofield	2.00	.80
10 Willie Stargell	10.00	4.00
11 Bob Veale	2.00	.80
12 Bill Virdon	2.50	1.00

1964 Pirates KDKA

This set featured members of the 1964 Pittsburgh Pirates. It was issued by radio station KDKA. The set can be dated to 1964 by the card of Rex Johnston, who only played for the Pirates in that season.

	NM	Ex
COMPLETE SET (28)	1200.00	475.00
1 Gene Alley	30.00	12.00
2 Bob Bailey	30.00	12.00
3 Frank Bork	30.00	12.00
4 Smoky Burgess	40.00	16.00
5 Tom Butters	30.00	12.00
6 Don Cardwell	30.00	12.00
7 Roberto Clemente	400.00	160.00
8 Donn Clendenon	40.00	16.00
9 Roy Face	50.00	20.00
10 Gene Freese	30.00	12.00
11 Bob Friend	40.00	16.00
12 Joe Gibbon	30.00	12.00
13 Julio Gotay	30.00	12.00
14 Rex Johnston	30.00	12.00
15 Vernon Law	50.00	20.00
16 Jerry Lynch	30.00	12.00
17 Bill Mazeroski	100.00	40.00
18 Al McBean	30.00	12.00
19 Orlando McFarlane	30.00	12.00
20 Manny Mota	50.00	20.00
21 Danny Murtaugh MG	40.00	16.00
22 Jim Pagliaroni	30.00	12.00
23 Dick Schofield	30.00	12.00
24 Don Schwall	30.00	12.00
25 Tommie Sisk	30.00	12.00
26 Willie Stargell	150.00	60.00
27 Bob Veale	30.00	12.00
28 Bill Virdon	40.00	16.00

1965 Pirates Jay Publishing

This 12-card set of the Pittsburgh Pirates measures approximately 5" by 7". The fronts feature black-and-white posed player photos with the player's and team name printed below in the white border. These cards were packaged 12 to a packet. The backs are blank. The cards are unnumbered and checklisted below in alphabetical order.

	NM	Ex
COMPLETE SET (12)	50.00	20.00
1 Bob Bailey	2.00	.80
2 Roberto Clemente	25.00	10.00
3 Donn Clendenon	2.50	1.00
4 Del Crandall	2.50	1.00
5 Vern Law	3.00	1.20
6 Bill Mazeroski	8.00	3.20
7 Manny Mota	2.50	1.00
8 Jim Pagliaroni	2.00	.80
9 Dick Schofield	2.00	.80
10 Willie Stargell	10.00	4.00
11 Bill Virdon	2.50	1.00
12 Harry Walker MG	2.00	.80

1965 Pirates KDKA Posters

These posters, which measure approximately 8" by 12" feature members of the 1965 Pirates and give the collector a chance to win an Emenee Electric Guitar. The top of the poster has the player's photo as well as his hame while the bottom half is dedicated to

information about the contest. We have sequenced the known players in alphabetical order but it would be suspected that there would be additions to this checklist.

	MINT	NRMT
COMPLETE SET	100.00	45.00
1 Tom Butters	50.00	22.00
2 Joe Gibbon	50.00	22.00

1966 Pirates East Hills

The 1966 East Hills Pirates set consists of 25 large (approximately 3 1/4" by 4 1/4"), full color photos of Pittsburgh Pirate ballplayers. These blank-backed cards are numbered in the lower right corner according to the uniform number of the individual depicted. The set was distributed by various stores located in the East Hills Shopping Center. The catalog number for this set is F405.

	NM	Ex
COMPLETE SET (25)	75.00	30.00
3 Harry Walker MG	.75	.30
7 Bob Bailey	.50	.20
8 Willie Stargell	25.00	10.00
9 Bill Mazeroski	5.00	2.00
10 Jim Pagliaroni	.50	.20
11 Jose Pagan	.50	.20
12 Jerry May	.50	.20
14 Gene Alley	1.00	.40
15 Manny Mota	1.00	.40
16 Andre Rodgers UER (Andy on card)	.50	.20
17 Donn Clendenon	1.00	.40
18 Matty Alou	3.00	1.20
19 Pete Mikkelsen	.50	.20
20 Jesse Gonder	.50	.20
21 Roberto Clemente	50.00	20.00
22 Woody Fryman	.75	.30
24 Jerry Lynch	.50	.20
25 Tommie Sisk	.50	.20
26 Roy Face	1.00	.40
28 Steve Blass	1.00	.40
32 Vernon Law	1.00	.40
34 Al McBean	.50	.20
39 Bob Veale	.75	.30
43 Don Cardwell	.50	.20
45 Gene Michael	.75	.30

1967 Pirate Stickers Topps

This was a limited production "test" issue for Topps. It is very similar to the Red Sox "test" issue following. The stickers are blank backed and measure 2 1/2" by 3 1/2". The stickers look like cards from the front and are somewhat attractive in spite of the "no neck" presentation of many of the players' photos. The cards are numbered on the front.

	NM	Ex
COMPLETE SET (33)	450.00	180.00
WRAPPER (5-CENT)	50.00	20.00
1 Gene Alley	8.00	3.20
2 Matty Alou	8.00	3.20
3 Dennis Ribant	6.00	2.40
4 Steve Blass	8.00	3.20
5 Juan Pizarro	6.00	2.40
6 Roberto Clemente	150.00	60.00
7 Donn Clendenon	8.00	3.20
8 Roy Face	10.00	4.00
9 Woodie Fryman	6.00	2.40
10 Jesse Gonder	6.00	2.40
11 Vern Law	8.00	3.20
12 Al McBean	6.00	2.40
13 Jerry May	6.00	2.40
14 Bill Mazeroski	20.00	8.00
15 Pete Mikkelsen	6.00	2.40
16 Manny Mota	8.00	3.20
17 Bill O'Dell	6.00	2.40
18 Jose Pagan	6.00	2.40
19 Jim Pagliaroni	6.00	2.40
20 Johnny Pesky CO	6.00	2.40
21 Tommie Sisk	6.00	2.40
22 Willie Stargell	50.00	20.00
23 Bob Veale	8.00	3.20
24 Harry Walker MG	6.00	2.40
25 I Love the Pirates	6.00	2.40
26 Let's Go Pirates	6.00	2.40
27 Roberto Clemente for Mayor	80.00	32.00
28 Matty Alou NL Batting Champ	8.00	3.20
29 Happiness is a Pirate Win	6.00	2.40
30 Donn Clendenon is my Hero	8.00	3.20
31 Willie Stargell Pirates HR Champ	30.00	12.00
32 Pirates Logo	6.00	2.40
33 Pirates Pennant	6.00	2.40

1967 Pirates Team Issue

This 24-card set of the Pittsburgh Pirates features color player photos with white borders and measures approximately 3 1/4" by 4 1/4". A facsimile autograph is printed in the wide bottom border. The backs are blank. The cards are unnumbered and checklisted below in alphabetical order. The complete set of 24 was available for $1 from Pitt Sportservice at time of issue.

	NM	Ex
COMPLETE SET (24)	80.00	32.00
1 Gene Alley	3.00	1.20
2 Matty Alou	4.00	1.60
3 Steve Blass	3.00	1.20
4 Roberto Clemente	20.00	8.00
5 Donn Clendenon	4.00	1.60
6 Roy Face	5.00	2.00
7 Woody Fryman	3.00	1.20
8 Jesse Gonder	3.00	1.20
9 Vernon Law	5.00	2.00
10 Jerry May	3.00	1.20
11 Bill Mazeroski	8.00	3.20
12 Al McBean	3.00	1.20
13 Pete Mikkelsen	3.00	1.20
14 Manny Mota	4.00	1.60
15 Jose Pagan	3.00	1.20
16 Jim Pagliaroni	3.00	1.20
17 Juan Pizarro	3.00	1.20
18 Dennis Ribant	3.00	1.20
19 Andy Rodgers	3.00	1.20
20 Tommie Sisk	3.00	1.20
21 Willie Stargell	10.00	4.00
22 Bob Veale	3.00	1.20
23 Harry Walker MG	4.00	1.60
24 Maury Wills	6.00	2.40

1967 Pirates Team Issue 8 by 10

These 24 blank-backed photos, which measure approximately 8" by 10", feature members of the 1967 Pittsburgh Pirates. From the description given, these were promotional shots mailed out to members of the press at the start of the 1967 season. Since these photos are unnumbered, we have sequenced them in alphabetical order.

	NM	Ex
COMPLETE SET (24)	150.00	60.00
1 Gene Alley	5.00	2.00
2 Matty Alou	6.00	2.40
3 Steve Blass	5.00	2.00
4 Roberto Clemente	30.00	12.00
5 Donn Clendenon	5.00	2.00
6 Roy Face	6.00	2.40
7 Woodie Fryman	5.00	2.00
8 Jesse Gonder	5.00	2.00
9 Vern Law	6.00	2.40
10 Jerry May	5.00	2.00
11 Bill Mazeroski	12.00	4.80
12 Al McBean	5.00	2.00
13 Pete Mikkelsen	5.00	2.00
14 Manny Mota	6.00	2.40
15 Billy O'Dell	5.00	2.00
16 Jose Pagan	5.00	2.00
17 Jim Pagliaroni	5.00	2.00
18 Juan Pizarro	5.00	2.00
19 Dennis Ribant	5.00	2.00
20 Tommie Sisk	5.00	2.00
21 Willie Stargell	15.00	6.00
22 Bob Veale	5.00	2.00
23 Harry Walker MG	5.00	2.00
24 Maury Wills	10.00	4.00

1968 Pirates KDKA

This 23-card set measures approximately 2 3/8" by 4" and was issued by radio and television station KDKA to promote the Pittsburgh Pirates, whom they were covering at the time. The fronts have the players' photo on the top 2/3 of the card and a facsimile autograph, the players name and position and uniform number on the lower left hand corner and an ad for KDKA on the lower right corner of the card. The back has an advertisment for both KDKA radio and television. The set is checklisted below by uniform number.

	NM	Ex
COMPLETE SET (23)	100.00	40.00
7 Larry Shepard MG	2.00	.80
8 Willie Stargell	20.00	8.00
9 Bill Mazeroski	10.00	4.00
10 Gary Kolb	2.00	.80
11 Jose Pagan	2.00	.80
12 Jerry May	2.00	.80
14 Jim Bunning	8.00	3.20
15 Manny Mota	3.00	1.20
17 Donn Clendenon	3.00	1.20
18 Matty Alou	3.00	1.20
21 Roberto Clemente	40.00	16.00
22 Gene Alley	3.00	1.20
25 Tommy Sisk	2.00	.80
26 Roy Face	4.00	1.60
27 Ron Kline	2.00	.80
28 Steve Blass	3.00	1.20
29 Juan Pizzaro	2.00	.80
30 Maury Wills	5.00	2.00
34 Al McBean	2.00	.80
35 Manny Sanguillen	4.00	1.60
38 Bob Moose	3.00	1.20
39 Bob Veale	2.00	.80
40 Dave Wickersham	2.00	.80

1968 Pirates Team Issue

This 24-card set of the Pittsburgh Pirates features color player photos with white borders and measures approximately 3 1/4" by 4 1/4". A facsimile autograph is printed in the wide bottom border. The backs are blank. The cards are unnumbered and checklisted below in alphabetical order.

	NM	Ex
COMPLETE SET (24)	100.00	40.00
1 Gene Alley	3.00	1.20
2 Matty Alou	5.00	2.00
3 Steve Blass	3.00	1.20
4 Jim Bunning	8.00	3.20
5 Roberto Clemente	20.00	8.00
6 Donn Clendenon	4.00	1.60
7 Roy Face	5.00	2.00
8 Ronnie Kline	3.00	1.20
9 Gary Kolb	3.00	1.20
10 Jerry May	3.00	1.20
11 Bill Mazeroski	8.00	3.20
12 Al McBean	3.00	1.20
13 Bob Moose	3.00	1.20
14 Manny Mota	4.00	1.60
15 Jose Pagan	3.00	1.20
16 Juan Pizarro	3.00	1.20
17 Manny Sanguillen	4.00	1.60
18 Jim Shellenback	3.00	1.20
19 Larry Shepard MG	3.00	1.20
20 Tommie Sisk	3.00	1.20
21 Willie Stargell	10.00	4.00
22 Bob Veale	3.00	1.20
23 Dave Wickersham	3.00	1.20
24 Maury Wills	6.00	2.40

1969 Pirates Jack in the Box

This 12-card set measures approximately 2 1/16" by 3 5/8" and features black-and-white player photos on a white card face. The player's name, team name, position, and batting or pitching record appear below the photo. The backs are blank. The cards are unnumbered and checklisted below in alphabetical order. Pittsburgh is misspelled Pittsburg on the front of the cards.

	NM	Ex
COMPLETE SET (12)	50.00	20.00
1 Gene Alley	3.00	1.20
2 Dave Cash	4.00	1.60
3 Dock Ellis	3.00	1.20
4 Dave Giusti	2.00	.80
5 Jerry May	2.00	.80
6 Bill Mazeroski	8.00	3.20
7 Al Oliver	6.00	2.40
8 Jose Pagan	2.00	.80
9 Fred Patek	3.00	1.20
10 Bob Robertson	2.00	.80
11 Manny Sanguillen	3.00	1.20
12 Willie Stargell	20.00	8.00

1969 Pirates Greiner

This eight-card set of the Pittsburgh Pirates, sponsored by Greiner Tire Service, measures approximately 5 1/2" by 8 1/2" and features black-and-white player portraits inside a white border. The player's name and team is printed with a "good luck" message in the wide bottom margin along with the sponsor name, address and phone number. The backs are blank. The cards are unnumbered and checklisted below in alphabetical order.

	NM	Ex
COMPLETE SET (8)	150.00	60.00
1 Gene Alley	10.00	4.00
2 Matty Alou	12.00	4.80
3 Steve Blass	8.00	3.20
4 Roberto Clemente	80.00	32.00
5 Jerry May	8.00	3.20
6 Bill Mazeroski	20.00	8.00
7 Larry Shepard MG	8.00	3.20
8 Willie Stargell	25.00	10.00

1969 Pirates Team Issue

This 26-card set of the Pittsburgh Pirates was issued in two series and measures approximately 3 1/4" by 4 1/4". The fronts feature color player photos in white borders with a facsimile autograph printed in the wide bottom margin. The backs are blank. The cards are unnumbered and checklisted below in alphabetical order.

	NM	Ex
COMPLETE SET (24)	90.00	36.00
1 Gene Alley	2.00	.80
2 Matty Alou	3.00	1.20
3 Steve Blass	2.00	.80
4 Jim Bunning	5.00	2.00
5 Roberto Clemente	20.00	8.00
6 Bruce Dal Canton	2.00	.80
7 Doc Ellis	2.50	1.00
8 Chuck Hartenstein	2.00	.80
9 Richie Hebner	2.50	1.00
10 Ronnie Kline	2.00	.80
11 Gary Kolb	2.00	.80
12 Vernon Law CO	2.50	1.00
13 Jose Martinez	2.00	.80
14 Jerry May	2.00	.80
15 Bill Mazeroski	6.00	2.40
16 Bob Moose	2.00	.80
17 Al Oliver	4.00	1.60
18 Jose Pagan	2.00	.80
19 Fred Patek	2.50	1.00
20 Manny Sanguillen	2.50	1.00
21 Larry Shepard MG	2.00	.80
22 Willie Stargell	10.00	4.00
23 Carl Taylor	2.00	.80
24 Bob Veale	2.00	.80
25 Bill Virdon CO	2.50	1.00
26 Luke Walker	2.00	.80

1970 Pirates Team Issue

This 20-card set of the Pittsburgh Pirates was issued in two series of 10 cards each measuring approximately 3 1/4" by 4 1/4". The fronts feature color player portraits in white borders. A facsimile autograph is printed in the wide bottom margin. The backs are blank. The cards are unnumbered and checklisted below in alphabetical order.

	NM	Ex
COMPLETE SET (20)	60.00	24.00
1 Gene Alley	2.00	.80
2 Matty Alou	3.00	1.20
3 Steve Blass	2.00	.80
4 Bob Clemente	15.00	6.00
5 Bruce Dal Canton	2.00	.80
6 Dock Ellis	2.00	.80
7 Chuck Hartenstein	2.00	.80
8 Richie Hebner	2.50	1.00
9 Gary Kolb	2.00	.80
10 Jerry May	2.00	.80
11 Bill Mazeroski	6.00	2.40
12 Bob Moose	2.00	.80
13 Al Oliver	4.00	1.60
14 Jose Pagan	2.00	.80
15 Fred Patek	2.50	1.00
16 Manny Sanguillen	2.50	1.00
17 Willie Stargell	8.00	3.20
18 Bob Veale	2.00	.80
19 Bill Virdon CO	2.50	1.00
20 Luke Walker	2.00	.80

1971 Pirates

The six blank-backed photos comprising this set "A" of the '71 Pirates measure approximately 7" by 8 3/4" and feature white-bordered posed color player shots. The player's name appears in black lettering within the bottom white margin. The pictures are unnumbered and checklisted below in alphabetical order.

	NM	Ex
COMPLETE SET (6)	30.00	12.00
1 Nelson Briles	5.00	2.00
2 Dave Cash	4.00	1.60
3 Roberto Clemente	20.00	8.00
4 Richie Hebner	5.00	2.00
5 Bob Robertson	4.00	1.60
6 Luke Walker	4.00	1.60

1971 Pirates Action Photos

These unnumbered cards feature members of the World Champion Pittsburgh Pirates. These cards were issued in two series (1-12, 13-24) and each group is sequenced into alphabetical order.

	NM	Ex
COMPLETE SET (24)	60.00	24.00
1 Gene Alley	1.50	.60
2 Nelson Briles	1.00	.40
3 Dave Cash	1.00	.40
4 Roberto Clemente	30.00	12.00
5 Dock Ellis	2.00	.80
6 Mudcat Grant	1.00	.40
7 Bob Johnson	1.00	.40
8 Milt May	1.00	.40
9 Jose Pagan	1.00	.40
10 Manny Sanguillen	2.00	.80
11 Bob Veale	1.00	.40
12 Luke Walker	1.00	.40
13 Steve Blass	1.50	.60
14 Gene Clines	1.00	.40
15 Vic Davalillo	1.00	.40
16 Dave Giusti	1.00	.40
17 Richie Hebner	1.50	.60
18 Jackie Hernandez	1.00	.40
19 Bill Mazeroski	4.00	1.60
20 Bob Moose	1.00	.40
21 Al Oliver	2.50	1.00
22 Bob Robertson	1.00	.40
23 Charlie Sands	1.00	.40
24 Willie Stargell	6.00	2.40

1971 Pirates Arco Oil

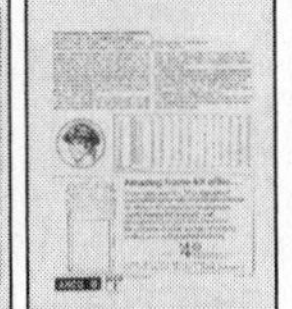

Sponsored by Arco Oil, this 12-card set features photos of the 1971 Pittsburgh Pirates. The cards are unnumbered and checklisted below in alphabetical order.

	NM	Ex
COMPLETE SET (12)	80.00	32.00
1 Gene Alley	5.00	2.00
2 Steve Blass	6.00	2.40
3 Roberto Clemente	25.00	10.00
4 Dave Giusti	5.00	2.00
5 Richie Hebner	5.00	2.00
6 Bill Mazeroski	12.00	4.80
7 Bob Moose	5.00	2.00
8 Al Oliver	8.00	3.20
9 Bob Robertson	5.00	2.00
10 Manny Sanguillen	8.00	3.20
11 Willie Stargell	15.00	6.00
12 Luke Walker	5.00	2.00

1971 Pirates Post-Gazette Inserts

These inserts, which feature members of the 1971 Pittsburgh Pirates, were inserted daily into the Post-Gazette newspaper. These inserts are numbered and this list may be incomplete so any further information is appreciated.

	NM	Ex
COMPLETE SET	60.00	24.00
5 Dave Cash	6.00	2.40
7 Bob Johnson	5.00	2.00
8 Nelson Briles	5.00	2.00
11 Dave Giusti	5.00	2.00
12 Luke Walker	5.00	2.00
13 Gene Clines	5.00	2.00
14 Milt May	5.00	2.00
15 Bob Robertson	5.00	2.00
17 Gene Alley	5.00	2.00
18 Bruce Kison	5.00	2.00
19 Jose Pagan	5.00	2.00
20 Dock Ellis	5.00	2.00
22 Bob Miller	5.00	2.00
23 Jackie Hernandez	5.00	2.00

1972 Pirates Team Issue

This eight-card set of the Pittsburgh Pirates measures approximately 3 1/4" by 4 1/4" and features color player portraits with a facsimile autograph in the wide bottom margin. The cards are unnumbered and checklisted below in alphabetical order.

	NM	Ex
COMPLETE SET	50.00	20.00
1 Steve Blass	3.00	1.20
2 Roberto Clemente	20.00	8.00
3 Dock Ellis	4.00	1.60
4 Richie Hebner	3.00	1.20
5 Dave Giusti	3.00	1.20
6 Bob Johnson	3.00	1.20
7 Bob Moose	3.00	1.20
8 Al Oliver	6.00	2.40
9 Jose Pagan	3.00	1.20
10 Bob Robertson	3.00	1.20
11 Manny Sanguillen	4.00	1.60
12 Willie Stargell	8.00	3.20

1973 Pirates Post/Gazette Inserts

These photos were inserted each day into the Pittsburgh Post Gazette. This listing is incomplete and any further information is appreciated. There may be other photos so all additional information is appreciated.

	NM	Ex
COMPLETE SET	50.00	20.00
6 Vic Davallilo	5.00	2.00
10 Ramon Hernandez	5.00	2.00
12 Bob Johnson	5.00	2.00
14 Milt May	5.00	2.00
15 Bob Miller	5.00	2.00
19 Charlie Sands	5.00	2.00
23 Luke Walker	5.00	2.00
24 Bill Virdon MG	5.00	2.00
NNO Steve Blass	5.00	2.00
NNO Nelson Briles	5.00	2.00
NNO Dave Cash	5.00	2.00
NNO Gene Alley	5.00	2.00

1974 Pirates 1938 Bra-Mac

These 26 photos, which measure 3 1/2" by 5" feature members of the 1938 Pittsburgh Pirates who lost the battle for the NL pennant very late in that season.

	NM	Ex
COMPLETE SET	15.00	6.00
1 Paul Waner	2.00	.80
2 Lloyd Waner	1.50	.60
3 Bill Swift	.50	.20
4 Woody Jensen	.50	.20
5 Jim Tobin	.50	.20
6 Ray Berres	.50	.20
7 Tommy Thevenow	.50	.20
8 Bob Klinger	.50	.20
9 Arky Vaughan	1.50	.60
10 Pep Young	.50	.20
11 Heinie Manush	1.50	.60
12 Bill Brubaker	.50	.20
13 Pie Traynor	2.00	.80
14 Lee Handley	.50	.20
15 Rip Sewell	.50	.20
16 Johnny Dickshot	.50	.20
17 Cy Blanton	.50	.20
18 Gus Suhr	.75	.30
19 Mace Brown	.50	.20
20 Johnny Rizzo	.50	.20
21 Al Todd	.50	.20
22 Russ Bauers	.50	.20
23 Ed Brandt	.50	.20
24 Red Lucas	.50	.20
25 Joe Bowman	.50	.20
26 Ken Heintzleman	.50	.20

1975 Pirates Postcards

This 29-card set of the Pittsburgh Pirates features player photos on postcard-size cards. The average size is 3 3/4" by 5 1/4". The fronts feature white-bordered black and white portraits. The player's name is printed in the wider bottom margin. Also a fascimile autograph in blue ink is inscribed across each picture. The backs are blank. The cards are unnumbered and checklisted below in alphabetical order.

	NM	Ex
COMPLETE SET (29)	20.00	8.00
1 Ken Brett	.50	.20
2 John Candelaria	1.50	.60
3 Larry Demery	.50	.20
4 Duffy Dyer	.50	.20
5 Dock Ellis	.50	.20
6 Dave Giusti	.50	.20
7 Richie Hebner	.75	.30
8 Ramon Hernandez	.50	.20
9 Art Howe	1.50	.60
10 Ed Kirkpatrick	.50	.20
11 Bruce Kison	.50	.20
12 Don Leppert CO	.50	.20
13 Mario Mendoza	.50	.20
14 Bob Moose	.50	.20
15 Danny Murtaugh MG	.50	.20
16 Al Oliver	1.50	.60
17 Don Osborne CO	.50	.20
18 Jose Pagan CO	.50	.20
19 Dave Parker	2.50	1.00
20 Paul Popovich	.50	.20
21 Jerry Reuss	1.00	.40
22 Bill Robinson	.50	.20
23 Bob Robertson	.50	.20
24 Jim Rooker	.75	.30
25 Manny Sanguillen	.75	.30
26 Willie Stargell	4.00	1.60
27 Rennie Stennett	.50	.20
28 Frank Taveras	.50	.20
29 Richie Zisk	.50	.20

1976 Pirates Postcards

This 27-card set of the Pittsburgh Pirates features player photos on postcard-size cards. The cards are unnumbered and checklisted below in alphabetical order.

	NM	Ex
COMPLETE SET (27)	15.00	6.00
1 John Candelaria	1.50	.60
2 Larry Demery	.50	.20
3 Dave Giusti	.50	.20
4 Richie Hebner	.75	.30
5 Tommy Helms	.50	.20
6 Ramon Hernandez	.50	.20
7 Ed Kirkpatrick	.50	.20
8 Bruce Kison	.50	.20
9 Don Leppert CO	.50	.20
10 George Medich	.50	.20
11 Mario Mendoza	.50	.20
12 Bob Moose	.50	.20
13 Danny Murtaugh MG	.50	.20
14 Al Oliver	1.50	.60
15 Ed Ott	.50	.20
16 Dave Parker	1.50	.60
17 Jerry Reuss	.75	.30
18 Bob Robertson	.50	.20
19 Bill Robinson	.50	.20
20 Jim Rooker	.50	.20
21 Manny Sanguillen	.50	.20
22 Bob Skinner CO	.50	.20
23 Willie Stargell	3.00	1.20
24 Rennie Stennett	.50	.20
25 Frank Taveras	.50	.20
26 Kent Tekulve	1.00	.40
27 Richie Zisk	.50	.20

1977 Pirates Post-Gazette Portraits

This 30-card set was distributed in an 8 1/2" by 11" book from the Pittsburgh Post-Gazette. The black-and-white player portraits were detachable and measured approximately 8" by 11". The backs are blank. The cards are unnumbered and checklisted below in alphabetical order.

	NM	Ex
COMPLETE SET (30)	20.00	8.00
1 John Candelaria	.75	.30
2 Larry Demery	.50	.20
3 Miguel Dilone	.50	.20
4 Duffy Dyer	.50	.20
5 Terry Forster	.50	.20
6 Jim Fregosi	.50	.20
7 Phil Garner	.50	.20
8 Fernando Gonzalez	.50	.20
9 Goose Gossage	1.50	.60
10 Grant Jackson	.50	.20
11 Odell Jones	.50	.20
12 Bruce Kison	.50	.20
13 Joe Lonnett CO	.50	.20
14 Mario Mendoza	.50	.20
15 Al Monchak CO	.50	.20
16 Omar Moreno	.75	.30
17 Al Oliver	1.50	.60
18 Ed Ott	.50	.20
19 Jose Pagan CO	.50	.20
20 Dave Parker	1.50	.60
21 Jerry Reuss	.75	.30
22 Bill Robinson	.50	.20
23 Jim Rooker	.50	.20
24 Larry Sherry CO	.50	.20
25 Willie Stargell	3.00	1.20
26 Rennie Stennett	.50	.20
27 Chuck Tanner MG	.50	.20
28 Frank Taveras	.50	.20
29 Kent Tekulve	.75	.30
30 Bobby Tolan	.50	.20

1977 Pirates 1960 World Champions TCMA

This 41-card set features black-and-white photos of the 1960 World Champion Pittsburgh Pirates in orange borders. The backs carry player information and statistics. (There is no card number 35 in the checklist.)

	NM	Ex
COMPLETE SET (41)	20.00	8.00
1 Danny Murtaugh MG	.50	.20
2 Dick Stuart	.50	.20
3 Bill Mazeroski	2.00	.80
4 Dick Groat	.75	.30
5 Don Hoak	.50	.20
6 Roberto Clemente	5.00	2.00
7 Bill Virdon	.75	.30
8 Bob Skinner	.50	.20
9 Smoky Burgess	.75	.30
10 Gino Cimoli	.50	.20
11 Rocky Nelson	.50	.20
12 Hal Smith	.50	.20
13 Dick Schofield	.50	.20
14 Joe Christopher	.50	.20
15 Gene Baker	.50	.20
16 Bob Oldis	.50	.20
17 Vern Law	.75	.30
18 Bob Friend	.50	.20
19 Vinegar Bend Mizell	.50	.20
20 Havey Haddix	.50	.20
21 Roy Face	.75	.30
22 Freddie Green	.50	.20
23 Joe Gibbon	.50	.20
24 Clem Labine	.50	.20
25 Paul Giel	.50	.20
26 Tom Chaney	.50	.20
27 Earl Francis	.50	.20
28 Jim Umbricht	.50	.20
29 George Witt	.50	.20
30 Bennie Daniels	.50	.20
31 Don Gross	.50	.20
32 Diomedes Olivo	.50	.20
33 Ramon Mejias	.50	.20
34 Mickey Vernon	.75	.30
36 Danny Kravitz	.50	.20
37 Harry Bright	.50	.20
38 Dick Barone	.50	.20
39 Bill Burwell CO	.50	.20
40 Lenny Levy	.50	.20
41 Sam Narron CO	.50	.20
42 Bob Friend	.75	.30

1980 Pirates Greats TCMA

This 12-card set features various all-time Pittsburgh Pirates greats. The fronts display a black-and-white player photo with blue borders. The backs carry player information.

	NM	Ex
COMPLETE SET (12)	8.00	3.20
1 Willie Stargell	1.00	.40
2 Bill Mazeroski	1.00	.40
3 Pie Traynor	.75	.30
4 Honus Wagner	1.00	.40
5 Roberto Clemente	2.00	.80
6 Paul Waner Lloyd Waner	1.00	.40
7 Ralph Kiner	1.00	.40
8 Manny Sanguillen	.25	.10
9 Deacon Phillippe	.25	.10
10 Bob Veale	.25	.10
11 Roy Face	.25	.10
12 Danny Murtaugh MG	.25	.10

1980 Pirates 1960 TCMA

This 41 card set was issued in 1980 and can be differentiated from the earlier 1960 Pirates set as the photos are clearer and the 1960 Pirates and player's name are on the front.

	MINT	NRMT
COMPLETE SET	20.00	9.00
1 Clem Labine	.50	.23
2 Bob Friend	.50	.23
3 Roy Face	.75	.35
4 Vern Law	.75	.35
5 Harvey Haddix	.50	.23
6 Wilmer Mizell	.25	.11
7 Bill Burwell	.25	.11
8 Diomedes Olivo	.25	.11
9 Don Gross	.25	.11
10 Fred Green	.25	.11
11 Jim Umbricht	.25	.11
12 George Witt	.25	.11
13 Tom Cheney	.25	.11
14 Bennie Daniels	.25	.11
15 Earl Francis	.25	.11
16 Joe Gibbon	.25	.11
17 Paul Giel	.25	.11
18 Danny Kravitz	.25	.11
19 R.C. Stevens	.25	.11
20 Roman Mejias	.25	.11
21 Dick Barone	.25	.11
22 Sam Narron	.25	.11
23 Harry Bright	.25	.11
24 Mickey Vernon	.50	.23
25 Bob Skinner	.25	.11
26 Smoky Burgess	.25	.11
27 Bill Virdon	.25	.11
28 Roberto Clemente No Number on back	5.00	2.20
29 Don Hoak	.50	.23
30 Bill Mazeroski	2.50	1.10
31 Dick Stuart	.75	.35
32 Dick Groat	1.00	.45
33 Bob Oldis	.25	.11
34 Gene Baker	.25	.11
35 Joe Christopher	.25	.11
36 Dick Schofield	.25	.11
37 Hal W. Smith	.25	.11
38 Rocky Nelson	.25	.11
39 Gino Cimoli	.25	.11
40 Danny Murtaugh MG	.25	.11
41 Leo Levy	.25	.11

1984 Pirates

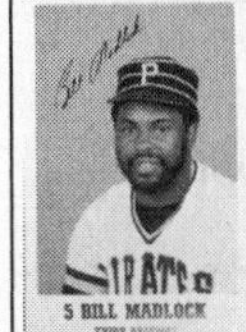

This 27-card set of the Pittsburgh Pirates measures approximately 3 3/8" by 5 1/4" and features white-bordered color player portraits with the player's name, jersey number, and position printed in the wide bottom margin. A facsimile autograph rounds out the front. The backs carry the dates of different games and name of the game sponsor. The cards are unnumbered and checklisted below in alphabetical order.

	Nm-Mt	Ex-Mt
COMPLETE SET (27)	8.00	3.20
1 Rafael Belliard	.25	.10
2 Dale Berra	.25	.10
3 John Candelaria	.50	.20
4 Jose DeLeon	.25	.10
5 Doug Frobel	.25	.10
6 Cecilio Guante	.25	.10
7 Brian Harper	.25	.10
8 Lee Lacy	.25	.10
9 Bill Madlock	.50	.20
10 Milt May	.25	.10
11 Lee Mazzilli	.50	.20
12 Larry McWilliams	.25	.10
13 Jim Morrison	.25	.10
14 Amos Otis	.25	.10
15 Tony Pena	.50	.20
16 Johnny Ray	.25	.10
17 Rick Rhoden	.25	.10
18 Don Robinson	.25	.10
19 Manny Sarmiento	.25	.10
20 Rod Scurry	.25	.10
21 Chuck Tanner MG	.50	.20
22 Kent Tekulve	.50	.20
23 Jason Thompson	.25	.10
24 John Tudor	.50	.20
25 Lee Tunnell	.25	.10
26 Hedi Vargas	.25	.10
27 Marvell Wynne	.25	.10

1985 Pirates

This 23-card set of the Pittsburgh Pirates measures approximately 3 3/8" by 5 1/4" and features white-bordered color player portraits with the player's name, jersey number, and position printed in the wide bottom margin. A facsimile autograph rounds out the front. The backs carry the dates of different games and name of the game sponsor. The cards are unnumbered and checklisted below in alphabetical order.

	Nm-Mt	Ex-Mt
COMPLETE SET (23)	6.00	2.40
1 Bill Almon	.25	.10
2 Rafael Belliard	.25	.10
3 Mike Bielecki	.25	.10
4 John Candelaria	.50	.20
5 Jose DeLeon	.25	.10
6 Tim Foli	.25	.10
7 George Hendrick	.25	.10
8 Steve Kemp	.25	.10
9 Sixto Lezcano	.25	.10
10 Bill Madlock	.50	.20
11 Lee Mazzilli	.50	.20
12 Larry McWilliams	.25	.10
13 Jim Morrison	.25	.10
14 Junior Ortiz	.25	.10
15 Tony Pena	.50	.20
16 Johnny Ray	.25	.10
17 Rick Rhoden	.25	.10
18 Don Robinson	.25	.10
19 Rod Scurry	.25	.10
20 Chuck Tanner MG	.50	.20
21 Jason Thompson	.25	.10
22 Lee Tunnell	.25	.10
23 Marvell Wynne	.25	.10

1986 Pirates Greats TCMA

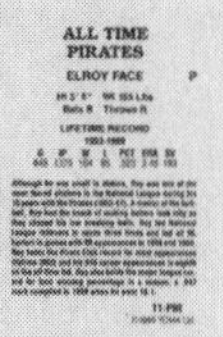

This 12-card standard-size set features all-time leading Pittsburgh Pirates. The player's photo and his name are featured on the front. The back gives more information about that player.

	Nm-Mt	Ex-Mt
COMPLETE SET (12)	7.50	3.00
1 Willie Stargell	1.00	.40
2 Bill Mazeroski	.75	.30

3 Honus Wagner 1.00 .40
4 Pie Traynor 1.00 .40
5 Ralph Kiner .75 .30
6 Paul Waner .75 .30
7 Roberto Clemente 2.50 1.00
8 Manny Sanguillen .25 .10
9 Vic Willis .50 .20
10 Wilbur Cooper .25 .10
11 Roy Face .25 .10
12 Danny Murtaugh MG .25 .10

1987 Pirates 1960 TCMA

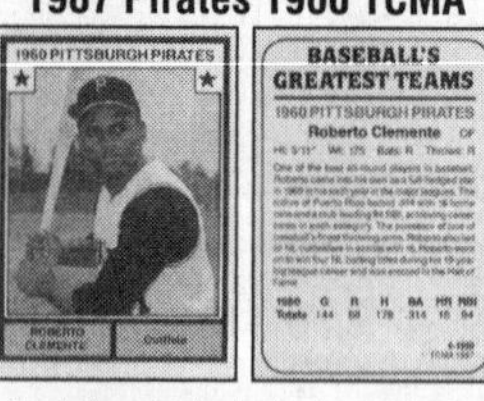

This nine-card standard-size set features members of the 1960 Pittsburgh Pirates. The player photo takes up most of the front with his name noted underneath. The backs give more information about the player as well as their 1960 stats.

	Nm-Mt	Ex-Mt
COMPLETE SET (9)	4.00	1.60
1 Dick Stuart	.25	.10
2 Bill Mazeroski	1.00	.40
3 Dick Groat	.50	.20
4 Roberto Clemente	2.50	1.00
5 Bob Skinner	.25	.10
6 Smoky Burgess	.25	.10
7 Roy Face	.50	.20
8 Bob Friend	.25	.10
9 Vernon Law	.50	.20

1988 Pirates Schedule Postcards

This 33-card set features color photos of the Pittsburgh Pirates measuring approximately 3 1/2" by 5 1/2". The cards are unnumbered and checklisted below in alphabetical order. The backs of these cards have basic player information and the Pirated 1988 home schedule.

	Nm-Mt	Ex-Mt
COMPLETE SET (33)	20.00	8.00
1 Rafael Belliard	.25	.10
2 Barry Bonds	10.00	4.00
3 Bobby Bonilla	.50	.20
4 Sid Bream	.25	.10
5 John Cangelosi	.25	.10
6 Darnell Coles	.25	.10
7 Mike Diaz	.25	.10
8 Rich Donnelly CO	.25	.10
9 Doug Drabek	.50	.20
10 Mike Dunne	.25	.10
11 Felix Fermin	.25	.10
12 Brian Fisher	.25	.10
13 Lanny Frattare ANN	.25	.10
14 Jim Gott	.25	.10
15 Barry Jones	.25	.10
16 Bob Kipper	.25	.10
17 Gene Lamont CO	.25	.10
18 Mike LaValliere	.25	.10
19 Jim Leyland MG	.50	.20
20 Jose Lind	.25	.10
21 Milt May CO	.25	.10
22 Ray Miller CO	.25	.10
23 Randy Milligan	.25	.10
24 Junior Ortiz	.25	.10
25 Al Pedrique	.25	.10
26 Pirate Parrot(Mascot)	.50	.20
27 R.J. Reynolds	.25	.10
28 Jeff Robinson	.25	.10
29 Jim Rooker ANN	.25	.10
30 Tommy Sandt CO	.25	.10
31 John Smiley	.25	.10
32 Andy Van Slyke	.50	.20
33 Bob Walk	.25	.10

1989 Pirates Very Fine Juice

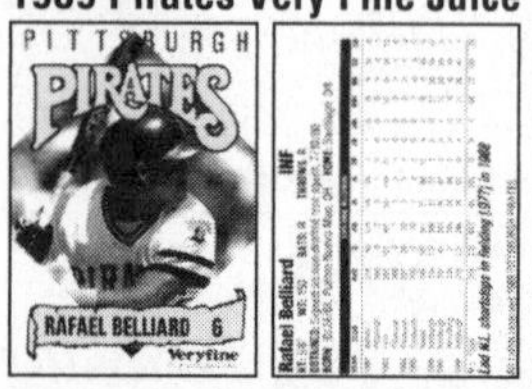

The 1989 Very Fine Juice Pittsburgh Pirates set is a 30-card set with cards measuring approximately 2 1/2" by 3 1/2" featuring the members of the 1989 Pittsburgh Pirates. This set was issued on three separate perforated sheets: two panels contain 15 player cards each, while the third panel serves as a cover for the set and displays color action photos of the Pirates. These panels were given away to fans attending the Pirates home game on April 23, 1989. There was a coupon (expiring on 10/31/89) on the back that could be redeemed for a free can of juice. The cards are numbered by uniform number in the list below. The cards are very colorful.

	Nm-Mt	Ex-Mt
COMPLETE SET (30)	20.00	8.00
0 Jumior Ortiz	.50	.20
2 Gary Redus	.50	.20
3 Jay Bell	.50	.20
5 Sid Bream	.50	.20
6 Rafael Belliard	.50	.20
10 Jim Leyland MG	.75	.30
11 Glenn Wilson	.50	.20
12 Mike LaValliere	.50	.20
13 Jose Lind	.50	.20
14 Ken Oberkfell	.50	.20
15 Doug Drabek	.75	.30
16 Bob Kipper	.50	.20
17 Bob Walk	.50	.20
18 Andy Van Slyke	.75	.30
23 R.J. Reynolds	.50	.20
24 Barry Bonds	6.00	2.40
25 Bobby Bonilla	.75	.30
26 Neal Heaton	.50	.20
30 Benny Distefano	.50	.20
31 Ray Miller CO and 37 Tommy Sandt CO	.50	.20
35 Jim Gott	.50	.20
36 Bruce Kimm CO and 32 Gene Lamont CO	.50	.20
39 Milt May CO and 45 Rich Donnelly CO	.50	.20
41 Mike Dunne	.50	.20
43 Bill Landrum	.50	.20
44 John Cangelosi	.50	.20
49 Jeff D. Robinson	.50	.20
52 Dorn Taylor	.50	.20
54 Brian Fisher	.50	.20
57 John Smiley	.50	.20

1990 Pirates Homers Cookies

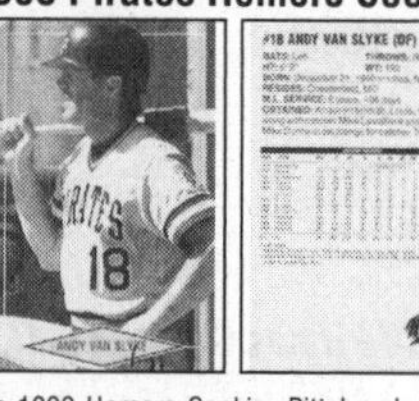

The 1990 Homers Cookies Pittsburgh Pirates set is an attractive 31-card set measuring approximately 4" by 6", used as a giveaway at a Pirates home game. It has been reported that 25,000 of these sets were produced. Four Homers Baseball trivia question cards were also included with the complete set. The fronts are full-color action photos with the backs containing complete statistical information. The set has been checklisted alphabetically below.

	Nm-Mt	Ex-Mt
COMPLETE SET (31)	18.00	5.50
1 Wally Backman	.25	.07
2 Doug Bair	.25	.07
3 Rafael Belliard	.25	.07
4 Jay Bell	.25	.07
5 Barry Bonds	10.00	3.00
6 Bobby Bonilla	.50	.15
7 Sid Bream	.25	.07
8 John Cangelosi	.25	.07
9 Rich Donnelly CO	.25	.07
10 Doug Drabek	.50	.15
11 Billy Hatcher	.25	.07
12 Neal Heaton	.25	.07
13 Jeff King	.25	.07
14 Bob Kipper	.25	.07
15 Randy Kramer	.25	.07
16 Gene Lamont CO	.25	.07
17 Bill Landrum	.25	.07
18 Mike LaValliere	.25	.07
19 Jim Leyland MG	.50	.15
20 Jose Lind	.25	.07
21 Milt May	.25	.07
22 Ray Miller CO	.25	.07
23 Ted Power	.25	.07
24 Gary Redus	.25	.07
25 R.J. Reynolds	.25	.07
26 Tommy Sandt CO	.25	.07
27 Don Slaught	.25	.07
28 Walt Terrell	.25	.07
29 Andy Van Slyke	.50	.15
30 John Smiley	.25	.07
31 Bob Walk	.25	.07

1992 Pirates Nationwide Insurance

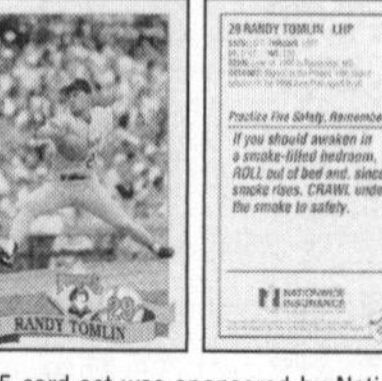

This 25-card set was sponsored by Nationwide Insurance, the Pittsburgh Bureau of Fire, and West Penn Hospital. The cards are oversized and measure 3 1/2" by 5 3/4". The color action player photos on the front are edged by a thin red and a wider white border. Superimposed at the bottom of the picture are the team logo, the player's name in a yellow banner, and his jersey number in a baseball icon. The backs feature statistical information about the player and fire safety tips. The cards are unnumbered and checklisted below in alphabetical order.

	Nm-Mt	Ex-Mt
COMPLETE SET (25)	15.00	4.50
1 Stan Belinda	.50	.15
2 Jay Bell	.75	.23
3 Barry Bonds	8.00	2.40
4 Steve Buechele	.50	.15
5 Terry Collins CO	.50	.15
6 Rich Donnelly CO	.50	.15
7 Doug Drabek	1.00	.30
8 Cecil Espy	.50	.15
9 Jeff King	.50	.15
10 Mike LaValliere	.50	.15
11 Jim Leyland MG	.75	.23
12 Jose Lind	.50	.15
13 Roger Mason	.50	.15
14 Milt May CO	.50	.15
15 Lloyd McClendon	.75	.23
16 Orlando Merced	.50	.15
17 Denny Neagle	1.50	.45
18 Bob Patterson	.50	.15
19 Gary Redus	.50	.15
20 Don Slaught	.50	.15
21 Zane Smith	.50	.15
22 Randy Tomlin	.50	.15
23 Andy Van Slyke	.75	.23
24 Gary Varsho	.50	.15
25 Bob Walk	.50	.15

1993 Pirates Hills

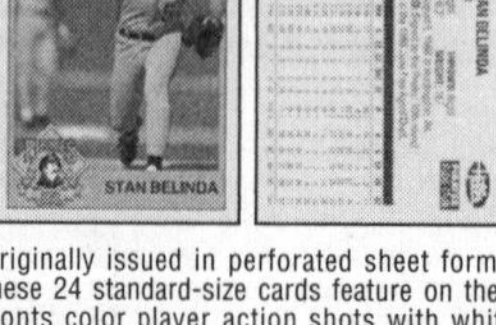

Originally issued in perforated sheet form , these 24 standard-size cards feature on their fronts color player action shots with white outer borders and yellow inner borders. The cards are unnumbered and checklisted below in alphabetical order.

	Nm-Mt	Ex-Mt
COMPLETE SET	20.00	6.00
1 Stan Belinda	.75	.23
2 Jay Bell	.75	.23
3 John Candelaria	1.00	.30
4 Dave Clark	.75	.23
5 Steve Cooke	.75	.23
6 Tom Foley	.75	.23
7 Carlos Garcia	.75	.23
8 Jeff King	.75	.23
9 Jim Leyland MG	1.00	.30
10 Al Martin	.75	.23
11 Lloyd McClendon	1.00	.30
12 Orlando Merced	.75	.23
13 Blas Minor	.75	.23
14 Denny Neagle	2.00	.60
15 Tom Prince	.75	.23
16 Don Slaught	.75	.23
17 Lonnie Smith	.75	.23
18 Zane Smith	.75	.23
19 Randy Tomlin	.75	.23
20 Andy Van Slyke	.75	.23
21 Paul Wagner	.75	.23
22 Tim Wakefield	1.50	.45
23 Bob Walk	.75	.23
24 Kevin Young	.75	.23

1993 Pirates Nationwide Insurance

These 40 oversized cards measure approximately 3 3/8" by 5 5/8". The color action player photos on the front are edged by a thin black line and a wide white border. The top of the card has a thin red border, and a red block carries the player's name printed in white and the Bucs' Three-Peat logo. The backs include biography and how the player was obtained. The Nationwide Insurance logo at the bottom rounds out the back. On Sunday June 27, children 14 and under were given a set at the Pirates-Phillies game at Three Rivers Stadium. Quintex Mobile Communications/Bell Atlantic is listed as the sponsor on the backs of the giveaway sets. The Parrot card and the Three Rivers card are not included in the Quintex sets.

	Nm-Mt	Ex-Mt
COMPLETE SET (40)	10.00	3.00
1 Stan Belinda	.25	.07
2 Jay Bell	.25	.07
3 Steve Blass ANN	.25	.07
4 John Candelaria	.50	.15
5 Dave Clark	.25	.07
6 Terry Collins CO	.25	.07
7 Steve Cooke	.25	.07
8 Kent Derdivannis ANN	.25	.07
9 Rich Donnelly CO	.25	.07
10 Tom Foley	.25	.07
11 Lanny Frattare ANN	.25	.07
12 Carlos Garcia	.25	.07
13 Jeff King	.25	.07
14 Jim Leyland MG	.50	.15
15 Al Martin	.25	.07
16 Milt May CO	.25	.07
17 Lloyd McClendon	.50	.15
18 Orlando Merced	.25	.07
19 Ray Miller CO	.25	.07
20 Blas Minor	.25	.07
21 Dennis Moeller	.25	.07
22 Denny Neagle	1.00	.30
23 Dave Otto	.25	.07
24 Pirate Parrot (Mascot)	.50	.15
25 Tom Prince	.25	.07
26 Jim Rooker ANN	.25	.07
27 Tommy Sandt CO	.25	.07
28 Ted Simmons XGM	.75	.23
29 Don Slaught	.25	.07
30 Lonnie Smith	.25	.07
31 Zane Smith	.25	.07
32 Randy Tomlin	.25	.07
33 Andy Van Slyke	.50	.15
34 Bill Virdon CO	.50	.15
35 Paul Wagner	.25	.07
36 Tim Wakefield	.75	.23
37 Bob Walk	.25	.07
38 John Wehner	.25	.07
39 Kevin Young	.25	.07
40 Three Rivers Stadium	.25	.07

1994 Pirates Quintex

These 29 oversized cards measure approximately 3 1/2" by 5 3/4". This set was passed out on July 31, 1994 at the Pirates' home game. A coupon for a cellular transportable bag phone at no charge came with it. The cards are unnumbered and checklisted below in alphabetical order. Cards are also known which say Nationwide Insurance. These cards have the same value as the Qunitex cards. The Jon Lieber card was issued later and is considered a Short Print since it was not included in the regular set.

	Nm-Mt	Ex-Mt
COMPLETE SET (30	12.00	3.60
COMMON CARD (1-30	.25	.07
COMMON SP		
1 Jay Bell	.25	.07
2 Dave Clark	.25	.07
3 Steve Cooke	.25	.07
4 Mark Dewey	.25	.07
5 Rich Donnelly CO	.25	.07
6 Tom Foley	.25	.07
7 Carlos Garcia	.25	.07
8 Brian Hunter	.25	.07
9 Jeff King	.25	.07
10 Jim Leyland MG	.50	.15
11 Jon Lieber SP	5.00	
12 Ravelo Manzanillo	.25	.07
13 Al Martin	.25	.07
14 Milt May CO	.25	.07
15 Lloyd McClendon	.50	.15
16 Orlando Merced	.25	.07
17 Dan Miceli	.25	.07
18 Ray Miller CO	.25	.07
19 Denny Neagle	.75	.23
20 Pirate Parrot (Mascot)	.50	.15
21 Tommy Sandt CO	.25	.07
22 Don Slaught	.25	.07
23 Zane Smith	.25	.07
24 Andy Van Slyke	.50	.15
25 Bill Virdon CO	.50	.15
26 Paul Wagner	.25	.07
27 Rick White	.25	.07
28 Spin Williams CO	.25	.07
29 Kevin Young	.25	.07
30 Three Rivers Stadium	.25	.07

1995 Pirates Coca-Cola Pogs

This set of 27 pogs commemorates the 25th anniversary of Three River Stadium where the Pirates play and was issued in three sheets of nine pogs each. The pogs measure approximately 11/16" in diameter. The fronts feature color and black-and-white photos of great moments that happened at the stadium. The backs carry the significance of the moment and the date it occurred along with either the Coke, Sprite, or Fruitopia logo.

	Nm-Mt	Ex-Mt
COMPLETE SET (25)	15.00	4.50
1 1994 All-Star Game 7/12/94	.25	.07
2 Roberto Clemente 3,000th Career Hit 9/30/72	3.00	.90
3 Roberto Clemente Uniform #21 Retired 4/6/73	3.00	.90
4 We Are Family Logo Pirates win NL Pennant 10/5/79	.25	.07
5 John Candelaria No-Hits the Dodgers 8/9/76	.25	.07
6 Willie Stargell Uniform #8 Retired 9/6/82	1.00	.30
7 Mike Schmidt 500th Home Run 4/18/87	2.00	.60
8 A Pirates' Pitcher First Game Played at Three Rivers 7/16/70	.25	.07
9 1971 World Series Game 4 First Ever Played at Night 10/13/71	.25	.07
10 Nellie Briles World Series Game Five 10/14/71	.25	.07
11 Pirates Win 1971 NL Pennant Pirates beat Giants 10/6/71	.25	.07
12 Pirates Clinch NL East 10/30/79	.25	.07
13 Pirates "Three-Peat" Clinch NL East 9/27/92	.25	.07
14 Bob Gibson No-Hits the Pirates 8/14/71	1.00	.30
15 1979 World Series Game 5 Bucs Battle Back vs Baltimore 10/14/79	.25	.07
16 Pirates Clinch NL East 9/27/70	.25	.07
17 Bob Walk Beats Braves NLCS Game Five 10/10/92	.25	.07
18 John Milner 9th Inning Grand Slam Beats Phillies 8/5/79	.25	.07
19 Barry Bonds 11th Inning Homer Beats St. Louis 8/12/91	3.00	.90
20 Pirates Score 5 Runs in 9th Beat Dodgers 5/28/90	.25	.07
21 Danny Murtaugh MG Joe Brown GM Retire 10/3/76	.25	.07
22 The Gunner Returns to Broadcast Booth 5/3/85	.25	.07
23 Pirates Sweep Phillies Doubleheader 9/29/78	.25	.07
24 Jim Leyland MG Makes Pittsburgh Debut 4/8/86	.25	.07
25 1974 All-Star Game 7/23/74	.25	.07
NNO Coke Logo	.25	.07
NNO Coke Logo Fruitopia Logo	.25	.07

1995 Pirates Filmet

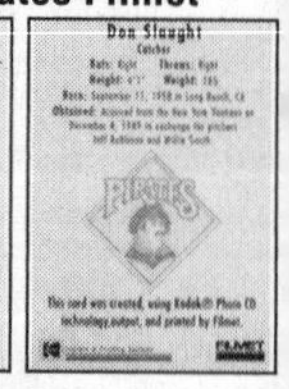

This 30-card set of the Pittsburgh Pirates was distributed on Picture Card Night as a perforated sheet measuring approximately 20 1/4" by 13 1/2". The cards themselves measure 2 1/4" by 3 1/4" and feature a color action player photo in a white border. The player's name is printed in yellow in a red banner at the top with the team name in gold running down the side margins. The white backs carry the player's name, position, biography and career information. The cards were created using Kodak Photo CD technology, output, and printed by Filmet Commercial Services. A coupon at the bottom could be used at Filmet locations for film processing. The cards are unnumbered and checklisted below in alphabetical order.

	Nm-Mt	Ex-Mt
COMPLETE SET (30)	8.00	2.40
1 Rich Aude	.25	.07
2 Jay Bell	.25	.07
3 Jacob Brumfield	.25	.07
4 Jason Christiansen	.25	.07
5 Dave Clark	.25	.07
6 Steve Cooke	.25	.07
7 Midre Cummings	.25	.07
8 Mike Dyer	.25	.07
9 Angelo Encarnacion	.25	.07
10 Carlos Garcia	.25	.07
11 Freddy A. Garcia	.25	.07
12 Jim Gott	.25	.07
13 Mark Johnson	.25	.07
14 Jeff King	.25	.07
15 Jim Leyland MG	.50	.15
16 Jon Lieber	.50	.15
17 Nelson Liriano	.25	.07
18 Esteban Loaiza	1.00	.30
19 Al Martin	.25	.07
20 Jeff McCurry	.25	.07
21 Orlando Merced	.25	.07
22 Dan Miceli	.25	.07
23 Denny Neagle	.25	.07
24 Mark Parent	.25	.07
25 Steve Pegues	.25	.07
26 Dan Plesac	.25	.07
27 Don Slaught	.25	.07
28 Paul Wagner	.25	.07
29 Rick White	.25	.07
30 Gary Wilson	.25	.07

1997 Pirates Post-Gazette

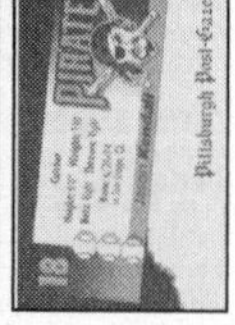

This one-card set measures approximately 3 1/2" by 5 3/4" and features a color photo of Pittsburgh Pirates catcher Jason Kendall in a paint-splashed border with a simulated autograph on the front. The back contains player information in a ticket format.

	Nm-Mt	Ex-Mt
1 Jason Kendall	5.00	1.50

1997 Pirates Postcards

This 45-card set of the 1997 Pittsburgh Pirates features color player portraits with the player's name, position, and jersey number printed on the front. The backs carry the team logo and player information. The cards are unnumbered and checklisted below in alphabetical order.

	Nm-Mt	Ex-Mt
COMPLETE SET (45)	12.00	3.60
1 Jermaine Allensworth	.25	.07
2 Steve Blass ANN	.50	.15
3 Adrian Brown	.25	.07
4 Emil Brown	.25	.07
5 Greg Brown ANN	.25	.07
6 Jason Christiansen	.25	.07
7 Lou Collier	.25	.07
8 Steve Cooke	.25	.07
9 Francisco Cordova	.25	.07
10 Midre Cummings	.25	.07

11 Kevin Elster .25 .07
12 John Ericks .25 .07
13 Lanny Frattare ANN .25 .07
13 Spin Williams CO .25 .07
14 Jeff Granger .25 .07
15 Jose Guillen 1.00 .30
16 Mark Johnson .25 .07
17 Joe Jones CO .25 .07
18 Jason Kendall 2.50 .75
19 Gene Lamont MG .25 .07
20 Jon Lieber .75 .23
21 Jack Lind CO .25 .07
22 Esteban Loaiza 1.00 .30
23 Rich Loiselle .25 .07
24 Al Martin .25 .07
25 Lloyd McClendon CO .50 .15
26 Keith Osik .25 .07
27 Chris Peters .25 .07
28 Kevin Polcovich .25 .07
29 Joe Randa .50 .15
30 Rick Renick CO .25 .07
31 Ricardo Rincon .25 .07
32 Matt Ruebel .25 .07
33 Jason Schmidt .75 .23
34 Jose Silva .25 .07
35 Mark Smith .25 .07
36 Clint Sodowsky .25 .07
37 Dale Sveum .25 .07
38 Pete Vuckovich CO .25 .07
39 Dave Wainhouse .25 .07
40 Bob Walk ANN .25 .07
41 Turner Ward .25 .07
42 Marc Wilkins .25 .07
44 Tony Womack .50 .15
45 Kevin Young .25 .07

1998 Pirates Postcards

These 3 5/8" by 4 3/4" color postcards feature members of the 1998 Pittsburgh Pirates. The fronts have the player photo, his name and position. The backs can have the Pirates logo, a brief bio and and an "Advance Auto Parts" logo. Since the cards are unnumbered we have sequenced them in alphabetical order.

Nm-Mt Ex-Mt
COMPLETE SET 15.00 4.50
1 Jermaine Allensworth .50 .15
2 Steve Blass ANN .75 .23
3 Greg Brown ANN .50 .15
4 Jason Christianson .50 .15
5 Lou Collier .50 .15
6 Francisco Cordorva .50 .15
7 Elmer Dessens .50 .15
8 Lanny Frattare ANN .50 .15
9 Jose Guillen 1.00 .30
10 Jason Kendall 1.50 .45
11 Gene Lamont MG .50 .15
12 Jon Lieber .75 .23
13 Jack Lind CO .50 .15
14 Scott Little CO .50 .15
15 Esteban Loaiza 1.50 .45
16 Rich Loiselle .50 .15
17 Al Martin .50 .15
18 Javier Martinez .50 .15
19 Manny Martinez .50 .15
20 Keith Osik .50 .15
21 Chris Peters .50 .15
22 Kevin Polcovich .50 .15
23 Aramis Ramirez 3.00 .90
24 Ricardo Rincon .50 .15
25 Chance Sanford .50 .15
26 Jason Schmidt 1.00 .30
27 Jose Silva .50 .15
28 Jeff Tabaka .50 .15
29 Turner Ward .50 .15
30 Marc Wilkins .50 .15
31 Mike Williams .50 .15
32 Tony Womack .50 .15
32 Kevin Young .50 .15

1999 Pirates Postcards Advance

This 36 card set measures 3 5/8" by 4 3/4" and features members of the 1999 Pittsburgh Pirates. The set was sponsored by Advance Auto Parts. The cards are unnumbered so we have sequenced them in alphabetical order

Nm-Mt Ex-Mt
COMPLETE SET 10.00 3.00
1 Jeff Banister .25 .07
2 Mike Benjamin .25 .07
3 Kris Benson .50 .15
4 Adrian Brown .25 .07
5 Brant Brown .25 .07
6 Jason Christiansen .25 .07
7 Brad Clontz .25 .07
8 Francisco Cordova .25 .07
9 Freddy Garcia .25 .07
10 Brian Giles 1.00 .30
11 Jose Guillen .25 .07
12 Joe Jones .25 .07
13 Jason Kendall 1.00 .30
14 Gene Lamont MG .25 .07
15 Jack Lind .25 .07
16 Rich Loiselle .25 .07
17 Al Martin .25 .07
18 Lloyd McClendon CO .25 .07
19 Pat Meares .25 .07
20 Warren Morris .25 .07
21 Abraham Nunez .25 .07
22 Keith Osik .25 .07
23 Chris Peters .25 .07
24 Rich Renick CO .25 .07
25 Todd Ritchie .25 .07
26 Scott Sauerbeck .25 .07
27 Pete Schourek .25 .07
28 Jason Schmidt .75 .23
29 Jose Silva .25 .07
30 Ed Sprague .25 .07
31 Chris Tremie .25 .07
32 Pete Vuckovich CO .25 .07
33 Jeff Wallace .25 .07
34 Turner Ward .25 .07
35 John Werner .25 .07
36 Marc Wilkins .25 .07
37 Mike Williams .25 .07
38 Spin Williams .25 .07
39 Kevin Young .25 .07

1999 Pirates Postcards Post-Gazette

These seven postcards measure 3 1/2" by 5 3/4" and are numbered by the uniform numbers. The backs feature the stats of the players featured.

Nm-Mt Ex-Mt
COMPLETE SET 10.00 3.00
1 Brian Giles 2.50 .75
2 Jason Kendall 2.50 .75
3 Pat Meares 1.00 .30
4 Warren Morris 1.00 .30
5 Jason Schmidt 2.00 .60
6 Ed Sprague 1.00 .30
7 Kevin Young 1.00 .30

2000 Pirates Postcards

These cards are similar to the 1999 Pirates cards. The fronts have the players photos on most of the card with the Pirates logo in the upper left and their name and position on the bottom. The cards were sponsored by "Advance Auto Parts". The cards are unnumbered, so we have sequenced them in alphabetical order.

Nm-Mt Ex-Mt
COMPLETE SET 15.00 4.50
1 Jimmy Anderson .50 .15
2 Bruce Aven .50 .15
3 Jeff Banister .50 .15
4 Mike Benjamin .50 .15
5 Kris Benson .75 .23
6 Adrian Brown .50 .15
7 Jason Christensen .50 .15
8 Wil Cordero .50 .15
9 Francisco Cordova .50 .15
10 Brian Giles 1.50 .45
11 Jason Kendall 1.50 .45
12 Gene Lamont MG .50 .15
13 Rich Loiselle .50 .15
14 Lloyd McClendon CO .50 .15
15 Pat Meares .50 .15
16 Warren Morris .50 .15
17 Abraham Nunez .50 .15
18 Keith Osik .50 .15
19 Rick Renick CO .50 .15
20 Todd Richie .50 .15
21 Scott Sauerbeck .50 .15
22 Jason Schmidt 1.00 .30
23 Jose Silva .50 .15
24 Luis Sojo .50 .15
25 John Vander Wal .50 .15
26 Pete Vuckovich CO .50 .15
27 Mike Williams .50 .15
28 Spin Williams CO .50 .15
29 Kevin Young .50 .15

2002 Pirates Outback

These full-color cards, which measure approximately 3 5/8" by 4 3/4" feature members of the 2002 Pittsburgh Pirates. The players are identified by their uniform numbers on the front of the cards, but since the cards are otherwise unnumbered, we have sequenced them in alphabetical order.

Nm-Mt Ex-Mt
COMPLETE SET 20.00 6.00
1 Jimmy Anderson .50 .15
2 Jeff Banister .50 .15
3 Joe Beimel .50 .15
4 Mike Benjamin .50 .15
5 Steve Blass ANN .75 .23
6 Brian Boehringer .50 .15
7 Adrian Brown .50 .15
8 Greg Brown ANN .50 .15
9 Dave Clark .50 .15
10 Mike Fetters .50 .15
11 Josh Fogg .75 .23
12 Lanny Frattare ANN .50 .15
13 Brian Giles 1.50 .45
14 Chad Hermansen .50 .15
15 Trent Jewett .50 .15
16 Jason Kendall 1.50 .45
17 Sean Lowe .50 .15
18 Rob Mackowiak .50 .15
19 Josias Manzanillo .50 .15
20 Lloyd McClendon MG .50 .15
21 Russ Nixon CO .50 .15
22 Abraham Nunez .50 .15
23 Keith Osik .50 .15
24 Aramis Ramirez 1.50 .45
25 Pokey Reese .50 .15
26 Armando Rios .50 .15
27 Tommy Sandt CO .50 .15
28 Scott Sauerbeck .50 .15
29 Bruce Tanner CO .50 .15
30 Ron Villone .50 .15
31 Bill Virdon CO .50 .15
32 Ryan Vogelsong .50 .15
33 Bob Walk ANN .50 .15
34 Dave Williams .50 .15
35 Mike Williams .50 .15
36 Spin Williams .50 .15
37 Craig Wilson .50 .15
38 Jack Wilson .50 .15
39 Kip Wells .75 .23
40 Kevin Young .50 .15
41 Pirate Parrot .50 .15
Mascot

2003 Pirates Outback

These cards, which measure approximately 3 5/8" by 4 3/4" have a player portrait on the front and a biography of the player on the back. An Outback Steakhouse logo is located in the right corner. Since these cards are unnumbered except for uniform number, we have sequenced them in alphabetical order.

MINT NRMT
COMPLETE SET 20.00 9.00
1 Joe Beimel .50 .23
2 Kris Benson .75 .35
3 Brian Boehringer .50 .23
4 Humberto Cota .50 .23
5 Jeff D'Amico .50 .23
6 Alvaro Espinoza CO .50 .23
7 Josh Fogg .50 .23
8 Lanny Frattare ANN .50 .23
9 Brian Giles 1.50 .70
10 Adam Hyzdu .50 .23
11 Jason Kendall 1.50 .70
12 Rusty Kuntz CO .50 .23
13 Mike Lincoln .50 .23
14 Dave Littlefield .50 .23
15 Kenny Lofton 1.00 .45
16 Pete Mackanin CO .50 .23
17 Rob Mackowiak .50 .23
18 Kevin McClatchy OWN .50 .23
19 Lloyd McClendon MG .50 .23
Outback Logo
20 Lloyd McClendon MG .50 .23
No Outback Logo
21 Brian Meadows .50 .23
22 Gerald Perry CO .50 .23
23 Aramis Ramirez 1.00 .45
24 Jeff Reboulet .50 .23
25 Pokey Reese .50 .23
26 Dennys Reyes .50 .23
27 Carlos Rivera .50 .23
28 John Russell .50 .23
29 Reggie Sanders .50 .23
30 Scott Sauerbeck .50 .23
31 Randall Simon .75 .35
32 Matt Stairs .50 .23
33 Jeff Suppan .50 .23
34 Bruce Tanner CO .50 .23
35 Julian Tavarez .50 .23
36 Salomon Torres .50 .23
37 Bob Walk ANN .50 .23
38 Kip Wells .75 .35
39 Dave Williams .50 .23
40 Mike Williams .50 .23
41 Spin Williams .50 .23
42 Craig Wilson .50 .23
43 Jack Wilson .50 .23
44 Kevin Young .50 .23
45 Pirate Parrot .50 .23
Mascot

1996 Pitch Postcards HOF

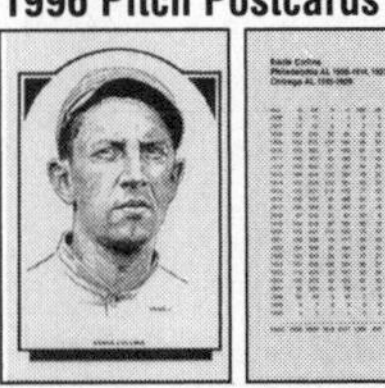

This 12-card set measures approximately 6" by 4" and features black-and-white player drawings. The backs carry player career stats. The cards are unnumbered and checklisted below in alphabetical order.

Nm-Mt Ex-Mt
COMPLETE SET (12) 6.00 1.80
1 Frank Baker .50 .15
2 Frank Chance .75 .23
3 Fred Clarke .50 .15
4 Eddie Collins 1.00 .30
5 Sam Crawford .50 .15
6 Johnny Evers .50 .15
7 Willie Keeler .50 .15
8 Nap Lajoie 1.00 .30
9 Rube Marquard .50 .15
10 Eddie Plank .75 .23
11 Joe Tinker .75 .23
12 Rube Waddell .50 .15

1996 Pizza Hut

This four card set was issued by Pizza Hut as a premium for ordering a special pizza. A person would receive a bat as well as a card for ordering this deal. The cards are numbered

and each features a hitter and a pitcher. We have sequenced the cards in alphabetical order of the hitter. We are pricing just the cards.

Nm-Mt Ex-Mt
COMPLETE SET (4) 8.00 2.40
1 Jeff Bagwell 1.25 .35
Orel Hershiser
2 Ken Griffey Jr. 5.00 1.50
Greg Maddux
3 Mike Piazza 3.00 .90
David Cone
4 Mo Vaughn .50 .15
Randy Johnson

1995 PKK Griffey National Promo

This card was given out at the 1995 National Sports Collectors Convention in St. Louis, Missouri and features a borderless color action photo of Ken Griffey Jr. The back displays the sponsor's and Convention's logos.

Nm-Mt Ex-Mt
1 Ken Griffey Jr. 1.00 .30

1995 PKK Griffey

This 10 card standard-size borderless set was issued by card supply manufacturer PKK and featured photos and highlights of Ken Griffey Jr.'s career.

Nm-Mt Ex-Mt
COMPLETE SET (10) 10.00 3.00
COMMON CARD (1-10) 1.00 .30

1939 Play Ball R334

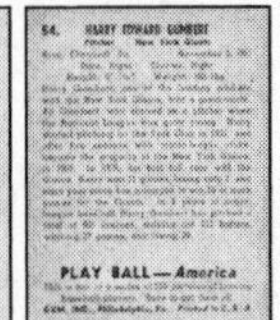

The cards in this 161-card set measure approximately 2 1/2" by 3 1/8". Gum Incorporated introduced a brief (war-shortened) but innovative era of baseball card production with its set of 1939. The combination of actual player photos (black and white), large card size, and extensive biography proved extremely popular. Player names are found either entirely capitalized or with initial caps only, and a "sample card" overprint is not uncommon. The "sample card" overprint variations are valued at double the prices below. Card number 126 was never issued, and cards 116-162 were produced in lesser quantities than cards 1-115. A card of Ted Williams in his rookie season as well as an early card of Joe DiMaggio are the key cards in the set.

Ex-Mt VG
COMPLETE SET (161) 10000.00 5000.00
COMMON CARD (1-115) 20.00 10.00
COMMON (116-162) 75.00 38.00
WRAPPER (1-CENT) 200.00 100.00
1 Jake Powell 60.00 18.00
2 Lee Grissom 20.00 10.00
3 Red Ruffing 75.00 38.00
4 Eldon Auker 20.00 10.00
5 Luke Sewell 25.00 12.50
6 Leo Durocher 100.00 50.00
7 Bobby Doerr 75.00 38.00
8 Henry Pippen 20.00 10.00
9 James Tobin 20.00 10.00
10 James DeShong 20.00 10.00
11 Johnny Rizzo 20.00 10.00
12 Hershel Martin 20.00 10.00
13 Luke Hamlin 20.00 10.00
14 Jim Tabor 20.00 10.00
15 Paul Derringer 30.00 15.00
16 John Peacock 20.00 10.00
17 Emerson Dickman 20.00 10.00
18 Harry Danning 20.00 10.00
19 Paul Dean 40.00 20.00
20 Joe Heving 20.00 10.00
21 Dutch Leonard 30.00 15.00
22 Bucky Walters 30.00 15.00
23 Burgess Whitehead 20.00 10.00
24 Richard Coffman 20.00 10.00
25 George Selkirk 40.00 20.00
26 Joe DiMaggio 1400.00 700.00
27 Fred Ostermueller 20.00 10.00
28 Sylvester Johnson 20.00 10.00
29 John(Jack) Wilson 20.00 10.00
30 Bill Dickey 125.00 60.00
31 Sam West 20.00 10.00
32 Bob Seeds 20.00 10.00
33 Del Young 20.00 10.00
34 Frank Demaree 20.00 10.00
35 Bill Jurges 20.00 10.00
36 Frank McCormick 20.00 10.00
37 Virgil Davis 20.00 10.00
38 Billy Myers 20.00 10.00
39 Rick Ferrell 75.00 38.00
40 James Bagby Jr. 20.00 10.00
41 Lon Warneke 25.00 12.50
42 Arndt Jorgens 20.00 10.00
43 Melo Almada 25.00 12.50
44 Don Heffner 20.00 10.00
45 Merrill May 20.00 10.00
46 Morris Arnovich 20.00 10.00
47 Buddy Lewis 20.00 10.00
48 Lefty Gomez 125.00 60.00
49 Eddie Miller 20.00 10.00
50 Charley Gehringer 125.00 60.00
51 Mel Ott 125.00 60.00
52 Tommy Henrich 40.00 20.00
53 Carl Hubbell 125.00 60.00
54 Harry Gumpert 20.00 10.00
55 Arky Vaughan 75.00 38.00
56 Hank Greenberg 150.00 75.00
57 Buddy Hassett 20.00 10.00
58 Lou Chiozza 20.00 10.00
59 Ken Chase 20.00 10.00
60 Schoolboy Rowe 40.00 20.00
61 Tony Cuccinello 25.00 12.50
62 Tom Carey 20.00 10.00
63 Emmett Mueller 20.00 10.00
64 Wally Moses 25.00 12.50
65 Harry Craft 25.00 12.50
66 Jimmy Ripple 20.00 10.00
67 Ed Joost 25.00 12.50
68 Fred Sington 20.00 10.00
69 Elbie Fletcher 20.00 10.00
70 Fred Frankhouse 20.00 10.00
71 Monte Pearson 30.00 15.00
72 Debs Garms 20.00 10.00
73 Hal Schumacher 25.00 12.50
74 Cookie Lavagetto 25.00 12.50
75 Stan Bordagaray 20.00 10.00
76 Goody Rosen 20.00 10.00
77 Lew Riggs 20.00 10.00
78 Julius Solters 20.00 10.00
79 Jo Jo Moore 20.00 10.00
80 Pete Fox 20.00 10.00
81 Babe Dahlgren 30.00 15.00
82 Chuck Klein 100.00 50.00
83 Gus Suhr 20.00 10.00
84 Skeeter Newsom 20.00 10.00
85 Johnny Cooney 20.00 10.00
86 Dolph Camilli 25.00 12.50
87 Milburn Shoffner 20.00 10.00
88 Charlie Keller 40.00 20.00
89 Lloyd Waner 75.00 38.00
90 Robert Klinger 20.00 10.00
91 John Knott 20.00 10.00
92 Ted Williams 1500.00 750.00
93 Charles Gelbert 20.00 10.00
94 Heinie Manush 75.00 38.00
95 Whit Wyatt 25.00 12.50
96 Babe Phelps 20.00 10.00
97 Bob Johnson 30.00 15.00
98 Pinky Whitney 20.00 10.00
99 Wally Berger 30.00 15.00
100 Buddy Myer 25.00 12.50
101 Roger Cramer 25.00 12.50
102 Lem Young 20.00 10.00
103 Moe Berg 125.00 60.00
104 Tom Bridges 25.00 12.50
105 Rabbit McNair 20.00 10.00
106 Dolly Stark UMP 30.00 15.00
107 Joe Vosmik 20.00 10.00
108 Frank Hayes 20.00 10.00
109 Myril Hoag 20.00 10.00
110 Fred Fitzsimmons 25.00 12.50
111 Van Lingle Mungo 30.00 15.00
112 Paul Waner 100.00 50.00
113 Al Schacht 30.00 15.00
114 Cecil Travis 25.00 12.50
115 Ralph Kress 20.00 10.00
116 Gene Desautels 75.00 38.00
117 Wayne Ambler 75.00 38.00
118 Lynn Nelson 75.00 38.00
119 Will Hershberger 100.00 50.00
120 Rabbit Warstler 75.00 38.00
121 Bill Posedel 75.00 38.00
122 George McQuinn 75.00 38.00
123 Ray T. Davis 75.00 38.00
124 Walter Brown 75.00 38.00
125 Cliff Melton 75.00 38.00
126 Not issued
127 Gil Brack 75.00 38.00
128 Joe Bowman 75.00 38.00
129 Bill Swift 75.00 38.00
130 Bill Brubaker 75.00 38.00
131 Mort Cooper 100.00 50.00
132 Jim Brown 75.00 38.00
133 Lynn Myers 75.00 38.00
134 Tot Presnell 75.00 38.00
135 Mickey Owen 100.00 50.00
136 Roy Bell 75.00 38.00
137 Pete Appleton 75.00 38.00
138 George Case 100.00 50.00
139 Vito Tamulis 75.00 38.00
140 Ray Hayworth 75.00 38.00
141 Pete Coscarart 75.00 38.00
142 Ira Hutchinson 75.00 38.00
143 Earl Averill 175.00 90.00
144 Zeke Bonura 100.00 50.00
145 Hugh Mulcahy 75.00 38.00
146 Tom Sunkel 75.00 38.00
147 George Coffman 75.00 38.00
148 Bill Trotter 75.00 38.00
149 Max West 75.00 38.00
150 James Walkup 75.00 38.00
151 Hugh Casey 100.00 50.00
152 Roy Weatherly 75.00 38.00
153 Dizzy Trout 100.00 50.00
154 Johnny Hudson 75.00 38.00
155 Jimmy Outlaw 75.00 38.00
156 Ray Berres 75.00 38.00
157 Don Padgett 75.00 38.00
158 Bud Thomas 75.00 38.00
159 Red Evans 75.00 38.00
160 Gene Moore 75.00 38.00
161 Lonnie Frey 75.00 38.00
162 Whitey Moore 100.00 50.00

1940 Play Ball R335

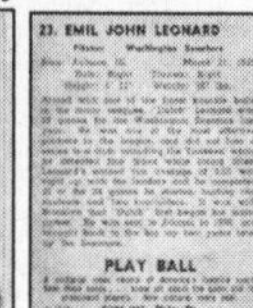
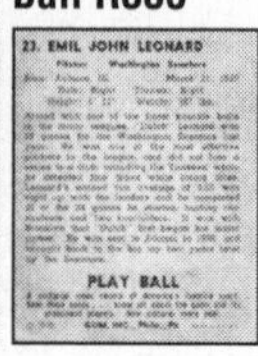

The cards in this 240-card series measure approximately 2 1/2" by 3 1/8". Gum Inc. improved upon its 1939 design by enclosing the 1940 black and white player photo with a frame line and printing the player's name in a panel below the picture (often using a nickname). The set included many Hall of Famers and Old Timers. Cards 1-114 are numbered in team groupings. Cards 181-240 are scarcer than cards 1-180. The backs contain an extensive biography and a dated copyright line. The key cards in the set are the cards of Joe DiMaggio, Shoeless Joe Jackson, and Ted Williams.

Ex-Mt VG
COMPLETE SET (240) 15000.00 7500.00
COMMON CARD (1-120) 20.00 10.00
COMMON (121-180) 20.00 10.00
COMMON (181-240) 70.00 35.00
WRAP.(1-CENT, DIFF. COLORS) 800.00 400.00
1 Joe DiMaggio 2500.00 1000.00
2 Art Jorgens 25.00 12.50
3 Babe Dahlgren 25.00 12.50
4 Tommy Henrich 35.00 17.50
5 Monte Pearson 25.00 12.50
6 Lefty Gomez 150.00 75.00
7 Bill Dickey 175.00 90.00
8 George Selkirk 25.00 12.50
9 Charlie Keller 35.00 17.50
10 Red Ruffing 90.00 45.00
11 Jake Powell 25.00 12.50
12 Johnny Schulte 20.00 10.00
13 Jack Knott 20.00 10.00
14 Rabbit McNair 20.00 10.00
15 George Case 25.00 12.50
16 Cecil Travis 25.00 12.50
17 Buddy Myer 25.00 12.50
18 Charlie Gelbert 20.00 10.00
19 Ken Chase 20.00 10.00
20 Buddy Lewis 20.00 10.00
21 Rick Ferrell 80.00 40.00
22 Sammy West 20.00 10.00
23 Dutch Leonard 25.00 12.50
24 Frank Hayes 20.00 10.00
25 Bob Johnson 25.00 12.50
26 Wally Moses 25.00 12.50
27 Ted Williams 1200.00 600.00
28 Gene Desautels 20.00 10.00
29 Doc Cramer 25.00 12.50
30 Moe Berg 150.00 75.00
31 Jack Wilson 20.00 10.00
32 Jim Bagby 20.00 10.00
33 Fritz Ostermueller 20.00 10.00
34 John Peacock 20.00 10.00
35 Joe Heving 20.00 10.00
36 Jim Tabor 20.00 10.00
37 Emerson Dickman 20.00 10.00
38 Bobby Doerr 90.00 45.00
39 Tom Carey 20.00 10.00
40 Hank Greenberg 200.00 100.00
41 Charley Gehringer 150.00 75.00
42 Bud Thomas 20.00 10.00
43 Pete Fox 20.00 10.00
44 Dizzy Trout 25.00 12.50
45 Red Kress 20.00 10.00
46 Earl Averill 90.00 45.00
47 Oscar Vitt 20.00 10.00
48 Luke Sewell 25.00 12.50
49 Stormy Weatherly 20.00 10.00
50 Hal Trosky 25.00 12.50
51 Don Heffner 20.00 10.00
52 Myril Hoag 20.00 10.00
53 George McQuinn 25.00 12.50
54 Bill Trotter 20.00 10.00
55 Slick Coffman 20.00 10.00
56 Eddie Miller 25.00 12.50
57 Max West 20.00 10.00
58 Bill Posedel 20.00 10.00
59 Rabbit Warstler 20.00 10.00
60 John Cooney 20.00 10.00
61 Tony Cuccinello 25.00 12.50
62 Buddy Hassett 20.00 10.00
63 Pete Coscarart 20.00 10.00
64 Van Lingle Mungo 25.00 12.50
65 Fred Fitzsimmons 25.00 12.50
66 Babe Phelps 25.00 12.50
67 Whit Wyatt 25.00 12.50
68 Dolph Camilli 25.00 12.50
69 Cookie Lavagetto 25.00 12.50
70 Luke Hamlin 20.00 10.00
(Hot Potato)
71 Mel Almada 20.00 10.00
72 Chuck Dressen 25.00 12.50
73 Bucky Walters 25.00 12.50
74 Paul(Duke) Derringer 25.00 12.50
75 Frank(Buck)McCormick 25.00 12.50
76 Lonny Frey 20.00 10.00
77 Willard Hershberger 25.00 12.50
78 Lew Riggs 20.00 10.00
79 Harry Craft 25.00 12.50
80 Billy Myers 20.00 10.00
81 Wally Berger 25.00 12.50
82 Hank Gowdy CO 25.00 12.50
83 Cliff Melton 20.00 10.00
84 Jo Jo Moore 20.00 10.00
85 Hal Schumacher 25.00 12.50
86 Harry Gumbert 20.00 10.00
87 Carl Hubbell 125.00 60.00
88 Mel Ott 175.00 90.00
89 Bill Jurges 20.00 10.00
90 Frank Demaree 20.00 10.00
91 Bob Seeds 20.00 10.00
92 Whitey Whitehead 20.00 10.00
93 Harry Danning 20.00 10.00
94 Gus Suhr 20.00 10.00
95 Hugh Mulcahy 20.00 10.00
96 Heinie Mueller 20.00 10.00
97 Morry Arnovich 20.00 10.00
98 Pinky May 20.00 10.00
99 Syl Johnson 20.00 10.00
100 Hersh Martin 20.00 10.00
101 Del Young 20.00 10.00
102 Chuck Klein 100.00 50.00
103 Elbie Fletcher 20.00 10.00
104 Paul Waner 90.00 45.00
105 Lloyd Waner 80.00 40.00
106 Pep Young 20.00 10.00
107 Arky Vaughan 80.00 40.00
108 Johnny Rizzo 20.00 10.00
109 Don Padgett 20.00 10.00
110 Tom Sunkel 20.00 10.00
111 Mickey Owen 25.00 12.50
112 Jimmy Brown 20.00 10.00
113 Mort Cooper 25.00 12.50
114 Lon Warneke 25.00 12.50
115 Mike Gonzalez CO 25.00 12.50
116 Al Schacht 25.00 12.50
117 Dolly Stark UMP 25.00 12.50
118 Waite Hoyt 90.00 45.00
119 Grover C. Alexander 175.00 90.00
120 Walter Johnson 200.00 100.00
121 Atley Donald 25.00 12.50
122 Sandy Sundra 25.00 12.50
123 Hildy Hildebrand 25.00 12.50
124 Earle Combs 100.00 50.00
125 Art Fletcher 25.00 12.50
126 Jake Solters 20.00 10.00
127 Muddy Ruel 20.00 10.00
128 Pete Appleton 20.00 10.00
129 Bucky Harris 80.00 40.00
130 Clyde Milan 25.00 12.50
131 Zeke Bonura 25.00 12.50
132 Connie Mack MG 150.00 75.00
133 Jimmie Foxx 200.00 100.00
134 Joe Cronin 100.00 50.00
135 Line Drive Nelson 20.00 10.00
136 Cotton Pippen 20.00 10.00
137 Bing Miller 20.00 10.00
138 Beau Bell 20.00 10.00
139 Elden Auker 20.00 10.00
140 Dick Coffman 20.00 10.00
141 Casey Stengel MG 175.00 90.00
142 George Kelly 90.00 45.00
143 Gene Moore 20.00 10.00
144 Joe Vosmik 20.00 10.00
145 Vito Tamulis 20.00 10.00
146 Tot Pressnell 20.00 10.00
147 Johnny Hudson 20.00 10.00
148 Hugh Casey 25.00 12.50
149 Pinky Shoffner 20.00 10.00
150 Whitey Moore 20.00 10.00
151 Edwin Joost 25.00 12.50
152 Jimmy Wilson 20.00 10.00
153 Bill McKechnie MG 80.00 40.00
154 Jumbo Brown 20.00 10.00
155 Ray Hayworth 20.00 10.00
156 Daffy Dean 35.00 17.50
157 Lou Chiozza 20.00 10.00
158 Travis Jackson 90.00 45.00
159 Pancho Snyder 20.00 10.00
160 Hans Lobert CO 20.00 10.00
161 Debs Garms 20.00 10.00
162 Joe Bowman 20.00 10.00
163 Spud Davis 20.00 10.00
164 Ray Berres 20.00 10.00
165 Bob Klinger 20.00 10.00
166 Bill Brubaker 20.00 10.00
167 Frankie Frisch MG 90.00 45.00
168 Honus Wagner CO 200.00 100.00
169 Gabby Street 20.00 10.00
170 Tris Speaker 175.00 90.00
171 Harry Heilmann 80.00 40.00
172 Chief Bender 80.00 40.00
173 Napoleon Lajoie 175.00 90.00
174 Johnny Evers 90.00 45.00
175 Christy Mathewson 250.00 125.00
176 Heinie Manush 90.00 45.00
177 Frank Baker 100.00 50.00
178 Max Carey 90.00 45.00
179 George Sisler 125.00 60.00
180 Mickey Cochrane 150.00 75.00
181 Spud Chandler 80.00 40.00
182 Knick Knickerbocker 70.00 35.00
183 Marvin Breuer 70.00 35.00
184 Mule Haas 70.00 35.00
185 Joe Kuhel 70.00 35.00
186 Taft Wright 70.00 35.00
187 Jimmy Dykes MG 80.00 40.00
188 Joe Krakauskas 70.00 35.00
189 Jim Bloodworth 70.00 35.00
190 Charley Berry 70.00 35.00
191 John Babich 70.00 35.00
192 Dick Siebert 70.00 35.00
193 Chubby Dean 70.00 35.00
194 Sam Chapman 70.00 35.00
195 Dee Miles 70.00 35.00
196 Red(Nonny)Nonnenkamp 70.00 35.00
197 Lou Finney 70.00 35.00
198 Denny Galehouse 70.00 35.00
199 Pinky Higgins 70.00 35.00
200 Soup Campbell 70.00 35.00
201 Barney McCosky 70.00 35.00
202 Al Milnar 70.00 35.00
203 Bad News Hale 70.00 35.00
204 Harry Eisenstat 70.00 35.00
205 Rollie Hemsley 70.00 35.00
206 Chet Laabs 70.00 35.00
207 Gus Mancuso 70.00 35.00
208 Lee Gamble 70.00 35.00
209 Hy Vandenberg 70.00 35.00
210 Bill Lohrman 70.00 35.00
211 Pop Joiner 70.00 35.00
212 Babe Young 70.00 35.00
213 John Rucker 70.00 35.00
214 Ken O'Dea 70.00 35.00
215 Johnnie McCarthy 70.00 35.00
216 Joe Marty 70.00 35.00
217 Walter Beck 70.00 35.00
218 Wally Millies 70.00 35.00
219 Russ Bauers 70.00 35.00
220 Mace Brown 70.00 35.00
221 Lee Handley 70.00 35.00
222 Max Butcher 70.00 35.00
223 Hughie Jennings 150.00 75.00
224 Pie Traynor 175.00 90.00
225 Joe Jackson 2500.00 1250.00
226 Harry Hooper 150.00 75.00
227 Jesse Haines 150.00 75.00
228 Charlie Grimm 80.00 40.00
229 Buck Herzog 70.00 35.00
230 Red Faber 175.00 90.00
231 Dolf Luque 100.00 50.00
232 Goose Goslin 150.00 75.00
233 George Earnshaw 80.00 40.00
234 Frank Chance 150.00 75.00
235 John McGraw 175.00 90.00
236 Jim Bottomley 150.00 75.00
237 Willie Keeler 175.00 90.00
238 Tony Lazzeri 175.00 90.00
239 George Uhle 70.00 35.00
240 Bill Atwood 100.00 50.00

1941 Play Ball R336

The cards in this 72-card set measure approximately 2 1/2" by 3 1/8". Many of the cards in the 1941 Play Ball series are simply color versions of pictures appearing in the 1940 set. This was the only color baseball card set produced by Gum, Inc.. Card numbers 49-72 are slightly more difficult to obtain as they were not issued until 1942. In 1942, numbers 1-48 were also reissued but without the copyright date. The cards were also printed on paper without a cardboard backing; these are generally encountered in sheets or strips. The set features a card of Pee Wee Reese in his rookie year.

Ex-Mt VG
COMPLETE SET (72) 10000.00 5000.00
COMMON CARD (1-48) 40.00 20.00
COMMON CARD (49-72) 60.00 30.00
WRAPPER (1-CENT) 800.00 400.00
1 Eddie Miller 125.00 60.00
2 Max West 40.00 20.00
3 Bucky Walters 45.00 22.00
4 Paul Derringer 50.00 25.00
5 Frank(Buck) McCormick 45.00 22.00
6 Carl Hubbell 175.00 90.00
7 Harry Danning 40.00 20.00
8 Mel Ott 225.00 110.00
9 Pinky May 40.00 20.00
10 Arky Vaughan 100.00 50.00
11 Debs Garms 40.00 20.00
12 Jimmy Brown 40.00 20.00
13 Jimmie Foxx 300.00 150.00
14 Ted Williams 1800.00 900.00
15 Joe Cronin 125.00 60.00
16 Hal Trosky 45.00 22.00
17 Roy Weatherly 40.00 20.00
18 Hank Greenberg 300.00 150.00
19 Charley Gehringer 200.00 100.00
20 Red Ruffing 125.00 60.00
21 Charlie Keller 60.00 30.00
22 Bob Johnson 50.00 25.00
23 George McQuinn 45.00 22.00
24 Dutch Leonard 45.00 22.00
25 Gene Moore 40.00 20.00
26 Harry Gumpert 40.00 20.00
27 Babe Young 40.00 20.00
28 Joe Marty 40.00 20.00
29 Jack Wilson 40.00 20.00
30 Lou Finney 40.00 20.00
31 Joe Kuhel 40.00 20.00
32 Taft Wright 40.00 20.00
33 Al Milnar 40.00 20.00
34 Rollie Hemsley 40.00 20.00
35 Pinky Higgins 45.00 22.00
36 Barney McCosky 45.00 22.00
37 Bruce Campbell 40.00 20.00
38 Atley Donald 50.00 25.00
39 Tommy Henrich 60.00 30.00
40 John Babich 40.00 20.00
41 Frank(Blimp) Hayes 40.00 20.00
42 Wally Moses 45.00 22.00
43 Al Brancato 40.00 20.00
44 Sam Chapman 40.00 20.00
45 Eldon Auker 40.00 20.00
46 Sid Hudson 40.00 20.00
47 Buddy Lewis 40.00 20.00
48 Cecil Travis 45.00 22.00
49 Babe Dahlgren 65.00 32.00
50 Johnny Cooney 60.00 30.00
51 Dolph Camilli 65.00 32.00
52 Kirby Higbe 60.00 30.00
53 Luke Hamlin 60.00 30.00
54 Pee Wee Reese 600.00 300.00
55 Whit Wyatt 65.00 32.00
56 Johnny VanderMeer 100.00 50.00
57 Moe Arnovich 60.00 30.00
58 Frank Demaree 60.00 30.00
59 Bill Jurges 60.00 30.00
60 Chuck Klein 150.00 75.00
61 Vince DiMaggio 225.00 110.00
62 Elbie Fletcher 60.00 30.00
63 Dom DiMaggio 250.00 125.00
64 Bobby Doerr 175.00 90.00
65 Tommy Bridges 65.00 32.00
66 Harland Clift 60.00 30.00
67 Walt Judnich 60.00 30.00
68 John Knott 60.00 30.00
69 George Case 65.00 32.00
70 Bill Dickey 400.00 200.00
71 Joe DiMaggio 2500.00 1250.00
72 Lefty Gomez 475.00 240.00

1991 Playball Will Clark

The numbering and card design indicates that this ten-card standard-size set is made up of two five-card sets. These single-player Playball sets were important as they were issued by Rob Broder, who had been associated with unliscenced cards in the 1980's and all of the variants had been given the "Broder" label. These cards were all given the OK by Major League Baseball as well as the player's team.

Nm-Mt Ex-Mt
COMPLETE SET (10) 6.00 1.80
COMMON CARD (21-25/39-43) .75 .23

1991 Playball Griffey Jr.

The glossy color player photos on the first five cards are full bleed without any border stripes. The glossy player photos on card numbers 1 and 49 bleed to the sides of the card but are bordered above and below by different color stripes. The photo on card number 50 is full bleed, while the unnumbered card has a gold-patterned border.

Nm-Mt Ex-Mt
COMPLETE SET 15.00 4.50
COMMON CARD 1.00 .30

1991 Playball Mattingly

The numbering and card design indicates that this ten-card standard-size set is made up of two five-card sets. The glossy player photos on the first five cards bleed to the sides of the card but are bordered above by a dark blue stripe and below by silver and dark blue stripes. The glossy color player photos on the second five cards are full bleed without any border stripes.

Nm-Mt Ex-Mt
COMPLETE SET (10) 5.00 1.50
COMMON CARD .50 .15

1991 Playball Mattingly Gold

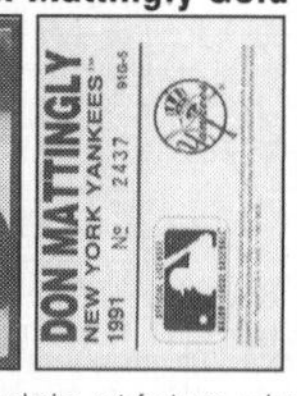

This two-card standard-size set features color action photos framed by gold foil borders. The team logo appears in the upper left corner, while the player's name and team name appear in white lettering at the lower left. The horizontal backs have the player's name, team name, serial number and card number ("91G-X") on the upper portion and MLB and team logos on the lower portion.

Nm-Mt Ex-Mt
COMPLETE SET 4.00 1.20
COMMON CARD 2.00 .60

1991 Playball Strawberry

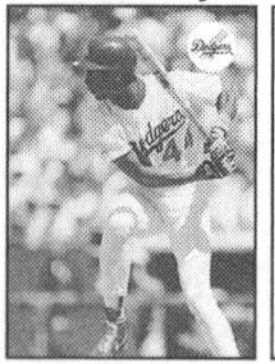

As with the other 1991 Playball sets, this seven-card standard-size set exhibits two different front designs. A blue border stripe above and silver and blue border stripes below frame the glossy color player photos on the first three cards, while the player photos on the last four cards are without any border stripes. The back design of all cards is horizontally oriented and features the player's name, team name, logo, year and MLB logo in black on a white card stock.

Nm-Mt Ex-Mt
COMPLETE SET (7) 3.00 .90
COMMON CARD (53-58/60) .50 .15

1992 Playball Griffey Jr.

This four-card standard-size set features color action shots of Ken Griffey Jr. These photos are edged in blue and bordered in prismatic gold foil. The cards are unnumbered.

Nm-Mt Ex-Mt
COMPLETE SET (4) 4.00 1.20
COMMON CARD (1-4) 1.00 .30

2001 Playoff Absolute Memorabilia

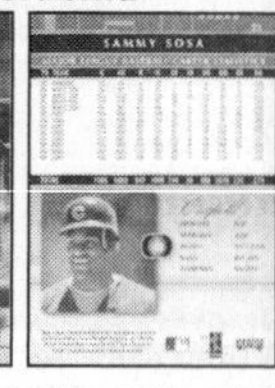

The 2001 Playoff Absolute Memorabilia set was issued in one series totally 200 cards. The set features color action player photos highlighted on metalized film board with the 50 rookie cards infused with a swatch of game-worn/used bat and jersey. The following cards were available via mail exchange cards (of which expired on June 1st, 2003): 151 - Bud Smith, 154 - Josh Beckett, 161 Ben Sheets, 164 - Carlos Garcia, 169 - Donaldo Mendez, 171 Jackson Melian, 173 Adrian Hernandez, 186 - C.C. Sabathia, 188 - Adam Pettyjohn, 193 - Alfonso Soriano, 196 - Billy Sylvester and 200 - Matt White.

Nm-Mt Ex-Mt
COMP.SET w/o SP's (150) 40.00 12.00
COMMON CARD (1-150) .75 .23
COMMON RPM (151-200) 10.00 3.00
1 Alex Rodriguez 3.00 .90
2 Barry Bonds 5.00 1.50
3 Cal Ripken 6.00 1.80
4 Chipper Jones 2.00 .60
5 Derek Jeter 5.00 1.50
6 Troy Glaus 1.25 .35
7 Frank Thomas 2.00 .60
8 Greg Maddux 3.00 .90
9 Ivan Rodriguez 2.00 .60
10 Jeff Bagwell 1.25 .35
11 Ryan Dempster .75 .23
12 Todd Helton 1.25 .35
13 Ken Griffey Jr. 3.00 .90
14 Manny Ramirez .75 .23
15 Mark McGwire 5.00 1.50
16 Mike Piazza 3.00 .90
17 Nomar Garciaparra 3.00 .90
18 Pedro Martinez 2.00 .60
19 Randy Johnson 2.00 .60
20 Rick Ankiel .75 .23
21 Rickey Henderson 2.00 .60
22 Roger Clemens 4.00 1.20
23 Sammy Sosa 3.00 .90
24 Tony Gwynn 2.50 .75
25 Vladimir Guerrero 2.00 .60
26 Kazuhiro Sasaki .75 .23
27 Roberto Alomar 2.00 .60
28 Barry Zito 2.00 .60
29 Pat Burrell .75 .23
30 Harold Baines .75 .23
31 Carlos Delgado .75 .23
32 J.D. Drew .75 .23
33 Jim Edmonds .75 .23
34 Darin Erstad .75 .23
35 Jason Giambi 2.00 .60
36 Tom Glavine 1.25 .35
37 Juan Gonzalez 2.00 .60
38 Mark Grace 1.25 .35
39 Shawn Green .75 .23
40 Tim Hudson .75 .23
41 Andruw Jones .75 .23
42 David Justice .75 .23
43 Jeff Kent .75 .23
44 Barry Larkin 2.00 .60
45 Rafael Furcal .75 .23
46 Mike Mussina 2.00 .60
47 Hideo Nomo 2.00 .60
48 Rafael Palmeiro 1.25 .35
49 Adam Piatt .75 .23
50 Scott Rolen 1.25 .35
51 Gary Sheffield .75 .23
52 Bernie Williams 1.25 .35
53 Bob Abreu .75 .23
54 Edgardo Alfonzo .75 .23
55 Edgar Renteria .75 .23
56 Phil Nevin .75 .23
57 Craig Biggio 1.25 .35
58 Andres Galarraga .75 .23
59 Edgar Martinez 1.25 .35
60 Fred McGriff 1.25 .35
61 Magglio Ordonez .75 .23
62 Jim Thome 2.00 .60
63 Matt Williams .75 .23
64 Kerry Wood 2.00 .60
65 Moises Alou .75 .23
66 Brady Anderson .75 .23
67 Garret Anderson .75 .23
68 Russell Branyan .75 .23
69 Tony Batista .75 .23
70 Vernon Wells .75 .23
71 Carlos Beltran .75 .23
72 Adrian Beltre .75 .23
73 Kris Benson .75 .23
74 Lance Berkman .75 .23
75 Kevin Brown .75 .23
76 Dee Brown .75 .23
77 Jeromy Burnitz .75 .23
78 Timo Perez .75 .23
79 Sean Casey .75 .23
80 Luis Castillo .75 .23
81 Eric Chavez .75 .23
82 Jeff Cirillo .75 .23
83 Bartolo Colon .75 .23
84 David Cone .75 .23
85 Freddy Garcia .75 .23
86 Johnny Damon .75 .23
87 Ray Durham .75 .23
88 Jermaine Dye .75 .23
89 Juan Encarnacion .75 .23
90 Terrence Long .75 .23
91 Carl Everett .75 .23
92 Steve Finley .75 .23
93 Cliff Floyd .75 .23

4 Brad Fullmer .75 .23
5 Brian Giles .75 .23
6 Luis Gonzalez .75 .23
7 Rusty Greer .75 .23
8 Jeffrey Hammonds .75 .23
9 Mike Hampton .75 .23
100 Orlando Hernandez .75 .23
101 Richard Hidalgo .75 .23
102 Geoff Jenkins .75 .23
103 Jacque Jones .75 .23
104 Brian Jordan .75 .23
105 Gabe Kapler .75 .23
106 Eric Karros .75 .23
107 Jason Kendall .75 .23
108 Adam Kennedy .75 .23
109 Deion Sanders 1.25 .35
110 Ryan Klesko .75 .23
111 Chuck Knoblauch .75 .23
112 Paul Konerko .75 .23
113 Carlos Lee .75 .23
114 Kenny Lofton .75 .23
115 Javy Lopez .75 .23
116 Tino Martinez 1.25 .35
117 Ruben Mateo .75 .23
118 Kevin Millwood .75 .23
119 Jimmy Rollins .75 .23
120 Raul Mondesi .75 .23
121 Trot Nixon 1.25 .35
122 John Olerud .75 .23
123 Paul O' Neill 1.25 .35
124 Chan Ho Park .75 .23
125 Andy Pettitte 1.25 .35
126 Jorge Posada 1.25 .35
127 Mark Quinn .75 .23
128 Aramis Ramirez .75 .23
129 Mariano Rivera 1.25 .35
130 Tim Salmon 1.25 .35
131 Curt Schilling 1.25 .35
132 Richie Sexson .75 .23
133 John Smoltz 1.25 .35
134 J.T. Snow .75 .23
135 Jay Payton .75 .23
136 Shannon Stewart .75 .23
137 B.J. Surhoff .75 .23
138 Mike Sweeney .75 .23
139 Fernando Tatis .75 .23
140 Miguel Tejada .75 .23
141 Jason Varitek .75 .23
142 Greg Vaughn .75 .23
143 Mo Vaughn .75 .23
144 Robin Ventura .75 .23
145 Jose Vidro .75 .23
146 Omar Vizquel .75 .23
147 Larry Walker 1.25 .35
148 David Wells .75 .23
149 Rondell White .75 .23
150 Preston Wilson .75 .23
151 Bud Smith RPM RC 10.00 3.00
152 C. Aldridge RPM RC 10.00 3.00
153 W.Caceres RPM RC 10.00 3.00
154 Josh Beckett RPM 12.00 3.60
155 W.Betemit RPM RC 10.00 3.00
156 J.Michaels RPM RC 10.00 3.00
157 Albert Pujols RPM RC 80.00 24.00
158 A.Torres RPM RC 10.00 3.00
159 Jack Wilson RPM RC 10.00 3.00
160 Alex Escobar RPM 10.00 3.00
161 Ben Sheets RPM 10.00 3.00
162 R.Soriano RPM RC 15.00 4.50
163 Nate Frese RPM RC 10.00 3.00
164 C. Garcia RPM EXCH 10.00 3.00
165 B.Larson RPM RC 10.00 3.00
166 A.Gomez RPM RC 10.00 3.00
167 Jason Hart RPM 10.00 3.00
168 Nick Johnson RPM 10.00 3.00
169 Donaldo Mendez RPM 10.00 3.00
170 C. Parker RPM RC 10.00 3.00
171 Jackson Melian RPM 10.00 3.00
172 Jack Cust RPM 10.00 3.00
173 Adrian Hernandez RPM 10.00 3.00
174 Joe Crede RPM 10.00 3.00
175 Jose Mieses RPM RC 10.00 3.00
176 Roy Oswalt RPM 12.00 3.60
177 Eric Munson RPM 10.00 3.00
178 Xavier Nady RPM 10.00 3.00
179 H. Ramirez RPM RC 12.00 3.60
180 Abraham Nunez RPM 10.00 3.00
181 Jose Ortiz RPM 10.00 3.00
182 J. Owens RPM RC 10.00 3.00
183 C. Vargas RPM RC 10.00 3.00
184 Marcus Giles RPM 10.00 3.00
185 Aubrey Huff RPM 10.00 3.00
186 C.C. Sabathia RPM 10.00 3.00
187 Adam Dunn RPM 10.00 3.00
188 Adam Pettyjohn RPM 10.00 3.00
189 El. Guzman RPM RC 10.00 3.00
190 Jay Gibbons RPM RC 12.00 3.60
191 Wilkin Ruan RPM RC 10.00 3.00
192 T. Shinjo RPM RC 12.00 3.60
193 Alfonso Soriano RPM 12.00 3.60
194 Corey Patterson RPM 10.00 3.00
195 Ichiro Suzuki RPM RC 60.00 18.00
196 Billy Sylvester RPM 10.00 3.00
197 Juan Uribe RPM RC 10.00 3.00
198 J. Estrada RPM RC 12.00 3.60
199 C. Valderrama RPM RC 10.00 3.00
200 Matt White RPM 10.00 3.00

2001 Playoff Absolute Memorabilia Ball Hoggs

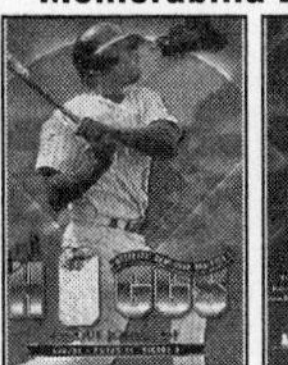

Randomly inserted in packs, this 46 card set features color action player photos with swatches of game-used baseballs embedded in the cards. Each card was sequentially numbered and the print runs are listed after the players' names in the checklist below. The first 25 of each card are spotlighted with a holo-foil stamp and labeled "Boss Hoggs." Exchange cards were seeded into packs for the following players: Jeff Bagwell, Darin Erstad, Chipper Jones, Magglio Ordonez, Cal Ripken and Alex Rodriguez. The deadline to redeem the cards was June 1st, 2003.

Nm-Mt Ex-Mt
BH1 Vladimir Guerrero/75 25.00 7.50
BH2 Troy Glaus/75 25.00 7.50
BH3 Tony Gwynn/75 40.00 12.00
BH4 Cal Ripken/175 100.00 30.00
BH5 Todd Helton/75 25.00 7.50
BH6 Jacque Jones/125 15.00 4.50
BH7 Shawn Green/100 15.00 4.50
BH8 Ichiro Suzuki/50 200.00 60.00
BH9 Scott Rolen/100 25.00 7.50
BH10 Roger Clemens/75 60.00 18.00
BH11 Ken Griffey Jr./25
BH14 Sammy Sosa/75 50.00 15.00
BH15 J.D. Drew/50 15.00 4.50
BH16 Barry Bonds/75 80.00 24.00
BH17 Pat Burrell/75 15.00 4.50
BH18 Mark McGwire/75 150.00 45.00
BH19 Mike Piazza/50 60.00 18.00
BH20 Maggio Ordonez/125 15.00 4.50
BH21 Miguel Tejada/75 15.00 4.50
BH22 Albert Pujols/75 150.00 45.00
BH23 Derek Jeter/50 100.00 30.00
BH24 Johnny Damon/125 15.00 4.50
BH25 Mike Sweeney/75 15.00 4.50
BH26 Ben Grieve/125 15.00 4.50
BH27 Jeff Kent/75 15.00 4.50
BH28 Andres Galarraga/75 15.00 4.50
BH29 Richie Sexson/25
BH30 J.Encarnacion/125 15.00 4.50
BH31 Ruben Mateo/75 15.00 4.50
BH33 Manny Ramirez/75 15.00 4.50
BH35 Ivan Rodriguez/75 25.00 7.50
BH36 D. Erstad/125 EXCH 15.00 4.50
BH37 Carlos Delgado/100 15.00 4.50
BH38 J. Bagwell/125 EXCH 25.00 7.50
BH39 Jermaine Dye/75 15.00 4.50
BH40 Jose Ortiz/50 15.00 4.50
BH41 Gary Sheffield/75 15.00 4.50
BH42 Eric Chavez/125 15.00 4.50
BH43 Mark Grace/75 25.00 7.50
BH44 Rafael Palmeiro/125 25.00 7.50
BH45 Tsuyoshi Shinjo/75 40.00 12.00
BH46 Terrence Long/75 15.00 4.50
BH47 Carlos Delgado/25
BH48 Frank Thomas/75 25.00 7.50
BH49 C. Jones/25 EXCH
BH50 Jason Giambi/75 25.00 7.50

2001 Playoff Absolute Memorabilia Boss Hoggs

Randomly inserted in packs, this 50-card set is a parallel version of the regular insert set with a holo-foil stamp and labeled "Boss Hoggs." Each card features a patch of a game-used baseball. This set is the first 25 of each card printed in the regular insert set. Exchange cards (with a redemption deadline of June 1st, 2003) were issued in packs for Jeff Bagwell, Darin Erstad, Chipper Jones, Maggio Ordonez, Cal Ripken and Alex Rodriguez. The Chipper and A-Rod cards were intended to be redeemed for autograph cards, the others were all for non-autographed cards.

Nm-Mt Ex-Mt
AU CL: 1-3/5/10/22/32/34/41/49

2001 Playoff Absolute Memorabilia Home Opener Souvenirs

Randomly inserted in packs at the rate of one per box, this 50-card set features color photos of top performers showcased on conventional board with foil featuring a swatch of an authentic game-used base embedded in the cards. Only 400 serially numbered sets were produced.

Nm-Mt Ex-Mt
*DOUBLE: .6X TO 1.5X BASIC SOUV..
DOUBLE: STATED PRINT RUN 200 SERIAL #'D SETS
RANDOM INSERTS IN PACKS
*TRIPLE: 1.25X TO 3X BASIC SOUV...
TRIPLE: STATED PRINT RUN 75 SERIAL #'D SETS
RANDOM INSERTS IN PACKS
*HOME RUN: NO PRICING DUE TO SCARCITY
HOME RUN: STATED PRINT RUN 25 SERIAL #'D SETS
RANDOM INSERTS IN PACKS
OD1 Barry Bonds 30.00 9.00
OD2 Cal Ripken 40.00 12.00
OD3 Pedro Martinez 10.00 3.00
OD4 Troy Glaus 10.00 3.00
OD5 Frank Thomas 10.00 3.00
OD6 Alex Rodriguez 20.00 6.00
OD7 Ivan Rodriguez 10.00 3.00
OD8 Jeff Bagwell 10.00 3.00
OD9 Mark McGwire 50.00 15.00
OD10 Todd Helton 10.00 3.00
OD11 Gary Sheffield 8.00 2.40
OD12 Manny Ramirez 8.00 2.40
OD13 Mike Piazza 20.00 6.00
OD14 Sammy Sosa 25.00 7.50
OD15 Preston Wilson 8.00 2.40
OD16 Tony Gwynn 15.00 4.50
OD17 Vladimir Guerrero 10.00 3.00
OD18 Carlos Delgado 8.00 2.40
OD19 Roberto Alomar 10.00 3.00
OD20 Todd Helton 10.00 3.00
OD21 Albert Pujols UER 50.00 15.00
Base shows a DiamondBacks logo
Dbacks did not play Cards opening day
OD22 Jason Giambi 10.00 3.00
OD23 Sammy Sosa 25.00 7.50
OD24 Ken Griffey Jr. 25.00 7.50
OD25 Darin Erstad 8.00 2.40
OD26 Mark McGwire 50.00 15.00
OD27 Carlos Delgado 8.00 2.40
OD28 Juan Gonzalez 10.00 3.00
OD29 Mike Sweeney 8.00 2.40
OD30 Alex Rodriguez 25.00 7.50
OD31 Roger Clemens 25.00 7.50
OD32 Tsuyoshi Shinjo 10.00 3.00
OD33 Ben Grieve 8.00 2.40
OD34 Jeff Kent 8.00 2.40
OD35 Vladimir Guerrero 10.00 3.00
OD36 Shawn Green 8.00 2.40
OD37 Rafael Palmeiro 10.00 3.00
OD38 Tony Gwynn 15.00 4.50
OD39 Scott Rolen 10.00 3.00
OD40 Ken Griffey Jr. 25.00 7.50
OD41 Albert Pujols 50.00 15.00
OD42 Barry Bonds 30.00 9.00
OD43 Mark Grace 10.00 3.00
OD44 Bernie Williams 10.00 3.00
OD45 Frank Thomas 10.00 3.00
OD46 Jermaine Dye 8.00 2.40
OD47 Mike Piazza 15.00 4.50
OD48 Chipper Jones 10.00 3.00
OD49 Richie Sexson 8.00 2.40
OD50 Maggio Ordonez 8.00 2.40

2001 Playoff Absolute Memorabilia Home Opener Souvenirs Autographs

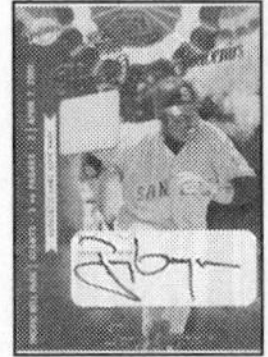

Randomly inserted in packs, this ten-card set features autographed action color photos of top players with a swatch of a game-used baseball and/or base embedded in the card. Only 25 serially numbered sets were produced but the cards are actually serial numbered out of 400 (whereby the first 25 of each card were signed by players participating in this program). No pricing is provided due to market scarcity. Exchange cards, with a redemption deadline of June 1st, 2003, were seeded into packs for Troy Glaus, Cal Ripken and Alex Rodriguez.

Nm-Mt Ex-Mt
OD2 Cal Ripken
OD4 Troy Glaus
OD6 Alex Rodriguez
OD16 Tony Gwynn
OD17 Vladimir Guerrero
OD19 Roberto Alomar
OD21 Albert Pujols
OD28 Juan Gonzalez
OD31 Roger Clemens
OD37 Rafael Palmeiro

2001 Playoff Absolute Memorabilia Home Opener Souvenirs Double

Randomly inserted in packs, this 50-card set is parallel to the regular insert set with two swatches of game-used bases embedded in the card. Only 200 serially numbered sets were produced.

Nm-Mt Ex-Mt
*DOUBLE: .6X TO 1.5X BASIC SOUV..

2001 Playoff Absolute Memorabilia Home Opener Souvenirs Triple

Randomly inserted in packs, this 50-card set is parallel to the regular insert set with three swatches of game-used bases embedded in the card. Only 75 serially numbered sets were produced.

Nm-Mt Ex-Mt
*TRIPLE: 1.25X TO 3X BASIC SOUV...

2001 Playoff Absolute Memorabilia Signing Bonus Baseballs

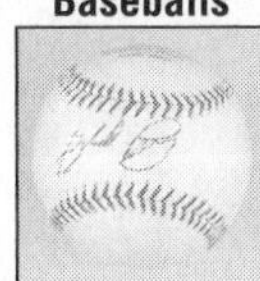

Randomly inserted one per box, this set features baseballs signed by a select group of stellar performers. The players' names are listed below in alphabetical order with the sequential numbering of the quantity signed following the names.

Nm-Mt Ex-Mt
1 Al Oliver/500 25.00 7.50
2 Andre Dawson/550 25.00 7.50
3 Barry Bonds/25
4 Bill Madlock/524 25.00 7.50
5 Bill Mazeroski/25
6 Billy Williams/325 25.00 7.50
7 Bob Feller/550 30.00 9.00
8 Bob Gibson/25
9 Bobby Doerr/300 30.00 9.00
10 Bobby Richardson/500 30.00 9.00
11 Boog Powell/500 40.00 12.00
12 Brian Jordan/25
13 Bucky Dent/500 25.00 7.50
14 Charles Johnson/25
15 Chipper Jones/25
16 Clete Boyer/500 25.00 7.50
17 Dale Murphy/25
18 Dave Concepcion/500 25.00 7.50
19 Dave Kingman/500 25.00 7.50
20 Don Larsen/200 50.00 15.00
21 Don Newcombe/500 25.00 7.50
22 Don Zimmer/500 25.00 7.50
23 Duke Snider/25
24 Earl Weaver/300 30.00 9.00
25 Enos Slaughter/525 30.00 9.00
26 Fergie Jenkins/1000 25.00 7.50
27 Frank Howard/500 25.00 7.50
28 Frank Robinson/25
29 Frank Thomas/25
30 Gary Carter/200 60.00 18.00
31 Gaylord Perry/1000 25.00 7.50
32 George Foster/500 25.00 7.50
33 George Kell/300 30.00 9.00
34 Goose Gossage/500 25.00 7.50
35 Greg Maddux/25
36 Hank Aaron/25
37 Hank Bauer/500 30.00 9.00
38 Harmon Killebrew/200 80.00 24.00
39 Henry Rodriguez/400 25.00 7.50
40 Herb Score/500 25.00 7.50
41 Hoyt Wilhelm/500 25.00 7.50
42 J.D. Drew/25
43 Javy Lopez/25
44 Jim Edmonds/25
45 Jim Palmer/500 25.00 7.50
46 Joe Pepitone/500 25.00 7.50
47 Johnny Bench/25
48 Johnny Podres/500 30.00 9.00
49 Juan Marichal/485 25.00 7.50
50 Kirby Puckett/25
51 Larry Doby/300 40.00 12.00
52 Lou Brock/25
53 Luis Tiant/500 25.00 7.50
54 Magglio Ordonez/200 25.00 7.50
55 Manny Ramirez/25
56 Maury Wills/500 30.00 9.00
57 Mike Schmidt/25
58 Minnie Minoso/1000 25.00 7.50
59 Monte Irvin/500 30.00 9.00
60 Moose Skowron/500 30.00 9.00
61 Nolan Ryan/25
62 Ozzie Smith/25
63 Phil Rizzuto/25
64 Ralph Kiner/100 50.00 15.00
65 Randy Johnson/25
66 Red Schoendienst/500 30.00 9.00
67 Reggie Jackson/25
68 Rickey Henderson/25
69 Robin Roberts/500 30.00 9.00
70 Roger Clemens/25
71 Rollie Fingers/575 25.00 7.50
72 Ryne Sandberg/25
73 Sean Casey/25
74 Stan Musial/25
75 Steve Carlton/25
76 Steve Garvey/1000 25.00 7.50
77 Todd Helton/25
78 Tom Glavine/25
79 Tom Seaver/25
80 Tommy John/1000 25.00 7.50
81 Tony Gwynn/25
82 Tony Perez/400 25.00 7.50
83 Wade Boggs/25
84 Warren Spahn/500 80.00 24.00
85 Whitey Ford/25
86 Willie Mays/25
87 Willie McCovey/25
88 Willie Stargell/25
89 Yogi Berra/25

2001 Playoff Absolute Memorabilia Tools of the Trade

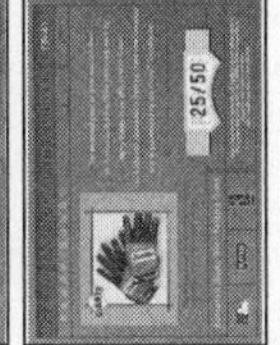

Randomly inserted in packs, this 50-card set features action color player images with game-worn/used jerseys, batting gloves, bats, and hats embedded in the cards. The cards with swatches of batting gloves were serially numbered to 50, with hats to 100, with bats to 100, and with jerseys to 300. Exchange cards with a redemption deadline of June 1st, 2003 were seeded into packs for the following cards: Roberto Alomar Bat, Roberto Alomar Glove, Jeff Bagwell Bat, Darin Erstad Bat, Troy Glaus Bat, Troy Glaus Hat, Troy Glaus Jsy, Tom Glavine Hat, Shawn Green Bat, Tony Gwynn Glove, David Justice Bat, Greg Maddux Hat, Kazuhiro Sasaki Jsy and Larry Walker Jsy.

Nm-Mt Ex-Mt
TT1 Vladimir Guerrero Jsy 15.00 4.50
TT2 Troy Glaus Jsy 15.00 4.50
TT3 Tony Gwynn Jsy 25.00 7.50
TT4 Todd Helton Jsy 15.00 4.50
TT5 Scott Rolen Jsy 15.00 4.50
TT6 Roger Clemens Jsy 40.00 12.00
TT7 Pedro Martinez Jsy 15.00 4.50
TT8 Richie Sexson Jsy 10.00 3.00
TT9 Magglio Ordonez Jsy 10.00 3.00
TT10 Ben Grieve Jsy 10.00 3.00
TT11 Jeff Bagwell Jsy 15.00 4.50
TT12 Edgar Martinez Jsy 15.00 4.50
TT13 Greg Maddux Jsy 25.00 7.50
TT14 Larry Walker Jsy 15.00 4.50
TT15 Frank Thomas Jsy 15.00 4.50
TT16 Edgardo Alfonzo Jsy 10.00 3.00
TT17 Cal Ripken Jsy 50.00 15.00
TT18 Jose Vidro Jsy 10.00 3.00
TT19 Andruw Jones Jsy 10.00 3.00
TT20 K. Sasaki Jsy EXCH 10.00 3.00
TT21 Barry Bonds Bat 80.00 24.00
TT22 Juan Gonzalez Bat 40.00 12.00
TT23 Andruw Jones Bat 25.00 7.50
TT24 Cal Ripken Bat 100.00 30.00
TT25 Greg Maddux Bat 40.00 12.00
TT26 Manny Ramirez Bat 25.00 7.50
TT27 Roberto Alomar Bat 40.00 12.00
TT28 S. Green Bat EXCH 25.00 7.50
TT29 Edgardo Alfonzo Bat 25.00 7.50
TT30 Rafael Palmeiro Bat 40.00 12.00
TT31 Hideo Nomo Bat 150.00 45.00
TT32 A. Galarraga Bat 25.00 7.50
TT33 Todd Helton Bat 40.00 12.00
TT34 Darin Erstad Bat 25.00 7.50
TT35 Ivan Rodriguez Bat 40.00 12.00
TT36 Sean Casey Bat 25.00 7.50
TT37 V. Guerrero Bat 40.00 12.00
TT38 David Justice Bat 25.00 7.50
TT39 Troy Glaus Bat 40.00 12.00
TT40 Jeff Bagwell Bat
TT41 Barry Bonds Glove 150.00 45.00
TT42 Cal Ripken Glove 200.00 60.00
TT43 Rob Alomar Glove 40.00 12.00
TT44 Sean Casey Glove 40.00 12.00
TT45 Tony Gwynn Glove
TT46 Bernie Williams Hat 40.00 12.00
TT47 Barry Zito Hat 40.00 12.00
TT48 Greg Maddux Hat
TT49 Tom Glavine Hat 40.00 12.00
TT50 Troy Glaus Hat 40.00 12.00

2001 Playoff Absolute Memorabilia Tools of the Trade Autographs

Randomly inserted in packs, this 10-card set is an autographed partial parallel version of the regular insert set. Only 25 serially numbered sets were produced. Due to market scarcity, no pricing is provided. An exchange card with a redemption deadline of June 1st, 2003 was placed into packs for the Troy Glaus Bat card.

Nm-Mt Ex-Mt
TT1 Vladimir Guerrero Jsy
TT3 Tony Gwynn Jsy
TT5 Scott Rolen Jsy
TT6 Roger Clemens Jsy
TT17 Cal Ripken Bat
TT22 Juan Gonzalez Bat
TT32 Andres Galarraga Bat
TT33 Todd Helton Bat
TT35 Ivan Rodriguez Bat
TT39 Troy Glaus Bat

2002 Playoff Absolute Memorabilia

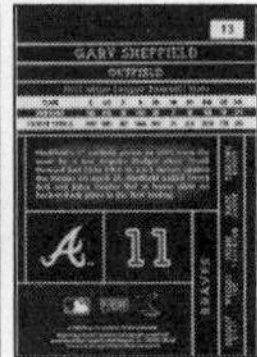

This 200 card standard-size set was issued in August, 2002. The set was released in a big box which contained two nine pack mini-boxes as well as a "Signing Bonus" framed piece. The first 150 cards of this set featured veterans while the final cards feature rookies and prospects with a stated print run of 1000 serial numbered sets.

Nm-Mt Ex-Mt
COMP.SET w/o SP's (150) 40.00 12.00
COMMON CARD (1-150) .75 .23
COMMON CARD (151-200) 5.00 1.50
1 David Eckstein .75 .23
2 Darin Erstad .75 .23
3 Troy Glaus 1.25 .35
4 Garret Anderson .75 .23
5 Tim Salmon 1.25 .35
6 Curt Schilling 1.25 .35
7 Randy Johnson 2.00 .60
8 Luis Gonzalez .75 .23
9 Mark Grace 1.25 .35
10 Tom Glavine 1.25 .35
11 Greg Maddux 3.00 .90
12 Chipper Jones 2.00 .60
13 Gary Sheffield .75 .23
14 John Smoltz 1.25 .35
15 Andruw Jones .75 .23
16 Wilson Betemit .75 .23
17 Tony Batista .75 .23
18 Javier Vazquez .75 .23
19 Scott Erickson .75 .23
20 Josh Towers .75 .23
21 Pedro Martinez 2.00 .60
22 Johnny Damon .75 .23
23 Manny Ramirez .75 .23
24 Rickey Henderson 2.00 .60
25 Trot Nixon 1.25 .35
26 Nomar Garciaparra 3.00 .90
27 Juan Cruz .75 .23
28 Kerry Wood 2.00 .60
29 Fred McGriff 1.25 .35
30 Moises Alou .75 .23

31 Sammy Sosa 3.00 .90
32 Corey Patterson .75 .23
33 Mark Buehrle .75 .23
34 Keith Foulke .75 .23
35 Frank Thomas 2.00 .60
36 Kenny Lofton .75 .23
37 Magglio Ordonez .75 .23
38 Barry Larkin 2.00 .60
39 Ken Griffey Jr. 3.00 .90
40 Adam Dunn .75 .23
41 Juan Encarnacion .75 .23
42 Sean Casey .75 .23
43 Bartolo Colon .75 .23
44 C.C. Sabathia .75 .23
45 Travis Fryman .75 .23
46 Jim Thome 2.00 .60
47 Omar Vizquel .75 .23
48 Ellis Burks .75 .23
49 Russell Branyan .75 .23
50 Mike Hampton .75 .23
51 Todd Helton 1.25 .35
52 Jose Ortiz .75 .23
53 Juan Uribe .75 .23
54 Juan Pierre .75 .23
55 Larry Walker 1.25 .35
56 Mike Rivera .75 .23
57 Robert Fick .75 .23
58 Bobby Higginson .75 .23
59 Josh Beckett 1.25 .35
60 Richard Hidalgo .75 .23
61 Cliff Floyd .75 .23
62 Mike Lowell .75 .23
63 Roy Oswalt .75 .23
64 Morgan Ensberg .75 .23
65 Jeff Bagwell 1.25 .35
66 Craig Biggio 1.25 .35
67 Lance Berkman .75 .23
68 Carlos Beltran .75 .23
69 Mike Sweeney .75 .23
70 Neifi Perez .75 .23
71 Kevin Brown .75 .23
72 Hideo Nomo 2.00 .60
73 Paul Lo Duca .75 .23
74 Adrian Beltre .75 .23
75 Shawn Green .75 .23
76 Eric Karros .75 .23
77 Brad Radke .75 .23
78 Corey Koskie .75 .23
79 Doug Mientkiewicz .75 .23
80 Torii Hunter .75 .23
81 Jacque Jones .75 .23
82 Ben Sheets .75 .23
83 Richie Sexson .75 .23
84 Geoff Jenkins .75 .23
85 Tony Armas Jr. .75 .23
86 Michael Barrett .75 .23
87 Jose Vidro .75 .23
88 Vladimir Guerrero 2.00 .60
89 Roger Clemens 4.00 1.20
90 Derek Jeter 5.00 1.50
91 Bernie Williams 1.25 .35
92 Jason Giambi 2.00 .60
93 Jorge Posada 1.25 .35
94 Mike Mussina 2.00 .60
95 Andy Pettitte 1.25 .35
96 Nick Johnson .75 .23
97 Alfonso Soriano 1.25 .35
98 Shawn Estes .75 .23
99 Al Leiter .75 .23
100 Mike Piazza 3.00 .90
101 Roberto Alomar 2.00 .60
102 Mo Vaughn .75 .23
103 Jeromy Burnitz .75 .23
104 Tim Hudson .75 .23
105 Barry Zito 1.25 .35
106 Mark Mulder .75 .23
107 Eric Chavez .75 .23
108 Miguel Tejada .75 .23
109 Carlos Pena .75 .23
110 Jermaine Dye .75 .23
111 Mike Lieberthal .75 .23
112 Scott Rolen 1.25 .35
113 Pat Burrell .75 .23
114 Brandon Duckworth .75 .23
115 Bobby Abreu .75 .23
116 Jason Kendall .75 .23
117 Aramis Ramirez .75 .23
118 Brian Giles .75 .23
119 Pokey Reese .75 .23
120 Phil Nevin .75 .23
121 Ryan Klesko .75 .23
122 Jeremy Giambi .75 .23
123 Trevor Hoffman .75 .23
124 Barry Bonds 5.00 1.50
125 Rich Aurilia .75 .23
126 Jeff Kent .75 .23
127 Tsuyoshi Shinjo .75 .23
128 Ichiro Suzuki 3.00 .90
129 Edgar Martinez 1.25 .35
130 Freddy Garcia .75 .23
131 Bret Boone .75 .23
132 Matt Morris .75 .23
133 Tino Martinez 1.25 .35
134 Albert Pujols 4.00 1.20
135 J.D. Drew .75 .23
136 Jim Edmonds .75 .23
137 Gabe Kapler .75 .23
138 Paul Wilson .75 .23
139 Ben Grieve .75 .23
140 Wade Miller .75 .23
141 Chan Ho Park .75 .23
142 Alex Rodriguez 3.00 .90
143 Rafael Palmeiro 1.25 .35
144 Juan Gonzalez 2.00 .60
145 Ivan Rodriguez 2.00 .60
146 Carlos Delgado .75 .23
147 Jose Cruz Jr. .75 .23
148 Shannon Stewart .75 .23
149 Raul Mondesi .75 .23
150 Vernon Wells .75 .23
151 So Taguchi RP RC 8.00 2.40
152 Kazuhisa Ishii RP RC 10.00 3.00
153 Hank Blalock RP 8.00 2.40
154 Sean Burroughs RP 5.00 1.50
155 Geronimo Gil RP 5.00 1.50
156 Jon Rauch RP 5.00 1.50
157 Fernando Rodney RP 5.00 1.50
158 Miguel Asencio RP RC 5.00 1.50
159 Franklyn German RP RC 5.00 1.50
160 Luis Ugueto RP RC 5.00 1.50
161 Jorge Sosa RP RC 5.00 1.50
162 Felix Escalona RP RC 5.00 1.50
163 Colby Lewis RP 5.00 1.50
164 Mark Teixeira RP 8.00 2.40
165 Mark Prior RP 15.00 4.50
166 Francis Beltran RP RC 5.00 1.50
167 Joe Thurston RP 5.00 1.50
168 Earl Snyder RP RC 5.00 1.50
169 Takahito Nomura RP RC 5.00 1.50
170 Bill Hall RP 5.00 1.50
171 Marlon Byrd RP 5.00 1.50
172 Dave Williams RP 5.00 1.50
173 Yorvit Torrealba RP 5.00 1.50
174 Brandon Backe RP RC 5.00 1.50
175 Jorge De La Rosa RP RC 5.00 1.50
176 Brian Mallette RP RC 5.00 1.50
177 Rodrigo Rosario RP RC 5.00 1.50
178 Anderson Machado RP RC 5.00 1.50
179 Jorge Padilla RP RC 5.00 1.50
180 Allan Simpson RP RC 5.00 1.50
181 Doug Devore RP RC 5.00 1.50
182 Steve Bechler RP RC 5.00 1.50
183 Raul Chavez RP RC 5.00 1.50
184 Tom Shearn RP RC 5.00 1.50
185 Ben Howard RP RC 5.00 1.50
186 Chris Baker RP RC 5.00 1.50
187 Travis Hughes RP RC 5.00 1.50
188 Kevin Mench RP 5.00 1.50
189 Drew Henson RP 5.00 1.50
190 Mike Moriarty RP RC 5.00 1.50
191 Corey Thurman RP RC 5.00 1.50
192 Bobby Hill RP 5.00 1.50
193 Steve Kent RP RC 5.00 1.50
194 Satoru Komiyama RP RC 5.00 1.50
195 Jason Lane RP 5.00 1.50
196 Angel Berroa RP 5.00 1.50
197 Brandon Puffer RP RC 5.00 1.50
198 Brian Fitzgerald RP RC 5.00 1.50
199 Rene Reyes RP RC 5.00 1.50
200 Hee Seop Choi RP 8.00 2.40

2002 Playoff Absolute Memorabilia Spectrum

Randomly inserted into packs, this is a parallel to the basic set. The veteran cards (1-150) were issued to a stated print run of 100 serial numbered sets while the rookies and prospects were issued to a stated print run of 50 serial numbered sets.

Nm-Mt Ex-Mt

*SPECTRUM 1-150: 2.5X TO 6X BASIC
72 Hideo Nomo 40.00 12.00
151 So Taguchi RP 15.00 4.50
152 Kazuhisa Ishii RP 40.00 12.00
153 Hank Blalock RP 25.00 7.50
154 Sean Burroughs RP 10.00 3.00
155 Geronimo Gil RP 10.00 3.00
156 Jon Rauch RP 10.00 3.00
157 Fernando Rodney RP 10.00 3.00
158 Miguel Asencio RP 10.00 3.00
159 Franklyn German RP 10.00 3.00
160 Luis Ugueto RP 10.00 3.00
161 Jorge Sosa RP 10.00 3.00
162 Felix Escalona RP 10.00 3.00
163 Colby Lewis RP 10.00 3.00
164 Mark Teixeira RP 25.00 7.50
165 Mark Prior RP 40.00 12.00
166 Francis Beltran RP 10.00 3.00
167 Joe Thurston RP 10.00 3.00
168 Earl Snyder RP 10.00 3.00
169 Takahito Nomura RP 25.00 7.50
170 Bill Hall RP 10.00 3.00
171 Marlon Byrd RP 10.00 3.00
172 Dave Williams RP 10.00 3.00
173 Yorvit Torrealba RP 10.00 3.00
174 Brandon Backe RP 10.00 3.00
175 Jorge De La Rosa RP 15.00 4.50
176 Brian Mallette RP 10.00 3.00
177 Rodrigo Rosario RP 10.00 3.00
178 Anderson Machado RP 10.00 3.00
179 Jorge Padilla RP 10.00 3.00
180 Allan Simpson RP 10.00 3.00
181 Doug Devore RP 10.00 3.00
182 Steve Bechler RP 10.00 3.00
183 Raul Chavez RP 10.00 3.00
184 Tom Shearn RP 10.00 3.00
185 Ben Howard RP 10.00 3.00
186 Chris Baker RP 10.00 3.00
187 Travis Hughes RP 10.00 3.00
188 Kevin Mench RP 10.00 3.00
189 Drew Henson RP 10.00 3.00
190 Mike Moriarty RP 10.00 3.00
191 Corey Thurman RP 10.00 3.00
192 Bobby Hill RP 10.00 3.00
193 Steve Kent RP 10.00 3.00
194 Satoru Komiyama RP 10.00 3.00
195 Jason Lane RP 10.00 3.00
196 Angel Berroa RP 10.00 3.00
197 Brandon Puffer RP 10.00 3.00
198 Brian Fitzgerald RP 10.00 3.00
199 Rene Reyes RP 10.00 3.00
200 Hee Seop Choi RP 15.00 4.50

2002 Playoff Absolute Memorabilia Absolutely Ink

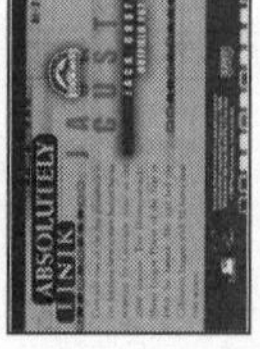

Inserted into packs at stated odds of one in 22 hobby and one in 36 retail, these 59 cards feature a mix of active player and retired superstars who signed cards for this set. Many players were printed to shorter supply and we have notated that information next to their name in our checklist. Cards with a stated print run of 50 or fewer are not priced due to market scarcity.

Nm-Mt Ex-Mt

1 Adrian Beltre 15.00 4.50
2 Alex Rodriguez SP/50
3 Ben Sheets 15.00 4.50
4 Bernie Williams SP/25
5 Bobby Doerr 20.00 6.00
6 Blaine Neal 10.00 3.00
7 Carlos Beltran 15.00 4.50
8 Carlos Pena 10.00 3.00
10 Corey Patterson SP/150 20.00 6.00
11 Curt Schilling SP/15
12 Dave Parker 15.00 4.50
13 David Justice SP/65 40.00 12.00
14 Don Mattingly SP/75 120.00 36.00
15 Duaner Sanchez 10.00 3.00
16 Eric Chavez SP/100 20.00 6.00
17 Freddy Garcia SP/200 20.00 6.00
18 Gary Carter SP/150 30.00 9.00
19 Gary Sheffield SP/25
20 George Brett SP/25
21 Greg Maddux SP/25
22 Ivan Rodriguez SP/50
23 J.D. Drew SP/100 20.00 6.00
24 Jack Cust 10.00 3.00
25 Jason Michaels 10.00 3.00
26 Jermaine Dye SP/125 20.00 6.00
27 Jim Palmer SP/150 20.00 6.00
28 Jose Vidro 15.00 4.50
29 Josh Towers 10.00 3.00
30 Kerry Wood SP/50 50.00 15.00
31 Kirby Puckett SP/50 100.00 30.00
32 Luis Gonzalez SP/75 40.00 12.00
33 Luis Rivera 10.00 3.00
34 Manny Ramirez SP/50 40.00 12.00
35 Marcus Giles 15.00 4.50
36 Mark Prior SP/100 60.00 18.00
37 Mark Teixeira SP/100 25.00 7.50
38 Marlon Byrd SP/250 20.00 6.00
39 Matt Ginter 10.00 3.00
40 Moises Alou SP/150 20.00 6.00
41 Nate Frese 10.00 3.00
42 Nick Johnson 15.00 4.50
43 Nomar Garciaparra SP/15
44 Pablo Ozuna 10.00 3.00
45 Paul Lo Duca SP/200 20.00 6.00
46 Richie Sexson 15.00 4.50
47 Roberto Alomar SP/100 50.00 15.00
48 Roy Oswalt SP/300 20.00 6.00
49 Ryan Klesko SP/75 30.00 9.00
50 Sean Casey SP/125 20.00 6.00
51 Shannon Stewart 15.00 4.50
52 So Taguchi 20.00 6.00
53 Terrence Long 15.00 4.50
54 Timo Perez 10.00 3.00
55 Todd Helton SP/25
56 Tony Gwynn SP/50 80.00 24.00
57 Troy Glaus SP/300 30.00 9.00
58 Vladimir Guerrero SP/225 50.00 15.00
59 Wade Miller 15.00 4.50
60 Wilson Betemit 10.00 3.00

2002 Playoff Absolute Memorabilia Absolutely Ink Gold

This is a partial parallel to the Absolutely Ink insert set. Each card can be identified by the gold foil printing as well as being issued to a stated print run of 25 serial numbered sets. Due to market scarcity, no pricing is provided for these cards.

Nm-Mt Ex-Mt

3 Ben Sheets
5 Bobby Doerr
7 Carlos Beltran
8 Carlos Pena
10 Corey Patterson
12 Dave Parker
15 Duaner Sanchez
16 Eric Chavez
18 Gary Carter
23 J.D. Drew
24 Jack Cust
28 Jose Vidro
33 Luis Rivera
37 Mark Teixeira
38 Marlon Byrd
41 Nate Frese
42 Nick Johnson
44 Pablo Ozuna
45 Paul Lo Duca
46 Richie Sexson
48 Roy Oswalt
52 So Taguchi
53 Terrence Long
54 Timo Perez
59 Wade Miller

2002 Playoff Absolute Memorabilia Absolutely Ink Numbers

This is a parallel to the Absolutely Ink insert set. Each card can be identified as they were issued to that player's print uniform number. If a player signed 25 or fewer or these cards, there is no pricing due to market scarcity.

Nm-Mt Ex-Mt

1 Adrian Beltre/29 30.00 9.00
2 Alex Rodriguez/3
3 Ben Sheets/15
5 Bobby Doerr/1
7 Carlos Beltran/15
8 Carlos Pena/15
10 Corey Patterson/20
12 Dave Parker/39 40.00 12.00
13 David Justice/23
14 Don Mattingly/23
16 Eric Chavez/3
17 Freddy Garcia/34 30.00 9.00
18 Gary Carter/8
19 Gary Sheffield/10
20 George Brett/5
21 Greg Maddux/31
22 Ivan Rodriguez/7
23 J.D. Drew/7
24 Jack Cust/67 15.00 4.50
25 Jason Michaels/22
26 Jermaine Dye/24
27 Jim Palmer/22
28 Jose Vidro/3
29 Josh Towers/35 25.00 7.50
30 Kerry Wood/34 80.00 24.00
31 Kirby Puckett/34 120.00 36.00
32 Luis Gonzalez/20
33 Luis Rivera/60 15.00 4.50
34 Manny Ramirez/24
35 Marcus Giles/22
36 Mark Prior/22
40 Moises Alou/18
42 Nick Johnson/36 30.00 9.00
43 Nomar Garciaparra/5
44 Pablo Ozuna/3
45 Paul Lo Duca/16
46 Richie Sexson/11
47 Roberto Alomar/12
48 Roy Oswalt/44 25.00 7.50
49 Ryan Klesko/30 30.00 9.00
50 Sean Casey/21
51 Shannon Stewart/24
52 So Taguchi/99 30.00 9.00
53 Terrence Long/12
54 Timo Perez/6
56 Tony Gwynn/19
57 Troy Glaus/25
58 Vladimir Guerrero/27
59 Wade Miller/52 25.00 7.50
60 Wilson Betemit/24

2002 Playoff Absolute Memorabilia Game-Used Bonus

Randomly inserted into packs, these 71 8" by 10" cards feature special pieces from a player's uniform. Each card was issued to a stated print run of one serial numbered set and thus there is no pricing due to market scarcity.

Nm-Mt Ex-Mt

1 Craig Biggio 7
2 Orlando Cabrera 18
3 Rod Carew 29
4 Rod Carew 25th Logo
5 Rod Carew CA Logo
6 Steve Carlton 32
7 Gary Carter 8
8 Sean Casey Logo
9 Roger Clemens Logo
10 Darin Erstad 40th Logo
11 Carlton Fisk 27
12 Carlton Fisk 72
13 Carlton Fisk Logo
14 Brian Giles Name
15 Juan Gonzalez Logo
16 Shawn Green 15
17 Shawn Green Logo
18 Vladimir Guerrero 27
19 Vladimir Guerrero Logo
20 Tony Gwynn Logo
21 Todd Helton 17
22 Todd Helton Logo
23 Rickey Henderson Mets 24
24 Rickey Henderson Mets Logo
25 Rickey Henderson Padres Logo
26 Rickey Henderson Padres Patch
27 Rickey Henderson Padres 24
28 Bo Jackson 6
29 Bo Jackson Patch
30 Randy Johnson Logo
31 Carlos Lee 45
32 Paul Lo Duca Gray/16
33 Paul Lo Duca White/16
34 Edgar Martinez Logo
35 Eddie Mathews Logo
36 Joe Mays TC Logo
37 Paul Molitor 4
38 Stan Musial Collar
39 Hideo Nomo 16
40 Magglio Ordonez Logo
41 Roy Oswalt Patch
42 Chan Ho Park Name
43 Mike Piazza Gray/31
44 Mike Piazza Gray/Logo
45 Mike Piazza Stripe/31
46 Mike Piazza Stripe/Logo
47 Aramis Ramirez 16
48 Cal Ripken 8
49 Brooks Robinson 5
50 Alex Rodriguez AL 100 Patch
51 Alex Rodriguez Flag Patch
52 Ivan Rodriguez Flag Patch
53 Nolan Ryan Angels 30
54 Nolan Ryan Angels Logo
55 Nolan Ryan Rangers 34
56 Ryne Sandberg Logo
57 Curt Schilling A Logo
58 Curt Schilling Patch
59 Tom Seaver Logo
60 Gary Sheffield 10
61 Warren Spahn 21
62 Warren Spahn Logo
63 Mike Sweeney 29
64 Frank Thomas 35
65 Frank Thomas AL 100 Patch
66 Joe Torre 15
67 Jose Vidro 3
68 Omar Vizquel AL 100 Patch
69 Matt Williams Logo
70 Robin Yount 19
71 Barry Zito 75

2002 Playoff Absolute Memorabilia Signing Bonus

Inserted into "full" boxes at one per box an with a SRP of $40 per frame, these 313 item was highlighted by a signature of the feature player. These frame have all different state print runs and we have notated that informatio in our checklist next to their names. Frame with a print run of 25 or less are not priced du to market scarcity.

Nm-Mt Ex-M

1 Bob Abreu Gray-N/53 60.00 18.00
2 Bob Abreu Stripe-N/53 60.00 18.00
3 Grover Alexander Gray/1
4 Rob Alomar Gray-N/12
5 Rob Alomar Gray-N/100 80.00 24.00
6 Rob Alomar Stripe-N/100 80.00 24.00
7 Moises Alou Blue-L/250 40.00 12.00
8 Moises Alou Blue-N/18
9 Moises Alou Gray-N/18
10 Moises Alou Stripe-L/250 40.00 12.00
11 Moises Alou Stripe-N/18
12 Jeff Bagwell Gray-N/5
13 Jeff Bagwell Red-N/5
14 Jeff Bagwell Stripe-N/5
15 Jeff Bagwell White-N/5
16 Carlos Beltran Black-N/15
17 Carlos Beltran Blue-N/50 60.00 18.00
18 Carlos Beltran Gray-N/50 60.00 18.00
19 Carlos Beltran White-N/15
20 Adrian Beltre Blue-N/150 40.00 12.00
21 Adrian Beltre Gray-N/150 40.00 12.00
22 Adrian Beltre White-N/29
23 Lance Berkman Gray-N/17
24 Lance Berkman Red-N/17
25 Lance Berkman Stripe-N/17
26 Lance Berkman White-N/17
27 Angel Berroa Black-N/100 30.00 9.00
28 Angel Berroa Blue-N/100 30.00 9.00
29 Angel Berroa Gray-N/50 40.00 12.00
30 Angel Berroa White-N/4
31 Wilson Betemit Gray-N/250 25.00 7.50
32 Wilson Betemit White-N/250 25.00 7.50
33 Craig Biggio Gray-N/7
34 Craig Biggio Red-N/7
35 Craig Biggio Stripe-N/7
36 Craig Biggio White-N/7
37 Hank Blalock Blue-N/12
38 Hank Blalock Gray-N/50 100.00 30.00
39 Hank Blalock White-N/100 60.00 18.00
40 George Brett Blue-N/5
41 George Brett Gray-N/5
42 George Brett White-N/5
43 Lou Brock Gray-N/100 60.00 18.00
44 Lou Brock White-N/200 50.00 15.00
45 Kevin Brown Blue-N/27 80.00 24.00
46 Kevin Brown Gray-N/150 40.00 12.00
47 Kevin Brown White-N/100 50.00 15.00
48 Mark Buehrle Black-N/200 40.00 12.00
49 Mark Buehrle Gray-N/200 40.00 12.00
50 Mark Buehrle Stripe-N/56 60.00 18.00
51 Sean Burroughs Blue-N/21
52 Sean Burroughs Gray-N/21
53 Sean Burroughs White-N/21
54 Marlon Byrd Gray-N/61 60.00 18.00
55 Marlon Byrd Stripe-N/61 60.00 18.00
56 Steve Carlton Gray-N/100 120.00 36.00
57 Steve Carlton Stripe-N/150 100.00 30.00
58 Sean Casey Gray-N/21
59 Sean Casey Stripe-L/100 50.00 15.00
60 Sean Casey Stripe-N/21
61 Eric Chavez Gray-N/25
62 Eric Chavez Green-N/3
63 Eric Chavez White-N/28 120.00 36.00
64 Roger Clemens Gray-N/10
65 Roger Clemens Stripe-N/10
66 Ty Cobb Gray/6
67 Eddie Collins Gray/1
68 Juan Cruz Blue-L/51 40.00 12.00
69 Juan Cruz Blue-N/51 40.00 12.00
70 Juan Cruz Gray-N/51 40.00 12.00
71 Juan Cruz Stripe-L/51 40.00 12.00
72 Juan Cruz Stripe-N/51 40.00 12.00
73 J.D. Drew Gray-N/100 50.00 15.00
74 J.D. Drew White-N/7
75 Bran Duckworth Gray-N/56 40.00 12.00
76 B.Duckworth Stripe-N/150 25.00 7.50
77 Adam Dunn Gray-N/10
78 Adam Dunn Stripe-L/10
79 Adam Dunn Stripe-N/44 100.00 30.00
80 Jermaine Dye Gray-N/250 40.00 12.00
81 Jermaine Dye Green-N/100 50.00 15.00
82 Jermaine Dye White-N/100 50.00 15.00
83 Morg Ensberg Gray-N/100 30.00 9.00
84 Morg Ensberg Red-N/100 30.00 9.00
85 Morg Ensberg Stripe-N/100 30.00 9.00
86 Morg Ensberg White-N/100 30.00 9.00
87 Darin Erstad Gray-N/5
88 Darin Erstad White-N/17
89 Cliff Floyd Gray-N/200 40.00 12.00
90 Cliff Floyd Stripe-N/200 40.00 12.00
91 Jimmie Foxx Gray/1
92 Freddy Garcia Blue-N/34 80.00 24.00
93 Freddy Garcia Gray-N/34 80.00 24.00
94 Freddy Garcia White-N/125 40.00 12.00
95 Nomar Garciaparra Gray-N/5
96 Nomar Garciaparra White-N/5
97 Troy Glaus Gray-N/50 100.00 30.00
98 Troy Glaus White-N/100 60.00 18.00
99 Tom Glavine Gray-N/25
100 Tom Glavine White-N/200 80.00 24.00
101 Luis Gonzalez Black-N/20

102 Luis Gonzalez Gray-N/125 .. 80.00 24.00
103 Luis Gonzalez Purple-N/125 80.00 24.00
104 Luis Gonzalez Stripe-N/125 80.00 24.00
105 Hank Greenberg Gray/1
106 Vlad Guerrero Gray-N/27
107 V.Guerrero Stripe-N/150 .. 150.00 45.00
108 Tony Gwynn Blue-N/19
109 Tony Gwynn Gray-N/19
110 Tony Gwynn White-N/19
111 Rich Hidalgo Gray-N/100 ... 50.00 15.00
112 Rich Hidalgo Red-N/135 ..... 40.00 12.00
113 Rich Hidalgo Stripe-N/15
114 Rich Hidalgo White-N/150 .. 40.00 12.00
115 Rogers Hornsby Gray/1
116 Tim Hudson Gray-N/50 .... 100.00 30.00
117 Tim Hudson Green-N/100 .. 60.00 18.00
118 Tim Hudson White-N/15
119 Kazuhisa Ishii Blue-N/17
120 Kazuhisa Ishii Gray-N/17
121 Kazuhisa Ishii White-N/17
122 Reg Jackson Gray-N/44 ... 120.00 36.00
123 Reg Jackson Stripe-N/44 . 150.00 45.00
124 Nick Johnson Gray-N/200 .. 40.00 12.00
125 Nick Johnson Stripe-N/200 40.00 12.00
126 Walter Johnson Gray/4
127 Andruw Jones Gray-N/75 . 100.00 30.00
128 Andruw Jones White-N/25
129 Chipper Jones Gray-N/10
130 Chipper Jones White-N/10
131 Al Kaline Gray-N/6
132 Al Kaline White-L/250 .... 80.00 24.00
133 Al Kaline White-N/6
134 Gabe Kapler Blue-N/125 ..... 25.00 7.50
135 Gabe Kapler Gray-N/18
136 Gabe Kapler White-N/175 ... 25.00 7.50
137 Ryan Klesko Blue-N/30 .... 80.00 24.00
138 Ryan Klesko Gray-N/30 ...... 80.00 24.00
139 Ryan Klesko White-N/30 .... 80.00 24.00
140 Nap Lajoie Gray/1
141 Jason Lane Gray-N/100 ...... 30.00 9.00
142 Jason Lane Red-N/100 .... 30.00 9.00
143 Jason Lane Stripe-N/100 .... 30.00 9.00
144 Jason Lane White-N/100 .... 30.00 9.00
145 Barry Larkin Gray-N/50 .... 100.00 30.00
146 Barry Larkin Stripe-L/100 ... 80.00 24.00
147 Barry Larkin Stripe-N/11
148 Paul LoDuca Blue-N/16
149 Paul LoDuca Gray-N/16
150 Paul LoDuca White-N/50 .... 60.00 18.00
151 Fred Lynn Gray-N/250 .... 40.00 12.00
152 Fred Lynn White-N/150 ...... 40.00 12.00
153 Connie Mack Gray/2
154 Greg Maddux Gray-N/31 .. 200.00 60.00
155 Greg Maddux White-N/31. 200.00 60.00
156 Roger Maris Gray/3
157 Edgar Martinez Blue-N/150 80.00 24.00
158 Edgar Martinez Gray-N/150 80.00 24.00
159 Edgar Martinez White-N/11
160 Pedro Martinez Gray-N/5
161 P.Martinez White-N/45 ..... 150.00 45.00
162 Don Mattingly Gray-N/100 200.00 60.00
163 D.Mattingly Stripe-N/100 . 200.00 60.00
164 Will McCovey Gray-N/190 .. 50.00 15.00
165 Will McCovey White-N/250 50.00 15.00
166 Wade Miller Gray-N/150 ..... 40.00 12.00
167 Wade Miller Stripe-N/250 ... 40.00 12.00
168 Wade Miller Red-N/52 .... 60.00 18.00
169 Wade Miller White-N/52 ..... 60.00 18.00
170 Paul Molitor Blue-N/75 ..... 100.00 30.00
171 Paul Molitor Gray-N/100 .... 60.00 18.00
172 Paul Molitor White-N/125 ... 80.00 24.00
173 Mark Mulder Gray-N/20
174 Mark Mulder Green-N/20
175 Mark Mulder White-N/40 .. 100.00 30.00
176 Mike Mussina Gray-N/5
177 Mike Mussina Stripe-N/5
178 Jose Ortiz Gray-N/125 .... 25.00 7.50
179 Jose Ortiz Purple-N/125 ..... 25.00 7.50
180 Jose Ortiz Stripe-L/125 ...... 25.00 7.50
181 Jose Ortiz Stripe-N/125 ...... 25.00 7.50
182 Roy Oswalt Gray-N/44 .... 60.00 18.00
183 Roy Oswalt Red-N/44 .... 60.00 18.00
184 Roy Oswalt Stripe-N/100 .... 50.00 15.00
185 Roy Oswalt White-N/100 .... 50.00 15.00
186 Mel Ott Gray/3
187 Rafael Palmeiro Blue-N/25
188 Rafael Palmeiro Gray-N/25
189 Rafael Palmeiro White-N/25
190 Jim Palmer Gray-N/250 ...... 40.00 12.00
191 Jim Palmer White-N/150 .... 40.00 12.00
192 Dave Parker Black-N/150 ... 50.00 15.00
193 Dave Parker White-N/150 ... 50.00 15.00
194 Cor Patterson Blue-L/250 ... 40.00 12.00
195 Cor Patterson Blue-N/20
196 Cor Patterson Gray-N/250 .. 40.00 12.00
197 Cor Patterson Stripe-L/250 40.00 12.00
198 Cor Patterson Stripe-N/250 40.00 12.00
199 Carlos Pena Gray-N/19
200 Carlos Pena Green-N/250 ... 25.00 7.50
201 Carlos Pena White-N/150 ... 25.00 7.50
202 Tony Perez Gray-N/24
203 Tony Perez Stripe-L/250 ..... 40.00 12.00
204 Tony Perez Stripe-N/24
205 Juan Pierre Gray-N/75 .... 60.00 18.00
206 Juan Pierre Purple-N/75 ..... 40.00 12.00
207 Juan Pierre White-L/75 ...... 40.00 12.00
208 Juan Pierre White-N/75 ...... 40.00 12.00
209 Mark Prior Blue-L/75 .... 150.00 45.00
210 Mark Prior Blue-N/125 ..... 120.00 36.00
211 Mark Prior Gray-N/75 .... 150.00 45.00
212 Mark Prior Stripe-L/50 ..... 200.00 60.00
213 Mark Prior Stripe-N/22
214 Kirby Puckett Blue-N/34 ... 150.00 45.00
215 Kirby Puckett Gray-N/34
216 Kirby Puckett Stripe-N/34. 150.00 45.00
217 Albert Pujols Gray-N/5
218 Albert Pujols White-N/100 200.00 60.00
219 Aram Ramirez Black-N/125 40.00 12.00
220 Aram Ramirez Gray-N/50 ... 60.00 18.00
221 Aram Ramirez White-N/16
222 Manny Ramirez Gray-N/24
223 Manny Ramirez White-N/5
224 Phil Rizzuto Gray-N/250 ... 100.00 30.00
225 Phil Rizzuto Stripe-N/10
226 B.Robinson Gray-N/250 ..... 80.00 24.00
227 B.Robinson White-N/150 . 100.00 30.00
227A Brooks Robinson ERR White-N/150
Card says in print it was signed by Jim Palmer
228 Jackie Robinson Gray/3
229 Alex Rodriguez Blue-N/3
230 Alex Rodriguez Gray-N/15
231 Alex Rodriguez White-N/15
232 Ivan Rodriguez Blue-N/7
233 Ivan Rodriguez Gray-N/7
234 Ivan Rodriguez White-N/7
235 Scott Rolen Gray-N/17
236 Scott Rolen Stripe-N/17
237 Babe Ruth Gray/8
238 N.Ryan Angel Gray-N/30 .. 250.00 75.00
239 N.Ryan Angel White-N/30 250.00 75.00
240 N.Ryan Astro Gray-N/34 ... 250.00 75.00
241 N.Ryan Astro White-N/34 . 250.00 75.00
242 N.Ryan Rgr Blue-N/34 ...... 250.00 75.00
243 N.Ryan Rgr Gray-N/34 ..... 250.00 75.00
244 N.Ryan Rgr White-N/34 .... 250.00 75.00
245 C.C. Sabathia Blue-N/15
246 C.C. Sabathia Gray-N/10
247 C.C. Sabathia White-N/10
248 Ryne Sandberg Blue-L/50 200.00 60.00
249 Ryne Sandberg Blue-N/23
250 Ryne Sandberg Gray-N/23
251 R.Sandberg Stripe-L/50 ... 200.00 60.00
252 Ryne Sandberg Stripe-N/23
253 Curt Schilling Black-N/10
254 Curt Schilling Gray-N/10
255 Curt Schilling Purple-N/10
256 Curt Schilling Stripe-N/5
257 Mike Schmidt Gray-N/100 120.00 36.00
258 M.Schmidt Stripe-N/100 .. 150.00 45.00
259 Richie Sexson Blue-N/100 .. 50.00 15.00
260 Richie Sexson Gray-N/100 . 50.00 15.00
261 Richie Sexson White-N/100 50.00 15.00
262 Ben Sheets Blue-N/150 ...... 40.00 12.00
263 Ben Sheets Gray-N/100 ...... 50.00 15.00
264 Ben Sheets White-N/100 .... 50.00 15.00
265 Gary Sheffield Gray-N/11
266 Gary Sheffield White-N/11
267 George Sisler Gray/3
268 Alfonso Soriano Gray-N/12
269 A.Soriano Stripe-N/100 ...... 80.00 24.00
270 Tris Speaker Gray/1
271 Shan Stewart Blue-N/150 ... 40.00 12.00
272 Shan Stewart Gray-N/100 ... 30.00 9.00
273 Shan Stewart White-N/24
274 Mike Sweeney Black-N/100 50.00 15.00
275 Mike Sweeney Blue-N/100 . 50.00 15.00
276 Mike Sweeney Gray-N/100 . 50.00 15.00
277 Mike Sweeney White-N/100 50.00 15.00
278 So Taguchi Gray-N/99 .... 60.00 18.00
279 So Taguchi White-N/99 ...... 60.00 18.00
280 Mark Teixeira Blue-N/100 ... 60.00 18.00
281 Mark Teixeira Gray-N/23
282 Mark Teixeira White-N/100. 60.00 18.00
283 Miguel Tejada Gray-N/50 ... 60.00 18.00
284 Miguel Tejada Green-N/4
285 Miguel Tejada White-N/40 .. 60.00 18.00
286 Frank Thomas Black-N/35 180.00 55.00
287 Frank Thomas Gray-N/10
288 Frank Thomas White-N/10
289 Juan Uribe Gray-N/25
290 Juan Uribe Purple-N/25
291 Juan Uribe White-L/4
292 Juan Uribe White-N/4
293 Jav Vazquez Gray-N/125 .... 40.00 12.00
294 Jav Vazquez Stripe-N/125 .. 40.00 12.00
295 Jose Vidro Gray-N/150 ...... 40.00 12.00
296 Jose Vidro Stripe-N/150 ..... 40.00 12.00
297 Honus Wagner Gray/11
298 Bernie Williams Gray-N/15
299 Bernie Williams Stripe-N/15
300 Ted Williams Gray/1
301 Hack Wilson Gray/1
302 Dave Winfield Gray-N/25
303 Dave Winfield Stripe-N/25
304 Kerry Wood Blue-L/34 ...... 150.00 45.00
305 Kerry Wood Blue-N/34 ..... 150.00 45.00
306 Kerry Wood Gray-N/34 ..... 150.00 45.00
307 Kerry Wood Stripe-L/34 ... 150.00 45.00
308 Kerry Wood Stripe-N/34 ... 150.00 45.00
309 Cy Young Gray/2
310 Barry Zito Gray-N/25
311 Barry Zito Green-N/25
312 Barry Zito White-N/50 ...... 100.00 30.00

2002 Playoff Absolute Memorabilia Signing Bonus Entry Cards

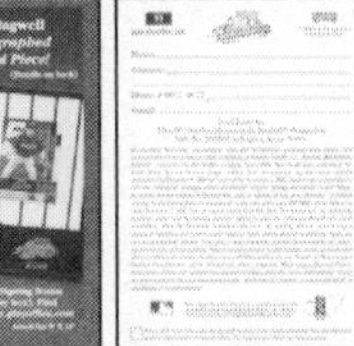

Issued one per pack, these 20 cards are "contest" cards which when sent in enabled collectors to win various items relating to the featured player.

Nm-Mt Ex-Mt
1 Chipper Jones
2 Mark Prior
3 Adam Dunn
5 Kazuhisa Ishii
6 Vladimir Guerrero
7 Greg Maddux
8 Nomar Garciaparra
10 Ryne Sandberg
11 Jeff Bagwell
12 Paul Molitor
13 George Brett
14 Kirby Puckett
16 Reggie Jackson
17 Roger Clemens
18 Tony Gwynn
19 Albert Pujols
20 Alex Rodriguez
DM Don Mattingly
LB Lance Berkman
PM Pedro Martinez

2002 Playoff Absolute Memorabilia Team Quads

Inserted into hobby packs at a stated rate of one in 18, these cards feature four players from 20 of the 30 different major league teams.

Nm-Mt Ex-Mt
*GOLD: .75X TO 2X BASIC QUADS
*SPECTRUM: .6X TO 1.5X BASIC QUADS
SPECTRUM ODDS 1:36 HOBBY
1 Troy Glaus 5.00 1.50
Darin Erstad
Garret Anderson
Troy Percival
2 Curt Schilling 5.00 1.50
Randy Johnson
Luis Gonzalez
Mark Grace
3 Chipper Jones 8.00 2.40
Andruw Jones
Greg Maddux
Tom Glavine
4 Nomar Garciaparra 8.00 2.40
Manny Ramirez
Trot Nixon
Pedro Martinez
5 Kerry Wood 8.00 2.40
Sammy Sosa
Fred McGriff
Moises Alou
6 Frank Thomas 5.00 1.50
Magglio Ordonez
Mark Buehrle
Kenny Lofton
7 Ken Griffey Jr. 8.00 2.40
Barry Larkin
Adam Dunn
Sean Casey
8 C.C Sabathia 5.00 1.50
Jim Thome
Bartolo Colon
Russell Branyan
9 Todd Helton 5.00 1.50
Larry Walker
Juan Pierre
Mike Hampton
10 Jeff Bagwell 5.00 1.50
Craig Biggio
Lance Berkman
Richard Hidalgo
11 Shawn Green 5.00 1.50
Adrian Beltre
Hideo Nomo
Paul Lo Duca
12 Mike Piazza 8.00 2.40
Roberto Alomar
Mo Vaughn
Roger Cedeno
13 Roger Clemens 12.00 3.60
Derek Jeter
Jason Giambi
Mike Mussina
14 Barry Zito 5.00 1.50
Tim Hudson
Eric Chavez
Miguel Tejada
15 Pat Burrell 5.00 1.50
Scott Rolen
Bobby Abreu
Marlon Byrd
16 Bernie Williams 5.00 1.50
Jorge Posada
Alfonso Soriano
Andy Pettitte
17 Barry Bonds 10.00 3.00
Rich Aurilia
Tsuyoshi Shinjo
Jeff Kent
18 Ichiro Suzuki 8.00 2.40
Kazuhiro Sasaki
Bret Boone
Edgar Martinez
19 Albert Pujols 10.00 3.00
J.D. Drew
Jim Edmonds
Tino Martinez
20 Alex Rodriguez 8.00 2.40
Ivan Rodriguez
Juan Gonzalez
Rafael Palmeiro

2002 Playoff Absolute Memorabilia Team Quads Materials

Randomly inserted into packs, these 19 cards parallel the Team Quads insert set. Each card be identified by both the four pieces of memorabilia on the card as well as having a stated print run of 100 serial numbered sets. Please note that card number 7 does not exist.

Nm-Mt Ex-Mt
1 Troy Glaus Jsy 40.00 12.00
Darin Erstad Jsy
Garret Anderson Jsy
Troy Percival Jsy
2 Curt Schilling Jsy 40.00 12.00
Randy Johnson Jsy
Luis Gonzalez Jsy
Mark Grace Jsy
3 Chipper Jones Jsy 50.00 15.00
Andruw Jones Jsy
Greg Maddux Jsy
Tom Glavine Jsy
4 Nomar Garciaparra Jsy 50.00 15.00
Manny Ramirez Jsy
Pedro Martinez Jsy
Trot Nixon Bat
5 Kerry Wood Base 40.00 12.00
Sammy Sosa Base
Fred McGriff Base
Moises Alou Base
6 Frank Thomas Jsy 40.00 12.00
Magglio Ordonez Jsy
Mark Buehrle Jsy
Kenny Lofton Bat
7 Does Not Exist
8 C.C Sabathia Jsy 40.00 12.00
Jim Thome Jsy
Bartolo Colon Jsy
Russell Branyan Jsy
9 Todd Helton Jsy 40.00 12.00
Larry Walker Jsy
Juan Pierre Jsy
Mike Hampton Jsy
10 Jeff Bagwell Jsy 40.00 12.00
Craig Biggio Jsy
Lance Berkman Jsy
Richard Hidalgo Pants
11 Shawn Green Jsy 60.00 18.00
Adrian Beltre Jsy
Hideo Nomo Jsy
Paul Lo Duca Jsy
12 Mike Piazza Jsy 40.00 12.00
Roberto Alomar Shoe
Mo Vaughn Bat
Roger Cedeno Bat
13 Roger Clemens Base 80.00 24.00
Derek Jeter Ball
Jason Giambi Ball
Mike Mussina Ball
14 Barry Zito Jsy 40.00 12.00
Tim Hudson Jsy
Eric Chavez Bat
Miguel Tejada Jsy
15 Pat Burrell Jsy 40.00 12.00
Scott Rolen Jsy
Bobby Abreu Jsy
Marlon Byrd Jsy
16 Bernie Williams Jsy 40.00 12.00
Jorge Posada Jsy
Alfonso Soriano Bat
Andy Pettitte Jsy
17 Barry Bonds Ball 50.00 15.00
Rich Aurilia Base
Tsuyoshi Shinjo Base
Jeff Kent Base
18 Ichiro Deck 80.00 24.00
Kazuhiro Sasaki Deck
Edgar Martinez Base
Bret Boone Base
19 Albert Pujols Ball 60.00 18.00
J.D. Drew Base
Jim Edmonds Base
Tino Martinez Base
20 Alex Rodriguez Jsy 40.00 12.00
Ivan Rodriguez Jsy
Juan Gonzalez Jsy
Rafael Palmeiro Jsy

2002 Playoff Absolute Memorabilia Team Tandems

Inserted into hobby packs at stated odds of one in 12 hobby and one in 36 retail packs, these 40 cards feature two stars who are also teammates.

Nm-Mt Ex-Mt
*GOLD: .75X TO 2X BASIC TANDEMS
GOLD ODDS 1:72 HOBBY, 1:216 RETAIL
*SPECTRUM: .6X TO 1.5X BASIC TANDEMS
SPECTRUM ODDS 1:36 HOBBY
1 Troy Glaus .... 3.00 .90
Darin Erstad
2 Curt Schilling 5.00 1.50
Randy Johnson
3 Chipper Jones 5.00 1.50
Andruw Jones
4 Greg Maddux 8.00 2.40
Tom Glavine
5 Nomar Garciaparra 8.00 2.40
Manny Ramirez
6 Pedro Martinez 5.00 1.50
Trot Nixon
7 Kerry Wood 8.00 2.40
Sammy Sosa
8 Frank Thomas 5.00 1.50
Magglio Ordonez
9 Ken Griffey Jr. 8.00 2.40
Barry Larkin
10 C.C Sabathia 5.00 1.50
Jim Thome
11 Todd Helton .... 3.00 .90
Larry Walker
12 Bobby Higginson .... 3.00 .90
Shane Halter
13 Cliff Floyd .... 3.00 .90
Brad Penny
14 Jeff Bagwell .... 3.00 .90
Craig Biggio
15 Shawn Green .... 3.00 .90
Adrian Beltre
16 Ben Sheets .... 3.00 .90
Richie Sexson
17 Vladimir Guerrero 5.00 1.50
Jose Vidro
18 Mike Piazza 8.00 2.40
Roberto Alomar
19 Roger Clemens 10.00 3.00
Mike Mussina
20 Derek Jeter 12.00 3.60
Jason Giambi
21 Barry Zito .... 3.00 .90
Tim Hudson
22 Eric Chavez .... 3.00 .90
Miguel Tejada
23 Pat Burrell .... 3.00 .90
Scott Rolen
24 Brian Giles .... 3.00 .90
Aramis Ramirez
25 Ryan Klesko .... 3.00 .90
Phil Nevin
26 Barry Bonds 10.00 3.00
Rich Aurilia
27 Ichiro Suzuki 8.00 2.40
Kazuhiro Sasaki
28 Albert Pujols 10.00 3.00
J.D. Drew
29 Alex Rodriguez 8.00 2.40
Ivan Rodriguez
30 Carlos Delgado .... 3.00 .90
Shannon Stewart
31 Mo Vaughn .... 3.00 .90
Roger Cedeno
32 Carlos Beltran .... 3.00 .90
Mike Sweeney
33 Edgar Martinez .... 3.00 .90
Bret Boone
34 Juan Gonzalez 5.00 1.50
Rafael Palmeiro
35 Johnny Damon 5.00 1.50
Rickey Henderson
36 Sean Casey .... 3.00 .90
Adam Dunn
37 Jeff Kent .... 3.00 .90
Tsuyoshi Shinjo
38 Lance Berkman .... 3.00 .90
Richard Hidalgo
39 So Taguchi .... 3.00 .90
Tino Martinez
40 Hideo Nomo 8.00 2.40
Kazuhisa Ishii

2002 Playoff Absolute Memorabilia Team Tandems Materials

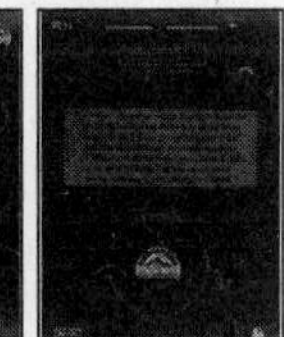

Inserted into hobby packs at a stated rate of one in 33 hobby and one in 164 retail, these 40 cards form a complete parallel to the Team Tandem insert set. These cards feature two pieces of memorabilia on each card. According to the manufacturer a few cards were printed in shorter supply and we have notated the announced print runs next to the card in our checklist. It was believed shortly after release that card 27 was not produced. Copies of the card eventually did surface but it's generally accepted to be one of the shortest cards in the set though a specific print run has never been divulged.

Nm-Mt Ex-Mt
1 Troy Glaus Jsy 15.00 4.50
Darin Erstad Bat
2 Curt Schilling Jsy 15.00 4.50
Randy Johnson Jsy
3 Chipper Jones Bat 15.00 4.50
Andruw Jones Bat
4 Greg Maddux Jsy 25.00 7.50
Tom Glavine Jsy
5 Nomar Garciaparra Bat 25.00 7.50
Manny Ramirez Bat SP/200
6 Pedro Martinez Jsy 20.00 6.00
Trot Nixon Bat SP/200
7 Kerry Wood Base 20.00 6.00
Sammy Sosa Base SP/250
8 Frank Thomas Bat 15.00 4.50
Magglio Ordonez Bat
9 Ken Griffey Jr. Base 15.00 4.50
Barry Larkin Base
10 C.C Sabathia Jsy 20.00 6.00
Jim Thome Bat SP/225
11 Todd Helton Bat 15.00 4.50
Larry Walker Bat
12 Bobby Higginson Bat 10.00 3.00
Shane Halter Bat
13 Cliff Floyd Bat 10.00 3.00
Brad Penny Jsy
14 Jeff Bagwell Bat 15.00 4.50
Craig Biggio Bat
15 Shawn Green Bat 10.00 3.00
Adrian Beltre Bat
16 Ben Sheets Jsy 10.00 3.00
Richie Sexson Bat
17 Vladimir Guerrero Bat 15.00 4.50
Jose Vidro Bat
18 Mike Piazza Bat 20.00 6.00
Roberto Alomar Bat SP/250
19 Roger Clemens Fld Glv 100.00 30.00
Mike Mussina Fld Glv SP/50
20 Derek Jeter Base 30.00 9.00
Jason Giambi Base SP/200
21 Barry Zito Jsy 20.00 6.00
Tim Hudson Shoe SP/200
22 Eric Chavez Bat 15.00 4.50

	Nm-Mt	Ex-Mt
Miguel Tejada Bat SP/200		
23 Pat Burrell Bat	15.00	4.50
Scott Rolen Bat		
24 Brian Giles Bat	10.00	3.00
Aramis Ramirez Bat		
25 Ryan Klesko Bat	15.00	4.50
Phil Nevin Jsy SP/250		
26 Barry Bonds Base	20.00	6.00
Rich Aurilia Base		
27 Ichiro Suzuki Deck		
Kazuhiro Sasaki Deck SP		
28 Albert Pujols Base	20.00	6.00
J.D. Drew Base SP/150		
29 Alex Rodriguez Bat	20.00	6.00
Ivan Rodriguez Bat		
30 Carlos Delgado Bat	10.00	3.00
Shannon Stewart Bat		
31 Mo Vaughn Bat	10.00	3.00
Roger Cedeno Bat		
32 Carlos Beltran Bat	10.00	3.00
Mike Sweeney Bat		
33 Edgar Martinez Bat	15.00	4.50
Bret Boone Bat		
34 Juan Gonzalez Bat	15.00	4.50
Rafael Palmeiro Bat		
35 Johnny Damon Bat	15.00	4.50
Rickey Henderson Bat		
36 Sean Casey Bat	15.00	4.50
Adam Dunn Shoe SP/100		
37 Jeff Kent Bat	15.00	4.50
Tsuyoshi Shinjo Bat SP/250		
38 Lance Berkman Bat	10.00	3.00
Richard Hidalgo Bat		
39 So Taguchi Bat	20.00	6.00
Tino Martinez Bat SP/100		
40 Hideo Nomo Jsy	60.00	18.00
Kazuhisa Ishii Jsy SP/50		

2002 Playoff Absolute Memorabilia Team Tandems Materials Gold

Randomly inserted into packs, this is a parallel to the Team Tandem insert set. Each card has gold foil and was issued to a stated print run of 50 serial numbered sets.

	Nm-Mt	Ex-Mt
1 Troy Glaus Jsy	40.00	12.00
Darin Erstad Jsy		
2 Curt Schilling Jsy	40.00	12.00
Randy Johnson Jsy		
3 Chipper Jones Jsy	40.00	12.00
Andruw Jones Jsy		
4 Greg Maddux Jsy	60.00	18.00
Tom Glavine Jsy		
5 Nomar Garciaparra Jsy	50.00	15.00
Manny Ramirez Jsy		
6 Pedro Martinez Jsy	40.00	12.00
Trot Nixon Bat		
7 Kerry Wood Base	40.00	12.00
Sammy Sosa Ball		
8 Frank Thomas Jsy	40.00	12.00
Magglio Ordonez Jsy		
9 Ken Griffey Jr. Base	40.00	12.00
Barry Larkin Base		
10 C.C Sabathia Jsy	40.00	12.00
Jim Thome Jsy		
11 Todd Helton Jsy	40.00	12.00
Larry Walker Jsy		
12 Bobby Higginson Bat	25.00	7.50
Shane Halter Bat		
13 Cliff Floyd Jsy	25.00	7.50
Brad Penny Jsy		
14 Jeff Bagwell Jsy	40.00	12.00
Craig Biggio Jsy		
15 Shawn Green Jsy	25.00	7.50
Adrian Beltre Jsy		
16 Ben Sheets Jsy	25.00	7.50
Richie Sexson Jsy		
17 Vladimir Guerrero Jsy	40.00	12.00
Jose Vidro Jsy		
18 Mike Piazza Jsy	40.00	12.00
Roberto Alomar Shoe		
19 Roger Clemens Jsy	120.00	36.00
Mike Mussina Shoe		
20 Derek Jeter Ball	60.00	18.00
Jason Giambi Ball		
21 Barry Zito Jsy	40.00	12.00
Tim Hudson Jsy		
22 Eric Chavez Bat	30.00	9.00
Miguel Tejada Jsy		
23 Pat Burrell Jsy	40.00	12.00
Scott Rolen Jsy		
24 Brian Giles Jsy	25.00	7.50
Aramis Ramirez Jsy		
25 Ryan Klesko Fld Glv	30.00	9.00
Phil Nevin Jsy		
26 Barry Bonds Ball	50.00	15.00
Rich Aurilia Base		
27 Ichiro Suzuki Ball	100.00	30.00
Kazuhiro Sasaki Deck		
28 Albert Pujols Ball	40.00	12.00
J.D. Drew Base		
29 Alex Rodriguez Jsy	50.00	15.00
Ivan Rodriguez Jsy		
30 Carlos Delgado Jsy	25.00	7.50
Shannon Stewart Jsy		
31 Mo Vaughn Bat	25.00	7.50
Roger Cedeno Bat		
32 Carlos Beltran Jsy	25.00	7.50
Mike Sweeney Jsy		
33 Edgar Martinez Jsy	40.00	12.00
Bret Boone Jsy		
34 Juan Gonzalez Jsy	40.00	12.00
Rafael Palmeiro Jsy		
35 Johnny Damon Bat	40.00	12.00
Rickey Henderson Bat		
36 Sean Casey Jsy	25.00	7.50
Adam Dunn Hat		
37 Jeff Kent Jsy	30.00	9.00
Tsuyoshi Shinjo Bat		
38 Lance Berkman Jsy	25.00	7.50
Richard Hidalgo Pants		
39 So Taguchi Jsy	30.00	9.00
Tino Martinez Bat		
40 Hideo Nomo Jsy		
Kazuhisa Ishii Jsy		

2002 Playoff Absolute Memorabilia Tools of the Trade

Issued in hobby packs at stated odds of one in nine hobby and one in 24 retail, these 95 cards feature many of the leading players in the game.

	Nm-Mt	Ex-Mt
*GOLD: .75X TO 2X BASIC TOOLS		
GOLD ODDS 1:45 HOBBY, 1:144 RETAIL		
1 Mike Mussina	6.00	1.80
2 Rickey Henderson	6.00	1.80
3 Raul Mondesi	2.50	.75
4 Nomar Garciaparra	10.00	3.00
5 Randy Johnson	6.00	1.80
6 Roger Clemens	12.00	3.60
7 Shawn Green	2.50	.75
8 Todd Helton	4.00	1.20
9 Aramis Ramirez	2.50	.75
10 Barry Larkin	6.00	1.80
11 Byung-Hyun Kim	2.50	.75
12 C.C. Sabathia	2.50	.75
13 Curt Schilling	4.00	1.20
14 Darin Erstad	2.50	.75
15 Eric Karros	2.50	.75
16 Freddy Garcia	2.50	.75
17 Greg Maddux	10.00	3.00
18 Jason Kendall	2.50	.75
19 Jim Thome	6.00	1.80
20 Juan Gonzalez	6.00	1.80
21 Kazuhiro Sasaki	2.50	.75
22 Kerry Wood	6.00	1.80
23 Luis Gonzalez	2.50	.75
24 Mark Mulder	2.50	.75
25 Rich Aurilia	2.50	.75
26 Ray Durham	2.50	.75
27 Ben Grieve	2.50	.75
28 Bret Boone	2.50	.75
29 Edgar Martinez	4.00	1.20
30 Ivan Rodriguez	6.00	1.80
31 Jorge Posada	4.00	1.20
32 Mike Piazza	10.00	3.00
33 Pat Burrell	2.50	.75
34 Robin Ventura	2.50	.75
35 Trot Nixon	4.00	1.20
36 Adrian Beltre	2.50	.75
37 Bernie Williams	4.00	1.20
38 Bobby Abreu	2.50	.75
39 Carlos Delgado	2.50	.75
40 Craig Biggio	4.00	1.20
41 Garret Anderson	2.50	.75
42 Jermaine Dye	2.50	.75
43 Johnny Damon	2.50	.75
44 Tim Salmon	4.00	1.20
45 Tino Martinez	4.00	1.20
46 Fred McGriff	4.00	1.20
47 Gary Sheffield	2.50	.75
48 Adam Dunn	2.50	.75
49 Joe Mays	2.50	.75
50 Kenny Lofton	2.50	.75
51 Josh Beckett	4.00	1.20
52 Bud Smith	2.50	.75
53 Johnny Estrada	2.50	.75
54 Charles Johnson	2.50	.75
55 Craig Wilson	2.50	.75
56 Terrence Long	2.50	.75
57 Andy Pettitte	4.00	1.20
58 Brian Giles	2.50	.75
59 Juan Pierre	2.50	.75
60 Cliff Floyd	2.50	.75
61 Ivan Rodriguez	6.00	1.80
62 Andruw Jones	2.50	.75
63 Lance Berkman	2.50	.75
64 Mark Buehrle	2.50	.75
65 Miguel Tejada	2.50	.75
66 Wade Miller	2.50	.75
67 Johnny Estrada	2.50	.75
68 Tsuyoshi Shinjo	2.50	.75
69 Scott Rolen	4.00	1.20
70 Roberto Alomar	6.00	1.80
71 Mark Grace	4.00	1.20
72 Larry Walker	4.00	1.20
73 Jim Edmonds	2.50	.75
74 Jeff Kent	2.50	.75
75 Frank Thomas	6.00	1.80
76 Carlos Beltran	2.50	.75
77 Barry Zito	4.00	1.20
78 Alex Rodriguez	10.00	3.00
79 Troy Glaus	4.00	1.20
80 Ryan Klesko	2.50	.75
81 Tom Glavine	4.00	1.20
82 Ben Sheets	2.50	.75
83 Manny Ramirez	2.50	.75
84 Shannon Stewart	2.50	.75
85 Vladimir Guerrero	6.00	1.80
86 Chipper Jones	6.00	1.80
87 Jeff Bagwell	4.00	1.20
88 Richie Sexson	2.50	.75
89 Sean Casey	2.50	.75
90 Tim Hudson	2.50	.75
91 J.D. Drew	2.50	.75
92 Ivan Rodriguez	6.00	1.80
93 Magglio Ordonez	2.50	.75
94 John Buck	2.50	.75
95 Paul Lo Duca	2.50	.75

2002 Playoff Absolute Memorabilia Tools of the Trade Materials

Randomly inserted into packs, this is a parallel to the Tools of the Trade insert set. Each card features a game worn piece(or pieces) of the featued player. Cards in this set were printed to

all sorts of different print runs which we have notated.

	Nm-Mt	Ex-Mt
1-32 PRINT RUN 300 SERIAL #'d SETS		
33-47 PRINT RUN 250 SERIAL #'d SETS		
48-55 PRINT RUN 150 SERIAL #'d SETS		
56-61 PRINT RUN 125 SERIAL #'d SETS		
62-66 PRINT RUN 50 SERIAL #'d SETS		
67 PRINT RUN 100 SERIAL #'d CARDS		
68-82 PRINT RUN 200 SERIAL #'d SETS		
83-87 PRINT RUN 75 SERIAL #'d SETS		
88-95 PRINT RUN 50 SERIAL #'d SETS		
1 Mike Mussina Jsy	10.00	3.00
2 Rickey Henderson Jsy	10.00	3.00
3 Raul Mondesi Jsy	8.00	2.40
4 Nomar Garciaparra Jsy	15.00	4.50
5 Randy Johnson Jsy	10.00	3.00
6 Roger Clemens Jsy	15.00	4.50
7 Shawn Green Jsy	8.00	2.40
8 Todd Helton Jsy	10.00	3.00
9 Aramis Ramirez Jsy	8.00	2.40
10 Barry Larkin Jsy	10.00	3.00
11 Byung-Hyun Kim Jsy	10.00	3.00
12 C.C. Sabathia Jsy	8.00	2.40
13 Curt Schilling Jsy	10.00	3.00
14 Darin Erstad Jsy	8.00	2.40
15 Eric Karros Jsy	8.00	2.40
16 Freddy Garcia Jsy	8.00	2.40
17 Greg Maddux Jsy	15.00	4.50
18 Jason Kendall Jsy	8.00	2.40
19 Jim Thome Jsy	10.00	3.00
20 Juan Gonzalez Jsy	10.00	3.00
21 Kazuhiro Sasaki Jsy	8.00	2.40
22 Kerry Wood Jsy	10.00	3.00
23 Luis Gonzalez Jsy	8.00	2.40
24 Mark Mulder Jsy	8.00	2.40
25 Rich Aurilia Jsy	8.00	2.40
26 Ray Durham Jsy	8.00	2.40
27 Ben Grieve Jsy	8.00	2.40
28 Bret Boone Jsy	8.00	2.40
29 Edgar Martinez Jsy	10.00	3.00
30 Ivan Rodriguez Jsy	10.00	3.00
31 Jorge Posada Jsy	10.00	3.00
32 Mike Piazza Jsy	15.00	4.50
33 Pat Burrell Bat	8.00	2.40
34 Robin Ventura Bat	8.00	2.40
35 Trot Nixon Bat	10.00	3.00
36 Adrian Beltre Bat	8.00	2.40
37 Bernie Williams Bat	10.00	3.00
38 Bobby Abreu Bat	8.00	2.40
39 Carlos Delgado Bat	8.00	2.40
40 Craig Biggio Bat	10.00	3.00
41 Garret Anderson Bat	8.00	2.40
42 Jermaine Dye Bat	8.00	2.40
43 Johnny Damon Bat	8.00	2.40
44 Tim Salmon Bat	10.00	3.00
45 Tino Martinez Bat	10.00	3.00
46 Fred McGriff Bat	10.00	3.00
47 Gary Sheffield Bat	8.00	2.40
48 Adam Dunn Shoe	10.00	3.00
49 Joe Mays Shoe	10.00	3.00
50 Kenny Lofton Shoe	10.00	3.00
51 Josh Beckett Shoe	15.00	4.50
52 Bud Smith Shoe	10.00	3.00
53 Johnny Estrada Shin	10.00	3.00
54 Charles Johnson Shin	10.00	3.00
55 Craig Wilson Shin	10.00	3.00
56 Terrence Long Fld Glv	10.00	3.00
57 Andy Pettitte Fld Glv	15.00	4.50
58 Brian Giles Fld Glv	10.00	3.00
59 Juan Pierre Fld Glv	10.00	3.00
60 Cliff Floyd Fld Glv	10.00	3.00
61 Ivan Rodriguez Fld Glv	25.00	7.50
62 Andruw Jones Hat	15.00	4.50
63 Lance Berkman Hat	15.00	4.50
64 Mark Buehrle Hat	15.00	4.50
65 Miguel Tejada Hat	15.00	4.50
66 Wade Miller Hat	15.00	4.50
67 Johnny Estrada Mask	10.00	3.00
68 Tsuyoshi Shinjo Bat-Shoe	15.00	4.50
69 Scott Rolen Jsy-Bat	20.00	6.00
70 Roberto Alomar Bat-Shoe	20.00	6.00
71 Mark Grace Jsy-Fld Glv	15.00	4.50
72 Larry Walker Jsy-Bat	20.00	6.00
73 Jim Edmonds Jsy-Bat	15.00	4.50
74 Jeff Kent Jsy-Bat	15.00	4.50
75 Frank Thomas Jsy-Bat	20.00	6.00
76 Carlos Beltran Jsy-Bat	15.00	4.50
77 Barry Zito Jsy-Shoe	20.00	6.00
78 Alex Rodriguez Jsy-Bat	25.00	7.50
79 Troy Glaus Jsy-Jsy	20.00	6.00
80 Ryan Klesko Bat-Fld Glv	15.00	4.50
81 Tom Glavine Jsy-Shoe	20.00	6.00
82 Ben Sheets Jsy-Bat	15.00	4.50
83 Manny Ramirez	25.00	7.50
Jsy-Fld Glv-Shoe		
84 Shannon Stewart Jsy-Bat-Hat	20.00	6.00
85 Vladimir Guerrero	50.00	15.00
Jsy-Bat-Fld Glv		
86 Chipper Jones Jsy-Bat-Fld Glv	50.00	15.00
87 Jeff Bagwell Jsy-Bat-Hat	40.00	12.00
88 Richie Sexson	40.00	12.00
Jsy-Bat-Shoe-Btg Glv		
89 Sean Casey Jsy-Bat-Shoe-Hat	40.00	12.00
90 Tim Hudson	40.00	12.00
Jsy-Hat-Shoe-Fld Glv		
91 J.D. Drew Jsy-Bat-Hat-Shoe.	40.00	12.00
92 Ivan Rodriguez	60.00	18.00
Glv-Chest-Jsy-Mask		
93 Magglio Ordonez	40.00	12.00
Jsy-Shoe-Hat-Btg Glv		
94 John Buck Glv-Chest-Shin-Mask	25.00	7.50
95 Paul Lo Duca	40.00	12.00
Jsy-Chest-Shin-Mask		

2003 Playoff Absolute Memorabilia

This 208-card set was issued in two separate series. The primary Absolute Memorabilia product - containing cards 1-200 from the basic set - was released in July, 2003. The cards were issued in six card packs with an approximate SRP of $7.50 which came 18 packs to a box and 16 boxes to a case. The first 150 cards feature veterans while the final 50 cards feature a mix of rookies and veterans. Those cards were issued to a stated print run of 1500 serial numbered sets. Cards 201-208 were randomly seeded into packs of DLP Rookies and Traded issued in December, 2003. Each card was serial-numbered to 1000 copies.

	MINT	NRMT
COMP.LO SET w/o SP's (150)	40.00	18.00
COMMON CARD (1-150)	.75	.35
COMMON CARD (151-208)	4.00	1.80
1 Nomar Garciaparra	3.00	1.35
2 Barry Bonds	5.00	2.20
3 Greg Maddux	3.00	1.35
4 Roger Clemens	4.00	1.80
5 Derek Jeter	5.00	2.20
6 Alex Rodriguez	3.00	1.35
7 Chipper Jones	2.00	.90
8 Sammy Sosa	3.00	1.35
9 Alfonso Soriano	1.25	.55
10 Albert Pujols	4.00	1.80
11 Adam Dunn	.75	.35
12 Tom Glavine	1.25	.55
13 Pedro Martinez	2.00	.90
14 Jim Thome	2.00	.90
15 Hideo Nomo	2.00	.90
16 Roberto Alomar	2.00	.90
17 Barry Zito	1.25	.55
18 Troy Glaus	1.25	.55
19 Kerry Wood	2.00	.90
20 Magglio Ordonez	.75	.35
21 Todd Helton	1.25	.55
22 Craig Biggio	1.25	.55
23 Roy Oswalt	.75	.35
24 Torii Hunter	.75	.35
25 Miguel Tejada	.75	.35
26 Tsuyoshi Shinjo	.75	.35
27 Scott Rolen	1.25	.55
28 Rafael Palmeiro	1.25	.55
29 Victor Martinez	.75	.35
30 Hank Blalock	1.25	.55
31 Jason Lane	.75	.35
32 Junior Spivey	.75	.35
33 Gary Sheffield	.75	.35
34 Corey Patterson	.75	.35
35 Corky Miller	.75	.35
36 Brian Tallet	.75	.35
37 Cliff Lee	.75	.35
38 Jason Jennings	.75	.35
39 Kirk Saarloos	.75	.35
40 Wade Miller	.75	.35
41 Angel Berroa	.75	.35
42 Mike Sweeney	.75	.35
43 Paul Lo Duca	.75	.35
44 A.J. Pierzynski	.75	.35
45 Drew Henson	.75	.35
46 Eric Chavez	.75	.35
47 Tim Hudson	.75	.35
48 Aramis Ramirez	.75	.35
49 Jack Wilson	.75	.35
50 Ryan Klesko	.75	.35
51 Antonio Perez	.75	.35
52 Dewon Brazelton	.75	.35
53 Mark Teixeira	1.25	.55
54 Eric Hinske	.75	.35
55 Freddy Sanchez	.75	.35
56 Mike Rivera	.75	.35
57 Alfredo Amezaga	.75	.35
58 Cliff Floyd	.75	.35
59 Brandon Larson	.75	.35
60 Richard Hidalgo	.75	.35
61 Cesar Izturis	.75	.35
62 Richie Sexson	.75	.35
63 Michael Cuddyer	.75	.35
64 Javier Vazquez	.75	.35
65 Brandon Claussen	.75	.35
66 Carlos Rivera	.75	.35
67 Vernon Wells	.75	.35
68 Kenny Lofton	.75	.35
69 Aubrey Huff	.75	.35
70 Adam LaRoche	1.25	.55
71 Jeff Baker	.75	.35
72 Jose Castillo	.75	.35
73 Joe Borchard	.75	.35
74 Walter Young	.75	.35
75 Jose Morban	.75	.35
76 Vinnie Chulk	.75	.35
77 Christian Parker	.75	.35
78 Mike Piazza	3.00	1.35
79 Ichiro Suzuki	3.00	1.35
80 Kazuhisa Ishii	.75	.35
81 Rickey Henderson	2.00	.90
82 Ken Griffey Jr.	3.00	1.35
83 Jason Giambi	2.00	.90
84 Randy Johnson	2.00	.90
85 Curt Schilling	1.25	.55
86 Manny Ramirez	.75	.35
87 Barry Larkin	2.00	.90
88 Jeff Bagwell	1.25	.55
89 Vladimir Guerrero	2.00	.90
90 Mike Mussina	2.00	.90
91 Juan Gonzalez	2.00	.90
92 Andruw Jones	.75	.35
93 Frank Thomas	2.00	.90
94 Sean Casey	.75	.35
95 Josh Beckett	1.25	.55
96 Lance Berkman	.75	.35
97 Shawn Green	.75	.35
98 Bernie Williams	1.25	.55
99 Pat Burrell	.75	.35
100 Edgar Martinez	1.25	.55
101 Ivan Rodriguez	2.00	.90
102 Jeremy Guthrie	.75	.35
103 Alexis Rios	3.00	1.35
104 Nic Jackson	.75	.35
105 Jason Anderson	.75	.35
106 Travis Chapman	.75	.35
107 Mac Suzuki	.75	.35
108 Toby Hall	.75	.35
109 Mark Prior	4.00	1.80
110 So Taguchi	.75	.35
111 Marlon Byrd	.75	.35
112 Garret Anderson	.75	.35
113 Luis Gonzalez	.75	.35
114 Jay Gibbons	.75	.35
115 Mark Buehrle	.75	.35
116 Wily Mo Pena	.75	.35
117 C.C. Sabathia	.75	.35
118 Ricardo Rodriguez	.75	.35
119 Robert Fick	.75	.35
120 Rodrigo Rosario	.75	.35
121 Alexis Gomez	.75	.35
122 Carlos Beltran	.75	.35
123 Joe Thurston	.75	.35
124 Ben Sheets	.75	.35
125 Jose Vidro	.75	.35
126 Nick Johnson	.75	.35
127 Mark Mulder	.75	.35
128 Bobby Abreu	.75	.35
129 Brian Giles	.75	.35
130 Brian Lawrence	.75	.35
131 Jeff Kent	.75	.35
132 Chris Snelling	.75	.35
133 Kevin Mench	.75	.35
134 Carlos Delgado	.75	.35
135 Orlando Hudson	.75	.35
136 Juan Cruz	.75	.35
137 Jim Edmonds	.75	.35
138 Geronimo Gil	.75	.35
139 Joe Crede	.75	.35
140 Wilson Valdez	.75	.35
141 Runelvys Hernandez	.75	.35
142 Nick Neugebauer	.75	.35
143 Takahito Nomura	.75	.35
144 Andres Galarraga	.75	.35
145 Mark Grace	1.25	.55
146 Brandon Duckworth	.75	.35
147 Oliver Perez	.75	.35
148 Xavier Nady	.75	.35
149 Rafael Soriano	.75	.35
150 Ben Kozlowski	.75	.35
151 Pr. Redman ROO RC	4.00	1.80
152 Craig Brazell ROO RC	5.00	2.20
153 Nook Logan ROO RC	4.00	1.80
154 Greg Aquino ROO RC	4.00	1.80
155 Matt Kata ROO RC	5.00	2.20
156 Ian Ferguson ROO RC	4.00	1.80
157 C.Wang ROO RC	6.00	2.70
158 Beau Kemp ROO RC	4.00	1.80
159 Alej. Machado ROO RC	4.00	1.80
160 Mi. Hessman ROO RC	4.00	1.80
161 Fran. Rosario ROO RC	4.00	1.80
162 Pedro Liriano ROO	4.00	1.80
163 Rich Fischer ROO RC	4.00	1.80
164 Franklin Perez ROO RC	4.00	1.80
165 Oscar Villarreal ROO RC	4.00	1.80
166 Arnie Munoz ROO RC	4.00	1.80
167 Tim Olson ROO RC	5.00	2.20
168 Jose Contreras ROO RC	6.00	2.70
169 Fran. Cruceta ROO RC	4.00	1.80
170 Jer. Bonderman ROO RC	5.00	2.20
171 Jeremy Griffiths ROO RC	5.00	2.20
172 John Webb ROO	4.00	1.80
173 Phil Seibel ROO RC	4.00	1.80
174 Aaron Looper ROO RC	4.00	1.80
175 Brian Stokes ROO RC	4.00	1.80
176 G.Quiroz ROO RC	5.00	2.20
177 Fern. Cabrera ROO RC	4.00	1.80
178 Josh Hall ROO RC	5.00	2.20
179 D. Markwell ROO RC	4.00	1.80
180 Andrew Brown ROO RC	4.00	1.80
181 Doug Waechter ROO RC	5.00	2.20
182 Felix Sanchez ROO RC	4.00	1.80
183 Gerardo Garcia ROO	4.00	1.80
184 Matt Bruback ROO RC	4.00	1.80
185 Mi. Hernandez ROO RC	4.00	1.80
186 Rett Johnson ROO RC	5.00	2.20
187 Ryan Cameron ROO RC	4.00	1.80
188 Rob Hammock ROO RC	5.00	2.20
189 Clint Barmes ROO RC	5.00	2.20
190 Brandon Webb ROO RC	8.00	3.60
191 Jon Leicester ROO RC	4.00	1.80
192 Shane Bazzell ROO RC	4.00	1.80
193 Joe Valentine ROO RC	4.00	1.80
194 Josh Stewart ROO RC	4.00	1.80
195 Pete LaForest ROO RC	5.00	2.20
196 Shane Victorino ROO RC	4.00	1.80
197 Terrmel Sledge ROO RC	5.00	2.20
198 Lew Ford ROO RC	5.00	2.20
199 T.Wellemeyer ROO RC	5.00	2.20
200 Hideki Matsui ROO RC	15.00	6.75
201 Adam Loewen ROO RC	8.00	3.60
202 Ramon Nivar ROO RC	5.00	2.20
203 Dan Haren ROO RC	5.00	2.20
204 Dontrelle Willis ROO	5.00	2.20
205 Chad Gaudin ROO RC	4.00	1.80
206 Rickie Weeks ROO RC	12.00	5.50
207 Ryan Wagner ROO RC	5.00	2.20
208 Delmon Young ROO RC	15.00	6.75

2003 Playoff Absolute Memorabilia Spectrum

	MINT	NRMT
*SPECTRUM 1-150: 2.5X TO 6X BASIC		
*SPECTRUM 151-208: .6X TO 1.5X BASIC		
1-200 RANDOM INSERTS IN PACKS..		
201-208 RANDOM IN DLP R/T PACKS		
STATED PRINT RUN 100 SERIAL #'d SETS		
190 Brandon Webb ROO	12.00	5.50
200 Hideki Matsui ROO	25.00	11.00
201 Adam Loewen ROO	12.00	5.50
206 Rickie Weeks ROO	20.00	9.00
208 Delmon Young ROO	25.00	11.00

2003 Playoff Absolute Memorabilia Spectrum Signatures

Randomly inserted into packs, these cards not only parallel the basic Playoff Absolute Memorabilia set but also were signed by the featured player. Cards 201-208 were randomly seeded into packs of DLP Rookies and Traded. Quantities of each card range from 5-304 copies per. Please note that we have put the stated print run next to the player's name in our checklist. If 25 or fewer of a card was signed, there is no pricing due to market scarcity.

	MINT	NRMT
3 Greg Maddux/10		
4 Roger Clemens/15		
6 Alex Rodriguez/15		
7 Chipper Jones/10		
9 Alfonso Soriano/15		
10 Albert Pujols/10		
11 Adam Dunn/15		
12 Tom Glavine/25		
13 Pedro Martinez/5		
14 Jim Thome/10		
15 Hideo Nomo/5		
16 Roberto Alomar/15		
17 Barry Zito/25		
18 Troy Glaus/10		
19 Kerry Wood/15		
20 Magglio Ordonez/25		
21 Todd Helton/10		
22 Craig Biggio/10		
23 Roy Oswalt/25		
24 Torii Hunter/25		
25 Miguel Tejada/25		
27 Scott Rolen/10		
28 Rafael Palmeiro/10		
29 Victor Martinez/100	25.00	11.00
30 Hank Blalock/50	40.00	18.00
31 Jason Lane/50		
32 Junior Spivey/50	15.00	6.75
33 Gary Sheffield/10		
34 Corey Patterson/50	25.00	11.00
35 Corky Miller/100		
36 Brian Tallet/100		
37 Cliff Lee/100		
38 Jason Jennings/100		
39 Kirk Saarloos/100		
40 Wade Miller/50	15.00	6.75
41 Angel Berroa/100	25.00	11.00
42 Mike Sweeney/50	25.00	11.00
43 Paul Lo Duca/50	25.00	11.00
44 A.J. Pierzynski/100	25.00	11.00
45 Drew Henson/50	40.00	18.00
46 Eric Chavez/10		
47 Tim Hudson/50	40.00	18.00
48 Aramis Ramirez/10		
49 Jack Wilson/25		
50 Ryan Klesko/25		
51 Antonio Perez/25		
52 Dewon Brazelton/50	15.00	6.75
53 Mark Teixeira/50	40.00	18.00
54 Eric Hinske/100	15.00	6.75
55 Freddy Sanchez/100	15.00	6.75
56 Mike Rivera/25		
57 Alfredo Amezaga/100	15.00	6.75
58 Cliff Floyd/25		
59 Brandon Larson/100		
60 Richard Hidalgo/100	25.00	11.00
61 Cesar Izturis/25		
62 Richie Sexson/25		
63 Michael Cuddyer/100	15.00	6.75
64 Javier Vazquez/25		
65 Brandon Claussen/25		
66 Carlos Rivera/100		
67 Vernon Wells/25		
68 Kenny Lofton/50	40.00	18.00
69 Aubrey Huff/100	25.00	11.00
70 Adam LaRoche/100	40.00	18.00
71 Jeff Baker/100	15.00	6.75
72 Jose Castillo/100	15.00	6.75
73 Joe Borchard/100	25.00	11.00
74 Walter Young/100	15.00	6.75
75 Jose Morban/100		
76 Vinnie Chulk/100	15.00	6.75
77 Christian Parker/25		
78 Mike Piazza/5		
80 Kazuhisa Ishii/25		
81 Rickey Henderson/5		
85 Curt Schilling/10		
86 Manny Ramirez/10		
87 Barry Larkin/50	80.00	36.00
88 Jeff Bagwell/5		
89 Vladimir Guerrero/50	50.00	22.00
90 Mike Mussina/10		
91 Juan Gonzalez/5		
92 Andruw Jones/25		
94 Sean Casey/10		
95 Josh Beckett/100	40.00	18.00
96 Lance Berkman/25		
97 Shawn Green/25		
98 Bernie Williams/10		
99 Pat Burrell/10		
100 Edgar Martinez/50	50.00	22.00
101 Ivan Rodriguez/5		
102 Jeremy Guthrie/100	15.00	6.75
103 Alexis Rios/100	50.00	22.00
104 Nic Jackson/100	15.00	6.75
105 Jason Anderson/100		
106 Travis Chapman/100	15.00	6.75
107 Mac Suzuki/304	25.00	11.00
108 Toby Hall/25		
109 Mark Prior/50	120.00	55.00
110 So Taguchi/25		
111 Marlon Byrd/100	25.00	11.00
112 Garret Anderson/10		
113 Luis Gonzalez/10		
114 Jay Gibbons/100	25.00	11.00
115 Mark Buehrle/25		
116 Wily Mo Pena/25		
117 C.C. Sabathia/25		
118 Ricardo Rodriguez/100	15.00	6.75
119 Robert Fick/100	25.00	11.00
120 Rodrigo Rosario/25		
121 Alexis Gomez/100	15.00	6.75
122 Carlos Beltran/25		
123 Joe Thurston/100		
124 Ben Sheets/50	25.00	11.00
125 Jose Vidro/25		
126 Nick Johnson/50	25.00	11.00
127 Mark Mulder/50	40.00	18.00
128 Bobby Abreu/25		
129 Brian Giles/10		
130 Brian Lawrence/25		
132 Chris Snelling/100	25.00	11.00
133 Kevin Mench/100	15.00	6.75
135 Orlando Hudson/50	15.00	6.75
136 Juan Cruz/100		
138 Geronimo Gil/25		
139 Joe Crede/100	15.00	6.75
140 Wilson Valdez/25		
141 Runelvys Hernandez/100	15.00	6.75
142 Nick Neugebauer/25		
143 Takahito Nomura/47	25.00	11.00
144 Andres Galarraga/25		
145 Mark Grace/25		
146 Brandon Duckworth/25		
147 Oliver Perez/50	15.00	6.75
148 Xavier Nady/100	15.00	6.75
149 Rafael Soriano/25		
150 Ben Kozlowski/100	15.00	6.75
151 Prentice Redman ROO/250	10.00	4.50
152 Craig Brazell ROO/250	15.00	6.75
153 Nook Logan ROO/250	10.00	4.50
154 Greg Aquino ROO/250	10.00	4.50
155 Matt Kata ROO/250	15.00	6.75
156 Ian Ferguson ROO/250	10.00	4.50
157 Chien Wang ROO/250	50.00	22.00
158 Beau Kemp ROO/250	10.00	4.50
159 Alej Machado ROO/250	10.00	4.50
160 Mike Hessman ROO/250	10.00	4.50
161 Franc Rosario ROO/250	10.00	4.50
162 Pedro Liriano ROO/250	10.00	4.50
163 Rich Fischer ROO/250	10.00	4.50
164 Franklin Perez ROO/250		
165 Oscar Villarreal ROO/250	10.00	4.50
166 Arnie Munoz ROO/250	10.00	4.50
167 Tim Olson ROO/250	15.00	6.75
168 Jose Contreras ROO/250	40.00	18.00
169 Franc Cruceta ROO/250	10.00	4.50
170 J.Bonderman ROO/250	20.00	9.00
171 Jeremy Griffiths ROO/250	15.00	6.75
172 John Webb ROO/250		
173 Phil Seibel ROO/250		
174 Aaron Looper ROO/250	10.00	4.50
175 Brian Stokes ROO/250	10.00	4.50
176 Guillermo Quiroz ROO/250	20.00	9.00
177 Francisco Cabrera ROO/250	10.00	4.50
178 Josh Hall ROO/250	15.00	6.75
179 Diego Markwell ROO/250	10.00	4.50
180 Andrew Brown ROO/250	10.00	4.50
181 Doug Waechter ROO/250	15.00	6.75
182 Felix Sanchez ROO/250	10.00	4.50
183 Gerardo Garcia ROO/250		
184 Matt Bruback ROO/250	10.00	4.50
185 Michel Hernandez ROO/250		
186 Rett Johnson ROO/250	15.00	6.75
187 Ryan Cameron ROO/250	10.00	4.50
188 Rob Hammock ROO/250	15.00	6.75
189 Clint Barmes ROO/250	15.00	6.75
190 Brandon Webb ROO/250	40.00	18.00
191 Jon Leicester ROO/250	10.00	4.50
192 Shane Bazzell ROO/250	10.00	4.50
193 Joe Valentine ROO/250	10.00	4.50
194 Josh Stewart ROO/250		
195 Pete LaForest ROO/250	15.00	6.75
196 Shane Victorino ROO/250	10.00	4.50
197 Terrmel Sledge ROO/250	15.00	6.75
198 Lew Ford ROO/250	15.00	6.75
199 Todd Wellemeyer ROO/250	15.00	6.75
201 Adam Loewen ROO/100	40.00	18.00
202 Ramon Nivar ROO/100	20.00	9.00
203 Dan Haren ROO/100	20.00	9.00
204 Dontrelle Willis ROO/25		
205 Chad Gaudin ROO/50	15.00	6.75
206 Rickie Weeks ROO/25		
207 Ryan Wagner ROO/100	25.00	11.00
208 Delmon Young ROO/25		

2003 Playoff Absolute Memorabilia Absolutely Ink

Inserted at a stated rate of one in 552, these 40 cards feature authentic autographs from a mix of established major leaguers and some of the best prospects. Due to market scarcity, no pricing is provided for these cards.

	MINT	NRMT
STATED ODDS 1:552		
NO PRICING DUE TO SCARCITY		
1 Vladimir Guerrero		
2 Adam Dunn		
3 Roy Oswalt		
4 Victor Martinez		
5 Edgar Martinez		
6 Eric Hinske		
7 Adam Johnson		
8 Jose Vidro		
9 Jeff Baker		
10 Jeremy Guthrie		
11 Wily Mo Pena		
12 Toby Hall		
13 Bobby Abreu		
14 Fernando Rodney		
15 Doug Nickle		
16 Rodrigo Rosario		
17 Brandon Claussen		
18 Jermaine Dye		
19 Rafael Soriano		
20 Dee Brown		
21 Donaldo Mendez		
22 Mark Prior		
23 Joe Borchard		
24 Brian Lawrence		
25 Nick Neugebauer		
26 Doug Davis		
27 Tim Hudson		
28 Christian Parker		
29 Barry Larkin		
30 Drew Henson		
31 Mike Maroth		
32 Corey Patterson		
33 Jeremy Giambi		
34 Cliff Bartosh		
35 Tom Glavine		
36 Mark Teixeira		
37 Jack Wilson		
38 Roberto Alomar		
39 Barry Zito		
40 Troy Glaus		

2003 Playoff Absolute Memorabilia Absolutely Ink Blue

	MINT	NRMT
RANDOM INSERTS IN PACKS		
PRINT RUNS B/WN 10-25 COPIES PER		
NO PRICING DUE TO SCARCITY		
1 Vladimir Guerrero/25		
2 Adam Dunn/10		
3 Roy Oswalt/25		
4 Victor Martinez/10		
5 Edgar Martinez/25		
6 Eric Hinske/25		
7 Adam Johnson/15		
8 Jose Vidro/25		
9 Jeff Baker/25		
10 Jeremy Guthrie/25		
11 Wily Mo Pena/15		
12 Toby Hall/15		
13 Bobby Abreu/25		
14 Fernando Rodney/15		
15 Doug Nickle/15		
16 Rodrigo Rosario/25		
17 Brandon Claussen/15		
18 Jermaine Dye/25		
19 Rafael Soriano/15		
20 Dee Brown/15		
21 Donaldo Mendez/15		
22 Mark Prior/10		
23 Joe Borchard/10		
24 Brian Lawrence/15		
25 Nick Neugebauer/15		
26 Doug Davis/15		
27 Tim Hudson/10		
28 Christian Parker/15		
29 Barry Larkin/10		
30 Drew Henson/10		
31 Mike Maroth/15		
32 Corey Patterson/10		
33 Jeremy Giambi/25		
34 Cliff Bartosh/15		
35 Tom Glavine/10		
36 Mark Teixeira/10		
37 Jack Wilson/15		
38 Roberto Alomar/10		
39 Barry Zito/10		
40 Troy Glaus/10		

2003 Playoff Absolute Memorabilia Absolutely Ink Gold

	MINT	NRMT
RANDOM INSERTS IN PACKS		
PRINT RUNS B/WN 5-10 COPIES PER		
NO PRICING DUE TO SCARCITY		
1 Vladimir Guerrero/10		
2 Adam Dunn/5		
3 Roy Oswalt/10		
4 Victor Martinez/5		
5 Edgar Martinez/10		
6 Eric Hinske/10		
7 Adam Johnson/10		
8 Jose Vidro/10		
9 Jeff Baker/10		
10 Jeremy Guthrie/10		
11 Wily Mo Pena/10		
12 Toby Hall/10		
13 Bobby Abreu/10		
14 Fernando Rodney/10		
15 Doug Nickle/10		
16 Rodrigo Rosario/10		
17 Brandon Claussen/10		
18 Jermaine Dye/10		
19 Rafael Soriano/10		
20 Dee Brown/10		
21 Donaldo Mendez/10		
22 Mark Prior/5		
23 Joe Borchard/5		
24 Brian Lawrence/10		
25 Nick Neugebauer/10		
26 Doug Davis/10		
27 Tim Hudson/5		
28 Christian Parker/10		
29 Barry Larkin/5		
30 Drew Henson/5		
31 Mike Maroth/10		
32 Corey Patterson/5		
33 Jeremy Giambi/10		
34 Cliff Bartosh/10		
35 Tom Glavine/5		
36 Mark Teixeira/5		
37 Jack Wilson/10		
38 Roberto Alomar/5		
39 Barry Zito/5		
40 Troy Glaus/5		

2003 Playoff Absolute Memorabilia Glass Plaques

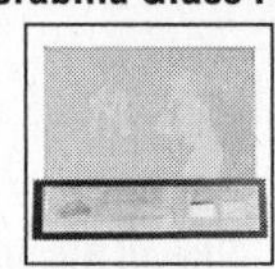

Inserted at the stated rate of one per sealed box, these 273 cards feature etched-glass collectibles with an autograph and/or a piece of game-used memorabilia. We have identified what comes with the card along with the stated print run in our checklist. Please note that for plaques with stated print runs of 25 or fewer no pricing is provided due to market scarcity.

	MINT	NRMT
1 Roberto Alomar AU/25		
2 Roberto Alomar AU-Jsy/25		
3 Roberto Alomar Bat-Jsy/100	60.00	27.00
4 Roberto Alomar Jsy/150	50.00	22.00
5 Jeff Bagwell AU/15		
6 Jeff Bagwell AU-Jsy/10		
7 Jeff Bagwell Bat-Jsy/100	60.00	27.00
8 Jeff Bagwell Jsy/150		
9 Ernie Banks AU/15		
10 Ernie Banks AU-Jsy/10		
11 Ernie Banks Bat-Jsy/25		
12 Ernie Banks Jsy/150	50.00	22.00
13 Lance Berkman AU/25		
14 Lance Berkman AU-Jsy/25		
15 Lance Berkman Bat-Jsy/100	50.00	22.00
16 Lance Berkman Jsy/150	40.00	18.00
17 Yogi Berra AU/25		
18 Yogi Berra AU-Jsy/25		
19 Yogi Berra Bat-Jsy/150		
20 Yogi Berra Jsy/150		
21 Barry Bonds Ball-Base/50	120.00	55.00
22 Barry Bonds Ball-Base/100	100.00	45.00
23 Barry Bonds Base/200	80.00	36.00
24 George Brett AU/15		
25 George Brett AU-Jsy/10		
26 George Brett Bat-Jsy/50	200.00	90.00
27 George Brett Jsy/200	80.00	36.00
28 Pat Burrell AU/25		
29 Pat Burrell AU-Jsy/25		
30 Pat Burrell Bat-Jsy/100	50.00	22.00
31 Pat Burrell Jsy/150	40.00	18.00
32 Steve Carlton AU/50	100.00	45.00
33 Steve Carlton AU-Jsy/25		
34 Steve Carlton Bat-Jsy/100		
35 Steve Carlton Jsy/150	40.00	18.00
36 R.Clemens Sox AU/15		
37 R.Clemens Sox AU-Jsy/25		
38 R.Clemens Sox Fld Glv-Jsy/50	200.00	90.00
39 R.Clemens Sox Jsy/150	80.00	36.00
40 R.Clemens Yanks AU/15		
41 R.Clemens Yanks AU-Jsy/10		
42 Clemens Yanks Glv-Jsy/50	200.00	90.00
43 R.Clemens Yanks Jsy/200	80.00	36.00
44 Roberto Clemente Bat-Jsy/50		
45 Roberto Clemente Bat-Jsy/150		
46 Roberto Clemente Jsy/200		
47 Jose Contreras AU/25		
48 Jose Contreras AU-Jsy/25		
49 Jose Contreras Jsy-Jsy/100		
50 Jose Contreras Jsy/150		
51 Adam Dunn AU/25		
52 Adam Dunn AU-Jsy/25		
53 Adam Dunn Bat-Jsy/100	50.00	22.00
54 Adam Dunn Jsy/150	40.00	18.00
55 Bob Feller AU/50	100.00	45.00
56 Bob Feller AU-Jsy/25		
57 Bob Feller Jsy-Jsy/50	80.00	36.00
58 Bob Feller Jsy/100	50.00	22.00
59 N.Garciaparra Bat-Jsy/100	80.00	36.00
60 N.Garciaparra Jsy/200	60.00	27.00
61 Jason Giambi Bat-Jsy/100	60.00	27.00
62 Jason Giambi Jsy/150	50.00	22.00
63 Troy Glaus AU/25		
64 Troy Glaus AU-Jsy/25		
65 Troy Glaus Bat-Jsy/100		
66 Troy Glaus Jsy/150	50.00	22.00
67 Juan Gonzalez AU/15		
68 Juan Gonzalez AU-Jsy/10		
69 Juan Gonzalez Bat-Jsy/100		
70 Juan Gonzalez Jsy/150		
71 Luis Gonzalez AU/25		
72 Luis Gonzalez AU-Jsy/25		
73 Luis Gonzalez Bat-Jsy/100	50.00	22.00
74 Luis Gonzalez Jsy/150	40.00	18.00
75 Mark Grace AU/50	120.00	55.00
76 Mark Grace AU-Jsy/25		
77 Mark Grace Bat-Jsy/100		
78 Mark Grace Jsy/150	50.00	22.00
79 Shawn Green AU/15		
80 Shawn Green AU-Jsy/10		
81 Shawn Green Bat-Jsy/100	50.00	22.00
82 Shawn Green Jsy/150	40.00	18.00
83 Ken Griffey Jr. Ball-Base/50		
84 Ken Griffey Jr. Ball-Base/100		
85 Ken Griffey Jr. Base/200		
86 Vladimir Guerrero AU/25		
87 Vladimir Guerrero AU-Jsy/25		
88 Vladimir Guerrero Bat-Jsy/100	60.00	27.00
89 Vladimir Guerrero Jsy/150		
90 Tony Gwynn AU/15		
91 Tony Gwynn AU-Jsy/10		
92 Tony Gwynn Bat-Jsy/150		
93 Tony Gwynn Jsy/200		
94 Todd Helton AU/25		
95 Todd Helton AU-Jsy/25		
96 Todd Helton Bat-Jsy/100		
97 Todd Helton Jsy/150		
98 R.Henderson AU/15		
99 R.Henderson AU-Jsy/10		
100 R.Henderson Bat-Jsy/100	60.00	27.00
101 R.Henderson Jsy/200	50.00	22.00
102 Tim Hudson AU/50	100.00	45.00
103 Tim Hudson AU-Jsy/25		
104 Tim Hudson Hat-Jsy/100	50.00	22.00
105 Tim Hudson Jsy/150	40.00	18.00
106 Torii Hunter AU/50	80.00	36.00
107 Torii Hunter AU-Jsy/25		
108 Torii Hunter Hat-Jsy/100	50.00	22.00
109 Torii Hunter Jsy/150		
110 Kazuhisa Ishii AU/15		
111 Kazuhisa Ishii AU-Jsy/10		
112 Kazuhisa Ishii Bat-Jsy/100	50.00	22.00
113 Kazuhisa Ishii Jsy/200	40.00	18.00
114 Derek Jeter Ball-Base/50		
115 Derek Jeter Ball-Base/150		
116 Derek Jeter Base/200		
117 Randy Johnson AU/15		
118 Randy Johnson AU-Jsy/10		
119 Randy Johnson Bat -Jsy/100	60.00	27.00
120 Randy Johnson Jsy/150	50.00	22.00
121 Andruw Jones AU/25		
122 Andruw Jones AU-Jsy/25		
123 Andruw Jones Bat-Jsy/100		
124 Andruw Jones Jsy/150	40.00	18.00
125 Chipper Jones AU/15		
126 Chipper Jones AU-Jsy/10		
127 Chipper Jones Bat-Jsy/100	60.00	27.00
128 Chipper Jones Jsy/150	50.00	22.00
129 Al Kaline AU/50		
130 Al Kaline AU-Jsy/25		
131 Al Kaline Bat-Jsy/100	60.00	27.00
132 Al Kaline Jsy/150	50.00	22.00
133 Barry Larkin AU/50	100.00	45.00
134 Barry Larkin AU-Jsy/25		
135 Barry Larkin Bat-Jsy/100	60.00	27.00
136 Barry Larkin Jsy/150	50.00	22.00
137 Greg Maddux AU/15		
138 Greg Maddux AU-Jsy/10		
139 Greg Maddux Bat -Jsy/100	60.00	27.00
140 Greg Maddux Jsy/200	50.00	22.00
141 Pedro Martinez AU/10		
142 Pedro Martinez AU-Jsy/10		
143 Pedro Martinez Bat-Jsy/100	60.00	27.00
144 Pedro Martinez Jsy/150	50.00	22.00
145 H.Matsui Ball-Base/50	150.00	70.00
146 H.Matsui Ball-Base/150	100.00	45.00
147 H.Matsui Base/200	60.00	27.00
148 Don Mattingly AU/25		
149 Don Mattingly AU-Jsy/25		
150 Don Mattingly Jsy/100		
151 Don Mattingly Jsy/200		
152 Mark Mulder AU/50	100.00	45.00
153 Mark Mulder AU-Jsy/25		
154 Mark Mulder Jsy/150	40.00	18.00
155 Mark Mulder Jsy-Jsy/100	50.00	22.00
156 Stan Musial AU/15		
157 Stan Musial AU-Jsy/10		
158 Stan Musial Bat-Jsy/150		
159 Stan Musial Jsy/200		
160 Hideo Nomo AU/15		
161 Hideo Nomo AU-Jsy/10		
162 Hideo Nomo Bat-Jsy/50	120.00	55.00
163 Hideo Nomo Bat-Jsy/100	60.00	27.00
164 Hideo Nomo Jsy/200	50.00	22.00
165 Magglio Ordonez AU/50	80.00	36.00
166 Magglio Ordonez AU-Jsy/25		
167 M.Ordonez Bat-Jsy/100	50.00	22.00
168 Magglio Ordonez Jsy/150	40.00	18.00
169 Roy Oswalt AU/50	80.00	36.00
170 Roy Oswalt AU-Jsy/25		
171 Roy Oswalt Bat-Jsy/100	50.00	22.00
172 Roy Oswalt Jsy/150	40.00	18.00
173 Rafael Palmeiro AU/25		
174 Rafael Palmeiro AU-Jsy/25		
175 Rafael Palmeiro Bat-Jsy/100	60.00	27.00
176 Rafael Palmeiro Jsy/150	50.00	22.00
177 Mike Piazza AU/15		
178 Mike Piazza AU-Jsy/10		
179 Mike Piazza Bat-Jsy/50	100.00	45.00
180 Mike Piazza Bat-Jsy/100	60.00	27.00
181 Mike Piazza Jsy/200	50.00	22.00
182 Mark Prior AU/25		
183 Mark Prior AU-Jsy/25		
184 Mark Prior Bat-Jsy/100	100.00	45.00
185 Mark Prior Jsy/150	80.00	36.00
186 Albert Pujols AU/25		
187 Albert Pujols AU-Jsy/25		
188 Albert Pujols Bat-Jsy/150	100.00	45.00
189 Albert Pujols Jsy/150	80.00	36.00
190 Manny Ramirez AU/15		
191 Manny Ramirez AU-Jsy 10		
192 Manny Ramirez Bat-Jsy/100	50.00	22.00
193 Manny Ramirez Jsy/150	40.00	18.00
194 Cal Ripken AU/15		
195 Cal Ripken AU-Jsy/10		
196 Cal Ripken Bat-Jsy/150	120.00	55.00
197 Cal Ripken Jsy/200	100.00	45.00
198 Frank Robinson AU/50	100.00	45.00
199 Frank Robinson AU-Jsy/25		
200 Frank Robinson Bat-Jsy/100	60.00	27.00
201 Frank Robinson Jsy/150	50.00	22.00
202 Alex Rodriguez AU/15		
203 Alex Rodriguez AU-Jsy/25		
204 Alex Rodriguez Bat-Jsy/100		
205 Alex Rodriguez Jsy/200		
206 N.Ryan Angels AU/15		
207 N.Ryan Angels AU-Jsy 25		
208 N.Ryan Angels Jacket-Jsy/150		
209 N.Ryan Angels Jsy/200	100.00	45.00
210 N.Ryan Astros AU/15		
211 N.Ryan Astros AU-Jsy/25		
212 N.Ryan Astros Fld Glv-Jsy/25		
213 N.Ryan Astros Jsy/200	100.00	45.00
214 N.Ryan Astros Jsy-Jsy/100	120.00	55.00
215 N.Ryan Rgr AU/15		
216 N.Ryan Rgr AU-Jsy/10		
217 N.Ryan Rgr Fld Glv-Jsy/25		
218 N.Ryan Rgr Jsy/200	100.00	45.00
219 N.Ryan Rgr Jsy-Jsy/100	120.00	55.00
220 R.Sandberg AU/15		
221 R.Sandberg AU-Jsy/10		
222 R.Sandberg Bat-Jsy G/50	150.00	70.00
223 R.Sandberg Bat-Jsy S/50	150.00	70.00
224 R.Sandberg Jsy/200	80.00	36.00
225 Curt Schilling AU/25		
226 Curt Schilling AU-Jsy/25		
227 Curt Schilling Fld Glv-Jsy/50		
228 Curt Schilling Jsy/150	50.00	22.00
229 Mike Schmidt AU/25		
230 Mike Schmidt AU-Jsy/25		
231 Mike Schmidt Bat-Jsy/100	100.00	45.00
232 Mike Schmidt Jsy/200	80.00	36.00
233 Ozzie Smith AU/15		
234 Ozzie Smith AU-Jsy/10		
235 Ozzie Smith Bat-Jsy/100	100.00	45.00
236 Ozzie Smith Jsy/150	80.00	36.00
237 A.Soriano AU/15		
238 A.Soriano AU-Jsy/10		
239 A.Soriano Bat-Jsy/150	60.00	27.00

240 A.Soriano Jsy/150 50.00 22.00
241 Sammy Sosa Bat-Jsy/150 80.00 36.00
242 Sammy Sosa Jsy/200 60.00 27.00
243 Junior Spivey AU/50
244 Junior Spivey AU-Jsy/25
245 Junior Spivey Bat-Jsy/100 50.00 22.00
246 Junior Spivey Jsy/150 40.00 18.00
247 I.Suzuki Ball-Base/50 120.00 55.00
248 I.Suzuki Ball-Base/150 100.00 45.00
249 I.Suzuki Base/200 60.00 27.00
250 Mark Teixeira AU/50
251 Mark Teixeira AU-Jsy/25
252 Mark Teixeira Bat-Jsy/100 60.00 27.00
253 Mark Teixeira Jsy/150 50.00 22.00
254 Miguel Tejada AU/50 80.00 36.00
255 Miguel Tejada AU-Jsy/25
256 Miguel Tejada Bat-Jsy/100 50.00 22.00
257 Miguel Tejada Jsy/150 40.00 18.00
258 Frank Thomas AU/25
259 Frank Thomas AU-Jsy/25
260 Frank Thomas Bat-Jsy/100 60.00 27.00
261 Frank Thomas Jsy/150 50.00 22.00
262 Bernie Williams AU/15
263 Bernie Williams AU-Jsy/10
264 Bernie Williams Bat-Jsy/100 60.00 27.00
265 Bernie Williams Jsy/150 50.00 22.00
266 Kerry Wood AU/50 100.00 45.00
267 Kerry Wood AU-Jsy/25
268 Kerry Wood Bat-Jsy/100 60.00 27.00
269 Kerry Wood Jsy/150 50.00 22.00
270 Barry Zito AU/50 80.00 36.00
271 Barry Zito AU-Jsy/25
272 Barry Zito Hat-Jsy/100 60.00 27.00
273 Barry Zito Jsy/150 50.00 22.00

2003 Playoff Absolute Memorabilia Player Collection

MINT NRMT
*PLAY.COLL: .75X TO 2X PRESTIGE PLAY.COLL
STATED PRINT RUN 75 SERIAL #'d SETS
SEE 2003 PRESTIGE PLAY.COLL FOR PRICING
SPECTRUM PRINT RUN 25 SERIAL #'d SETS
NO SPECTRUM PRICING DUE TO SCARCITY
RANDOM INSERTS IN PACKS

2003 Playoff Absolute Memorabilia Portraits Promos

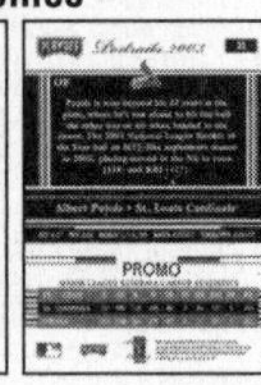

MINT NRMT
STATED ODDS ONE PER BOX
1 Vladimir Guerrero 2.50 1.10
2 Luis Gonzalez 1.00 .45
3 Andruw Jones 1.00 .45
4 Manny Ramirez 1.00 .45
5 Derek Jeter 6.00 2.70
6 Eric Hinske 1.00 .45
7 Curt Schilling 1.50 .70
8 Adam Dunn 1.00 .45
9 Jason Jennings 1.00 .45
10 Mike Piazza 4.00 1.80
11 Jason Giambi 2.50 1.10
12 Jeff Bagwell 1.50 .70
13 Rickey Henderson 2.50 1.10
14 Randy Johnson 2.50 1.10
15 Roger Clemens 5.00 2.20
16 Troy Glaus 1.50 .70
17 Hideo Nomo 2.50 1.10
18 Joe Borchard 1.00 .45
19 Torii Hunter 1.00 .45
20 Lance Berkman 1.00 .45
21 Todd Helton 1.50 .70
22 Mike Mussina 1.50 .70
23 Vernon Wells 1.00 .45
24 Pat Burrell 1.00 .45
25 Ichiro Suzuki 4.00 1.80
26 Shawn Green 1.00 .45
27 Frank Thomas 2.50 1.10
28 Barry Zito 1.50 .70
29 Barry Bonds 6.00 2.70
30 Ken Griffey Jr. 4.00 1.80
31 Albert Pujols 5.00 2.20
32 Roberto Alomar 2.50 1.10
33 Barry Larkin 2.50 1.10
34 Tony Gwynn 3.00 1.35
35 Chipper Jones 2.50 1.10
36 Pedro Martinez 2.50 1.10
37 Juan Gonzalez 2.50 1.10
38 Greg Maddux 4.00 1.80
39 Tim Hudson 1.00 .45
40 Sammy Sosa 4.00 1.80
41 Victor Martinez 1.00 .45
42 Mark Buehrle 1.00 .45
43 Austin Kearns 1.00 .45
44 Kerry Wood 2.50 1.10
45 Nomar Garciaparra 4.00 1.80
46 Alfonso Soriano 1.50 .70
47 Mark Prior 5.00 2.20
48 Richie Sexson 1.00 .45
49 Mark Teixeira 1.50 .70
50 Craig Biggio 1.50 .70
51 Rafael Palmeiro 1.50 .70
52 Carlos Beltran 1.00 .45
53 Bernie Williams 1.50 .70
54 Eric Chavez 1.00 .45
55 Paul Konerko 1.00 .45
56 Nolan Ryan 6.00 2.70
57 Mark Mulder 1.00 .45
58 Miguel Tejada 1.00 .45
59 Roy Oswalt 1.00 .45
60 Jim Edmonds 1.00 .45
61 Ryan Klesko 1.00 .45
62 Cal Ripken 8.00 3.60
63 Josh Beckett 1.50 .70
64 Kazuhisa Ishii 1.00 .45
65 Alex Rodriguez 4.00 1.80
66 Mike Sweeney 1.00 .45
67 C.C. Sabathia 1.00 .45
68 Jose Vidro 1.00 .45
69 Magglio Ordonez 1.00 .45
70 Carlos Delgado 1.00 .45
71 Jorge Posada 1.50 .70
72 Bobby Abreu 1.00 .45

2003 Playoff Absolute Memorabilia Rookie Materials Jersey Number

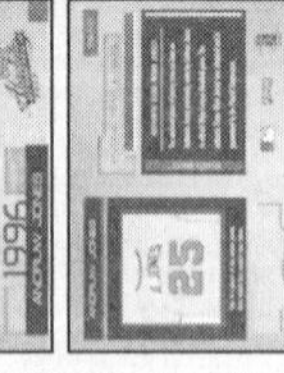

Randomly inserted into packs, these 15 cards feature not only game-worn jersey swatches but were printed to a stated print run which matched the player's jersey number. For cards with a print run of 25 or fewer, no pricing is provided due to market scarcity.

MINT NRMT
RANDOM INSERTS IN PACKS
PRINT RUNS B/WN 5-51 COPIES PER
NO PRICING ON QTY OF 25 OR LESS.
1 Stan Musial Jsy/6
2 Yogi Berra Jsy/35 50.00 22.00
3 Vladimir Guerrero Jsy/27 50.00 22.00
4 Randy Johnson Jsy/51 50.00 22.00
5 Andruw Jones Jsy/25
6 Jeff Kent Jsy/11
7 Nomar Garciaparra Jsy/5
8 Hideo Nomo Jsy/16
9 Ivan Rodriguez Jsy/7
10 Alfonso Soriano Jsy/33 50.00 22.00
11 Scott Rolen Jsy/17
12 Juan Gonzalez Jsy/19
13 Rafael Palmeiro Bat/25
14 Mike Schmidt Bat/20
15 Cal Ripken Bat/8

2003 Playoff Absolute Memorabilia Rookie Materials Season

Randomly inserted into packs, these 15 cards feature not only game-worn jersey swatches but were printed to a stated print run which matched the player's debut season.

MINT NRMT
RANDOM INSERTS IN PACKS
PRINT RUNS B/WN 42-101 COPIES PER
1 Stan Musial Jsy/42 120.00 55.00
2 Yogi Berra Jsy/47 60.00 27.00
3 Vladimir Guerrero Jsy/97 25.00 11.00
4 Randy Johnson Jsy/89 25.00 11.00
5 Andruw Jones Jsy/96 15.00 6.75
6 Jeff Kent Jsy/92 15.00 6.75
8 Hideo Nomo Jsy/95 40.00 18.00
9 Ivan Rodriguez Jsy/91 25.00 11.00
10 Alfonso Soriano Jsy/101 25.00 11.00
11 Scott Rolen Jsy/96 25.00 11.00
12 Juan Gonzalez Jsy/89 25.00 11.00
13 Rafael Palmeiro Bat/86 25.00 11.00
14 Mike Schmidt Bat/73 60.00 27.00
15 Cal Ripken Bat/82 80.00 36.00

2003 Playoff Absolute Memorabilia Signing Bonus

Randomly inserted into packs, these 10 cards feature authentic autographs of baseball legends. Each of these cards were issued to a stated print run of 15 serial numbered sets and no pricing is provided due to market scarcity.

MINT NRMT
RANDOM INSERTS IN PACKS
STATED PRINT RUN 15 SERIAL #'d SETS
NO PRICING DUE TO SCARCITY
1 Nolan Ryan
2 Cal Ripken
3 Don Mattingly
4 Kirby Puckett
5 Tony Gwynn
6 Ozzie Smith
7 Mike Schmidt
8 Reggie Jackson
9 Yogi Berra
10 Stan Musial

2003 Playoff Absolute Memorabilia Signing Bonus Blue

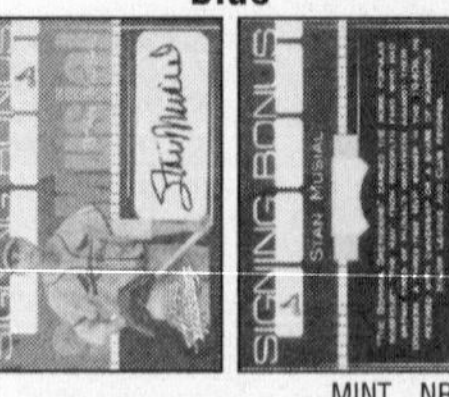

MINT NRMT
RANDOM INSERTS IN PACKS
STATED PRINT RUN 10 SERIAL #'d SETS
NO PRICING DUE TO SCARCITY

2003 Playoff Absolute Memorabilia Signing Bonus Gold

MINT NRMT
RANDOM INSERTS IN PACKS
STATED PRINT RUN 5 SERIAL #'d SETS
NO PRICING DUE TO SCARCITY

2003 Playoff Absolute Memorabilia Team Tandems

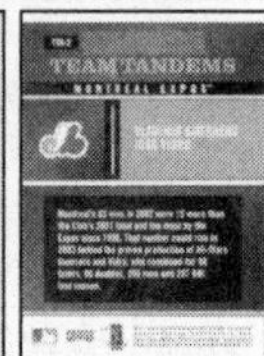

MINT NRMT
STATED ODDS 1:48
*SPECTRUM: 1.25X TO 3X BASIC
SPECTRUM RANDOM INSERTS IN PACKS
SPECTRUM PRINT RUN 100 #'d SETS
1 Sammy Sosa 10.00 4.50
Mark Prior
2 Vladimir Guerrero 5.00 2.20
Jose Vidro
3 Bernie Williams 5.00 2.20
Alfonso Soriano
4 Mike Sweeney 3.00 1.35
Carlos Beltran
5 Magglio Ordonez 3.00 1.35
Paul Konerko
6 Adam Dunn 3.00 1.35
Austin Kearns
7 Randy Johnson 5.00 2.20
Curt Schilling
8 Hideo Nomo 5.00 2.20
Kazuhisa Ishii
9 Pat Burrell 3.00 1.35
Bobby Abreu
10 Todd Helton 5.00 2.20
Larry Walker

2003 Playoff Absolute Memorabilia Team Tandems Materials

MINT NRMT
1-7/10 PRINT RUN 100 SERIAL #'d SETS
8-9 PRINT RUN 40 SERIAL #'d SETS
SPECTRUM 1-7/10 PRINT RUN 25 #'d SETS
SPECTRUM 8-9 PRINT RUN 10 #'d SETS
NO SPECTRUM PRICING DUE TO SCARCITY
RANDOM INSERTS IN PACKS
ALL FEATURE DUAL JERSEY SWATCHES
1 Sammy Sosa 40.00 18.00
Mark Prior
2 Vladimir Guerrero 25.00 11.00
Jose Vidro
3 Bernie Williams 25.00 11.00
Alfonso Soriano
4 Mike Sweeney 15.00 6.75
Carlos Beltran
5 Magglio Ordonez 15.00 6.75
Paul Konerko
6 Adam Dunn 15.00 6.75
Austin Kearns
7 Randy Johnson 25.00 11.00
Curt Schilling
8 Hideo Nomo 80.00 36.00
Kazuhisa Ishii/40
9 Pat Burrell 25.00 11.00
Bobby Abreu/40
10 Todd Helton 25.00 11.00
Larry Walker

2003 Playoff Absolute Memorabilia Team Trios

MINT NRMT
STATED ODDS 1:88
*SPECTRUM: 1X TO 2.5X BASIC
SPECTRUM RANDOM INSERTS IN PACKS
SPECTRUM PRINT RUN 50 SERIAL #'d SETS
1 Greg Maddux 15.00 6.75
Chipper Jones
Andruw Jones
2 Sammy Sosa 15.00 6.75
Mark Prior
Kerry Wood
3 Pedro Martinez 15.00 6.75
Nomar Garciaparra
Manny Ramirez
4 Jason Giambi 15.00 6.75
Alfonso Soriano
Roger Clemens
5 Alex Rodriguez 15.00 6.75
Rafael Palmeiro
Mark Teixeira
6 Mike Piazza 15.00 6.75
Roberto Alomar
Tsuyoshi Shinjo
7 Jeff Bagwell 10.00 4.50
Craig Biggio
Lance Berkman
8 Troy Glaus 10.00 4.50
Garret Anderson
Troy Percival
9 Miguel Tejada 10.00 4.50
Eric Chavez
Barry Zito
10 Luis Gonzalez 10.00 4.50
Randy Johnson
Curt Schilling

2003 Playoff Absolute Memorabilia Team Trios Materials

MINT NRMT
1-2/4-5/7/9-10 PRINT RUN 100 #'d SETS
3/6/8 PRINT RUNS B/WN 40-50 COPIES PER
SPECTRUM 1-2/4-5/7/9-10 PRINT 25 #'d SETS
SPECTRUM 3/6/8 PRINT RUN 10 #'d SETS
NO SPECTRUM PRICING DUE TO SCARCITY
RANDOM INSERTS IN PACKS
ALL FEATURE THREE JERSEY SWATCHES
1 Greg Maddux 40.00 18.00
Chipper Jones
Andruw Jones
2 Sammy Sosa 50.00 22.00
Mark Prior
Kerry Wood
3 Pedro Martinez 80.00 36.00
Nomar Garciaparra
Manny Ramirez/50
4 Jason Giambi 50.00 22.00
Alfonso Soriano
Roger Clemens
5 Alex Rodriguez 40.00 18.00
Rafael Palmeiro
Mark Teixeira
6 Mike Piazza 60.00 27.00
Roberto Alomar
Tsuyoshi Shinjo/40
7 Jeff Bagwell 40.00 18.00
Craig Biggio
Lance Berkman
8 Troy Glaus 40.00 18.00
Garret Anderson
Troy Percival/40
9 Miguel Tejada 40.00 18.00
Eric Chavez
Barry Zito
10 Luis Gonzalez 40.00 18.00
Randy Johnson
Curt Schilling

2003 Playoff Absolute Memorabilia Tools of the Trade

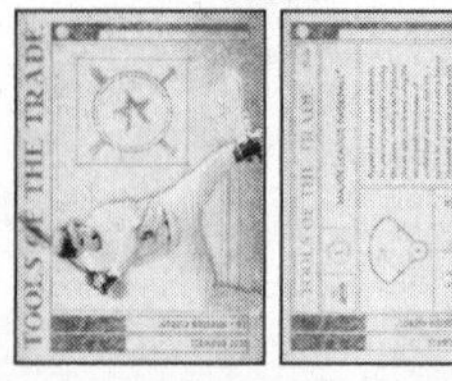

MINT NRMT
STATED ODDS 1:5
*SPECTRUM: 1X TO 2.5X BASIC
SPECTRUM RANDOM INSERTS IN PACKS
SPECTRUM PRINT RUN 100 #'d SETS
1 Sammy Sosa 6.00 2.70
2 Nomar Garciaparra 6.00 2.70
3 Andruw Jones 1.50 .70
4 Troy Glaus 2.50 1.10
5 Greg Maddux 6.00 2.70
6 Rickey Henderson 4.00 1.80
7 Alex Rodriguez 6.00 2.70
8 Manny Ramirez 1.50 .70
9 Lance Berkman 1.50 .70
10 Roger Clemens 8.00 3.60
11 Ivan Rodriguez 4.00 1.80
12 Kazuhisa Ishii 1.50 .70
13 Alfonso Soriano 2.50 1.10
14 Austin Kearns 1.50 .70
15 Mike Piazza 6.00 2.70
16 Curt Schilling 2.50 1.10
17 Jeff Bagwell 2.50 1.10
18 Todd Helton 2.50 1.10
19 Randy Johnson 4.00 1.80
20 Vladimir Guerrero 4.00 1.80
21 Kerry Wood 4.00 1.80
22 Rafael Palmeiro 2.50 1.10
23 Roy Oswalt 1.50 .70
24 Chipper Jones 4.00 1.80
25 Pat Burrell 1.50 .70
26 Jason Giambi 4.00 1.80
27 Pedro Martinez 4.00 1.80
28 Roberto Alomar 4.00 1.80
29 Shawn Green 2.50 1.10
30 Adam Dunn 1.50 .70
31 Juan Gonzalez 4.00 1.80
32 Mark Prior 8.00 3.60
33 Hideo Nomo 4.00 1.80
34 Torii Hunter 1.50 .70
35 Mark Teixeira 2.50 1.10
36 Craig Biggio 2.50 1.10
37 Rafael Palmeiro 2.50 1.10
38 Jeff Bagwell 2.50 1.10
39 Albert Pujols 8.00 3.60
40 Richie Sexson 1.50 .70
41 Alex Rodriguez 6.00 2.70
42 Carlos Delgado 1.50 .70
43 Frank Thomas 4.00 1.80
44 Sammy Sosa 6.00 2.70
45 Marlon Byrd 1.50 .70
46 Mark Prior 8.00 3.60
47 Adrian Beltre 1.50 .70
48 Tom Glavine 2.50 1.10
49 So Taguchi 1.50 .70
50 Jeff Bagwell 2.50 1.10
51 Mike Sweeney 1.50 .70
52 Luis Gonzalez 1.50 .70
53 Chipper Jones 4.00 1.80
54 Jason Giambi 4.00 1.80
55 Miguel Tejada 1.50 .70
56 Todd Helton 2.50 1.10
57 Andruw Jones 1.50 .70
58 Mike Piazza 6.00 2.70
59 Manny Ramirez 1.50 .70
60 Randy Johnson 4.00 1.80
61 Carlos Beltran 1.50 .70
62 Victor Martinez 1.50 .70
63 Orlando Hudson 1.50 .70
64 Jeff Kent 1.50 .70
65 Greg Maddux 6.00 2.70
66 Garret Anderson 1.50 .70
67 Joe Thurston 1.50 .70
68 Mark Teixeira 2.50 1.10
69 Kazuhisa Ishii 1.50 .70
70 Austin Kearns 1.50 .70
71 Pat Burrell 1.50 .70
72 Joe Borchard 1.50 .70
73 Josh Phelps 1.50 .70
74 Travis Hafner 1.50 .70
75 So Taguchi 1.50 .70
76 Victor Martinez 1.50 .70
77 Paul Lo Duca 1.50 .70
78 Bernie Williams 2.50 1.10
79 Josh Phelps 1.50 .70
80 Marlon Byrd 1.50 .70
81 Manny Ramirez 1.50 .70
82 Jason Giambi 4.00 1.80
83 Jeff Bagwell 2.50 1.10
84 Sammy Sosa 6.00 2.70
85 Josh Phelps 1.50 .70
86 Tim Hudson 1.50 .70
87 Randy Johnson 4.00 1.80
88 Troy Glaus 2.50 1.10
89 Joe Thurston 1.50 .70
90 Miguel Tejada 1.50 .70
91 Adam Dunn 1.50 .70
92 Magglio Ordonez 1.50 .70
93 Mike Sweeney 1.50 .70
94 Andruw Jones 1.50 .70
95 Carlos Beltran 1.50 .70
96 Joe Borchard 1.50 .70
97 Austin Kearns 1.50 .70
98 Richie Sexson 1.50 .70
99 Mark Prior 8.00 3.60
100 Mark Teixeira 2.50 1.10
101 Ryan Klesko 1.50 .70
102 Jason Jennings 1.50 .70
103 Travis Hafner 1.50 .70
104 Mark Buehrle 1.50 .70
105 Eric Hinske 1.50 .70
106 Rafael Palmeiro 2.50 1.10
107 Roy Oswalt 1.50 .70
108 Kerry Wood 4.00 1.80
109 Brian Giles 1.50 .70
110 Ivan Rodriguez 4.00 1.80

2003 Playoff Absolute Memorabilia Tools of the Trade Materials

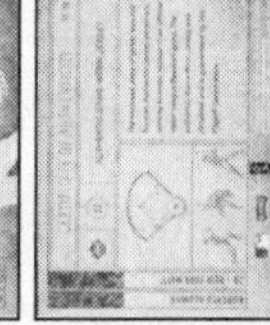

MINT NRMT
1-74 PRINT RUNS B/WN 40-250 COPIES PER

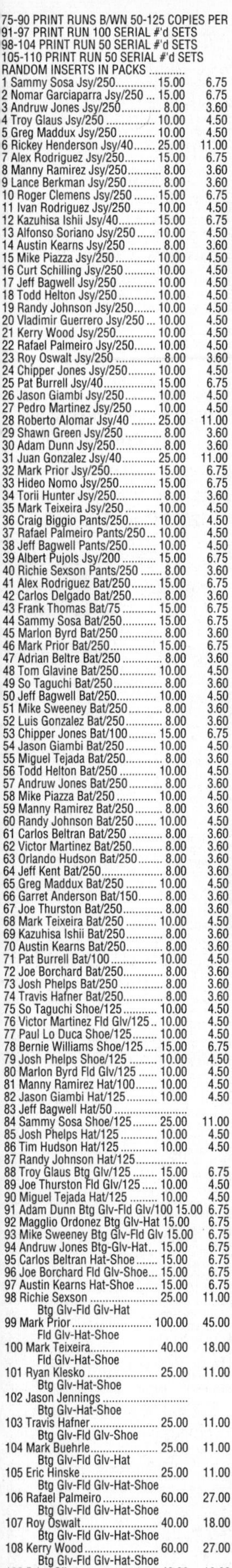

75-90 PRINT RUNS B/WN 50-125 COPIES PER
91-97 PRINT RUN 100 SERIAL #'d SETS
98-104 PRINT RUN 50 SERIAL #'d SETS
105-110 PRINT RUN 50 SERIAL #'d SETS
RANDOM INSERTS IN PACKS
1 Sammy Sosa Jsy/250 15.00 6.75
2 Nomar Garciaparra Jsy/250 15.00 6.75
3 Andruw Jones Jsy/250 8.00 3.60
4 Troy Glaus Jsy/250 10.00 4.50
5 Greg Maddux Jsy/250 10.00 4.50
6 Rickey Henderson Jsy/40 25.00 11.00
7 Alex Rodriguez Jsy/250 15.00 6.75
8 Manny Ramirez Jsy/250 8.00 3.60
9 Lance Berkman Jsy/250 8.00 3.60
10 Roger Clemens Jsy/250 15.00 6.75
11 Ivan Rodriguez Jsy/250 10.00 4.50
12 Kazuhisa Ishii Jsy/40 15.00 6.75
13 Alfonso Soriano Jsy/250 10.00 4.50
14 Austin Kearns Jsy/250 8.00 3.60
15 Mike Piazza Jsy/250 10.00 4.50
16 Curt Schilling Jsy/250 10.00 4.50
17 Jeff Bagwell Jsy/250 10.00 4.50
18 Todd Helton Jsy/250 10.00 4.50
19 Randy Johnson Jsy/250 10.00 4.50
20 Vladimir Guerrero Jsy/250 10.00 4.50
21 Kerry Wood Jsy/250 10.00 4.50
22 Rafael Palmeiro Jsy/250 10.00 4.50
23 Roy Oswalt Jsy/250 8.00 3.60
24 Chipper Jones Jsy/250 10.00 4.50
25 Pat Burrell Jsy/40 15.00 6.75
26 Jason Giambi Jsy/250 10.00 4.50
27 Pedro Martinez Jsy/250 10.00 4.50
28 Roberto Alomar Jsy/40 25.00 11.00
29 Shawn Green Jsy/250 8.00 3.60
30 Adam Dunn Jsy/250 8.00 3.60
31 Juan Gonzalez Jsy/40 25.00 11.00
32 Mark Prior Jsy/250 15.00 6.75
33 Hideo Nomo Jsy/250 15.00 6.75
34 Torii Hunter Jsy/250 8.00 3.60
35 Mark Teixeira Jsy/250 10.00 4.50
36 Craig Biggio Pants/250 10.00 4.50
37 Rafael Palmeiro Pants/250 10.00 4.50
38 Jeff Bagwell Pants/250 10.00 4.50
39 Albert Pujols Jsy/200 15.00 6.75
40 Richie Sexson Pants/250 8.00 3.60
41 Alex Rodriguez Bat/250 15.00 6.75
42 Carlos Delgado Bat/250 8.00 3.60
43 Frank Thomas Bat/75 15.00 6.75
44 Sammy Sosa Bat/250 15.00 6.75
45 Marlon Byrd Bat/250 8.00 3.60
46 Mark Prior Bat/250 15.00 6.75
47 Adrian Beltre Bat/250 8.00 3.60
48 Tom Glavine Bat/250 10.00 4.50
49 So Taguchi Bat/250 8.00 3.60
50 Jeff Bagwell Bat/250 10.00 4.50
51 Mike Sweeney Bat/250 8.00 3.60
52 Luis Gonzalez Bat/250 8.00 3.60
53 Chipper Jones Bat/100 15.00 6.75
54 Jason Giambi Bat/250 10.00 4.50
55 Miguel Tejada Bat/250 8.00 3.60
56 Todd Helton Bat/250 10.00 4.50
57 Andruw Jones Bat/250 8.00 3.60
58 Mike Piazza Bat/250 10.00 4.50
59 Manny Ramirez Bat/250 8.00 3.60
60 Randy Johnson Bat/250 10.00 4.50
61 Carlos Beltran Bat/250 8.00 3.60
62 Victor Martinez Bat/250 8.00 3.60
63 Orlando Hudson Bat/250 8.00 3.60
64 Jeff Kent Bat/250 8.00 3.60
65 Greg Maddux Bat/250 10.00 4.50
66 Garret Anderson Bat/150 8.00 3.60
67 Joe Thurston Bat/250 8.00 3.60
68 Mark Teixeira Bat/250 10.00 4.50
69 Kazuhisa Ishii Bat/250 8.00 3.60
70 Austin Kearns Bat/250 8.00 3.60
71 Pat Burrell Bat/100 10.00 4.50
72 Joe Borchard Bat/250 8.00 3.60
73 Josh Phelps Bat/250 8.00 3.60
74 Travis Hafner Bat/250 8.00 3.60
75 So Taguchi Shoe/125 10.00 4.50
76 Victor Martinez Fld Glv/125 10.00 4.50
77 Paul Lo Duca Shoe/125 10.00 4.50
78 Bernie Williams Shoe/125 15.00 6.75
79 Josh Phelps Shoe/125 10.00 4.50
80 Marlon Byrd Fld Glv/125 10.00 4.50
81 Manny Ramirez Hat/100 10.00 4.50
82 Jason Giambi Hat/125 10.00 4.50
83 Jeff Bagwell Hat/50
84 Sammy Sosa Shoe/125 25.00 11.00
85 Josh Phelps Hat/125 10.00 4.50
86 Tim Hudson Hat/125 10.00 4.50
87 Randy Johnson Hat/125
88 Troy Glaus Btg Glv/125 15.00 6.75
89 Joe Thurston Fld Glv/125 10.00 4.50
90 Miguel Tejada Hat/125 10.00 4.50
91 Adam Dunn Btg Glv-Fld Glv/100 15.00 6.75
92 Magglio Ordonez Btg Glv-Hat 15.00 6.75
93 Mike Sweeney Btg Glv-Fld Glv 15.00 6.75
94 Andruw Jones Btg-Glv-Hat 15.00 6.75
95 Carlos Beltran Hat-Shoe 15.00 6.75
96 Joe Borchard Fld Glv-Shoe 15.00 6.75
97 Austin Kearns Hat-Shoe 15.00 6.75
98 Richie Sexson 25.00 11.00
Btg Glv-Fld Glv-Hat
99 Mark Prior 100.00 45.00
Fld Glv-Hat-Shoe
100 Mark Teixeira 40.00 18.00
Fld Glv-Hat-Shoe
101 Ryan Klesko 25.00 11.00
Btg Glv-Hat-Shoe
102 Jason Jennings
Btg Glv-Hat-Shoe
103 Travis Hafner 25.00 11.00
Btg Glv-Fld Glv-Shoe
104 Mark Buehrle 25.00 11.00
Btg Glv-Fld Glv-Hat
105 Eric Hinske 25.00 11.00
Btg Glv-Fld Glv-Hat-Shoe
106 Rafael Palmeiro 60.00 27.00
Btg Glv-Fld Glv-Hat-Shoe
107 Roy Oswalt 40.00 18.00
Btg Glv-Fld Glv-Hat-Shoe
108 Kerry Wood 60.00 27.00
Btg Glv-Fld Glv-Hat-Shoe
109 Brian Giles 40.00 18.00
Btg Glv-Fld Glv-Hat-Shoe
110 Ivan Rodriguez 60.00 27.00
Btg Glv-Fld Glv-Hat-Shoe

2003 Playoff Absolute Memorabilia Tools of the Trade Materials Spectrum

MINT NRMT
*SPECTRUM p/r 40-50: 1.25X TO 3X BASIC
PRINT RUNS B/WN 10-50 COPIES PER
NO PRICING ON QTY OF 25 OR LESS.

2003 Playoff Absolute Memorabilia Total Bases

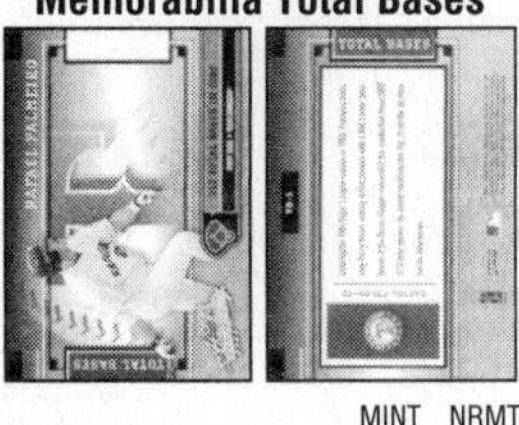

MINT NRMT
STATED ODDS 1:16
1 Albert Pujols 8.00 3.60
2 Nomar Garciaparra 6.00 2.70
3 Jason Giambi 4.00 1.80
4 Miguel Tejada 1.50 .70
5 Rafael Palmeiro 2.50 1.10
6 Sammy Sosa 6.00 2.70
7 Pat Burrell 1.50 .70
8 Lance Berkman 1.50 .70
9 Bernie Williams 2.50 1.10
10 Jim Thome 4.00 1.80
11 Carlos Beltran 1.50 .70
12 Eric Chavez 1.50 .70
13 Alex Rodriguez 6.00 2.70
14 Magglio Ordonez 1.50 .70
15 Brian Giles 1.50 .70
16 Alfonso Soriano 2.50 1.10
17 Shawn Green 1.50 .70
18 Vladimir Guerrero 4.00 1.80
19 Garret Anderson 1.50 .70
20 Todd Helton 2.50 1.10
21 Barry Bonds 10.00 4.50
22 Jeff Kent 1.50 .70
23 Torii Hunter 1.50 .70
24 Ichiro Suzuki 6.00 2.70
25 Derek Jeter 10.00 4.50
26 Chipper Jones 4.00 1.80
27 Jeff Bagwell 2.50 1.10
28 Mike Piazza 6.00 2.70
29 Rickey Henderson 4.00 1.80
30 Ken Griffey Jr. 6.00 2.70

2003 Playoff Absolute Memorabilia Total Bases Materials 1B

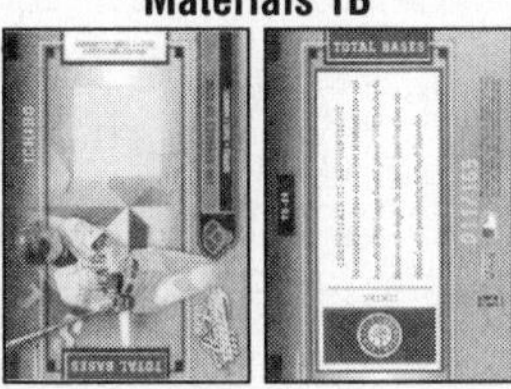

MINT NRMT
RANDOM INSERTS IN PACKS
PRINT RUNS B/WN 28-165 COPIES PER
1 Albert Pujols/109 20.00 9.00
2 Nomar Garciaparra/112 20.00 9.00
3 Jason Giambi/100 15.00 6.75
4 Miguel Tejada/140 10.00 4.50
5 Rafael Palmeiro/58 25.00 11.00
6 Sammy Sosa/90 20.00 9.00
7 Pat Burrell/87 10.00 4.50
8 Lance Berkman/90 10.00 4.50
9 Bernie Williams/146 10.00 4.50
10 Jim Thome/73 15.00 6.75
11 Carlos Beltran/94 10.00 4.50
12 Eric Chavez/93 10.00 4.50
13 Alex Rodriguez/101 20.00 9.00
14 Magglio Ordonez/103 10.00 4.50
15 Brian Giles/68 10.00 4.50
16 Alfonso Soriano/117 15.00 6.75
17 Shawn Green/92 10.00 4.50
18 Vladimir Guerrero/128 10.00 4.50
19 Garret Anderson/107 10.00 4.50
20 Todd Helton/109 15.00 6.75
21 Barry Bonds/70 30.00 13.50
22 Jeff Kent/114 10.00 4.50
23 Torii Hunter/92 10.00 4.50
24 Ichiro Suzuki/165 40.00 18.00
25 Derek Jeter/147 40.00 18.00
26 Chipper Jones/117 15.00 6.75
27 Jeff Bagwell/100 15.00 6.75
28 Mike Piazza/76
29 Rickey Henderson/28 40.00 18.00
30 Ken Griffey Jr./36

2003 Playoff Absolute Memorabilia Total Bases Materials 2B

MINT NRMT
RANDOM INSERTS IN PACKS
PRINT RUNS B/WN 6-56 COPIES PER
NO PRICING ON QTY OF 25 OR LESS.
1 Albert Pujols/40 50.00 22.00
2 Nomar Garciaparra/56 40.00 18.00
3 Jason Giambi/34
4 Miguel Tejada/30
5 Rafael Palmeiro/34
6 Sammy Sosa/19
7 Pat Burrell/39 15.00 6.75
8 Lance Berkman/35 25.00 11.00
9 Bernie Williams/37
10 Jim Thome/19
11 Carlos Beltran/44 15.00 6.75
12 Eric Chavez/31
13 Alex Rodriguez/27 80.00 36.00
14 Magglio Ordonez/47 15.00 6.75
15 Brian Giles/37
16 Alfonso Soriano/51 25.00 11.00
17 Shawn Green/31 25.00 11.00
18 Vladimir Guerrero/37 25.00 11.00
19 Garret Anderson/56 15.00 6.75
20 Todd Helton/39 25.00 11.00
21 Barry Bonds/31 60.00 27.00
22 Jeff Kent/42 15.00 6.75
23 Torii Hunter/37 15.00 6.75
24 Ichiro Suzuki/27
25 Derek Jeter/26 80.00 36.00
26 Chipper Jones/35 40.00 18.00
27 Jeff Bagwell/33 40.00 18.00
28 Mike Piazza/23
29 Rickey Henderson/6
30 Ken Griffey Jr./8

2003 Playoff Absolute Memorabilia Total Bases Materials 3B

MINT NRMT
RANDOM INSERTS IN PACKS
PRINT RUNS B/WN 1-8 COPIES PER
NO PRICING DUE TO SCARCITY

2003 Playoff Absolute Memorabilia Total Bases Materials HR

MINT NRMT
RANDOM INSERTS IN PACKS
PRINT RUNS B/WN 5-57 COPIES PER
NO PRICING ON QTY OF 25 OR LESS.
1 Albert Pujols/34 60.00 27.00
2 Nomar Garciaparra/24
3 Jason Giambi/41 25.00 11.00
4 Miguel Tejada/34 25.00 11.00
5 Rafael Palmeiro/43 25.00 11.00
6 Sammy Sosa/49
7 Pat Burrell/37 15.00 6.75
8 Lance Berkman/42 15.00 6.75
9 Bernie Williams/19
10 Jim Thome/52 25.00 11.00
11 Carlos Beltran/29
12 Eric Chavez/34 25.00 11.00
13 Alex Rodriguez/57 40.00 18.00
14 Magglio Ordonez/38 15.00 6.75
15 Brian Giles/38 15.00 6.75
16 Alfonso Soriano/39 25.00 11.00
17 Shawn Green/42 15.00 6.75
18 Vladimir Guerrero/39 25.00 11.00
19 Garret Anderson/29 25.00 11.00
20 Todd Helton/30
21 Barry Bonds/46 50.00 22.00
22 Jeff Kent/37 15.00 6.75
23 Torii Hunter/29 25.00 11.00
24 Ichiro Suzuki/8
25 Derek Jeter/18
26 Chipper Jones 26 40.00 18.00
27 Jeff Bagwell/31 40.00 18.00
28 Mike Piazza/33 50.00 22.00
29 Rickey Henderson/5
30 Ken Griffey Jr./8

2003 Playoff Absolute Memorabilia Atlantic City National

Collectors attending the 2003 Atlantic City National who opened Donruss Product while at their corporate booth were able to receive these specially produced cards. These cards parallel the regular Playoff Absolute Memorabilia set but have a special Atlantic City National embossing on the front and were printed to a stated print run of five serial numbers which is visible on the back. Due to market scarcity, no pricing is provided for these cards.

MINT NRMT
PRINT RUN 5 SERIAL #'d SETS

2002 Playoff Piece of the Game

This 100 card set was issued in November, 2002. It was released in six card packs, issued six packs to a box and 24 boxes to a case, which retailed for $16.99 per pack. The first 50 cards of the set featured veterans while the final 50 cards featured Rookie Cards. All the cards from 51 through 100 were issued to a stated print run of 500 serial·numbered sets.

Nm-Mt Ex-Mt
COMP.SET w/o SP's (50) 40.00 12.00
COMMON CARD (1-50) .75 .23
COMMON CARD (51-100) 8.00 2.40
1 Vladimir Guerrero 2.00 .60
2 Troy Glaus 1.25 .35
3 Ichiro Suzuki 3.00 .90
4 Chipper Jones 2.00 .60
5 Roberto Alomar 2.00 .60
6 Scott Rolen 1.25 .35
7 Randy Johnson 2.00 .60
8 Roger Clemens 4.00 1.20
9 Nomar Garciaparra 3.00 .90
10 Greg Maddux 3.00 .90
11 Barry Bonds 5.00 1.50
12 Derek Jeter 5.00 1.50
13 Albert Pujols 4.00 1.20
14 Kerry Wood 2.00 .60
15 Jim Thome 2.00 .60
16 Manny Ramirez .75 .23
17 Carlos Delgado .75 .23
18 Magglio Ordonez .75 .23
19 Torii Hunter .75 .23
20 Garret Anderson .75 .23
21 Eric Chavez .75 .23
22 Rafael Palmeiro 1.25 .35
23 Andruw Jones .75 .23
24 Cliff Floyd .75 .23
25 Sammy Sosa 3.00 .90
26 Mike Mussina 2.00 .60
27 Jeff Bagwell 1.25 .35
28 Miguel Tejada .75 .23
29 Curt Schilling 1.25 .35
30 Tom Glavine 1.25 .35
31 Frank Thomas 2.00 .60
32 Jim Edmonds .75 .23
33 Juan Gonzalez 2.00 .60
34 Todd Helton 1.25 .35
35 Shawn Green .75 .23
36 Alfonso Soriano 1.25 .35
37 Lance Berkman .75 .23
38 Barry Zito 1.25 .35
39 Ryan Klesko .75 .23
40 Larry Walker 1.25 .35
41 Craig Biggio 1.25 .35
42 Luis Gonzalez .75 .23
43 Ivan Rodriguez 2.00 .60
44 J.D. Drew .75 .23
45 Roy Oswalt .75 .23
46 Jason Giambi 2.00 .60
47 Brian Giles .75 .23
48 Richie Sexson .75 .23
49 Pat Burrell .75 .23
50 Alex Rodriguez 3.00 .90
51 So Taguchi ROO RC 10.00 3.00
52 Allan Simpson ROO RC 8.00 2.40
53 Oliver Perez ROO RC 10.00 3.00
54 Ben Howard ROO RC 8.00 2.40
55 Kirk Saarloos ROO RC 8.00 2.40
56 Francis Beltran ROO RC 8.00 2.40
57 Jorge Padilla ROO RC 8.00 2.40
58 Brandon Puffer ROO RC 8.00 2.40
59 Brian Mallette ROO RC 8.00 2.40
60 Kyle Kane ROO RC 8.00 2.40
61 Travis Driskill ROO RC 8.00 2.40
62 Jeremy Lambert ROO RC 8.00 2.40
63 Steve Kent ROO RC 8.00 2.40
64 Julius Matos ROO RC 8.00 2.40
65 Julio Mateo ROO RC 8.00 2.40
66 Kazuhisa Ishii ROO RC 12.00 3.60
67 Franklyn German ROO RC 8.00 2.40
68 John Foster ROO RC 8.00 2.40
69 Luis Ugueto ROO RC 8.00 2.40
70 Shawn Sedlacek ROO RC 8.00 2.40
71 Earl Snyder ROO RC 8.00 2.40
72 J.Simontacchi ROO RC 8.00 2.40
73 Victor Alvarez ROO RC 8.00 2.40
74 Tom Shearn ROO RC 8.00 2.40
75 Corey Thurman ROO RC 8.00 2.40
76 Eric Junge ROO RC 8.00 2.40
77 Hansel Izquierdo ROO RC 8.00 2.40
78 Elio Serrano ROO RC 8.00 2.40
79 J.J. Trujillo ROO RC 8.00 2.40
80 Chris Snelling ROO RC 10.00 3.00
81 S.Komiyama ROO RC 8.00 2.40
82 Brandon Backe ROO RC 8.00 2.40
83 An. Machado ROO RC 8.00 2.40
84 Doug Devore ROO RC 8.00 2.40
85 Steve Bechler ROO RC 8.00 2.40
86 John Ennis ROO RC 8.00 2.40
87 Rodrigo Rosario ROO RC 8.00 2.40
88 Jorge Sosa ROO RC 8.00 2.40
89 Ken Huckaby ROO RC 8.00 2.40
90 Mike Moriarty ROO RC 8.00 2.40
91 Mike Crudale ROO RC 8.00 2.40
92 Kevin Frederick ROO RC 8.00 2.40
93 Aaron Guiel ROO RC 8.00 2.40
94 Jose Rodriguez ROO RC 8.00 2.40
95 Andy Shibilo ROO RC 8.00 2.40
96 Deivis Santos ROO 8.00 2.40
97 Felix Escalona ROO RC 8.00 2.40
98 Miguel Asencio ROO RC 8.00 2.40
99 Takahito Nomura ROO RC 8.00 2.40
100 Cam Esslinger ROO RC 8.00 2.40

2002 Playoff Piece of the Game Materials

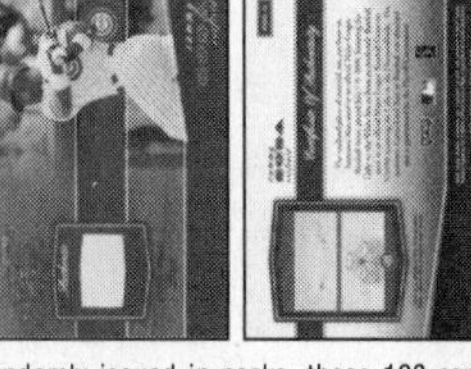

Randomly issued in packs, these 193 cards featured game-used memorabilia from many of today's leading players as well as a few retired superstars. Cards numbered from 91 through 95 were issued to a stated print run of 500 serial numbered sets and cards numbered from 96 through 100 were issued to a stated print run of 250 serial numbered sets. In addition, there were a whole number of short-printed cards between numbers 1 and 90 and we have put the print run of those cards next to the card in our checklist.

Nm-Mt Ex-Mt
1A Adam Dunn Bat 8.00 2.40
1B Adam Dunn Jsy/50 25.00 7.50
1C Adam Dunn Btg Glv/50 25.00 7.50
2A Adrian Beltre Bat 8.00 2.40
2B Adrian Beltre Jsy/100 15.00 4.50
3A Albert Pujols Base 15.00 4.50
3B Albert Pujols Ball/50 40.00 12.00
4A Alex Rodriguez Jsy 15.00 4.50
5A Alex Rodriguez Bat 15.00 4.50
5B Alex Rodriguez Fld Glv/50 60.00 18.00
6A Andruw Jones Jsy 8.00 2.40
6B Andruw Jones Fld Glv/50 25.00 7.50
6C Andruw Jones Hat/50 25.00 7.50
7A Andruw Jones Bat 8.00 2.40
7B Andruw Jones Shoe/50 25.00 7.50
7C Andruw Jones Btg Glv/50 25.00 7.50
8A Barry Bonds Base 20.00 6.00
8B Barry Bonds Ball/50 50.00 15.00
9A Barry Larkin Bat 10.00 3.00
9B Barry Larkin Jsy/100 20.00 6.00
10A Juan Gonzalez Jsy 10.00 3.00
11A Bernie Williams Bat 10.00 3.00
11B Bernie Williams Shoe/50
11C Bernie Williams Jsy/50 30.00 9.00
12A Carlos Delgado Jsy 8.00 2.40
12B Carlos Delgado Bat/100 15.00 4.50
13A Chipper Jones Jsy 10.00 3.00
14A Chipper Jones Bat 10.00 3.00
14B Chipper Jones Fld Glv/50 40.00 12.00
15A Craig Biggio Jsy 10.00 3.00
15B Craig Biggio Btg Glv/50 30.00 9.00
16A Craig Biggio Bat 10.00 3.00
16B Craig Biggio Shoe/100 20.00 6.00
17A Cristian Guzman Jsy 8.00 2.40
18A Curt Schilling Jsy 10.00 3.00
19A Derek Jeter Base 20.00 6.00
19B Derek Jeter Ball/50 50.00 15.00
20A Edgar Martinez Jsy 10.00 3.00
20B Edgar Martinez Bat/100 20.00 6.00
21A Edgardo Alfonzo Jsy 8.00 2.40
21B Edgardo Alfonzo Bat/100 15.00 4.50
22A Ellis Burks Jsy 8.00 2.40
23A Frank Thomas Bat 10.00 3.00
23B Frank Thomas Jsy/100 20.00 6.00
24A Freddy Garcia Jsy 8.00 2.40
25A Greg Maddux Jsy 15.00 4.50
25B Greg Maddux Bat/50 60.00 18.00
25B Greg Maddux Shoe/50 60.00 18.00
26A Harmon Killebrew Pants 10.00 3.00
26B Harmon Killebrew Bat/50 40.00 12.00
26C Harmon Killebrew Jsy/50 40.00 12.00
27A Hideo Nomo Jsy 20.00 6.00
27B Hideo Nomo Bat/50 100.00 30.00
28A Ichiro Suzuki Base 20.00 6.00
28B Ichiro Suzuki Ball/50 60.00 18.00
29A Ivan Rodriguez Jsy 10.00 3.00
29B Ivan Rodriguez Fld Glv/50 40.00 12.00
29C Ivan Rodriguez Btg Glv/50 40.00 12.00
30A Ivan Rodriguez Bat 10.00 3.00
30B Ivan Rodriguez Hat/50 40.00 12.00
30C Ivan Rodriguez Shoe/50 40.00 12.00
31A J.D. Drew Bat 8.00 2.40
31B J.D. Drew Shoe/100 15.00 4.50
32A J.D. Drew Jsy 8.00 2.40
33A Javy Lopez Jsy 8.00 2.40
33B Javy Lopez Bat/100 15.00 4.50
34A Jeff Bagwell Jsy 10.00 3.00
34B Jeff Bagwell Bat/50
34C Jeff Bagwell Hat/50
35A Jim Edmonds Jsy 8.00 2.40
35B Jim Edmonds Btg Glv/50 25.00 7.50
36A Jim Edmonds Bat 8.00 2.40
36B Jim Edmonds Shoe/50 25.00 7.50
36C Jim Edmonds Wristband/50 25.00 7.50
37A John Olerud Jsy 8.00 2.40
37B John Olerud Bat/100 15.00 4.50
38A John Smoltz Jsy 10.00 3.00
39A Jose Cruz Jr. Jsy 8.00 2.40
39B Jose Cruz Jr. Bat/100 15.00 4.50
40A Jose Vidro Jsy 8.00 2.40
40B Jose Vidro Bat/100 15.00 4.50
41A Juan Gonzalez Bat 10.00 3.00
42A Juan Pierre Jsy 8.00 2.40
42B Juan Pierre Shoe/50 25.00 7.50
42C Juan Pierre Btg Glv/50 25.00 7.50
43A Ken Griffey Jr. Base 15.00 4.50
44A Kenny Lofton Bat 8.00 2.40
44B Kenny Lofton Shoe/50 25.00 7.50
44C Kenny Lofton Btg Glv/50 25.00 7.50
45A Kerry Wood Bat 10.00 3.00
45B Kerry Wood Fld Glv/50
45C Kerry Wood Btg Glv/50 40.00 12.00
46A Kevin Brown Jsy 8.00 2.40
47A Lance Berkman Jsy 8.00 2.40
47B Lance Berkman Btg Glv/50. 25.00 7.50
48A Lance Berkman Bat 8.00 2.40
48B Lance Berkman Shoe/50
48C Lance Berkman Fld Glv/50 25.00 7.50
49A Larry Walker Jsy 10.00 3.00
49B Larry Walker Bat/50 30.00 9.00
50A Luis Gonzalez Jsy 8.00 2.40
50B Luis Gonzalez Bat/100 15.00 4.50
51A Magglio Ordonez Jsy 8.00 2.40
51B Magglio Ordonez Btg Glv/50 25.00 7.50
52A Magglio Ordonez Bat 8.00 2.40
52B Magglio Ordonez Shoe/50 25.00 7.50
52C Magglio Ordonez Hat/50 25.00 7.50
53A Manny Ramirez Jsy 8.00 2.40
54A Manny Ramirez Bat 8.00 2.40
54B Manny Ramirez Hat/50
54C Manny Ramirez Fld Glv/50 25.00 7.50
55A Vladimir Guerrero White Jsy 10.00 3.00
56A Mark Grace Bat 10.00 3.00
56B Mark Grace Fld Glv/50 30.00 9.00
57A Michael Barrett Jsy 8.00 2.40
58A Miguel Tejada Jsy 8.00 2.40
58B Miguel Tejada Hat/50 25.00 7.50
58C Miguel Tejada Bat/50 25.00 7.50
59A Mike Piazza Jsy 15.00 4.50
60A Mike Piazza Bat 15.00 4.50
60B Mike Piazza Shoe/100 50.00 15.00
61A Mike Schmidt Bat 20.00 6.00
61B Mike Schmidt Fld Glv/50
61C Mike Schmidt Jsy/50
62A Mike Sweeney Jsy 8.00 2.40
63A Nolan Ryan Jsy 40.00 12.00
63B Nolan Ryan Fld Glv/50
64A Nomar Garciaparra Jsy 15.00 4.50
64B Nomar Garciaparra Bat/50 50.00 15.00
65A Paul Lo Duca Jsy 8.00 2.40
65B Paul Lo Duca Chest Pro/50
65C Paul Lo Duca Fld Glv/50 25.00 7.50
66A Rafael Palmeiro Jsy 10.00 3.00
66B Rafael Palmeiro Btg Glv/50
67A Rafael Palmeiro Bat 10.00 3.00
67B Rafael Palmeiro Shoe/50 30.00 9.00
67C Rafael Palmeiro Fld Glv/50 30.00 9.00
68A Jose Canseco Bat 10.00 3.00
68B Jose Canseco Jsy/50 40.00 12.00
68C Jose Canseco Btg Glv/50
69A Raul Mondesi Jsy 8.00 2.40
70A Reggie Jackson Bat 10.00 3.00
70B Reggie Jackson Jsy/50 30.00 9.00
71A Rickey Henderson Bat 10.00 3.00
71B Rickey Henderson Jsy/100. 20.00 6.00

72A Roberto Alomar Bat 10.00 3.00
73A Robin Ventura Jsy 8.00 2.40
74A Rod Carew Bat 10.00 3.00
74B Rod Carew Hat/50
74C Rod Carew Jsy/50 30.00 9.00
75A Roger Clemens Jsy 15.00 4.50
75B Roger Clemens Fld Glv/50 60.00 18.00
76A Sammy Sosa Base 15.00 4.50
76B Sammy Sosa Ball/50 40.00 12.00
77A Sean Casey Jsy 8.00 2.40
77B Sean Casey Bat/100 15.00 4.50
78A Shannon Stewart Jsy 8.00 2.40
78B Shannon Stewart Hat/100 15.00 4.50
79A Shawn Green Jsy 8.00 2.40
80A Shawn Green Bat 8.00 2.40
81A Tim Hudson Jsy 8.00 2.40
81B Tim Hudson Shoe/50 25.00 7.50
81C Tim Hudson Fld Glv/50 25.00 7.50
82A Todd Helton Bat 10.00 3.00
82B Todd Helton Jsy/100 20.00 6.00
83A Tom Glavine Jsy 10.00 3.00
83B Tom Glavine Btg Glv/50 30.00 9.00
84A Tony Gwynn Grey Jsy 15.00 4.50
84B Tony Gwynn Fld Glv/50 80.00 24.00
85A Tony Gwynn Blue Jsy 15.00 4.50
85B Tony Gwynn Hat/100 50.00 15.00
86A Tony Gwynn Bat 15.00 4.50
86B Tony Gwynn Shoe/50 80.00 24.00
86C Tony Gwynn Btg Glv/50
87A Troy Glaus Jsy 10.00 3.00
87B Troy Glaus Bat/50 30.00 9.00
87C Troy Glaus Shoe/50 30.00 9.00
88A Tsuyoshi Shinjo Bat 8.00 2.40
88B Tsuyoshi Shinjo Hat/50 25.00 7.50
88C Tsuyoshi Shinjo Btg Glv/50 25.00 7.50
89A Vladimir Guerrero Grey Jsy 10.00 3.00
89B Vladimir Guerrero Fld Glv/50
90A Vladimir Guerrero Bat 10.00 3.00
91 Nomar Garciaparra Jsy 40.00 12.00
Pedro Martinez Jsy
92 Randy Johnson Jsy 20.00 6.00
Curt Schilling Jsy
93 Andruw Jones Jsy 20.00 6.00
Chipper Jones Jsy
94 Todd Helton Jsy 20.00 6.00
Larry Walker Jsy
95 Jeff Bagwell Pants 20.00 6.00
Craig Biggio Pants
96 Alex Rodriguez Bat-Jsy 40.00 12.00
97 Greg Maddux Bat-Jsy 40.00 12.00
98 Mike Piazza Bat-Jsy 40.00 12.00
99 Lance Berkman Bat-Jsy 20.00 6.00
100 Vladimir Guerrero Bat-Jsy 25.00 7.50

2002 Playoff Piece of the Game Materials Bronze

This 100 card set parallels the basic Materials insert set. Each card numbered 1-90 was issued to a stated print run of 250 sets while cards numbered 91 through 95 were issued to a stated print run of 100 sets and cards numbered 96 through 100 were issued to a stated print run of 50 serial numbered sets.

Nm-Mt Ex-Mt
*BRONZE 1-90: .6X TO 1.5X BASIC MATERIAL
*BRONZE 91-95: .5X TO 1.2X BASIC MATERIAL
*BRONZE 96-100: .6X TO 1.5X BASIC MATERIAL

2002 Playoff Piece of the Game Materials Gold

This 100 card set parallels the basic Materials insert set. Each card numbered 1-90 was issued to a stated print run of 50 sets while cards numbered 91 through 95 were issued to a stated print run of 25 sets and cards numbered 96 through 100 were issued to a stated print run of 10 serial numbered sets. Due to market scarcity, no pricing is provided for cards numbered 91 through 100.

Nm-Mt Ex-Mt
*GOLD 1-90: 1.25X TO 3X BASIC MATERIAL

2002 Playoff Piece of the Game Materials Silver

This 100 card set parallels the basic Materials insert set. Each card numbered 1-90 was issued to a stated print run of 100 sets while cards numbered 91 through 95 were issued to a stated print run of 50 sets and cards numbered 96 through 100 were issued to a stated print run of 25 serial numbered sets. Due to market scarcity, no pricing for cards numbered 96 through 100.

Nm-Mt Ex-Mt
*SILVER 1-90: .75X TO 2X BASIC MATERIAL
*SILVER 91-95: .75X TO 2X BASIC MATERIAL

2003 Playoff Piece of the Game

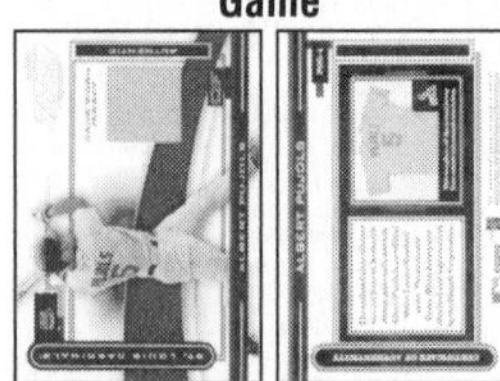

This 179 card set was released in September, 2003. The set was issued in one card packs with an $120 SRP. Each card contains a game-used memorabilia piece used by the featured player. These cards were issued to stated print runs between 10 and 200 serial numbered copies and we have notated that information in our checklist.

MINT NRMT
STATED ODDS 1:1.5
SERIAL #'d PRINTS B/WN 10-200 COPIES PER
NO PRICING ON QTY OF 25 OR LESS.
1A Adam Dunn Bat 8.00 3.60
1B Adam Dunn Btg Glv/40 15.00 6.75
2 Adam Dunn Jsy 8.00 3.60
3A Adrian Beltre Bat 8.00 3.60
3B Adrian Beltre Jsy/100 10.00 4.50
3C Adrian Beltre Hat/50 15.00 6.75
3D Adrian Beltre Shoe/50 15.00 6.75
4 Albert Pujols Jsy 20.00 9.00
5 Albert Pujols Bat 20.00 9.00
6 Alex Rodriguez Bat 10.00 4.50
7 Alex Rodriguez Blue Jsy 10.00 4.50
8 Alex Rodriguez White Jsy 10.00 4.50
9 Alfonso Soriano Bat 10.00 4.50
10 Alfonso Soriano Gray Jsy 10.00 4.50
11 Alfonso Soriano White Jsy 10.00 4.50
12 Brett Myers Jsy/50 15.00 6.75
13 Andruw Jones Jsy 8.00 3.60
14A Austin Kearns Jsy 8.00 3.60
14B Austin Kearns Bat/195 8.00 3.60
15A Barry Larkin Jsy 10.00 4.50
15B Barry Larkin Bat/200 10.00 4.50
16A Barry Zito Jsy 10.00 4.50
16B Barry Zito Hat/40 25.00 11.00
17A Bernie Williams Jsy 10.00 4.50
17B Bernie Williams Bat/95 15.00 6.75
17C Bernie Williams Shoe/45 25.00 11.00
18A Brian Giles Bat 8.00 3.60
18B Brian Giles Hat/85 10.00 4.50
18C Brian Giles Btg Glv/40 15.00 6.75
18D Brian Giles Shoe/45 15.00 6.75
19 Zach Day Jsy/50 15.00 6.75
20A Carlos Beltran Bat 8.00 3.60
20B Carlos Beltran Jsy/75 10.00 4.50
20C Carlos Beltran Hat/45 15.00 6.75
20D Carlos Beltran Shoe/25
21 Brandon Phillips Bat/50 15.00 6.75
22 Carlos Lee Bat/50 15.00 6.75
23A Casey Fossum Jsy/75 10.00 4.50
23B Casey Fossum Hat/25
23C Casey Fossum Fld Glv/25
23D Casey Fossum Shoe/25
24A Chipper Jones Jsy 10.00 4.50
24B Chipper Jones Bat/195 10.00 4.50
25 Marcus Giles Jsy/50 15.00 6.75
26A Craig Biggio Bat 10.00 4.50
26B Craig Biggio Jsy/100 15.00 6.75
26C Craig Biggio Hat/50 25.00 11.00
26D Craig Biggio Shoe/50 25.00 11.00
27 Curt Schilling Jsy 10.00 4.50
28 Derek Jeter Base 20.00 9.00
29A Edgar Martinez Jsy 10.00 4.50
29B Edgar Martinez Bat/150 10.00 4.50
30A Eric Chavez Jsy 8.00 3.60
30B Eric Chavez Bat/175 8.00 3.60
31A Eric Hinske Bat/25
31B Eric Hinske Hat/25
31C Eric Hinske Shoe/10
32A Frank Thomas Jsy 10.00 4.50
32B Frank Thomas Bat/190 10.00 4.50
33 Aubrey Huff Jsy/50 15.00 6.75
34A Gary Carter Jacket 8.00 3.60
34B Gary Carter Fld Glv/40 25.00 11.00
34C Gary Carter Bat/40 25.00 11.00
35 Greg Maddux Gray Jsy 10.00 4.50
36 Greg Maddux White Jsy 10.00 4.50
37 Hideki Matsui Base RC 20.00 9.00
38 Hideo Nomo White Jsy 15.00 6.75
39A Rod Carew Jacket 10.00 4.50
39B Rod Carew Shoe/100 15.00 6.75
39C Rod Carew Hat/50 25.00 11.00
40 Ichiro Suzuki Base 15.00 6.75
41A Ivan Rodriguez Bat 10.00 4.50
41B Ivan Rodriguez Btg Glv/10
41C Ivan Rodriguez Fld Glv/25
41D Ivan Rodriguez Shoe/25
42A Jason Giambi A's Bat 10.00 4.50
42B J.Giambi A's Hat/200 10.00 4.50
43 Jason Giambi Yanks Bat 10.00 4.50
44 J.C. Romero Jsy/50 15.00 6.75
45 Jason Giambi Yanks Jsy 10.00 4.50
46A Jeff Bagwell Jsy 10.00 4.50
46B Jeff Bagwell Bat/195 10.00 4.50
47 Josh Bard Jsy/50 15.00 6.75
48A Jim Thome Jsy 10.00 4.50
48B Jim Thome Bat/200 10.00 4.50
49 Jay Gibbons Jsy/200 8.00 3.60
50A Jorge Posada Jsy 10.00 4.50
50B Jorge Posada Bat/200 10.00 4.50
51A Juan Gonzalez Bat 10.00 4.50
51B Juan Gonzalez Jsy/40 25.00 11.00
52A Kazuhisa Ishii Bat 8.00 3.60
52B Kazuhisa Ishii Jsy/200 8.00 3.60
53 George Brett Bat 15.00 6.75
54A Kenny Lofton Bat 10.00 4.50
54B Kenny Lofton Hat/90 15.00 6.75
54C Kenny Lofton Fld Glv/45 25.00 11.00
54D Kenny Lofton Shoe/45 25.00 11.00
55A Kerry Wood Jsy 10.00 4.50
55B Kerry Wood Hat/90 15.00 6.75
55C Kerry Wood Fld Glv/45 25.00 11.00
55D Kerry Wood Shoe/45 25.00 11.00
56 Kevin Brown Jsy 8.00 3.60
57 Kirk Saarloos Jsy 8.00 3.60
58A Lance Berkman Jsy 8.00 3.60
58B Lance Berkman Bat/90 10.00 4.50
58C L.Berkman Btg Glv/45 15.00 6.75
58D Lance Berkman Shoe/45 15.00 6.75
59A Larry Walker Jsy 10.00 4.50
59B Larry Walker Bat/200 10.00 4.50
60A Magglio Ordonez Jsy 8.00 3.60
60B Magglio Ordonez Hat/100 10.00 4.50
60C Magglio Ordonez Bat/50 15.00 6.75
60D Mag.Ordonez Shoe/50 15.00 6.75
61A Manny Ramirez Jsy 8.00 3.60
61B Manny Ramirez Bat/200 8.00 3.60
62 Mark Mulder Jsy 8.00 3.60
63A Mark Prior Jsy 20.00 9.00
63B Mark Prior Hat/95 30.00 13.50
63C Mark Prior Fld Glv/45 60.00 27.00
63D Mark Prior Shoe/45 40.00 18.00
64 Matt Williams Jsy/50 25.00 11.00
65A Miguel Tejada Jsy 8.00 3.60
65B Miguel Tejada Bat/100 10.00 4.50
65C Miguel Tejada Hat/50 15.00 6.75
66A Mike Mussina Jsy 10.00 4.50
66B Mike Mussina Fld Glv/45 25.00 11.00
67 Mike Piazza Bat 10.00 4.50
68 Mike Piazza Black Jsy 10.00 4.50
69 Mike Piazza White Jsy 10.00 4.50
70 Nomar Garciaparra Bat 15.00 6.75
71 N.Garciaparra Gray Jsy 15.00 6.75
72 N.Garciaparra White Jsy 15.00 6.75
73 Paul Lo Duca Jsy/50 15.00 6.75
74 Pedro Martinez Jsy 10.00 4.50
75A Rafael Palmeiro Jsy 10.00 4.50
75B Rafael Palmeiro Hat/95 15.00 6.75
75C R.Palmeiro Fld Glv/45 25.00 11.00
75D R.Palmeiro Btg Glv/45 25.00 11.00
76 Randy Johnson Gray Jsy 10.00 4.50
77 Randy Johnson White Jsy 10.00 4.50
78A Rickey Henderson Jsy 10.00 4.50
78B Ri. Henderson Bat/195 10.00 4.50
79A Roberto Alomar Jsy 10.00 4.50
79B Roberto Alomar Bat/90 15.00 6.75
79C Rob.Alomar Btg Glv/45 25.00 11.00
80 Rod Carew Pants 10.00 4.50
81 Roger Clemens Gray Jsy 15.00 6.75
82 Roger Clemens White Jsy 15.00 6.75
83 Cal Ripken Jsy 25.00 11.00
84A Roy Oswalt Jsy 8.00 3.60
84B Roy Oswalt Fld Glv/95 10.00 4.50
84C Roy Oswalt Shoe/45 15.00 6.75
85 Jer Bonderman Jsy/50 RC 15.00 6.75
86 Ryne Sandberg Bat 15.00 6.75
87 Sammy Sosa Bat 15.00 6.75
88 Sammy Sosa Gray Jsy 15.00 6.75
89 Sammy Sosa White Jsy 15.00 6.75
90A Scott Rolen Jsy 10.00 4.50
90B Scott Rolen Bat/185 10.00 4.50
91 Frank Catalanotto Jsy/50 15.00 6.75
92A Shawn Green Jsy 8.00 3.60
92B Shawn Green Bat/195 8.00 3.60
93A Tim Hudson Jsy 8.00 3.60
93B Tim Hudson Hat/100 10.00 4.50
93C Tim Hudson Shoe/50 15.00 6.75
94A Todd Helton Jsy 10.00 4.50
94B Todd Helton Bat/195 10.00 4.50
95A Tony Gwynn Pants 10.00 4.50
95B Tony Gwynn Bat/95 15.00 6.75
95C Tony Gwynn Btg Glv/45 30.00 13.50
95D Tony Gwynn Hat/45
96A Torii Hunter Jsy 8.00 3.60
96B Torii Hunter Bat/150 8.00 3.60
97A Troy Glaus Jsy 10.00 4.50
97B Troy Glaus Bat/195 10.00 4.50
98 Run.Hernandez Jsy/50 15.00 6.75
99 Vernon Wells Jsy 8.00 3.60
100A Vladimir Guerrero Jsy 10.00 4.50
100B Vlad. Guerrero Bat/150 10.00 4.50

2003 Playoff Piece of the Game Bronze

MINT NRMT
*BRONZE ACTIVE: .4X TO 1X BASIC
*BRONZE RETIRED: .6X TO 1.5X BASIC
*BRONZE: .5X TO 1.2X BASIC RC's
*BRONZE: .4X TO 1X BASIC p/r 200
*BRONZE: .2X TO .5X BASIC p/r 50-75
*BRONZE: .2X TO .5X BASIC p/r 50 RC's
RANDOM INSERTS IN PACKS
STATED PRINT RUN 150 SERIAL #'d SETS
CARDS 21 AND 22 DO NOT EXIST

2003 Playoff Piece of the Game Gold

MINT NRMT
*GOLD ACTIVE: .75X TO 2X BASIC
*GOLD RETIRED: 1.25X TO 3X BASIC
*GOLD: 1X TO 2.5X BASIC RC's
*GOLD: .75X TO 2X BASIC p/r 200
*GOLD: .4X TO 1X BASIC p/r 50-75
*GOLD: .4X TO 1X BASIC p/r 50 RC's
RANDOM INSERTS IN PACKS
STATED PRINT RUN 50 SERIAL #'d SETS

2003 Playoff Piece of the Game Platinum

MINT NRMT
RANDOM INSERTS IN PACKS
STATED PRINT RUN 25 SERIAL #'d SETS
NO PRICING DUE TO SCARCITY

2003 Playoff Piece of the Game Prime

MINT NRMT
RANDOM INSERTS IN PACKS
STATED PRINT RUN 25 SERIAL #'d SETS
NO PRICING DUE TO SCARCITY
66-CARD SKIP-NUMBERED SET

2003 Playoff Piece of the Game Silver

MINT NRMT
*SILVER ACTIVE: .6X TO 1.5X BASIC
*SILVER RETIRED: 1X TO 2.5X BASIC
*SILVER: .75X TO 2X BASIC RC's
*SILVER: .6X TO 1.5X BASIC p/r 200
*SILVER: .3X TO .8X BASIC p/r 50-75
*SILVER: .3X TO .8X BASIC p/r 50 RC's
RANDOM INSERTS IN PACKS
STATED PRINT RUN 75 SERIAL #'d SETS

2003 Playoff Piece of the Game Autographs

MINT NRMT
RANDOM INSERTS IN PACKS
SERIAL #'d PRINTS B/WN 5-150 COPIES PER
1A Adam Dunn Bat/10
1B Adam Dunn Btg Glv/10
5 Albert Pujols Bat/5
6 Alex Rodriguez/10
12 Brett Myers Jsy 15.00 6.75
13 Andruw Jones Jsy/50 50.00 22.00
14A Austin Kearns Jsy/25
14B Austin Kearns Bat/5
17A Bernie Williams Jsy/10
17B Bernie Williams Bat/5
17C Bernie Williams Shoe/5
18A Brian Giles Bat/30 40.00 18.00
18B Brian Giles Hat/15
18C Brian Giles Btg Glv/10
18D Brian Giles Shoe/5
19 Zach Day Jsy 10.00 4.50
20A Carlos Beltran Bat/5
20B Carlos Beltran Jsy/25
20C Carlos Beltran Hat/5
20D Carlos Beltran Shoe/5
21 Brandon Phillips Bat 10.00 4.50
22 Carlos Lee Bat 15.00 6.75
23A Casey Fossum Jsy 10.00 4.50
23B Casey Fossum Hat/75 20.00 9.00
23C Casey Fossum Fld Glv/25
23D Casey Fossum Shoe/25
25 Marcus Giles Jsy 15.00 6.75
29A Edgar Martinez Jsy/100 50.00 22.00
29B Edgar Martinez Bat/50 60.00 27.00
30A Eric Chavez Jsy/75 30.00 13.50
30B Eric Chavez Bat/25
31A Eric Hinske Bat 10.00 4.50
31B Eric Hinske Hat/75 20.00 9.00
31C Eric Hinske Shoe/40 25.00 11.00
32A Frank Thomas Jsy/25
32B Frank Thomas Bat/10
33 Aubrey Huff Jsy 15.00 6.75
34A Gary Carter Jacket/15
34B Gary Carter Jsy/10
34C Gary Carter Fld Glv/10
34D Gary Carter Bat/10
38 Hideo Nomo White Jsy/5
41A Ivan Rodriguez Bat/75 50.00 22.00
41B Ivan Rodriguez Btg Glv/50 60.00 27.00
41C Ivan Rodriguez Fld Glv/25
41D Ivan Rodriguez Shoe/25
44 J.C. Romero Jsy 10.00 4.50
46A Jeff Bagwell Jsy/10
46B Jeff Bagwell Bat/5
47 Josh Bard Jsy 10.00 4.50
49 Jay Gibbons Jsy 15.00 6.75
51A Juan Gonzalez Bat/50 60.00 27.00
51B Juan Gonzalez Jsy/10
54A Kenny Lofton Bat/20
54B Kenny Lofton Hat/10
54C Kenny Lofton Fld Glv/5
54D Kenny Lofton Shoe/5
55A Kerry Wood Jsy/15
55B Kerry Wood Hat/10
55C Kerry Wood Fld Glv/5
55D Kerry Wood Shoe/5
57 Kirk Saarloos Jsy 10.00 4.50
58A Lance Berkman Jsy/15
58B Lance Berkman Bat/10
58C Lance Berkman Btg Glv/5
58D Lance Berkman Shoe/5
62 Mark Mulder Jsy/100 30.00 13.50
63A Mark Prior Jsy/25
63B Mark Prior Hat/5
63C Mark Prior Field Glove/5
63D Mark Prior Shoe/5
64 Matt Williams Jsy 15.00 6.75
67 Mike Piazza Bat/5
68 Mike Piazza Black Jsy/5
69 Mike Piazza White Jsy/5
73 Paul Lo Duca Jsy 15.00 6.75
74 Pedro Martinez Jsy/10
75A Rafael Palmeiro Jsy/10
75B Rafael Palmeiro Hat/5
75C Rafael Palmeiro Fld Glv/5
75D Rafael Palmeiro Btg Glv/5
76 Randy Johnson Gray/10
77 Randy Johnson White/10
78A Rickey Henderson Jsy/10
78B Rickey Henderson Bat/5
79A Roberto Alomar Jsy/25
79B Roberto Alomar Bat/10
79C Roberto Alomar Btg Glv/5
81 Roger Clemens Gray Jsy/10
82 Roger Clemens White Jsy/10
83 Cal Ripken Jsy/5
84A Roy Oswalt Jsy/50 40.00 18.00
84B Roy Oswalt Fld Glv/5
84C Roy Oswalt Shoe/5
85 Jeremy Bonderman Jsy 15.00 6.75
86 Ryne Sandberg Bat/40 120.00 55.00
90A Scott Rolen Jsy/50 50.00 22.00
90B Scott Rolen Bat/15
91 Frank Catalanotto Jsy 10.00 4.50
92A Shawn Green Jsy/10
92B Shawn Green Bat/5
95A Tony Gwynn Pants/5
95B Tony Gwynn Bat/5
95C Tony Gwynn Btg Glv/5
95D Tony Gwynn Hat/5
96A Torii Hunter Jsy/140 25.00 11.00
96B Torii Hunter Bat/50 40.00 18.00
97A Troy Glaus Jsy/15
97B Troy Glaus Bat/5
98 Runelvys Hernandez Jsy 10.00 4.50
100A Vladimir Guerrero Jsy/150 40.00 18.00
100B Vladimir Guerrero Bat/50 60.00 27.00

2003 Playoff Piece of the Game Prime Autographs

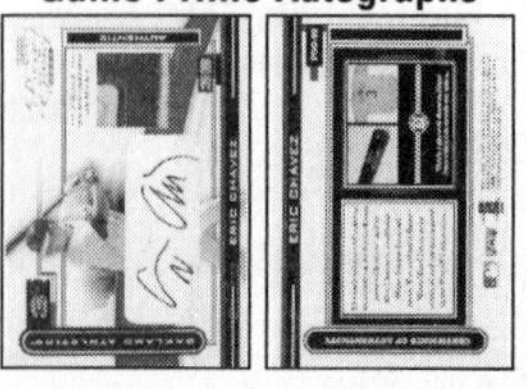

MINT NRMT
RANDOM INSERTS IN PACKS
NO PRICING DUE TO SCARCITY
2 Adam Dunn/10
4 Albert Pujols/5
8 Alex Rodriguez White/5
13 Andruw Jones/15
14 Austin Kearns/10
17 Bernie Williams/5
23 Casey Fossum/25
29 Edgar Martinez/25
30 Eric Chavez/10
32 Frank Thomas/5
46 Jeff Bagwell/5
55 Kerry Wood/10
58 Lance Berkman/5
62 Mark Mulder/25
63 Mark Prior/10
64 Matt Williams/25
68 Mike Piazza Black/5
69 Mike Piazza White/5
73 Paul Lo Duca/25
74 Pedro Martinez/5
75 Rafael Palmeiro/5
76 Randy Johnson Gray/5
77 Randy Johnson White/5
78 Rickey Henderson/5
79 Roberto Alomar/10
81 Roger Clemens Gray/5
82 Roger Clemens White/5
83 Cal Ripken/3
84 Roy Oswalt/25
90 Scott Rolen/10
92 Shawn Green/5
96 Torii Hunter/15
97 Troy Glaus/10
100 Vladimir Guerrero/25

2003 Playoff Piece of the Game Player Collection

MINT NRMT
*PLAY.COLL: .6X TO 1.5X PRESTIGE P.COLL.
RANDOM INSERTS IN PACKS
STATED PRINT RUN 100 SERIAL #'d SETS

2003 Playoff Portraits

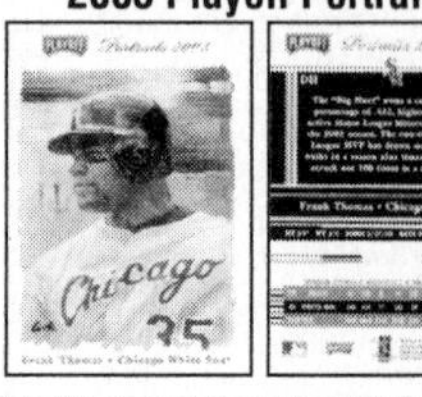

This 144 card set was released in September, 2003. The cards were issued in seven card packs with an $10 SRP which came 20 packs to a box and 12 boxes to a case. Randomly inserted in packs were exchange cards for original artwork in which collectors could be eligible to get the original painting that these cards are based on. The exchange deadline for these cards was April 1, 2005.

MINT NRMT
COMPLETE SET (144) 50.00 22.00
1 Vladimir Guerrero 2.00 .90
2 Luis Gonzalez .75 .35
3 Andruw Jones .75 .35
4 Manny Ramirez .75 .35
5 Derek Jeter 5.00 2.20
6 Eric Hinske .75 .35
7 Curt Schilling 1.25 .55
8 Adam Dunn .75 .35
9 Jason Jennings .75 .35
10 Mike Piazza Mets 3.00 1.35
11 Jason Giambi Yanks 2.00 .90
12 Jeff Bagwell 1.25 .55
13 Rickey Henderson Sox 2.00 .90
14 Randy Johnson D'backs 2.00 .90
15 Roger Clemens Yanks 4.00 1.80
16 Troy Glaus 1.25 .55
17 Hideo Nomo Dodgers 2.00 .90
18 Joe Borchard .75 .35
19 Torii Hunter .75 .35
20 Lance Berkman .75 .35
21 Todd Helton 1.25 .55
22 Mike Mussina 2.00 .90
23 Vernon Wells .75 .35
24 Pat Burrell .75 .35
25 Ichiro Suzuki 3.00 1.35
26 Shawn Green .75 .35
27 Frank Thomas 2.00 .90
28 Barry Zito 1.25 .55
29 Barry Bonds 5.00 2.20
30 Ken Griffey Jr. 3.00 1.35
31 Albert Pujols 4.00 1.80
32 Roberto Alomar 2.00 .90
33 Barry Larkin 2.00 .90
34 Tony Gwynn 3.00 1.35
35 Chipper Jones 2.00 .90
36 Pedro Martinez Sox 2.00 .90
37 Juan Gonzalez 2.00 .90
38 Greg Maddux 3.00 1.35
39 Tim Hudson .75 .35
40 Sammy Sosa 3.00 1.35
41 Victor Martinez .75 .35
42 Mark Buehrle .75 .35
43 Austin Kearns .75 .35
44 Kerry Wood 2.00 .90
45 Nomar Garciaparra 3.00 1.35
46 Alfonso Soriano 1.25 .55
47 Mark Prior 4.00 1.80
48 Richie Sexson .75 .35
49 Mark Teixeira 1.25 .55
50 Craig Biggio 1.25 .55
51 Rafael Palmeiro 1.25 .55
52 Carlos Beltran .75 .35
53 Bernie Williams 1.25 .55
54 Eric Chavez .75 .35
55 Paul Konerko .75 .35
56 Nolan Ryan Rgr 6.00 2.70
57 Mark Mulder .75 .35
58 Miguel Tejada .75 .35
59 Roy Oswalt .75 .35
60 Jim Edmonds .75 .35
61 Ryan Klesko .75 .35
62 Cal Ripken 8.00 3.60
63 Josh Beckett 1.25 .55
64 Kazuhisa Ishii .75 .35
65 Alex Rodriguez Rgr 3.00 1.35

66 Mike Sweeney .75 .35
67 C.C. Sabathia .75 .35
68 Jose Vidro .75 .35
69 Magglio Ordonez .75 .35
70 Carlos Delgado .75 .35
71 Jorge Posada 1.25 .55
72 Bobby Abreu .75 .35
73 Brian Giles .75 .35
74 Kirby Puckett 2.50 1.10
75 Yogi Berra 2.50 1.10
76 Ryne Sandberg 5.00 2.20
77 Tom Glavine 1.25 .55
78 Jim Thome 2.00 .90
79 Chris Snelling .75 .35
80 Drew Henson .75 .35
81 Junior Spivey .75 .35
82 Mike Schmidt 5.00 2.20
83 Jeff Kent .75 .35
84 Stan Musial 4.00 1.80
85 Garret Anderson .75 .35
86 Jose Contreras RC 5.00 2.20
87 Ivan Rodriguez 2.00 .90
88 Hideki Matsui RC 8.00 3.60
89 Don Mattingly 6.00 2.70
90 Angel Berroa .75 .35
91 George Brett 6.00 2.70
92 Jermaine Dye .75 .35
93 John Olerud .75 .35
94 Josh Phelps .75 .35
95 Sean Casey .75 .35
96 Larry Walker 1.25 .55
97 Jason Lane .75 .35
98 Travis Hafner .75 .35
99 Terrence Long .75 .35
100 Shannon Stewart .75 .35
101 Richard Hidalgo .75 .35
102 Joe Thurston .75 .35
103 Ben Sheets .75 .35
104 Orlando Cabrera .75 .35
105 Aramis Ramirez .75 .35
106 So Taguchi .75 .35
107 Frank Robinson 1.50 .70
108 Phil Nevin .75 .35
109 Dennis Tankersley .75 .35
110 J.D. Drew .75 .35
111 Paul Lo Duca .75 .35
112 Ozzie Smith 4.00 1.80
113 Carlos Lee .75 .35
114 Nick Johnson .75 .35
115 Edgar Martinez 1.25 .55
116 Hank Blalock 1.25 .55
117 Orlando Hudson .75 .35
118 Corey Patterson .75 .35
119 Steve Carlton 1.00 .45
120 Wade Miller .75 .35
121 Adrian Beltre .75 .35
122 Scott Rolen 1.25 .55
123 Brian Lawrence .75 .35
124 Rich Aurilia .75 .35
125 Tsuyoshi Shinjo .75 .35
126 John Buck .75 .35
127 Marlon Byrd .75 .35
128 Michael Cuddyer .75 .35
129 Marshall McDougall .75 .35
130 Travis Chapman .75 .35
131 Jose Morban .75 .35
132 Adam LaRoche 1.25 .55
133 Jose Castillo .75 .35
134 Walter Young .75 .35
135 Jeff Baker .75 .35
136 Jeremy Guthrie .75 .35
137 Pedro Martinez Expos 2.00 .90
138 Randy Johnson M's 2.00 .90
139 Alex Rodriguez M's 3.00 1.35
140 Hideo Nomo Mets 2.00 .90
141 Roger Clemens Sox 4.00 1.80
142 Rickey Henderson A's 2.00 .90
143 Jason Giambi A's 2.00 .90
144 Mike Piazza Dodgers 3.00 1.35
NNO Original Artwork EXCH/144

2003 Playoff Portraits Beige

MINT NRMT

*BEIGE: 1X TO 2.5X BASIC
*BEIGE RC'S: .75X TO 2X BASIC
RANDOM INSERTS IN PACKS
ONE BEIGE GLUED TO EACH SEALED BOX
STATED PRINT RUN 250 SERIAL #'d SETS

2003 Playoff Portraits Bronze

MINT NRMT

*BRONZE: 2X TO 5X BASIC
*BRONZE RC'S: 1.25X TO 3X BASIC
RANDOM INSERTS IN PACKS
STATED PRINT RUN 100 SERIAL #'d SETS

2003 Playoff Portraits Gold

MINT NRMT

RANDOM INSERTS IN PACKS
STATED PRINT RUN 10 SERIAL #'d SETS
NO PRICING DUE TO SCARCITY

2003 Playoff Portraits Silver

MINT NRMT

*SILVER ACTIVE: 2.5X TO 6X BASIC
*SILVER RETIRED: 3X TO 8X BASIC
*SILVER RC'S: 2.5X TO 6X BASIC
RANDOM INSERTS IN PACKS
STATED PRINT RUN 50 SERIAL #'d SETS

2003 Playoff Portraits Autographs Bronze

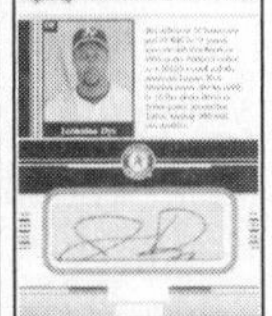

Randomly inserted in packs were these autographs from 128 of the players in the Playoff Portraits set. Since these cards have varying print runs, we have notated next to the player's name the print run. Please note that for cards with print run of 29 or fewer, no pricing is provided due to market scarcity.

MINT NRMT

RANDOM INSERTS IN PACKS
PRINT RUNS B/WN 2-100 COPIES PER
NO PRICING ON QTY OF 29 OR LESS.
1 Vladimir Guerrero/100 40.00 18.00
2 Luis Gonzalez/15
3 Andruw Jones/25
4 Manny Ramirez/15
6 Eric Hinske/100 10.00 4.50
7 Curt Schilling/2
8 Adam Dunn/50 40.00 18.00
9 Jason Jennings/100 10.00 4.50
10 Mike Piazza Mets/2
12 Jeff Bagwell/9
13 Rickey Henderson Sox/15
14 Randy Johnson D'backs/10
15 Roger Clemens Yanks/9
16 Troy Glaus/60 40.00 18.00
17 Hideo Nomo Dodgers/2
18 Joe Borchard/100 15.00 6.75
19 Torii Hunter/25
20 Lance Berkman/25
21 Todd Helton/10
22 Mike Mussina/4
23 Vernon Wells/20
24 Pat Burrell/10
26 Shawn Green/10
27 Frank Thomas/2
28 Barry Zito/10
31 Albert Pujols/25
32 Roberto Alomar/100 40.00 18.00
33 Barry Larkin/95 40.00 18.00
34 Tony Gwynn/60 80.00 36.00
35 Chipper Jones/25
36 Pedro Martinez Sox/2
37 Juan Gonzalez/50 60.00 27.00
38 Greg Maddux/9
39 Tim Hudson/5
41 Victor Martinez/100 15.00 6.75
42 Mark Buehrle/100 15.00 6.75
43 Austin Kearns/25
44 Kerry Wood/40 50.00 22.00
46 Alfonso Soriano/2
47 Mark Prior/25
48 Richie Sexson/100 15.00 6.75
49 Mark Teixeira/25
50 Craig Biggio/25
51 Rafael Palmeiro/25
52 Carlos Beltran/25
53 Bernie Williams/25
54 Eric Chavez/25
55 Paul Konerko/25
56 Nolan Ryan Rgr/25
57 Mark Mulder/100 25.00 11.00
58 Miguel Tejada/2
59 Roy Oswalt/40 25.00 11.00
60 Jim Edmonds/9
61 Ryan Klesko/40 25.00 11.00
62 Cal Ripken/25
63 Josh Beckett/10
64 Kazuhisa Ishii/10
65 Alex Rodriguez Rgr/10
66 Mike Sweeney/25
67 C.C. Sabathia/50 25.00 11.00
68 Jose Vidro/25
69 Magglio Ordonez/25
72 Bobby Abreu/100 15.00 6.75
73 Brian Giles/50 25.00 11.00
74 Kirby Puckett/50 80.00 36.00
75 Yogi Berra/25
76 Ryne Sandberg/25
77 Tom Glavine/100 40.00 18.00
79 Chris Snelling/100 15.00 6.75
80 Drew Henson/25
81 Junior Spivey/100 10.00 4.50
82 Mike Schmidt/50 100.00 45.00
83 Jeff Kent/50 25.00 11.00
84 Stan Musial/50 80.00 36.00
85 Garret Anderson/25
86 Jose Contreras/50 50.00 22.00
87 Ivan Rodriguez/20
89 Don Mattingly/50 100.00 45.00
90 Angel Berroa/100 15.00 6.75
91 George Brett/9
92 Jermaine Dye/100 15.00 6.75
94 Josh Phelps/100 10.00 4.50
95 Sean Casey/15
97 Jason Lane/100 10.00 4.50
98 Travis Hafner/100 15.00 6.75
99 Terrence Long/100 15.00 6.75
100 Shannon Stewart/100 15.00 6.75
101 Richard Hidalgo/25
102 Joe Thurston/100 10.00 4.50
103 Ben Sheets/100 15.00 6.75
105 Aramis Ramirez/40 15.00 6.75
106 So Taguchi/29
107 Frank Robinson/15
108 Phil Nevin/100 15.00 6.75
109 Dennis Tankersley/100 10.00 4.50
110 J.D. Drew/25
111 Paul Lo Duca/100 15.00 6.75
112 Ozzie Smith/25
113 Carlos Lee/100 15.00 6.75
114 Nick Johnson/100 25.00 11.00
115 Edgar Martinez/100 40.00 18.00
116 Hank Blalock/25
117 Orlando Hudson/100 10.00 4.50
118 Corey Patterson/100 15.00 6.75
119 Steve Carlton/25
120 Wade Miller/100 15.00 6.75
121 Adrian Beltre/25
122 Scott Rolen/100 40.00 18.00
123 Brian Lawrence/100 10.00 4.50
124 Rich Aurilia/15
126 John Buck/100 10.00 4.50
127 Marlon Byrd/100 15.00 6.75
128 Michael Cuddyer/100 10.00 4.50
129 Marshall McDougall/100 10.00 4.50
130 Travis Chapman/100 10.00 4.50
131 Jose Morban/100 10.00 4.50
132 Adam LaRoche/100 25.00 11.00
133 Jose Castillo/100 15.00 6.75
134 Walter Young/100 10.00 4.50
135 Jeff Baker/100 10.00 4.50
136 Jeremy Guthrie/100 10.00 4.50
137 Pedro Martinez Expos/2
138 Randy Johnson M's/9
139 Alex Rodriguez M's/9
140 Hideo Nomo Mets/2
141 Roger Clemens Sox/9
142 Rickey Henderson A's/10
144 Mike Piazza Dodgers/2

2003 Playoff Portraits Autographs Gold

MINT NRMT

RANDOM INSERTS IN PACKS
PRINT RUNS B/WN 1-25 COPIES PER
NO PRICING DUE TO SCARCITY

2003 Playoff Portraits Autographs Silver

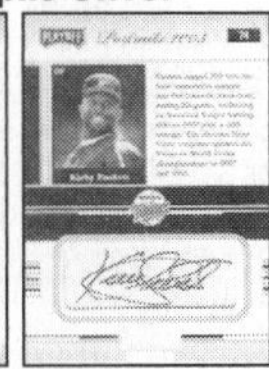

MINT NRMT

RANDOM INSERTS IN PACKS
PRINT RUNS B/WN 2-50 COPIES PER
NO PRICING ON QTY OF 25 OR LESS.
1 Vladimir Guerrero/50 50.00 22.00
2 Luis Gonzalez/14
3 Andruw Jones/15
4 Manny Ramirez/10
6 Eric Hinske/50 15.00 6.75
7 Curt Schilling/2
8 Adam Dunn/25
9 Jason Jennings/50 15.00 6.75
10 Mike Piazza Mets/2
12 Jeff Bagwell/5
13 Rickey Henderson Sox/10
14 Randy Johnson D'backs/10
15 Roger Clemens Yanks/5
16 Troy Glaus/25
17 Hideo Nomo Dodgers/2
18 Joe Borchard/50 25.00 11.00
19 Torii Hunter/15
20 Lance Berkman/15
21 Todd Helton/10
22 Mike Mussina/4
23 Vernon Wells/4
24 Pat Burrell/4
26 Shawn Green/5
27 Frank Thomas/2
28 Barry Zito/10
31 Albert Pujols/15
32 Roberto Alomar/35 50.00 22.00
33 Barry Larkin/15
34 Tony Gwynn/25
35 Chipper Jones/15
36 Pedro Martinez Sox/2
37 Juan Gonzalez/35 80.00 36.00
38 Greg Maddux/5
39 Tim Hudson/2
41 Victor Martinez/50 25.00 11.00
42 Mark Buehrle/50 25.00 11.00
43 Austin Kearns/15
44 Kerry Wood/25
46 Alfonso Soriano/2
47 Mark Prior/15
48 Richie Sexson/35 25.00 11.00
49 Mark Teixeira/15
50 Craig Biggio/15
51 Rafael Palmeiro/15
52 Carlos Beltran/15
53 Bernie Williams/15
54 Eric Chavez/15
55 Paul Konerko/15
56 Nolan Ryan Rgr/15
57 Mark Mulder/35 40.00 18.00
58 Miguel Tejada/2
59 Roy Oswalt/25
60 Jim Edmonds/5
61 Ryan Klesko/25
62 Cal Ripken/15
63 Josh Beckett/4
64 Kazuhisa Ishii/10
65 Alex Rodriguez Rgr/10
66 Mike Sweeney/15
67 C.C. Sabathia/25
68 Jose Vidro/15
69 Magglio Ordonez/15
72 Bobby Abreu/50 25.00 11.00
73 Brian Giles/35 25.00 11.00
74 Kirby Puckett/35 100.00 45.00
75 Yogi Berra/15
76 Ryne Sandberg/10
77 Tom Glavine/35 50.00 22.00
79 Chris Snelling/50 25.00 11.00
80 Drew Henson/15
81 Junior Spivey/50 15.00 6.75
82 Mike Schmidt/15
83 Jeff Kent/25
84 Stan Musial/35 100.00 45.00
85 Garret Anderson/15
86 Jose Contreras/35 60.00 27.00
87 Ivan Rodriguez/4
89 Don Mattingly/35 120.00 55.00
90 Angel Berroa/50 25.00 11.00
91 George Brett/5
92 Jermaine Dye/50 25.00 11.00
94 Josh Phelps/50 15.00 6.75
95 Sean Casey/10
97 Jason Lane/50
98 Travis Hafner/50 25.00 11.00
99 Terrence Long/50 25.00 11.00
100 Shannon Stewart/50 25.00 11.00
101 Richard Hidalgo/15
102 Joe Thurston/50 15.00 6.75
103 Ben Sheets/50 25.00 11.00
105 Aramis Ramirez/25
106 So Taguchi/15
107 Frank Robinson/5
108 Phil Nevin/50 25.00 11.00
109 Dennis Tankersley/50 15.00 6.75
110 J.D. Drew/15
111 Paul Lo Duca/35 25.00 11.00
112 Ozzie Smith/15
113 Carlos Lee/50 25.00 11.00
114 Nick Johnson/50 40.00 18.00
115 Edgar Martinez/35 50.00 22.00
116 Hank Blalock/15
117 Orlando Hudson/50 15.00 6.75
118 Corey Patterson/50 25.00 11.00
119 Steve Carlton/15
120 Wade Miller/50 25.00 11.00
121 Adrian Beltre/15
122 Scott Rolen/35 50.00 22.00
123 Brian Lawrence/50 15.00 6.75
124 Rich Aurilia/10
126 John Buck/50 15.00 6.75
127 Marlon Byrd/50 25.00 11.00
128 Michael Cuddyer/50 15.00 6.75
129 Marshall McDougall/50 15.00 6.75
130 Travis Chapman/50 15.00 6.75
131 Jose Morban/50
132 Adam LaRoche/50 40.00 18.00
133 Jose Castillo/50 25.00 11.00
134 Walter Young/50 15.00 6.75
135 Jeff Baker/50 15.00 6.75
136 Jeremy Guthrie/50 15.00 6.75
137 Pedro Martinez Expos/2
138 Randy Johnson M's/5
139 Alex Rodriguez M's/5
140 Hideo Nomo Mets/2
141 Roger Clemens Sox/5
142 Rickey Henderson A's/5
144 Mike Piazza Dodgers/2

2003 Playoff Portraits Materials Bronze

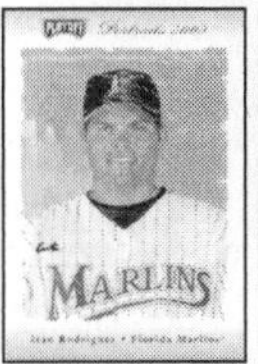

Randomly inserted into packs are these cards featuring game-used memorabilia of the featured player. Please note that since there are varying amounts of cards printed, we have placed the print run next to the player's name in our checklist. Please note that for cards with print runs of 25 or fewer, no pricing is available due to market scarcity.

MINT NRMT

1 Vladimir Guerrero Jsy/100 15.00 6.75
2 Luis Gonzalez Jsy/100 8.00 3.60
3 Andruw Jones Jsy/100 8.00 3.60
4 Manny Ramirez Jsy/50 10.00 4.50
5A Derek Jeter Ball/25
5B Derek Jeter Base/100 30.00 13.50
6 Eric Hinske Jsy/100 8.00 3.60
7A Curt Schilling Bat/50 15.00 6.75
7B Curt Schilling Jsy/100 10.00 4.50
8A Adam Dunn Bat/50 10.00 4.50
8B Adam Dunn Jsy/50 10.00 4.50
9 Jason Jennings Jsy/100 8.00 3.60
10 Mike Piazza Mets Jsy/100 15.00 6.75
11 Jason Giambi Yanks Jsy/100 15.00 6.75
12A Jeff Bagwell Bat/50 15.00 6.75
12B Jeff Bagwell Jsy/50 15.00 6.75
13A R.Henderson Sox Bat/50 25.00 11.00
13B R.Henderson Sox Jsy/50 25.00 11.00
14 R.Johnson D'backs Jsy/100 15.00 6.75
15A R.Clemens Yanks Bat/50 40.00 18.00
15B R.Clemens Yanks Jsy/100 25.00 11.00
16 Troy Glaus Jsy/100 10.00 4.50
17 H.Nomo Dodgers Jsy/100 25.00 11.00
18 Joe Borchard Jsy/20
19 Torii Hunter Jsy/100 8.00 3.60
20 Lance Berkman Jsy/100 8.00 3.60
21A Todd Helton Bat/50 15.00 6.75
21B Todd Helton Jsy/50 15.00 6.75
22A Mike Mussina Bat/50 40.00 18.00
22B Mike Mussina Jsy/100 25.00 11.00
23 Vernon Wells Jsy/100 8.00 3.60
24A Pat Burrell Bat/50 10.00 4.50
24B Pat Burrell Jsy/100 8.00 3.60
25A Ichiro Suzuki Ball/50 40.00 18.00
25B Ichiro Suzuki Base/100 25.00 11.00
26 Shawn Green Jsy/100 8.00 3.60
27 Frank Thomas Jsy/100 15.00 6.75
28 Barry Zito Jsy/100 10.00 4.50
29 Barry Bonds Ball/50 40.00 18.00
29 Barry Bonds Base/100 25.00 11.00
30 Ken Griffey Jr. Base/100 20.00 9.00
31 Albert Pujols Jsy/100 25.00 11.00
32A Roberto Alomar Bat/50 25.00 11.00
32B Roberto Alomar Jsy/50 25.00 11.00
33 Barry Larkin Jsy/50 25.00 11.00
34 Tony Gwynn Jsy/100 25.00 11.00
35 Chipper Jones Jsy/100 15.00 6.75
36A Pedro Martinez Sox Bat/50 25.00 11.00
36B P.Martinez Sox Jsy/100 15.00 6.75
37A Juan Gonzalez Bat/50 25.00 11.00
37B Juan Gonzalez Jsy/50 25.00 11.00
38A Greg Maddux Bat/50 25.00 11.00
38B Greg Maddux Jsy/100 15.00 6.75
39 Tim Hudson Jsy/100 8.00 3.60
40 Sammy Sosa Jsy/100 20.00 9.00
41 Victor Martinez Jsy/100 8.00 3.60
42A Mark Buehrle Bat/50 10.00 4.50
42B Mark Buehrle Jsy/50 10.00 4.50
43A Austin Kearns Bat/50 10.00 4.50
43B Austin Kearns Jsy/100 8.00 3.60
44A Kerry Wood Bat/50 25.00 11.00
44B Kerry Wood Jsy/50 25.00 11.00
45 Nomar Garciaparra Jsy/100 20.00 9.00
46 Alfonso Soriano Jsy/100 10.00 4.50
47 Mark Prior Jsy/100 25.00 11.00
48 Richie Sexson Jsy/100 8.00 3.60
49A Mark Teixeira Bat/50 15.00 6.75
49B Mark Teixeira Jsy/50 15.00 6.75
50A Craig Biggio Bat/50 15.00 6.75
50B Craig Biggio Jsy/50 15.00 6.75
51A Rafael Palmeiro Bat/50 15.00 6.75
51B Rafael Palmeiro Jsy/50
52 Carlos Beltran Jsy/50 10.00 4.50
53A Bernie Williams Bat/50 15.00 6.75
53B Bernie Williams Jsy/50 15.00 6.75
54 Eric Chavez Jsy/100 8.00 3.60
55 Paul Konerko Jsy/100 8.00 3.60
56A Nolan Ryan Rgr Bat/50 80.00 36.00
56B Nolan Ryan Rgr Jsy/100 50.00 22.00
57 Mark Mulder Jsy/100 8.00 3.60
58 Miguel Tejada Jsy/100 8.00 3.60
59A Roy Oswalt Bat/50
59B Roy Oswalt Jsy/50 10.00 4.50
60A Jim Edmonds Bat/50
60B Jim Edmonds Jsy/50 10.00 4.50
61A Ryan Klesko Bat/50 10.00 4.50
61B Ryan Klesko Jsy/100 8.00 3.60
62 Cal Ripken Jsy/100 50.00 22.00
63A Josh Beckett Bat/50 15.00 6.75
63B Josh Beckett Jsy/100 10.00 4.50
64 Kazuhisa Ishii Jsy/50 10.00 4.50
65 Alex Rodriguez Rgr Jsy/100 20.00 9.00
66A Mike Sweeney Bat/50 10.00 4.50
66B Mike Sweeney Jsy/100 8.00 3.60
67 C.C. Sabathia Jsy/100 8.00 3.60
68 Jose Vidro Jsy/100 8.00 3.60
69A Magglio Ordonez Bat/50 10.00 4.50
69B Magglio Ordonez Jsy/50 10.00 4.50
70A Carlos Delgado Bat/50 10.00 4.50
70B Carlos Delgado Jsy/50 10.00 4.50
71 Jorge Posada Jsy/100 10.00 4.50
72 Bobby Abreu Jsy/100 8.00 3.60
73 Brian Giles Jsy/20
74A Kirby Puckett Bat/50 40.00 18.00
74B Kirby Puckett Jsy/50 40.00 18.00
75A Yogi Berra Bat/50 25.00 11.00
75B Yogi Berra Jsy/50 25.00 11.00
76 Ryne Sandberg Jsy/50 60.00 27.00
77A Tom Glavine Bat/50 15.00 6.75
77B Tom Glavine Jsy/50 15.00 6.75
78 Jim Thome Jsy/100 15.00 6.75
79 Chris Snelling Bat/50 10.00 4.50
80 Drew Henson Bat/50 10.00 4.50
81A Junior Spivey Bat/50 10.00 4.50
81B Junior Spivey Jsy/50 10.00 4.50
82A Mike Schmidt Bat/50 50.00 22.00
82B Mike Schmidt Jsy/50 50.00 22.00
83 Jeff Kent Bat/50 10.00 4.50
84 Stan Musial Jsy/100 40.00 18.00
85 Garret Anderson Bat/50 10.00 4.50
85 Garret Anderson Jsy/50 10.00 4.50
86 Jose Contreras Base/50 20.00 9.00
87 Ivan Rodriguez Bat/50 25.00 11.00
88A Hideki Matsui Ball/50 50.00 22.00
88B Hideki Matsui Base/100 40.00 18.00
89 Don Mattingly Jsy/100 50.00 22.00
90 Angel Berroa Pants/100 8.00 3.60
91A George Brett Bat/50 80.00 36.00
91B George Brett Jsy/50 80.00 36.00
92 Jermaine Dye Bat/50 10.00 4.50
93 John Olerud Jsy/100 8.00 3.60
94A Josh Phelps Bat/50 10.00 4.50
94B Josh Phelps Jsy/50 10.00 4.50
95A Sean Casey Bat/50 10.00 4.50
95B Sean Casey Jsy/50 10.00 4.50
96 Larry Walker Jsy/50 15.00 6.75
97 Jason Lane Bat/50 10.00 4.50
98 Travis Hafner Bat/100 8.00 3.60
99A Terrence Long Bat/50 10.00 4.50
99B Terrence Long Jsy/50 10.00 4.50
100A Shannon Stewart Bat/50 10.00 4.50
100B Shannon Stewart Jsy/100 8.00 3.60
101A Richard Hidalgo Bat/50 10.00 4.50
101B Richard Hidalgo Pants/50 10.00 4.50
102 Joe Thurston Bat/100 8.00 3.60
103 Ben Sheets Jsy/100 8.00 3.60
104A Orlando Cabrera Bat/50 10.00 4.50
104B Orlando Cabrera Jsy/50 10.00 4.50
105 Aramis Ramirez Jsy/100 8.00 3.60
106A So Taguchi Bat/50 10.00 4.50
106B So Taguchi Jsy/50
107A Frank Robinson Bat/50 15.00 6.75
107B Frank Robinson Jsy/50 15.00 6.75
109 Dennis Tankersley Jsy/100 8.00 3.60
110 J.D. Drew Jsy/100 8.00 3.60
111A Paul Lo Duca Bat/50 10.00 4.50
111B Paul Lo Duca Jsy/50 10.00 4.50
112A Ozzie Smith Bat/50 50.00 22.00
112B Ozzie Smith Jsy/50 50.00 22.00
113 Carlos Lee Jsy/100 8.00 3.60
114 Nick Johnson Jsy/100 8.00 3.60
115 Edgar Martinez Jsy/100 10.00 4.50
116A Hank Blalock Bat/50 15.00 6.75
116B Hank Blalock Jsy/50 15.00 6.75
117 Orlando Hudson Bat/50 10.00 4.50
118 Corey Patterson Pants/100 8.00 3.60
119 Steve Carlton Bat/50 10.00 4.50
120 Wade Miller Jsy/50 10.00 4.50
121A Adrian Beltre Bat/50 10.00 4.50
121B Adrian Beltre Jsy/50 10.00 4.50
122 Scott Rolen Bat/50 15.00 6.75
123 Brian Lawrence Bat/50 10.00 4.50
124 Rich Aurilia Jsy/50 10.00 4.50
125A Tsuyoshi Shinjo Bat/50 10.00 4.50
125B Tsuyoshi Shinjo Jsy/50 10.00 4.50
126A John Buck Bat/50 10.00 4.50
126B John Buck Jsy/50 10.00 4.50
127 Marlon Byrd Jsy/100 8.00 3.60
128A Michael Cuddyer Bat/50 10.00 4.50
128B Michael Cuddyer Jsy/50 10.00 4.50
130 Travis Chapman Bat/100 8.00 3.60
131 Jose Morban Bat/100 8.00 3.60
132 Adam LaRoche Bat/100 10.00 4.50
133 Jose Castillo Bat/100 8.00 3.60
134 Walter Young Bat/100 8.00 3.60
137 P.Martinez Expos Jsy/100 15.00 6.75
138 R.Johnson M's Jsy/100 15.00 6.75
139 Alex Rodriguez M's Jsy/100 20.00 9.00

140A Hideo Nomo Mets Bat/50. 40.00 18.00
140B Hideo Nomo Mets Jsy/50. 40.00 18.00
141A R.Clemens Sox Bat/50 40.00 18.00
141B R.Clemens Sox Jsy/100 25.00 11.00
142A R.Henderson A's Bat/50 25.00 11.00
142B R.Henderson A's Jsy/50 25.00 11.00
143 Jason Giambi A's Jsy/100 15.00 6.75
144 Mike Piazza Dodgers Jsy/50 25.00 11.00

2003 Playoff Portraits Materials Gold

MINT NRMT
RANDOM INSERTS IN PACKS
PRINT RUNS B/WN 10-25 COPIES PER
NO PRICING DUE TO SCARCITY

2003 Playoff Portraits Materials Silver

MINT NRMT
1 Vladimir Guerrero Jsy/50 25.00 11.00
2 Luis Gonzalez Jsy/50 10.00 4.50
3 Andruw Jones Jsy/50 10.00 4.50
4 Manny Ramirez Jsy/50 10.00 4.50
5 Derek Jeter Base/50 50.00 22.00
6 Eric Hinske Jsy/50 10.00 4.50
7 Curt Schilling Jsy/50 15.00 6.75
8 Adam Dunn Jsy/50 10.00 4.50
9 Jason Jennings Jsy/50 10.00 4.50
10 Mike Piazza Mets Jsy/50 25.00 11.00
11 Jason Giambi Yanks Jsy/50 25.00 11.00
12 Jeff Bagwell Jsy/50 15.00 6.75
13 R.Henderson Sox Jsy/50 25.00 11.00
14 R.Johnson D'backs Jsy/50 25.00 11.00
15 R.Clemens Yanks Jsy/50 40.00 18.00
16 Troy Glaus Jsy/50 15.00 6.75
17 H.Nomo Dodgers Jsy/50 40.00 18.00
18 Joe Borchard Jsy/10
19 Torii Hunter Jsy/50 10.00 4.50
20 Lance Berkman Jsy/50 10.00 4.50
21 Todd Helton Jsy/50 15.00 6.75
22 Mike Mussina Jsy/50 40.00 18.00
23 Vernon Wells Jsy/50 10.00 4.50
24 Pat Burrell Jsy/50 10.00 4.50
25 Ichiro Suzuki Base/50 40.00 18.00
26 Shawn Green Jsy/50 10.00 4.50
27 Frank Thomas Jsy/50 25.00 11.00
28 Barry Zito Jsy/50 15.00 6.75
29 Barry Bonds Base/50 40.00 18.00
30 Ken Griffey Jr. Base/50 30.00 13.50
31 Albert Pujols Jsy/50 40.00 18.00
32 Roberto Alomar Jsy/50 25.00 11.00
33 Barry Larkin Jsy/50 25.00 11.00
34 Tony Gwynn Jsy/50 40.00 18.00
35 Chipper Jones Jsy/50 25.00 11.00
36 P.Martinez Sox Jsy/50 25.00 11.00
37 Juan Gonzalez Jsy/50 25.00 11.00
38 Greg Maddux Jsy/50 25.00 11.00
39 Tim Hudson Jsy/50 10.00 4.50
40 Sammy Sosa Jsy/50 30.00 13.50
41 Victor Martinez Jsy/50 10.00 4.50
42 Mark Buehrle Jsy/50 10.00 4.50
43 Austin Kearns Jsy/50 10.00 4.50
44 Kerry Wood Jsy/50 25.00 11.00
45 Nomar Garciaparra Jsy/50 30.00 13.50
46 Alfonso Soriano Jsy/50 15.00 6.75
47 Mark Prior Jsy/50 40.00 18.00
48 Richie Sexson Jsy/50 10.00 4.50
49 Mark Teixeira Jsy/50 15.00 6.75
50 Craig Biggio Jsy/50 15.00 6.75
51 Rafael Palmeiro Jsy/50 15.00 6.75
52 Carlos Beltran Jsy/50 10.00 4.50
53 Bernie Williams Jsy/50 15.00 6.75
54 Eric Chavez Jsy/50 10.00 4.50
55 Paul Konerko Jsy/50 10.00 4.50
56 Nolan Ryan Rgr Jsy/50 80.00 36.00
57 Mark Mulder Jsy/50 10.00 4.50
58 Miguel Tejada Jsy/50 10.00 4.50
59 Roy Oswalt Jsy/50 10.00 4.50
60 Jim Edmonds Jsy/50 10.00 4.50
61 Ryan Klesko Jsy/50 10.00 4.50
62 Cal Ripken Jsy/50 80.00 36.00
63 Josh Beckett Jsy/50 15.00 6.75
64 Kazuhisa Ishii Jsy/50 10.00 4.50
65 Alex Rodriguez Rgr Jsy/50 30.00 13.50
66 Mike Sweeney Jsy/50 10.00 4.50
67 C.C. Sabathia Jsy/50 10.00 4.50
68 Jose Vidro Jsy/50 10.00 4.50
69 Magglio Ordonez Jsy/50 10.00 4.50
70 Carlos Delgado Jsy/50 10.00 4.50
71 Jorge Posada Jsy/50 15.00 6.75
72 Bobby Abreu Jsy/50 10.00 4.50
73 Brian Giles Jsy/10
74 Kirby Puckett Jsy/25
75 Yogi Berra Jsy/50 25.00 11.00
76 Ryne Sandberg Jsy/50 60.00 27.00
77 Tom Glavine Jsy/25
78 Jim Thome Jsy/50 25.00 11.00
79 Chris Snelling Bat/25
80 Drew Henson Bat/25
81 Junior Spivey Bat/25
82 Mike Schmidt Jsy/50 50.00 22.00
83 Jeff Kent Bat/25
84 Stan Musial Jsy/50 60.00 27.00
85 Garret Anderson Jsy/50 10.00 4.50
86 Jose Contreras Base/25
88 Hideki Matsui Base/50 50.00 22.00
89 Don Mattingly Jsy/50 80.00 36.00
90 Angel Berroa Pants/50 10.00 4.50
91 George Brett Jsy/50 80.00 36.00
92 Jermaine Dye Bat/25
93 John Olerud Jsy/50 10.00 4.50
94 Josh Phelps Jsy/50 10.00 4.50
95 Sean Casey Jsy/50 10.00 4.50
96 Larry Walker Jsy/50 15.00 6.75
97 Jason Lane Bat/25
99 Terrence Long Jsy/50 10.00 4.50
100 Shannon Stewart Jsy/50 10.00 4.50
101 Richard Hidalgo Pants/50 10.00 4.50
102 Joe Thurston Bat/25
103 Ben Sheets Jsy/50 10.00 4.50
104 Orlando Cabrera Jsy/50 10.00 4.50
105 Aramis Ramirez Jsy/50 10.00 4.50
106 So Taguchi Jsy/50 10.00 4.50
107 Frank Robinson Jsy/50 15.00 6.75
109 Dennis Tankersley Jsy/50 10.00 4.50
110 J.D. Drew Jsy/50 10.00 4.50
111 Paul Lo Duca Jsy/50 10.00 4.50
112 Ozzie Smith Jsy/50 50.00 22.00
113 Carlos Lee Jsy/50 10.00 4.50
114 Nick Johnson Jsy/50 10.00 4.50
115 Edgar Martinez Jsy/50 15.00 6.75
116 Hank Blalock Jsy/50 15.00 6.75
117 Orlando Hudson Bat/25
118 Corey Patterson Pants/50 10.00 4.50
119 Steve Carlton Bat/25
120 Wade Miller Jsy/50 10.00 4.50
121 Adrian Beltre Jsy/50 10.00 4.50
122 Scott Rolen Bat/25
123 Brian Lawrence Bat/25
124 Rich Aurilia Jsy/25
125 Tsuyoshi Shinjo Jsy/50 10.00 4.50
126 John Buck Jsy/50 10.00 4.50
127 Marlon Byrd Jsy/50 10.00 4.50
128 Michael Cuddyer Jsy/50 10.00 4.50
130 Travis Chapman Bat/25
131 Jose Morban Bat/25
132 Adam LaRoche Bat/25
133 Jose Castillo Bat/25
134 Walter Young Bat/25
137 P.Martinez Expos Jsy/50 25.00 11.00
138 R.Johnson M's Jsy/50 25.00 11.00
139 Alex Rodriguez M's Jsy/50. 30.00 13.50
140 Hideo Nomo Mets Jsy/50 40.00 18.00
141 R.Clemens Sox Jsy/50 40.00 18.00
142 R.Henderson A's Jsy/50 25.00 11.00
143 Jason Giambi A's Jsy/50 25.00 11.00
144 Mike Piazza Dodgers Jsy/50 25.00 11.00

2003 Playoff Portraits Materials Combo Bronze

Randomly inserted into packs, these cards feature two pieces of game-used memorabilia. Please note that for cards with a print run of 25 or fewer, no pricing information is provided.

MINT NRMT
RANDOM INSERTS IN PACKS
PRINT RUNS B/WN 10-50 COPIES PER
NO PRICING ON QTY OF 25 OR LESS.
1 Vladimir Guerrero Bat-Jsy 30.00 13.50
2 Luis Gonzalez Bat-Jsy 15.00 6.75
3 Andruw Jones Bat-Jsy 15.00 6.75
4 Manny Ramirez Bat-Jsy 15.00 6.75
5 Derek Jeter Ball-Base/10
6 Eric Hinske Bat-Jsy 15.00 6.75
7 Curt Schilling Bat-Jsy 20.00 9.00
8 Adam Dunn Bat-Jsy 15.00 6.75
9 Jason Jennings Bat-Jsy 15.00 6.75
10 Mike Piazza Mets Bat-Jsy 40.00 18.00
11 Jason Giambi Yanks Bat-Jsy 30.00 13.50
12 Jeff Bagwell Bat-Jsy 20.00 9.00
13 R.Henderson Sox Bat-Jsy 30.00 13.50
14 R.Johnson D'backs Bat-Jsy 30.00 13.50
15 R.Clemens Yanks Bat-Jsy 50.00 22.00
16 Troy Glaus Bat-Jsy 20.00 9.00
17 H.Nomo Dodgers Bat-Jsy 50.00 22.00
18 Joe Borchard Bat-Jsy/25
19 Torii Hunter Bat-Jsy 15.00 6.75
20 Lance Berkman Bat-Jsy 15.00 6.75
21 Todd Helton Bat-Jsy 20.00 9.00
22 Mike Mussina Bat-Jsy 50.00 22.00
23 Vernon Wells Bat-Jsy 15.00 6.75
24 Pat Burrell Bat-Jsy 15.00 6.75
25 Ichiro Suzuki Ball-Base 50.00 22.00
26 Shawn Green Bat-Jsy 15.00 6.75
27 Frank Thomas Bat-Jsy 30.00 13.50
28 Barry Zito Bat-Jsy 20.00 9.00
29 Barry Bonds Ball-Base 50.00 22.00
31 Albert Pujols Bat-Jsy 50.00 22.00
32 Roberto Alomar Bat-Jsy 30.00 13.50
33 Barry Larkin Bat-Jsy 30.00 13.50
34 Tony Gwynn Bat-Jsy 50.00 22.00
35 Chipper Jones Bat-Jsy 30.00 13.50
36 P.Martinez Sox Bat-Jsy 30.00 13.50
37 Juan Gonzalez Bat-Jsy 30.00 13.50
38 Greg Maddux Bat-Jsy 40.00 18.00
40 Sammy Sosa Bat-Jsy 40.00 18.00
41 Victor Martinez Bat-Jsy 15.00 6.75
42 Mark Buehrle Bat-Jsy 15.00 6.75
43 Austin Kearns Bat-Jsy 15.00 6.75
44 Kerry Wood Bat-Jsy 30.00 13.50
45 Nomar Garciaparra Bat-Jsy 40.00 18.00
46 Alfonso Soriano Bat-Jsy 20.00 9.00
47 Mark Prior Bat-Jsy 50.00 22.00
48 Richie Sexson Bat-Jsy 15.00 6.75
49 Mark Teixeira Bat-Jsy 20.00 9.00
50 Craig Biggio Bat-Jsy 20.00 9.00
51 Rafael Palmeiro Bat-Jsy 20.00 9.00
52 Carlos Beltran Bat-Jsy 15.00 6.75
53 Bernie Williams Bat-Jsy 20.00 9.00
54 Eric Chavez Bat-Jsy 15.00 6.75
55 Paul Konerko Bat-Jsy 15.00 6.75
56 Nolan Ryan Rgr Bat-Jsy 100.00 45.00
57 Mark Mulder Bat-Jsy 15.00 6.75
58 Miguel Tejada Bat-Jsy 15.00 6.75
59 Roy Oswalt Bat-Jsy 15.00 6.75
60 Jim Edmonds Bat-Jsy 15.00 6.75
61 Ryan Klesko Bat-Jsy 15.00 6.75
62 Cal Ripken Bat-Jsy 100.00 45.00
63 Josh Beckett Bat-Jsy 20.00 9.00
64 Kazuhisa Ishii Bat-Jsy 15.00 6.75
65 Alex Rodriguez Rgr Bat-Jsy 40.00 18.00
66 Mike Sweeney Bat-Jsy 15.00 6.75
68 Jose Vidro Bat-Jsy 15.00 6.75
69 Magglio Ordonez Bat-Jsy 15.00 6.75
70 Carlos Delgado Bat-Jsy 15.00 6.75
71 Jorge Posada Bat-Jsy 20.00 9.00
72 Bobby Abreu Bat-Jsy 15.00 6.75
73 Brian Giles Bat-Jsy/25
74 Kirby Puckett Bat-Jsy 50.00 22.00
75 Yogi Berra Bat-Jsy 30.00 13.50
76 Ryne Sandberg Bat-Jsy 80.00 36.00
77 Tom Glavine Bat-Jsy 20.00 9.00
78 Jim Thome Bat-Jsy 30.00 13.50
81 Junior Spivey Bat-Jsy 15.00 6.75
82 Mike Schmidt Bat-Jsy 60.00 27.00
84 Stan Musial Bat-Jsy 80.00 36.00
85 Garret Anderson Bat-Jsy 15.00 6.75
88 Hideki Matsui Ball-Base 80.00 36.00
89 Don Mattingly Bat-Jsy 100.00 45.00
90 Angel Berroa Bat-Pants 15.00 6.75
91 George Brett Bat-Jsy 100.00 45.00
93 John Olerud Bat-Jsy 15.00 6.75
94 Josh Phelps Bat-Jsy 15.00 6.75
95 Sean Casey Bat-Jsy 15.00 6.75
96 Larry Walker Bat-Jsy 20.00 9.00
99 Terrence Long Bat-Jsy 15.00 6.75
100 Shannon Stewart Bat-Jsy 15.00 6.75
101 Richard Hidalgo Bat-Pants 15.00 6.75
103 Ben Sheets Bat-Jsy 15.00 6.75
104 Orlando Cabrera Bat-Jsy 15.00 6.75
105 Aramis Ramirez Bat-Jsy 15.00 6.75
106 So Taguchi Bat-Jsy 15.00 6.75
107 Frank Robinson Bat-Jsy 20.00 9.00
109 Dennis Tankersley Bat-Jsy 15.00 6.75
110 J.D. Drew Bat-Jsy 15.00 6.75
111 Paul Lo Duca Bat-Jsy 15.00 6.75
112 Ozzie Smith Bat-Jsy 60.00 27.00
113 Carlos Lee Bat-Jsy 15.00 6.75
114 Nick Johnson Bat-Jsy 15.00 6.75
115 Edgar Martinez Bat-Jsy 20.00 9.00
116 Hank Blalock Bat-Jsy 20.00 9.00
118 Corey Patterson Bat-Pants 15.00 6.75
120 Wade Miller Bat-Jsy 15.00 6.75
121 Adrian Beltre Bat-Jsy 15.00 6.75
122 Scott Rolen Bat-Jsy 20.00 9.00
125 Tsuyoshi Shinjo Bat-Jsy 15.00 6.75
126 John Buck Bat-Jsy 15.00 6.75
127 Marlon Byrd Bat-Jsy 15.00 6.75
128 Michael Cuddyer Bat-Jsy 15.00 6.75
137 P.Martinez Expos Bat-Jsy 30.00 13.50
138 R.Johnson M's Bat-Jsy 30.00 13.50
139 Alex Rodriguez M's Bat-Jsy 40.00 18.00
140 Hideo Nomo Mets Bat-Jsy 50.00 22.00
141 R.Clemens Sox Bat-Jsy 50.00 22.00
142 R.Henderson A's Bat-Jsy 30.00 13.50
143 Jason Giambi A's Bat-Jsy 30.00 13.50
144 M.Piazza Dodgers Bat-Jsy 40.00 18.00

2003 Playoff Portraits Materials Combo Gold

MINT NRMT
RANDOM INSERTS IN PACKS
STATED PRINT RUN 10 SERIAL #'d SETS
NO PRICING DUE TO SCARCITY

2003 Playoff Portraits Materials Combo Silver

MINT NRMT
RANDOM INSERTS IN PACKS
STATED PRINT RUN 25 SERIAL #'d SETS
NO PRICING DUE TO SCARCITY

2003 Playoff Prestige

This 210 card set was issued in two separate series. The primary product - containing cards 1-200 from the basic set - was released in May, 2003. The set was issued in six-card packs which were issued 24 packs to a box and 20 boxes to a case. The first 180 cards in the set featured veterans while the final 20 cards featured leading rookies and prospects. Those final 20 cards were inserted at a stated rate of one in three. Cards 201-210 were issued in DLP Rookies and Traded packs of which was distributed in December, 2003.

Nm-Mt Ex-Mt
COMP.LO SET (200) 40.00 12.00
COMP.LO SET w/o SP's (180) 25.00 7.50
COMP.UPDATE SET (10) 8.00 2.40
COMMON CARD (1-180) .40 .12
COMMON CARD (181-200) 1.50 .45
COMMON CARD (201-210) .50 .15
201-210 ISSUED IN DLP R/T PACKS
1 Darin Erstad .40 .12
2 David Eckstein .40 .12
3 Garret Anderson .40 .12
4 Jarrod Washburn .40 .12
5 Tim Salmon .60 .18
6 Troy Glaus .60 .18
7 Jay Gibbons .40 .12
8 Marty Cordova .40 .12
9 Melvin Mora .40 .12
10 Rodrigo Lopez .40 .12
11 Tony Batista .40 .12
12 Cliff Floyd .40 .12
13 Derek Lowe .40 .12
14 Johnny Damon .40 .12
15 Manny Ramirez .40 .12
16 Nomar Garciaparra 1.50 .45
17 Pedro Martinez 1.00 .30
18 Rickey Henderson 1.00 .30
19 Shea Hillenbrand .40 .12
20 Carlos Lee .40 .12
21 Frank Thomas 1.00 .30
22 Magglio Ordonez .40 .12
23 Mark Buehrle .40 .12
24 Paul Konerko .40 .12
25 C.C. Sabathia .40 .12
26 Danys Baez .40 .12
27 Ellis Burks .40 .12
28 Travis Hafner .40 .12
29 Omar Vizquel .40 .12
30 Bobby Higginson .40 .12
31 Carlos Pena .40 .12
32 Mark Redman .40 .12
33 Robert Fick .40 .12
34 Steve Sparks .40 .12
35 Carlos Beltran .40 .12
36 Joe Randa .40 .12
37 Mike Sweeney .40 .12
38 Paul Byrd .40 .12
39 Raul Ibanez .40 .12
40 Runelvys Hernandez .40 .12
41 Brad Radke .40 .12
42 Corey Koskie .40 .12
43 Cristian Guzman .40 .12
44 David Ortiz .40 .12
45 Doug Mientkiewicz .40 .12
46 Dustin Mohr .40 .12
47 Jacque Jones .40 .12
48 Torii Hunter .40 .12
49 Alfonso Soriano .60 .18
50 Andy Pettitte .60 .18
51 Bernie Williams .60 .18
52 David Wells .40 .12
53 Derek Jeter 2.50 .75
54 Jason Giambi 1.00 .30
55 Jeff Weaver .40 .12
56 Jorge Posada .60 .18
57 Mike Mussina 1.00 .30
58 Roger Clemens 2.00 .60
59 Barry Zito .60 .18
60 David Justice .40 .12
61 Eric Chavez .40 .12
62 Jermaine Dye .40 .12
63 Mark Mulder .40 .12
64 Miguel Tejada .40 .12
65 Ray Durham .40 .12
66 Tim Hudson .40 .12
67 Bret Boone .40 .12
68 Chris Snelling .40 .12
69 Edgar Martinez .60 .18
70 Freddy Garcia .40 .12
71 Ichiro Suzuki 2.00 .60
72 Jamie Moyer .40 .12
73 John Olerud .40 .12
74 Kazuhiro Sasaki .40 .12
75 Aubrey Huff .40 .12
76 Joe Kennedy .40 .12
77 Paul Wilson .40 .12
78 Alex Rodriguez 2.00 .60
79 Chan Ho Park .40 .12
80 Hank Blalock .60 .18
81 Ivan Rodriguez 1.00 .30
82 Juan Gonzalez .60 .18
83 Kevin Mench .40 .12
84 Rafael Palmeiro .60 .18
85 Carlos Delgado .40 .12
86 Eric Hinske .40 .12
87 Jose Cruz Jr. .40 .12
88 Josh Phelps .40 .12
89 Roy Halladay .40 .12
90 Shannon Stewart .40 .12
91 Vernon Wells .40 .12
92 Curt Schilling .60 .18
93 Junior Spivey .40 .12
94 Luis Gonzalez .40 .12
95 Mark Grace .60 .18
96 Randy Johnson 1.00 .30
97 Andruw Jones .40 .12
98 Chipper Jones 1.00 .30
99 Gary Sheffield .40 .12
100 Greg Maddux 1.50 .45
101 John Smoltz .60 .18
102 Kevin Millwood .40 .12
103 Mike Hampton .40 .12
104 Corey Patterson .40 .12
105 Fred McGriff .60 .18
106 Kerry Wood 1.00 .30
107 Mark Prior 2.00 .60
108 Moises Alou .40 .12
109 Sammy Sosa 1.50 .45
110 Adam Dunn .40 .12
111 Austin Kearns .40 .12
112 Barry Larkin 1.00 .30
113 Ken Griffey Jr. 1.50 .45
114 Sean Casey .40 .12
115 Jason Jennings .40 .12
116 Jay Payton .40 .12
117 Larry Walker .60 .18
118 Todd Helton .60 .18
119 A.J. Burnett .40 .12
120 Josh Beckett .60 .18
121 Juan Encarnacion .40 .12
122 Mike Lowell .40 .12
123 Craig Biggio .60 .18
124 Daryle Ward .40 .12
125 Jeff Bagwell .60 .18
126 Lance Berkman .40 .12
127 Roy Oswalt .40 .12
128 Adrian Beltre .40 .12
129 Hideo Nomo 1.00 .30
130 Kazuhisa Ishii .40 .12
131 Kevin Brown .40 .12
132 Odalis Perez .40 .12
133 Paul Lo Duca .40 .12
134 Shawn Green .40 .12
135 Jeff Kent .40 .12
136 Ben Sheets .40 .12
137 Jeffrey Hammonds .40 .12
138 Jose Hernandez .40 .12
139 Richie Sexson .40 .12
140 Bartolo Colon .40 .12
141 Brad Wilkerson .40 .12
142 Javier Vazquez .40 .12
143 Jose Vidro .40 .12
144 Michael Barrett .40 .12
145 Vladimir Guerrero 1.00 .30
146 Al Leiter .40 .12
147 Mike Piazza 1.50 .45
148 Mo Vaughn .40 .12
149 Pedro Astacio .40 .12
150 Roberto Alomar 1.00 .30
151 Roger Cedeno .40 .12
152 Tom Glavine .60 .18
153 Bobby Abreu .40 .12
154 Jimmy Rollins .40 .12
155 Mike Lieberthal .40 .12
156 Pat Burrell .40 .12
157 Vicente Padilla .40 .12
158 Jim Thome 1.00 .30
159 Aramis Ramirez .40 .12
160 Brian Giles .40 .12
161 Jason Kendall .40 .12
162 Josh Fogg .40 .12
163 Kip Wells .40 .12
164 Mark Kotsay .40 .12
165 Oliver Perez .40 .12
166 Phil Nevin .40 .12
167 Ryan Klesko .40 .12
168 Sean Burroughs .40 .12
169 Trevor Hoffman .40 .12
170 Barry Bonds 2.50 .75
171 Benito Santiago .40 .12
172 Reggie Sanders .40 .12
173 Rich Aurilia .40 .12
174 Russ Ortiz .40 .12
175 Albert Pujols 2.00 .60
176 J.D. Drew .40 .12
177 Jim Edmonds .40 .12
178 Matt Morris .40 .12
179 Tino Martinez .60 .18
180 Scott Rolen .60 .18
181 Joe Borchard ROO 1.50 .45
182 Freddy Sanchez ROO 1.50 .45
183 Jose Contreras ROO RC 3.00 .90
184 Jeff Baker ROO 1.50 .45
185 Ryan Church ROO 1.50 .45
186 Mario Ramos ROO 1.50 .45
187 Corwin Malone ROO 1.50 .45
188 Jimmy Gobble ROO 1.50 .45
189 Jon Adkins ROO 1.50 .45
190 Tim Kalita ROO 1.50 .45
191 Nelson Castro ROO 1.50 .45
192 Colin Young ROO 1.50 .45
193 Luis Martinez ROO 1.50 .45
194 Todd Donovan ROO 1.50 .45
195 Jeremy Ward ROO 1.50 .45
196 Wilson Valdez ROO 1.50 .45
197 Hideki Matsui ROO RC 6.00 1.80
198 Mitch Wylie ROO 1.50 .45
199 Adam Walker ROO 1.50 .45
200 Cliff Bartosh ROO 1.50 .45
201 Jeremy Bonderman ROO RC .60 .18
202 Brandon Webb ROO RC 1.25 .35
203 Adam Loewen ROO RC 1.25 .35
204 Chien-Ming Wang ROO RC 1.00 .30
205 Hong-Chih Kuo ROO RC .50 .15
206 Delmon Young ROO RC 3.00 .90
207 Ryan Wagner ROO RC .75 .23
208 Dan Haren ROO RC .60 .18
209 Rickie Weeks ROO RC 2.50 .75
210 Ramon Nivar ROO RC .50 .15

2003 Playoff Prestige Autographs

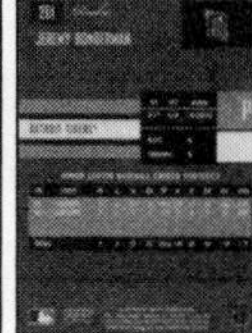

These 10 cards were inserted into the DLP Update Packs. It is interesting to note that although the Rookie Cards were issued in a parallel autograph form for the updates, there were no "parallel" autogaph cards issued as part of the regular issue.

MINT NRMT
201 Jeremy Bonderman ROO/100 20.00 9.00
202 Brandon Webb ROO/100 40.00 18.00
203 Adam Loewen ROO/100 40.00 18.00
204 Chien-Ming Wang ROO/50. 60.00 27.00
205 Hong-Chih Kuo ROO/100 30.00 13.50
206 Delmon Young ROO/25
207 Ryan Wagner ROO/100 25.00 11.00
208 Dan Haren ROO/100 20.00 9.00
209 Rickie Weeks ROO/10
210 Ramon Nivar ROO/100 20.00 9.00

2003 Playoff Prestige Xtra Points Green

Nm-Mt Ex-Mt
*GREEN 1-180: 3X TO 8X BASIC
1-180 PRINT RUN 150 SERIAL #'d SETS
*GREEN 181-200: 1.25X TO 3X BASIC
*GREEN 201-210: 6X TO 15X BASIC
181-210 PRINT RUN 50 SERIAL #'d SETS
1-200 RANDOM INSERTS IN RETAIL PACKS
201-210 RANDOM IN DLP R/T PACKS

2003 Playoff Prestige Xtra Points Purple

Nm-Mt Ex-Mt
*PURPLE 1-180: 3X TO 8X BASIC
1-180 PRINT RUN 150 SERIAL #'d SETS
*PURPLE 181-200: 1.25X TO 3X BASIC
*PURPLE 201-210: 6X TO 15X BASIC
181-200 PRINT RUN 50 SERIAL #'d SETS
RANDOM INSERTS IN RETAIL PACKS

2003 Playoff Prestige Award Winners

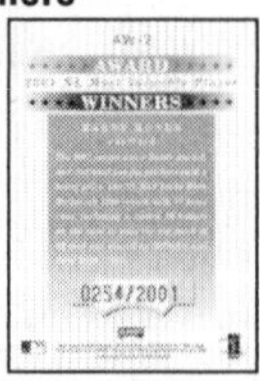

Nm-Mt Ex-Mt
RANDOM INSERTS IN PACKS
SERIAL NUMBERED TO YEAR OF AWARD
1 Barry Zito CY/2002 3.00 .90
2 Barry Bonds MVP/2001 8.00 2.40
3 Randy Johnson CY/2002 3.00 .90
4 Roger Clemens CY/2001 6.00 1.80
5 Ichiro Suzuki MVP/2001 5.00 1.50
6 Chipper Jones MVP/1999 3.00 .90
7 Ken Griffey Jr. MVP/1997 5.00 1.50
8 Miguel Tejada MVP/2002 3.00 .90
9 Greg Maddux CY/1995 5.00 1.50
10 Jeff Bagwell MVP/1994 3.00 .90
11 Rickey Henderson MVP/1990. 3.00 .90
12 Tom Glavine CY/1998 3.00 .90

Card	Nm-Mt	Ex-Mt
13 Albert Pujols ROY/2001	6.00	1.80
14 Nomar Garciaparra ROY/1997	5.00	1.50
15 Derek Jeter ROY/1996	8.00	2.40

2003 Playoff Prestige Connections

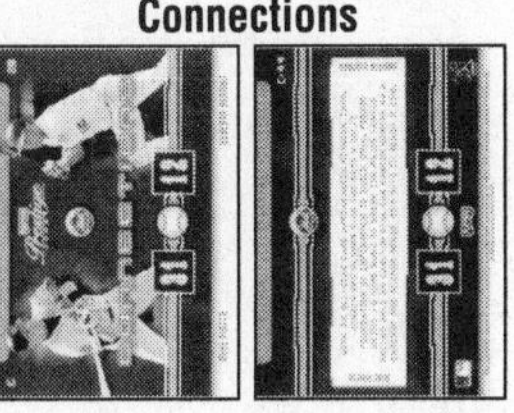

STATED ODDS 1:8 HOBBY/RETAIL.....
*PARALLEL 100: 1.5X TO 4X BASIC...
PARALLEL 100 RANDOM IN PACKS...
PARALLEL 100 PRINT RUN 100 #'d SETS

Card	Nm-Mt	Ex-Mt
1 Troy Glaus	2.00	.60
Garret Anderson		
2 Troy Glaus	2.00	.60
Tim Salmon		
3 Randy Johnson	2.50	.75
Curt Schilling		
4 Matt Williams	2.00	.60
Luis Gonzalez		
5 Greg Maddux	4.00	1.20
John Smoltz		
6 Andruw Jones	2.50	.75
Chipper Jones		
7 Greg Maddux	4.00	1.20
Kevin Millwood		
8 Tony Batista	2.00	.60
Geronimo Gil		
9 Pedro Martinez	4.00	1.20
Nomar Garciaparra		
10 Manny Ramirez	4.00	1.20
Nomar Garciaparra		
11 Nomar Garciaparra	4.00	1.20
Rickey Henderson		
12 Trot Nixon	2.00	.60
Manny Ramirez		
13 Kerry Wood	5.00	1.50
Mark Prior		
14 Sammy Sosa	4.00	1.20
Fred McGriff		
15 Sammy Sosa	4.00	1.20
Corey Patterson		
16 Frank Thomas	2.50	.75
Magglio Ordonez		
17 Joe Borchard	2.00	.60
Magglio Ordonez		
18 Adam Dunn	2.00	.60
Austin Kearns		
19 Barry Larkin	4.00	1.20
Ken Griffey Jr.		
20 Adam Dunn	2.50	.75
Barry Larkin		
21 Adam Dunn	4.00	1.20
Ken Griffey Jr.		
22 Victor Martinez	2.00	.60
Omar Vizquel		
23 C.C. Sabathia	2.00	.60
Victor Martinez		
24 Larry Walker	2.00	.60
Todd Helton		
25 Carlos Pena	2.00	.60
Robert Fick		
26 Josh Beckett	2.00	.60
Juan Encarnacion		
27 Jeff Bagwell	2.00	.60
Craig Biggio		
28 Lance Berkman	2.00	.60
Roy Oswalt		
29 Lance Berkman	2.00	.60
Jeff Bagwell		
30 Mike Sweeney	2.00	.60
Carlos Beltran		
31 Mike Sweeney	2.00	.60
Angel Berroa		
32 Kazuhisa Ishii	2.00	.60
Shawn Green		
33 Adrian Beltre	2.00	.60
Shawn Green		
34 Kazuhisa Ishii	5.00	1.50
Hideo Nomo		
35 Richie Sexson	2.00	.60
Ben Sheets		
36 Jacque Jones	2.00	.60
Torii Hunter		
37 Doug Mientkiewicz	2.00	.60
David Ortiz		
38 Vladimir Guerrero	2.50	.75
Jose Vidro		
39 Derek Jeter	6.00	1.80
Jason Giambi		
40 Derek Jeter	6.00	1.80
Bernie Williams		
41 Roger Clemens	5.00	1.50
Mike Mussina		
42 Alfonso Soriano	2.00	.60
Jorge Posada		
43 Derek Jeter	6.00	1.80
Alfonso Soriano		
44 Mike Piazza	4.00	1.20
Roberto Alomar		
45 Mike Piazza	4.00	1.20
Mo Vaughn		
46 Eric Chavez	2.00	.60
Miguel Tejada		
47 Mark Mulder	2.00	.60
Barry Zito		
48 Tim Hudson	2.00	.60
Barry Zito		
49 Pat Burrell	2.00	.60
Bobby Abreu		
50 Jim Thome	2.50	.75
Pat Burrell		
51 Jim Thome	2.50	.75
Marlon Byrd		
52 Brian Giles	2.00	.60
Aramis Ramirez		
53 Ryan Klesko	2.00	.60
Phil Nevin		
54 Barry Bonds	6.00	1.80
Benito Santiago		
55 Jeff Kent	2.00	.60
Rich Aurilia		
56 Barry Bonds	6.00	1.80
Jeff Kent		
57 Ichiro Suzuki	4.00	1.20
Kazuhiro Sasaki		
58 Edgar Martinez	2.00	.60
John Olerud		
59 Albert Pujols	5.00	1.50
Scott Rolen		
60 Jim Edmonds	2.00	.60
J.D. Drew		
61 Albert Pujols	5.00	1.50
Jim Edmonds		
62 Dewon Brazelton	2.00	.60
Joe Kennedy		
63 Alex Rodriguez	4.00	1.20
Ivan Rodriguez		
64 Juan Gonzalez	2.50	.75
Rafael Palmeiro		
65 Mark Teixeira	2.00	.60
Hank Blalock		
66 Alex Rodriguez	4.00	1.20
Rafael Palmeiro		
67 Alex Rodriguez	4.00	1.20
Juan Gonzalez		
68 Shannon Stewart	2.00	.60
Carlos Delgado		
69 Josh Phelps	2.00	.60
Eric Hinske		
70 Vernon Wells	2.00	.60
Roy Halladay		

2003 Playoff Prestige Connections Materials

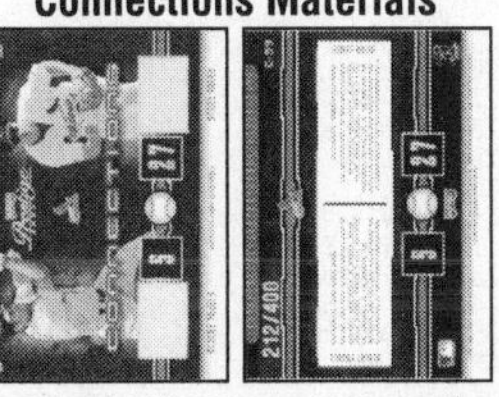

Randomly inserted into packs, this is a parallel to the Connections insert set. These cards feature a game-used memorabilia piece from each player pictured and were issued to a stated print run of 400 serial numbered sets.

Card	Nm-Mt	Ex-Mt
1 Troy Glaus Jsy	10.00	3.00
Garret Anderson Bat		
2 Troy Glaus Jsy	10.00	3.00
Tim Salmon Bat		
4 Matt Williams Jsy	10.00	3.00
Luis Gonzalez Bat		
5 Greg Maddux Jsy	15.00	4.50
John Smoltz Jsy		
6 Andruw Jones Bat	10.00	3.00
Chipper Jones Bat		
7 Greg Maddux Jsy	15.00	4.50
Kevin Millwood Jsy		
8 Tony Batista Jsy	10.00	3.00
Geronimo Gil Bat		
9 Pedro Martinez Jsy	20.00	6.00
Nomar Garciaparra Jsy		
10 Manny Ramirez Bat	15.00	4.50
Nomar Garciaparra Bat		
11 Nomar Garciaparra Bat	20.00	6.00
Rickey Henderson Bat		
12 Trot Nixon Bat	10.00	3.00
Manny Ramirez Bat		
13 Kerry Wood Jsy	30.00	9.00
Mark Prior Jsy		
14 Sammy Sosa Base	10.00	3.00
Fred McGriff Base		
15 Sammy Sosa Base	10.00	3.00
Corey Patterson Base		
16 Frank Thomas Jsy	10.00	3.00
Magglio Ordonez Jsy		
17 Joe Borchard Jsy	10.00	3.00
Magglio Ordonez Bat		
18 Adam Dunn Bat	10.00	3.00
Austin Kearns Jsy		
20 Adam Dunn Jsy	10.00	3.00
Barry Larkin Bat		
22 Victor Martinez Bat	10.00	3.00
Omar Vizquel Bat		
23 C.C. Sabathia Jsy	10.00	3.00
Victor Martinez Bat		
24 Larry Walker Jsy	10.00	3.00
Todd Helton Bat		
26 Josh Beckett Jsy	10.00	3.00
Juan Encarnacion Bat		
27 Jeff Bagwell Pants	10.00	3.00
Craig Biggio Pants		
28 Lance Berkman Jsy	10.00	3.00
Roy Oswalt Jsy		
29 Lance Berkman Jsy	10.00	3.00
Jeff Bagwell Pants		
30 Mike Sweeney Bat	10.00	3.00
Carlos Beltran Bat		
31 Mike Sweeney Bat	10.00	3.00
Angel Berroa Pants		
32 Kazuhisa Ishii Jsy	10.00	3.00
Shawn Green Bat		
33 Adrian Beltre Bat	10.00	3.00
Shawn Green Jsy		
34 Kazuhisa Ishii Jsy	25.00	7.50
Hideo Nomo Jsy		
35 Richie Sexson Jsy	10.00	3.00
Ben Sheets Jsy		
36 Jacque Jones Jsy	10.00	3.00
Torii Hunter Bat		
37 Doug Mientkiewicz Bat	10.00	3.00
David Ortiz Jsy		
38 Vladimir Guerrero Bat	10.00	3.00
Jose Vidro Jsy		
39 Derek Jeter Base	15.00	4.50
Jason Giambi Bat		
40 Derek Jeter Base	15.00	4.50
Bernie Williams Base		
41 Roger Clemens Jsy	25.00	7.50
Mike Mussina Jsy		
42 Alfonso Soriano Jsy	10.00	3.00
Jorge Posada Jsy		
43 Derek Jeter Base	25.00	7.50
Alfonso Soriano Base		
44 Mike Piazza Bat	15.00	4.50
Roberto Alomar Jsy		
45 Mike Piazza Bat	15.00	4.50
Mo Vaughn Bat		
46 Eric Chavez Jsy	10.00	3.00
Miguel Tejada Jsy		
47 Mark Mulder Jsy	10.00	3.00
Barry Zito Jsy		
48 Tim Hudson Jsy	10.00	3.00
Barry Zito Jsy		
49 Pat Burrell Bat	10.00	3.00
Bobby Abreu Bat		
50 Jim Thome Bat	10.00	3.00
Pat Burrell Bat		
51 Jim Thome Bat	10.00	3.00
Marlon Byrd Jsy		
52 Brian Giles Bat	10.00	3.00
Aramis Ramirez Jsy		
53 Ryan Klesko Jsy	10.00	3.00
Phil Nevin Jsy		
54 Barry Bonds Base	15.00	4.50
Benito Santiago Base		
55 Jeff Kent Jsy	10.00	3.00
Rich Aurilia Jsy		
56 Barry Bonds Base	15.00	4.50
Jeff Kent Base		
57 Ichiro Suzuki Base	25.00	7.50
Kazuhiro Sasaki Base		
58 Edgar Martinez Bat	10.00	3.00
John Olerud Jsy		
59 Albert Pujols Base	15.00	4.50
Scott Rolen Base		
60 Jim Edmonds Bat	10.00	3.00
J.D. Drew Jsy		
61 Albert Pujols Base	15.00	4.50
Jim Edmonds Base		
62 Dewon Brazelton Jsy	10.00	3.00
Joe Kennedy Jsy		
63 Alex Rodriguez Jsy	15.00	4.50
Ivan Rodriguez Bat		
64 Juan Gonzalez Pants	10.00	3.00
Rafael Palmeiro Pants		
65 Mark Teixeira Bat	10.00	3.00
Hank Blalock Bat		
66 Alex Rodriguez Jsy	15.00	4.50
Rafael Palmeiro Pants		
67 Alex Rodriguez Bat	15.00	4.50
Juan Gonzalez Pants		
68 Shannon Stewart Bat	10.00	3.00
Carlos Delgado Jsy		
69 Josh Phelps Bat	10.00	3.00
Eric Hinske Bat		
70 Vernon Wells Jsy	10.00	3.00
Roy Halladay Jsy		

2003 Playoff Prestige Diamond Heritage

STATED ODDS 1:21 HOBBY, 1:43 RETAIL
*GOLDEN: 1.25X TO 3X BASIC
GOLDEN RANDOM INSERTS IN PACKS
GOLDEN PRINT RUN 50 SERIAL #'d SETS

Card	Nm-Mt	Ex-Mt
1 Larry Walker	4.00	1.20
2 Troy Glaus	4.00	1.20
3 Magglio Ordonez	4.00	1.20
4 Roy Oswalt	4.00	1.20
5 Barry Zito	4.00	1.20
6 Nomar Garciaparra	6.00	1.80
7 Kerry Wood	4.00	1.20
8 Roger Clemens	8.00	2.40
9 Pedro Martinez	4.00	1.20
10 Mark Prior	8.00	2.40
11 Sammy Sosa	6.00	1.80
12 Randy Johnson	4.00	1.20
13 Greg Maddux	6.00	1.80
14 Manny Ramirez	4.00	1.20
15 Torii Hunter	4.00	1.20
16 Alex Rodriguez	6.00	1.80
17 Mike Piazza	6.00	1.80
18 Vladimir Guerrero	4.00	1.20
19 Ivan Rodriguez	4.00	1.20
20 Lance Berkman	4.00	1.20
21 Miguel Tejada	4.00	1.20
22 Chipper Jones	4.00	1.20
23 Todd Helton	4.00	1.20
24 Shawn Green	4.00	1.20
25 Scott Rolen	4.00	1.20
26 Adam Dunn	4.00	1.20
27 Jim Thome	4.00	1.20
28 Rafael Palmeiro	4.00	1.20
29 Eric Chavez	4.00	1.20
30 Andruw Jones	4.00	1.20

2003 Playoff Prestige Diamond Heritage Material

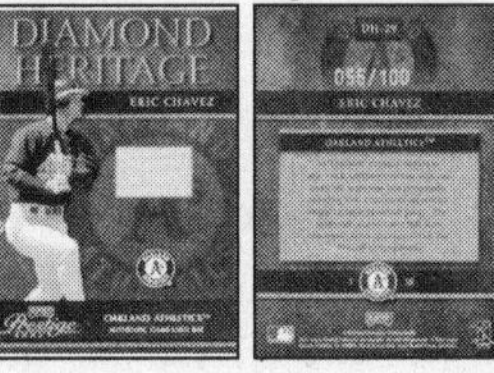

Randomly inserted into packs, this is a parallel ot the Diamond Heritage insert set. These cards were issued to a stated print run of 200 serial numbered sets for the jersey cards and 100 serial numbered sets for the bat cards.

*MULTI-COLOR PATCH 1-15: 1X TO 1.5X HI

Card	Nm-Mt	Ex-Mt
1 Larry Walker Jsy	10.00	3.00
2 Troy Glaus Jsy	10.00	3.00
3 Magglio Ordonez Jsy	10.00	3.00
4 Roy Oswalt Jsy	10.00	3.00
5 Barry Zito Jsy	10.00	3.00
6 Nomar Garciaparra Jsy	15.00	4.50
7 Kerry Wood Jsy	10.00	3.00
8 Roger Clemens Jsy	20.00	6.00
9 Pedro Martinez Jsy	10.00	3.00
10 Mark Prior Jsy	20.00	6.00
11 Sammy Sosa Jsy	15.00	4.50
12 Randy Johnson Jsy	10.00	3.00
13 Greg Maddux Jsy	15.00	4.50
14 Manny Ramirez Jsy	10.00	3.00
15 Torii Hunter Jsy	10.00	3.00
16 Alex Rodriguez Bat	20.00	6.00
17 Mike Piazza Bat	15.00	4.50
18 Vladimir Guerrero Bat	15.00	4.50
19 Ivan Rodriguez Bat	15.00	4.50
20 Lance Berkman Bat	15.00	4.50
21 Miguel Tejada Bat	10.00	3.00
22 Chipper Jones Bat	15.00	4.50
23 Todd Helton Bat	15.00	4.50
24 Shawn Green Bat	10.00	3.00
25 Scott Rolen Bat	15.00	4.50
26 Adam Dunn Bat	10.00	3.00
27 Jim Thome Bat	15.00	4.50
28 Rafael Palmeiro Bat	15.00	4.50
29 Eric Chavez Bat	10.00	3.00
30 Andruw Jones Bat	10.00	3.00

2003 Playoff Prestige Diamond Heritage Material Autographs

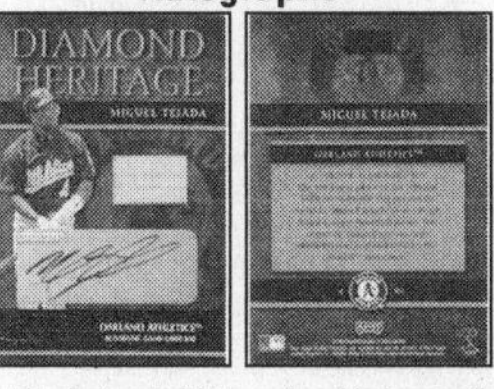

Randomly inserted into packs, this is a partial parallel to the Heritage Material insert set. These 10 cards feature not only a memorabilia piece but also an authentic signature from the player. Please note that since no card was issued to a stated print run of more than 25 cards, there is no pricing for this set.

Card	Nm-Mt	Ex-Mt
2 Troy Glaus Jsy/15		
3 Magglio Ordonez Jsy/25		
7 Kerry Wood Jsy/15		
15 Torii Hunter Jsy/25		
20 Lance Berkman Bat/15		
21 Miguel Tejada Bat/25		
25 Scott Rolen Bat/15		
26 Adam Dunn Bat/25		
27 Jim Thome Bat/15		
29 Eric Chavez Bat/25		

2003 Playoff Prestige Draft Class Reunion

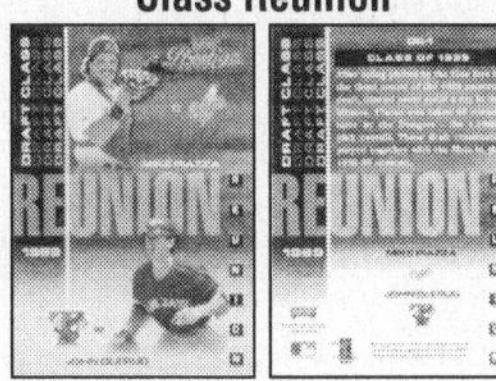

STATED ODDS 1:24 HOBBY, 1:42 RETAIL

Card	Nm-Mt	Ex-Mt
1 Mike Piazza	5.00	1.50
John Olerud		
2 Derek Jeter	8.00	2.40
Shannon Stewart		
3 Alex Rodriguez	5.00	1.50
Torii Hunter		
4 Nomar Garciaparra	5.00	1.50
Paul Konerko		
5 Kerry Wood	3.00	.90
Todd Helton		
6 Eric Chavez	3.00	.90
Billy Koch		
7 Lance Berkman	3.00	.90
Troy Glaus		
8 Pat Burrell	3.00	.90
Mark Mulder		
9 Barry Zito	3.00	.90
Jason Jennings		
10 Mark Prior	6.00	1.80
Mark Teixeira		

2003 Playoff Prestige Infield/Outfield Tandems Materials

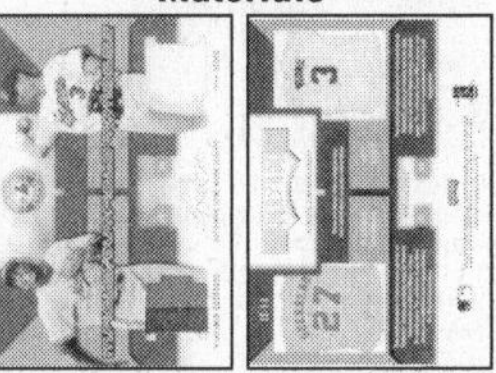

Randomly inserted into packs, these cards feature an outfielder and infielder from the same team along with a game-used memorabilia piece from each player. These cards were issued to a stated print run of 100 serial numbered sets.

Card	Nm-Mt	Ex-Mt
1 Troy Glaus Jsy	15.00	4.50
Garret Anderson Bat		
2 Mark Grace Bat	15.00	4.50
Luis Gonzalez Jsy		
3 Nomar Garciaparra Jsy	25.00	7.50
Manny Ramirez Jsy		
4 Alfonso Soriano Jsy	15.00	4.50
Bernie Williams Jsy		
5 Jeff Bagwell Jsy	15.00	4.50
Lance Berkman Jsy		
6 Alex Rodriguez Jsy	25.00	7.50
Juan Gonzalez Jsy		
7 Barry Larkin Jsy	15.00	4.50
Adam Dunn Jsy		
8 Scott Rolen Bat	25.00	7.50
Jim Edmonds Jsy		
9 Todd Helton Jsy	15.00	4.50
Larry Walker Jsy		
10 Adrian Beltre Jsy	10.00	3.00
Shawn Green Jsy		
11 Jose Vidro Jsy	15.00	4.50
Vladimir Guerrero Jsy		
12 Mike Sweeney Jsy	10.00	3.00
Carlos Beltran Jsy		
13 Josh Phelps Jsy	10.00	3.00
Vernon Wells Jsy		
14 Paul Konerko Jsy	10.00	3.00
Magglio Ordonez Jsy		
15 Phil Nevin Jsy	10.00	3.00
Ryan Klesko Jsy		

2003 Playoff Prestige Inside the Numbers

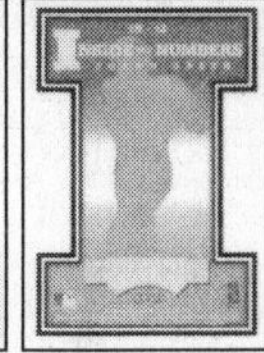

STATED PRINT RUN 2002 SERIAL #'d SETS
*DIE CUT p/r 45-75: 2X TO 5X BASIC
*DIE CUT p/r 27-38: 2.5X TO 6X BASIC
DIE CUT PRINT RUN BASED ON UNIFORM
NO DIE CUT PRICING ON QTY OF 25 OR LESS
RANDOM INSERTS IN PACKS ....

Card	Nm-Mt	Ex-Mt
1 Roger Clemens	6.00	1.80
2 Greg Maddux	5.00	1.50
3 Miguel Tejada	3.00	.90
4 Alex Rodriguez	5.00	1.50
5 Ichiro Suzuki	5.00	1.50
6 Sammy Sosa	5.00	1.50
7 Jim Thome	3.00	.90
8 Derek Jeter	8.00	2.40
9 Randy Johnson	3.00	.90
10 Barry Zito	3.00	.90
11 Jason Giambi	3.00	.90
12 Shawn Green	3.00	.90
13 Curt Schilling	3.00	.90
14 Albert Pujols	6.00	1.80
15 Vladimir Guerrero	3.00	.90
16 Pedro Martinez	3.00	.90
17 Alfonso Soriano	3.00	.90
18 Barry Bonds	8.00	2.40
19 Magglio Ordonez	3.00	.90
20 Chipper Jones	3.00	.90
21 Pat Burrell	3.00	.90
22 Luis Gonzalez	3.00	.90
23 Jeff Bagwell	3.00	.90
24 Garret Anderson	3.00	.90
25 Larry Walker	3.00	.90

2003 Playoff Prestige League Leaders

RANDOM INSERTS IN PACKS ....
STATED PRINT RUN 2002 SERIAL #'d SETS

Card	Nm-Mt	Ex-Mt
1 Manny Ramirez AVG	3.00	.90
2 Sammy Sosa HR	5.00	1.50
3 Alex Rodriguez RBI	5.00	1.50
4 Alfonso Soriano Runs	3.00	.90
5 Vladimir Guerrero Hits	3.00	.90
6 Nomar Garciaparra 2B	5.00	1.50
7 Johnny Damon 3B	3.00	.90
8 Alfonso Soriano SB	3.00	.90
9 Barry Bonds Walks	8.00	2.40
10 Barry Zito Wins	3.00	.90
11 Pedro Martinez ERA	3.00	.90
12 John Smoltz SV	3.00	.90
13 Randy Johnson CG	3.00	.90
14 Lance Berkman RBI	3.00	.90
15 Randy Johnson SO	3.00	.90

2003 Playoff Prestige League Leaders Materials

RANDOM INSERTS IN PACKS ....
STATED PRINT RUN 250 SERIAL #'d SETS

Card	Nm-Mt	Ex-Mt
1 Manny Ramirez AVG Jsy	8.00	2.40
2 Sammy Sosa HR Base	10.00	3.00
3 Alex Rodriguez RBI Jsy	15.00	4.50
4 Alfonso Soriano Runs Jsy	10.00	3.00

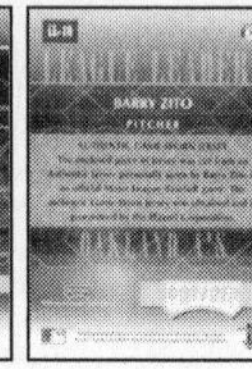

Card	Nm-Mt	Ex-Mt
5 Vladimir Guerrero Hits Jsy	10.00	3.00
6 Nomar Garciaparra 2B Jsy	20.00	6.00
7 Johnny Damon 3B Bat	8.00	2.40
8 Alfonso Soriano SB Jsy	10.00	3.00
9 Barry Bonds Walks Base	15.00	4.50
10 Barry Zito Wins Jsy	10.00	3.00
11 Pedro Martinez ERA Jsy	10.00	3.00
12 John Smoltz SV Jsy	10.00	3.00
13 Randy Johnson CG Jsy	10.00	3.00
14 Lance Berkman RBI Jsy	8.00	2.40
15 Randy Johnson SO Jsy	10.00	3.00

2003 Playoff Prestige Patches of MLB

Randomly inserted into packs, these 20 cards feature patch pieces from the game-used jerseys used in this product. These cards were issued to a stated print run of 25 serial numbered sets and no pricing is available due to market scarcity.

Nm-Mt Ex-Mt

1 Roger Clemens
2 Randy Johnson
3 Sammy Sosa
4 Vladimir Guerrero
5 Lance Berkman
6 Alfonso Soriano
7 Alex Rodriguez
8 Roberto Alomar
9 Miguel Tejada
10 Pedro Martinez
11 Greg Maddux
12 Barry Zito
13 Magglio Ordonez
14 Chipper Jones
15 Manny Ramirez
16 Troy Glaus
17 Pat Burrell
18 Roy Oswalt
19 Mike Piazza
20 Nomar Garciaparra

2003 Playoff Prestige Patches of MLB Autographs

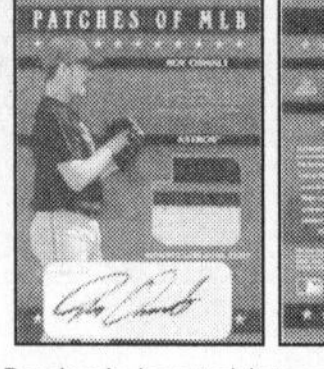

Randomly inserted into packs, these cards feature not only a game-used patch piece but also an authentic autograph from the featured player. Please note that since no card was issued to a stated print run of more than 10 copies, there is no pricing due to market scarcity.

Nm-Mt Ex-Mt

1 Roger Clemens/5
4 Vladimir Guerrero/5
5 Lance Berkman/10
6 Alfonso Soriano/5
7 Alex Rodriguez/5
9 Miguel Tejada/10
10 Pedro Martinez/5
11 Greg Maddux/5
12 Barry Zito/10
13 Magglio Ordonez/10
14 Chipper Jones/5
16 Troy Glaus/5
17 Pat Burrell/5
18 Roy Oswalt/10

2003 Playoff Prestige Player Collection

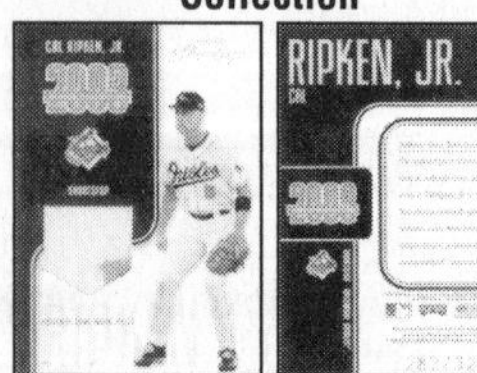

Randomly inserted into packs, these 100 cards feature leading players as well as various memorabilia pieces. Each of these cards was issued to a stated print run of 325 serial numbered sets. It is believed that this design on card style was used on more than one product issued by Playoff/Donruss during 2003 but each card was easily identifiable from what product it was pulled from.

Card	Nm-Mt	Ex-Mt
*MULTI-COLOR PATCH: 1.25X TO 3X HI		
1 Roberto Alomar Bat	10.00	3.00
2 Jeff Bagwell Bat	10.00	3.00
3 Jeff Bagwell Jsy	10.00	3.00
4 Jeff Bagwell Pants	10.00	3.00
5 Jay Bell Jsy	8.00	2.40
6 Adrian Beltre Jsy	8.00	2.40
7 Lance Berkman Jsy	8.00	2.40
8 Craig Biggio Bat	10.00	3.00
9 Craig Biggio Jsy	10.00	3.00
10 Bret Boone Jsy	8.00	2.40
11 Joe Borchard Jsy	8.00	2.40
12 Kevin Brown Jsy	8.00	2.40
13 Jeromy Burnitz Jsy	8.00	2.40
14 Pat Burrell Bat	8.00	2.40
15 Marlon Byrd Bat	8.00	2.40
16 Marlon Byrd Jsy	8.00	2.40
17 Roger Clemens Stand Jsy	15.00	4.50
18 Roger Clemens Throw Jsy	15.00	4.50
19 Doug Davis Jsy	8.00	2.40
20 Carlos Delgado Jsy	8.00	2.40
21 J.D. Drew Jsy	8.00	2.40
22 Adam Dunn Jsy	8.00	2.40
23 Jim Edmonds Jsy	8.00	2.40
24 Steve Finley Jsy	8.00	2.40
25 Freddy Garcia Jsy	8.00	2.40
26 Nomar Garciaparra Jsy	15.00	4.50
27 Jason Giambi Bat	10.00	3.00
28 Jason Giambi Jsy	10.00	3.00
29 Troy Glaus Jsy	10.00	3.00
30 Juan Gonzalez Bat	10.00	3.00
31 Juan Gonzalez Jsy	10.00	3.00
32 Luis Gonzalez Bat	8.00	2.40
33 Shawn Green Jsy	8.00	2.40
34 Ben Grieve Jsy	8.00	2.40
35 Vladimir Guerrero Jsy	10.00	3.00
36 Tony Gwynn Jsy	10.00	3.00
37 Toby Hall Jsy	8.00	2.40
38 Wes Helms Jsy	8.00	2.40
39 Todd Helton Bat	10.00	3.00
40 Todd Helton Jsy	10.00	3.00
41 Rickey Henderson Bat	10.00	3.00
42 Rickey Henderson Jsy	10.00	3.00
43 Rickey Henderson Pants	10.00	3.00
44 Tim Hudson Jsy	8.00	2.40
45 Jason Jennings Jsy	8.00	2.40
46 Andruw Jones Bat	8.00	2.40
47 Andruw Jones Jsy	8.00	2.40
48 Chipper Jones Jsy	10.00	3.00
49 Ryan Klesko Jsy	8.00	2.40
50 Paul Konerko Jsy	8.00	2.40
51 Barry Larkin Bat	10.00	3.00
52 Barry Larkin Jsy	10.00	3.00
53 Travis Lee Jsy	8.00	2.40
54 Paul Lo Duca Jsy	8.00	2.40
55 Terrence Long Jsy	8.00	2.40
56 Pedro Martinez Jsy	10.00	3.00
57 Joe Mays Jsy	8.00	2.40
58 Mark Mulder Jsy	8.00	2.40
59 John Olerud Jsy	8.00	2.40
60 Magglio Ordonez Bat	8.00	2.40
61 Magglio Ordonez Jsy	8.00	2.40
62 Roy Oswalt Jsy	8.00	2.40
63 Rafael Palmeiro Pants	10.00	3.00
64 Chan Ho Park Jsy	8.00	2.40
65 Jay Payton Jsy	8.00	2.40
66 Robert Person Jsy	8.00	2.40
67 Andy Pettitte Jsy	10.00	3.00
68 Mike Piazza Bat	10.00	3.00
69 Mike Piazza Jsy	10.00	3.00
70 Mark Prior Bat	15.00	4.50
71 Mark Prior Jsy	15.00	4.50
72 Manny Ramirez Bat	8.00	2.40
73 Manny Ramirez Jsy	8.00	2.40
74 Cal Ripken Jsy	40.00	12.00
75 Alex Rodriguez Bat	10.00	3.00
76 Alex Rodriguez M's Jsy	10.00	3.00
77 Alex Rodriguez Rgr Jsy	10.00	3.00
78 Ivan Rodriguez Bat	10.00	3.00
79 Ivan Rodriguez Jsy	10.00	3.00
80 C.C. Sabathia Jsy	8.00	2.40
81 Reggie Sanders Jsy	8.00	2.40
82 Kazuhiro Sasaki Jsy	8.00	2.40
83 Curt Schilling Jsy	10.00	3.00
84 Richie Sexson Jsy	8.00	2.40
85 Tsuyoshi Shinjo Jsy	8.00	2.40
86 Alfonso Soriano Bat	10.00	3.00
87 Alfonso Soriano Jsy	10.00	3.00
88 Sammy Sosa Jsy	15.00	4.50
89 Miguel Tejada Jsy	8.00	2.40
90 Frank Thomas Jsy	10.00	3.00
91 Jim Thome Jsy	10.00	3.00
92 Larry Walker Bat	10.00	3.00
93 Larry Walker Jsy	10.00	3.00
94 David Wells Jsy	8.00	2.40
95 Vernon Wells Jsy	8.00	2.40
96 Bernie Williams Jsy	10.00	3.00
97 Matt Williams Jsy	8.00	2.40
98 Preston Wilson Jsy	8.00	2.40
99 Kerry Wood Jsy	10.00	3.00
100 Barry Zito Jsy	10.00	3.00

2003 Playoff Prestige Signature Impressions

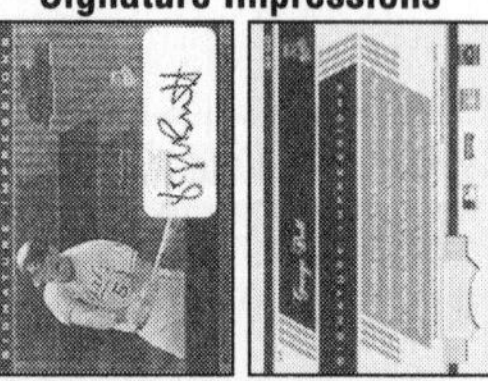

Randomly inserted into packs, these 50 cards feature authentic autographs from the player pictured on the card. These cards were printed to varying quantities and we have notated that information next to the player's name in our checklist.

Card	Nm-Mt	Ex-Mt
1 A.J. Pierzynski/50	25.00	7.50
2 Adam Dunn/25		
3 Barry Zito/25		
4 Bobby Abreu/20		
5 Brandon Phillips/25		
6 Chipper Jones/5		
7 Don Mattingly/15		
8 Edgar Martinez/25		
9 Eric Hinske/25		
10 Greg Maddux/5		
11 Joe Borchard/25		
12 John Candelaria/50		
13 Jose Canseco/10		
14 Kerry Wood/5		
15 Kevin Mench/25		
16 Lance Berkman/25		
17 Magglio Ordonez/5		
18 Miguel Tejada/25		
19 Nolan Ryan/5		
20 Rafael Palmeiro/5		
21 Roberto Alomar/5		
22 Roy Oswalt/25		
23 Bobby Doerr/25		
24 Scott Rolen/5		
25 Tim Hudson/15		
26 Will Clark/10		
27 Yogi Berra/15		
28 Joe Kennedy/50	15.00	4.50
29 Johnny Bench/10		
30 Lenny Dykstra/50	25.00	7.50
31 Mark Mulder/5		
32 Mark Prior/25		
33 Mike Schmidt/5		
34 Ozzie Smith/5		
35 Paul Lo Duca/25		
36 Reggie Jackson/5		
37 Roger Clemens/5		
38 Steve Garvey/25		
39 Toby Hall/50	15.00	4.50
40 Victor Martinez/25		
41 Vladimir Guerrero/5		
42 Adrian Beltre/15		
43 Al Kaline/15		
44 Albert Pujols/15		
45 Barry Larkin/15		
46 Brian Giles/15		
47 C.C. Sabathia/15		
48 Dale Murphy/15		
49 George Brett/5		
50 Jeremy Bonderman/100	20.00	6.00

2003 Playoff Prestige Stars of MLB Jersey

Randomly inserted into packs, these 20 cards feature game-used jersey swatches of the featured players. Each of these cards were issued to a stated print run of 150 serial numbered sets.

Card	Nm-Mt	Ex-Mt
1 Roger Clemens	20.00	6.00
2 Randy Johnson	10.00	3.00
3 Sammy Sosa	20.00	6.00
4 Vladimir Guerrero	10.00	3.00
5 Lance Berkman	8.00	2.40
6 Alfonso Soriano	10.00	3.00
7 Alex Rodriguez	15.00	4.50
8 Roberto Alomar	10.00	3.00
9 Miguel Tejada	8.00	2.40
10 Pedro Martinez	10.00	3.00
11 Greg Maddux	15.00	4.50
12 Barry Zito	10.00	3.00
13 Magglio Ordonez	8.00	2.40
14 Chipper Jones	10.00	3.00
15 Manny Ramirez	8.00	2.40
16 Troy Glaus	10.00	3.00
17 Pat Burrell	8.00	2.40
18 Roy Oswalt	8.00	2.40
19 Mike Piazza	15.00	4.50
20 Nomar Garciaparra	20.00	6.00

2003 Playoff Prestige Stars of MLB Jersey Autographs

Randomly inserted into packs, these eight cards feature not only game-used jersey swatches but authentic autographs from the player. Each of these cards were issued to a stated print run of 25 serial numbered sets and no pricing is available due to market scarcity.

Nm-Mt Ex-Mt

4 Vladimir Guerrero
5 Lance Berkman
9 Miguel Tejada
12 Barry Zito
13 Magglio Ordonez
14 Chipper Jones
16 Troy Glaus
18 Roy Oswalt

2004 Playoff Prestige

This 200 card set was released in March, 2004. The set was issued in six card packs with an $3 SRP which came 24 packs to a box and 12 boxes to a case. Interspersed into this set are various prospect cards which were printed to the same quantity as the other cards.

Card	Nm-Mt	Ex-Mt
COMPLETE SET (200)	40.00	12.00
1 Bengie Molina	.40	.12
2 Garret Anderson	.40	.12
3 Jarrod Washburn	.40	.12
4 Scott Spiezio	.40	.12
5 Tim Salmon	.60	.18
6 Troy Glaus	.60	.18
7 Alex Cintron	.40	.12
8 Brandon Webb	.40	.12
9 Curt Schilling	.60	.18
10 Edgar Gonzalez PROS	.75	.23
11 Luis Gonzalez	.40	.12
12 Randy Johnson	1.00	.30
13 Steve Finley	.40	.12
14 Andruw Jones	.40	.12
15 Bubba Nelson PROS	1.00	.30
16 Chipper Jones	1.00	.30
17 Gary Sheffield	.40	.12
18 Greg Maddux	1.50	.45
19 Javy Lopez	.40	.12
20 John Smoltz	.60	.18
21 Marcus Giles	.40	.12
22 Rafael Furcal	.40	.12
23 Brian Roberts	.40	.12
24 Jason Johnson	.40	.12
25 Jay Gibbons	.40	.12
26 Luis Matos	.40	.12
27 Melvin Mora	.40	.12
28 Tony Batista	.40	.12
29 Bill Mueller	.40	.12
30 David Ortiz	.40	.12
31 Johnny Damon	.40	.12
32 Kevin Youkilis PROS	1.50	.45
33 Manny Ramirez	.40	.12
34 Nomar Garciaparra	1.50	.45
35 Pedro Martinez	1.00	.30
36 Trot Nixon	.60	.18
37 Aramis Ramirez	.40	.12
38 Brendan Harris PROS	.75	.23
39 Carlos Zambrano	.40	.12
40 Corey Patterson	.40	.12
41 Kenny Lofton	.40	.12
42 Kerry Wood	1.00	.30
43 Mark Prior	2.00	.60
44 Sammy Sosa	1.50	.45
45 Bartolo Colon	.40	.12
46 Carlos Lee	.40	.12
47 Esteban Loaiza	.40	.12
48 Frank Thomas	1.00	.30
49 Joe Crede	.40	.12
50 Magglio Ordonez	.40	.12
51 Roberto Alomar	1.00	.30
52 Adam Dunn	.40	.12
53 Austin Kearns	.40	.12
54 Josh Hall	.40	.12
55 Ken Griffey Jr.	1.50	.45
56 Sean Casey	.40	.12
57 Mike Nakamura	.40	.12
58 C.C. Sabathia	.40	.12
59 Casey Blake	.40	.12
60 Jody Gerut	.40	.12
61 Matt Lawton	.40	.12
62 Milton Bradley	.40	.12
63 Omar Vizquel	.40	.12
64 Jason Jennings	.40	.12
65 Jay Payton	.40	.12
66 Larry Walker	.60	.18
67 Preston Wilson	.40	.12
68 Todd Helton	.60	.18
69 Bobby Higginson	.40	.12
70 Carlos Pena	.40	.12
71 Dmitri Young	.40	.12
72 Jeremy Bonderman	.40	.12
73 Preston Larrison PROS	.75	.23
74 Derrek Lee	.40	.12
75 Dontrelle Willis	.40	.12
76 Ivan Rodriguez	1.00	.30
77 Josh Beckett	.60	.18
78 Juan Pierre	.40	.12
79 Miguel Cabrera	1.00	.30
80 Mike Lowell	.40	.12
81 Chris Burke PROS	.75	.23
82 Craig Biggio	.60	.18
83 Jeff Bagwell	.60	.18
84 Jeff Kent	.40	.12
85 Lance Berkman	.40	.12
86 Richard Hidalgo	.40	.12
87 Roy Oswalt	.40	.12
88 Aaron Guiel	.40	.12
89 Angel Berroa	.40	.12
90 Carlos Beltran	.40	.12
91 Jeremy Affeldt	.40	.12
92 Mike Sweeney	.40	.12
93 Runelvys Hernandez	.40	.12
94 Dave Roberts	.40	.12
95 Eric Gagne	.60	.18
96 Hideo Nomo	1.00	.30
97 Kevin Brown	.40	.12
98 Paul Lo Duca	.40	.12
99 Shawn Green	.40	.12
100 Ben Sheets	.40	.12
101 Geoff Jenkins	.40	.12
102 Richie Sexson	.40	.12
103 Rickie Weeks PROS	2.00	.60
104 Scott Podsednik	1.00	.30
105 J.D. Durbin PROS	1.00	.30
106 Jacque Jones	.40	.12
107 Jason Kubel PROS	1.00	.30
108 Shannon Stewart	.40	.12
109 Torii Hunter	.40	.12
110 Chad Cordero PROS	.75	.23
111 Javier Vazquez	.40	.12
112 Jose Vidro	.40	.12
113 Livan Hernandez	.40	.12
114 Orlando Cabrera	.40	.12
115 Tony Armas Jr.	.40	.12
116 Vladimir Guerrero	1.00	.30
117 Al Leiter	.40	.12
118 Cliff Floyd	.40	.12
119 Jae Weong Seo	.40	.12
120 Jose Reyes	.60	.18
121 Mike Piazza	1.50	.45
122 Tom Glavine	.60	.18
123 Aaron Boone	.40	.12
124 Alfonso Soriano	.60	.18
125 Andy Pettitte	.60	.18
126 Derek Jeter	2.50	.75
127 Hideki Matsui	1.50	.45
128 Jason Giambi	1.00	.30
129 Jorge Posada	.60	.18
130 Jose Contreras	.40	.12
131 Mike Mussina	1.00	.30
132 Barry Zito	.60	.18
133 Eric Byrnes	.40	.12
134 Eric Chavez	.40	.12
135 Jose Guillen	.40	.12
136 Mark Mulder	.40	.12
137 Miguel Tejada	.40	.12
138 Ramon Hernandez	.40	.12
139 Rich Harden	.40	.12
140 Tim Hudson	.40	.12
141 Bobby Abreu	.40	.12
142 Brett Myers	.40	.12
143 Jim Thome	1.00	.30
144 Kevin Millwood	.40	.12
145 Mike Lieberthal	.40	.12
146 Ryan Howard PROS	.75	.23
147 Craig Wilson	.40	.12
148 Jack Wilson	.40	.12
149 Jason Kendall	.40	.12
150 Kip Wells	.40	.12
151 Reggie Sanders	.40	.12
152 Albert Pujols	2.00	.60
153 Edgar Renteria	.40	.12
154 Jim Edmonds	.40	.12
155 Matt Morris	.40	.12
156 Scott Rolen	.60	.18
157 Tino Martinez	.60	.18
158 Woody Williams	.40	.12
159 Brian Giles	.40	.12
160 Freddy Guzman PROS RC	1.00	.30
161 Jake Peavy	.40	.12
162 Khalil Greene PROS	1.00	.30
163 Phil Nevin	.40	.12
164 Ryan Klesko	.40	.12
165 Ray Durham	.40	.12
166 Jason Schmidt	.40	.12
167 Jerome Williams PROS	1.00	.30
168 Jesse Foppert	.40	.12
169 Jose Cruz Jr.	.40	.12
170 Marquis Grissom	.40	.12
171 Merkin Valdez PROS RC	3.00	.90
172 Rich Aurilia	.40	.12
173 Bret Boone	.40	.12
174 Freddy Garcia	.40	.12
175 Ichiro Suzuki	1.50	.45
176 Jamie Moyer	.40	.12
177 John Olerud	.40	.12
178 Mike Cameron	.40	.12
179 Randy Winn	.40	.12
180 Aubrey Huff	.40	.12
181 Carl Crawford	.40	.12
182 Chad Gaudin PROS	.75	.23
183 Rocco Baldelli	1.00	.30
184 Toby Hall	.40	.12
185 Travis Lee	.40	.12
186 Alex Rodriguez	1.50	.45
187 Hank Blalock	.40	.12
188 John Thomson	.40	.12
189 Juan Gonzalez	1.00	.30
190 Mark Teixeira	.40	.12
191 Michael Young	.40	.12
192 Rafael Palmeiro	.60	.18
193 Ramon Nivar PROS	.75	.23
194 Carlos Delgado	.40	.12
195 Dustin McGowan PROS	1.00	.30
196 Frank Catalanotto	.40	.12
197 Vinny Chulk	.40	.12
198 Orlando Hudson	.40	.12
199 Roy Halladay	.40	.12
200 Vernon Wells	.40	.12

2004 Playoff Prestige Autographs

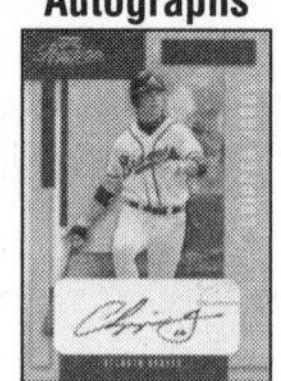

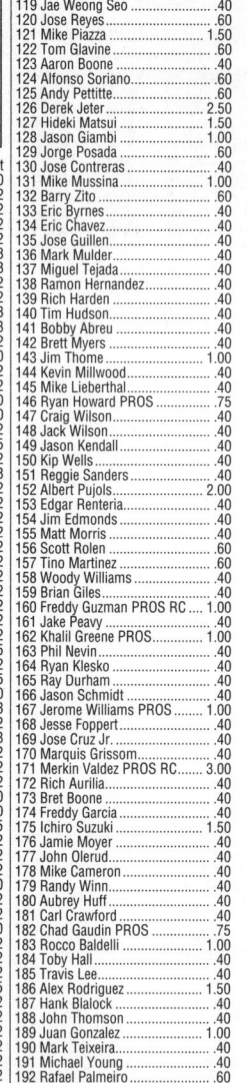

Card	Nm-Mt	Ex-Mt
RANDOM INSERTS IN PACKS		
PRINT RUNS B/WN 4-500 COPIES PER		
PRINT RUNS PROVIDED BY DONRUSS		
CARDS ARE NOT SERIAL-NUMBERED		
SEE BECKETT.COM OPG FOR PRINT RUNS		
NO PRICING ON QTY OF 25 OR LESS.		
8 Brandon Webb/100	15.00	4.50
10 Edgar Gonzalez PROS/150	10.00	3.00
15 Bubba Nelson PROS/250	15.00	4.50
25 Jay Gibbons/50	25.00	7.50
32 Kevin Youkilis PROS/100	25.00	7.50
38 Brendan Harris PROS/400	10.00	3.00
57 Mike Nakamura/250	10.00	3.00
60 Jody Gerut/50	25.00	7.50
73 Preston Larrison PROS/250	10.00	3.00
79 Miguel Cabrera/100	40.00	12.00
81 Chris Burke PROS/250	15.00	4.50
93 Runelvys Hernandez/50	15.00	4.50
105 J.D. Durbin PROS/500	10.00	3.00
106 Jacque Jones/50	15.00	4.50
107 Jason Kubel PROS/400	10.00	3.00
108 Shannon Stewart/50	15.00	4.50
133 Eric Byrnes/50	15.00	4.50
139 Rich Harden/50	40.00	12.00
146 Ryan Howard PROS/400	10.00	3.00
193 Ramon Nivar PROS/100	10.00	3.00
195 Dustin McGowan PROS/100	15.00	4.50
197 Vinny Chulk/112	10.00	3.00
198 Orlando Hudson/100	10.00	3.00

2004 Playoff Prestige Xtra Bases Black

Nm-Mt Ex-Mt
*XB BLACK: 5X TO 12X BASIC
*XB BLACK: 5X TO 12X BASIC PROS
RANDOM INSERTS IN HOBBY PACKS
STATED PRINT RUN 75 SERIAL #'d SETS

2004 Playoff Prestige Xtra Bases Black Autographs

Nm-Mt Ex-Mt
RANDOM INSERTS IN HOBBY PACKS
STATED PRINT RUN 25 SERIAL #'d SETS
NO PRICING DUE TO SCARCITY

2004 Playoff Prestige Xtra Bases Green

Nm-Mt Ex-Mt
*XB GREEN: 3X TO 8X BASIC
*XB GREEN: 3X TO 8X BASIC PROS
RANDOM INSERTS IN RETAIL PACKS
STATED PRINT RUN 150 SERIAL #'d SETS

2004 Playoff Prestige Xtra Bases Green Autographs

Nm-Mt Ex-Mt
RANDOM INSERTS IN RETAIL PACKS
STATED PRINT RUN 100 SERIAL #'d SETS
10 Edgar Gonzalez PROS 10.00 3.00
15 Bubba Nelson PROS 15.00 4.50
38 Brendan Harris PROS 10.00 3.00
57 Mike Nakamura 10.00 3.00
81 Chris Burke PROS 15.00 4.50
105 J.D. Durbin PROS 15.00 4.50
107 Jason Kubel PROS 15.00 4.50
146 Ryan Howard PROS 10.00 3.00
195 Dustin McGowan PROS 15.00 4.50

2004 Playoff Prestige Xtra Bases Purple

Nm-Mt Ex-Mt
*XB PURPLE: 3X TO 8X BASIC
*XB PURPLE: 3X TO 8X BASIC PROS
RANDOM INSERTS IN HOBBY PACKS
STATED PRINT RUN 150 SERIAL #'d SETS

2004 Playoff Prestige Xtra Bases Purple Autographs

Nm-Mt Ex-Mt
RANDOM INSERTS IN HOBBY PACKS
STATED PRINT RUN 100 SERIAL #'d SETS
10 Edgar Gonzalez PROS 10.00 3.00
15 Bubba Nelson PROS 15.00 4.50
32 Kevin Youkilis PROS 25.00 7.50
38 Brendan Harris PROS 10.00 3.00
57 Mike Nakamura 10.00 3.00
73 Preston Larrison PROS 10.00 3.00
79 Miguel Cabrera 40.00 12.00
81 Chris Burke PROS 15.00 4.50
105 J.D. Durbin PROS 15.00 4.50
107 Jason Kubel PROS 15.00 4.50
146 Ryan Howard PROS 10.00 3.00
193 Ramon Nivar PROS 10.00 3.00
195 Dustin McGowan PROS 15.00 4.50
198 Orlando Hudson 10.00 3.00

2004 Playoff Prestige Xtra Bases Red

Nm-Mt Ex-Mt
RANDOM INSERTS IN RETAIL PACKS
STATED PRINT RUN 25 SERIAL #'d SETS
NO PRICING DUE TO SCARCITY

2004 Playoff Prestige Xtra Bases Red Autographs

Nm-Mt Ex-Mt
RANDOM INSERTS IN RETAIL PACKS
STATED PRINT RUN 25 SERIAL #'d SETS
NO PRICING DUE TO SCARCITY

2004 Playoff Prestige Achievements

Nm-Mt Ex-Mt
COMPLETE SET (15)
STATED ODDS 1:8
1 Hideo Nomo 95 ROY 3.00 .90
2 Don Mattingly 85 MVP 10.00 3.00
3 Roger Clemens 86 CY/MVP 6.00 1.80
4 Greg Maddux 95 CY 5.00 1.50
5 Stan Musial 43 MVP 6.00 1.80
6 Roberto Clemente 66 MVP 10.00 3.00
7 Derek Jeter 96 ROY 8.00 2.40
8 Albert Pujols 01 ROY 6.00 1.80
9 Cal Ripken 91 MVP 12.00 3.60
10 George Brett 80 MVP 10.00 3.00
11 Carl Yastrzemski 67 MVP 6.00 1.80
12 Rickey Henderson 90 MVP 3.00 .90
13 Sammy Sosa 98 MVP 5.00 1.50
14 Randy Johnson 02 CY 3.00 .90
15 Bob Gibson 68 CY/MVP 4.00 1.20

2004 Playoff Prestige Changing Stripes

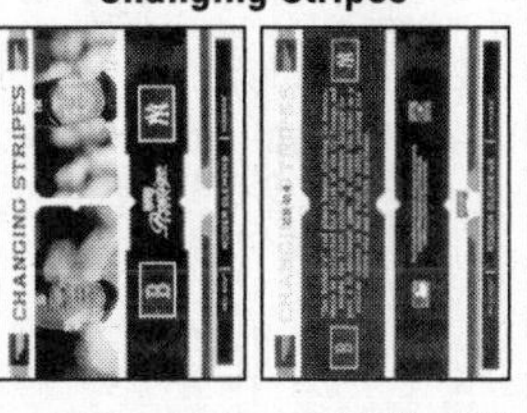

Nm-Mt Ex-Mt
STATED ODDS 1:11
*FOIL: .75X TO 2X BASIC
FOIL PRINT RUN 150 SERIAL #'d SETS
*HOLO-FOIL: 1.5X TO 4X BASIC
HOLO-FOIL PRINT RUN 50 SERIAL #'d SETS
FOIL/HOLO-FOIL RANDOM IN PACKS.
1 Rickey Henderson A's-Yanks 4.00 1.20
2 Mike Mussina O's-Yanks 4.00 1.20
3 Jim Thome Indians-Phils 4.00 1.20
4 Hideo Nomo Sox-Dodgers 4.00 1.20
5 Scott Rolen Phils-Cards 4.00 1.20
6 Jason Giambi A's-Yanks 4.00 1.20
7 R.Johnson Astros-D'backs 4.00 1.20
8 Shawn Green Jays-Dodgers 4.00 1.20
9 Curt Schilling Phils-D'backs 4.00 1.20
10 Alex Rodriguez M's-Rangers 6.00 1.80
11 Greg Maddux Cubs-Braves 6.00 1.80
12 Randy Johnson M's-Astros 4.00 1.20
13 Hideo Nomo Dodgers-Mets 4.00 1.20
14 Ivan Rodriguez Rgr-Marlins 4.00 1.20
15 Juan Gonzalez Indians-Rangers 4.00 1.20
16 Manny Ramirez Indians-Sox 4.00 1.20
17 Mike Piazza Dodgers-Mets 6.00 1.80
18 Nolan Ryan Angels-Astros 10.00 3.00
19 Nolan Ryan Astros-Rangers 10.00 3.00
20 Pedro Martinez Expos-Sox 4.00 1.20
21 Reg Jackson Yanks-Angels 4.00 1.20
22 Roberto Alomar Mets-Sox 4.00 1.20
23 Rod Carew Twins-Angels 4.00 1.20
24 Roger Clemens Sox-Yanks 8.00 2.40
25 Sammy Sosa Sox-Cubs 6.00 1.80

2004 Playoff Prestige Changing Stripes Dual Jersey

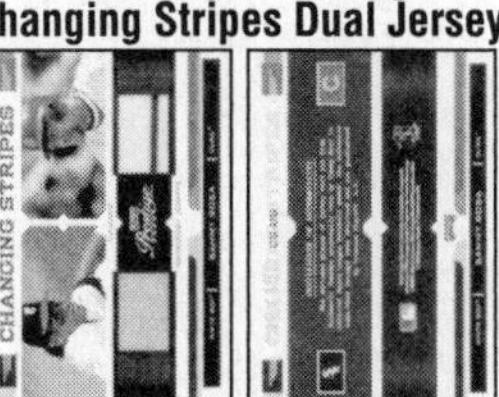

Nm-Mt Ex-Mt
STATED PRINT RUN 150 SERIAL #'d SETS
PRIME PRINT RUN 25 SERIAL #'d SETS
NO PRIME PRICING DUE TO SCARCITY
RANDOM INSERTS IN PACKS
1 Rickey Henderson A's-Yanks 15.00 4.50
2 Mike Mussina O's-Yanks 15.00 4.50
3 Jim Thome Indians-Phils 15.00 4.50
4 Hideo Nomo Sox-Dodgers 25.00 7.50
5 Scott Rolen Phils-Cards 15.00 4.50
6 Jason Giambi A's-Yanks 15.00 4.50
7 R.Johnson Astros-D'backs 15.00 4.50
8 Shawn Green Jays-Dodgers 10.00 3.00
9 Curt Schilling Phils-D'backs 15.00 4.50
10 Alex Rodriguez M's-Rangers 15.00 4.50
12 Randy Johnson M's-Astros 15.00 4.50
13 Hideo Nomo Dodgers-Mets 25.00 7.50
14 Ivan Rodriguez Rgr-Marlins 15.00 4.50
15 Juan Gonzalez Indians-Rangers 15.00 4.50
16 Manny Ramirez Indians-Sox 10.00 3.00
17 Mike Piazza Dodgers-Mets 15.00 4.50
18 Nolan Ryan Angels-Astros 50.00 15.00
19 Nolan Ryan Astros-Rangers 50.00 15.00
20 Pedro Martinez Expos-Sox 15.00 4.50
22 Roberto Alomar Mets-Sox 15.00 4.50
23 Rod Carew Twins-Angels 15.00 4.50
24 Roger Clemens Sox-Yanks 20.00 6.00
25 Sammy Sosa Sox-Cubs 20.00 6.00

2004 Playoff Prestige Connections

Nm-Mt Ex-Mt
STATED ODDS 1:9
*FOIL: 1.5X TO 4X BASIC
FOIL PRINT RUN 100 SERIAL #'d SETS
HOLO-FOIL PRINT RUN 21 SERIAL #'d SETS
NO HOLO-FOIL PRICING DUE TO SCARCITY
FOIL/HOLO-FOIL RANDOM IN PACKS.
1 Derek Jeter 6.00 1.80
Alfonso Soriano
2 Greg Maddux 4.00 1.20
Chipper Jones
3 Albert Pujols 5.00 1.50
Scott Rolen
4 Randy Johnson 2.50 .75
Curt Schilling
5 Nomar Garciaparra 4.00 1.20
Manny Ramirez
6 Alex Rodriguez 4.00 1.20
Mark Teixeira
7 Barry Zito 2.00 .60
Tim Hudson
8 Sammy Sosa 5.00 1.50
Mark Prior
9 Derek Jeter 6.00 1.80
Jason Giambi
10 Roger Clemens 5.00 1.50
Mike Mussina
11 Mark Prior 5.00 1.50
Kerry Wood
12 Alex Rodriguez 4.00 1.20
Hank Blalock
13 Frank Thomas 2.50 .75
Magglio Ordonez
14 Nomar Garciaparra 4.00 1.20
Pedro Martinez
15 Carlos Delgado 2.00 .60
Vernon Wells
16 Miguel Tejada 2.00 .60
Eric Chavez
17 Jeff Bagwell 2.00 .60
Lance Berkman
18 Jim Thome 2.50 .75
Bobby Abreu
19 Todd Helton 2.00 .60
Preston Wilson
20 Vladimir Guerrero 2.50 .75
Javier Vazquez

2004 Playoff Prestige Connections Material

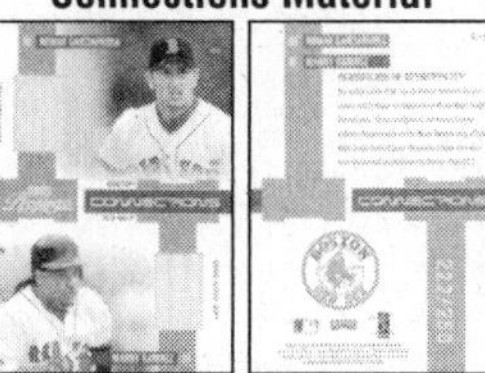

Nm-Mt Ex-Mt
RANDOM INSERTS IN PACKS
STATED PRINT RUN 250 SERIAL #'d SETS
1 Derek Jeter Bat 25.00 7.50
Alfonso Soriano Bat
2 Greg Maddux Bat 15.00 4.50
Chipper Jones Jsy
3 Albert Pujols Bat 20.00 6.00
Scott Rolen Bat
4 Randy Johnson Bat 15.00 4.50
Curt Schilling Bat
5 Nomar Garciaparra Bat 15.00 4.50
Manny Ramirez Bat
6 Alex Rodriguez Bat 15.00 4.50
Mark Texeira Bat
7 Barry Zito Bat 15.00 4.50
Tim Hudson Bat
8 Sammy Sosa Bat 25.00 7.50
Mark Prior Bat
9 Derek Jeter Bat 25.00 7.50
Jason Giambi Bat
10 Roger Clemens Jsy 20.00 6.00
Mike Mussina Bat
11 Mark Prior Bat 25.00 7.50
Kerry Wood Bat
12 Alex Rodriguez Bat 15.00 4.50
Hank Blalock Bat
13 Frank Thomas Bat 15.00 4.50
Magglio Ordonez Bat
14 Nomar Garciaparra Bat 25.00 7.50
Pedro Martinez Bat
15 Carlos Delgado Bat 10.00 3.00
Vernon Wells Bat
16 Miguel Tejada Bat 10.00 3.00
Eric Chavez Bat
17 Jeff Bagwell Bat 15.00 4.50
Lance Berkman Bat
18 Jim Thome Jsy 15.00 4.50
Bobby Abreu Bat
19 Todd Helton Bat 15.00 4.50
Preston Wilson Bat
20 Vladimir Guerrero Bat 15.00 4.50
Javier Vazquez Jsy

2004 Playoff Prestige Diamond Heritage

Nm-Mt Ex-Mt
STATED ODDS 1:13
1 Mike Piazza 5.00 1.50

2 Greg Maddux 5.00 1.50
3 Nomar Garciaparra 5.00 1.50
4 Chipper Jones 3.00 .90
5 Albert Pujols 6.00 1.80
6 Derek Jeter 8.00 2.40
7 Shawn Green 3.00 .90
8 Alex Rodriguez 5.00 1.50
9 Jim Thome 3.00 .90
10 Jason Giambi 3.00 .90
11 Sammy Sosa 5.00 1.50
12 Hank Blalock 3.00 .90
13 Garret Anderson 3.00 .90
14 Manny Ramirez 3.00 .90
15 Scott Rolen 3.00 .90
16 Jeff Bagwell 3.00 .90
17 Randy Johnson 3.00 .90
18 Ichiro Suzuki 5.00 1.50
19 Ivan Rodriguez 3.00 .90
20 Alfonso Soriano 3.00 .90

2004 Playoff Prestige Diamond Heritage Material

Nm-Mt Ex-Mt
STATED ODDS 1:92
1 Mike Piazza Bat 15.00 4.50
2 Greg Maddux Bat 15.00 4.50
3 Nomar Garciaparra Bat 15.00 4.50
4 Chipper Jones Jsy 10.00 3.00
5 Albert Pujols Bat 20.00 6.00
6 Derek Jeter Jsy 25.00 7.50
7 Shawn Green Bat 8.00 2.40
8 Alex Rodriguez Bat 15.00 4.50
9 Jim Thome Jsy 10.00 3.00
10 Jason Giambi Bat 10.00 3.00
11 Sammy Sosa Bat 15.00 4.50
12 Hank Blalock Bat 8.00 2.40
13 Garret Anderson Bat 8.00 2.40
14 Manny Ramirez Bat 8.00 2.40
15 Scott Rolen Bat 10.00 3.00
16 Jeff Bagwell Bat 10.00 3.00
17 Randy Johnson Bat 10.00 3.00
19 Ivan Rodriguez Bat 10.00 3.00
20 Alfonso Soriano Bat 10.00 3.00

2004 Playoff Prestige League Leaders Single

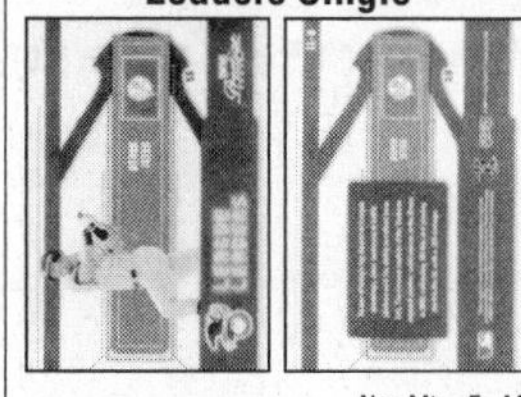

Nm-Mt Ex-Mt
STATED ODDS 1:18
*FOIL: 1.5X TO 4X BASIC
FOIL PRINT RUN 100 SERIAL #'d SETS
HOLO-FOIL PRINT RUN 25 SERIAL #'d SETS
NO HOLO-FOIL PRICING DUE TO SCARCITY
FOIL/HOLO-FOIL RANDOM IN PACKS.
1 Alex Rodriguez AL HR 4.00 1.20
2 Albert Pujols NL Hit 5.00 1.50
3 Albert Pujols NL Avg 5.00 1.50
4 Nomar Garciaparra AL Hit 4.00 1.20
5 Mark Prior NL ERA 5.00 1.50
6 Pedro Martinez AL ERA 2.50 .75
7 Kerry Wood NL SO 2.50 .75
8 Derek Jeter AL Avg 6.00 1.80
9 Jason Giambi AL BB 2.50 .75
10 Roger Clemens AL SO 5.00 1.50

2004 Playoff Prestige League Leaders Single Material

Nm-Mt Ex-Mt
RANDOM INSERTS IN PACKS
STATED PRINT RUN 250 SERIAL #'d SETS
1 Alex Rodriguez AL HR Bat 10.00 3.00
2 Albert Pujols NL Hit Bat 15.00 4.50
3 Albert Pujols NL Avg Bat 15.00 4.50
4 Nomar Garciaparra AL Hit Bat 10.00 3.00
5 Mark Prior NL ERA Jsy 15.00 4.50
6 Pedro Martinez AL ERA Jsy 10.00 3.00
7 Kerry Wood NL SO Jsy 10.00 3.00
8 Derek Jeter AL Avg Jsy 20.00 6.00
9 Jason Giambi AL BB Jsy 10.00 3.00
10 Roger Clemens AL SO Jsy

2004 Playoff Prestige League Leaders Double

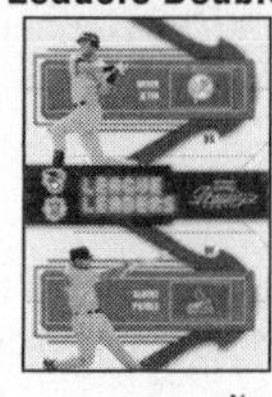

Nm-Mt Ex-Mt
STATED PRINT RUN 500 SERIAL #'d SETS
*FOIL: .75X TO 2X BASIC
FOIL PRINT RUN 75 SERIAL #'d SETS
HOLO-FOIL PRINT RUN 10 SERIAL #'d SETS
NO HOLO-FOIL PRICING DUE TO SCARCITY
RANDOM INSERTS IN PACKS
1 Alex Rodriguez 10.00 3.00
Jim Thome HR
2 Mark Prior 12.00 3.60
Pedro Martinez ERA
3 Roger Clemens 12.00 3.60
Kerry Wood SO
4 Nomar Garciaparra 12.00 3.60
Albert Pujols Hit
5 Derek Jeter 15.00 4.50
Albert Pujols Avg

2004 Playoff Prestige League Leaders Double Material

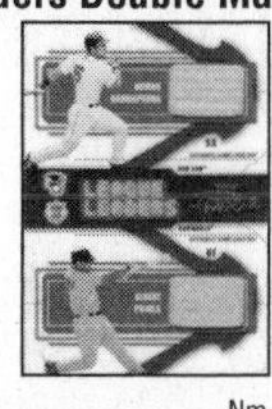

Nm-Mt Ex-Mt
RANDOM INSERTS IN PACKS
STATED PRINT RUN 100 SERIAL #'d SETS
1 Alex Rodriguez Bat 25.00 7.50
Jim Thome Bat HR
2 Mark Prior Jsy 30.00 9.00
Pedro Martinez Jsy ERA
3 Roger Clemens Jsy 30.00 9.00
Kerry Wood Jsy SO
4 Nomar Garciaparra Bat 30.00 9.00
Albert Pujols Bat Hits
5 Derek Jeter Jsy 40.00 12.00
Albert Pujols Bat Avg

2004 Playoff Prestige League Leaders Quad

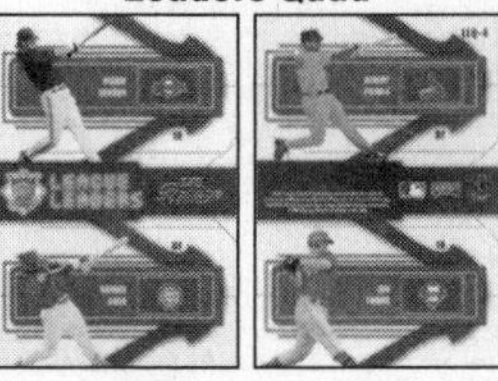

Nm-Mt Ex-Mt
STATED PRINT RUN 250 SERIAL #'d SETS
*FOIL: .75X TO 2X BASIC
FOIL PRINT RUN 50 SERIAL #'d SETS
HOLO-FOIL PRINT RUN 5 SERIAL #'d SETS
NO HOLO-FOIL PRICING DUE TO SCARCITY
RANDOM INSERTS IN PACKS
1 Albert Pujols 15.00 4.50
Todd Helton
Edgar Renteria
Gary Sheffield NL Avg
2 Derek Jeter 20.00 6.00
Manny Ramirez
Nomar Garciaparra
Ichiro Suzuki AL Avg
3 Mark PriorCurt Schilling 15.00 4.50
Hideo Nomo
Kevin Brown NL ERA
4 Richie Sexson 12.00 3.60
Sammy Sosa
Albert Pujols
Jim Thome NL HR
5 Alex Rodriguez 12.00 3.60
Frank Thomas
Jason Giambi
Carlos Delgado AL HR

2004 Playoff Prestige League Leaders Quad Material

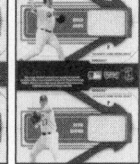

Nm-Mt Ex-Mt
RANDOM INSERTS IN PACKS
STATED PRINT RUN 50 SERIAL #'d SETS
1 Albert Pujols Bat 40.00 12.00

Todd Helton Bat
Edgar Renteria Jsy
Gary Sheffield Jsy NL Avg
3 Mark Prior Jsy 40.00 12.00
Curt Schilling Jsy
Hideo Nomo Jsy
Kevin Brown Jsy NL ERA
4 Richie Sexson Jsy 50.00 15.00
Sammy Sosa Bat
Albert Pujols Bat
Jim Thome Bat NL HR
5 Alex Rodriguez Jsy 40.00 12.00
Frank Thomas Jsy
Jason Giambi Jsy
Carlos Delgado Jsy AL HR

2004 Playoff Prestige Players Collection Jersey

Nm-Mt Ex-Mt
STATED ODDS 1:79
*PLATINUM: .75X TO 2X BASIC
PLATINUM RANDOM INSERTS IN PACKS
PLATINUM PRINT RUN 50 SERIAL #'d SETS
1 Adam Dunn AS 8.00 2.40
2 Adam Dunn Gray 8.00 2.40
3 Adam Dunn White 8.00 2.40
4 Alex Rodriguez M's 10.00 3.00
5 Alex Rodriguez Rgr AS 10.00 3.00
6 Alex Rodriguez Rgr Blue 10.00 3.00
7 Alex Rodriguez Rgr White 10.00 3.00
8 Andruw Jones Home 8.00 2.40
9 Andruw Jones Road 8.00 2.40
10 Austin Kearns 8.00 2.40
11 Brandon Webb 8.00 2.40
12 C.C. Sabathia 8.00 2.40
13 Cal Ripken 40.00 12.00
14 Carlos Beltran 8.00 2.40
15 Carlos Delgado 8.00 2.40
16 Carlos Lee 8.00 2.40
17 Chipper Jones Home 10.00 3.00
18 Chipper Jones Road 10.00 3.00
19 Craig Biggio 10.00 3.00
20 Curt Schilling 10.00 3.00
21 David Wells 8.00 2.40
22 Don Mattingly 25.00 7.50
23 Dontrelle Willis 8.00 2.40
24 Frank Thomas Black 10.00 3.00
25 Frank Thomas White 10.00 3.00
26 Fred McGriff 10.00 3.00
27 Garret Anderson AS 8.00 2.40
28 Gary Sheffield Braves 8.00 2.40
29 Gary Sheffield Dodgers 8.00 2.40
30 Greg Maddux Gray 10.00 3.00
31 Hank Blalock Home 8.00 2.40
32 Hank Blalock Road 8.00 2.40
33 Hee Seop Choi 8.00 2.40
34 Hideo Nomo Mets 10.00 3.00
35 Hideo Nomo Dodgers Gray .. 10.00 3.00
36 Hideo Nomo Dodgers White. 10.00 3.00
37 Ivan Rodriguez Marlins 10.00 3.00
38 Ivan Rodriguez Rgr 10.00 3.00
39 Jason Giambi Home 10.00 3.00
40 Jim Edmonds 8.00 2.40
41 Jim Thome 10.00 3.00
42 John Olerud 8.00 2.40
43 John Smoltz 10.00 3.00
44 Josh Beckett 10.00 3.00
45 Josh Phelps 8.00 2.40
46 Juan Gonzalez Rgr 10.00 3.00
47 Juan Gonzalez Indians 10.00 3.00
48 Kazuhisa Ishii 8.00 2.40
49 Lance Berkman White 8.00 2.40
50 Larry Walker Home 10.00 3.00
51 Larry Walker Road 10.00 3.00
52 Luis Gonzalez AS 8.00 2.40
53 Magglio Ordonez Home 8.00 2.40
54 Magglio Ordonez Road 8.00 2.40
55 Manny Ramirez 8.00 2.40
56 Manny Ramirez AS 8.00 2.40
57 Mark Prior Home 15.00 4.50
58 Mark Prior Road 15.00 4.50
59 Mark Teixeira 8.00 2.40
60 Mike Mussina 10.00 3.00
61 Mike Piazza AS 10.00 3.00
62 Mike Piazza Black 10.00 3.00
63 Mike Piazza White 10.00 3.00
64 Nomar Garciaparra Gray 10.00 3.00
65 Nomar Garciaparra White 10.00 3.00
66 Pat Burrell 8.00 2.40
67 Paul Konerko 8.00 2.40
68 Paul Lo Duca 8.00 2.40
69 Pedro Martinez 10.00 3.00
70 Rafael Furcal 8.00 2.40
71 Rafael Palmeiro Blue 10.00 3.00
72 Rafael Palmeiro Gray 10.00 3.00
73 Ramon Hernandez 8.00 2.40
74 Rickey Henderson 10.00 3.00
75 Rickey Henderson Black 10.00 3.00
76 Rickey Henderson White 10.00 3.00
77 Roberto Alomar Indians 10.00 3.00
78 Roberto Alomar Mets 10.00 3.00
79 Robin Ventura AS 8.00 2.40
80 Roger Clemens Away 15.00 4.50
81 Roger Clemens Home 15.00 4.50
82 Roy Halladay 8.00 2.40
83 Sammy Sosa AS 10.00 3.00
84 Sammy Sosa Gray 10.00 3.00
85 Sammy Sosa White 10.00 3.00
86 Scott Rolen 10.00 3.00
87 Shannon Stewart 8.00 2.40
88 Shawn Green Blue 8.00 2.40
89 Shawn Green Gray 8.00 2.40
90 Shawn Green White 8.00 2.40
91 Terrence Long 8.00 2.40
92 Tim Hudson 8.00 2.40
93 Todd Helton Away 10.00 3.00
94 Todd Helton Home 10.00 3.00
95 Tom Glavine Braves 10.00 3.00
96 Tom Glavine Mets 10.00 3.00
97 Torii Hunter 8.00 2.40
98 Vernon Wells 8.00 2.40
99 Vladimir Guerrero 10.00 3.00
100 Vladimir Guerrero AS 10.00 3.00

2004 Playoff Prestige Prestigious Pros

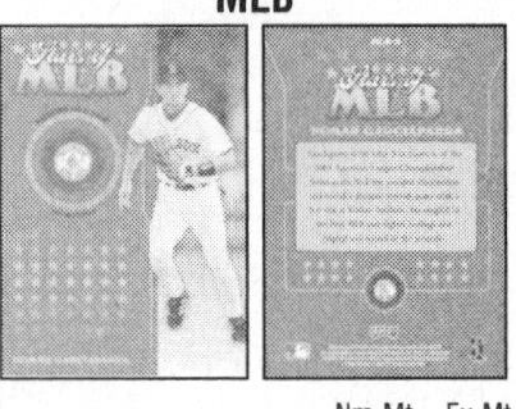

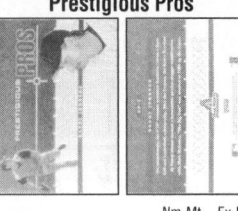

Nm-Mt Ex-Mt
STATED ODDS 1:23
1 Mark Prior 8.00 2.40
2 Derek Jeter 10.00 3.00
3 Mike Mussina 4.00 1.20
4 Nomar Garciaparra 6.00 1.80
5 Roger Clemens 8.00 2.40
6 Jason Giambi 4.00 1.20
7 Randy Johnson 4.00 1.20
8 Rafael Palmeiro 4.00 1.20
9 Barry Zito 4.00 1.20
10 Pat Burrell 4.00 1.20

2004 Playoff Prestige Stars of MLB

Nm-Mt Ex-Mt
STATED ODDS 1:36
*FOIL: .75X TO 2X BASIC
FOIL PRINT RUN 100 SERIAL #'d SETS
HOLO-FOIL PRINT RUN 25 SERIAL #'d SETS
NO HOLO-FOIL PRICING DUE TO SCARCITY
FOIL/HOLO-FOIL RANDOM IN PACKS.
1 Albert Pujols 10.00 3.00
2 Derek Jeter 12.00 3.60
3 Mike Piazza 8.00 2.40
4 Greg Maddux 8.00 2.40
5 Ichiro Suzuki 8.00 2.40
6 Nomar Garciaparra 8.00 2.40
7 Ivan Rodriguez 5.00 1.50
8 Randy Johnson 5.00 1.50
9 Alex Rodriguez 8.00 2.40
10 Sammy Sosa 8.00 2.40
11 Alfonso Soriano 5.00 1.50
12 Vladimir Guerrero 5.00 1.50
13 Jason Giambi 5.00 1.50
14 Mark Prior 10.00 3.00
15 Chipper Jones 5.00 1.50

2004 Playoff Prestige Stars of MLB Jersey

Nm-Mt Ex-Mt
STATED PRINT RUN 250 SERIAL #'d SETS
*PRIME: 1X TO 2.5X BASIC
PRIME PRINT RUN 50 SERIAL #'d SETS
RANDOM INSERTS IN PACKS
1 Albert Pujols 15.00 4.50
2 Derek Jeter 20.00 6.00
3 Mike Piazza 10.00 3.00
4 Greg Maddux 10.00 3.00
6 Nomar Garciaparra 10.00 3.00
7 Ivan Rodriguez 10.00 3.00
8 Randy Johnson 10.00 3.00
9 Alex Rodriguez 10.00 3.00
10 Sammy Sosa 15.00 4.50
11 Alfonso Soriano 10.00 3.00
12 Vladimir Guerrero 10.00 3.00
13 Jason Giambi 10.00 3.00
14 Mark Prior 15.00 4.50
15 Chipper Jones 10.00 3.00

2004 Playoff Prestige Stars of MLB Jersey Autographs

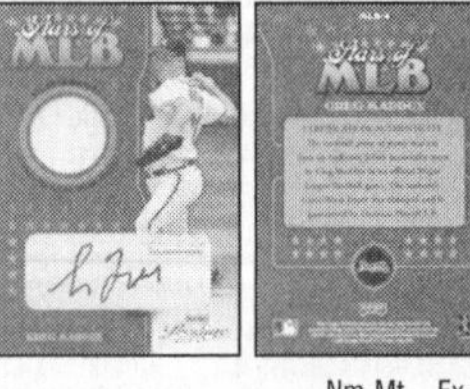

Nm-Mt Ex-Mt
RANDOM INSERTS IN PACKS
PRINT RUNS B/WN 1-50 COPIES PER
NO PRICING ON QTY OF 25 OR LESS.
14 Mark Prior/50 .... 150.00 45.00

2004 Playoff Prime Cuts

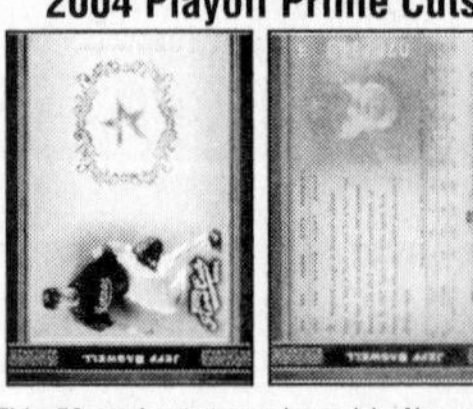

This 50-card set was released in November, 2003. Each four-card pack retailed for $150 and contained four cards per pack along with an encased (but not Graded) BGS card. Each case continued fifteen of these one-pack boxes. Please note a Babe Ruth "Santa" card was randomly inserted into packs and is not considered part of the basic set.

MINT NRMT
COMPLETE SET (50) 225.00 100.00
STATED PRINT RUN 949 SERIAL #'d SETS
B.RUTH SANTA STATED ODDS 1:15...
1 Roger Clemens Yanks 10.00 4.50
2 Nomar Garciaparra 8.00 3.60
3 Albert Pujols 10.00 4.50
4 Sammy Sosa 8.00 3.60
5 Greg Maddux Braves 8.00 3.60
6 Jason Giambi 5.00 2.20
7 Hideo Nomo Dodgers 5.00 2.20
8 Mike Piazza Mets 8.00 3.60
9 Ichiro Suzuki 8.00 3.60
10 Jeff Bagwell 5.00 2.20
11 Derek Jeter 12.00 5.50
12 Manny Ramirez 5.00 2.20
13 R.Henderson Dodgers 5.00 2.20
14 Alex Rodriguez Rgr 8.00 3.60
15 Troy Glaus 5.00 2.20
16 Mike Mussina 5.00 2.20
17 Kerry Wood 5.00 2.20
18 Kazuhisa Ishii 5.00 2.20
19 Hideki Matsui 8.00 3.60
20 Frank Thomas 5.00 2.20
21 Barry Bonds Giants 12.00 5.50
22 Adam Dunn 5.00 2.20
23 Randy Johnson D'backs 5.00 2.20
24 Alfonso Soriano 5.00 2.20
25 Pedro Martinez Sox 5.00 2.20
26 Andruw Jones 5.00 2.20
27 Mark Prior 10.00 4.50
28 Vladimir Guerrero 5.00 2.20
29 Chipper Jones 5.00 2.20
30 Todd Helton 5.00 2.20
31 Rafael Palmeiro 5.00 2.20
32 Mark Grace 5.00 2.20
33 Pedro Martinez Dodgers 5.00 2.20
34 Randy Johnson M's 5.00 2.20
35 Randy Johnson Astros 5.00 2.20
36 Roger Clemens Sox 10.00 4.50
37 Roger Clemens Jays 10.00 4.50
38 Alex Rodriguez M's 8.00 3.60
39 Greg Maddux Cubs 8.00 3.60
40 Mike Piazza Dodgers 8.00 3.60
41 Mike Piazza Marlins 8.00 3.60
42 Hideo Nomo Mets 5.00 2.20
43 R.Henderson Yanks 5.00 2.20
44 Rickey Henderson A's 5.00 2.20
45 Barry Bonds Pirates 12.00 5.50
46 Ivan Rodriguez 5.00 2.20
47 George Brett 10.00 4.50
48 Cal Ripken 12.00 5.50
49 Nolan Ryan 10.00 4.50
50 Don Mattingly 10.00 4.50
BRS1 Babe Ruth Santa 15.00 6.75

2004 Playoff Prime Cuts Century

MINT NRMT
*CENTURY 1-45: .75X TO 2X BASIC...
*CENTURY MATSUI: 1X TO 2.5X BASIC
*CENTURY 47-50: 1.25X TO 3X BASIC
RANDOM INSERTS IN PACKS
STATED PRINT RUN 100 SERIAL #'d SETS

2004 Playoff Prime Cuts Century Gold

MINT NRMT
RANDOM INSERTS IN PACKS
STATED PRINT RUN 10 SERIAL #'d SETS
NO PRICING DUE TO SCARCITY

2004 Playoff Prime Cuts Century Proofs

MINT NRMT
RANDOM INSERTS IN PACKS
STATED PRINT RUN 1 SERIAL #'d SET
NO PRICING DUE TO SCARCITY

2004 Playoff Prime Cuts Material

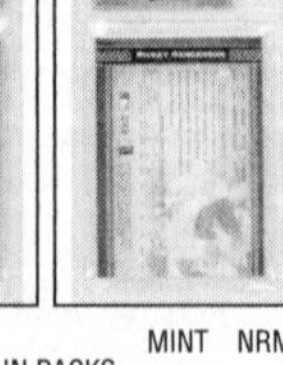

MINT NRMT
RANDOM INSERTS IN PACKS
PRINT RUNS B/WN 10-50 COPIES PER
NO PRICING ON QTY OF 10 OR LESS.
ALL CARDS FEATURE PRIME SWATCHES
1 Roger Clemens Yanks Jsy/50. 50.00 22.00
2 Nomar Garciaparra Jsy/50 ..... 50.00 22.00
3 Albert Pujols Jsy/50 .... 80.00 36.00
4 Sammy Sosa Jsy/50 .... 50.00 22.00
5 Greg Maddux Jsy/50 .... 50.00 22.00
6 Jason Giambi Jsy/25 .... 50.00 22.00
7 H.Nomo Dodgers Jsy/50 .... 50.00 22.00
8 Mike Piazza Mets Jsy/50 .... 40.00 18.00
9 Ichiro Suzuki Base/25 .... 80.00 36.00
10 Jeff Bagwell Jsy/25 .... 50.00 22.00
11 Derek Jeter Base/25 .... 80.00 36.00
12 Manny Ramirez Jsy/25 .... 40.00 18.00
13 R.Henderson Dodgers Jsy/50 40.00 18.00
14 Alex Rodriguez Rgr Jsy/25 ... 60.00 27.00
15 Troy Glaus Jsy/25 .... 40.00 18.00
16 Mike Mussina Jsy/10
17 Kerry Wood Jsy/25 .... 50.00 22.00
18 Kazuhisa Ishii Jsy/25 .... 40.00 18.00
19 Hideki Matsui Base/25 .... 100.00 45.00
20 Frank Thomas Jsy/25 .... 50.00 22.00
21 Barry Bonds Base/25 .... 80.00 36.00
22 Adam Dunn Jsy/25 .... 40.00 18.00
23 R.Johnson D'backs Jsy/25 ... 50.00 22.00
24 Alfonso Soriano Jsy/35 .... 40.00 18.00
25 Pedro Martinez Sox Jsy/25 .. 50.00 22.00
26 Andruw Jones Jsy/25 .... 40.00 18.00
27 Mark Prior Jsy/50 .... 60.00 27.00
28 Vladimir Guerrero Jsy/25 .... 50.00 22.00
29 Chipper Jones Jsy/25 .... 50.00 22.00
30 Todd Helton Jsy/25 .... 50.00 22.00
31 Rafael Palmeiro Jsy/25 .... 50.00 22.00
32 Mark Grace Jsy/25 .... 50.00 22.00
33 P.Martinez Dodgers Jsy/25 .. 50.00 22.00
34 Randy Johnson M's Jsy/25 .. 50.00 22.00
35 R.Johnson Astros Jsy/25 .... 50.00 22.00
36 Roger Clemens Sox Jsy/50 .. 50.00 22.00
38 Alex Rodriguez M's Jsy/25 ... 60.00 27.00
40 Mike Piazza Dodgers Jsy/50. 40.00 18.00
42 Hideo Nomo Mets Jsy/50 .... 60.00 27.00
43 R.Henderson Yanks Jsy/50 .. 40.00 18.00
44 R.Henderson A's Jsy/50 .... 40.00 18.00
46 Ivan Rodriguez Jsy/25 .... 50.00 22.00
47 George Brett Jsy/50 .... 80.00 36.00
48 Cal Ripken Jsy/50 .... 100.00 45.00
49 Nolan Ryan Jsy/50 .... 80.00 36.00
50 Don Mattingly Jsy/50 .... 80.00 36.00

2004 Playoff Prime Cuts Material Combos

MINT NRMT
RANDOM INSERTS IN PACKS
STATED PRINT RUN 25 SERIAL #'d SETS
ALL CARDS FEATURE PRIME SWATCHES
1 R.Clemens Yanks Bat-Jsy 80.00 36.00
2 Nomar Garciaparra Bat-Jsy ... 80.00 36.00
3 Albert Pujols Bat-Jsy 120.00 55.00
4 Sammy Sosa Bat-Jsy 80.00 36.00
5 Greg Maddux Bat-Jsy 80.00 36.00
6 Jason Giambi Bat-Jsy 60.00 27.00
7 H.Nomo Dodgers Bat-Jsy 80.00 36.00
8 Mike Piazza Mets Bat-Jsy 60.00 27.00
9 Ichiro Suzuki Ball-Base 100.00 45.00
10 Jeff Bagwell Bat-Jsy 60.00 27.00
11 Derek Jeter Ball-Base 100.00 45.00
12 Manny Ramirez Bat-Jsy 50.00 22.00
13 R.Henderson Dodgers Bat-Jsy 60.00 27.00
14 Alex Rodriguez Rgr Bat-Jsy.. 80.00 36.00
15 Troy Glaus Bat-Jsy 50.00 22.00
16 Mike Mussina Bat-Jsy 60.00 27.00
17 Kerry Wood Bat-Jsy 60.00 27.00
18 Kazuhisa Ishii Bat-Jsy 50.00 22.00
19 Hideki Matsui Ball-Base 120.00 55.00
20 Frank Thomas Bat-Jsy 60.00 27.00
21 Barry Bonds Ball-Base 100.00 45.00
22 Adam Dunn Bat-Jsy 50.00 22.00
23 R.Johnson D'backs Bat-Jsy . 60.00 27.00
24 Alfonso Soriano Bat-Jsy 60.00 27.00
25 Pedro Martinez Sox Bat-Jsy . 60.00 27.00
26 Andruw Jones Bat-Jsy 50.00 22.00
27 Mark Prior Bat-Jsy 100.00 45.00
28 Vladimir Guerrero Bat-Jsy ... 60.00 27.00
29 Chipper Jones Bat-Jsy 60.00 27.00
30 Todd Helton Bat-Jsy 60.00 27.00
31 Rafael Palmeiro Bat-Jsy 60.00 27.00
32 Mark Grace Bat-Jsy 60.00 27.00
33 P.Martinez Dodgers Bat-Jsy. 60.00 27.00
34 Randy Johnson M's Bat-Jsy. 60.00 27.00
35 R.Johnson Astros Bat-Jsy .. 60.00 27.00
36 Roger Clemens Sox Bat-Jsy. 80.00 36.00
38 Alex Rodriguez M's Bat-Jsy . 80.00 36.00
40 M.Piazza Dodgers Bat-Jsy... 60.00 27.00
42 Hideo Nomo Mets Bat-Jsy.. 100.00 45.00
43 R.Henderson Yanks Bat-Jsy. 60.00 27.00
44 R.Henderson A's Bat-Jsy 60.00 27.00
46 Ivan Rodriguez Bat-Jsy 60.00 27.00
47 George Brett Bat-Jsy 150.00 70.00
48 Cal Ripken Bat-Jsy 200.00 90.00
49 Nolan Ryan Bat-Jsy 120.00 55.00
50 Don Mattingly Bat-Jsy 150.00 70.00

2004 Playoff Prime Cuts Material Signature

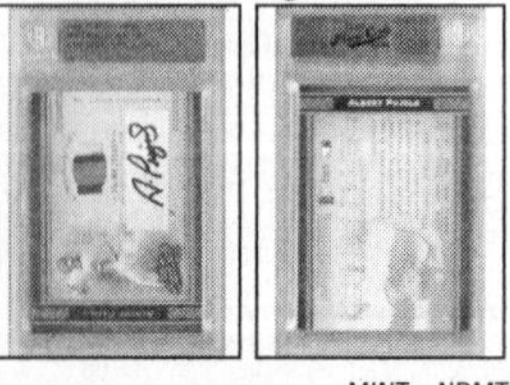

MINT NRMT
RANDOM INSERTS IN PACKS
PRINT RUNS B/WN 5-50 COPIES PER
NO PRICING ON QTY OF 10 OR LESS.
ALL CARDS FEATURE PRIME SWATCHES
1 R.Clemens Yanks Jsy/25 ...... 250.00 110.00
3 Albert Pujols Jsy/25 .... 250.00 110.00
5 Greg Maddux Jsy/25 .... 250.00 110.00
7 H.Nomo Dodgers Jsy/10
8 Mike Piazza Mets Jsy/10
10 Jeff Bagwell Jsy/25 .... 120.00 55.00
12 Manny Ramirez Jsy/25 .... 120.00 55.00
13 R.Hend Dodgers Jsy/25 .... 200.00 90.00
14 Alex Rodriguez Rgr Jsy/25 . 300.00 135.00
15 Troy Glaus Jsy/50 .... 60.00 27.00
16 Mike Mussina Jsy/25 .... 120.00 55.00
17 Kerry Wood Jsy/25 .... 150.00 70.00
18 Kazuhisa Ishii Jsy/50 .... 60.00 27.00
20 Frank Thomas Jsy/25 .... 120.00 55.00
22 Adam Dunn Jsy/50 .... 100.00 45.00
23 R.Johnson D'backs Jsy/10
24 Alfonso Soriano Jsy/25 ...... 120.00 55.00
25 Pedro Martinez Sox Jsy/10
26 Andruw Jones Jsy/25 .... 80.00 36.00
27 Mark Prior Jsy/50 .... 200.00 90.00
28 Vladimir Guerrero Jsy/50 ... 100.00 45.00
29 Chipper Jones Jsy/50 .... 120.00 55.00
30 Todd Helton Jsy/50 .... 100.00 45.00
31 Rafael Palmeiro Jsy/25 .... 120.00 55.00
32 Mark Grace Jsy/50 .... 100.00 45.00
33 P.Martinez Dodgers Jsy/10
34 Randy Johnson M's Jsy/10
35 R.Johnson Astros Jsy/10
36 Roger Clemens Sox Jsy/25 250.00 110.00
38 Alex Rodriguez M's Jsy/25. 300.00 135.00
40 Mike Piazza Dodgers Jsy/10
42 Hideo Nomo Mets Jsy/5
43 R.Henderson Yanks Jsy/5
44 R.Henderson A's Jsy/25 ..... 200.00 90.00
46 Ivan Rodriguez Jsy/25 .... 120.00 55.00
47 George Brett Jsy/50 .... 150.00 70.00
48 Cal Ripken Jsy/50 .... 250.00 110.00
49 Nolan Ryan Jsy/50 .... 200.00 90.00
50 Don Mattingly Jsy/50 .... 150.00 70.00

2004 Playoff Prime Cuts Signature

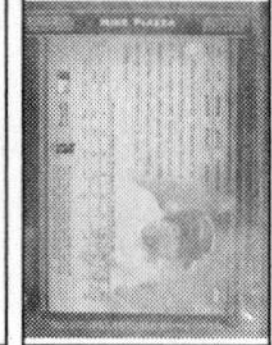

MINT NRMT
RANDOM INSERTS IN PACKS
PRINT RUNS B/WN 5-25 COPIES PER
NO PRICING ON QTY OF 14 OR LESS.
1 Roger Clemens Yanks/25 ..... 150.00 70.00
3 Albert Pujols/25 .... 200.00 90.00
5 Greg Maddux Braves/10
7 Hideo Nomo Dodgers/10
8 Mike Piazza Mets/10
10 Jeff Bagwell/25 .... 100.00 45.00
12 Manny Ramirez/14
13 R.Henderson Dodgers/25 ... 120.00 55.00
14 Alex Rodriguez Rgr/25 .... 200.00 90.00
15 Troy Glaus/25 .... 60.00 27.00
16 Mike Mussina/25 .... 100.00 45.00
17 Kerry Wood/25 .... 120.00 55.00
18 Kazuhisa Ishii/25 .... 60.00 27.00
20 Frank Thomas/25 .... 100.00 45.00
22 Adam Dunn/25 .... 100.00 45.00
23 Randy Johnson D'backs/10
24 Alfonso Soriano/25 .... 100.00 45.00
25 Pedro Martinez Sox/10
26 Andruw Jones/25 .... 60.00 27.00
27 Mark Prior/25 .... 200.00 90.00
28 Vladimir Guerrero/25 .... 100.00 45.00
29 Chipper Jones/25 .... 100.00 45.00
30 Todd Helton/17 .... 100.00 45.00
31 Rafael Palmeiro/25 .... 100.00 45.00
32 Mark Grace/25 .... 100.00 45.00
33 Pedro Martinez Dodgers/10
34 Randy Johnson M's/10
35 Randy Johnson Astros/10
36 Roger Clemens Sox/25 .... 150.00 70.00
37 Roger Clemens Jays/25 .... 150.00 70.00
38 Alex Rodriguez M's/25 .... 200.00 90.00
39 Greg Maddux Cubs/10
40 Mike Piazza Dodgers/10
41 Mike Piazza Marlins/5
42 Hideo Nomo Mets/5
43 Rickey Henderson Yanks/25 120.00 55.00
44 Rickey Henderson A's/25 ... 120.00 55.00
46 Ivan Rodriguez/25 .... 100.00 45.00
47 George Brett/25 .... 150.00 70.00
48 Cal Ripken/25 .... 250.00 110.00
49 Nolan Ryan/25 .... 150.00 70.00
50 Don Mattingly/25 .... 120.00 55.00

2004 Playoff Prime Cuts Signature Proofs

MINT NRMT
RANDOM INSERTS IN PACKS
STATED PRINT RUN 1 SERIAL #'d SET
NO PRICING DUE TO SCARCITY

2004 Playoff Prime Cuts MLB Icons Material

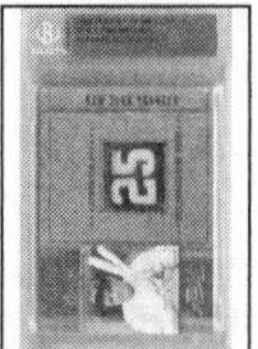
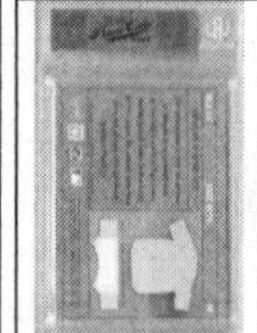

MINT NRMT
RANDOM INSERTS IN PACKS
PRINT RUNS B/WN 9-50 COPIES PER
NO PRICING ON QTY OF 9 OR LESS...
1 Ty Cobb Pants/9

2 Babe Ruth Pants/9
3 Lou Gehrig Pants/9
4 Johnny Bench Jsy/50 50.00 22.00
5 Lefty Grove A's Hat/25 120.00 55.00
6 Carlton Fisk Jsy/50 40.00 18.00
7 Mel Ott Jsy/25 100.00 45.00
8 Bob Feller Jsy/25 50.00 22.00
9 Jackie Robinson Jsy/25 120.00 55.00
10 Ted Williams Jsy/50 150.00 70.00
11 Roy Campanella Pants/50 60.00 27.00
12 Stan Musial Jsy/50 60.00 27.00
13 Yogi Berra Jsy/50 50.00 22.00
14 Babe Ruth Jsy/25 1500.00 700.00
15 Roberto Clemente Jsy/50 150.00 70.00
16 Warren Spahn Jsy/50 50.00 22.00
17 Ernie Banks Jsy/50 50.00 22.00
18 Eddie Mathews Jsy/50 50.00 22.00
19 Ryne Sandberg Jsy/50 60.00 27.00
20 Rod Carew Angels Jsy/50 40.00 18.00
21 Duke Snider Jsy/50 40.00 18.00
22 Jim Palmer Jsy/50 30.00 13.50
24 Frank Robinson Jsy/50 30.00 13.50
25 Brooks Robinson Jsy/50 50.00 22.00
26 Harmon Killebrew Jsy/50 50.00 22.00
27 Carl Yastrzemski Jsy/50 60.00 27.00
28 Reggie Jackson A's Jsy/50 40.00 18.00
29 Mike Schmidt Jsy/50 50.00 22.00
30 Robin Yount Jsy/50 50.00 22.00
31 George Brett Jsy/50 60.00 27.00
32 Nolan Ryan Rgr Jsy/50 60.00 27.00
33 Kirby Puckett Jsy/50 50.00 22.00
34 Cal Ripken Jsy/50 80.00 36.00
35 Don Mattingly Jsy/50 60.00 27.00
36 Tony Gwynn Jsy/19 80.00 36.00
37 Deion Sanders Jsy/19 50.00 22.00
38 Dave Winfield Yanks Jsy/19 40.00 18.00
39 Eddie Murray Jsy/19 60.00 27.00
40 Tom Seaver Jsy/19 50.00 22.00
41 Willie Stargell Jsy/19 50.00 22.00
42 Wade Boggs Yanks Jsy/19 50.00 22.00
43 Ozzie Smith Jsy/19 60.00 27.00
44 Willie McCovey Jsy/19 50.00 22.00
45 R.Jackson Angels Jsy/19 50.00 22.00
46 Whitey Ford Jsy/19 50.00 22.00
47 Lou Brock Jsy/19 50.00 22.00
48 Lou Boudreau Jsy/19 40.00 18.00
49 Steve Carlton Jsy/19 40.00 18.00
50 Rod Carew Twins Jsy/19 50.00 22.00
51 Bob Gibson Jsy/19 50.00 22.00
52 Thurman Munson Jsy/19 80.00 36.00
53 Roger Maris Jsy/19 120.00 55.00
54 Nolan Ryan Astros Jsy/50 60.00 27.00
55 Nolan Ryan Angels Jsy/50 60.00 27.00
56 Bo Jackson Jsy/19 60.00 27.00
57 Joe Morgan Jsy/19 40.00 18.00
58 Phil Rizzuto Jsy/19 50.00 22.00
59 Gary Carter Jsy/19 40.00 18.00
60 Paul Molitor Jsy/19 50.00 22.00
61 Don Drysdale Jsy/19 60.00 27.00
62 Catfish Hunter Jsy/19 50.00 22.00
63 Fergie Jenkins Pants/19 40.00 18.00
64 Pee Wee Reese Jsy/19 50.00 22.00
65 Dave Winfield Padres Jsy/19 40.00 18.00
66 Wade Boggs Sox Jsy/19 50.00 22.00
67 Lefty Grove Sox Hat/19 120.00 55.00
68 Rickey Henderson Jsy/19 60.00 27.00
69 Roger Clemens Sox Jsy/19 60.00 27.00
70 R.Clemens Yanks Jsy/19 60.00 27.00

2004 Playoff Prime Cuts MLB Icons Material Prime

MINT NRMT
RANDOM INSERTS IN PACKS
PRINT RUNS B/WN 1-25 COPIES PER
NO PRICING ON QTY OF 9 OR LESS
1 Ty Cobb Pants/9
2 Babe Ruth Pants/9
3 Lou Gehrig Pants/9
4 Johnny Bench Jsy/1
5 Lefty Grove A's Hat/9
6 Carlton Fisk Jsy/25 60.00 27.00
7 Mel Ott Jsy/25 200.00 90.00
8 Bob Feller Jsy/5
9 Jackie Robinson Jsy/9
10 Ted Williams Jsy/9
11 Roy Campanella Pants/25 80.00 36.00
12 Stan Musial Jsy/1
13 Yogi Berra Jsy/1
15 Roberto Clemente Jsy/25
16 Warren Spahn Jsy/25 120.00 55.00
17 Ernie Banks Jsy/25 80.00 36.00
18 Eddie Mathews Jsy/25 80.00 36.00
19 Ryne Sandberg Jsy/25 100.00 45.00
20 Rod Carew Angels Jsy/25 60.00 27.00
21 Duke Snider Jsy/9
22 Jim Palmer Jsy/25 50.00 22.00
24 Frank Robinson Jsy/25 50.00 22.00
25 Brooks Robinson Jsy/25 100.00 45.00
26 Harmon Killebrew Jsy/8
27 Carl Yastrzemski Jsy/25 100.00 45.00
28 Reggie Jackson A's Jsy/25 60.00 27.00
29 Mike Schmidt Jsy/25 100.00 45.00
30 Robin Yount Jsy/25 80.00 36.00
31 George Brett Jsy/25 100.00 45.00
32 Nolan Ryan Rgr Jsy/25 100.00 45.00
33 Kirby Puckett Jsy/25 80.00 36.00
34 Cal Ripken Jsy/25 120.00 55.00
35 Don Mattingly Jsy/25 80.00 36.00
36 Tony Gwynn Jsy/19 100.00 45.00
37 Deion Sanders Jsy/19 60.00 27.00
38 Dave Winfield Yanks Jsy/19 50.00 22.00
39 Eddie Murray Jsy/19 100.00 45.00
40 Tom Seaver Jsy/19 60.00 27.00
41 Willie Stargell Jsy/19 60.00 27.00
42 Wade Boggs Yanks Jsy/19 60.00 27.00
43 Ozzie Smith Jsy/19 80.00 36.00
44 Willie McCovey Jsy/19 60.00 27.00
45 R.Jackson Angels Jsy/19 60.00 27.00
46 Whitey Ford Jsy/19 60.00 27.00
47 Lou Brock Jsy/19 80.00 36.00
48 Lou Boudreau Jsy/19 50.00 22.00
49 Steve Carlton Jsy/19 50.00 22.00
50 Rod Carew Twins Jsy/19 60.00 27.00
51 Bob Gibson Jsy/19 80.00 36.00
52 Thurman Munson Jsy/19 120.00 55.00
53 Roger Maris Jsy/19 150.00 70.00
54 Nolan Ryan Astros Jsy/19 100.00 45.00
55 Nolan Ryan Angels Jsy/19 100.00 45.00
56 Bo Jackson Jsy/19 80.00 36.00

57 Joe Morgan Jsy/19 50.00 22.00
58 Phil Rizzuto Jsy/5
59 Gary Carter Jsy/19 50.00 22.00
60 Paul Molitor Jsy/19 60.00 27.00
61 Don Drysdale Jsy/19 100.00 45.00
62 Catfish Hunter Jsy/19 80.00 36.00
63 Fergie Jenkins Pants/19 50.00 22.00
64 Pee Wee Reese Jsy/19 60.00 27.00
65 Dave Winfield Padres Jsy/19 50.00 22.00
66 Wade Boggs Sox Jsy/19 60.00 27.00
67 Lefty Grove Sox Hat/19 150.00 70.00
68 Rickey Henderson Jsy/19 80.00 36.00
69 Roger Clemens Sox Jsy/19 80.00 36.00
70 R.Clemens Yanks Jsy/19 80.00 36.00

2004 Playoff Prime Cuts MLB Icons Material Combos Prime

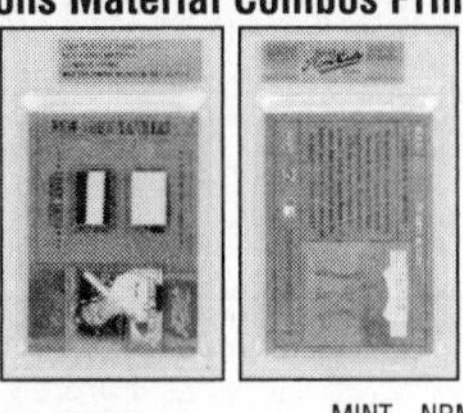

MINT NRMT
RANDOM INSERTS IN PACKS
PRINT RUNS B/WN 1-25 COPIES PER
NO PRICING ON QTY OF 15 OR LESS.
1 Ty Cobb Bat-Pants/9
2 Babe Ruth Bat-Pants/9
3 Lou Gehrig Bat-Pants/9
4 Johnny Bench Bat-Jsy/5
6 Carlton Fisk Bat-Jsy/25 80.00 36.00
7 Mel Ott Bat-Jsy/25
10 Ted Williams Bat-Jsy/9
11 R.Campanella Bat-Pants/25 100.00 45.00
12 Stan Musial Bat-Jsy/1
13 Yogi Berra Bat-Jsy/1
15 R.Clemente Bat-Jsy/25
17 Ernie Banks Bat-Jsy/25 100.00 45.00
18 Eddie Mathews Bat-Jsy/25 100.00 45.00
19 Ryne Sandberg Bat-Jsy/25 120.00 55.00
20 R.Carew Angels Bat-Jsy/25 80.00 36.00
21 Duke Snider Bat-Jsy/15
24 Frank Robinson Bat-Jsy/25 60.00 27.00
25 Brooks Robinson Bat-Jsy/25 120.00 55.00
26 Harmon Killebrew Bat-Jsy/5
27 Carl Yastrzemski Bat-Jsy/25 150.00 70.00
28 R.Jackson A's Bat-Jsy/25 80.00 36.00
29 Mike Schmidt Bat-Jsy/25 100.00 45.00
30 Robin Yount Bat-Jsy/25 100.00 45.00
31 George Brett Bat-Jsy/25 120.00 55.00
32 Nolan Ryan Rgr Bat-Jsy/25 120.00 55.00
33 Kirby Puckett Bat-Jsy/25 100.00 45.00
34 Cal Ripken Bat-Jsy/25 150.00 70.00
35 Don Mattingly Bat-Jsy/25 120.00 55.00
36 Tony Gwynn Bat-Jsy/19 120.00 55.00
37 Deion Sanders Bat-Jsy/19 80.00 36.00
38 D.Winfield Yanks Bat-Jsy/19 60.00 27.00
39 Eddie Murray Bat-Jsy/19 120.00 55.00
41 Willie Stargell Bat-Jsy/19 80.00 36.00
42 W.Boggs Yanks Bat-Jsy/19 80.00 36.00
43 Ozzie Smith Bat-Jsy/19 150.00 70.00
44 Willie McCovey Bat-Jsy/19 80.00 36.00
45 R.Jackson Angels Bat-Jsy/19 80.00 36.00
46 Whitey Ford Jsy-Pants/19 80.00 36.00
47 Lou Brock Bat-Jsy/19 100.00 45.00
48 Lou Boudreau Bat-Jsy/19 60.00 27.00
49 Steve Carlton Bat-Jsy/19 60.00 27.00
50 Rod Carew Twins Bat-Jsy/19 80.00 36.00
52 Thurman Munson Bat-Jsy/19 150.00 70.00
53 Roger Maris Bat-Jsy/19 200.00 90.00
54 N.Ryan Astros Bat-Jsy/19 150.00 70.00
55 N.Ryan Angels Bat-Jsy/19 150.00 70.00
56 Bo Jackson Bat-Jsy/19 100.00 45.00
57 Joe Morgan Bat-Jsy/19 60.00 27.00
58 Phil Rizzuto Bat-Pants/19 80.00 36.00
59 Gary Carter Bat-Jsy/19 60.00 27.00
60 Paul Molitor Bat-Jsy/19 80.00 36.00
63 F.Jenkins Fld Glv-Pants/19 60.00 27.00
64 P.Reese Bat-Jsy/19 100.00 45.00
65 D.Winfield Padres Bat-Jsy/19 60.00 27.00
66 W.Boggs Sox Bat-Jsy/19 80.00 36.00
68 R.Henderson Bat-Jsy/19 100.00 45.00
69 R.Clemens Sox Bat-Jsy/19 100.00 45.00
70 R.Clemens Yanks Bat-Jsy/19 100.00 45.00

2004 Playoff Prime Cuts MLB Icons Material Signature

MINT NRMT
RANDOM INSERTS IN PACKS
PRINT RUNS B/WN 16-45 COPIES PER
4 Johnny Bench Jsy/18 150.00 70.00
8 Bob Feller Jsy/45 100.00 45.00
12 Stan Musial Jsy/30 150.00 70.00
13 Yogi Berra Jsy/42 120.00 55.00
21 Duke Snider Jsy/35 100.00 45.00
26 Harmon Killebrew Jsy/30 120.00 55.00
33 Kirby Puckett Jsy/16 150.00 70.00
69 Roger Clemens Sox Jsy/25 200.00 90.00

2004 Playoff Prime Cuts MLB Icons Material Signature Prime

MINT NRMT
RANDOM INSERTS IN PACKS
PRINT RUNS B/WN 1-50 COPIES PER
NO PRICING ON QTY OF 15 OR LESS.

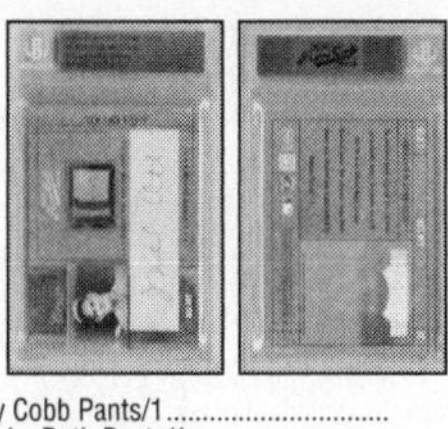

1 Ty Cobb Pants/1
2 Babe Ruth Pants/1
3 Lou Gehrig Pants/1
4 Johnny Bench Jsy/5
5 Lefty Grove A's Hat/1
6 Carlton Fisk Jsy/50 80.00 36.00
7 Mel Ott Jsy/1
8 Bob Feller Jsy/5
9 Jackie Robinson Jsy/1
10 Ted Williams Jsy/1
11 Roy Campanella Pants/1
12 Stan Musial Jsy/20 200.00 90.00
13 Yogi Berra Jsy/8
16 Warren Spahn Jsy/25 200.00 90.00
17 Ernie Banks Jsy/50 120.00 55.00
18 Eddie Mathews Jsy/1
19 Ryne Sandberg Jsy/50 150.00 70.00
20 Rod Carew Angels Jsy/50 80.00 36.00
21 Duke Snider Jsy/15
22 Jim Palmer Jsy/50 60.00 27.00
24 Frank Robinson Jsy/50 60.00 27.00
25 Brooks Robinson Jsy/50 120.00 55.00
26 Harmon Killebrew Jsy/20 150.00 70.00
27 Carl Yastrzemski Jsy/50 150.00 70.00
28 Reggie Jackson A's Jsy/50 100.00 45.00
29 Mike Schmidt Jsy/20 200.00 90.00
30 Robin Yount Jsy/50 120.00 55.00
31 George Brett Jsy/50 150.00 70.00
32 Nolan Ryan Rgr Jsy/50 200.00 90.00
33 Kirby Puckett Jsy/34 100.00 45.00
34 Cal Ripken Jsy/50 250.00 110.00
35 Don Mattingly Jsy/50 150.00 70.00
36 Tony Gwynn Jsy/50 100.00 45.00
37 Deion Sanders Jsy/50 120.00 55.00
38 Dave Winfield Yanks Jsy/50 80.00 36.00
39 Eddie Murray Jsy/50 120.00 55.00
40 Tom Seaver Jsy/10
41 Willie Stargell Jsy/1
42 Wade Boggs Yanks Jsy/50 100.00 45.00
43 Ozzie Smith Jsy/50 150.00 70.00
44 Willie McCovey Jsy/50 80.00 36.00
45 R.Jackson Angels Jsy/50 100.00 45.00
46 Whitey Ford Jsy/50 100.00 45.00
47 Lou Brock Jsy/25 100.00 45.00
48 Lou Boudreau Jsy/50 150.00 70.00
49 Steve Carlton Jsy/50 80.00 36.00
50 Rod Carew Twins Jsy/50 80.00 36.00
51 Bob Gibson Jsy/50 120.00 55.00
52 Thurman Munson Jsy/1
53 Roger Maris Jsy/1
54 Nolan Ryan Astros Jsy/50 200.00 90.00
55 Nolan Ryan Angels Jsy/50 200.00 90.00
56 Bo Jackson Jsy/50 120.00 55.00
57 Joe Morgan Jsy/50 60.00 27.00
58 Phil Rizzuto Pants/50 80.00 36.00
59 Gary Carter Jsy/50 80.00 36.00
60 Paul Molitor Jsy/50 80.00 36.00
61 Don Drysdale Jsy/1
62 Catfish Hunter Jsy/1
63 Fergie Jenkins Pants/50 60.00 27.00
64 Pee Wee Reese Jsy/1
65 D.Winfield Padres Jsy/50 80.00 36.00
66 Wade Boggs Sox Jsy/50 100.00 45.00
67 Lefty Grove Sox Hat/1
68 Rickey Henderson Jsy/50 150.00 70.00
69 Roger Clemens Sox Jsy/25 250.00 110.00
70 R.Clemens Yanks Jsy/50 200.00 90.00

2004 Playoff Prime Cuts MLB Icons Signature

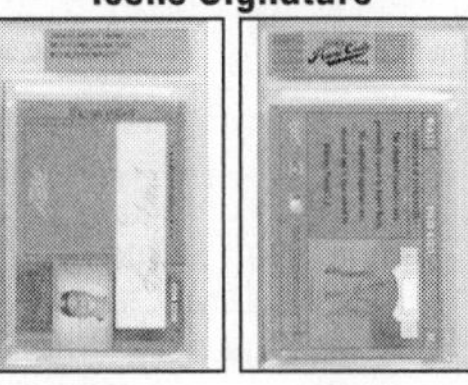

MINT NRMT
RANDOM INSERTS IN PACKS
PRINT RUNS B/WN 1-50 COPIES PER
NO PRICING ON QTY OF 12 OR LESS.
4 Johnny Bench/50 80.00 36.00
6 Carlton Fisk/50 60.00 27.00
8 Bob Feller/50 60.00 27.00
12 Stan Musial/50 100.00 45.00
13 Yogi Berra/50 80.00 36.00
16 Warren Spahn/25 150.00 70.00
17 Ernie Banks/50 100.00 45.00
18 Eddie Mathews/12
19 Ryne Sandberg/50 120.00 55.00
20 Rod Carew Angels/5
21 Duke Snider/25 80.00 36.00
22 Jim Palmer/25 60.00 27.00
24 Frank Robinson/50 50.00 22.00
25 Brooks Robinson/50 80.00 36.00
26 Harmon Killebrew/25 120.00 55.00
27 Carl Yastrzemski/50 100.00 45.00
28 Reggie Jackson A's/50 80.00 36.00
29 Mike Schmidt/20 120.00 55.00
30 Robin Yount/25 120.00 55.00
31 George Brett/25 150.00 70.00
32 Nolan Ryan Rgr/50 150.00 70.00
33 Kirby Puckett/25 100.00 45.00
34 Cal Ripken/25 250.00 110.00
35 Don Mattingly/50 120.00 55.00
36 Tony Gwynn/25 100.00 45.00
37 Deion Sanders/25
38 Dave Winfield Yanks/25 80.00 36.00
39 Eddie Murray/25 120.00 55.00
40 Tom Seaver/25

42 Wade Boggs Yanks/25 100.00 45.00
43 Ozzie Smith/25 150.00 70.00
44 Willie McCovey/25 80.00 36.00
45 Reggie Jackson Angels/25 100.00 45.00
46 Whitey Ford/10
47 Lou Brock/25 80.00 36.00
48 Lou Boudreau/25 150.00 70.00
49 Steve Carlton/10
50 Rod Carew Twins/5
51 Bob Gibson/25 80.00 36.00
53 Roger Maris/1
54 Nolan Ryan Astros/10
55 Nolan Ryan Angels/10
56 Bo Jackson/25 120.00 55.00
57 Joe Morgan/25 60.00 27.00
58 Phil Rizzuto/10
59 Gary Carter/25 80.00 36.00
60 Paul Molitor/25 80.00 36.00
61 Don Drysdale/1
62 Catfish Hunter/1
63 Fergie Jenkins/10
64 Pee Wee Reese/1
65 Dave Winfield Padres/25 80.00 36.00
66 Wade Boggs Sox/25 100.00 45.00
67 Lefty Grove/1
68 Rickey Henderson A's/10
69 Roger Clemens Sox/10
70 Roger Clemens Yanks/10

2004 Playoff Prime Cuts MLB Icons Signature Proofs

MINT NRMT
RANDOM INSERTS IN PACKS
STATED PRINT RUN 1 SERIAL #'d SET
NO PRICING DUE TO SCARCITY

2004 Playoff Prime Cuts Timeline Material

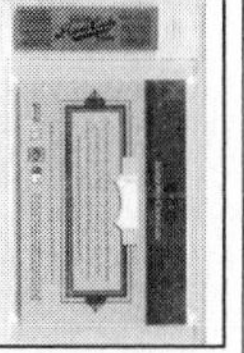

MINT NRMT
RANDOM INSERTS IN PACKS
NO PRICING ON QTY OF 9 OR LESS
1 Ty Cobb Pants/9
2 Babe Ruth Pants/9
3 Lou Gehrig Pants/9
4 Ted Williams TC Jsy/50 150.00 70.00
5 Roy Campanella Pants/50 60.00 27.00
6 Stan Musial MVP Jsy/50 60.00 27.00
7 Yogi Berra 51M Jsy/50 50.00 22.00
9 R.Clemente MVP Jsy/50 150.00 70.00
10 Will Clark Jsy/25 60.00 27.00
12 Carl Yastrzemski Jsy/50 60.00 27.00
13 Mike Schmidt Jsy/50 50.00 22.00
14 George Brett MVP Jsy/50 60.00 27.00
15 Nolan Ryan WIN Jsy/50 60.00 27.00
16 Stan Musial BA Jsy/50 60.00 27.00
17 Ted Williams BA Jsy/50 150.00 70.00
18 R.Clemente BTG Jsy/50 150.00 70.00
19 Greg Maddux Jsy/50 50.00 22.00
21 Robin Yount Jsy/50 50.00 22.00
22 Nolan Ryan HOF Jsy/50 60.00 27.00
23 Ted Williams RET Jsy/50 150.00 70.00
24 George Brett RET Jsy/50 60.00 27.00
25 Yogi Berra 55M Jsy/50 50.00 22.00
26 Rod Carew Jsy/50 40.00 18.00
27 Dale Murphy Jsy/25 60.00 27.00

2004 Playoff Prime Cuts Timeline Material Prime

MINT NRMT
RANDOM INSERTS IN PACKS
PRINT RUNS B/WN 1-25 COPIES PER
NO PRICING ON QTY OF 9 OR LESS
1 Ty Cobb Pants/9
2 Babe Ruth Pants/9
3 Lou Gehrig Pants/9
4 Ted Williams TC Jsy/9
5 Roy Campanella Pants/25 80.00 36.00
6 Stan Musial MVP Jsy/2
7 Yogi Berra 51M Jsy/1
9 R.Clemente MVP Jsy/25
10 Will Clark Jsy/25 80.00 36.00
12 Carl Yastrzemski Jsy/25 120.00 55.00
13 Mike Schmidt Jsy/25 100.00 45.00
14 George Brett MVP Jsy/25 100.00 45.00
15 Nolan Ryan WIN Jsy/25 100.00 45.00
16 Stan Musial BA Jsy/2
17 Ted Williams BA Jsy/9
18 R.Clemente BTG Jsy/25 150.00 70.00
19 Greg Maddux Jsy/25 80.00 36.00
21 Robin Yount Jsy/25 80.00 36.00
22 Nolan Ryan HOF Jsy/25 100.00 45.00
23 Ted Williams RET Jsy/9
24 George Brett RET Jsy/25 100.00 45.00
25 Yogi Berra 55M Jsy/1
26 Rod Carew Jsy/25 80.00 36.00
27 Dale Murphy Jsy/25 80.00 36.00

2004 Playoff Prime Cuts Timeline Material Combos

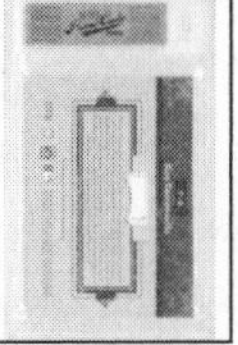

MINT NRMT
RANDOM INSERTS IN PACKS
PRINT RUNS B/WN 1-19 COPIES PER
NO PRICING ON QTY OF 9 OR LESS
1 Ty Cobb Bat-Pants/9
2 Babe Ruth Bat-Pants/9
3 Lou Gehrig Bat-Pants/9
4 Ted Williams TC Bat-Jsy/9
5 Roy Campanella Bat-Pants/9
6 Stan Musial MVP Bat-Jsy/1
7 Yogi Berra 51M Bat-Jsy/2
9 R.Clemente MVP Bat-Jsy/9
10 Will Clark Bat-Jsy/19 180.00 80.00
12 Carl Yastrzemski Bat-Jsy/19 150.00 70.00
13 Mike Schmidt Bat-Jsy/19 120.00 55.00
14 G.Brett MVP Bat-Jsy/19 150.00 70.00
15 N.Ryan WIN Bat-Jsy/19 150.00 70.00
16 Stan Musial BA Bat-Jsy/1
17 Ted Williams BA Bat-Jsy/9
18 R.Clemente BTG Bat-Jsy/9
19 Greg Maddux Bat-Jsy/19 100.00 45.00
21 Robin Yount Bat-Jsy/19 120.00 55.00
22 N.Ryan HOF Bat-Jsy/19 150.00 70.00
23 Ted Williams RET Bat-Jsy/9
24 G.Brett RET Bat-Jsy/19 150.00 70.00
25 Yogi Berra 55M Bat-Jsy/2
26 Rod Carew Bat-Jsy/19 80.00 36.00
27 Dale Murphy Bat-Jsy/19 100.00 45.00

2004 Playoff Prime Cuts Timeline Material Signature

MINT NRMT
RANDOM INSERTS IN PACKS
PRINT RUNS B/WN 33-42 COPIES PER
6 Stan Musial MVP Jsy/33 150.00 70.00
7 Yogi Berra 51M Jsy/42 120.00 55.00
16 Stan Musial BA Jsy/38 150.00 70.00
25 Yogi Berra 55M Jsy/42 120.00 55.00

2004 Playoff Prime Cuts Timeline Material Signature Prime

MINT NRMT
RANDOM INSERTS IN PACKS
PRINT RUNS B/WN 1-50 COPIES PER
NO PRICING ON QTY OF 10 OR LESS.
1 Ty Cobb Pants/1
2 Babe Ruth Pants/1
3 Lou Gehrig Pants/1
6 Stan Musial MVP Jsy/10
7 Yogi Berra 51M Jsy/8
9 Roberto Clemente Jsy/1
10 Will Clark Jsy/50 120.00 55.00
12 Carl Yastrzemski Jsy/50 150.00 70.00
13 Mike Schmidt Jsy/20 200.00 90.00
14 George Brett MVP Jsy/25 200.00 90.00
15 Nolan Ryan WIN Jsy/50 200.00 90.00
16 Stan Musial BA Jsy/10
19 Greg Maddux Jsy/50 200.00 90.00
21 Robin Yount Jsy/50 120.00 55.00
22 Nolan Ryan HOF Jsy/50 200.00 90.00
24 George Brett RET Jsy/25 200.00 90.00
25 Yogi Berra 55M Jsy/8
26 Rod Carew Jsy/50 80.00 36.00
27 Dale Murphy Jsy/50 100.00 45.00

2004 Playoff Prime Cuts Timeline Signature

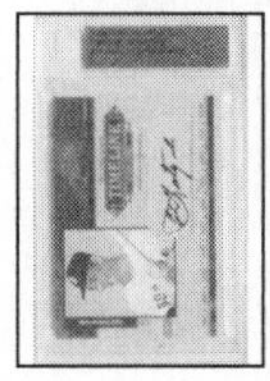
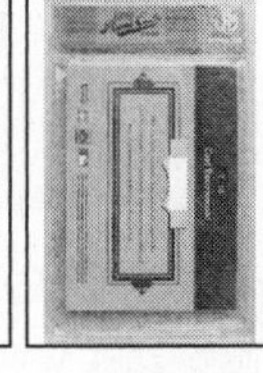

MINT NRMT
RANDOM INSERTS IN PACKS
PRINT RUNS B/WN 10-50 COPIES PER
NO PRICING ON QTY OF 20 OR LESS.
6 Stan Musial MVP/50 100.00 45.00
7 Yogi Berra 51M/50 80.00 36.00
10 Will Clark/25 150.00 70.00
12 Carl Yastrzemski/50 100.00 45.00
13 Mike Schmidt/20 120.00 55.00
14 George Brett MVP/25 150.00 70.00
15 Nolan Ryan WIN/50 150.00 70.00
16 Stan Musial BA/50 100.00 45.00
19 Greg Maddux/31 150.00 70.00
21 Robin Yount/25 120.00 55.00
22 Nolan Ryan HOF/50 150.00 70.00
24 George Brett RET/25 150.00 70.00
25 Yogi Berra 55M/50 80.00 36.00
26 Rod Carew/10
27 Dale Murphy/25 100.00 45.00

2004 Playoff Prime Cuts Timeline Signature Proofs

MINT NRMT
RANDOM INSERTS IN PACKS
STATED PRINT RUN 1 SERIAL #'d SET
NO PRICING DUE TO SCARCITY

2004 Playoff Prime Cuts Timeline Dual Achievements Material

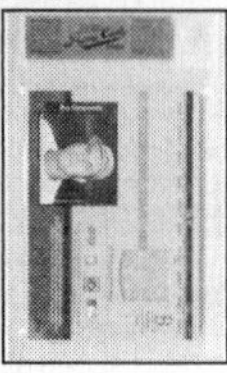

MINT NRMT
RANDOM INSERTS IN PACKS ....
PRINT RUNS B/WN 9-19 COPIES PER
NO PRICING ON QTY OF 9 OR LESS...
1 Roy Campanella Pants ....
Yogi Berra Jsy/9
2 Jackie Robinson Jsy........................
Ted Williams Jsy/9
3 Stan Musial Jsy.................... 250.00 110.00
Ted Williams Jsy/19
4 Mike Schmidt Jsy................. 120.00 55.00
George Brett Jsy/19
5 Dale Murphy Jsy 120.00 55.00
Cal Ripken Jsy/19
6 Roger Clemens Jsy 100.00 45.00
Mike Schmidt Jsy/19
7 Ty Cobb Pants..................................
Babe Ruth Pants/9
8 Roy Campanella Pants ....
Stan Musial Jsy/9
10 George Brett Jsy................. 120.00 55.00
Nolan Ryan Jsy/19
11 Jackie Robinson Jsy.......................
Roy Campanella Pants/9
12 Al Kaline Pants 80.00 36.00
Duke Snider Jsy/19

2004 Playoff Prime Cuts Timeline Dual Achievements Material Prime

MINT NRMT
RANDOM INSERTS IN PACKS ....
PRINT RUNS B/WN 1-19 COPIES PER
NO PRICING ON QTY OF 15 OR LESS.
1 Roy Campanella Pants ....
Yogi Berra Jsy/1
2 Jackie Robinson Jsy........................
Ted Williams Jsy/9
3 Stan Musial Jsy...............................
Ted Williams Jsy/2
4 Mike Schmidt Jsy................. 200.00 90.00
George Brett Jsy/19
5 Dale Murphy Jsy 200.00 90.00
Cal Ripken Jsy/19
6 Roger Clemens Jsy 150.00 70.00
Mike Schmidt Jsy/19
7 Ty Cobb Pants..................................
Babe Ruth Pants/9
8 Roy Campanella Pants ....
Stan Musial Jsy/2
10 George Brett Jsy................. 200.00 90.00
Nolan Ryan Jsy/19
11 Jackie Robinson Jsy.......................
Roy Campanella Pants/9
12 Al Kaline Pants ....
Duke Snider Jsy/15

2004 Playoff Prime Cuts Timeline Dual Achievements Material Combos

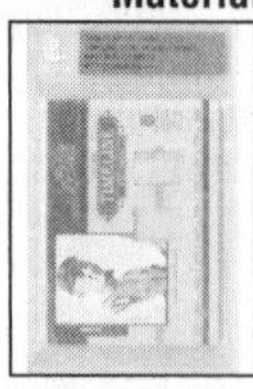

MINT NRMT
RANDOM INSERTS IN PACKS ....
PRINT RUNS B/WN 1-19 COPIES PER
NO PRICING ON QTY OF 15 OR LESS.
1 Roy Campanella Bat-Pants ....
Yogi Berra Bat-Jsy/1
3 Stan Musial Bat-Jsy ....
Ted Williams Bat-Jsy/1
4 Mike Schmidt Bat-Jsy 250.00 110.00
George Brett Bat-Jsy/19
5 Dale Murphy Bat-Jsy........... 200.00 90.00
Cal Ripken Bat-Jsy/19
6 Roger Clemens Bat-Jsy........ 150.00 70.00
Mike Schmidt Bat-Jsy/19
7 Ty Cobb Bat-Pants ....
Babe Ruth Bat-Pants/9
8 Roy Campanella Bat-Pants...............
Stan Musial Bat-Jsy/2
10 George Brett Bat-Jsy 250.00 110.00
Nolan Ryan Bat-Jsy/19
12 Al Kaline Bat-Pants.........................
Duke Snider Bat-Jsy/15

2004 Playoff Prime Cuts Timeline Dual Achievements Material Signature

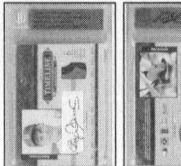

MINT NRMT
RANDOM INSERTS IN PACKS ....
PRINT RUNS B/WN 1-25 COPIES PER
NO PRICING ON QTY OF 15 OR LESS.
2 Jackie Robinson Jsy........................
Ted Williams Jsy/1
3 Stan Musial Jsy...............................
Ted Williams Jsy/1
4 Mike Schmidt Jsy................. 300.00 135.00
George Brett Jsy/24
5 Dale Murphy Jsy 300.00 135.00
Cal Ripken Jsy/25
6 Roger Clemens Jsy 300.00 135.00
Mike Schmidt Jsy/24
7 Ty Cobb Pants..................................
Babe Ruth Pants/1
10 George Brett Jsy................. 350.00 160.00
Nolan Ryan Jsy/25
12 Al Kaline Pants ....
Duke Snider Jsy/15

2004 Playoff Prime Cuts Timeline Dual Achievements Signature

MINT NRMT
RANDOM INSERTS IN PACKS ....
PRINT RUNS B/WN 24-25 COPIES PER
4 Mike Schmidt 250.00 110.00
George Brett/24
5 Dale Murphy.......................... 250.00 110.00
Cal Ripken/25
6 Roger Clemens...................... 250.00 110.00
Mike Schmidt/24
10 George Brett 300.00 135.00
Nolan Ryan/25
12 Al Kaline 150.00 70.00
Duke Snider/25

2004 Playoff Prime Cuts Timeline Dual Achievements Signature Proofs

MINT NRMT
RANDOM INSERTS IN PACKS ....
STATED PRINT RUN 1 SERIAL #'d SET
NO PRICING DUE TO SCARCITY.........

2004 Playoff Prime Cuts Timeline Dual League Leaders Material

MINT NRMT
RANDOM INSERTS IN PACKS ....
PRINT RUNS B/WN 9-19 COPIES PER
NO PRICING ON QTY OF 9 OR LESS...
1 Mel Ott Jsy.....................................
Lou Gehrig Pants/9
2 Mel Ott Jsy.....................................
Ted Williams Jsy/9
4 Steve Carlton Jsy 60.00 27.00
Jim Palmer Jsy/19
6 Roberto Clemente Jsy ....
Carl Yastrzemski Jsy/9
7 Steve Carlton Jsy 100.00 45.00
Nolan Ryan Jsy/19
8 Don Mattingly Jsy 120.00 55.00
Tony Gwynn Jsy/19
9 Roger Clemens Jsy 120.00 55.00
Nolan Ryan Jsy/19
10 Babe Ruth Pants.............................
Lou Gehrig Pants/9

2004 Playoff Prime Cuts Timeline Dual League Leaders Material Prime

MINT NRMT
RANDOM INSERTS IN PACKS ....
PRINT RUNS B/WN 9-19 COPIES PER
NO PRICING DUE TO SCARCITY.........
1 Mel Ott Jsy.....................................
Lou Gehrig Pants/9
2 Mel Ott Jsy.....................................
Ted Williams Jsy/9
4 Steve Carlton Jsy 100.00 45.00
Jim Palmer Jsy/19
6 Roberto Clemente Jsy ....
Carl Yastrzemski Jsy/9
7 Steve Carlton Jsy 150.00 70.00
Nolan Ryan Jsy/19
8 Don Mattingly Jsy 200.00 90.00
Tony Gwynn Jsy/19
9 Roger Clemens Jsy 200.00 90.00
Nolan Ryan Jsy/19
10 Babe Ruth Pants.............................
Lou Gehrig Pants/9

2004 Playoff Prime Cuts Timeline Dual League Leaders Material Combos

MINT NRMT
RANDOM INSERTS IN PACKS ....
PRINT RUNS B/WN 9-19 COPIES PER
NO PRICING ON QTY OF 9 OR LESS...
1 Mel Ott Bat-Jsy..............................
Lou Gehrig Bat-Pants/9
2 Mel Ott Bat-Jsy..............................
Ted Williams Bat-Jsy/9
6 Roberto Clemente Bat-Jsy...............
Carl Yastrzemski Bat-Jsy/9
7 Steve Carlton Bat-Jsy 150.00 70.00
Nolan Ryan Bat-Jsy/19
8 Don Mattingly Bat-Jsy.......... 200.00 90.00
Tony Gwynn Bat-Jsy/19
9 Roger Clemens Bat-Jsy........ 200.00 90.00
Nolan Ryan Bat-Jsy/19
10 Babe Ruth Bat-Pants......................
Lou Gehrig Bat-Pants/9

2004 Playoff Prime Cuts Timeline Dual League Leaders Material Signature

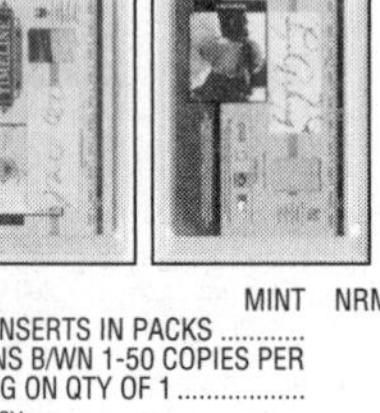

MINT NRMT
RANDOM INSERTS IN PACKS ....
PRINT RUNS B/WN 1-50 COPIES PER
NO PRICING ON QTY OF 1 ....
1 Mel Ott Jsy.....................................
Lou Gehrig Pants/1
2 Mel Ott Jsy.....................................
Ted Williams Jsy/1
4 Steve Carlton Jsy 120.00 55.00
Jim Palmer Jsy/50
6 Roberto Clemente Jsy ....
Carl Yastrzemski Jsy/1
7 Steve Carlton Jsy 300.00 135.00
Nolan Ryan Jsy/25
8 Don Mattingly Jsy 300.00 135.00
Tony Gwynn Jsy/25
9 Roger Clemens Jsy 500.00 220.00
Nolan Ryan Jsy/25
10 Babe Ruth Pants.............................
Lou Gehrig Pants/1

2004 Playoff Prime Cuts Timeline Dual League Leaders Signature

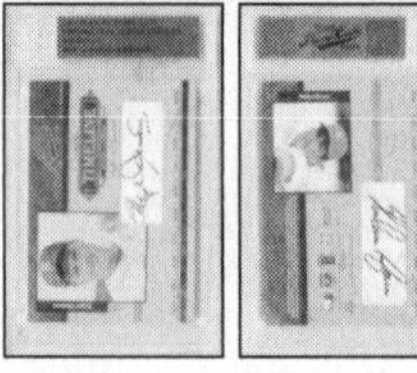

MINT NRMT
RANDOM INSERTS IN PACKS ....
PRINT RUNS B/WN 25-50 COPIES PER
4 Steve Carlton........................ 100.00 45.00
Jim Palmer/50
7 Steve Carlton........................ 250.00 110.00
Nolan Ryan/25
8 Don Mattingly........................ 250.00 110.00
Tony Gwynn/25
9 Roger Clemens...................... 400.00 180.00
Nolan Ryan/25

2004 Playoff Prime Cuts Timeline Dual League Leaders Signature Proofs

MINT NRMT
RANDOM INSERTS IN PACKS ....
STATED PRINT RUN 1 SERIAL #'d SET
NO PRICING DUE TO SCARCITY.........

1911 Plow's Candy E300

The cards in this set measure 3" X 4" with a sepia photograph measuring 2 1/4" X 3 5/16". This set was issued by Plow's Candy Company circa 1911 on thin cardboard with wide borders. The subject's name is printed in block letters outside the bottom frame, and his team is listed directly beneath. The title "Plow's Candy Collection" is printed at the top; the cards are unnumbered and blank-backed. A few cards have been discovered with "premium or offer" backs. Those cards do trade at a premium. The cards have been alphabetized and numbered in the checklist below. The Doyle card was just discovered recently, leading many to believe that there might be other additions to this checklist. Any additions are therefore appreciated.

Ex-Mt VG
COMPLETE SET 30000.00 15000.00
1 Babe Adams........................ 500.00 250.00
2 Frank Baker 800.00 400.00
3 Cy Barger 400.00 200.00
4 Jack Barry 400.00 200.00
5 Johnny Bates...................... 400.00 200.00
6 Chief Bender...................... 800.00 400.00
7 Joe Benz............................. 400.00 200.00
8 Bill Bergen.......................... 400.00 200.00
9 Roger Breshnahan.............. 800.00 400.00
10 Mordecai Brown................ 800.00 400.00
11 Donie Bush........................ 400.00 200.00
12 Bobby Byrne..................... 400.00 200.00
13 Nixey Callahan.................. 400.00 200.00
14 Hal Chase 600.00 300.00
15 Fred Clarke 800.00 400.00
16 Ty Cobb............................ 3000.00 1500.00
17 King Cole.......................... 400.00 800.00
18 Eddie Collins 800.00 400.00
19 Jack Coombs..................... 400.00 200.00
20 Bill Dahlen 400.00 200.00
21 Bert Daniels...................... 400.00 200.00
22 George Davis..................... 800.00 400.00
23 Jim Delahanty 400.00 200.00
24 Josh Devore 400.00 200.00
25 Bill Donovan...................... 500.00 250.00
26 Red Dooin 400.00 200.00
27 Larry Doyle....................... 500.00 250.00
28 Johnny Evers..................... 800.00 400.00
29 Russ Ford.......................... 400.00 200.00
30 Del Gainor......................... 400.00 200.00
31 Vean Gregg 400.00 200.00
32 Robert Harmon 400.00 200.00
33 Arnold Hauser 400.00 200.00
34 Dick Hoblitzell................... 400.00 200.00
35 Solly Hoffman 400.00 200.00
36 Miller Huggins................... 800.00 400.00
37 John Hummel.................... 400.00 200.00
38 Walter Johnson 1500.00 750.00
39 Johnny Kling 400.00 200.00
40 Nap Lajoie......................... 800.00 400.00
41 John Lapp 400.00 200.00
42 Fred Luderus..................... 400.00 200.00
43 Sherry Magee.................... 500.00 250.00
44 Rube Marquard 800.00 400.00
45 Christy Mathewson 1500.00 750.00
46 Stuffy McInnis 500.00 250.00
47 Larry McLean.................... 400.00 200.00
48 Fred Merkle 600.00 300.00
49 Cy Morgan......................... 400.00 200.00
50 George Moriarity 400.00 200.00
51 Harry Mowrey 400.00 200.00
52 Chief Meyers..................... 500.00 250.00
53 Rube Oldring..................... 400.00 200.00
54 Martin O'Toole 400.00 200.00
55 Nap Rucker 500.00 250.00
56 Slim Sallee 400.00 200.00
57 Boss Schmidt.................... 400.00 200.00
58 Jimmy Sheckard 400.00 200.00
59 Tris Speaker 800.00 400.00
60 Billy Sullivan.................... 400.00 200.00
61 Ira Thomas........................ 400.00 200.00
62 Joe Tinker 800.00 400.00
63 John Titus......................... 400.00 200.00
64 Hippo Vaughn 400.00 200.00
65 Honus Wagner 1500.00 750.00
66 Ed Walsh........................... 800.00 400.00
67 Harry Williams.................. 400.00 200.00

1991 PM Gold Card Prototype

This standard-size card is a prototype for PM cards. Each card contains one gram of pure 999.9 gold (24 karat) and will feature baseball, basketball, football and hockey players (some promos were also printed that do not contain gold). The front design features a color player photo of a fictional player, with a yellow/orange inner border and a gold outer border. The back has the serial number, player biography and an advertisement for PM cards.

Nm-Mt Ex-Mt
1 Ken Katcher.............................. 1.00 .30

1992 PM Gold

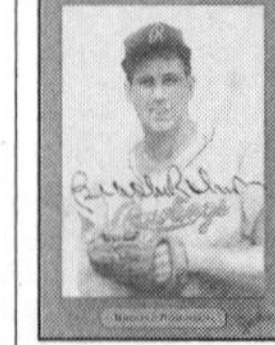
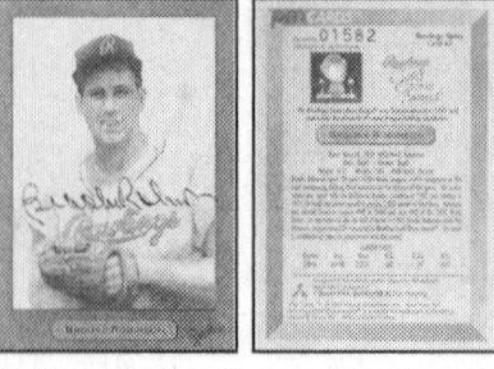

Distributed by Powell Associates, these PM ("precious metal") cards each contain one gram of pure 24K (999.9 percent) fine gold. These standard-size cards are the product of a technological break through developed by Mitsubishi that makes it possible to put a full color picture on precious metals. Artist Gregory Perillo created the oil paintings of the players reproduced on the card fronts. Production quantities vary for each card. Only 1,000 of card number 1 (a prototype) were produced and distributed to attendees of the Gold Glove charity dinner. The production run of cards number 2 and 3 were 10,000 and 1,200 respectively. The card front also has gold borders and the player's name appears in a gold plaque in the bottom gold border. The back has the serial number and career summary. The cards are numbered on the back by "Rawling Series Card number X."

Nm-Mt Ex-Mt
COMPLETE SET (3)................... 40.00 12.00
1 Brooks Robinson.................... 20.00 6.00
Defensive posture, Prototype
2 Brooks Robinson...................... 3.00 .90
Portrait
3 Roberto Clemente 25.00 7.50

1992 PM Gold Ruth Prototype

Distributed by Powell Associates, this Babe Ruth Precious Metal card contains one gram of pure 24K (999.9 percent) fine gold. The card measures the standard size. Artist Gregory Perillo created the oil painting of Ruth that was reproduced on the card front. The card front also has gold borders and the player's name appears in a gold plaque in the bottom gold border. The back has the serial number and career summary. The card is numbered on the back by "Baseball Series Card Number 1."

Nm-Mt Ex-Mt
1 Babe Ruth .... 3.00 .90

1993 PM Gold Bench

A one-gram, 24-K gold card featuring former Reds catcher Johnny Bench was given to each attendee at the Third Annual Rawlings Gold Glove Award Charity Dinner held Nov. 18, 1993 at the Sheraton New York. The card was created from an original painting by sports artist Daniel Fruend. The back features a brief biography of the baseball legend.

Nm-Mt Ex-Mt
1 Johnny Bench 50.00 15.00

1906-16 Police Gazette Supplements

These 11" by 16" premiums were issued with copies of the "Police Gazette" magazine. The high quality photos have the police gazette ID on the top and an ID of the athlete as well as some information about him on the bottom. We have just listed the Baseball players here but it is believed many more should exist.

Ex-Mt VG
COMPLETE SET 5000.00 2500.00
1 Harry Bay 200.00 100.00
2 Hal Chase........................... 500.00 250.00
3 Ty Cobb.............................. 2000.00 1000.00
4 Harry Coveleski 200.00 100.00
5 Mike Donlin........................ 200.00 100.00
6 Dave Fultz.......................... 200.00 100.00
7 Danny Hoffman 200.00 100.00
8 Joe Jackson 2000.00 1000.00
9 Sherry Magee..................... 250.00 125.00
10 Clarence Mitchell.............. 200.00 100.00

1985 Police Mets/Yankees

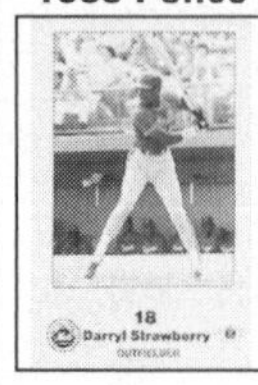
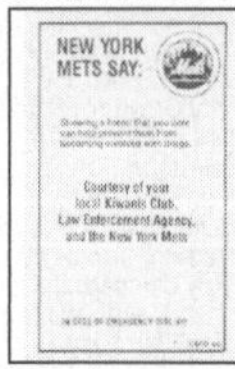

This 12-card set was supposedly issued courtesy of the Kiwanis Club, a local law enforcement agency, and the New York Mets and New York Yankees. The cards measure approximately 2 9/16" by 4 1/16". The cards are numbered on the back and are indicated below by a prefix for Mets or Yankees.

Nm-Mt Ex-Mt
COMPLETE SET (12).................. 6.00 2.40
M1 George Foster and.................. .50 .20
Bill Robinson CO
M2 Davey Johnson MG .... 1.00 .40
and Gary Carter
M3 Dwight Gooden .... 1.50 .60
M4 Mookie Wilson........................ .75 .30
M5 Keith Hernandez .... 1.00 .40
M6 Darryl Strawberry.................... .75 .30
Y1 Willie Randolph........................ .75 .30
Y2 Phil Niekro .... 1.50 .60
Y3 Ron Guidry............................... .75 .30
Y4 Dave Winfield......................... 2.50 1.00
Y5 Dave Righetti........................... .75 .30
Y6 Billy Martin MG .... 1.00 .40

1914 Polo Grounds WG4

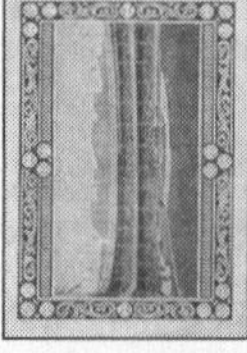

These cards were distributed as part of a baseball game produced around 1913. The cards each measure approximately 2 1/2" by 3 1/2" and have rounded corners. The card fronts show a photo of the player, his name, his team, and the game outcome associated with that particular card. The card backs are printed in green and white and are all the same each showing a panoramic picture of the Polo Grounds inside an ornate frame with a white outer border. Since the cards are unnumbered, they are listed below in alphabetical order.

	Ex-Mt	VG
COMPLETE SET (30)	1500.00	750.00
1 Jimmy Archer	40.00	20.00
2 Frank Baker	80.00	40.00
3 Frank Chance	100.00	50.00
4 Larry Cheney	40.00	20.00
5 Ty Cobb	300.00	150.00
6 Eddie Collins	80.00	40.00
7 Larry Doyle	50.00	25.00
8 Art Fletcher	40.00	20.00
9 Claude Hendrix	40.00	20.00
10 Joe Jackson	500.00	250.00
11 Hugh Jennings MG	80.00	40.00
12 Nap Lajoie	120.00	60.00
13 Jimmy Lavender	40.00	20.00
14 Fritz Maisel	40.00	20.00
15 Rabbit Maranville	80.00	40.00
16 Rube Marquard	80.00	40.00
17 Christy Mathewson	150.00	75.00
18 John McGraw MG	120.00	60.00
19 Stuffy McInnis sic,McInnes	50.00	25.00
20 Chief Meyers	50.00	25.00
21 Red Murray	40.00	20.00
22 Eddie Plank	80.00	40.00
23 Nap Rucker	50.00	25.00
24 Reb Russell	40.00	20.00
25 Frank Schulte	50.00	25.00
26 Jim Scott	40.00	20.00
27 Tris Speaker	120.00	60.00
28 Honus Wagner	150.00	75.00
29 Ed Walsh	80.00	40.00
30 Joe Wood	60.00	30.00

1928 Portraits and Action R315

This listing is actually an amalgamation of different issued sets. The cards all measure 3 1/4" by 5 1/4" and are all blank-backed. Cissell, Clancy, Hendrick, Jolley and Traynor were all issued in a sepia toned version which are both made of thicker stock than the regular photos and are considerably more difficult to acquire than the other cards in the set,

	Ex-Mt	VG
COMPLETE SET (88)	5000.00	2500.00
COMMON CARD A/B	20.00	10.00
COMMON CARD C/D	25.00	12.50
A1 Earl Averill	50.00	25.00
A2 Benny Bengough	20.00	10.00
A3 Laurence Benton	20.00	10.00
A4 Max Bishop	20.00	10.00
A5 Jim Bottomley	50.00	25.00
A6 Freddy Fitzsimmons	20.00	10.00
A7 Jimmie Foxx	200.00	100.00
A8 Johnny Fredericks	20.00	10.00
A9 Frank Frisch	80.00	40.00
A10 Lou Gehrig	400.00	200.00
A11 Goose Goslin	50.00	25.00
A12 Burleigh Grimes	50.00	25.00
A13 Lefty Grove	120.00	60.00
A14 Mule Haas	20.00	10.00
A15 Babe Herman	25.00	12.50
A16 Rogers Hornsby	200.00	100.00
A17 Carl Hubbell	80.00	40.00
A18 Travis Jackson	40.00	20.00
A19 Chuck Klein	80.00	40.00
A20 Mark Koenig	20.00	10.00
A21 Tony Lazzeri	40.00	20.00
A22 Fred Leach	20.00	10.00
A23 Fred Lindstrom	40.00	20.00
A24 Fred Marberry	20.00	10.00
A25 Bing Miller	20.00	10.00
A26 Lefty O'Doul	30.00	15.00
A27 Bob O'Farrell	20.00	10.00
A28 Herb Pennock	50.00	25.00
A29 George Pipgras	20.00	10.00
A30 Andrew Reese	20.00	10.00
A31 Babe Ruth	500.00	250.00
A32 Bob Shawkey	25.00	12.50
A33 Al Simmons	50.00	25.00
A34 Riggs Stephenson	30.00	15.00
A35 Bill Terry	80.00	40.00
A36 Pie Traynor	100.00	50.00
A37 Dazzy Vance	50.00	25.00
A38 Paul Waner	50.00	25.00
A39 Hack Wilson	80.00	40.00
A40 Tom Zachary	20.00	10.00
B1 Earl Averill	50.00	25.00
B2 Benny Bengough	20.00	10.00
B3 Laurence Benton	20.00	10.00
B4 Max Bishop	20.00	10.00
B5 Jim Bottomley	50.00	25.00
B6 Freddy Fitzsimmons	20.00	10.00
B7 Jimmie Foxx	150.00	75.00
B8 Johnny Fredericks	20.00	10.00
B9 Frank Frisch	120.00	60.00
B10 Lou Gehrig	400.00	200.00
B11 Goose Goslin	50.00	25.00
B12 Burleigh Grimes	50.00	25.00
B13 Lefty Grove	120.00	60.00
B14 Mule Haas	20.00	10.00
B15 Babe Herman	25.00	12.50
B16 Rogers Hornsby	200.00	100.00
B17 Carl Hubbell	100.00	50.00
B18 Travis Jackson	50.00	25.00
B19 Chuck Klein	80.00	40.00
B20 Mark Koenig	20.00	10.00
B21 Tony Lazzeri	40.00	20.00
B22 Fred Leach	20.00	10.00
B23 Fred Lindstrom	50.00	25.00
B24 Fred Marberry	20.00	10.00
B25 Bing Miller	20.00	10.00
B26 Lefty O'Doul	30.00	15.00
B27 Bob O'Farrell	20.00	10.00
B28 Herb Pennock	50.00	25.00
B29 George Pipgras	20.00	10.00
B30 Andrew Reese	20.00	10.00
B31 Babe Ruth	500.00	250.00
B32 Bob Shawkey	20.00	10.00
B33 Al Simmons	50.00	25.00
B34 Riggs Stephenson	30.00	15.00
B35 Bill Terry	100.00	50.00
B36 Pie Traynor	80.00	40.00
B37 Dazzy Vance	50.00	25.00
B38 Paul Waner	50.00	25.00
B39 Hack Wilson	80.00	40.00
B40 Tom Zachary	20.00	10.00
C1 Bill Cissell	25.00	12.50
C2 Harvey Hendricks	25.00	12.50
C3 Smead Jolley	25.00	12.50
C4 Carl Reynolds	25.00	12.50
C5 Art Shires	25.00	12.50
D1 Bill Cissell	25.00	12.50
D2 Bud Clancy	25.00	12.50
D3 Smead Jolley	25.00	12.50

1929 Portraits and Action R316

The 1929 R316 Portraits and Action Baseball set features 101 unnumbered, blank backed, black and white cards each measuring 3 1/2" by 4 1/2". The name of the player is written in script at the bottom of the card. The Hadley, Haines, Siebold and Todt cards are considered scarce. The Babe Ruth card seems to be one of the more plentiful cards in the set. These cards were issued in 25 count boxes which had the checklist printed on the reverse. There were four different boxes issued: Orange, Blue, Coral and Canary and Babe Ruth is the only player included in all four of these boxes. This set was issued by Kashin Publications.

	Ex-Mt	VG
COMPLETE SET (101)	4500.00	2200.00
1 Ethan N. Allen	30.00	15.00
2 Dale Alexander	30.00	15.00
3 Larry Benton	30.00	15.00
4 Moe Berg	60.00	30.00
5 Max Bishop	30.00	15.00
6 Del Bissonette	30.00	15.00
7 Lucerne A. Blue	30.00	15.00
8 Jim Bottomley	50.00	25.00
9 Guy T. Bush	30.00	15.00
10 Harold G. Carlson	30.00	15.00
11 Owen Carroll	30.00	15.00
12 Chalmers W. Cissell	30.00	15.00
13 Earle Combs	50.00	25.00
14 Hugh M. Critz	30.00	15.00
15 H.J. DeBerry	30.00	15.00
16 Pete Donohue	30.00	15.00
17 Taylor Douthit	30.00	15.00
18 Chuck Dressen	40.00	20.00
19 Jimmy Dykes	40.00	20.00
20 Howard Ehmke	30.00	15.00
21 Woody English	30.00	15.00
22 Urban Faber	50.00	25.00
23 Fred Fitzsimmons	40.00	20.00
24 Lewis A. Fonseca	30.00	15.00
25 Horace H. Ford	30.00	15.00
26 Jimmie Foxx	80.00	40.00
27 Frankie Frisch	60.00	30.00
28 Lou Gehrig	400.00	200.00
29 Charley Gehringer	60.00	30.00
30 Goose Goslin	50.00	25.00
31 George Grantham	30.00	15.00
32 Burleigh Grimes	50.00	25.00
33 Lefty Grove	60.00	30.00
34 Bump Hadley	200.00	100.00
35 Chick Hafey	50.00	25.00
36 Jesse Haines	250.00	125.00
37 Harvey Hendrick	30.00	15.00
38 Babe Herman	40.00	20.00
39 Andy High	30.00	15.00
40 Urban J. Hodapp	30.00	15.00
41 Frank Hogan	30.00	15.00
42 Rogers Hornsby	80.00	40.00
43 Waite Hoyt	50.00	25.00
44 Willis Hudlin	30.00	15.00
45 Frank O. Hurst	30.00	15.00
46 Charlie Jamieson	30.00	15.00
47 Roy C. Johnson	30.00	15.00
48 Percy Jones	30.00	15.00
49 Sam Jones	40.00	20.00
50 Joseph Judge	30.00	15.00
51 Willie Kamm	30.00	15.00
52 Chuck Klein	50.00	25.00
53 Mark Koenig	30.00	15.00
54 Ralph Kress	30.00	15.00
55 Fred M. Leach	30.00	15.00
56 Fred Lindstrom	50.00	25.00
57 Ad Liska	30.00	15.00
58 Fred Lucas	30.00	15.00
59 Fred Maguire	30.00	15.00
60 Perce L. Malone	30.00	15.00
61 Heinie Manush	50.00	25.00
62 Rabbit Maranville	50.00	25.00
63 Douglas McWeeney	30.00	15.00
64 Oscar Melillo	30.00	15.00
65 Bing Miller	30.00	15.00
66 Lefty O'Doul	40.00	20.00
67 Mel Ott	80.00	40.00
68 Herb Pennock	50.00	25.00
69 William W. Regan	30.00	15.00
70 Harry F. Rice	30.00	15.00
71 Sam Rice	50.00	25.00
72 Lance Richbourg	30.00	15.00
73 Eddie Rommel	30.00	15.00
74 Chas. H. Root	30.00	15.00
75 Ed Roush	50.00	25.00
76 Harold Ruel	30.00	15.00
77 Red Ruffing	50.00	25.00
78 Jack Russell	30.00	15.00
79 Babe Ruth QP	400.00	200.00
80 Fred Schulte	30.00	15.00
81 Joe Sewell	50.00	25.00
82 Luke Sewell	40.00	20.00
83 Art Shires	30.00	15.00
84 Henry Seibold	200.00	100.00
85 Al Simmons	50.00	25.00
86 Bob Smith	30.00	15.00
87 Riggs Stephenson	40.00	20.00
88 Bill Terry	60.00	30.00
89 Alphonse Thomas	30.00	15.00
90 Lafayette Thompson	30.00	15.00
91 Phil Todt	200.00	100.00
92 Pie Traynor	50.00	25.00
93 Dazzy Vance	50.00	25.00
94 Lloyd Waner	50.00	25.00
95 Paul Waner	50.00	25.00
96 Jimmy Welsh	30.00	15.00
97 Earl Whitehill	30.00	15.00
98 A.C. Whitney	30.00	15.00
99 Claude Willoughby	30.00	15.00
100 Hack Wilson	60.00	30.00
101 Tom Zachary	30.00	15.00

1930 Post Famous North Americans

This blank-backed card, which measures approximately 2 3/8" by 3 3/8" was cut from a strip of 4 cards and features a photo of Christy Mathewson on the front. Mathewson is the only sports personage featured in this set of 32 cards.

	Ex-Mt	VG
1 Christy Mathewson	150.00	75.00

1960 Post *

These large cards measure approximately 7" by 8 3/4". The 1960 Post Cereal Sports Stars set contains nine cards depicting current baseball, football and basketball players. Each card comprised the entire back of a Grape Nuts Flakes Box and is blank backed. The color player photos are set on a colored background surrounded by a wooden frame design and they are unnumbered (assigned numbers below for reference). The catalog designation is F278-26.

	NM	Ex
COMPLETE SET (9)	4500.00	1800.00
4 Al Kaline Detroit Tigers (baseball)	400.00	160.00
5 Harmon Killebrew Minnesota Twins (baseball)	300.00	120.00
6 Eddie Mathews Milwaukee Braves (baseball)	300.00	120.00
7 Mickey Mantle New York Yankees (baseball)	2000.00	800.00

1961 Post

The cards in this 200-card set measure 2 1/2" by 3 1/2". The 1961 Post set was this company's first major set. The cards were available on thick cardbox stock, singly or in various panel sizes from cereal boxes (BOX), or in team sheets, printed on thinner cardboard stock, directly from the Post Cereal Company (COM). It is difficult to differentiate the COM cards from the BOX cards; the thickness of the card stock is the best indicator. Many variations exist and are noted in the checklist below. There are many cards which were produced in lesser quantities; the prices below reflect the relative scarcity of the cards. Cards 10, 23, 70, 73, 94, 113, 135, 163, and 183 are examples of cards printed in limited quantities and hence commanding premium prices. The cards are numbered essentially in team groups, i.e., New York Yankees (1-18), Chicago White Sox (19-34), Detroit (35-46), Boston (47-56), Cleveland (57-67), Baltimore (68-80), Kansas City (81-90), Minnesota (91-100), Milwaukee (101-114), Philadelphia (115-124), Pittsburgh (125-140), San Francisco (141-155), Los Angeles Dodgers (156-170), St. Louis (171-180), Cincinnati (181-190), and Chicago Cubs (191-200). The catalog number is F278-33. The complete set price refers to the set with all variations (357). There was also an album produced by Post to hold the cards.

	NM	Ex
COMP. MASTER SET (357)	3000.00	1200.00
1A Yogi Berra COM	30.00	12.00
1B Yogi Berra BOX	30.00	12.00
2A Elston Howard COM	5.00	2.00
2B Elston Howard BOX	5.00	2.00
3A Bill Skowron COM	5.00	2.00
3B Bill Skowron BOX	5.00	2.00
4A Mickey Mantle COM	150.00	60.00
4B Mickey Mantle BOX	150.00	60.00
5 Bob Turley COM only	20.00	8.00
6A Whitey Ford COM	12.00	4.80
6B Whitey Ford BOX	12.00	4.80
7A Roger Maris COM	30.00	12.00
7B Roger Maris BOX	30.00	12.00
8A B.Richardson COM	5.00	2.00
8B Bobby Richardson BOX	5.00	2.00
9A Tony Kubek COM	5.00	2.00
9B Tony Kubek BOX	5.00	2.00
10 G.McDougald BOX only	50.00	20.00
11 Cletis Boyer BOX only	5.00	2.00
12A Hector Lopez COM	3.00	1.20
12B Hector Lopez BOX	3.00	1.20
13 Bob Cerv BOX only	3.00	1.20
14 Ryne Duren BOX only	3.00	1.20
15 Bobby Shantz BOX only	3.00	1.20
16 Art Ditmar BOX only	3.00	1.20
17 Jim Coates BOX only	3.00	1.20
18 Johnny Blanchard BOX only	3.00	1.20
19A Luis Aparicio COM	8.00	3.20
19B Luis Aparicio BOX	8.00	3.20
20A Nellie Fox COM	8.00	3.20
20B Nellie Fox BOX	8.00	3.20
21A Billy Pierce COM	5.00	2.00
21B Billy Pierce BOX	5.00	2.00
22A Early Wynn COM	15.00	6.00
22B Early Wynn BOX	15.00	6.00
23 Bob Shaw BOX only	100.00	40.00
24A Al Smith COM	5.00	2.00
24B Al Smith BOX	5.00	2.00
25A Minnie Minoso COM	6.00	2.40
25B Minnie Minoso BOX	6.00	2.40
26A Roy Sievers COM	3.00	1.20
26B Roy Sievers BOX	3.00	1.20
27A Jim Landis COM	3.00	1.20
27B Jim Landis BOX	3.00	1.20
28A Sherm Lollar COM	3.00	1.20
28B Sherm Lollar BOX	3.00	1.20
29 Gerry Staley BOX only	3.00	1.20
30A Gene Freese COM (Reds)	12.00	4.80
30B Gene Freese BOX (White Sox)	3.00	1.20
31 Ted Kluszewski BOX only	6.00	2.40
32 Turk Lown BOX only	3.00	1.20
33A Jim Rivera COM	3.00	1.20
33B Jim Rivera BOX	3.00	1.20
34 F.Baumann BOX only	3.00	1.20
35A Al Kaline COM	20.00	8.00
35B Al Kaline BOX	20.00	8.00
36A Rocky Colavito COM	10.00	4.00
36B Rocky Colavito BOX	10.00	4.00
37A Charlie Maxwell COM	5.00	2.00
37B Charlie Maxwell BOX	5.00	2.00
38A Frank Lary COM	5.00	2.00
38B Frank Lary BOX	5.00	2.00
39A Jim Bunning COM	8.00	3.20
39B Jim Bunning BOX	8.00	3.20
40A Norm Cash COM	5.00	2.00
40B Norm Cash BOX	5.00	2.00
41A Frank Bolling COM (Braves, Charlie Gehringer in bio)	5.00	2.00
41B Frank Bolling BOX (Tigers, Charlie Derringer in bio)	8.00	3.20
42A Don Mossi COM	3.00	1.20
42B Don Mossi BOX	3.00	1.20
43A Lou Berberet COM	3.00	1.20
43B Lou Berberet BOX	3.00	1.20
44 Dave Sisler BOX only	3.00	1.20
45 Eddie Yost BOX only	3.00	1.20
46 Pete Burnside BOX only	3.00	1.20
47A Pete Runnels COM	5.00	2.00
47B Pete Runnels BOX	5.00	2.00
48A Frank Malzone COM	3.00	1.20
48B Frank Malzone BOX	3.00	1.20
49A Vic Wertz COM	5.00	2.00
49B Vic Wertz BOX	5.00	2.00
50A Tom Brewer COM	3.00	1.20
50B Tom Brewer BOX	3.00	1.20
51A Willie Tasby COM (Sold to Wash.)	8.00	3.20
51B Willie Tasby BOX (No sale mention)	5.00	2.00
52A Russ Nixon COM	3.00	1.20
52B Russ Nixon BOX	3.00	1.20
53A Don Buddin COM	3.00	1.20
53B Don Buddin BOX	3.00	1.20
54A B.Monbouquette COM	3.00	1.20
54B B.Monbouquette BOX	3.00	1.20
55A Frank Sullivan COM (Phillies)	10.00	4.00
55B Frank Sullivan BOX (Red Sox)	3.00	1.20
56A H.Sullivan COM	3.00	1.20
56B H.Sullivan BOX	3.00	1.20
57A Harvey Kuenn COM (Giants)	8.00	3.20
57B Harvey Kuenn BOX (Indians)	6.00	2.40
58A Gary Bell COM	5.00	2.00
58B Gary Bell BOX	5.00	2.00
59A Jim Perry COM	3.00	1.20
59B Jim Perry BOX	3.00	1.20
60A Jim Grant COM	5.00	2.00
60B Jim Grant BOX	5.00	2.00
61A Johnny Temple COM	5.00	2.00
61B Johnny Temple BOX	5.00	2.00
62A Paul Foytack COM	3.00	1.20
62B Paul Foytack BOX	3.00	1.20
63A Vic Power COM	3.00	1.20
63B Vic Power BOX	3.00	1.20
64A Tito Francona COM	3.00	1.20
64B Tito Francona BOX	3.00	1.20
65A K.Aspromonte COM Sold to L.A.	8.00	3.20
65B Ken Aspromonte BOX (No sale mention)	8.00	3.20
66 Bob Wilson BOX only	3.00	1.20
67A John Romano COM	5.00	2.00
67B John Romano BOX	5.00	2.00
68A Jim Gentile COM	5.00	2.00
68B Jim Gentile BOX	5.00	2.00
69A Gus Triandos COM	5.00	2.00
69B Gus Triandos BOX	5.00	2.00
70 G.Woodling BOX only	30.00	12.00
71A Milt Pappas COM	5.00	2.00
71B Milt Pappas BOX	5.00	2.00
72A Ron Hansen COM	3.00	1.20
72B Ron Hansen BOX	3.00	1.20
73 Chuck Estrada COM only	125.00	50.00
74A Steve Barber COM	3.00	1.20
74B Steve Barber BOX	3.00	1.20
75A B.Robinson COM	25.00	10.00
75B B.Robinson BOX	25.00	10.00
76A Jackie Brandt COM	3.00	1.20
76B Jackie Brandt BOX	3.00	1.20
77A Marv Breeding COM	3.00	1.20
77B Marv Breeding BOX	3.00	1.20
78 Hal Brown BOX only	3.00	1.20
79 Billy Klaus BOX only	3.00	1.20
80A Hoyt Wilhelm COM	8.00	3.20
80B Hoyt Wilhelm BOX	8.00	3.20
81A Jerry Lumpe COM	5.00	2.00
81B Jerry Lumpe BOX	5.00	2.00
82A Norm Siebern COM	3.00	1.20
82B Norm Siebern BOX	3.00	1.20
83A Bud Daley COM	5.00	2.00
83B Bud Daley BOX	5.00	2.00
84A Bill Tuttle COM	3.00	1.20
84B Bill Tuttle BOX	3.00	1.20
85A M.Throneberry COM	5.00	2.00
85B M.Throneberry BOX	5.00	2.00
86A Dick Williams COM	5.00	2.00
86B Dick Williams BOX	5.00	2.00
87A Ray Herbert COM	3.00	1.20
87B Ray Herbert BOX	3.00	1.20
88A Whitey Herzog COM	6.00	2.40
88B Whitey Herzog BOX	6.00	2.40
89A Ken Hamlin COM (Sold to L.A.)	20.00	8.00
89B Ken Hamlin BOX (No sale mention)	3.00	1.20
90A Hank Bauer COM	5.00	2.00
90B Hank Bauer BOX	5.00	2.00
91A Bob Allison COM (Minnesota)	6.00	2.40
91B Bob Allison BOX (Minneapolis)	6.00	2.40
92A Harmon Killebrew (Minnesota) COM	50.00	20.00
92B Harmon Killebrew (Minneapolis) BOX	40.00	16.00
93A Jim Lemon COM (Minnesota)	25.00	10.00
93B Jim Lemon BOX (Minneapolis)	80.00	32.00
94A Chuck Stobbs (Minnesota) COM only	200.00	80.00
95A Reno Bertoia COM (Minnesota)	5.00	2.00
95B Reno Bertoia BOX (Minneapolis)	3.00	1.20
96A Billy Gardner COM (Minnesota)	5.00	2.00
96B Billy Gardner BOX (Minneapolis)	3.00	1.20
97A Earl Battey COM (Minnesota)	5.00	2.00
97B Earl Battey BOX (Minneapolis)	3.00	1.20
98A Pedro Ramos COM (Minnesota)	5.00	2.00
98B Pedro Ramos BOX (Minneapolis)	3.00	1.20
99A Camilo Pascual COM (Minnesota)	5.00	2.00
99B Camilo Pascual BOX (Minneapolis)	3.00	1.20
100A Billy Consolo COM (Minnesota)	5.00	2.00
100B Billy Consolo BOX (Minneapolis)	3.00	1.20
101A Warren Spahn COM	25.00	10.00
101B Warren Spahn BOX	25.00	10.00
102A Lew Burdette COM	5.00	2.00
102B Lew Burdette BOX	5.00	2.00
103A Bob Buhl COM	3.00	1.20
103B Bob Buhl BOX	3.00	1.20
104A Joe Adcock COM	5.00	2.00
104B Joe Adcock BOX	5.00	2.00
105A Johnny Logan COM	5.00	2.00
105B Johnny Logan BOX	5.00	2.00
106 E.Mathews COM only	40.00	16.00
107A Hank Aaron COM	30.00	12.00
107B Hank Aaron BOX	30.00	12.00
108A Wes Covington COM	3.00	1.20
108B Wes Covington BOX	3.00	1.20
109A Bill Bruton COM (Tigers)	6.00	2.40
109B Bill Bruton BOX (Braves)	6.00	2.40
110A Del Crandall COM	5.00	2.00
110B Del Crandall BOX	5.00	2.00
111 Red Schoendienst BOX only	6.00	2.40
112 Juan Pizarro BOX only	3.00	1.20
113 Chuck Cottier BOX only	15.00	6.00
114 Al Spangler BOX only	3.00	1.20
115A Dick Farrell COM	5.00	2.00
115B Dick Farrell BOX	5.00	2.00
116A Jim Owens COM	5.00	2.00
116B Jim Owens BOX	5.00	2.00
117A Robin Roberts COM	10.00	4.00
117B Robin Roberts BOX	8.00	3.20
118A Tony Taylor COM	3.00	1.20
118B Tony Taylor BOX	3.00	1.20
119A Lee Walls COM	3.00	1.20
119B Lee Walls BOX	3.00	1.20
120A Tony Curry COM	3.00	1.20
120B Tony Curry BOX	3.00	1.20
121A P.Herrera COM	5.00	2.00
121B Pancho Herrera BOX	5.00	2.00
122A Ken Walters COM	5.00	2.00
122B Ken Walters BOX	5.00	2.00
123A John Callison COM	5.00	2.00
123B John Callison BOX	5.00	2.00
124A Gene Conley COM (Red Sox)	12.00	4.80
124B Gene Conley BOX (Phillies)	3.00	1.20
125A Bob Friend COM	5.00	2.00
125B Bob Friend BOX	5.00	2.00
126A Vern Law COM	5.00	2.00
126B Vern Law BOX	5.00	2.00
127A Dick Stuart COM	5.00	2.00

1962 Post

127B Dick Stuart BOX 5.00 2.00
128A Bill Mazeroski COM 6.00 2.40
128B Bill Mazeroski BOX 6.00 2.40
129A Dick Groat COM 5.00 2.00
129B Dick Groat BOX 5.00 2.00
130A Don Hoak COM 3.00 1.20
130B Don Hoak BOX 3.00 1.20
131A Bob Skinner COM 3.00 1.20
131B Bob Skinner BOX 3.00 1.20
132A R.Clemente COM 60.00 24.00
132B R.Clemente BOX 60.00 24.00
133 Roy Face BOX only 5.00 2.00
134 H.Haddix BOX only 3.00 1.20
135 Bill Virdon BOX only 40.00 16.00
136A Gino Cimoli COM 3.00 1.20
136B Gino Cimoli BOX 3.00 1.20
137 Rocky Nelson 3.00 1.20
BOX only
138A S.Burgess COM 5.00 2.00
138B Smoky Burgess BOX 5.00 2.00
139 Hal W. Smith 3.00 1.20
BOX only
140 Wilmer Mizell 3.00 1.20
BOX only
141A M.McCormick COM 3.00 1.20
141B M.McCormick BOX 3.00 1.20
142A John Antonelli COM 6.00 2.40
(Cleveland)
142B John Antonelli BOX 5.00 2.00
(San Francisco)
143A Sam Jones COM 5.00 2.00
143B Sam Jones BOX 5.00 2.00
144A O.Cepeda COM 10.00 4.00
144B Orlando Cepeda BOX 10.00 4.00
145A Willie Mays COM 40.00 16.00
145B Willie Mays BOX 40.00 16.00
146A Willie Kirkland 8.00 3.20
(Cleveland) COM
146B Willie Kirkland 6.00 2.40
(San Francisco) BOX
147A Willie McCovey COM 10.00 4.00
147B Willie McCovey BOX 10.00 4.00
148A D.Blasingame COM 3.00 1.20
148B D.Blasingame BOX 3.00 1.20
149A Jim Davenport COM 5.00 2.00
149B Jim Davenport BOX 5.00 2.00
150A Hobie Landrith COM 3.00 1.20
150B Hobie Landrith BOX 3.00 1.20
151 B.Schmidt BOX only 3.00 1.20
152A Ed Bressoud COM 3.00 1.20
152B Ed Bressoud BOX 3.00 1.20
153A Andre Rodgers 20.00 8.00
no trade mention
BOX only
153B Andre Rodgers 5.00 2.00
(Traded to Milw.)
BOX only
154 Jack Sanford 3.00 1.20
BOX only
155 Billy O'Dell 3.00 1.20
BOX only
156A Norm Larker COM 3.00 1.20
156B Norm Larker BOX 3.00 1.20
157A Charlie Neal COM 5.00 2.00
157B Charlie Neal BOX 5.00 2.00
158A Jim Gilliam COM 8.00 3.20
158B Jim Gilliam BOX 8.00 3.20
159A Wally Moon COM 6.00 2.40
159B Wally Moon BOX 6.00 2.40
160A Don Drysdale COM 15.00 6.00
160B Don Drysdale BOX 15.00 6.00
161A Larry Sherry COM 5.00 2.00
161B Larry Sherry BOX 5.00 2.00
162 Stan Williams 8.00 3.20
BOX only
163 Mel Roach BOX only 100.00 40.00
164A Maury Wills COM 10.00 4.00
164B Maury Wills BOX 10.00 4.00
165 T.Davis BOX only 5.00 2.00
166A John Roseboro COM 3.00 1.20
166B John Roseboro BOX 3.00 1.20
167A Duke Snider COM 8.00 3.20
167B Duke Snider BOX 8.00 3.20
168A Gil Hodges COM 8.00 3.20
168B Gil Hodges BOX 8.00 3.20
169 J.Podres BOX only 5.00 2.00
170 Ed Roebuck BOX only 5.00 2.00
171A Ken Boyer COM 10.00 4.00
171B Ken Boyer BOX 10.00 4.00
172A J.Cunningham COM 3.00 1.20
172B J.Cunningham BOX 3.00 1.20
173A Daryl Spencer COM 3.00 1.20
173B Daryl Spencer BOX 3.00 1.20
174A Larry Jackson COM 5.00 2.00
174B Larry Jackson BOX 5.00 2.00
175A Lindy McDaniel COM 3.00 1.20
175B Lindy McDaniel BOX 3.00 1.20
176A Bill White COM 5.00 2.00
176B Bill White BOX 5.00 2.00
177A Alex Grammas COM 3.00 1.20
177B Alex Grammas BOX 3.00 1.20
178A Curt Flood COM 6.00 2.40
178B Curt Flood BOX 6.00 2.40
179A Ernie Broglio COM 3.00 1.20
179B Ernie Broglio BOX 3.00 1.20
180A Hal Smith COM 3.00 1.20
180B Hal Smith BOX 3.00 1.20
181A Vada Pinson COM 5.00 2.00
181B Vada Pinson BOX 5.00 2.00
182A Fr. Robinson COM 35.00 14.00
182B Frank Robinson BOX 35.00 14.00
183 Roy McMillan 90.00 36.00
BOX only
184A Bob Purkey COM 3.00 1.20
184B Bob Purkey BOX 3.00 1.20
185A Ed Kasko COM 3.00 1.20
185B Ed Kasko BOX 3.00 1.20
186A Gus Bell COM 3.00 1.20
186B Gus Bell BOX 3.00 1.20
187A Jerry Lynch COM 3.00 1.20
187B Jerry Lynch BOX 3.00 1.20
188A Ed Bailey COM 3.00 1.20
188B Ed Bailey BOX 3.00 1.20
189A Jim O'Toole COM 3.00 1.20
189B Jim O'Toole BOX 3.00 1.20
190A Billy Martin COM 10.00 4.00
Sold to Milwaukee
190B Billy Martin BOX 6.00 2.40
(No sale mention)
191A Ernie Banks COM 30.00 12.00
191B Ernie Banks BOX 30.00 12.00
192A Richie Ashburn COM 10.00 4.00
192B Richie Ashburn BOX 10.00 4.00
193A Frank Thomas COM 50.00 20.00
193B Frank Thomas BOX 50.00 20.00
194A Don Cardwell COM 5.00 2.00
194B Don Cardwell BOX 5.00 2.00
195A George Altman COM 3.00 1.20
195B George Altman BOX 3.00 1.20
196A Ron Santo COM 6.00 2.40
196B Ron Santo BOX 6.00 2.40
197A Glen Hobbie COM 3.00 1.20
197B Glen Hobbie BOX 3.00 1.20
198A Sam Taylor COM 3.00 1.20
198B Sam Taylor BOX 3.00 1.20
199A Jerry Kindall COM 3.00 1.20
199B Jerry Kindall BOX 3.00 1.20
200A Don Elston COM 5.00 2.00
200B Don Elston BOX 5.00 2.00
XX Album

1962 Post

The cards in this 200-player series measure 2 1/2" by 3 1/2" and are oriented horizontally. The 1962 Post set is the easiest of the Post sets to complete. The cards are grouped numerically by team, for example, New York Yankees (1-13), Detroit (14-26), Baltimore (27-36), Cleveland (37-45), Chicago White Sox (46-55), Boston (56-64), Washington (65-73), Los Angeles Angels (74-82), Minnesota (83-91), Kansas City (92-100), Los Angeles Dodgers (101-115), Cincinnati (116-130), San Francisco (131-144), Milwaukee (145-157), St. Louis (158-168), Pittsburgh (169-181), Chicago Cubs (182-191) and Philadelphia (192-200). Cards 5B and 6B were printed on thin stock in a two-card panel and distributed in a Life magazine promotion. The scarce cards are 55, 69, 83, 92, 101, 103, 113, 116, 122, 125, 127, 131, 140, 144, and 158. The checklist for this set is the same as that of 1962 Jello and 1962 Post Canadian, but those sets are considered separate issues. The catalog number for this set is F278-37.

NM Ex
COMP. MASTER SET (210) 2000.00 800.00
1 Bill Skowron 6.00 2.40
2 Bobby Richardson 6.00 2.40
3 Cletis Boyer 5.00 2.00
4 Tony Kubek 6.00 2.40
5A Mickey Mantle 150.00 60.00
5B Mickey Mantle AD 150.00 60.00
6A Roger Maris 25.00 10.00
6B Roger Maris AD 25.00 10.00
7 Yogi Berra 25.00 10.00
8 Elston Howard 5.00 2.00
9 Whitey Ford 10.00 4.00
10 Ralph Terry 4.00 1.60
11 John Blanchard 3.00 1.20
12 Luis Arroyo 4.00 1.60
13 Bill Stafford 3.00 1.20
14A Norm Cash ERR 20.00 8.00
Throws: right
14B Norm Cash COR 6.00 2.40
(Throws: left)
15 Jake Wood 3.00 1.20
16 Steve Boros 3.00 1.20
17 Chico Fernandez 3.00 1.20
18 Bill Bruton 3.00 1.20
19 Rocky Colavito 8.00 3.20
20 Al Kaline 15.00 6.00
21 Dick Brown 3.00 1.20
22 Frank Lary 3.00 1.20
23 Don Mossi 3.00 1.20
24 Phil Regan 3.00 1.20
25 Charley Maxwell 3.00 1.20
26 Jim Bunning 8.00 3.20
27A Jim Gentile 4.00 1.60
(Home: Baltimore)
27B Jim Gentile 20.00 8.00
(Home: San Lorenzo)
28 Marv Breeding 3.00 1.20
29 Brooks Robinson 15.00 6.00
30A Ron Hansen 5.00 2.00
(At-Bats)
30B Ron Hansen 5.00 2.00
(At Bats)
31 Jackie Brandt 3.00 1.20
32 Dick Williams 4.00 1.60
33 Gus Triandos 3.00 1.20
34 Milt Pappas 4.00 1.60
35 Hoyt Wilhelm 8.00 3.20
36 Chuck Estrada 10.00 4.00
37 Vic Power 3.00 1.20
38 Johnny Temple 3.00 1.20
39 Bubba Phillips 3.00 1.20
40 Tito Francona 3.00 1.20
41 Willie Kirkland 3.00 1.20
42 John Romano 3.00 1.20
43 Jim Perry 3.00 1.20
44 Woodie Held 3.00 1.20
45 Chuck Essegian 3.00 1.20
46 Roy Sievers 3.00 1.20
47 Nellie Fox 8.00 3.20
48 Al Smith 3.00 1.20
49 Luis Aparicio 8.00 3.20
50 Jim Landis 3.00 1.20
51 Minnie Minoso 5.00 2.00
52 Andy Carey 3.00 1.20
53 Sherman Lollar 3.00 1.20
54 Billy Pierce 4.00 1.60
55 Early Wynn 30.00 12.00
56 Chuck Schilling 4.00 1.60
57 Pete Runnels 3.00 1.20
58 Frank Malzone 3.00 1.20
59 Don Buddin 3.00 1.20
60 Gary Geiger 3.00 1.20
61 Carl Yastrzemski 40.00 16.00
62 Jackie Jensen 4.00 1.60
63 Jim Pagliaroni 3.00 1.20
64 Don Schwall 3.00 1.20
65 Dale Long 3.00 1.20
66 Chuck Cottier 3.00 1.20
67 Billy Klaus 3.00 1.20
68 Coot Veal 4.00 1.60
69 Marty Keough 40.00 16.00
70 Willie Tasby 3.00 1.20
71 Gene Woodling 3.00 1.20
72 Gene Green 4.00 1.60
73 Dick Donovan 3.00 1.20
74 Steve Bilko 3.00 1.20
75 Rocky Bridges 3.00 1.20
76 Eddie Yost 3.00 1.20
77 Leon Wagner 3.00 1.20
78 Albie Pearson 4.00 1.60
79 Ken Hunt 3.00 1.20
80 Earl Averill 3.00 1.20
81 Ryne Duren 3.00 1.20
82 Ted Kluszewski 10.00 4.00
83 Bob Allison 30.00 12.00
84 Billy Martin 8.00 3.20
85 Harmon Killebrew 10.00 4.00
86 Zoilo Versalles 3.00 1.20
87 Lenny Green 3.00 1.20
88 Bill Tuttle 3.00 1.20
89 Jim Lemon 3.00 1.20
90 Earl Battey 3.00 1.20
91 Camilo Pascual 3.00 1.20
92 Norm Siebern 75.00 30.00
93 Jerry Lumpe 3.00 1.20
94 Dick Howser 4.00 1.60
95A Gene Stephens 5.00 2.00
(Born: Jan. 5)
95B Gene Stephens 20.00 8.00
(Born: Jan. 20)
96 Leo Posada 3.00 1.20
97 Joe Pignatano 3.00 1.20
98 Jim Archer 3.00 1.20
99 Haywood Sullivan 3.00 1.20
100 Art Ditmar 3.00 1.20
101 Gil Hodges 100.00 40.00
102 Charlie Neal 3.00 1.20
103 Daryl Spencer 30.00 12.00
104 Maury Wills 10.00 4.00
105 Tommy Davis 4.00 1.60
106 Willie Davis 4.00 1.60
107 John Roseboro 3.00 1.20
108 Johnny Podres 4.00 1.60
109A Sandy Koufax 40.00 16.00
109B Sandy Koufax 150.00 60.00
With blue lines
110 Don Drysdale 12.00 4.80
111 Larry Sherry 4.00 1.60
112 Jim Gilliam 5.00 2.00
113 Norm Larker 40.00 16.00
114 Duke Snider 8.00 3.20
115 Stan Williams 3.00 1.20
116 Gordy Coleman 100.00 40.00
117 Don Blasingame 3.00 1.20
118 Gene Freese 3.00 1.20
119 Ed Kasko 3.00 1.20
120 Gus Bell 3.00 1.20
121 Vada Pinson 4.00 1.60
122 Frank Robinson 30.00 12.00
123 Bob Purkey 3.00 1.20
124A Joey Jay 4.00 1.60
124B Joey Jay 20.00 8.00
(With blue lines)
125 Jim Brosnan 30.00 12.00
126 Jim O'Toole 3.00 1.20
127 Jerry Lynch 80.00 32.00
128 Wally Post 3.00 1.20
129 Ken Hunt 3.00 1.20
130 Jerry Zimmerman 3.00 1.20
131 Willie McCovey 100.00 40.00
132 Jose Pagan 3.00 1.20
133 Felipe Alou UER 4.00 1.60
(Misspelled Filipe
in text)
134 Jim Davenport 3.00 1.20
135 Harvey Kuenn 4.00 1.60
136 Orlando Cepeda 6.00 2.40
137 Ed Bailey 3.00 1.20
138 Sam Jones 3.00 1.20
139 Mike McCormick 4.00 1.60
140 Juan Marichal 125.00 50.00
141 Jack Sanford 3.00 1.20
142 Willie Mays 50.00 20.00
143 Stu Miller 6.00 2.40
144 Joe Amalfitano 25.00 10.00
145A Joe Adock (sic) ERR 80.00 32.00
145B Joe Adcock COR 5.00 2.00
146 Frank Bolling 3.00 1.20
147 Eddie Mathews 12.00 4.80
148 Roy McMillan 3.00 1.20
149 Hank Aaron 50.00 20.00
150 Gino Cimoli 3.00 1.20
151 Frank Thomas 3.00 1.20
152 Joe Torre 6.00 2.40
153 Lew Burdette 4.00 1.60
154 Bob Buhl 3.00 1.20
155 Carlton Willey 3.00 1.20
156 Lee Maye 3.00 1.20
157 Al Spangler 3.00 1.20
158 Bill White 40.00 16.00
159 Ken Boyer 6.00 2.40
160 Joe Cunningham 3.00 1.20
161 Carl Warwick 3.00 1.20
162 Carl Sawatski 3.00 1.20
163 Lindy McDaniel 3.00 1.20
164 Ernie Broglio 3.00 1.20
165 Larry Jackson 3.00 1.20
166 Curt Flood 4.00 1.60
167 Curt Simmons 4.00 1.60
168 Alex Grammas 3.00 1.20
169 Dick Stuart 5.00 2.00
170 Bill Mazeroski UER 6.00 2.40
(Bio reads 1959,
should read 1960)
171 Don Hoak 3.00 1.20
172 Dick Groat 4.00 1.60
173A Roberto Clemente 60.00 24.00
173B Roberto Clemente 250.00 100.00
With blue lines
174 Bob Skinner 3.00 1.20
175 Bill Virdon 4.00 1.60
176 Smoky Burgess 3.00 1.20
177 Roy Face 4.00 1.60
178 Bob Friend 3.00 1.20
179 Vernon Law 3.00 1.20
180 Harvey Haddix 3.00 1.20
181 Hal Smith 3.00 1.20
182 Ed Bouchee 3.00 1.20
183 Don Zimmer 3.00 1.20
184 Ron Santo 5.00 2.00
185 Andre Rodgers 3.00 1.20
186 Richie Ashburn 8.00 3.20
187 George Altman 3.00 1.20
188 Ernie Banks 15.00 6.00
189 Sam Taylor 4.00 1.60
190 Don Elston 3.00 1.20
191 Jerry Kindall 3.00 1.20
192 Pancho Herrera 4.00 1.60
193 Tony Taylor 3.00 1.20
194 Ruben Amaro 3.00 1.20
195 Don Demeter 3.00 1.20
196 Bobby Gene Smith 3.00 1.20
197 Clay Dalrymple 3.00 1.20
198 Robin Roberts 8.00 3.20
199 Art Mahaffey 4.00 1.60
200 John Buzhardt 10.00 4.00

1962 Post Canadian

The 200 blank-backed cards comprising the 1962 Post Canadian set measure approximately 2 1/2" by 3 1/2". The set is similar in appearance to the Jell-O set released in the U.S. that same year. The fronts feature a posed color player photo at the upper right. To the left of the photo, the player's name appears in blue cursive lettering, followed below by bilingual biography and career highlights. The cards are numbered on the front. The cards are grouped by team as follows: New York Yankees (1-13), Detroit (14-26), Baltimore (27-36), Cleveland (37-45), Chicago White Sox (46-55), Boston (56-64), Washington (65-73), Los Angeles Angels (74-82), Minnesota (83-91), Kansas City (92-100), Los Angeles Dodgers (101-115), Cincinnati (116-130), San Francisco (131-144), Milwaukee (145-157), St. Louis (158-168), Pittsburgh (169-181), Chicago Cubs (182-191) and Philadelphia (192-200). Maris (6) and Mays (142) are somewhat scarce. Whitey Ford is listed incorrectly with the Dodgers and correctly with the Yankees. The complete set price includes both Whitey Ford variations.

NM Ex
COMPLETE SET (201) 3000.00 1200.00
1 Bill Skowron 12.00 4.80
2 Bobby Richardson 12.00 4.80
3 Cletis Boyer 10.00 4.00
4 Tony Kubek 12.00 4.80
5 Mickey Mantle 400.00 160.00
6 Roger Maris 125.00 50.00
7 Yogi Berra 60.00 24.00
8 Elston Howard 12.00 4.80
9A Whitey Ford ERR 80.00 32.00
(Los Angeles Dodgers)
9B Whitey Ford COR 80.00 32.00
(New York Yankees)
10 Ralph Terry 8.00 3.20
11 John Blanchard 8.00 3.20
12 Luis Arroyo 6.00 2.40
13 Bill Stafford 6.00 2.40
14 Norm Cash 12.00 4.80
15 Jake Wood 6.00 2.40
16 Steve Boros 6.00 2.40
17 Chico Fernandez 6.00 2.40
18 Bill Bruton 6.00 2.40
19A Rocky Colavito 20.00 8.00
Colavito spelled in Large Letter
19B Rocky Colavito 20.00 8.00
Name is in small letter
20 Al Kaline 40.00 16.00
21 Dick Brown 6.00 2.40
22A Frank Lary 20.00 8.00
The word residence is in his vital stats
22B Frank Lary 20.00 8.00
No word residence in french vital stats
23 Don Mossi 8.00 3.20
24 Phil Regan 6.00 2.40
25 Charlie Maxwell 6.00 2.40
26 Jim Bunning 15.00 6.00
27A Jim Gentile 15.00 6.00
Partie is in third line
27B Jim Gentile 15.00 6.00
Partie in on final line of French text
28 Marv Breeding 6.00 2.40
29 Brooks Robinson 40.00 16.00
30 Ron Hansen 6.00 2.40
31 Jackie Brandt 6.00 2.40
32 Dick Williams 12.00 4.80
33 Gus Triandos 6.00 2.40
34 Milt Pappas 10.00 4.00
35 Hoyt Wilhelm 50.00 20.00
36 Chuck Estrada 6.00 2.40
37 Vic Power 6.00 2.40
38 Johnny Temple 6.00 2.40
39 Bubba Phillips 6.00 2.40
40 Tito Francona 20.00 8.00
41 Willie Kirkland 6.00 2.40
42 John Romano 6.00 2.40
43 Jim Perry 10.00 4.00
44 Woodie Held 6.00 2.40
45 Chuck Essegian 6.00 2.40
46 Roy Sievers 10.00 4.00
47 Nellie Fox 15.00 6.00
48 Al Smith 6.00 2.40
49 Luis Aparicio 50.00 20.00
50 Jim Landis 6.00 2.40
51 Minnie Minoso 12.00 4.80
52 Andy Carey 6.00 2.40
53 Sherman Lollar 6.00 2.40
54 Bill Pierce 10.00 4.00
55 Early Wynn 15.00 6.00
56 Chuck Schilling 6.00 2.40
57 Pete Runnels 8.00 3.20
58 Frank Malzone 8.00 3.20
59 Don Buddin 6.00 2.40
60 Gary Geiger 6.00 2.40
61 Carl Yastrzemski 60.00 24.00
62 Jackie Jensen 10.00 4.00
63 Jim Pagliaroni 6.00 2.40
64 Don Schwall 20.00 8.00
65 Dale Long 6.00 2.40
66 Chuck Cottier 6.00 2.40
67 Billy Klaus 6.00 2.40
68 Coot Veal 6.00 2.40
69 Marty Keough 6.00 2.40
70 Willie Tasby 6.00 2.40
71 Gene Woodling 8.00 3.20
72 Gene Green 6.00 2.40
73 Dick Donovan 6.00 2.40
74 Steve Bilko 6.00 2.40
75 Rocky Bridges 6.00 2.40
76 Eddie Yost 6.00 2.40
77 Leon Wagner 20.00 8.00
78 Albie Pearson 6.00 2.40
79 Ken L. Hunt 6.00 2.40
80 Earl Averill 6.00 2.40
81 Ryne Duren 8.00 3.20
82 Ted Kluszewski 12.00 4.80
83 Bob Allison 6.00 2.40
84 Billy Martin 12.00 4.80
85 Harmon Killebrew 30.00 12.00
86 Zoilo Versalles 10.00 4.00
87 Lenny Green 20.00 8.00
88 Bill Tuttle 6.00 2.40
89 Jim Lemon 6.00 2.40
90 Earl Battey 6.00 2.40
91 Camilo Pascual 8.00 3.20
92 Norm Siebern 6.00 2.40
93 Jerry Lumpe 6.00 2.40
94 Dick Howser 8.00 3.20
95 Gene Stephens 6.00 2.40
96 Leo Posada 6.00 2.40
97 Joe Pignatano 6.00 2.40
98 Jim Archer 6.00 2.40
99 Haywood Sullivan 6.00 2.40
100 Art Ditmar 6.00 2.40
101 Gil Hodges 30.00 12.00
102 Charlie Neal 6.00 2.40
103 Daryl Spencer 6.00 2.40
104 Maury Wills 15.00 6.00
105 Tommy Davis 25.00 10.00
106 Willie Davis 8.00 3.20
107 John Roseboro 8.00 3.20
108 John Podres 10.00 4.00
109 Sandy Koufax 60.00 24.00
110 Don Drysdale 30.00 12.00
111 Larry Sherry 8.00 3.20
112 Jim Gilliam 25.00 10.00
113 Norm Larker 6.00 2.40
114 Duke Snider 40.00 16.00
115 Stan Williams 6.00 2.40
116 Gordy Coleman 6.00 2.40
117 Don Blasingame 20.00 8.00
118 Gene Freese 6.00 2.40
119 Ed Kasko 6.00 2.40
120 Gus Bell 6.00 2.40
121 Vada Pinson 10.00 4.00
122 Frank Robinson 30.00 12.00
123 Bob Purkey 20.00 8.00
124 Joey Jay 6.00 2.40
125 Jim Brosnan 8.00 3.20
126 Jim O'Toole 6.00 2.40
127 Jerry Lynch 6.00 2.40
128 Wally Post 8.00 3.20
129 Ken R. Hunt 6.00 2.40
130 Jerry Zimmerman 8.00 3.20
131 Willie McCovey 30.00 12.00
132 Jose Pagan 6.00 2.40
133 Felipe Alou 12.00 4.80
134 Jim Davenport 6.00 2.40
135 Harvey Kuenn 8.00 3.20
136 Orlando Cepeda 20.00 8.00
137 Ed Bailey 20.00 8.00
138 Sam Jones 6.00 2.40
139 Mike McCormick 6.00 2.40
140 Juan Marichal 30.00 12.00
141 Jack Sanford 6.00 2.40
142 Willie Mays 100.00 40.00
143 Stu Miller 6.00 2.40
144 Joe Amalfitano 40.00 16.00
145 Joe Adcock 8.00 3.20
146 Frank Bolling 6.00 2.40
147 Eddie Mathews 25.00 10.00
148 Roy McMillan 6.00 2.40
149 Hank Aaron 100.00 40.00
150 Gino Cimoli 6.00 2.40
151 Frank Thomas 8.00 3.20
152 Joe Torre 20.00 8.00
153 Lew Burdette 10.00 4.00
154 Bob Buhl 6.00 2.40
155 Carlton Willey 6.00 2.40
156 Lee Maye 6.00 2.40
157 Al Spangler 6.00 2.40
158 Bill White 10.00 4.00
159 Ken Boyer 12.00 4.80
160 Joe Cunningham 8.00 3.20
161 Carl Warwick 20.00 8.00
162 Carl Sawatski 6.00 2.40
163 Lindy McDaniel 6.00 2.40
164 Ernie Broglio 6.00 2.40
165 Larry Jackson 6.00 2.40
166 Curt Flood 10.00 4.00
167 Curt Simmons 6.00 2.40
168 Alex Grammas 6.00 2.40
169 Dick Stuart 6.00 2.40
170 Bill Mazeroski 15.00 6.00
171 Don Hoak 6.00 2.40
172 Dick Groat 10.00 4.00
173 Roberto Clemente 150.00 60.00
174 Bob Skinner 6.00 2.40
175 Bill Virdon 6.00 2.40
176 Smoky Burgess 20.00 8.00
177 Roy Face 10.00 4.00
178 Bob Friend 6.00 2.40
179 Vernon Law 8.00 3.20
180 Harvey Haddix 6.00 2.40
181 Hal Smith 6.00 2.40
182 Ed Bouchee 20.00 8.00
183 Don Zimmer 8.00 3.20
184 Ron Santo 15.00 6.00
185 Andre Rodgers 6.00 2.40
186 Richie Ashburn 15.00 6.00
187 George Altman 6.00 2.40
188 Ernie Banks 40.00 16.00
189 Sam Taylor 6.00 2.40
190 Don Elston 6.00 2.40
191 Jerry Kindall 6.00 2.40
192 Pancho Herrera 6.00 2.40
193 Tony Taylor 8.00 3.20
194 Ruben Amaro 6.00 2.40
195 Don Demeter 6.00 2.40
196 Bobby Gene Smith 6.00 2.40
197 Clay Dalrymple 6.00 2.40

198 Robin Roberts 25.00 10.00
199 Art Mahaffey 6.00 2.40
200 John Buzhardt 6.00 2.40

1963 Post

The cards in this 200-card set measure 2 1/2" by 3 1/2". The players are grouped by team with American Leaguers comprising 1-100 and National Leaguers 101-200. The ordering of teams is as follows: Minnesota (1-11), New York Yankees, Los Angeles Angels (24-34), Chicago White Sox (35-45), Detroit (46-56), Baltimore (57-66), Cleveland (67-76), Boston (77-84), Kansas City (85-92), Washington (93-100), San Francisco (101-112), Los Angeles Dodgers (113-124), Cincinnati (125-136), Pittsburgh (137-147), Milwaukee (148-157), St. Louis (158-168), Chicago Cubs (169-176), Philadelphia (177-184), Houston (185-192), and New York Mets (193-200). In contrast to the 1962 issue, the 1963 Post baseball card series is very difficult to complete. There are many card scarcities reflected in the price list below. Cards of the Post set are easily confused with those of the 1963 Jello set, which are 1/4" narrower (a difference which is often eliminated by bad cutting). The catalog designation is F278-38. There was also an album produced by Post to hold the cards. The album could only hold 120 cards.

NM Ex
COMP. MASTER SET (206) 4250.00 1700.00
1 Vic Power 6.00 2.40
2 Bernie Allen 3.50 1.40
3 Zoilo Versalles 3.50 1.40
4 Rich Rollins 3.50 1.40
5 Harmon Killebrew 20.00 8.00
6 Lenny Green 50.00 20.00
7 Bob Allison 5.00 2.00
8 Earl Battey 5.00 2.00
9 Camilo Pascual 3.50 1.40
10 Jim Kaat 6.00 2.40
11 Jack Kralick 3.50 1.40
12 Bill Skowron 6.00 2.40
13 Bobby Richardson 10.00 4.00
14 Cletis Boyer 3.50 1.40
15 Mickey Mantle 350.00 140.00
16 Roger Maris 200.00 80.00
17 Yogi Berra ERR 25.00 10.00
Living in Monclair, N.Y.
18 Elston Howard 6.00 2.40
19 Whitey Ford 15.00 6.00
20 Ralph Terry 3.50 1.40
21 John Blanchard 5.00 2.00
22 Bill Stafford 3.50 1.40
23 Tom Tresh 3.50 1.40
24 Steve Bilko 5.00 2.00
25 Bill Moran 3.50 1.40
26A Joe Koppe 5.00 2.00
(BA: .277)
26B Joe Koppe 20.00 8.00
(BA: .227)
27 Felix Torres 3.50 1.40
28A Leon Wagner 3.50 1.40
(BA: .278)
28B Leon Wagner 20.00 8.00
(BA: .272)
29 Albie Pearson 3.50 1.40
30 Lee Thomas UER 120.00 47.50
(Photo actually George Thomas)
31 Bob Rodgers 3.50 1.40
32 Dean Chance 3.50 1.40
33 Ken McBride 3.50 1.40
34 George Thomas UER 3.50 1.40
(Photo actually Lee Thomas)
35 Joe Cunningham 3.50 1.40
36 Nellie Fox 10.00 4.00
37 Luis Aparicio 8.00 3.20
38 Al Smith 50.00 20.00
39 Floyd Robinson 125.00 50.00
40 Jim Landis 3.50 1.40
41 Charlie Maxwell 3.50 1.40
42 Sherman Lollar 3.50 1.40
43 Early Wynn 8.00 3.20
44 Juan Pizarro 3.50 1.40
45 Ray Herbert 5.00 2.00
46 Norm Cash 5.00 2.00
47 Steve Boros 3.50 1.40
48 Dick McAuliffe 25.00 10.00
49 Bill Bruton 5.00 2.00
50 Rocky Colavito 6.00 2.40
51 Al Kaline 25.00 10.00
52 Dick Brown 3.50 1.40
53 Jim Bunning 200.00 80.00
54 Hank Aguirre 3.50 1.40
55 Frank Lary 3.50 1.40
56 Don Mossi 3.50 1.40
57 Jim Gentile 3.50 1.40
58 Jackie Brandt 3.50 1.40
59 Brooks Robinson 25.00 10.00
60 Ron Hansen 5.00 2.00
61 Jerry Adair 200.00 80.00
62 Boog Powell 6.00 2.40
63 Russ Snyder 3.50 1.40
64 Steve Barber 3.50 1.40
65 Milt Pappas 3.50 1.40
66 Robin Roberts 8.00 3.20
67 Tito Francona 3.50 1.40
68 Jerry Kindall 3.50 1.40
69 Woody Held 3.50 1.40
70 Bubba Phillips 15.00 6.00
71 Chuck Essegian 3.50 1.40
72 Willie Kirkland 3.50 1.40
73 Al Luplow 3.50 1.40
74 Ty Cline 3.50 1.40
75 Dick Donovan 3.50 1.40
76 John Romano 3.50 1.40
77 Pete Runnels 3.50 1.40
78 Ed Bressoud 3.50 1.40
79 Frank Malzone 3.50 1.40
80 Carl Yastrzemski 300.00 120.00
81 Gary Geiger 3.50 1.40
82 Lou Clinton 3.50 1.40
83 Earl Wilson 3.50 1.40
84 Bill Monbouquette 3.50 1.40
85 Norm Siebern 3.50 1.40
86 Jerry Lumpe 125.00 50.00
87 Manny Jimenez 125.00 50.00
88 Gino Cimoli 3.50 1.40
89 Ed Charles 3.50 1.40
90 Ed Rakow 3.50 1.40
91 Bob Del Greco 3.50 1.40
92 Haywood Sullivan 3.50 1.40
93 Chuck Hinton 3.50 1.40
94 Ken Retzer 3.50 1.40
95 Harry Bright 3.50 1.40
96 Bob Johnson 3.50 1.40
97 Dave Stenhouse 15.00 6.00
98 Chuck Cottier 25.00 10.00
99 Tom Cheney 3.50 1.40
100 Claude Osteen 15.00 6.00
101 Orlando Cepeda 8.00 3.20
102 Chuck Hiller 3.50 1.40
103 Jose Pagan 3.50 1.40
104 Jim Davenport 3.50 1.40
105 Harvey Kuenn 5.00 2.00
106 Willie Mays 50.00 20.00
107 Felipe Alou 5.00 2.00
108 Tom Haller 125.00 50.00
109 Juan Marichal 10.00 4.00
110 Jack Sanford 3.50 1.40
111 Bill O'Dell 3.50 1.40
112 Willie McCovey 10.00 4.00
113 Lee Walls 3.50 1.40
114 Jim Gilliam 6.00 2.40
115 Maury Wills 6.00 2.40
116 Ron Fairly 5.00 2.00
117 Tommy Davis 5.00 2.00
118 Duke Snider 10.00 4.00
119 Willie Davis 200.00 80.00
120 John Roseboro 3.50 1.40
121 Sandy Koufax 50.00 20.00
122 Stan Williams 3.50 1.40
123 Don Drysdale 10.00 4.00
124 Daryl Spencer 3.50 1.40
125 Gordy Coleman 3.50 1.40
126 Don Blasingame 3.50 1.40
127 Leo Cardenas 3.50 1.40
128 Eddie Kasko 200.00 80.00
129 Jerry Lynch 15.00 6.00
130 Vada Pinson 6.00 2.40
131A Frank Robinson 25.00 10.00
(No stripes)
131B Frank Robinson 50.00 20.00
(Stripes on hat)
132 John Edwards 5.00 2.00
133 Joey Jay 3.50 1.40
134 Bob Purkey 3.50 1.40
135 Marty Keough 30.00 12.00
136 Jim O'Toole 3.50 1.40
137 Dick Stuart 3.50 1.40
138 Bill Mazeroski 10.00 4.00
139 Dick Groat 5.00 2.00
140 Don Hoak 40.00 16.00
141 Bob Skinner 20.00 8.00
142 Bill Virdon 5.00 2.00
143 Roberto Clemente 100.00 40.00
144 Smoky Burgess 5.00 2.00
145 Bob Friend 3.50 1.40
146 Al McBean 3.50 1.40
147 Roy Face 5.00 2.00
148 Joe Adcock 5.00 2.00
149 Frank Bolling 3.50 1.40
150 Roy McMillan 3.50 1.40
151 Eddie Mathews 20.00 8.00
152 Hank Aaron 150.00 60.00
153 Del Crandall 40.00 16.00
154A Bob Shaw COR 3.50 1.40
154B Bob Shaw ERR 15.00 6.00
(Two "in 1959" in same sentence)
155 Lew Burdette 6.00 2.40
156 Joe Torre 6.00 2.40
157 Tony Cloninger 3.50 1.40
158A Bill White 5.00 2.00
(Ht. 6'0")
158B Bill White 5.00 2.00
(Ht. 6';)
159 Julian Javier 3.50 1.40
160 Ken Boyer 8.00 3.20
161 Julio Gotay 3.50 1.40
162 Curt Flood 125.00 50.00
163 Charlie James 3.50 1.40
164 Gene Oliver 3.50 1.40
165 Ernie Broglio 3.50 1.40
166 Bob Gibson 10.00 4.00
167A Lindy McDaniel 8.00 3.20
(No asterisk)
167B Lindy McDaniel 8.00 3.20
(Asterisk traded line)
168 Ray Washburn 3.50 1.40
169 Ernie Banks 20.00 8.00
170 Ron Santo 6.00 2.40
171 George Altman 3.50 1.40
172 Billy Williams 175.00 70.00
173 Andre Rodgers 15.00 6.00
174 Ken Hubbs 30.00 12.00
175 Don Landrum 3.50 1.40
176 Dick Bertell 20.00 8.00
177 Roy Sievers 3.50 1.40
178 Tony Taylor 5.00 2.00
179 John Callison 3.50 1.40
180 Don Demeter 5.00 2.00
181 Tony Gonzalez 15.00 6.00
182 Wes Covington 25.00 10.00
183 Art Mahaffey 3.50 1.40
184 Clay Dalrymple 3.50 1.40
185 Al Spangler 3.50 1.40
186 Roman Mejias 3.50 1.40
187 Bob Aspromonte 400.00 160.00
188 Norm Larker 40.00 16.00
189 Johnny Temple 3.50 1.40
190 Carl Warwick 3.50 1.40
191 Bob Lillis 3.50 1.40
192 Dick Farrell 3.50 1.40
193 Gil Hodges 10.00 4.00
194 Marv Throneberry 5.00 2.00
195 Charlie Neal 10.00 4.00
196 Frank Thomas 225.00 90.00
197 Richie Ashburn 30.00 12.00
198 Felix Mantilla 3.50 1.40
199 Rod Kanehl 20.00 8.00
200 Roger Craig 5.00 2.00
XX Album

1979 Post Garvey Tips

These "Baseball Tips" were printed on boxes of Post Raisin Bran cereal in 1979. Cards 1-6 were on 15 oz. boxes and cards 7-12 were on the larger 20 oz. boxes. The cards are blank backed and feature a lime green background color with a red stitching border around the card. The cards measure approximately 7" by 2 1/16" although as with most cereal cards they are frequently found badly cut. The set essentially consists of Steve Garvey's advice or tips on various segments and aspects of the game of baseball. Each card shows a crude line drawing demonstrating the skill discussed in the narrative on the card. Each card contains a color drawing of Steve Garvey in the upper left corner of the card along with his facsimile autograph.

NM Ex
COMPLETE SET (12) 15.00 6.00
COMMON CARD (1-6) 1.50 .60
COMMON CARD (7-12) 2.00 .80

1990 Post

1990 Post Cereal is a 30-card standard-size set issued with the assistance of Mike Schechter Associates. The sets do not have either team logos or other uniform identification on them. There is also a facsimile autograph on the back of the cards. The cards were inserted randomly as a cello pack (with three cards) inside specially marked boxes of Post cereals. The cards feature red, white, and blue fronts with the words, "First Collector Series". Card backs feature a facsimile autograph.

Nm-Mt Ex-Mt
COMPLETE SET (30) 10.00 3.00
1 Don Mattingly 1.25 .35
2 Roger Clemens 1.25 .35
3 Kirby Puckett .50 .15
4 George Brett 1.00 .30
5 Tony Gwynn 1.25 .35
6 Ozzie Smith .75 .23
7 Will Clark .30 .09
8 Orel Hershiser .10 .03
9 Ryne Sandberg .75 .23
10 Darryl Strawberry .10 .03
11 Nolan Ryan 2.50 .75
12 Mark McGwire 2.00 .60
13 Jim Abbott .20 .06
14 Bo Jackson .30 .09
15 Kevin Mitchell .05 .02
16 Jose Canseco .40 .12
17 Wade Boggs .50 .15
18 Dale Murphy .30 .09
19 Mark Grace .30 .09
20 Mike Scott .05 .02
21 Cal Ripken 2.50 .75
22 Pedro Guerrero .05 .02
23 Ken Griffey Jr. 1.50 .45
24 Eric Davis .10 .03
25 Rickey Henderson .75 .23
26 Robin Yount .40 .12
27 Von Hayes .05 .02
28 Alan Trammell .30 .09
29 Dwight Gooden .10 .03
30 Joe Carter .10 .03

1991 Post

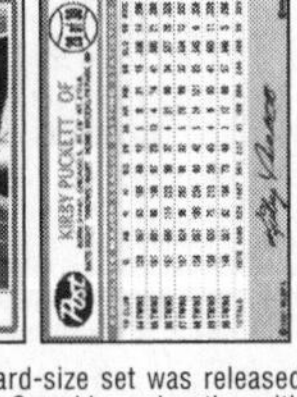

This 30-card standard-size set was released early in 1991 by Post Cereal in conjunction with Michael Schechter Associates (MSA). The players pictured are some of the star players of baseball entering the 1991 season. The cards were inserted three-at-a-time in boxes of the following cereals: Post Honeycomb, Super Golden Crisp, Cocoa Pebbles, Fruity Pebbles, Alpha-Bits, and Marshmallow Alpha-Bits. Some cards (numbers 1, 6, 25, and 30) have a banner at the top that reads "Rookie Star".

Nm-Mt Ex-Mt
COMPLETE SET (30) 8.00 2.40
1 Dave Justice .30 .09
2 Mark McGwire 2.00 .60
3 Will Clark .30 .09
4 Jose Canseco .40 .12
5 Vince Coleman .05 .02
6 Sandy Alomar Jr. .10 .03
7 Darryl Strawberry .10 .03
8 Len Dykstra .10 .03
9 Gregg Jefferies .05 .02
10 Tony Gwynn 1.25 .35
11 Ken Griffey Jr. 1.50 .45
12 Roger Clemens 1.25 .35
13 Chris Sabo .05 .02
14 Bobby Bonilla .05 .02
15 Gary Sheffield .40 .12
16 Ryne Sandberg .75 .23
17 Nolan Ryan 2.50 .75
18 Barry Larkin .30 .09
19 Cal Ripken 2.50 .75
20 Jim Abbott .10 .03
21 Barry Bonds 1.25 .35
22 Mark Grace .30 .09
23 Cecil Fielder .10 .03
24 Kevin Mitchell .05 .02
25 Todd Zeile .10 .03
26 George Brett 1.25 .35
27 Rickey Henderson .50 .15
28 Kirby Puckett .50 .15
29 Don Mattingly 1.25 .35
30 Kevin Maas .05 .02

1991 Post Canadian

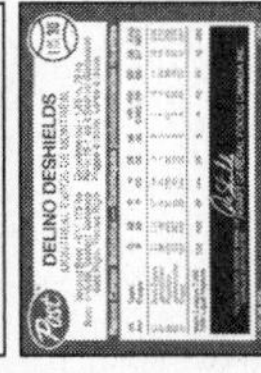

This 30-card Super Stars set was sponsored by Post and features 14 National League and 16 American League players. Two cards were inserted in specially marked boxes of Post Alpha-Bits, Sugar Crisp and Honeycomb sold in Canada. The cards measure the standard size and are bilingual (French and English) on both sides. While all the cards feature color player photos (action or posed) on the fronts, the NL cards (1-14) are accentuated with red stripes while the AL cards (15-30) have royal blue stripes.

Nm-Mt Ex-Mt
COMPLETE SET (30) 15.00 4.50
1 Delino DeShields .20 .06
2 Tim Wallach .10 .03
3 Andres Galarraga .40 .12
4 Dave Magadan .10 .03
5 Barry Bonds UER 1.50 .45
(Career BA .256, should be .265)
6 Len Dykstra .20 .06
7 Andre Dawson .40 .12
8 Ozzie Smith 1.00 .30
9 Will Clark .40 .12
10 Chris Sabo .10 .03
11 Eddie Murray .50 .15
12 Dave Justice .40 .12
13 Benito Santiago .20 .06
14 Glenn Davis .10 .03
15 Kelly Gruber .10 .03
16 Dave Stieb .20 .06
17 John Olerud .20 .06
18 Roger Clemens 1.50 .45
19 Cecil Fielder .20 .06
20 Kevin Maas .10 .03
21 Robin Yount .50 .15
22 Cal Ripken 3.00 .90
23 Sandy Alomar Jr. .20 .06
24 Rickey Henderson .75 .23
25 Bobby Thigpen .10 .03
26 Ken Griffey Jr. 2.00 .60
27 Nolan Ryan 3.00 .90
28 Dave Winfield .50 .15
29 George Brett 1.25 .35
30 Kirby Puckett .50 .15

1992 Post

This 30-card standard-size set was manufactured by MSA (Michael Schechter Associates) for Post Cereal. Three-card packs were inserted in the following Post cereals: Honeycomb, Super Golden Crisp, Cocoa Pebbles, Fruity Pebbles, Alpha-Bits, Marshmallow Alpha-Bits and, for the first time, Raisin Bran. In the last-mentioned cereal, the cards were protected in cello packs that also had a 50 cent manufacturers coupon good on the next purchase. The other cereals contained tan paper wrapped packs. The complete set could also be obtained via a mail-in offer for 1.00 and five UPC symbols. The Bagwell and Knoblauch cards display the words "Rookie Star" in a yellow banner at the card top.

Nm-Mt Ex-Mt
COMPLETE SET (30) 6.00 1.80
1 Jeff Bagwell .50 .15
2 Ryne Sandberg .60 .18
3 Don Mattingly 1.00 .30
4 Wally Joyner .10 .03
5 Dwight Gooden .10 .03
6 Chuck Knoblauch .20 .06
7 Kirby Puckett .40 .12
8 Ozzie Smith .60 .18
9 Cal Ripken 2.00 .60
10 Darryl Strawberry .10 .03
11 George Brett .75 .23
12 Joe Carter .10 .03
13 Cecil Fielder .10 .03
14 Will Clark .20 .06
15 Barry Bonds 1.00 .30
16 Roger Clemens 1.00 .30
17 Paul Molitor .40 .12
18 Scott Erickson .10 .03
19 Wade Boggs .60 .18
20 Ken Griffey Jr. 1.25 .35
21 Bobby Bonilla .05 .02
22 Terry Pendleton .05 .02
23 Barry Larkin .20 .06
24 Frank Thomas .50 .15
25 Jose Canseco .30 .09
26 Tony Gwynn 1.00 .30
27 Nolan Ryan 2.00 .60
28 Howard Johnson .05 .02
29 Dave Justice .20 .06
30 Danny Tartabull .05 .02

1992 Post Canadian

This 18-card Post Super Star II stand-up set was sponsored by Post and measures the standard size. The set features nine American League and nine National League players and is bilingual (French and English) on both sides. The NL cards (1-9) are accented with a red stripe at the top and bottom of the photo and the AL cards (10-18) are accented with blue stripes.

Nm-Mt Ex-Mt
COMPLETE SET (18) 15.00 4.50
1 Dennis Martinez .40 .12
2 Benito Santiago .40 .12
3 Will Clark 1.00 .30
4 Ryne Sandberg 1.50 .45
5 Tim Wallach .20 .06
6 Ozzie Smith 1.50 .45
7 Darryl Strawberry .40 .12
8 Brett Butler .40 .12
9 Barry Bonds 2.00 .60
10 Roger Clemens 2.00 .60
11 Sandy Alomar Jr. .40 .12
12 Cecil Fielder .40 .12
13 Roberto Alomar .75 .23
14 Kelly Gruber .20 .06
15 Cal Ripken 4.00 1.20
16 Jose Canseco 1.00 .30
17 Kirby Puckett 1.00 .30
18 Rickey Henderson 1.25 .35

1993 Post

This 30-card standard-size set features full-bleed action color player photos. Three-packs of cards were found in specially marked boxes of Post Cereal during this promotion. In addition, complete sets were available as a mail-in for five proofs of purchase from any Post Cereal plus 1.00.

Nm-Mt Ex-Mt
COMPLETE SET (30) 6.00 1.80
1 Dave Fleming .05 .02
2 Will Clark .30 .09
3 Kirby Puckett .40 .12
4 Roger Clemens 1.00 .30
5 Fred McGriff .20 .06
6 Eric Karros .20 .06
7 Ken Griffey Jr. 1.25 .35
8 Tony Gwynn .75 .23
9 Cal Ripken 2.00 .60
10 Cecil Fielder .10 .03
11 Gary Sheffield .40 .12
12 Don Mattingly 1.00 .30
13 Ryne Sandberg .75 .23
14 Frank Thomas .50 .15
15 Barry Bonds 1.00 .30
16 Paul Molitor .40 .12
17 Terry Pendleton .05 .02
18 Darren Daulton .10 .03
19 Mark McGwire 1.50 .45
20 Nolan Ryan 2.00 .60
21 Tom Glavine .40 .12
22 Roberto Alomar .30 .09
23 Juan Gonzalez .50 .15
24 Bobby Bonilla .05 .02
25 George Brett .75 .23
26 Ozzie Smith .75 .23
27 Andy Van Slyke .10 .03
28 Barry Larkin .30 .09
29 John Kruk .10 .03
30 Robin Yount .40 .12

1993 Post Canadian

This 18-card limited edition stand-up set was sponsored by Post and measures the standard size. The set features American League (1-9) and National League (10-18) players and is printed in French and English. The cards are numbered on the front.

Nm-Mt Ex-Mt
COMPLETE SET (18) 20.00 6.00
1 Pat Borders .25 .07
2 Juan Guzman .25 .07

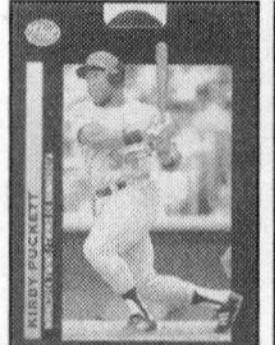

3 Roger Clemens	2.50	.75
4 Joe Carter	.50	.15
5 Roberto Alomar	1.00	.30
6 Robin Yount	1.25	.35
7 Cal Ripken	5.00	1.50
8 Kirby Puckett	1.25	.35
9 Ken Griffey Jr.	3.00	.90
10 Darren Daulton	.50	.15
11 Andy Van Slyke	.50	.15
12 Bobby Bonilla	.25	.07
13 Larry Walker	.50	.15
14 Ryne Sandberg	1.50	.45
15 Barry Larkin	1.00	.30
16 Gary Sheffield	1.25	.35
17 Ozzie Smith	1.25	.35
18 Terry Pendleton	.25	.07

1994 Post

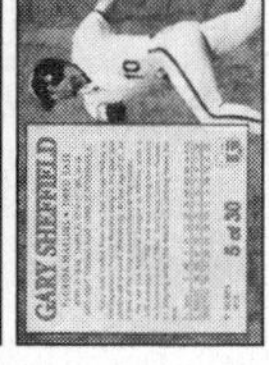

This 30-card standard-size set was sponsored by Post and produced by MSA (Michael Schlechter Associates). The cards are numbered on the back "X of 30."

	Nm-Mt	Ex-Mt
COMPLETE SET (30)	5.00	1.50
1 Mike Piazza	1.25	.35
2 Don Mattingly	1.00	.30
3 Juan Gonzalez	.25	.07
4 Kirby Puckett	.30	.09
5 Gary Sheffield	.40	.12
6 Dave Justice	.25	.07
7 Jack McDowell	.05	.02
8 Mo Vaughn	.10	.03
9 Darren Daulton	.10	.03
10 Bobby Bonilla	.05	.02
11 Barry Bonds	1.00	.30
12 Barry Larkin	.25	.07
13 Tony Gwynn	1.00	.30
14 Mark Grace	.15	.04
15 Ken Griffey Jr.	1.25	.35
16 Tom Glavine	.30	.09
17 Cecil Fielder	.10	.03
18 Roberto Alomar	.10	.03
19 Mark Whiten	.05	.02
20 Lenny Dykstra	.10	.03
21 Frank Thomas	.50	.15
22 Will Clark	.25	.07
23 Andres Galarraga	.25	.07
24 John Olerud	.10	.03
25 Cal Ripken	2.00	.60
26 Tim Salmon	.25	.07
27 Albert Belle	.10	.03
28 Gregg Jefferies	.05	.02
29 Jeff Bagwell	.75	.23
30 Orlando Merced	.05	.02

1994 Post Canadian

This 18-card set was distributed as single cello-wrapped cards in Canadian Post Alpha-Bits, Honeycomb, Sugar-Crisp, and Marshmallow Alpha-Bits. The cards are slightly smaller than standard-size, measuring 2 1/2" by 3 3/8". Randomly inserted throughout the boxes were Joe Carter HERO cards; 1,000 of these were personally signed. Odds of finding a HERO card were about 1 in 16; odds for finding a signed HERO card were 1 in 3,000. The entire set was available through a mail-in offer for 7 UPC's and $3.49 for postage and handling. An album to display the cards was offered for 2 UPC's and $5.99, plus $4.50 for postage and handling. The cards are numbered on the back as "X of 18." It is believed that only Joe Carter comes in a gold version.

	Nm-Mt	Ex-Mt
COMPLETE SET (18)	20.00	6.00
1 Joe Carter	.50	.15
1G Joe Carter Gold	5.00	1.50
2 Paul Molitor	1.25	.35
3 Roberto Alomar	1.00	.30
4 John Olerud	.50	.15
5 Dave Stewart	.25	.07
6 Juan Guzman	.25	.07
7 Pat Borders	.25	.07
8 Larry Walker	.50	.15
9 Moises Alou	.50	.15
10 Ken Griffey Jr.	3.00	.90
11 Barry Bonds	2.50	.75
12 Frank Thomas	1.25	.35
13 Cal Ripken	5.00	1.50
14 Mike Piazza	4.00	1.20
15 Juan Gonzalez	1.50	.45
16 Len Dykstra	.50	.15
17 David Justice	.75	.23
18 Kirby Puckett	1.25	.35
NNO Joe Carter AU Hero Card	20.00	6.00

1995 Post

This 16-card standard-size set was distributed solely in limited in-store promotions. Unlike previous years, the cards were not available in cereal boxes nor directly from the company.

	Nm-Mt	Ex-Mt
COMPLETE SET (16)	10.00	3.00
1 Wade Boggs	.75	.23
2 Jeff Bagwell	.50	.15
3 Greg Maddux	2.00	.60
4 Ken Griffey Jr.	2.00	.60
5 Roberto Alomar	.40	.12
6 Kirby Puckett	.60	.18
7 Tony Gwynn	1.50	.45
8 Cal Ripken Jr.	3.00	.90
9 Matt Williams	.30	.09
10 David Justice	.40	.12
11 Barry Bonds	1.50	.45
12 Mike Piazza	2.00	.60
13 Albert Belle	.20	.06
14 Frank Thomas	.75	.23
15 Len Dykstra	.10	.03
16 Will Clark	.40	.12

1995 Post Canadian

This 18-card standard-size set was produced by Upper Deck and issued one per box and was also available via mail-order from the company. The cards carry both English and French printing and were designed to fit into a marblized design black book with the words "1995 Anniversary Edition" printed in gold foil in English and French on the front.

	Nm-Mt	Ex-Mt
COMPLETE SET (18)	30.00	9.00
1 Ken Griffey Jr.	6.00	1.80
2 Roberto Alomar	2.50	.75
3 Paul Molitor	3.00	.90
4 Devon White	1.00	.30
5 Moises Alou	1.50	.45
6 Ken Hill	1.00	.30
7 Paul O'Neill	1.50	.45
8 Joe Carter	1.50	.45
9 Kirby Puckett	3.00	.90
10 Jimmy Key	1.50	.45
11 Frank Thomas	3.00	.90
12 David Cone	2.00	.60
13 Tony Gwynn	5.00	1.50
14 Matt Williams	2.00	.60
15 Greg Maddux	6.00	1.80
16 Jeff Bagwell	3.00	.90
17 Barry Bonds	5.00	1.50
18 Cal Ripken Jr.	10.00	3.00
XX Album	5.00	1.50

2001 Post

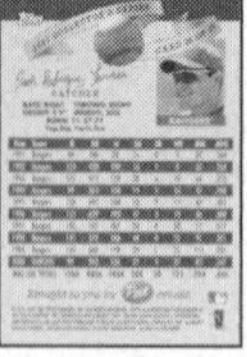

This 18-card set was issued in Post cereal products from April through June 2001. The set features many modern-day superstars. Card backs state "Brought to you by Post Cereal", while the card fronts have the "Topps 50 Years emblem in the top left-hand.

	Nm-Mt	Ex-Mt
COMPLETE SET (18)	25.00	7.50
1 Alex Rodriguez	2.50	.75
2 Barry Bonds	2.50	.75
3 Bernie Williams	1.00	.30
4 Frank Thomas	1.25	.35
5 Greg Maddux	3.00	.90
6 Mark McGwire	3.00	.90
7 Manny Ramirez	1.00	.30
8 Orlando Hernandez	.25	.07
9 Pedro Martinez	1.25	.35
10 Gary Sheffield	1.25	.35
11 Jermaine Dye	.25	.07
12 Mike Piazza	3.00	.90
13 Barry Larkin	1.00	.30
14 Brad Radke	.25	.07
15 Ivan Rodriguez	1.25	.35
16 Moises Alou	.50	.15
17 Tony Gwynn	2.50	.75
18 Todd Helton	1.50	.45

2001 Post 500 Club

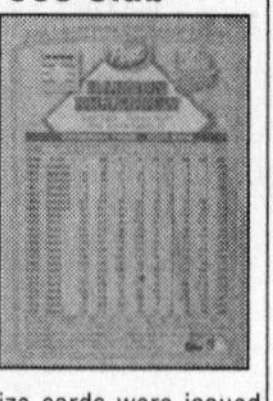

These eight standard-size cards were issued two to a Post cereal box. The collector could see the front of one of these cards through the front of the cereal box. These cards were produced by Topps and have the Topps Logo, the Hall of Fame Logo and a "500 Home Run Club" logo.

	Nm-Mt	Ex-Mt
COMPLETE SET (8)	8.00	2.40
1 Babe Ruth	3.00	.90
2 Ernie Banks	1.00	.30
3 Jimmie Foxx	1.50	.45
4 Willie McCovey	.75	.23
5 Frank Robinson	1.00	.30
6 Harmon Killebrew	.75	.23
7 Mike Schmidt	1.50	.45
8 Reggie Jackson	1.50	.45

2002 Post

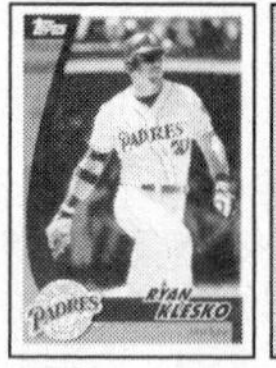

In conjunction with Post Cereal, Topps created a special 30-card baseball set for the 2002 MLB season. Each specially marked box of Post Brand Cereals featured two exclusively designed Topps baseball trading cards. The standard-sized cards have a white border set around a color action photo of the featured player. The player's name is in the lower right-hand corner with his team logo in the lower left-hand corner. The backs offer the featured player's MLB stats as well as his personal stats.

	Nm-Mt	Ex-Mt
COMPLETE SET (30)	30.00	9.00
1 Alex Rodriguez	3.00	.90
2 Pedro Martinez	1.25	.35
3 Bernie Williams	1.25	.35
4 Mike Piazza	4.00	1.20
5 Jim Edmonds	.75	.23
6 Rich Aurilia	.50	.15
7 Sammy Sosa	3.00	.90
8 Sean Casey	.75	.23
9 Ichiro Suzuki	5.00	1.50
10 Jason Giambi	1.25	.35
11 Todd Helton	1.25	.35
12 Chipper Jones	1.50	.45
13 Frank Thomas	1.50	.45
14 Scott Rolen	1.25	.35
15 Carlos Delgado	1.25	.35
16 Jeff Bagwell	1.50	.45
17 Jim Thome	1.25	.35
18 Shawn Green	1.25	.35
19 Luis Gonzalez	1.25	.35
20 Vladimir Guerrero	1.50	.45
21 Troy Glaus	1.25	.35
22 Ryan Klesko	.75	.23
23 Jeromy Burnitz	.75	.23
24 Bobby Higginson	.50	.15
25 Jason Kendall	.75	.23
26 Cliff Floyd	.75	.23
27 Greg Vaughn	.75	.23
28 Brad Radke	.50	.15
29 Mike Sweeney	.75	.23
30 Jeff Conine	.50	.15

2003 Post

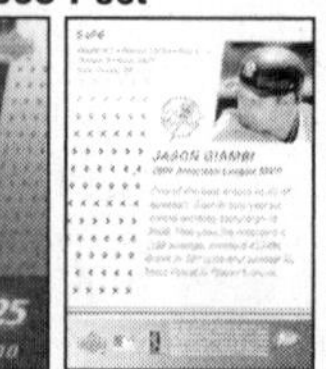

This six-card set was produced by Upper Deck for Post Cereal. These cards feature a 3D photo of the featured player along with the player's name, team affiliation and which league he won the MVP in. The back has biographical information as well as a brief blurb.

	MINT	NRMT
COMPLETE SET (6)	12.00	5.50
1 Barry Bonds	2.00	.90
2 Miguel Tejada	1.50	.70
3 Ichiro Suzuki	4.00	1.80
4 Ken Griffey Jr	2.00	.90
5 Jason Giambi	1.50	.70
6 Sammy Sosa	1.50	.70

1997 Premier Concepts

This 30-card set produced and distributed by Premier Concepts, Inc. features color action player photos on lenticular cards with a thin white inner border and black outer border with gold foil lettering. When held, these motion cards show the player swinging the bat with a twist of the wrist. The cards measure approximately 7 1/8" by 6 1/4". The backs carry

a checklist of the set. Only 5,000 numbered editions of each framed motion print were made and sequentially numbered on the back. The cards were separated into four divisions: East (1-7), Central (8-14), West (15-21), and Rookies (22-30). The cards are unnumbered and checklisted below alphabetically within each division.

	Nm-Mt	Ex-Mt
COMPLETE SET (30)	125.00	38.00
1 Roberto Alomar	3.00	.90
2 Derek Jeter	10.00	3.00
3 Chipper Jones	6.00	1.80
4 Greg Maddux	6.00	1.80
5 Cal Ripken	10.00	3.00
6 Gary Sheffield	4.00	1.20
7 Mo Vaughn	2.00	.60
8 Jeff Bagwell	4.00	1.20
9 Albert Belle	2.00	.60
10 Brian Jordan	2.00	.60
11 Manny Ramirez	4.00	1.20
12 Ryne Sandberg	5.00	1.50
13 Sammy Sosa	5.00	1.50
14 Frank Thomas	4.00	1.20
15 Barry Bonds	5.00	1.50
16 Juan Gonzalez	2.00	.60
17 Ken Griffey Jr.	6.00	1.80
18 Tony Gwynn	5.00	1.50
19 Mark McGwire	8.00	2.40
20 Mike Piazza	6.00	1.80
21 Alex Rodriguez	8.00	2.40
22 Tony Clark	1.50	.45
23 Darin Erstad	3.00	.90
24 Nomar Garciaparra	5.00	1.50
25 Vladimir Guerrero	5.00	1.50
26 Todd Hollandsworth	1.50	.45
27 Andruw Jones(1)	5.00	1.50
28 Andruw Jones(2)	5.00	1.50
29 Scott Rolen	4.00	1.20
30 Dmitri Young	2.00	.60

1998 Premier Concepts

This 20-card set produced and distributed by Premier Concepts, Inc. features color action player photos on lenticular cards set in a plastic black frame with a suggested retail price of $6. When held, these motion cards show the player swinging the bat with a twist of the wrist. The cards measure approximately 6 1/2" by 8" including the frame and were distributed in a blister package which included a tripod to display the Replay card. Twelve of the cards show only single players (1-12), while eight picture two players (13-20). The cards are unnumbered and checklisted below in alphabetical order within the single and by the first player listed in the double divisions.

	Nm-Mt	Ex-Mt
COMPLETE SET (20)	80.00	24.00
1 Jeff Bagwell	2.50	.75
2 Barry Bonds	5.00	1.50
3 Nomar Garciaparra	6.00	1.80
4 Ken Griffey Jr.(1)	6.00	1.80
5 Ken Griffey Jr.(2)	6.00	1.80
6 Tony Gwynn	5.00	1.50
7 Chipper Jones	5.00	1.50
8 Mike Piazza	6.00	1.80
9 Cal Ripken	10.00	3.00
10 Alex Rodriguez	5.00	1.50
11 Frank Thomas	4.00	1.20
12 Larry Walker	1.00	.30
13 Sandy Alomar Jr. Omar Vizquel	1.00	.30
14 Brady Anderson Mike Mussina	2.00	.60
15 Juan Gonzalez Ivan Rodriguez	4.00	1.20
16 Charles Johnson Livan Hernandez	1.00	.30
17 Dave Justice Jim Thome	2.00	.60
18 Tino Martinez Bernie Williams	2.00	.60
19 Mark McGwire Ray Lankford	8.00	2.40
20 Andy Pettite Derek Jeter	10.00	3.00

1972 Pro Stars Postcards

Printed in Canada by Pro Star Promotions, these 37 blank-backed postcards measure approximately 3 1/2" by 5 1/2" and feature white-bordered color player photos. The player's name appears within the lower white border and also as a facsimile autograph across the bottom of the photo. The postcards are unnumbered and checklisted below in alphabetical order within the Expos team (1-12), National League (13-24) and American League (25-36). In addition to the 36 players listed below, the checklist also carries a listing for 12 posters of major league players.

	NM	Ex
COMPLETE SET (37)	100.00	40.00
COMMON EXPOS (1-12)	1.50	.60
COMMON ALL-STAR (13-36)	2.00	.80
1 Bob Bailey	2.00	.80
2 John Boccabella	2.00	.80
3 Boots Day	1.50	.60
4 Jim Fairey	1.50	.60
5 Tim Foli	1.50	.60
6 Ron Hunt	1.50	.60
7 Mike Jorgensen	1.50	.60
8 Ernie McAnally	1.50	.60
9 Carl Morton	1.50	.60
10 Steve Renko	1.50	.60
11 Ken Singleton	3.00	1.20
12 Bill Stoneman	2.00	.80
13 Hank Aaron	10.00	4.00
14 Johnny Bench	10.00	4.00
15 Roberto Clemente	15.00	6.00
16 Ferguson Jenkins	4.00	1.60
17 Juan Marichal	4.00	1.60
18 Willie Mays	10.00	4.00
19 Willie McCovey	6.00	2.40
20 Frank Robinson	6.00	2.40
21 Pete Rose	6.00	2.40
22 Tom Seaver	6.00	2.40
23 Willie Stargell	4.00	1.60
24 Joe Torre	3.00	1.20
25 Vida Blue	3.00	1.20
26 Reggie Jackson	6.00	2.40
27 Al Kaline	6.00	2.40
28 Harmon Killebrew	4.00	1.60
29 Mickey Lolich	3.00	1.20
30 Dave McNally	3.00	1.20
31 Bill Melton	2.00	.80
32 Bobby Murcer	3.00	1.20
33 Fritz Peterson	2.00	.80
34 Boog Powell	3.00	1.20
35 Merv Rettenmund	2.00	.80
36 Brooks Robinson	6.00	2.40
37 Checklist Card	2.00	.80

1994 Pro Mags Promo

These three cards were issued to introduce Pro Mags to the collectible market. They measure 2 1/8" by 3 3/8" and have blank backs. The cards are numbered with a "Promo Mag" logo near the bottom.

	Nm-Mt	Ex-Mt
COMPLETE SET (3)	8.00	2.40
1 Ken Griffey	4.00	1.20
2 Greg Maddux	3.00	.90
3 Frank Thomas	2.50	.75

1994-95 Pro Mags

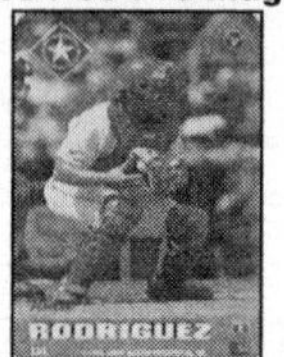

1994-95 Pro Mags were distributed in rack packs containing five random player magnets, one team magnet, and a checklist. Each player mag has rounded corners and measures 2 1/8" by 3 3/8" (team mags measure 2 1/8" by 3/4"). Fronts feature borderless color player action shots with name at the bottom and a team logo at upper left. The black magnetized backs are blank. The magnets are numbered on the front. Five hundred Joe Carter autograph magnets were randomly inserted into packs as well.

	Nm-Mt	Ex-Mt
COMPLETE SET (140)	80.00	24.00
1 Terry Pendleton	.25	.07
2 Ryan Klesko	.50	.15
3 Fred McGriff	.75	.23
4 David Justice	1.00	.30
5 Greg Maddux	4.00	1.20
6 Brady Anderson	.75	.23
7 Ben McDonald	.25	.07
8 Cal Ripken	6.00	1.80
9 Mike Mussina	1.00	.30
10 Jeffrey Hammonds	.25	.07
11 Roger Clemens	3.00	.90
12 Andre Dawson	.75	.23
13 Mike Greenwell	.25	.07
14 Mo Vaughn	.50	.15
15 Otis Nixon	.50	.15
16 Chad Curtis	.25	.07
17 Mark Langston	.25	.07
18 Tim Salmon	1.00	.30
19 Chuck Finley	.25	.07
20 Eduardo Perez	.25	.07
21 Steve Buechele	.25	.07
22 Mark Grace	1.00	.30
23 Sammy Sosa	3.00	.90
24 Derrick May	.25	.07
25 Shawon Dunston	.25	.07
26 Jack McDowell	.25	.07
27 Tim Raines	.50	.15
28 Frank Thomas	1.50	.45

29 Robin Ventura .75 .23
30 Julio Franco .50 .15
31 John Smiley .25 .07
32 Barry Larkin 1.00 .30
33 Jose Rijo .25 .07
34 Reggie Sanders .50 .15
35 Kevin Mitchell .25 .07
36 Sandy Alomar .50 .15
37 Carlos Baerga .50 .15
38 Albert Belle .50 .15
39 Manny Ramirez 1.00 .30
40 Eddie Murray 1.50 .45
41 Dante Bichette .50 .15
42 Ellis Burks .50 .15
43 Andres Galarraga 1.00 .30
44 Greg Harris .25 .07
45 David Nied .25 .07
46 Cecil Fielder .50 .15
47 Kirk Gibson .50 .15
48 Mickey Tettleton .25 .07
49 Lou Whitaker .50 .15
50 Travis Fryman .50 .15
51 Jeff Conine .50 .15
52 Charlie Hough .50 .15
53 Benito Santiago .50 .15
54 Gary Sheffield 1.25 .35
55 Dave Magadan .25 .07
56 Jeff Bagwell 1.50 .45
57 Luis Gonzalez 1.00 .30
58 Andujar Cedeno .25 .07
59 Craig Biggio .75 .23
60 Doug Drabek .25 .07
61 Tom Gordon .25 .07
62 Brian McRae .25 .07
63 David Cone .75 .23
64 Wally Joyner .50 .15
65 Jeff Montgomery .25 .07
66 Eric Karros .75 .23
67 Tom Candiotti .25 .07
68 Delino DeShields .25 .07
69 Orel Hershiser .50 .15
70 Mike Piazza 4.00 1.20
71 Darryl Hamilton .25 .07
72 Kevin Seitzer .25 .07
73 B.J. Surhoff .50 .15
74 John Jaha .25 .07
75 Greg Vaughn .25 .07
76 Kent Hrbek .25 .07
77 Kirby Puckett 1.50 .45
78 Kevin Tapani .25 .07
79 Dave Winfield 1.25 .35
80 Chuck Knoblauch .50 .15
81 Moises Alou .50 .15
82 Wil Cordero .25 .07
83 Marquis Grissom .50 .15
84 Pedro Martinez 1.50 .45
85 Larry Walker .50 .15
86 Jim Abbott .25 .07
87 Wade Boggs 1.50 .45
88 Don Mattingly 3.00 .90
89 Luis Polonia .25 .07
90 Danny Tartabull .25 .07
91 Bobby Bonilla .25 .07
92 Todd Hundley .50 .15
93 Dwight Gooden .50 .15
94 Jeromy Burnitz .50 .15
95 Bret Saberhagen .25 .07
96 Dennis Eckersley 1.25 .35
97 Mark McGwire 5.00 1.50
98 Ruben Sierra .50 .15
99 Terry Steinbach .25 .07
100 Rickey Henderson 2.00 .60
101 Darren Daulton .50 .15
102 Lenny Dykstra .50 .15
103 Dave Hollins .25 .07
104 John Kruk .50 .15
105 Curt Schilling 1.50 .45
106 Carlos Garcia .25 .07
107 Jay Bell .25 .07
108 Don Slaught .25 .07
109 Andy Van Slyke .50 .15
110 Orlando Merced .25 .07
111 Ray Lankford .50 .15
112 Mark Whiten .25 .07
113 Todd Zeile .25 .07
114 Ozzie Smith 2.50 .75
115 Gregg Jefferies .50 .15
116 Derek Bell .25 .07
117 Andy Benes .25 .07
118 Phil Plantier .25 .07
119 Tony Gwynn 3.00 .90
120 Bip Roberts .25 .07
121 Barry Bonds 3.00 .90
122 John Burkett .25 .07
123 Robby Thompson .25 .07
124 Darren Lewis .25 .07
125 Willie McGee .25 .07
126 Jay Buhner .75 .23
127 Ken Griffey Jr. 5.00 1.50
128 Randy Johnson 1.50 .45
129 Eric Anthony .25 .07
130 Edgar Martinez .75 .23
131 Kevin Brown .75 .23
132 Jose Canseco 1.50 .45
133 Juan Gonzalez 1.50 .45
134 Will Clark 1.00 .30
135 Ivan Rodriguez 1.50 .45
136 Roberto Alomar 1.00 .30
137 Joe Carter .50 .15
138 Juan Guzman .25 .07
139 Paul Molitor 1.50 .45
140 John Olerud .75 .23
AU137 Joe Carter AU 20.00 6.00

1996 Pro Mags All-Stars

These 24 magnet cards measure approximately 2" by 3 1/4". The set was distributed in 12-card packs for each league, including 10 players plus an All-Star Game logo and league logo card. The cards have rounded corners and the garish fronts feature the players portrait against either the National or American League background. There is also a league logo and a 1996 All-Star game logo on the front of the card. These cards are numbered in very small print in the lower left hand corner. The American League cards are 1-10, while the National League cards are #11-20.

Nm-Mt Ex-Mt
COMPLETE SET (24) 50.00 15.00
1 Brady Anderson 1.00 .30
2 Jose Canseco 2.50 .75
3 Ken Griffey Jr. UER NNO 6.00 1.80
4 Kenny Lofton 1.50 .45
5 Cal Ripken 10.00 3.00
6 Frank Thomas 2.50 .75
7 Ivan Rodriguez 2.50 .75
8 Mo Vaughn 1.00 .30
9 Albert Belle 1.00 .30
10 Alex Rodriguez 6.00 1.80
11 Hideo Nomo 2.00 .60
12 Greg Maddux 6.00 1.80
13 Jeff Bagwell 2.50 .75
14 Barry Bonds 5.00 1.50
15 Ryan Klesko 1.00 .30
16 Mike Piazza 6.00 1.80
17 David Justice 2.00 .60
18 Dante Bichette 1.00 .30
19 Barry Larkin 2.00 .60
20 Tony Gwynn 5.00 1.50
NNO American League Logo .50 .15
NNO National League Logo .50 .15
NNO All-Star Game Logo .50 .15
NNO All-Star Game Logo .50 .15

1996 Pro Mags Die Cuts

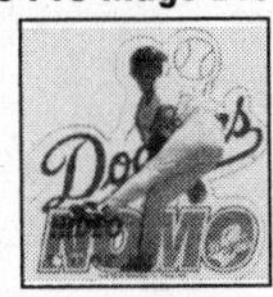

This 25-card set was issued by Chris Martin Enterprises and features color action figures of some of the stars of Major League Baseball on a die-cut magnet.

Nm-Mt Ex-Mt
COMPLETE SET (25) 60.00 18.00
1 David Justice 1.50 .45
2 Ryan Klesko 1.50 .45
3 Fred McGriff 2.00 .60
4 Cal Ripken Jr. 10.00 3.00
5 Bobby Bonilla 1.00 .30
6 Mo Vaughn 1.50 .45
7 Tim Salmon 2.50 .75
8 Frank Thomas 3.00 .90
9 Barry Larkin 2.50 .75
10 Albert Belle 1.50 .45
11 Eddie Murray 3.00 .90
12 Dante Bichette 1.50 .45
13 Andres Galarraga 2.50 .75
14 Cecil Fielder 1.50 .45
15 Hideo Nomo 2.50 .75
16 Mike Piazza 6.00 1.80
17 Kirby Puckett 3.00 .90
18 Don Mattingly 5.00 1.50
19 Tony Gwynn 5.00 1.50
20 Barry Bonds 5.00 1.50
21 Ken Griffey Jr. 6.00 1.80
22 Randy Johnson 3.00 .90
23 Will Clark 2.50 .75
24 Juan Gonzalez 3.00 .90
25 Joe Carter 1.50 .45

1996 Pro Stamps

This 140-stamp set was issued by Chris Martin Enterprises and distributed on 3" by 7 1/2" sheets of six stamps, five players of the same team and team logo. The team logo stamps are unnumbered and not included in the checklist below. Each stamp measures approximately 1 1/2" by 1 15/16". A collector could receive more stamps and become an official Pro Stamps Club member by mailing in the form found on the back of the stamp sheets.

Nm-Mt Ex-Mt
COMPLETE SET (140) 80.00 24.00
1 Gary DiScarcina .25 .07
2 Tim Salmon 1.00 .30
3 J.T. Snow .50 .01
4 Brian Anderson .25 .07
5 Chili Davis .50 .15
6 Mark McGwire 4.00 1.20
7 Terry Steinbach .25 .07
8 Danny Tartabull .25 .07
9 Todd Stottlemyre .25 .07
10 Geronimo Berroa .25 .07
11 Derek Bell .25 .07
12 Craig Biggio .75 .23
13 Jeff Bagwell 1.25 .35
14 Doug Drabek .25 .07
15 Shane Reynolds .25 .07
16 Ed Sprague .25 .07
17 Pat Hentgen .50 .15
18 Joe Carter .50 .15
19 John Olerud .75 .23
20 Carlos Delgado 1.25 .35
21 Fred McGriff .75 .23
22 Ryan Klesko .50 .15
23 David Justice .50 .15
24 Greg Maddux 3.00 .90
25 Tom Glavine 1.00 .30
26 Kevin Seitzer .25 .07
27 Greg Vaughn .25 .07
28 John Jaha .25 .07
29 Pat Listach .25 .07
30 Bill Wegman .25 .07
31 Brian Jordan .50 .15
32 Ray Lankford .50 .15
33 Tom Pagnozzi .25 .07
34 Bernard Gilkey .25 .07
35 Ozzie Smith 2.00 .60
36 Mark Grace 1.00 .30
37 Shawon Dunston .25 .07
38 Brian McRae .25 .07
39 Jaime Navarro .25 .07
40 Sammy Sosa 2.50 .75
41 Mike Piazza 3.00 .90
42 Eric Karros .50 .15
43 Raul Mondesi 1.00 .30
44 Delino DeShields .25 .07
45 Hideo Nomo 1.25 .35
46 Wilfredo Cordero .25 .07
47 Darrin Fletcher .25 .07
48 David Segui .25 .07
49 Pedro Martinez 1.25 .35
50 Rondell White .50 .15
51 Matt Williams .75 .23
52 Barry Bonds 2.50 .75
53 Deion Sanders 1.00 .30
54 Mark Leiter .25 .07
55 Glenallen Hill .25 .07
56 Kenny Lofton .75 .23
57 Albert Belle .50 .15
58 Eddie Murray 1.25 .35
59 Manny Ramirez 1.25 .35
60 Charles Nagy .25 .07
61 Ken Griffey Jr. 3.00 .90
62 Randy Johnson 1.25 .35
63 Jay Buhner .50 .15
64 Edgar Martinez .75 .23
65 Alex Rodriguez 3.00 .90
66 Gary Sheffield 1.25 .35
67 Jeff Conine .50 .15
68 Terry Pendleton .25 .07
69 Chris Hammond .25 .07
70 Greg Colbrunn .25 .07
71 Todd Hundley .50 .15
72 Jose Vizcaino .25 .07
73 Jeff Kent 1.00 .30
74 Rico Brogna .25 .07
75 Bobby Jones .25 .07
76 Cal Ripken 5.00 1.50
77 Bobby Bonilla .25 .07
78 Brady Anderson .50 .15
79 Mike Mussina 1.00 .30
80 Rafael Palmeiro 1.00 .30
81 Tony Gwynn 2.00 .60
82 Ken Caminiti .50 .15
83 Andujar Cedeno .25 .07
84 Andy Ashby .25 .07
85 Jody Reed .25 .07
86 Jim Eisenreich .25 .07
87 Gregg Jefferies .25 .07
88 Mickey Morandini .25 .07
89 Paul Quantrill .25 .07
90 Darren Daulton .50 .15
91 Orlando Merced .25 .07
92 Carlos Garcia .25 .07
93 Jay Bell .25 .07
94 Al Martin .25 .07
95 Denny Neagle .25 .07
96 Benji Gil .25 .07
97 Will Clark 1.00 .30
98 Juan Gonzalez 1.50 .45
99 Ivan Rodriguez 1.25 .35
100 Dean Palmer .25 .07
101 Barry Larkin 1.00 .30
102 Reggie Sanders .25 .07
103 Benito Santiago .50 .15
104 Jose Rijo .25 .07
105 Bret Boone .75 .23
106 Mo Vaughn .50 .15
107 Jose Canseco 1.25 .35
108 Mike Greenwell .25 .07
109 John Valentin .25 .07
110 Roger Clemens 2.50 .75
111 Dante Bichette .50 .15
112 Vinny Castilla .50 .15
113 Andres Galarraga 1.00 .30
114 Larry Walker .50 .15
115 Walt Weiss .25 .07
116 Tom Goodwin .25 .07
117 Keith Lockhart .25 .07
118 Mark Gubicza .25 .07
119 Jon Nunnally .25 .07
120 Kevin Appier .50 .15
121 Chad Curtis .25 .07
122 Phil Nevin .25 .07
123 Travis Fryman .50 .15
124 Alan Trammell .75 .23
125 Cecil Fielder .50 .15
126 Chuck Knoblauch 1.00 .30
127 Kirby Puckett 2.50 .75
128 Marty Cordova .25 .07
129 Pedro Munoz .25 .07
130 Rich Aguilera .25 .07
131 Frank Thomas 1.50 .45
132 Ozzie Guillen .50 .15
133 Robin Ventura .75 .23
134 Ron Karkovice .25 .07
135 Alex Fernandez .25 .07
136 Wade Boggs 1.25 .35
137 Jimmy Key .50 .15
138 Paul O'Neill .50 .15
139 David Cone .75 .23
140 Bernie Williams 1.00 .30

1995 ProMint

This set of 15 diamond cards was produced by ProMint. The embossed gold-foil cards feature 22-karat gold on their fronts and a five-point diamond next to the player's name at the bottom. Each card is individually numbered and packaged in an acrylic holder.

Nm-Mt Ex-Mt
COMPLETE SET (15) 375.00 110.00
1 Jeff Bagwell 25.00 7.50
2 Albert Belle 15.00 4.50
3 Barry Bonds 25.00 7.50
4 George Brett 25.00 7.50
5 Roger Clemens 25.00 7.50
6 Ken Griffey Jr. 25.00 7.50
7 Tony Gwynn 25.00 7.50
8 Greg Maddux 30.00 9.00
9 Don Mattingly 25.00 7.50
10 Mike Piazza 25.00 7.50
11 Kirby Puckett 20.00 6.00
12 Cal Ripken 40.00 12.00
13 Nolan Ryan 40.00 12.00
14 Ozzie Smith 25.00 7.50
15 Frank Thomas 25.00 7.50

1998 ProMint

These two cards honor the participants in the great home run chase of 1998.

Nm-Mt Ex-Mt
COMPLETE SET 20.00 6.00
1 Mark McGwire 10.00 3.00
70 Homers
2 Sammy Sosa 10.00 3.00
66 Homers

1998 ProMint McGwire Fleer

Issued by ProMint and liscenced by Fleers, this 24K card commemorates Mark McGwire breaking the single season home run record

Nm-Mt Ex-Mt
1 Mark McGwire 10.00 3.00
Smashing the Record

1993 ProMint 22K Gold

This 22 karat gold cards measure the standard size and features an embossed image of the player bordered by an embossed arrow design. The player's name, along with the ProMint logo, appear near the bottom. The horizontal back carries the player's name within a motion-streaked baseball icon at the upper left. Career highlights appear in the "outfield" of a baseball field design. The card carries its production number at the bottom right, but is otherwise unnumbered.

Nm-Mt Ex-Mt
1 Barry Bonds 25.00 7.50
2 Nolan Ryan 50.00 15.00

1967 Pro's Pizza

This set, which features members of both Chicago teams features a square design with the words "The Pro's Pizza" in a black box in the upper right. These photos are in black and white. Since these cards are unnumbered, we have sequenced them in alphabetical order. Ron Santo was involved in management of Pro's Pizza at the time this set was issued.

NM Ex
COMPLETE SET 1800.00 700.00
1 Ted Abernathy 50.00 20.00
2 George Altman 50.00 20.00
3 Joe Amalfitano 50.00 20.00
4 Ernie Banks 400.00 160.00
5 Glenn Beckert 75.00 30.00
6 Ernie Broglio 50.00 20.00
7 Byron Browne 50.00 20.00
8 Don Buford 50.00 20.00
9 Billy Connors 50.00 20.00
10 Dick Ellsworth 50.00 20.00
11 Billy Hoeft 50.00 20.00
12 Ken Holtzman 100.00 40.00
13 Joel Horlen 50.00 20.00
14 Randy Hundley 75.00 30.00
15 Fergie Jenkins 250.00 100.00
16 Don Kessinger 75.00 30.00
17 Chris Krug 50.00 20.00
18 Gary Peters 50.00 20.00
19 Ron Santo 150.00 60.00
20 Carl Warwick 50.00 20.00
21 Billy Williams 250.00 100.00

1998-00 ProTalk Griffey

These four items, which feature a talking card and a displayable piece feature various highlights from the career of Ken Griffey Jr. Each card has about 45 seconds of actual game highlights which can be heard. These were originally available directly from ProTalk on their website for $4.99 each.

Nm-Mt Ex-Mt
COMPLETE SET (4) 20.00 6.00
COMMON CARD (1-4) 5.00 1.50

1998-00 Protalk Talking Cards

Issued as a combination of talking card and displayable portrait, these items were available through stores as well as through the Fanaticsonline.com web site at a direct cost of $4.99 per. Each card features approximately 45 seconds of actual game highlights.

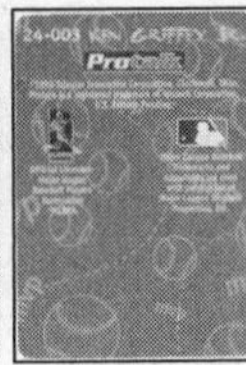

Nm-Mt Ex-Mt
COMPLETE SET 80.00 24.00
1 Mark McGwire 8.00 2.40
500th career homer
2 Mark McGwire 8.00 2.40
70th homer
3 Sammy Sosa 6.00 1.80
300th career homer
4 Sammy Sosa 6.00 1.80
66th homer
5 Ken Griffey Jr. 6.00 1.80
Grand slam homer
6 Ken Griffey Jr. 6.00 1.80
Amazing Catch
7 New York Yankees 5.00 1.50
World Champions
8 Mike Piazza 6.00 1.80
Game Winning Homer
9 Chipper Jones 6.00 1.80
World Series Homer
10 Cal Ripken Jr. 8.00 2.40
400th career homer
11 Derek Jeter 8.00 2.40
World Series Play
12 Derek Jeter 8.00 2.40
Spectactular Leaping Catch
13 Nomar Garciaparra 6.00 1.80
10 RBI Game
14 Ivan Rodriguez 5.00 1.50
Texas Ranger RBI Record
15 Alex Rodriguez 6.00 1.80
Joins the 40/40 Club

1990 Publications International Stickers

The 1990 Publications International baseball stickers set contains 648 stickers bound in a book. Subsets of the 648-sticker set include All-Stars from each league, and young stars from each league. The stickers are put into the album over a question which pertains to each player pictured as a clue for where the sticker goes. Good stat information is available on this set in the album/book. The set numbering is ordered by teams. The album spaces are numbered and contain a trivia question answered by the players name. The set/book was licensed by Major League Baseball and MLBPA and was produced by Publications International.

Nm-Mt Ex-Mt
COMPLETE SET (648) 40.00 12.00
1 Dave Anderson .05 .02
2 Tim Belcher .05 .02
3 Mike Davis .05 .02
4 Rick Dempsey .10 .03
5 Kirk Gibson .15 .04
6 Alfredo Griffin .05 .02
7 Jeff Hamilton .05 .02
8 Mickey Hatcher .05 .02
9 Orel Hershiser .10 .03
10 Ricky Horton .05 .02
11 Jay Howell .05 .02
12 Tim Leary .05 .02
13 Mike Marshall .05 .02
14 Eddie Murray .50 .15
15 Alejandro Pena .05 .02
16 Willie Randolph .10 .03
17 Mike Scioscia .15 .04
18 John Shelby .05 .02
19 Franklin Stubbs .05 .02
20 John Tudor .05 .02
21 Fernando Valenzuela .10 .03
22 Todd Benzinger .05 .02
23 Tom Browning .05 .02
24 Norm Charlton .05 .02
25 Kal Daniels .05 .02
26 Eric Davis .10 .03
27 Bo Diaz .05 .02
28 Rob Dibble .05 .02
29 John Franco .10 .03
30 Ken Griffey Sr. .10 .03
31 Lenny Harris .05 .02
32 Danny Jackson .05 .02
33 Barry Larkin .25 .07
34 Rick Mahler .05 .02
35 Ron Oester .05 .02
36 Paul O'Neill .10 .03
37 Jeff Reed .05 .02
38 Jose Rijo .05 .02
39 Chris Sabo .05 .02
40 Kent Tekulve .10 .03
41 Manny Trillo .05 .02
42 Joel Youngblood .05 .02
43 Roberto Alomar .50 .15
44 Greg Booker .05 .02
45 Jack Clark .10 .03
46 Jerald Clark .05 .02
47 Mark Davis .05 .02
48 Tim Flannery .05 .02
49 Mark Grant .05 .02
50 Tony Gwynn 1.25 .35
51 Bruce Hurst .05 .02
52 John Kruk .10 .03
53 Dave Leiper .05 .02
54 Carmelo Martinez .05 .02
55 Mark Parent .05 .02
56 Dennis Rasmussen .05 .02
57 Randy Ready .05 .02
58 Benito Santiago .10 .03
59 Eric Show .05 .02
60 Garry Templeton .05 .02
61 Walt Terrell .05 .02
62 Ed Whitson .05 .02
63 Marvell Wynne .05 .02
64 Brett Butler .10 .03

65 Will Clark .25 .07
66 Kelly Downs .05 .02
67 Scott Garrelts .05 .02
68 Rich(Goose) Gossage .10 .03
69 Atlee Hammaker .05 .02
70 Tracy Jones .05 .02
71 Terry Kennedy .05 .02
72 Mike Krukow .05 .02
73 Mike LaCoss .05 .02
74 Craig Lefferts .05 .02
75 Candy Maldonado .05 .02
76 Kirt Manwaring .05 .02
77 Kevin Mitchell .05 .02
78 Donell Nixon .05 .02
79 Rick Reuschel .10 .03
80 Ernest Riles .05 .02
81 Don Robinson .05 .02
82 Chris Speier .05 .02
83 Robby Thompson .05 .02
84 Jose Uribe .05 .02
85 Juan Agosto .05 .02
86 Larry Andersen .05 .02
87 Kevin Bass .05 .02
88 Craig Biggio .50 .15
89 Ken Caminiti .10 .03
90 Jim Clancy .05 .02
91 Danny Darwin .05 .02
92 Glenn Davis .05 .02
93 Jim Deshaies .05 .02
94 Bill Doran .05 .02
95 Bob Forsch .05 .02
96 Billy Hatcher .05 .02
97 Bob Knepper .05 .02
98 Terry Puhl .05 .02
99 Rafael Ramirez .05 .02
100 Craig Reynolds .05 .02
101 Rick Rhoden .05 .02
102 Mike Scott .05 .02
103 Dave Smith .05 .02
104 Alex Trevino .05 .02
105 Gerald Young .05 .02
106 Jose Alvarez .05 .02
107 Paul Assenmacher .05 .02
108 Bruce Benedict .05 .02
109 Jeff Blauser .05 .02
110 Joe Boever .05 .02
111 Jody Davis .05 .02
112 Darrell Evans .10 .03
113 Ron Gant .10 .03
114 Tommy Gregg .05 .02
115 Dion James .05 .02
116 Derek Lilliquist .05 .02
117 Dale Murphy .25 .07
118 Gerald Perry .05 .02
119 Charlie Puleo .05 .02
120 John Russell .05 .02
121 Lonnie Smith .05 .02
122 Pete Smith .05 .02
123 Zane Smith .05 .02
124 John Smoltz .25 .07
125 Bruce Sutter .10 .03
126 Andres Thomas .05 .02
127 Rick Aguilera .10 .03
128 Gary Carter .50 .15
129 David Cone .15 .04
130 Ron Darling .05 .02
131 Len Dykstra .10 .03
132 Kevin Elster .05 .02
133 Sid Fernandez .05 .02
134 Dwight Gooden .10 .03
135 Keith Hernandez .10 .03
136 Gregg Jefferies .05 .02
137 Howard Johnson .05 .02
138 Dave Magadan .05 .02
139 Lee Mazzilli .10 .03
140 Roger McDowell .05 .02
141 Kevin McReynolds .05 .02
142 Randy Myers .10 .03
143 Bob Ojeda .05 .02
144 Mackey Sasser .05 .02
145 Darryl Strawberry .10 .03
146 Tim Teufel .05 .02
147 Mookie Wilson .10 .03
148 Rafael Belliard .05 .02
149 Barry Bonds 1.00 .30
150 Bobby Bonilla .10 .03
151 Sid Bream .05 .02
152 Benny Distefano .05 .02
153 Doug Drabek .05 .02
154 Brian Fisher .05 .02
155 Jim Gott .05 .02
156 Neal Heaton .05 .02
157 Bill Landrum .05 .02
158 Mike LaValliere .05 .02
159 Jose Lind .05 .02
160 Junior Ortiz .05 .02
161 Tom Prince .05 .02
162 Gary Redus .05 .02
163 R.J. Reynolds .05 .02
164 Jeff Robinson .05 .02
165 John Smiley .05 .02
166 Andy Van Slyke .10 .03
167 Bob Walk .05 .02
168 Glenn Wilson .05 .02
169 Hubie Brooks .05 .02
170 Tim Burke .05 .02
171 Mike Fitzgerald .05 .02
172 Tom Foley .05 .02
173 Andres Galarraga .25 .07
174 Kevin Gross .05 .02
175 Joe Hesketh .05 .02
176 Brian Holman .05 .02
177 Rex Hudler .05 .02
178 Wallace Johnson .05 .02
179 Mark Langston .05 .02
180 Dave Martinez .05 .02
181 Dennis Martinez .10 .03
182 Andy McGaffigan .05 .02
183 Otis Nixon .05 .02
184 Spike Owen .05 .02
185 Pascual Perez .05 .02
186 Tim Raines .10 .03
187 Nelson Santovenia .05 .02
188 Bryn Smith .05 .02
189 Tim Wallach .05 .02
190 Damon Berryhill .05 .02
191 Mike Bielecki .05 .02
192 Andre Dawson .25 .07
193 Shawon Dunston .05 .02
194 Mark Grace .25 .07
195 Darrin Jackson .05 .02
196 Paul Kilgus .05 .02
197 Vance Law .05 .02
198 Greg Maddux 1.25 .35
199 Pat Perry .05 .02
200 Jeff Pico .05 .02
201 Ryne Sandberg .50 .15
202 Scott Sanderson .05 .02
203 Calvin Schiraldi .05 .02
204 Dwight Smith .05 .02
205 Rick Sutcliffe .10 .03
206 Gary Varsho .05 .02
207 Jerome Walton .05 .02
208 Mitch Webster .05 .02
209 Curtis Wilkerson .05 .02
210 Mitch Williams .05 .02
211 Tom Brunansky .05 .02
212 Cris Carpenter .05 .02
213 Vince Coleman .05 .02
214 John Costello .05 .02
215 Danny Cox .05 .02
216 Ken Dayley .05 .02
217 Jose DeLeon .05 .02
218 Frank DiPino .05 .02
219 Pedro Guerrero .10 .03
220 Joe Magrane .05 .02
221 Greg Mathews .05 .02
222 Willie McGee .10 .03
223 Jose Oquendo .05 .02
224 Tom Pagnozzi .05 .02
225 Tony Pena .10 .03
226 Terry Pendleton .10 .03
227 Dan Quisenberry .05 .02
228 Ozzie Smith .75 .23
229 Scott Terry .05 .02
230 Milt Thompson .05 .02
231 Todd Worrell .05 .02
232 Steve Bedrosian .05 .02
233 Don Carman .05 .02
234 Darren Daulton .10 .03
235 Bob Dernier .05 .02
236 Marvin Freeman .05 .02
237 Greg Harris .05 .02
238 Von Hayes .05 .02
239 Tom Herr .05 .02
240 Ken Howell .05 .02
241 Chris James .05 .02
242 Steve Jeltz .05 .02
243 Ron Jones .05 .02
244 Ricky Jordan .05 .02
245 Steve Lake .05 .02
246 Mike Maddux .05 .02
247 Larry McWilliams .05 .02
248 Jeff Parrett .05 .02
249 Juan Samuel .05 .02
250 Mike Schmidt .60 .18
251 Dickie Thon .05 .02
252 Floyd Youmans .05 .02
253 Bobby Bonilla .10 .03
254 Will Clark .25 .07
255 Eric Davis .10 .03
256 Andre Dawson .25 .07
257 Bill Doran .05 .02
258 John Franco .10 .03
259 Kirk Gibson .10 .03
260 Dwight Gooden .10 .03
261 Tony Gwynn 1.00 .30
262 Keith Hernandez .10 .03
263 Orel Hershiser .10 .03
264 Danny Jackson .05 .02
265 Howard Johnson .05 .02
266 Barry Larkin .25 .07
267 Joe Magrane .05 .02
268 Kevin McReynolds .05 .02
269 Tony Pena .10 .03
270 Ryne Sandberg .75 .23
271 Benito Santiago .10 .03
272 Ozzie Smith .75 .23
273 Darryl Strawberry .10 .03
274 Todd Worrell .05 .02
275 Harold Baines .10 .03
276 George Bell .05 .02
277 Wade Boggs .50 .15
278 Bob Boone .10 .03
279 Jose Canseco .40 .12
280 Joe Carter .10 .03
281 Roger Clemens 1.00 .30
282 Dennis Eckersley .40 .12
283 Tony Fernandez .10 .03
284 Carlton Fisk .50 .15
285 Julio Franco .10 .03
286 Gary Gaetti .10 .03
287 Mike Greenwell .05 .02
288 Rickey Henderson .75 .23
289 Ted Higuera .05 .02
290 Kent Hrbek .10 .03
291 Don Mattingly 1.00 .30
292 Kirby Puckett .30 .09
293 Jeff Reardon .10 .03
294 Harold Reynolds .10 .03
295 Dave Stewart .10 .03
296 Alan Trammell .15 .04
297 Frank Viola .05 .02
298 Dave Winfield .50 .15
299 Todd Burns .05 .02
300 Greg Cadaret .05 .02
301 Jose Canseco .40 .12
302 Storm Davis .05 .02
303 Dennis Eckersley .40 .12
304 Mike Gallego .05 .02
305 Ron Hassey .05 .02
306 Dave Henderson .05 .02
307 Rick Honeycutt .05 .02
308 Stan Javier .05 .02
309 Carney Lansford .10 .03
310 Mark McGwire 1.50 .45
311 Mike Moore .05 .02
312 Dave Parker .10 .03
313 Eric Plunk .05 .02
314 Luis Polonia .05 .02
315 Terry Steinbach .05 .02
316 Dave Stewart .10 .03
317 Walt Weiss .05 .02
318 Bob Welch .05 .02
319 Curt Young .05 .02
320 Allan Anderson .05 .02
321 Wally Backman .05 .02
322 Doug Baker .05 .02
323 Juan Berenguer .05 .02
324 Randy Bush .05 .02
325 Jim Dwyer .05 .02
326 Gary Gaetti .10 .03
327 Greg Gagne .05 .02
328 Dan Gladden .05 .02
329 Brian Harper .05 .02
330 Kent Hrbek .10 .03
331 Gene Larkin .05 .02
332 Tim Laudner .05 .02
333 John Moses .05 .02
334 Al Newman .05 .02
335 Kirby Puckett .30 .09
336 Shane Rawley .05 .02
337 Jeff Reardon .10 .03
338 Steve Shields .05 .02
339 Frank Viola .05 .02
340 Gary Wayne .05 .02
341 Luis Aquino .05 .02
342 Floyd Bannister .05 .02
343 Bob Boone .10 .03
344 George Brett .75 .23
345 Bill Buckner .10 .03
346 Jim Eisenreich .05 .02
347 Steve Farr .05 .02
348 Tom Gordon .10 .03
349 Mark Gubicza .05 .02
350 Bo Jackson .25 .07
351 Charlie Leibrandt .05 .02
352 Mike Macfarlane .05 .02
353 Jeff Montgomery .10 .03
354 Bret Saberhagen .10 .03
355 Kevin Seitzer .05 .02
356 Kurt Stillwell .05 .02
357 Pat Tabler .05 .02
358 Danny Tartabull .05 .02
359 Gary Thurman .05 .02
360 Frank White .10 .03
361 Willie Wilson .05 .02
362 Jim Abbott .15 .04
363 Kent Anderson .05 .02
364 Tony Armas .05 .02
365 Dante Bichette .10 .03
366 Bert Blyleven .10 .03
367 Chili Davis .10 .03
368 Brian Downing .05 .02
369 Chuck Finley .10 .03
370 Willie Fraser .05 .02
371 Jack Howell .05 .02
372 Wally Joyner .10 .03
373 Kirk McCaskill .05 .02
374 Bob McClure .05 .02
375 Greg Minton .05 .02
376 Lance Parrish .05 .02
377 Dan Petry .05 .02
378 Johnny Ray .05 .02
379 Dick Schofield .05 .02
380 Claudell Washington .05 .02
381 Devon White .05 .02
382 Mike Witt .05 .02
383 Harold Baines .10 .03
384 Daryl Boston .05 .02
385 Ivan Calderon .05 .02
386 Carlton Fisk .50 .15
387 Dave Gallagher .05 .02
388 Ozzie Guillen .10 .03
389 Shawn Hillegas .05 .02
390 Barry Jones .05 .02
391 Ron Karkovice .05 .02
392 Eric King .05 .02
393 Ron Kittle .05 .02
394 Bill Long .05 .02
395 Steve Lyons .10 .03
396 Fred Manrique .05 .02
397 Donn Pall .05 .02
398 Dan Pasqua .05 .02
399 Melido Perez .05 .02
400 Jerry Reuss .05 .02
401 Bobby Thigpen .05 .02
402 Greg Walker .05 .02
403 Eddie Williams .05 .02
404 Buddy Bell .10 .03
405 Kevin Brown .25 .07
406 Steve Buechele .05 .02
407 Cecil Espy .05 .02
408 Scott Fletcher .05 .02
409 Julio Franco .10 .03
410 Cecilio Guante .05 .02
411 Jose Guzman .05 .02
412 Charlie Hough .10 .03
413 Pete Incaviglia .05 .02
414 Chad Kreuter .05 .02
415 Jeff Kunkel .05 .02
416 Rick Leach .05 .02
417 Jamie Moyer .15 .04
418 Rafael Palmeiro .25 .07
419 Geno Petralli .05 .02
420 Jeff Russell .05 .02
421 Nolan Ryan 2.00 .60
422 Ruben Sierra .10 .03
423 Jim Sundberg .05 .02
424 Bobby Witt .05 .02
425 Steve Balboni .05 .02
426 Scott Bankhead .05 .02
427 Scott Bradley .05 .02
428 Mickey Brantley .05 .02
429 Darnell Coles .05 .02
430 Henry Cotto .05 .02
431 Alvin Davis .05 .02
432 Mario Diaz .05 .02
433 Ken Griffey Jr. 1.50 .45
434 Erik Hanson .05 .02
435 Mike Jackson .10 .03
436 Jeffrey Leonard .05 .02
437 Edgar Martinez .15 .04
438 Tom Niedenfuer .05 .02
439 Jim Presley .05 .02
440 Jerry Reed .05 .02
441 Harold Reynolds .10 .03
442 Bill Swift .05 .02
443 Steve Trout .05 .02
444 David Valle .05 .02
445 Omar Vizquel .25 .07
446 Marty Barrett .05 .02
447 Mike Boddicker .05 .02
448 Wade Boggs .50 .15
449 Dennis(Oil Can) Boyd .05 .02
450 Ellis Burks .15 .04
451 Rick Cerone .05 .02
452 Roger Clemens 1.00 .30
453 Nick Esasky .05 .02
454 Dwight Evans .10 .03
455 Wes Gardner .05 .02
456 Rich Gedman .05 .02
457 Mike Greenwell .05 .02
458 Sam Horn .05 .02
459 Randy Kutcher .05 .02
460 Dennis Lamp .05 .02
461 Rob Murphy .05 .02
462 Jody Reed .05 .02
463 Jim Rice .10 .03
464 Lee Smith .10 .03
465 Mike Smithson .05 .02
466 Bob Stanley .05 .02
467 Doyle Alexander .05 .02
468 Dave Bergman .05 .02
469 Chris Brown .05 .02
470 Paul Gibson .05 .02
471 Mike Heath .05 .02
472 Mike Henneman .05 .02
473 Guillermo Hernandez .05 .02
474 Charles Hudson .05 .02
475 Chet Lemon .05 .02
476 Fred Lynn .05 .02
477 Keith Moreland .05 .02
478 Jack Morris .10 .03
479 Matt Nokes .05 .02
480 Gary Pettis .05 .02
481 Jeff Robinson .05 .02
482 Pat Sheridan .05 .02
483 Frank Tanana .05 .02
484 Alan Trammell .15 .04
485 Lou Whitaker .10 .03
486 Frank Williams .05 .02
487 Kenny Williams .10 .03
488 Don August .05 .02
489 Mike Birkbeck .05 .02
490 Chris Bosio .05 .02
491 Glenn Braggs .05 .02
492 Greg Brock .05 .02
493 Chuck Crim .05 .02
494 Rob Deer .05 .02
495 Mike Felder .05 .02
496 Jim Gantner .05 .02
497 Ted Higuera .05 .02
498 Joey Meyer .05 .02
499 Paul Mirabella .05 .02
500 Paul Molitor .25 .07
501 Juan Nieves .05 .02
502 Charlie O'Brien .05 .02
503 Dan Plesac .05 .02
504 Gary Sheffield .50 .15
505 B.J. Surhoff .10 .03
506 Dale Sveum .05 .02
507 Bill Wegman .05 .02
508 Robin Yount .50 .15
509 George Bell .05 .02
510 Pat Borders .05 .02
511 John Cerutti .05 .02
512 Rob Ducey .05 .02
513 Tony Fernandez .10 .03
514 Mike Flanagan .05 .02
515 Kelly Gruber .05 .02
516 Tom Henke .05 .02
517 Alexis Infante .05 .02
518 Jimmy Key .10 .03
519 Tom Lawless .05 .02
520 Manny Lee .05 .02
521 Al Leiter .25 .07
522 Nelson Liriano .05 .02
523 Fred McGriff .25 .07
524 Lloyd Moseby .05 .02
525 Rance Mulliniks .05 .02
526 Dave Stieb .10 .03
527 Todd Stottlemyre .05 .02
528 Duane Ward .05 .02
529 Ernie Whitt .05 .02
530 Jesse Barfield .05 .02
531 Bob Brower .05 .02
532 John Candelaria .05 .02
533 Richard Dotson .05 .02
534 Lee Guetterman .05 .02
535 Mel Hall .05 .02
536 Andy Hawkins .05 .02
537 Rickey Henderson .75 .23
538 Roberto Kelly .05 .02
539 Dave LaPoint .05 .02
540 Don Mattingly 1.00 .30
541 Lance McCullers .05 .02
542 Mike Pagliarulo .05 .02
543 Clay Parker .05 .02
544 Ken Phelps .05 .02
545 Dave Righetti .05 .02
546 Rafael Santana .05 .02
547 Steve Sax .05 .02
548 Don Slaught .05 .02
549 Wayne Tolleson .05 .02
550 Dave Winfield .50 .15
551 Andy Allanson .05 .02
552 Keith Atherton .05 .02
553 Scott Bailes .05 .02
554 Bud Black .05 .02
555 Jerry Browne .05 .02
556 Tom Candiotti .05 .02
557 Joe Carter .10 .03
558 David Clark .05 .02
559 John Farrell .05 .02
560 Felix Fermin .05 .02
561 Brook Jacoby .05 .02
562 Doug Jones .05 .02
563 Oddibe McDowell .05 .02
564 Luis Medina .05 .02
565 Pete O'Brien .05 .02
566 Jesse Orosco .10 .03
567 Joel Skinner .05 .02
568 Cory Snyder .05 .02
569 Greg Swindell .05 .02
570 Rich Yett .05 .02
571 Mike Young .05 .02
572 Brady Anderson .25 .07
573 Jeff Ballard .05 .02
574 Jose Bautista .05 .02
575 Phil Bradley .05 .02
576 Mike Devereaux .05 .02
577 Kevin Hickey .05 .02
578 Brian Holton .05 .02
579 Bob Melvin .10 .03
580 Bob Milacki .05 .02
581 Gregg Olson .05 .02
582 Joe Orsulak .05 .02
583 Bill Ripken .05 .02
584 Cal Ripken Jr. 2.00 .60
585 Dave Schmidt .05 .02
586 Larry Sheets .05 .02
587 Mickey Tettleton .10 .03
588 Mark Thurmond .05 .02
589 Jay Tibbs .05 .02
590 Jim Traber .05 .02
591 Mark Williamson .05 .02
592 Craig Worthington .05 .02
593 Allan Anderson .05 .02
594 Ellis Burks .15 .04
595 Ken Griffey Jr. 1.50 .45
596 Bo Jackson .25 .07
597 Roberto Kelly .05 .02
598 Kirk McCaskill .05 .02
599 Fred McGriff .25 .07
600 Mark McGwire 1.50 .45
601 Bob Milacki .05 .02
602 Melido Perez .05 .02
603 Jeff Robinson .05 .02
604 Gary Sheffield .50 .15
605 Ruben Sierra .10 .03
606 Greg Swindell .05 .02
607 Roberto Alomar .75 .23
608 Tim Belcher .05 .02
609 Vince Coleman .05 .02
610 Kal Daniels .05 .02
611 Andres Galarraga .25 .07
612 Ron Gant .10 .03
613 Mark Grace .25 .07
614 Gregg Jefferies .05 .02
615 Ricky Jordan .05 .02
616 Jose Lind .05 .02
617 Kevin Mitchell .05 .02
618 Gerald Young .05 .02
619 Base .05 .02
620 Batting helmets .05 .02
621 Bats .05 .02
622 Batting gloves .05 .02
623 Los Angeles Dodgers .05 .02
624 Cincinnati Reds .05 .02
625 San Diego Padres .05 .02
626 San Francisco Giants .05 .02
627 Houston Astros .05 .02
628 Atlanta Braves .05 .02
629 New York Mets .05 .02
630 Pittsburgh Pirates .05 .02
631 Montreal Expos .05 .02
632 Chicago Cubs .05 .02
633 St. Louis Cardinals .05 .02
634 Philadelphia Phillies .05 .02
635 Oakland Athletics .05 .02
636 Minnesota Twins .05 .02
637 Kansas City Royals .05 .02
638 California Angels .05 .02
639 Chicago White Sox .05 .02
640 Texas Rangers .05 .02
641 Seattle Mariners .05 .02
642 Boston Red Sox .05 .02
643 Detroit Tigers .05 .02
644 Milwaukee Brewers .05 .02
645 Toronto Blue Jays .05 .02
646 New York Yankees .05 .02
647 Cleveland Indians .05 .02
648 Baltimore Orioles .05 .02

1997 Puckett Glaucoma

This one card oversized set featured Kirby Puckett and information about Glaucoma. The front has an action shot of Kirby with the words "Don't Be Blindsided" on top and the sponsorship information on the bottom. The back has information about Glaucoma and information about two more sponsors: Allina Health System and Phillips Eye Institute.

	Nm-Mt	Ex-Mt
1 Kirby Puckett	5.00	1.50

1997 Puckett Sight Night

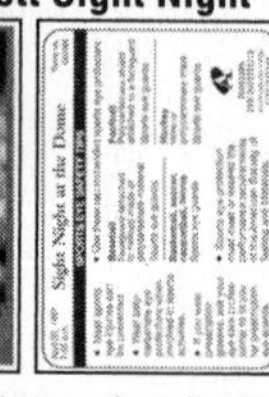

This one-card set features a color action photo of Kirby Puckett in a red frame with a white border. The card was distributed at the April 30, 1997 Game between the Twins and the Orioles. The back displays sports eye safety tips and was sponsored by the Phillips Eye Institute.

	Nm-Mt	Ex-Mt
1 Kirby Puckett	5.00	1.50

1986 Quaker Granola

This set of 33 standard-size cards was available in packages of Quaker Oats Chewy Granola, three player cards plus a complete set offer card in each package. The set was also available through a mail-in offer where anyone sending in four UPC seals from Chewy Granola (before 12/31/86) would receive a complete set. The cards were produced by Topps for Quaker Oats. Card backs are printed in red and blue on gray card stock. The cards are numbered on the front and the back. Cards 1-17 feature National League players and cards 18-33 feature American League players. The first three cards in each sequence depict that league's MVP, Cy Young, and Rookie of the Year, respectively. The rest of the cards in each sequence are ordered alphabetically.

Nm-Mt Ex-Mt

COMPLETE SET (33) 6.00 2.40
1 Willie McGee .20 .08
2 Dwight Gooden .30 .12
3 Vince Coleman .20 .08
4 Gary Carter .50 .20
5 Jack Clark .10 .04
6 Steve Garvey .30 .12
7 Tony Gwynn 1.00 .40
8 Dale Murphy .40 .16
9 Dave Parker .20 .08
10 Tim Raines .20 .08
11 Pete Rose .50 .20
12 Nolan Ryan 2.00 .80
13 Ryne Sandberg .40 .16
14 Mike Schmidt .50 .20
15 Ozzie Smith .50 .20
16 Darryl Strawberry .10 .04
17 Fernando Valenzuela .20 .08
18 Don Mattingly 1.00 .40
19 Bret Saberhagen .20 .08
20 Ozzie Guillen .30 .12
21 Bert Blyleven .20 .08
22 Wade Boggs .40 .16
23 George Brett 1.00 .40
24 Darrell Evans .10 .04
25 Rickey Henderson .60 .24
26 Reggie Jackson .50 .20
27 Eddie Murray .50 .20
28 Phil Niekro .50 .20
29 Dan Quisenberry .10 .04
30 Jim Rice .20 .08
31 Cal Ripken 2.00 .80
32 Tom Seaver .50 .20
33 Dave Winfield .50 .20
NNO Offer Card for .10 .04
the complete set

1938 Quaker Oats Ruth

This 8" by 10" blank backed poster of Babe Ruth was produced in the 1930's by the Quaker Oats company.The poster features Ruth swinging and has a facsimile autograph with the words "To My Pal from "Babe" Ruth. The bottom of the poster has the words "Presented to Members of the the Babe Ruth Base Ball Clun by the Quaker Oats Company, Makers of the Quaker Puffed Wheat and Puffed Rice." Like most promotional photos, it was sent in a mailing envelope to insure delivery in good condition

Ex-Mt VG
1 Babe Ruth 250.00 125.00

1997 R and N Ted Williams Porcelain

This 18-card limited edition set honors Ted Williams with previous card images of him printed on porcelain. Each card was hand numbered and came packaged in a plexi case with a display easel and a certificate of authenticity. The set was available in several versions besides just the white porcelain card version: white porcelain with a 23kt. gold trim, white porcelain with a .999 pure platinum trim, porcelain with gold covered surface (only 750 produced), porcelain with platinum covered surface (only 500 produced), and in a Collector Series Mug version. The cards are listed below according to the year they were produced by the card manufacturers also listed.

Nm-Mt Ex-Mt
COMPLETE SET (18) 450.00 135.00
COMMON CARD (1-18) 25.00 7.50

1936 R311 Premiums

The 1936 R311 set of Portraits and Team Baseball Photos exist in two different forms, each measuring 6" by 8". Fifteen leather-like or uneven surface cards comprise the first type; these are indicated by the prefix L in the checklist below and are listed first. Twenty eight glossy surface, sepia or black and white cards comprise the second type. These glossy cards are indicated by the prefix G in the checklist below. The Boston Red Sox team exists with or without a sky above the building at the right of the card. Scarcities within the glossy subset include Pepper Martin, Mel Harder, Schoolboy Rowe, and the Dodgers, Pirates, Braves and Columbus team cards; these are asterisked in the checklist below.

Ex-Mt VG
COMPLETE SET (44) 2400.00 1200.00
COMMON GLOSSY (G1-G28) 20.00 10.00
COMMON LEATHER (L1-L15) 30.00 15.00
G1 Earl Averill 40.00 20.00
G2 Jim Bottomley 40.00 20.00
G3 Mickey Cochrane 50.00 25.00
G4 Joe Cronin 40.00 20.00
G5 Dizzy Dean 80.00 40.00
G6 Jimmy Dykes 20.00 10.00
G7 Jimmie Foxx 80.00 40.00
G8 Frankie Frisch 50.00 25.00
G9 Hank Greenberg 50.00 25.00
G10 Mel Harder 30.00 15.00
G11 Ken Keltner 25.00 12.50
G12 Pepper Martin 150.00 75.00
G13 Schoolboy Rowe 25.00 12.50
G14 Bill Terry 40.00 20.00
G15 Pie Traynor 40.00 20.00
G16 American League All 20.00 10.00
Stars 1935
G17 American League 40.00 20.00
Pennant Winners 1934
(Detroit Tigers)
G18 Boston Braves 1935 200.00 100.00
G19A Boston Red Sox 20.00 10.00
with sky above
building at right
of the card
G19B Boston Red Sox 80.00 40.00
without sky
G20 Brooklyn Dodgers 200.00 100.00
1935 *
G21 Chicago White Sox 20.00 10.00
1935
G22 Columbus Red Birds 20.00 10.00
1934 Pennant Winners
of Amer. Assoc.
G23 National League All 20.00 10.00
Stars 1934
G24 National League 20.00 10.00
Champions 1935
Chicago Cubs
G25 New York Yankees 40.00 20.00
1935
G26 Pittsburgh Pirates 40.00 20.00
1935 *
G27 St. Louis Browns 20.00 10.00
1935
G28 World Champions 1934 20.00 10.00
St. Louis Cardinals
L1 Paul Derringer 30.00 15.00
L2 Wes Ferrell 30.00 15.00
L3 Jimmie Foxx 100.00 50.00
L4 Charley Gehringer 60.00 30.00
L5 Mel Harder 30.00 15.00
L6 Gabby Hartnett 60.00 30.00
L7 Rogers Hornsby 100.00 50.00
L8 Connie Mack MG 80.00 40.00
L9 Van Mungo 30.00 15.00
L10 Steve O'Neill 30.00 15.00
L11 Red Ruffing 60.00 30.00
L12 Joe DiMaggio 400.00 200.00
Frank Crosetti
Tony Lazzeri
L13 Arky Vaughan 100.00 50.00
Honus Wagner CO
L14 American League 30.00 15.00
Pennant Winners 1935
Detroit Tigers
L15 National League 30.00 15.00
Pennant Winners 1935
Chicago Cubs

1936 R312 Pastel Photos

The 1936 R312 Baseball Photos set contains 25 color tinted, single player cards, listed with the letter A in the checklist; 14 multiple player cards, listed with the letter B in the checklist; 6 action cards with handwritten signatures, listed with the letter C in the checklist; and 5 action cards with printed titles, listed with the letter D in the checklist. The pictures are reminiscent of a water-color type painting in soft pastels. The Allen card is reportedly more difficult to obtain than other cards in the set.

Ex-Mt VG
COMPLETE SET (50) 2000.00 1000.00
1 Johnny Allen 100.00 50.00
2 Cy Blanton 25.00 12.50
3 Mace Brown 25.00 12.50
4 Dolph Camilli 25.00 12.50
5 Mickey Cochrane 60.00 30.00
6 Rip Collins 25.00 12.50
7 KiKi Cuyler 50.00 25.00
8 Bill Dickey 60.00 30.00
9 Joe DiMaggio 500.00 250.00
(misspelled DiMagio)
10 Chuck Dressen 30.00 15.00
11 Benny Frey 25.00 12.50
12 Hank Greenberg 60.00 30.00
13 Mel Harder 30.00 15.00
14 Rogers Hornsby 100.00 50.00
15 Ernie Lombardi 50.00 25.00
16 Pepper Martin 30.00 15.00
17 Johnny Mize 60.00 30.00
18 Van Lingle Mungo 25.00 12.50
19 Bud Parmalee 25.00 12.50
20 Red Ruffing
21 Eugene Schott 25.00 12.50
22 Casey Stengel MG 100.00 50.00
23 Billy Sullivan 25.00 12.50
24 Bill Swift 25.00 12.50
25 Ralph Winegarner 25.00 12.50
26 Ollie Bejma and 25.00 12.50
Rollie Hemsley
27 Cliff Bolton and 25.00 12.50
Earl Whitehill
28 Stan Bordagaray 25.00 12.50
George Earnshaw
29 Billy Herman 30.00 15.00
Phil Cavarretta
Stan Hack
Bill Jurges
30 Pete Fox 30.00 15.00
Jo Jo White
Goose Goslin
31 Augie Galan 30.00 15.00
Billy Herman
Fred Lindstrom
Gabby Hartnett
Frank Demare
Phil Cavarretta
Stan Hack
Billy Jurges
Chuck Klein
32 Bucky Harris MG 50.00 25.00
Joe Cronin
33 Gabby Hartnett and 30.00 15.00
Lon Warnecke
sic, Warneke
34 Myril Hoag and 50.00 25.00
Lefty Gomez
35 Allen Sothoron and 50.00 25.00
Rogers Hornsby
36 Connie Mack MG and 75.00 38.00
Lefty Grove
37 Taylor 50.00 25.00
Tris Speaker
Kiki Cuyler
38 Dixie Walker 25.00 12.50
Mule Haas
Mike Kreevich
39 Paul Waner 50.00 25.00
Lloyd Waner
Big Jim Weaver
40 Nick Altrock 30.00 15.00
Al Schacht
Clowning on the Diamond
41 Beau Bell 25.00 12.50
Out At First
Zeke Bonura
first baseman
42 Jim Collins (Safe) 25.00 12.50
and Stan Hack
43 Jimmie Foxx batting 50.00 25.00
with Luke Sewell
catching
44 Al Lopez Traps Two 50.00 25.00
Cubs on Third Base
45 Pie Traynor 50.00 25.00
Augie Galan
46 Alvin Crowder 25.00 12.50
after victory in
the World Series
48 Gabby Hartnett 50.00 25.00
(crossing home plate
after hitting homer...
49 Kids flock around 25.00 12.50
Schoolboy Rowe as he
leaves Cubs park...
50 Russ Van Atta 25.00 12.50
St. Louis pitcher out at plate
Rick Ferrell
Boston, catching

1932 R337 Series Of 24

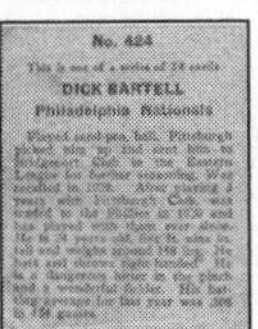
No. 424
DICK BARTELL
Philadelphia Nationals

The cards in this 24-card set measure 2 5/16" by 2 13/16". The "Series of 24" is similar to the MP and Co. issues in terms of style and quality. Produced about 1932, this set is numbered 401-424. The three missing numbers, 403, 413, and 414, probably correspond to the three known unnumbered players. Some dealers believe this is known as the "Eclipse Import" set.

Ex-Mt VG
COMPLETE SET (24) 2400.00 1200.00
401 Johnny Vergez 50.00 25.00
402 Babe Ruth 1000.00 500.00
404 George Pipgras 50.00 25.00
405 Bill Terry 100.00 50.00
406 George Connally 50.00 25.00
407 Wilson Clark 50.00 25.00
408 Lefty Grove 150.00 75.00
409 Henry Johnson 50.00 25.00
410 Jimmy Dykes 50.00 25.00
411 Henry Hine Schuble 50.00 25.00
412 Dave Harris 80.00 40.00
Washington
Makes Home Run
415 Al Simmons 100.00 50.00
416 Heinie Manush 80.00 40.00
417 Glen Myatt 50.00 25.00
418 Babe Herman 80.00 40.00
419 Frank Frisch 100.00 50.00
420 A Safe Slide to 50.00 25.00
the Home Plate
421 Paul Waner 80.00 40.00
422 Jimmy Wilson 50.00 25.00
423 Charles Grimm 80.00 40.00
424 Dick Bartell 50.00 25.00
xx Jimmy Fox 150.00 75.00
sic, Jimmie Foxx
unnumbered
xx Roy Johnson 50.00 25.00
unnumbered
xx Pie Traynor 100.00 50.00
Pitss,sic, Pittsburgh
unnumbered

1951 R423 Small Strip

Many numbers of these small and unattractive cards are either unknown or do not exist for this issue of the early 1950s. The cards are printed on thin stock and measure 5/8" by 3/4"; sometimes they are found as a long horizontal strip of 13 cards connected by a perforation. Complete strips intact are worth 50 percent more than the sum of the individual players on the strip. The cards were available with a variety of back colors, red, green, blue, or purple. The cards on the strip are in no apparent order, numerically or alphabetically. The producer's numbering of the cards in the set is very close to alphabetical order. Cards are so small they are sometimes lost. These strips were premiums or prizes in one-cent bubblegum machines; they were folded accordion style and held together by a small metal clip. Obviously, all additions to this list are greatly appreciated.

NM Ex
COMPLETE SET 250.00 125.00
1 Richie Ashburn 1.50 .75
3 Frank Baumholtz .50 .25
4 Ralph Branca .75 .35
5 Yogi Berra 8.00 4.00
7 Lou Boudreau 1.50 .75
8 Harry Brecheen .50 .25
9 Chico Carrasquel .50 .25
10 Jerry Coleman .50 .25
11 Walker Cooper .50 .25
12 Roy Campanella 8.00 4.00
13 Phil Cavarretta .75 .35
14A Ty Cobb 15.00 7.50
Has Fascimile Autograph
14B Ty Cobb 15.00 7.50
No Autograph
15 Mickey Cochrane 1.50 .75
16 Eddie Collins 1.50 .75
17 Frank Crosetti .75 .35
18 Larry Doby 1.50 .75
19 Walter Dropo .50 .25
20 Alvin Dark .75 .35
21 Dizzy Dean 6.00 3.00
22 Bill Dickey 1.50 .75
23 Murray Dickson .50 .25
24 Dom DiMaggio 1.50 .75
25 Joe DiMaggio 15.00 7.50
28 Bob Elliott .75 .35
29 Del Ennis .50 .25
31 Bob Feller 6.00 3.00
32 Frank Frisch 1.50 .75
33 Billy Goodman .50 .25
35 Lou Gehrig 15.00 7.50
36 Joe Gordon .75 .35
38 Hank Greenberg 1.50 .75
39 Lefty Grove 1.50 .75
42 Ken Heintzelman .50 .25
44 Jim Hearn .50 .25
45 Gil Hodges 3.00 1.50
46 Harry Heilman 1.50 .75
47 Tommy Henrich 1.00 .50
48 Roger Hornsby 5.00 2.50
49 Carl Hubbell 1.50 .75
50 Eddie Joost .50 .25
51 Nippy Jones .50 .25
53 Nippy Jones .50 .25
54 Walter Johnson 5.00 2.50
55 Ellis Kinder .50 .25
56 Jim Konstanty .75 .35
57 George Kell 1.50 .75
58 Ralph Kiner 1.50 .75
59 Bob Lemon 1.50 .75
60 Whitey Lockman .75 .35
61 Ed Lopat .75 .35
62 Tony Lazzeri 1.50 .75
63 Cass Michaels .50 .25
64 Cliff Mapes .50 .25
65 Willard Marshall .50 .25
66 Clyde McCullough .50 .25
67 Connie Mack 1.50 .75
68 Christy Mathewson 5.00 2.50
69 Joe Medwick 1.50 .75
70 Johnny Mize 1.50 .75
71 Terry Moore .50 .25
72 Stan Musial 10.00 5.00
73 Hal Newhouser 1.50 .75
74 Don Newcombe 1.00 .50
75 Lefty O'Doul .75 .35
76 Mel Ott 1.50 .75
77 Mel Parnell .50 .25
79 Gerald Priddy .50 .25
80 Dave Philley .50 .25
81 Bob Porterfield .50 .25
82 Andy Pafko .50 .25
83 Howie Pollet .50 .25
84 Herb Pennock 1.50 .75
85 Al Rosen .75 .35
86 Pee Wee Reese 1.50 .75
87 Del Rice .50 .25
89 Allie Reynolds .75 .35
90 Phil Rizzuto 1.50 .75
91 Jackie Robinson 15.00 7.50
92 Babe Ruth 20.00 10.00
93 Casey Stengel 1.50 .75
94 Vern Stephens .75 .35
95 Duke Snider 3.00 1.50
96 Enos Slaughter 1.50 .75
97 Al Schoendienst 1.50 .75
98 Gerald Staley .50 .25
99 Clyde Shoun .50 .25
102 Al Simmons 1.50 .75
103 George Sisler 1.50 .75
104 Tris Speaker 1.50 .75
105 Ed Stanky .75 .35
106 Virgil Trucks .50 .25
107 Henry Thompson .50 .25
109 Dazzy Vance 1.50 .75
110 Lloyd Waner 1.50 .75
111 Paul Waner 1.50 .75
112 Gene Woodling .50 .25
113 Ted Williams 15.00 7.50
114 Vic Wertz .50 .25
115 Wes Westrum .50 .25
116 Johnny Wyrostek .50 .25
117 Eddie Yost .50 .25
118 Al Zarilla .50 .25
119 Gus Zernial .50 .25
120 Sam Zoldak .50 .25
XX Strip of 13 cards 20.00 10.00

1984 Ralston Purina

The cards in this 33-card set measure the standard size. In 1984 the Ralston Purina Company issued what it has entitled "The First Annual Collectors Edition of Baseball Cards." The cards feature portrait photos of the players rather than batting action shots. The Topps logo appears along with the Ralston logo on the front of the card. The backs are completely different from the Topps cards of this year; in fact, they contain neither a Topps logo nor a Topps copyright. Large quantities of these cards were obtained by card dealers for direct distribution into the organized hobby, hence the relatively low price of the set. These cards are very similar to the Topps Cereal issue of the same year -- note that the only difference is the Ralston Purina logo on the front.

Nm-Mt Ex-Mt
COMPLETE SET (33) 5.00 2.00
1 Eddie Murray .40 .16
2 Ozzie Smith .75 .30
3 Ted Simmons .05 .02
4 Pete Rose .40 .16
5 Greg Luzinski .05 .02
6 Andre Dawson .30 .12
7 Dave Winfield .40 .16
8 Tom Seaver .40 .16
9 Jim Rice .10 .04
10 Fernando Valenzuela .10 .04
11 Wade Boggs .40 .16
12 Dale Murphy .30 .12
13 George Brett .75 .30
14 Nolan Ryan 1.50 .60
15 Rickey Henderson .60 .24
16 Steve Carlton .40 .16
17 Rod Carew .40 .16
18 Steve Garvey .20 .08
19 Reggie Jackson .40 .16
20 Dave Concepcion .10 .04
21 Robin Yount .40 .16
22 Mike Schmidt .40 .16
23 Jim Palmer .40 .16
24 Bruce Sutter .05 .02
25 Dan Quisenberry .05 .02
26 Bill Madlock .10 .04
27 Cecil Cooper .10 .04
28 Gary Carter .40 .16
29 Fred Lynn .10 .04
30 Pedro Guerrero .05 .02
31 Ron Guidry .10 .04
32 Keith Hernandez .10 .04
33 Carlton Fisk .40 .16

1987 Ralston Purina

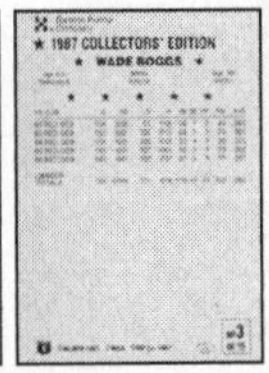

The Ralston Purina Company issued a set of 15 cards picturing players without their respective team logos. The cards measure approximately 2 1/2" by 3 3/8" and are in full-color on the front. The cards are numbered on the back in the lower right hand corner; the player's uniform number is prominently displayed on the front. The cards were distributed as inserts inside packages of certain flavors of Ralston Purina's breakfast cereals. Three cards and a contest card were packaged in cellophane and inserted within the cereal box. The set was also available as an uncut sheet through a mail-in offer. Since the uncut sheets are relatively common, the value of the sheet is essentially the same as the value of the sum of the individual cards. In fact there were two uncut sheets issued, one had "Honey Graham Chex" printed at the top and the other had "Cookie Crisp" printed at the top. Also cards were issued with (cards from cereal boxes) and without (cards cut from the uncut sheets) the words "1987 Collectors Edition" printed in blue on the front. Reportedly 100,000 of the uncut sheets were given away free via instant win certificates inserted in with the cereal or collectors could send in two non-winning contest cards plus 1.00 for each uncut sheet.

Nm-Mt Ex-Mt
COMPLETE SET (15) 18.00 7.25
1 Nolan Ryan 5.00 2.00
2 Steve Garvey .75 .30
3 Wade Boggs 2.00 .80
4 Dave Winfield 1.25 .50
5 Don Mattingly 2.50 1.00
6 Don Sutton 1.25 .50
7 Dave Parker .25 .10
8 Eddie Murray 1.25 .50
9 Gary Carter 1.25 .50
10 Roger Clemens 2.50 1.00
11 Fernando Valenzuela .50 .20
12 Cal Ripken 5.00 2.00
13 Ozzie Smith 2.50 1.00
14 Mike Schmidt 1.25 .50
15 Ryne Sandberg 2.50 1.00

1909 Ramly T204

The cards in this 121-card set measure approximately 2" by 2 1/2". The Ramly baseball series, designated T204 in the catalog, contains unnumbered cards. This set is one of the most distinguished ever produced, containing ornate gold borders around a black and white portrait of each player. There are spelling errors, and two distinct backs, "Ramly" and "TTT", are known. There is a premium of up to 25 percent for the "TTT" back. Much of the obverse card detail is actually embossed. The players have been alphabetized and numbered for reference in the checklist below. A few players (so far only six are confirmed, and a seventh is rumored) are known with square frames with blank backs. It is possible that these are proofs. The confirmed square players are John Anderson, Frank Bancroft, Kitty Bransfield, Jesse Burkett, Bill Dineen and Pat Moran.

	Ex-Mt	VG
COMPLETE SET (121)	60000.00	30000.00
1 Whitey Alperman	400.00	200.00
2 John J. Anderson	400.00	200.00
3 Jimmy Archer	400.00	200.00
4 Frank Arrelanes UER	400.00	200.00
5 Jim Ball (Boston NL)	400.00	200.00
6 Neal Ball (N.Y. AL)	400.00	200.00
7 Frank Bancroft	500.00	250.00
8 Johnny Bates	400.00	200.00
9 Fred Beebe	400.00	200.00
10 George Bell	400.00	200.00
11 Chief Bender	1200.00	600.00
12 Walter Blair	400.00	200.00
13 Cliff Blankenship	400.00	200.00
14 Frank Bowerman	400.00	200.00
15 Kitty Bransfield	400.00	200.00
16 Roger Bresnahan	1200.00	600.00
17 Al Bridwell	400.00	200.00
18 Mordecai Brown	1200.00	600.00
19 Fred Burchell	400.00	200.00
20 Jesse Burkett	1200.00	600.00
21 Bobby Byrnes UER	400.00	200.00
22 Bill Carrigan	400.00	200.00
23 Frank Chance	1500.00	750.00
24 Charles Chech	400.00	200.00
25 Eddie Cicolte	800.00	400.00
26 Otis Clymer	400.00	200.00
27 Andrew Coakley	400.00	200.00
28 Eddie Collins	1200.00	600.00
29 Jimmy Collins	1200.00	600.00
30 Wid Conroy	400.00	200.00
31 Jack Coombs	600.00	300.00
32 Doc Crandall	400.00	200.00
33 Lou Criger	400.00	200.00
34 Harry Davis	400.00	200.00
35 Art Devlin	400.00	200.00
36 Bill Dineen UER	400.00	200.00
37 Pat Donahue	400.00	200.00
38 Mike Donlin	500.00	250.00
39 Bill Donovan	400.00	200.00
40 Gus Dorner	400.00	200.00
41 Joe Dunn	400.00	200.00
42 Kid Elberfield	400.00	200.00
43 Johnny Evers	1500.00	750.00
44 Bob Ewing	400.00	200.00
45 George Ferguson	400.00	200.00
46 Hobe Ferris	400.00	200.00
47 Jerry Freeman	400.00	200.00
48 Art Fromme	400.00	200.00
49 Bob Ganley	400.00	200.00
50 Doc Gessler	400.00	200.00
51 Peaches Graham	400.00	200.00
52 Clark Griffith	1200.00	600.00
53 Roy Hartzell	400.00	200.00
54 Charlie Hemphill	400.00	200.00
55 Dick Hoblitzell UER	400.00	200.00
56 George Howard	400.00	200.00
57 Harry Howell	400.00	200.00
58 Miller Huggins	1200.00	600.00
59 John Hummel	400.00	200.00
60 Walter Johnson	8000.00	4000.00
61 Tom Jones	400.00	200.00
62 Mike Kahoe	400.00	200.00
63 Ed Kargar UER	400.00	200.00
64 Willie Keeler	1500.00	750.00
65 Ed Konetchey UER	400.00	200.00
66 Red Kleinonw	400.00	200.00
67 John Knight	400.00	200.00
68 Vive Lindaman	400.00	200.00
69 Hans Loebert UER	400.00	200.00
70 Harry Lord	400.00	200.00
71 Harry Lumley	400.00	200.00
72 Ernie Lush	400.00	200.00
73 Rube Manning	400.00	200.00
74 Jimmy McAleer	400.00	200.00
75 Amby McConnell	400.00	200.00
76 Moose McCormick	400.00	200.00
77 Matty McIntyre	400.00	200.00
78 Larry McLean	400.00	200.00
79 Fred Merkle	600.00	300.00
80 Clyde Milan	500.00	250.00
81 Mike Mitchell	400.00	200.00
82 Pat Moran	400.00	200.00
83 Harry Cy Morgan	400.00	200.00
84 Tim Murname UER	400.00	200.00
85 Danny Murphy	400.00	200.00
86 Red Murray	400.00	200.00
87 Doc Newton	400.00	200.00
88 Simon Nichols UER	400.00	200.00
89 Harry Niles	400.00	200.00
90 Bill O'Hare UER	400.00	200.00
91 Charley O'Leary	400.00	200.00
92 Dode Paskert	400.00	200.00
93 Barney Pelty	400.00	200.00
94 Jack Pfeister UER	400.00	200.00
95 Eddie Plank	2500.00	1250.00
96 Jack Powell	400.00	200.00
97 Bugs Raymond	500.00	250.00
98 Tom Reilly	400.00	200.00
99 Claude Ritchey	400.00	200.00
100 Nap Rucker	500.00	250.00
101 Ed Ruelbach UER	500.00	250.00
102 Slim Sallee	400.00	200.00
103 Germany Schaefer	500.00	250.00
104 Jimmy Schekard UER	400.00	200.00
105 Admiral Schlei	400.00	200.00
106 Wildfire Schulte	500.00	250.00
107 Jimmy Sebring	400.00	200.00
108 Bill Shipke	400.00	200.00
109 Charlie Smith	400.00	200.00
110 Tubby Spencer	400.00	200.00
111 Jake Stahl	600.00	300.00
112 Harry Stienfeldt UER	600.00	300.00
113 Jim Stephens	400.00	200.00
114 Gabby Street	400.00	200.00
115 Bill Sweeney	400.00	200.00
116 Fred Tenney	400.00	200.00
117 Ira Thomas	400.00	200.00
118 Joe Tinker	1500.00	750.00
119 Bob Unglane UER	400.00	200.00
120 Heinie Wagner	400.00	200.00
121 Bobby Wallace	1200.00	600.00

1909 Ramly T204 Square Frames

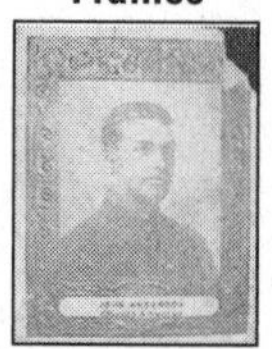

These few cards are known to exist with square picture frames. They can also be identified as the players full name is printed on the card. It is believed that a few other players in this set may exist but no confirmation is known at this time.

	Ex-Mt	VG
COMPLETE SET	25000.00	12500.00
1 John Anderson	3000.00	1500.00
2 Frank Bancroft	3000.00	1500.00
3 Kitty Bransfield	3000.00	1500.00
4 Jesse Burkett	8000.00	4000.00
5 Bill Dineen	3000.00	1500.00
6 Pat Moran	5000.00	2500.00

1972 Rangers Team Issue

This 32-card set of the 1972 Texas Rangers measures approximately 3 1/2" by 5 3/4" and features black-and-white player portraits with white borders. A facsimile autograph is printed on the photo. Name, position, and Texas Rangers are printed across the bottom of the photo. The backs are blank. The cards are unnumbered and checklisted below in alphabetical order.

	NM	Ex
COMPLETE SET (32)	80.00	32.00
1 Larry Biittner	2.00	.80
2 Dick Billings	2.00	.80
3 Dick Bosman	3.00	1.20
4 Pete Broberg	2.00	.80
5 Jeff Burroughs	5.00	2.00
6 Casey Cox	2.00	.80
7 Jim Driscoll	2.00	.80
8 Ted Ford	2.00	.80
9 Bill Gogolewski	2.00	.80
10 Tom Grieve	4.00	1.60
11 Rich Hand	2.00	.80
12 Toby Harrah	5.00	2.00
13 Frank Howard	5.00	2.00
14 Sid Hudson CO	2.00	.80
15 Dalton Jones	2.00	.80
16 Hal King	2.00	.80
17 Ted Kubiak	2.00	.80
18 Paul Lindblad	2.00	.80
19 Joe Lovitto	2.00	.80
20 Elliott Maddox	2.00	.80
21 Don Mincher	2.00	.80
22 Dave Nelson	2.00	.80
23 Jim Panther	2.00	.80
24 Mike Paul	2.00	.80
25 Horacio Pina	2.00	.80
26 Lenny Randle	2.00	.80
27 Jim Shellenback	2.00	.80
28 Don Stanhouse	3.00	1.20
29 Ken Suarez	2.00	.80
30 George Susce CO	2.00	.80
31 Wayne Terwilliger CO	2.00	.80
32 Ted Williams MG	15.00	6.00

1973 Rangers Team Issue

This set of the Texas Rangers measures approximately 3 1/2" by 5 3/4" and features black-and-white player portraits in a white border. The backs are blank. The cards are unnumbered and checklisted below in alphabetical order. Since the Rangers changed managers during the 1973 season, both Whitey Herzog and Billy Martin are listed as managers in our checklist.

	NM	Ex
COMPLETE SET	40.00	16.00
1 Lloyd Allen	1.00	.40
2 Jim Bibby	2.00	.80
3 Larry Biittner	1.00	.40
4 Rich Billings	1.00	.40
5 Pete Broberg	1.00	.40
6 Jeff Burroughs	4.00	1.60
7 Rico Carty	2.00	.80
8 David Clyde	2.00	.80
9 Steve Dunning	1.00	.40
10 Chuck Estrada CO	1.00	.40
11 Steve Foucalt	1.00	.40
12 Bill Gogolewski	1.00	.40
13 Rich Hand	1.00	.40
14 Toby Harrah	3.00	1.20
15 Vic Harris	1.00	.40
16 Whitey Herzog MG	2.00	.80
17 Chuck Hiller CO	1.00	.40
18 Charlie Hudson	1.00	.40
19 Alex Johnson	2.00	.80
20 Elliot Maddox	1.00	.40
21 Billy Martin MG	5.00	2.00
22 Jim Mason	1.00	.40
23 Jim Merritt	1.00	.40
24 Dave Nelson	1.00	.40
25 Mike Paul	1.00	.40
26 Lenny Randle	1.00	.40
27 Sonny Siebert	1.00	.40
28 Don Stanhouse	1.00	.40
29 Ken Suarez	1.00	.40

1974 Rangers Team Issue

This set, which measured 3 1/2" by 5 3/4" featured members of the 1974 Texas Rangers. These black and white blank-backed cards feature the player's photo along with their name, position and Texas Rangers name on the bottom. Since these cards are unnumbered, we have sequenced them in alphabetical order. It is believed but not confirmed that cards were issued for Dick Billings and Don Stanhouse.

	NM	Ex
COMPLETE SET	30.00	12.00
1 Jim Bibby	1.00	.40
2 Pete Broberg	1.00	.40
3 Jackie Brown	1.00	.40
4 Larry Brown	1.00	.40
5 Jeff Burroughs	1.50	.60
6 Leo Cardenas	1.00	.40
7 David Clyde	1.00	.40
8 Merrill Combs CO	1.00	.40
9 Mike Cubbage	1.00	.40
10 Don Durham	1.00	.40
11 Steve Dunning	1.00	.40
12 Chuck Estrada CO	1.00	.40
13 Steve Foucault	1.00	.40
14 Art Fowler CO	1.00	.40
15 Jim Fregosi	1.00	.40
16 Tom Grieve	1.50	.60
17 Toby Harrah	1.00	.40
18 Steve Hargan	1.00	.40
19 Mike Hargrove	2.50	1.00
20 Fergie Jenkins	3.00	1.20
21 Alex Johnson	1.00	.40
22 Joe Lovitto	1.00	.40
23 Frank Lucchesi CO	1.00	.40
24 Billy Martin MG	3.00	1.20
25 Jim Merritt	1.00	.40
26 Jackie Moore	1.00	.40
27 Dave Nelson	1.00	.40
28 Lenny Randle	1.00	.40
29 Jim Shellenback	1.00	.40
30 Charlie Silvera CO	1.00	.40
31 Jim Spencer	1.00	.40
32 Jim Sundberg	2.50	1.00
33 Cesar Tovar	1.00	.40

1975 Rangers Postcards

This 37-card set of the Texas Rangers features player photos on postcard-size cards. The cards are unnumbered and checklisted below in alphabetical order.

	NM	Ex
COMPLETE SET (37)	20.00	8.00
1 Mike Bacsik	.50	.20
2 Jim Bibby	.50	.20
3 Jackie Brown	.50	.20
4 Jeff Burroughs	.75	.30
5 Leo Cardenas	.50	.20
6 Merrill Combs CO	.50	.20
7 Mike Cubbage	.50	.20
8 Bill Fahey	.50	.20
9 Steve Foucault	.50	.20
10 Art Fowler CO	.50	.20
11 Jim Fregosi	.75	.30
12 Tom Grieve	.75	.30
13 Bill Hands	.50	.20
14 Steve Hargan	.50	.20
15 Mike Hargrove	1.50	.60
16 Toby Harrah	.75	.30
17 Roy Howell	.50	.20
18 Fergie Jenkins	1.50	.60
19 Joe Lovitto	.50	.20
20 Frank Lucchesi CO	.50	.20
21 Billy Martin MG	1.50	.60
22 Jim Merritt	.50	.20
23 Dave Moates		
24 Jackie Moore	.50	.20
25 Tommy Joe Moore		
26 Dave Nelson	.50	.20
27 Dave Nelson (Autographed)	.50	.20
28 Gaylord Perry	1.50	.60
29 Lenny Randle	.50	.20
30 Lenny Randle (Autographed)	.50	.20
31 Charlie Silvera CO	.50	.20
32 Roy Smalley	.75	.30
33 Jim Spencer	.50	.20
34 Jim Sundberg	.75	.30
35 Jim Sundberg Older Picture	.75	.30
36 Stan Thomas	.50	.20
37 Cesar Tovar	.50	.20
38 Jim Umbarger	.50	.20
39 Clyde Wright	.50	.20

1976 Rangers Team Issue

This photo card set featured members of the 1976 Texas Rangers. The 3 1/2" by 5 3/4" blank-backed cards black and white cards feature player photos surrounded by a white border. The player's name is identified at the bottom of the card. Since the cards are unnumbered, we have sequenced them in alphabetical order.

	NM	Ex
COMPLETE SET	30.00	12.00
1 Steve Barr	1.00	.40
2 Juan Beniquez	1.00	.40
3 Bert Blyleven	2.50	1.00
4 Nelson Briles	1.00	.40
5 Jeff Burroughs	1.00	.40
6 Gene Clines	1.00	.40
7 Pat Corrales CO	1.00	.40
8 John Ellis	1.00	.40
9 Bill Fahey	1.00	.40
10 Steve Foucault	1.00	.40
11 Jim Fregosi	1.00	.40
12 Dick Gernert CO	1.00	.40
13 Tom Grieve	1.50	.60
14 Steve Hargan	1.00	.40
15 Mike Hargrove	1.50	.60
16 Toby Harrah	1.00	.40
17 Joe Hoerner	1.00	.40
18 Roy Lee Howell	1.00	.40
19 Sid Hudson CO	1.00	.40
20 Joe Lahoud	1.00	.40
21 Dave Moates	1.00	.40
22 Jackie Moore	1.00	.40
23 Gaylord Perry	3.00	1.20
24 Lenny Randle	1.00	.40
25 Jim Sundberg	1.50	.60
26 Danny Thompson	1.00	.40
27 Jim Umbarger	1.00	.40
28 Bill Zeigler	1.00	.40

1977 Rangers Team Issue

This set was issued to promote the members of the 1977 Texas Rangers. The black and white blank-backed cards measures approximately 3 1/2" by 5 3/4". The player's photo are surrounded by white borders. This checklist may be incomplete and any additions are appreciated. Since these cards are unnumbered, we have sequenced them in alphabetical order.

	NM	Ex
COMPLETE SET	25.00	10.00
1 Doyle Alexander	1.00	.40
2 Bert Blyleven	2.00	.80
3 Nelson Briles	1.00	.40
4 Bert Campaneris	2.00	.80
5 Adrian Devine	1.00	.40
6 Dock Ellis	1.00	.40
7 Bill Fahey	1.00	.40
8 Tom Grieve	1.50	.60
9 Mike Hargrove	1.50	.60
10 Toby Harrah	1.00	.40
11 Ken Henderson	1.00	.40
12 Willie Horton	1.50	.60
13 Billy Hunter MG	1.00	.40
14 Darold Knowles	1.00	.40
15 Paul Lindblad	1.00	.40
16 Mike Marshall	1.00	.40
17 Jim Mason	1.00	.40
18 Dave May	1.00	.40
19 Gaylord Perry	3.00	1.20
20 Jim Sundberg	1.50	.60
21 Claudell Washington	1.00	.40
22 Bump Wills	1.50	.60

1978 Rangers Burger King

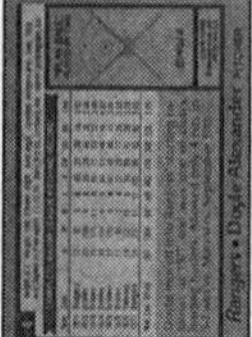

The cards in this 23-card set measure 2 1/2" by 3 1/2". This set of 22 numbered player cards (featuring the Texas Rangers) and one unnumbered checklist was issued regionally by Burger King in 1978. Asterisks denote poses different from those found in the regular Topps cards of this year.

	NM	Ex
COMPLETE SET (23)	15.00	6.00
1 Billy Hunter MG	.50	.20
2 Jim Sundberg	1.00	.40
3 John Ellis	.50	.20
4 Doyle Alexander	.75	.30
5 Jon Matlack *	.75	.30
6 Dock Ellis	.50	.20
7 Doc Medich	.50	.20
8 Fergie Jenkins *	4.00	1.60
9 Len Barker	.50	.20
10 Reggie Cleveland *	.50	.20
11 Mike Hargrove	1.50	.60
12 Bump Wills	.50	.20
13 Toby Harrah	1.00	.40
14 Bert Campaneris	1.00	.40
15 Sandy Alomar	.75	.30
16 Kurt Bevacqua	.50	.20
17 Al Oliver *	1.50	.60
18 Juan Beniquez	.50	.20
19 Claudell Washington	1.00	.40
20 Richie Zisk	.75	.30
21 John Lowenstein *	.50	.20
22 Bobby Thompson *	.50	.20
NNO Checklist Card TP	.25	.10

1978-79 Rangers Team Issue

Issued over a period of years, these cards feature members of the late 1970's Texas Rangers. These black and white blank-backed cards measure 3 1/2" by 5 1/2". The player's photo is surrounded by white borders while his name is located at the bottom. Since the cards are unnumbered, we have sequenced this set in alphabetical order.

	NM	Ex
COMPLETE SET	30.00	12.00
1 Doyle Alexander	1.00	.40
2 Sandy Alomar	1.00	.40
3 Len Barker	1.50	.60
4 Buddy Bell	1.50	.60
5 Juan Beniquez	1.00	.40
6 Kurt Bevacqua	1.00	.40
7 Bobby Bonds	2.50	1.00
8 Bert Campaneris	1.50	.60
9 Reggie Cleveland	1.00	.40
10 Steve Comer	1.00	.40
11 Pat Corrales CO	1.00	.40
12 John Ellis	1.00	.40
13 Bill Fahey	1.00	.40
14 Mike Hargrove	1.50	.60
15 Toby Harrah	1.00	.40
16 Sid Hudson CO	1.00	.40
17 Billy Hunter MG	1.00	.40
18 Mike Jorgensen	1.00	.40
19 Jim Kern	1.00	.40
20 Fred Koenig CO	1.00	.40
21 Paul Lindblad	1.00	.40
22 John Lowenstein	1.00	.40
23 Sparky Lyle	1.50	.60
24 Jim Mason	1.00	.40
25 Jon Matlack	1.00	.40
26 George Doc Medich	1.00	.40
27 Roger Moret	1.00	.40
28 Al Oliver	2.00	.80
29 Jim Sundberg	1.50	.60
30 Jim Umbarger	1.00	.40
31 Bump Wills	1.00	.40
32 Richie Zisk	1.00	.40

1980 Rangers Postcards

These postcards came in black and white with the player's name in a white border on the bottom. For some unexplained reason, both Billy Sample and Bump Wills have two poses. These cards are not numbered so we have sequenced them in alphabetical order.

	NM	Ex
COMPLETE SET	20.00	8.00
1 Buddy Bell	1.00	.40
2 Steve Comer	.50	.20
3 Pat Corrales MG	.50	.20
4 Danny Darwin	.50	.20
5 Adrian Devine	.50	.20
6 Rich Donnelly CO	.50	.20
7 John Ellis	.50	.20
8 Pepe Frias	.50	.20
9 John Grubb	.50	.20
10 Bud Harrelson	.50	.20
11 Fergie Jenkins	2.00	.80
12 Jim Kern	.50	.20
13 Fred Koenig CO	.50	.20
14 Sparky Lyle	.75	.30
15 Jon Matlack	.50	.20
16 Doc Medich	.50	.20
17 Jackie Moore CO	.50	.20
18 Nelson Norman	.50	.20
19 Jim Norris	.50	.20
20 Al Oliver	1.00	.40
21 Gaylord Perry	2.00	.80
22 Pat Putnam	.50	.20
23 Dave Rajsich	.50	.20
24 Mickey Rivers	.75	.30
25 Dave Roberts	.50	.20
26 Billy Sample Patch on Uniform	.50	.20
27 Billy Sample No Patch	.50	.20
28 Rusty Staub	1.50	.60
29 Jim Sundberg	.50	.20
30 Jim Umbarger	.50	.20
31 Bump Wills With facial hair	.50	.20
32 Bump Wills Clean shaven	.50	.20
33 Richie Zisk	.75	.30

1983 Rangers Affiliated Food

The cards in this 28-card set measure 2 3/8" by 3 1/2". The Affiliated Food Stores chain of Arlington, Texas, produced this set of Texas Rangers late during the 1983 baseball season. Complete sets were given to children 13 and under at the September 3, 1983, Rangers game. The cards are numbered by uniform number and feature the player's name, card number, and the words "1983 Rangers" on the bottom front. The backs contain biographical data, career totals, a small black and white insert picture of the player, and the Affiliated Food Stores' logo. The coaches card is unnumbered.

	Nm-Mt	Ex-Mt
COMPLETE SET (28)	5.00	2.00
1 Bill Stein	.25	.10
2 Mike Richardt	.25	.10
3 Wayne Tolleson	.25	.10
5 Billy Sample	.25	.10
6 Bobby Jones	.25	.10
7 Bucky Dent	.50	.20
8 Bobby Johnson	.25	.10
9 Pete O'Brien	.50	.20
10 Jim Sundberg	.50	.20
11 Doug Rader MG	.25	.10
12 Dave Hostetler	.25	.10
14 Larry Biittner	.25	.10
15 Larry Parrish	.50	.20
17 Mickey Rivers	.25	.10
21 Odell Jones	.25	.10
24 Dave Schmidt	.25	.10
25 Buddy Bell	1.00	.40
26 George Wright	.25	.10
28 Frank Tanana	.75	.30
29 John Butcher	.25	.10
32 Jon Matlack	.25	.10
40 Rick Honeycutt	.25	.10
41 Dave Tobik	.25	.10

44 Danny Darwin .25 .10
46 Jim Anderson .25 .10
48 Mike Smithson .25 .10
49 Charlie Hough .75 .30
NNO Wayne Terwilliger CO .25 .10
Merv Rettenmund CO
Dick Such CO
Glenn Ezell CO
Rich Donnelly CO

1984 Rangers Jarvis Press

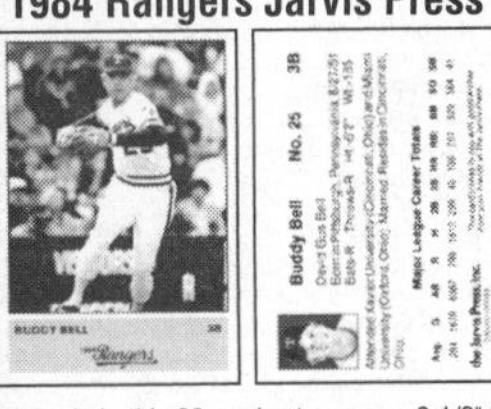

The cards in this 30-card set measure 2 1/2" by 3 1/2". The Jarvis Press of Dallas issued this full-color regional set of Texas Rangers. Cards are numbered on the front by the players uniform number. The cards were issued on an uncut sheet. Twenty-seven player cards, a manager card, a trainer card (unnumbered) and a coaches card (unnumbered) comprise this set. The backs are black and white and contain biographical information, statistics, and an additional photo of the player.

	Nm-Mt	Ex-Mt
COMPLETE SET (30)	5.00	2.00
1 Bill Stein	.25	.10
2 Alan Bannister	.25	.10
3 Wayne Tolleson	.25	.10
5 Billy Sample	.25	.10
6 Bobby Jones	.25	.10
7 Ned Yost	.25	.10
9 Pete O'Brien	.50	.20
11 Doug Rader MG	.25	.10
13 Tommy Dunbar	.25	.10
14 Jim Anderson	.25	.10
15 Larry Parrish	.50	.20
16 Mike Mason	.25	.10
17 Mickey Rivers	.50	.20
19 Curtis Wilkerson	.25	.10
20 Jeff Kunkel	.25	.10
21 Odell Jones	.25	.10
24 Dave Schmidt	.25	.10
25 Buddy Bell	1.00	.40
26 George Wright	.25	.10
28 Frank Tanana	.75	.30
30 Marv Foley	.25	.10
31 Dave Stewart	1.00	.40
32 Gary Ward	.25	.10
36 Dickie Noles	.25	.10
43 Donnie Scott	.25	.10
44 Danny Darwin	.50	.20
49 Charlie Hough	.75	.30
53 Joey McLaughlin	.25	.10
NNO Bill Ziegler TR	.25	.10
NNO Merv Rettenmund CO	.25	.10
Rich Donnelly CO		
Glenn Ezell CO		
Dick Such CO		
Wayne Terwilliger CO		

1984 Rangers Team Issue 4 X 6

This 31-card set features members of the 1984 Texas Rangers. These black and white blank-backed cards measure approximately 4 1/8" by 6 1/2" and have the player's photo surrounded by a white border. The bottom is dedicated to the player's name as well as the Rangers logo. Since these cards are unnumbered, we have sequenced them in alphabetical order.

	Nm-Mt	Ex-Mt
COMPLETE SET	15.00	6.00
1 Jim Anderson	.50	.20
2 Alan Bannister	.50	.20
3 Buddy Bell	.75	.30
4 Danny Darwin	.50	.20
5 Rich Donnelly	.50	.20
6 Glenn Ezell	.50	.20
7 Marv Foley	.50	.20
8 Tom Henke	1.50	.60
9 Charlie Hough	.75	.30
10 Bobby Jones	.50	.20
11 Odell Jones	.50	.20
12 Mike Mason	.50	.20
13 Pete O'Brien	.50	.20
14 Larry Parrish	.50	.20
15 Doug Rader MG	.50	.20
16 Merv Rettenmund	.50	.20
17 Mickey Rivers	.75	.30
18 Billy Sample	.50	.20
19 Dave Schmidt	.50	.20
20 Donnie Scott	.50	.20
21 Bill Stein	.50	.20
22 Dave Stewart	.50	.20
23 Dick Such CO	.50	.20
24 Frank Tanana	.75	.30
25 Wayne Terwilliger CO	.50	.20
26 Dave Tobik	.50	.20
27 Wayne Tolleson	.50	.20
28 Gary Ward	.50	.20
29 Curtis Wilkerson	.50	.20
30 George Wright	.50	.20
31 Ned Yost	.50	.20

1984-85 Rangers Team Issue 3 X 5

These cards, issued over at least a two-year period, feature members of the mid-1980's Texas Rangers. These blank-back black and white cards measure approximately 3" by 5" and feature black and white photos surrounded by white borders. The bottom left has the player's name while the bottom right has the Rangers logo. Since these cards are unnumbered, we have checklisted them in alphabetical order.

	Nm-Mt	Ex-Mt
COMPLETE SET	20.00	8.00
1 Jim Anderson	.50	.20
2 Alan Bannister	.50	.20
3 Buddy Bell	.75	.30
4 Bobby Bragan	.75	.30
5 Glenn Brummer	.50	.20
6 Glen Cook	.50	.20
7 Danny Darwin	.50	.20
8 Rich Donnelly	.50	.20
9 Tommy Dunbar	.50	.20
10 Glenn Ezell	.50	.20
11 Toby Harrah	.50	.20
12 Greg Harris	.50	.20
13 Burt Hooton	.50	.20
14 Charlie Hough	.75	.30
15 Tom House	.50	.20
16 Art Howe	.75	.30
17 Cliff Johnson	.50	.20
18 Bobby Jones	.50	.20
19 Mike Mason	.50	.20
20 Oddibe McDowell	1.00	.40
21 Dickie Noles	.50	.20
22 Pete O'Brien	.50	.20
23 Larry Parrish	.50	.20
24 Luis Pujols	.50	.20
25 Doug Rader MG	.50	.20
26 Dave Rozema	.50	.20
27 Billy Sample	.50	.20
28 Dave Schmidt	.50	.20
29 Don Slaught	.50	.20
30 Bill Stein	.50	.20
31 Dave Stewart	1.00	.40
32 Frank Tanana	.75	.30
33 Wayne Terwilliger CO	.50	.20
34 Wayne Tolleson	.50	.20
35 Gary Ward	.50	.20
36 Chris Welsh	.50	.20
37 Curtis Wilkerson	.50	.20
38 Bobby Valentine MG	.50	.20
39 George Wright	.50	.20
40 Ned Yost	.75	.30

1985 Rangers Performance

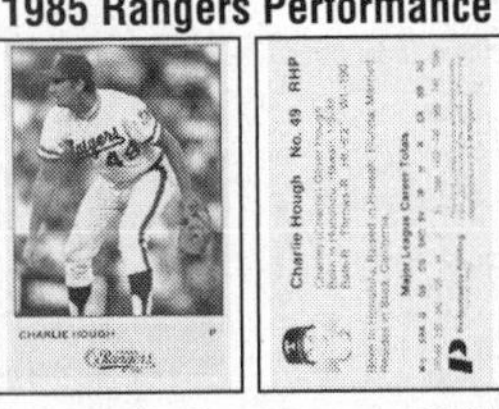

The cards in this 28-card set measure 2 3/8" by 3 1/2". Performance Printing sponsored this full-color regional set of Texas Rangers. Cards are numbered on the back by the players uniform number. The cards were also issued on an uncut sheet. Twenty-five player cards, a manager card, a trainer card (unnumbered) and a coaches card (unnumbered) comprise this set. The backs are black and white and contain biographical information, statistics, and an additional photo of the player.

	Nm-Mt	Ex-Mt
COMPLETE SET (28)	5.00	2.00
0 Oddibe McDowell	.75	.30
1 Bill Stein	.25	.10
2 Bobby Valentine MG	.50	.20
3 Wayne Tolleson	.25	.10
4 Don Slaught	.25	.10
5 Alan Bannister	.25	.10
6 Bobby Jones	.25	.10
7 Glenn Brummer	.25	.10
8 Luis Pujols	.25	.10
9 Pete O'Brien	.50	.20
11 Toby Harrah	.50	.20
13 Tommy Dunbar	.25	.10
15 Larry Parrish	.50	.20
16 Mike Mason	.25	.10
19 Curtis Wilkerson	.25	.10
24 Dave Schmidt	.25	.10
25 Buddy Bell	1.00	.40
27 Greg A. Harris	.25	.10
30 Dave Rozema	.25	.10
32 Gary Ward	.25	.10
36 Dickie Noles	.25	.10
41 Chris Welsh	.25	.10
44 Cliff Johnson	.50	.20
46 Burt Hooton	.25	.10
48 Dave Stewart	1.00	.40
49 Charlie Hough	.75	.30
NNO Bill Ziegler TR	.25	.10
Danny Wheat TR		
NNO Art Howe CO	.25	.10
Rich Donnelly CO		
Glenn Ezell CO		
Tom House CO		
Wayne Terwilliger CO		

1986 Rangers Greats TCMA

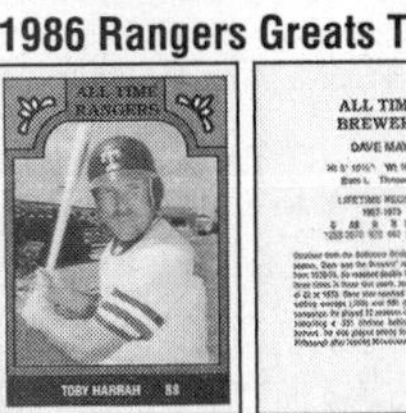

This 12-card standard-size set honors some of the leading Texas Rangers from their first 15 seasons. The player's photo, name and position are noted on the front. The backs have career information, vital statistics as well as a biography.

	Nm-Mt	Ex-Mt
COMPLETE SET (12)	3.00	1.20
1 Gaylord Perry	1.00	.40
2 Jon Matlack	.25	.10
3 Jim Kern	.25	.10
4 Billy Hunter MG	.25	.10
5 Mike Hargrove	.50	.20
6 Bump Wills	.25	.10
7 Toby Harrah	.50	.20
8 Lenny Randle	.25	.10
9 Al Oliver	.50	.20
10 Mickey Rivers	.50	.20
11 Jeff Burroughs	.25	.10
12 Dick Billings	.25	.10

1986 Rangers Lite

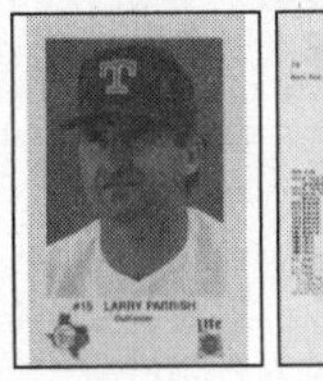

This seven-card set of the Texas Rangers features color player portraits with white borders and measures approximately 4" by 6". The backs carry player biographical information and career statistics. The cards are unnumbered and checklisted below in alphabetical order. These cards are known with our without stats on the back, however all values are the same for cards no matter what the back.

	Nm-Mt	Ex-Mt
COMPLETE SET	20.00	8.00
1 Bob Brower	.50	.20
2 Steve Buechele	1.00	.40
3 Edwin Correa	.50	.20
4 Joe Ferguson	.50	.20
5 Scott Fletcher	.50	.20
6 Tim Foli CO	.50	.20
7 Jose Guzman	.75	.30
8 Toby Harrah	.75	.30
9 Greg Harris	.50	.20
10 Dwayne Henry	.50	.20
11 Charlie Hough	1.00	.40
12 Tom House CO	.50	.20
13 Art Howe	.50	.20
14 Pete Incaviglia	1.50	.60
15 Mickey Mahler	.50	.20
16 Mike Mason	.50	.20
17 Oddibe McDowell	.75	.30
18 Pete O'Brien	.50	.20
19 Tom Paciorek	.50	.20
20 Larry Parrish	.75	.30
21 Geno Petralli	.50	.20
22 Darrell Porter	.75	.30
23 Tom Robson	.50	.20
24 Don Slaught	.50	.20
25 Bobby Valentine MG	.75	.30
26 Gary Ward	.50	.20
27 Curtis Wilkerson	.50	.20
28 Mitch Williams	1.00	.40
29 Bobby Witt	1.00	.40
30 George Wright	.50	.20
31 Ricky Wright	.50	.20
32 Arlington Stadium	.50	.20

1986 Rangers Performance

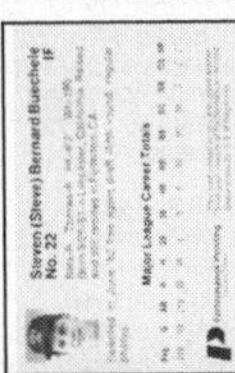

Performance Printing of Dallas produced a 28-card set of Texas Rangers which were given out at the stadium on August 23rd. Cards measure approximately 2 3/8" by 3 1/2" and are in full color. The cards are unnumbered except for uniform number which is given on the card back. Card backs feature black printing on white card stock with a small picture of the player's head in the upper left corner. The set seems to be more desirable than the previous Ranger sets due to the Rangers' 1986 success which was directly related to their outstanding rookie crop including Jose Guzman, Pete Incaviglia, Ruben Sierra, Mitch Williams, and Bobby Witt.

	Nm-Mt	Ex-Mt
COMPLETE SET (28)	10.00	4.00
0 Oddibe McDowell	.50	.20
1 Scott Fletcher	.25	.10
2 Bobby Valentine MG	.50	.20
3 Ruben Sierra	1.50	.60
4 Don Slaught	.25	.10
9 Pete O'Brien	.50	.20
11 Toby Harrah	.50	.20
12 Geno Petralli	.25	.10
15 Larry Parrish	.50	.20
16 Mike Mason	.25	.10
17 Darrell Porter	.50	.20
18 Edwin Correa	.25	.10
19 Curtis Wilkerson	.25	.10
22 Steve Buechele	.50	.20
23 Jose Guzman	.25	.10
24 Ricky Wright	.25	.10
27 Greg A. Harris	.25	.10
28 Mitch Williams	.75	.30
29 Pete Incaviglia	.75	.30
32 Gary Ward	.25	.10
34 Dale Mohorcic	.25	.10
40 Jeff Russell	.25	.10
44 Tom Paciorek	.25	.10
46 Mike Loynd	.25	.10
48 Bobby Witt	1.00	.40
49 Charlie Hough	1.00	.40
NNO Art Howe CO	.25	.10
Joe Ferguson CO		
Tim Foli CO		
Tom Robson CO		
Tom House CO		
NNO Bill Ziegler TR	.25	.10
Danny Wheat TR		

1987 Rangers Mother's

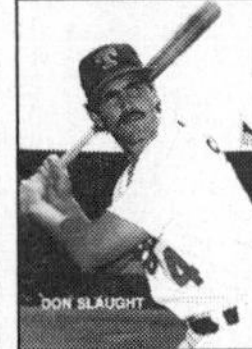

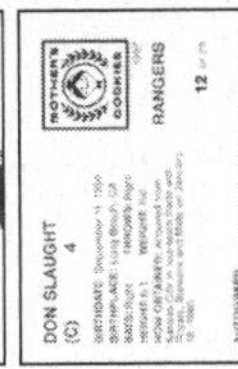

This set consists of 28 full-color, rounded-corner cards each measuring 2 1/2" by 3 1/2". Starter sets (only 20 cards but also including a certificate for eight more cards) were given out at the ballpark and collectors were encouraged to trade to fill in the rest of their set. Cards were originally given out on July 17th during the game against the Yankees. Photos were taken by Barry Colla. The sets were reportedly given out free to the first 25,000 paid admissions at the game.

	Nm-Mt	Ex-Mt
COMPLETE SET (28)	12.00	4.80
1 Bobby Valentine MG	.50	.20
2 Pete Incaviglia	.75	.30
3 Charlie Hough	.75	.30
4 Oddibe McDowell	.50	.20
5 Larry Parrish	.50	.20
6 Scott Fletcher	.25	.10
7 Steve Buechele	.25	.10
8 Tom Paciorek	.25	.10
9 Pete O'Brien	.50	.20
10 Darrell Porter	.50	.20
11 Greg A. Harris	.25	.10
12 Don Slaught	.25	.10
13 Ruben Sierra	1.50	.60
14 Curtis Wilkerson	.25	.10
15 Dale Mohorcic	.25	.10
16 Ron Meridith	.25	.10
17 Mitch Williams	1.00	.40
18 Bob Brower	.25	.10
19 Edwin Correa	.25	.10
20 Geno Petralli	.25	.10
21 Mike Loynd	.25	.10
22 Jerry Browne	.50	.20
23 Jose Guzman	.25	.10
24 Jeff Kunkel	.25	.10
25 Bobby Witt	1.00	.40
26 Jeff Russell	.50	.20
27 Bill Ziegler TR	.25	.10
Danny Wheat TR		
28 Tom Robson CO	.25	.10
Art Howe CO		
Joe Ferguson CO		
Tim Foli CO		
Tom House CO		
Dave Oliver CO CL		

1987 Rangers Smokey

The U.S. Forestry Service (in conjunction with the Texas Rangers) produced this large, attractive 32-card set. The cards feature Smokey the Bear pictured in the upper-right corner of every player's card. The card backs give a cartoon fire safety tip. The cards measure approximately 4 1/4" by 6" and are subtitled "Wildfire Prevention" on the front. Card numbers 4 Mike Mason and 14 Tom Paciorek were withdrawn and were never formally released as part of the set and hence are quite scarce.

	Nm-Mt	Ex-Mt
COMPLETE SET (32)	90.00	36.00
COMMON CARD (1-32)	.25	.10
COMMON SP	40.00	16.00
1 Charlie Hough	1.00	.40
2 Greg A. Harris	.25	.10
3 Jose Guzman	.25	.10
4 Mike Mason SP	40.00	16.00
5 Dale Mohorcic	.25	.10
6 Bobby Witt	1.00	.40
7 Mitch Williams	1.00	.40
8 Geno Petralli	.25	.10
9 Don Slaught	.25	.10
10 Darrell Porter	.25	.10
11 Steve Buechele	.25	.10
12 Pete O'Brien	.50	.20
13 Scott Fletcher	.25	.10
14 Tom Paciorek SP	40.00	16.00
15 Pete Incaviglia	1.00	.40
16 Oddibe McDowell	.50	.20
17 Ruben Sierra	1.50	.60
18 Larry Parrish	.50	.20
19 Bobby Valentine MG	.50	.20
20 Tom House CO	.25	.10
21 Tom Robson CO	.25	.10
22 Edwin Correa	.25	.10
23 Mike Stanley	2.00	.80
24 Joe Ferguson CO	.25	.10
25 Art Howe CO	.25	.10
26 Bob Brower	.25	.10
27 Mike Loynd	.25	.10
28 Curtis Wilkerson	.25	.10
29 Tim Foli CO	.25	.10
30 Dave Oliver CO	.25	.10
31 Jerry Browne	.25	.10
32 Jeff Russell	.25	.10

1988 Rangers Mother's

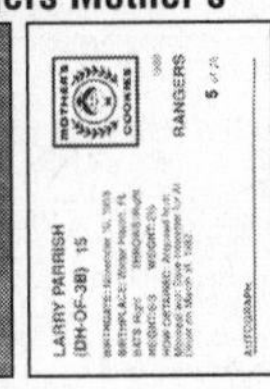

This set consists of 28 full-color, rounded-corner cards each measuring 2 1/2" by 3 1/2". Starter sets (only 20 cards but also including a certificate for eight more cards) were given out at the ballpark and collectors were encouraged to trade to fill in the rest of their set. Cards were originally given out on August 7th. Photos were taken by Barry Colla. The sets were reportedly given out free to the first 25,000 paid admissions at the game.

	Nm-Mt	Ex-Mt
COMPLETE SET (28)	8.00	3.20
1 Bobby Valentine MG	.50	.20
2 Pete Incaviglia	.50	.20
3 Charlie Hough	.75	.30
4 Oddibe McDowell	.50	.20
5 Larry Parrish	.50	.20
6 Scott Fletcher	.25	.10
7 Steve Buechele	.25	.10
8 Steve Kemp	.25	.10
9 Pete O'Brien	.50	.20
10 Ruben Sierra	1.00	.40
11 Mike Stanley	.25	.10
12 Jose Cecena	.25	.10
13 Cecil Espy	.25	.10
14 Curtis Wilkerson	.25	.10
15 Dale Mohorcic	.25	.10
16 Ray Hayward	.25	.10
17 Mitch Williams	.75	.30
18 Bob Brower	.25	.10
19 Paul Kilgus	.25	.10
20 Geno Petralli	.25	.10
21 James Steels	.25	.10
22 Jerry Browne	.25	.10
23 Jose Guzman	.25	.10
24 DeWayne Vaughn	.25	.10
25 Bobby Witt	.25	.10
26 Jeff Russell	.25	.10
27 Richard Egan CO	.25	.10
Tom House CO		
Art Howe CO		
Davey Lopes CO		
David Oliver CO		
Tom Robson CO		
28 Danny Wheat TR	.25	.10
Bill Zeigler TR CL		

1988 Rangers Smokey

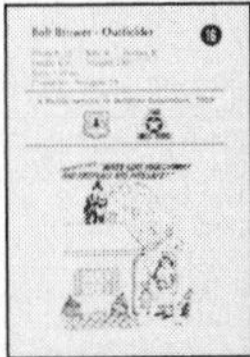

The cards in this 21-card set measure approximately 3 1/2" by 5". This numbered, full color set features the Fire Prevention Bear, Smokey, and a Rangers player (or manager) on each card. The set was given out at Arlington Stadium to fans during the Smokey Bear Day game promotion on August 7th. The logos of the Texas Forest Service and the U.S. Forestry Service appear on the reverse in conjunction with a Smokey the Bear logo on the obverse. The backs contain short biographical data and a fire prevention hint from Smokey.

	Nm-Mt	Ex-Mt
COMPLETE SET (21)	12.00	4.80
1 Tom O'Malley	.50	.20
2 Pete O'Brien	.75	.30
3 Geno Petralli	.50	.20
4 Pete Incaviglia	.75	.30
5 Oddibe McDowell	.75	.30
6 Dale Mohorcic	.50	.20
7 Bobby Witt	.50	.20
8 Bobby Valentine MG	.75	.30
9 Ruben Sierra	1.50	.60
10 Scott Fletcher	.50	.20
11 Mike Stanley	.50	.20
12 Steve Buechele	.50	.20
13 Charlie Hough	1.00	.40
14 Larry Parrish	.75	.30
15 Jerry Browne	.50	.20
16 Bob Brower	.50	.20
17 Jeff Russell	.50	.20
18 Edwin Correa	.50	.20
19 Mitch Williams	.75	.30
20 Jose Guzman	.50	.20
21 Curtis Wilkerson	.50	.20

1989 Rangers Mother's

The 1989 Mother's Cookies Texas Rangers set contains 28 standard-size cards with rounded corners. The fronts have borderless color photos, and the horizontally oriented backs have biographical information. Starter sets containing 20 of these cards were given away at a Rangers home game during the 1989 season.

	Nm-Mt	Ex-Mt
COMPLETE SET (28)	15.00	6.00
1 Bobby Valentine MG	.50	.20
2 Nolan Ryan	8.00	3.20
3 Julio Franco	1.00	.40
4 Charlie Hough	.75	.30
5 Rafael Palmeiro	2.50	1.00
6 Jeff Russell	.25	.10
7 Ruben Sierra	1.00	.40
8 Steve Buechele	.25	.10
9 Buddy Bell	.75	.30
10 Pete Incaviglia	.50	.20
11 Geno Petralli	.25	.10
12 Cecil Espy	.25	.10
13 Scott Fletcher	.25	.10
14 Bobby Witt	.25	.10
15 Brad Arnsberg	.25	.10
16 Rick Leach	.25	.10
17 Jamie Moyer	1.00	.40
18 Kevin Brown	2.00	.80
19 Jeff Kunkel	.25	.10
20 Craig McMurtry	.25	.10
21 Kenny Rogers	1.00	.40
22 Mike Stanley	.25	.10
23 Cecilio Guante	.25	.10
24 Jim Sundberg	.50	.20
25 Jose Guzman	.25	.10
26 Jeff Stone	.25	.10
27 Dick Egan CO Tom House CO Toby Harrah CO Davey Lopes CO Dave Oliver CO Tom Robson CO	.25	.10
28 Danny Wheat TR Bill Ziegler TR CL	.25	.10

1989 Rangers Smokey

The 1989 Smokey Rangers set features 34 unnumbered cards measuring approximately 4 1/4" by 6". The fronts feature mugshot photos with white borders. The backs feature biographical information and fire prevention tips. The set was given away at a 1989 Rangers' home game.

	Nm-Mt	Ex-Mt
COMPLETE SET (34)	25.00	10.00
1 Darrel Akerfelds	.50	.20
2 Brad Arnsberg	.50	.20
3 Buddy Bell	1.00	.40
4 Kevin Brown	2.50	1.00
5 Steve Buechele	.50	.20
6 Dick Egan CO	.50	.20
7 Cecil Espy	.50	.20
8 Scott Fletcher	.50	.20
9 Julio Franco	1.00	.40
10 Cecilio Guante	.50	.20
11 Jose Guzman	.50	.20
12 Drew Hall	.50	.20
13 Toby Harrah CO	.50	.20
14 Charlie Hough	1.00	.40
15 Tom House CO	.50	.20
16 Pete Incaviglia	.75	.30
17 Chad Kreuter	.50	.20
18 Jeff Kunkel	.50	.20
19 Rick Leach	.50	.20
20 Davey Lopes CO	.75	.30
21 Craig McMurtry	.50	.20
22 Jamie Moyer	1.50	.60
23 Dave Oliver CO	.50	.20
24 Rafael Palmeiro	5.00	2.00
25 Geno Petralli	.50	.20
26 Tom Robson CO	.50	.20
27 Kenny Rogers	1.50	.60
28 Jeff Russell	.50	.20
29 Nolan Ryan	12.00	4.80
30 Ruben Sierra	1.50	.60
31 Mike Stanley	.50	.20
32 Jim Sundberg	.75	.30
33 Bobby Valentine MG	.75	.30
34 Bobby Witt	.50	.20

1990 Rangers Mother's

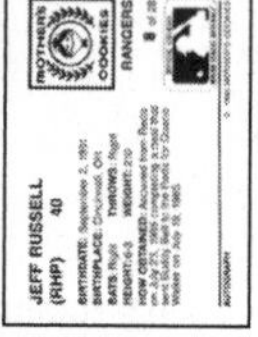

This 28-card, standard-size set features members of the 1990 Texas Rangers. The set has beautiful full-color photos on the front along with biographical information on the back. The set also features the now traditional Mother's Cookies rounded corners. The Rangers cards were distributed on July 22nd to the first 25,000 game attendees in Arlington. They were distributed in 20-card random packets at the game and eight more at the redemption booths. However, both groups of cards were random and there was no guarantee of getting a complete set in the cards. The promotional idea was that the only way one could finish the set was to trade for them. The redemption certificates (for eight more cards) were also able to be redeemed at the 17th Annual Dallas Card Convention on August 18-19, 1990.

	Nm-Mt	Ex-Mt
COMPLETE SET (28)	15.00	4.50
1 Bobby Valentine MG	.75	.23
2 Nolan Ryan	8.00	2.40
3 Ruben Sierra	1.00	.30
4 Pete Incaviglia	.50	.15
5 Charlie Hough	.50	.15
6 Harold Baines	.75	.23
7 Gino Petralli	.25	.07
8 Jeff Russell	.25	.07
9 Rafael Palmeiro	2.00	.60
10 Julio Franco	1.00	.30
11 Jack Daugherty	.25	.07
12 Gary Pettis	.25	.07
13 Brian Bohanon	.25	.07
14 Steve Buechele	.25	.07
15 Bobby Witt	.25	.07
16 Thad Bosley	.25	.07
17 Gary Mielke	.25	.07
18 Jeff Kunkel	.25	.07
19 Mike Jeffcoat	.25	.07
20 Mike Stanley	.25	.07
21 Kevin Brown	3.00	.90
22 Kenny Rogers	1.00	.30
23 Jeff Huson	.25	.07
24 Jamie Moyer	1.00	.30
25 Cecil Espy	.25	.07
26 John Russell	.25	.07
27 Dave Oliver CO Davey Lopes CO Tom Robson CO Tom House CO Toby Harrah CO	.25	.07
28 Bill Zeigler TR Joe Macko EQ.MG. Marty Stajduhar, Strength and Cond. Danny Wheat ATR	.25	.07

1990 Rangers Smokey

These oversize cards, which measure approximately 3 1/2" by 5" were given away at Rangers games in 1990. The cards were issued with the player photos in the middle, the Rangers logo on the upper left and the Smokey logo on the upper right. The backs have biographical information as well as a safety tip.

	Nm-Mt	Ex-Mt
COMPLETE SET	20.00	6.00
1 Harold Baines	1.00	.30
2 Brian Bohanon	.50	.15
3 Thad Bosley	.50	.15
4 Kevin Brown	1.50	.45
5 Jack Daugherty	.50	.15
6 Cecil Espy	.50	.15
7 Julio Franco	1.50	.45
8 Jeff Huson	.50	.15
9 Pete Incaviglia	.75	.23
10 Mike Jeffcoat	.50	.15
11 Chad Kreuter	.50	.15
12 Jeff Kunkel	.50	.15
13 Gary Mielke	.50	.15
14 Jamie Moyer	1.50	.45
15 Rafael Palmeiro	2.50	.75
16 Gary Pettis	.50	.15
17 Kenny Rogers	1.50	.45
18 Jeff Russell	.50	.15
19 John Russell	.50	.15
20 Nolan Ryan	5.00	1.50
21 Ruben Sierra	1.00	.30
22 Bobby Valentine MG	.75	.23
23 Bobby Witt	.50	.15
24 Arlington Stadium	.50	.15

1991 Rangers Mother's

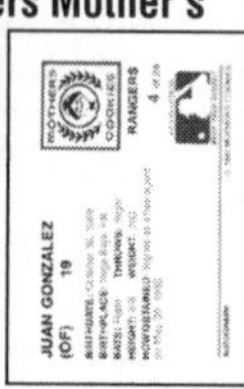

The 1991 Mother's Cookies Texas Rangers set contains 28 cards with rounded corners measuring the standard size.

	Nm-Mt	Ex-Mt
COMPLETE SET (28)	15.00	4.50
1 Bobby Valentine MG	.75	.23
2 Nolan Ryan	8.00	2.40
3 Ruben Sierra	.75	.23
4 Juan Gonzalez	8.00	2.40
5 Steve Buechele	.25	.07
6 Bobby Witt	.25	.07
7 Geno Petralli	.25	.07
8 Jeff Russell	.25	.07
9 Rafael Palmeiro	2.00	.60
10 Julio Franco	.75	.23
11 Jack Daugherty	.25	.07
12 Gary Pettis	.25	.07
13 John Barfield	.25	.07
14 Scott Chiamparino	.25	.07
15 Kevin Reimer	.25	.07
16 Rich Gossage	1.00	.30
17 Brian Downing	.50	.15
18 Denny Walling	.25	.07
19 Mike Jeffcoat	.25	.07
20 Mike Stanley	.25	.07
21 Kevin Brown	2.00	.60
22 Kenny Rogers	.75	.23
23 Jeff Huson	.25	.07
24 Mario Diaz	.25	.07
25 Brad Arnsberg	.25	.07
26 John Russell	.25	.07
27 Gerald Alexander	.25	.07
28 Tom Robson CO Toby Harrah CO Orlando Gomez CO Tom House CO Dave Oliver CO Davey Lopes CO CL	.25	.07

1992 Rangers Mother's

The 1992 Mother's Cookies Rangers set contains 28 cards with rounded corners measuring the standard size.

	Nm-Mt	Ex-Mt
COMPLETE SET (28)	15.00	4.50
1 Bobby Valentine MG	.75	.23
2 Nolan Ryan	5.00	1.50
3 Ruben Sierra	1.00	.30
4 Juan Gonzalez	3.00	.90
5 Ivan Rodriguez	4.00	1.20
6 Bobby Witt	.25	.07
7 Geno Petralli	.25	.07
8 Jeff Russell	.25	.07
9 Rafael Palmeiro	2.00	.60
10 Julio Franco	.75	.23
11 Jack Daugherty	.25	.07
12 Dickie Thon	.25	.07
13 Floyd Bannister	.25	.07
14 Scott Chiamparino	.25	.07
15 Kevin Reimer	.25	.07
16 Jeff M. Robinson	.25	.07
17 Brian Downing	.50	.15
18 Brian Bohanon	.25	.07
19 Jose Guzman	.25	.07
20 Terry Mathews	.25	.07
21 Kevin Brown	2.00	.60
22 Kenny Rogers	.75	.23
23 Jeff Huson	.25	.07
24 Monty Fariss	.25	.07
25 Al Newman	.25	.07
26 Dean Palmer	1.00	.30
27 John Cangelosi	.25	.07
28 Tom Robson CO Ray Burris CO Toby Harrah CO Dave Oliver CO Tom House CO Orlando Gomez CO	.25	.07

1992 Rangers Team Issue

This 27-card team photo set measures approximately 3" by 5". The fronts feature posed color player photos against a variegated gray studio background. The backs are blank. The cards are unnumbered and checklisted below in alphabetical order. Julio Franco, Brian Downing and Edwin Nunez all have a blue background.

	Nm-Mt	Ex-Mt
COMPLETE SET (27)	10.00	3.00
1 Floyd Bannister	.25	.07
2 Kevin Brown	1.50	.45
3 John Cangelosi	.25	.07
4 Scott Chiamparino	.25	.07
5 Jack Daugherty	.25	.07
6 Brian Downing	.50	.15
7 Julio Franco	.75	.23
8 Juan Gonzalez	1.50	.45
9 Jose Guzman	.25	.07
10 Jeff Huson	.25	.07
11 Mike Jeffcoat	.25	.07
12 Terry Mathews	.25	.07
13 Al Newman	.25	.07
14 Edwin Nunez	.25	.07
15 Rafael Palmeiro	1.50	.45
16 Dean Palmer	1.00	.30
17 Geno Petralli	.25	.07
18 Kevin Reimer	.25	.07
19 Ivan Rodriguez	2.00	.60
20 Kenny Rogers	.75	.23
21 Jeff Russell	.25	.07
22 Nolan Ryan	3.00	.90
23 Ruben Sierra	1.00	.30
24 Dickie Thon	.25	.07
25 Bobby Valentine MG	.50	.15
26 Bobby Witt	.25	.07
27 Model of New Ballpark	.25	.07

1993 Rangers Dr. Pepper

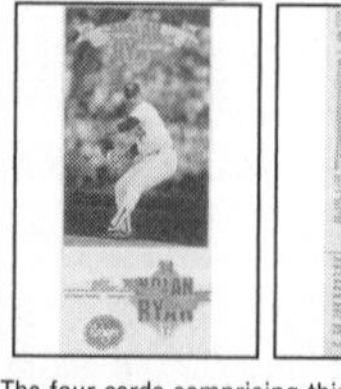

The four cards comprising this set were issued with metal pins which came attached to cardboard tabs beneath the perforated card bottoms. The cards measure approximately 2 1/2" by 3 7/8" and feature white-bordered color photos on their fronts. Other than the card of Nolan Ryan; the other pin/card combinations feature a picture of Arlington Stadium and some highlights from the history there. The back of Nolan Ryan's card features his career statistics. The attached pin carries his name and uniform number and bids "Farewell to a Legend." The backs of the Arlington Stadium cards feature text that explains the history of the ballpark. The backs of the Arlington Stadium pins carry Rangers logos. Though the cards are unnumbered, the pins are numbered "X of 4" on the cardboard tabs and checklisted below accordingly.

	Nm-Mt	Ex-Mt
COMPLETE SET (4)	15.00	4.50
COMMON CARD (1-4)	1.50	.45
3 Nolan Ryan	12.00	3.60

1993 Rangers Decker

These blank-backed full-color cards were sponsored by Decker foods and featured members of the 1993 Texas Rangers. These cards measure approximately 3" by 5" and since the cards are not numbered, we have sequenced them in alphabetical order. Please note that this set was originally available from the Rangers for $6.50.

	Nm-Mt	Ex-Mt
COMPLETE SET	20.00	6.00
1 Brian Bohanon	.50	.15
2 Jeff Bronkey	.50	.15
3 Kevin Brown	.50	.15
4 Todd Burns	.50	.15
5 Jose Canseco	.50	.15
6 Doug Dascenzo	.50	.15
7 Butch Davis	.50	.15
8 Julio Franco	.50	.15
9 Jeff Frye	.50	.15
10 Juan Gonzalez	.50	.15
11 Mickey Hatcher	.50	.15
12 Tom Henke	.75	.23
13 Perry Hill CO	.50	.15
14 David Hulse	.50	.15
15 Jeff Huson	.50	.15
16 Kevin Kennedy MG	.50	.15
17 Manuel Lee	.50	.15
18 Craig Lefferts	.50	.15
19 Charlie Leibrandt	.50	.15
20 Jackie Moore CO	.50	.15
21 Robb Nen	1.00	.30
22 Dave Oliver CO	.50	.15
23 Claude Osteen CO	.50	.15
24 Rafael Palmeiro	2.50	.75
25 Dean Palmer	1.00	.30
26 Bob Patterson	.50	.15
27 Roger Pavlik	.50	.15
28 Geno Petralli	.50	.15
29 Gary Redus	.50	.15
30 Bill Ripken	.50	.15
31 Ivan Rodriguez	2.50	.75
32 Kenny Rogers	1.00	.30
33 Nolan Ryan	4.00	1.20
34 Doug Strange	.50	.15
35 Willie Upshaw	.50	.15
36 Matt Whiteside	.50	.15

1993 Rangers Keebler

The Keebler All-Time Texas Rangers Card Series was a 468-card set (446 player cards plus 22 stat cards that have SP prefixes) issued in eight series booklets of perforated card sheets that honored everyone who ever wore a Rangers uniform during its 22-year history. The set was sponsored by Keebler and Albertsons food stores. Booklets of perforated sheets were distributed free to 35,000 fans as an in-stadium promotion at specific games. The exception was on April 9, when 42,000 booklets were distributed. Series I highlights 1972 team members, while Series VIII features the 1993 team, with the balance of the Rangers appearing in alphabetical order in Series II-VII.

	Nm-Mt	Ex-Mt
COMPLETE SET (468)	50.00	15.00
1 Ted Williams MG	4.00	1.20
2 Larry Biittner	.10	.03
3 Rich Billings	.10	.03
4 Dick Bosman	.10	.03
5 Pete Broberg	.10	.03
6 Jeff Burroughs	.25	.07
7 Casey Cox	.10	.03
8 Jim Driscoll	.10	.03
9 Jan Dukes	.10	.03
10 Bill Fahey	.10	.03
11 Ted Ford	.10	.03
12 Bill Gogolewski	.10	.03
13 Tom Grieve	.75	.23
14 Rich Hand	.10	.03
15 Toby Harrah	.25	.07
16 Vic Harris	.10	.03
17 Rich Hinton	.10	.03
18 Frank Howard	.75	.23
19 Gerry Janeski	.10	.03
20 Dalton Jones	.10	.03
21 Hal King	.10	.03
22 Ted Kubiak	.10	.03
23 Steve Lawson	.10	.03
24 Paul Lindblad	.10	.03
25 Joe Lovitto	.10	.03
26 Elliott Maddox	.10	.03
27 Marty Martinez	.10	.03
28 Jim Mason	.10	.03
29 Don Mincher	.10	.03
30 Dave Nelson	.10	.03
31 Jim Panther	.10	.03
32 Mike Paul	.10	.03
33 Horacio Pina	.10	.03
34 Tom Ragland	.10	.03
35 Lenny Randle	.25	.07
36 Jim Roland	.10	.03
37 Jim Shellenback	.10	.03
38 Don Stanhouse	.10	.03
39 Ken Suarez	.10	.03
40 Joe Camacho CO	.10	.03
41 Nellie Fox CO	1.50	.45
42 Sid Hudson CO	.10	.03
43 George Susce CO	.10	.03
44 Wayne Terwilliger CO	.10	.03
45 Darrel Akerfelds	.10	.03
46 Doyle Alexander	.25	.07
47 Gerald Alexander	.10	.03
48 Brian Allard	.10	.03
49 Lloyd Allen	.10	.03
50 Sandy Alomar	.25	.07
51 Wilson Alvarez	.75	.23
52 Jim Anderson	.10	.03
53 Scott Anderson	.10	.03
54 Brad Arnsberg	.10	.03
55 Tucker Ashford	.10	.03
56 Doug Ault	.10	.03
57 Bob Babcock	.10	.03
58 Mike Bacsik	.10	.03
59 Harold Baines	.75	.23
60 Alan Bannister	.10	.03
61 Floyd Bannister	.10	.03
62 John Barfield	.10	.03
63 Len Barker	.25	.07
64 Steve Barr	.10	.03
65 Randy Bass	.10	.03
66 Lew Beasley	.10	.03
67 Kevin Belcher	.10	.03
68 Buddy Bell	.75	.23
69 Juan Beniquez	.10	.03
70 Kurt Bevacqua	.25	.07
71 Jim Bibby	.10	.03
72 Joe Bitker	.10	.03
73 Larvell Blanks	.10	.03
74 Bert Blyleven	.75	.23
75 Terry Bogener	.10	.03
76 Tommy Boggs	.10	.03
77 Dan Boitano	.10	.03
78 Bobby Bonds	.75	.23
79 Thad Bosley	.10	.03
80 Dennis Boyd	.10	.03
81 Nelson Briles	.10	.03
82 Ed Brinkman	.10	.03
83 Bob Brower	.10	.03
84 Jackie Brown	.10	.03
85 Larry Brown	.10	.03
86 Jerry Browne	.10	.03
87 Glenn Brummer	.10	.03
88 Kevin Buckley	.10	.03
89 Steve Buechele	.10	.03
90 Ray Burris	.10	.03
91 John Butcher	.10	.03
92 Bert Campaneris	.25	.07
93 Mike Campbell	.10	.03
94 John Cangelosi	.10	.03
95 Nick Capra	.10	.03
96 Leo Cardenas	.25	.07
97 Don Carman	.10	.03
98 Rico Carty	.25	.07
99 Don Castle	.10	.03
100 Jose Cecena	.10	.03
101 Dave Chalk	.10	.03
102 Scott Chiamparino	.10	.03
103 Ken Clay	.10	.03
104 Reggie Cleveland	.10	.03
105 Gene Clines	.10	.03
106 David Clyde	.25	.07
107 Cris Colon	.10	.03
108 Merrill Combs CO	.10	.03
109 Steve Comer	.10	.03
110 Glen Cook	.10	.03
111 Scott Coolbaugh	.10	.03
112 Pat Corrales MG	.10	.03
113 Edwin Correa	.10	.03
114 Larry Cox	.10	.03
115 Keith Creel	.10	.03
116 Victor Cruz	.10	.03
117 Mike Cubbage	.10	.03
118 Bobby Cuellar	.10	.03
119 Danny Darwin	.10	.03
120 Jack Daugherty	.10	.03
121 Doug Davis	.10	.03
122 Odie Davis	.10	.03
123 Willie Davis	.25	.07
124 Bucky Dent	.25	.07
125 Adrian Devine	.10	.03
126 Mario Diaz	.10	.03
127 Rich Donnelly CO	.10	.03
128 Brian Downing	.25	.07
129 Tommy Dunbar	.10	.03
130 Steve Dunning	.10	.03
131 Dan Duran	.10	.03
132 Don Durham	.10	.03
133 Dick Egan CO	.10	.03
134 Dock Ellis	.25	.07
135 John Ellis	.10	.03
136 Mike Epstein	.10	.03
137 Cecil Espy	.10	.03
138 Chuck Estrada CO	.10	.03
139 Glenn Ezell CO	.10	.03
140 Hector Fajardo	.10	.03
141 Monty Fariss	.10	.03
142 Ed Farmer	.10	.03
143 Jim Farr	.10	.03
144 Joe Ferguson	.25	.07
145 Ed Figueroa	.10	.03
146 Steve Fireovid	.10	.03
147 Scott Fletcher	.10	.03
148 Doug Flynn	.10	.03
149 Marv Foley	.10	.03
150 Tim Foli	.10	.03
151 Tony Fossas	.10	.03
152 Steve Foucault	.10	.03
153 Art Fowler CO	.10	.03
154 Jim Fregosi	.25	.07
155 Pepe Frias	.10	.03
156 Oscar Gamble	.25	.07
157 Barbaro Garbey	.10	.03
158 Dick Gernert CO	.10	.03
159 Jim Gideon	.10	.03
160 Jerry Don Gleaton	.10	.03
161 Orlando Gomez CO	.10	.03
162 Rich Gossage	.75	.23
163 Gary Gray	.10	.03
164 Gary Green	.10	.03
165 John Grubb	.10	.03
166 Cecilio Guante	.10	.03
167 Jose Guzman	.10	.03
168 Drew Hall	.10	.03
169 Bill Hands	.10	.03
170 Steve Hargan	.10	.03

171 Mike Hargrove .50 .15
172 Toby Harrah .50 .15
173 Bud Harrelson .25 .07
174 Donald Harris .10 .03
175 Greg A. Harris .10 .03
176 Mike Hart .10 .03
177 Bill Haselman .10 .03
178 Ray Hayward .10 .03
179 Tommy Helms .10 .03
180 Ken Henderson .10 .03
181 Rick Henninger .10 .03
182 Dwayne Henry .10 .03
183 Jose Hernandez .10 .03
184 Whitey Herzog MG .50 .15
185 Chuck Hiller CO .10 .03
186 Joe Hoerner .10 .03
187 Guy Hoffman .10 .03
188 Gary Holle .10 .03
189 Rick Honeycutt .10 .03
190 Burt Hooton .25 .07
191 John Hoover .10 .03
192 Willie Horton .50 .15
193 Dave Hostetler .10 .03
194 Charlie Hough .50 .15
195 Tom House .10 .03
196 Art Howe CO .25 .07
197 Steve Howe .10 .03
198 Roy Howell .10 .03
199 Charles Hudson .10 .03
200 Billy Hunter MG .10 .03
201 Pete Incaviglia .50 .15
202 Mike Jeffcoat .10 .03
203 Ferguson Jenkins 1.50 .45
204 Alex Johnson .25 .07
205 Bobby Johnson .10 .03
206 Cliff Johnson .25 .07
207 Darrell Johnson MG .10 .03
208 John Henry Johnson .10 .03
209 Lamar Johnson .10 .03
210 Bobby Jones .10 .03
211 Odell Jones .10 .03
212 Mike Jorgensen .10 .03
213 Don Kainer .10 .03
214 Mike Kekich .10 .03
215 Steve Kemp .25 .07
216 Jim Kern .10 .03
217 Paul Kilgus .10 .03
218 Ed Kirkpatrick .10 .03
219 Darold Knowles .10 .03
220 Fred Koenig CO .10 .03
221 Jim Kremmel .10 .03
222 Chad Kreuter .10 .03
223 Jeff Kunkel .10 .03
224 Bob Lacey .10 .03
225 Al Lachowicz .10 .03
226 Joe Lahoud .10 .03
227 Rick Leach .10 .03
228 Danny Leon .10 .03
229 Dennis Lewallyn .10 .03
230 Rick Lisi .10 .03
231 Davey Lopes .25 .07
232 John Lowenstein .10 .03
233 Mike Loynd .10 .03
234 Frank Lucchesi MG .10 .03
235 Sparky Lyle .50 .15
236 Pete Mackanin .10 .03
237 Bill Madlock .25 .07
238 Greg Mahlberg .10 .03
239 Mickey Mahler .10 .03
240 Bob Malloy .10 .03
241 Ramon Manon .10 .03
242 Fred Manrique .10 .03
243 Barry Manuel .10 .03
244 Mike Marshall .25 .07
245 Billy Martin MG .75 .23
246 Mike Mason .10 .03
247 Terry Mathews .10 .03
248 Jon Matlack .10 .03
249 Rob Maurer .10 .03
250 Dave May .10 .03
251 Scott May .10 .03
252 Lee Mazzilli .25 .07
253 Larry McCall .10 .03
254 Lance McCullers .10 .03
255 Oddibe McDowell .25 .07
256 Russ McGinnis .10 .03
257 Joey McLaughlin .10 .03
258 Craig McMurtry .10 .03
259 Doc Medich .10 .03
260 Dave Meier .10 .03
261 Mario Mendoza .10 .03
262 Orlando Mercado .10 .03
263 Mark Mercer .10 .03
264 Ron Meridith .10 .03
265 Jim Merritt .10 .03
266 Gary Mielke .10 .03
267 Eddie Miller .10 .03
268 Paul Mirabella .10 .03
269 Dave Moates .10 .03
270 Dale Mohorcic .10 .03
271 Willie Montanez .10 .03
272 Tommy Moore .10 .03
273 Roger Moret .10 .03
274 Jamie Moyer 1.00 .30
275 Dale Murray .10 .03
276 Al Newman .10 .03
277 Dickie Noles .10 .03
278 Eric Nolte .10 .03
279 Nelson Norman .10 .03
280 Jim Norris .10 .03
281 Edwin Nunez .10 .03
282 Pete O'Brien .25 .07
283 Al Oliver .75 .23
284 Tom O'Malley .10 .03
285 Tom Paciorek .10 .03
286 Ken Pape .10 .03
287 Mark Parent .10 .03
288 Larry Parrish .25 .07
289 Gaylord Perry 1.50 .45
290 Stan Perzanowski .10 .03
291 Fritz Peterson .10 .03
292 Mark Petkovsek .10 .03
293 Gary Pettis .10 .03
294 Jim Piersall CO .25 .07
295 John Poloni .10 .03
296 Jim Poole .10 .03
297 Tom Poquette .10 .03
298 Darrell Porter .25 .07
299 Ron Pruitt .10 .03
300 Greg Pryor .10 .03
301 Luis Pujols .10 .03
302 Pat Putnam .10 .03
303 Doug Rader MG .10 .03
304 Dave Rajsich .10 .03
305 Kevin Reimer .10 .03
306 Merv Rettenmund CO .10 .03
307 Mike Richardt .10 .03
308 Mickey Rivers .25 .07
309 Dave Roberts .10 .03
310 Leon Roberts .10 .03
311 Jeff M. Robinson .10 .03
312 Tom Robson .10 .03
313 Wayne Rosenthal .10 .03
314 Dave Rozema .10 .03
315 Jeff Russell .25 .07
316 Connie Ryan MG .10 .03
317 Billy Sample .25 .07
318 Jim Schaffer CO .10 .03
319 Calvin Schiraldi .10 .03
320 Dave Schmidt .10 .03
321 Donnie Scott .10 .03
322 Tony Scruggs .10 .03
323 Bob Sebra .10 .03
324 Larry See .10 .03
325 Sonny Siebert .10 .03
326 Ruben Sierra 1.50 .45
327 Charlie Silvera CO .10 .03
328 Duke Sims .10 .03
329 Bill Singer .10 .03
330 Craig Skok .10 .03
331 Don Slaught .10 .03
332 Roy Smalley .25 .07
333 Dan Smith .10 .03
334 Keith Smith .10 .03
335 Mike Smithson .10 .03
336 Eric Soderholm .10 .03
337 Sammy Sosa 10.00 3.00
338 Jim Spencer .10 .03
339 Dick Such CO .10 .03
340 Eddie Stanky MG .25 .07
341 Mike Stanley .10 .03
342 Rusty Staub .75 .23
343 James Steels .10 .03
344 Bill Stein .10 .03
345 Rick Stelmaszek .10 .03
346 Ray Stephens .10 .03
347 Dave Stewart .50 .15
348 Jeff Stone .10 .03
349 Bill Sudakis .10 .03
350 Jim Sundberg .25 .07
351 Rich Surhoff .10 .03
352 Greg Tabor .10 .03
353 Frank Tanana .25 .07
354 Jeff Terpko .10 .03
355 Stan Thomas .10 .03
356 Bobby Thompson .10 .03
357 Danny Thompson .10 .03
358 Dickie Thon .10 .03
359 Dave Tobik .10 .03
360 Wayne Tolleson .10 .03
361 Cesar Tovar .10 .03
362 Jim Umbarger .10 .03
363 Bobby Valentine MG .50 .15
364 Ellis Valentine .10 .03
365 Ed Vande Berg .10 .03
366 DeWayne Vaughn .10 .03
367 Mark Wagner .10 .03
368 Rick Waits .10 .03
369 Duane Walker .10 .03
370 Mike Wallace .10 .03
371 Denny Walling .10 .03
372 Danny Walton .10 .03
373 Gary Ward .25 .07
374 Claudell Washington .25 .07
375 LaRue Washington UER .10 .03
(Misspelled Wasington on card back)
376 Chris Welsh .10 .03
377 Don Werner .10 .03
378 Len Whitehouse .10 .03
379 Del Wilber MG .10 .03
380 Curtis Wilkerson .10 .03
381 Matt Williams .10 .03
382 Mitch Williams .50 .15
383 Bump Wills .10 .03
384 Paul Wilmet .10 .03
385 Steve Wilson .10 .03
386 Bobby Witt .50 .15
387 Clyde Wright .10 .03
388 George Wright .10 .03
389 Ricky Wright .10 .03
390 Ned Yost .10 .03
391 Don Zimmer MG .25 .07
392 Richie Zisk .25 .07
393 Kevin Kennedy MG .10 .03
394 Steve Balboni .10 .03
395 Brian Bohanon .10 .03
396 Jeff Bronkey .10 .03
397 Kevin Brown 2.00 .60
398 Todd Burns .10 .03
399 Jose Canseco 3.00 .90
400 Cris Carpenter .10 .03
401 Doug Dascenzo .10 .03
402 Butch Davis .10 .03
403 Steve Dreyer .10 .03
404 Rob Ducey .10 .03
405 Julio Franco .50 .15
406 Jeff Frye .10 .03
407 Benji Gil .10 .03
408 Juan Gonzalez 2.50 .75
409 Tom Henke .50 .15
410 David Hulse .10 .03
411 Jeff Huson .10 .03
412 Chris James .10 .03
413 Manuel Lee .10 .03
414 Craig Lefferts .10 .03
415 Charlie Leibrandt .10 .03
416 Gene Nelson .10 .03
417 Robb Nen 1.00 .30
418 Darren Oliver .10 .03
419 Rafael Palmeiro 4.00 1.20
420 Dean Palmer 1.00 .30
421 Bob Patterson .10 .03
422 Roger Pavlik .10 .03
423 Dan Peltier .10 .03
424 Geno Petralli .10 .03
425 Gary Redus .10 .03
426 Rick Reed .50 .15
427 Bill Ripken .10 .03
428 Ivan Rodriguez 6.00 1.80
429 Kenny Rogers .50 .15
430 John Russell .10 .03
431 Nolan Ryan 12.00 3.60
432 Mike Schooler .10 .03
433 Jon Shave .10 .03
434 Doug Strange .10 .03
435 Matt Whiteside .10 .03
436 Mickey Hatcher CO .10 .03
437 Perry Hill CO .10 .03
438 Jackie Moore CO .10 .03
439 Dave Oliver CO .10 .03
440 Claude Osteen CO .10 .03
441 Willie Upshaw CO .10 .03
442 Checklist 1-112 .10 .03
443 Checklist 113-224 .10 .03
444 Checklist 225-336 .10 .03
445 Checklist 337-446 .10 .03
446 Arlington Stadium .10 .03
SP1 1972 Team Photo .25 .07
SP2 Logo .10 .03
SP3 Logo .10 .03
SP4 Logo .10 .03
SP5 Logo .10 .03
SP6 Home Run Leaders .10 .03
SP7 RBI Leaders .10 .03
SP9 Win Leaders .10 .03
SP10 Save Leaders .10 .03
SP11 Hit Leaders .10 .03
SP12 Stolen Base Leaders .10 .03
SP13 Games Played Leaders .10 .03
SP14 Strikeout Leaders .10 .03
SP15 ERA Leaders .10 .03
SP16 Games Pitched Leaders .10 .03
SP17 Innings Pitched Leaders .10 .03
SP18 Attendance Records .10 .03
SP19 Top 20 Crowds .10 .03
SP20 Hitting Streaks .10 .03
SP21 All-Stars .10 .03
SP22 Top Draft Picks .10 .03

1993 Rangers Stadium Club

This 30-card standard-size set features the 1993 Texas Rangers. The set was issued in hobby (plastic box) and retail (blister) form.

Nm-Mt Ex-Mt
COMP. FACT SET (30) 8.00 2.40
1 Nolan Ryan 4.00 1.20
2 Ritchie Moody .10 .03
3 Matt Whiteside .10 .03
4 David Hulse .10 .03
5 Roger Pavlik .10 .03
6 Dan Smith .10 .03
7 Donald Harris .10 .03
8 Butch Davis .10 .03
9 Benji Gil .10 .03
10 Ivan Rodriguez 2.00 .60
11 Dean Palmer .75 .23
12 Jeff Huson .10 .03
13 Rob Maurer .10 .03
14 Gary Redus .10 .03
15 Doug Dascenzo .10 .03
16 Charlie Leibrandt .10 .03
17 Tom Henke .10 .03
18 Manuel Lee .10 .03
19 Kenny Rogers .50 .15
20 Kevin Brown .75 .23
21 Juan Gonzalez 1.50 .45
22 Geno Petralli .10 .03
23 John Russell .10 .03
24 Robb Nen .75 .23
25 Julio Franco .75 .23
26 Rafael Palmeiro 1.50 .45
27 Todd Burns .10 .03
28 Jose Canseco 1.00 .30
29 Billy Ripken .10 .03
30 Dan Peltier .10 .03

1994 Rangers Magic Marker

This 40-card set was sponsored by Magic Marker and measures approximately 3" by 4 15/16". The fronts feature borderless color portraits of the 1994 Texas Rangers. The backs are blank. The cards are unnumbered and checklisted below in alphabetical order.

Nm-Mt Ex-Mt
COMPLETE SET (40) 15.00 4.50
1 Jack Armstrong .25 .07
2 Esteban Beltre .25 .07
3 Kevin Brown 1.00 .30
4 Jose Canseco 1.25 .35
5 Cris Carpenter .25 .07
6 Will Clark 1.50 .45
7 Steve Dreyer .25 .07
8 Rob Ducey .25 .07
9 Jeff Frye .25 .07
10 Juan Gonzalez 1.50 .45
11 Mickey Hatcher CO .25 .07
12 Rick Helling 1.00 .30
13 Tom Henke .50 .15
14 Perry Hill CO .25 .07
15 Rick Honeycutt .25 .07
16 Jay Howell .25 .07
17 David Hulse .25 .07
18 Bruce Hurst .25 .07
19 James Hurst .25 .07
20 Jeff Huson .25 .07
21 Chris James .25 .07
22 Kevin Kennedy MG .25 .07
23 Manuel Lee .25 .07
24 Oddibe McDowell .25 .07
25 Jackie Moore CO .25 .07
26 Darren Oliver .50 .15
27 Dave Oliver CO .25 .07
28 Junior Ortiz .25 .07
29 Claude Osteen CO .25 .07
30 Dean Palmer 1.00 .30
31 Roger Pavlik .25 .07
32 Gary Redus .25 .07
33 Rick Reed .50 .15
34 Bill Ripken .25 .07
35 Ivan Rodriguez 2.50 .75
36 Kenny Rogers .75 .23
37 Doug Strange .25 .07
38 Willie Upshaw CO .25 .07
39 Matt Whiteside .25 .07
40 The Ballpark in Arlington .25 .07

1995 Rangers Crayola

This 36-card set measures approximately 3" by 5". The fronts feature full-bleed color posed player portraits with the team logo, sponsor name, player's name and position in a blue bar across the bottom. The backs are blank. The cards are unnumbered and checklisted below in alphabetical order. This set was originally available from the Ragers for $6.50.

Nm-Mt Ex-Mt
COMPLETE SET (36) 10.00 3.00
1 The Ballpark in Arlington .25 .07
2 Jose Alberro .25 .07
3 Esteban Beltre .25 .07
4 Dick Bosman CO .25 .07
5 Terry Burrows .25 .07
6 Will Clark 1.50 .45
7 Bucky Dent CO .50 .15
8 Hector Fajardo .25 .07
9 Jeff Frye .25 .07
10 Benji Gil .25 .07
11 Juan Gonzalez 1.50 .45
12 Rusty Greer 1.50 .45
13 Kevin Gross .25 .07
14 Larry Hardy CO .25 .07
15 Shawn Hare .25 .07
16 Rudy Jaramillo CO .25 .07
17 Roger McDowell .25 .07
18 Mark McLemore .50 .15
19 Ed Napoleon CO .25 .07
20 Jerry Narron CO .25 .07
21 Chris Nichting .25 .07
22 Otis Nixon .25 .07
23 Johnny Oates MG .25 .07
24 Darren Oliver .50 .15
25 Mike Pagliarulo .25 .07
26 Dean Palmer 1.00 .30
27 Roger Pavlik .50 .15
28 Ivan Rodriguez 2.00 .60
29 Kenny Rogers .50 .15
30 Jeff Russell .25 .07
31 Mickey Tettleton .50 .15
32 Bob Tewksbury .25 .07
33 David Valle .25 .07
34 Jack Voigt .25 .07
35 Ed Vosberg .25 .07
36 Matt Whiteside .25 .07

1996 Rangers Dr Pepper

This 39-card set of the 1996 Texas Rangers was sponsored by the Dr. Pepper Bottling Co. of Texas and measures approximately 3" by 5". The fronts feature color player portraits on a blue background with the team logo, sponsor's name, player's name and position in a white box at the bottom. The backs are blank. The cards are unnumbered and checklisted below in alphabetical order. During the season, cards of Rene Gonzales, Rick Helling and Mike Stanton were pulled; however there is no real extra value for these cards.

Nm-Mt Ex-Mt
COMPLETE SET (39) 12.00 3.60
1 Dick Bosman CO .25 .07
2 Mark Brandenburg .25 .07
3 Damon Buford .25 .07
4 Will Clark 1.00 .30
5 Dennis Cook .25 .07
6 Bucky Dent CO .50 .15
7 Kevin Elster .25 .07
8 Lou Frazier .25 .07
9 Benji Gil .25 .07
10 Rene Gonzales .50 .15
11 Juan Gonzalez 1.25 .35
12 Rusty Greer 1.00 .30
13 Kevin Gross .25 .07
14 Darryl Hamilton .25 .07
15 Larry Hardy CO .25 .07
16 Rick Helling .75 .23
17 Gil Heredia .25 .07
18 Mike Henneman .25 .07
19 Ken Hill .25 .07
20 Rudy Jaramillo CO .25 .07
21 Mark McLemore .50 .15
22 Ed Napoleon CO .25 .07
23 Jerry Narron CO .25 .07
24 Warren Newson .25 .07
25 Johnny Oates MG .25 .07
26 Darren Oliver .25 .07
27 Dean Palmer 1.00 .30
28 Roger Pavlik .25 .07
29 Ivan Rodriguez 1.50 .45
30 Jeff Russell .25 .07
31 Mike Stanton .50 .15
32 Kurt Stillwell .25 .07
33 Mickey Tettleton .50 .15
34 David Valle .25 .07
35 Ed Vosberg .25 .07
36 Matt Whiteside .25 .07
37 Bobby Witt .25 .07
38 Craig Worthington .25 .07
39 The Ballpark in Arlington .25 .07

1996 Rangers Fleer

These 20 standard-size cards have the same design as the regular Fleer issue, except they are UV coated, use silver foil and are numbered "x of 20". The team set packs were available at retail locations and hobby shops in 10-card packs for a suggested price of $1.99.

Nm-Mt Ex-Mt
COMPLETE SET (20) 3.00 .90
1 Mark Brandenburg .10 .03
2 Damon Buford .10 .03
3 Will Clark .40 .12
4 Kevin Elster .10 .03
5 Benji Gil .10 .03
6 Juan Gonzalez .50 .15
7 Rusty Greer .30 .09
8 Kevin Gross .10 .03
9 Darryl Hamilton .10 .03
10 Ken Hill .10 .03
11 Mark McLemore .20 .06
12 Dean Palmer .20 .06
13 Roger Pavlik .10 .03
14 Ivan Rodriguez .75 .23
15 Mickey Tettleton .20 .06
16 Dave Valle .10 .03
17 Ed Vosberg .10 .03
18 Matt Whiteside .10 .03
19 Logo card .10 .03
20 Checklist .10 .03

1996 Rangers Mother's

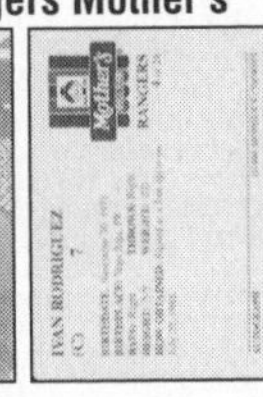

This 28-card set consists of borderless posed color player portraits in stadium settings. The player's and team's names appear in one of the top rounded corners. The backs carry biographical information and the sponsor's logo on a white background in red and purple print. A blank slot for the player's autograph rounds out the back.

Nm-Mt Ex-Mt
COMPLETE SET (28) 10.00 3.00
1 Johnny Oates MG .25 .07
2 Will Clark 1.25 .35
3 Juan Gonzalez 1.00 .30
4 Ivan Rodriguez 1.50 .45
5 Darryl Hamilton .25 .07
6 Dean Palmer .75 .23
7 Mickey Tettleton .50 .15
8 Craig Worthington .25 .07
9 Rusty Greer 1.00 .30
10 Kevin Gross .25 .07
11 Rick Helling .25 .07
12 Kevin Elster .25 .07
13 Bobby Witt .25 .07
14 Mark McLemore .50 .15
15 Warren Newson .25 .07
16 Mike Henneman .25 .07
17 Ken Hill .25 .07
18 Gil Heredia .25 .07
19 Roger Pavlik .25 .07
20 David Valle .25 .07
21 Mark Brandenburg .25 .07
22 Kurt Stillwell .25 .07
23 Ed Vosberg .25 .07
24 Dennis Cook .25 .07
25 Damon Buford .25 .07
26 Benji Gil .25 .07
27 Darren Oliver .25 .07
28 Dick Bosman CO .25 .07
Bucky Dent CO
Larry Hardy CO
Rudy Jaramillo CO
Ed Napoleon CO
Jerry Narron CO

1997 Rangers Commemorative Sheet

This 11" by 8 1/2" card was given away at the April 21, 1997, game between the Texas

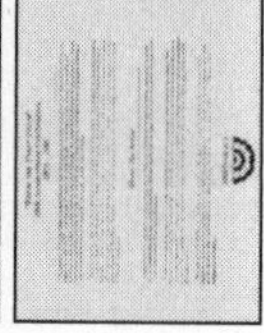

Rangers and the Detroit Tigers and commemorates the 25th Anniversary of the Rangers' first game at Arlington Stadium. It also honors former Arlington Mayor, Judge Tom Vandergriff, who was instrumental in biringing Major League Baseball to the North Texas area. The front features art work by sports artist, Vernon Wells, and depicts various present and former Texas Rangers. The back displays information about the 25th anniversary and the artist. Only 50,000 of this card was produced and are sequentially numbered.

Nm-Mt Ex-Mt
1 From the First Pitch 5.00 1.50

1997 Rangers Dr Pepper

This 34-card set sponsored by the Dr. Pepper Bottling Co. of Texas measures approximately 3" by 5" and features borderless color player portraits. The backs are blank. The cards are unnumbered and checklisted below in alphabetical order. During the season, the Dean Palmer card was pulled and was replaced by a card of Mark Sagmoen. This set was available from the Rangers for $5.

Nm-Mt Ex-Mt
COMPLETE SET (34) 12.00 3.60
1 Dick Bosman CO .... .25 .07
2 Damon Buford .... .25 .07
3 John Burkett .... .25 .07
4 Domingo Cedeno .... .25 .07
5 Will Clark .... 1.00 .30
6 Bucky Dent CO .... .25 .07
7 Mike Devereaux .... .25 .07
8 Benji Gil .... .25 .07
9 Juan Gonzalez .... 1.00 .30
10 Rusty Greer .... 1.00 .30
11 Eric Gunderson .... .25 .07
12 Xavier Hernandez .... .25 .07
13 Larry Hardy CO .... .25 .07
14 Ken Hill .... .25 .07
15 Rudy Jaramillo CO .... .25 .07
16 Mark McLemore .... .50 .15
17 Henry Mercedes .... .25 .07
18 Ed Napoleon CO .... .25 .07
19 Jerry Narron CO .... .25 .07
20 Warren Newson .... .25 .07
21 Johnny Oates MG .... .25 .07
22 Darren Oliver .... .25 .07
23 Dean Palmer .... 1.00 .30
24 Danny Patterson .... .25 .07
25 Roger Pavlik .... .25 .07
26 Bill Ripken .... .25 .07
27 Ivan Rodriguez .... 1.50 .45
28 Marc Sagmoen .... .25 .07
29 Julio Santana .... .25 .07
30 Lee Stevens .... .25 .07
31 Mickey Tettleton .... .50 .15
32 Ed Vosberg .... .25 .07
33 John Wetteland .... .75 .23
34 Bobby Witt .... .25 .07
35 The Ballpark in Arlington .... .25 .07

1997 Rangers 1st Interleague Game

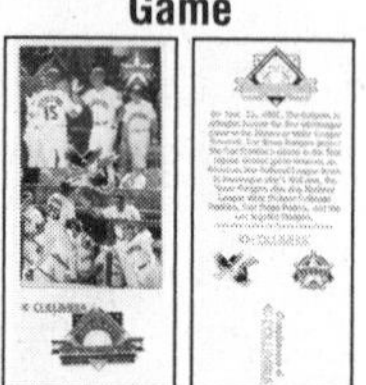

This one-card set and pin sponsored by Columbia Healthcare Systems was issued to commemorate the first regular season interleague game played in Major League Baseball on June 12, 1997. The American League Texas Rangers played the National League San Francisco Giants.

Nm-Mt Ex-Mt
1 Mickey Tettleton 4.00 1.20
Will Clark
Barry Bonds
Dusty Baker

1997 Rangers Minyard Magnets

This six-card set sponsored by Minyard Food Stores and Powerade Thirst Quencher features action color player photos printed on die-cut magnets. The magnets are unnumbered and checklisted below in alphabetical order.

Nm-Mt Ex-Mt
COMPLETE SET (6) 12.00 3.60
1 John Burkett .... 2.00 .60
2 Will Clark 4.00 1.20

3 Rusty Greer 4.00 1.20
4 Ken Hill .... 2.00 .60
5 Johnny Oates MG .... 2.00 .60
6 Mickey Tettleton .... 2.00 .60

1997 Rangers Mother's

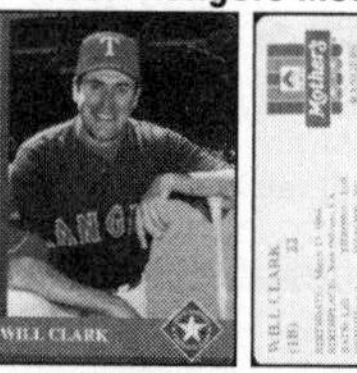

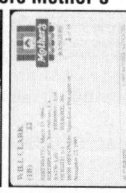

This 28-card set of the Texas Rangers sponsored by Mother's Cookies consists of posed color player photos with rounded corners. The backs carry biographical information and the sponsor's logo on a white background in red and purple print. A blank slot for the player's autograph rounds out the back.

Nm-Mt Ex-Mt
COMPLETE SET (28) 10.00 3.00
1 Johnny Oates MG .... .25 .07
2 Will Clark .... 1.00 .30
3 Juan Gonzalez .... 1.25 .35
4 Ivan Rodriguez .... 1.50 .45
5 John Wetteland .... .75 .23
6 Mickey Tettleton .... .50 .15
7 Dean Palmer .... .50 .15
8 Rusty Greer .... 1.00 .30
9 Ed Vosberg .... .25 .07
10 Lee Stevens .... .25 .07
11 Benji Gil .... .25 .07
12 Mike Devereaux .... .25 .07
13 Bobby Witt .... .25 .07
14 Mark McLemore .... .50 .15
15 Warren Newson .... .25 .07
16 Eric Gunderson .... .25 .07
17 Ken Hill .... .25 .07
18 Damon Buford .... .25 .07
19 Roger Pavlik .... .25 .07
20 Bill Ripken .... .25 .07
21 John Burkett .... .25 .07
22 Darren Oliver .... .25 .07
23 Mike Simms .... .25 .07
24 Julio Santana .... .25 .07
25 Henry Mercedes .... .25 .07
26 Xavier Hernandez .... .25 .07
27 Danny Patterson .... .25 .07
28 Dick Bosman CO .... .25 .07
Bucky Dent CO
Larry Hardy CO
Rudy Jaramillo CO
Ed Napoleon CO
Jerry Narron CO

1997 Rangers Score

This 15-card set of the Texas Rangers was issued in five-card packs with a suggested retail price of $1.30 each. The fronts feature color player photos with special team specific color foil stamping. The backs carry player information. Only 100 cases were made for each team. Platinum parallel cards were inserted at a rate of 1:6, Premier parallel cards at a rate of 1:31.

Nm-Mt Ex-Mt
COMPLETE SET (15) 5.00 1.50
*PLATINUM: 5X BASIC CARDS ....
*PREMIER: 20X BASIC CARDS ....
1 Mickey Tettleton .... .50 .15
2 Will Clark .... 1.00 .30
3 Ken Hill .... .25 .07
4 Rusty Greer .... .75 .23
5 Kevin Elster .... .25 .07
6 Darren Oliver .... .25 .07
7 Mark McLemore .... .50 .15
8 Roger Pavlik .... .25 .07
9 Dean Palmer .... .75 .23
10 Bobby Witt .... .25 .07
11 Juan Gonzalez .... 1.25 .35
12 Ivan Rodriguez .... 1.50 .45
13 Darryl Hamilton .... .25 .07
14 John Burkett .... .25 .07
15 Warren Newson .... .25 .07

1998 Rangers Dr. Pepper

This 34 card postcard set was issued by the Texas Rangers and was available to all fans through a mail in offer in the Rangers Program. The fronts feature posed shots against a blue background and blank banks. The backs are blank so we have sequenced them in alphabetical order. This set was available from the Rangers for a $5 cost.

Nm-Mt Ex-Mt
COMPLETE SET (34) 12.00 3.60
1 Luis Alicea .... .25 .07
2 Scott Bailes .... .25 .07
3 Dick Bosman CO .... .25 .07
4 John Burkett .... .25 .07
5 Domingo Cedeno .... .25 .07
6 Will Clark .... 1.00 .30
7 Tim Crabtree .... .25 .07
8 Bucky Dent CO .... .25 .07
9 Kevin Elster .... .25 .07
10 Juan Gonzalez .... 1.25 .35
11 Tom Goodwin .... .25 .07
12 Rusty Greer .... 1.00 .30
13 Eric Gunderson .... .25 .07
14 Larry Hardy CO .... .25 .07
15 Bill Haselman .... .25 .07
16 Rick Helling .... .25 .07
17 Xavier Hernandez .... .25 .07
18 Rudy Jarmaillo CO .... .25 .07
19 Roberto Kelly .... .25 .07
20 Mark McLemore .... .50 .15
21 Ed Napoleon CO .... .25 .07
22 Jerry Narron CO .... .25 .07
23 Johnny Oates MG .... .25 .07
24 Darren Oliver .... .25 .07
25 Danny Patterson .... .25 .07
26 Roger Pavlik .... .25 .07
27 Ivan Rodriguez .... 1.50 .45
28 Aaron Sele .... .50 .15
29 Mike Simms .... .25 .07
30 Lee Stevens .... .25 .07
31 Fernando Tatis .... .50 .15
32 John Wetteland .... .75 .23
33 Bobby Witt .... .25 .07
34 Ballpark in Arlington .... .25 .07

1999 Rangers Postcards Dr Pepper

These postcards were available directly from the Texas Rangers and cost $7 when ordered from the program. The fronts are a player portrait against a solid blue background except for the Johnny Oates cards and the players name along with the Rangers logo and an ad for Dr. Pepper is on the bottom of the card. The cards are blank backed and we have sequenced them in alphabetical order.

Nm-Mt Ex-Mt
COMPLETE SET 12.00 3.60
1 Luis Alicea .... .25 .07
2 Dick Bosman CO .... .25 .07
3 John Burkett .... .25 .07
4 Mark Clark .... .25 .07
5 Royce Clayton .... .25 .07
6 Tim Crabtree .... .25 .07
7 Bucky Dent CO .... .25 .07
8 Juan Gonzalez .... 1.25 .35
9 Tom Goodwin .... .25 .07
10 Rusty Greer .... .75 .23
11 Ryan Glynn .... .25 .07
12 Eric Gunderson .... .25 .07
13 Larry Hardy CO .... .25 .07
14 Rick Helling .... .25 .07
15 Rudy Jaramillo CO .... .25 .07
16 Roberto Kelly .... .25 .07
17 Danny Kolb .... .25 .07
18 Esteban Loiaza .... .75 .23
19 Ruben Mateo .... .50 .15
20 Mark McLemore .... .50 .15
21 Mike Morgan .... .25 .07
22 Mike Munoz .... .25 .07
23 Ed Napoleon CO .... .25 .07
24 Jerry Narron CO .... .25 .07
25 Johnny Oates MG .... .25 .07
26 Rafael Palmeiro .... 1.50 .45
27 Danny Patterson .... .25 .07
28 Ivan Rodriguez .... 1.50 .45
29 Aaron Sele .... .50 .15
30 Jon Shave .... .25 .07
31 Mike Simms .... .25 .07
32 Lee Stevens .... .25 .07
33 Mike Venafro .... .25 .07
34 John Wetteland .... .75 .23
35 Gregg Zaun .... .25 .07
36 Todd Zeile .... .50 .15
37 Jeff Zimmerman .... .25 .07
38 The Ballpark in Arlington .... .25 .07

2000 Rangers Clayton Sickle-Cell

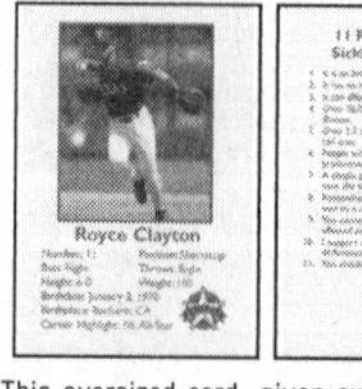

This oversized card, given away at a Texas Ranger game, features Rangers Shortstop Royce Clayton. The front has a color photo of Clayton along with his vital statistics. The back has 11 informative backs about sickle-cell anemia and includes information about how to help fight the disease.

Nm-Mt Ex-Mt
1 Royce Clayton .... 1.00 .30

2000 Rangers Postcards Dr. Pepper

Issued in conjunction with Dr. Pepper, these blank-backed postcards feature members of the 2000 Texas Rangers. Since these are unnumbered, we have sequenced them in alphabetical order. These cards were available from the Rangers public relations department for a $5 charge.

Nm-Mt Ex-Mt
COMPLETE SET (37) 12.00 3.60
1 Luis Alicea .... .25 .07
2 Dick Bosman CO .... .25 .07
3 Frank Catalanotto .... .50 .15
4 Mark Clark .... .25 .07
5 Royce Clayton .... .25 .07
6 Francisco Cordero .... .25 .07
7 Tim Crabtree .... .25 .07
8 Chad Curtis .... .25 .07
9 Doug Davis .... .25 .07
10 Bucky Dent CO .... .25 .07
11 Tom Evans .... .25 .07
12 Ryan Glynn .... .25 .07
13 Rusty Greer .... .75 .23
14 Bill Haselman .... .25 .07
15 Rick Helling .... .25 .07
16 Rudy Jaramillo CO .... .25 .07
17 Bobby Jones CO .... .25 .07
18 Gabe Kapler .... .50 .15
19 Mike Lamb .... .25 .07
20 Esteban Loaiza .... .75 .23
21 Ruben Mateo .... .50 .15
22 Jason McDonald .... .25 .07
23 Mike Munoz .... .25 .07
24 Jerry Narron CO .... .25 .07
25 Johnny Oates MG .... .25 .07
Card does not have a Dr. Pepper logo on it
26 Darren Oliver .... .25 .07
27 Rafael Palmeiro .... 1.50 .45
28 Matt Perisho .... .25 .07
29 Ivan Rodriguez .... 1.50 .45
30 Kenny Rogers .... .50 .15
31 David Segui .... .50 .15
32 Scott Sheldon .... .25 .07
33 Justin Thompson .... .25 .07
34 Mike Venafro .... .25 .07
35 John Wetteland .... .75 .23
36 Jeff Zimmerman .... .25 .07
37 The Ballpark in Arlington .... .25 .07

2000 Rangers Southwest Airline

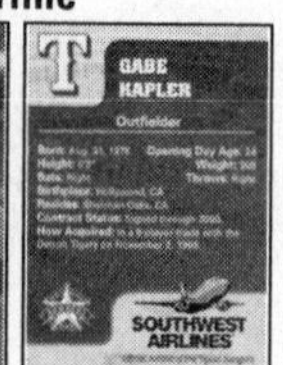

These 33 standard-size cards were handed out at the June 24th Texas Rangers game. Unlike previous Rangers set handed out at games, these sets were handed out in complete set fashion to all fans who wanted one. Since the sets are unnumbered except for uniform numbers we have sequenced them alphabetically.

Nm-Mt Ex-Mt
COMPLETE SET (33) 10.00 3.00
1 Luis Alicea .... .25 .07
2 Frank Catalanotto .... .75 .23
3 Royce Clayton .... .25 .07
4 Francisco Cordero .... .25 .07
5 Tim Crabtree .... .25 .07
6 Mark Clark .... .25 .07
7 Chad Curtis .... .25 .07
8 Tom Evans .... .25 .07
9 Scarborough Green .... .25 .07
10 Rusty Greer .... .75 .23
11 Bill Haselman .... .25 .07
12 Rick Helling .... .25 .07
13 Gabe Kapler .... .50 .15
14 Mike Lamb .... .25 .07
15 Esteban Loiaza .... .75 .23
16 Ruben Mateo .... .50 .15
17 Jason McDonald .... .25 .07
18 Mike Munoz .... .25 .07
19 Johnny Oates MG .... .25 .07
20 Darren Oliver .... .25 .07
21 Rafael Palmeiro .... 1.50 .45
22 Matt Perisho .... .25 .07
23 Ivan Rodriguez .... 1.50 .45
24 Kenny Rogers .... .25 .07
25 David Segui .... .50 .15
26 Mike Simms .... .25 .07
27 Scott Sheldon .... .25 .07
28 Justin Thompson .... .25 .07
29 Mike Venafro .... .25 .07
30 John Wetteland .... .75 .23
31 Jeff Zimmerman .... .25 .07
32 Rudy Jaramillo CO .... .25 .07
Bucky Dent CO
Jerry Narron CO
Johnny Oates CO
Dick Bosman CO
Bobby Jones CO
Larry Hardy CO
Coaches Card
33 Southwest Airline .... .25 .07

2001 Rangers Mrs Baird

This 10 card standard-size set was inserted into special loaves of Mrs Baird bread. In addition to these cards, lucky collectors had the chance to win discount Ranger tickets, a special "Breadwinners" set, autographed memorabilia and a chance to win use of a luxury suite at the Ballpark in Arlington. These cards were issued over two distinct series: Cards 1-5 from April to June and Cards 6-10 from July to August.

Nm-Mt Ex-Mt
COMPLETE SET (10) 8.00 2.40
1 Ivan Rodriguez .... 1.50 .45
2 Gabe Kapler .... .50 .15
3 Rusty Greer .... .75 .23
4 Rafael Palmeiro .... 1.50 .45
5 Kenny Rogers .... .50 .15
6 Alex Rodriguez .... 3.00 .90
7 Ruben Mateo .... .50 .15
8 Rick Helling .... .25 .07
9 Ken Caminiti .... .25 .07
10 Andres Galarraga .... 1.00 .30

2001 Rangers Postcards

Issued in conjunction with Dr. Pepper, these blank-backed postcards feature members of the 2001 Texas Rangers. Since these are unnumbered, we have sequenced them in alphabetical order. A savvy collector could order this set from the Rangerds public relations department for $5.

Nm-Mt Ex-Mt
COMPLETE SET 12.00 3.60
1 Jeff Brantley .... .50 .15
2 Ken Caminiti .... .25 .07
3 Frank Catalanotto .... .50 .15
4 Tim Crabtree .... .25 .07
5 Bobby Cuellar CO .... .25 .07
6 Chad Curtis .... .25 .07
7 Doug Davis .... .25 .07
8 Bucky Dent CO .... .25 .07
9 Andres Galarraga .... .50 .15
10 Ryan Glynn .... .25 .07
11 Rusty Greer .... .75 .23
12 Larry Hardy CO .... .25 .07
13 Bill Haselman .... .25 .07
14 Rick Helling .... .25 .07
15 Rudy Jaramillo CO .... .25 .07
16 Jonathan Johnson .... .25 .07
17 Bobby Jones CO .... .25 .07
18 Gabe Kapler .... .50 .15
19 Ricky Ledee .... .25 .07
20 Joe Macko TRIB .... .25 .07
21 Pat Mahomes .... .25 .07
22 Ruben Mateo .... .50 .15
23 Doug Mirabelli .... .25 .07
24 Jerry Narron CO .... .25 .07
25 Darren Oliver .... .25 .07
26 Rafael Palmeiro .... 1.25 .35
27 Mark Petkovsek .... .25 .07
28 Bo Porter .... .25 .07
29 Alex Rodriguez .... 2.50 .75
30 Ivan Rodriguez .... 1.25 .35
31 Kenny Rogers .... .75 .23
32 Scott Sheldon .... .25 .07
33 Justin Thompson .... .25 .07
34 Randy Velarde .... .25 .07
35 Mike Venafro .... .25 .07
36 Jeff Zimmerman .... .25 .07
37 The Ballpark in Arlington .... .25 .07

2001 Rangers Upper Deck Collectibles

This 20-card standard-size set was issued by Upper Deck and was a special set issued through the Texas Rangers gift shop. This set retailed for $15 at the gift shop and features mainly active players with the addition of retired great Nolan Ryan. Please note that these cards have a "TR" prefix before the number

MINT NRMT
COMPLETE SET 15.00 6.75
1 Alex Rodriguez 2.50 1.10
2 Rafael Palmeiro .... 1.50 .70
3 Ivan Rodriguez .... 1.50 .70
4 Andres Galarraga .... 1.00 .45
5 Ken Caminiti .... .50 .23
6 Ruben Mateo .... .25 .11
7 Rusty Greer .... .50 .23
8 Rick Helling .... .25 .11

9 Gabe Kapler .25 .11
10 Kenny Rogers .25 .11
11 Randy Velarde .25 .11
12 Doug Davis .25 .11
13 Bill Haselman .25 .11
14 Tim Crabtree .25 .11
15 Darren Oliver .25 .11
16 Jeff Zimmerman .25 .11
17 Ricky Ledee .25 .11
18 Mark Petkovsek .25 .11
19 Frank Catalanotto .25 .11
20 Nolan Ryan 5.00 2.20

2002 Rangers Postcards

Issued in conjunction with Dr. Pepper, these blank-backed postcards feature members of the 2002 Texas Rangers. Since these are unnumbered, we have sequenced them in alphabetical order.

	Nm-Mt	Ex-Mt
COMPLETE SET	15.00	4.50
1 Oscar Acosta CO	.25	.07
2 Hank Blalock	2.00	.60
3 Dave Burba	.25	.07
4 Frank Catalanotto	.75	.23
5 Doug Davis	.25	.07
6 Carl Everett	.50	.15
7 Terry Francona CO	.25	.07
8 Juan Gonzalez	1.25	.35
9 Rusty Greer	.75	.23
10 DeMarlo Hale CO	.25	.07
11 Bill Haselman	.25	.07
12 Hideki Irabu	.25	.07
13 Gabe Kapler	.50	.15
14 Rudy Jaramillo CO	.25	.07
15 Mike Lamb	.25	.07
16 Colby Lewis	.25	.07
17 Kevin Mench	1.00	.30
18 Chris Michalak	.25	.07
19 Jerry Narron MG	.25	.07
20 Rafael Palmeiro	1.25	.35
21 Chan Ho Park	.25	.07
22 Herbert Perry	.25	.07
23 Jay Powell	.25	.07
24 Jamie Quirk CO	.25	.07
25 John Rocker	.50	.15
26 Alex Rodriguez	2.50	.75
27 Ivan Rodriguez	1.25	.35
28 Rich Rodriguez	.25	.07
29 Kenny Rogers	.50	.15
30 Rudy Seanez	.25	.07
31 Steve Smith CO	.25	.07
32 Ismael Valdes	.25	.07
33 Todd Van Poppel	.25	.07
34 Steve Woodard	.25	.07
35 Michael Young	.75	.23
36 Jeff Zimmerman	.25	.07
37 The Ballpark in Arlington	.25	.07

2003 Rangers Dr. Pepper

This 38 card set was sold by the Rangers to their fans for $7 postpaid. Since these cards are not numbered, we have sequenced them in alphabetical order.

	MINT	NRMT
COMPLETE SET	15.00	6.75
1 Joacquin Benoit	.50	.23
2 Hank Blalock	1.50	.70
3 Ryan Christenson	.25	.11
4 Mark Connor CO	.25	.11
5 Francisco Cordero	.50	.23
6 Einar Diaz	.25	.11
7 R.A. Dickey	.25	.11
8 Ryan Drese	.25	.11
9 Carl Everett	.50	.23
10 Aaron Fultz	.25	.11
11 Rosman Garcia	.25	.11
12 Doug Glanville	.25	.11
13 Juan Gonzalez	1.00	.45
14 Todd Greene	.25	.11
15 Rusty Greer	.75	.35
16 DeMarlo Hale CO	.25	.11
17 Orel Hershiser CO	.25	.11
18 Rudy Jaramillo CO	.25	.11
19 Colby Lewis	.25	.11
20 Kevin Mench	.50	.23
21 Chan Ho Park	.25	.11
22 Rafael Palmeiro	1.50	.70
23 Herbert Perry	.25	.11
24 Jay Powell	.25	.11
25 Alex Rodriguez	2.50	1.10
26 Buck Showalter MG	.25	.11
27 Brian Shouse	.25	.11
28 Ruben Sierra	.50	.23
29 Steve Smith CO	.25	.11
30 Mark Teixeira	2.00	.90
31 John Thomson	.25	.11
32 Ugueth Urbina	.25	.11
33 Ismael Valdes	.25	.11
34 Todd Van Poppel	.25	.11
35 Don Wakamatsu CO	.25	.11
36 Esteban Yan	.25	.11
37 Michael Young	.25	.11
38 Jeff Zimmerman	.25	.11

1955 Rawlings Musial

This six-card set was actually the side panels of the box containing a Rawlings baseball glove. Rawlings Sporting Goods was headquartered in St. Louis. The cards are numbered and come in two sizes. Cards 1-4 are larger, 2 5/8" by 3 3/4" whereas numbers 1A and 2A are smaller, 2 1/8" by 3 1/8". The cards are blank backed and have a black and white picture on a light blue background.

	NM	Ex
COMPLETE SET (6)	1500.00	750.00
1 Stan Musial portrait	300.00	150.00
1A Stan Musial portrait with hand and bat visible	200.00	100.00
2 Stan Musial kneeling	300.00	150.00
2A Stan Musial portrait, same picture as number 1	200.00	100.00
3 Stan Musial swinging HOR	300.00	150.00
4 Stan Musial batting stance	300.00	150.00

1961 Rawlings

This set measures approximately 8 1/8" by 10 1/8" and features white-bordered, black-and-white player photos. A facsimile autograph and sponsor name is printed in a white box on one side of the picture. The backs are blank. The cards are unnumbered and checklisted below in alphabetical order. More photos, from more years, are believed to exist so any additions to this checklist are appreciated.

	NM	Ex
COMPLETE SET	500.00	200.00
1 Joe Adcock	20.00	8.00
2 Ed Bailey	10.00	4.00
3 John Blanchard	10.00	4.00
4 Clete Boyer	20.00	8.00
5 Ken Boyer 2 different photos known	25.00	10.00
6 Lew Burdette	15.00	6.00
7 Bob Cerv	10.00	4.00
8 Wes Covington	10.00	4.00
9 Joe Cunningham	10.00	4.00
10 Tommy Davis	15.00	6.00
11 Don Demeter	10.00	4.00
12 Jim Grant	10.00	4.00
13 Dick Groat	10.00	4.00
14 Harvey Haddix	10.00	4.00
15 Elston Howard	25.00	10.00
16 Larry Jackson	10.00	4.00
17 Tony Kubek	25.00	10.00
18 Vern Law	10.00	4.00
19 Sherm Lollar	10.00	4.00
20 Mickey Mantle	80.00	32.00
21 Eddie Mathews	30.00	12.00
22 Wilmer Mizell	10.00	4.00
23 Wally Moon	15.00	6.00
24 Stan Musial	40.00	16.00
25 Charlie Neal	10.00	4.00
26 Rocky Nelson	10.00	4.00
27 Brooks Robinson	30.00	12.00
28 Herb Score	15.00	6.00
29 Roy Sievers	15.00	6.00
30 Bob Skinner	10.00	4.00
31 Duke Snider	30.00	12.00
32 Warren Spahn	30.00	12.00
33 Bob Turley	15.00	6.00

1964-66 Rawlings

This set features borderless color player photos that measure 2 3/8" by 4" when properly cut off the glove boxes on which they were printed. The photos are of stars of the day posing with their Rawlings glove prominently displayed, and a facsimile autograph is printed across the bottom of the picture. The cards are unnumbered and checklisted below in alphabetical order. There was also a picture issue of 8" by 9 1/2" Advisory Staff photos given away upon purchase. The same players featured on the boxes were featured on these photos.

	NM	Ex
COMPLETE SET	150.00	60.00
1 Ken Boyer Cards	15.00	6.00
2 Ken Boyer Mets	15.00	6.00
3 Gordy Coleman	10.00	4.00
4 Tommy Davis	10.00	4.00
5 Willie Davis	12.00	4.80
6 Dick Groat	15.00	6.00
7 Mickey Mantle	50.00	20.00
8 Dal Maxvill	10.00	4.00
9 Brooks Robinson	25.00	10.00
10 Warren Spahn	20.00	8.00
11 Tom Tresh	12.00	4.80
12 Bill White Phillies	15.00	6.00
13 Billy Williams	20.00	8.00

1976 Rawlings

This card was distributed by Rawlings Sporting Goods Company honoring Cesar Cedeno on the winning of his 4th consecutive Golden Glove Award. It measures approximately 5" by 7" and features a color photo in a white border with a white facsimile autograph. The back displays player information and career statistics. This set may be incomplete.

	NM	Ex
1 Cesar Cedeno	3.00	1.20

1998 Rawlings

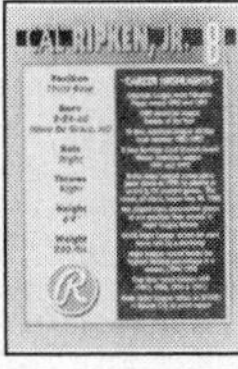

This 10 card standard-size set was issued by Rawlings to promote their line of gloves. Each card has the player's photo on the front surrounded by brown borders while the back has biographical information as well as career highlights. Since these cards are unnumbered, we have sequenced them in alphabetical order.

	MINT	NRMT
COMPLETE SET	15.00	6.75
1 Craig Biggio	.75	.35
2 Ken Griffey Jr.	1.50	.70
3 Tony Gwynn	2.00	.90
4 Derek Jeter	4.00	1.80
5 Randy Johnson	1.25	.55
6 Mark McGwire	2.50	1.10
7 Mike Piazza	2.50	1.10
8 Cal Ripken Jr.	4.00	1.80
9 Larry Walker	1.00	.45
10 Bernie Williams	1.00	.45

1976 Red Barn Discs

These are the toughest discs issued in 1976. They are valued at a significantly higher multiplier than any of the other Disc sets. They have a Red Barn back.

	NM	Ex
COMPLETE SET (70)	300.00	120.00
1 Hank Aaron	40.00	16.00
2 Johnny Bench	30.00	12.00
3 Vida Blue	4.00	1.60
4 Larry Bowa	4.00	1.60
5 Lou Brock	30.00	12.00
6 Jeff Burroughs	1.50	.60
7 John Candelaria	1.50	.60
8 Jose Cardenal	1.50	.60
9 Rod Carew	30.00	12.00
10 Steve Carlton	30.00	12.00
11 Dave Cash	1.50	.60
12 Cesar Cedeno	4.00	1.60
13 Ron Cey	4.00	1.60
14 Carlton Fisk	30.00	12.00
15 Tito Fuentes	1.50	.60
16 Steve Garvey	15.00	6.00
17 Ken Griffey	4.00	1.60
18 Don Gullett	1.50	.60
19 Willie Horton	1.50	.60
20 Al Hrabosky	1.50	.60
21 Catfish Hunter	20.00	8.00
22A Reggie Jackson Oakland Athletics	75.00	30.00
22B Reggie Jackson Baltimore Orioles	20.00	8.00
23 Randy Jones	1.50	.60
24 Jim Kaat	8.00	3.20
25 Don Kessinger	1.50	.60
26 Dave Kingman	8.00	3.20
27 Jerry Koosman	4.00	1.60
28 Mickey Lolich	4.00	1.60
29 Greg Luzinski	8.00	3.20
30 Fred Lynn	8.00	3.20
31 Bill Madlock	4.00	1.60
32A Carlos May Chicago White Sox	15.00	6.00
32B Carlos May New York Yankees	1.50	.60
33 John Mayberry	1.50	.60
34 Bake McBride	1.50	.60
35 Doc Medich	1.50	.60
36A Andy Messersmith Los Angeles Dodgers	15.00	6.00
36B Andy Messersmith Atlanta Braves	1.50	.60
37 Rick Monday	1.50	.60
38 John Montefusco	1.50	.60
39 Jerry Morales	1.50	.60
40 Joe Morgan	20.00	8.00
41 Thurman Munson	15.00	6.00
42 Bobby Murcer	8.00	3.20
43 Al Oliver	8.00	3.20
44 Jim Palmer	20.00	8.00
45 Dave Parker	10.00	4.00
46 Tony Perez	15.00	6.00
47 Jerry Reuss	1.50	.60
48 Brooks Robinson	20.00	8.00
49 Frank Robinson	20.00	8.00
50 Steve Rogers	1.50	.60
51 Pete Rose	30.00	12.00
52 Nolan Ryan	60.00	24.00
53 Manny Sanguillen	1.50	.60
54 Mike Schmidt	40.00	16.00
55 Tom Seaver	30.00	12.00
56 Ted Simmons	8.00	3.20
57 Reggie Smith	4.00	1.60
58 Willie Stargell	20.00	8.00
59 Rusty Staub	8.00	3.20
60 Rennie Stennett	1.50	.60
61 Don Sutton	20.00	8.00
62A Andre Thornton Chicago Cubs	15.00	6.00
62B Andre Thornton Montreal Expos	1.50	.60
63 Luis Tiant	8.00	3.20
64 Joe Torre	10.00	4.00
65 Mike Tyson	1.50	.60
66 Bob Watson	4.00	1.60
67 Wilbur Wood	1.50	.60
68 Jimmy Wynn	1.50	.60
69 Carl Yastrzemski	20.00	8.00
70 Richie Zisk	1.50	.60

1910-13 Red Cross T215

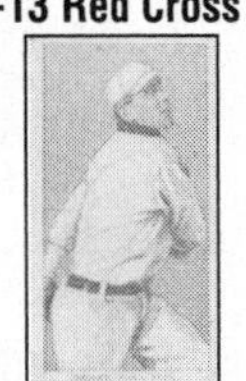

The cards in this 167-card set measure 1 1/2" by 2 5/8." There are actually three distinct groupings or types. Type 1 cards have brown captions. Type 2 cards have blue captions. Type 3 cards are distinguished by their "Pirate Cigarettes" backs printed in green ink. The type 3 cards, are so thinly traded that there is no pricing information available on them. According to leading dealers and collectors, these cards were produced for Americans serving their country in the South Seas. The players have been alphabetized within Type and numbered for reference in the checklist below.

	Ex-Mt	VG
COMMON TYPE 1 (1-88)	120.00	60.00
COMMON TYPE 2 (89-167)	80.00	40.00
COMMON TYPE 3 (168-259)		
1 Red Ames	120.00	60.00
2 Frank Baker	250.00	125.00
3 Neal Ball	120.00	60.00
4 Chief Bender (2)	250.00	125.00
5 Chief Bender (2)	250.00	125.00
6 Al Bridwell	120.00	60.00
7 Bobby Byrne	120.00	60.00
8 Howie Camnitz	120.00	60.00
9 Frank Chance	400.00	200.00
10 Hal Chase	250.00	125.00
11 Ty Cobb	2000.00	1000.00
12 Eddie Collins	250.00	125.00
13 Wid Conroy	120.00	60.00
14 Doc Crandall	120.00	60.00
15 Sam Crawford	250.00	125.00
16 Birdie Cree	120.00	60.00
17 Harry Davis	120.00	60.00
18 Josh Devore	120.00	60.00
19 Mike Donlin	150.00	75.00
20 Mickey Doolan	120.00	60.00
21 Patsy Dougherty	120.00	60.00
22 Larry Doyle	150.00	75.00
23 Larry Doyle	150.00	75.00
24 Kid Elberfeld	120.00	60.00
25 Russ Ford	120.00	60.00
26 Art Fromme	120.00	60.00
27 Clark Griffith	250.00	125.00
28 Topsy Hartsel	120.00	60.00
29 Doc Hoblitzell	120.00	60.00
30 Danny Hofman	120.00	60.00
31 Del Howard	120.00	60.00
32 Miller Huggins	250.00	125.00
33 John Hummell	120.00	60.00
34 Hugh Jennings (2)	250.00	125.00
35 Hugh Jennings (2)	250.00	125.00
36 Walter Johnson	600.00	300.00
37 Ed Konetchy	120.00	60.00
38 Harry Krause	120.00	60.00
39 Nap Lajoie	500.00	250.00
40 Arlie Latham	120.00	60.00
41 Tommy Leach	120.00	60.00
42 Lefty Leifield	120.00	60.00
43 Harry Lord	120.00	60.00
44 Sherry Magee	200.00	100.00
45 Rube Marquard (2)	250.00	125.00
46 Rube Marquard (2)	250.00	125.00
47 Christy Mathewson	600.00	300.00
48 Christy Mathewson	600.00	300.00
49 Joe McGinnity	250.00	125.00
50 John McGraw (2)	400.00	200.00
51 John McGraw (2)	400.00	200.00
52 Matty McIntyre	120.00	60.00
53 Fred Merkle	200.00	100.00
54 Chief Meyers	150.00	75.00
55 Dots Miller	120.00	60.00
56 George Mullin	150.00	75.00
57 Danny Murphy	120.00	60.00
58 Red Murray	120.00	60.00
59 Rebel Oakes	120.00	60.00
60 Charley O'Leary	120.00	60.00
61 Dode Paskert	120.00	60.00
62 Barney Pelty	120.00	60.00
63 Jack Quinn	120.00	60.00
64 Ed Reulbach	150.00	75.00
65 Nap Rucker	150.00	75.00
66 Germany Schaefer	200.00	100.00
67 Frank Schulte	150.00	75.00
68 Jimmy Sheckard	120.00	60.00
69 Frank Smith	120.00	60.00
70 Smither	120.00	60.00
71 Tris Speaker	500.00	250.00
72 Jake Stahl	150.00	75.00
73 Harry Steinfeldt	150.00	75.00
74 Gabby Street (2)	120.00	60.00
75 Gabby Street (2)	120.00	60.00
76 William Sweeney	120.00	60.00
77 Lee Tannehill	120.00	60.00
78 Joe Tinker (2)	250.00	125.00
79 Joe Tinker (2)	250.00	125.00
80 Honus Wagner	600.00	300.00
81 Jack Warhop	120.00	60.00
82 Zach Wheat	250.00	125.00
83 Doc White	120.00	60.00
84 Ed Willett	120.00	60.00
85 Owen Wilson	120.00	60.00
86 Hooks Wiltse (2)	120.00	60.00
87 Hooks Wiltse (2)	120.00	60.00
88 Cy Young	500.00	250.00
89 Red Ames	80.00	40.00
90 Chief Bender (2)	150.00	75.00
91 Chief Bender (2)	150.00	75.00
92 Roger Bresnahan	150.00	75.00
93 Mordecai Brown	150.00	75.00
94 Bobby Byrne	80.00	40.00
95 Howie Camnitz	80.00	40.00
96 Frank Chance	300.00	150.00
97 Ty Cobb	1500.00	750.00
98 Eddie Collins	150.00	75.00
99 Doc Crandall	80.00	40.00
100 Birdie Cree	80.00	40.00
101 Harry Davis	80.00	40.00
102 Josh Devore	80.00	40.00
103 Mike Donlin	100.00	50.00
104 Mickey Doolan (2)	80.00	40.00
105 Mickey Doolan (2)	80.00	40.00
106 Patsy Dougherty	80.00	40.00
107 Larry Doyle (2)	100.00	50.00
108 Larry Doyle (2)	100.00	50.00
109 Jean Dubuc	80.00	40.00
110 Kid Elberfeld	80.00	40.00
111 Johnny Evers	150.00	75.00
112 Russ Ford	80.00	40.00
113 Art Fromme	80.00	40.00
114 Clark Griffith	150.00	75.00
115 Bob Groom	80.00	40.00
116 Topsy Hartsel	80.00	40.00
117 Buck Herzog	80.00	40.00
118 Doc Hoblitzell	80.00	40.00
119 Solly Hofman	80.00	40.00
120 Miller Huggins (2)	300.00	150.00
121 Miller Huggins (2)	300.00	150.00
122 John Hummel	80.00	40.00
123 Hugh Jennings	150.00	75.00
124 Walter Johnson	500.00	250.00
125 Joe Kelley	150.00	75.00
126 Ed Konetchy	80.00	40.00
127 Harry Krause	80.00	40.00
128 Napolean Lajoie	400.00	200.00
129 Joe Lake	80.00	40.00
130 Tommy Leach	80.00	40.00
131 Lefty Leifield	80.00	40.00
132 Harry Lord	80.00	40.00
133 Rube Marquard	150.00	75.00
134 Christy Mathewson	500.00	250.00
135 John McGraw (2)	250.00	125.00
136 John McGraw (2)	250.00	125.00
137 Larry McLean	80.00	40.00
138 Dots Miller	80.00	40.00
139 Michael Mitchell	80.00	40.00
140 Mike Mowrey	80.00	40.00
141 George Mullin	100.00	50.00
142 Danny Murphy	80.00	40.00
143 Red Murray	80.00	40.00
144 Rebel Oakes	80.00	40.00
145 Rube Oldring	80.00	40.00
146 Charley O'Leary	80.00	40.00
147 Dode Paskert	80.00	40.00
148 Barney Pelty	80.00	40.00
149 William Purtell	80.00	40.00
150 Ed Reulbach	100.00	50.00
151 Nap Rucker	100.00	50.00
152 Germany Schaefer (2)	100.00	50.00
153 Germany Schaefer (2)	100.00	50.00
154 Frank Schulte	100.00	50.00
155 Frank Smith (2)	80.00	40.00
156 Frank Smith (2)	80.00	40.00
157 Tris Speaker	400.00	200.00
158 Jake Stahl	80.00	40.00
159 Harry Steinfeldt	100.00	50.00
160 Ed Summers	80.00	40.00
161 William Sweeney	80.00	40.00
162 Joe Tinker	150.00	75.00
163 Honus Wagner	500.00	250.00
164 Jack Warhop	80.00	40.00
165 Doc White	80.00	40.00
166 Hooks Wiltse (2)	80.00	40.00
167 Hooks Wiltse (2)	80.00	40.00
168 Red Ames		
169 Frank Baker		
170 Neal Ball		
171 Chief Bender		
172 Al Bridwell		
173 Bobby Byrne		
174 Howie Camnitz		
175 Frank Chance		
176 Hal Chase		
177 Eddie Collins		
178 Doc Crandall		
179 Sam Crawford		
180 Birdie Cree		
181 Harry Davis		
182 Josh Devore		
183 Mike Donlin		
184 Mickey Doolan		
185 Mickey Doolan		
186 Patsy Dougherty		
187 Larry Doyle		
188 Larry Doyle		
189 Jean Dubuc		
190 Kid Eberfeld		
191 Steve Evans		
192 Johnny Evers		
193 Russ Ford		

194 Art Fromme
195 Clark Griffith
196 Bob Groom
197 Topsy Hartsell
198 Buck Herzog
199 Dick Hoblitzell
200 Solly Hofman
201 Del Howard
202 Miller Huggins
203 Miller Huggins
204 John Hummel
205 Hugh Jennings
206 Hugh Jennings
207 Walter Johnson
208 Joe Kelley
209 Ed Konetchy
210 Harry Krause
211 Nap Lajoie
212 Joe Lake
213 Lefty Leifield
214 Harry Lord
215 Sherry Magee
216 Rube Marquard
217 Rube Marquard
218 Joe McGinnity
219 John McGraw
220 John McGraw
221 Matty McIntyre
Chicago Nat'l
222 Matty McIntyre
Bkln. and Chicago Nat'l
223 Larry McLean
224 Fred Merkle
225 Chief Meyers
226 Michael Mitchell
227 Mike Mowrey
228 George Mullin
229 Danny Murphy
230 Red Murray
231 Rebel Oakes
232 Rube Oldring
233 Charley O'Leary
234 Dode Paskert
235 Barney Pelty
236 William Purtell
237 Jack Quinn
238 Ed Reulbach
239 Nap Rucker
240 Germany Schaefer
241 Frank Schulte
242 Jimmy Sheckard
243 Frank Smith
244 Tris Speaker
245 Jake Stahl
246 Harry Steinfeldt
247 Gabby Street
248 Ed Summers
249 William Sweeney
250 Lee Tannehill
251 Ira Thomas
252 Joe Tinker
253 Heinie Wagner
254 Jack Warhop
255 Zack Wheat
256 Ed Willett
257 Owen Wilson
258 Hooks Wiltse
259 Hooks Wiltse

1954 Red Heart

The cards in this 33-card set measure approximately 2 5/8" by 3 3/4". The 1954 Red Heart baseball series was marketed by Red Heart dog food, which, incidentally, was a subsidiary of Morrell Meats. The set consists of three series of eleven unnumbered cards each of which could be ordered from the company via an offer (two can labels plus ten cents for each series) on the can label. Each series has a specific color background (red, green or blue) behind the color player photo. Cards with red backgrounds are considered scarcer and are marked with SP in the checklist (which has been alphabetized and numbered for reference). The catalog designation is F156.

	NM	Ex
COMPLETE SET (33)	2000.00	1000.00
COMMON CARD (1-33)	30.00	15.00
COMMON CARD SP	40.00	20.00
1 Richie Ashburn SP	80.00	40.00
2 Frank Baumholtz SP	40.00	20.00
3 Gus Bell	30.00	15.00
4 Billy Cox	40.00	20.00
5 Alvin Dark	35.00	17.50
6 Carl Erskine SP	60.00	30.00
7 Ferris Fain	35.00	17.50
8 Dee Fondy	30.00	15.00
9 Nellie Fox	80.00	40.00
10 Jim Gilliam	40.00	20.00
11 Jim Hegan SP	60.00	30.00
12 George Kell	50.00	25.00
13 Ralph Kiner SP	80.00	40.00
14 Ted Kluszewski SP	80.00	40.00
15 Harvey Kuenn	40.00	20.00
16 Bob Lemon SP	60.00	30.00
17 Sherman Lollar	35.00	17.50
18 Mickey Mantle	500.00	250.00
19 Billy Martin	50.00	25.00
20 Gil McDougald SP	50.00	25.00
21 Roy McMillan	35.00	17.50
22 Minnie Minoso	50.00	25.00
23 Stan Musial SP	400.00	200.00
24 Billy Pierce	35.00	17.50
25 Al Rosen SP	60.00	30.00
26 Hank Sauer	35.00	17.50
27 Red Schoendienst SP	80.00	40.00
28 Enos Slaughter	50.00	25.00
29 Duke Snider	150.00	75.00
30 Warren Spahn	60.00	30.00
31 Sammy White	30.00	15.00
32 Eddie Yost	30.00	15.00
33 Gus Zernial	35.00	17.50

1952 Red Man

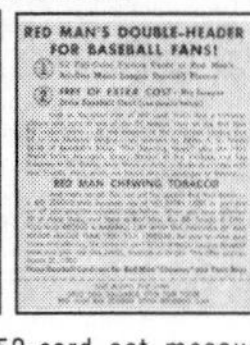

The cards in this 52-card set measure approximately 3 1/2" by 4" (or 3 1/2" by 3 5/8" without the tab). This Red Man issue was the first nationally available tobacco issue since the T cards of the teens early in this century. This 52-card set contains 26 top players from each league. Cards that have the tab (coupon) attached are generally worth a multiplier of cards without tabs. Please refer to multiplier line below. The 1952 Red Man cards are considered to be the most difficult (of the Red Man sets) to find with tabs. Card numbers are located on the tabs. The prices listed below refer to cards without tabs. The numbering of the set is alphabetical by player within league with the exception of the managers who are listed first.

	NM	Ex
COMPLETE SET (52)	800.00	400.00
*CARDS WITH TABS:3X VALUES		
AL1 Casey Stengel MG	25.00	12.50
AL2 Bobby Avila	8.00	4.00
AL3 Yogi Berra	40.00	20.00
AL4 Gil Coan	8.00	4.00
AL5 Dom DiMaggio	15.00	7.50
AL6 Larry Doby	20.00	10.00
AL7 Ferris Fain	8.00	4.00
AL8 Bob Feller	25.00	12.50
AL9 Nellie Fox	20.00	10.00
AL10 Johnny Groth	8.00	4.00
AL11 Jim Hegan	8.00	4.00
AL12 Eddie Joost	8.00	4.00
AL13 George Kell	20.00	10.00
AL14 Gil McDougald	12.00	6.00
AL15 Minnie Minoso	12.00	6.00
AL16 Billy Pierce	10.00	5.00
AL17 Bob Porterfield	8.00	4.00
AL18 Eddie Robinson	8.00	4.00
AL19 Saul Rogovin	8.00	4.00
AL20 Bobby Shantz	10.00	5.00
AL21 Vern Stephens	8.00	4.00
AL22 Vic Wertz	8.00	4.00
AL23 Ted Williams	100.00	50.00
AL24 Early Wynn	20.00	10.00
AL25 Eddie Yost	8.00	4.00
AL26 Gus Zernial	10.00	5.00
NL1 Leo Durocher MG	20.00	10.00
NL2 Richie Ashburn	20.00	10.00
NL3 Ewell Blackwell	8.00	4.00
NL4 Cliff Chambers	8.00	4.00
NL5 Murry Dickson	8.00	4.00
NL6 Sid Gordon	8.00	4.00
NL7 Granny Hamner	8.00	4.00
NL8 Jim Hearn	8.00	4.00
NL9 Monte Irvin	20.00	10.00
NL10 Larry Jansen	8.00	4.00
NL11 Willie Jones	8.00	4.00
NL12 Ralph Kiner	20.00	10.00
NL13 Whitey Lockman	8.00	4.00
NL14 Sal Maglie	10.00	5.00
NL15 Willie Mays	80.00	40.00
NL16 Stan Musial	80.00	40.00
NL17 Pee Wee Reese	25.00	12.50
NL18 Robin Roberts	20.00	10.00
NL19 Red Schoendienst	20.00	10.00
NL20 Enos Slaughter	20.00	10.00
NL21 Duke Snider	50.00	25.00
NL22 Warren Spahn	25.00	12.50
NL23 Eddie Stanky	10.00	5.00
NL24 Bobby Thomson	12.00	6.00
NL25 Earl Torgeson	8.00	4.00
NL26 Wes Westrum	8.00	4.00

1953 Red Man

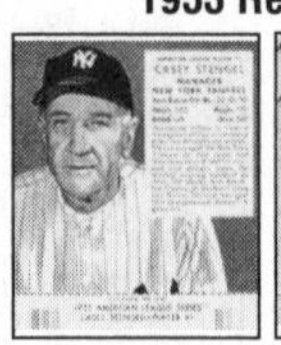
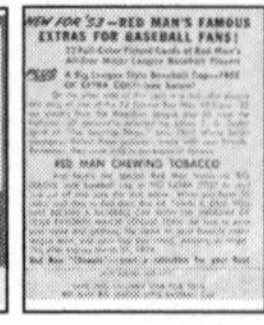

The cards in this 52-card set measure approximately 3 1/2" by 4" (or 3 1/2" by 3 5/8" without the tab). The 1953 Red Man set contains 26 National League stars and 26 American League stars. Card numbers are located both on the write-up of the player and on the tab. Cards that have the tab (coupon) attached are worth a multiplier of cards without tabs. Please refer to the multiplier line below. The prices listed below refer to cards without tabs.

	NM	Ex
COMPLETE SET (52)	600.00	300.00
*CARDS WITH TABS: 2.5X VALUES		
AL1 Casey Stengel MG	25.00	12.50
AL2 Hank Bauer	8.00	4.00
AL3 Yogi Berra	40.00	20.00
AL4 Walt Dropo	6.00	3.00
AL5 Nellie Fox	20.00	10.00
AL6 Jackie Jensen	8.00	4.00
AL7 Eddie Joost	6.00	3.00
AL8 George Kell	15.00	7.50
AL9 Dale Mitchell	6.00	3.00
AL10 Phil Rizzuto	25.00	12.50
AL11 Eddie Robinson	6.00	3.00
AL12 Gene Woodling	10.00	5.00
AL13 Gus Zernial	10.00	5.00
AL14 Early Wynn	15.00	7.50
AL15 Joe Dobson	6.00	3.00
AL16 Billy Pierce	10.00	5.00
AL17 Bob Lemon	15.00	7.50
AL18 Johnny Mize	15.00	7.50
AL19 Bob Porterfield	6.00	3.00
AL20 Bobby Shantz	10.00	5.00
AL21 Mickey Vernon	10.00	5.00
AL22 Dom DiMaggio	12.00	6.00
AL23 Gil McDougald	8.00	4.00
AL24 Al Rosen	8.00	4.00
AL25 Mel Parnell	6.00	3.00
AL26 Bobby Avila	6.00	3.00
NL1 Charlie Dressen MG	6.00	3.00
NL2 Bobby Adams	6.00	3.00
NL3 Richie Ashburn	20.00	10.00
NL4 Joe Black	8.00	4.00
NL5 Roy Campanella	50.00	25.00
NL6 Ted Kluszewski	12.00	6.00
NL7 Whitey Lockman	6.00	3.00
NL8 Sal Maglie	8.00	4.00
NL9 Andy Pafko	6.00	3.00
NL10 Pee Wee Reese	25.00	12.50
NL11 Robin Roberts	15.00	7.50
NL12 Red Schoendienst	15.00	7.50
NL13 Enos Slaughter	15.00	7.50
NL14 Duke Snider	50.00	25.00
NL15 Ralph Kiner	15.00	7.50
NL16 Hank Sauer	8.00	4.00
NL17 Del Ennis	8.00	4.00
NL18 Granny Hamner	8.00	4.00
NL19 Warren Spahn	25.00	12.50
NL20 Wes Westrum	6.00	3.00
NL21 Hoyt Wilhelm	15.00	7.50
NL22 Murry Dickson	6.00	3.00
NL23 Warren Hacker	6.00	3.00
NL24 Gerry Staley	6.00	3.00
NL25 Bobby Thomson	12.00	6.00
NL26 Stan Musial	80.00	40.00

1954 Red Man

The cards in this 50-card set measure approximately 3 1/2" by 4" (or 3 1/2" by 3 5/8" without the tab). The 1954 Red Man set witnessed a reduction to 25 players from each league. George Kell, Sam Mele, and Dave Philley are known to exist with two different teams. Card number 19 of the National League exists as Enos Slaughter and as Gus Bell. Card numbers are on the write-ups of the players. Cards that have the tab (coupon) attached are worth a multiple of cards without tabs. Please refer to the values below for cards with tabs. The prices listed below refer to cards without tabs. The complete set price below refers to all 54 cards including the four variations.

	NM	Ex
COMPLETE SET (54)	800.00	400.00
*CARDS WITH TABS:2.5X VALUES		
AL1 Bobby Avila	6.00	3.00
AL2 Jim Busby	6.00	3.00
AL3 Nellie Fox	20.00	10.00
AL4A George Kell (Boston)	25.00	12.50
AL4B George Kell (Chicago)	60.00	30.00
AL5 Sherman Lollar	6.00	3.00
AL6A Sam Mele (Baltimore)	12.00	6.00
AL6B Sam Mele (Chicago)	40.00	20.00
AL7 Minnie Minoso	10.00	5.00
AL8 Mel Parnell	6.00	3.00
AL9A Dave Philley (Cleveland)	12.00	6.00
AL9B Dave Philley (Philadelphia)	40.00	20.00
AL10 Billy Pierce	10.00	5.00
AL11 Jimmy Piersall	10.00	5.00
AL12 Al Rosen	10.00	5.00
AL13 Mickey Vernon	10.00	5.00
AL14 Sammy White	6.00	3.00
AL15 Gene Woodling	10.00	5.00
AL16 Whitey Ford	25.00	12.50
AL17 Phil Rizzuto	20.00	10.00
AL18 Bob Porterfield	6.00	3.00
AL19 Chico Carrasquel	6.00	3.00
AL20 Yogi Berra	40.00	20.00
AL21 Bob Lemon	15.00	7.50
AL22 Ferris Fain	6.00	3.00
AL23 Hank Bauer	10.00	5.00
AL24 Jim Delsing	6.00	3.00
AL25 Gil McDougald	10.00	5.00
NL1 Richie Ashburn	20.00	10.00
NL2 Billy Cox	10.00	5.00
NL3 Del Crandall	10.00	5.00
NL4 Carl Erskine	10.00	5.00
NL5 Monte Irvin	12.00	6.00
NL6 Ted Kluszewski	12.00	6.00
NL7 Don Mueller	6.00	3.00
NL8 Andy Pafko	6.00	3.00
NL9 Del Rice	6.00	3.00
NL10 Red Schoendienst	15.00	7.50
NL11 Warren Spahn	20.00	10.00
NL12 Curt Simmons	10.00	5.00
NL13 Roy Campanella	50.00	25.00
NL14 Jim Gilliam	10.00	5.00
NL15 Pee Wee Reese	25.00	12.50
NL16 Duke Snider	50.00	25.00
NL17 Rip Repulski	6.00	3.00
NL18 Robin Roberts	15.00	7.50
NL19A Enos Slaughter	60.00	30.00
NL19B Gus Bell	25.00	12.50
NL20 Johnny Logan	6.00	3.00
NL21 John Antonelli	6.00	3.00
NL22 Gil Hodges	20.00	10.00
NL23 Eddie Mathews	20.00	10.00
NL24 Lew Burdette	10.00	5.00
NL25 Willie Mays	80.00	40.00

1955 Red Man

The cards in this 50-card set measure approximately 3 1/2" by 4" (or 3 1/2" by 3 5/8" without the tab). The 1955 Red Man set contains 25 players from each league. Card numbers are on the write-ups of the players. Cards that have the tab (coupon) attached are generally worth a multiple of cards which have had their tabs removed. Please see multiplier values below. The prices listed below refer to cards without tabs.

	NM	Ex
COMPLETE SET (50)	500.00	250.00
*CARDS WITH TABS:2.5X VALUES		
AL1 Ray Boone	6.00	3.00
AL2 Jim Busby	6.00	3.00
AL3 Whitey Ford	25.00	12.50
AL4 Nellie Fox	20.00	10.00
AL5 Bob Grim	6.00	3.00
AL6 Jack Harshman	6.00	3.00
AL7 Jim Hegan	6.00	3.00
AL8 Bob Lemon	15.00	7.50
AL9 Irv Noren	6.00	3.00
AL10 Bob Porterfield	6.00	3.00
AL11 Al Rosen	8.00	4.00
AL12 Mickey Vernon	10.00	5.00
AL13 Vic Wertz	6.00	3.00
AL14 Early Wynn	15.00	7.50
AL15 Bobby Avila	6.00	3.00
AL16 Yogi Berra	40.00	20.00
AL17 Joe Coleman	6.00	3.00
AL18 Larry Doby	15.00	7.50
AL19 Jackie Jensen	10.00	5.00
AL20 Pete Runnels	6.00	3.00
AL21 Jimmy Piersall	8.00	4.00
AL22 Hank Bauer	8.00	4.00
AL23 Chico Carrasquel	6.00	3.00
AL24 Minnie Minoso	10.00	5.00
AL25 Sandy Consuegra	6.00	3.00
NL1 Richie Ashburn	20.00	10.00
NL2 Del Crandall	6.00	3.00
NL3 Gil Hodges	20.00	10.00
NL4 Brooks Lawrence	6.00	3.00
NL5 Johnny Logan	6.00	3.00
NL6 Sal Maglie	8.00	4.00
NL7 Willie Mays	80.00	40.00
NL8 Don Mueller	6.00	3.00
NL9 Bill Sarni	6.00	3.00
NL10 Warren Spahn	20.00	10.00
NL11 Hank Thompson	6.00	3.00
NL12 Hoyt Wilhelm	15.00	7.50
NL13 John Antonelli	6.00	3.00
NL14 Carl Erskine	10.00	5.00
NL15 Granny Hamner	6.00	3.00
NL16 Ted Kluszewski	12.00	6.00
NL17 Pee Wee Reese	25.00	12.50
NL18 Red Schoendienst	15.00	7.50
NL19 Duke Snider	50.00	25.00
NL20 Frank Thomas	8.00	4.00
NL21 Ray Jablonski	6.00	3.00
NL22 Dusty Rhodes	8.00	4.00
NL23 Gus Bell	8.00	4.00
NL24 Curt Simmons	8.00	4.00
NL25 Marv Grissom	6.00	3.00

1912 Red Sox Boston American Series PC742-1

These cream-colored cards with sepia photo and printing were issued in 1912 by the Boston American newspaper. The set features players from the 1912 Red Sox, who won the World Series. It is reasonable to assume that additional cards will be found. All additions to this checklist are appreciated. Unlike the PC 742-2 Boston Daily American Souvenir set, this set features excellent quality photos. The two most commonly found postcards from this set are Tris Speaker and Joe Wood, the others are found only on rare occassions.

	Ex-Mt	VG
COMPLETE SET (6)	1000.00	500.00
1 Forest Cady	150.00	75.00
2 Hub Perdue	150.00	75.00
3 Tris Speaker	300.00	150.00
4 Jake Stahl	150.00	75.00
5 Heinie Wagner	150.00	75.00
6 Joe Wood	250.00	125.00

1912 Red Sox Boston Daily American Souvenir PC742-2

This black and white postcard set was issued in 1912 and features players from the World Champion Boston Red Sox of that year. The printing quality of the cards are rather poor. It is thought that this checklist may be incomplete, so any additions are appreciated.

	Ex-Mt	VG
COMPLETE SET (4)	600.00	300.00
1 Forest Cady	150.00	75.00
2 Ray Collins	150.00	75.00
3 Hub Perdue	150.00	75.00
4 Heinie Wagner	150.00	75.00

1940 Red Sox Team Issue

These 25 blank-backed cards, which measure 6 1/2" by 9" feature the players photo along with a facsimile autograph. The cards are unnumbered, so we have sequenced them in alphabetical order.

	Ex-Mt	VG
COMPLETE SET	250.00	125.00
1 Jim Bagby Jr	8.00	4.00
2 Bull Butland	8.00	4.00
3 Tom Carey	8.00	4.00
4 Doc Cramer	10.00	5.00
5 Joe Cronin	15.00	7.50
6 Gene Desautels	8.00	4.00
7 Emerson Dickman	8.00	4.00
8 Dom DiMaggio	20.00	10.00
9 Bobby Doerr	15.00	7.50
10 Lou Finney	8.00	4.00
11 Jimmie Foxx	30.00	15.00
12 Denny Galehouse	8.00	4.00
13 Joe Glenn	8.00	4.00
14 Lefty Grove	25.00	12.50
15 Mickey Harris	8.00	4.00
16 Herb Hash	8.00	4.00
17 Joe Hevering	8.00	4.00
18 Leo Nonnenkamp	8.00	4.00
19 Fritz Ostermueller	8.00	4.00
20 Marv Owen	8.00	4.00
21 John Peacock	8.00	4.00
22 Jim Tabor	8.00	4.00
23 Charlie Wagner	8.00	4.00
24 Ted Williams	50.00	25.00
25 Jack Wilson	8.00	4.00

1941 Red Sox Team Issue

These 25 blank-backed cards, which measure 6 1/2" by 9" feature the players photo along with a facsimile autograph. Since these cards are unnumbered, we have sequenced them in alphabetical order.

	Ex-Mt	VG
1 Tom Carey	6.00	3.00
2 Joe Cronin	12.00	6.00
3 Emerson Dickman	6.00	3.00
4 Dom DiMaggio	12.00	6.00
5 Joe Dobson	6.00	3.00
6 Bobby Doerr	12.00	6.00
7 Lou Finney	6.00	3.00
8 Bill Fleming	6.00	3.00
9 Pete Fox	6.00	3.00
10 Jimmie Foxx	20.00	10.00
11 Lefty Grove	15.00	7.50
12 Odell Hale	6.00	3.00
13 Mickey Harris	6.00	3.00
14 Earl Johnson	6.00	3.00
15 Lefty Judd	6.00	3.00
16 Skeeter Newsome	6.00	3.00
17 Dick Newsome	6.00	3.00
18 John Peacock	6.00	3.00
19 Frank Pytlak	6.00	3.00
20 Mike Ryba	6.00	3.00
21 Stan Spence	6.00	3.00
22 Jim Tabor	6.00	3.00
23 Charlie Wagner	6.00	3.00
24 Ted Williams	50.00	25.00
25 Jack Wilson	6.00	3.00

1942 Red Sox Team Issue

This set of the Boston Red Sox measures approximately 6 1/2" by 9". The black and white photos display fascimile autographs. The backs are blank. The cards are unnumbered and are checklisted below in alphabetical order.

	Ex-Mt	VG
COMPLETE SET (25)	160.00	80.00
1 Mace Brown	5.00	2.50
2 Bill Butland	5.00	2.50
3 Paul Campbell	5.00	2.50
4 Tom Carey	5.00	2.50
5 Ken Chase	5.00	2.50
6 Bill Conroy	5.00	2.50
7 Joe Cronin	10.00	5.00
8 Dominic DiMaggio	10.00	5.00
9 Joe Dobson	5.00	2.50
10 Bob Doerr	10.00	5.00
11 Lou Finney	5.00	2.50
12 Pete Fox	5.00	2.50
13 Jimmie Foxx	20.00	10.00
14 Tex Hughson	5.00	2.50
15 Oscar Judd	5.00	2.50
16 Tony Lupien	5.00	2.50
17 Dick Newsome	5.00	2.50
18 Skeeter Newsome	5.00	2.50
19 John Peacock	5.00	2.50
20 Johnny Pesky	8.00	4.00
21 Mike Ryba	5.00	2.50
22 Jim Tabor	5.00	2.50
23 Yank Terry	5.00	2.50
24 Charles Wagner	5.00	2.50
25 Ted Williams	40.00	20.00

1943 Red Sox Team Issue

This 24-card set of the Boston Red Sox measures approximately 6 1/2" by 9" and features black-and-white player portraits with a facsimile autograph. The cards are unnumbered and checklisted below in alphabetical order.

	Ex-Mt	VG
COMPLETE SET (24)	100.00	50.00
1 Mace Brown	4.00	2.00
2 Ken Chase	4.00	2.00
3 Bill Conroy	4.00	2.00
4 Joe Cronin	8.00	4.00
5 Joe Dobson	4.00	2.00
6 Bob Doerr	8.00	4.00
7 Pete Fox	4.00	2.00
8 Ford Garrison	4.00	2.00
9 Tex Hughson	4.00	2.00
10 Oscar Judd	4.00	2.00
11 Andy Karl	4.00	2.00
12 Eddie Lake	4.00	2.00
13 John Lazor	4.00	2.00
14 Lou Luceer	4.00	2.00
15 Tony Lupien	4.00	2.00
16 Dee Miles	4.00	2.00
17 Dick Newsome	4.00	2.00
18 Skeeter Newsome	4.00	2.00
19 Roy Partee	4.00	2.00

20 John Peacock	4.00	2.00
21 Mike Ryba	4.00	2.00
22 Al Simmons	20.00	10.00
23 Jim Tabor	4.00	2.00
24 Yank Terry	4.00	2.00

1946 Red Sox Team Issue

These 25 cards measure approximately 6 1/2" by 9". They feature members of the 1946 American League pennant winners Red Sox. The set can be dated by Ernie Andres whose only year in the majors was 1946.

	Ex-Mt	VG
COMPLETE SET (25)	120.00	60.00
1 Ernie Andres	3.00	1.50
2 Jim Bagby Jr.	3.00	1.50
3 Mace Brown	3.00	1.50
4 Joe Cronin	10.00	5.00
5 Leon Culberson	3.00	1.50
6 Mel Deutsch	3.00	1.50
7 Dom DiMaggio	10.00	5.00
8 Joe Dobson	3.00	1.50
9 Bob Doerr	10.00	5.00
10 Dave Ferriss	3.00	1.50
11 Mickey Harris	3.00	1.50
12 Randy Heflin	3.00	1.50
13 Tex Hughson	3.00	1.50
14 Earl Johnson	3.00	1.50
15 Ed McGah	3.00	1.50
16 George Metkovich	3.00	1.50
17 Roy Partee	3.00	1.50
18 Eddie Pellagrini	3.00	1.50
19 Johnny Pesky	5.00	2.50
20 Rip Russell	3.00	1.50
21 Mike Ryba	3.00	1.50
22 Charlie Wagner	3.00	1.50
23 Hal Wagner	3.00	1.50
24 Ted Williams	40.00	20.00
25 Rudy York	5.00	2.50

1947 Red Sox Team Issue

This 25-card set of the Boston Red Sox team measures approximately 6 1/2" by 9" and features black-and-white player portraits. A fascimile autograph is printed on each photo. The backs are blank. The cards are unnumbered and checklisted below in alphabetical order.

	Ex-Mt	VG
COMPLETE SET (25)	150.00	75.00
1 Joe Cronin MG	8.00	4.00
2 Leon Culberson	4.00	2.00
3 Dom DiMaggio	8.00	4.00
4 Joseph Dobson	4.00	2.00
5 Bob Doerr	8.00	4.00
6 Harry Dorish	4.00	2.00
7 David"Boo" Ferriss	4.00	2.00
8 Tommy Fine	4.00	2.00
9 Don Gutteridge	4.00	2.00
10 Mickey Harris	4.00	2.00
11 Tex Hughson	4.00	2.00
12 Earl Johnson	4.00	2.00
13 Bob Klinger	4.00	2.00
14 Sam Mele	4.00	2.00
15 Wally Moses	5.00	2.50
16 Johnny Murphy	4.00	2.00
17 Mel Parnell	5.00	2.50
18 Roy Partee	4.00	2.00
19 Eddie Pellagrini	4.00	2.00
20 Johnny Pesky	6.00	3.00
21 Rip Russell	4.00	2.00
22 Birdie Tebbetts	5.00	2.50
23 Ted Williams	40.00	20.00
24 Rudy York	6.00	3.00
25 Bill Zuber	4.00	2.00

1948 Red Sox Team Issue

These 25 photos measure approximately 6 1/2" by 9". They feature members of the 1948 Boston Red Sox. The photos take up almost the entire surface and are surrounded by white borders. A fascimile autograph is also on each photo. The backs are blank and we have sequenced this set in alphabetical order.

	NM	Ex
COMPLETE SET (25)	150.00	75.00
1 Matt Batts	4.00	2.00
2 Dom DiMaggio	10.00	5.00
3 Joe Dobson	4.00	2.00
4 Bobby Doerr	10.00	5.00
5 Harry Dorish	4.00	2.00
6 Dave "Boo" Ferriss	4.00	2.00
7 Denny Galehouse	4.00	2.00
8 Bill Goodman	6.00	3.00
9 Mickey Harris	4.00	2.00
10 Billy Hitchcock	4.00	2.00
11 Earl Johnson	4.00	2.00
12 Jake Jones	4.00	2.00
13 Ellis Kinder	4.00	2.00
14 Jack Kramer	4.00	2.00
15 Joe McCarthy MG	10.00	5.00
16 Maurice McDermott	4.00	2.00
17 Sam Mele	5.00	2.50
18 Wally Moses	5.00	2.50
19 Mel Parnell	6.00	3.00
20 Johnny Pesky	6.00	3.00
21 Stan Spence	4.00	2.00
22 Vern Stephens	6.00	3.00
23 Chuck Stobbs	4.00	2.00
24 Birdie Tebbetts	5.00	2.50
25 Ted Williams	40.00	20.00

1949 Red Sox Team Issue

This 25-card set of the Boston Red Sox team measures approximately 6 1/2" by 9" and features black-and-white player portraits with white borders. A fascimile autograph is printed on each photo. The backs are blank. The cards are unnumbered and checklisted below in alphabetical order.

	NM	Ex
COMPLETE SET (25)	150.00	75.00
1 Matt Batts	4.00	2.00
2 Merrill Combs	4.00	2.00
3 Dom DiMaggio	8.00	4.00
4 Joe Dobson	4.00	2.00
5 Bob Doerr	8.00	4.00
6 David"Boo" Ferriss	4.00	2.00
7 Bill Goodman	6.00	3.00
8 Mickey Harris	4.00	2.00
9 Billy Hitchcock	4.00	2.00
10 Tex Hughson	4.00	2.00
11 Earl Johnson	4.00	2.00
12 Ellis Kinder	4.00	2.00
13 Jack Kramer	4.00	2.00
14 Joe McCarthy MG	8.00	4.00
15 Sam Mele	4.00	2.00
16 Tommy O'Brien	4.00	2.00
17 Mel Parnell	6.00	3.00
18 Johnny Pesky	6.00	3.00
19 Frank Quinn	4.00	2.00
20 Vern Stephens	6.00	3.00
21 Chuck Stobbs	4.00	2.00
22 Lou Stringer	4.00	2.00
23 Birdie Tebbetts	5.00	2.50
24 Ted Williams	40.00	20.00
25 Al Zarilla	4.00	2.00

1950 Red Sox Clark Locksmith

This four-card set features black-and-white photos of Boston Red Sox players and measures approximately 2 3/4" bvy 3 3/4".

	NM	Ex
COMPLETE SET (4)	50.00	25.00
1 Bobby Doerr	10.00	5.00
2 Ted Williams	25.00	12.50
3 Dom DiMaggio	15.00	7.50
4 Johnny Pesky	5.00	2.50

1950 Red Sox Team Issue

This 30-card set of the Boston Red Sox team measures approximately 6 1/2" by 9" and features black-and-white player portraits with white borders. A fascimile autograph is printed on each photo. The backs are blank. The cards are unnumbered and checklisted below in alphabetical order. Earl Johnson, Ken Keltner, Joe McCarthy, Al Papai and Charley Schanz were issued originally and were replaced in the second series with Dick Littlefield, Williard Nixon, Steve O'Neill, George Susce, and Clyde Vollmer. All of these 10 people are notated with SP's below.

	NM	Ex
COMPLETE SET (30)	250.00	125.00
COMMON CARD (1-30)	4.00	2.00
COMMON SP	10.00	5.00
1 Matt Batts	4.00	2.00
2 Earle Combs CO	8.00	4.00
3 Dom DiMaggio	8.00	4.00
4 Joe Dobson	4.00	2.00
5 Bob Doerr	8.00	4.00
6 Walter Dropo	5.00	2.50
7 Bill Goodman	4.00	2.00
8 Earl Johnson SP	10.00	5.00
9 Ken Keltner SP	12.00	6.00
10 Ellis Kinder	4.00	2.00
11 Dick Littlefield SP	10.00	5.00
12 Walter Masterson	4.00	2.00
13 Joe McCarthy MG SP	20.00	10.00
14 Maurice McDermott	4.00	2.00
15 Willard Nixon SP	10.00	5.00
16 Steve O'Neill MG SP	12.00	6.00
17 Al Papai SP	10.00	5.00
18 Mel Parnell	6.00	3.00
19 Johnny Pesky	6.00	3.00
20 Buddy Rosar	4.00	2.00
21 Charley Schanz SP	10.00	5.00
22 Vern Stephens	6.00	3.00
23 Chuck Stobbs	4.00	2.00
24 Lou Stringer	4.00	2.00
25 George Susce SP	10.00	5.00
26 Birdie Tebbetts	5.00	2.50
27 Clyde Vollmer SP	20.00	10.00
28 Ted Williams	40.00	20.00
29 Tom Wright	4.00	2.00
30 Al Zarilla	4.00	2.00

1953 Red Sox First National Super Market Stores

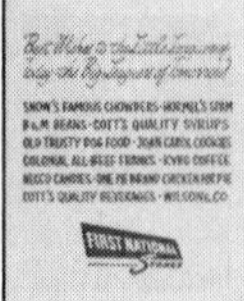

This four-card set features black-and-white player photos and measures approximately 3 3/4" by 5". The backs carry advertising for the stores. The cards are unnumbered and checklisted below in alphabetical order. A reprint of this set was made in the early 80's.

	NM	Ex
COMPLETE SET (4)	300.00	150.00
1 Bill Goodman	80.00	40.00
2 Ellis Kinder	80.00	40.00
3 Mel Parnell	100.00	50.00
4 Sammy White	80.00	40.00

1953 Red Sox Team Issue

This set of the Boston Red Sox measures approximately 6 1/2" by 9". The black-and-white player photos display fascimile autographs. The backs are blank. The cards are unnumbered and checklisted below in alphabetical order.

	NM	Ex
COMPLETE SET (30)	125.00	60.00
1 Milt Bolling	4.00	2.00
2 Lou Boudreau MG	8.00	4.00
3 Harold Brown	4.00	2.00
4 Bill Consolo	4.00	2.00
5 Dom DiMaggio	8.00	4.00
6 Hoot Evers	4.00	2.00
7 Ben Flowers	4.00	2.00
8 Hershell Freeman	4.00	2.00
9 Dick Gernert	4.00	2.00
10 Bill Goodman	6.00	3.00
11 Marv Grissom	4.00	2.00
12 Ken Holcombe	4.00	2.00
13 Sid Hudson	4.00	2.00
14 George Kell	8.00	4.00
15 Bill Kennedy	4.00	2.00
16 Ellis Kinder	6.00	3.00
17 Ted Lepcio	4.00	2.00
18 Johnny Lipon	4.00	2.00
19 Maurice McDermott	4.00	2.00
20 John Merson	4.00	2.00
21 Gus Niarhos	4.00	2.00
22 Willard Nixon	4.00	2.00
23 Mel Parnell	6.00	3.00
24 Jimmy Piersall	8.00	4.00
25 Gene Stephens	4.00	2.00
26 Tommy Umphlett	4.00	2.00
27 Bill Werle	4.00	2.00
28 Sam White	4.00	2.00
29 Del Wilber	4.00	2.00
30 Al Zarilla	4.00	2.00

1954 Red Sox Team Issue

These 30 blank-backed cards, which measure 6 1/2" by 9" feature members of the 1954 Boston Red Sox. The fronts feature the players photo along with a fascimile autograph. Since these cards are unnumbered, we have sequenced them in alphabetical order. One of the very few Harry Agganis cards printed during his short career is in this set.

	NM	Ex
COMPLETE SET	150.00	75.00
1 Harry Agganis	15.00	7.50
2 Milt Bolling	4.00	2.00
3 Lou Boudreau MG	8.00	4.00
4 Tom Brewer	4.00	2.00
5 Hal Brown	4.00	2.00
6 Tex Clevenger	4.00	2.00
7 Billy Consolo	4.00	2.00
8 Joe Dobson	4.00	2.00
9 Hoot Evers	4.00	2.00
10 Dick Gernert	4.00	2.00
11 Billy Goodman	5.00	2.50
12 Bill Henry	4.00	2.00
13 Tom Herrin	4.00	2.00
14 Sid Hudson	4.00	2.00
15 Jackie Jensen	6.00	3.00
16 George Kell	8.00	4.00
17 Leo Kiely	4.00	2.00
18 Ellis Kinder	4.00	2.00
19 Ted Lepcio	4.00	2.00
20 Charlie Maxwell	4.00	2.00
21 Willard Nixon	4.00	2.00
22 Karl Olson	4.00	2.00
23 Mickey Owen CO	4.00	2.00
24 Mel Parnell	5.00	2.50
25 Jimmy Piersall	6.00	3.00
26 Frank Sullivan	4.00	2.00
27 Bill Werle	4.00	2.00
28 Sammy White	4.00	2.00
29 Del Wilber	4.00	2.00
30 Ted Williams	40.00	20.00

1958 Red Sox Jay Publishing

This 12-card set of the Boston Red Sox measures approximately 5" by 7" and features black-and-white player photos in a white border. These cards were packaged 12 to a packet. The backs are blank. The cards are unnumbered and checklisted below in alphabetical order.

	NM	Ex
COMPLETE SET (12)	60.00	30.00
1 Tom Brewer	3.00	1.50
2 Don Buddin	3.00	1.50
3 Dick Gernert	3.00	1.50
4 Mike Higgins MG	3.00	1.50
5 Jack Jensen	5.00	2.50
6 Frank Malzone	5.00	2.50
7 Jim Piersall	5.00	2.50
8 Pete Runnels	4.00	2.00
9 Gene Stephens	3.00	1.50
10 Frank Sullivan	3.00	1.50
11 Sam White	3.00	1.50
12 Ted Williams	25.00	12.50

1959 Red Sox Jay Publishing

This 12-card set of the Boston Red Sox measures approximately 5" by 7" and features black-and-white player photos in a white border. These cards were packaged 12 to a packet and originally sold for 25 cents. The backs are blank. The cards are unnumbered and checklisted below in alphabetical order.

	NM	Ex
COMPLETE SET (12)	60.00	30.00
1 Tom Brewer	3.00	1.50
2 Dick Gernert	3.00	1.50
3 Mike Higgins MG	3.00	1.50
4 Jackie Jensen	5.00	2.50
5 Frank Malzone	5.00	2.50
6 Gene Mauch	3.00	1.50
7 Jimmy Piersall	5.00	2.50
8 Dave Sisler	3.00	1.50
9 Gene Stephens	3.00	1.50
10 Frank Sullivan	3.00	1.50
11 Sammy White	3.00	1.50
12 Ted Williams	25.00	12.50

1960 Red Sox Jay Publishing

This 12-card set of the Boston Red Sox measures approximately 5" by 7" and features black-and-white player photos in a white border. These cards were packaged 12 to a packet. The backs are blank. The cards are unnumbered and checklisted below in alphabetical order.

	NM	Ex
COMPLETE SET (12)	40.00	16.00
1 Tom Brewer	2.00	.80
2 Don Buddin	2.00	.80
3 Jerry Casale	2.00	.80
4 Ike Delock	2.00	.80
5 Jerry(Pumpsie) Green	2.00	.80
6 Bill Jurges MG	2.00	.80
7 Frank Malzone	3.00	1.20
8 Pete Runnels	2.50	1.00
9 Gene Stephens	2.00	.80
10 Bobby Thomson	4.00	1.60
11 Vic Wertz	2.00	.80
12 Ted Williams	25.00	10.00

1962 Red Sox Jay Publishing

Like other Jay Publishing issues these black-and-white, blank-backed, white-bordered, 5" X 7" photos. The player's name and team are printed in black within the lower margin. The photos are unnumbered and checklisted below in alphabetical order. This set has more than 12 cards since two different versions were issued during 1962.

	NM	Ex
COMPLETE SET	35.00	14.00
1 Ed Bressoud	2.00	.80
2 Lou Clinton	2.00	.80
3 Gene Conley	2.50	1.00
4 Gary Geiger	2.00	.80
5 Carroll Hardy	2.00	.80
6 Mike Higgins MG	2.00	.80
7 Frank Malzone	3.00	1.20
8 Bill Monbouquette	2.00	.80
9 Russ Nixon	2.00	.80
10 Pete Runnels	2.00	.80
11 Chuck Schilling	2.00	.80
12 Don Schwall	2.00	.80
13 Carl Yastrzemski UER (Misspelled Yastremski)	20.00	8.00

1963 Red Sox Jay Publishing

This 12-card set of the Boston Red Sox measures approximately 5" by 7". The fronts feature black-and-white posed player photos with the player's and team name printed below in the white border. These cards were packaged 12 to a packet. The backs are blank. The cards are unnumbered and checklisted below in alphabetical order.

	NM	Ex
COMPLETE SET (12)	40.00	16.00
1 Ed Bressoud	2.00	.80
2 Lou Clinton	2.00	.80
3 Gary Geiger	2.00	.80
4 Frank Malzone	3.00	1.20
5 Roman Mejias	2.00	.80
6 Bill Monbouquette	2.00	.80
7 Johnny Pesky MG	2.50	1.00
8 Dick Radatz	2.50	1.00
9 Chuck Schilling	2.00	.80
10 Dick Stuart	2.00	.80
11 Bob Tillman	2.00	.80
12 Carl Yastrzemski	20.00	8.00

1964 Red Sox Jay Publishing

This 12-card set of the Boston Red Sox measures approximately 5" by 7". The fronts feature black-and-white posed player photos with the player's and team name printed below in the white border. These cards were packaged 12 to a packet. The backs are blank. The cards are unnumbered and checklisted below in alphabetical order.

	NM	Ex
COMPLETE SET (12)	40.00	16.00
1 Ed Bressoud	2.00	.80
2 Lou Clinton	2.00	.80
3 Gary Geiger	2.00	.80
4 Frank Malzone	3.00	1.20
5 Felix Mantilla	2.00	.80
6 Bill Monbouquette	2.00	.80
7 Russ Nixon	2.00	.80
8 Johnny Pesky MG	2.50	1.00
9 Dick Radatz	2.50	1.00
10 Chuck Schilling	2.00	.80
11 Dick Stuart	2.50	1.00
12 Carl Yastrzemski	20.00	8.00

1964 Red Sox Team Issue

This eight-card set of the Boston Red Sox measures approximately 8" by 10" and features color portraits with a white border and a facsimile autograph. The backs are blank. The photos were packaged eight to a clear plastic packet and originally sold for 50 cents at the park or through the mail. They were also inserted one to each Red Sox year book. The cards are unnumbered and checklisted below in alphabetical order.

	NM	Ex
COMPLETE SET (8)	40.00	16.00
1 Ed Bressoud	4.00	1.60
2 Jack Lamabe	4.00	1.60
3 Frank Malzone	6.00	2.40
4 Bill Monbouquette	5.00	2.00
5 Johnny Pesky MG	5.00	2.00
6 Dick Radatz	5.00	2.00
7 Dick Stuart	5.00	2.00
8 Carl Yastrzemski	20.00	8.00

1965 Red Sox Jay Publishing

This 12-card set of the Boston Red Sox measures approximately 5" by 7". The fronts feature black-and-white posed player photos with the player's and team name printed below in the white border. These cards were packaged 12 to a packet. The backs are blank. The cards are unnumbered and checklisted below in alphabetical order.

	NM	Ex
COMPLETE SET (12)	40.00	16.00
1 Dennis Bennett	2.00	.80
2 Ed Bressoud	2.00	.80
3 Tony Conigliaro	4.00	1.60
4 Billy Herman MG	4.00	1.60
5 Frank Malzone	3.00	1.20
6 Felix Mantilla	2.00	.80
7 Bill Monbouquette	2.00	.80
8 Dick Radatz	2.50	1.00
9 Lee Thomas	2.00	.80
10 John Tillman	2.00	.80
11 Earl Wilson	2.00	.80
12 Carl Yastrzemski	20.00	8.00

1965 Red Sox Team Issue

This 16-card set of the 1965 Boston Red Sox features color player photos measuring approximately 7 7/8" by 9 7/8" with a white border. A facsimile autograph is printed across the bottom of the photo. The cards were packaged in a clear plastic packet and was originally sold for $1 at the park or through the mail. They were also inserted one to each Red Sox year book. The backs are blank. The cards are unnumbered and checklisted below in alphabetical order.

	NM	Ex
COMPLETE SET (16)	80.00	32.00
1 Dennis Bennett	4.00	1.60
2 Ed Bressoud	4.00	1.60
3 Tony Conigliaro	12.00	4.80
4 Bob Heffner	4.00	1.60
5 Billy Herman MG	8.00	3.20
6 Jack Lamabe	4.00	1.60
7 Frank Malzone	6.00	2.40
8 Felix Mantilla	4.00	1.60
9 Bill Monbouquette	4.00	1.60
10 Dave Morehead	4.00	1.60
11 Dick Radatz	5.00	2.00
12 Jerry Stephenson	4.00	1.60
13 Lee Thomas	4.00	1.60
14 Bob Tillman	4.00	1.60
15 Earl Wilson	4.00	1.60
16 Carl Yastrzemski	30.00	12.00

1966 Red Sox Team Issue

This 16-card set of the 1966 Boston Red Sox features color player photos measuring approximately 7 3/4" by 9 7/8" with a white border. A facsimile autograph is printed at the bottom of the photo. The photos were packaged in a clear plastic packet and was originally sold for $1 at the park or through the mail. They were also inserted one to each Red Sox year book. The backs are blank. The cards are unnumbered and checklisted below in alphabetical order.

	NM	Ex
COMPLETE SET (16)	80.00	32.00
1 Dennis Bennett	4.00	1.60
2 Tony Conigliaro	8.00	3.20
3 Joe Foy	4.00	1.60
4 Jim Gosger	4.00	1.60
5 Tony Horton	5.00	2.00
6 Jim Lonborg	6.00	2.40
7 Dave Morehead	4.00	1.60
8 Dan Osinski	4.00	1.60
9 Rico Petrocelli	6.00	2.40

10 Dick Radatz	4.00	1.60
11 Mike Ryan	4.00	1.60
12 Bob Sadowski	4.00	1.60
13 George Smith	4.00	1.60
14 George Thomas	4.00	1.60
15 Earl Wilson	4.00	1.60
16 Carl Yastrzemski	25.00	10.00

1967 Red Sox Stickers Topps

This was a limited production "test" issue for Topps. It is very similar to the Pirates "test" issue preceding. The stickers are blank backed and measure 2 1/2" by 3 1/2". The stickers look like cards from the front and are somewhat attractive in spite of the "no neck" presentation of many of the players' photos. The cards are numbered on the front.

	NM	Ex
COMPLETE SET (33)	250.00	100.00
WRAPPER (5-CENT)	50.00	20.00
1 Dennis Bennett	4.00	1.60
2 Darrell Brandon	4.00	1.60
3 Tony Conigliaro	10.00	4.00
4 Don Demeter	4.00	1.60
5 Hank Fischer	4.00	1.60
6 Joe Foy	4.00	1.60
7 Mike Andrews	4.00	1.60
8 Dalton Jones	4.00	1.60
9 Jim Lonborg	8.00	3.20
10 Don McMahon	4.00	1.60
11 Dave Morehead	4.00	1.60
12 Reggie Smith	10.00	4.00
13 Rico Petrocelli	8.00	3.20
14 Mike Ryan	4.00	1.60
15 Jose Santiago	4.00	1.60
16 George Scott	8.00	3.20
17 Sal Maglie CO	8.00	3.20
18 George Smith	4.00	1.60
19 Lee Stange	4.00	1.60
20 Jerry Stephenson	4.00	1.60
21 Jose Tartabull	4.00	1.60
22 George Thomas	4.00	1.60
23 Bob Tillman	4.00	1.60
24 John Wyatt	4.00	1.60
25 Carl Yastrzemski	80.00	32.00
26 Dick Williams MG	10.00	4.00
27 I Love the Red Sox	4.00	1.60
28 Let's Go Red Sox	4.00	1.60
29 Carl Yastrzemski for Mayor	40.00	16.00
30 Tony Conigliaro is my Hero	10.00	4.00
31 Happiness is a Boston Win	4.00	1.60
32 Red Sox Logo	4.00	1.60
33 Red Sox Pennant	4.00	1.60

1967 Red Sox Team Issue

These 16 blank backed cards measure approximately 4" by 5 5/8" and have white borders. They were issued in two series and were available at the ball park or via the mail for 50 cents per pack. They were issued in two series and we have sequenced them alphabetically by series.

	NM	Ex
COMPLETE SET (16)	40.00	16.00
1 Tony Conigliaro A	4.00	1.60
2 Joe Foy A	2.00	.80
3 Jim Lonborg A	3.00	1.20
4 Don McMahon A	2.00	.80
5 Rico Petrocelli A	3.00	1.20
6 George Scott A	2.50	1.00
7 Lee Stange A	2.00	.80
8 Carl Yastrzemski A	10.00	4.00
9 Darrell Brandon B	2.00	.80
10 Russ Gibson B	2.00	.80
11 Bill Rohr B	2.00	.80
12 Mike Ryan B	2.00	.80
13 Reggie Smith B	6.00	2.40
14 Jose Tartabull B	2.00	.80
15 George Thomas B	2.00	.80
16 John Wyatt B	2.00	.80

1968 Red Sox Team Issue

This eight-card set of the 1968 Boston Red Sox measures approximately 5 1/2" by 7 1/2". The fronts feature black-and-white player portraits with facsimile autographs and white borders. The backs are blank. The cards are unnumbered and checklisted below in alphabetical order. The set may be incomplete and any confirmed additions would be appreciated.

	NM	Ex
COMPLETE SET (8)	25.00	10.00
1 Mike Andrews	2.00	.80
2 Darrell Brandon	2.00	.80
3 Bobby Doerr CO	5.00	2.00
4 Ken Harrelson	5.00	2.00
5 Jim Lonborg	4.00	1.60
6 Rico Petrocelli	5.00	2.00
7 Reggie Smith	5.00	2.00
8 Dick Williams MG	5.00	2.00

1969 Red Sox Arco Oil

Sponsored by Arco Oil, this 12-card set features photos of the 1969 Boston Red Sox. The cards are unnumbered and checklisted below in alphabetical order.

	NM	Ex
COMPLETE SET (12)	80.00	32.00
1 Mike Andrews	5.00	2.00
2 Tony Conigliaro	10.00	4.00
3 Ray Culp	5.00	2.00
4 Russ Gibson	5.00	2.00
5 Dalton Jones	5.00	2.00
6 Jim Lonborg	8.00	3.20
7 Sparky Lyle	10.00	4.00
8 Syd O'Brien	5.00	2.00
9 Rico Petrocelli	8.00	3.20
10 George Scott	6.00	2.40
11 Reggie Smith	8.00	3.20
12 Carl Yastrzemski	20.00	8.00

1969 Red Sox Team Issue

This 12-card set of the Boston Red Sox measures approximately 4 1/4" by 7". The fronts display black-and-white player portraits bordered in white. The player's name and team are printed in the top margin. The backs are blank. The cards are unnumbered and checklisted below in alphabetical order.

	NM	Ex
COMPLETE SET (12)	30.00	12.00
1 Mike Andrews	2.00	.80
2 Tony Conigliaro	4.00	1.60
3 Russ Gibson	2.00	.80
4 Dalton Jones	2.00	.80
5 Bill Landis	2.00	.80
6 Jim Lonborg	3.00	1.20
7 Sparky Lyle	4.00	1.60
8 Rico Petrocelli	3.00	1.20
9 George Scott	2.50	1.00
10 Reggie Smith	2.50	1.00
11 Dick Williams MG	2.50	1.00
12 Carl Yastrzemski	8.00	3.20

1969 Red Sox Team Issue Color

This 10-card set features color portraits of the Boston Red Sox with white borders and measures approximately 7" by 8 3/4". The backs are blank. The cards are unnumbered and checklisted below in alphabetical order.

	NM	Ex
COMPLETE SET (10)	35.00	14.00
1 Mike Andrews	3.00	1.20
2 Tony Conigliaro	6.00	2.40
3 Ray Culp	3.00	1.20
4 Russ Gibson	3.00	1.20
5 Jim Lonborg	5.00	2.00
6 Rico Petrocelli	5.00	2.00
7 George Scott	4.00	1.60
8 Reggie Smith	5.00	2.00
9 Dick Williams MG	4.00	1.60
10 Carl Yastrzemski	10.00	4.00

1970 Red Sox Color Photo Post Cards

This set features members of the 1970 Boston Red Sox. These color post cards are unnumbered and we have sequenced them in alphabetical order.

	NM	Ex
COMPLETE SET (17)	30.00	12.00
1 Luis Alvarado	1.00	.40
2 Mike Andrews	1.00	.40
3 Ken Brett	1.50	.60
4 Bill Conigliaro	1.50	.60
5 Tony Conigliaro	2.50	1.00
6 Ray Culp	1.00	.40
7 Sparky Lyle	2.50	1.00
8 Gerry Moses	1.00	.40
9 Mike Nagy	1.00	.40
10 Gary Peters	1.50	.60
11 Rico Petrocelli	2.00	.80
12 George Scott	1.50	.60
13 Sonny Siebert	1.00	.40
14 Reggie Smith	2.00	.80
15 Lee Stange	1.00	.40
16 Carl Yastrzemski	8.00	3.20
17 Jim Lonborg (oversize)	2.00	.80

1971 Red Sox Arco Oil

Sponsored by Arco Oil, these 12 pictures of the 1971 Boston Red Sox measure approximately 8" by 10" and feature on their fronts white-bordered posed color player photos. The player's name is shown in black lettering within the white margin below the photo. His facsimile autograph appears across the picture. The white back carries the team's and player's names at the top, followed below by position, biography, career highlights, and statistics. An

ad at the bottom for picture frames rounds out the back. The cards are unnumbered and checklisted below in alphabetical order.

	NM	Ex
COMPLETE SET (12)	60.00	24.00
1 Luis Aparicio	10.00	4.00
2 Ken Brett	5.00	2.00
3 Billy Conigliaro	6.00	2.40
4 Ray Culp	5.00	2.00
5 Doug Griffin	5.00	2.00
6 Bob Montgomery	5.00	2.00
7 Gary Peters	5.00	2.00
8 George Scott	6.00	2.40
9 Sonny Siebert	5.00	2.00
10 Reggie Smith	6.00	2.40
11 Ken Tatum	5.00	2.00
12 Carl Yastrzemski	12.00	4.80

1971 Red Sox Team Issue

These 12 photos measure approximately 4 1/4" by 7". The player's name and team are noted on the top with the rest of the front dedicated to a photo. The backs are blank. We have sequenced this set in alphabetical order. The set is dated 1971 as that was Luis Aparicio's first year with the Red Sox and Sparky Lyle's last season with the club.

	NM	Ex
COMPLETE SET (12)	25.00	10.00
1 Luis Aparicio	3.00	1.20
2 Billy Conigliaro	2.00	.80
3 Ray Culp	1.50	.60
4 Duane Josephson	1.50	.60
5 Jim Lonborg	2.50	1.00
6 Sparky Lyle	2.50	1.00
7 Gary Peters	1.50	.60
8 Rico Petrocelli	2.50	1.00
9 George Scott	2.00	.80
10 Sonny Siebert	1.50	.60
11 Reggie Smith	2.00	.80
12 Carl Yastrzemski	5.00	2.00

1972 Red Sox Team Issue

This 23-card set of the Boston Red Sox features borderless black-and-white player portraits with a facsimile autograph. The backs are blank. The cards are unnumbered and checklisted below in alphabetical order. Carlton Fisk has a card in his Rookie Card year.

	NM	Ex
COMPLETE SET (23)	20.00	8.00
1 Juan Beniquez	.50	.20
2 Bob Bolin	.50	.20
3 Danny Cater	.50	.20
4 John Curtis	.50	.20
5 Mike Fiore	.50	.20
6 Carlton Fisk	8.00	3.20
7 Phil Gagliano	.50	.20
8 Doug Griffin	.50	.20
9 Tommy Harper	.75	.30
10 John Kennedy	.50	.20
11 Lew Krausse	.50	.20
12 Joe Lahoud	.50	.20
13 Bill Lee	1.00	.40
14 Lynn McGlothlin	.50	.20
15 Rick Miller	.75	.30
16 Bob Montgomery	.50	.20
17 Roger Moret	.50	.20
18 Ben Oglivie	.75	.30
19 Marty Pattin	.50	.20
20 Don Pavletich	.50	.20
21 Ken Tatum	.50	.20
22 Luis Tiant	1.00	.40
23 Carl Yastrzemski	8.00	3.20

1975 Red Sox Herald

This 26 card set was issued as an insert in the two Boston Herald papers over a period of time and featured drawings by sports artist Phil Bissell.

	NM	Ex
COMPLETE SET	30.00	12.00
1 Carl Yastrzemski	5.00	2.00
2 Fred Lynn	5.00	2.00
3 Jim Rice	5.00	2.00
4 Carlton Fisk	5.00	2.00
5 Bill Lee	1.00	.40
6 Rick Wise	.50	.20
7 Rico Petrocelli	1.00	.40
8 Luis Tiant	2.00	.80
9 Bernie Carbo	.50	.20
10 Bob Heise	.50	.20
11 Juan Beniquez	.50	.20
12 Jim Willoughby	.50	.20
13 Jim Burton	.50	.20
14 Dick Pole	.50	.20
15 Reggie Cleveland	.50	.20
16 Tim Blackwell	.50	.20
17 Cecil Cooper	1.00	.40
18 Dick Drago	.50	.20
19 Dwight Evans	2.00	.80
20 Rick Burleson	1.50	.60
21 Doug Griffin	.50	.20
22 Rick Miller	.50	.20
23 Roger Moret	.50	.20
24 Diego Segui	.50	.20
25 Bob Montgomery	.50	.20
26 Denny Doyle	.50	.20

1975 Red Sox 1946 TCMA

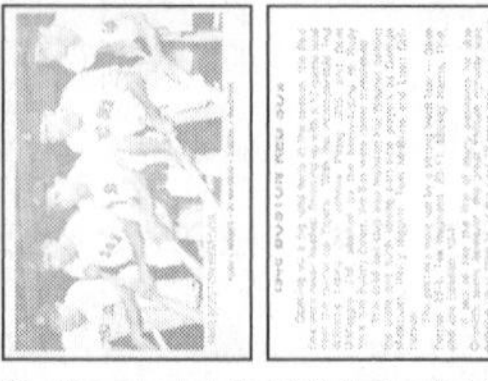

This 43-card set of the 1946 Boston Red Sox team was printed in 1975 by TCMA and features white-and-blue tinted player photos with red lettering. The backs carry player information. The cards are unnumbered and checklisted below in alphabetical order. Card number 43 pictures five players and measures 3 1/2" by 5" instead of the standard size.

	NM	Ex
COMPLETE SET (43)	25.00	10.00
1 Jim Bagby	.50	.20
2 Floyd Baker	.50	.20
3 Mace Brown	.50	.20
4 Bill Butland	.50	.20
5 Paul Campbell	.50	.20
6 Tom Carey	.50	.20
7 Joe Cronin P/MG	2.00	.80
8 Leon Culbertson	.50	.20
9 Tom Daly CO	.50	.20
10 Dom DiMaggio	1.50	.60
11 Joe Dobson	.50	.20
12 Bob Doerr	2.00	.80
13 Clem Dreisewerd	.50	.20
14 Boo Ferriss	.50	.20
15 Andy Gilbert	.50	.20
16 Don Gutteridge	.50	.20
17 Mickey Harris	.50	.20
18 Randy Heflin	.50	.20
19 Pinky Higgins	.50	.20
20 Tex Hughson	.50	.20
21 Earl Johnson	.50	.20
22 Bob Klinger	.50	.20
23 John Lazor	.50	.20
24 Thomas McBride	.50	.20
25 Ed McGah	.50	.20
26 Catfish Metkovich	.50	.20
27 Wally Moses	1.00	.40
28 Roy Partee	.50	.20
29 Eddie Pellagrini	.50	.20
30 Johnny Pesky	1.50	.60
31 Frank Pytlak	.50	.20
32 Rip Russell	.50	.20
33 Mike Ryba	.50	.20
34 Ben Steiner	.50	.20
35 Charlie Wagner	.50	.20
36 Hal Wagner	.50	.20
37 Ted Williams	5.00	2.00
38 Larry Woodall CO	.50	.20
39 Larry Woodall CO, Charlie Wagner, Floyd Baker	.50	.20
40 Rudy York	1.00	.40
41 Bill Zuber	.50	.20
42 Six player card	1.00	.40
43 Rudy York, Wally Moses, Dom DiMaggio, Bobby Doerr, Hal Wagner	1.00	.40

1976 Red Sox Star Market

This 16-card set of the Boston Red Sox measures approximately 5 7/8" by 9". The white-bordered fronts feature color player head photos with a facsimile autograph. The backs are blank. The cards are unnumbered and checklisted below in alphabetical order.

	NM	Ex
COMPLETE SET (16)	35.00	14.00
1 Rick Burleson	2.00	.80
2 Reggie Cleveland	1.00	.40
3 Cecil Cooper	2.50	1.00
4 Denny Doyle	1.00	.40
5 Dwight Evans	4.00	1.60
6 Carlton Fisk	8.00	3.20
7 Tom House	1.00	.40
8 Fergie Jenkins	4.00	1.60
9 Bill Lee	2.00	.80
10 Fred Lynn	2.50	1.00
11 Rick Miller	1.00	.40
12 Rico Petrocelli	2.00	.80
13 Jim Rice	4.00	1.60
14 Luis Tiant	2.50	1.00
15 Rick Wise	1.00	.40
16 Carl Yastrzemski	8.00	3.20

1976-77 Red Sox

This nine-card set of the Boston Red Sox measures approximately 7" by 8 1/2". The fronts feature white-bordered color player action photos with the player's name printed in black in the bottom margin. The backs are blank. The cards are unnumbered and checklisted below in alphabetical order. These cards were issued over a two year period as eight card sets. They are listed together since there is no difference other than Rico Petrocelli retired after the 1976 season and was replaced by George Scott.

	NM	Ex
COMPLETE SET (9)	18.00	7.25
1 Rick Burleson	2.00	.80
2 Denny Doyle	1.50	.60
3 Dwight Evans	3.00	1.20
4 Carlton Fisk	5.00	2.00
5 Fred Lynn	3.00	1.20
6 Rico Petrocelli '76	2.50	1.00
7 Jim Rice	3.00	1.20
8 George Scott '77	2.50	1.00
9 Carl Yastrzemski	3.00	1.20

1979 Red Sox Early Favorites

This 25-card set measures 2 1/2" by 3 3/4". The set covers the early years of Tom Yawkey's ownership. The photos are all black and white.

	NM	Ex
COMPLETE SET (25)	20.00	8.00
1 New Fenway Park	1.00	.40
2 Mrs. Tom Yawkey, Mrs. Eddie Collins	.75	.30
3 Tom Oliver, Earl Webb, Jack Rothrock	.75	.30
4 John Marcum, Wes Ferrell, Lefty Grove, Fritz Ostermueller	.75	.30
5 John Gooch	.75	.30
6 Joe Cronin, Lee Rogers, Bud Buetter, Walter Ripley, Jim Henry, Alex Mustaikis, Stewart Bowers	1.00	.40
7 Danny MacFayden	.75	.30
8 Dale Alexander	.75	.30
9 Robert Fothergill (Fatsy)	.75	.30
10 Sunday Morning Workout	.75	.30
11 Jimmy Foxx signs ball for Mrs. Tom Yawkey	1.00	.40
12 Lefty Grove receiving key for new car	1.00	.40
13 Lefty Grove Fireball	1.00	.40
14 Jack Rothrock Urbane Pickering	.75	.30
15 Tom Daly CO, Al Schact CO, Herb Pennock CO	.75	.30
16 Heinie Manush, Eddie Collins	1.00	.40
17 Tris Speaker	1.50	.60
18 Jimmy Foxx	2.00	.80
19 Smead Jolley	.75	.30
20 Hal Trosky, James Foxx	.75	.30
21 Harold (Muddy) Ruel, Wilcy (Fireman) Moore	.75	.30
22 Bob Quinn PR, Shano Collins MG	.75	.30
23 Tom Oliver	.75	.30
24 Joe Cronin CO, Herb Pennock CO, Bud Buetter	1.00	.40
25 Jimmie Foxx	5.00	2.00

1979 Red Sox Vendor Cards

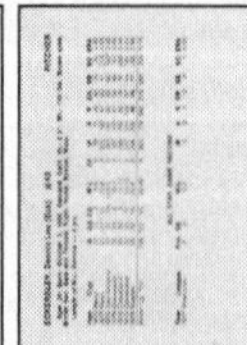

This standard-size set of the Boston Red Sox features black-and-white player portraits with biographical and statistical information on the backs except for one card which displays a picture of Garry Hancodk on one side and Stan Papi on the other. There are three other double player cards who need identifying. For now they are listed as two player cards. Any help on hese three other cards is appreciated. ccording to the back, The Phantom Co. issued ese cards. The cards came in a white packet ith a picture of a Red Sox (apparently Yaz) ounding the bases.

NM Ex
OMPLETE SET 25.00 10.00
Gary Allenson .50 .20
Jack Brohamer .50 .20
Tom Burgmeier .50 .20
Rick Burleson .75 .30
Bill Campbell .50 .20
Dick Drago .50 .20
Dennis Eckersley 3.00 1.20
Dwight Evans 1.50 .60
Carlton Fisk 5.00 2.00
0 Andy Hassler .50 .20
1 Butch Hobson .50 .20
2 Fred Lynn 1.50 .60
3 Bob Montgomery .50 .20
4 Mike O'Berry .50 .20
5 Jerry Remy .50 .20
6 Steve Renko .50 .20
7 Jim Rice 2.00 .80
8 George Scott .75 .30
9 Bob Stanley .50 .20
0 Mike Torrez .50 .20
1 Larry Wolfe .50 .20
2 Jim Wright .50 .20
3 Carl Yastrzemski 5.00 2.00
4 Garry Hancock .50 .20
Stan Papi
5 Two Player Card .50 .20
6 Two Player Card .50 .20
7 Two Player Card .50 .20

1980 Red Sox Postcards

ssued by the team, these 19 cards are black nd white and are postcard sized. Some of ese cards were known to come with facsimile utographs. Since these cards are unnumbered e have sequenced them in alphabetical order.

NM Ex
OMPLETE SET 20.00 8.00
Gary Allenson .50 .20
Jack Billingham .50 .20
Jack Brohamer .50 .20
Rick Burleson .50 .20
Dick Drago .50 .20
Dennis Eckersley 2.00 .80
Dwight Evans 1.50 .60
Carlton Fisk 3.00 1.20
Butch Hobson .50 .20
0 Glenn Hoffman .50 .20
1 Fred Lynn 1.50 .60
2 Tony Perez 2.00 .80
3 Chuck Rainey .50 .20
4 Jerry Remy .50 .20
5 Steve Renko .50 .20
6 Jim Rice 1.50 .60
7 Bob Stanley .50 .20
8 Mike Torrez .50 .20
9 Carl Yastrzemski 5.00 2.00

1981 Red Sox Boston Globe

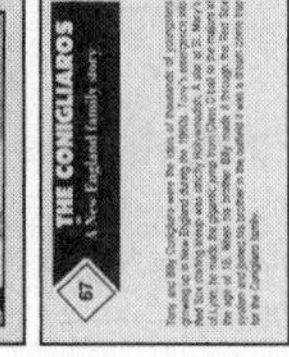

his standard size 128-card set consists of the oston Globe's series featuring black-and-hite photos surrounded by white borders of amous Boston Red Sox players. The cards were ssued in two series with cards 1-64 making up e first series and cards 65-128 being the econd series. The horizontal backs have player formation as well as career statistics. This set oncentrates on players from the 60's. These hotos were never intended to be issued as ards until a Globe employee got a hold of the rinting plated and illegally produced this set in wo series of 64 cards each. Series one eatured players of the 50's while series two eatured the 60's Red Sox players.

Nm-Mt Ex-Mt
OMPLETE SET (128) 40.00 16.00
Harry Agganis 1.00 .40
Ken Aspromonte .25 .10
Bobby Avila .25 .10
Frank Baumann .25 .10
Lou Berberet .25 .10
Milt Bolling .25 .10
Lou Boudreau 1.00 .40
Ted Bowsfield .25 .10
Tom Brewer .25 .10
0 Don Buddin .25 .10
1 Jerry Casale .25 .10
2 Billy Consolo UER .75 .30
Harry Agganis pictured
3 Pete Daley .25 .10
4 Ike Delock .25 .10
5 Dom DiMaggio 1.00 .40
6 Bobby Doerr 1.00 .40
7 Walt Dropo .50 .20
8 Arnie Earley .25 .10
9 Hoot Evers .25 .10
0 Mike Fornieles .25 .10
1 Gary Geiger .25 .10
2 Don Gile .25 .10
3 Joe Ginsburg .25 .10
4 Billy Goodman .25 .10
5 Pumpsie Green .25 .10
6 Grady Hatton .25 .10
7 Mike Higgins MG .25 .10
8 Jackie Jensen .75 .30
9 George Kell 1.00 .40
0 Marty Keough .25 .10
1 Leo Kiely .25 .10
2 Ellis Kinder .25 .10
3 Billy Klaus .25 .10
34 Don Lenhardt .25 .10
35 Ted Lepcio .25 .10
36 Frank Malzone .75 .30
37 Gene Mauch .25 .10
38 Maury McDermott .25 .10
39 Bill Monbouquette .25 .10
40 Chet Nichols .25 .10
41 Willard Nixon .25 .10
42 Jim Pagliaroni .25 .10
43 Mel Parnell .75 .30
44 Johnny Pesky .75 .30
45 Jimmy Piersall .50 .20
46 Bob Porterfield .25 .10
47 Pete Runnels .25 .10
48 Dave Sisler .25 .10
49 Riverboat Smith .25 .10
50 Gene Stephens .25 .10
51 Vern Stephens .25 .10
52 Chuck Stobbs .25 .10
53 Dean Stone .25 .10
54 Frank Sullivan .25 .10
55 Haywood Sullivan .25 .10
56 Birdie Tebbetts .25 .10
57 Mickey Vernon .75 .30
58 Vic Wertz .25 .10
59 Sammy White .25 .10
60 Ted Williams 5.00 2.00
61 Ted Wills .25 .10
62 Earl Wilson .25 .10
63 Al Zarilla .25 .10
64 Norm Zauchin .25 .10
65 Ted Williams 2.50 1.00
Carl Yastrzemski
66 Dick Williams MG 1.00 .40
Carl Yastrzemski
Jim Lonborg
George Scott
67 Tony Conigliaro .25 .10
Billy Conigliaro
68 Jerry Adair .25 .10
69 Mike Andrews .25 .10
70 Gary Bell .25 .10
71 Dennis Bennett .25 .10
72 Ed Bressoud .25 .10
73 Ken Brett .25 .10
74 Lu Clinton .25 .10
75 Tony Conigliaro 1.00 .40
76 Billy Conigliaro .25 .10
77 Gene Conley .25 .10
78 Ray Culp .25 .10
79 Dick Ellsworth .25 .10
80 Joe Foy .25 .10
81 Russ Gibson .25 .10
82 Jim Gosger .25 .10
83 Lennie Green .25 .10
84 Ken Harrelson .50 .20
85 Tony Horton .25 .10
86 Elston Howard 1.00 .40
87 Dalton Jones .25 .10
88 Eddie Kasko .25 .10
89 Joe Lahoud .25 .10
90 Jack Lamabe .25 .10
91 Jim Lonborg .75 .30
92 Sparky Lyle .75 .30
93 Felix Mantilla .25 .10
94 Roman Mejias .25 .10
95 Don McMahon .25 .10
96 Dave Morehead .25 .10
97 Gerry Moses .25 .10
98 Mike Nagy .25 .10
99 Russ Nixon .25 .10
100 Gene Oliver .25 .10
101 Dan Osinski .25 .10
102 Rico Petrocelli .50 .20
103 Juan Pizarro .25 .10
104 Dick Radatz .25 .10
105 Vicente Romo .25 .10
106 Mike Ryan .25 .10
107 Jose Santiago .25 .10
108 Chuck Schilling .25 .10
109 Dick Schofield .25 .10
110 Don Schwall .25 .10
111 George Scott .50 .20
112 Norm Siebern .25 .10
113 Sonny Seibert .25 .10
114 Reggie Smith .50 .20
115 Bill Spanswick .25 .10
116 Tracy Stallard .25 .10
117 Lee Stange .25 .10
118 Jerry Stephenson .25 .10
119 Dick Stuart .50 .20
120 Tom Sturdivant .25 .10
121 Jose Tartabull .25 .10
122 George Thomas .25 .10
123 Lee Thomas .25 .10
124 Bob Tillman .25 .10
125 Gary Waslewski .25 .10
126 Dick Williams .50 .20
127 John Wyatt .25 .10
128 Carl Yastrzemski 2.50 1.00

1982 Red Sox Coke

The cards in this 23-card set measure the standard size. This set of Boston Red Sox ballplayers was issued locally in the Boston area as a joint promotion by Brigham's Ice Cream Stores and Coca-Cola. The pictures are identical to those in the Topps regular 1982 issue, except that the colors are brighter and the Brigham and Coke logos appear inside the frame line. The reverses are done in red, black and gray, in contrast to the Topps set, and the number appears to the right of the position listing. The cards were initally distributed in three-card cello packs with an ice cream or Coca-Cola purchase but later became available as sets within the hobby. The unnumbered title or advertising card carries a premium offer on the reverse. The set numbering is in alphabetical order by player's name.

Nm-Mt Ex-Mt
COMPLETE SET (23) 8.00 3.20
1 Gary Allenson .25 .10
2 Tom Burgmeier .25 .10
3 Mark Clear .25 .10
4 Steve Crawford .25 .10
5 Dennis Eckersley 2.00 .80
6 Dwight Evans 1.00 .40
7 Rich Gedman .25 .10
8 Garry Hancock .25 .10
9 Glenn Hoffman .25 .10
10 Carney Lansford .50 .20
11 Rick Miller .25 .10
12 Reid Nichols .50 .20
13 Bob Ojeda .75 .30
14 Tony Perez 2.00 .80
15 Chuck Rainey .25 .10
16 Jerry Remy .25 .10
17 Jim Rice 1.00 .40
18 Bob Stanley .50 .20
19 Dave Stapleton .25 .10
20 Mike Torrez .25 .10
21 John Tudor .50 .20
22 Carl Yastrzemski 3.00 1.20
NNO Title Card .15 .06

1982 Red Sox Herald Stamps

These stamps, which feature a mix of active and retired players for the Red Sox were issued by the Boston Herald. Stamps 1 through 26 feature players from the 1982 Red Sox, 39 through 42 feature prospect and the others feature all-time Red Sox greats.

Nm-Mt Ex-Mt
COMPLETE SET 40.00 16.00
1 Jerry Remy .25 .10
2 Glenn Hoffman .25 .10
3 Luis Aponte .25 .10
4 Jim Rice 1.25 .50
5 Mark Clear .25 .10
6 Reid Nichols .25 .10
7 Wade Boggs 5.00 2.00
8 Dennis Eckersley 1.50 .60
9 Jeff Newman .25 .10
10 Bob Ojeda .25 .10
11 Ed Jurak .25 .10
12 Rick Miller .25 .10
13 Carl Yastrzemski 2.50 1.00
14 Mike Brown .25 .10
15 Bob Stanley .25 .10
16 John Tudor .25 .10
17 Gary Allenson .25 .10
18 Rich Gedman .25 .10
19 Tony Armas .50 .20
20 Doug Bird .25 .10
21 Bruce Hurst .25 .10
22 Dave Stapleton .25 .10
23 Dwight Evans 1.00 .40
24 Julio Valdez .25 .10
25 John Henry Johnson .25 .10
26 Ralph Houk MG .25 .10
27 George Scott .50 .20
28 Bobby Doerr 1.00 .40
29 Frank Malzone .50 .20
30 Rico Petrocelli .50 .20
31 Carl Yastrzemski 1.50 .60
32 Ted Williams 5.00 2.00
33 Dwight Evans 1.25 .50
34 Carlton Fisk 2.00 .80
35 Dick Radatz .50 .20
36 Luis Tiant 1.00 .40
37 Mel Parnell .50 .20
38 Jim Rice 1.25 .50
39 Dennis Boyd .50 .20
40 Marty Barrett .50 .20
41 Brian Denman .25 .10
42 Steve Crawford .25 .10
43 Cy Young 1.25 .50
44 Jimmy Collins 1.25 .50
45 Tris Speaker 1.50 .60
46 Harry Hooper 1.00 .40
47 Lefty Grove 2.00 .80
48 Joe Cronin 1.50 .60
49 Jimmy Foxx 2.00 .80
50 Ted Williams 5.00 2.00

1986 Red Sox Greats TCMA

This 12-card standard-size set features all-time leading Red Sox. The player's photo and his name are featured on the front. The back gives more information about that player.

Nm-Mt Ex-Mt
COMPLETE SET (12) 7.50 3.00
1 Sammy White .25 .10
2 Lefty Grove 1.00 .40
3 Cy Young 1.00 .40
4 Jimmie Foxx 1.00 .40
5 Bobby Doerr .50 .20
6 Joe Cronin .50 .20
7 Frank Malzone .25 .10
8 Ted Williams 2.50 1.00
9 Carl Yastrzemski 1.00 .40
10 Tris Speaker .75 .30
11 Dick Radatz .25 .10
12 Dick Williams MG .25 .10

1987 Red Sox 1946 TCMA

This nine-card standard-size set honors players on the 1946 Red Sox. This team would prove to be the only time Ted Williams would participate in post season play.

Nm-Mt Ex-Mt
COMPLETE SET (9) 5.00 2.00
1 Joe Cronin MG .50 .20
2 Rudy York .25 .10
3 Bobby Doerr .75 .30
4 Johnny Pesky .50 .20
5 Dom DiMaggio .75 .30
6 Ted Williams 2.50 1.00
7 Dave "Boo" Ferriss .25 .10
8 Tex Hughson .25 .10
9 Mickey Harris .25 .10

1987 Red Sox Postcards

This 22-card set features photos of the 1987 Boston Red Sox printed on postcard-size cards. The cards are unnumbered and checklisted below in alphabetical order.

Nm-Mt Ex-Mt
COMPLETE SET (22) 18.00 7.25
1 Marty Barrett .50 .20
2 Don Baylor 1.00 .40
3 Wade Boggs 2.00 .80
4 Dennis Boyd .50 .20
5 Ellis Burks 2.00 .80
6 Roger Clemens 4.00 1.60
7 Steve Crawford .50 .20
8 Dwight Evans 1.50 .60
9 Wes Gardner .50 .20
10 Rich Gedman .50 .20
11 Mike Greenwell 1.50 .60
12 Dave Henderson .50 .20
13 Bruce Hurst .50 .20
14 Al Nipper .50 .20
15 Spike Owen .50 .20
16 Jim Rice 1.00 .40
17 Ed Romero .50 .20
18 Joe Sambito .50 .20
19 Calvin Schiraldi .50 .20
20 Jeff Sellers .50 .20
21 Bob Stanley .50 .20
22 Marc Sullivan .50 .20

1987 Red Sox Sports Action Postcards

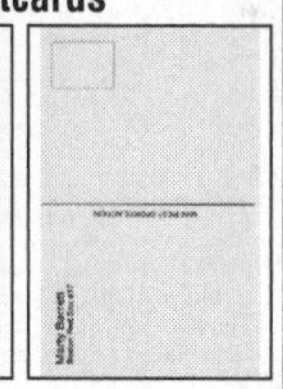

These color postcards featured members of the 1987 Boston Red Sox. They were issued in sets of all ten players.

Nm-Mt Ex-Mt
COMPLETE SET (10) 8.00 3.20
1 Marty Barrett .50 .20
2 Don Baylor 1.00 .40
3 Wade Boggs 2.00 .80
4 Dennis Boyd .50 .20
5 Bill Buckner .75 .30
6 Roger Clemens 4.00 1.60
7 Dwight Evans 1.50 .60
8 Bruce Hurst .50 .20
9 Spike Owen .50 .20
10 Jim Rice 1.00 .40

1988 Red Sox Donruss Team Book

The 1988 Donruss Red Sox Team Book set features 27 cards (three pages with nine cards on each page) plus a large full-page puzzle of Stan Musial. Cards are in full color and are standard size. The set was distributed as a four-page book; although the puzzle page was perforated, the card pages were not. The cover of the "Team Collection" book is primarily bright red. Card fronts are very similar in design to the 1988 Donruss regular issue. The card numbers on the backs are the same for those players that are the same as in the regular Donruss set; the new players pictured are numbered on the back as "NEW." The book is usually sold intact. When cut from the book into individual cards, these cards are distinguishable from the regular 1988 Donruss cards since these have a 1988 copyright on the back whereas the regular issue has a 1987 copyright on the back.

Nm-Mt Ex-Mt
COMPLETE SET (27) 4.00 1.60
41 Jody Reed RR .25 .10
51 Roger Clemens 2.00 .80
92 Bob Stanley .10 .04
129 Rich Gedman .10 .04
153 Wade Boggs 1.50 .60
174 Ellis Burks 1.00 .40
216 Dwight Evans .25 .10
252 Bruce Hurst .10 .04
276 Marty Barrett .10 .04
297 Todd Benzinger .10 .04
339 Mike Greenwell .10 .04
399 Jim Rice .25 .10
421 John Marzano .10 .04
462 Oil Can Boyd .10 .04
498 Sam Horn .10 .04
544 Spike Owen .10 .04
585 Jeff Sellers .10 .04
623 Ed Romero .10 .04
634 Wes Gardner .10 .04
NEW Brady Anderson 1.00 .40
NEW Rick Cerone .10 .04
NEW Steve Ellsworth .10 .04
NEW Dennis Lamp .10 .04
NEW Kevin Romine .10 .04
NEW Lee Smith .25 .10
NEW Mike Smithson .10 .04
NEW John Trautwein .10 .04

1990 Red Sox Pepsi

The 1990 Pepsi Boston Red Sox set is a 20-card standard-size set, which is checklisted alphabetically below. This set was apparently prepared very early in the 1990 season as Bill Buckner and Lee Smith were still members of the Red Sox in this set. The cards were supposedly available as a store promotion with one card per specially marked 12-pack of Pepsi. The cards were difficult to remove from the boxes, thus making perfect mint cards worth an extra premium.

Nm-Mt Ex-Mt
COMPLETE SET (20) 40.00 12.00
1 Marty Barrett 1.00 .30
2 Mike Boddicker 1.00 .30
3 Wade Boggs 10.00 3.00
4 Bill Buckner 1.50 .45
5 Ellis Burks 6.00 1.80
6 Roger Clemens 20.00 6.00
7 John Dopson 1.00 .30
8 Dwight Evans 2.50 .75
9 Wes Gardner 1.00 .30
10 Rich Gedman 1.00 .30
11 Mike Greenwell 2.00 .60
12 Dennis Lamp 1.00 .30
13 Rob Murphy 1.00 .30
14 Tony Pena 1.50 .45
15 Carlos Quintana 1.00 .30
16 Jeff Reardon 1.50 .45
17 Jody Reed 1.00 .30
18 Luis Rivera 1.00 .30
19 Kevin Romine 1.00 .30
20 Lee Smith 2.50 .75

1990 Red Sox Topps TV

This Red Sox team set contains 66 cards measuring the standard size. Cards numbered 1-33 were with the parent club, while cards 34-66 were in the farm system. The set features an early card of Mo Vaughn.

Nm-Mt Ex-Mt
COMPLETE FACT. SET (66) 80.00 24.00
1 Joe Morgan MG .25 .07
2 Dick Berardino CO .25 .07
3 Al Bumbry CO .25 .07
4 Bill Fischer CO .25 .07
5 Richie Hebner CO .25 .07
6 Rac Slider CO .25 .07
7 Mike Boddicker .25 .07
8 Roger Clemens 40.00 12.00
9 John Dopson .25 .07
10 Wes Gardner .25 .07
11 Greg A. Harris .25 .07
12 Dana Kiecker .25 .07
13 Dennis Lamp .25 .07
14 Rob Murphy .25 .07
15 Jeff Reardon .50 .15
16 Mike Rochford .25 .07
17 Lee Smith 1.50 .45
18 Rich Gedman .25 .07
19 John Marzano .25 .07
20 Tony Pena .50 .15
21 Marty Barrett .25 .07
22 Wade Boggs 20.00 6.00
23 Bill Buckner .50 .15
24 Danny Heep .25 .07
25 Jody Reed .25 .07
26 Luis Rivera .25 .07
27 Billy Joe Robidoux .25 .07
28 Ellis Burks 3.00 .90

29 Dwight Evans	1.50	.45
30 Mike Greenwell	.50	.15
31 Randy Kutcher	.25	.07
32 Carlos Quintana	.25	.07
33 Kevin Romine	.25	.07
34 Ed Nottle MG	.25	.07
35 Mark Meleski CO	.25	.07
36 Steve Bast	.25	.07
37 Greg Blosser	.25	.07
38 Tom Bolton	.25	.07
39 Scott Cooper	.25	.07
40 Zach Crouch	.25	.07
41 Steve Curry	.25	.07
42 Mike Dalton	.25	.07
43 John Flaherty	.25	.07
44 Angel Gonzalez	.25	.07
45 Eric Hetzel	.25	.07
46 Daryl Irvine	.25	.07
47 Joe Johnson	.25	.07
48 Rick Lancellotti	.25	.07
49 John Leister	.25	.07
50 Derek Livernois	.25	.07
51 Josias Manzanillo	.25	.07
52 Kevin Morton	.25	.07
53 Julius McDougal	.25	.07
54 Tim Naehring	.50	.15
55 Jim Pankovits	.25	.07
56 Mickey Pina	.25	.07
57 Phil Plantier	.50	.15
58 Jerry Reed	.25	.07
59 Larry Shikles	.25	.07
60 Tito Stewart	.25	.07
61 Jeff Stone	.25	.07
62 John Trautwein	.25	.07
63 Gary Tremblay	.25	.07
64 Mo Vaughn	10.00	3.00
65 Scott Wade	.25	.07
66 Eric Wedge	1.50	.45

1991 Red Sox Pepsi

This 20-card set was sponsored by Pepsi and officially licensed by Mike Schechter Associates on behalf of the MLBPA. The 1991 edition consists of 100,000 sets that were available from July 1 through August 10, 1991 in the New England area, with one card per specially marked pack of Pepsi and Diet Pepsi. The promotion also includes a sweepstakes offering a grand prize trip for four to Red Sox Spring training camp. The cards are unnumbered and checklisted below in alphabetical order.

	Nm-Mt	Ex-Mt
COMPLETE SET (20)	20.00	6.00
1 Tom Bolton	.75	.23
2 Tom Brunansky	.75	.23
3 Ellis Burks	2.50	.75
4 Jack Clark	1.00	.30
5 Roger Clemens	10.00	3.00
6 Danny Darwin	.75	.23
7 Jeff Gray	.75	.23
8 Mike Greenwell	1.25	.35
9 Greg A. Harris	.75	.23
10 Dana Kiecker	.75	.23
11 Dennis Lamp	.75	.23
12 John Marzano	.75	.23
13 Tim Naehring	.75	.23
14 Tony Pena	1.00	.30
15 Phil Plantier	.75	.23
16 Carlos Quintana	.75	.23
17 Jeff Reardon	1.25	.35
18 Jody Reed	.75	.23
19 Luis Rivera	.75	.23
20 Matt Young	.75	.23

1991 Red Sox Postcards

This 29-card set features photos of the 1991 Boston Red Sox printed on postcard-size cards. The cards are unnumbered and checklisted below in alphabetical order.

	Nm-Mt	Ex-Mt
COMPLETE SET (29)	20.00	6.00
1 Wade Boggs	2.00	.60
2 Tom Bolton	.50	.15
3 Mike Brumley	.50	.15
4 Tom Brunansky	.75	.23
5 Ellis Burks	1.50	.45
6 Jack Clark	.75	.23
7 Roger Clemens	4.00	1.20
8 Danny Darwin	.50	.15
9 John Dopson	.50	.15
10 Tony Fossas	.50	.15
11 Mike Gardiner	.50	.15
12 Jeff Gray	.50	.15
13 Mike Greenwell	.75	.23
14 Greg Harris	.50	.15
15 Joe Hesketh	.50	.15
16 Dana Kiechker	.50	.15
17 Dennis Lamp	.50	.15
18 Steve Lyons	.75	.23
19 John Marzano	.50	.15
20 Kevin Morton	.50	.15
21 Tim Naehring	.50	.15
22 Carlos Quintana	.50	.15
23 Tony Pena	.75	.23
24 Jeff Reardon	.75	.23
25 Jody Reed	.50	.15
26 Luis Rivera	.50	.15
27 Kevin Romine	.50	.15
28 Mo Vaughn	3.00	.90
29 Matt Young	.50	.15

1992 Red Sox Dunkin' Donuts

The 1992 Boston Red Sox Player Photo Collection was sponsored by Dunkin' Donuts and WVIT Channel 30 (Connecticut's NBC Station). It consists of three large sheets (each

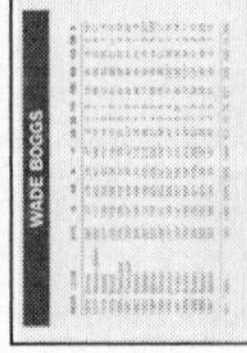

measuring approximately 9 3/8" by 10 3/4") joined together to form one continuous sheet. The first panel displays a color picture of Fenway Park and a WVIT Red Sox Schedule. The second and third panels, which are perforated, feature 15 player cards each. After perforation, the cards measure approximately 2 1/8" by 3 1/8". The set was also available sponsored by WJAR-10 TV in Providence, Rhode Island and by Rookie Red Sox Coke via a mail-in offer on 12-packs of Coke in the Boston area for 7.00.

	Nm-Mt	Ex-Mt
COMPLETE SET (30)	12.00	3.60
1 Gary Allenson CO	.25	.07
2 Wade Boggs	2.00	.60
3 Tom Bolton	.25	.07
4 Tom Brunansky	.25	.07
5 Al Bumbry CO	.25	.07
6 Ellis Burks	.75	.23
7 Rick Burleson CO	.25	.07
8 Jack Clark	.50	.15
9 Roger Clemens	5.00	1.50
10 Danny Darwin	.25	.07
11 Tony Fossas	.25	.07
12 Rich Gale CO	.25	.07
13 Mike Gardiner	.25	.07
14 Mike Greenwell	.50	.15
15 Greg A. Harris	.25	.07
16 Joe Hesketh	.25	.07
17 Butch Hobson MG	.25	.07
18 John Marzano	.25	.07
19 Kevin Morton	.25	.07
20 Tim Naehring	.25	.07
21 Tony Pena	.50	.15
22 Phil Plantier	.25	.07
23 Carlos Quintana	.25	.07
24 Jeff Reardon	.50	.15
25 Jody Reed	.25	.07
26 Luis Rivera	.25	.07
27 Mo Vaughn	3.00	.90
28 Frank Viola	.50	.15
29 Matt Young	.25	.07
30 Don Zimmer CO	.50	.15

1993 Red Sox Postcards

This 33-card set features photos of the 1993 Boston Red Sox printed on postcard-size cards. The cards are unnumbered and checklisted below in alphabetical order.

	Nm-Mt	Ex-Mt
COMPLETE SET (33)	20.00	6.00
1 Gary Allenson CO	.50	.15
2 Scott Bankhead	.50	.15
3 Al Bumbry	.50	.15
4 Rick Burleson CO	.50	.15
5 Ivan Calderon	.50	.15
6 Roger Clemens	4.00	1.20
7 Scott Cooper	.50	.15
8 Danny Darwin	.50	.15
9 Andre Dawson	1.50	.45
10 John Dopson	.50	.15
11 Mike Easler CO	.50	.15
12 John Flaherty	.50	.15
13 Scott Fletcher	.50	.15
14 Tony Fossas	.50	.15
15 Rich Gale	.50	.15
16 Mike Greenwell	.75	.23
17 Greg Harris	.50	.15
18 Billy Hatcher	.50	.15
19 Joe Hesketh	.50	.15
20 Butch Hobson MG	.50	.15
21 Jose Melendez	.50	.15
22 Bob Melvin	.75	.23
23 Tim Naehring	.50	.15
24 Tony Pena	.75	.23
25 Paul Quantrill	.50	.15
26 Carlos Quintana	.50	.15
27 Ernest Riles	.50	.15
28 Luis Rivera	.50	.15
29 Jeff Russell	.50	.15
30 John Valentin	.50	.15
31 Mo Vaughn	2.00	.60
32 Frank Viola	.75	.23
33 Bob Zupcic	.50	.15

1993 Red Sox Winter Haven Police

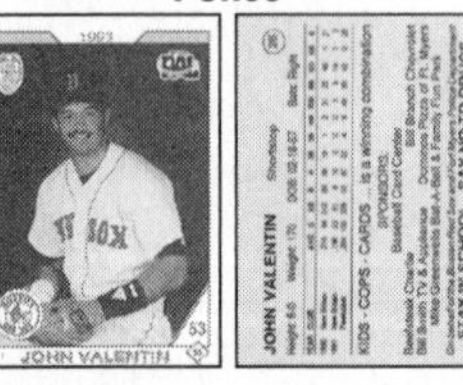

This 28-card standard-size set features players who were invited to the 1993 Red Sox spring training camp. The fronts feature posed studio shots while the backs feature recent stats as well as listing the various sponsors. Many of the stats only go through the 1991 season.

	Nm-Mt	Ex-Mt
COMPLETE SET (28)	10.00	3.00
1 Checklist	.25	.07
2 Scott Bankhead	.25	.07
3 Danny Darwin	.25	.07
4 Andre Dawson	1.00	.30
5 Scott Fletcher	.25	.07
6 Billy Hatcher	.25	.07
7 Jack Clark	.50	.15
8 Roger Clemens	3.00	.90
9 Scott Cooper	.25	.07
10 John Dopson	.25	.07
11 Paul Quantrill	.25	.07
12 Mike Greenwell	.50	.15
13 Greg A. Harris	.25	.07
14 Joe Hesketh	.25	.07
15 Peter Hoy	.25	.07
16 Daryl Irvine	.25	.07
17 John Marzano	.25	.07
18 Jeff McNeely	.25	.07
19 Tim Naehring	.25	.07
20 Matt Young	.25	.07
21 Jeff Plympton	.25	.07
22 Bob Melvin	.50	.15
23 Tony Pena	.50	.15
24 Luis Rivera	.25	.07
25 Scott Taylor	.25	.07
26 John Valentin	.25	.07
27 Mo Vaughn	1.50	.45
28 Frank Viola	.50	.15

1996 Red Sox Fleer

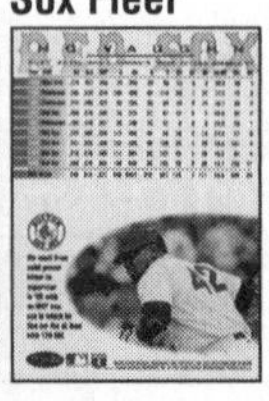

These 20 standard-size cards feature the same design as the regular Fleer issue, except they are UV coated, use silver foil and are numbered "x of 20". The team set packs were available at retail locations and hobby shops in 10-card packs for a suggested retail price of $1.99.

	Nm-Mt	Ex-Mt
COMPLETE SET (20)	4.00	1.20
1 Stan Belinda	.10	.03
2 Jose Canseco	.50	.15
3 Roger Clemens	2.00	.60
4 Wil Cordero	.10	.03
5 Vaughn Eshelman	.10	.03
6 Tom Gordon	.30	.09
7 Mike Greenwell	.10	.03
8 Dwayne Hosey	.10	.03
9 Kevin Mitchell	.10	.03
10 Tim Naehring	.10	.03
11 Troy O'Leary	.10	.03
12 Aaron Sele	.20	.06
13 Heathcliff Slocumb	.10	.03
14 Mike Stanley	.10	.03
15 Jeff Suppan	.10	.03
16 John Valentin	.10	.03
17 Mo Vaughn	.20	.06
18 Tim Wakefield	.30	.09
19 Logo card	.10	.03
20 Checklist	.10	.03

1997 Red Sox Score

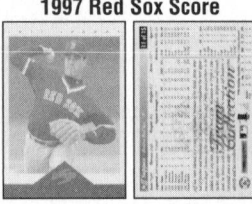

This 15-card set of the Boston Red Sox was issued in five-card packs with a suggested retail price of $1.30 each. The fronts feature color player photos with special team specific color foil stamping. The backs carry player information. Only 100 cases were made for each team. Platinum parallel cards were inserted at a rate of 1:6, Premier parallel cards at a rate of 1:31.

	Nm-Mt	Ex-Mt
COMPLETE SET (15)	5.00	1.50
*PLATINUM: 5X BASIC CARDS		
*PREMIER: 20X BASIC CARDS		
1 Wil Cordero	.25	.07
2 Mo Vaughn	.50	.15
3 John Valentin	.25	.07
4 Reggie Jefferson	.25	.07
5 Tom Gordon	.50	.15
6 Mike Stanley	.25	.07
7 Jose Canseco	1.25	.35
8 Roger Clemens	2.00	.60
9 Darren Bragg	.25	.07
10 Jeff Frye	.25	.07
11 Jeff Suppan	.25	.07
12 Mike Greenwell	.25	.07
13 Arquimedez Pozo	.25	.07
14 Tim Naehring	.25	.07
15 Troy O'Leary	.25	.07

1998 Red Sox Postcards

These 37 blank backed postcards measure 4" by 5 3/4". They are unnumbered so we have sequenced them in alphabetical order.

	Nm-Mt	Ex-Mt
COMPLETE SET (37)	12.00	3.60
1 Steve Avery	.25	.07
2 Mike Benjamin	.25	.07
3 Darren Bragg	.25	.07
4 Damon Buford	.25	.07
5 Jin Ho Cho	1.00	.30
6 Jim Corsi	.25	.07
7 Midre Cummings	.25	.07
8 Dennis Eckersley	1.50	.45
9 Nomar Garciaparra	3.00	.90
10 Tom Gordon	.50	.15
11 Scott Hattenberg	.25	.07
12 Butch Henry	.25	.07
13 Joe Hudson	.25	.07
14 Dave Jauss CO	.25	.07
15 Reggie Jefferson	.25	.07
16 Wendell Kim CO	.25	.07
17 Joe Kerrigan CO	.25	.07
18 Mark Lemke	.25	.07
19 Darren Lewis	.25	.07
20 Grady Little CO	.50	.15
21 Derek Lowe	.75	.23
22 Ron Mahay	.25	.07
23 Pedro Martinez	1.50	.45
24 Lou Merloni	.25	.07
25 Tim Naehring	.25	.07
26 Troy O'Leary	.25	.07
27 Dick Pole CO	.25	.07
28 Jim Rice CO	.50	.15
29 Brian Rose	.25	.07
30 Bret Saberhagen	.50	.15
31 Donnie Sadler	.25	.07
32 John Valentin	.25	.07
33 Jason Varitek	.75	.23
34 Mo Vaughn	.50	.15
35 Tim Wakefield	.75	.23
36 John Wasdin	.25	.07
37 Jimy Williams MG	.25	.07

1998 Red Sox Score

This 15-card set was issued in special retail packs and features color photos of the Boston Red Sox team. The backs carry player information. A special platinum parallel set was also issued and randomly inserted in packs.

	Nm-Mt	Ex-Mt
COMPLETE SET (15)	6.00	1.80
*PLATINUM: 5X BASIC CARDS		
1 Steve Avery	.25	.07
2 Aaron Sele	.50	.15
3 Tim Wakefield	.25	.07
4 Darren Bragg	.25	.07
5 Scott Hatteberg	.25	.07
6 Jeff Suppan	.25	.07
7 Nomar Garciaparra	3.00	.90
8 Tim Naehring	.25	.07
9 Reggie Jefferson	.25	.07
10 John Valentin	.25	.07
11 Jeff Frye	.25	.07
12 Wil Cordero	.25	.07
13 Troy O'Leary	.25	.07
14 Mo Vaughn	.50	.15
15 Shane Mack	.25	.07

2001 Red Sox Commemorative Set

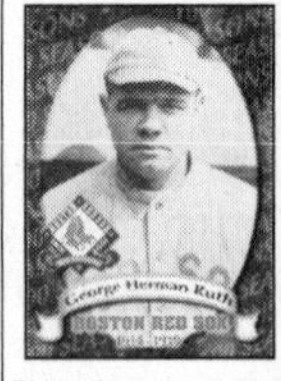

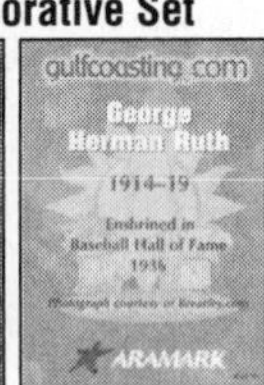

This 16-card set was issued in Fort Myers during 2001 Boston Red Sox spring training games. One card was issued to the first 4000 fans that entered the ballpark before each spring training game. A total of 5000 sets were produced. These cards feature some of the all-time great Red Sox players. These cards were produced by Aramark and Gulfcoast.com, and feature the "Aramark" symbol on the back of each card.

	Nm-Mt	Ex-Mt
COMPLETE SET (16)	12.00	3.60
1 Jimmy Collins	.25	.07
2 Cy Young	1.00	.30
3 Tris Speaker	.50	.15
4 Babe Ruth	3.00	.90
5 Lefty Grove	.50	.15
6 Joe Cronin	.50	.15
7 Jimmie Foxx	.75	.23
8 Bobby Doerr	.50	.15
9 Ted Williams	2.50	.75
10 Dom DiMaggio	.50	.15
11 Johnny Pesky	.25	.07
12 Carl Yastrzemski	1.00	.30
13 Carlton Fisk	1.00	.30
14 Jim Rice	.50	.15
15 Nomar Garciaparra	1.50	.45
16 Pedro Martinez	1.25	.35

2001 Red Sox Team Issue

Same size as colored cards a year ago, but wider borders and larger names. Red Sox logo appears on the front. Back is blank as with previous years. Cards were free, but there were no sets available directly from the team..

	Nm-Mt	Ex-Mt
COMPLETE SET (19)	10.00	3.00
1 Rolando Arrojo	.25	.07
2 Rod Beck	.25	.07
3 Dante Bichette	.25	.07
4 Frank Castillo	.25	.07
5 Paxton Crawford	.25	.07
6 Brian Daubach	.25	.07
7 Carl Everett	.50	.15
8 Shea Hillenbrand	1.00	.30
9 Mike Lansing	.25	.07
10 Pedro Martinez	2.00	.60
11 Lou Merloni	.25	.07
12 Hideo Nomo	2.00	.60
13 Tomo Ohka	.25	.07
14 Manny Ramirez	2.00	.60
15 Pete Schourek	.25	.07
16 Chris Stynes	.25	.07
17 John Valentin	.25	.07
18 Tim Wakefield	.75	.23
19 Wilton Veras	.25	.07

2002 Red Sox Polish Spring

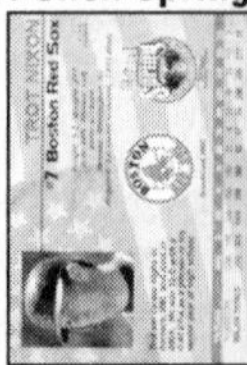

This 23-card standard-size set was issued as a stadium giveaway and featured members of the 2002 Boston Red Sox. The UV-coated fronts have the player's photo surrounded by white borders. There is a Polish Spring logo on the upper right corner. The horizontal backs have biographical information, a brief blurb as well as 2001 and career stats. The back's upper left also has a photo. Since these cards are not numbered, we have sequenced them in alphabetical order.

	Nm-Mt	Ex-Mt
COMPLETE SET	10.00	3.00
1 Rolando Arrojo	.25	.07
2 Carlos Baerga	.50	.15
3 John Burkett	.25	.07
4 Frank Castillo	.25	.07
5 Tony Clark	.25	.07
6 Johnny Damon	.75	.23
7 Brian Daubach	.25	.07
8 Rich Garces	.25	.07
9 Nomar Garciaparra	2.00	.60
10 Rickey Henderson	1.50	.45
11 Shea Hillenbrand	.25	.07
12 Grady Little MG	.25	.07
13 Derek Lowe	.75	.23
14 Pedro Martinez	1.50	.45
15 Lou Merloni	.25	.07
16 Doug Mirabelli	.25	.07
17 Trot Nixon	.75	.23
18 Jose Offerman	.25	.07
19 Manny Ramirez	1.50	.45
20 Ugueth Urbina	.50	.15
21 Jason Varitek	.75	.23
22 Tim Wakefield	.75	.23
23 Wally Mascot	.25	.07
XX Polish Spring Promo	.10	.02

2003 Red Sox Team Issue

These color cards, which measure approximately 4" by 6" feature members of the 2003 Boston Red Sox. There are reports that these were sold by the team (however, not through their web site) for $5 for the set. It is believed that the Robert Person card was issued in much shorter supply. Since these cards are unnumbered, we have sequenced them in alphabetical order. As there are cards of both Shea Hillenbrand and Byung-Hyun Kim it is evident that this set was continually updated during the 2003 as those two players were traded for each other during the season.

	MINT	NRMT
COMPLETE SET	10.00	4.50
1 John Burkett	.25	.11
2 Tony Cloninger CO	.25	.11
3 Mike Cubbage CO	.25	.11
4 Johnny Damon	.75	.35
5 Alan Embree	.25	.11
6 Casey Fossum	.25	.11
7 Nomar Garciaparra	2.00	.90
8 Shea Hillenbrand	.50	.23
9 Damian Jackson	.25	.11
10 Ron Jackson CO	.25	.11
11 Byung-Hyun Kim	.50	.23
12 Grady Little MG	.25	.11
13 Brandon Lyon	.25	.11
14 Derek Lowe	.75	.35
15 Pedro Martinez	1.50	.70
16 Ramiro Mendoza	.25	.11
17 Lou Merloni	.25	.11
18 Kevin Millar	.75	.35
19 Doug Mirabelli	.25	.11
20 Bill Mueller	.75	.35
21 Jerry Narron CO	.25	.11
22 Trot Nixon	1.00	.45
23 David Ortiz	1.00	.45
24 Robert Person	1.00	.45
25 Euclidies Rojas	.25	.11
26 Manny Ramirez	1.50	.70
27 Freddy Sanchez	.25	.11
28 Mike Timlin	.25	.11
29 Tim Wakefield	.75	.35
30 Todd Walker	.50	.23
31 Dallas Williams	.25	.11

1869 Red Stockings Peck and Snyder

This card was issued by Peck and Snyder as an advertising trade piece. It comes in two versions (either with red or black borders). The black version is usually larger than the red version. Most of these cards are found trimmed to fit into CdV albums. The front features a photo of the 1869 Red Stockings while the

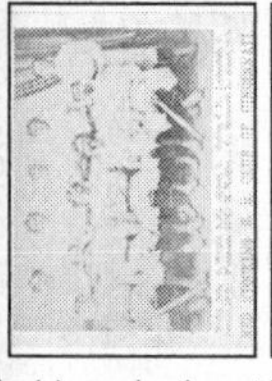

back is an advertisment for Peck and Snyder.

	Ex-Mt	VG
1 Red Stockings Team	10000.00	5000.00

1891 Reds Cabinets Conly

These Cabinets feature members of the 1891 Cincinnati Reds. The players are all pictured in suit and tie. The back features an ad for Conly studios. This set is not numbered so we have sequenced them in alphabetical order.

	Ex-Mt	VG
COMPLETE SET	15000.00	7500.00
1 Tom Brown	1500.00	750.00
2 Charlie Buffington	1500.00	750.00
3 Bill Daley	1500.00	750.00
4 Duke Farrell	1500.00	750.00
5 Arthur Irwin	1500.00	750.00
6 John Irwin	1500.00	750.00
7 Morgan Murphy	1500.00	750.00
8 Darby O'Brien	1500.00	750.00
9 Paul Radford	1500.00	750.00
10 Hardy Richardson	1500.00	750.00
11 John Striker	1500.00	750.00

1920 Reds World's Champions PCs

This black and white set of Cincinnati players was issued in 1920 and appears with either of two captions in the border on the front of the card -- World Champions 1919 or National League Champions 1919. A glossy version of this set also exists.

	Ex-Mt	VG
COMPLETE SET	1800.00	900.00
1 Nick Allen	80.00	40.00
2 Rube Bressler	80.00	40.00
3 Jake Daubert	80.00	40.00
4 Pat Duncan	80.00	40.00
5 Hod Eller	80.00	40.00
6 Ray Fisher	80.00	40.00
7 Eddie Gerner	80.00	40.00
8 Heine Groh	120.00	60.00
9 Larry Kopf	80.00	40.00
10 Adolfo Luque	120.00	60.00
11 Sherwood Magee	100.00	50.00
12 Roy Mitchell	80.00	40.00
13 Pat Moran MG	80.00	40.00
14 Greasy Neale	120.00	60.00
15 Bill Rariden	80.00	40.00
16 Morris Rath	80.00	40.00
17 Jimmy Ring	80.00	40.00
18 Edd Roush	150.00	75.00
19 Walter Reuther	80.00	40.00
20 Harry Sallee	80.00	40.00
21 Hank Schreiber	80.00	40.00
22 Charles See	80.00	40.00
23 Jimmy Smith	80.00	40.00
24 Ivy Wingo	80.00	40.00
25 Team Card	500.00	250.00

1938-39 Reds Orange/Gray W711-1

The cards in this 32-card set measure approximately 2" by 3". The 1938-39 Cincinnati Reds Baseball player set was printed in orange and gray tones. Many back variations exist and there are two poses of Johnny VanderMeer, portrait (PORT) and an action (ACT) poses. The set was sold at the ballpark and was printed on thin cardboard stock. The cards are unnumbered but have been alphabetized and numbered in the checklist below.

	Ex-Mt	VG
COMPLETE SET (32)	750.00	375.00
1 Wally Berger (2)	25.00	12.50
2 Nino Bongiovanni (39)	50.00	25.00
3 Stanley Bordagaray Frenchy (39)	50.00	25.00
4 Joe Cascarella (38)	15.00	7.50
5 Allen Dusty Cooke (38)	15.00	7.50
6 Harry Craft	20.00	10.00
7 Ray(Peaches) Davis	15.00	7.50
8 Paul Derringer (2)	30.00	15.00
9 Linus Frey (2)	15.00	7.50
10 Lee Gamble (2)	15.00	7.50
11 Ival Goodman (2)	15.00	7.50
12 Hank Gowdy CO	20.00	10.00
13 Lee Grissom (2)	15.00	7.50
14 Willard Hershberger (2)	20.00	10.00
15 Eddie Joost (39)	20.00	10.00
16 Wes Livengood (39)	100.00	50.00
17 Ernie Lombardi (2)	60.00	30.00
18 Frank McCormick	25.00	12.50
19 Bill McKechnie (2) MG	30.00	15.00
20 Lloyd Whitey Moore (2)	15.00	7.50
21 Billy Myers (2)	15.00	7.50
22 Lew Riggs (2)	15.00	7.50
23 Eddie Roush CO (38)	50.00	25.00
24 Les Scarsella (39)	15.00	7.50
25 Gene Schott (38)	15.00	7.50
26 Eugene Thompson	15.00	7.50
27 Johnny VanderMeer PORT	30.00	15.00
28 Johnny VanderMeer ACT	30.00	15.00
29 Wm.(Bucky) Walters (2)	25.00	12.50
30 Jim Weaver	15.00	7.50
31 Bill Werber (39)	15.00	7.50
32 Jimmy Wilson (39)	15.00	7.50

1939 Reds Team Issue

This 25-card set of the Cincinnati Reds features player photos printed on cards with blank backs. The cards are unnumbered and checklisted below in alphabetical order. The cards measure approximately 2" by 3", were printed in grey sepia and the players' name is printed in orange. It is believed that this set was issued by Kroger's.

	Ex-Mt	VG
COMPLETE SET (25)	150.00	75.00
1 Wally Berger	6.00	3.00
2 Nino Bongiovanni	5.00	2.50
3 Frenchy Bordagaray	5.00	2.50
4 Joe Cascarella	5.00	2.50
5 Harry Craft	5.00	2.50
6 Paul Derringer	5.00	2.50
7 Linus Frey	5.00	2.50
8 Lee Gamble	5.00	2.50
9 Ival Goodman	5.00	2.50
10 Hank Gowdy CO	5.00	2.50
11 Willard Hershberger	6.00	3.00
12 Eddie Joost	5.00	2.50
13 Ernie Lombardi	10.00	5.00
14 Frank McCormick	6.00	3.00
15 Bill McKechnie MG	10.00	5.00
16 Whitey Moore	5.00	2.50
17 Billy Myers	5.00	2.50
18 Lew Riggs	5.00	2.50
19 Eddie Roush CO	10.00	5.00
20 Les Scarsella	5.00	2.50
21 Junior Thompson	5.00	2.50
22 Johnny VanderMeer	10.00	5.00
23 Jimmy Wilson CO	5.00	2.50
24 Bill Werber	6.00	3.00
25 Bucky Walters	10.00	5.00

1941 Reds Harry Hartman W711-2

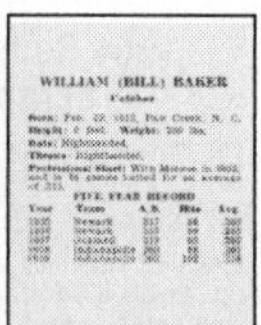

The cards in this 34-card set measure approximately 2 1/8" by 2 5/8". The W711-2 Cincinnati Reds set contains unnumbered, black and white cards and was issued in boxes which had a reverse side resembling a mailing label. This issue is sometimes called the "Harry Hartman" set. The cards are numbered below in alphabetical order by player's name with non-player cards listed at the end. The set is worth about $100 more when it is in the original mailing box. The set originally cost 20 cents when ordered in 1940.

	Ex-Mt	VG
COMPLETE SET (34)	500.00	250.00
COMMON CARD (1-28)	15.00	7.50
COMMON CARD (29-34)	12.00	6.00
1 Morris Arnovich	15.00	7.50
2 William(Bill) Baker	15.00	7.50
3 Joseph Beggs	15.00	7.50
4 Harry Craft	20.00	10.00
5 Paul Derringer	30.00	15.00
6 Linus Frey	15.00	7.50
7 Ival Goodman	15.00	7.50
8 Hank Gowdy CO	20.00	10.00
9 Witt Guise	15.00	7.50
10 Willard Hershberger	20.00	10.00
11 John Hutchings	15.00	7.50
12 Edwin Joost	20.00	10.00
13 Ernie Lombardi	50.00	25.00
14 Frank McCormick	25.00	12.50
15 Myron McCormick	15.00	7.50
16 Bill McKechnie MG	30.00	15.00
17 Whitey Moore	15.00	7.50
18 William(Bill) Myers	15.00	7.50
19 Elmer Riddle	15.00	7.50
20 Lewis Riggs	15.00	7.50
21 James A. Ripple	15.00	7.50
22 Milburn Shoffner	15.00	7.50
23 Eugene Thompson	15.00	7.50
24 James Turner	20.00	10.00
25 John VanderMeer	30.00	15.00
26 Bucky Walters	25.00	12.50
27 Bill Werber	20.00	10.00
28 James Wilson	15.00	7.50
29 Results 1940 World Series	12.00	6.00
30 The Cincinnati Reds (Title Card)	12.00	6.00
31 The Cincinnati Reds World's Champions (Title Card)	12.00	6.00
32 Debt of Gratitude to Wm. Koehl Co.	12.00	6.00
33 Tell the World About Our Reds	12.00	6.00
34 Harry Hartman ANN	12.00	6.00

1954-55 Reds Postcards

These cards, which were issued over a two year period, have four distinct styles to them. They are: no name in the white 3/4" inch space at the bottom; no name in the box but a blue fascimile autograph; printed name and fascimile autograph in the bottom white box and printed name, Cincinnati Redleg in white space plus the blue fascimile autograph. This set carries a catalog naming of PC746. These cards are unnumbered, so we have sequenced them in alphabetical order. At least 20 more players are considered to be possible additions to this set so any help is appreciated.

	NM	Ex
COMPLETE SET	400.00	200.00
1 Bobby Adams Portrait	5.00	2.50
2 Bobby Adams Fielding	5.00	2.50
3 Fred Baczewski	5.00	2.50
4 Ed Bailey	5.00	2.50
5 Dick Bartell CO Neck Shows	5.00	2.50
6 Dick Bartell CO No-Neck	5.00	2.50
7 Matt Batts	5.00	2.50
8 Gus Bell Hitting	6.00	3.00
9 Gus Bell Portrait	6.00	3.00
10 Joe Black	6.00	3.00
11 Bob Borbowski	5.00	2.50
12 Rocky Bridges	5.00	2.50
13 Smoky Burgess	5.00	2.50
14 Jackie Collum Portrait	5.00	2.50
15 Jackie Collum Pitching	5.00	2.50
16 Powell Crosley Jr. PRES.	5.00	2.50
17 Jimmy Dykes MG	6.00	3.00
18 Nico Escalera	5.00	2.50
19 Tom Ferrick	5.00	2.50
20 Art Fowler Portrait	5.00	2.50
21 Art Fowler Pitching	5.00	2.50
22 Herschel Freeman	5.00	2.50
23 Jim Greengrass	5.00	2.50
24 Don Gross	5.00	2.50
25 Charley Harmon	5.00	2.50
26 Ray Jablonski	5.00	2.50
27 Howie Judson	5.00	2.50
28 Johnny Klippstein	5.00	2.50
29 Ted Kluszewski Neck Shows, looking right	15.00	7.50
30 Ted Kluszewski No-Beck, leaning right	15.00	7.50
31 Ted Kluszewski Standing, holding 4 bats	15.00	7.50
32 Ted Kluszewski Ready to hit; cut-out sleeves	15.00	7.50
33 Ted Kluszewski Uniform number visible	15.00	7.50
34 Ted Kluszewski Stretching at 1st	15.00	7.50
35 Ted Kluszewski Ready to hit; hands at belt	15.00	7.50
36 Ted Kluszewski Batting follow-through, lookin up	15.00	7.50
37 Ted Kluszewski Batting follow-through; stands visible	15.00	7.50
38 Hobie Landrith	5.00	2.50
39 Bill McKechnie Jr.	5.00	2.50
40 Roy McMillian Portrait	6.00	3.00
41 Roy McMillian Batting	6.00	3.00
42 Lloyd Merriman	5.00	2.50
43 Rudy Minarcin Neck shows	5.00	2.50
44 Rudy Minarcin No-Neck	5.00	2.50
45 Joe Nuxhall Portrait	6.00	3.00
46 Joe Nuxhall Pitching	6.00	3.00
47 Stan Palys	5.00	2.50
48 Bud Podbielan No Belt	5.00	2.50
49 Bud Podbielan Belt	5.00	2.50
50 Wally Post Ready to hit; only to hips	6.00	3.00
51 Wally Post Ready to hit; belt shows	6.00	3.00
52 Wally Post Follow-through; one pole	6.00	3.00
53 Wally Post Follow-through; two posts	6.00	3.00
54 Wally Post Portrait	6.00	3.00
56 Ken Raffensberger	5.00	2.50
57 Steve Ridzik	5.00	2.50
58 Connie Ryan	5.00	2.50
59 Andy Seminick	5.00	2.50
60 Al Silvera	5.00	2.50
61 Frank Smith	5.00	2.50
62 Milt Smith	5.00	2.50
63 Gerry Staley	5.00	2.50
64 Birdie Tebbetts Neck	5.00	2.50
65 Birdie Tebbetts No-Neck	5.00	2.50
66 Johnny Temple Mouth closed	5.00	2.50
67 Johnny Temple Mouth open	5.00	2.50
68 Corky Valentine	5.00	2.50
69 George Zuverink	5.00	2.50
70 Crosley Field	5.00	2.50

1956-65 Reds Burger Beer

This 23-card set features 8 1/2" by 11" black-and-white photos of various Cincinnati Reds from 1956 through 1965. Most of the backs are blank, but the 1959 photos have a Burger Beer ad on them. The cards are unnumbered and checklisted below in alphabetical order.

	NM	Ex
COMPLETE SET	500.00	250.00
1 Ed Bailey 60-61	10.00	5.00
2 Mel Bailey 57-58	15.00	7.50
3 Gus Bell 59-61	15.00	7.50
4 Smoky Burgess 56	25.00	12.50
5 Gordon Coleman 60-65	10.00	5.00
6 John Edwards 61-65	10.00	5.00
7 Gene Freese 61-63	10.00	5.00
8 Waite Hoyt ANN 60-65 Black Suit	15.00	7.50
9 Waite Hoyt ANN 60-65 Checkered Suit	15.00	7.50
10 Fred Hutchinson MG 60-64	10.00	5.00
11 Joey Jay 60-65	10.00	5.00
12 Hal Jeffcoat 57-58	15.00	7.50
13 Eddie Kasko 60-63	10.00	5.00
14 Gene Kelly ANN 60-65	10.00	5.00
15 Jerry Lynch 59	15.00	7.50
16 Jim Maloney 60-65	10.00	5.00
17 Ray McMillan 56-58	20.00	10.00
18 Joe Nuxhall 60, 62-65	10.00	5.00
19 Jim O'Toole 60-65 Winding Up	10.00	5.00
20 Jim O'Toole 60-65 Follow Through	10.00	5.00
21 Vada Pinson 60-65 Hands on Knee	25.00	12.50
22 Vada Pinson 60-65 Catching Fly Ball	25.00	12.50
23 Vada Pinson 60-65 Batting	25.00	12.50
24 Wally Post 56	20.00	10.00
25 Bob Purkey 59-64 Portrait	15.00	7.50
26 Bob Purkey 59-64 Pitching	15.00	7.50
27 Frank Robinson 59-65 Portrait	40.00	20.00
28 Frank Robinson 59-65 Fielding	40.00	20.00
29 Pete Rose 63-65	50.00	25.00
30 Johnny Temple 58-59	10.00	5.00
31 Frank Thomas 58-59	15.00	7.50

1957 Reds Sohio

The 1957 Sohio Cincinnati Reds set consists of 18 perforated photos, approximately 5" by 7", in black and white with facsimile autographs on the front which were designed to be pasted into a special photo album issued by SOHIO (Standard Oil of Ohio). The set features an early Frank Robinson card. These unnumbered cards are listed below in alphabetical order for convenience.

	NM	Ex
COMPLETE SET (18)	200.00	100.00
1 Ed Bailey	8.00	4.00
2 Gus Bell	10.00	5.00
3 Rocky Bridges	8.00	4.00
4 Smoky Burgess	10.00	5.00
5 Hersh Freeman	8.00	4.00
6 Alex Grammas	8.00	4.00
7 Don Gross	8.00	4.00
8 Warren Hacker	8.00	4.00
9 Don Hoak	10.00	5.00
10 Hal Jeffcoat	8.00	4.00
11 Johnny Klippstein	8.00	4.00
12 Ted Kluszewski	50.00	25.00
13 Brooks Lawrence	8.00	4.00
14 Roy McMillan	8.00	4.00
15 Joe Nuxhall	10.00	5.00
16 Wally Post	10.00	5.00
17 Frank Robinson	100.00	50.00
18 John Temple	10.00	5.00

1957 Reds Team Issue

These 8" by 10" photos feature members of the 1957 Cincinnati Reds. The fronts have the players photo along with their name on the bottom. The backs are blank so we have sequenced these photos in alphabetical order. Some of these photos are also know with the Cincinnati Baseball Club stamp on the back.

	NM	Ex
COMPLETE SET	80.00	40.00
1 Tom Acker	4.00	2.00
2 Gus Bell	4.00	2.00
3 George Crowe	4.00	2.00
4 Jimmy Dykes CO	5.00	2.50
5 Tom Ferrick	4.00	2.00
6 Art Fowler	4.00	2.00
7 Hersh Freeman	4.00	2.00
8 Alex Grammas	4.00	2.00
9 Don Gross	4.00	2.00
10 Bobby Henrich	4.00	2.00
11 Don Hoak	4.00	2.00
12 Johnny Klippstein	4.00	2.00
13 Brooks Lawrence	4.00	2.00
14 Frank McCormick CO	4.00	2.00
15 Roy McMillan	4.00	2.00
16 Joe Nuxhall	5.00	2.50
17 Gabe Paul GM	4.00	2.00
18 Frank Robinson	15.00	7.50
19 Raul Sanchez	4.00	2.00
20 Birdie Tebbetts MG	4.00	2.00
21 Pete Whisenant	4.00	2.00

1958 Reds Enquirer

This set consists of Lou Smith's Redleg Scrapbook newspaper clippings from the Cincinnati Enquirer and features black-and-white photos of the members of the 1958 Cincinnati Reds team with information about the players. The clippings were designed to be placed in an album. They are unnumbered and

checklisted below in alphabetical order.

	NM	Ex
COMPLETE SET (44)	75.00	38.00
1 Tom Acker	1.50	.75
2 Chico Alvarez	1.50	.75
3 Ed Bailey	1.50	.75
4 Gus Bell	1.50	.75
5 Steve Bilko	1.50	.75
6 Smoky Burgess	2.00	1.00
7 Jerry Cade	1.50	.75
8 George Crowe	2.00	1.00
9 Dutch Dotterer	1.50	.75
10 Jimmy Dykes CO	2.50	1.25
11 Tom Ferrick CO	1.50	.75
12 Dee Fondy	1.50	.75
13 Hersh Freeman	1.50	.75
14 Buddy Gilbert	1.50	.75
15 Harvey Haddix	2.50	1.25
16 Bob Henrich	1.50	.75
17 Don Hoak	2.00	1.00
18 Ken Hommel	1.50	.75
19 Jay Hook	1.50	.75
20 Hal Jeffcoat	1.50	.75
21 Bob Kelly	1.50	.75
22 John Klippstein	1.50	.75
23 Marty Kutyna	1.50	.75
24 Brooks Lawrence	2.00	1.00
25 Jerry Lynch	1.50	.75
26 Roy McMillan	1.50	.75
27 Joe Nuxhall	3.00	1.50
28 Jim O'Toole	1.50	.75
29 Stan Palys	1.50	.75
30 Bob Purkey	1.50	.75
31 Charley Rabe	1.50	.75
32 Johnny Riddle CO	1.50	.75
33 Frank Robinson	10.00	5.00
34 Haven Schmidt	1.50	.75
35 Willard Schmidt	1.50	.75
36 Dave Skaugstad	1.50	.75
37 John Smith	1.50	.75
38 Birdie Tebbetts MG	1.50	.75
39 John Temple	1.50	.75
40 Bob Thurman	1.50	.75
41 Pete Whisenant	1.50	.75
42 Ted Wieand	1.50	.75
43 Bill Wight	1.50	.75
44 Album	15.00	7.50

1958 Reds Jay Publishing

This 12-card set of the Cincinnati Reds measures approximately 5" by 7" and features black-and-white player photos in a white border. These cards were packaged 12 to a packet. The backs are blank. The cards are unnumbered and checklisted below in alphabetical order.

	NM	Ex
COMPLETE SET (12)	40.00	20.00
1 Ed Bailey	3.00	1.50
2 Gus Bell	3.00	1.50
3 Steve Bilko	3.00	1.50
4 Smoky Burgess	4.00	2.00
5 George Crowe	4.00	2.00
6 Harvey Haddix	4.00	2.00
7 Don Hoak	3.00	1.50
8 Hal Jeffcoat	3.00	1.50
9 Roy McMillan	5.00	2.50
10 Bob Purkey	3.00	1.50
11 Frank Robinson	10.00	5.00
12 Birdie Tebbetts MG	4.00	2.00

1959 Reds Enquirer

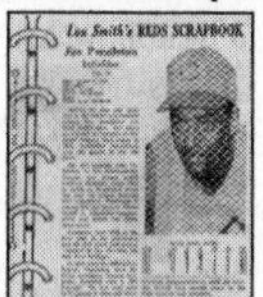

This set consists of Lou Smith's Reds Scrapbook newspaper clippings from the Cincinnati Enquirer and features black-and-white photos of the members of the 1959 Cincinnati Reds team with information about the players. The clippings are unnumbered and checklisted below in alphabetical order.

	NM	Ex
COMPLETE SET (28)	35.00	17.50
1 Tom Acker	1.50	.75
2 Ed Bailey	1.50	.75
3 Chuck Coles	1.50	.75
4 Dutch Dotterer	1.50	.75
5 Walt Dropo	1.50	.75
6 Del Ennis	2.00	1.00
7 Jim Fridley	1.50	.75
8 Buddy Gilbert	1.50	.75
9 Jesse Gonder	1.50	.75
10 Bob Henrich	1.50	.75
11 Hal Jeffcoat	1.50	.75
12 Brooks Lawrence	1.50	.75
13 Bobbie Mabe	1.50	.75
14 Roy McMillan	1.50	.75
15 Don Newcombe	3.00	1.50
16 Joe Nuxhall	2.50	1.25
17 Claude Osteen	2.50	1.25
18 Don Pavletich	1.50	.75
19 Orlando Pena	1.50	.75
20 Jim Pendleton	1.50	.75
21 John Powers	1.50	.75
22 Charley Rabe	1.50	.75
23 Willard Schmidt	1.50	.75
24 Mayo Smith MG	2.00	1.00
25 Johnny Temple	1.50	.75
26 Frank Thomas	2.50	1.25

27 Bob Thurman	1.50	.75
28 Ted Wieand	1.50	.75

1959 Reds Jay Publishing

This 12-card set of the Cincinnati Reds measures approximately 5" by 7" and features black-and-white player photos in a white border. These cards were packaged 12 to a packet. The backs are blank. The cards are unnumbered and checklisted below in alphabetical order.

	NM	Ex
COMPLETE SET	40.00	20.00
1 Ed Bailey	3.00	1.50
2 Gus Bell	3.00	1.50
3 Brooks Lawrence	3.00	1.50
4 Jerry Lynch	3.00	1.50
5 Roy McMillan	4.00	2.00
6 Don Newcombe	4.00	2.00
7 Joe Nuxhall	4.00	2.00
8 Vada Pinson	6.00	3.00
9 Bob Purkey	3.00	1.50
10 Johnny Temple	3.00	1.50
11 Frank Robinson	12.00	6.00
12 Frank Thomas	3.00	1.50

1960 Reds Jay Publishing

This 12-card set of the Cincinnati Reds measures approximately 5" by 7". The fronts feature black-and-white posed player photos with the player's and team name printed below in the white border. These cards were packaged 12 in a packet and originally sold for 25 cents. The backs are blank. The cards are unnumbered and checklisted below in alphabetical order.

	NM	Ex
COMPLETE SET (12)	30.00	12.00
1 Gus Bell	3.00	1.20
2 Dutch Dotterer	2.00	.80
3 Jay Hook	2.00	.80
4 Fred Hutchinson MG	3.00	1.20
5 Roy McMillan	3.00	1.20
6 Don Newcombe	4.00	1.60
7 Joe Nuxhall	3.00	1.20
8 Jim O'Toole	2.00	.80
9 Orlanda Pena	2.00	.80
10 Vada Pinson	4.00	1.60
11 Bob Purkey	2.00	.80
12 Frank Robinson	12.00	4.80

1961 Reds Jay Publishing

This 12-card set of the Cincinnati Reds measures approximately 5" by 7". The fronts feature black-and-white posed player photos with the player's and team name printed below in the white border. These cards were packaged 12 in a packet. The backs are blank. The cards are unnumbered and checklisted below in alphabetical order.

	NM	Ex
COMPLETE SET (12)	35.00	14.00
1 Ed Bailey	2.00	.80
2 Jim Baumer	2.00	.80
3 Gus Bell	3.00	1.20
4 Gordon Coleman	2.00	.80
5 Fred Hutchinson MG	3.00	1.20
6 Joey Jay	2.50	1.00
7 Willie Jones	2.00	.80
8 Eddie Kasko	2.00	.80
9 Jerry Lynch	2.00	.80
10 Claude Osteen	2.50	1.00
11 Vada Pinson	4.00	1.60
12 Frank Robinson	12.00	4.80

1961 Reds Postcards

These postcards feature members of the NL Champion Cincinnati Reds. Many of these cards have stamped blue signatures which appear to be the only year this approach was used. Since these cards are unnumbered, we have sequenced them in alphabetical order.

	MINT	NRMT
COMPLETE SET	150.00	70.00
1 Gus Bell	5.00	2.20
2 Don Blasingame	5.00	2.20
3 Marshall Bridges	5.00	2.20
4 Jim Brosnan	5.00	2.20
5 Leo Cardenas	5.00	2.20
6 Elio Chacon	5.00	2.20
7 Gordy Coleman	5.00	2.20
8 Otis Douglas	5.00	2.20
9 John Edwards	5.00	2.20
10 Gene Freese	5.00	2.20
11 Dick Gernert	5.00	2.20
12 Bill Henry	5.00	2.20
13 Ken Hunt	5.00	2.20
14 Fred Hutchinson MG Black Background	5.00	2.20
15 Fred Hutchinson MG Smiling	5.00	2.20
16 Joey Jay	5.00	2.20
17 Ken Johnson	5.00	2.20
18 Sherman Jones	5.00	2.20
19 Eddie Kasko	5.00	2.20
20 Jerry Lynch Dark Background	5.00	2.20
21 Jerry Lynch number 4 on back	5.00	2.20
22 Jim Maloney	8.00	3.60
23 Howie Nunn	5.00	2.20
24 Reggie Otero	5.00	2.20
25 Jim O'Toole	5.00	2.20
26 Vada Pinson	10.00	4.50
27 Wally Post	5.00	2.20
28 Bob Purkey	5.00	2.20
29 Frank Robinson	15.00	6.75
30 Dick Sisler	5.00	2.20
31 Bob Schmidt	5.00	2.20
32 Jim Turner CO	5.00	2.20
33 Pete Whisenant	5.00	2.20
34 Jerry Zimmerman	5.00	2.20

1962 Reds Enquirer

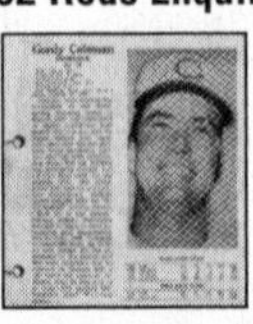

This set consists of newspaper clippings from the Cincinnati Enquirer and features black-and-white photos of the members of the 1962 Cincinnati Reds team with information about the players. They are unnumbered and checklisted below in alphabetical order.

	NM	Ex
COMPLETE SET (32)	50.00	20.00
1 Don Blasingame	1.50	.60
2 Jim Brosnan	1.50	.60
3 Leo Cardenas	2.00	.80
4 Gordy Coleman	1.50	.60
5 Cliff Cook	1.50	.60
6 Myron Drabowsky	1.50	.60
7 John Edwards	1.50	.60
8 Gene Freese	1.50	.60
9 Joe Gaines	1.50	.60
10 Jesse Gonder	1.50	.60
11 Tom Harper	2.00	.80
12 Bill Henry	1.50	.60
13 Dave Hillman	1.50	.60
14 Ken Hunt	1.50	.60
15 Fred Hutchinson MG	2.50	1.00
16 Joey Jay	1.50	.60
17 Darrell Johnson	1.50	.60
18 Eddie Kasko	1.50	.60
19 Marty Keough	1.50	.60
20 John Klippstein	1.50	.60
21 Jerry Lynch	1.50	.60
22 Jim Maloney	2.50	1.00
23 Bob Miller	1.50	.60
24 Jim O'Toole	1.50	.60
25 Don Pavletich	1.50	.60
26 Vada Pinson	3.00	1.20
27 Wally Post	2.00	.80
28 Bob Purkey	1.50	.60
29 Frank Robinson	10.00	4.00
30 Octavio Rojas	3.00	1.20
31 Hiraldo Ruiz	1.50	.60
32 Dave Sisler	1.50	.60

1962 Reds Jay Publishing

This 12-card set features members of the Cincinnati Reds. Originally, this set came in a brown envelope that included a "picture pak order form". Printed on thin stock paper, the cards measure approximately 5" by 7". On a white background the fronts have a black-and-white posed player photo. The player's name and team appear in black letters under the photo. The backs are blank. The cards are unnumbered and checklisted below in alphabetical order.

	NM	Ex
COMPLETE SET (12)	35.00	14.00
1 Jim Brosnan	2.00	.80
2 Leo Cardenas	2.50	1.00
3 Gordon Coleman	2.00	.80
4 Jess Gonder	2.00	.80
5 Fred Hutchinson MG	3.00	1.20
6 Joey Jay	3.00	1.20
7 Eddie Kasko	2.00	.80
8 Jerry Lynch	2.00	.80
9 Jim O'Toole	2.50	1.00
10 Vada Pinson	4.00	1.60
11 Wally Post	3.00	1.20
12 Frank Robinson	12.00	4.80

1962 Reds Postcards

These cards feature members of the 1962 Cincinnati Reds. For the first time, the stamped autographs are no longer on the card. Since these cards are unnumbered, we have sequenced them in alphabetical order.

	MINT	NRMT
COMPLETE SET	150.00	70.00
1 Don Blasingame	5.00	2.20
2 Jim Brosnan	5.00	2.20
3 Leo Cardenas	5.00	2.20
4 Gordy Coleman	5.00	2.20
5 Otis Douglas	5.00	2.20
6 Moe Drabowsky	5.00	2.20
7 John Edwards	5.00	2.20
8 Sammy Ellis	5.00	2.20
9 Hank Foiles	5.00	2.20
10 Gene Freese	5.00	2.20
11 Joe Gaines	5.00	2.20
12 Bill Henry	5.00	2.20
13 Fred Hutchinson MG	5.00	2.20
14 Joey Jay	5.00	2.20
15 Eddie Kasko	5.00	2.20
16 Marty Keough	5.00	2.20
17 Johnny Klippstein	5.00	2.20
18 Jerry Lynch	5.00	2.20
19 Howie Nunn	5.00	2.20
20 Reggie Otero CO	5.00	2.20
21 Jim O'Toole	5.00	2.20
22 Don Pavletich	5.00	2.20
23 Vada Pinson	10.00	4.50
24 Bob Purkey	5.00	2.20
25 Dr. Richard Rohde	5.00	2.20
26 Cookie Rojas	6.00	2.70
27 Ray Shore	5.00	2.20
28 Dave Sisler	5.00	2.20
29 Dick Sisler	5.00	2.20
30 Jim Turner CO	5.00	2.20
31 Pete Whisenant	5.00	2.20
32 Ted Wills	5.00	2.20
33 Don Zimmer	8.00	3.60

1963 Reds Enquirer

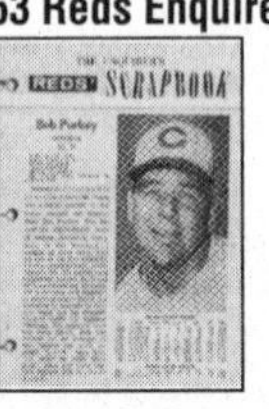

This set consists of newspaper clippings from the Reds' Scrapbook found in the Cincinnati Enquirer and features black-and-white photos of the members of the 1963 Cincinnati Reds team with information about the players. They are unnumbered and checklisted below in alphabetical order. Pete Rose appears in his rookie year.

	NM	Ex
COMPLETE SET (33)	75.00	30.00
1 Don Blasingame	1.50	.60
2 Harry Bright	1.50	.60
3 Jim Brosnan	1.50	.60
4 Leo Cardenas	2.00	.80
5 Gordy Coleman	1.50	.60
6 John Edwards	1.50	.60
7 Sam Ellis	1.50	.60
8 Hank Foiles	1.50	.60
9 Gene Freese	1.50	.60
10 Jesse Gonder	1.50	.60
11 Tom Harper	2.00	.80
12 Bill Henry	1.50	.60
13 Ken Hunt	1.50	.60
14 Fred Hutchinson MG	2.50	1.00
15 Joey Jay	1.50	.60
16 Eddie Kasko	1.50	.60
17 Marty Keough	1.50	.60
18 John Klippstein	1.50	.60
19 Jerry Lynch	1.50	.60
20 Jim Maloney	2.50	1.00
21 Joe Nuxall	2.50	1.00
22 Jim O'Toole	1.50	.60
23 Jim Owens	1.50	.60
24 Don Pavletich	1.50	.60
25 Vada Pinson	3.00	1.20
26 Wally Post	2.00	.80
27 Bob Purkey	1.50	.60
28 Frank Robinson	12.00	4.80
29 Dave Sisler	1.50	.60
30 John Tsitouris	1.50	.60
31 Ken Walters	1.50	.60
32 Pete Rose	30.00	12.00
33 Al Worthington	1.50	.60

1963 Reds French Bauer Caps

These are a 32 "card" set of (cardboard) milk bottle caps featuring personnel of the Cincinnati Reds. These unattractive cardboard caps are blank-backed and unnumbered; they are numbered below for convenience in alphabetical order. The caps are approximately 1 1/4" in diameter. Blasingame was traded to the Senators early in the '63 season and Spencer was picked up from the Dodgers early in the '63 season; hence their caps are tougher to find than the others. Ken Walters and Don Pavletich also seem to be harder to find. We are listing those caps as SP's. Pete Rose has a cap in his rookie year.

	NM	Ex
COMPLETE SET (32)	400.00	160.00
COMMON CAP	5.00	2.00
COMMON SP	12.00	4.80
1 Don Blasingame SP	12.00	4.80
2 Leo Cardenas	6.00	2.40
3 Gordon Coleman	5.00	2.00
4 Wm. O. DeWitt OWN	5.00	2.00
5 John Edwards	5.00	2.00
6 Jesse Gonder	5.00	2.00
7 Tommy Harper	6.00	2.40
8 Bill Henry	5.00	2.00
9 Fred Hutchinson MG	8.00	3.20
10 Joey Jay	6.00	2.40
11 Eddie Kasko	5.00	2.00
12 Marty Keough	5.00	2.00
13 Jim Maloney	8.00	3.20
14 Joe Nuxhall	8.00	3.20
15 Reggie Otero CO	5.00	2.00
16 Jim O'Toole	6.00	2.40
17 Jim Owens	5.00	2.00
18 Don Pavletich SP	12.00	4.80
19 Vada Pinson	10.00	4.00
20 Bob Purkey	5.00	2.00
21 Dr. Richard Rohde	5.00	2.00
22 Frank Robinson	50.00	20.00
23 Pete Rose	200.00	80.00
24 Ray Shore CO	5.00	2.00
25 Dick Sisler CO	5.00	2.00
26 Bob Skinner	5.00	2.00
27 Daryl Spencer SP	25.00	10.00
28 John Tsitouris	5.00	2.00
29 Jim Turner CO	6.00	2.40
30 Ken Walters SP	12.00	4.80
31 Al Worthington	5.00	2.00
32 Dom Zanni	5.00	2.00

1963 Reds Jay Publishing

This 12-card set features members of the Cincinnati Reds. Printed on thin stock paper, the cards measure approximately 5" by 7". On a white background the fronts have a black-and-white posed player photo. The player's name and team appear in black letters under the photo. The backs are blank. The cards are unnumbered and checklisted below in alphabetical order.

	NM	Ex
COMPLETE SET (12)	30.00	12.00
1 Jim Brosnan	2.00	.80
2 Gordy Coleman	2.00	.80
3 Fred Hutchinson MG	3.00	1.20
4 Joey Jay	2.50	1.00
5 Eddie Kasko	2.00	.80
6 Marty Keough	2.00	.80
7 Jerry Lynch	2.00	.80
8 Jim O'Toole	2.50	1.00
9 Don Pavletich	2.00	.80
10 Vada Pinson	4.00	1.60
11 Bob Purkey	2.00	.80
12 Frank Robinson	12.00	4.80

1964 Reds Enquirer Scrapbook

These newspaper "clippings" measure about 5" by 7" when cut from the Cincinnati Enquirer Newspaper. Each time, a different member of the 1964 Reds was featured with some biographical information, his statistics as well as a brief biography. Since these are unnumbered, we have sequenced them in alphabetical order.

	MINT	NRMT
COMPLETE SET	80.00	36.00
1 Steve Boros	2.00	.90
2 Leo Cardenas	2.00	.90
3 Gordy Coleman	2.00	.90
4 Lincoln Curtis	2.00	.90
5 Jim Dickson	2.00	.90
6 John Edwards	2.00	.90
7 Sam Ellis	2.00	.90
8 Tommy Harper	2.00	.90
9 Bill Henry	2.00	.90
10 Fred Hutchinson MG	2.00	.90
11 Joey Jay	2.00	.90
12 Deron Johnson	2.00	.90
13 Marty Keough	2.00	.90
14 Jim Maloney	2.50	1.10
15 Billy McCool	2.00	.90
16 Charley Neal	2.00	.90
17 Chet Nichols	2.00	.90
18 Joe Nuxhall	3.00	1.35
19 Vada Pinson	4.00	1.80
20 Bob Purkey	2.00	.90
21 Mel Queen	2.00	.90
22 Frank Robinson	8.00	3.60
23 Pete Rose	25.00	11.00
24 Chico Ruiz	2.00	.90
25 Bob Skinner	2.00	.90
26 Hal Smith	2.00	.90
27 John Tsitouris	2.00	.90
28 Al Worthington	2.00	.90

1964 Reds Jay Publishing

This 12-card set of the Cincinnati Reds measures approximately 5" by 7". The fronts feature black-and-white posed player photos with the player's and team name printed below in the white border. These cards were packaged 12 in a packet. The backs are blank. The cards are unnumbered and checklisted below in alphabetical order.

	NM	Ex
COMPLETE SET (12)	60.00	24.00
1 Leo Cardenas	2.00	.80
2 Gordy Coleman	2.00	.80
3 Tommy Harper	2.50	1.00
4 Fred Hutchinson MG	2.00	.80
5 Joey Jay	2.50	1.00
6 Jim Maloney	3.00	1.20
7 Joe Nuxhall	3.00	1.20
8 Jim O'Toole	2.50	1.00
9 Vada Pinson	4.00	1.60
10 Bob Purkey	2.00	.80
11 Frank Robinson	12.00	4.80
12 Pete Rose	25.00	10.00

1964 Reds Postcards

This set features members of the 1964 Cincinnati Reds. These cards had no PC markings on the back. Since these cards were unnumbered, we have sequenced them in alphabetical order. A Pre-Rookie Card Tony Perez is in this set.

	MINT	NRMT
COMPLETE SET	250.00	110.00
1 Steve Boros	5.00	2.20
2 Leo Cardenas	5.00	2.20
3 Jim Coker Arms Crossed	5.00	2.20
4 Jim Coker Near the dugout	5.00	2.20
5 Gordy Coleman	5.00	2.20
6 Ryne Duren	5.00	2.20
7 John Edwards	5.00	2.20
8 Sam Ellis	5.00	2.20
9 Tommy Harper	5.00	2.20
10 Bill Henry	5.00	2.20
11 Fred Hutchinson MG	5.00	2.20
12 Joey Jay	5.00	2.20
13 Deron Johnson	5.00	2.20
14 Marty Keough	5.00	2.20
15 Bobby Klaus	5.00	2.20
16 Jim Maloney	6.00	2.70
17 Billy McCool	5.00	2.20
18 Tom Murphy TR	5.00	2.20
19 Joe Nuxhall	8.00	3.60
20 Reggie Otero CO	5.00	2.20
21 Jim O'Toole	5.00	2.20
22 Don Pavletich	5.00	2.20
23 Tony Perez	20.00	9.00
24 Vada Pinson	10.00	4.50
25 Bob Purkey	5.00	2.20
26 Mel Queen	5.00	2.20
27 Frank Robinson	15.00	6.75
28 Pete Rose	60.00	27.00
29 Chico Ruiz	5.00	2.20
30 Ray Shore	5.00	2.20
31 Dick Sisler CO	5.00	2.20
32 Johnny Temple	5.00	2.20
33 John Tsitouris	5.00	2.20
34 Jim Turner CO	5.00	2.20

1965 Reds Enquirer

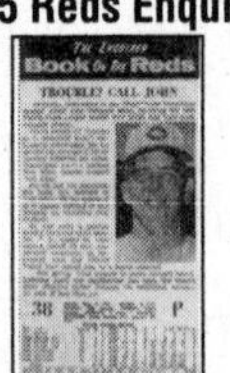

This set consists of newspaper clippings from the Cincinnati Enquirer and features black-and-white photos of the members of the 1965 Cincinnati Reds team with information about the players. They are unnumbered and checklisted below in alphabetical order.

	NM	Ex
COMPLETE SET (29)	60.00	24.00
1 Gerry Arrigo	1.50	.60
2 Steve Boros	1.50	.60
3 Leo Cardenas	1.50	.60
4 Jim Coker	1.50	.60
5 Gordy Coleman	1.50	.60
6 Roger Craig	2.00	.80
7 Ryne Duren	2.00	.80
8 John Edwards	1.50	.60
9 Sammy Ellis	1.50	.60
10 Tommy Harper	2.00	.80
11 Tommy Helms	2.00	.80
12 Bill Henry	1.50	.60
13 Charley James	1.50	.60
14 Joey Jay	1.50	.60
15 Deron Johnson	1.50	.60
16 Marty Keough	1.50	.60
17 Jim Maloney	2.50	1.00
18 Bill McCool	1.50	.60
19 Joe Nuxhall	2.50	1.00
20 Jim O'Toole	1.50	.60
21 Don Pavletich	1.50	.60
22 Tony Perez	8.00	3.20
23 Vada Pinson	3.00	1.20
24 Frank Robinson	10.00	4.00
25 Pete Rose	20.00	8.00
26 Hiraldo S.(Chico) Ruiz	1.50	.60
27 Art Shamsky	1.50	.60
28 Dick Sisler MG	1.50	.60
29 John Tsitouris	1.50	.60

1965 Reds Jay Publishing

This 12-card set of the Cincinnati Reds measures approximately 5" by 7". The fronts feature black-and-white posed player photos with the player's and team name printed below in the white border. These cards were packaged 12 to a packet. The backs are blank. The cards are unnumbered and checklisted below in alphabetical order.

	NM	Ex
COMPLETE SET (12)	50.00	20.00
1 Gerry Arrigo	2.00	.80
2 Gordy Coleman	2.00	.80
3 Sammy Ellis	2.00	.80

4 Joey Jay	2.50	1.00
5 Marty Keough	2.00	.80
6 Jim Maloney	3.00	1.20
7 Jim O'Toole	2.50	1.00
8 Vada Pinson	4.00	1.60
9 Mel Queen	2.00	.80
10 Frank Robinson	12.00	4.80
11 Pete Rose	25.00	10.00
12 Dick Sisler MG	2.00	.80

1965 Reds Postcards

Issued by the team, these postcards feature members of the 1965 Cincinnati Reds. Since these are unnumbered, we have sequenced them in alphabetical order. A Tony Perez card is in this series, which is also his Rookie Card year.

	NM	Ex
COMPLETE SET	200.00	80.00
1 Gerry Arrigo	5.00	2.00
2 Leo Cardenas	5.00	2.00
3 Jimmy Coker	5.00	2.00
4 Gordy Coleman	5.00	2.00
5 Roger Craig	5.00	2.00
6 Jim Duffalo	5.00	2.00
7 Johnny Edwards	5.00	2.00
8 Sammy Ellis	5.00	2.00
9 Tommy Harper	6.00	2.40
10 Charlie James	5.00	2.00
11 Joey Jay	5.00	2.00
12 Deron Johnson	5.00	2.00
13 Marty Keough	5.00	2.00
14 Jim Maloney	6.00	2.40
15 Billy McCool	5.00	2.00
16 Joe Nuxhall	8.00	3.20
17 Frank Oceak	5.00	2.00
18 Reggie Otero CO	5.00	2.00
19 Jim O'Toole	5.00	2.00
20 Don Pavletich	5.00	2.00
21 Tony Perez	30.00	12.00
22 Vada Pinson	10.00	4.00
23 Frank Robinson	20.00	8.00
24 Pete Rose	50.00	20.00
25 Chico Ruiz	5.00	2.00
26 Art Shamsky	5.00	2.00
27 Ray Shore	5.00	2.00
28 Dick Sisler MG	5.00	2.00
29 John Tsitouris	5.00	2.00
30 Jim Turner CO Portrait to Belt	5.00	2.00
31 Jim Turner CO Portrait shows entire right shoulder	5.00	2.00

1966 Reds Postcards

These 33 postcards were issued by the Cincinnati Reds and featured members of the 1966 Reds. Since they are unnumbered, we have sequenced them in alphabetical order. These cards can be identified as they were the last year the Reds printed cards on glossy stock.

	NM	Ex
COMPLETE SET	200.00	80.00
1 Jack Baldschun	5.00	2.00
2 Dave Bristol CO	5.00	2.00
3 Leo Cardenas	5.00	2.00
4 Jimmie Coker	5.00	2.00
5 Gordy Coleman	5.00	2.00
6 Ted Davidson	5.00	2.00
7 Johnny Edwards	5.00	2.00
8 Sammy Ellis	5.00	2.00
9 Bill Fischer	5.00	2.00
10 Mel Harder CO	5.00	2.00
11 Tommy Harper	6.00	2.40
12 Don Heffner MG	5.00	2.00
13 Tommy Helms	5.00	2.00
14 Joey Jay	5.00	2.00
15 Alex Johnson	5.00	2.00
16 Jim Maloney	6.00	2.40
17 Bill McCool	5.00	2.00
18 Don Nottebart	5.00	2.00
19 Joe Nuxhall	8.00	3.20
20 Darrell Osteen	5.00	2.00
21 Jim O'Toole	5.00	2.00
22 Milt Pappas	6.00	2.40
23 Don Pavletich	5.00	2.00
24 Tony Perez	15.00	6.00
25 Vada Pinson	10.00	4.00
26 Mel Queen	5.00	2.00
27 Pete Rose	40.00	16.00
28 Chico Ruiz	5.00	2.00
29 Art Shamsky	5.00	2.00
30 Ray Shore CO	5.00	2.00
31 Roy Sievers	6.00	2.40
32 Dick Simpson	5.00	2.00
33 Whitey Wietelmann CO	5.00	2.00

1966 Reds Team Issue

These 5" by 7" black and white glossy photos featured members of the 1966 Cincinnati Reds. Since they are unnumbered, we have sequenced them in alphabetical order. It is possible that there are more photos so any additions are greatly appreciated.

	NM	Ex
COMPLETE SET	80.00	32.00
1 Gerry Arrigo	4.00	1.60
2 Jack Baldschun	4.00	1.60
3 Leo Cardenas	4.00	1.60
4 Jim Coker	4.00	1.60
5 Gordy Coleman	4.00	1.60
6 Ted Davidson	4.00	1.60
7 Johnny Edwards	4.00	1.60
8 Sammy Ellis	4.00	1.60
9 Tommy Helms	4.00	1.60
10 Deron Johnson	4.00	1.60
11 Jim Maloney	5.00	2.00
12 Billy McCool	4.00	1.60
13 Don Nottebart	4.00	1.60
14 Milt Pappas	5.00	2.00
15 Vada Pinson	8.00	3.20
16 Pete Rose	20.00	8.00

1967 Reds Postcards

These 38 blank-backed black and white postcards measure 3 1/2" by 5 1/2" and feature members of the 1967 Reds. The fronts have a player photo, a blue fascimile autograph as well

as the Cincinnati Reds in red lettering. Since the photos are unnumbered, we have sequenced them in alphabetical order. Darrell Osteen, who was pictured in the special folder made available to put these photos in, was not published as a postcard. A Johnny Bench postcard is known in this series which predates his Rookie Card.

	NM	Ex
COMPLETE SET (38)	150.00	60.00
1 Ted Abernathy	4.00	1.60
2 Gerry Arrigo	4.00	1.60
3 Jack Baldschun	4.00	1.60
4 Johnny Bench	30.00	12.00
5 Vern Benson CO	4.00	1.60
6 Jimmy Bragan CO	4.00	1.60
7 Dave Bristol MG	4.00	1.60
8 Leo Cardenas	4.00	1.60
9 Jim Coker	4.00	1.60
10 Ted Davidson	4.00	1.60
11 John Edwards	4.00	1.60
12 Sammy Ellis	4.00	1.60
13 Ray Evans CP	4.00	1.60
14 Mel Harder CO	5.00	2.00
15 Tommy Harper	4.00	1.60
16 Tommy Helms	4.00	1.60
17 Deron Johnson	4.00	1.60
18 Bob Lee	4.00	1.60
19 Jim Maloney	5.00	2.00
20 Lee May	5.00	2.00
21 Bill McCool	4.00	1.60
22 Tom Murphy CP	4.00	1.60
23 Gary Nolan	4.00	1.60
24 Don Nottebart	4.00	1.60
25 Don Pavletich	4.00	1.60
26 Milt Pappas	5.00	2.00
27 Tony Perez	10.00	4.00
28 Vada Pinson	8.00	3.20
29 Mel Queen	4.00	1.60
30 Floyd Robinson	4.00	1.60
31 Pete Rose	20.00	8.00
32 Chico Ruiz	4.00	1.60
33 Art Shamsky	4.00	1.60
34 Ray Shore CO	4.00	1.60
35 Dick Simpson	4.00	1.60
36 Jake Wood	4.00	1.60
37 Whitey Wietelmann CO	4.00	1.60
38 Al Wylder CP	4.00	1.60

1968 Reds Postcards

These 30 blank-backed black and white postcards features members of the 1968 Reds. The fronts have a player photo, a blue fascimile signature and "Cincinnati Reds" in red lettering. Since the cards are unnumbered, we have sequenced them in alphabetical order. John Bench is featured during his rookie season.

	NM	Ex
COMPLETE SET (30)	150.00	60.00
1 Ted Abernathy	4.00	1.60
2 Gerry Arrigo	4.00	1.60
3 Johnny Bench	20.00	8.00
4 Vern Benson CO	4.00	1.60
5 Jimmy Bragan CO	4.00	1.60
6 Dave Bristol MG	4.00	1.60
7 Leo Cardenas	4.00	1.60
8 Clay Carroll	4.00	1.60
9 Tony Cloninger	4.00	1.60
10 George Culver	4.00	1.60
11 Tommy Helms	4.00	1.60
12 Alex Johnson	4.00	1.60
13 Mack Jones	4.00	1.60
14 Bill Kelso	4.00	1.60
15 Bob Lee	4.00	1.60
16 Jim Maloney	5.00	2.00
17 Lee May	5.00	2.00
18 Bill McCool	4.00	1.60
19 Gary Nolan	4.00	1.60
20 Don Pavletich	4.00	1.60
21 Tony Perez	10.00	4.00
22 Vada Pinson	8.00	3.20
23 Mel Queen	4.00	1.60
24 Jay Ritchie	4.00	1.60
25 Pete Rose	20.00	8.00
26 Chico Ruiz	4.00	1.60
27 Jim Schaffer	4.00	1.60
28 Hal Smith CO	4.00	1.60
29 Fred Whitfield	4.00	1.60
30 Woody Woodward	4.00	1.60

1969 Reds Postcards

These 28 blank-backed black and white postcards feature members of the 1969 Cincinnati Reds. These postcards have a player photo, a black fascimile autograph and "Cincinnati Reds" in red lettering. Since these are unnumbered, we have sequenced them in alphabetical order.

	NM	Ex
COMPLETE SET (28)	100.00	40.00
1 Gerry Arrigo	3.00	1.20
2 Johnny Bench	15.00	6.00
3 Jim Beauchamp	3.00	1.20
4 Vern Benson CO	3.00	1.20
5 Jimmy Bragan CO	3.00	1.20
6 Dave Bristol MG	3.00	1.20
7 Clay Carroll	3.00	1.20
8 Darrel Chaney	3.00	1.20
9 Tony Cloninger	3.00	1.20
10 Pat Corrales	3.00	1.20
11 George Culver	3.00	1.20
12 Jack Fisher	3.00	1.20
13 Wayne Granger	3.00	1.20
14 Harvey Haddix CO	3.00	1.20
15 Tommy Helms	3.00	1.20
16 Alex Johnson	3.00	1.20
17 Jim Maloney	3.00	1.20
18 Lee May	4.00	1.60
19 Jim Merritt	3.00	1.20
20 Tony Perez	8.00	3.20
21 Pete Rose	15.00	6.00
22 Chico Ruiz	3.00	1.20
23 Ted Savage	3.00	1.20
24 Hal Smith CO	3.00	1.20
25 Jim Stewart	3.00	1.20
26 Bob Tolan	3.00	1.20
27 Fred Whitfield	3.00	1.20
28 Woody Woodward	3.00	1.20

1970 Reds Team Issue

These two 5" by 7" blank-backed cards feature members of the Cincinnati Reds circa 1970. It is probable that there are many more cards in this set and grouping so all additional information is appreciated. These cards are unnumbered so we have put them in alphabetical order. Interestingly enough, these are the same photos used in Partridge meats set around the same era.

	NM	Ex
COMPLETE SET	20.00	8.00
1 Johnny Bench	10.00	4.00
2 Pete Rose	10.00	4.00

1971 Reds Postcards

These 33 black and white blank-backed postcards feature members of the 1971 Cincinnati Reds. The fronts have a player photo, a black fascimile autograph and "Cincinnati Reds" in black lettering. Since these cards are unnumbered, we have sequenced them in alphabetical order.

	NM	Ex
COMPLETE SET	80.00	32.00
1 Sparky Anderson MG	5.00	2.00
2 Johnny Bench	10.00	4.00
3 Buddy Bradford	2.00	.80
4 Bernie Carbo	2.00	.80
5 Clay Carroll	2.00	.80
6 Ty Cline	2.00	.80
7 Tony Cloninger	2.00	.80
8 Dave Concepcion	5.00	2.00
9 Pat Corrales	2.00	.80
10 Al Ferrara	2.00	.80
11 George Foster	6.00	2.40
12 Joe Gibbon	2.00	.80
13 Alex Grammas CO	2.00	.80
14 Wayne Granger	2.00	.80
15 Ross Grimsley	2.00	.80
16 Don Gullett	3.00	1.20
17 Tommy Helms	2.00	.80
18 Ted Kluszewski CO	5.00	2.00
19 Lee May	3.00	1.20
20 Jim McGlothlin	2.00	.80
21 Hal McRae	2.00	.80
22 Jim Merritt	2.00	.80
23 Gary Nolan	2.00	.80
24 Tony Perez	6.00	2.40
25 Pete Rose	15.00	6.00
26 George Scherger CO	2.00	.80
27 Larry Shepard	2.00	.80
28 Willie Smith	2.00	.80
29 Wayne Simpson	2.00	.80
30 Jim Stewart	2.00	.80
31 Bobby Tolan	2.00	.80
32 Milt Wilcox	2.00	.80
33 Woody Woodward	2.00	.80

1973 Reds Postcards

These blank-backed cards feature members of the 1973 Cincinnati Reds. Each of the cards have the player's fascimile autograph in a white box with a Cincinnati Reds logo below the signature. It is believed that many of these cards were also issued during the 1974 season. Since these cards are unnumbered, we have sequenced them in alphabetical order.

	MINT	NRMT
COMPLETE SET	60.00	27.00
1 Sparky Anderson MG	2.50	1.10
2 Dick Baney	1.00	.45
3 Bob Barton	1.00	.45
4 Johnny Bench	5.00	2.20
5 Jack Billingham	1.00	.45
6 Jack Billingham Photo credit given	1.00	.45
7 Pedro Borbon	1.00	.45
8 Clay Carroll	1.00	.45
9 Darrel Chaney	1.00	.45
10 Dave Concepcion	2.50	1.10
11 Ed Crosby	1.00	.45
12 Dan Driessen	1.00	.45
13 Phil Gagliano	1.00	.45
14 Cesar Geronimo	1.00	.45
15 Alex Grammas CO	1.00	.45
16 Ken Griffey	2.50	1.10
17 Ross Grimsley	1.00	.45
18 Don Gullett	1.50	.70
19 Joe Hague	1.00	.45
20 Tom Hall	1.00	.45
21 Hal King	1.00	.45
22 Ted Kluszewski CO	2.50	1.10
23 Andy Kosco	1.00	.45
24 Gene Locklear	1.00	.45
25 Jim McGlothlin	1.00	.45
26 Denis Menke	1.00	.45
27 Joe Morgan	4.00	1.80
28 Roger Nelson	1.00	.45
29 Gary Nolan	1.00	.45
30 Fred Norman	1.00	.45
31 Tony Perez	3.00	1.35
32 Bill Plummer	1.00	.45
33 Pete Rose	8.00	3.60
34 Richie Scheinblum	1.00	.45
35 George Scherger CO	1.00	.45
36 Larry Shepard CO	1.00	.45
37 Ed Sprague	1.00	.45
38 Larry Stahl	1.00	.45
39 Bobby Tolan	1.00	.45
40 Dave Tomlin	1.00	.45

1974 Reds 1939-40 Bra-Mac

This 48 card set, which measured 3 1/2" by 5" featured members of the NL Champions Cincinnati Reds and were issued by Bra-Mac using their extensive photo library. The 1939-40 Reds won consecutive NL pennants during that period.

	NM	Ex
COMPLETE SET	25.00	10.00
1 John Vander Meer	1.50	.60
2 Jimmie Wilson	.75	.30
3 Wally Berger	.75	.30
4 Bucky Walters	1.50	.60
5 Vince DiMaggio	.75	.30
6 Johnny Rizzo	.50	.20
7 Ival Goodman	.50	.20
8 Junior Thompson	.50	.20
9 Jim Turner	.50	.20
10 Milt Shoffner	.50	.20
11 Whitey Moore	.50	.20
12 Moe Arnovich	.50	.20
13 Ernie Lombardi	2.00	.80
14 Mike Dejan	.50	.20
15 Dick West	.50	.20
16 Johnny Ripple	.50	.20
17 Joe Beggs	.50	.20
18 Harry Craft	.50	.20
19 Lew Riggs	.50	.20
20 Mike McCormick	.75	.30
21 Red Barrett	.50	.20
22 Paul Derringer	1.00	.40
23 Johnny Riddle	.50	.20
24 Witt Guise	.50	.20
25 Billy Werber	.75	.30
26 Johnny Hutchings	.50	.20
27 Billy Myers	.50	.20
28 Williard Hershberger	.75	.30
29 Lonnie Frey	.50	.20
30 Frank McCormick	.75	.30
31 Bill Baker	.50	.20
32 Lee Gamble	.50	.20
33 Eddie Joost	.75	.30
34 Nino Bongiovani	.50	.20
35 French Bordagaray	.50	.20
36 Peaches Davis	.50	.20
37 Johnny Niggeling	.50	.20
38 Les Scarsella	.50	.20
39 Lee Grissom	.50	.20
40 Wes Livengood	.50	.20
41 Milt Galatzer	.50	.20
42 Pete Noktenis	.50	.20
43 Jim Weaver	.50	.20
44 Art Jacobs	.50	.20
45 Nolen Richardson	.50	.20
46 Al Simmons	2.00	.80
47 Hank Johnson	.50	.20
48 Bill McKechnie MG	1.50	.60

1976 Reds Icee Lids

This unnumbered and blank-backed set of "lids" is complete at 12. Cards are listed below in alphabetical order. They are circular cards with the bottom squared off. The circle is approximately 2" in diameter. The fronts contain the MLB logo as well as the player's name, position and team. The player photo is in black and white with the cap logo removed. If a collector acquired all 12 of these discs, they were then eligible to win free tickets to a Cincinnati Reds game. These discs were on the bottom of 12 ounce Icee drinks.

	NM	Ex
COMPLETE SET	50.00	20.00
1 Johnny Bench	15.00	6.00
2 Dave Concepcion	2.50	1.00
3 Rawley Eastwick	.50	.20
4 George Foster	1.50	.60
5 Cesar Geronimo	.50	.20
6 Ken Griffey	1.50	.60
7 Don Gullett	.50	.20
8 Will McEnaney	.50	.20
9 Joe Morgan	8.00	3.20
10 Gary Nolan	.50	.20
11 Tony Perez	5.00	2.00
12 Pete Rose	25.00	10.00

1976 Reds Kroger

This 16-card set of the Cincinnati Reds measures approximately 5 7/8" by 9". The white-bordered fronts feature color player head photos with a facsimile autograph below. The backs are blank. The cards are unnumbered and checklisted below in alphabetical order. They were printed on thin glossy paper.

	NM	Ex
COMPLETE SET (16)	25.00	10.00
1 Ed Armbrister	1.00	.40
2 Bob Bailey	1.00	.40
3 Johnny Bench	5.00	2.00
4 Jack Billingham	1.00	.40
5 Dave Concepcion	2.00	.80
6 Dan Driessen	1.00	.40
7 Rawly Eastwick	1.00	.40
8 George Foster	2.00	.80
9 Cesar Geronimo	1.00	.40
10 Ken Griffey	2.50	1.00
11 Don Gullett	1.00	.40
12 Joe Morgan	4.00	1.60
13 Gary Nolan	1.00	.40
14 Fred Norman	1.00	.40
15 Tony Perez	2.50	1.00
16 Pete Rose	8.00	3.20

1976 Reds Parker Classic

These 24 cartoons honor various people who have been involved with the Reds as either a player or manager. These cartoons were drawn by noted sports artist Bob Parker.

	NM	Ex
COMPLETE SET (24)	10.00	4.00
1 Sparky Anderson MG	1.50	.60
2 Wally Berger	.50	.20
3 Pedro Borbon	.50	.20
4 Rube Bressler	.50	.20
5 Gordy Coleman	.50	.20
6 Dave Concepcion	1.00	.40
7 Harry Craft	.50	.20
8 Hugh Critz	.50	.20
9 Dan Driessen	.50	.20
10 Pat Duncan	.50	.20
11 Lonnie Frey	.50	.20
12 Ival Goodman	.50	.20
13 Heinie Groh	.50	.20
14 Noodles Hahn	.75	.30
15 Mike Lum	.50	.20
16 Bill McKechnie	1.50	.60
17 Pat Moran	.50	.20
18 Billy Myers	.50	.20
19 Gary Nolan	.50	.20
20 Fred Norman	.50	.20
21 Jim O'Toole	.50	.20
22 Vada Pinson	1.00	.40
23 Bucky Walters	1.00	.40
24 Checklist	.50	.20

1977 Reds Cartoons Parker

This 24-card set features drawings of famous Cincinnati Reds players by cartoonist and photographer, Bob Parker. The set displays player head drawings along with cartoon illustrated player facts and could be obtained by mail for $3.50.

	NM	Ex
COMPLETE SET (24)	25.00	10.00
1 Ted Kluszewski	1.50	.60
2 Johnny Bench	5.00	2.00
3 Jim Maloney	.50	.20
4 Bub Hargrave	.50	.20
5 Don Gullett	.50	.20
6 Joe Nuxhall	.50	.20
7 Eddie Roush	1.00	.40
8 Wally Post	.50	.20
9 George Wright	1.50	.60
10 George Foster	.75	.30
11 Pete Rose	5.00	2.00
12 Red Lucas	.50	.20
13 Joe Morgan	4.00	1.60
14 Eppa Rixey	1.00	.40
15 Bill Werber	.50	.20
16 Frank Robinson	4.00	1.60
17 Dolf Luque	.50	.20
18 Frank McCormick	.50	.20
19 Paul Derringer	.50	.20
20 Ken Griffey	.75	.30
21 Jack Billingham	.50	.20
22 Larry Kopf	.50	.20

23 Ernie Lombardi 1.00 .40
24 John Vandermeer .75 .30

1977 Reds 1939-40 TCMA

This 45-card set features black-and-white player photos of the 1939-40 Cincinnati Reds in red borders. The backs carry 1939 and 1940 player statistics.

	NM	Ex
COMPLETE SET (45)	20.00	8.00
1 Vince DiMaggio	1.00	.40
2 Wally Berger	1.00	.40
3 Nolen Richardson	.50	.20
4 Ernie Lombardi	2.00	.80
5 Ival Goodman	.50	.20
6 Jim Turner	1.00	.40
7 Bucky Walters	1.50	.60
8 Jimmy Ripple	.50	.20
9 Hank Johnson	.50	.20
10 Bill Baker	.50	.20
11 Al Simmons	2.00	.80
12 Johnny Hutchings	.50	.20
13 Peaches Davis	.50	.20
14 Willard Hershberger	1.00	.40
15 Bill Werber	1.00	.40
16 Harry Craft	.50	.20
17 Milt Galatzer	.50	.20
18 Dick West	.50	.20
19 Art Jacobs	.50	.20
20 Joe Beggs	.50	.20
21 Frenchy Bordagary	.50	.20
22 Lee Gamble	.50	.20
23 Lee Grissom	.50	.20
24 Eddie Joost	1.00	.40
25 Milt Shofner	.50	.20
26 Morrie Arnovich	.50	.20
27 Pete Naktenis	.50	.20
28 Jim Weaver	.50	.20
30 Johnny Niggeling	.50	.20
31 Les Scarsella	.50	.20
32 Lonny Frey	.50	.20
33 Billy Myers	.50	.20
34 Frank McCormick	1.00	.40
35 Lew Riggs	.50	.20
36 Nino Bongiovanni	.50	.20
37 Johnny Rizzo	.50	.20
38 Wes Livengood	.50	.20
39 Junior Thompson	.50	.20
40 Mike Dejan	.50	.20
41 Jimmy Wilson	.50	.20
42 Paul Derringer	1.00	.40
43 Johnny VanderMeer	1.00	.40
44 Whitey Moore	.50	.20
45 Bill McKechnie MG	1.00	.40

1980 Reds Enquirer

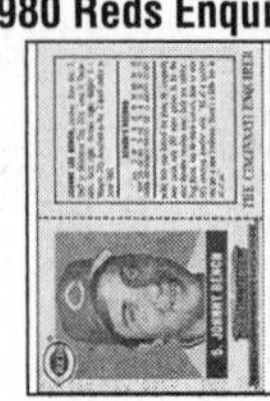

This set features members of the 1980 Cincinnati Reds. The cards are sequenced by uniform numbers of the organization. When cut out, these cards measure 3" by 4 7/16".

	NM	Ex
COMPLETE SET	12.50	5.00
2 Russ Nixon CO	.25	.10
3 John McNamara MG	.25	.10
4 Harry Dunlop CO	.25	.10
5 Johnny Bench	4.00	1.60
6 Bill Fischer CO	.25	.10
7 Hector Cruz	.25	.10
9 Vic Correll	.25	.10
11 Ron Plaza CO	.25	.10
12 Harry Spilman	.25	.10
13 Dave Concepcion	1.00	.40
15 George Foster	1.00	.40
16 Ron Oester	.25	.10
19 Don Werner	.25	.10
20 Cesar Geronimo	.25	.10
22 Dan Driessen	.25	.10
23 Rick Auerbach	.25	.10
25 Ray Knight	.50	.20
26 Junior Kennedy	.25	.10
28 Sam Mejias	.25	.10
29 Dave Collins	.25	.10
30 Ken Griffey	1.00	.40
31 Paul Moskau	.25	.10
34 Sheldon Burnside	.25	.10
35 Frank Pastore	.25	.10
36 Mario Soto	.50	.20
37 Dave Tomlin	.25	.10
40 Doug Bair	.25	.10
41 Tom Seaver	2.50	1.00
42 Bill Bonham	.25	.10
44 Charlie Leibrandt	.25	.10
47 Tom Hume	.25	.10
51 Mike LaCoss	.25	.10

1980 Reds 1961 TCMA

This 41-card set features photos of the 1961 Cincinnati Reds team with red lettering. The backs carry player information and statistics.

	NM	Ex
COMPLETE SET (41)	10.00	4.00
1 Eddie Kasko	.25	.10
2 Wally Post	.25	.10

3 Vada Pinson	.75	.30
4 Frank Robinson	1.00	.40
5 Pete Whisenant	.25	.10
6 Reggie Otero CO	.25	.10
7 Dick Sisler CO	.25	.10
8 Jim Turner CO	.50	.20
9 Fred Hutchinson MG	.25	.10
10 Gene Freese	.25	.10
11 Gordy Coleman	.25	.10
12 Don Blasingame	.25	.10
13 Gus Bell	.25	.10
14 Leo Cardenas	.25	.10
15 Elio Chacon	.25	.10
16 Dick Gernert	.25	.10
17 Jim Baumer	.25	.10
18 Willie Jones	.25	.10
19 Joe Gaines	.25	.10
20 Cliff Cook	.25	.10
21 Harry Anderson	.25	.10
22 Jerry Zimmerman	.25	.10
23 Johnny Edwards	.25	.10
24 Bob Schmidt	.25	.10
25 Darrell Johnson	.25	.10
26 Ed Bailey	.25	.10
27 Joey Jay	.25	.10
28 Jim O'Toole	.25	.10
29 Bob Purkey	.25	.10
30 Jim Brosnan	.25	.10
31 Ken Hunt	.25	.10
32 Ken Johnson	.25	.10
33 Jim Maloney	.50	.20
34 Bill Henry	.25	.10
35 Jerry Lynch	.25	.10
36 Hal Bevan	.25	.10
37 Howie Nunn	.25	.10
38 Sherman Jones	.25	.10
39 Jay Hook	.25	.10
40 Claude Osteen	.25	.10
41 Marshall Bridges	.25	.10

1982 Reds Coke

The cards in this 23-card set measure the standard size. The 1982 Coca-Cola Cincinnati Reds set, issued in conjunction with Topps, contains 22 cards of current Reds players. Although the cards of 15 players feature the exact photo used in the Topps' regular issue, the Coke photos have better coloration and appear sharper than their Topps counterparts. Six players, Cedeno, Harris, Hurdle, Kern, Krenchicki, and Trevino are new to the Reds uniform via trades, while Paul Householder had formerly appeared on the Reds' 1982 Topps "Future Stars" card. The cards are numbered 1 to 22 on the red and gray reverse, and the Coke logo appears on both sides of the card. There is an unnumbered title card which contains a premium offer on the reverse. The set numbering is in alphabetical order by player's name.

	Nm-Mt	Ex-Mt
COMPLETE SET (23)	8.00	3.20
1 Johnny Bench	3.00	1.20
2 Bruce Berenyi	.25	.10
3 Larry Biittner	.25	.10
4 Cesar Cedeno	.50	.20
5 Dave Concepcion	.75	.30
6 Dan Driessen	.25	.10
7 Greg A. Harris	.50	.20
8 Paul Householder	.25	.10
9 Tom Hume	.25	.10
10 Clint Hurdle	.50	.20
11 Jim Kern	.25	.10
12 Wayne Krenchicki	.25	.10
13 Rafael Landestoy	.25	.10
14 Charlie Leibrandt	.25	.10
15 Mike O'Berry	.25	.10
16 Ron Oester	.25	.10
17 Frank Pastore	.25	.10
18 Joe Price	.25	.10
19 Tom Seaver	3.00	1.20
20 Mario Soto	.50	.20
21 Alex Trevino	.25	.10
22 Mike Vail	.25	.10
NNO Title Card	.15	.06

1983 Reds Yearbook

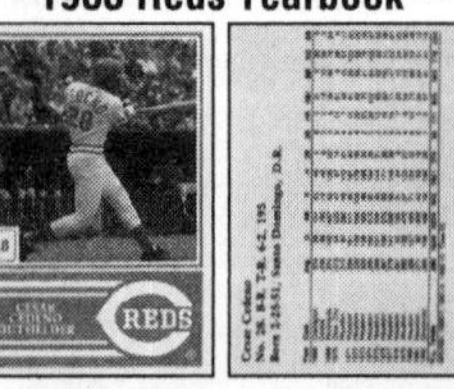

These perforated cards are found in the center of the 1983 Reds Yearbook; they are numbered by uniform number; cards are in full color; backs contain year by year statistical information. The yearbook itself originally sold (cover price) for $3.00. The cards are sequenced in uniform number order.

	Nm-Mt	Ex-Mt
COMPLETE SET	5.00	2.00
2 Gary Redus	.25	.10
5 Johnny Bench	2.50	1.00
7 Russ Nixon MG	.25	.10
13 Dave Concepcion	.75	.30
16 Ron Oester	.25	.10
20 Eddie Milner	.25	.10
21 Paul Householder	.25	.10
22 Dan Driessen	.25	.10
25 Charlie Puleo	.25	.10
28 Cesar Cedeno	.50	.20
29 Alex Trevino	.25	.10
32 Rich Gale	.25	.10
35 Frank Pastore	.25	.10
36 Mario Soto	.50	.20
38 Bruce Berenyi	.25	.10
47 Tom Hume	.25	.10
49 Joe Price	.25	.10
xx Riverfront Stadium	.25	.10

1984 Reds Borden's

This set of eight stickers featuring Eric Davis' first Cincinnati card, was produced as two sheets of four by Borden's Dairy. The sheets are perforated so that the individual stickers may be separated. The sheet of four stickers measures approximately 5 1/2" by 8" whereas the individual stickers measure 2 1/2" by 3 7/8". The backs of the stickers feature discount "cents off" coupons applicable to Borden's products. The fronts feature a full color photo of the player in a bold red border. The stickers are not numbered except that each player's uniform number is given prominently on the front. The sheets are arbitrarily numbered one and two and designated in the checklist below. We have noted either a 1 or a 2 after the player's name to notate which sheet their visage appeared on.

	Nm-Mt	Ex-Mt
COMPLETE SET (8)	8.00	3.20
2 Gary Redus 2	.25	.10
16 Ron Oester 1	.25	.10
20 Eddie Milner 2	.25	.10
24 Tony Perez 2	2.50	1.00
36 Mario Soto 1	.25	.10
39 Dave Parker 1	1.00	.40
44 Eric Davis 1	4.00	1.60
46 Jeff Russell 2	.50	.20

1984 Reds Enquirer

This set consists of newspaper clippings from the Cincinnati Enquirer and features black-and-white head photos of the members of the 1984 Cincinnati Reds team with information about the players.

	Nm-Mt	Ex-Mt
COMPLETE SET (32)	15.00	6.00
1 Tony Perez	1.00	.40
2 Dan Driessen	.25	.10
3 Ron Oester	.25	.10
4 Tom Lawless	.25	.10
5 Dave Concepcion	.75	.30
6 Tom Foley	.25	.10
7 Nick Esasky	.25	.10
8 Wayne Krenchicki	.25	.10
9 Gary Redus	.25	.10
10 Duane Walker	.25	.10
11 Eddie Milner	.25	.10
12 Dave Parker	1.00	.40
13 Cesar Cedeno	.50	.20
14 Dann Bilardello	.25	.10
15 Brad Gulden	.25	.10
16 Jeff Russell	.25	.10
17 Joe Price	.25	.10
18 Bill Scherrer	.25	.10
19 Tom Hume	.25	.10
20 Bruce Berenyi	.25	.10
21 Bob Owchinko	.25	.10
22 Ted Power	.25	.10
23 Frank Pastore	.25	.10
24 John Franco	2.00	.80
25 Mario Soto	.50	.20
26 Eric Davis	5.00	2.00
27 Tommy Helms CO	.25	.10
28 Bruce Kimm CO	.25	.10
29 George Scherger CO	.25	.10
30 Joe Sparks CO	.25	.10
31 Stan Williams CO	.25	.10
32 Vern Rapp MG	.25	.10

1984 Reds Yearbook

These 18 standard-size cards were inserted into the 1984 Cincinnati Reds yearbook. The cards were issued in two nine-card sheets and could be perforated into standard-size cards. The player photo is surrounded by red trim with the player's name on top and the position on the bottom. The backs have biographical information and career statistics. Since the cards are unnumbered, we have sequenced them in alphabetical order.

	Nm-Mt	Ex-Mt
COMPLETE SET (18)	10.00	4.00
1 Bruce Berenyi	.50	.20
2 Dann Billardello	.50	.20
3 Dave Concepcion	2.00	.80
4 Dan Driessen	.50	.20
5 Nick Esasky	.50	.20
6 Bob Howsam PRES	.50	.20
7 Tom Hume	.50	.20
8 Eddie Milner	.50	.20
9 Ron Oester	.50	.20
10 Dave Parker	2.00	.80
11 Frank Pastore	.50	.20
12 Tony Perez	3.00	1.20
13 Joe Price	.50	.20
14 Vern Rapp MG	.50	.20
15 Gary Redus	.50	.20
16 Bill Schrerrer	.50	.20
17 Mario Soto	.50	.20
18 Duane Walker	.50	.20

1985 Reds Yearbook

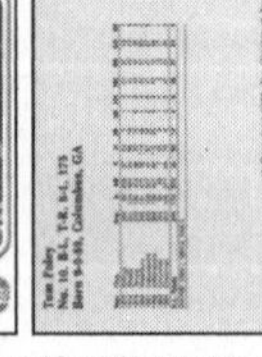

When perforated, these 18 cards measure the standard size. These cards were included as an insert in the 1985 Cincinnati Reds Yearbook. The fronts feature photos, the player's name and his position. The horizontal backs feature vital statistics and career information. We have sequenced this set in alphabetical order.

	Nm-Mt	Ex-Mt
COMPLETE SET (18)	8.00	3.20
1 Cesar Cedeno	.50	.20
2 Dave Concepcion	.75	.30
3 Eric Davis	2.50	1.00
4 Nick Esasky	.25	.10
5 Tom Foley	.25	.10
6 John Franco	1.50	.60
7 Brad Gulden	.25	.10
8 Wayne Krenchicki	.25	.10
9 Eddie Milner	.25	.10
10 Ron Oester	.25	.10
11 Dave Parker	1.00	.40
12 Ted Power	.25	.10
13 Joe Price	.25	.10
14 Pete Rose P/MG	2.00	.80
15 Jeff Russell	.25	.10
16 Mario Soto	.25	.10
17 Jay Tibbs	.25	.10
18 Duane Walker	.25	.10

1986 Reds Greats TCMA

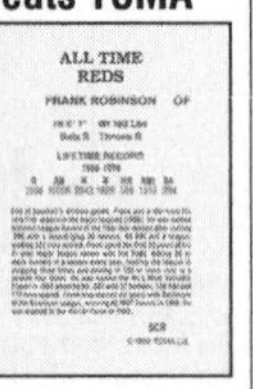

This 12-card standard-size set features some all-time leading Red players. The player's photo, name and position are on the front. The back contains more information about that player.

	Nm-Mt	Ex-Mt
COMPLETE SET (12)	8.00	3.20
1 Clay Carroll	.25	.10
2 Bill McKechnie MG	.50	.20
3 Paul Derringer	.50	.20
4 Eppa Rixey	.75	.30
5 Frank Robinson	1.00	.40
6 Vada Pinson	.50	.20
7 Leo Cardenas	.25	.10
8 Heinie Groh	.25	.10
9 Ted Kluszewski	1.00	.40
10 Joe Morgan	1.00	.40
11 Edd Roush	.75	.30
12 Johnny Bench	2.00	.80

1986 Reds Texas Gold

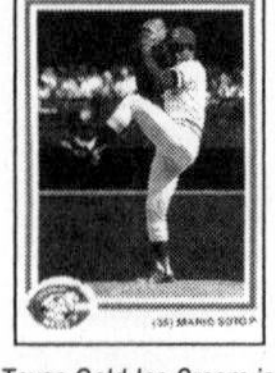

Texas Gold Ice Cream is the sponsor of this 28-card set of Cincinnati Reds. The standard-size cards feature player photos in full color with a red and white border on the front of the card. The set was distributed to fans attending the Reds game at Riverfront Stadium on September 19th. The card backs contain the player's career statistics, uniform number, name, position, and the Texas Gold logo.

	Nm-Mt	Ex-Mt
COMPLETE SET (28)	50.00	20.00
6 Bo Diaz	1.00	.40
9 Max Venable	1.00	.40
11 Kurt Stillwell	1.00	.40
12 Nick Esasky	1.00	.40
13 Dave Concepcion	2.00	.80
14A Pete Rose INF	10.00	4.00
14B Pete Rose MG	10.00	4.00
14C Pete Rose (Commemorative)	10.00	4.00
16 Ron Oester	1.00	.40
20 Eddie Milner	1.00	.40
22 Sal Butera	1.00	.40
24 Tony Perez	5.00	2.00
25 Buddy Bell	1.50	.60
28 Kal Daniels	1.25	.50
29 Tracy Jones	1.00	.40
31 John Franco	2.00	.80
32 Tom Browning	1.25	.50
33 Ron Robinson	1.00	.40
34 Bill Gullickson	1.00	.40
36 Mario Soto	1.25	.50
39 Dave Parker	2.00	.80
40 John Denny	1.25	.50
44 Eric Davis	4.00	1.60
45 Chris Welsh	1.00	.40
48 Ted Power	1.00	.40
49 Joe Price	1.00	.40
NNO George Scherger CO, Bruce Kimm CO, Billy DeMars CO, Tommy Helms CO, Scott Breeden CO, Jim Lett CO	1.00	.40
NNO Coupon Card	1.00	.40

1987 Reds Kahn's

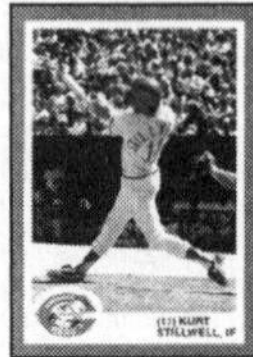

This 28-card standard-size set was issued to the first 20,000 fans at the August 2nd game between the Reds and the San Francisco Giants at Riverfront Stadium by Kahn's Wieners. The cards are unnumbered except for uniform number and feature full-color photos bordered in red and white on the front. The Kahn's logo is printed in red in the corner of the reverse. The set features a card of Barry Larkin in his Rookie Card year.

	Nm-Mt	Ex-Mt
COMPLETE SET (28)	25.00	10.00
6 Bo Diaz	.50	.20
10 Terry Francona	.75	.30
11 Kurt Stillwell	.50	.20
12 Nick Esasky	.50	.20
13 Dave Concepcion	1.25	.50
15 Barry Larkin	10.00	4.00
16 Ron Oester	.50	.20
21 Paul O'Neill	4.00	1.60
23 Lloyd McClendon	1.00	.40
25 Buddy Bell	1.00	.40
28 Kal Daniels	.75	.30
29 Tracy Jones	.50	.20
30 Guy Hoffman	.50	.20
31 John Franco	1.25	.50
32 Tom Browning	.75	.30
33 Ron Robinson	.50	.20
34 Bill Gullickson	.50	.20
35 Pat Pacillo	.50	.20
39 Dave Parker	1.25	.50
43 Bill Landrum	.50	.20
44 Eric Davis	4.00	1.60
46 Rob Murphy	.50	.20
47 Frank Williams	.50	.20
48 Ted Power	.50	.20
NNO Pete Rose MG	4.00	1.60
NNO Scott Breeden CO, Billy DeMars CO, Tommy Helms CO, Bruce Kimm CO, Jim Lett CO, Tony Perez CO	.75	.30
NNO Ad Card, Save 25 cents on Corn Dogs	.25	.10
NNO Ad Card, Save 30 cents on Smokeys	.25	.10

1988 Reds Kahn's

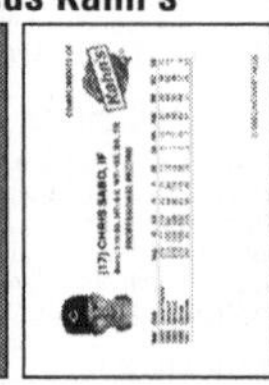

These 26-card standard-size sets were issued to fans at the August 14th game between the Cincinnati Reds and the Atlanta Braves at Riverfront Stadium. The cards are unnumbered except for uniform number and feature full-color photos bordered in red and white on the front. The Kahn's logo is printed in red in the corner of the reverse. The cards are numbered below by uniform number which is listed parenthetically on the front of the cards.

	Nm-Mt	Ex-Mt
COMPLETE SET (26)	15.00	6.00
6 Bo Diaz	.25	.10
8 Terry McGriff	.25	.10
9 Eddie Milner	.25	.10
10 Leon Durham	.25	.10
11 Barry Larkin	5.00	2.00
12 Nick Esasky	.25	.10
13 Dave Concepcion	1.00	.40
14 Pete Rose MG	2.50	1.00
15 Jeff Treadway	.25	.10
17 Chris Sabo	1.00	.40

Card	Nm-Mt	Ex-Mt
20 Danny Jackson	.25	.10
21 Paul O'Neill	1.25	.50
22 Dave Collins	.25	.10
27 Jose Rijo	.25	.10
28 Kal Daniels	.25	.10
29 Tracy Jones	.25	.10
30 Lloyd McClendon	.50	.20
31 John Franco	1.00	.40
32 Tom Browning	.50	.20
33 Ron Robinson	.25	.10
40 Jack Armstrong	.25	.10
44 Eric Davis	1.00	.40
46 Rob Murphy	.25	.10
47 Frank Williams	.25	.10
48 Tim Birtsas	.25	.10
NNO Lee May CO	.75	.30
Tony Perez CO		
Bruce Kimm CO		
Tommy Helms CO		
Jim Lett CO		
Scott Breeden CO		

1989 Reds Kahn's

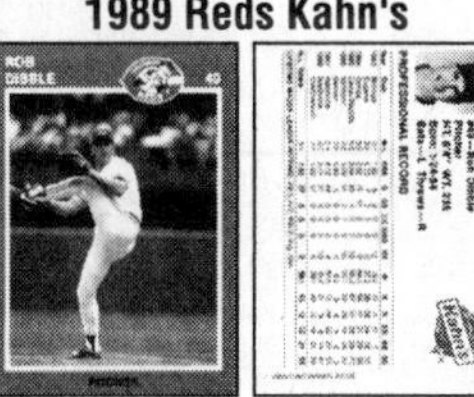

The 1989 Kahn's Reds set contains 28 standard-size cards; each card features a member of the Cincinnati Reds. The fronts have color photos with red borders. The horizontally oriented backs have career stats. The card numbering below is according to uniform number.

	Nm-Mt	Ex-Mt
COMPLETE SET (28)	12.00	4.80
6 Bo Diaz	.25	.10
7 Lenny Harris	.50	.20
11 Barry Larkin	3.00	1.20
12 Joel Youngblood	.25	.10
14 Pete Rose MG	2.00	.80
16 Ron Oester	.25	.10
17 Chris Sabo	.50	.20
20 Danny Jackson	.25	.10
21 Paul O'Neill	1.25	.50
25 Todd Benzinger	.25	.10
27 Jose Rijo	.50	.20
28 Kal Daniels	.25	.10
29 Herm Winningham	.25	.10
30 Ken Griffey	.75	.30
31 John Franco	1.00	.40
32 Tom Browning	.50	.20
33 Ron Robinson	.25	.10
34 Jeff Reed	.25	.10
36 Rolando Roomes	.25	.10
37 Norm Charlton	.50	.20
42 Rick Mahler	.25	.10
43 Kent Tekulve	.50	.20
44 Eric Davis	1.00	.40
48 Tim Birtsas	.25	.10
49 Rob Dibble	.75	.30
XX Scott Breeden CO	.50	.20
Dave Bristol CO		
Tommy Helms CO		
Jim Lett CO		
Lee May CO		
Tony Perez CO		
xx Sponsor Coupon	.15	.06
Kahn's Corndogs		
xx Sponsor Coupon	.15	.06
Kahn's Wieners		

1990 Reds Kahn's

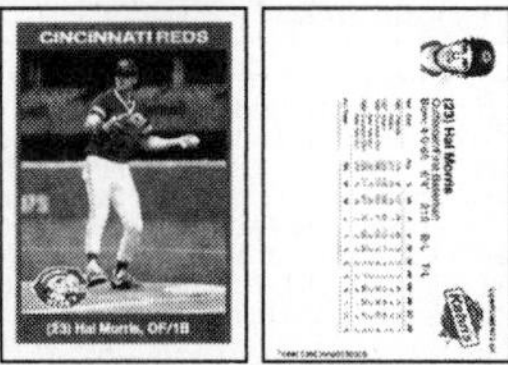

This 27-card, standard size set of Cincinnati Reds was issued by Kahn's Meats. This set which continued a more than 30-year tradition of Kahn's issuing Cincinnati Reds cards had the player's photos framed by red and white borders. The front have full-color photos while the back have a small black and white photo in the upper left hand corner and complete career statistics on the back of the card. The set is checklisted alphabetically since the cards are unnumbered.

	Nm-Mt	Ex-Mt
COMPLETE SET (27)	10.00	3.00
1 Jack Armstrong	.25	.07
2 Todd Benzinger	.25	.07
3 Tim Birtsas	.25	.07
4 Glenn Braggs	.25	.07
5 Tom Browning	.50	.15
6 Norm Charlton	.25	.07
7 Eric Davis	1.25	.35
8 Rob Dibble	.50	.15
9 Mariano Duncan	.25	.07
10 Ken Griffey	.75	.23
11 Billy Hatcher	.25	.07
12 Barry Larkin	2.50	.75
13 Danny Jackson	.25	.07
14 Tim Layana	.25	.07
15 Rick Mahler	.25	.07
16 Hal Morris	.25	.07
17 Randy Myers	.75	.23
18 Ron Oester	.25	.07
19 Joe Oliver	.25	.07
20 Paul O'Neill	1.00	.30
21 Lou Piniella MG	.75	.23
22 Luis Quinones	.25	.07
23 Jeff Reed	.25	.07
24 Jose Rijo	.50	.15
25 Chris Sabo	.25	.07
26 Herm Winningham	.25	.07
27 Jackie Moore CO	.75	.23
Tony Perez CO		
Sam Perlozzo CO		
Larry Rothschild CO		
Stan Williams CO		

1991 Reds Kahn's

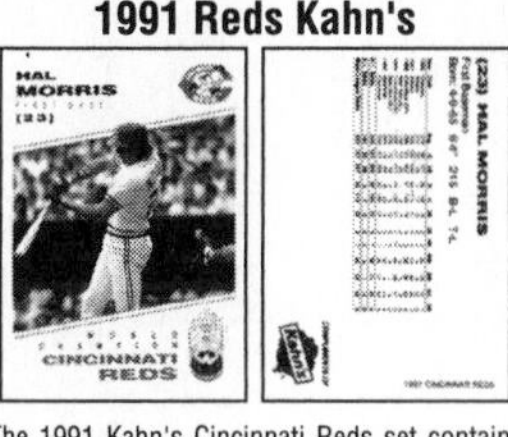

The 1991 Kahn's Cincinnati Reds set contains 28 standard-size cards. The set is skip-numbered by uniform number and includes two Kahn's coupon cards.

	Nm-Mt	Ex-Mt
COMPLETE SET (28)	8.00	2.40
0 Schottzie	.25	.07
Mascot		
7 Mariano Duncan	.25	.07
9 Joe Oliver	.25	.07
10 Luis Quinones	.25	.07
11 Barry Larkin	2.50	.75
15 Glenn Braggs	.25	.07
17 Chris Sabo	.25	.07
19 Bill Doran	.25	.07
21 Paul O'Neill	1.00	.30
22 Billy Hatcher	.25	.07
23 Hal Morris	.25	.07
25 Todd Benzinger	.25	.07
27 Jose Rijo	.50	.15
28 Randy Myers	.50	.15
29 Herm Winningham	.25	.07
32 Tom Browning	.50	.15
34 Jeff Reed	.25	.07
36 Don Carman	.25	.07
37 Norm Charlton	.25	.07
40 Jack Armstrong	.25	.07
41 Lou Piniella MG	.75	.23
44 Eric Davis	1.00	.30
45 Chris Hammond	.75	.23
47 Scott Scudder	.25	.07
48 Ted Power	.25	.07
49 Rob Dibble	.50	.15
57 Freddie Benavides	.25	.07
NNO Jackie Moore CO	.50	.15
Tony Perez CO		
Sam Perlozzo CO		
Larry Rothschild CO		
Stan Williams CO		

1991 Reds Pepsi

This 20-card standard-size set was produced by MSA (Michael Schechter Associates) for Pepsi-Cola of Ohio, and Pepsi logos adorn the upper corners of the card face. The cards were placed inside of 24-soda packs of Pepsi, Diet Pepsi, Caffeine-Free Pepsi, Caffeine Free Diet-Pepsi, Mountain Dew, and Diet Mountain Dew.

	Nm-Mt	Ex-Mt
COMPLETE SET (20)	12.00	3.60
1 Jack Armstrong	.50	.15
2 Todd Benzinger	.50	.15
3 Glenn Braggs	.50	.15
4 Tom Browning	.75	.23
5 Norm Charlton	.50	.15
6 Eric Davis	1.50	.45
7 Rob Dibble	.75	.23
8 Bill Doran	.50	.15
9 Mariano Duncan	.50	.15
10 Billy Hatcher	.50	.15
11 Barry Larkin	2.50	.75
12 Hal Morris	.50	.15
13 Randy Myers	1.00	.30
14 Joe Oliver	.50	.15
15 Paul O'Neill	1.50	.45
16 Lou Piniella MG	1.00	.30
17 Jeff Reed	.50	.15
18 Jose Rijo	.75	.23
19 Chris Sabo	.50	.15
20 Herm Winningham	.50	.15

1992 Reds Kahn's

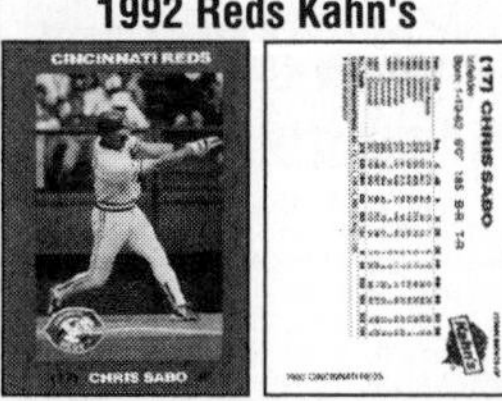

The 1992 Kahn's Cincinnati Reds set consists of 29 standard-size cards. The set included two manufacturer's coupons (one for 50 cents off Kahn's Wieners and another for the same amount off Kahn's Corn Dogs). The cards are skip-numbered by uniform number on both sides and checklisted below accordingly.

	Nm-Mt	Ex-Mt
COMPLETE SET (29)	8.00	2.40
2 Schottzie	.25	.07
(Mascot)		
9 Joe Oliver	.25	.07
10 Bip Roberts	.25	.07
11 Barry Larkin	2.00	.60
12 Freddie Benavides	.25	.07
15 Glenn Braggs	.25	.07
16 Reggie Sanders	.75	.23
17 Chris Sabo	.25	.07
19 Bill Doran	.25	.07
21 Paul O'Neill	1.00	.30
23 Hal Morris	.25	.07
25 Scott Bankhead	.25	.07
26 Darnell Coles	.25	.07
27 Jose Rijo	.25	.07
28 Scott Ruskin	.25	.07
29 Greg Swindell	.25	.07
30 Dave Martinez	.25	.07
31 Tim Belcher	.25	.07
32 Tom Browning	.50	.15
34 Jeff Reed	.25	.07
37 Norm Charlton	.25	.07
38 Troy Afenir	.25	.07
41 Lou Piniella MG	.75	.23
45 Chris Hammond	.25	.07
48 Dwayne Henry	.25	.07
49 Rob Dibble	.50	.15
NNO Jackie Moore CO	.50	.15
John McLaren CO		
Sam Perlozzo CO		
Tony Perez CO		
Larry Rothschild CO		
NNO Manufacturer's Coupon	.15	.04
Kahn's Corn Dogs		
NNO Manufacturer's Coupon	.15	.04
Kahn's Beef Franks		

1993 Reds Kahn's

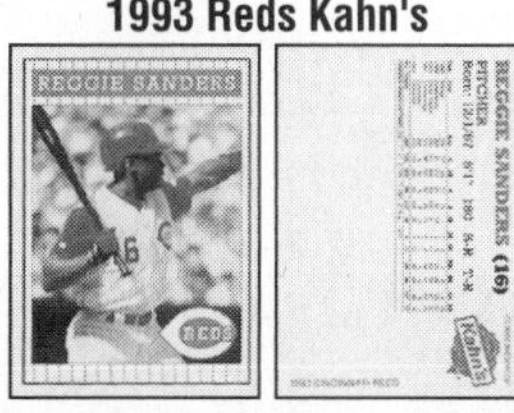

This 27-card standard-size set was issued by Kahn's Meats. The cards are unnumbered and checklisted below in alphabetical order.

	Nm-Mt	Ex-Mt
COMPLETE SET (30)	8.00	2.40
1 Bobby Ayala	.25	.07
2 Tim Belcher	.25	.07
3 Jeff Branson	.25	.07
4 Marty Brennaman ANN	.50	.15
Joe Nuxhall ANN		
5 Tom Browning	.50	.15
6 Jacob Brumfield	.25	.07
7 Greg Cadaret	.25	.07
8 Jose Cardenal CO	.25	.07
Don Gullett CO		
Ray Knight CO		
Dave Miley CO		
Bobby Valentine CO		
9 Rob Dibble	.50	.15
10 Davey Johnson MG	.50	.15
11 Roberto Kelly	.25	.07
12 Bill Landrum	.25	.07
13 Barry Larkin	2.00	.60
14 Randy Milligan	.25	.07
15 Kevin Mitchell	.50	.15
16 Hal Morris	.25	.07
17 Joe Oliver	.25	.07
18 Tim Pugh	.25	.07
19 Jeff Reardon	.50	.15
20 Jose Rijo	.50	.15
21 Bip Roberts	.25	.07
22 Chris Sabo	.25	.07
23 Juan Samuel	.25	.07
24 Reggie Sanders	.50	.15
25 Schottzie (mascot)	.25	.07
Marge Schott		
26 John Smiley	.25	.07
27 Gary Varsho	.25	.07
28 Kevin Wickander	.25	.07
NNO Manufacturer's Coupon	.15	.04
(Kahn's hot dogs)		
NNO Manufacturer's Coupon	.15	.04
(Kahn's corn dogs)		

1994 Reds Kahn's

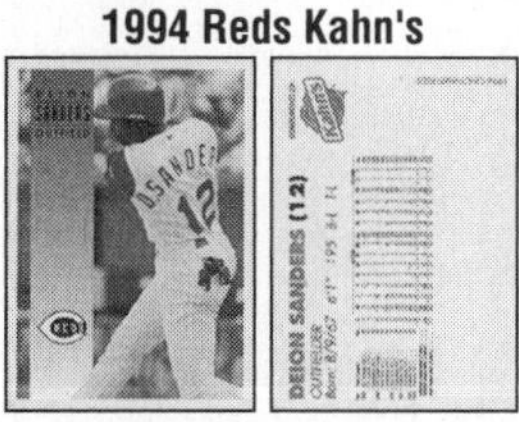

These 33 standard-size cards were handed out at Riverfront Stadium to fans attending a Reds' home game on August 7. The cards are unnumbered and checklisted below in alphabetical order.

	Nm-Mt	Ex-Mt
COMPLETE SET (35)	7.50	2.20
1 Bret Boone UER	.75	.23
(Misspelled Brett on front and back)		
2 Jeff Branson	.25	.07
3 Jeff Brantley	.50	.15
4 Tom Browning	.50	.15
5 Jacob Brumfield	.25	.07
6 Hector Carrasco	.25	.07
7 Rob Dibble	.25	.07
8 Brian Dorsett	.25	.07
9 Tony Fernandez	.50	.15
10 Tim Fortugno UER	.50	.15
(Misspelled Fortungo on back)		
11 Steve Foster	.25	.07
12 Ron Gant	.50	.15
13 Erik Hanson	.25	.07
14 Lenny Harris	.25	.07
15 Thomas Howard	.25	.07
16 Davey Johnson MG	.50	.15
17 Barry Larkin	2.00	.60
18 Chuck McElroy	.25	.07
19 Kevin Mitchell	.50	.15
20 Hal Morris	.25	.07
21 Joe Oliver	.25	.07
22 Tim Pugh	.25	.07
23 Jose Rijo	.50	.15
24 John Roper	.25	.07
25 Johnny Ruffin	.25	.07
26 Deion Sanders	1.00	.30
27 Reggie Sanders	.50	.15
28 Schottzie (Mascot)	.25	.07
29 Pete Schourek	.25	.07
30 John Smiley UER	.25	.07
(Front photo is Erik Hanson)		
31 Eddie Taubensee	.25	.07
32 Jerome Walton	.25	.07
33 Bob Boone CO	.25	.07
Don Gullett CO		
Grant Jackson CO		
Ray Knight CO		
Joel Youngblood CO		
NNO Manufacturer's Coupon	.15	.04
Kahn's Wieners		
NNO Manufacturer's Coupon	.15	.04
Kahn's Corn Dogs		

1995 Reds Kahn's

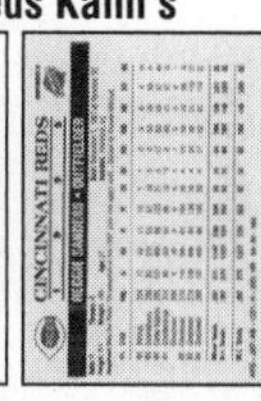

This 34-card standard-size set has white-bordered fronts feature color player action photos. The cards are unnumbered and checklisted below in alphabetical order.

	Nm-Mt	Ex-Mt
COMPLETE SET (36)	6.00	1.80
1 Eric Anthony	.10	.03
2 Damon Berryhill	.10	.03
3 Bret Boone	.75	.23
4 Jeff Branson	.10	.03
5 Jeff Brantley	.25	.07
6 Hector Carrasco	.10	.03
7 Ron Gant	.25	.07
8 Willie Greene	.10	.03
9 Lenny Harris	.10	.03
10 Xavier Hernandez	.10	.03
11 Thomas Howard	.10	.03
12 Brian Hunter	.10	.03
13 Mike Jackson	.25	.07
14 Kevin Jarvis	.10	.03
15 Davey Johnson MG	.25	.07
16 Barry Larkin	1.50	.45
17 Mark Lewis	.10	.03
18 Chuck McElroy	.10	.03
19 Hal Morris	.10	.03
20 C.J. Nitkowski	.10	.03
21 Brad Pennington	.10	.03
22 Tim Pugh	.10	.03
23 Jose Rijo	.25	.07
24 John Roper	.10	.03
25 Johnny Ruffin	.10	.03
26 Deion Sanders	.75	.23
27 Reggie Sanders	.25	.07
28 Benito Santiago	.25	.07
29 Schottzie (Mascot)	.10	.03
30 Pete Schourek	.10	.03
31 John Smiley	.10	.03
32 Eddie Taubensee	.10	.03
33 Jerome Walton	.10	.03
34 Ray Knight CO	.10	.03
Don Gullett CO		
Grant Jackson CO		
Hal McRae CO		
Joel Youngblood CO		
NNO Manufacturer's Coupon	.05	.02
Kahn's Corn Dogs		
NNO Manufacturer's Coupon	.05	.02
Kahn's Hot Dogs		

1996 Reds Kahn's

This 36 card standard-size set features members of the 1996 Cincinnati Reds. Since the cards are unnumbered, we have sequenced them in alphabetical order.

	Nm-Mt	Ex-Mt
COMPLETE SET (36)	10.00	3.00
1 Eric Anthony	.25	.07
2 Tim Belk	.25	.07
3 Bret Boone	1.00	.30
4 Jeff Branson	.25	.07
5 Jeff Brantley	.50	.15
6 Dave Burba	.25	.07
7 Hector Carrasco	.25	.07
8 Eric Davis	.75	.23
9 Curtis Goodwin	.25	.07
10 Willie Greene	.25	.07
11 Lenny Harris	.25	.07
12 Thomas Howard	.25	.07
13 Kevin Jarvis	.25	.07
14 Mike Kelly	.25	.07
15 Ray Knight MG	.25	.07
16 Barry Larkin	1.50	.45
17 Hal Morris	.25	.07
18 Joe Oliver	.25	.07
19 Eric Owens	.25	.07
20 Eduardo Perez	.25	.07
21 Mark Portugal	.25	.07
22 Jose Rijo	.25	.07
23 Johnny Ruffin	.25	.07
24 Chris Sabo	.25	.07
25 Roger Salkeld	.25	.07
26 Reggie Sanders	.50	.15
27 Pete Schourek	.25	.07
28 Scott Service	.25	.07
29 Jeff Shaw	.50	.15
30 John Smiley	.25	.07
31 Bernie Stowe EQMG	.25	.07
32 Eddie Taubensee	.25	.07
33 Marc Bombard CO	.25	.07
Don Gullett CO		
Jim Lett CO		
Hal McRae CO		
Joel Youngblood CO		
Tom Hume CO		
34 Schottzie 02	.25	.07
Mascot		
35 Coupon	.15	.04
36 Coupon	.15	.04

1996 Reds '76 Klosterman

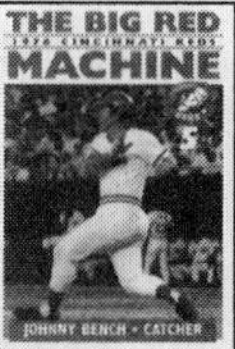

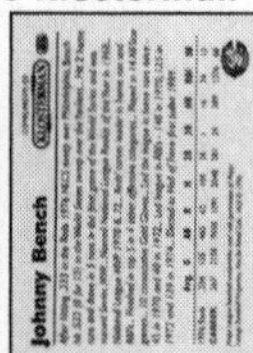

This 10-card set celebrates the 20th anniversary of the Cincinnati Reds 1976 World Championship team. Distributed by Klosterman Baking Co., one card was inserted in bags of Big White Bread product and released to participating Cincinnati-area grocery stores.

	Nm-Mt	Ex-Mt
COMPLETE SET (10)	5.00	1.50
1 Sparky Anderson MG	.50	.15
2 Johnny Bench	1.00	.30
3 Johnny Bench	2.50	.75
Joe Morgan		
Tony Perez		
Pete Rose		
4 Dave Concepcion	.75	.23
5 George Foster	.50	.15
6 Cesar Geronimo	.25	.07
7 Ken Griffey	.75	.23
8 Don Gullett	.25	.07
9 Joe Morgan	1.00	.30
10 Tony Perez	1.00	.30

1997 Reds Kahn's

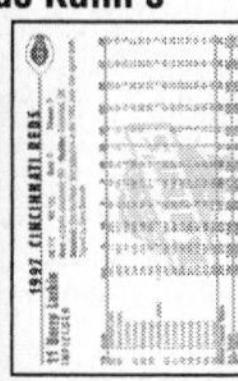

This 36 card standard-size set features members of the 1997 Cincinnati Reds. The players and uniform number are on the left of the card while the rest of the card is devoted to a borderless photo.

	Nm-Mt	Ex-Mt
COMPLETE SET (36)	10.00	3.00
1 Stan Belinda	.25	.07
2 Aaron Boone	.25	.07
3 Bret Boone	1.00	.30
4 Jeff Branson	.25	.07
5 Jeff Brantley	.50	.15
6 Dave Burba	.25	.07
7 Brook Fordyce	.25	.07
8 Steve Gibralter	.25	.07
9 Curtis Goodwin	.25	.07
10 Willie Greene	.25	.07
11 Lenny Harris	.25	.07
12 Mike Kelly	.25	.07
13 Ray Knight MG	.25	.07
14 Barry Larkin	1.50	.45
15 Kent Mercker	.25	.07
16 Mike Morgan	.25	.07
17 Hal Morris	.25	.07
18 Joe Oliver	.25	.07
19 Terry Pendleton	.25	.07
20 Eduardo Perez	.25	.07
21 Pokey Reese	.25	.07
22 Mike Remlinger	.25	.07
23 Jose Rijo	.50	.15
24 Felix Rodriguez	.50	.15
25 Deion Sanders	1.00	.30
26 Reggie Sanders	.50	.15
27 Pete Schourek	.25	.07
28 Jeff Shaw	.50	.15
29 John Smiley	.25	.07
30 Scott Sullivan	.25	.07
31 Eddie Taubensee	.25	.07
32 Brett Tomko	.25	.07
33 Ken Griffey Sr CO	.25	.07
Don Gullett CO		
Tom Hume CO		
Denis Menke CO		
Ron Oester CO		
Joel Youngblood CO		
34 Schottzie 02	.25	.07
Mascot		

	Nm-Mt	Ex-Mt
35 Coupon	.15	.04
36 Coupon	.15	.04

1998 Reds Kahn's

This 36 card standard-size set features members of the 1998 Cincinnati Reds. Since the cards are unnumbered, we have sequenced them in alphabetical order.

	Nm-Mt	Ex-Mt
COMPLETE SET (36)	12.00	3.60
1 Stan Belinda	.25	.07
2 Aaron Boone	1.00	.30
3 Bret Boone	1.00	.30
4 Sean Casey	1.50	.45
5 Steve Cooke	.25	.07
6 Brook Fordyce	.25	.07
7 Mike Frank	.25	.07
8 Danny Graves	.75	.23
9 Willie Greene	.25	.07
10 Pete Harnisch	.25	.07
11 John Hudek	.25	.07
12 Damian Jackson	.50	.15
13 Paul Konerko	1.50	.45
14 Rick Krivda	.25	.07
15 Barry Larkin	1.50	.45
16 Jack McKeon MG	.50	.15
17 Melvin Nieves	.25	.07
18 Jon Nunnally	.25	.07
19 Steve Parris	.25	.07
20 Eduardo Perez	.25	.07
21 Pokey Reese	.25	.07
22 Mike Remlinger	.25	.07
23 Reggie Sanders	.50	.15
24 Chris Stynes	.25	.07
25 Scott Sullivan	.25	.07
26 Eddie Taubensee	.25	.07
27 Brett Tomko	.25	.07
28 Pat Watkins	.25	.07
29 Gabe White	.25	.07
30 Todd Williams	.25	.07
31 Scott Winchester	.25	.07
32 Dmitri Young	.50	.15
33 Ken Griffey Sr. CO	.25	.07
Tom Hume CO		
Ron Oester CO		
Don Gullett CO		
Denis Menke CO		
Harry Dunlop CO		
34 Schottzie 02	.25	.07
Mascot		
35 Coupon	.15	.04
36 Coupon	.15	.04

1999 Reds Kahns

This 34 card standard-size set features members of the 1999 Cincinnati Reds. The cards have the player's name and position running down the left side with the words, "1999 Cincinnati Reds" on the bottom. The rest of the borderless cards feature an action shot of the player. The back has biographical stats and complete career statistics. Other than the uniform numbers on the back, the cards are unnumbered, and therefore we have sequenced the cards in alphabetical order.

	Nm-Mt	Ex-Mt
COMPLETE SET (34)	10.00	3.00
1 Steve Avery	.25	.07
2 Stan Belinda	.25	.07
3 Jason Bere	.25	.07
4 Aaron Boone	1.00	.30
5 Mike Cameron	.25	.07
6 Sean Casey	1.00	.30
7 Danny Graves	.75	.23
8 Jeffrey Hammonds	.25	.07
9 Pete Harnisch	.25	.07
10 Brian Johnson	.25	.07
11 Barry Larkin	1.00	.30
12 Jason LaRue	.25	.07
13 Mark Lewis	.25	.07
14 Jack McKeon MG	.50	.15
15 Hal Morris	.25	.07
16 Denny Neagle	.25	.07
17 Steve Parris	.25	.07
18 Pokey Reese	.25	.07
19 Dennis Reyes	.25	.07
20 Chris Stynes	.25	.07
21 Scott Sullivan	.25	.07
22 Eddie Taubensee	.25	.07
23 Brett Tomko	.25	.07
24 Michael Tucker	.50	.15
25 Greg Vaughn	.50	.15
26 Ron Villone	.25	.07
27 Gabe White	.25	.07
28 Scott Williamson	.25	.07
29 Mark Wohlers	.25	.07
30 Dmitri Young	.50	.15
31 Schottzie	.25	.07
Mascot		
32 Marty Brennaman ANN	.50	.15
Joe Nuxhall ANN		
33 Ken Griffey Sr. CO	.25	.07
Ron Oester CO		
Denis Menke CO		
Dave Collins CO		
34 Don Gullett CO	.25	.07
Tom Hume CO		
Harry Dunlop INS		
Mark Berry CO		
XX Kanh's Coupon	.15	.04
Hot Dogs		
XX Kahn's Coupon	.15	.04
Corn Dogs		

2000 Reds Kahn's

This 34 card standard-size set features members of the 2000 Cincinnati Reds. The cards have the words 2000 Cincinnati Reds down the left horizontal border with the rest of the front devoted to a player photo. The Reds logo in in the upper left part of the photo with the player's name in the upper right and his uniform number and position in the lower right. The horizontal back has vital statistics and career statistics. Since the cards are unnumbered we have sequenced them in alphabetical order.

	Nm-Mt	Ex-Mt
COMPLETE SET (34)	10.00	3.00
1 Manny Aybar	.25	.07
2 Rob Bell	.25	.07
3 Dante Bichette	.50	.15
4 Aaron Boone	1.00	.30
5 Sean Casey	1.00	.30
6 Juan Castro	.25	.07
7 Elmer Dessens	.25	.07
8 Osvaldo Fernandez	.25	.07
9 Danny Graves	.75	.23
10 Ken Griffey Jr.	3.00	.90
11 Pete Harnisch	.25	.07
12 Barry Larkin	1.50	.45
13 Jack McKeon MG	.50	.15
14 Hal Morris	.25	.07
15 Denny Neagle	.50	.15
16 Alex Ochoa	.25	.07
17 Steve Parris	.25	.07
18 Pokey Reese	.25	.07
19 Dennys Reyes	.25	.07
20 Benito Santiago	.50	.15
21 Chris Stynes	.25	.07
22 Scott Sullivan	.25	.07
23 Eddie Taubensee	.25	.07
24 Michael Tucker	.50	.15
25 Ron Villone	.25	.07
26 Scott Williamson	.25	.07
27 Dmitri Young	.50	.15
28 Ken Griffey Sr. CO	.25	.07
Ron Oester CO		
Denis Menke CO		
Dave Collins CO		
29 Don Gullett CO	.25	.07
Tom Hume CO		
Harry Dunlop CO		
Mark Berry CO		
30 Marty Brennaman ANN	.50	.15
Joe Nuxhall ANN		
31 Red	.25	.07
Mascot		
32 Kahnlee	.25	.07
Mascot		
33 Coupon	.15	.04
34 Coupon	.15	.04

2000 Reds Perez Sheet Pepsi

This sheet was given away at the May 27, 2000 game in which the Cincinnati Reds retired 2000 HOF inductee Tony Perez's uniform. The front of the sheet has tghreew drawings of Perez along with the notation of the date. The perforated side has the "Pepsi-Cola" logo along with a note of congratulations. The back is blank.

	Nm-Mt	Ex-Mt
1 Tony Perez	3.00	.90

2001 Reds Kahn

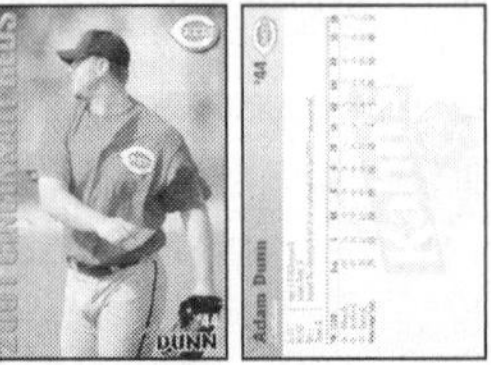

This 33 card standard-size set featured members of the 2001 Cincinnati Reds. The full-bleed fronts have the team name going vertically on the left side with the player's name on the bottom. The horizontal backs have biographical information as well as career stats. An ad for Kahn's is apparent in the background. Since these cards are unnumbered, we have sequenced them in alphabetical order

	Nm-Mt	Ex-Mt
COMPLETE SET (33)	10.00	3.00
1 Juan Acevedo	.25	.07
2 Aaron Boone	1.00	.30
3 Bob Boone MG	.50	.15
4 Jim Brower	.25	.07
5 Sean Casey	1.00	.30
6 Juan Castro	.25	.07
7 Brady Clark	.25	.07
8 Lance Davis	.25	.07
9 Elmer Dessens	.25	.07
10 Adam Dunn	2.00	.60
11 Osvaldo Fernandez	.25	.07
12 Danny Graves	.25	.07
13 Ken Griffey Jr	2.00	.60
14 Pete Harnisch	.25	.07
15 Barry Larkin	1.00	.30
16 Jason Larue	.25	.07
17 Hector Mercado	.25	.07
18 Chris Nichting	.25	.07
19 Pokey Reese	.25	.07
20 Chris Reitsma	.25	.07
21 Dennys Reyes	.25	.07
22 John Riedling	.25	.07
23 Ruben Rivera	.25	.07
24 Bill Selby	.25	.07
25 Kelly Stinnett	.25	.07
26 Scott Sullivan	.25	.07
27 Michael Tucker	.50	.15
28 Scott Williamson	.25	.07
29 Dmitri Young	.25	.07
30 Marty Brennaman ANN	.50	.15
Joe Nuxhall ANN		
31 Mr. Red	.25	.07
Mascot		
32 Ken Griffey Sr. CO	.25	.07
Ron Oester CO		
Tim Foli CO		
Bill Doran CO		
33 Don Gullett CO	.25	.07
Tom Hume CO		
Mark Berry CO		
XX Manufacturer Coupon	.10	.03
Hot Dogs		
XX Manufacturer Coupon	.10	.03
Corn Dogs		

2002 Reds Kahn

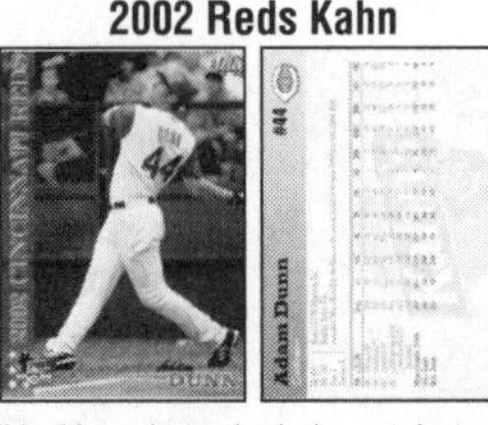

This 33 card standard-size set featured members of the 2002 Cincinnati Reds. The full-bleed fronts have the team name going vertically on the left side with the player's name on the bottom. The horizontal backs have biographical information as well as career stats. An ad for Kahn's is apparent in the background. Since these cards are unnumbered, we have sequenced them in alphabetical order

	Nm-Mt	Ex-Mt
COMPLETE SET	10.00	3.00
1 Aaron Boone	1.00	.30
2 Bob Boone MG	.25	.07
3 Russell Branyan	.50	.15
4 Sean Casey	1.00	.30
5 Juan Castro	.25	.07
6 Bruce Chen	.25	.07
7 Ryan Dempster	.50	.15
8 Elmer Dessens	.25	.07
9 Adam Dunn	1.50	.45
10 Jared Fernandez	.25	.07
11 Danny Graves	.50	.15
12 Ken Griffey Jr.	3.00	.90
13 Joey Hamilton	.25	.07
14 Jimmy Haynes	.25	.07
15 Austin Kearns	1.50	.45
16 Barry Larkin	1.25	.35
17 Jason Larue	.25	.07
18 Corky Miller	.25	.07
19 Luis Pineda	.25	.07
20 Chris Reitsma	.25	.07
21 John Riedling	.25	.07
22 Jose Rijo	.50	.15
23 Jose Silva	.25	.07
24 Kelly Stinnett	.25	.07
25 Scott Sullivan	.25	.07
26 Reggie Taylor	.25	.07
27 Todd Walker	.75	.23
28 Gabe White	.25	.07
29 Scott Williamson	.25	.07
30 Don Gullett CO	.25	.07
Tom Hume CO		
Mark Berry CO		
31 Jim Lefebvre CO	.25	.07
Tim Foli CO		
Ray Knight CO		
Jose Cardenal CO		
32 Joe Nuxhall ANN	.50	.15
Marty Brennaman ANN		
33 Cinergy Field	.25	.07
XX Corn Dog Coupon	.10	.03
XX Hot Dog Coupon	.10	.03

2003 Reds Kahn's

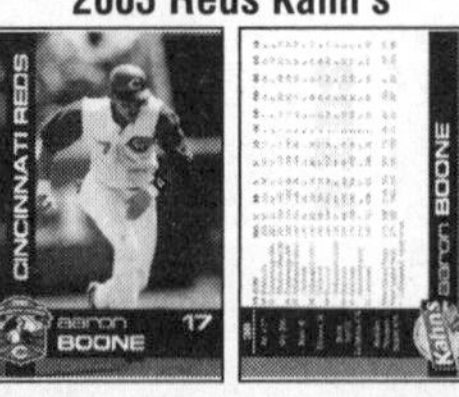

This 30 card standard-size set was given away at a Cincinnati Reds game during the 2003 season. The fronts feature full-bleed red borders on the left and the bottom with the photo going to the right of the card. The player's name and uniform number is at the bottom. The horizontal backs include biographical information as well as complete major and minor league stats. Since these cards are unnunmbered, we have sequenced them in alphabetical order.

	MINT	NRMT
COMPLETE SET	10.00	4.50
1 Aaron Boone	1.00	.45
2 Bob Boone MG	.25	.11
3 Russell Branyan	.50	.23
4 Sean Casey	.75	.35
5 Juan Castro	.25	.11
6 Ryan Dempster	.25	.11
7 Adam Dunn	1.00	.45
8 Danny Graves	.50	.23
9 Ken Griffey Jr.	1.50	.70
10 Jose Guillen	.75	.35
11 Jimmy Haynes	.25	.11
12 Felix Heredia	.25	.11
13 Austin Kearns	1.00	.45
14 Barry Larkin	1.00	.45
15 Jason LaRue	.25	.11
16 Kent Mercker	.25	.11
17 Wily Mo Pena	.25	.11
18 Brian Reith	.25	.11
19 Chris Reitsma	.25	.11
20 John Riedling	.25	.11
21 Kelly Stinnett	.25	.11
22 Scott Sullivan	.25	.11
23 Reggie Taylor	.25	.11
24 Gabe White	.25	.11
25 Scott Williamson	.25	.11
26 Paul Wilson	.25	.11
27 Tom Robson CO	.25	.11
Tim Foli CO		
Ray Knight CO		
Jose Cardenal CO		
28 Don Gullett CO	.25	.11
Tom Hume CO		
Mark Berry CO		
29 Coupon Card (50 cents off)	.25	.11
30 Coupon Card (75 cents off)	.25	.11

1992 Rembrandt Ultra-Pro Promos

The 1992 Rembrandt Ultra-Pro set of 19 standard-size cards was issued one-per-package inside specially marked packages of Rembrandt Ultra-Pro sheets. The cards are numbered with a "P" prefix. The cards contain a high-gloss UV coating and feature an exclusive anti-counterfeiting hologram on the back. The set of the first 18 cards was also available direct from Rembrandt for $35.95 ($37.95 or $39.95) plus $4 shipping and handling along with three (two or one) UPC's or other proofs of purchase.

	Nm-Mt	Ex-Mt
COMPLETE SET (19)	30.00	9.00
P1 Bobby Bonilla	1.00	.30
P2 Bobby Bonilla	1.00	.30
P3 Bobby Bonilla	1.00	.30
P4 Jose Canseco	2.50	.75
P5 Jose Canseco	2.50	.75
P6 Jose Canseco	2.50	.75
P7 Hal Morris#	1.00	.30
P8 Hal Morris	1.00	.30
P9 Hal Morris	1.00	.30
P10 Scott Erickson	1.00	.30
P11 Scott Erickson	1.00	.30
P12 Scott Erickson	1.00	.30
P13 Danny Tartabull	1.00	.30
P14 Danny Tartabull	1.00	.30
P15 Danny Tartabull	1.00	.30
P16 Danny Tartabull	1.00	.30
Bobby Bonilla		
P17 Bobby Bonilla	1.00	.30
P18 Danny Tartabull	5.00	1.50
Bobby Bonilla		
P19 Jose Canseco	2.50	.75

1993 Rembrandt Ultra-Pro Karros

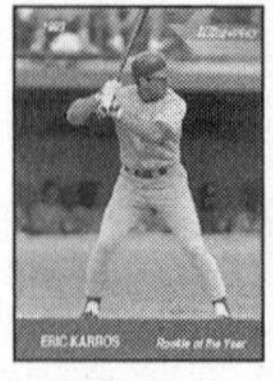

Eric Karros is the exclusive subject of this five-card, standard-size set that celebrates his National League Rookie of the Year award. The full-bleed action photos have a blue bar across the bottom with Karros' name and "Rookie of the Year" in white lettering. The borderless backs carry a head shot in the left with career highlights on the right. Below the picture, Karros' 1992 statistics are listed. The Rembrandt logo appears on a blue bar in the lower left.

	Nm-Mt	Ex-Mt
COMPLETE SET (5)	4.00	1.20
COMMON CARD (1-5)	1.00	.30

1994 Rembrandt Ultra-Pro Piazza Promos

Issued to promote Ultra-Pro's card storage products, these two standard-size cards feature on their borderless fronts color photos of Mike Piazza posed in front of a purple background and holding Ultra-Pro products. His name and the words "1993 Rookie of the Year" appear at the bottom. The pink back carries product information and a facsimile Mike Piazza autograph. The cards are unnumbered.

	Nm-Mt	Ex-Mt
COMPLETE SET (2)	2.00	.60
COMMON CARD (1-2)	1.00	.30

1994 Rembrandt Ultra-Pro Piazza

These six standard-size cards feature on their borderless fronts color photos of Mike Piazza in various game and non-game situations. His name and "1993 Rookie of the Year" appear at the bottom. The pink back has a color head shot of Piazza, with career highlights and statistics below. One of these cards was inserted in each 200-count box of Ultra-Pro Mini Top Loaders. A black vinyl binder for displaying all six cards was also available. The cards are numbered on the back as "X of 6." There were refractors of these cards issued -- however they are thinly traded so no prices can be established at this time.

	Nm-Mt	Ex-Mt
COMPLETE SET (6)	12.00	3.60
COMMON CARD (1-6)	2.00	.60

1996 Rembrandt Ultra Pro Piazza

This nine-card set is actually a puzzle with each of the cards featuring a different portion of an action photo of Mike Piazza. The complete set could be mailed in for an uncut version of the photo. Gold and silver versions of the puzzle were also produced which, when completed, could be mailed in for monetary prizes. The gold version is distinguished by a gold foil emblem on each piece and could be exchanged for a prize of $250. The silver version displays a silver foil emblem and could be exchanged for $100. The mail-in prize offer expired April 1, 1997.

	Nm-Mt	Ex-Mt
COMPLETE SET (9)	5.00	1.50
COMMON CARD (1-9)	.75	.23

1985 Reuss Cystic Fibrosis

This one-card set measures approximately 3 1/2" by 5 1/2" and features a color photo of Jerry Reuss in a white border. The back displays information and a form for ordering the photo in a full color personally autographed 8" by 10" version which could be purchased by mail for $5 along with a 16" by 20" poster for $8. A portion of the proceeds was to be donated to the Cystic Fibrosis Foundation.

	Nm-Mt	Ex-Mt
1 Jerry Reuss	5.00	2.00

1998 Revolution

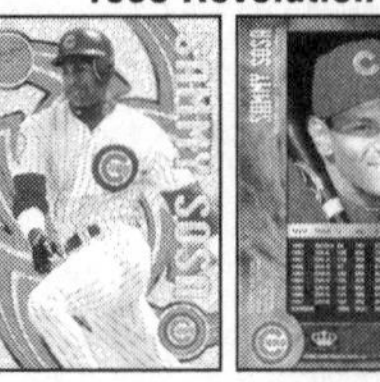

The 1998 Revolution set (produced by Pacific) consists of 150 standard size cards. The three card packs retailed for a suggested price of $5.99. The fronts feature a color action photo atop a state-of-the-art silver foil sparkling background. The backs provide collectors with full year-by-year statistics of the featured player. The set release date was September, 1998. Rookie Cards inlcude Magglio Ordonez.

	Nm-Mt	Ex-Mt
COMPLETE SET (150)	100.00	30.00
1 Garret Anderson	1.00	.30
2 Jim Edmonds	1.00	.30
3 Darin Erstad	1.00	.30
4 Chuck Finley	1.00	.30
5 Tim Salmon	1.50	.45
6 Jay Bell	1.00	.30
7 Travis Lee	.60	.18
8 Devon White	.60	.18
9 Matt Williams	1.00	.30

10 Andres Galarraga 1.00 .30
11 Tom Glavine 1.50 .45
12 Andruw Jones 1.00 .30
13 Chipper Jones 2.50 .75
14 Ryan Klesko 1.00 .30
15 Javy Lopez 1.00 .30
16 Greg Maddux 4.00 1.20
17 Walt Weiss 1.00 .30
18 Roberto Alomar 2.50 .75
19 Joe Carter 1.00 .30
20 Mike Mussina 2.50 .75
21 Rafael Palmeiro 1.50 .45
22 Cal Ripken 8.00 2.40
23 B.J. Surhoff 1.00 .30
24 Nomar Garciaparra 4.00 1.20
25 Reggie Jefferson .60 .18
26 Pedro Martinez 2.50 .75
27 Troy O'Leary .60 .18
28 Mo Vaughn 1.00 .30
29 Mark Grace 1.50 .45
30 Mickey Morandini .60 .18
31 Henry Rodriguez .60 .18
32 Sammy Sosa 4.00 1.20
33 Kerry Wood 2.50 .75
34 Albert Belle 1.00 .30
35 Ray Durham 1.00 .30
36 Magglio Ordonez RC 5.00 1.50
37 Frank Thomas 2.50 .75
38 Robin Ventura 1.00 .30
39 Bret Boone 1.00 .30
40 Barry Larkin 2.50 .75
41 Reggie Sanders 1.00 .30
42 Brett Tomko .60 .18
43 Sandy Alomar Jr. .60 .18
44 David Justice 1.00 .30
45 Kenny Lofton 1.00 .30
46 Manny Ramirez 1.00 .30
47 Jim Thome 2.50 .75
48 Omar Vizquel 1.00 .30
49 Jaret Wright .60 .18
50 Dante Bichette 1.00 .30
51 Ellis Burks 1.00 .30
52 Vinny Castilla 1.00 .30
53 Todd Helton 1.50 .45
54 Larry Walker 1.50 .45
55 Tony Clark .60 .18
56 Deivi Cruz .60 .18
57 Damion Easley .60 .18
58 Bobby Higginson 1.00 .30
59 Brian Hunter .60 .18
60 Cliff Floyd 1.00 .30
61 Livan Hernandez .60 .18
62 Derrek Lee 1.00 .30
63 Edgar Renteria 1.00 .30
64 Moises Alou 1.00 .30
65 Jeff Bagwell 1.50 .45
66 Derek Bell .60 .18
67 Craig Biggio 1.50 .45
68 Richard Hidalgo 1.00 .30
69 Johnny Damon 1.00 .30
70 Jeff King .60 .18
71 Hal Morris .60 .18
72 Dean Palmer 1.00 .30
73 Bobby Bonilla 1.00 .30
74 Charles Johnson 1.00 .30
75 Eric Karros 1.00 .30
76 Raul Mondesi 1.00 .30
77 Gary Sheffield 1.00 .30
78 Jeromy Burnitz 1.00 .30
79 Marquis Grissom .60 .18
80 Dave Nilsson .60 .18
81 Fernando Vina 1.00 .30
82 Marty Cordova .60 .18
83 Pat Meares .60 .18
84 Paul Molitor 1.50 .45
85 Brad Radke 1.00 .30
86 Terry Steinbach .60 .18
87 Todd Walker 1.00 .30
88 Brad Fullmer .60 .18
89 Vladimir Guerrero 2.50 .75
90 Carl Pavano .60 .18
91 Rondell White 1.00 .30
92 Bernard Gilkey .60 .18
93 Hideo Nomo 2.50 .75
94 John Olerud 1.00 .30
95 Rey Ordonez .60 .18
96 Mike Piazza 4.00 1.20
97 Masato Yoshii RC 1.50 .45
98 Hideki Irabu .60 .18
99 Derek Jeter 6.00 1.80
100 Chuck Knoblauch 1.00 .30
101 Tino Martinez 1.50 .45
102 Paul O'Neill 1.50 .45
103 Darryl Strawberry 1.50 .45
104 Bernie Williams 1.50 .45
105 Jason Giambi 2.50 .75
106 Ben Grieve .60 .18
107 Rickey Henderson 2.50 .75
108 Matt Stairs .60 .18
109 Doug Glanville .60 .18
110 Desi Relaford .60 .18
111 Scott Rolen 1.50 .45
112 Curt Schilling 1.50 .45
113 Jason Kendall 1.00 .30
114 Al Martin .60 .18
115 Jason Schmidt 1.00 .30
116 Kevin Young 1.00 .30
117 Delino DeShields .60 .18
118 Gary Gaetti 1.00 .30
119 Brian Jordan 1.00 .30
120 Ray Lankford .60 .18
121 Mark McGwire 6.00 1.80
122 Kevin Brown 1.50 .45
123 Steve Finley 1.00 .30
124 Tony Gwynn 3.00 .90
125 Wally Joyner 1.00 .30
126 Greg Vaughn 1.00 .30
127 Barry Bonds 6.00 1.80
128 Orel Hershiser 1.00 .30
129 Jeff Kent 1.00 .30
130 Bill Mueller 1.00 .30
131 Jay Buhner 1.00 .30
132 Ken Griffey Jr. 4.00 1.20
133 Randy Johnson 2.50 .75
134 Edgar Martinez 1.50 .45
135 Alex Rodriguez 4.00 1.20
136 David Segui .60 .18
137 Rolando Arrojo RC 1.00 .30
138 Wade Boggs 1.50 .45
139 Quinton McCracken .60 .18
140 Fred McGriff 1.50 .45
141 Will Clark 2.50 .75
142 Juan Gonzalez 2.50 .75
143 Tom Goodwin .60 .18
144 Ivan Rodriguez 2.50 .75
145 Aaron Sele .60 .18
146 John Wetteland 1.00 .30
147 Jose Canseco 2.50 .75
148 Roger Clemens 5.00 1.50
149 Jose Cruz Jr. 1.00 .30
150 Carlos Delgado 1.00 .30

1998 Revolution Shadow Series

The 1998 Revolution Shadow Series consists of 150 cards and is a parallel to the 1998 Revolution base set. The cards are randomly inserted in hobby packs. Only 99 sets were produced and each card is embossed with the words "Shadow Series" and is serial numbered "X of 99" in thin small, black print on back.

Nm-Mt Ex-Mt
*STARS: 4X TO 10X BASIC CARDS ....
*ROOKIES: 3X TO 8X BASIC CARDS ..

1998 Revolution Foul Pole

The 1998 Revolution Foul Pole Laser Cuts set consists of 20 cards and is an insert to the 1998 Revolution base set. The cards are randomly inserted in packs at a rate of one in 49. The fronts feature color action photography with a unique laser-cut design recreating the look of an actual foul pole.

Nm-Mt Ex-Mt
COMPLETE SET (20) 300.00 90.00
1 Cal Ripken 50.00 15.00
2 Nomar Garciaparra 25.00 7.50
3 Mo Vaughn 6.00 1.80
4 Frank Thomas 15.00 4.50
5 Manny Ramirez 6.00 1.80
6 Bernie Williams 10.00 3.00
7 Ben Grieve 4.00 1.20
8 Ken Griffey Jr. 25.00 7.50
9 Alex Rodriguez 25.00 7.50
10 Juan Gonzalez 15.00 4.50
11 Ivan Rodriguez 15.00 4.50
12 Travis Lee 4.00 1.20
13 Chipper Jones 15.00 4.50
14 Sammy Sosa 25.00 7.50
15 Vinny Castilla 6.00 1.80
16 Moises Alou 6.00 1.80
17 Gary Sheffield 6.00 1.80
18 Mike Piazza 25.00 7.50
19 Mark McGwire 40.00 12.00
20 Barry Bonds 40.00 12.00

1998 Revolution Major League Icons

The 1998 Revolution Major League Icons set consists of 10 cards and is an insert to the 1998 Revolution base set. The cards are randomly inserted in packs at a rate of one 121. The fronts feature color action photos of the MLB's best atop a die-cut "shield of honor" design.

Nm-Mt Ex-Mt
COMPLETE SET (10) 100.00 30.00
1 Cal Ripken 40.00 12.00
2 Nomar Garciaparra 20.00 6.00
3 Frank Thomas 12.00 3.60
4 Ken Griffey Jr. 20.00 6.00
5 Alex Rodriguez 20.00 6.00
6 Chipper Jones 12.00 3.60
7 Kerry Wood 12.00 3.60
8 Mike Piazza 20.00 6.00
9 Mark McGwire 30.00 9.00
10 Tony Gwynn 15.00 4.50

1998 Revolution Prime Time Performers

The 1998 Revolution Prime Time Performers Laser-Cuts set consists of 20 card and is an insert to the 1998 Revolution base set. The cards are randomly inserted in packs at a rate of one in 25. The fronts feature color action photography, a laser-cut logo in the upper left corner and an eye-catching "television" and "Prime Time" television schedule design.

Nm-Mt Ex-Mt
COMPLETE SET (20) 150.00 45.00
1 Cal Ripken 25.00 7.50
2 Nomar Garciaparra 12.00 3.60
3 Frank Thomas 8.00 2.40
4 Jim Thome 8.00 2.40
5 Hideki Irabu 2.00 .60
6 Derek Jeter 20.00 6.00
7 Ben Grieve 2.00 .60
8 Ken Griffey Jr. 12.00 3.60
9 Alex Rodriguez 12.00 3.60
10 Juan Gonzalez 8.00 2.40
11 Ivan Rodriguez 8.00 2.40
12 Travis Lee 2.00 .60
13 Chipper Jones 8.00 2.40
14 Greg Maddux 12.00 3.60
15 Kerry Wood 8.00 2.40
16 Larry Walker 5.00 1.50
17 Jeff Bagwell 5.00 1.50
18 Mike Piazza 12.00 3.60
19 Mark McGwire 20.00 6.00
20 Tony Gwynn 10.00 3.00

1998 Revolution Rookies and Hardball Heroes

This 30 card set was inserted one every six hobby packs. This set features 30 of either the leading players in baseball or some of the most promising young stars.

Nm-Mt Ex-Mt
COMPLETE SET (30) 50.00 15.00
*GOLD 1-20: 6X TO 15X BASIC ROOK/HARDBALL ....
GOLD 1-20 RANDOM INSERTS IN HOBBY PACKS
GOLD 1-20 PRINT RUN 50 SERIAL #'d SETS
1 Justin Baughman 1.00 .30
2 Jarrod Washburn 1.00 .30
3 Travis Lee 1.00 .30
4 Kerry Wood 4.00 1.20
5 Magglio Ordonez 6.00 1.80
6 Todd Helton 2.50 .75
7 Derrek Lee 1.50 .45
8 Richard Hidalgo 1.50 .45
9 Mike Caruso 1.00 .30
10 David Ortiz 1.50 .45
11 Brad Fullmer 1.00 .30
12 Masato Yoshii 1.00 .30
13 Orlando Hernandez 2.50 .75
14 Ricky Ledee 1.50 .45
15 Ben Grieve 1.00 .30
16 Carlton Loewer 1.00 .30
17 Desi Relaford 1.00 .30
18 Ruben Rivera 1.50 .45
19 Rolando Arrojo 1.00 .30
20 Matt Perisho 1.00 .30
21 Chipper Jones 4.00 1.20
22 Greg Maddux 6.00 1.80
23 Cal Ripken 12.00 3.60
24 Nomar Garciaparra 6.00 1.80
25 Frank Thomas 4.00 1.20
26 Mark McGwire 10.00 3.00
27 Tony Gwynn 5.00 1.50
28 Ken Griffey Jr. 6.00 1.80
29 Alex Rodriguez 6.00 1.80
30 Juan Gonzalez 4.00 1.20

1998 Revolution Showstoppers

The 1998 Revolution Showstoppers set consists of 36 cards and is an insert to the 1998 Revolution base set. The cards are randomly inserted in packs at a rate of two in 25. The fronts feature color action photos of 36 of the most exciting stars in the MLB.

Nm-Mt Ex-Mt
COMPLETE SET (36) 200.00 60.00
1 Cal Ripken 20.00 6.00
2 Nomar Garciaparra 10.00 3.00
3 Pedro Martinez 6.00 1.80
4 Mo Vaughn 2.50 .75
5 Frank Thomas 6.00 1.80
6 Manny Ramirez 2.50 .75
7 Jim Thome 6.00 1.80
8 Jaret Wright 1.50 .45
9 Paul Molitor 4.00 1.20
10 Orlando Hernandez 5.00 1.50
11 Derek Jeter 15.00 4.50
12 Bernie Williams 4.00 1.20
13 Ben Grieve 1.50 .45
14 Ken Griffey Jr. 10.00 3.00
15 Alex Rodriguez 10.00 3.00
16 Wade Boggs 4.00 1.20
17 Juan Gonzalez 6.00 1.80
18 Ivan Rodriguez 6.00 1.80
19 Jose Canseco 6.00 1.80
20 Roger Clemens 12.00 3.60
21 Travis Lee 1.50 .45
22 Andres Galarraga 2.50 .75
23 Chipper Jones 6.00 1.80
24 Greg Maddux 10.00 3.00
25 Sammy Sosa 10.00 3.00
26 Kerry Wood 6.00 1.80
27 Vinny Castilla 2.50 .75
28 Larry Walker 4.00 1.20
29 Moises Alou 2.50 .75
30 Raul Mondesi 2.50 .75
31 Gary Sheffield 2.50 .75
32 Hideki Irabu 1.50 .45
33 Mike Piazza 10.00 3.00
34 Mark McGwire 15.00 4.50
35 Tony Gwynn 8.00 2.40
36 Barry Bonds 15.00 4.50

1999 Revolution

The 1999 Revolution set (produced by Pacific) was issued in one series totalling 150 cards and distributed in three-card packs with a suggested retail price of $3.99. The set features color action player photos on dual-foiled, etched and embossed cards. The set contains a short-printed 25-card rookies subset inserted in packs at the rate of one in four. Rookie Cards include Freddy Garcia.

Nm-Mt Ex-Mt
COMPLETE SET (150) 80.00 24.00
COMMON CARD (1-150) .60 .18
COMMON SP 2.00 .60
1 Jim Edmonds 1.00 .30
2 Darin Erstad 1.00 .30
3 Troy Glaus 1.50 .45
4 Tim Salmon 1.50 .45
5 Mo Vaughn 1.00 .30
6 Steve Finley 1.00 .30
7 Luis Gonzalez 1.00 .30
8 Randy Johnson 2.50 .75
9 Travis Lee .60 .18
10 Matt Williams 1.00 .30
11 Andruw Jones 1.00 .30
12 Chipper Jones 2.50 .75
13 Brian Jordan 1.00 .30
14 Javy Lopez 1.00 .30
15 Greg Maddux 4.00 1.20
16 Kevin McGlinchy SP 2.00 .60
17 John Smoltz 1.50 .45
18 Brady Anderson 1.00 .30
19 Albert Belle 1.00 .30
20 Will Clark 2.50 .75
21 Willis Otanez SP 2.00 .60
22 Calvin Pickering SP 2.00 .60
23 Cal Ripken 8.00 2.40
24 Nomar Garciaparra 4.00 1.20
25 Pedro Martinez 2.50 .75
26 Troy O'Leary .60 .18
27 Jose Offerman .60 .18
28 Mark Grace 1.50 .45
29 Mickey Morandini .60 .18
30 Henry Rodriguez .60 .18
31 Sammy Sosa 4.00 1.20
32 Ray Durham 1.00 .30
33 Carlos Lee SP 2.00 .60
34 Jeff Liefer SP 2.00 .60
35 Magglio Ordonez 1.00 .30
36 Frank Thomas 2.50 .75
37 Mike Cameron 1.00 .30
38 Sean Casey 1.00 .30
39 Barry Larkin 2.50 .75
40 Greg Vaughn 1.00 .30
41 Roberto Alomar 2.50 .75
42 Sandy Alomar Jr. .60 .18
43 David Justice 1.00 .30
44 Kenny Lofton 1.00 .30
45 Manny Ramirez 1.00 .30
46 Richie Sexson 1.00 .30
47 Jim Thome 2.50 .75
48 Dante Bichette 1.00 .30
49 Vinny Castilla 1.00 .30
50 Darryl Hamilton .60 .18
51 Todd Helton 1.50 .45
52 Larry Walker 1.50 .45
53 Tony Clark .60 .18
54 Damion Easley .60 .18
55 Bob Higginson 1.00 .30
56 Gabe Kapler SP 2.00 .60
57 Alex Gonzalez SP 2.00 .60
58 Mark Kotsay .60 .18
59 Kevin Orie .60 .18
60 Preston Wilson SP 2.00 .60
61 Jeff Bagwell 1.50 .45
62 Derek Bell .60 .18
63 Craig Biggio 1.50 .45
64 Ken Caminiti 1.00 .30
65 Carlos Beltran SP 2.00 .60
66 Johnny Damon 1.00 .30
67 Jermaine Dye 1.00 .30
68 Carlos Febles SP 2.00 .60
69 Kevin Brown 1.50 .45
70 Todd Hundley .60 .18
71 Eric Karros 1.00 .30
72 Raul Mondesi 1.00 .30
73 Gary Sheffield 1.00 .30
74 Jeromy Burnitz 1.00 .30
75 Jeff Cirillo .60 .18
76 Marquis Grissom .60 .18
77 Fernando Vina 1.00 .30
78 Chad Allen SP RC 2.00 .60
79 Corey Koskie SP 2.00 .60
80 D.Mientkiewicz SP RC 4.00 1.20
81 Brad Radke 1.00 .30
82 Todd Walker 1.00 .30
83 Michael Barrett SP 2.00 .60
84 Vladimir Guerrero 2.50 .75
85 Wilton Guerrero .60 .18
86 Guillermo Mota SP RC 2.00 .60
87 Rondell White 1.00 .30
88 Edgardo Alfonzo 1.00 .30
89 Rickey Henderson 2.50 .75
90 John Olerud 1.00 .30
91 Mike Piazza 4.00 1.20
92 Robin Ventura 1.00 .30
93 Roger Clemens 5.00 1.50
94 Chili Davis 1.00 .30
95 Derek Jeter 6.00 1.80
96 Chuck Knoblauch 1.00 .30
97 Tino Martinez 1.50 .45
98 Paul O'Neill 1.50 .45
99 Bernie Williams 1.50 .45
100 Eric Chavez SP 2.00 .60
101 Jason Giambi 2.50 .75
102 Ben Grieve .60 .18
103 John Jaha .60 .18
104 Olmedo Saenz SP 2.00 .60
105 Bobby Abreu 1.00 .30
106 Doug Glanville .60 .18
107 Desi Relaford .60 .18
108 Scott Rolen 1.50 .45
109 Curt Schilling 1.50 .45
110 Brian Giles 1.00 .30
111 Jason Kendall 1.00 .30
112 Pat Meares .60 .18
113 Kevin Young 1.00 .30
114 J.D. Drew SP 2.00 .60
115 Ray Lankford .60 .18
116 Eli Marrero .60 .18
117 Joe McEwing SP RC 2.00 .60
118 Mark McGwire 6.00 1.80
119 Fernando Tatis .60 .18
120 Tony Gwynn 3.00 .90
121 Trevor Hoffman 1.00 .30
122 Wally Joyner 1.00 .30
123 Reggie Sanders 1.00 .30
124 Barry Bonds 6.00 1.80
125 Ellis Burks 1.00 .30
126 Jeff Kent 1.00 .30
127 Ramon E.Martinez SP RC 2.00 .60
128 Joe Nathan SP RC 2.00 .60
129 Freddy Garcia SP RC 3.00 .90
130 Ken Griffey Jr. 4.00 1.20
131 Brian Hunter .60 .18
132 Edgar Martinez 1.50 .45
133 Alex Rodriguez 4.00 1.20
134 David Segui .60 .18
135 Wade Boggs 1.50 .45
136 Jose Canseco 2.50 .75
137 Quinton McCracken .60 .18
138 Fred McGriff 1.50 .45
139 K.Dransfeldt SP RC 2.00 .60
140 Juan Gonzalez 2.50 .75
141 Rusty Greer 1.00 .30
142 Rafael Palmeiro 1.50 .45
143 Ivan Rodriguez 2.50 .75
144 Lee Stevens .60 .18
145 Jose Cruz Jr. 1.00 .30
146 Carlos Delgado 1.00 .30
147 Shawn Green 1.00 .30
148 Roy Halladay SP 2.00 .60
149 Shannon Stewart 1.00 .30
150 Kevin Witt SP 2.00 .60

1999 Revolution Premiere Date

Randomly inserted in hobby packs only at the rate of one in 25, this 150-card set is parallel to the base set. Only 49 serial-numbered sets were produced.

Nm-Mt Ex-Mt
*STARS: 5X TO 12X BASIC CARDS ....
*SP'S: 2X TO 5X BASIC SP'S
*SP RC'S: 2X TO 5X BASIC SP RC'S ..

1999 Revolution Red

Randomly inserted in retail packs only, this 150-card set is a red foil parallel version of the base set. Only 299 serial-numbered sets were produced.

Nm-Mt Ex-Mt
*STARS: 2X TO 5X BASIC CARDS ......
*SP'S: .75X TO 2X BASIC SP'S ....
*SP RC'S: .6X TO 1.5X BASIC SP RC'S

1999 Revolution Shadow Series

Randomly inserted in hobby packs only, this 150-card set is a gold foil parallel version of the base set. Only 99 serial-numbered sets were produced.

Nm-Mt Ex-Mt
*STARS: 4X TO 10X BASIC CARDS ....
*SP'S: 1.5X TO 4X BASIC SP'S ....
*SP RC'S: 1.25X TO 3X BASIC SP RC'S

1999 Revolution Diamond Legacy

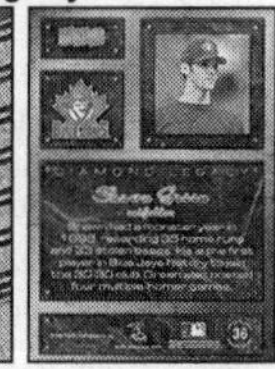

Randomly inserted in packs at the rate of two in 25, this 36-card set features color action photos of some of the league's elite players printed on cards with a new holographic patterned foil design.

Nm-Mt Ex-Mt
COMPLETE SET (36) 250.00 75.00
1 Troy Glaus 4.00 1.20
2 Mo Vaughn 2.50 .75
3 Matt Williams 2.50 .75
4 Chipper Jones 6.00 1.80
5 Andruw Jones 2.50 .75
6 Greg Maddux 10.00 3.00
7 Albert Belle 2.50 .75
8 Cal Ripken 20.00 6.00
9 Nomar Garciaparra 10.00 3.00
10 Sammy Sosa 10.00 3.00
11 Frank Thomas 6.00 1.80
12 Manny Ramirez 2.50 .75

13 Todd Helton	4.00	1.20
14 Larry Walker	4.00	1.20
15 Gabe Kapler	2.00	.60
16 Jeff Bagwell	4.00	1.20
17 Craig Biggio	4.00	1.20
18 Raul Mondesi	2.50	.75
19 Vladimir Guerrero	6.00	1.80
20 Mike Piazza	10.00	3.00
21 Roger Clemens	12.00	3.60
22 Derek Jeter	15.00	4.50
23 Bernie Williams	4.00	1.20
24 Ben Grieve	1.50	.45
25 Scott Rolen	4.00	1.20
26 J.D. Drew	2.00	.60
27 Mark McGwire	15.00	4.50
28 Fernando Tatis	1.50	.45
29 Tony Gwynn	8.00	2.40
30 Barry Bonds	15.00	4.50
31 Ken Griffey Jr.	10.00	3.00
32 Alex Rodriguez	10.00	3.00
33 Jose Canseco	6.00	1.80
34 Juan Gonzalez	6.00	1.80
35 Ivan Rodriguez	6.00	1.80
36 Shawn Green	2.50	.75

1999 Revolution Foul Pole

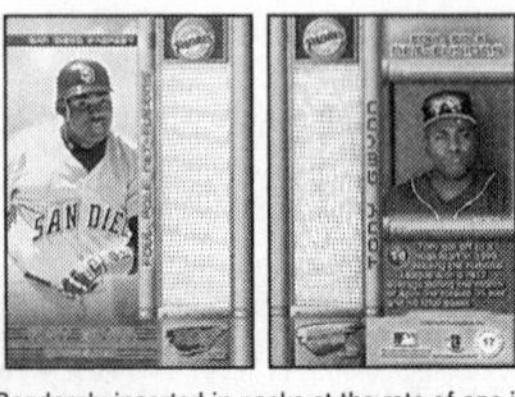

Randomly inserted in packs at the rate of one in 49, this 20-card set features color photos of MLB hitting stars printed on partially foiled cards with an all-new net-fusion technology using actual netting.

	Nm-Mt	Ex-Mt
COMPLETE SET (20)	400.00	120.00
1 Chipper Jones	15.00	4.50
2 Andruw Jones	6.00	1.80
3 Cal Ripken	50.00	15.00
4 Nomar Garciaparra	25.00	7.50
5 Sammy Sosa	25.00	7.50
6 Frank Thomas	15.00	4.50
7 Manny Ramirez	6.00	1.80
8 Jeff Bagwell	10.00	3.00
9 Raul Mondesi	6.00	1.80
10 Vladimir Guerrero	15.00	4.50
11 Mike Piazza	25.00	7.50
12 Derek Jeter	40.00	12.00
13 Bernie Williams	10.00	3.00
14 Scott Rolen	10.00	3.00
15 J.D. Drew	5.00	1.50
16 Mark McGwire	40.00	12.00
17 Tony Gwynn	20.00	6.00
18 Ken Griffey Jr.	25.00	7.50
19 Alex Rodriguez	25.00	7.50
20 Juan Gonzalez	15.00	4.50

1999 Revolution MLB Icons

Randomly inserted in packs at the rate of one in 121, this 10-card set features color action photos of some of the hottest players printed on fully silver foiled and etched cards die-cut in the shape of a shield of honor.

	Nm-Mt	Ex-Mt
COMPLETE SET (10)	500.00	150.00
1 Cal Ripken	80.00	24.00
2 Nomar Garciaparra	40.00	12.00
3 Sammy Sosa	40.00	12.00
4 Frank Thomas	25.00	7.50
5 Mike Piazza	40.00	12.00
6 Derek Jeter	60.00	18.00
7 Mark McGwire	60.00	18.00
8 Tony Gwynn	30.00	9.00
9 Ken Griffey Jr.	40.00	12.00
10 Alex Rodriguez	40.00	12.00

1999 Revolution Thorn in the Side

Randomly inserted in packs at the rate of one in 25, this 20-card set features color action player photos printed on full holographic silver foil die-cut cards.

	Nm-Mt	Ex-Mt
COMPLETE SET (20)	200.00	60.00
1 Mo Vaughn	3.00	.90
2 Chipper Jones	8.00	2.40
3 Greg Maddux	12.00	3.60
4 Cal Ripken	25.00	7.50
5 Nomar Garciaparra	12.00	3.60
6 Sammy Sosa	12.00	3.60
7 Frank Thomas	8.00	2.40
8 Manny Ramirez	3.00	.90
9 Jeff Bagwell	5.00	1.50
10 Mike Piazza	12.00	3.60
11 Derek Jeter	20.00	6.00
12 Bernie Williams	5.00	1.50
13 J.D. Drew	2.50	.75
14 Mark McGwire	20.00	6.00
15 Tony Gwynn	10.00	3.00
16 Barry Bonds	20.00	6.00
17 Ken Griffey Jr.	12.00	3.60
18 Alex Rodriguez	12.00	3.60
19 Juan Gonzalez	8.00	2.40
20 Ivan Rodriguez	8.00	2.40

1999 Revolution Tripleheader

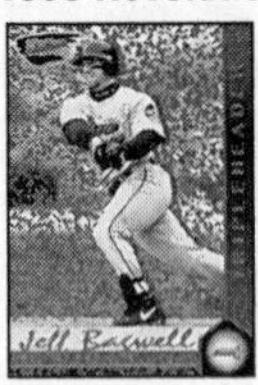

Randomly inserted in hobby packs only at the rate of four in 25, this 30-card set features color photos of top stars and rookies printed on cards with a gold foil design. A three tier serial-numbered parallel silver foil set was also produced. Only 99 serial-numbered sets of Tier 1 which consists of cards 1-10 was produced; 199 serial-numbered Tier 2 sets were produced which consists of cards 11-20; and 299 serial-numbered Tier 3 sets, which consist of cards 21-30, were also produced.

	Nm-Mt	Ex-Mt
COMPLETE SET (30)	120.00	36.00
*TIER 1 (1-10): 3X TO 8X BASIC TRIPLEHEADER		
TIER 1 PRINT RUN 99 SERIAL #'d SETS		
*TIER 2 (11-20): 2X TO 5X BASIC TRIPLEHEADER		
*TIER 2 DREW: 1X TO 2.5X BASE SP HI		
TIER 2 PRINT RUN 199 SERIAL #'d SETS		
*TIER 3: 1.25X TO 3X BASIC TRIPLEHEADER		
TIER 3 PRINT RUN 299 SERIAL #'d SETS		
TIER CARDS RANDOM IN HOBBY PACKS		
1 Greg Maddux	5.00	1.50
2 Cal Ripken	10.00	3.00
3 Nomar Garciaparra	5.00	1.50
4 Sammy Sosa	5.00	1.50
5 Frank Thomas	3.00	.90
6 Mike Piazza	5.00	1.50
7 Mark McGwire	8.00	2.40
8 Tony Gwynn	4.00	1.20
9 Ken Griffey Jr.	5.00	1.50
10 Alex Rodriguez	5.00	1.50
11 Mo Vaughn	1.25	.35
12 Chipper Jones	3.00	.90
13 Manny Ramirez	1.25	.35
14 Larry Walker	2.00	.60
15 Jeff Bagwell	2.00	.60
16 Vladimir Guerrero	3.00	.90
17 Derek Jeter	8.00	2.40
18 J.D. Drew	1.00	.30
19 Barry Bonds	8.00	2.40
20 Juan Gonzalez	3.00	.90
21 Troy Glaus	2.00	.60
22 Andruw Jones	1.25	.35
23 Matt Williams	1.25	.35
24 Craig Biggio	2.00	.60
25 Raul Mondesi	1.25	.35
26 Roger Clemens	6.00	1.80
27 Bernie Williams	2.00	.60
28 Scott Rolen	2.00	.60
29 Jose Canseco	3.00	.90
30 Ivan Rodriguez	3.00	.90

2000 Revolution

The 2000 Revolution product (produced by Pacific) was released in July, 2000. The product featured a 150-card base set with short-printed prospects (1:4). Each pack contained three cards and carried a suggested retail price of $3.99.

	Nm-Mt	Ex-Mt
COMPLETE SET (150)	100.00	30.00
COMMON CARD (1-150)	1.00	.30
COMMON SP	3.00	.90
1 Darin Erstad	1.00	.30
2 Troy Glaus	1.50	.45
3 Adam Kennedy SP	3.00	.90
4 Mo Vaughn	1.00	.30
5 Erubiel Durazo	1.00	.30
6 Steve Finley	1.00	.30
7 Luis Gonzalez	1.00	.30
8 Randy Johnson	2.50	.75
9 Travis Lee	1.00	.30
10 Vicente Padilla SP RC	5.00	1.50
11 Matt Williams	1.00	.30
12 Rafael Furcal SP	3.00	.90
13 Andres Galarraga	1.00	.30
14 Andruw Jones	1.00	.30
15 Chipper Jones	2.50	.75
16 Greg Maddux	4.00	1.20
17 Luis Rivera SP RC	3.00	.90
18 Albert Belle	1.00	.30
19 Mike Bordick	1.00	.30
20 Will Clark	2.50	.75
21 Mike Mussina	2.50	.75
22 Cal Ripken	8.00	2.40
23 B.J. Surhoff	1.00	.30
24 Carl Everett	1.00	.30
25 Nomar Garciaparra	4.00	1.20
26 Pedro Martinez	2.50	.75
27 Jason Varitek	1.00	.30
28 Wilton Veras SP	3.00	.90
29 Shane Andrews	1.00	.30
30 Scott Downs SP RC	3.00	.90
31 Mark Grace	1.50	.45
32 Sammy Sosa	4.00	1.20
33 Kerry Wood	2.50	.75
34 Ray Durham	1.00	.30
35 Paul Konerko	1.00	.30
36 Carlos Lee	1.00	.30
37 Magglio Ordonez	1.00	.30
38 Frank Thomas	2.50	.75
39 Rob Bell SP	3.00	.90
40 Sean Casey	1.00	.30
41 Ken Griffey Jr.	4.00	1.20
42 Barry Larkin	2.50	.75
43 Pokey Reese	1.00	.30
44 Roberto Alomar	2.50	.75
45 David Justice	1.00	.30
46 Kenny Lofton	1.00	.30
47 Manny Ramirez	1.00	.30
48 Richie Sexson	1.00	.30
49 Jim Thome	2.50	.75
50 Jeff Cirillo	1.00	.30
51 Jeffrey Hammonds	1.00	.30
52 Todd Helton	1.50	.45
53 Larry Walker	1.50	.45
54 Tony Clark	1.00	.30
55 Juan Gonzalez	2.50	.75
56 Hideo Nomo	2.50	.75
57 Dean Palmer	1.00	.30
58 Alex Gonzalez	1.00	.30
59 Mike Lowell	1.00	.30
60 Pablo Ozuna SP	3.00	.90
61 Brad Penny SP	3.00	.90
62 Preston Wilson	1.00	.30
63 Moises Alou	1.00	.30
64 Jeff Bagwell	1.50	.45
65 Craig Biggio	1.50	.45
66 Ken Caminiti	1.00	.30
67 Julio Lugo SP	3.00	.90
68 Carlos Beltran	1.00	.30
69 Johnny Damon UER Carlos Beltran pictured on front	1.00	.30
70 Jermaine Dye	1.00	.30
71 Carlos Febles	1.00	.30
72 Mark Quinn SP	3.00	.90
73 Kevin Brown	1.00	.30
74 Shawn Green	1.00	.30
75 Chan Ho Park	1.00	.30
76 Gary Sheffield	1.00	.30
77 Kevin Barker SP	3.00	.90
78 Ron Belliard	1.00	.30
79 Jeromy Burnitz	1.00	.30
80 Geoff Jenkins	1.00	.30
81 Cristian Guzman	1.00	.30
82 Jacque Jones	1.00	.30
83 Corey Koskie	1.00	.30
84 Matt Lawton	1.00	.30
85 Peter Bergeron SP	3.00	.90
86 Vladimir Guerrero	2.50	.75
87 Andy Tracy SP RC	3.00	.90
88 Jose Vidro	1.00	.30
89 Rondell White	1.00	.30
90 Edgardo Alfonzo	1.00	.30
91 Derek Bell	1.00	.30
92 Eric Cammack SP RC	3.00	.90
93 Mike Piazza	4.00	1.20
94 Robin Ventura	1.00	.30
95 Roger Clemens	5.00	1.50
96 Orlando Hernandez	1.00	.30
97 Derek Jeter	6.00	1.80
98 Tino Martinez	1.50	.45
99 Alfonso Soriano SP	5.00	1.50
100 Bernie Williams	1.50	.45
101 Eric Chavez	1.00	.30
102 Jason Giambi	2.50	.75
103 Ben Grieve	1.00	.30
104 Terrence Long SP	3.00	.90
105 Mark Mulder SP	5.00	1.50
106 Adam Piatt SP	3.00	.90
107 Bobby Abreu	1.00	.30
108 Pat Burrell SP	5.00	1.50
109 Rico Brogna	1.00	.30
110 Doug Glanville	1.00	.30
111 Mike Lieberthal	1.00	.30
112 Scott Rolen	1.50	.45
113 Brian Giles	1.00	.30
114 Jason Kendall	1.00	.30
115 Warren Morris	1.00	.30
116 Rick Ankiel SP	3.00	.90
117 J.D. Drew	1.00	.30
118 Jim Edmonds	1.00	.30
119 Mark McGwire	6.00	1.80
120 Fernando Tatis	1.00	.30
121 Fernando Vina	1.00	.30
122 Tony Gwynn	3.00	.90
123 Trevor Hoffman	1.00	.30
124 Ryan Klesko	1.00	.30
125 Eric Owens	1.00	.30
126 Barry Bonds	6.00	1.80
127 Ellis Burks	1.00	.30
128 Bobby Estalella	1.00	.30
129 Jeff Kent	1.00	.30
130 Scott Linebrink SP RC	3.00	.90
131 Jay Buhner	1.00	.30
132 Stan Javier	1.00	.30
133 Edgar Martinez	1.50	.45
134 John Olerud	1.00	.30
135 Alex Rodriguez	4.00	1.20
136 K.Sasaki SP RC	5.00	1.50
137 Jose Canseco	2.50	.75
138 Vinny Castilla	1.00	.30
139 Fred McGriff	1.50	.45
140 Greg Vaughn	1.00	.30
141 Gabe Kapler	1.00	.30
142 Mike Lamb SP RC	3.00	.90
143 Ruben Mateo SP	3.00	.90
144 Rafael Palmeiro	1.50	.45
145 Ivan Rodriguez	2.50	.75
146 Tony Batista	1.00	.30
147 Jose Cruz Jr.	1.00	.30
148 Carlos Delgado	1.00	.30
149 Brad Fullmer	1.00	.30
150 Raul Mondesi	1.00	.30

2000 Revolution Premiere Date

Randomly inserted in hobby packs at one in 25 packs, this 150-card set is a parallel version of the base set. Only 99 serial-numbered sets were produced.

	Nm-Mt	Ex-Mt
*STARS: 3X TO 8X BASIC CARDS		
*SP's: 1X TO 2.5X BASIC SP's		
*RC SP's: 3X TO 8X BASIC RC SP's		

2000 Revolution Red

Randomly inserted in retail packs only, this 150-card set is a red foil parallel version of the base set. Only 63 serial-numbered sets were produced.

	Nm-Mt	Ex-Mt
*STARS: 4X TO 10X BASIC CARDS		
*SP's: 1.25X TO 3X BASIC SP's		
*SP RC's: 5X TO 12X BASIC RC SP's		

2000 Revolution Shadow Series

Randomly inserted in hobby packs at one in 25, this 150-card set is a parallel version of the base set. Only 99 serial-numbered sets were produced.

	Nm-Mt	Ex-Mt
*STARS: 3X TO 8X BASIC CARDS		
*SP's: 1X TO 2.5X BASIC SP's		
*RC SP's: 3X TO 8X BASIC RC SP's		

2000 Revolution Foul Pole

Inserted one every 49 packs, these 20 cards feature players who hit the longball. These cards feature a swatch of netting.

	Nm-Mt	Ex-Mt
COMPLETE SET (20)	400.00	120.00
1 Chipper Jones	12.00	3.60
2 Cal Ripken	40.00	12.00
3 Nomar Garciaparra	20.00	6.00
4 Pedro Martinez	12.00	3.60
5 Sammy Sosa	20.00	6.00
6 Frank Thomas	12.00	3.60
7 Ken Griffey Jr.	20.00	6.00
8 Manny Ramirez	5.00	1.50
9 Jeff Bagwell	8.00	2.40
10 Shawn Green	5.00	1.50
11 Vladimir Guerrero	12.00	3.60
12 Mike Piazza	20.00	6.00
13 Derek Jeter	30.00	9.00
14 Pat Burrell	25.00	7.50
15 Rick Ankiel	15.00	4.50
16 Mark McGwire	30.00	9.00
17 Tony Gwynn	15.00	4.50
18 Barry Bonds	30.00	9.00
19 Alex Rodriguez	20.00	6.00
20 Ivan Rodriguez	12.00	3.60

2000 Revolution MLB Game Ball Signatures

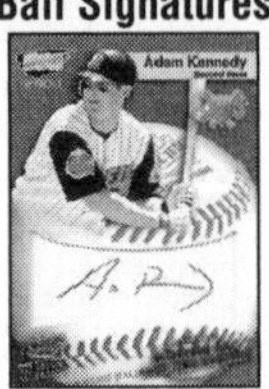

Randomly inserted into packs, these 25 cards feature MLB player's autographs on actual swatches of baseball. A couple of players are not priced due to lack of market information.

	Nm-Mt	Ex-Mt
1 Randy Johnson	80.00	24.00
2 Greg Maddux	100.00	30.00
3 Rafael Furcal	15.00	4.50
4 Shane Andrews	10.00	3.00
5 Sean Casey	15.00	4.50
6 Travis Dawkins	10.00	3.00
7 Alex Gonzalez	10.00	3.00
8 Shane Reynolds	10.00	3.00
9 Eric Gagne	40.00	12.00
10 Kevin Barker	10.00	3.00
11 Eric Milton	10.00	3.00
12 Mark Quinn	10.00	3.00
13 Alfonso Soriano	40.00	12.00
14 Brian Giles	15.00	4.50
15 Mark Mulder	25.00	7.50
16 Adam Piatt	10.00	3.00
17 Warren Morris	10.00	3.00
18 Rick Ankiel	10.00	3.00
19 Adam Kennedy	15.00	4.50
20 Fernando Tatis	10.00	3.00
21 Barry Bonds	175.00	52.50
22 Alex Rodriguez	100.00	30.00
23 Ruben Mateo	10.00	3.00
24 Billy Koch	15.00	4.50
25 Brad Penny	15.00	4.50

2000 Revolution MLB Icons

Inserted one every 121 packs, these 20 cards feature players that are looked upon as icons of their community.

	Nm-Mt	Ex-Mt
COMPLETE SET (20)	500.00	150.00
1 Randy Johnson	15.00	4.50
2 Chipper Jones	15.00	4.50
3 Greg Maddux	25.00	7.50
4 Cal Ripken	50.00	15.00
5 Nomar Garciaparra	25.00	7.50
6 Pedro Martinez	15.00	4.50
7 Sammy Sosa	25.00	7.50
8 Frank Thomas	15.00	4.50
9 Ken Griffey Jr.	25.00	7.50
10 Juan Gonzalez	15.00	4.50
11 Jeff Bagwell	10.00	3.00
12 Vladimir Guerrero	15.00	4.50
13 Mike Piazza	25.00	7.50
14 Roger Clemens	30.00	9.00
15 Derek Jeter	40.00	12.00
16 Mark McGwire	40.00	12.00
17 Tony Gwynn	20.00	6.00
18 Barry Bonds	40.00	12.00
19 Alex Rodriguez	25.00	7.50
20 Ivan Rodriguez	15.00	4.50

2000 Revolution On Deck

Inserted one in every 25 packs, these 20 cards feature players who strike fear into the hearts of pitchers that see them on deck.

	Nm-Mt	Ex-Mt
COMPLETE SET (20)	200.00	60.00
1 Chipper Jones	8.00	2.40
2 Cal Ripken	25.00	7.50
3 Nomar Garciaparra	12.00	3.60
4 Sammy Sosa	12.00	3.60
5 Frank Thomas	8.00	2.40
6 Ken Griffey Jr.	12.00	3.60
7 Manny Ramirez	3.00	.90
8 Larry Walker	5.00	1.50
9 Juan Gonzalez	8.00	2.40
10 Jeff Bagwell	5.00	1.50
11 Shawn Green	3.00	.90
12 Vladimir Guerrero	8.00	2.40
13 Mike Piazza	12.00	3.60
14 Derek Jeter	20.00	6.00
15 Scott Rolen	5.00	1.50
16 Mark McGwire	20.00	6.00
17 Tony Gwynn	10.00	3.00
18 Alex Rodriguez	12.00	3.60
19 Jose Canseco	8.00	2.40
20 Ivan Rodriguez	8.00	2.40

2000 Revolution Season Opener

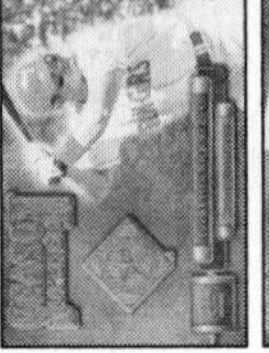
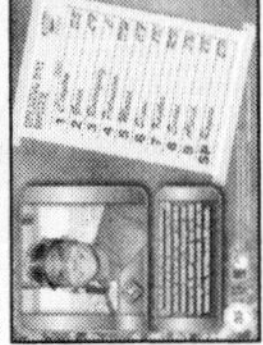

Inserted two in every 25 packs, these 36 cards feature players who will be starting come opening day.

	Nm-Mt	Ex-Mt
COMPLETE SET (36)	200.00	60.00
1 Erubiel Durazo	2.50	.75
2 Randy Johnson	6.00	1.80
3 Andruw Jones	2.50	.75
4 Chipper Jones	6.00	1.80
5 Greg Maddux	10.00	3.00
6 Cal Ripken	20.00	6.00
7 Nomar Garciaparra	10.00	3.00
8 Pedro Martinez	6.00	1.80
9 Sammy Sosa	10.00	3.00
10 Frank Thomas	6.00	1.80
11 Magglio Ordonez	2.50	.75
12 Ken Griffey Jr.	10.00	3.00
13 Barry Larkin	6.00	1.80
14 Kenny Lofton	2.50	.75
15 Manny Ramirez	2.50	.75
16 Jim Thome	6.00	1.80
17 Larry Walker	4.00	1.20
18 Juan Gonzalez	6.00	1.80
19 Jeff Bagwell	4.00	1.20
20 Craig Biggio	4.00	1.20
21 Carlos Beltran	2.50	.75
22 Shawn Green	2.50	.75
23 Vladimir Guerrero	6.00	1.80
24 Mike Piazza	10.00	3.00
25 Orlando Hernandez	2.50	.75
26 Derek Jeter	15.00	4.50
27 Bernie Williams	4.00	1.20
28 Eric Chavez	2.50	.75
29 Scott Rolen	4.00	1.20
30 Jim Edmonds	2.50	.75
31 Tony Gwynn	8.00	2.40
32 Barry Bonds	15.00	4.50
33 Alex Rodriguez	10.00	3.00
34 Jose Canseco	6.00	1.80
35 Ivan Rodriguez	6.00	1.80
36 Rafael Palmeiro	4.00	1.20

2000 Revolution Triple Header

Inserted four in every 25 packs, these 30 cards feature players that lead the league in just about every statistical category.

	Nm-Mt	Ex-Mt
COMPLETE SET (30)	80.00	24.00
1 Chipper Jones	5.00	1.50
2 Cal Ripken	8.00	2.40
3 Nomar Garciaparra	6.00	1.80
4 Frank Thomas	4.00	1.20
5 Larry Walker	1.00	.30
6 Vladimir Guerrero	3.00	.90
7 Mike Piazza	6.00	1.80
8 Derek Jeter	8.00	2.40
9 Tony Gwynn	4.00	1.20
10 Ivan Rodriguez	2.50	.75
11 Sammy Sosa	4.00	1.20
12 Ken Griffey Jr.	8.00	2.40
13 Manny Ramirez	2.50	.75
14 Jeff Bagwell	2.50	.75
15 Shawn Green	2.00	.60
16 Mark McGwire	8.00	2.40
17 Barry Bonds	2.50	.75
18 Alex Rodriguez	6.00	1.80
19 Jose Canseco	2.50	.75
20 Rafael Palmeiro	2.00	.60
21 Randy Johnson	2.50	.75
22 Tom Glavine	2.00	.60
23 Greg Maddux	5.00	1.50
24 Mike Mussina	2.00	.60
25 Pedro Martinez	2.50	.75
26 Kerry Wood	1.00	.30
27 Chuck Finley	1.00	.30
28 Kevin Brown	1.25	.35
29 Roger Clemens	4.00	1.20
30 Rick Ankiel	3.00	.90

2000 Revolution Triple Header Holographic Gold

Randomly inserted into packs, this 30-card insert is a complete parallel of the Triple Header insert. Please note that these cards are stamped with gold foil, and that cards (1-10) are serial numbered to 99, cards (11-20) are serial numbered to 99, and cards (21-30) are serial numbered to 599.

Nm-Mt Ex-Mt
*BTG.AVG. 1-10: 3X TO 8X BASIC TRIPLE HDR
*HR'S 11-20: 3X TO 8X BASIC TRIPLE HDR
*K'S 21-30: 1.25X TO 3X BASIC TRIPLE HDR

2000 Revolution Triple Header Holographic Silver

Randomly inserted into packs, this 10-card insert is a partial parallel of the Triple Header insert. Please note that these cards are stamped with silver foil, and that cards (21-30) are serial numbered to 299.

Nm-Mt Ex-Mt
*K'S 21-30: 1.5X TO 4X BASIC TRIPLE HDR

2000 Revolution Triple Header Platinum Blue

Randomly inserted into packs, this 30-card insert is a complete parallel of the Triple Header insert. Please note that these cards are stamped with platinum blue foil, and that cards (1-10) are serial numbered to 359, cards (11-20) are serial numbered to 199, and cards (21-30) are serial numbered to 799.

Nm-Mt Ex-Mt
*BTG.AVG. 1-10: 1.5X TO 4X BASIC TRIPLE
*HR'S 11-20: 2.5X TO 6X BASIC TRIPLE HDR
*K'S 21-30: .75X TO 2X BASIC TRIPLE HDR

2000 Revolution Triple Header Silver

Randomly inserted into packs, this 30-card insert is a complete parallel of the Triple Header insert. Please note that these cards are stamped with silver foil, and that cards (1-10) are serial numbered to 899, cards (11-20) are serial numbered to 399, and cards (21-30) are serial numbered to 999.

Nm-Mt Ex-Mt
*BTG.AVG. 1-10: .75X TO 2X BASIC TRIPLE
*HR'S 11-20: 1.5X TO 4X BASIC TRIPLE HDR
*K'S 21-30: .75X TO 2X BASIC TRIPLE HDR

1992-93 Revolutionary Legends 1

Revolutionary Comics released this Series one card set and inserted three cards within each issue of Baseball Legends magazine. The individual cards measure approximately 2 1/2" by 3 5/8" but are combined on one strip and stapled to the center of the magazine. The strip measures 10 1/2" by 2 1/2". These are unauthorized cards according to Revolutionary Comics. The fronts display graphic illustrations by Scott Penzer on a red and black background within an irregular yellow and black border. The black and white backs carry biography, career highlights and career summary.

	Nm-Mt	Ex-Mt
COMPLETE SET (15)	10.00	3.00
1 Willie Mays	1.00	.30
2 Willie Mays	1.00	.30
3 Willie Mays	1.00	.30
4 Honus Wagner	.75	.23
5 Honus Wagner	.75	.23
6 Honus Wagner	.75	.23
7 Roberto Clemente	1.50	.45
8 Roberto Clemente	1.50	.45
9 Roberto Clemente	1.50	.45
10 Yogi Berra	.75	.23
11 Yogi Berra	.75	.23
12 Yogi Berra	.75	.23
13 Billy Martin	.50	.15
14 Billy Martin	.50	.15
15 Billy Martin	.50	.15

1992-93 Revolutionary Superstars 1

1992-93 Baseball Superstars Series one was issued by Revolutionary Comics. The cards were inserted in the magazine Baseball Superstars. The cards measure approximately 2 1/2" by 3 5/8" individually and the strip of three measures 10 1/2" by 2 1/2". The graphic illustrations of these superstar players was by Scott Penzer. The fronts display a black background with black and white mottled corner design. The white backs have black print and include biography, career highlights and career summary.

	Nm-Mt	Ex-Mt
COMPLETE SET (15)	12.00	3.60
1 Darryl Strawberry	.50	.15
2 Darryl Strawberry	.50	.15
3 Darryl Strawberry	.50	.15
4 Frank Thomas	2.00	.60
5 Frank Thomas	2.00	.60
6 Frank Thomas	2.00	.60
7 Ryne Sandberg	1.00	.30
8 Ryne Sandberg	1.00	.30
9 Ryne Sandberg	1.00	.30
10 Kirby Puckett	1.00	.30
11 Kirby Puckett	1.00	.30
12 Kirby Puckett	1.00	.30
13 Roberto Alomar Sandy Alomar	.75	.23
14 Roberto Alomar Sandy Alomar	.75	.23
15 Roberto Alomar Sandy Alomar	.75	.23

1997 Bobby Richardson

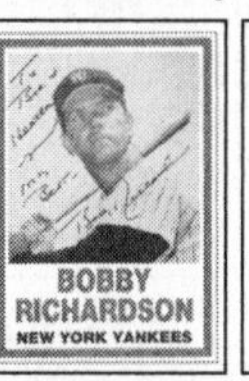

This one card standard-size set was given out by Bobby Richardson, former star second baseman for the New York Yankees, as a promotional card he handed out to fans.

	Nm-Mt	Ex-Mt
1 Bobby Richardson	1.00	.30

1989 Rini Postcards Gehrig

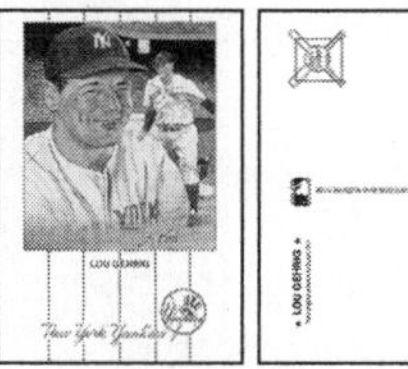

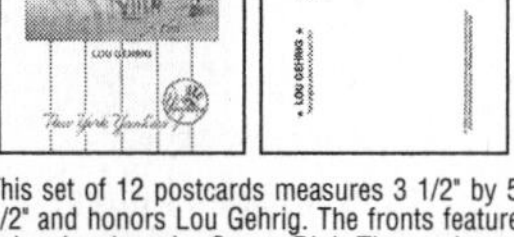

This set of 12 postcards measures 3 1/2" by 5 1/2" and honors Lou Gehrig. The fronts feature color drawings by Susan Rini. The cards are numbered on the back.

	Nm-Mt	Ex-Mt
COMPLETE SET (10)	5.00	2.00
COMMON CARD (1-10)	.50	.20
4 Lou Gehrig Babe Ruth Sitting Together	1.00	.40

1989 Rini Postcards Mattingly 1

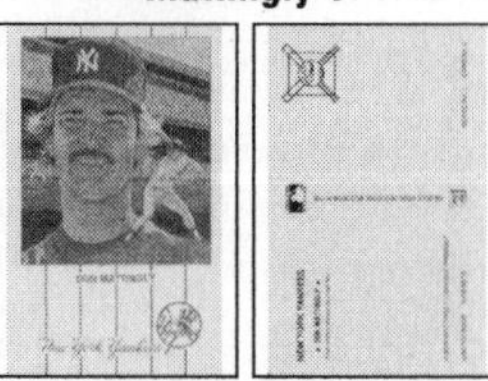

This set of 12 postcards measures 3 1/2" by 5 1/2" and honors Don Mattingly. The fronts feature color drawings by Susan Rini.

	Nm-Mt	Ex-Mt
COMPLETE SET (12)	5.00	2.00
COMMON CARD (1-12)	.50	.20

1990 Rini Postcards Clemente

This 12-card set measures approximately 3 1/2" by 5 1/2" and honors Roberto Clemente. The

fronts of the postcards feature the artwork of Susan Rini while the back notes that the set is limited to 5,000 copies of each postcard made.

	Nm-Mt	Ex-Mt
COMPLETE SET (12)	5.00	1.50
COMMON CARD (1-12)	.50	.15

1990 Rini Postcards Munson

This set of 12 postcards measures 3 1/2" by 5 1/2" and honors Thurman Munson. The fronts feature color drawings by Susan Rini.

	Nm-Mt	Ex-Mt
COMPLETE SET (12)	5.00	1.50
COMMON CARD (1-12)	.50	.15

1990 Rini Postcards Ryan 1

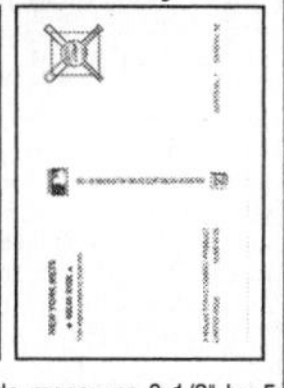

This set of 12 postcards measures 3 1/2" by 5 1/2" and honors Nolan Ryan. On a light blue background, the fronts feature color drawings by Susan Rini.

	Nm-Mt	Ex-Mt
COMPLETE SET (12)	5.00	1.50
COMMON CARD (1-12)	.50	.15

1990 Rini Postcards Ryan 2

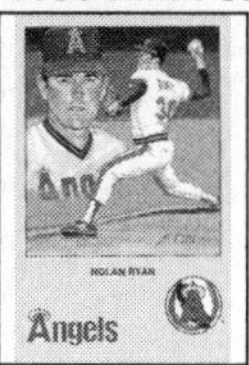

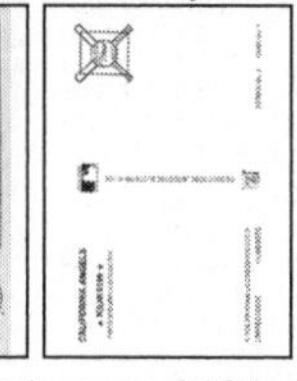

This set of 12 postcards measures 3 1/2" by 5 1/2" and honors Nolan Ryan. On a peach colored background, the fronts feature color drawings by Susan Rini.

	Nm-Mt	Ex-Mt
COMPLETE SET (12)	5.00	1.50
COMMON CARD (1-12)	.50	.15

1991 Rini Postcards Mattingly 2

This set of 12 postcards measures approximately 3 1/2" by 5 1/2" and honors Don Mattingly. On a white background with blue stripes, the fronts feature color drawings by Susan Rini. The backs carry a postcard format.

	Nm-Mt	Ex-Mt
COMPLETE SET (12)	5.00	1.50
COMMON CARD (1-12)	.50	.15

2001 Ripken Essay

This one card standard-size set was issued to all people who responded and entered a contest through www.dadsdayessay.com with the grand prize of a day with Cal Ripken Jr. The brown-bordered front has an action photo of Ripken with his name on the bottom and the "Cal Ripken Baseball" logo in the upper left. The back has biographical information, a photo, career stats and explanation about the contest. The card also was sponsored by "The Sports Authority" and "US Airways".

	Nm-Mt	Ex-Mt
1 Cal Ripken Jr	2.00	.60

1933 Rittenhouse Candy E285

These cards measure 2 1/4" by 1 7/16" and are found in three colors: red, green or blue. The fronts feature a player photo in the middle surrounded by the suits symbol. The backs either feature one alphabetical character from the words "Rittnehouse Candy Co" or a description of the premium offers. We have sequenced the set in playing order by suit and numbers are assigned to Aces (1), Jacks (11A), Queens (12) and Kings (13).

	Ex-Mt	VG
COMPLETE SET (52)	3750.00	1900.00
1C Doc Cramer	40.00	20.00
1D Babe Herman	80.00	40.00
1H Mule Haas	40.00	20.00
1S Babe Ruth	400.00	200.00
2C Bing Miller	40.00	20.00
2D Chick Hafey	80.00	40.00
2H Gus Mancuso	40.00	20.00
2S Billy Herman	80.00	40.00
3C Lefty O'Doul	80.00	40.00
3D Chuck Klein	80.00	40.00
3H George Earnshaw	50.00	25.00
3S Frankie Frisch	120.00	60.00
4C Mel Ott	120.00	60.00
4D Fred Brickell	40.00	20.00
4H Leroy Mahaffey	40.00	20.00
4S Dick Bartell	40.00	20.00
5C Kiki Cuyler	80.00	40.00
5D George Davis	40.00	20.00
5H Jimmy Dykes	50.00	25.00
5S Paul Waner	80.00	40.00
6C Hugh Critz	40.00	20.00
6D Paul Waner	80.00	40.00
6H Rogers Hornsby	150.00	75.00
6S Don Hurst	40.00	20.00
7C Walter Berger	50.00	25.00
7D Sugar Cain	40.00	20.00
7H Joe Cronin	80.00	40.00
7S Frankie Frisch	80.00	40.00
8C Dib Williams	40.00	20.00
8D Lefty Grove	120.00	60.00
8H Lou Finney	40.00	20.00
8S Ed. Cihocki	40.00	20.00
9C Hack Wilson	80.00	40.00
9D Al Simmons	80.00	40.00
9H Spud Davis	40.00	20.00
9S Hack Wilson	80.00	40.00
10C Pie Traynor	80.00	40.00
10D Bill Terry	80.00	40.00
10H Lloyd Waner	80.00	40.00
10S Jimmy Foxx	120.00	60.00
11C Jumbo Elliott	40.00	20.00
11D Don Hurst	40.00	20.00
11H Pinky Higgins	40.00	20.00
11S Jim Bottomley	80.00	40.00
12C Pinky Whitney	40.00	20.00
12D Lloyd Waner	80.00	40.00
12H Eric McNair	40.00	20.00
12S Rube Walberg	40.00	20.00
13C Babe Ruth	400.00	200.00
13D Phil Collins	40.00	20.00
13H Gabby Hartnett	80.00	40.00
13S Max Bishop	40.00	20.00

1955 Robert Gould W605

The cards in this 28-card set measure 2 1/2" by 3 1/2". The 1955 Robert F. Gould set of black and white on green cards were toy store cardboard holders for small plastic statues. The statues were attached to the card by a rubber band through two holes on the side of the card. The catalog designation is W605. The cards are numbered in the bottom right corner of the obverse and are blank-backed.

	NM	Ex
COMPLETE SET (28)	1500.00	750.00
1 Willie Mays	400.00	200.00
2 Gus Zernial	30.00	15.00
3 Red Schoendienst	60.00	30.00
4 Chico Carrasquel	30.00	15.00
5 Jim Hegan	30.00	15.00
6 Curt Simmons	40.00	20.00
7 Bob Porterfield	30.00	15.00
8 Jim Busby	30.00	15.00
9 Don Mueller	30.00	15.00
10 Ted Kluszewski	60.00	30.00
11 Ray Boone	30.00	15.00
12 Smoky Burgess	40.00	20.00
13 Bob Rush	30.00	15.00
14 Early Wynn	60.00	30.00
15 Bill Bruton	30.00	15.00
16 Gus Bell	30.00	15.00
17 Jim Finigan	30.00	15.00
18 Granny Hamner	30.00	15.00
19 Hank Thompson	30.00	15.00
20 Joe Coleman	30.00	15.00
21 Don Newcombe	50.00	25.00
22 Richie Ashburn	100.00	50.00
23 Bobby Thomson	50.00	25.00
24 Sid Gordon	30.00	15.00
25 Gerry Coleman	40.00	20.00
26 Ernie Banks	200.00	100.00
27 Billy Pierce	40.00	20.00
28 Mel Parnell	40.00	20.00

1993 Brooks Robinson Country Time Legends

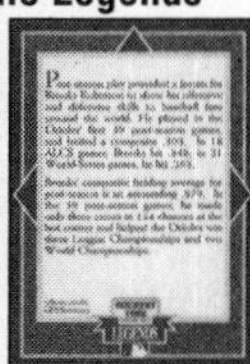

These eight cards measure approximately 2 1/2" by 3 5/8" and feature restored "colorized" black-and-white photos highlighting the 23-season career of HOFer Brooks Robinson. Each photo is overlaid upon a black diamond. The border around the photo is green, red, and black, and the set's logo rests at the lower right. The back carries career highlights within a white rectangle framed in yellow and bordered in gray, yellow and black. The cards are unnumbered and checklisted below chronologically and distinguished by pose descriptions.

	Nm-Mt	Ex-Mt
COMPLETE SET	6.00	1.80
COMMON CARD (1-7)	1.00	.30

1947 Jackie Robinson Bond Bread

The 1947 Bond Bread Jackie Robinson set features 13 unnumbered cards of Jackie in different action or portrait poses; each card measures approximately 2 1/4" by 3 1/2". Card number 7, which is the only card in the set to contain a facsimile autograph, was apparently issued in greater quantity than other cards in the set and has been noted as a double print (DP) in the checklist below. Several of the cards have a horizontal format; these are marked in the checklist below by HOR. The catalog designation for this set is D302.

	Ex-Mt	VG
COMPLETE SET (13)	8000.00	4000.00
COMMON DP	450.00	225.00
1 Jackie Robinson Sliding into base cap, ump in photo, HOR	750.00	375.00
2 Jackie Robinson Running down 3rd base line	750.00	375.00
3 Jackie Robinson Batting bat behind head facing camera	750.00	375.00
4 Jackie Robinson Moving towards second throw almost to glove HOR	750.00	375.00
5 Jackie Robinson Taking throw at first, HOR	750.00	375.00
6 Jackie Robinson Jumping high in the air for ball	750.00	375.00
7 Jackie Robinson Profile with glove in front of head facsimile autograph DP	450.00	225.00
8 Jackie Robinson Leaping over second base ready to throw	750.00	375.00
9 Jackie Robinson Portrait holding glove over head	750.00	375.00
10 Jackie Robinson Portrait holding bat perpendicular to body	750.00	375.00
11 Jackie Robinson Reaching for throw glove near ankle	750.00	375.00
12 Jackie Robinson Leaping for throw no scoreboard in background	750.00	375.00
13 Jackie Robinson Portrait holding bat parallel to body	750.00	375.00
XX Jackie Robinson 6 1/2" by 9" Premium Photo	1500.00	750.00

1993 Rockies Stadium Club

This 30-card standard-size set features the 1993 Colorado Rockies. The set was issued in hobby (plastic box) and retail (blister) form as well as being distributed in shrinkwrapped cardboard boxes with a manager card pictured on it.

	Nm-Mt	Ex-Mt
COMP. FACT SET (30)	5.00	1.50

1 David Nied .10 .03
2 Quinton McCracken .10 .03
3 Charlie Hayes .10 .03
4 Bryn Smith .10 .03
5 Dante Bichette .75 .23
6 Alex Cole .10 .03
7 Scott Aldred .10 .03
8 Roberto Mejia .10 .03
9 Jeff Parrett .10 .03
10 Joe Girardi .25 .07
11 Andres Galarraga 1.50 .45
12 Daryl Boston .10 .03
13 Jerald Clark .10 .03
14 Gerald Young .10 .03
15 Bruce Ruffin .10 .03
16 Rudy Seanez .10 .03
17 Darren Holmes .10 .03
18 Andy Ashby .10 .03
19 Chris Jones .10 .03
20 Mark Thompson .10 .03
21 Freddie Benavides .10 .03
22 Eric Wedge .25 .07
23 Vinny Castilla .75 .23
24 Butch Henry .10 .03
25 Jim Tatum .10 .03
26 Steve Reed .10 .03
27 Eric Young .50 .15
28 Danny Sheaffer .10 .03
29 Roger Bailey .10 .03
30 Brad Ausmus .10 .03

1993 Rockies U.S. Playing Cards

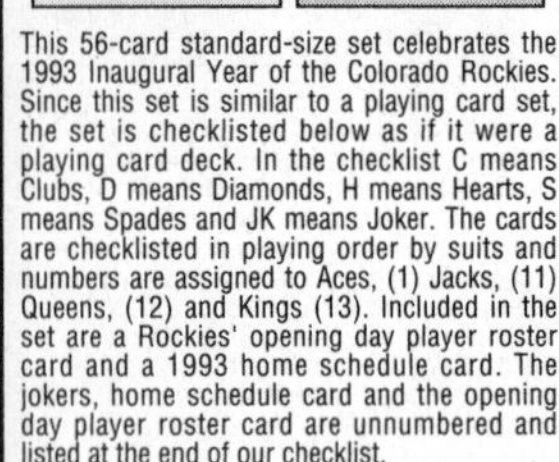

This 56-card standard-size set celebrates the 1993 Inaugural Year of the Colorado Rockies. Since this set is similar to a playing card set, the set is checklisted below as if it were a playing card deck. In the checklist C means Clubs, D means Diamonds, H means Hearts, S means Spades and JK means Joker. The cards are checklisted in playing order by suits and numbers are assigned to Aces, (1) Jacks, (11) Queens, (12) and Kings (13). Included in the set are a Rockies' opening day player roster card and a 1993 home schedule card. The jokers, home schedule card and the opening day player roster card are unnumbered and listed at the end of our checklist.

Nm-Mt Ex-Mt
COMP. FACT SET (56) 4.00 1.20
1C Jim Tatum .05 .02
1D Andres Galarraga .50 .15
1H Charlie Hayes .05 .02
1S David Nied .05 .02
2C Charlie Hayes .05 .02
2D David Nied .05 .02
2H Jim Tatum .05 .02
2S Andres Galarraga .50 .15
3C Dale Murphy .50 .15
3D Dante Bichette .25 .07
3H Andy Ashby .05 .02
3S Gary Wayne .05 .02
4C Scott Aldred .05 .02
4D Joe Girardi .10 .03
4H Vinny Castilla .25 .07
4S Freddie Benavides .05 .02
5C Braulio Castillo .05 .02
5D Bryn Smith .05 .02
5H Steve Reed .05 .02
5S Butch Henry .05 .02
6C Danny Sheaffer .05 .02
6D Darren Holmes .05 .02
6H Daryl Boston .05 .02
6S Gerald Young .05 .02
7C Jerald Clark .05 .02
7D Bruce Ruffin .05 .02
7H Alex Cole .05 .02
7S Jeff Parrett .05 .02
8C Willie Blair .05 .02
8D Eric Young .15 .04
8H Bryn Smith .05 .02
8S Braulio Castillo .05 .02
9C Daryl Boston .05 .02
9D Gerald Young .05 .02
9H Danny Sheaffer .05 .02
9S Darren Holmes .05 .02
10C Andy Ashby .05 .02
10D Gary Wayne .05 .02
10H Willie Blair .05 .02
10S Dale Murphy .50 .15
11C Butch Henry .05 .02
11D Steve Reed .05 .02
11H Dante Bichette .40 .12
11S Eric Young .15 .04
12C Alex Cole .05 .02
12D Jeff Parrett .05 .02
12H Jerald Clark .05 .02
12S Bruce Ruffin .05 .02
13C Vinny Castilla .25 .07
13D Freddie Benavides .05 .02
13H Scott Aldred .05 .02
13S Joe Girardi .10 .03
JKO National League Logo .05 .02
NNO 1993 Home Schedule .05 .02

1993 Rockies Upper Deck

This 27-card set of the Colorado Rockies features the same design as the players' 1993 regular Upper Deck cards. The difference is found in the gold foil stamping of the team's logo on the front. The cards are checklisted below according to their corresponding numbers in the regular Upper Deck set. These cards were issued in special "team sets" form.

Nm-Mt Ex-Mt
COMPLETE SET 8.00 2.40
27 David Nied .10 .03
444 John Burke .10 .03
478 Dante Bichette .25 .07
David Nied
Andres Galarraga
521 Eric Young .25 .07
529 Jeff Parrett .10 .03
538 Alex Cole .10 .03
560 Vinny Castilla .40 .12
571 Joe Girardi .10 .03
593 Andres Galarraga .25 .07
647 Charlie Hayes .10 .03
653 Eric Wedge .25 .07
668 Darren Holmes .10 .03
670 Bruce Ruffin .10 .03
683 Dante Bichette .25 .07
706 Dale Murphy 6.00 1.80
720 Willie Blair .10 .03
723 Bryn Smith .10 .03
732 Freddie Benavides .10 .03
737 Daryl Boston .10 .03
740 Gerald Young .10 .03
752 Steve Reed .10 .03
761 Jim Tatum .10 .03
763 Andy Ashby .10 .03
770 Butch Henry .10 .03
793 Armando Reynoso .10 .03
797 Jerald Clark .10 .03
834 David Nied CL .10 .03

1994 Rockies Police

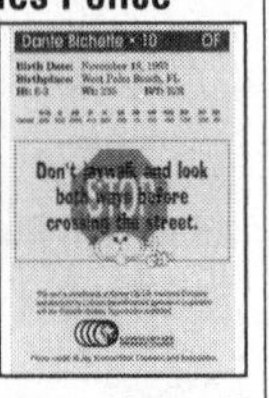

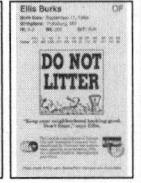

These 27 cards measure approximately 2 5/8" by 4" and feature color action and posed player photos on their yellow-bordered fronts. The cards are unnumbered and checklisted below in alphabetical order.

Nm-Mt Ex-Mt
COMPLETE SET (27) 10.00 3.00
1 Don Baylor MG .75 .23
2 Dante Bichette 1.00 .30
3 Willie Blair .25 .07
4 Kent Bottenfield .25 .07
5 Ellis Burks 1.00 .30
6 Vinny Castilla 1.00 .30
7 Marvin Freeman .25 .07
8 Andres Galarraga 2.00 .60
9 Andres Galarraga 2.00 .60
1993 Batting Champ
10 Joe Girardi .50 .15
11 Mike Harkey .25 .07
12 Greg W. Harris .25 .07
13 Charlie Hayes .25 .07
14 Darren Holmes .25 .07
15 Howard Johnson .25 .07
16 Nelson Liriano .25 .07
17 Roberto Mejia .25 .07
18 Mike Munoz .25 .07
19 David Nied .25 .07
20 Steve Reed .25 .07
21 Armando Reynoso .25 .07
22 Bruce Ruffin .25 .07
23 Danny Sheaffer .25 .07
24 Darrell Sherman .25 .07
25 Walt Weiss .25 .07
26 Eric Young .50 .15
27 Larry Bearnarth CO .25 .07
Dwight Evans CO
Gene Glynn CO
Ron Hassey CO
Bill Plummer CO
Don Zimmer CO

1995 Rockies Police

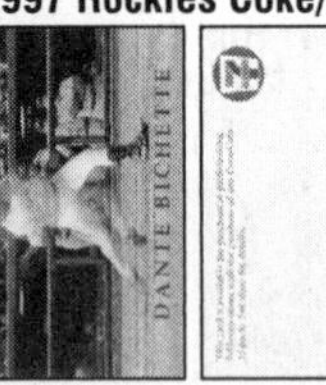

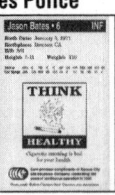

This 12-card set of the Colorado Rockies measures 2 5/8" by 4" and was sponsored by the Kansas City Life Insurance Company. The cards are unnumbered and checklisted below in alphabetical order.

Nm-Mt Ex-Mt
COMPLETE SET (12) 6.00 1.80
1 Jason Bates .25 .07
2 Don Baylor MG .50 .15
3 Dante Bichette 1.00 .30
4 Ellis Burks 1.00 .30
5 Vinny Castilla 1.00 .30
6 Andres Galarraga 1.50 .45
7 Joe Girardi .25 .07
8 Mike Kingery .25 .07
9 Bill Swift .25 .07
10 Larry Walker .75 .23
11 Walt Weiss .25 .07
12 Eric Young .50 .15

1996 Rockies Fleer

These 20 standard-size cards are same as the regular Fleer issue, except they are UV coated, they use silver foil and they are numbered "x of 20". The team set packs were available at retail locations and hobby shops in 10-card packs for a suggested price of $1.99.

Nm-Mt Ex-Mt
COMPLETE SET (20) 2.00 .60
1 Jason Bates .10 .03

2 Dante Bichette .20 .06
3 Ellis Burks .30 .09
4 Vinny Castilla .20 .06
5 Andres Galarraga .40 .12
6 Darren Holmes .10 .03
7 Curt Leskanic .10 .03
8 Quinton McCracken .10 .03
9 Mike Munoz .10 .03
10 Jayhawk Owens .10 .03
11 Steve Reed .10 .03
12 Kevin Ritz .10 .03
13 Bret Saberhagen .20 .06
14 Bill Swift .10 .03
15 John Vander Wal .10 .03
16 Larry Walker .30 .09
17 Walt Weiss .10 .03
18 Eric Young .20 .06
19 Logo card .10 .03
20 Checklist .10 .03

1996 Rockies Police

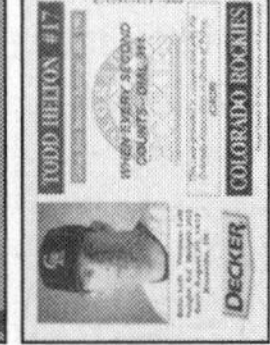

This 27-card set measures approximately 2 5/8" by 4". This set features members of the 1996 Colorado Rockies. The cards are unnumbered and we have sequenced them in alphabetical order. The set was sponsored by Kansas City Life Insurance Company and the back features various safety tips.

Nm-Mt Ex-Mt
COMPLETE SET (27) 8.00 2.40
1 Roger Bailey .25 .07
2 Jason Bates .25 .07
3 Don Baylor MG .50 .15
4 Dante Bichette .50 .15
5 Ellis Burks 1.00 .30
6 Vinny Castilla .50 .15
7 Marvin Freeman .25 .07
8 Andres Galarraga 1.00 .30
9 Darren Holmes .25 .07
10 Trenidad Hubbard .25 .07
11 Curt Leskanic .25 .07
12 Quinton McCracken .25 .07
13 Mike Munoz .25 .07
14 Jayhawk Owens .25 .07
15 Lance Painter .25 .07
16 Steve Reed .25 .07
17 Bryan Rekar .25 .07
18 Armando Reynoso .25 .07
19 Kevin Ritz .25 .07
20 Bruce Ruffin .25 .07
21 Bret Saberhagen .50 .15
22 Bill Swift .25 .07
23 Mark Thompson .25 .07
24 John Vander Wal .25 .07
25 Larry Walker 1.00 .30
26 Walt Weiss .25 .07
27 Eric Young .50 .15

1997 Rockies Coke/7-11

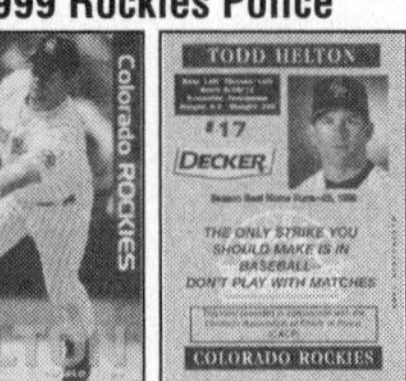

This four-card set was produced by World Holographics and was available for purchase at participating 7-Eleven stores with the purchase of any Coca-Cola 12-pack. The set measures approximately 3" by 4" and features 3-D lenticular color action player photos. The cards are unnumbered and checklisted below alphabetically.

Nm-Mt Ex-Mt
COMPLETE SET (4) 8.00 2.40
1 Dante Bichette 2.00 .60
2 Dante Bichette 2.00 .60
3 Ellis Burks 2.50 .75
4 Ellis Burks 2.50 .75

1997 Rockies Police

This 12-card set of the Colorado Rockies was sponsored by the Colorado Association of Chiefs of Police (CACP) and Decker. The fronts feature color action player photos in a thin white border. The backs carry player information and a safety message. The cards are unnumbered and checklisted below in alphabetical order.

Nm-Mt Ex-Mt
COMPLETE SET (12) 10.00 3.00
1 Don Baylor MG .75 .23
2 Dante Bichette .75 .23
3 Ellis Burks 1.50 .45
4 Vinny Castilla .75 .23
5 Dinger(Mascot) .50 .15
6 Andres Galarraga 2.00 .60
7 Kirt Manwaring .50 .15
8 Quinton McCracken .50 .15
9 Bill Swift .50 .15
10 Larry Walker 1.50 .45
11 Walt Weiss .50 .15
12 Eric Young .75 .23

1997 Rockies Score

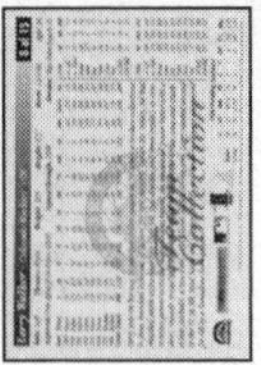

This 15-card set of the Colorado Rockies was issued in five-card packs with a suggested retail price of $1.30 each. The fronts feature color player photos with special team specific color foil stamping. The backs carry player information. Only 100 cases were made for each team. Platinum parallel cards were inserted at a rate of 1:6, Premier parallel cards at a rate of 1:31.

Nm-Mt Ex-Mt
COMPLETE SET (15) 5.00 1.50
*PLATINUM: 5X BASIC CARDS
*PREMIER: 20X BASIC CARDS
1 Dante Bichette .50 .15
2 Kevin Ritz .25 .07
3 Walt Weiss .25 .07
4 Ellis Burks .75 .23
5 Jamey Wright .25 .07
6 Andres Galarraga 1.00 .30
7 Eric Young .50 .15
8 Larry Walker 1.00 .30
9 Vinny Castilla .75 .23
10 Quinton McCracken .25 .07
11 Armando Reynoso .25 .07
12 Jayhawk Owens .25 .07
13 Mark Thompson .25 .07
14 Bruce Ruffin .25 .07
15 John Burke .25 .07

1998 Rockies Police

This 12 card standard-size set was issued by the Colorado Rockies and produced by Grandstand. The borderless cards feature a player portrait along with the player's name going down the side. The horizontal back has a player portrait, vital information and a safety tip. The cards were sponsored by "Decker", the hot dog manufacturer. The cards are unnumbered so we have sequenced them alphabetically.

Nm-Mt Ex-Mt
COMPLETE SET 8.00 2.40
1 Pedro Astacio .50 .15
2 Don Baylor MG .75 .23
3 Dante Bichette .75 .23
4 Ellis Burks 1.00 .30
5 Vinny Castilla .75 .23
6 Todd Helton 2.00 .60
7 Darryl Kile .50 .15
8 Mike Lansing .50 .15
9 Kirt Manwaring .50 .15
10 Neifi Perez .50 .15
11 Larry Walker 1.50 .45
12 Dinger .50 .15
Mascot

1999 Rockies Police

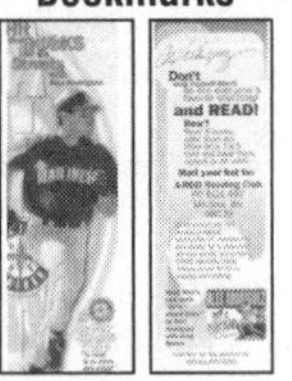

These 12 standard-size cards feature members of the 1999 Colorado Rockies. The borderless fronts have player photos with the player's name and position on the bottom and the words "Colorado Rockies" running along the side. The backs have a smaller player photo, biographical information and a safety tip. Since the cards are unnumbered, we have sequenced them in alphabetical order.

Nm-Mt Ex-Mt
COMPLETE SET (12) 8.00 2.40
1 Dante Bichette .75 .23
2 Vinny Castilla .75 .23
3 Dinger .50 .15
Mascot
4 Jerry DiPoto .50 .15
5 Darryl Hamilton .50 .15
6 Todd Helton 2.00 .60
7 Darryl Kile .50 .15
8 Mike Lansing .50 .15
9 Jim Leyland MG .50 .15
10 Kirt Manwaring .50 .15
11 Neifi Perez .50 .15
12 Larry Walker 1.50 .45

2000 Rockies Police

These 12 standard-size cards feature members of the 2000 Colorado Rockies. The borderless fronts have actions shots with the players name and position on the bottom. The words "Rockies 2000" appear on the side. The horizontal backs have a player portrait, biographical information and a safety tip. The cards were sponsored by Decker. Since the cards are unnumbered, we have sequenced them in alphabetical order.

Nm-Mt Ex-Mt
COMPLETE SET (12) 8.00 2.40
1 Rolando Arrojo .50 .15
2 Buddy Bell MG .75 .23
3 Jeff Cirillo .50 .15
4 Tom Goodwin .50 .15
5 Jeffrey Hammonds .50 .15
6 Todd Helton 2.00 .60
7 Mike Lansing .50 .15
8 Brent Mayne .50 .15
9 Neifi Perez .50 .15
10 Larry Walker 1.50 .45
11 Dinger .50 .15
Mascot
12 Coors Field .50 .15

2002 Rockies Police

This 12-card standard-size set features members of the 2002 Colorado Rockies. These cards have player photos surrounded by white borders. The horizontal backs have a player photo, biographical information, a safety tip, 2001 Colorado stats and a brief blurb. Since these cards are unnumbered, we have sequenced them in alphabetical order.

Nm-Mt Ex-Mt
COMPLETE SET 6.00 1.80
1 Gary Bennett .25 .07
2 Mike Hampton .50 .15
3 Todd Helton 2.00 .60
4 Todd Hollandsworth .25 .07
5 Clint Hurdle MG .25 .07
6 Denny Neagle .25 .07
7 Jose Ortiz .50 .15
8 Juan Pierre 1.00 .30
9 Juan Uribe .25 .07
10 Larry Walker 1.00 .30
11 Todd Zeile .50 .15
12 Dinger .25 .07
Mascot
XX Armour Coupon .25 .07

1999 Alex Rodriguez Bookmarks

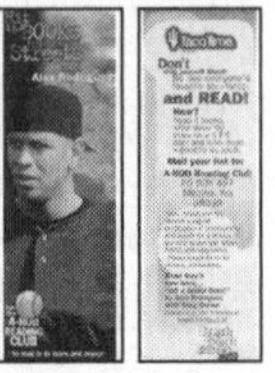

These five bookmarks feature star shortstop Alex Rodriguez and publicize his a-rod reading club program

Nm-Mt Ex-Mt
COMPLETE SET 10.00 3.00
COMMON CARD 2.00 .60

1998 Alex Rodriguez Taco Time Bookmarks

These four bookmarks feature Alex Rodriguez and promote the A-Rod reading club which encourage young kids to read at least five books. The fronts feature photos of Alex along with the message, "Hit the Books, not the streets". The backs have the Taco Time logo on the top and information on how to join the A-Rod reading club as well as information about his web site.

Nm-Mt Ex-Mt
COMPLETE SET (4) 5.00 1.50
COMMON CARD (1-4) 1.50 .45

1964 Rollins Sheels Hardware

This blank-backed photograph, which measures approximately 7 1/2" by 9 1/2" features Twins star third baseman Rich Rollins. The front has a photo of Rollins along with a note at the bottom for Sheels Hardware which then had 3 locations in the Fargo-Moorehead, North Dakota area.

	MINT	NRMT
1 Rich Rollins	10.00	4.50

1908-09 Rose Company PC760

One of the most attractive postcards ever issued, The Rose Company postcards were issued during the end of the 20th century's first decade. The set features a black and white photo in a circle surrounded by a yellow and green baseball field, crossed bats and small figures. Imprints on the reverse contain the letters TRC, with the loop around the bottom of the C possibly accounting for a lower case "o," giving Co. The Rose Co. baseball series is listed in alphabetical order by teams in the checklist below-research indicates that each of the 16 major league teams is represented by 12 Rose postcards (to date not all have been found). And several minor league franchises are now believed to have 10 or more cards for them as well. The cards we currently list as 192 through 204 all feature members of the Springfield Mass baseball team. Although it is not confirmed that these are Rose postcards, the similarities are obvious enough that to add these to these listings makes sense.

	Ex-Mt	VG
COMPLETE SET	35000.00	17500.00
1 Ralph Glaze	150.00	75.00
2 Dad Hale	150.00	75.00
3 Frank LaPorte	150.00	75.00
4 Bris Lord	150.00	75.00
5 Tex Pruiett	150.00	75.00
6 Jack Thoney	150.00	75.00
7 Bob Unglaub	150.00	75.00
8 Heinie Wagner	150.00	75.00
9 George Winter	150.00	75.00
10 Cy Young	800.00	400.00
11 Nick Altrock	200.00	100.00
12 John Anderson	150.00	75.00
13 Jiggs Donohue	150.00	75.00
14 Fielder Jones	150.00	75.00
15 Freddy Parent	150.00	75.00
16 Frank Smith	150.00	75.00
17 Billy Sullivan	150.00	75.00
18 Lee Tannehill	150.00	75.00
19 Doc White	150.00	75.00
20 Harry Bemis	150.00	75.00
21 Joe Birmingham	150.00	75.00
22 Bill Bradley	150.00	75.00
23 Josh Clarke	150.00	75.00
24 Bill Hinchman	150.00	75.00
25 Addie Joss	500.00	250.00
26 Nap Lajoie	300.00	150.00
27 Glen Liebhardt	150.00	75.00
28 Bob Rhoads	150.00	75.00
Spelled Rhoades on card		
29 George Stovall	150.00	75.00
30 Terry Turner	150.00	75.00
31 Ty Cobb	1500.00	750.00
32 Bill Coughlin	150.00	75.00
33 Sam Crawford	300.00	150.00
34 Bill Donovan	200.00	100.00
35 Ed Killian	150.00	75.00
36 Matty McIntyre	150.00	75.00
37 George Mullin	200.00	100.00
38 Charley O'Leary	150.00	75.00
39 Claude Rossman	150.00	75.00
40 Germany Schaefer	200.00	100.00
41 Boss Schmidt	150.00	75.00
42 Ed Summers	150.00	75.00
43 Hal Chase	300.00	150.00
44 Jack Chesbro	300.00	150.00
45 Wid Conroy	150.00	75.00
46 Kid Elberfeld	150.00	75.00
47 Fred Glade	150.00	75.00
48 Charlie Hemphill	150.00	75.00
49 Willie Keeler	300.00	150.00
50 Red Kleinow	150.00	75.00
51 Doc Newton	150.00	75.00
52 Harry Niles	150.00	75.00
53 Al Orth	150.00	75.00
54 Jake Stahl	150.00	75.00
55 Chief Bender	300.00	150.00
56 Jimmy Collins	300.00	150.00
57 Jack Coombs	150.00	75.00
58 Harry Davis	150.00	75.00
59 Jimmy Dygert	150.00	75.00
60 Topsy Hartsel	150.00	75.00
61 Danny Murphy	150.00	75.00
62 Simon Nicholls	150.00	75.00
63 Rube Oldring	150.00	75.00
64 Eddie Plank	300.00	150.00
65 Ossee Schreck	150.00	75.00
66 Socks Seybold	150.00	75.00
67 Hobe Ferris	150.00	75.00
68 Danny Hoffman	150.00	75.00
69 Harry Howell	150.00	75.00
70 Tom Jones	150.00	75.00
71 Jack Powell	150.00	75.00
72 Tubby Spencer	150.00	75.00
73 George Stone	150.00	75.00
74 Rube Waddell	300.00	150.00
75 Jimmy Williams	150.00	75.00
76 Otis Clymer	150.00	75.00
77 Frank Delahanty	150.00	75.00
78 Bob Ganley	150.00	75.00
79 Jerry Freeman	150.00	75.00
80 Tom Hughes	150.00	75.00
81 Walter Johnson	1000.00	500.00
82 George McBride	150.00	75.00
83 Casey Patten	150.00	75.00
84 Clyde Milan	200.00	100.00
85 Bill Shipke	150.00	75.00
86 Charlie Smith	150.00	75.00
87 Jack Warner	150.00	75.00
88 Ginger Beaumont	150.00	75.00
89 Sam Brown	150.00	75.00
90 Bill Dahlen	150.00	75.00
91 George Ferguson	150.00	75.00
92 Vive Lindaman	150.00	75.00
93 Claude Ritchey	150.00	75.00
94 Whitey Alperman	150.00	75.00
95 John Hummel	150.00	75.00
96 Phil Lewis		
97 Harry Lumley	150.00	75.00
98 Billy Maloney	150.00	75.00
99 Harry MacIntyre	150.00	75.00
100 Nap Rucker	150.00	75.00
101 Tommy Sheehan	150.00	75.00
102 Mordecai Brown	300.00	150.00
103 Frank Chance	500.00	250.00
104 Johnny Evers	500.00	250.00
105 Solly Hofman	150.00	75.00
106 John Kling	150.00	75.00
107 Orvall Overall	150.00	75.00
108 Ed Reulbach	150.00	75.00
109 Frank Schulte	200.00	100.00
110 Jimmy Sheckard	150.00	75.00
111 Jimmy Slagle	150.00	75.00
112 Harry Steinfeldt	200.00	100.00
113 Joe Tinker	500.00	250.00
114 Billy Campbell	150.00	75.00
115 Andy Coakley	150.00	75.00
116 Bob Ewing	150.00	75.00
117 John Ganzel	150.00	75.00
118 Miller Huggins	300.00	150.00
119 Rudy Hulswitt	150.00	75.00
120 Hans Lobert	150.00	75.00
121 Larry McLean	150.00	75.00
122 Mike Mitchell	150.00	75.00
123 Mike Mowery	150.00	75.00
124 Dode Paskert	150.00	75.00
125 Jake Weimer	150.00	75.00
126 Roger Bresnahan	300.00	150.00
127 Al Bridwell	150.00	75.00
128 Art Devlin	150.00	75.00
129 Mike Donlin	200.00	100.00
130 Larry Doyle	200.00	100.00
131 Christy Mathewson	1000.00	500.00
132 Joe McGinnity	300.00	150.00
133 Cy Seymour	150.00	75.00
134 Spike Shannon	150.00	75.00
135 Dummy Taylor	200.00	100.00
136 Fred Tenney	150.00	75.00
137 Hooks Wiltse	150.00	75.00
138 Kitty Bransfield	150.00	75.00
139 Buster Brown	150.00	75.00
140 Frank Corridon	150.00	75.00
141 Red Dooin	150.00	75.00
142 Mickey Doolan	150.00	75.00
143 Eddie Grant	200.00	100.00
144 Otto Knabe	150.00	75.00
145 Sherry Magee	250.00	125.00
146 George McQuillan	150.00	75.00
Spelled McQuillen on card		
147 Fred Osborn	150.00	75.00
148 Tully Sparks	150.00	75.00
149 John Titus	150.00	75.00
150 Ed Abbaticchio	150.00	75.00
151 Howie Camnitz	150.00	75.00
152 Fred Clarke	300.00	150.00
153 George Gibson	150.00	75.00
154 Jim Kane	150.00	75.00
155 Tommy Leach	150.00	75.00
156 Nick Maddox	150.00	75.00
157 Deacon Philippe	200.00	100.00
158 Roy Thomas	150.00	75.00
159 Honus Wagner	1000.00	500.00
160 Owen Wilson	200.00	100.00
161 Irv Young	150.00	75.00
162 Shad Barry	150.00	75.00
163 Fred Beebe	150.00	75.00
164 Bobby Byrne	150.00	75.00
165 Joe Delahanty	150.00	75.00
166 Billy Gilbert	150.00	75.00
167 Art Hoelskoetter	150.00	75.00
168 Ed Karger	150.00	75.00
169 Ed Konetchy	150.00	75.00
170 Johnny Lush	150.00	75.00
171 Stoney McGlynn	150.00	75.00
172 Red Murray	150.00	75.00
173 Patsy O'Rourke	150.00	75.00
174 Beckendorf	150.00	75.00
Scranton		
175 Bills	150.00	75.00
176 Graham	150.00	75.00
177 Groh	150.00	75.00
Scranton		
178 Halligan	150.00	75.00
179 Houser	150.00	75.00
180 Isbel	150.00	75.00
181 Kellogg	150.00	75.00
Scranton		
182 Kittredge	150.00	75.00
Scranton		
183 Moran	150.00	75.00
184 Schultz	150.00	75.00
185 Steele	150.00	75.00
186 Andy Coakley	150.00	75.00
187 Knight	150.00	75.00
188 Schlei	150.00	75.00
189 Spade	150.00	75.00
190 Tris Speaker	300.00	150.00
191 Thomas	150.00	75.00
192 Harl Maggert	150.00	75.00
193 Parker	150.00	75.00
194 James Burns	150.00	75.00
195 Edwin Warner	150.00	75.00
196 Rising	150.00	75.00
197 Connor	150.00	75.00
198 Wachob	150.00	75.00
199 McLean	150.00	75.00
200 Chet Waite	150.00	75.00
201 Luby	150.00	75.00
202 George Tacy	150.00	75.00
203 Collins	150.00	75.00
204 Louis Barbour	150.00	75.00

2001 Rose Ballpark Café

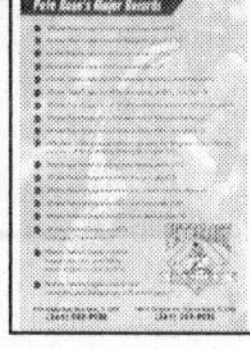

This one card postcard size set features several photos of Pete Rose on the front and information about his major league records on the back. There is also information about his two restaurants.

	Nm-Mt	Ex-Mt
1 Pete Rose	5.00	1.50

1992 Rose Dynasty

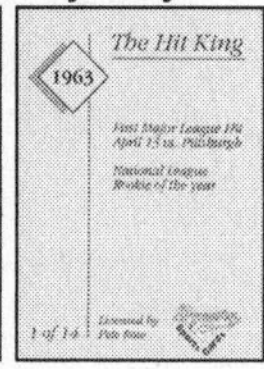

Produced by Dynasty Sports Cards, this 15-card, standard-size set is aptly titled "The Hit King" and showcases Pete Rose. The white-bordered color pictures on the fronts were painted by artist Tim Seeberger. A gold foil crown and a card subtitle are printed in the wider white border below the picture. On a white background in black print, backs carry the year in a diamond icon and running narrative summarizing Rose's illustrious career.

	Nm-Mt	Ex-Mt
COMPLETE SET (15)	10.00	3.00
COMMON CARD (1-14)	.75	.23

1968 Rose Jamesway Trucking

This one card set, which measures 4" by 5 1/4" featured a batting pose of Pete Rose and the "Jamesway Trucking Logo" on the bottom.

	NM	Ex
1 Pete Rose	400.00	160.00

1905 Rotograph Co. PC782

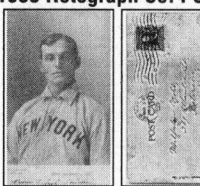

This rather distinguished looking set mesaures 3 1/4" by 5 3/8" and was printed by the Rotograph Company of New York in 1905. Some of the cards are numbered while others are not. The Clark Griffith card was initially issued with the name misspelled and was later corrected. The Rotograph identification is printed on the back of the card. Only New York teams are portrayed.

	Ex-Mt	VG
COMPLETE SET (9)	1750.00	900.00
1 Ambrose Puttman	100.00	50.00
2 Jack Chesbro (2)	200.00	100.00
3 George Brown	100.00	50.00
4 Bill Dahlen	100.00	50.00
5 John McGraw	300.00	150.00
6 Clark Griffill	200.00	100.00
Sic, Griffith		
7 Clark Griffith	200.00	100.00
8 Joe McGinnity	200.00	100.00
Spelled Josep		
9 Joe McGinnity	200.00	100.00
Spelled Joseph		
10 Luther Taylor	100.00	50.00

1976 Rowe Exhibits

These collector issued exhibits feature the best major leaguers of the pre- World War 2 era. The cards are unnumbered and we have sequenced in alphabetical order by who appears in the upper left corner.

	NM	Ex
COMPLETE SET (16)	9.00	3.60
1 Luke Appling	.40	.16
Ted Lyons		
Red Ruffing		
Red Faber		
2 Jim Bottomley	.50	.20
Earle Combs		
George Sisler		
Roger Hornsby		
3 Dizzy Dean	.75	.30
Stan Musial		
Jesse Haines		
Frank Frisch		
4 Joe DiMaggio	1.00	.40
Lou Gehrig		
Lefty Gomez		
Bill Dickey		
5 Bob Feller	.50	.20
Lou Boudreau		
Earl Averill		
Bob Lemon		
6 Jimmie Foxx	.40	.16
Grover C. Alexander		
Robin Roberts		
Eppa Rixey		
7 Hank Greenberg	1.00	.40
Charlie Gehringer		
Ty Cobb		
Goose Goslin		
8 Chick Hafey	.40	.16
Edd Roush		
Bill McKechnie		
George Kelly		
9 Fred Lindstrom	.40	.16
Billy Herman		
Kiki Cuyler		
Gabby Hartnett		
10 Heinie Manush	.50	.20
Walter Johnson		
Bucky Harris		
Sam Rice		
11 Joe Medwick	.40	.16
Max Carey		
Dazzy Vance		
Burleigh Grimes		
12 Mel Ott	.50	.20
Carl Hubbell		
Dave Bancroft		
Bill Terry		
13 Al Simmons	.50	.20
Lefty Grove		
Mickey Cochrane		
Eddie Collins		
14 Warren Spahn	.50	.20
Al Lopez		
Casey Stengel		
Rabbit Maranville		
15 Pie Traynor	.50	.20
Lloyd Waner		
Honus Wagner		
Paul Waner		
16 Ted Williams	1.00	.40
Herb Pennock		
Babe Ruth		
Joe Cronin		

1950-53 Royal Desserts

These cards were issued by Royal desserts over a period of years. These cards measure 2 1/2" by 3 1/2" and even though the same players are featured, variations exist when biographies were changed to keep the cards current. The backs are blank but the cards are numbered on the front. A set is considered complete with only one of each variation. These items were also made in blue. They have a value of 1X to2X the values listed below.

	NM	Ex
COMPLETE SET	1200.00	600.00
COMMON CARD (1-24)	25.00	12.50
COMMON DP	100.00	50.00
1 Stan Musial DP	250.00	125.00
2 Pee Wee Reese DP	10.00	50.00
3 George Kell	80.00	40.00
4 Dom DiMaggio	50.00	25.00
5 Warren Spahn	100.00	50.00
6A Andy Pafko	25.00	12.50
Chicago Cubs		
6B Andy Pafko	100.00	50.00
Brooklyn Dodgers		
7A Andy Seminick	25.00	12.50
Philadelphia Phillies		
7B Andy Seminick	25.00	12.50
Cincinnati Reds		
8A Lou Brissie	25.00	12.50
Philadelphia A's		
8B Lou Brissie	100.00	50.00
Cleveland Indians		
9 Ewell Blackwell	25.00	12.50
10 Bobby Thomson	50.00	25.00
11 Phil Rizzuto DP	100.00	50.00
12 Tommy Henrich	50.00	25.00
13 Joe Gordon	50.00	25.00
14A Ray Scarborough	25.00	12.50
Washington Senators		
14B Ray Scarborough	100.00	50.00
Chicago White Sox		
14C Ray Scarborough	25.00	12.50
Boston Red Sox		
15A Stan Rojek	25.00	12.50
Pittsburgh Pirates		
15B Stan Rojek	100.00	50.00
St. Louis Browns		
16 Luke Appling	80.00	40.00
17 Willard Marshall	25.00	12.50
18 Alvin Dark	50.00	25.00
19A Dick Sisler	25.00	12.50
Philadelphia Phillies		
19B Dick Sisler	25.00	12.50
Cincinnati Reds		
20 Johnny Ostrowski	25.00	12.50
21A Virgil Trucks	25.00	12.50
Detroit Tigers		
21B Virgil Trucks	100.00	50.00
St. Louis Browns		
22 Eddie Robinson	25.00	12.50
23 Nanny Fernandez	100.00	50.00
24 Ferris Fain	25.00	12.50

1952 Royal Premiums

These 16 photos measure approximately 5" by 7". These black and white photos are all facsimile signed with the expression "To a Royal Fan". The backs are blank and sequenced in alphabetical order.

	NM	Ex
COMPLETE SET (16)	400.00	200.00
1 Ewell Blackwell	15.00	7.50
2 Leland Brissie Jr.	15.00	7.50
3 Alvin Dark	20.00	10.00
4 Dom DiMaggio	30.00	15.00
5 Ferris Fain	15.00	7.50
6 George Kell	30.00	15.00
7 Stan Musial	100.00	50.00
8 Andy Pafko	15.00	7.50
9 Pee Wee Reese	50.00	25.00
10 Phil Rizzuto	50.00	25.00
11 Eddie Robinson	15.00	7.50
12 Ray Scarborough	15.00	7.50
13 Andy Seminick	15.00	7.50
14 Dick Sisler	15.00	7.50
15 Warren Spahn	50.00	25.00
16 Bobby Thomson	20.00	10.00

1969 Royals Solon

These 15 blank-backed cards measure approximately 2 1/8" by 3 3/8" and feature blue-screened posed player photos on their white-bordered fronts. The player's name and position, along with the Royals logo, appear in blue lettering in the lower white margin. The cards are unnumbered and checklisted below in alphabetical order.

	NM	Ex
COMPLETE SET (15)	15.00	6.00
1 Jerry Adair	1.00	.40
2 Wally Bunker	1.00	.40
3 Moe Drabowsky	1.00	.40
4 Dick Drago	1.00	.40
5 Joe Foy	1.00	.40
6 Joe Gordon MG	1.50	.60
7 Chuck Harrison	1.00	.40
8 Mike Hedlund	1.00	.40
9 Jack Hernandez	1.00	.40
10 Pat Kelly	1.00	.40
11 Roger Nelson	1.00	.40
12 Bob Oliver	1.00	.40
13 Lou Piniella	4.00	1.60
14 Ellie Rodriguez	1.00	.40
15 Dave Wickersham	1.00	.40

1969 Royals Team Issue

This 12-card set of the Kansas City Royals measures approximately 4 1/4" by 7". The fronts display black-and-white player portraits bordered in white. The player's name and team are printed in the top margin. The backs are blank. The cards are unnumbered and checklisted below in alphabetical order.

	NM	Ex
COMPLETE SET	20.00	8.00
1 Jerry Adair	1.50	.60
2 Jimmy Campanis	1.50	.60
3 Moe Drabowsky	1.50	.60
4 Mike Fiore	1.50	.60
5 Joe Foy	1.50	.60
6 Joe Gordon MG	2.50	1.00
7 Pat Kelly	1.50	.60
8 Joe Keough	1.50	.60
9 Roger Nelson	1.50	.60
10 Bob Oliver	1.50	.60

Card		
11 Juan Rios	1.50	.60
12 Dave Wickersham	1.50	.60

1970 Royals Team Issue

This 38-card set measures approximately 3 3/8" by 5" and features black-and-white player portraits in a white border. A facsimile autograph across the bottom of the picture. The backs are blank. The cards are unnumbered and checklisted below in alphabetical order.

	NM	Ex
COMPLETE SET (38)	20.00	8.00
1 Ted Abernathy	1.00	.40
2 Jerry Adair	1.00	.40
3 Luis Alcaraz	1.00	.40
4 Wally Bunker	1.00	.40
5 Tom Burgmeier	1.00	.40
6 Bill Butler	1.00	.40
7 Jim Campanis	1.00	.40
8 Dan Carnevale CO	1.00	.40
9 Moe Drabowsky	1.00	.40
10 Dick Drago	1.00	.40
11 Harry Dunlop CO	1.00	.40
12 Mike Fiore	1.00	.40
13 Al Fitzmorris	1.00	.40
14 Jack Hernandez	1.00	.40
15 Bob Johnson	1.00	.40
16 Pat Kelly	1.00	.40
17 Joe Keough	1.00	.40
18 Ed Kirkpatrick	1.00	.40
19 Bob Lemon MG	2.50	1.00
20 Pat Locanto	1.00	.40
21 Tommy Matchick	1.00	.40
22 Charlie Metro CO	1.00	.40
23 Aurelio Monteagudo	1.00	.40
24 Dave Morehead	1.00	.40
25 Bob Oliver	1.00	.40
26 Amos Otis	1.50	.60
27 Lou Piniella	2.50	1.00
28 Ellie Rodriguez	1.00	.40
29 Cookie Rojas	1.50	.60
30 Jim Rooker	1.00	.40
31 Paul Schaal	1.00	.40
32 Joe Schultz CO	1.50	.60
33 Bill Sorrell	1.00	.40
34 Rich Stevenson	1.00	.40
35 George Strickland CO	1.00	.40
36 Cedric Tallis GM	1.00	.40
37 Bob"Hawk" Taylor	1.00	.40
38 Ken Wright	1.00	.40

1971 Royals Signature Series Team

These photos feature members of the 1971 Kansas City Royals. The photos are unnumbered and feature fascimile signatures on them and we have sequenced them in alphabetical order.

	NM	Ex
COMPLETE SET	30.00	12.00
1 Ted Abernathy	1.00	.40
2 Wally Bunker	1.00	.40
3 Galen Cisco	1.00	.40
4 Bruce Dal Canton	1.00	.40
5 Dick Drago	1.00	.40
6 Harry Dunlop CO	1.00	.40
7 Al Fitzmorris	1.50	.60
8 Mike Hedlund	1.00	.40
9 Chuck Harrison	1.00	.40
10 Gail Hopkins	1.00	.40
11 Pat Kelly	1.00	.40
12 Ed Kirkpatrick	1.00	.40
13 Bobby Knoop	1.00	.40
14 Charley Lau CO	1.50	.60
15 Bob Lemon MG	2.50	1.00
16 Jerry May	1.00	.40
17 Dave Morehead	1.00	.40
18 Roger Nelson	1.00	.40
19 Bob Oliver	2.00	.80
20 Amos Otis	2.50	1.00
21 Dennis Paepke	1.00	.40
22 Fred Patek	2.00	.80
23 Lou Piniella	2.50	1.00
24 Lou Piniella	2.50	1.00
25 Cookie Rojas	1.50	.60
26 Ted Savage	1.00	.40
27 Paul Splittorff	1.50	.60
28 George Strickland CO	1.00	.40
29 Cedric Talles GM	1.00	.40
30 Carl Taylor	1.00	.40
31 Ken Wright	1.00	.40
32 Jim York	1.00	.40

1972 Royals Team Issue

These photos feature members of the 1972 Kansas City Royals. They are unnumbered so we have sequenced them in alphabetical order.

	NM	Ex
COMPLETE SET	20.00	8.00
1 Ted Abernathy	.50	.20
2 Tom Burgmeier	.50	.20
3 Harry Dunlop GM	.50	.20
4 Al Fitzmorris	.50	.20
5 Bob Floyd	.50	.20
6 Mike Hedlund	.50	.20
7 Gail Hopkins	.50	.20
8 Steve Hovley	.50	.20
9 Joe Keough	.50	.20
10 Ed Kirkpatrick	.50	.20
11 Bobby Knoop	.50	.20
12 Charley Lau CO	1.00	.40
13 Bob Lemon MG	1.50	.60
14 Jerry May	.50	.20
15 John Mayberry	1.00	.40
16 Roger Nelson	.50	.20
17 Amos Otis	1.50	.60
18 Fred Patek	1.00	.40
19 Lou Pinella	1.50	.60
20 Cookie Rojas	.75	.30
21 Jim Rooker	.50	.20
22 Paul Schaal	.50	.20
23 Richie Scheinblum	.50	.20
24 Paul Splittorff	.75	.30
25 George Strickland CO	.50	.20
26 Carl Taylor	.50	.20
27 Ken Wright	.50	.20

1974 Royals Postcards

This 29-card set of the Kansas City Royals features black-and-white player protraits measuring approximately 3 1/4" by 5" with a facsimile autograph. The set could originally be bought from the team for $2 or 10 cards for $1. The cards are unnumbered and checklisted below in alphabetical order. George Brett has a postcard in this set, a year before his Rookie Card.

	NM	Ex
COMPLETE SET (29)	40.00	16.00
1 Kurt Bevacqua	.75	.30
2 Doug Bird	.50	.20
3 George Brett	25.00	10.00
4 Nelson Briles	.50	.20
5 Steve Busby	.50	.20
6 Orlando Cepeda	5.00	2.00
7 Galen Cisco CO	.50	.20
8 Al Cowens	.75	.30
9 Bruce Dal Canton	.50	.20
10 Harry Dunlop CO	.50	.20
11 Al Fitzmorris	.50	.20
12 Fran Healy	1.00	.40
13 Joe Hoerner	.50	.20
14 Charley Lau CO	.75	.30
Card does not have a fascimile autograph		
15 Buck Martinez	.75	.30
16 John Mayberry	1.00	.40
17 Lindy McDaniel	.50	.20
18 Jack McKeon MG	.50	.20
19 Hal McRae	1.00	.40
20 Steve Mingori	.50	.20
21 Amos Otis	1.00	.40
22 Fred Patek	.75	.30
23 Marty Pattin	.50	.20
24 Vada Pinson	1.50	.60
25 Cookie Rojas	.75	.30
26 Tony Solaita	.50	.20
27 Paul Spittorff	.50	.20
28 Frank White	3.00	1.20
29 Jim Wohlford	.50	.20

1975 Royals Postcards

This 32-card set of the Kansas City Royals features player photos on postcard-size cards. The cards are unnumbered and checklisted below in alphabetical order.

	NM	Ex
COMPLETE SET (32)	25.00	10.00
1 Doug Bird	.50	.20
2 George Brett	10.00	4.00
3 Steve Boros CO	.50	.20
4 Nelson Briles	.50	.20
5 Joe Burke GM	.50	.20
6 Steve Busby	.50	.20
7 Bruce Dal Canton	.50	.20
8 Galen Cisco CO	.50	.20
9 Al Cowens	.50	.20
10 Harry Dunlop CO	.50	.20
11 Al Fitzmorris	.50	.20
12 Fran Healy	.50	.20
13 Whitey Herzog MG	.50	.20
14 Harmon Killebrew	3.00	1.20
15 Charlie Lau CO	.50	.20
16 Dennis Leonard	.50	.20
17 Burck Martinez	.75	.30
18 John Mayberry	.50	.20
19 Lindy McDaniel	.75	.30
20 Jack McKeon FO	.75	.30
21 Hal McRae	1.00	.40
22 Steve Mingori	.50	.20
23 Amos Otis	1.00	.40
24 Fred Patek	.75	.30
25 Marty Pattin	.50	.20
26 Vada Pinson	1.50	.60
27 Cookie Rojas	.75	.30
28 Tony Solaita	.50	.20
29 Paul Splittorff	.50	.20
30 Bob Stinson	.50	.20
31 Frank White	1.50	.60
32 Jim Wohlford	.50	.20

1976 Royals A and P

This 16-card set features color photos of the Kansas City Royals and is believed to measure approximately 5 7/8" by 9". The set was produced by the Atlantic and Pacific Tea Company and distributed in Missouri and surrounding areas. The cards are unnumbered and checklisted below in alphabetical order. These cards were issued over a four week period at a rate of four each week. The cards were available when a customer bought two specially priced items at the A and P.

	NM	Ex
COMPLETE SET (16)	20.00	8.00
1 Doug Bird	1.00	.40
2 George Brett	8.00	3.20
3 Steve Busby	1.00	.40
4 Al Cowens	1.00	.40
5 Al Fitzmorris	1.00	.40
6 Dennis Leonard	1.00	.40
7 Buck Martinez	1.50	.60
8 John Mayberry	1.00	.40
9 Hal McRae	2.00	.80
10 Amos Otis	2.00	.80
11 Fred Patek	1.50	.60
12 Tom Poquette	1.00	.40
13 Cookie Rojas	1.50	.60
14 Tony Solaita	1.00	.40
15 Paul Splittorff	1.00	.40
16 Jim Wohlford	1.00	.40

1976 Royals Postcards

This 33-card set of the Kansas City Royals features player photos on postcard-size cards. The cards are unnumbered and checklisted below in alphabetical order.

	NM	Ex
COMPLETE SET (33)	20.00	8.00
1 Doug Bird	.50	.20
2 Steve Boros CO	.50	.20
3 George Brett	6.00	2.40
4 Joe Burke GM	.50	.20
5 Steve Busby	.50	.20
6 Galen Cisco CO	.50	.20
7 Al Cowens	.50	.20
8 Al Fitzsimmons	.50	.20
9 Larry Gura	.50	.20
10 Tom Hall	.50	.20
11 Fran Healy	.50	.20
12 Whitey Herzog MG	1.50	.60
13 Chuck Hiller CO	.50	.20
14 Charley Lau CO	.50	.20
15 Dennis Leonard	.50	.20
16 Mark Littell	.50	.20
17 Buck Martinez	.50	.20
18 John Mayberry	.75	.30
19 Hal McRae	1.00	.40
20 Steve Mingori	.50	.20
21 Dave Nelson	.50	.20
22 Amos Otis	1.00	.40
23 Fred Patek	.75	.30
24 Marty Pattin	.50	.20
25 Tom Poquette	.50	.20
26 Jamie Quirk	.50	.20
27 Cookie Rojas	.75	.30
28 Tony Solaita	.50	.20
29 Paul Splittorff	.50	.20
30 Bob Stinson	.50	.20
31 John Wathan	.75	.30
32 Frank White	1.00	.40
33 Jim Wohlford	.50	.20

1978 Royals

This 27-card set features the Kansas City Royals. The cards measure approximately 3 1/4" by 5". The fronts have black-and-white player portraits with a thin white border. The player's name, position, and team name are printed in a wider border beneath the picture. The backs are blank. The cards are unnumbered and checklisted below in alphabetical order.

	NM	Ex
COMPLETE SET (27)	25.00	10.00
1 Doug Bird	.75	.30
2 Steve Braun	.75	.30
3 George Brett	5.00	2.00
4 Al Cowens	.75	.30
5 Rich Gale	.75	.30
6 Larry Gura	.75	.30
7 Whitey Herzog MG	1.50	.60
8 Al Hrabosky	1.00	.40
9 Clint Hurdle	1.50	.60
10 Pete LaCock	.75	.30
11 Dennis Leonard	.75	.30
12 John Mayberry	1.00	.40
13 Hal McRae	1.50	.60
14 Steve Mingori	.75	.30
15 Dave Nelson	.75	.30
16 Amos Otis	1.50	.60
17 Fred Patek	.75	.30
18 Marty Pattin	.75	.30
19 Tom Poquette	.75	.30
20 Darrell Porter	1.50	.60
21 Paul Splittorff	.75	.30
22 Jerry Terrell	.75	.30
23 U.L. Washington	.75	.30
24 John Wathan	.75	.30
25 Frank White	1.50	.60
26 Willie Wilson	2.00	.80
27 Joe Zdeb	.75	.30

1979-80 Royals Team Issue

These color photos feature members of the Kansas City Royals. The photos measure approximately 4" by 5 1/4" and have blank backs. A fascimile signature is on each photo and we have sequenced these photos in alphabetical order.

	NM	Ex
COMPLETE SET (13)	20.00	8.00
1 Willie Mays Aikens	.75	.30
2 Steve Braun	.50	.20
3 George Brett	5.00	2.00
4 Steve Busby	.50	.20
5 Al Cowens	.50	.20
6 Rich Gale	.50	.20
7 Larry Gura	.50	.20
8 Whitey Herzog MG	1.00	.40
9 Al Hrabosky	.50	.20
10 Clint Hurdle	.75	.30
11 Pete LaCock	.50	.20
12 Dennis Leonard	.75	.30
13 Renie Martin	.50	.20
14 Hal McRae	1.00	.40
15 Steve Mingori	.50	.20
16 Amos Otis	1.00	.40
17 Fred Patek	.50	.20
18 Marty Pattin	.50	.20
19 Tom Poquette	.50	.20
20 Darrell Porter	.75	.30
21 Jamie Quirk	.50	.20
22 Dan Quisenberry	1.50	.60
23 Ed Rodriquez	.50	.20
24 Paul Splitorff	.50	.20
25 Jerry Terrell	.50	.20
26 U.L Washington	.50	.20
27 John Wathan	.50	.20
28 Frank White	1.00	.40
29 Willie Wilson	1.00	.40
30 Joe Zdeb	.50	.20
31 Steve Boros CO Galen Cisco CO	.50	.20
32 John Sullivan CO Chuck Hiller CO	.50	.20

1981 Royals Police

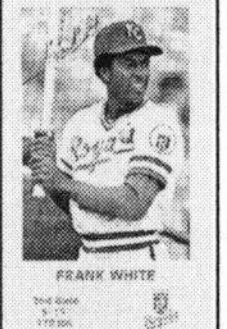

The cards in this ten-card set measure approximately 2 1/2" by 4 1/8". The 1981 Police Kansas City Royals set features full color cards of Royals players. The fronts feature the player's name, position, height and weight, and the Royals' logo in addition to the photo and facsimile autograph of the player. The backs feature player statistics, Tips from the Royals, and identification of the sponsoring organizations. This set can be distinguished from the 1983 Police Royals set by the statistics on the backs of these 1981 cards, whereas the 1983 cards only show a biographical paragraph in the same space.

	Nm-Mt	Ex-Mt
COMPLETE SET (10)	30.00	12.00
1 Willie Aikens	1.50	.60
2 George Brett	15.00	6.00
3 Rich Gale	1.50	.60
4 Clint Hurdle	2.00	.80
5 Dennis Leonard	2.00	.80
6 Hal McRae	2.50	1.00
7 Amos Otis	2.50	1.00
8 U.L. Washington	1.50	.60
9 Frank White	3.00	1.20
10 Willie Wilson	3.00	1.20

1982 Royals

This set features members of the 1982 Kansas City Royals. Since the cards are unnumbered we have checklisted them below in alphabetical order.

	Nm-Mt	Ex-Mt
COMPLETE SET (25)	8.00	3.20
1 Willie Aikens	.25	.10
2 Mike Armstrong	.25	.10
3 Vida Blue	.50	.20
4 George Brett	4.00	1.60
5 Scott Brown	.25	.10
6 Onix Concepcion	.25	.10
7 Dave Frost	.25	.10
8 Cesar Geronimo	.25	.10
9 Larry Gura	.25	.10
10 Dick Howser MG	.25	.10
11 Dennis Leonard	.25	.10
12 Jerry Martin	.25	.10
13 Hal McRae	.75	.30
14 Amos Otis	.75	.30
15 Tom Poquette	.25	.10
16 Greg Pryor	.25	.10
17 Jamie Quirk	.25	.10
18 Dan Quisenberry	.75	.30
19 John Schuerholz GM	.25	.10
20 Paul Splittorff	.25	.10
21 U.L. Washington	.25	.10
22 John Wathan	.25	.10
23 Dennis Werth	.25	.10
24 Frank White	.75	.30
25 Willie Wilson	.75	.30

1983 Royals Police

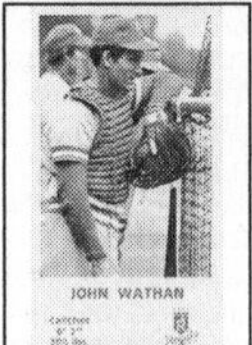

The cards in this ten-card set measure approximately 2 1/2" by 4 1/8". The 1983 Police Kansas City Royals set features full color cards of Royals players. The fronts feature the player's name, height and weight, and the Royals' logo in addition to the player's photo and a facsimile autograph. The backs feature Kids and Cops Facts about the players, Tips from the Royals, and identification of the sponsors of the set. The cards are unnumbered. This set can be distinguished from the 1981 Police Royals set by the absence of statistics on the backs of these 1983 cards, since these 1983 cards only show a brief biographical paragraph.

	Nm-Mt	Ex-Mt
COMPLETE SET (10)	25.00	10.00
1 Willie Aikens	1.50	.60
2 George Brett	12.00	4.80
3 Dennis Leonard	2.00	.80
4 Hal McRae	2.50	1.00
5 Amos Otis	2.50	1.00
6 Dan Quisenberry	2.50	1.00
7 U.L. Washington	1.50	.60
8 John Wathan	2.00	.80
9 Frank White	3.00	1.20
10 Willie Wilson	2.00	.80

1983 Royals Postcards

This 33-card set features photos of the 1983 Kansas City Royals printed on postcard-size cards. The cards are unnumbered and checklisted below in alphabetical order.

	Nm-Mt	Ex-Mt
COMPLETE SET (33)	20.00	8.00
1 Willie Aikens	.50	.20
2 Mike Armstrong	.50	.20
3 Bud Black	.50	.20
4 Vida Blue	.75	.30
5 Cloyd Boyer CO	.50	.20
6 George Brett	5.00	2.00
7 Bill Castro	.50	.20
8 Rocky Colavito CO	2.50	1.00
9 Onix Concepcion	.50	.20
10 Keith Creel	.50	.20
11 Cesar Geronimo	.50	.20
12 Larry Gura	.50	.20
13 Don Hood	.50	.20
14 Dick Howser MG	.50	.20
15 Ron Johnson	.50	.20
16 Dennis Leonard	.50	.20
17 Jose Martinez CO	.50	.20
18 Jerry Martin	.50	.20
19 Hal McRae	.75	.30
20 Joe Nossek CO	.50	.20
21 Amos Otis	.75	.30
22 Greg Pryor	.50	.20
23 Dan Quisenberry	1.00	.40
24 Steve Renko	.50	.20
25 Leon Roberts	.50	.20
26 Jim Schaffer CO	.50	.20
27 John Scherholz GM	.50	.20
28 Joe Simpson	.50	.20
29 Don Slaught	.50	.20
30 Paul Splittorff	.50	.20
31 Bob Tufts	.50	.20
32 U.L. Washington	.50	.20
33 John Wathan	.50	.20
34 Frank White	1.00	.40
35 Willie Wilson	.75	.30

1984 Royals Postcards

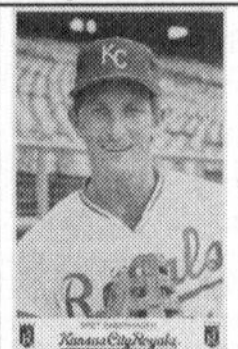

This 37-card set features black-and-white portraits of the 1984 Kansas City Royals in white borders printed on postcard-size cards. The backs are blank. The cards are unnumbered and checklisted below in alphabetical order.

	Nm-Mt	Ex-Mt
COMPLETE SET (37)	15.00	6.00
1 Steve Balboni	.25	.10
2 Howie Bedell CO	.25	.10
3 Joe Beckwith	.25	.10
4 Buddy Biancalana	.25	.10
5 Bud Black	.25	.10
6 Gary Blaylock CO	.25	.10

7 George Brett	5.00	2.00
8 Onix Concepcion	.25	.10
9 Butch Davis	.25	.10
10 Mike Ferraro CO	.25	.10
11 Mark Gubicza	1.00	.40
12 Larry Gura	.25	.10
13 Dick Howser MG	.25	.10
14 Mark Huismann	.25	.10
15 Dane Iorg	.25	.10
16 Danny Jackson	.25	.10
17 Lynn Jones	.25	.10
18 Charlie Leibrandt	.25	.10
19 Dennis Leonard	.25	.10
20 Jose Martinez CO	.25	.10
21 Lee May	.50	.20
22 Hal McRae	.75	.30
23 Darryl Motley	.25	.10
24 Jorge Orta	.25	.10
25 Greg Pryor	.25	.10
26 Dan Quisenberry	.75	.30
27 Leon Roberts	.25	.10
28 Bret Saberhagen	2.00	.80
29 Jim Schaffer CO	.25	.10
30 John Schuerholz GM	.25	.10
31 Pat Sheridan	.25	.10
32 Don Slaught	.25	.10
33 Paul Splittorff	.25	.10
34 U.L. Washington	.25	.10
35 John Wathan	.25	.10
36 Frank White	.75	.30
37 Willie Wilson	.50	.20

1985 Royals Team Issue

This 33-card set features black-and-white photos of the Kansas City Royals measuring approximately 3 1/4" by 5". The cards are unnumbered and checklisted below in alphabetical order.

	Nm-Mt	Ex-Mt
COMPLETE SET (33)	12.00	4.80
1 Steve Balboni	.25	.10
2 Joe Beckwith	.25	.10
3 Buddy Biancalana	.25	.10
4 Bud Black	.25	.10
5 Gary Blaylock CO	.25	.10
6 George Brett	5.00	2.00
7 Onix Concepcion	.25	.10
8 Mike Ferraro CO	.25	.10
9 Mark Gubicza	.50	.20
10 Larry Gura	.25	.10
11 Dick Howser MG	.25	.10
12 Dane Iorg	.25	.10
13 Danny Jackson	.25	.10
14 Lynn Jones	.25	.10
15 Mike Jones	.25	.10
16 Mike LaCoss	.25	.10
17 Charlie Liebrandt	.25	.10
18 Dennis Leonard	.25	.10
19 Jose Martinez CO	.25	.10
20 Lee May CO	.25	.10
21 Hal McRae	.75	.30
22 Darryl Motley	.25	.10
23 Jorge Orta	.25	.10
24 Dan Quisenberry	.75	.30
25 Greg Pryor	.25	.10
26 Bret Saberhagen	1.00	.40
27 Jim Schaffer CO	.25	.10
28 John Schuerholz GM	.25	.10
29 Pat Sheridan	.25	.10
30 Jim Sundberg	.25	.10
31 John Wathan	.25	.10
32 Frank White	.75	.30
33 Willie Wilson	.50	.20

1986 Royals Greats TCMA

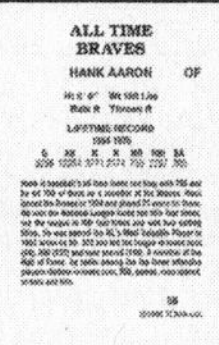

This 12-card standard-size set features some of the best Kansas City Royals from their first two decades. The player's photo, name and position are noted on the front. There is more personal information about the player on the back.

	Nm-Mt	Ex-Mt
COMPLETE SET (12)	3.00	1.20
1 John Mayberry	.50	.20
2 Cookie Rojas	.25	.10
3 Fred Patek	.25	.10
4 Paul Schall	.25	.10
5 Lou Piniella	.75	.30
6 Amos Otis	.50	.20
7 Tom Poquette	.25	.10
8 Ed Kirkpatrick	.25	.10
9 Steve Busby	.25	.10
10 Paul Splittorff	.25	.10
11 Mark Littell	.25	.10
12 Jim Frey MG	.25	.10

1986 Royals Kitty Clover Discs

This set of discs was distributed by Kitty Clover in 1986 to commemorate the Kansas City Royals' World Championship in 1985. Each disc measures 2 3/4" in diameter. Each disc has a white border on the front. Inside this white border is a full color photo of the player with his hat on. However the hat's team emblem has been deleted from the picture. The statistics on back of the disc give the player's 1985 pitching or hitting record as well as his vital statistics.

	Nm-Mt	Ex-Mt
COMPLETE SET (20)	20.00	8.00
1 Lonnie Smith	.50	.20
2 Buddy Biancalana	.50	.20
3 Bret Saberhagen	1.50	.60
4 Hal McRae	1.00	.40
5 Onix Concepcion	.50	.20
6 Jorge Orta	.50	.20
7 Bud Black	.50	.20
8 Dan Quisenberry	1.00	.40
9 Dane Iorg	.50	.20
10 Charlie Leibrandt	.50	.20
11 Pat Sheridan	.50	.20
12 John Wathan	.50	.20
13 Frank White	1.00	.40
14 Darryl Motley	.50	.20
15 Willie Wilson	.75	.30
16 Danny Jackson	.50	.20
17 Steve Balboni	.50	.20
18 Jim Sundberg	.75	.30
19 Mark Gubicza	.50	.20
20 George Brett	10.00	4.00

1986 Royals National Photo

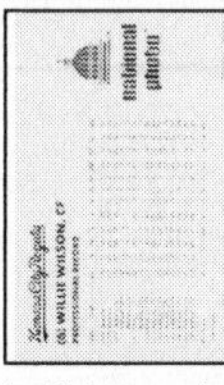

The set contains 24 cards which are numbered only by uniform number except for the checklist card and discount card, which entitles the bearer to a 40 percent discount at National Photo. Cards measure approximately 2 7/8" by 4 1/4". Cards were distributed at the stadium on August 14th. The set was supposedly later available for 3.00 directly from the Royals.

	Nm-Mt	Ex-Mt
COMPLETE SET (24)	12.00	4.80
1 Buddy Biancalana	.25	.10
3 Jorge Orta	.25	.10
4 Greg Pryor	.25	.10
5 George Brett	6.00	2.40
6 Willie Wilson	1.00	.40
8 Jim Sundberg	.25	.10
10 Dick Howser MG	.50	.20
11 Hal McRae	.75	.30
20 Frank White	.75	.30
21 Lonnie Smith	.25	.10
22 Dennis Leonard	.50	.20
23 Mark Gubicza	.25	.10
24 Darryl Motley	.25	.10
25 Danny Jackson	.25	.10
26 Steve Farr	.25	.10
29 Dan Quisenberry	.75	.30
31 Bret Saberhagen	1.00	.40
35 Lynn Jones	.25	.10
37 Charlie Leibrandt	.25	.10
38 Mark Huismann	.25	.10
40 Bud Black	.25	.10
45 Steve Balboni	.25	.10
NNO Discount card	.25	.10
NNO Checklist card	.25	.10

1986 Royals Team Issue

This 27-card set of the Kansas City Royals measures approximately 3 1/4" by 5" and features black-and-white player portraits with white borders. The backs are blank. The cards are unnumbered and checklisted. David Cone has a postcard in this set which predates his Rookie Card.

	Nm-Mt	Ex-Mt
COMPLETE SET (27)	10.00	4.00
1 Steve Balboni	.25	.10
2 Scott Bankhead	.25	.10
3 Buddy Biancalana	.25	.10
4 Bud Black	.25	.10
5 George Brett	2.50	1.00
6 David Cone	2.50	1.00
7 Steve Farr	.25	.10
8 Mark Gubicza	.25	.10
9 Dick Howser MG	.25	.10
10 Danny Jackson	.25	.10
11 Lynn Jones	.25	.10
12 Mike Kingery	.25	.10
13 Rudy Law	.25	.10
14 Charlie Leibrandt	.25	.10
15 Dennis Leonard	.25	.10
16 Hal McRae	.75	.30
17 Darryl Motley	.25	.10
18 Jorge Orta	.25	.10
19 Greg Pryor	.25	.10
20 Jamie Quirk	.25	.10
21 Dan Quisenberry	.50	.20
22 Bret Saberhagen	.75	.30
23 Angel Salazar	.25	.10
24 Lonnie Smith	.25	.10
25 Jim Sundberg	.25	.10
26 Willie Wilson	.50	.20
27 Frank White	.75	.30

1988 Royals Smokey

This set of 28 cards features caricatures of the Kansas City Royals players. The cards are numbered on the back except for the unnumbered title/checklist card. The card set

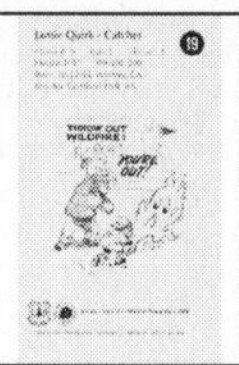

was distributed as a giveaway item at the stadium on August 14th to kids age 14 and under. The cards are approximately 3" by 5" and are in full color on the card fronts. The Smokey logo is in the upper right corner of every obverse.

	Nm-Mt	Ex-Mt
COMPLETE SET (28)	12.00	4.80
1 John Wathan MG	.25	.10
2 Royals Coaches	.50	.20
3 Willie Wilson	.50	.20
4 Danny Tartabull	.50	.20
5 Bo Jackson	1.50	.60
6 Gary Thurman	.25	.10
7 Jerry Don Gleaton	.25	.10
8 Floyd Bannister	.25	.10
9 Bud Black	.25	.10
10 Steve Farr	.25	.10
11 Gene Garber	.50	.20
12 Mark Gubicza	.25	.10
13 Charlie Leibrandt	.25	.10
14 Ted Power	.25	.10
15 Dan Quisenberry	.75	.30
16 Bret Saberhagen	1.00	.40
17 Mike Macfarlane	.50	.20
18 Scotti Madison	.25	.10
19 Jamie Quirk	.25	.10
20 George Brett	4.00	1.60
21 Kevin Seitzer	1.00	.40
22 Bill Pecota	.25	.10
23 Kurt Stillwell	.25	.10
24 Brad Wellman	.25	.10
25 Frank White	.75	.30
26 Jim Eisenreich	.50	.20
27 Smokey Bear	.25	.10
NNO Checklist Card	.25	.10

1988 Royals Team Issue

This 38-card set features black-and-white photos of the Kansas City Royals measuring approximately 3 1/4" by 5". The cards are unnumbered and checklisted below in alphabetical order.

	Nm-Mt	Ex-Mt
COMPLETE SET (38)	12.00	4.80
1 Rick Anderson	.25	.10
2 Steve Balboni	.25	.10
3 Floyd Bannister	.25	.10
4 Bud Black	.25	.10
5 Thad Bosley	.25	.10
6 George Brett	3.00	1.20
7 Bill Buckner	.50	.20
8 Jim Eisenreich	.50	.20
9 Steve Farr	.25	.10
10 Frank Funk CO	.25	.10
11 Gene Garber	.50	.20
12 Adrian Garrett CO	.25	.10
13 Jerry Don Gleaton	.25	.10
14 Mark Gubicza	.25	.10
15 Ed Hearn	.25	.10
16 Bo Jackson	1.00	.40
17 Charlie Liebrandt	.25	.10
18 Mike Lum CO	.25	.10
19 Mike Macfarlane	.50	.20
20 Jeff Montgomery	1.00	.40
21 Ed Napoleon CO	.25	.10
22 Larry Owen	.25	.10
23 Bill Pecota	.25	.10
24 Ted Power	.25	.10
25 Jamie Quirk	.25	.10
26 Dan Quisenberry	.75	.30
27 Bret Saberhagen	.75	.30
28 Bob Schaefer CO	.25	.10
29 Jim Schaffer CO	.25	.10
30 Kevin Seitzer	.25	.10
31 Kurt Stillwell	.25	.10
32 Pat Tabler	.25	.10
33 Danny Tartabull	.25	.10
34 Gary Thurman	.25	.10
35 John Wathan MG	.25	.10
36 Brad Wellman	.25	.10
37 Frank White	.75	.30
38 Willie Wilson	.50	.20

1989 Royals Tastee Discs

This set features members of the 1989 Kansas City Royals. These discs were issued by Tastee-Freez.

	Nm-Mt	Ex-Mt
COMPLETE SET (12)	12.00	4.80
1 George Brett	8.00	3.20
2 Kevin Seitzer	.75	.30
3 Pat Tabler	.50	.20
4 Danny Tartabull	.75	.30
5 Willie Wilson	.75	.30
6 Bo Jackson	1.50	.60
7 Frank White	1.00	.40
8 Kurt Stillwell	.50	.20
9 Mark Gubicza	.50	.20
10 Charlie Leibrandt	.50	.20
11 Bret Saberhagen	1.50	.60
12 Steve Farr	.50	.20

1990 Royals Postcards

This 29-card set features photos of the 1990 Kansas City Royals printed on postcard-size cards. The cards are unnumbered and checklisted below in alphabetical order.

	Nm-Mt	Ex-Mt
COMPLETE SET (29)	10.00	3.00
1 Kevin Appier	1.00	.30
2 Luis Aquino	.25	.07
3 Bob Boone	.75	.23
4 George Brett	3.00	.90
5 Steve Crawford	.25	.07
6 Mark Davis	.25	.07
7 Jim Eisenreich	.50	.15
8 Glenn Ezell CO	.25	.07
9 Steve Farr	.25	.07
10 Frank Funk CO	.25	.07
11 Adrian Garrett CO	.25	.07
12 Tom Gordon	.75	.23
13 Bo Jackson	1.00	.30
14 Steve Jeltz	.25	.07
15 Mike Macfarlane	.25	.07
16 John Mayberry CO	.25	.07
17 Jeff Montgomery	.50	.15
18 Rey Palacios	.25	.07
19 Bill Pecota	.25	.07
20 Gerald Perry	.25	.07
21 Bret Saberhagen	1.00	.30
22 Kevin Seitzer	.50	.15
23 Terry Shumpert	.50	.15
24 Kurt Stillwell	.25	.07
25 Pat Tabler	.25	.07
26 Danny Tartabull	.50	.15
27 John Wathan	.25	.07
28 Frank White	.75	.23
29 Willie Wilson	.50	.15

1991 Royals Police

This 27-card set, measuring 2 5/*' by 4 1/8" was distributed by the Metropolitan Chiefs and Sheriffs Association. The cards are unnumbered and checklisted below in alphabetical order, with the coaches' cards listed at the end of our checklist. Supposedly many of the Bo Jackson cards were burned after Bo was released from the Royals.

	Nm-Mt	Ex-Mt
COMPLETE SET (27)	15.00	4.50
COMMON SP	5.00	1.50
1 Kevin Appier	1.00	.30
2 Luis Aquino	.25	.07
3 Mike Boddicker	.25	.07
4 George Brett	4.00	1.20
5 Steve Crawford	.25	.07
6 Mark Davis	.50	.15
7 Storm Davis	.25	.07
8 Jim Eisenreich	.50	.15
9 Kirk Gibson	.75	.23
10 Tom Gordon	.50	.15
11 Mark Gubicza	.25	.07
12 Bo Jackson SP	5.00	1.50
13 Mike Macfarlane	.25	.07
14 Andy McGaffigan	.25	.07
15 Brian McRae	1.00	.30
16 Jeff Montgomery	.75	.23
17 Bill Pecota	.25	.07
18 Bret Saberhagen	1.00	.30
19 Kevin Seitzer	.50	.15
20 Terry Shumpert	.25	.07
21 Kurt Stillwell	.25	.07
22 Danny Tartabull	.50	.15
23 Gary Thurman	.25	.07
24 John Wathan MG	.25	.07
25 Pat Dobson CO	.25	.07
Adrian Garrett CO		
26 Glenn Ezell CO	.25	.07
Lynn Jones CO		
Bob Schaefer CO		
27 Checklist Card	.25	.07

1992 Royals Police

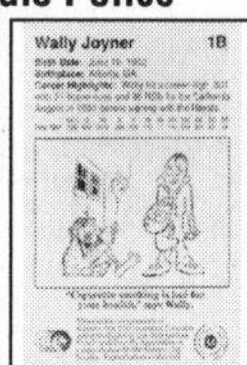

This 27-card set, given out as a promotion at the stadium, was sponsored by the Kansas City Life Insurance Company and distributed by the Metropolitan Chiefs and Sheriffs Association. It is rumored that two cards were pulled prior to release (the cards of Kevin Seitzer, who went to Milwaukee, and Kirk Gibson, who went to Pittsburgh). The cards are unnumbered and checklisted below in alphabetical order.

	Nm-Mt	Ex-Mt
COMPLETE SET (27)	10.00	3.00
1 Kevin Appier	1.00	.30
2 Luis Aquino	.25	.07
3 Mike Boddicker	.25	.07
4 George Brett	3.00	.90
5 Mark Davis	.25	.07
6 Jim Eisenreich	.50	.15
7 Kirk Gibson	.75	.23
8 Tom Gordon	.50	.15
9 Mark Gubicza	.25	.07
10 Chris Gwynn	.25	.07
11 David Howard	.25	.07
12 Gregg Jefferies	.25	.07
13 Joel Johnston	.25	.07
14 Wally Joyner	.50	.15
15 Mike Macfarlane	.25	.07
16 Mike Magnante	.25	.07
17 Brent Mayne	.25	.07
18 Brian McRae	.25	.07
19 Hal McRae MG	.50	.15
20 Kevin McReynolds	.25	.07
21 Bob Melvin CO	.25	.07
22 Keith Miller	.25	.07
23 Jeff Montgomery	.75	.23
24 Kevin Seitzer	.50	.15
25 Terry Shumpert	.25	.07
26 Gary Thurman	.25	.07
27 Glenn Ezell CO	.25	.07
Adrian Garrett CO		
Guy Hansen CO		
Lynn Jones CO		
Bruce Kison CO		
Lee May CO		

1993 Royals Police

This 27-card set was given away to fans attending the Royals-Twins game of April 10. The set was sponsored by Kansas City Life Insurance and distributed by the Metropolitan Chiefs and Sheriffs Association. The cards are unnumbered and checklisted below in alphabetical order.

	Nm-Mt	Ex-Mt
COMPLETE SET (27)	10.00	3.00
1 Hal McRae MG	.50	.15
2 Kevin Appier	.75	.23
3 Luis Aquino	.25	.07
4 Mike Boddicker	.25	.07
5 George Brett	3.00	.90
6 David Cone	1.00	.30
7 Greg Gagne	.25	.07
8 Mark Gardner	.25	.07
9 Tom Gordon	.50	.15
10 Mark Gubicza	.25	.07
11 Chris Gwynn	.25	.07
12 Chris Haney	.25	.07
13 Felix Jose	.25	.07
14 Wally Joyner	.50	.15
15 Kevin Koslofski	.25	.07
16 Jose Lind	.25	.07
17 Mike Macfarlane	.25	.07
18 Brent Mayne	.25	.07
19 Brian McRae	.25	.07
20 Kevin McReynolds	.25	.07
21 Rusty Meacham	.25	.07
22 Keith Miller	.25	.07
23 Jeff Montgomery	.50	.15
24 Hipolito Pichardo	.25	.07
25 Curtis Wilkerson	.25	.07
26 Craig Wilson	.25	.07
27 Steve Boros CO	.25	.07
Glenn Ezell CO		
Guy Hansen CO		
Bruce Kison CO		
Lee May CO		

1993 Royals Stadium Club

This 30-card standard-size set features the 1993 Kansas City Royals. The set was issued in hobby (plastic box) and retail (blister) form.

	Nm-Mt	Ex-Mt
COMP. FACT SET (30)	4.00	1.20
1 George Brett	2.00	.60
2 Mike Macfarlane	.10	.03
3 Tom Gordon	.25	.07
4 Wally Joyner	.25	.07
5 Kevin Appier	.25	.07
6 Phil Hiatt	.10	.03
7 Keith Miller	.10	.03
8 Hipolito Pichardo	.10	.03
9 Chris Gwynn	.10	.03
10 Jose Lind	.10	.03
11 Mark Gubicza	.10	.03
12 Dennis Rasmussen	.10	.03
13 Mike Magnante	.10	.03
14 Joe Vitiello	.10	.03
15 Kevin McReynolds	.10	.03
16 Greg Gagne	.10	.03
17 David Cone	.75	.23
18 Brent Mayne	.10	.03
19 Jeff Montgomery	.25	.07
20 Joe Randa	.10	.03
21 Felix Jose	.10	.03
22 Bill Sampen	.10	.03
23 Curt Wilkerson	.10	.03
24 Mark Gardner	.10	.03
25 Brian McRae	.10	.03
26 Hubie Brooks	.10	.03
27 Chris Eddy	.10	.03
28 Harvey Pulliam	.10	.03
29 Rusty Meacham	.10	.03
30 Danny Miceli	.10	.03

1993 Royals Star 25th

Subtitled "Royals All-Time Team" this 16-card set celebrates the Royals' 25th Anniversary (1969-1993), features great Royals of the past, and was originally issued in a perforated sheet. The sheet measures approximately 10 3/8" by

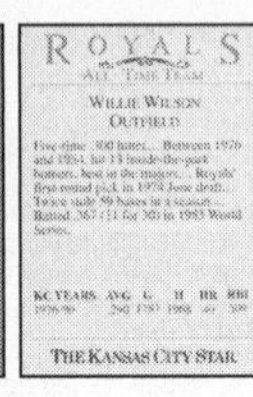

14 3/8"; after perforation, each card would measure the standard size. The individual cards measure the standard size. The cards are unnumbered and checklisted below in alphabetical order.

	Nm-Mt	Ex-Mt
COMPLETE SET (16)	20.00	6.00
1 George Brett	10.00	3.00
2 Steve Busby	1.00	.30
3 Al Cowens	1.00	.30
4 Dick Howser MG	1.50	.45
5 Dennis Leonard	1.50	.45
6 John Mayberry	1.50	.45
7 Hal McRae	2.00	.60
8 Amos Otis	2.00	.60
9 Fred Patek	1.50	.45
10 Darrell Porter	1.50	.45
11 Dan Quisenberry	2.00	.60
12 Bret Saberhagen	2.00	.60
13 Paul Splittorff	1.00	.30
14 Frank White	1.50	.45
15 Willie Wilson	1.50	.45
16 Title card	1.00	.30

1995 Royals Postcards

These 5" by 7" blank-backed postcards feature members of the 1995 Kansas City Royals. The fronts have white borders, a color photo and the players name and team logo on the bottom. Since they are unnumbered we have sequenced them in alphabetical order.

	Nm-Mt	Ex-Mt
COMPLETE SET (31)	8.00	2.40
1 Kevin Appier	.50	.15
2 Bob Boone MG	.50	.15
3 Pat Borders	.25	.07
4 Billy Brewer	.25	.07
5 Melvin Bunch	.25	.07
6 Edgar Caceres	.25	.07
7 Vince Coleman	.50	.15
8 Gary Gaetti	.50	.15
9 Greg Gagne	.25	.07
10 Tom Goodwin	.25	.07
11 Tom Gordon	.50	.15
12 Jeff Grotewold	.25	.07
13 Mark Gubicza	.25	.07
14 Bob Hamelin	.25	.07
15 Chris Haney	.25	.07
16 Phil Hiatt	.25	.07
17 David Howard	.25	.07
18 Wally Joyner	.50	.15
19 Keith Lockhart	.25	.07
20 Brent Mayne	.25	.07
21 Rusty Meacham	.25	.07
22 Jeff Montgomery	.50	.15
23 Les Norman	.25	.07
24 Jon Nunnally	.25	.07
25 Hipolito Pichardo	.25	.07
26 Joe Randa	.75	.23
27 Dennis Rasmussen	.25	.07
28 Dilson Torres	.25	.07
29 Michael Tucker	.50	.15
30 Chris Stynes	.25	.07
31 Joe Vitiello	.25	.07

1996 Royals Police

This 26-card set of the Kansas City Royals measures 2 5/8" by 4" and was sponsored by the Kansas City Life Insurance Company. The fronts feature color action player photos in a thin white border. The backs carry player information, statistics, and a safety message. The cards are unnumbered and checklisted below in alphabetical order.

	Nm-Mt	Ex-Mt
COMPLETE SET (26)	4.00	1.20
1 Kevin Appier	.25	.07
2 Tim Belcher	.10	.03
3 Bob Boone MG	.25	.07
4 Melvin Bunch	.10	.03
5 Terry Clark	.10	.03
6 Jim Converse	.10	.03
7 Johnny Damon	1.50	.45
8 Tom Goodwin	.25	.07
9 Mark Gubicza	.10	.03
10 Bob Hamelin	.10	.03
11 Chris Haney	.10	.03
12 David Howard	.10	.03
13 Rick Huisman	.10	.03
14 Jason Jacome	.10	.03
15 Keith Lockhart	.10	.03
16 Mike Macfarlane	.10	.03
17 Rusty Meacham	.10	.03
18 Jeff Montgomery	.25	.07
19 Les Norman	.10	.03
20 Jon Nunnally	.10	.03
21 Jose Offerman	.10	.03
22 Hipolito Pichardo	.10	.03
23 Joe Randa	.50	.15
24 Bip Roberts	.10	.03
25 Michael Tucker	.25	.07
26 Joe Vitiello	.10	.03

1997 Royals Police

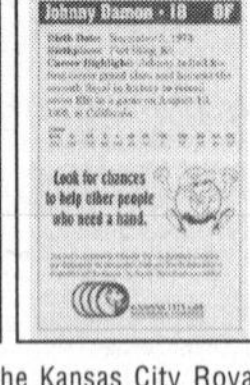

This 23-card set of the Kansas City Royals measures 2 5/8" by 4" and was sponsored by the Kansas City Life Insurance Company. The fronts feature color action player photos in a white border. The backs carry player information, statistics, and a safety message. The cards are unnumbered and checklisted below in alphabetical order.

	Nm-Mt	Ex-Mt
COMPLETE SET (23)	8.00	2.40
1 Kevin Appier	.50	.15
2 Tim Belcher	.25	.07
3 Jay Bell	.25	.07
4 Jaime Bluma	.25	.07
5 Bob Boone MG	.25	.07
6 Johnny Damon	1.00	.30
7 Chili Davis	.75	.23
8 Tom Goodwin	.50	.15
9 Chris Haney	.25	.07
10 David Howard	.25	.07
11 Rick Huisman	.25	.07
12 Jason Jacome	.25	.07
13 Jeff King	.25	.07
14 Mike Macfarlane	.25	.07
15 Jeff Montgomery	.50	.15
16 Jose Offerman	.25	.07
17 Craig Paquette	.25	.07
18 Hipolito Pichardo	.25	.07
19 Bip Roberts	.25	.07
20 Jose Rosado	.25	.07
21 Mike Sweeney	1.50	.45
22 Joe Vitiello	.25	.07
23 Sluggerrr(Mascot)	.25	.07

1999 Royals Postcards

These postcars measure 3" by 5" and feature members of the 1999 Kansas City Royals. The fronts have a player photo and identification and some cards were issued with the "Conoco" logo. No matter in what version these cards exist, the values are the same. Since the cards are not numbered we have sequenced them in alphabetical order.

	Nm-Mt	Ex-Mt
COMPLETE SET	10.00	3.00
1 Kevin Appier	.50	.15
2 Carlos Beltran	1.00	.30
3 Tim Byrdak	.25	.07
4 Johnny Damon	1.50	.45
5 Jermaine Dye	.50	.15
6 Carlos Febles	.25	.07
7 Jeremy Giambi	.25	.07
8 Jed Hansen	.25	.07
9 Jeff King	.25	.07
10 Chad Krueter	.25	.07
11 Mendy Lopez	.25	.07
12 Jeff Montgomery	.50	.15
13 Alvin Morman	.25	.07
14 Tony Muser MG	.25	.07
15 Hipolito Pichardo	.25	.07
16 Jim Pittsley	.25	.07
17 Scott Pose	.25	.07
18 Jamie Quirk	.25	.07
19 Joe Randa	.25	.07
20 Jose Rosado	.25	.07
21 Glendon Rusch	.25	.07
22 Rey Sanchez	.25	.07
23 Scott Service	.25	.07
24 Tim Spehr	.25	.07
25 Jeff Suppan	.25	.07
26 Larry Sutton	.25	.07
27 Mac Suzuki	.25	.07
28 Mike Sweeney	1.00	.30
29 Matt Whisenant	.25	.07
30 Frank White CO	.50	.15
31 Jay Witasick	.25	.07
32 Kauffman Stadium	.25	.07

2000 Royals Safety

This set, sponsored by the Kansas City Life Insurance Company and featuring safety hints, features members of the 2000 Kansas City Royals team. Since the oversize cards are unnumbered, we have sequenced them in alphabetical order.

	Nm-Mt	Ex-Mt
COMPLETE SET	15.00	4.50
1 Carlos Beltran	1.50	.45
2 Ricky Bottalico	.50	.15
3 Johnny Damon	1.50	.45
4 Todd Dunwoody	.50	.15
5 Chad Durbin	.50	.15
6 Jermaine Dye	.75	.23
7 Carlos Febles	.50	.15
8 Chris Fussell	.50	.15
9 Ray Holbert	.50	.15
10 Brian Johnson	.50	.15
11 Tony Muser MG	.50	.15
12 Scott Pose	.50	.15
13 Mark Quinn	.50	.15
14 Joe Randa	.50	.15
15 Jeff Reboulet	.50	.15
16 Dan Reichert	.50	.15
17 Jose Rosado	.50	.15
18 Rey Sanchez	.50	.15
19 Jose Santiago	.50	.15
20 Jerry Spradlin	.50	.15
21 Blake Stein	.50	.15
22 Jeff Suppan	.50	.15
23 Mike Sweeney	2.00	.60
24 Jay Witasik	.50	.15
25 Slugger Mascot	.50	.15

2002 Royals KC Life

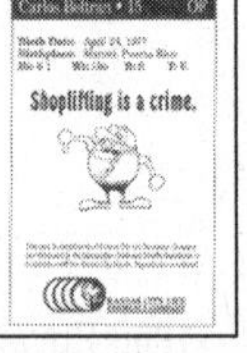

This set, which measures 2 5/8" by 4" features members of the 2002 K.C. Royals. The fronts features a player's photo with the same photo repeated in the background as if it were a mirror effect. The back features player biographical information along with a safety tip. This set was sponsored by the Kansas City Life Insurance Companies. Since these cards are not numbered, we have sequenced them in alphabetical order.

	Nm-Mt	Ex-Mt
COMPLETE SET	8.00	2.40
1 Luis Alicea	.25	.07
2 Cory Bailey	.25	.07
3 Carlos Beltran	1.50	.45
4 Dee Brown	.75	.23
5 Paul Byrd	.25	.07
6 Chad Durbin	.25	.07
7 Carlos Febles	.25	.07
8 Jason Grimsley	.25	.07
9 Roberto Hernandez	.50	.15
10 A.J. Hinch	.25	.07
11 Raul Ibanez	.50	.15
12 Chuck Knoblauch	.50	.15
13 Darrell May	.25	.07
14 Brent Mayne	.25	.07
15 Dave McCarty	.25	.07
16 Tony Muser MG	.25	.07
17 Neifi Perez	.25	.07
18 Mark Quinn	.25	.07
19 Joe Randa	.25	.07
20 Dan Reichert	.25	.07
21 Donnie Sadler	.25	.07
22 Blake Stein	.25	.07
23 Jeff Suppan	.25	.07
24 Mike Sweeney	1.50	.45
25 Michael Tucker	.50	.15
26 Sluggerr Mascot	.25	.07

2003 Royals Police

This set, which measures 2 5/8" by 4" features members of the 2003 K.C. Royals. The fronts features a player's photo with the same photo repeated in the background as if it were a mirror effect. The back features player biographical information along with a safety tip. This set was sponsored by the Kansas City Life Insurance Companies. Since these cards are not numbered, we have sequenced them in alphabetical order.

	MINT	NRMT
COMPLETE SET (27)	8.00	3.60
1 Jeremy Affeldt	.25	.11
2 Miguel Asencio	.25	.11
3 James Baldwin	.25	.11
4 Carlos Beltran	1.00	.45
5 Brandon Berger	.25	.11
6 Angel Berroa	1.00	.45
7 Ryan Bukvich	.25	.11
8 Mike DiFelice	.25	.11
9 Carlos Febles	.25	.11
10 Chris George	.25	.11
11 Jason Grimsley	.25	.11
12 Aaron Guiel	.25	.11
13 Ken Harvey	.50	.23
14 Runelvys Hernandez	.25	.11
15 Raul Ibanez	.50	.23
16 Albie Lopez	.25	.11
17 Mike MacDougal	.75	.35
18 Darrell May	.25	.11
19 Brent Mayne	.25	.11
20 Scott Mullen	.25	.11
21 Tony Pena MG	.25	.11
22 Joe Randa	.25	.11
23 Desi Relaford	.25	.11
24 Mike Sweeney	1.00	.45
25 Michael Tucker	.50	.23
26 Kris Wilson	.25	.11
27 Sluggerrr Mascot	.25	.11

2003 Royals Team Issue

These blank-backed color cards, which measure approximately 4" by 6" feature members of the 2003 Kansas City Royals. Each of these cards has the player's name and uniform number in a silver strip on the bottom. Since these cards are unnumbered except for uniform information, we have sequenced them in alphabetical order. It is possible that more cards exist so any additional information is appreciated.

	MINT	NRMT
COMPLETE SET	10.00	4.50
1 Jeremy Affeldt	.50	.23
2 Carlos Beltran	1.50	.70
3 Angel Berroa	1.50	.70
4 Dee Brown	.75	.35
5 Mike DiFelice	.50	.23
6 Jimmy Gobble	.50	.23
7 Aaron Guiel	.50	.23
8 Ken Harvey	.75	.35
9 Raul Ibanez	.75	.35
10 Mike MacDougal	1.00	.45
11 Darrell May	.50	.23
12 Scott Mullen	.50	.23
13 Tony Pena MG	.50	.23
14 Desi Relaford	.50	.23
15 Mike Sweeney	1.50	.70
16 Michael Tucker	.75	.35

1933 Ruth Blue Bird

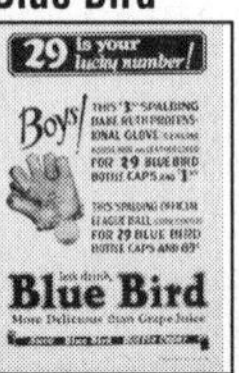

This card, which measures approximately 3 7/8" by 5 7/" features all-time slugger Babe Ruth. The photo shows the Babe in a batting pose, while the back has an advertisment for Blue Bird drink.

	Ex-Mt	VG
1 Babe Ruth	1000.00	500.00

1996 Ruth Danbury Mint

This one card standard-size set features a card of Babe Ruth set against a gold relief border. The front has a photo of Ruth along with his name, team affiliation and position. The back has his vital stats along with his career stats. We suspect there might be more Danbury Mint cards so any further cards known would be appreciated.

	Nm-Mt	Ex-Mt
1 Babe Ruth	10.00	3.00

1992 Ruth Delphi

This standard size card was issued to promote the Legends of Baseball plates released by the Delphi company. With each plate in the series, collectors received a free old-fashioned Baseball Legends card depicting the player and recounting the milestones of his career. The front features the artwork of Brent Benger showing Babe Ruth in the batter's box watching the flight of the ball. The card is unnumbered.

	Nm-Mt	Ex-Mt
1 Babe Ruth	2.00	.60

1992 Ruth Gold Entertainment

Gold Entertainment produced this five-card holographic set celebrating the life and legend of Babe Ruth, along with Lou Gehrig and Roger Maris. The artwork for these cards was created by Hollywood artists Mike Butkus and Alan Hunter. This standard-size set was sold in box

cases containing 20 five-card sets (16 in silver and four in gold) and four bonus holograms (of a surprise player). The gold sets are valued at one and a half times the (silver) values listed below. The production run is reported to be 12,500 boxes, with each box carrying a numbered holographic seal. Each set features two double-sided full-bleed holograms and three full-color backs presenting biography, statistics, and quotes. The cards are numbered on the front in a diamond in the upper left corner (the cards with the color backs also carry a number on the back).

	Nm-Mt	Ex-Mt
COMPLETE SET (5)	10.00	3.00
2 Babe Ruth Lou Gehrig Two-sided hologram Ruth's stats on front Gehrig's stats on back	3.00	.90
4 Babe Ruth Roger Maris 61 in 1961 - 60 in 1927 Two-sided hologram Ruth and Maris on front	3.00	.90

1920 Ruth Heading Home

This six card blank-back set, which measure approximately 1 1/2" by 2 3/8", was issued to promote Babe Ruth in his first starring movie vehichle. That film was titled "Heading Home" and each card shows the Babe with a bat in his hand

	Ex-Mt	VG
COMPLETE SET (6)	4000.00	2000.00
COMMON CARD	750.00	375.00

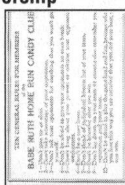

1928 Ruth Home Run Candy Membership

This one card set was issued to people who purchased a ruth's home run candy which cost a nickel and featured a photo of the Babe on the front and ten general rules for members on the back. Very few copies are known to exist of this card and any additional information is greatly appreciated. A few wrappers are also known to exist of this product.

	Ex-Mt	VG
1 Babe Ruth	2000.00	1000.00

1921 Ruth Pathe

This 7" by 9" card was issued as a premium card by the Pathe Freres Phonograph Company. This card is printed in green and gray tones and shows the Babe with his hands at the waist. The back describes his 1920 season when he set a then record with 54 homers in a season.

	Ex-Mt	VG
1 Babe Ruth	2000.00	1000.00

1995 Ruth Stamp Cards.

These 12 standard-size cards were issued by the Sport Stamps Collectors Association to

honor the 100th anniversary of Babe ruth's birth. The fronts feature pitcures of Babe Ruth surrounded by a frame. In the upper left corner is the word "Guyana" while on the right corner there is a $160 price tag. The backs describe various parts of Babe's life and also have a montage of some of the photos shown on the fronts. This set was issued in a special box and was a full reprint of the stamps issued in Guyana.

	Nm-Mt	Ex-Mt
COMP.FACT SET	10.00	3.00
COMMON CARD	1.00	.30
6 Babe Ruth Lou Gehrig	2.00	.60

1990 Ryan Arlington Yellow Pages

This card was distributed by the Greater Arlington/Mansfield Spotlight Yellow Pages and measures approximately 5 1/4" by 6 3/4". The front displays a color action picture of Nolan Ryan pitching, and his 17 Major League strike out records are printed on the back.

	Nm-Mt	Ex-Mt
1 Nolan Ryan	5.00	1.50

1989 Ryan Best Western

This one-card standard-size set was sponsored by Best Western in conjunction with American Express to commemorate the 50th anniversary of Little League Baseball. The cards were distributed at a Texas Rangers home game in 1989. This card has a black and white photo of Nolan Ryan in his Little League uniform.

	Nm-Mt	Ex-Mt
NNO0 Nolan Ryan Little League photo	3.00	1.20

1994 Ryan Legends Postcard

This postcard features Texas Ranger great Nolan Ryan. This was issued after Ryan's career finished and is a tribute to his long and fabled career which included more than 300 wins and the shattering of the exisitng strikeout record.

	Nm-Mt	Ex-Mt
1 Nolan Ryan	2.00	.60

1994 Ryan SSCA

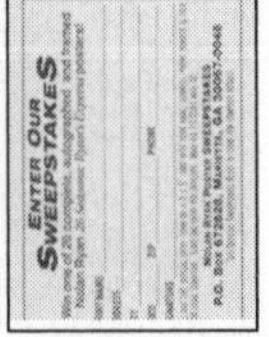

This 12-card set was distributed in sealed factory boxes and are actually official postage stamp cards issued by the Government of Guyana. The fronts feature color photos of Nolan Ryan with a gold foil simulated autograph. The backs carry information about Ryan's career. 1000 redemption cards were randomly seeded into sets which could be redeemed for a special card autographed by Nolan Ryan himself.

	Nm-Mt	Ex-Mt
COMPLETE SET (12)	20.00	6.00
COMMON CARD (1-12)	2.00	.60

1993 Ryan Texas Supermarket Stickers

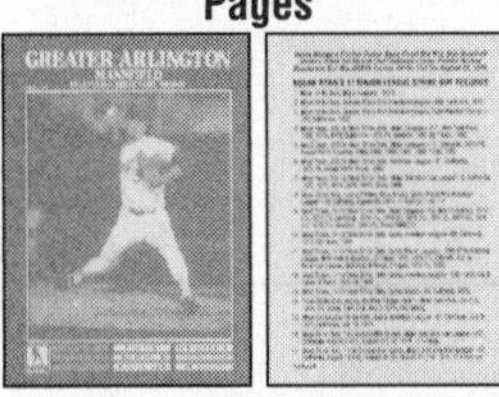

These stickers featured reprints of Nolan Ryan Topps cards. They were regionally issued in various Texas Supermarkets: Minyards, Super S, Brookshire Borthers and Budget Chopper. over a period of ten weeks. Each sticker sheet contained three "reprint" cards. These stickers were issued by Big League Collectibles and measure 98 percent of the regular card size.

	Nm-Mt	Ex-Mt
COMPLETE SET (30)	10.00	3.00
COMMON STICKER (1-30)	.50	.15

1993 Ryan Whataburger

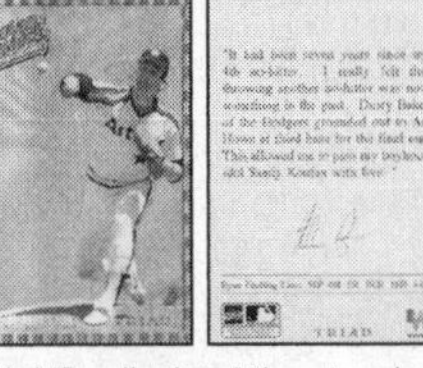

Subtitled "Recollections," these ten plastic-coated cards were produced by Triad and distributed by Whataburger. The standard-size fronts have a prismatic border and color action shots of Ryan, which lay under the diffraction grating plastic coating that gives a 3-D appearance. The cards are unnumbered.

	Nm-Mt	Ex-Mt
COMPLETE SET (10)	5.00	1.50
COMMON CARD (1-10)	.50	.15

1936 S and S WG8

These cards were distributed as part of a baseball game produced in 1936. The cards each measure approximately 2 1/4" by 3 1/2" and have rounded corners. The card fronts are all oriented horizontally and show a small black and white photo of the player, his name, position, his team, vital statistics and the game outcome associated with that particular card. The card backs are evenly split between a plain green back with a thin white border or a plain back on a tannish paper stock. Since the cards are unnumbered, they are listed below in alphabetical order.

	Ex-Mt	VG
COMPLETE SET (52)	800.00	400.00
1 Luke Appling	25.00	12.50
2 Earl Averill	25.00	12.50
3 Zeke Bonura	10.00	5.00
4 Dolph Camilli	15.00	7.50
5 Ben Cantwell	10.00	5.00
6 Phil Cavarretta	20.00	10.00
7 Rip Collins	15.00	7.50
8 Joe Cronin	50.00	25.00
9 Frank Crosetti	20.00	10.00
10 Kiki Cuyler	25.00	12.50
11 Virgil Davis	10.00	5.00
12 Frank Demaree	15.00	7.50
13 Paul Derringer	25.00	12.50
14 Bill Dickey	60.00	30.00
15 Woody English	10.00	5.00
16 Fred Fitzsimmons	15.00	7.50
17 Rick Ferrell	25.00	12.50
18 Pete Fox	10.00	5.00
19 Jimmy Foxx	60.00	30.00
20 Larry French	10.00	5.00
21 Frank Frisch	50.00	25.00
22 August Galan	15.00	7.50
23 Charlie Gehringer	50.00	25.00
24 John Gill	10.00	5.00
25 Charles Grimm	20.00	10.00
26 Mule Haas	15.00	7.50
27 Stan Hack	20.00	10.00
28 Bill Hallahan	15.00	7.50
29 Mel Harder	20.00	10.00
30 Gabby Hartnett	25.00	12.50
31 Ray Hayworth	10.00	5.00
32 Ralston Hemsley	10.00	5.00
33 Bill Herman	25.00	12.50
34 Frank Higgins	10.00	5.00
35 Carl Hubbell	50.00	25.00
36 Bill Jurges	10.00	5.00
37 Vernon Kennedy	10.00	5.00
38 Chuck Klein	25.00	12.50
39 Mike Kreevich	10.00	5.00
40 Bill Lee	10.00	5.00
41 Joe Medwick	25.00	12.50
42 Van Mungo	15.00	7.50
43 James O'Dea	10.00	5.00
44 Mel Ott	50.00	25.00
45 Rip Radcliff	10.00	5.00
46 Pie Traynor	25.00	12.50
47 Arky Vaughan	25.00	12.50
48 Joe Vosmik	10.00	5.00
49 Lloyd Waner	25.00	12.50
50 Paul Waner	25.00	12.50
51 Lon Warneke	15.00	7.50
52 Floyd Young	10.00	5.00

1911 S74 Silks

Issued around 1911, these silk fabric collectibles have designs similar to the designs in the T205 Cigarette card set. The silk itself is 2" by 3" and the image is 1 1/4" by 2 3/8". The line work on the silks is in one color only, with colors of blue, red, brown and several variations between red and brown known to exist. The field or stock color is known in white and several pastel tints. The cards are unnumbered but have been numbered and listed by team alphabetical order and then player alphabetical order within the teams in the checklist below. Turkey Red and Old Mill Cigarettes are among the issuers of these silks. These silks were produced in more than one year and in fact may possibly be broken into two distinct sets. Silks with Helmar and Red Sun backs can also be found; although the Red Sun variations seem to be very scarce. White backgroung silks ave valued 25% higher. Silks which still have the paper ad backing attached are worth double the prices listed below.

	Ex-Mt	VG
COMPLETE SET (122)	8000.00	4000.00
1 Bill Carrigan	40.00	20.00
2 Ed Cicotte	150.00	75.00
3 Tris Speaker	200.00	100.00
4 Jake Stahl	40.00	20.00
5 Hugh Duffy	120.00	60.00
6 Amby McConnell	40.00	20.00
7 Freddie Parent	40.00	20.00
8 Fred Payne	40.00	20.00
9 Lee Tannehill	40.00	20.00
10 Doc White	40.00	20.00
11 Terry Turner	40.00	20.00
12 Cy Young	200.00	100.00
13 Ty Cobb	800.00	400.00
14 Jim Delahanty	40.00	20.00
15 Davy Jones	40.00	20.00
16 George Moriarity	40.00	20.00
17 George Mullin	50.00	25.00
18 Ed Summers	40.00	20.00
19 Ed Willett	40.00	20.00
20 Hal Chase	80.00	40.00
21 Russ Ford	40.00	20.00
22 Charlie Hemphill	40.00	20.00
23 John Knight	40.00	20.00
24 John Quinn	50.00	25.00
25 Harry Wolter	40.00	20.00
26 Frank Baker	120.00	60.00
27 Jack Barry	40.00	20.00
28 Chief Bender	120.00	60.00
29 Eddie Collins	120.00	60.00
30 Jimmy Dygert	40.00	20.00
31 Topsy Hartsel	40.00	20.00
32 Harry Krause	40.00	20.00
33 Danny Murphy	40.00	20.00
34 Rube Oldring	40.00	20.00
35 Barney Pelty	40.00	20.00
36 George Stone	40.00	20.00
37 Bobby Wallace	120.00	60.00
38 Kid Elberfeld	40.00	20.00
39 Walter Johnson	400.00	200.00
40 Germany Schaefer	50.00	25.00
41 Gabby Street	40.00	20.00
42 Fred Beck	40.00	20.00
43 Peaches Graham	40.00	20.00
44 Buck Herzog	40.00	20.00
45 Al Mattern	40.00	20.00
46 Dave Shean	40.00	20.00
47 Harry Steinfeldt	50.00	25.00
48 Cy Barger (2)	40.00	20.00
49 George Bell	40.00	20.00
50 Bill Bergen	40.00	20.00
51 Bill Dahlen	50.00	25.00
52 Jake Daubert	50.00	25.00
53 John Hummel	40.00	20.00
54 Nap Rucker	50.00	25.00
55 Doc Scanlan	40.00	20.00
56 Red Smith	40.00	20.00
57 Zach Wheat	120.00	60.00
58 Mordecai Brown	120.00	60.00
59 Frank Chance	150.00	75.00
60 Johnny Evers	150.00	75.00
61 Bill Foxen	40.00	20.00
62 Peaches Graham	40.00	20.00
63 Johnny Kling	50.00	25.00
64 Harry McIntire	40.00	20.00
65 Tom Needham	40.00	20.00
66 Orval Overall	50.00	25.00
67 Ed Reulbach	50.00	25.00
68 Frank Schulte	50.00	25.00
69 Jimmy Sheckard	40.00	20.00
70 Harry Steinfeldt	50.00	25.00
71 Joe Tinker	150.00	75.00
72 Bob Bescher	40.00	20.00
73 Tom Downey	40.00	20.00
74 Art Fromme	40.00	20.00
75 Eddie Grant	40.00	20.00
76 Clark Griffith	120.00	60.00
77 Dick Hoblitzell	40.00	20.00
78 Mike Mitchell	40.00	20.00
79 Red Ames	40.00	20.00
80 Beals Becker	40.00	20.00
81 Al Bridwell	40.00	20.00
82 Doc Crandall	40.00	20.00
83 Art Devlin	40.00	20.00
84 Josh Devore	40.00	20.00
85 Larry Doyle	50.00	25.00
86 Art Fletcher	40.00	20.00
87 Rube Marquard	120.00	60.00
88 Christy Mathewson	400.00	200.00
89 John McGraw MG	150.00	75.00
90 Fred Merkle	50.00	25.00
91 Chief Meyers	50.00	25.00
92 Red Murray	40.00	20.00
93 Bugs Raymond	40.00	20.00
94 Admiral Schlei	40.00	20.00
95 Fred Snodgrass	40.00	20.00
96 Hooks Wiltse (2)	40.00	20.00
97 Johnny Bates	40.00	20.00
98 Red Dooin	40.00	20.00
99 Mickey Doolan	40.00	20.00
100 Bob Ewing	40.00	20.00
101 Hans Lobert	40.00	20.00
102 Pat Moran	40.00	20.00
103 Dode Paskert	40.00	20.00
104 Jack Rowan	40.00	20.00
105 John Titus	40.00	20.00
106 Bobby Byrne	40.00	20.00
107 Howie Camnitz	40.00	20.00
108 Fred Clarke	120.00	60.00
109 John Flynn	40.00	20.00
110 George Gibson	40.00	20.00
111 Tommy Leach	40.00	20.00
112 Lefty Leifield	40.00	20.00
113 Dots Miller	40.00	20.00
114 Deacon Phillippe	50.00	25.00
115 Kirby White	40.00	20.00
116 Owen Wilson	40.00	20.00
117 Roger Bresnahan (2)	120.00	60.00
118 Steve Evans	40.00	20.00
119 Arnold Hauser	40.00	20.00
120 Miller Huggins	120.00	60.00
121 Ed Konetchy	40.00	20.00
122 Rebel Oakes	40.00	20.00

1911 S81 Large Silks

These large and attractive silks are found in two sizes, approximately 5" by 7" or 7" by 9". Unlike the smaller S74 Baseball Silks, these silks are numbered, beginning with number 86 and ending at number 110. The pose of the picture is the same as that of the T3 Turkey Red baseball cards. The silks were issued in 1911 and are frequently found grouped on pillow covers. For some reason the silk of Mathewson appears to be the most plentiful member of this admittedly scarce issue. Therefore no premium typically associated with a Hall of Famer exists for this card.

	Ex-Mt	VG
COMPLETE SET (25)	35000.00	17500.00
86 Rube Marquard	1500.00	750.00
87 Marty O'Toole	800.00	400.00
88 Rube Benton	800.00	400.00
89 Grover C. Alexander	1500.00	750.00
90 Russ Ford	800.00	400.00
91 John McGraw MG	1500.00	750.00
92 Nap Rucker	800.00	400.00
93 Mike Mitchell	800.00	400.00
94 Chief Bender	1500.00	750.00
95 Frank Baker	1500.00	750.00
96 Napoleon Lajoie	1500.00	750.00
97 Joe Tinker	1500.00	750.00
98 Sherry Magee	1000.00	500.00
99 Howie Camnitz	800.00	400.00
100 Eddie Collins	1500.00	750.00
101 Red Dooin	800.00	400.00
102 Ty Cobb	8000.00	4000.00
103 Hugh Jennings MG	1500.00	750.00
104 Roger Bresnahan	1500.00	750.00
105 Jake Stahl	800.00	400.00
106 Tris Speaker	1500.00	750.00
107 Ed Walsh	1500.00	750.00
108 Christy Mathewson	1200.00	600.00
109 Johnny Evers	1500.00	750.00
110 Walter Johnson	4000.00	2000.00

1889 S.F.Hess and Co. N338-1

In contrast to the color drawings in Hess' California League set N321, the players in this series of big league ballplayers are shown in sepia photographs. The cards are blank-backed and unnumbered; they have no printed detail except for the player's name and the advertisement for S.F. Hess and Co.'s Cigarettes found below the picture. Cards denoted by SPOT are "Spotted Ties".

	Ex-Mt	VG
COMPLETE SET	60000.00	30000.00
1 Bill Brown: New York	2500.00	1250.00
2 Roger Conner (sic) New York	5000.00	2500.00
3 Ed Crane: New York	2500.00	1250.00
4 Buck Ewing: New York SPOT	5000.00	2500.00
5 Elmer Foster: New York	2500.00	1250.00
6 William George: New York	2500.00	1250.00
7 Joe Gerhardt: New York SPOT	2500.00	1250.00
8 Charles Getzein: Detroit	2500.00	1250.00
9 George Gore: New York	2500.00	1250.00
10 Gil Hatfield: New York	2500.00	1250.00
11 Arlie Latham: St.Louis	4000.00	2000.00
12 Pat Murphy: New York	2500.00	1250.00
13 Jim Mutrie: New York	4000.00	2000.00
14 Dave Orr: New York SPOT	2500.00	1250.00
15 Danny Richardson: New York	2500.00	1250.00
16 Mike Slattery: New York	2500.00	1250.00
17 Lidell Titcomb: New York	2500.00	1250.00
18 John M. Ward: New York	5000.00	2500.00
19 Curt Welch: St. Louis	3000.00	1500.00
20 Mickey Welch: New York SPOT	5000.00	2500.00
21 Arthur Whitney: New York	2500.00	1250.00

1976 Safelon Discs

These discs are another variety of discs issued in 1976. These have a Safelon back and are valued as a multiple of the Crane Discs.

	NM	Ex
COMPLETE SET (70)	40.00	16.00
1 Hank Aaron	5.00	2.00
2 Johnny Bench	3.00	1.20
3 Vida Blue	.50	.20
4 Larry Bowa	.50	.20
5 Lou Brock	3.00	1.20
6 Jeff Burroughs	.25	.10
7 John Candelaria	.25	.10
8 Jose Cardenal	.25	.10
9 Rod Carew	3.00	1.20
10 Steve Carlton	3.00	1.20
11 Dave Cash	.25	.10
12 Cesar Cedeno	.50	.20
13 Ron Cey	.50	.20
14 Carlton Fisk	4.00	1.60
15 Tito Fuentes	.25	.10
16 Steve Garvey	2.00	.80
17 Ken Griffey	.50	.20
18 Don Gullett	.25	.10
19 Willie Horton	.25	.10
20 Al Hrabosky	.25	.10
21 Catfish Hunter	3.00	1.20
22A Reggie Jackson Oakland Athletics	10.00	4.00
22B Reggie Jackson Baltimore Orioles	3.00	1.20
23 Randy Jones	.25	.10
24 Jim Kaat	1.00	.40
25 Don Kessinger	.25	.10
26 Dave Kingman	1.00	.40
27 Jerry Koosman	.50	.20
28 Mickey Lolich	.50	.20
29 Greg Luzinski	1.00	.40
30 Fred Lynn	1.00	.40
31 Bill Madlock	.50	.20
32A Carlos May Chicago White Sox	2.00	.80
32B Carlos May New York Yankees	.25	.10
33 John Mayberry	.25	.10
34 Bake McBride	.25	.10
35 Doc Medich	.25	.10
36A Andy Messersmith Los Angeles Dodgers	2.00	.80
36B Andy Messersmith Atlanta Braves	.25	.10
37 Rick Monday	.25	.10
38 John Montefusco	.25	.10
39 Jerry Morales	.25	.10
40 Joe Morgan	3.00	1.20
41 Thurman Munson	2.00	.80
42 Bobby Murcer	1.00	.40
43 Al Oliver	1.00	.40
44 Jim Palmer	3.00	1.20
45 Dave Parker	1.50	.60
46 Tony Perez	2.00	.80
47 Jerry Reuss	.25	.10
48 Brooks Robinson	3.00	1.20
49 Frank Robinson	3.00	1.20
50 Steve Rogers	.25	.10
51 Pete Rose	4.00	1.60
52 Nolan Ryan	8.00	3.20
53 Manny Sanguillen	.25	.10
54 Mike Schmidt	5.00	2.00
55 Tom Seaver	4.00	1.60
56 Ted Simmons	1.00	.40
57 Reggie Smith	.50	.20
58 Willie Stargell	3.00	1.20
59 Rusty Staub	1.00	.40
60 Rennie Stennett	.25	.10
61 Don Sutton	3.00	1.20
62A Andre Thornton Chicago Cubs	2.00	.80
62B Andre Thornton Montreal Expos	.25	.10
63 Luis Tiant	1.00	.40
64 Joe Torre	1.50	.60
65 Mike Tyson	.25	.10
66 Bob Watson	.50	.20
67 Wilbur Wood	.25	.10
68 Jimmy Wynn	.25	.10
69 Carl Yastrzemski	3.00	1.20
70 Richie Zisk	.25	.10

1977 Saga Discs

As they had done the previous year in Football, Saga was one of the distributors of player discs. While not as difficult to obtain as the Football discs, these are not that easy to acquire.

	NM	Ex
COMPLETE SET (70)	30.00	12.00
1 Sal Bando	.25	.10
2 Buddy Bell	.50	.20
3 Johnny Bench	4.00	1.60
4 Lou Brock	3.00	1.20
5 Larry Bowa	.50	.20
6 Steve Braun	.25	.10
7 George Brett	6.00	2.40
8 Jeff Burroughs	.25	.10
9 Campy Campaneris	.50	.20
10 John Candelaria	.25	.10
11 Jose Cardenal	.25	.10
12 Rod Carew	3.00	1.20
13 Steve Carlton	3.00	1.20
14 Dave Cash	.25	.10
15 Cesar Cedeno	.25	.10
16 Ron Cey	.50	.20
17 Dave Concepcion	.75	.30
18 Dennis Eckersley	3.00	1.20
19 Mark Fidrych	3.00	1.20
20 Rollie Fingers	2.00	.80
21 Carlton Fisk	3.00	1.20
22 George Foster	.75	.30
23 Wayne Garland	.25	.10
24 Ralph Garr	.50	.20
25 Steve Garvey	1.00	.40
26 Cesar Geronimo	.25	.10
27 Bobby Grich	.50	.20
28 Ken Griffey	.75	.30
29 Don Gullett	.25	.10
30 Mike Hargrove	.50	.20
31 Al Hrabosky	.25	.10
32 Catfish Hunter	2.00	.80

33 Reggie Jackson	4.00	1.60
34 Randy Jones	.25	.10
35 Dave Kingman	1.00	.40
36 Jerry Koosman	.50	.20
37 Dave LaRoche	.25	.10
38 Greg Luzinski	.75	.30
39 Fred Lynn	.50	.20
40 Bill Madlock	.50	.20
41 Rick Manning	.25	.10
42 Jon Matlack	.25	.10
43 John Mayberry	.25	.10
44 Hal McRae	.50	.20
45 Andy Messersmith	.25	.10
46 Rick Monday	.25	.10
47 John Montefusco	.25	.10
48 Joe Morgan	2.00	.80
49 Thurman Munson	1.00	.40
50 Bobby Murcer	.75	.30
51 Bill North	.25	.10
52 Jim Palmer	2.00	.80
53 Tony Perez	2.00	.80
54 Jerry Reuss	.25	.10
55 Brooks Robinson	3.00	1.20
56 Pete Rose	4.00	1.60
57 Joe Rudi	.25	.10
58 Nolan Ryan	8.00	3.20
59 Manny Sanguillen	.25	.10
60 Mike Schmidt	4.00	1.60
61 Tom Seaver	4.00	1.60
62 Bill Singer	.25	.10
63 Willie Stargell	2.00	.80
64 Rusty Staub	.75	.30
65 Luis Tiant	.50	.20
66 Bob Watson	.50	.20
67 Butch Wynegar	.25	.10
68 Carl Yastrzemski	3.00	1.20
69 Robin Yount	3.00	1.20
70 Richie Zisk	.25	.10

1978 Saga Discs

This set is a parallel to the 1978 Tastee-Freez discs. They were issued through Saga and are significantly more difficult than the regular Tastee-Freez discs.

	NM	Ex
COMPLETE SET (26)	175.00	70.00
1 Buddy Bell	5.00	2.00
2 Jim Palmer	20.00	8.00
3 Steve Garvey	8.00	3.20
4 Jeff Burroughs	2.50	1.00
5 Greg Luzinski	5.00	2.00
6 Lou Brock	15.00	6.00
7 Thurman Munson	10.00	4.00
8 Rod Carew	15.00	6.00
9 George Brett	50.00	20.00
10 Tom Seaver	20.00	8.00
11 Willie Stargell	15.00	6.00
12 Jerry Koosman	2.50	1.00
13 Bill North	2.50	1.00
14 Richie Zisk	2.50	1.00
15 Bill Madlock	5.00	2.00
16 Carl Yastrzemski	15.00	6.00
17 Dave Cash	2.50	1.00
18 Bob Watson	5.00	2.00
19 Dave Kingman	10.00	4.00
20 Gene Tenace	2.50	1.00
21 Ralph Garr	2.50	1.00
22 Mark Fidrych	15.00	6.00
23 Frank Tanana	5.00	2.00
24 Larry Hisle	2.50	1.00
25 Bruce Bochte	2.50	1.00
26 Bob Bailor	2.50	1.00

1962 Sain Spinner Postcard

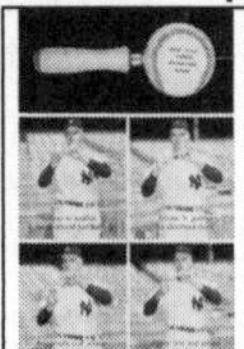
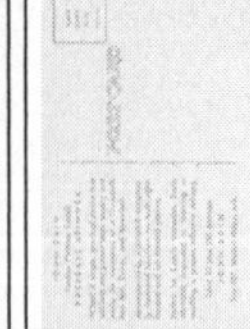

This one-card set features four small color photos of the New York Yankee's pitching coach, John Sain, demonstrating how to use the Spinner, a device to teach the mechanics of a Curveball, Fast Ball, Sinker, and Screwball. The back displays a postcard format with an ad for the Spinner and instructions on how to obtain it.

	NM	Ex
1 John Sain	20.00	8.00

1995 Tim Salmon

This one card standard-sized set features star outfielder Tim Salmon. Issued as a testimonial to his religious beliefs, the card has his player portrait surrounded by yellow borders. The back has some biographical information and also has further explanation of his religious beliefs. While the card shown is signed, not all of these cards come autographed.

	Nm-Mt	Ex-Mt
1 Tim Salmon	5.00	1.50

1981 San Diego Sports Collectors

This 20-card standard-size rounded-corner set was presented by the San Diego Sports Collectors Association at the San Diego Show

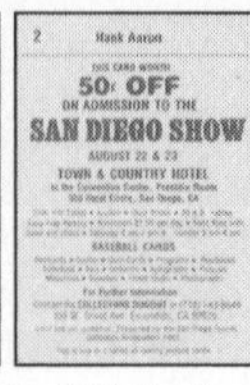

held August 22 and 23, 1981. The fronts feature borderless, glossy, black-and-white player photos. The backs are white and carry the player's name, advertisement information and an offer for 50 cents off admission to the show with the card.

	Nm-Mt	Ex-Mt
COMPLETE SET (20)	17.50	7.00
1 Gary Butcher	.25	.10
2 Hank Aaron	1.50	.60
3 Duke Snider	1.00	.40
4 Al Kaline	1.00	.40
5 Vic Power	.50	.20
6 Jackie Robinson	1.00	.40
7 Carl Erskine	.50	.20
8 Ted Williams	2.00	.80
(Batting)		
9 Ted Williams	2.00	.80
(Portrait)		
10 Mickey Mantle	2.50	1.00
(Portrait)		
11 Mickey Mantle	2.50	1.00
(Holding bat)		
12 Mickey Mantle	1.00	.40
Willie Mays		
13 Mickey Mantle	1.00	.40
Stan Musial		
14 Joe DiMaggio	2.00	.80
15 Roger Maris	1.00	.40
(Portrait)		
16 Roger Maris	1.00	.40
(Holding bat)		
17 Lou Gehrig	2.00	.80
18 Bill Dickey	1.00	.40
Lou Gehrig		
19 Lou Gehrig	.75	.30
Joe Cronin		
Bill Dickey		
Joe DiMaggio		
20 Gary Butcher	.25	.10

1997 Sandberg Commemorative

This one-card set was given away by the Chicago Cubs on Ryne Sandberg day. The card measures approximately 6 1/4" by 9" and features color images of Ryne Sandberg on the front with a postcard format on the back and a message to group leaders about ticket discounts.

	Nm-Mt	Ex-Mt
1 Ryne Sandberg	10.00	3.00

1968 SCFS Old Timers

This 72-card set measures 3 1/2" X 4 1/4" and features black-and-white artistic renderings of old time baseball players. The player's name, position and years played are printed at the bottom. The backs are blank except for a small stamp at the bottom with the 1968 copywrite date. The cards are numbered on the front. The cards were produced by long time hobbyist Mike Aronstein. This set was available from the producer at time of issue for $6.50.

	NM	Ex
COMPLETE SET	25.00	10.00
1 Babe Ruth	5.00	2.00
2 Rube Marquard	.75	.30
3 Zack Wheat	.75	.30
4 John Clarkson	.75	.30
5 Honus Wagner	1.00	.40
6 Crab Evers	.75	.30
7 Bill Dickey	.75	.30
8 Elmer Smith	.25	.10
9 Ty Cobb	2.50	1.00
10 Happy Jack Chesbro	.75	.30
11 Moon Gibson	.25	.10
12 Bullet Joe Bush	.25	.10
13 George Mullin	.25	.10
14 Buddy Myer	.25	.10
15 James Collins	.75	.30
16 William Wambsganss	.25	.10
17 Jack Barry	.25	.10
18 Dickie Kerr	.25	.10
19 Connie Mack	.75	.30
20 Rabbit Maranville	.75	.30
21 Roger Peckinpaugh	.25	.10
22 Mickey Cochrane	.75	.30
23 George Kelly	.75	.30
24 John Baker	.25	.10
25 Wally Schang	.25	.10
26 Eddie Plank	.75	.30
27 Bill Donovan	.25	.10
28 Red Faber	.75	.30
29 Hack Wilson	.75	.30
30 Three Fingered Brown	.75	.30
31 Frederick Merkle	.25	.10
32 Heinie Groh	.25	.10
33 Stuffy McInnis	.25	.10
34 Prince Hal Chase	.75	.30
35 Kenesaw Mountain	.50	.20
Landis COMM		
36 Chief Bender	.75	.30
50 Jimmy Wilson	.25	.10
55 Jim Thorpe	2.50	1.00

1930 Schutter-Johnson R332

This set of 50 cards was issued by the Schutter-Johnson Candy Corporation around 1930. Each card measures 2 1/4" by 2 7/8". While each card in the series is numbered, the ones in the checklist below are the only ones known at the present time. These black line-drawing cards on a red field are entitled "Major League Secrets" and feature tips from major league players on the reverse.

	Ex-Mt	VG
COMPLETE SET (50)	4000.00	2000.00
1 Al Simmons	60.00	30.00
2 Lloyd Waner	60.00	30.00
3 Kiki Cuyler	60.00	30.00
4 Frank Frisch	80.00	40.00
5 Chick Hafey	60.00	30.00
6 Bill Klem UMP	80.00	40.00
7 Rogers Hornsby	125.00	60.00
8 Carl Mays	40.00	20.00
9 Charles Wrigley UMP	40.00	20.00
10 Christy Mathewson	150.00	75.00
11 Bill Dickey	80.00	40.00
12 Walter Berger	40.00	20.00
13 George Earnshaw	40.00	20.00
14 Hack Wilson	80.00	40.00
15 Charley Grimm	40.00	20.00
16 Paul Waner	60.00	30.00
Lloyd Waner		
17 Chuck Klein	60.00	30.00
18 Woody English	40.00	20.00
19 Grover Alexander	80.00	40.00
20 Lou Gehrig	400.00	200.00
21 Wes Ferrell	40.00	20.00
22 Carl Hubbell	80.00	40.00
23 Pie Traynor	60.00	30.00
24 Gus Mancuso	40.00	20.00
25 Ben Cantwell	40.00	20.00
26 Babe Ruth	800.00	400.00
27 Goose Goslin	60.00	30.00
28 Earle Combs	60.00	30.00
29 Kiki Cuyler	60.00	30.00
30 Jimmy Wilson	40.00	20.00
31 Dizzy Dean	120.00	60.00
32 Mickey Cochrane	80.00	40.00
33 Ted Lyons	80.00	40.00
34 Si Johnson	40.00	20.00
35 Dizzy Dean	120.00	60.00
36 Pepper Martin	40.00	20.00
37 Joe Cronin	60.00	30.00
38 Gabby Hartnett	60.00	30.00
39 Oscar Melillo	40.00	20.00
40 Ben Chapman	40.00	20.00
41 John McGraw MG	80.00	40.00
42 Babe Ruth	800.00	400.00
43 Red Lucas	40.00	20.00
44 Charley Root	40.00	20.00
45 Dazzy Vance	60.00	30.00
46 Hugh Critz	40.00	20.00
47 Firpo Marberry	40.00	20.00
48 Grover Alexander	80.00	40.00
49 Lefty Grove	80.00	40.00
50 Heine Meine	40.00	20.00

1996 Schwebels Discs

This 20-disc set measures approximately 2 3/4" in diameter. The fronts feature color player portraits in a blue-and-red border with fading stars. The player's name is printied in the top blue border with the year "1996" in the bottom red border. The backs carry the player's name, team, position, biographical information, season and career statistics.

	Nm-Mt	Ex-Mt
COMPLETE SET (20)	20.00	6.00
1 Jim Thome	1.25	.35
2 Orel Hershiser	.50	.15
3 Greg Maddux	3.00	.90
4 Charles Nagy	.25	.07
5 Omar Vizquel	1.00	.30
6 Manny Ramirez	1.25	.35
7 Dennis Martinez	.50	.15
8 Eddie Murray	1.55	.45
9 Albert Belle	.50	.15
10 Fred McGriff	.75	.23
11 Jack McDowell	.25	.07
12 Kenny Lofton	.75	.23
13 Cal Ripken	5.00	1.50
14 Jose Mesa	.25	.07
15 Randy Johnson	1.25	.35
16 Ken Griffey Jr.	3.00	.90
17 Carlos Baerga	.50	.15
18 Frank Thomas	1.25	.35
19 Sandy Alomar	.25	.07
20 Barry Bonds	2.50	.75

1988 Score Samples

Early in 1988, Score prepared some samples to show prospective dealers and buyers of the new Score cards what they would look like. These sample cards are distinguished by the fact that there is a row of zeroes for the 1987 season statistics since the season was not over when these sample cards were being printed. The cards are standard size and are virtually indistinguishable from the regular 1988 Score cards of the same players except for border color variations in a few instances.

	Nm-Mt	Ex-Mt
COMPLETE SET (6)	40.00	16.00
30 Mark Langston	5.00	2.00
48 Tony Pena	8.00	3.20
71 Keith Moreland	5.00	2.00
72 Barry Larkin	20.00	8.00
121 Dennis Boyd	5.00	2.00
145 Denny Walling	5.00	2.00

1988 Score

This set consists of 660 standard-size cards. The set was distributed by Major League Marketing and features six distinctive border colors on the front. Subsets include Reggie Jackson Tribute (500-504), Highlights (652-660) and Rookie Prospects (623-647). Card number 501, showing Reggie as a member of the Baltimore Orioles, is one of the few opportunities collectors have to visually remember Reggie's one-year stay with the Orioles. The set is distinguished by the fact that each card back shows a full-color picture of the player. Rookie Cards in this set include Ellis Burks, Ken Caminiti, Tom Glavine and Matt Williams.

	Nm-Mt	Ex-Mt
COMPLETE SET (660)	10.00	4.00
COMP.FACT.SET (660)	12.00	4.80
1 Don Mattingly	.60	.24
2 Wade Boggs	.15	.06
3 Tim Raines	.10	.04
4 Andre Dawson	.10	.04
5 Mark McGwire	1.50	.60
6 Kevin Seitzer	.10	.04
7 Wally Joyner	.15	.06
8 Jesse Barfield	.05	.02
9 Pedro Guerrero	.05	.02
10 Eric Davis	.10	.04
11 George Brett	.50	.20
12 Ozzie Smith	.30	.12
13 Rickey Henderson	.20	.08
14 Jim Rice	.10	.04
15 Matt Nokes RC*	.05	.02
16 Mike Schmidt	.50	.20
17 Dave Parker	.10	.04
18 Eddie Murray	.20	.08
19 Andres Galarraga	.10	.04
20 Tony Fernandez	.05	.02
21 Kevin McReynolds	.05	.02
22 B.J. Surhoff	.10	.04
23 Pat Tabler	.05	.02
24 Kirby Puckett	.20	.08
25 Benny Santiago	.15	.06
26 Ryne Sandberg	.40	.16
27 Kelly Downs	.05	.02
(Will Clark in back-ground, out of focus)		
28 Jose Cruz	.05	.02
29 Pete O'Brien	.05	.02
30 Mark Langston	.05	.02
31 Lee Smith	.10	.04
32 Juan Samuel	.05	.02
33 Kevin Bass	.05	.02
34 R.J. Reynolds	.05	.02
35 Steve Sax	.05	.02
36 John Kruk	.10	.04
37 Alan Trammell	.15	.06
38 Chris Bosio	.05	.02
39 Brook Jacoby	.05	.02
40 Willie McGee UER	.10	.04
(Excited misspelled as excitd)		
41 Dave Magadan	.05	.02
42 Fred Lynn	.05	.02
43 Kent Hrbek	.10	.04
44 Brian Downing	.05	.02
45 Jose Canseco	.20	.08
46 Jim Presley	.05	.02
47 Mike Stanley	.10	.04
48 Tony Pena	.05	.02
49 David Cone	.10	.04
50 Rick Sutcliffe	.10	.04
51 Doug Drabek	.05	.02
52 Bill Doran	.05	.02
53 Mike Scioscia	.05	.02
54 Candy Maldonado	.05	.02
55 Dave Winfield	.10	.04
56 Lou Whitaker	.10	.04
57 Tom Henke	.05	.02
58 Ken Gerhart	.05	.02
59 Glenn Braggs	.05	.02
60 Julio Franco	.05	.02
61 Charlie Leibrandt	.05	.02
62 Gary Gaetti	.10	.04
63 Bob Boone	.10	.04
64 Luis Polonia RC*	.10	.04
65 Dwight Evans	.10	.04
66 Phil Bradley	.05	.02
67 Mike Boddicker	.05	.02
68 Vince Coleman	.05	.02
69 Howard Johnson	.05	.02
70 Tim Wallach	.05	.02
71 Keith Moreland	.05	.02
72 Barry Larkin	.20	.08
73 Alan Ashby	.05	.02
74 Rick Rhoden	.05	.02
75 Darrell Evans	.10	.04
76 Dave Stieb	.05	.02
77 Dan Plesac	.05	.02
78 Will Clark UER	.20	.08
(Born 3/17/64, should be 3/13/64)		
79 Frank White	.10	.04
80 Joe Carter	.20	.08
81 Mike Witt	.05	.02
82 Terry Steinbach	.10	.04
83 Alvin Davis	.05	.02
84 Tommy Herr	.10	.04
(Will Clark shown sliding into second)		
85 Vance Law	.05	.02
86 Kal Daniels	.05	.02
87 Rick Honeycutt UER	.05	.02
(Wrong years for stats on back)		
88 Alfredo Griffin	.05	.02
89 Bret Saberhagen	.10	.04
90 Bert Blyleven	.10	.04
91 Jeff Reardon	.10	.04
92 Cory Snyder	.05	.02
93A Greg Walker ERR	2.00	.80
(93 of 66)		
93B Greg Walker COR	.05	.02
(93 of 660)		
94 Joe Magrane RC*	.05	.02
95 Rob Deer	.05	.02
96 Ray Knight	.05	.02
97 Casey Candaele	.05	.02
98 John Cerutti	.05	.02
99 Buddy Bell	.10	.04
100 Jack Clark	.10	.04
101 Eric Bell	.05	.02
102 Willie Wilson	.05	.02
103 Dave Schmidt	.05	.02
104 Dennis Eckersley UER	.10	.04
(Complete games stats are wrong)		
105 Don Sutton	.20	.08
106 Danny Tartabull	.05	.02
107 Fred McGriff	.20	.08
108 Les Straker	.05	.02
109 Lloyd Moseby	.05	.02
110 Roger Clemens	.50	.20
111 Glenn Hubbard	.05	.02
112 Ken Williams RC	.05	.02
113 Ruben Sierra	.05	.02
114 Stan Jefferson	.05	.02
115 Milt Thompson	.05	.02
116 Bobby Bonilla	.10	.04
117 Wayne Tolleson	.05	.02
118 Matt Williams RC	.75	.30
119 Chet Lemon	.05	.02
120 Dale Sveum	.05	.02
121 Dennis Boyd	.05	.02
122 Brett Butler	.10	.04
123 Terry Kennedy	.05	.02
124 Jack Howell	.05	.02
125 Curt Young	.05	.02
126A Dave Valle ERR	.10	.04
(Misspelled Dale on card front)		
126B Dave Valle COR	.05	.02
127 Curt Wilkerson	.05	.02
128 Tim Teufel	.05	.02
129 Ozzie Virgil	.05	.02
130 Brian Fisher	.05	.02
131 Lance Parrish	.05	.02
132 Tom Browning	.05	.02
133A Larry Andersen ERR	.10	.04
(Misspelled Anderson on card front)		
133B Larry Andersen COR	.05	.02
134A Bob Brenly ERR	.10	.04
(Misspelled Brenley on card front)		
134B Bob Brenly COR	.05	.02
135 Mike Marshall	.05	.02
136 Gerald Perry	.05	.02
137 Bobby Meacham	.05	.02
138 Larry Herndon	.05	.02
139 Fred Manrique	.05	.02
140 Charlie Hough	.10	.04
141 Ron Darling	.05	.02
142 Herm Winningham	.05	.02
143 Mike Diaz	.05	.02
144 Mike Jackson RC*	.10	.04
145 Denny Walling	.05	.02
146 Robby Thompson	.05	.02
147 Franklin Stubbs	.05	.02
148 Albert Hall	.05	.02
149 Bobby Witt	.05	.02
150 Lance McCullers	.05	.02
151 Scott Bradley	.05	.02
152 Mark McLemore	.05	.02
153 Tim Laudner	.05	.02
154 Greg Swindell	.05	.02
155 Marty Barrett	.05	.02
156 Mike Heath	.05	.02
157 Gary Ward	.05	.02
158A Lee Mazzilli ERR	.10	.04
(Misspelled Mazilli on card front)		
158B Lee Mazzilli COR	.05	.02
159 Tom Foley	.05	.02
160 Robin Yount	.30	.12
161 Steve Bedrosian	.05	.02
162 Bob Walk	.05	.02
163 Nick Esasky	.05	.02
164 Ken Caminiti RC	.40	.16
165 Jose Uribe	.05	.02
166 Dave Anderson	.05	.02
167 Ed Whitson	.05	.02
168 Ernie Whitt	.05	.02
169 Cecil Cooper	.10	.04
170 Mike Pagliarulo	.05	.02
171 Pat Sheridan	.05	.02
172 Chris Bando	.05	.02
173 Lee Lacy	.05	.02
174 Steve Lombardozzi	.05	.02
175 Mike Greenwell	.05	.02
176 Greg Minton	.05	.02
177 Moose Haas	.05	.02
178 Mike Kingery	.05	.02
179 Greg A. Harris	.05	.02
180 Bo Jackson	.20	.08
181 Carmelo Martinez	.05	.02
182 Alex Trevino	.05	.02
183 Ron Oester	.05	.02
184 Danny Darwin	.05	.02
185 Mike Krukow	.05	.02
186 Rafael Palmeiro	.40	.16
187 Tim Burke	.05	.02
188 Roger McDowell	.05	.02
189 Garry Templeton	.05	.02

190 Terry Pendleton .10 .04
191 Larry Parrish .05 .02
192 Rey Quinones .05 .02
193 Joaquin Andujar .05 .02
194 Tom Brunansky .05 .02
195 Donnie Moore .05 .02
196 Dan Pasqua .05 .02
197 Jim Gantner .05 .02
198 Mark Eichhorn .05 .02
199 John Grubb .05 .02
200 Bill Ripken RC* .05 .02
201 Sam Horn RC .05 .02
202 Todd Worrell .10 .04
203 Terry Leach .05 .02
204 Garth Iorg .05 .02
205 Brian Dayett .05 .02
206 Bo Diaz .05 .02
207 Craig Reynolds .05 .02
208 Brian Holton .05 .02
209 Marvell Wynne UER .05 .02
(Misspelled Marvelle
on card front)
210 Dave Concepcion .10 .04
211 Mike Davis .05 .02
212 Devon White .10 .04
213 Mickey Brantley .05 .02
214 Greg Gagne .05 .02
215 Oddibe McDowell .05 .02
216 Jimmy Key .10 .04
217 Dave Bergman .05 .02
218 Calvin Schiraldi .05 .02
219 Larry Sheets .05 .02
220 Mike Easler .05 .02
221 Kurt Stillwell .05 .02
222 Chuck Jackson .05 .02
223 Dave Martinez .05 .02
224 Tim Leary .05 .02
225 Steve Garvey .10 .04
226 Greg Mathews .05 .02
227 Doug Sisk .05 .02
228 Dave Henderson .05 .02
(Wearing Red Sox uniform;
Red Sox logo on back)
229 Jimmy Dwyer .05 .02
230 Larry Owen .05 .02
231 Andre Thornton .10 .04
232 Mark Salas .05 .02
233 Tom Brookens .05 .02
234 Greg Brock .05 .02
235 Rance Mulliniks .05 .02
236 Bob Brower .05 .02
237 Joe Niekro .05 .02
238 Scott Bankhead .05 .02
239 Doug DeCinces .05 .02
240 Tommy John .10 .04
241 Rich Gedman .05 .02
242 Ted Power .05 .02
243 Dave Meads .05 .02
244 Jim Sundberg .05 .02
245 Ken Oberkfell .05 .02
246 Jimmy Jones .05 .02
247 Ken Landreaux .05 .02
248 Jose Oquendo .05 .02
249 John Mitchell RC .05 .02
250 Don Baylor .10 .04
251 Scott Fletcher .05 .02
252 Al Newman .05 .02
253 Carney Lansford .10 .04
254 Johnny Ray .05 .02
255 Gary Pettis .05 .02
256 Ken Phelps .05 .02
257 Rick Leach .05 .02
258 Tim Stoddard .05 .02
259 Ed Romero .05 .02
260 Sid Bream .05 .02
261A T.Niedenfuer ERR .10 .04
Misspelled Neidenfuer
on card front
261B T.Niedenfuer COR .05 .02
262 Rick Dempsey .05 .02
263 Lonnie Smith .05 .02
264 Bob Forsch .05 .02
265 Barry Bonds 2.00 .80
266 Willie Randolph .10 .04
267 Mike Ramsey .05 .02
268 Don Slaught .05 .02
269 Mickey Tettleton .05 .02
270 Jerry Reuss .05 .02
271 Marc Sullivan .05 .02
272 Jim Morrison .05 .02
273 Steve Balboni .05 .02
274 Dick Schofield .05 .02
275 John Tudor .05 .02
276 Gene Larkin RC* .05 .02
277 Harold Reynolds .10 .04
278 Jerry Browne .05 .02
279 Willie Upshaw .05 .02
280 Ted Higuera .05 .02
281 Terry McGriff .05 .02
282 Terry Puhl .05 .02
283 Mark Wasinger .05 .02
284 Luis Salazar .05 .02
285 Ted Simmons .10 .04
286 John Shelby .05 .02
287 John Smiley RC* .10 .04
288 Curt Ford .05 .02
289 Steve Crawford .05 .02
290 Dan Quisenberry .05 .02
291 Alan Wiggins .05 .02
292 Randy Bush .05 .02
293 John Candelaria .05 .02
294 Tony Phillips .05 .02
295 Mike Morgan .10 .04
296 Bill Wegman .05 .02
297A Terry Francona ERR .10 .04
(Misspelled Franconia
on card front)
297B Terry Francona COR .05 .02
298 Mickey Hatcher .05 .02
299 Andres Thomas .05 .02
300 Bob Stanley .05 .02
301 Al Pedrique .05 .02
302 Jim Lindeman .05 .02
303 Wally Backman .05 .02
304 Paul O'Neill .15 .06
305 Hubie Brooks .05 .02
306 Steve Buechele .05 .02
307 Bobby Thigpen .05 .02
308 George Hendrick .05 .02
309 John Moses .05 .02
310 Ron Guidry .10 .04
311 Bill Schroeder .05 .02
312 Jose Nunez .05 .02
313 Bud Black .05 .02
314 Joe Sambito .05 .02
315 Scott McGregor .05 .02
316 Rafael Santana .05 .02
317 Frank Williams .05 .02
318 Mike Fitzgerald .05 .02
319 Rick Mahler .05 .02
320 Jim Gott .05 .02
321 Mariano Duncan .05 .02
322 Jose Guzman .05 .02
323 Lee Guetterman .05 .02
324 Dan Gladden .05 .02
325 Gary Carter .15 .06
326 Tracy Jones .05 .02
327 Floyd Youmans .05 .02
328 Bill Dawley .05 .02
329 Paul Noce .05 .02
330 Angel Salazar .05 .02
331 Goose Gossage .15 .06
332 George Frazier .05 .02
333 Ruppert Jones .05 .02
334 Billy Joe Robidoux .05 .02
335 Mike Scott .05 .02
336 Randy Myers .15 .06
337 Bob Sebra .05 .02
338 Eric Show .05 .02
339 Mitch Williams .05 .02
340 Paul Molitor .15 .06
341 Gus Polidor .05 .02
342 Steve Trout .05 .02
343 Jerry Don Gleaton .05 .02
344 Bob Knepper .05 .02
345 Mitch Webster .05 .02
346 John Morris .05 .02
347 Andy Hawkins .05 .02
348 Dave Leiper .05 .02
349 Ernest Riles .05 .02
350 Dwight Gooden .15 .06
351 Dave Righetti .05 .02
352 Pat Dodson .05 .02
353 John Habyan .05 .02
354 Jim Deshaies .05 .02
355 Butch Wynegar .05 .02
356 Bryn Smith .05 .02
357 Matt Young .05 .02
358 Tom Pagnozzi RC .05 .02
359 Floyd Rayford .05 .02
360 Darryl Strawberry .15 .06
361 Sal Butera .05 .02
362 Domingo Ramos .05 .02
363 Chris Brown .05 .02
364 Jose Gonzalez .05 .02
365 Dave Smith .05 .02
366 Andy McGaffigan .05 .02
367 Stan Javier .05 .02
368 Henry Cotto .05 .02
369 Mike Birkbeck .05 .02
370 Len Dykstra .10 .04
371 Dave Collins .05 .02
372 Spike Owen .05 .02
373 Geno Petralli .05 .02
374 Ron Karkovice .05 .02
375 Shane Rawley .05 .02
376 DeWayne Buice .05 .02
377 Bill Pecota RC* .05 .02
378 Leon Durham .05 .02
379 Ed Olwine .05 .02
380 Bruce Hurst .05 .02
381 Bob McClure .05 .02
382 Mark Thurmond .05 .02
383 Buddy Biancalana .05 .02
384 Tim Conroy .05 .02
385 Tony Gwynn .30 .12
386 Greg Gross .05 .02
387 Barry Lyons .05 .02
388 Mike Felder .05 .02
389 Pat Clements .05 .02
390 Ken Griffey .10 .04
391 Mark Davis .05 .02
392 Jose Rijo .05 .02
393 Mike Young .05 .02
394 Willie Fraser .05 .02
395 Dion James .05 .02
396 Steve Shields .05 .02
397 Randy St.Claire .05 .02
398 Danny Jackson .05 .02
399 Cecil Fielder .15 .06
400 Keith Hernandez .15 .06
401 Don Carman .05 .02
402 Chuck Crim .05 .02
403 Rob Woodward .05 .02
404 Junior Ortiz .05 .02
405 Glenn Wilson .05 .02
406 Ken Howell .05 .02
407 Jeff Kunkel .05 .02
408 Jeff Reed .05 .02
409 Chris James .05 .02
410 Zane Smith .05 .02
411 Ken Dixon .05 .02
412 Ricky Horton .05 .02
413 Frank DiPino .05 .02
414 Shane Mack .05 .02
415 Danny Cox .05 .02
416 Andy Van Slyke .10 .04
417 Danny Heep .05 .02
418 John Cangelosi .05 .02
419A J.Christensen ERR .10 .04
Christiansen
on card front
419B J.Christensen COR .05 .02
420 Joey Cora RC .20 .08
421 Mike LaValliere .05 .02
422 Kelly Gruber .05 .02
423 Bruce Benedict .05 .02
424 Len Matuszek .05 .02
425 Kent Tekulve .05 .02
426 Rafael Ramirez .05 .02
427 Mike Flanagan .05 .02
428 Mike Gallego .05 .02
429 Juan Castillo .05 .02
430 Neal Heaton .05 .02
431 Phil Garner .05 .02
432 Mike Dunne .05 .02
433 Wallace Johnson .05 .02
434 Jack O'Connor .05 .02
435 Steve Jeltz .05 .02
436 Donell Nixon .05 .02
437 Jack Lazorko .05 .02
438 Keith Comstock .05 .02
439 Jeff D. Robinson .05 .02
440 Graig Nettles .10 .04
441 Mel Hall .05 .02
442 Gerald Young .05 .02
443 Gary Redus .05 .02
444 Charlie Moore .05 .02
445 Bill Madlock .10 .04
446 Mark Clear .05 .02
447 Greg Booker .05 .02
448 Rick Schu .05 .02
449 Ron Kittle .05 .02
450 Dale Murphy .20 .08
451 Bob Dernier .05 .02
452 Dale Mohorcic .05 .02
453 Rafael Belliard .05 .02
454 Charlie Puleo .05 .02
455 Dwayne Murphy .05 .02
456 Jim Eisenreich .20 .08
457 David Palmer .05 .02
458 Dave Stewart .10 .04
459 Pascual Perez .05 .02
460 Glenn Davis .05 .02
461 Dan Petry .05 .02
462 Jim Winn .05 .02
463 Darrell Miller .05 .02
464 Mike Moore .05 .02
465 Mike LaCoss .05 .02
466 Steve Farr .05 .02
467 Jerry Mumphrey .05 .02
468 Kevin Gross .05 .02
469 Bruce Bochy .05 .02
470 Orel Hershiser .10 .04
471 Eric King .05 .02
472 Ellis Burks RC .40 .16
473 Darren Daulton .10 .04
474 Mookie Wilson .10 .04
475 Frank Viola .05 .02
476 Ron Robinson .05 .02
477 Bob Melvin .05 .02
478 Jeff Musselman .05 .02
479 Charlie Kerfeld .05 .02
480 Richard Dotson .05 .02
481 Kevin Mitchell .10 .04
482 Gary Roenicke .05 .02
483 Tim Flannery .05 .02
484 Rich Yett .05 .02
485 Pete Incaviglia .05 .02
486 Rick Cerone .05 .02
487 Tony Armas .05 .02
488 Jerry Reed .05 .02
489 Dave Lopes .10 .04
490 Frank Tanana .05 .02
491 Mike Loynd .05 .02
492 Bruce Ruffin .05 .02
493 Chris Speier .05 .02
494 Tom Hume .05 .02
495 Jesse Orosco .05 .02
496 Robbie Wine UER .05 .02
(Misspelled Robby
on card front)
497 Jeff Montgomery RC .20 .08
498 Jeff Dedmon .05 .02
499 Luis Aguayo .05 .02
500 Reggie Jackson A's .15 .06
501 Reggie Jackson O's .15 .06
502 Reggie Jackson Yanks .15 .06
503 Reggie Jackson Angels .15 .06
504 Reggie Jackson A's .15 .06
505 Billy Hatcher .05 .02
506 Ed Lynch .05 .02
507 Willie Hernandez .05 .02
508 Jose DeLeon .05 .02
509 Joel Youngblood .05 .02
510 Bob Welch .05 .02
511 Steve Ontiveros .05 .02
512 Randy Ready .05 .02
513 Juan Nieves .05 .02
514 Jeff Russell .05 .02
515 Von Hayes .05 .02
516 Mark Gubicza .05 .02
517 Ken Dayley .05 .02
518 Don Aase .05 .02
519 Rick Reuschel .05 .02
520 Mike Henneman RC* .10 .04
521 Rick Aguilera .10 .04
522 Jay Howell .05 .02
523 Ed Correa .05 .02
524 Manny Trillo .05 .02
525 Kirk Gibson .10 .04
526 Wally Ritchie .05 .02
527 Al Nipper .05 .02
528 Atlee Hammaker .05 .02
529 Shawon Dunston .05 .02
530 Jim Clancy .05 .02
531 Tom Paciorek .10 .04
532 Joel Skinner .05 .02
533 Scott Garrelts .05 .02
534 Tom O'Malley .05 .02
535 John Franco .10 .04
536 Paul Kilgus .05 .02
537 Darrell Porter .05 .02
538 Walt Terrell .05 .02
539 Bill Long .05 .02
540 George Bell .05 .02
541 Jeff Sellers .05 .02
542 Joe Boever .05 .02
543 Steve Howe .05 .02
544 Scott Sanderson .05 .02
545 Jack Morris .10 .04
546 Todd Benzinger RC* .05 .02
547 Steve Henderson .05 .02
548 Eddie Milner .05 .02
549 Jeff M. Robinson .05 .02
550 Cal Ripken .75 .30
551 Jody Davis .05 .02
552 Kirk McCaskill .05 .02
553 Craig Lefferts .05 .02
554 Darnell Coles .05 .02
555 Phil Niekro .10 .04
556 Mike Aldrete .05 .02
557 Pat Perry .05 .02
558 Juan Agosto .05 .02
559 Rob Murphy .05 .02
560 Dennis Rasmussen .05 .02
561 Manny Lee .05 .02
562 Jeff Blauser RC .20 .08
563 Bob Ojeda .05 .02
564 Dave Dravecky .10 .04
565 Gene Garber .05 .02
566 Ron Roenicke .05 .02
567 Tommy Hinzo .05 .02
568 Eric Nolte .05 .02
569 Ed Hearn .05 .02
570 Mark Davidson .05 .02
571 Jim Walewander .05 .02
572 Donnie Hill UER .05 .02
(84 Stolen Base
total listed as 7)
573 Jamie Moyer .20 .08
574 Ken Schrom .05 .02
575 Nolan Ryan 1.00 .40
576 Jim Acker .05 .02
577 Jamie Quirk .05 .02
578 Jay Aldrich .05 .02
579 Claudell Washington .05 .02
580 Jeff Leonard .05 .02
581 Carmen Castillo .05 .02
582 Daryl Boston .05 .02
583 Jeff DeWillis .05 .02
584 John Marzano .05 .02
585 Bill Gullickson .05 .02
586 Andy Allanson .05 .02
587 Lee Tunnell UER .05 .02
(1987 stat line
reads .4.84 ERA)
588 Gene Nelson .05 .02
589 Dave LaPoint .05 .02
590 Harold Baines .10 .04
591 Bill Buckner .10 .04
592 Carlton Fisk .15 .06
593 Rick Manning .05 .02
594 Doug Jones RC .20 .08
595 Tom Candiotti .05 .02
596 Steve Lake .05 .02
597 Jose Lind RC .05 .02
598 Ross Jones .05 .02
599 Gary Matthews .05 .02
600 Fernando Valenzuela .10 .04
601 Dennis Martinez .10 .04
602 Les Lancaster .05 .02
603 Ozzie Guillen .05 .02
604 Tony Bernazard .05 .02
605 Chili Davis .15 .06
606 Roy Smalley .05 .02
607 Ivan Calderon .05 .02
608 Jay Tibbs .05 .02
609 Guy Hoffman .05 .02
610 Doyle Alexander .05 .02
611 Mike Bielecki .05 .02
612 Shawn Hillegas .05 .02
613 Keith Atherton .05 .02
614 Eric Plunk .05 .02
615 Sid Fernandez .05 .02
616 Dennis Lamp .05 .02
617 Dave Engle .05 .02
618 Harry Spilman .05 .02
619 Don Robinson .05 .02
620 John Farrell RC .05 .02
621 Nelson Liriano .05 .02
622 Floyd Bannister .05 .02
623 Randy Milligan RC .05 .02
624 Kevin Elster .05 .02
625 Jody Reed RC .10 .04
626 Shawn Abner .05 .02
627 Kirt Manwaring RC .05 .02
628 Pete Stanicek .05 .02
629 Rob Ducey .05 .02
630 Steve Kiefer .05 .02
631 Gary Thurman .05 .02
632 Darrel Akerfelds .05 .02
633 Dave Clark .05 .02
634 Roberto Kelly RC .20 .08
635 Keith Hughes .05 .02
636 John Davis .05 .02
637 Mike Devereaux RC .10 .04
638 Tom Glavine RC 1.50 .60
639 Keith A. Miller RC .05 .02
640 Chris Gwynn RC UER .10 .04
(Wrong batting and
throwing on back)
641 Tim Crews RC .05 .02
642 Mackey Sasser RC .05 .02
643 Vicente Palacios .05 .02
644 Kevin Romine .05 .02
645 Gregg Jefferies RC .20 .08
646 Jeff Treadway RC .05 .02
647 Ron Gant RC .40 .16
648 Mark McGwire .75 .30
Matt Nokes
649 Eric Davis .10 .04
Tim Raines
650 Don Mattingly .30 .12
Jack Clark
651 Tony Fernandez .25 .10
Alan Trammell
Cal Ripken
652 Vince Coleman HL .05 .02
653 Kirby Puckett HL .15 .06
654 Benito Santiago HL .10 .04
655 Juan Nieves HL .05 .02
656 Steve Bedrosian HL .05 .02
657 Mike Schmidt HL .20 .08
658 Don Mattingly HL .30 .12
659 Mark McGwire HL .75 .30
660 Paul Molitor HL .10 .04

1988 Score Glossy

This 660 card set is a parallel to the regular 1988 Score set. According to the manufacturer, 5,000 of these sets were produced. These sets are considered glossy as "UV Coating" was added to the front of the card. These sets were issued in factory set versions only and released solely through Major League Marketing's hobby accounts.

	Nm-Mt	Ex-Mt
COMP.FACT.SET (660)	120.00	47.50

*STARS: 6X TO 15X BASIC CARDS
*ROOKIES: 6X TO 15X BASIC CARDS

1988 Score Box Cards

There are six different wax box bottom panels each featuring three players and a trivia (related to a particular stadium for a given year) question. The players and trivia question cards are individually numbered. The trivia are numbered below with the prefix T in order to avoid confusion. The trivia cards are very unpopular with collectors since they do not picture any players. When panels of four are cut into individuals, the cards are standard size. The card backs of the players feature the respective League logos most prominently.

	Nm-Mt	Ex-Mt
COMPLETE SET (24)	10.00	4.00
1 Terry Kennedy	.10	.04
2 Don Mattingly	1.50	.60
3 Willie Randolph	.20	.08
4 Wade Boggs	1.00	.40
5 Cal Ripken	3.00	1.20
6 George Bell	.10	.04
7 Rickey Henderson	1.25	.50
8 Dave Winfield	.75	.30
9 Bret Saberhagen	.20	.08
10 Gary Carter	.75	.30
11 Jack Clark	.20	.08
12 Ryne Sandberg	1.50	.60
13 Mike Schmidt	.75	.30
14 Ozzie Smith	1.50	.60
15 Eric Davis	.20	.08
16 Andre Dawson	.50	.20
17 Darryl Strawberry	.20	.08
18 Mike Scott	.10	.04
T1 Ted Williams Fenway Park '60	2.00	.80
T2 Fred Lynn Comiskey Park '83	.20	.08
T3 Mark McGwire Anaheim Stadium '87	2.00	.80
T4 Gabby Hartnett Wrigley Field '38	.20	.08
T5 Red Schoendienst Comiskey Park '50	.20	.08
T6 John Farrell Paul Molitor County Stadium '87	.50	.20

1988 Score Rookie/Traded

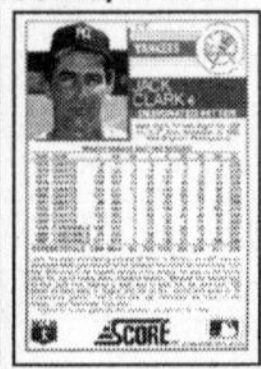

This 110-card standard-size set issued exclusively in a boxes factory-set form features traded players (1-65) and rookies (66-110) for the 1988 season. The cards are distinguishable from the regular Score set by the orange borders and by the fact that the numbering on the back has a T suffix. Apparently Score's first attempt at a Rookie/Traded set was produced very conservatively, resulting in a set which is now recognized as being much tougher to find than the other Rookie/Traded sets from the other major companies of that year. Extended Rookie Cards in this set include Roberto Alomar, Brady Anderson, Craig Biggio, Jay Buhner and Mark Grace.

	Nm-Mt	Ex-Mt
COMP.FACT.SET (110)	40.00	16.00
1T Jack Clark	.75	.30
2T Danny Jackson	.25	.10
3T Brett Butler	.75	.30
4T Kurt Stillwell	.25	.10
5T Tom Brunansky	.25	.10
6T Dennis Lamp	.25	.10
7T Jose DeLeon	.25	.10
8T Tom Herr	.25	.10
9T Keith Moreland	.25	.10
10T Kirk Gibson	2.00	.80
11T Bud Black	.25	.10
12T Rafael Ramirez	.25	.10
13T Luis Salazar	.25	.10
14T Goose Gossage	1.25	.50
15T Bob Welch	.25	.10
16T Vance Law	.25	.10
17T Ray Knight	.25	.10
18T Dan Quisenberry	.25	.10
19T Don Slaught	.25	.10
20T Lee Smith	.75	.30
21T Rick Cerone	.25	.10
22T Pat Tabler	.25	.10
23T Larry McWilliams	.25	.10
24T Ricky Horton	.25	.10
25T Graig Nettles	.75	.30
26T Dan Petry	.25	.10
27T Jose Rijo	.25	.10
28T Chili Davis	1.25	.50
29T Dickie Thon	.25	.10
30T Mackey Sasser	.25	.10
31T Mickey Tettleton	.25	.10
32T Rick Dempsey	.25	.10
33T Ron Hassey	.25	.10
34T Phil Bradley	.25	.10
35T Jay Howell	.25	.10
36T Bill Buckner	.75	.30
37T Alfredo Griffin	.25	.10
38T Gary Pettis	.25	.10
39T Calvin Schiraldi	.25	.10
40T John Candelaria	.25	.10
41T Joe Orsulak	.25	.10
42T Willie Upshaw	.25	.10
43T Herm Winningham	.25	.10
44T Ron Kittle	.25	.10
45T Bob Dernier	.25	.10
46T Steve Balboni	.25	.10

47T Steve Shields .25 .10
48T Henry Cotto .25 .10
49T Dave Henderson .25 .10
50T Dave Parker .75 .30
51T Mike Young .25 .10
52T Mark Salas .25 .10
53T Mike Davis .25 .10
54T Rafael Santana .25 .10
55T Don Baylor .75 .30
56T Dan Pasqua .25 .10
57T Ernest Riles .25 .10
58T Glenn Hubbard .25 .10
59T Mike Smithson .25 .10
60T Richard Dotson .25 .10
61T Jerry Reuss .25 .10
62T Mike Jackson .75 .30
63T Floyd Bannister .25 .10
64T Jesse Orosco .25 .10
65T Larry Parrish .25 .10
66T Jeff Bittiger .25 .10
67T Ray Hayward .25 .10
68T Ricky Jordan XRC .75 .30
69T Tommy Gregg .25 .10
70T Brady Anderson XRC 1.50 .60
71T Jeff Montgomery 2.00 .80
72T Darryl Hamilton XRC .75 .30
73T Cecil Espy .25 .10
74T Greg Briley XRC .25 .10
75T Joey Meyer .25 .10
76T Mike Macfarlane XRC .25 .10
77T Oswald Peraza .25 .10
78T Jack Armstrong XRC .25 .10
79T Don Heinkel .25 .10
80T Mark Grace XRC 8.00 3.20
81T Steve Curry .25 .10
82T Damon Berryhill XRC .25 .10
83T Steve Ellsworth .25 .10
84T Pete Smith XRC* .25 .10
85T Jack McDowell XRC 2.00 .80
86T Rob Dibble XRC 1.50 .60
87T Bryan Harvey UER .75 .30
(Games Pitched 47, Innings 5) XRC
88T John Dopson .25 .10
89T Dave Gallagher .25 .10
90T Todd Stottlemyre XRC 1.25 .50
91T Mike Schooler .25 .10
92T Don Gordon .25 .10
93T Sil Campusano .25 .10
94T Jeff Pico .25 .10
95T Jay Buhner XRC 3.00 1.20
96T Nelson Santovenia .25 .10
97T Al Leiter XRC* 3.00 1.20
98T Luis Alicea XRC .75 .30
99T Pat Borders XRC .75 .30
100T Chris Sabo XRC .75 .30
101T Tim Belcher .75 .30
102T Walt Weiss XRC* .75 .30
103T Craig Biggio XRC 8.00 3.20
104T Don August .25 .10
105T Roberto Alomar XRC 20.00 8.00
106T Todd Burns .25 .10
107T John Costello .25 .10
108T Melido Perez XRC* .25 .10
109T Darrin Jackson XRC .25 .10
110T O.Destrade XRC .75 .30

1988 Score Rookie/Traded Glossy

This 110-card standard-size set was issued as a parallel vesion to the regular Score Rookie/Traded set. This set was issued only in boxed factory-set form. According to published reports, only 3,000 of these sets were created. The sets were sold solely through Score's dealer's accounts of the time.

Nm-Mt Ex-Mt
COMP.FACT.SET (110) 150.00 60.00
*STARS: 1.25X TO 3X BASIC CARDS
*ROOKIES: 1X TO 2.5X BASIC CARDS

1988 Score Young Superstars I

This attractive high-gloss 40-card standard-size set of "Young Superstars" was distributed in a small blue box which had the checklist of the set on a side panel of the box. The cards were also distributed as an insert, one per rack pack. These attractive cards are in full color on the front and also have a full-color small portrait on the card back. The cards in this series are distinguishable from the cards in Series II by the fact that this series has a blue and green border on the card front instead of the (Series II) blue and pink border.

Nm-Mt Ex-Mt
COMPLETE SET (40) 8.00 3.20
1 Mark McGwire 4.00 1.60
2 Benito Santiago .10 .04
3 Sam Horn .05 .02
4 Chris Bosio .05 .02
5 Matt Nokes .05 .02
6 Ken Williams .10 .04
7 Dion James .05 .02
8 B.J. Surhoff .15 .06
9 Joe Magrane .05 .02
10 Kevin Seitzer .05 .02
11 Stanley Jefferson .05 .02
12 Devon White .10 .04
13 Nelson Liriano .05 .02
14 Chris James .05 .02
15 Mike Henneman .10 .04
16 Terry Steinbach .05 .02
17 John Kruk .10 .04
18 Matt Williams 1.00 .40
19 Kelly Downs .05 .02

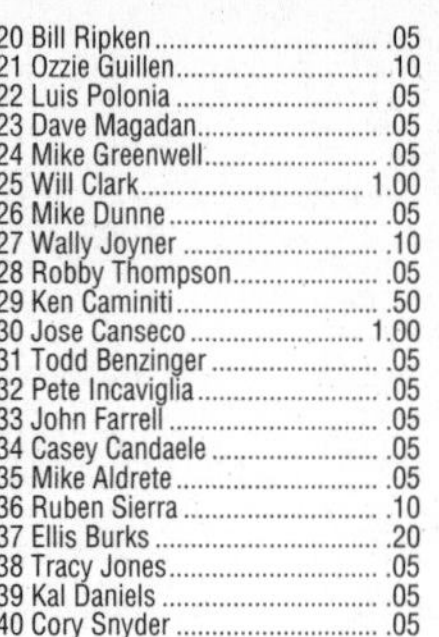

20 Bill Ripken .05 .02
21 Ozzie Guillen .10 .04
22 Luis Polonia .05 .02
23 Dave Magadan .05 .02
24 Mike Greenwell .05 .02
25 Will Clark 1.00 .40
26 Mike Dunne .05 .02
27 Wally Joyner .10 .04
28 Robby Thompson .05 .02
29 Ken Caminiti .50 .20
30 Jose Canseco 1.00 .40
31 Todd Benzinger .05 .02
32 Pete Incaviglia .05 .02
33 John Farrell .05 .02
34 Casey Candaele .05 .02
35 Mike Aldrete .05 .02
36 Ruben Sierra .10 .04
37 Ellis Burks .20 .08
38 Tracy Jones .05 .02
39 Kal Daniels .05 .02
40 Cory Snyder .05 .02

1988 Score Young Superstars II

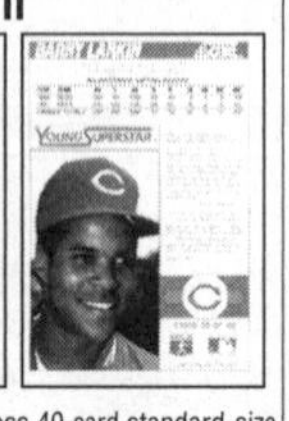

This attractive high-gloss 40-card standard-size set of "Young Superstars" was distributed in a small purple box which had the checklist of the set on a side panel of the box. The cards were not distributed as an insert with rak paks as the first series was, but were only available as a complete set from hobby dealers or through a mail-in offer direct from the company. These attractive cards are in full color on the front and also have a full-color small portrait on the card back. The cards in this series are distinguishable from the cards in Series I by the fact that this series has a blue and pink border on the card front instead of the (Series I) blue and green border.

Nm-Mt Ex-Mt
COMP.FACT SET (40) 5.00 2.00
1 Don Mattingly 1.00 .40
2 Glenn Braggs .05 .02
3 Dwight Gooden .15 .06
4 Jose Lind .05 .02
5 Danny Tartabull .05 .02
6 Tony Fernandez .15 .06
7 Julio Franco .15 .06
8 Andres Galarraga .20 .08
9 Bobby Bonilla .05 .02
10 Eric Davis .15 .06
11 Gerald Young .05 .02
12 Barry Bonds 1.00 .40
13 Jerry Browne .05 .02
14 Jeff Blauser .15 .06
15 Mickey Brantley .05 .02
16 Floyd Youmans .05 .02
17 Bret Saberhagen .15 .06
18 Shawon Dunston .05 .02
19 Len Dykstra .15 .06
20 Darryl Strawberry .15 .06
21 Rick Aguilera .15 .06
22 Ivan Calderon .05 .02
23 Roger Clemens 1.00 .40
24 Vince Coleman .05 .02
25 Gary Thurman .05 .02
26 Jeff Treadway .05 .02
27 Oddibe McDowell .05 .02
28 Fred McGriff .20 .08
29 Mark McLemore .15 .06
30 Jeff Musselman .05 .02
31 Mitch Williams .05 .02
32 Dan Plesac .05 .02
33 Juan Nieves .05 .02
34 Barry Larkin .20 .08
35 Greg Mathews .05 .02
36 Shane Mack .05 .02
37 Scott Bankhead .05 .02
38 Eric Bell .05 .02
39 Greg Swindell .05 .02
40 Kevin Elster .05 .02

1989 Score

This 660-card standard-size set was distributed by Major League Marketing. Cards were issued primarily in fin-wrapped plastic packs and factory sets. Cards feature six distinctive inner border (inside a white outer border) colors on the front. Subsets include Highlights (652-660) and Rookie Prospects (621-651). Rookie Cards in this set include Brady Anderson, Craig Biggio, Randy Johnson, Gary Sheffield, and John Smoltz.

Nm-Mt Ex-Mt
COMPLETE SET (660) 10.00 4.00
COMP.FACT.SET (660) 10.00 4.00
1 Jose Canseco .25 .10
2 Andre Dawson .10 .04
3 Mark McGwire UER 1.00 .40
4 Benito Santiago .10 .04
5 Rick Reuschel .05 .02
6 Fred McGriff .25 .10
7 Kal Daniels .05 .02
8 Gary Gaetti .10 .04
9 Ellis Burks .15 .06
10 Darryl Strawberry .15 .06
11 Julio Franco .05 .02
12 Lloyd Moseby .05 .02
13 Jeff Pico .05 .02
14 Johnny Ray .05 .02
15 Cal Ripken .75 .30
16 Dick Schofield .05 .02
17 Mel Hall .05 .02
18 Bill Ripken .05 .02
19 Brook Jacoby .05 .02
20 Kirby Puckett .25 .10
21 Bill Doran .05 .02
22 Pete O'Brien .05 .02
23 Matt Nokes .05 .02
24 Brian Fisher .05 .02
25 Jack Clark .05 .02
26 Gary Pettis .05 .02
27 Dave Valle .05 .02
28 Willie Wilson .05 .02
29 Curt Young .05 .02
30 Dale Murphy .25 .10
31 Barry Larkin .25 .10
32 Dave Stewart .10 .04
33 Mike LaValliere .05 .02
34 Glenn Hubbard .05 .02
35 Ryne Sandberg .40 .16
36 Tony Pena .05 .02
37 Greg Walker .05 .02
38 Von Hayes .05 .02
39 Kevin Mitchell .10 .04
40 Tim Raines .10 .04
41 Keith Hernandez .15 .06
42 Keith Moreland .05 .02
43 Ruben Sierra .05 .02
44 Chet Lemon .05 .02
45 Willie Randolph .10 .04
46 Andy Allanson .05 .02
47 Candy Maldonado .05 .02
48 Sid Bream .05 .02
49 Denny Walling .05 .02
50 Dave Winfield .10 .04
51 Alvin Davis .05 .02
52 Cory Snyder .05 .02
53 Hubie Brooks .05 .02
54 Chili Davis .10 .04
55 Kevin Seitzer .05 .02
56 Jose Uribe .05 .02
57 Tony Fernandez .05 .02
58 Tim Teufel .05 .02
59 Oddibe McDowell .05 .02
60 Les Lancaster .05 .02
61 Billy Hatcher .05 .02
62 Dan Gladden .05 .02
63 Marty Barrett .05 .02
64 Nick Esasky .05 .02
65 Wally Joyner .10 .04
66 Mike Greenwell .05 .02
67 Ken Williams .05 .02
68 Bob Horner .05 .02
69 Steve Sax .05 .02
70 Rickey Henderson .25 .10
71 Mitch Webster .05 .02
72 Rob Deer .05 .02
73 Jim Presley .05 .02
74 Albert Hall .05 .02
75 George Brett COR .60 .24
(At age 35)
75A George Brett ERR 1.00 .40
(At age 33)
76 Brian Downing .05 .02
77 Dave Martinez .05 .02
78 Scott Fletcher .05 .02
79 Phil Bradley .05 .02
80 Ozzie Smith .40 .16
81 Larry Sheets .05 .02
82 Mike Aldrete .05 .02
83 Darnell Coles .05 .02
84 Len Dykstra .10 .04
85 Jim Rice .10 .04
86 Jeff Treadway .05 .02
87 Jose Lind .05 .02
88 Willie McGee .10 .04
89 Mickey Brantley .05 .02
90 Tony Gwynn .30 .12
91 R.J. Reynolds .05 .02
92 Milt Thompson .05 .02
93 Kevin McReynolds .05 .02
94 Eddie Murray UER .25 .10
('86 batting .205, should be .305)
95 Lance Parrish .05 .02
96 Ron Kittle .05 .02
97 Gerald Young .05 .02
98 Ernie Whitt .05 .02
99 Jeff Reed .05 .02
100 Don Mattingly .60 .24
101 Gerald Perry .05 .02
102 Vance Law .05 .02
103 John Shelby .05 .02
104 Chris Sabo RC * .40 .16
105 Danny Tartabull .05 .02
106 Glenn Wilson .05 .02
107 Mark Davidson .05 .02
108 Dave Parker .10 .04
109 Eric Davis .10 .04
110 Alan Trammell .15 .06
111 Ozzie Virgil .05 .02
112 Frank Tanana .05 .02
113 Rafael Ramirez .05 .02
114 Dennis Martinez .10 .04
115 Jose DeLeon .05 .02
116 Bob Ojeda .05 .02
117 Doug Drabek .05 .02
118 Andy Hawkins .05 .02
119 Greg Maddux .50 .20
120 Cecil Fielder UER .10 .04
Reversed Photo on back
121 Mike Scioscia .05 .02
122 Dan Petry .05 .02
123 Terry Kennedy .05 .02
124 Kelly Downs .05 .02
125 Greg Gross UER .05 .02
(Gregg on back)
126 Fred Lynn .05 .02
127 Barry Bonds 1.25 .50
128 Harold Baines .10 .04
129 Doyle Alexander .05 .02
130 Kevin Elster .05 .02
131 Mike Heath .05 .02
132 Teddy Higuera .05 .02
133 Charlie Leibrandt .05 .02
134 Tim Laudner .05 .02
135A Ray Knight ERR .15 .06
(Reverse negative)
135B Ray Knight COR .05 .02
136 Howard Johnson .05 .02
137 Terry Pendleton .10 .04
138 Andy McGaffigan .05 .02
139 Ken Oberkfell .05 .02
140 Butch Wynegar .05 .02
141 Rob Murphy .05 .02
142 Rich Renteria .05 .02
143 Jose Guzman .05 .02
144 Andres Galarraga .10 .04
145 Ricky Horton .05 .02
146 Frank DiPino .05 .02
147 Glenn Braggs .05 .02
148 John Kruk .10 .04
149 Mike Schmidt .50 .20
150 Lee Smith .10 .04
151 Robin Yount .40 .16
152 Mark Eichhorn .05 .02
153 DeWayne Buice .05 .02
154 B.J. Surhoff .10 .04
155 Vince Coleman .05 .02
156 Tony Phillips .05 .02
157 Willie Fraser .05 .02
158 Lance McCullers .05 .02
159 Greg Gagne .05 .02
160 Jesse Barfield .05 .02
161 Mark Langston .05 .02
162 Kurt Stillwell .05 .02
163 Dion James .05 .02
164 Glenn Davis .05 .02
165 Walt Weiss .05 .02
166 Dave Concepcion .10 .04
167 Alfredo Griffin .05 .02
168 Don Heinkel .05 .02
169 Luis Rivera .05 .02
170 Shane Rawley .05 .02
171 Darrell Evans .10 .04
172 Robby Thompson .05 .02
173 Jody Davis .05 .02
174 Andy Van Slyke .10 .04
175 Wade Boggs UER .15 .06
(Bio says .364, should be .356)
176 Garry Templeton .05 .02
('85 stats off-centered)
177 Gary Redus .05 .02
178 Craig Lefferts .05 .02
179 Carney Lansford .10 .04
180 Ron Darling .05 .02
181 Kirk McCaskill .05 .02
182 Tony Armas .05 .02
183 Steve Farr .05 .02
184 Tom Brunansky .05 .02
185 B.Harvey RC UER .25 .10
'87 games 47, should be 3
186 Mike Marshall .05 .02
187 Bo Diaz .05 .02
188 Willie Upshaw .05 .02
189 Mike Pagliarulo .05 .02
190 Mike Krukow .05 .02
191 Tommy Herr .05 .02
192 Jim Pankovits .05 .02
193 Dwight Evans .10 .04
194 Kelly Gruber .05 .02
195 Bobby Bonilla .10 .04
196 Wallace Johnson .05 .02
197 Dave Stieb .05 .02
198 Pat Borders RC * .25 .10
199 Rafael Palmeiro .25 .10
200 Dwight Gooden .15 .06
201 Pete Incaviglia .05 .02
202 Chris James .05 .02
203 Marvell Wynne .05 .02
204 Pat Sheridan .05 .02
205 Don Baylor .10 .04
206 Paul O'Neill .15 .06
207 Pete Smith .05 .02
208 Mark McLemore .05 .02
209 Henry Cotto .05 .02
210 Kirk Gibson .10 .04
211 Claudell Washington .05 .02
212 Randy Bush .05 .02
213 Joe Carter .15 .06
214 Bill Buckner .10 .04
215 Bert Blyleven UER .10 .04
(Wrong birth year)
216 Brett Butler .10 .04
217 Lee Mazzilli .05 .02
218 Spike Owen .05 .02
219 Bill Swift .05 .02
220 Tim Wallach .05 .02
221 David Cone .10 .04
222 Don Carman .05 .02
223 Rich Gossage .10 .04
224 Bob Walk .05 .02
225 Dave Righetti .05 .02
226 Kevin Bass .05 .02
227 Kevin Gross .05 .02
228 Tim Burke .05 .02
229 Rick Mahler .05 .02
230 Lou Whitaker UER .10 .04
(252 games in '85, should be 152)
231 Luis Alicea RC * .25 .10
232 Roberto Alomar .30 .12
233 Bob Boone .10 .04
234 Dickie Thon .05 .02
235 Shawon Dunston .05 .02
236 Pete Stanicek .05 .02
237 Craig Biggio RC .75 .30
(Inconsistent design, portrait on front)
238 Dennis Boyd .05 .02
239 Tom Candiotti .05 .02
240 Gary Carter .15 .06
241 Mike Stanley .05 .02
242 Ken Phelps .05 .02
243 Chris Bosio .05 .02
244 Les Straker .05 .02
245 Dave Smith .05 .02
246 John Candelaria .05 .02
247 Joe Orsulak .05 .02
248 Storm Davis .05 .02
249 Floyd Bannister UER .05 .02
(ML Batting Record)
250 Jack Morris .10 .04
251 Bret Saberhagen .10 .04
252 Tom Niedenfuer .05 .02
253 Neal Heaton .05 .02
254 Eric Show .05 .02
255 Juan Samuel .05 .02
256 Dale Sveum .05 .02
257 Jim Gott .05 .02
258 Scott Garrelts .05 .02
259 Larry McWilliams .05 .02
260 Steve Bedrosian .05 .02
261 Jack Howell .05 .02
262 Jay Tibbs .05 .02
263 Jamie Moyer .10 .04
264 Doug Sisk .05 .02
265 Todd Worrell .05 .02
266 John Farrell .05 .02
267 Dave Collins .05 .02
268 Sid Fernandez .05 .02
269 Tom Brookens .05 .02
270 Shane Mack .05 .02
271 Paul Kilgus .05 .02
272 Chuck Crim .05 .02
273 Bob Knepper .05 .02
274 Mike Moore .05 .02
275 Guillermo Hernandez .05 .02
276 Dennis Eckersley .10 .04
277 Graig Nettles .10 .04
278 Rich Dotson .05 .02
279 Larry Herndon .05 .02
280 Gene Larkin .05 .02
281 Roger McDowell .05 .02
282 Greg Swindell .05 .02
283 Juan Agosto .05 .02
284 Jeff M. Robinson .05 .02
285 Mike Dunne .05 .02
286 Greg Mathews .05 .02
287 Kent Tekulve .05 .02
288 Jerry Mumphrey .05 .02
289 Jack McDowell .10 .04
290 Frank Viola .05 .02
291 Mark Gubicza .05 .02
292 Dave Schmidt .05 .02
293 Mike Henneman .05 .02
294 Jimmy Jones .05 .02
295 Charlie Hough .10 .04
296 Rafael Santana .05 .02
297 Chris Speier .05 .02
298 Mike Witt .05 .02
299 Pascual Perez .05 .02
300 Nolan Ryan 1.00 .40
301 Mitch Williams .05 .02
302 Mookie Wilson .10 .04
303 Mackey Sasser .05 .02
304 John Cerutti .05 .02
305 Jeff Reardon .10 .04
306 Randy Myers UER .10 .04
(6 hits in '87, should be 61)
307 Greg Brock .05 .02
308 Bob Welch .05 .02
309 Jeff D. Robinson .05 .02
310 Harold Reynolds .10 .04
311 Jim Walewander .05 .02
312 Dave Magadan .05 .02
313 Jim Gantner .05 .02
314 Walt Terrell .05 .02
315 Wally Backman .05 .02
316 Luis Salazar .05 .02
317 Rick Rhoden .05 .02
318 Tom Henke .05 .02
319 Mike Macfarlane RC * .25 .10
320 Dan Plesac .05 .02
321 Calvin Schiraldi .05 .02
322 Stan Javier .05 .02
323 Devon White .10 .04
324 Scott Bradley .05 .02
325 Bruce Hurst .05 .02
326 Manny Lee .05 .02
327 Rick Aguilera .10 .04
328 Bruce Ruffin .05 .02
329 Ed Whitson .05 .02
330 Bo Jackson .25 .10
331 Ivan Calderon .05 .02
332 Mickey Hatcher .05 .02
333 Barry Jones .05 .02
334 Ron Hassey .05 .02
335 Bill Wegman .05 .02
336 Damon Berryhill .05 .02
337 Steve Ontiveros .05 .02
338 Dan Pasqua .05 .02
339 Bill Pecota .05 .02
340 Greg Cadaret .05 .02
341 Scott Bankhead .05 .02
342 Ron Guidry .10 .04
343 Danny Heep .05 .02
344 Bob Brower .05 .02
345 Rich Gedman .05 .02
346 Nelson Santovenia .05 .02
347 George Bell .05 .02
348 Ted Power .05 .02
349 Mark Grant .05 .02
350 Roger Clemens COR .50 .20
(78 career wins)
350A Roger Clemens ERR 1.25 .50
(778 career wins)
351 Bill Long .05 .02
352 Jay Bell .15 .06
353 Steve Balboni .05 .02
354 Bob Kipper .05 .02
355 Steve Jeltz .05 .02
356 Jesse Orosco .05 .02
357 Bob Dernier .05 .02
358 Mickey Tettleton .05 .02
359 Duane Ward .05 .02
360 Darrin Jackson .05 .02
361 Rey Quinones .05 .02
362 Mark Grace .25 .10
363 Steve Lake .05 .02
364 Pat Perry .05 .02
365 Terry Steinbach .10 .04
366 Alan Ashby .05 .02
367 Jeff Montgomery .10 .04
368 Steve Buechele .05 .02
369 Chris Brown .05 .02
370 Orel Hershiser .10 .04
371 Todd Benzinger .05 .02
372 Ron Gant .10 .04
373 Paul Assenmacher .05 .02
374 Joey Meyer .05 .02
375 Neil Allen .05 .02

376 Mike Davis .05 .02
377 Jeff Parrett .05 .02
378 Jay Howell .05 .02
379 Rafael Belliard .05 .02
380 Luis Polonia UER .05 .02
(2 triples in '87,
should be 10)
381 Keith Atherton .05 .02
382 Kent Hrbek .10 .04
383 Bob Stanley .05 .02
384 Dave LaPoint .05 .02
385 Rance Mulliniks .05 .02
386 Melido Perez .05 .02
387 Doug Jones .05 .02
388 Steve Lyons .05 .02
389 Alejandro Pena .05 .02
390 Frank White .10 .04
391 Pat Tabler .05 .02
392 Eric Plunk .05 .02
393 Mike Maddux .05 .02
394 Allan Anderson .05 .02
395 Bob Brenly .05 .02
396 Rick Cerone .05 .02
397 Scott Terry .05 .02
398 Mike Jackson .05 .02
399 Bobby Thigpen UER .05 .02
Bio says 37 saves in
'88, should be 34
400 Don Sutton .25 .10
401 Cecil Espy .05 .02
402 Junior Ortiz .05 .02
403 Mike Smithson .05 .02
404 Bud Black .05 .02
405 Tom Foley .05 .02
406 Andres Thomas .05 .02
407 Rick Sutcliffe .10 .04
408 Brian Harper .05 .02
409 John Smiley .05 .02
410 Juan Nieves .05 .02
411 Shawn Abner .05 .02
412 Wes Gardner .05 .02
413 Darren Daulton .10 .04
414 Juan Berenguer .05 .02
415 Charles Hudson .05 .02
416 Rick Honeycutt .05 .02
417 Greg Booker .05 .02
418 Tim Belcher .05 .02
419 Don August .05 .02
420 Dale Mohorcic .05 .02
421 Steve Lombardozzi .05 .02
422 Atlee Hammaker .05 .02
423 Jerry Don Gleaton .05 .02
424 Scott Bailes .05 .02
425 Bruce Sutter .05 .02
426 Randy Ready .05 .02
427 Jerry Reed .05 .02
428 Bryn Smith .05 .02
429 Tim Leary .05 .02
430 Mark Clear .05 .02
431 Terry Leach .05 .02
432 John Moses .05 .02
433 Ozzie Guillen .05 .02
434 Gene Nelson .05 .02
435 Gary Ward .05 .02
436 Luis Aguayo .05 .02
437 Fernando Valenzuela .10 .04
438 Jeff Russell UER .05 .02
(Saves total does
not add up correctly)
439 Cecilio Guante .05 .02
440 Don Robinson .05 .02
441 Rick Anderson .05 .02
442 Tom Glavine .25 .10
443 Daryl Boston .05 .02
444 Joe Price .05 .02
445 Stu Cliburn .05 .02
446 Manny Trillo .05 .02
447 Joel Skinner .05 .02
448 Charlie Puleo .05 .02
449 Carlton Fisk .15 .06
450 Will Clark .25 .10
451 Otis Nixon .05 .02
452 Rick Schu .05 .02
453 Todd Stottlemyre UER .15 .06
(ML Batting Record)
454 Tim Birtsas .05 .02
455 Dave Gallagher .05 .02
456 Barry Lyons .05 .02
457 Fred Manrique .05 .02
458 Ernest Riles .05 .02
459 Doug Jennings .05 .02
460 Joe Magrane .05 .02
461 Jamie Quirk .05 .02
462 Jack Armstrong RC * .25 .10
463 Bobby Witt .05 .02
464 Keith A. Miller .05 .02
465 Todd Burns .05 .02
466 John Dopson .05 .02
467 Rich Yett .05 .02
468 Craig Reynolds .05 .02
469 Dave Bergman .05 .02
470 Rex Hudler .05 .02
471 Eric King .05 .02
472 Joaquin Andujar .05 .02
473 Sil Campusano .05 .02
474 Terry Mulholland .05 .02
475 Mike Flanagan .05 .02
476 Greg A. Harris .05 .02
477 Tommy John .10 .04
478 Dave Anderson .05 .02
479 Fred Toliver .05 .02
480 Jimmy Key .10 .04
481 Donell Nixon .05 .02
482 Mark Portugal .05 .02
483 Tom Pagnozzi .05 .02
484 Jeff Kunkel .05 .02
485 Frank Williams .05 .02
486 Jody Reed .05 .02
487 Roberto Kelly .10 .04
488 Shawn Hillegas UER .05 .02
(165 innings in '87,
should be 165.2)
489 Jerry Reuss .05 .02
490 Mark Davis .05 .02
491 Jeff Sellers .05 .02
492 Zane Smith .05 .02
493 Al Newman .05 .02
494 Mike Young .05 .02
495 Larry Parrish .05 .02
496 Herm Winningham .05 .02
497 Carmen Castillo .05 .02
498 Joe Hesketh .05 .02
499 Darrell Miller .05 .02
500 Mike LaCoss .05 .02
501 Charlie Lea .05 .02
502 Bruce Benedict .05 .02
503 Chuck Finley .10 .04
504 Brad Wellman .05 .02
505 Tim Crews .05 .02
506 Ken Gerhart .05 .02
507A Brian Holton ERR .05 .02
(Born 1/25/65 Denver,
should be 11/29/59
in McKeesport)
507B Brian Holton COR 2.00 .80
508 Dennis Lamp .05 .02
509 Bobby Meacham UER .05 .02
('84 games 099)
510 Tracy Jones .05 .02
511 Mike R. Fitzgerald .05 .02
512 Jeff Bittiger .05 .02
513 Tim Flannery .05 .02
514 Ray Hayward .05 .02
515 Dave Leiper .05 .02
516 Rod Scurry .05 .02
517 Carmelo Martinez .05 .02
518 Curtis Wilkerson .05 .02
519 Stan Jefferson .05 .02
520 Dan Quisenberry .05 .02
521 Lloyd McClendon .05 .02
522 Steve Trout .05 .02
523 Larry Andersen .05 .02
524 Don Aase .05 .02
525 Bob Forsch .05 .02
526 Geno Petralli .05 .02
527 Angel Salazar .05 .02
528 Mike Schooler .05 .02
529 Jose Oquendo .05 .02
530 Jay Buhner UER .10 .04
(Wearing 43 on front,
listed as 34 on back)
531 Tom Bolton .05 .02
532 Al Nipper .05 .02
533 Dave Henderson .05 .02
534 John Costello .05 .02
535 Donnie Moore .05 .02
536 Mike Laga .05 .02
537 Mike Gallego .05 .02
538 Jim Clancy .05 .02
539 Joel Youngblood .05 .02
540 Rick Leach .05 .02
541 Kevin Romine .05 .02
542 Mark Salas .05 .02
543 Greg Minton .05 .02
544 Dave Palmer .05 .02
545 Dwayne Murphy UER .05 .02
(Game-sinning)
546 Jim Deshaies .05 .02
547 Don Gordon .05 .02
548 Ricky Jordan RC * .25 .10
549 Mike Boddicker .05 .02
550 Mike Scott .05 .02
551 Jeff Ballard .05 .02
552A Jose Rijo ERR .15 .06
(Uniform listed as
27 on back)
552B Jose Rijo COR .15 .06
(Uniform listed as
24 on back)
553 Danny Darwin .05 .02
554 Tom Browning .05 .02
555 Danny Jackson .05 .02
556 Rick Dempsey .05 .02
557 Jeffrey Leonard .05 .02
558 Jeff Musselman .05 .02
559 Ron Robinson .05 .02
560 John Tudor .05 .02
561 Don Slaught UER .05 .02
(237 games in 1987)
562 Dennis Rasmussen .05 .02
563 Brady Anderson RC .50 .20
564 Pedro Guerrero .05 .02
565 Paul Molitor .15 .06
566 Terry Clark .05 .02
567 Terry Puhl .05 .02
568 Mike Campbell .05 .02
569 Paul Mirabella .05 .02
570 Jeff Hamilton .05 .02
571 Oswald Peraza .05 .02
572 Bob McClure .05 .02
573 Jose Bautista RC .10 .04
574 Alex Trevino .05 .02
575 John Franco .10 .04
576 Mark Parent .05 .02
577 Nelson Liriano .05 .02
578 Steve Shields .05 .02
579 Odell Jones .05 .02
580 Al Leiter .25 .10
581 Dave Stapleton .05 .02
582 Orel Hershiser .10 .04
Jose Canseco
Kirk Gibson
Dave Stewart WS
583 Donnie Hill .05 .02
584 Chuck Jackson .05 .02
585 Rene Gonzales .05 .02
586 Tracy Woodson .05 .02
587 Jim Adduci .05 .02
588 Mario Soto .05 .02
589 Jeff Blauser .10 .04
590 Jim Traber .05 .02
591 Jon Perlman .05 .02
592 Mark Williamson .05 .02
593 Dave Meads .05 .02
594 Jim Eisenreich .05 .02
595A Paul Gibson P1 1.00 .40
595B Paul Gibson P2 .05 .02
(Airbrushed leg on
player in background)
596 Mike Birkbeck .05 .02
597 Terry Francona .10 .04
598 Paul Zuvella .05 .02
599 Franklin Stubbs .05 .02
600 Gregg Jefferies .10 .04
601 John Cangelosi .05 .02
602 Mike Sharperson .05 .02
603 Mike Diaz .05 .02
604 Gary Varsho .05 .02
605 Terry Blocker .05 .02
606 Charlie O'Brien .05 .02
607 Jim Eppard .05 .02
608 John Davis .05 .02
609 Ken Griffey Sr. .10 .04
610 Buddy Bell .10 .04
611 Ted Simmons UER .10 .04
('78 stats Cardinal)
612 Matt Williams .25 .10
613 Danny Cox .05 .02
614 Al Pedrique .05 .02
615 Ron Oester .05 .02
616 John Smoltz RC 1.00 .40
617 Bob Melvin .05 .02
618 Rob Dibble RC * .50 .20
619 Kirt Manwaring .05 .02
620 Felix Fermin .05 .02
621 Doug Dascenzo .05 .02
622 Bill Brennan .05 .02
623 Carlos Quintana RC .10 .04
624 Mike Harkey RC UER .10 .04
(13 and 31 walks in '88,
should be 35 and 33
625 Gary Sheffield RC 1.50 .60
626 Tom Prince .05 .02
627 Steve Searcy .05 .02
628 Charlie Hayes RC .25 .10
(Listed as outfielder)
629 Felix Jose RC UER .10 .04
(Modesto misspelled
as Modesta)
630 Sandy Alomar Jr. RC .40 .16
(Inconsistent design,
portrait on front)
631 Derek Lilliquist RC .10 .04
632 Geronimo Berroa .05 .02
633 Luis Medina .05 .02
634 Tom Gordon RC UER .25 .10
Height 6'0"
635 Ramon Martinez RC .25 .10
636 Craig Worthington .05 .02
637 Edgar Martinez .25 .10
638 Chad Kreuter RC .25 .10
639 Ron Jones .05 .02
640 Van Snider RC .10 .04
641 Lance Blankenship RC .10 .04
642 Dwight Smith RC UER .25 .10
10 HR's in '87, should be 18
643 Cameron Drew .05 .02
644 Jerald Clark RC .10 .04
645 Randy Johnson RC 3.00 1.20
646 Norm Charlton RC .25 .10
647 Todd Frohwirth UER .05 .02
(Southpaw on back)
648 Luis De Los Santos .05 .02
649 Tim Jones .05 .02
650 Dave West RC UER .10 .04
ML hits 3
should be 6
651 Bob Milacki .05 .02
652 Wrigley Field HL .10 .04
653 Orel Hershiser HL .10 .04
654A W.Boggs HL ERR .15 .06
("seaason" on back
654B W.Boggs HL COR .10 .04
655 Jose Canseco HL .10 .04
656 Doug Jones HL .05 .02
657 Rickey Henderson HL .15 .06
658 Tom Browning HL .05 .02
659 Mike Greenwell HL .05 .02
660 Boston Red Sox HL .05 .02

1989 Score Rookie/Traded

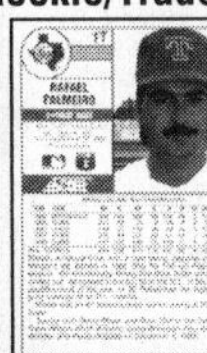

The 1989 Score Rookie and Traded set contains 110 standard-size cards. The set was issued exclusively in factory set form through hobby dealers. The set was distributed in a blue box with 10 Magic Motion trivia cards. The fronts have coral green borders with pink diamonds at the bottom. Cards 1-80 feature traded players; cards 81-110 feature 1989 rookies. Rookie Cards in this set include Jim Abbott, Joey (Albert) Belle, Ken Griffey Jr. and John Wetteland.

Nm-Mt Ex-Mt
COMP.FACT.SET (110) 15.00 6.00
1T Rafael Palmeiro .25 .10
2T Nolan Ryan 1.50 .60
3T Jack Clark .05 .02
4T Dave LaPoint .05 .02
5T Mike Moore .05 .02
6T Pete O'Brien .05 .02
7T Jeffrey Leonard .05 .02
8T Rob Murphy .05 .02
9T Tom Herr .05 .02
10T Claudell Washington .05 .02
11T Mike Pagliarulo .05 .02
12T Steve Lake .05 .02
13T Spike Owen .05 .02
14T Andy Hawkins .05 .02
15T Todd Benzinger .05 .02
16T Mookie Wilson .10 .04
17T Bert Blyleven .10 .04
18T Jeff Treadway .05 .02
19T Bruce Hurst .05 .02
20T Steve Sax .05 .02
21T Juan Samuel .05 .02
22T Jesse Barfield .05 .02
23T Carmen Castillo .05 .02
24T Terry Leach .05 .02
25T Mark Langston .05 .02
26T Eric King .05 .02
27T Steve Balboni .05 .02
28T Len Dykstra .10 .04
29T Keith Moreland .05 .02
30T Terry Kennedy .05 .02
31T Eddie Murray .25 .10
32T Mitch Williams .05 .02
33T Jeff Parrett .05 .02
34T Wally Backman .05 .02
35T Julio Franco .05 .02
36T Lance Parrish .05 .02
37T Nick Esasky .05 .02
38T Luis Polonia .05 .02
39T Kevin Gross .05 .02
40T John Dopson .05 .02
41T Willie Randolph .10 .04
42T Jim Clancy .05 .02
43T Tracy Jones .05 .02
44T Phil Bradley .05 .02
45T Milt Thompson .05 .02
46T Chris James .05 .02
47T Scott Fletcher .05 .02
48T Kal Daniels .05 .02
49T Steve Bedrosian .05 .02
50T Rickey Henderson .25 .10
51T Dion James .05 .02
52T Tim Leary .05 .02
53T Roger McDowell .05 .02
54T Mel Hall .05 .02
55T Dickie Thon .05 .02
56T Zane Smith .05 .02
57T Danny Heep .05 .02
58T Bob McClure .05 .02
59T Brian Holton .05 .02
60T Randy Ready .05 .02
61T Bob Melvin .05 .02
62T Harold Baines .10 .04
63T Lance McCullers .05 .02
64T Jody Davis .05 .02
65T Darrell Evans .10 .04
66T Joel Youngblood .05 .02
67T Frank Viola .05 .02
68T Mike Aldrete .05 .02
69T Greg Cadaret .05 .02
70T John Kruk .10 .04
71T Pat Sheridan .05 .02
72T Oddibe McDowell .05 .02
73T Tom Brookens .05 .02
74T Bob Boone .10 .04
75T Walt Terrell .05 .02
76T Joel Skinner .05 .02
77T Randy Johnson 2.00 .80
78T Felix Fermin .05 .02
79T Rick Mahler .05 .02
80T Richard Dotson .05 .02
81T Cris Carpenter RC * .10 .04
82T Bill Spiers RC .25 .10
83T Junior Felix RC .10 .04
84T Joe Girardi RC .40 .16
85T Jerome Walton .25 .10
86T Greg Litton .05 .02
87T Greg W.Harris RC .10 .04
88T Jim Abbott RC* .50 .20
89T Kevin Brown .25 .10
90T John Wetteland RC .40 .16
91T Gary Wayne .05 .02
92T Rich Monteleone .05 .02
93T Bob Geren RC .05 .02
94T Clay Parker .05 .02
95T Steve Finley RC .50 .20
96T Gregg Olson RC .25 .10
97T Ken Patterson .05 .02
98T Ken Hill RC .25 .10
99T Scott Scudder RC .10 .04
100T Ken Griffey Jr. RC 8.00 3.20
101T Jeff Brantley RC .25 .10
102T Donn Pall .05 .02
103T Carlos Martinez RC .10 .04
104T Joe Oliver RC .25 .10
105T Omar Vizquel RC .50 .20
106T Joey Belle RC .75 .30
107T Kenny Rogers RC .50 .20
108T Mark Carreon .05 .02
109T Rolando Roomes .05 .02
110T Pete Harnisch RC .25 .10

1989 Score Hottest 100 Rookies

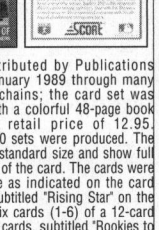

This set was distributed by Publications International in January 1989 through many retail stores and chains; the card set was packaged along with a colorful 48-page book for a suggested retail price of 12.95. Supposedly 225,000 sets were produced. The cards measure the standard size and show full color on both sides of the card. The cards were produced by Score as indicated on the card backs. The set is subtitled "Rising Star" on the reverse. The first six cards (1-6) of a 12-card set of Score's trivia cards, subtitled "Rookies to Remember" is included along with each set. This set is distinguished by the sharp blue borders and the player's first initial inside a yellow triangle in the lower left corner of the obverse. The set features Dave Justice appearing one year before his Rookie Card year.

Nm-Mt Ex-Mt
COMP.FACT SET (100) 10.00 4.00
1 Gregg Jefferies .05 .02
2 Vicente Palacios .05 .02
3 Cameron Drew .05 .02
4 Doug Dascenzo .05 .02
5 Luis Medina .05 .02
6 Craig Worthington .05 .02
7 Rob Ducey .05 .02
8 Hal Morris .15 .06
9 Bill Brennan .05 .02
10 Gary Sheffield .75 .30
11 Mike Devereaux .05 .02
12 Hensley Meulens .05 .02
13 Carlos Quintana .05 .02
14 Todd Frohwirth .05 .02
15 Scott Lusader .05 .02
16 Mark Carreon .05 .02
17 Torey Lovullo .05 .02
18 Randy Velarde .15 .06
19 Billy Bean .15 .06
20 Lance Blankenship .05 .02
21 Chris Gwynn .05 .02
22 Felix Jose .05 .02
23 Derek Lilliquist .05 .02
24 Gary Thurman .05 .02
25 Ron Jones .05 .02
26 Dave Justice 2.00 .80
27 Johnny Paredes .05 .02
28 Tim Jones .05 .02
29 Jose Gonzalez .05 .02
30 Geronimo Berroa .05 .02
31 Trevor Wilson .05 .02
32 Morris Madden .05 .02
33 Lance Johnson .05 .02
34 Marvin Freeman .05 .02
35 Jose Cecena .05 .02
36 Jim Corsi .05 .02
37 Rolando Roomes .05 .02
38 Scott Medvin .05 .02
39 Charlie Hayes .05 .02
40 Edgar Martinez .50 .20
41 Van Snider .05 .02
42 John Fishel .05 .02
43 Bruce Fields .05 .02
44 Darryl Hamilton .05 .02
45 Tom Prince .05 .02
46 Kirt Manwaring .05 .02
47 Steve Searcy .05 .02
48 Mike Harkey .05 .02
49 German Gonzalez .05 .02
50 Tony Perezchica .05 .02
51 Chad Kreuter .05 .02
52 Luis DeLosSantos .05 .02
53 Steve Curry .05 .02
54 Greg Briley .05 .02
55 Ramon Martinez .25 .10
56 Ron Tingley .05 .02
57 Randy Kramer .05 .02
58 Alex Madrid .05 .02
59 Kevin Reimer .05 .02
60 Dave Otto .05 .02
61 Ken Patterson .05 .02
62 Keith Miller .05 .02
63 Randy Johnson 3.00 1.20
64 Dwight Smith .15 .06
65 Eric Yelding .05 .02
66 Bob Geren .05 .02
67 Shane Turner .05 .02
68 Tom Gordon .40 .16
69 Jeff Huson .05 .02
70 Marty Brown .05 .02
71 Nelson Santovenia .05 .02
72 Roberto Alomar 1.00 .40
73 Mike Schooler .05 .02
74 Pete Smith .05 .02
75 John Costello .05 .02
76 Chris Sabo .05 .02
77 Damon Berryhill .05 .02
78 Mark Grace 2.00 .80
79 Melido Perez .05 .02
80 Al Leiter .40 .16
81 Todd Stottlemyre .05 .02
82 Mackey Sasser .05 .02
83 Don August .05 .02
84 Jeff Treadway .05 .02
85 Jody Reed .05 .02
86 Mike Campbell .05 .02
87 Ron Gant .15 .06
88 Ricky Jordan .05 .02
89 Terry Clark .05 .02
90 Roberto Kelly .05 .02
91 Pat Borders .15 .06
92 Bryan Harvey .05 .02
93 Joey Meyer .05 .02
94 Tim Belcher .05 .02
95 Walt Weiss .05 .02
96 Dave Gallagher .05 .02
97 Mike Macfarlane .05 .02
98 Craig Biggio 2.50 1.00
99 Jack Armstrong .05 .02
100 Todd Burns .05 .02

1989 Score Hottest 100 Stars

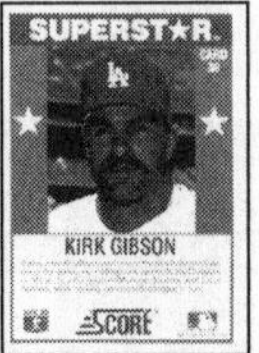

This set was distributed by Publications International in January 1989 through many retail stores and chains; the card set was packaged along with a colorful 48-page book for a suggested retail price of 12.95. Supposedly 225,000 sets were produced. The cards measure the standard size and show full color on both sides of the card. The cards were produced by Score as indicated on the card backs. The set is subtitled "Superstar" on the reverse. The last six cards (7-12) of a 12-card set of Score's trivia cards, subtitled "Rookies to Remember" is included along with each set. This set is distinguished by the sharp red borders and the player's first initial inside a yellow triangle in the upper left corner of the obverse.

Nm-Mt Ex-Mt
COMP. FACT SET (100) 10.00 4.00
1 Jose Canseco .60 .24
2 David Cone .50 .20
3 Dave Winfield .75 .30
4 George Brett 1.00 .40
5 Frank Viola .05 .02
6 Cory Snyder .05 .02
7 Alan Trammell .30 .12
8 Dwight Evans .15 .06
9 Tim Leary .05 .02
10 Don Mattingly 1.50 .60
11 Kirby Puckett .60 .24

12 Carney Lansford .15 .06
13 Dennis Martinez .15 .06
14 Kent Hrbek .15 .06
15 Dwight Gooden .15 .06
16 Dennis Eckersley .60 .24
17 Kevin Seitzer .05 .02
18 Lee Smith .15 .06
19 Danny Tartabull .05 .02
20 Gerald Perry .05 .02
21 Gary Gaetti .15 .06
22 Rick Reuschel .15 .06
23 Keith Hernandez .15 .06
24 Jeff Reardon .15 .06
25 Mark McGwire 2.00 .80
26 Juan Samuel .05 .02
27 Jack Clark .05 .02
28 Robin Yount .75 .30
29 Steve Bedrosian .05 .02
30 Kirk Gibson .15 .06
31 Barry Bonds 1.50 .60
32 Dan Plesac .05 .02
33 Steve Sax .05 .02
34 Jeff M. Robinson .05 .02
35 Orel Hershiser .15 .06
36 Julio Franco .15 .06
37 Dave Righetti .05 .02
38 Bob Knepper .05 .02
39 Carlton Fisk .75 .30
40 Tony Gwynn 1.25 .50
41 Doug Jones .05 .02
42 Bobby Bonilla .15 .06
43 Ellis Burks .30 .12
44 Pedro Guerrero .05 .02
45 Rickey Henderson 1.00 .40
46 Glenn Davis .05 .02
47 Benito Santiago .15 .06
48 Greg Maddux 2.00 .80
49 Teddy Higuera .05 .02
50 Darryl Strawberry .15 .06
51 Ozzie Guillen .15 .06
52 Barry Larkin .50 .20
53 Tony Fernandez .15 .06
54 Ryne Sandberg 1.00 .40
55 Joe Carter .30 .12
56 Rafael Palmeiro .50 .20
57 Paul Molitor .75 .30
58 Eric Davis .15 .06
59 Mike Henneman .05 .02
60 Mike Scott .15 .06
61 Tom Browning .05 .02
62 Mark Davis .05 .02
63 Tom Henke .05 .02
64 Nolan Ryan 3.00 1.20
65 Fred McGriff .50 .20
66 Dale Murphy .50 .20
67 Mark Langston .05 .02
68 Bobby Thigpen .05 .02
69 Mark Gubicza .05 .02
70 Mike Greenwell .05 .02
71 Ron Darling .05 .02
72 Gerald Young .05 .02
73 Wally Joyner .15 .06
74 Andres Galarraga .50 .20
75 Danny Jackson .05 .02
76 Mike Schmidt .75 .30
77 Cal Ripken 3.00 1.20
78 Alvin Davis .05 .02
79 Bruce Hurst .05 .02
80 Andre Dawson .50 .20
81 Bob Boone .15 .06
82 Harold Reynolds .15 .06
83 Eddie Murray .75 .30
84 Robby Thompson .05 .02
85 Will Clark .50 .20
86 Vince Coleman .05 .02
87 Doug Drabek .05 .02
88 Ozzie Smith 1.00 .40
89 Bob Welch .05 .02
90 Roger Clemens 1.50 .60
91 George Bell .05 .02
92 Andy Van Slyke .15 .06
93 Willie McGee .15 .06
94 Todd Worrell .05 .02
95 Tim Raines .15 .06
96 Kevin McReynolds .05 .02
97 John Franco .15 .06
98 Jim Gott .05 .02
99 Johnny Ray .05 .02
100 Wade Boggs .75 .30

1989 Scoremasters

The 1989 Scoremasters set contains 42 standard-size cards. The fronts are "pure" with attractively drawn action portraits. The backs feature write-ups of the players' careers. The set was issued in factory set form only. A first year card of Ken Griffey Jr. highlights the set.

Nm-Mt Ex-Mt
COMP.FACT.SET (42) 10.00 4.00
1 Bo Jackson .25 .10
2 Jerome Walton .15 .06
3 Cal Ripken .75 .30
4 Mike Scott .05 .02
5 Nolan Ryan 1.00 .40
6 Don Mattingly .60 .24
7 Tom Gordon .25 .10
8 Jack Morris .10 .04
9 Carlton Fisk .20 .08
10 Will Clark .25 .10
11 George Brett .60 .24
12 Kevin Mitchell .10 .04
13 Mark Langston .05 .02
14 Dave Stewart .10 .04
15 Dale Murphy .25 .10
16 Gary Gaetti .10 .04
17 Wade Boggs .15 .06
18 Eric Davis .10 .04
19 Kirby Puckett .25 .10
20 Roger Clemens .50 .20
21 Orel Hershiser .10 .04
22 Mark Grace .25 .10
23 Ryne Sandberg .40 .16
24 Barry Larkin .40 .16
25 Ellis Burks .15 .06
26 Dwight Gooden .15 .06
27 Ozzie Smith .40 .16
28 Andre Dawson .10 .04
29 Julio Franco .05 .02
30 Ken Griffey Jr. 8.00 3.20
31 Ruben Sierra .05 .02
32 Mark McGwire .75 .30
33 Andres Galarraga .10 .04
34 Joe Carter .15 .06
35 Vince Coleman .05 .02
36 Mike Greenwell .05 .02
37 Tony Gwynn .30 .12
38 Andy Van Slyke .10 .04
39 Gregg Jefferies .10 .04
40 Jose Canseco .25 .10
41 Dave Winfield .10 .04
42 Darryl Strawberry .15 .06
NNO Don Mattingly Promo 5.00 2.00
Issued for National Convention

1989 Score Young Superstars I

The 1989 Score Young Superstars I set contains 42 standard-size cards. The fronts are pink, white and blue. The vertically oriented backs have color facial shots, 1988 and career stats, and biographical information. One card was included in each 1989 Score rack pack, and the cards were also distributed as a boxed set with five Magic Motion trivia cards.

Nm-Mt Ex-Mt
COMPLETE SET (42) 8.00 3.20
1 Gregg Jefferies .40 .16
2 Jody Reed .25 .10
3 Mark Grace 1.00 .40
4 Dave Gallagher .25 .10
5 Bo Jackson 1.00 .40
6 Jay Buhner .40 .16
7 Melido Perez .25 .10
8 Bobby Witt .25 .10
9 David Cone .40 .16
10 Chris Sabo .25 .10
11 Pat Borders .25 .10
12 Mark Grant .25 .10
13 Mike Macfarlane .25 .10
14 Mike Jackson .25 .10
15 Ricky Jordan .25 .10
16 Ron Gant .40 .16
17 Al Leiter 1.00 .40
18 Jeff Parrett .25 .10
19 Pete Smith .25 .10
20 Walt Weiss .40 .16
21 Doug Drabek .25 .10
22 Kirt Manwaring .25 .10
23 Keith Miller .25 .10
24 Damon Berryhill .25 .10
25 Gary Sheffield 4.00 1.60
26 Brady Anderson 1.00 .40
27 Mitch Williams .25 .10
28 Roberto Alomar 1.25 .50
29 Bobby Thigpen .25 .10
30 Bryan Harvey UER .25 .10
(47 games in '87)
31 Jose Rijo .25 .10
32 Dave West .25 .10
33 Joey Meyer .25 .10
34 Allan Anderson .25 .10
35 Rafael Palmeiro 1.00 .40
36 Tim Belcher .25 .10
37 John Smiley .25 .10
38 Mackey Sasser .25 .10
39 Greg Maddux 2.00 .80
40 Ramon Martinez .40 .16
41 Randy Myers .40 .16
42 Scott Bankhead .25 .10

1989 Score Young Superstars II

The 1989 Score Young Superstars II set contains 42 standard-size cards. The fronts are orange, white and purple. The vertically oriented backs have color facial shots, 1988 and career stats, and biographical information. The cards were distributed as a boxed set with five Magic Motion trivia cards. A first year card of Ken Griffey Jr. highlights the set.

Nm-Mt Ex-Mt
COMP.FACT.SET (42) 25.00 10.00
1 Sandy Alomar Jr. .60 .24
2 Tom Gordon 1.00 .40
3 Ron Jones .25 .10
4 Todd Burns .25 .10
5 Paul O'Neill .60 .24
6 Gene Larkin .25 .10
7 Eric King .25 .10
8 Jeff M. Robinson .25 .10
9 Bill Wegman .25 .10
10 Cecil Espy .25 .10
11 Jose Guzman .25 .10
12 Kelly Gruber .25 .10
13 Duane Ward .25 .10
14 Mark Gubicza .25 .10
15 Norm Charlton .40 .16
16 Jose Oquendo .25 .10
17 Geronimo Berroa .25 .10
18 Ken Griffey Jr. 15.00 6.00
19 Lance McCullers .25 .10
20 Todd Stottlemyre .60 .24
21 Craig Worthington .25 .10
22 Mike Devereaux .25 .10
23 Tom Glavine 1.00 .40
24 Dale Sveum .25 .10
25 Roberto Kelly .40 .16
26 Luis Medina .25 .10
27 Steve Searcy .25 .10
28 Don August .25 .10
29 Shawn Hillegas .25 .10
30 Mike Campbell .25 .10
31 Mike Harkey .25 .10
32 Randy Johnson 8.00 3.20
33 Craig Biggio 3.00 1.20
34 Mike Schooler .25 .10
35 Andres Thomas .25 .10
36 Jerome Walton 1.00 .40
37 Cris Carpenter .25 .10
38 Kevin Mitchell .40 .16
39 Eddie Williams .25 .10
40 Chad Kreuter .25 .10
41 Danny Jackson .25 .10
42 Kurt Stillwell .25 .10

1990 Score Promos

These 110 different cards were randomly sent to dealers to promote the 1990 Score issue. The cards may be distinguished from their regular issue counterparts by the absence of the previous season's statistics and the fact that the career stats are not updated.

Nm-Mt Ex-Mt
*PROMOS: 10X BASIC CARDS

1990 Score

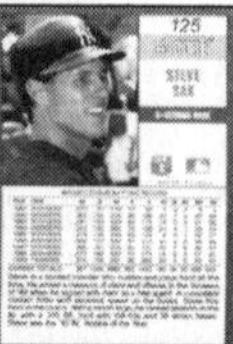

The 1990 Score set contains 704 standard-size cards. Cards were distributed in plastic-wrap packs and factory sets. The front borders are red, blue, green or white. The vertically oriented backs are white with borders that match the fronts, and feature color mugshots. Subsets include Draft Picks (661-682) and Dream Team (683-695). A special black and white horizontal-designed card of Bo Jackson in football pads holding a bat above his shoulders was a big hit in 1990. That card traded for as much as $10 but has since cooled off. Nevertheless, it remains one of the most noteworthy cards issued in the early 1990's. Rookie Cards of note include Juan Gonzalez, Dave Justice, Chuck Knoblauch, Dean Palmer, Sammy Sosa, Frank Thomas, Mo Vaughn, Larry Walker and Bernie Williams. A ten-card set of Dream Team Rookies was inserted into each hobby factory set, but was not included in retail factory sets.

Nm-Mt Ex-Mt
COMPLETE SET (704) 15.00 4.50
COMP.RETAIL SET (704) 15.00 4.50
COMP.HOBBY SET (714) 15.00 4.50
1 Don Mattingly .60 .18
2 Cal Ripken .75 .23
3 Dwight Evans .10 .03
4 Barry Bonds .60 .18
5 Kevin McReynolds .05 .02
6 Ozzie Guillen .05 .02
7 Terry Kennedy .05 .02
8 Bryan Harvey .05 .02
9 Alan Trammell .15 .04
10 Cory Snyder .05 .02
11 Jody Reed .05 .02
12 Roberto Alomar .25 .07
13 Pedro Guerrero .05 .02
14 Gary Redus .05 .02
15 Marty Barrett .05 .02
16 Ricky Jordan .05 .02
17 Joe Magrane .05 .02
18 Sid Fernandez .05 .02
19 Richard Dotson .05 .02
20 Jack Clark .10 .03
21 Bob Walk .05 .02
22 Ron Karkovice .05 .02
23 Lenny Harris .05 .02
24 Phil Bradley .05 .02
25 Andres Galarraga .10 .03
26 Brian Downing .05 .02
27 Dave Martinez .05 .02
28 Eric King .05 .02
29 Barry Lyons .05 .02
30 Dave Schmidt .05 .02
31 Mike Boddicker .05 .02
32 Tom Foley .05 .02
33 Brady Anderson .10 .03
34 Jim Presley .05 .02
35 Lance Parrish .05 .02
36 Von Hayes .05 .02
37 Lee Smith .10 .03
38 Herm Winningham .05 .02
39 Alejandro Pena .05 .02
40 Mike Scott .05 .02
41 Joe Orsulak .05 .02
42 Rafael Ramirez .05 .02
43 Gerald Young .05 .02
44 Dick Schofield .05 .02
45 Dave Smith .05 .02
46 Dave Magadan .05 .02
47 Dennis Martinez .10 .03
48 Greg Minton .05 .02
49 Milt Thompson .05 .02
50 Orel Hershiser .10 .03
51 Bip Roberts .10 .03
52 Jerry Browne .05 .02
53 Bob Ojeda .05 .02
54 Fernando Valenzuela .10 .03
55 Matt Nokes .05 .02
56 Brook Jacoby .05 .02
57 Frank Tanana .05 .02
58 Scott Fletcher .05 .02
59 Ron Oester .05 .02
60 Bob Boone .10 .03
61 Dan Gladden .05 .02
62 Darnell Coles .05 .02
63 Gregg Olson .10 .03
64 Todd Burns .05 .02
65 Todd Benzinger .05 .02
66 Dale Murphy .25 .07
67 Mike Flanagan .05 .02
68 Jose Oquendo .05 .02
69 Cecil Espy .05 .02
70 Chris Sabo .05 .02
71 Shane Rawley .05 .02
72 Tom Brunansky .05 .02
73 Vance Law .05 .02
74 B.J. Surhoff .10 .03
75 Lou Whitaker .10 .03
76 Ken Caminiti UER .10 .03
Euclid and Ohio should be Hanford and California
77 Nelson Liriano .05 .02
78 Tommy Gregg .05 .02
79 Don Slaught .05 .02
80 Eddie Murray .25 .07
81 Joe Boever .05 .02
82 Charlie Leibrandt .05 .02
83 Jose Lind .05 .02
84 Tony Phillips .05 .02
85 Mitch Webster .05 .02
86 Dan Plesac .05 .02
87 Rick Mahler .05 .02
88 Steve Lyons .05 .02
89 Tony Fernandez .05 .02
90 Ryne Sandberg .40 .12
91 Nick Esasky .05 .02
92 Luis Salazar .05 .02
93 Pete Incaviglia .05 .02
94 Ivan Calderon .05 .02
95 Jeff Treadway .05 .02
96 Kurt Stillwell .05 .02
97 Gary Sheffield .25 .07
98 Jeffrey Leonard .05 .02
99 Andres Thomas .05 .02
100 Roberto Kelly .05 .02
101 Alvaro Espinoza .05 .02
102 Greg Gagne .05 .02
103 John Farrell .05 .02
104 Willie Wilson .05 .02
105 Glenn Braggs .05 .02
106 Chet Lemon .05 .02
107A Jamie Moyer ERR .10 .03
(Scintilating)
107B Jamie Moyer COR .50 .15
(Scintillating)
108 Chuck Crim .05 .02
109 Dave Valle .05 .02
110 Walt Weiss .05 .02
111 Larry Sheets .05 .02
112 Don Robinson .05 .02
113 Danny Heep .05 .02
114 Carmelo Martinez .05 .02
115 Dave Gallagher .05 .02
116 Mike LaValliere .05 .02
117 Bob McClure .05 .02
118 Rene Gonzales .05 .02
119 Mark Parent .05 .02
120 Wally Joyner .10 .03
121 Mark Gubicza .05 .02
122 Tony Pena .05 .02
123 Carmelo Castillo .05 .02
124 Howard Johnson .05 .02
125 Steve Sax .05 .02
126 Tim Belcher .05 .02
127 Tim Burke .05 .02
128 Al Newman .05 .02
129 Dennis Rasmussen .05 .02
130 Doug Jones .05 .02
131 Fred Lynn .05 .02
132 Jeff Hamilton .05 .02
133 German Gonzalez .05 .02
134 John Morris .05 .02
135 Dave Parker .10 .03
136 Gary Pettis .05 .02
137 Dennis Boyd .05 .02
138 Candy Maldonado .05 .02
139 Rick Cerone .05 .02
140 George Brett .60 .18
141 Dave Clark .05 .02
142 Dickie Thon .05 .02
143 Junior Ortiz .05 .02
144 Don August .05 .02
145 Gary Gaetti .10 .03
146 Kirt Manwaring .05 .02
147 Jeff Reed .05 .02
148 Jose Alvarez .05 .02
149 Mike Schooler .05 .02
150 Mark Grace .15 .04
151 Geronimo Berroa .05 .02
152 Barry Jones .05 .02
153 Geno Petralli .05 .02
154 Jim Deshaies .05 .02
155 Barry Larkin .25 .07
156 Alfredo Griffin .05 .02
157 Tom Henke .05 .02
158 Mike Jeffcoat .05 .02
159 Bob Welch .05 .02
160 Julio Franco .05 .02
161 Henry Cotto .05 .02
162 Terry Steinbach .05 .02
163 Damon Berryhill .05 .02
164 Tim Crews .05 .02
165 Tom Browning .05 .02
166 Fred Manrique .05 .02
167 Harold Reynolds .10 .03
168A Ron Hassey ERR .10 .03
(27 on back)
168B Ron Hassey COR .50 .15
(24 on back)
169 Shawon Dunston .05 .02
170 Bobby Bonilla .10 .03
171 Tommy Herr .05 .02
172 Mike Heath .05 .02
173 Rich Gedman .05 .02
174 Bill Ripken .05 .02
175 Pete O'Brien .05 .02
176A L.McClendon ERR .05 .02
Uniform number on back listed as 1
176B L.McClendon COR .50 .15
Uniform number on back listed as 10
177 Brian Holton .05 .02
178 Jeff Blauser .05 .02
179 Jim Eisenreich .05 .02
180 Bert Blyleven .10 .03
181 Rob Murphy .05 .02
182 Bill Doran .05 .02
183 Curt Ford .05 .02
184 Mike Henneman .05 .02
185 Eric Davis .10 .03
186 Lance McCullers .05 .02
187 Steve Davis .05 .02
188 Bill Wegman .05 .02
189 Brian Harper .05 .02
190 Mike Moore .05 .02
191 Dale Mohorcic .05 .02
192 Tim Wallach .05 .02
193 Keith Hernandez .15 .04
194 Dave Righetti .05 .02
195A B.Saberhagen ERR .10 .03
Joke
195B B.Saberhagen COR .50 .15
Joker
196 Paul Kilgus .05 .02
197 Bud Black .05 .02
198 Juan Samuel .05 .02
199 Kevin Seitzer .05 .02
200 Darryl Strawberry .15 .04
201 Dave Stieb .10 .03
202 Charlie Hough .10 .03
203 Jack Morris .10 .03
204 Rance Mulliniks .05 .02
205 Alvin Davis .05 .02
206 Jack Howell .05 .02
207 Ken Patterson .05 .02
208 Terry Pendleton .10 .03
209 Craig Lefferts .05 .02
210 Kevin Brown UER .10 .03
(First mention of '89 Rangers should be '88)
211 Dan Petry .05 .02
212 Dave Leiper .05 .02
213 Daryl Boston .05 .02
214 Kevin Hickey .05 .02
215 Mike Krukow .05 .02
216 Terry Francona .10 .03
217 Kirk McCaskill .05 .02
218 Scott Bailes .05 .02
219 Bob Forsch .05 .02
220A Mike Aldrete ERR .05 .02
(25 on back)
220B Mike Aldrete COR .50 .15
(24 on back)
221 Steve Buechele .05 .02
222 Jesse Barfield .05 .02
223 Juan Berenguer .05 .02
224 Andy McGaffigan .05 .02
225 Pete Smith .05 .02
226 Mike Witt .05 .02
227 Jay Howell .05 .02
228 Scott Bradley .05 .02
229 Jerome Walton .05 .02
230 Greg Swindell .05 .02
231 Atlee Hammaker .05 .02
232A Mike Devereaux ERR .05 .02
(RF on front)
232B M.Devereaux COR .50 .15
CF on front
233 Ken Hill .10 .03
234 Craig Worthington .05 .02
235 Scott Terry .05 .02
236 Brett Butler .10 .03
237 Doyle Alexander .05 .02
238 Dave Anderson .05 .02
239 Bob Milacki .05 .02
240 Dwight Smith .05 .02
241 Otis Nixon .05 .02
242 Pat Tabler .05 .02
243 Derek Lilliquist .05 .02
244 Danny Tartabull .05 .02
245 Wade Boggs .15 .04
246 Scott Garrelts .05 .02
(Should say Relief Pitcher on front)
247 Spike Owen .05 .02
248 Norm Charlton .05 .02
249 Gerald Perry .05 .02
250 Nolan Ryan 1.00 .30
251 Kevin Gross .05 .02
252 Randy Milligan .05 .02
253 Mike LaCoss .05 .02
254 Dave Bergman .05 .02
255 Tony Gwynn .30 .09
256 Felix Fermin .05 .02
257 Greg W. Harris .05 .02
258 Junior Felix .05 .02
259 Mark Davis .05 .02
260 Vince Coleman .05 .02
261 Paul Gibson .05 .02
262 Mitch Williams .05 .02
263 Jeff Russell .05 .02
264 Omar Vizquel .25 .07
265 Andre Dawson .10 .03
266 Storm Davis .05 .02
267 Guillermo Hernandez .05 .02
268 Mike Felder .05 .02
269 Tom Candiotti .05 .02
270 Bruce Hurst .05 .02
271 Fred McGriff .25 .07
272 Glenn Davis .05 .02
273 John Franco .10 .03
274 Rich Yett .05 .02
275 Craig Biggio .15 .04
276 Gene Larkin .05 .02
277 Rob Dibble .10 .03
278 Randy Bush .05 .02
279 Kevin Bass .05 .02
280A Bo Jackson ERR .25 .07
(Watham)
280B Bo Jackson COR .75 .23

(Wathan)
281 Wally Backman .05 .02
282 Larry Andersen .05 .02
283 Chris Bosio .05 .02
284 Juan Agosto .05 .02
285 Ozzie Smith .40 .12
286 George Bell .05 .02
287 Rex Hudler .05 .02
288 Pat Borders .05 .02
289 Danny Jackson .05 .02
290 Carlton Fisk .15 .04
291 Tracy Jones .05 .02
292 Allan Anderson .05 .02
293 Johnny Ray .05 .02
294 Lee Guetterman .05 .02
295 Paul O'Neill .15 .04
296 Carney Lansford .10 .03
297 Tom Brookens .05 .02
298 Claudell Washington .05 .02
299 Hubie Brooks .05 .02
300 Will Clark .25 .07
301 Kenny Rogers .10 .03
302 Darrell Evans .10 .03
303 Greg Briley .05 .02
304 Donn Pall .05 .02
305 Teddy Higuera .05 .02
306 Dan Pasqua .05 .02
307 Dave Winfield .10 .03
308 Dennis Powell .05 .02
309 Jose DeLeon .05 .02
310 Roger Clemens UER .50 .15
(Dominate, should say dominant)
311 Melido Perez .05 .02
312 Devon White .05 .02
313 Dwight Gooden .15 .04
314 Carlos Martinez .05 .02
315 Dennis Eckersley .10 .03
316 Clay Parker UER .05 .02
(Height 6'11")
317 Rick Honeycutt .05 .02
318 Tim Laudner .05 .02
319 Joe Carter .10 .03
320 Robin Yount .40 .12
321 Felix Jose .05 .02
322 Mickey Tettleton .05 .02
323 Mike Gallego .05 .02
324 Edgar Martinez .15 .04
325 Dave Henderson .05 .02
326 Chili Davis .10 .03
327 Steve Balboni .05 .02
328 Jody Davis .05 .02
329 Shawn Hillegas .05 .02
330 Jim Abbott .15 .04
331 John Dopson .05 .02
332 Mark Williamson .05 .02
333 Jeff D. Robinson .05 .02
334 John Smiley .05 .02
335 Bobby Thigpen .05 .02
336 Garry Templeton .05 .02
337 Marvell Wynne .05 .02
338A Ken Griffey Sr. ERR .10 .03
(Uniform number on back listed as 25)
338B Ken Griffey Sr. COR .50 .15
(Uniform number on back listed as 30)
339 Steve Finley .10 .03
340 Ellis Burks .15 .04
341 Frank Williams .05 .02
342 Mike Morgan .05 .02
343 Kevin Mitchell .05 .02
344 Joel Youngblood .05 .02
345 Mike Greenwell .05 .02
346 Glenn Wilson .05 .02
347 John Costello .05 .02
348 Wes Gardner .05 .02
349 Jeff Ballard .05 .02
350 Mark Thurmond UER .05 .02
(ERA is 192, should be 1.92)
351 Randy Myers .10 .03
352 Shawn Abner .05 .02
353 Jesse Orosco .05 .02
354 Greg Walker .05 .02
355 Pete Harnisch .05 .02
356 Steve Farr .05 .02
357 Dave LaPoint .05 .02
358 Willie Fraser .05 .02
359 Mickey Hatcher .05 .02
360 Rickey Henderson .25 .07
361 Mike Fitzgerald .05 .02
362 Bill Schroeder .05 .02
363 Mark Carreon .05 .02
364 Ron Jones .05 .02
365 Jeff Montgomery .10 .03
366 Bill Krueger .05 .02
367 John Cangelosi .05 .02
368 Jose Gonzalez .05 .02
369 Greg Hibbard RC .10 .03
370 John Smoltz .25 .07
371 Jeff Brantley .05 .02
372 Frank White .10 .03
373 Ed Whitson .05 .02
374 Willie McGee .10 .03
375 Jose Canseco .25 .07
376 Randy Ready .05 .02
377 Don Aase .05 .02
378 Tony Armas .05 .02
379 Steve Bedrosian .05 .02
380 Chuck Finley .10 .03
381 Kent Hrbek .10 .03
382 Jim Gantner .05 .02
383 Mel Hall .05 .02
384 Mike Marshall .05 .02
385 Mark McGwire .60 .18
386 Wayne Tolleson .05 .02
387 Brian Holman .05 .02
388 John Wetteland .25 .07
389 Darren Daulton .10 .03
390 Rob Deer .05 .02
391 John Moses .05 .02
392 Todd Worrell .05 .02
393 Chuck Cary .05 .02
394 Stan Javier .05 .02
395 Willie Randolph .10 .03
396 Bill Buckner .05 .02
397 Robby Thompson .05 .02
398 Mike Scioscia .05 .02
399 Lonnie Smith .05 .02
400 Kirby Puckett .25 .07
401 Mark Langston .05 .02
402 Danny Darwin .05 .02
403 Greg Maddux .40 .12
404 Lloyd Moseby .05 .02
405 Rafael Palmeiro .15 .04
406 Chad Kreuter .05 .02
407 Jimmy Key .10 .03
408 Tim Birtsas .05 .02
409 Tim Raines .10 .03
410 Dave Stewart .10 .03
411 Eric Yelding .05 .02
412 Kent Anderson .05 .02
413 Les Lancaster .05 .02
414 Rick Dempsey .05 .02
415 Randy Johnson .40 .12
416 Gary Carter .15 .04
417 Rolando Roomes .05 .02
418 Dan Schatzeder .05 .02
419 Bryn Smith .05 .02
420 Ruben Sierra .05 .02
421 Steve Jeltz .05 .02
422 Ken Oberkfell .05 .02
423 Sid Bream .05 .02
424 Jim Clancy .05 .02
425 Kelly Gruber .05 .02
426 Rick Leach .05 .02
427 Len Dykstra .10 .03
428 Jeff Pico .05 .02
429 John Cerutti .05 .02
430 David Cone .10 .03
431 Jeff Kunkel .05 .02
432 Luis Aquino .05 .02
433 Ernie Whitt .05 .02
434 Bo Diaz .05 .02
435 Steve Lake .05 .02
436 Pat Perry .05 .02
437 Mike Davis .05 .02
438 Cecilio Guante .05 .02
439 Duane Ward .05 .02
440 Andy Van Slyke .10 .03
441 Gene Nelson .05 .02
442 Luis Polonia .05 .02
443 Kevin Elster .05 .02
444 Keith Moreland .05 .02
445 Roger McDowell .05 .02
446 Ron Darling .05 .02
447 Ernest Riles .05 .02
448 Mookie Wilson .10 .03
449A Billy Spiers ERR .05 .02
(No birth year)
449B Billy Spiers COR .50 .15
(Born in 1966)
450 Rick Sutcliffe .10 .03
451 Nelson Santovenia .05 .02
452 Andy Allanson .05 .02
453 Bob Melvin .05 .02
454 Benito Santiago .10 .03
455 Jose Uribe .05 .02
456 Bill Landrum .05 .02
457 Bobby Witt .05 .02
458 Kevin Romine .05 .02
459 Lee Mazzilli .05 .02
460 Paul Molitor .15 .04
461 Ramon Martinez .05 .02
462 Frank DiPino .05 .02
463 Walt Terrell .05 .02
464 Bob Geren .05 .02
465 Rick Reuschel .05 .02
466 Mark Grant .05 .02
467 John Kruk .10 .03
468 Gregg Jefferies .10 .03
469 R.J. Reynolds .05 .02
470 Harold Baines .10 .03
471 Dennis Lamp .05 .02
472 Tom Gordon .10 .03
473 Terry Puhl .05 .02
474 Curt Wilkerson .05 .02
475 Dan Quisenberry .05 .02
476 Oddibe McDowell .05 .02
477A Zane Smith ERR .05 .02
(Career ERA .393)
477B Zane Smith COR .50 .15
(career ERA 3.93)
478 Franklin Stubbs .05 .02
479 Wallace Johnson .05 .02
480 Jay Tibbs .05 .02
481 Tom Glavine .15 .04
482 Manny Lee .05 .02
483 Joe Hesketh UER .05 .02
Says Rookiess on back, should say Rookies
484 Mike Bielecki .05 .02
485 Greg Brock .05 .02
486 Pascual Perez .05 .02
487 Kirk Gibson .10 .03
488 Scott Sanderson .05 .02
489 Domingo Ramos .05 .02
490 Kal Daniels .05 .02
491A David Wells ERR .10 .03
(Reverse negative photo on card back)
491B David Wells COR .50 .15
492 Jerry Reed .05 .02
493 Eric Show .05 .02
494 Mike Pagliarulo .05 .02
495 Ron Robinson .05 .02
496 Brad Komminsk .05 .02
497 Greg Litton .05 .02
498 Chris James .05 .02
499 Luis Quinones .05 .02
500 Frank Viola .05 .02
501 Tim Teufel UER .05 .02
(Twins '85, the s is lower case, should be upper case)
502 Terry Leach .05 .02
503 Matt Williams UER .10 .03
(Wearing 10 on front, listed as 9 on back)
504 Tim Leary .05 .02
505 Doug Drabek .05 .02
506 Mariano Duncan .05 .02
507 Charlie Hayes .05 .02
508 Joey Belle .15 .04
509 Pat Sheridan .05 .02
510 Mackey Sasser .05 .02
511 Jose Rijo .05 .02
512 Mike Smithson .05 .02
513 Gary Ward .05 .02
514 Dion James .05 .02
515 Jim Gott .05 .02
516 Drew Hall .05 .02
517 Doug Bair .05 .02
518 Scott Scudder .05 .02
519 Rick Aguilera .10 .03
520 Rafael Belliard .05 .02
521 Jay Buhner .10 .03
522 Jeff Reardon .10 .03
523 Steve Rosenberg .05 .02
524 Randy Velarde .05 .02
525 Jeff Musselman .05 .02
526 Bill Long .05 .02
527 Gary Wayne .05 .02
528 Dave Johnson (P) .05 .02
529 Ron Kittle .05 .02
530 Erik Hanson UER .05 .02
(5th line on back says seson, should say season)
531 Steve Wilson .05 .02
532 Joey Meyer .05 .02
533 Curt Young .05 .02
534 Kelly Downs .05 .02
535 Joe Girardi .15 .04
536 Lance Blankenship .05 .02
537 Greg Mathews .05 .02
538 Donell Nixon .05 .02
539 Mark Knudson .05 .02
540 Jeff Wetherby .05 .02
541 Darrin Jackson .05 .02
542 Terry Mulholland .05 .02
543 Eric Hetzel .05 .02
544 Rick Reed RC .25 .07
545 Dennis Cook .05 .02
546 Mike Jackson .05 .02
547 Brian Fisher .05 .02
548 Gene Harris .05 .02
549 Jeff King .05 .02
550 Dave Dravecky .25 .07
551 Randy Kutcher .05 .02
552 Mark Portugal .05 .02
553 Jim Corsi .05 .02
554 Todd Stottlemyre .10 .03
555 Scott Bankhead .05 .02
556 Ken Dayley .05 .02
557 Rick Wrona .05 .02
558 Sammy Sosa RC 8.00 2.40
559 Keith Miller .05 .02
560 Ken Griffey Jr. .75 .23
561A R.Sandberg HL ERR 8.00 2.40
Position on front listed as 3B
561B R.Sandberg HL COR .25 .07
562 Billy Hatcher .05 .02
563 Jay Bell .10 .03
564 Jack Daugherty .05 .02
565 Rich Monteleone .05 .02
566 Bo Jackson AS-MVP .10 .03
567 Tony Fossas .05 .02
568 Roy Smith .05 .02
569 Jaime Navarro .05 .02
570 Lance Johnson .05 .02
571 Mike Dyer RC .05 .02
572 Kevin Ritz .05 .02
573 Dave West .05 .02
574 Gary Mielke .05 .02
575 Scott Lusader .05 .02
576 Joe Oliver .05 .02
577 Sandy Alomar Jr. .10 .03
578 Andy Benes UER .10 .03
(Extra comma between day and year)
579 Tim Jones .05 .02
580 Randy McCament .05 .02
581 Curt Schilling 1.00 .30
582 John Orton RC .10 .03
583A Milt Cuyler ERR RC .10 .03
(998 games)
583B Milt Cuyler RC COR .50 .15
(98 games; the extra 9 was ghosted out and may still be visible)
584 Eric Anthony RC .10 .03
585 Greg Vaughn .10 .03
586 Deion Sanders .25 .07
587 Jose DeJesus .05 .02
588 Chip Hale .05 .02
589 John Olerud RC .50 .15
590 Steve Olin RC .25 .07
591 Marquis Grissom RC .25 .07
592 Moises Alou RC .50 .15
593 Mark Lemke .05 .02
594 Dean Palmer RC .25 .07
595 Robin Ventura .25 .07
596 Tino Martinez .25 .07
597 Mike Huff .05 .02
598 Scott Hemond RC .10 .03
599 Wally Whitehurst .05 .02
600 Todd Zeile .10 .03
601 Glenallen Hill .05 .02
602 Hal Morris .05 .02
603 Juan Bell .05 .02
604 Bobby Rose .05 .02
605 Matt Merullo .05 .02
606 Kevin Maas RC .25 .07
607 Randy Nosek .05 .02
608A Billy Bates .05 .02
(Text mentions 12 triples in tenth line)
608B Billy Bates .05 .02
(Text has no mention of triples)
609 Mike Stanton RC .25 .07
610 Mauro Gozzo .05 .02
611 Charles Nagy .05 .02
612 Scott Coolbaugh .05 .02
613 Jose Vizcaino RC .25 .07
614 Greg Smith .05 .02
615 Jeff Huson RC .10 .03
616 Mickey Weston .05 .02
617 John Pawlowski .05 .02
618A Joe Skalski ERR .05 .02
(27 on back)
618B Joe Skalski COR .50 .15
(67 on back)
619 Bernie Williams RC 1.00 .30
620 Shawn Holman .05 .02
621 Gary Eave .05 .02
622 Darrin Fletcher UER .10 .03
Elmherst, should be Elmhurst
623 Pat Combs .05 .02
624 Mike Blowers RC .10 .03
625 Kevin Appier .25 .07
626 Pat Austin .05 .02
627 Kelly Mann .05 .02
628 Matt Kinzer .05 .02
629 Chris Hammond RC .10 .03
630 Dean Wilkins .05 .02
631 Larry Walker RC UER 1.00 .30
Uniform number 55 on front and 33 on back; Home is Maple Ridge, not Maple River
632 Blaine Beatty .05 .02
633A Tommy Barrett ERR .05 .02
(29 on back)
633B Tommy Barrett COR .50 .15
(14 on back)
634 Stan Belinda RC .10 .03
635 Mike (Tex) Smith .05 .02
636 Hensley Meulens .05 .02
637 J.Gonzalez RC UER 1.50 .45
Sarasots on back, should be Sarasota
638 Lenny Webster RC .10 .03
639 Mark Gardner RC .10 .03
640 Tommy Greene RC .10 .03
641 Mike Hartley .05 .02
642 Phil Stephenson .05 .02
643 Kevin Mmahat .05 .02
644 Ed Whited .05 .02
645 Delino DeShields RC .25 .07
646 Kevin Blankenship .05 .02
647 Paul Sorrento RC .25 .07
648 Mike Roesler .05 .02
649 Jason Grimsley RC .10 .03
650 Dave Justice RC .50 .15
651 Scott Cooper RC .10 .03
652 Dave Eiland .05 .02
653 Mike Munoz .05 .02
654 Jeff Fischer .05 .02
655 Terry Jorgensen .05 .02
656 George Canale .05 .02
657 Brian DuBois UER .05 .02
(Misspelled Dubois on card)
658 Carlos Quintana .05 .02
659 Luis de los Santos .05 .02
660 Jerald Clark .05 .02
661 Donald Harris DC .05 .02
662 Paul Coleman DC RC .10 .03
663 Frank Thomas DC RC 1.50 .45
664 Brent Mayne DC RC .25 .07
665 Eddie Zosky DC RC .10 .03
666 Steve Hosey DC RC .10 .03
667 Scott Bryant DC .10 .03
668 Tom Goodwin DC RC .25 .07
669 Cal Eldred DC RC .25 .07
670 E.Cunningham DC RC .10 .03
671 Alan Zinter DC RC .10 .03
672 C.Knoblauch DC RC .40 .12
673 Kyle Abbott DC .05 .02
674 Roger Salkeld DC RC .05 .02
675 M.Vaughn DC RC .50 .15
676 Keith (Kiki) Jones DC .05 .02
677 Tyler Houston DC RC .25 .07
678 Jeff Jackson DC RC .10 .03
679 Greg Gohr DC RC .10 .03
680 Ben McDonald DC RC .25 .07
681 Greg Blosser DC RC .10 .03
682 W.Greene RC DC UER .25 .07
Name spelled as Green
683A W.Boggs DT ERR .10 .03
Text says 215 hits in '89, should be 205
683B W.Boggs DT COR .50 .15
Text says 205 hits in '89
684 Will Clark DT .10 .03
685 Tony Gwynn DT UER .15 .04
(Text reads battling instead of batting)
686 Rickey Henderson DT .15 .04
687 Bo Jackson DT .10 .03
688 Mark Langston DT .05 .02
689 Barry Larkin DT .10 .03
690 Kirby Puckett DT .15 .04
691 Ryne Sandberg DT .25 .07
692 Mike Scott DT .05 .02
693A Terry Steinbach DT .05 .02
ERR (cathers)
693B Terry Steinbach DT .05 .02
COR (catchers)
694 Bobby Thigpen DT .05 .02
695 Mitch Williams DT .05 .02
696 Nolan Ryan HL .40 .12
697 Bo Jackson FB/BB .50 .15
698 Rickey Henderson .15 .04
ALCS-MVP
699 Will Clark .10 .03
NLCS-MVP
700 Dave Stewart .10 .03
Mike Moore WS
701 Lights Out .25 .07
702 Carney Lansford .15 .04
Rickey Henderson
Jose Canseco
Dave Henderson WS
703 WS Game 4/Wrap-up .05 .02
704 Wade Boggs HL .10 .03

1990 Score Rookie Dream Team

A ten-card set of Dream Team Rookies was inserted only into hobby factory sets. These standard size cards carry a B prefix on the card number and include a player at each position plus a commemorative card honoring the late Baseball Commissioner A. Bartlett Giamatti.

Nm-Mt Ex-Mt
COMPLETE SET (10) 4.00 1.20
B1 A.Bartlett Giamatti 1.00 .30
COMM MEM
B2 Pat Combs .20 .06
B3 Todd Zeile .40 .12
B4 Luis de los Santos .20 .06
B5 Mark Lemke .20 .06
B6 Robin Ventura 1.00 .30
B7 Jeff Huson .40 .12
B8 Greg Vaughn .40 .12
B9 Marquis Grissom 1.00 .30
B10 Eric Anthony .40 .12

1990 Score Rookie/Traded

The standard-size 110-card 1990 Score Rookie and Traded set marked the third consecutive year Score had issued an end of the year set to note trades and give rookies early cards. The set was issued through hobby accounts and only in factory set form. The first 66 cards are traded players while the last 44 cards are rookie cards. Hockey star Eric Lindros is included in this set. Rookie Cards in the set include Derek Bell, Todd Hundley and Ray Lankford.

Nm-Mt Ex-Mt
COMP.FACT.SET (110) 3.00 .90
1T Dave Winfield .10 .03
2T Kevin Bass .05 .02
3T Nick Esasky .05 .02
4T Mitch Webster .05 .02
5T Pascual Perez .05 .02
6T Gary Pettis .05 .02
7T Tony Pena .05 .02
8T Candy Maldonado .05 .02
9T Cecil Fielder .10 .03
10T Carmelo Martinez .05 .02
11T Mark Langston .05 .02
12T Dave Parker .10 .03
13T Don Slaught .05 .02
14T Tony Phillips .05 .02
15T John Franco .10 .03
16T Randy Myers .10 .03
17T Jeff Reardon .10 .03
18T Sandy Alomar Jr. .10 .03
19T Joe Carter .10 .03
20T Fred Lynn .05 .02
21T Storm Davis .05 .02
22T Craig Lefferts .05 .02
23T Pete O'Brien .05 .02
24T Dennis Boyd .05 .02
25T Lloyd Moseby .05 .02
26T Mark Davis .05 .02
27T Tim Leary .05 .02
28T Gerald Perry .05 .02
29T Don Aase .05 .02
30T Ernie Whitt .05 .02
31T Dale Murphy .25 .07
32T Alejandro Pena .05 .02
33T Juan Samuel .05 .02
34T Hubie Brooks .05 .02
35T Gary Carter .15 .04
36T Jim Presley .05 .02
37T Wally Backman .05 .02
38T Matt Nokes .05 .02
39T Dan Petry .05 .02
40T Franklin Stubbs .05 .02
41T Jeff Huson .05 .02
42T Billy Hatcher .05 .02
43T Terry Leach .05 .02
44T Phil Bradley .05 .02
45T Claudell Washington .05 .02
46T Luis Polonia .05 .02
47T Daryl Boston .05 .02
48T Lee Smith .10 .03
49T Tom Brunansky .05 .02
50T Mike Witt .05 .02
51T Willie Randolph .10 .03
52T Stan Javier .05 .02
53T Brad Komminsk .05 .02
54T John Candelaria .05 .02
55T Bryn Smith .05 .02
56T Glenn Braggs .05 .02
57T Keith Hernandez .15 .04
58T Ken Oberkfell .05 .02
59T Steve Jeltz .05 .02
60T Chris James .05 .02
61T Scott Sanderson .05 .02
62T Bill Long .05 .02
63T Rick Cerone .05 .02
64T Scott Bailes .05 .02
65T Larry Sheets .05 .02
66T Junior Ortiz .05 .02
67T Francisco Cabrera .05 .02
68T Gary DiSarcina RC .25 .07
69T Greg Olson .05 .02
70T Beau Allred RC .05 .02
71T Oscar Azocar .05 .02
72T Kent Mercker RC .25 .07
73T John Burkett .05 .02
74T Carlos Baerga RC .25 .07
75T Dave Hollins RC .25 .07
76T Todd Hundley RC .25 .07
77T Rick Parker .05 .02
78T Steve Cummings RC .05 .02
79T Bill Sampen .05 .02
80T Jerry Kutzler .05 .02
81T Derek Bell RC .25 .07
82T Kevin Tapani RC .25 .07
83T Jim Leyritz RC .25 .07
84T Ray Lankford RC .25 .07
85T Wayne Edwards .05 .02
86T Frank Thomas 1.50 .45

87T Tim Naehring RC .10 .03
88T Willie Blair RC .10 .03
89T Alan Mills RC .10 .03
90T Scott Radinsky RC .10 .03
91T Howard Farmer .05 .02
92T Julio Machado .05 .02
93T Rafael Valdez .05 .02
94T Shawn Boskie RC .10 .03
95T David Segui RC .25 .07
96T Chris Hoiles RC .25 .07
97T D.J. Dozier RC .10 .03
98T Hector Villanueva .05 .02
99T Eric Gunderson .05 .02
100T Eric Lindros 1.00 .30
101T Dave Otto .05 .02
102T Dana Kiecker .05 .02
103T Tim Drummond .05 .02
104T Mickey Pina .05 .02
105T Craig Grebeck RC .10 .03
106T Bernard Gilkey RC .25 .07
107T Tim Layana .05 .02
108T Scott Chiamparino .05 .02
109T Steve Avery .05 .02
110T Terry Shumpert .05 .02

1990 Score 100 Superstars

The 1990 Score Superstars set contains 100 standard size cards. The fronts are red, white, blue and purple. The vertically oriented backs feature a large color facial shot and career highlights. The cards were distributed as a set in a blister pack, which also included a full color booklet with more information about each player.

Nm-Mt Ex-Mt
COMP.FACT SET (100) 10.00 3.00
1 Kirby Puckett .50 .15
2 Steve Sax .05 .02
3 Tony Gwynn 1.50 .45
4 Willie Randolph .10 .03
5 Jose Canseco .50 .15
6 Ozzie Smith 1.25 .35
7 Rick Reuschel .05 .02
8 Bill Doran .05 .02
9 Mickey Tettleton .10 .03
10 Don Mattingly 1.25 .35
11 Greg Swindell .05 .02
12 Bert Blyleven .10 .03
13 Dave Stewart .10 .03
14 Andres Galarraga .30 .09
15 Darryl Strawberry .10 .03
16 Ellis Burks .20 .06
17 Paul O'Neill .10 .03
18 Bruce Hurst .05 .02
19 Dave Smith .05 .02
20 Carney Lansford .10 .03
21 Robby Thompson .05 .02
22 Gary Gaetti .10 .03
23 Jeff Russell .05 .02
24 Chuck Finley .10 .03
25 Mark McGwire 2.00 .60
26 Alvin Davis .05 .02
27 George Bell .05 .02
28 Cory Snyder .05 .02
29 Keith Hernandez .10 .03
30 Will Clark .30 .09
31 Steve Bedrosian .05 .02
32 Ryne Sandberg 1.00 .30
33 Tom Browning .05 .02
34 Tim Burke .05 .02
35 John Smoltz .20 .06
36 Phil Bradley .05 .02
37 Bobby Bonilla .10 .03
38 Kirk McCaskill .05 .02
39 Dave Righetti .05 .02
40 Bo Jackson .30 .09
41 Alan Trammell .20 .06
42 Mike Moore UER .05 .02
Uniform number is 21, not 23 as on front
43 Harold Reynolds .10 .03
44 Nolan Ryan 3.00 .90
45 Fred McGriff .20 .06
46 Brian Downing .05 .02
47 Brett Butler .10 .03
48 Mike Scioscia .10 .03
49 John Franco .10 .03
50 Kevin Mitchell .05 .02
51 Mark Davis .05 .02
52 Glenn Davis .05 .02
53 Barry Bonds 1.50 .45
54 Dwight Evans .10 .03
55 Terry Steinbach .05 .02
56 Dave Gallagher .05 .02
57 Roberto Kelly .05 .02
58 Rafael Palmeiro .30 .09
59 Joe Carter .10 .03
60 Mark Grace .30 .09
61 Pedro Guerrero .05 .02
62 Von Hayes .05 .02
63 Benito Santiago .10 .03
64 Dale Murphy .30 .09
65 John Smiley .05 .02
66 Cal Ripken 3.00 .90
67 Mike Greenwell .05 .02
68 Devon White .05 .02
69 Ed Whitson .05 .02
70 Carlton Fisk .50 .15
71 Lou Whitaker .10 .03
72 Danny Tartabull .05 .02
73 Vince Coleman .05 .02
74 Andre Dawson .50 .15
75 Tim Raines .10 .03
76 George Brett 1.00 .30
77 Tom Herr .05 .02
78 Andy Van Slyke .10 .03
79 Roger Clemens 1.50 .45
80 Wade Boggs .75 .23
81 Wally Joyner .10 .03
82 Lonnie Smith .05 .02
83 Howard Johnson .05 .02
84 Julio Franco .10 .03
85 Ruben Sierra .10 .03
86 Dan Plesac .05 .02
87 Bobby Thigpen .05 .02
88 Kevin Seitzer .05 .02
89 Dave Stieb .05 .02
90 Rickey Henderson 1.00 .30
91 Jeffrey Leonard .05 .02
92 Robin Yount .50 .15
93 Mitch Williams .05 .02
94 Orel Hershiser .10 .03
95 Eric Davis .10 .03
96 Mark Langston .05 .02
97 Mike Scott .05 .02
98 Paul Molitor .75 .23
99 Dwight Gooden .10 .03
100 Kevin Bass .05 .02

1990 Score McDonald's

This 25-card standard-size set was produced by Score for McDonald's restaurants; included with the set were 15 World Series Trivia cards. The player cards were given away four to a pack and free with the purchase of fries and a drink, at only 11 McDonald's in the United States (in Idaho and Eastern Oregon) during a special promotion which lasted approximately three weeks. The front has color action player photos, with white and yellow borders on a purple card face that fades as one moves toward the middle of the card. The upper left corner of the picture is cut off to allow space for the McDonald's logo; the player's name and team logo at the bottom round out the card face. The backs have color mugshots, biography, statistics, and career summary.

Nm-Mt Ex-Mt
COMPLETE SET (25) 800.00 240.00
1 Will Clark 60.00 18.00
2 Sandy Alomar Jr. 15.00 4.50
3 Julio Franco 15.00 4.50
4 Carlton Fisk 60.00 18.00
5 Rickey Henderson 80.00 24.00
6 Matt Williams 25.00 7.50
7 John Franco 15.00 4.50
8 Ryne Sandberg 80.00 24.00
9 Kelly Gruber 5.00 1.50
10 Andre Dawson 40.00 12.00
11 Barry Bonds 80.00 24.00
12 Gary Sheffield 50.00 15.00
13 Ramon Martinez 15.00 4.50
14 Len Dykstra 15.00 4.50
15 Benito Santiago 15.00 4.50
16 Cecil Fielder 15.00 4.50
17 John Olerud 40.00 12.00
18 Roger Clemens 100.00 30.00
19 George Brett 80.00 24.00
20 George Bell 5.00 1.50
21 Ozzie Guillen 15.00 4.50
22 Steve Sax 5.00 1.50
23 Dave Stewart 15.00 4.50
24 Ozzie Smith 80.00 24.00
25 Robin Yount 60.00 18.00

1990 Score Rising Stars

The 1990 Score Rising Stars set contains 100 standard size cards. The fronts are green, blue and white. The vertically oriented backs feature a large color facial shot and career highlights. The cards were distributed as a set in a blister pack, which also included a full color booklet with more information about each player.

Nm-Mt Ex-Mt
COMP.FACT.SET (100) 15.00 4.50
1 Tom Gordon .25 .07
2 Jerome Walton .10 .03
3 Ken Griffey Jr. 2.00 .60
4 Dwight Smith .10 .03
5 Jim Abbott .40 .12
6 Todd Zeile .25 .07
7 Donn Pall .10 .03
8 Rick Reed .60 .18
9 Joey Belle .60 .18
10 Gregg Jefferies .25 .07
11 Kevin Ritz .10 .03
12 Charlie Hayes .10 .03
13 Kevin Appier .60 .18
14 Jeff Huson .10 .03
15 Gary Wayne .10 .03
16 Eric Yelding .10 .03
17 Clay Parker .10 .03
18 Junior Felix .10 .03
19 Derek Lilliquist .10 .03
20 Gary Sheffield .60 .18
21 Craig Worthington .10 .03
22 Jeff Brantley .10 .03
23 Eric Hetzel .10 .03
24 Greg W.Harris .10 .03
25 John Wetteland .60 .18
26 Joe Oliver .10 .03
27 Kevin Maas .25 .07
28 Kevin Brown .25 .07
29 Mike Stanton .10 .03
30 Greg Vaughn .25 .07
31 Ron Jones .10 .03
32 Gregg Olson .25 .07
33 Joe Girardi .40 .12
34 Ken Hill .25 .07
35 Sammy Sosa 10.00 3.00
36 Geronimo Berroa .10 .03
37 Omar Vizquel .60 .18
38 Dean Palmer .60 .18
39 John Olerud .75 .23
40 Deion Sanders .60 .18
41 Randy Kramer .10 .03
42 Scott Lusader .10 .03
43 Dave Johnson (P) .10 .03
44 Jeff Wetherby .10 .03
45 Eric Anthony .10 .03
46 Kenny Rogers .25 .07
47 Matt Winters .10 .03
48 Mauro Gozzo .10 .03
49 Carlos Quintana .10 .03
50 Bob Geren .10 .03
51 Chad Kreuter .10 .03
52 Randy Johnson 1.00 .30
53 Hensley Meulens .10 .03
54 Gene Harris .10 .03
55 Bill Spiers .10 .03
56 Kelly Mann .10 .03
57 Tom McCarthy .10 .03
58 Steve Finley .25 .07
59 Ramon Martinez .10 .03
60 Greg Briley .10 .03
61 Jack Daugherty .10 .03
62 Tim Jones .10 .03
63 Doug Strange .10 .03
64 John Orton .10 .03
65 Scott Scudder .10 .03
66 Mark Gardner .10 .03
67 Mark Carreon .10 .03
68 Bob Milacki .10 .03
69 Andy Benes .25 .07
70 Carlos Martinez .10 .03
71 Jeff King .10 .03
72 Brad Arnsberg .10 .03
73 Rick Wrona .10 .03
74 Cris Carpenter .10 .03
75 Dennis Cook .10 .03
76 Pete Harnisch .10 .03
77 Greg Hibbard .10 .03
78 Ed Whited .10 .03
79 Scott Coolbaugh .10 .03
80 Billy Bates .10 .03
81 German Gonzalez .10 .03
82 Lance Blankenship .10 .03
83 Lenny Harris .10 .03
84 Milt Cuyler .10 .03
85 Erik Hanson .10 .03
86 Kent Anderson .10 .03
87 Hal Morris .10 .03
88 Mike Brumley .10 .03
89 Ken Patterson .10 .03
90 Mike Devereaux .10 .03
91 Greg Litton .10 .03
92 Rolando Roomes .10 .03
93 Ben McDonald .10 .03
94 Curt Schilling 2.00 .60
95 Jose DeJesus .10 .03
96 Robin Ventura .60 .18
97 Steve Searcy .10 .03
98 Chip Hale .10 .03
99 Marquis Grissom .60 .18
100 Luis de los Santos .10 .03

1990 Score Sportflics Ryan

This standard-size card was issued by Optigraphics (producer of Score and Sportflics) to commemorate the 11th National Sports Card Collectors Convention held in Arlington, Texas in July of 1990. This card featured a Score front similar to the Ryan 1990 Score highlight card except for the 11th National Convention Logo on the bottom right of the card. On the other side a Ryan Sportflics card was printed that stated (reflected) either Sportflics or 1990 National Sports Collectors Convention on the bottom of the card. This issue was limited to a printing of 600 cards with Ryan himself destroying the printing plates.

Nm-Mt Ex-Mt
NNO Nolan Ryan 300.00 90.00
(No number on back; card back is actually another front in Sportflics style)

1990 Score Young Superstars I

1990 Score Young Superstars I are glossy full color cards featuring 42 standard-size cards of popular young players. The first series was issued with 1990 Score baseball rack packs while the second series was available only via a mailaway from the company.

Nm-Mt Ex-Mt
COMPLETE SET (42) 10.00 3.00
1 Bo Jackson 1.25 .35
2 Dwight Smith .25 .07
3 Albert Belle 1.25 .35
4 Gregg Olson .50 .15
5 Jim Abbott .75 .23
6 Felix Fermin .25 .07
7 Brian Holman .25 .07
8 Clay Parker .25 .07
9 Junior Felix .25 .07
10 Joe Oliver .25 .07
11 Steve Finley .50 .15
12 Greg Briley .25 .07
13 Greg Vaughn .50 .15
14 Bill Spiers .25 .07
15 Eric Yelding .25 .07
16 Jose Gonzalez .25 .07
17 Mark Carreon .25 .07
18 Greg W. Harris .25 .07
19 Felix Jose .25 .07
20 Bob Milacki .25 .07
21 Kenny Rogers .50 .15
22 Rolando Roomes .25 .07
23 Bip Roberts .25 .07
24 Jeff Brantley .25 .07
25 Jeff Ballard .25 .07
26 John Dopson .25 .07
27 Ken Patterson .25 .07
28 Omar Vizquel 1.25 .35
29 Kevin Brown .50 .15
30 Derek Lilliquist .25 .07
31 David Wells .50 .15
32 Ken Hill .50 .15
33 Greg Litton .25 .07
34 Rob Ducey .25 .07
35 Carlos Martinez .25 .07
36 John Smoltz 1.25 .35
37 Lenny Harris .25 .07
38 Charlie Hayes .25 .07
39 Tommy Gregg .25 .07
40 John Wetteland 1.25 .35
41 Jeff Huson .25 .07
42 Eric Anthony .25 .07

1990 Score Young Superstars II

1990 Score Young Superstars II are glossy full color cards featuring 42 standard-size cards of popular young players. Whereas the first series was issued with 1990 Score baseball rack packs, this second series was available only via a mailaway from the company.

Nm-Mt Ex-Mt
COMP.FACT.SET (42) 25.00 7.50
1 Todd Zeile .50 .15
2 Ben McDonald .25 .07
3 Delino DeShields 1.50 .45
4 Pat Combs .25 .07
5 John Olerud 3.00 .90
6 Marquis Grissom 1.50 .45
7 Mike Stanton .25 .07
8 Robin Ventura 1.50 .45
9 Larry Walker 5.00 1.50
10 Dante Bichette 1.50 .45
11 Jack Armstrong .25 .07
12 Jay Bell .50 .15
13 Andy Benes .50 .15
14 Joey Cora .50 .15
15 Rob Dibble .50 .15
16 Jeff King .25 .07
17 Jeff Hamilton .25 .07
18 Erik Hanson .25 .07
19 Pete Harnisch .25 .07
20 Greg Hibbard .25 .07
21 Stan Javier .25 .07
22 Mark Lemke .25 .07
23 Steve Olin .50 .15
24 Tommy Greene .25 .07
25 Sammy Sosa 20.00 6.00
26 Gary Wayne .25 .07
27 Deion Sanders 1.50 .45
28 Steve Wilson .25 .07
29 Joe Girardi .75 .23
30 John Orton .25 .07
31 Kevin Tapani 1.50 .45
32 Carlos Baerga .50 .15
33 Glenallen Hill .25 .07
34 Mike Blowers .50 .15
35 Dave Hollins 1.50 .45
36 Lance Blankenship .25 .07
37 Hal Morris .25 .07
38 Lance Johnson .25 .07
39 Chris Gwynn .25 .07
40 Doug Dascenzo .25 .07
41 Jerald Clark .25 .07
42 Carlos Quintana .25 .07

1991 Score Promos

These cards may be distinguished from their regular issue counterparts by the absence of the last season's statistics and the fact that career stats are not updated. To date, 46 of the 110 cards numbered between 111 and 220 have been verified as promos. No set price has been provided.

Nm-Mt Ex-Mt
*PROMOS: 10X BASIC CARDS

1991 Score

The 1991 Score set contains 893 standard-size cards issued in two separate series of 441 and 452 cards each. This set marks the fourth consecutive year that Score issued a major set but the first time Score issued the set in two series. Cards were distributed in plastic-wrap packs, blister packs and factory sets. The card fronts feature one of four different solid color borders (black, blue, teal and white) framing the full-color photo of the cards. Subsets include Rookie Prospects (331-379), First Draft Picks (380-391, 671-682), AL All-Stars (392-401), Master Blasters (402-406, 689-693), K-Men (407-411, 684-688), Rifleman (412-416, 694-698), NL All-Stars (661-670), No-Hitters (699-707), Franchise (849-874), Award Winners (875-881) and Dream Team (882-893). An American Flag card (737) was issued to honor the American soldiers involved in Desert Storm. Rookie Cards in the set include Carl Everett, Jeff Conine, Chipper Jones, Mike Mussina and Rondell White. There are a number of pitchers whose card backs show Innings Pitched totals which do not equal the added year-by-year total; the following card numbers were affected, 4, 24, 29, 30, 51, 81, 109, 111, 118, 141, 150, 156, 177, 204, 218, 232, 235, 255, 287, 289, 311, and 328.

Nm-Mt Ex-Mt
COMPLETE SET (893) 20.00 6.00
COMP.FACT.SET (900) 25.00 7.50
1 Jose Canseco .25 .07
2 Ken Griffey Jr. .50 .15
3 Ryne Sandberg .40 .12
4 Nolan Ryan 1.00 .30
5 Bo Jackson .25 .07
6 Bret Saberhagen UER .05 .02
(In bio, missed misspelled as mised)
7 Will Clark .25 .07
8 Ellis Burks .10 .03
9 Joe Carter .10 .03
10 Rickey Henderson .25 .07
11 Ozzie Guillen .05 .02
12 Wade Boggs .15 .04
13 Jerome Walton .05 .02
14 John Franco .10 .03
15 Ricky Jordan UER .05 .02
(League misspelled as legue)
16 Wally Backman .05 .02
17 Rob Dibble .10 .03
18 Glenn Braggs .05 .02
19 Cory Snyder .05 .02
20 Kal Daniels .05 .02
21 Mark Langston .05 .02
22 Kevin Gross .05 .02
23 Don Mattingly UER .60 .18
First line, ' is missing from Yankee
24 Dave Righetti .10 .03
25 Roberto Alomar .25 .07
26 Robby Thompson .05 .02
27 Jack McDowell .05 .02
28 Bip Roberts UER .05 .02
(Bio reads playd)
29 Jay Howell .05 .02
30 Dave Stieb UER .05 .02
(17 wins in bio, 18 in stats)
31 Johnny Ray .05 .02
32 Steve Sax .05 .02
33 Terry Mulholland .05 .02
34 Lee Guetterman .05 .02
35 Tim Raines .10 .03
36 Scott Fletcher .05 .02
37 Lance Parrish .05 .02
38 Tony Phillips UER .05 .02
(Born 4/15 should be 4/25)
39 Todd Stottlemyre .05 .02
40 Alan Trammell .15 .04
41 Todd Burns .05 .02
42 Mookie Wilson .10 .03
43 Chris Bosio .05 .02
44 Jeffrey Leonard .05 .02
45 Doug Jones .05 .02
46 Mike Scott UER .05 .02
(In first line, dominate should read dominating)
47 Andy Hawkins .05 .02
48 Harold Reynolds .10 .03
49 Paul Molitor .15 .04
50 John Farrell .05 .02
51 Danny Darwin .05 .02
52 Jeff Blauser .05 .02
53 John Tudor UER .05 .02
(41 wins in '81)
54 Milt Thompson .05 .02
55 Dave Justice .10 .03
56 Greg Olson .05 .02
57 Willie Blair .05 .02
58 Rick Parker .05 .02
59 Shawn Boskie .05 .02
60 Kevin Tapani .05 .02
61 Dave Hollins .05 .02
62 Scott Radinsky .05 .02
63 Francisco Cabrera .05 .02
64 Tim Layana .05 .02
65 Jim Leyritz .05 .02
66 Wayne Edwards .05 .02
67 Lee Stevens .05 .02
68 Bill Sampen UER .05 .02
Fourth line, long is spelled along
69 Craig Grebeck UER .05 .02
Born in Cerritos, not Johnstown
70 John Burkett .05 .02
71 Hector Villanueva .05 .02
72 Oscar Azocar .05 .02
73 Alan Mills .05 .02
74 Carlos Baerga .05 .02

75 Charles Nagy .05 .02
76 Tim Drummond .05 .02
77 Dana Kiecker .05 .02
78 Tom Edens .05 .02
79 Kent Mercker .05 .02
80 Steve Avery .05 .02
81 Lee Smith .10 .03
82 Dave Martinez .05 .02
83 Dave Winfield .10 .03
84 Bill Spiers .05 .02
85 Dan Pasqua .05 .02
86 Randy Milligan .05 .02
87 Tracy Jones .05 .02
88 Greg Myers .05 .02
89 Keith Hernandez .15 .04
90 Todd Benzinger .05 .02
91 Mike Jackson .05 .02
92 Mike Stanley .05 .02
93 Candy Maldonado .05 .02
94 John Kruk UER .10 .03
(No decimal point before 1990 BA)
95 Cal Ripken UER .75 .23
(Genius spelled genuis)
96 Willie Fraser .05 .02
97 Mike Felder .05 .02
98 Bill Landrum .05 .02
99 Chuck Crim .05 .02
100 Chuck Finley .10 .03
101 Kirt Manwaring .05 .02
102 Jaime Navarro .05 .02
103 Dickie Thon .05 .02
104 Brian Downing .05 .02
105 Jim Abbott .15 .04
106 Tom Brookens .05 .02
107 Darryl Hamilton UER .05 .02
(Bio info is for Jeff Hamilton)
108 Bryan Harvey .05 .02
109 Greg A. Harris UER .05 .02
Shown pitching lefty, bio says righty
110 Greg Swindell .05 .02
111 Juan Berenguer .05 .02
112 Mike Heath .05 .02
113 Scott Bradley .05 .02
114 Jack Morris .10 .03
115 Barry Jones .05 .02
116 Kevin Romine .05 .02
117 Garry Templeton .05 .02
118 Scott Sanderson .05 .02
119 Roberto Kelly .05 .02
120 George Brett .60 .18
121 Oddibe McDowell .05 .02
122 Jim Acker .05 .02
123 Bill Swift UER .05 .02
(Born 12/27/61, should be 10/27)
124 Eric King .05 .02
125 Jay Buhner .10 .03
126 Matt Young .05 .02
127 Alvaro Espinoza .05 .02
128 Greg Hibbard .05 .02
129 Jeff M. Robinson .05 .02
130 Mike Greenwell .05 .02
131 Dion James .05 .02
132 Donn Pall UER .05 .02
(1988 ERA in stats 0.00)
133 Lloyd Moseby .05 .02
134 Randy Velarde .05 .02
135 Allan Anderson .05 .02
136 Mark Davis .05 .02
137 Eric Davis .10 .03
138 Phil Stephenson .05 .02
139 Felix Fermin .05 .02
140 Pedro Guerrero .10 .03
141 Charlie Hough .10 .03
142 Mike Henneman .05 .02
143 Jeff Montgomery .05 .02
144 Lenny Harris .05 .02
145 Bruce Hurst .05 .02
146 Eric Anthony .05 .02
147 Paul Assenmacher .05 .02
148 Jesse Barfield .05 .02
149 Carlos Quintana .05 .02
150 Dave Stewart .10 .03
151 Roy Smith .05 .02
152 Paul Gibson .05 .02
153 Mickey Hatcher .05 .02
154 Jim Eisenreich .05 .02
155 Kenny Rogers .10 .03
156 Dave Schmidt .05 .02
157 Lance Johnson .05 .02
158 Dave West .05 .02
159 Steve Balboni .05 .02
160 Jeff Brantley .05 .02
161 Craig Biggio .15 .04
162 Brook Jacoby .05 .02
163 Dan Gladden .05 .02
164 Jeff Reardon UER .10 .03
(Total IP shown as 943.2, should be 943.1)
165 Mark Carreon .05 .02
166 Mel Hall .05 .02
167 Gary Mielke .05 .02
168 Cecil Fielder .10 .03
169 Darrin Jackson .05 .02
170 Rick Aguilera .10 .03
171 Walt Weiss .05 .02
172 Steve Farr .05 .02
173 Jody Reed .05 .02
174 Mike Jeffcoat .05 .02
175 Mark Grace .15 .04
176 Larry Sheets .05 .02
177 Bill Gullickson .05 .02
178 Chris Gwynn .05 .02
179 Melido Perez .05 .02
180 Sid Fernandez UER .05 .02
(779 runs in 1990)
181 Tim Burke .05 .02
182 Gary Pettis .05 .02
183 Rob Murphy .05 .02
184 Craig Lefferts .05 .02
185 Howard Johnson .05 .02
186 Ken Caminiti .10 .03
187 Tim Belcher .05 .02
188 Greg Cadaret .05 .02
189 Matt Williams .10 .03
190 Dave Magadan .05 .02
191 Geno Petralli .05 .02
192 Jeff D. Robinson .05 .02
193 Jim Deshaies .05 .02
194 Willie Randolph .10 .03
195 George Bell .05 .02
196 Hubie Brooks .05 .02
197 Tom Gordon .05 .02
198 Mike Fitzgerald .05 .02
199 Mike Pagliarulo .05 .02
200 Kirby Puckett .25 .07
201 Shawon Dunston .05 .02
202 Dennis Boyd .05 .02
203 Junior Felix UER .05 .02
(Text has him in NL)
204 Alejandro Pena .05 .02
205 Pete Smith .05 .02
206 Tom Glavine UER .15 .04
(Lefty spelled leftie)
207 Luis Salazar .05 .02
208 John Smoltz .15 .04
209 Doug Dascenzo .05 .02
210 Tim Wallach .05 .02
211 Greg Gagne .05 .02
212 Mark Gubicza .05 .02
213 Mark Parent .05 .02
214 Ken Oberkfell .05 .02
215 Gary Carter .15 .04
216 Rafael Palmeiro .15 .04
217 Tom Niedenfuer .05 .02
218 Dave LaPoint .05 .02
219 Jeff Treadway .05 .02
220 Mitch Williams UER .05 .02
('89 ERA shown as 2.76, should be 2.64)
221 Jose DeLeon .05 .02
222 Mike LaValliere .05 .02
223 Darrel Akerfelds .05 .02
224A Kent Anderson ERR .10 .03
(First line& flachy should read flashy)
224B Kent Anderson COR .10 .03
(Corrected in factory sets)
225 Dwight Evans .10 .03
226 Gary Redus .05 .02
227 Paul O'Neill .15 .04
228 Marty Barrett .05 .02
229 Tom Browning .05 .02
230 Terry Pendleton .10 .03
231 Jack Armstrong .05 .02
232 Mike Boddicker .05 .02
233 Neal Heaton .05 .02
234 Marquis Grissom .05 .02
235 Bert Blyleven .10 .03
236 Curt Young .05 .02
237 Don Carman .05 .02
238 Charlie Hayes .05 .02
239 Mark Knudson .05 .02
240 Todd Zeile .05 .02
241 Larry Walker UER .25 .07
(Maple River, should be Maple Ridge)
242 Jerald Clark .05 .02
243 Jeff Ballard .05 .02
244 Jeff King .05 .02
245 Tom Brunansky .05 .02
246 Darren Daulton .10 .03
247 Scott Terry .05 .02
248 Rob Deer .05 .02
249 Brady Anderson UER .10 .03
(1990 Hagerstown 1 hit, should say 13 hits)
250 Len Dykstra .10 .03
251 Greg W. Harris .05 .02
252 Mike Hartley .05 .02
253 Joey Cora .05 .02
254 Ivan Calderon .05 .02
255 Ted Power .05 .02
256 Sammy Sosa .50 .15
257 Steve Buechele .05 .02
258 Mike Devereaux UER .05 .02
(No comma between city and state)
259 Brad Komminsk UER .05 .02
(Last text line, Ba should be BA)
260 Ted Higuera .05 .02
261 Shawn Abner .05 .02
262 Dave Valle .05 .02
263 Jeff Huson .05 .02
264 Edgar Martinez .15 .04
265 Carlton Fisk .15 .04
266 Steve Finley .10 .03
267 John Wetteland .10 .03
268 Kevin Appier .10 .03
269 Steve Lyons .05 .02
270 Mickey Tettleton .05 .02
271 Luis Rivera .05 .02
272 Steve Jeltz .05 .02
273 R.J. Reynolds .05 .02
274 Carlos Martinez .05 .02
275 Dan Plesac .05 .02
276 Mike Morgan UER .05 .02
Total IP shown as 1149.1, should be 1149
277 Jeff Russell .05 .02
278 Pete Incaviglia .05 .02
279 Kevin Seitzer UER .05 .02
Bio has 200 hits twice and .300 four times, should be once and three times
280 Bobby Thigpen .05 .02
281 Stan Javier UER .05 .02
(Born 1/9, should say 9/1)
282 Henry Cotto .05 .02
283 Gary Wayne .05 .02
284 Shane Mack .05 .02
285 Brian Holman .05 .02
286 Gerald Perry .05 .02
287 Steve Crawford .05 .02
288 Nelson Liriano .05 .02
289 Don Aase .05 .02
290 Randy Johnson .30 .09
291 Harold Baines .10 .03
292 Kent Hrbek .10 .03
293A Les Lancaster ERR .05 .02
(No comma between Dallas and Texas)
293B Les Lancaster COR .05 .02
(Corrected in factory sets)
294 Jeff Musselman .05 .02
295 Kurt Stillwell .05 .02
296 Stan Belinda .05 .02
297 Lou Whitaker .10 .03
298 Glenn Wilson .05 .02
299 Omar Vizquel UER .10 .03
Born 5/15, should be 4/24, there is a decimal before GP total for '90
300 Ramon Martinez .05 .02
301 Dwight Smith .05 .02
302 Tim Crews .05 .02
303 Lance Blankenship .05 .02
304 Sid Bream .05 .02
305 Rafael Ramirez .05 .02
306 Steve Wilson .05 .02
307 Mackey Sasser .05 .02
308 Franklin Stubbs .05 .02
309 Jack Daugherty UER .05 .02
(Born 6/3/60, should say July)
310 Eddie Murray .25 .07
311 Bob Welch .05 .02
312 Brian Harper .05 .02
313 Lance McCullers .05 .02
314 Dave Smith .05 .02
315 Bobby Bonilla .10 .03
316 Jerry Don Gleaton .05 .02
317 Greg Maddux .40 .12
318 Keith Miller .05 .02
319 Mark Portugal .05 .02
320 Robin Ventura .10 .03
321 Bob Ojeda .05 .02
322 Mike Harkey .05 .02
323 Jay Bell .10 .03
324 Mark McGwire .60 .18
325 Gary Gaetti .10 .03
326 Jeff Pico .05 .02
327 Kevin McReynolds .05 .02
328 Frank Tanana .05 .02
329 Eric Yelding UER .05 .02
(Listed as 6'3" should be 5'11")
330 Barry Bonds .60 .18
331 Brian McRae RC UER .25 .07
(No comma between city and state)
332 Pedro Munoz RC .10 .03
333 Daryl Irvine .05 .02
334 Chris Hoiles .05 .02
335 Thomas Howard .05 .02
336 Jeff Schulz .05 .02
337 Jeff Manto .05 .02
338 Beau Allred .05 .02
339 Mike Bordick RC .40 .12
340 Todd Hundley .05 .02
341 Jim Vatcher UER .05 .02
(Height 6'9", should be 5'9")
342 Luis Sojo .05 .02
343 Jose Offerman UER .05 .02
(Born 1969, should say 1968)
344 Pete Coachman .05 .02
345 Mike Benjamin .05 .02
346 Ozzie Canseco .05 .02
347 Tim McIntosh .05 .02
348 Phil Plantier RC .10 .03
349 Terry Shumpert .05 .02
350 Darren Lewis .05 .02
351 David Walsh RC .05 .02
352A Scott Chiamparino .10 .03
ERR
Bats left, should be right
352B Scott Chiamparino .10 .03
COR
corrected in factory sets
353 Julio Valera .05 .02
UER (Progressed mis-spelled as progessed)
354 Anthony Telford .05 .02
355 Kevin Wickander .05 .02
356 Tim Naehring .05 .02
357 Jim Poole .05 .02
358 Mark Whiten UER .05 .02
Shown hitting lefty, bio says righty
359 Terry Wells .05 .02
360 Rafael Valdez .05 .02
361 Mel Stottlemyre Jr. .05 .02
362 David Segui .05 .02
363 Paul Abbott RC .10 .03
364 Steve Howard .05 .02
365 Karl Rhodes .05 .02
366 Rafael Novoa .05 .02
367 Joe Grahe RC .05 .02
368 Darren Reed .05 .02
369 Jeff McKnight .05 .02
370 Scott Leius .05 .02
371 Mark Dewey .05 .02
372 Mark Lee UER RC .10 .03
(Shown hitting left, bio says righty, born in Dakota, should say North Dakota
373 Rosario Rodriguez UER .05 .02
Shown hitting lefty, bio says righty
374 Chuck McElroy .05 .02
375 Mike Bell .05 .02
376 Mickey Morandini .05 .02
377 Bill Haselman .05 .02
378 Dave Pavlas .05 .02
379 Derrick May .05 .02
380 J.Burnitz FDP RC .40 .12
381 Donald Peters FDP .05 .02
382 Alex Fernandez FDP .05 .02
383 Mike Mussina FDP RC 1.50 .45
384 Dan Smith FDP RC .10 .03
385 L.Dickson FDP RC .10 .03
386 Carl Everett FDP RC .50 .15
387 Tom Nevers FDP RC .10 .03
388 Adam Hyzdu FDP RC .25 .07
389 T.Van Poppel FDP RC .25 .07
390 R.White FDP RC .40 .12
391 M.Newfield FDP RC .10 .03
392 Julio Franco AS .05 .02
393 Wade Boggs AS .10 .03
394 Ozzie Guillen AS .05 .02
395 Cecil Fielder AS .05 .02
396 Ken Griffey Jr. AS .25 .07
397 Rickey Henderson AS .15 .04
398 Jose Canseco AS .10 .03
399 Roger Clemens AS .25 .07
400 Sandy Alomar Jr. AS .05 .02
401 Bobby Thigpen AS .05 .02
402 Bobby Bonilla MB .05 .02
403 Eric Davis MB .05 .02
404 Fred McGriff MB .10 .03
405 Glenn Davis MB .05 .02
406 Kevin Mitchell MB .05 .02
407 Rob Dibble KM .05 .02
408 Ramon Martinez KM .05 .02
409 David Cone KM .05 .02
410 Bobby Witt KM .05 .02
411 Mark Langston KM .05 .02
412 Bo Jackson RIF .10 .03
413 Shawon Dunston RIF .05 .02
UER
In the baseball, should say in baseball
414 Jesse Barfield RIF .05 .02
415 Ken Caminiti RIF .05 .02
416 Benito Santiago RIF .05 .02
417 Nolan Ryan HL .50 .15
418 B.Thigpen HL UER .05 .02
Back refers to Hal McRae Jr., should say Brian McRae
419 Ramon Martinez HL .05 .02
420 Bo Jackson HL .10 .03
421 Carlton Fisk HL .10 .03
422 Jimmy Key .10 .03
423 Junior Noboa .05 .02
424 Al Newman .05 .02
425 Pat Borders .05 .02
426 Von Hayes .05 .02
427 Tim Teufel .05 .02
428 Eric Plunk UER .05 .02
Text says Eric's had, no apostrophe needed
429 John Moses .05 .02
430 Mike Witt .05 .02
431 Otis Nixon .05 .02
432 Tony Fernandez .05 .02
433 Rance Mulliniks .05 .02
434 Dan Petry .05 .02
435 Bob Geren .05 .02
436 Steve Frey .05 .02
437 Jamie Moyer .10 .03
438 Junior Ortiz .05 .02
439 Tom O'Malley .05 .02
440 Pat Combs .05 .02
441 Jose Canseco DT .25 .07
442 Alfredo Griffin .05 .02
443 Andres Galarraga .10 .03
444 Bryn Smith .05 .02
445 Andre Dawson .10 .03
446 Juan Samuel .05 .02
447 Mike Aldrete .05 .02
448 Ron Gant .10 .03
449 Fernando Valenzuela .10 .03
450 Vince Coleman UER .05 .02
Should say topped majors in steals four times, not three times
451 Kevin Mitchell .05 .02
452 Spike Owen .05 .02
453 Mike Bielecki .05 .02
454 Dennis Martinez .10 .03
455 Brett Butler .10 .03
456 Ron Darling .05 .02
457 Dennis Rasmussen .05 .02
458 Ken Howell .05 .02
459 Steve Bedrosian .05 .02
460 Frank Viola .10 .03
461 Jose Lind .05 .02
462 Chris Sabo .05 .02
463 Dante Bichette .10 .03
464 Rick Mahler .05 .02
465 John Smiley .05 .02
466 Devon White .05 .02
467 John Orton .05 .02
468 Mike Stanton .05 .02
469 Billy Hatcher .05 .02
470 Wally Joyner .10 .03
471 Gene Larkin .05 .02
472 Doug Drabek .05 .02
473 Gary Sheffield .10 .03
474 David Wells .10 .03
475 Andy Van Slyke .10 .03
476 Mike Gallego .05 .02
477 B.J. Surhoff .10 .03
478 Gene Nelson .05 .02
479 Mariano Duncan .05 .02
480 Fred McGriff .15 .04
481 Jerry Browne .05 .02
482 Alvin Davis .05 .02
483 Bill Wegman .05 .02
484 Dave Parker .10 .03
485 Dennis Eckersley .10 .03
486 Erik Hanson UER .05 .02
(Basketball misspelled as baseketball)
487 Bill Ripken .05 .02
488 Tom Candiotti .05 .02
489 Mike Schooler .05 .02
490 Gregg Olson .05 .02
491 Chris James .05 .02
492 Pete Harnisch .05 .02
493 Julio Franco .10 .03
494 Greg Briley .05 .02
495 Ruben Sierra .05 .02
496 Steve Olin .05 .02
497 Mike Fetters .05 .02
498 Mark Williamson .05 .02
499 Bob Tewksbury .05 .02
500 Tony Gwynn .30 .09
501 Randy Myers .05 .02
502 Keith Comstock .05 .02
503 C.Worthington UER .05 .02
DeCinces misspelled DiCinces on back
504 Mark Eichhorn UER .05 .02
Stats incomplete, doesn't have '89 Braves stint
505 Barry Larkin .25 .07
506 Dave Johnson .05 .02
507 Bobby Witt .05 .02
508 Joe Orsulak .05 .02
509 Pete O'Brien .05 .02
510 Brad Arnsberg .05 .02
511 Storm Davis .05 .02
512 Bob Milacki .05 .02
513 Bill Pecota .05 .02
514 Glenallen Hill .05 .02
515 Danny Tartabull .05 .02
516 Mike Moore .05 .02
517 Ron Robinson UER .05 .02
(577 K's in 1990)
518 Mark Gardner .05 .02
519 Rick Wrona .05 .02
520 Mike Scioscia .05 .02
521 Frank Wills .05 .02
522 Greg Brock .05 .02
523 Jack Clark .10 .03
524 Bruce Ruffin .05 .02
525 Robin Yount .40 .12
526 Tom Foley .05 .02
527 Pat Perry .05 .02
528 Greg Vaughn .10 .03
529 Wally Whitehurst .05 .02
530 Norm Charlton .05 .02
531 Marvell Wynne .05 .02
532 Jim Gantner .05 .02
533 Greg Litton .05 .02
534 Manny Lee .05 .02
535 Scott Bailes .05 .02
536 Charlie Leibrandt .05 .02
537 Roger McDowell .05 .02
538 Andy Benes .05 .02
539 Rick Honeycutt .05 .02
540 Dwight Gooden .15 .04
541 Scott Garrelts .05 .02
542 Dave Clark .05 .02
543 Lonnie Smith .05 .02
544 Rick Reuschel .05 .02
545 Delino DeShields UER .10 .03
(Rockford misspelled as Rock Ford in '88)
546 Mike Sharperson .05 .02
547 Mike Kingery .05 .02
548 Terry Kennedy .05 .02
549 David Cone .10 .03
550 Orel Hershiser .10 .03
551 Matt Nokes .05 .02
552 Eddie Williams .05 .02
553 Frank DiPino .05 .02
554 Fred Lynn .05 .02
555 Alex Cole .05 .02
556 Terry Leach .05 .02
557 Chet Lemon .05 .02
558 Paul Mirabella .05 .02
559 Bill Long .05 .02
560 Phil Bradley .05 .02
561 Duane Ward .05 .02
562 Dave Bergman .05 .02
563 Eric Show .05 .02
564 Xavier Hernandez .05 .02
565 Jeff Parrett .05 .02
566 Chuck Cary .05 .02
567 Ken Hill .05 .02
568 Bob Welch Hand .05 .02
(Complement should be compliment) UER
569 John Mitchell .05 .02
570 Travis Fryman .10 .03
571 Derek Lilliquist .05 .02
572 Steve Lake .05 .02
573 John Barfield .05 .02
574 Randy Bush .05 .02
575 Joe Magrane .05 .02
576 Eddie Diaz .05 .02
577 Casey Candaele .05 .02
578 Jesse Orosco .05 .02
579 Tom Henke .05 .02
580 Rick Cerone UER .05 .02
(Actually his third go-round with Yankees)
581 Drew Hall .05 .02
582 Tony Castillo .05 .02
583 Jimmy Jones .05 .02
584 Rick Reed .05 .02
585 Joe Girardi .05 .02
586 Jeff Gray .05 .02
587 Luis Polonia .05 .02
588 Joe Klink .05 .02
589 Rex Hudler .05 .02
590 Kirk McCaskill .05 .02
591 Juan Agosto .05 .02
592 Wes Gardner .05 .02
593 Rich Rodriguez .05 .02
594 Mitch Webster .05 .02
595 Kelly Gruber .05 .02
596 Dale Mohorcic .05 .02
597 Willie McGee .10 .03
598 Bill Krueger .05 .02
599 Bob Walk UER .05 .02
Cards says he's 33, but actually he's 34
600 Kevin Maas .05 .02
601 Danny Jackson .05 .02
602 Craig McMurtry UER .05 .02
(Anonymously misspelled anonimously)
603 Curtis Wilkerson .05 .02
604 Adam Peterson .05 .02
605 Sam Horn .05 .02
606 Tommy Gregg .05 .02
607 Ken Dayley .05 .02
608 Carmelo Castillo .05 .02
609 John Shelby .05 .02
610 Don Slaught .05 .02
611 Calvin Schiraldi .05 .02
612 Dennis Lamp .05 .02
613 Andres Thomas .05 .02
614 Jose Gonzalez .05 .02
615 Randy Ready .05 .02
616 Kevin Bass .05 .02
617 Mike Marshall .05 .02
618 Daryl Boston .05 .02
619 Andy McGaffigan .05 .02
620 Joe Oliver .05 .02
621 Jim Gott .05 .02
622 Jose Oquendo .05 .02
623 Jose DeJesus .05 .02
624 Mike Brumley .05 .02
625 John Olerud .10 .03
626 Ernest Riles .05 .02
627 Gene Harris .05 .02
628 Jose Uribe .05 .02
629 Darnell Coles .05 .02

630 Carney Lansford .10 .03
631 Tim Leary .05 .02
632 Tim Hulett .05 .02
633 Kevin Elster .05 .02
634 Tony Fossas .05 .02
635 Francisco Oliveras .05 .02
636 Bob Patterson .05 .02
637 Gary Ward .05 .02
638 Rene Gonzales .05 .02
639 Don Robinson .05 .02
640 Darryl Strawberry .15 .04
641 Dave Anderson .05 .02
642 Scott Scudder .05 .02
643 Reggie Harris UER .05 .02
(Hepatitis misspelled as hepititis)
644 Dave Henderson .05 .02
645 Ben McDonald .05 .02
646 Bob Kipper .05 .02
647 Hal Morris UER .05 .02
(It's should be its)
648 Tim Birtsas .05 .02
649 Steve Searcy .05 .02
650 Dale Murphy .25 .07
651 Ron Oester .05 .02
652 Mike LaCoss .05 .02
653 Ron Jones .05 .02
654 Kelly Downs .05 .02
655 Roger Clemens .50 .15
656 Herm Winningham .05 .02
657 Trevor Wilson .05 .02
658 Jose Rijo .05 .02
659 Dann Bilardello UER .05 .02
Bio has 13 games, 1 hit, and 32 AB, stats show 19, 2, and 37
660 Gregg Jefferies .05 .02
661 Doug Drabek AS UER .05 .02
(Through is mis-spelled though)
662 Randy Myers AS .05 .02
663 Benny Santiago AS .05 .02
664 Will Clark AS .10 .03
665 Ryne Sandberg AS .25 .07
666 Barry Larkin AS UER .10 .03
Line 13, coolly misspelled cooly
667 Matt Williams AS .05 .02
668 Barry Bonds AS .30 .09
669 Eric Davis AS .05 .02
670 Bobby Bonilla AS .05 .02
671 C.Jones FDP RC 4.00 1.20
672 E.Christopherson RC .10 .03
FDP
673 R.Beckett FDP RC .10 .03
674 S.Andrews FDP RC .25 .07
675 Steve Karsay FDP RC .25 .07
676 Aaron Holbert FDP RC .10 .03
677 D.Osborne FDP RC .10 .03
678 Todd Ritchie FDP RC .25 .07
679 Ron Walden FDP RC .10 .03
680 Tim Costo FDP RC .10 .03
681 Dan Wilson FDP RC .25 .07
682 Kurt Miller FDP RC .10 .03
683 M.Lieberthal FDP RC .40 .12
684 Roger Clemens KM .25 .07
685 Dwight Gooden KM .10 .03
686 Nolan Ryan KM .50 .15
687 Frank Viola KM .05 .02
688 Erik Hanson KM .05 .02
689 Matt Williams MB .05 .02
690 J.Canseco MB UER .10 .03
Mammoth misspelled as monmouth
691 Darryl Strawberry MB .10 .03
692 Bo Jackson MB .10 .03
693 Cecil Fielder MB .05 .02
694 Sandy Alomar Jr. RF .05 .02
695 Cory Snyder RF .05 .02
696 Eric Davis RF .05 .02
697 Ken Griffey Jr. RF .25 .07
698 A.Van Slyke RF UER .05 .02
Line 2, outfielders does not need
699 Mark Langston NH .05 .02
Mike Witt
700 Randy Johnson NH .15 .04
701 Nolan Ryan NH .50 .15
702 Dave Stewart NH .05 .02
703 F.Valenzuela NH .05 .02
704 Andy Hawkins NH .05 .02
705 Melido Perez NH .05 .02
706 Terry Mulholland NH .05 .02
707 Dave Stieb NH .05 .02
708 Brian Barnes RC .05 .02
709 Bernard Gilkey .05 .02
710 Steve Decker .05 .02
711 Paul Faries .05 .02
712 Paul Marak .05 .02
713 Wes Chamberlain RC .10 .03
714 Kevin Belcher .05 .02
715 Dan Boone UER .05 .02
(IP adds up to 101, but card has 101.2)
716 Steve Adkins .05 .02
717 Geronimo Pena .05 .02
718 Howard Farmer .05 .02
719 Mark Leonard .05 .02
720 Tom Lampkin .05 .02
721 Mike Gardiner .05 .02
722 Jeff Conine RC .50 .15
723 Efrain Valdez .05 .02
724 Chuck Malone .05 .02
725 Leo Gomez .05 .02
726 Paul McClellan .05 .02
727 Mark Leiter RC .10 .03
728 Rich DeLucia UER .05 .02
(Line 2, all told is written alltold)
729 Mel Rojas .05 .02
730 Hector Wagner .05 .02
731 Ray Lankford .05 .02
732 Turner Ward RC .10 .03
733 Gerald Alexander .05 .02
734 Scott Anderson .05 .02
735 Tony Perezchica .05 .02
736 Jimmy Kremers .05 .02
737 American Flag .25 .07
(Pray for Peace)
738 Mike York .05 .02
739 Mike Rochford .05 .02
740 Scott Aldred .05 .02
741 Rico Brogna .05 .02
742 Dave Burba RC .25 .07
743 Ray Stephens .05 .02
744 Eric Gunderson .05 .02
745 Troy Afenir .05 .02
746 Jeff Shaw .05 .02
747 Orlando Merced RC .10 .03
748 O.Olivares UER RC .10 .03
Line 9, league is misspelled legaue
749 Jerry Kutzler .05 .02
750 Mo Vaughn UER .10 .03
(44 SB's in 1990)
751 Matt Stark .05 .02
752 Randy Hennis .05 .02
753 Andujar Cedeno .05 .02
754 Kelvin Torve .05 .02
755 Joe Kraemer .05 .02
756 Phil Clark RC .10 .03
757 Ed Vosberg .05 .02
758 Mike Perez RC .10 .03
759 Scott Lewis .05 .02
760 Steve Chitren .05 .02
761 Ray Young .05 .02
762 Andres Santana .05 .02
763 Rodney McCray .05 .02
764 Sean Berry UER RC .10 .03
(Name misspelled Barry on card front)
765 Brent Mayne .05 .02
766 Mike Simms .05 .02
767 Glenn Sutko .05 .02
768 Gary DiSarcina .05 .02
769 George Brett HL .25 .07
770 Cecil Fielder HL .05 .02
771 Jim Presley .05 .02
772 John Dopson .05 .02
773 Bo Jackson Breaker .10 .03
774 Brent Knackert UER .05 .02
Born in 1954, shown throwing righty, but bio says lefty
775 Bill Doran UER .05 .02
(Reds in NL East)
776 Dick Schofield .05 .02
777 Nelson Santovenia .05 .02
778 Mark Guthrie .05 .02
779 Mark Lemke .05 .02
780 Terry Steinbach .05 .02
781 Tom Bolton .05 .02
782 Randy Tomlin RC .10 .03
783 Jeff Kunkel .05 .02
784 Felix Jose .05 .02
785 Rick Sutcliffe .10 .03
786 John Cerutti .05 .02
787 Jose Vizcaino UER .05 .02
(Offerman, not Opperman)
788 Curt Schilling .15 .04
789 Ed Whitson .05 .02
790 Tony Pena .05 .02
791 John Candelaria .05 .02
792 Carmelo Martinez .05 .02
793 Sandy Alomar Jr. UER .05 .02
(Indian's should say Indians')
794 Jim Neidlinger .05 .02
795 Barry Larkin WS .10 .03
and Chris Sabo
796 Paul Sorrento .05 .02
797 Tom Pagnozzi .05 .02
798 Tino Martinez .15 .04
799 Scott Ruskin UER .05 .02
(Text says first three seasons but lists averages for four)
800 Kirk Gibson .10 .03
801 Walt Terrell .05 .02
802 John Russell .05 .02
803 Chili Davis .10 .03
804 Chris Nabholz .05 .02
805 Juan Gonzalez .25 .07
806 Ron Hassey .05 .02
807 Todd Worrell .05 .02
808 Tommy Greene .05 .02
809 Joel Skinner UER .05 .02
Joel, not Bob, was drafted in 1979
810 Benito Santiago .10 .03
811 Pat Tabler UER .05 .02
Line 3, always misspelled always
812 Scott Erickson UER .05 .02
(Record spelled rcord)
813 Moises Alou .10 .03
814 Dale Sveum .05 .02
815 R.Sandberg MANYR .25 .07
816 Rick Dempsey .05 .02
817 Scott Bankhead .05 .02
818 Jason Grimsley .05 .02
819 Doug Jennings .05 .02
820 Tom Herr .05 .02
821 Rob Ducey .05 .02
822 Luis Quinones .05 .02
823 Greg Minton .05 .02
824 Mark Grant .05 .02
825 Ozzie Smith UER .40 .12
(Shortstop misspelled shortsop)
826 Dave Eiland .05 .02
827 Danny Heep .05 .02
828 Hensley Meulens .05 .02
829 Charlie O'Brien .05 .02
830 Glenn Davis .05 .02
831 John Marzano UER .05 .02
(International mis-spelled Internaional)
832 Steve Ontiveros .05 .02
833 Ron Karkovice .05 .02
834 Jerry Goff .05 .02
835 Ken Griffey Sr. .10 .03
836 Kevin Reimer .05 .02
837 Randy Kutcher UER .05 .02
(Infectious mis-spelled infectous)
838 Mike Blowers .05 .02
839 Mike Macfarlane .05 .02
840 Frank Thomas UER .25 .07
1989 Sarasota stats, 15 games but 188 AB
841 Ken Griffey Jr. .40 .12
Ken Griffey Sr.
842 Jack Howell .05 .02
843 Goose Gozzo .05 .02
844 Gerald Young .05 .02
845 Zane Smith .05 .02
846 Kevin Brown .10 .03
847 Sil Campusano .05 .02
848 Larry Andersen .05 .02
849 Cal Ripken FRAN .40 .12
850 Roger Clemens FRAN .25 .07
851 S.Alomar Jr. FRAN .05 .02
852 Alan Trammell FRAN .10 .03
853 George Brett FRAN .25 .07
854 Robin Yount FRAN .25 .07
855 Kirby Puckett FRAN .15 .04
856 Don Mattingly FRAN .30 .09
857 R.Henderson FRAN .15 .04
858 Ken Griffey Jr. FRAN .25 .07
859 Ruben Sierra FRAN .05 .02
860 John Olerud FRAN .05 .02
861 Dave Justice FRAN .05 .02
862 Ryne Sandberg FRAN .25 .07
863 Eric Davis FRAN .05 .02
864 D.Strawberry FRAN .10 .03
865 Tim Wallach FRAN .05 .02
866 Dwight Gooden FRAN .10 .03
867 Len Dykstra FRAN .05 .02
868 Barry Bonds FRAN .30 .09
869 Todd Zeile FRAN UER .05 .02
(Powerful misspelled as poweful)
870 Benito Santiago FRAN .05 .02
871 Will Clark FRAN .10 .03
872 Craig Biggio FRAN .10 .03
873 Wally Joyner FRAN .05 .02
874 Frank Thomas FRAN .15 .04
875 R.Henderson MVP .15 .04
876 Barry Bonds MVP .30 .09
877 Bob Welch CY .05 .02
878 Doug Drabek CY .05 .02
879 S.Alomar Jr. ROY .05 .02
880 Dave Justice ROY .05 .02
881 Damon Berryhill .05 .02
882 Frank Viola DT .05 .02
883 Dave Stewart DT .05 .02
884 Doug Jones DT .05 .02
885 Randy Myers DT .05 .02
886 Will Clark DT .10 .03
887 Roberto Alomar DT .10 .03
888 Barry Larkin DT .10 .03
889 Wade Boggs DT .15 .04
890 Rickey Henderson DT .25 .07
891 Kirby Puckett DT .15 .04
892 Ken Griffey Jr DT .50 .15
893 Benny Santiago DT .10 .03

1991 Score Cooperstown

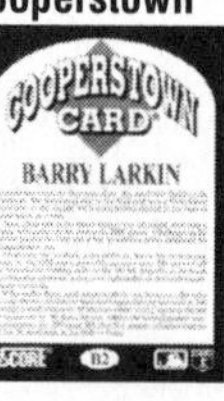

This seven-card standard-size set was available only in complete set form as an insert with 1991 Score factory sets. The card design is not like the regular 1991 Score cards. The card front features a portrait of the player in an oval on a white background. The words "Cooperstown Card" are prominently displayed on the front. The cards are numbered on the back with a B prefix.

	Nm-Mt	Ex-Mt
COMPLETE SET (7)	6.00	1.80
B1 Wade Boggs	.60	.18
B2 Barry Larkin	1.00	.30
B3 Ken Griffey Jr.	2.00	.60
B4 Rickey Henderson	1.00	.30
B5 George Brett	2.50	.75
B6 Will Clark	1.00	.30
B7 Nolan Ryan	4.00	1.20

1991 Score Hot Rookies

This ten-card standard-size set was inserted in the one per 1991 Score 100-card blister pack. The front features a color action player photo, with white borders and the words "Hot Rookie" in yellow above the picture. The card background shades from orange to yellow to orange as one moves down the card face. In a horizontal format, the left half of the back has a color head shot, while the right half has career summary.

	Nm-Mt	Ex-Mt
COMPLETE SET (10)	8.00	2.40
1 Dave Justice	1.00	.30
2 Kevin Maas	.50	.15
3 Hal Morris	.50	.15
4 Frank Thomas	2.00	.60
5 Jeff Conine	1.00	.30
6 Sandy Alomar Jr.	.50	.15
7 Ray Lankford	.50	.15
8 Steve Decker	.50	.15
9 Juan Gonzalez	2.00	.60
10 Jose Offerman	.50	.15

1991 Score Mantle

This seven-card standard-size set features Mickey Mantle at various points in his career. The fronts are full-color glossy shots of Mantle while the backs are in a horizontal format with a full-color photo and some narrative information. The cards were randomly inserted in second series packs. 2,500 serial numbered cards were actually signed by Mantle and stamped with certification press. A similar version of this set was also released to dealers and media members on Score's mailing list and was individually to 5,000 numbered on the back. The cards were sent in seven-card packs. The card number and the set serial number appear on the back.

	Nm-Mt	Ex-Mt
COMPLETE SET (7)	100.00	30.00
COMMON MANTLE (1-7)	15.00	4.50
AU Mickey Mantle AU (Autographed with certified signature)	500.00	150.00

1991 Score Rookie/Traded

The 1991 Score Rookie and Traded contains 110 standard-size player cards and was issued exclusively in factory set form along with 10 "World Series II" magic motion trivia cards through hobby dealers. The front design is identical to the regular issue 1991 Score set except for the distinctive mauve borders and T-suffixed numbering. Cards 1T-80T feature traded players, while cards 81T-110T focus on rookies. Rookie Cards in the set include Jeff Bagwell and Ivan Rodriguez.

	Nm-Mt	Ex-Mt
COMP.FACT.SET (110)	5.00	1.50
1T Bo Jackson	.25	.07
2T Mike Flanagan	.05	.02
3T Pete Incaviglia	.05	.02
4T Jack Clark	.10	.03
5T Hubie Brooks	.05	.02
6T Ivan Calderon	.05	.02
7T Glenn Davis	.05	.02
8T Wally Backman	.05	.02
9T Dave Smith	.05	.02
10T Tim Raines	.10	.03
11T Joe Carter	.10	.03
12T Sid Bream	.05	.02
13T George Bell	.05	.02
14T Steve Bedrosian	.05	.02
15T Willie Wilson	.05	.02
16T Darryl Strawberry	.15	.04
17T Danny Jackson	.05	.02
18T Kirk Gibson	.10	.03
19T Willie McGee	.10	.03
20T Junior Felix	.05	.02
21T Steve Farr	.05	.02
22T Pat Tabler	.05	.02
23T Brett Butler	.10	.03
24T Danny Darwin	.05	.02
25T Mickey Tettleton	.05	.02
26T Gary Carter	.15	.04
27T Mitch Williams	.05	.02
28T Candy Maldonado	.05	.02
29T Otis Nixon	.05	.02
30T Brian Downing	.05	.02
31T Tom Candiotti	.05	.02
32T John Candelaria	.05	.02
33T Rob Murphy	.05	.02
34T Deion Sanders	.15	.04
35T Willie Randolph	.10	.03
36T Pete Harnisch	.05	.02
37T Dante Bichette	.10	.03
38T Garry Templeton	.05	.02
39T Gary Gaetti	.10	.03
40T John Cerutti	.05	.02
41T Rick Cerone	.05	.02
42T Mike Pagliarulo	.05	.02
43T Ron Hassey	.05	.02
44T Roberto Alomar	.25	.07
45T Mike Boddicker	.05	.02
46T Bud Black	.05	.02
47T Rob Deer	.05	.02
48T Devon White	.05	.02
49T Luis Sojo	.05	.02
50T Terry Pendleton	.10	.03
51T Kevin Gross	.05	.02
52T Mike Huff	.05	.02
53T Dave Righetti	.10	.03
54T Matt Young	.05	.02
55T Earnest Riles	.05	.02
56T Bill Gullickson	.05	.02
57T Vince Coleman	.05	.02
58T Fred McGriff	.15	.04
59T Franklin Stubbs	.05	.02
60T Eric King	.05	.02
61T Cory Snyder	.05	.02
62T Dwight Evans	.10	.03
63T Gerald Perry	.05	.02
64T Eric Show	.05	.02
65T Shawn Hillegas	.05	.02
66T Tony Fernandez	.05	.02
67T Tim Teufel	.05	.02
68T Mitch Webster	.05	.02
69T Mike Heath	.05	.02
70T Chili Davis	.10	.03
71T Larry Andersen	.05	.02
72T Gary Varsho	.05	.02
73T Juan Berenguer	.05	.02
74T Jack Morris	.10	.03
75T Barry Jones	.05	.02
76T Rafael Belliard	.05	.02
77T Steve Buechele	.05	.02
78T Scott Sanderson	.05	.02
79T Bob Ojeda	.05	.02
80T Curt Schilling	.15	.04
81T Brian Drahman	.05	.02
82T Ivan Rodriguez RC	2.00	.60
83T David Howard	.05	.02
84T H.Slocumb RC	.10	.03
85T Mike Timlin RC	.10	.03
86T Darryl Kile	.10	.03
87T Pete Schourek RC	.05	.02
88T Bruce Walton	.05	.02
89T Al Osuna RC	.05	.02
90T Gary Scott RC	.05	.02
91T Doug Simons	.05	.02
92T Chris Jones RC	.05	.02
93T Chuck Knoblauch	.10	.03
94T Dana Allison RC	.05	.02
95T Erik Pappas	.05	.02
96T Jeff Bagwell RC	1.50	.45
97T K.Dressendorfer RC	.05	.02
98T Freddie Benavides	.05	.02
99T Luis Gonzalez RC	1.00	.30
100T Wade Taylor	.05	.02
101T Ed Sprague	.05	.02
102T Bob Scanlan	.05	.02
103T Rick Wilkins RC	.05	.02
104T Chris Donnels	.05	.02
105T Joe Slusarski	.05	.02
106T Mark Lewis	.05	.02
107T Pat Kelly RC	.05	.02
108T John Briscoe	.05	.02
109T Luis Lopez RC	.05	.02
110T Jeff Johnson	.05	.02

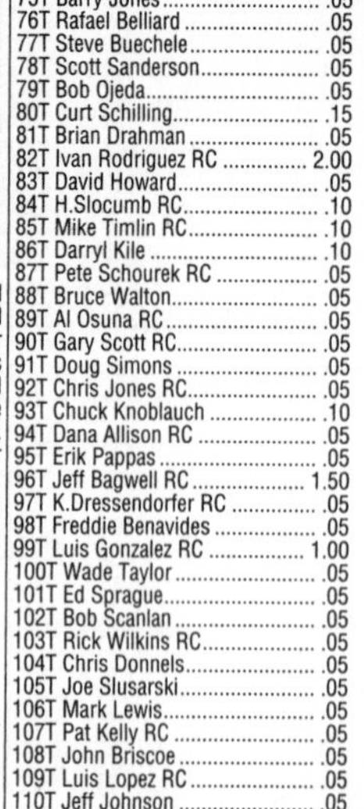

1991 Score All-Star Fanfest

This 11-card standard-size set was issued with a 3-D 1946 World Series trivia card. The cards feature on the fronts color action player photos, with red borders above and below the pictures. The card face is lime green with miniature yellow baseballs and blue player icons, and it can be seen at the top and bottom of the card front. The backs have a similar pattern on a white background and present biographical information as well as career highlights. The set features young players, who were apparently projected by Score to be future All-Stars. The cards are numbered on the back as "X of 10."

	Nm-Mt	Ex-Mt
COMPLETE SET (10)	5.00	1.50
1 Ray Lankford	1.50	.45
2 Steve Decker	.25	.07
3 Gary Scott	.25	.07
4 Hensley Meulens	.25	.07
5 Tim Naehring	.25	.07
6 Mark Whiten	.25	.07
7 Ed Sprague	.25	.07
8 Charles Nagy	.25	.07
9 Terry Shumpert	.25	.07
10 Chuck Knoblauch	2.50	.75
NNO Title Card	.25	.07

1991 Score 100 Rising Stars

The 1991 Score 100 Rising Stars sets were issued by Score with or without special books which goes with the cards. The standard-size cards feature 100 of the most popular rising stars. The sets (with the special book with brief biography on the players) are marketed for retail purposes at a suggested price of 12.95.

	Nm-Mt	Ex-Mt
COMP. FACT SET (100)	8.00	2.40
1 Sandy Alomar Jr.	.10	.03
2 Tom Edens	.05	.02
3 Terry Shumpert	.05	.02
4 Shawn Boskie	.05	.02
5 Steve Avery	.05	.02
6 Deion Sanders	.25	.07
7 John Burkett	.05	.02
8 Stan Belinda	.05	.02
9 Thomas Howard	.05	.02
10 Wayne Edwards	.05	.02
11 Rick Parker	.05	.02
12 Randy Veres	.05	.02
13 Alex Cole	.05	.02
14 Scott Chiamparino	.05	.02
15 Greg Olson	.05	.02
16 Jose DeJesus	.05	.02
17 Mike Blowers	.05	.02
18 Jeff Huson	.05	.02
19 Willie Blair	.05	.02
20 Howard Farmer	.05	.02
21 Larry Walker	.25	.07
22 Scott Kremers	.05	.02
23 Mel Stottlemyre Jr.	.05	.02
24 Mark Whiten	.05	.02
25 Jeff Schulz	.05	.02
26 Gary DiSarcina	.05	.02
27 George Canale	.05	.02
28 Dean Palmer	.20	.06

29 Jim Leyritz .05 .02
30 Carlos Baerga .10 .03
31 Rafael Valdez .05 .02
32 Derek Bell .05 .02
33 Francisco Cabrera .05 .02
34 Chris Hoiles .05 .02
35 Craig Grebeck .05 .02
36 Scott Coolbaugh .05 .02
37 Kevin Wickander .05 .02
38 Marquis Grissom .15 .04
39 Chip Hale .05 .02
40 Kevin Maas .05 .02
41 Juan Gonzalez .75 .23
42 Eric Anthony .05 .02
43 Luis Sojo .05 .02
44 Paul Sorrento .05 .02
45 Dave Justice .20 .06
46 Oscar Azocar .05 .02
47 Charles Nagy .05 .02
48 Robin Ventura .20 .06
49 Reggie Harris .05 .02
50 Ben McDonald .05 .02
51 Hector Villanueva .05 .02
52 Kevin Tapani .05 .02
53 Brian Bohanon .05 .02
54 Tim Layana .05 .02
55 Delino DeShields .10 .03
56 Beau Allred .05 .02
57 Eric Gunderson .05 .02
58 Kent Mercker .05 .02
59 Juan Bell .05 .02
60 Glenallen Hill .05 .02
61 David Segui .10 .03
62 Alan Mills .05 .02
63 Mike Harkey .05 .02
64 Bill Sampen .05 .02
65 Greg Vaughn .20 .06
66 Alex Fernandez .05 .02
67 Mike Hartley .05 .02
68 Travis Fryman .20 .06
69 Dave Rohde .05 .02
70 Tom Lampkin .05 .02
71 Mark Gardner .05 .02
72 Pat Combs .05 .02
73 Kevin Appier .10 .03
74 Mike Fetters .05 .02
75 Greg Myers .05 .02
76 Steve Searcy .05 .02
77 Tim Naehring .05 .02
78 Frank Thomas 1.00 .30
79 Todd Hundley .20 .06
80 Ed Vosberg .05 .02
81 Todd Zeile .10 .03
82 Lee Stevens .05 .02
83 Scott Radinsky .05 .02
84 Hensley Meulens .05 .02
85 Brian DuBois .05 .02
86 Steve Olin .05 .02
87 Julio Machado .05 .02
88 Jose Vizcaino .05 .02
89 Mark Lemke .05 .02
90 Felix Jose .05 .02
91 Wally Whitehurst .05 .02
92 Dana Kiecker .05 .02
93 Mike Munoz .05 .02
94 Adam Peterson .05 .02
95 Tim Drummond .05 .02
96 Dave Hollins .05 .02
97 Craig Wilson .05 .02
98 Hal Morris .05 .02
99 Jose Offerman .05 .02
100 John Olerud .20 .06

1991 Score 100 Superstars

The 1991 Score 100 Superstars sets were issued by Score with or without special books that came with the cards. The standard-size cards feature 100 of the most popular superstars. The sets (with the special book with brief biography on the players) are marketed for retail purposes at a suggested price of 12.95.

	Nm-Mt	Ex-Mt
COMP. FACT SET (100)	8.00	2.40
1 Jose Canseco	.40	.12
2 Bo Jackson	.20	.06
3 Wade Boggs	.50	.15
4 Will Clark	.20	.06
5 Ken Griffey Jr.	1.25	.35
6 Doug Drabek	.05	.02
7 Kirby Puckett	.50	.15
8 Joe Orsulak	.05	.02
9 Eric Davis	.10	.03
10 Rickey Henderson	.75	.23
11 Len Dykstra	.10	.03
12 Ruben Sierra	.10	.03
13 Paul Molitor	.50	.15
14 Ron Gant	.10	.03
15 Ozzie Guillen	.10	.03
16 Ramon Martinez	.05	.02
17 Edgar Martinez	.15	.04
18 Ozzie Smith	.75	.23
19 Charlie Hayes	.05	.02
20 Barry Larkin	.20	.06
21 Cal Ripken	2.00	.60
22 Andy Van Slyke	.10	.03
23 Don Mattingly	1.00	.30
24 Dave Stewart	.10	.03
25 Nolan Ryan	2.00	.60
26 Barry Bonds	1.00	.30
27 Gregg Olson	.05	.02
28 Chris Sabo	.05	.02
29 John Franco	.10	.03
30 Gary Sheffield	.30	.09
31 Jeff Treadway	.05	.02
32 Tom Browning	.05	.02
33 Jose Lind	.05	.02
34 Dave Magadan	.05	.02
35 Dale Murphy	.20	.06
36 Tom Candiotti	.05	.02
37 Willie McGee	.10	.03
38 Robin Yount	.50	.15
39 Mark McGwire	1.50	.45
40 George Bell	.10	.03
41 Carlton Fisk	.50	.15
42 Bobby Bonilla	.10	.03
43 Randy Milligan	.05	.02
44 Dave Parker	.10	.03
45 Shawon Dunston	.05	.02
46 Brian Harper	.05	.02
47 John Tudor	.05	.02
48 Ellis Burks	.10	.03
49 Bob Welch	.05	.02
50 Roger Clemens	1.00	.30
51 Mike Henneman	.05	.02
52 Eddie Murray	.40	.12
53 Kal Daniels	.05	.02
54 Doug Jones	.05	.02
55 Craig Biggio	.15	.04
56 Rafael Palmeiro	.20	.06
57 Wally Joyner	.10	.03
58 Tim Wallach	.05	.02
59 Bret Saberhagen	.10	.03
60 Ryne Sandberg	.75	.23
61 Benito Santiago	.10	.03
62 Darryl Strawberry	.10	.03
63 Alan Trammell	.15	.04
64 Kelly Gruber	.05	.02
65 Dwight Gooden	.10	.03
66 Dave Winfield	.50	.15
67 Rick Aguilera	.10	.03
68 Dave Righetti	.05	.02
69 Jim Abbott	.10	.03
70 Frank Viola	.05	.02
71 Fred McGriff	.15	.04
72 Steve Sax	.05	.02
73 Dennis Eckersley	.40	.12
74 Cory Snyder	.05	.02
75 Mackey Sasser	.05	.02
76 Candy Maldonado	.05	.02
77 Matt Williams	.15	.04
78 Kent Hrbek	.10	.03
79 Randy Myers	.10	.03
80 Gregg Jefferies	.05	.02
81 Joe Carter	.10	.03
82 Mike Greenwell	.05	.02
83 Jack Armstrong	.05	.02
84 Julio Franco	.10	.03
85 George Brett	.75	.23
86 Howard Johnson	.05	.02
87 Andre Dawson	.20	.06
88 Cecil Fielder	.10	.03
89 Tim Raines	.10	.03
90 Chuck Finley	.10	.03
91 Mark Grace	.20	.06
92 Brook Jacoby	.05	.02
93 Dave Stieb	.05	.02
94 Tony Gwynn	1.00	.30
95 Bobby Thigpen	.05	.02
96 Roberto Kelly	.05	.02
97 Kevin Seitzer	.05	.02
98 Kevin Mitchell	.05	.02
99 Dwight Evans	.10	.03
100 Roberto Alomar	.20	.06

1991 Score Rookies

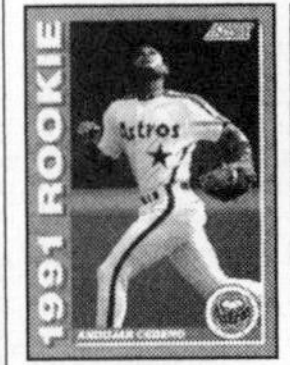

This 40-card standard-sized set was distributed with five magic motion trivia cards. The fronts feature high glossy color action player photos, on a blue card face with meandering green lines.

	Nm-Mt	Ex-Mt
COMP.FACT SET (40)	4.00	1.20
1 Mel Rojas	.05	.02
2 Ray Lankford	.30	.09
3 Scott Aldred	.05	.02
4 Turner Ward	.05	.02
5 Omar Olivares	.05	.02
6 Mo Vaughn	1.50	.45
7 Phil Clark	.05	.02
8 Brent Mayne	.05	.02
9 Scott Lewis	.05	.02
10 Brian Barnes	.05	.02
11 Bernard Gilkey	.05	.02
12 Steve Decker	.05	.02
13 Paul Marak	.05	.02
14 Wes Chamberlain	.05	.02
15 Kevin Belcher	.05	.02
16 Steve Adkins	.05	.02
17 Geronimo Pena	.05	.02
18 Mark Leonard	.05	.02
19 Jeff Conine	.10	.03
20 Leo Gomez	.05	.02
21 Chuck Malone	.05	.02
22 Beau Allred	.05	.02
23 Todd Hundley	.30	.09
24 Lance Dickson	.05	.02
25 Mike Benjamin	.05	.02
26 Jose Offerman	.05	.02
27 Terry Shumpert	.05	.02
28 Darren Lewis	.05	.02
29 Scott Chiamparino	.05	.02
30 Tim Naehring	.05	.02
31 David Segui	.10	.03
32 Karl Rhodes	.05	.02
33 Mickey Morandini	.05	.02
34 Chuck McElroy	.05	.02
35 Tim McIntosh	.05	.02
36 Derrick May	.05	.02
37 Rich DeLucia	.05	.02
38 Tino Martinez	1.00	.30
39 Hensley Meulens	.05	.02
40 Andujar Cedeno	.05	.02

1991 Score Ryan Life and Times

This four-card standard-size set was manufactured by Score to commemorate four significant milestones in Nolan Ryan's illustrious career beginning with his years growing up in Alvin, Texas, his years with the Mets and Angels, with the Astros and Rangers, and his career statistics. Each card commemorates a career milestone (all occur with the Rangers) and features Ryan's color photo on the front. They are part of "The Life and Times of Nolan Ryan," by Tarrant Printing, a special collector set that consists of four volumes (8 1/2" by 11" booklets) along with the cards packaged in a folder.

	Nm-Mt	Ex-Mt
COMPLETE SET (4)	20.00	6.00
COMMON CARD (1-4)	5.00	1.50

1992 Score Samples

The 1992 Score Preview set contains six standard-size cards done in the same style as the 1992 Score baseball cards. Supposedly the Sandberg and Mack cards are tougher as they were only available at the St. Louis card show that Score attended in November 1991.

	Nm-Mt	Ex-Mt
COMPLETE SET (6)	20.00	6.00
COMMON CARD (1-6)	.50	.15
COMMON SP	1.00	.30
1 Ken Griffey Jr.	8.00	2.40
2 Dave Justice	2.00	.60
3 Robin Ventura	2.00	.60
4 Steve Avery	.50	.15
5 Ryne Sandberg SP	8.00	2.40
6 Shane Mack SP	1.00	.30

1992 Score

The 1992 Score set marked the second year that Score released their set in two different series. The first series contains 442 cards while the second series contains 451 cards. Cards were distributed in plastic wrapped packs, blister packs, jumbo packs and factory sets. Each pack included a special "World Series II" trivia card. Topical subsets include Rookie Prospects (395-424/736-772/814-877), No-Hit Club (425-428/784-787), Highlights (429-430), AL All-Stars (431-440; with color montages displaying Chris Greco's player caricatures), Dream Team (441-442/883-893), NL All-Stars (773-782), Highlights (783, 795-797), Draft Picks (799-810), and Memorabilia (878-882). All of the Rookie Prospects (736-772) can be found with or without the Rookie Prospect stripe. Rookie Cards in the set include Vinny Castilla and Manny Ramirez. Chuck Knoblauch, 1991 American League Rookie of the Year, autographed 3,000 of his own 1990 Score Draft Pick cards (card number 672) in gold ink, 2,989 were randomly inserted in Series two poly packs, while the other 11 were given away in a sweepstakes. The backs of these Knoblauch autograph cards have special holograms to differentiate them.

	Nm-Mt	Ex-Mt
COMPLETE SET (893)	15.00	4.50
COMP.FACT.SET (910)	20.00	6.00
COMP. SERIES 1 (442)	8.00	2.40
COMP. SERIES 2 (451)	8.00	2.40
1 Ken Griffey Jr.	.40	.12
2 Nolan Ryan	1.00	.30
3 Will Clark	.25	.07
4 Dave Justice	.10	.03
5 Dave Henderson	.05	.02
6 Bret Saberhagen	.10	.03
7 Fred McGriff	.15	.04
8 Erik Hanson	.05	.02
9 Darryl Strawberry	.15	.04
10 Dwight Gooden	.15	.04
11 Juan Gonzalez	.25	.07
12 Mark Langston	.05	.02
13 Lonnie Smith	.05	.02
14 Jeff Montgomery	.05	.02
15 Roberto Alomar	.25	.07
16 Delino DeShields	.05	.02
17 Steve Bedrosian	.05	.02
18 Terry Pendleton	.10	.03
19 Mark Carreon	.05	.02
20 Mark McGwire	.60	.18
21 Roger Clemens	.50	.15
22 Chuck Crim	.05	.02
23 Don Mattingly	.60	.18
24 Dickie Thon	.05	.02
25 Ron Gant	.10	.03
26 Milt Cuyler	.05	.02
27 Mike Macfarlane	.05	.02
28 Dan Gladden	.05	.02
29 Melido Perez	.05	.02
30 Willie Randolph	.10	.03
31 Albert Belle	.10	.03
32 Dave Winfield	.10	.03
33 Jimmy Jones	.05	.02
34 Kevin Gross	.05	.02
35 Andres Galarraga	.10	.03
36 Mike Devereaux	.05	.02
37 Chris Bosio	.05	.02
38 Mike LaValliere	.05	.02
39 Gary Gaetti	.10	.03
40 Felix Jose	.05	.02
41 Alvaro Espinoza	.05	.02
42 Rick Aguilera	.10	.03
43 Mike Gallego	.05	.02
44 Eric Davis	.10	.03
45 George Bell	.05	.02
46 Tom Brunansky	.05	.02
47 Steve Farr	.05	.02
48 Duane Ward	.05	.02
49 David Wells	.10	.03
50 Cecil Fielder	.10	.03
51 Walt Weiss	.05	.02
52 Todd Zeile	.05	.02
53 Doug Jones	.05	.02
54 Bob Walk	.05	.02
55 Rafael Palmeiro	.15	.04
56 Rob Deer	.05	.02
57 Paul O'Neill	.15	.04
58 Jeff Reardon	.10	.03
59 Randy Ready	.05	.02
60 Scott Erickson	.05	.02
61 Paul Molitor	.15	.04
62 Jack McDowell	.05	.02
63 Jim Acker	.05	.02
64 Jay Buhner	.10	.03
65 Travis Fryman	.10	.03
66 Marquis Grissom	.05	.02
67 Mike Harkey	.05	.02
68 Luis Polonia	.05	.02
69 Ken Caminiti	.10	.03
70 Chris Sabo	.05	.02
71 Gregg Olson	.05	.02
72 Carlton Fisk	.15	.04
73 Juan Samuel	.05	.02
74 Todd Stottlemyre	.05	.02
75 Andre Dawson	.10	.03
76 Alvin Davis	.05	.02
77 Bill Doran	.05	.02
78 B.J. Surhoff	.10	.03
79 Kirk McCaskill	.05	.02
80 Dale Murphy	.25	.07
81 Jose DeLeon	.05	.02
82 Alex Fernandez	.05	.02
83 Ivan Calderon	.05	.02
84 Brent Mayne	.05	.02
85 Jody Reed	.05	.02
86 Randy Tomlin	.05	.02
87 Randy Milligan	.05	.02
88 Pascual Perez	.05	.02
89 Hensley Meulens	.05	.02
90 Joe Carter	.10	.03
91 Mike Moore	.05	.02
92 Ozzie Guillen	.05	.02
93 Shawn Hillegas	.05	.02
94 Chili Davis	.10	.03
95 Vince Coleman	.05	.02
96 Jimmy Key	.10	.03
97 Billy Ripken	.05	.02
98 Dave Smith	.05	.02
99 Tom Bolton	.05	.02
100 Barry Larkin	.25	.07
101 Kenny Rogers	.10	.03
102 Mike Boddicker	.05	.02
103 Kevin Elster	.05	.02
104 Ken Hill	.05	.02
105 Charlie Leibrandt	.05	.02
106 Pat Combs	.05	.02
107 Hubie Brooks	.05	.02
108 Julio Franco	.10	.03
109 Vicente Palacios	.05	.02
110 Kal Daniels	.05	.02
111 Bruce Hurst	.05	.02
112 Willie McGee	.10	.03
113 Ted Power	.05	.02
114 Milt Thompson	.05	.02
115 Doug Drabek	.05	.02
116 Rafael Belliard	.05	.02
117 Scott Garrelts	.05	.02
118 Terry Mulholland	.05	.02
119 Jay Howell	.05	.02
120 Danny Jackson	.05	.02
121 Scott Ruskin	.05	.02
122 Robin Ventura	.10	.03
123 Bip Roberts	.05	.02
124 Jeff Russell	.05	.02
125 Hal Morris	.05	.02
126 Teddy Higuera	.05	.02
127 Luis Sojo	.05	.02
128 Carlos Baerga	.05	.02
129 Jeff Ballard	.05	.02
130 Tom Gordon	.05	.02
131 Sid Bream	.05	.02
132 Rance Mulliniks	.05	.02
133 Andy Benes	.05	.02
134 Mickey Tettleton	.05	.02
135 Rich DeLucia	.05	.02
136 Tom Pagnozzi	.05	.02
137 Harold Baines	.10	.03
138 Danny Darwin	.05	.02
139 Kevin Bass	.05	.02
140 Chris Nabholz	.05	.02
141 Pete O'Brien	.05	.02
142 Jeff Treadway	.05	.02
143 Mickey Morandini	.05	.02
144 Eric King	.05	.02
145 Danny Tartabull	.05	.02
146 Lance Johnson	.05	.02
147 Casey Candaele	.05	.02
148 Felix Fermin	.05	.02
149 Rich Rodriguez	.05	.02
150 Dwight Evans	.10	.03
151 Joe Klink	.05	.02
152 Kevin Reimer	.05	.02
153 Orlando Merced	.05	.02
154 Mel Hall	.05	.02
155 Randy Myers	.05	.02
156 Greg A. Harris	.05	.02
157 Jeff Brantley	.05	.02
158 Jim Eisenreich	.05	.02
159 Luis Rivera	.05	.02
160 Cris Carpenter	.05	.02
161 Bruce Ruffin	.05	.02
162 Omar Vizquel	.10	.03
163 Gerald Alexander	.05	.02
164 Mark Guthrie	.05	.02
165 Scott Lewis	.05	.02
166 Bill Sampen	.05	.02
167 Dave Anderson	.05	.02
168 Kevin McReynolds	.05	.02
169 Jose Vizcaino	.05	.02
170 Bob Geren	.05	.02
171 Mike Morgan	.05	.02
172 Jim Gott	.05	.02
173 Mike Pagliarulo	.05	.02
174 Mike Jeffcoat	.05	.02
175 Craig Lefferts	.05	.02
176 Steve Finley	.10	.03
177 Wally Backman	.05	.02
178 Kent Mercker	.05	.02
179 John Cerutti	.05	.02
180 Jay Bell	.10	.03
181 Dale Sveum	.05	.02
182 Greg Gagne	.05	.02
183 Donnie Hill	.05	.02
184 Rex Hudler	.05	.02
185 Pat Kelly	.05	.02
186 Jeff D. Robinson	.05	.02
187 Jeff Gray	.05	.02
188 Jerry Willard	.05	.02
189 Carlos Quintana	.05	.02
190 Dennis Eckersley	.10	.03
191 Kelly Downs	.05	.02
192 Gregg Jefferies	.05	.02
193 Darrin Fletcher	.05	.02
194 Mike Jackson	.05	.02
195 Eddie Murray	.25	.07
196 Bill Landrum	.05	.02
197 Eric Yelding	.05	.02
198 Devon White	.05	.02
199 Larry Walker	.15	.04
200 Ryne Sandberg	.40	.12
201 Dave Magadan	.05	.02
202 Steve Chitren	.05	.02
203 Scott Fletcher	.05	.02
204 Dwayne Henry	.05	.02
205 Scott Coolbaugh	.05	.02
206 Tracy Jones	.05	.02
207 Von Hayes	.05	.02
208 Bob Melvin	.05	.02
209 Scott Scudder	.05	.02
210 Luis Gonzalez	.15	.04
211 Scott Sanderson	.05	.02
212 Chris Donnels	.05	.02
213 Heathcliff Slocumb	.05	.02
214 Mike Timlin	.05	.02
215 Brian Harper	.05	.02
216 Juan Berenguer UER (Decimal point missing in IP total)	.05	.02
217 Mike Henneman	.05	.02
218 Bill Spiers	.05	.02
219 Scott Terry	.05	.02
220 Frank Viola	.10	.03
221 Mark Eichhorn	.05	.02
222 Ernest Riles	.05	.02
223 Ray Lankford	.05	.02
224 Pete Harnisch	.05	.02
225 Bobby Bonilla	.10	.03
226 Mike Scioscia	.05	.02
227 Joel Skinner	.05	.02
228 Brian Holman	.05	.02
229 Gilberto Reyes	.05	.02
230 Matt Williams	.10	.03
231 Jaime Navarro	.05	.02
232 Jose Rijo	.05	.02
233 Atlee Hammaker	.05	.02
234 Tim Teufel	.05	.02
235 John Kruk	.10	.03
236 Kurt Stillwell	.05	.02
237 Dan Pasqua	.05	.02
238 Tim Crews	.05	.02
239 Dave Gallagher	.05	.02
240 Leo Gomez	.05	.02
241 Steve Avery	.05	.02
242 Bill Gullickson	.05	.02
243 Mark Portugal	.05	.02
244 Lee Guetterman	.05	.02
245 Benito Santiago	.10	.03
246 Jim Gantner	.05	.02
247 Robby Thompson	.05	.02
248 Terry Shumpert	.05	.02
249 Mike Bell	.05	.02
250 Harold Reynolds	.10	.03
251 Mike Felder	.05	.02
252 Bill Pecota	.05	.02
253 Bill Krueger	.05	.02
254 Alfredo Griffin	.05	.02
255 Lou Whitaker	.10	.03
256 Roy Smith	.05	.02
257 Jerald Clark	.05	.02
258 Sammy Sosa	.40	.12
259 Tim Naehring	.05	.02
260 Dave Righetti	.10	.03
261 Paul Gibson	.05	.02
262 Chris James	.05	.02
263 Larry Andersen	.05	.02
264 Storm Davis	.05	.02
265 Jose Lind	.05	.02
266 Greg Hibbard	.05	.02
267 Norm Charlton	.05	.02
268 Paul Kilgus	.05	.02
269 Greg Maddux	.40	.12
270 Ellis Burks	.10	.03
271 Frank Tanana	.05	.02
272 Gene Larkin	.05	.02
273 Ron Hassey	.05	.02
274 Jeff M. Robinson	.05	.02
275 Steve Howe	.05	.02
276 Daryl Boston	.05	.02
277 Mark Lee	.05	.02
278 Jose Segura	.05	.02
279 Lance Blankenship	.05	.02
280 Don Slaught	.05	.02
281 Russ Swan	.05	.02
282 Bob Tewksbury	.05	.02
283 Geno Petralli	.05	.02
284 Shane Mack	.05	.02
285 Bob Scanlan	.05	.02
286 Tim Leary	.05	.02
287 John Smoltz	.15	.04
288 Pat Borders	.05	.02
289 Mark Davidson	.05	.02

290 Sam Horn .05 .02
291 Lenny Harris .05 .02
292 Franklin Stubbs .05 .02
293 Thomas Howard .05 .02
294 Steve Lyons .05 .02
295 Francisco Oliveras .05 .02
296 Terry Leach .05 .02
297 Barry Jones .05 .02
298 Lance Parrish .10 .03
299 Wally Whitehurst .05 .02
300 Bob Welch .05 .02
301 Charlie Hayes .05 .02
302 Charlie Hough .10 .03
303 Gary Redus .05 .02
304 Scott Bradley .05 .02
305 Jose Oquendo .05 .02
306 Pete Incaviglia .05 .02
307 Marvin Freeman .05 .02
308 Gary Pettis .05 .02
309 Joe Slusarski .05 .02
310 Kevin Seitzer .05 .02
311 Jeff Reed .05 .02
312 Pat Tabler .05 .02
313 Mike Maddux .05 .02
314 Bob Milacki .05 .02
315 Eric Anthony .05 .02
316 Dante Bichette .10 .03
317 Steve Decker .05 .02
318 Jack Clark .10 .03
319 Doug Dascenzo .05 .02
320 Scott Leius .05 .02
321 Jim Lindeman .05 .02
322 Bryan Harvey .05 .02
323 Spike Owen .05 .02
324 Roberto Kelly .05 .02
325 Stan Belinda .05 .02
326 Joey Cora .05 .02
327 Jeff Innis .05 .02
328 Willie Wilson .05 .02
329 Juan Agosto .05 .02
330 Charles Nagy .05 .02
331 Scott Bailes .05 .02
332 Pete Schourek .05 .02
333 Mike Flanagan .05 .02
334 Omar Olivares .05 .02
335 Dennis Lamp .05 .02
336 Tommy Greene .05 .02
337 Randy Velarde .05 .02
338 Tom Lampkin .05 .02
339 John Russell .05 .02
340 Bob Kipper .05 .02
341 Todd Burns .05 .02
342 Ron Jones .05 .02
343 Dave Valle .05 .02
344 Mike Heath .05 .02
345 John Olerud .10 .03
346 Gerald Young .05 .02
347 Ken Patterson .05 .02
348 Les Lancaster .05 .02
349 Steve Crawford .05 .02
350 John Candelaria .05 .02
351 Mike Aldrete .05 .02
352 Mariano Duncan .05 .02
353 Julio Machado .05 .02
354 Ken Williams .05 .02
355 Walt Terrell .05 .02
356 Mitch Williams .05 .02
357 Al Newman .05 .02
358 Bud Black .05 .02
359 Joe Hesketh .05 .02
360 Paul Assenmacher .05 .02
361 Bo Jackson .25 .07
362 Jeff Blauser .05 .02
363 Mike Brumley .05 .02
364 Jim Deshaies .05 .02
365 Brady Anderson .10 .03
366 Chuck McElroy .05 .02
367 Matt Merullo .05 .02
368 Tim Belcher .05 .02
369 Luis Aquino .05 .02
370 Joe Oliver .05 .02
371 Greg Swindell .05 .02
372 Lee Stevens .05 .02
373 Mark Knudson .05 .02
374 Bill Wegman .05 .02
375 Jerry Don Gleaton .05 .02
376 Pedro Guerrero .10 .03
377 Randy Bush .05 .02
378 Greg W. Harris .05 .02
379 Eric Plunk .05 .02
380 Jose DeJesus .05 .02
381 Bobby Witt .05 .02
382 Curtis Wilkerson .05 .02
383 Gene Nelson .05 .02
384 Wes Chamberlain .05 .02
385 Tom Henke .05 .02
386 Mark Lemke .05 .02
387 Greg Briley .05 .02
388 Rafael Ramirez .05 .02
389 Tony Fossas .05 .02
390 Henry Cotto .05 .02
391 Tim Hulett .05 .02
392 Dean Palmer .10 .03
393 Glenn Braggs .05 .02
394 Mark Salas .05 .02
395 Rusty Meacham .05 .02
396 Andy Ashby .05 .02
397 Jose Melendez .05 .02
398 Warren Newson .05 .02
399 Frank Castillo .05 .02
400 Chito Martinez .05 .02
401 Bernie Williams .15 .04
402 Derek Bell .10 .03
403 Javier Ortiz .05 .02
404 Tim Sherrill .05 .02
405 Rob MacDonald .05 .02
406 Phil Plantier .05 .02
407 Troy Afenir .05 .02
408 Gino Minutelli .05 .02
409 Reggie Jefferson .05 .02
410 Mike Remlinger .05 .02
411 Carlos Rodriguez .05 .02
412 Joe Redfield .05 .02
413 Alonzo Powell .05 .02
414 S.Livingstone UER .05 .02
(Travis Fryman, not Woodie, should be referenced on back)
415 Scott Kamieniecki .05 .02
416 Tim Spehr .05 .02
417 Brian Hunter .05 .02
418 Ced Landrum .05 .02
419 Bret Barberie .05 .02
420 Kevin Morton .05 .02
421 Doug Henry RC .10 .03
422 Doug Piatt .05 .02
423 Pat Rice .05 .02
424 Juan Guzman .05 .02
425 Nolan Ryan NH .50 .15
426 Tommy Greene NH .05 .02
427 Bob Milacki and .05 .02
Mike Flanagan NH
(Mark Williamson and Gregg Olson)
428 Wilson Alvarez NH .05 .02
429 Otis Nixon HL .05 .02
430 Rickey Henderson HL .15 .04
431 Cecil Fielder AS .05 .02
432 Julio Franco AS .05 .02
433 Cal Ripken AS .40 .12
434 Wade Boggs AS .10 .03
435 Joe Carter AS .05 .02
436 Ken Griffey Jr. AS .25 .07
437 Ruben Sierra AS .05 .02
438 Scott Erickson AS .05 .02
439 Tom Henke AS .05 .02
440 Terry Steinbach AS .05 .02
441 Rickey Henderson DT .25 .07
442 Ryne Sandberg DT .40 .12
443 Otis Nixon .05 .02
444 Scott Radinsky .05 .02
445 Mark Grace .15 .04
446 Tony Pena .05 .02
447 Billy Hatcher .05 .02
448 Glenallen Hill .05 .02
449 Chris Gwynn .05 .02
450 Tom Glavine .15 .04
451 John Habyan .05 .02
452 Al Osuna .05 .02
453 Tony Phillips .05 .02
454 Greg Cadaret .05 .02
455 Rob Dibble .10 .03
456 Rick Honeycutt .05 .02
457 Jerome Walton .05 .02
458 Mookie Wilson .10 .03
459 Mark Gubicza .05 .02
460 Craig Biggio .15 .04
461 Dave Cochrane .05 .02
462 Keith Miller .05 .02
463 Alex Cole .05 .02
464 Pete Smith .05 .02
465 Brett Butler .10 .03
466 Jeff Huson .05 .02
467 Steve Lake .05 .02
468 Lloyd Moseby .05 .02
469 Tim McIntosh .05 .02
470 Dennis Martinez .10 .03
471 Greg Myers .05 .02
472 Mackey Sasser .05 .02
473 Junior Ortiz .05 .02
474 Greg Olson .05 .02
475 Steve Sax .05 .02
476 Ricky Jordan .05 .02
477 Max Venable .05 .02
478 Brian McRae .05 .02
479 Doug Simons .05 .02
480 Rickey Henderson .25 .07
481 Gary Varsho .05 .02
482 Carl Willis .05 .02
483 Rick Wilkins .05 .02
484 Donn Pall .05 .02
485 Edgar Martinez .15 .04
486 Tom Foley .05 .02
487 Mark Williamson .05 .02
488 Jack Armstrong .05 .02
489 Gary Carter .15 .04
490 Ruben Sierra .05 .02
491 Gerald Perry .05 .02
492 Rob Murphy .05 .02
493 Zane Smith .05 .02
494 Darryl Kile .10 .03
495 Kelly Gruber .05 .02
496 Jerry Browne .05 .02
497 Darryl Hamilton .05 .02
498 Mike Stanton .05 .02
499 Mark Leonard .05 .02
500 Jose Canseco .25 .07
501 Dave Martinez .05 .02
502 Jose Guzman .05 .02
503 Terry Kennedy .05 .02
504 Ed Sprague .10 .03
505 Frank Thomas UER .25 .07
(His Gulf Coast League stats are wrong)
506 Darren Daulton .10 .03
507 Kevin Tapani .05 .02
508 Luis Salazar .05 .02
509 Paul Faries .05 .02
510 Sandy Alomar Jr. .05 .02
511 Jeff King .05 .02
512 Gary Thurman .05 .02
513 Chris Hammond .05 .02
514 Pedro Munoz .05 .02
515 Alan Trammell .15 .04
516 Geronimo Pena .05 .02
517 Rodney McCray UER .05 .02
Stole 6 bases in 1990, not 5; career totals are correct at 7
518 Manny Lee .05 .02
519 Junior Felix .05 .02
520 Kirk Gibson .10 .03
521 Darrin Jackson .05 .02
522 John Burkett .05 .02
523 Jeff Johnson .05 .02
524 Jim Corsi .05 .02
525 Robin Yount .40 .12
526 Jamie Quirk .05 .02
527 Bob Ojeda .05 .02
528 Mark Lewis .05 .02
529 Bryn Smith .05 .02
530 Kent Hrbek .10 .03
531 Dennis Boyd .05 .02
532 Ron Karkovice .05 .02
533 Don August .05 .02
534 Todd Frohwirth .05 .02
535 Wally Joyner .10 .03
536 Dennis Rasmussen .05 .02
537 Andy Allanson .05 .02
538 Rich Gossage .10 .03
539 John Marzano .05 .02
540 Cal Ripken .75 .23
541 Bill Swift UER .05 .02
(Brewers logo on front)
542 Kevin Appier .10 .03
543 Dave Bergman .05 .02
544 Bernard Gilkey .05 .02
545 Mike Greenwell .05 .02
546 Jose Uribe .05 .02
547 Jesse Orosco .05 .02
548 Bob Patterson .05 .02
549 Mike Stanley .05 .02
550 Howard Johnson .05 .02
551 Joe Orsulak .05 .02
552 Dick Schofield .05 .02
553 Dave Hollins .05 .02
554 David Segui .05 .02
555 Barry Bonds .60 .18
556 Mo Vaughn .10 .03
557 Craig Wilson .05 .02
558 Bobby Rose .05 .02
559 Rod Nichols .05 .02
560 Len Dykstra .10 .03
561 Craig Grebeck .05 .02
562 Darren Lewis .05 .02
563 Todd Benzinger .05 .02
564 Ed Whitson .05 .02
565 Jesse Barfield .05 .02
566 Lloyd McClendon .05 .02
567 Dan Plesac .05 .02
568 Danny Cox .05 .02
569 Skeeter Barnes .05 .02
570 Bobby Thigpen .05 .02
571 Deion Sanders .15 .04
572 Chuck Knoblauch .10 .03
573 Matt Nokes .05 .02
574 Herm Winningham .05 .02
575 Tom Candiotti .05 .02
576 Jeff Bagwell .25 .07
577 Brook Jacoby .05 .02
578 Chico Walker .05 .02
579 Brian Downing .05 .02
580 Dave Stewart .10 .03
581 Francisco Cabrera .05 .02
582 Rene Gonzales .05 .02
583 Stan Javier .05 .02
584 Randy Johnson .25 .07
585 Chuck Finley .10 .03
586 Mark Gardner .05 .02
587 Mark Whiten .05 .02
588 Garry Templeton .05 .02
589 Gary Sheffield .10 .03
590 Ozzie Smith .40 .12
591 Candy Maldonado .05 .02
592 Mike Sharperson .05 .02
593 Carlos Martinez .05 .02
594 Scott Bankhead .05 .02
595 Tim Wallach .05 .02
596 Tino Martinez .15 .04
597 Roger McDowell .05 .02
598 Cory Snyder .05 .02
599 Andujar Cedeno .05 .02
600 Kirby Puckett .25 .07
601 Rick Parker .05 .02
602 Todd Hundley .05 .02
603 Greg Litton .05 .02
604 Dave Johnson .05 .02
605 John Franco .10 .03
606 Mike Fetters .05 .02
607 Luis Alicea .05 .02
608 Trevor Wilson .05 .02
609 Rob Ducey .05 .02
610 Ramon Martinez .05 .02
611 Dave Burba .05 .02
612 Dwight Smith .05 .02
613 Kevin Maas .05 .02
614 John Costello .05 .02
615 Glenn Davis .05 .02
616 Shawn Abner .05 .02
617 Scott Hemond .05 .02
618 Tom Prince .05 .02
619 Wally Ritchie .05 .02
620 Jim Abbott .15 .04
621 Charlie O'Brien .05 .02
622 Jack Daugherty .05 .02
623 Tommy Gregg .05 .02
624 Jeff Shaw .05 .02
625 Tony Gwynn .30 .09
626 Mark Leiter .05 .02
627 Jim Clancy .05 .02
628 Tim Layana .05 .02
629 Jeff Schaefer .05 .02
630 Lee Smith .10 .03
631 Wade Taylor .05 .02
632 Mike Simms .05 .02
633 Terry Steinbach .05 .02
634 Shawon Dunston .05 .02
635 Tim Raines .10 .03
636 Kirt Manwaring .05 .02
637 Warren Cromartie .05 .02
638 Luis Quinones .05 .02
639 Greg Vaughn .10 .03
640 Kevin Mitchell .05 .02
641 Chris Hoiles .05 .02
642 Tom Browning .05 .02
643 Mitch Webster .05 .02
644 Steve Olin .05 .02
645 Tony Fernandez .05 .02
646 Juan Bell .05 .02
647 Joe Boever .05 .02
648 Carney Lansford .10 .03
649 Mike Benjamin .05 .02
650 George Brett .60 .18
651 Tim Burke .05 .02
652 Jack Morris .10 .03
653 Orel Hershiser .10 .03
654 Mike Schooler .05 .02
655 Andy Van Slyke .10 .03
656 Dave Stieb .05 .02
657 Dave Clark .05 .02
658 Ben McDonald .05 .02
659 John Smiley .05 .02
660 Wade Boggs .15 .04
661 Eric Bullock .05 .02
662 Eric Show .05 .02
663 Lenny Webster .05 .02
664 Mike Huff .05 .02
665 Rick Sutcliffe .10 .03
666 Jeff Manto .05 .02
667 Mike Fitzgerald .05 .02
668 Matt Young .05 .02
669 Dave West .05 .02
670 Mike Hartley .05 .02
671 Curt Schilling .15 .04
672 Brian Bohanon .05 .02
673 Cecil Espy .05 .02
674 Joe Grahe .05 .02
675 Sid Fernandez .05 .02
676 Edwin Nunez .05 .02
677 Hector Villanueva .05 .02
678 Sean Berry .05 .02
679 Dave Eiland .05 .02
680 David Cone .10 .03
681 Mike Bordick .05 .02
682 Tony Castillo .05 .02
683 John Barfield .05 .02
684 Jeff Hamilton .05 .02
685 Ken Dayley .05 .02
686 Carmelo Martinez .05 .02
687 Mike Capel .05 .02
688 Scott Chiamparino .05 .02
689 Rich Gedman .05 .02
690 Rich Monteleone .05 .02
691 Alejandro Pena .05 .02
692 Oscar Azocar .05 .02
693 Jim Poole .05 .02
694 Mike Gardiner .05 .02
695 Steve Buechele .05 .02
696 Rudy Seanez .05 .02
697 Paul Abbott .05 .02
698 Steve Searcy .05 .02
699 Jose Offerman .05 .02
700 Ivan Rodriguez .25 .07
701 Joe Girardi .05 .02
702 Tony Perezchica .05 .02
703 Paul McClellan .05 .02
704 David Howard .05 .02
705 Dan Petry .05 .02
706 Jack Howell .05 .02
707 Jose Mesa .05 .02
708 Randy St. Claire .05 .02
709 Kevin Brown .10 .03
710 Ron Darling .05 .02
711 Jason Grimsley .05 .02
712 John Orton .05 .02
713 Shawn Boskie .05 .02
714 Pat Clements .05 .02
715 Brian Barnes .05 .02
716 Luis Lopez .05 .02
717 Bob McClure .05 .02
718 Mark Davis .05 .02
719 Dann Bilardello .05 .02
720 Tom Edens .05 .02
721 Willie Fraser .05 .02
722 Curt Young .05 .02
723 Neal Heaton .05 .02
724 Craig Worthington .05 .02
725 Mel Rojas .05 .02
726 Daryl Irvine .05 .02
727 Roger Mason .05 .02
728 Kirk Dressendorfer .05 .02
729 Scott Aldred .05 .02
730 Willie Blair .05 .02
731 Allan Anderson .05 .02
732 Dana Kiecker .05 .02
733 Jose Gonzalez .05 .02
734 Brian Drahman .05 .02
735 Brad Komminsk .05 .02
736 Arthur Rhodes .05 .02
737 Terry Mathews .05 .02
738 Jeff Fassero .05 .02
739 Mike Magnante RC .10 .03
740 Kip Gross .05 .02
741 Jim Hunter .05 .02
742 Jose Mota .05 .02
743 Joe Bitker .05 .02
744 Tim Mauser .05 .02
745 Ramon Garcia .05 .02
746 Rod Beck RC .25 .07
747 Jim Austin RC .05 .02
748 Keith Mitchell .05 .02
749 Wayne Rosenthal .05 .02
750 Bryan Hickerson RC .10 .03
751 Bruce Egloff .05 .02
752 John Wehner .05 .02
753 Darren Holmes .05 .02
754 Dave Hansen .05 .02
755 Mike Mussina .25 .07
756 Anthony Young .05 .02
757 Ron Tingley .05 .02
758 Ricky Bones .05 .02
759 Mark Wohlers .05 .02
760 Wilson Alvarez .05 .02
761 Harvey Pulliam .05 .02
762 Ryan Bowen .05 .02
763 Terry Bross .05 .02
764 Joel Johnston .05 .02
765 Terry McDaniel .05 .02
766 Esteban Beltre .05 .02
767 Rob Maurer .05 .02
768 Ted Wood .05 .02
769 Mo Sanford .05 .02
770 Jeff Carter .05 .02
771 Gil Heredia RC .25 .07
772 Monty Fariss .05 .02
773 Will Clark AS .10 .03
774 Ryne Sandberg AS .25 .07
775 Barry Larkin AS .10 .03
776 Howard Johnson AS .05 .02
777 Barry Bonds AS .30 .09
778 Brett Butler AS .05 .02
779 Tony Gwynn AS .10 .03
780 Ramon Martinez AS .05 .02
781 Lee Smith AS .05 .02
782 Mike Scioscia AS .05 .02
783 D.Martinez HL UER .05 .02
Card has both 13th and 15th perfect game in Major League history
784 Dennis Martinez NH .05 .02
785 Mark Gardner NH .05 .02
786 Bret Saberhagen NH .05 .02
787 Kent Mercker NH .05 .02
Mark Wohlers
Alejandro Pena
788 Cal Ripken MVP .40 .12
789 Terry Pendleton MVP .05 .02
790 Roger Clemens CY .25 .07
791 Tom Glavine CY .10 .03
792 C.Knoblauch ROY .05 .02
793 Jeff Bagwell ROY .15 .04
794 Cal Ripken MANYR .40 .12
795 David Cone HL .05 .02
796 Kirby Puckett HL .15 .04
797 Steve Avery HL .05 .02
798 Jack Morris HL .05 .02
799 Allen Watson DC RC .10 .03
800 M.Ramirez DC RC 1.50 .45
801 Cliff Floyd DC RC .75 .23
802 Al Shirley DC RC .10 .03
803 Brian Barber DC RC .10 .03
804 Jon Farrell DC RC .10 .03
805 Brent Gates DC RC .10 .03
806 Scott Ruffcorn DC RC .10 .03
807 Tyrone Hill DC RC .10 .03
808 Benji Gil DC RC .25 .07
809 Aaron Sele DC RC .40 .12
810 Tyler Green DC RC .10 .03
811 Chris Jones .05 .02
812 Steve Wilson .05 .02
813 Freddie Benavides .05 .02
814 Don Wakamatsu .05 .02
815 Mike Humphreys .05 .02
816 Scott Servais .05 .02
817 Rico Rossy .05 .02
818 John Ramos .05 .02
819 Rob Mallicoat .05 .02
820 Milt Hill .05 .02
821 Carlos Garcia .05 .02
822 Stan Royer .05 .02
823 Jeff Plympton .05 .02
824 Braulio Castillo .05 .02
825 David Haas .05 .02
826 Luis Mercedes .05 .02
827 Eric Karros .10 .03
828 Shawn Hare RC .10 .03
829 Reggie Sanders .10 .03
830 Tom Goodwin .05 .02
831 Dan Gakeler .05 .02
832 Stacy Jones .05 .02
833 Kim Batiste .05 .02
834 Cal Eldred .05 .02
835 Chris George .05 .02
836 Wayne Housie .05 .02
837 Mike Ignasiak .05 .02
838 Josias Manzanillo RC .10 .03
839 Jim Olander .05 .02
840 Gary Cooper .05 .02
841 Royce Clayton .05 .02
842 Hector Fajardo RC .10 .03
843 Blaine Beatty .05 .02
844 Jorge Pedre .05 .02
845 Kenny Lofton .25 .07
846 Scott Brosius RC .50 .15
847 Chris Cron .05 .02
848 Denis Boucher .05 .02
849 Kyle Abbott .05 .02
850 Bob Zupcic RC .10 .03
851 Rheal Cormier .05 .02
852 Jimmy Lewis RC .05 .02
853 Anthony Telford .05 .02
854 Cliff Brantley .05 .02
855 Kevin Campbell .05 .02
856 Craig Shipley .05 .02
857 Chuck Carr .05 .02
858 Tony Eusebio .10 .03
859 Jim Thome .25 .07
860 Vinny Castilla RC .50 .15
861 Dann Howitt .05 .02
862 Kevin Ward .05 .02
863 Steve Wapnick .05 .02
864 Rod Brewer RC .10 .03
865 Todd Van Poppel .05 .02
866 Jose Hernandez RC .40 .12
867 Amalio Carreno .05 .02
868 Calvin Jones .05 .02
869 Jeff Gardner .05 .02
870 Jarvis Brown .05 .02
871 Eddie Taubensee RC .25 .07
872 Andy Mota .05 .02
873 Chris Haney .05 .02
874 Roberto Hernandez .05 .02
875 Laddie Renfroe .05 .02
876 Scott Cooper .05 .02
877 Armando Reynoso RC .25 .07
878 Ty Cobb MEMO .25 .07
879 Babe Ruth MEMO .50 .15
880 Honus Wagner MEMO .25 .07
881 Lou Gehrig MEMO .40 .12
882 Satchel Paige MEMO .25 .07
883 Will Clark DT .10 .03
884 Cal Ripken DT 2.00 .60
885 Wade Boggs DT .10 .03
886 Kirby Puckett DT .15 .04
887 Tony Gwynn DT .15 .04
888 Craig Biggio DT .10 .03
889 Scott Erickson DT .05 .02
890 Tom Glavine DT .10 .03
891 Rob Dibble DT .10 .03
892 Mitch Williams DT .05 .02
893 Frank Thomas DT .15 .04
X672 Chuck Knoblauch AU 25.00 7.50
1990 Score card,
3000 copies signed

1992 Score DiMaggio

This five-card standard-size insert set was issued in honor of one of baseball's all-time greats, Joe DiMaggio. These cards were randomly inserted in first series packs. According to sources at Score, 30,000 of each card were produced. On a white card face, the fronts have vintage photos that have been colorized and accented by red, white, and blue border stripes. DiMaggio autographed 2,500 cards for this promotion. 2,495 of these cards were inserted in packs while the other five were used as prizes in a mail-in sweepstakes. The autographed cards are individually numbered out of 2,500.

Nm-Mt Ex-Mt
COMPLETE SET (5) 80.00 24.00

	Nm-Mt	Ex-Mt
COMMON CARD (1-5)	15.00	4.50
AU Joe DiMaggio AU (Autographed with certified signature)	400.00	120.00

1992 Score Factory Inserts

This 17-card insert standard-size set was distributed only in 1992 Score factory sets and consists of four topical subsets. Cards B1-B7 capture a moment from each game of the 1991 World Series. Cards B8-B11 are Cooperstown cards, honoring future Hall of Famers. Cards B12-B14 form a "Joe D" subset paying tribute to Joe DiMaggio. Cards B15-B17, subtitled "Yaz", conclude the set by commemorating Carl Yastrzemski's heroic feats twenty-five years ago in winning the Triple Crown and lifting the Red Sox to their first American League pennant in 21 years. Each subset displayed a different front design. The World Series cards carry full-bleed color action photos except for a blue stripe at the bottom, while the Cooperstown cards have a color portrait on a white card face. Both the DiMaggio and Yastrzemski subsets have action photos with silver borders; they differ in that the DiMaggio photos are black and white, the Yastrzemski photos color. The DiMaggio and Yastrzemski subsets are numbered on the back within each subset (e.g., "1 of 3") and as a part of the 17-card insert set (e.g., "B1"). In the DiMaggio and Yastrzemski subsets, Score varied the insert set slightly in retail versus hobby factory sets. In the hobby set, the DiMaggio cards display different black-and-white photos that are bordered beneath by a dark blue stripe (the stripe is green in the retail factory insert). On the backs, these hobby inserts have a red stripe at the bottom; the same stripe is dark blue on the retail inserts. The Yastrzemski cards in the hobby set have different color photos on their fronts than the retail inserts.

	Nm-Mt	Ex-Mt
COMPLETE SET (17)	6.00	1.80
B1 Greg Gagne WS	.40	.12
B2 Scott Leius WS	.40	.12
B3 Mark Lemke WS David Justice	.40	.12
B4 Lonnie Smith WS Brian Harper	.40	.12
B5 David Justice WS	.75	.23
B6 Kirby Puckett WS	2.00	.60
B7 Gene Larkin WS	.40	.12
B8 Carlton Fisk	1.25	.35
B9 Ozzie Smith	3.00	.90
B10 Dave Winfield	.75	.23
B11 Robin Yount	3.00	.90
B12 Joe DiMaggio The Hard Hitter	1.00	.30
B13 Joe DiMaggio The Stylish Fielder	1.00	.30
B14 Joe DiMaggio The Championship Player	1.00	.30
B15 Carl Yastrzemski The Impossible Dream	.50	.15
B16 Carl Yastrzemski The Triple Crown	.50	.15
B17 Carl Yastrzemski The World Series	.50	.15

1992 Score Franchise

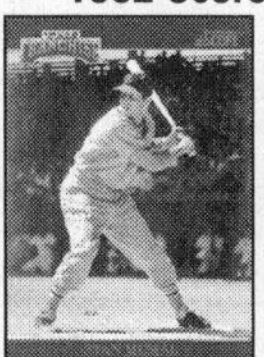

This four-card standard-size set features three all-time greats, Stan Musial, Mickey Mantle, and Carl Yastrzemski. Each former player autographed 2,000 of his 1992 Score cards, and 500 of the combo cards were signed by all three. In addition to these signed cards, Score produced 150,000 of each Franchise card, and both signed and unsigned cards were randomly inserted in 1992 Score Series II poly packs, blister packs, and cello packs.

	Nm-Mt	Ex-Mt
COMPLETE SET (4)	30.00	9.00
1 Stan Musial	5.00	1.50
2 Mickey Mantle	12.00	3.60
3 Carl Yastrzemski	5.00	1.50
4 The Franchise Players Stan Musial Mickey Mantle Carl Yastrzemski	10.00	3.00
AU1 Stan Musial (Autographed with certified signature)	80.00	24.00
AU2 Mickey Mantle (Autographed with certified signature)	500.00	150.00
AU3 Carl Yastrzemski (Autographed with certified signature)	80.00	24.00
AU4 Franchise Players Stan Musial Mickey Mantle Carl Yastrzemski (Autographed with certified signatures of all three)	800.00	240.00

1992 Score Hot Rookies

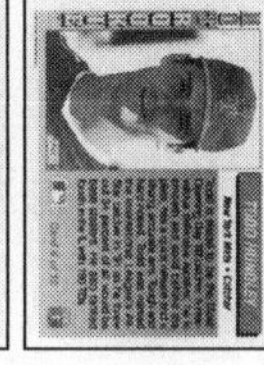

This ten-card standard-size set features color action player photos on a white face. These cards were inserted one per blister pack.

	Nm-Mt	Ex-Mt
COMPLETE SET (10)	8.00	2.40
1 Cal Eldred	.50	.15
2 Royce Clayton	.50	.15
3 Kenny Lofton	2.00	.60
4 Todd Van Poppel	.50	.15
5 Scott Cooper	.50	.15
6 Todd Hundley	.50	.15
7 Tino Martinez	2.00	.60
8 Anthony Telford	.50	.15
9 Derek Bell	.50	.15
10 Reggie Jefferson	.50	.15

1992 Score Impact Players

The 1992 Score Impact Players insert set was issued in two series each with 45 standard-size cards with the respective series of the 1992 regular issue Score cards. Five of these cards were inserted in each 1992 Score jumbo pack.

	Nm-Mt	Ex-Mt
COMPLETE SERIES 1 (45)	12.00	3.60
COMPLETE SERIES 2 (45)	6.00	1.80
1 Chuck Knoblauch	.30	.09
2 Jeff Bagwell	.75	.23
3 Juan Guzman	.15	.04
4 Milt Cuyler	.15	.04
5 Ivan Rodriguez	.75	.23
6 Rich DeLucia	.15	.04
7 Orlando Merced	.15	.04
8 Ray Lankford	.15	.04
9 Brian Hunter	.15	.04
10 Roberto Alomar	.75	.23
11 Wes Chamberlain	.15	.04
12 Steve Avery	.15	.04
13 Scott Erickson	.15	.04
14 Jim Abbott	.50	.15
15 Mark Whiten	.15	.04
16 Leo Gomez	.15	.04
17 Doug Henry	.30	.09
18 Brent Mayne	.15	.04
19 Charles Nagy	.15	.04
20 Phil Plantier	.15	.04
21 Mo Vaughn	.30	.09
22 Craig Biggio	.50	.15
23 Derek Bell	.30	.09
24 Royce Clayton	.15	.04
25 Gary Cooper	.15	.04
26 Scott Cooper	.15	.04
27 Juan Gonzalez	.75	.23
28 Ken Griffey Jr.	1.25	.35
29 Larry Walker	.50	.15
30 John Smoltz	.50	.15
31 Todd Hundley	.50	.15
32 Kenny Lofton	.75	.23
33 Andy Mota	.15	.04
34 Todd Zeile	.15	.04
35 Arthur Rhodes	.15	.04
36 Jim Thome	.75	.23
37 Todd Van Poppel	.15	.04
38 Mark Wohlers	.15	.04
39 Anthony Young	.15	.04
40 Sandy Alomar Jr.	.15	.04
41 John Olerud	.30	.09
42 Robin Ventura	.30	.09
43 Frank Thomas	.75	.23
44 Dave Justice	.30	.09
45 Hal Morris	.15	.04
46 Ruben Sierra	.15	.04
47 Travis Fryman	.30	.09
48 Mike Mussina	.75	.23
49 Tom Glavine	.50	.15
50 Barry Larkin	.75	.23
51 Will Clark UER Career Totals spelled To als	.75	.23
52 Jose Canseco	.75	.23
53 Bo Jackson	.30	.09
54 Dwight Gooden	.50	.15
55 Barry Bonds	2.00	.60
56 Fred McGriff	.50	.15
57 Roger Clemens	1.50	.45
58 Benito Santiago	.30	.09
59 Darryl Strawberry	.50	.15
60 Cecil Fielder	.30	.09
61 John Franco	.30	.09
62 Matt Williams	.30	.09
63 Marquis Grissom	.15	.04
64 Danny Tartabull	.15	.04
65 Ron Gant	.30	.09
66 Paul O'Neill	.50	.15
67 Devon White	.15	.04
68 Rafael Palmeiro	.50	.15
69 Tom Gordon	.15	.04
70 Shawon Dunston	.15	.04
71 Rob Dibble	.30	.09
72 Eddie Zosky	.15	.04
73 Jack McDowell	.15	.04
74 Len Dykstra	.30	.09
75 Ramon Martinez	.15	.04
76 Reggie Sanders	.30	.09
77 Greg Maddux	1.25	.35
78 Ellis Burks	.30	.09
79 John Smiley	.15	.04
80 Roberto Kelly	.15	.04
81 Ben McDonald	.15	.04
82 Mark Lewis	.15	.04
83 Jose Rijo	.15	.04
84 Ozzie Guillen	.15	.04
85 Lance Dickson	.15	.04
86 Kim Batiste	.15	.04
87 Gregg Olson	.15	.04
88 Andy Benes	.15	.04
89 Cal Eldred	.15	.04
90 David Cone	.30	.09

1992 Score Rookie/Traded

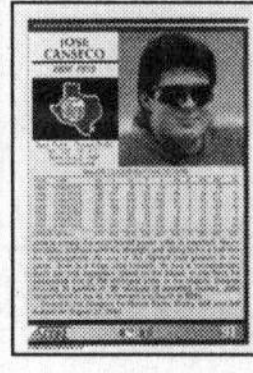

The 1992 Score Rookie and Traded set contains 110 standard-size cards featuring traded veterans and rookies. This set was issued in complete set form and was released through hobby dealers. The set is arranged numerically such that cards 1T-79T are traded players and cards 80T-110T feature rookies. Notable Rookie Cards in this set include Brian Jordan and Jeff Kent.

	Nm-Mt	Ex-Mt
COMP.FACT.SET (110)	8.00	2.40
1T Gary Sheffield	.30	.09
2T Kevin Seitzer	.20	.06
3T Danny Tartabull	.20	.06
4T Steve Sax	.20	.06
5T Bobby Bonilla	.30	.09
6T Frank Viola	.30	.09
7T Dave Winfield	.30	.09
8T Rick Sutcliffe	.30	.09
9T Jose Canseco	.75	.23
10T Greg Swindell	.20	.06
11T Eddie Murray	.75	.23
12T Randy Myers	.20	.06
13T Wally Joyner	.30	.09
14T Kenny Lofton	.50	.15
15T Jack Morris	.30	.09
16T Charlie Hayes	.20	.06
17T Pete Incaviglia	.20	.06
18T Kevin Mitchell	.20	.06
19T Kurt Stillwell	.20	.06
20T Bret Saberhagen	.30	.09
21T Steve Buechele	.20	.06
22T John Smiley	.20	.06
23T Sammy Sosa	1.25	.35
24T George Bell	.20	.06
25T Curt Schilling	.50	.15
26T Dick Schofield	.20	.06
27T David Cone	.30	.09
28T Dan Gladden	.20	.06
29T Kirk McCaskill	.20	.06
30T Mike Gallego	.20	.06
31T Kevin McReynolds	.20	.06
32T Bill Swift	.20	.06
33T Dave Martinez	.20	.06
34T Storm Davis	.20	.06
35T Willie Randolph	.30	.09
36T Melido Perez	.20	.06
37T Mark Carreon	.20	.06
38T Doug Jones	.20	.06
39T Gregg Jefferies	.20	.06
40T Mike Jackson	.20	.06
41T Dickie Thon	.20	.06
42T Eric King	.20	.06
43T Herm Winningham	.20	.06
44T Derek Lilliquist	.20	.06
45T Dave Anderson	.20	.06
46T Jeff Reardon	.30	.09
47T Scott Bankhead	.20	.06
48T Cory Snyder	.20	.06
49T Al Newman	.20	.06
50T Keith Miller	.20	.06
51T Dave Burba	.20	.06
52T Bill Pecota	.20	.06
53T Chuck Crim	.20	.06
54T Mariano Duncan	.20	.06
55T Dave Gallagher	.20	.06
56T Chris Gwynn	.20	.06
57T Scott Ruskin	.20	.06
58T Jack Armstrong	.20	.06
59T Gary Carter	.50	.15
60T Andres Galarraga	.30	.09
61T Ken Hill	.20	.06
62T Eric Davis	.30	.09
63T Ruben Sierra	.20	.06
64T Darrin Fletcher	.20	.06
65T Tim Belcher	.20	.06
66T Mike Morgan	.20	.06
67T Scott Scudder	.20	.06
68T Tom Candiotti	.20	.06
69T Hubie Brooks	.20	.06
70T Kal Daniels	.20	.06
71T Bruce Ruffin	.20	.06
72T Billy Hatcher	.20	.06
73T Bob Melvin	.20	.06
74T Lee Guetterman	.20	.06
75T Rene Gonzales	.20	.06
76T Kevin Bass	.20	.06
77T Tom Bolton	.20	.06
78T John Wetteland	.30	.09
79T Bip Roberts	.20	.06
80T Pat Listach RC	.40	.12
81T John Doherty RC	.20	.06
82T Sam Militello	.20	.06
83T Brian Jordan RC	1.00	.30
84T Jeff Kent RC	2.00	.60
85T Dave Fleming	.20	.06
86T Jeff Tackett	.20	.06
87T Chad Curtis RC	.40	.12
88T Eric Fox RC	.20	.06
89T Denny Neagle	.30	.09
90T Donovan Osborne	.20	.06
91T Carlos Hernandez	.20	.06
92T Tim Wakefield RC	1.00	.30
93T Tim Salmon	.75	.23
94T Dave Nilsson	.20	.06
95T Mike Perez	.20	.06
96T Pat Hentgen	.20	.06
97T Frank Seminara RC	.20	.06
98T Ruben Amaro	.20	.06
99T Archi Cianfrocco RC	.20	.06
100T Andy Stankiewicz	.20	.06
101T Jim Bullinger	.20	.06
102T Pat Mahomes RC	.40	.12
103T Hipolito Pichardo RC	.20	.06
104T Bret Boone	.75	.23
105T John Vander Wal	.20	.06
106T Vince Horsman	.20	.06
107T Jim Austin	.20	.06
108T Brian Williams RC	.20	.06
109T Dan Walters	.20	.06
110T Wil Cordero	.20	.06

1992 Score 100 Rising Stars

The 1992 Score Rising Stars set contains 100 standard size player cards and six "Magic Motion" trivia cards.

	Nm-Mt	Ex-Mt
COMPLETE SET (100)	8.00	2.40
1 Milt Cuyler	.05	.02
2 David Howard	.05	.02
3 Brian R. Hunter	.05	.02
4 Darryl Kile	.10	.03
5 Pat Kelly	.05	.02
6 Luis Gonzalez	.25	.07
7 Mike Benjamin	.05	.02
8 Eric Anthony	.05	.02
9 Moises Alou	.15	.04
10 Darren Lewis	.05	.02
11 Chuck Knoblauch	.25	.07
12 Geronimo Pena	.05	.02
13 Jeff Plympton	.05	.02
14 Bret Barberie	.05	.02
15 Chris Haney	.05	.02
16 Rick Wilkins	.05	.02
17 Julio Valera	.05	.02
18 Joe Slusarski	.05	.02
19 Jose Melendez	.05	.02
20 Pete Schourek	.05	.02
21 Jeff Conine	.10	.03
22 Paul Faries	.05	.02
23 Scott Kamieniecki	.05	.02
24 Bernard Gilkey	.05	.02
25 Wes Chamberlain	.05	.02
26 Charles Nagy	.10	.03
27 Juan Guzman	.05	.02
28 Heath Slocumb	.05	.02
29 Eddie Taubensee	.10	.03
30 Cedric Landrum	.05	.02
31 Jose Offerman	.05	.02
32 Andres Santana	.05	.02
33 David Segui	.10	.03
34 Bernie Williams	1.25	.35
35 Jeff Bagwell	2.50	.75
36 Kevin Morton	.05	.02
37 Kirk Dressendorfer	.05	.02
38 Mike Fetters	.05	.02
39 Darren Holmes	.05	.02
40 Jeff Johnson	.05	.02
41 Scott Aldred	.05	.02
42 Kevin Ward	.05	.02
43 Ray Lankford	.25	.07
44 Terry Shumpert	.05	.02
45 Wade Taylor	.05	.02
46 Rob MacDonald	.05	.02
47 Jose Mota	.05	.02
48 Reggie Harris	.05	.02
49 Mike Remlinger	.05	.02
50 Mark Lewis	.05	.02
51 Tino Martinez	.25	.07
52 Ed Sprague	.05	.02
53 Freddie Benavides	.05	.02
54 Rich DeLucia	.05	.02
55 Brian Drahman	.05	.02
56 Steve Decker	.05	.02
57 Scott Livingstone	.05	.02
58 Mike Timlin	.05	.02
59 Bob Scanlan	.05	.02
60 Dean Palmer	.15	.04
61 Frank Castillo	.05	.02
62 Mark Leonard	.05	.02
63 Chuck McElroy	.05	.02
64 Derek Bell	.05	.02
65 Andujar Cedeno	.05	.02
66 Leo Gomez	.05	.02
67 Rusty Meacham	.05	.02
68 Dann Howitt	.05	.02
69 Chris Jones	.05	.02
70 Dave Cochrane	.05	.02
71 Carlos Martinez	.05	.02
72 Hensley Meulens	.05	.02
73 Rich Reed	.10	.03
74 Pedro Munoz	.05	.02
75 Orlando Merced	.05	.02
76 Chito Martinez	.05	.02
77 Ivan Rodriguez	2.50	.75
78 Brian Barnes	.05	.02
79 Chris Donnels	.05	.02
80 Todd Hundley	.10	.03
81 Gary Scott	.05	.02
82 John Wehner	.05	.02
83 Al Osuna	.05	.02
84 Luis Lopez	.05	.02
85 Brent Mayne	.05	.02
86 Phil Plantier	.05	.02
87 Joe Bitker	.05	.02
88 Scott Cooper	.05	.02
89 Chris Hammond	.05	.02
90 Tim Sherrill	.05	.02
91 Doug Simons	.05	.02
92 Kip Gross	.05	.02
93 Tim McIntosh	.05	.02
94 Larry Casian	.05	.02
95 Mike Dalton	.05	.02
96 Lance Dickson	.05	.02
97 Joe Grahe	.05	.02
98 Glenn Sutko	.05	.02
99 Gerald Alexander	.05	.02
100 Mo Vaughn	.25	.07

1992 Score 100 Superstars

The 1992 Score Superstars set contains 100 standard-size player cards and six "Magic Motion" trivia cards.

	Nm-Mt	Ex-Mt
COMPLETE SET (100)	12.00	3.60
1 Ken Griffey Jr.	2.00	.60
2 Scott Erickson	.05	.02
3 John Smiley	.05	.02
4 Rick Aguilera	.10	.03
5 Jeff Reardon	.10	.03
6 Chuck Finley	.10	.03
7 Kirby Puckett	.50	.15
8 Paul Molitor	.40	.12
9 Dave Winfield	.40	.12
10 Mike Greenwell	.05	.02
11 Bret Saberhagen	.10	.03
12 Pete Harnisch	.05	.02
13 Ozzie Guillen	.10	.03
14 Hal Morris	.05	.02
15 Tom Glavine	.40	.12
16 David Cone	.15	.04
17 Edgar Martinez	.15	.04
18 Willie McGee	.10	.03
19 Jim Abbott	.10	.03
20 Mark Grace	.15	.04
21 George Brett	1.25	.35
22 Jack McDowell	.05	.02
23 Don Mattingly	1.50	.45
24 Will Clark	.25	.07
25 Dwight Gooden	.10	.03
26 Barry Bonds	1.50	.45
27 Rafael Palmeiro	.25	.07
28 Lee Smith	.10	.03
29 Wally Joyner	.10	.03
30 Wade Boggs	.75	.23
31 Tom Henke	.05	.02
32 Mark Langston	.05	.02
33 Robin Ventura	.25	.07
34 Steve Avery	.05	.02
35 Joe Carter	.10	.03
36 Benito Santiago	.10	.03
37 Dave Stieb	.05	.02
38 Julio Franco	.10	.03
39 Albert Belle	.10	.03
40 Dale Murphy	.25	.07
41 Rob Dibble	.05	.02
42 Dave Justice	.25	.07
43 Jose Rijo	.05	.02
44 Eric Davis	.10	.03
45 Terry Pendleton	.05	.02
46 Kevin Maas	.05	.02
47 Ozzie Smith	1.00	.30
48 Andre Dawson	.15	.04
49 Sandy Alomar Jr.	.05	.02
50 Nolan Ryan	3.00	.90
51 Frank Thomas	.75	.23
52 Craig Biggio	.15	.04
53 Doug Drabek	.05	.02
54 Bobby Thigpen	.05	.02
55 Darryl Strawberry	.15	.04
56 Dennis Eckersley	.40	.12
57 John Franco	.10	.03
58 Paul O'Neill	.15	.04
59 Scott Sanderson	.05	.02
60 Dave Stewart	.10	.03
61 Ivan Calderon	.05	.02
62 Frank Viola	.05	.02
63 Mark McGwire	2.50	.75
64 Kelly Gruber	.05	.02
65 Fred McGriff	.15	.04
66 Cecil Fielder	.10	.03
67 Jose Canseco	.25	.07
68 Howard Johnson	.05	.02
69 Juan Gonzalez	.75	.23
70 Tim Wallach	.05	.02
71 John Olerud	.25	.07
72 Carlton Fisk	.40	.12
73 Otis Nixon	.05	.02
74 Roger Clemens	1.50	.45
75 Ramon Martinez	.10	.03
76 Ron Gant	.10	.03
77 Barry Larkin	.25	.07
78 Eddie Murray	.40	.12
79 Vince Coleman	.05	.02
80 Bobby Bonilla	.05	.02
81 Tony Gwynn	1.25	.35
82 Roberto Alomar	.25	.07
83 Ellis Burks	.10	.03
84 Robin Yount	.50	.15
85 Ryne Sandberg	.50	.15
86 Len Dykstra	.10	.03
87 Ruben Sierra	.10	.03
88 George Bell	.05	.02
89 Cal Ripken	3.00	.90
90 Danny Tartabull	.05	.02
91 Gregg Olson	.05	.02
92 Dave Henderson	.05	.02
93 Kevin Mitchell	.05	.02
94 Ben McDonald	.05	.02
95 Matt Williams	.15	.04
96 Roberto Kelly	.05	.02
97 Dennis Martinez	.05	.02
98 Kent Hrbek	.10	.03

99 Felix Jose .05 .02
100 Rickey Henderson .75 .23

1992 Score/Pinnacle Promo Panels

These promo panels were issued by Score to illustrate the design of the 1992 Score and 1992 Pinnacle series cards. The Score card is in the upper left of the panel, with a second Score card placed diagonally across in the lower right corner. The Pinnacle cards are diagonally placed in the upper right, and lower left of the promo panel. The promo panel measures approximately 5" by 7". If cut, each of the four cards would measure the standard size. The Score fronts feature a glossy color action photo bordered above and below by a blue bar. Along the left side is a wider green border. The Score backs carry a close-up shot in the upper right corner, with biography, complete career statistics, and player profile printed on a yellow background. The Pinnacle fronts display a glossy color player photos on a black background accented by thin white borders. On a black background the horizontal backs have a close-up player portrait, statistics, and a player profile. An anti-counterfeit device appears in the bottom border of each back. The cards for each set are numbered on the back as in the regular series; the panels themselves, however, are unnumbered. We have sequenced this set according to the player's card number in the upper left corner.

	Nm-Mt	Ex-Mt
COMPLETE SET (25)	50.00	15.00
1 Nolan Ryan Terry Pendleton Willie McGee Lonnie Smith	10.00	3.00
2 Will Clark Mark Langston Paul Molitor Devon White	2.00	.60
3 Frank Thomas David Justice Mark Carreon Dave Henderson	8.00	2.40
4 Kirby Puckett Ryne Sandberg Roberto Alomar Dave Henderson	6.00	1.80
5 Ozzie Smith Darryl Strawberry Kevin Seitzer Jeff Montgomery	4.00	1.20
6 Robin Yount Jay Buhner Chuck Crim Jimmy Jones	2.00	.60
7 Don Mattingly Matt Williams Dave Winfield George Bell	4.00	1.20
8 Orel Hershiser Wes Chamberlain Gary Gaetti Dickie Thon	1.00	.30
9 Ron Gant Andres Galarraga Bruce Hurst Alex Fernandez	2.00	.60
10 Albert Belle Ellis Burks Melido Perez Kevin Gross	1.50	.45
11 Ivan Calderon Bill Doran Rick Aguilera Doug Jones	1.00	.30
12 Todd Zeile Mike Gallego Lenny Harris Jack Clark	1.00	.30
13 Harold Baines Walt Weiss Eric Davis Randy Ready	1.00	.30
14 Nolan Ryan George Brett George Bell Rafael Palmeiro	15.00	4.50
15 Chili Davis Phil Plantier David Wells Bob Walk	1.00	.30
16 John Olerud Dave Hollins Jack McDowell Juan Samuel	1.00	.30
17 Carlton Fisk Kent Hrbek Dennis Martinez Jim Acker	1.50	.45
18 Jay Buhner Greg Olson Terry Steinbach Kirk McCaskill	1.50	.45
19 Jeff Bagwell Darryl Strawberry Travis Fryman Andre Dawson	4.00	1.20
20 Alex Cole Jim Gantner Ken Caminiti Todd Stottlemyre	1.50	.45
21 Alex Fernandez Bill Gullickson Jose Guzman Shawn Hillegas	1.00	.30
22 Bernard Gilkey Omar Vizquel Ivan Calderon Ozzie Guillen	1.00	.30
23 Gary Gaetti Doug Drabek Brent Mayne Tom Bolton	1.00	.30
24 David Justice Kevin Maas Jody Reed Vince Coleman	2.00	.60
25 Chili Davis Hensley Meulens David Howard Mark Lewis	1.00	.30

1992 Score Proctor and Gamble

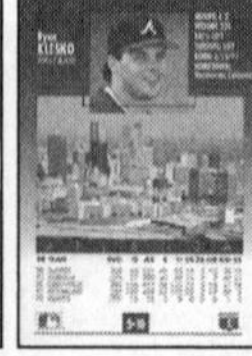

This 18-card standard-size set was produced by Score for Proctor and Gamble as a mail-in premium and contains 18 players from the 1992 All-Star Game line-up. The production run comprised 2,000,000 sets and 25 uncut sheets. A three-card sample set was also produced for sales representatives with a print run of 5,000,000 sets and 25 uncut sheets. The three sample cards, featuring Griffey, Sandberg, and Henderson, are stamped "sample" on the back. Collectors could obtain the set by sending in a required certificate, 99 cents, three UPC symbols from three different Proctor and Gamble products, and 50 cents for postage and handling. The certificate was published in a flyer inserted in Sunday, August 16 newspapers. The card fronts feature color action player cutouts superimposed on a diagonally striped background showing a large star behind the player. Card numbers 1-9 have a blue star on a graded magenta background, while card numbers 10-18 show a red star on blue-green. The backs display a close-up photo, biographical and statistical information, and career summary on a graded yellow-orange background. The cards are numbered "X/18" at the lower right corner.

	Nm-Mt	Ex-Mt
COMPLETE SET (18)	5.00	1.50
1 Sandy Alomar Jr.	.15	.04
2 Mark McGwire	1.50	.45
3 Roberto Alomar	.25	.07
4 Wade Boggs	.40	.12
5 Cal Ripken	2.00	.60
6 Kirby Puckett	.50	.15
7 Ken Griffey Jr.	1.25	.35
8 Jose Canseco	.30	.09
9 Kevin Brown	.20	.06
10 Benito Santiago	.15	.04
11 Fred McGriff	.20	.06
12 Ryne Sandberg	.75	.23
13 Terry Pendleton	.10	.03
14 Ozzie Smith	.75	.23
15 Barry Bonds	1.00	.30
16 Tony Gwynn	1.00	.30
17 Andy Van Slyke	.10	.03
18 Tom Glavine	.25	.07

1992 Score Rookies

This 40-card boxed set measures the standard size and features glossy color action player photos on a kelly green face with meandering purple stripes.

	Nm-Mt	Ex-Mt
COMP.FACT SET (40)	4.00	1.20
1 Todd Van Poppel	.05	.02
2 Kyle Abbott	.05	.02
3 Derek Bell	.05	.02
4 Jim Thome	1.50	.45
5 Mark Wohlers	.05	.02
6 Todd Hundley	.25	.07
7 Arthur Lee Rhodes	.05	.02
8 John Ramos	.05	.02
9 Chris George	.05	.02
10 Kenny Lofton	1.00	.30
11 Ted Wood	.05	.02
12 Royce Clayton	.05	.02
13 Scott Cooper	.05	.02
14 Anthony Young	.05	.02
15 Joel Johnston	.05	.02
16 Andy Mota	.05	.02
17 Lenny Webster	.05	.02
18 Andy Ashby	.05	.02
19 Jose Mota	.05	.02
20 Tim McIntosh	.05	.02
21 Terry Bross	.05	.02
22 Harvey Pulliam	.05	.02
23 Hector Fajardo	.05	.02
24 Esteban Beltre	.05	.02
25 Gary DiSarcina	.05	.02
26 Mike Humphreys	.05	.02
27 Jarvis Brown	.05	.02
28 Gary Cooper	.05	.02
29 Chris Donnels	.05	.02
30 Monty Fariss	.05	.02
31 Eric Karros	.75	.23
32 Braulio Castillo	.05	.02
33 Cal Eldred	.05	.02
34 Tom Goodwin	.05	.02
35 Reggie Sanders	.50	.15
36 Scott Servais	.05	.02
37 Kim Batiste	.05	.02
38 Eric Wedge	.25	.07
39 Willie Banks	.05	.02
40 Mo Sanford	.05	.02

1993 Score

The 1993 Score baseball set consists of 660 standard-size cards issued in one single series. The cards were distributed in 16-card poly packs and 35-card jumbo superpacks. Topical subsets featured are Award Winners (481-486), Draft Picks (487-501), All-Star Caricature (502-512 [AL], 522-531 [NL]), Highlights (513-519), World Series Highlights (520-521), Dream Team (532-542) and Rookies (sprinkled throughout the set). Rookie Cards in this set include Derek Jeter, Jason Kendall and Shannon Stewart.

	Nm-Mt	Ex-Mt
COMPLETE SET (660)	40.00	12.00
1 Ken Griffey Jr.	.75	.23
2 Gary Sheffield	.20	.06
3 Frank Thomas	.50	.15
4 Ryne Sandberg	.75	.23
5 Larry Walker	.30	.09
6 Cal Ripken Jr.	1.50	.45
7 Roger Clemens	1.00	.30
8 Bobby Bonilla	.20	.06
9 Carlos Baerga	.10	.03
10 Darren Daulton	.20	.06
11 Travis Fryman	.20	.06
12 Andy Van Slyke	.20	.06
13 Jose Canseco	.50	.15
14 Roberto Alomar	.50	.15
15 Tom Glavine	.30	.09
16 Barry Larkin	.50	.15
17 Gregg Jefferies	.10	.03
18 Craig Biggio	.30	.09
19 Shane Mack	.10	.03
20 Brett Butler	.20	.06
21 Dennis Eckersley	.20	.06
22 Will Clark	.50	.15
23 Don Mattingly	1.25	.35
24 Tony Gwynn	.60	.18
25 Ivan Rodriguez	.50	.15
26 Shawon Dunston	.10	.03
27 Mike Mussina	.50	.15
28 Marquis Grissom	.10	.03
29 Charles Nagy	.10	.03
30 Len Dykstra	.20	.06
31 Cecil Fielder	.20	.06
32 Jay Bell	.20	.06
33 B.J. Surhoff	.20	.06
34 Bob Tewksbury	.10	.03
35 Danny Tartabull	.10	.03
36 Terry Pendleton	.20	.06
37 Jack Morris	.20	.06
38 Hal Morris	.10	.03
39 Luis Polonia	.10	.03
40 Ken Caminiti	.20	.06
41 Robin Ventura	.20	.06
42 Darryl Strawberry	.30	.09
43 Wally Joyner	.20	.06
44 Fred McGriff	.30	.09
45 Kevin Tapani	.10	.03
46 Matt Williams	.20	.06
47 Robin Yount	.75	.23
48 Ken Hill	.10	.03
49 Edgar Martinez	.30	.09
50 Mark Grace	.30	.09
51 Juan Gonzalez	.50	.15
52 Curt Schilling	.30	.09
53 Dwight Gooden	.30	.09
54 Chris Hoiles	.10	.03
55 Frank Viola	.20	.06
56 Ray Lankford	.10	.03
57 George Brett	1.25	.35
58 Kenny Lofton	.20	.06
59 Nolan Ryan	2.00	.60
60 Mickey Tettleton	.10	.03
61 John Smoltz	.30	.09
62 Howard Johnson	.10	.03
63 Eric Karros	.20	.06
64 Rick Aguilera	.10	.03
65 Steve Finley	.20	.06
66 Mark Langston	.10	.03
67 Bill Swift	.10	.03
68 John Olerud	.20	.06
69 Kevin McReynolds	.10	.03
70 Jack McDowell	.10	.03
71 Rickey Henderson	.50	.15
72 Brian Harper	.10	.03
73 Mike Morgan	.10	.03
74 Rafael Palmeiro	.30	.09
75 Dennis Martinez	.20	.06
76 Tino Martinez	.30	.09
77 Eddie Murray	.50	.15
78 Ellis Burks	.20	.06
79 John Kruk	.20	.06
80 Gregg Olson	.10	.03
81 Bernard Gilkey	.10	.03
82 Milt Cuyler	.10	.03
83 Mike LaValliere	.10	.03
84 Albert Belle	.20	.06
85 Bip Roberts	.10	.03
86 Melido Perez	.10	.03
87 Otis Nixon	.10	.03
88 Bill Spiers	.10	.03
89 Jeff Bagwell	.30	.09
90 Orel Hershiser	.20	.06
91 Andy Benes	.10	.03
92 Devon White	.10	.03
93 Willie McGee	.20	.06
94 Ozzie Guillen	.10	.03
95 Ivan Calderon	.10	.03
96 Keith Miller	.10	.03
97 Steve Buechele	.10	.03
98 Kent Hrbek	.20	.06
99 Dave Hollins	.10	.03
100 Mike Bordick	.10	.03
101 Randy Tomlin	.10	.03
102 Omar Vizquel	.20	.06
103 Lee Smith	.20	.06
104 Leo Gomez	.10	.03
105 Jose Rijo	.10	.03
106 Mark Whiten	.10	.03
107 Dave Justice	.20	.06
108 Eddie Taubensee	.10	.03
109 Lance Johnson	.10	.03
110 Felix Jose	.10	.03
111 Mike Harkey	.10	.03
112 Randy Milligan	.10	.03
113 Anthony Young	.10	.03
114 Rico Brogna	.10	.03
115 Bret Saberhagen	.20	.06
116 Sandy Alomar Jr.	.10	.03
117 Terry Mulholland	.10	.03
118 Darryl Hamilton	.10	.03
119 Todd Zeile	.10	.03
120 Bernie Williams	.30	.09
121 Zane Smith	.10	.03
122 Derek Bell	.10	.03
123 Deion Sanders	.30	.09
124 Luis Sojo	.10	.03
125 Joe Oliver	.10	.03
126 Craig Grebeck	.10	.03
127 Andujar Cedeno	.10	.03
128 Brian McRae	.10	.03
129 Jose Offerman	.10	.03
130 Pedro Munoz	.10	.03
131 Bud Black	.10	.03
132 Mo Vaughn	.20	.06
133 Bruce Hurst	.10	.03
134 Dave Henderson	.10	.03
135 Tom Pagnozzi	.10	.03
136 Erik Hanson	.10	.03
137 Orlando Merced	.10	.03
138 Dean Palmer	.20	.06
139 John Franco	.20	.06
140 Brady Anderson	.20	.06
141 Ricky Jordan	.10	.03
142 Jeff Blauser	.10	.03
143 Sammy Sosa	.75	.23
144 Bob Walk	.10	.03
145 Delino DeShields	.10	.03
146 Kevin Brown	.20	.06
147 Mark Lemke	.10	.03
148 Chuck Knoblauch	.20	.06
149 Chris Sabo	.10	.03
150 Bobby Witt	.10	.03
151 Luis Gonzalez	.20	.06
152 Ron Karkovice	.10	.03
153 Jeff Brantley	.10	.03
154 Kevin Appier	.20	.06
155 Darrin Jackson	.10	.03
156 Kelly Gruber	.10	.03
157 Royce Clayton	.10	.03
158 Chuck Finley	.20	.06
159 Jeff King	.10	.03
160 Greg Vaughn	.20	.06
161 Geronimo Pena	.10	.03
162 Steve Farr	.10	.03
163 Jose Oquendo	.10	.03
164 Mark Lewis	.10	.03
165 John Wetteland	.20	.06
166 Mike Henneman	.10	.03
167 Todd Hundley	.10	.03
168 Wes Chamberlain	.10	.03
169 Steve Avery	.10	.03
170 Mike Devereaux	.10	.03
171 Reggie Sanders	.20	.06
172 Jay Buhner	.20	.06
173 Eric Anthony	.10	.03
174 John Burkett	.10	.03
175 Tom Candiotti	.10	.03
176 Phil Plantier	.10	.03
177 Doug Henry	.10	.03
178 Scott Leius	.10	.03
179 Kirt Manwaring	.10	.03
180 Jeff Parrett	.10	.03
181 Don Slaught	.10	.03
182 Scott Radinsky	.10	.03
183 Luis Alicea	.10	.03
184 Tom Gordon	.10	.03
185 Rick Wilkins	.10	.03
186 Todd Stottlemyre	.10	.03
187 Moises Alou	.20	.06
188 Joe Grahe	.10	.03
189 Jeff Kent	.50	.15
190 Bill Wegman	.10	.03
191 Kim Batiste	.10	.03
192 Matt Nokes	.10	.03
193 Mark Wohlers	.10	.03
194 Paul Sorrento	.10	.03
195 Chris Hammond	.10	.03
196 Scott Livingstone	.10	.03
197 Doug Jones	.10	.03
198 Scott Cooper	.10	.03
199 Ramon Martinez	.10	.03
200 Dave Valle	.10	.03
201 Mariano Duncan	.10	.03
202 Ben McDonald	.10	.03
203 Darren Lewis	.10	.03
204 Kenny Rogers	.20	.06
205 Manuel Lee	.10	.03
206 Scott Erickson	.10	.03
207 Dan Gladden	.10	.03
208 Bob Welch	.10	.03
209 Greg Olson	.10	.03
210 Dan Pasqua	.10	.03
211 Tim Wallach	.10	.03
212 Jeff Montgomery	.10	.03
213 Derrick May	.10	.03
214 Ed Sprague	.10	.03
215 David Haas	.10	.03
216 Darrin Fletcher	.10	.03
217 Brian Jordan	.20	.06
218 Jaime Navarro	.10	.03
219 Randy Velarde	.10	.03
220 Ron Gant	.20	.06
221 Paul Quantrill	.10	.03
222 Damion Easley	.10	.03
223 Charlie Hough	.20	.06
224 Brad Brink	.10	.03
225 Barry Manuel	.10	.03
226 Kevin Koslofski	.10	.03
227 Ryan Thompson	.10	.03
228 Mike Munoz	.10	.03
229 Dan Wilson	.20	.06
230 Peter Hoy	.10	.03
231 Pedro Astacio	.10	.03
232 Matt Stairs	.10	.03
233 Jeff Reboulet	.10	.03
234 Manny Alexander	.10	.03
235 Willie Banks	.10	.03
236 John Jaha	.10	.03
237 Scooter Tucker	.10	.03
238 Russ Springer	.10	.03
239 Paul Miller	.10	.03
240 Dan Peltier	.10	.03
241 Ozzie Canseco	.10	.03
242 Ben Rivera	.10	.03
243 John Valentin	.10	.03
244 Henry Rodriguez	.10	.03
245 Derek Parks	.10	.03
246 Carlos Garcia	.10	.03
247 Tim Pugh RC	.10	.03
248 Melvin Nieves	.10	.03
249 Rich Amaral	.10	.03
250 Willie Greene	.10	.03
251 Tim Scott	.10	.03
252 Dave Silvestri	.10	.03
253 Rob Mallicoat	.10	.03
254 Donald Harris	.10	.03
255 Craig Colbert	.10	.03
256 Jose Guzman	.10	.03
257 Domingo Martinez RC	.10	.03
258 William Suero	.10	.03
259 Juan Guerrero	.10	.03
260 J.T. Snow RC	.50	.15
261 Tony Pena	.10	.03
262 Tim Fortugno	.10	.03
263 Tom Marsh	.10	.03
264 Kurt Knudsen	.10	.03
265 Tim Costo	.10	.03
266 Steve Shifflett	.10	.03
267 Billy Ashley	.10	.03
268 Jerry Nielsen	.10	.03
269 Pete Young	.10	.03
270 Johnny Guzman	.10	.03
271 Greg Colbrunn	.10	.03
272 Jeff Nelson	.10	.03
273 Kevin Young	.20	.06
274 Jeff Frye	.10	.03
275 J.T. Bruett	.10	.03
276 Todd Pratt RC	.20	.06
277 Mike Butcher	.10	.03
278 John Flaherty	.10	.03
279 John Patterson	.10	.03
280 Eric Hillman	.10	.03
281 Bien Figueroa	.10	.03
282 Shane Reynolds	.10	.03
283 Rich Rowland	.10	.03
284 Steve Foster	.10	.03
285 Dave Milicki	.10	.03
286 Mike Piazza	1.25	.35
287 Mike Trombley	.10	.03
288 Jim Pena	.10	.03
289 Bob Ayrault	.10	.03
290 Henry Mercedes	.10	.03
291 Bob Wickman	.10	.03
292 Jacob Brumfield	.10	.03
293 David Hulse RC	.10	.03
294 Ryan Klesko	.20	.06
295 Doug Linton	.10	.03
296 Steve Cooke	.10	.03
297 Eddie Zosky	.10	.03
298 Gerald Williams	.10	.03
299 Jonathan Hurst	.10	.03
300 Larry Carter RC	.10	.03
301 William Pennyfeather	.10	.03
302 Cesar Hernandez	.10	.03
303 Steve Hosey	.10	.03
304 Blas Minor	.10	.03
305 Jeff Grotewald	.10	.03
306 Bernardo Brito	.10	.03
307 Rafael Bournigal	.10	.03
308 Jeff Branson	.10	.03
309 Tom Quinlan RC	.10	.03
310 Pat Gomez RC	.10	.03
311 Sterling Hitchcock RC	.20	.06
312 Kent Bottenfield	.10	.03
313 Alan Trammell	.30	.09
314 Cris Colon	.10	.03
315 Paul Wagner	.10	.03
316 Matt Maysey	.10	.03
317 Mike Stanton	.10	.03
318 Rick Trlicek	.10	.03
319 Kevin Rogers	.10	.03
320 Mark Clark	.10	.03
321 Pedro Martinez	1.00	.30
322 Al Martin	.10	.03
323 Mike Macfarlane	.10	.03
324 Rey Sanchez	.10	.03
325 Roger Pavlik	.10	.03
326 Troy Neel	.10	.03
327 Kerry Woodson	.10	.03
328 Wayne Kirby	.10	.03
329 Ken Ryan RC	.10	.03
330 Jesse Levis	.10	.03
331 Jim Austin	.10	.03
332 Dan Walters	.10	.03
333 Brian Williams	.10	.03
334 Wil Cordero	.10	.03
335 Bret Boone	.30	.09
336 Hipolito Pichardo	.10	.03
337 Pat Mahomes	.10	.03
338 Andy Stankiewicz	.10	.03
339 Jim Bullinger	.10	.03
340 Archi Cianfrocco	.10	.03
341 Ruben Amaro	.10	.03
342 Frank Seminara	.10	.03
343 Pat Hentgen	.10	.03
344 Dave Nilsson	.10	.03
345 Mike Perez	.10	.03
346 Tim Salmon	.30	.09
347 Tim Wakefield	.20	.06
348 Carlos Hernandez	.10	.03
349 Donovan Osborne	.10	.03
350 Denny Neagle	.20	.06
351 Sam Militello	.10	.03

352 Eric Fox .10 .03
353 John Doherty .10 .03
354 Chad Curtis .10 .03
355 Jeff Tackett .10 .03
356 Dave Fleming .10 .03
357 Pat Listach .10 .03
358 Kevin Wickander .10 .03
359 John Vander Wal .10 .03
360 Arthur Rhodes .10 .03
361 Bob Scanlan .10 .03
362 Bob Zupcic .10 .03
363 Mel Rojas .10 .03
364 Jim Thome .50 .15
365 Bill Pecota .10 .03
366 Mark Carreon .10 .03
367 Mitch Williams .10 .03
368 Cal Eldred .10 .03
369 Stan Belinda .10 .03
370 Pat Kelly .10 .03
371 Rheal Cormier .10 .03
372 Juan Guzman .10 .03
373 Damon Berryhill .10 .03
374 Gary DiSarcina .10 .03
375 Norm Charlton .10 .03
376 Roberto Hernandez .10 .03
377 Scott Kamieniecki .10 .03
378 Rusty Meacham .10 .03
379 Kurt Stillwell .10 .03
380 Lloyd McClendon .10 .03
381 Mark Leonard .10 .03
382 Jerry Browne .10 .03
383 Glenn Davis .10 .03
384 Randy Johnson .50 .15
385 Mike Greenwell .10 .03
386 Scott Chiamparino .10 .03
387 George Bell .10 .03
388 Steve Olin .10 .03
389 Chuck McElroy .10 .03
390 Mark Gardner .10 .03
391 Rod Beck .10 .03
392 Dennis Rasmussen .10 .03
393 Charlie Leibrandt .10 .03
394 Julio Franco .20 .06
395 Pete Harnisch .10 .03
396 Sid Bream .10 .03
397 Milt Thompson .10 .03
398 Glenallen Hill .10 .03
399 Chico Walker .10 .03
400 Alex Cole .10 .03
401 Trevor Wilson .10 .03
402 Jeff Conine .20 .06
403 Kyle Abbott .10 .03
404 Tom Browning .10 .03
405 Jerald Clark .10 .03
406 Vince Horsman .10 .03
407 Kevin Mitchell .10 .03
408 Pete Smith .10 .03
409 Jeff Innis .10 .03
410 Mike Timlin .10 .03
411 Charlie Hayes .10 .03
412 Alex Fernandez .10 .03
413 Jeff Russell .10 .03
414 Jody Reed .10 .03
415 Mickey Morandini .10 .03
416 Darnell Coles .10 .03
417 Xavier Hernandez .10 .03
418 Steve Sax .10 .03
419 Joe Girardi .10 .03
420 Mike Fetters .10 .03
421 Danny Jackson .10 .03
422 Jim Gott .10 .03
423 Tim Belcher .10 .03
424 Jose Mesa .10 .03
425 Junior Felix .10 .03
426 Thomas Howard .10 .03
427 Julio Valera .10 .03
428 Dante Bichette .20 .06
429 Mike Sharperson .10 .03
430 Darryl Kile .20 .06
431 Lonnie Smith .10 .03
432 Monty Fariss .10 .03
433 Reggie Jefferson .10 .03
434 Bob McClure .10 .03
435 Craig Lefferts .10 .03
436 Duane Ward .10 .03
437 Shawn Abner .10 .03
438 Roberto Kelly .10 .03
439 Paul O'Neill .30 .09
440 Alan Mills .10 .03
441 Roger Mason .10 .03
442 Gary Pettis .10 .03
443 Steve Lake .10 .03
444 Gene Larkin .10 .03
445 Larry Andersen .10 .03
446 Doug Dascenzo .10 .03
447 Daryl Boston .10 .03
448 John Candelaria .10 .03
449 Storm Davis .10 .03
450 Tom Edens .10 .03
451 Mike Maddux .10 .03
452 Tim Naehring .10 .03
453 John Orton .10 .03
454 Joey Cora .10 .03
455 Chuck Crim .10 .03
456 Dan Plesac .10 .03
457 Mike Bielecki .10 .03
458 Terry Jorgensen .10 .03
459 John Habyan .10 .03
460 Pete O'Brien .10 .03
461 Jeff Treadway .10 .03
462 Frank Castillo .10 .03
463 Jimmy Jones .10 .03
464 Tommy Greene .10 .03
465 Tracy Woodson .10 .03
466 Rich Rodriguez .10 .03
467 Joe Hesketh .10 .03
468 Greg Myers .10 .03
469 Kirk McCaskill .10 .03
470 Ricky Bones .10 .03
471 Lenny Webster .10 .03
472 Francisco Cabrera .10 .03
473 Turner Ward .10 .03
474 Dwayne Henry .10 .03
475 Al Osuna .10 .03
476 Craig Wilson .10 .03
477 Chris Nabholz .10 .03
478 Rafael Belliard .10 .03
479 Terry Leach .10 .03
480 Tim Teufel .10 .03
481 Dennis Eckersley AW .20 .06
482 Barry Bonds AW .60 .18
483 Dennis Eckersley AW .20 .06
484 Greg Maddux AW .50 .15
485 Pat Listach AW .10 .03
486 Eric Karros AW .10 .03
487 Jamie Arnold DP RC .10 .03
488 B.J. Wallace DP .10 .03
489 Derek Jeter DP RC 10.00 3.00
490 Jason Kendall DP RC .75 .23
491 Rick Helling DP .10 .03
492 Derek Wallace DP RC .10 .03
493 Sean Lowe DP RC .10 .03
494 S.Stewart DP RC .75 .23
495 Benji Grigsby DP RC .10 .03
496 T.Steverson DP RC .10 .03
497 Dan Serafini DP RC .10 .03
498 Michael Tucker DP .10 .03
499 Chris Roberts DP .10 .03
500 Pete Janicki DP RC .10 .03
501 Jeff Schmidt DP RC .10 .03
502 Edgar Martinez AS .20 .06
503 Omar Vizquel AS .20 .06
504 Ken Griffey Jr. AS .50 .15
505 Kirby Puckett AS .30 .09
506 Joe Carter AS .10 .03
507 Ivan Rodriguez AS .30 .09
508 Jack Morris AS .10 .03
509 Dennis Eckersley AS .20 .06
510 Frank Thomas AS .30 .09
511 Roberto Alomar AS .20 .06
512 Mickey Morandini AS .10 .03
513 Dennis Eckersley HL .20 .06
514 Jeff Reardon HL .10 .03
515 Danny Tartabull HL .10 .03
516 Bip Roberts HL .10 .03
517 George Brett HL .60 .18
518 Robin Yount HL .50 .15
519 Kevin Gross HL .10 .03
520 Ed Sprague WS .10 .03
521 Dave Winfield WS .10 .03
522 Ozzie Smith AS .50 .15
523 Barry Bonds AS .60 .18
524 Andy Van Slyke AS .10 .03
525 Tony Gwynn AS .30 .09
526 Darren Daulton AS .10 .03
527 Greg Maddux AS .50 .15
528 Fred McGriff AS .30 .09
529 Lee Smith AS .10 .03
530 Ryne Sandberg AS .50 .15
531 Gary Sheffield AS .10 .03
532 Ozzie Smith DT .50 .15
533 Kirby Puckett DT .30 .09
534 Gary Sheffield DT .10 .03
535 Andy Van Slyke DT .10 .03
536 Ken Griffey Jr. DT .50 .15
537 Ivan Rodriguez DT .30 .09
538 Charles Nagy DT .10 .03
539 Tom Glavine DT .20 .06
540 Dennis Eckersley DT .20 .06
541 Frank Thomas DT .30 .09
542 Roberto Alomar DT .20 .06
543 Sean Berry .10 .03
544 Mike Schooler .10 .03
545 Chuck Carr .10 .03
546 Lenny Harris .10 .03
547 Gary Scott .10 .03
548 Derek Lilliquist .10 .03
549 Brian Hunter .10 .03
550 Kirby Puckett MOY .30 .09
551 Jim Eisenreich .10 .03
552 Andre Dawson .20 .06
553 David Nied .10 .03
554 Spike Owen .10 .03
555 Greg Gagne .10 .03
556 Sid Fernandez .10 .03
557 Mark McGwire 1.25 .35
558 Bryan Harvey .10 .03
559 Harold Reynolds .20 .06
560 Barry Bonds 1.25 .35
561 Eric Wedge RC .10 .03
562 Ozzie Smith .75 .23
563 Rick Sutcliffe .20 .06
564 Jeff Reardon .20 .06
565 Alex Arias .10 .03
566 Greg Swindell .10 .03
567 Brook Jacoby .10 .03
568 Pete Incaviglia .10 .03
569 Butch Henry .10 .03
570 Eric Davis .20 .06
571 Kevin Seitzer .10 .03
572 Tony Fernandez .10 .03
573 Steve Reed RC .10 .03
574 Cory Snyder .10 .03
575 Joe Carter .20 .06
576 Greg Maddux .75 .23
577 Bert Blyleven UER .20 .06
(Should say 3701
career strikeouts)
578 Kevin Bass .10 .03
579 Carlton Fisk .30 .09
580 Doug Drabek .10 .03
581 Mark Gubicza .10 .03
582 Bobby Thigpen .10 .03
583 Chili Davis .20 .06
584 Scott Bankhead .10 .03
585 Harold Baines .20 .06
586 Eric Young .10 .03
587 Lance Parrish .20 .06
588 Juan Bell .10 .03
589 Bob Ojeda .10 .03
590 Joe Orsulak .10 .03
591 Benito Santiago .20 .06
592 Wade Boggs .30 .09
593 Robby Thompson .10 .03
594 Eric Plunk .10 .03
595 Hensley Meulens .10 .03
596 Lou Whitaker .20 .06
597 Dale Murphy .50 .15
598 Paul Molitor .30 .09
599 Greg W. Harris .10 .03
600 Darren Holmes .10 .03
601 Dave Martinez .10 .03
602 Tom Henke .10 .03
603 Mike Benjamin .10 .03
604 Rene Gonzales .10 .03
605 Roger McDowell .10 .03
606 Kirby Puckett .50 .15
607 Randy Myers .10 .03
608 Ruben Sierra .10 .03
609 Wilson Alvarez .10 .03
610 David Segui .10 .03
611 Juan Samuel .10 .03
612 Tom Brunansky .10 .03
613 Willie Randolph .20 .06
614 Tony Phillips .10 .03
615 Candy Maldonado .10 .03
616 Chris Bosio .10 .03
617 Bret Barberie .10 .03
618 Scott Sanderson .10 .03
619 Ron Darling .10 .03
620 Dave Winfield .20 .06
621 Mike Felder .10 .03
622 Greg Hibbard .10 .03
623 Mike Scioscia .10 .03
624 John Smiley .10 .03
625 Alejandro Pena .10 .03
626 Terry Steinbach .10 .03
627 Freddie Benavides .10 .03
628 Kevin Reimer .10 .03
629 Braulio Castillo .10 .03
630 Dave Stieb .10 .03
631 Dave Magadan .10 .03
632 Scott Fletcher .10 .03
633 Cris Carpenter .10 .03
634 Kevin Maas .10 .03
635 Todd Worrell .10 .03
636 Rob Deer .10 .03
637 Dwight Smith .10 .03
638 Chito Martinez .10 .03
639 Jimmy Key .20 .06
640 Greg A. Harris .10 .03
641 Mike Moore .10 .03
642 Pat Borders .10 .03
643 Bill Gullickson .10 .03
644 Gary Gaetti .20 .06
645 David Howard .10 .03
646 Jim Abbott .30 .09
647 Willie Wilson .10 .03
648 David Wells .20 .06
649 Andres Galarraga .20 .06
650 Vince Coleman .10 .03
651 Rob Dibble .20 .06
652 Frank Tanana .10 .03
653 Steve Decker .10 .03
654 David Cone .20 .06
655 Jack Armstrong .10 .03
656 Dave Stewart .20 .06
657 Billy Hatcher .10 .03
658 Tim Raines .20 .06
659 Walt Weiss .10 .03
660 Jose Lind .10 .03

1993 Score Boys of Summer

Randomly inserted exclusively into one in every four 1993 Score 35-card super packs, cards from this standard-size set feature 30 rookies expected to be the best in their class. Early cards of Pedro Martinez and Mike Piazza highlight this set.

Nm-Mt Ex-Mt
COMPLETE SET (30) 50.00 15.00
1 Billy Ashley 1.50 .45
2 Tim Salmon 3.00 .90
3 Pedro Martinez 10.00 3.00
4 Luis Mercedes 1.50 .45
5 Mike Piazza 10.00 3.00
6 Troy Neel 1.50 .45
7 Melvin Nieves 1.50 .45
8 Ryan Klesko 2.00 .60
9 Ryan Thompson 1.50 .45
10 Kevin Young 2.00 .60
11 Gerald Williams 1.50 .45
12 Willie Greene 1.50 .45
13 John Patterson 1.50 .45
14 Carlos Garcia 1.50 .45
15 Ed Zosky 1.50 .45
16 Sean Berry 1.50 .45
17 Rico Brogna 1.50 .45
18 Larry Carter 1.50 .45
19 Bobby Ayala 1.50 .45
20 Alan Embree 1.50 .45
21 Donald Harris 1.50 .45
22 Sterling Hitchcock 2.00 .60
23 David Nied 1.50 .45
24 Henry Mercedes 1.50 .45
25 Ozzie Canseco 1.50 .45
26 David Hulse 1.50 .45
27 Al Martin 1.50 .45
28 Dan Wilson 1.50 .45
29 Paul Miller 1.50 .45
30 Rich Rowland 1.50 .45

1993 Score Franchise

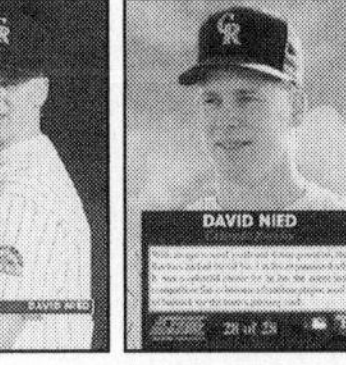

This 28-card set honors the top player on each of the major league teams. These cards were randomly inserted into one in every 24 16-card packs.

Nm-Mt Ex-Mt
COMPLETE SET (28) 120.00 36.00
1 Cal Ripken 25.00 7.50
2 Roger Clemens 15.00 4.50
3 Mark Langston 1.50 .45
4 Frank Thomas 8.00 2.40
5 Carlos Baerga 1.50 .45
6 Cecil Fielder 3.00 .90
7 Gregg Jefferies 1.50 .45
8 Robin Yount 12.00 3.60
9 Kirby Puckett 8.00 2.40
10 Don Mattingly 20.00 6.00
11 Dennis Eckersley 3.00 .90
12 Ken Griffey Jr. 12.00 3.60
13 Juan Gonzalez 8.00 2.40
14 Roberto Alomar 8.00 2.40
15 Terry Pendleton 3.00 .90
16 Ryne Sandberg 12.00 3.60
17 Barry Larkin 8.00 2.40
18 Jeff Bagwell 5.00 1.50
19 Brett Butler 3.00 .90
20 Larry Walker 5.00 1.50
21 Bobby Bonilla 3.00 .90
22 Darren Daulton 3.00 .90
23 Andy Van Slyke 3.00 .90
24 Ray Lankford 1.50 .45
25 Gary Sheffield 3.00 .90
26 Will Clark 8.00 2.40
27 Bryan Harvey 1.50 .45
28 David Nied 1.50 .45

1993 Score Gold Dream Team

Cards from this 12-card standard-size set feature Score's selection of the best players in baseball at each position. The cards were available only through a mail-in offer. Each card front features sepia tone photos of the players out of uniform, with the exception of Griffey's card (of whom is pictured in his Mariners togs). The photo edges are rounded with an airbrush effect.

Nm-Mt Ex-Mt
COMPLETE SET (12) 5.00 1.50
1 Ozzie Smith .75 .23
2 Kirby Puckett .50 .15
3 Gary Sheffield .20 .06
4 Andy Van Slyke .20 .06
5 Ken Griffey Jr. .75 .23
6 Ivan Rodriguez .50 .15
7 Charles Nagy .10 .03
8 Tom Glavine .30 .09
9 Dennis Eckersley .20 .06
10 Frank Thomas .50 .15
11 Roberto Alomar .50 .15
NNO Header Card .10 .03

1993 Score Proctor and Gamble

This ten-card standard-size set was produced by Score as a promotion for Proctor and Gamble. The set was advertised through store displays; the set could be acquired by sending in three UPC symbols and money to cover postage and handling.

Nm-Mt Ex-Mt
COMPLETE SET (10) 6.00 1.80
1 Wil Cordero .25 .07
2 Pedro Martinez 4.00 1.20
3 Bret Boone 2.00 .60
4 Melvin Nieves .25 .07
5 Ryan Klesko 1.00 .30
6 Ryan Thompson .25 .07
7 Kevin Young .25 .07
8 Willie Greene .25 .07
9 Eric Wedge .50 .15
10 David Nied .25 .07

1994 Score Samples

This 19-card standard-size promo set features dark blue-bordered color player action shots on its fronts. Each dealer received one basic promo and one "Gold Rush" promo with their order form. The word "SAMPLE" is printed diagonally across the front and back of each card.

Nm-Mt Ex-Mt
COMPLETE SET (19) 35.00 10.50
1 Barry Bonds 2.00 .60
1GR Barry Bonds 3.00 .90
2 John Olerud .50 .15
2GR John Olerud 1.50 .45
3 Ken Griffey Jr. 2.50 .75
3GR Ken Griffey Jr. 8.00 2.40
4 Jeff Bagwell 1.25 .35
4GR Jeff Bagwell 5.00 1.50
5 John Burkett .25 .07
5GR John Burkett 1.00 .30
6 Jack McDowell .25 .07
6GR Jack McDowell 1.00 .30
7 Albert Belle .50 .15
7GR Albert Belle 1.50 .45
8 Andres Galarraga 1.00 .30
8GR Andres Galarraga 2.50 .75
DT5 Barry Larkin 4.00 1.20
NNO Hobby Ad Card .25 .07
NNO Retail Ad Card .25 .07

1994 Score

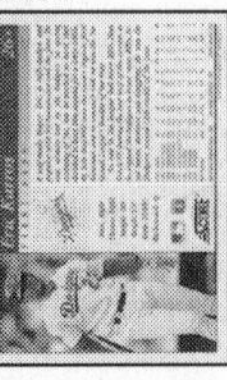

The 1994 Score set of 660 standard-size cards was issued in two series of 330. Cards were distributed in 14-card hobby and retail packs. Each pack contained 13 basic cards plus one Gold Rush parallel card. Cards were also distributed in retail Jumbo packs. 4,875 cases of 1994 Score baseball were printed for the hobby. This figure does not take into account additional product printed for retail outlets. Among the subsets are American League stadiums (317-330) and National League stadiums (647-660). Rookie Cards include Trot Nixon and Billy Wagner.

Nm-Mt Ex-Mt
COMPLETE SET (660) 24.00 7.25
COMP.SERIES 1 (330) 12.00 3.60
COMP.SERIES 2 (330) 12.00 3.60
1 Barry Bonds 1.25 .35
2 John Olerud .20 .06
3 Ken Griffey Jr. .75 .23
4 Jeff Bagwell .30 .09
5 John Burkett .10 .03
6 Jack McDowell .10 .03
7 Albert Belle .20 .06
8 Andres Galarraga .20 .06
9 Mike Mussina .50 .15
10 Will Clark .50 .15
11 Travis Fryman .20 .06
12 Tony Gwynn .60 .18
13 Robin Yount .75 .23
14 Dave Magadan .10 .03
15 Paul O'Neill .30 .09
16 Ray Lankford .10 .03
17 Damion Easley .10 .03
18 Andy Van Slyke .20 .06
19 Brian McRae .10 .03
20 Ryne Sandberg .75 .23
21 Kirby Puckett .50 .15
22 Dwight Gooden .30 .09
23 Don Mattingly 1.25 .35
24 Kevin Mitchell .10 .03
25 Roger Clemens 1.00 .30
26 Eric Karros .20 .06
27 Juan Gonzalez .50 .15
28 John Kruk .20 .06
29 Gregg Jefferies .10 .03
30 Tom Glavine .30 .09
31 Ivan Rodriguez .50 .15
32 Jay Bell .20 .06
33 Randy Johnson .50 .15
34 Darren Daulton .20 .06
35 Rickey Henderson .50 .15
36 Eddie Murray .50 .15
37 Brian Harper .10 .03
38 Delino DeShields .10 .03
39 Jose Lind .10 .03
40 Benito Santiago .20 .06
41 Frank Thomas .50 .15
42 Mark Grace .30 .09
43 Roberto Alomar .50 .15
44 Andy Benes .10 .03
45 Luis Polonia .10 .03
46 Brett Butler .20 .06
47 Terry Steinbach .10 .03
48 Craig Biggio .30 .09
49 Greg Vaughn .20 .06
50 Charlie Hayes .10 .03
51 Mickey Tettleton .10 .03
52 Jose Rijo .10 .03
53 Carlos Baerga .10 .03
54 Jeff Blauser .10 .03
55 Leo Gomez .10 .03
56 Bob Tewksbury .10 .03
57 Mo Vaughn .20 .06
58 Orlando Merced .10 .03
59 Tino Martinez .30 .09
60 Lenny Dykstra .20 .06
61 Jose Canseco .50 .15
62 Tony Fernandez .10 .03
63 Donovan Osborne .10 .03
64 Ken Hill .10 .03
65 Kent Hrbek .20 .06
66 Bryan Harvey .10 .03
67 Wally Joyner .20 .06
68 Derrick May .10 .03
69 Lance Johnson .10 .03
70 Willie McGee .20 .06
71 Mark Langston .10 .03
72 Terry Pendleton .20 .06
73 Joe Carter .20 .06
74 Barry Larkin .50 .15
75 Jimmy Key .20 .06
76 Joe Girardi .10 .03
77 B.J. Surhoff .20 .06
78 Pete Harnisch .10 .03
79 Lou Whitaker UER .20 .06
(Milt Cuyler
pictured on front)
80 Cory Snyder .10 .03
81 Kenny Lofton .20 .06
82 Fred McGriff .30 .09
83 Mike Greenwell .10 .03
84 Mike Perez .10 .03
85 Cal Ripken 1.50 .45
86 Don Slaught .10 .03
87 Omar Vizquel .20 .06
88 Curt Schilling .30 .09
89 Chuck Knoblauch .20 .06
90 Moises Alou .20 .06
91 Greg Gagne .10 .03
92 Bret Saberhagen .20 .06
93 Ozzie Guillen .20 .06
94 Matt Williams .20 .06
95 Chad Curtis .10 .03
96 Mike Harkey .10 .03
97 Devon White .10 .03

98 Walt Weiss .10 .03
99 Kevin Brown .20 .06
100 Gary Sheffield .20 .06
101 Wade Boggs .30 .09
102 Orel Hershiser .20 .06
103 Tony Phillips .10 .03
104 Andujar Cedeno .10 .03
105 Bill Spiers .10 .03
106 Otis Nixon .10 .03
107 Felix Fermin .10 .03
108 Bip Roberts .10 .03
109 Dennis Eckersley .20 .06
110 Dante Bichette .20 .06
111 Ben McDonald .10 .03
112 Jim Poole .10 .03
113 John Dopson .10 .03
114 Rob Dibble .20 .06
115 Jeff Treadway .10 .03
116 Ricky Jordan .10 .03
117 Mike Henneman .10 .03
118 Willie Blair .10 .03
119 Doug Henry .10 .03
120 Gerald Perry .10 .03
121 Greg Myers .10 .03
122 John Franco .20 .06
123 Roger Mason .10 .03
124 Chris Hammond .10 .03
125 Hubie Brooks .10 .03
126 Kent Mercker .10 .03
127 Jim Abbott .30 .09
128 Kevin Bass .10 .03
129 Rick Aguilera .10 .03
130 Mitch Webster .10 .03
131 Eric Plunk .10 .03
132 Mark Carreon .10 .03
133 Dave Stewart .20 .06
134 Willie Wilson .10 .03
135 Dave Fleming .10 .03
136 Jeff Tackett .10 .03
137 Geno Petralli .10 .03
138 Gene Harris .10 .03
139 Scott Bankhead .10 .03
140 Trevor Wilson .10 .03
141 Alvaro Espinoza .10 .03
142 Ryan Bowen .10 .03
143 Mike Moore .10 .03
144 Bill Pecota .10 .03
145 Jaime Navarro .10 .03
146 Jack Daugherty .10 .03
147 Bob Wickman .10 .03
148 Chris Jones .10 .03
149 Todd Stottlemyre .10 .03
150 Brian Williams .10 .03
151 Chuck Finley .20 .06
152 Lenny Harris .10 .03
153 Alex Fernandez .10 .03
154 Candy Maldonado .10 .03
155 Jeff Montgomery .10 .03
156 David West .10 .03
157 Mark Williamson .10 .03
158 Milt Thompson .10 .03
159 Ron Darling .10 .03
160 Stan Belinda .10 .03
161 Henry Cotto .10 .03
162 Mel Rojas .10 .03
163 Doug Strange .10 .03
164 Rene Arocha .10 .03
165 Tim Hulett .10 .03
166 Steve Avery .10 .03
167 Jim Thome .50 .15
168 Tom Browning .10 .03
169 Mario Diaz .10 .03
170 Steve Reed .10 .03
171 Scott Livingstone .10 .03
172 Chris Donnels .10 .03
173 John Jaha .10 .03
174 Carlos Hernandez .10 .03
175 Dion James .10 .03
176 Bud Black .10 .03
177 Tony Castillo .10 .03
178 Jose Guzman .10 .03
179 Torey Lovullo .10 .03
180 John Vander Wal .10 .03
181 Mike LaValliere .10 .03
182 Sid Fernandez .10 .03
183 Brent Mayne .10 .03
184 Terry Mulholland .10 .03
185 Willie Banks .10 .03
186 Steve Cooke .10 .03
187 Brent Gates .10 .03
188 Erik Pappas .10 .03
189 Bill Haselman .10 .03
190 Fernando Valenzuela .20 .06
191 Gary Redus .10 .03
192 Danny Darwin .10 .03
193 Mark Portugal .10 .03
194 Derek Lilliquist .10 .03
195 Charlie O'Brien .10 .03
196 Matt Nokes .10 .03
197 Danny Sheaffer .10 .03
198 Bill Gullickson .10 .03
199 Alex Arias .10 .03
200 Mike Fetters .10 .03
201 Brian Jordan .20 .06
202 Joe Grahe .10 .03
203 Tom Candiotti .10 .03
204 Jeremy Hernandez .10 .03
205 Mike Stanton .10 .03
206 David Howard .10 .03
207 Darren Holmes .10 .03
208 Rick Honeycutt .10 .03
209 Danny Jackson .10 .03
210 Rich Amaral .10 .03
211 Blas Minor .10 .03
212 Kenny Rogers .20 .06
213 Jim Leyritz .10 .03
214 Mike Morgan .10 .03
215 Dan Gladden .10 .03
216 Randy Velarde .10 .03
217 Mitch Williams .10 .03
218 Hipolito Pichardo .10 .03
219 Dave Burba .10 .03
220 Wilson Alvarez .10 .03
221 Bob Zupcic .10 .03
222 Francisco Cabrera .10 .03
223 Julio Valera .10 .03
224 Paul Assenmacher .10 .03
225 Jeff Branson .10 .03
226 Todd Frohwirth .10 .03
227 Armando Reynoso .10 .03
228 Rich Rowland .10 .03
229 Freddie Benavides .10 .03
230 Wayne Kirby .10 .03
231 Darryl Kile .20 .06
232 Skeeter Barnes .10 .03
233 Ramon Martinez .10 .03
234 Tom Gordon .10 .03
235 Dave Gallagher .10 .03
236 Ricky Bones .10 .03
237 Larry Andersen .10 .03
238 Pat Meares .10 .03
239 Zane Smith .10 .03
240 Tim Leary .10 .03
241 Phil Clark .10 .03
242 Danny Cox .10 .03
243 Mike Jackson .10 .03
244 Mike Gallego .10 .03
245 Lee Smith .20 .06
246 Todd Jones .10 .03
247 Steve Bedrosian .10 .03
248 Troy Neel .10 .03
249 Jose Bautista .10 .03
250 Steve Frey .10 .03
251 Jeff Reardon .20 .06
252 Stan Javier .10 .03
253 Mo Sanford .10 .03
254 Steve Sax .10 .03
255 Luis Aquino .10 .03
256 Domingo Jean .10 .03
257 Scott Servais .10 .03
258 Brad Pennington .10 .03
259 Dave Hansen .10 .03
260 Rich Gossage .20 .06
261 Jeff Fassero .10 .03
262 Junior Ortiz .10 .03
263 Anthony Young .10 .03
264 Chris Bosio .10 .03
265 Ruben Amaro .10 .03
266 Mark Eichhorn .10 .03
267 Dave Clark .10 .03
268 Gary Thurman .10 .03
269 Les Lancaster .10 .03
270 Jamie Moyer .20 .06
271 Ricky Gutierrez .10 .03
272 Greg A. Harris .10 .03
273 Mike Benjamin .10 .03
274 Gene Nelson .10 .03
275 Damon Berryhill .10 .03
276 Scott Radinsky .10 .03
277 Mike Aldrete .10 .03
278 Jerry DiPoto .10 .03
279 Chris Haney .10 .03
280 Richie Lewis .10 .03
281 Jarvis Brown .10 .03
282 Juan Bell .10 .03
283 Joe Klink .10 .03
284 Graeme Lloyd .10 .03
285 Casey Candaele .10 .03
286 Bob MacDonald .10 .03
287 Mike Sharperson .10 .03
288 Gene Larkin .10 .03
289 Brian Barnes .10 .03
290 David McCarty .10 .03
291 Jeff Innis .10 .03
292 Bob Patterson .10 .03
293 Ben Rivera .10 .03
294 John Habyan .10 .03
295 Rich Rodriguez .10 .03
296 Edwin Nunez .10 .03
297 Rod Brewer .10 .03
298 Mike Timlin .10 .03
299 Jesse Orosco .10 .03
300 Gary Gaetti .20 .06
301 Todd Benzinger .10 .03
302 Jeff Nelson .10 .03
303 Rafael Belliard .10 .03
304 Matt Whiteside .10 .03
305 Vinny Castilla .20 .06
306 Matt Turner .10 .03
307 Eduardo Perez .10 .03
308 Joel Johnston .10 .03
309 Chris Gomez .10 .03
310 Pat Rapp .10 .03
311 Jim Tatum .10 .03
312 Kirk Rueter .20 .06
313 John Flaherty .10 .03
314 Tom Kramer .10 .03
315 Mark Whiten .10 .03
316 Chris Bosio .10 .03
317 Baltimore Orioles CL .10 .03
318 Bos.Red Sox CL UER .10 .03
Viola listed as 316; should be 331
319 California Angels CL .10 .03
320 Chicago White Sox CL .10 .03
321 Cleveland Indians CL .10 .03
322 Detroit Tigers CL .10 .03
323 KC Royals CL .10 .03
324 Milw. Brewers CL .10 .03
325 Minnesota Twins CL .10 .03
326 New York Yankees CL .10 .03
327 Oakland Athletics CL .10 .03
328 Seattle Mariners CL .10 .03
329 Texas Rangers CL .10 .03
330 Toronto Blue Jays CL .10 .03
331 Frank Viola .20 .06
332 Ron Gant .20 .06
333 Charles Nagy .10 .03
334 Roberto Kelly .10 .03
335 Brady Anderson .20 .06
336 Alex Cole .10 .03
337 Alan Trammell .30 .09
338 Derek Bell .10 .03
339 Bernie Williams .30 .09
340 Jose Offerman .10 .03
341 Bill Wegman .10 .03
342 Ken Caminiti .20 .06
343 Pat Borders .10 .03
344 Kirt Manwaring .10 .03
345 Chili Davis .20 .06
346 Steve Buechele .10 .03
347 Robin Ventura .20 .06
348 Teddy Higuera .10 .03
349 Jerry Browne .10 .03
350 Scott Kamieniecki .10 .03
351 Kevin Tapani .10 .03
352 Marquis Grissom .20 .06
353 Jay Buhner .20 .06
354 Dave Hollins .10 .03
355 Dan Wilson .10 .03
356 Bob Walk .10 .03
357 Chris Hoiles .10 .03
358 Todd Zeile .10 .03
359 Kevin Appier .20 .06
360 Chris Sabo .10 .03
361 David Segui .10 .03
362 Jerald Clark .10 .03
363 Tony Pena .10 .03
364 Steve Finley .20 .06
365 Roger Pavlik .10 .03
366 John Smoltz .30 .09
367 Scott Fletcher .10 .03
368 Jody Reed .10 .03
369 David Wells .20 .06
370 Jose Vizcaino .10 .03
371 Pat Listach .10 .03
372 Orestes Destrade .10 .03
373 Danny Tartabull .10 .03
374 Greg W. Harris .10 .03
375 Juan Guzman .10 .03
376 Larry Walker .30 .09
377 Gary DiSarcina .10 .03
378 Bobby Bonilla .20 .06
379 Tim Raines .20 .06
380 Tommy Greene .10 .03
381 Chris Gwynn .10 .03
382 Jeff King .10 .03
383 Shane Mack .10 .03
384 Ozzie Smith .75 .23
385 Eddie Zambrano RC .10 .03
386 Mike Devereaux .10 .03
387 Erik Hanson .10 .03
388 Scott Cooper .10 .03
389 Dean Palmer .20 .06
390 John Wetteland .20 .06
391 Reggie Jefferson .10 .03
392 Mark Lemke .10 .03
393 Cecil Fielder .20 .06
394 Reggie Sanders .20 .06
395 Darryl Hamilton .10 .03
396 Daryl Boston .10 .03
397 Pat Kelly .10 .03
398 Joe Orsulak .10 .03
399 Ed Sprague .10 .03
400 Eric Anthony .10 .03
401 Scott Sanderson .10 .03
402 Jim Gott .10 .03
403 Ron Karkovice .10 .03
404 Phil Plantier .10 .03
405 David Cone .20 .06
406 Robby Thompson .10 .03
407 Dave Winfield .20 .06
408 Dwight Smith .10 .03
409 Ruben Sierra .10 .03
410 Jack Armstrong .10 .03
411 Mike Felder .10 .03
412 Wil Cordero .10 .03
413 Julio Franco .20 .06
414 Howard Johnson .10 .03
415 Mark McLemore .10 .03
416 Pete Incaviglia .10 .03
417 John Valentin .10 .03
418 Tim Wakefield .20 .06
419 Jose Mesa .10 .03
420 Bernard Gilkey .10 .03
421 Kirk Gibson .20 .06
422 Dave Justice .20 .06
423 Tom Brunansky .10 .03
424 John Smiley .10 .03
425 Kevin Maas .10 .03
426 Doug Drabek .10 .03
427 Paul Molitor .30 .09
428 Darryl Strawberry .30 .09
429 Tim Naehring .10 .03
430 Bill Swift .10 .03
431 Ellis Burks .20 .06
432 Greg Hibbard .10 .03
433 Felix Jose .10 .03
434 Bret Barberie .10 .03
435 Pedro Munoz .10 .03
436 Darrin Fletcher .10 .03
437 Bobby Witt .10 .03
438 Wes Chamberlain .10 .03
439 Mackey Sasser .10 .03
440 Mark Whiten .10 .03
441 Harold Reynolds .20 .06
442 Greg Olson .10 .03
443 Billy Hatcher .10 .03
444 Joe Oliver .10 .03
445 Sandy Alomar Jr. .10 .03
446 Tim Wallach .10 .03
447 Karl Rhodes .10 .03
448 Royce Clayton .10 .03
449 Cal Eldred .10 .03
450 Rick Wilkins .10 .03
451 Mike Stanley .10 .03
452 Charlie Hough .20 .06
453 Jack Morris .20 .06
454 Jon Ratliff RC .10 .03
455 Rene Gonzales .10 .03
456 Eddie Taubensee .10 .03
457 Roberto Hernandez .10 .03
458 Todd Hundley .10 .03
459 Mike Macfarlane .10 .03
460 Mickey Morandini .10 .03
461 Scott Erickson .10 .03
462 Lonnie Smith .10 .03
463 Dave Henderson .10 .03
464 Ryan Klesko .20 .06
465 Edgar Martinez .30 .09
466 Tom Pagnozzi .10 .03
467 Charlie Leibrandt .10 .03
468 Brian Anderson RC .25 .07
469 Harold Baines .20 .06
470 Tim Belcher .10 .03
471 Andre Dawson .20 .06
472 Eric Young .10 .03
473 Paul Sorrento .10 .03
474 Luis Gonzalez .20 .06
475 Rob Deer .10 .03
476 Mike Piazza 1.00 .30
477 Kevin Reimer .10 .03
478 Jeff Gardner .10 .03
479 Melido Perez .10 .03
480 Darren Lewis .10 .03
481 Duane Ward .10 .03
482 Rey Sanchez .10 .03
483 Mark Lewis .10 .03
484 Jeff Conine .20 .06
485 Joey Cora .10 .03
486 Trot Nixon RC .50 .15
487 Kevin McReynolds .10 .03
488 Mike Lansing .10 .03
489 Mike Pagliarulo .10 .03
490 Mariano Duncan .10 .03
491 Mike Bordick .10 .03
492 Kevin Young .10 .03
493 Dave Valle .10 .03
494 Wayne Gomes RC .10 .03
495 Rafael Palmeiro .30 .09
496 Deion Sanders .30 .09
497 Rick Sutcliffe .20 .06
498 Randy Milligan .10 .03
499 Carlos Quintana .10 .03
500 Chris Turner .10 .03
501 Thomas Howard .10 .03
502 Greg Swindell .10 .03
503 Chad Kreuter .10 .03
504 Eric Davis .20 .06
505 Dickie Thon .10 .03
506 Matt Drews RC .10 .03
507 Spike Owen .10 .03
508 Rod Beck .10 .03
509 Pat Hentgen .10 .03
510 Sammy Sosa .75 .23
511 J.T. Snow .20 .06
512 Chuck Carr .10 .03
513 Bo Jackson .50 .15
514 Dennis Martinez .20 .06
515 Phil Hiatt .10 .03
516 Jeff Kent .20 .06
517 Brooks Kieschnick RC .25 .07
518 Kirk Presley RC .10 .03
519 Kevin Seitzer .10 .03
520 Carlos Garcia .10 .03
521 Mike Blowers .10 .03
522 Luis Alicea .10 .03
523 David Hulse .10 .03
524 Greg Maddux UER .75 .23
(career strikeout totals listed as 113; should be 1134)
525 Gregg Olson .10 .03
526 Hal Morris .10 .03
527 Daron Kirkreit .10 .03
528 David Nied .10 .03
529 Jeff Russell .10 .03
530 Kevin Gross .10 .03
531 John Doherty .10 .03
532 Matt Brunson RC .10 .03
533 Dave Nilsson .10 .03
534 Randy Myers .20 .06
535 Steve Farr .10 .03
536 Billy Wagner RC .50 .15
537 Darnell Coles .10 .03
538 Frank Tanana .10 .03
539 Tim Salmon .30 .09
540 Kim Batiste .10 .03
541 George Bell .10 .03
542 Tom Henke .10 .03
543 Sam Horn .10 .03
544 Doug Jones .10 .03
545 Scott Leius .10 .03
546 Al Martin .10 .03
547 Bob Welch .10 .03
548 Scott Christman RC .10 .03
549 Norm Charlton .10 .03
550 Mark McGwire 1.25 .35
551 Greg McMichael .10 .03
552 Tim Costo .10 .03
553 Rodney Bolton .10 .03
554 Pedro Martinez .50 .15
555 Marc Valdes .10 .03
556 Darrell Whitmore .10 .03
557 Tim Bogar .10 .03
558 Steve Karsay .10 .03
559 Danny Bautista .10 .03
560 Jeffrey Hammonds .10 .03
561 Aaron Sele .10 .03
562 Russ Springer .10 .03
563 Jason Bere .10 .03
564 Billy Brewer .10 .03
565 Sterling Hitchcock .10 .03
566 Bobby Munoz .10 .03
567 Craig Paquette .10 .03
568 Bret Boone .20 .06
569 Dan Peltier .10 .03
570 Jeromy Burnitz .20 .06
571 John Wasdin RC .10 .03
572 Chipper Jones .50 .15
573 Jamey Wright RC .10 .03
574 Jeff Granger .10 .03
575 Jay Powell RC .10 .03
576 Ryan Thompson .10 .03
577 Lou Frazier .10 .03
578 Paul Wagner .10 .03
579 Brad Ausmus .10 .03
580 Jack Voigt .10 .03
581 Kevin Rogers .10 .03
582 Damon Buford .10 .03
583 Paul Quantrill .10 .03
584 Marc Newfield .10 .03
585 Derrek Lee RC .60 .18
586 Shane Reynolds .10 .03
587 Cliff Floyd .20 .06
588 Jeff Schwarz .10 .03
589 Ross Powell RC .10 .03
590 Gerald Williams .10 .03
591 Mike Trombley .10 .03
592 Ken Ryan .10 .03
593 John O'Donoghue .10 .03
594 Rod Correia .10 .03
595 Darrell Sherman .10 .03
596 Steve Scarsone .10 .03
597 Sherman Obando .10 .03
598 Kurt Abbott RC .25 .07
599 Dave Telgheder .10 .03
600 Rick Trlicek .10 .03
601 Carl Everett .20 .06
602 Luis Ortiz .10 .03
603 Larry Luebbers .10 .03
604 Kevin Roberson .10 .03
605 Butch Huskey .10 .03
606 Benji Gil .10 .03
607 Todd Van Poppel .10 .03
608 Mark Hutton .10 .03
609 Chip Hale .10 .03
610 Matt Maysey .10 .03
611 Scott Ruffcorn .10 .03
612 Hilly Hathaway .10 .03
613 Allen Watson .10 .03
614 Carlos Delgado .30 .09
615 Roberto Mejia .10 .03
616 Turk Wendell .10 .03
617 Tony Tarasco .10 .03
618 Raul Mondesi .20 .06
619 Kevin Stocker .10 .03
620 Javier Lopez .20 .06
621 Keith Kessinger .10 .03
622 Bob Hamelin .10 .03
623 John Roper .10 .03
624 Lenny Dykstra WS .10 .03
625 Joe Carter WS .10 .03
626 Jim Abbott HL .20 .06
627 Lee Smith HL .10 .03
628 Ken Griffey Jr. HL .50 .15
629 Dave Winfield HL .10 .03
630 Darryl Kile HL .10 .03
631 F.Thomas AL MVP .30 .09
632 Barry Bonds NL MVP .60 .18
633 Jack McDowell AL CY .10 .03
634 Greg Maddux NL CY .50 .15
635 Tim Salmon AL ROY .20 .06
636 Mike Piazza NL ROY .50 .15
637 Brian Turang RC .10 .03
638 Rondell White .20 .06
639 Nigel Wilson .10 .03
640 Torii Hunter RC 2.00 .60
641 Salomon Torres .10 .03
642 Kevin Higgins .10 .03
643 Eric Wedge .10 .03
644 Roger Salkeld .10 .03
645 Manny Ramirez .30 .09
646 Jeff McNeely .10 .03
647 Atlanta Braves CL .10 .03
648 Chicago Cubs CL .10 .03
649 Cincinnati Reds CL .10 .03
650 Colorado Rockies CL .10 .03
651 Florida Marlins CL .10 .03
652 Houston Astros CL .10 .03
653 L.A. Dodgers CL .10 .03
654 Montreal Expos CL .10 .03
655 New York Mets CL .10 .03
656 Phi. Phillies CL .10 .03
657 Pittsburgh Pirates CL .10 .03
658 St. Louis Cardinals CL .10 .03
659 San Diego Padres CL .10 .03
660 S.F. Giants CL .10 .03

1994 Score Gold Rush

This 660-card standard-size set is parallel to the basic Score issue. This set features metallicized and gold-bordered fronts. Gold Rush cards came one per 14-card pack or super pack. They were also issued two per jumbo. These cards were inserted into both hobby and retail packs.

	Nm-Mt	Ex-Mt
COMPLETE SET (660)	120.00	36.00
COMP. SERIES 1 (330)	60.00	18.00
COMP. SERIES 2 (330)	60.00	18.00
*STARS: 1.5X to 4X BASIC CARDS		
*ROOKIES: 1.25X TO 3X BASIC		

1994 Score Boys of Summer

Randomly inserted in super packs at a rate of one in four, this 60-card set features top young stars and hopefuls. The set was issued in two series of 30 cards.

	Nm-Mt	Ex-Mt
COMPLETE SET (60)	60.00	18.00
COMPLETE SERIES 1 (30)	25.00	7.50
COMPLETE SERIES 2 (30)	35.00	10.50
1 Jeff Conine	2.00	.60
2 Aaron Sele	1.00	.30
3 Kevin Stocker	1.00	.30
4 Pat Meares	1.00	.30
5 Jeromy Burnitz	2.00	.60
6 Mike Piazza	8.00	2.40
7 Allen Watson	1.00	.30
8 Jeffrey Hammonds	1.00	.30
9 Kevin Roberson	1.00	.30
10 Hilly Hathaway	1.00	.30
11 Kirk Rueter	2.00	.60
12 Eduardo Perez	1.00	.30
13 Ricky Gutierrez	1.00	.30
14 Domingo Jean	1.00	.30
15 David Nied	1.00	.30
16 Wayne Kirby	1.00	.30
17 Mike Lansing	1.00	.30
18 Jason Bere	1.00	.30
19 Brent Gates	1.00	.30
20 Javier Lopez	2.00	.60
21 Greg McMichael	1.00	.30
22 David Hulse	1.00	.30
23 Roberto Mejia	1.00	.30
24 Tim Salmon	3.00	.90
25 Rene Arocha	1.00	.30
26 Bret Boone	2.00	.60
27 David McCarty	1.00	.30
28 Todd Van Poppel	1.00	.30
29 Lance Painter	1.00	.30
30 Erik Pappas	1.00	.30
31 Chuck Carr	1.00	.30
32 Mark Hutton	1.00	.30
33 Jeff McNeely	1.00	.30
34 Willie Greene	1.00	.30
35 Nigel Wilson	1.00	.30
36 Rondell White	2.00	.60
37 Brian Turang	1.00	.30
38 Manny Ramirez	3.00	.90
39 Salomon Torres	1.00	.30
40 Melvin Nieves	1.00	.30
41 Ryan Klesko	2.00	.60
42 Keith Kessinger	1.00	.30
43 Brad Ausmus	1.00	.30
44 Bob Hamelin	1.00	.30
45 Carlos Delgado	3.00	.90
46 Marc Newfield	1.00	.30
47 Raul Mondesi	2.00	.60
48 Tim Costo	1.00	.30
49 Pedro Martinez	5.00	1.50

50 Steve Karsay 1.00 .30
51 Danny Bautista 1.00 .30
52 Butch Huskey 1.00 .30
53 Kurt Abbott 2.00 .60
54 Darrell Sherman 1.00 .30
55 Damon Buford 1.00 .30
56 Ross Powell 1.00 .30
57 Darrell Whitmore 1.00 .30
58 Chipper Jones 5.00 1.50
59 Jeff Granger 1.00 .30
60 Cliff Floyd 2.00 .60

1994 Score Cycle

This 20-card set was randomly inserted in second series foil at a rate of one in 72 and jumbo packs at a rate of one in 36. The set is arranged according to players with the most singles (1-5), doubles (6-10), triples (11-15) and home runs (16-20). The cards are number with a "TC" prefix.

	Nm-Mt	Ex-Mt
COMPLETE SET (20)	150.00	45.00
TC1 Brett Butler	5.00	1.50
TC2 Kenny Lofton	5.00	1.50
TC3 Paul Molitor	8.00	2.40
TC4 Carlos Baerga	2.50	.75
TC5 Gregg Jefferies Tony Phillips	2.50	.75
TC6 John Olerud	5.00	1.50
TC7 Charlie Hayes	2.50	.75
TC8 Lenny Dykstra	5.00	1.50
TC9 Dante Bichette	5.00	1.50
TC10 Devon White	2.50	.75
TC11 Lance Johnson	2.50	.75
TC12 Joey Cora Steve Finley	5.00	1.50
TC13 Tony Fernandez	2.50	.75
TC14 David Hulse Brett Butler	5.00	1.50
TC15 Jay Bell Brian McRae Mickey Morandini	5.00	1.50
TC16 Juan Gonzalez Barry Bonds	30.00	9.00
TC17 Ken Griffey Jr.	20.00	6.00
TC18 Frank Thomas	12.00	3.60
TC19 Dave Justice	5.00	1.50
TC20 Matt Williams Albert Belle	5.00	1.50

1994 Score Dream Team

Randomly inserted in first series foil and jumbo packs at a rate of one in 72, this ten-card set feature's baseball's Dream Team as selected by Pinnacle Brands. Banded by forest green stripes above and below, the player photos on the fronts feature ten of baseball's best players sporting historical team uniforms from the 1930's. A Barry Larkin promo card was distributed to dealers and hobby media to preview the set.

	Nm-Mt	Ex-Mt
COMPLETE SET (10)	60.00	18.00
1 Mike Mussina	12.00	3.60
2 Tom Glavine	8.00	2.40
3 Don Mattingly	30.00	9.00
4 Carlos Baerga	2.50	.75
5 Barry Larkin	12.00	3.60
6 Matt Williams	5.00	1.50
7 Juan Gonzalez	12.00	3.60
8 Andy Van Slyke	5.00	1.50
9 Larry Walker	8.00	2.40
10 Mike Stanley	2.50	.75
S5 Barry Larkin Sample	1.00	.30

1994 Score Gold Stars

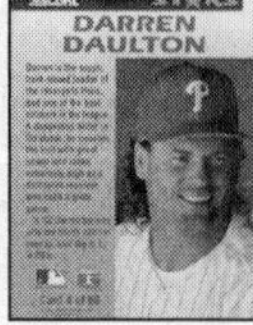

Randomly inserted at a rate of one in every 18 hobby packs, this 60-card set features National and American stars. Split into two series of 30 cards, the first series (1-30) comprises of National League players and the second series (31-60) American Leaguers.

	Nm-Mt	Ex-Mt
COMPLETE SET (60)	250.00	75.00
COMPLETE NL (30)	100.00	30.00
COMPLETE AL (30)	150.00	45.00
1 Barry Bonds	20.00	6.00
2 Orlando Merced	1.50	.45
3 Mark Grace	5.00	1.50
4 Darren Daulton	3.00	.90
5 Jeff Blauser	1.50	.45
6 Deion Sanders	5.00	1.50
7 John Kruk	3.00	.90
8 Jeff Bagwell	5.00	1.50
9 Gregg Jefferies	1.50	.45
10 Matt Williams	3.00	.90
11 Andres Galarraga	3.00	.90
12 Jay Bell	3.00	.90
13 Mike Piazza	15.00	4.50
14 Ron Gant	3.00	.90
15 Barry Larkin	8.00	2.40
16 Tom Glavine	5.00	1.50
17 Lenny Dykstra	3.00	.90
18 Fred McGriff	5.00	1.50
19 Andy Van Slyke	3.00	.90
20 Gary Sheffield	3.00	.90
21 John Burkett	1.50	.45
22 Dante Bichette	3.00	.90
23 Tony Gwynn	10.00	3.00
24 Dave Justice	3.00	.90
25 Marquis Grissom	1.50	.45
26 Bobby Bonilla	3.00	.90
27 Larry Walker	5.00	1.50
28 Brett Butler	3.00	.90
29 Robby Thompson	1.50	.45
30 Jeff Conine	3.00	.90
31 Joe Carter	3.00	.90
32 Ken Griffey Jr.	12.00	3.60
33 Juan Gonzalez	8.00	2.40
34 Rickey Henderson	8.00	2.40
35 Bo Jackson	8.00	2.40
36 Cal Ripken	25.00	7.50
37 John Olerud	3.00	.90
38 Carlos Baerga	1.50	.45
39 Jack McDowell	1.50	.45
40 Cecil Fielder	3.00	.90
41 Kenny Lofton	3.00	.90
42 Roberto Alomar	8.00	2.40
43 Randy Johnson	8.00	2.40
44 Tim Salmon	5.00	1.50
45 Frank Thomas	8.00	2.40
46 Albert Belle	3.00	.90
47 Greg Vaughn	3.00	.90
48 Travis Fryman	3.00	.90
49 Don Mattingly	20.00	6.00
50 Wade Boggs	5.00	1.50
51 Mo Vaughn	3.00	.90
52 Kirby Puckett	8.00	2.40
53 Devon White	1.50	.45
54 Tony Phillips	1.50	.45
55 Brian Harper	1.50	.45
56 Chad Curtis	1.50	.45
57 Paul Molitor	5.00	1.50
58 Ivan Rodriguez	8.00	2.40
59 Rafael Palmeiro	5.00	1.50
60 Brian McRae	1.50	.45

1994 Score Rookie/Traded Samples

Issued to preview the designs of Score's 1994 Rookie/Traded set and its inserts, these 11 standard-size cards feature color player action shots on their fronts. The Jackson card is from the one-per-pack Gold Rush insert set. The Palmeiro card represents the randomly inserted Changing Places insert set, and the Ramirez card is an example of the randomly inserted Super Rookies set. Except for the title card, all the cards carry the word "Sample" in diagonal white lettering on their fronts and backs. The cards are numbered on the back with prefixes as shown below.

	Nm-Mt	Ex-Mt
COMPLETE SET (11)	12.00	3.60
CP2 Rafael Palmeiro	1.25	.35
RT1 Will Clark	2.00	.60
RT2 Lee Smith	.75	.23
RT3 Bo Jackson	2.00	.60
RT4 Ellis Burks	.75	.23
RT5 Eddie Murray	2.50	.75
RT6 Delino DeShields	.50	.15
RT102 Carlos Delgado	2.50	.75
SU2 Manny Ramirez	2.50	.75
NNO Title Card	.50	.15
NNO September Call-Up Redemption Sample	.50	.15

1994 Score Rookie/Traded

The 1994 Score Rookie and Traded set consists of 165 standard-size cards featuring rookie standouts, traded players, and new young prospects. The set is delineated by traded players (RT1-RT70) and rookies/young prospects (RT71-RT163). The set closes with checklists (RT164-RT165). Each foil pack contained one Gold Rush card. The cards are numbered on the back with an "RT" prefix. Several leading dealers are under the belief that Jose Lima's card (number RT158) was short-printed. Conversely, extra cards of John Mabry are typically found in place of the short Lima's. A special unnumbered September Call-Up Redemption card could be exchanged for an Alex Rodriguez card. The expiration date was January 31, 1995. Odds of finding a redemption card were approximately one in 240 retail and hobby packs. Rookie Cards include Jose Lima and Chan Ho Park.

	Nm-Mt	Ex-Mt
COMPLETE SET (165)	15.00	4.50
RT1 Will Clark	.75	.23
RT2 Lee Smith	.30	.09
RT3 Bo Jackson	.75	.23
RT4 Ellis Burks	.30	.09
RT5 Eddie Murray	.75	.23
RT6 Delino DeShields	.15	.04
RT7 Erik Hanson	.15	.04
RT8 Rafael Palmeiro	.50	.15
RT9 Luis Polonia	.15	.04
RT10 Omar Vizquel	.30	.09
RT11 Kurt Abbott	.30	.09
RT12 Vince Coleman	.15	.04
RT13 Rickey Henderson	.75	.23
RT14 Terry Mulholland	.15	.04
RT15 Greg Hibbard	.15	.04
RT16 Walt Weiss	.15	.04
RT17 Chris Sabo	.15	.04
RT18 Dave Henderson	.15	.04
RT19 Rick Sutcliffe	.30	.09
RT20 Harold Reynolds	.30	.09
RT21 Jack Morris	.30	.09
RT22 Dan Wilson	.15	.04
RT23 Dave Magadan	.15	.04
RT24 Dennis Martinez	.30	.09
RT25 Wes Chamberlain	.15	.04
RT26 Otis Nixon	.15	.04
RT27 Eric Anthony	.15	.04
RT28 Randy Milligan	.15	.04
RT29 Julio Franco	.30	.09
RT30 Kevin McReynolds	.15	.04
RT31 Anthony Young	.15	.04
RT32 Brian Harper	.15	.04
RT33 Gene Harris	.15	.04
RT34 Eddie Taubensee	.15	.04
RT35 David Segui	.15	.04
RT36 Stan Javier	.15	.04
RT37 Felix Fermin	.15	.04
RT38 Darrin Jackson	.15	.04
RT39 Tony Fernandez	.15	.04
RT40 Jose Vizcaino	.15	.04
RT41 Willie Banks	.15	.04
RT42 Brian Hunter	.15	.04
RT43 Reggie Jefferson	.15	.04
RT44 Junior Felix	.15	.04
RT45 Jack Armstrong	.15	.04
RT46 Bip Roberts	.15	.04
RT47 Jerry Browne	.15	.04
RT48 Marvin Freeman	.15	.04
RT49 Jody Reed	.15	.04
RT50 Alex Cole	.15	.04
RT51 Sid Fernandez	.15	.04
RT52 Pete Smith	.15	.04
RT53 Xavier Hernandez	.15	.04
RT54 Scott Sanderson	.15	.04
RT55 Turner Ward	.15	.04
RT56 Rex Hudler	.15	.04
RT57 Deion Sanders	.50	.15
RT58 Sid Bream	.15	.04
RT59 Tony Pena	.15	.04
RT60 Bret Boone	.30	.09
RT61 Bobby Ayala	.15	.04
RT62 Pedro Martinez	.75	.23
RT63 Howard Johnson	.15	.04
RT64 Mark Portugal	.15	.04
RT65 Roberto Kelly	.15	.04
RT66 Spike Owen	.15	.04
RT67 Jeff Treadway	.15	.04
RT68 Mike Harkey	.15	.04
RT69 Doug Jones	.15	.04
RT70 Steve Farr	.15	.04
RT71 Billy Taylor RC	.15	.04
RT72 Manny Ramirez	.50	.15
RT73 Bob Hamelin	.15	.04
RT74 Steve Karsay	.15	.04
RT75 Ryan Klesko	.30	.09
RT76 Cliff Floyd	.30	.09
RT77 Jeffrey Hammonds	.15	.04
RT78 Javier Lopez	.30	.09
RT79 Roger Salkeld	.15	.04
RT80 Hector Carrasco	.15	.04
RT81 Gerald Williams	.15	.04
RT82 Raul Mondesi	.30	.09
RT83 Sterling Hitchcock	.15	.04
RT84 Danny Bautista	.15	.04
RT85 Chris Turner	.15	.04
RT86 Shane Reynolds	.15	.04
RT87 Rondell White	.30	.09
RT88 Salomon Torres	.15	.04
RT89 Turk Wendell	.15	.04
RT90 Tony Tarasco	.15	.04
RT91 Shawn Green	.75	.23
RT92 Greg Colbrunn	.15	.04
RT93 Eddie Zambrano	.15	.04
RT94 Rich Becker	.15	.04
RT95 Chris Gomez	.15	.04
RT96 John Patterson	.15	.04
RT97 Derek Parks	.15	.04
RT98 Rich Rowland	.15	.04
RT99 James Mouton	.15	.04
RT100 Tim Hyers RC	.15	.04
RT101 Jose Valentin	.15	.04
RT102 Carlos Delgado	.50	.15
RT103 Robert Eenhoorn	.15	.04
RT104 John Hudek RC	.15	.04
RT105 Domingo Cedeno	.15	.04
RT106 Denny Hocking	.15	.04
RT107 Greg Pirkl	.15	.04
RT108 Mark Smith	.15	.04
RT109 Paul Shuey	.15	.04
RT110 Jorge Fabregas	.15	.04
RT111 Rikkert Faneyte RC	.15	.04
RT112 Rob Butler	.15	.04
RT113 Darren Oliver RC	.30	.09
RT114 Troy O'Leary	.15	.04
RT115 Scott Brow	.15	.04
RT116 Tony Eusebio	.15	.04
RT117 Carlos Reyes	.15	.04
RT118 J.R. Phillips	.15	.04
RT119 Alex Diaz	.15	.04
RT120 Charles Johnson	.30	.09
RT121 Nate Minchey	.15	.04
RT122 Scott Sanders	.15	.04
RT123 Daryl Boston	.15	.04
RT124 Joey Hamilton	.15	.04
RT125 Brian Anderson	.30	.09
RT126 Dan Miceli	.15	.04
RT127 Tom Brunansky	.15	.04
RT128 Dave Staton	.15	.04
RT129 Mike Oquist	.15	.04
RT130 John Mabry RC	.30	.09
RT131 Norberto Martin	.15	.04
RT132 Hector Fajardo	.15	.04
RT133 Mark Hutton	.15	.04
RT134 Fernando Vina	.50	.15
RT135 Lee Tinsley	.15	.04
RT136 Chan Ho Park RC	.75	.23
RT137 Paul Spoljaric	.15	.04
RT138 Matias Carrillo	.15	.04
RT139 Mark Kiefer	.15	.04
RT140 Stan Royer	.15	.04
RT141 Bryan Eversgerd	.15	.04
RT142 Brian L. Hunter	.15	.04
RT143 Joe Hall	.15	.04
RT144 Johnny Ruffin	.15	.04
RT145 Alex Gonzalez	.15	.04
RT146 Keith Lockhart RC	.30	.09
RT147 Tom Marsh	.15	.04
RT148 Tony Longmire	.15	.04
RT149 Keith Mitchell	.15	.04
RT150 Melvin Nieves	.15	.04
RT151 Kelly Stinnett RC	.15	.04
RT152 Miguel Jimenez	.15	.04
RT153 Jeff Juden	.15	.04
RT154 Matt Walbeck	.15	.04
RT155 Marc Newfield	.15	.04
RT156 Matt Mieske	.15	.04
RT157 Marcus Moore	.15	.04
RT158 Jose Lima RC SP	5.00	1.50
RT159 Mike Kelly	.15	.04
RT160 Jim Edmonds	.50	.15
RT161 Steve Trachsel	.15	.04
RT162 Greg Blosser	.15	.04
RT163 Marc Acre RC	.15	.04
RT164 AL Checklist	.15	.04
RT165 NL Checklist	.15	.04
HC1 Alex Rodriguez Call-Up Redemption	450.00	135.00
NNO Sept. Call-Up Trade EXP	2.00	.60

1994 Score Rookie/Traded Gold Rush

Issued one per pack, these cards are a gold foil version of the 165-card Rookie/Traded set. The differences between the basic card and Gold Rush version are the gold foil borders that surround a metallicized player photo. The only difference on the back is a Gold Rush logo.

	Nm-Mt	Ex-Mt
COMPLETE SET (165)	50.00	15.00

*STARS: 1X TO 2.5X BASIC CARDS ...
*ROOKIES: 1X TO 2.5X BASIC CARDS

1994 Score Rookie/Traded Changing Places

Randomly inserted in both retail and hobby packs at a rate of one in 36 Rookie/Traded packs, this 10-card standard-size set focuses on ten veteran superstar players who were traded prior to or during the 1994 season. Cards fronts feature a color photo with a slanted design. The backs have a short write-up and a distorted photo.

	Nm-Mt	Ex-Mt
COMPLETE SET (10)	30.00	9.00
CP1 Will Clark	10.00	3.00
CP2 Rafael Palmeiro	6.00	1.80
CP3 Roberto Kelly	2.00	.60
CP4 Bo Jackson	10.00	3.00
CP5 Otis Nixon	2.00	.60
CP6 Rickey Henderson	10.00	3.00
CP7 Ellis Burks	4.00	1.20
CP8 Lee Smith	4.00	1.20
CP9 Delino DeShields	2.00	.60
CP10 Deion Sanders	6.00	1.80

1994 Score Rookie/Traded Super Rookies

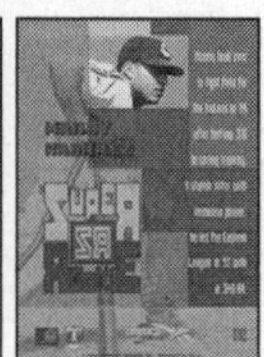

Randomly inserted in hobby packs at a rate of one in 36, this 18-card standard-size set focuses on top rookies of 1994. Odds of finding one of these cards is approximately one in 36 hobby packs. Designed much like the Gold Rush, the cards have an all-foil design. The fronts have a player photo and the backs have a photo that serves as background to the Super Rookies logo and text.

	Nm-Mt	Ex-Mt
COMPLETE SET (18)	60.00	18.00
SU1 Carlos Delgado	8.00	2.40
SU2 Manny Ramirez	8.00	2.40
SU3 Ryan Klesko	5.00	1.50
SU4 Raul Mondesi	5.00	1.50
SU5 Bob Hamelin	2.50	.75
SU6 Steve Karsay	2.50	.75
SU7 Jeffrey Hammonds	2.50	.75
SU8 Cliff Floyd	5.00	1.50
SU9 Kurt Abbott	5.00	1.50
SU10 Marc Newfield	2.50	.75
SU11 Javier Lopez	5.00	1.50
SU12 Rich Becker	2.50	.75
SU13 Greg Pirkl	2.50	.75
SU14 Rondell White	5.00	1.50
SU15 James Mouton	2.50	.75
SU16 Tony Tarasco	2.50	.75
SU17 Brian Anderson	5.00	1.50
SU18 Jim Edmonds	8.00	2.40

1995 Score Samples

These ten sample cards were issued to herald the release of the 1995 Score baseball series. The standard-size cards feature on their horizontal and vertical fronts color action player shots with irregular dark green and sand brown borders. The player's name, position and the team logo appear in a blue bar under the picture. The word "Sample" is printed diagonally over the photo. The horizontal backs have the same design as the fronts. They carry another small color headshot on the left, with the player's name, short biography, career highlights and statistics on the right. The word "Sample" is also printed diagonally across the backs.

	Nm-Mt	Ex-Mt
COMPLETE SET (10)	10.00	3.00
2 Roberto Alomar	1.00	.30
4 Jose Canseco	1.25	.35
5 Matt Williams	.75	.23
221 Jeff Bagwell	1.50	.45
223 Albert Belle	.50	.15
224 Chuck Carr	.25	.07
288 Jorge Fabregas	.25	.07
DP8 McKay Christensen	.25	.07
HG5 Cal Ripken	5.00	1.50
NNO Title Card	.25	.07

1995 Score

The 1995 Score set consists of 605 standard-size cards issued in hobby, retail and jumbo packs. Hobby packs featured a special signed Ryan Klesko (RG1)card. Retail packs also had a Klesko card (SG1) but these were not signed.

	Nm-Mt	Ex-Mt
COMPLETE SET (605)	24.00	7.25
COMP. SERIES 1 (330)	12.00	3.60
COMP. SERIES 2 (275)	12.00	3.60
1 Frank Thomas	.50	.15
2 Roberto Alomar	.50	.15
3 Cal Ripken	1.50	.45
4 Jose Canseco	.50	.15
5 Matt Williams	.20	.06
6 Esteban Beltre	.10	.03
7 Domingo Cedeno	.10	.03
8 John Valentin	.10	.03
9 Glenallen Hill	.10	.03
10 Rafael Belliard	.10	.03
11 Randy Myers	.10	.03
12 Mo Vaughn	.20	.06
13 Hector Carrasco	.10	.03
14 Chili Davis	.20	.06
15 Dante Bichette	.20	.06
16 Darrin Jackson	.10	.03
17 Mike Piazza	.75	.23
18 Junior Felix	.10	.03
19 Moises Alou	.20	.06
20 Mark Gubicza	.10	.03
21 Bret Saberhagen	.20	.06
22 Lenny Dykstra	.20	.06
23 Steve Howe	.10	.03
24 Mark Dewey	.10	.03
25 Brian Harper	.10	.03
26 Ozzie Smith	.75	.23
27 Scott Erickson	.10	.03
28 Tony Gwynn	.60	.18
29 Bob Welch	.10	.03
30 Barry Bonds	1.25	.35
31 Leo Gomez	.10	.03
32 Greg Maddux	.75	.23
33 Mike Greenwell	.10	.03
34 Sammy Sosa	.75	.23
35 Darnell Coles	.10	.03
36 Tommy Greene	.10	.03
37 Will Clark	.50	.15
38 Steve Ontiveros	.10	.03
39 Stan Javier	.10	.03
40 Bip Roberts	.10	.03
41 Paul O'Neill	.30	.09
42 Bill Haselman	.10	.03
43 Shane Mack	.10	.03
44 Orlando Merced	.10	.03
45 Kevin Seitzer	.10	.03
46 Trevor Hoffman	.20	.06
47 Greg Gagne	.10	.03
48 Jeff Kent	.20	.06
49 Tony Phillips	.10	.03
50 Ken Hill	.10	.03
51 Carlos Baerga	.10	.03
52 Henry Rodriguez	.10	.03
53 Scott Sanderson	.10	.03
54 Jeff Conine	.20	.06
55 Chris Turner	.10	.03
56 Ken Caminiti	.20	.06
57 Harold Baines	.20	.06
58 Charlie Hayes	.10	.03
59 Roberto Kelly	.10	.03
60 John Olerud	.20	.06
61 Tim Davis	.10	.03
62 Rich Rowland	.10	.03
63 Rey Sanchez	.10	.03
64 Junior Ortiz	.10	.03
65 Ricky Gutierrez	.10	.03
66 Rex Hudler	.10	.03
67 Johnny Ruffin	.10	.03
68 Jay Buhner	.20	.06
69 Tom Pagnozzi	.10	.03
70 Julio Franco	.20	.06
71 Eric Young	.10	.03
72 Mike Bordick	.10	.03
73 Don Slaught	.10	.03
74 Goose Gossage	.20	.06
75 Lonnie Smith	.10	.03
76 Jimmy Key	.20	.06
77 Dave Hollins	.10	.03

1995 Score

78 Mickey Tettleton .10 .03
79 Luis Gonzalez .20 .06
80 Dave Winfield .20 .06
81 Ryan Thompson .10 .03
82 Felix Jose .10 .03
83 Rusty Meacham .10 .03
84 Darryl Hamilton .10 .03
85 John Wetteland .20 .06
86 Tom Brunansky .10 .03
87 Mark Lemke .10 .03
88 Spike Owen .10 .03
89 Shawon Dunston .10 .03
90 Wilson Alvarez .10 .03
91 Lee Smith .20 .06
92 Scott Kamieniecki .10 .03
93 Jacob Brumfield .10 .03
94 Kirk Gibson .20 .06
95 Joe Girardi .10 .03
96 Mike Macfarlane .10 .03
97 Greg Colbrunn .10 .03
98 Ricky Bones .10 .03
99 Delino DeShields .10 .03
100 Pat Meares .10 .03
101 Jeff Fassero .10 .03
102 Jim Leyritz .10 .03
103 Gary Redus .10 .03
104 Terry Steinbach .10 .03
105 Kevin McReynolds .10 .03
106 Felix Fermin .10 .03
107 Danny Jackson .10 .03
108 Chris James .10 .03
109 Jeff King .10 .03
110 Pat Hentgen .10 .03
111 Gerald Perry .10 .03
112 Tim Raines .20 .06
113 Eddie Williams .10 .03
114 Jamie Moyer .20 .06
115 Bud Black .10 .03
116 Chris Gomez .10 .03
117 Luis Lopez .10 .03
118 Roger Clemens 1.00 .30
119 Javier Lopez .20 .06
120 Dave Nilsson .10 .03
121 Karl Rhodes .10 .03
122 Rick Aguilera .10 .03
123 Tony Fernandez .10 .03
124 Bernie Williams .30 .09
125 James Mouton .10 .03
126 Mark Langston .10 .03
127 Mike Lansing .10 .03
128 Tino Martinez .30 .09
129 Joe Orsulak .10 .03
130 Dave Hulse .10 .03
131 Pete Incaviglia .10 .03
132 Mark Clark .10 .03
133 Tony Eusebio .10 .03
134 Chuck Finley .20 .06
135 Lou Frazier .10 .03
136 Craig Grebeck .10 .03
137 Kelly Stinnett .10 .03
138 Paul Shuey .10 .03
139 David Nied .10 .03
140 Billy Brewer .10 .03
141 Dave Weathers .10 .03
142 Scott Leius .10 .03
143 Brian Jordan .20 .06
144 Melido Perez .10 .03
145 Tony Tarasco .10 .03
146 Dan Wilson .10 .03
147 Rondell White .20 .06
148 Mike Henneman .10 .03
149 Brian Johnson .10 .03
150 Tom Henke .10 .03
151 John Patterson .10 .03
152 Bobby Witt .10 .03
153 Eddie Taubensee .10 .03
154 Pat Borders .10 .03
155 Ramon Martinez .10 .03
156 Mike Kingery .10 .03
157 Zane Smith .10 .03
158 Benito Santiago .20 .06
159 Matias Carrillo .10 .03
160 Scott Brosius .20 .06
161 Dave Clark .10 .03
162 Mark McLemore .10 .03
163 Curt Schilling .30 .09
164 J.T. Snow .20 .06
165 Rod Beck .10 .03
166 Scott Fletcher .10 .03
167 Bob Tewksbury .10 .03
168 Mike LaValliere .10 .03
169 Dave Hansen .10 .03
170 Pedro Martinez .50 .15
171 Kirk Rueter .10 .03
172 Jose Lind .10 .03
173 Luis Alicea .10 .03
174 Mike Moore .10 .03
175 Andy Ashby .10 .03
176 Jody Reed .10 .03
177 Darryl Kile .20 .06
178 Carl Willis .10 .03
179 Jeromy Burnitz .20 .06
180 Mike Gallego .10 .03
181 Bill VanLandingham .10 .03
182 Sid Fernandez .10 .03
183 Kim Batiste .10 .03
184 Greg Myers .10 .03
185 Steve Avery .10 .03
186 Steve Farr .10 .03
187 Robb Nen .20 .06
188 Dan Pasqua .10 .03
189 Bruce Ruffin .10 .03
190 Jose Valentin .10 .03
191 Willie Banks .10 .03
192 Mike Aldrete .10 .03
193 Randy Milligan .10 .03
194 Steve Karsay .10 .03
195 Mike Stanley .10 .03
196 Jose Mesa .10 .03
197 Tom Browning .10 .03
198 John Vander Wal .10 .03
199 Kevin Brown .20 .06
200 Mike Oquist .10 .03
201 Greg Swindell .10 .03
202 Eddie Zambrano .10 .03
203 Joe Boever .10 .03
204 Gary Varsho .10 .03
205 Chris Gwynn .10 .03
206 David Howard .10 .03
207 Jerome Walton .10 .03
208 Danny Darwin .10 .03
209 Darryl Strawberry .30 .09
210 Todd Van Poppel .10 .03
211 Scott Livingstone .10 .03
212 Dave Fleming .10 .03
213 Todd Worrell .10 .03
214 Carlos Delgado .20 .06
215 Bill Pecota .10 .03
216 Jim Lindeman .10 .03
217 Rick White .10 .03
218 Jose Oquendo .10 .03
219 Tony Castillo .10 .03
220 Fernando Vina .20 .06
221 Jeff Bagwell .30 .09
222 Randy Johnson .50 .15
223 Albert Belle .20 .06
224 Chuck Carr .10 .03
225 Mark Leiter .10 .03
226 Hal Morris .10 .03
227 Robin Ventura .20 .06
228 Mike Munoz .10 .03
229 Jim Thome .50 .15
230 Mario Diaz .10 .03
231 John Doherty .10 .03
232 Bobby Jones .10 .03
233 Raul Mondesi .20 .06
234 Ricky Jordan .10 .03
235 John Jaha .10 .03
236 Carlos Garcia .10 .03
237 Kirby Puckett .50 .15
238 Orel Hershiser .20 .06
239 Don Mattingly 1.25 .35
240 Sid Bream .10 .03
241 Brent Gates .10 .03
242 Tony Longmire .10 .03
243 Robby Thompson .10 .03
244 Rick Sutcliffe .20 .06
245 Dean Palmer .20 .06
246 Marquis Grissom .10 .03
247 Paul Molitor .30 .09
248 Mark Carreon .10 .03
249 Jack Voigt .10 .03
250 Greg McMichael UER .10 .03
(photo on front is Mike Stanton)
251 Damon Berryhill .10 .03
252 Brian Dorsett .10 .03
253 Jim Edmonds .20 .06
254 Barry Larkin .50 .15
255 Jack McDowell .10 .03
256 Wally Joyner .20 .06
257 Eddie Murray .50 .15
258 Lenny Webster .10 .03
259 Milt Cuyler .10 .03
260 Todd Benzinger .10 .03
261 Vince Coleman .10 .03
262 Todd Stottlemyre .10 .03
263 Turner Ward .10 .03
264 Ray Lankford .10 .03
265 Matt Walbeck .10 .03
266 Deion Sanders .30 .09
267 Gerald Williams .10 .03
268 Jim Gott .10 .03
269 Jeff Frye .10 .03
270 Jose Rijo .10 .03
271 Dave Justice .20 .06
272 Ismael Valdes .10 .03
273 Ben McDonald .10 .03
274 Darren Lewis .10 .03
275 Graeme Lloyd .10 .03
276 Luis Ortiz .10 .03
277 Julian Tavarez .10 .03
278 Mark Dalesandro .10 .03
279 Brett Merriman .10 .03
280 Ricky Bottalico .10 .03
281 Robert Eenhoorn .10 .03
282 Rikkert Faneyte .10 .03
283 Mike Kelly .10 .03
284 Mark Smith .10 .03
285 Turk Wendell .10 .03
286 Greg Blosser .10 .03
287 Garey Ingram .10 .03
288 Jorge Fabregas .10 .03
289 Blaise Ilsley .10 .03
290 Joe Hall .10 .03
291 Orlando Miller .10 .03
292 Jose Lima .10 .03
293 Greg O'Halloran RC .10 .03
294 Mark Kiefer .10 .03
295 Jose Oliva .10 .03
296 Rich Becker .10 .03
297 Brian L. Hunter .10 .03
298 Dave Silvestri .10 .03
299 Armando Benitez .20 .06
300 Darren Dreifort .10 .03
301 John Mabry .10 .03
302 Greg Pirkl .10 .03
303 J.R. Phillips .10 .03
304 Shawn Green .20 .06
305 Roberto Petagine .10 .03
306 Keith Lockhart .10 .03
307 Jonathan Hurst .10 .03
308 Paul Spoljaric .10 .03
309 Mike Lieberthal .20 .06
310 Garret Anderson .20 .06
311 John Johnstone .10 .03
312 Alex Rodriguez 1.25 .35
313 Kent Mercker HL .10 .03
314 John Valentin HL .10 .03
315 Kenny Rogers HL .20 .06
316 Fred McGriff HL .20 .06
317 Team Checklists .10 .03
318 Team Checklists .10 .03
319 Team Checklists .10 .03
320 Team Checklists .10 .03
321 Team Checklists .10 .03
322 Team Checklists .10 .03
323 Team Checklists .10 .03
324 Team Checklists .10 .03
325 Team Checklists .10 .03
326 Team Checklists .10 .03
327 Team Checklists .10 .03
328 Team Checklists .10 .03
329 Team Checklists .10 .03
330 Team Checklists .10 .03
331 Pedro Munoz .10 .03
332 Ryan Klesko .20 .06
333 Andre Dawson .20 .06
334 Derrick May .10 .03
335 Aaron Sele .10 .03
336 Kevin Mitchell .10 .03
337 Steve Trachsel .10 .03
338 Andres Galarraga .20 .06
339 Terry Pendleton .20 .06
340 Gary Sheffield .20 .06
341 Travis Fryman .20 .06
342 Bo Jackson .50 .15
343 Gary Gaetti .20 .06
344 Brett Butler .20 .06
345 B.J. Surhoff .20 .06
346 Larry Walker .30 .09
347 Kevin Tapani .10 .03
348 Rick Wilkins .10 .03
349 Wade Boggs .30 .09
350 Mariano Duncan .10 .03
351 Ruben Sierra .10 .03
352 Andy Van Slyke .20 .06
353 Reggie Jefferson .10 .03
354 Gregg Jefferies .10 .03
355 Tim Naehring .10 .03
356 John Roper .10 .03
357 Joe Carter .20 .06
358 Kurt Abbott .10 .03
359 Lenny Harris .10 .03
360 Lance Johnson .10 .03
361 Brian Anderson .10 .03
362 Jim Eisenreich .10 .03
363 Jerry Browne .10 .03
364 Mark Grace .30 .09
365 Devon White .20 .06
366 Reggie Sanders .20 .06
367 Ivan Rodriguez .50 .15
368 Kirt Manwaring .10 .03
369 Pat Kelly .10 .03
370 Ellis Burks .20 .06
371 Charles Nagy .10 .03
372 Kevin Bass .10 .03
373 Lou Whitaker .20 .06
374 Rene Arocha .10 .03
375 Derek Parks .10 .03
376 Mark Whiten .10 .03
377 Mark McGwire 1.25 .35
378 Doug Drabek .10 .03
379 Greg Vaughn .20 .06
380 Al Martin .10 .03
381 Ron Darling .10 .03
382 Tim Wallach .10 .03
383 Alan Trammell .30 .09
384 Randy Velarde .10 .03
385 Chris Sabo .10 .03
386 Wil Cordero .10 .03
387 Darrin Fletcher .10 .03
388 David Segui .10 .03
389 Steve Buechele .10 .03
390 Dave Gallagher .10 .03
391 Thomas Howard .10 .03
392 Chad Curtis .10 .03
393 Cal Eldred .10 .03
394 Jason Bere .10 .03
395 Bret Barberie .10 .03
396 Paul Sorrento .10 .03
397 Steve Finley .20 .06
398 Cecil Fielder .20 .06
399 Eric Karros .20 .06
400 Jeff Montgomery .10 .03
401 Cliff Floyd .20 .06
402 Matt Mieske .10 .03
403 Brian Hunter .10 .03
404 Alex Cole .10 .03
405 Kevin Stocker .10 .03
406 Eric Davis .20 .06
407 Marvin Freeman .10 .03
408 Dennis Eckersley .20 .06
409 Todd Zeile .10 .03
410 Keith Mitchell .10 .03
411 Andy Benes .10 .03
412 Juan Bell .10 .03
413 Royce Clayton .10 .03
414 Ed Sprague .10 .03
415 Mike Mussina .50 .15
416 Todd Hundley .10 .03
417 Pat Listach .10 .03
418 Joe Oliver .10 .03
419 Rafael Palmeiro .30 .09
420 Tim Salmon .30 .09
421 Brady Anderson .20 .06
422 Kenny Lofton .20 .06
423 Craig Biggio .30 .09
424 Bobby Bonilla .20 .06
425 Kenny Rogers .20 .06
426 Derek Bell .10 .03
427 Scott Cooper .10 .03
428 Ozzie Guillen .10 .03
429 Omar Vizquel .20 .06
430 Phil Plantier .10 .03
431 Chuck Knoblauch .20 .06
432 Darren Daulton .20 .06
433 Bob Hamelin .10 .03
434 Tom Glavine .30 .09
435 Walt Weiss .10 .03
436 Jose Vizcaino .10 .03
437 Ken Griffey Jr. .75 .23
438 Jay Bell .20 .06
439 Juan Gonzalez .50 .15
440 Jeff Blauser .10 .03
441 Rickey Henderson .50 .15
442 Bobby Ayala .10 .03
443 David Cone .20 .06
444 Pedro Martinez .50 .15
445 Manny Ramirez .20 .06
446 Mark Portugal .10 .03
447 Damion Easley .10 .03
448 Gary DiSarcina .10 .03
449 Roberto Hernandez .10 .03
450 Jeffrey Hammonds .10 .03
451 Jeff Treadway .10 .03
452 Jim Abbott .30 .09
453 Carlos Rodriguez .10 .03
454 Joey Cora .10 .03
455 Bret Boone .20 .06
456 Danny Tartabull .10 .03
457 John Franco .20 .06
458 Roger Salkeld .10 .03
459 Fred McGriff .30 .09
460 Pedro Astacio .10 .03
461 Jon Lieber .10 .03
462 Luis Polonia .10 .03
463 Geronimo Pena .10 .03
464 Tom Gordon .10 .03
465 Brad Ausmus .10 .03
466 Willie McGee .20 .06
467 Doug Jones .10 .03
468 John Smoltz .30 .09
469 Troy Neel .10 .03
470 Luis Sojo .10 .03
471 John Smiley .10 .03
472 Rafael Bournigal .10 .03
473 Bill Taylor .10 .03
474 Juan Guzman .10 .03
475 Dave Magadan .10 .03
476 Mike Devereaux .10 .03
477 Andujar Cedeno .10 .03
478 Edgar Martinez .30 .09
479 Milt Thompson .10 .03
480 Allen Watson .10 .03
481 Ron Karkovice .10 .03
482 Joey Hamilton .10 .03
483 Vinny Castilla .20 .06
484 Tim Belcher .10 .03
485 Bernard Gilkey .10 .03
486 Scott Servais .10 .03
487 Cory Snyder .10 .03
488 Mel Rojas .10 .03
489 Carlos Reyes .10 .03
490 Chip Hale .10 .03
491 Bill Swift .10 .03
492 Pat Rapp .10 .03
493 Brian McRae .10 .03
494 Mickey Morandini .10 .03
495 Tony Pena .10 .03
496 Danny Bautista .10 .03
497 Armando Reynoso .10 .03
498 Ken Ryan .10 .03
499 Billy Ripken .10 .03
500 Pat Mahomes .10 .03
501 Mark Acre .10 .03
502 Geronimo Berroa .10 .03
503 Norberto Martin .10 .03
504 Chad Kreuter .10 .03
505 Howard Johnson .10 .03
506 Eric Anthony .10 .03
507 Mark Wohlers .10 .03
508 Scott Sanders .10 .03
509 Pete Harnisch .10 .03
510 Wes Chamberlain .10 .03
511 Tom Candiotti .10 .03
512 Albie Lopez .10 .03
513 Denny Neagle .20 .06
514 Sean Berry .10 .03
515 Billy Hatcher .10 .03
516 Todd Jones .10 .03
517 Wayne Kirby .10 .03
518 Butch Henry .10 .03
519 Sandy Alomar Jr. .10 .03
520 Kevin Appier .20 .06
521 Roberto Mejia .10 .03
522 Steve Cooke .10 .03
523 Terry Shumpert .10 .03
524 Mike Jackson .10 .03
525 Kent Mercker .10 .03
526 David Wells .20 .06
527 Juan Samuel .10 .03
528 Salomon Torres .10 .03
529 Duane Ward .10 .03
530 Rob Dibble .20 .06
531 Mike Blowers .10 .03
532 Mark Eichhorn .10 .03
533 Alex Diaz .10 .03
534 Dan Miceli .10 .03
535 Jeff Branson .10 .03
536 Dave Stevens .10 .03
537 Charlie O'Brien .10 .03
538 Shane Reynolds .10 .03
539 Rich Amaral .10 .03
540 Rusty Greer .20 .06
541 Alex Arias .10 .03
542 Eric Plunk .10 .03
543 John Hudek .10 .03
544 Kirk McCaskill .10 .03
545 Jeff Reboulet .10 .03
546 Sterling Hitchcock .10 .03
547 Warren Newson .10 .03
548 Bryan Harvey .10 .03
549 Mike Huff .10 .03
550 Lance Parrish .20 .06
551 Ken Griffey Jr. HIT .50 .15
552 Matt Williams HIT .10 .03
553 R.Alomar HIT UER .20 .06
Card says he's a NL All-Star
He plays in the AL
554 Jeff Bagwell HIT .20 .06
555 Dave Justice HIT .10 .03
556 Cal Ripken Jr. HIT .75 .23
557 Albert Belle HIT .10 .03
558 Mike Piazza HIT .40 .12
559 Kirby Puckett HIT .30 .09
560 Wade Boggs HIT .20 .06
561 Tony Gwynn HIT UER .30 .09
card has him winning AL batting titles
he's played whole career in the NL
562 Barry Bonds HIT .60 .18
563 Mo Vaughn HIT .10 .03
564 Don Mattingly HIT .60 .18
565 Carlos Baerga HIT .10 .03
566 Paul Molitor HIT .20 .06
567 Raul Mondesi HIT .10 .03
568 Manny Ramirez HIT .20 .06
569 Alex Rodriguez HIT .50 .15
570 Will Clark HIT .20 .06
571 Frank Thomas HIT .30 .09
572 Moises Alou HIT .10 .03
573 Jeff Conine HIT .10 .03
574 Joe Ausanio .10 .03
575 Charles Johnson .20 .06
576 Ernie Young .10 .03
577 Jeff Granger .10 .03
578 Robert Perez .10 .03
579 Melvin Nieves .10 .03
580 Gar Finnvold .10 .03
581 Duane Singleton .10 .03
582 Chan Ho Park .20 .06
583 Fausto Cruz .10 .03
584 Dave Staton .10 .03
585 Denny Hocking .10 .03
586 Nate Minchey .10 .03
587 Marc Newfield .10 .03
588 Jayhawk Owens UER .10 .03
Front Photo is Jim Tatum
589 Darren Bragg .10 .03
590 Kevin King .10 .03
591 Kurt Miller .10 .03
592 Aaron Small .10 .03
593 Troy O'Leary .10 .03
594 Phil Stidham .10 .03
595 Steve Dunn .10 .03
596 Cory Bailey .10 .03
597 Alex Gonzalez .10 .03
598 Jim Bowie RC .10 .03
599 Jeff Cirillo .10 .03
600 Mark Hutton .10 .03
601 Russ Davis .10 .03
602 Checklist .10 .03
603 Checklist .10 .03
604 Checklist .10 .03
605 Checklist .10 .03
RG1 R.Klesko Rook.Great. 1.00 .30
SG1 Ryan Klesko AU/6100 10.00 3.00
NNO Trade Hall of Gold 1.00 .30

1995 Score Gold Rush

Parallel to the basic Score issue, these cards were inserted one per foil pack and two per jumbo pack. The fronts were printed in gold foil and the backs contain the Gold Rush logo. As part of the Gold Rush program, one Platinum Team Redemption card was randomly inserted in Score packs at a rate of one in 36. This redemption card and up to four Gold Rush team sets (and $2) could be redeemed for platinum versions of the team set(s). The Gold Rush sets that were sent in would be returned with a stamp indicating they were already used for redemption purposes. The Platinum Upgrade offer was good through 7/13/95 for series 1, 10/1/95 for series 2.

Nm-Mt Ex-Mt
COMPLETE SET (605) 100.00 30.00
COMP. SERIES 1 (330) 50.00 15.00
COMP. SERIES 2 (275) 50.00 15.00
*STARS: 2X TO 5X BASIC CARDS

1995 Score Platinum Team Sets

After completing a Score Gold Rush team set in either series, a collector could mail in those cards along with a platinum redemption card. In return, the collector would receive a complete Platinum Team Set. The cards are similar to the gold cards except they have sparkling platinum-foil fronts and come in a small card case. The top card is the certificate for the team set. Only 4,950 of each platinum team set was produced.

Nm-Mt Ex-Mt
*STARS: 5X TO 12X BASIC CARDS

1995 Score You Trade Em

This skip-numbered 11-card set was available only by redeeming the randomly inserted Score You Trade Em redemption card. The set features a selection of veteran players that were traded to new teams at the beginning of the 1995 season. The numbering and card design parallel the corresponding cards within the regular issue 1995 Score set, but these Trade cards feature the players in their new uniforms.

Nm-Mt Ex-Mt
COMPLETE SET (11) 1.50 .45
333T Andre Dawson UER .40 .12
position listed as DH
339T Terry Pendleton .40 .12
344T Brett Butler .40 .12
346T Larry Walker .60 .18
352T Andy Van Slyke .40 .12
392T Chad Curtis .20 .06
427T Scott Cooper .20 .06
443T David Cone .40 .12
452T Jim Abbott .60 .18
493T Brian McRae .20 .06
530T Rob Dibble .40 .12
NNO Expired Trade Card .50 .15

1995 Score Airmail

This 18-card set was randomly inserted in series two jumbo packs at a rate of one in 24.

Nm-Mt Ex-Mt
COMPLETE SET (18) 50.00 15.00
AM1 Bob Hamelin 1.50 .45
AM2 John Mabry 1.50 .45
AM3 Marc Newfield 1.50 .45
AM4 Jose Oliva 1.50 .45
AM5 Charles Johnson 2.50 .75
AM6 Russ Davis 1.50 .45
AM7 Ernie Young 1.50 .45
AM8 Billy Ashley 1.50 .45
AM9 Ryan Klesko 2.50 .75
AM10 J.R. Phillips 1.50 .45
AM11 Cliff Floyd 2.50 .75
AM12 Carlos Delgado 2.50 .75
AM13 Melvin Nieves 1.50 .45
AM14 Raul Mondesi 2.50 .75
AM15 Manny Ramirez 2.50 .75
AM16 Mike Kelly 1.50 .45
AM17 Alex Rodriguez 15.00 4.50
AM18 Rusty Greer 2.50 .75

1995 Score Contest Redemption

These cards were mailed to collectors who correctly identified intentional errors in two Pinnacle print ads depicting baseball scenes. The Alex Rodriguez card was the prize for the first ad, the Ivan Rodriguez card for the second ad.

	Nm-Mt	Ex-Mt
COMPLETE SET (2)	8.00	2.40
AD1 Alex Rodriguez	6.00	1.80
AD2 Ivan Rodriguez	3.00	.90

1995 Score Double Gold Champs

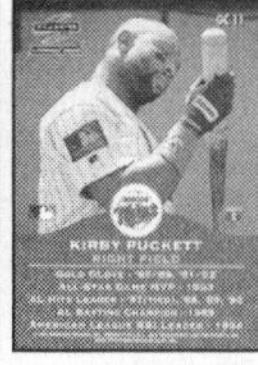

This 12-card set was randomly inserted in second series hobby packs at a rate of one in 36.

	Nm-Mt	Ex-Mt
COMPLETE SET (12)	80.00	24.00
GC1 Frank Thomas	5.00	1.50
GC2 Ken Griffey Jr.	8.00	2.40
GC3 Barry Bonds	12.00	3.60
GC4 Tony Gwynn	6.00	1.80
GC5 Don Mattingly	12.00	3.60
GC6 Greg Maddux	8.00	2.40
GC7 Roger Clemens	10.00	3.00
GC8 Kenny Lofton	2.00	.60
GC9 Jeff Bagwell	3.00	.90
GC10 Matt Williams	2.00	.60
GC11 Kirby Puckett	5.00	1.50
GC12 Cal Ripken	15.00	4.50

1995 Score Draft Picks

Randomly inserted in first series hobby packs at a rate of one in 36, this 18-card set takes a look at top picks selected in June of 1994. The cards are numbered with a "DP" prefix.

	Nm-Mt	Ex-Mt
COMPLETE SET (18)	25.00	7.50
DP1 McKay Christensen	1.00	.30
DP2 Bret Wagner	1.00	.30
DP3 Paul Wilson	1.00	.30
DP4 C.J. Nitkowski	1.00	.30
DP5 Josh Booty	1.50	.45
DP6 Antone Williamson	1.00	.30
DP7 Paul Konerko	1.50	.45
DP8 Scott Elarton	1.50	.45
DP9 Jacob Shumate	1.00	.30
DP10 Terrence Long	1.50	.45
DP11 Mark Johnson	1.50	.45
DP12 Ben Grieve	1.50	.45
DP13 Doug Million	1.00	.30
DP14 Jayson Peterson	1.00	.30
DP15 Dustin Hermanson	1.00	.30
DP16 Matt Smith	1.00	.30
DP17 Kevin Witt	1.00	.30
DP18 Brian Buchanan	1.50	.45

1995 Score Dream Team

Randomly inserted in first series hobby and retail packs at a rate of one in 72 packs, this 12-card hologram set showcases top performers from the 1994 season. The cards are numbered with a "DG" prefix.

	Nm-Mt	Ex-Mt
COMPLETE SET (12)	100.00	30.00
DG1 Frank Thomas	8.00	2.40
DG2 Roberto Alomar	8.00	2.40
DG3 Cal Ripken	25.00	7.50
DG4 Matt Williams	3.00	.90
DG5 Mike Piazza	12.00	3.60
DG6 Albert Belle	3.00	.90
DG7 Ken Griffey Jr.	12.00	3.60
DG8 Tony Gwynn	10.00	3.00
DG9 Paul Molitor	5.00	1.50
DG10 Jimmy Key	3.00	.90
DG11 Greg Maddux	12.00	3.60
DG12 Lee Smith	3.00	.90

1995 Score Hall of Gold

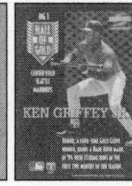

Randomly inserted in packs at a rate one in six, this 110-card multi-series set is a collection of top stars and young hopefuls. Cards numbered one through 55 were seeded in first series packs and cards 56-100 were seeded in second series packs.

	Nm-Mt	Ex-Mt
COMP. SERIES 1 (55)	50.00	15.00
COMP.SERIES 2 (55)	30.00	9.00
*YTE CARDS: .4X TO 1X BASIC HALL		
ONE YTE SET VIA MAIL PER YTE TRADE CARD		
HG1 Ken Griffey Jr.	5.00	1.50
HG2 Matt Williams	1.25	.35
HG3 Roberto Alomar	3.00	.90
HG4 Jeff Bagwell	2.00	.60
HG5 Dave Justice	1.25	.35
HG6 Cal Ripken	10.00	3.00
HG7 Randy Johnson	3.00	.90
HG8 Barry Larkin	3.00	.90
HG9 Albert Belle	1.25	.35
HG10 Mike Piazza	5.00	1.50
HG11 Kirby Puckett	3.00	.90
HG12 Moises Alou	1.25	.35
HG13 Jose Canseco	3.00	.90
HG14 Tony Gwynn	4.00	1.20
HG15 Roger Clemens	6.00	1.80
HG16 Barry Bonds	8.00	2.40
HG17 Mo Vaughn	1.25	.35
HG18 Greg Maddux	5.00	1.50
HG19 Dante Bichette	1.25	.35
HG20 Will Clark	3.00	.90
HG21 Lenny Dykstra	1.25	.35
HG22 Don Mattingly	8.00	2.40
HG23 Carlos Baerga	.60	.18
HG24 Ozzie Smith	5.00	1.50
HG25 Paul Molitor	2.00	.60
HG26 Paul O'Neill	2.00	.60
HG27 Deion Sanders	2.00	.60
HG28 Jeff Conine	1.25	.35
HG29 John Olerud	1.25	.35
HG30 Jose Rijo	.60	.18
HG31 Sammy Sosa	5.00	1.50
HG32 Robin Ventura	1.25	.35
HG33 Raul Mondesi	1.25	.35
HG34 Eddie Murray	3.00	.90
HG35 Marquis Grissom	.60	.18
HG36 Darryl Strawberry	2.00	.60
HG37 Dave Nilsson	.60	.18
HG38 Manny Ramirez	1.25	.35
HG39 Delino DeShields	.60	.18
HG40 Lee Smith	1.25	.35
HG41 Alex Rodriguez	8.00	2.40
HG42 Julio Franco	1.25	.35
HG43 Bret Saberhagen	1.25	.35
HG44 Ken Hill	.60	.18
HG45 Roberto Kelly	.60	.18
HG46 Hal Morris	.60	.18
HG47 Jimmy Key	1.25	.35
HG48 Terry Steinbach	.60	.18
HG49 Mickey Tettleton	.60	.18
HG50 Tony Phillips	.60	.18
HG51 Carlos Garcia	.60	.18
HG52 Jim Edmonds	1.25	.35
HG53 Rod Beck	.60	.18
HG54 Shane Mack	.60	.18
HG55 Ken Caminiti	1.25	.35
HG56 Frank Thomas	3.00	.90
HG57 Kenny Lofton	1.25	.35
HG58 Juan Gonzalez	3.00	.90
HG59 Jason Bere	.60	.18
HG60 Joe Carter	1.25	.35
HG61 Gary Sheffield	1.25	.35
HG62 Andres Galarraga	1.25	.35
HG63 Ellis Burks	1.25	.35
HG64 Bobby Bonilla	1.25	.35
HG65 Tom Glavine	2.00	.60
HG66 John Smoltz	2.00	.60
HG67 Fred McGriff	2.00	.60
HG68 Craig Biggio	2.00	.60
HG69 Reggie Sanders	1.25	.35
HG70 Kevin Mitchell	.60	.18
HG71 Larry Walker	2.00	.60
HG72 Carlos Delgado	1.25	.35
HG73 Alex Gonzalez	.60	.18
HG74 Ivan Rodriguez	3.00	.90
HG75 Ryan Klesko	1.25	.35
HG76 John Kruk	.60	.18
HG77 Brian McRae	.60	.18
HG78 Tim Salmon	2.00	.60
HG79 Travis Fryman	1.25	.35
HG80 Chuck Knoblauch	1.25	.35
HG81 Jay Bell	1.25	.35
HG82 Cecil Fielder	1.25	.35
HG83 Cliff Floyd	1.25	.35
HG84 Ruben Sierra	.60	.18
HG85 Mike Mussina	3.00	.90
HG86 Mark Grace	2.00	.60
HG87 Dennis Eckersley	1.25	.35
HG88 Dennis Martinez	.60	.18
HG89 Rafael Palmeiro	2.00	.60
HG90 Ben McDonald	.60	.18
HG91 Dave Hollins	.60	.18
HG92 Steve Avery	.60	.18
HG93 David Cone	1.25	.35
HG94 Darren Daulton	1.25	.35
HG95 Bret Boone	1.25	.35
HG96 Wade Boggs	2.00	.60
HG97 Doug Drabek	.60	.18
HG98 Andy Benes	.60	.18
HG99 Jim Thome	3.00	.90
HG100 Chili Davis	1.25	.35
HG101 J.Hammonds	.60	.18
HG102 R.Henderson	3.00	.90
HG103 Brett Butler	1.25	.35
HG104 Tim Wallach	.60	.18
HG105 Wil Cordero	.60	.18
HG106 Mark Whiten	.60	.18
HG107 Bob Hamelin	.60	.18
HG108 Rondell White	1.25	.35
HG109 Devon White	1.25	.35
HG110 Tony Tarasco	.60	.18

1995 Score Rookie Dream Team

This 12-card set was randomly inserted in second series retail and hobby packs at a rate of one in 12. The cards are numbered with a "RDT" prefix.

	Nm-Mt	Ex-Mt
COMPLETE SET (12)	60.00	18.00
RDT1 J.R. Phillips	2.50	.75
RDT2 Alex Gonzalez	2.50	.75
RDT3 Alex Rodriguez	20.00	6.00
RDT4 Jose Oliva	2.50	.75
RDT5 Charles Johnson	5.00	1.50
RDT6 Shawn Green	5.00	1.50
RDT7 Brian Hunter	2.50	.75
RDT8 Garret Anderson	5.00	1.50
RDT9 Julian Tavarez	2.50	.75
RDT10 Jose Lima	2.50	.75
RDT11 Armando Benitez	5.00	1.50
RDT12 Ricky Bottalico	2.50	.75

1995 Score Rules

Randomly inserted in first series jumbo packs, this 30-card standard-size set features top big league players. The cards are numbered with an "SR" prefix.

	Nm-Mt	Ex-Mt
COMPLETE SET (30)	120.00	36.00
*JUMBO'S: .5X TO 1.2X		
JUMBOS ISSUED ONE PER COLLECTOR KIT		
SR1 Ken Griffey Jr.	8.00	2.40
SR2 Frank Thomas	5.00	1.50
SR3 Mike Piazza	8.00	2.40
SR4 Jeff Bagwell	3.00	.90
SR5 Alex Rodriguez	12.00	3.60
SR6 Albert Belle	2.00	.60
SR7 Matt Williams	2.00	.60
SR8 Roberto Alomar	5.00	1.50
SR9 Barry Bonds	12.00	3.60
SR10 Raul Mondesi	2.00	.60
SR11 Jose Canseco	5.00	1.50
SR12 Kirby Puckett	5.00	1.50
SR13 Fred McGriff	3.00	.90
SR14 Kenny Lofton	2.00	.60
SR15 Greg Maddux	8.00	2.40
SR16 Juan Gonzalez	5.00	1.50
SR17 Cliff Floyd	2.00	.60
SR18 Cal Ripken Jr.	15.00	4.50
SR19 Will Clark	5.00	1.50
SR20 Tim Salmon	3.00	.90
SR21 Paul O'Neill	3.00	.90
SR22 Jason Bere	1.00	.30
SR23 Tony Gwynn	6.00	1.80
SR24 Manny Ramirez	2.00	.60
SR25 Don Mattingly	12.00	3.60
SR26 Dave Justice	2.00	.60
SR27 Javier Lopez	2.00	.60
SR28 Ryan Klesko	2.00	.60
SR29 Carlos Delgado	2.00	.60
SR30 Mike Mussina	5.00	1.50

1996 Score Samples

This eight-card set was issued to preview the 1996 Score series. Inside white borders, the fronts feature color action photos with the upper left corner torn off to allow space for the "96 Score" logo. The backs carry a second color closeup photo, biography, statistics, and player profile. The final two cards listed belong to the Rookie subset and have a different front design. All cards have "SAMPLE" stamped diagonally across their front and back. The cards were distributed in complete set form within 9-card cello wrappers. A full 8-card basic Sample set was included with one of eight differnet Dugout Collection Sample parallels.

	Nm-Mt	Ex-Mt
COMPLETE SET (8)	8.00	2.40
3 Ryan Klesko	.50	.15
4 Jim Edmonds	1.00	.30
5 Barry Larkin	1.00	.30
6 Jim Thome	1.25	.35
7 Raul Mondesi	.75	.23
110 Derek Bell	.25	.07
240 Derek Jeter	5.00	1.50
241 Michael Tucker	.50	.15

1996 Score

This set consists of 517 standard-size cards. These cards were issued in packs of 10 that retailed for 99 cents per pack. The fronts feature an action photo surrounded by white borders. The "Score 96" logo is in the upper left, while the player is identified on the bottom. The backs have season and career stats as well as a player photo and some text. A Cal Ripken tribute card was issued at a rate of 1 every 300 packs.

	Nm-Mt	Ex-Mt
COMPLETE SET (517)	24.00	7.25
COMP. SERIES 1 (275)	12.00	3.60
COMP. SERIES 2 (242)	12.00	3.60
1 Will Clark	.50	.15
2 Rich Becker	.20	.06
3 Ryan Klesko	.20	.06
4 Jim Edmonds	.20	.06
5 Barry Larkin	.50	.15
6 Jim Thome	.50	.15
7 Raul Mondesi	.20	.06
8 Don Mattingly	1.25	.35
9 Jeff Conine	.20	.06
10 Rickey Henderson	.50	.15
11 Chad Curtis	.20	.06
12 Darren Daulton	.20	.06
13 Larry Walker	.30	.09
14 Carlos Garcia	.20	.06
15 Carlos Baerga	.20	.06
16 Tony Gwynn	.60	.18
17 Jon Nunnally	.20	.06
18 Deion Sanders	.30	.09
19 Mark Grace	.30	.09
20 Alex Rodriguez	1.00	.30
21 Frank Thomas	.50	.15
22 Brian Jordan	.20	.06
23 J.T. Snow	.20	.06
24 Shawn Green	.20	.06
25 Tim Wakefield	.20	.06
26 Curtis Goodwin	.20	.06
27 John Smoltz	.30	.09
28 Devon White	.20	.06
29 Brian L. Hunter	.20	.06
30 Tim Salmon	.30	.09
31 Rafael Palmeiro	.30	.09
32 Bernard Gilkey	.20	.06
33 John Valentin	.20	.06
34 Randy Johnson	.50	.15
35 Garret Anderson	.20	.06
36 Rikkert Faneyte	.20	.06
37 Ray Durham	.20	.06
38 Bip Roberts	.20	.06
39 Jaime Navarro	.20	.06
40 Mark Johnson	.20	.06
41 Darren Lewis	.20	.06
42 Tyler Green	.20	.06
43 Bill Pulsipher	.20	.06
44 Jason Giambi	.50	.15
45 Kevin Ritz	.20	.06
46 Jack McDowell	.20	.06
47 Felipe Lira	.20	.06
48 Rico Brogna	.20	.06
49 Terry Pendleton	.20	.06
50 Rondell White	.20	.06
51 Andre Dawson	.20	.06
52 Kirby Puckett	.50	.15
53 Wally Joyner	.20	.06
54 B.J. Surhoff	.20	.06
55 Randy Velarde	.20	.06
56 Greg Vaughn	.20	.06
57 Roberto Alomar	.50	.15
58 David Justice	.20	.06
59 Kevin Seitzer	.20	.06
60 Cal Ripken	1.50	.45
61 Ozzie Smith	.75	.23
62 Mo Vaughn	.20	.06
63 Ricky Bones	.20	.06
64 Gary DiSarcina	.20	.06
65 Matt Williams	.20	.06
66 Wilson Alvarez	.20	.06
67 Lenny Dykstra	.20	.06
68 Brian McRae	.20	.06
69 Todd Stottlemyre	.20	.06
70 Bret Boone	.20	.06
71 Sterling Hitchcock	.20	.06
72 Albert Belle	.20	.06
73 Todd Hundley	.20	.06
74 Vinny Castilla	.20	.06
75 Moises Alou	.20	.06
76 Cecil Fielder	.20	.06
77 Brad Radke	.20	.06
78 Quilvio Veras	.20	.06
79 Eddie Murray	.50	.15
80 James Mouton	.20	.06
81 Pat Listach	.20	.06
82 Mark Gubicza	.20	.06
83 Dave Winfield	.20	.06
84 Fred McGriff	.30	.09
85 Darryl Hamilton	.20	.06
86 Jeffrey Hammonds	.20	.06
87 Pedro Munoz	.20	.06
88 Craig Biggio	.30	.09
89 Cliff Floyd	.20	.06
90 Tim Naehring	.20	.06
91 Brett Butler	.20	.06
92 Kevin Foster	.20	.06
93 Pat Kelly	.20	.06
94 John Smiley	.20	.06
95 Terry Steinbach	.20	.06
96 Orel Hershiser	.20	.06
97 Darrin Fletcher	.20	.06
98 Walt Weiss	.20	.06
99 John Wetteland	.20	.06
100 Alan Trammell	.30	.09
101 Steve Avery	.20	.06
102 Tony Eusebio	.20	.06
103 Sandy Alomar Jr.	.20	.06
104 Joe Girardi	.20	.06
105 Rick Aguilera	.20	.06
106 Tony Tarasco	.20	.06
107 Chris Hammond	.20	.06
108 Mike Macfarlane	.20	.06
109 Doug Drabek	.20	.06
110 Derek Bell	.20	.06
111 Ed Sprague	.20	.06
112 Todd Hollandsworth	.20	.06
113 Otis Nixon	.20	.06
114 Keith Lockhart	.20	.06
115 Donovan Osborne	.20	.06
116 Dave Magadan	.20	.06
117 Edgar Martinez	.30	.09
118 Chuck Carr	.20	.06
119 J.R. Phillips	.20	.06
120 Sean Bergman	.20	.06
121 Andujar Cedeno	.20	.06
122 Eric Young	.20	.06
123 Al Martin	.20	.06
124 Mark Lemke	.20	.06
125 Jim Eisenreich	.20	.06
126 Benito Santiago	.20	.06
127 Ariel Prieto	.20	.06
128 Jim Bullinger	.20	.06
129 Russ Davis	.20	.06
130 Jim Abbott	.30	.09
131 Jason Isringhausen	.20	.06
132 Carlos Perez	.20	.06
133 David Segui	.20	.06
134 Troy O'Leary	.20	.06
135 Pat Meares	.20	.06
136 Chris Hoiles	.20	.06
137 Ismael Valdes	.20	.06
138 Jose Oliva	.20	.06
139 Carlos Delgado	.20	.06
140 Tom Goodwin	.20	.06
141 Bob Tewksbury	.20	.06
142 Chris Gomez	.20	.06
143 Jose Oquendo	.20	.06
144 Mark Lewis	.20	.06
145 Salomon Torres	.20	.06
146 Luis Gonzalez	.20	.06
147 Mark Carreon	.20	.06
148 Lance Johnson	.20	.06
149 Melvin Nieves	.20	.06
150 Lee Smith	.20	.06
151 Jacob Brumfield	.20	.06
152 Armando Benitez	.20	.06
153 Curt Schilling	.30	.09
154 Javier Lopez	.20	.06
155 Frank Rodriguez	.20	.06
156 Alex Gonzalez	.20	.06
157 Todd Worrell	.20	.06
158 Benji Gil	.20	.06
159 Greg Gagne	.20	.06
160 Tom Henke	.20	.06
161 Randy Myers	.20	.06
162 Joey Cora	.20	.06
163 Scott Ruffcorn	.20	.06
164 W. VanLandingham	.20	.06
165 Tony Phillips	.20	.06
166 Eddie Williams	.20	.06
167 Bobby Bonilla	.20	.06
168 Denny Neagle	.20	.06
169 Troy Percival	.20	.06
170 Billy Ashley	.20	.06
171 Andy Van Slyke	.20	.06
172 Jose Offerman	.20	.06
173 Mark Parent	.20	.06
174 Edgardo Alfonzo	.20	.06
175 Trevor Hoffman	.20	.06
176 David Cone	.20	.06
177 Dan Wilson	.20	.06
178 Steve Ontiveros	.20	.06
179 Dean Palmer	.20	.06
180 Mike Kelly	.20	.06
181 Jim Leyritz	.20	.06
182 Ron Karkovice	.20	.06
183 Kevin Brown	.20	.06
184 Jose Valentin	.20	.06
185 Jorge Fabregas	.20	.06
186 Jose Mesa	.20	.06
187 Brent Mayne	.20	.06
188 Carl Everett	.20	.06
189 Paul Sorrento	.20	.06
190 Pete Schourek	.20	.06
191 Scott Kamieniecki	.20	.06
192 Roberto Hernandez	.20	.06
193 Randy Johnson RR	.30	.09
194 Greg Maddux RR	.50	.15
195 Hideo Nomo RR	.30	.09
196 David Cone RR	.20	.06
197 Mike Mussina RR	.30	.09
198 Andy Benes RR	.20	.06
199 Kevin Appier RR	.20	.06
200 John Smoltz RR	.20	.06
201 John Wetteland RR	.20	.06
202 Mark Wohlers RR	.20	.06
203 Stan Belinda	.20	.06
204 Brian Anderson	.20	.06
205 Mike Devereaux	.20	.06
206 Mark Wohlers	.20	.06
207 Omar Vizquel	.20	.06
208 Jose Rijo	.20	.06
209 Willie Blair	.20	.06
210 Jamie Moyer	.20	.06
211 Craig Shipley	.20	.06
212 Shane Reynolds	.20	.06
213 Chad Fonville	.20	.06
214 Jose Vizcaino	.20	.06
215 Sid Fernandez	.20	.06
216 Andy Ashby	.20	.06
217 Frank Castillo	.20	.06
218 Kevin Tapani	.20	.06
219 Kent Mercker	.20	.06
220 Karim Garcia	.20	.06
221 Antonio Osuna	.20	.06
222 Tim Unroe	.20	.06
223 Johnny Damon	.20	.06
224 LaTroy Hawkins	.20	.06
225 Mariano Rivera	.30	.09
226 Jose Alberro	.20	.06
227 Angel Martinez	.20	.06
228 Jason Schmidt	.20	.06
229 Tony Clark	.20	.06
230 Kevin Jordan UER	.20	.06
Ricky Jordan pictured on both sides		
231 Mark Thompson	.20	.06
232 Jim Dougherty	.20	.06
233 Roger Cedeno	.20	.06
234 Ugueth Urbina	.20	.06

1996 Score

235 Ricky Otero .20 .06
236 Mark Smith .20 .06
237 Brian Barber .20 .06
238 Kevin Flora .20 .06
239 Joe Rosselli .20 .06
240 Derek Jeter 1.25 .35
241 Michael Tucker .20 .06
242 Ben Blomdahl .20 .06
243 Joe Vitiello .20 .06
244 Todd Steverson .20 .06
245 James Baldwin .20 .06
246 Alan Embree .20 .06
247 Shannon Penn .20 .06
248 Chris Stynes .20 .06
249 Oscar Munoz .20 .06
250 Jose Herrera .20 .06
251 Scott Sullivan .20 .06
252 Reggie Williams .20 .06
253 Mark Grudzielanek .20 .06
254 Steve Rodriguez .20 .06
255 Terry Bradshaw .20 .06
256 F.P. Santangelo .20 .06
257 Lyle Mouton .20 .06
258 George Williams .20 .06
259 Larry Thomas .20 .06
260 Rudy Pemberton .20 .06
261 Jim Pittsley .20 .06
262 Les Norman .20 .06
263 Ruben Rivera .20 .06
264 Cesar Devarez .20 .06
265 Greg Zaun .20 .06
266 Dustin Hermanson .20 .06
267 John Frascatore .20 .06
268 Joe Randa .20 .06
269 Jeff Bagwell CL .20 .06
270 Mike Piazza CL .50 .15
271 Dante Bichette CL .20 .06
272 Frank Thomas CL .30 .09
273 Ken Griffey Jr. CL .50 .15
274 Cal Ripken CL .75 .23
275 Greg Maddux CL .20 .06
Albert Belle
276 Greg Maddux .75 .23
277 Pedro Martinez .50 .15
278 Bobby Higginson .20 .06
279 Ray Lankford .20 .06
280 Shawon Dunston .20 .06
281 Gary Sheffield .20 .06
282 Ken Griffey Jr. .75 .23
283 Paul Molitor .30 .09
284 Kevin Appier .20 .06
285 Chuck Knoblauch .20 .06
286 Alex Fernandez .20 .06
287 Steve Finley .20 .06
288 Jeff Blauser .20 .06
289 Charles Johnson .20 .06
290 John Franco .20 .06
291 Mark Langston .20 .06
292 Bret Saberhagen .20 .06
293 John Mabry .20 .06
294 Ramon Martinez .20 .06
295 Mike Blowers .20 .06
296 Paul O'Neill .30 .09
297 Dave Nilsson .20 .06
298 Dante Bichette .20 .06
299 Marty Cordova .20 .06
300 Jay Bell .20 .06
301 Mike Mussina .50 .15
302 Ivan Rodriguez .50 .15
303 Jose Canseco .50 .15
304 Jeff Bagwell .30 .09
305 Manny Ramirez .20 .06
306 Dennis Martinez .20 .06
307 Charlie Hayes .20 .06
308 Joe Carter .20 .06
309 Travis Fryman .20 .06
310 Mark McGwire 1.25 .35
311 Reggie Sanders UER .20 .06
Photo on front is John Roper
312 Julian Tavarez .20 .06
313 Jeff Montgomery .20 .06
314 Andy Benes .20 .06
315 John Jaha .20 .06
316 Jeff Kent .20 .06
317 Mike Piazza .75 .23
318 Erik Hanson .20 .06
319 Kenny Rogers .20 .06
320 Hideo Nomo .50 .15
321 Gregg Jefferies .20 .06
322 Chipper Jones .50 .15
323 Jay Buhner .20 .06
324 Dennis Eckersley .20 .06
325 Kenny Lofton .20 .06
326 Robin Ventura .20 .06
327 Tom Glavine .30 .09
328 Tim Salmon .30 .09
329 Andres Galarraga .20 .06
330 Hal Morris .20 .06
331 Brady Anderson .20 .06
332 Chili Davis .20 .06
333 Roger Clemens 1.00 .30
334 Marquis Grissom .20 .06
335 Mike Greenwell UER .20 .06
Name spelled Jeff on Front
336 Sammy Sosa .75 .23
337 Ron Gant .20 .06
338 Ken Caminiti .20 .06
339 Danny Tartabull .20 .06
340 Barry Bonds 1.25 .35
341 Ben McDonald .20 .06
342 Ruben Sierra .20 .06
343 Bernie Williams .30 .09
344 Wil Cordero .20 .06
345 Wade Boggs .30 .09
346 Gary Gaetti .20 .06
347 Greg Colbrunn .20 .06
348 Juan Gonzalez .50 .15
349 Marc Newfield .20 .06
350 Charles Nagy .20 .06
351 Robby Thompson .20 .06
352 Roberto Petagine .20 .06
353 Darryl Strawberry .30 .09
354 Tino Martinez .30 .09
355 Eric Karros .20 .06
356 Cal Ripken SS .75 .23
357 Cecil Fielder SS .20 .06
358 Kirby Puckett SS .30 .09
359 Jim Edmonds SS .20 .06
360 Matt Williams SS .20 .06
361 Alex Rodriguez SS .50 .15
362 Barry Larkin SS .20 .06
363 Rafael Palmeiro SS .20 .06
364 David Cone SS .20 .06
365 Roberto Alomar SS .20 .06
366 Eddie Murray SS .30 .09
367 Randy Johnson SS .30 .09
368 Ryan Klesko SS .20 .06
369 Raul Mondesi SS .20 .06
370 Mo Vaughn SS .20 .06
371 Will Clark SS .20 .06
372 Carlos Baerga SS .20 .06
373 Frank Thomas SS .30 .09
374 Larry Walker SS .20 .06
375 Garret Anderson SS .20 .06
376 Edgar Martinez SS .20 .06
377 Don Mattingly SS .60 .18
378 Tony Gwynn SS .30 .09
379 Albert Belle SS .20 .06
380 J.Isringhausen SS .20 .06
381 Ruben Rivera SS .20 .06
382 Johnny Damon SS .20 .06
383 Karim Garcia SS .20 .06
384 Derek Jeter SS .60 .18
385 David Justice SS .20 .06
386 Royce Clayton .20 .06
387 Mark Whiten .20 .06
388 Mickey Tettleton .20 .06
389 Steve Trachsel .20 .06
390 Danny Bautista .20 .06
391 Midre Cummings .20 .06
392 Scott Leius .20 .06
393 Manny Alexander .20 .06
394 Brent Gates .20 .06
395 Rey Sanchez .20 .06
396 Andy Pettitte .30 .09
397 Jeff Cirillo .20 .06
398 Kurt Abbott .20 .06
399 Lee Tinsley .20 .06
400 Paul Assenmacher .20 .06
401 Scott Erickson .20 .06
402 Todd Zeile .20 .06
403 Tom Pagnozzi .20 .06
404 Ozzie Guillen .20 .06
405 Jeff Frye .20 .06
406 Kirt Manwaring .20 .06
407 Chad Ogea .20 .06
408 Harold Baines .20 .06
409 Jason Bere .20 .06
410 Chuck Finley .20 .06
411 Jeff Fassero .20 .06
412 Joey Hamilton .20 .06
413 John Olerud .20 .06
414 Kevin Stocker .20 .06
415 Eric Anthony .20 .06
416 Aaron Sele .20 .06
417 Chris Bosio .20 .06
418 Michael Mimbs .20 .06
419 Orlando Miller .20 .06
420 Stan Javier .20 .06
421 Matt Mieske .20 .06
422 Jason Bates .20 .06
423 Orlando Merced .20 .06
424 John Flaherty .20 .06
425 Reggie Jefferson .20 .06
426 Scott Stahoviak .20 .06
427 John Burkett .20 .06
428 Rod Beck .20 .06
429 Bill Swift .20 .06
430 Scott Cooper .20 .06
431 Mel Rojas .20 .06
432 Todd Van Poppel .20 .06
433 Bobby Jones .20 .06
434 Mike Harkey .20 .06
435 Sean Berry .20 .06
436 Glenallen Hill .20 .06
437 Ryan Thompson .20 .06
438 Luis Alicea .20 .06
439 Esteban Loaiza .20 .06
440 Jeff Reboulet .20 .06
441 Vince Coleman .20 .06
442 Ellis Burks .20 .06
443 Allen Battle .20 .06
444 Jimmy Key .20 .06
445 Ricky Bottalico .20 .06
446 Delino DeShields .20 .06
447 Albie Lopez .20 .06
448 Mark Petkovsek .20 .06
449 Tim Raines .20 .06
450 Bryan Harvey .20 .06
451 Pat Hentgen .20 .06
452 Tim Laker .20 .06
453 Tom Gordon .20 .06
454 Phil Plantier .20 .06
455 Ernie Young .20 .06
456 Pete Harnisch .20 .06
457 Roberto Kelly .20 .06
458 Mark Portugal .20 .06
459 Mark Leiter .20 .06
460 Tony Pena .20 .06
461 Roger Pavlik .20 .06
462 Jeff King .20 .06
463 Bryan Rekar .20 .06
464 Al Leiter .20 .06
465 Phil Nevin .20 .06
466 Jose Lima .20 .06
467 Mike Stanley .20 .06
468 David McCarty .20 .06
469 Herb Perry .20 .06
470 Geronimo Berroa .20 .06
471 David Wells .20 .06
472 Vaughn Eshelman .20 .06
473 Greg Swindell .20 .06
474 Steve Sparks .20 .06
475 Luis Sojo .20 .06
476 Derrick May .20 .06
477 Joe Oliver .20 .06
478 Alex Arias .20 .06
479 Brad Ausmus .20 .06
480 Gabe White .20 .06
481 Pat Rapp .20 .06
482 Damon Buford .20 .06
483 Turk Wendell .20 .06
484 Jeff Brantley .20 .06
485 Curtis Leskanic .20 .06
486 Robb Nen .20 .06
487 Lou Whitaker .20 .06
488 Melido Perez .20 .06
489 Luis Polonia .20 .06
490 Scott Brosius .20 .06
491 Robert Perez .20 .06
492 Mike Sweeney RC 1.25 .35
493 Mark Loretta .20 .06
494 Alex Ochoa .20 .06
495 Matt Lawton RC .20 .06
496 Shawn Estes .20 .06
497 John Wasdin .20 .06
498 Marc Kroon .20 .06
499 Chris Snopek .20 .06
500 Jeff Suppan .20 .06
501 Terrell Wade .20 .06
502 Marvin Benard RC .20 .06
503 Chris Widger .20 .06
504 Quinton McCracken .20 .06
505 Bob Wolcott .20 .06
506 C.J. Nitkowski .20 .06
507 Aaron Ledesma .20 .06
508 Scott Hatteberg .20 .06
509 Jimmy Haynes .20 .06
510 Howard Battle .20 .06
511 Marty Cordova CL .20 .06
512 Randy Johnson CL .30 .09
513 Mo Vaughn CL .20 .06
514 Hideo Nomo CL .20 .06
515 Greg Maddux CL .50 .15
516 Barry Larkin CL .20 .06
517 Tom Glavine CL .20 .06
NNO Cal Ripken 2131 20.00 6.00

1996 Score All-Stars

Randomly inserted in second series jumbo packs at a rate of one in nine, this 20-card set was printed in rainbow holographic prismatic foil.

Nm-Mt Ex-Mt
COMPLETE SET (20) 60.00 18.00
1 Frank Thomas 3.00 .90
2 Albert Belle 1.25 .35
3 Ken Griffey Jr. 5.00 1.50
4 Cal Ripken 10.00 3.00
5 Mo Vaughn 1.25 .35
6 Matt Williams 1.25 .35
7 Barry Bonds 8.00 2.40
8 Dante Bichette 1.25 .35
9 Tony Gwynn 4.00 1.20
10 Greg Maddux 5.00 1.50
11 Randy Johnson 3.00 .90
12 Hideo Nomo 3.00 .90
13 Tim Salmon 2.00 .60
14 Jeff Bagwell 2.00 .60
15 Edgar Martinez 2.00 .60
16 Reggie Sanders 1.25 .35
17 Larry Walker 2.00 .60
18 Chipper Jones 3.00 .90
19 Manny Ramirez 1.25 .35
20 Eddie Murray 3.00 .90

1996 Score Big Bats

This 20-card set was randomly inserted in retail packs at a rate of approximately one in 31. The cards are numbered "X" of 20 in the upper left corner.

Nm-Mt Ex-Mt
COMPLETE SET (20) 100.00 30.00
1 Cal Ripken 15.00 4.50
2 Ken Griffey Jr. 8.00 2.40
3 Frank Thomas 5.00 1.50
4 Jeff Bagwell 3.00 .90
5 Mike Piazza 8.00 2.40
6 Barry Bonds 12.00 3.60
7 Matt Williams 2.00 .60
8 Raul Mondesi 2.00 .60
9 Tony Gwynn 6.00 1.80
10 Albert Belle 2.00 .60
11 Manny Ramirez 2.00 .60
12 Carlos Baerga 2.00 .60
13 Mo Vaughn 2.00 .60
14 Derek Bell 2.00 .60
15 Larry Walker 3.00 .90
16 Kenny Lofton 2.00 .60
17 Edgar Martinez 3.00 .90
18 Reggie Sanders 2.00 .60
19 Eddie Murray 5.00 1.50
20 Chipper Jones 5.00 1.50

1996 Score Diamond Aces

This 30-card set features some of baseball's best players. These cards were inserted approximately one every eight jumbo packs.

Nm-Mt Ex-Mt
COMPLETE SET (30) 120.00 36.00
1 Hideo Nomo 5.00 1.50
2 Brian L.Hunter 2.00 .60
3 Ray Durham 2.00 .60
4 Frank Thomas 5.00 1.50
5 Cal Ripken 15.00 4.50
6 Barry Bonds 12.00 3.60
7 Greg Maddux 8.00 2.40
8 Chipper Jones 5.00 1.50
9 Raul Mondesi 2.00 .60
10 Mike Piazza 8.00 2.40
11 Derek Jeter 12.00 3.60
12 Bill Pulsipher 2.00 .60
13 Larry Walker 3.00 .90
14 Ken Griffey Jr. 8.00 2.40
15 Alex Rodriguez 10.00 3.00
16 Manny Ramirez 2.00 .60
17 Mo Vaughn 2.00 .60
18 Reggie Sanders 2.00 .60
19 Derek Bell 2.00 .60
20 Jim Edmonds 2.00 .60
21 Albert Belle 2.00 .60
22 Eddie Murray 5.00 1.50
23 Tony Gwynn 6.00 1.80
24 Jeff Bagwell 3.00 .90
25 Carlos Baerga 2.00 .60
26 Matt Williams 2.00 .60
27 Garret Anderson 2.00 .60
28 Todd Hollandsworth 2.00 .60
29 Johnny Damon 2.00 .60
30 Tim Salmon 3.00 .90

1996 Score Dream Team

This nine-card set was randomly inserted in approximately one in 72 packs. This set features a leading player at each position. The cards are numbered in the upper right as "X" of nine.

Nm-Mt Ex-Mt
COMPLETE SET (9) 60.00 18.00
1 Cal Ripken 15.00 4.50
2 Frank Thomas 5.00 1.50
3 Carlos Baerga 2.00 .60
4 Matt Williams 2.00 .60
5 Mike Piazza 8.00 2.40
6 Barry Bonds 12.00 3.60
7 Ken Griffey Jr. 8.00 2.40
8 Manny Ramirez 2.00 .60
9 Greg Maddux 8.00 2.40

1996 Score Dugout Collection Samples

These cards were distributed to dealers and hobby media prior to the release of 1996 Score baseball. The cards are similar in design to basic Dugout Collection cards, except for the "SAMPLE" text running diagonally across the front and back. The Dugout Collection Samples were seeded at a rate of one per nine-card 1996 Score Sample cello pack.

Nm-Mt Ex-Mt
COMPLETE SET (8) 6.00 1.80
3 Ryan Klesko .50 .15
4 Jim Edmonds 1.00 .30
5 Barry Larkin 1.00 .30
6 Jim Thome 1.25 .35
7 Raul Mondesi .50 .15
110 Derek Bell .25 .07
240 Derek Jeter 3.00 .90
241 Michael Tucker .25 .07

1996 Score Dugout Collection

This set is a mini-parallel to the regular issue. Only 110 cards of each Series 1 and Series 2 were selected. Randomly inserted approximately one in every three packs, these cards have all gold foil printing that gives them a shiny copper cast. The words "Dugout Collection" are printed on the back.

Nm-Mt Ex-Mt
COMP. SERIES 1 (110) 50.00 15.00
COMP. SERIES 2 (110) 50.00 15.00
*DUGOUT: 1.5X TO 4X BASIC
STATED ODDS 1:3 HOB/RET
*AP DUGOUT: 10X TO 25X BASIC
AP STATED ODDS 1:36 HOB/RET

1996 Score Dugout Collection Artist's Proofs

This set is a parallel to the Dugout Collection set. These cards are different from the regular Dugout Collection as they have the words Artist Proof printed on the front. Randomly inserted one in every 36 packs, this set was printed using Gold Rush all gold-foil card technology.

Nm-Mt Ex-Mt
*STARS: 2.5X TO 6X BASIC DUGOUT

1996 Score Future Franchise

Randomly inserted in retail packs at a rate of one in 72, this 16-card set honors young stars of the game.

Nm-Mt Ex-Mt
COMPLETE SET (16) 100.00 30.00
1 Jason Isringhausen 4.00 1.20
2 Chipper Jones 10.00 3.00
3 Derek Jeter 25.00 7.50
4 Alex Rodriguez 20.00 6.00
5 Alex Ochoa 4.00 1.20
6 Manny Ramirez 4.00 1.20
7 Johnny Damon 4.00 1.20
8 Ruben Rivera 4.00 1.20
9 Karim Garcia 4.00 1.20
10 Garret Anderson 4.00 1.20
11 Marty Cordova 4.00 1.20
12 Bill Pulsipher 4.00 1.20
13 Hideo Nomo 10.00 3.00
14 Marc Newfield 4.00 1.20
15 Charles Johnson 4.00 1.20
16 Raul Mondesi 4.00 1.20

1996 Score Gold Stars

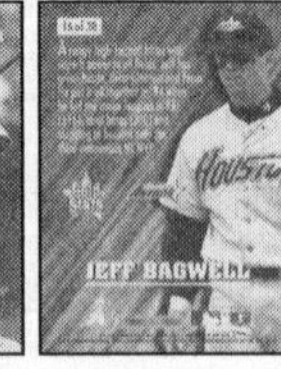

Randomly inserted in packs at a rate of one in 15, this 30-card set features borderless color action player photos with a special sepia player cutout inserted behind a gold foil stamp designating the star player.

Nm-Mt Ex-Mt
COMPLETE SET (30) 50.00 15.00
1 Ken Griffey Jr. 4.00 1.20
2 Frank Thomas 2.50 .75
3 Reggie Sanders 1.00 .30
4 Tim Salmon 1.50 .45
5 Mike Piazza 4.00 1.20
6 Tony Gwynn 3.00 .90
7 Gary Sheffield 1.00 .30
8 Matt Williams 1.00 .30
9 Bernie Williams 1.50 .45
10 Jason Isringhausen 1.00 .30
11 Albert Belle 1.00 .30
12 Chipper Jones 2.50 .75
13 Edgar Martinez 1.50 .45
14 Barry Larkin 2.50 .75
15 Barry Bonds 6.00 1.80
16 Jeff Bagwell 1.50 .45
17 Greg Maddux 4.00 1.20
18 Mo Vaughn 1.00 .30
19 Ryan Klesko 1.00 .30
20 Sammy Sosa 4.00 1.20
21 Darren Daulton 1.00 .30
22 Ivan Rodriguez 2.50 .75
23 Dante Bichette 1.00 .30
24 Hideo Nomo 2.50 .75
25 Cal Ripken 8.00 2.40
26 Rafael Palmeiro 1.50 .45
27 Larry Walker 1.50 .45
28 Carlos Baerga 1.00 .30
29 Randy Johnson 2.50 .75
30 Manny Ramirez 1.00 .30

1996 Score Numbers Game

This 30-card set was inserted approximately one in every 15 packs. The cards are numbered as "X" of 30 in the upper left corner.

Nm-Mt Ex-Mt
COMPLETE SET (30) 60.00 18.00
1 Cal Ripken 8.00 2.40
2 Frank Thomas 2.50 .75
3 Ken Griffey Jr. 4.00 1.20
4 Mike Piazza 4.00 1.20
5 Barry Bonds 6.00 1.80
6 Greg Maddux 4.00 1.20
7 Jeff Bagwell 1.50 .45
8 Derek Bell 1.00 .30
9 Tony Gwynn 3.00 .90
10 Hideo Nomo 2.50 .75
11 Raul Mondesi 1.00 .30
12 Manny Ramirez 1.00 .30
13 Albert Belle 1.00 .30
14 Matt Williams 1.00 .30
15 Jim Edmonds 1.00 .30
16 Edgar Martinez 1.50 .45
17 Mo Vaughn 1.00 .30
18 Reggie Sanders 1.00 .30
19 Chipper Jones 2.50 .75
20 Larry Walker 1.50 .45
21 Juan Gonzalez 2.50 .75
22 Kenny Lofton 1.00 .30
23 Don Mattingly 6.00 1.80
24 Ivan Rodriguez 2.50 .75
25 Randy Johnson 2.50 .75
26 Derek Jeter 6.00 1.80
27 J.T. Snow 1.00 .30
28 Will Clark 2.50 .75
29 Rafael Palmeiro 1.50 .45
30 Alex Rodriguez 5.00 1.50

1996 Score Power Pace

Randomly inserted in retail packs at a rate of one in 31, this 18-card set features homerun hitters.

Nm-Mt Ex-Mt
COMPLETE SET (18) 60.00 18.00
1 Mark McGwire 10.00 3.00
2 Albert Belle 1.50 .45
3 Jay Buhner 1.50 .45
4 Frank Thomas 4.00 1.20
5 Matt Williams 1.50 .45

6 Gary Sheffield 1.50 .45
7 Mike Piazza 6.00 1.80
8 Larry Walker 2.50 .75
9 Mo Vaughn 1.50 .45
10 Rafael Palmeiro 2.50 .75
11 Dante Bichette 1.50 .45
12 Ken Griffey Jr. 6.00 1.80
13 Barry Bonds 10.00 3.00
14 Manny Ramirez 1.50 .45
15 Sammy Sosa 6.00 1.80
16 Tim Salmon 2.50 .75
17 Dave Justice 1.50 .45
18 Eric Karros 1.50 .45

1996 Score Reflextions

This 20-card set was randomly inserted approximately one in every 31 hobby packs. Two players per card are featured, a veteran player and a younger star playing the same position.

	Nm-Mt	Ex-Mt
COMPLETE SET (20)	100.00	30.00
1 Cal Ripken Chipper Jones	15.00	4.50
2 Ken Griffey Jr. Alex Rodriguez	8.00	2.40
3 Frank Thomas Mo Vaughn	5.00	1.50
4 Kenny Lofton Brian L.Hunter	2.00	.60
5 Don Mattingly J.T.Snow	12.00	3.60
6 Manny Ramirez Raul Mondesi	2.00	.60
7 Tony Gwynn Garret Anderson	6.00	1.80
8 Roberto Alomar Carlos Baerga	5.00	1.50
9 Andre Dawson Larry Walker	2.00	.60
10 Barry Larkin Derek Jeter	12.00	3.60
11 Barry Bonds Reggie Sanders	12.00	3.60
12 Mike Piazza Albert Belle	8.00	2.40
13 Wade Boggs Edgar Martinez	3.00	.90
14 David Cone John Smoltz	2.00	.60
15 Will Clark Jeff Bagwell	3.00	.90
16 Mark McGwire Cecil Fielder	12.00	3.60
17 Greg Maddux Mike Mussina	8.00	2.40
18 Randy Johnson Hideo Nomo	5.00	1.50
19 Jim Thome Dean Palmer	5.00	1.50
20 Chuck Knoblauch Craig Biggio	3.00	.90

1996 Score Titanic Taters

Randomly inserted in hobby packs at a rate of one in 31, this 18-card set features long home run hitters.

	Nm-Mt	Ex-Mt
COMPLETE SET (18)	80.00	24.00
1 Albert Belle	2.00	.60
2 Frank Thomas	5.00	1.50
3 Mo Vaughn	2.00	.60
4 Ken Griffey Jr.	8.00	2.40
5 Matt Williams	2.00	.60
6 Mark McGwire	12.00	3.60
7 Dante Bichette	2.00	.60
8 Tim Salmon	3.00	.90
9 Jeff Bagwell	3.00	.90
10 Rafael Palmeiro	3.00	.90
11 Mike Piazza	8.00	2.40
12 Cecil Fielder	2.00	.60
13 Larry Walker	3.00	.90
14 Sammy Sosa	8.00	2.40
15 Manny Ramirez	2.00	.60
16 Gary Sheffield	2.00	.60
17 Barry Bonds	12.00	3.60
18 Jay Buhner	2.00	.60

1997 Score

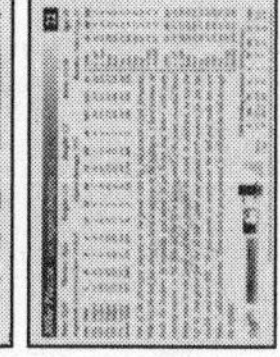

The 1997 Score set has a total of 550 cards. With cards 1-330 distributed in series one packs and cards 331-550 in series two packs. The 10-card Series one packs and the 12-card Series two packs carried a suggested retail price of $.99 each and were distributed exclusively to retail outlets. The fronts feature color player action photos in a white border. The backs carry player information and career statistics. The Hideki Irabu card (551A and B) is shortprinted (about twice as tough to pull as a basic card). One final note on the Irabu card, in the retail packs and factory sets, the card text is in English. In the Hobby Reserve packs, text is in Japanese. Notable Rookie Cards include Brian Giles.

	Nm-Mt	Ex-Mt
COMPLETE SET (551)	40.00	12.00
COMP.FACT.SET (551)	40.00	12.00
COMP.SERIES 1 (330)	15.00	4.50
COMP.SERIES 2 (221)	25.00	7.50
1 Jeff Bagwell	.30	.09
2 Mickey Tettleton	.20	.06
3 Johnny Damon	.20	.06
4 Jeff Conine	.20	.06
5 Bernie Williams	.30	.09
6 Will Clark	.50	.15
7 Ryan Klesko	.20	.06
8 Cecil Fielder	.20	.06
9 Paul Wilson	.20	.06
10 Gregg Jefferies	.20	.06
11 Chili Davis	.20	.06
12 Albert Belle	.20	.06
13 Ken Hill	.20	.06
14 Cliff Floyd	.20	.06
15 Jaime Navarro	.20	.06
16 Ismael Valdes	.20	.06
17 Jeff King	.20	.06
18 Chris Bosio	.20	.06
19 Reggie Sanders	.20	.06
20 Darren Daulton	.20	.06
21 Ken Caminiti	.20	.06
22 Mike Piazza	.75	.23
23 Chad Mottola	.20	.06
24 Darin Erstad	.20	.06
25 Dante Bichette	.20	.06
26 Frank Thomas	.50	.15
27 Ben McDonald	.20	.06
28 Raul Casanova	.20	.06
29 Kevin Ritz	.20	.06
30 Garret Anderson	.20	.06
31 Jason Kendall	.20	.06
32 Billy Wagner	.20	.06
33 Dave Justice	.20	.06
34 Marty Cordova	.20	.06
35 Derek Jeter	1.25	.35
36 Trevor Hoffman	.20	.06
37 Geronimo Berroa	.20	.06
38 Walt Weiss	.20	.06
39 Kirt Manwaring	.20	.06
40 Alex Gonzalez	.20	.06
41 Sean Berry	.20	.06
42 Kevin Appier	.20	.06
43 Rusty Greer	.20	.06
44 Pete Incaviglia	.20	.06
45 Rafael Palmeiro	.30	.09
46 Eddie Murray	.50	.15
47 Moises Alou	.20	.06
48 Mark Lewis	.20	.06
49 Hal Morris	.20	.06
50 Edgar Renteria	.20	.06
51 Rickey Henderson	.50	.15
52 Pat Listach	.20	.06
53 John Wasdin	.20	.06
54 James Baldwin	.20	.06
55 Brian Jordan	.20	.06
56 Edgar Martinez	.30	.09
57 Wil Cordero	.20	.06
58 Danny Tartabull	.20	.06
59 Keith Lockhart	.20	.06
60 Rico Brogna	.20	.06
61 Ricky Bottalico	.20	.06
62 Terry Pendleton	.20	.06
63 Bret Boone	.20	.06
64 Charlie Hayes	.20	.06
65 Marc Newfield	.20	.06
66 Sterling Hitchcock	.20	.06
67 Roberto Alomar	.50	.15
68 John Jaha	.20	.06
69 Greg Colbrunn	.20	.06
70 Sal Fasano	.20	.06
71 Brooks Kieschnick	.20	.06
72 Pedro Martinez	.50	.15
73 Kevin Elster	.20	.06
74 Ellis Burks	.20	.06
75 Chuck Finley	.20	.06
76 John Olerud	.20	.06
77 Jay Bell	.20	.06
78 Allen Watson	.20	.06
79 Darryl Strawberry	.30	.09
80 Orlando Miller	.20	.06
81 Jose Herrera	.20	.06
82 Andy Pettitte	.30	.09
83 Juan Guzman	.20	.06
84 Alan Benes	.20	.06
85 Jack McDowell	.20	.06
86 Ugueth Urbina	.20	.06
87 Rocky Coppinger	.20	.06
88 Jeff Cirillo	.20	.06
89 Tom Glavine	.30	.09
90 Robby Thompson	.20	.06
91 Barry Bonds	1.25	.35
92 Carlos Delgado	.20	.06
93 Mo Vaughn	.20	.06
94 Ryne Sandberg	.75	.23
95 Alex Rodriguez	.75	.23
96 Brady Anderson	.20	.06
97 Scott Brosius	.20	.06
98 Dennis Eckersley	.20	.06
99 Brian McRae	.20	.06
100 Rey Ordonez	.20	.06
101 John Valentin	.20	.06
102 Brett Butler	.20	.06
103 Eric Karros	.20	.06
104 Harold Baines	.20	.06
105 Javier Lopez	.20	.06
106 Alan Trammell	.30	.09
107 Jim Thome	.50	.15
108 Frank Rodriguez	.20	.06
109 Bernard Gilkey	.20	.06
110 Reggie Jefferson	.20	.06
111 Scott Stahoviak	.20	.06
112 Steve Gibralter	.20	.06
113 Todd Hollandsworth	.20	.06
114 Ruben Rivera	.20	.06
115 Dennis Martinez	.20	.06
116 Mariano Rivera	.30	.09
117 John Smoltz	.30	.09
118 John Mabry	.20	.06
119 Tom Gordon	.20	.06
120 Alex Ochoa	.20	.06
121 Jamey Wright	.20	.06
122 Dave Nilsson	.20	.06
123 Bobby Bonilla	.20	.06
124 Al Leiter	.20	.06
125 Rick Aguilera	.20	.06
126 Jeff Brantley	.20	.06
127 Kevin Brown	.20	.06
128 George Arias	.20	.06
129 Darren Oliver	.20	.06
130 Bill Pulsipher	.20	.06
131 Roberto Hernandez	.20	.06
132 Delino DeShields	.20	.06
133 Mark Grudzielanek	.20	.06
134 John Wetteland	.20	.06
135 Carlos Baerga	.20	.06
136 Paul Sorrento	.20	.06
137 Leo Gomez	.20	.06
138 Andy Ashby	.20	.06
139 Julio Franco	.20	.06
140 Brian Hunter	.20	.06
141 Jermaine Dye	.20	.06
142 Tony Clark	.20	.06
143 Ruben Sierra	.20	.06
144 Donovan Osborne	.20	.06
145 Mark McLemore	.20	.06
146 Terry Steinbach	.20	.06
147 Bob Wells	.20	.06
148 Chan Ho Park	.20	.06
149 Tim Salmon	.30	.09
150 Paul O'Neill	.30	.09
151 Cal Ripken	1.50	.45
152 Wally Joyner	.20	.06
153 Omar Vizquel	.20	.06
154 Mike Mussina	.50	.15
155 Andres Galarraga	.20	.06
156 Ken Griffey Jr.	.75	.23
157 Kenny Lofton	.20	.06
158 Ray Durham	.20	.06
159 Hideo Nomo	.50	.15
160 Ozzie Guillen	.20	.06
161 Roger Pavlik	.20	.06
162 Manny Ramirez	.20	.06
163 Mark Lemke	.20	.06
164 Mike Stanley	.20	.06
165 Chuck Knoblauch	.20	.06
166 Kimera Bartee	.20	.06
167 Wade Boggs	.30	.09
168 Jay Buhner	.20	.06
169 Eric Young	.20	.06
170 Jose Canseco	.50	.15
171 Dwight Gooden	.30	.09
172 Fred McGriff	.30	.09
173 Sandy Alomar Jr.	.20	.06
174 Andy Benes	.20	.06
175 Dean Palmer	.20	.06
176 Larry Walker	.30	.09
177 Charles Nagy	.20	.06
178 David Cone	.20	.06
179 Mark Grace	.30	.09
180 Robin Ventura	.20	.06
181 Roger Clemens	1.00	.30
182 Bobby Witt	.20	.06
183 Vinny Castilla	.20	.06
184 Gary Sheffield	.20	.06
185 Dan Wilson	.20	.06
186 Roger Cedeno	.20	.06
187 Mark McGwire	1.25	.35
188 Darren Bragg	.20	.06
189 Quinton McCracken	.20	.06
190 Randy Myers	.20	.06
191 Jeromy Burnitz	.20	.06
192 Randy Johnson	.50	.15
193 Chipper Jones	.50	.15
194 Greg Vaughn	.20	.06
195 Travis Fryman	.20	.06
196 Tim Naehring	.20	.06
197 B.J. Surhoff	.20	.06
198 Juan Gonzalez	.50	.15
199 Terrell Wade	.20	.06
200 Jeff Frye	.20	.06
201 Joey Cora	.20	.06
202 Raul Mondesi	.20	.06
203 Ivan Rodriguez	.50	.15
204 Armando Reynoso	.20	.06
205 Jeffrey Hammonds	.20	.06
206 Darren Dreifort	.20	.06
207 Kevin Seitzer	.20	.06
208 Tino Martinez	.30	.09
209 Jim Bruske	.20	.06
210 Jeff Suppan	.20	.06
211 Mark Carreon	.20	.06
212 Wilson Alvarez	.20	.06
213 John Burkett	.20	.06
214 Tony Phillips	.20	.06
215 Greg Maddux	.75	.23
216 Mark Whiten	.20	.06
217 Curtis Pride	.20	.06
218 Lyle Mouton	.20	.06
219 Todd Hundley	.30	.09
220 Greg Gagne	.20	.06
221 Rich Amaral	.20	.06
222 Tom Goodwin	.20	.06
223 Chris Hoiles	.20	.06
224 Jayhawk Owens	.20	.06
225 Kenny Rogers	.20	.06
226 Mike Greenwell	.20	.06
227 Mark Wohlers	.20	.06
228 Henry Rodriguez	.20	.06
229 Robert Perez	.20	.06
230 Jeff Kent	.20	.06
231 Darryl Hamilton	.20	.06
232 Alex Fernandez	.20	.06
233 Ron Karkovice	.20	.06
234 Jimmy Haynes	.20	.06
235 Craig Biggio	.30	.09
236 Ray Lankford	.20	.06
237 Lance Johnson	.20	.06
238 Matt Williams	.20	.06
239 Chad Curtis	.20	.06
240 Mark Thompson	.20	.06
241 Jason Giambi	.50	.15
242 Barry Larkin	.50	.15
243 Paul Molitor	.30	.09
244 Sammy Sosa	.75	.23
245 Kevin Tapani	.20	.06
246 Marquis Grissom	.20	.06
247 Joe Carter	.20	.06
248 Ramon Martinez	.20	.06
249 Tony Gwynn	.60	.18
250 Andy Fox	.20	.06
251 Troy O'Leary	.20	.06
252 Warren Newson	.20	.06
253 Troy Percival	.20	.06
254 Jamie Moyer	.20	.06
255 Danny Graves	.20	.06
256 David Wells	.20	.06
257 Todd Zeile	.20	.06
258 Raul Ibanez	.20	.06
259 Tyler Houston	.20	.06
260 LaTroy Hawkins	.20	.06
261 Joey Hamilton	.20	.06
262 Mike Sweeney	.20	.06
263 Brant Brown	.20	.06
264 Pat Hentgen	.20	.06
265 Mark Johnson	.20	.06
266 Robb Nen	.20	.06
267 Justin Thompson	.20	.06
268 Ron Gant	.20	.06
269 Jeff D'Amico	.20	.06
270 Shawn Estes	.20	.06
271 Derek Bell	.20	.06
272 Fernando Valenzuela	.20	.06
273 Tom Pagnozzi	.20	.06
274 John Burke	.20	.06
275 Ed Sprague	.20	.06
276 F.P. Santangelo	.20	.06
277 Todd Greene	.20	.06
278 Butch Huskey	.20	.06
279 Steve Finley	.20	.06
280 Eric Davis	.20	.06
281 Shawn Green	.20	.06
282 Al Martin	.20	.06
283 Michael Tucker	.20	.06
284 Shane Reynolds	.20	.06
285 Matt Mieske	.20	.06
286 Jose Rosado	.20	.06
287 Mark Langston	.20	.06
288 Ralph Milliard	.20	.06
289 Mike Lansing	.20	.06
290 Scott Servais	.20	.06
291 Royce Clayton	.20	.06
292 Mike Grace	.20	.06
293 James Mouton	.20	.06
294 Charles Johnson	.20	.06
295 Gary Gaetti	.20	.06
296 Kevin Mitchell	.20	.06
297 Carlos Garcia	.20	.06
298 Desi Relaford	.20	.06
299 Jason Thompson	.20	.06
300 Osvaldo Fernandez	.20	.06
301 Fernando Vina	.20	.06
302 Jose Offerman	.20	.06
303 Yamil Benitez	.20	.06
304 J.T. Snow	.20	.06
305 Rafael Bournigal	.20	.06
306 Jason Isringhausen	.20	.06
307 Bobby Higginson	.20	.06
308 Nerio Rodriguez RC	.20	.06
309 Brian Giles RC	1.00	.30
310 Andruw Jones	.20	.06
311 Tony Graffanino	.20	.06
312 Arquimedez Pozo	.20	.06
313 Jermaine Allensworth	.20	.06
314 Jeff Darwin	.20	.06
315 George Williams	.20	.06
316 Karim Garcia	.20	.06
317 Trey Beamon	.20	.06
318 Mac Suzuki	.20	.06
319 Robin Jennings	.20	.06
320 Danny Patterson	.20	.06
321 Damon Mashore	.20	.06
322 Wendell Magee	.20	.06
323 Dax Jones	.20	.06
324 Kevin Brown	.20	.06
325 Marvin Benard	.20	.06
326 Mike Cameron	.20	.06
327 Marcus Jensen	.20	.06
328 Eddie Murray CL	.30	.09
329 Paul Molitor CL	.20	.06
330 Todd Hundley CL	.20	.06
331 Norm Charlton	.20	.06
332 Bruce Ruffin	.20	.06
333 John Wetteland	.20	.06
334 Marquis Grissom	.20	.06
335 Sterling Hitchcock	.20	.06
336 John Olerud	.20	.06
337 David Wells	.20	.06
338 Chili Davis	.20	.06
339 Mark Lewis	.20	.06
340 Kenny Lofton	.20	.06
341 Alex Fernandez	.20	.06
342 Ruben Sierra	.20	.06
343 Delino DeShields	.20	.06
344 John Wasdin	.20	.06
345 Dennis Martinez	.20	.06
346 Kevin Elster	.20	.06
347 Bobby Bonilla	.20	.06
348 Jaime Navarro	.20	.06
349 Chad Curtis	.20	.06
350 Terry Steinbach	.20	.06
351 Ariel Prieto	.20	.06
352 Jeff Kent	.20	.06
353 Carlos Garcia	.20	.06
354 Mark Whiten	.20	.06
355 Todd Zeile	.20	.06
356 Eric Davis	.20	.06
357 Greg Colbrunn	.20	.06
358 Moises Alou	.20	.06
359 Allen Watson	.20	.06
360 Jose Canseco	.50	.15
361 Matt Williams	.20	.06
362 Jeff King	.20	.06
363 Darryl Hamilton	.20	.06
364 Mark Clark	.20	.06
365 J.T. Snow	.20	.06
366 Kevin Mitchell	.20	.06
367 Orlando Miller	.20	.06
368 Rico Brogna	.20	.06
369 Mike James	.20	.06
370 Brad Ausmus	.20	.06
371 Darryl Kile	.20	.06
372 Edgardo Alfonzo	.20	.06
373 Julian Tavarez	.20	.06
374 Darren Lewis	.20	.06
375 Steve Karsay	.20	.06
376 Lee Stevens	.20	.06
377 Albie Lopez	.20	.06
378 Orel Hershiser	.20	.06
379 Lee Smith	.20	.06
380 Rick Helling	.20	.06
381 Carlos Perez	.20	.06
382 Tony Tarasco	.20	.06
383 Melvin Nieves	.20	.06
384 Benji Gil	.20	.06
385 Devon White	.20	.06
386 Armando Benitez	.20	.06
387 Bill Swift	.20	.06
388 John Smiley	.20	.06
389 Midre Cummings	.20	.06
390 Tim Belcher	.20	.06
391 Tim Raines	.20	.06
392 Todd Worrell	.20	.06
393 Quilvio Veras	.20	.06
394 Matt Lawton	.20	.06
395 Aaron Sele	.20	.06
396 Bip Roberts	.20	.06
397 Denny Neagle	.20	.06
398 Tyler Green	.20	.06
399 Hipolito Pichardo	.20	.06
400 Scott Erickson	.20	.06
401 Bobby Jones	.20	.06
402 Jim Edmonds	.20	.06
403 Chad Ogea	.20	.06
404 Cal Eldred	.20	.06
405 Pat Listach	.20	.06
406 Todd Stottlemyre	.20	.06
407 Phil Nevin	.20	.06
408 Otis Nixon	.20	.06
409 Billy Ashley	.20	.06
410 Jimmy Key	.20	.06
411 Mike Timlin	.20	.06
412 Joe Vitiello	.20	.06
413 Rondell White	.20	.06
414 Jeff Fassero	.20	.06
415 Rex Hudler	.20	.06
416 Curt Schilling	.30	.09
417 Rich Becker	.20	.06
418 W.Van Landingham	.20	.06
419 Chris Snopek	.20	.06
420 David Segui	.20	.06
421 Eddie Murray	.50	.15
422 Shane Andrews	.20	.06
423 Gary DiSarcina	.20	.06
424 Brian Hunter	.20	.06
425 Willie Greene	.20	.06
426 Felipe Crespo	.20	.06
427 Jason Bates	.20	.06
428 Albert Belle	.20	.06
429 Rey Sanchez	.20	.06
430 Roger Clemens	1.00	.30
431 Deion Sanders	.30	.09
432 Ernie Young	.20	.06
433 Jay Bell	.20	.06
434 Jeff Blauser	.20	.06
435 Lenny Dykstra	.20	.06
436 Chuck Carr	.20	.06
437 Russ Davis	.20	.06
438 Carl Everett	.20	.06
439 Damion Easley	.20	.06
440 Pat Kelly	.20	.06
441 Pat Rapp	.20	.06
442 Dave Justice	.20	.06
443 Graeme Lloyd	.20	.06
444 Damon Buford	.20	.06
445 Jose Valentin	.20	.06
446 Jason Schmidt	.20	.06
447 Dave Martinez	.20	.06
448 Danny Tartabull	.20	.06
449 Jose Vizcaino	.20	.06
450 Steve Avery	.20	.06
451 Mike Devereaux	.20	.06
452 Jim Eisenreich	.20	.06
453 Mark Leiter	.20	.06
454 Roberto Kelly	.20	.06
455 Benito Santiago	.20	.06
456 Steve Trachsel	.20	.06
457 Gerald Williams	.20	.06
458 Pete Schourek	.20	.06
459 Esteban Loaiza	.20	.06
460 Mel Rojas	.20	.06
461 Tim Wakefield	.20	.06
462 Tony Fernandez	.20	.06
463 Doug Drabek	.20	.06
464 Joe Girardi	.20	.06
465 Mike Bordick	.20	.06
466 Jim Leyritz	.20	.06
467 Erik Hanson	.20	.06
468 Michael Tucker	.20	.06
469 Tony Womack RC	.20	.06
470 Doug Glanville	.20	.06
471 Rudy Pemberton	.20	.06
472 Keith Lockhart	.20	.06
473 Nomar Garciaparra	.75	.23
474 Scott Rolen	.30	.09
475 Jason Dickson	.20	.06
476 Glendon Rusch	.20	.06
477 Todd Walker	.20	.06
478 Dmitri Young	.20	.06
479 Rod Myers	.20	.06
480 Wilton Guerrero	.20	.06
481 Jorge Posada	.30	.09
482 Brant Brown	.20	.06
483 Bubba Trammell RC	.20	.06
484 Jose Guillen	.20	.06
485 Scott Spiezio	.20	.06

486 Bob Abreu .20 .06
487 Chris Holt .20 .06
488 Deivi Cruz RC .20 .06
489 Vladimir Guerrero .50 .15
490 Julio Santana .20 .06
491 Ray Montgomery RC .20 .06
492 Kevin Orie .20 .06
493 Todd Hundley GY .20 .06
494 Tim Salmon GY .20 .06
495 Albert Belle GY .20 .06
496 Manny Ramirez GY .20 .06
497 Rafael Palmeiro GY .20 .06
498 Juan Gonzalez GY .30 .09
499 Ken Griffey Jr. GY .50 .15
500 Andruw Jones GY .20 .06
501 Mike Piazza GY .50 .15
502 Jeff Bagwell GY .20 .06
503 Bernie Williams GY .20 .06
504 Barry Bonds GY .50 .15
505 Ken Caminiti GY .20 .06
506 Darin Erstad GY .20 .06
507 Alex Rodriguez GY .50 .15
508 Frank Thomas GY .30 .09
509 Chipper Jones GY .30 .09
510 Mo Vaughn GY .20 .06
511 Mark McGwire GY .60 .18
512 Fred McGriff GY .20 .06
513 Jay Buhner GY .20 .06
514 Gary Sheffield GY .20 .06
515 Jim Thome GY .30 .09
516 Dean Palmer GY .20 .06
517 Henry Rodriguez GY .20 .06
518 Andy Pettitte RF .20 .06
519 Mike Mussina RF .30 .09
520 Greg Maddux RF .50 .15
521 John Smoltz RF .20 .06
522 Hideo Nomo RF .20 .06
523 Troy Percival RF .20 .06
524 John Wetteland RF .20 .06
525 Roger Clemens RF .50 .15
526 Charles Nagy RF .20 .06
527 Mariano Rivera RF .20 .06
528 Tom Glavine RF .20 .06
529 Randy Johnson RF .30 .09
530 J.Isringhausen RF .20 .06
531 Alex Fernandez RF .20 .06
532 Kevin Brown RF .20 .06
533 Chuck Knoblauch TG .20 .06
534 Rusty Greer TG .20 .06
535 Tony Gwynn TG .30 .09
536 Ryan Klesko TG .20 .06
537 Ryne Sandberg TG .50 .15
538 Barry Larkin TG .20 .06
539 Will Clark TG .20 .06
540 Kenny Lofton TG .20 .06
541 Paul Molitor TG .20 .06
542 Roberto Alomar TG .20 .06
543 Rey Ordonez TG .20 .06
544 Jason Giambi TG .20 .06
545 Derek Jeter TG .60 .18
546 Cal Ripken TG .75 .23
547 Ivan Rodriguez TG .30 .09
548 Ken Griffey Jr. CL .50 .15
549 Frank Thomas CL .30 .09
550 Mike Piazza CL .50 .15
551A Hideki Irabu SP 2.50 .75
551B Hideki Irabu 2.50 .75
Japenese SP

1997 Score Artist's Proofs White Border

Artist's Proofs White Border cards were randomly inserted exclusively into Score Series 1 retail packs. The cards share the similar "Artist's Proof" logo as seen on the more commonly traded Showcase Series Artist's Proofs. Unlike the silver-foiled Showcase Series Artist's Proofs, however, the White Border cards have plain white stock card fronts - making them easy to misidentify with a basic issue Score card. Please note that Series 2 Artist Proofs do not exist.

Nm-Mt Ex-Mt
*STARS: 12.5X TO 30X BASIC CARDS
*ROOKIES: 4X TO 10X BASIC CARDS

1997 Score Premium Stock

A special Premium Stock version of the base series one set was produced exclusively for hobby outlets. The cards parallel the regular issue set except for a grey border, thicker card stock and a prominent gold foil "Premium Stock" logo on front. The cards were distributed in Premium Stock hobby packs. Second series Premium Stock cards were called "Hobby Reserve."

Nm-Mt Ex-Mt
COMPLETE SET (551) 80.00 24.00
COMP.SERIES 1 (330) 40.00 12.00
COMP.SERIES 2 (221) 40.00 12.00
*STARS: .75X TO 2X BASIC CARDS ...
*ROOKIES: .6X TO 1.5X BASIC CARDS
*IRABU: .4X TO 1X BASIC IRABU ....

1997 Score Reserve Collection

Randomly inserted in second series hobby reserve packs only at a rate of one in 11, this set is parallel to the regular second series set. The cards are printed on thick 20 pt. foil card stock with screen printing for a raised ink effect. A large grey "Reserve Collection" logo is printed on each card back.

Nm-Mt Ex-Mt
*STARS: 5X TO 12X BASIC CARDS ....
*ROOKIES: 2.5X TO 6X BASIC CARDS
*IRABU: 1.5X TO 3X BASIC IRABU .....

1997 Score Showcase Series

Randomly inserted in first series packs at a rate of one in seven hobby packs, one in two jumbo packs, one in four magazine and one in seven retail packs, and second series packs at a rate of one in five hobby packs and one in seven retail packs, cards from this set are silver-coated parallel versions of the regular Score set.

Nm-Mt Ex-Mt
*STARS: 3X TO 8X BASIC CARDS ......
*ROOKIES: 1.5X TO 4X BASIC CARDS
*IRABU: .5X TO 1.2X BASIC IRABU ....

1997 Score Showcase Series Artist's Proofs

Randomly inserted in first series hobby and retail packs at a rate of one in 35, and second series hobby 1:23 and second series retail 1:35, cards from this 551-card set are parallel to the more common Showcase Series set. The cards are printed on holographic laminated card stock with a prismatic foil background and stamped with an Artist's Proof logo on front.

Nm-Mt Ex-Mt
*STARS: 10X TO 25X BASIC CARDS ..
*ROOKIES: 4X TO 10X BASIC CARDS
*IRABU: 2X TO 5X BASIC IRABU ....

1997 Score All-Star Fanfest

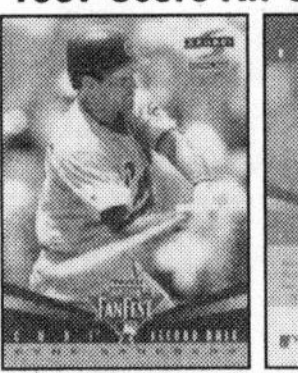

This 20-card insert set features players that were involved in the 1996 All-Star game. The cards were available at a rate of 1:29 in special retail Score I boxes.

Nm-Mt Ex-Mt
COMPLETE SET (20) 80.00 24.00
1 Frank Thomas 5.00 1.50
2 Jeff Bagwell 5.00 1.50
3 Chuck Knoblauch 3.00 .90
4 Ryne Sandberg 5.00 1.50
5 Alex Rodriguez 10.00 3.00
6 Chipper Jones 8.00 2.40
7 Jim Thome 4.00 1.20
8 Ken Caminiti 2.00 .60
9 Albert Belle 2.00 .60
10 Tony Gwynn 8.00 2.40
11 Ken Griffey Jr. 12.00 3.60
12 Andruw Jones 6.00 1.80
13 Juan Gonzalez 5.00 1.50
14 Brian Jordan 2.00 .60
15 Ivan Rodriguez 5.00 1.50
16 Mike Piazza 10.00 3.00
17 Andy Pettitte 2.00 .60
18 John Smoltz 2.00 .60
19 John Wetteland 2.00 .60
20 Mark Wohlers 1.00 .30

1997 Score Blast Masters

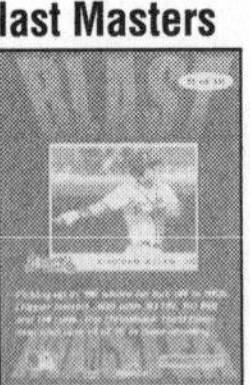

Randomly inserted in second series packs at a rate of 1:35 (retail) and 1:23 (hobby reserve), this 18-card set features color player photos on a gold prismatic foil card.

Nm-Mt Ex-Mt
COMPLETE SET (18) 100.00 30.00
1 Mo Vaughn 2.00 .60
2 Mark McGwire 12.00 3.60
3 Juan Gonzalez 5.00 1.50
4 Albert Belle 2.00 .60
5 Barry Bonds 12.00 3.60
6 Ken Griffey Jr. 8.00 2.40
7 Andruw Jones 2.00 .60
8 Chipper Jones 5.00 1.50
9 Mike Piazza 8.00 2.40
10 Jeff Bagwell 3.00 .90
11 Dante Bichette 2.00 .60
12 Alex Rodriguez 8.00 2.40
13 Gary Sheffield 2.00 .60
14 Ken Caminiti 2.00 .60
15 Sammy Sosa 8.00 2.40
16 Vladimir Guerrero 5.00 1.50
17 Brian Jordan 2.00 .60
18 Tim Salmon 3.00 .90

1997 Score Franchise

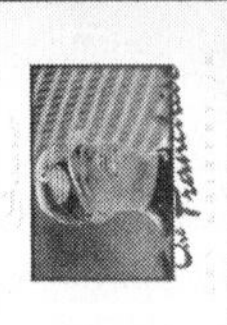

Randomly inserted in series one hobby packs only at a rate of one in 72, this nine-card set honors superstar players for their irreplaceable contribution to their team. The fronts display sepia player portraits on a white baseball replica background. The backs carry an action player photo with a sentence about the player which explains why he was selected for this set.

Nm-Mt Ex-Mt
COMPLETE SET (9) 20.00 6.00
*GLOWING: 1.25X TO 3X BASIC FRANCHISE
GLOW.SER.1 ODDS 1:240H/R, 1:79J, 1:120M
1 Ken Griffey Jr. 2.00 .60
2 John Smoltz .75 .23
3 Cal Ripken 4.00 1.20
4 Chipper Jones 1.25 .35
5 Mike Piazza 2.00 .60
6 Albert Belle .50 .15
7 Frank Thomas 1.25 .35
8 Sammy Sosa 2.00 .60
9 Roberto Alomar 1.25 .35

1997 Score Heart of the Order

Randomly inserted in packs at a rate of 1:23 (retail) and 1:15 (hobby reserve), this 36-card set features color photos of players on six teams with a panorama of the stadium in the background. Each team's three cards form one collectible unit. Eighteen of these cards are found in retail packs, and eighteen in Hobby Reserve packs.

Nm-Mt Ex-Mt
COMPLETE SET (36) 100.00 30.00
1 Will Clark 4.00 1.20
2 Ivan Rodriguez 4.00 1.20
3 Juan Gonzalez 4.00 1.20
4 Frank Thomas 4.00 1.20
5 Albert Belle 1.50 .45
6 Robin Ventura 1.50 .45
7 Alex Rodriguez 6.00 1.80
8 Jay Buhner 1.50 .45
9 Ken Griffey Jr. 6.00 1.80
10 Rafael Palmeiro 2.50 .75
11 Roberto Alomar 4.00 1.20
12 Cal Ripken 12.00 3.60
13 Manny Ramirez 1.50 .45
14 Matt Williams 1.50 .45
15 Jim Thome 4.00 1.20
16 Derek Jeter 10.00 3.00
17 Wade Boggs 2.50 .75
18 Bernie Williams 2.50 .75
19 Chipper Jones 4.00 1.20
20 Andruw Jones 1.50 .45
21 Ryan Klesko 1.50 .45
22 Mike Piazza 6.00 1.80
23 Wilton Guerrero 1.50 .45
24 Raul Mondesi 1.50 .45
25 Tony Gwynn 5.00 1.50
26 Greg Vaughn 1.50 .45
27 Ken Caminiti 1.50 .45
28 Brian Jordan 1.50 .45
29 Ron Gant 1.50 .45
30 Dmitri Young 1.50 .45
31 Darin Erstad 1.50 .45
32 Tim Salmon 2.50 .75
33 Jim Edmonds 1.50 .45
34 Chuck Knoblauch 1.50 .45
35 Paul Molitor 2.50 .75
36 Todd Walker 1.50 .45

1997 Score Highlight Zone

Randomly inserted in series one hobby packs only at a rate of one in 35, this 18-card set honors those mega-stars who have the incredible ability to consistently make the highlight films. The set is printed on thicker card stock with special foil stamping and a dot matrix holographic background.

Nm-Mt Ex-Mt
COMPLETE SET (18) 150.00 45.00
1 Frank Thomas 6.00 1.80
2 Ken Griffey Jr. 10.00 3.00
3 Mo Vaughn 2.50 .75
4 Albert Belle 2.50 .75
5 Mike Piazza 10.00 3.00
6 Barry Bonds 15.00 4.50
7 Greg Maddux 10.00 3.00
8 Sammy Sosa 10.00 3.00
9 Jeff Bagwell 4.00 1.20
10 Alex Rodriguez 10.00 3.00
11 Chipper Jones 6.00 1.80
12 Brady Anderson 2.50 .75
13 Ozzie Smith 2.50 .75
14 Edgar Martinez 4.00 1.20
15 Cal Ripken 20.00 6.00
16 Ryan Klesko 2.50 .75
17 Randy Johnson 6.00 1.80
18 Eddie Murray 6.00 1.80

1997 Score Pitcher Perfect

Randomly inserted in series one packs at a rate of one in 23, this 15-card set features players photographed by Randy Johnson in unique poses and foil stamping. The backs carry player information.

Nm-Mt Ex-Mt
COMPLETE SET (15) 5.00 1.50
1 Cal Ripken 1.50 .45
2 Alex Rodriguez .75 .23
3 Alex Rodriguez 3.00 .90
Cal Ripken
4 Edgar Martinez .30 .09
5 Ivan Rodriguez .50 .15
6 Mark McGwire 1.25 .35
7 Tim Salmon .30 .09
8 Chili Davis .20 .06
9 Joe Carter .20 .06
10 Frank Thomas .50 .15
11 Will Clark .50 .15
12 Mo Vaughn .20 .06
13 Wade Boggs .30 .09
14 Ken Griffey Jr. .75 .23
15 Randy Johnson .50 .15

1997 Score Stand and Deliver

Randomly inserted in series two packs at a rate of 1:71 (retail) and 1:47 (hobby reserve), this 24-card set features color player photos printed on silver foil card stock. The set is broken into six separate 4-card groupings. Groups contain players from the following teams: 1-4 (Braves), 5-8 (Mariners), 9-12 (Yankees), 13-16 (Dodgers), 17-20 (Indians) and 21-24 (Wild Card). The four players featured within the Wild Card group are from "lesser" teams not given a shot at winning the World Series. Each of these cards, unlike cards 1-20, has a "Wild Card" logo stamped on front. Collectors were then supposed to gather up the particular group that won the 1997 World Series, in this case - the Florida Marlins. Since none of the featured teams won, the 4-card Wild Card group was designated as the winner. The winning cards could then be mailed into Pinnacle for a special gold upgrade version of the set, framed in glass.

Nm-Mt Ex-Mt
COMPLETE SET (24) 250.00 75.00
1 Andruw Jones 4.00 1.20
2 Greg Maddux 15.00 4.50
3 Chipper Jones 10.00 3.00
4 John Smoltz 6.00 1.80
5 Ken Griffey Jr. 15.00 4.50
6 Alex Rodriguez 15.00 4.50
7 Jay Buhner 4.00 1.20
8 Randy Johnson 10.00 3.00
9 Derek Jeter 25.00 7.50
10 Andy Pettitte 6.00 1.80
11 Bernie Williams 6.00 1.80
12 Mariano Rivera 6.00 1.80
13 Mike Piazza 15.00 4.50
14 Hideo Nomo 10.00 3.00
15 Raul Mondesi 4.00 1.20
16 Todd Hollandsworth 4.00 1.20
17 Manny Ramirez 4.00 1.20
18 Jim Thome 10.00 3.00
19 Dave Justice 4.00 1.20
20 Matt Williams 4.00 1.20
21 Juan Gonzalez W 10.00 3.00
22 Jeff Bagwell W 6.00 1.80
23 Cal Ripken W 30.00 9.00
24 Frank Thomas W 10.00 3.00

1997 Score Stellar Season

Randomly inserted in series one pre-priced magazine packs only at a rate of one in 35, this 18-card set features players who had a star season. The cards are printed using dot matrix holographic printing.

Nm-Mt Ex-Mt
COMPLETE SET (18) 60.00 18.00
1 Juan Gonzalez 4.00 1.20
2 Chuck Knoblauch 1.50 .45
3 Jeff Bagwell 2.50 .75
4 John Smoltz 2.50 .75
5 Mark McGwire 10.00 3.00
6 Ken Griffey Jr. 6.00 1.80
7 Frank Thomas 4.00 1.20
8 Alex Rodriguez 6.00 1.80
9 Mike Piazza 6.00 1.80
10 Albert Belle 1.50 .45
11 Roberto Alomar 4.00 1.20
12 Sammy Sosa 6.00 1.80
13 Mo Vaughn 1.50 .45
14 Brady Anderson 1.50 .45
15 Henry Rodriguez 1.50 .45
16 Eric Young 1.50 .45
17 Gary Sheffield 1.50 .45
18 Ryan Klesko 1.50 .45

1997 Score Titanic Taters

Randomly inserted in series one retail packs only at a rate of one in 35, this 18-card set honors the long-ball ability of some of the league's top sluggers and uses dot matrix holographic printing.

Nm-Mt Ex-Mt
COMPLETE SET (18) 120.00 36.00

1 Mark McGwire 15.00 4.50
2 Mike Piazza 10.00 3.00
3 Ken Griffey Jr. 10.00 3.00
4 Juan Gonzalez 6.00 1.80
5 Frank Thomas 6.00 1.80
6 Albert Belle 2.50 .75
7 Sammy Sosa 10.00 3.00
8 Jeff Bagwell 4.00 1.20
9 Todd Hundley 2.50 .75
10 Ryan Klesko 2.50 .75
11 Brady Anderson 2.50 .75
12 Mo Vaughn 2.50 .75
13 Jay Buhner 2.50 .75
14 Chipper Jones 6.00 1.80
15 Barry Bonds 15.00 4.50
16 Gary Sheffield 2.50 .75
17 Alex Rodriguez 10.00 3.00
18 Cecil Fielder 2.50 .75

1997 Score Andruw Jones Blister Pack Special

This one-card set features a white bordered color photo of Andruw Jones batting with the distance of his home runs displayed in the background. The card was always inserted on the top of the prepriced 1997 Score Series II jumbo packs. The backs carry a "Thank you for buying Score Baseball Series II" sentence with a list and description of insert sets found in Score Series II. The rules for the Stand and Deliver Promotion rounded out the backs.

Nm-Mt Ex-Mt
1 Andruw Jones 2.00 .60

1998 Score Samples

These six cards were distributed to dealers to preview the upcoming 1998 Score baseball release. These samples are parallel to the basic issue cards except for the large, black "SAMPLE" text running diagonally across the back of the card and the lack of any 1997 statistics (all replaced by 000's).

Nm-Mt Ex-Mt
COMPLETE SET (6) 12.00 3.60
10 Alex Rodriguez 2.00 .60
24 Mike Piazza 2.50 .75
34 Ken Griffey Jr. 2.50 .75
43 Cal Ripken 4.00 1.20
51 Chipper Jones 2.00 .60
60 Carlos Delgado 1.00 .30

1998 Score

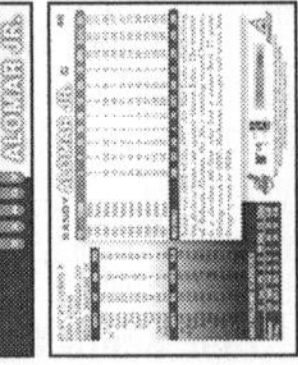

This 270-card set was distributed in 10-card packs exclusively to retail outlets with a suggested retail price of $.99. The fronts feature color player photos in a thin white border. The backs carry player information and statistics. In addition, two unnumbered checklist cards were created. The first card was available only in regular issue packs and provided listings for the standard 270-card set. A blank-backed checklist card was randomly seeded exclusively into All-Star Edition packs (released about three months after the regular packs went live). This checklist card provided listings only for the three insert sets exclusively distributed in All-Star Edition packs (First Pitch, Loaded Lineup and New Season).

Nm-Mt Ex-Mt
COMPLETE SET (270) 40.00 12.00
1 Andruw Jones .20 .06
2 Dan Wilson .20 .06
3 Hideo Nomo .50 .15
4 Chuck Carr .20 .06
5 Barry Bonds 1.25 .35
6 Jack McDowell .20 .06
7 Albert Belle .20 .06
8 Francisco Cordova .20 .06
9 Greg Maddux .75 .23
10 Alex Rodriguez .75 .23
11 Steve Avery .20 .06
12 Chuck McElroy .20 .06
13 Larry Walker .30 .09
14 Hideki Irabu .20 .06
15 Roberto Alomar .50 .15
16 Neifi Perez .20 .06
17 Jim Thome .50 .15
18 Rickey Henderson .50 .15
19 Andres Galarraga .20 .06
20 Jeff Fassero .20 .06

21 Kevin Young .20 .06
22 Derek Jeter 1.25 .35
23 Andy Benes .20 .06
24 Mike Piazza .75 .23
25 Todd Stottlemyre .20 .06
26 Michael Tucker .20 .06
27 Denny Neagle .20 .06
28 Javier Lopez .20 .06
29 Aaron Sele .20 .06
30 Ryan Klesko .20 .06
31 Dennis Eckersley .20 .06
32 Quinton McCracken .20 .06
33 Brian Anderson .20 .06
34 Ken Griffey Jr. .75 .23
35 Shawn Estes .20 .06
36 Tim Wakefield .20 .06
37 Jimmy Key .20 .06
38 Jeff Bagwell .30 .09
39 Edgardo Alfonzo .20 .06
40 Mike Cameron .20 .06
41 Mark McGwire 1.25 .35
42 Tino Martinez .30 .09
43 Cal Ripken 1.50 .45
44 Curtis Goodwin .20 .06
45 Bobby Ayala .20 .06
46 Sandy Alomar Jr. .20 .06
47 Bobby Jones .20 .06
48 Omar Vizquel .20 .06
49 Roger Clemens 1.00 .30
50 Tony Gwynn .60 .18
51 Chipper Jones .50 .15
52 Ron Coomer .20 .06
53 Dmitri Young .20 .06
54 Brian Giles .20 .06
55 Steve Finley .20 .06
56 David Cone .20 .06
57 Andy Pettitte .30 .09
58 Wilton Guerrero .20 .06
59 Deion Sanders .30 .09
60 Carlos Delgado .20 .06
61 Jason Giambi .50 .15
62 Ozzie Guillen .20 .06
63 Jay Bell .20 .06
64 Barry Larkin .50 .15
65 Sammy Sosa .75 .23
66 Bernie Williams .30 .09
67 Terry Steinbach .20 .06
68 Scott Rolen .30 .09
69 Melvin Nieves .20 .06
70 Craig Biggio .30 .09
71 Todd Greene .20 .06
72 Greg Gagne .20 .06
73 Shigetoshi Hasegawa .20 .06
74 Mark McLemore .20 .06
75 Darren Bragg .20 .06
76 Brett Butler .20 .06
77 Ron Gant .20 .06
78 Mike Difelice RC .20 .06
79 Charles Nagy .20 .06
80 Scott Hatteberg .20 .06
81 Brady Anderson .20 .06
82 Jay Buhner .20 .06
83 Todd Hollandsworth .20 .06
84 Geronimo Berroa .20 .06
85 Jeff Suppan .20 .06
86 Pedro Martinez .50 .15
87 Roger Cedeno .20 .06
88 Ivan Rodriguez .50 .15
89 Jaime Navarro .20 .06
90 Chris Hoiles .20 .06
91 Nomar Garciaparra .75 .23
92 Rafael Palmeiro .30 .09
93 Darin Erstad .20 .06
94 Kenny Lofton .20 .06
95 Mike Timlin .20 .06
96 Chris Clemons .20 .06
97 Vinny Castilla .20 .06
98 Charlie Hayes .20 .06
99 Lyle Mouton .20 .06
100 Jason Dickson .20 .06
101 Justin Thompson .20 .06
102 Pat Kelly .20 .06
103 Chan Ho Park .20 .06
104 Ray Lankford .20 .06
105 Frank Thomas .50 .15
106 Jermaine Allensworth .20 .06
107 Doug Drabek .20 .06
108 Todd Hundley .20 .06
109 Carl Everett .20 .06
110 Edgar Martinez .30 .09
111 Robin Ventura .20 .06
112 John Wetteland .20 .06
113 Mariano Rivera .30 .09
114 Jose Rosado .20 .06
115 Ken Caminiti .20 .06
116 Paul O'Neill .30 .09
117 Tim Salmon .30 .09
118 Eduardo Perez .20 .06
119 Mike Jackson .20 .06
120 John Smoltz .30 .09
121 Brant Brown .20 .06
122 John Mabry .20 .06
123 Chuck Knoblauch .20 .06
124 Reggie Sanders .20 .06
125 Ken Hill .20 .06
126 Mike Mussina .50 .15
127 Chad Curtis .20 .06
128 Todd Worrell .20 .06
129 Chris Widger .20 .06
130 Damon Mashore .20 .06
131 Kevin Brown .30 .09
132 Bip Roberts .20 .06
133 Tim Naehring .20 .06
134 Dave Martinez .20 .06
135 Jeff Blauser .20 .06
136 David Justice .20 .06
137 Dave Hollins .20 .06
138 Pat Hentgen .20 .06
139 Darren Daulton .20 .06
140 Ramon Martinez .20 .06
141 Raul Casanova .20 .06
142 Tom Glavine .30 .09
143 J.T. Snow .20 .06
144 Tony Graffanino .20 .06
145 Randy Johnson .50 .15
146 Orlando Merced .20 .06
147 Jeff Juden .20 .06
148 Darryl Kile .20 .06
149 Ray Durham .20 .06
150 Alex Fernandez .20 .06
151 Joey Cora .20 .06
152 Royce Clayton .20 .06
153 Randy Myers .20 .06
154 Charles Johnson .20 .06
155 Alan Benes .20 .06
156 Mike Bordick .20 .06
157 Heathcliff Slocumb .20 .06
158 Roger Bailey .20 .06
159 Reggie Jefferson .20 .06
160 Ricky Bottalico .20 .06
161 Scott Erickson .20 .06
162 Matt Williams .20 .06
163 Robb Nen .20 .06
164 Matt Stairs .20 .06
165 Ismael Valdes .20 .06
166 Lee Stevens .20 .06
167 Gary DiSarcina .20 .06
168 Brad Radke .20 .06
169 Mike Lansing .20 .06
170 Armando Benitez .20 .06
171 Mike James .20 .06
172 Russ Davis .20 .06
173 Lance Johnson .20 .06
174 Joey Hamilton .20 .06
175 John Valentin .20 .06
176 David Segui .20 .06
177 David Wells .20 .06
178 Delino DeShields .20 .06
179 Eric Karros .20 .06
180 Jim Leyritz .20 .06
181 Raul Mondesi .20 .06
182 Travis Fryman .20 .06
183 Todd Zeile .20 .06
184 Brian Jordan .20 .06
185 Rey Ordonez .20 .06
186 Jim Edmonds .20 .06
187 Terrell Wade .20 .06
188 Marquis Grissom .20 .06
189 Chris Snopek .20 .06
190 Shane Reynolds .20 .06
191 Jeff Frye .20 .06
192 Paul Sorrento .20 .06
193 James Baldwin .20 .06
194 Brian McRae .20 .06
195 Fred McGriff .30 .09
196 Troy Percival .20 .06
197 Rich Amaral .20 .06
198 Juan Guzman .20 .06
199 Cecil Fielder .20 .06
200 Willie Blair .20 .06
201 Chili Davis .20 .06
202 Gary Gaetti .20 .06
203 B.J. Surhoff .20 .06
204 Steve Cooke .20 .06
205 Chuck Finley .20 .06
206 Jeff Kent .20 .06
207 Ben McDonald .20 .06
208 Jeffrey Hammonds .20 .06
209 Tom Goodwin .20 .06
210 Billy Ashley .20 .06
211 Wil Cordero .20 .06
212 Shawon Dunston .20 .06
213 Tony Phillips .20 .06
214 Jamie Moyer .20 .06
215 John Jaha .20 .06
216 Troy O'Leary .20 .06
217 Brad Ausmus .20 .06
218 Garret Anderson .20 .06
219 Wilson Alvarez .20 .06
220 Kent Mercker .20 .06
221 Wade Boggs .30 .09
222 Mark Wohlers .20 .06
223 Kevin Appier .20 .06
224 Tony Fernandez .20 .06
225 Ugueth Urbina .20 .06
226 Gregg Jefferies .20 .06
227 Mo Vaughn .20 .06
228 Arthur Rhodes .20 .06
229 Jorge Fabregas .20 .06
230 Mark Gardner .20 .06
231 Shane Mack .20 .06
232 Jorge Posada .30 .09
233 Jose Cruz Jr. .20 .06
234 Paul Konerko .20 .06
235 Derrek Lee .20 .06
236 Steve Woodard .20 .06
237 Todd Dunwoody .20 .06
238 Fernando Tatis .20 .06
239 Jacob Cruz .20 .06
240 Pokey Reese .20 .06
241 Mark Kotsay .20 .06
242 Matt Morris .20 .06
243 Antone Williamson .20 .06
244 Ben Grieve .20 .06
245 Ryan McGuire .20 .06
246 Lou Collier .20 .06
247 Shannon Stewart .20 .06
248 Brett Tomko .20 .06
249 Bobby Estalella .20 .06
250 Livan Hernandez .20 .06
251 Todd Helton .30 .09
252 Jaret Wright .20 .06
253 Darryl Hamilton IM .20 .06
254 Stan Javier IM .20 .06
255 Glenallen Hill IM .20 .06
256 Mark Gardner IM .20 .06
257 Cal Ripken IM .75 .23
258 Mike Mussina IM .30 .09
259 Mike Piazza IM .50 .15
260 Sammy Sosa IM .50 .15
261 Todd Hundley IM .20 .06
262 Eric Karros IM .20 .06
263 Denny Neagle IM .20 .06
264 Jeromy Burnitz IM .20 .06
265 Greg Maddux IM .50 .15
266 Tony Clark IM .20 .06
267 Vladimir Guerrero IM .30 .09
268 Cal Ripken CL UER .75 .23
269 Ken Griffey Jr. CL .50 .15
270 Mark McGwire CL .60 .18
NNO CL Regular Issue .20 .06
NNO CL All-Star Edition .30 .09

1998 Score Showcase Series

Randomly inserted in packs at the rate of one in seven, this 160-card set is an all silver-foil partial parallel rendition of the base set.

Nm-Mt Ex-Mt
*SHOWCASE: 2X TO 5X BASIC CARDS
STATED ODDS 1:7

1998 Score Showcase Series Artist's Proofs

Randomly inserted in packs at the rate of one in 35, this 160-card set is a partial parallel to the base set and features color player photos printed on full prismatic foil with the "Artist Proof" stamp on the fronts.

Nm-Mt Ex-Mt
*STARS: 1.5X TO 4X BASIC SHOWCASE
STATED ODDS 1:35

1998 Score All Score Team

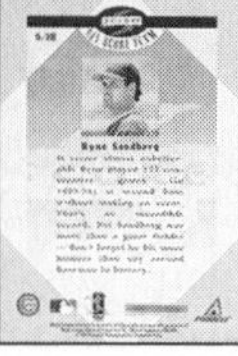

Randomly inserted in packs at the rate of one in 35, this 20-card set features color player images on a metallic foil background. The backs carry a small player head photo with information stating why the player was selected to this appear in this set.

Nm-Mt Ex-Mt
COMPLETE SET (20) 100.00 30.00
1 Mike Piazza 8.00 2.40
2 Ivan Rodriguez 5.00 1.50
3 Frank Thomas 5.00 1.50
4 Mark McGwire 12.00 3.60
5 Ryne Sandberg 5.00 1.50
6 Roberto Alomar 5.00 1.50
7 Cal Ripken 15.00 4.50
8 Barry Larkin 5.00 1.50
9 Paul Molitor 5.00 1.50
10 Travis Fryman 2.00 .60
11 Kirby Puckett 10.00 3.00
12 Tony Gwynn 6.00 1.80
13 Ken Griffey Jr. 8.00 2.40
14 Juan Gonzalez 5.00 1.50
15 Barry Bonds 12.00 3.60
16 Andruw Jones 2.00 .60
17 Roger Clemens 10.00 3.00
18 Randy Johnson 5.00 1.50
19 Greg Maddux 8.00 2.40
20 Dennis Eckersley 2.00 .60

1998 Score All-Score Team Gold Jones Autograph

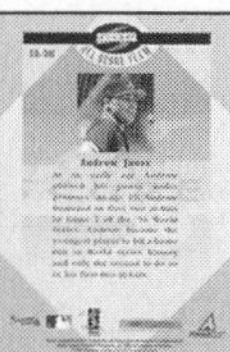

This special autographed card was created as a prize for Pinnacle's 1998 "Score with Score" hobby shop promotion. Dealers that ordered 1998 Score 1 baseball direct from Pinnacle or through one of their distributors were automatically entered into Pinnacle's hobby shop locator program. In December of 1997, all eligible shops were mailed a "Score with Score" contest ballot box and collector entry forms. Over the next several months, store customers could then fill out and submit forms. In the Spring of 1998, 600 lucky collectors were randomly selected winners. 100 people won actual Interleague game-used baseballs and 500 people won this special Andruw Jones autographed All-Score Team Gold card. The card is easy to differentiate from the more common All-Score Team inserts by it's bold gold (rather than silver) foil front and Jones' black ink signature.

Nm-Mt Ex-Mt
1 Andruw Jones Gold AU 50.00 15.00

1998 Score Complete Players

Randomly inserted in packs at the rate of one in 23, this 30-card set features three photos of each of the ten listed players with full holographic foil stamping.

Nm-Mt Ex-Mt
COMPLETE SET (30) 150.00 45.00
*GOLD: .4X TO 1X BASIC COMP.PLAY.
GOLD: RANDOM IN SCORE TEAM SETS
1A Ken Griffey Jr. 6.00 1.80
2A Mark McGwire 10.00 3.00
3A Derek Jeter 10.00 3.00
4A Cal Ripken 12.00 3.60
5A Mike Piazza 6.00 1.80
6A Darin Erstad 1.50 .45
7A Frank Thomas 4.00 1.20
8A Andruw Jones 1.50 .45
9A Nomar Garciaparra 6.00 1.80
10A Manny Ramirez 4.00 1.20

1998 Score First Pitch

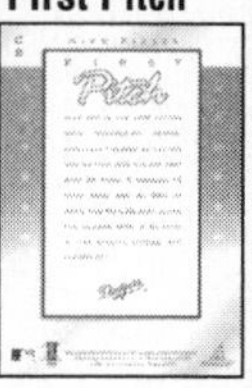

This 20 card insert set features star players anxiously awaiting opening day. The player's name is at top with the "First Pitch" words on the bottom of the card. These cards were inserted one every 11 All-Star Edition packs.

Nm-Mt Ex-Mt
COMPLETE SET (20) 60.00 18.00
1 Ken Griffey Jr. 4.00 1.20
2 Frank Thomas 2.50 .75
3 Alex Rodriguez 4.00 1.20
4 Cal Ripken 8.00 2.40
5 Chipper Jones 2.50 .75
6 Juan Gonzalez 2.50 .75
7 Derek Jeter 6.00 1.80
8 Mike Piazza 4.00 1.20
9 Andruw Jones 1.00 .30
10 Nomar Garciaparra 4.00 1.20
11 Barry Bonds 6.00 1.80
12 Jeff Bagwell 1.50 .45
13 Scott Rolen 1.50 .45
14 Hideo Nomo 2.50 .75
15 Roger Clemens 5.00 1.50
16 Mark McGwire 6.00 1.80
17 Greg Maddux 4.00 1.20
18 Albert Belle 1.00 .30
19 Ivan Rodriguez 2.50 .75
20 Mo Vaughn 1.00 .30

1998 Score Andruw Jones Icon Order Card

This one-card set features a white bordered color photo of Andruw Jones kneeling with his right arm resting on his bat. The card was always inserted on the top of the prepriced 1998 Score 27-card blister packs. The backs carry instructions on how to order a Pinnacle Icon display.

Nm-Mt Ex-Mt
1 Andruw Jones 1.00 .30

1998 Score Loaded Lineup

This 10-card set was inserted one every 45 Score All-Star Edition packs. The cards feature a player for each position and the cards are printed on all-foil micro etched cards.

Nm-Mt Ex-Mt
COMPLETE SET (10) 60.00 18.00
LL1 Chuck Knoblauch 2.00 .60
LL2 Tony Gwynn 6.00 1.80
LL3 Frank Thomas 5.00 1.50
LL4 Ken Griffey Jr. 8.00 2.40
LL5 Mike Piazza 8.00 2.40
LL6 Barry Bonds 12.00 3.60
LL7 Cal Ripken 15.00 4.50
LL8 Paul Molitor 5.00 1.50
LL9 Nomar Garciaparra 8.00 2.40
LL10 Greg Maddux 8.00 2.40

1998 Score New Season

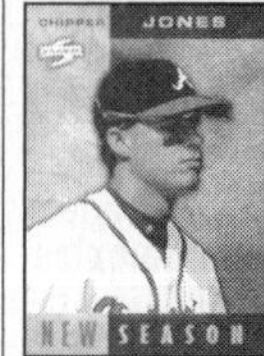

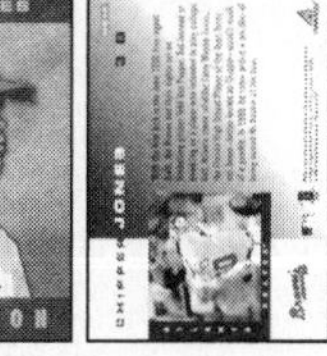

This 15 card insert set features a mix of young and veteran players waiting for the new season to begin. The players photo take up most of the borderless cards with his name on top and the words "New Season" on the bottom.

Nm-Mt Ex-Mt
COMPLETE SET (15) 50.00 15.00
NS1 Kenny Lofton 2.00 .60
NS2 Nomar Garciaparra 6.00 1.80
NS3 Todd Helton 2.50 .75
NS4 Miguel Tejada 2.50 .75
NS5 Jaret Wright 1.50 .45
NS6 Alex Rodriguez 6.00 1.80
NS7 Vladimir Guerrero 3.00 .90
NS8 Ken Griffey Jr. 8.00 2.40
NS9 Ben Grieve 1.50 .45
NS10 Travis Lee 1.50 .45
NS11 Jose Cruz Jr. 2.00 .60
NS12 Paul Konerko 2.00 .60
NS13 Frank Thomas 3.00 .90
NS14 Chipper Jones 3.00 .90
NS15 Cal Ripken 12.00 3.60

1998 Score Rookie Traded

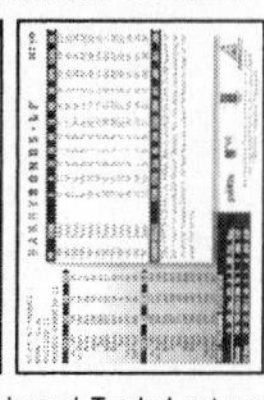

The 1998 Score Rookie and Traded set was issued in one series totalling 270 cards. The 10-card packs retail for $.99 each. The set contains the subset: Spring Training (253-267). Cards numbered one through 50 were inserted one per pack making them short prints compared to the other cards in the set. Paul Konerko signed 500 cards which were also randomly seeded into packs. Notable Rookie Cards include Maggio Ordonez.

Nm-Mt Ex-Mt
COMPLETE SET (270) 40.00 12.00
COMMON SP (1-50) .30 .09
COMMON CARD (51-270) .20 .06
1 Tony Clark .30 .09
2 Juan Gonzalez .75 .23
3 Frank Thomas .75 .23
4 Greg Maddux 1.25 .35
5 Barry Larkin .75 .23
6 Derek Jeter 2.00 .60
7 Randy Johnson .75 .23
8 Roger Clemens 1.50 .45
9 Tony Gwynn 1.00 .30
10 Barry Bonds 2.00 .60
11 Jim Edmonds .30 .09
12 Bernie Williams .50 .15
13 Ken Griffey Jr. 1.25 .35
14 Tim Salmon .50 .15
15 Mo Vaughn .30 .09
16 David Justice .30 .09
17 Jose Cruz Jr. .30 .09
18 Andruw Jones .30 .09
19 Sammy Sosa 1.25 .35
20 Jeff Bagwell .50 .15
21 Scott Rolen .50 .15
22 Darin Erstad .30 .09
23 Andy Pettitte .50 .15
24 Mike Mussina .75 .23
25 Mark McGwire 2.00 .60
26 Hideo Nomo .75 .23
27 Chipper Jones .75 .23
28 Cal Ripken 2.50 .75
29 Chuck Knoblauch .30 .09
30 Alex Rodriguez 1.25 .35
31 Jim Thome .75 .23
32 Mike Piazza 1.25 .35
33 Ivan Rodriguez .75 .23
34 Roberto Alomar .75 .23
35 Nomar Garciaparra 1.25 .35
36 Albert Belle .30 .09
37 Vladimir Guerrero .75 .23
38 Raul Mondesi .30 .09
39 Larry Walker .50 .15
40 Manny Ramirez .30 .09
41 Tino Martinez .50 .15
42 Craig Biggio .50 .15
43 Jay Buhner .30 .09
44 Kenny Lofton .30 .09
45 Pedro Martinez .75 .23
46 Edgar Martinez .50 .15
47 Gary Sheffield .30 .09
48 Jose Guillen .30 .09
49 Ken Caminiti .30 .09
50 Bobby Higginson .30 .09
51 Alan Benes .20 .06
52 Shawn Green .20 .06
53 Ron Coomer .20 .06
54 Charles Nagy .20 .06
55 Steve Karsay .20 .06
56 Matt Morris .20 .06
57 Bobby Jones .20 .06
58 Jason Kendall .20 .06
59 Jeff Conine .20 .06
60 Joe Girardi .20 .06
61 Mark Kotsay .20 .06
62 Eric Karros .20 .06
63 Bartolo Colon .20 .06
64 Mariano Rivera .30 .09
65 Alex Gonzalez .20 .06
66 Scott Spiezio .20 .06
67 Luis Castillo .20 .06
68 Joey Cora .20 .06
69 Mark McLemore .20 .06
70 Reggie Jefferson .20 .06
71 Lance Johnson .20 .06
72 Damian Jackson .20 .06
73 Jeff D'Amico .20 .06
74 David Ortiz .20 .06
75 J.T. Snow .20 .06
76 Todd Hundley .20 .06
77 Billy Wagner .20 .06
78 Vinny Castilla .20 .06
79 Ismael Valdes .20 .06
80 Neifi Perez .20 .06
81 Derek Bell .20 .06
82 Ryan Klesko .20 .06
83 Rey Ordonez .20 .06
84 Carlos Garcia .20 .06
85 Curt Schilling .30 .09
86 Robin Ventura .20 .06
87 Pat Hentgen .20 .06
88 Glendon Rusch .20 .06
89 Hideki Irabu .20 .06
90 Antone Williamson .20 .06
91 Denny Neagle .20 .06
92 Kevin Orie .20 .06
93 Reggie Sanders .20 .06
94 Brady Anderson .20 .06
95 Andy Benes .20 .06

96 John Valentin .20 .06
97 Bobby Bonilla .20 .06
98 Walt Weiss .20 .06
99 Robin Jennings .20 .06
100 Marty Cordova .20 .06
101 Brad Ausmus .20 .06
102 Brian Rose .20 .06
103 Calvin Maduro .20 .06
104 Raul Casanova .20 .06
105 Jeff King .20 .06
106 Sandy Alomar Jr. .20 .06
107 Tim Naehring .20 .06
108 Mike Cameron .20 .06
109 Omar Vizquel .20 .06
110 Brad Radke .20 .06
111 Jeff Fassero .20 .06
112 Deivi Cruz .20 .06
113 Dave Hollins .20 .06
114 Dean Palmer .20 .06
115 Esteban Loaiza .20 .06
116 Brian Giles .20 .06
117 Steve Finley .20 .06
118 Jose Canseco .50 .15
119 Al Martin .20 .06
120 Eric Young .20 .06
121 Curtis Goodwin .20 .06
122 Ellis Burks .20 .06
123 Mike Hampton .20 .06
124 Lou Collier .20 .06
125 John Olerud .20 .06
126 Ramon Martinez .20 .06
127 Todd Dunwoody .20 .06
128 Jermaine Allensworth .20 .06
129 Eduardo Perez .20 .06
130 Dante Bichette .20 .06
131 Edgar Renteria .20 .06
132 Bob Abreu .20 .06
133 Rondell White .20 .06
134 Michael Coleman .20 .06
135 Jason Giambi .50 .15
136 Brant Brown .20 .06
137 Michael Tucker .20 .06
138 Dave Nilsson .20 .06
139 Benito Santiago .20 .06
140 Ray Durham .20 .06
141 Jeff Kent .20 .06
142 Matt Stairs .20 .06
143 Kevin Young .20 .06
144 Eric Davis .20 .06
145 John Wetteland .20 .06
146 Esteban Yan RC .20 .06
147 Wilton Guerrero .20 .06
148 Moises Alou .20 .06
149 Edgardo Alfonzo .20 .06
150 Andy Ashby .20 .06
151 Todd Walker .20 .06
152 Jermaine Dye .20 .06
153 Brian Hunter .20 .06
154 Shawn Estes .20 .06
155 Bernard Gilkey .20 .06
156 Tony Womack .20 .06
157 John Smoltz .30 .09
158 Delino DeShields .20 .06
159 Jacob Cruz .20 .06
160 Javier Valentin .20 .06
161 Chris Hoiles .20 .06
162 Garret Anderson .20 .06
163 Dan Wilson .20 .06
164 Paul O'Neill .30 .09
165 Matt Williams .20 .06
166 Travis Fryman .20 .06
167 Javier Lopez .20 .06
168 Ray Lankford .20 .06
169 Bobby Estalella .20 .06
170 Henry Rodriguez .20 .06
171 Quinton McCracken .20 .06
172 Jaret Wright .20 .06
173 Darryl Kile .20 .06
174 Wade Boggs .50 .15
175 Orel Hershiser .20 .06
176 B.J. Surhoff .20 .06
177 Fernando Tatis .20 .06
178 Carlos Delgado .20 .06
179 Jorge Fabregas .20 .06
180 Tony Saunders .20 .06
181 Devon White .20 .06
182 Dmitri Young .20 .06
183 Ryan McGuire .20 .06
184 Mark Bellhorn .20 .06
185 Joe Carter .20 .06
186 Kevin Stocker .20 .06
187 Mike Lansing .20 .06
188 Jason Dickson .20 .06
189 Charles Johnson .20 .06
190 Will Clark .50 .15
191 Shannon Stewart .20 .06
192 Johnny Damon .20 .06
193 Todd Greene .20 .06
194 Carlos Baerga .20 .06
195 David Cone .20 .06
196 Pokey Reese .20 .06
197 Livan Hernandez .20 .06
198 Tom Glavine .30 .09
199 Geronimo Berroa .20 .06
200 Darryl Hamilton .20 .06
201 Terry Steinbach .20 .06
202 Robb Nen .20 .06
203 Ron Gant .20 .06
204 Rafael Palmeiro .30 .09
205 Rickey Henderson .50 .15
206 Justin Thompson .20 .06
207 Jeff Suppan .20 .06
208 Kevin Brown .30 .09
209 Jimmy Key .20 .06
210 Brian Jordan .20 .06
211 Aaron Sele .20 .06
212 Fred McGriff .30 .09
213 Jay Bell .20 .06
214 Andres Galarraga .20 .06
215 Mark Grace .30 .09
216 Brett Tomko .20 .06
217 Francisco Cordova .20 .06
218 Rusty Greer .20 .06
219 Bubba Trammell .20 .06
220 Derrek Lee .20 .06
221 Brian Anderson .20 .06
222 Mark Grudzielanek .20 .06
223 Marquis Grissom .20 .06
224 Gary DiSarcina .20 .06
225 Jim Leyritz .20 .06
226 Jeffrey Hammonds .20 .06
227 Karim Garcia .20 .06
228 Chan Ho Park .20 .06
229 Brooks Kieschnick .20 .06
230 Trey Beamon .20 .06
231 Kevin Appier .20 .06
232 Wally Joyner .20 .06
233 Richie Sexson .20 .06
234 Frank Catalanotto RC .30 .09
235 Rafael Medina .20 .06
236 Travis Lee .20 .06
237 Eli Marrero .20 .06
238 Carl Pavano .20 .06
239 Enrique Wilson .20 .06
240 Richard Hidalgo .20 .06
241 Todd Helton .30 .09
242 Ben Grieve .20 .06
243 Mario Valdez .20 .06
244 Magglio Ordonez RC 1.00 .30
245 Juan Encarnacion .20 .06
246 Russell Branyan .20 .06
247 Sean Casey .20 .06
248 Abraham Nunez .20 .06
249 Brad Fullmer .20 .06
250 Paul Konerko .20 .06
251 Miguel Tejada .30 .09
252 Mike Lowell RC 1.00 .30
253 Ken Griffey Jr. ST .50 .15
254 Frank Thomas ST .30 .09
255 Alex Rodriguez ST .50 .15
256 Jose Cruz Jr. ST .20 .06
257 Jeff Bagwell ST .50 .15
258 Chipper Jones ST .30 .09
259 Mo Vaughn ST .20 .06
260 Nomar Garciaparra ST .50 .15
261 Jim Thome ST .30 .09
262 Derek Jeter ST .60 .18
263 Mike Piazza ST .50 .15
264 Tony Gwynn ST .30 .09
265 Scott Rolen ST .20 .06
266 Andruw Jones ST .20 .06
267 Cal Ripken ST .75 .23
268 Checklist 1 .20 .06
269 Checklist 2 .20 .06
270 Checklist 3 .20 .06
S250 Paul Konerko AU/500 10.00 3.00

1998 Score Rookie Traded Showcase Series

Randomly inserted in packs at a rate of one in seven, this 160-card set is a parallel to the Score Rookie Traded base set.

Nm-Mt Ex-Mt
*STARS 1-50: 1.25X TO 3X BASIC CARDS
*SHOWCASE 51-270: 2X TO 5X BASIC
*SHOWCASE RC'S 51-270: 1.5X TO 4X BASIC
STATED ODDS 1:7

1998 Score Rookie Traded Showcase Series Artist's Proofs

Randomly inserted in packs at a rate of one in 35, this 160-card set is a parallel to the Score Rookie Traded base set.

Nm-Mt Ex-Mt
*SHOWCASE AP 1-50: 5X TO 12X BASIC
*SHOWCASE AP 51-270: 8X TO 20X BASIC
*SHOWCASE AP RC'S 51-270: 3X TO 8X BASIC
STATED ODDS 1:35

1998 Score Rookie Traded Showcase Series Artist's Proofs 1 of 1's

These extremely scarce parallel Artist's Proofs cards were randomly seeded into Rookie Traded hobby packs. Only one of each card was produced. They're easy to spot due to the gold foil circular logo directly on the middle of the card front that says "SCORE ONE OF ONE . . . 001/001". Due to scarcity no pricing is provided.

Nm-Mt Ex-Mt
RANDOM INSERTS IN HOBBY PACKS
STATED PRINT RUN 1 SET
NO PRICING DUE TO SCARCITY

1998 Score Rookie Traded All-Star Epix

Randomly inserted in packs at a rate of one in 61, these cards are an insert to the Score Rookie Traded brand. The fronts feature 12 top players in color action photos printed on high-tech dot matrix orange, purple, and emerald variations. The cards were actually seeded in both Score Rookie Traded and Pinnacle Plus in a cross-brand promotion. Please see 1998 Pinnacle Plus All-Star Epix for pricing.

Nm-Mt Ex-Mt
PLEASE SEE 1998 PINNACLE PLUS AS EPIX

1998 Score Rookie Traded Complete Players Samples

These cards were issued to preview the Score Rookie Traded Complete Players set. The cards have the word sample written on them so they can be easily differentiated from the regular Complete Player cards.

Nm-Mt Ex-Mt
COMPLETE SET (30) 50.00 15.00
THREE CARDS PER PLAYER
1A Ken Griffey Jr. 5.00 1.50
2A Larry Walker .50 .15
3A Alex Rodriguez 2.50 .75
4A Jose Cruz Jr. .50 .15
5A Jeff Bagwell 1.25 .35
6A Greg Maddux 3.00 .90
7A Ivan Rodriguez 1.25 .35
8A Roger Clemens 2.50 .75
9A Chipper Jones 2.50 .75
10A Hideo Nomo 1.00 .30

1998 Score Rookie Traded Complete Players

Randomly inserted in packs at a rate of one in 11, this 30-card set is an insert to the Score Rookie Traded base set. The card fronts feature special holographic foil stamping. Each player has three different cards highlighting his own power, speed and approach to the game. Put them together and form the Complete Player.

Nm-Mt Ex-Mt
COMPLETE SET (30) 50.00 15.00
1A Ken Griffey Jr. 3.00 .90
2A Larry Walker 1.25 .35
3A Alex Rodriguez 3.00 .90
4A Jose Cruz Jr. .75 .23
5A Jeff Bagwell 1.25 .35
6A Greg Maddux 3.00 .90
7A Ivan Rodriguez 2.00 .60
8A Roger Clemens 4.00 1.20
9A Chipper Jones 2.00 .60
10A Hideo Nomo 2.00 .60

1998 Score Rookie Traded Star Gazing

Randomly inserted in packs at a rate of one in 35, this 20-card set is an insert to the Score Rookie Traded base set. The fronts feature color action photos printed on a diamond-shaped star-gazing background. The player's name sits atop the player photo with the Score logo in the upper right corner.

Nm-Mt Ex-Mt
COMPLETE SET (20) 25.00 7.50
1 Ken Griffey Jr. 2.50 .75
2 Frank Thomas 1.50 .45
3 Chipper Jones 1.50 .45
4 Mark McGwire 4.00 1.20
5 Cal Ripken 5.00 1.50
6 Mike Piazza 2.50 .75
7 Nomar Garciaparra 2.50 .75
8 Derek Jeter 4.00 1.20
9 Juan Gonzalez 1.50 .45
10 Vladimir Guerrero 1.50 .45
11 Alex Rodriguez 2.50 .75
12 Tony Gwynn 2.00 .60
13 Andruw Jones .60 .18
14 Scott Rolen 1.00 .30
15 Jose Cruz Jr. .60 .18
16 Mo Vaughn .60 .18
17 Bernie Williams 1.00 .30
18 Greg Maddux 2.50 .75
19 Tony Clark .60 .18
20 Ben Grieve .40 .12

1997 Scoreboard Mantle

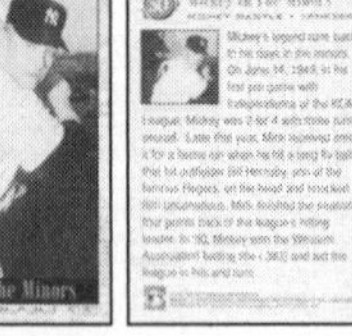

This 75-card set features color and blue-and-white photos of Baseball great Mickey Mantle and some special events that occurred in his life. Cards numbers 1, 6, 7, 70, and 74 are die cut with special gold foil enhancements. Cards numbers 51-69 are replicas of his 1951-1969 trading cards.

Nm-Mt Ex-Mt
COMPLETE SET (75) 50.00 15.00
COMMON CARD (1-50) .50 .15
COMMON REPLICA CARD
COMMON DIE CUT
28 Mickey Mantle 1.50 .45
Roger Maris
Cleanup Hitter
71 Mickey Mantle 1.50 .45
Bobby Kennedy
Mickey Mantle Day 1965
P1 Mickey Mantle 1.50 .45
Summary of the Legend
P7 Mickey Mantle 1.50 .45
Uniform #7

1997 Scoreboard Mantle 7

The first six cards of this seven-card set were randomly inserted in packs of Mickey Mantle Shoe Box Collection cards at the rate of one in 16 with card number 7 having an insertion rate of one in 320. The complete set could be mailed in for a chance to win a $7,000 Mickey Mantle prepaid phone card or a $700 one. The fronts feature color photos of Mickey Mantle. The backs display the game rules.

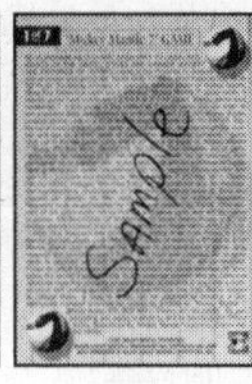

Nm-Mt Ex-Mt
COMPLETE SET (7) 75.00 22.00
COMMON CARD (1-7) 8.00 2.40
5 Mickey Mantle 10.00 3.00
Head and shoulder view while batting
7 Mickey Mantle 50.00 15.00
Hand on hip

1998 Scoreboard 23K Collection

These cards, issued in the style of the Bleachers cards, were produced by Scoreboard in their final days as a company in 1998. These cards are produced in 23K and feature photos on the front along with player information on the back. These cards are all credited to the Score Board Inc. but as Scoreboard in the process of declaring bankruptcy during this period, any further information would be greatly appreciated.

Nm-Mt Ex-Mt
1 Reggie Jackson 15.00 4.50
500 Home Run Club
2 Mark McGwire 20.00 6.00
Numbered to 6262
3 Mark McGwire 15.00 4.50
Chasing Sixty-One, Numbered to 9861
4 Mark McGwire 20.00 6.00
History Breaking in Black, Numbered to 4500
5 Mark McGwire 30.00 9.00
History Breaking in Black, Individually numbered

1887 Scrapps Die Cuts

These cards are unnumbered; they are ordered below alphabetially within team. The first nine players (1-9) are St. Louis and the second nine (10-18) are Detroit players.

Ex-Mt VG
COMPLETE SET (18) 6000.00 3000.00
1 Doc Bushong 300.00 150.00
2 Bob Caruthers 300.00 150.00
3 Charles Comiskey 800.00 400.00
4 Dave Foutz 300.00 150.00
5 Bill Gleason 500.00 250.00
6 Arlie Latham 400.00 200.00
7 Tip O'Neill 300.00 150.00
8 Yank Robinson 300.00 150.00
9 Curt Welch 400.00 200.00
10 C.W. Bennett 300.00 150.00
11 Dan Brouthers 800.00 400.00
12 Fred Dunlap 300.00 150.00
13 Charlie Getzen (sic) 300.00 150.00
14 Ned Hanlon 600.00 300.00
15 Hardie Richardson 300.00 150.00
16 Jack Rowe 300.00 150.00
17 Sam Thompson 800.00 400.00
18 Deacon White 300.00 150.00

1946 Sears-East St. Louis PC783

This black and white blank-backed set measures 3 1/2" by 5 3/8" and was issued in 1946 and given away by Sears at their East St. Louis location. The set features players from St. Louis teams. Two poses of John Miller exist. The cards are unnumbered so we have listed them alphabetically. Famed broadcaster Joe Garagiola has an early card in this set.

Ex-Mt VG
COMPLETE SET 6000.00 3000.00
1 Buster Adams 80.00 40.00
2 Red Barrett 80.00 40.00
3 Johnny Beazley 80.00 40.00
4 John Berardino 120.00 60.00
5 Frank Biscan 80.00 40.00
6 Al Brazle 80.00 40.00
7 Harry Breechen 100.00 50.00
8 Ken Burkhardt 80.00 40.00
9 Jerry Burmeister 80.00 40.00
10 Mark Christman 80.00 40.00
11 Joffre Cross 80.00 40.00
12 Babe Dahlgren 100.00 50.00
13 Murray Dickson 80.00 40.00
14 Bob Dillinger 100.00 50.00
15 George Duckins 80.00 40.00
16 Blix Donnelly 80.00 40.00
17 Erv Dusak 80.00 40.00
18 Eddie Dyer MG 80.00 40.00
19 Bill Endicott 80.00 40.00
20 Stanley Ferens 80.00 40.00
21 Denny Galehouse 80.00 40.00
22 Joe Garagiola 200.00 100.00
23 Mike Gonzales CO 80.00 40.00
24 Joe Grace 80.00 40.00
25 Jeff Heath 80.00 40.00
26 Henry Helf 80.00 40.00
27 Fred Hoffman 80.00 40.00
28 Walt Judnich 80.00 40.00
29 Ellis Kinder 80.00 40.00
30 Lou Klein 80.00 40.00
31 Clyde Kluttz 80.00 40.00
32 Jack Kramer 80.00 40.00
33 Howard Krist 80.00 40.00
34 Whitey Kurowski 100.00 50.00
35 Chet Laabs 80.00 40.00
36 Al LaMacchia 80.00 40.00
37 John Lucadello 80.00 40.00
38 Frank Mancuso 80.00 40.00
39 Marty Marion 120.00 60.00
40 Fred Martin 80.00 40.00
41 George McQuillen 80.00 40.00
42 John Miller (2) 80.00 40.00
43 Al Milnar 80.00 40.00
44 Terry Moore 120.00 60.00
45 Bob Muncrief 80.00 40.00
46 Stan Musial 300.00 150.00
47 Ken O'Dea 80.00 40.00
48 Howie Pollet 80.00 40.00
49 Nelson Potter 80.00 40.00
50 Del Rice 80.00 40.00
51 Len Schulte 80.00 40.00
51 Red Schoendienst 150.00 75.00
53 Ken Sears 80.00 40.00
54 Walt Sessi 80.00 40.00
55 Luke Sewell MG 100.00 50.00
56 Joe Schultz 80.00 40.00
57 Tex Shirley 80.00 40.00
58 Dick Sisler 80.00 40.00
59 Enos Slaughter 150.00 75.00
60 Vern Stephens 120.00 60.00
61 Chuck Stevens 80.00 40.00
62 Max Surkont 80.00 40.00
63 Zack Taylor MG 80.00 40.00
64 Harry Walker 100.00 50.00
65 Buzzy Wares 80.00 40.00
66 Ernie White 80.00 40.00
67 Ted Wilks 80.00 40.00
68 Al Zarilla 80.00 40.00
69 Sam Zoldak 80.00 40.00

1993 Seaver Chemical Bank

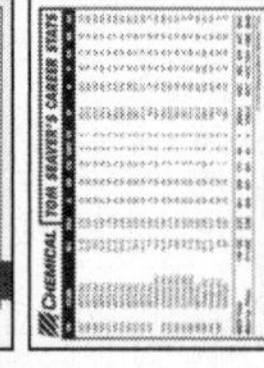

This one card standard-size set was issued by Chemical Bank and featured their spokesman Tom Seaver. Seaver is nattily attired in a business suit holding a baseball on the front while the back has complete career statistics.

Nm-Mt Ex-Mt
1 Tom Seaver 5.00 1.50

1993 Select Samples

These eight promo cards were issued to provide dealers with a preview of Score's new Select series cards. The cards measure the standard size feature glossy color player photos edged on two sides by a two-toned green border area. The back design is similar to the fronts but with a smaller player photo to create space for player profile and statistics. These promo cards are distinguished from the regular issue by the zeroes in the statistic lines.

Nm-Mt Ex-Mt
COMPLETE SET (8) 25.00 7.50
22 Robin Yount 6.00 1.80
24 Don Mattingly 10.00 3.00
26 Sandy Alomar Jr. 2.00 .60
41 Gary Sheffield 6.00 1.80
56 Brady Anderson 2.00 .60
65 Rob Dibble 2.00 .60
75 John Smiley 1.00 .30
79 Mitch Williams 1.00 .30

1993 Select

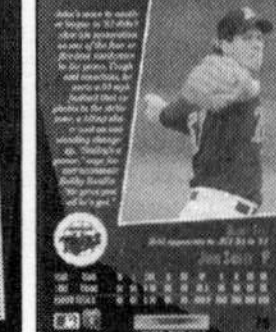

Seeking a niche in the premium, mid-price market, Score produced a new 405-card standard-size set entitled Select in 1993. The set includes regular players, rookies, and draft picks, and was sold in 15-card hobby and retail packs and 28-card super packs. Subset cards include Draft Picks and Rookies, both sprinkled throughout the latter part of the set. Rookie Cards in this set include Derek Jeter, Jason Kendall and Shannon Stewart.

Nm-Mt Ex-Mt
COMPLETE SET (405) 25.00 7.50
1 Barry Bonds 1.25 .35
2 Ken Griffey Jr. .75 .23
3 Will Clark .50 .15
4 Kirby Puckett .50 .15
5 Tony Gwynn .60 .18
6 Frank Thomas .50 .15

7 Tom Glavine .30 .09
8 Roberto Alomar .50 .15
9 Andre Dawson .20 .06
10 Ron Darling .15 .04
11 Bobby Bonilla .20 .06
12 Danny Tartabull .15 .04
13 Darren Daulton .20 .06
14 Roger Clemens 1.00 .30
15 Ozzie Smith .75 .23
16 Mark McGwire 1.25 .35
17 Terry Pendleton .20 .06
18 Cal Ripken 1.50 .45
19 Fred McGriff .30 .09
20 Cecil Fielder .20 .06
21 Darryl Strawberry .30 .09
22 Robin Yount .75 .23
23 Barry Larkin .50 .15
24 Don Mattingly 1.25 .35
25 Craig Biggio .30 .09
26 Sandy Alomar Jr. .15 .04
27 Larry Walker .30 .09
28 Junior Felix .15 .04
29 Eddie Murray .50 .15
30 Robin Ventura .20 .06
31 Greg Maddux .75 .23
32 Dave Winfield .20 .06
33 John Kruk .20 .06
34 Wally Joyner .20 .06
35 Andy Van Slyke .20 .06
36 Chuck Knoblauch .20 .06
37 Tom Pagnozzi .15 .04
38 Dennis Eckersley .20 .06
39 Dave Justice .20 .06
40 Juan Gonzalez .50 .15
41 Gary Sheffield .20 .06
42 Paul Molitor .30 .09
43 Delino DeShields .15 .04
44 Travis Fryman .20 .06
45 Hal Morris .15 .04
46 Greg Olson .15 .04
47 Ken Caminiti .20 .06
48 Wade Boggs .30 .09
49 Orel Hershiser .20 .06
50 Albert Belle .20 .06
51 Bill Swift .15 .04
52 Mark Langston .15 .04
53 Joe Girardi .15 .04
54 Keith Miller .15 .04
55 Gary Carter .30 .09
56 Brady Anderson .20 .06
57 Dwight Gooden .30 .09
58 Julio Franco .20 .06
59 Lenny Dykstra .20 .06
60 Mickey Tettleton .20 .06
61 Randy Tomlin .15 .04
62 B.J. Surhoff .20 .06
63 Todd Zeile .15 .04
64 Roberto Kelly .15 .04
65 Rob Dibble .20 .06
66 Leo Gomez .15 .04
67 Doug Jones .15 .04
68 Ellis Burks .20 .06
69 Mike Scioscia .15 .04
70 Charles Nagy .15 .04
71 Cory Snyder .15 .04
72 Devon White .15 .04
73 Mark Grace .30 .09
74 Luis Polonia .15 .04
75 John Smiley 2X .15 .04
76 Carlton Fisk .30 .09
77 Luis Sojo .15 .04
78 George Brett 1.25 .35
79 Mitch Williams .15 .04
80 Kent Hrbek .20 .06
81 Jay Bell .20 .06
82 Edgar Martinez .30 .09
83 Lee Smith .20 .06
84 Deion Sanders .30 .09
85 Bill Gullickson .15 .04
86 Paul O'Neill .30 .09
87 Kevin Seitzer .15 .04
88 Steve Finley .20 .06
89 Mel Hall .15 .04
90 Nolan Ryan 2.00 .60
91 Eric Davis .20 .06
92 Mike Mussina .50 .15
93 Tony Fernandez .15 .04
94 Frank Viola .20 .06
95 Matt Williams .20 .06
96 Joe Carter .20 .06
97 Ryne Sandberg .75 .23
98 Jim Abbott .30 .09
99 Marquis Grissom .15 .04
100 George Bell .15 .04
101 Howard Johnson .15 .04
102 Kevin Appier .15 .04
103 Dale Murphy .50 .15
104 Shane Mack .15 .04
105 Jose Lind .15 .04
106 Rickey Henderson .50 .15
107 Bob Tewksbury .15 .04
108 Kevin Mitchell .15 .04
109 Steve Avery .15 .04
110 Candy Maldonado .15 .04
111 Bip Roberts .15 .04
112 Lou Whitaker .20 .06
113 Jeff Bagwell .30 .09
114 Dante Bichette .20 .06
115 Brett Butler .20 .06
116 Melido Perez .15 .04
117 Andy Benes .15 .04
118 Randy Johnson .50 .15
119 Willie McGee .20 .06
120 Jody Reed .15 .04
121 Shawon Dunston .15 .04
122 Carlos Baerga .15 .04
123 Bret Saberhagen .20 .06
124 John Olerud .20 .06
125 Ivan Calderon .15 .04
126 Bryan Harvey .15 .04
127 Terry Mulholland .15 .04
128 Ozzie Guillen .15 .04
129 Steve Buechele .15 .04
130 Kevin Tapani .15 .04
131 Felix Jose .15 .04
132 Terry Steinbach .15 .04
133 Ron Gant .20 .06
134 Harold Reynolds .20 .06
135 Chris Sabo .15 .04
136 Ivan Rodriguez .50 .15
137 Eric Anthony .15 .04
138 Mike Henneman .15 .04
139 Robby Thompson .15 .04
140 Scott Fletcher .15 .04
141 Bruce Hurst .15 .04
142 Kevin Maas .15 .04
143 Tom Candiotti .15 .04
144 Chris Hoiles .15 .04
145 Mike Morgan .15 .04
146 Mark Whiten .15 .04
147 Dennis Martinez .20 .06
148 Tony Pena .15 .04
149 Dave Magadan .15 .04
150 Mark Lewis .15 .04
151 Mariano Duncan .15 .04
152 Gregg Jefferies .15 .04
153 Doug Drabek .15 .04
154 Brian Harper .15 .04
155 Ray Lankford .15 .04
156 Carney Lansford .20 .06
157 Mike Sharperson .15 .04
158 Jack Morris .20 .06
159 Otis Nixon .15 .04
160 Steve Sax .15 .04
161 Mark Lemke .15 .04
162 Rafael Palmeiro .30 .09
163 Jose Rijo .15 .04
164 Omar Vizquel .20 .06
165 Sammy Sosa .75 .23
166 Milt Cuyler .15 .04
167 John Franco .20 .06
168 Darryl Hamilton .15 .04
169 Ken Hill .15 .04
170 Mike Devereaux .15 .04
171 Don Slaught .15 .04
172 Steve Farr .15 .04
173 Bernard Gilkey .15 .04
174 Mike Fetters .15 .04
175 Vince Coleman .15 .04
176 Kevin McReynolds .15 .04
177 John Smoltz .30 .09
178 Greg Gagne .15 .04
179 Greg Swindell .15 .04
180 Juan Guzman .15 .04
181 Kal Daniels .15 .04
182 Rick Sutcliffe .20 .06
183 Orlando Merced .15 .04
184 Bill Wegman .15 .04
185 Mark Gardner .15 .04
186 Rob Deer .15 .04
187 Dave Hollins .15 .04
188 Jack Clark .20 .06
189 Brian Hunter .15 .04
190 Tim Wallach .15 .04
191 Tim Belcher .15 .04
192 Walt Weiss .15 .04
193 Kurt Stillwell .15 .04
194 Charlie Hayes .15 .04
195 Willie Randolph .20 .06
196 Jack McDowell .15 .04
197 Jose Offerman .15 .04
198 Chuck Finley .20 .06
199 Darrin Jackson .15 .04
200 Kelly Gruber .15 .04
201 John Wetteland .20 .06
202 Jay Buhner .20 .06
203 Mike LaValliere .15 .04
204 Kevin Brown .20 .06
205 Luis Gonzalez .20 .06
206 Rick Aguilera .15 .04
207 Norm Charlton .15 .04
208 Mike Bordick .15 .04
209 Charlie Leibrandt .15 .04
210 Tom Brunansky .15 .04
211 Tom Henke .15 .04
212 Randy Milligan .15 .04
213 Ramon Martinez .15 .04
214 Mo Vaughn .20 .06
215 Randy Myers .15 .04
216 Greg Hibbard .15 .04
217 Wes Chamberlain .15 .04
218 Tony Phillips .15 .04
219 Pete Harnisch .15 .04
220 Mike Gallego .15 .04
221 Bud Black .15 .04
222 Greg Vaughn .20 .06
223 Milt Thompson .15 .04
224 Ben McDonald .15 .04
225 Billy Hatcher .15 .04
226 Paul Sorrento .15 .04
227 Mark Gubicza .15 .04
228 Mike Greenwell .15 .04
229 Curt Schilling .30 .09
230 Alan Trammell .30 .09
231 Zane Smith .15 .04
232 Bobby Thigpen .15 .04
233 Greg Olson .15 .04
234 Joe Orsulak .15 .04
235 Joe Oliver .15 .04
236 Tim Raines .20 .06
237 Juan Samuel .15 .04
238 Chili Davis .20 .06
239 Spike Owen .15 .04
240 Dave Stewart .20 .06
241 Jim Eisenreich .15 .04
242 Phil Plantier .15 .04
243 Sid Fernandez .15 .04
244 Dan Gladden .15 .04
245 Mickey Morandini .15 .04
246 Tino Martinez .30 .09
247 Kirt Manwaring .15 .04
248 Dean Palmer .20 .06
249 Tom Browning .15 .04
250 Brian McRae .15 .04
251 Scott Leius .15 .04
252 Bert Blyleven .20 .06
253 Scott Erickson .15 .04
254 Bob Welch .15 .04
255 Pat Kelly .15 .04
256 Felix Fermin .15 .04
257 Harold Baines .20 .06
258 Duane Ward .15 .04
259 Bill Spiers .15 .04
260 Jaime Navarro .15 .04
261 Scott Sanderson .15 .04
262 Gary Gaetti .20 .06
263 Bob Ojeda .15 .04
264 Jeff Montgomery .15 .04
265 Scott Bankhead .15 .04
266 Lance Johnson .15 .04
267 Rafael Belliard .15 .04
268 Kevin Reimer .15 .04
269 Benito Santiago .20 .06
270 Mike Moore .15 .04
271 Dave Fleming .15 .04
272 Moises Alou .20 .06
273 Pat Listach .15 .04
274 Reggie Sanders .20 .06
275 Kenny Lofton .20 .06
276 Donovan Osborne .15 .04
277 Rusty Meacham .15 .04
278 Eric Karros .20 .06
279 Andy Stankiewicz .15 .04
280 Brian Jordan .20 .06
281 Gary DiSarcina .15 .04
282 Mark Wohlers .15 .04
283 Dave Nilsson .15 .04
284 Anthony Young .15 .04
285 Jim Bullinger .15 .04
286 Derek Bell .15 .04
287 Brian Williams .15 .04
288 Julio Valera .15 .04
289 Dan Walters .15 .04
290 Chad Curtis .15 .04
291 Michael Tucker DP .15 .04
292 Bob Zupcic .15 .04
293 Todd Hundley .15 .04
294 Jeff Tackett .15 .04
295 Greg Colbrunn .15 .04
296 Cal Eldred .15 .04
297 Chris Roberts DP .15 .04
298 John Doherty .15 .04
299 Denny Neagle .20 .06
300 Arthur Rhodes .15 .04
301 Mark Clark .15 .04
302 Scott Cooper .15 .04
303 Jamie Arnold DP RC .15 .04
304 Jim Thome .50 .15
305 Frank Seminara .15 .04
306 Kurt Knudsen .15 .04
307 Tim Wakefield .20 .06
308 John Jaha .15 .04
309 Pat Hentgen .15 .04
310 B.J. Wallace DP .15 .04
311 Roberto Hernandez .15 .04
312 Hipolito Pichardo .15 .04
313 Eric Fox .15 .04
314 Willie Banks .15 .04
315 Sam Militello .15 .04
316 Vince Horsman .15 .04
317 Carlos Hernandez .15 .04
318 Jeff Kent .50 .15
319 Mike Perez .15 .04
320 Scott Livingstone .15 .04
321 Jeff Conine .20 .06
322 Jim Austin .15 .04
323 John Vander Wal .15 .04
324 Pat Mahomes .15 .04
325 Pedro Astacio .15 .04
326 Bret Boone UER .30 .09
(Misspelled Brett)
327 Matt Stairs .15 .04
328 Damion Easley .15 .04
329 Ben Rivera .15 .04
330 Reggie Jefferson .15 .04
331 Luis Mercedes .15 .04
332 Kyle Abbott .15 .04
333 Eddie Taubensee .15 .04
334 Tim McIntosh .15 .04
335 Phil Clark .15 .04
336 Wil Cordero .15 .04
337 Russ Springer .15 .04
338 Craig Colbert .15 .04
339 Tim Salmon .30 .09
340 Braulio Castillo .15 .04
341 Donald Harris .15 .04
342 Eric Young .15 .04
343 Bob Wickman .15 .04
344 John Valentin .15 .04
345 Dan Wilson .20 .06
346 Steve Hosey .15 .04
347 Mike Piazza 1.25 .35
348 Willie Greene .15 .04
349 Tom Goodwin .15 .04
350 Eric Hillman .15 .04
351 Steve Reed RC .15 .04
352 Dan Serafini DP RC .15 .04
353 T.Steverson DP RC .15 .04
354 Benji Grigsby DP RC .15 .04
355 S.Stewart DP RC .75 .23
356 Sean Lowe DP RC .15 .04
357 Derek Wallace DP RC .15 .04
358 Rick Helling DP .15 .04
359 Jason Kendall DP RC .30 .09
360 Derek Jeter DP RC 10.00 3.00
361 David Cone .20 .06
362 Jeff Reardon .20 .06
363 Bobby Witt .15 .04
364 Jose Canseco .50 .15
365 Jeff Russell .15 .04
366 Ruben Sierra .15 .04
367 Alan Mills .15 .04
368 Matt Nokes .15 .04
369 Pat Borders .15 .04
370 Pedro Munoz .15 .04
371 Danny Jackson .15 .04
372 Geronimo Pena .15 .04
373 Craig Lefferts .15 .04
374 Joe Grahe .15 .04
375 Roger McDowell .15 .04
376 Jimmy Key .20 .06
377 Steve Olin .15 .04
378 Glenn Davis .15 .04
379 Rene Gonzales .15 .04
380 Manuel Lee .15 .04
381 Ron Karkovice .15 .04
382 Sid Bream .15 .04
383 Gerald Williams .15 .04
384 Lenny Harris .15 .04
385 J.T. Snow RC .50 .15
386 Dave Stieb .15 .04
387 Kirk McCaskill .15 .04
388 Lance Parrish .20 .06
389 Craig Grebeck .15 .04
390 Rick Wilkins .15 .04
391 Manny Alexander .15 .04
392 Mike Schooler .15 .04
393 Bernie Williams .30 .09
394 Kevin Koslofski .15 .04
395 Willie Wilson .15 .04
396 Jeff Parrett .15 .04
397 Mike Harkey .15 .04
398 Frank Tanana .15 .04
399 Doug Henry .15 .04
400 Royce Clayton .15 .04
401 Eric Wedge RC .15 .04
402 Derrick May .15 .04
403 Carlos Garcia .15 .04
404 Henry Rodriguez .15 .04
405 Ryan Klesko .20 .06

1993 Select Aces

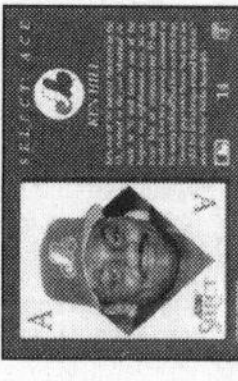

This 24-card standard-size set features some of the top starting pitchers in both leagues. The cards were randomly inserted into one in every eight 28-card super packs.

	Nm-Mt	Ex-Mt
COMPLETE SET (24)	50.00	15.00
1 Roger Clemens	15.00	4.50
2 Tom Glavine	5.00	1.50
3 Jack McDowell	2.50	.75
4 Greg Maddux	12.00	3.60
5 Jack Morris	3.00	.90
6 Dennis Martinez	3.00	.90
7 Kevin Brown	3.00	.90
8 Dwight Gooden	5.00	1.50
9 Kevin Appier	3.00	.90
10 Mike Morgan	2.50	.75
11 Juan Guzman	2.50	.75
12 Charles Nagy	2.50	.75
13 John Smiley	2.50	.75
14 Ken Hill	2.50	.75
15 Bob Tewksbury	2.50	.75
16 Doug Drabek	2.50	.75
17 John Smoltz	5.00	1.50
18 Greg Swindell	2.50	.75
19 Bruce Hurst	2.50	.75
20 Mike Mussina	8.00	2.40
21 Cal Eldred	2.50	.75
22 Melido Perez	2.50	.75
23 Dave Fleming	2.50	.75
24 Kevin Tapani	2.50	.75

1993 Select Chase Rookies

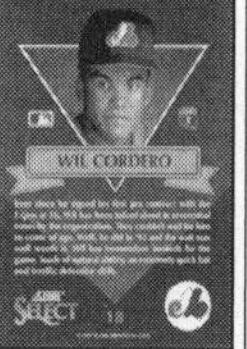

This 21-card standard-size set showcases 1992's best rookies. The cards were randomly inserted into one in every eighteen 15-card hobby packs.

	Nm-Mt	Ex-Mt
COMPLETE SET (21)	50.00	15.00
1 Pat Listach	2.50	.75
2 Moises Alou	5.00	1.50
3 Reggie Sanders	5.00	1.50
4 Kenny Lofton	5.00	1.50
5 Eric Karros	5.00	1.50
6 Brian Williams	2.50	.75
7 Donovan Osborne	2.50	.75
8 Sam Militello	2.50	.75
9 Chad Curtis	2.50	.75
10 Bob Zupcic	2.50	.75
11 Tim Salmon	8.00	2.40
12 Jeff Conine	5.00	1.50
13 Pedro Astacio	2.50	.75
14 Arthur Rhodes	2.50	.75
15 Cal Eldred	2.50	.75
16 Tim Wakefield	5.00	1.50
17 Andy Stankiewicz	2.50	.75
18 Wil Cordero	2.50	.75
19 Todd Hundley	2.50	.75
20 Dave Fleming	2.50	.75
21 Bret Boone	8.00	2.40

1993 Select Chase Stars

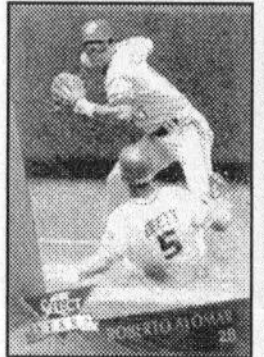

This 24-card standard-size set showcases the top players in Major League Baseball. The cards were randomly inserted into one in every eighteen retail 15-card packs. The fronts exhibit Score's "dufex" printing process, in which a color photo is printed on a metallic base creating an unusual, three-dimensional look.

	Nm-Mt	Ex-Mt
COMPLETE SET (24)	100.00	30.00
1 Fred McGriff	4.00	1.20
2 Ryne Sandberg	10.00	3.00
3 Ozzie Smith	10.00	3.00
4 Gary Sheffield	2.50	.75
5 Darren Daulton	2.50	.75
6 Andy Van Slyke	2.50	.75
7 Barry Bonds	15.00	4.50
8 Tony Gwynn	8.00	2.40
9 Greg Maddux	10.00	3.00
10 Tom Glavine	4.00	1.20
11 John Franco	2.50	.75
12 Lee Smith	2.50	.75
13 Cecil Fielder	2.50	.75
14 Roberto Alomar	6.00	1.80
15 Cal Ripken	20.00	6.00
16 Edgar Martinez	4.00	1.20
17 Ivan Rodriguez	6.00	1.80
18 Kirby Puckett	6.00	1.80
19 Ken Griffey Jr.	10.00	3.00
20 Joe Carter	2.50	.75
21 Roger Clemens	12.00	3.60
22 Dave Fleming	2.00	.60
23 Paul Molitor	4.00	1.20
24 Dennis Eckersley	2.50	.75

1993 Select Stat Leaders

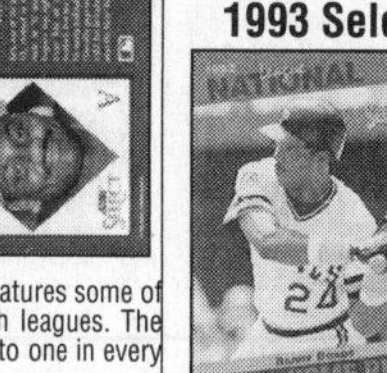
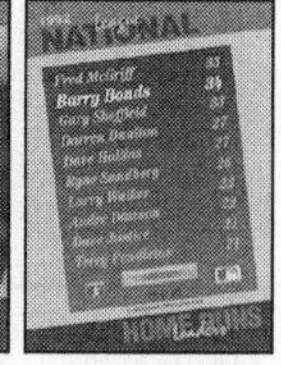

Featuring 45 cards from each league, these 90 Stat Leaders were inserted one per 1993 Score pack in every regular pack and super pack.

	Nm-Mt	Ex-Mt
COMPLETE SET (90)	8.00	2.40
1 Edgar Martinez	.20	.06
2 Kirby Puckett	.30	.09
3 Frank Thomas	.30	.09
4 Gary Sheffield	.10	.03
5 Andy Van Slyke	.10	.03
6 John Kruk	.10	.03
7 Kirby Puckett	.30	.09
8 Carlos Baerga	.10	.03
9 Paul Molitor	.20	.06
10 Terry Pendleton Andy Van Slyke	.10	.03
11 Ryne Sandberg	.50	.15
12 Mark Grace	.20	.06
13 Frank Thomas Edgar Martinez	.30	.09
14 Don Mattingly Robin Yount	.75	.23
15 Ken Griffey	.50	.15
16 Andy Van Slyke	.10	.03
17 Mariano Duncan Will Clark Ray Lankford	.10	.03
18 Marquis Grissom Terry Pendleton	.10	.03
19 Lance Johnson	.10	.03
20 Mike Devereaux	.10	.03
21 Brady Anderson	.10	.03
22 Deion Sanders	.20	.06
23 Steve Finley	.10	.03
24 Andy Van Slyke	.10	.03
25 Juan Gonzalez	.30	.09
26 Mark McGwire	.75	.23
27 Cecil Fielder	.10	.03
28 Fred McGriff	.20	.06
29 Barry Bonds	.75	.23
30 Gary Sheffield	.10	.03
31 Cecil Fielder	.10	.03
32 Joe Carter	.10	.03
33 Frank Thomas	.30	.09
34 Darren Daulton	.10	.03
35 Terry Pendleton	.10	.03
36 Fred McGriff	.20	.06
37 Tony Phillips	.10	.03
38 Frank Thomas	.30	.09
39 Roberto Alomar	.30	.09
40 Barry Bonds	.75	.23
41 Dave Hollins	.10	.03
42 Andy Van Slyke	.10	.03
43 Mark McGwire	.75	.23
44 Edgar Martinez	.20	.06
45 Frank Thomas	.30	.09
46 Barry Bonds	.75	.23
47 Gary Sheffield	.10	.03
48 Fred McGriff	.20	.06
49 Frank Thomas	.30	.09
50 Danny Tartabull	.10	.03
51 Roberto Alomar	.30	.09
52 Barry Bonds	.75	.23
53 John Kruk	.10	.03
54 Brett Butler	.10	.03
55 Kenny Lofton	.10	.03
56 Pat Listach	.10	.03
57 Brady Anderson	.10	.03
58 Marquis Grissom	.10	.03
59 Delino DeShields	.10	.03
60 Bip Roberts Steve Finley	.10	.03
61 Jack McDowell	.10	.03
62 Kevin Brown Roger Clemens	.60	.18
63 Charles Nagy Melido Perez	.10	.03
64 Terry Mulholland	.10	.03
65 Curt Schilling Doug Drabek	.10	.03
66 Greg Maddux John Smoltz	.50	.15
67 Dennis Eckersley	.10	.03
68 Rick Aguilera	.10	.03
69 Jeff Montgomery	.10	.03
70 Lee Smith	.10	.03
71 Randy Myers	.10	.03
72 John Wetteland	.10	.03
73 Randy Johnson	.30	.09
74 Melido Perez	.10	.03
75 Roger Clemens	.60	.18
76 John Smoltz	.20	.06
77 David Cone	.10	.03
78 Greg Maddux	.50	.15
79 Roger Clemens	.60	.18
80 Kevin Appier	.10	.03
81 Mike Mussina	.30	.09
82 Bill Swift	.10	.03
83 Bob Tewksbury	.10	.03
84 Greg Maddux	.50	.15

85 Jack Morris	.10	.03
Kevin Brown		
86 Jack McDowell	.10	.03
87 Roger Clemens	.60	.18
Mike Mussina		
88 Tom Glavine	.50	.15
Greg Maddux		
89 Ken Hill	.10	.03
Bob Tewksbury		
90 Mike Morgan	.10	.03
Dennis Martinez		

1993 Select Triple Crown

Honoring the three most recent Triple Crown winners since 1993, cards from this three-card standard-size set were randomly inserted in 15-card hobby packs.

	Nm-Mt	Ex-Mt
COMPLETE SET (3)	50.00	15.00
1 Mickey Mantle	40.00	12.00
2 Frank Robinson	10.00	3.00
3 Carl Yastrzemski	10.00	3.00

1993 Select Rookie/Traded

These 150 standard-size cards feature rookies and traded veteran players. The production run comprised 1,950 individually numbered cases. Cards were distributed in foil packs. Card design is similar to the regular 1993 Select cards excpt for the dramatic royal blue borders (instead of emerald green for the regular cards) and T-suffixed numbering. There are no key Rookie Cards in this set. Two Rookie of the Year insert cards and a Nolan Ryan Tribute card were randomly inserted in the foil packs. The chances of finding a Nolan Ryan card was listed at not less than one per 288 packs. The two ROY cards, featuring American League Rookie of the Year, Tim Salmon and National League Rookie of the Year, Mike Piazza were randomly inserted into one in every 576 packs.

	Nm-Mt	Ex-Mt
COMPLETE SET (150)	15.00	4.50
COMMON CARD (1T-150T)	.40	.12
COMMON RC	.40	.12
1T Rickey Henderson	1.50	.45
2T Rob Deer	.40	.12
3T Tim Belcher	.40	.12
4T Gary Sheffield	.60	.18
5T Fred McGriff	1.00	.30
6T Mark Whiten	.40	.12
7T Jeff Russell	.40	.12
8T Harold Baines	.60	.18
9T Dave Winfield	.60	.18
10T Ellis Burks	.60	.18
11T Andre Dawson	.60	.18
12T Gregg Jefferies	.40	.12
13T Jimmy Key	.60	.18
14T Harold Reynolds	.60	.18
15T Tom Henke	.40	.12
16T Paul Molitor	1.00	.30
17T Wade Boggs	1.00	.30
18T David Cone	.60	.18
19T Tony Fernandez	.40	.12
20T Roberto Kelly	.40	.12
21T Paul O'Neill	1.00	.30
22T Jose Lind	.40	.12
23T Barry Bonds	4.00	1.20
24T Dave Stewart	.60	.18
25T Randy Myers	.40	.12
26T Benito Santiago	.60	.18
27T Tim Wallach	.40	.12
28T Greg Gagne	.40	.12
29T Kevin Mitchell	.40	.12
30T Jim Abbott	1.00	.30
31T Lee Smith	.60	.18
32T Bobby Munoz	.40	.12
33T Mo Sanford	.40	.12
34T John Roper	.40	.12
35T David Hulse RC	.40	.12
36T Pedro Martinez	3.00	.90
37T Chuck Carr	.40	.12
38T Armando Reynoso	.40	.12
39T Ryan Thompson	.40	.12
40T Carlos Garcia	.40	.12
41T Matt Whiteside RC	.40	.12
42T Benji Gil	.40	.12
43T Rodney Bolton	.40	.12
44T J.T. Snow	1.50	.45
45T David McCarty	.40	.12
46T Paul Quantrill	.40	.12
47T Al Martin	.40	.12
48T Lance Painter RC	.40	.12
49T Lou Frazier RC	.40	.12
50T Eduardo Perez	.40	.12
51T Kevin Young	.60	.18
52T Mike Trombley	.40	.12
53T Sterling Hitchcock RC	.60	.18
54T Tim Bogar RC	.40	.12
55T Hilly Hathaway RC	.40	.12
56T Wayne Kirby	.40	.12
57T Craig Paquette	.40	.12
58T Bret Boone	1.00	.30
59T Greg McMichael RC	.40	.12
60T Mike Lansing RC	.60	.18
61T Brent Gates	.40	.12
62T Rene Arocha RC	.60	.18
63T Ricky Gutierrez	.40	.12
64T Kevin Rogers	.40	.12
65T Ken Ryan RC	.40	.12
66T Phil Hiatt	.40	.12
67T Pat Meares RC	.60	.18
68T Troy Neel	.40	.12
69T Steve Cooke	.40	.12
70T Sherman Obando RC	.40	.12
71T Blas Minor	.40	.12
72T Angel Miranda	.40	.12
73T Tom Kramer RC	.40	.12
74T Chip Hale	.40	.12
75T Brad Pennington	.40	.12
76T Graeme Lloyd RC	.60	.18
77T Darrell Whitmore RC	.40	.12
78T David Nied	.40	.12
79T Todd Van Poppel	.40	.12
80T Chris Gomez RC	.60	.18
81T Jason Bere	.40	.12
82T Jeffrey Hammonds	.40	.12
83T Brad Ausmus	.40	.12
84T Kevin Stocker	.40	.12
85T Jeromy Burnitz	.60	.18
86T Aaron Sele	.40	.12
87T Roberto Mejia RC	.40	.12
88T Kirk Rueter RC	1.00	.30
89T Kevin Roberson RC	.40	.12
90T Allen Watson	.40	.12
91T Charlie Leibrandt	.40	.12
92T Eric Davis	.60	.18
93T Jody Reed	.40	.12
94T Danny Jackson	.40	.12
95T Gary Gaetti	.60	.18
96T Norm Charlton	.40	.12
97T Doug Drabek	.40	.12
98T Scott Fletcher	.40	.12
99T Greg Swindell	.40	.12
100T John Smiley	.40	.12
101T Kevin Reimer	.40	.12
102T Andres Galarraga	.60	.18
103T Greg Hibbard	.40	.12
104T Chris Hammond	.40	.12
105T Darnell Coles	.40	.12
106T Mike Felder	.40	.12
107T Jose Guzman	.40	.12
108T Chris Bosio	.40	.12
109T Spike Owen	.40	.12
110T Felix Jose	.40	.12
111T Cory Snyder	.40	.12
112T Craig Lefferts	.40	.12
113T David Wells	.60	.18
114T Pete Incaviglia	.40	.12
115T Mike Pagliarulo	.40	.12
116T Dave Magadan	.40	.12
117T Charlie Hough	.60	.18
118T Ivan Calderon	.40	.12
119T Manuel Lee	.40	.12
120T Bob Patterson	.40	.12
121T Bob Ojeda	.40	.12
122T Scott Bankhead	.40	.12
123T Greg Maddux	2.50	.75
124T Chili Davis	.60	.18
125T Milt Thompson	.40	.12
126T Dave Martinez	.40	.12
127T Frank Tanana	.40	.12
128T Phil Plantier	.40	.12
129T Juan Samuel	.40	.12
130T Eric Young	.40	.12
131T Joe Orsulak	.40	.12
132T Derek Bell	.40	.12
133T Darrin Jackson	.40	.12
134T Tom Brunansky	.40	.12
135T Jeff Reardon	.60	.18
136T Kevin Higgins	.40	.12
137T Joel Johnston	.40	.12
138T Rick Trlicek	.40	.12
139T Richie Lewis RC	.40	.12
140T Jeff Gardner	.40	.12
141T Jack Voigt RC	.40	.12
142T Rod Correia RC	.40	.12
143T Billy Brewer	.40	.12
144T Terry Jorgensen	.40	.12
145T Rich Amaral	.40	.12
146T Sean Berry	.40	.12
147T Dan Peltier	.40	.12
148T Paul Wagner	.40	.12
149T Damon Buford	.40	.12
150T Wil Cordero	.40	.12
NR1 Nolan Ryan Tribute	40.00	12.00
ROY1 T.Salmon AL ROY	5.00	1.50
ROY2 Mike Piazza NL ROY	25.00	7.50

1993 Select Rookie/Traded All-Star Rookies

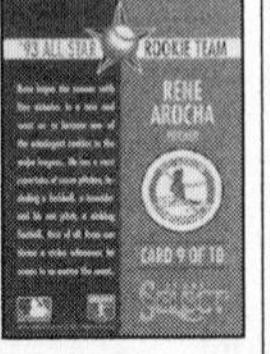

This ten-card standard-size set was randomly inserted in foil packs of 1993 Select Rookie and Traded. The insertion rate was reportedly not less than one in 36 packs.

	Nm-Mt	Ex-Mt
COMPLETE SET (10)	100.00	30.00
1 Jeff Conine	10.00	3.00
2 Brent Gates	5.00	1.50
3 Mike Lansing	10.00	3.00
4 Kevin Stocker	5.00	1.50
5 Mike Piazza	40.00	12.00
6 Jeffrey Hammonds	5.00	1.50
7 David Hulse	5.00	1.50
8 Tim Salmon	10.00	3.00
9 Rene Arocha	10.00	3.00
10 Greg McMichael	5.00	1.50

1994 Select Samples

Issued to preview the designs of the 1994 Score Select set and its inserts, these nine standard-size cards feature color player action shots on their fronts -- except for the Kruk card (24), which pictures him dozing, and so could hardly qualify as an "action shot." The cards are from the regular series, except for the Dykstra card, the Floyd card, and the Klesko card. Except for the title card, all the cards carry the word "Sample" in diagonal black lettering on their fronts and backs.

	Nm-Mt	Ex-Mt
COMPLETE SET (9)	8.00	2.40
3 Paul Molitor	2.00	.60
17 Kirby Puckett	2.00	.60
19 Randy Johnson	2.00	.60
24 John Kruk	.50	.15
51 Jose Lind	.25	.07
197 Ryan Klesko	.50	.15
94 Rookie Prospect		
CC1 Lenny Dykstra	1.50	.45
Crown Contenders		
RS1 Cliff Floyd	1.50	.45
Rookie Surge '94		
NNO Title Card	.25	.07

1994 Select

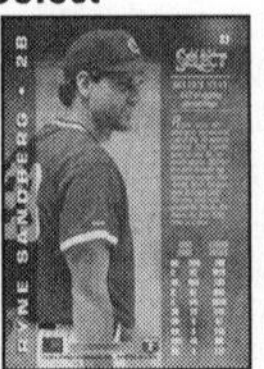

Measuring the standard size, the 1994 Select set consists of 420 cards that were issued in two series of 210. The horizontal fronts feature a color player action photo and a duo-tone player shot. The backs are vertical and contain a photo, 1993 and career statistics and highlights. Special Dave Winfield and Cal Ripken cards were inserted in first series packs. A Paul Molitor MVP card and a Carlos Delgado Rookie of the Year card were inserted in second series packs. The insertion rate for each card was one in 360 packs. Rookie Cards include Chan Ho Park.

	Nm-Mt	Ex-Mt
COMPLETE SET (420)	25.00	7.50
COMP. SERIES 1 (210)	15.00	4.50
COMP. SERIES 2 (210)	10.00	3.00
1 Ken Griffey Jr.	1.25	.35
2 Greg Maddux	1.25	.35
3 Paul Molitor	.50	.15
4 Mike Piazza	1.50	.45
5 Jay Bell	.30	.09
6 Frank Thomas	.75	.23
7 Barry Larkin	.75	.23
8 Paul O'Neill	.50	.15
9 Darren Daulton	.30	.09
10 Mike Greenwell	.15	.04
11 Chuck Carr	.15	.04
12 Joe Carter	.30	.09
13 Lance Johnson	.15	.04
14 Jeff Blauser	.15	.04
15 Chris Hoiles	.15	.04
16 Rick Wilkins	.15	.04
17 Kirby Puckett	.75	.23
18 Larry Walker	.50	.15
19 Randy Johnson	.75	.23
20 Bernard Gilkey	.15	.04
21 Devon White	.15	.04
22 Randy Myers	.15	.04
23 Don Mattingly	2.00	.60
24 John Kruk	.30	.09
25 Ozzie Guillen	.15	.04
26 Jeff Conine	.30	.09
27 Mike Macfarlane	.15	.04
28 Dave Hollins	.15	.04
29 Chuck Knoblauch	.30	.09
30 Ozzie Smith	1.25	.35
31 Harold Baines	.30	.09
32 Ryne Sandberg	1.25	.35
33 Ron Karkovice	.15	.04
34 Terry Pendleton	.30	.09
35 Wally Joyner	.30	.09
36 Mike Mussina	.75	.23
37 Felix Jose	.15	.04
38 Derrick May	.15	.04
39 Scott Cooper	.15	.04
40 Jose Rijo	.15	.04
41 Robin Ventura	.30	.09
42 Charlie Hayes	.15	.04
43 Jimmy Key	.30	.09
44 Eric Karros	.30	.09
45 Ruben Sierra	.15	.04
46 Ryan Thompson	.15	.04
47 Brian McRae	.15	.04
48 Pat Hentgen	.15	.04
49 John Valentin	.15	.04
50 Al Martin	.15	.04
51 Jose Lind	.15	.04
52 Kevin Stocker	.15	.04
53 Mike Gallego	.15	.04
54 Dwight Gooden	.50	.15
55 Brady Anderson	.30	.09
56 Jeff King	.15	.04
57 Mark McGwire	2.00	.60
58 Sammy Sosa	1.25	.35
59 Ryan Bowen	.15	.04
60 Mark Lemke	.15	.04
61 Roger Clemens	1.50	.45
62 Brian Jordan	.30	.09
63 Andres Galarraga	.30	.09
64 Kevin Appier	.30	.09
65 Don Slaught	.15	.04
66 Mike Blowers	.15	.04
67 Wes Chamberlain	.15	.04
68 Troy Neel	.15	.04
69 John Wetteland	.30	.09
70 Joe Girardi	.15	.04
71 Reggie Sanders	.30	.09
72 Edgar Martinez	.50	.15
73 Todd Hundley	.15	.04
74 Pat Borders	.15	.04
75 Roberto Mejia	.15	.04
76 David Cone	.30	.09
77 Tony Gwynn	1.00	.30
78 Jim Abbott	.50	.15
79 Jay Buhner	.30	.09
80 Mark McLemore	.15	.04
81 Wil Cordero	.15	.04
82 Pedro Astacio	.15	.04
83 Bob Tewksbury	.15	.04
84 Dave Winfield	.30	.09
85 Jeff Kent	.30	.09
86 Todd Van Poppel	.15	.04
87 Steve Avery	.15	.04
88 Mike Lansing	.15	.04
89 Lenny Dykstra	.30	.09
90 Jose Guzman	.15	.04
91 Brian R. Hunter	.15	.04
92 Tim Raines	.30	.09
93 Andre Dawson	.30	.09
94 Joe Orsulak	.15	.04
95 Ricky Jordan	.15	.04
96 Billy Hatcher	.15	.04
97 Jack McDowell	.15	.04
98 Tom Pagnozzi	.15	.04
99 Darryl Strawberry	.50	.15
100 Mike Stanley	.15	.04
101 Bret Saberhagen	.30	.09
102 Willie Greene	.15	.04
103 Bryan Harvey	.15	.04
104 Tim Bogar	.15	.04
105 Jack Voigt	.15	.04
106 Brad Ausmus	.15	.04
107 Ramon Martinez	.15	.04
108 Mike Perez	.15	.04
109 Jeff Montgomery	.15	.04
110 Danny Darwin	.15	.04
111 Wilson Alvarez	.15	.04
112 Kevin Mitchell	.15	.04
113 David Nied	.15	.04
114 Rich Amaral	.15	.04
115 Stan Javier	.15	.04
116 Mo Vaughn	.30	.09
117 Ben McDonald	.15	.04
118 Tom Gordon	.15	.04
119 Carlos Garcia	.15	.04
120 Phil Plantier	.15	.04
121 Mike Morgan	.15	.04
122 Pat Meares	.15	.04
123 Kevin Young	.15	.04
124 Jeff Fassero	.15	.04
125 Gene Harris	.15	.04
126 Bob Welch	.15	.04
127 Walt Weiss	.15	.04
128 Bobby Witt	.15	.04
129 Andy Van Slyke	.30	.09
130 Steve Cooke	.15	.04
131 Mike Devereaux	.15	.04
132 Joey Cora	.15	.04
133 Bret Barberie	.15	.04
134 Orel Hershiser	.30	.09
135 Ed Sprague	.15	.04
136 Shawon Dunston	.15	.04
137 Alex Arias	.15	.04
138 Archi Cianfrocco	.15	.04
139 Tim Wallach	.15	.04
140 Bernie Williams	.50	.15
141 Karl Rhodes	.15	.04
142 Pat Kelly	.15	.04
143 Dave Magadan	.15	.04
144 Kevin Tapani	.15	.04
145 Eric Young	.15	.04
146 Derek Bell	.15	.04
147 Dante Bichette	.30	.09
148 Geronimo Pena	.15	.04
149 Joe Oliver	.15	.04
150 Orestes Destrade	.15	.04
151 Tim Naehring	.15	.04
152 Ray Lankford	.15	.04
153 Phil Clark	.15	.04
154 David McCarty	.15	.04
155 Tommy Greene	.15	.04
156 Wade Boggs	.50	.15
157 Kevin Gross	.15	.04
158 Hal Morris	.15	.04
159 Moises Alou	.30	.09
160 Rick Aguilera	.15	.04
161 Curt Schilling	.50	.15
162 Chip Hale	.15	.04
163 Tino Martinez	.50	.15
164 Mark Whiten	.15	.04
165 Dave Stewart	.30	.09
166 Steve Buechele	.15	.04
167 Bobby Jones	.15	.04
168 Darrin Fletcher	.15	.04
169 John Smiley	.15	.04
170 Cory Snyder	.15	.04
171 Scott Erickson	.15	.04
172 Kirk Rueter	.30	.09
173 Dave Fleming	.15	.04
174 John Smoltz	.50	.15
175 Ricky Gutierrez	.15	.04
176 Mike Bordick	.15	.04
177 Chan Ho Park RC	.75	.23
178 Alex Gonzalez	.15	.04
179 Steve Karsay	.15	.04
180 Jeffrey Hammonds	.15	.04
181 Manny Ramirez	.50	.15
182 Salomon Torres	.15	.04
183 Raul Mondesi	.30	.09
184 James Mouton	.15	.04
185 Cliff Floyd	.30	.09
186 Danny Bautista	.15	.04
187 Kurt Abbott RC	.30	.09
188 Javier Lopez	.30	.09
189 John Patterson	.15	.04
190 Greg Blosser	.15	.04
191 Bob Hamelin	.15	.04
192 Tony Eusebio	.15	.04
193 Carlos Delgado	.50	.15
194 Chris Gomez	.15	.04
195 Kelly Stinnett RC	.30	.09
196 Shane Reynolds	.15	.04
197 Ryan Klesko	.30	.09
198 Jim Edmonds UER	.50	.15
Mark Dalesandro pictured on front		
199 James Hurst RC	.15	.04
200 Dave Staton	.15	.04
201 Rondell White	.30	.09
202 Keith Mitchell	.15	.04
203 Darren Oliver RC	.30	.09
204 Mike Matheny RC	.30	.09
205 Chris Turner	.15	.04
206 Matt Mieske	.15	.04
207 NL Team Checklist	.15	.04
208 NL Team Checklist	.15	.04
209 AL Team Checklist	.15	.04
210 AL Team Checklist	.15	.04
211 Barry Bonds	2.00	.60
212 Juan Gonzalez	.75	.23
213 Jim Eisenreich	.15	.04
214 Ivan Rodriguez	.75	.23
215 Tony Phillips	.15	.04
216 John Jaha	.15	.04
217 Lee Smith	.30	.09
218 Bip Roberts	.15	.04
219 Dave Hansen	.15	.04
220 Pat Listach	.15	.04
221 Willie McGee	.30	.09
222 Damion Easley	.15	.04
223 Dean Palmer	.30	.09
224 Mike Moore	.15	.04
225 Brian Harper	.15	.04
226 Gary DiSarcina	.15	.04
227 Delino DeShields	.15	.04
228 Otis Nixon	.15	.04
229 Roberto Alomar	.75	.23
230 Mark Grace	.50	.15
231 Kenny Lofton	.30	.09
232 Gregg Jefferies	.15	.04
233 Cecil Fielder	.30	.09
234 Jeff Bagwell	.50	.15
235 Albert Belle	.30	.09
236 Dave Justice	.30	.09
237 Tom Henke	.15	.04
238 Bobby Bonilla	.30	.09
239 John Olerud	.30	.09
240 Robby Thompson	.15	.04
241 Dave Valle	.15	.04
242 Marquis Grissom	.15	.04
243 Greg Swindell	.15	.04
244 Todd Zeile	.15	.04
245 Dennis Eckersley	.30	.09
246 Jose Offerman	.15	.04
247 Greg McMichael	.15	.04
248 Tim Belcher	.15	.04
249 Cal Ripken Jr.	2.50	.75
250 Tom Glavine	.50	.15
251 Luis Polonia	.15	.04
252 Bill Swift	.15	.04
253 Juan Guzman	.15	.04
254 Rickey Henderson	.75	.23
255 Terry Mulholland	.15	.04
256 Gary Sheffield	.30	.09
257 Terry Steinbach	.15	.04
258 Brett Butler	.30	.09
259 Jason Bere	.15	.04
260 Doug Strange	.15	.04
261 Kent Hrbek	.30	.09
262 Graeme Lloyd	.15	.04
263 Lou Frazier	.15	.04
264 Charles Nagy	.15	.04
265 Bret Boone	.30	.09
266 Kirk Gibson	.30	.09
267 Kevin Brown	.30	.09
268 Fred McGriff	.50	.15
269 Matt Williams	.30	.09
270 Greg Gagne	.15	.04
271 Mariano Duncan	.15	.04
272 Jeff Russell	.15	.04
273 Eric Davis	.30	.09
274 Shane Mack	.15	.04
275 Jose Vizcaino	.15	.04
276 Jose Canseco	.75	.23
277 Roberto Hernandez	.15	.04
278 Royce Clayton	.15	.04
279 Carlos Baerga	.15	.04
280 Pete Incaviglia	.15	.04
281 Brent Gates	.15	.04
282 Jeromy Burnitz	.30	.09
283 Chili Davis	.30	.09
284 Pete Harnisch	.15	.04
285 Alan Trammell	.50	.15
286 Eric Anthony	.15	.04
287 Ellis Burks	.30	.09
288 Julio Franco	.30	.09
289 Jack Morris	.30	.09
290 Erik Hanson	.15	.04
291 Chuck Finley	.30	.09
292 Reggie Jefferson	.15	.04
293 Kevin McReynolds	.15	.04
294 Greg Hibbard	.15	.04
295 Travis Fryman	.30	.09
296 Craig Biggio	.50	.15
297 Kenny Rogers	.30	.09
298 Dave Henderson	.15	.04
299 Jim Thome	.75	.23
300 Rene Arocha	.15	.04
301 Pedro Munoz	.15	.04
302 David Hulse	.15	.04
303 Greg Vaughn	.30	.09
304 Darren Lewis	.15	.04
305 Deion Sanders	.50	.15
306 Danny Tartabull	.15	.04
307 Darryl Hamilton	.15	.04
308 Andujar Cedeno	.15	.04
309 Tim Salmon	.50	.15
310 Tony Fernandez	.15	.04
311 Alex Fernandez	.15	.04
312 Roberto Kelly	.15	.04
313 Harold Reynolds	.30	.09
314 Chris Sabo	.15	.04
315 Howard Johnson	.15	.04
316 Mark Portugal	.15	.04
317 Rafael Palmeiro	.50	.15
318 Pete Smith	.15	.04
319 Will Clark	.75	.23
320 Henry Rodriguez	.15	.04
321 Omar Vizquel	.30	.09
322 David Segui	.15	.04
323 Lou Whitaker	.30	.09
324 Felix Fermin	.15	.04
325 Spike Owen	.15	.04
326 Darryl Kile	.30	.09
327 Chad Kreuter	.15	.04
328 Rod Beck	.15	.04
329 Eddie Murray	.75	.23
330 B.J. Surhoff	.30	.09
331 Mickey Tettleton	.15	.04
332 Pedro Martinez	.75	.23
333 Roger Pavlik	.15	.04
334 Eddie Taubensee	.15	.04
335 John Doherty	.15	.04

336 Jody Reed .15 .04
337 Aaron Sele .15 .04
338 Leo Gomez .15 .04
339 Dave Nilsson .15 .04
340 Rob Dibble .30 .09
341 John Burkett .15 .04
342 Wayne Kirby .15 .04
343 Dan Wilson .15 .04
344 Armando Reynoso .15 .04
345 Chad Curtis .15 .04
346 Dennis Martinez .30 .09
347 Cal Eldred .15 .04
348 Luis Gonzalez .30 .09
349 Doug Drabek .15 .04
350 Jim Leyritz .15 .04
351 Mark Langston .15 .04
352 Darrin Jackson .15 .04
353 Sid Fernandez .15 .04
354 Benito Santiago .30 .09
355 Kevin Seitzer .15 .04
356 Bo Jackson .75 .23
357 David Wells .30 .09
358 Paul Sorrento .15 .04
359 Ken Caminiti .30 .09
360 Eduardo Perez .15 .04
361 Orlando Merced .15 .04
362 Steve Finley .30 .09
363 Andy Benes .15 .04
364 Manuel Lee .15 .04
365 Todd Benzinger .15 .04
366 Sandy Alomar Jr. .15 .04
367 Rex Hudler .15 .04
368 Mike Henneman .15 .04
369 Vince Coleman .15 .04
370 Kirt Manwaring .15 .04
371 Ken Hill .15 .04
372 Glenallen Hill .15 .04
373 Sean Berry .15 .04
374 Geronimo Berroa .15 .04
375 Duane Ward .15 .04
376 Allen Watson .15 .04
377 Marc Newfield .15 .04
378 Dan Miceli .15 .04
379 Denny Hocking .15 .04
380 Mark Kiefer .15 .04
381 Tony Tarasco .15 .04
382 Tony Longmire .15 .04
383 Brian Anderson RC .30 .09
384 Fernando Vina .50 .15
385 Hector Carrasco .15 .04
386 Mike Kelly .15 .04
387 Greg Colbrunn .15 .04
388 Roger Salkeld .15 .04
389 Steve Trachsel .15 .04
390 Rich Becker .15 .04
391 Billy Taylor RC .30 .09
392 Rich Rowland .15 .04
393 Carl Everett .30 .09
394 Johnny Ruffin .15 .04
395 Keith Lockhart RC .30 .09
396 J.R. Phillips .15 .04
397 Sterling Hitchcock .15 .04
398 Jorge Fabregas .15 .04
399 Jeff Granger .15 .04
400 Eddie Zambrano RC .15 .04
401 Rikkert Faneyte RC .15 .04
402 Gerald Williams .15 .04
403 Joey Hamilton .15 .04
404 Joe Hall RC .15 .04
405 John Hudek RC .15 .04
406 Roberto Petagine .15 .04
407 Charles Johnson .30 .09
408 Mark Smith .15 .04
409 Jeff Juden .15 .04
410 Carlos Pulido RC .15 .04
411 Paul Shuey .15 .04
412 Rob Butler .15 .04
413 Mark Acre RC .15 .04
414 Greg Pirkl .15 .04
415 Melvin Nieves .15 .04
416 Tim Hyers RC .15 .04
417 NL Checklist .15 .04
418 NL Checklist .15 .04
419 AL Checklist .15 .04
420 AL Checklist .15 .04
RY1 Carlos Delgado 5.00 1.50
SS1 Cal Ripken Jr. Salute 20.00 6.00
SS2 Dave Winfield Salute 4.00 1.20
MVP1 Paul Molitor 5.00 1.50

1994 Select Crown Contenders

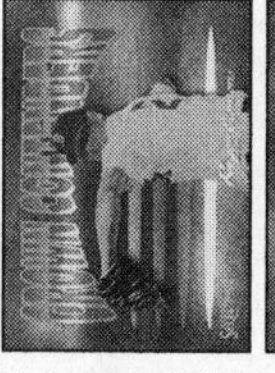

This ten-card set showcases top contenders for various awards such as batting champion, Cy Young Award winner and Most Valuable Player. The cards were inserted in first series packs at a rate of one in 24 and measure the standard size.

Nm-Mt Ex-Mt
COMPLETE SET (10) 60.00 18.00
CC1 Lenny Dykstra 2.00 .60
CC2 Greg Maddux 8.00 2.40
CC3 Roger Clemens 10.00 3.00
CC4 Randy Johnson 5.00 1.50
CC5 Frank Thomas 5.00 1.50
CC6 Barry Bonds 12.00 3.60
CC7 Juan Gonzalez 5.00 1.50
CC8 John Olerud 2.00 .60
CC9 Mike Piazza 10.00 3.00
CC10 Ken Griffey Jr. 8.00 2.40

1994 Select Rookie Surge

This 18-card standard-size set showcases potential top rookies for 1994. The set was

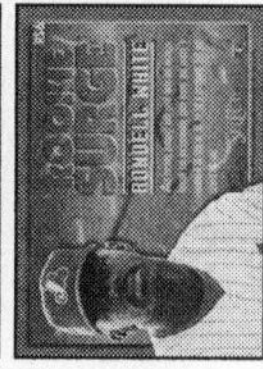

divided into two series of nine cards. The cards were randomly inserted in packs at a rate of one in 48. The fronts exhibit Score's "dufex" printing process, in which a color photo is printed on a metallic base creating an unusual, three-dimensional look.

Nm-Mt Ex-Mt
COMPLETE SET (18) 80.00 24.00
COMPLETE SERIES 1 (9) 30.00 9.00
COMPLETE SERIES 2 (9) 50.00 15.00
RS1 Cliff Floyd 6.00 1.80
RS2 Bob Hamelin 4.00 1.20
RS3 Ryan Klesko 6.00 1.80
RS4 Carlos Delgado 10.00 3.00
RS5 Jeffrey Hammonds 4.00 1.20
RS6 Rondell White 6.00 1.80
RS7 Salomon Torres 4.00 1.20
RS8 Steve Karsay 4.00 1.20
RS9 Javier Lopez 6.00 1.80
RS10 Manny Ramirez 10.00 3.00
RS11 Tony Tarasco 4.00 1.20
RS12 Kurt Abbott 6.00 1.80
RS13 Chan Ho Park 15.00 4.50
RS14 Rich Becker 4.00 1.20
RS15 James Mouton 4.00 1.20
RS16 Alex Gonzalez 4.00 1.20
RS17 Raul Mondesi 6.00 1.80
RS18 Steve Trachsel 4.00 1.20

1994 Select Skills

This 10-card standard-size set takes an up close look at the leagues top statistical leaders. The cards were randomly inserted in second series packs at a rate of approximately one in 24.

Nm-Mt Ex-Mt
COMPLETE SET (10) 50.00 15.00
SK1 Randy Johnson 12.00 3.60
SK2 Barry Larkin 12.00 3.60
SK3 Lenny Dykstra 5.00 1.50
SK4 Kenny Lofton 5.00 1.50
SK5 Juan Gonzalez 12.00 3.60
SK6 Barry Bonds 30.00 9.00
SK7 Marquis Grissom 2.50 .75
SK8 Ivan Rodriguez 12.00 3.60
SK9 Larry Walker 8.00 2.40
SK10 Travis Fryman 5.00 1.50

1995 Select Samples

This four-card set was issued to preview the 1995 Select series. Both sides of each card have the disclaimer "SAMPLE" diagonally stamped across the pictures.

Nm-Mt Ex-Mt
COMPLETE SET (4) 12.00 3.60
34 Roberto Alomar 2.00 .60
37 Jeff Bagwell 3.00 .90
241 Alex Rodriguez 8.00 2.40
NNO Title Card .50 .15

1995 Select

This 250-card set was issued in 12-card packs with 24 packs per box and 24 boxes per case. There was an announced production run of 4,950 cases. A special card of Hideo Nomo (number 251) was issued to hobby dealers who had bought cases of the Select product.

Nm-Mt Ex-Mt
COMPLETE SET (250) 15.00 4.50
1 Cal Ripken Jr. 1.50 .45
2 Robin Ventura .20 .06
3 Al Martin .10 .03
4 Jeff Frye .10 .03
5 Darryl Strawberry .30 .09
6 Chan Ho Park .20 .06
7 Steve Avery .10 .03
8 Bret Boone .20 .06
9 Danny Tartabull .10 .03
10 Dante Bichette .20 .06
11 Rondell White .20 .06
12 Dave McCarty .10 .03
13 Bernard Gilkey .10 .03
14 Mark McGwire 1.25 .35
15 Ruben Sierra .10 .03
16 Wade Boggs .30 .09
17 Mike Piazza .75 .23
18 Jeffrey Hammonds .10 .03
19 Mike Mussina .50 .15
20 Darryl Kile .20 .06
21 Greg Maddux .75 .23
22 Frank Thomas .50 .15
23 Kevin Appier .20 .06
24 Jay Bell .20 .06
25 Kirk Gibson .20 .06
26 Pat Hentgen .10 .03
27 Joey Hamilton .10 .03
28 Bernie Williams .30 .09
29 Aaron Sele .10 .03
30 Delino DeShields .10 .03
31 Danny Bautista .10 .03
32 Jim Thome .50 .15
33 Rikkert Faneyte .10 .03
34 Roberto Alomar .50 .15
35 Paul Molitor .30 .09
36 Allen Watson .10 .03
37 Jeff Bagwell .30 .09
38 Jay Buhner .20 .06
39 Marquis Grissom .20 .06
40 Jim Edmonds .20 .06
41 Ryan Klesko .20 .06
42 Fred McGriff .30 .09
43 Tony Tarasco .10 .03
44 Darren Daulton .20 .06
45 Marc Newfield .10 .03
46 Barry Bonds 1.25 .35
47 Bobby Bonilla .20 .06
48 Greg Pirkl .10 .03
49 Steve Karsay .10 .03
50 Bob Hamelin .10 .03
51 Javier Lopez .20 .06
52 Barry Larkin .50 .15
53 Kevin Young .10 .03
54 Sterling Hitchcock .10 .03
55 Tom Glavine .30 .09
56 Carlos Delgado .20 .06
57 Darren Oliver .10 .03
58 Cliff Floyd .20 .06
59 Tim Salmon .30 .09
60 Albert Belle .20 .06
61 Salomon Torres .10 .03
62 Gary Sheffield .20 .06
63 Ivan Rodriguez .50 .15
64 Charles Nagy .10 .03
65 Eduardo Perez .10 .03
66 Terry Steinbach .10 .03
67 Dave Justice .20 .06
68 Jason Bere .10 .03
69 Dave Nilsson .10 .03
70 Brian Anderson .10 .03
71 Billy Ashley .10 .03
72 Roger Clemens 1.00 .30
73 Jimmy Key .20 .06
74 Wally Joyner .20 .06
75 Andy Benes .10 .03
76 Ray Lankford .10 .03
77 Jeff Kent .20 .06
78 Moises Alou .20 .06
79 Kirby Puckett .50 .15
80 Joe Carter .20 .06
81 Manny Ramirez .20 .06
82 J.R. Phillips .10 .03
83 Matt Mieske .10 .03
84 John Olerud .20 .06
85 Andres Galarraga .10 .03
86 Juan Gonzalez .50 .15
87 Pedro Martinez .50 .15
88 Dean Palmer .20 .06
89 Ken Griffey Jr. .75 .23
90 Brian Jordan .20 .06
91 Hal Morris .10 .03
92 Lenny Dykstra .20 .06
93 Wil Cordero .10 .03
94 Tony Gwynn .60 .18
95 Alex Gonzalez .10 .03
96 Cecil Fielder .20 .06
97 Mo Vaughn .20 .06
98 John Valentin .10 .03
99 Will Clark .50 .15
100 Geronimo Pena .10 .03
101 Don Mattingly 1.25 .35
102 Charles Johnson .20 .06
103 Raul Mondesi .20 .06
104 Reggie Sanders .20 .06
105 Royce Clayton .10 .03
106 Reggie Jefferson .10 .03
107 Craig Biggio .30 .09
108 Jack McDowell .10 .03
109 James Mouton .10 .03
110 Mike Greenwell .10 .03
111 David Cone .10 .03
112 Matt Williams .20 .06
113 Garret Anderson .20 .06
114 Carlos Garcia .10 .03
115 Alex Fernandez .10 .03
116 Deion Sanders .30 .09
117 Chili Davis .20 .06
118 Mike Kelly .10 .03
119 Jeff Conine .20 .06
120 Kenny Lofton .20 .06
121 Rafael Palmeiro .30 .09
122 Chuck Knoblauch .20 .06
123 Ozzie Smith .75 .23
124 Carlos Baerga .20 .06
125 Brett Butler .20 .06
126 Sammy Sosa .75 .23
127 Ellis Burks .20 .06
128 Bret Saberhagen .20 .06
129 Doug Drabek .10 .03
130 Dennis Martinez .20 .06
131 Paul O'Neill .30 .09
132 Travis Fryman .20 .06
133 Brent Gates .10 .03
134 Rickey Henderson .50 .15
135 Randy Johnson .50 .15
136 Mark Langston .10 .03
137 Greg Colbrunn .10 .03
138 Jose Rijo .10 .03
139 Bryan Harvey .10 .03
140 Dennis Eckersley .20 .06
141 Ron Gant .20 .06
142 Carl Everett .20 .06
143 Jeff Granger .10 .03
144 Ben McDonald .10 .03
145 Kurt Abbott UER .10 .03
(Mariners logo on front
146 Jim Abbott .30 .09
147 Jason Jacome .10 .03
148 Rico Brogna .10 .03
149 Cal Eldred .10 .03
150 Rich Becker .10 .03
151 Pete Harnisch .10 .03
152 Roberto Petagine .10 .03
153 Jacob Brumfield .10 .03
154 Todd Hundley .10 .03
155 Roger Cedeno .10 .03
156 Harold Baines .20 .06
157 Steve Dunn .10 .03
158 Tim Belk .10 .03
159 Marty Cordova .10 .03
160 Russ Davis .10 .03
161 Jose Malave .10 .03
162 Brian Hunter .10 .03
163 Andy Pettitte .30 .09
164 Brooks Kieschnick .10 .03
165 Midre Cummings .10 .03
166 Frank Rodriguez .10 .03
167 Chad Mottola .10 .03
168 Brian Barber .10 .03
169 Tim Unroe RC .10 .03
170 Shane Andrews .10 .03
171 Kevin Flora .10 .03
172 Ray Durham .20 .06
173 Chipper Jones .50 .15
174 Butch Huskey .10 .03
175 Ray McDavid .10 .03
176 Jeff Cirillo .10 .03
177 Terry Pendleton .20 .06
178 Scott Ruffcorn .10 .03
179 Ray Holbert .10 .03
180 Joe Randa .10 .03
181 Jose Oliva .10 .03
182 Andy Van Slyke .20 .06
183 Albie Lopez .10 .03
184 Chad Curtis .10 .03
185 Ozzie Guillen .10 .03
186 Chad Ogea .10 .03
187 Dan Wilson .10 .03
188 Tony Fernandez .10 .03
189 John Smoltz .30 .09
190 Willie Greene .10 .03
191 Darren Lewis .10 .03
192 Orlando Miller .10 .03
193 Kurt Miller .10 .03
194 Andrew Lorraine .10 .03
195 Ernie Young .10 .03
196 Jimmy Haynes .10 .03
197 Raul Casanova RC .10 .03
198 Joe Vitiello .10 .03
199 Brad Woodall RC .10 .03
200 Juan Acevedo RC .10 .03
201 Michael Tucker .10 .03
202 Shawn Green .20 .06
203 Alex Rodriguez 1.25 .35
204 Julian Tavarez .10 .03
205 Jose Lima .10 .03
206 Wilson Alvarez .10 .03
207 Rich Aude .10 .03
208 Armando Benitez .20 .06
209 Dwayne Hosey .10 .03
210 Gabe White .10 .03
211 Joey Eischen .10 .03
212 Bill Pulsipher .10 .03
213 Robby Thompson .10 .03
214 Toby Borland .10 .03
215 Rusty Greer .20 .06
216 Fausto Cruz .10 .03
217 Luis Ortiz .10 .03
218 Duane Singleton .10 .03
219 Troy Percival .20 .06
220 Gregg Jefferies .10 .03
221 Mark Grace .30 .09
222 Mickey Tettleton .10 .03
223 Phil Plantier .10 .03
224 Larry Walker .30 .09
225 Ken Caminiti .20 .06
226 Dave Winfield .20 .06
227 Brady Anderson .20 .06
228 Kevin Brown .20 .06
229 Andujar Cedeno .10 .03
230 Roberto Kelly .10 .03
231 Jose Canseco .50 .15
232 Scott Ruffcorn ST .10 .03
233 Billy Ashley ST .10 .03
234 J.R. Phillips ST .10 .03
235 Chipper Jones ST .30 .09
236 Charles Johnson ST .10 .03
237 Midre Cummings ST .10 .03
238 Brian L.Hunter ST .10 .03
239 Garret Anderson ST .10 .03
240 Shawn Green ST .10 .03
241 Alex Rodriguez ST .50 .15
242 Frank Thomas CL .30 .09
243 Ken Griffey Jr. CL .50 .15
244 Albert Belle CL .10 .03
245 Cal Ripken Jr. CL .75 .23
246 Barry Bonds CL .60 .18
247 Raul Mondesi CL .10 .03
248 Mike Piazza CL .50 .15
249 Jeff Bagwell CL .20 .06
250 Jeff Bagwell .50 .15
Ken Griffey Jr.
Frank Thomas
Mike Piazza CL
251S Hideo Nomo 1.50 .45

1995 Select Artist's Proofs

This 250-card set is parallel to the regular Select set. These cards were inserted at a rate of one per 24 packs. The only difference between these cards and the regular issue cards are the words "Artist's Proof" printed in the lower left corner. Based upon the announced print run of 4,950 cases, approximately 238 complete sets of Artist's Proofs were produced. Please note, however, that these cards are not serial numbered and that number has never been verified by the manufacturer. The Hideo Nomo card was randomly distributed directly to hobby dealers and never inserted in packs.

Nm-Mt Ex-Mt
*STARS: 12.5X TO 30X BASIC CARDS

1995 Select Big Sticks

Randomly inserted in packs, these 12 cards feature leading hitters. The cards are numbered in the upper right corner with a "BS" prefix.

Nm-Mt Ex-Mt
COMPLETE SET (12) 120.00 36.00
BS1 Frank Thomas 8.00 2.40
BS2 Ken Griffey Jr. 12.00 3.60
BS3 Cal Ripken Jr. 25.00 7.50
BS4 Mike Piazza 12.00 3.60
BS5 Don Mattingly 20.00 6.00
BS6 Will Clark 8.00 2.40
BS7 Tony Gwynn 10.00 3.00
BS8 Jeff Bagwell 5.00 1.50
BS9 Barry Bonds 20.00 6.00
BS10 Paul Molitor 5.00 1.50
BS11 Matt Williams 3.00 .90
BS12 Albert Belle 3.00 .90

1995 Select Can't Miss

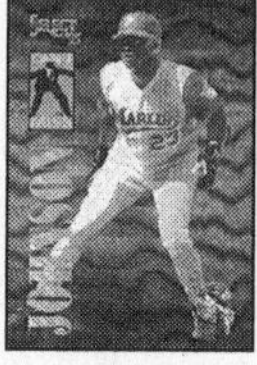
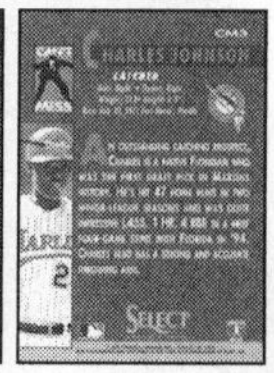

These 12 cards featuring promising young players were inserted one per 24 packs. The cards are numbered with a "CM" prefix in the upper right corner.

Nm-Mt Ex-Mt
COMPLETE SET (12) 50.00 15.00
CM1 Cliff Floyd 2.50 .75
CM2 Ryan Klesko 2.50 .75
CM3 Charles Johnson 2.50 .75
CM4 Raul Mondesi 2.50 .75
CM5 Manny Ramirez 2.50 .75
CM6 Billy Ashley 1.50 .45
CM7 Alex Gonzalez 1.50 .45
CM8 Carlos Delgado 2.50 .75
CM9 Garret Anderson 2.50 .75
CM10 Alex Rodriguez 12.00 3.60
CM11 Chipper Jones 5.00 1.50
CM12 Shawn Green 2.50 .75

1995 Select Sure Shots

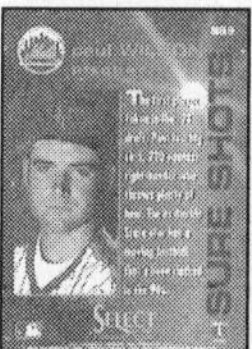

These ten cards were randomly inserted into packs at a rate of one in 90. This set features some of the top 1994 draft picks. The cards are numbered with an "SS" prefix in the upper right corner.

Nm-Mt Ex-Mt
COMPLETE SET (10) 30.00 9.00
SS1 Ben Grieve 3.00 .90
SS2 Kevin Witt 3.00 .90
SS3 Mark Farris 3.00 .90
SS4 Paul Konerko 3.00 .90
SS5 Dustin Hermanson 3.00 .90
SS6 Ramon Castro 3.00 .90
SS7 McKay Christensen 3.00 .90
SS8 Brian Buchanan 3.00 .90
SS9 Paul Wilson 3.00 .90
SS10 Terrence Long 3.00 .90

1996 Select

The 1996 Select set was issued in one series totalling 200 cards. The 10-card packs retailed for $1.99 each. The fronts feature a color action player photo over most of the card with a small player photo framed and name in gold foil printing. The backs carry another player photo, player information and statistics. The set contains the topical subsets: Lineup Leaders (151-160) and Rookies (161-195).

Nm-Mt Ex-Mt
COMPLETE SET (200) 15.00 4.50
1 Wade Boggs .30 .09
2 Shawn Green .20 .06
3 Andres Galarraga .20 .06
4 Bill Pulsipher .20 .06
5 Chuck Knoblauch .20 .06
6 Ken Griffey Jr. .75 .23
7 Greg Maddux .75 .23
8 Manny Ramirez .20 .06
9 Ivan Rodriguez .50 .15
10 Tim Salmon .30 .09
11 Frank Thomas .50 .15
12 Jeff Bagwell .30 .09

13 Travis Fryman .20 .06
14 Kenny Lofton .20 .06
15 Matt Williams .20 .06
16 Jay Bell .20 .06
17 Ken Caminiti .20 .06
18 Ray Lankford .20 .06
19 Cal Ripken 1.50 .45
20 Roger Clemens 1.00 .30
21 Carlos Baerga .20 .06
22 Mike Piazza .75 .23
23 Gregg Jefferies .20 .06
24 Reggie Sanders .20 .06
25 Rondell White .20 .06
26 Sammy Sosa .75 .23
27 Kevin Appier .20 .06
28 Kevin Seitzer .20 .06
29 Gary Sheffield .20 .06
30 Mike Mussina .50 .15
31 Mark McGwire 1.25 .35
32 Barry Larkin .50 .15
33 Marc Newfield .20 .06
34 Ismael Valdes .20 .06
35 Marty Cordova .20 .06
36 Albert Belle .20 .06
37 Johnny Damon .20 .06
38 Garret Anderson .20 .06
39 Cecil Fielder .20 .06
40 John Mabry .20 .06
41 Chipper Jones .50 .15
42 Omar Vizquel .20 .06
43 Jose Rijo .20 .06
44 Charles Johnson .20 .06
45 Alex Rodriguez 1.00 .30
46 Rico Brogna .20 .06
47 Joe Carter .20 .06
48 Mo Vaughn .20 .06
49 Moises Alou .20 .06
50 Raul Mondesi .20 .06
51 Robin Ventura .20 .06
52 Jim Thome .50 .15
53 David Justice .20 .06
54 Jeff King .20 .06
55 Brian L.Hunter .20 .06
56 Juan Gonzalez .50 .15
57 John Olerud .20 .06
58 Rafael Palmeiro .30 .09
59 Tony Gwynn .60 .18
60 Eddie Murray .50 .15
61 Jason Isringhausen .20 .06
62 Dante Bichette .20 .06
63 Randy Johnson .50 .15
64 Kirby Puckett .50 .15
65 Jim Edmonds .20 .06
66 David Cone .20 .06
67 Ozzie Smith .75 .23
68 Fred McGriff .30 .09
69 Darren Daulton .20 .06
70 Edgar Martinez .30 .09
71 J.T. Snow .20 .06
72 Butch Huskey .20 .06
73 Hideo Nomo .50 .15
74 Pedro Martinez .50 .15
75 Bobby Bonilla .20 .06
76 Jeff Conine .20 .06
77 Ryan Klesko .20 .06
78 Bernie Williams .30 .09
79 Andre Dawson .20 .06
80 Trevor Hoffman .20 .06
81 Mark Grace .30 .09
82 Benji Gil .20 .06
83 Eric Karros .20 .06
84 Pete Schourek .20 .06
85 Edgardo Alfonzo .20 .06
86 Jay Buhner .20 .06
87 Vinny Castilla .20 .06
88 Bret Boone .20 .06
89 Ray Durham .20 .06
90 Brian Jordan .20 .06
91 Jose Canseco .50 .15
92 Paul O'Neill .30 .09
93 Chili Davis .20 .06
94 Tom Glavine .30 .09
95 Julian Tavarez .20 .06
96 Derek Bell .20 .06
97 Will Clark .50 .15
98 Larry Walker .30 .09
99 Denny Neagle .20 .06
100 Alex Fernandez .20 .06
101 Barry Bonds 1.25 .35
102 Ben McDonald .20 .06
103 Andy Pettitte .30 .09
104 Tino Martinez .30 .09
105 Sterling Hitchcock .20 .06
106 Royce Clayton .20 .06
107 Jim Abbott .30 .09
108 Rickey Henderson .50 .15
109 Ramon Martinez .20 .06
110 Paul Molitor .30 .09
111 Dennis Eckersley .20 .06
112 Alex Gonzalez .20 .06
113 Marquis Grissom .20 .06
114 Greg Vaughn .20 .06
115 Lance Johnson .20 .06
116 Todd Stottlemyre .20 .06
117 Jack McDowell .20 .06
118 Ruben Sierra .20 .06
119 Brady Anderson .20 .06
120 Julio Franco .20 .06
121 Brooks Kieschnick .20 .06
122 Roberto Alomar .50 .15
123 Greg Gagne .20 .06
124 Wally Joyner .20 .06
125 John Smoltz .30 .09
126 John Valentin .20 .06
127 Russ Davis .20 .06
128 Joe Vitiello .20 .06
129 Shawon Dunston .20 .06
130 Frank Rodriguez .20 .06
131 Charlie Hayes .20 .06
132 Andy Benes .20 .06
133 B.J. Surhoff .20 .06
134 Dave Nilsson .20 .06
135 Carlos Delgado .20 .06
136 Walt Weiss .20 .06
137 Mike Stanley .20 .06
138 Greg Colbrunn .20 .06
139 Mike Kelly .20 .06
140 Ryne Sandberg .75 .23
141 Lee Smith .20 .06
142 Dennis Martinez .20 .06
143 Bernard Gilkey .20 .06
144 Lenny Dykstra .20 .06
145 Danny Tartabull .20 .06
146 Dean Palmer .20 .06
147 Craig Biggio .30 .09
148 Juan Acevedo .20 .06
149 Michael Tucker .20 .06
150 Bobby Higginson .20 .06
151 Ken Griffey Jr. LUL .50 .15
152 Frank Thomas LUL .30 .09
153 Cal Ripken LUL .75 .23
154 Albert Belle LUL .20 .06
155 Mike Piazza LUL .50 .15
156 Barry Bonds LUL .50 .15
157 Sammy Sosa LUL .50 .15
158 Mo Vaughn LUL .20 .06
159 Greg Maddux LUL .50 .15
160 Jeff Bagwell LUL .20 .06
161 Derek Jeter 1.25 .35
162 Paul Wilson .20 .06
163 Chris Snopek .20 .06
164 Jason Schmidt .20 .06
165 Jimmy Haynes .20 .06
166 George Arias .20 .06
167 Steve Gibralter .20 .06
168 Bob Wolcott .20 .06
169 Jason Kendall .20 .06
170 Greg Zaun .20 .06
171 Quinton McCracken .20 .06
172 Alan Benes .20 .06
173 Rey Ordonez .20 .06
174 Livan Hernandez RC .50 .15
175 Osvaldo Fernandez .20 .06
176 Marc Barcelo .20 .06
177 Sal Fasano .20 .06
178 Mike Grace .20 .06
179 Chan Ho Park .20 .06
180 Robert Perez .20 .06
181 Todd Hollandsworth .20 .06
182 Wilton Guerrero RC .20 .06
183 John Wasdin .20 .06
184 Jim Pittsley .20 .06
185 LaTroy Hawkins .20 .06
186 Jay Powell .20 .06
187 Felipe Crespo .20 .06
188 Jermaine Dye .20 .06
189 Bob Abreu .20 .06
190 Matt Luke .20 .06
191 Richard Hidalgo .20 .06
192 Karim Garcia .20 .06
193 Marvin Benard RC .20 .06
194 Andy Fox .20 .06
195 Terrell Wade .20 .06
196 Frank Thomas CL .30 .09
197 Ken Griffey Jr. CL .50 .15
198 Greg Maddux CL .50 .15
199 Mike Piazza CL .50 .15
200 Cal Ripken CL .75 .23

1996 Select Artist's Proofs

Randomly inserted one in 35 packs, this 200-card set is parallel and similar in design to the regular set. The difference is the holographic foil-stamped Artist's Proof logo on the card front.

Nm-Mt Ex-Mt
*STARS: 12.5X TO 30X BASIC CARDS
*ROOKIES: 8X TO 20X BASIC CARDS

1996 Select Claim To Fame

Randomly inserted in packs at a rate of one in 72, this 20-card set features potential Hall of Famers. The fronts display a color player portrait on a diecut plaque similar to the ones that enshrine Hall of Famers. The backs carry information about the player's claim to fame. Only 2100 of these sets were produced. A Sammy Sosa Sample card was distributed to dealers and hobby media to preview the set.

Nm-Mt Ex-Mt
COMPLETE SET (20) 250.00 75.00
1 Cal Ripken 30.00 9.00
2 Greg Maddux 15.00 4.50
3 Ken Griffey Jr. 15.00 4.50
4 Frank Thomas 10.00 3.00
5 Mo Vaughn 4.00 1.20
6 Albert Belle 4.00 1.20
7 Jeff Bagwell 6.00 1.80
8 Sammy Sosa 15.00 4.50
9 Reggie Sanders 4.00 1.20
10 Hideo Nomo 10.00 3.00
11 Chipper Jones 10.00 3.00
12 Mike Piazza 15.00 4.50
13 Matt Williams 4.00 1.20
14 Tony Gwynn 12.00 3.60
15 Johnny Damon 4.00 1.20
16 Dante Bichette 4.00 1.20
17 Kirby Puckett 10.00 3.00
18 Barry Bonds 25.00 7.50
19 Randy Johnson 10.00 3.00
20 Eddie Murray 10.00 3.00
S8 Sammy Sosa Sample 2.00 .60

1996 Select En Fuego

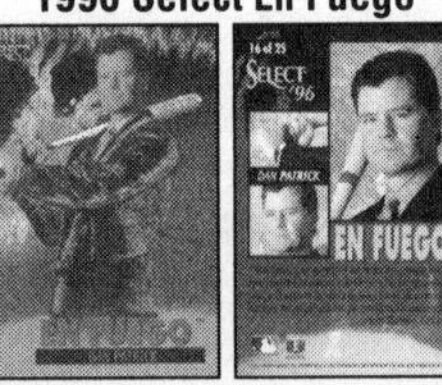

Randomly inserted in packs at a rate of one in 48, this 25-card set is printed with all-foil Dufex technology, etched highlights and transparent inks that make each card shine. Spanish for "on fire," En Fuego is an expression popularized by ESPN sportscaster Dan Patrick, who provides the commentary for each player on the card back. The fronts feature color action player photos while the backs display more player photos and the commentary.

Nm-Mt Ex-Mt
COMPLETE SET (25) 200.00 60.00
1 Ken Griffey Jr. 12.00 3.60
2 Frank Thomas 8.00 2.40
3 Cal Ripken 25.00 7.50
4 Greg Maddux 12.00 3.60
5 Jeff Bagwell 5.00 1.50
6 Barry Bonds 20.00 6.00
7 Mo Vaughn 3.00 .90
8 Albert Belle 3.00 .90
9 Sammy Sosa 12.00 3.60
10 Reggie Sanders 3.00 .90
11 Mike Piazza 12.00 3.60
12 Chipper Jones 8.00 2.40
13 Tony Gwynn 10.00 3.00
14 Kirby Puckett 8.00 2.40
15 Wade Boggs 5.00 1.50
16 Dan Patrick ANN 3.00 .90
17 Gary Sheffield 3.00 .90
18 Dante Bichette 3.00 .90
19 Randy Johnson 8.00 2.40
20 Matt Williams 3.00 .90
21 Alex Rodriguez 15.00 4.50
22 Tim Salmon 5.00 1.50
23 Johnny Damon 3.00 .90
24 Manny Ramirez 3.00 .90
25 Hideo Nomo 8.00 2.40

1996 Select Team Nucleus

Randomly inserted in packs at a rate of one in 18, this 28-card set is printed on clear plastic with holographic and micro-etched highlights and gold foil stamping.

Nm-Mt Ex-Mt
COMPLETE SET (28) 100.00 30.00
1 Albert Belle 1.50 .45
Manny Ramirez
Carlos Baerga
2 Ray Lankford 6.00 1.80
Brian Jordan
Ozzie Smith
3 Jay Bell 1.50 .45
Jeff King
Denny Neagle
4 Dante Bichette 1.50 .45
Andres Galarraga
Larry Walker
5 Mark McGwire 10.00 3.00
Mike Bordick
Terry Steinbach
6 Bernie Williams 2.50 .75
Wade Boggs
David Cone
7 Joe Carter 1.50 .45
Alex Gonzalez
Shawn Green
8 Roger Clemens 8.00 2.40
Mo Vaughn
Jose Canseco
9 Ken Griffey Jr. 6.00 1.80
Edgar Martinez
Randy Johnson
10 Gregg Jefferies 1.50 .45
Darren Daulton
Len Dykstra
11 Mike Piazza 6.00 1.80
Raul Mondesi
Hideo Nomo
12 Greg Maddux 6.00 1.80
Chipper Jones
Ryan Klesko
13 Cecil Fielder 1.50 .45
Travis Fryman
Phil Nevin
14 Ivan Rodriguez 4.00 1.20
Will Clark
Juan Gonzalez
15 Ryne Sandberg 6.00 1.80
Sammy Sosa
Mark Grace
16 Gary Sheffield 1.50 .45
Charles Johnson
Andre Dawson
17 Johnny Damon 1.50 .45
Michael Tucker
Kevin Appier
18 Barry Bonds 10.00 3.00
Matt Williams
Rod Beck
19 Kirby Puckett 4.00 1.20
Chuck Knoblauch
Marty Cordova
20 Cal Ripken 12.00 3.60
Barry Bonilla
Mike Mussina
21 Jason Isringhausen 1.50 .45
Bill Pulsipher
Rico Brogna
22 Tony Gwynn 5.00 1.50
Ken Caminiti
Mark Newfield
23 Tim Salmon 1.50 .45
Garret Anderson
Jim Edmonds
24 Moises Alou 1.50 .45
Rondell White
Cliff Floyd
25 Barry Larkin 4.00 1.20
Reggie Sanders
Bret Boone
26 Jeff Bagwell 2.50 .75
Craig Biggio
Derek Bell
27 Frank Thomas 4.00 1.20
Robin Ventura
Alex Fernandez
28 John Jaha 1.50 .45
Greg Vaughn
Kevin Seitzer

1997 Select Samples

This set was issued to preview the 1997 Select set. These cards have Sample written on the front to differentiate them from the regular cards. There may be more cards in this set so any additions are appreciated.

Nm-Mt Ex-Mt
COMPLETE SET 20.00 6.00
1 Juan Gonzalez 1.25 .35
3 Tony Gwynn 2.00 .60
8 Frank Thomas 1.25 .35
15 Paul Molitor 1.00 .30
23 Greg Maddux 3.00 .90
47 Ken Griffey Jr. 3.00 .90
50 Rickey Henderson 1.25 .35
53 Alex Rodriguez 3.00 .90
71 Cal Ripken 5.00 1.50
107 Danny Patterson .25 .07
124 J.J. Johnson .25 .07

1997 Select

The 1997 Select set was issued in two series totalling 200 cards and was distributed in hobby only six-card packs with a suggested retail price of $2.99. The 150-card first series set contains 100 common "Red" cards and 50 short-printed Blue cards. Each card featues a distinctive silver-foil treatment with either a red or blue foil accent. The red cards are twice as easy to find than the blue cards. The fronts display a color action player photo over most of the card with a small player photo at the bottom. The backs carry another player photo, player information and statistics.

Nm-Mt Ex-Mt
COMPLETE SET (200) 65.00 19.50
COMP. SERIES 1 (150) 40.00 12.00
COMP. HI SERIES (50) 25.00 7.50
COMMON RED (1-150) .30 .09
COMMON BLUE (1-150) .60 .18
COMMON (151-200) .60 .18
1 Juan Gonzalez B 1.50 .45
2 Mo Vaughn B .60 .18
3 Tony Gwynn R 1.00 .30
4 Manny Ramirez B .60 .18
5 Jose Canseco R .75 .23
6 David Cone R .30 .09
7 Chan Ho Park R .30 .09
8 Frank Thomas B 1.50 .45
9 Todd Hollandsworth R .30 .09
10 Marty Cordova R .30 .09
11 Gary Sheffield B .60 .18
12 John Smoltz B 1.00 .30
13 Mark Grudzielanek R .30 .09
14 Sammy Sosa B 2.50 .75
15 Paul Molitor R .50 .15
16 Kevin Brown R .30 .09
17 Albert Belle B .60 .18
18 Eric Young R .30 .09
19 John Wetteland R .30 .09
20 Ryan Klesko B .60 .18
21 Joe Carter R .30 .09
22 Alex Ochoa R .30 .09
23 Greg Maddux B 2.50 .75
24 Roger Clemens B 3.00 .90
25 Ivan Rodriguez B 1.50 .45
26 Barry Bonds B 4.00 1.20
27 Kenny Lofton B .60 .18
28 Javy Lopez R .30 .09
29 Hideo Nomo B 1.50 .45
30 Rusty Greer R .30 .09
31 Rafael Palmeiro R .50 .15
32 Mike Piazza B 2.50 .75
33 Ryne Sandberg R 1.25 .35
34 Wade Boggs R .50 .15
35 Jim Thome B 1.50 .45
36 Ken Caminiti B .60 .18
37 Mark Grace R .50 .15
38 Brian Jordan B .60 .18
39 Craig Biggio R .50 .15
40 Henry Rodriguez R .30 .09
41 Dean Palmer R .30 .09
42 Jason Kendall R .30 .09
43 Bill Pulsipher R .30 .09
44 Tim Salmon B 1.00 .30
45 Marc Newfield R .30 .09
46 Pat Hentgen R .30 .09
47 Ken Griffey Jr. B 2.50 .75
48 Paul Wilson R .30 .09
49 Jay Buhner B .60 .18
50 Rickey Henderson R .75 .23
51 Jeff Bagwell B 1.00 .30
52 Cecil Fielder R .30 .09
53 Alex Rodriguez B 2.00 .60
54 John Jaha R .30 .09
55 Brady Anderson B .60 .18
56 Andres Galarraga R .30 .09
57 Raul Mondesi R .30 .09
58 Andy Pettitte R .50 .15
59 Roberto Alomar B 1.50 .45
60 Derek Jeter B 4.00 1.20
61 Charles Johnson R .30 .09
62 Travis Fryman R .30 .09
63 Chipper Jones B 1.50 .45
64 Edgar Martinez R .50 .15
65 Bobby Bonilla R .30 .09
66 Greg Vaughn R .30 .09
67 Bobby Higginson R .30 .09
68 Garret Anderson R .30 .09
69 Chuck Knoblauch B .60 .18
70 Jermaine Dye R .30 .09
71 Cal Ripken B 5.00 1.50
72 Jason Giambi R .75 .23
73 Trey Beamon R .30 .09
74 Shawn Green R .30 .09
75 Mark McGwire B 4.00 1.20
76 Carlos Delgado R .30 .09
77 Jason Isringhausen R .30 .09
78 Randy Johnson B 1.50 .45
79 Troy Percival B .60 .18
80 Ron Gant R .30 .09
81 Ellis Burks R .30 .09
82 Mike Mussina B 1.50 .45
83 Todd Hundley R .30 .09
84 Jim Edmonds R .30 .09
85 Charles Nagy R .30 .09
86 Dante Bichette B .60 .18
87 Mariano Rivera R .50 .15
88 Matt Williams B .60 .18
89 Rondell White R .30 .09
90 Steve Finley R .30 .09
91 Alex Fernandez R .30 .09
92 Barry Larkin R .75 .23
93 Tom Goodwin R .30 .09
94 Will Clark R .75 .23
95 Michael Tucker R .30 .09
96 Derek Bell R .30 .09
97 Larry Walker R .50 .15
98 Alan Benes R .30 .09
99 Tom Glavine R .50 .15
100 Darin Erstad B .60 .18
101 Andruw Jones B .60 .18
102 Scott Rolen R .50 .15
103 Todd Walker B .60 .18
104 Dmitri Young R .30 .09
105 Vladimir Guerrero B 1.50 .45
106 Nomar Garciaparra R 1.25 .35
107 Danny Patterson R .30 .09
108 Karim Garcia R .30 .09
109 Todd Greene R .30 .09
110 Ruben Rivera R .30 .09
111 Raul Casanova R .30 .09
112 Mike Cameron R .30 .09
113 Bartolo Colon R .30 .09
114 Rod Myers R .30 .09
115 Todd Dunn R .30 .09
116 Torii Hunter R .30 .09
117 Jason Dickson R .30 .09
118 Eugene Kingsale R .30 .09
119 Rafael Medina R .30 .09
120 Raul Ibanez R .30 .09
121 Bobby Henley R RC .30 .09
122 Scott Spiezio R .30 .09
123 Bobby Smith R .30 .09
124 J.J. Johnson R .30 .09
125 Bubba Trammell R RC .30 .09
126 Jeff Abbott R .30 .09
127 Neifi Perez R .30 .09
128 Derrek Lee R .30 .09
129 Kevin Brown C R .30 .09
130 Mendy Lopez R .30 .09
131 Kevin Orie R .30 .09
132 Ryan Jones R .30 .09
133 Juan Encarnacion R .30 .09
134 Jose Guillen B .30 .09
135 Greg Norton R .30 .09
136 Richie Sexson R .30 .09
137 Jay Payton R .30 .09
138 Bob Abreu R .30 .09
139 Ron Belliard R RC .30 .09
140 Wilton Guerrero B .60 .18
141 Alex Rodriguez SS B 1.25 .35
142 Juan Gonzalez SS B 1.00 .30
143 Ken Caminiti SS B .60 .18
144 Frank Thomas SS B 1.50 .45
145 Ken Griffey Jr. SS B 1.50 .45
146 John Smoltz SS B 1.00 .30
147 Mike Piazza SS B .75 .23
148 Derek Jeter SS B 2.00 .60
149 Frank Thomas CL R .50 .15
150 Ken Griffey Jr. CL R .75 .23
151 Jose Cruz Jr. RC 4.00 1.20
152 Moises Alou .60 .18
153 Hideki Irabu RC .60 .18
154 Glendon Rusch .60 .18
155 Ron Coomer .60 .18
156 Jeremi Gonzalez RC .60 .18
157 Fernando Tatis RC 2.00 .60
158 John Olerud .60 .18
159 Rickey Henderson .75 .23
160 Shannon Stewart .60 .18
161 Kevin Polcovich RC .60 .18
162 Jose Rosado .60 .18
163 Ray Lankford .60 .18
164 David Justice .60 .18
165 Mark Kotsay RC .60 .18
166 Deivi Cruz RC .60 .18
167 Billy Wagner .60 .18
168 Jacob Cruz .60 .18
169 Matt Morris .30 .09
170 Brian Banks .60 .18
171 Brett Tomko .60 .18
172 Todd Helton 1.50 .45
173 Eric Young .60 .18
174 Bernie Williams 1.00 .30
175 Jeff Fassero .60 .18
176 Ryan McGuire .60 .18
177 Darryl Kile .60 .18
178 Kelvim Escobar RC .60 .18
179 Dave Nilsson .60 .18
180 Geronimo Berroa .60 .18
181 Livan Hernandez .60 .18
182 Tony Womack RC .60 .18
183 Deion Sanders 1.00 .30
184 Jeff Kent .60 .18
185 Brian Hunter .60 .18
186 Jose Malave .60 .18
187 Steve Woodard RC .60 .18
188 Brad Radke .60 .18
189 Todd Dunwoody .60 .18
190 Joey Hamilton .60 .18
191 Denny Neagle .60 .18
192 Bobby Jones .60 .18
193 Tony Clark .60 .18
194 Jaret Wright RC .60 .18

195 Matt Stairs .60 .18
196 Francisco Cordova .60 .18
197 Justin Thompson .60 .18
198 Pokey Reese .60 .18
199 Garrett Stephenson .60 .18
200 Carl Everett .60 .18

1997 Select Artist's Proofs

Randomly inserted in packs at the rate of one in 71 for red cards and one in 355 for blue cards, this 150-card set is a holographic foil rendition of the Series 1 base set with either red or blue foil treatment and the unique Artist's Proof logo.

Nm-Mt Ex-Mt
*STARS: 5X TO 12X BASIC CARDS ....

1997 Select Company

Randomly inserted one in every Select Hi Series pack, this 200-card set is a fractured parallel version of the Select base set. The difference is found in the full foil card stock with puffed ink accented highlights. The first level features 100 players from the base set with a red bordered design. The second level features the 50 players found only in the Select High Series. The final level features 50 parallel cards of top superstars utilizing a blue puffed ink border.

Nm-Mt Ex-Mt
*BLUE 1-150: .4X TO 1X BASIC.........
*RED 1-150: .75X TO 2X BASIC.........
*HI SERIES 151-200: .4X TO 1X BASIC
P121 B.Henley PROMO .50 .15

1997 Select Registered Gold

Randomly inserted in packs at the rate of one in 11 for red cards and one in 47 for blue cards, this 150-card set is parallel to the regular Select Series 1 set. The difference is found in the fractured gold foil treatment which replaces the silver foil treatment of the regular set.

Nm-Mt Ex-Mt
*STARS: 1.25X TO 3X BASIC CARDS .

1997 Select Rookie Autographs

This four-card set features color player photos of potential Rookie of the Year candidates with their autographs. Each player signed 3000 cards except for Andruw Jones who only signed 2500.

Nm-Mt Ex-Mt
1 Jose Guillen 15.00 4.50
2 Wilton Guerrero 8.00 2.40
3 Andruw Jones 25.00 7.50
4 Todd Walker 15.00 4.50

1997 Select Rookie Revolution

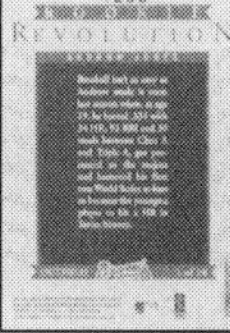

Randomly inserted in packs at a rate of one in 56, this 20-card set features color photos of top rookies on a micro-etched, full mylar card.

Nm-Mt Ex-Mt
COMPLETE SET (20) 100.00 30.00
1 Andruw Jones 3.00 .90
2 Derek Jeter 15.00 4.50
3 Todd Hollandsworth 2.00 .60
4 Edgar Renteria 3.00 .90
5 Jason Kendall 3.00 .90
6 Rey Ordonez 2.00 .60
7 F.P. Santangelo 2.00 .60
8 Jermaine Dye 3.00 .90
9 Alex Ochoa 2.00 .60
10 Vladimir Guererro 6.00 1.80
11 Dmitri Young 3.00 .90
12 Todd Walker 3.00 .90
13 Scott Rolen 5.00 1.50
14 Nomar Garciaparra 10.00 3.00
15 Ruben Rivera 2.00 .60
16 Darin Erstad 3.00 .90
17 Todd Greene 2.00 .60
18 Mariano Rivera 5.00 1.50
19 Trey Beamon 2.00 .60
20 Karim Garcia 2.00 .60

1997 Select Tools of the Trade

Randomly inserted in packs at a rate of one in nine, this 25-card set matches color photos of 25 young players with 25 veteran superstars printed back-to-back on a double-fronted full silver foil card stock with gold foil stamping.

Nm-Mt Ex-Mt
COMPLETE SET (25) 120.00 36.00
*MIRROR BLUE: 2X TO 5X BASIC MIRROR
MIRROR BLUE STATED ODDS 1:240..
1 Ken Griffey Jr. 6.00 1.80
Andruw Jones
2 Greg Maddux 6.00 1.80

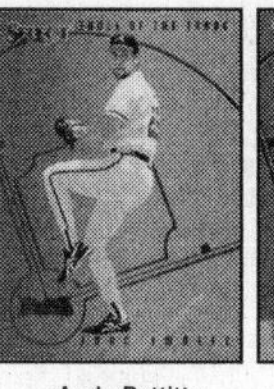

Andy Pettitte
3 Cal Ripken 8.00 2.40
Chipper Jones
4 Mike Piazza 6.00 1.80
Jason Kendall
5 Albert Belle 1.25 .35
Karim Garcia
6 Mo Vaughn 1.25 .35
Dmitri Young
7 Juan Gonzalez 3.00 .90
Vladimir Guerrero
8 Tony Gwynn 5.00 1.50
Jermaine Dye
9 Barry Bonds 10.00 3.00
Alex Ochoa
10 Jeff Bagwell 3.00 .90
Jason Giambi
11 Kenny Lofton 1.25 .35
Darin Erstad
12 Gary Sheffield 1.25 .35
Manny Ramirez
13 Tim Salmon 2.00 .60
Todd Hollandsworth
14 Sammy Sosa 6.00 1.80
Ruben Rivera
15 Paul Molitor 2.00 .60
George Arias
16 Jim Thome 3.00 .90
Todd Walker
17 Wade Boggs 2.00 .60
Scott Rolen
18 Ryne Sandberg 6.00 1.80
Chuck Knoblauch
19 Mark McGwire 8.00 2.40
Frank Thomas
20 Ivan Rodriguez 3.00 .90
Charles Johnson
21 Brian Jordan 1.25 .35
Rusty Greer
22 Roger Clemens 8.00 2.40
Troy Percival
23 John Smoltz 3.00 .90
Mike Mussina
24 Alex Rodriguez 6.00 1.80
Rey Ordonez
25 Derek Jeter 8.00 2.40
Nomar Garciaparra

2002 Select Rookies and Prospects

These cards were issued as part of special "retail" promotions late in 2002. All of these cards featured Donruss/Playoff "band-aid" autographs and the cards feature the return of the Select trading line. Please note that this set is sequenced in alphabetical order by first name. The blue autograph versions are believed to be much tougher, we can use any help gathering information as to which players signed in both blue and black ink. Card number 59 is not believed to exist. We'd like to thank Bruce DeVlieger for his generous help in compiling this checklist for our use.

Nm-Mt Ex-Mt
COMPLETE SET 500.00 150.00
1 Abraham Nunez 5.00 1.50
2 Adam Bernero 5.00 1.50
3 Adam Pettyjohn 5.00 1.50
4 Alex Escobar 5.00 1.50
5 Allan Simpson 5.00 1.50
6 Andres Torres 5.00 1.50
7 Andy Pratt 5.00 1.50
8 Bert Snow 5.00 1.50
Black Aut
8A Bert Snow 5.00 1.50
Blue Autograph
9 Bill Ortega 5.00 1.50
10 Billy Sylvester 5.00 1.50
11 Brad Voyles 5.00 1.50
12 Brandon Backe 5.00 1.50
13 Brent Abernathy 5.00 1.50
14 Brian Mallette 5.00 1.50
15 Brian Rogers 5.00 1.50
16 Cam Esslinger 5.00 1.50
17 Carlos Garcia 5.00 1.50
18 Carlos Valderrama 5.00 1.50
19 Cesar Izturis 5.00 1.50
20 Chad Durbin 5.00 1.50
21 Chris Baker 5.00 1.50
22 Claudio Vargas 5.00 1.50
23 Cory Aldridge 5.00 1.50
24 Craig Monroe 6.00 1.80
25 David Elder 5.00 1.50
26 David Brous 5.00 1.50
27 David Espinosa 5.00 1.50
28 Derrick Lewis 5.00 1.50
29 Elio Serrano 5.00 1.50
30 Elpidio Guzman 5.00 1.50
31 Eric Cyr 5.00 1.50
32 Eric Valent 5.00 1.50
33 Erik Bedard 10.00 3.00
34 Esix Snead 5.00 1.50
35 Francis Beltran 5.00 1.50
36 George Perez 5.00 1.50
37 Gene Altman 5.00 1.50
38 Greg Miller 5.00 1.50
39 Horacio Ramirez 5.00 1.50
40 Jason Hart 5.00 1.50
41 Jason Karnuth 5.00 1.50
42 Jason Romano 5.00 1.50
43 Jeff Deardorff 5.00 1.50
44 Jeremy Affeldt 6.00 1.80
45 Jeremy Lambert 5.00 1.50
46 John Ennis 5.00 1.50
47 John Grabow 5.00 1.50
48 Jose Cueto 5.00 1.50
49 Jose Mieses 5.00 1.50
50 Jose Ortiz 6.00 1.80
51 Josh Pearce 5.00 1.50
52 Josue Perez 5.00 1.50
53 Juan Diaz 5.00 1.50
54 Juan Pena 5.00 1.50
55 Keith Ginter 6.00 1.80
56 Kevin Frederick 5.00 1.50
57 Kevin Joseph 5.00 1.50
58 Kevin Olsen 5.00 1.50
60 Kris Keller 5.00 1.50
61 Larry Bigbie 8.00 2.40
62 Les Walrond 5.00 1.50
63 Luis Pineda 5.00 1.50
64 Luis Rivas 5.00 1.50
65 Luis Rivera 5.00 1.50
66 Luke Hudson 5.00 1.50
67 Marcus Giles 10.00 3.00
68 Mark Ellis 5.00 1.50
69 Martin Vargas 5.00 1.50
70 Matt Childers 5.00 1.50
71 Matt Guerrier 5.00 1.50
72 Matt Thornton 5.00 1.50
73 Matt White 5.00 1.50
74 Mike Penney 5.00 1.50
75 Nate Teut 5.00 1.50
76 Nick Maness 5.00 1.50
77 Orlando Woodards 5.00 1.50
78 Paul Phillips 5.00 1.50
79 Pedro Feliz 6.00 1.80
80 Ramon Vazquez 5.00 1.50
81 Raul Chavez 5.00 1.50
82 Reed Johnson 5.00 1.50
83 Ryan Freel 5.00 1.50
84 Ryan Jamison 5.00 1.50
85 Ryan Ludwick 5.00 1.50
86 Saul Rivera 5.00 1.50
87 Steve Bechler 8.00 2.40
88 Steve Green 5.00 1.50
89 Steve Smyth 5.00 1.50
90 Tike Redman 5.00 1.50
91 Tom Shearn 5.00 1.50
92 Tomas De La Rosa 5.00 1.50
93 Tony Cogan 5.00 1.50
94 Travis Hafner 6.00 1.80
95 Travis Hughes 5.00 1.50
96 Wilkin Ruan 5.00 1.50
97 Will Ohman 5.00 1.50
98 Wilmy Caceras 5.00 1.50
99 Wilson Guzman 5.00 1.50
100 Winston Abreu 5.00 1.50

1995 Select Certified Samples

This eight-card set was issued to preview the premier edition of the Select Certified series. This hobby-only issue is distinguished by 24-point cardstock, a metallic sheen, and double lamination. The cards have the word "SAMPLE" stamped diagonally across both sides.

Nm-Mt Ex-Mt
COMPLETE SET (8) 20.00 6.00
2 Reggie Sanders .50 .15
3 Cal Ripken 10.00 3.00
Gold Team
10 Mo Vaughn .50 .15
39 Mike Piazza 6.00 1.80
50 Mark McGwire 8.00 2.40
75 Roberto Alomar 1.25 .35
89 Larry Walker .50 .15
110 Ray Durham .75 .23

1995 Select Certified

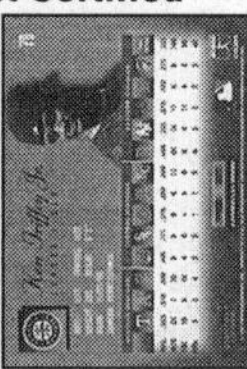

This 135-card standard-size set was issued through hobby outlets only. This product was issued in six-card packs. The cards are made with 24-point stock and are all metallic and double laminated. Rookie Cards in this set include Bobby Higginson and Hideo Nomo. Card number 18 was never printed; Cal Ripken is featured on a special card numbered 2131, which is included in the complete set of 135.

Nm-Mt Ex-Mt
COMPLETE SET (135) 40.00 12.00
1 Barry Bonds 3.00 .90
2 Reggie Sanders .50 .15
3 Terry Steinbach .25 .07
4 Eduardo Perez .25 .07
5 Frank Thomas 1.25 .35
6 Wil Cordero .25 .07
7 John Olerud .50 .15
8 Deion Sanders .75 .23
9 Mike Mussina 1.25 .35
10 Mo Vaughn .50 .15
11 Will Clark 1.25 .35
12 Chili Davis .50 .15
13 Jimmy Key .50 .15
14 Eddie Murray 1.25 .35
15 Bernard Gilkey .25 .07
16 David Cone .50 .15
17 Tim Salmon .75 .23
19 Steve Ontiveros .25 .07
20 Andres Galarraga .50 .15
21 Don Mattingly 3.00 .90
22 Kevin Appier .50 .15
23 Paul Molitor .75 .23
24 Edgar Martinez .75 .23
25 Andy Benes .25 .07
26 Rafael Palmeiro .75 .23
27 Barry Larkin 1.25 .35
28 Gary Sheffield .50 .15
29 Wally Joyner .50 .15
30 Wade Boggs .75 .23
31 Rico Brogna .25 .07
32 Eddie Murray .75 .23
3000th Hit
33 Kirby Puckett 1.25 .35
34 Bobby Bonilla .50 .15
35 Hal Morris .25 .07
36 Moises Alou .50 .15
37 Javier Lopez .50 .15
38 Chuck Knoblauch .50 .15
39 Mike Piazza 2.00 .60
40 Travis Fryman .50 .15
41 Rickey Henderson 1.25 .35
42 Jim Thome 1.25 .35
43 Carlos Baerga .25 .07
44 Dean Palmer .50 .15
45 Kirk Gibson .50 .15
46 Bret Saberhagen .50 .15
47 Cecil Fielder .50 .15
48 Manny Ramirez .50 .15
49 Derek Bell .25 .07
50 Mark McGwire 3.00 .90
51 Jim Edmonds .50 .15
52 Robin Ventura .50 .15
53 Ryan Klesko .50 .15
54 Jeff Bagwell .75 .23
55 Ozzie Smith 2.00 .60
56 Albert Belle .50 .15
57 Darren Daulton .50 .15
58 Jeff Conine .50 .15
59 Greg Maddux 2.00 .60
60 Lenny Dykstra .50 .15
61 Randy Johnson 1.25 .35
62 Fred McGriff .75 .23
63 Ray Lankford .25 .07
64 David Justice .50 .15
65 Paul O'Neill .75 .23
66 Tony Gwynn 1.50 .45
67 Matt Williams .50 .15
68 Dante Bichette .50 .15
69 Craig Biggio .75 .23
70 Ken Griffey Jr. 2.00 .60
71 J.T. Snow .50 .15
72 Cal Ripken 4.00 1.20
73 Jay Bell .50 .15
74 Joe Carter .50 .15
75 Roberto Alomar 1.25 .35
76 Benji Gil .25 .07
77 Ivan Rodriguez 1.25 .35
78 Raul Mondesi .50 .15
79 Cliff Floyd .50 .15
80 Eric Karros 1.25 .35
Mike Piazza
Raul Mondesi
81 Royce Clayton .25 .07
82 Billy Ashley .25 .07
83 Joey Hamilton .25 .07
84 Sammy Sosa 2.00 .60
85 Jason Bere .25 .07
86 Dennis Martinez .50 .15
87 Greg Vaughn .50 .15
88 Roger Clemens 2.50 .75
89 Larry Walker .75 .23
90 Mark Grace .75 .23
91 Kenny Lofton .50 .15
92 Carlos Perez RC .50 .15
93 Roger Cedeno .25 .07
94 Scott Ruffcorn .25 .07
95 Jim Pittsley .25 .07
96 Andy Pettitte .75 .23
97 James Baldwin .25 .07
98 Hideo Nomo RC 3.00 .90
99 Ismael Valdes .25 .07
100 Armando Benitez .50 .15
101 Jose Malave .25 .07
102 Bob Higginson RC 1.25 .35
103 LaTroy Hawkins .25 .07
104 Russ Davis .25 .07
105 Shawn Green .50 .15
106 Joe Vitiello .25 .07
107 Chipper Jones 1.25 .35
108 Shane Andrews .25 .07
109 Jose Oliva .25 .07
110 Ray Durham .50 .15
111 Jon Nunnally .25 .07
112 Alex Gonzalez .25 .07
113 Vaughn Eshelman .25 .07
114 Marty Cordova .25 .07
115 Mark Grudzielanek RC .75 .23
116 Brian L.Hunter .25 .07
117 Charles Johnson .50 .15
118 Alex Rodriguez 3.00 .90
119 David Bell .25 .07
120 Todd Hollandsworth .25 .07
121 Joe Randa .25 .07
122 Derek Jeter 3.00 .90
123 Frank Rodriguez .25 .07
124 Curtis Goodwin .25 .07
125 Bill Pulsipher .25 .07
126 John Mabry .25 .07
127 Julian Tavarez .25 .07
128 Edgardo Alfonzo .50 .15
129 Orlando Miller .25 .07
130 Juan Acevedo RC .25 .07
131 Jeff Cirillo .25 .07
132 Roberto Petagine .25 .07
133 Antonio Osuna .25 .07
134 Michael Tucker .25 .07
135 Garret Anderson .50 .15
2131 Cal Ripken TRIB 4.00 1.20

1995 Select Certified Mirror Gold

This 135-card set is a parallel to the regular issue. Pinnacle used their all-holographic foil technology on the fronts. The backs are identical to the regular issue but the words "Mirror Gold" are in the middle. These cards were inserted approximately one every five packs.

Nm-Mt Ex-Mt
*STARS: 4X TO 10X BASIC CARDS ....
*ROOKIES: 5X TO 12X BASIC.........

1995 Select Certified Checklists

This seven-card standard-size set was inserted one per Select Certified pack. These cards were not made of the same card stock as the regular Certified cards.

Nm-Mt Ex-Mt
COMPLETE SET (7) 3.00 .90
1 Ken Griffey Jr. .50 .15
2 Frank Thomas .30 .09
3 Cal Ripken 1.00 .30
4 Jeff Bagwell .20 .06
5 Mike Piazza .50 .15
6 Barry Bonds .75 .23
7 Manny Ramirez .15 .04
Raul Mondesi

1995 Select Certified Future

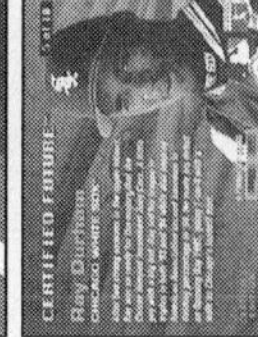

This ten-card set was inserted approximately one in every 19 packs. Ten leading 1995 rookie players are included in this set. These cards were produced using Pinnacle's Dufex technology.

Nm-Mt Ex-Mt
COMPLETE SET (10) 40.00 12.00
1 Chipper Jones 5.00 1.50
2 Curtis Goodwin 1.00 .30
3 Hideo Nomo 6.00 1.80
4 Shawn Green 2.00 .60
5 Ray Durham 2.00 .60
6 Todd Hollandsworth 1.00 .30
7 Brian L.Hunter 1.00 .30
8 Carlos Delgado 2.00 .60
9 Michael Tucker UER 1.00 .30
(Front photo is Jon Nunnally)
10 Alex Rodriguez 12.00 3.60

1995 Select Certified Gold Team

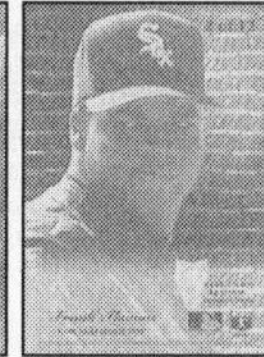

This 12-card was inserted approximately one in every 41 packs. This set features some of the leading players in baseball. These cards feature double-sided all-gold-foil Dufex technology.

Nm-Mt Ex-Mt
COMPLETE SET (12) 200.00 60.00
1 Ken Griffey Jr. 20.00 6.00
2 Frank Thomas 12.00 3.60
3 Cal Ripken 40.00 12.00
4 Jeff Bagwell 8.00 2.40
5 Mike Piazza 20.00 6.00
6 Barry Bonds 30.00 9.00
7 Matt Williams 5.00 1.50
8 Don Mattingly 30.00 9.00
9 Will Clark 12.00 3.60
10 Tony Gwynn 15.00 4.50
11 Kirby Puckett 12.00 3.60
12 Jose Canseco 12.00 3.60

1995 Select Certified Potential Unlimited 1975

Cards from this 20-card set were randomly inserted into one in every 29 packs. The cards feature Pinnacle's all-foil Dufex printing technology. Only 1,975 sets were made and each card is numbered 1 of 1,975 at the bottom right.

Nm-Mt Ex-Mt
COMPLETE SET (20) 120.00 36.00
*903 CARDS: .6X TO 1.5X 1975 CARDS
ONE 903 CARD PER SEALED BOX......
STATED PRINT RUN 903 SETS..........
1 Cliff Floyd 4.00 1.20

2 Manny Ramirez 4.00 1.20
3 Raul Mondesi 4.00 1.20
4 Scott Ruffcorn 4.00 1.20
5 Billy Ashley 4.00 1.20
6 Alex Gonzalez 4.00 1.20
7 Midre Cummings 4.00 1.20
8 Charles Johnson 4.00 1.20
9 Garret Anderson 4.00 1.20
10 Hideo Nomo 15.00 4.50
11 Chipper Jones 10.00 3.00
12 Curtis Goodwin 4.00 1.20
13 Frank Rodriguez 4.00 1.20
14 Shawn Green 4.00 1.20
15 Ray Durham 4.00 1.20
16 Todd Hollandsworth 4.00 1.20
17 Brian L.Hunter 4.00 1.20
18 Carlos Delgado 4.00 1.20
19 Michael Tucker 4.00 1.20
20 Alex Rodriguez 30.00 9.00

1996 Select Certified

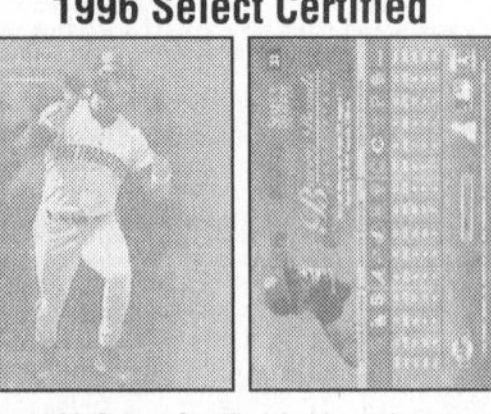

The 1996 Select Certified hobby only set was issued in one series totalling 144 cards. Each six-card pack carried a suggested retail price of $4.99. Printed on special 24-point silver mirror mylar card stock, the fronts feature a color player photo on a gray and black background. The backs carry another color player photo with information about his playing abilities.

Nm-Mt Ex-Mt
COMPLETE SET (144) 40.00 12.00
1 Frank Thomas 1.00 .30
2 Tino Martinez .60 .18
3 Gary Sheffield .40 .12
4 Kenny Lofton .40 .12
5 Joe Carter .40 .12
6 Alex Rodriguez 2.00 .60
7 Chipper Jones 1.00 .30
8 Roger Clemens 2.00 .60
9 Jay Bell .40 .12
10 Eddie Murray 1.00 .30
11 Will Clark 1.00 .30
12 Mike Mussina 1.00 .30
13 Hideo Nomo 1.00 .30
14 Andres Galarraga .40 .12
15 Marc Newfield .25 .07
16 Jason Isringhausen .40 .12
17 Randy Johnson 1.00 .30
18 Chuck Knoblauch .40 .12
19 J.T. Snow .40 .12
20 Mark McGwire 2.50 .75
21 Tony Gwynn 1.25 .35
22 Albert Belle .40 .12
23 Gregg Jefferies .25 .07
24 Reggie Sanders .40 .12
25 Bernie Williams .60 .18
26 Ray Lankford .25 .07
27 Johnny Damon .40 .12
28 Ryne Sandberg 1.50 .45
29 Rondell White .40 .12
30 Mike Piazza 1.50 .45
31 Barry Bonds 2.50 .75
32 Greg Maddux 1.50 .45
33 Craig Biggio .60 .18
34 John Valentin .25 .07
35 Ivan Rodriguez 1.00 .30
36 Rico Brogna .25 .07
37 Tim Salmon .60 .18
38 Sterling Hitchcock .25 .07
39 Charles Johnson .40 .12
40 Travis Fryman .40 .12
41 Barry Larkin 1.00 .30
42 Tom Glavine .60 .18
43 Marty Cordova .25 .07
44 Shawn Green .40 .12
45 Ben McDonald .25 .07
46 Robin Ventura .40 .12
47 Ken Griffey Jr. 1.50 .45
48 Orlando Merced .25 .07
49 Paul O'Neill .60 .18
50 Ozzie Smith 1.50 .45
51 Manny Ramirez .40 .12
52 Ismael Valdes .25 .07
53 Cal Ripken 3.00 .90
54 Jeff Bagwell .60 .18
55 Greg Vaughn .40 .12
56 Juan Gonzalez 1.00 .30
57 Raul Mondesi .40 .12
58 Carlos Baerga .25 .07
59 Sammy Sosa 1.50 .45
60 Mike Kelly .25 .07
61 Edgar Martinez .60 .18
62 Kirby Puckett 1.00 .30
63 Cecil Fielder .40 .12
64 David Cone .40 .12
65 Moises Alou .40 .12
66 Fred McGriff .60 .18
67 Mo Vaughn .40 .12
68 Edgardo Alfonzo .40 .12
69 Jim Thome 1.00 .30
70 Rickey Henderson 1.00 .30
71 Dante Bichette .40 .12
72 Lenny Dykstra .40 .12
73 Benji Gil .25 .07
74 Wade Boggs .60 .18
75 Jim Edmonds .40 .12
76 Michael Tucker .25 .07
77 Carlos Delgado .40 .12
78 Butch Huskey .25 .07
79 Billy Ashley .25 .07
80 Dean Palmer .40 .12
81 Paul Molitor .60 .18
82 Ryan Klesko .40 .12
83 Brian L.Hunter .25 .07
84 Jay Buhner .40 .12
85 Larry Walker .60 .18
86 Mike Bordick .25 .07
87 Matt Williams .40 .12
88 Jack McDowell .25 .07
89 Hal Morris .25 .07
90 Brian Jordan .40 .12
91 Andy Pettitte .60 .18
92 Melvin Nieves .25 .07
93 Pedro Martinez 1.00 .30
94 Mark Grace .60 .18
95 Garret Anderson .40 .12
96 Andre Dawson .40 .12
97 Ray Durham .40 .12
98 Jose Canseco 1.00 .30
99 Roberto Alomar 1.00 .30
100 Derek Jeter 2.50 .75
101 Alan Benes .25 .07
102 Karim Garcia .25 .07
103 Robin Jennings .25 .07
104 Bob Abreu .40 .12
105 Sal Fasano UER .25 .07
(name on front is Livan Hernandez)
105A Sal Fasano
Correct Name on Front of Card
106 Steve Gibralter .25 .07
107 Jermaine Dye .40 .12
108 Jason Kendall .40 .12
109 Mike Grace RC .25 .07
110 Jason Schmidt .40 .12
111 Paul Wilson .25 .07
112 Rey Ordonez .25 .07
113 Wilton Guerrero RC .40 .12
114 Brooks Kieschnick .25 .07
115 George Arias .25 .07
116 O.Fernandez RC .25 .07
117 Todd Hollandsworth .25 .07
118 John Wasdin .25 .07
119 Eric Owens .25 .07
120 Chan Ho Park .40 .12
121 Mark Loretta .25 .07
122 Richard Hidalgo .40 .12
123 Jeff Suppan .25 .07
124 Jim Pittsley .25 .07
125 LaTroy Hawkins .25 .07
126 Chris Snopek .25 .07
127 Justin Thompson .25 .07
128 Jay Powell .25 .07
129 Alex Ochoa .25 .07
130 Felipe Crespo .25 .07
131 Matt Lawton RC .40 .12
132 Jimmy Haynes .25 .07
133 Terrell Wade .25 .07
134 Ruben Rivera .25 .07
135 Frank Thomas PP .60 .18
136 Ken Griffey Jr. PP 1.00 .30
137 Greg Maddux PP 1.00 .30
138 Mike Piazza PP 1.00 .30
139 Cal Ripken PP 1.50 .45
140 Albert Belle PP .40 .12
141 Mo Vaughn PP .25 .07
142 Chipper Jones PP .60 .18
143 Hideo Nomo PP .60 .18
144 Ryan Klesko PP .25 .07

1996 Select Certified Artist's Proofs

Randomly inserted in packs at a rate of one in 18, this 144-card set is parallel to the base set with only 500 sets being produced. The design is similar to the regular set with the exception of a holographic gold foil Artist's proof stamp on the front.

Nm-Mt Ex-Mt
*STARS: 2.5X TO 6X BASIC CARDS ...

1996 Select Certified Certified Blue

Randomly inserted in packs at a rate of one in 50, this 144-card set is parallel to the base set with only 180 sets being produced. This set is a blue all-foil rendition of the base set.

Nm-Mt Ex-Mt
*STARS: 5X TO 12X BASIC CARDS ....
*ROOKIES: 2.5X TO 6X BASIC CARDS

1996 Select Certified Certified Red

Randomly inserted in packs at a rate of one in five, this 144-card set is parallel to the base set with only 1,800 sets being produced. This set is a red all-foil rendition of the base set.

Nm-Mt Ex-Mt
*STARS: 1X TO 2.5X BASIC CARDS ...

1996 Select Certified Mirror Blue

Randomly inserted in packs at a rate of one in 200, this 144-card set is parallel to the base set with only 45 sets being produced. This set is a blue holographic foil rendition of the base set. No set price has been provided due to scarcity.

Nm-Mt Ex-Mt
*STARS: 20X TO 50X BASIC CARDS
*PP STARS 135-144: 15X TO 40X BASIC
*ROOKIES: 10X TO 25X BASIC..........

1996 Select Certified Mirror Gold

Randomly inserted in packs at a rate of one in 300, this 144-card set is parallel to the base set with only 30 sets being produced. This set is a gold holographic foil rendition of the base set. No set price has been provided due to scarcity.

Nm-Mt Ex-Mt
*STARS: 75X TO 150X BASIC CARDS
*PP STARS 135-144: 75X TO 150X BASIC
*ROOKIES: 40X TO 80X BASIC CARDS

1996 Select Certified Mirror Red

Randomly inserted in packs at a rate of one in 100, this 144-card set is parallel to the base set with only 90 sets being produced. This set is a red holographic foil rendition of the base set. No set price has been provided due to scarcity.

Nm-Mt Ex-Mt
*STARS: 12.5X TO 30X BASIC CARDS
*ROOKIES: 6X TO 15X BASIC CARDS

1996 Select Certified Interleague Preview

Randomly inserted in packs at a rate of one in 42, this 25-card set gets ready for the start of interleague play in the 1997 season. Printed on Silver Prime Frost foil stock with gold lettering, the fronts feature color player cutouts of two opposing players. The backs carry another color cutout of the two players with information as to why they are a great matchup.

Nm-Mt Ex-Mt
COMPLETE SET (25) 200.00 60.00
1 Ken Griffey Jr. 8.00 2.40
Hideo Nomo
2 Greg Maddux 8.00 2.40
Mo Vaughn
3 Frank Thomas 8.00 2.40
Sammy Sosa
4 Mike Piazza 8.00 2.40
Jim Edmonds
5 Ryan Klesko 10.00 3.00
Roger Clemens
6 Derek Jeter 12.00 3.60
Rey Ordonez
7 Johnny Damon 2.00 .60
Ray Lankford
8 Manny Ramirez 2.00 .60
Reggie Sanders
9 Barry Bonds 12.00 3.60
Jay Buhner
10 Jason Isringhausen 3.00 .90
Wade Boggs
11 David Cone 5.00 1.50
Chipper Jones
12 Jeff Bagwell 3.00 .90
Will Clark
13 Tony Gwynn 6.00 1.80
Randy Johnson
14 Cal Ripken 15.00 4.50
Tom Glavine
15 Kirby Puckett 5.00 1.50
Andy Benes
16 Gary Sheffield 5.00 1.50
Mike Mussina
17 Raul Mondesi 3.00 .90
Tim Salmon
18 Rondell White 2.00 .60
Carlos Delgado
19 Cecil Fielder 8.00 2.40
Ryne Sandberg
20 Kenny Lofton 2.00 .60
Brian L.Hunter
21 Paul Wilson 3.00 .90
Paul O'Neill
22 Ismael Valdes 3.00 .90
Edgar Martinez
23 Matt Williams 12.00 3.60
Mark McGwire
24 Albert Belle 5.00 1.50
Barry Larkin
25 Brady Anderson 2.00 .60
Marquis Grissom
S7 Johnny Damon
Ray Lankford SAMPLE

1996 Select Certified Select Few

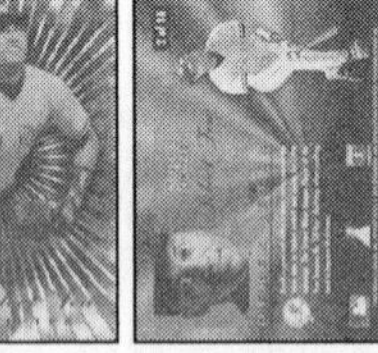

Randomly inserted in packs at a rate of one in 60, this 18-card set honors superstar athletes with unmatched playing field talents. Utilizing the all-new Dot Matrix hologram technology, the fronts feature color action player cutouts. Several of the cards were erroneously printed without player's name on the front. These uncorrected errors are worth the same as the corrected cards.

Nm-Mt Ex-Mt
COMPLETE SET (18) 100.00 30.00
1 Sammy Sosa 8.00 2.40
2 Derek Jeter 12.00 3.60
3 Ken Griffey Jr. 8.00 2.40
4 Albert Belle 2.00 .60
5 Cal Ripken 15.00 4.50
6 Greg Maddux 8.00 2.40
7 Frank Thomas 5.00 1.50
8 Mo Vaughn 2.00 .60
9 Chipper Jones 5.00 1.50
10 Mike Piazza 8.00 2.40
11 Ryan Klesko 2.00 .60
12 Hideo Nomo 5.00 1.50
13 Alan Benes 1.25 .35
14 Manny Ramirez 2.00 .60
15 Gary Sheffield 2.00 .60
16 Barry Bonds 12.00 3.60
17 Matt Williams 2.00 .60
18 Johnny Damon 2.00 .60

1894 Senators Cabinets Bell

These cabinets feature members of the 19th century Washington Senators and were produced at the Bell Studio on Pennsylvania Avenue. These cabinets feature mainly players in uniform but a couple of players are posed in suit and tie. Since these cabinets are unnumbered, we have sequenced them in alphabetical order.

Ex-Mt VG
COMPLETE SET 12000.00 6000.00
1 Charles Abbey 1500.00 750.00
2 Ed Cartwright 1500.00 750.00
3 Dan Dugdale 1500.00 750.00
4 Jim McGuire 1500.00 750.00
5 Tim O'Rourke 1500.00 750.00
6 Al Selbach 1500.00 750.00
7 Otis Stocksdale 1500.00 750.00
8 Mike Sullivan 1500.00 750.00
9 George Tebeau 1500.00 750.00
10 Frank Ward 1500.00 750.00

1909 Senators Barr-Farnham Postcards

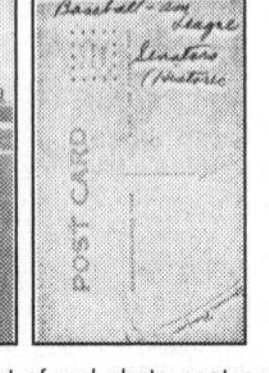

This extremely rare set of real photo postcards was produced by Barr-Farnham Picture Postcards Co. located in Washington, DC in 1909. Ten cards have been positively identified but there are undoubtedly others, probably every member of the team. There is a strong possibility there is a team postcard as well. All additions to this checklist are greatly appreciated. All views show a full body close up of the player taken on the outfield grass with the ball park in the background.

Ex-Mt VG
COMPLETE SET (10) 1500.00 750.00
1 Otis Clymer 200.00 100.00
2 Wid Conroy 200.00 100.00
3 Bob Ganley 200.00 100.00
4 Dolly Gray 200.00 100.00
5 Bob Groom 200.00 100.00
6 Walter Johnson 800.00 400.00
7 George McBride 200.00 100.00
8 Charlie Smith 200.00 100.00
9 Jesse Tannehill 200.00 100.00
10 Bob Unglaub 200.00 100.00

1912 Senators National Photo Company

The National Photo Company located in Washington, DC published a rare set of real photo postcards. The Postcards were also titled "The Climbers" and was probably produced in 1912 when the Senators climbed to second place from a seventh place finish the season before. The two known players are all time great pitcher Walter Johnson and fleet outfielder Clyde Milan. Both players had superb seasons in 1912. There might be other players in this set so additions to the checklist are appreciated.

Ex-Mt VG
COMPLETE SET (2) 700.00 350.00
1 Walter Johnson 600.00 300.00
2 Clyde Milan 200.00 100.00

1925 Senators Holland Creameries

These 18 cards, which feature members of the Washington Senators, were issued in Canada by an ice cream company. These cards, which measure approximately 1 1/2" by 3", feature the players photo and his position on the front and the back describes the prize is all 18 cards are returned. Roger Peckinpaugh, number 16, is believed to have been deliberately short printed to make winning the prize extremely hard.

Ex-Mt VG
COMPLETE SET (18) 3000.00 1500.00
COMMON CARD (1-18) 100.00 50.00
COMMON SP
1 Ralph Miller 100.00 50.00
2 Earl McNeely 100.00 50.00
3 Allan Russell 100.00 50.00
4 Ernest Shirley 100.00 50.00
5 Sam Rice 250.00 125.00
6 Muddy Ruel 100.00 50.00
7 Ossie Bluege 150.00 75.00
8 Nemo Leibold 100.00 50.00
9 Paul Zahniser 100.00 50.00
10 Firpo Marberry 150.00 75.00
11 Warren Ogden 100.00 50.00
12 George Mogridge 100.00 50.00
13 Tom Zachary 100.00 50.00
14 Goose Goslin 250.00 125.00
15 Joe Judge 150.00 75.00
16 Roger Peckinpaugh SP 400.00
17 Bucky Harris 250.00 125.00
18 Walter Johnson 800.00 400.00

1925 Senators Oakland Tribune

This one-card set measures approximately 3" by 4 3/4" and was issued to commemorate the Washington Senators 1924 Series victory. The card features a blue tinted photo of Walter Johnson who was close to purchasing the Oakland minor league team at the time.

Ex-Mt VG
1 Walter Johnson 1000.00 500.00

1931 Senators Team Issue Photos W-UNC

This 30-card team set of the Washington Senators measures approximately 6 1/8" by 9 3/8" and features sepia-toned player photos printed on thin paper stock. The backs are blank. The cards are unnumbered and checklisted below in alphabetical order.

Ex-Mt VG
COMPLETE SET (30) 250.00 125.00
1 Nick Altrock CO 6.00 3.00
2 Oswald Bluege 8.00 4.00
3 Cliff Bolton 5.00 2.50
4 Lloyd Brown 5.00 2.50
5 Robert Burke 5.00 2.50
6 Joe Cronin 20.00 10.00
7 Alvin Crowder 5.00 2.50
8 E.B. Eynon Jr. 5.00 2.50
9 Charles Fischer 5.00 2.50
10 Edward Gharrity 5.00 2.50
11 Clark Griffith OWN 20.00 10.00
12 Irving Hadley 5.00 2.50
13 William Hargrave 5.00 2.50
14 David Harris 5.00 2.50
15 Jack Hayes 5.00 2.50
16 Walter Johnson MG 80.00 40.00
17 Sam Jones 6.00 3.00
18 Baxter Jordan 5.00 2.50
19 Joe Judge 5.00 2.50
20 Joe Kuhel 5.00 2.50
21 Henry Manush 10.00 5.00
22 Fred Marberry 6.00 3.00
23 Mike Martin 5.00 2.50
24 Walter Masters 5.00 2.50
25 Charles Myer 6.00 3.00
26 Harry Rice 5.00 2.50
27 Sam Rice 20.00 10.00
28 Al Schacht CO 10.00 5.00
29 Ray Spencer 5.00 2.50
30 Sam West 5.00 2.50

1947 Senators Gunther Beer PC

These postcards usually featuring two players on the front were issued around 1947-48 based on the players in the set. The cards feature the players photos on the front along with their names in big bold black letters on the bottom. The backs have room for messages to be sent, usually from the Senators annoucer of the time, Arch MacDonald. This listing may be incomplete so additions are welcome.

Ex-Mt VG
COMPLETE SET (11) 750.00 375.00
1 Joe Kuhel 80.00 40.00
2 Al Evans 80.00 40.00
Scott Cary
3 Tom Ferrick 80.00 40.00
Harold Keller
4 Mickey Haefner 80.00 40.00
Forrest Thompson
5 Sid Hudson 80.00 40.00
Al Kozar
6 Walter Masterson 100.00 50.00
Rick Ferrell
7 Tom McBride 80.00 40.00
Milo Candini
8 Marino Pieretti 80.00 40.00
Leon Culberson
9 Sherrard Robertson 80.00 40.00
Eddie Lyons
10 Ray Scarborough 80.00 40.00
Kenneth McCreight
11 Mickey Vernon 100.00 50.00
Gil Coan

1958 Senators Jay Publishing

This 12-card set of the Washington Senators measures approximately 5" by 7" and features black-and-white player photos in a white border. These cards were packaged 12 to a packet. The backs are blank. The cards are unnumbered and checklisted below in alphabetical order.

NM Ex
COMPLETE SET (12) 40.00 20.00
1 Rocky Bridges 4.00 2.00
2 Truman Clevenger 3.00 1.50
3 Clint Courtney 3.00 1.50
4 Dick Hyde 3.00 1.50
5 Cookie Lavagetto MG 4.00 2.00
6 Jim Lemon 3.00 1.50
7 Camilo Pascual 5.00 2.50
8 Albie Pearson 4.00 2.00
9 Herb Plews 3.00 1.50
10 Pedro Ramos 3.00 1.50
11 Roy Sievers 4.00 2.00
12 Eddie Yost 4.00 2.00

1958 Senators Team Issue

This 29-card set of the Washington Senators measures approximately 4" by 5" and features black-and-white player photos in a white border with a facsimile autograph printed on the front. These cards were originally sold through the mail by the club for 10 cents each. The cards are unnumbered and checklisted below in alphabetical order.

NM Ex
COMPLETE SET (29) 150.00 75.00
1 Ozzie Alvarez 5.00 2.50

2 Ken Aspromonte	5.00	2.50
3 Boom-Boom Beck CO	5.00	2.50
4 Julio Becquer	5.00	2.50
5 Rocky Bridges	6.00	3.00
6 Neil Chrisley	5.00	2.50
7 Ellis Clary CO	5.00	2.50
8 Truman Clevenger	5.00	2.50
9 Clint Courtney	5.00	2.50
10 Ed Fitzgerald	5.00	2.50
11 Hal Griggs	5.00	2.50
12 Dick Hyde	5.00	2.50
13 Walter Johnson	10.00	5.00
14 Bill Jurges CO	5.00	2.50
15 Russ Kemmerer	5.00	2.50
16 Steve Korcheck	5.00	2.50
17 Cookie Lavagetto MG	6.00	3.00
18 Jim Lemon	5.00	2.50
19 Bob Malkmus	5.00	2.50
20 Camilio Pascual	8.00	4.00
21 Albie Pearson	6.00	3.00
22 Herb Plews	5.00	2.50
23 Pedro Ramos	5.00	2.50
24 Roy Sievers	8.00	4.00
25 Faye Throneberry	5.00	2.50
26 Vito Valentinetti	5.00	2.50
27 Eddie Yost	6.00	3.00
28 Norm Zauchin	5.00	2.50
29 Team Picture	20.00	10.00

1959 Senators Team Issue

This Washington Senators team set features black-and-white player photos in a white border and measures approximately 4" by 5". The cards are unnumbered and checklisted below in alphabetical order. This checklist may be incomplete and any known additions are welcomed.

	NM	Ex
COMPLETE SET	80.00	40.00
1 Ken Aspromonte	5.00	2.50
2 Julio Becquer	5.00	2.50
3 Reno Bertoia	5.00	2.50
4 Tex Clevenger	5.00	2.50
5 Billy Consolo	5.00	2.50
6 Clint Courtney	5.00	2.50
7 Bill Fischer	5.00	2.50
8 Hal Griggs	5.00	2.50
9 Russ Kemmerer	5.00	2.50
10 Ralph Lumenti	5.00	2.50
11 Hal Naragon	5.00	2.50
12 Camilo Pascual	8.00	4.00
13 J.W. Porter	5.00	2.50
14 Pedro Ramos	5.00	2.50
15 John Romonosky	5.00	2.50
16 Ron Samford	5.00	2.50
17 Jose Valdivielso	5.00	2.50
18 Hal Woodeshick	5.00	2.50

1959 Senators Team Issue 5 by 7

Measuring 5" by 7", these photos were issued by the Senators in 1959. Since these photos are unnumbered, we have sequenced them in alphabetical order.

	NM	Ex
COMPLETE SET	30.00	15.00
1 Reno Bertoia	3.00	1.50
2 Clint Courtney	3.00	1.50
3 Ed Fitzgerald	3.00	1.50
4 Dick Hyde	3.00	1.50
5 Cookie Lavagetto MG	3.00	1.50
6 Jim Lemon	3.00	1.50
7 Camilio Pascual	4.00	2.00
8 Albie Pearson	3.00	1.50
9 Herb Plews	3.00	1.50
10 Pedro Ramos	3.00	1.50
11 Roy Sievers	4.00	2.00
12 Norm Zauchin	3.00	1.50

1960 Senators Universal Match Corp.

This 20-cover set produced by the Universal Match Corp. of Washington, D.C. titled "Famous Senators" features a facial cut-out of a player on a cream. The "Mr. Senator" logo is printed in red, blue and black. The set was sponsored by 1st Federal Savings and Loan Associatiion. Complete matchbooks carry a fifty percent premium.

	NM	Ex
COMPLETE SET (20)	150.00	60.00
1 Nick Altrock	8.00	3.20
2 Ossie Bluege	8.00	3.20
3 Joe Cronin	15.00	6.00
4 Alvin Crowder	8.00	3.20
5 Goose Goslin	15.00	6.00
6 Clark Griffith	15.00	6.00
7 Bucky Harris	15.00	6.00
8 Walter Johnson	20.00	8.00
9 Joe Judge	8.00	3.20
10 Harmon Killebrew	20.00	8.00
11 Joe Kuhel	8.00	3.20
12 Buddy Lewis	8.00	3.20
13 Clyde Milan	8.00	3.20
14 Buddy Myer	8.00	3.20
15 Roger Peckinpaugh	8.00	3.20
16 Sam Rice	15.00	6.00
17 Roy Sievers	10.00	4.00
18 Stan Spence	8.00	3.20
19 Mickey Vernon	10.00	4.00
20 Sam West	8.00	3.20

1960 Senators Jay Publishing

This 12-card set of the Washington Senators measures approximately 5" by 7" and features black-and-white player photos in a white border. These cards were packaged 12 to a packet. The backs are blank. The cards are unnumbered and checklisted below in alphabetical order.

	NM	Ex
COMPLETE SET (12)	30.00	12.00
1 Bob Allison	3.00	1.20
2 Julio Becquer	2.00	.80
3 Truman Clevenger	2.00	.80
4 Billy Consolo	2.00	.80
5 Dan Dobbek	2.00	.80
6 William(Billy) Gardner	2.00	.80
7 Harmon Killebrew	10.00	4.00
8 Steve Korchek	2.00	.80
9 Cookie Lavagetto MG	2.50	1.00
10 Jim Lemon	2.00	.80
11 Camilo Pascual	3.00	1.20
12 Pedro Ramos	2.00	.80

1962 Senators Jay Publishing

Produced by Jay Publishing, this 12-card set features members of the Washington Senators. Originally, this set came in a plastic sack that included a "picture pak order form" and sold for 25 cents. Printed on thin stock paper, the cards measure approximately 5" by 7". On a white background the fronts have a black-and-white posed player photo. The player's name and team appear in black letters under the photo. The backs are blank. The cards are unnumbered and checklisted below in alphabetical order.

	NM	Ex
COMPLETE SET (12)	20.00	8.00
1 Pete Burnside	2.00	.80
2 Chuck Cottier	2.00	.80
3 Bernie Daniels	2.00	.80
4 Bob Johnson	2.00	.80
5 Marty Kutyna	2.00	.80
6 Joe McClain	2.00	.80
7 Danny O'Connell	2.00	.80
8 Ken Retzer	2.00	.80
9 Willie Tasby	2.00	.80
10 Mickey Vernon MG	3.00	1.20
11 Gene Wooding	2.50	1.00
12 Bud Zipfel	2.00	.80

1962 Senators Newberrys Little Pro

This one-card set was a promotional card for a batting practice device. The card measures approximately 4" by 5" and features a photo of Jimmy Piersall. The back displays a statement by Roger Maris as to the effectiveness of the device as a batting aid and a list of six reasons as to why it is a good batting tool.

	NM	Ex
1 Jimmy Piersall	15.00	6.00

1963 Senators Jay Publishing

This 12-card set of the Washington Senators measures approximately 5" by 7". The fronts feature black-and-white posed player photos with the player's and team name printed below in the white border. These cards were packaged 12 to a packet. The backs are blank. The cards are unnumbered and checklisted below in alphabetical order.

	NM	Ex
COMPLETE SET (12)	20.00	8.00
1 Tom Cheney	2.00	.80
2 Bennie Daniels	2.00	.80
3 Ken Hamlin	2.00	.80
4 Chuck Hinton	2.00	.80
5 Don Lock	2.00	.80
6 Claude Osteen	3.00	1.20
7 Jim Piersall	4.00	1.60
8 Ken Retzer	2.00	.80
9 Don Rudolph	2.00	.80
10 Bob Schmidt	2.00	.80
11 Dave Stenhouse	2.00	.80
12 Mickey Vernon MG	2.50	1.00

1964 Senators Jay Publishing

This 12-card set of the Washington Senators measures approximately 5" by 7". The fronts feature black-and-white posed player photos with the player's and team name printed below in the white border. These cards were packaged 12 to a packet. The backs are blank. The cards are unnumbered and checklisted below in alphabetical order.

	NM	Ex
COMPLETE SET (12)	25.00	10.00
1 Don Blasingame	2.00	.80
2 Tom Cheney	2.00	.80
3 Chuck Cottier	2.00	.80
4 Chuck Hinton	2.00	.80
5 Gil Hodges MG	5.00	2.00
6 Jim King	2.00	.80
7 Ron Kline	2.00	.80
8 Don Leppert	2.00	.80
9 Don Lock	2.00	.80
10 Claude Osteen	3.00	1.20
11 Ed Roebuck	2.00	.80
12 Don Rudolph	2.00	.80

1965 Senators Jay Publishing

This 12-card set of the Washington Senators measures approximately 5" by 7". The fronts feature black-and-white posed player photos with the player's and team name printed below in the white border. These cards were packaged 12 to a packet. The backs are blank. The cards are unnumbered and checklisted below in alphabetical order.

	NM	Ex
COMPLETE SET (12)	20.00	8.00
1 Don Blasingame	2.00	.80
2 Ed Brinkman	2.00	.80
3 Mike Brumley	2.00	.80
4 Woodie Held	2.00	.80
5 Gil Hodges MG	5.00	2.00
6 Frank Howard	4.00	1.60
7 Jim King	2.00	.80
8 Don Lock	2.00	.80
9 Ken McMullen	2.00	.80
10 Buster Narum	2.00	.80
11 Phil Ortega	2.00	.80
12 Pete Richert	2.00	.80

1966 Senators Team Issue

This 12-card set of the Washington Senators measures approximately 5" by 7" and is printed on textured paper stock. The fronts feature black-and-white posed player photos with the player's and team name printed below in the white border. These cards were packaged 12 to a packet and could be obtained from the team through a mail-in offer. The twelfth player in the pack is unknown. The backs are blank. The cards are unnumbered and checklisted below in alphabetical order.

	NM	Ex
COMPLETE SET (12)	30.00	12.00
1 Don Blasingame	2.50	1.00
2 Ed Brinkman (Without hat)	2.50	1.00
3 Mike Brumley	2.50	1.00
4 Bob Chance	2.50	1.00
5 Bennie Daniels	2.50	1.00
6 Woodie Held	2.50	1.00
7 Gil Hodges MG	6.00	2.40
8 Frank Howard	5.00	2.00
9 Don Lock	2.50	1.00
10 Phil Ortega	2.50	1.00
11 Pete Richert (With plain cap)	2.50	1.00
12 Unknown player		

1967 Senators Postcards

This 22-card set of the Washington Senators features borderless black-and-white player photos with a facsimile autograph in a white bar at the bottom. The cards measure approximately 3 1/2" by 5 13/16". The backs are blank. The cards are unnumbered and checklisted below in alphabetical order.

	NM	Ex
COMPLETE SET (22)	20.00	8.00
1 Bernie Allen	1.00	.40
2 Hank Allen	1.00	.40
3 Dave Baldwin	1.00	.40
4 Frank Bertaina	1.00	.40
5 Ed Brinkman	1.00	.40
6 Doug Camilli	1.00	.40
7 Paul Casanova	1.00	.40
8 Joe Coleman	1.00	.40
9 Tim Cullen	1.00	.40
10 Mike Epstein	1.00	.40
11 Frank Howard	5.00	2.00
12 Bob Humphreys	1.00	.40
13 Darold Knowles	1.00	.40
14 Dick Lines	1.00	.40
15 Ken McMullen	1.00	.40
16 Dick Nen	1.00	.40
17 Phil Ortega	1.00	.40
18 Camilo Pascual	1.50	.60
19 Cap Peterson	1.00	.40
20 Bob Priddy	1.00	.40
21 Bob Saverine	1.00	.40
22 Fred Valentine	1.00	.40

1967 Senators Team Issue

This 12-card set of the Washington Senators measures approximately 5" by 7" and is printed on textured paper stock. The fronts feature black-and-white posed player photos with the player's and team name printed below in the white border. These cards were packaged 12 to a packet and could be obtained from the team through a mail-in offer. The backs are blank. The cards are unnumbered and checklisted below in alphabetical order.

	NM	Ex
COMPLETE SET (12)	25.00	10.00
1 Bernie Allen	2.00	.80
2 Ed Brinkman (With hat)	2.00	.80
3 Paul Casanova	2.00	.80
4 Ken Harrelson	4.00	1.60
5 Gil Hodges MG	6.00	2.40
6 Frank Howard	5.00	2.00
7 Jim Lemon CO	2.00	.80
8 Ken McMullen	2.00	.80
9 Phil Ortega	2.00	.80
10 Camilo Pascual	3.00	1.20
11 Pete Richert (With Senators cap)	2.00	.80
12 Fred Valentine	2.00	.80

1968 Senators Team Issue

This 12-card set of the Washington Senators measures approximately 5" by 7" and is printed on textured paper stock. The fronts feature black-and-white posed player photos with the player's and team name printed below in the white border. These cards were packaged 12 to a packet and could be obtained from the team through a mail-in offer. The backs are blank. The cards are unnumbered and checklisted below in alphabetical order.

	NM	Ex
COMPLETE SET (12)	25.00	10.00
1 Frank Bertaina	2.50	1.00
2 Paul Casanova	2.50	1.00
3 Frank Coggins	2.50	1.00
4 Mike Epstein	2.50	1.00
5 Ron Hansen	2.50	1.00
6 Frank Howard	5.00	2.00
7 Jim Lemon MG	2.50	1.00
8 Ken McMullen	2.50	1.00
9 Phil Ortega	2.50	1.00
10 Camilo Pascual	3.00	1.20
11 Cap Peterson	2.50	1.00
12 Fred Valentine	2.50	1.00

1968 Senators Team Issue 8 1/2x 11

This set features black-and-white player photos in white borders and measures 8 1/2" by 11". The backs are blank. The cards are unnumbered and checklisted below in alphabetical order. The checklist is incomplete and any known additions are welcomed.

	NM	Ex
COMPLETE SET	20.00	8.00
1 Ed Brinkman	10.00	4.00
2 Sid Hudson CO	10.00	4.00

1969-70 Senators Team Issue

This 16-card set of the Washington Senators measures approximately 4 1/4" by 7". The fronts display black-and-white player portraits bordered in white and printed on a grainy, textured card stock. The player's name and team are printed in the top margin. The backs are blank. The cards are unnumbered and checklisted below in alphabetical order.

	NM	Ex
COMPLETE SET (16)	25.00	10.00
1 Hank Allen	2.00	.80
2 Dick Bosman	2.00	.80
3 Ed Brinkman	2.00	.80
4 George Brunet	2.00	.80
5 Paul Casanova	2.00	.80
6 Joe Coleman	2.50	1.00
7 Mike Epstein	2.00	.80
8 Jim Hannan	2.00	.80
9 Frank Howard	4.00	1.60
10 Lee Maye	2.00	.80
11 Ken McMullen	2.00	.80
12 Camilo Pascual	3.00	1.20
13 Aurelio Rodriguez	2.00	.80
14 Ed Stroud	2.00	.80
15 Del Unser	2.00	.80
16 Ted Williams MG	15.00	6.00

1969 Senators Team Issue 8x10

This 20-card set features black-and-white player photos in white borders and measuring 8" by 10". The backs are blank. The cards are unnumbered and checklisted below in alphabetical order.

	NM	Ex
COMPLETE SET (20)	80.00	32.00
1 Bernie Allen	3.00	1.20
2 Hank Allen	3.00	1.20
3 Dave Baldwin	3.00	1.20
4 Dick Bosman	3.00	1.20
5 Ed Brinkman (Batting)	3.00	1.20
6 Ed Brinkman (Throwing)	3.00	1.20
7 Doug Camilli	3.00	1.20
8 Joe Coleman	4.00	1.60
9 Casey Cox	3.00	1.20
10 Mike Epstein	3.00	1.20
11 Nellie Fox CO	10.00	4.00
12 Frank Howard	6.00	2.40
13 Darold Knowles	3.00	1.20
14 Ken McMullen	3.00	1.20
15 Phil Ortega	3.00	1.20
16 Camilo Pascual	5.00	2.00
17 Cap Peterson	3.00	1.20
18 Del Unser	3.00	1.20
19 Fred Valentine	3.00	1.20
20 Ted Williams MG	20.00	8.00

1970 Senators Police Yellow

The 1970 Washington Senators Police set was issued on a thin unperforated cardboard sheet measuring approximately 12 1/2" by 8". The sheet is divided into ten cards by thin black lines. When the players are cut into individual cards, they measure approximately 2 1/2" by 4". The color of the sheet is yellow, and consequently the black and white borderless player photos have a similar cast. The player's name, position, and team name appear below the pictures. The backs have different safety messages sponsored by the Office of Traffic Safety, D.C. Department of Motor Vehicles. The cards are unnumbered and checklisted below in alphabetical order.

	NM	Ex
COMPLETE SET (10)	30.00	12.00
1 Dick Bosman	3.00	1.20
2 Eddie Brinkman	3.00	1.20
3 Paul Casanova	2.50	1.00
4 Mike Epstein	3.00	1.20
5 Frank Howard	8.00	3.20
6 Darold Knowles	2.50	1.00
7 Lee Maye	2.50	1.00
8 Aurelio Rodriguez	3.00	1.20
9 John Roseboro	3.00	1.20
10 Ed Stroud	2.50	1.00

1971 Senators Police Pink

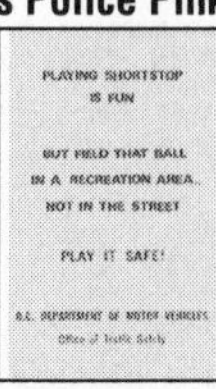

The 1971 Washington Senators Police set was issued on a thin unperforated cardboard sheet measuring approximately 12 1/2" by 8". In contrast to the previous year's issue, the sheet is not divided up into separate cards by thin black lines. If the sheet were cut into individual player cards, each player's card would measure approximately 2 1/2" by 4". The color of the sheet ranges from pink to peach, and consequently the black and white borderless player photos have a similar cast. The player's name, position, and team name appear below the pictures. The backs have different safety messages sponsored by the Office of Traffic Safety, D.C. Department of Motor Vehicles. The cards are unnumbered and checklisted below in alphabetical order. The set is dated by the fact that it is Denny McLain's only year on the Senators.

	NM	Ex
COMPLETE SET (10)	30.00	12.00
1 Dick Bosman	3.00	1.20
2 Paul Casanova	2.50	1.00
3 Tim Cullen	2.50	1.00
4 Joe Foy	2.50	1.00
5 Toby Harrah	5.00	2.00
6 Frank Howard	8.00	3.20
7 Elliott Maddox	3.00	1.20
8 Tom McCraw	2.50	1.00
9 Denny McLain	5.00	2.00
10 Don Wert	2.50	1.00

1971 Senators Team Issue W-UNC

This 24-card set of the Washington Senators features black-and-white player photos with a facsimile autograph in the bottom margin. The cards measure approximately 3 1/2" by 5 3/4" and have blank backs. The cards are unnumbered and checklisted below in alphabetical order.

	NM	Ex
COMPLETE SET (24)	80.00	32.00
1 Bernie Allen	3.00	1.20
2 Larry Biittner	3.00	1.20
3 Dick Billings	3.00	1.20
4 Dick Bosman	4.00	1.60
5 Pete Broberg	3.00	1.20
6 Jackie Brown	3.00	1.20
7 Paul Casanova	3.00	1.20
8 Casey Cox	3.00	1.20
9 Tim Cullen	3.00	1.20
10 Bill Gogolewski	3.00	1.20
11 Joe Grzenda	3.00	1.20
12 Toby Harrah	6.00	2.40
13 Frank Howard	6.00	2.40
14 Paul Lindblad	3.00	1.20
15 Elliott Maddox	3.00	1.20
16 Denny McLain	6.00	2.40
17 Don Mincher	3.00	1.20
18 Dave Nelson	3.00	1.20
19 Horacio Pina	3.00	1.20
20 Lenny Randle	3.00	1.20
21 Denny Riddleberger	3.00	1.20
22 Jim Shellenback	3.00	1.20
23 Mike Thompson	3.00	1.20
24 Del Unser	3.00	1.20

1975 Senators 1924-25 TCMA

This 40-card set features black-and-white photos of the 1924-25 Washington Senators in white borders. The cards measure approximately 2 3/8" by 3 3/8". The backs carry player information and statistics. The cards are unnumbered and checklisted below in alphabetical order except for cards 38-40 which are jumbo cards.

	NM	Ex
COMPLETE SET (40)	25.00	10.00
1 Spencer Adams	.50	.20
2 Nick Altrock	2.00	.80
3 Ossie Bluege	1.00	.40

4 Stan Coveleski 2.00 .80
5 Alex Fergeson .50 .20
6 Showboat Fischer .50 .20
7 Goose Goslin 2.00 .80
8 Bert Griffith .50 .20
9 Pinky Hargrave .50 .20
10 Bucky Harris P/MG 2.00 .80
11 Joe Harris .50 .20
12 Tex Jeans .50 .20
13 Walter Johnson 4.00 1.60
14 Joe Judge 1.50 .60
15 Wade Lefler .50 .20
16 Nemo Leibold .50 .20
17 Firpo Marberry .50 .20
18 Joe Martina .50 .20
19 Wid Matthews .50 .20
20 Mike McNally .50 .20
21 Ralph Miller .50 .20
22 Beorge Mogridge .50 .20
23 Buddy Myer .50 .20
24 Curly Ogden .50 .20
25 Roger Peckinpaugh 1.00 .40
26 Sam Rice .50 .20
27 Muddy Ruel .50 .20
28 Dutch Ruether .50 .20
29 Allen Russell .50 .20
30 Hank Severeid .50 .20
31 Everett Scott .50 .20
32 Mule Shirley .50 .20
33 By Speece .50 .20
34 Bennie Tate .50 .20
35 Bobby Veach .50 .20
36 Tom Zachary .50 .20
37 Paul Zahniser .50 .20
38 Bucky Harris MG 1.00 .40
Bill McKechnie MG
39 Ossie Bluege 1.00 .40
Roger Peckinpaugh
Bucky Harris
Joe Judge
40 Tom Zachary 2.00 .80
Firpo Marberry
Alex Fergeson
Walter Johnson

1999 Senators 69 Reunion

These 28 cards feature members of the 1969 Washington Senators and was issued by the Washington Senators Historical Society. These cards measure 2" by 2 1/2" and feature commentary on each player as if it were written at the end of the 1969 season.

Nm-Mt Ex-Mt
COMPLETE SET (28) 10.00 3.00
1 Bernie Allen .25 .07
2 Hank Allen .25 .07
3 Frank Bertania .25 .07
4 Dick Billings .25 .07
5 Dick Bosman .25 .07
6 Ed Brinkman .25 .07
7 Johnny Holliday ANN .25 .07
8 Joe Camacho CO .25 .07
9 Casey Cox .25 .07
10 Tim Cullen .25 .07
11 Mike Epstein .25 .07
12 Jim French .25 .07
13 Jim Hannan .25 .07
14 Ron Menchine ANN .25 .07
15 Denny Higgins .25 .07
16 Frank Howard 1.00 .30
17 Sid Hudson CO .50 .15
18 Bob Humphreys .25 .07
19 Frank Kruetzer .25 .07
20 Lee Maye .25 .07
21 Shelby Whitfield ANN .25 .07
22 Ken McMullen .25 .07
23 Ed Stroud .25 .07
24 Wayne Terwillger CO .25 .07
25 Del Unser .25 .07
26 Fred Valentine .25 .07
27 Ted Williams MG 5.00 1.50
28 Checklist Card .50 .15
All Players printed in front

1910 Sepia Anon PC796

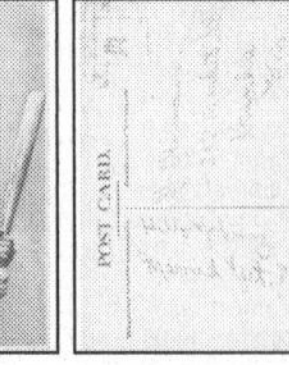

This sepia with white border set measures 3 1/2" by 5 1/2", was issued circa 1910 and features 25 cards of popular players of the era. No markings are found either on the front or on the backs to indicate a manufacturer or issuer. The Cobb and Wagner card spells Honus' name as Honas. The same checklist is also used for the PC Novelty Cultery Co set. The pictures in that set have been reduced and enclosed in an ornate frame border. Postcards by either issuer are valued the same.

Ex-Mt VG
COMPLETE SET (25) 7500.00 3800.00
1 Roger Bresnahan 300.00 150.00
2 Al Bridwell 150.00 75.00
3 Mordecai Brown 250.00 125.00
4 Ty Cobb 1200.00 600.00
5 Ty Cobb 800.00 400.00
Honus Wagner
6 Frank Chance MG 300.00 150.00
7 Hal Chase 250.00 125.00
8 Eddie Collins 250.00 125.00
9 Sam Crawford 250.00 125.00
10 Johnny Evers 300.00 150.00
Germany Schaefer
11 Art Devlin 150.00 75.00
12 Red Dooin 150.00 75.00
13 Sam Frock 150.00 75.00
14 George Gibson 150.00 75.00
15 Artie Hoffman 150.00 75.00
16 Walter Johnson 600.00 300.00
17 Nap Lajoie 300.00 150.00
18 Harry Lord 150.00 75.00
19 Christy Mathewson 600.00 300.00
20 Orvall Overall 150.00 75.00
21 Eddie Plank 250.00 125.00
22 Tris Speaker 300.00 150.00
23 Charley Street 150.00 75.00
24 Honus Wagner 600.00 300.00
25 Ed Walsh 250.00 125.00

1977 Sertoma Stars

This 25-card set measures approximately 2 3/4" by 4 1/4". The fronts feature a black-and-white player portrait in a black-framed circle on a yellow background. The player's name, position, sponsor logo, and card name are printed in black and red between a top and bottom row of black stars which border the card. The backs carry a puzzle piece which, when placed in the right position, form a picture of the 1913 Pittsburgh Nationals. The cards are unnumbered and checklisted below in alphabetical order.

NM Ex
COMPLETE SET (25) 25.00 10.00
1 Bernie Allen .25 .10
2 Frank(Home Run) Baker 1.00 .40
3 Ted Beard .25 .10
4 Don Buford .25 .10
5 Eddie Cicotte 1.00 .40
6 Roberto Clemente 3.00 1.20
7 Dom Dallessandro .25 .10
8 Carl Erskine .50 .20
9 Nellie Fox 1.00 .40
10 Lou Gehrig 3.00 1.20
11 Joe Jackson 3.00 1.20
12 Len Johnston .25 .10
13 Benny Kauff .25 .10
14 Dick Kenworthy .25 .10
15 Harmon Killebrew 1.00 .40
16 Bob(Lefty) Logan .25 .10
17 Willie Mays 3.00 1.20
18 Satchell Paige 3.00 1.20
19 Edd Roush 1.00 .40
20 Chico Ruiz .25 .10
21 Babe Ruth 5.00 2.00
22 Herb Score .50 .20
23 George Sisler 1.00 .40
24 George(Buck) Weaver 1.00 .40
25 Early Wynn 1.00 .40

1961 Seven-Eleven

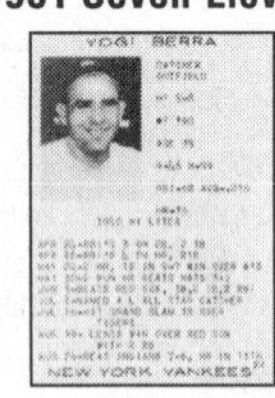

The 1961 7-Eleven set consists of 30 cards, each measuring approximately 2 7/16" by 3 3/8". The checklist card states that this is the first series, and that a new series was to be released every two weeks (though apparently no other series were issued). The cards are printed on pink cardboard stock and the backs are blank and were available as seven cards for five cents. The fronts have a black and white headshot in the upper left portion and brief biographical information to the right of the picture. The player's name appears across the top of each front. The remainder of the front carries "1960 Hi Lites," which consist of a list of dates and the player's achievements on those dates. The team name across the bottom of the card rounds out the front. The cards are numbered on the front in the lower right corner.

NM Ex
COMPLETE SET (30) 500.00 200.00
1 Dave Sisler 5.00 2.00
2 Don Mossi 8.00 3.20
3 Joey Jay 5.00 2.00
4 Bob Purkey 5.00 2.00
5 Jack Fisher 5.00 2.00
6 John Romano 5.00 2.00
7 Russ Snyder 5.00 2.00
8 Johnny Temple 5.00 2.00
9 Roy Sievers 8.00 3.20
10 Ron Hansen 5.00 2.00
11 Pete Runnels 8.00 3.20
12 Gene Woodling 8.00 3.20
13 Clint Courtney 5.00 2.00
14 Whitey Herzog 10.00 4.00
15 Warren Spahn 30.00 12.00
16 Stan Musial 60.00 24.00
17 Willie Mays 80.00 32.00
18 Ken Boyer 10.00 4.00
19 Joe Cunningham 8.00 3.20
20 Orlando Cepeda 20.00 8.00
21 Gil Hodges 15.00 6.00
22 Yogi Berra 40.00 16.00
23 Ernie Banks 40.00 16.00
24 Lou Burdette 10.00 4.00
25 Roger Maris 50.00 20.00
26 Charlie Smith 5.00 2.00
27 Jimmie Foxx 20.00 8.00
28 Mel Ott 20.00 8.00
29 Don Nottebart 5.00 2.00
NNO Checklist Card 15.00 6.00

1975 Shakey's Pizza

This 18-card set measures 2 3/4" by 3 1/2" and features black-and-white players photos on a white card face. The red Shakey's Pizza logo overlaps the lower left corner of the picture. The phrase "West Coast Greats" cuts diagonally across the upper left corner of the picture. The player's name is printed below the photo in red. Red and brown stars accent the margins. The backs carry a Shakey's Pizza advertisement encouraging consumers to visit Shakey's Pizza parlors in Bellevue, Lake City, Aurora and West Seattle. The DiMaggio back has an offer for $1.00 off on a family-size pizza and were given away to the 1st 1,000 attendees at a Seattle card convention. The cards are numbered on the front below the picture.

NM Ex
COMPLETE SET (18) 60.00 24.00
1 Joe DiMaggio 15.00 6.00
2 Paul Waner 4.00 1.60
3 Lefty Gomez 4.00 1.60
4 Earl Averill 4.00 1.60
5 Ernie Lombardi 4.00 1.60
6 Joe Cronin 4.00 1.60
7 George Burns 3.00 1.20
8 Casey Stengel 6.00 2.40
9 Sam Crawford 4.00 1.60
10 Ted Williams 15.00 6.00
11 Fred Hutchinson 3.00 1.20
12 Duke Snider 6.00 2.40
13 Hal Chase 3.00 1.20
14 Bobby Doerr 4.00 1.60
15 Arky Vaughan 4.00 1.60
16 Tony Lazzeri 4.00 1.60
17 Lefty O'Doul 3.00 1.20
18 Stan Hack 3.00 1.20

1976 Shakey's Pizza

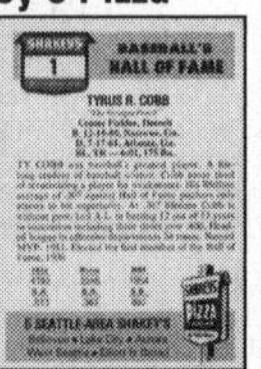

The 1976 Shakey's Pizza set contains 159 standard-size cards. The cards were part of a promotion at five Seattle-area Shakey's restaurants, and the "A" card could be exchanged for $1.00 off on any family-size pizza. The set is arranged according to year of induction into the Baseball Hall of Fame. The fronts feature vintage black and white player photos framed by red and white border stripes against a blue card face. The player's name appears in a baseball icon at the bottom of the picture. The backs have biography, career summary and player statistics.

NM Ex
COMPLETE SET (159) 50.00 20.00
1 Ty Cobb 5.00 2.00
2 Babe Ruth 8.00 3.20
3 Walter Johnson 1.50 .60
4 Christy Mathewson 1.50 .60
5 Honus Wagner 2.00 .80
6 Nap Lajoie 1.50 .60
7 Tris Speaker .75 .30
8 Cy Young 1.50 .60
9 Morgan G. Bulkeley .10 .04
10 Ban Johnson PRES .10 .04
11 John McGraw 1.00 .40
12 Connie Mack 1.00 .40
13 George Wright .20 .08
14 Grover C. Alexander .75 .30
15 Alexander Cartwright .10 .04
16 Henry Chadwick .10 .04
17 Eddie Collins .75 .30
18 Lou Gehrig 5.00 2.00
19 Willie Keeler .20 .08
20 George Sisler .75 .30
21 Cap Anson .75 .30
22 Charles Comiskey .20 .08
23 Candy Cummings .20 .08
24 Buck Ewing .20 .08
25 Old Hoss Radbourne .20 .08
26 Al Spalding .20 .08
27 Rogers Hornsby 1.00 .40
28 Kenesaw Landis COMM .10 .04
29 Roger Bresnahan .20 .08
30 Dan Brouthers .20 .08
31 Fred Clarke .20 .08
32 Jimmy Collins .20 .08
33 Ed Delahanty .20 .08
34 Hugh Duffy .20 .08
35 Hugh Jennings .20 .08
36 Mike(King) Kelly .20 .08
37 Jim O'Rourke .20 .08
38 Wilbert Robinson .20 .08
39 Jesse Burkett .20 .08
40 Frank Chance .75 .30
41 Jack Chesbro .20 .08
42 Johnny Evers .75 .30
43 Clark Griffith .75 .30
44 Tommy McCarthy .20 .08
45 Joe McGinnity .20 .08
46 Eddie Plank .20 .08
47 Joe Tinker .75 .30
48 Rube Waddell .20 .08
49 Ed Walsh .20 .08
50 Mickey Cochrane .75 .30
51 Frankie Frisch .20 .08
52 Lefty Grove .75 .30
53 Carl Hubbell .20 .08
54 Herb Pennock .20 .08
55 Pie Traynor .75 .30
56 Charley Gehringer .20 .08
57 Mordecai Brown .20 .08
58 Kid Nichols .20 .08
59 Jimmie Foxx 1.00 .40
60 Mel Ott .75 .30
61 Harry Heilmann .20 .08
62 Paul Waner .20 .08
63 Dizzy Dean 1.00 .40
64 Al Simmons .20 .08
65 Ed Barrow .10 .04
66 Chief Bender .20 .08
67 Tommy Connolly .10 .04
68 Bill Klem .10 .04
69 Bobby Wallace .20 .08
70 Harry Wright .20 .08
71 Bill Dickey .75 .30
72 Rabbit Maranville .20 .08
73 Bill Terry .20 .08
74 Joe DiMaggio 5.00 2.00
75 Gabby Hartnett .20 .08
76 Ted Lyons .20 .08
77 Dazzy Vance .20 .08
78 Home Run Baker .20 .08
79 Ray Schalk .20 .08
80 Joe Cronin .20 .08
81 Hank Greenberg .75 .30
82 Sam Crawford .20 .08
83 Joe McCarthy MG .10 .04
84 Zack Wheat .20 .08
85 Max Carey .20 .08
86 Billy Hamilton .20 .08
87 Bob Feller 1.00 .40
88 Jackie Robinson 5.00 2.00
89 Bill McKechnie .10 .04
90 Edd Roush .20 .08
91 John Clarkson .20 .08
92 Elmer Flick .20 .08
93 Sam Rice .20 .08
94 Eppa Rixey .20 .08
95 Luke Appling .20 .08
96 Red Faber .20 .08
97 Burleigh Grimes .20 .08
98 Miller Huggins .20 .08
99 Tim Keefe .20 .08
100 Heinie Manush .20 .08
101 Monte Ward .20 .08
102 Pud Galvin .20 .08
103 Ted Williams 5.00 2.00
104 Casey Stengel 1.00 .40
105 Red Ruffing .20 .08
106 Branch Rickey .10 .04
107 Lloyd Waner .20 .08
108 Joe Medwick .20 .08
109 Kiki Cuyler .20 .08
110 Goose Goslin .20 .08
111 Roy Campanella 1.00 .40
112 Stan Musial 2.00 .80
113 Stan Coveleski .20 .08
114 Waite Hoyt .20 .08
115 Lou Boudreau .20 .08
116 Earle Combs .20 .08
117 Ford Frick COMM .10 .04
118 Jesse Haines .20 .08
119 Dave Bancroft .20 .08
120 Jake Beckley .20 .08
121 Chick Hafey .20 .08
122 Harry Hooper .20 .08
123 Joe Kelley .20 .08
124 Rube Marquard .20 .08
125 Satchel Paige 2.00 .80
126 George Weiss GM .10 .04
127 Yogi Berra 1.00 .40
128 Josh Gibson 2.00 .80
129 Lefty Gomez .20 .08
130 Will Harridge PRES .10 .04
131 Sandy Koufax 1.00 .40
132 Buck Leonard .20 .08
133 Early Wynn .20 .08
134 Ross Youngs .20 .08
135 Roberto Clemente 5.00 2.00
136 Billy Evans .10 .04
137 Monte Irvin .20 .08
138 George Kelly .20 .08
139 Warren Spahn .20 .08
140 Mickey Welch .10 .04
141 Cool Papa Bell .10 .04
142 Jim Bottomley .10 .04
143 Jocko Conlan .10 .04
144 Whitey Ford .10 .04
145 Mickey Mantle 8.00 3.20
146 Sam Thompson .20 .08
147 Earl Averill .20 .08
148 Bucky Harris .20 .08
149 Billy Herman .20 .08
150 Judy Johnson .20 .08
151 Ralph Kiner .50 .20
152 Oscar Charleston .20 .08
153 Roger Connor .20 .08
154 Cal Hubbard .20 .08
155 Bob Lemon .20 .08
156 Fred Lindstrom .20 .08
157 Robin Roberts .50 .20
158 Robin Roberts .50 .20
Same picture and text
as previous card
A Earl Averill .10 .04

1977 Shakey's Pizza

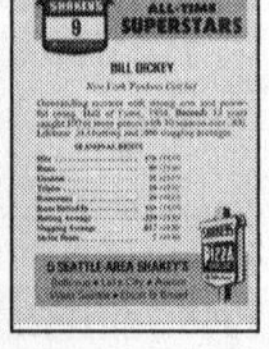

In this 28-card commemorative set, cards A-C were issued in honor of baseball's "1977 WASSCA Convention Superstars." Cards 1-25 honor "All-Time Superstars." They were available at five Seattle area Shakey's: Bellevue, Lake City, Aurora, West Seattle and at Elliott and Broad. The cards measure 2 1/4" by 3" and feature posed and action black-and-white player photos with faded maroon borders. A blue facsimile autograph runs across the bottom of each picture. The backs carry the player's name, career highlights and statistics in the form of "Seasonal Bests."

NM Ex
COMPLETE SET (28) 50.00 20.00
1 Connie Mack 1.50 .60
2 John McGraw 1.00 .40
3 Cy Young 1.50 .60
4 Walter Johnson 1.50 .60
5 Grover C. Alexander 1.50 .60
6 Christy Mathewson 1.50 .60
7 Lefty Grove 1.50 .60
8 Mickey Cochrane 1.00 .40
9 Bill Dickey 1.00 .40
10 Lou Gehrig 6.00 2.40
11 George Sisler 1.00 .40
12 Cap Anson 1.00 .40
13 Jimmie Foxx 1.50 .60
14 Rogers Hornsby 2.50 1.00
15 Nap Lajoie 1.50 .60
16 Eddie Collins 1.00 .40
17 Pie Traynor 1.00 .40
18 Honus Wagner 1.50 .60
19 Ty Cobb 6.00 2.40
20 Babe Ruth 8.00 3.20
21 Joe Jackson 5.00 2.00
22 Tris Speaker 1.50 .60
23 Ted Williams 5.00 2.00
24 Joe DiMaggio 5.00 2.00
25 Stan Musial 2.50 1.00
A Earl Averill .75 .30
B Johnny Mize .75 .30
C Bob Johnson .50 .20

1990 Mike Shannon Restaurant

This 5" by 7" blank-backed card features three photos of Mike Shannon (two from his playing career and one as an announcer) and has some information about his restaurant (location, hours and specialities).

Nm-Mt Ex-Mt
1 Mike Shannon 3.00 .90

1998 Monty Sheldon Promos Tri-Fold

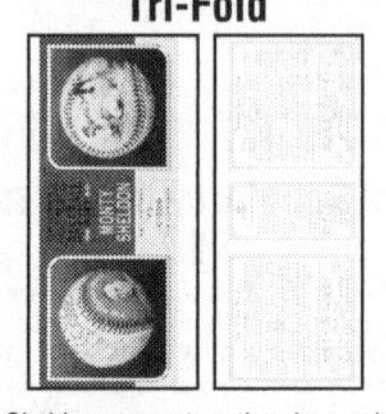

Monty Sheldon, a sports artist, draws elaborate hand-painted baseballs. These 12 cards, issued in the stule of the T202 Hassan Triple Folder set, were produced to show what these baseballs look like upon completion. Since these cards are unnumbered, we have sequenced them in alphabetical order.

Nm-Mt Ex-Mt
COMPLETE SET (12) 60.00 18.00
1 Ty Cobb 6.00 1.80
2 Joe DiMaggio 8.00 2.40
3 Joe Jackson 8.00 2.40
4 Walter Johnson 5.00 1.50
5 Sadaharu Oh 4.00 1.20
6 Satchel Paige 4.00 1.20
7 Cal Ripken 8.00 2.40
8 Babe Ruth 10.00 3.00
9 Rube Waddell 4.00 1.20
10 Honus Wagner 5.00 1.50
11 Ted Williams 8.00 2.40
12 Artie Wilson 1.00 .30

1998-99 Monty Sheldon Promos

These small sized cards, which measure approximately 2" by 2" feature the artwork of Monty Sheldon who creates special art baseballs featuring requested players. Since these cards are unnumbered, we have sequenced them in alphabetical order.

Nm-Mt Ex-Mt
COMPLETE SET 150.00 45.00
1 Hank Aaron 6.00 1.80
2 Grover C. Alexander 4.00 1.20
3 Roger Clemens 5.00 1.50
4 Ty Cobb 6.00 1.80
5 Eddie Collins 4.00 1.20
6 Joe DiMaggio 8.00 2.40
7 Whitey Ford 5.00 1.50
8 Eddie Gaedel 2.00 .60
9 Lou Gehrig 8.00 2.40
10 Josh Gibson 8.00 2.40
11 Ken Griffey Jr 6.00 1.80
12 Tony Gwynn 5.00 1.50
13 Joe Jackson 8.00 2.40
14 Walter Johnson 6.00 1.80
15 Michael Jordan 10.00 3.00
16 Sandy Koufax 6.00 1.80
17 Mickey Mantle 10.00 3.00
18 Christy Mathewson 5.00 1.50
19 Willie Mays 8.00 2.40
20 Mark McGwire 8.00 2.40
21 Stan Musial 6.00 1.80
22 Bill Raimondi 1.00 .30
23 Cal Ripken Jr 8.00 2.40
24 Alex Rodriguez 8.00 2.40
25 Pete Rose 5.00 1.50
26 Babe Ruth 10.00 3.00
27 Duke Snider 5.00 1.50
28 Sammy Sosa 5.00 1.50
29 Warren Spahn 4.00 1.20
30 Rube Waddell 4.00 1.20
31 Honus Wagner 5.00 1.50

32 Ted Williams 8.00 2.40
33 Artie Wilson 1.00 .30
34 Carl Yastrzemski 4.00 1.20

1991 Sierra United Way

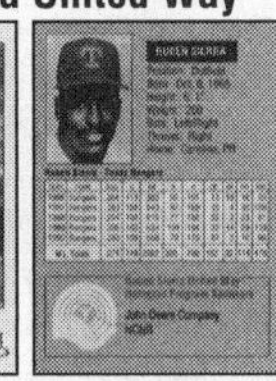

This one-card standard-size set features star outfielder Ruben Sierra. An United Way logo is in the upper left corner. There is also a photo and the player and his team is identified on the bottom. The back has vital statistics and career information about Sierra. This card was issued with six different sponsors; Etheridge Printing Company, National Semi-Conductor Corporation and Pier 1 Imports, Electro-Com Automation and General Dynamics; Stripling and Cox and the Tandy Corporation; John Deere Company and NCNB, and County Seat Stores, Inc. and Dallas Times-Herald. Each card has two different sponsors except for the ones with Etheridge.

Nm-Mt Ex-Mt
1 Ruben Sierra 1.00 .30

1991 SilverStar Holograms

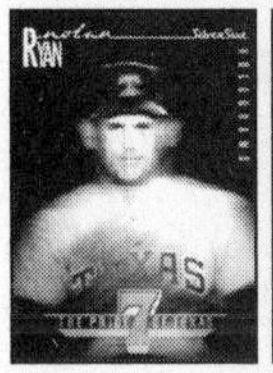
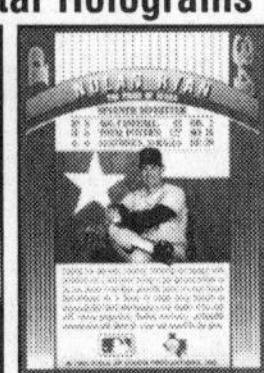

These hologram cards measure the standard size and were issued to commemorate outstanding achievements of the players. The backs of the hologram cards are brightly colored and have statistics as well as a player profile. Each card also comes with a 2 1/16" by 5 3/8" blank-backed ticket. The tickets have a color player photo, serial number, and a description of the achievement honored. The Henderson hologram honors him as the all-time stolen base leader; the Ryan hologram celebrates his 7th no-hitter; and the Justice hologram commemorates his two-run homer against the Reds on October 1 that led to a 7-6 Braves' victory during the NL West pennant race. The cards are unnumbered and checklisted below chronologically by release dates. Cards numbered 5 though 8 were released later and are unnumbered. These cards are sequenced in alphabetical order.

Nm-Mt Ex-Mt
COMPLETE SET (8) 10.00 3.00
1 Rickey Henderson 1.25 .35
2 Nolan Ryan 3.00 .90
3 Dave Justice .75 .23
4 Cal Ripken 3.00 .90
5 Will Clark 1.00 .30
6 Roger Clemens 1.50 .45
7 Rawlings Gold Glove .25 .07
8 Darryl Strawberry .50 .15

1991 Simon and Schuster More Little Big Leaguers

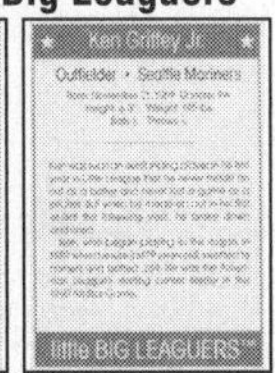

This 96-page album was published by Simon and Schuster and includes boyhood stories of today's pro baseball players. Moreover, five 8 1/2" by 11" sheets of cards (9 cards per sheet) are inserted at the end of the album; after perforation, the cards measure the standard size. The fronts feature black and white photos of these players as kids. The pictures are bordered in green on a white card face. The backs have the same design, only with biography and career summary in place of the picture. The cards are unnumbered and checklisted below in alphabetical order.

Nm-Mt Ex-Mt
COMPLETE SET (45) 8.00 2.40
1 Jim Abbott .10 .03
2 Jesse Barfield .10 .03
3 Kevin Bass .10 .03
4 Craig Biggio .30 .09
5 Phil Bradley .10 .03
6 Jeff Brantley .20 .06
7 Tom Brunansky .10 .03
8 Ken Caminiti .30 .09
9 Will Clark .40 .12
10 Vince Coleman .10 .03
11 David Cone .20 .06
12 Alvin Davis .10 .03
13 Andre Dawson .30 .09
14 Bill Doran .10 .03
15 Nick Esasky .10 .03
16 Dwight Gooden .20 .06
17 Tom Gordon .10 .03
18 Ken Griffey Jr. 1.25 .35
19 Kevin Gross .10 .03
20 Kelly Gruber .10 .03
21 Lee Guetterman .10 .03
22 Terry Kennedy .10 .03
23 John Kruk .20 .06
24 Bill Landrum .10 .03
25 Mark Langston .10 .03
26 Barry Larkin .30 .09
27 Dave Magadan .10 .03
28 Don Mattingly 1.00 .30
29 Mark McGwire 1.50 .45
30 Kevin Mitchell .10 .03
31 Bob Ojeda .10 .03
32 Gregg Olson .10 .03
33 Terry Pendleton .10 .03
34 Ted Power .10 .03
35 Kirby Puckett .50 .15
36 Terry Puhl .10 .03
37 Bret Saberhagen .10 .03
38 Chris Sabo .10 .03
39 Kevin Seitzer .10 .03
40 Don Slaught .10 .03
41 Lonnie Smith .10 .03
42 Darryl Strawberry .20 .06
43 Mickey Tettleton .10 .03
44 Bobby Thigpen .10 .03
45 Frank White .20 .06

1995 Skin Bracer

Sponsored by Colgate-Palmolive Co., this three-card standard-size set was included in specially marked Skin Bracer toiletries bags and five-ounce Skin Bracer gift cartons. Also autographed 8" by 10" photos commemorating the same players and events were available for $7.99 with a proof-of-purchase from Skin Bracer, Afta skin conditioner or Colgate shave cream. The autographed photo offer was available via in-store tear pads and on-pack. The cards are unnumbered and checklisted below in alphabetical order.

Nm-Mt Ex-Mt
COMPLETE SET (3) 15.00 4.50
1 Don Larsen 5.00 1.50
2 Bill Mazeroski 5.00 1.50
3 Bobby Thomson 5.00 1.50

2000 SkyBox

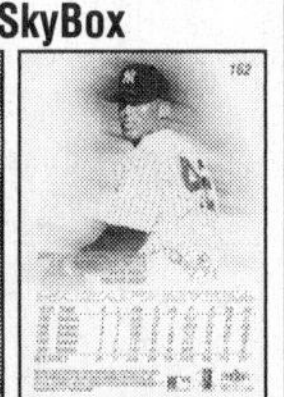

The 2000 SkyBox product was released in late May, 2000 as a 250-card set that featured 200-player cards, and 50-short printed prospect cards. The set also includes a horizontal parallel version of each of the 50 prospect cards (1:8). The last ten cards in the set feature dual player cards of some of the hottest prospects in baseball. The horizontal parallel version of these ten cards were inserted at one in 12 packs. Each pack contained 10-cards and carried a suggested retail price of 2.99.

Nm-Mt Ex-Mt
COMP.MASTER SET (300) 120.00 36.00
COMP.SET w/o SP's (250) 40.00 12.00
COMMON CARD (1-200) .30 .09
COMMON (201S-240S) 2.00 .60
COMMON (241S-250S) .75 .23
1 Cal Ripken 2.50 .75
2 Ivan Rodriguez .75 .23
3 Chipper Jones .75 .23
4 Dean Palmer .30 .09
5 Devon White .30 .09
6 Ugueth Urbina .30 .09
7 Doug Glanville .30 .09
8 Damian Jackson .30 .09
9 Jose Canseco .75 .23
10 Billy Koch .30 .09
11 Brady Anderson .30 .09
12 Vladimir Guerrero .75 .23
13 Dan Wilson .30 .09
14 Kevin Brown .50 .15
15 Eddie Taubensee .30 .09
16 Jose Lima .30 .09
17 Greg Maddux 1.25 .35
18 Manny Ramirez .30 .09
19 Brad Fullmer .30 .09
20 Ron Gant .30 .09
21 Edgar Martinez .50 .15
22 Pokey Reese .30 .09
23 Jason Varitek .30 .09
24 Neifi Perez .30 .09
25 Shane Reynolds .30 .09
26 Robin Ventura .50 .15
27 Scott Rolen .50 .15
28 Trevor Hoffman .30 .09
29 John Valentin .30 .09
30 Shannon Stewart .30 .09
31 Troy Glaus .50 .15
32 Kerry Wood .75 .23
33 Jim Thome .75 .23
34 Rafael Roque .30 .09
35 Tino Martinez .50 .15
36 Jeffrey Hammonds .30 .09
37 Orlando Hernandez .30 .09
38 Kris Benson .30 .09
39 Fred McGriff .50 .15
40 Brian Jordan .30 .09
41 Trot Nixon .50 .15
42 Matt Clement .30 .09
43 Ray Durham .30 .09
44 Johnny Damon .30 .09
45 Todd Hollandsworth .30 .09
46 Edgardo Alfonzo .30 .09
47 Tim Hudson .50 .15
48 Tony Gwynn 1.00 .30
49 Barry Bonds 2.00 .60
50 Andruw Jones .30 .09
51 Pedro Martinez .75 .23
52 Mike Hampton .30 .09
53 Miguel Tejada .30 .09
54 Kevin Young .30 .09
55 J.T. Snow .30 .09
56 Carlos Delgado .30 .09
57 Bobby Howry .30 .09
58 Andres Galarraga .30 .09
59 Paul Konerko .30 .09
60 Mike Cameron .30 .09
61 Jeremy Giambi .30 .09
62 Todd Hundley .30 .09
63 Al Leiter .30 .09
64 Matt Stairs .30 .09
65 Edgar Renteria .30 .09
66 Jeff Kent .30 .09
67 John Wetteland .30 .09
68 Nomar Garciaparra 1.25 .35
69 Jeff Weaver .30 .09
70 Matt Williams .30 .09
71 Kyle Farnsworth .30 .09
72 Brad Radke .30 .09
73 Eric Chavez .30 .09
74 J.D. Drew .30 .09
75 Steve Finley .30 .09
76 Pete Harnisch .30 .09
77 Chad Kreuter .30 .09
78 Todd Pratt .30 .09
79 John Jaha .30 .09
80 Armando Rios .30 .09
81 Luis Gonzalez .30 .09
82 Ryan Minor .30 .09
83 Juan Gonzalez .75 .23
84 Rickey Henderson .75 .23
85 Jason Giambi .75 .23
86 Shawn Estes .30 .09
87 Chad Curtis .30 .09
88 Jeff Cirillo .30 .09
89 Juan Encarnacion .30 .09
90 Tony Womack .30 .09
91 Mike Mussina .75 .23
92 Jeff Bagwell .50 .15
93 Rey Ordonez .30 .09
94 Joe McEwing .30 .09
95 Robb Nen .30 .09
96 Will Clark .75 .23
97 Chris Singleton .30 .09
98 Jason Kendall .30 .09
99 Ken Griffey Jr. 1.25 .35
100 Rusty Greer .30 .09
101 Charles Johnson .30 .09
102 Carlos Lee .30 .09
103 Brad Ausmus .30 .09
104 Preston Wilson .30 .09
105 Ronnie Belliard .30 .09
106 Mike Lieberthal .30 .09
107 Alex Rodriguez 1.25 .35
108 Jay Bell .30 .09
109 Frank Thomas .75 .23
110 Adrian Beltre .30 .09
111 Ron Coomer .30 .09
112 Ben Grieve .30 .09
113 Darryl Kile .30 .09
114 Erubiel Durazo .30 .09
115 Magglio Ordonez .30 .09
116 Gary Sheffield .30 .09
117 Joe Mays .30 .09
118 Fernando Tatis .30 .09
119 David Wells .30 .09
120 Tim Salmon .50 .15
121 Troy O'Leary .30 .09
122 Roberto Alomar .75 .23
123 Damion Easley .30 .09
124 Brant Brown .30 .09
125 Carlos Beltran .30 .09
126 Eric Karros .30 .09
127 Geoff Jenkins .30 .09
128 Roger Clemens 1.50 .45
129 Warren Morris .30 .09
130 Eric Owens .30 .09
131 Jose Cruz Jr. .30 .09
132 Mo Vaughn .30 .09
133 Eric Young .30 .09
134 Kenny Lofton .30 .09
135 Marquis Grissom .30 .09
136 A.J. Burnett .30 .09
137 Bernie Williams .50 .15
138 Javy Lopez .30 .09
139 Jose Offerman .30 .09
140 Sean Casey .30 .09
141 Alex Gonzalez .30 .09
142 Carlos Febles .30 .09
143 Mike Piazza 1.25 .35
144 Curt Schilling .50 .15
145 Ben Davis .30 .09
146 Rafael Palmeiro .50 .15
147 Scott Williamson .30 .09
148 Darin Erstad .30 .09
149 Joe Girardi .30 .09
150 Gerald Williams .30 .09
151 Richie Sexson .30 .09
152 Corey Koskie .30 .09
153 Paul O'Neill .50 .15
154 Chad Hermansen .30 .09
155 Randy Johnson .75 .23
156 Henry Rodriguez .30 .09
157 Bartolo Colon .30 .09
158 Tony Clark .30 .09
159 Mike Lowell .30 .09
160 Moises Alou .30 .09
161 Todd Walker .30 .09
162 Mariano Rivera .50 .15
163 Mark McGwire 2.00 .60
164 Roberto Hernandez .30 .09
165 Larry Walker .50 .15
166 Albert Belle .30 .09
167 Barry Larkin .75 .23
168 Rolando Arrojo .30 .09
169 Mark Kotsay .30 .09
170 Ken Caminiti .30 .09
171 Dermal Brown .30 .09
172 Michael Barrett .30 .09
173 Jay Buhner .30 .09
174 Ruben Mateo .30 .09
175 Jim Edmonds .30 .09
176 Sammy Sosa 1.25 .35
177 Omar Vizquel .30 .09
178 Todd Helton .50 .15
179 Kevin Barker .30 .09
180 Derek Jeter 2.00 .60
181 Brian Giles .30 .09
182 Greg Vaughn .30 .09
183 Roy Halladay .30 .09
184 Tom Glavine .50 .15
185 Craig Biggio .50 .15
186 Jose Vidro .30 .09
187 Andy Ashby .30 .09
188 Freddy Garcia .30 .09
189 Garret Anderson .30 .09
190 Mark Grace .50 .15
191 Travis Fryman .30 .09
192 Jeromy Burnitz .30 .09
193 Jacque Jones .30 .09
194 David Cone .30 .09
195 Ryan Rupe .30 .09
196 John Smoltz .50 .15
197 Daryle Ward .30 .09
198 Rondell White .30 .09
199 Bobby Abreu .30 .09
200 Justin Thompson .30 .09
201 Norm Hutchins .30 .09
201S Norm Hutchins SP 2.00 .60
202 Ramon Ortiz .30 .09
202S Ramon Ortiz SP 2.00 .60
203 Dan Wheeler .30 .09
203S Dan Wheeler SP 2.00 .60
204 Matt Riley .30 .09
204S Matt Riley SP 2.00 .60
205 Steve Lomasney .30 .09
205S Steve Lomasney SP 2.00 .60
206 Chad Meyers .30 .09
206S Chad Meyers SP 2.00 .60
207 Gary Glover RC .50 .15
207S Gary Glover SP 2.00 .60
208 Joe Crede .30 .09
208S Joe Crede SP 2.00 .60
209 Kip Wells .30 .09
209S Kip Wells SP 2.00 .60
210 Travis Dawkins .30 .09
210S Travis Dawkins SP 2.00 .60
211 Denny Stark RC .50 .15
211S Denny Stark SP 2.00 .60
212 Ben Petrick .30 .09
212S Ben Petrick SP 2.00 .60
213 Eric Munson .30 .09
213S Eric Munson SP 2.00 .60
214 Josh Beckett 1.00 .30
214S Josh Beckett SP 5.00 1.50
215 Pablo Ozuna .30 .09
215S Pablo Ozuna SP 2.00 .60
216 Brad Penny .30 .09
216S Brad Penny SP 2.00 .60
217 Julio Ramirez .30 .09
217S Julio Ramirez SP 2.00 .60
218 Danny Peoples .30 .09
218S Danny Peoples SP 2.00 .60
219 W.Rodriguez RC .50 .15
219S W.Rodriguez SP 2.00 .60
220 Julio Lugo .30 .09
220S Julio Lugo SP 2.00 .60
221 Mark Quinn .30 .09
221S Mark Quinn SP 2.00 .60
222 Eric Gagne .75 .23
222S Eric Gagne SP 4.00 1.20
223 Chad Green .30 .09
223S Chad Green SP 2.00 .60
224 Tony Armas Jr. .30 .09
224S Tony Armas Jr. SP 2.00 .60
225 Milton Bradley .30 .09
225S Milton Bradley SP 2.00 .60
226 Rob Bell .30 .09
226S Rob Bell SP 2.00 .60
227 Alfonso Soriano .75 .23
227S Alfonso Soriano SP 4.00 1.20
228 Wily Pena .30 .09
228S Wily Pena SP 2.00 .60
229 Nick Johnson .30 .09
229S Nick Johnson SP 2.00 .60
230 Ed Yarnall .30 .09
230S Ed Yarnall SP 2.00 .60
231 Ryan Bradley .30 .09
231S Ryan Bradley SP 2.00 .60
232 Adam Piatt .30 .09
232S Adam Piatt SP 2.00 .60
233 Chad Harville .30 .09
233S Chad Harville SP 2.00 .60
234 Alex Sanchez .30 .09
234S Alex Sanchez SP 2.00 .60
235 Michael Coleman .30 .09
235S Michael Coleman SP 2.00 .60
236 Pat Burrell .75 .23
236S Pat Burrell SP .75 .23
237 Wascar Serrano RC .50 .15
237S Wascar Serrano SP 2.00 .60
238 Rick Ankiel .30 .09
238S Rick Ankiel SP 2.00 .60
239 Mike Lamb RC .50 .15
239S Mike Lamb SP 2.00 .60
240 Vernon Wells .30 .09
240S Vernon Wells SP 2.00 .60
241 Jorge Toca .30 .09
Geoffrey Tomlinson
241S Jorge Toca .75 .23
Geoffrey Tomlinson SP
242 Josh Phelps RC 1.50 .45
Shea Hillenbrand
242S Josh Phelps 3.00 .90
Shea Hillenbrand SP
243 Aaron Myette .30 .09
Doug Davis
243S Aaron Myette .75 .23
Doug Davis SP
244 Brett Laxton .30 .09
Rob Ramsay
244S Brett Laxton .75 .23
Rob Ramsay SP
245 B.J. Ryan .30 .09
Corey Lee
245S B.J.Ryan .75 .23
Corey Lee SP
246 Chris Haas .30 .09
Wilton Veras
246S Chris Haas .75 .23
Wilton Veras SP
247 Jimmy Anderson .30 .09
Kyle Peterson
247S Jimmy Anderson .75 .23
Kyle Peterson SP
248 Jason Dewey .30 .09
Giuseppe Chiaramonte
248S Jason Dewey .75 .23
Giuseppe Chiaramonte SP
249 Guillermo Mota .30 .09
Orber Moreno
249S Guillermo Mota .75 .23
Orber Moreno SP
250 Julio Zuleta RC .50 .15
Steve Cox
250S Julio Zuleta 1.25 .35
Steve Cox SP

2000 SkyBox Star Rubies

Randomly inserted into packs at one in 12, this set parallels the 250-card base issued Skybox set. Card fronts feature red foil. Card backs carry a "SR" prefix.

Nm-Mt Ex-Mt
*STARS: 4X TO 10X BASIC CARDS ....
*ROOKIES: 2X TO 5X BASIC VERTICAL

2000 SkyBox Star Rubies Extreme

Randomly inserted into packs, this set parallels the 250-card base issued Skybox set. There were 50 serial numbered sets produced. Card fronts feature red foil. Card backs carry a "SRE" prefix.

Nm-Mt Ex-Mt
*STARS: 15X TO 40X BASIC CARDS ..
*ROOKIES: 8X TO 20X BASIC CARDS

2000 SkyBox Autographics

Randomly inserted in numerous Fleer/SkyBox brands insert set features autographed cards of a wide array of major league veterans and youngsters. Stated odds per brand are as follows: Dominion 1:144, E-X 1:24, Impact 1:216, Metal 1:96 and SkyBox 1:72.

Nm-Mt Ex-Mt
1 Bobby Abreu EX-IM-MT 15.00 4.50
2 Chad Allen MT 10.00 3.00
3 Moises Alou EX 15.00 4.50
4 Marlon Anderson IM-MT 10.00 3.00
5 Rick Ankiel 10.00 3.00
DM-EX-IM-MT-SB
6 Glen Barker MT 10.00 3.00
7 Michael Barrett EX-SB 10.00 3.00
8 Josh Beckett EX-SB 40.00 12.00
9 Rob Bell EX-IM-MT-SB 10.00 3.00
10 Mark Bellhorn MT 10.00 3.00
11 Carlos Beltran EX-IM 15.00 4.50
12 Adrian Beltre EX-SB 15.00 4.50
13 Peter Bergeron 10.00 3.00
DM-MT-SB
14 Lance Berkman MT-SB 15.00 4.50
15 Wade Boggs 40.00 12.00
DM-EX-IM-MT
16 Barry Bonds 175.00 52.50
DM-EX-IM-MT
17 Kent Bottenfield EX-MT 10.00 3.00
18 Milton Bradley EX-IM 15.00 4.50
19 Rico Brogna SB 10.00 3.00
20 Pat Burrell 25.00 7.50
DM-EX-IM-MT-SB
21 Orlando Cabrera IM-SB 10.00 3.00
22 Miguel Cairo DM-MT 10.00 3.00
23 Mike Cameron 15.00 4.50
DM-MT-SB
24 Chris Carpenter 10.00 3.00
EX-IM-MT
25 Sean Casey EX-IM 15.00 4.50
26 Roger Cedeno MT-SB 10.00 3.00
27 Eric Chavez EX-SB 15.00 4.50
28 Bruce Chen SB 10.00 3.00
29 Will Clark EX 40.00 12.00
30 Johnny Damon EX-SB 15.00 4.50
31 Mike Darr EX-MT 10.00 3.00
32 Ben Davis EX-DM-SB 10.00 3.00
33 Russ Davis EX-DM 10.00 3.00
34 Carlos Delgado EX-IM 25.00 7.50
35 Jason Dewey EX-SB 10.00 3.00
36 Einar Diaz DM-MT 10.00 3.00
37 Octavio Dotel EX-SB 10.00 3.00
38 J.D. Drew 15.00 4.50
EX-IM-MT-SB
39 Erubiel Durazo MT-SB 15.00 4.50
40 Ray Durham EX-IM-MT 15.00 4.50
41 Damion Easley EX-MT 10.00 3.00
42 Scott Elarton DM-MT 10.00 3.00
43 Kelvim Escobar EX-IM 10.00 3.00
44 Carlos Febles EX 10.00 3.00
45 Freddy Garcia EX 15.00 4.50
46 Jason Giambi SB 40.00 12.00
47 Jeremy Giambi 10.00 3.00
DM-EX-MT
48 Doug Glanville MT-SB 10.00 3.00
49 Troy Glaus SB 25.00 7.50
50 Alex Gonzalez SB 10.00 3.00
51 Shawn Green MT-SB 15.00 4.50
52 Todd Greene DM-EX 10.00 3.00
53 Jason Grilli EX-SB 10.00 3.00
54 Vladimir Guerrero 40.00 12.00
DM-EX-IM
55 Tony Gwynn 50.00 15.00

DM-EX-IM-SB
56 Jerry Hairston Jr. 10.00 3.00
EX-IM-MT
57 Mike Hampton EX-SB.......... 15.00 4.50
58 Todd Helton EX-IM.............. 25.00 7.50
59 Trevor Hoffman EX.............. 15.00 4.50
60 Bobby Howry DM-MT.......... 10.00 3.00
61 Tim Hudson DM-EX-SB....... 25.00 7.50
62 Norm Hutchins MT-SB........ 10.00 3.00
63 John Jaha EX-SB............... 10.00 3.00
64 Derek Jeter EX-SB............ 120.00 36.00
65 D'Angelo Jimenez.............. 10.00 3.00
EX-SB
66 Nick Johnson IM 15.00 4.50
67 Russ Johnson 80.00 24.00
DM-EX-MT-SB
68 Andruw Jones DM-SB.......... 25.00 7.50
69 Jacque Jones DM-MT 15.00 4.50
70 Gabe Kapler MT-SB............. 10.00 3.00
71 Jason Kendall..................... 15.00 4.50
EX-IM-SB
72 Adam Kennedy EX-SB.......... 10.00 3.00
73 Cesar King EX-MT-SB.......... 10.00 3.00
74 Paul Konerko EX-SB............ 15.00 4.50
75 Mark Kotsay 10.00 3.00
EX-IM-MT-SB
76 Ray Lankford EX.................. 10.00 3.00
77 Jason LaRue DM-EX............ 10.00 3.00
78 Matt Lawton DM-EX............. 10.00 3.00
79 Carlos Lee EX-SB................ 15.00 4.50
80 Mike Lieberthal EX-SB......... 15.00 4.50
81 Cole Liniak EX-IM-MT.......... 10.00 3.00
82 Steve Lomasney EX-SB........ 10.00 3.00
83 Jose Macias EX-IM............... 10.00 3.00
84 Greg Maddux....................... 80.00 24.00
DM-EX-MT-SB-IM
85 Edgar Martinez EX-SB......... 40.00 12.00
86 Pedro Martinez.................. 100.00 30.00
DM-EX-MT
87 Ruben Mateo....................... 10.00 3.00
EX-IM-MT
88 Gary Matthews Jr. EX.......... 10.00 3.00
89 Aaron McNeal EX-SB............ 10.00 3.00
90 Kevin Millwood SB............... 15.00 4.50
91 Raul Mondesi EX-SB............ 15.00 4.50
92 Orber Moreno EX-IM............ 10.00 3.00
93 Warren Morris EX-MT.......... 10.00 3.00
94 Eric Munson EX-IM............... 15.00 4.50
95 Heath Murray EX-MT............ 10.00 3.00
96 Mike Mussina EX.................. 40.00 12.00
97 Joe Nathan 10.00 3.00
EX-IM-MT-SB
98 Magglio Ordonez SB............. 15.00 4.50
99 Eric Owens SB...................... 10.00 3.00
100 Rafael Palmeiro................. 40.00 12.00
EX-SB
101 Jim Parque EX-MT 10.00 3.00
102 Angel Pena 10.00 3.00
EX-IM-MT-SB
103 Adam Piatt IM 10.00 3.00
104 Wily Pena EX-SB................. 10.00 3.00
105 Pokey Reese DM-EX............ 10.00 3.00
106 Matt Riley EX-IM................. 15.00 4.50
107 Cal Ripken 120.00 36.00
EX-IM-MT-SB
108 Alex Rodriguez................. 100.00 30.00
DM-EX-IM-MT-SB
109 Scott Rolen EX-IM-SB......... 25.00 7.50
110 Jimmy Rollins 15.00 4.50
EX-IM-SB
111 Ryan Rupe DM-MT.............. 10.00 3.00
112 B.J. Ryan EX-IM-SB 10.00 3.00
113 Tim Salmon SB 25.00 7.50
114 Randall Simon EX-MT 10.00 3.00
115 Chris Singleton.................. 10.00 3.00
EX-MT-SB
116 J.T. Snow DM-SB................ 15.00 4.50
117 Alfonso Soriano................. 40.00 12.00
EX-IM
118 Shannon Stewart EX 15.00 4.50
119 Mike Sweeney 15.00 4.50
EX-MT-SB
120 Miguel Tejada EX................ 15.00 4.50
121 Frank Thomas EX-IM........... 40.00 12.00
122 Wilton Veras...................... 10.00 3.00
EX-IM-MT
123 Jose Vidro DM-SB............... 15.00 4.50
124 Billy Wagner EX-IM............. 25.00 7.50
125 Jeff Weaver EX-IM.............. 15.00 4.50
126 Rondell White EX-SB........... 15.00 4.50
127 Scott Williamson 10.00 3.00
EX-IM-MT
128 Randy Wolf EX-MT.............. 15.00 4.50
129 Tony Womack 10.00 3.00
DM-MT
130 Jaret Wright EX-SB 10.00 3.00
131 Ed Yarnall DM-EX................ 10.00 3.00
132 Kevin Young DM-EX............. 10.00 3.00

2000 SkyBox Autographics Purple Foil

Randomly inserted in numerous 2000 Fleer/SkyBox brands, this set is a parallel of the standard Autographics insert. These cards can be quickly differentiated from their base card counterparts by the purple foil logos and player names on the card front coupled with the fact that each card is hand-numbered to 50 on front.

Nm-Mt Ex-Mt
2 Chad Allen MT..................... 25.00 7.50
3 Moises Alou EX..................... 40.00 12.00
4 Marlon Anderson.................. 25.00 7.50
IM-MT
5 Rick Ankiel 25.00 7.50
EX-IM-MT-SB
6 Glen Barker MT 25.00 7.50
7 Michael Barrett EX-SB.......... 25.00 7.50
8 Josh Beckett EX-SB............ 100.00 30.00
9 Rob Bell EX-IM-MT-SB.......... 25.00 7.50
11 Adrian Beltre EX-SB 40.00 12.00
12 Carlos Beltran EX-IM........... 40.00 12.00
13 Peter Bergeron 25.00 7.50
DM-MT-SB
14 Lance Berkman MT-SB......... 40.00 12.00
15 Wade Boggs EX-IM-MT...... 100.00 30.00
16 Barry Bonds EX-IM-MT 400.00 120.00
17 Kent Bottenfield EX-MT 25.00 7.50
18 Milton Bradley EX................ 40.00 12.00
19 Rico Brogna SB.................... 25.00 7.50
20 Pat Burrell 60.00 18.00
EX-IM-MT-SB
21 Orlando Cabrera IM-SB........ 25.00 7.50
22 Miguel Cairo DM-MT............ 25.00 7.50
23 Mike Cameron 40.00 12.00
DM-MT-SB
24 Chris Carpenter 25.00 7.50
EX-IM-MT
25 Sean Casey EX-IM............... 40.00 12.00
26 Roger Cedeno MT-SB........... 25.00 7.50
27 Eric Chavez EX-SB............... 40.00 12.00
28 Bruce Chen SB 25.00 7.50
29 Will Clark EX...................... 100.00 30.00
30 Johnny Damon EX-SB.......... 40.00 12.00
31 Ben Davis EX-SB.................. 25.00 7.50
33 Russ Davis EX-DM 25.00 7.50
34 Carlos Delgado EX-IM.......... 60.00 18.00
35 Jason Dewey EX-SB............. 25.00 7.50
36 Einar Diaz DM-MT................ 25.00 7.50
37 Octavio Dotel EX-SB............ 25.00 7.50
38 J.D. Drew 40.00 12.00
EX-IM-MT-SB
39 Erubiel Durazo MT-SB.......... 40.00 12.00
40 Ray Durham EX-IM-MT......... 40.00 12.00
41 Damion Easley EX-MT.......... 25.00 7.50
42 Scott Elarton DM-MT 25.00 7.50
43 Kelvim Escobar EX............... 25.00 7.50
44 Carlos Febles EX................. 25.00 7.50
45 Freddy Garcia EX................. 40.00 12.00
46 Jason Giambi EX-SB 100.00 30.00
47 Jeremy Giambi 25.00 7.50
DM-MT
48 Doug Glanville MT-SB 25.00 7.50
49 Troy Glaus SB...................... 60.00 18.00
50 Alex Gonzalez SB................. 25.00 7.50
51 Shawn Green MT-SB............ 40.00 12.00
52 Todd Greene DM-EX............ 25.00 7.50
53 Jason Grilli EX-SB 25.00 7.50
54 Vladimir Guerrero.............. 100.00 30.00
EX-IM
55 Tony Gwynn 120.00 36.00
EX-IM-SB
57 Mike Hampton EX-SB........... 40.00 12.00
58 Todd Helton EX-IM.............. 60.00 18.00
59 Trevor Hoffman EX.............. 40.00 12.00
60 Bobby Howry DM-MT............ 25.00 7.50
61 Tim Hudson......................... 60.00 18.00
DM-EX-SB
62 Norm Hutchins..................... 25.00 7.50
MT-SB
63 John Jaha SB 25.00 7.50
64 Derek Jeter EX-SB............. 300.00 90.00
65 D'Angelo Jiminez 25.00 7.50
EX-SB
66 Nick Johnson EX-IM............. 40.00 12.00
67 Randy Johnson 200.00 60.00
EX-MT-SB
68 Andruw Jones SB................. 60.00 18.00
69 Jacque Jones DM-MT 40.00 12.00
70 Gabe Kapler MT-SB.............. 25.00 7.50
71 Jason Kendall...................... 40.00 12.00
EX-IM-SB
72 Adam Kennedy EX-SB........... 25.00 7.50
73 Cesar King EX-MT-SB........... 25.00 7.50
74 Paul Konerko EX-SB............. 40.00 12.00
75 Mark Kotsay 25.00 7.50
EX-IM-MT-SB
76 Ray Lankford EX.................. 25.00 7.50
77 Jason LaRue DM-EX 25.00 7.50
78 Matt Lawton DM-EX 25.00 7.50
79 Carlos Lee EX-SB................. 40.00 12.00
80 Mike Lieberthal.................... 40.00 12.00
EX-SB
81 Cole Liniak EX-IM-MT 25.00 7.50
82 Steve Lomasney................... 25.00 7.50
EX-SB
83 Jose Macias EX.................... 25.00 7.50
84 Greg Maddux..................... 200.00 60.00
EX-IM-MT-SB
85 Edgar Martinez EX-SB 100.00 30.00
86 Pedro Martinez................. 250.00 75.00
EX-MT
87 Ruben Mateo....................... 25.00 7.50
EX-IM-MT
88 Gary Matthews Jr. EX........... 25.00 7.50
89 Aaron McNeal EX-SB............ 25.00 7.50
90 Kevin Millwood SB 40.00 12.00
91 Raul Mondesi EX-SB 40.00 12.00
92 Orber Moreno EX-IM............ 25.00 7.50
93 Warren Morris EX-MT........... 25.00 7.50
94 Eric Munson EX-IM 40.00 12.00
96 Mike Mussina EX................ 100.00 30.00
97 Joe Nathan.......................... 25.00 7.50
EX-IM-MT-SB
98 Magglio Ordonez SB............. 40.00 12.00
99 Eric Owens SB...................... 25.00 7.50
100 Rafael Palmeiro 100.00 30.00
EX-SB
102 Angel Pena EX-MT-SB......... 25.00 7.50
103 Adam Piatt IM 25.00 7.50
105 Pokey Reese DM 25.00 7.50
106 Matt Riley EX-IM................. 40.00 12.00
107 Cal Ripken 300.00 90.00
EX-IM-MT-SB
108 Alex Rodriguez................. 250.00 75.00
EX-IM-MT-SB
109 Scott Rolen EX-IM-SB......... 60.00 18.00
110 Jimmy Rollins 40.00 12.00
EX-IM-SB
111 Ryan Rupe DM-MT.............. 25.00 7.50
112 B.J. Ryan EX-IM-SB 25.00 7.50
113 Tim Salmon SB 60.00 18.00
114 Randall Simon EX-MT 25.00 7.50
115 Chris Singleton.................. 25.00 7.50
EX-MT-SB
116 J.T. Snow DM-SB................ 40.00 12.00
117 Alfonso Soriano............... 100.00 30.00
EX-IM
118 Shannon Stewart EX 40.00 12.00
119 Mike Sweeney 40.00 12.00
EX-MT-SB
120 Miguel Tejada EX................ 40.00 12.00
121 Frank Thomas EX-IM......... 100.00 30.00
122 Wilton Veras...................... 25.00 7.50
EX-IM-MT
123 Jose Vidro DM-SB............... 40.00 12.00
124 Billy Wagner EX-IM............. 60.00 18.00
126 Rondell White EX-SB........... 40.00 12.00
128 Randy Wolf EX-MT.............. 40.00 12.00
129 Tony Womack 25.00 7.50
DM-MT
130 Jaret Wright EX-SB 25.00 7.50
131 Ed Yarnall EX-DM............... 25.00 7.50
132 Kevin Young EX-DM............ 25.00 7.50

2000 SkyBox E-Ticket

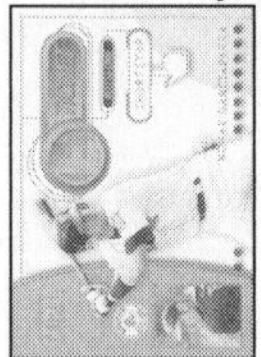

Randomly inserted into packs at one in four, this 15-card insert features players that are Hall of Fame bound. Card backs carry an "ET" prefix.

Nm-Mt Ex-Mt
COMPLETE SET (15)................ 20.00 6.00
*STAR RUBY: 8X TO 20X BASIC E-TICKET
STAR RUBIES: RANDOM IN HOBBY PACKS
STAR RUBIES PR.RUN 100 SERIAL #'d SETS
ET1 Alex Rodriguez .... 1.50 .45
ET2 Derek Jeter.......................... 2.50 .75
ET3 Nomar Garciaparra .... 1.50 .45
ET4 Cal Ripken .... 3.00 .90
ET5 Sean Casey............................ .40 .12
ET6 Mark McGwire...................... 2.50 .75
ET7 Sammy Sosa .... 1.50 .45
ET8 Ken Griffey Jr. .... 1.50 .45
ET9 Tony Gwynn......................... 1.25 .35
ET10 Pedro Martinez................... 1.00 .30
ET11 Chipper Jones .... 1.00 .30
ET12 Vladimir Guerrero................ 1.00 .30
ET13 Roger Clemens.................... 2.00 .60
ET14 Mike Piazza .... 1.50 .45
ET15 Randy Johnson .... 1.00 .30

2000 SkyBox Genuine Coverage

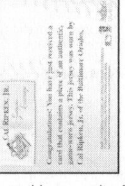

This insert features game-used jersey cards of 10 of the major league's top athletes. All cards are unnumbered and checklisted below alphabetically by player name. The set was split into two five card groups for hobby and retail distribution. The five "common" cards - tagged with an "HR" in the checklist below - were distributed in both hobby and retail packs at a rate of 1:399. The five "hobby-only" cards - tagged with an "H" in the checklist below - were seeded hobby packs at a rate of 1:144. In addition, Cal Ripken and Alex Rodriguez each signed 20 serial numbered copies of their jersey cards. These rare cards were seeded exclusively into hobby packs and are listed at the end of the checklist.

Nm-Mt Ex-Mt
1 Jose Canseco H.................... 15.00 4.50
2 J.D. Drew H......................... 10.00 3.00
3 Troy Glaus HR...................... 15.00 4.50
4 Manny Ramirez H................. 10.00 3.00
5 Cal Ripken HR...................... 40.00 12.00
6 Alex Rodriguez HR 25.00 7.50
7 Ivan Rodriguez H.................. 15.00 4.50
8 Frank Thomas H 15.00 4.50
9 Robin Ventura HR 10.00 3.00
10 Matt Williams HR................ 10.00 3.00
AU1 Cal Ripken AU/20..........................
AU2 Alex Rodriguez AU 20..................

2000 SkyBox Higher Level

Randomly inserted into packs at one in 24, this insert features 10 players that take their game to the next level. Card backs carry a "HL" prefix.

Nm-Mt Ex-Mt
COMPLETE SET (10)................ 50.00 15.00
*STAR RUBIES: 5X TO 12X BASIC HIGH.LEVEL
STAR RUBIES: RANDOM IN HOBBY PACKS
STAR RUBIES PRINT RUN 50 SERIAL #'d
SETS ....
HL1 Cal Ripken......................... 10.00 3.00
HL2 Derek Jeter 10.00 3.00
HL3 Nomar Garciaparra 8.00 2.40
HL4 Chipper Jones..................... 6.00 1.80
HL5 Mike Piazza 8.00 2.40
HL6 Ivan Rodriguez.................... 3.00 .90
HL7 Ken Griffey Jr.................... 10.00 3.00
HL8 Sammy Sosa........................ 5.00 1.50
HL9 Alex Rodriguez.................... 8.00 2.40
HL10 Mark McGwire 10.00 3.00

2000 SkyBox Preeminence

Randomly inserted into packs at one in 24, this insert set features 10 of major league baseball's top athletes. Card backs carry a "P" prefix.

Nm-Mt Ex-Mt
COMPLETE SET (10)................. 40.00 12.00
*STAR RUBIES: 5X TO 12X BASIC PRE-EM
STAR RUBIES: RANDOM IN HOBBY PACKS
STAR RUBIES PRINT RUN 50 SERIAL #'d
SETS ....
P1 Pedro Martinez..................... 3.00 .90
P2 Derek Jeter........................... 8.00 2.40
P3 Nomar Garciaparra 5.00 1.50
P4 Alex Rodriguez...................... 5.00 1.50
P5 Mark McGwire....................... 8.00 2.40
P6 Sammy Sosa......................... 5.00 1.50
P7 Sean Casey .... 1.25 .35
P8 Mike Piazza 5.00 1.50
P9 Chipper Jones .... 3.00 .90
P10 Ivan Rodriguez.................... 3.00 .90

2000 SkyBox Skylines

Randomly inserted into packs at one in 11, this insert set features ten MLB stars against the backdrop of the city they play in. Card backs carry a "SL" prefix.

Nm-Mt Ex-Mt
COMPLETE SET (10)................ 25.00 7.50
*STAR RUBIES: 10X TO 25X BASIC SKYLINES
STAR RUBIES: RANDOM IN HOBBY PACKS
STAR RUBIES PRINT RUN 50 SERIAL #'d
SETS ....
SL1 Cal Ripken........................... 5.00 1.50
SL2 Mark McGwire...................... 4.00 1.20
SL3 Alex Rodriguez .... 2.50 .75
SL4 Sammy Sosa......................... 2.50 .75
SL5 Derek Jeter.......................... 4.00 1.20
SL6 Mike Piazza .... 2.50 .75
SL7 Nomar Garciaparra............... 2.50 .75
SL8 Chipper Jones .... 1.50 .45
SL9 Ken Griffey Jr. .... 2.50 .75
SL10 Manny Ramirez................... .60 .18

2000 SkyBox Speed Merchants

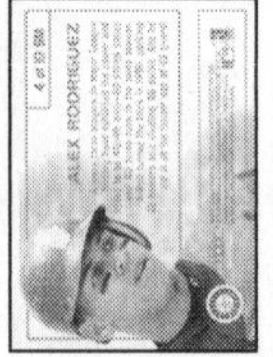

Randomly inserted into packs at one in 8, this set features 10 players who exhibit speed including baserunning, bat speed, pitching and fielding. Card backs carry a "SM" prefix.

Nm-Mt Ex-Mt
COMPLETE SET (10)................. 20.00 6.00
*STAR RUBIES: 6X TO 15X BASIC MERCHANT
STAR RUBIES: RANDOM IN HOBBY PACKS
STAR RUBIES PRINT RUN 100 SERIAL #'d
SETS ....
SM1 Derek Jeter......................... 3.00 .90
SM2 Sammy Sosa........................ 2.00 .60
SM3 Nomar Garciaparra............... 2.00 .60
SM4 Alex Rodriguez.................... 2.00 .60
SM5 Randy Johnson.................... 1.25 .35
SM6 Ken Griffey Jr. .... 2.00 .60
SM7 Pedro Martinez.................... 1.25 .35
SM8 Pat Burrell .... 1.25 .35
SM9 Barry Bonds .... 3.00 .90
SM10 Mark McGwire .... 3.00 .90

2000 SkyBox Technique

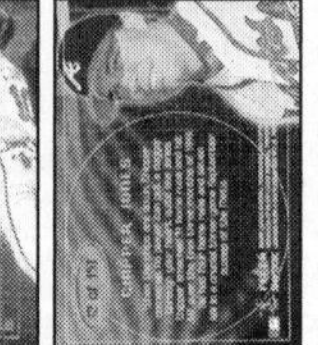

Randomly inserted into packs at one in 11, this insert set features 15 players that get the job done with their exceptional fundamentals and technique. Card backs carry a "T" prefix.

Nm-Mt Ex-Mt
COMPLETE SET (15)................. 40.00 12.00
*STAR RUBIES: 8X TO 20X BASIC TECHNIQUE
STAR RUBIES: RANDOM IN HOBBY PACKS
STAR RUBIES PRINT RUN 50 SERIAL #'d
SETS ....
T1 Alex Rodriguez....................... 3.00 .90
T2 Tony Gwynn........................... 2.50 .75
T3 Sean Casey.............................. .75 .23
T4 Mark McGwire........................ 5.00 1.50
T5 Sammy Sosa........................... 3.00 .90
T6 Ken Griffey Jr. .... 3.00 .90
T7 Mike Piazza .... 3.00 .90
T8 Nomar Garciaparra.................. 3.00 .90
T9 Derek Jeter 5.00 1.50
T10 Vladimir Guerrero.................. 2.00 .60
T11 Cal Ripken.............................. 6.00 1.80
T12 Chipper Jones .... 2.00 .60
T13 Frank Thomas .... 2.00 .60
T14 Manny Ramirez .... .75 .23
T15 Jeff Bagwell............................ 1.25 .35

2000 SkyBox Hobby Bullpen

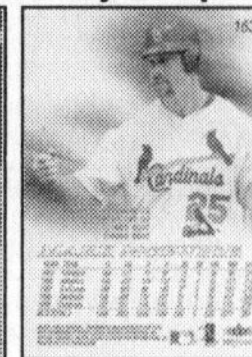

These 15 standard-size cards were given away by Fleer executives at 15 different promotional stops as part of the Fleer Traveling Road Show. These are parallel cards to the regular SkyBox cards and they feature a red "Fleer Hobby Bullpen" logo.

Nm-Mt Ex-Mt
COMPLETE SET (15)................ 30.00 9.00
1 Cal Ripken............................. 5.00 1.50
2 Ivan Rodriguez....................... 1.25 .35
3 Chipper Jones .... 2.00 .60
12 Vladimir Guerrero.................. 1.50 .45
17 Greg Maddux......................... 2.50 .75
18 Manny Ramirez..................... 1.25 .35
48 Tony Gwynn .... 2.50 .75
49 Barry Bonds .... 2.50 .75
51 Pedro Martinez...................... 1.25 .35
68 Nomar Garciaparra................. 2.00 .60
98 Jason Kendall......................... 1.00 .30
99 Ken Griffey Jr. .... 3.00 .90
163 Mark McGwire...................... 4.00 1.20
176 Sammy Sosa......................... 2.50 .75
180 Derek Jeter........................... 5.00 1.50

2000 SkyBox National

This six-card standard-size set was distributed at the 2000 National Convention in Anaheim,CA in July, 2000. The set features cards from the 2000 SkyBox set with a special "NSCC" stamp on the front right corner.

Nm-Mt Ex-Mt
COMPLETE SET (6).................. 20.00 6.00
1 Cal Ripken............................. 5.00 1.50
2 Ken Griffey Jr. .... 3.00 .90
3 Derek Jeter............................ 5.00 1.50
4 Alex Rodriguez....................... 3.00 .90
5 Mark McGwire........................ 4.00 1.20
6 Mike Piazza .... 3.00 .90

2000 SkyBox Dominion

This 300 card set was issued in 10 cards packs with a SRP of $1.49. The following subsets are included in this set: League Leaders (1-8), Highlights (9-23), Prospects (251-270), Future Stars (271-300). The Future Star cards feature two players from each team. The regular cards have color photos against a black and white background. An Alex Rodriguez Promo card was distributed to dealers and hobby media several weeks prior to the product's release. The promo is easy to distinguish by the text "PROMOTIONAL SAMPLE" running diagonally across the card front.

Nm-Mt Ex-Mt
COMPLETE SET (300).............. 40.00 12.00
COMMON CARD (1-250)................ .20 .06
COMMON (251-300).................... .40 .12
1 Mark McGwire LL....................... .50 .15
Ken.Griffey Jr.
2 Mark McGwire LL....................... .50 .15
Manny Ramirez
3 Larry Walker LL......................... .50 .15
Nomar Garciaparra
4 Tony Womack LL .... .20 .06
Brian Hunter
5 Mike Hampton LL....................... .30 .09
Pedro Martinez
6 Randy Johnson LL .... .30 .09
Pedro Martinez
7 Randy Johnson LL .... .30 .09
Pedro Martinez
8 Ugueth Urbina LL .... .20 .06
Mariano Rivera
9 Vinny Castilla HL........................ .20 .06
10 Orioles/Cuban Nat'l HL.............. .20 .06
11 Jose Canseco HL....................... .30 .09
12 Fernando Tatis HL..................... .20 .06
13 Robin Ventura HL...................... .20 .06

14 Roger Clemens HL .50 .15
15 Jose Jimenez HL .20 .06
16 David Cone HL .20 .06
17 Mark McGwire HL .60 .18
18 Cal Ripken HL .75 .23
19 Tony Gwynn HL .30 .09
20 Wade Boggs HL .20 .06
21 Ivan Rodriguez HL .30 .09
22 Chuck Finley HL UER .20 .06
23 Eric Milton HL .20 .06
24 Adrian Beltre .20 .06
25 Brad Radke .20 .06
26 Derek Bell .20 .06
27 Garret Anderson .20 .06
28 Ivan Rodriguez .50 .15
29 Jeff Kent .20 .06
30 Jeremy Giambi .20 .06
31 John Franco .20 .06
32 Jose Hernandez .20 .06
33 Jose Offerman .20 .06
34 Jose Rosado .20 .06
35 Kevin Appier .20 .06
36 Kris Benson .20 .06
37 Mark McGwire 1.25 .35
38 Matt Williams .20 .06
39 Paul O'Neill .30 .09
40 Rickey Henderson .50 .15
41 Todd Greene .20 .06
42 Russ Ortiz .20 .06
43 Sean Casey .20 .06
44 Tony Womack .20 .06
45 Troy O'Leary .20 .06
46 Ugueth Urbina .20 .06
47 Tom Glavine .30 .09
48 Mike Mussina .50 .15
49 Carlos Febles .20 .06
50 Jon Lieber .20 .06
51 Juan Gonzalez .50 .15
52 Matt Clement .20 .06
53 Moises Alou .20 .06
54 Ray Durham .20 .06
55 Robb Nen .20 .06
56 Tino Martinez .30 .09
57 Troy Glaus .30 .09
58 Curt Schilling .30 .09
59 Mike Sweeney .20 .06
60 Steve Finley .20 .06
61 Roger Cedeno .20 .06
62 Bobby Jones .20 .06
63 John Smoltz .30 .09
64 Darin Erstad .20 .06
65 Carlos Delgado .20 .06
66 Ray Lankford .20 .06
67 Todd Stottlemyre .20 .06
68 Andy Ashby .20 .06
69 Bob Abreu .20 .06
70 Chuck Finley .20 .06
71 Damion Easley .20 .06
72 Dustin Hermanson .20 .06
73 Frank Thomas .50 .15
74 Kevin Brown .30 .09
75 Kevin Millwood .20 .06
76 Mark Grace .30 .09
77 Matt Stairs .20 .06
78 Mike Hampton .20 .06
79 Omar Vizquel .20 .06
80 Preston Wilson .20 .06
81 Robin Ventura .30 .09
82 Todd Helton .30 .09
83 Tony Clark .20 .06
84 Al Leiter .20 .06
85 Alex Fernandez .20 .06
86 Bernie Williams .30 .09
87 Edgar Martinez .30 .09
88 Edgar Renteria .20 .06
89 Fred McGriff .30 .09
90 Jermaine Dye .20 .06
91 Joe McEwing .20 .06
92 John Halama .20 .06
93 Lee Stevens .20 .06
94 Matt Lawton .20 .06
95 Mike Piazza .75 .23
96 Pete Harnisch .20 .06
97 Scott Karl .20 .06
98 Tony Fernandez .20 .06
99 Sammy Sosa .75 .23
100 Bobby Higginson .20 .06
101 Tony Gwynn .60 .18
102 J.D. Drew .20 .06
103 Roberto Hernandez .20 .06
104 Rondell White .20 .06
105 David Nilsson .20 .06
106 Shane Reynolds .20 .06
107 Jaret Wright .20 .06
108 Jeff Bagwell .30 .09
109 Jay Bell .20 .06
110 Kevin Tapani .20 .06
111 Michael Barrett .20 .06
112 Neifi Perez .20 .06
113 Pat Hengen .20 .06
114 Roger Clemens 1.00 .30
115 Travis Fryman .20 .06
116 Aaron Sele .20 .06
117 Eric Davis .20 .06
118 Trevor Hoffman .20 .06
119 Chris Singleton .20 .06
120 Ryan Klesko .20 .06
121 Scott Rolen .30 .09
122 Jorge Posada .30 .09
123 Abraham Nunez .20 .06
124 Alex Gonzalez .20 .06
125 B.J. Surhoff .20 .06
126 Barry Bonds 1.25 .35
127 Billy Koch .20 .06
128 Billy Wagner .20 .06
129 Brad Ausmus .20 .06
130 Bret Boone .20 .06
131 Cal Ripken 1.50 .45
132 Chad Allen .20 .06
133 Chris Carpenter .20 .06
134 Craig Biggio .30 .09
135 Dante Bichette .20 .06
136 Dean Palmer .20 .06
137 Derek Jeter 1.25 .35
138 Ellis Burks .20 .06
139 Freddy Garcia .20 .06
140 Gabe Kapler .20 .06
141 Greg Maddux .75 .23
142 Greg Vaughn .20 .06
143 Jason Kendall .20 .06
144 Jim Parque .20 .06
145 John Valentin .20 .06
146 Jose Vidro .20 .06
147 Ken Griffey Jr. .75 .23
148 Kenny Lofton .20 .06
149 Kenny Rogers .20 .06
150 Kent Bottenfield .20 .06
151 Chuck Knoblauch .20 .06
152 Larry Walker .30 .09
153 Manny Ramirez .20 .06
154 Mickey Morandini .20 .06
155 Mike Cameron .20 .06
156 Mike Lieberthal .20 .06
157 Mo Vaughn .20 .06
158 Randy Johnson .50 .15
159 Rey Ordonez .20 .06
160 Roberto Alomar .50 .15
161 Scott Williamson .20 .06
162 Shawn Estes .20 .06
163 Tim Wakefield .20 .06
164 Tony Batista .20 .06
165 Will Clark .50 .15
166 Wade Boggs .30 .09
167 David Cone .20 .06
168 Doug Glanville .20 .06
169 Jeff Cirillo .20 .06
170 John Jaha .20 .06
171 Mariano Rivera .30 .09
172 Tom Gordon .20 .06
173 Wally Joyner .20 .06
174 Alex Gonzalez .20 .06
175 Andruw Jones .20 .06
176 Barry Larkin .50 .15
177 Bartolo Colon .20 .06
178 Brian Giles .20 .06
179 Carlos Lee .20 .06
180 Darren Dreifort .20 .06
181 Eric Chavez .20 .06
182 Henry Rodriguez .20 .06
183 Ismael Valdes .20 .06
184 Jason Giambi .50 .15
185 John Wetteland .20 .06
186 Juan Encarnacion .20 .06
187 Luis Gonzalez .20 .06
188 Reggie Sanders .20 .06
189 Richard Hidalgo .20 .06
190 Ryan Rupe .20 .06
191 Sean Berry .20 .06
192 Rick Helling .20 .06
193 Randy Wolf .20 .06
194 Cliff Floyd .20 .06
195 Jose Lima .20 .06
196 Chipper Jones .50 .15
197 Charles Johnson .20 .06
198 Nomar Garciaparra .75 .23
199 Magglio Ordonez .20 .06
200 Shawn Green .20 .06
201 Travis Lee .20 .06
202 Jose Canseco .50 .15
203 Fernando Tatis .20 .06
204 Bruce Aven .20 .06
205 Johnny Damon .20 .06
206 Gary Sheffield .20 .06
207 Ken Caminiti .20 .06
208 Ben Grieve .20 .06
209 Sidney Ponson .20 .06
210 Vinny Castilla .20 .06
211 Alex Rodriguez .75 .23
212 Chris Widger .20 .06
213 Carl Pavano .20 .06
214 J.T. Snow .20 .06
215 Jim Thome .50 .15
216 Kevin Young .20 .06
217 Mike Sirotka .20 .06
218 Rafael Palmeiro .30 .09
219 Rico Brogna .20 .06
220 Todd Walker .20 .06
221 Todd Zeile .20 .06
222 Brian Rose .20 .06
223 Chris Fussell .20 .06
224 Corey Koskie .20 .06
225 Rich Aurilia .20 .06
226 Geoff Jenkins .20 .06
227 Pedro Martinez .50 .15
228 Todd Hundley .20 .06
229 Brian Jordan .20 .06
230 Cristian Guzman .20 .06
231 Raul Mondesi .20 .06
232 Tim Hudson .30 .09
233 Albert Belle .20 .06
234 Andy Pettitte .30 .09
235 Brady Anderson .20 .06
236 Brian Bohanon .20 .06
237 Carlos Beltran .20 .06
238 Doug Mientkiewicz .20 .06
239 Jason Schmidt .20 .06
240 Jeff Zimmerman .20 .06
241 John Olerud .20 .06
242 Paul Byrd .20 .06
243 Vladimir Guerrero .50 .15
244 Warren Morris .20 .06
245 Eric Karros .20 .06
246 Jeff Weaver .20 .06
247 Jeromy Burnitz .20 .06
248 David Bell .20 .06
249 Rusty Greer .20 .06
250 Kevin Stocker .20 .06
251 S.Hillenbrand PROS .40 .12
252 A.Soriano PROS .75 .23
253 Micah Bowie PROS .40 .12
254 G.Matthews Jr. PROS .40 .12
255 Lance Berkman PROS .40 .12
256 Pat Burrell PROS .50 .15
257 Ruben Mateo PROS .40 .12
258 Kip Wells PROS .40 .12
259 Wilton Veras PROS .40 .12
260 Ben Davis PROS .40 .12
261 Eric Munson PROS .40 .12
262 R.Hernandez PROS .40 .12
263 Tony Armas Jr. PROS .40 .12
264 Erubiel Durazo PROS .40 .12
265 Chad Meyers PROS .40 .12
266 Rick Ankiel PROS .40 .12
267 Ramon Ortiz PROS .40 .12
268 Adam Kennedy PROS .40 .12
269 Vernon Wells PROS .40 .12
270 C.Hermansen PROS .40 .12
271 Norm Hutchins .40 .12
Trent Durrington
272 Gabe Molina .40 .12
B.J. Ryan
273 Juan Pena .40 .12
Tomakazu Ohka RC
274 Pat Daneker .40 .12
Aaron Myette
275 Jason Rakers .40 .12
Russ Branyan
276 Beiker Graterol .40 .12
Dave Borkowski
277 Mark Quinn .40 .12
Dan Reichert
278 Mark Redman .40 .12
Jacque Jones
279 Ed Yarnall .40 .12
Wily Pena
280 Chad Harville .40 .12
Brett Laxton
281 Aaron Scheffer .40 .12
Gil Meche
282 Jim Morris 1.25 .35
Dan Wheeler
283 Danny Kolb .40 .12
Kelly Dransfeldt
284 Peter Munro .40 .12
Casey Blake
285 Rob Ryan .40 .12
Byung-Hyun Kim
286 Derrin Ebert .40 .12
Pascual Matos
287 Richard Barker .40 .12
Kyle Farnsworth
288 Jason LaRue .40 .12
Travis Dawkins
289 Chris Sexton .40 .12
Edgard Clemente
290 Amaury Garcia .40 .12
A.J. Burnett
291 Carlos Hernandez .40 .12
Daryle Ward
292 Eric Gagne .75 .23
Jeff R.Williams RC
293 Kyle Peterson .40 .12
Kevin Barker
294 Fernando Seguignol .40 .12
Guillermo Mota
295 Melvin Mora .40 .12
Octavio Dotel
296 Anthony Shumaker .40 .12
Cliff Politte
297 Yamid Haad .40 .12
Jimmy Anderson
298 Rick Heiserman .40 .12
Chad Hutchinson
299 Mike Darr .40 .12
Wiki Gonzalez
300 Joe Nathan .40 .12
Calvin Murray
P211 A.Rodriguez Promo 2.00 .60

2000 Skybox Dominion Double Play

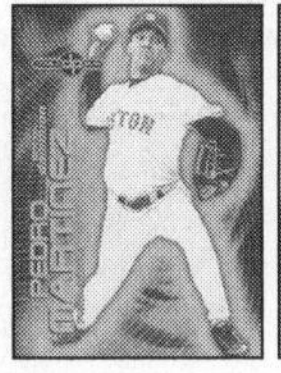

Inserted one every nine packs, this 10 card set highlights two stars on each card. The cards are double-sided with one of the players featured on each side.

Nm-Mt Ex-Mt
COMPLETE SET (10) 25.00 7.50
*PLUS: 1.5X TO 4X BASIC DOUBLE PLAY
PLUS STATED ODDS 1:90
*WARP TEK: 8X TO 20X BASIC DOUBLE PLAY
WARP TEK STATED ODDS 1:900
DP1 Nomar Garciaparra 2.50 .75
Alex Rodriguez
DP2 Pedro Martinez 1.50 .45
Randy Johnson
DP3 Chipper Jones 1.50 .45
Scott Rolen
DP4 Mark McGwire 4.00 1.20
Ken Griffey Jr.
DP5 Cal Ripken 4.00 1.20
Derek Jeter
DP6 Roger Clemens 2.50 .75
Greg Maddux
DP7 Juan Gonzalez 1.50 .45
Manny Ramirez
DP8 Tony Gwynn 2.00 .60
Shawn Green
DP9 Sammy Sosa 1.50 .45
Frank Thomas
DP10 Mike Piazza 2.50 .75
Ivan Rodriguez

2000 Skybox Dominion Eye on October

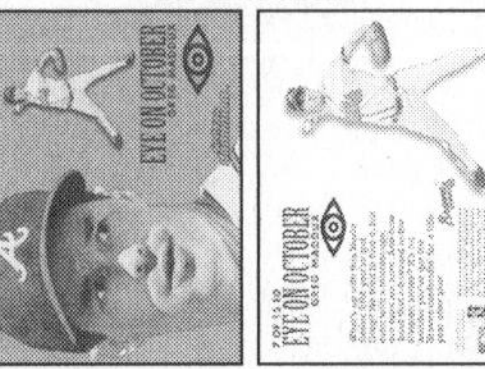

Inserted one every 24 packs, these 15 cards feature players who are striving to appear in the post season. Card backs carry an "EO" prefix.

Nm-Mt Ex-Mt
COMPLETE SET (15) 80.00 24.00
*PLUS: 2X TO 5X BASIC OCTOBER
PLUS STATED ODDS 1:240
EO1 Ken Griffey Jr. 5.00 1.50
EO2 Mark McGwire 8.00 2.40
EO3 Derek Jeter 8.00 2.40
EO4 Juan Gonzalez 3.00 .90
EO5 Chipper Jones 3.00 .90
EO6 Sammy Sosa 5.00 1.50
EO7 Greg Maddux 5.00 1.50
EO8 Frank Thomas 3.00 .90
EO9 Nomar Garciaparra 5.00 1.50
EO10 Shawn Green 1.25 .35
EO11 Cal Ripken 10.00 3.00
EO12 Manny Ramirez 1.25 .35
EO13 Scott Rolen 2.00 .60
EO14 Mike Piazza 5.00 1.50
EO15 Alex Rodriguez 5.00 1.50

2000 Skybox Dominion Eye on October Warp Tek

Randomly inserted into packs, these cards parallel the Eye on October insert set. These cards, are printed on lenticular, three dimensional stock and are serial numbered to the players uniform number. Due to the scarcity of these cards, no pricing is provided.

Nm-Mt Ex-Mt
EO1 Ken Griffey Jr./24
EO2 Mark McGwire/25
EO3 Derek Jeter/2
EO4 Juan Gonzalez/19
EO5 Chipper Jones/10
EO6 Sammy Sosa/21
EO7 Greg Maddux/31
EO8 Frank Thomas/35
EO9 Nomar Garciaparra/5
EO10 Shawn Green/15
EO11 Cal Ripken/8
EO12 Manny Ramirez/24
EO13 Scott Rolen/17
EO14 Mike Piazza/31
EO15 Alex Rodriguez/3

2000 Skybox Dominion Hats Off

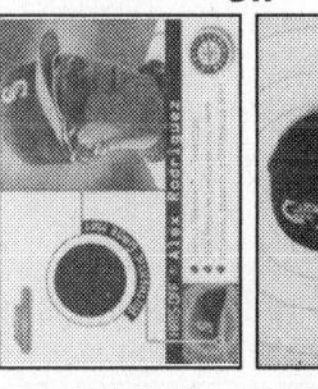

Inserted into hobby packs at a rate of one in 467, these 15 cards feature a piece of a a game worn hat along with a picture of that player.

Nm-Mt Ex-Mt
1 Wade Boggs 25.00 7.50
2 Barry Bonds 60.00 18.00
3 J.D. Drew 15.00 4.50
4 Shawn Green 15.00 4.50
5 Vladimir Guerrero 25.00 7.50
6 Randy Johnson 25.00 7.50
7 Andruw Jones 15.00 4.50
8 Greg Maddux 50.00 15.00
9 Pedro Martinez 25.00 7.50
10 Mike Mussina 25.00 7.50
11 Rafael Palmeiro 25.00 7.50
12 Alex Rodriguez 50.00 15.00
13 Scott Rolen 25.00 7.50
14 Tim Salmon 25.00 7.50
15 Robin Ventura 15.00 4.50

2000 Skybox Dominion Milestones

Issued one every 1999 packs, these six cards feature players who reached important career milestones during the 1999 season. The horizontal cards have the players photo against a background in which the milestone is identified.

Nm-Mt Ex-Mt
COMPLETE SET (6) 300.00 90.00
M1 Mark McGwire 80.00 24.00
M2 Roger Clemens 60.00 18.00
M3 Tony Gwynn 40.00 12.00
M4 Wade Boggs 20.00 6.00
M5 Cal Ripken 100.00 30.00
M6 Jose Canseco 30.00 9.00

2000 SkyBox Dominion New Era

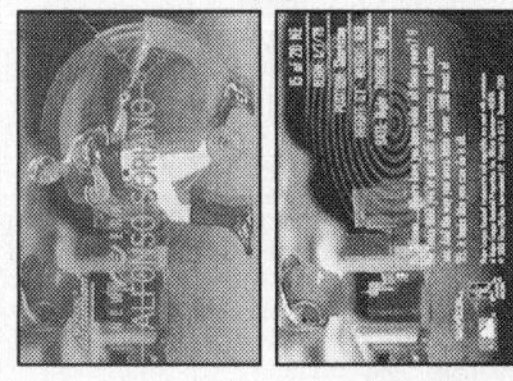

Issued one every three packs these 20 cards feature some of the leading young players who are expected to be stars in the 21st century. These cards are printed on silver foil board.

Nm-Mt Ex-Mt
COMPLETE SET (20) 10.00 3.00
*PLUS: 1.5X TO 4X BASIC NEW ERA
PLUS STATED ODDS 1:30
*WARP TEK: 5X TO 12X BASIC NEW ERA
WARP TEK STATED ODDS 1:300
N1 Pat Burrell 1.00 .30
N2 Ruben Mateo 1.00 .30
N3 Wilton Veras 1.00 .30
N4 Eric Munson 1.00 .30
N5 Jeff Weaver 1.00 .30
N6 Tim Hudson 1.00 .30
N7 Carlos Beltran 1.00 .30
N8 Chris Singleton 1.00 .30
N9 Lance Berkman 1.00 .30
N10 Freddy Garcia 1.00 .30
N11 Erubiel Durazo 1.00 .30
N12 Randy Wolf 1.00 .30
N13 Shea Hillenbrand 1.00 .30
N14 Kip Wells 1.00 .30
N15 Alfonso Soriano 1.50 .45
N16 Rick Ankiel 1.00 .30
N17 Ramon Ortiz 1.00 .30
N18 Adam Kennedy 1.00 .30
N19 Vernon Wells 1.00 .30
N20 Chad Hermansen 1.00 .30

1998 SkyBox Dugout Axcess

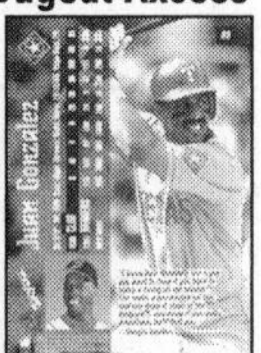

The 1998 SkyBox Dugout Axcess set was issued in one series totalling 150 cards. The 12-card packs retailed for $1.59 each. The set contains the topical subsets: The Insiders (1-90), Little Dawgs (91-120), 7th Inning Sketch (121-132), Name Plates (133-140), and Trivia Cards (141-150). Notable Rookie Cards include Magglio Ordonez. In addition, an Alex Rodriguez sample card was distributed to dealers and hobby media a few months prior to the release of the product. The card is identical to the standard 1998 SkyBox Axcess Alex Rodriguez except for the text 'PROMOTIONAL SAMPLE' diagonally written across the front and back. Also, Todd Helton signed 800 copies of his Little Dawgs subset card (number 120) for the 1999 Fleer Baseball Card Flipping Challenge. A total of 380 hobby shops participated in the program and each shop received two cards. One copy was intended to be given to the winner of each shop's card flipping tournament and the other one was to be kept by the shop owner as a gift for participating. Though the cards lack any serial numbering, they do feature an embossed SkyBox seal of authenticity and the print run was publicly released by the manufacturer. The additional 40 cards not used in the Flipping Challenge were mostly used as grab bag prizes at the 1999 MLB All-Star Fanfest in Boston.

Nm-Mt Ex-Mt
COMPLETE SET (150) 15.00 4.50
1 Travis Lee .20 .06
2 Matt Williams .20 .06
3 Andy Benes .20 .06
4 Chipper Jones .50 .15
5 Ryan Klesko .20 .06
6 Greg Maddux .75 .23
7 Sammy Sosa .75 .23
8 Henry Rodriguez .20 .06
9 Mark Grace .30 .09
10 Barry Larkin .30 .09
11 Bret Boone .20 .06
12 Reggie Sanders .20 .06
13 Vinny Castilla .20 .06
14 Larry Walker .30 .09
15 Darryl Kile .20 .06
16 Charles Johnson .20 .06
17 Edgar Renteria .20 .06
18 Gary Sheffield .20 .06
19 Jeff Bagwell .30 .09
20 Craig Biggio .30 .09
21 Moises Alou .30 .09
22 Mike Piazza .75 .23
23 Hideo Nomo .50 .15
24 Raul Mondesi .20 .06
25 John Jaha .20 .06
26 Jeff Cirillo .20 .06
27 Jeromy Burnitz .20 .06
28 Mark Grudzielanek .20 .06
29 Vladimir Guerrero .50 .15
30 Rondell White .20 .06
31 Edgardo Alfonzo .20 .06
32 Rey Ordonez .20 .06
33 Bernard Gilkey .20 .06
34 Scott Rolen .30 .09
35 Curt Schilling .30 .09
36 Ricky Bottalico .20 .06
37 Tony Womack .20 .06
38 Al Martin .20 .06
39 Jason Kendall .20 .06
40 Ron Gant .20 .06
41 Mark McGwire 1.25 .35
42 Ray Lankford .20 .06
43 Tony Gwynn .60 .18
44 Ken Caminiti .20 .06
45 Kevin Brown .30 .09
46 Barry Bonds 1.25 .35
47 J.T. Snow .20 .06
48 Shawn Estes .20 .06
49 Jim Edmonds .20 .06
50 Tim Salmon .30 .09
51 Jason Dickson .20 .06
52 Cal Ripken 1.50 .45
53 Mike Mussina .50 .15
54 Roberto Alomar .50 .15
55 Mo Vaughn .20 .06
56 Pedro Martinez .50 .15
57 Nomar Garciaparra .75 .23
58 Albert Belle .20 .06
59 Frank Thomas .50 .15
60 Robin Ventura .20 .06
61 Jim Thome .50 .15

62 Sandy Alomar Jr. .20 .06
63 Jaret Wright .20 .06
64 Bobby Higginson .30 .09
65 Tony Clark .20 .06
66 Justin Thompson .20 .06
67 Dean Palmer .20 .06
68 Kevin Appier .20 .06
69 Johnny Damon .20 .06
70 Paul Molitor .30 .09
71 Marty Cordova .20 .06
72 Brad Radke .20 .06
73 Derek Jeter 1.25 .35
74 Bernie Williams .30 .09
75 Andy Pettitte .30 .09
76 Matt Stairs .20 .06
77 Ben Grieve .50 .15
78 Jason Giambi .50 .15
79 Randy Johnson .50 .15
80 Ken Griffey Jr. .75 .23
81 Alex Rodriguez .75 .23
82 Fred McGriff .30 .09
83 Wade Boggs .30 .09
84 Wilson Alvarez .20 .06
85 Juan Gonzalez .50 .15
86 Ivan Rodriguez .50 .15
87 Fernando Tatis .20 .06
88 Roger Clemens 1.00 .30
89 Jose Cruz Jr. .20 .06
90 Shawn Green .20 .06
91 Jeff Suppan .20 .06
92 Eli Marrero .20 .06
93 Mike Lowell RC 1.00 .30
94 Ben Grieve .50 .15
95 Cliff Politte .20 .06
96 Rolando Arrojo RC .20 .06
97 Mike Caruso .20 .06
98 Miguel Tejada .30 .09
99 Rod Myers .20 .06
100 Juan Encarnacion .20 .06
101 Enrique Wilson .20 .06
102 Brian Giles .20 .06
103 Magglio Ordonez RC 1.00 .30
104 Brian Rose .20 .06
105 Ryan Jackson RC .20 .06
106 Mark Kotsay .20 .06
107 Desi Relaford .20 .06
108 A.J. Hinch .20 .06
109 Eric Milton .20 .06
110 Ricky Ledee .20 .06
111 Karim Garcia .20 .06
112 Derrek Lee .20 .06
113 Brad Fullmer .20 .06
114 Travis Lee .50 .15
115 Greg Norton .20 .06
116 Rich Butler RC .20 .06
117 Masato Yoshii RC .30 .09
118 Paul Konerko .20 .06
119 Richard Hidalgo .20 .06
120 Todd Helton .30 .09
121 N.Garciaparra 7TH .50 .15
122 Scott Rolen 7TH .20 .06
123 Cal Ripken 7TH .75 .23
124 Derek Jeter 7TH .60 .18
125 Mike Piazza 7TH .50 .15
126 Tony Gwynn 7TH .30 .09
127 Mark McGwire 7TH .60 .18
128 Kenny Lofton 7TH .20 .06
129 Greg Maddux 7TH .50 .15
130 Jeff Bagwell 7TH .20 .06
131 Randy Johnson 7TH .30 .09
132 Alex Rodriguez 7TH .50 .15
133 Mo Vaughn NAME .20 .06
134 Chipper Jones NAME .30 .09
135 Juan Gonzalez NAME .30 .09
136 Tony Clark NAME .20 .06
137 Fred McGriff NAME .20 .06
138 Roger Clemens NAME .50 .15
139 Ken Griffey Jr. NAME .50 .15
140 Ivan Rodriguez NAME .30 .09
141 Vinny Castilla TRIV .20 .06
142 Livan Hernandez TRIV .20 .06
143 Jose Cruz Jr. TRIV .20 .06
144 Andruw Jones TRIV .20 .06
145 Rafael Palmeiro TRIV .20 .06
146 C.Knoblauch TRIV .20 .06
147 Jay Buhner TRIV .20 .06
148 A.Galarraga TRIV .20 .06
149 Frank Thomas TRIV .30 .09
150 Todd Hundley TRIV .20 .06
S120 Todd Helton AU/800 30.00 9.00
NNO A.Rodriguez Sample 2.00 .60

1998 SkyBox Dugout Axcess Inside Axcess

These cards were randomly inserted in SkyBox Dugout Axcess packs. This 150-card set is a parallel to the SkyBox Dugout Axcess base set and the cards are serially numbered to 50.

Nm-Mt Ex-Mt
*STARS: 10X TO 25X BASIC CARDS ..
*ROOKIES: 12.5X TO 30X BASIC CARDS

1998 SkyBox Dugout Axcess Autograph Redemptions

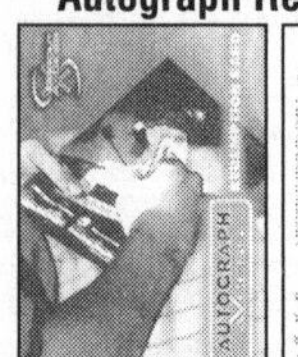

Randomly seeded exclusively into hobby packs at a rate of 1:96, these redemption cards could be exchanged for fifteen different items (either baseballs or fielding gloves) signed by a collection of fourteen major league stars. The exchange deadline for all fifteen cards was March 31st, 1999. The glove redemption cards were immeasurably scarcer to pull from packs than the ball redemption cards. Since the cards lack any player images (they're simply a shot of someone's arm signing a piece of memorabilia) - the expired cards carry little value.

Nm-Mt Ex-Mt
1 Jay Buhner Ball 1.00 .30
2 Roger Clemens Ball 1.00 .30
3 Jose Cruz Jr. Ball 1.00 .30
4 Darin Erstad Glove 1.00 .30
5 Nomar Garciaparra Ball 1.00 .30
6 Tony Gwynn Ball 1.00 .30
7 Roberto Hernandez Ball 1.00 .30
8 T.Hollandsworth Glove 1.00 .30
9 Greg Maddux Ball 1.00 .30
10 Alex Ochoa Glove 1.00 .30
11 Alex Rodriguez Ball 1.00 .30
12 Scott Rolen Ball 1.00 .30
13 Scott Rolen Glove 1.00 .30
14 Todd Walker Glove 1.00 .30
15 Tony Womack Ball 1.00 .30

1998 SkyBox Dugout Axcess Dishwashers

Randomly inserted in packs at a rate of one in eight, this 10-card set is an insert to the SkyBox Dugout Axcess base set. The fronts feature color action photos on silver foil. The featured player's jersey number sits in the upper left corner. The player's name and team runs vertically along the right side.

Nm-Mt Ex-Mt
COMPLETE SET (10) 10.00 3.00
D1 Greg Maddux 2.00 .60
D2 Kevin Brown .75 .23
D3 Pedro Martinez 1.25 .35
D4 Randy Johnson 1.25 .35
D5 Curt Schilling .75 .23
D6 John Smoltz .50 .15
D7 Darryl Kile .50 .15
D8 Roger Clemens 2.50 .75
D9 Andy Pettitte .75 .23
D10 Mike Mussina 1.25 .35

1998 SkyBox Dugout Axcess Double Header

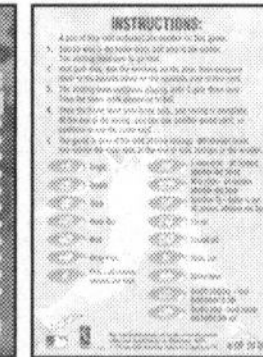

Randomly inserted in packs at a rate of two in 1, this 20-card set is an insert to the SkyBox Dugout Axcess base set. Each card not only features a star player, but is also an interactive game with instructions on how to play. Please make note that a pair of dice is needed to play; however, dice are not included.

Nm-Mt Ex-Mt
COMPLETE SET (20) 5.00 1.50
DH1 Jeff Bagwell .15 .04
DH2 Albert Belle .10 .03
DH3 Barry Bonds .60 .18
DH4 Derek Jeter .60 .18
DH5 Tony Clark .10 .03
DH6 Nomar Garciaparra .40 .12
DH7 Juan Gonzalez .25 .07
DH8 Ken Griffey Jr. .40 .12
DH9 Chipper Jones .25 .07
DH10 Kenny Lofton .10 .03
DH11 Mark McGwire .60 .18
DH12 Mo Vaughn .10 .03
DH13 Mike Piazza .40 .12
DH14 Cal Ripken .75 .23
DH15 Ivan Rodriguez .25 .07
DH16 Scott Rolen .15 .04
DH17 Frank Thomas .25 .07
DH18 Tony Gwynn .30 .09
DH19 Travis Lee .10 .03
DH20 Jose Cruz Jr. .10 .03

1998 SkyBox Dugout Axcess Frequent Flyers

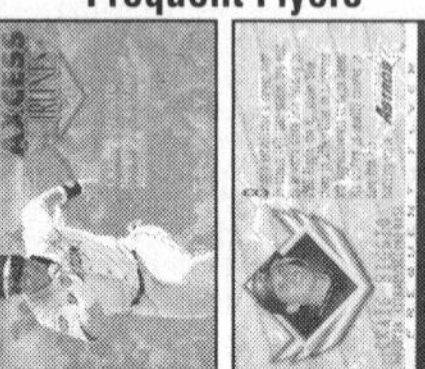

Randomly inserted in packs at a rate of one in four, this 10-card set is an insert to the SkyBox Dugout Axcess base set. The cards, with rounded edges, are designed to resemble a frequent flyer card. The fronts feature a color player photo on a background of floating clouds and a SkyBox logo "Axcess Airlines" in the upper right corner.

Nm-Mt Ex-Mt
COMPLETE SET (10) 2.50 .75
FF1 Brian Hunter .20 .06
FF2 Kenny Lofton .30 .09
FF3 Chuck Knoblauch .30 .09
FF4 Tony Womack .20 .06
FF5 Marquis Grissom .20 .06
FF6 Craig Biggio .40 .12
FF7 Barry Bonds 1.00 .30
FF8 Tom Goodwin .20 .06
FF9 Delino DeShields .20 .06
UER front DeSheilds
FF10 Eric Young .20 .06

1998 SkyBox Dugout Axcess Gronks

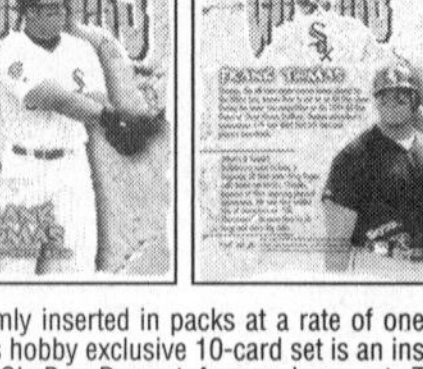

Randomly inserted in packs at a rate of one in 72, this hobby exclusive 10-card set is an insert to the SkyBox Dugout Axcess base set. The fronts feature game action photography of today's "Gronks", diamond lingo for home run hitters, on a grainy pattern to give the card the authentic look and feel of stone.

Nm-Mt Ex-Mt
COMPLETE SET (10) 60.00 18.00
G1 Jeff Bagwell 5.00 1.50
G2 Albert Belle 3.00 .90
G3 Juan Gonzalez 8.00 2.40
G4 Ken Griffey Jr. 12.00 3.60
G5 Mark McGwire 20.00 6.00
G6 Mike Piazza 12.00 3.60
G7 Frank Thomas 8.00 2.40
G8 Mo Vaughn 3.00 .90
G9 Ken Caminiti 3.00 .90
G10 Tony Clark 3.00 .90

1998 SkyBox Dugout Axcess SuperHeroes

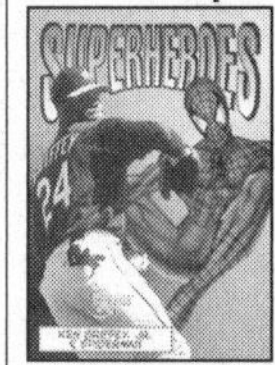

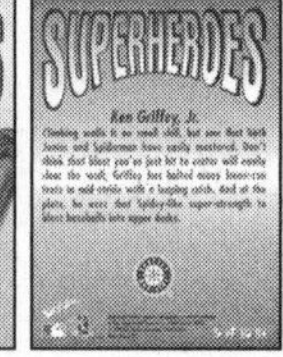

Randomly inserted in packs at a rate of one in 20, this 10-card set is an insert to the SkyBox Dugout Axcess base set. The card fronts showcase some of MLB's most popular superstars and their Marvel Comics counterparts. This insert appeals to both card and comic enthusiasts.

Nm-Mt Ex-Mt
COMPLETE SET (10) 30.00 9.00
SH1 Barry Bonds 8.00 2.40
SH2 Andres Galarraga 1.25 .35
SH3 Ken Griffey Jr. 5.00 1.50
SH4 Chipper Jones 3.00 .90
SH5 Andruw Jones 1.25 .35
SH6 Hideo Nomo 3.00 .90
SH7 Cal Ripken 10.00 3.00
SH8 Alex Rodriguez 5.00 1.50
SH9 Frank Thomas 3.00 .90
SH10 Mo Vaughn 1.25 .35

2004 Skybox LE

This 160 card set was released in March, 2004. This set was issued in three-card packs which came in both hobby and retail versions. The hobby packs were issued with an $3 SRP and came 18 packs to a box and 16 boxes to a case. Retail packs had a $2 SRP and were not as insert laden as the hobby packs. The first 110 cards of this set featured veterans while cards number 111 through 160 featured leading prospects. Please note that these cards were all issued to a print run of 99 or 299.

Nm-Mt Ex-Mt
COMP.SET w/o SP'S (110) 40.00 12.00
COMMON CARD (1-110) .75 .23
1-110 HOBBY CARDS ARE ALL DIE-CUT
COMMON CARD p/r 299 8.00 2.40
COMMON CARD p/r 99 10.00 3.00
111-160 ODDS 1:18 HOBBY, 1:144 RETAIL
111-160 PRINTS B/WN 99-299 COPIES PER
1 Juan Pierre .75 .23
2 Derek Jeter 5.00 1.50
3 Brandon Webb .75 .23
4 Jeff Bagwell 1.25 .35
5 Jason Schmidt .75 .23
6 Marlon Byrd .75 .23
7 Garret Anderson .75 .23
8 Miguel Cabrera 2.00 .60
9 Jose Reyes 1.25 .35
10 Rocco Baldelli 2.00 .60
11 Tony Batista .75 .23
12 Carlos Beltran .75 .23
13 Nomar Garciaparra 3.00 .90
14 Shawn Green .75 .23
15 Albert Pujols 4.00 1.20
16 Magglio Ordonez .75 .23
17 Kip Wells .75 .23
18 Andruw Jones .75 .23
19 Ryan Wagner .75 .23
20 Alex Rodriguez 3.00 .90
21 Vernon Wells .75 .23
22 Todd Helton 1.25 .35
23 David Ortiz .75 .23
24 Troy Glaus 1.25 .35
25 Jim Thome 2.00 .60
26 Greg Maddux 3.00 .90
27 Roberto Alomar 2.00 .60
28 Edgardo Alfonzo .75 .23
29 Hee Seop Choi .75 .23
30 Ken Griffey Jr. 3.00 .90
31 Tim Hudson .75 .23
32 Shannon Stewart .75 .23
33 Ichiro Suzuki 3.00 .90
34 Luis Gonzalez .75 .23
35 Darin Erstad .75 .23
36 Dmitri Young .75 .23
37 Ivan Rodriguez 2.00 .60
38 Scott Podsednik 2.00 .60
39 Jose Vidro .75 .23
40 Mark Prior 4.00 1.20
41 Mike Mussina 2.00 .60
42 Gary Sheffield .75 .23
43 Manny Ramirez .75 .23
44 C.C. Sabathia .75 .23
45 Curt Schilling 1.25 .35
46 Scott Rolen 1.25 .35
47 Hideo Nomo 2.00 .60
48 Torii Hunter .75 .23
49 Aubrey Huff .75 .23
50 Javy Lopez .75 .23
51 Austin Kearns .75 .23
52 Mike Piazza 3.00 .90
53 Sean Burroughs .75 .23
54 Kerry Wood 2.00 .60
55 Marquis Grissom .75 .23
56 Preston Wilson .75 .23
57 Angel Berroa .75 .23
58 Jason Kendall .75 .23
59 Rafael Palmeiro 1.25 .35
60 Mike Lowell .75 .23
61 Eric Chavez .75 .23
62 Bartolo Colon .75 .23
63 Adam Dunn .75 .23
64 Pedro Martinez 2.00 .60
65 Lance Berkman .75 .23
66 Bret Boone .75 .23
67 Eric Gagne 1.25 .35
68 Vladimir Guerrero 2.00 .60
69 Jay Gibbons .75 .23
70 Larry Walker 1.25 .35
71 Orlando Cabrera .75 .23
72 Jorge Posada 1.25 .35
73 Jamie Moyer .75 .23
74 Carl Crawford .75 .23
75 Hank Blalock .75 .23
76 Josh Beckett 1.25 .35
77 Jody Gerut .75 .23
78 Kevin Brown .75 .23
79 Sammy Sosa 3.00 .90
80 Chipper Jones 2.00 .60
81 Tom Glavine 1.25 .35
82 Barry Zito 1.25 .35
83 Edgar Renteria .75 .23
84 Esteban Loaiza .75 .23
85 Jason Giambi 2.00 .60
86 Miguel Tejada .75 .23
87 Randy Johnson 2.00 .60
88 A.J. Burnett .75 .23
89 Richie Sexson .75 .23
90 Reggie Sanders .75 .23
91 Carlos Delgado .75 .23
92 Pat Burrell .75 .23
93 Jacque Jones .75 .23
94 Roy Oswalt .75 .23
95 Frank Thomas 2.00 .60
96 Melvin Mora .75 .23
97 Jeremy Bonderman .75 .23
98 Mike Sweeney .75 .23
99 Brian Giles .75 .23
100 Edgar Martinez 1.25 .35
101 Mark Teixeira .75 .23
102 Sean Casey .75 .23
103 Javier Vazquez .75 .23
104 Hideki Matsui 3.00 .90
105 Jim Edmonds .75 .23
106 Roy Halladay .75 .23
107 Craig Biggio 1.25 .35
108 Geoff Jenkins .75 .23
109 Alfonso Soriano 1.25 .35
110 Barry Larkin 2.00 .60
111 Chris Bootcheck PR/299 8.00 2.40
112 Dallas McPherson PR/99 10.00 3.00
113 Matt Kata PR/99 10.00 3.00
114 Scott Hairston PR/299 8.00 2.40
115 Bobby Crosby PR/299 8.00 2.40
116 Adam Wainright PR/99 10.00 3.00
117 Daniel Cabrera PR/299 8.00 2.40
118 Kevin Youkilis PR/299 8.00 2.40
119 Ronny Cedeno PR/299 RC 8.00 2.40
120 Ruddy Yan PR/299 8.00 2.40
121 Ryan Wing PR/299 8.00 2.40
122 William Bergolla PR/299 RC 8.00 2.40
123 Edwin Encarnacion PR/299 8.00 2.40
124 Jonny Gomes PR/299 8.00 2.40
125 Garrett Atkins PR/299 8.00 2.40
126 Clint Barmes PR/299 8.00 2.40
127 Wilfredo Ledezma PR/299 8.00 2.40
128 Cody Ross PR/299 8.00 2.40
129 Josh Willingham PR/99 10.00 3.00
130 Chin-Hui Tsao PR/299 8.00 2.40
131 Hector Gimenez PR/299 RC 8.00 2.40
132 David DeJesus PR/299 8.00 2.40
133 Jimmy Gobble PR/299 8.00 2.40
134 Edwin Jackson PR/99 15.00 4.50
135 Koyie Hill PR/299 8.00 2.40
136 Rickie Weeks PR/99 15.00 4.50
137 Graham Koonce PR/299 10.00 3.00
138 Rob Bowen PR/299 8.00 2.40
139 Shawn Hill PR/299 RC 8.00 2.40
140 Craig Brazell PR/299 8.00 2.40
141 Mike Hessman PR/299 8.00 2.40
142 Jorge De Paula PR/299 8.00 2.40
143 Chien-Ming Wang PR/99 10.00 3.00
144 Rich Harden PR/299 8.00 2.40
145 Ryan Howard PR/99 10.00 3.00
146 Alfredo Simon PR/299 RC 8.00 2.40
147 Ian Snell PR RC/299 RC 10.00 3.00
148 Ryan Doumit PR/299 8.00 2.40
149 Khalil Greene PR/99 10.00 3.00
150 Angel Chavez PR/299 RC 8.00 2.40
151 Dan Haren PR/299 8.00 2.40
152 Chris Snelling PR/299 8.00 2.40
153 Aaron Miles PR/299 8.00 2.40
154 John Gall PR/299 RC 8.00 2.40
155 Chris Narveson PR/299 8.00 2.40
156 Delmon Young PR/99 15.00 4.50
157 Chad Gaudin PR/299 8.00 2.40
158 Gerald Laird PR/299 8.00 2.40
159 Alexis Rios PR/299 10.00 3.00
160 Jason Arnold PR/299 8.00 2.40

2004 Skybox LE Artist Proof

Nm-Mt Ex-Mt
*AP 1-110: 2.5X TO 6X BASIC
*AP 111-160: .5X TO 1.2X BASIC p/r 299
*AP 111-160: .4X TO 1X BASIC p/r 99
OVERALL PARALLEL ODDS 1:6 H, 1:48 R
STATED PRINT RUN 50 SERIAL #'d SETS

2004 Skybox LE Executive Proof

Nm-Mt Ex-Mt
OVERALL PARALLEL ODDS 1:6 H, 1:48 R
STATED PRINT RUN 1 SERIAL #'d SET
NO PRICING DUE TO SCARCITY

2004 Skybox LE Gold Proof

Nm-Mt Ex-Mt
*GOLD 1-110: 1.25X TO 3X BASIC
*GOLD 111-160: .3X TO .8X BASIC p/r 299
*GOLD 111-160: .25X TO .6X BASIC p/r 99
OVERALL PARALLEL ODDS 1:6 H, 1:48 R
STATED PRINT RUN 150 SERIAL #'d SETS

2004 Skybox LE Photographer Proof

Nm-Mt Ex-Mt
*PHOTO 1-110: 5X TO 12X BASIC
*PHOTO 111-160: .75X TO 2X BASIC p/r 299
*PHOTO 111-160: .6X TO 1.5X BASIC p/r 99
OVERALL PARALLEL ODDS 1:6 H, 1:48 R
STATED PRINT RUN 25 SERIAL #'d SETS

2004 SkyBox LE Retail

Nm-Mt Ex-Mt
*RETAIL 1-110: .15X TO .4X BASIC
ISSUED ONLY IN RETAIL PACKS
RETAIL CARDS ARE NOT DIE CUT

2004 Skybox LE Jersey Proof

Nm-Mt Ex-Mt
STATED PRINT RUN 299 SERIAL #'d SETS
GOLD PRINT RUN 10 SERIAL #'d SETS
NO GOLD PRICING DUE TO SCARCITY
*SILVER: .6X TO 1.5X BASIC
SILVER PRINT RUN 50 SERIAL #'d SETS
OVERALL GU ODDS 1:9 H, 1:48 R
1 Troy Glaus 10.00 3.00
2 Curt Schilling 10.00 3.00
3 Randy Johnson 10.00 3.00
4 Brandon Webb 8.00 2.40
5 Gary Sheffield 8.00 2.40
6 Greg Maddux 15.00 4.50
7 Chipper Jones 10.00 3.00
8 David Ortiz 8.00 2.40
9 Nomar Garciaparra 15.00 4.50
10 Pedro Martinez 10.00 3.00
11 Manny Ramirez 8.00 2.40
12 Kerry Wood 10.00 3.00
13 Mark Prior 20.00 6.00
14 Sammy Sosa 15.00 4.50
15 Frank Thomas 10.00 3.00
16 Austin Kearns
17 Todd Helton 10.00 3.00
18 Preston Wilson 8.00 2.40
19 Juan Pierre 8.00 2.40
20 Josh Beckett 10.00 3.00
21 Ivan Rodriguez 10.00 3.00
22 Miguel Cabrera 10.00 3.00
23 Mike Lowell 8.00 2.40
24 Lance Berkman 8.00 2.40
25 Jeff Bagwell 10.00 3.00
26 Angel Berroa 8.00 2.40
27 Hideo Nomo 15.00 4.50
28 Eric Gagne 10.00 3.00
29 Scott Podsednik 12.00 3.60
30 Richie Sexson 8.00 2.40
31 Torii Hunter 8.00 2.40
32 Mike Piazza 15.00 4.50
33 Jose Reyes 10.00 3.00
34 Tom Glavine 10.00 3.00
35 Derek Jeter 30.00 9.00
36 Jorge Posada 10.00 3.00
37 Jason Giambi 10.00 3.00
38 Alfonso Soriano 10.00 3.00
39 Eric Chavez 8.00 2.40
40 Miguel Tejada 8.00 2.40
41 Jim Thome 8.00 2.40
42 Albert Pujols 20.00 6.00
43 Scott Rolen 10.00 3.00
44 Rocco Baldelli 10.00 3.00
45 Alex Rodriguez 12.00 3.60
46 Hank Blalock 8.00 2.40
47 Mark Teixeira 8.00 2.40
48 Rafael Palmeiro 10.00 3.00
49 Carlos Delgado 8.00 2.40
50 Roy Halladay 8.00 2.40

2004 Skybox LE History Draft 90's Autograph Black

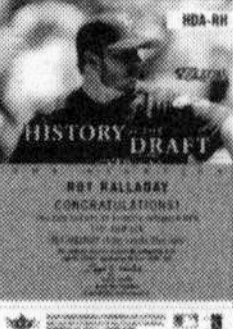

Nm-Mt Ex-Mt
STATED PRINT RUN 199 SERIAL #'d SETS
*COPPER: .4X TO 1X BASIC

COPPER PRINTS B/WN 93-99 COPIES PER
GOLD PRINT RUN 10 SERIAL #'d SETS
NO GOLD PRICING DUE TO SCARCITY
*SILVER: .5X TO 1.2X BASIC............
SILVER PRINT RUN 50 SERIAL #'d SETS
OVERALL AUTO ODDS 1:18 HOBBY...
AH Aubrey Huff........................ 15.00 4.50
AK Austin Kearns..................... 15.00 4.50
AP Albert Pujols...................... 120.00 36.00
CP Corey Patterson.................. 15.00 4.50
HB Hank Blalock....................... 25.00 7.50
JP Juan Pierre.......................... 15.00 4.50
MB Marlon Byrd......................... 10.00 3.00
ML Mike Lowell......................... 15.00 4.50
RH Roy Halladay....................... 15.00 4.50
SP Scott Podsednik.................. 25.00 7.50
SR Scott Rolen.......................... 25.00 7.50
TH Torii Hunter......................... 15.00 4.50
VW Vernon Wells....................... 15.00 4.50

2004 Skybox LE History Draft 90's Jersey

Nm-Mt Ex-Mt
PRINT RUNS B/WN 90-99 COPIES PER
GOLD PRINT RUN 10 SERIAL #'d SETS
NO GOLD PRICING DUE TO SCARCITY
*SILVER: .5X TO 1.2X BASIC............
SILVER PRINT RUN 50 SERIAL #'d SETS
OVERALL GU ODDS 1:9 H, 1:48 R......
AB A.J. Burnett/95................... 10.00 3.00
AD Adam Dunn/98.................... 10.00 3.00
AH Aubrey Huff/98................... 10.00 3.00
AK Austin Kearns/98................ 10.00 3.00
AP Albert Pujols/99................. 25.00 7.50
AR Alex Rodriguez/93.............. 15.00 4.50
BB Bret Boone/90.................... 10.00 3.00
BZ Barry Zito/99...................... 12.00 3.60
CB Carlos Beltran/95............... 10.00 3.00
CJ Chipper Jones/90................ 12.00 3.60
CP Corey Patterson/98............ 10.00 3.00
DE Darin Erstad/95.................. 10.00 3.00
DJ Derek Jeter/92.................... 40.00 12.00
EC Eric Chavez/96................... 10.00 3.00
GA Garret Anderson/90............ 10.00 3.00
HB Hank Blalock/99................. 10.00 3.00
JB Josh Beckett/99.................. 12.00 3.60
JG Jason Giambi/92................ 12.00 3.60
JPI Juan Pierre/98................... 10.00 3.00
JPO Jorge Posada/90.............. 12.00 3.60
JS Jason Schmidt/91............... 10.00 3.00
JV Javier Vazquez/94.............. 10.00 3.00
KW Kerry Wood/95.................. 12.00 3.60
LB Lance Berkman/97............. 10.00 3.00
MB Marlon Byrd/99................. 10.00 3.00
ML Mike Lowell/95.................. 10.00 3.00
MM Mike Mussina/90.............. 12.00 3.60
MR Manny Ramirez/91............ 10.00 3.00
NG Nomar Garciaparra/94........ 20.00 6.00
PB Pat Burrell/98.................... 10.00 3.00
RH Roy Halladay/95................ 10.00 3.00
RS Richie Sexson/93.............. 10.00 3.00
SG Shawn Green/91................ 10.00 3.00
SP Scott Podsednik/94............ 15.00 4.50
SR Scott Rolen/93.................. 12.00 3.60
SS Shannon Stewart/92.......... 10.00 3.00
THE Todd Helton/95............... 12.00 3.60
THN Torii Hunter/93............... 10.00 3.00
THU Tim Hudson/97............... 10.00 3.00
VW Vernon Wells/97............... 10.00 3.00

2004 Skybox LE League Leaders

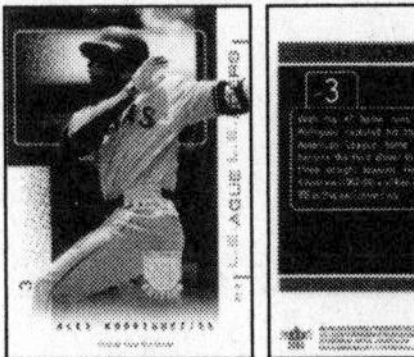

Nm-Mt Ex-Mt
STATED ODDS 1:18 HOBBY, 1:12 RETAIL
EXECUTIVE RANDOM INSERTS IN PACKS
EXECUTIVE PRINT RUN 1 SERIAL #'d SET
NO EXECUTIVE PRICING DUE TO SCARCITY
1 Alex Rodriguez........................ 6.00 1.80
2 Jim Thome.............................. 4.00 1.20
3 Albert Pujols........................... 8.00 2.40
4 Pedro Martinez........................ 4.00 1.20
5 Roy Halladay........................... 3.00 .90
6 Jason Schmidt......................... 3.00 .90
7 Kerry Wood............................. 4.00 1.20
8 Juan Pierre............................. 3.00 .90
9 Preston Wilson........................ 3.00 .90
10 Carlos Delgado...................... 3.00 .90

2004 Skybox LE League Leaders Jersey

Nm-Mt Ex-Mt
STATED PRINT RUN 75 SERIAL #'d SETS
GOLD PRINT RUN 10 SERIAL #'d SETS
NO GOLD PRICING DUE TO SCARCITY
*SILVER: .5X TO 1.2X BASIC............
SILVER PRINT RUN 50 SERIAL #'d SETS
OVERALL GU ODDS 1:9 H, 1:48 R......
AP Albert Pujols....................... 25.00 7.50
AR Alex Rodriguez.................... 15.00 4.50
CD Carlos Delgado.................... 10.00 3.00
JP Juan Pierre.......................... 10.00 3.00

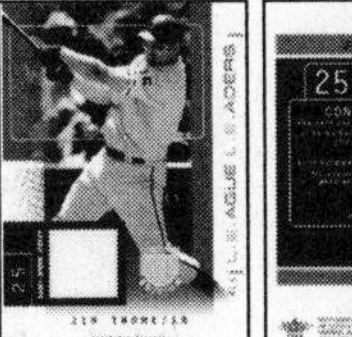

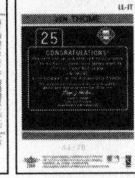

JS Jason Schmidt...................... 10.00 3.00
JT Jim Thome........................... 12.00 3.60
KW Kerry Wood......................... 12.00 3.60
PM Pedro Martinez.................... 12.00 3.60
PW Preston Wilson.................... 10.00 3.00
RH Roy Halladay....................... 10.00 3.00

2004 Skybox LE Rare Form

Nm-Mt Ex-Mt
STATED ODDS 1:288 HOBBY, 1:576 RETAIL
NO MORE THAN 130 SETS PRODUCED
PRINT RUN INFO PROVIDED BY FLEER
EXECUTIVE RANDOM INSERTS IN PACKS
EXECUTIVE PRINT RUN 1 SERIAL #'d SET
NO EXECUTIVE PRICING DUE TO SCARCITY
1 Albert Pujols.......................... 30.00 9.00
2 Miguel Cabrera....................... 15.00 4.50
3 Jim Thome.............................. 15.00 4.50
4 Derek Jeter............................ 40.00 12.00
5 Nomar Garciaparra.................. 25.00 7.50
6 Mike Piazza............................ 25.00 7.50
7 Alex Rodriguez....................... 25.00 7.50
8 Delmon Young........................ 15.00 4.50
9 Chipper Jones......................... 15.00 4.50
10 Rickie Weeks........................ 15.00 4.50

2004 Skybox LE Rare Form Autograph Black

Nm-Mt Ex-Mt
STATED PRINT RUN 299 SERIAL #'d SETS
*COPPER: .5X TO 1.2X BASIC...........
COPPER PRINT RUN 99 SERIAL #'d SETS
GOLD PRINT RUN 10 SERIAL #'d SETS
NO GOLD PRICING DUE TO SCARCITY
*SILVER: .6X TO 1.5X BASIC.............
SILVER PRINT RUN 50 SERIAL #'d SETS
OVERALL AUTO ODDS 1:18 HOBBY...
1 Dallas McPherson.................. 15.00 4.50
2 Delmon Young....................... 30.00 9.00
3 Rickie Weeks........................ 30.00 9.00
4 Brandon Webb....................... 15.00 4.50
5 Matt Kata.............................. 15.00 4.50
6 Edwin Jackson....................... 20.00 6.00
7 Rocco Baldelli........................ 30.00 9.00
8 Angel Berroa......................... 15.00 4.50
9 Rich Harden.......................... 20.00 6.00

2004 Skybox LE Rare Form Game Used Silver

Nm-Mt Ex-Mt
STATED PRINT RUN 50 SERIAL #'d SETS
GOLD PRINT RUN 10 SERIAL #'d SETS
NO GOLD PRICING DUE TO SCARCITY
*NUMBER p/r 31: .5X TO 1.2X BASIC.
*NUMBER p/r 20-25: .6X TO 1.5X BASIC
NUMBER PRINTS B/WN 2-31 COPIES PER
NO NUMBER PRICING ON 25 OR LESS
OVERALL GU ODDS 1:9 H, 1:48 R......
AP Albert Pujols Jsy................. 30.00 9.00
AR Alex Rodriguez Jsy.............. 20.00 6.00
CJ Chipper Jones Jsy............... 15.00 4.50
DJ Derek Jeter Jsy.................. 50.00 15.00
JT Jim Thome Jsy................... 15.00 4.50
MC Miguel Cabrera Jsy............ 15.00 4.50
MP Mike Piazza Jsy................. 25.00 7.50
NG Nomar Garciaparra Jsy....... 25.00 7.50
RB Rocco Baldelli Jsy.............. 15.00 4.50
RW Rickie Weeks Bat.............. 15.00 4.50

2004 Skybox LE Sky's the Limit

Nm-Mt Ex-Mt
STATED ODDS 1:6 HOBBY, 1:8 RETAIL
EXECUTIVE RANDOM INSERTS IN PACKS
EXECUTIVE PRINT RUN 1 SERIAL #'d SET

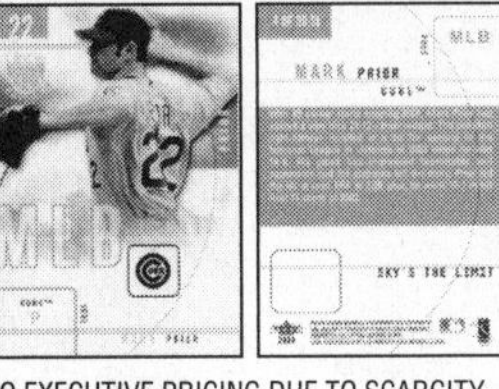

NO EXECUTIVE PRICING DUE TO SCARCITY
1 Dontrelle Willis...................... 2.00 .60
2 Rocco Baldelli........................ 3.00 .90
3 Miguel Cabrera....................... 3.00 .90
4 Mark Prior............................. 6.00 1.80
5 Hideki Matsui......................... 5.00 1.50
6 Kerry Wood........................... 3.00 .90
7 Alfonso Soriano..................... 3.00 .90
8 Ichiro Suzuki......................... 5.00 1.50
9 Brandon Webb....................... 2.00 .60
10 Alex Rodriguez..................... 5.00 1.50
11 Barry Zito............................ 3.00 .90
12 Hank Blalock........................ 2.00 .60
13 Jose Reyes.......................... 3.00 .90
14 Torii Hunter.......................... 2.00 .60
15 Josh Beckett........................ 3.00 .90
16 Manny Ramirez.................... 2.00 .60
17 Andruw Jones...................... 2.00 .60
18 Vladimir Guerrero................. 3.00 .90
19 Miguel Tejada....................... 2.00 .60
20 Carlos Delgado..................... 2.00 .60

2004 Skybox LE Sky's the Limit Jersey

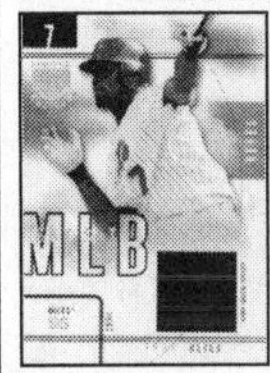

Nm-Mt Ex-Mt
STATED PRINT RUN 99 SERIAL #'d SETS
GOLD PRINT RUN 10 SERIAL #'d SETS
NO GOLD PRICING DUE TO SCARCITY
*SILVER: .5X TO 1.2X BASIC............
SILVER PRINT RUN 50 SERIAL #'d SETS
OVERALL GU ODDS 1:9 H, 1:48 R......
AJ Andruw Jones..................... 10.00 3.00
AR Alex Rodriguez.................. 15.00 4.50
AS Alfonso Soriano................. 12.00 3.60
BW Brandon Webb.................. 10.00 3.00
BZ Barry Zito......................... 12.00 3.60
CD Carlos Delgado.................. 10.00 3.00
DW Dontrelle Willis................. 10.00 3.00
HB Hank Blalock..................... 10.00 3.00
JB Josh Beckett...................... 12.00 3.60
JR Jose Reyes........................ 12.00 3.60
KW Kerry Wood....................... 12.00 3.60
MC Miguel Cabrera.................. 12.00 3.60
MP Mark Prior......................... 25.00 7.50
MR Manny Ramirez.................. 10.00 3.00
MT Miguel Tejada.................... 10.00 3.00
RB Rocco Baldelli.................... 12.00 3.60
TH Torii Hunter....................... 10.00 3.00
VG Vladimir Guerrero............... 12.00 3.60

1999 SkyBox Molten Metal

The 1999 SkyBox Molten Metal set was issued in one series and distributed in six-card packs with a suggested retail price of $4.99. The set features 100 of the game's top veterans in the Metal Smiths (cards 1-100) subset with an insertion rate of 4:1 pack; 30 of today's power hitters in the Heavy Metal subset (101-130) inserted one per pack; and 20 of 1999's hottest rookies in the Supernatural subset(131-150) with an insertion rate of 1:2 packs. The cards are silver-foil on 24-point stock and enhanced with additional holofoil and wet laminate. Rookie Cards inlcude Pat Burrell and Freddy Garcia. Finally, special National Edition boxes were printed and distributed exclusively at the National Sportscard Collectors Convention in Atlanta in July 1999.

Nm-Mt Ex-Mt
COMPLETE SET (150)............ 100.00 30.00
COMMON CARD (1-100)............. .40 .12
COMMON (101-130).................. .40 .12
COMMON (131-150).................. .75 .23
1 Larry Walker MS..................... .60 .18
2 Jose Canseco MS.................. 1.00 .30
3 Brian Jordan MS..................... .40 .12
4 Rafael Palmeiro MS................ .60 .18
5 Edgar Renteria MS................. .40 .12
6 Dante Bichette MS................. .40 .12
7 Mark Kotsay MS..................... .40 .12
8 Denny Neagle MS.................. .40 .12
9 Ellis Burks MS....................... .40 .12
10 Paul O'Neill MS.................... .60 .18
11 Miguel Tejada MS................. .40 .12
12 Ken Caminiti MS................... .40 .12
13 David Cone MS..................... .40 .12
14 Jason Kendall MS................. .40 .12
15 Ruben Rivera MS.................. .40 .12
16 Todd Walker MS................... .40 .12
17 Bobby Higginson MS............. .40 .12
18 Derrek Lee MS...................... .40 .12
19 Rondell White MS................. .40 .12
20 Pedro Martinez MS............... 1.00 .30
21 Jeff Kent MS........................ .40 .12
22 Randy Johnson MS.............. 1.00 .30
23 Matt Williams MS.................. .40 .12
24 Sean Casey MS.................... .40 .12
25 Eric Davis MS....................... .40 .12
26 Ryan Klesko MS................... .40 .12
27 Curt Schilling MS.................. .60 .18
28 Geoff Jenkins MS................. .40 .12
29 Bob Abreu MS...................... .40 .12
30 Vinny Castilla MS................. .40 .12
31 Will Clark MS...................... 1.00 .30
32 Ray Durham MS................... .40 .12
33 Ray Lankford MS.................. .40 .12
34 Richie Sexson MS................. .40 .12
35 Derrick Gibson MS................ .40 .12
36 Mark Grace MS..................... .60 .18
37 Greg Vaughn MS................... .40 .12
38 Bartolo Colon MS.................. .40 .12
39 Steve Finley MS.................... .40 .12
40 Chuck Knoblauch MS............. .40 .12
41 Ricky Ledee MS.................... .40 .12
42 John Smoltz MS.................... .60 .18
43 Moises Alou MS.................... .40 .12
44 Jim Edmonds MS.................. .40 .12
45 Cliff Floyd MS....................... .40 .12
46 Javy Lopez MS..................... .40 .12
47 Jim Thome MS..................... 1.00 .30
48 J.T. Snow MS....................... .40 .12
49 Sandy Alomar Jr. MS............. .40 .12
50 Andy Pettitte MS................... .60 .18
51 Juan Encarnacion MS............. .40 .12
52 Travis Fryman MS................. .40 .12
53 Eli Marrero MS...................... .40 .12
54 Jeff Cirillo MS....................... .40 .12
55 Brady Anderson MS............... .40 .12
56 Jose Cruz Jr. MS.................. .40 .12
57 Edgar Martinez MS................ .60 .18
58 Garret Anderson MS.............. .40 .12
59 Paul Konerko MS.................. .40 .12
60 Eric Milton MS...................... .40 .12
61 Jason Giambi MS................. 1.00 .30
62 Tom Glavine MS.................... .60 .18
63 Justin Thompson MS............. .40 .12
64 Brad Fullmer MS................... .40 .12
65 Marquis Grissom MS............. .40 .12
66 Fernando Tatis MS................ .40 .12
67 Carlos Beltran MS................. .40 .12
68 Charles Johnson MS............. .40 .12
69 Raul Mondesi MS.................. .40 .12
70 Richard Hildago MS.............. .40 .12
71 Barry Larkin MS.................. 1.00 .30
72 David Wells MS.................... .40 .12
73 Jay Buhner MS..................... .40 .12
74 Matt Clement MS.................. .40 .12
75 Eric Karros MS..................... .40 .12
76 Carl Pavano MS.................... .40 .12
77 Mariano Rivera MS................ .60 .18
78 Livan Hernandez MS............. .40 .12
79 A.J. Hinch MS...................... .40 .12
80 Tino Martinez MS.................. .60 .18
81 Rusty Greer MS.................... .40 .12
82 Jose Guillen MS................... .40 .12
83 Robin Ventura MS................. .40 .12
84 Kevin Brown MS.................... .60 .18
85 Chan Ho Park MS.................. .40 .12
86 John Olerud MS.................... .40 .12
87 Johnny Damon MS................ .40 .12
88 Todd Hundley MS.................. .40 .12
89 Fred McGriff MS................... .60 .18
90 Wade Boggs MS................... .60 .18
91 Mike Cameron MS................. .40 .12
92 Gary Sheffield MS................. .40 .12
93 Rickey Henderson MS........... 1.00 .30
94 Pat Hentgen MS.................... .40 .12
95 Omar Vizquel MS.................. .40 .12
96 Craig Biggio MS.................... .60 .18
97 Mike Caruso MS.................... .40 .12
98 Neifi Perez MS..................... .40 .12
99 Mike Mussina MS................. 1.00 .30
100 Carlos Delgado MS.............. .40 .12
101 Andruw Jones HM............... .40 .12
102 Pat Burrell HM RC.............. 2.50 .75
103 O.Hernandez HM................ .40 .12
104 Darin Erstad HM................. .40 .12
105 Roberto Alomar HM........... 1.00 .30
106 Tim Salmon HM.................. .60 .18
107 Albert Belle HM.................. .40 .12
108 Chad Allen HM RC.............. .40 .12
109 Travis Lee HM.................... .40 .12
110 Jesse Garcia HM RC........... .40 .12
111 Tony Clark HM.................... .40 .12
112 Ivan Rodriguez HM............ 1.00 .30
113 Troy Glaus HM.................... .60 .18
114 A.J. Burnett HM RC........... 1.00 .30
115 David Justice HM................ .40 .12
116 Adrian Beltre HM................ .40 .12
117 Eric Chavez HM.................. .40 .12
118 Kenny Lofton HM................ .40 .12
119 Michael Barrett HM............. .40 .12
120 Jeff Weaver HM RC............ .60 .18
121 Manny Ramirez HM............. .40 .12
122 Barry Bonds HM................ 3.00 .90
123 Bernie Williams HM............ .60 .18
124 Freddy Garcia HM RC........ 1.00 .30
125 Scott Hunter HM RC............ .40 .12
126 Jeremy Giambi HM.............. .40 .12
127 Masao Kida HM RC............. .40 .12
128 Todd Helton HM.................. .60 .18
129 Mike Figga HM.................... .40 .12
130 Mo Vaughn HM................... .40 .12
131 J.D. Drew SN..................... .75 .23
132 Cal Ripken SN................... 5.00 1.50
133 Ken Griffey Jr. SN............. 2.50 .75
134 Mark McGwire SN.............. 4.00 1.20
135 N.Garciaparra SN.............. 2.50 .75
136 Greg Maddux SN................ 2.50 .75
137 Mike Piazza SN.................. 2.50 .75
138 Alex Rodriguez SN............. 2.50 .75
139 Frank Thomas SN.............. 1.50 .45
140 Juan Gonzalez SN.............. 1.50 .45
141 Tony Gwynn SN................. 2.00 .60
142 Derek Jeter SN.................. 4.00 1.20
143 Chipper Jones SN.............. 1.50 .45
144 Scott Rolen SN.................. 1.00 .30
145 Sammy Sosa SN................ 2.50 .75
146 Kerry Wood SN.................. 1.50 .45
147 Roger Clemens SN............. 3.00 .90
148 Jeff Bagwell SN................. 1.00 .30
149 Vladimir Guerrero SN......... 1.50 .45
150 Ben Grieve SN.................... .75 .23

1999 SkyBox Molten Metal Xplosion

Randomly inserted in packs at the rate of one in two, this 150-card set if parallel to the base set printed on metal stock with added etching, rounded corners and foil stamping. A promotional card featuring Kerry Wood was distributed to dealers and hobby media several weeks prior to the product's national release. This unnumbered card can be readily identified by the text "PROMOTIONAL SAMPLE" running diagonally across the back.

Nm-Mt Ex-Mt
*METALSMITHS 1-100: 2.5X TO 6X BASIC
*HEAVY METAL 101-130: 2X TO 5X BASIC
*HVY.MTL RC'S 101-130: 1.25X TO 3X BASIC
*S'NATURAL 131-150: 1.5X TO 4X BASIC
NNO Kerry Wood Sample........... 1.00 .30

1999 SkyBox Molten Metal Fusion

Randomly inserted in packs, this 50-card set consists of two subsets. Cards 1-30 were inserted at the rate of one in 12 and features a laser die-cut version of the Heavy Metal subset from the base set with additional silver-foil stamping. Cards 31-50 were inserted 1:24 packs and consists of a laser die-cut version of the Supernatural subset from the base set. These cards parallel cards numbered 101 through 150 in the regular SkyBox Molten Metal set

Nm-Mt Ex-Mt
COMPLETE SET (50)............. 400.00 120.00
COMMON CARD (1-30).............. 2.00 .60
COMMON CARD (31-50)............ 5.00 1.50
1 Andruw Jones HM.................. 2.00 .60
2 Pat Burrell HM..................... 10.00 3.00
3 Orlando Hernandez HM.......... 2.00 .60
4 Darin Erstad HM.................... 2.00 .60
5 Roberto Alomar HM............... 3.00 .90
6 Tim Salmon HM..................... 2.00 .60
7 Albert Belle HM..................... 2.00 .60
8 Chad Allen HM...................... 2.00 .60
9 Travis Lee HM....................... 2.00 .60
10 Jesse Garcia HM.................. 2.00 .60
11 Tony Clark HM..................... 2.00 .60
12 Ivan Rodriguez HM............... 3.00 .90
13 Troy Glaus HM..................... 2.00 .60
14 A.J. Burnett HM................... 3.00 .90
15 David Justice HM................. 2.00 .60
16 Adrian Beltre HM................. 2.00 .60
17 Eric Chavez HM................... 2.00 .60
18 Kenny Lofton HM................. 2.00 .60
19 Michael Barrett HM.............. 2.00 .60
20 Jeff Weaver HM................... 2.00 .60
21 Manny Ramirez HM.............. 2.00 .60
22 Barry Bonds HM.................. 15.00 4.50
23 Bernie Williams HM.............. 2.00 .60
24 Freddy Garcia HM................ 3.00 .90
25 Scott Hunter HM.................. 2.00 .60
26 Jeremy Giambi HM............... 2.00 .60
27 Masao Kida HM................... 2.00 .60
28 Todd Helton HM................... 2.00 .60
29 Mike Figga HM..................... 2.00 .60
30 Mo Vaughn HM..................... 2.00 .60
31 J.D. Drew SN....................... 5.00 1.50
32 Cal Ripken SN.................... 25.00 7.50
33 Ken Griffey Jr. SN.............. 12.00 3.60
34 Mark McGwire SN............... 20.00 6.00
35 Nomar Garciaparra SN......... 12.00 3.60
36 Greg Maddux SN................. 12.00 3.60
37 Mike Piazza SN................... 12.00 3.60
38 Alex Rodriguez SN.............. 12.00 3.60
39 Frank Thomas SN................. 5.00 1.50
40 Juan Gonzalez SN................ 5.00 1.50
41 Tony Gwynn SN.................. 10.00 3.00
42 Derek Jeter SN................... 20.00 6.00
43 Chipper Jones SN................. 5.00 1.50
44 Scott Rolen SN..................... 5.00 1.50
45 Sammy Sosa SN.................. 12.00 3.60
46 Kerry Wood SN..................... 5.00 1.50
47 Roger Clemens SN.............. 15.00 4.50
48 Jeff Bagwell SN.................... 5.00 1.50
49 Vladimir Guerrero SN............ 5.00 1.50
50 Ben Grieve SN...................... 5.00 1.50

1999 SkyBox Molten Metal Autograph Redemption

300 special exchange cards were randomly seeded exclusively into National Edition packs. These packs were distributed to tableholders of the 1999 National Convention in Atlanta to be sold at the show. Two types of autograph exchange cards were available. Fifty of these cards allowed the lucky collector to choose a free autograph from any of the athlete's signing at that year's National Convention. 250 additional cards could be exchanged for an autographed item from an athlete specifically chosen by the NSCC board.

Nm-Mt Ex-Mt
NNO Their Choice EXCH/250....... 1.00 .30
NNO Your Choice EXCH/50.......... 2.00 .60

1999 SkyBox Molten Metal Oh Atlanta

Inserted one per National Editon pack, this 30-card set die cut in the shape of the "A" logo for

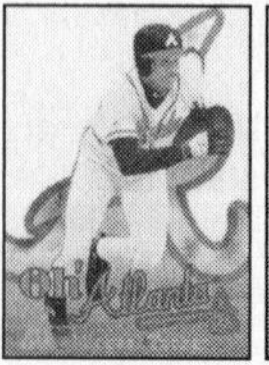

Atlanta features color photos of current and former Atlanta Braves players.

	Nm-Mt	Ex-Mt
COMPLETE SET (30)	100.00	30.00
1 Kenny Lofton	3.00	.90
2 Kevin Millwood	3.00	.90
3 Bret Boone	3.00	.90
4 Otis Nixon	2.00	.60
5 Vinny Castilla	3.00	.90
6 Brian Jordan	3.00	.90
7 Chipper Jones	8.00	2.40
8 David Justice	3.00	.90
9 Micah Bowie	2.00	.60
10 Fred McGriff	5.00	1.50
11 Ron Gant	3.00	.90
12 Andruw Jones	3.00	.90
13 Kent Mercker	2.00	.60
14 Greg McMichael	2.00	.60
15 Steve Avery	2.00	.60
16 Marquis Grissom	2.00	.60
17 Jason Schmidt	3.00	.90
18 Ryan Klesko	3.00	.90
19 Charlie O'Brien	2.00	.60
20 Terry Pendleton	3.00	.90
21 Denny Neagle	2.00	.60
22 Greg Maddux	15.00	4.50
23 Tom Glavine	5.00	1.50
24 Javy Lopez	3.00	.90
25 John Rocker	2.00	.60
26 Walt Weiss	2.00	.60
27 John Smoltz	5.00	1.50
28 Michael Tucker	2.00	.60
29 Odalis Perez	2.00	.60
30 Andres Galarraga	3.00	.90

1999 SkyBox Premium

The 1999 SkyBox Premium set was issued in one series for a total of 350 cards and distributed in eight-card packs with a suggested retail price of $2.69. The set features color action player photos with a team colored action-trail and gold-foil stamping. The set contains the following subsets: Spring Fling (273-297) and two versions of the 50 Rookies. In an effoty to satisfy fans of both complete sets and short-printed Rookie Cards, dual version rookie and prospect cards were created. The commonly available versions feature close-up shots of the players and these are considered the true Rookie Card. The short-printed versions feature full-body action shots and are seeded at a rate of one in eight packs. Both versions of these cards are numbered but we've added an "S" suffix on the short-prints for checklisting purposes. Notable Rookie Cards include Pat Burrell and Freddy Garcia.

	Nm-Mt	Ex-Mt
COMP.MASTER SET (350)	200.00	60.00
COMP.SET w/o SP's (300)	25.00	7.50
COMMON (1-222/273-300)	.20	.06
COMMON (223-272)	.30	.09
COMMON SP (223-272)	2.00	.60
1 Alex Rodriguez	1.25	.35
2 Sidney Ponson	.30	.09
3 Shawn Green	.30	.09
4 Dan Wilson	.20	.06
5 Rolando Arrojo	.20	.06
6 Roberto Alomar	.75	.23
7 Matt Anderson	.20	.06
8 David Segui	.20	.06
9 Alex Gonzalez	.20	.06
10 Edgar Renteria	.30	.09
11 Benito Santiago	.30	.09
12 Todd Stottlemyre	.20	.06
13 Rico Brogna	.20	.06
14 Troy Glaus	.50	.15
15 Al Leiter	.30	.09
16 Pedro Martinez	.75	.23
17 Paul O'Neill	.50	.15
18 Manny Ramirez	.30	.09
19 Scott Rolen	.50	.15
20 Curt Schilling	.50	.15
21 Bob Abreu	.30	.09
22 Robb Nen	.30	.09
23 Andy Pettitte	.50	.15
24 John Wetteland	.30	.09
25 Bobby Bonilla	.30	.09
26 Darin Erstad	.30	.09
27 Shawn Estes	.20	.06
28 John Franco	.30	.09
29 Nomar Garciaparra	1.25	.35
30 Rick Helling	.20	.06
31 David Justice	.30	.09
32 Chuck Knoblauch	.30	.09
33 Quinton McCracken	.20	.06
34 Kenny Rogers	.30	.09
35 Brian Giles	.30	.09
36 Armando Benitez	.20	.06
37 Trevor Hoffman	.30	.09
38 Charles Johnson	.30	.09
39 Travis Lee	.20	.06
40 Tom Glavine	.50	.15
41 Rondell White	.30	.09
42 Orlando Hernandez	.30	.09
43 Mickey Morandini	.20	.06
44 Darryl Kile	.30	.09
45 Greg Vaughn	.30	.09
46 Gregg Jefferies	.20	.06
47 Mark McGwire	2.00	.60
48 Kerry Wood	.75	.23
49 Jeromy Burnitz	.30	.09
50 Ron Gant	.30	.09
51 Vinny Castilla	.30	.09
52 Doug Glanville	.20	.06
53 Juan Guzman	.20	.06
54 Dustin Hermanson	.20	.06
55 Jose Hernandez	.20	.06
56 Bobby Higginson	.30	.09
57 A.J. Hinch	.20	.06
58 Randy Johnson	.75	.23
59 Eli Marrero	.20	.06
60 Rafael Palmeiro	.50	.15
61 Carl Pavano	.20	.06
62 Brett Tomko	.20	.06
63 Jose Guillen	.20	.06
64 Mike Lieberthal	.30	.09
65 Jim Abbott	.50	.15
66 Dante Bichette	.30	.09
67 Jeff Cirillo	.20	.06
68 Eric Davis	.30	.09
69 Delino DeShields	.20	.06
70 Steve Finley	.30	.09
71 Mark Grace	.50	.15
72 Jason Kendall	.30	.09
73 Jeff Kent	.30	.09
74 Desi Relaford	.20	.06
75 Ivan Rodriguez	.75	.23
76 Shannon Stewart	.30	.09
77 Geoff Jenkins	.30	.09
78 Ben Grieve	.20	.06
79 Cliff Floyd	.30	.09
80 Jason Giambi	.75	.23
81 Rod Beck	.20	.06
82 Derek Bell	.20	.06
83 Will Clark	.75	.23
84 David Dellucci	.20	.06
85 Joey Hamilton	.20	.06
86 Livan Hernandez	.20	.06
87 Barry Larkin	.75	.23
88 Matt Mantei	.20	.06
89 Dean Palmer	.30	.09
90 Chan Ho Park	.30	.09
91 Jim Thome	.75	.23
92 Miguel Tejada	.30	.09
93 Justin Thompson	.20	.06
94 David Wells	.30	.09
95 Bernie Williams	.50	.15
96 Jeff Bagwell	.50	.15
97 Derrek Lee	.30	.09
98 Devon White	.20	.06
99 Jeff Shaw	.20	.06
100 Brad Radke	.30	.09
101 Mark Grudzielanek	.20	.06
102 Javy Lopez	.30	.09
103 Mike Sirotka	.20	.06
104 Robin Ventura	.30	.09
105 Andy Ashby	.30	.09
106 Juan Gonzalez	.75	.23
107 Albert Belle	.30	.09
108 Andy Benes	.30	.09
109 Jay Buhner	.30	.09
110 Ken Caminiti	.30	.09
111 Roger Clemens	1.50	.45
112 Mike Hampton	.30	.09
113 Pete Harnisch	.20	.06
114 Mike Piazza	1.25	.35
115 J.T. Snow	.30	.09
116 John Olerud	.30	.09
117 Tony Womack	.20	.06
118 Todd Zeile	.30	.09
119 Tony Gwynn	1.00	.30
120 Brady Anderson	.30	.09
121 Sean Casey	.30	.09
122 Jose Cruz Jr.	.30	.09
123 Carlos Delgado	.30	.09
124 Edgar Martinez	.50	.15
125 Jose Mesa	.20	.06
126 Shane Reynolds	.20	.06
127 John Valentin	.20	.06
128 Mo Vaughn	.30	.09
129 Kevin Young	.30	.09
130 Jay Bell	.30	.09
131 Aaron Boone	.30	.09
132 John Smoltz	.50	.15
133 Mike Stanley	.20	.06
134 Bret Saberhagen	.30	.09
135 Tim Salmon	.50	.15
136 Mariano Rivera	.50	.15
137 Ken Griffey Jr.	1.25	.35
138 Jose Offerman	.20	.06
139 Troy Percival	.30	.09
140 Greg Maddux	1.25	.35
141 Frank Thomas	.75	.23
142 Steve Avery	.20	.06
143 Kevin Millwood	.30	.09
144 Sammy Sosa	1.25	.35
145 Larry Walker	.50	.15
146 Matt Williams	.30	.09
147 Mike Caruso	.20	.06
148 Todd Helton	.50	.15
149 Andruw Jones	.30	.09
150 Ray Lankford	.20	.06
151 Craig Biggio	.50	.15
152 Ugueth Urbina	.20	.06
153 Wade Boggs	.50	.15
154 Derek Jeter	2.00	.60
155 Wally Joyner	.30	.09
156 Mike Mussina	.75	.23
157 Gregg Olson	.20	.06
158 Henry Rodriguez	.20	.06
159 Reggie Sanders	.30	.09
160 Fernando Tatis	.20	.06
161 Dmitri Young	.30	.09
162 Rick Aguilera	.20	.06
163 Marty Cordova	.20	.06
164 Johnny Damon	.30	.09
165 Ray Durham	.30	.09
166 Brad Fullmer	.20	.06
167 Chipper Jones	.75	.23
168 Bobby Smith	.20	.06
169 Omar Vizquel	.30	.09
170 Todd Hundley	.20	.06
171 David Cone	.30	.09
172 Royce Clayton	.20	.06
173 Ryan Klesko	.30	.09
174 Jeff Montgomery	.20	.06
175 Maglio Ordonez	.30	.09
176 Billy Wagner	.30	.09
177 Masato Yoshii	.20	.06
178 Jason Christiansen	.20	.06
179 Chuck Finley	.30	.09
180 Tom Gordon	.20	.06
181 Wilton Guerrero	.20	.06
182 Rickey Henderson	.75	.23
183 Sterling Hitchcock	.20	.06
184 Kenny Lofton	.30	.09
185 Tino Martinez	.50	.15
186 Fred McGriff	.50	.15
187 Matt Stairs	.20	.06
188 Neifi Perez	.20	.06
189 Bob Wickman	.20	.06
190 Barry Bonds	2.00	.60
191 Jose Canseco	.75	.23
192 Damion Easley	.20	.06
193 Jim Edmonds	.30	.09
194 Juan Encarnacion	.20	.06
195 Travis Fryman	.30	.09
196 Tom Goodwin	.20	.06
197 Rusty Greer	.30	.09
198 Roberto Hernandez	.20	.06
199 B.J. Surhoff	.30	.09
200 Scott Brosius	.30	.09
201 Brian Jordan	.30	.09
202 Paul Konerko	.30	.09
203 Ismael Valdes	.30	.09
204 Eric Milton	.20	.06
205 Adrian Beltre	.30	.09
206 Tony Clark	.20	.06
207 Bartolo Colon	.30	.09
208 Cal Ripken	2.50	.75
209 Moises Alou	.30	.09
210 Wilson Alvarez	.20	.06
211 Kevin Brown	.50	.15
212 Orlando Cabrera	.20	.06
213 Vladimir Guerrero	.75	.23
214 Jose Rosado	.20	.06
215 Raul Mondesi	.30	.09
216 David Nilsson	.20	.06
217 Carlos Perez	.20	.06
218 Jason Schmidt	.30	.09
219 Richie Sexson	.30	.09
220 Gary Sheffield	.30	.09
221 Fernando Vina	.30	.09
222 Todd Walker	.30	.09
223 Scott Sauerbeck RC	.30	.09
223S Scott Sauerbeck SP	2.00	.60
224 Pascual Matos RC	.30	.09
224S Pascual Matos SP	2.00	.60
225 Kyle Farnsworth RC	.75	.23
225S Kyle Farnsworth SP	3.00	.90
226 Freddy Garcia RC	.75	.23
226S Freddy Garcia SP	3.00	.90
227 David Lundquist RC	.30	.09
227S David Lundquist SP	2.00	.60
228 Jolbert Cabrera RC	.30	.09
228S Jolbert Cabrera SP	2.00	.60
229 Dan Perkins RC	.30	.09
229S Dan Perkins SP	2.00	.60
230 Warren Morris	.30	.09
230S Warren Morris SP	2.00	.60
231 Carlos Febles	.30	.09
231S Carlos Febles SP	2.00	.60
232 Brett Hinchliffe RC	.30	.09
232S Brett Hinchliffe SP	2.00	.60
233 Jason Phillips RC	.30	.09
233S Jason Phillips SP	2.00	.60
234 Glen Barker RC	.30	.09
234S Glen Barker SP	2.00	.60
235 Jose Macias RC	.30	.09
235S Jose Macias SP	2.00	.60
236 Joe Mays RC	.50	.15
236S Joe Mays SP	2.00	.60
237 Chad Allen RC	.30	.09
237S Chad Allen SP	2.00	.60
238 Miguel Del Toro RC	.30	.09
238S Miguel Del Toro SP	2.00	.60
239 Chris Singleton	.30	.09
239S Chris Singleton SP	2.00	.60
240 Jesse Garcia RC	.30	.09
240S Jesse Garcia SP	2.00	.60
241 Kris Benson	.30	.09
241S Kris Benson SP	2.00	.60
242 Clay Bellinger RC	.30	.09
242S Clay Bellinger SP	2.00	.60
243 Scott Williamson	.30	.09
243S Scott Williamson SP	2.00	.60
244 Masao Kida RC	.30	.09
244S Masao Kida SP	2.00	.60
245 Guillermo Garcia RC	.30	.09
245S Guillermo Garcia SP	2.00	.60
246 A.J. Burnett RC	.75	.23
246S A.J. Burnett SP	3.00	.90
247 Bo Porter RC	.30	.09
247S Bo Porter SP	2.00	.60
248 Pat Burrell RC	2.00	.60
248S Pat Burrell SP	10.00	3.00
249 Carlos Lee	.30	.09
249S Carlos Lee SP	2.00	.60
250 Jeff Weaver RC	.50	.15
250S Jeff Weaver SP	2.00	.60
251 Ruben Mateo	.30	.09
251S Ruben Mateo SP	2.00	.60
252 J.D. Drew	.30	.09
252S J.D. Drew SP	2.00	.60
253 Jeremy Giambi	.30	.09
253S Jeremy Giambi SP	2.00	.60
254 Gary Bennett RC	.30	.09
254S Gary Bennett SP	2.00	.60
255 Edwards Guzman RC	.30	.09
255S Edwards Guzman SP	2.00	.60
256 Ramon E.Martinez RC	.30	.09
256S RamonE.Martinez SP	2.00	.60
257 Giomar Guevara RC	.30	.09
257S Giomar Guevara SP	2.00	.60
258 Joe McEwing RC	.30	.09
258S Joe McEwing SP	2.00	.60
259 Tom Davey RC	.30	.09
259S Tom Davey SP	2.00	.60
260 Gabe Kapler	.30	.09
260S Gabe Kapler SP	2.00	.60
261 Ryan Rupe RC	.30	.09
261S Ryan Rupe SP	2.00	.60
262 Kelly Dransfeldt RC	.30	.09
262S Kelly Dransfeldt SP	2.00	.60
263 Michael Barrett	.30	.09
263S Michael Barrett SP	2.00	.60
264 Eric Chavez	.30	.09
264S Eric Chavez SP	2.00	.60
265 Orber Moreno RC	.30	.09
265S Orber Moreno SP	2.00	.60
266 Marlon Anderson	.30	.09
266S Marlon Anderson SP	2.00	.60
267 Carlos Beltran	.30	.09
267S Carlos Beltran SP	2.00	.60
268 D.Mientkiewicz RC	.75	.23
268S D.Mientkiewicz SP	4.00	1.20
269 Roy Halladay	.30	.09
269S Roy Halladay SP	2.00	.60
270 Torii Hunter	.30	.09
270S Torii Hunter SP	2.00	.60
271 Stan Spencer	.30	.09
271S Stan Spencer SP	2.00	.60
272 Alex Gonzalez	.30	.09
272S Alex Gonzalez SP	2.00	.60
273 Mark McGwire SF	1.00	.30
274 Scott Rolen SF	.30	.09
275 Jeff Bagwell SF	.30	.09
276 Derek Jeter SF	1.00	.30
277 Tony Gwynn SF	.50	.15
278 Frank Thomas SF	.50	.15
279 Sammy Sosa SF	.75	.23
280 Nomar Garciaparra SF	.75	.23
281 Cal Ripken SF	1.25	.35
282 Albert Belle SF	.20	.06
283 Kerry Wood SF	.50	.15
284 Greg Maddux SF	.75	.23
285 Barry Bonds SF	.75	.23
286 Juan Gonzalez SF	.50	.15
287 Ken Griffey Jr. SF	.75	.23
288 Alex Rodriguez SF	.75	.23
289 Ben Grieve SF	.20	.06
290 Travis Lee SF	.20	.06
291 Mo Vaughn SF	.20	.06
292 Mike Piazza SF	.75	.23
293 Roger Clemens SF	.75	.23
294 J.D. Drew SF	.20	.06
295 Randy Johnson SF	.50	.15
296 Chipper Jones SF	.50	.15
297 Vladimir Guerrero SF	.50	.15
298 Nomar Garciaparra CL	.75	.23
299 Ken Griffey Jr. CL	.75	.23
300 Mark McGwire CL	1.00	.30
S83 Ben Grieve Sample	1.00	.30

1999 SkyBox Premium Star Rubies

Randomly inserted into packs, this 300-card set is parallel to the base set. Only 50 serial-numbered sets were produced with the short-printed full-body action shot rookie and prospect cards sequentially numbered to just 15. Like the rest of the cards in this set, the close-up rookie and prospect cards are serial numbered to 50.

	Nm-Mt	Ex-Mt
COMMON CARD (1-300)	8.00	2.40

*STARS 1-300: 12.5X TO 30X BASIC CARDS
*PROSPECTS 223-272: 12.5X TO 30X BASIC
*ROOKIES 223-272: 8X TO 20X BASIC RC'S

1999 SkyBox Premium Autographics

Randomly inserted in packs at the rate of one in 68, this 52-card set features autographed color photos of top players. The cards are unnumbered and checklisted in alphabetical order.

	Nm-Mt	Ex-Mt
1 Roberto Alomar	40.00	12.00
2 Paul Bako	10.00	3.00
3 Michael Barrett	10.00	3.00
4 Kris Benson	10.00	3.00
5 Micah Bowie	10.00	3.00
6 Roosevelt Brown	15.00	4.50
7 A.J. Burnett	15.00	4.50
8 Pat Burrell	30.00	9.00
9 Ken Caminiti	15.00	4.50
10 Royce Clayton	10.00	3.00
11 Edgard Clemente	10.00	3.00
12 Bartolo Colon	15.00	4.50
13 J.D. Drew	15.00	4.50
14 Damion Easley	10.00	3.00
15 Derrin Ebert	10.00	3.00
16 Mario Encarnacion	10.00	3.00
17 Juan Encarnacion	10.00	3.00
18 Troy Glaus	25.00	7.50
19 Tom Glavine	40.00	12.00
20 Juan Gonzalez SP	150.00	45.00
21 Shawn Green	15.00	4.50
22 Wilton Guerrero	10.00	3.00
23 Jose Guillen	10.00	3.00
24 Tony Gwynn	50.00	15.00
25 Mark Harriger	10.00	3.00
26 Todd Hollandsworth	10.00	3.00
27 Scott Hunter	10.00	3.00
28 Gabe Kapler	10.00	3.00
29 Scott Karl	10.00	3.00
30 Mike Kinkade	10.00	3.00
31 Ray Lankford	10.00	3.00
32 Barry Larkin	40.00	12.00
33 Matt Lawton	10.00	3.00
34 Ricky Ledee	10.00	3.00
35 Travis Lee	10.00	3.00
36 Eli Marrero	10.00	3.00
37 Ruben Mateo	10.00	3.00
38 Joe McEwing	15.00	4.50
39 Doug Mientkiewicz	15.00	4.50
40 Russ Ortiz	15.00	4.50
41 Jim Parque	10.00	3.00
42 Robert Person	10.00	3.00
43 Alex Rodriguez	100.00	30.00
44 Scott Rolen	25.00	7.50
45 Benj Sampson	10.00	3.00
46 Luis Saturria	10.00	3.00
47 Curt Schilling	25.00	7.50
48 David Segui	10.00	3.00
49 Fernando Tatis	10.00	3.00
50 Peter Tucci	10.00	3.00
51 Javier Vazquez	25.00	7.50
52 Robin Ventura	15.00	4.50

1999 SkyBox Premium Autographics Blue Ink

Randomly inserted in packs, this 52-card set is a blue ink parallel version of the regular insert set. Only 50 serial-numbered sets were produced.

Nm-Mt Ex-Mt

*BLUE INK STARS: 1X TO 2.5X BASIC AU'S
*BLUE INK RC's: .75X TO 2X BASIC AU'S

1999 SkyBox Premium Diamond Debuts

Randomly inserted in packs at the rate of one in 49, this 15-card set features color photos of the best rookies of 1999 printed on silver rainbow holo-foil and etched cards.

	Nm-Mt	Ex-Mt
COMPLETE SET (15)	80.00	24.00
1 Eric Chavez	8.00	2.40
2 Kyle Farnsworth	20.00	6.00
3 Ryan Rupe	8.00	2.40
4 Jeremy Giambi	8.00	2.40
5 Marlon Anderson	8.00	2.40
6 J.D. Drew	8.00	2.40
7 Carlos Febles	8.00	2.40
8 Joe McEwing	8.00	2.40
9 Jeff Weaver	12.00	3.60
10 Alex Gonzalez	5.00	1.50
11 Chad Allen	8.00	2.40
12 Michael Barrett	8.00	2.40
13 Gabe Kapler	8.00	2.40
14 Carlos Lee	8.00	2.40
15 Edwards Guzman	8.00	2.40

1999 SkyBox Premium Intimidation Nation

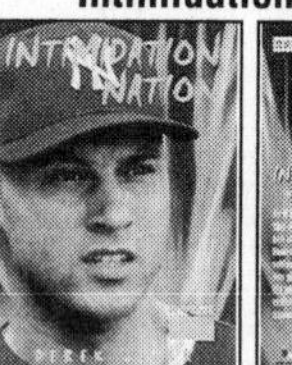

Randomly inserted in packs, this 15-card set features color photos of top players stamped on gold rainbow holo-foil cards. Only 99 serial-numbered sets were produced.

	Nm-Mt	Ex-Mt
COMPLETE SET (15)	800.00	240.00
1 Cal Ripken	100.00	30.00
2 Tony Gwynn	40.00	12.00
3 Nomar Garciaparra	50.00	15.00
4 Frank Thomas	30.00	9.00
5 Mike Piazza	50.00	15.00
6 Mark McGwire	80.00	24.00
7 Scott Rolen	20.00	6.00
8 Chipper Jones	30.00	9.00
9 Greg Maddux	50.00	15.00
10 Ken Griffey Jr.	50.00	15.00
11 Juan Gonzalez	30.00	9.00
12 Derek Jeter	80.00	24.00
13 J.D. Drew	20.00	6.00
14 Roger Clemens	60.00	18.00
15 Alex Rodriguez	50.00	15.00

1999 SkyBox Premium Live Bats

Randomly inserted in packs at the rate of one in seven, this 15-card set features color photos of some of baseball's best hitters on foil stamped cards.

	Nm-Mt	Ex-Mt
COMPLETE SET (15)	25.00	7.50
1 Juan Gonzalez	1.25	.35
2 Mark McGwire	3.00	.90
3 Jeff Bagwell	.75	.23
4 Frank Thomas	1.25	.35
5 Mike Piazza	2.00	.60
6 Nomar Garciaparra	2.00	.60
7 Alex Rodriguez	2.00	.60
8 Scott Rolen	.75	.23
9 Travis Lee	.30	.09
10 Tony Gwynn	1.50	.45
11 Derek Jeter	3.00	.90
12 Ben Grieve	.30	.09
13 Chipper Jones	1.25	.35

14 Ken Griffey Jr. 2.00 .60
15 Cal Ripken 4.00 1.20

1999 SkyBox Premium Show Business

Randomly inserted in packs at the rate of one in 70, this 15-card set features top players printed on double foil-stamped cards.

Nm-Mt Ex-Mt
COMPLETE SET (15) 200.00 60.00
1 Mark McGwire 20.00 6.00
2 Tony Gwynn 10.00 3.00
3 Nomar Garciaparra 12.00 3.60
4 Juan Gonzalez 8.00 2.40
5 Roger Clemens 15.00 4.50
6 Chipper Jones 8.00 2.40
7 Cal Ripken 25.00 7.50
8 Alex Rodriguez 12.00 3.60
9 Orlando Hernandez 3.00 .90
10 Greg Maddux 12.00 3.60
11 Mike Piazza 12.00 3.60
12 Frank Thomas 8.00 2.40
13 Ken Griffey Jr. 12.00 3.60
14 Scott Rolen 5.00 1.50
15 Derek Jeter 20.00 6.00

1999 SkyBox Premium Soul of the Game

Randomly inserted into packs at the rate of one in 14, this 15-card set features players who are fan favorites printed on rainbow foil stamped cards.

Nm-Mt Ex-Mt
COMPLETE SET (15) 60.00 18.00
1 Alex Rodriguez 4.00 1.20
2 Vladimir Guerrero 2.50 .75
3 Chipper Jones 2.50 .75
4 Derek Jeter 6.00 1.80
5 Tony Gwynn 3.00 .90
6 Scott Rolen 1.50 .45
7 Juan Gonzalez 2.50 .75
8 Mark McGwire 6.00 1.80
9 Ken Griffey Jr. 4.00 1.20
10 Jeff Bagwell 1.50 .45
11 Cal Ripken 8.00 2.40
12 Frank Thomas 2.50 .75
13 Mike Piazza 4.00 1.20
14 Nomar Garciaparra 4.00 1.20
15 Sammy Sosa 4.00 1.20

1999 SkyBox Thunder

The 1999 SkyBox Thunder set was issued in one series totalling 300 cards. The set was distributed in eight-card packs with a suggested retail price of $1.59. The fronts feature color action player photos with computer-enhanced graphics. The backs carry player information. The regular player cards (1-140) have an insertion rate of four or five per pack. Veteran stars (141-240) come two per pack. Superstars (241-300) are seeded 1:1. A sample card featuring Ben Grieve was distributed to dealers and hobby media several weeks prior to the product shipping. The card can be easily distinguished by the text "Promotional Sample" running diagonally across the front and back.

Nm-Mt Ex-Mt
COMPLETE SET (300) 40.00 12.00
COMMON (1-140) .20 .06
COMMON (141-240) .30 .09
COMMON (241-300) .40 .12
1 John Smoltz .30 .09
2 Garret Anderson .20 .06
3 Matt Williams .20 .06
4 Daryle Ward .20 .06
5 Andy Ashby .20 .06
6 Miguel Tejada .20 .06
7 Dmitri Young .20 .06
8 Roberto Alomar .50 .15
9 Kevin Brown .30 .09
10 Eric Young .20 .06
11 Odalis Perez .20 .06
12 Preston Wilson .20 .06
13 Jeff Abbott .20 .06
14 Bret Boone .20 .06
15 Mendy Lopez .20 .06
16 B.J. Surhoff .20 .06
17 Steve Woodard .20 .06
18 Ron Coomer .20 .06
19 Rondell White .20 .06
20 Edgardo Alfonzo .20 .06
21 Kevin Millwood .20 .06
22 Jose Canseco .50 .15
23 Blake Stein .20 .06
24 Quilvio Veras .20 .06
25 Chuck Knoblauch .20 .06
26 David Segui .20 .06
27 Eric Davis .20 .06
28 Francisco Cordova .20 .06
29 Randy Winn .20 .06
30 Will Clark .50 .15
31 Billy Wagner .20 .06
32 Kevin Witt .20 .06
33 Jim Edmonds .20 .06
34 Todd Stottlemyre .20 .06
35 Shane Andrews .20 .06
36 Michael Tucker .20 .06
37 Sandy Alomar Jr. .20 .06
38 Neifi Perez .20 .06
39 Jaret Wright .20 .06
40 Devon White .20 .06
41 Edgar Renteria .20 .06
42 Shane Reynolds .20 .06
43 Jeff King .20 .06
44 Darren Dreifort .20 .06
45 Fernando Vina .20 .06
46 Marty Cordova .20 .06
47 Ugueth Urbina .20 .06
48 Bobby Bonilla .20 .06
49 Omar Vizquel .20 .06
50 Tom Gordon .20 .06
51 Ryan Christenson .20 .06
52 Aaron Boone .20 .06
53 Jamie Moyer .20 .06
54 Brian Giles .20 .06
55 Kevin Tapani .20 .06
56 Scott Brosius .20 .06
57 Ellis Burks .20 .06
58 Al Leiter .20 .06
59 Royce Clayton .20 .06
60 Chris Carpenter .20 .06
61 Bubba Trammell .20 .06
62 Tom Glavine .30 .09
63 Shannon Stewart .20 .06
64 Todd Zeile .20 .06
65 J.T. Snow .20 .06
66 Matt Clement .20 .06
67 Matt Stairs .20 .06
68 Ismael Valdes .20 .06
69 Todd Walker .20 .06
70 Jose Lima .20 .06
71 Mike Caruso .20 .06
72 Brett Tomko .20 .06
73 Mike Lansing .20 .06
74 Justin Thompson .20 .06
75 Damion Easley .20 .06
76 Derrek Lee .20 .06
77 Derek Bell .20 .06
78 Brady Anderson .20 .06
79 Charles Johnson .20 .06
80 Rafael Roque RC .20 .06
81 Corey Koskie .20 .06
82 Fernando Seguignol .20 .06
83 Jay Tessmer .20 .06
84 Jason Giambi .50 .15
85 Mike Lieberthal .20 .06
86 Jose Guillen .20 .06
87 Jim Leyritz .20 .06
88 Shawn Estes .20 .06
89 Ray Lankford .20 .06
90 Paul Sorrento .20 .06
91 Javy Lopez .20 .06
92 John Wetteland .20 .06
93 Sean Casey .20 .06
94 Chuck Finley .20 .06
95 Trot Nixon .30 .09
96 Ray Durham .20 .06
97 Reggie Sanders .20 .06
98 Bartolo Colon .20 .06
99 Henry Rodriguez .20 .06
100 Rolando Arrojo .20 .06
101 Geoff Jenkins .20 .06
102 Darryl Kile .20 .06
103 Mark Kotsay .20 .06
104 Craig Biggio .30 .09
105 Omar Daal .20 .06
106 Carlos Febles .20 .06
107 Eric Karros .20 .06
108 Matt Lawton .20 .06
109 Carl Pavano .20 .06
110 Brian McRae .20 .06
111 Mariano Rivera .30 .09
112 Jay Buhner .20 .06
113 Doug Glanville .20 .06
114 Jason Kendall .20 .06
115 Wally Joyner .20 .06
116 Jeff Kent .20 .06
117 Shane Monahan .20 .06
118 Eli Marrero .20 .06
119 Bobby Smith .20 .06
120 Shawn Green .20 .06
121 Kirk Rueter .20 .06
122 Tom Goodwin .20 .06
123 Andy Benes .20 .06
124 Ed Sprague .20 .06
125 Mike Mussina .50 .15
126 Jose Offerman .20 .06
127 Mickey Morandini .20 .06
128 Paul Konerko .20 .06
129 Denny Neagle .20 .06
130 Travis Fryman .20 .06
131 John Rocker .20 .06
132 Robert Fick .20 .06
133 Livan Hernandez .20 .06
134 Ken Caminiti .20 .06
135 Johnny Damon .20 .06
136 Jeff Kubenka .20 .06
137 Marquis Grissom .20 .06
138 D.Mientkiewicz RC .60 .18
139 Dustin Hermanson .20 .06
140 Carl Everett .20 .06
141 Hideo Nomo .75 .23
142 Jorge Posada .50 .15
143 Rickey Henderson .75 .23
144 Robb Nen .30 .09
145 Ron Gant .30 .09
146 Aramis Ramirez .30 .09
147 Trevor Hoffman .30 .09
148 Bill Mueller .30 .09
149 Edgar Martinez .50 .15
150 Fred McGriff .50 .15
151 Rusty Greer .30 .09
152 Tom Evans .30 .09
153 Todd Greene .30 .09
154 Jay Bell .30 .09
155 Mike Lowell .30 .09
156 Orlando Cabrera .30 .09
157 Troy O'Leary .30 .09
158 Jose Hernandez .30 .09
159 Maggio Ordonez .30 .09
160 Barry Larkin .75 .23
161 David Justice .30 .09
162 Derrick Gibson .30 .09
163 Luis Gonzalez .30 .09
164 Alex Gonzalez .30 .09
165 Scott Elarton .30 .09
166 Dermal Brown .30 .09
167 Eric Milton .30 .09
168 Raul Mondesi .30 .09
169 Jeff Cirillo .30 .09
170 Benj Sampson .30 .09
171 John Olerud .30 .09
172 Andy Pettitte .50 .15
173 A.J. Hinch .30 .09
174 Rico Brogna .30 .09
175 Jason Schmidt .30 .09
176 Dean Palmer .30 .09
177 Matt Morris .30 .09
178 Quinton McCracken .30 .09
179 Rick Helling .30 .09
180 Walt Weiss .30 .09
181 Troy Percival .30 .09
182 Tony Batista .30 .09
183 Brian Jordan .30 .09
184 Jerry Hairston Jr. .30 .09
185 Bret Saberhagen .30 .09
186 Mark Grace .50 .15
187 Brian Simmons .30 .09
188 Pete Harnisch .30 .09
189 Kenny Lofton .30 .09
190 Vinny Castilla .30 .09
191 Bobby Higginson .30 .09
192 Joey Hamilton .30 .09
193 Cliff Floyd .30 .09
194 Andres Galarraga .30 .09
195 Chan Ho Park .30 .09
196 Jeromy Burnitz .30 .09
197 David Ortiz .30 .09
198 Wilton Guerrero .30 .09
199 Rey Ordonez .30 .09
200 Paul O'Neill .50 .15
201 Kenny Rogers .30 .09
202 Marlon Anderson .30 .09
203 Tony Womack .30 .09
204 Robin Ventura .30 .09
205 Russ Ortiz .30 .09
206 Mike Frank .30 .09
207 Fernando Tatis .30 .09
208 Miguel Cairo .30 .09
209 Ivan Rodriguez .75 .23
210 Carlos Delgado .30 .09
211 Tim Salmon .50 .15
212 Brian Anderson .30 .09
213 Ryan Klesko .30 .09
214 Scott Erickson .30 .09
215 Mike Stanley .30 .09
216 Brant Brown .30 .09
217 Rod Beck .30 .09
218 Guillermo Garcia RC .30 .09
219 David Wells .30 .09
220 Dante Bichette .30 .09
221 Armando Benitez .30 .09
222 Todd Dunwoody .30 .09
223 Kelvim Escobar .30 .09
224 Richard Hidalgo .30 .09
225 Angel Pena .30 .09
226 Ronnie Belliard .30 .09
227 Brad Radke .30 .09
228 Brad Fullmer .30 .09
229 Jay Payton .30 .09
230 Tino Martinez .50 .15
231 Scott Spiezio .30 .09
232 Bob Abreu .30 .09
233 John Valentin .30 .09
234 Kevin Young .30 .09
235 Steve Finley .30 .09
236 David Cone .30 .09
237 Armando Rios .30 .09
238 Russ Davis .30 .09
239 Wade Boggs .50 .15
240 Aaron Sele .30 .09
241 Jose Cruz Jr. .40 .12
242 George Lombard .40 .12
243 Todd Helton .60 .18
244 Andruw Jones .40 .12
245 Troy Glaus .60 .18
246 Manny Ramirez .40 .12
247 Ben Grieve .40 .12
248 Richie Sexson .40 .12
249 Juan Encarnacion .40 .12
250 Randy Johnson 1.00 .30
251 Gary Sheffield .40 .12
252 Rafael Palmeiro .60 .18
253 Roy Halladay .40 .12
254 Mike Piazza 1.50 .45
255 Tony Gwynn 1.25 .35
256 Juan Gonzalez 1.00 .30
257 Jeremy Giambi .40 .12
258 Ben Davis .40 .12
259 Russ Branyan .40 .12
260 Pedro Martinez 1.00 .30
261 Frank Thomas 1.00 .30
262 Calvin Pickering .40 .12
263 Chipper Jones 1.00 .30
264 Ryan Minor .40 .12
265 Roger Clemens 2.00 .60
266 Sammy Sosa 1.50 .45
267 Mo Vaughn .40 .12
268 Carlos Beltran .40 .12
269 Jim Thome 1.00 .30
270 Mark McGwire 2.50 .75
271 Travis Lee .40 .12
272 Darin Erstad .40 .12
273 Derek Jeter 2.50 .75
274 Greg Maddux 1.50 .45
275 Ricky Ledee .40 .12
276 Alex Rodriguez 1.50 .45
277 Vladimir Guerrero 1.00 .30
278 Greg Vaughn .40 .12
279 Scott Rolen .60 .18
280 Carlos Guillen .40 .12
281 Jeff Bagwell .60 .18
282 Bruce Chen .40 .12
283 Tony Clark .40 .12
284 Albert Belle .40 .12
285 Cal Ripken 3.00 .90
286 Barry Bonds 2.50 .75
287 Curt Schilling .60 .18
288 Eric Chavez .40 .12
289 Larry Walker .60 .18
290 Orlando Hernandez .40 .12
291 Moises Alou .40 .12
292 Ken Griffey Jr. 1.50 .45
293 Kerry Wood 1.00 .30
294 Nomar Garciaparra 1.50 .45
295 Gabe Kapler .40 .12
296 Bernie Williams .60 .18
297 Matt Anderson .40 .12
298 Adrian Beltre .40 .12
299 J.D. Drew .40 .12
300 Ryan Bradley .40 .12
S247 Ben Grieve Sample 1.00 .30

1999 SkyBox Thunder Rant

Randomly inserted in retail packs only at the rate of one in two, this 300-card set is a parallel version of the base set.

Nm-Mt Ex-Mt
*RANT 1-140: 4X TO 10X BASIC 1-140
*RANT 141-240: 2.5X TO 6X BASIC 141-240
*RANT 241-300: 2X TO 5X BASIC 241-300

1999 SkyBox Thunder Rave

Randomly inserted in hobby packs only, this 300-card set is a different foil parallel version of the base set. Only 150 serially numbered sets were produced.

Nm-Mt Ex-Mt
*RAVE 1-140: 15X TO 40X BASIC 1-140
*RAVE 141-240: 10X TO 25X BASIC 141-240
*RAVE 241-300: 8X TO 20X BASIC 241-300

1999 SkyBox Thunder Super Rave

Randomly inserted in hobby packs only, this 300-card set is a parallel verion of the regular base set. Only 25 serially numbered sets were produced.

Nm-Mt Ex-Mt
*S.RAVE 1-140: 30X TO 80X BASIC ...
*S.RAVE 141-240: 20X TO 50X BASIC
*S.RAVE 241-300: 15X TO 40X BASIC

1999 SkyBox Thunder Dial 1

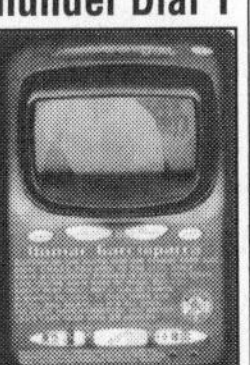

Randomly inserted in packs at the rate of one in 300, this 10-card set features color photos of long-distance hitters printed on black plastic cards with rounded corners designed to look like a mobile phone.

Nm-Mt Ex-Mt
COMPLETE SET (10) 200.00 60.00
D1 Nomar Garciaparra 25.00 7.50
D2 Juan Gonzalez 15.00 4.50
D3 Ken Griffey Jr. 25.00 7.50
D4 Chipper Jones 15.00 4.50
D5 Mark McGwire 40.00 12.00
D6 Mike Piazza 25.00 7.50
D7 Manny Ramirez 6.00 1.80
D8 Alex Rodriguez 25.00 7.50
D9 Sammy Sosa 25.00 7.50
D10 Mo Vaughn 6.00 1.80

1999 SkyBox Thunder Hip-No-Tized

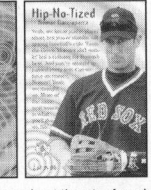

Randomly inserted in packs at the rate of one in 36, this 15-card set features color action photos of position players and pitchers who have a "mesmerizing" effect on opponents.

Nm-Mt Ex-Mt
COMPLETE SET (15) 100.00 30.00
H1 J.D. Drew 1.50 .45
H2 Nomar Garciaparra 6.00 1.80
H3 Juan Gonzalez 4.00 1.20
H4 Ken Griffey Jr. 6.00 1.80
H5 Derek Jeter 10.00 3.00
H6 Randy Johnson 4.00 1.20
H7 Chipper Jones 4.00 1.20
H8 Mark McGwire 10.00 3.00
H9 Mike Piazza 6.00 1.80
H10 Cal Ripken 12.00 3.60
H11 Alex Rodriguez 6.00 1.80
H12 Sammy Sosa 6.00 1.80
H13 Frank Thomas 4.00 1.20
H14 Jim Thome 4.00 1.20
H15 Kerry Wood 4.00 1.20

1999 SkyBox Thunder In Depth

Randomly inserted in packs at the rate of one in 24, this 10-card set features color action photos of players with key statistical achievements printed on cards highlighted with rainbow holofoil treatment.

Nm-Mt Ex-Mt
COMPLETE SET (10) 30.00 9.00
ID1 Albert Belle 1.00 .30
ID2 Barry Bonds 6.00 1.80
ID3 Roger Clemens 5.00 1.50
ID4 Juan Gonzalez 2.50 .75
ID5 Ken Griffey Jr. 4.00 1.20
ID6 Mark McGwire 6.00 1.80
ID7 Mike Piazza 4.00 1.20
ID8 Sammy Sosa 4.00 1.20
ID9 Mo Vaughn 1.00 .30
ID10 Kerry Wood 2.50 .75

1999 SkyBox Thunder Turbo-Charged

Randomly inserted in packs at the rate of one in 72, this 10-card set features action color photos of long-ball hitters printed on see-through plastic cards enhanced with rainbow holofoil.

Nm-Mt Ex-Mt
COMPLETE SET (10) 60.00 18.00
TC1 Jose Canseco 2.50 .75
TC2 Juan Gonzalez 5.00 1.50
TC3 Ken Griffey Jr. 8.00 2.40
TC4 Vladimir Guerrero 5.00 1.50
TC5 Mark McGwire 12.00 3.60
TC6 Mike Piazza 8.00 2.40
TC7 Manny Ramirez 2.00 .60
TC8 Alex Rodriguez 8.00 2.40
TC9 Sammy Sosa 8.00 2.40
TC10 Mo Vaughn 2.00 .60

1999 SkyBox Thunder Unleashed

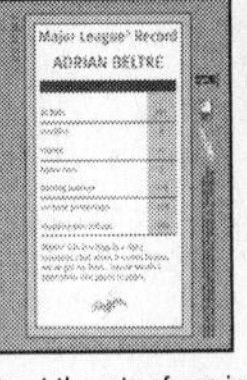

Randomly inserted in packs at the rate of one in six, this 15-card set features action color photos of new star players printed on cards designed to resemble a cereal box.

Nm-Mt Ex-Mt
COMPLETE SET (15) 15.00 4.50
U1 Carlos Beltran 1.00 .30
U2 Adrian Beltre 1.00 .30
U3 Eric Chavez 1.00 .30
U4 J.D. Drew 1.00 .30
U5 Juan Encarnacion 1.00 .30
U6 Jeremy Giambi 1.00 .30
U7 Troy Glaus 1.50 .45
U8 Ben Grieve 1.00 .30
U9 Todd Helton 1.50 .45
U10 Orlando Hernandez 1.00 .30
U11 Gabe Kapler 1.00 .30
U12 Travis Lee 1.00 .30
U13 Calvin Pickering 1.00 .30
U14 Richie Sexson 1.00 .30
U15 Kerry Wood 2.50 .75

1999 SkyBox Thunder www.batterz.com

Randomly inserted in packs at the rate of one in 18, this 10-card set features color action photos of the game's best hitters printed on these computer-inspired cards.

Nm-Mt Ex-Mt
COMPLETE SET (10) 30.00 9.00
WB1 J.D. Drew .75 .23
WB2 Nomar Garciaparra 3.00 .90
WB3 Ken Griffey Jr. 3.00 .90

Card	Nm-Mt	Ex-Mt
WB4 Tony Gwynn	2.50	.75
WB5 Derek Jeter	5.00	1.50
WB6 Mark McGwire	5.00	1.50
WB7 Alex Rodriguez	3.00	.90
WB8 Scott Rolen	1.25	.35
WB9 Sammy Sosa	3.00	.90
WB10 Bernie Williams	1.25	.35

1987 Smokey American League

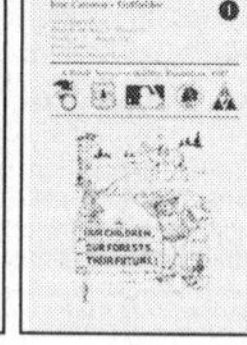

The U.S. Forestry Service (in conjunction with Major League Baseball) produced this large, attractive 14-player card set to commemorate the 43rd birthday of Smokey. The cards feature Smokey the Bear pictured on every card with the player. The card backs give a fire safety tip. The cards measure approximately 4" by 6" and are subtitled "National Smokey Bear Day 1987" on the front. The cards were printed on an uncut (but perforated) sheet that measured 18" by 24".

	Nm-Mt	Ex-Mt
COMPLETE SET (16)	8.00	3.20
1 Jose Canseco	1.50	.60
2 Dennis Oil Can Boyd	.25	.10
3 John Candelaria	.25	.10
4 Harold Baines	.50	.20
5 Joe Carter	.75	.30
6 Jack Morris	.50	.20
7 Buddy Biancalana	.25	.10
8 Kirby Puckett	2.00	.80
9 Mike Pagliarulo	.25	.10
10 Larry Sheets	.25	.10
11 Mike Moore	.25	.10
12 Charlie Hough	.25	.10
13 National Smokey	.25	.10
Bear Day 1987		
14 Tom Henke	.50	.20
15 Jim Gantner	.25	.10
16 American League	.25	.10
Smokey Bear Day 1987		

1987 Smokey National League

The U.S. Forestry Service (in conjunction with Major League Baseball) produced this large, attractive 14 player card set to commemorate the 43rd birthday of Smokey. The cards feature Smokey the Bear pictured on every card with the player. The card backs give a fire safety tip. The cards measure approximately 4" by 6" and are subtitled "National Smokey Bear Day 1987" on the front. The set price below does not include the more difficult variation cards.

	Nm-Mt	Ex-Mt
COMPLETE SET (15)	8.00	3.20
1 Steve Sax	.25	.10
2A Dale Murphy	3.00	1.20
Holding bat		
2B Dale Murphy	12.00	4.80
No bat		
arm around Smokey		
3A Jody Davis	.50	.20
Kneeling with Smokey		
3B Jody Davis	8.00	3.20
Standing, shaking Smokey's hand		
4 Bill Gullickson	.25	.10
5 Mike Scott	.25	.10
6 Roger McDowell	.25	.10
7 Steve Bedrosian	.25	.10
8 Johnny Ray	.25	.10
9 Ozzie Smith	2.50	1.00
10 Steve Garvey	.75	.30
11 National Smokey	.25	.10
Bear Day		
12 Mike Krukow	.25	.10
13 Smokey the Bear	.25	.10
14 Mike Fitzgerald	.25	.10
15 National League Logo	.25	.10

1995 Sonic/Pepsi Greats

This 12-card standard-size set was released at Sonic restaurants which served Pepsi products. Some players apparently signed cards for this set. The cards were issued in three-card cello packs. The fronts display color player photos inside red borders. Team logos have been airbrushed off hats and jerseys. In blue print on a white background, the backs present career summary, honors received, player profile, and career statistics. The cards are unnumbered and checklisted below in alphabetical order.

	Nm-Mt	Ex-Mt
COMPLETE SET (12)	7.00	2.10
1 Bert Campaneris	.50	.15
2 George Foster	.50	.15
3 Steve Garvey	.75	.23
4 Ferguson Jenkins	1.00	.30
5 Tommy John	.50	.15
6 Harmon Killebrew	1.00	.30
7 Sparky Lyle	.50	.15
8 Fred Lynn	.50	.15
9 Joe Morgan	1.00	.30
10 Graig Nettles	.50	.15
11 Warren Spahn	1.00	.30
12 Maury Wills	.75	.23

1999 Sotheby's Halper Auction

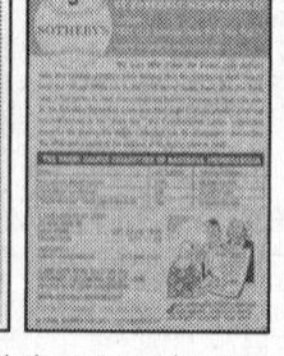

This 15-card standard-size set was issued to preview the auction of Barry Halper's collection through the Sotheby's auction house. This set features some of the most important moments or people in baseball history and what lots in the auction feature items apropos to that event. The fronts feature black and white photos with white borders with the words, "The Barry Halper Collection of Baseball Memorabilia" on the front. At the bottom is a description of the moment or person pictured. The back, styled similarly to the 1953 Topps set, features more information about the items. These sets were first displayed at the Atlanta National in 1999.

	Nm-Mt	Ex-Mt
COMPLETE SET (15)	20.00	6.00
1 Babe Ruth	5.00	1.50
Auction Catalogue Information		
2 Babe Ruth	5.00	1.50
Last Bat		
3 Lou Gehrig	3.00	.90
Day		
4 Joe DiMaggio	3.00	.90
PCL Rookie		
5 Joe Jackson	3.00	.90
Black Sox Scandal		
6 Mookie Wilson	.50	.15
Bill Buckner		
1986 World Series		
7 Bobby Thomson	.50	.15
Ralph Branca		
Shot Heard Round the World		
8 1888 World Tour	.25	.07
9 Henry Chadwick	.25	.07
Father of Baseball		
10 Ty Cobb	3.00	.90
Famous Slide into 3rd		
11 George Brett	1.00	.30
Don Slaught		
Pine Tar Outburst		
12 Mickey Mantle	5.00	1.50
Roger Maris		
The M and M Boys		
13 Willie Mays	3.00	.90
The Catch		
14 Autographed Baseball	.25	.07
Babe Ruth Ball against a computer		
XX Header Card	.25	.07

1999 Sotheby's Halper Auction Amazon

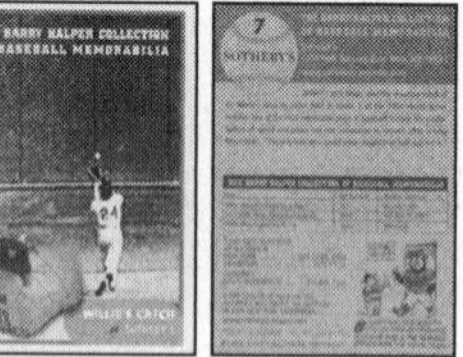

This 16 card set was one of the two sets issued to preview the sale of the Barry Halper collection. This set was issued in conjunction with Amazon.com and is slightly different from the set issued directly from Sotheby's.

	Nm-Mt	Ex-Mt
COMPLETE SET (16)	25.00	7.50
1 Header	.25	.07
Card is numbered		
2 Babe Ruth	5.00	1.50
Last Bat		
3 Lou Gehrig	3.00	.90
Day		
4 Joe DiMaggio	3.00	.90
Rookie Year		
5 Joe Jackson	3.00	.90
1919 World Series		
6 Roger Maris	3.00	.90
Mickey Mantle		
1961 Yankees		
7 Willie Mays	3.00	.90
1954 World Series Catch		
8 Bobby Thomson	.50	.15
Ralph Branca		
1951 Playoff Game		
9 Ty Cobb	3.00	.90
Famous Slide into 3rd		
10 George Brett	1.00	.30
Pine Tar Game		
11 Babe Ruth Ball	.25	.07
Shown against computer screen		
12 Pete Rose	2.00	.60
4,000 Hit		
13 Babe Ruth	5.00	1.50
Shows kids how to play		
14 Babe Ruth	5.00	1.50
Newspaperman		
15 Bob Feller	1.00	.30
Satchel Paige		
Barnstormers		
16 Jackie Robinson	3.00	.90
Keeps his promise		

1993 SP

This 290-card standard-size set, produced by Upper Deck, features fronts with action color player photos. Special subsets include All Star players (1-18) and Foil Prospects (271-290). Cards 19-270 are in alphabetical order by team nickname. Notable Rookie Cards include Johnny Damon and Derek Jeter.

	Nm-Mt	Ex-Mt
COMPLETE SET (290)	100.00	30.00
COMMON CARD (1-270)	.50	.15
COMMON FOIL (271-290)	1.00	.30
1 Roberto Alomar AS	2.00	.60
2 Wade Boggs AS	1.25	.35
3 Joe Carter AS	.50	.15
4 Ken Griffey Jr. AS	3.00	.90
5 Mark Langston AS	.50	.15
6 John Olerud AS	.75	.23
7 Kirby Puckett AS	2.00	.60
8 Cal Ripken Jr. AS	6.00	1.80
9 Ivan Rodriguez AS	2.00	.60
10 Barry Bonds AS	5.00	1.50
11 Darren Daulton AS	.75	.23
12 Marquis Grissom AS	.50	.15
13 David Justice AS	.75	.23
14 John Kruk AS	.75	.23
15 Barry Larkin AS	2.00	.60
16 Terry Mulholland AS	.50	.15
17 Ryne Sandberg AS	3.00	.90
18 Gary Sheffield AS	.75	.23
19 Chad Curtis	.50	.15
20 Chili Davis	.75	.23
21 Gary DiSarcina	.50	.15
22 Damion Easley	.50	.15
23 Chuck Finley	.75	.23
24 Luis Polonia	.50	.15
25 Tim Salmon	1.25	.35
26 J.T. Snow RC	2.00	.60
27 Russ Springer	.50	.15
28 Jeff Bagwell	1.25	.35
29 Craig Biggio	1.25	.35
30 Ken Caminiti	.75	.23
31 Andujar Cedeno	.50	.15
32 Doug Drabek	.50	.15
33 Steve Finley	.75	.23
34 Luis Gonzalez	.75	.23
35 Pete Harnisch	.50	.15
36 Darryl Kile	.75	.23
37 Mike Bordick	.50	.15
38 Dennis Eckersley	.75	.23
39 Brent Gates	.50	.15
40 Rickey Henderson	2.00	.60
41 Mark McGwire	5.00	1.50
42 Craig Paquette	.50	.15
43 Ruben Sierra	.50	.15
44 Terry Steinbach	.50	.15
45 Todd Van Poppel	.50	.15
46 Pat Borders	.50	.15
47 Tony Fernandez	.50	.15
48 Juan Guzman	.50	.15
49 Pat Hentgen	.50	.15
50 Paul Molitor	1.25	.35
51 Jack Morris	.75	.23
52 Ed Sprague	.50	.15
53 Duane Ward	.50	.15
54 Devon White	.50	.15
55 Steve Avery	.50	.15
56 Jeff Blauser	.50	.15
57 Ron Gant	.75	.23
58 Tom Glavine	1.25	.35
59 Greg Maddux	3.00	.90
60 Fred McGriff	1.25	.35
61 Terry Pendleton	.75	.23
62 Deion Sanders	1.25	.35
63 John Smoltz	1.25	.35
64 Cal Eldred	.50	.15
65 Darryl Hamilton	.50	.15
66 John Jaha	.50	.15
67 Pat Listach	.50	.15
68 Jaime Navarro	.50	.15
69 Kevin Reimer	.50	.15
70 B.J. Surhoff	.75	.23
71 Greg Vaughn	.75	.23
72 Robin Yount	3.00	.90
73 Rene Arocha RC	.75	.23
74 Bernard Gilkey	.50	.15
75 Gregg Jefferies	.50	.15
76 Ray Lankford	.50	.15
77 Tom Pagnozzi	.50	.15
78 Lee Smith	.75	.23
79 Ozzie Smith	3.00	.90
80 Bob Tewksbury	.50	.15
81 Mark Whiten	.50	.15
82 Steve Buechele	.50	.15
83 Mark Grace	1.25	.35
84 Jose Guzman	.50	.15
85 Derrick May	.50	.15
86 Mike Morgan	.50	.15
87 Randy Myers	.50	.15
88 Kevin Roberson RC	.50	.15
89 Sammy Sosa	3.00	.90
90 Rick Wilkins	.50	.15
91 Brett Butler	.75	.23
92 Eric Davis	.75	.23
93 Orel Hershiser	.75	.23
94 Eric Karros	.75	.23
95 Ramon Martinez	.50	.15
96 Raul Mondesi	.75	.23
97 Jose Offerman	.50	.15
98 Mike Piazza	5.00	1.50
99 Darryl Strawberry	1.25	.35
100 Moises Alou	.75	.23
101 Wil Cordero	.50	.15
102 Delino DeShields	.50	.15
103 Darrin Fletcher	.50	.15
104 Ken Hill	.50	.15
105 Mike Lansing RC	.75	.23
106 Dennis Martinez	.75	.23
107 Larry Walker	1.25	.35
108 John Wetteland	.75	.23
109 Rod Beck	.50	.15
110 John Burkett	.50	.15
111 Will Clark	2.00	.60
112 Royce Clayton	.50	.15
113 Darren Lewis	.50	.15
114 Willie McGee	.75	.23
115 Bill Swift	.50	.15
116 Robby Thompson	.50	.15
117 Matt Williams	.75	.23
118 Sandy Alomar Jr.	.50	.15
119 Carlos Baerga	.50	.15
120 Albert Belle	.75	.23
121 Reggie Jefferson	.50	.15
122 Wayne Kirby	.50	.15
123 Kenny Lofton	.75	.23
124 Carlos Martinez	.50	.15
125 Charles Nagy	.50	.15
126 Paul Sorrento	.50	.15
127 Rich Amaral	.50	.15
128 Jay Buhner	.75	.23
129 Norm Charlton	.50	.15
130 Dave Fleming	.50	.15
131 Erik Hanson	.50	.15
132 Randy Johnson	2.00	.60
133 Edgar Martinez	1.25	.35
134 Tino Martinez	1.25	.35
135 Omar Vizquel	.75	.23
136 Bret Barberie	.50	.15
137 Chuck Carr	.50	.15
138 Jeff Conine	.75	.23
139 Orestes Destrade	.50	.15
140 Chris Hammond	.50	.15
141 Bryan Harvey	.50	.15
142 Benito Santiago	.75	.23
143 Walt Weiss	.50	.15
144 Darrell Whitmore RC	.50	.15
145 Tim Bogar RC	.50	.15
146 Bobby Bonilla	.75	.23
147 Jeromy Burnitz	.75	.23
148 Vince Coleman	.50	.15
149 Dwight Gooden	1.25	.35
150 Todd Hundley	.50	.15
151 Howard Johnson	.50	.15
152 Eddie Murray	2.00	.60
153 Bret Saberhagen	.75	.23
154 Brady Anderson	.75	.23
155 Mike Devereaux	.50	.15
156 Jeffrey Hammonds	.50	.15
157 Chris Hoiles	.50	.15
158 Ben McDonald	.50	.15
159 Mark McLemore	.50	.15
160 Mike Mussina	2.00	.60
161 Gregg Olson	.50	.15
162 David Segui	.50	.15
163 Derek Bell	.50	.15
164 Andy Benes	.50	.15
165 Archi Cianfrocco	.50	.15
166 Ricky Gutierrez	.50	.15
167 Tony Gwynn	2.50	.75
168 Gene Harris	.50	.15
169 Trevor Hoffman	.75	.23
170 Ray McDavid RC	.50	.15
171 Phil Plantier	.50	.15
172 Mariano Duncan	.50	.15
173 Len Dykstra	.75	.23
174 Tommy Greene	.50	.15
175 Dave Hollins	.50	.15
176 Pete Incaviglia	.50	.15
177 Mickey Morandini	.50	.15
178 Curt Schilling	1.25	.35
179 Kevin Stocker	.50	.15
180 Mitch Williams	.50	.15
181 Stan Belinda	.50	.15
182 Jay Bell	.75	.23
183 Steve Cooke	.50	.15
184 Carlos Garcia	.50	.15
185 Jeff King	.50	.15
186 Orlando Merced	.50	.15
187 Don Slaught	.50	.15
188 Andy Van Slyke	.75	.23
189 Kevin Young	.75	.23
190 Kevin Brown	.75	.23
191 Jose Canseco	2.00	.60
192 Julio Franco	.75	.23
193 Benji Gil	.50	.15
194 Juan Gonzalez	2.00	.60
195 Tom Henke	.50	.15
196 Rafael Palmeiro	1.25	.35
197 Dean Palmer	.75	.23
198 Nolan Ryan	8.00	2.40
199 Roger Clemens	4.00	1.20
200 Scott Cooper	.50	.15
201 Andre Dawson	.75	.23
202 Mike Greenwell	.50	.15
203 Carlos Quintana	.50	.15
204 Jeff Russell	.50	.15
205 Aaron Sele	.50	.15
206 Mo Vaughn	.75	.23
207 Frank Viola	.75	.23
208 Rob Dibble	.75	.23
209 Roberto Kelly	.50	.15
210 Kevin Mitchell	.50	.15
211 Hal Morris	.50	.15
212 Joe Oliver	.50	.15
213 Jose Rijo	.50	.15
214 Bip Roberts	.50	.15
215 Chris Sabo	.50	.15
216 Reggie Sanders	.75	.23
217 Dante Bichette	.75	.23
218 Jerald Clark	.50	.15
219 Alex Cole	.50	.15
220 Andres Galarraga	.75	.23
221 Joe Girardi	.50	.15
222 Charlie Hayes	.50	.15
223 Roberto Mejia RC	.50	.15
224 Armando Reynoso	.50	.15
225 Eric Young	.50	.15
226 Kevin Appier	.75	.23
227 George Brett	5.00	1.50
228 David Cone	.75	.23
229 Phil Hiatt	.50	.15
230 Felix Jose	.50	.15
231 Wally Joyner	.75	.23
232 Mike Macfarlane	.50	.15
233 Brian McRae	.50	.15
234 Jeff Montgomery	.50	.15
235 Rob Deer	.50	.15
236 Cecil Fielder	.75	.23
237 Travis Fryman	.75	.23
238 Mike Henneman	.50	.15
239 Tony Phillips	.50	.15
240 Mickey Tettleton	.50	.15
241 Alan Trammell	1.25	.35
242 David Wells	.75	.23
243 Lou Whitaker	.75	.23
244 Rick Aguilera	.50	.15
245 Scott Erickson	.50	.15
246 Brian Harper	.50	.15
247 Kent Hrbek	.75	.23
248 Chuck Knoblauch	.75	.23
249 Shane Mack	.50	.15
250 David McCarty	.50	.15
251 Pedro Munoz	.50	.15
252 Dave Winfield	.75	.23
253 Alex Fernandez	.50	.15
254 Ozzie Guillen	.50	.15
255 Bo Jackson	2.00	.60
256 Lance Johnson	.50	.15
257 Ron Karkovice	.50	.15
258 Jack McDowell	.50	.15
259 Tim Raines	.75	.23
260 Frank Thomas	2.00	.60
261 Robin Ventura	.75	.23
262 Jim Abbott	1.25	.35
263 Steve Farr	.50	.15
264 Jimmy Key	.75	.23
265 Don Mattingly	5.00	1.50
266 Paul O'Neill	1.25	.35
267 Mike Stanley	.50	.15
268 Danny Tartabull	.50	.15
269 Bob Wickman	.50	.15
270 Bernie Williams	1.25	.35
271 Jason Bere FOIL	1.00	.30
272 R.Cedeno FOIL RC	1.50	.45
273 J.Damon FOIL RC	8.00	2.40
274 Russ Davis FOIL RC	1.50	.45
275 Carlos Delgado FOIL	4.00	1.20
276 Carl Everett FOIL	1.50	.45
277 Cliff Floyd FOIL	2.50	.75
278 Alex Gonzalez FOIL	1.00	.30
279 Derek Jeter FOIL RC	80.00	24.00
280 Chipper Jones FOIL	4.00	1.20
281 Javier Lopez FOIL	1.25	.35
282 Chad Mottola FOIL RC	1.00	.30
283 Marc Newfield FOIL	1.00	.30
284 Eduardo Perez FOIL	1.00	.30
285 Manny Ramirez FOIL	4.00	1.20
286 T.Steverson FOIL RC	1.00	.30
287 Michael Tucker FOIL	1.00	.30
288 Allen Watson FOIL	1.00	.30
289 Rondell White FOIL	1.50	.45
290 Dmitri Young FOIL	1.50	.45

1993 SP Platinum Power

Cards from this 20-card standard-size were inserted one every nine packs and feature power hitters from the American and National Leagues.

	Nm-Mt	Ex-Mt
COMPLETE SET (20)	80.00	24.00
PP1 Albert Belle	2.00	.60
PP2 Barry Bonds	12.00	3.60
PP3 Joe Carter	1.25	.35
PP4 Will Clark	5.00	1.50
PP5 Darren Daulton	2.00	.60
PP6 Cecil Fielder	2.00	.60
PP7 Ron Gant	2.00	.60
PP8 Juan Gonzalez	5.00	1.50
PP9 Ken Griffey Jr.	8.00	2.40
PP10 Dave Hollins	1.25	.35
PP11 David Justice	2.00	.60
PP12 Fred McGriff	3.00	.90
PP13 Mark McGwire	12.00	3.60
PP14 Dean Palmer	2.00	.60
PP15 Mike Piazza	12.00	3.60
PP16 Tim Salmon	3.00	.90
PP17 Ryne Sandberg	8.00	2.40
PP18 Gary Sheffield	2.00	.60
PP19 Frank Thomas	5.00	1.50
PP20 Matt Williams	2.00	.60

1994 SP Previews

These 15 cards were distributed regionally as inserts in second series Upper Deck hobby packs. They were inserted at a rate of one in 35. The manner of distribution was five cards per Central, East and West region. The cards are nearly identical to the basic SP issue. Card fronts differ in that the region is at bottom right where the team name is located on the SP cards.

	Nm-Mt	Ex-Mt
COMPLETE SET (15)	160.00	47.50
COMPLETE CENTRAL (5)	60.00	18.00
COMPLETE EAST (5)	40.00	12.00
COMPLETE WEST (5)	60.00	18.00
CR1 Jeff Bagwell	5.00	1.50
CR2 Michael Jordan	30.00	9.00
CR3 Kirby Puckett	8.00	2.40
CR4 Manny Ramirez	5.00	1.50
CR5 Frank Thomas	8.00	2.40
ER1 Roberto Alomar	8.00	2.40
ER2 Cliff Floyd	3.00	.90
ER3 Javier Lopez	3.00	.90
ER4 Don Mattingly	20.00	6.00

Card	Nm-Mt	Ex-Mt
ER5 Cal Ripken	25.00	7.50
WR1 Barry Bonds	20.00	6.00
WR2 Juan Gonzalez	8.00	2.40
WR3 Ken Griffey Jr.	12.00	3.60
WR4 Mike Piazza	15.00	4.50
WR5 Tim Salmon	5.00	1.50

1994 SP

This 200-card standard-size set distributed in foil packs contains the game's top players and prospects. The first 20 cards in the set are Foil Prospects which are brighter and more metallic than the rest of the set. These cards therefore are highly condition sensitive. Cards 21-200 are in alphabetical order by team nickname. Rookie Cards include Brad Fullmer, Derrek Lee, Chan Ho Park and Alex Rodriguez.

Card	Nm-Mt	Ex-Mt
COMPLETE SET (200)	150.00	45.00
COMMON CARD (21-200)	.20	.06
COMMON FOIL (1-20)	.50	.15
1 Mike Bell FOIL RC	.50	.15
2 D.J. Boston FOIL RC	.50	.15
3 Johnny Damon FOIL	.75	.23
4 Brad Fullmer FOIL RC	2.00	.60
5 Joey Hamilton FOIL	.50	.15
6 T.Hollandsworth FOIL	.50	.15
7 Brian L. Hunter FOIL	.50	.15
8 L.Hawkins FOIL RC	.75	.23
9 B.Kieschnick FOIL RC	.75	.23
10 Derrek Lee FOIL RC	2.50	.75
11 Trot Nixon FOIL RC	2.00	.60
12 Alex Ochoa FOIL	.50	.15
13 Chan Ho Park FOIL RC	2.00	.60
14 Kirk Presley FOIL RC	.50	.15
15 A.Rodriguez FOIL RC	120.00	36.00
16 Jose Silva FOIL RC	.50	.15
17 Terrell Wade FOIL RC	.50	.15
18 Billy Wagner FOIL RC	2.00	.60
19 G.Williams FOIL RC	.50	.15
20 Preston Wilson FOIL	1.25	.35
21 Brian Anderson RC	.40	.12
22 Chad Curtis	.20	.06
23 Chili Davis	.40	.12
24 Bo Jackson	1.00	.30
25 Mark Langston	.20	.06
26 Tim Salmon	.60	.18
27 Jeff Bagwell	.60	.18
28 Craig Biggio	.60	.18
29 Ken Caminiti	.40	.12
30 Doug Drabek	.20	.06
31 John Hudek RC	.20	.06
32 Greg Swindell	.20	.06
33 Brent Gates	.20	.06
34 Rickey Henderson	1.00	.30
35 Steve Karsay	.20	.06
36 Mark McGwire	2.50	.75
37 Ruben Sierra	.20	.06
38 Terry Steinbach	.20	.06
39 Roberto Alomar	1.00	.30
40 Joe Carter	.40	.12
41 Carlos Delgado	.60	.18
42 Alex Gonzalez	.20	.06
43 Juan Guzman	.20	.06
44 Paul Molitor	.60	.18
45 John Olerud	.40	.12
46 Devon White	.20	.06
47 Steve Avery	.20	.06
48 Jeff Blauser	.20	.06
49 Tom Glavine	.60	.18
50 David Justice	.40	.12
51 Roberto Kelly	.20	.06
52 Ryan Klesko	.40	.12
53 Javier Lopez	.40	.12
54 Greg Maddux	1.50	.45
55 Fred McGriff	.60	.18
56 Ricky Bones	.20	.06
57 Cal Eldred	.20	.06
58 Brian Harper	.20	.06
59 Pat Listach	.20	.06
60 B.J. Surhoff	.40	.12
61 Greg Vaughn	.40	.12
62 Bernard Gilkey	.20	.06
63 Gregg Jefferies	.20	.06
64 Ray Lankford	.20	.06
65 Ozzie Smith	1.50	.45
66 Bob Tewksbury	.20	.06
67 Mark Whiten	.20	.06
68 Todd Zeile	.20	.06
69 Mark Grace	.60	.18
70 Randy Myers	.20	.06
71 Ryne Sandberg	1.50	.45
72 Sammy Sosa	1.50	.45
73 Steve Trachsel	.20	.06
74 Rick Wilkins	.20	.06
75 Brett Butler	.40	.12
76 Delino DeShields	.20	.06
77 Orel Hershiser	.40	.12
78 Eric Karros	.40	.12
79 Raul Mondesi	.40	.12
80 Mike Piazza	2.00	.60
81 Tim Wallach	.20	.06
82 Moises Alou	.40	.12
83 Cliff Floyd	.40	.12
84 Marquis Grissom	.20	.06
85 Pedro Martinez	1.00	.30
86 Larry Walker	.60	.18
87 John Wetteland	.40	.12
88 Rondell White	.40	.12
89 Rod Beck	.20	.06
90 Barry Bonds	2.50	.75
91 John Burkett	.20	.06
92 Royce Clayton	.20	.06
93 Billy Swift	.20	.06
94 Robby Thompson	.20	.06
95 Matt Williams	.40	.12
96 Carlos Baerga	.20	.06
97 Albert Belle	.40	.12
98 Kenny Lofton	.40	.12
99 Dennis Martinez	.40	.12
100 Eddie Murray	1.00	.30
101 Manny Ramirez	.60	.18
102 Eric Anthony	.20	.06
103 Chris Bosio	.20	.06
104 Jay Buhner	.40	.12
105 Ken Griffey Jr.	1.50	.45
106 Randy Johnson	1.00	.30
107 Edgar Martinez	.60	.18
108 Chuck Carr	.20	.06
109 Jeff Conine	.40	.12
110 Carl Everett	.40	.12
111 Chris Hammond	.20	.06
112 Bryan Harvey	.20	.06
113 Charles Johnson	.40	.12
114 Gary Sheffield	.40	.12
115 Bobby Bonilla	.40	.12
116 Dwight Gooden	.60	.18
117 Todd Hundley	.20	.06
118 Bobby Jones	.20	.06
119 Jeff Kent	.40	.12
120 Bret Saberhagen	.40	.12
121 Jeffrey Hammonds	.20	.06
122 Chris Hoiles	.20	.06
123 Ben McDonald	.20	.06
124 Mike Mussina	1.00	.30
125 Rafael Palmeiro	.60	.18
126 Cal Ripken Jr.	3.00	.90
127 Lee Smith	.40	.12
128 Derek Bell	.20	.06
129 Andy Benes	.20	.06
130 Tony Gwynn	1.25	.35
131 Trevor Hoffman	.40	.12
132 Phil Plantier	.20	.06
133 Bip Roberts	.20	.06
134 Darren Daulton	.40	.12
135 Lenny Dykstra	.40	.12
136 Dave Hollins	.20	.06
137 Danny Jackson	.20	.06
138 John Kruk	.40	.12
139 Kevin Stocker	.20	.06
140 Jay Bell	.40	.12
141 Carlos Garcia	.20	.06
142 Jeff King	.20	.06
143 Orlando Merced	.20	.06
144 Andy Van Slyke	.40	.12
145 Rick White	.20	.06
146 Jose Canseco	1.00	.30
147 Will Clark	1.00	.30
148 Juan Gonzalez	1.00	.30
149 Rick Helling	.20	.06
150 Dean Palmer	.40	.12
151 Ivan Rodriguez	1.00	.30
152 Roger Clemens	2.00	.60
153 Scott Cooper	.20	.06
154 Andre Dawson	.40	.12
155 Mike Greenwell	.20	.06
156 Aaron Sele	.20	.06
157 Mo Vaughn	.40	.12
158 Bret Boone	.40	.12
159 Barry Larkin	1.00	.30
160 Kevin Mitchell	.20	.06
161 Jose Rijo	.20	.06
162 Deion Sanders	.60	.18
163 Reggie Sanders	.40	.12
164 Dante Bichette	.40	.12
165 Ellis Burks	.40	.12
166 Andres Galarraga	.40	.12
167 Charlie Hayes	.20	.06
168 David Nied	.20	.06
169 Walt Weiss	.20	.06
170 Kevin Appier	.40	.12
171 David Cone	.40	.12
172 Jeff Granger	.20	.06
173 Felix Jose	.20	.06
174 Wally Joyner	.40	.12
175 Brian McRae	.20	.06
176 Cecil Fielder	.40	.12
177 Travis Fryman	.40	.12
178 Mike Henneman	.20	.06
179 Tony Phillips	.20	.06
180 Mickey Tettleton	.20	.06
181 Alan Trammell	.60	.18
182 Rick Aguilera	.20	.06
183 Rich Becker	.20	.06
184 Scott Erickson	.20	.06
185 Chuck Knoblauch	.40	.12
186 Kirby Puckett	1.00	.30
187 Dave Winfield	.40	.12
188 Wilson Alvarez	.20	.06
189 Jason Bere	.20	.06
190 Alex Fernandez	.20	.06
191 Julio Franco	.40	.12
192 Jack McDowell	.20	.06
193 Frank Thomas	1.00	.30
194 Robin Ventura	.40	.12
195 Jim Abbott	.60	.18
196 Wade Boggs	.60	.18
197 Jimmy Key	.40	.12
198 Don Mattingly	2.50	.75
199 Paul O'Neill	.60	.18
200 Danny Tartabull	.20	.06
P24 Ken Griffey Jr. Promo	2.00	.60

1994 SP Die Cuts

This 200-card die-cut set is parallel to that of the basic SP issue. The cards were inserted one per SP pack. The difference, of course, is the unique die-cut shape. The backs have a silver Upper Deck hologram as opposed to gold on the basic issue.

Card	Nm-Mt	Ex-Mt
COMPLETE SET (200)	200.00	60.00
*STARS: .75X TO 2X BASIC CARDS ...		
*ROOKIES: .5X TO 1.2X BASIC CARDS		
15 Alex Rodriguez FOIL	150.00	45.00

1994 SP Holoviews

Randomly inserted in SP foil packs at a rate of one in five, this 38-card set contains top stars and prospects.

Card	Nm-Mt	Ex-Mt
1 Roberto Alomar	5.00	1.50
2 Kevin Appier	2.00	.60
3 Jeff Bagwell	3.00	.90
4 Jose Canseco	5.00	1.50
5 Roger Clemens	10.00	3.00
6 Carlos Delgado	2.00	.60
7 Cecil Fielder	2.00	.60
8 Cliff Floyd	2.00	.60
9 Travis Fryman	2.00	.60
10 Andres Galarraga	2.00	.60
11 Juan Gonzalez	5.00	1.50
12 Ken Griffey Jr.	8.00	2.40
13 Tony Gwynn	6.00	1.80
14 Jeffrey Hammonds	1.50	.45
15 Bo Jackson	5.00	1.50
16 Michael Jordan	25.00	7.50
17 David Justice	2.00	.60
18 Steve Karsay	1.50	.45
19 Jeff Kent	2.00	.60
20 Brooks Kieschnick	2.00	.60
21 Ryan Klesko	2.00	.60
22 John Kruk	2.00	.60
23 Barry Larkin	5.00	1.50
24 Pat Listach	1.50	.45
25 Don Mattingly	12.00	3.60
26 Mark McGwire	12.00	3.60
27 Raul Mondesi	2.00	.60
28 Trot Nixon	5.00	1.50
29 Mike Piazza	8.00	2.40
30 Kirby Puckett	5.00	1.50
31 Manny Ramirez	2.00	.60
32 Cal Ripken	15.00	4.50
33 Alex Rodriguez	60.00	18.00
34 Tim Salmon	3.00	.90
35 Gary Sheffield	2.00	.60
36 Ozzie Smith	8.00	2.40
37 Sammy Sosa	8.00	2.40
38 Andy Van Slyke	2.00	.60

1994 SP Holoviews Die Cuts

Parallel to the blue Holoview set, this 38-card red-bordered issue was also randomly inserted in SP packs. They are much more difficult to pull than the blue version with an insertion rate of one in 75.

Card	Nm-Mt	Ex-Mt
*DIE CUTS: 4X TO 10X BASIC HOLO ..		
*DIE CUTS: 2.5X TO 6X BASIC HOLO RC YR		
16 Michael Jordan	150.00	45.00
28 Trot Nixon	30.00	9.00
33 Alex Rodriguez	500.00	150.00

1995 SP

This set consists of 207 cards being sold in eight-card, hobby-only packs with a suggested retail price of $3.99. Subsets featured are Salute (1-4) and Premier Prospects (5-24). The only notable Rookie Card in this set is Hideo Nomo. Dealers who ordered a certain quantity of Upper Deck baseball cases received as a bonus, a certified autographed SP card of Ken Griffey Jr.

Card	Nm-Mt	Ex-Mt
COMPLETE SET (207)	40.00	12.00
COMMON CARD (1-207)	.20	.06
COMMON FOIL (5-24)	.50	.15
1 Cal Ripken Salute	3.00	.90
2 Nolan Ryan Salute	4.00	1.20
3 George Brett Salute	2.50	.75
4 Mike Schmidt Salute	1.50	.45
5 Dustin Hermanson FOIL	.50	.15
6 Antonio Osuna FOIL	.50	.15
7 M.Grudzielanek FOIL RC	1.25	.35
8 Ray Durham FOIL	.75	.23
9 Ugueth Urbina FOIL	.50	.15
10 Ruben Rivera FOIL	.50	.15
11 Curtis Goodwin FOIL	.50	.15
12 Jimmy Hurst FOIL	.50	.15
13 Jose Malave FOIL	.50	.15
14 Hideo Nomo FOIL RC	3.00	.90
15 Juan Acevedo RC FOIL	.50	.15
16 Tony Clark FOIL	.50	.15
17 Jim Pittsley FOIL	.50	.15
18 Freddy A. Garcia RC FOIL	.50	.15
19 Carlos Perez RC FOIL	.75	.23
20 R.Casanova FOIL RC	.50	.15
21 Quilvio Veras FOIL	.50	.15
22 Edgardo Alfonzo FOIL	.75	.23
23 Marty Cordova FOIL	.50	.15
24 C.J. Nitkowski FOIL	.50	.15
25 Wade Boggs CL	.40	.12
26 Dave Winfield CL	.20	.06
27 Eddie Murray CL	.60	.18
28 David Justice	.40	.12
29 Marquis Grissom	.20	.06
30 Fred McGriff	.60	.18
31 Greg Maddux	1.50	.45
32 Tom Glavine	.60	.18
33 Steve Avery	.20	.06
34 Chipper Jones	1.00	.30
35 Sammy Sosa	1.50	.45
36 Jaime Navarro	.20	.06
37 Randy Myers	.20	.06
38 Mark Grace	.60	.18
39 Todd Zeile	.20	.06
40 Brian McRae	.20	.06
41 Reggie Sanders	.40	.12
42 Ron Gant	.40	.12
43 Deion Sanders	.60	.18
44 Bret Boone	.40	.12
45 Barry Larkin	1.00	.30
46 Jose Rijo	.20	.06
47 Jason Bates	.20	.06
48 Andres Galarraga	.40	.12
49 Bill Swift	.20	.06
50 Larry Walker	.60	.18
51 Vinny Castilla	.40	.12
52 Dante Bichette	.40	.12
53 Jeff Conine	.40	.12
54 John Burkett	.20	.06
55 Gary Sheffield	.40	.12
56 Andre Dawson	.40	.12
57 Terry Pendleton	.40	.12
58 Charles Johnson	.40	.12
59 Brian L. Hunter	.20	.06
60 Jeff Bagwell	.60	.18
61 Craig Biggio	.60	.18
62 Phil Nevin	.40	.12
63 Doug Drabek	.20	.06
64 Derek Bell	.20	.06
65 Raul Mondesi	.40	.12
66 Eric Karros	.40	.12
67 Roger Cedeno	.20	.06
68 Delino DeShields	.20	.06
69 Ramon Martinez	.20	.06
70 Mike Piazza	1.50	.45
71 Billy Ashley	.20	.06
72 Jeff Fassero	.20	.06
73 Shane Andrews	.20	.06
74 Wil Cordero	.20	.06
75 Tony Tarasco	.20	.06
76 Rondell White	.40	.12
77 Pedro Martinez	1.00	.30
78 Moises Alou	.40	.12
79 Rico Brogna	.20	.06
80 Bobby Bonilla	.40	.12
81 Jeff Kent	.40	.12
82 Brett Butler	.40	.12
83 Bobby Jones	.20	.06
84 Bill Pulsipher	.20	.06
85 Bret Saberhagen	.40	.12
86 Gregg Jefferies	.20	.06
87 Lenny Dykstra	.40	.12
88 Dave Hollins	.20	.06
89 Charlie Hayes	.20	.06
90 Darren Daulton	.40	.12
91 Curt Schilling	.60	.18
92 Heathcliff Slocumb	.20	.06
93 Carlos Garcia	.20	.06
94 Denny Neagle	.40	.12
95 Jay Bell	.40	.12
96 Orlando Merced	.20	.06
97 Dave Clark	.20	.06
98 Bernard Gilkey	.20	.06
99 Scott Cooper	.20	.06
100 Ozzie Smith	1.50	.45
101 Tom Henke	.20	.06
102 Ken Hill	.20	.06
103 Brian Jordan	.40	.12
104 Ray Lankford	.20	.06
105 Tony Gwynn	1.25	.35
106 Andy Benes	.20	.06
107 Ken Caminiti	.40	.12
108 Steve Finley	.40	.12
109 Joey Hamilton	.20	.06
110 Bip Roberts	.20	.06
111 Eddie Williams	.20	.06
112 Rod Beck	.20	.06
113 Matt Williams	.40	.12
114 Glenallen Hill	.20	.06
115 Barry Bonds	2.50	.75
116 Robby Thompson	.20	.06
117 Mark Portugal	.20	.06
118 Brady Anderson	.40	.12
119 Mike Mussina	1.00	.30
120 Rafael Palmeiro	.60	.18
121 Chris Hoiles	.20	.06
122 Harold Baines	.40	.12
123 Jeffrey Hammonds	.20	.06
124 Tim Naehring	.20	.06
125 Mo Vaughn	.40	.12
126 Mike Macfarlane	.20	.06
127 Roger Clemens	2.00	.60
128 John Valentin	.20	.06
129 Aaron Sele	.20	.06
130 Jose Canseco	1.00	.30
131 J.T. Snow	.40	.12
132 Mark Langston	.20	.06
133 Chili Davis	.40	.12
134 Chuck Finley	.40	.12
135 Tim Salmon	.60	.18
136 Tony Phillips	.20	.06
137 Jason Bere	.20	.06
138 Robin Ventura	.40	.12
139 Tim Raines	.40	.12
140 Frank Thomas COR	1.00	.30
140A Frank Thomas ERR	1.00	.30
141 Alex Fernandez	.20	.06
142 Jim Abbott	.60	.18
143 Wilson Alvarez	.20	.06
144 Carlos Baerga	.20	.06
145 Albert Belle	.40	.12
146 Jim Thome	1.00	.30
147 Dennis Martinez	.40	.12
148 Eddie Murray	1.00	.30
149 Dave Winfield	.40	.12
150 Kenny Lofton	.40	.12
151 Manny Ramirez	.60	.18
152 Chad Curtis	.20	.06
153 Lou Whitaker	.40	.12
154 Alan Trammell	.60	.18
155 Cecil Fielder	.40	.12
156 Kirk Gibson	.40	.12
157 Michael Tucker	.20	.06
158 Jon Nunnally	.20	.06
159 Wally Joyner	.40	.12
160 Kevin Appier	.40	.12
161 Jeff Montgomery	.20	.06
162 Greg Gagne	.20	.06
163 Ricky Bones	.20	.06
164 Cal Eldred	.20	.06
165 Greg Vaughn	.40	.12
166 Kevin Seitzer	.20	.06
167 Jose Valentin	.20	.06
168 Joe Oliver	.20	.06
169 Rick Aguilera	.20	.06
170 Kirby Puckett	1.00	.30
171 Scott Stahoviak	.20	.06
172 Kevin Tapani	.20	.06
173 Chuck Knoblauch	.40	.12
174 Rich Becker	.20	.06
175 Don Mattingly	2.50	.75
176 Jack McDowell	.20	.06
177 Jimmy Key	.40	.12
178 Paul O'Neill	.60	.18
179 John Wetteland	.40	.12
180 Wade Boggs	.60	.18
181 Derek Jeter	2.50	.75
182 Rickey Henderson	1.00	.30
183 Terry Steinbach	.20	.06
184 Ruben Sierra	.20	.06
185 Mark McGwire	2.50	.75
186 Todd Stottlemyre	.20	.06
187 Dennis Eckersley	.40	.12
188 Alex Rodriguez	2.50	.75
189 Randy Johnson	1.00	.30
190 Ken Griffey Jr.	1.50	.45
191 Tino Martinez UER	.60	.18
Mike Blowers pictured on back		
192 Jay Buhner	.40	.12
193 Edgar Martinez	.60	.18
194 Mickey Tettleton	.20	.06
195 Juan Gonzalez	1.00	.30
196 Benji Gil	.20	.06
197 Dean Palmer	.40	.12
198 Ivan Rodriguez	1.00	.30
199 Kenny Rogers	.40	.12
200 Will Clark	1.00	.30
201 Roberto Alomar	1.00	.30
202 David Cone	.40	.12
203 Paul Molitor	.60	.18
204 Shawn Green	.40	.12
205 Joe Carter	.40	.12
206 Alex Gonzalez	.20	.06
207 Pat Hentgen	.20	.06
P100 K.Griffey Jr. Promo	2.00	.60
AU190 Ken Griffey Jr. AU	150.00	45.00

1995 SP Silver

This 207-card set parallels that of the regular SP set and was inserted one per pack. The only difference between the regular 180 cards in the two sets is that the chevron of the parallel version on the left side of the front uses rainbow-colored foil instead of blue or red. The subset cards have a die-cut design to differentiate them from the regular edition cards. The only other difference is the silver (rather than gold) hologram on the back.

Card	Nm-Mt	Ex-Mt
COMPLETE SET (207)	100.00	30.00
*STARS: 1X to 2.5X BASIC CARDS		
*ROOKIES: .6X to 1.5X BASIC CARDS		

1995 SP Platinum Power

This 20-card set was randomly inserted in packs at a rate of one in five. This die-cut set is comprised of the top home run hitters in baseball.

Card	Nm-Mt	Ex-Mt
COMPLETE SET (20)	20.00	6.00
PP1 Jeff Bagwell	.75	.23
PP2 Barry Bonds	3.00	.90
PP3 Ron Gant	.50	.15
PP4 Fred McGriff	.75	.23
PP5 Raul Mondesi	.50	.15
PP6 Mike Piazza	2.00	.60
PP7 Larry Walker	.75	.23
PP8 Matt Williams	.50	.15
PP9 Albert Belle	.50	.15
PP10 Cecil Fielder	.50	.15
PP11 Juan Gonzalez	1.25	.35
PP12 Ken Griffey Jr.	2.00	.60
PP13 Mark McGwire	3.00	.90
PP14 Eddie Murray	1.25	.35
PP15 Manny Ramirez	.50	.15
PP16 Cal Ripken	4.00	1.20
PP17 Tim Salmon	.75	.23
PP18 Frank Thomas	1.25	.35
PP19 Jim Thome	1.25	.35
PP20 Mo Vaughn	.50	.15

1995 SP Special FX

This 48-card set was randomly inserted in packs at a rate of one in 75. The set is comprised of the top names in baseball. The cards are numbered on the back "X/48."

Card	Nm-Mt	Ex-Mt
COMPLETE SET (48)	400.00	120.00
1 Jose Canseco	15.00	4.50
2 Roger Clemens	30.00	9.00
3 Mo Vaughn	6.00	1.80
4 Tim Salmon	10.00	3.00
5 Chuck Finley	6.00	1.80
6 Robin Ventura	6.00	1.80
7 Jason Bere	3.00	.90
8 Carlos Baerga	3.00	.90
9 Albert Belle	6.00	1.80
10 Kenny Lofton	10.00	3.00
11 Manny Ramirez	6.00	1.80
12 Jeff Montgomery	3.00	.90

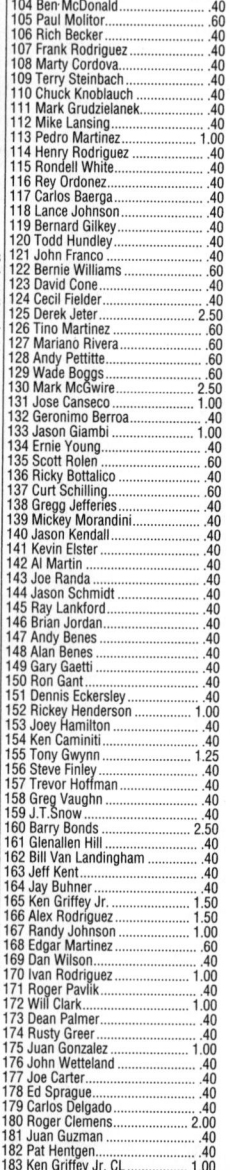

13 Kirby Puckett 15.00 4.50
14 Wade Boggs 10.00 3.00
15 Don Mattingly 40.00 12.00
16 Cal Ripken 50.00 15.00
17 Ruben Sierra 3.00 .90
18 Ken Griffey Jr. 25.00 7.50
19 Randy Johnson 15.00 4.50
20 Alex Rodriguez 40.00 12.00
21 Will Clark 15.00 4.50
22 Juan Gonzalez 15.00 4.50
23 Roberto Alomar 15.00 4.50
24 Joe Carter 6.00 1.80
25 Alex Gonzalez 3.00 .90
26 Paul Molitor 10.00 3.00
27 Ryan Klesko 6.00 1.80
28 Fred McGriff 10.00 3.00
29 Greg Maddux 25.00 7.50
30 Sammy Sosa 25.00 7.50
31 Bret Boone 6.00 1.80
32 Barry Larkin 15.00 4.50
33 Reggie Sanders 6.00 1.80
34 Dante Bichette 6.00 1.80
35 Andres Galarraga 6.00 1.80
36 Charles Johnson 6.00 1.80
37 Gary Sheffield 6.00 1.80
38 Jeff Bagwell 10.00 3.00
39 Craig Biggio 10.00 3.00
40 Eric Karros 6.00 1.80
41 Billy Ashley 3.00 .90
42 Raul Mondesi 6.00 1.80
43 Mike Piazza 25.00 7.50
44 Rondell White 6.00 1.80
45 Bret Saberhagen 6.00 1.80
46 Tony Gwynn 20.00 6.00
47 Melvin Nieves 3.00 .90
48 Matt Williams 6.00 1.80

1996 SP Previews FanFest

These eight standard-size cards were issued to promote the 1996 Upper Deck SP Issue. The fronts feature a color action photo as well as a small inset player shot. The 1996 All-Star game logo as well as the SP logo are on the bottom left corner. The backs have another photo as well as some biographical information.

Nm-Mt Ex-Mt
COMPLETE SET (8) 40.00 12.00
1 Ken Griffey Jr. 10.00 3.00
2 Frank Thomas 4.00 1.20
3 Albert Belle 2.50 .75
4 Mo Vaughn 2.50 .75
5 Barry Bonds 8.00 2.40
6 Mike Piazza 10.00 3.00
7 Matt Williams 3.00 .90
8 Sammy Sosa 8.00 2.40

1996 SP

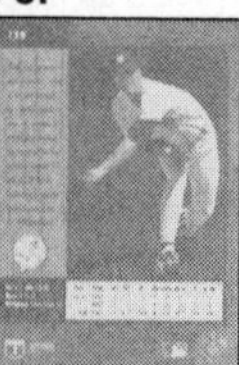

The 1996 SP set was issued in one series totalling 188 cards. The eight-card packs retailed for $4.19 each. Cards number 1-20 feature color action player photos with "Premier Prospects" printed in silver foil across the top and the player's name and team at the bottom in the border. The backs carry player information and statistics. Cards number 21-185 display unique player photos with an outer wood-grain border and inner thin platinum foil border as well as a small inset player shot. The only notable Rookie Card in this set is Darin Erstad.

Nm-Mt Ex-Mt
COMPLETE SET (188) 40.00 12.00
1 Rey Ordonez FOIL .40 .12
2 George Arias FOIL .40 .12
3 Osvaldo Fernandez FOIL .40 .12
4 Darin Erstad FOIL RC 8.00 2.40
5 Paul Wilson FOIL .40 .12
6 Richard Hidalgo FOIL .40 .12
7 Justin Thompson FOIL .40 .12
8 Jimmy Haynes FOIL .40 .12
9 Edgar Renteria FOIL .40 .12
10 Ruben Rivera FOIL .40 .12
11 Chris Snopek FOIL .40 .12
12 Billy Wagner FOIL .40 .12
13 Mike Grace FOIL RC .40 .12
14 Todd Greene FOIL .40 .12
15 Karim Garcia FOIL .40 .12
16 John Wasdin FOIL .40 .12
17 Jason Kendall FOIL .40 .12
18 Bob Abreu FOIL .40 .12
19 Jermaine Dye FOIL .40 .12
20 Jason Schmidt FOIL .40 .12
21 Javy Lopez .40 .12
22 Ryan Klesko .40 .12
23 Tom Glavine .60 .18
24 John Smoltz .60 .18
25 Greg Maddux 1.50 .45
26 Chipper Jones 1.00 .30
27 Fred McGriff .60 .18
28 David Justice .40 .12
29 Roberto Alomar 1.00 .30
30 Cal Ripken 3.00 .90
31 B.J. Surhoff .40 .12
32 Bobby Bonilla .40 .12
33 Mike Mussina 1.00 .30
34 Randy Myers .40 .12
35 Rafael Palmeiro .60 .18
36 Brady Anderson .40 .12
37 Tim Naehring .40 .12
38 Jose Canseco 1.00 .30
39 Roger Clemens 2.00 .60
40 Mo Vaughn .40 .12
41 John Valentin .40 .12
42 Kevin Mitchell .40 .12
43 Chili Davis .40 .12
44 Garret Anderson .40 .12
45 Tim Salmon .60 .18
46 Chuck Finley .40 .12
47 Troy Percival .40 .12
48 Jim Abbott .60 .18
49 J.T. Snow .40 .12
50 Jim Edmonds .40 .12
51 Sammy Sosa 1.50 .45
52 Brian McRae .40 .12
53 Ryne Sandberg 1.50 .45
54 Jaime Navarro .40 .12
55 Mark Grace .60 .18
56 Harold Baines .40 .12
57 Robin Ventura .40 .12
58 Tony Phillips .40 .12
59 Alex Fernandez .40 .12
60 Frank Thomas 1.00 .30
61 Ray Durham .40 .12
62 Bret Boone .40 .12
63 Reggie Sanders .40 .12
64 Pete Schourek .40 .12
65 Barry Larkin 1.00 .30
66 John Smiley .40 .12
67 Carlos Baerga .40 .12
68 Jim Thome 1.00 .30
69 Eddie Murray 1.00 .30
70 Albert Belle .40 .12
71 Dennis Martinez .40 .12
72 Jack McDowell .40 .12
73 Kenny Lofton .40 .12
74 Manny Ramirez .40 .12
75 Dante Bichette .40 .12
76 Vinny Castilla .40 .12
77 Andres Galarraga .40 .12
78 Walt Weiss .40 .12
79 Ellis Burks .40 .12
80 Larry Walker .60 .18
81 Cecil Fielder .40 .12
82 Melvin Nieves .40 .12
83 Travis Fryman .40 .12
84 Chad Curtis .40 .12
85 Alan Trammell .60 .18
86 Gary Sheffield .40 .12
87 Charles Johnson .40 .12
88 Andre Dawson .40 .12
89 Jeff Conine .40 .12
90 Greg Colbrunn .40 .12
91 Derek Bell .40 .12
92 Brian L.Hunter .40 .12
93 Doug Drabek .40 .12
94 Craig Biggio .60 .18
95 Jeff Bagwell .60 .18
96 Kevin Appier .40 .12
97 Jeff Montgomery .40 .12
98 Michael Tucker .40 .12
99 Bip Roberts .40 .12
100 Johnny Damon .40 .12
101 Eric Karros .40 .12
102 Raul Mondesi .40 .12
103 Ramon Martinez .40 .12
104 Ismael Valdes .40 .12
105 Mike Piazza 1.50 .45
106 Hideo Nomo 1.00 .30
107 Chan Ho Park .40 .12
108 Ben McDonald .40 .12
109 Kevin Seitzer .40 .12
110 Greg Vaughn .40 .12
111 Jose Valentin .40 .12
112 Rick Aguilera .40 .12
113 Marty Cordova .40 .12
114 Brad Radke .40 .12
115 Kirby Puckett 1.00 .30
116 Chuck Knoblauch .40 .12
117 Paul Molitor .60 .18
118 Pedro Martinez 1.00 .30
119 Mike Lansing .40 .12
120 Rondell White .40 .12
121 Moises Alou .40 .12
122 Mark Grudzielanek .40 .12
123 Jeff Fassero .40 .12
124 Rico Brogna .40 .12
125 Jason Isringhausen .40 .12
126 Jeff Kent .40 .12
127 Bernard Gilkey .40 .12
128 Todd Hundley .40 .12
129 David Cone .40 .12
130 Andy Pettitte .60 .18
131 Wade Boggs .60 .18
132 Paul O'Neill .60 .18
133 Ruben Sierra .40 .12
134 John Wetteland .40 .12
135 Derek Jeter 2.50 .75
136 Geronimo Berroa .40 .12
137 Terry Steinbach .40 .12
138 Ariel Prieto .40 .12
139 Scott Brosius .40 .12
140 Mark McGwire 2.50 .75
141 Lenny Dykstra .40 .12
142 Todd Zeile .40 .12
143 Benito Santiago .40 .12
144 Mickey Morandini .40 .12
145 Gregg Jefferies .40 .12
146 Denny Neagle .40 .12
147 Orlando Merced .40 .12
148 Charlie Hayes .40 .12
149 Carlos Garcia .40 .12
150 Jay Bell .40 .12
151 Ray Lankford .40 .12
152 Alan Benes .40 .12
Andy Benes
153 Dennis Eckersley .40 .12
154 Gary Gaetti .40 .12
155 Ozzie Smith 1.50 .45
156 Ron Gant .40 .12
157 Brian Jordan .40 .12
158 Ken Caminiti .40 .12
159 Rickey Henderson 1.00 .30
160 Tony Gwynn 1.25 .35
161 Wally Joyner .40 .12
162 Andy Ashby .40 .12
163 Steve Finley .40 .12
164 Glenallen Hill .40 .12
165 Matt Williams .40 .12
166 Barry Bonds 2.50 .75
167 W. VanLandingham .40 .12
168 Rod Beck .40 .12
169 Randy Johnson 1.00 .30
170 Ken Griffey Jr. 1.50 .45
171 Alex Rodriguez 2.00 .60
172 Edgar Martinez .60 .18
173 Jay Buhner .40 .12
174 Russ Davis .40 .12
175 Juan Gonzalez 1.00 .30
176 Mickey Tettleton .40 .12
177 Will Clark 1.00 .30
178 Ken Hill .40 .12
179 Dean Palmer .40 .12
180 Ivan Rodriguez 1.00 .30
181 Carlos Delgado .40 .12
182 Alex Gonzalez .40 .12
183 Shawn Green .40 .12
184 Juan Guzman .40 .12
185 Joe Carter .40 .12
186 Hideo Nomo CL UER .60 .18
Checklist lists Livan Hernandez as #4
187 Cal Ripken CL 1.50 .45
188 Ken Griffey Jr. CL 1.00 .30

1996 SP Baseball Heroes

This 10-card set was randomly inserted at the rate of one in 96 packs. It continues the insert set that was started in 1990 featuring ten of the top players in baseball. Please note these cards are condition sensitive and trade for premiums in Mint.

Nm-Mt Ex-Mt
COMPLETE SET (10) 150.00 45.00
82 Frank Thomas 12.00 3.60
83 Albert Belle 5.00 1.50
84 Barry Bonds 30.00 9.00
85 Chipper Jones 12.00 3.60
86 Hideo Nomo 12.00 3.60
87 Mike Piazza 20.00 6.00
88 Manny Ramirez 5.00 1.50
89 Greg Maddux 20.00 6.00
90 Ken Griffey Jr. 20.00 6.00
NNO Ken Griffey Jr. HDR 20.00 6.00

1996 SP Marquee Matchups

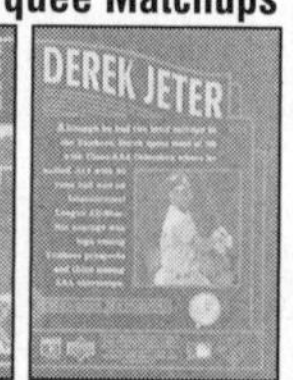

Randomly inserted at the rate of one in five packs, this 20-card set highlights two superstars' cards with a common matching stadium background photograph in a blue border.

Nm-Mt Ex-Mt
COMPLETE SET (20) 40.00 12.00
*DIE CUTS: 2X TO 5X BASIC MARQUEE
DC STATED ODDS 1:61
MM1 Ken Griffey Jr. 3.00 .90
MM2 Hideo Nomo 2.00 .60
MM3 Derek Jeter 5.00 1.50
MM4 Rey Ordonez .75 .23
MM5 Tim Salmon 1.25 .35
MM6 Mike Piazza 3.00 .90
MM7 Mark McGwire 5.00 1.50
MM8 Barry Bonds 5.00 1.50
MM9 Cal Ripken 6.00 1.80
MM10 Greg Maddux 3.00 .90
MM11 Albert Belle .75 .23
MM12 Barry Larkin 2.00 .60
MM13 Jeff Bagwell 1.25 .35
MM14 Juan Gonzalez 2.00 .60
MM15 Frank Thomas 2.00 .60
MM16 Sammy Sosa 3.00 .90
MM17 Mike Mussina 2.00 .60
MM18 Chipper Jones 2.00 .60
MM19 Roger Clemens 4.00 1.20
MM20 Fred McGriff 1.25 .35

1996 SP Special FX

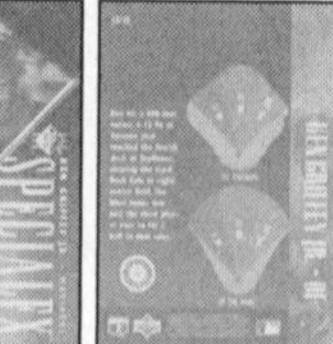

Randomly inserted at the rate of one in five packs, this 48-card set features a color action player cutout on a gold foil background with a holoview diamond shaped insert containing a black-and-white player portrait.

Nm-Mt Ex-Mt
COMPLETE SET (48) 150.00 45.00
*DIE CUTS: 2X TO 5X BASIC SPECIAL FX
DIE CUTS STATED ODDS 1:75
1 Greg Maddux 8.00 2.40
2 Eric Karros 2.00 .60
3 Mike Piazza 8.00 2.40
4 Raul Mondesi 2.00 .60
5 Hideo Nomo 5.00 1.50
6 Jim Edmonds 2.00 .60
7 Jason Isringhausen 2.00 .60
8 Jay Buhner 2.00 .60
9 Barry Larkin 5.00 1.50
10 Ken Griffey Jr. 8.00 2.40
11 Gary Sheffield 2.00 .60
12 Craig Biggio 3.00 .90
13 Paul Wilson 2.00 .60
14 Rondell White 2.00 .60
15 Chipper Jones 5.00 1.50
16 Kirby Puckett 5.00 1.50
17 Ron Gant 2.00 .60
18 Wade Boggs 3.00 .90
19 Fred McGriff 3.00 .90
20 Cal Ripken 15.00 4.50
21 Jason Kendall 2.00 .60
22 Johnny Damon 2.00 .60
23 Kenny Lofton 2.00 .60
24 Roberto Alomar 5.00 1.50
25 Barry Bonds 12.00 3.60
26 Dante Bichette 2.00 .60
27 Mark McGwire 12.00 3.60
28 Rafael Palmeiro 3.00 .90
29 Juan Gonzalez 5.00 1.50
30 Albert Belle 2.00 .60
31 Randy Johnson 5.00 1.50
32 Jose Canseco 5.00 1.50
33 Sammy Sosa 8.00 2.40
34 Eddie Murray 5.00 1.50
35 Frank Thomas 5.00 1.50
36 Tom Glavine 3.00 .90
37 Matt Williams 2.00 .60
38 Roger Clemens 10.00 3.00
39 Paul Molitor 3.00 .90
40 Tony Gwynn 6.00 1.80
41 Mo Vaughn 2.00 .60
42 Tim Salmon 3.00 .90
43 Manny Ramirez 2.00 .60
44 Jeff Bagwell 3.00 .90
45 Edgar Martinez 3.00 .90
46 Rey Ordonez 2.00 .60
47 Osvaldo Fernandez 2.00 .60
48 Derek Jeter 12.00 3.60

1997 SP

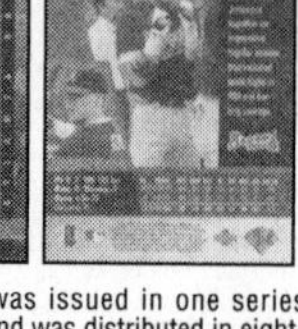

The 1997 SP set was issued in one series totalling 183 cards and was distributed in eight-card packs with a suggested retail of $4.39. Athough unconfirmed by the manufacturer, it is perceived in some circles that cards numbered between 160 and 180 are in slightly shorter supply. Notable Rookie Cards include Jose Cruz Jr. and Hideki Irabu.

Nm-Mt Ex-Mt
COMPLETE SET (184) 40.00 12.00
1 Andruw Jones FOIL .40 .12
2 Kevin Orie FOIL .40 .12
3 Nomar Garciaparra FOIL 1.50 .45
4 Jose Guillen FOIL .40 .12
5 Todd Walker FOIL .40 .12
6 Derrick Gibson FOIL .40 .12
7 Aaron Boone FOIL .40 .12
8 Bartolo Colon FOIL .40 .12
9 Derrek Lee FOIL .40 .12
10 Vladimir Guerrero FOIL 1.00 .30
11 Wilton Guerrero FOIL .40 .12
12 Luis Castillo FOIL .40 .12
13 Jason Dickson FOIL .40 .12
14 B.Trammell FOIL RC .40 .12
15 Jose Cruz Jr. FOIL RC 1.00 .30
16 Eddie Murray 1.00 .30
17 Darin Erstad .40 .12
18 Garret Anderson .40 .12
19 Jim Edmonds .40 .12
20 Tim Salmon .60 .18
21 Chuck Finley .40 .12
22 John Smoltz .60 .18
23 Greg Maddux 1.50 .45
24 Kenny Lofton .40 .12
25 Chipper Jones 1.00 .30
26 Ryan Klesko .40 .12
27 Javy Lopez .40 .12
28 Fred McGriff .60 .18
29 Roberto Alomar 1.00 .30
30 Rafael Palmeiro .60 .18
31 Mike Mussina 1.00 .30
32 Brady Anderson .40 .12
33 Rocky Coppinger .40 .12
34 Cal Ripken 3.00 .90
35 Mo Vaughn .40 .12
36 Steve Avery .40 .12
37 Tom Gordon .40 .12
38 Tim Naehring .40 .12
39 Troy O'Leary .40 .12
40 Sammy Sosa 1.50 .45
41 Brian McRae .40 .12
42 Mel Rojas .40 .12
43 Ryne Sandberg 1.50 .45
44 Mark Grace .60 .18
45 Albert Belle .40 .12
46 Robin Ventura .40 .12
47 Roberto Hernandez .40 .12
48 Ray Durham .40 .12
49 Harold Baines .40 .12
50 Frank Thomas 1.00 .30
51 Bret Boone .40 .12
52 Reggie Sanders .40 .12
53 Deion Sanders .60 .18
54 Hal Morris .40 .12
55 Barry Larkin 1.00 .30
56 Jim Thome 1.00 .30
57 Marquis Grissom .40 .12
58 David Justice .40 .12
59 Charles Nagy .40 .12
60 Manny Ramirez .40 .12
61 Matt Williams .40 .12
62 Jack McDowell .40 .12
63 Vinny Castilla .40 .12
64 Dante Bichette .40 .12
65 Andres Galarraga .40 .12
66 Ellis Burks .40 .12
67 Larry Walker .60 .18
68 Eric Young .40 .12
69 Brian L. Hunter .40 .12
70 Travis Fryman .40 .12
71 Tony Clark .40 .12
72 Bobby Higginson .40 .12
73 Melvin Nieves .40 .12
74 Jeff Conine .40 .12
75 Gary Sheffield .40 .12
76 Moises Alou .40 .12
77 Edgar Renteria .40 .12
78 Alex Fernandez .40 .12
79 Charles Johnson .40 .12
80 Bobby Bonilla .40 .12
81 Darryl Kile .40 .12
82 Derek Bell .40 .12
83 Shane Reynolds .40 .12
84 Craig Biggio .60 .18
85 Jeff Bagwell .60 .18
86 Billy Wagner .40 .12
87 Chili Davis .40 .12
88 Kevin Appier .40 .12
89 Jay Bell .40 .12
90 Johnny Damon .40 .12
91 Jeff King .40 .12
92 Hideo Nomo 1.00 .30
93 Todd Hollandsworth .40 .12
94 Eric Karros .40 .12
95 Mike Piazza 1.50 .45
96 Ramon Martinez .40 .12
97 Todd Worrell .40 .12
98 Raul Mondesi .40 .12
99 Dave Nilsson .40 .12
100 John Jaha .40 .12
101 Jose Valentin .40 .12
102 Jeff Cirillo .40 .12
103 Jeff D'Amico .40 .12
104 Ben McDonald .40 .12
105 Paul Molitor .60 .18
106 Rich Becker .40 .12
107 Frank Rodriguez .40 .12
108 Marty Cordova .40 .12
109 Terry Steinbach .40 .12
110 Chuck Knoblauch .40 .12
111 Mark Grudzielanek .40 .12
112 Mike Lansing .40 .12
113 Pedro Martinez 1.00 .30
114 Henry Rodriguez .40 .12
115 Rondell White .40 .12
116 Rey Ordonez .40 .12
117 Carlos Baerga .40 .12
118 Lance Johnson .40 .12
119 Bernard Gilkey .40 .12
120 Todd Hundley .40 .12
121 John Franco .40 .12
122 Bernie Williams .60 .18
123 David Cone .40 .12
124 Cecil Fielder .40 .12
125 Derek Jeter 2.50 .75
126 Tino Martinez .60 .18
127 Mariano Rivera .60 .18
128 Andy Pettitte .60 .18
129 Wade Boggs .60 .18
130 Mark McGwire 2.50 .75
131 Jose Canseco 1.00 .30
132 Geronimo Berroa .40 .12
133 Jason Giambi 1.00 .30
134 Ernie Young .40 .12
135 Scott Rolen .60 .18
136 Ricky Bottalico .40 .12
137 Curt Schilling .60 .18
138 Gregg Jefferies .40 .12
139 Mickey Morandini .40 .12
140 Jason Kendall .40 .12
141 Kevin Elster .40 .12
142 Al Martin .40 .12
143 Joe Randa .40 .12
144 Jason Schmidt .40 .12
145 Ray Lankford .40 .12
146 Brian Jordan .40 .12
147 Andy Benes .40 .12
148 Alan Benes .40 .12
149 Gary Gaetti .40 .12
150 Ron Gant .40 .12
151 Dennis Eckersley .40 .12
152 Rickey Henderson 1.00 .30
153 Joey Hamilton .40 .12
154 Ken Caminiti .40 .12
155 Tony Gwynn 1.25 .35
156 Steve Finley .40 .12
157 Trevor Hoffman .40 .12
158 Greg Vaughn .40 .12
159 J.T.Snow .40 .12
160 Barry Bonds 2.50 .75
161 Glenallen Hill .40 .12
162 Bill Van Landingham .40 .12
163 Jeff Kent .40 .12
164 Jay Buhner .40 .12
165 Ken Griffey Jr. 1.50 .45
166 Alex Rodriguez 1.50 .45
167 Randy Johnson 1.00 .30
168 Edgar Martinez .60 .18
169 Dan Wilson .40 .12
170 Ivan Rodriguez 1.00 .30
171 Roger Pavlik .40 .12
172 Will Clark 1.00 .30
173 Dean Palmer .40 .12
174 Rusty Greer .40 .12
175 Juan Gonzalez 1.00 .30
176 John Wetteland .40 .12
177 Joe Carter .40 .12
178 Ed Sprague .40 .12
179 Carlos Delgado .40 .12
180 Roger Clemens 2.00 .60
181 Juan Guzman .40 .12
182 Pat Hentgen .40 .12
183 Ken Griffey Jr. CL 1.00 .30
184 Hideki Irabu RC .40 .12

1997 SP Game Film

Randomly inserted in packs, this 10-card set features actual game film that highlights the accomplishments of some of the League's greatest players. Only 500 of each card in this crash numbered, limited edition set were produced.

	Nm-Mt	Ex-Mt
COMPLETE SET (10)	250.00	75.00
GF1 Alex Rodriguez	25.00	7.50
GF2 Frank Thomas	15.00	4.50
GF3 Andruw Jones	6.00	1.80
GF4 Cal Ripken	50.00	15.00
GF5 Mike Piazza	25.00	7.50
GF6 Derek Jeter	40.00	12.00
GF7 Mark McGwire	40.00	12.00
GF8 Chipper Jones	15.00	4.50
GF9 Barry Bonds	40.00	12.00
GF10 Ken Griffey Jr.	25.00	7.50

1997 SP Griffey Heroes

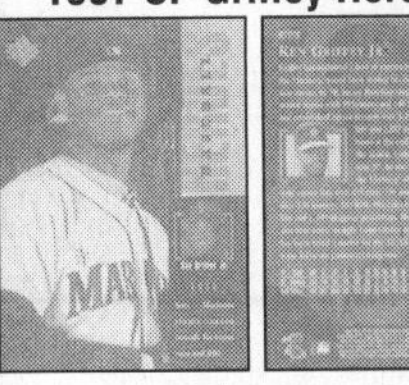
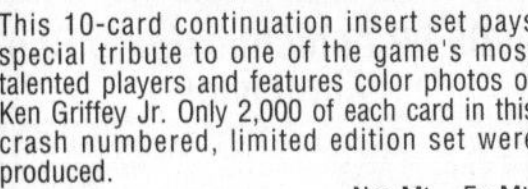

This 10-card continuation insert set pays special tribute to one of the game's most talented players and features color photos of Ken Griffey Jr. Only 2,000 of each card in this crash numbered, limited edition set were produced.

	Nm-Mt	Ex-Mt
COMPLETE SET (10)	50.00	15.00
COMMON CARD (91-100)	8.00	2.40

1997 SP Inside Info

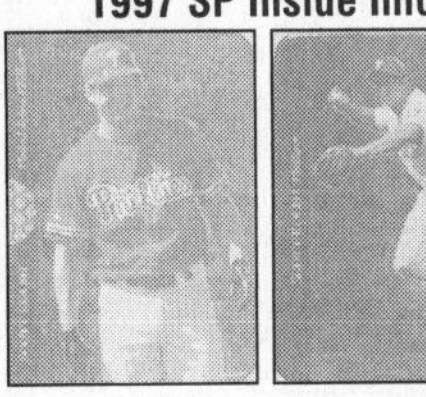

Inserted one in every 30-pack box, this 25-card set features color player photos on original cards with an exclusive pull-out panel that details the accomplishments of the League's brightest stars. Please note these cards are condition sensitive and trade for premium values in Mint condition.

	Nm-Mt	Ex-Mt
COMPLETE SET (25)	150.00	45.00
1 Ken Griffey Jr.	10.00	3.00
2 Mark McGwire	15.00	4.50
3 Kenny Lofton	2.50	.75
4 Paul Molitor	4.00	1.20
5 Frank Thomas	6.00	1.80
6 Greg Maddux	10.00	3.00
7 Mo Vaughn	2.50	.75
8 Cal Ripken	20.00	6.00
9 Jeff Bagwell	4.00	1.20
10 Alex Rodriguez	10.00	3.00
11 John Smoltz	4.00	1.20
12 Manny Ramirez	2.50	.75
13 Sammy Sosa	10.00	3.00
14 Vladimir Guerrero	6.00	1.80
15 Albert Belle	2.50	.75
16 Mike Piazza	10.00	3.00
17 Derek Jeter	15.00	4.50
18 Scott Rolen	4.00	1.20
19 Tony Gwynn	8.00	2.40
20 Barry Bonds	15.00	4.50
21 Ken Caminiti	2.50	.75
22 Chipper Jones	6.00	1.80
23 Juan Gonzalez	6.00	1.80
24 Roger Clemens	12.00	3.60
25 Andruw Jones	2.50	.75

1997 SP Marquee Matchups

Randomly inserted in packs at a rate of one in five, this 20-card set features color player images on die-cut cards that match-up the best pitchers and hitters from around the League.

	Nm-Mt	Ex-Mt
COMPLETE SET (20)	50.00	15.00
MM1 Ken Griffey Jr.	3.00	.90
MM2 Andres Galarraga	.75	.23
MM3 Barry Bonds	5.00	1.50
MM4 Mark McGwire	5.00	1.50
MM5 Mike Piazza	3.00	.90
MM6 Tim Salmon	1.25	.35
MM7 Tony Gwynn	2.50	.75
MM8 Alex Rodriguez	3.00	.90
MM9 Chipper Jones	2.00	.60
MM10 Derek Jeter	5.00	1.50
MM11 Manny Ramirez	.75	.23
MM12 Jeff Bagwell	1.25	.35
MM13 Greg Maddux	3.00	.90
MM14 Cal Ripken	6.00	1.80
MM15 Mo Vaughn	.75	.23
MM16 Gary Sheffield	.75	.23
MM17 Jim Thome	2.00	.60
MM18 Barry Larkin	2.00	.60
MM19 Frank Thomas	2.00	.60
MM20 Sammy Sosa	3.00	.90

1997 SP Special FX

Randomly inserted in packs at a rate of one in nine, this 48-card set features color player photos on Holoview cards with the Special F/X die-cut design. Cards numbers 1-47 are from 1997 with card number 49 featuring a design from 1996. There is no card number 48.

	Nm-Mt	Ex-Mt
COMPLETE SET (48)	200.00	60.00
1 Ken Griffey Jr.	8.00	2.40
2 Frank Thomas	5.00	1.50
3 Barry Bonds	12.00	3.60
4 Albert Belle	2.00	.60
5 Mike Piazza	8.00	2.40
6 Greg Maddux	8.00	2.40
7 Chipper Jones	5.00	1.50
8 Cal Ripken	15.00	4.50
9 Jeff Bagwell	3.00	.90
10 Alex Rodriguez	8.00	2.40
11 Mark McGwire	12.00	3.60
12 Kenny Lofton	2.00	.60
13 Juan Gonzalez	5.00	1.50
14 Mo Vaughn	2.00	.60
15 John Smoltz	3.00	.90
16 Derek Jeter	12.00	3.60
17 Tony Gwynn	6.00	1.80
18 Ivan Rodriguez	5.00	1.50
19 Barry Larkin	5.00	1.50
20 Sammy Sosa	8.00	2.40
21 Mike Mussina	5.00	1.50
22 Gary Sheffield	2.00	.60
23 Brady Anderson	2.00	.60
24 Roger Clemens	10.00	3.00
25 Ken Caminiti	2.00	.60
26 Roberto Alomar	5.00	1.50
27 Hideo Nomo	5.00	1.50
28 Bernie Williams	3.00	.90
29 Todd Hundley	2.00	.60
30 Manny Ramirez	2.00	.60
31 Eric Karros	2.00	.60
32 Tim Salmon	3.00	.90
33 Jay Buhner	2.00	.60
34 Andy Pettitte	3.00	.90
35 Jim Thome	5.00	1.50
36 Ryne Sandberg	8.00	2.40
37 Matt Williams	2.00	.60
38 Ryan Klesko	2.00	.60
39 Jose Canseco	5.00	1.50
40 Paul Molitor	3.00	.90
41 Eddie Murray	5.00	1.50
42 Darin Erstad	2.00	.60
43 Todd Walker	2.00	.60
44 Wade Boggs	3.00	.90
45 Andruw Jones	2.00	.60
46 Scott Rolen	3.00	.90
47 Vladimir Guerrero	5.00	1.50
49 Alex Rodriguez '96	10.00	3.00

1997 SP SPx Force

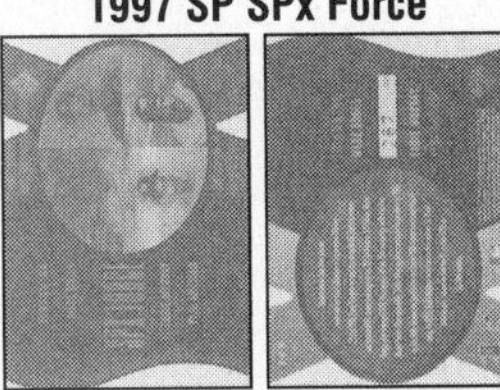

Randomly inserted in packs, this 10-card die-cut set features head photos of four of the very best players on each card with an "X" in the background and players' and teams' names on one side. Only 500 of each card in this crash numbered, limited edition set were produced.

	Nm-Mt	Ex-Mt
COMPLETE SET (10)	200.00	60.00
1 Ken Griffey Jr. Jay Buhner Andres Galarraga Dante Bichette	25.00	7.50
2 Albert Belle Brady Anderson Mark McGwire Cecil Fielder	40.00	12.00
3 Mo Vaughn Ken Caminiti Frank Thomas Jeff Bagwell	15.00	4.50
4 Gary Sheffield Sammy Sosa Barry Bonds Jose Canseco	25.00	7.50
5 Greg Maddux Roger Clemens John Smoltz Randy Johnson	25.00	7.50
6 Alex Rodriguez Derek Jeter Chipper Jones Rey Ordonez	40.00	12.00
7 Todd Hollandsworth Mike Piazza Raul Mondesi Hideo Nomo	25.00	7.50
8 Juan Gonzalez Manny Ramirez Roberto Alomar Ivan Rodriguez	15.00	4.50
9 Tony Gwynn Wade Boggs Eddie Murray Paul Molitor	20.00	6.00
10 Andruw Jones Vladimir Guerrero Todd Walker Scott Rolen	15.00	4.50

1997 SP SPx Force Autographs

Randomly inserted in packs, this 10-card set is an autographed parallel version of the regular SPx Force set. Only 100 of each card in this crash numbered, limited edition set were produced. Mo Vaughn packed out as an exchange card.

	Nm-Mt	Ex-Mt
1 Ken Griffey Jr.	200.00	60.00
2 Albert Belle	50.00	15.00
3 Mo Vaughn	50.00	15.00
4 Gary Sheffield	80.00	24.00
5 Greg Maddux	200.00	60.00
6 Alex Rodriguez	200.00	60.00
7 Todd Hollandsworth	30.00	9.00
8 Roberto Alomar	100.00	30.00
9 Tony Gwynn	100.00	30.00
10 Andruw Jones	80.00	24.00

1997 SP Vintage Autographs

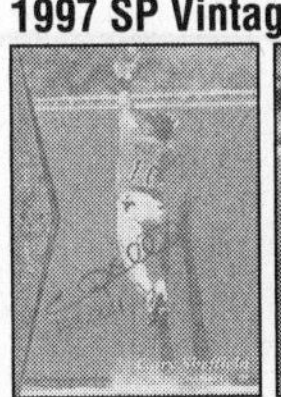

Randomly inserted in packs, this set features authenticated original 1993-1996 SP cards that have been autographed by the pictured player. The print runs are listed after year following the player's name in our checklist. Some of the very short printed autographs are listed but not priced. Each card came in the pack along with a standard size certificate of authenticity. These certificates are usually included when these autographed cards are traded. The 1997 Mo Vaughn card was available only as a mail-in exchange. Upper Deck seeded 250 '97 SP Vaughn cards into packs each carrying a large circular sticker on front. UD sent Mo 300 cards to sign, hoping that he'd sign at least 250 cards and actually received 293 cards back. The additional 43 cards were sent to UD's Quality Assurance area. An additional Mo Vaughn card, hailing from 1995, surfaced in early 2001. This set now stands as one of the most important issues of the 1990's in that it was the first to feature the popular "buy-back" concept widely used in the 2000's.

	Nm-Mt	Ex-Mt
1 Jeff Bagwell 93/7		
2 Jeff Bagwell 95/173	40.00	12.00
3 Jeff Bagwell 96/292	40.00	12.00
4 Jeff Bagwell 96 MM/23		
5 Jay Buhner 95/57	60.00	18.00
6 Jay Buhner 96/79	60.00	18.00
7 Jay Buhner 96 FX/27	100.00	30.00
8 Ken Griffey Jr. 93/16		
9 Ken Griffey Jr. 93 PP/5		
10 Ken Griffey Jr. 94/103	150.00	45.00
11 Ken Griffey Jr. 95/38	250.00	75.00
12 Ken Griffey Jr. 96/312	120.00	36.00
13 Tony Gwynn 93/17		
14 Tony Gwynn 94/367	40.00	12.00
15 Tony Gwynn 94 HV/31	150.00	45.00
16 Tony Gwynn 95/64	60.00	18.00
17 Tony Gwynn 96/20		
18 Todd Hollandsworth 94/167	15.00	4.50
19 Chipper Jones 93/34	150.00	45.00
20 Chipper Jones 95/60	80.00	24.00
21 Chipper Jones 96/102	60.00	18.00
22 Rey Ordonez 96/111	15.00	4.50
23 R.Ordonez '96 MM/40	25.00	7.50
24 Alex Rodriguez 94/94	1600.00	475.00
25 Alex Rodriguez 95/63	150.00	45.00
26 Alex Rodriguez 96/73	150.00	45.00
27 Gary Sheffield 94/130	40.00	12.00
28 Gary Sheffield 94 HVDC/4		
29 Gary Sheffield 95/221	25.00	7.50
30 Gary Sheffield 96/58	60.00	18.00
31 Mo Vaughn 95/75	40.00	12.00
32 Mo Vaughn 97/293	15.00	4.50

1998 SP Authentic

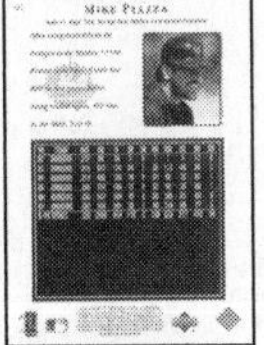

The 1998 SP Authentic set was issued in one series totalling 198 cards. The five-card packs retailed for $4.99 each. The set contains the topical subset: Future Watch (1-30). Rookie Cards include Magglio Ordonez. A sample card featuring Ken Griffey Jr. was issued prior to the product's release and distributed along with dealer order forms. The card is identical to the basic issue Griffey Jr. card (number 123) except for the term "SAMPLE" in red print running diagonally against the card back.

	Nm-Mt	Ex-Mt
COMPLETE SET (198)	40.00	12.00
1 Travis Lee FOIL	.40	.12
2 Mike Caruso FOIL	.40	.12
3 Kerry Wood FOIL	2.00	.60
4 Mark Kotsay FOIL	.40	.12
5 M.Ordonez FOIL RC	8.00	2.40
6 Scott Elarton FOIL	.40	.12
7 Carl Pavano FOIL	.40	.12
8 A.J. Hinch FOIL	.40	.12
9 Rolando Arrojo FOIL RC	.40	.12
10 Ben Grieve FOIL	.40	.12
11 Gabe Alvarez FOIL	.40	.12
12 Mike Kinkade FOIL RC	.40	.12
13 Bruce Chen FOIL	.40	.12
14 Juan Encarnacion FOIL	.40	.12
15 Todd Helton FOIL	.60	.18
16 Aaron Boone FOIL	.40	.12
17 Sean Casey FOIL	.40	.12
18 R.Hernandez FOIL	.40	.12
19 Daryle Ward FOIL	.40	.12
20 Paul Konerko FOIL	.40	.12
21 David Ortiz FOIL	.40	.12
22 Derrek Lee FOIL	.40	.12
23 Brad Fullmer FOIL	.40	.12
24 Javier Vazquez FOIL	.40	.12
25 Miguel Tejada FOIL	.60	.18
26 Dave Dellucci FOIL RC	.40	.12
27 Alex Gonzalez FOIL	.40	.12
28 Matt Clement FOIL	.40	.12
29 Masato Yoshii FOIL RC	.60	.18
30 Russell Branyan FOIL	.40	.12
31 Chuck Finley	.40	.12
32 Jim Edmonds	.40	.12
33 Darin Erstad	.40	.12
34 Jason Dickson	.40	.12
35 Tim Salmon	.60	.18
36 Cecil Fielder	.40	.12
37 Todd Greene	.40	.12
38 Andy Benes	.40	.12
39 Jay Bell	.40	.12
40 Matt Williams	.40	.12
41 Brian Anderson	.40	.12
42 Karim Garcia	.40	.12
43 Javy Lopez	.40	.12
44 Tom Glavine	.60	.18
45 Greg Maddux	1.50	.45
46 Andruw Jones	.40	.12
47 Chipper Jones	1.00	.30
48 Ryan Klesko	.40	.12
49 John Smoltz	.60	.18
50 Andres Galarraga	.40	.12
51 Rafael Palmeiro	.60	.18
52 Mike Mussina	1.00	.30
53 Roberto Alomar	1.00	.30
54 Joe Carter	.40	.12
55 Cal Ripken	3.00	.90
56 Brady Anderson	.40	.12
57 Mo Vaughn	.40	.12
58 John Valentin	.40	.12
59 Dennis Eckersley	.40	.12
60 Nomar Garciaparra	1.50	.45
61 Pedro Martinez	1.00	.30
62 Jeff Blauser	.40	.12
63 Kevin Orie	.40	.12
64 Henry Rodriguez	.40	.12
65 Mark Grace	.60	.18
66 Albert Belle	.40	.12
67 Mike Cameron	.40	.12
68 Robin Ventura	.40	.12
69 Frank Thomas	1.00	.30
70 Barry Larkin	1.00	.30
71 Brett Tomko UER 1 Yr Total is Wrong	.40	.12
72 Willie Greene	.40	.12
73 Reggie Sanders	.40	.12
74 Sandy Alomar Jr.	.40	.12
75 Kenny Lofton	.40	.12
76 Jaret Wright	.40	.12
77 David Justice	.40	.12
78 Omar Vizquel	.40	.12
79 Manny Ramirez	.40	.12
80 Jim Thome	1.00	.30
81 Travis Fryman	.40	.12
82 Neifi Perez	.40	.12
83 Mike Lansing	.40	.12
84 Vinny Castilla	.40	.12
85 Larry Walker	.60	.18
86 Dante Bichette	.40	.12
87 Darryl Kile	.40	.12
88 Justin Thompson	.40	.12
89 Damion Easley	.40	.12
90 Tony Clark	.40	.12
91 Bobby Higginson	.40	.12
92 Brian Hunter	.40	.12
93 Edgar Renteria	.40	.12
94 Craig Counsell	.40	.12
95 Mike Piazza	1.50	.45
96 Livan Hernandez	.40	.12
97 Todd Zeile	.40	.12
98 Richard Hidalgo	.40	.12
99 Moises Alou	.40	.12
100 Jeff Bagwell	.60	.18
101 Mike Hampton	.40	.12
102 Craig Biggio	.60	.18
103 Dean Palmer	.40	.12
104 Tim Belcher	.40	.12
105 Jeff King	.40	.12
106 Jeff Conine	.40	.12
107 Johnny Damon	.40	.12
108 Hideo Nomo	1.00	.30
109 Raul Mondesi	.40	.12
110 Gary Sheffield	.40	.12
111 Ramon Martinez	.40	.12
112 Chan Ho Park	.40	.12
113 Eric Young	.40	.12
114 Charles Johnson	.40	.12
115 Eric Karros	.40	.12
116 Bobby Bonilla	.40	.12
117 Jeromy Burnitz	.40	.12
118 Cal Eldred	.40	.12
119 Jeff D'Amico	.40	.12
120 Marquis Grissom	.40	.12
121 Dave Nilsson	.40	.12
122 Brad Radke	.40	.12
123 Marty Cordova	.40	.12
124 Ron Coomer	.40	.12
125 Paul Molitor	.60	.18
126 Todd Walker	.40	.12
127 Rondell White	.40	.12
128 Mark Grudzielanek	.40	.12
129 Carlos Perez	.40	.12
130 Vladimir Guerrero	1.00	.30
131 Dustin Hermanson	.40	.12
132 Butch Huskey	.40	.12
133 John Franco	.40	.12
134 Rey Ordonez	.40	.12
135 Todd Hundley	.40	.12
136 Edgardo Alfonzo	.40	.12
137 Bobby Jones	.40	.12
138 John Olerud	.40	.12
139 Chili Davis	.40	.12
140 Tino Martinez	.60	.18
141 Andy Pettitte	.60	.18
142 Chuck Knoblauch	.40	.12
143 Bernie Williams	.60	.18
144 David Cone	.40	.12
145 Derek Jeter	2.50	.75
146 Paul O'Neill	.60	.18
147 Rickey Henderson	1.00	.30
148 Jason Giambi	1.00	.30
149 Kenny Rogers	.40	.12
150 Scott Rolen	.60	.18
151 Curt Schilling	.60	.18
152 Ricky Bottalico	.40	.12
153 Mike Lieberthal	.40	.12
154 Francisco Cordova	.40	.12
155 Jose Guillen	.40	.12
156 Jason Schmidt	.40	.12
157 Jason Kendall	.40	.12
158 Kevin Young	.40	.12
159 Delino DeShields	.40	.12
160 Mark McGwire	2.50	.75
161 Ray Lankford	.40	.12
162 Brian Jordan	.40	.12
163 Ron Gant	.40	.12
164 Todd Stottlemyre	.40	.12
165 Ken Caminiti	.40	.12
166 Kevin Brown	.60	.18
167 Trevor Hoffman	.40	.12
168 Steve Finley	.40	.12
169 Wally Joyner	.40	.12
170 Tony Gwynn	1.25	.35
171 Shawn Estes	.40	.12
172 J.T. Snow	.40	.12
173 Jeff Kent	.40	.12
174 Robb Nen	.40	.12
175 Barry Bonds	2.50	.75
176 Randy Johnson	1.00	.30
177 Edgar Martinez	.60	.18
178 Jay Buhner	.40	.12
179 Alex Rodriguez	1.50	.45
180 Ken Griffey Jr.	1.50	.45
181 Ken Cloude	.40	.12
182 Wade Boggs	.60	.18
183 Tony Saunders	.40	.12
184 Wilson Alvarez	.40	.12
185 Fred McGriff	.60	.18
186 Roberto Hernandez	.40	.12
187 Kevin Stocker	.40	.12
188 Fernando Tatis	.40	.12
189 Will Clark	1.00	.30
190 Juan Gonzalez	1.00	.30
191 Rusty Greer	.40	.12
192 Ivan Rodriguez	1.00	.30
193 Jose Canseco	1.00	.30
194 Carlos Delgado	.40	.12
195 Roger Clemens	2.00	.60
196 Pat Hentgen	.40	.12
197 Randy Myers	.40	.12
198 Ken Griffey Jr. CL	1.00	.30
S123 Ken Griffey Jr. Sample	2.00	.60

1998 SP Authentic Chirography

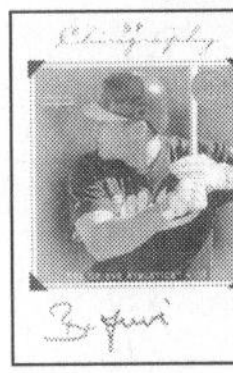

Randomly inserted in packs at a rate of one in 25, this 31-card set is autographed by the league's top players. The Ken Griffey Jr. card was actually not available in packs. Instead, an exchange card was printed and seeded into packs. Collectors had until July 27th, 1999 to redeem these Griffey exchange cards. A selection of players were short-printed to 400 or 800 copies. These cards, however, are not serial numbered.

	Nm-Mt	Ex-Mt
AJ Andruw Jones	25.00	7.50
AR Alex Rodriguez SP/800	100.00	30.00
BG Ben Grieve	15.00	4.50
CJ Charles Johnson	15.00	4.50
CP Chipper Jones SP/800	40.00	12.00
DE Darin Erstad	15.00	4.50
GS Gary Sheffield	25.00	7.50
IR Ivan Rodriguez	40.00	12.00
JC Jose Cruz Jr.	15.00	4.50
JW Jaret Wright	15.00	4.50
KG Ken Griffey Jr. SP/400	150.00	45.00
KG-EX K.Griffey Jr. EXCH	20.00	6.00
LH Livan Hernandez	15.00	4.50
MK Mark Kotsay	15.00	4.50
MM Mike Mussina	40.00	12.00
MT Miguel Tejada	25.00	7.50
MV Mo Vaughn SP800	15.00	4.50
NG N. Garciaparra SP400	150.00	45.00
PK Paul Konerko	15.00	4.50
PM Paul Molitor SP/800	25.00	7.50
RA R. Alomar SP/800	40.00	12.00
RB Russell Branyan	15.00	4.50
RC R. Clemens SP/400	120.00	36.00
RL Ray Lankford	15.00	4.50
SC Sean Casey	15.00	4.50
SR Scott Rolen	25.00	7.50
TC Tony Clark	15.00	4.50
TG Tony Gwynn SP/850	50.00	15.00
TH Todd Helton	25.00	7.50
TL Travis Lee	15.00	4.50
VG Vladimir Guerrero	40.00	12.00

1998 SP Authentic Griffey 300th HR Redemption

This 5" by 7" card is the redemption one received for mailing in the Ken Griffey Jr. 300

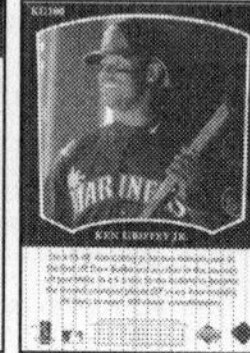

Home Run card available in the SP Authentic packs.

	Nm-Mt	Ex-Mt
300 Ken Griffey Jr.	30.00	9.00

1998 SP Authentic Game Jersey 5 x 7

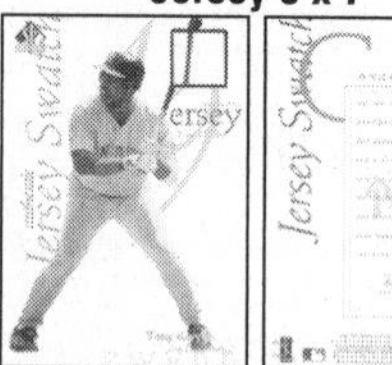
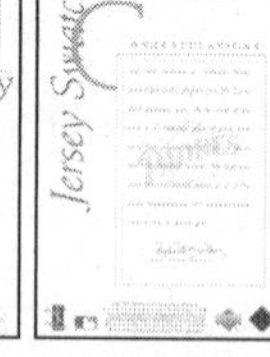

These attractive 5" by 7" memorabilia cards are the items one received when redeeming the SP Authentic Trade Cards (of which were randomly seeded into 1998 SP Authentic packs at a rate of 1:291). The 5 x 7 cards feature a larger swatch of the jersey on them as compared to a standard size Game Jersey card. The exchange deadline expired back on August 1st, 1999.

	Nm-Mt	Ex-Mt
1 Ken Griffey Jr./125	80.00	24.00
2 Gary Sheffield/125	25.00	7.50
3 Greg Maddux/125	100.00	30.00
4 Alex Rodriguez/125	80.00	24.00
5 Tony Gwynn/415	50.00	15.00
6 Jay Buhner/125	25.00	7.50

1998 SP Authentic Sheer Dominance

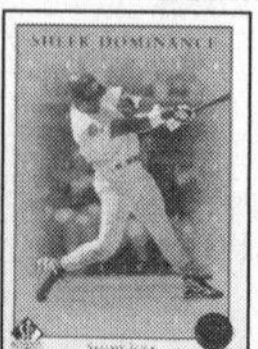
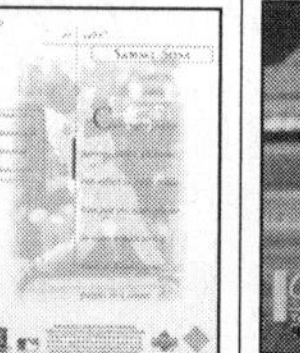

Randomly inserted in packs at a rate of one in three, this 42-card set has a mix of stars and young players and were issued in three different versions.

	Nm-Mt	Ex-Mt
COMPLETE SET (42)	100.00	30.00
*GOLD: 1.25X TO 3X BASIC DOMINANCE		
GOLD: RANDOM INSERTS IN PACKS		
GOLD PRINT RUN 2000 SERIAL #'d SETS		
*TITANIUM: 3X TO 8X BASIC DOMINANCE		
TITANIUM: RANDOM INSERTS IN PACKS		
TITANIUM PRINT RUN 100 SERIAL #'d SETS		
SD1 Ken Griffey Jr.	4.00	1.20
SD2 Rickey Henderson	2.50	.75
SD3 Jaret Wright	1.00	.30
SD4 Craig Biggio	1.50	.45
SD5 Travis Lee	1.00	.30
SD6 Kenny Lofton	1.00	.30
SD7 Raul Mondesi	1.00	.30
SD8 Cal Ripken	8.00	2.40
SD9 Matt Williams	1.00	.30
SD10 Mark McGwire	6.00	1.80
SD11 Alex Rodriguez	4.00	1.20
SD12 Fred McGriff	1.50	.45
SD13 Scott Rolen	1.50	.45
SD14 Paul Molitor	1.50	.45
SD15 Nomar Garciaparra	4.00	1.20
SD16 Vladimir Guerrero	2.50	.75
SD17 Andruw Jones	1.00	.30
SD18 Manny Ramirez	1.00	.30
SD19 Tony Gwynn	3.00	.90
SD20 Barry Bonds	6.00	1.80
SD21 Ben Grieve	1.00	.30
SD22 Ivan Rodriguez	2.50	.75
SD23 Jose Cruz Jr.	2.50	.75
SD24 Pedro Martinez	2.50	.75
SD25 Chipper Jones	2.50	.75
SD26 Albert Belle	1.00	.30
SD27 Todd Helton	1.50	.45
SD28 Paul Konerko	1.00	.30
SD29 Sammy Sosa	2.50	.75
SD30 Frank Thomas	2.50	.75
SD31 Greg Maddux	4.00	1.20
SD32 Randy Johnson	2.50	.75
SD33 Larry Walker	1.50	.45
SD34 Roberto Alomar	1.50	.45
SD35 Roger Clemens	5.00	1.50
SD36 Mo Vaughn	1.00	.30
SD37 Jim Thome	2.50	.75
SD38 Jeff Bagwell	1.50	.45
SD39 Tino Martinez	1.50	.45
SD40 Mike Piazza	4.00	1.20
SD41 Derek Jeter	6.00	1.80
SD42 Juan Gonzalez	2.50	.75

1998 SP Authentic Trade Cards

Randomly seeded into packs at a rate of 1:291, these fifteen different trade cards could be redeemed for an assortion of UDA material. Specific quantities for each item are detailed below after each player name. The deadline to redeem these cards was August 1st, 1999. It is important to note that the redemption items came from UDA back stock and in many cases the card is far mor valuable than the redemption prize.

	Nm-Mt	Ex-Mt
COMMON CARD (B1-B5)	15.00	4.50
COMMON CARD (J1-J6)	15.00	4.50
COMMON CARD (KG1-KG4)	15.00	4.50
B1 Roberto Alomar Ball 100	30.00	9.00
B2 Albert Belle Ball 100	15.00	4.50
B3 Brian Jordan Ball 50	25.00	7.50
B4 Raul Mondesi Ball 100	15.00	4.50
B5 Robin Ventura Ball 50	25.00	7.50
J1 Jay Buhner Jersey Card 125	15.00	4.50
J2 Ken Griffey Jr. Jersey Card 125	60.00	18.00
J3 Tony Gwynn Jersey Card 415	25.00	7.50
J4 Greg Maddux Jersey Card 125	60.00	18.00
J5 Alex Rodriguez Jersey Card 125	50.00	15.00
J6 Gary Sheffield Jersey Card 125	15.00	4.50
KG1 Ken Griffey Jr. 300 Card 1000 made	15.00	4.50
KG2 Ken Griffey Jr. Auto Glove 30		
KG3 Ken Griffey Jr. Auto Jersey 30		
KG4 Ken Griffey Jr. Standee 200	25.00	7.50

1999 SP Authentic

The 1999 SP Authentic set was issued in one series totalling 135 cards and distributed in five-card packs with a suggested retail price of $4.99. The fronts feature color action player photos with player information printed on the backs. The set features the following limited edition subsets: Future Watch (91-120) serially numbered to 2700 and Season to Remember (121-135) numbered to 2700 also. 350 Ernie Banks A Piece of History 500 Club bat cards were randomly seeded into packs. Also, Banks signed and numbered two additional copies. Pricing for these bat cards can be referenced under 1999 Upper Deck A Piece of History 500 Club.

	Nm-Mt	Ex-Mt
COMP.SET w/o SP's (90)	25.00	7.50
COMMON CARD (1-90)	.40	.12
COMMON FW (91-120)	10.00	3.00
COMMON STR (121-135)	3.00	.90
1 Mo Vaughn	.40	.12
2 Jim Edmonds	.40	.12
3 Darin Erstad	.40	.12
4 Travis Lee	.40	.12
5 Matt Williams	.40	.12
6 Randy Johnson	1.00	.30
7 Chipper Jones	1.00	.30
8 Greg Maddux	1.50	.45
9 Andruw Jones	.40	.12
10 Andres Galarraga	.40	.12
11 Tom Glavine	.60	.18
12 Cal Ripken	3.00	.90
13 Brady Anderson	.40	.12
14 Albert Belle	.40	.12
15 Nomar Garciaparra	1.50	.45
16 Donnie Sadler	.40	.12
17 Pedro Martinez	1.00	.30
18 Sammy Sosa	1.50	.45
19 Kerry Wood	1.00	.30
20 Mark Grace	.60	.18
21 Mike Caruso	.40	.12
22 Frank Thomas	1.00	.30
23 Paul Konerko	.40	.12
24 Sean Casey	.40	.12
25 Barry Larkin	1.00	.30
26 Kenny Lofton	.40	.12
27 Manny Ramirez	.40	.12
28 Jim Thome	1.00	.30
29 Bartolo Colon	.40	.12
30 Jaret Wright	.40	.12
31 Larry Walker	.60	.18
32 Todd Helton	.60	.18
33 Tony Clark	.40	.12
34 Dean Palmer	.40	.12
35 Mark Kotsay	.40	.12
36 Cliff Floyd	.40	.12
37 Ken Caminiti	.40	.12
38 Craig Biggio	.60	.18
39 Jeff Bagwell	.60	.18
40 Moises Alou	.40	.12
41 Johnny Damon	.40	.12
42 Larry Sutton	.40	.12
43 Kevin Brown	.60	.18
44 Gary Sheffield	.40	.12
45 Raul Mondesi	.40	.12
46 Jeromy Burnitz	.40	.12
47 Jeff Cirillo	.40	.12
48 Todd Walker	.40	.12
49 David Ortiz	.40	.12
50 Brad Radke	.40	.12
51 Vladimir Guerrero	1.00	.30
52 Rondell White	.40	.12
53 Brad Fullmer	.40	.12
54 Mike Piazza	1.50	.45
55 Robin Ventura	.40	.12
56 John Olerud	.40	.12
57 Derek Jeter	2.50	.75
58 Tino Martinez	.60	.18
59 Bernie Williams	.60	.18
60 Roger Clemens	2.00	.60
61 Ben Grieve	.40	.12
62 Miguel Tejada	.40	.12
63 A.J. Hinch	.40	.12
64 Scott Rolen	.60	.18
65 Curt Schilling	.60	.18
66 Doug Glanville	.40	.12
67 Aramis Ramirez	.40	.12
68 Tony Womack	.40	.12
69 Jason Kendall	.40	.12
70 Tony Gwynn	1.25	.35
71 Wally Joyner	.40	.12
72 Greg Vaughn	.40	.12
73 Barry Bonds	2.50	.75
74 Ellis Burks	.40	.12
75 Jeff Kent	.40	.12
76 Ken Griffey Jr.	1.50	.45
77 Alex Rodriguez	1.50	.45
78 Edgar Martinez	.60	.18
79 Mark McGwire	2.50	.75
80 Eli Marrero	.40	.12
81 Matt Morris	.40	.12
82 Rolando Arrojo	.40	.12
83 Quinton McCracken	.40	.12
84 Jose Canseco	1.00	.30
85 Ivan Rodriguez	1.00	.30
86 Juan Gonzalez	1.00	.30
87 Royce Clayton	.40	.12
88 Shawn Green	.40	.12
89 Jose Cruz Jr.	.40	.12
90 Carlos Delgado	.40	.12
91 Troy Glaus FW	12.00	3.60
92 George Lombard FW	10.00	3.00
93 Ryan Minor FW	10.00	3.00
94 Calvin Pickering FW	10.00	3.00
95 Jin Ho Cho FW	10.00	3.00
96 Russ Branyan FW	10.00	3.00
97 Derrick Gibson FW	10.00	3.00
98 Gabe Kapler FW	10.00	3.00
99 Matt Anderson FW	10.00	3.00
100 Preston Wilson FW	10.00	3.00
101 Alex Gonzalez FW	10.00	3.00
102 Carlos Beltran FW	10.00	3.00
103 Dee Brown FW	10.00	3.00
104 Jeremy Giambi FW	10.00	3.00
105 Angel Pena FW	10.00	3.00
106 Geoff Jenkins FW	10.00	3.00
107 Corey Koskie FW	10.00	3.00
108 A.J. Pierzynski FW	10.00	3.00
109 Michael Barrett FW	10.00	3.00
110 F.Seguignol FW	10.00	3.00
111 Mike Kinkade FW	10.00	3.00
112 Ricky Ledee FW	10.00	3.00
113 Mike Lowell FW	10.00	3.00
114 Eric Chavez FW	10.00	3.00
115 Matt Clement FW	10.00	3.00
116 Shane Monahan FW	10.00	3.00
117 J.D. Drew FW	10.00	3.00
118 Bubba Trammell FW	10.00	3.00
119 Kevin Witt FW	10.00	3.00
120 Roy Halladay FW	10.00	3.00
121 Mark McGwire STR	12.00	3.60
122 Mark McGwire STR Sammy Sosa	10.00	3.00
123 Sammy Sosa STR	8.00	2.40
124 Ken Griffey Jr. STR	8.00	2.40
125 Cal Ripken STR	15.00	4.50
126 Juan Gonzalez STR	5.00	1.50
127 Kerry Wood STR	5.00	1.50
128 Trevor Hoffman STR	3.00	.90
129 Barry Bonds STR	12.00	3.60
130 Alex Rodriguez STR	8.00	2.40
131 Ben Grieve STR	3.00	.90
132 Tom Glavine STR	3.00	.90
133 David Wells STR	3.00	.90
134 Mike Piazza STR	8.00	2.40
135 Scott Brosius STR	3.00	.90

1999 SP Authentic Chirography

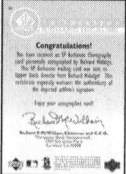

Randomly inserted in packs at the rate of one in 24, this 39-card set features color player photos with the pictured player's autograph at the bottom of the photo. Exchange cards for Ken Griffey Jr., Cal Ripken, Ruben Rivera and Scott Rolen were seeded into packs. The expiration date for the exchange cards was February 24th, 2000. Prices in our checklist refer to the actual autograph cards.

	Nm-Mt	Ex-Mt
AG Alex Gonzalez	10.00	3.00
BC Bruce Chen	10.00	3.00
BF Brad Fullmer	10.00	3.00
BG Ben Grieve	10.00	3.00
CB Carlos Beltran	15.00	4.50
CJ Chipper Jones	40.00	12.00
CK Corey Koskie	15.00	4.50
CP Calvin Pickering	10.00	3.00
CR Cal Ripken	150.00	45.00
EC Eric Chavez	15.00	4.50
GK Gabe Kapler	10.00	3.00
GL George Lombard	10.00	3.00
GM Greg Maddux	100.00	30.00
GMJ Gary Matthews Jr.	10.00	3.00
GV Greg Vaughn	15.00	4.50
IR Ivan Rodriguez	40.00	12.00
JD J.D. Drew	15.00	4.50
JG Jeremy Giambi	10.00	3.00
JR Ken Griffey Jr.	120.00	36.00
JT Jim Thome	40.00	12.00
KW Kevin Witt	10.00	3.00
KW Kerry Wood	40.00	12.00
MA Matt Anderson	10.00	3.00
MK Mike Kinkade	10.00	3.00
ML Mike Lowell	15.00	4.50
NG Nomar Garciaparra	120.00	36.00
RB Russell Branyan	10.00	3.00
RH Richard Hidalgo	15.00	4.50
RL Ricky Ledee	10.00	3.00
RM Ryan Minor	10.00	3.00
RR Ruben Rivera	10.00	3.00
SM Shane Monahan	10.00	3.00
SR Scott Rolen	25.00	7.50
TG Tony Gwynn	40.00	12.00
TGL Troy Glaus	25.00	7.50
TH Todd Helton	25.00	7.50
TL Travis Lee	10.00	3.00
TW Todd Walker	15.00	4.50
VG Vladimir Guerrero	40.00	12.00
CR-X Cal Ripken EXCH	20.00	6.00
JR-X Ken Griffey Jr. EXCH	12.00	3.60
RR-X Ruben Rivera EXCH	1.00	.30
SR-X Scott Rolen EXCH	2.50	.75

1999 SP Authentic Chirography Gold

These scarce parallel versions of the Chirography cards were all serial numbered to the featured player's jersey number. The serial numbering was done by hand and is on the front of the card. In addition, gold ink was used on the card fronts (a flat grey front was used on the more common basic Chirography cards). While we only have pricing on some of the cards in this set, we are printing the checklist so collectors can know how many cards are available of each player. The same four players featured on exchange cards in the basic chirography (Griffey, Ripken, Rivera and Rolen) also had exchange cards in this set. The deadline for redeeming these cards was February 24th, 2000. Our listed price refers to the actual autograph cards.

	Nm-Mt	Ex-Mt
AG Alex Gonzalez/22		
BC Bruce Chen/48	25.00	7.50
BF Brad Fullmer/20		
BG Ben Grieve/14		
CB Carlos Beltran/36	40.00	12.00
CJ Chipper Jones/10		
CK Corey Koskie/47	40.00	12.00
CP Calvin Pickering/6		
CR Cal Ripken/8		
EC Eric Chavez/30	40.00	12.00
GK Gabe Kapler/51	25.00	7.50
GL George Lombard/26	25.00	7.50
GM Greg Maddux/31	250.00	75.00
GMJ G.Matthews Jr./68	25.00	7.50
GV Greg Vaughn/23		
IR Ivan Rodriguez/7		
JD J.D. Drew/8		
JG Jeremy Giambi/15		
JR Ken Griffey Jr./24		
JT Jim Thome/25		
KW Kevin Witt/6		
KW Kerry Wood/34	120.00	36.00
MA Matt Anderson/14		
MK Mike Kinkade/33	25.00	7.50
ML Mike Lowell/60	40.00	12.00
NG Nomar Garciaparra/5		
RB Russ Branyan/66	25.00	7.50
RH Richard Hidalgo/15		
RL Ricky Ledee/38	25.00	7.50
RM Ryan Minor/10		
RR Ruben Rivera/28	25.00	7.50
SM Shane Monahan/12		
SR Scott Rolen/17		
TG Tony Gwynn/19		
TGL Troy Glaus/14		
TH Todd Helton/17		
TL Travis Lee/16		
TW Todd Walker/12		
VG Vladimir Guerrero/27	120.00	36.00
CR-X Cal Ripken EXCH		
JR-X Ken Griffey Jr. EXCH	50.00	15.00
RR-X Ruben Rivera EXCH	4.00	1.20
SR-X Scott Rolen EXCH	15.00	4.50

1999 SP Authentic Epic Figures

Randomly inserted in packs at the rate of one in seven, this 30-card set features action color photos of some of the game's most impressive players.

	Nm-Mt	Ex-Mt
COMPLETE SET (30)	100.00	30.00
E1 Mo Vaughn	1.50	.45
E2 Travis Lee	1.50	.45
E3 Andres Galarraga	1.50	.45
E4 Andruw Jones	1.50	.45
E5 Chipper Jones	4.00	1.20
E6 Greg Maddux	6.00	1.80
E7 Cal Ripken	12.00	3.60
E8 Nomar Garciaparra	6.00	1.80
E9 Sammy Sosa	6.00	1.80
E10 Frank Thomas	4.00	1.20
E11 Kerry Wood	4.00	1.20
E12 Kenny Lofton	1.50	.45
E13 Manny Ramirez	1.50	.45
E14 Larry Walker	2.50	.75
E15 Jeff Bagwell	2.50	.75
E16 Paul Molitor	4.00	1.20
E17 Vladimir Guerrero	4.00	1.20
E18 Derek Jeter	10.00	3.00
E19 Tino Martinez	2.50	.75
E20 Mike Piazza	6.00	1.80
E21 Ben Grieve	1.50	.45
E22 Scott Rolen	2.50	.75
E23 Mark McGwire	10.00	3.00
E24 Tony Gwynn	5.00	1.50
E25 Barry Bonds	10.00	3.00
E26 Ken Griffey Jr.	6.00	1.80
E27 Alex Rodriguez	6.00	1.80
E28 J.D. Drew	1.50	.45
E29 Juan Gonzalez	4.00	1.20
E30 Kevin Brown	2.50	.75

1999 SP Authentic Home Run Chronicles

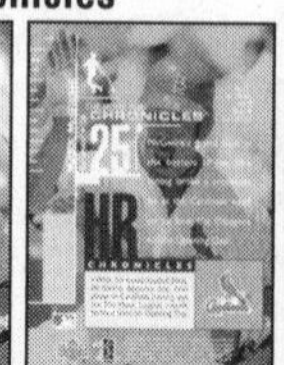

Inserted one per pack, this 70-card set features action color photos of players who were the leading sluggers of the 1998 season.

	Nm-Mt	Ex-Mt
COMPLETE SET (70)	120.00	36.00
*DIE CUTS: 8X TO 20X BASIC HR CHRON.		
DIE CUTS RANDOM INSERTS IN PACKS		
DIE CUT PRINT RUN 70 SERIAL #'d SETS		
HR1 Mark McGwire	4.00	1.20
HR2 Sammy Sosa	1.50	.45
HR3 Ken Griffey Jr.	1.50	.45
HR4 Mark McGwire	2.50	.75
HR5 Mark McGwire	2.50	.75
HR6 Albert Belle	.40	.12
HR7 Jose Canseco	1.00	.30
HR8 Juan Gonzalez	1.00	.30
HR9 Manny Ramirez	.40	.12
HR10 Rafael Palmeiro	1.00	.30
HR11 Mo Vaughn	.40	.12
HR12 Carlos Delgado	.40	.12
HR13 Nomar Garciaparra	1.50	.45
HR14 Barry Bonds	2.50	.75
HR15 Alex Rodriguez	1.50	.45
HR16 Tony Clark	.40	.12
HR17 Jim Thome	1.00	.30
HR18 Edgar Martinez	.60	.18
HR19 Frank Thomas	1.00	.30
HR20 Greg Vaughn	.40	.12
HR21 Vinny Castilla	.40	.12
HR22 Andres Galarraga	.40	.12
HR23 Moises Alou	.40	.12
HR24 Jeromy Burnitz	.40	.12
HR25 Vladimir Guerrero	1.00	.30
HR26 Jeff Bagwell	.60	.18
HR27 Chipper Jones	1.00	.30
HR28 Javier Lopez	.40	.12
HR29 Mike Piazza	1.50	.45
HR30 Andruw Jones	.40	.12
HR31 Henry Rodriguez	.40	.12
HR32 Jeff Kent	.40	.12
HR33 Ray Lankford	.40	.12
HR34 Scott Rolen	.60	.18
HR35 Raul Mondesi	.40	.12
HR36 Ken Caminiti	.40	.12
HR37 J.D. Drew	.40	.12
HR38 Troy Glaus	.50	.15
HR39 Gabe Kapler	.40	.12
HR40 Alex Rodriguez	1.50	.45
HR41 Ken Griffey Jr.	1.50	.45
HR42 Sammy Sosa	1.50	.45
HR43 Mark McGwire	2.50	.75
HR44 Sammy Sosa	1.50	.45
HR45 Mark McGwire	2.50	.75
HR46 Vinny Castilla	.40	.12
HR47 Sammy Sosa	1.50	.45
HR48 Mark McGwire	2.50	.75
HR49 Sammy Sosa	1.50	.45
HR50 Greg Vaughn	.40	.12
HR51 Sammy Sosa	1.50	.45
HR52 Mark McGwire	2.50	.75
HR53 Sammy Sosa	1.50	.45
HR54 Mark McGwire	2.50	.75
HR55 Sammy Sosa	1.50	.45
HR56 Ken Griffey Jr.	1.50	.45
HR57 Sammy Sosa	1.50	.45
HR58 Mark McGwire	2.50	.75
HR59 Sammy Sosa	1.50	.45
HR60 Mark McGwire	2.50	.75
HR61 Mark McGwire	4.00	1.20
HR62 Mark McGwire	5.00	1.50
HR63 Mark McGwire	2.50	.75
HR64 Mark McGwire	2.50	.75
HR65 Mark McGwire	2.50	.75
HR66 Sammy Sosa	8.00	2.40
HR67 Mark McGwire	2.50	.75
HR68 Mark McGwire	2.50	.75
HR69 Mark McGwire	2.50	.75
HR70 Mark McGwire	10.00	3.00

1999 SP Authentic Redemption Cards

Randomly inserted in packs at the rate of one in 864, this 10-card set features hand-numbered

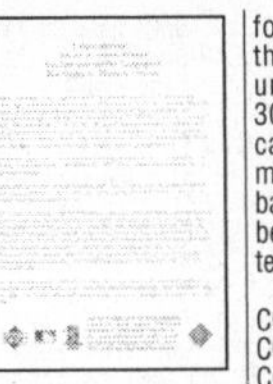

cards that could be redeemed for various items autographed by the player named on the card. The expiration date for these cards was March 1st, 2000.

	Nm-Mt	Ex-Mt
1 K.Griffey Jr. AU Jersey/25		
2 K.Griffey Jr. AU Baseball/75		
3 K.Griffey Jr. AU SI Cover/75		
4 K.Griffey Jr. AU Mini Helmet/75		
5 M.McGwire AU 62 Ticket/1		
6 M.McGwire AU 70 Ticket/3		
7 Ken Griffey Jr. Standee/300	12.00	3.60
8 Ken Griffey Jr. Glove Card/200	40.00	12.00
9 Ken Griffey Jr. HE Cel Card/346	25.00	7.50
10 Ken Griffey Jr. SI Cover/200	20.00	6.00

1999 SP Authentic Reflections

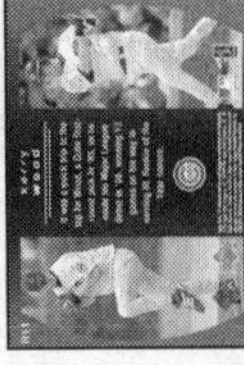

Randomly inserted in packs at the rate of one in 23, this 30-card set features color action photos of some of the game's best players and printed using Dot Matrix technology.

	Nm-Mt	Ex-Mt
COMPLETE SET (30)	300.00	90.00
R1 Mo Vaughn	3.00	.90
R2 Travis Lee	3.00	.90
R3 Andres Galarraga	3.00	.90
R4 Andruw Jones	3.00	.90
R5 Chipper Jones	8.00	2.40
R6 Greg Maddux	12.00	3.60
R7 Cal Ripken	25.00	7.50
R8 Nomar Garciaparra	12.00	3.60
R9 Sammy Sosa	12.00	3.60
R10 Frank Thomas	8.00	2.40
R11 Kerry Wood	8.00	2.40
R12 Kenny Lofton	3.00	.90
R13 Manny Ramirez	3.00	.90
R14 Larry Walker	5.00	1.50
R15 Jeff Bagwell	5.00	1.50
R16 Paul Molitor	8.00	2.40
R17 Vladimir Guerrero	8.00	2.40
R18 Derek Jeter	20.00	6.00
R19 Tino Martinez	5.00	1.50
R20 Mike Piazza	12.00	3.60
R21 Ben Grieve	3.00	.90
R22 Scott Rolen	5.00	1.50
R23 Mark McGwire	20.00	6.00
R24 Tony Gwynn	10.00	3.00
R25 Barry Bonds	20.00	6.00
R26 Ken Griffey Jr.	12.00	3.60
R27 Alex Rodriguez	12.00	3.60
R28 J.D. Drew	3.00	.90
R29 Juan Gonzalez	8.00	2.40
R30 Roger Clemens	15.00	4.50

2000 SP Authentic

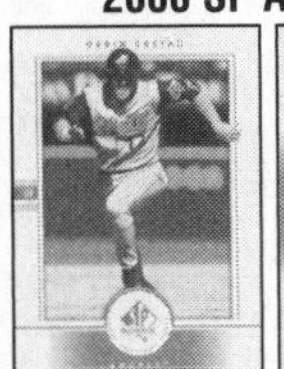
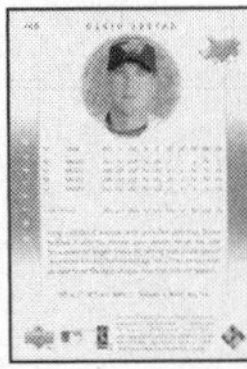

The 2000 SP Authentic product was initially released in late July, 2000 as a 135-card set. Each pack contained five cards and carried a suggested retail price of $4.99. The basic set features 90 veteran players, a 15-card SP Superstars subset serial numbered to 2500, and a 30-card Future Watch subset also serial numbered to 2500. In late December, Upper Deck released their UD Rookie Update brand, which contained a selection of cards to append the 2000 SP Authentic, SPx and UD Pros and Prospects brands. For SP Authentic, sixty new cards were intended, but card number 165 was never created due to problems at the manufacturer. Cards 136-164 are devoted to an extension of the Future Watch prospect subset established in the basic set. Similar to the basic set's FW cards, these Update cards are serial numbered, but only 1,700 copies of each card were produced (as compared to the 2,500 print run for the "first series" cards). Cards 166-195 feature a selection of established veterans either initially not included in the basic set or traded to new teams. Notable Rookie Cards include Xavier Nady, Kazuhiro Sasaki and Barry Zito. Also, a selection of A Piece of History 3000 Club Tris Speaker and Paul Waner memorabilia cards were randomly seeded into packs. 350 bat cards and five hand-numbered, combination bat chip and autograph cut cards for each player were produced. Pricing for these memorabilia cards can be referenced under 2000 Upper Deck A Piece of History 3000 Club. Finally, a Ken Griffey Jr. sample card was distributed to dealers and hobby media in June, 2000 (several weeks prior to the basic product's national release). The card can be readily distinguished by the large "SAMPLE" text running diagonally across the back.

	Nm-Mt	Ex-Mt
COMP.BASIC w/o SP's (90)	25.00	7.50
COMP.UPDATE w/o SP'S (30)	10.00	3.00
COMMON CARD (1-90)	.40	.12
COMMON SUP (91-105)	3.00	.90
COMMON FW (106-135)	5.00	1.50
COMMON FW (136-164)	6.00	1.80
COMMON (166-195)	.60	.18
1 Mo Vaughn	.40	.12
2 Troy Glaus	.60	.18
3 Jason Giambi	1.00	.30
4 Tim Hudson	.60	.18
5 Eric Chavez	.40	.12
6 Shannon Stewart	.40	.12
7 Raul Mondesi	.40	.12
8 Carlos Delgado	.40	.12
9 Jose Canseco	1.00	.30
10 Vinny Castilla	.40	.12
11 Greg Vaughn	.40	.12
12 Manny Ramirez	.40	.12
13 Roberto Alomar	1.00	.30
14 Jim Thome	1.00	.30
15 Richie Sexson	.40	.12
16 Alex Rodriguez	1.50	.45
17 Freddy Garcia	.40	.12
18 John Olerud	.40	.12
19 Albert Belle	.40	.12
20 Cal Ripken	3.00	.90
21 Mike Mussina	1.00	.30
22 Ivan Rodriguez	1.00	.30
23 Gabe Kapler	.40	.12
24 Rafael Palmeiro	.60	.18
25 Nomar Garciaparra	1.50	.45
26 Pedro Martinez	1.00	.30
27 Carl Everett	.40	.12
28 Carlos Beltran	.40	.12
29 Jermaine Dye	.40	.12
30 Juan Gonzalez	1.00	.30
31 Dean Palmer	.40	.12
32 Corey Koskie	.40	.12
33 Jacque Jones	.40	.12
34 Frank Thomas	1.00	.30
35 Paul Konerko	.40	.12
36 Magglio Ordonez	.40	.12
37 Bernie Williams	.60	.18
38 Derek Jeter	2.50	.75
39 Roger Clemens	2.00	.60
40 Mariano Rivera	.60	.18
41 Jeff Bagwell	.60	.18
42 Craig Biggio	.60	.18
43 Jose Lima	.40	.12
44 Moises Alou	.40	.12
45 Chipper Jones	1.00	.30
46 Greg Maddux	1.50	.45
47 Andruw Jones	.40	.12
48 Andres Galarraga	.40	.12
49 Jeromy Burnitz	.40	.12
50 Geoff Jenkins	.40	.12
51 Mark McGwire	2.50	.75
52 Fernando Tatis	.40	.12
53 J.D. Drew	.40	.12
54 Sammy Sosa	1.50	.45
55 Kerry Wood	1.00	.30
56 Mark Grace	.60	.18
57 Matt Williams	.40	.12
58 Randy Johnson	1.00	.30
59 Erubiel Durazo	.40	.12
60 Gary Sheffield	.40	.12
61 Kevin Brown	.60	.18
62 Shawn Green	.40	.12
63 Vladimir Guerrero	1.00	.30
64 Michael Barrett	.40	.12
65 Barry Bonds	2.50	.75
66 Jeff Kent	.40	.12
67 Russ Ortiz	.40	.12
68 Preston Wilson	.40	.12
69 Mike Lowell	.40	.12
70 Mike Piazza	1.50	.45
71 Mike Hampton	.40	.12
72 Robin Ventura	.40	.12
73 Edgardo Alfonzo	.40	.12
74 Tony Gwynn	1.25	.35
75 Ryan Klesko	.40	.12
76 Trevor Hoffman	.40	.12
77 Scott Rolen	.60	.18
78 Bob Abreu	.40	.12
79 Mike Lieberthal	.40	.12
80 Curt Schilling	.60	.18
81 Jason Kendall	.40	.12
82 Brian Giles	.40	.12
83 Kris Benson	.40	.12
84 Ken Griffey Jr.	1.50	.45
85 Sean Casey	.40	.12
86 Pokey Reese	.40	.12
87 Barry Larkin	1.00	.30
88 Larry Walker	.60	.18
89 Todd Helton	.60	.18
90 Jeff Cirillo	.40	.12
91 Ken Griffey Jr. SUP	8.00	2.40
92 Mark McGwire SUP	12.00	3.60
93 Chipper Jones SUP	5.00	1.50
94 Derek Jeter SUP	12.00	3.60
95 Shawn Green SUP	3.00	.90
96 Pedro Martinez SUP	5.00	1.50
97 Mike Piazza SUP	8.00	2.40
98 Alex Rodriguez SUP	8.00	2.40
99 Jeff Bagwell SUP	3.00	.90
100 Cal Ripken SUP	15.00	4.50
101 Sammy Sosa SUP	8.00	2.40
102 Barry Bonds SUP	12.00	3.60
103 Jose Canseco SUP	5.00	1.50
104 N.Garciaparra SUP	8.00	2.40
105 Ivan Rodriguez SUP	5.00	1.50
106 Rick Ankiel FW	5.00	1.50
107 Pat Burrell FW	3.00	.90
108 Vernon Wells FW	5.00	1.50
109 Nick Johnson FW	5.00	1.50
110 Kip Wells FW	5.00	1.50
111 Matt Riley FW	5.00	1.50
112 Alfonso Soriano FW	8.00	2.40
113 Josh Beckett FW	20.00	6.00
114 Danys Baez FW RC	8.00	2.40
115 Travis Dawkins FW	5.00	1.50
116 Eric Gagne FW	10.00	3.00
117 Mike Lamb FW RC	5.00	1.50
118 Eric Munson FW	5.00	1.50
119 W.Rodriguez FW RC	5.00	1.50
120 K.Sasaki FW RC	10.00	3.00
121 Chad Hutchinson FW	5.00	1.50
122 Peter Bergeron FW	5.00	1.50
123 W.Serrano FW RC	5.00	1.50
124 Tony Armas Jr. FW	5.00	1.50
125 Ramon Ortiz FW	5.00	1.50
126 Adam Kennedy FW	5.00	1.50
127 Joe Crede FW	5.00	1.50
128 Roosevelt Brown FW	5.00	1.50
129 Mark Mulder FW	8.00	2.40
130 Brad Penny FW	5.00	1.50
131 Terrence Long FW	5.00	1.50
132 Ruben Mateo FW	5.00	1.50
133 Wily Mo Pena FW	5.00	1.50
134 Rafael Furcal FW	5.00	1.50
135 M.Encarnacion FW	5.00	1.50
136 Barry Zito FW RC	40.00	12.00
137 Aaron McNeal FW RC	6.00	1.80
138 Timo Perez FW RC	6.00	1.80
139 Sun Woo Kim FW RC	6.00	1.80
140 Xavier Nady FW RC	10.00	3.00
141 M.Wheatland FW RC	6.00	1.80
142 B.Abernathy FW RC	6.00	1.80
143 Cory Vance FW RC	6.00	1.80
144 Scott Heard FW RC	6.00	1.80
145 Mike Meyers FW RC	6.00	1.80
146 Ben Diggins FW RC	6.00	1.80
147 Luis Matos FW RC	10.00	3.00
148 Ben Sheets FW RC	10.00	3.00
149 K.Ainsworth FW RC	10.00	3.00
150 Dave Krynzel FW RC	6.00	1.80
151 Alex Cabrera FW RC	6.00	1.80
152 Mike Tonis FW RC	10.00	3.00
153 Dane Sardinha FW RC	6.00	1.80
154 Keith Ginter FW RC	6.00	1.80
155 D.Espinosa FW RC	6.00	1.80
156 Joe Torres FW RC	6.00	1.80
157 Daylan Holt FW RC	6.00	1.80
158 Koyie Hill FW RC	10.00	3.00
159 B.Wilkerson FW RC	10.00	3.00
160 Juan Pierre FW RC	10.00	3.00
161 Matt Ginter FW RC	6.00	1.80
162 Dane Artman FW RC	6.00	1.80
163 Jon Rauch FW RC	6.00	1.80
164 Sean Burnett FW RC	10.00	3.00
165 Does Not Exist		
166 Darin Erstad	.60	.18
167 Ben Grieve	.60	.18
168 David Wells	.60	.18
169 Fred McGriff	1.00	.30
170 Bob Wickman	.60	.18
171 Al Martin	.60	.18
172 Melvin Mora	.60	.18
173 Ricky Ledee	.60	.18
174 Dante Bichette	.60	.18
175 Mike Sweeney	.60	.18
176 Bobby Higginson	.60	.18
177 Matt Lawton	.60	.18
178 Charles Johnson	.60	.18
179 David Justice	.60	.18
180 Richard Hidalgo	.60	.18
181 B.J. Surhoff	.60	.18
182 Richie Sexson	.60	.18
183 Jim Edmonds	.60	.18
184 Rondell White	.60	.18
185 Curt Schilling	1.00	.30
186 Tom Goodwin	.60	.18
187 Jose Vidro	.60	.18
188 Ellis Burks	.60	.18
189 Henry Rodriguez	.60	.18
190 Mike Bordick	.60	.18
191 Eric Owens	.60	.18
192 Travis Lee	.60	.18
193 Kevin Young	.60	.18
194 Aaron Boone	.60	.18
195 Todd Hollandsworth	.60	.18
SPA K.Griffey Jr. Sample	2.00	.60

2000 SP Authentic Limited

Randomly inserted into packs, this 135-card set is a complete parallel of the 2000 SP Authentic base set. These cards are individually serial numbered to 100.

Nm-Mt Ex-Mt

*STARS 1-90: 8X TO 20X BASIC CARDS
*SUP 91-105: 1.25X TO 3X BASIC SUP
*FW 106-135: 1X TO 2.5X BASIC FW .
*FW 106-135 RC: 1X TO 2.5X BASIC FW RC

2000 SP Authentic Buybacks

Representatives at Upper Deck purchased back a selection of vintage SP brand trading cards from 1993-1999, featuring 29 different players. The "vintage" cards were all purchased in 2000 through hobby dealers. Each card was then hand-numbered in blue ink sharpie on front (please see listings for print runs), affixed with a serial numbered UDA hologram on back and packaged with a 2 1/2" by 3 1/2" UDA Certificate of Authenticity (of which had a hologram with a matching serial number of the signed card). The Certificate of Authenticity and the signed card were placed together in a soft plastic "penny" sleeve and then randomly seeded into 2000 SP Authentic packs at a rate of 1:95. Jeff Bagwell, Ken Griffey, Andruw Jones, Chipper Jones, Manny Ramirez and Alex Rodriguez did not manage to sign their cards in time for packout, thus exchange cards were created and seeded into packs for these players. The exchange cards did NOT specify the actual vintage card that the bearer would receive back in the mail. The deadline to redeem the exchange cards was March 30th, 2001. Pricing for cards with production of 25 or fewer cards is not provided due to scarcity.

	Nm-Mt	Ex-Mt
1 Jeff Bagwell 93/58	60.00	18.00
2 Jeff Bagwell 94/46	80.00	24.00
3 Jeff Bagwell 95/60	60.00	18.00
4 Jeff Bagwell 96/74	50.00	15.00
5 Jeff Bagwell 97/53	60.00	18.00
6 Jeff Bagwell 98/38	80.00	24.00
7 Jeff Bagwell 99/539	40.00	12.00
8 Jeff Bagwell EXCH	3.00	.90
9 Craig Biggio 93/59	60.00	18.00
10 Craig Biggio 94/69	60.00	18.00
11 Craig Biggio 95/171	50.00	15.00
12 Craig Biggio 96/71	60.00	18.00
13 Craig Biggio 97/46	80.00	24.00
14 Craig Biggio 98/40	80.00	24.00
15 Craig Biggio 99/125	50.00	15.00
16 Barry Bonds 93/12		
17 Barry Bonds 94/12		
18 Barry Bonds 95/21		
19 Barry Bonds 96/9		
20 Barry Bonds 97/5		
21 Barry Bonds 98/22		
22 Barry Bonds 99/520	175.00	52.50
23 Jose Canseco 93/29	120.00	36.00
24 Jose Canseco 94/20		
25 Jose Canseco 95/6		
26 Jose Canseco 96/23		
27 Jose Canseco 97/23		
28 Jose Canseco 98/24		
29 Jose Canseco 99/502	40.00	12.00
30 Sean Casey 98/5		
31 Sean Casey 99/139	15.00	4.50
32 Roger Clemens 93/68	120.00	36.00
33 Roger Clemens 94/60	120.00	36.00
34 Roger Clemens 95/68	120.00	36.00
35 Roger Clemens 96/68	120.00	36.00
36 Roger Clemens 97/7		
37 Roger Clemens 98/25		
38 Roger Clemens 99/134	100.00	30.00
39 Jason Giambi 97/34	120.00	36.00
40 Jason Giambi 98/25		
41 Tom Glavine 93/99	50.00	15.00
42 Tom Glavine 94/107	50.00	15.00
43 Tom Glavine 95/97	50.00	15.00
44 Tom Glavine 96/42	80.00	24.00
45 Tom Glavine 98/40	80.00	24.00
46 Tom Glavine 99/138	40.00	12.00
47 Shawn Green 96/55	30.00	9.00
48 Shawn Green 99/530	15.00	4.50
49 Ken Griffey Jr. 93/19		
50 Ken Griffey Jr. 94/8		
51 Ken Griffey Jr. 95/9		
52 Ken Griffey Jr. 96/12		
53 Ken Griffey Jr. 97/10		
54 Ken Griffey Jr. 98/22		
55 Ken Griffey Jr. 99/403	120.00	36.00
56 Ken Griffey Jr. EXCH	10.00	3.00
57 Tony Gwynn 93/17		
58 Tony Gwynn 94/7		
59 Tony Gwynn 95/11		
60 Tony Gwynn 96/11		
61 Tony Gwynn 97/24		
62 Tony Gwynn 98/21		
63 Tony Gwynn 99/129	50.00	15.00
64 Tony Gwynn 99/369	40.00	12.00
65 Derek Jeter 93/5		
66 Derek Jeter 95/17		
67 Derek Jeter 96/10		
68 Derek Jeter 97/12		
69 Derek Jeter 98/11		
70 Derek Jeter 99/119	200.00	60.00
71 Randy Johnson 93/60	120.00	36.00
72 Randy Johnson 94/45	120.00	36.00
73 Randy Johnson 95/70	100.00	30.00
74 Randy Johnson 96/60	120.00	36.00
75 Randy Johnson 97/10		
76 Randy Johnson 98/21		
77 Randy Johnson 99/113	80.00	24.00
78 Andruw Jones 97/70	40.00	12.00
79 Andruw Jones 98/56	50.00	15.00
80 Andruw Jones 99/531	25.00	7.50
81 Andruw Jones EXCH	4.00	1.20
82 Chipper Jones 93/3		
83 Chipper Jones 95/9		
84 Chipper Jones 96/17		
85 Chipper Jones 97/63	100.00	30.00
86 Chipper Jones 98/23		
87 Chipper Jones 99/541	40.00	12.00
88 Chipper Jones EXCH	5.00	1.50
89 Kenny Lofton 94/100	25.00	7.50
90 Kenny Lofton 95/84	25.00	7.50
91 Kenny Lofton 96/34	60.00	18.00
92 Kenny Lofton 97/82	25.00	7.50
93 Kenny Lofton 98/21		
94 Kenny Lofton 99/109	25.00	7.50
95 Javy Lopez 93/106	25.00	7.50
96 Javy Lopez 94/160	15.00	4.50
97 Javy Lopez 96/99	25.00	7.50
98 Javy Lopez 97/61	30.00	9.00
99 Javy Lopez 98/26	60.00	18.00
100 Greg Maddux 93/22		
101 Greg Maddux 94/19		
102 Greg Maddux 95/14		
103 Greg Maddux 96/13		
104 Greg Maddux 97/8		
105 Greg Maddux 98/11		
106 Greg Maddux 99/504	80.00	24.00
107 Paul O'Neill 93/110	40.00	12.00
108 Paul O'Neill 94/97	40.00	12.00
109 Paul O'Neill 95/142	25.00	7.50
110 Paul O'Neill 96/70	40.00	12.00
111 Paul O'Neill 98/23		
112 Manny Ramirez 93/6		
113 Manny Ramirez 94/7		
114 Manny Ramirez 95/22		
115 Manny Ramirez 96/13		
116 Manny Ramirez 97/42	60.00	18.00
117 Manny Ramirez 98/36	60.00	18.00
118 M. Ramirez 99/532	15.00	4.50
119 Manny Ramirez EXCH	4.00	1.20
120 Cal Ripken 93/7		
121 Cal Ripken 94/22		
122 Cal Ripken 95/10		
123 Cal Ripken 96/12		
124 Cal Ripken 97/12		
125 Cal Ripken 98/13		
126 Cal Ripken 99/510	120.00	36.00
127 Alex Rodriguez 94/5		
128 Alex Rodriguez 95/57	200.00	60.00
129 Alex Rodriguez 96/37	200.00	60.00
130 Alex Rodriguez 97/10		
131 Alex Rodriguez 98/22		
132 A.Rodriguez 99/408	100.00	30.00
133 Alex Rodriguez EXCH	8.00	2.40
134 Ivan Rodriguez 93/29	120.00	36.00
135 Ivan Rodriguez 94/16		
136 Ivan Rodriguez 95/18		
137 Ivan Rodriguez 96/22		
138 Ivan Rodriguez 97/14		
139 Ivan Rodriguez 98/27	120.00	36.00
140 Ivan Rodriguez 99/2		
141 Scott Rolen 97/23		
142 Scott Rolen 98/31	100.00	30.00
143 Frank Thomas 93/1		
144 Frank Thomas 94/20		
145 Frank Thomas 95/5		
146 Frank Thomas 96/10		
147 Frank Thomas 97/20		
148 Frank Thomas 98/29	120.00	36.00
149 F.Thomas 99/100	50.00	15.00
150 Greg Vaughn 93/79	25.00	7.50
151 Greg Vaughn 94/75	25.00	7.50
152 Greg Vaughn 95/155	15.00	4.50
153 Greg Vaughn 96/113	25.00	7.50
154 Greg Vaughn 97/29	60.00	18.00
155 Greg Vaughn 99/527	15.00	4.50
156 Mo Vaughn 93/119	25.00	7.50
157 Mo Vaughn 94/96	25.00	7.50
158 Mo Vaughn 95/121	15.00	4.50
159 Mo Vaughn 96/114	25.00	7.50
160 Mo Vaughn 97/61	30.00	9.00
161 Mo Vaughn 98/29	60.00	18.00
162 Mo Vaughn 99/537	15.00	4.50
163 Robin Ventura 93/59	30.00	9.00
164 Robin Ventura 94/49	40.00	12.00
165 R.Ventura 95/125	15.00	4.50
166 Robin Ventura 96/55	30.00	9.00
167 Robin Ventura 97/44	40.00	12.00
168 Robin Ventura 98/28	60.00	18.00
169 R.Ventura 99/370	15.00	4.50
170 Matt Williams 93/55	30.00	9.00
171 Matt Williams 94/50	30.00	9.00
172 Matt Williams 95/137	15.00	4.50
173 Matt Williams 96/77	25.00	7.50
174 Matt Williams 97/54	30.00	9.00
175 Matt Williams 98/29	60.00	18.00
176 Matt Williams 99/529	15.00	4.50
177 P.Wilson 94/249	15.00	4.50
178 P.Wilson 99/195	15.00	4.50
179 Authentication Card	.50	.15

2000 SP Authentic Chirography

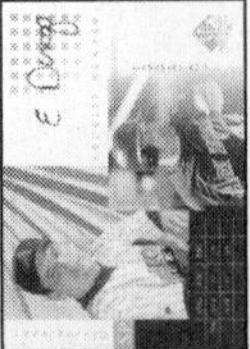
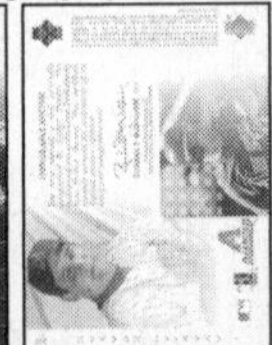

Randomly inserted into packs at one in 23, this 42-card insert features autographed cards of modern superstar players. Please note that there were also autographs of Sandy Koufax inserted into this set. There were a number of cards in this set that packed out as exchange cards, the exchange cards must be sent to Upper Deck by 03/30/01.

	Nm-Mt	Ex-Mt
AJ Andruw Jones	25.00	7.50
AR Alex Rodriguez	100.00	30.00
AS Alfonso Soriano	40.00	12.00
BB Barry Bonds	200.00	60.00
BP Ben Petrick	10.00	3.00
CBE Carlos Beltran	15.00	4.50
CJ Chipper Jones	40.00	12.00
CR Cal Ripken	120.00	36.00
DJ Derek Jeter	150.00	45.00
EC Eric Chavez	15.00	4.50
ED Erubiel Durazo	15.00	4.50
EM Eric Munson	15.00	4.50
EY Ed Yarnall	10.00	3.00
IR Ivan Rodriguez	30.00	9.00
JB Jeff Bagwell	30.00	9.00
JC Jose Canseco	30.00	9.00
JD J.D. Drew	15.00	4.50
JG Jason Giambi	30.00	9.00
JK Josh Kalinowski	10.00	3.00
JL Jose Lima	10.00	3.00
JMA Joe Mays	10.00	3.00
JMO Jim Morris	30.00	9.00
JOB John Bale	10.00	3.00
KL Kenny Lofton	15.00	4.50
MQ Mark Quinn	10.00	3.00
MR Manny Ramirez	25.00	7.50
MRI Matt Riley	15.00	4.50
MV Mo Vaughn	15.00	4.50
NJ Nick Johnson	15.00	4.50
PB Pat Burrell	25.00	7.50
RA Rick Ankiel	10.00	3.00
RC Roger Clemens	100.00	30.00
RF Rafael Furcal	15.00	4.50
RP Robert Person	10.00	3.00
SC Sean Casey	15.00	4.50
SK Sandy Koufax	250.00	75.00
SR Scott Rolen	25.00	7.50
TG Tony Gwynn	50.00	15.00
TGL Troy Glaus	25.00	7.50
VG Vladimir Guerrero	30.00	9.00
VW Vernon Wells	15.00	4.50
WG Wilton Guerrero	10.00	3.00

2000 SP Authentic Chirography Gold

Randomly inserted into packs, this 42-card insert is a complete parallel of the SP Authentic

Chirography set. All Gold cards have a G suffix on the card number (for example Rick Ankiel's card is number G-RA). For the handful of exchange cards that were seeded into packs, this was the key manner to differentiate them from basic Chirography cards. Please note exchange cards (with a redemtpion deadline of 03/30/01) were seeded into packs for Andruw Jones, Alex Rodriguez, Chipper Jones, Jeff Bagwell, Manny Ramirez, Pat Burrell, Rick Ankiel and Scott Rolen. In addition, about 50% of Jose Lima's cards went into packs as real autographs and the remainder packed out as exchange cards.

	Nm-Mt	Ex-Mt
G-AJ Andruw Jones/25		
G-AR Alex Rodriguez/3		
G-AS Alfonso Soriano/53	80.00	24.00
G-BB Barry Bonds/25		
G-BP Ben Petrick/15		
G-CJ Cal Ripken/8		
G-CR Chipper Jones/10		
G-DJ Derek Jeter/2		
G-EC Eric Chavez/3		
G-ED Erubiel Durazo/44	40.00	12.00
G-EM Eric Munson/17		
G-EY Ed Yarnall/41	25.00	7.50
G-IR Ivan Rodriguez/7		
G-JB Jeff Bagwell/5		
G-JC Jose Canseco/33	120.00	36.00
G-JD J.D. Drew/7		
G-JG Jason Giambi/16		
G-JK Josh Kalinowski/62	25.00	7.50
G-JL Jose Lima/42	25.00	7.50
G-JMA Joe Mays/53	25.00	7.50
G-JMO Jim Morris/63	40.00	12.00
G-JOB John Bale/49	25.00	7.50
G-KL Kenny Lofton/7		
G-MQ Mark Quinn/14		
G-MR Manny Ramirez/24		
G-MRI Matt Riley/25		
G-MV Mo Vaughn/42	40.00	12.00
G-NJ Nick Johnson/63	40.00	12.00
G-PB Pat Burrell/33	60.00	18.00
G-RA Rick Ankiel/66	25.00	7.50
G-RC Roger Clemens/22		
G-RF Rafael Furcal/1		
G-RP Robert Person/31	40.00	12.00
G-SC Sean Casey/21		
G-SK Sandy Koufax/32		
G-SR Scott Rolen/17		
G-TG Tony Gwynn/19		
G-TGL Troy Glaus/14		
G-VG V.Guerrero/27	120.00	36.00
G-VW Vernon Wells/10		
G-WG Wilton Guerrero/4		
GCBE Carlos Beltran/15		

2000 SP Authentic Cornerstones

Randomly inserted into packs at one in 23, this seven-card insert features players that are the cornerstones of their teams. Card backs carry a "C" prefix.

	Nm-Mt	Ex-Mt
COMPLETE SET (7)	60.00	18.00
C1 Ken Griffey Jr	6.00	1.80
C2 Cal Ripken	12.00	3.60
C3 Mike Piazza	6.00	1.80
C4 Derek Jeter	10.00	3.00
C5 Mark McGwire	10.00	3.00
C6 Nomar Garciaparra	6.00	1.80
C7 Sammy Sosa	6.00	1.80

2000 SP Authentic DiMaggio Memorabilia

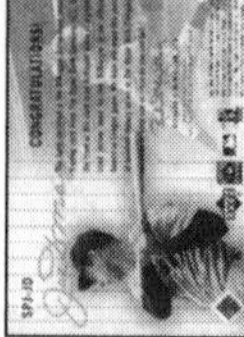

Randomly inserted into packs, this three-card insert features game-used memorabilia cards of Joe DiMaggio. This set features a Game-Used Jersey card (numbered to 500), a Game-Used Jersey card Gold (numbered to 56), and a Game-Used Jersey/Cut Autograph card (numbered to 5).

	Nm-Mt	Ex-Mt
1 Joe DiMaggio Jsy/500	120.00	36.00
2 Joe DiMaggio Jsy Gold/56	250.00	75.00
3 Joe DiMaggio Jsy-Cut AU/5		

2000 SP Authentic Midsummer Classics

Randomly inserted into packs at one in 12, this 10-card insert features perennial All-Stars. Card backs carry a "MC" prefix.

	Nm-Mt	Ex-Mt
COMPLETE SET (10)	30.00	9.00
MC1 Cal Ripken	8.00	2.40
MC2 Roger Clemens	5.00	1.50
MC3 Jeff Bagwell	1.50	.45
MC4 Barry Bonds	6.00	1.80
MC5 Jose Canseco	2.50	.75
MC6 Frank Thomas	2.50	.75
MC7 Mike Piazza	4.00	1.20
MC8 Tony Gwynn	3.00	.90
MC9 Juan Gonzalez	2.50	.75
MC10 Greg Maddux	4.00	1.20

2000 SP Authentic Premier Performers

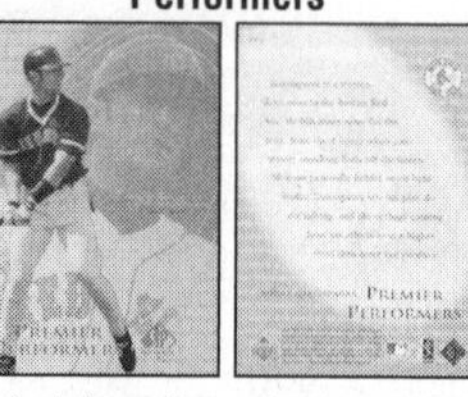

Randomly inserted into packs at one in 12, this 10-card insert features prime-time players that leave it all on the field and hold nothing back. Card backs carry a "PP" prefix.

	Nm-Mt	Ex-Mt
COMPLETE SET (10)	50.00	15.00
PP1 Mark McGwire	6.00	1.80
PP2 Alex Rodriguez	4.00	1.20
PP3 Cal Ripken	8.00	2.40
PP4 Nomar Garciaparra	4.00	1.20
PP5 Ken Griffey Jr.	4.00	1.20
PP6 Chipper Jones	2.50	.75
PP7 Derek Jeter	6.00	1.80
PP8 Ivan Rodriguez	2.50	.75
PP9 Vladimir Guerrero	2.50	.75
PP10 Sammy Sosa	4.00	1.20

2000 SP Authentic Supremacy

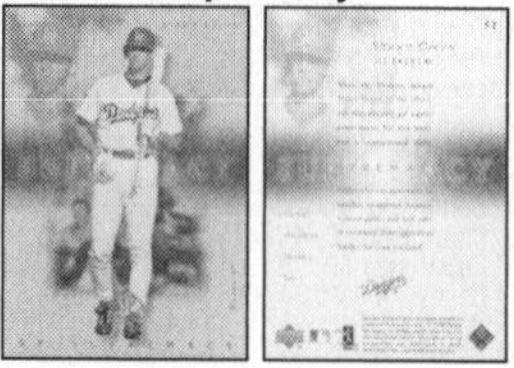

Randomly inserted into packs at one in 23, this seven-card insert features players that any team would like to have. Card backs carry a "S" prefix.

	Nm-Mt	Ex-Mt
COMPLETE SET (7)	30.00	9.00
S1 Alex Rodriguez	6.00	1.80
S2 Shawn Green	1.50	.45
S3 Pedro Martinez	4.00	1.20
S4 Chipper Jones	4.00	1.20
S5 Tony Gwynn	5.00	1.50
S6 Ivan Rodriguez	4.00	1.20
S7 Jeff Bagwell	2.50	.75

2000 SP Authentic United Nations

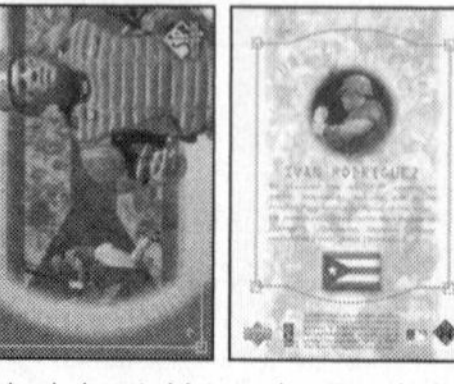

Randomly inserted into packs at one in four, this 10-card insert features players that have come from other countries to play in the Major Leagues. Card backs carry a "UN" prefix.

	Nm-Mt	Ex-Mt
COMPLETE SET (10)	10.00	3.00
UN1 Sammy Sosa	2.00	.60
UN2 Ken Griffey Jr.	2.00	.60
UN3 Orlando Hernandez	.50	.15
UN4 Andres Galarraga	.50	.15
UN5 Kazuhiro Sasaki	1.50	.45
UN6 Larry Walker	.75	.23
UN7 Vinny Castilla	.50	.15
UN8 Andruw Jones	.50	.15
UN9 Ivan Rodriguez	1.25	.35
UN10 Chan Ho Park	.50	.15

2001 SP Authentic

SP Authentic was initially released as a 180-card set in September, 2001. An additional 60-

card Update set was distributed within Upper Deck Rookie Update packs in late December, 2001. Each basic sealed box contained 24 packs plus two three-card bonus packs (one entitled Stars of Japan and another entitled Mantle Pinstripe Exclusives). Each basic pack of SP Authentic contained five cards and carried a suggested retail price of $4.99. Upper Deck Rookie Update packs contained four cards and carried an SRP of $4.99. The basic set is broken into the following components: basic veterans (1-90), Future Watch (91-135) and Superstars (136-180). Each Future Watch and Superstar subset card from the first series is serial numbered of 1250 copies. Though odds were not released by the manufacturer, information supplied by dealers breaking several cases indicate on average one in every 18 basic packs contains one of these serial-numbered cards. The Update set is broken down as follows: basic veterans (181-210) and Future Watch (211-240). Each Update Future Watch is serial numbered to 1500 copies. Notable Rookie Cards in the basic set include Albert Pujols, Tsuyoshi Shinjo and Ichiro Suzuki. Notable Rookie Cards in the Update set include Mark Prior and Mark Teixeira.

	Nm-Mt	Ex-Mt
COMP.BASIC w/o SP's (90)	25.00	7.50
COMP.UPDATE w/o SP's (30)	10.00	3.00
COMMON CARD (1-90)	.40	.12
COMMON FW (91-135)	8.00	2.40
COMMON SS (136-180)	5.00	1.50
COMMON (181-210)	.60	.18
COMMON (211-240)	6.00	1.80
1 Troy Glaus	.60	.18
2 Darin Erstad	.40	.12
3 Jason Giambi	1.00	.30
4 Tim Hudson	.40	.12
5 Eric Chavez	.40	.12
6 Miguel Tejada	.40	.12
7 Jose Ortiz	.40	.12
8 Carlos Delgado	.40	.12
9 Tony Batista	.40	.12
10 Raul Mondesi	.40	.12
11 Aubrey Huff	.40	.12
12 Greg Vaughn	.40	.12
13 Roberto Alomar	1.00	.30
14 Juan Gonzalez	1.00	.30
15 Jim Thome	1.00	.30
16 Omar Vizquel	.40	.12
17 Edgar Martinez	.60	.18
18 Freddy Garcia	.40	.12
19 Cal Ripken	3.00	.90
20 Ivan Rodriguez	1.00	.30
21 Rafael Palmeiro	.60	.18
22 Alex Rodriguez	1.50	.45
23 Manny Ramirez	.40	.12
24 Pedro Martinez	1.00	.30
25 Nomar Garciaparra	1.50	.45
26 Mike Sweeney	.40	.12
27 Jermaine Dye	.40	.12
28 Bobby Higginson	.40	.12
29 Dean Palmer	.40	.12
30 Matt Lawton	.40	.12
31 Eric Milton	.40	.12
32 Frank Thomas	1.00	.30
33 Magglio Ordonez	.40	.12
34 David Wells	.40	.12
35 Paul Konerko	.40	.12
36 Derek Jeter	2.50	.75
37 Bernie Williams	.60	.18
38 Roger Clemens	2.00	.60
39 Mike Mussina	1.00	.30
40 Jorge Posada	.60	.18
41 Jeff Bagwell	.60	.18
42 Richard Hidalgo	.40	.12
43 Craig Biggio	.60	.18
44 Greg Maddux	1.50	.45
45 Chipper Jones	1.00	.30
46 Andruw Jones	.40	.12
47 Rafael Furcal	.40	.12
48 Tom Glavine	.60	.18
49 Jeromy Burnitz	.40	.12
50 Jeffrey Hammonds	.40	.12
51 Mark McGwire	2.50	.75
52 Jim Edmonds	.40	.12
53 Rick Ankiel	.40	.12
54 J.D. Drew	.40	.12
55 Sammy Sosa	1.50	.45
56 Corey Patterson	.40	.12
57 Kerry Wood	1.00	.30
58 Randy Johnson	1.00	.30
59 Luis Gonzalez	.40	.12
60 Curt Schilling	.60	.18
61 Gary Sheffield	.40	.12
62 Shawn Green	.40	.12
63 Kevin Brown	.40	.12
64 Vladimir Guerrero	1.00	.30
65 Jose Vidro	.40	.12
66 Barry Bonds	2.50	.75
67 Jeff Kent	.40	.12
68 Livan Hernandez	.40	.12
69 Preston Wilson	.40	.12
70 Charles Johnson	.40	.12
71 Ryan Dempster	.40	.12
72 Mike Piazza	1.50	.45
73 Al Leiter	.40	.12
74 Edgardo Alfonzo	.40	.12
75 Robin Ventura	.40	.12
76 Tony Gwynn	1.25	.35
77 Phil Nevin	.40	.12
78 Trevor Hoffman	.40	.12
79 Scott Rolen	.60	.18
80 Pat Burrell	.40	.12
81 Bob Abreu	.40	.12
82 Jason Kendall	.40	.12
83 Brian Giles	.40	.12
84 Kris Benson	.40	.12
85 Ken Griffey Jr.	1.50	.45
86 Barry Larkin	1.00	.30
87 Sean Casey	.40	.12
88 Todd Helton	.60	.18
89 Mike Hampton	.40	.12
90 Larry Walker	.60	.18
91 Ichiro Suzuki FW RC	80.00	24.00
92 Wilson Betemit FW RC	8.00	2.40
93 A. Hernandez FW RC	8.00	2.40
94 Juan Uribe FW RC	8.00	2.40
95 Travis Hafner FW RC	15.00	4.50
96 M. Ensberg FW RC	15.00	4.50
97 Sean Douglass FW RC	8.00	2.40
98 Juan Diaz FW RC	8.00	2.40
99 Erick Almonte FW RC	8.00	2.40
100 Ryan Freel FW RC	8.00	2.40
101 E. Guzman FW RC	8.00	2.40
102 C. Parker FW RC	8.00	2.40
103 Josh Fogg FW RC	8.00	2.40
104 Bert Snow FW RC	8.00	2.40
105 H. Ramirez FW RC	12.00	3.60
106 R. Rodriguez FW RC	8.00	2.40
107 Tyler Walker FW RC	8.00	2.40
108 Jose Mieses FW RC	8.00	2.40
109 Billy Sylvester FW RC	8.00	2.40
110 Martin Vargas FW RC	8.00	2.40
111 Andres Torres FW RC	8.00	2.40
112 Greg Miller FW RC	8.00	2.40
113 Alexis Gomez FW RC	8.00	2.40
114 Grant Balfour FW RC	8.00	2.40
115 Henry Mateo FW RC	8.00	2.40
116 Esix Snead FW RC	8.00	2.40
117 J. Melian FW RC	8.00	2.40
118 Nate Teut FW RC	8.00	2.40
119 T. Shinjo FW RC	15.00	4.50
120 C. Valderrama FW RC	8.00	2.40
121 J. Estrada FW RC	10.00	3.00
122 J. Michaels FW RC	8.00	2.40
123 William Ortega FW RC	8.00	2.40
124 Jason Smith FW RC	8.00	2.40
125 B. Lawrence FW RC	8.00	2.40
126 Albert Pujols FW RC	200.00	60.00
127 Wilkin Ruan FW RC	8.00	2.40
128 Josh Towers FW RC	8.00	2.40
129 Kris Keller FW RC	8.00	2.40
130 Nick Maness FW RC	8.00	2.40
131 Jack Wilson FW RC	8.00	2.40
132 B. Duckworth FW RC	8.00	2.40
133 Mike Penney FW RC	8.00	2.40
134 Jay Gibbons FW RC	15.00	4.50
135 Cesar Crespo FW RC	8.00	2.40
136 Ken Griffey Jr. SS	10.00	3.00
137 Mark McGwire SS	15.00	4.50
138 Derek Jeter SS	15.00	4.50
139 Alex Rodriguez SS	10.00	3.00
140 Sammy Sosa SS	10.00	3.00
141 Carlos Delgado SS	5.00	1.50
142 Cal Ripken SS	20.00	6.00
143 Pedro Martinez SS	6.00	1.80
144 Frank Thomas SS	6.00	1.80
145 Juan Gonzalez SS	6.00	1.80
146 Troy Glaus SS	5.00	1.50
147 Jason Giambi SS	6.00	1.80
148 Ivan Rodriguez SS	6.00	1.80
149 Chipper Jones SS	6.00	1.80
150 Vladimir Guerrero SS	6.00	1.80
151 Mike Piazza SS	10.00	3.00
152 Jeff Bagwell SS	5.00	1.50
153 Randy Johnson SS	6.00	1.80
154 Todd Helton SS	5.00	1.50
155 Gary Sheffield SS	5.00	1.50
156 Tony Gwynn SS	8.00	2.40
157 Barry Bonds SS	15.00	4.50
158 N. Garciaparra SS	10.00	3.00
159 Bernie Williams SS	5.00	1.50
160 Greg Vaughn SS	5.00	1.50
161 David Wells SS	5.00	1.50
162 Roberto Alomar SS	6.00	1.80
163 Jermaine Dye SS	5.00	1.50
164 Rafael Palmeiro SS	5.00	1.50
165 Andruw Jones SS	5.00	1.50
166 Preston Wilson SS	5.00	1.50
167 Edgardo Alfonzo SS	5.00	1.50
168 Pat Burrell SS	5.00	1.50
169 Jim Edmonds SS	5.00	1.50
170 Mike Hampton SS	5.00	1.50
171 Jeff Kent SS	5.00	1.50
172 Kevin Brown SS	5.00	1.50
173 Manny Ramirez SS	5.00	1.50
174 Magglio Ordonez SS	5.00	1.50
175 Roger Clemens SS	12.00	3.60
176 Jim Thome SS	6.00	1.80
177 Barry Zito SS	5.00	1.50
178 Brian Giles SS	5.00	1.50
179 Rick Ankiel SS	5.00	1.50
180 Corey Patterson SS	5.00	1.50
181 Garret Anderson	.60	.18
182 Jermaine Dye	.60	.18
183 Shannon Stewart	.60	.18
184 Ben Grieve	.60	.18
185 Ellis Burks	.60	.18
186 John Olerud	.60	.18
187 Tony Batista	.60	.18
188 Ruben Sierra	.60	.18
189 Carl Everett	.60	.18
190 Neifi Perez	.60	.18
191 Tony Clark	.60	.18
192 Doug Mientkiewicz	.60	.18
193 Carlos Lee	.60	.18
194 Jorge Posada	1.00	.30
195 Lance Berkman	5.00	1.50
196 Ken Caminiti	.60	.18
197 Ben Sheets	.60	.18
198 Matt Morris	.60	.18
199 Fred McGriff	1.00	.30
200 Mark Grace	1.00	.30
201 Paul LoDuca	.60	.18
202 Tony Armas Jr.	.60	.18
203 Andres Galarraga	.60	.18
204 Cliff Floyd	.60	.18
205 Matt Lawton	.60	.18
206 Ryan Klesko	.60	.18
207 Jimmy Rollins	.60	.18
208 Aramis Ramirez	.60	.18
209 Aaron Boone	.60	.18
210 Jose Ortiz	.60	.18
211 Mark Prior FW RC	200.00	60.00
212 Mark Teixeira FW RC	80.00	24.00
213 Bud Smith FW RC	6.00	1.80
214 W.Caceres FW RC	6.00	1.80
215 Dave Williams FW RC	6.00	1.80
216 Delvin James FW RC	6.00	1.80
217 Endy Chavez FW RC	6.00	1.80
218 Doug Nickle FW RC	6.00	1.80
219 Bret Prinz FW RC	6.00	1.80
220 Troy Mattes FW RC	6.00	1.80
221 D.Sanchez FW RC	6.00	1.80
222 D.Brazelton FW RC	8.00	2.40
223 Brian Bowles FW RC	6.00	1.80
224 D.Mendez FW RC	6.00	1.80
225 Jorge Julio FW RC	6.00	1.80
226 Matt White FW RC	6.00	1.80
227 Casey Fossum FW RC	6.00	1.80
228 Mike Rivera FW RC	6.00	1.80
229 Joe Kennedy FW RC	6.00	1.80
230 Kyle Lohse FW RC	10.00	3.00
231 Juan Cruz FW RC	6.00	1.80
232 Jeremy Affeldt FW RC	10.00	3.00
233 Brandon Lyon FW RC	6.00	1.80
234 Brian Roberts FW RC	6.00	1.80
235 Willie Harris FW RC	6.00	1.80
236 Pedro Santana FW RC	6.00	1.80
237 Rafael Soriano FW RC	15.00	4.50
238 Steve Green FW RC	6.00	1.80
239 Junior Spivey FW RC	10.00	3.00
240 R.Mackowiak FW RC	6.00	1.80
NNO K.Griffey Jr. Promo	2.00	.60

2001 SP Authentic Limited

This 180-card set is a straight parallel of the basic set. Only fifty sets were produced and each card features serial-numbering in thin gold foil on front and a gold foil brand logo (basic cards feature silver foil brand logos).

	Nm-Mt	Ex-Mt
*STARS 1-90: 10X TO 25X BASIC 1-90		
*FW 91-135: .75X TO 2X BASIC 91-135		
*SS 136-180: 1.5X TO 4X BASIC 136-180		

2001 SP Authentic BuyBacks

For the third time in the history of the brand (including 1997 and 2000), Upper Deck incorporated Buyback cards into SP Authentic packs. Representatives from UD purchased varying quantities of actual previously released SP Authentic cards ranging from 1993 to 2000. The cards were then signed by the featured ballplayer, hand-numbered in blue ink on front and affixed with a serial-numbered hologram sticker on back (note: it's believed all 2001 hologram sticker numbers begin with the letters "AAA"). In addition to the actual signed card, each Buyback was distributed with a 2 1/2" by 3 1/2" Authenticity Guarantee card. Each of these cards featured a hologram with a matching serial-number and a note of congratulations from Upper Deck's CEO Richard McWilliam. Our listings for these cards feature the year of the card followed by the quantity produced. Thus, "Edgardo Alfonzo 95/77" indicates a 1995 SP Authentic Edgardo Alfonzo card of which 77 copies were made. Please note that several Buyback cards are too scarce for us to provide accurate pricing. Please see our magazine or website for pricing information on these cards as it's made available. The following players were seeded into packs as exchange cards: Roger Clemens, Cal Ripken and Frank Thomas. Collectors did not know which card of these players they would receive until it was mailed to them.

	Nm-Mt	Ex-Mt
1 Edgardo Alfonzo 95/77	20.00	6.00
2 Edgardo Alfonzo 98/15		
3 Edgardo Alfonzo 00/280	10.00	3.00
4 Barry Bonds 93/75	200.00	60.00
5 Barry Bonds 94/103	175.00	52.50
6 Barry Bonds 95/31		
7 Barry Bonds 95 Silver/2		
8 Barry Bonds 96/49	200.00	60.00
9 Barry Bonds 97/15		
10 Barry Bonds 98/15		
11 Barry Bonds 00/146	175.00	52.50
12 Roger Clemens 00/145	120.00	36.00
13 R.Clemens 99/150 EXCH	120.00	36.00
14 Carlos Delgado 93/24		
15 Carlos Delgado 94/272	20.00	6.00
16 Carlos Delgado 96/81	30.00	9.00
17 Carlos Delgado 97/8		
18 Carlos Delgado 98/29	80.00	24.00
19 Carlos Delgado 00/169	25.00	7.50
20 Jim Edmonds 96/72	30.00	9.00
21 Jim Edmonds 97/38	50.00	15.00
22 Jim Edmonds 98/23		
23 Jason Giambi 97/14		
24 Jason Giambi 98/6		
25 Jason Giambi 00/290	40.00	12.00
26 Troy Glaus 00/340	30.00	9.00
27 Shawn Green 00/340	20.00	6.00
28 Ken Griffey Jr. 93/34	200.00	60.00
29 Ken Griffey Jr. 94/182	120.00	36.00
30 Ken Griffey Jr. 95/116	120.00	36.00
31 Ken Griffey Jr. 95 Silver/2		
32 Ken Griffey Jr. 96/53	175.00	52.50
33 Ken Griffey Jr. 97/7		
34 Ken Griffey Jr. 98/8		
35 Ken Griffey Jr. 00/333	100.00	30.00
36 Tony Gwynn 93/101	60.00	18.00
37 Tony Gwynn 94/88	60.00	18.00
38 Tony Gwynn 95/179	50.00	15.00
39 Tony Gwynn 96/92	60.00	18.00
40 Tony Gwynn 97/9		
41 Tony Gwynn 98/16		
42 Tony Gwynn 00/95	60.00	18.00
43 Todd Helton 00/194	40.00	12.00
44 Tim Hudson 00/291	30.00	9.00
45 Randy Johnson 93/97	100.00	30.00

46 Randy Johnson 94/146 ... 60.00 18.00
47 Randy Johnson 95/121 ... 60.00 18.00
48 Randy Johnson 95 Silver/6 ...
49 Randy Johnson 96/78 ... 100.00 30.00
50 Randy Johnson 97/8 ...
51 Randy Johnson 98/12 ...
52 Randy Johnson 00/213 ... 60.00 18.00
53 Andruw Jones 97/20 ...
54 Andruw Jones 98/12 ...
55 Andruw Jones 00/336 ... 30.00 9.00
56 Chipper Jones 93/13 ...
57 Chipper Jones 95/118 ... 60.00 18.00
58 Chipper Jones 96/72 ... 60.00 18.00
59 Chipper Jones 97/15 ...
60 Chipper Jones 98/11 ...
61 Chipper Jones 00/303 ... 40.00 12.00
62 Cal Ripken 93/22 ...
63 Cal Ripken 94/99 ... 120.00 36.00
64 Cal Ripken 95/37 ... 200.00 60.00
65 Cal Ripken 96/16 ...
66 Cal Ripken 96 CL/10 ...
67 Cal Ripken 97/23 ...
68 Cal Ripken 98/11 ...
69 Cal Ripken 00/266 ... 120.00 36.00
70 Cal Ripken EXCH ...
71 Alex Rodriguez 95/117 ... 120.00 36.00
72 Alex Rodriguez 95 Silver/2 ...
73 Alex Rodriguez 96/72 ... 150.00 45.00
74 Alex Rodriguez 97/14 ...
75 Alex Rodriguez 98/11 ...
76 Alex Rodriguez 00/332 ... 100.00 30.00
77 Ivan Rodriguez 93/89 ... 60.00 18.00
78 Ivan Rodriguez 95/16 ...
79 Ivan Rodriguez 95 Silver/2 ...
80 Ivan Rodriguez 96/64 ... 80.00 24.00
81 Ivan Rodriguez 97/8 ...
82 Ivan Rodriguez 98/13 ...
83 Ivan Rodriguez 00/163 ... 50.00 15.00
84 Gary Sheffield 93/82 ... 30.00 9.00
85 Gary Sheffield 94/2 ...
86 Gary Sheffield 95/70 ... 30.00 9.00
87 Gary Sheffield 96/67 ... 30.00 9.00
88 Gary Sheffield 97/43 ... 50.00 15.00
89 Gary Sheffield 98/27 ... 80.00 24.00
90 Gary Sheffield 00/146 ... 25.00 7.50
91 Sammy Sosa 93/73 ... 200.00 60.00
92 Sammy Sosa 94/19 ...
93 Sammy Sosa 95/30 ... 250.00 75.00
94 Sammy Sosa 96/9 ...
95 Sammy Sosa 97/14 ...
96 Fernando Tatis 00/267 ... 10.00 3.00
97 Frank Thomas 93/79 ... 60.00 18.00
98 Frank Thomas 94/165 ... 50.00 15.00
99 Frank Thomas 95/3 ...
100 Frank Thomas 97/34 ... 150.00 45.00
101 Frank Thomas 98/10 ...
102 Frank Thomas 00/302 ... 40.00 12.00
103 Frank Thomas EXCH ...
104 Mo Vaughn 93/94 ... 30.00 9.00
105 Mo Vaughn 94/102 ... 30.00 9.00
106 Mo Vaughn 95/129 ... 25.00 7.50
107 Mo Vaughn 95 Silver/3 ...
108 Mo Vaughn 96/81 ... 30.00 9.00
109 Mo Vaughn 97/36 ... 50.00 15.00
110 Mo Vaughn 98/23 ...
111 Mo Vaughn 00/309 ... 20.00 6.00
112 Robin Ventura 00/340 ... 20.00 6.00
113 Matt Williams 00/340 ... 20.00 6.00
114 Authentication Card ...

2001 SP Authentic Chirography

Signed Chirography inserts were brought back for the fourth straight year within SP Authentic. Over 40 players were featured in the 2001 issue, with announced odds of 1:72 packs. Each card features a horizontal design and a small black and white action photo of the player at the side to allow the maximum amount of room for the featured player's autograph (of which is typically found signed in blue ink). Quantities produced for each card varied dramatically and shortly after the product was released, representatives at Upper Deck publicly announced print runs on a selection of the toughest cards to obtain. Those quantities have been added to our checklist following the featured player's name.

Nm-Mt Ex-Mt
AB Albert Belle ... 15.00 4.50
AJ Andruw Jones ... 25.00 7.50
ALP Albert Pujols ... 200.00 60.00
AR Alex Rodriguez SP/229 ... 120.00 36.00
BS Ben Sheets ... 15.00 4.50
CB Carlos Beltran ... 15.00 4.50
CD Carlos Delgado ... 15.00 4.50
CF Cliff Floyd ... 15.00 4.50
CJ Chipper Jones SP/184 ... 40.00 12.00
CR Cal Ripken SP/109 ... 150.00 45.00
DD Darren Dreifort SP/206 ... 10.00 3.00
DER Darin Erstad ... 15.00 4.50
DES David Espinosa ... 10.00 3.00
DJ David Justice ... 15.00 4.50
DS Dane Sardinha ... 10.00 3.00
DW David Wells ... 15.00 4.50
EA Edgardo Alfonzo ... 15.00 4.50
JC Jose Canseco ... 40.00 12.00
JD J.D. Drew ... 15.00 4.50
JE Jim Edmonds ... 15.00 4.50
JG Jason Giambi ... 40.00 12.00
KG Ken Griffey Jr. SP/126 ... 150.00 45.00
LG Luis Gonzalez SP/271 ... 25.00 7.50
MB Milton Bradley ... 15.00 4.50
MK Mark Kotsay SP/228 ... 10.00 3.00
MS Mike Sweeney ... 15.00 4.50
MV Mo Vaughn SP/103 ... 15.00 4.50
MW Matt Williams ... 15.00 4.50
PB Pat Burrell ... 15.00 4.50
RF Rafael Furcal SP/222 ... 15.00 4.50
RH Rick Helling SP/211 ... 10.00 3.00
RJ R. Johnson SP/143 ... 50.00 15.00
RV Robin Ventura SP/92 ...
RW Rondell White ... 15.00 4.50
SG Shawn Green SP/82 ... 40.00 12.00
SS Sammy Sosa SP/76 ... 200.00 60.00
TIH Tim Hudson ... 25.00 7.50
TL Travis Lee SP/226 ... 10.00 3.00
TOG Tony Gwynn SP/76 ... 60.00 18.00
TOH Todd Helton SP/152 ... 40.00 12.00
TRG Troy Glaus ... 25.00 7.50

2001 SP Authentic Chirography Gold

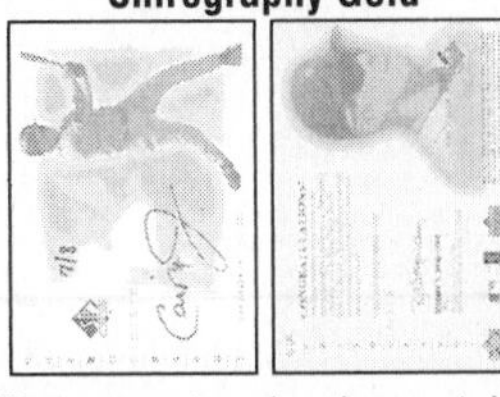

These scarce autograph cards are a straight parallel of the more commonly available Chirography cards. The Gold cards, however, were all produced to quantities mirroring the featured player's uniform number. Furthermore, the cards are individually numbered on front in blue ink and the imagery and design accents are printed in a subdued gold color (rather than the black and white design used on the basic Chirography cards). Many of these cards are too scarce for us to provide accurate pricing on.

Nm-Mt Ex-Mt
G-AB Albert Belle/88 ... 50.00 15.00
G-AJ Andruw Jones/25 ...
G-ALP Albert Pujols/5 ...
G-AR Alex Rodriguez/3 ...
G-BS Ben Sheets/15 ...
G-CB Carlos Beltran/15 ...
G-CD Carlos Delgado/25 ...
G-CF Cliff Floyd/30 ...
G-CJ Chipper Jones/10 ...
G-CR Cal Ripken/8 ...
G-DD Darren Dreifort/37 ... 25.00 7.50
G-DER Darin Erstad/17 ...
G-DES David Espinosa/79 ... 25.00 7.50
G-DJ David Justice/28 ... 50.00 15.00
G-DS Dane Sardinha/50 ... 25.00 7.50
G-DW David Wells/33 ... 50.00 15.00
G-EA Edgardo Alfonzo/13 ...
G-JD J.D. Drew/7 ...
G-JE Jim Edmonds/15 ...
G-JG Jason Giambi/16 ...
G-KG Ken Griffey Jr./30 ... 400.00 120.00
G-LG Luis Gonzalez/20 ...
G-MB Milton Bradley/24 ...
G-MK Mark Kotsay/14 ...
G-MS Mike Sweeney/29 ... 50.00 15.00
G-MV Mo Vaughn/42 ... 50.00 15.00
G-MW Matt Williams/9 ...
G-PB Pat Burrell/5 ...
G-RF Rafael Furcal/1 ...
G-RH Rick Helling/32 ... 25.00 7.50
G-RJ Randy Johnson/51 ... 120.00 36.00
G-RV Robin Ventura/4 ...
G-RW Rondell White/22 ...
G-SG Shawn Green/15 ...
G-SS Sammy Sosa/21 ...
G-TIH Tim Hudson/15 ...
G-TL Travis Lee/16 ...
G-TOG Tony Gwynn/21 ...
G-TOH Todd Helton/17 ...
G-TRG Troy Glaus/25 ...

2001 SP Authentic Chirography Update

Randomly inserted into Upper Deck Rookie Update packs, thse eight cards feature autographs from leading players in the game. Cal Ripken Jr. and Ichiro Suuzki did not return their cards in time for inclusion in these packs and these cards are available as exchange cards. Those cards could be redeemed until September 13th, 2004. These cards are serial numbered to 250.

Nm-Mt Ex-Mt
SP-CR Cal Ripken EXCH ... 150.00 45.00
SP-DM Doug Mientkiewicz ... 15.00 4.50
SP-IS Ichiro Suzuki EXCH ... 400.00 120.00
SP-JP Jorge Posada ... 40.00 12.00
SP-KG Ken Griffey Jr. ... 120.00 36.00
SP-LB Lance Berkman ... 15.00 4.50
SP-MS Mike Sweeney ... 15.00 4.50
SP-TG Tony Gwynn ... 40.00 12.00

2001 SP Authentic Chirography Update Silver

Randomly inserted into Upper Deck Rookie Update packs, thse eight cards parallel the Chirography Update insert set and feature autographs from leading players in the game. Cal Ripken Jr. and Ichiro Suuzki did not return their cards in time for inclusion in these packs

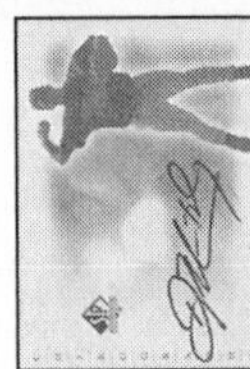

and these cards are available as exchange cards. These cards are serial numbered to 100.

Nm-Mt Ex-Mt
SPCR Cal Ripken EXCH ...
SPDM Doug Mientkiewicz ... 25.00 7.50
SPIS Ichiro Suzuki EXCH ...
SPJP Jorge Posada ... 60.00 18.00
SPKG Ken Griffey Jr. ... 150.00 45.00
SPLB Lance Berkman ... 25.00 7.50
SPMS Mike Sweeney ... 25.00 7.50
SPTG Tony Gwynn ... 60.00 18.00

2001 SP Authentic Cooperstown Calling Game Jersey

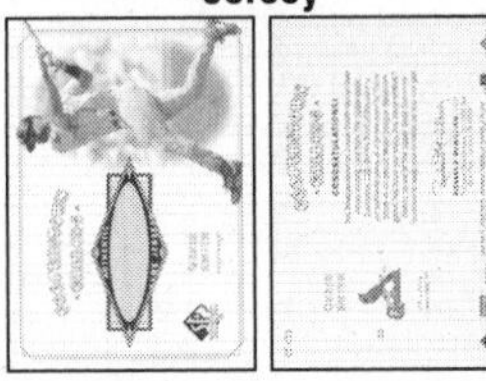

This 22-card set features a selection of players that were voted in (or were soon to be voted in) to the baseball Hall of Fame in Cooperstown, NY. Each card features a swatch of game-used jersey incorporated into an attractive horizontal design. Though specific odds per pack were not released for this set, Upper Deck did release cumulative odds of 1:24 packs for finding a game-used jersey card from either of the Cooperstown Calling, UD Exclusives or UD Exclusives Combos sets within the SP Authentic product.

Nm-Mt Ex-Mt
CC-AD Andre Dawson ... 10.00 3.00
CC-BM Bill Mazeroski ... 15.00 4.50
CC-CR Cal Ripken ... 40.00 12.00
CC-DM Don Mattingly ... 40.00 12.00
CC-DW Dave Winfield ... 10.00 3.00
CC-EM Eddie Murray ... 15.00 4.50
CC-GC Gary Carter ... 15.00 4.50
CC-GG Goose Gossage ... 10.00 3.00
CC-JB Jeff Bagwell ... 15.00 4.50
CC-KP Kirby Puckett ... 15.00 4.50
CC-KS Kazuhiro Sasaki ... 10.00 3.00
CC-MP Mike Piazza SP ... 25.00 7.50
CC-MR M. Ramirez SP ... 10.00 3.00
CC-OS Ozzie Smith ... 15.00 4.50
CC-PM Pedro Martinez SP ... 15.00 4.50
CC-PM Paul Molitor ... 15.00 4.50
CC-RC Roger Clemens ... 40.00 12.00
CC-RM R. Maris SP/243 ... 100.00 30.00
CC-RS Ryne Sandberg ... 30.00 9.00
CC-SG Steve Garvey ... 10.00 3.00
CC-TG Tony Gwynn ... 20.00 6.00
CC-WB Wade Boggs ... 15.00 4.50

2001 SP Authentic Stars of Japan

This 30-card dual player set features a selection of Japanese stars active in Major League baseball at the time of issue. The cards were distributed in special Stars of Japan packs of which were available as a bonus pack within each sealed box of 2001 SP Authentic baseball. Each Stars of Japan pack contained three cards and one in every 12 packs contained a memorabilia card.

Nm-Mt Ex-Mt
COMPLETE SET (30) ... 80.00 24.00
RS1 Ichiro Suzuki ... 8.00 2.40
Tsuyoshi Shinjo
RS2 Shigetoshi Hasegawa ... 2.00 .60
Hideki Irabu
RS3 Tomo Ohka ... 2.00 .60
Mac Suzuki
RS4 Tsuyoshi Shinjo ... 2.00 .60
Hideki Irabu
RS5 Ichiro Suzuki ... 10.00 3.00
Hideo Nomo
RS6 Tsuyoshi Shinjo ... 2.00 .60
Mac Suzuki
RS7 Tsuyoshi Shinjo ... 2.00 .60
Kazuhiro Sasaki
RS8 Hideo Nomo ... 2.00 .60
Tomo Ohka
RS9 Ichiro Suzuki ... 8.00 2.40
Mac Suzuki
RS10 Hideo Nomo ... 2.00 .60
Shigetoshi Hasegawa
RS11 Hideo Nomo ... 2.00 .60
Masato Yoshii
RS12 Hideo Nomo ... 2.00 .60
Hideki Irabu
RS13 Shig. Hasegawa ... 2.00 .60
Kazuhiro Sasaki
RS14 Shig. Hasegawa ... 2.00 .60
Mac Suzuki
RS15 Tsuyoshi Shinjo ... 2.00 .60
Hideo Nomo
RS16 Tsuyoshi Shinjo ... 2.00 .60
Tomo Ohka
RS17 Ichiro Suzuki ... 10.00 3.00
Kazuhiro Sasaki
RS18 Masato Yoshii ... 2.00 .60
Hideki Irabu
RS19 Ichiro Suzuki ... 8.00 2.40
Tomo Ohka
RS20 Hideki Irabu ... 2.00 .60
Kazuhiro Sasaki
RS21 Tsuyoshi Shinjo ... 2.00 .60
Masato Yoshii
RS22 Ichiro Suzuki ... 8.00 2.40
Shigetoshi Hasegawa
RS23 Mac Suzuki ... 2.00 .60
Kazuhiro Sasaki
RS24 Ichiro Suzuki ... 8.00 2.40
Hideki Irabu
RS25 Tomo Ohka ... 2.00 .60
Kazuhiro Sasaki
RS26 Tsuyoshi Shinjo ... 2.00 .60
Shigetoshi Hasegawa
RS27 Masato Yoshii ... 2.00 .60
Kazuhiro Sasaki
RS28 Hideo Nomo ... 2.00 .60
Kazuhiro Sasaki
RS29 Ichiro Suzuki ... 8.00 2.40
Masato Yoshii
RS30 Hideo Nomo ... 2.00 .60
Mac Suzuki

2001 SP Authentic Stars of Japan Game Ball

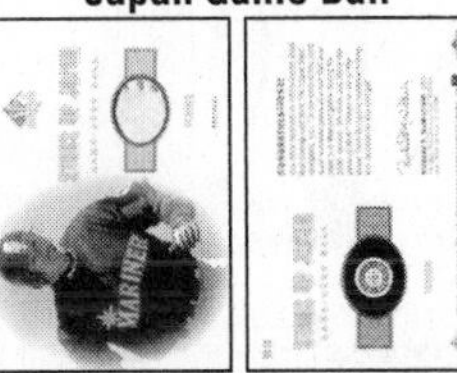

This six-card set features a selection of Japanese stars actively playing in the Major Leagues at the time of issue. Each card features a patch of game-used baseball. The cards were distributed in special Stars of Japan packs. Each sealed box of 2001 SP Authentic contained one three-card Stars of Japan pack inside.Though individual Jersey card odds were not announced, the cumulative odds of finding a memorabilia card (ball, base, bat or jersey) from a Stars of Japan packs was 1:12.

Nm-Mt Ex-Mt
GOLD RANDOM INSERTS IN PACKS ..
GOLD PRINT RUN 25 SERIAL #'d SETS
GOLD NO PRICING DUE TO SCARCITY
BB-HI Hideki Irabu ... 10.00 3.00
BB-IS Ichiro Suzuki ... 80.00 24.00
BB-KS Kazuhiro Sasaki ... 10.00 3.00
BB-MY Masato Yoshii ... 10.00 3.00
BB-SH Shig. Hasegawa SP/30 ...
BB-TS T. Shinjo SP/50 ... 40.00 12.00

2001 SP Authentic Stars of Japan Game Ball-Base Combos

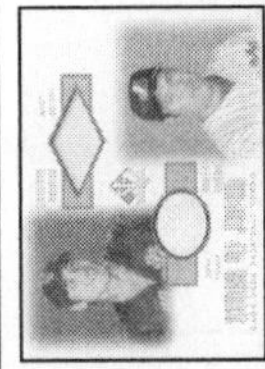

This 14-card dual player set features a selection of Japanese stars actively playing in the Major Leagues at the time of issue. Each card features a piece of a game-used baseball coupled with a piece of game-used base. The cards were distributed in special Stars of Japan packs. Each sealed box of 2001 SP Authentic contained one three-card Stars of Japan pack inside.Though individual Jersey card odds were not announced, the cumulative odds of finding a memorabilia card (ball, base, bat or jersey) from a Stars of Japan packs was 1:12.

Nm-Mt Ex-Mt
GOLD RANDOM INSERTS IN PACKS ..
GOLD PRINT RUN 25 SERIAL #'d SETS
GOLD NO PRICING DUE TO SCARCITY
HI-KS Hideki Irabu ...
Kazuhiro Sasaki SP/30
HN-KS Hideo Nomo ... 80.00 24.00
Kazuhiro Sasaki SP/50
HN-SH Hideo Nomo ... 25.00 7.50
Shigetosi Hasegawa
IS-KS Ichiro Suzuki ...
Kazuhiro Sasaki SP/30
IS-MY Ichiro Suzuki ... 80.00 24.00
Masato Yoshii
IS-SH Ichiro Suzuki ... 120.00 36.00
Shigestosi Hasegawa SP/72
IS-TS Ichiro Suzuki ...
Tsuyoshi Shinjo SP/40
MS-KS Mac Suzuki ...
Kazuhiro Sasaki SP/30
MY-KS Masato Yoshii ...
Kazuhiro Sasaki SP/30
SH-KS S. Hasegawa ...
Kazuhiro Sasaki SP/30
TO-KS Tomokazu Ohka ... 10.00 3.00
Kazuhiro Sasaki
TS-HI Tsuyoshi Shinjo ...
Hideki Irabu SP/30
TS-KS Tsuyoshi Shinjo ...
Kazuhiro Sasaki SP/30
TS-SH Tsuyoshi Shinjo ...
Shigetosi Hasegawa SP/30

2001 SP Authentic Stars of Japan Game Ball-Base Trio

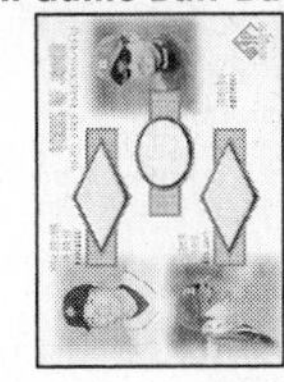

This card features the three greatest Japanese stars actively playing in the Major Leagues at the time of issue. The card features two pieces of game-used bases and one piece of a game-used baseball from the highlighted players. The card was distributed in special Stars of Japan packs. Each sealed box of 2001 SP Authentic contained one three-card Stars of Japan pack inside.Though individual Jersey card odds were not announced, the cumulative odds of finding a memorabilia card (ball, base, bat or jersey) from a Stars of Japan packs was 1:12.

Nm-Mt Ex-Mt
GOLD RANDOM INSERTS IN PACKS ..
GOLD PRINT RUN 25 SERIAL #'d SETS
GOLD NO PRICING DUE TO SCARCITY
RS Kazuhiro Sasaki ...
Ichiro Suzuki
Hideo Nomo SP/30

2001 SP Authentic Stars of Japan Game Base

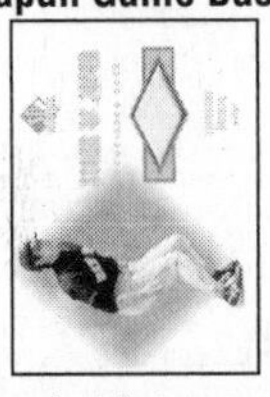

This eight-card set features a selection of Japanese stars actively playing in the Major Leagues at the time of issue. Each card features a piece of game used base. The cards were distributed in special Stars of Japan packs. Each sealed box of 2001 SP Authentic contained one three-card Stars of Japan pack inside.Though individual Jersey card odds were not announced, the cumulative odds of finding a memorabilia card (ball, base, bat or jersey) from a Stars of Japan packs was 1:12.

Nm-Mt Ex-Mt
GOLD RANDOM INSERTS IN PACKS ..
GOLD PRINT RUN 25 SERIAL #'d SETS
GOLD NO PRICING DUE TO SCARCITY
HI Hideki Irabu SP/33 ...
IS Ichiro Suzuki SP/23 ...
KS Kazuhiro Sasaki SP/33 ...
MS Mac Suzuki SP/23 ...
MY Masato Yoshii SP/33 ...
SH S. Hasegawa SP/33 ...
TO Tomokazu Ohka SP/33 ...
TS Tsuyoshi Shinjo SP/33 ...

2001 SP Authentic Stars of Japan Game Bat

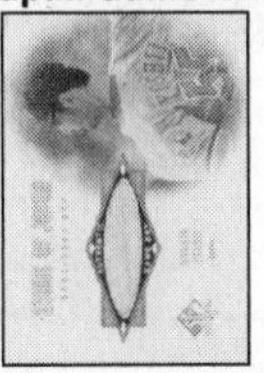

This three-card set features a selection of Japanese stars actively playing in the Major Leagues at the time of issue. Each card features a piece of game-used bat. The cards were distributed in special Stars of Japan packs. Each sealed box of 2001 SP Authentic contained one three-card Stars of Japan pack inside.Though individual Jersey card odds were not announced, the cumulative odds of finding a memorabilia card (ball, base, bat or jersey) from a Stars of Japan packs was 1:12.

Nm-Mt Ex-Mt
GOLD RANDOM INSERTS IN PACKS ..
GOLD PRINT RUN 25 SERIAL #'d SETS
GOLD NO PRICING DUE TO SCARCITY
B-HN Hideo Nomo SP/30 ...
B-MY Masato Yoshii ... 10.00 3.00
B-TS T. Shinjo SP/30 ...

2001 SP Authentic Stars of Japan Game Bat-Jersey Combos

This 4-card dual player set features a selection of Japanese stars actively playing in the Major Leagues at the time of issue. Each card features a combination of a game-used bat chip or game-used jersey swatch from the featured players. The cards were distributed in special Stars of Japan packs. Each sealed box of 2001 SP Authentic contained one 3-card Stars of Japan pack inside.Though individual Jersey

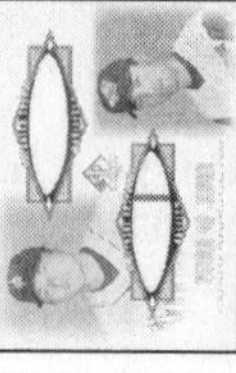

card odds were not announced, the cumulative odds of finding a memorabilia card (ball, base, bat or jersey) from a Stars of Japan packs was 1:12.

	Nm-Mt	Ex-Mt
GOLD RANDOM INSERTS IN PACKS ..		
GOLD PRINT RUN 25 SERIAL #'d SETS		
GOLD NO PRICING DUE TO SCARCITY		
BB-HS S. Hasegawa / Tsuyoshi Shinjo	25.00	7.50
JB-NN Hideo Nomo / Hideo Nomo	60.00	18.00
JB-SN Kazuhiro Sasaki / Hideo Nomo	25.00	7.50
JJ-SH Kazuhiro Sasaki / Shigetosi Hasegawa	15.00	4.50

2001 SP Authentic Stars of Japan Game Jersey

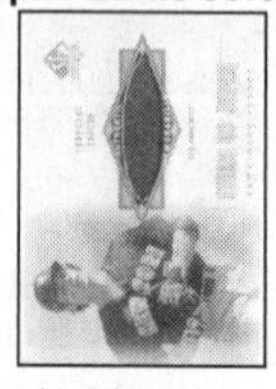

This six-card set features a selection of Japanese stars actively playing in the Major Leagues at the time of issue. Each card features a swatch of game-used jersey. The cards were distributed in special Stars of Japan packs. Each sealed box of 2001 SP Authentic contained one three-card Stars of Japan pack inside.Though individual Jersey card odds were not announced, the cumulative odds of finding a memorabilia card (ball, base, bat or jersey) from a Stars of Japan packs was 1:12.

	Nm-Mt	Ex-Mt
GOLD RANDOM INSERTS IN PACKS ..		
GOLD PRINT RUN 25 SERIAL #'d SETS		
NO GOLD PRICING DUE TO SCARCITY		
J-HN Hideo Nomo	40.00	12.00
J-IS I. Suzuki SP/260 EXCH	100.00	30.00
J-KS Kazuhiro Sasaki	10.00	3.00
J-MY Masato Yoshii	10.00	3.00
J-SH S. Hasegawa	10.00	3.00
J-TS Tsuyoshi Shinjo	15.00	4.50

2001 SP Authentic Sultan of Swatch Memorabilia

This 21-card set features a selection of significant achievements from legendary slugger Babe Ruth's storied career. Each card features a swatch of game-used uniform (most likely pants) and is hand-numbered in blue ink on front to the year or statisitical figure of the featured event (i.e. card SOS3 highlights Ruth's 94 career wins as a pitcher, thus only 94 hand-numbered copies of that card were produced). Quantities on each card vary from as many as 94 copies to as few as 14 copies. The cards were randomly inserted into packs at an unspecified ratio.

	Nm-Mt	Ex-Mt
SOS1 B.Ruth Red Sox/14		
SOS2 B.Ruth 29.2 Inn/29	400.00	120.00
SOS3 B.Ruth 94 Wins/94	400.00	120.00
SOS4 B.Ruth 54 HRs/54	400.00	120.00
SOS5 B.Ruth 59 HRs/59	400.00	120.00
SOS6 Babe Ruth / 3 HRs WS/26	400.00	120.00
SOS7 B.Ruth 60 HRs/27	400.00	120.00
SOS8 Babe Ruth / Called Shot/32	400.00	120.00
SOS9 B.Ruth HR Title/20		
SOS10 B.Ruth HR Title/21		
SOS11 B.Ruth Christens/23		
SOS12 B.Ruth 46 HRs/24		
SOS13 B.Ruth 40 HRs/26	400.00	120.00
SOS14 B.Ruth HR Title/27	400.00	120.00
SOS15 B.Ruth 50 HRs/28	400.00	120.00
SOS16 Babe Ruth / Leads Way/29	400.00	120.00
SOS17 B.Ruth 49 HRs/30	400.00	120.00
SOS18 Babe Ruth / Last Title/31	400.00	120.00
SOS19 Babe Ruth / 1st AS/33	400.00	120.00
SOS20 B.Ruth 1st HOF/36	400.00	120.00
SOS21 B.Ruth House/48	400.00	120.00

2001 SP Authentic Sultan of Swatch Memorabilia Signature Cuts

Each of these cards features an actual Babe Ruth autograph taken from an autographed "cut" (an industry term for a signed piece of paper - often old checks or 3 x 5 note cards) incorporated directly into the card through a window of cardboard. Though only one copy of each card was made for this set, three cards are actually identical parallels of each other save for the SOS-prefixed card numbering on back and the variations in the cut signatures used for each. The signature on card SOS2 has been verified as "Babe Ruth" and for card SOS3 as "G.H. Ruth". Due to the extreme scarcity of these cards, we cannot provide an accurate value as they rarely are seen for public sale.

	Nm-Mt	Ex-Mt
SOS-JC1 Babe Ruth Jsy-Cut AU/1		
SOS-JC2 Babe Ruth Jsy-Cut AU / Cut signed as "Babe Ruth"		
SOS-JC3 Babe Ruth Jsy-Cut AU / Cut signed as G.H. Ruth"		

2001 SP Authentic UD Exclusives Game Jersey

This 6-card set features a selection of superstars signed exclusively to Upper Deck for the rights to produce game-used jersey cards. Each card features a swatch of game-used jersey incorporated into an attractive horizontal design. Though specific odds per pack were not released for this set, Upper Deck did release cumulative odds of 1:24 packs for finding a game-used jersey card from either of the Cooperstown Calling, UD Exclusives or UD Exclusives Combos sets within the SP Authentic product. Shortly after release, representatives at Upper Deck publicly released print run information on several short prints. These quantities have been added to the end of the card description within our checklist.

	Nm-Mt	Ex-Mt
AR Alex Rodriguez	15.00	4.50
GS Gary Sheffield	10.00	3.00
JD J.DiMaggio SP/243	120.00	36.00
KG Ken Griffey Jr.	20.00	6.00
MM M.Mantle SP/243	250.00	75.00
SS Sammy Sosa	20.00	6.00

2001 SP Authentic UD Exclusives Game Jersey Combos

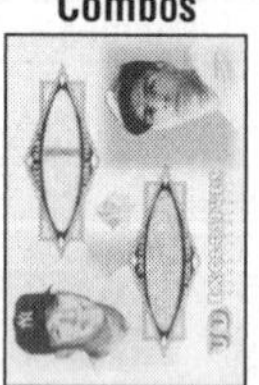

This six-card set features a selection of superstars signed exclusively to Upper Deck for the rights to produce game-used jersey cards. Each card features a swatch of game-used jersey from each featured player incorporated into an attractive horizontal design. Though specific odds per pack were not released for this set, Upper Deck did release cumulative odds of 1:24 packs for finding a game-used jersey card from either of the Cooperstown Calling, UD Exclusives or UD Exclusives Combos sets within the SP Authentic product. Shortly after release, representatives at Upper Deck publicly released print run information on several short prints. These quantities have been added to the end of the card description within our checklist.

	Nm-Mt	Ex-Mt
GD Ken Griffey Jr. / Joe DiMaggio SP/98	150.00	45.00
MD Mickey Mantle / Joe DiMaggio SP/98	400.00	120.00
MG Mickey Mantle / Ken Griffey Jr. SP/98	250.00	75.00
RS Alex Rodriguez / Ozzie Smith	50.00	15.00
SD Sammy Sosa / Andre Dawson	40.00	12.00
SW Gary Sheffiel / Dave Winfield	25.00	7.50

2002 SP Authentic

This 230 card set was released in two separate series. The basic SP Authentic product (containing cards 1-170) was issued in September, 2002. Update cards 171-230 were distributed within packs of 2002 Upper Deck Rookie Update in mid-December, 2002. SP Authentic packs were issued in five card packs with a $5 SRP. Boxes contained 24 packs and were packed five to a case. Cards numbered 1 through 90 featured veterans while cards number 91 through 135 were part of the Future Watch subset and were printed to a stated print run of 1999 serial numbered sets. Cards numbered 136 through 170 were signed by the player and most of the cards were printed to a stated print run of 999 serial numbered sets. Cards number 146, 152 and 157 were printed to a stated print run of 249 serial numbered sets. Update cards 201-230 continued the Future Watch subset (focusing on rookies and prospects) and each card was serial numbered to 1999. Though pack odds for these cards was never released, we estimate the cards were seeded at an approximate rate of 1:7 Rookie Update packs. In addition, an exchange card good for a signed Joe DiMaggio poster was randomly inserted into SP Authentic packs.

	Nm-Mt	Ex-Mt
COMP.LOW w/o SP's (90)	15.00	4.50
COMP.UPDATE w/o SP's (30)	10.00	3.00
COMMON CARD (1-90)	.40	.12
COMMON (91-135/201-230)	8.00	2.40
COMMON CARD (136-170)	15.00	4.50
COMMON CARD (171-200)	.60	.18
1 Troy Glaus	.60	.18
2 Darin Erstad	.40	.12
3 Barry Zito	.60	.18
4 Eric Chavez	.40	.12
5 Tim Hudson	.40	.12
6 Miguel Tejada	.40	.12
7 Carlos Delgado	.40	.12
8 Shannon Stewart	.40	.12
9 Ben Grieve	.40	.12
10 Jim Thome	1.00	.30
11 C.C. Sabathia	.40	.12
12 Ichiro Suzuki	1.50	.45
13 Freddy Garcia	.40	.12
14 Edgar Martinez	.60	.18
15 Bret Boone	.40	.12
16 Jeff Conine	.40	.12
17 Alex Rodriguez	1.50	.45
18 Juan Gonzalez	1.00	.30
19 Ivan Rodriguez	1.00	.30
20 Rafael Palmeiro	.60	.18
21 Hank Blalock	1.00	.30
22 Pedro Martinez	1.00	.30
23 Manny Ramirez	.40	.12
24 Nomar Garciaparra	1.50	.45
25 Carlos Beltran	.40	.12
26 Mike Sweeney	.40	.12
27 Randall Simon	.40	.12
28 Dmitri Young	.40	.12
29 Bobby Higginson	.40	.12
30 Corey Koskie	.40	.12
31 Eric Milton	.40	.12
32 Torii Hunter	.40	.12
33 Joe Mays	.40	.12
34 Frank Thomas	1.00	.30
35 Mark Buehrle	.40	.12
36 Magglio Ordonez	.40	.12
37 Kenny Lofton	.40	.12
38 Roger Clemens	2.00	.60
39 Derek Jeter	2.50	.75
40 Jason Giambi	1.00	.30
41 Bernie Williams	.60	.18
42 Alfonso Soriano	.60	.18
43 Lance Berkman	.40	.12
44 Roy Oswalt	.40	.12
45 Jeff Bagwell	.60	.18
46 Craig Biggio	.60	.18
47 Chipper Jones	1.00	.30
48 Greg Maddux	1.50	.45
49 Gary Sheffield	.40	.12
50 Andruw Jones	.40	.12
51 Ben Sheets	.40	.12
52 Richie Sexson	.40	.12
53 Albert Pujols	2.00	.60
54 Matt Morris	.40	.12
55 J.D. Drew	.40	.12
56 Sammy Sosa	1.50	.45
57 Kerry Wood	1.00	.30
58 Corey Patterson	.40	.12
59 Mark Prior	2.00	.60
60 Randy Johnson	1.00	.30
61 Luis Gonzalez	.40	.12
62 Curt Schilling	.60	.18
63 Shawn Green	.40	.12
64 Kevin Brown	.40	.12
65 Hideo Nomo	1.00	.30
66 Vladimir Guerrero	1.00	.30
67 Jose Vidro	.40	.12
68 Barry Bonds	2.50	.75
69 Jeff Kent	.40	.12
70 Rich Aurilia	.40	.12
71 Preston Wilson	.40	.12
72 Josh Beckett	.60	.18
73 Mike Lowell	.40	.12
74 Roberto Alomar	1.00	.30
75 Mo Vaughn	.40	.12
76 Jeromy Burnitz	.40	.12
77 Mike Piazza	1.50	.45
78 Sean Burroughs	.40	.12
79 Phil Nevin	.40	.12
80 Bobby Abreu	.40	.12
81 Pat Burrell	.40	.12
82 Scott Rolen	.60	.18
83 Jason Kendall	.40	.12
84 Brian Giles	.40	.12
85 Ken Griffey Jr.	1.50	.45
86 Adam Dunn	.40	.12
87 Sean Casey	.40	.12
88 Todd Helton	.60	.18
89 Larry Walker	.60	.18
90 Mike Hampton	.40	.12
91 Brandon Puffer FW	8.00	2.40
92 Tom Shearn FW RC	8.00	2.40
93 Chris Baker FW RC	8.00	2.40
94 Gustavo Chacin FW RC	8.00	2.40
95 Joe Orloski FW RC	8.00	2.40
96 Mike Smith FW RC	8.00	2.40
97 John Ennis FW RC	8.00	2.40
98 John Foster FW RC	8.00	2.40
99 Kevin Gryboski FW RC	8.00	2.40
100 Brian Mallette FW RC	8.00	2.40
101 Takahito Nomura FW RC	8.00	2.40
102 So Taguchi FW RC	10.00	3.00
103 Jeremy Lambert FW RC	8.00	2.40
104 J.Simontacchi FW RC	8.00	2.40
105 Jorge Sosa FW RC	8.00	2.40
106 Brandon Backe FW RC	8.00	2.40
107 P.J. Bevis FW RC	8.00	2.40
108 Jeremy Ward FW RC	8.00	2.40
109 Doug Devore FW RC	8.00	2.40
110 Ron Chiavacci FW	8.00	2.40
111 Ron Calloway FW RC	8.00	2.40
112 Nelson Castro FW RC	8.00	2.40
113 Deivis Santos FW	8.00	2.40
114 Earl Snyder FW RC	8.00	2.40
115 Julio Mateo FW RC	8.00	2.40
116 J.J. Putz FW RC	8.00	2.40
117 Allan Simpson FW RC	8.00	2.40
118 Satoru Komiyama FW RC	8.00	2.40
119 Adam Walker FW RC	8.00	2.40
120 Oliver Perez FW RC	10.00	3.00
121 Cliff Bartosh FW RC	8.00	2.40
122 Todd Donovan FW RC	8.00	2.40
123 Elio Serrano FW RC	8.00	2.40
124 Pete Zamora FW RC	8.00	2.40
125 Mike Gonzalez FW RC	8.00	2.40
126 Travis Hughes FW RC	8.00	2.40
127 J.De La Rosa FW RC	8.00	2.40
128 An.Martinez FW RC	8.00	2.40
129 Colin Young FW RC	8.00	2.40
130 Nate Field FW RC	8.00	2.40
131 Tim Kalita FW RC	8.00	2.40
132 Julius Matos FW RC	8.00	2.40
133 Terry Pearson FW RC	8.00	2.40
134 Kyle Kane FW RC	8.00	2.40
135 Mitch Wylie FW RC	8.00	2.40
136 Rodrigo Rosario AU RC	15.00	4.50
137 Franklyn German AU RC	15.00	4.50
138 Reed Johnson AU RC	20.00	6.00
139 Luis Martinez AU RC	15.00	4.50
140 Michael Crudale AU RC	15.00	4.50
141 Francis Beltran AU RC	15.00	4.50
142 Steve Kent AU RC	15.00	4.50
143 Felix Escalona AU RC	15.00	4.50
144 Jose Valverde AU RC	20.00	6.00
145 Victor Alvarez AU RC	15.00	4.50
146 Kazuhisa Ishii AU/249 RC	50.00	15.00
147 Jorge Nunez AU RC	15.00	4.50
148 Eric Good AU RC	15.00	4.50
149 Luis Ugueto AU RC	15.00	4.50
150 Matt Thornton AU RC	15.00	4.50
151 Wilson Valdez AU RC	15.00	4.50
152 Han Izquierdo AU/249 RC	40.00	12.00
153 Jaime Cerda AU RC	15.00	4.50
154 Mark Corey AU RC	15.00	4.50
155 Tyler Yates AU RC	20.00	6.00
156 Steve Bechler AU RC	15.00	4.50
157 Ben Howard AU/249 RC	40.00	12.00
158 And. Machado AU RC	15.00	4.50
159 Jorge Padilla AU RC	15.00	4.50
160 Eric Junge AU RC	15.00	4.50
161 Adrian Burnside AU RC	15.00	4.50
162 Josh Hancock AU RC	15.00	4.50
163 Chris Booker AU RC	15.00	4.50
164 Cam Esslinger AU RC	15.00	4.50
165 Rene Reyes AU RC	15.00	4.50
166 Aaron Cook AU RC	15.00	4.50
167 Juan Brito AU RC	15.00	4.50
168 Miguel Ascencio AU RC	15.00	4.50
169 Kevin Frederick AU RC	15.00	4.50
170 Edwin Almonte AU RC	15.00	4.50
171 Erubiel Durazo	.60	.18
172 Junior Spivey	.60	.18
173 Geronimo Gil	.60	.18
174 Cliff Floyd	.60	.18
175 Brandon Larson	.60	.18
176 Aaron Boone	.60	.18
177 Shawn Estes	.60	.18
178 Austin Kearns	.60	.18
179 Joe Borchard	.60	.18
180 Russell Branyan	.60	.18
181 Jay Payton	.60	.18
182 Andres Torres	.60	.18
183 Andy Van Hekken	.60	.18
184 Alex Sanchez	.60	.18
185 Endy Chavez	.60	.18
186 Bartolo Colon	.60	.18
187 Raul Mondesi	.60	.18
188 Robin Ventura	.60	.18
189 Mike Mussina	1.50	.45
190 Jorge Posada	1.00	.30
191 Ted Lilly	.60	.18
192 Ray Durham	.60	.18
193 Brett Myers	.60	.18
194 Marlon Byrd	.60	.18
195 Vicente Padilla	.60	.18
196 Josh Fogg	.60	.18
197 Kenny Lofton	.60	.18
198 Scott Rolen	1.00	.30
199 Jason Lane	.60	.18
200 Josh Phelps	.60	.18
201 Travis Driskill FW RC	8.00	2.40
202 Howie Clark FW RC	8.00	2.40
203 Mike Mahoney FW	8.00	2.40
204 Brian Tallet FW RC	10.00	3.00
205 Kirk Saarloos FW RC	8.00	2.40
206 Barry Wesson FW RC	8.00	2.40
207 Aaron Guiel FW RC	8.00	2.40
208 Shawn Sedlacek FW RC	8.00	2.40
209 Jose Diaz FW RC	8.00	2.40
210 Jorge Nunez FW	8.00	2.40
211 Danny Mota FW RC	8.00	2.40
212 David Ross FW RC	8.00	2.40
213 Jayson Durocher FW RC	8.00	2.40
214 Shane Nance FW RC	8.00	2.40
215 Wil Nieves FW RC	8.00	2.40
216 Freddy Sanchez FW RC	8.00	2.40
217 Alex Pelaez FW RC	8.00	2.40
218 Jamey Carroll FW RC	8.00	2.40
219 J.J. Trujillo FW RC	8.00	2.40
220 Kevin Pickford FW RC	8.00	2.40
221 Clay Condrey FW RC	8.00	2.40
222 Chris Snelling FW RC	10.00	3.00
223 Cliff Lee FW RC	10.00	3.00
224 Jeremy Hill FW RC	8.00	2.40
225 Jose Rodriguez FW RC	8.00	2.40
226 Lance Carter FW RC	8.00	2.40
227 Ken Huckaby FW RC	8.00	2.40
228 Scott Wiggins FW RC	8.00	2.40
229 Corey Thurman FW RC	8.00	2.40
230 Kevin Cash FW RC	8.00	2.40
RJ-D J.DiMaggio Poster AU EX	200.00	60.00

2002 SP Authentic Limited

Randomly inserted into packs, this is a parallel to the basic 170-card SP Authentic first series set. These cards have a stated print run of 125 serial numbered sets.

	Nm-Mt	Ex-Mt
*LTD 1-90: 5X TO 12X BASIC		
*LTD 91-135: .4X TO 1X BASIC		
*LTD 136-170: .4X TO 1X BASIC		
*LTD 146/152/157: .3X TO .8X BASIC		
104 Jason Simontacchi FW	8.00	2.40
120 Oliver Perez FW	10.00	3.00
146 Kazuhisa Ishii FW AU	50.00	15.00

2002 SP Authentic Limited Gold

Randomly inserted into packs, this is a parallel to the basic 170-card SP Authentic first series set. These cards have a stated print run of 50 serial numbered sets.

	Nm-Mt	Ex-Mt
*GOLD 1-90: 10X TO 25X BASIC		
*GOLD 91-135: .6X TO 1.5X BASIC		
*GOLD 136-170: .6X TO 1.5X BASIC		
*GOLD 146/152/157: .5X TO 1.2X BASIC		

2002 SP Authentic Big Mac Missing Link

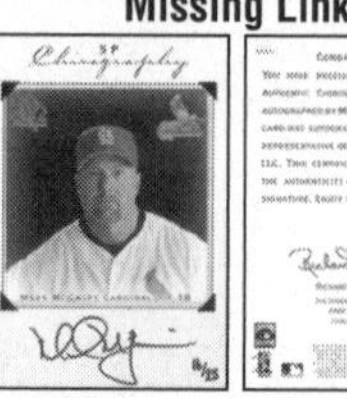
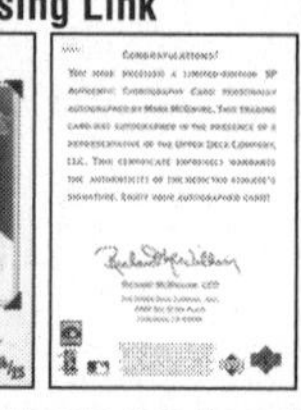

Randomly inserted into packs, these five cards feature autographs of Mark McGwire. Each card was issued to a stated print run of 25 serial numbered sets and thus no pricing is available due to market scarcity.

	Nm-Mt	Ex-Mt
MMC Mark McGwire 98		
MM Mark McGwire 99		
MAM Mark McGwire 00		
SP-MM Mark McGwire 01		
MAMC Mark McGwire 02		

2002 SP Authentic Chirography

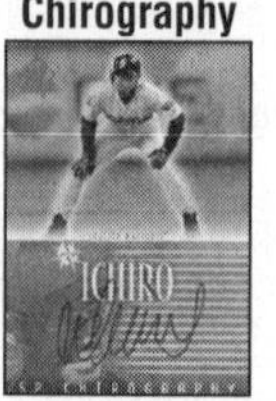

Bret Boone and Tony Gwynn are available only in the basic Chirography set. No Gold parallels were created for them. The following players packed out as redemption cards: Alex Rodriguez, Bret Boone, Sammy Sosa and Tony Gwynn. The deadline for exchange cards to be received by Upper Deck was September 10th, 2005.

	Nm-Mt	Ex-Mt
AD Adam Dunn/348	30.00	9.00
AG Alex Graman/418	15.00	4.50
AR Alex Rodriguez/391 EXCH	120.00	36.00
BB Barry Bonds/112	175.00	52.50
BBo Bret Boone/500 EXCH	20.00	6.00
BZ Barry Zito/419	40.00	12.00
CF Cliff Floyd/313	15.00	4.50
CS C.C. Sabathia/442	20.00	6.00
DE Darin Erstad/80	25.00	7.50
DM Doug Mientkiewicz/478	20.00	6.00
FG Freddy Garcia/456	20.00	6.00
HB Hank Blalock/282	30.00	9.00
IS Ichiro Suzuki/78	400.00	120.00
JB John Buck/427	15.00	4.50
JG Jason Giambi/244	60.00	18.00
JL Jon Lieber/462	15.00	4.50
JM Joe Mays/469	15.00	4.50
KG Ken Griffey Jr./238	120.00	36.00
MBr Milton Bradley/470	20.00	6.00
MBu Mark Buehrle/438	20.00	6.00
MM Mark McGwire/50	300.00	90.00
MS Mike Sweeney/265	20.00	6.00
RS Richie Sexson/483	20.00	6.00
SB Sean Burroughs/275	20.00	6.00
SS Sammy Sosa/247 EXCH	150.00	45.00
TG Tom Glavine/376	40.00	12.00
TGw Tony Gwynn/75 EXCH	50.00	15.00

2002 SP Authentic Chirography Gold

Gold parallel cards were not created for Tony Gwynn and Bret Boone. Sammy Sosa and Alex Rodriguez packed out as exchange cards with a redemption deadline of September 10th, 2005.

	Nm-Mt	Ex-Mt
AD Adam Dunn/44	50.00	15.00
AG Alex Graman/76	25.00	7.50
AR Alex Rodriguez/3 EXCH		
BB Barry Bonds/25		
BZ Barry Zito/75	60.00	18.00

F Cliff Floyd/30	30.00	9.00
S C.C. Sabathia/52	30.00	9.00
E Darin Erstad/17		
M Doug Mientkiewicz/16		
G Freddy Garcia/34	50.00	15.00
B Hank Blalock/12		
Ichiro Suzuki/51		
B John Buck/67		
G Jason Giambi/25		
L Jon Lieber/32	30.00	9.00
M Joe Mays/25		
G Ken Griffey Jr./30	300.00	90.00
Br Milton Bradley/24		
Bu Mark Buehrle/56	30.00	9.00
M Mark McGwire/25		
S Mike Sweeney/29	50.00	15.00
S Richie Sexson/11		
B Sean Burroughs/21		
S Sammy Sosa/21 EXCH		
G Tom Glavine/47	80.00	24.00

2002 SP Authentic Excellence

Randomly inserted into packs, theis card featues signatures of many of Upper Deck's spokespeople. This card was issued to a stated print run of 25 serial numbered sets and no pricing is available due to market scarcity. Please note that this card was issued as an exchange card and was redeemable until September 10, 2005.

	Nm-Mt	Ex-Mt
E Ken Griffey Jr. Sammy Sosa Cal Ripken Jason Giambi Mark McGwire Ichiro Suzuki		

2002 SP Authentic Game Jersey

Inserted into packs at stated odds of one in 24, these 38 cards feature some of the leading players along with a game-used memorabila swatch. A few cards were issued in shorter supply and we have notated that in our checklist along with a stated print run when available.

	Nm-Mt	Ex-Mt
J-AJ Andruw Jones	10.00	3.00
J-AP Andy Pettitte	15.00	4.50
J-AR Alex Rodriguez	20.00	6.00
J-BW Bernie Williams	15.00	4.50
J-BZ Barry Zito	15.00	4.50
J-CC C.C. Sabathia	10.00	3.00
J-CD Carlos Delgado	10.00	3.00
J-CJ Chipper Jones	15.00	4.50
J-CS Curt Schilling	15.00	4.50
J-DE Darin Erstad	10.00	3.00
J-GM Greg Maddux	15.00	4.50
J-GS Gary Sheffield	10.00	3.00
J-IR Ivan Rodriguez	15.00	4.50
J-IS Ichiro Suzuki SP	60.00	18.00
J-JBA Jeff Bagwell	15.00	4.50
J-JBU Jeromy Burnitz SP	15.00	4.50
J-JE Jim Edmonds	10.00	3.00
J-JGO Juan Gonzalez	15.00	4.50
J-JGR Jason Giambi	15.00	4.50
J-JK Jason Kendall	10.00	3.00
J-JT Jim Thome	15.00	4.50
J-KG Ken Griffey Jr. SP/95	40.00	12.00
J-KI Kazuhisa Ishii	15.00	4.50
J-MM Mark McGwire SP	150.00	45.00
J-MO Magglio Ordonez	10.00	3.00
J-MP Mike Piazza	15.00	4.50
J-MR Manny Ramirez	10.00	3.00
J-OV Omar Vizquel	10.00	3.00
J-PW Preston Wilson	10.00	3.00
J-RA Roberto Alomar	15.00	4.50
J-RC Roger Clemens	20.00	6.00
J-RJ Randy Johnson	15.00	4.50
J-RV Robin Ventura	10.00	3.00
J-SG Shawn Green	10.00	3.00
J-SR Scott Rolen	15.00	4.50
J-SS Sammy Sosa	20.00	6.00
J-TH Todd Helton	15.00	4.50
J-TS Tsuyoshi Shinjo	10.00	3.00

2002 SP Authentic Game Jersey Gold

Randomly inserted into packs, this is a parallel to the Game Jersey insert set. Each of these cards have a stated print run which matches the featured player's uniform number and we have notated that information in our checklist. If a card was issued to a stated print run of 25 or fewer, it is not priced due to market scarcity.

	Nm-Mt	Ex-Mt
J-AJ Andruw Jones/25		
J-AP Andy Pettitte/46	30.00	9.00
J-AR Alex Rodriguez/3		
J-BW Bernie Williams/51	30.00	9.00
J-BZ Barry Zito/75	30.00	9.00
J-CC C.C. Sabathia/52	20.00	6.00
J-CD Carlos Delgado/25		
J-CJ Chipper Jones/10		
J-CS Curt Schilling/38	40.00	12.00
J-DE Darin Erstad/17		
J-GM Greg Maddux/31	80.00	24.00
J-GS Gary Sheffield/11		
J-IR Ivan Rodriguez/7		
J-IS Ichiro Suzuki/51	120.00	36.00
J-JBA Jeff Bagwell/5		
J-JBU Jeromy Burnitz/20		
J-JE Jim Edmonds/15		
J-JGO Juan Gonzalez/19		
J-JGR Jason Giambi/25		
J-JK Jason Kendall/18		
J-JT Jim Thome/25		
J-KG Ken Griffey Jr./30	100.00	30.00
J-KI Kazuhisa Ishii/17		
J-MM Mark McGwire/25		
J-MO Magglio Ordonez/30	25.00	7.50
J-MP Mike Piazza/31	80.00	24.00
J-MR Manny Ramirez/24		
J-OV Omar Vizquel/13		
J-PW Preston Wilson/44	20.00	6.00
J-RA Roberto Alomar/12		
J-RC Roger Clemens/22		
J-RJ Randy Johnson/51	40.00	12.00
J-RV Robin Ventura/19		
J-SG Shawn Green/15		
J-SR Scott Rolen/17		
J-SS Sammy Sosa/21		
J-TH Todd Helton/17		
J-TS Tsuyoshi Shinjo/5		

2002 SP Authentic Prospects Signatures

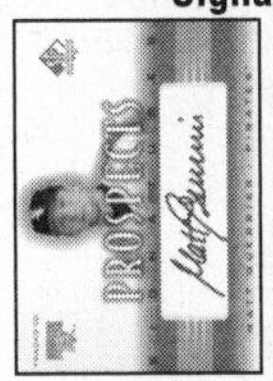

Inserted into packs at a stated rate of one in 36, these 12 cards feature signed cards of some leading baseball prospects.

	Nm-Mt	Ex-Mt
P-AG Alex Graman	10.00	3.00
P-BH Bill Hall	10.00	3.00
P-DM Dustan Mohr	10.00	3.00
P-DW Danny Wright	10.00	3.00
P-JC Jose Cueto	10.00	3.00
P-JDE Jeff Deardorff	10.00	3.00
P-JDI Jose Diaz	15.00	4.50
P-KH Ken Huckaby	10.00	3.00
P-MG Matt Guerrier	10.00	3.00
P-MS Marcos Scutaro	10.00	3.00
P-ST Steve Torrealba	10.00	3.00
P-XN Xavier Nady	10.00	3.00

2002 SP Authentic Signed Big Mac

Randomly inserted into packs, these 10 cards feature authentic autographs of retired superstar Mark McGwire. Each of these cards were signed to a different stated print run and we have notated that information in our checklist. If a card was signed to 25 or fewer copies, there is no pricing provided due to market scarcity.

	Nm-Mt	Ex-Mt
MM1 Mark McGwire/1		
MM2 Mark McGwire/25		
MM3 Mark McGwire/5		
MM4 Mark McGwire/4		
MM5 Mark McGwire/12		
MM6 Mark McGwire/70	300.00	90.00
MM7 Mark McGwire/4		
MM8 Mark McGwire/7		
MM9 Mark McGwire/5		
MM10 Mark McGwire/16		

2002 SP Authentic Signs of Greatness

Randomly inserted into packs, this is a one card set featuring five autograph on the same card. Since only one of these cards was produced, there is no pricing due to market scarcity.

	Nm-Mt	Ex-Mt
SOG Babe Ruth Joe DiMaggio Mickey Mantle Ken Griffey Jr. Sammy Sosa Mark McGwire		

2002 SP Authentic USA Future Watch

Randomly inserted into packs, these 22 cards feature players from the USA National Team. Each card was issued to a stated print run of 1999 serial numbered sets.

	Nm-Mt	Ex-Mt
USA1 Chad Cordero	8.00	2.40
USA2 Philip Humber	10.00	3.00
USA3 Grant Johnson	8.00	2.40

USA4 Wes Littleton	12.00	3.60
USA5 Kyle Sleeth	25.00	7.50
USA6 Huston Street	10.00	3.00
USA7 Brad Sullivan	12.00	3.60
USA8 Bob Zimmermann	8.00	2.40
USA9 Abe Alvarez	10.00	3.00
USA10 Kyle Bakker	8.00	2.40
USA11 Landon Powell	8.00	2.40
USA12 Clint Sammons	8.00	2.40
USA13 Michael Aubrey	60.00	18.00
USA14 Aaron Hill	25.00	7.50
USA15 Conor Jackson	20.00	6.00
USA16 Eric Patterson	10.00	3.00
USA17 Dustin Pedroia	8.00	2.40
USA18 Rickie Weeks	80.00	24.00
USA19 Shane Costa	10.00	3.00
USA20 Mark Jurich	8.00	2.40
USA21 Sam Fuld	8.00	2.40
USA22 Carlos Quentin	15.00	4.50

2002 SP Authentic Hawaii Sign of the Times Duke Snider

This card was distributed on February 27th, 2002 at Upper Deck's poolside reception during the Hawaii Trade Conference. Each attendee received either this signed Duke Snider card or a signed card of NFL legend John Riggins, both of which were hand-numbered to 500 copies in blue ink. Snider signed each card in blue ink sharpie across the front.

	Nm-Mt	Ex-Mt
DS Duke Snider/500	20.00	6.00

2003 SP Authentic

This 239-card set was distributed in two separate series. The primary SP Authentic product was originally issued as a 189-card set released in May, 2003. These cards were issued in five card packs with an $5 SRP which were issued 24 packs to a box and 12 boxes to a case. Update cards 190-239 were issued randomly within packs of 2003 Upper Deck Finite and released in December, 2003. Cards numbered 1-90 featured commonly seeded veterans while cards 91-123 featured what was titled SP Rookie Archives (RA) and those cards were issued to a stated print run of 2500 serial numbered sets. Cards numbered 124 to 150 feature a subset called Back to 93 and those cards were issued to a stated print run of 1993 serial numbered sets. Cards numbered 151 through 189 feature Future Watch prospects (with 181 to 189 being autographed). Please note that cards numbered 151-180 were also issued to a stated print run of 2003 serial numbered sets and cards numbered 181-189 were issued to a stated print run of 500 serial numbered sets. The Jose Contreras signed card was issued either as a live card or an exchange card. The Contreras exchange card could be redeemed until May 21, 2006. Cards 190-239 (released at year's end) continued the Future Watch subset but each card was serial numbered to 699 copies.

	Nm-Mt	Ex-Mt
COMP.LO SET w/o SP's (90)	15.00	4.50
COMMON CARD (1-90)	.40	.12
COMMON CARD (91-123)	3.00	.90
COMMON CARD (124-150)	3.00	.90
COMMON CARD (151-180)	5.00	1.50
COMMON CARD (181-189)	15.00	4.50
91-189 RANDOM INSERTS IN PACKS		
COMMON CARD (190-239)	5.00	1.50
190-239 RANDOM IN 03 UD FINITE PACKS		
190-239 PRINT RUN 699 SERIAL #'d SETS		
1 Darin Erstad	.40	.12
2 Garret Anderson	.40	.12
3 Troy Glaus	.60	.18
4 Eric Chavez	.40	.12
5 Barry Zito	.60	.18
6 Miguel Tejada	.40	.12
7 Eric Hinske	.40	.12
8 Carlos Delgado	.40	.12
9 Josh Phelps	.40	.12
10 Ben Grieve	.40	.12
11 Carl Crawford	.40	.12
12 Omar Vizquel	.40	.12
13 Matt Lawton	.40	.12
14 C.C. Sabathia	.40	.12
15 Ichiro Suzuki	1.50	.45
16 John Olerud	.40	.12
17 Freddy Garcia	.40	.12
18 Jay Gibbons	.40	.12
19 Tony Batista	.40	.12
20 Melvin Mora	.40	.12
21 Alex Rodriguez	1.50	.45
22 Rafael Palmeiro	.60	.18
23 Hank Blalock	.60	.18
24 Nomar Garciaparra	1.50	.45
25 Pedro Martinez	1.00	.30
26 Johnny Damon	.40	.12
27 Mike Sweeney	.40	.12
28 Carlos Febles	.40	.12
29 Carlos Beltran	.40	.12
30 Carlos Pena	.40	.12
31 Eric Munson	.40	.12
32 Bobby Higginson	.40	.12
33 Torii Hunter	.40	.12
34 Doug Mientkiewicz	.40	.12
35 Jacque Jones	.40	.12
36 Paul Konerko	.40	.12
37 Bartolo Colon	.40	.12
38 Magglio Ordonez	.40	.12
39 Derek Jeter	2.50	.75
40 Bernie Williams	.60	.18
41 Jason Giambi	1.00	.30
42 Alfonso Soriano	.60	.18
43 Roger Clemens	2.00	.60
44 Jeff Bagwell	.60	.18
45 Jeff Kent	.40	.12
46 Lance Berkman	.40	.12
47 Chipper Jones	1.00	.30
48 Andruw Jones	.40	.12
49 Gary Sheffield	.40	.12
50 Ben Sheets	.40	.12
51 Richie Sexson	.40	.12
52 Geoff Jenkins	.40	.12
53 Jim Edmonds	.40	.12
54 Albert Pujols	2.00	.60
55 Scott Rolen	.60	.18
56 Sammy Sosa	1.50	.45
57 Kerry Wood	1.00	.30
58 Eric Karros	.40	.12
59 Luis Gonzalez	.40	.12
60 Randy Johnson	1.00	.30
61 Curt Schilling	.60	.18
62 Fred McGriff	.60	.18
63 Shawn Green	.40	.12
64 Paul Lo Duca	.40	.12
65 Vladimir Guerrero	1.00	.30
66 Jose Vidro	.40	.12
67 Barry Bonds	2.50	.75
68 Rich Aurilia	.40	.12
69 Edgardo Alfonzo	.40	.12
70 Ivan Rodriguez	1.00	.30
71 Mike Lowell	.40	.12
72 Derrek Lee	.40	.12
73 Tom Glavine	.60	.18
74 Mike Piazza	1.50	.45
75 Roberto Alomar	1.00	.30
76 Ryan Klesko	.40	.12
77 Phil Nevin	.40	.12
78 Mark Kotsay	.40	.12
79 Jim Thome	1.00	.30
80 Pat Burrell	.40	.12
81 Bobby Abreu	.40	.12
82 Jason Kendall	.40	.12
83 Brian Giles	.40	.12
84 Aramis Ramirez	.40	.12
85 Austin Kearns	.40	.12
86 Ken Griffey Jr.	1.50	.45
87 Adam Dunn	.40	.12
88 Larry Walker	.60	.18
89 Todd Helton	.60	.18
90 Preston Wilson	.40	.12
91 Derek Jeter RA	8.00	2.40
92 Johnny Damon RA	3.00	.90
93 Chipper Jones RA	3.00	.90
94 Manny Ramirez RA	3.00	.90
95 Trot Nixon RA	3.00	.90
96 Alex Rodriguez RA	5.00	1.50
97 Chan Ho Park RA	3.00	.90
98 Brad Fullmer RA	3.00	.90
99 Billy Wagner RA	3.00	.90
100 Hideo Nomo RA	3.00	.90
101 Freddy Garcia RA	3.00	.90
102 Darin Erstad RA	3.00	.90
103 Jose Cruz Jr. RA	3.00	.90
104 Nomar Garciaparra RA	5.00	1.50
105 Magglio Ordonez RA	3.00	.90
106 Kerry Wood RA	3.00	.90
107 Troy Glaus RA	3.00	.90
108 J.D. Drew RA	3.00	.90
109 Alfonso Soriano RA	3.00	.90
110 Danys Baez RA	3.00	.90
111 Kazuhiro Sasaki RA	3.00	.90
112 Barry Zito RA	3.00	.90
113 Brent Abernathy RA	3.00	.90
114 Ben Diggins RA	3.00	.90
115 Ben Sheets RA	3.00	.90
116 Brad Wilkerson RA	3.00	.90
117 Juan Pierre RA	3.00	.90
118 Jon Rauch RA	3.00	.90
119 Ichiro Suzuki RA	5.00	1.50
120 Albert Pujols RA	6.00	1.80
121 Mark Prior RA	6.00	1.80
122 Mark Teixeira RA	3.00	.90
123 Kazuhisa Ishii RA	3.00	.90
124 Troy Glaus B93	3.00	.90
125 Randy Johnson B93	3.00	.90
126 Curt Schilling B93	3.00	.90
127 Chipper Jones B93	3.00	.90
128 Greg Maddux B93	5.00	1.50
129 Nomar Garciaparra B93	5.00	1.50
130 Pedro Martinez B93	3.00	.90
131 Sammy Sosa B93	5.00	1.50
132 Mark Prior B93	6.00	1.80
133 Ken Griffey Jr. B93	5.00	1.50
134 Adam Dunn B93	3.00	.90
135 Jeff Bagwell B93	3.00	.90
136 Vladimir Guerrero B93	3.00	.90
137 Mike Piazza B93	5.00	1.50
138 Tom Glavine B93	3.00	.90
139 Derek Jeter B93	8.00	2.40
140 Roger Clemens B93	6.00	1.80
141 Jason Giambi B93	3.00	.90
142 Alfonso Soriano B93	3.00	.90
143 Miguel Tejada B93	3.00	.90
144 Barry Zito B93	3.00	.90
145 Jim Thome B93	3.00	.90
146 Barry Bonds B93	8.00	2.40
147 Ichiro Suzuki B93	5.00	1.50
148 Albert Pujols B93	6.00	1.80
149 Alex Rodriguez B93	5.00	1.50
150 Carlos Delgado B93	3.00	.90
151 Rich Fischer FW RC	5.00	1.50
152 Brandon Webb FW RC	20.00	6.00
153 Rob Hammock FW RC	8.00	2.40
154 Matt Kata FW RC	8.00	2.40
155 Tim Olson FW RC	8.00	2.40
156 Oscar Villarreal FW RC	5.00	1.50
157 Michael Hessman FW RC	5.00	1.50
158 Daniel Cabrera FW RC	5.00	1.50
159 Jon Leicester FW RC	5.00	1.50
160 Todd Wellemeyer FW RC	8.00	2.40
161 Felix Sanchez FW RC	5.00	1.50
162 David Sanders FW RC	5.00	1.50
163 Josh Stewart FW RC	5.00	1.50
164 Arnie Munoz FW RC	5.00	1.50
165 Ryan Cameron FW RC	5.00	1.50
166 Clint Barmes FW RC	8.00	2.40
167 Josh Willingham FW RC	10.00	3.00
169 Willie Eyre FW RC	5.00	1.50
170 Brent Hoard FW RC	5.00	1.50
171 Terrmel Sledge FW RC	8.00	2.40
172 Phil Seibel FW RC	5.00	1.50
173 Craig Brazell FW RC	8.00	2.40
174 Jeff Duncan FW RC	8.00	2.40
176 Bernie Castro FW RC	5.00	1.50
177 Mike Nicolas FW RC	5.00	1.50
178 Rett Johnson FW RC	8.00	2.40
179 Bobby Madritsch FW RC	5.00	1.50
180 Chris Capuano FW RC	5.00	1.50
181 Hideki Matsui FW AU RC	250.00	75.00
182 J.Contreras FW AU RC	50.00	15.00
183 Lew Ford FW AU RC	25.00	7.50
184 Jer. Griffiths FW AU RC	25.00	7.50
185 G. Quiroz FW AU RC	50.00	15.00
186 Alej Machado FW AU RC	15.00	4.50
187 Fran Cruceta FW AU RC	15.00	4.50
188 Pr. Redman FW AU RC	15.00	4.50
189 S.Bazzell FW AU RC	15.00	4.50
190 Aaron Looper FW RC	5.00	1.50
191 Alex Prieto FW RC	5.00	1.50
192 Alfredo Gonzalez FW RC	5.00	1.50
193 Andrew Brown FW RC	5.00	1.50
194 Anthony Ferrari FW RC	5.00	1.50
195 Aquilino Lopez FW RC	5.00	1.50
196 Beau Kemp FW RC	5.00	1.50
197 Bo Hart FW RC	15.00	4.50
198 Chad Gaudin FW RC	5.00	1.50
199 Colin Porter FW RC	5.00	1.50
200 D.J. Carrasco FW RC	5.00	1.50
201 Dan Haren FW RC	8.00	2.40
202 Danny Garcia FW RC	5.00	1.50
203 Jon Switzer FW	5.00	1.50
204 Edwin Jackson FW RC	25.00	7.50
205 Fernando Cabrera FW RC	5.00	1.50
206 Garrett Atkins FW	5.00	1.50
207 Gerald Laird FW	5.00	1.50
208 Greg Jones FW RC	5.00	1.50
209 Ian Ferguson FW RC	5.00	1.50
210 Jason Roach FW RC	5.00	1.50
211 Jason Shiell FW RC	5.00	1.50
212 Jeremy Bonderman FW RC	8.00	2.40
213 Jeremy Wedel FW RC	5.00	1.50
214 Jhonny Peralta FW RC	5.00	1.50
215 Delmon Young FW RC	50.00	15.00
216 Jorge DePaula FW	5.00	1.50
217 Josh Hall FW RC	8.00	2.40
218 Julio Manon FW RC	5.00	1.50
219 Kevin Correia FW RC	5.00	1.50
220 Kevin Ohme FW RC	5.00	1.50
221 Kevin Tolar FW RC	5.00	1.50
222 Luis Ayala FW RC	5.00	1.50
223 Luis De Los Santos FW	5.00	1.50
224 Chad Cordero FW RC	5.00	1.50
225 Mark Malaska FW RC	5.00	1.50
226 Khalil Greene FW	8.00	2.40
227 Michael Nakamura FW RC	5.00	1.50
228 Michel Hernandez FW RC	5.00	1.50
229 Miguel Ojeda FW RC	5.00	1.50
230 Mike Neu FW RC	5.00	1.50
231 Nate Bland FW RC	5.00	1.50
232 Pete LaForest FW RC	8.00	2.40
233 Rickie Weeks FW RC	40.00	12.00
234 Rosman Garcia FW RC	5.00	1.50
235 Ryan Wagner FW RC	8.00	2.40
236 Lance Niekro FW	5.00	1.50
237 Tom Gregorio FW RC	5.00	1.50
238 Tommy Phelps FW	5.00	1.50
239 Wilfredo Ledezma FW RC	5.00	1.50

2003 SP Authentic Matsui Future Watch Autograph Parallel

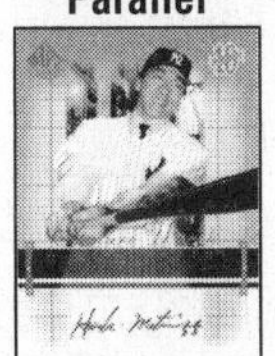

	Nm-Mt	Ex-Mt
RANDOM INSERTS IN PACKS		
PRINT RUNS B/WN 10-75 COPIES PER		
NO PRICING ON QTY OF 25 OR LESS.		
181A H.Matsui Bronze/75	400.00	120.00
181B H.Matsui Silver/25		
181C H.Matsui Gold/10		

2003 SP Authentic 500 HR Club

Randomly inserted into packs, this card featured members of the 500 homer club along with a game-used memorablia piece from each player. A gold parallel was also issued for this card and that card was issued to a stated print run of 25 serial numbered sets. The gold version is not priced due to market scarcity.

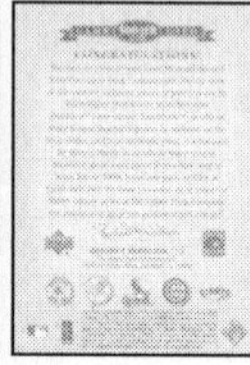

	Nm-Mt	Ex-Mt
500 Sammy Sosa Jsy/Pants Ted Williams Pants Mickey Mantle Jsy/Pants Mark McGwire Jsy/Pants Barry Bonds Base	400.00	120.00
500G Sammy Sosa Jsy/Pants Ted Williams Pants Mickey Mantle Jsy/Pants Mark McGwire Jsy/Pants Barry Bonds Base Gold/25		

2003 SP Authentic Chirography

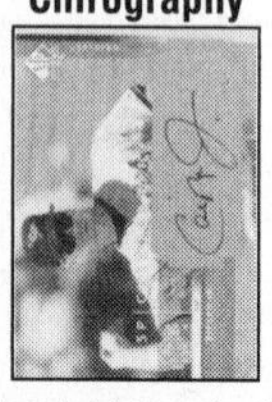

Randomly inserted into packs, these cards feature authentic autographs from the player pictured on the card. These cards marked the debut of Upper Deck using the "Band-Aid" approach to putting autographs on cards. What that means is that the player does not actually sign the card, instead the player signs a sticker which is then attached to the card. Please note that since these cards were issued to varying print runs, we have notated the stated print run next to the player's name in our checklist. Several players did not get their cards signed in time for inclusion in this product and those exchange cards could be redeemed until April 21, 2006. Please note that many cards in the various sets have notations but neither Mark Prior nor Corey Patterson used whatever notations they were supposed to throughout the course of this product.

	Nm-Mt	Ex-Mt
AD Adam Dunn/170	30.00	9.00
BA Jeff Bagwell/175	60.00	18.00
CR Cal Ripken/250	120.00	36.00
FC Rafael Furcal/150	20.00	6.00
FG Freddy Garcia/345	15.00	4.50
FL Cliff Floyd/125	15.00	4.50
GA1 Garret Anderson/350	15.00	4.50
GI Jason Giambi/250	50.00	15.00
GJ Ken Griffey Jr./350 EXCH	120.00	36.00
GL Brian Giles/225	15.00	4.50
IC Ichiro Suzuki/85	350.00	105.00
IS Ichiro Suzuki/75	350.00	105.00
JD Johnny Damon/245	15.00	4.50
JE2 Jim Edmonds/350	25.00	7.50
JM Joe Mays/245	10.00	3.00
JR Ken Griffey Jr./350 EXCH	120.00	36.00
JT1 Jim Thome/250 EXCH	40.00	12.00
KE Jason Kendall/145	20.00	6.00
LG1 Luis Gonzalez/195	20.00	6.00
MM Mark McGwire/50	300.00	90.00
RO Scott Rolen/345	40.00	12.00
RS Richie Sexson/245	15.00	4.50
SA Sammy Sosa/335 EXCH	150.00	45.00
SO Sammy Sosa/335 EXCH	150.00	45.00
SW Mike Sweeney/125	20.00	6.00
TO Torii Hunter/245	15.00	4.50
TS Tim Salmon/350	25.00	7.50

2003 SP Authentic Chirography Bronze

Randomly inserted into packs, this is a partial parallel to the Chirography insert set. A few of these cards have special notations and we have noted that information in our checklist. Again, a few cards were issued as exchange cards and those cards could be redeemed until May 21, 2006.

	Nm-Mt	Ex-Mt
AD Adam Dunn/50	50.00	15.00
BA Jeff Bagwell/50	100.00	30.00
CR Cal Ripken/75	200.00	60.00
FC Rafael Furcal/50	30.00	9.00
FG Freddy Garcia/100	25.00	7.50
FL Cliff Floyd/50	25.00	7.50
GI Jason Giambi/50	80.00	24.00
GJ Ken Griffey Jr./100 EXCH	120.00	36.00
GL Brian Giles/50	25.00	7.50
IC Ichiro Suzuki ROY/50	500.00	150.00
IS Ichiro Suzuki MVP/50	500.00	150.00
JD Johnny Damon/100	25.00	7.50
JM Joe Mays/100	15.00	4.50
JR Ken Griffey Jr./100 EXCH	120.00	36.00
KE Jason Kendall/50	30.00	9.00
MM Mark McGwire/25		
RO Scott Rolen/100	60.00	18.00
RS Richie Sexson	25.00	7.50
Milwaukee Notation/100		
SA Sammy Sosa/100 EXCH	150.00	45.00
SO Sammy Sosa/100 EXCH	150.00	45.00
SW Mike Sweeney/75 EXCH	30.00	9.00
TO Torii Hunter/100 Gold Glove Notation	25.00	7.50

2003 SP Authentic Chirography Silver

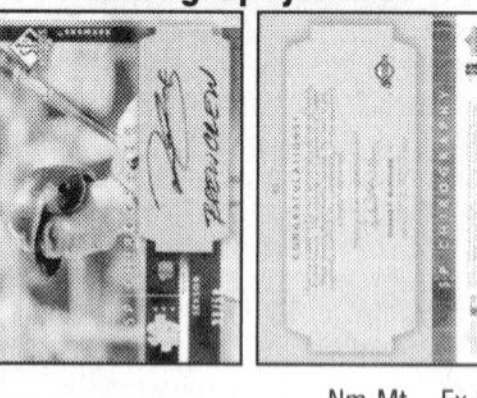

	Nm-Mt	Ex-Mt
AD Adam Dunn/25		
BA Jeff Bagwell/25		
CR Cal Ripken/25		
FC Rafael Furcal/25		
FG Freddy Garcia/50	40.00	12.00
FL Cliff Floyd/25		
GI Jason Giambi/25		
GJ Ken Griffey Jr./25 EXCH		
GL Brian Giles/25		
IC Ichiro Suzuki/25		
IS Ichiro Suzuki/25		
JD Johnny Damon/50	40.00	12.00
JM Joe Mays/50	25.00	7.50
JR Ken Griffey Jr./25 EXCH		
KE Jason Kendall/25		
MM Mark McGwire/15		
RO Scott Rolen/50	100.00	30.00
RS Richie Sexson/50	40.00	12.00
SA Sammy Sosa/50 EXCH	200.00	60.00
SO Sammy Sosa/50 EXCH	200.00	60.00
SW Mike Sweeney/25 EXCH		
TO Torii Hunter/50	40.00	12.00

2003 SP Authentic Chirography Dodgers Stars

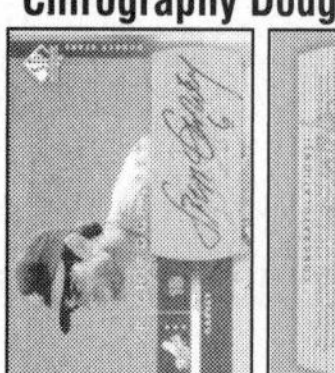

Randomly inserted into packs, these 11 cards feature retired Dodger stars and were issued to varying print runs. We have noted the stated print run in our checklist next to the player's name.

	Nm-Mt	Ex-Mt
BB Bill Buckner/245	15.00	4.50
BI Bill Russell/245	15.00	4.50
CE Ron Cey/345	15.00	4.50
DL Davey Lopes/245	15.00	4.50
DN Don Newcombe/345	15.00	4.50
DS Duke Snider/345	40.00	12.00
JN Tommy John/170	15.00	4.50
MW Maury Wills/320	15.00	4.50
SG Steve Garvey/320	25.00	7.50
SU Don Sutton/245	15.00	4.50
SY Steve Yeager/345	15.00	4.50

2003 SP Authentic Chirography Dodgers Stars Bronze

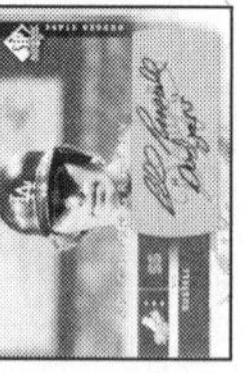

Randomly inserted into packs, this is a partial parallel to the Dodgers Stars insert set. Please note that all of these cards have the word "Dodgers" as an inscription.

	Nm-Mt	Ex-Mt
*BRONZE: .6X TO 1.5X BASIC DODGER		

2003 SP Authentic Chirography Dodgers Stars Silver

Randomly inserted into packs, this is a partial parallel to the Dodgers Stars insert set. Each of these cards were issued to a stated print run of 50 serial numbered sets and most of these cards had a 1981 WS Champs Notation. Please note that the player's who signed cards for this set and were not on the 81 Dodgers used different notations which we have identified in our checklist.

	Nm-Mt	Ex-Mt
*SILVER: .75X TO 2X BASIC DODGER		

2003 SP Authentic Chirography Doubles

Randomly inserted into packs, these 15 cards feature signatures from two different players, who had a reason for commonality. These cards were issued to a stated print run of anywhere from 10 to 150 copies and we have placed that information next to the player's name in our checklist. Please note that cards with a stated print run of 25 or fewer are not priced due to market scarcity. In addition, a few cards were issued as exchange cards and those cards could be redeemed until May 21, 2006.

	Nm-Mt	Ex-Mt
FB Whitey Ford Yogi Berra/75	150.00	45.00
FE Carlton Fisk Dwight Evans/75	80.00	24.00
FM Carlton Fisk Bill Mazeroski/75	60.00	18.00
GG Ken Griffey Jr. Jason Giambi/75 EXCH	150.00	45.00
GR Steve Garvey Ron Cey/75	60.00	18.00
JI Ken Griffey Jr. Ichiro Suzuki/125 EXCH	500.00	150.00
KR Tony Kubek Bobby Richardson/75	100.00	30.00
KT Jerry Koosman Tom Seaver/75	80.00	24.00
MG Don Mattingly Jason Giambi/25		
MJ Mark McGwire Ken Griffey Jr./10		
MS Mark McGwire Sammy Sosa/15 EXCH		
RT Nolan Ryan Tom Seaver/25		
SE Tim Salmon Darin Erstad/25		
SJ Sammy Sosa Jason Giambi/75 EXCH	200.00	60.00
WB Mookie Wilson Bill Buckner/150	50.00	15.00

2003 SP Authentic Chirography Flashback

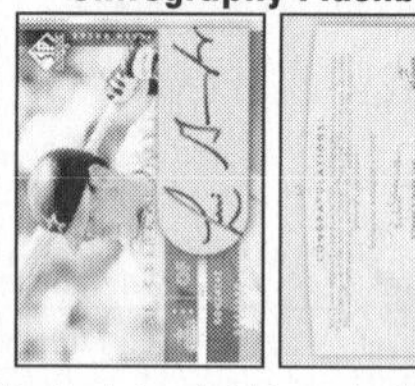

Randomly inserted into packs, these cards feature an important moment from the player's career as well as authentic autograph. Most of these cards were issued to a stated print run of 350 copies but a few were issued to differing amounts so we have noted the print run information next to the player's name in our checklist. In addition, some players did not return their autograph in time and those cards could be exchanged until May 21, 2006.

	Nm-Mt	Ex-Mt
BN Brian Giles/245	15.00	4.50
CF1 Cliff Floyd/350	15.00	4.50
GM Ken Griffey Jr./350 EXCH	120.00	36.00
JA Jason Giambi/350	40.00	12.00
JE1 Jim Edmonds/350	15.00	4.50
LA Luis Gonzalez/200	20.00	6.00
MA Mark McGwire/55	300.00	90.00
SR Sammy Sosa/245 EXCH	150.00	45.00

2003 SP Authentic Chirography Flashback Bronze

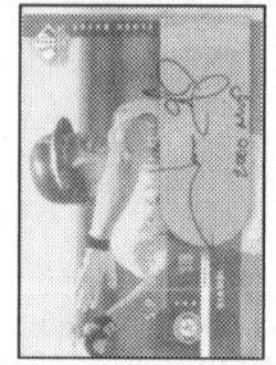

Randomly inserted in packs, this is a partial parallel to the Flashback insert set. All of the cards live at the time of issue had special notations and we have noted those notations in our checklist. These cards were issued to varying print runs and we have identified the stated print runs in our checklist. Ken Griffey Jr and Sammy Sosa did not return their autographs in time for inclusion and those exchange cards could be redeemed until May 21, 2006.

	Nm-Mt	Ex-Mt
BN Brian Giles/50	25.00	7.50
GM Ken Griffey Jr./100 EXCH	120.00	36.00
JA Jason Giambi 2000 MVP/100	60.00	18.00
LA Luis Gonzalez 2001 Champs/75	30.00	9.00
MA Mark McGwire 500 HR Club/25		
SR Sammy Sosa/100 EXCH	150.00	45.00

2003 SP Authentic Chirography Flashback Silver

Randomly inserted into packs, this is a partial parallel to the Flashback insert set. These cards were issued to stated print runs of between 15 and 50 copies and for those copies with stated print runs fo 25 or fewer, no pricing is provided due to market scarcity.

	Nm-Mt	Ex-Mt
BN Brian Giles/25		
GM Ken Griffey Jr./25 EXCH		
JA0 Jason Giambi A's/50	80.00	24.00
LA Luis Gonzalez 25		
MA Mark McGwire/15		
SR Sammy Sosa/50 EXCH	200.00	60.00

2003 SP Authentic Chirography Hall of Famers

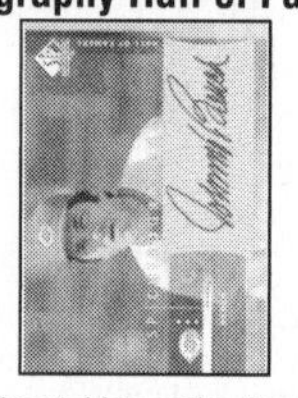

Randomly inserted into packs, these 14 cards feature autographs of Hall of Famers. Since these cards were issued to varying print runs, we have identified the stated print run next to the player's name in our checklist.

	Nm-Mt	Ex-Mt
BG Bob Gibson/245	40.00	12.00
CF Carlton Fisk/240	40.00	12.00
DS Duke Snider/250	40.00	12.00
DW2 Dave Winfield/350	25.00	7.50
GC1 Gary Carter/350	25.00	7.50
JB1 Johnny Bench/350	50.00	15.00
NR Nolan Ryan/170	150.00	45.00
OC Orlando Cepeda/245	25.00	7.50
RF Rollie Fingers/170	25.00	7.50
RR Robin Roberts/170	40.00	12.00
RY Robin Yount/350	50.00	15.00
TP Tony Perez/320	25.00	7.50
TS Tom Seaver/170	40.00	12.00
WF Whitey Ford/150	40.00	12.00

2003 SP Authentic Chirography Hall of Famers Bronze

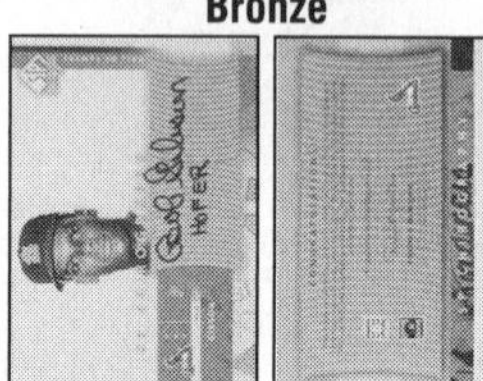

Randomly inserted into packs, this is a partial parallel to the Hall of Famers insert set. These cards all feature an HOF (or some close variation) notation as part of the autograph. These cards were issued to stated print runs between 50 and 100 copies and we have noted the specific information next to the player's name in our checklist.

	Nm-Mt	Ex-Mt
BG Bob Gibson/100	60.00	18.00
CF Carlton Fisk/100	60.00	18.00
DS Duke Snider/100	60.00	18.00
NR Nolan Ryan/50	200.00	60.00
OC Orlando Cepeda/100	40.00	12.00
RF Rollie Fingers/50	40.00	12.00
RR Robin Roberts/50	60.00	18.00
TP Tony Perez/100	40.00	12.00
TS Tom Seaver/75	60.00	18.00
WF Whitey Ford/75	60.00	18.00

2003 SP Authentic Chirography Hall of Famers Silver

Randomly inserted into packs, this is a partial parallel to the Hall of Famers insert set. All of these cards have the HOF (and specific year of the player's induction) notation. These cards were issued to a stated print run of either 25 or 50 copies. Please note that for cards with stated print run of 25 copies there is no pricing due to market scarcity.

	Nm-Mt	Ex-Mt
BG Bob Gibson/50	80.00	24.00
CF Carlton Fisk/50	80.00	24.00
DS Duke Snider/50	80.00	24.00
NR Nolan Ryan/25		
OC Orlando Cepeda/50	50.00	15.00
RF Rollie Fingers/25		
RR Robin Roberts/25		
TP Tony Perez/50	50.00	15.00
TS Tom Seaver/50	80.00	24.00
WF Whitey Ford/25		

2003 SP Authentic Chirography Triples

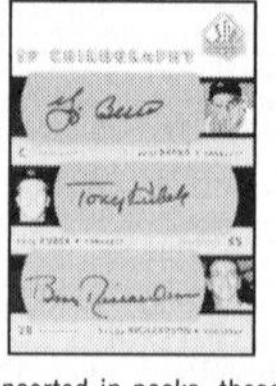

Randomly inserted in packs, these 12 cards feature autographs from three leading players. These cards were issued to stated print runs of anywhere from 10 to 75 copies and we are only providing pricing for cards with a stated print run of more than 10 copies. The following cards were available only as an exchange and those cards could be redeemed until May 21 2006: Berra/Kubek/Richardson Fisk/Carter/Gibson, Griffey Jr./Ichiro/Sosa Griffey Jr./Sosa/Giambi, Giambi/Sosa/Griffey Jr., Ichiro/Sosa/Giambi, McGwire/Sosa/Griffey Jr., McGwire/Sosa/Ichiro and Seaver/Koosman/McGraw.

	Nm-Mt	Ex-Mt
BKR Yogi Berra Tony Kubek Bobby Richardson/75	200.00	60.00
FCG Carlton Fisk Gary Carter Kirk Gibson/75 EXCH	120.00	36.00
GIS Ken Griffey Jr. Ichiro Suzuki Sammy Sosa/75 EXCH	600.00	180.00
GLC Steve Garvey Davy Lopes Ron Cey/75	100.00	30.00
GRC Steve Garvey Bill Russell Ron Cey/75	100.00	30.00
GSG Ken Griffey Jr. Sammy Sosa Jason Giambi/75 EXCH	300.00	90.00
GSJ Jason Giambi Sammy Sosa Ken Griffey Jr./75	300.00	90.00
ISG Ichiro Suzuki Sammy Sosa Jason Giambi/75	500.00	150.00
MSG Mark McGwire Sammy Sosa Ken Griffey Jr./10		
MSI Mark McGwire Sammy Sosa Ichiro Suzuki/10		
SEA Tim Salmon Darin Erstad Garret Anderson/75	120.00	36.00
SKM Tom Seaver Jerry Koosman Tug McGraw/75 EXCH		

2003 SP Authentic Chirography World Series Heroes

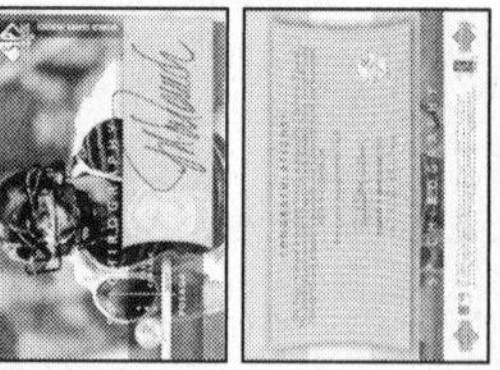

Randomly inserted into packs, these 17 cards feature players who were leading players in at least one World Series. Each of these cards were issued to varying print runs and we have identified the stated print run next to the player's name in our checklist. Andruw Jones did not return his cards in time for inclusion in this product so those exchange cards could be redeemed until May 21, 2006.

	Nm-Mt	Ex-Mt
AJ1 Andruw Jones/350 EXCH	40.00	12.00
BM Bill Mazeroski/245	25.00	7.50
CF Carlton Fisk/200	40.00	12.00
CR Cal Ripken/295	120.00	36.00
CS Curt Schilling/345	40.00	12.00
DE Darin Erstad/245	20.00	6.00
DJ David Justice/170	25.00	7.50
ER Edgar Renteria/220	20.00	6.00
GA Garret Anderson/245	25.00	7.50
GC Gary Carter/345	25.00	7.50
GO Luis Gonzalez/225	20.00	6.00
GS Ken Griffey Sr./295	20.00	6.00
JK Jerry Koosman/170	25.00	7.50
JP Jorge Posada/350	40.00	12.00
KG Kirk Gibson/145	25.00	7.50
TI Tim Salmon/245	25.00	7.50
TM Tug McGraw/170	50.00	15.00

2003 SP Authentic Chirography World Series Heroes Bronze

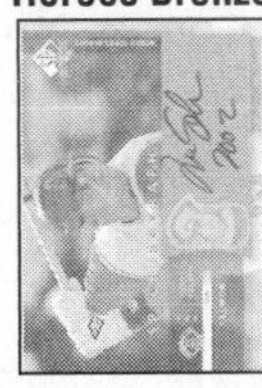

Randomly inserted into packs, this is a partial parallel to the World Series Heroes insert set. Each of these cards have not only an autograph but a notation identifying a key world series this player's career. Each of these cards were issued to a stated print run of between 50 and 100 copies.

	Nm-Mt	Ex-Mt
BM Bill Mazeroski/100	40.00	12.00
CF Carlton Fisk/75	60.00	18.00
CS Curt Schilling/100	60.00	18.00
DE Darin Erstad/100	30.00	9.00
DJ David Justice/75 EXCH	40.00	12.00
ER Edgar Renteria/75	30.00	9.00
GA Garret Anderson/100	40.00	12.00
GC Gary Carter/100	40.00	12.00
GO Luis Gonzalez/100	30.00	9.00
GS Ken Griffey Sr./100	30.00	9.00
JK Jerry Koosman/75	40.00	12.00
KG Kirk Gibson/50	40.00	12.00
TI Tim Salmon/100	40.00	12.00
TM Tug McGraw/100	80.00	24.00

2003 SP Authentic Chirography World Series Heroes Silver

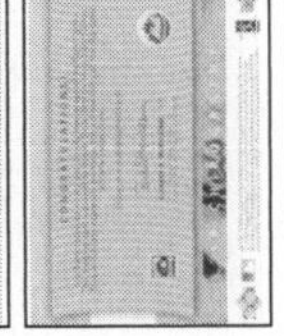

Randomly inserted into packs, this is a partial parallel to the World Series Heroes insert set. These cards feature not only the player's autograph but also in most cases a notation which we have identified in our checklist. Please note that these cards have stated print runs of either 25 or 50 cards. Cards with stated print runs of 25 are not printed due to market scarcity. Of note, Tug McGraw's card, inscribed "Ya Gotta Believe" took on a much deeper meaning after his unfortunate death less than a year after the card was issued.

	Nm-Mt	Ex-Mt
BM Bill Mazeroski Buc's 60/50	50.00	15.00
CF Carlton Fisk Home Run/25		
CS Curt Schilling/50	80.00	24.00
DE Darin Erstad/50	40.00	12.00
DJ David Justice/50	50.00	15.00
ER Edgar Renteria Marlins 97/25		
GA Garret Anderson/50	50.00	15.00
GC Gary Carter Mets Champs/50	50.00	15.00
GO Luis Gonzalez D-Backs 01/50	40.00	12.00
GS Ken Griffey Sr. Big Red Machine/50	40.00	12.00
JK Jerry Koosman/50	50.00	15.00
KG Kirk Gibson Home Run/25		
TI Tim Salmon 2002 Champs/50	50.00	15.00
TM Tug McGraw Ya Gotta Believe/50	100.00	30.00

2003 SP Authentic Chirography Yankees Stars

Randomly inserted into packs, these 14 cards feature not only Yankee stars of the past and present but also authentic autographs of the featured players. Since these cards were issued to varying print runs, we have identified the stated print run next to the player's name in our checklist.

	Nm-Mt	Ex-Mt
BR Bobby Richardson/320	25.00	7.50
DM Don Mattingly/295	60.00	18.00
DW1 Dave Winfield/350	25.00	7.50
HK Ralph Houk/245	15.00	4.50
JB Jim Bouton/345	15.00	4.50
JG Jason Giambi/275	50.00	15.00
KS Ken Griffey Sr./350	15.00	4.50
RC Roger Clemens/210	150.00	45.00
SL Sparky Lyle/350	15.00	4.50
ST Mel Stottlemyre/345	15.00	4.50
TH Tommy Henrich/345	15.00	4.50
TJ Tommy John/245	15.00	4.50
TK Tony Kubek/345	25.00	7.50
YB Yogi Berra/320	40.00	12.00

2003 SP Authentic Chirography Yankees Stars Bronze

Randomly inserted into packs, this is a partial parallel to the Yankee Stars insert set. Most of these cards were issued to a stated print run of 100 copies and most have an "Yankees" inscription. Please note that for the few players who did not put an Yankees inscription we put a NO next to the player's name. In addition, since a few cards have a print run of fewer than 100 copies we have noted all print runs in our checklist.

	Nm-Mt	Ex-Mt
BR Bobby Richardson/100	40.00	12.00
DM Don Mattingly NO/100	100.00	30.00
HK Ralph Houk/100	25.00	7.50
JB Jim Bouton/100	25.00	7.50
JG Jason Giambi/60	80.00	24.00
KS Ken Griffey Sr./100	25.00	7.50
RC Roger Clemens NO/75	200.00	60.00
SL Sparky Lyle/100	25.00	7.50
ST Mel Stottlemyre/100	25.00	7.50
TH Tommy Henrich/100	25.00	7.50
TJ Tommy John/100	25.00	7.50
TK Tony Kubek/100	40.00	12.00
YB Yogi Berra NO/100	60.00	18.00

2003 SP Authentic Chirography Yankees Stars Silver

Randomly inserted into packs, this is a partial parallel to the Yankee Stars insert set. Each of these cards were issued to a stated print run of either 25 or 50 copies and we have noted that information in our checklist. Since there is a mix in this set about cards with notations, what the notations are -- we have put the notation information, when it exists, in our checklist.

	Nm-Mt	Ex-Mt
BR Bobby Richardson New York/50	50.00	15.00
DM Don Mattingly/50	120.00	36.00
HK Ralph Houk New York/50	30.00	9.00
JB Jim Bouton New York/50	30.00	9.00
JG Jason Giambi/25		
KS Ken Griffey Sr./25		
RC Roger Clemens/50	200.00	60.00
SL Sparky Lyle/50	30.00	9.00
ST Mel Stottlemyre/50	30.00	9.00
TH Tommy Henrich Yankees/50	30.00	9.00
TJ Tommy John/50	30.00	9.00
TK Tony Kubek New York/50	50.00	15.00
YB Yogi Berra/75	80.00	24.00

2003 SP Authentic Chirography Young Stars

Randomly inserted into packs, these 25 cards feature autographs of some of the leading young stars in baseball. These cards were issued to stated print runs of between 150 and 350 cards and we have notated that information in our checklist. Please note that Hee Seop Choi did not return his autographs in time for pack out and those exchange cards could be redeemed until May 21, 2006.

	Nm-Mt	Ex-Mt
AP A.J. Pierzynski/245	15.00	4.50
BO Joe Borchard/245	15.00	4.50
BP1 Brandon Phillips/350	10.00	3.00
BZ Barry Zito/350	40.00	12.00
CP Corey Patterson/245	25.00	7.50
DH Drew Henson/245	25.00	7.50
DI1 Ben Diggins/350	10.00	3.00
EH Eric Hinske/245	10.00	3.00
FS Freddy Sanchez/350	10.00	3.00
HB Hank Blalock/245	25.00	7.50
HC Hee Seop Choi/245 EXCH	60.00	18.00
JJ Jacque Jones/245	15.00	4.50
JJ1 Jimmy Journell/350	10.00	3.00
JL Jason Lane/245	10.00	3.00
JP Josh Phelps/245	10.00	3.00
JS Jayson Werth/350	10.00	3.00
MB Marlon Byrd/245	15.00	4.50
MI Doug Mientkiewicz/245	15.00	4.50
MP Mark Prior/150	80.00	24.00
MY Brett Myers/245	15.00	4.50
OH Orlando Hudson/245	10.00	3.00
OP Oliver Perez/245	10.00	3.00
PE Carlos Pena/245	10.00	3.00
SB Sean Burroughs/245	15.00	4.50
TX Mark Teixeira/245	25.00	7.50

2003 SP Authentic Chirography Young Stars Bronze

Randomly inserted into packs, this is a partial parallel to the Young Stars insert set. Please note that most of these cards (with the exception of the Mark Prior card) were issued to a stated print run of 100 serial numbered sets and most of these cards had a notation of what city the player was playing in at the time of issue for this set. We have put the city information when applicable in our checklist.

Nm-Mt Ex-Mt

*BRONZE: .6X TO 1.5X BASIC YS

2003 SP Authentic Chirography Young Stars Silver

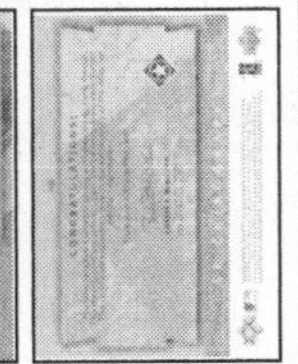

Randomly inserted into packs, this is a partial parallel to the Young Stars insert set. Most of these cards have a team notation and we have put that information next to tha players name in our checklist. Please note that most of these cards, with the exception of Mark Prior was issued to a stated print run of 50 serial numbered sets. The Prior card was issued to a stated print run of 25 serial numbered sets and there is no pricing due to market scarcity on that card.

Nm-Mt Ex-Mt

*SILVER: .75X TO 2X BASIC YS

2003 SP Authentic Simply Splendid

	Nm-Mt	Ex-Mt
COMMON CARD (TW1-TW30)	10.00	3.00

RANDOM INSERTS IN PACKS
STATED PRINT RUN 406 SERIAL #'d SETS

2003 SP Authentic Splendid Jerseys

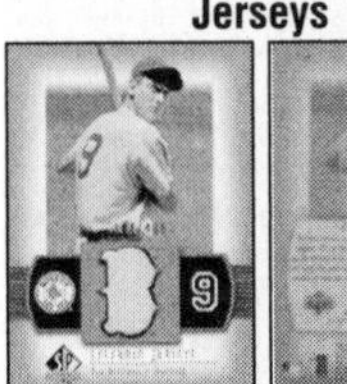

	Nm-Mt	Ex-Mt

RANDOM INSERTS IN PACKS
STATED PRINT RUN 406 SERIAL #'d SETS

SJTW Ted Williams	100.00	30.00

2003 SP Authentic Splendid Signatures

Randomly inserted in packs, these two cards feature autographs of current Red Sox star Nomar Garciaparra and retired Red Sox legend Ted Williams. Please note, that since these cards were issued after Williams passed on, that the Williams autographs are "cuts" while the Nomar autographs were signed for this product. Since the Williams card was issued to a stated print run of five serial numbered copies, no pricing is available for that card.

	Nm-Mt	Ex-Mt
GA Nomar Garciaparra/406	150.00	45.00
TWSIG Ted Williams/5		

2003 SP Authentic Splendid Signatures Pairs

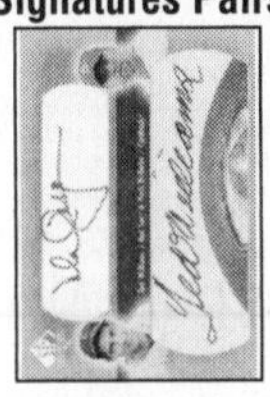

Randomly inserted into packs, these six cards feature a Ted Williams autograph "cut" to go with an autograph of an modern star. Each of these cards were issued to a stated print run of 3 serial numbered copies and no pricing is available due to market scarcity. Of note, all three copies of the Ken Griffey Jr./Ted Williams combo signature actually packed erroneously featuring Ken Griffey Sr. signatures. It's been verified that at least one of the three copies was returned to Upper Deck by a dealer and a Griffey Jr. signature was switched out.

	Nm-Mt	Ex-Mt
IS2 Ted Williams Ichiro Suzuki		
JG2 Ted Williams Jason Giambi		
KG2 Ted Williams Ken Griffey Jr.		
MM2 Ted Williams Mark McGwire		
NM3 Ted Williams Nomar Garciaparra		
SS2 Ted Williams Sammy Sosa		

2003 SP Authentic Splendid Swatches Pairs

Randomly inserted into packs, these nine cards feature a game-worn jersey swatch of retired Red Sox legend Ted Williams along with a game-used jersey swatch of another star. Each of the these cards were issued to a stated print run of 406 serial numbered sets. The two Williams/Nomar cards were not ready for pack-out and those were issued as a exchange cards with a redemption date of May 21, 2006.

	Nm-Mt	Ex-Mt
IS Ted Williams Ichiro Suzuki	100.00	30.00
JG Ted Williams Jason Giambi	60.00	18.00
KG Ted Williams Ken Griffey Jr.	100.00	30.00
MM Ted Williams Mark McGwire	120.00	36.00
NM1 Ted Williams Nomar Garciaparra EXCH	100.00	30.00
NM2 Ted Williams Nomar Garciaparra EXCH	120.00	36.00
SS Ted Williams Sammy Sosa	100.00	30.00
TW Ted Williams Mickey Mantle	200.00	60.00

2003 SP Authentic Superstar Flashback

Nm-Mt Ex-Mt

RANDOM INSERTS IN PACKS
STATED PRINT RUN 2003 SERIAL #'d SETS

	Nm-Mt	Ex-Mt
SF1 Tim Salmon	3.00	.90
SF2 Darin Erstad	3.00	.90
SF3 Troy Glaus	3.00	.90
SF4 Randy Johnson	3.00	.90
SF5 Curt Schilling	3.00	.90
SF6 Steve Finley	3.00	.90
SF7 Greg Maddux	5.00	1.50
SF8 Chipper Jones	3.00	.90
SF9 Andruw Jones	3.00	.90
SF10 Gary Sheffield	3.00	.90
SF11 Manny Ramirez	3.00	.90
SF12 Pedro Martinez	3.00	.90
SF13 Nomar Garciaparra	5.00	1.50
SF14 Sammy Sosa	5.00	1.50
SF15 Frank Thomas	3.00	.90
SF16 Kerry Wood	3.00	.90
SF17 Paul Konerko	3.00	.90
SF18 Corey Patterson	3.00	.90
SF19 Mark Prior	6.00	1.80
SF20 Ken Griffey Jr.	5.00	1.50
SF21 Adam Dunn	3.00	.90
SF22 Larry Walker	3.00	.90
SF23 Preston Wilson	3.00	.90
SF24 Todd Helton	3.00	.90
SF25 Ivan Rodriguez	3.00	.90
SF26 Josh Beckett	3.00	.90
SF27 Jeff Bagwell	3.00	.90
SF28 Jeff Kent	3.00	.90
SF29 Lance Berkman	3.00	.90
SF30 Carlos Beltran	3.00	.90
SF31 Shawn Green	3.00	.90
SF32 Richie Sexson	3.00	.90
SF33 Vladimir Guerrero	3.00	.90
SF34 Mike Piazza	5.00	1.50
SF35 Roberto Alomar	3.00	.90
SF36 Roger Clemens	6.00	1.80
SF37 Derek Jeter	8.00	2.40
SF38 Jason Giambi	3.00	.90
SF39 Bernie Williams	3.00	.90
SF40 Nick Johnson	3.00	.90
SF41 Alfonso Soriano	3.00	.90
SF42 Miguel Tejada	3.00	.90
SF43 Eric Chavez	3.00	.90
SF44 Barry Zito	3.00	.90
SF45 Jim Thome	3.00	.90
SF46 Pat Burrell	3.00	.90
SF47 Marlon Byrd	3.00	.90
SF48 Jason Kendall	3.00	.90
SF49 Aramis Ramirez	3.00	.90
SF50 Brian Giles	3.00	.90
SF51 Phil Nevin	3.00	.90
SF52 Barry Bonds	8.00	2.40
SF53 Ichiro Suzuki	5.00	1.50
SF54 Scott Rolen	3.00	.90
SF55 J.D. Drew	3.00	.90
SF56 Albert Pujols	6.00	1.80
SF57 Mark Teixeira	3.00	.90
SF58 Hank Blalock	3.00	.90
SF59 Carlos Delgado	3.00	.90
SF60 Roy Halladay	3.00	.90

1995 SP Championship

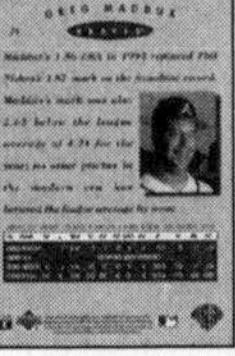

This set contains 200 cards that were sold in six-card retail packs for a suggested price of $2.99. The fronts have a full-bleed action photo with the words "SP Championship Series" in gold-foil in the bottom left-hand corner. In the bottom right-hand corner is the team's name in blue (National League) and red (American League) foil. The backs have a small head shot and player information. Statistics and team name are also on the back in blue or red just like on the front. Subsets featured are Diamonds in the Rough (1-20), October Legends (100-114) and Major League Profiles. Rookie Cards in this set include Bobby Higginson and Hideo Nomo. In addition, two special "one-shot" Cal Ripken cards (a basic design and a scarcer parallel die cut version) were randomly seeded into packs to commemorate his consecutive games streak record.

	Nm-Mt	Ex-Mt
COMPLETE SET (200)	40.00	12.00
1 Hideo Nomo RC	2.00	.60
2 Roger Cedeno	.20	.06
3 Curtis Goodwin	.20	.06
4 Jon Nunnally	.20	.06
5 Bill Pulsipher	.20	.06
6 Garret Anderson	.40	.12
7 Dustin Hermanson	.20	.06
8 Marty Cordova	.20	.06
9 Ruben Rivera	.20	.06
10 Ariel Prieto RC	.20	.06
11 Edgardo Alfonzo	.40	.12
12 Ray Durham	.40	.12
13 Quilvio Veras	.20	.06
14 Ugueth Urbina	.20	.06
15 Carlos Perez RC	.40	.12
16 Glenn Dishman RC	.20	.06
17 Jeff Suppan	.20	.06
18 Jason Bates	.20	.06
19 Jason Isringhausen	.40	.12
20 Derek Jeter	2.50	.75
21 Fred McGriff MLP	.40	.12
22 Marquis Grissom	.20	.06
23 Fred McGriff	.60	.18
24 Tom Glavine	.60	.18
25 Greg Maddux	1.50	.45
26 Chipper Jones	1.00	.30
27 Sammy Sosa MLP	1.00	.30
28 Randy Myers	.20	.06
29 Mark Grace	.60	.18
30 Sammy Sosa	1.50	.45
31 Todd Zeile	.20	.06
32 Brian McRae	.20	.06
33 Ron Gant MLP	.20	.06
34 Reggie Sanders	.40	.12
35 Ron Gant	.40	.12
36 Barry Larkin	1.00	.30
37 Bret Boone	.40	.12
38 John Smiley	.20	.06
39 Larry Walker MLP	.20	.06
40 Andres Galarraga	.40	.12
41 Bill Swift	.20	.06
42 Larry Walker	.60	.18
43 Vinny Castilla	.40	.12
44 Dante Bichette	.40	.12
45 Jeff Conine MLP	.20	.06
46 Charles Johnson	.40	.12

1995 SP Championship

47 Gary Sheffield .40 .12
48 Andre Dawson .40 .12
49 Jeff Conine .40 .12
50 Jeff Bagwell MLP .40 .12
51 Phil Nevin .40 .12
52 Craig Biggio .60 .18
53 Brian L. Hunter .20 .06
54 Doug Drabek .20 .06
55 Jeff Bagwell .60 .18
56 Derek Bell .20 .06
57 Mike Piazza MLP 1.00 .30
58 Raul Mondesi .40 .12
59 Eric Karros .40 .12
60 Mike Piazza 1.50 .45
61 Ramon Martinez .20 .06
62 Billy Ashley .20 .06
63 Rondell White MLP .20 .06
64 Jeff Fassero .20 .06
65 Moises Alou .40 .12
66 Tony Tarasco .20 .06
67 Rondell White .40 .12
68 Pedro Martinez 1.00 .30
69 Bobby Jones MLP .20 .06
70 Bobby Bonilla .40 .12
71 Bobby Jones .20 .06
72 Bret Saberhagen .40 .12
73 Darren Daulton MLP .20 .06
74 Darren Daulton .40 .12
75 Gregg Jefferies .20 .06
76 Tyler Green .20 .06
77 Heathcliff Slocumb .20 .06
78 Lenny Dykstra .40 .12
79 Jay Bell MLP .40 .12
80 Denny Neagle .40 .12
81 Orlando Merced .20 .06
82 Jay Bell .40 .12
83 Ozzie Smith MLP 1.00 .30
84 Ken Hill .20 .06
85 Ozzie Smith 1.50 .45
86 Bernard Gilkey .20 .06
87 Ray Lankford .20 .06
88 Tony Gwynn MLP .60 .18
89 Ken Caminiti .40 .12
90 Tony Gwynn 1.25 .35
91 Joey Hamilton .20 .06
92 Bip Roberts .20 .06
93 Deion Sanders MLP .40 .12
94 Glenallen Hill .20 .06
95 Matt Williams .40 .12
96 Barry Bonds 2.50 .75
97 Rod Beck .20 .06
98 Eddie Murray CL .60 .18
99 Cal Ripken Jr. CL 1.50 .45
100 Roberto Alomar OL .40 .12
101 George Brett OL 2.50 .75
102 Joe Carter OL .20 .06
103 Will Clark OL .40 .12
104 Dennis Eckersley OL .40 .12
105 Whitey Ford OL .60 .18
106 Steve Garvey OL .20 .06
107 Kirk Gibson OL .20 .06
108 Orel Hershiser OL .20 .06
109 Reggie Jackson OL .60 .18
110 Paul Molitor OL .40 .12
111 Kirby Puckett OL .60 .18
112 Mike Schmidt OL 1.50 .45
113 Dave Stewart OL .20 .06
114 Alan Trammell OL .40 .12
115 Cal Ripken Jr. MLP 1.50 .45
116 Brady Anderson .40 .12
117 Mike Mussina 1.00 .30
118 Rafael Palmeiro .60 .18
119 Chris Hoiles .20 .06
120 Cal Ripken 3.00 .90
121 Mo Vaughn MLP .20 .06
122 Roger Clemens 2.00 .60
123 Tim Naehring .20 .06
124 John Valentin .20 .06
125 Mo Vaughn .40 .12
126 Tim Wakefield .40 .12
127 Jose Canseco 1.00 .30
128 Rick Aguilera .20 .06
129 Chili Davis MLP .20 .06
130 Lee Smith .40 .12
131 Jim Edmonds .40 .12
132 Chuck Finley .40 .12
133 Chili Davis .40 .12
134 J.T. Snow .40 .12
135 Tim Salmon .60 .18
136 Frank Thomas MLP .60 .18
137 Jason Bere .20 .06
138 Robin Ventura .40 .12
139 Tim Raines .40 .12
140 Frank Thomas 1.00 .30
141 Alex Fernandez .20 .06
142 Eddie Murray MLP .60 .18
143 Carlos Baerga .20 .06
144 Eddie Murray 1.00 .30
145 Albert Belle .40 .12
146 Jim Thome 1.00 .30
147 Dennis Martinez .40 .12
148 Dave Winfield .40 .12
149 Kenny Lofton .40 .12
150 Manny Ramirez .40 .12
151 Cecil Fielder MLP .20 .06
152 Lou Whitaker .40 .12
153 Alan Trammell .60 .18
154 Kirk Gibson .40 .12
155 Cecil Fielder .40 .12
156 Bobby Higginson RC 1.00 .30
157 Kevin Appier MLP .20 .06
158 Wally Joyner .40 .12
159 Jeff Montgomery .20 .06
160 Kevin Appier .40 .12
161 Gary Gaetti .40 .12
162 Greg Gagne .20 .06
163 Ricky Bones MLP .20 .06
164 Greg Vaughn .40 .12
165 Kevin Seitzer .20 .06
166 Ricky Bones .20 .06
167 Kirby Puckett MLP .60 .18
168 Pedro Munoz .20 .06
169 Chuck Knoblauch .40 .12
170 Kirby Puckett 1.00 .30
171 Don Mattingly MLP 1.25 .35
172 Wade Boggs .60 .18
173 Paul O'Neill .60 .18
174 John Wetteland .40 .12
175 Don Mattingly 2.50 .75
176 Jack McDowell .20 .06
177 Mark McGwire MLP 1.25 .35
178 Rickey Henderson 1.00 .30
179 Terry Steinbach .20 .06
180 Ruben Sierra .20 .06
181 Mark McGwire 2.50 .75
182 Dennis Eckersley .40 .12
183 Ken Griffey Jr. MLP 1.00 .30
184 Alex Rodriguez 2.50 .75
185 Ken Griffey Jr. 1.50 .45
186 Randy Johnson 1.00 .30
187 Jay Buhner .40 .12
188 Edgar Martinez .60 .18
189 Will Clark MLP .40 .12
190 Juan Gonzalez 1.00 .30
191 Benji Gil .20 .06
192 Ivan Rodriguez 1.00 .30
193 Kenny Rogers .40 .12
194 Will Clark 1.00 .30
195 Paul Molitor MLP .40 .12
196 Roberto Alomar 1.00 .30
197 David Cone .40 .12
198 Paul Molitor .60 .18
199 Shawn Green .40 .12
200 Joe Carter .40 .12
CR1 Cal Ripken Jr. TRIB 10.00 3.00
CR1 C.Ripken 2131 DC 40.00 12.00

1995 SP Championship Die Cuts

This 200-card set parallels the regular SP Championship set and was inserted one per pack. The only difference between the sets is the die-cut bordered design.

Nm-Mt Ex-Mt
COMPLETE SET (200) 120.00 36.00
*STARS: 1X TO 2.5X BASIC CARDS ...
*ROOKIES: .75X TO 2X BASIC CARDS

1995 SP Championship Classic Performances

Cards from this 10-card set were randomly inserted in packs at a rate of one in 15. The set consists of 10 of the most memorable highlights since the 1969 Miracle Mets. The fronts have a series action photo highlighted with the words "Classic Performances" at the top in gold-foil enclosed by red. The backs have a color head shot with information and statistics from the series.

Nm-Mt Ex-Mt
COMPLETE SET (10) 40.00 12.00
*DIE CUTS: 2X TO 5X BASIC CARDS..
DC STATED ODDS 1:75
CP1 Reggie Jackson 3.00 .90
CP2 Nolan Ryan 20.00 6.00
CP3 Kirk Gibson 2.00 .60
CP4 Joe Carter 2.00 .60
CP5 George Brett 12.00 3.60
CP6 Roberto Alomar 5.00 1.50
CP7 Ozzie Smith 8.00 2.40
CP8 Kirby Puckett 5.00 1.50
CP9 Bret Saberhagen 2.00 .60
CP10 Steve Garvey 2.00 .60

1995 SP Championship Fall Classic

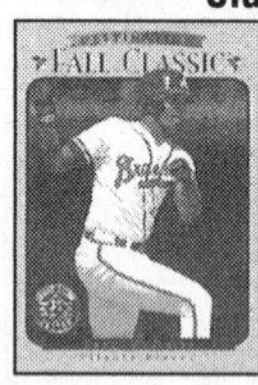
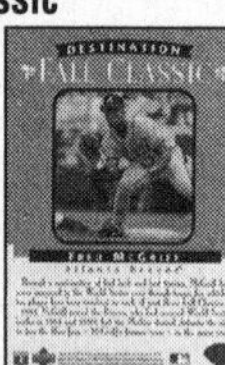

This nine-card set was randomly inserted in packs at a rate of one in 40. The set is comprised of players who had never been to the World Series prior to the 1995 Fall Classic. The fronts have a color-action photo with the game background in foil. There is a grain-colored border with the word "Destination" at the top in bronze-foil and "Fall Classic" underneath in black. The backs have a small, color picture inside a black box with player information underneath.

Nm-Mt Ex-Mt
COMPLETE SET (9) 100.00 30.00
*DIE CUTS: .6X TO 1.5X BASIC FALL CLASSIC
DC STATED ODDS 1:75
1 Ken Griffey Jr. 12.00 3.60
2 Frank Thomas 8.00 2.40
3 Albert Belle 3.00 .90
4 Mike Piazza 12.00 3.60
5 Don Mattingly 20.00 6.00
6 Hideo Nomo 15.00 4.50
7 Greg Maddux 12.00 3.60
8 Fred McGriff 5.00 1.50
9 Barry Bonds 20.00 6.00

2001 SP Game Bat Edition

The 2001 SP Game Bat Edition product was released in late December, 2000 and featured a 90-card base set. Each pack contained four cards and carried a suggested retail price of $19.99 per pack. Please note that each pack contained one game-used memorabilia card.

Nm-Mt Ex-Mt
COMPLETE SET (90) 50.00 15.00
1 Troy Glaus 1.50 .45
2 Darin Erstad 1.00 .30

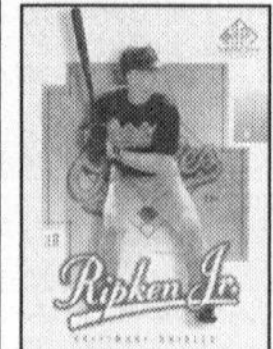
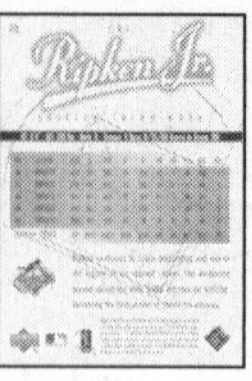

3 Mo Vaughn 1.00 .30
4 Jason Giambi 2.50 .75
5 Ben Grieve 1.00 .30
6 Eric Chavez 1.00 .30
7 Carlos Delgado 1.00 .30
8 Tony Batista 1.00 .30
9 Shannon Stewart 1.00 .30
10 Jose Cruz Jr. 1.00 .30
11 Fred McGriff 1.50 .45
12 Greg Vaughn 1.00 .30
13 Roberto Alomar 2.50 .75
14 Manny Ramirez 1.00 .30
15 Jim Thome 2.50 .75
16 Russell Branyan 1.00 .30
17 Alex Rodriguez 4.00 1.20
18 John Olerud 1.00 .30
19 Edgar Martinez 1.50 .45
20 Cal Ripken 8.00 2.40
21 Albert Belle 1.00 .30
22 Ivan Rodriguez 2.50 .75
23 Rafael Palmeiro 1.50 .45
24 Nomar Garciaparra 4.00 1.20
25 Carl Everett 1.00 .30
26 Dante Bichette 1.00 .30
27 Mike Sweeney 1.00 .30
28 Jermaine Dye 1.00 .30
29 Carlos Beltran 1.00 .30
30 Juan Gonzalez 2.50 .75
31 Dean Palmer 1.00 .30
32 Bobby Higginson 1.00 .30
33 Matt Lawton 1.00 .30
34 Jacque Jones 1.00 .30
35 Frank Thomas 2.50 .75
36 Magglio Ordonez 1.00 .30
37 Paul Konerko 1.00 .30
38 Carlos Lee 1.00 .30
39 Bernie Williams 1.50 .45
40 Derek Jeter 6.00 1.80
41 Paul O'Neill 1.50 .45
42 Jose Canseco 2.50 .75
43 Ken Caminiti 1.00 .30
44 Jeff Bagwell 1.50 .45
45 Craig Biggio 1.50 .45
46 Richard Hidalgo 1.00 .30
47 Andruw Jones 1.00 .30
48 Chipper Jones 2.50 .75
49 Andres Galarraga 1.00 .30
50 B.J. Surhoff 1.00 .30
51 Jeromy Burnitz 1.00 .30
52 Geoff Jenkins 1.00 .30
53 Richie Sexson 1.00 .30
54 Mark McGwire 6.00 1.80
55 Jim Edmonds 1.00 .30
56 J.D. Drew 1.00 .30
57 Fernando Tatis 1.00 .30
58 Sammy Sosa 4.00 1.20
59 Mark Grace 1.50 .45
60 Eric Young 1.00 .30
61 Matt Williams 1.00 .30
62 Luis Gonzalez 1.00 .30
63 Steve Finley 1.00 .30
64 Shawn Green 1.00 .30
65 Gary Sheffield 1.00 .30
66 Eric Karros 1.00 .30
67 Vladimir Guerrero 2.50 .75
68 Jose Vidro 1.00 .30
69 Barry Bonds 6.00 1.80
70 Jeff Kent 1.00 .30
71 Preston Wilson 1.00 .30
72 Mike Lowell 1.00 .30
73 Luis Castillo 1.00 .30
74 Mike Piazza 4.00 1.20
75 Robin Ventura 1.00 .30
76 Edgardo Alfonzo 1.00 .30
77 Tony Gwynn 3.00 .90
78 Eric Owens 1.00 .30
79 Ryan Klesko 1.00 .30
80 Scott Rolen 1.50 .45
81 Bobby Abreu 1.00 .30
82 Pat Burrell 1.00 .30
83 Brian Giles 1.00 .30
84 Jason Kendall 1.00 .30
85 Aaron Boone 1.00 .30
86 Ken Griffey Jr. 4.00 1.20
87 Barry Larkin 2.50 .75
88 Todd Helton 1.50 .45
89 Larry Walker 1.50 .45
90 Jeffrey Hammonds 1.00 .30

2001 SP Game Bat Edition Big League Hit Parade

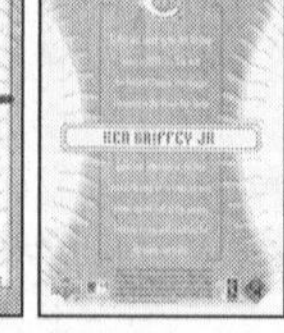

Randomly inserted into packs at one in 15, this six-card set features some of the Major League's top hitters. Card backs carry a "HP" prefix.

Nm-Mt Ex-Mt
COMPLETE SET (6) 30.00 9.00
HP1 Nomar Garciaparra 5.00 1.50
HP2 Ken Griffey Jr. 5.00 1.50
HP3 Sammy Sosa 5.00 1.50
HP4 Alex Rodriguez 5.00 1.50
HP5 Mark McGwire 8.00 2.40
HP6 Ivan Rodriguez 3.00 .90

2001 SP Game Bat Edition In the Swing

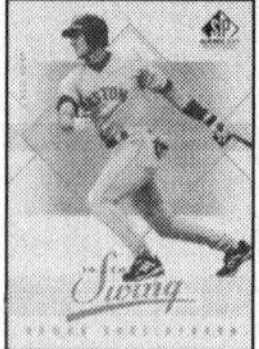
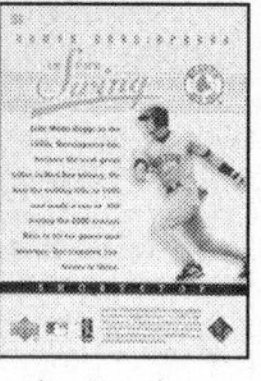

Randomly inserted into packs at one in seven, this 15-card set features some sweetest swings in Major League Baseball. Card backs carry a "IS" prefix.

Nm-Mt Ex-Mt
COMPLETE SET (15) 60.00 18.00
IS1 Ken Griffey Jr. 5.00 1.50
IS2 Jim Edmonds 1.25 .35
IS3 Carlos Delgado 1.25 .35
IS4 Frank Thomas 3.00 .90
IS5 Barry Bonds 8.00 2.40
IS6 Nomar Garciaparra 5.00 1.50
IS7 Gary Sheffield 1.25 .35
IS8 Vladimir Guerrero 3.00 .90
IS9 Alex Rodriguez 5.00 1.50
IS10 Todd Helton 2.00 .60
IS11 Darin Erstad 1.25 .35
IS12 Derek Jeter 8.00 2.40
IS13 Sammy Sosa 5.00 1.50
IS14 Mark McGwire 8.00 2.40
IS15 Jason Giambi 3.00 .90

2001 SP Game Bat Edition Line Up Time

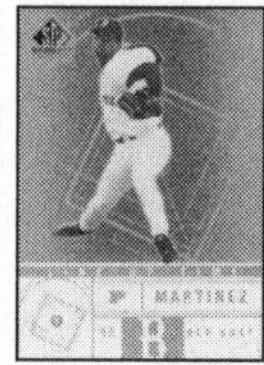

Randomly inserted into packs at one in eight, this 11-card set features players that are always in the starting line up. Card backs carry a "LT" prefix.

Nm-Mt Ex-Mt
COMPLETE SET (11) 50.00 15.00
LT1 Mark McGwire 8.00 2.40
LT2 Roberto Alomar 3.00 .90
LT3 Alex Rodriguez 5.00 1.50
LT4 Chipper Jones 3.00 .90
LT5 Ivan Rodriguez 3.00 .90
LT6 Ken Griffey Jr. 5.00 1.50
LT7 Sammy Sosa 5.00 1.50
LT8 Barry Bonds 8.00 2.40
LT9 Frank Thomas 3.00 .90
LT10 Pedro Martinez 3.00 .90
LT11 Derek Jeter 8.00 2.40

2001 SP Game Bat Edition Lumber Yard

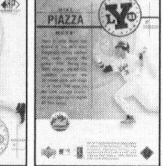

Randomly inserted into packs at one in 10, this 10-card set features some of the Major League's top power hitters. Card backs carry a "Y" prefix.

Nm-Mt Ex-Mt
COMPLETE SET (10) 40.00 12.00
Y1 Jason Giambi 3.00 .90
Y2 Chipper Jones 3.00 .90
Y3 Carl Everett 1.25 .35
Y4 Alex Rodriguez 5.00 1.50
Y5 Frank Thomas 3.00 .90
Y6 Barry Bonds 8.00 2.40
Y7 Jeff Bagwell 2.00 .60
Y8 Sammy Sosa 5.00 1.50
Y9 Carlos Delgado 1.25 .35
Y10 Mike Piazza 5.00 1.50

2001 SP Game Bat Edition Piece of History

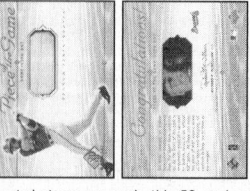

Inserted at one per pack, this 58-card set features actual game-used pieces of bat. Card backs carry the player's initials as numbering. Cards are listed below in alphabetical order for convenience. Upper Deck announced shortly after the product went live that fifteen cards were short-printed in comparison to others in the set. According to Upper Deck, all short-print cards have a production of 1,500 or fewer cards.

Nm-Mt Ex-Mt
AJ Andruw Jones 10.00 3.00
AR Alex Rodriguez 15.00 4.50
BB Barry Bonds 25.00 7.50
BG Bob Gibson SP 40.00 12.00
BW Bernie Williams 15.00 4.50
CB Carlos Beltran 10.00 3.00
CD Carlos Delgado 10.00 3.00
CJ Chipper Jones 15.00 4.50
CR Cal Ripken SP 50.00 15.00
DE Darin Erstad SP 25.00 7.50
DJ David Justice 10.00 3.00
EA Edgardo Alfonzo SP 25.00 7.50
EM Edgar Martinez 15.00 4.50
FM Fred McGriff SP 40.00 12.00
FT Frank Thomas 15.00 4.50
GM Greg Maddux 15.00 4.50
GS Gary Sheffield 10.00 3.00
GV Greg Vaughn 10.00 3.00
IR Ivan Rodriguez 15.00 4.50
JB Jeff Bagwell SP 40.00 12.00
JB Johnny Bench SP 40.00 12.00
JC Jose Canseco 15.00 4.50
JD J.D. Drew 10.00 3.00
JE Jim Edmonds 10.00 3.00
JO John Olerud 10.00 3.00
JOD Joe DiMaggio SP 120.00 36.00
KB Kevin Brown SP 25.00 7.50
KG Ken Griffey Jr. 15.00 4.50
KL Kenny Lofton 10.00 3.00
MG Mark Grace 15.00 4.50
MO Magglio Ordonez 10.00 3.00
MQ Mark Quinn SP 25.00 7.50
MR Manny Ramirez 10.00 3.00
MV Mo Vaughn 10.00 3.00
MW Matt Williams 10.00 3.00
NR Nolan Ryan SP 40.00 12.00
PB Pat Burrell 10.00 3.00
PN Phil Nevin SP 25.00 7.50
PO Paul O'Neill 15.00 4.50
PW Preston Wilson 10.00 3.00
RA Rick Ankiel 10.00 3.00
RA Roberto Alomar 15.00 4.50
REJ Reggie Jackson SP 40.00 12.00
RF Rafael Furcal 10.00 3.00
RJ Randy Johnson 15.00 4.50
RV Robin Ventura 10.00 3.00
SA Sandy Alomar Jr. 10.00 3.00
SAS Sammy Sosa SP 25.00 7.50
SG Shawn Green 10.00 3.00
SR Scott Rolen 15.00 4.50
SS Shannon Stewart 10.00 3.00
TGL Tom Glavine SP 40.00 12.00
TGW Tony Gwynn 15.00 4.50
TH Todd Helton 15.00 4.50
TH Todd Hundley SP 25.00 7.50
TM Tino Martinez 15.00 4.50
TS Tim Salmon SP 40.00 12.00
WC Will Clark 15.00 4.50

2001 SP Game Bat Edition Piece of History Autograph

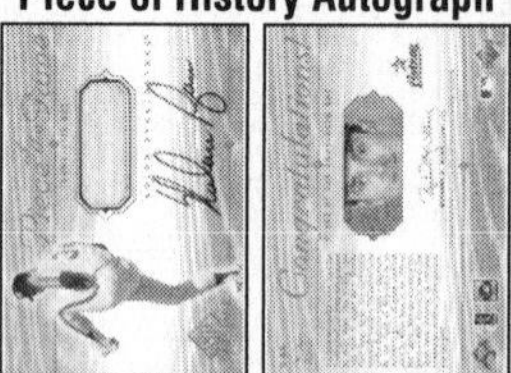

Inserted into packs at one in 96, this nine-card insert features actual game-used pieces of bats, and are autographed by the players. Card backs carry a "S" prefix followed by the players initials. Please note that Frank Thomas, Ken Griffey Jr. and Sammy Sosa packed out as exchange cards. The deadline to exchange these cards is 09/22/01.

Nm-Mt Ex-Mt
S-AJ Andruw Jones 50.00 15.00
S-AR Alex Rodriguez 150.00 45.00
S-BB Barry Bonds 300.00 90.00
S-FT Frank Thomas 80.00 24.00
S-JC Jose Canseco 50.00 15.00
S-KG Ken Griffey Jr. 150.00 45.00
S-NR Nolan Ryan 150.00 45.00
S-SS Sammy Sosa 200.00 60.00
S-TGW Tony Gwynn 80.00 24.00

2001 SP Game Bat Milestone

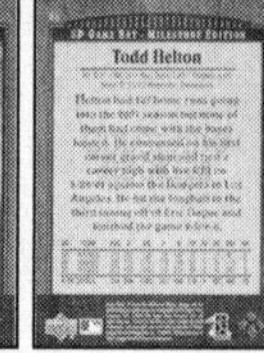

This ninety-six card set was issued in October, 2001. This set was issued in four-card packs with an SRP of $19.99 per pack. Cards numbered 91-96 were short printed and these cards were serial numbered to 500.

Nm-Mt Ex-Mt
COMP.SET w/o SP's (90) 80.00 24.00
COMMON CARD (1-90) 1.00 .30
COMMON BAT (91-96) 10.00 3.00
1 Troy Glaus 1.50 .45
2 Darin Erstad 1.00 .30
3 Jason Giambi 2.50 .75
4 Jermaine Dye 1.00 .30
5 Eric Chavez 1.00 .30
6 Carlos Delgado 1.00 .30
7 Raul Mondesi 1.00 .30
8 Shannon Stewart 1.00 .30
9 Greg Vaughn 1.00 .30
10 Aubrey Huff 1.00 .30
11 Juan Gonzalez 2.50 .75
12 Roberto Alomar 2.50 .75
13 Jim Thome 2.50 .75

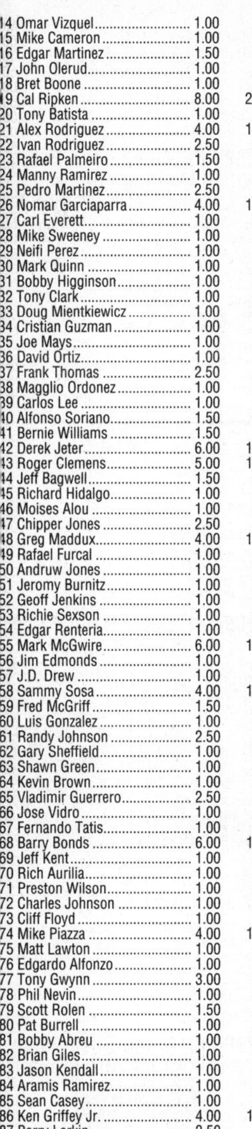

14 Omar Vizquel	1.00	.30
15 Mike Cameron	1.00	.30
16 Edgar Martinez	1.50	.45
17 John Olerud	1.00	.30
18 Bret Boone	1.00	.30
19 Cal Ripken	8.00	2.40
20 Tony Batista	1.00	.30
21 Alex Rodriguez	4.00	1.20
22 Ivan Rodriguez	2.50	.75
23 Rafael Palmeiro	1.50	.45
24 Manny Ramirez	1.00	.30
25 Pedro Martinez	2.50	.75
26 Nomar Garciaparra	4.00	1.20
27 Carl Everett	1.00	.30
28 Mike Sweeney	1.00	.30
29 Neifi Perez	1.00	.30
30 Mark Quinn	1.00	.30
31 Bobby Higginson	1.00	.30
32 Tony Clark	1.00	.30
33 Doug Mientkiewicz	1.00	.30
34 Cristian Guzman	1.00	.30
35 Joe Mays	1.00	.30
36 David Ortiz	1.00	.30
37 Frank Thomas	2.50	.75
38 Magglio Ordonez	1.00	.30
39 Carlos Lee	1.00	.30
40 Alfonso Soriano	1.50	.45
41 Bernie Williams	1.50	.45
42 Derek Jeter	6.00	1.80
43 Roger Clemens	5.00	1.50
44 Jeff Bagwell	1.50	.45
45 Richard Hidalgo	1.00	.30
46 Moises Alou	1.00	.30
47 Chipper Jones	2.50	.75
48 Greg Maddux	4.00	1.20
49 Rafael Furcal	1.00	.30
50 Andruw Jones	1.00	.30
51 Jeromy Burnitz	1.00	.30
52 Geoff Jenkins	1.00	.30
53 Richie Sexson	1.00	.30
54 Edgar Renteria	1.00	.30
55 Mark McGwire	6.00	1.80
56 Jim Edmonds	1.00	.30
57 J.D. Drew	1.00	.30
58 Sammy Sosa	4.00	1.20
59 Fred McGriff	1.50	.45
60 Luis Gonzalez	1.00	.30
61 Randy Johnson	2.50	.75
62 Gary Sheffield	1.00	.30
63 Shawn Green	1.00	.30
64 Kevin Brown	1.00	.30
65 Vladimir Guerrero	2.50	.75
66 Jose Vidro	1.00	.30
67 Fernando Tatis	1.00	.30
68 Barry Bonds	6.00	1.80
69 Jeff Kent	1.00	.30
70 Rich Aurilia	1.00	.30
71 Preston Wilson	1.00	.30
72 Charles Johnson	1.00	.30
73 Cliff Floyd	1.00	.30
74 Mike Piazza	4.00	1.20
75 Matt Lawton	1.00	.30
76 Edgardo Alfonzo	1.00	.30
77 Tony Gwynn	3.00	.90
78 Phil Nevin	1.00	.30
79 Scott Rolen	1.50	.45
80 Pat Burrell	1.00	.30
81 Bobby Abreu	1.00	.30
82 Brian Giles	1.00	.30
83 Jason Kendall	1.00	.30
84 Aramis Ramirez	1.00	.30
85 Sean Casey	1.00	.30
86 Ken Griffey Jr.	4.00	1.20
87 Barry Larkin	2.50	.75
88 Todd Helton	1.50	.45
89 Mike Hampton	1.00	.30
90 Larry Walker	1.50	.45
91 Ichiro Suzuki BAT RC	40.00	12.00
92 Albert Pujols BAT RC	50.00	15.00
93 T. Shinjo BAT RC	15.00	4.50
94 Jack Wilson BAT RC	10.00	3.00
95 D. Mendez BAT RC	10.00	3.00
96 Junior Spivey BAT RC	15.00	4.50

2001 SP Game Bat Milestone Art of Hitting

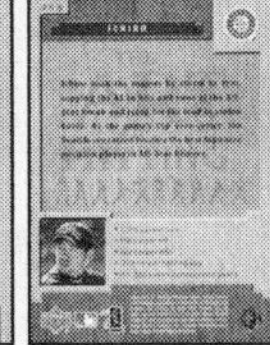

Inserted at a rate of one in five and featured a mix of batting champions and other leading hitters who made hitting an art.

	Nm-Mt	Ex-Mt
COMPLETE SET (12)	50.00	15.00
AH1 Tony Gwynn	4.00	1.20
AH2 Manny Ramirez	2.00	.60
AH3 Todd Helton	2.00	.60
AH4 Nomar Garciaparra	5.00	1.50
AH5 Vladimir Guerrero	3.00	.90
AH6 Ichiro Suzuki	20.00	6.00
AH7 Darin Erstad	2.00	.60
AH8 Alex Rodriguez	5.00	1.50
AH9 Carlos Delgado	2.00	.60
AH10 Edgar Martinez	2.00	.60
AH11 Luis Gonzalez	2.00	.60
AH12 Barry Bonds	8.00	2.40

2001 SP Game Bat Milestone Piece of Action Autographs

Inserted at a rate of one per 100 packs, these 13 cards feature signed cards of some of the leading players in the game. A few players were printed in lower quantities than the others and we have notated those players with both and SP and officially released print information from Upper Deck. Jose Vidro did not return his cards in time for inclusion in this product,

these cards were available via exchange until October 12, 2004.

	Nm-Mt	Ex-Mt
S-AR A. Rodriguez SP/97	150.00	45.00
S-CD C. Delgado SP/97	50.00	15.00
S-GS G. Sheffield SP/194	50.00	15.00
S-IS Ichiro Suzuki SP/53	1200.00	350.00
S-JD J.D. Drew	40.00	12.00
S-JD Jermaine Dye	40.00	12.00
S-JK Jason Kendall	40.00	12.00
S-JK Jeff Kent SP/194	60.00	18.00
S-JV Jose Vidro EXCH	40.00	12.00
S-LG Luis Gonzalez	40.00	12.00
S-MT Miguel Tejada	40.00	12.00
S-PW Preston Wilson	40.00	12.00
S-RB Russell Branyan	25.00	7.50

2001 SP Game Bat Milestone Piece of Action Bound for the Hall

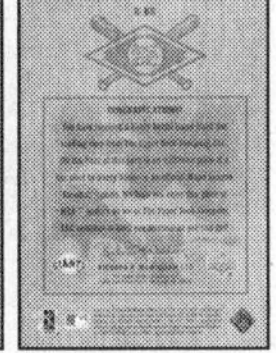

Randomly inserted in packs, these 16 cards feature bat clippings of players who look like they are on their way to enshriment in Cooperstown. A few players seemed to be available in larger supply, we have notated those players with an asterisk next to their name.

	Nm-Mt	Ex-Mt
BAR A.Rodriguez Rangers	15.00	4.50
BBB Barry Bonds	25.00	7.50
BCD Carlos Delgado	10.00	3.00
BCR Cal Ripken	40.00	12.00
BEM Edgar Martinez	15.00	4.50
BFM Fred McGriff	15.00	4.50
BGM Greg Maddux	15.00	4.50
BIR Ivan Rodriguez	15.00	4.50
BJG Jason Giambi	15.00	4.50
BMP Mike Piazza	15.00	4.50
BRC R.Clemens SP/203	40.00	12.00
BRP Rafael Palmeiro	15.00	4.50
BSS Sammy Sosa	20.00	6.00
BTG Tony Gwynn	15.00	4.50
BKGM Ken Griffey Jr. M's*	20.00	6.00
BKGR K.Griffey Jr. Reds	20.00	6.00

2001 SP Game Bat Milestone Piece of Action Bound for the Hall Gold

Randomly inserted in packs, these 16 cards parallel the Piece of History Bound for the Hall insert set. These cards are serial numbered to 35.

	Nm-Mt	Ex-Mt
BAR Alex Rodriguez	60.00	18.00
BBB Barry Bonds	80.00	24.00
BCD Carlos Delgado	25.00	7.50
BCR Cal Ripken	100.00	30.00
BEM Edgar Martinez	40.00	12.00
BFM Fred McGriff	40.00	12.00
BGM Greg Maddux	60.00	18.00
BIR Ivan Rodriguez	40.00	12.00
BJG Jason Giambi	40.00	12.00
BMP Mike Piazza	60.00	18.00
BRC Roger Clemens	80.00	24.00
BRP Rafael Palmeiro	40.00	12.00
BSS Sammy Sosa	60.00	18.00
BTG Tony Gwynn	60.00	18.00
BKGM K.Griffey Jr. Mariners	60.00	18.00
BKGR K.Griffey Jr. Reds	60.00	18.00

2001 SP Game Bat Milestone Piece of Action International

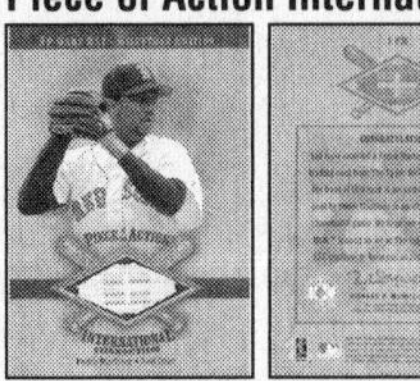

Randomly inserted into packs, these 16 cards feature bat pieces of some of the finest imports playing major league baseball. A couple of players were printed in lesser quantity then the other cards in this set and we have notated those with an SP as well as the print information. Omar Vizquel seems to have been printed in larger quantites and we have notated that with an asterisk.

	Nm-Mt	Ex-Mt
IAB Adrian Beltre	10.00	3.00
IAJ Andruw Jones	10.00	3.00
IAP Albert Pujols	50.00	15.00
ICP Chan Ho Park	10.00	3.00
IHN Hideo Nomo SP/275	40.00	12.00
IIS Ichiro Suzuki SP/203	100.00	30.00
IJG Juan Gonzalez	15.00	4.50
IJP Jorge Posada	15.00	4.50
IMO Magglio Ordonez	10.00	3.00
IMR Manny Ramirez	10.00	3.00
IMT Miguel Tejada	10.00	3.00
IOV Omar Vizquel *	10.00	3.00
IPM Pedro Martinez	15.00	4.50
IRA Roberto Alomar	15.00	4.50
IRF Rafael Furcal	10.00	3.00
ITS Tsuyoshi Shinjo	15.00	4.50

2001 SP Game Bat Milestone Piece of Action International Gold

Randomly inserted in packs, these 16 cards parallel the Piece of History International insert set. These cards are serial numbered to 35.

	Nm-Mt	Ex-Mt
I-AB Adrian Beltre	25.00	7.50
I-AJ Andruw Jones	25.00	7.50
I-AP Albert Pujols	150.00	45.00
I-CP Chan Ho Park	25.00	7.50
I-HN Hideo Nomo	100.00	30.00
I-IS Ichiro Suzuki	150.00	45.00
I-JG Juan Gonzalez	40.00	12.00
I-JP Jorge Posada	40.00	12.00
I-MO Magglio Ordonez	25.00	7.50
I-MR Manny Ramirez	25.00	7.50
I-MT Miguel Tejada	25.00	7.50
I-OV Omar Vizquel	25.00	7.50
I-PM Pedro Martinez	40.00	12.00
I-RA Roberto Alomar	40.00	12.00
I-RF Rafael Furcal	25.00	7.50
I-TS Tsuyoshi Shinjo	50.00	15.00

2001 SP Game Bat Milestone Piece of Action Milestone

Randomly inserted into packs, these 18 cards feature some of the best hitters in baseball. Each card features a bat sliver on it.

	Nm-Mt	Ex-Mt
MAR A.Rodriguez Mariners	15.00	4.50
MBB Barry Bonds	25.00	7.50
MCJ Chipper Jones	15.00	4.50
MCR Cal Ripken	40.00	12.00
MDE Darin Erstad	10.00	3.00
MFT Frank Thomas *	15.00	4.50
MGS Gary Sheffield	10.00	3.00
MIS Ichiro Suzuki SP/203	100.00	30.00
MJB Jeff Bagwell	15.00	4.50
MJB Jeromy Burnitz	10.00	3.00
MJT Jim Thome	15.00	4.50
MKG Ken Griffey Jr.	20.00	6.00
MLG Luis Gonzalez *	10.00	3.00
MMP Mike Piazza	15.00	4.50
MRB Russell Branyan	10.00	3.00
MRC Roger Clemens	20.00	6.00
MSS Sammy Sosa *	15.00	4.50
MTH Todd Helton	15.00	4.50

2001 SP Game Bat Milestone Piece of Action Milestone Gold

Randomly inserted in packs, these 16 cards parallel the Piece of History Milestone set. These cards are serial numbered to 35.

	Nm-Mt	Ex-Mt
MAR Alex Rodriguez	60.00	18.00
MBB Barry Bonds	80.00	24.00
MCJ Chipper Jones	40.00	12.00
MCR Cal Ripken	100.00	30.00
MDE Darin Erstad	25.00	7.50
MFT Frank Thomas	40.00	12.00
MGS Gary Sheffield	25.00	7.50
MIS Ichiro Suzuki	150.00	45.00
MJB Jeromy Burnitz	25.00	7.50
MJB Jeff Bagwell	40.00	12.00
MJT Jim Thome	40.00	12.00
MKG Ken Griffey Jr.	60.00	18.00
MLG Luis Gonzalez	25.00	7.50
MMP Mike Piazza	80.00	24.00
MRB Russell Branyan	25.00	7.50
MRC Roger Clemens	80.00	24.00
MSS Sammy Sosa	60.00	18.00
MTH Todd Helton	40.00	12.00

2001 SP Game Bat Milestone Piece of Action Quads

Inserted in packs at a rate of one in 50, these 15 cards feature four pieces of game-used bats from four different major league stars.

	Nm-Mt	Ex-Mt
GDBS Ken Griffey Jr.	50.00	15.00
J.D. Drew		
Jeromy Burnitz		
Sammy Sosa		
GGRR Ken Griffey Jr.	80.00	24.00
Ken Griffey Jr.		
Alex Rodriguez		
Alex Rodriguez		
GHSK Luis Gonzalez	40.00	12.00
Todd Helton		
Gary Sheffield		
Jeff Kent		
GRBM Tony Gwynn	100.00	30.00
Cal Ripken		
Barry Bonds		
Fred McGriff		
GRSB Ken Griffey Jr.	100.00	30.00
Alex Rodriguez		
Sammy Sosa		
Barry Bonds		
JJFM Chipper Jones	40.00	12.00
Andruw Jones		
Rafael Furcal		
Greg Maddux		
JVBW Chipper Jones	40.00	12.00
Robin Ventura		
Pat Burrell		
Preston Wilson		
OJCP Paul O'Neill	100.00	30.00
David Justice		
Roger Clemens		
Jorge Posada		
ONRD Paul O'Neill	100.00	30.00
Hideo Nomo		
Cal Ripken		
Carlos Delgado		
PWSG Kirby Puckett	40.00	12.00
Dave Winfield		
Ozzie Smith		
Steve Garvey		
RGGM Alex Rodriguez	50.00	15.00
Troy Glaus		
Jason Giambi		
Edgar Martinez		
RRPM Alex Rodriguez	50.00	15.00
Ivan Rodriguez		
Rafael Palmeiro		
Ruben Mateo		
SGBP Gary Sheffield	25.00	7.50
Shawn Green		
Adrian Beltre		
Chan Ho Park		
TDTA Frank Thomas	40.00	12.00
Jermaine Dye		
Jim Thome		
Roberto Alomar		
TVAL Jim Thome	40.00	12.00
Omar Vizquel		
Roberto Alomar		
Kenny Lofton		

2001 SP Game Bat Milestone Piece of Action Trios

Inserted in packs at a rate of one in 50, these 14 cards feature four pieces of game-used bats from three different major league stars.

	Nm-Mt	Ex-Mt
CMG Roger Clemens	50.00	15.00
Greg Maddux		
Tom Glavine		
GBM Ken Griffey Jr.	40.00	12.00
Barry Bonds		
Fred McGriff		
GRB Tony Gwynn	80.00	24.00
Cal Ripken		
Barry Bonds		
GRS Ken Griffey Jr.	40.00	12.00
Alex Rodriguez		
Sammy Sosa		
JJF Chipper Jones	40.00	12.00
Andruw Jones		
Rafael Furcal		
KGR Jason Kendall	25.00	7.50
Brian Giles		
Aramis Ramirez		
OJC Paul O'Neill	50.00	15.00
David Justice		
Roger Clemens		
OTA Rey Ordonez	40.00	12.00
Frank Thomas		
Sandy Alomar Jr.		
PWS Kirby Puckett	40.00	12.00
Dave Winfield		
Ozzie Smith		
RRP Alex Rodriguez	50.00	15.00
Ivan Rodriguez		
Rafael Palmeiro		
SFR Alfonso Soriano	40.00	12.00
Rafael Furcal		
Aramis Ramirez		
SGB Gary Sheffield	25.00	7.50
Shawn Green		
Adrian Beltre		
TVA Jim Thome	40.00	12.00
Omar Vizquel		
Roberto Alomar		
VSA Robin Ventura	40.00	12.00
Tsuyoshi Shinjo		
Edgardo Alfonzo		

2001 SP Game Bat Milestone Slugging Sensations

Inserted in packs at a rate of one in five, these 12 cards feature the players who hit a baseball harder and farther than other players.

	Nm-Mt	Ex-Mt
COMPLETE SET (12)	40.00	12.00
SS1 Troy Glaus	2.00	.60
SS2 Mark McGwire	8.00	2.40
SS3 Sammy Sosa	5.00	1.50
SS4 Juan Gonzalez	3.00	.90

SS5 Barry Bonds	8.00	2.40
SS6 Jeff Bagwell	2.00	.60
SS7 Jason Giambi	3.00	.90
SS8 Ivan Rodriguez	3.00	.90
SS9 Mike Piazza	5.00	1.50
SS10 Chipper Jones	3.00	.90
SS11 Ken Griffey Jr.	5.00	1.50
SS12 Gary Sheffield	1.25	.35

2001 SP Game Bat Milestone Trophy Room

Inserted at a rate of one in ten, these six cards feature players who have won key awards during their career.

	Nm-Mt	Ex-Mt
COMPLETE SET (6)	30.00	9.00
TR1 Sammy Sosa	5.00	1.50
TR2 Jason Giambi	3.00	.90
TR3 Todd Helton	3.00	.90
TR4 Alex Rodriguez	5.00	1.50
TR5 Mark McGwire	8.00	2.40
TR6 Ken Griffey Jr.	5.00	1.50

2001 SP Game-Used Edition

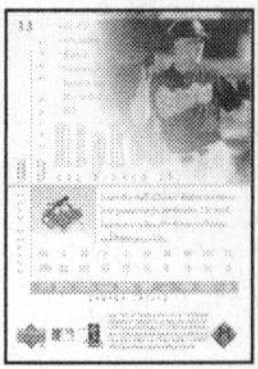

This 90-card set was distributed in three-card packs with a suggested retail value of $29.99 and features color action player photos. The set includes the following subset: Super Prospects (61-90).

	Nm-Mt	Ex-Mt
COMP.SET w/o SP's (60)	80.00	24.00
COMMON CARD (1-60)	1.25	.35
COMMON CARD (61-90)	10.00	3.00
1 Garret Anderson	1.25	.35
2 Troy Glaus	2.00	.60
3 Darin Erstad	1.25	.35
4 Jason Giambi	3.00	.90
5 Tim Hudson	1.25	.35
6 Johnny Damon	1.25	.35
7 Carlos Delgado	1.25	.35
8 Greg Vaughn	1.25	.35
9 Juan Gonzalez	3.00	.90
10 Roberto Alomar	3.00	.90
11 Jim Thome	3.00	.90
12 Edgar Martinez	2.00	.60
13 Cal Ripken	10.00	3.00
14 Andres Galarraga	1.25	.35
15 Alex Rodriguez	5.00	1.50
16 Rafael Palmeiro	2.00	.60
17 Ivan Rodriguez	3.00	.90
18 Manny Ramirez	1.25	.35
19 Nomar Garciaparra	5.00	1.50
20 Pedro Martinez	3.00	.90
21 Jermaine Dye	1.25	.35
22 Dean Palmer	1.25	.35
23 Matt Lawton	1.25	.35
24 Frank Thomas	3.00	.90
25 David Wells	1.25	.35
26 Magglio Ordonez	1.25	.35
27 Derek Jeter	8.00	2.40
28 Bernie Williams	2.00	.60
29 Roger Clemens	6.00	1.80
30 Jeff Bagwell	2.00	.60
31 Richard Hidalgo	1.25	.35
32 Chipper Jones	3.00	.90
33 Andruw Jones	1.25	.35
34 Greg Maddux	5.00	1.50
35 Jeffrey Hammonds	1.25	.35
36 Mark McGwire	8.00	2.40
37 Jim Edmonds	1.25	.35
38 Sammy Sosa	5.00	1.50
39 Corey Patterson	1.25	.35
40 Randy Johnson	3.00	.90
41 Luis Gonzalez	1.25	.35
42 Gary Sheffield	1.25	.35
43 Shawn Green	1.25	.35
44 Kevin Brown	1.25	.35
45 Vladimir Guerrero	3.00	.90
46 Barry Bonds	8.00	2.40
47 Jeff Kent	1.25	.35
48 Preston Wilson	1.25	.35
49 Charles Johnson	1.25	.35
50 Mike Piazza	5.00	1.50
51 Edgardo Alfonzo	1.25	.35
52 Tony Gwynn	4.00	1.20
53 Scott Rolen	2.00	.60
54 Pat Burrell	1.25	.35
55 Brian Giles	1.25	.35
56 Jason Kendall	1.25	.35
57 Ken Griffey Jr.	5.00	1.50

58 Mike Hampton 1.25 .35
59 Todd Helton 2.00 .60
60 Larry Walker 2.00 .60
61 Wilson Betemit RC 10.00 3.00
62 Travis Hafner RC 15.00 4.50
63 Ichiro Suzuki RC 60.00 18.00
64 Juan Diaz RC 10.00 3.00
65 Morgan Ensberg RC 15.00 4.50
66 Horacio Ramirez RC 15.00 4.50
67 Ricardo Rodriguez RC 10.00 3.00
68 Sean Douglass RC 10.00 3.00
69 Brandon Duckworth RC 10.00 3.00
70 Jackson Melian RC 10.00 3.00
71 Adrian Hernandez RC 10.00 3.00
72 Kyle Kessel RC 10.00 3.00
73 Jason Michaels RC 10.00 3.00
74 Esix Snead RC 10.00 3.00
75 Jason Smith RC 10.00 3.00
76 Tyler Walker RC 10.00 3.00
77 Juan Uribe RC 10.00 3.00
78 Adam Pettyjohn RC 10.00 3.00
79 Tsuyoshi Shinjo RC 15.00 4.50
80 Mike Penney RC 10.00 3.00
81 Josh Towers RC 10.00 3.00
82 Erick Almonte RC 10.00 3.00
83 Ryan Freel RC 10.00 3.00
84 Juan Pena 10.00 3.00
85 Albert Pujols RC 80.00 24.00
86 Henry Mateo RC 10.00 3.00
87 Greg Miller RC 10.00 3.00
88 Jose Mieses RC 10.00 3.00
89 Jack Wilson RC 10.00 3.00
90 Carlos Valderrama RC 10.00 3.00

2001 SP Game-Used Edition Authentic Fabric

Randomly inserted one in every pack, this 82-card set features color player portraits with a swatch of a game-used jersey embedded in the card.

Nm-Mt Ex-Mt
AH Aubrey Huff 10.00 3.00
AJ Andruw Jones 10.00 3.00
AL Al Leiter 10.00 3.00
AP Adam Piatt 10.00 3.00
ARH A.Rodriguez Rangers 15.00 4.50
ARM A.Rodriguez Mariners* 15.00 4.50
BB Barry Bonds 25.00 7.50
BG Brian Giles SP 25.00 7.50
BL Barry Larkin 15.00 4.50
CD Carlos Delgado SP 25.00 7.50
CJ Chipper Jones 15.00 4.50
CJO Charles Johnson 10.00 3.00
CR Cal Ripken 40.00 12.00
DE Darin Erstad 10.00 3.00
DW David Wells SP 25.00 7.50
DY Dmitri Young 10.00 3.00
EA Edgardo Alfonzo 10.00 3.00
EC Eric Chavez 10.00 3.00
EM Edgar Martinez * 15.00 4.50
FM Fred McGriff 15.00 4.50
FTA Fernando Tatis 10.00 3.00
FTH Frank Thomas 15.00 4.50
GM Greg Maddux * 15.00 4.50
GS Gary Sheffield 10.00 3.00
GV Greg Vaughn 10.00 3.00
IR Ivan Rodriguez 15.00 4.50
JB Jeromy Burnitz 10.00 3.00
JCB Jose Canseco BLC
JCH Jose Canseco 15.00 4.50
JCI Jeff Cirillo 10.00 3.00
JDI Joe DiMaggio SP/50
JDR J.D. Drew * 10.00 3.00
JDY Jermaine Dye SP 25.00 7.50
JE Jim Edmonds * 10.00 3.00
JG Jason Giambi 15.00 4.50
JI Jason Isringhausen SP 15.00 4.50
JK Jason Kendall 10.00 3.00
JK Jeff Kent 10.00 3.00
JO John Olerud 10.00 3.00
JT Jim Thome 15.00 4.50
JV Jose Vidro 10.00 3.00
KB Kevin Brown 10.00 3.00
KGH Ken Griffey Jr. Reds 15.00 4.50
KGM K.Griffey Jr. Mariners* 15.00 4.50
KGR Ken Griffey Jr. Road
KL Kenny Lofton 10.00 3.00
KM Kevin Millwood 10.00 3.00
LG Luis Gonzalez 10.00 3.00
MG Mark Grace 15.00 4.50
MH Mike Hampton 10.00 3.00
MM Mickey Mantle SP/50 300.00 90.00
MO Magglio Ordonez 10.00 3.00
MR Mariano Rivera 15.00 4.50
MT Miguel Tejada 10.00 3.00
MW Matt Williams 10.00 3.00
NR Nolan Ryan 100.00 30.00
Rangers SP/50
NRA Nolan Ryan Astros 100.00 30.00
SP/50
PB Pat Burrell 10.00 3.00
PN Phil Nevin 10.00 3.00
PW Preston Wilson 10.00 3.00
RA Roberto Alomar 15.00 4.50
RA Rick Ankiel * 10.00 3.00
RC Roger Clemens 15.00 4.50
RJ Randy Johnson 15.00 4.50
RM Roger Maris SP 100.00 30.00
RV Robin Ventura 10.00 3.00
SG Shawn Green 10.00 3.00
SR Scott Rolen 15.00 4.50
SSH Sammy Sosa Home 15.00 4.50
SSR Sammy Sosa Road 15.00 4.50
TB Tony Batista SP 25.00 7.50
TGL Troy Glaus 15.00 4.50
TGW Tony Gwynn * 15.00 4.50
TH Tim Hudson 10.00 3.00

THE Todd Helton 15.00 4.50
TL Terrence Long 10.00 3.00
TM Tino Martinez 15.00 4.50
TOG Tom Glavine 15.00 4.50
TRH Trevor Hoffman 10.00 3.00
TS Tom Seaver 40.00 12.00
Mets SP/50
TSR Tom Seaver 40.00 12.00
Reds SP/50
TZ Todd Zeile 10.00 3.00

2001 SP Game-Used Edition Authentic Fabric Autographs

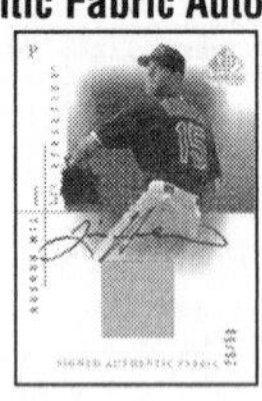

Randomly inserted in packs, this 21-card set is an autographed, partial parallel version of the regular insert set. Only 50 serially numbered sets were produced. An exchange card was seeded into packs for Alex Rodriguez.

Nm-Mt Ex-Mt
S-AJ Andruw Jones 80.00 24.00
S-AR A.Rodriguez EXCH 200.00 60.00
S-BB Barry Bonds 300.00 90.00
S-CD Carlos Delgado 50.00 15.00
S-CJ Chipper Jones 120.00 36.00
S-CR Cal Ripken 250.00 75.00
S-DW David Wells 50.00 15.00
S-EA Edgardo Alfonzo 50.00 15.00
S-FTH Frank Thomas 120.00 36.00
S-IR Ivan Rodriguez 120.00 36.00
S-JC Jose Canseco 120.00 36.00
S-JDR J.D. Drew 50.00 15.00
S-JG Jason Giambi 120.00 36.00
S-KG Ken Griffey Jr. 200.00 60.00
S-NR Nolan Ryan 250.00 75.00
S-RA Rick Ankiel 50.00 15.00
S-RJ Randy Johnson 120.00 36.00
S-SS Sammy Sosa 250.00 75.00
S-TGL Troy Glaus 80.00 24.00
S-TH Tim Hudson 80.00 24.00
S-TS Tom Seaver Mets

2001 SP Game-Used Edition Authentic Fabric Duos

Randomly inserted in packs, this 14-card set features color photos of two players to a card with two game jersey swatches embedded in each card. Only 50 serially numbered sets were produced.

Nm-Mt Ex-Mt
B-C Barry Bonds 120.00 36.00
Jose Canseco
C-W Roger Clemens 100.00 30.00
Bernie Williams
G-R Ken Griffey Jr. 80.00 24.00
Alex Rodriguez
G-S Ken Griffey Jr. 80.00 24.00
Sammy Sosa
H-G Tim Hudson 50.00 15.00
Jason Giambi
J-J Chipper Jones 50.00 15.00
Andruw Jones
J-R Randy Johnson 150.00 45.00
Nolan Ryan
M-D Mickey Mantle 700.00 210.00
Joe DiMaggio
M-M Mickey Mantle 600.00 180.00
Roger Maris
R-R Alex Rodriguez 100.00 30.00
Ivan Rodriguez
R-S Nolan Ryan 200.00 60.00
Tom Seaver
S-G Gary Sheffield 40.00 12.00
Shawn Green
S-R Sammy Sosa 80.00 24.00
Alex Rodriguez
S-T Sammy Sosa 60.00 18.00
Frank Thomas

2001 SP Game-Used Edition Authentic Fabric Trios

Randomly inserted in packs, this six-card set features color photos of three players to a card with three game jersey swatches embedded in each card. Only 25 serially numbered sets were produced. Due to market scarcity, no pricing is provided for these cards.

Nm-Mt Ex-Mt
D-G-S Joe DiMaggio
Ken Griffey Jr.
Sammy Sosa
D-M-M Joe DiMaggio
Mickey Mantle
Roger Maris
G-R-S Ken Griffey Jr.
Alex Rodriguez
Sammy Sosa
J-B-S Andruw Jones
Barry Bonds
Sammy Sosa
J-S-M Randy Johnson
Tom Seaver
Greg Maddux
M-J-J Greg Maddux
Chipper Jones
Andruw Jones

2004 SP Game Used Patch

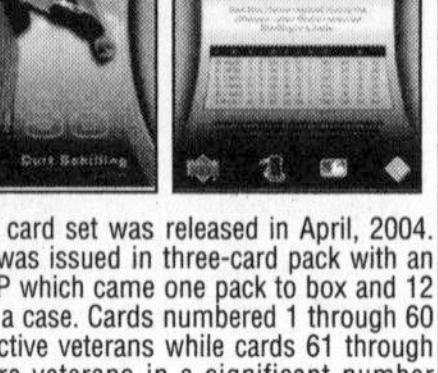

This 119 card set was released in April, 2004. This set was issued in three-card pack with an $150 SRP which came one pack to box and 12 boxes to a case. Cards numbered 1 through 60 feature active veterans while cards 61 through 90 feature veterans in a significant number subset in which cards were issued to an important number of their career. Cards numbered 91 through 119 feature rookies and those cards were issued to a stated print run of 375 serial numbered sets.

Nm-Mt Ex-Mt
COMMON CARD 1-60 4.00 1.20
61-90 PRINT RUN B/WN 86-684 COPIES PER
COMMON CARD (91-119) 8.00 2.40
1 Miguel Cabrera 5.00 1.50
2 Alex Rodriguez Yanks 15.00 4.50
3 Edgar Renteria 4.00 1.20
4 Juan Gonzalez 5.00 1.50
5 Mike Lowell 4.00 1.20
6 Andruw Jones 4.00 1.20
7 Eric Chavez 4.00 1.20
8 Jim Edmonds 4.00 1.20
9 Mike Piazza 8.00 2.40
10 Angel Berroa 4.00 1.20
11 Eric Gagne 4.00 1.20
12 Jody Gerut 4.00 1.20
13 Orlando Cabrera 4.00 1.20
14 Austin Kearns 4.00 1.20
15 Frank Thomas 5.00 1.50
16 Johan Santana 4.00 1.20
17 Randy Johnson 5.00 1.50
18 Preston Wilson 4.00 1.20
19 Garret Anderson 4.00 1.20
20 Jorge Posada 4.00 1.20
21 Rich Harden 4.00 1.20
22 Barry Zito 4.00 1.20
23 Gary Sheffield 4.00 1.20
24 Jose Reyes 4.00 1.20
25 Roy Halladay 4.00 1.20
26 Ben Sheets 4.00 1.20
27 Geoff Jenkins 4.00 1.20
28 Josh Beckett 4.00 1.20
29 Roy Oswalt 4.00 1.20
30 Bobby Abreu 4.00 1.20
31 Hank Blalock 4.00 1.20
32 Kerry Wood 5.00 1.50
33 Ryan Klesko 4.00 1.20
34 Rafael Furcal 4.00 1.20
35 Tom Glavine 4.00 1.20
36 Kevin Brown 4.00 1.20
37 Scott Rolen 4.00 1.20
38 Bret Boone 4.00 1.20
39 Ichiro Suzuki 8.00 2.40
40 Lance Berkman 4.00 1.20
41 Tim Hudson 4.00 1.20
42 Carlos Delgado 4.00 1.20
43 Ivan Rodriguez 5.00 1.50
44 Luis Gonzalez 4.00 1.20
45 Torii Hunter 4.00 1.20
46 Carlos Lee 4.00 1.20
47 Jacque Jones 4.00 1.20
48 Manny Ramirez 4.00 1.20
49 Troy Glaus 4.00 1.20
50 Corey Patterson 4.00 1.20
51 Jason Schmidt 4.00 1.20
52 Mark Mulder 4.00 1.20
53 Vernon Wells 4.00 1.20
54 Curt Schilling 4.00 1.20
55 Javy Lopez 4.00 1.20
56 Mark Prior 10.00 3.00
57 Dontrelle Willis 4.00 1.20
58 Derek Jeter 12.00 3.60
59 Jeff Bagwell 4.00 1.20
60 Marlon Byrd 4.00 1.20
61 Rafael Palmeiro SN/500 5.00 1.50
62 Kevin Millwood SN/165 5.00 1.50
63 Greg Maddux SN/273 10.00 3.00
64 Adam Dunn SN/400 5.00 1.50
65 Richie Sexson SN/469 5.00 1.50
66 Magglio Ordonez SN/567 5.00 1.50
67 Hideo Nomo SN/236 6.00 1.80
68 Albert Pujols SN/194 12.00 3.60
69 Rocco Baldelli SN/368 6.00 1.80
70 Mark Teixeira SN/86 6.00 1.80
71 Jason Giambi SN/660 6.00 1.80
72 Alfonso Soriano SN/230 5.00 1.50
73 Roger Clemens SN/300 12.00 3.60
74 Miguel Tejada SN/359 5.00 1.50
75 Jeff Kent SN/684 5.00 1.50
76 Bernie Williams SN/342 5.00 1.50
77 Sammy Sosa SN/479 10.00 3.00
78 Mike Mussina SN/641 6.00 1.80
79 Jim Thome SN/334 6.00 1.80
80 Brian Giles SN/506 5.00 1.50
81 Shawn Green SN/234 5.00 1.50
82 Mike Sweeney SN/340 5.00 1.50
83 John Smoltz SN/262 5.00 1.50
84 Carlos Beltran SN/319 5.00 1.50
85 Todd Helton SN/384 5.00 1.50
86 Nomar Garciaparra SN/372 10.00 3.00
87 Ken Griffey Jr. SN/481 10.00 3.00
88 Chipper Jones SN/633 6.00 1.80
89 Vladimir Guerrero SN/226 6.00 1.80
90 Pedro Martinez SN/313 6.00 1.80
91 Brandon Medders RD RC 8.00 2.40
92 Colby Miller RD RC 8.00 2.40
93 Dave Crouthers RD RC 8.00 2.40
94 Dennis Sarfate RD RC 10.00 3.00
95 Donald Kelly RD RC 8.00 2.40
96 Alec Zumwalt RD RC 8.00 2.40
97 Chris Aguila RD RC 8.00 2.40
98 Greg Dobbs RD RC 8.00 2.40
99 Ian Snell RD RC 10.00 3.00
100 Jake Woods RD RC 8.00 2.40
101 Jamie Brown RD RC 8.00 2.40
102 Jason Frasor RD RC 8.00 2.40
103 Jerome Gamble RD RC 8.00 2.40
104 Jesse Harper RD RC 8.00 2.40
105 Josh Labandeira RD RC 8.00 2.40
106 Justin Hampson RD RC 8.00 2.40
107 Justin Huisman RD RC 8.00 2.40
108 Justin Leone RD RC 8.00 2.40
109 Lincoln Holdzkom RD RC 8.00 2.40
110 Mike Bumatay RD RC 8.00 2.40
111 Mike Gosling RD RC 8.00 2.40
112 Mike Johnston RD RC 8.00 2.40
113 Mike Rouse RD RC 8.00 2.40
114 Nick Regilio RD RC 8.00 2.40
115 Ryan Meaux RD RC 8.00 2.40
116 Scott Dohmann RD RC 8.00 2.40
117 Sean Henn RD RC 10.00 3.00
118 Tim Bausher RD RC 8.00 2.40
119 Tim Bittner RD RC 8.00 2.40

2004 SP Game Used Patch 1 of 1

Nm-Mt Ex-Mt
RANDOM INSERTS IN PACKS
STATED PRINT RUN 1 SERIAL #'d SET
NO PRICING DUE TO SCARCITY

2004 SP Game Used Patch 300 Win Club

Nm-Mt Ex-Mt
RANDOM INSERTS IN PACKS
STATED PRINT RUN 10 SERIAL #'d SETS
NO PRICING DUE TO SCARCITY
DS Don Sutton
LG Lefty Grove
NR Nolan Ryan
RC Roger Clemens
SC Steve Carlton
TS Tom Seaver
WS Warren Spahn

2004 SP Game Used Patch 300 Win Club Autograph

Nm-Mt Ex-Mt
RANDOM INSERTS IN PACKS
STATED PRINT RUN 10 SERIAL #'d SETS
NO PRICING DUE TO SCARCITY
DS Don Sutton
GP Gaylord Perry
NR Nolan Ryan Astros
NR1 Nolan Ryan Mets
NR2 Nolan Ryan Angels
NR3 Nolan Ryan Rgr
PN Phil Niekro
SC Steve Carlton
TS Tom Seaver Mets
TS1 Tom Seaver W.Sox

2004 SP Game Used Patch 3000 Hit Club

Nm-Mt Ex-Mt
RANDOM INSERTS IN PACKS
STATED PRINT RUN 10 SERIAL #'d SETS
NO PRICING DUE TO SCARCITY
CR Cal Ripken
CY Carl Yastrzemski
SM Stan Musial
TG Tony Gwynn

2004 SP Game Used Patch 3000 Hit Club Autograph

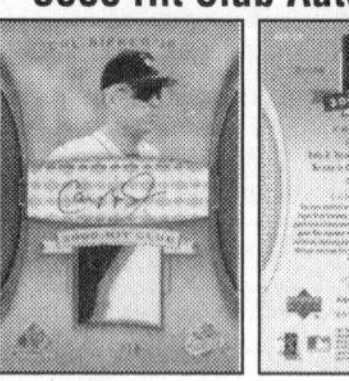

Nm-Mt Ex-Mt
RANDOM INSERTS IN PACKS
STATED PRINT RUN 10 SERIAL #'d SETS
NO PRICING DUE TO SCARCITY
CR Cal Ripken
CY Carl Yastrzemski
LB Lou Brock Cards
LB1 Lou Brock Cubs
PM Paul Molitor Brewers
PM1 Paul Molitor Jays
PM2 Paul Molitor Twins
RY Robin Yount
TG Tony Gwynn
WB Wade Boggs

2004 SP Game Used Patch 500 HR Club

Nm-Mt Ex-Mt
RANDOM INSERTS IN PACKS
STATED PRINT RUN 10 SERIAL #'d SETS
NO PRICING DUE TO SCARCITY
EM Eddie Mathews
FR Frank Robinson
HK Harmon Killebrew
MS Mike Schmidt
RP Rafael Palmeiro
SS Sammy Sosa
TW Ted Williams

2004 SP Game Used Patch 500 HR Club Autograph

Nm-Mt Ex-Mt
RANDOM INSERTS IN PACKS
STATED PRINT RUN 10 SERIAL #'d SETS
NO PRICING DUE TO SCARCITY
FR Frank Robinson Reds
FR1 Frank Robinson O's
HK Harmon Killebrew Twins
HK1 Harmon Killebrew Royals
HK2 Harmon Killebrew Senators
RP Rafael Palmeiro Rgr
RP1 Rafael Palmeiro O's

2004 SP Game Used Patch 500 HR Club Triple

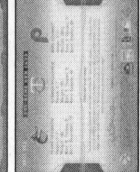

Nm-Mt Ex-Mt
RANDOM INSERTS IN PACKS
STATED PRINT RUN 10 SERIAL #'d SETS
NO PRICING DUE TO SCARCITY
MSW Eddie Mathews
Sammy Sosa
Ted Williams
RKS Frank Robinson
Harmon Killebrew
Mike Schmidt

2004 SP Game Used Patch All-Star

Nm-Mt Ex-Mt
RANDOM INSERTS IN PACKS
STATED PRINT RUN 50 SERIAL #'d SETS
AP Albert Pujols 80.00 24.00
AR Alex Rodriguez 60.00 18.00

AS Alfonso Soriano 40.00 12.00
BZ Barry Zito 40.00 12.00
CD Carlos Delgado 25.00 7.50
CJ Chipper Jones 40.00 12.00
CS Curt Schilling 40.00 12.00
DJ Derek Jeter 100.00 30.00
EC Eric Chavez 25.00 7.50
FT Frank Thomas 40.00 12.00
GS Gary Sheffield 25.00 7.50
HE Todd Helton 40.00 12.00
HN Hideo Nomo 80.00 24.00
IS Ichiro Suzuki 100.00 30.00
JG Juan Gonzalez 40.00 12.00
JT Jim Thome 40.00 12.00
KG Ken Griffey Jr. 60.00 18.00
MP Mark Prior 60.00 18.00
SS Sammy Sosa 50.00 15.00
TH Tim Hudson 25.00 7.50
VW Vernon Wells 25.00 7.50

2004 SP Game Used Patch All-Star Number

Nm-Mt Ex-Mt
RANDOM INSERTS IN PACKS
PRINT RUNS B/WN 3-50 COPIES PER
NO PRICING ON QTY OF 12 OR LESS.
AJ Andruw Jones/25 40.00 12.00
AP Andy Pettitte/42 40.00 12.00
AR Alex Rodriguez/3
AS Alfonso Soriano/12
BZ Barry Zito/50 40.00 12.00
CD Carlos Delgado/25 40.00 12.00
CD1 Carlos Delgado/25 40.00 12.00
CJ Chipper Jones/10
CS Curt Schilling Sox/38 40.00 12.00
CS1 Curt Schilling D'backs/38 40.00 12.00
CY Carl Yastrzemski/8
EC Eric Chavez/3
EC1 Eric Chavez/3
FT Frank Thomas/35 40.00 12.00
GA Garret Anderson/16 40.00 12.00
GM Greg Maddux Braves/31 60.00 18.00
GM1 Greg Maddux Cubs/31 60.00 18.00
GS Gary Sheffield/11
HE Todd Helton/17 50.00 15.00
HN Hideo Nomo/10
IR Ivan Rodriguez/7
IS Ichiro Suzuki/50 100.00 30.00
JG Juan Gonzalez/19 50.00 15.00
JP Jorge Posada/20 50.00 15.00
JT Jim Thome/25 50.00 15.00
KG Ken Griffey Jr./30 80.00 24.00
MM Mike Mussina/35 40.00 12.00
MO Maggio Ordonez/30 25.00 7.50
MP Mark Prior/5
MT Miguel Tejada/4
PM Pedro Martinez/45 40.00 12.00
PU Albert Pujols/7
RC Roger Clemens/22 80.00 24.00
RH Roy Halladay/32 25.00 7.50
RP Rafael Palmeiro/25 50.00 15.00
SG Shawn Green/15 40.00 12.00
SR Scott Rolen/27 40.00 12.00
SS Sammy Sosa Cubs/21 100.00 30.00
SS1 Sammy Sosa Sox/21 100.00 30.00
TH Tim Hudson/15 40.00 12.00
TH1 Tim Hudson/15 40.00 12.00
VW Vernon Wells/10

2004 SP Game Used Patch All-Star Autograph

Nm-Mt Ex-Mt
RANDOM INSERTS IN PACKS
STATED PRINT RUN 10 SERIAL #'d SETS
NO PRICING DUE TO SCARCITY

2004 SP Game Used Patch All-Star Autograph Dual

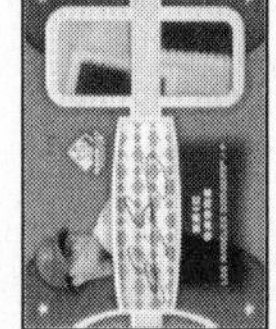

Nm-Mt Ex-Mt
RANDOM INSERTS IN PACKS
STATED PRINT RUN 10 SERIAL #'d SETS
NO PRICING DUE TO SCARCITY

2004 SP Game Used Patch Cut Signatures

Nm-Mt Ex-Mt
RANDOM INSERTS IN PACKS
PRINT RUNS B/WN 1-2 COPIES PER
NO PRICING DUE TO SCARCITY
AD John Adams/1
AE Albert Einstein/1
DE1 Dwight Eisenhower/1
HH Herbert Hoover/1
JA James Monroe/1
JPG Jean Paul Getty/2
MLK Martin Luther King Jr./1
OW Orville Wright/1
REL Robert E. Lee/1
SH William Sherman/1
TE Thomas Edison/1

2004 SP Game Used Patch Cut Signatures Dual

Nm-Mt Ex-Mt
RANDOM INSERTS IN PACKS
STATED PRINT RUN 1 SERIAL #'d SET
NO PRICING DUE TO SCARCITY
AECL Amelia Earhart
Charles Lindberg
BRMM Babe Ruth
Mickey Mantle
ERFR Eleanor Roosevelt
Franklin D.Roosevelt
GWTJ George Washington
Thomas Jefferson
JKRK John F. Kennedy
Robert Kennedy

2004 SP Game Used Patch Famous Nicknames

Nm-Mt Ex-Mt
RANDOM INSERTS IN PACKS
PRINT RUNS B/WN 1-27 COPIES PER
NO PRICING ON QTY OF 14 OR LESS.
AR Alex Rodriguez/10
BM Bill Mazeroski/1
BR Brooks Robinson/23 80.00 24.00
CR Cal Ripken Glove Down/21 200.00 60.00
CR1 Cal Ripken Glove Up/21 200.00 60.00
CY Carl Yastrzemski/23 80.00 24.00
DM Don Mattingly/14
DS Darryl Strawberry/17 50.00 15.00
DW Dontrelle Willis/1
ES Duke Snider/18 50.00 15.00
FT Frank Thomas/14
GA Sparky Anderson/27 25.00 7.50
GC Gary Carter/19 50.00 15.00
HK Harmon Killebrew/22 100.00 30.00
HM Hideki Matsui/1
IR Ivan Rodriguez/13
JB Jeff Bagwell/13
JD Joe DiMaggio/13
JF Nellie Fox/19 200.00 60.00
JG Juan Gonzalez/15 50.00 15.00
JH Catfish Hunter/15 50.00 15.00
KG Ken Griffey Jr./15 150.00 45.00
LB Yogi Berra/19 100.00 30.00
LJ Chipper Jones Hand Up/10
LJ1 Chipper Jones Arms Out/10
MU Mike Mussina Yanks/13
MU1 Mike Mussina O's/13
NR Nolan Ryan Astros/27 100.00 30.00
NR1 Nolan Ryan Rgr/27 100.00 30.00
OC Orlando Cepeda/17 40.00 12.00
OS Ozzie Smith/19 80.00 24.00
PN Phil Niekro/24 40.00 12.00
RC Roger Clemens/20 80.00 24.00
RI Phil Rizzuto/13
RJ Randy Johnson/16 50.00 15.00
RR Red Rolfe/10
RY Robin Yount/20 80.00 24.00
SM Stan Musial/22 150.00 45.00
SS Sammy Sosa Cubs/15 120.00 36.00
SS1 Sammy Sosa Sox/15 120.00 36.00
TS Tom Seaver/20 50.00 15.00
WS Willie Stargell/21 50.00 15.00

2004 SP Game Used Patch Famous Nicknames Autograph

Nm-Mt Ex-Mt
RANDOM INSERTS IN PACKS
STATED PRINT RUN 50 SERIAL #'d SETS
AD Andre Dawson 60.00 18.00
AR Alex Rodriguez Rgr 200.00 60.00
AR1 Alex Rodriguez M's 200.00 60.00
BM Bill Mazeroski 80.00 24.00
BR Brooks Robinson 100.00 30.00

DM Don Mattingly 150.00 45.00
FT Frank Thomas 100.00 30.00
HK Harmon Killebrew 100.00 30.00
HM Hideki Matsui 500.00 150.00
JB Jeff Bagwell 100.00 30.00
JG Juan Gonzalez 80.00 24.00
KG Ken Griffey Jr. 250.00 75.00
LJ Chipper Jones Hand Up 100.00 30.00
MM Mike Mussina 80.00 24.00
NR Nolan Ryan 200.00 60.00
OS Ozzie Smith 120.00 36.00
PN Phil Niekro 60.00 18.00
RC Roger Clemens 175.00 52.50
RY Robin Yount 120.00 36.00
TS Tom Seaver 80.00 24.00
WI Dontrelle Willis 80.00 24.00

2004 SP Game Used Patch HOF Numbers

Nm-Mt Ex-Mt
RANDOM INSERTS IN PACKS
PRINT RUNS B/WN 1-50 COPIES PER
NO PRICING ON QTY OF 11 OR LESS.
AJ Andruw Jones/25 40.00 12.00
AP Albert Pujols/5
AR Alex Rodriguez/3
BE Johnny Bench/5
BG Bob Gibson/45 40.00 12.00
BM Bill Mazeroski/1
BR Brooks Robinson/5
BW Billy Williams/26 40.00 12.00
CD Carlos Delgado/25 40.00 12.00
CH Catfish Hunter/27 40.00 12.00
CJ Chipper Jones/10
CL Roger Clemens/22 80.00 24.00
CR Cal Ripken/8
CS Curt Schilling/38 40.00 12.00
CY Carl Yastrzemski/8
DD Don Drysdale/50 60.00 18.00
DJ Derek Jeter Cap/2
DJ1 Derek Jeter No Cap/2
DS Don Sutton/20 40.00 12.00
EC Eric Chavez/3
EG Eric Gagne/38 40.00 12.00
EM Eddie Mathews/41 80.00 24.00
FR Frank Robinson/20 40.00 12.00
FT Frank Thomas/35 40.00 12.00
GC Gary Carter/8
GL Tom Glavine/47 40.00 12.00
GM Greg Maddux/31 60.00 18.00
GO Juan Gonzalez Royals/19 50.00 15.00
GO1 Juan Gonzalez Rgr/19 50.00 15.00
GP Gaylord Perry/36 25.00 7.50
GS Gary Sheffield/11
HE Todd Helton/17 50.00 15.00
HK Harmon Killebrew/3
HN Hideo Nomo/10
IR Ivan Rodriguez/7
IS Ichiro Suzuki/50 100.00 30.00
JB Jeff Bagwell/5
JC Jose Canseco/33 40.00 12.00
JD Joe DiMaggio/5
JG Jason Giambi/25 50.00 15.00
JI Jim Thome/25 50.00 15.00
JM Joe Morgan/8
JP Jim Palmer/22 40.00 12.00
JT Joe Torre/9
KG Ken Griffey Jr./30 80.00 24.00
LA Luis Aparicio/11
LD Leo Durocher/2
MA Juan Marichal/27 40.00 12.00
MP Mike Piazza/31 60.00 18.00
MR Manny Ramirez/24 40.00 12.00
MS Mike Schmidt/20 80.00 24.00
MZ Pedro Martinez/45 40.00 12.00
NF Nellie Fox/2
NG Nomar Garciaparra/5
NR Nolan Ryan/34 80.00 24.00
OC Orlando Cepeda/30 25.00 7.50
OS Ozzie Smith/1
PI Mark Prior Look Right/22 80.00 24.00
PI1 Mark Prior Look Left/22 80.00 24.00
PM Paul Molitor/4
PR Phil Rizzuto/10
RC Roberto Clemente/21 350.00 105.00
RF Rollie Fingers/34 25.00 7.50
RH Rickey Henderson/25 50.00 15.00
RP Rafael Palmeiro O's/25 50.00 15.00
RP1 Rafael Palmeiro Rgr/25 50.00 15.00
RY Robin Yount/19 80.00 24.00
SA Sparky Anderson/2
SC Steve Carlton/32 25.00 7.50
SG Shawn Green/15 40.00 12.00
SM Stan Musial/6
SN Duke Snider/4
SR Scott Rolen/27 40.00 12.00
SS Sammy Sosa Cubs/21 100.00 30.00
SS1 Sammy Sosa Sox/21 100.00 30.00
ST Willie Stargell/8
TG Tony Gwynn/19
TH Tim Hudson/15 40.00 12.00
TS Tom Seaver/41 40.00 12.00
WB Wade Boggs/26 40.00 12.00
WS Warren Spahn/21 80.00 24.00
YB Yogi Berra/8

2004 SP Game Used Patch HOF Numbers Autograph

Nm-Mt Ex-Mt
RANDOM INSERTS IN PACKS
STATED PRINT RUN 10 SERIAL #'d SETS
PUCKETT PRINT RUN 3 SERIAL #'d CARDS
NO PRICING DUE TO SCARCITY

2004 SP Game Used Patch HOF Numbers Autograph Dual

Nm-Mt Ex-Mt
RANDOM INSERTS IN PACKS
STATED PRINT RUN 10 SERIAL #'d SETS
NO PRICING DUE TO SCARCITY

2004 SP Game Used Patch Legendary Fabrics

Nm-Mt Ex-Mt
RANDOM INSERTS IN PACKS
PRINT RUNS B/WN 6-50 COPIES PER
NO PRICING ON QTY OF 10 OR LESS.
BE Johnny Bench w/Mask/50 40.00 12.00
BE1 Johnny Bench Hitting/50 40.00 12.00
BG Bob Gibson/50 40.00 12.00
BR Brooks Robinson/9
BR1 Brooks Robinson/10
BW Billy Williams/50 25.00 7.50
CH Catfish Hunter/50 40.00 12.00
CR Cal Ripken Fielding/50 100.00 30.00
CR1 Cal Ripken Running/50 100.00 30.00
CY Carl Yastrzemski/31 60.00 18.00
EM Eddie Mathews/50 80.00 24.00
FR Frank Robinson O's/50 40.00 12.00
FR1 Frank Robinson Reds/50 40.00 12.00
GP Gaylord Perry/50 25.00 7.50
HK Harmon Killebrew Twins/50 80.00 24.00
HK1 H.Killebrew Senators/50 80.00 24.00
JC Jose Canseco/50 40.00 12.00
JM Joe Morgan Reds/50 25.00 7.50
JM1 Joe Morgan Giants/50 25.00 7.50
JP Jim Palmer/6
JP1 Jim Palmer/7
JT Joe Torre/50 40.00 12.00
LA Luis Aparicio/50 25.00 7.50
LD Leo Durocher/50 40.00 12.00
MS Mike Schmidt Bat Hand/50 60.00 18.00
MS1 Mike Schmidt Swing/50 60.00 18.00
NR Nolan Ryan Astros/50 60.00 18.00
NR1 Nolan Ryan Rgr/50 60.00 18.00
OC Orlando Cepeda/50 25.00 7.50
OS Ozzie Smith/50 50.00 15.00
PO Paul O'Neill/50 40.00 12.00
RF Rollie Fingers/50 25.00 7.50
RY Robin Yount Bat Up/50 50.00 15.00
RY1 Robin Yount Bat Down/50 50.00 15.00
SC Steve Carlton/50 25.00 7.50
TS Tom Seaver Mets/50 40.00 12.00
TS1 Tom Seaver Reds/50 40.00 12.00
WS W.Spahn Arms Down/50 50.00 15.00
WS1 W.Spahn Arms Up/50 50.00 15.00

2004 SP Game Used Patch Legendary Fabrics Autograph Dual

Nm-Mt Ex-Mt
RANDOM INSERTS IN PACKS
PRINT RUNS B/WN 10-25 COPIES PER
NO PRICING ON QTY OF 13 OR LESS.
AD Andre Dawson/25 100.00 30.00
BE Johnny Bench/25 150.00 45.00
BM Bill Mazeroski/10
BR Brooks Robinson/25 150.00 45.00
BW Billy Williams/25 120.00 36.00
CR Cal Ripken/25 350.00 105.00
CY Carl Yastrzemski/17 200.00 60.00
DE Dwight Evans/25 100.00 30.00
DM Don Mattingly/25 250.00 75.00
DS Don Sutton/25 80.00 24.00
FL Fred Lynn/25 80.00 24.00
FR Frank Robinson/25 120.00 36.00
GP Gaylord Perry/25 80.00 24.00
HK Harmon Killebrew/25 150.00 45.00
JC Jose Canseco/25 150.00 45.00
JM Joe Morgan/25 100.00 30.00
JP Jim Palmer/25 100.00 30.00
JT Joe Torre Cards 25 120.00 36.00
JT1 Joe Torre Braves/25 120.00 36.00
KP Kirby Puckett/25 150.00 45.00
KP1 Kirby Puckett/12
LA Luis Aparicio/25 80.00 24.00
LB Lou Brock/13
NR Nolan Ryan Astros/25 250.00 75.00
NR1 Nolan Ryan Rgr/25 250.00 75.00
OC Orlando Cepeda/25 100.00 30.00
OS Ozzie Smith/25 175.00 52.50
PM Paul Molitor/25 120.00 36.00
PO Paul O'Neill/25 120.00 36.00
RC Roger Clemens/25 250.00 75.00
RF Rollie Fingers/25 100.00 30.00
RY Robin Yount Look Ahead/25 175.00 52.50
SG Steve Garvey/25 100.00 30.00
ST Darryl Strawberry/25 120.00 36.00
TG Tony Gwynn Look Left/25 150.00 45.00
TG1 Tony Gwynn Look Right/25 150.00 45.00
TS Tom Seaver Mets/25 120.00 36.00
TS1 Tom Seaver Reds/25 120.00 36.00
WB Wade Boggs Yanks/25 120.00 36.00
WB1 Wade Boggs Sox/25 120.00 36.00
WI Maury Wills/25 80.00 24.00
YO Robin Yount Look Right/25 175.00 52.50

2004 SP Game Used Patch Logo Threads

Nm-Mt Ex-Mt
RANDOM INSERTS IN PACKS
STATED PRINT RUN 1 SERIAL #'d SET
NO PRICING DUE TON SCARCITY

2004 SP Game Used Patch Logo Threads Autograph

Nm-Mt Ex-Mt
RANDOM INSERTS IN PACKS
STATED PRINT RUN 1 SERIAL #'d SET
NO PRICING DUE TO SCARCITY

2004 SP Game Used Patch Logo Threads Autograph Dual

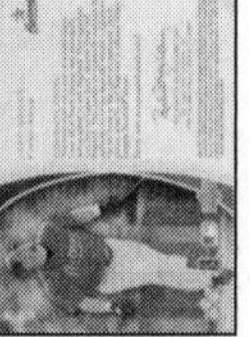

Nm-Mt Ex-Mt
RANDOM INSERTS IN PACKS
STATED PRINT RUN 1 SERIAL #'d SET
NO PRICING DUE TO SCARCITY

2004 SP Game Used Patch MLB Masters

Nm-Mt Ex-Mt
RANDOM INSERTS IN PACKS
PRINT RUNS B/WN 3-50 COPIES PER
NO PRICING ON QTY OF 12 OR LESS.
AJ Andruw Jones/25 40.00 12.00
AP Albert Pujols/5
AR Alex Rodriguez/3
AS Alfonso Soriano/12
BE Josh Beckett/25 50.00 15.00
CD Carlos Delgado/25 40.00 12.00
CJ Chipper Jones/10

CS Curt Schilling/38 .... 40.00 12.00
EC Eric Chavez/3
FT Frank Thomas/35 .... 40.00 12.00
GM Greg Maddux Braves/31 ..... 60.00 18.00
GM1 Greg Maddux Cubs/31 ..... 60.00 18.00
GO Juan Gonzalez/19 .... 50.00 15.00
GS Gary Sheffield/11
HE Todd Helton/17 .... 50.00 15.00
HN Hideo Nomo Dodgers/10
HN1 Hideo Nomo Sox/10
IR Ivan Rodriguez/7
IS Ichiro Suzuki/50 .... 100.00 30.00
JB Jeff Bagwell/5
JG Jason Giambi/25 .... 50.00 15.00
JP Jorge Posada/20 .... 50.00 15.00
JT Jim Thome Phils/25 .... 50.00 15.00
JT1 Jim Thome Indians/25 .... 50.00 15.00
KG Ken Griffey Jr./30 .... 80.00 24.00
MO Magglio Ordonez/30 .... 25.00 7.50
MP Mark Prior/22 .... 80.00 24.00
MR Manny Ramirez/24 .... 40.00 12.00
PI Mike Piazza/31 .... 60.00 18.00
PM Pedro Martinez/45 .... 40.00 12.00
RC Roger Clemens/22 .... 80.00 24.00
RH Roy Halladay/32 .... 25.00 7.50
SG Shawn Green/15 .... 40.00 12.00
SR Scott Rolen/27 .... 40.00 12.00
SS Sammy Sosa/21 .... 100.00 30.00
TH Tim Hudson Glove Up/15 .... 40.00 12.00
TH1 Tim Hudson Glove Down/15 40.00 12.00
VW Vernon Wells/10

2004 SP Game Used Patch MVP

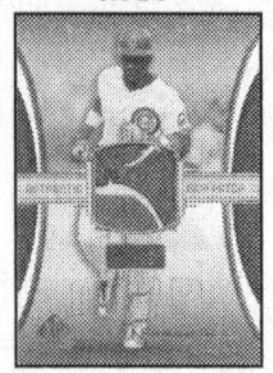

Nm-Mt Ex-Mt
RANDOM INSERTS IN PACKS
STATED PRINT RUN 25 SERIAL #'d SETS
AR Alex Rodriguez 60.00 18.00
BR Brooks Robinson 80.00 24.00
BW Bernie Williams 50.00 15.00
CJ Chipper Jones 50.00 15.00
CR Cal Ripken 150.00 45.00
CS Curt Schilling 50.00 15.00
DJ Derek Jeter 120.00 36.00
FT Frank Thomas 50.00 15.00
GA Garret Anderson 40.00 12.00
IS Ichiro Suzuki 120.00 36.00
IV Ivan Rodriguez 50.00 15.00
JB Josh Beckett 50.00 15.00
JG Jason Giambi 50.00 15.00
KG Ken Griffey Jr. 80.00 24.00
MP Mike Piazza 60.00 18.00
MT Miguel Tejada 40.00 12.00
PM Pedro Martinez 50.00 15.00
RC Roger Clemens 80.00 24.00
RJ Randy Johnson 50.00 15.00
SS Sammy Sosa 60.00 18.00
TG Troy Glaus 50.00 15.00

2004 SP Game Used Patch Premium

Nm-Mt Ex-Mt
RANDOM INSERTS IN PACKS
STATED PRINT RUN 50 SERIAL #'d SETS
GARCIAPARRA PRINT RUN 11 #'d CARDS
MATSUI PRINT RUN 17 #'d CARDS ...
SORIANO PRINT RUN 34 #'d CARDS .
NO PRICING ON QTY OF 11 OR LESS.
AD Adam Dunn 25.00 7.50
AP Albert Pujols 80.00 24.00
AR Alex Rodriguez Rgr 60.00 18.00
AR1 A.Rodriguez Yanks Cap 80.00 24.00
AR2 A.Rodriguez Yanks Helmet 80.00 24.00
AS Alfonso Soriano/34 .... 40.00 12.00
BE Josh Beckett 40.00 12.00
BW Bernie Williams 40.00 12.00
BZ Barry Zito 40.00 12.00
CD Carlos Delgado 25.00 7.50
CJ Chipper Jones 40.00 12.00
CS Curt Schilling Glove Up 40.00 12.00
CS1 Curt Schilling Hand in Air... 40.00 12.00
DJ Derek Jeter 100.00 30.00
DW Dontrelle Willis 25.00 7.50
EC Eric Chavez 25.00 7.50
FT Frank Thomas 40.00 12.00
GM Greg Maddux Braves 50.00 15.00
GM1 Greg Maddux Cubs 50.00 15.00
GO Juan Gonzalez 40.00 12.00
HM Hideki Matsui/17 .... 200.00 60.00
IR Ivan Rodriguez 40.00 12.00
IS Ichiro Suzuki Profile 100.00 30.00
IS1 Ichiro Suzuki Arm Out 100.00 30.00
JB Jeff Bagwell 40.00 12.00
JG Jason Giambi 40.00 12.00
JP Jorge Posada 40.00 12.00
JT Jim Thome 40.00 12.00
KB Kevin Brown 25.00 7.50
KG Ken Griffey Jr. Arm Out 60.00 18.00
KG1 K.Griffey Jr. Red Helmet 60.00 18.00
MO Magglio Ordonez 25.00 7.50
MP Mark Prior 60.00 18.00
MR Manny Ramirez 25.00 7.50
MT Miguel Tejada 25.00 7.50
NG Nomar Garciaparra/11
NR Nolan Ryan 60.00 18.00
PI Mike Piazza 50.00 15.00
PM Pedro Martinez 40.00 12.00
RC Roger Clemens 50.00 15.00
RH Roy Halladay 25.00 7.50
RI Mariano Rivera 40.00 12.00
RJ Randy Johnson 40.00 12.00
RP Rafael Palmeiro 40.00 12.00
SG Shawn Green 25.00 7.50
SR Scott Rolen 40.00 12.00
SS Sammy Sosa Swing 50.00 15.00
SS1 Sammy Sosa Bat Down 50.00 15.00
TE Mark Teixeira 25.00 7.50
TG Tom Glavine 40.00 12.00
TH Tim Hudson 25.00 7.50

2004 SP Game Used Patch Premium Autograph

Nm-Mt Ex-Mt
RANDOM INSERTS IN PACKS ....
STATED PRINT RUN 50 SERIAL #'d SETS
GARCIAPARRA PRINT 33 SERIAL #'d CARDS
AK Austin Kearns 60.00 18.00
AR Alex Rodriguez 200.00 60.00
BZ Barry Zito 80.00 24.00
CD Carlos Delgado 60.00 18.00
DW Dontrelle Willis 80.00 24.00
EC Eric Chavez 60.00 18.00
EG Eric Gagne 80.00 24.00
HM Hideki Matsui 500.00 150.00
IR Ivan Rodriguez 100.00 30.00
IS Ichiro Suzuki 400.00 120.00
KB Kevin Brown 60.00 18.00
KG Ken Griffey Jr. Reds 250.00 75.00
KG1 Ken Griffey Jr. M's 250.00 75.00
MP Mark Prior 150.00 45.00
MT Miguel Tejada 60.00 18.00
NG Nomar Garciaparra/33 .... 250.00 75.00
RC Roger Clemens 175.00 52.50
SG Shawn Green 60.00 18.00
TG Troy Glaus
TH Tim Hudson 80.00 24.00
VG Vladimir Guerrero 100.00 30.00

2004 SP Game Used Patch Significant Numbers

Nm-Mt Ex-Mt
RANDOM INSERTS IN PACKS ....
PRINT RUNS B/WN 1-27 COPIES PER
NO PRICING ON QTY OF 14 OR LESS.
AJ Andruw Jones/8
AP Albert Pujols/3
AR Alex Rodriguez/10
BE Josh Beckett/3
BW Brandon Webb/1
CD Carlos Delgado/11
CJ Chipper Jones/10
CR Cal Ripken/21 .... 200.00 60.00
CS Curt Schilling/16 .... 50.00 15.00
CY Carl Yastrzemski/23 .... 80.00 24.00
DJ Derek Jeter/9
DS Darryl Strawberry/17 .... 50.00 15.00
EC Eric Chavez/6
EG Eric Gagne/5
EM Eddie Mathews/17 .... 120.00 36.00
FT Frank Thomas/14
GM Greg Maddux/18 .... 80.00 24.00
GO Juan Gonzalez/15 .... 50.00 15.00
GS Gary Sheffield/16 .... 40.00 12.00
HM Hideki Matsui/1
IS Ichiro Suzuki/3
JB Jeff Bagwell/13
JG Jason Giambi/9
KG Ken Griffey Jr./15 .... 150.00 45.00
MM Mike Mussina/13
MP Mike Piazza/12
MR Manny Ramirez/11
MT Mark Teixeira/1
NR Nolan Ryan/27 .... 100.00 30.00
PM Pedro Martinez/12
PO Paul O'Neill/17 .... 50.00 15.00
PR Mark Prior/2
RC Roger Clemens/20 .... 80.00 24.00
RF Rollie Fingers/17 .... 40.00 12.00
RH Roy Halladay/6
RJ Randy Johnson/16 .... 50.00 15.00
RP Rafael Palmeiro/18 .... 50.00 15.00
SG Shawn Green/11
SN Duke Snider/18 .... 50.00 15.00
SS Sammy Sosa/15 .... 120.00 36.00
TG Tom Glavine/17 .... 50.00 15.00
TS Tom Seaver/20 .... 50.00 15.00

2004 SP Game Used Patch Significant Numbers Autograph

Nm-Mt Ex-Mt
RANDOM INSERTS IN PACKS
STATED PRINT RUN 50 SERIAL #'d SETS
BROCK PRINT RUN 16 SERIAL #'d CARDS

PUCKETT PRINT RUN 3 SERIAL #'d CARDS
NO PUCKETT PRICING DUE TO SCARCITY
AR Alex Rodriguez Rgr 200.00 60.00
AR1 Alex Rodriguez M's 200.00 60.00
BA Bobby Abreu 60.00 18.00
BG Brian Giles 60.00 18.00
BW Bernie Williams 120.00 36.00
BZ Barry Zito 80.00 24.00
CD Carlos Delgado 60.00 18.00
CJ Chipper Jones 100.00 30.00
EC Eric Chavez 60.00 18.00
EG Eric Gagne 80.00 24.00
GM Greg Maddux 150.00 45.00
HE Todd Helton 80.00 24.00
HM Hideki Matsui 500.00 150.00
JG Juan Gonzalez Royals 80.00 24.00
JG1 Juan Gonzalez Rgr 80.00 24.00
KB Kevin Brown 60.00 18.00
KG Ken Griffey Jr. Reds 250.00 75.00
KG1 Ken Griffey Jr. M's 250.00 75.00
KP Kirby Puckett/3
LB Lou Brock/16 .... 100.00 30.00
LG Luis Gonzalez 60.00 18.00
MM Mike Mussina Yanks 80.00 24.00
MM1 Mike Mussina O's 80.00 24.00
MP Mike Piazza 250.00 75.00
MS Mike Schmidt 120.00 36.00
MT Miguel Tejada O's 60.00 18.00
MT1 Miguel Tejada A's 60.00 18.00
NR Nolan Ryan 200.00 60.00
PB Pat Burrell 60.00 18.00
PO Paul O'Neill 80.00 24.00
PR Mark Prior 150.00 45.00
RA Roberto Alomar 100.00 30.00
RB Rocco Baldelli 100.00 30.00
RF Rollie Fingers 60.00 18.00
RO Roy Oswalt Arm Up 60.00 18.00
RO1 Roy Oswalt Elbow Out 60.00 18.00
RP Rafael Palmeiro 100.00 30.00
RS Ryne Sandberg 120.00 36.00
SG Shawn Green 60.00 18.00
TG Tom Glavine 80.00 24.00
TH Tim Hudson 80.00 24.00
VG Vladimir Guerrero 100.00 30.00

2004 SP Game Used Patch Significant Numbers Autograph Dual

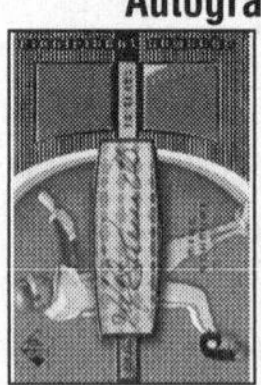

Nm-Mt Ex-Mt
RANDOM INSERTS IN PACKS
STATED PRINT RUN 25 SERIAL #'d SETS
BROCK PRINT RUN 14 SERIAL #'d CARDS
NO BROCK PRICING DUE TO SCARCITY
AR Alex Rodriguez Rgr 300.00 90.00
BA Bobby Abreu 80.00 24.00
BG Brian Giles 80.00 24.00
BW Bernie Williams 200.00 60.00
BZ Barry Zito 120.00 36.00
CD Carlos Delgado 100.00 30.00
CJ Chipper Jones 150.00 45.00
DW Dontrelle Willis 120.00 36.00
EC Eric Chavez 100.00 30.00
EG Eric Gagne 120.00 36.00
GI Bob Gibson 120.00 36.00
GM Greg Maddux 200.00 60.00
HE Todd Helton 120.00 36.00
HM Hideki Matsui 600.00 180.00
JG Juan Gonzalez Royals 120.00 36.00
JG1 Juan Gonzalez Rgr 120.00 36.00
KB Kevin Brown 100.00 30.00
KG Ken Griffey Jr. Reds 400.00 120.00
KP Kirby Puckett 150.00 45.00
LB Lou Brock/14
LG Luis Gonzalez 80.00 24.00
MM Mike Mussina Yanks 120.00 36.00
MM1 Mike Mussina O's 120.00 36.00
MP Mike Piazza 350.00 105.00
MR Troy Glaus 120.00 36.00
MS Mike Schmidt 250.00 75.00
MT Miguel Tejada O's 80.00 24.00
MT1 Miguel Tejada A's 80.00 24.00
NR Nolan Ryan 250.00 75.00
PB Pat Burrell 100.00 30.00
PO Paul O'Neill 120.00 36.00
RA Roberto Alomar 150.00 45.00
RF Rollie Fingers 100.00 30.00
RP Rafael Palmeiro 150.00 45.00
RS Ryne Sandberg 250.00 75.00
SG Shawn Green Dodgers 100.00 30.00
SG1 Shawn Green Jays 100.00 30.00
TG Tom Glavine 120.00 36.00
TH Tim Hudson 120.00 36.00
TO Tony Gwynn 150.00 45.00
TS Tom Seaver 120.00 36.00
VG Vladimir Guerrero 150.00 45.00

2004 SP Game Used Patch Star Potential

Nm-Mt Ex-Mt
RANDOM INSERTS IN PACKS ....
PRINT RUNS B/WN 3-50 COPIES PER
NO PRICING ON QTY OF 12 OR LESS.

AS Alfonso Soriano/12
BW Brandon Webb/50 .... 25.00 7.50
CP Corey Patterson/20 .... 40.00 12.00
DWO D.Willis Arm Up/35 .... 25.00 7.50
DW1 D.Willis Arm Down/35 .... 25.00 7.50
EC Eric Chavez/3
HA Roy Halladay/32 .... 25.00 7.50
HB Hank Blalock/9
IS Ichiro Suzuki/50 .... 100.00 30.00
JB Josh Beckett/21 .... 50.00 15.00
JR Jose Reyes/7
LB Lance Berkman/17 .... 40.00 12.00
MM Mark Mulder/20 .... 40.00 12.00
MPO M.Prior Hand in Glove/22 . 80.00 24.00
MP1 Mark Prior Throwing/22 .... 80.00 24.00
MT M.Teixeira Hands Back/23 .. 40.00 12.00
MT1 M.Teixeira Hands Fwd/23 .. 40.00 12.00
RB Rocco Baldelli/5
RH Rich Harden/40 .... 25.00 7.50
RO Roy Oswalt/44 .... 25.00 7.50
RS Richie Sexson/11
RW Rickie Weeks/23 .... 50.00 15.00
TE Miguel Tejada/4
TG Troy Glaus/25 .... 50.00 15.00
TH Tim Hudson/15 .... 40.00 12.00
VW Vernon Wells/10

2004 SP Game Used Patch Stellar Combos Dual

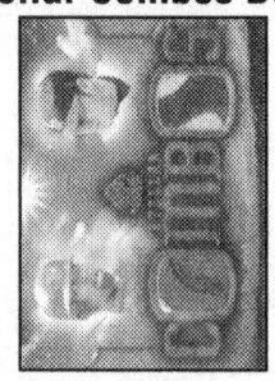

Nm-Mt Ex-Mt
RANDOM INSERTS IN PACKS ....
PRINT RUNS B/WN 1-25 COPIES PER
NO PRICING ON QTY OF 8 OR LESS...
AD Alfonso Soriano 120.00 36.00
Derek Jeter/8
AJ Alex Rodriguez 80.00 24.00
Juan Gonzalez/25
AT Bobby Abreu 60.00 18.00
Jim Thome/25
BK Jeff Bagwell 60.00 18.00
Jeff Kent/25
BT Hank Blalock 50.00 15.00
Mark Teixeira/25
CA Joe Carter 60.00 18.00
Roberto Alomar/25
CO Roger Clemens 80.00 24.00
Roy Oswalt/25
CR Curt Schilling 60.00 18.00
Randy Johnson/25
DG Carlos Delgado 60.00 18.00
Jason Giambi/25
DK Adam Dunn 50.00 15.00
Austin Kearns/25
DL Derek Jeter
Lou Gehrig/25
GH Eric Gagne 60.00 18.00
Trevor Hoffman/25
GT Greg Maddux 100.00 30.00
Tom Glavine/25
JD Derek Jeter
Joe DiMaggio/10
JG Derek Jeter
Nomar Garciaparra/3
JJ Andruw Jones 60.00 18.00
Chipper Jones/25
KR Jerry Koosman 175.00 52.50
Nolan Ryan/25
LP Al Leiter 80.00 24.00
Mike Piazza/25
LS Fred Lynn 120.00 36.00
Ichiro Suzuki/25
MG Don Mattingly 100.00 30.00
Jason Giambi/25
MM Hideki Matsui
Mickey Mantle/1
MN Hideki Matsui
Hideo Nomo/5
MT Edgar Martinez 60.00 18.00
Frank Thomas/25
MY Paul Molitor 100.00 30.00
Robin Yount/25
NB Hideo Nomo 60.00 18.00
Kevin Brown/25
NY Alfonso Soriano 60.00 18.00
Jose Reyes/25
PC Mark Prior 100.00 30.00
Roger Clemens/25
PE Albert Pujols 120.00 36.00
Jim Edmonds/25
PM Andy Pettitte 60.00 18.00
Mike Mussina/25
PP Jorge Posada 80.00 24.00
Mike Piazza/25
PS Rafael Palmeiro 80.00 24.00
Sammy Sosa/25
RB Ivan Rodriguez 60.00 18.00
Josh Beckett/25
RG1 Manny Ramirez
Nomar Garciaparra/3
RG2 Cal Ripken 500.00 150.00
Lou Gehrig/25
RJ1 Alex Rodriguez Rgr 150.00 45.00
Derek Jeter/25
RJ2 Alex Rodriguez Yanks

Derek Jeter/25
RR Alex Rodriguez 250.00 75.00
Cal Ripken/25
RS Brooks Robinson 150.00 45.00
Mike Schmidt/25
SC Ichiro Suzuki 250.00 75.00
Ty Cobb/25
SG Duke Snider 60.00 18.00
Shawn Green/25
SJ Gary Sheffield 60.00 18.00
Randy Johnson/25
SM Curt Schilling 60.00 18.00
Pedro Martinez/25
SR Curt Schilling 100.00 30.00
Nolan Ryan/25
TO Frank Thomas 60.00 18.00
Magglio Ordonez/25
WC David Wells 80.00 24.00
Roger Clemens/25
WH Larry Walker 60.00 18.00
Todd Helton/25
WS Billy Williams 80.00 24.00
Sammy Sosa/25
WW Honus Wagner
Ted Williams/1
ZH Barry Zito 60.00 18.00
Tim Hudson/25

2004 SP Game Used Patch Team Threads Triple

Nm-Mt Ex-Mt
RANDOM INSERTS IN PACKS
STATED PRINT RUN 10 SERIAL #'d SETS
MANNY/NOMAR/PEDRO PRINT 3 #'d CARDS
A.ROD/JETER/MATSUI PRINT 5 #'d CARDS
NO PRICING DUE TO SCARCITY ....
AB Andruw Jones
Chipper Jones
Gary Sheffield
AD Curt Schilling
Luis Gonzalez
Randy Johnson
BR Manny Ramirez
Nomar Garciaparra
Pedro Martinez/3
CC Kerry Wood
Mark Prior
Sammy Sosa
CW Frank Thomas
Magglio Ordonez
Roberto Alomar
HA Craig Biggio
Jeff Bagwell
Lance Berkman
NY Bernie Williams
Hideki Matsui
Jason Giambi
PP Bobby Abreu
Jim Thome
Kevin Millwood
RJG Alex Rodriguez
Derek Jeter
Jason Giambi
RJM Alex Rodriguez
Derek Jeter
Hideki Matsui/5
RSB Alex Rodriguez
Gary Sheffield
Kevin Brown
SC Albert Pujols
Jim Edmonds
Scott Rolen
SM Bret Boone
Edgar Martinez
Ichiro Suzuki
WSM Honus Wagner
Ichiro Suzuki
Mickey Mantle

2004 SP Game Used Patch Triple Authentic

Nm-Mt Ex-Mt
RANDOM INSERTS IN PACKS ....
STATED PRINT RUN 10 SERIAL #'d SETS
A.ROD/JETER/NOMAR PRINT 3 #'d CARDS
A.ROD/MANNY/NOMAR PRINT 3 #'d CARDS
NO PRICING DUE TO SCARCITY ....
BTH Jeff Bagwell
Jim Thome
Todd Helton
CBG Eric Chavez
Hank Blalock
Troy Glaus
CRB Eric Chavez
Scott Rolen
Tony Batista
DGP Carlos Delgado
Jason Giambi
Rafael Palmeiro
DHW Carlos Delgado
Roy Halladay
Vernon Wells
DKG Adam Dunn

Austin Kearns
Ken Griffey Jr.
FCB Carlton Fisk
Gary Carter
Johnny Bench
GNG Eric Gagne
Hideo Nomo
Shawn Green
GPS Ken Griffey Jr.
Rafael Palmeiro
Sammy Sosa
JAB Andruw Jones
Bobby Abreu
Pat Burrell
JBJ Jason Jennings
Kevin Brown
Randy Johnson
JJP Randy Johnson
Jacque Jones
Mark Prior
KSB Adam Kennedy
Alfonso Soriano
Bret Boone
LHG Al Leiter
Mike Hampton
Tom Glavine
LTP Javy Lopez
Miguel Tejada
Rafael Palmeiro
MMG Greg Maddux
Kevin Millwood
Tom Glavine
MYW Paul Molitor
Robin Yount
Rickie Weeks
PBS Albert Pujols
Lance Berkman
Sammy Sosa
PDH Albert Pujols
Carlos Delgado
Todd Helton
PMO Mark Prior
Matt Morris
Roy Oswalt
RJG Alex Rodriguez
Derek Jeter
Nomar Garciaparra/3
RPP Ivan Rodriguez
Jorge Posada
Mike Piazza
RRG Alex Rodriguez
Manny Ramirez
Nomar Garciaparra/3
RVS Cal Ripken
Omar Vizquel
Ozzie Smith
SCM Ichiro Suzuki
Roberto Clemente
Stan Musial
SJM Alfonso Soriano
Derek Jeter
Hideki Matsui
SSB Curt Schilling
Gary Sheffield
Kevin Brown
WWP Brandon Webb
Dontrelle Willis
Mark Prior
ZMC Barry Zito
Pedro Martinez
Roger Clemens
ZMH Barry Zito
Mark Mulder
Tim Hudson

2004 SP Game Used Patch World Series

	Nm-Mt	Ex-Mt
RANDOM INSERTS IN PACKS		
PRINT RUNS B/WN 15-50 COPIES PER		
AJ Andruw Jones/50	25.00	7.50
AP Andy Pettitte/15	50.00	15.00
ASO A.Soriano Hands on Bat/15	50.00	15.00
AS1 A.Soriano Hands Apart/15	50.00	15.00
BL Barry Larkin/50	40.00	12.00
BW Bernie Williams/50	40.00	12.00
CA Jose Canseco/50	40.00	12.00
CJ Chipper Jones/50	40.00	12.00
CS Curt Schilling D'backs/50	40.00	12.00
CS1 Curt Schilling Sox/50	40.00	12.00
CY Carl Yastrzemski/31	60.00	18.00
DW Dontrelle Willis/50	25.00	7.50
GA Garret Anderson/50	25.00	7.50
GL Troy Glaus Run/50	40.00	12.00
GL1 Troy Glaus Walk/50	40.00	12.00
GM Greg Maddux Arm Up/50	50.00	15.00
GM1 Greg Maddux Cubs/50	50.00	15.00
GM2 G.Maddux Glove Out/50	50.00	15.00
HM Hideki Matsui/17	200.00	60.00
IR Ivan Rodriguez/50	40.00	12.00
JB Josh Beckett Leaning/50	40.00	12.00
JB1 Josh Beckett Leg Kick/50	40.00	12.00
JE Derek Jeter Gray/50	100.00	30.00
JE1 Derek Jeter Stripes/50	100.00	30.00
JM Joe Morgan/50	25.00	7.50
JP Jorge Posada/50	40.00	12.00
JT Jim Thome Indians/50	40.00	12.00
JT1 Jim Thome Phils/50	40.00	12.00
KB Kevin Brown/50	25.00	7.50
MM Mike Mussina Yanks/50	40.00	12.00
MM1 Mike Mussina O's/43	40.00	12.00
MP Mike Piazza Mets/50	50.00	15.00
MP1 Mike Piazza Dodgers/50	50.00	15.00
MR Mariano Rivera/50	40.00	12.00
MS Mike Schmidt/50	60.00	18.00
PM Paul Molitor/50	40.00	12.00
PO Paul O'Neill/50	40.00	12.00
RC Roger Clemens/50	50.00	15.00
RF Rollie Fingers/50	40.00	12.00
RJ Randy Johnson/50	40.00	12.00
TG Tom Glavine/50	40.00	12.00

2004 SP Game Used Patch World Series Autograph

Nm-Mt Ex-Mt
RANDOM INSERTS IN PACKS
STATED PRINT RUN 1 SERIAL #'d SET
NO PRICING DUE TO SCARCITY

2004 SP Game Used Patch World Series Autograph Dual

Nm-Mt Ex-Mt
RANDOM INSERTS IN PACKS
STATED PRINT RUN 1 SERIAL #'d SET
NO PRICING DUE TO SCARCITY

2001 SP Legendary Cuts

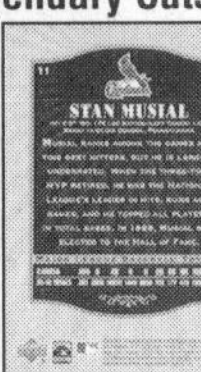

The SP Lengendary Cuts product was released in October, 2001 and featured a 90-card base set. Each pack contained four cards and carried a suggested retail price of $9.99.

	Nm-Mt	Ex-Mt
COMPLETE SET (90)	25.00	7.50
1 Al Simmons	.30	.09
2 Jimmie Foxx	.75	.23
3 Mickey Cochrane	.50	.15
4 Phil Niekro	.30	.09
5 Eddie Mathews	.75	.23
6 Gary Matthews	.30	.09
7 Hank Aaron	1.50	.45
8 Joe Adcock	.30	.09
9 Warren Spahn	.50	.15
10 George Sisler	.30	.09
11 Stan Musial	1.25	.35
12 Dizzy Dean	.75	.23
13 Frankie Frisch	.30	.09
14 Harvey Haddix	.30	.09
15 Johnny Mize	.50	.15
16 Ken Boyer	.30	.09
17 Rogers Hornsby	.75	.23
18 Cap Anson	.75	.23
19 Andre Dawson	.30	.09
20 Billy Williams	.30	.09
21 Billy Herman	.30	.09
22 Hack Wilson	.50	.15
23 Ron Santo	.50	.15
24 Ryne Sandberg	1.25	.35
25 Ernie Banks	.75	.23
26 Burleigh Grimes	.30	.09
27 Don Drysdale	.75	.23
28 Gil Hodges	.75	.23
29 Jackie Robinson	1.00	.30
30 Tommy Lasorda	.30	.09
31 Pee Wee Reese	.75	.23
32 Roy Campanella	.75	.23
33 Tommy Davis	.30	.09
34 Branch Rickey	.30	.09
35 Leo Durocher	.50	.15
36 Walt Alston	.30	.09
37 Bill Terry	.30	.09
38 Carl Hubbell	.50	.15
39 Eddie Stanky	.30	.09
40 George Kelly	.30	.09
41 Mel Ott	.75	.23
42 Juan Marichal	.30	.09
43 Rube Marquard	.30	.09
44 Travis Jackson	.30	.09
45 Bob Feller	.50	.15
46 Earl Averill	.30	.09
47 Elmer Flick	.30	.09
48 Ken Keltner	.30	.09
49 Lou Boudreau	.50	.15
50 Early Wynn	.50	.15
51 Satchel Paige	.75	.23
52 Ron Hunt	.30	.09
53 Tom Seaver	.50	.15
54 Richie Ashburn	.50	.15
55 Mike Schmidt	1.50	.45
56 Honus Wagner	1.00	.30
57 Lloyd Waner	.50	.15
58 Max Carey	.30	.09
59 Paul Waner	.50	.15
60 Roberto Clemente	2.00	.60
61 Nolan Ryan	2.00	.60
62 Bobby Doerr	.50	.15
63 Carlton Fisk	.50	.15
64 Joe Cronin	.30	.09
65 Joe Wood	.50	.15
66 Tony Conigliaro	.50	.15
67 Edd Roush	.30	.09
68 Johnny VanderMeer	.30	.09
69 Walter Johnson	.75	.23
70 Charlie Gehringer	.30	.09
71 Al Kaline	.75	.23
72 Ty Cobb	1.25	.35
73 Tony Oliva	.30	.09
74 Luke Appling	.30	.09
75 Minnie Minoso	.30	.09
76 Nellie Fox	.50	.15
77 Joe Jackson	1.50	.45
78 Babe Ruth	2.50	.75
79 Bill Dickey	.50	.15
80 Elston Howard	.50	.15
81 Joe DiMaggio	1.50	.45
82 Lefty Gomez	.75	.23
83 Lou Gehrig	1.50	.45
84 Mickey Mantle	3.00	.90
85 Reggie Jackson	.50	.15
86 Roger Maris	1.25	.35
87 Whitey Ford	.50	.15
88 Waite Hoyt	.30	.09
89 Yogi Berra	.75	.23
90 Casey Stengel	.75	.23

2001 SP Legendary Cuts Autographs

Randomly inserted into packs at a rate of one in 252 (a.k.a. - one per case), this 85-card set features more than 3,300 autographs of deceased legends that were cut off of checks, contracts, letters, etc that Upper Deck purchased on the secondary market. The card backs carry the players initials as numbering. Cards with a print run of less than 25 are not priced due to scarcity. A couple of players: Joe DiMaggio and Ted Lyons were printed to different quantities.

	Nm-Mt	Ex-Mt
C-BD Bill Dickey/28	400.00	120.00
C-BG Burleigh Grimes/18		
C-BHA Bucky Harris/10		
C-BHE Billy Herman/88	150.00	45.00
C-BL Bob Lemon/23		
C-BM Bob Meusel/23		
C-BRI Branch Rickey/16		
C-BRU Babe Ruth/7		
C-BS Bob Shawkey/39	200.00	60.00
C-BT Bill Terry/184	250.00	75.00
C-BW Bucky Walters/13		
C-CA Cap Anson/2		
C-CH Carl Hubbell/30	600.00	180.00
C-CK Charlie Keller/16		
C-CS Casey Stengel/10		
C-DDE Dizzy Dean/56	900.00	275.00
C-DDR Don Drysdale/12		
C-EA Earl Averill/189	120.00	36.00
C-EB Ed Barrow/16		
C-EF Elmer Flick/22		
C-EL Eddie Lopat/22		
C-ER Edd Roush/83	150.00	45.00
C-FF Ford Frick/21		
C-FF Frankie Frisch/3		
C-FL Freddy Lindstrom/2		
C-GA Grover Alexander/1		
C-GH Gil Hodges/6		
C-GH Gabby Hartnett/32	400.00	120.00
C-GK George Kelly/52	200.00	60.00
C-GS George Selkirk/15		
C-GS George Sisler/1		
C-HH Harvey Haddix/4		
C-HH Harry Hooper/14		
C-HM Heinie Manush/50	350.00	105.00
C-HW Honus Wagner/24		
C-HW Hack Wilson/4		
C-JC Jocko Conlan/26	450.00	135.00
C-JC Joe Cronin/12		
C-JD1 Joe DiMaggio/25		
C-JD2 Joe DiMaggio/50	500.00	150.00
C-JD3 Joe DiMaggio/150	500.00	150.00
C-JD4 Joe DiMaggio/275	400.00	120.00
C-JF Jimmie Foxx/16		
C-JJ Judy Johnson/9		
C-JM Joe Medwick/18		
C-JMC Joe McCarthy/40	500.00	150.00
C-JMI Johnny Mize/84	300.00	90.00
C-JR Jackie Robinson/147	900.00	275.00
C-JS Joe Sewell/55	300.00	90.00
C-JW Joe Wood/43	600.00	180.00
C-KC Kiki Cuyler/6		
C-KK Ken Keltner/11		
C-KL Kenesaw Landis/4		
C-LA Luke Appling/45	300.00	90.00
C-LD Leo Durocher/45	500.00	150.00
C-LG Lefty Grove/34	600.00	180.00
C-LGE Lou Gehrig/7		
C-LGO Lefty Gomez/85	300.00	90.00
C-LW Lloyd Waner/213	200.00	60.00
C-MC Max Carey/73	300.00	90.00
C-MK Mark Koenig/30	400.00	120.00
C-MM Mickey Mantle/8		
C-MO Mel Ott/8		
C-NF Nellie Fox/9		
C-PW Paul Waner/4		
C-RC Roberto Clemente/4		
C-RF Rick Ferrell/8		
C-RH Rogers Hornsby/4		
C-ROM Roger Maris/73	1500.00	450.00
C-RP R.Peckinpaugh/45	250.00	75.00
C-RR Red Ruffing/5		
C-RS Rip Sewell/39	300.00	90.00
C-RUM Rube Marquard/23		
C-SC Stanley Coveleski/42	250.00	75.00
C-SM Sal Maglie/19		
C-SP Satchel Paige/36	2000.00	600.00
C-TC Ty Cobb/24		
C-TJ Travis Jackson/35	300.00	90.00
C-TL1 Ted Lyons/2		
C-TL2 Ted Lyons/59	300.00	90.00
C-VM J. VanderMeer/65	250.00	75.00
C-VR Vic Raschi/26	500.00	150.00
C-WA Walt Alston/34	400.00	120.00
C-WG Warren Giles/10		
C-WH Waite Hoyt/38	400.00	120.00
C-WJ Walter Johnson/113	1000.00	300.00

2001 SP Legendary Cuts Debut Game Bat

Randomly inserted into packs at one in 18, this 35-card set features the first game-used pieces of bat cards for each player. Card backs carry the player's intials as numbering. Cards with a perceived larger supply carry an asterisk and all short-print cards carry an SP designation.

	Nm-Mt	Ex-Mt
B-AT Alan Trammell *	15.00	4.50
B-BB Bobby Bonds	10.00	3.00
B-BF Bill Freehan	10.00	3.00
B-GL Greg Luzinski	10.00	3.00
B-SS Steve Sax *	10.00	3.00
B-SY Steve Yeager	10.00	3.00
B-WH Willie Horton	10.00	3.00
B-WP Wes Parker *	10.00	3.00
D-BB Bill Buckner *	10.00	3.00
D-BD Bobby Doerr SP	25.00	7.50
D-BF Bob Feller SP	25.00	7.50
D-BH Billy Herman SP	25.00	7.50
D-BM Bill Mazeroski	15.00	4.50
D-BR B.Richardson SP	25.00	7.50
D-CG Charlie Gehringer	25.00	7.50
D-EH Elston Howard SP	25.00	7.50
D-ES Eddie Stanky	10.00	3.00
D-FF Frankie Frisch SP	25.00	7.50
D-GM Gary Matthews	10.00	3.00
D-GS George Sisler	25.00	7.50
D-HW Hack Wilson SP	60.00	18.00
D-JA Joe Adcock SP	25.00	7.50
D-JC Joe Cronin	15.00	4.50
D-JJ Joe Jackson	200.00	60.00
D-KB Ken Boyer SP	25.00	7.50
D-LA Luke Appling SP	40.00	12.00
D-LB Lou Boudreau	15.00	4.50
D-LW Lou Whitaker	10.00	3.00
D-MC Mickey Cochrane	40.00	12.00
D-MM Minnie Minoso SP	25.00	7.50
D-PW Paul Waner SP	50.00	15.00
D-RA Richie Ashburn SP	40.00	12.00
D-RH Ron Hunt	10.00	3.00
D-TC Tony Conigliaro SP	25.00	7.50
D-TO Tony Oliva	10.00	3.00

2001 SP Legendary Cuts Game Bat

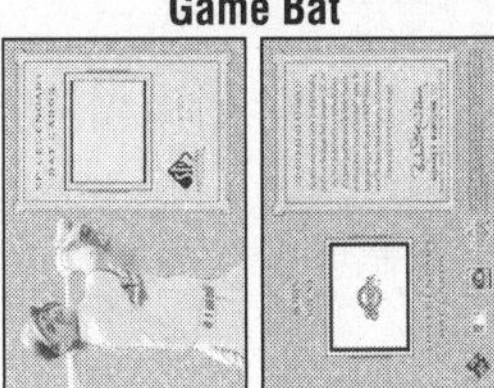

Randomly inserted into packs at one in 18, this 36-card set features game-used pieces of bat cards for each player. Card backs carry the player's intials as numbering. Cards with a perceived larger supply carry an asterisk and all short-print cards carry an SP designation.

	Nm-Mt	Ex-Mt
B-AD Andre Dawson *	10.00	3.00
B-AS Al Simmons SP	40.00	12.00
B-BR Babe Ruth SP	200.00	60.00
B-BT Bill Terry SP	40.00	12.00
B-CF Carlton Fisk	15.00	4.50
B-DD Don Drysdale SP	40.00	12.00
B-DJ Davey Johnson	10.00	3.00
B-EM Eddie Mathews	15.00	4.50
B-GB George Brett *	15.00	4.50
B-GH Gil Hodges SP	60.00	18.00
B-HA Hank Aaron SP	60.00	18.00
B-JD Joe DiMaggio SP	120.00	36.00
B-JF Jimmie Foxx	50.00	15.00
B-JR Jackie Robinson SP	100.00	30.00
B-KC Kiki Cuyler	25.00	7.50
B-MM Mickey Mantle SP	150.00	45.00
B-MM Manny Mota	10.00	3.00
B-MO Mel Ott SP	60.00	18.00
B-MW Maury Wills *	10.00	3.00
B-NF Nellie Fox	15.00	4.50
B-NR Nolan Ryan SP	50.00	15.00
B-PM Paul Molitor	15.00	4.50
B-RC Rico Carty	10.00	3.00
B-RCA R.Campanella SP	50.00	15.00
B-RCL Roberto Clemente	80.00	24.00
B-RJ Reggie Jackson *	15.00	4.50
B-RM Roger Maris SP	80.00	24.00
B-RS Ryne Sandberg *	25.00	7.50
B-RY Robin Yount *	15.00	4.50
B-TC Ty Cobb SP	175.00	52.50
B-TD Tommy Davis SP	100.00	30.00
B-THO Tommy Holmes UER	10.00	3.00
Eddie Mathews pictured		
B-VP Vada Pinson	10.00	3.00
B-WB Wade Boggs *	15.00	4.50
B-WMC Willie McCovey *	10.00	3.00
B-YB Yogi Berra	15.00	4.50

2001 SP Legendary Cuts Game Bat Combo

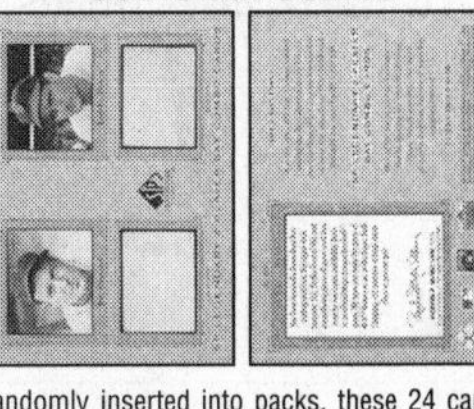

Randomly inserted into packs, these 24 cards feature dual player game-used bat pieces from some of the games greatest stars. Card backs carry both players' initials as numbering. Please note that there were only 25 serial numbered sets produced. Due to market scarcity, no pricing is provided for these cards.

Nm-Mt Ex-Mt
BMRC Bill Mazeroski
Roberto Clemente
BRMM Babe Ruth
Mickey Mantle
GSBT George Sisler
Bill Terry
HABR Hank Aaron
Babe Ruth
HWBH Hack Wilson
Billy Herman
JCBD Joe Cronin
Bobby Doerr
JDMM Joe DiMaggio
Mickey Mantle
JFAS Jimmie Foxx
Al Simmons
JFBR Jimmie Foxx
Babe Ruth
JRRC Jackie Robinson
Roy Campanella
LBBF Lou Boudreau
Bob Feller
MMNF Minnie Minoso
Nellie Fox
MOBT Mel Ott
Bill Terry
MOJD Mel Ott
Joe DiMaggio
NRBF Nolan Ryan
Bob Feller
RJMM Reggie Jackson
Mickey Mantle
RMMM Roger Maris
Mickey Mantle
RSAD Ryne Sandberg
Andre Dawson
SJPW Joe Jackson
Paul Waner
TCBR Ty Cobb
Babe Ruth
TCCG Ty Cobb
Charlie Gehringer
TDDD Tommy Davis
Don Drysdale
TORC Tony Oliva
Roberto Clemente
YBEH Yogi Berra
Elston Howard

2001 SP Legendary Cuts Game Jersey

Randomly inserted into packs at one in 18, this 35-card set features game-worn jersey or uniform pieces for each player. Card backs carry the player's intials as numbering. Cards with a perceived larger supply carry an asterisk and all short-print cards carry an SP designation.

	Nm-Mt	Ex-Mt
J-BD Bill Dickey Uni	40.00	12.00
J-BL Bob Lemon Uni	15.00	4.50
J-BM B.Mazeroski Uni SP	80.00	24.00
J-BR B.Richardson Uni	10.00	3.00
J-BR Babe Ruth Uni SP		
J-BRO B.Robinson Uni	15.00	4.50
J-BT Bobby Thomson Uni	15.00	4.50
J-BW Billy Williams Jsy	10.00	3.00
J-CS Casey Stengel Uni	15.00	4.50
J-GH Gil Hodges Jsy	15.00	4.50
J-GP Gaylord Perry Jsy	10.00	3.00
J-HW H.Wagner Uni SP		
J-JD Joe DiMaggio Uni SP		
J-JF Jim Fregosi Jsy	10.00	3.00
J-JM Juan Marichal Jsy *	10.00	3.00
J-JN Joe Nuxhall Jsy	15.00	4.50
J-LD Leo Durocher Jsy	15.00	4.50
J-MM M. Mantle Uni SP		
J-MW Maury Wills Jsy	10.00	3.00
J-NF Nellie Fox Uni	15.00	4.50
J-NR Nolan Ryan Jsy	50.00	15.00
J-RC R. Clemente Jsy	100.00	30.00
J-RJ Reggie Jackson Jsy	15.00	4.50
J-RM Roger Maris Uni SP	250.00	75.00
J-RY Robin Yount Jsy	15.00	4.50
J-TC Tony Conigliaro Jsy	15.00	4.50
J-TC Ty Cobb Uni SP		
J-THO T.Holmes Uni*	10.00	3.00
J-TK Ted Kluszewski Jsy	15.00	4.50
J-TS Tom Seaver Jsy SP	150.00	45.00
J-VL Vic Lombardi Jsy	10.00	3.00

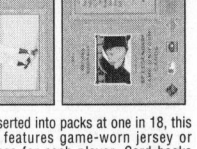

J-WB Wade Boggs Jsy............ 15.00 4.50
J-WF Whitey Ford Uni............ 15.00 4.50
J-WM Willie McCovey Uni*....... 10.00 3.00
J-YB Yogi Berra Uni.................. 15.00 4.50

2002 SP Legendary Cuts

This 90 card set was released in October, 2002. The set was issued in four card packs which came 12 packs to a box and 16 boxes to a case. In addition to these basic cards, an exchange card for a Mark McGwire "private signings" card was randomly inserted into packs. That card has a stated print run of 100 copies inserted and a redemption deadline of 09/12/03.

Nm-Mt Ex-Mt
COMPLETE SET (90)................ 30.00 9.00
1 Al Kaline.............................. 1.50 .45
2 Alvin Dark............................. .60 .18
3 Andre Dawson......................... .60 .18
4 Babe Ruth............................. 5.00 1.50
5 Ernie Banks........................... 1.50 .45
6 Bob Lemon............................. 1.00 .30
7 Bobby Bonds........................... .60 .18
8 Carl Erskine........................... .60 .18
9 Carl Hubbell........................... 1.00 .30
10 Casey Stengel........................ 1.50 .45
11 Charlie Gehringer................... 1.00 .30
12 Christy Mathewson.................. 1.50 .45
13 Dale Murphy.......................... 1.50 .45
14 Dave Concepcion.................... .60 .18
15 Dave Parker........................... .60 .18
16 Dazzy Vance.......................... .60 .18
17 Dizzy Dean............................ 1.00 .30
18 Don Baylor............................ .60 .18
19 Don Drysdale......................... 1.50 .45
20 Duke Snider........................... 1.00 .30
21 Earl Averill............................ .60 .18
22 Early Wynn............................ .60 .18
23 Edd Roush............................. .60 .18
24 Elston Howard........................ .60 .18
25 Ferguson Jenkins................... .60 .18
26 Frank Crosetti........................ .60 .18
27 Frankie Frisch........................ .60 .18
28 Gaylord Perry......................... .60 .18
29 George Foster........................ .60 .18
30 George Kell............................ .60 .18
31 Gil Hodges............................. 1.00 .30
32 Hank Greenberg..................... 1.50 .45
33 Phil Niekro............................ .60 .18
34 Harvey Haddix....................... .60 .18
35 Harvey Kuenn........................ .60 .18
36 Honus Wagner........................ 2.50 .75
37 Jackie Robinson..................... 2.00 .60
38 Orlando Cepeda...................... .60 .18
39 Joe Adcock............................. .60 .18
40 Joe Cronin.............................. .60 .18
41 Joe DiMaggio.......................... 3.00 .90
42 Joe Morgan............................. .60 .18
43 Johnny Mize............................ .60 .18
44 Lefty Gomez........................... 1.00 .30
45 Lefty Grove............................. 1.00 .30
46 Jim Palmer.............................. .60 .18
47 Lou Boudreau.......................... .60 .18
48 Lou Gehrig.............................. 3.00 .90
49 Luke Appling........................... .60 .18
50 Mark McGwire........................ 5.00 1.50
51 Mel Ott................................... 1.50 .45
52 Mickey Cochrane..................... 1.00 .30
53 Mickey Mantle......................... 6.00 1.80
54 Minnie Minoso......................... .60 .18
55 Brooks Robinson...................... 1.50 .45
56 Nellie Fox................................ 1.00 .30
57 Nolan Ryan.............................. 4.00 1.20
58 Rollie Fingers........................... .60 .18
59 Pee Wee Reese......................... 1.00 .30
60 Phil Rizzuto.............................. 1.00 .30
61 Ralph Kiner.............................. .60 .18
62 Ray Dandridge.......................... .60 .18
63 Richie Ashburn......................... 1.00 .30
64 Robin Yount............................. 2.50 .75
65 Rocky Colavito.......................... 1.00 .30
66 Roger Maris.............................. 2.50 .75
67 Rogers Hornsby........................ 1.50 .45
68 Ron Santo................................. .60 .18
69 Ryne Sandberg.......................... 3.00 .90
70 Stan Musial.............................. 2.50 .75
71 Sam McDowell.......................... .60 .18
72 Satchel Paige............................ 1.50 .45
73 Willie McCovey.......................... .60 .18
74 Steve Garvey............................. .60 .18
75 Ted Kluszewski.......................... 1.00 .30
76 Catfish Hunter........................... 1.00 .30
77 Terry Moore.............................. .40 .12
78 Thurman Munson........................ 2.00 .60
79 Tom Seaver................................ 1.00 .30
80 Tommy John.............................. .60 .18
81 Tony Gwynn.............................. 2.00 .60
82 Tony Kubek................................ 1.00 .30
83 Tony Lazzeri............................... .60 .18
84 Ty Cobb..................................... 2.50 .75
85 Wade Boggs................................ 1.00 .30
86 Waite Hoyt.................................. .60 .18
87 Walter Johnson............................ 1.50 .45
88 Willie Stargell.............................. 1.00 .30
89 Yogi Berra................................... 1.50 .45
90 Zack Wheat................................. .60 .18
MM M.McGwire AU/100 EX 600.00 180.00

2002 SP Legendary Cuts Autographs

Inserted in packs at stated odds of one in 128, these 97 cards feature "cut" autographs of a mix of retired greats and tough to track down early players dating back to the 1910's. Each card has a different stated serial numbered

print run and we have notated that information next to the player's name in our checklist. Edd Roush has two different varieties issued. Also, if a player has a stated print run of 25 or fewer copies, there is no pricing provided due to market scarcity.

Nm-Mt Ex-Mt
BDA Babe Dahlgren/51........... 250.00 75.00
BFA Bibb Falk/44................. 200.00 60.00
BGO Bill Goodman/53............ 150.00 45.00
BHA Buddy Hassett/56........... 250.00 75.00
BIL Bill Lee/40..................... 200.00 60.00
BKA Bob Kahle/53................. 150.00 45.00
BOL Bob Lemon/91................ 200.00 60.00
BRU Babe Ruth/3..........................
BSC Bob Scheffing/19....................
BSE Bill Serena/16........................
BSH Bill Sherdel/10.......................
BSH Bob Shawkey/118 .... 150.00 45.00
BSZ Billy Shantz/17........................
BVE Bill Veeck/11...........................
BWA Bucky Walters/31 .... 250.00 75.00
CGE Charlie Gehringer/3..................
CHM Chet Morgan/27............. 300.00 90.00
CHRM Christy Mathewson/2..............
CHU Carl Hubbell/17.........................
CKE Charlie Keller/29 .... 250.00 75.00
CLA Cookie Lavagetto/22...................
CST Casey Stengel/8..........................
DDE Dizzy Dean/4..............................
DDO Dick Donovan/23........................
DDR Don Drysdale/14.........................
DVA Dazzy Vance/5............................
EAV Earl Averill/22.............................
EJO Earl Johnson/31............. 250.00 75.00
ELO Ed Lopat/58.................. 200.00 60.00
ERO Edd Roush/101.............. 120.00 36.00
ERO2 Edd Roush/155............. 120.00 36.00
EWY Early Wynn/4...............................
FFR Frankie Frisch/35............ 400.00 120.00
FOF Ford Frick/1.................................
GBU Guy Bush/38................. 150.00 45.00
GCA George Case/35............ 200.00 60.00
GHO Gil Hodges/1...............................
GPI George Pipgras/34.......... 200.00 60.00
HCH Happy Chandler/96......... 150.00 45.00
HGR Hank Greenberg/94........ 400.00 120.00
HHA Harvey Haddix/37........... 250.00 75.00
HKU Harvey Kuenn/23...........................
HMA Hank Majeski/21............................
HNE Hal Newhouser/81.......... 150.00 45.00
HSC Hal Schumacher/17........................
HWA Honus Wagner/6............................
JAD Joe Adcock/48................ 250.00 75.00
JBE Johnny Berardino/12.......................
JCO Johnny Cooney/64........... 150.00 45.00
JCR Joe Cronin/185............... 200.00 60.00
JDI Joe DiMaggio/103............ 450.00 135.00
JDU Joe Dugan/39................. 200.00 60.00
JJO Judy Johnson/86.............. 250.00 75.00
JMI Johnny Mize/3.................................
JMO Johnny Moore/22............................
JSE Joe Sewell/136................. 150.00 45.00
KKE Ken Keltner/11................................
LAP Luke Appling/53............... 200.00 60.00
LBO Lou Boudreau/85............. 150.00 45.00
LGE Lou Gehrig/3...................................
LGO Lefty Gomez/3.................................
LGR Lefty Grove/194.............. 300.00 90.00
LJA Larry Jackson/37.............. 200.00 60.00
LRI Lance Richbourg/3...........................
LSE Luke Sewell/2..................................
MCO Mickey Cochrane/2.........................
MKO Mark Koenig/22..............................
MMA Mickey Mantle/2.............................
NFO Nellie Fox/1....................................
NJA Bucky Jacobs/44.............. 200.00 60.00
ORO Oscar Roettger/9.............................
PRE Pete Reiser/73................. 200.00 60.00
PWE Pee Wee Reese/23..........................
PWI Pete Whisenant/13..........................
RAS Richie Ashburn/10...........................
RDA Ray Dandridge/179.......... 120.00 36.00
RFE Rick Ferrell/19.................................
RHO Rogers Hornsby/1............................
RMA Roger Maris/1.................................
RMC Roy McMillan/18.............................
RRE Rip Repulski/19...............................
SCH Spud Chandler/17............................
SCO Stan Coveleski/85............ 200.00 60.00
SHA Stan Hack/36.................. 250.00 75.00
SMA Sal Maglie/29.................. 250.00 75.00
TDO Taylor Douthit/60............ 200.00 60.00
TKL Ted Kluszewski/23............................
TMO Terry Moore/86................ 150.00 45.00
TYC Ty Cobb/2..
VRA Vic Raschi/98................... 150.00 45.00
VWE Vic Wertz/17....................................
WHO Waite Hoyt/61................. 300.00 90.00
WJO Walter Johnson/20............................
WKA Willie Kamm/57................. 150.00 45.00
WSC Willard Schmidt/10............................
WST Willie Stargell/153............ 120.00 36.00
ZWH Zack Wheat/127............... 200.00 60.00

2002 SP Legendary Cuts Bat Barrel

Randomly inserted into packs, these 26 cards feature "barrel" pieces of the featured player. Each card has a stated print run of 11 or fewer and there is no pricing provided due to market scarcity.

Nm-Mt Ex-Mt
BB-ADA Alvin Dark/4..............................
BB-AND Andre Dawson/4.........................
BB-BBO Bobby Bonds/3...........................

BB-BRU Babe Ruth/3..............................
BB-DBA Don Baylor/5..............................
BB-DMU Dale Murphy/3...........................
BB-DPA Dave Parker/6.............................
BB-DSN Duke Snider/2.............................
BB-EWY Early Wynn/1..............................
BB-GFO George Foster/5...........................
BB-HGR Hank Greenberg/1........................
BB-JAR Jackie Robinson/1.........................
BB-JMI Johnny Mize/2..............................
BB-LGR Lefty Grove/1...............................
BB-MMA Mickey Mantle/7..........................
BB-MMC Mark McGwire/4...........................
BB-NRY Nolan Ryan/9................................
BB-PWE Pee Wee Reese/4..........................
BB-RCO Rocky Colavito/2...........................
BB-RMA Roger Maris/1...............................
BB-RSA Ryne Sandberg/3............................
BB-RYO Robin Yount/8................................
BB-TGW Tony Gwynn/11..............................
BB-TLA Tony Lazzeri/1.................................
BB-TMU Thurman Munson/4..........................
BB-WST Willie Stargell/5..............................

2002 SP Legendary Cuts Buybacks

Randomly inserted into packs, this is a one card set featuring "bought-back" signed cards from the 1992 Upper Deck Heroes set featuring Ted Williams autograph. These bought back cards have a stated print run of nine serial numbered sets and there is no pricing due to market scarcity.

Nm-Mt Ex-Mt
NNO Ted Williams 92 Heroes AU/9.....

2002 SP Legendary Cuts Game Bat

Inserted in packs at a stated rate of one in eight, these 36 cards feature game-used bat chips of some leading retired superstars. A few cards were issued in shorter supply and we have either notated that information with an SP next to the players name or an asterisk.

Nm-Mt Ex-Mt
B-ADA Alvin Dark *.................. 10.00 3.00
B-AND Andre Dawson *............. 8.00 2.40
B-BBO Bobby Bonds *.............. 8.00 2.40
B-BRU Babe Ruth SP............. 200.00 60.00
B-CRI Cal Ripken..................... 30.00 9.00
B-DBA Don Baylor *................... 8.00 2.40
B-DMU Dale Murphy *.............. 15.00 4.50
B-DPA Dave Parker *................ 8.00 2.40
B-DSN Duke Snider................... 15.00 4.50
B-EHO Elston Howard SP *....... 15.00 4.50
B-EWY Early Wynn................... 10.00 3.00
B-GFO George Foster *............. 8.00 2.40
B-GKE George Kell.................... 10.00 3.00
B-GPE Gaylord Perry................. 8.00 2.40
B-HGR Hank Greenberg SP....... 50.00 15.00
B-JAR Jackie Robinson SP *...... 50.00 15.00
B-JMI Johnny Mize SP *........... 15.00 4.50
B-LGR Lefty Grove.................... 25.00 7.50
B-MMA Mickey Mantle SP........ 150.00 45.00
B-MMC Mark McGwire *............ 80.00 24.00
B-NFO Nellie Fox...................... 15.00 4.50
B-NRY Nolan Ryan.................... 40.00 12.00
B-PWE Pee Wee Reese *........... 15.00 4.50
B-RCO Rocky Colavito *............ 15.00 4.50
B-RKI Ralph Kiner..................... 10.00 3.00
B-RMA Roger Maris SP *.......... 60.00 18.00
B-RSA Ryne Sandberg *............ 15.00 4.50
B-RYO Robin Yount *................ 15.00 4.50
B-SGA Steve Garvey.................. 8.00 2.40
B-TGW Tony Gwynn SP *.......... 20.00 6.00
B-TKU Tony Kubek UER............. 15.00 4.50
Name spelled Tonk on the front
B-TLA Tony Lazzeri.................. 10.00 3.00
B-TMU Thurman Munson........... 25.00 7.50
B-TSE Tom Seaver SP............... 20.00 6.00
B-WST Willie Stargell................ 10.00 3.00
B-YBE Yogi Berra SP................. 25.00 7.50

2002 SP Legendary Cuts Game Jersey

Inserted in packs at stated odds of one in 24, these 15 cards feature pieces of game-worn jerseys. A few players cards actually feature pant pieces and we have notated that next to

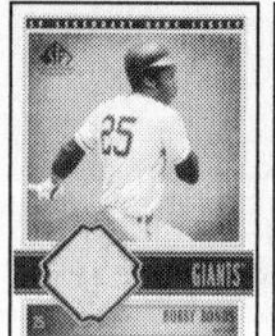
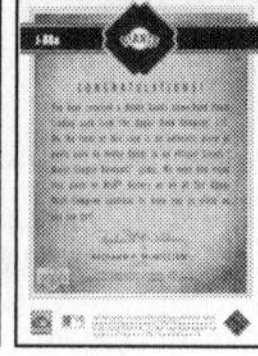

their name in our checklist. In addition, a few cards were issued in shorter supply and we have notated that information in our checklist as well.

Nm-Mt Ex-Mt
J-AND Andre Dawson................. 8.00 2.40
J-BBO Bobby Bonds Pants.......... 8.00 2.40
J-DBA Don Baylor...................... 8.00 2.40
J-DPA Dave Parker Pants *......... 8.00 2.40
J-FCR Frank Crosetti................. 10.00 3.00
J-GFO George Foster................. 8.00 2.40
J-JRO J.Robinson Pants SP *... 50.00 15.00
J-MMA M.Mantle Pants SP * .. 120.00 36.00
J-NRY Nolan Ryan Pants........... 40.00 12.00
J-PWE Pee Wee Reese.............. 15.00 4.50
J-RMA Roger Maris Pants.......... 50.00 15.00
J-RSA Ryne Sandberg SP *...... 25.00 7.50
J-SGA Steve Garvey................... 8.00 2.40
J-TSE Tom Seaver..................... 10.00 3.00
J-YBE Yogi Berra Pants *.......... 25.00 7.50

2002 SP Legendary Cuts Game Swatches

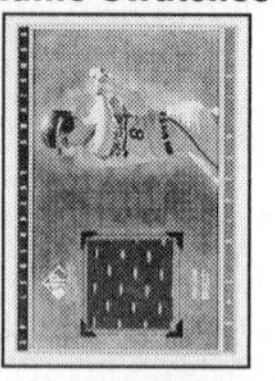

Inserted in packs at stated odds of one in 24, these 15 cards feature game-used memorabilia swatches of the featured players.

Nm-Mt Ex-Mt
S-CER Carl Erskine Pants.......... 10.00 3.00
S-CRJ Cal Ripken..................... 30.00 9.00
S-DBA Don Baylor..................... 8.00 2.40
S-DDR Don Drysdale Pants......... 25.00 7.50
S-DPA Dave Parker.................... 8.00 2.40
S-FCR Frank Crosetti................. 10.00 3.00
S-FJE Ferguson Jenkins Pants.... 8.00 2.40
S-JMO Joe Morgan..................... 8.00 2.40
S-MMI Minnie Minoso................ 10.00 3.00
S-MOT Mel Ott Pants................. 25.00 7.50
S-RSA Ron Santo...................... 15.00 4.50
S-SMC Sam McDowell................ 8.00 2.40
S-TGW Tony Gwynn.................. 15.00 4.50
S-TJO Tommy John.................... 8.00 2.40
S-WBO Wade Boggs.................. 10.00 3.00

2003 SP Legendary Cuts

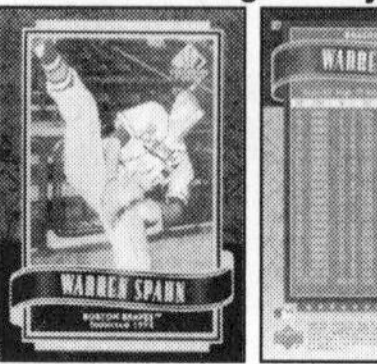

This 130-card set was released in December, 2003. This set was issued in four-card packs with an $10 SRP which came 12 packs to a box and 16 boxes to a case. Thirty cards in this set were short printed and each of those cards were issued to a stated print run of 1299 serial numbered sets and were inserted at a stated rate of one in 12.

MINT NRMT
COMP.SET w/o SP's (100)........ 40.00 18.00
COMMON CARD........................... .40 .18
COMMON SP.............................. 8.00 3.60
1 Luis Aparicio............................. .60 .25
2 Al Barlick.................................. .40 .18
3 Al Lopez.................................... .60 .25
4 Ernie Banks.............................. 1.50 .70
5 Alexander Cartwright................. .60 .25
6 Lou Brock.................................. 1.00 .45
7 Babe Ruth/1299....................... 15.00 6.75
8 Bill Dickey................................. 1.00 .45
9 Bill Mazeroski............................ 1.00 .45
10 Bob Feller................................ 1.00 .45
11 Billy Herman............................ .60 .25
12 Billy Williams........................... .60 .25
13 Bob Gibson/1299.................... 10.00 4.50
14 Bob Lemon.............................. .60 .25
15 Bobby Doerr............................ .60 .25
16 Branch Rickey.......................... .60 .25
17 Gary Carter.............................. .60 .25
18 Burleigh Grimes....................... .60 .25
19 Cap Anson................................ 1.00 .45
20 Carl Hubbell............................. 1.00 .45
21 Carlton Fisk............................. 1.00 .45
22 Casey Stengel.......................... 1.00 .45
23 Charlie Gehringer..................... .60 .25
24 Chief Bender............................ .60 .25
25 Christy Mathewson/1299...... 10.00 4.50
26 Cy Young................................. 1.50 .70
27 Dave Winfield........................... .60 .25
28 Dazzy Vance............................. .60 .25
29 Dizzy Dean/1299................... 10.00 4.50
30 Don Drysdale/1299................ 10.00 4.50
31 Duke Snider/1299.................. 10.00 4.50
32 Earl Averill............................... .60 .25
33 Earle Combs............................. .60 .25
34 Edd Roush............................... .60 .25
35 Earl Weaver.............................. .60 .25
36 Eddie Collins............................ .60 .25
37 Eddie Plank.............................. .60 .25
38 Elmer Flick............................... .60 .25
39 Enos Slaughter......................... .60 .25
40 Ernie Lombardi......................... .60 .25
41 Ford Frick................................. .40 .18
42 Jim Hunter................................ 1.00 .45
43 Frankie Frisch........................... .60 .25
44 Gabby Hartnett......................... .60 .25
45 George Kell............................... .60 .25
46 Early Wynn................................ .60 .25
47 Ferguson Jenkins....................... .60 .25
48 Al Kaline................................... 1.50 .70
49 Harmon Killebrew..................... 1.50 .70
50 Hal Newhouser.......................... .60 .25
51 Hank Greenberg/1299.......... 10.00 4.50
52 Harry Caray.............................. 1.00 .45
53 Tommy Lasorda......................... .60 .25
54 Honus Wagner/1299............ 10.00 4.50
55 Hoyt Wilhelm/1299................ 8.00 3.60
56 Jackie Robinson/1299.......... 10.00 4.50
57 Jim Bottomley........................... .60 .25
58 Jim Bunning/1299................. 10.00 4.50
59 Jimmie Foxx/1299................. 10.00 4.50
60 Eddie Mathews......................... 1.50 .70
61 Joe Cronin................................. .60 .25
62 Joe DiMaggio/1299............... 10.00 4.50
63 Joe McCarthy/1299................. 8.00 3.60
64 Joe Morgan/1299.................... 8.00 3.60
65 Willie McCovey......................... 1.00 .45
66 Joe Tinker.................................. .60 .25
67 Johnny Bench/1299.............. 10.00 4.50
68 Johnny Evers/1299................. 8.00 3.60
69 Johnny Mize/1299.................. 8.00 3.60
70 Josh Gibson/1299................. 10.00 4.50
71 Juan Marichal............................ .60 .25
72 Judy Johnson............................ .60 .25
73 Stan Musial............................... 2.50 1.10
74 Kiki Cuyler................................ .60 .25
75 Larry Doby................................ .60 .25
76 Nap Lajoie................................. 1.00 .45
77 Larry MacPhail........................... .40 .18
78 Phil Niekro................................. .60 .25
79 Lefty Gomez/1299................. 10.00 4.50
80 Lefty Grove/1299.................. 10.00 4.50
81 Leo Durocher/1299................. 8.00 3.60
82 Leon Day.................................... .60 .25
83 Gaylord Perry/1299................. 8.00 3.60
84 Lou Boudreau............................. .60 .25
85 Lou Gehrig.................................. 3.00 1.35
86 Luke Appling.............................. .60 .25
87 Max Carey.................................. .60 .25
88 Mel Allen/1299.......................... 8.00 3.60
89 Mel Ott/1299............................ 10.00 4.50
90 Mickey Cochrane........................ .60 .25
91 Mickey Mantle............................ 5.00 2.20
92 Brooks Robinson........................ 1.50 .70
93 Monte Irvin................................ .60 .25
94 Nellie Fox................................... 1.00 .45
95 Nolan Ryan/1299...................... 12.00 5.50
96 Ozzie Smith/1299...................... 10.00 4.50
97 Mike Schmidt.............................. 3.00 1.35
98 Pee Wee Reese/1299................ 10.00 4.50
99 Phil Rizzuto................................ 1.00 .45
100 Ralph Kiner............................... .60 .25
101 Ray Dandridge........................... .60 .25
102 Richie Ashburn.......................... 1.00 .45
103 Rick Ferrell................................ .60 .25
104 Roberto Clemente..................... 4.00 1.80
105 Robin Roberts........................... .60 .25
106 Robin Yount.............................. 2.50 1.10
107 Rogers Hornsby......................... 1.50 .70
108 Rollie Fingers............................. .60 .25
109 Roy Campanella......................... 1.50 .70
110 Rube Marquard.......................... .60 .25
111 Sam Crawford............................ .60 .25
112 Steve Carlton............................. .60 .25
113 Satchel Paige/1299.................. 10.00 4.50
114 Sparky Anderson........................ .60 .25
115 Stan Coveleski............................ .60 .25
116 Red Schoendienst........................ 1.00 .45
117 Ted Williams............................... 4.00 1.80
118 Tom Seaver................................. 1.00 .45
119 Tom Yawkey................................ .40 .18
120 Tony Lazzeri................................ .60 .25
121 Tony Perez.................................. .60 .25
122 Tris Speaker................................ 1.50 .70
123 Ty Cobb...................................... 2.50 1.10
124 Waite Hoyt/1299......................... 8.00 3.60
125 Walter Alston............................... .60 .25
126 Walter Johnson............................ 1.50 .70
127 Warren Spahn.............................. 1.00 .45
128 Whitey Ford................................. 1.00 .45
129 Willie Stargell............................... 1.00 .45
130 Yogi Berra.................................... 1.50 .70

2003 SP Legendary Cuts Blue

MINT NRMT
*BLUE POST-WAR: 2X TO 5X BASIC..
*BLUE PRE-WAR: 1.5X TO 4X BASIC.
*BLUE POST-WAR: .6X TO 1.5X BASIC SP
*BLUE PRE-WAR: .5X TO 1.2X BASIC SP
RANDOM INSERTS IN PACKS
STATED PRINT RUN 275 SERIAL #'d SETS

2003 SP Legendary Cuts Green

MINT NRMT
RANDOM INSERTS IN PACKS...........
STATED PRINT RUN 25 SERIAL #'d SETS
NO PRICING DUE TO SCARCITY........

2003 SP Legendary Cuts Autographs

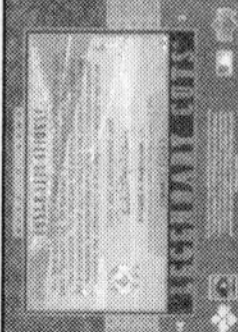

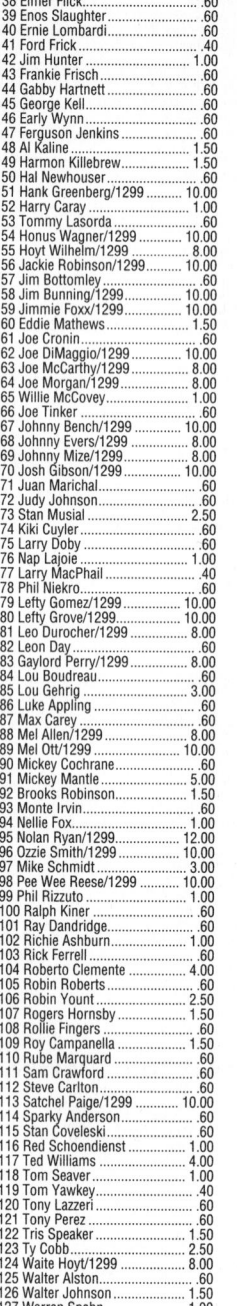

All the autograph cards in this insert set feature HOFers. After having a mix in 2002 of HOFers and retired players of varying note, Upper Deck decided that this product was better off with only HOFers involved in the cut signature insert set. Please note that several players: Bob Lemon, Charlie Gehringer, Carl Hubbell, Hal Newhouser, Joe DiMaggio and Ray Dandridge had two different varities in the main autograph set. In addition, for the first time, Upper Deck made some "color" variations in the autograph cut insert set. This set includes a "cut" signature of Alexander Cartwright who is believed by most historians to be the true founder of baseball.

MINT NRMT
OVERALL CUT SIG ODDS 1:196
PRINT RUNS B/WN 1-96 COPIES PER
NO PRICING ON QTY OF 25 OR LESS.
AL Alexander Cartwright/1
BD Bill Dickey/25
BG Burleigh Grimes/34 300.00 135.00
BI Billy Herman/30 200.00 90.00
BL Bob Lemon/34 200.00 90.00
BL1 Bob Lemon/41 200.00 90.00
CG Charlie Gehringer/17
CG1 Charlie Gehringer/20
CH Carl Hubbell/47 300.00 135.00
CH1 Carl Hubbell/63 300.00 135.00
CS Casey Stengel/3
CY Cy Young/2
DD Dizzy Dean/8
DO Don Drysdale/12
DV Dazzy Vance/2
EA Earl Averill/96 120.00 55.00
EC Earle Combs/45 250.00 110.00
EF Elmer Flick/6
EL Ernie Lombardi/1
ER Edd Roush/15
ER1 Edd Roush/14
ES Enos Slaughter/30 250.00 110.00
FF Ford Frick/10
FR Frankie Frisch/4
GH Gabby Hartnett/20
HC Harry Caray/29 300.00 135.00
HC1 Harry Caray/35 300.00 135.00
HG Hank Greenberg/30 500.00 220.00
HN Hal Newhouser TC/22
HN1 Hal Newhouser B2B/22
HW Honus Wagner/1
JB Jim Bottomley/2
JC Joe Cronin/15
JD Joe DiMaggio/50 500.00 220.00
JD1 Joe DiMaggio/28 600.00 275.00
JF Jimmie Foxx/3
JJ Judy Johnson/23
JM Johnny Mize/18
JM1 Johnny Mize/12
JO Joe McCarthy/22
JR Jackie Robinson/4
LA Leon Day/6
LB Lou Boudreau/82 150.00 70.00
LB1 Lou Boudreau/49 150.00 70.00
LD Leo Durocher/20
LE Lefty Grove/9
LG Lefty Gomez/21
LM Larry MacPhail/2
LU Luke Appling/52 150.00 70.00
MA Mel Allen/2
MC Max Carey/18
MI Mickey Cochrane/3
MM Mickey Mantle/2
NF Nellie Fox/5
NL Nap Lajoie/2
RA Richie Ashburn/10
RD Ray Dandridge Hands/20
RD1 Ray Dandridge MVP/20
RH Rogers Hornsby/1
RM Rube Marquard/40 250.00 110.00
RO Roy Campanella/1
SC Sam Crawford/3
SP Satchel Paige/11
ST Stanley Coveleski/19
ST1 Stan Coveleski/20
TC Ty Cobb/6
TJ Travis Jackson/19
TO Tony Lazzeri/8
TS Tris Speaker/2
TW Ted Williams/7
TY Tom Yawkey/1
WA Walter Alston/30
WJ Walter Johnson/1
WS Willie Stargell/4
ZW Zack Wheat/19

2003 SP Legendary Cuts Autographs Blue

MINT NRMT
OVERALL CUT SIG ODDS 1:196
PRINT RUNS B/WN 1-50 COPIES PER
NO PRICING ON QTY OF 25 OR LESS.
BD Bill Dickey/12
BG Burleigh Grimes/22
BI Billy Herman/15
BL1 Bob Lemon/25
BR Branch Rickey/1
CG1 Charlie Gehringer/4
CH1 Carl Hubbell/25
CS Casey Stengel/1
CY Cy Young/1
DD Dizzy Dean/4
DO Don Drysdale/6
DV Dazzy Vance/1
EA Earl Averill/50 150.00 70.00
EC Earle Combs/16
ED Eddie Collins/1
EF Elmer Flick/4
EL Ernie Lombardi/1
ER Edd Roush/15
ES Enos Slaughter/11
FF Ford Frick/7
FR Frankie Frisch/2
GH Gabby Hartnett/5
HC1 Harry Caray/35 300.00 135.00
HG Hank Greenberg/15
HN1 Hal Newhouser B2B/29 200.00 90.00
HW Honus Wagner/1
JB Jim Bottomley/2
JC Joe Cronin/5
JD1 Joe DiMaggio/40 500.00 220.00
JE Johnny Evers/1
JF Jimmie Foxx/2
JJ Judy Johnson/8
JM Johnny Mize/15
JO Joe McCarthy/15
JR Jackie Robinson/2
JT Joe Tinker/1
LA Leon Day/15
LB Lou Boudreau/25
LD Leo Durocher/5
LE Lefty Grove/4
LG Lefty Gomez/14
LM Larry MacPhail/1
LO Lou Gehrig/1
LU Luke Appling/18
MA Mel Allen/1
MC Max Carey/5
MI Mickey Cochrane/2
MM Mickey Mantle/1
MO Mel Ott/1
NF Nellie Fox/1
NL Nap Lajoie/1
RA Richie Asburn/1
RC Roberto Clemente/1
RD1 Ray Dandridge MVP/9
RH Rogers Hornsby/1
RM Rube Marquard/16
RO Roy Campanella/1
SC Sam Crawford/2
SP Satchel Paige/4
ST1 Stan Coveleski/20
TC Ty Cobb/2
TJ Travis Jackson/5
TO Tony Lazzeri/3
TS Tris Speaker/1
TW Ted Williams/1
TY Tom Yawkey/1
WA Walter Alston/10
WJ Walter Johnson/1
WS Willie Stargell/1
ZW Zack Wheat/5

2003 SP Legendary Cuts Autographs Green

MINT NRMT
OVERALL CUT SIG ODDS 1:196
PRINT RUNS B/WN 1-5 COPIES PER
NO PRICING DUE TO SCARCITY

2003 SP Legendary Cuts Combo Autographs

MINT NRMT
OVERALL CUT SIG ODDS 1:196
STATED PRINT RUN 1 SERIAL #'d SET
NO PRICING DUE TO SCARCITY
BJ Branch Rickey
Jackie Robinson
BL Babe Ruth
Lou Gehrig
HM Harry Caray
Mel Allen
HT Honus Wagner
Ty Cobb
JC Jackie Robinson
Roy Campanella
JM Joe DiMaggio
Mickey Mantle
JT Joe DiMaggio
Ted Williams
SJ Satchel Paige
Jackie Robinson

2003 SP Legendary Cuts Etched in Time 400

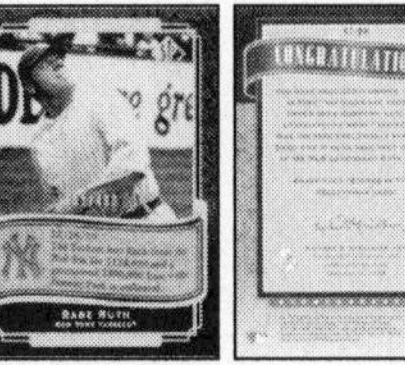

MINT NRMT
STATED PRINT RUN 400 SERIAL #'d SETS
*ETCHED 300: .4X TO 1X BASIC 400..
ETCHED 300 PRINT RUN 300 #'d SETS
*ETCHED 175: .5X TO 1.2X BASIC 400
ETCHED 175 PRINT RUN 175 #'d SETS
OVERALL ETCHED ODDS 1:12
AB Al Barlick 5.00 2.20
AC Alexander Cartwright 5.00 2.20
BR Babe Ruth 15.00 6.75
CG Charlie Gehringer 5.00 2.20
CH Carl Hubbell 8.00 3.60
CM Christy Mathewson 8.00 3.60
CS Casey Stengel 8.00 3.60
CY Cy Young 8.00 3.60
DD Dizzy Dean 8.00 3.60
DO Don Drysdale 8.00 3.60
EC Eddie Collins 5.00 2.20
EL Ernie Lombardi 5.00 2.20
GH Gabby Hartnett 5.00 2.20
HC Harry Caray 8.00 3.60
HG Hank Greenberg 8.00 3.60
HW Honus Wagner 8.00 3.60
JD Joe DiMaggio 10.00 4.50
JF Jimmie Foxx 8.00 3.60
JG Josh Gibson 8.00 3.60
JM Joe McCarthy 5.00 2.20
JO Johnny Mize 5.00 2.20
JR Jackie Robinson 10.00 4.50
LB Lou Boudreau 5.00 2.20
LD Leo Durocher 5.00 2.20
LE Lefty Grove 8.00 3.60
LG Lefty Gomez 8.00 3.60
LO Lou Gehrig 12.00 5.50
ME Mel Allen 5.00 2.20
MM Mickey Mantle 25.00 11.00
MO Mel Ott 8.00 3.60
PR Pee Wee Reese 8.00 3.60
RA Richie Ashburn 8.00 3.60
RC Roberto Clemente 20.00 9.00
RH Rogers Hornsby 8.00 3.60
RO Roy Campanella 8.00 3.60
SP Satchel Paige 8.00 3.60
TC Ty Cobb 10.00 4.50
TL Tony Lazzeri 5.00 2.20
TS Tris Speaker 8.00 3.60
TW Ted Williams 12.00 5.50

2003 SP Legendary Cuts Hall Marks Autographs

MINT NRMT
OVERALL HALL MARKS ODDS 1:196.
BLACK INK PRINTS B/WN 10-99 COPIES PER
BLUE INK PRINTS B/WN 10-15 COPIES PER
RED INK PRINT RUN 5 #'d COPIES PER
NO PRICING ON QTY OF 15 OR LESS.
BD1 Bobby Doerr Black/50 40.00 18.00
BD2 Bobby Doerr Blue/15
BD3 Bobby Doerr Red/5
BG1 Bob Gibson Black/30
BG2 Bob Gibson Blue/15
BG3 Bob Gibson Red/5
BM1 Bill Mazeroski Black/50 60.00 27.00
BM2 Bill Mazeroski Blue/15
BM3 Bill Mazeroski Red/5
CF1 Carlton Fisk Black/50 60.00 27.00
CF2 Carlton Fisk Blue/15
CF3 Carlton Fisk Red/5
CY1 Carl Yastrzemski Black/45 100.00 45.00
CY2 Carl Yastrzemski Blue/15
CY3 Carl Yastrzemski Red/5
DS1 Duke Snider Black/50 60.00 27.00
DS2 Duke Snider Blue/15
DS3 Duke Snider Red/5
DW1 Dave Winfield Black/10
DW2 Dave Winfield Blue/15
DW3 Dave Winfield Red/5
GC1 Gary Carter Black/50 40.00 18.00
GC2 Gary Carter Blue/15
GC3 Gary Carter Red/5
GK1 George Kell Black/50 25.00 11.00
GK2 George Kell Blue/15
GK3 George Kell Red/5
JB2 Johnny Bench Blue/10
JB3 Johnny Bench Red/5
JM1 Juan Marichal Black/50 40.00 18.00
JM2 Juan Marichal Blue/15
JM3 Juan Marichal Red/5
JO1 Joe Morgan Black/75 40.00 18.00
JO2 Joe Morgan Blue/15
JO3 Joe Morgan Red/5
LA1 Luis Aparicio Black/45 40.00 18.00
LA2 Luis Aparicio Blue/15
LA3 Luis Aparicio Red/5
MI1 Monte Irvin Black/85 50.00 22.00
MI2 Monte Irvin Blue/15
MI3 Monte Irvin Red/5
NR3 Nolan Ryan Red/5
OS1 Ozzie Smith Black/45 100.00 45.00
OS2 Ozzie Smith Blue/15
OS3 Ozzie Smith Red/5
PR1 Phil Rizzuto Black/50 60.00 27.00
PR2 Phil Rizzuto Blue/15
PR3 Phil Rizzuto Red/5
RF1 Rollie Fingers Black/99 25.00 11.00
RF2 Rollie Fingers Blue/15
RF3 Rollie Fingers Red/5
RK1 Ralph Kiner Black/50 40.00 18.00
RK2 Ralph Kiner Blue/15
RK3 Ralph Kiner Red/5
RR1 Robin Roberts Black/65 60.00 27.00
RR2 Robin Roberts Blue/15
RR3 Robin Roberts Red/5
RY1 Robin Yount Black/45 100.00 45.00
RY2 Robin Yount Blue/15
RY3 Robin Yount Red/5
SA1 Sparky Anderson Black/30. 40.00 18.00
SA2 Sparky Anderson Blue/15
SA3 Sparky Anderson Red/5
TP1 Tony Perez Black/50 40.00 18.00
TP2 Tony Perez Blue/15
TP3 Tony Perez Red/5
TS2 Tom Seaver Blue/10
TS3 Tom Seaver Red/5
WS1 Warren Spahn Black/35 80.00 36.00
WS2 Warren Spahn Blue/15
WS3 Warren Spahn Red/5
YB1 Yogi Berra Black/50 80.00 36.00
YB2 Yogi Berra Blue/15
YB3 Yogi Berra Red/5

2003 SP Legendary Cuts Hall Marks Autographs Blue

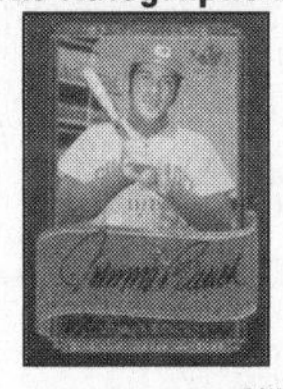

MINT NRMT
OVERALL HALL MARKS ODD 1:196
STATED PRINT RUN 25 SERIAL #'d SETS
NO PRICING DUE TO SCARCITY

2003 SP Legendary Cuts Hall Marks Autographs Green

MINT NRMT
OVERALL HALL MARKS ODDS 1:196.
STATED PRINT RUN 10 SERIAL #'d SETS
NO PRICING DUE TO SCARCITY

2003 SP Legendary Cuts Historic Lumber

MINT NRMT
OVERALL GAME USED ODDS 1:12
PRINT RUNS B/WN 50-350 COPIES PER
BR Babe Ruth Away/150 150.00 70.00
BR1 Babe Ruth Home/150 150.00 70.00
CF Carlton Fisk R.Sox/50 25.00 11.00
CF1 Carlton Fisk W.Sox/50 25.00 11.00
CY C.Yastrzemski w/Bat/300 30.00 13.50
CY1 C.Yastrzemski w/Cap/350 30.00 13.50
CY2 C.Yaz w/Helmet/350 30.00 13.50
DW Dave Winfield Padres/350 10.00 4.50
DW1 Dave Winfield Yanks/350 10.00 4.50
FR Frank Robinson O's/300 15.00 6.75
FR1 Frank Robinson Reds/350 15.00 6.75
FR2 Frank Robinson Angels/350 15.00 6.75
GC Gary Carter Mets/300 10.00 4.50
GC1 G.Carter Helmet Expos/100 10.00 4.50
GC2 G.Carter Cap Expos/100 10.00 4.50
HK Harmon Killebrew/350 15.00 6.75
JB Johnny Bench w/Bat/350 15.00 6.75
JB1 Johnny Bench Swing/350 15.00 6.75
JM Joe Morgan Reds/350 10.00 4.50
JM1 Joe Morgan Astros/350 10.00 4.50
MM Mickey Mantle/300 120.00 55.00
NR Nolan Ryan Rgr/225 30.00 13.50
OS Ozzie Smith Cards/300 25.00 11.00
OS1 Ozzie Smith Padres/350 25.00 11.00
RS R.Schoen Look Right/165 15.00 6.75
RS1 R.Schoen Look Left/165 15.00 6.75
SC Steve Carlton/350 10.00 4.50
TP Tony Perez Swing/350 10.00 4.50
TP1 Tony Perez Portrait/350 10.00 4.50
TS Tom Seaver/100 15.00 6.75
TW Ted Williams w/3 Bats/150 80.00 36.00
TW1 Ted Williams Portrait/150 80.00 36.00
WS W.Stargell Arms Down/150 15.00 6.75
WS1 W.Stargell Arms Up/150 15.00 6.75
YB Yogi Berra Shout/350 15.00 6.75
YB1 Yogi Berra w/Bat/350 15.00 6.75

2003 SP Legendary Cuts Historic Lumber Green

MINT NRMT
OVERALL GAME USED ODDS 1:12
PRINT RUNS BETWEEN 50-125 COPIES PER
BR Babe Ruth Away/75 200.00 90.00
BR1 Babe Ruth Home/75 200.00 90.00
CY C.Yastrzemski w/Bat/125 40.00 18.00
CY1 C.Yastrzemski w/Cap/125 40.00 18.00
CY2 C.Yaz w/Helmet/125 40.00 18.00
DW Dave Winfield Padres/125 10.00 4.50
DW1 Dave Winfield Yanks/125 10.00 4.50
FR Frank Robinson O's/125 15.00 6.75
FR1 Frank Robinson Reds/125 15.00 6.75
FR2 Frank Robinson Angels/125 15.00 6.75
GC Gary Carter Mets/125 10.00 4.50
GC1 G.Carter Helmet Expos/125 10.00 4.50
GC2 G.Carter Cap Expos/125 10.00 4.50
HK Harmon Killebrew/125 15.00 6.75
JB Johnny Bench w/Bat/125 15.00 6.75
JB1 Johnny Bench Swing/125 15.00 6.75
JM Joe Morgan Reds/125 10.00 4.50
JM1 Joe Morgan Astros/125 10.00 4.50
MM Mickey Mantle/75 150.00 70.00
NR Nolan Ryan Astros/50 60.00 27.00
OS Ozzie Smith Cards/125 30.00 13.50
OS1 Ozzie Smith Padres/125 30.00 13.50
RS R.Schoen Look Right/125 15.00 6.75
RS1 R.Schoen Look Left/125 15.00 6.75
SC Steve Carlton/125 10.00 4.50
TP Tony Perez Swing/125 10.00 4.50
TP1 Tony Perez Portrait/125 10.00 4.50
TS Tom Seaver/50 25.00 11.00
TW Ted Williams w/3 Bats/75 100.00 45.00
TW1 Ted Williams Portrait/75 100.00 45.00
WS W.Stargell Arms Down/125 15.00 6.75
WS1 W.Stargell Arms Up/125 15.00 6.75
YB Yogi Berra Shout/125 15.00 6.75
YB1 Yogi Berra w/Bat/125 15.00 6.75

2003 SP Legendary Cuts Historic Swatches

MINT NRMT
OVERALL GAME USED ODDS 1:12
PRINT RUNS B/WN 48-350 COPIES PER
BG Bob Gibson CO Jsy/350 15.00 6.75
BM Bill Mazeroski Pants/50 25.00 11.00
BW Billy Williams Jsy/190 10.00 4.50
CF Carlton Fisk Pants/350 15.00 6.75
CM C.Mathewson Pants/300 100.00 45.00
CS Casey Stengel Jsy/275 15.00 6.75
CY Carl Yastrzemski Jsy/350 25.00 11.00
CY1 C.Yastrzemski Pants/350 25.00 11.00
DS Duke Snider Jsy/350 15.00 6.75
DW1 D.Winfield Twins Jsy/300 10.00 4.50
FR F.Robinson O's Jsy/350 15.00 6.75
FR1 F.Robinson Angels Jsy/350 15.00 6.75
GC G.Carter Mets Jsy/350 10.00 4.50
GC1 G.Carter Expos Jsy/350 10.00 4.50
HW Honus Wagner Pants/275 100.00 45.00
JB Johnny Bench Jsy/150 15.00 6.75
JM Joe Morgan Jsy/350 10.00 4.50
JN Juan Marichal Pants/225 10.00 4.50
JN1 Juan Marichal Jsy/48 15.00 6.75
LA Luis Aparicio Jsy/230 10.00 4.50
LB Lou Boudreau Jsy/265 10.00 4.50
MM Mickey Mantle Pants/350 120.00 55.00
NR N.Ryan Rgr Pants/350 30.00 13.50
NR1 N.Ryan Astros Pants/350 30.00 13.50
OS Ozzie Smith Jsy/85 40.00 18.00
RF Rollie Fingers Jsy/105 10.00 4.50
RY R.Yount Portrait Jsy/350 15.00 6.75
RY1 R.Yount Swing Jsy/350 15.00 6.75
SA Sparky Anderson Jsy/350 10.00 4.50
SC Steve Carlton Jsy/350 10.00 4.50
SM Stan Musial Jsy/350 40.00 18.00
TC Ty Cobb Pants/300 100.00 45.00
TP Tony Perez Jsy/350 10.00 4.50
TS Tom Seaver Jsy/350 15.00 6.75
TS1 Tom Seaver Pants/350 15.00 6.75
TW Ted Williams Jsy/250 80.00 36.00
WA W.Alston Look Left Jsy/350 10.00 4.50
WA1 W.Alston Ahead Jsy/350 10.00 4.50
WI Willie Stargell Jsy/55 25.00 11.00
WS Warren Spahn CO Jsy/350 15.00 6.75
YB Yogi Berra Jsy/300 15.00 6.75

2003 SP Legendary Cuts Historic Swatches Blue

MINT NRMT
*BLUE: .6X TO 1.5X BASIC p/r 225-350
*BLUE: .6X TO 1.5X BASIC p/r 150-190
OVERALL GAME USED ODDS 1:12
STATED PRINT RUN 50 SERIAL #'d SETS

2003 SP Legendary Cuts Historic Swatches Green

MINT NRMT
*GREEN: .5X TO 1.2X BASIC SWATCH
OVERALL GAME USED ODDS 1:12
PRINT RUNS B/WN 160-250 COPIES PER
DW D.Winfield Yanks Jsy/160 10.00 4.50

2003 SP Legendary Cuts Historic Swatches Purple

MINT NRMT
*PURPLE p/r 150: .5X TO 1.2X BASIC
*PURPLE p/r 75-100: .6X TO 1.5X BASIC
OVERALL GAME USED ODDS 1:12
PRINT RUNS B/WN 75-150 COPIES PER

2003 SP Legendary Cuts Historical Impressions

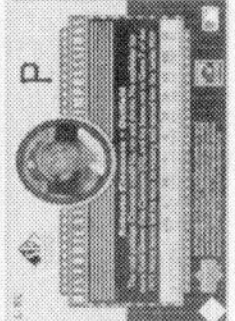

MINT NRMT
STATED PRINT RUN 350 SERIAL #'d SETS
*GOLD 200: .6X TO 1.5X BASIC

GOLD 200 PRINT RUN 200 SERIAL #'d SETS
*GOLD 75: 1.25X TO 3X BASIC
GOLD 75 PRINT RUN 75 SERIAL #'d SETS
*SILVER: .75X TO 2X BASIC
SILVER PRINT RUN 250 SERIAL #'d SETS
OVERALL HIST.IMP.ODDS 1:12
AC Alexander Cartwright 8.00 3.60
BR Babe Ruth 20.00 9.00
CG Charlie Gehringer 8.00 3.60
CH Carl Hubbell 10.00 4.50
CM Christy Mathewson 10.00 4.50
CS Casey Stengel 10.00 4.50
CY Cy Young 10.00 4.50
DD Dizzy Dean 10.00 4.50
DO Don Drysdale 10.00 4.50
EC Eddie Collins 8.00 3.60
ES Enos Slaughter 8.00 3.60
GH Gabby Hartnett 8.00 3.60
HC Harry Caray 10.00 4.50
HG Hank Greenberg 10.00 4.50
HO Hoyt Wilhelm 8.00 3.60
HW Honus Wagner 10.00 4.50
JD Joe DiMaggio 12.00 5.50
JF Jimmie Foxx 10.00 4.50
JM Johnny Mize 8.00 3.60
JO Joe McCarthy 8.00 3.60
JR Jackie Robinson 12.00 5.50
LB Lou Boudreau 8.00 3.60
LD Leo Durocher 8.00 3.60
LE Lefty Grove 10.00 4.50
LG Lefty Gomez 10.00 4.50
LO Lou Gehrig 12.00 5.50
MA Mel Allen 8.00 3.60
MC Mickey Cochrane 8.00 3.60
MM Mickey Mantle 30.00 13.50
MO Mel Ott 10.00 4.50
PR Pee Wee Reese 10.00 4.50
RA Richie Ashburn 10.00 4.50
RC Roberto Clemente 25.00 11.00
RH Rogers Hornsby 10.00 4.50
RO Roy Campanella 10.00 4.50
SP Satchel Paige 10.00 4.50
TL Tony Lazzeri 8.00 3.60
TS Tris Speaker 10.00 4.50
TW Ted Williams 15.00 6.75
TY Ty Cobb 12.00 5.50

2003 SP Legendary Cuts Presidential Cut Signatures

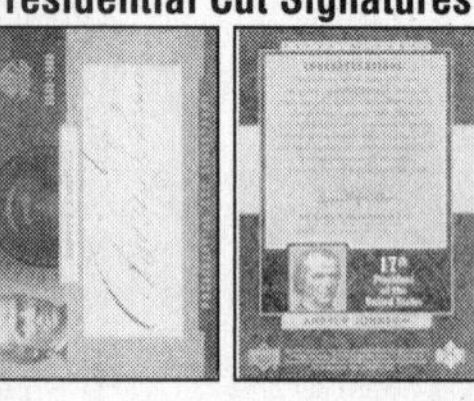

Randomly inserted into packs, these cards featured autographs of deceased United States Presidents. It is believed that these cards were originally supposed to be included in the 2003 Upper Deck "American History" set which was never produced. We have put the stated print runs for these cards next to the President's name in our checklist. Please note that due to market scarcity, no pricing is provided for these cards. Many collectors were somewhat dismayed to discover that Upper Deck actually put their serial numbering on the cut itself.

MINT NRMT
AJ Andrew Johnson/2
BH Benjamin Harrison/2
CA Chester Arthur/3
CC Calvin Coolidge/2
DE Dwight Eisenhower/2
FDR Franklin D. Roosevelt/3
GW George Washington /1
HT Harry Truman/2
JK John F. Kennedy /2
LJ Lyndon Johnson/2
RN Richard Nixon/2
UG Ulysses S. Grant/2
WT William Taft/2
WW Woodrow Wilson/2

1999 SP Signature

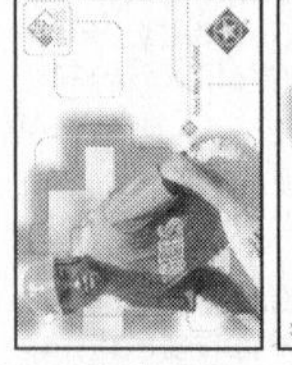

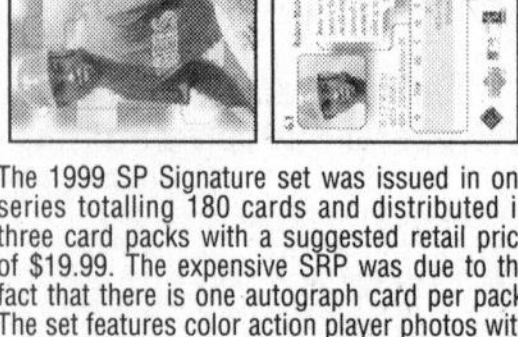

The 1999 SP Signature set was issued in one series totalling 180 cards and distributed in three card packs with a suggested retail price of $19.99. The expensive SRP was due to the fact that there is one autograph card per pack. The set features color action player photos with player information on the cardback. Rookie Cards include A.J. Burnett and Pat Burrell. 350 Mel Ott A Piece of History 500 Club bat cards were randomly seeded into packs. Pricing for these bat cards can be referenced under 1999 Upper Deck A Piece of History 500 Club.

Nm-Mt Ex-Mt
COMPLETE SET (180) 150.00 45.00
1 Nomar Garciaparra 4.00 1.20
2 Ken Griffey Jr. 4.00 1.20
3 J.D. Drew 1.00 .30
4 Alex Rodriguez 4.00 1.20
5 Juan Gonzalez 2.50 .75
6 Mo Vaughn 1.00 .30
7 Greg Maddux 4.00 1.20
8 Chipper Jones 2.50 .75
9 Frank Thomas 2.50 .75
10 Vladimir Guerrero 2.50 .75
11 Mike Piazza 4.00 1.20
12 Eric Chavez 1.00 .30
13 Tony Gwynn 3.00 .90
14 Orlando Hernandez 1.00 .30
15 Pat Burrell RC 12.00 3.60
16 Darin Erstad 1.00 .30
17 Greg Vaughn 1.00 .30
18 Russ Branyan .75 .23
19 Gabe Kapler .75 .23
20 Craig Biggio 1.50 .45
21 Troy Glaus 1.50 .45
22 Pedro Martinez 2.50 .75
23 Carlos Beltran 1.00 .30
24 Derrek Lee 1.00 .30
25 Manny Ramirez 1.00 .30
26 Shea Hillenbrand RC 6.00 1.80
27 Carlos Lee 1.00 .30
28 Angel Pena .75 .23
29 Rafael Roque RC 1.00 .30
30 Octavio Dotel .75 .23
31 Jeromy Burnitz 1.00 .30
32 Jeremy Giambi .75 .23
33 Andruw Jones 1.00 .30
34 Todd Helton 1.50 .45
35 Scott Rolen 1.50 .45
36 Jason Kendall 1.00 .30
37 Trevor Hoffman 1.00 .30
38 Barry Bonds 6.00 1.80
39 Ivan Rodriguez 2.50 .75
40 Roy Halladay 1.00 .30
41 Rickey Henderson 2.50 .75
42 Ryan Minor .75 .23
43 Brian Jordan 1.00 .30
44 Alex Gonzalez .75 .23
45 Raul Mondesi 1.00 .30
46 Corey Koskie 1.00 .30
47 Paul O'Neill 1.50 .45
48 Todd Walker 1.00 .30
49 Carlos Febles .75 .23
50 Travis Fryman 1.00 .30
51 Albert Belle 1.00 .30
52 Travis Lee .75 .23
53 Bruce Chen .75 .23
54 Reggie Taylor .75 .23
55 Jerry Hairston Jr. 1.00 .30
56 Carlos Guillen .75 .23
57 Michael Barrett .75 .23
58 Jason Conti .75 .23
59 Joe Lawrence .75 .23
60 Jeff Cirillo .75 .23
61 Juan Melo .75 .23
62 Chad Hermansen .75 .23
63 Ruben Mateo .75 .23
64 Ben Davis .75 .23
65 Mike Caruso .75 .23
66 Jason Giambi 2.50 .75
67 Jose Canseco 2.50 .75
68 Chad Hutchinson RC 1.50 .45
69 Mitch Meluskey .75 .23
70 Adrian Beltre 1.00 .30
71 Mark Kotsay 1.00 .30
72 Juan Encarnacion 1.00 .30
73 Dermal Brown .75 .23
74 Kevin Witt .75 .23
75 Vinny Castilla 1.00 .30
76 Aramis Ramirez 1.00 .30
77 Marlon Anderson .75 .23
78 Mike Kinkade .75 .23
79 Kevin Barker .75 .23
80 Ron Belliard .75 .23
81 Chris Haas .75 .23
82 Bob Henley .75 .23
83 Fernando Seguignol .75 .23
84 Damon Minor .75 .23
85 A.J. Burnett RC 4.00 1.20
86 Calvin Pickering .75 .23
87 Mike Darr .75 .23
88 Cesar King .75 .23
89 Rob Bell .75 .23
90 Derrick Gibson .75 .23
91 Orber Moreno RC 1.00 .30
92 Robert Fick 1.00 .30
93 Doug Mientkiewicz RC 5.00 1.50
94 A.J. Pierzynski 1.00 .30
95 Orlando Palmeiro .75 .23
96 Sidney Ponson 1.00 .30
97 Ivanon Coffie RC 1.00 .30
98 Juan Pena RC 1.00 .30
99 Matt Karchner .75 .23
100 Carlos Castillo .75 .23
101 Bryan Ward RC 1.00 .30
102 Mario Valdez .75 .23
103 Billy Wagner 1.00 .30
104 Miguel Tejada 1.00 .30
105 Jose Cruz Jr. 1.00 .30
106 George Lombard .75 .23
107 Geoff Jenkins 1.00 .30
108 Ray Lankford 1.00 .30
109 Todd Stottlemyre .75 .23
110 Mike Lowell 1.00 .30
111 Matt Clement 1.00 .30
112 Scott Brosius 1.00 .30
113 Preston Wilson 1.00 .30
114 Bartolo Colon 1.00 .30
115 Rolando Arrojo .75 .23
116 Jose Guillen .75 .23
117 Ron Gant 1.00 .30
118 Ricky Ledee .75 .23
119 Carlos Delgado 1.00 .30
120 Abraham Nunez .75 .23
121 John Olerud 1.00 .30
122 Chan Ho Park 1.00 .30
123 Brad Radke 1.00 .30
124 Al Leiter 1.00 .30
125 Gary Matthews Jr. .75 .23
126 F.P. Santangelo .75 .23
127 Brad Fullmer .75 .23
128 Matt Anderson .75 .23
129 A.J. Hinch .75 .23
130 Sterling Hitchcock .75 .23
131 Edgar Martinez 1.50 .45
132 Fernando Tatis .75 .23
133 Bobby Smith .75 .23
134 Paul Konerko 1.00 .30
135 Sean Casey 1.00 .30
136 Donnie Sadler .75 .23
137 Denny Neagle .75 .23
138 Sandy Alomar Jr. .75 .23
139 Mariano Rivera 1.50 .45
140 Emil Brown .75 .23
141 J.T. Snow 1.00 .30
142 Eli Marrero .75 .23
143 Rusty Greer 1.00 .30
144 Johnny Damon 1.00 .30
145 Damion Easley .75 .23
146 Eric Milton .75 .23
147 Rico Brogna .75 .23
148 Ray Durham 1.00 .30
149 Wally Joyner 1.00 .30
150 Royce Clayton .75 .23
151 David Ortiz 1.00 .30
152 Wade Boggs 1.50 .45
153 Ugueth Urbina .75 .23
154 Richard Hidalgo 1.00 .30
155 Bob Abreu 1.00 .30
156 Robb Nen 1.00 .30
157 David Segui .75 .23
158 Sean Berry .75 .23
159 Kevin Tapani .75 .23
160 Jason Varitek 1.00 .30
161 Fernando Vina 1.00 .30
162 Jim Leyritz .75 .23
163 Enrique Wilson .75 .23
164 Jim Parque .75 .23
165 Doug Glanville .75 .23
166 Jesus Sanchez .75 .23
167 Nolan Ryan 6.00 1.80
168 Robin Yount 4.00 1.20
169 Stan Musial 4.00 1.20
170 Tom Seaver 1.50 .45
171 Mike Schmidt 5.00 1.50
172 Willie Stargell 1.50 .45
173 Rollie Fingers 1.00 .30
174 Willie McCovey 1.00 .30
175 Harmon Killebrew 2.50 .75
176 Eddie Mathews 2.50 .75
177 Reggie Jackson 1.50 .45
178 Frank Robinson 1.50 .45
179 Ken Griffey Sr. 1.00 .30
180 Eddie Murray 2.50 .75
S1 Ken Griffey Jr. Sample 2.00 .60

1999 SP Signature Autographs

Inserted one per pack, this 150-card set is a partial parallel autographed version of the base set. Though print runs were not released, the amount of cards each player signed varied greatly. Many of the active veteran stars are noticeably tougher to find than the other cards in the set. In addition, several players had exchange cards of which expired on May 12th, 2000. The following players originally packed out as exchange cards: A.J. Burnett, Sean Casey, Vinny Castilla, Bartolo Colon, Pedro Martinez, Ruben Mateo, Jim Parque, Mike Piazza, Scott Rolen, J.T. Snow and Willie Stargell.

Nm-Mt Ex-Mt
AB Albert Belle 25.00 7.50
ABE Adrian Beltre 15.00 4.50
AG Alex Gonzalez 8.00 2.40
AJ Andruw Jones 25.00 7.50
AJB A.J. Burnett 15.00 4.50
AJP A.J. Pierzynski 15.00 4.50
AL Al Leiter 15.00 4.50
AN Abraham Nunez 8.00 2.40
AP Angel Pena 8.00 2.40
AR Alex Rodriguez 150.00 45.00
ARA Aramis Ramirez 15.00 4.50
BA Bob Abreu 15.00 4.50
BB Barry Bonds 200.00 60.00
BC Bruce Chen 8.00 2.40
BCO Bartolo Colon 15.00 4.50
BD Ben Davis 8.00 2.40
BF Brad Fullmer 8.00 2.40
BH Bob Henley 8.00 2.40
BR Brad Radke 15.00 4.50
BS Bobby Smith 8.00 2.40
BW Bryan Ward 8.00 2.40
BWA Billy Wagner 25.00 7.50
CBE Carlos Beltran 15.00 4.50
CC Carlos Castillo 8.00 2.40
CD Carlos Delgado 25.00 7.50
CF Carlos Febles 8.00 2.40
CH Chad Hermansen 8.00 2.40
CHA Chris Haas 8.00 2.40
CHU Chad Hutchinson 8.00 2.40
CJ Chipper Jones 40.00 12.00
CK Corey Koskie 15.00 4.50
CKI Cesar King 8.00 2.40
CL Carlos Lee 15.00 4.50
CP Calvin Pickering 8.00 2.40
DAM Damon Minor 8.00 2.40
DB Dermal Brown 8.00 2.40
DE Darin Erstad 15.00 4.50
DEA Damion Easley 8.00 2.40
DG Derrick Gibson 8.00 2.40
DGL Doug Glanville 8.00 2.40
DL Derrek Lee 15.00 4.50
DO David Ortiz 15.00 4.50
DOM Doug Mientkiewicz 15.00 4.50
DS Donnie Sadler 8.00 2.40
DSE David Segui 8.00 2.40
EB Emil Brown 8.00 2.40
EC Eric Chavez 15.00 4.50
ED Orlando Hernandez SP 50.00 15.00
ELI Eli Marrero 8.00 2.40
EM Edgar Martinez 40.00 12.00
EMA Eddie Mathews 50.00 15.00
EMI Eric Milton 8.00 2.40
EW Enrique Wilson 8.00 2.40
FR Frank Robinson 25.00 7.50
FS Fernando Seguignol 8.00 2.40
FT Frank Thomas 60.00 18.00
FTA Fernando Tatis 8.00 2.40
FV Fernando Vina 15.00 4.50
GJ Geoff Jenkins 15.00 4.50
GK Gabe Kapler 8.00 2.40
GM Greg Maddux 120.00 36.00
GMJ Gary Matthews Jr. 8.00 2.40
GV Greg Vaughn 15.00 4.50
HK Harmon Killebrew 40.00 12.00
IC Ivanon Coffie 8.00 2.40
JAG Jason Giambi 40.00 12.00
JC Jason Conti 8.00 2.40
JCI Jeff Cirillo 8.00 2.40
JD J.D. Drew 15.00 4.50
JDA Johnny Damon 15.00 4.50
JE Juan Encarnacion 8.00 2.40
JEG Jeremy Giambi 8.00 2.40
JG Jose Guillen 8.00 2.40
JHJ Jerry Hairston Jr. 8.00 2.40
JK Jason Kendall 15.00 4.50
JLA Joe Lawrence 8.00 2.40
JLE Jim Leyritz 8.00 2.40
JM Juan Melo 8.00 2.40
JO John Olerud 25.00 7.50
JOC Jose Canseco 40.00 12.00
JP Jim Parque 8.00 2.40
JR Ken Griffey Jr. 150.00 45.00
JS Jesus Sanchez 8.00 2.40
JT J.T. Snow 15.00 4.50
JV Jason Varitek 25.00 7.50
KB Kevin Barker 8.00 2.40
KW Kevin Witt 8.00 2.40
MA Marlon Anderson 8.00 2.40
MB Michael Barrett 8.00 2.40
MC Mike Caruso 8.00 2.40
MCL Matt Clement 15.00 4.50
MK Mark Kotsay 8.00 2.40
MKA Matt Karchner 8.00 2.40
MKI Mike Kinkade 8.00 2.40
MME Mitch Meluskey 8.00 2.40
MO Mo Vaughn 15.00 4.50
MP Mike Piazza 300.00 90.00
MR Manny Ramirez 25.00 7.50
MRI Mariano Rivera 60.00 18.00
MS Mike Schmidt 80.00 24.00
MT Miguel Tejada 25.00 7.50
MV Mario Valdez 8.00 2.40
NG Nomar Garciaparra 150.00 45.00
NR Nolan Ryan 150.00 45.00
OD Octavio Dotel 8.00 2.40
OP Orlando Palmeiro 8.00 2.40
PB Pat Burrell 30.00 9.00
PG Ivan Rodriguez 40.00 12.00
PK Paul Konerko 15.00 4.50
PM Pedro Martinez 120.00 36.00
PO Paul O'Neill 25.00 7.50
POP Willie Stargell 50.00 15.00
RB Russ Branyan 8.00 2.40
RBE Ron Belliard 8.00 2.40
RC Royce Clayton 8.00 2.40
RD Ray Durham 15.00 4.50
RGA Ron Gant SP 50.00 15.00
RGR Rusty Greer 15.00 4.50
RH Roy Halladay 25.00 7.50
RJ Reggie Jackson SP 80.00 24.00
RL Ray Lankford 8.00 2.40
RM Ryan Minor 8.00 2.40
RMA Ruben Mateo 8.00 2.40
RN Robb Nen 15.00 4.50
ROB Rob Bell 8.00 2.40
ROB Robert Fick 15.00 4.50
ROL Rollie Fingers 15.00 4.50
RR Rafael Roque 8.00 2.40
RT Reggie Taylor 8.00 2.40
RY Robin Yount 50.00 15.00
SA Sandy Alomar Jr. 8.00 2.40
SB Scott Brosius SP 60.00 18.00
SC Sean Casey 15.00 4.50
SHH Shea Hillenbrand 15.00 4.50
SM Stan Musial 60.00 18.00
SP Sidney Ponson 15.00 4.50
SR Ken Griffey Sr. 15.00 4.50
SR Scott Rolen 25.00 7.50
STH Sterling Hitchcock 8.00 2.40
TG Tony Gwynn 50.00 15.00
TGL Troy Glaus 25.00 7.50
THE Todd Helton 25.00 7.50
THO Trevor Hoffman 15.00 4.50
TSE Tom Seaver 25.00 7.50
TST Todd Stottlemyre 8.00 2.40
TW Todd Walker 15.00 4.50
VC Vinny Castilla 15.00 4.50
VG Vladimir Guerrero 40.00 12.00
WJ Wally Joyner 15.00 4.50
WMC Willie McCovey 40.00 12.00

1999 SP Signature Autographs Gold

Randomly inserted into packs, this 90-card set is a gold signature style partial parallel version of the base set. The only difference in design is a thin strip of gold foil squares on the card front. According to Upper Deck, 11 players did not sign their cards and are marked "NO AU" in the checklist below. Only 50 serial-numbered sets were produced. In addition, the following players had exchange cards of which expired on May 12th, 2000: Mike Piazza, Pedro Martinez, Scott Rolen and Vinny Castilla. Finally, a mere 20 copies of A.J. Burnett's cards packed out. All twenty made their way into packs as exchange cards with a May 12th, 2000 deadline. The Burnett card is not priced due to scarcity.

Nm-Mt Ex-Mt
AB Albert Belle 60.00 18.00
ABE Adrian Beltre 40.00 12.00
AG Alex Gonzalez 25.00 7.50
AJ Andruw Jones 60.00 18.00
AJB A.J. Burnett SP/20
AP Angel Pena 25.00 7.50
AR Alex Rodriguez 250.00 75.00
ARA Aramis Ramirez 40.00 12.00
BB Barry Bonds 300.00 90.00
BC Bruce Chen 25.00 7.50
BD Ben Davis 25.00 7.50
BH Bob Henley 25.00 7.50
CBE Carlos Beltran 40.00 12.00
CF Carlos Febles 25.00 7.50
CH Chad Hermansen 25.00 7.50
CHA Chris Haas 25.00 7.50
CHU Chad Hutchinson 25.00 7.50
CJ Chipper Jones 100.00 30.00
CK Corey Koskie 40.00 12.00
CKI Cesar King 25.00 7.50
CL Carlos Lee 40.00 12.00
CP Calvin Pickering 25.00 7.50
DAM Damon Minor 25.00 7.50
DB Dermal Brown 25.00 7.50
DE Darin Erstad 40.00 12.00
DG Derrick Gibson 25.00 7.50
DL Derrek Lee 40.00 12.00
EC Eric Chavez 40.00 12.00
ED Orlando Hernandez 40.00 12.00
FS Fernando Seguignol 25.00 7.50
FT Frank Thomas 100.00 30.00
GK Gabe Kapler 25.00 7.50
GM Greg Maddux 250.00 75.00
GV Greg Vaughn 40.00 12.00
JAG Jason Giambi 100.00 30.00
JC Jason Conti 25.00 7.50
JCI Jeff Cirillo 25.00 7.50
JD J.D. Drew 40.00 12.00
JE Juan Encarnacion 25.00 7.50
JHJ Jerry Hairston Jr. 25.00 7.50
JK Jason Kendall 40.00 12.00
JLA Joe Lawrence 25.00 7.50
JM Juan Melo 25.00 7.50
JOC Jose Canseco 100.00 30.00
JR Ken Griffey Jr. 300.00 90.00
KB Kevin Barker 25.00 7.50
KW Kevin Witt 25.00 7.50
MA Marlon Anderson 25.00 7.50
MB Michael Barrett 25.00 7.50
MC Mike Caruso 25.00 7.50
MK Mark Kotsay 25.00 7.50
MKI Mike Kinkade 25.00 7.50
MME Mitch Meluskey 25.00 7.50
MO Mo Vaughn 40.00 12.00
MP Mike Piazza 400.00 120.00
MR Manny Ramirez 60.00 18.00
NG Nomar Garciaparra 300.00 90.00
OD Octavio Dotel 25.00 7.50
PB Pat Burrell 120.00 36.00
PG Ivan Rodriguez 100.00 30.00
PM Pedro Martinez 200.00 60.00
PO Paul O'Neill 60.00 18.00
RB Russ Branyan 25.00 7.50
RBE Ron Belliard 25.00 7.50
RH Roy Halladay 60.00 18.00
RM Ryan Minor 25.00 7.50
RMA Ruben Mateo 25.00 7.50
ROB Rob Bell 25.00 7.50
RR Rafael Roque 25.00 7.50
RT Reggie Taylor 25.00 7.50
SHH Shea Hillenbrand 40.00 12.00
SR Scott Rolen 60.00 18.00
TG Tony Gwynn 120.00 36.00
TGL Troy Glaus 60.00 18.00
THE Todd Helton 60.00 18.00
THO Trevor Hoffman 40.00 12.00
TW Todd Walker 40.00 12.00
VC Vinny Castilla 40.00 12.00
VG Vladimir Guerrero 100.00 30.00

1999 SP Signature Legendary Cuts

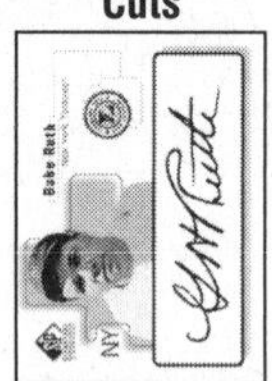

Randomly inserted into packs, this eight-card set features a "cut" signature from one of baseball's legends. Only one of each card was produced. No pricing is available due to scarcity but a checklist is provided.

Nm-Mt Ex-Mt
ROY Roy Campanella
XX Jimmie Foxx
LG Lefty Grove
W Walter Johnson
MEL1 Mel Ott
MEL2 Mel Ott
BR Babe Ruth
CY Cy Young

1993 Spectrum Gold Signature Griffey Jr.

This standard-size card features Ken Griffey Jr. Each of the 4,000 gold signature cards comes with a certificate of authenticity.

Nm-Mt Ex-Mt
1 Ken Griffey Jr. 8.00 2.40

1993 Spectrum Gold Signature Herman

This card honors Hall of Fame second baseman Billy Herman. Each of the 4,000 gold signature cards comes with a certificate of authenticity.

Nm-Mt Ex-Mt
1 Billy Herman 2.00 .60

1993 Spectrum Gold Signature Seaver

This card honors Tom Seaver, whose career 311 wins and 3,640 strikeouts earned him a first year induction into the Hall of Fame. Each of the 5,000 gold signature cards comes with a certificate of authenticity.

Nm-Mt Ex-Mt
1 Tom Seaver 4.00 1.20

1993 Spectrum HOF I

This five-card standard-size set features on its fronts borderless black-and-white vintage player photos that are trimmed in gold foil. The set includes an official certificate of authenticity giving the set serial number and the production run figures (5,000). The cards are numbered on the back. There was also a Gold Signature version (5,000 sets produced) of the cards which are similar to the regular 1993 Spectrum

86 John Cerutti .20 .06
87 Dave Winfield .30 .09
88 Dave Righetti .30 .09
89 Danny Jackson .20 .06
90 Andy Benes .30 .09
91 Tom Browning .20 .06
92 Pete O'Brien .20 .06
93 Roberto Alomar .75 .23
94 Bret Saberhagen .30 .09
95 Phil Bradley .20 .06
96 Doug Jones .20 .06
97 Eric Davis .30 .09
98 Tony Gwynn 1.00 .30
99 Jim Abbott .50 .15
100 Cal Ripken 2.50 .75
101 Andy Van Slyke .30 .09
102 Dan Plesac .20 .06
103 Lou Whitaker .30 .09
104 Steve Bedrosian .20 .06
105 Dave Gallagher .20 .06
106 Keith Hernandez .50 .15
107 Duane Ward .20 .06
108 Andre Dawson .30 .09
109 Howard Johnson .20 .06
110 Mark Langston .20 .06
111 Jerry Browne .20 .06
112 Alvin Davis .20 .06
113 Sid Fernandez .20 .06
114 Mike Devereaux .20 .06
115 Benito Santiago .30 .09
116 Bip Roberts .20 .06
117 Craig Worthington .20 .06
118 Kevin Elster .20 .06
119 Harold Reynolds .30 .09
120 Joe Carter .30 .09
121 Brian Harper .20 .06
122 Frank Viola .30 .09
123 Jeff Ballard .20 .06
124 John Kruk .30 .09
125 Harold Baines .30 .09
126 Tom Candiotti .20 .06
127 Kevin McReynolds .20 .06
128 Mookie Wilson .30 .09
129 Danny Tartabull .20 .06
130 Craig Lefferts .20 .06
131 Jose DeJesus .20 .06
132 John Orton .20 .06
133 Curt Schilling 1.50 .45
134 Marquis Grissom .75 .23
135 Greg Vaughn .30 .09
136 Brett Butler .30 .09
137 Rob Deer .20 .06
138 John Franco .30 .09
139 Keith Moreland .20 .06
140 Dave Smith .20 .06
141 Mark McGwire 2.50 .75
142 Vince Coleman .20 .06
143 Barry Bonds 2.00 .60
144 Mike Henneman .20 .06
145 Dwight Gooden .50 .15
146 Darryl Strawberry .50 .15
147 Von Hayes .20 .06
148 Andres Galarraga .30 .09
149 Roger Clemens 1.50 .45
150 Don Mattingly 2.00 .60
151 Joe Magrane .20 .06
152 Dwight Smith .20 .06
153 Ricky Jordan .20 .06
154 Alan Trammell .50 .15
155 Brook Jacoby .20 .06
156 Len Dykstra .30 .09
157 Mike LaValliere .20 .06
158 Julio Franco .30 .09
159 Joey Belle .75 .23
160 Barry Larkin .75 .23
161 Rick Reuschel .20 .06
162 Nelson Santovenia .20 .06
163 Mike Scioscia .20 .06
164 Damon Berryhill .20 .06
165 Todd Worrell .20 .06
166 Jim Eisenreich .20 .06
167 Ivan Calderon .20 .06
168 Mauro Gozzo .20 .06
169 Kirk McCaskill .20 .06
170 Dennis Eckersley .30 .09
171 Mickey Tettleton .20 .06
172 Chuck Finley .30 .09
173 Dave Magadan .20 .06
174 Terry Pendleton .30 .09
175 Willie Randolph .30 .09
176 Jeff Huson .20 .06
177 Todd Zeile .30 .09
178 Steve Olin .20 .06
179 Eric Anthony .20 .06
180 Scott Coolbaugh .20 .06
181 Rick Sutcliffe .30 .09
182 Tim Wallach .20 .06
183 Paul Molitor .50 .15
184 Roberto Kelly .20 .06
185 Mike Moore .20 .06
186 Junior Felix .20 .06
187 Mike Schooler .20 .06
188 Ruben Sierra .20 .06
189 Dale Murphy .75 .23
190 Dan Gladden .20 .06
191 John Smiley .20 .06
192 Jeff Russell .20 .06
193 Bert Blyleven .30 .09
194 Dave Stewart .30 .09
195 Bobby Bonilla .30 .09
196 Mitch Williams .20 .06
197 Orel Hershiser .30 .09
198 Kevin Bass .20 .06
199 Tim Burke .20 .06
200 Bo Jackson .75 .23
201 David Cone .30 .09
202 Gary Pettis .20 .06
203 Kent Hrbek .30 .09
204 Carlton Fisk .50 .15
205 Bob Geren .20 .06
206 Bill Spiers .20 .06
207 Oddibe McDowell .20 .06
208 Rickey Henderson .75 .23
209 Ken Caminiti .30 .09
210 Devon White .20 .06
211 Greg Maddux 1.25 .35
212 Ed Whitson .20 .06
213 Carlos Martinez .20 .06
214 George Brett 2.00 .60
215 Gregg Olson .20 .06
216 Kenny Rogers .30 .09
217 Dwight Evans .30 .09
218 Pat Tabler .20 .06
219 Jeff Treadway .20 .06
220 Scott Fletcher .20 .06
221 Deion Sanders .75 .23
222 Robin Ventura .75 .23
223 Chip Hale .20 .06
224 Tommy Greene .20 .06
225 Dean Palmer .75 .23

1994 Sportflics Samples

Enclosed in a cello pack, this four-card standard-size set was issued to give dealers a preview of the design of the forthcoming 1994 Sportflics 2000 series. The disclaimer "SAMPLE" is stenciled diagonally across the front and back of each card. In addition to the whole set being sent to dealers, all Wal-Mart greeters were given Len Dykstra cards to give out to promote this product.

Nm-Mt Ex-Mt
COMPLETE SET (4) 6.00 1.80
1 Len Dykstra .75 .23
7 Javier Lopez 1.50 .45
193 Greg Maddux 5.00 1.50
NNO Sportflics 2000 .50 .15
'94 Hobby Baseball
(Ad card)

1994 Sportflics

After a three-year hiatus, Pinnacle resumed producing these lenticular "three-dimensional" cards, issued in hobby and retail packs. Each of the 193 "Magic Motion" cards features two images, which alternate when the card is viewed from different angles and creates the illusion of movement. Cards 176-193 are Starflics featuring top stars. The two commemorative cards, featuring Cliff Floyd and Paul Molitor, were inserted at a rate of one in every 360 packs.

Nm-Mt Ex-Mt
COMPLETE SET (193) 25.00 7.50
1 Lenny Dykstra .30 .09
2 Mike Stanley .15 .04
3 Alex Fernandez .15 .04
4 Mark McGwire UER 2.00 .60
(name spelled McGuire on front)
5 Eric Karros .30 .09
6 Dave Justice .30 .09
7 Jeff Bagwell .50 .15
8 Darren Lewis .15 .04
9 David McCarty .15 .04
10 Albert Belle .30 .09
11 Ben McDonald .15 .04
12 Joe Carter .30 .09
13 Benito Santiago .30 .09
14 Rob Dibble .30 .09
15 Roger Clemens 1.50 .45
16 Travis Fryman .30 .09
17 Doug Drabek .15 .04
18 Jay Buhner .30 .09
19 Orlando Merced .15 .04
20 Ryan Klesko .30 .09
21 Chuck Finley .30 .09
22 Dante Bichette .30 .09
23 Wally Joyner .30 .09
24 Robin Yount 1.25 .35
25 Tony Gwynn 1.00 .30
26 Allen Watson .15 .04
27 Rick Wilkins .15 .04
28 Gary Sheffield .30 .09
29 John Burkett .15 .04
30 Randy Johnson .75 .23
31 Roberto Alomar .75 .23
32 Fred McGriff .50 .15
33 Ozzie Guillen .15 .04
34 Jimmy Key .30 .09
35 Juan Gonzalez .75 .23
36 Wil Cordero .15 .04
37 Aaron Sele .15 .04
38 Mark Langston .15 .04
39 David Cone .30 .09
40 John Jaha .15 .04
41 Ozzie Smith 1.25 .35
42 Kirby Puckett .75 .23
43 Kenny Lofton .30 .09
44 Mike Mussina .75 .23
45 Ryne Sandberg 1.25 .35
46 Robby Thompson .15 .04
47 Bryan Harvey .15 .04
48 Marquis Grissom .15 .04
49 Bobby Bonilla .30 .09
50 Dennis Eckersley .30 .09
51 Curt Schilling .50 .15
52 Andy Benes .15 .04
53 Greg Maddux 1.25 .35
54 Bill Swift .15 .04
55 Andres Galarraga .30 .09
56 Tony Phillips .15 .04
57 Darryl Hamilton .15 .04
58 Duane Ward .15 .04
59 Bernie Williams .50 .15
60 Steve Avery .15 .04
61 Eduardo Perez .15 .04
62 Jeff Conine .30 .09
63 Dave Winfield .30 .09
64 Phil Plantier .15 .04
65 Ray Lankford .15 .04
66 Robin Ventura .30 .09
67 Mike Piazza 1.50 .45
68 Jason Bere .15 .04
69 Cal Ripken 2.50 .75
70 Frank Thomas .75 .23
71 Carlos Baerga .15 .04
72 Darryl Kile .30 .09
73 Ruben Sierra .15 .04
74 Gregg Jefferies UER .15 .04
Name spelled Jeffries on front
75 John Olerud .30 .09
76 Andy Van Slyke .30 .09
77 Larry Walker .50 .15
78 Cecil Fielder .30 .09
79 Andre Dawson .30 .09
80 Tom Glavine .50 .15
81 Sammy Sosa 1.25 .35
82 Charlie Hayes .15 .04
83 Chuck Knoblauch .30 .09
84 Kevin Appier .30 .09
85 Dean Palmer .30 .09
86 Royce Clayton .15 .04
87 Moises Alou .30 .09
88 Ivan Rodriguez .75 .23
89 Tim Salmon .50 .15
90 Ron Gant .30 .09
91 Barry Bonds 2.00 .60
92 Jack McDowell .15 .04
93 Alan Trammell .50 .15
94 Dwight Gooden .50 .15
95 Jay Bell .30 .09
96 Devon White .15 .04
97 Wilson Alvarez .15 .04
98 Jim Thome .75 .23
99 Ramon Martinez .15 .04
100 Kent Hrbek .30 .09
101 John Kruk .30 .09
102 Wade Boggs .50 .15
103 Greg Vaughn .30 .09
104 Tom Henke .15 .04
105 Brian Jordan .30 .09
106 Paul Molitor .50 .15
107 Cal Eldred .15 .04
108 Deion Sanders .50 .15
109 Barry Larkin .75 .23
110 Mike Greenwell .15 .04
111 Jeff Blauser .15 .04
112 Jose Rijo .15 .04
113 Pete Harnisch .15 .04
114 Chris Hoiles .15 .04
115 Edgar Martinez .50 .15
116 Juan Guzman .15 .04
117 Todd Zeile .15 .04
118 Danny Tartabull .15 .04
119 Chad Curtis .15 .04
120 Mark Grace .50 .15
121 J.T. Snow .30 .09
122 Mo Vaughn .30 .09
123 Lance Johnson .15 .04
124 Eric Davis .30 .09
125 Orel Hershiser .30 .09
126 Kevin Mitchell .15 .04
127 Don Mattingly 2.00 .60
128 Darren Daulton .30 .09
129 Rod Beck .15 .04
130 Charles Nagy .15 .04
131 Mickey Tettleton .15 .04
132 Kevin Brown .30 .09
133 Pat Hentgen .15 .04
134 Terry Mulholland .15 .04
135 Steve Finley .30 .09
136 John Smoltz .50 .15
137 Frank Viola .30 .09
138 Jim Abbott .50 .15
139 Matt Williams .30 .09
140 Bernard Gilkey .15 .04
141 Jose Canseco .75 .23
142 Mark Whiten .15 .04
143 Ken Griffey Jr. 1.25 .35
144 Rafael Palmeiro .50 .15
145 Dave Hollins .15 .04
146 Will Clark .75 .23
147 Paul O'Neill .50 .15
148 Bobby Jones .15 .04
149 Butch Huskey .15 .04
150 Jeffrey Hammonds .15 .04
151 Manny Ramirez .50 .15
152 Bob Hamelin .15 .04
153 Kurt Abbott RC .30 .09
154 Scott Stahoviak .15 .04
155 Steve Hosey .15 .04
156 Salomon Torres .15 .04
157 Sterling Hitchcock .15 .04
158 Nigel Wilson .15 .04
159 Luis Lopez .15 .04
160 Chipper Jones .75 .23
161 Norberto Martin .15 .04
162 Raul Mondesi .30 .09
163 Steve Karsay .15 .04
164 J.R. Phillips .15 .04
165 Marc Newfield .15 .04
166 Mark Hutton .15 .04
167 Curtis Pride RC .30 .09
168 Carl Everett .30 .09
169 Scott Ruffcorn .15 .04
170 Turk Wendell .15 .04
171 Jeff McNeely .15 .04
172 Javier Lopez .30 .09
173 Cliff Floyd .30 .09
174 Rondell White .30 .09
175 Scott Lydy .15 .04
176 Frank Thomas AS .50 .15
177 Roberto Alomar AS .30 .09
178 Travis Fryman AS .15 .04
179 Cal Ripken AS 1.25 .35
180 Chris Hoiles AS .15 .04
181 Ken Griffey Jr. AS .75 .23
182 Juan Gonzalez AS .50 .15
183 Joe Carter AS .15 .04
184 Jack McDowell AS .15 .04
185 Fred McGriff AS .30 .09
186 Robby Thompson AS .15 .04
187 Matt Williams AS .15 .04
188 Jay Bell AS .15 .04
189 Mike Piazza AS .75 .23
190 Barry Bonds AS 1.00 .30
191 Lenny Dykstra AS .15 .04
192 Dave Justice AS .15 .04
193 Greg Maddux AS .75 .23
NNO Cliff Floyd SPEC 3.00 .90
NNO Paul Molitor SPEC 8.00 2.40

1994 Sportflics Movers

These 12 standard-size chase cards were randomly inserted in retail foil packs and

picture the game's top veterans. The insertion rate was one in every 24 packs. Fronts feature the dual image effect with the player's name appearing in dual image. The name "Movers" appears in a circular design off to the left of the player's name.

Nm-Mt Ex-Mt
COMPLETE SET (12) 50.00 15.00
MM1 Gregg Jefferies 1.25 .35
MM2 Ryne Sandberg 10.00 3.00
MM3 Cecil Fielder 2.50 .75
MM4 Kirby Puckett 6.00 1.80
MM5 Tony Gwynn 8.00 2.40
MM6 Andres Galarraga 2.50 .75
MM7 Sammy Sosa 10.00 3.00
MM8 Rickey Henderson 5.00 1.50
MM9 Don Mattingly 15.00 4.50
MM10 Joe Carter 2.50 .75
MM11 Carlos Baerga 1.25 .35
MM12 Lenny Dykstra 2.50 .75

1994 Sportflics Shakers

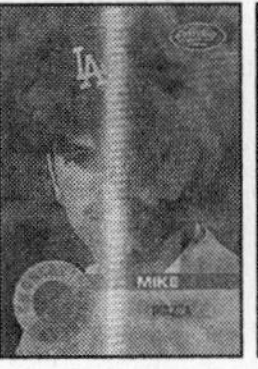

These 12 standard-size chase cards were randomly inserted in hobby foil packs and picture baseball's elite young players. The insertion rate was one in every 24 packs. Fronts feature the dual image effect with the player's name also appearing as dual image. The name "Shakers" appears in a circular design off to the left of the player's name.

Nm-Mt Ex-Mt
COMPLETE SET (12) 60.00 18.00
SH1 Kenny Lofton 6.00 1.80
SH2 Tim Salmon 6.00 1.80
SH3 Jeff Bagwell 6.00 1.80
SH4 Jason Bere 1.50 .45
SH5 Salomon Torres 1.50 .45
SH6 Rondell White 2.50 .75
SH7 Javier Lopez 4.00 1.20
SH8 Dean Palmer 2.50 .75
SH9 Jim Thome 6.00 1.80
SH10 J.T. Snow 2.50 .75
SH11 Mike Piazza 20.00 6.00
SH12 Manny Ramirez 6.00 1.80

1994 Sportflics Rookie/Traded Samples

This set of nine standard-size sample cards previews the 1994 Sportflics Rookie/Traded series. On the fronts, two color game-action photos are overlayed to create a multi-dimensional card that changes images when the card is rotated. On a red and black geometric design, the backs carry a color head shot, biography, and statistics. Both sides have the word "SAMPLE" running diagonally from the lower left to the upper right corner.

Nm-Mt Ex-Mt
COMPLETE SET (9) 8.00 2.40
1 Will Clark 2.50 .75
14 Bret Boone 1.00 .30
20 Ellis Burks 1.00 .30
25 Deion Sanders 1.00 .30
65 Chris Turner .50 .15
82 Tony Tarasco .50 .15
102 Rich Becker .50 .15
GG1 Gary Sheffield 3.00 .90
Going, Going, Gone
NNO Title Card .50 .15

1994 Sportflics Rookie/Traded

This set of 150 standard-size cards was distributed in five-card retail packs at a suggested price of $1.89. The set features top rookies and traded players. This set was released only through retail (non-hobby) outlets. The fronts feature the "Magic Motion" printing with two action views of the player which change with the tilting of the card. The player's name is printed in red and expands and contracts with the tilting of the card. Numbered backs include a player biography and career stats and the 1994 performance of the rookie or how the player was acquired in a trade. A full-color photo of the player is framed at an angle with a red and black background. Rookie Cards in this set include Chan Ho Park and Alex Rodriguez.

Nm-Mt Ex-Mt
COMPLETE SET (150) 25.00 7.50
1 Will Clark 1.25 .35
2 Sid Fernandez .25 .07
3 Joe Magrane .25 .07
4 Pete Smith .25 .07
5 Roberto Kelly .25 .07
6 Delino DeShields .25 .07
7 Brian Harper .25 .07
8 Darrin Jackson .25 .07
9 Omar Vizquel .50 .15
10 Luis Polonia .25 .07
11 Reggie Jefferson .25 .07
12 Geronimo Berroa .25 .07
13 Mike Harkey .25 .07
14 Bret Boone .50 .15
15 Dave Henderson .25 .07
16 Pedro Martinez 1.25 .35
17 Jose Vizcaino .25 .07
18 Xavier Hernandez .25 .07
19 Eddie Taubensee .25 .07
20 Ellis Burks .50 .15
21 Turner Ward .25 .07
22 Terry Mulholland .25 .07
23 Howard Johnson .25 .07
24 Vince Coleman .25 .07
25 Deion Sanders .75 .23
26 Rafael Palmeiro .75 .23
27 Dave Weathers .25 .07
28 Kent Mercker .25 .07
29 Gregg Olson .25 .07
30 Cory Bailey RC .25 .07
31 Brian L. Hunter .25 .07
32 Garey Ingram RC .25 .07
33 Daniel Smith .25 .07
34 Denny Hocking .25 .07
35 Charles Johnson .50 .15
36 Otis Nixon .25 .07
37 Hector Fajardo .25 .07
38 Lee Smith .50 .15
39 Phil Stidham .25 .07
40 Melvin Nieves .25 .07
41 Julio Franco .50 .15
42 Greg Gohr .25 .07
43 Steve Dunn .25 .07
44 Tony Fernandez .25 .07
45 Toby Borland RC .25 .07
46 Paul Shuey .25 .07
47 Shawn Hare .25 .07
48 Shawn Green 1.25 .35
49 Julian Tavarez RC .50 .15
50 Ernie Young RC .50 .15
51 Chris Sabo .25 .07
52 Greg O'Halloran .25 .07
53 Donnie Elliott .25 .07
54 Jim Converse .25 .07
55 Ray Holbert .25 .07
56 Keith Lockhart RC .50 .15
57 Tony Longmire .25 .07
58 Jorge Fabregas .25 .07
59 Ravelo Manzanillo .25 .07
60 Marcus Moore .25 .07
61 Carlos Rodriguez .25 .07
62 Mark Portugal .25 .07
63 Yorkis Perez .25 .07
64 Dan Miceli .25 .07
65 Chris Turner .25 .07
66 Mike Oquist .25 .07
67 Tom Quinlan .25 .07
68 Matt Walbeck .25 .07
69 Dave Staton .25 .07
70 W.VanLandingham RC .25 .07
71 Dave Stevens .25 .07
72 Domingo Cedeno .25 .07
73 Alex Diaz .25 .07
74 Darren Bragg RC .25 .07
75 James Hurst .25 .07
76 Alex Gonzalez .25 .07
77 Steve Dreyer .25 .07
78 Robert Eenhoorn .25 .07
79 Derek Parks .25 .07
80 Jose Valentin .25 .07
81 Wes Chamberlain .25 .07
82 Tony Tarasco .25 .07
83 Steve Traschel .25 .07
84 Willie Banks .25 .07
85 Rob Butler .25 .07
86 Miguel Jimenez .25 .07
87 Gerald Williams .25 .07
88 Aaron Small .25 .07
89 Matt Mieske .25 .07
90 Tim Hyers RC .25 .07
91 Eddie Murray 1.25 .35
92 Dennis Martinez .50 .15
93 Tony Eusebio .25 .07
94 Brian Anderson RC .50 .15
95 Blaise Ilsley .25 .07
96 Johnny Ruffin .25 .07
97 Carlos Reyes .25 .07
98 Greg Pirkl .25 .07
99 Jack Morris .50 .15
100 John Mabry RC .50 .15
101 Mike Kelly .25 .07
102 Rich Becker .25 .07
103 Chris Gomez .25 .07
104 Jim Edmonds .75 .23
105 Rich Rowland .25 .07
106 Damon Buford .25 .07
107 Mark Kiefer .25 .07
108 Matias Carrillo .25 .07
109 James Mouton .25 .07
110 Kelly Stinnett RC .25 .07
111 Billy Ashley .25 .07
112 Fausto Cruz RC .25 .07
113 Roberto Petagine .25 .07
114 Joe Hall .25 .07
115 Brian Johnson RC .25 .07
116 Kevin Jarvis .25 .07
117 Tim Davis .25 .07
118 John Patterson .25 .07
119 Stan Royer .25 .07
120 Jeff Juden .25 .07
121 Bryan Eversgerd .25 .07
122 Chan Ho Park RC 1.50 .45
123 Shane Reynolds .25 .07
124 Danny Bautista .25 .07
125 Rikkert Faneyte RC .25 .07
126 Carlos Pulido .25 .07
127 Mike Matheny RC .50 .15
128 Hector Carrasco .25 .07

129 Eddie Zambrano .25 .07
130 Lee Tinsley .25 .07
131 Roger Salkeld .25 .07
132 Carlos Delgado .75 .23
133 Troy O'Leary .25 .07
134 Keith Mitchell .25 .07
135 Lance Painter .25 .07
136 Nate Minchey .25 .07
137 Eric Anthony .25 .07
138 Rafael Bournigal .25 .07
139 Joey Hamilton .25 .07
140 Bobby Munoz .25 .07
141 Rex Hudler .25 .07
142 Alex Cole .25 .07
143 Stan Javier .25 .07
144 Jose Oliva .25 .07
145 Tom Brunansky .25 .07
146 Greg Colbrunn .25 .07
147 Luis Lopez .25 .07
148 Alex Rodriguez RC 20.00 6.00
149 Darryl Strawberry .75 .23
150 Bo Jackson 1.25 .35
RO1 Ryan Klesko ROY 4.00 1.20
Manny Ramirez

1994 Sportflics Rookie/Traded Artist's Proofs

This set of cards parallels the 150 regular issue Rookie/Traded cards and are embellished with the gold foil "Artist's Proof" stamp. They were randomly inserted in at a rate of one in 24 packs.

Nm-Mt Ex-Mt
*STARS: 10X TO 25X BASIC CARDS..
*ROOKIES: 10X TO 25X BASIC CARDS

1994 Sportflics Rookie/Traded Going Going Gone

Randomly inserted in packs at a rate of one in 18, this 12-card set features big hitters. Sportflics used its "Magic Mirror" technology to produce two images when the card is tilted. Borderless backs are numbered with the prefix "GG" and have a dark background containing a blurred stadium.

Nm-Mt Ex-Mt
COMPLETE SET (12) 60.00 18.00
GG1 Gary Sheffield 2.50 .75
GG2 Matt Williams 2.50 .75
GG3 Juan Gonzalez 6.00 1.80
GG4 Ken Griffey Jr. 10.00 3.00
GG5 Mike Piazza 12.00 3.60
GG6 Frank Thomas 6.00 1.80
GG7 Tim Salmon 4.00 1.20
GG8 Barry Bonds 15.00 4.50
GG9 Fred McGriff 4.00 1.20
GG10 Cecil Fielder 2.50 .75
GG11 Albert Belle 2.50 .75
GG12 Joe Carter 2.50 .75

1994 Sportflics Rookie/Traded Rookie Starflics

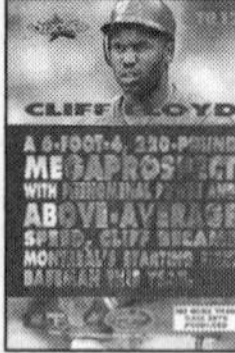

Randomly inserted in packs at a rate of one in 36, these 3-D cards highlight the rookie sensations of 1994. A first year card of Alex Rodriguez highlights this set.

Nm-Mt Ex-Mt
COMPLETE SET (18) 150.00 45.00
TR1 John Hudek 5.00 1.50
TR2 Manny Ramirez 10.00 3.00
TR3 Jeffrey Hammonds 5.00 1.50
TR4 Carlos Delgado 10.00 3.00
TR5 Javier Lopez 8.00 2.40
TR6 Alex Gonzalez 5.00 1.50
TR7 Raul Mondesi 8.00 2.40
TR8 Bob Hamelin 5.00 1.50
TR9 Ryan Klesko 8.00 2.40
TR10 Brian Anderson 8.00 2.40
TR11 Alex Rodriguez 80.00 24.00
TR12 Cliff Floyd 8.00 2.40
TR13 Chan Ho Park 15.00 4.50
TR14 Steve Karsay 5.00 1.50
TR15 Rondell White 8.00 2.40
TR16 Shawn Green 15.00 4.50
TR17 Rich Becker 5.00 1.50
TR18 Charles Johnson 8.00 2.40

1994 Sportflics FanFest All-Stars

At Fanfest, collectors received redemption coupons at various locations. These redemption coupons could be turned in at certain distribution centers for the Sportflics cards. It is noted on the backs that 10,000 sets were produced. The cards measure the standard size. The borderless fronts carry two-dimensional color action photos featuring an American League player and a National League

player. The player's names appear in the upper left and bottom right corners. The backs carry headshots and statistics for each player. According to reports, between 10-20 percent of the mintage of this set was destroyed at the end of fanfest.

Nm-Mt Ex-Mt
COMPLETE SET (9) 100.00 30.00
AS1 Fred McGriff 10.00 3.00
Frank Thomas
AS2 Ryne Sandberg 8.00 2.40
Roberto Alomar
AS3 Matt Williams 4.00 1.20
Travis Fryman
AS4 Ozzie Smith 25.00 7.50
Cal Ripken Jr.
AS5 Mike Piazza 15.00 4.50
Ivan Rodriguez
AS6 Barry Bonds 10.00 3.00
Juan Gonzalez
AS7 Lenny Dykstra 20.00 6.00
Ken Griffey Jr.
AS8 Gary Sheffield 10.00 3.00
Kirby Puckett
AS9 Greg Maddux 12.00 3.60
Mike Mussina

1995 Sportflix Samples

This nine-card set features samples of the 1995 Sportlix series. The cards are numbered below according to their numbers in the regular series. It is rumored that only 200 to 300 of each card were produced.

Nm-Mt Ex-Mt
COMPLETE SET (9) 200.00 60.00
3 Fred McGriff 12.00 3.60
20 Frank Thomas 20.00 6.00
105 Manny Ramirez 20.00 6.00
122 Cal Ripken 80.00 24.00
128 Roberto Alomar 15.00 4.50
152 Russ Davis 8.00 2.40
162 Chipper Jones 40.00 12.00
DE2 Matt Williams 12.00 3.60
Detonator
NNO Title card 8.00 2.40

1995 Sportflix

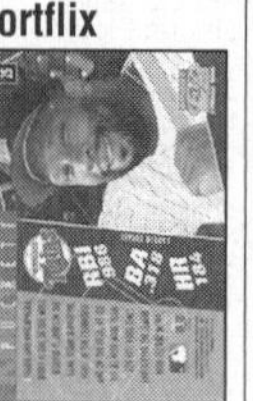

This 170 card standard-size set was released by Pinnacle brands. The set was issued in five card packs that had a suggested retail price of $1.89 per pack. Thirty-six of these packs are contained in a full box. Jumbo packs were also issued: these packs contained eight cards per pack and had 36 packs in a box. Card fronts feature Pinnacle's "Magic Motion" printing which shows the player in two different action shots when the card is tilted. The player's position is printed diagonally on the top right with the team logo underneath. Horizontal backs feature a full-color player photo on the right. Subsets include a rookies section (141-165) and a checklist grouping (166-170).

Nm-Mt Ex-Mt
COMPLETE SET (170) 20.00 6.00
1 Ken Griffey Jr. 1.25 .35
2 Jeffrey Hammonds .15 .04
3 Fred McGriff .50 .15
4 Rickey Henderson .75 .23
5 Derrick May .15 .04
6 Robin Ventura .30 .09
7 Royce Clayton .15 .04
8 Paul Molitor .50 .15
9 Charlie Hayes .15 .04
10 David Nied .15 .04
11 Ellis Burks .30 .09
12 Bernard Gilkey .15 .04
13 Don Mattingly 2.00 .60
14 Albert Belle .30 .09
15 Doug Drabek .15 .04
16 Tony Gwynn 1.00 .30
17 Delino DeShields .15 .04
18 Bobby Bonilla .30 .09
19 Cliff Floyd .30 .09
20 Frank Thomas .75 .23
21 Raul Mondesi .30 .09
22 Dave Nilsson .15 .04
23 Todd Zeile .15 .04
24 Bernie Williams .50 .15
25 Kirby Puckett .75 .23
26 David Cone .30 .09
27 Darren Daulton .30 .09
28 Marquis Grissom .15 .04
29 Randy Johnson .75 .23
30 Jeff Kent .30 .09
31 Orlando Merced .15 .04
32 Dave Justice .30 .09
33 Ivan Rodriguez .75 .23
34 Kirk Gibson .30 .09
35 Alex Fernandez .15 .04
36 Rick Wilkins .15 .04
37 Andy Benes .15 .04
38 Bret Saberhagen .30 .09
39 Billy Ashley .15 .04
40 Jose Rijo .15 .04
41 Matt Williams .30 .09
42 Lenny Dykstra .30 .09
43 Jay Bell .30 .09
44 Reggie Jefferson .15 .04
45 Greg Maddux 1.25 .35
46 Gary Sheffield .30 .09
47 Bret Boone .30 .09
48 Jeff Bagwell .50 .15
49 Ben McDonald .15 .04
50 Eric Karros .30 .09
51 Roger Clemens 1.50 .45
52 Sammy Sosa 1.25 .35
53 Barry Bonds 2.00 .60
54 Joey Hamilton .15 .04
55 Brian Jordan .30 .09
56 Wil Cordero .15 .04
57 Aaron Sele .15 .04
58 Paul O'Neill .50 .15
59 Carlos Garcia .15 .04
60 Mike Mussina .75 .23
61 John Olerud .30 .09
62 Kevin Appier .30 .09
63 Matt Mieske .15 .04
64 Carlos Baerga .15 .04
65 Ryan Klesko .30 .09
66 Jimmy Key .30 .09
67 James Mouton .15 .04
68 Tim Salmon .50 .15
69 Hal Morris .15 .04
70 Albie Lopez .15 .04
71 Dave Hollins .15 .04
72 Greg Colbrunn .15 .04
73 Juan Gonzalez .75 .23
74 Wally Joyner .30 .09
75 Bob Hamelin .15 .04
76 Brady Anderson .30 .09
77 Deion Sanders .50 .15
78 Javier Lopez .30 .09
79 Brian McRae .15 .04
80 Craig Biggio .50 .15
81 Kenny Lofton .30 .09
82 Cecil Fielder .30 .09
83 Mike Piazza 1.25 .35
84 Rafael Palmeiro .50 .15
85 Jim Thome .75 .23
86 Ruben Sierra .15 .04
87 Mark Langston .15 .04
88 John Valentin .15 .04
89 Shawon Dunston .15 .04
90 Travis Fryman .30 .09
91 Chuck Knoblauch .30 .09
92 Dean Palmer .30 .09
93 Robby Thompson .15 .04
94 Barry Larkin .75 .23
95 Darren Lewis .15 .04
96 Andres Galarraga .30 .09
97 Tony Phillips .15 .04
98 Mo Vaughn .30 .09
99 Pedro Martinez .75 .23
100 Chad Curtis .15 .04
101 Brent Gates .15 .04
102 Pat Hentgen .15 .04
103 Rico Brogna .15 .04
104 Carlos Delgado .30 .09
105 Manny Ramirez .30 .09
106 Mike Greenwell .15 .04
107 Wade Boggs .50 .15
108 Ozzie Smith 1.25 .35
109 Rusty Greer .30 .09
110 Willie Greene .15 .04
111 Chili Davis .30 .09
112 Reggie Sanders .30 .09
113 Roberto Kelly .15 .04
114 Tom Glavine .50 .15
115 Moises Alou .30 .09
116 Dennis Eckersley .30 .09
117 Danny Tartabull .15 .04
118 Jeff Conine .30 .09
119 Will Clark .75 .23
120 Joe Carter .30 .09
121 Mark McGwire 2.00 .60
122 Cal Ripken Jr. 2.50 .75
123 Danny Jackson .15 .04
124 Phil Plantier .15 .04
125 Dante Bichette .30 .09
126 Jack McDowell .15 .04
127 Jose Canseco .75 .23
128 Roberto Alomar .75 .23
129 Rondell White .30 .09
130 Ray Lankford .15 .04
131 Ryan Thompson .15 .04
132 Ken Caminiti .30 .09
133 Gregg Jefferies .15 .04
134 Omar Vizquel .30 .09
135 Mark Grace .50 .15
136 Derek Bell .15 .04
137 Mickey Tettleton .15 .04
138 Wilson Alvarez .15 .04
139 Larry Walker .50 .15
140 Bo Jackson .75 .23
141 Alex Rodriguez 2.00 .60
142 Orlando Miller .15 .04
143 Shawn Green .30 .09
144 Steve Dunn .15 .04
145 Midre Cummings .15 .04
146 Chan Ho Park .30 .09
147 Jose Oliva .15 .04
148 Armando Benitez .30 .09
149 J.R. Phillips .15 .04
150 Charles Johnson .30 .09
151 Garret Anderson .30 .09
152 Russ Davis .15 .04
153 Brian L.Hunter .15 .04
154 Ernie Young .15 .04
155 Marc Newfield .15 .04
156 Greg Pirkl .15 .04
157 Scott Ruffcorn .15 .04
158 Rikkert Faneyte .15 .04
159 Duane Singleton .15 .04
160 Gabe White .15 .04
161 Alex Gonzalez .15 .04
162 Chipper Jones .75 .23
163 Mike Kelly .15 .04
164 Kurt Miller .15 .04
165 Roberto Petagine .15 .04
166 Jeff Bagwell CL .30 .09
167 Mike Piazza CL .75 .23
168 Ken Griffey Jr. CL .75 .23
169 Frank Thomas CL .50 .15
170 Barry Bonds CL 2.50 .75
Cal Ripken

1995 Sportflix Artist's Proofs

Cards from this 170-card parallel set were randomly inserted in packs at a rate of one in 36. Only 700 sets were printed. The "Artist's Proof" logo is printed in gold foil at the bottom right and the player's last name expands and contracts with the tilting of the card.

Nm-Mt Ex-Mt
*STARS: 6X TO 15X BASIC CARDS ....

1995 Sportflix Detonators

Randomly inserted in packs at a rate of one in 16, this nine-card set highlights power hitters. Backs are numbered with the prefix "DE".

Nm-Mt Ex-Mt
COMPLETE SET (9) 20.00 6.00
DE1 Jeff Bagwell 1.50 .45
DE2 Matt Williams 1.00 .30
DE3 Ken Griffey Jr. 4.00 1.20
DE4 Frank Thomas 2.50 .75
DE5 Mike Piazza 4.00 1.20
DE6 Barry Bonds 6.00 1.80
DE7 Albert Belle 1.00 .30
DE8 Cliff Floyd 1.00 .30
DE9 Juan Gonzalez 2.50 .75

1995 Sportflix Double Take

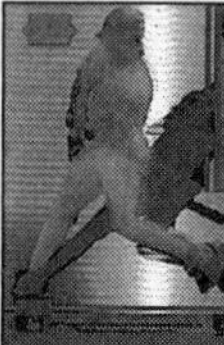

Randomly inserted in packs at a rate of one in 48, this 12-card set features two stars in one see-through 3-D card. Fronts feature the Sportflix "Magic Motion" process that allows the viewer to see two different images when the card is tilted.

Nm-Mt Ex-Mt
COMPLETE SET (12) 100.00 30.00
1 Jeff Bagwell 6.00 1.80
Frank Thomas
2 Will Clark 6.00 1.80
Fred McGriff
3 Roberto Alomar 6.00 1.80
Jeff Kent
4 Matt Williams 4.00 1.20
Wade Boggs
5 Cal Ripken Jr. 20.00 6.00
Ozzie Smith
6 Alex Rodriguez 15.00 4.50
Wil Cordero
7 Mike Piazza 10.00 3.00
Carlos Delgado
8 Kenny Lofton 2.50 .75
Dave Justice
9 Barry Bonds 10.00 3.00
Ken Griffey Jr.
10 Albert Belle 2.50 .75
Raul Mondesi
11 Tony Gwynn 6.00 1.80
Kirby Puckett
12 Jimmy Key 10.00 3.00
Greg Maddux

1995 Sportflix Hammer Team

This 18-card set was inserted randomly in packs at a rate of one in 48 and looks at the league's top hitters. Full-bleed, horizontal backs are numbered with the prefix "HT" and picture the player in full color.

Nm-Mt Ex-Mt
COMPLETE SET (18) 25.00 7.50
HT1 Ken Griffey Jr. 2.00 .60
HT2 Frank Thomas 1.25 .35
HT3 Jeff Bagwell .75 .23
HT4 Mike Piazza 2.00 .60
HT5 Cal Ripken Jr. 4.00 1.20
HT6 Albert Belle .50 .15
HT7 Barry Bonds 3.00 .90
HT8 Don Mattingly 3.00 .90
HT9 Will Clark 1.25 .35
HT10 Tony Gwynn 1.50 .45
HT11 Matt Williams .50 .15
HT12 Kirby Puckett 1.25 .35
HT13 Manny Ramirez .50 .15
HT14 Fred McGriff .75 .23
HT15 Juan Gonzalez 1.25 .35
HT16 Kenny Lofton .50 .15
HT17 Raul Mondesi .50 .15
HT18 Tim Salmon .75 .23

1995 Sportflix ProMotion

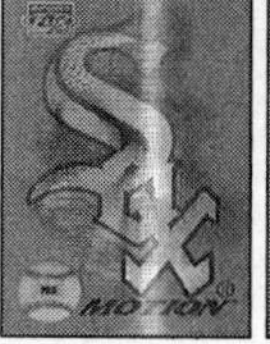

Randomly inserted in jumbo packs at a rate of one in 18, this 12-card set features top stars in the "Magic Motion" technology. The horizontal backs feature the player in an action shot and are numbered with the prefix "PM".

Nm-Mt Ex-Mt
COMPLETE SET (12) 100.00 30.00
PM1 Ken Griffey Jr. 10.00 3.00
PM2 Frank Thomas 6.00 1.80
PM3 Cal Ripken Jr. 20.00 6.00
PM4 Jeff Bagwell 4.00 1.20
PM5 Mike Piazza 10.00 3.00
PM6 Matt Williams 2.50 .75
PM7 Albert Belle 2.50 .75
PM8 Jose Canseco 6.00 1.80
PM9 Don Mattingly 15.00 4.50
PM10 Barry Bonds 15.00 4.50
PM11 Will Clark 6.00 1.80
PM12 Kirby Puckett 6.00 1.80

1996 Sportflix

With retail only distribution, this 144 card set comes in five card packs that retail for $1.99. Regular cards picture two different pieces of photography. The set contains the UC3 Subset (97-120), Rookies Subset (121-141), and Checklists (142-144). The UC3 Subset features veteran superstars in 3-D animation. The 21-card Rookie subset carries color player photos on a background of part of a baseball that changes into a wooden baseball bat section when moved.

Nm-Mt Ex-Mt
COMPLETE SET (144) 25.00 7.50
1 Wade Boggs .50 .15
2 Tim Salmon .50 .15
3 Will Clark .75 .23
4 Dante Bichette .30 .09
5 Barry Bonds 2.00 .60
6 Kirby Puckett .75 .23
7 Albert Belle .30 .09
8 Greg Maddux 1.25 .35
9 Tony Gwynn 1.00 .30
10 Mike Piazza 1.25 .35
11 Ivan Rodriguez .75 .23
12 Marty Cordova .30 .09
13 Frank Thomas .75 .23
14 Raul Mondesi .30 .09
15 Johnny Damon .30 .09
16 Mark McGwire 2.00 .60
17 Len Dykstra .30 .09
18 Ken Griffey Jr. 1.25 .35
19 Chipper Jones .75 .23
20 Alex Rodriguez 1.50 .45
21 Jeff Bagwell .50 .15
22 Jim Edmonds .30 .09
23 Edgar Martinez .50 .15
24 David Cone .30 .09
25 Tom Glavine .50 .15
26 Eddie Murray .75 .23
27 Paul Molitor .50 .15
28 Ryan Klesko .30 .09
29 Rafael Palmeiro .50 .15
30 Manny Ramirez .30 .09
31 Mo Vaughn .30 .09
32 Rico Brogna .30 .09
33 Marc Newfield .30 .09
34 J.T. Snow .30 .09
35 Reggie Sanders .30 .09
36 Fred McGriff .50 .15
37 Craig Biggio .50 .15
38 Jeff King .30 .09
39 Kenny Lofton .30 .09
40 Gary Gaetti .30 .09
41 Eric Karros .30 .09
42 Jason Isringhausen .30 .09
43 B.J. Surhoff .30 .09
44 Michael Tucker .30 .09
45 Gary Sheffield .30 .09
46 Chili Davis .30 .09
47 Bobby Bonilla .30 .09
48 Hideo Nomo .75 .23
49 Ray Durham .30 .09
50 Phil Nevin .30 .09
51 Randy Johnson .75 .23
52 Bill Pulsipher .30 .09
53 Ozzie Smith 1.25 .35
54 Cal Ripken 2.50 .75
55 Cecil Fielder .30 .09
56 Matt Williams .30 .09
57 Sammy Sosa 1.25 .35
58 Roger Clemens 1.50 .45
59 Brian L.Hunter .30 .09
60 Barry Larkin .75 .23
61 Charles Johnson .30 .09
62 David Justice .30 .09
63 Garret Anderson .30 .09
64 Rondell White .30 .09
65 Derek Bell .30 .09
66 Andres Galarraga .30 .09
67 Moises Alou .30 .09
68 Travis Fryman .30 .09
69 Pedro Martinez .75 .23

70 Carlos Baerga .30 .09
71 John Valentin .30 .09
72 Larry Walker .50 .15
73 Roberto Alomar .75 .23
74 Mike Mussina .75 .23
75 Kevin Appier .30 .09
76 Bernie Williams .50 .15
77 Ray Lankford .30 .09
78 Gregg Jefferies .30 .09
79 Robin Ventura .30 .09
80 Kenny Rogers .30 .09
81 Paul O'Neill .50 .15
82 Mark Grace .50 .15
83 Deion Sanders .50 .15
84 Tino Martinez .50 .15
85 Joe Carter .30 .09
86 Pete Schourek .30 .09
87 Jack McDowell .30 .09
88 John Mabry .30 .09
89 Darren Daulton .30 .09
90 Jim Thome .75 .23
91 Jay Buhner .30 .09
92 Jay Bell .30 .09
93 Kevin Seitzer .30 .09
94 Jose Canseco .75 .23
95 Juan Gonzalez .75 .23
96 Jeff Conine .30 .09
97 Chipper Jones UC3 .50 .15
98 Ken Griffey Jr. UC3 .75 .23
99 Frank Thomas UC3 .50 .15
100 Cal Ripken UC3 1.25 .35
101 Albert Belle UC3 .30 .09
102 Mike Piazza UC3 .75 .23
103 Dante Bichette UC3 .30 .09
104 Sammy Sosa UC3 .75 .23
105 Mo Vaughn UC3 .30 .09
106 Tim Salmon UC3 .30 .09
107 Reggie Sanders UC3 .30 .09
108 Gary Sheffield UC3 .30 .09
109 Ruben Rivera UC3 .30 .09
110 Rafael Palmeiro UC3 .30 .09
111 Edgar Martinez UC3 .30 .09
112 Barry Bonds UC3 .75 .23
113 Manny Ramirez UC3 .30 .09
114 Larry Walker UC3 .30 .09
115 Jeff Bagwell UC3 .30 .09
116 Matt Williams UC3 .30 .09
117 Mark McGwire UC3 1.00 .30
118 Johnny Damon UC3 .30 .09
119 Eddie Murray UC3 .50 .15
120 Jay Buhner UC3 .30 .09
121 Tim Unroe .30 .09
122 Todd Hollandsworth .30 .09
123 Tony Clark .30 .09
124 Roger Cedeno .30 .09
125 Jim Pittsley .30 .09
126 Ruben Rivera .30 .09
127 Bob Wolcott .30 .09
128 Chan Ho Park .30 .09
129 Chris Snopek .30 .09
130 Alex Ochoa .30 .09
131 Yamil Benitez .30 .09
132 Jimmy Haynes .30 .09
133 Dustin Hermanson .30 .09
134 Shawn Estes .30 .09
135 Howard Battle .30 .09
136 Matt Lawton RC .30 .09
137 Terrell Wade .30 .09
138 Jason Schmidt .30 .09
139 Derek Jeter 2.00 .60
140 Shannon Stewart .30 .09
141 Chris Stynes .30 .09
142 Ken Griffey Jr. CL .75 .23
143 Greg Maddux CL .75 .23
144 Cal Ripken CL 1.25 .35

1996 Sportflix Artist's Proofs

Inserted at the rate of one in 48, cards from this 144-card set are parallel to the regular set. A gold-foil stamped Artist's Proof logo distinguish them from their regular issue counterparts.

Nm-Mt Ex-Mt
*STARS: 10X TO 25X BASIC CARDS
*ROOKIES: 6X TO 15X BASIC CARDS

1996 Sportflix Double Take

Randomly inserted in jumbo packs, this 12-card set features color player photos of two players per card that play the same position.

Nm-Mt Ex-Mt
COMPLETE SET (12) 60.00 18.00
1 Barry Larkin 12.00 3.60
Cal Ripken
2 Roberto Alomar 4.00 1.20
Craig Biggio
3 Chipper Jones 4.00 1.20
Matt Williams
4 Ken Griffey 6.00 1.80
Ruben Rivera
5 Greg Maddux 6.00 1.80
Hideo Nomo
6 Frank Thomas 4.00 1.20
Mo Vaughn
7 Ivan Rodriguez 6.00 1.80
Mike Piazza
8 Albert Belle 10.00 3.00
Barry Bonds
9 Alex Rodriguez 8.00 2.40
Derek Jeter
10 Kirby Puckett 5.00 1.50
Tony Gwynn
11 Sammy Sosa 6.00 1.80
Manny Ramirez
12 Jeff Bagwell 2.50 .75
Rico Brogna

1996 Sportflix Hit Parade

With an insertion rate of one in 35, this 16-card set features color player photos of hitters in 3D with a background scene in full-motion animation.

Nm-Mt Ex-Mt
COMPLETE SET (16) 80.00 24.00
1 Ken Griffey Jr. 6.00 1.80
2 Cal Ripken 12.00 3.60
3 Frank Thomas 4.00 1.20
4 Mike Piazza 6.00 1.80
5 Mo Vaughn 1.50 .45
6 Albert Belle 1.50 .45
7 Jeff Bagwell 2.50 .75
8 Matt Williams 1.50 .45
9 Sammy Sosa 6.00 1.80
10 Kirby Puckett 4.00 1.20
11 Dante Bichette 1.50 .45
12 Gary Sheffield 1.50 .45
13 Tony Gwynn 5.00 1.50
14 Wade Boggs 2.50 .75
15 Chipper Jones 4.00 1.20
16 Barry Bonds 10.00 3.00

1996 Sportflix Power Surge

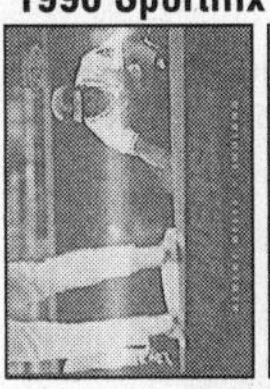

With an insertion rate of one in 35, this retail only 24-card set is printed on clear plastic and is a 3-D parallel rendition of the UC3 subset found in the regular Sportflix set.

Nm-Mt Ex-Mt
COMPLETE SET (24) 120.00 36.00
1 Chipper Jones 6.00 1.80
2 Ken Griffey Jr. 10.00 3.00
3 Frank Thomas 6.00 1.80
4 Cal Ripken 20.00 6.00
5 Albert Belle 2.50 .75
6 Mike Piazza 10.00 3.00
7 Dante Bichette 2.50 .75
8 Sammy Sosa 10.00 3.00
9 Mo Vaughn 2.50 .75
10 Tim Salmon 4.00 1.20
11 Reggie Sanders 2.50 .75
12 Gary Sheffield 2.50 .75
13 Ruben Rivera 2.50 .75
14 Rafael Palmeiro 4.00 1.20
15 Edgar Martinez 4.00 1.20
16 Barry Bonds 15.00 4.50
17 Manny Ramirez 2.50 .75
18 Larry Walker 4.00 1.20
19 Jeff Bagwell 4.00 1.20
20 Matt Williams 2.50 .75
21 Mark McGwire 15.00 4.50
22 Johnny Damon 2.50 .75
23 Eddie Murray 6.00 1.80
24 Jay Buhner 2.50 .75

1996 Sportflix ProMotion

Inserted at the rate of one in 17, this 20-card set uses morphing technology and multi-phase animation to turn a player's photo into a bat, a ball, a glove, or a catcher's mask.

Nm-Mt Ex-Mt
COMPLETE SET (20) 50.00 15.00
1 Cal Ripken 8.00 2.40
2 Greg Maddux 4.00 1.20
3 Mo Vaughn 1.00 .30
4 Albert Belle 1.00 .30
5 Mike Piazza 4.00 1.20
6 Ken Griffey Jr. 4.00 1.20
7 Frank Thomas 2.50 .75
8 Jeff Bagwell 1.50 .45
9 Hideo Nomo 2.50 .75
10 Chipper Jones 2.50 .75
11 Tony Gwynn 3.00 .90
12 Don Mattingly 5.00 1.50
13 Dante Bichette 1.00 .30
14 Matt Williams 1.00 .30
15 Manny Ramirez 1.00 .30
16 Barry Bonds 6.00 1.80
17 Reggie Sanders 1.00 .30
18 Tim Salmon 1.50 .45
19 Ruben Rivera 1.00 .30
20 Garret Anderson 1.00 .30

1996 Sportflix Rookie Jumbos

These eight 5" by 7" cards were issued as chiptoppers in retail Sportflix boxes. They are numbered out of eight but otherwise are reprints of the regular Sportflix cards.

Nm-Mt Ex-Mt
COMPLETE SET 30.00 9.00
1 Jason Schmidt 5.00 1.50
2 Chris Snopek 2.00 .60
3 Tony Clark 2.00 .60
4 Todd Hollandsworth 2.00 .60
5 Alex Ochoa 2.00 .60
6 Derek Jeter 25.00 7.50
7 Howard Battle 2.00 .60
8 Bob Wolcott 2.00 .60

1910-11 Sporting Life M116

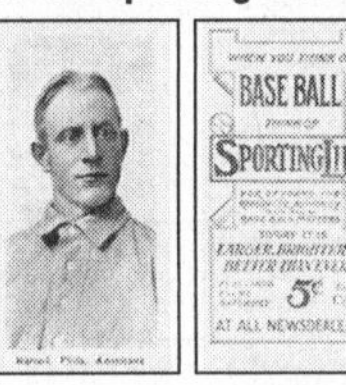

The cards in this 288-card set (326 with all variations) measure approximately 1 1/2" by 2 5/8". The Sporting Life set was offered as a premium to the publication's subscribers in 1910 and 1911. Each of the 24 series of 12 cards came in an envelope printed with a list of the players within. Cards marked with S1 or S2 followed by an asterisk can be found with both a blue background and a more common pastel background. Cards marked with S3 followed with an asterisk are found with either a blue or black printed Sporting Life advertisement on the reverse. McConnell appears with both Boston AL (common) and Chicago White Sox (scarce); McQuillan appears with Phillies (common) and Cincinnati (scarce). After the players name the letter S followed by a number indicates which series the card was issued with. Cards are numbered in the checklist below alphabetically within team. Teams are ordered alphabetically within league: Boston AL (1-19), Chicago AL (20-36), Cleveland (37-52), Detroit (53-73), New York AL (74-84), Philadelphia AL (85-105), St. Louis AL (106-120), Washington (121-134), Boston NL (135-147), Brooklyn (148-164), Chicago NL (165-185), Cincinnati (186-203), New York NL (204-223), Philadelphia NL (224-242), Pittsburgh (243-261), and St. Louis (262-279). Cards 280-288 feature minor leaguers and are somewhat more difficult to find since most are from the tougher higher series.

Ex-Mt VG
COMPLETE SET (290) 35000.00 17500.00
COMMON MAJOR (1-280) 60.00 30.00
COMMON MINOR (280-288) 60.00 30.00
COMMON S19-S24 120.00 60.00
1 Frank Arellanes S9 60.00 30.00
2 Bill Carrigan S5 60.00 30.00
3 Ed Cicotte S18 200.00 100.00
4 Ray Collins S24 120.00 60.00
5 Pat Donahue S13 60.00 30.00
6 Patsy Donovan MG S21 120.00 60.00
7 Arthur Engle S4 60.00 30.00
8 Larry Gardner S24 120.00 60.00
9 Charles Hall S14 60.00 30.00
10 Harry Hooper S23 350.00 180.00
11 Edwin Karger S9 60.00 30.00
12 Harry Lord S2* 60.00 30.00
13 Thomas Madden S24 120.00 60.00
14A Amby McConnell S6 60.00 30.00
(Boston AL)
14B Amby McConnell 2500.00 1250.00
(Chicago AL)
15 Tris Speaker S23 700.00 350.00
16 Jake Stahl S8 80.00 40.00
17 John Thoney S7 60.00 30.00
18 Heinie Wagner S4 80.00 40.00
19 Joe Wood S23 250.00 125.00
20 Lena Blackburn UER S15 60.00 30.00
(Sic, Blackburne)
21 James J. Block S21 120.00 60.00
22 Patsy Dougherty S10 60.00 30.00
23 Hugh Duffy MG S17 150.00 75.00
24 Ed Hahn S9 60.00 30.00
25 Paul Meloan S24 120.00 60.00
26 Fred Parent S18 60.00 30.00
27 Frederick Payne S21 120.00 60.00
28 William Purtell S11 60.00 30.00
29 James Scott S23 120.00 60.00
30 Frank Smith S7 60.00 30.00
31 Billy Sullivan S5 80.00 40.00
32 Lee Tannehill S14 60.00 30.00
33 Ed Walsh S8 150.00 75.00
34 Guy(Doc) White S4 60.00 30.00
35 Irv Young S13 60.00 30.00
36 Dutch Zwilling S24 120.00 60.00
37 Harry Bemis S13 60.00 30.00
38 Charles Berger S12 60.00 30.00
39 Joseph Birmingham S17 60.00 30.00
40 Hugh Bradley S8 60.00 30.00
41 Nig Clarke S18 60.00 30.00
42 Cy Falkenberg S11 60.00 30.00
43 Elmer Flick S15 200.00 100.00
44 Addie Joss S7 250.00 125.00
45 Napoleon Lajoie S2* 350.00 180.00
46 Frederick Link S20 120.00 60.00
47 Bris Lord S9 60.00 30.00
48 Deacon McGuire MG S16 60.00 30.00
49 Harry Niles S17 60.00 30.00
50 George Stovall S18 60.00 30.00
51 Terry Turner S10 60.00 30.00
52 Cy Young S3* 500.00 250.00
53 Heine Beckendorf S16 60.00 30.00
54 Donie Bush S4 60.00 30.00
55 Ty Cobb S1* 2500.00 1250.00
56 Sam Crawford S2* 200.00 100.00
57 Jim Delehanty S8 80.00 40.00
58 Bill Donovan S2* 60.00 30.00
59 Hugh Jennings MG S1* 150.00 75.00
60 Davy Jones S2* 60.00 30.00
61 Tom Jones S12 60.00 30.00
62 Chick Lathers S21 120.00 60.00
63 Matty McIntyre S9 60.00 30.00
64 George Moriarty S6 80.00 40.00
65 George Mullin S3* 60.00 30.00
66 Charley O'Leary S10 60.00 30.00
67 Hub Pernoll S22 120.00 60.00
68 Boss Schmidt S14 60.00 30.00
69 Oscar Stanage S11 60.00 30.00
70 Sailor Stroud S21 120.00 60.00
71 Ed Summers S3* 60.00 30.00
72 Ed Willett S5 60.00 30.00
73 Ralph Works S15 60.00 30.00
74 Jimmy Austin S19 120.00 60.00
75 Hal Chase S1* 120.00 60.00
76 Birdie Cree S18 60.00 30.00
77 Lou Criger S17 60.00 30.00
78 Russ Ford S23 120.00 60.00
79 Earle Gardner S23 120.00 60.00
80 John Knight S19 120.00 60.00
81 Frank LaPorte S13 60.00 30.00
82 George Stallings MG S15 60.00 30.00
83 Jeff Sweeney S19 120.00 60.00
84 Harry Wolter S12 60.00 30.00
85 Tommy Atkins S24 120.00 60.00
86 Frank Baker S3* 200.00 100.00
87 Jack Barry S6 80.00 40.00
88 Chief Bender S1* 120.00 60.00
89 Eddie Collins S1* 200.00 100.00
90 Jack Coombs S8 120.00 60.00
91 Harry Davis S1* 60.00 30.00
92 Jimmy Dygert S16 60.00 30.00
93 Topsy Hartsel S6 60.00 30.00
94 Heinie Heitmuller S13 60.00 30.00
95 Harry Krause S7 60.00 30.00
96 Jack Lapp S24 120.00 60.00
97 Paddy Livingstone S11 60.00 30.00
98 Connie Mack MG S17 300.00 150.00
99 Stuffy McInnis S24 150.00 75.00
UER (Misspelled
McInnes on card)
100 Cy Morgan S12 60.00 30.00
101 Danny Murphy S4 60.00 30.00
102 Rube Oldring S14 60.00 30.00
103 Eddie Plank S5 350.00 180.00
104 Amos Strunk S24 120.00 60.00
105 Ira Thomas S2* 60.00 30.00
106 Bill Bailey S13 60.00 30.00
107 Dode Criss S19 120.00 60.00
108 Bert Graham S12 60.00 30.00
109 Roy Hartzell S11 60.00 30.00
110 Danny Hoffman S6 60.00 30.00
111 Harry Howell S16 60.00 30.00
112 Joe Lake S19 120.00 60.00
113 Jack O'Conner S13 60.00 30.00
114 Barney Pelty S9 60.00 30.00
115 Jack Powell S17 60.00 30.00
116 Al Schweitzer S16 60.00 30.00
117 Jim Stephens S10 60.00 30.00
118 George Stone S7 60.00 30.00
119 Rube Waddell S3* 200.00 100.00
120 Bobby Wallace S5 120.00 60.00
121 Wid Conroy S12 60.00 30.00
122 Kid Elberfeld S4 60.00 30.00
123 Doc Gessler S8 60.00 30.00
124 Walter Johnson S7 800.00 400.00
125 Red Killifer S22 120.00 60.00
126 Jimmy McAleer MG S15 60.00 30.00
127 George McBride S21 120.00 60.00
128 Clyde Milan S15 80.00 40.00
129 Warren Miller S22 120.00 60.00
130 Doc Reisling S10 60.00 30.00
131 Germany Schaefer S11 80.00 40.00
132 Gabby Street S5 60.00 30.00
133 Bob Unglaub S18 60.00 30.00
134 Fred Beck S17 60.00 30.00
135 Buster Brown S18 60.00 30.00
136 Cliff Curtis S23 120.00 60.00
137 George Ferguson S13 60.00 30.00
138 Samuel Frock S20 120.00 60.00
139 Peaches Graham S14 60.00 30.00
140 Buck Herzog S11 60.00 30.00
141 Fred Lake MG S16 60.00 30.00
142 Bayard Sharpe S22 120.00 60.00
142 David Shean S20 120.00 60.00
144 Charlie Smith S22 120.00 60.00
145 Harry Smith S5 60.00 30.00
146 Bill Sweeney S6 60.00 30.00
147 Cy Barger S13 60.00 30.00
148 George Bell S6 60.00 30.00
149 Bill Bergen S9 60.00 30.00
150 Al Burch S14 60.00 30.00
151 Bill Dahlen MG S9 80.00 40.00
152 William Davidson S21 120.00 60.00
153 Frank Dessau S21 120.00 60.00
154 Tex Erwin S20 120.00 60.00
155 John Hummel S18 60.00 30.00
156 George Hunter S15 60.00 30.00
157 Tim Jordan S2* 60.00 30.00
158 Ed Lennox S4 60.00 30.00
159 Pryor McElveen S16 60.00 30.00
160 Tommy McMillan S16 60.00 30.00
161 Nap Rucker S3* 80.00 40.00
162 Doc Scanlon UER S12 60.00 30.00
(Sic, Scanlan)
163 Kaiser Wilhelm S14 60.00 30.00
164 Jimmy Archer S22 120.00 60.00
165 Ginger Beaumont S11 60.00 30.00
166 Mordecai Brown S2* 200.00 100.00
167 Frank Chance S1* 250.00 125.00
168 Johnny Evers S3* 200.00 100.00
169 Solly Hofman S5 60.00 30.00
170 John Kane S12 60.00 30.00
171 Johnny Kling S7 60.00 30.00
172 Rube Kroh S17 60.00 30.00
173 Harry McIntire S16 60.00 30.00
174 Tom Needham S10 60.00 30.00
175 Orvie Overall S4 60.00 30.00
176 Big Jeff Pfeffer S23 120.00 60.00
177 Jack Pfiester S10 60.00 30.00
178 Ed Reulbach S7 80.00 40.00
179 Lew Richie S15 60.00 30.00
180 Frank Schulte S6 60.00 30.00
181 Jimmy Sheckard S9 60.00 30.00
182 Harry Steinfeldt S8 80.00 40.00
183 Joe Tinker S3* 200.00 100.00
184 He. Zimmerman S19 120.00 60.00
185 Fred Beebe S14 60.00 30.00
186 Bob Bescher S6 60.00 30.00
187 Chappy Charles S15 60.00 30.00
188 Tommy Clarke S20 120.00 60.00
189 Tom Downey S13 60.00 30.00
190 Jim Doyle S10 60.00 30.00
191 Dick Eagan UER S11 60.00 30.00
(Sic, Egan)
192 Art Fromme S16 60.00 30.00
193 Harry Gaspar S19 120.00 60.00
194 Clark Griffith MG S8 150.00 75.00
195 Doc Hoblitzel S15 60.00 30.00
196 Hans Lobert S5 60.00 30.00
197 Larry McLean S9 60.00 30.00
198 Mike Mitchell S7 60.00 30.00
199 Art Phelan S23 120.00 60.00
200 Jack Rowan S17 60.00 30.00
201 Bob Space UER S10 60.00 30.00
(Sic& Spade)
202 George Suggs S18 60.00 30.00
203 Red Ames S22 120.00 60.00
204 Al Bridwell S10 60.00 30.00
205 Doc Crandall S17 60.00 30.00
206 Art Devlin S3* 60.00 30.00
207 Josh Devore S19 120.00 60.00
208 Larry Doyle S1* 80.00 40.00
209 Art Fletcher S22 120.00 60.00
210 Christy Mathewson S1* 800.00 400.00
211 John McGraw MG S8 250.00 125.00
212 Fred Merkle S6 100.00 50.00
213 Red Murray S11 60.00 30.00
214 Chief Meyers S23 150.00 75.00
UER (Misspelled
Myers on card)
215 Bugs Raymond S18 80.00 40.00
216 Admiral Schlei S4 60.00 30.00
217 James Seymour S7 60.00 30.00
218 Tillie Shafer S19 120.00 60.00
219 Fred Snodgrass S15 80.00 40.00
220 Fred Tenney S2* 60.00 30.00
221 Art Wilson S23 120.00 60.00
222 Hooks Wiltse S5 60.00 30.00
223 Johnny Bates S8 60.00 30.00
224 Kitty Bransfield S4 60.00 30.00
225 Red Dooin S1* 60.00 30.00
226 Mickey Doolan S6 60.00 30.00
227 Bob Ewing S14 60.00 30.00
228 Bill Foxen S16 60.00 30.00
229 Eddie Grant S5 60.00 30.00
230 Fred Jacklitsch S17 60.00 30.00
231 Otto Knabe S14 60.00 30.00
232 Sherry Magee S7 60.00 30.00
233A Geo.McQuillan S1* 60.00 30.00
(Philadelphia NL)
233B Geo.McQuillan 2500.00 1250.00
(Cincinnati NL)
234 Earl Moore S18 60.00 30.00
235 Pat Moran S12 60.00 30.00
236 Lew Moren S3* 60.00 30.00
237 Dode Paskert S19 120.00 60.00
238 Lou Schettler S20 120.00 60.00
239 Tully Sparks S13 60.00 30.00
240 John Titus S22 120.00 60.00
241 Jimmy Walsh S20 200.00 100.00
(Dark background)
242 Jimmy Walsh S22 200.00 100.00
(White background)
243 Ed Abbaticchio S16 60.00 30.00
244 Babe Adams S3 80.00 40.00
245 Bobby Byrne S6 60.00 30.00
246 Howie Camnitz S5 60.00 30.00
247 Vin Campbell S21 120.00 60.00
248 Fred Clarke S3* 150.00 75.00
249 John Flynn S20 120.00 60.00
250 George Gibson S2* 60.00 30.00
251 Ham Hyatt S14 60.00 30.00
252 Tommy Leach S2* 60.00 30.00
253 Sam Leever S8 60.00 30.00
254 Lefty Leifield S10 60.00 30.00
255 Nick Maddox S11 60.00 30.00
256 Dots Miller S4 60.00 30.00
257 Paddy O'Connor S10 60.00 30.00
258 Deacon Phillipe S9 80.00 40.00
259 Mike Simon S21 120.00 60.00
260 Hans Wagner S1* 1000.00 500.00
261 Chief Wilson S12 60.00 30.00
262 Les Bachman UER S15 60.00 30.00
(Sic, Backman)
263 Jack Bliss S21 120.00 60.00
264 Roger Bresnahan S2* 150.00 75.00
265 Frank Corridon S8 60.00 30.00
266 Ray Demmitt S22 120.00 60.00
267 Rube Ellis S12 60.00 30.00
268 Steve Evans S23 120.00 60.00
269 Bob Harmon S20 120.00 60.00
270 Miller Huggins S4 150.00 75.00
271 Rudy Hulswitt S11 60.00 30.00
272 Ed Konetchy S7 60.00 30.00
273 Johnny Lush S9 60.00 30.00
274 Al Mattern S12 60.00 30.00
275 Mike Mowery S21 120.00 60.00
276 Rebel Oakes S24 120.00 60.00
277 Ed Phelps S14 60.00 30.00
278 Slim Sallee S13 60.00 30.00
279 Vic Willis S18 150.00 75.00
280 Coveleski: Louisville S22 200.00 100.00
UER (Misspelled
Coveleskie on card)
281 Foster: Rochester S19 120.00 60.00
282 Frill: Jersey City S20 120.00 60.00
283 Hughes: Rochester S23 120.00 60.00
284 Krueger: Sacramento S20 120.00 60.00
285 Mitchell: Rochester S19 120.00 60.00
286 O'Hara: Toronto S17 60.00 30.00
287 Perring: Columbus S20 120.00 60.00
288 Ray: Western League S24 120.00 60.00

1911 Sporting Life M116 Cabinets

This six-card set which measures approximately 5 5/8" by 7 1/2" was issued as a premium offer to the Sporting Life card set. These cards have a player photo surrounded by green borders with the players name on the bottom. The backs contain an advertisement for the Sporting Life newspaper. Since the cards are unnumbered, we have put them in alphabetical order.

Ex-Mt VG
COMPLETE SET (6) 7000.00 3500.00
1 Frank Chance 1000.00 500.00
2 Hal Chase 800.00 400.00
3 Ty Cobb 2500.00 1250.00
4 Larry Lajoie 1500.00 750.00
5 Christy Mathewson 2000.00 1000.00
6 Honus Wagner 2000.00 1000.00

1903-11 Sporting Life Cabinets W600

These large and attractive cabinet-type cards were issued by the Sporting Life Publishing Company over a period of years between 1903 and 1911. The exact number of cards in the set is not known but is estimated to be about 450. The cards are not numbered and might appear to have a slight reddish or sepia tinit. Many are found still in the glassine envelope in which they were issued. The backs are blank.

Ex-Mt VG
COMPLETE SET 100000.00 50000.00
1 Bill Abstein 250.00 125.00
2 Babe Adams 250.00 125.00
3 Whitey Alperman 250.00 125.00
4 Nick Altrock 300.00 150.00
5 Red Ames 250.00 125.00
6 Frank Arelanes 250.00 125.00
7 Charlie Armbruster 250.00 125.00
8 Bill Armour MG 250.00 125.00
9 Harry Arndt 250.00 125.00
10 Harry Aubrey 250.00 125.00
11 Jimmy Austin 300.00 150.00
12 Charlie Babb 250.00 125.00
13 Frank Baker 800.00 400.00
14 Jap Barbeau 250.00 125.00
15 George Barclay 250.00 125.00
16 Cy Barger 250.00 125.00
17 Jimmy Barrett 250.00 125.00
18 Shad Barry 250.00 125.00
19 Jack Barry 250.00 125.00
20 Harry Barton 250.00 125.00
21 Emil Batch 250.00 125.00
22 Johnny Bates 250.00 125.00
23 Harry Bay 250.00 125.00
24 Ginger Beaumont 250.00 125.00
25 Fred Beck 250.00 125.00
26 Henie Beckendorf 250.00 125.00
27 Fred Beebe 250.00 125.00
28 George Bell 250.00 125.00
29 Harry Bemis 250.00 125.00
30 Chief Bender 500.00 250.00
31 Pug Bennett 250.00 125.00
32 Bill Bergen 250.00 125.00
33 C. Berger 250.00 125.00
34 Bill Bernhard 250.00 125.00
35 Bob Bescher 250.00 125.00
36 W. Beville 250.00 125.00
37 Lena Blackburne 250.00 125.00
38 Elmer Bliss 250.00 125.00
39 Frank Bowerman 250.00 125.00
40 Bill Bradley 250.00 125.00
41 W. Bradley 250.00 125.00
42 Dave Brain 250.00 125.00
43 Kitty Bransfield 250.00 125.00
44 Roger Bresnahan 500.00 250.00
45 Al Bridwell 250.00 125.00
46 Buster Brown 250.00 125.00
47 Mordecai Brown 500.00 250.00
48 Sam Brown 250.00 125.00
49 George Browne 250.00 125.00
50 Jimmy Burke 250.00 125.00
51 Nixey Callahan 250.00 125.00
52 Howie Camnitz 250.00 125.00
53 Rip Cannell 250.00 125.00
54 Joe Cantillon MG 250.00 125.00
55 Pat Carney 250.00 125.00
56 Charlie Carr 250.00 125.00
57 Bill Carrigan 250.00 125.00
58 Doc Casey 250.00 125.00
59 Frank Chance 1200.00 600.00
60 Hal Chase 400.00 200.00
61 Jack Chesbro 500.00 250.00
62 Eddie Cicotte 500.00 250.00
63 Fred Clarke 800.00 400.00
64 Nig Clarke 250.00 125.00
65 T. Clarke 250.00 125.00
66 Walter Clarkson 250.00 125.00
67 Otis Clymer 250.00 125.00
68 Andy Coakley 250.00 125.00
69 Ty Cobb 4000.00 2000.00
70 Eddie Collins 500.00 250.00
71 Jimmy Collins 800.00 400.00
72 Bunk Congalton 250.00 125.00
73 Wid Conroy 250.00 125.00
74 Duff Cooley 250.00 125.00
75 Jack Coombs 300.00 150.00
76 Frank Corridon 250.00 125.00
77 Bill Coughlin 250.00 125.00
78 Ernie Courtney 250.00 125.00
79 Doc Crandall 250.00 125.00
80 Sam Crawford 500.00 250.00
81 Lou Criger 250.00 125.00
82 Dode Criss 250.00 125.00
83 John Cronin 300.00 150.00
84 Lave Cross 250.00 125.00
85 Monte Cross 250.00 125.00
86 Clarence Currie 250.00 125.00
87 Bill Dahlen 300.00 150.00
88 George Davis 800.00 400.00
89 Harry Davis 250.00 125.00
90 Jim Delehanty 300.00 150.00
91 Art Devlin 300.00 150.00
92 Pop Dillon 250.00 125.00
93 Bill Dineen 250.00 125.00
94 John Dobbs 250.00 125.00
95 Ed Doheny 250.00 125.00
96 Cozy Dolan 250.00 125.00
97 Jiggs Donahue 250.00 125.00
98 Mike Donlin 400.00 200.00
99 Patsy Donovan 250.00 125.00
100 Bill Donovan 250.00 125.00
101 Red Dooin 250.00 125.00
102 Mickey Doolan 250.00 125.00
103 Tom Doran 250.00 125.00
104 Gus Dorner 250.00 125.00
105 Patsy Dougherty 250.00 125.00
106 Tom Downey 250.00 125.00
107 Red Downs 250.00 125.00
108 Jim Doyle 250.00 125.00
109 Joe Doyle 250.00 125.00
110 Larry Doyle 300.00 150.00
111 Hugh Duffy 500.00 250.00
112 Bill Duggleby 250.00 125.00
113 Gus Dundon 250.00 125.00
114 Jack Dunleavy 250.00 125.00
115 Jack Dunn 300.00 150.00
116 Jimmy Dygert 250.00 125.00
117 Dick Egan 250.00 125.00
118 Kid Elberfeld 300.00 150.00
119 Claude Elliott 250.00 125.00
120 Rube Ellis 250.00 125.00
121 Johnny Evers 800.00 400.00
122 Bob Ewing 250.00 125.00
123 Cy Falkenberg 250.00 125.00
124 John Farrell 250.00 125.00
125 George Ferguson 250.00 125.00
126 Hobe Ferris 250.00 125.00
127 Tom Fisher 250.00 125.00
128 Patsy Flaherty 250.00 125.00
129 Elmer Flick 500.00 250.00
130 John Flynn 250.00 125.00
131 Bill Foxen 250.00 125.00
132 Chick Fraser 250.00 125.00
133 Bill Friel 250.00 125.00
134 Art Fromme 250.00 125.00
135 Dave Fultz 250.00 125.00
136 Bob Ganley 250.00 125.00
137 John Ganzel 250.00 125.00
138 Ned Garvin 250.00 125.00
139 Harry Gasper 250.00 125.00
140 Phil Geier 250.00 125.00
141 Doc Gessler 250.00 125.00
142 George Gibson 250.00 125.00
143 Norwood Gibson 250.00 125.00
144 Billy Gilbert 250.00 125.00
145 Fred Glade 250.00 125.00
146 Harry Gleason 300.00 150.00
147 Eddie Grant 300.00 150.00
148 Danny Green 250.00 125.00
149 Ed Gremminger 250.00 125.00
150 Clark Griffith 500.00 250.00
151 Moose Grimshaw 250.00 125.00
152 H. Hackett 250.00 125.00
153 Ed Hahn 250.00 125.00
154 Noodles Hahn 300.00 150.00
155 Charley Hall 250.00 125.00
156 Bill Hallman 250.00 125.00
157 Ned Hanlon MG 500.00 250.00
158 Bob Harmon 250.00 125.00
159 Jack Harper 250.00 125.00
160 Hub Hart 250.00 125.00
161 Topsy Hartsel 250.00 125.00
162 Roy Hartzell 250.00 125.00
163 Charlie Hemphill 250.00 125.00
164 Weldon Henley 250.00 125.00
165 Otto Hess 250.00 125.00
166 Mike Heydon 250.00 125.00
167 Piano Legs Hickman 250.00 125.00
168 Hunter Hill 250.00 125.00
169 Homer Hillebrand 250.00 125.00
170 Harry Hinchman 250.00 125.00
171 Bill Hinchman 250.00 125.00
172 Dick Hoblitzel 250.00 125.00
173 Danny Hoffman 250.00 125.00
174 Solly Hofman 250.00 125.00
175 Bill Hogg 250.00 125.00
176 A. Holesketter 250.00 125.00
177 Ducky Holmes 250.00 125.00
178 Del Howard 250.00 125.00
179 Harry Howell 250.00 125.00
180 J. Huelsman 250.00 125.00
181 Miller Huggins 500.00 250.00
182 Jim Hughes 250.00 125.00
183 Tom Hughes 250.00 125.00
184 Rudy Hulswitt 250.00 125.00
185 John Hummell 250.00 125.00
186 Ham Hyatt 250.00 125.00
187 Frank Isbell 250.00 125.00
188 Fred Jacklitsch 250.00 125.00
189 Joe Jackson 2500.00 1250.00
190 H. Jacobson 250.00 125.00
191 Hugh Jennings MG 500.00 250.00
192 Charlie Jones 250.00 125.00
193 Davy Jones 250.00 125.00
194 Oscar Jones 250.00 125.00
195 Tom Jones 250.00 125.00
196 Dutch Jordan 250.00 125.00
197 Addie Joss 500.00 250.00
198 Mike Kahoe 250.00 125.00
199 Ed Karger 250.00 125.00
200 Bob Keefe 250.00 125.00
201 Willie Keeler 1000.00 500.00
202 Bill Keister 250.00 125.00
203 Joe Kelley 500.00 250.00
204 Brickyard Kennedy 250.00 125.00
205 Ed Killian 250.00 125.00
206 J. Kissinger 250.00 125.00
207 Frank Kitson 250.00 125.00
208 Mal Kittridge 250.00 125.00
209 Red Kleinrow 250.00 125.00
210 Johnny Kling 300.00 150.00
211 Ben Koehler 250.00 125.00
212 Ed Konetchy 250.00 125.00
213 Harry Krause 250.00 125.00
214 Otto Krueger 250.00 125.00
215 Candy LaChance 250.00 125.00
216 Nap Lajoie 1200.00 600.00
217 Joe Lake 250.00 125.00
218 Frank Laporte 250.00 125.00
219 L. Laroy 250.00 125.00
220 Tommy Leach 300.00 150.00
221 Watty Lee 250.00 125.00
222 Sam Leever 250.00 125.00
223 Phil Lewis 250.00 125.00
224 Vive Lindaman 250.00 125.00
225 Paddy Livingstone 250.00 125.00
226 Hans Lobert 300.00 150.00
227 Herman Long 250.00 125.00
228 Bris Lord 250.00 125.00
229 Harry Lord 300.00 150.00
230 Harry Lumley 250.00 125.00
231 Carl Lundgren 250.00 125.00
232 Johnny Lush 250.00 125.00
233 Connie Mack MG 1000.00 500.00
234 Nick Maddox 250.00 125.00
235 Sherry Magee 400.00 200.00
236 George Magoon 250.00 125.00
237 John Malarkey 250.00 125.00
238 Billy Maloney 250.00 125.00
239 Doc Marshall 250.00 125.00
240 Christy Mathewson 2000.00 1000.00
241 Jimmy McAleer 250.00 125.00
242 Sport McAlister 250.00 125.00
243 Jack McCarthy 250.00 125.00
244 John McCloskey 250.00 125.00
245 Amby McConnell 250.00 125.00
246 Moose McCormick 250.00 125.00
247 Chappie McFarland 250.00 125.00
248 Herm McFarland 250.00 125.00
249 Dan McGann 250.00 125.00
250 Joe McGinnity 500.00 250.00
251 John McGraw MG 1000.00 500.00
252 Deacon McGuire 300.00 150.00
253 Harry McIntyre 250.00 125.00
254 Matty McIntyre 250.00 125.00
255 Larry McLean 250.00 125.00
256 Fred Merkle 400.00 200.00
257 Sam Mertes 250.00 125.00
258 Clyde Milan 300.00 150.00
259 Dots Miller 250.00 125.00
260 Billy Milligan 250.00 125.00
261 Fred Mitchell 250.00 125.00
262 Mike Mitchell 250.00 125.00
263 Earl Moore 250.00 125.00
264 Pat Moran 300.00 150.00
265 Lew Moren 250.00 125.00
266 Cy Morgan 250.00 125.00
267 E. Moriarty 250.00 125.00
268 Jack Morrissey 250.00 125.00
269 Mike Mowery 250.00 125.00
270 George Mullin 300.00 150.00
271 Danny Murphy 250.00 125.00
272 Red Murray 250.00 125.00
273 W. Murray 250.00 125.00
274 Jim Nealon 250.00 125.00
275 D. Needham 250.00 125.00
276 Doc Newton 250.00 125.00
277 Harry Niles 250.00 125.00
278 Rabbit Nill 250.00 125.00
279 Pete Noonan 250.00 125.00
280 Jack O'Brien 250.00 125.00
281 Pete O'Brien 250.00 125.00
282 Rube Oldring 250.00 125.00
283 Charley O'Leary 250.00 125.00
284 Jack O'Neil 250.00 125.00
285 Mike O'Neil 250.00 125.00
286 Al Orth 250.00 125.00
287 Orvie Overall 250.00 125.00
288 Frank Owens 250.00 125.00
289 Freddie Parent 250.00 125.00
290 Dode Paskert 250.00 125.00
291 Jim Pastorious 250.00 125.00
292 Roy Paterson 250.00 125.00
293 Fred Payne 250.00 125.00
294 Barney Pelty 250.00 125.00
295 Big Jeff Pfeiffer 250.00 125.00
296 Jack Pfiester 250.00 125.00
297 Ed Phelps 250.00 125.00
298 Deacon Phillippe 300.00 150.00
299 Bill Phillips 250.00 125.00
300 Ollie Pickering 250.00 125.00
301 Eddie Plank 1000.00 500.00
302 Ed Poole 250.00 125.00
303 Jack Powell 250.00 125.00
304 Billy Purtell 250.00 125.00
305 Ambrose Puttman 250.00 125.00
306 Tommy Raub 250.00 125.00
307 Fred Raymer 250.00 125.00
308 Bill Reidy 250.00 125.00
309 Ed Reulbach 400.00 200.00
310 Bob Rhoads 250.00 125.00
311 D. Richie 250.00 125.00
312 Claude Ritchey 250.00 125.00
313 Lew Ritter 250.00 125.00
314 C. Robinson 250.00 125.00
315 George Rohe 250.00 125.00
316 Claude Rossman 250.00 125.00
317 Frank Roth 250.00 125.00
318 Jack Rowan 250.00 125.00
319 Slim Sallee 250.00 125.00
320 Germany Schaefer 300.00 150.00
321 Admiral Schiel 250.00 125.00
322 Boss Schmidt 250.00 125.00
323 Frank Schulte 250.00 125.00
324 Al Schweitzer 250.00 125.00
325 T. Sebring 250.00 125.00
326 Kip Selbach 250.00 125.00
327 Cy Seymour 250.00 125.00
328 Spike Shannon 250.00 125.00
329 Danny Shay 250.00 125.00
330 Dave Shean 250.00 125.00
331 Jimmy Sheckard 250.00 125.00
332 Ed Siever 250.00 125.00
333 Jimmy Slagle 250.00 125.00
334 Jack Slattery 250.00 125.00
335 Charlie Smith 250.00 125.00
336 E. Smith 250.00 125.00
337 Frank Smith 250.00 125.00
338 Harry Smith 250.00 125.00
339 Homer Smoot 250.00 125.00
340 Tully Sparks 250.00 125.00
341 Chick Stahl 300.00 150.00
342 Jake Stahl 300.00 150.00
343 Joe Stanley 250.00 125.00
344 Harry Steinfeldt 300.00 150.00
345 George Stone 250.00 125.00
346 George Stovall 250.00 125.00
347 Jesss Stovall 250.00 125.00
348 Sammy Strang 250.00 125.00
349 Elmer Stricklett 250.00 125.00
350 Willie Sudhoff 250.00 125.00
351 Joe Sugden 250.00 125.00
352 Billy Sullivan 250.00 125.00
353 Ed Summers 250.00 125.00
354 Bill Sweeney 250.00 125.00
355 Lee Tannehill 250.00 125.00
356 Jack Taylor 250.00 125.00
357 Dummy Taylor 250.00 125.00
358 Fred Tenney 250.00 125.00
359 Ira Thomas 250.00 125.00
360 Jack Thoney 250.00 125.00
361 Joe Tinker 500.00 250.00
362 Terry Turner 250.00 125.00
363 Bob Unglaub 250.00 125.00
364 George Van Haltren 250.00 125.00
365 Bucky Veil 250.00 125.00
366 Rube Waddell 800.00 400.00
367 Heinie Wagner 250.00 125.00
368 Honus Wagner 1500.00 750.00
369 Bobby Wallace 500.00 250.00
370 Ed Walsh 800.00 400.00
371 Jack Warner 250.00 125.00
372 Art Weaver 250.00 125.00
373 Jake Weimer 250.00 125.00
374 Kirby White 250.00 125.00
375 Bob Wicker 250.00 125.00
376 F. Wilhelm 250.00 125.00
377 Ed Willett 250.00 125.00
378 Jimmy Williams 250.00 125.00
379 Otto Williams 250.00 125.00
380 Hooks Wiltse 300.00 150.00
381 George Winter 250.00 125.00
382 Bill Wolfe 250.00 125.00
383 Harry Wolverton 250.00 125.00
384 Joe Yeager 250.00 125.00
385 Cy Young 1500.00 750.00
386 Irv Young 250.00 125.00
387 Chief Zimmer 250.00 125.00
388 Henie Zimmerman 250.00 125.00

1899-00 Sporting News Supplements M101-1

Measuring approximately 9" by 11", these photos were issued as supplements in the Sporting News. This list is far from complete, so any additions are appreciated.

Ex-Mt VG
COMPLETE SET 3000.00 1500.00
1 Ted Breitenstein 400.00 200.00
2 Tom Corcoran 300.00 150.00
3 Bill Dahlen 400.00 200.00
4 Patsy Donovan 300.00 150.00
5 Deacon Phillippe 400.00 200.00
6 Roy Thomas 300.00 150.00
7 Honus Wagner 1500.00 750.00

1909-13 Sporting News Supplements M101-2

These 100 8" x 10" sepia supplements were inserted in various issues of the Sporting News. We have identified the player and then given the date of the issue in which this supplement appears. The set is sequenced in order of appearence. No photos were issued between 4/14 and 8/25 in 1910. No photos were issued between 3/30 and 10/19 in 1911. No photos were issued between 1/18 and 10/03 in 1912.

Ex-Mt VG
COMPLETE SET (101) 10000.00 5000.00
1 Roger Bresnahan 150.00 75.00
St. Louis NL
7/22/09
2 Denton T. Young 200.00 100.00
Cleveland AL
and Louis Criger&
St. Louis AL
7/29/09
3 Christopher Mathewson 400.00 200.00
New York-N
8/5/09
4 Nap Lajoie 250.00 125.00
Cleve
8/10/09
5 Tyrus R. Cobb 600.00 300.00
Detroit
8/12/09
6 Nap Lajoie 250.00 125.00
Cleveland
8/19/09
7 Sherwood N. Magee 60.00 30.00
Philadelphia-N
8/26/09
8 Frank L. Chance 250.00 125.00
Chicago-N
9/02/09
9 Edward Walsh 100.00 50.00
Chicago-A
9/9/09
10 Nap Rucker 40.00 20.00
Brooklyn
9/16/09
11 Honus Wagner 400.00 200.00
Pittsburgh
9/23/09
12 Hugh Jennings MG 100.00 50.00
Detroit
9/30/09
13 Fred C. Clarke 200.00 100.00
Pittsburgh
10/07/09
14 Ban Johnson AL PRES 200.00 100.00
10/14/09
15 Charles A. Comiskey OWN 150.00 75.00
Chicago White Sox
10/21/09
16 Eddie Collins 150.00 75.00
Philadelphia-A
10/28/09
17 James A. McAleer 40.00 20.00
Washington
11/04/09
18 Pittsburgh Pirates 100.00 50.00
11/11/09
19 Detroit Team 100.00 50.00
11/18/09
20 George Bell 40.00 20.00
Brooklyn
11/25/09
21 Tris Speaker 300.00 150.00
Boston-A
12/02/09
22 Mordecai Brown 200.00 100.00
Chicago-N
12/09/09
23 Hal Chase 100.00 50.00
New York-A
12/16/09
24 Thomas W. Leach 60.00 30.00
Pittsburgh
12/23/09
25 Owen Bush 40.00 20.00
Detroit
12/30/09
26 John J. Evers 150.00 75.00
Chicago-N
1/6/10
27 Harry Krause 40.00 20.00
Philadelphia-A
1/13/10
28 Babe Adams 60.00 30.00
Pittsburgh
1/20/10
29 Addie Joss 250.00 125.00
Cleveland
1/27/10
30 Orval Overall 40.00 20.00
Chicago-N
2/3/10
31 Samuel E. Crawford 200.00 100.00
Detroit
2/10/10
32 Fred Merkle 60.00 30.00
New York-N
2/17/10
33 George Mullin 60.00 30.00
Detroit
2/24/10
34 Edward Konetchy 40.00 20.00
St. Louis-N
3/3/10
35 George Gibson 40.00 20.00
Pitt.
Bugs Raymond
NY NL
3/10/10
36 Ty Cobb 400.00 200.00
Detroit
Hans Wagner
Pittsburgh
3/17/10
37 Connie Mack MG 300.00 150.00
Phila.-AL
3/24/10
38 Bill Evans UMP 40.00 20.00
Silk O'Loughlin UMP
Bill Klem UMP
Bill Johnston UMP
3/31/10
39 Edward Plank 150.00 75.00
Philadelphia-AL
4/7/10
40 Walter Johnson 300.00 150.00
Gabby Street
Wash.
9/1/10
41 John C. Kling 40.00 20.00
Chicago-N
9/8/10
42 Frank Baker 150.00 75.00
Philadelphia-A
9/15/10
43 Charles S. Dooin 40.00 20.00
Philadelphia-A
9/22/10
44 Wm. F. Carrigan 40.00 20.00
Boston-A
9/29/10
45 John B. McLean 40.00 20.00
Cincinnati
10/06/10
46 John W. Coombs 60.00 30.00
Philadelphia-A
10/13/10
47 Jos. B. Tinker 200.00 100.00
Chicago-N
10/20/10
48 John I. Taylor OWN 40.00 20.00
Boston-A
10/27/10
49 Russell Ford 40.00 20.00
New York-A
11/03/10
50 Leonard L. Cole 40.00 20.00
Chicago-N
11/10/10
51 Harry Lord 40.00 20.00
Chicago-A
11/17/10
52 Philadelphia-A Team 100.00 50.00
11/24/10
53 Chicago-N Team 100.00 50.00
12/1/10
54 Charles A. Bender 100.00 50.00
Philadelphia-A
12/08/10

55 Arthur Hofman 40.00 20.00
Chicago-N
12/15/10
56 Bobby Wallace 100.00 50.00
St. Louis-A
12/21/10
57 John J. McGraw MG 300.00 150.00
New York-N
12/28/10
58 Harry H. Davis 40.00 20.00
1/5/11
Philadelphia-A
59 James P. Archer 40.00 20.00
Chicago-N
1/12/11
60 Ira Thomas 40.00 20.00
Philadelphia-A
1/19/11
61 Robert Byrnes 40.00 20.00
Pittsbutrgh
1/26/11
62 Clyde Milan 60.00 30.00
Washington
2/2/11
63 John T. Meyer 60.00 30.00
New York-N
2/9/11
64 Robert Bescher 40.00 20.00
Cincinnati
2/16/11
65 John J. Barry 40.00 20.00
Philadelphia-A
2/23/11
66 Frank Schulte 60.00 30.00
Chicago-N
3/2/11
67 C. Harris White 40.00 20.00
Chicago-A
3/9/11
68 Lawrence Doyle 60.00 30.00
New York-N
3/16/11
69 Joe Jackson 800.00 400.00
Cleveland
3/23/11
70 Martin J. O'Toole 40.00 20.00
William Kelly
Pittsburgh
10/26/11
71 Vean Gregg 40.00 20.00
Cleveland
11/2/11
72 Richard W. Marquard 150.00 75.00
New York-N
11/9/11
73 John E. McInnis 60.00 30.00
Philadelphia-N
11/16/11
74 Grover C. Alexander 250.00 125.00
Philadelphia-N
11/23/11
75 Del Gainor 40.00 20.00
Detroit
11/30/11
76 Fred Snodgrass 60.00 30.00
New York-N
12/7/11
77 James J. Callahan 60.00 30.00
Chicago-A
12/14/11
78 Robert Harmon 40.00 20.00
St. Louis-N
12/21/11
79 George Stovall 40.00 20.00
Cleveland
12/28/11
80 Zack D. Wheat 150.00 75.00
Brooklyn
1/4/12
81 Frank 'Ping' Bodie 40.00 20.00
Chicago-A
1/11/12
82 Boston-A Team 100.00 50.00
10/10/1912
83 New York-NTeam 100.00 50.00
10/17/1912
84 Jake Stahl MG 60.00 30.00
Boston-A
10/24/12
85 Joe Wood 80.00 40.00
Boston-A
10/31/12
86 Charles Wagner 40.00 20.00
Boston-A
11/07/12
87 Lew Ritchie 40.00 20.00
Chicago-N
11/14/12
88 Clark Griffith MG 100.00 50.00
Washington
11/21/12
89 Arnold Houser 40.00 20.00
St. Louis-N
11/28/12
90 Charles Herzog 40.00 20.00
New York-N
12/05/12
91 James Lavender 40.00 20.00
Chicago-N
12/12/12
92 Jeff Tesreau 40.00 20.00
New York-N
12/19/12
93 August Herrmann OWN 60.00 30.00
Cinc
chairman, National Commission
94 Jake Daubert 60.00 30.00
Brooklyn
10/23/13
95 Heinie Zimmerman 40.00 20.00
Chicago-N
10/30/13
96 Ray Schalk 150.00 75.00
Chicago-A
11/07/13
97 Hans Lobert 40.00 20.00
Philadelphia-N
11/13/13
98 Albert W. Demaree 40.00 20.00
New York-N
11/20/13
99 Arthur Fletcher 40.00 20.00
New York-N
11/27/13
100 Charles A. Somers OWN 40.00 20.00
Cleveland
12/04/13
101 Joe Birmingham MG 40.00 20.00
Cleveland
12/11/13

1916 Sporting News M101-5

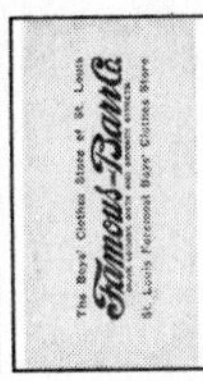

The cards in this 200-card set measure approximately 1 5/8 by 3". The 1915 M101-5 series of black and white, numbered baseball cards is very similar in style to M101-4. The set was offered as a marketing promotion by C.C. Spink and Son, publishers of The Sporting News ("The Baseball Paper of the World"). Most of the players in this also appear in the M101-4 set. Those cards which are asterisked in the checklist below are those cards which do not appear in the companion M101-4 set issued the next year.

	Ex-Mt	VG
COMPLETE SET (200)	25000.00	12500.00
1 Babe Adams	60.00	30.00
2 Sam Agnew	50.00	25.00
3 Ed Ainsmith	50.00	25.00
4 Grover C. Alexander	250.00	125.00
5 Leon Ames	50.00	25.00
6 Jimmy Archer	50.00	25.00
7 Jimmy Austin	50.00	25.00
8 Frank Baker	100.00	50.00
9 Dave Bancroft	100.00	50.00
10 Jack Barry	60.00	30.00
11 Zinn Beck	50.00	25.00
12 Luke Boone *	60.00	30.00
13 Joe Benz	50.00	25.00
14 Bob Bescher	50.00	25.00
15 Al Betzel	50.00	25.00
16 Roger Bresnahan *	100.00	50.00
17 Eddie Burns	50.00	25.00
18 George J. Burns	50.00	25.00
19 Joe Bush	60.00	30.00
20 Owen Bush	60.00	30.00
21 Art Butler	50.00	25.00
22 Bobby Byrne	50.00	25.00
23 Mordecai Brown	100.00	50.00
24 Jimmy Callahan	50.00	25.00
25 Ray Caldwell	50.00	25.00
26 Max Carey	100.00	50.00
27 George Chalmers	50.00	25.00
28 Frank Chance *	150.00	75.00
29 Ray Chapman	60.00	30.00
30 Larry Cheney	50.00	25.00
31 Ed Cicotte	150.00	75.00
32 Tommy Clarke	50.00	25.00
33 Eddie Collins	100.00	50.00
34 Shano Collins	50.00	25.00
35 Chas. Comiskey OWN	100.00	50.00
36 Joe Connolly	50.00	25.00
37 L.(Doc) Cook *	60.00	30.00
38 Jack Coombs *	100.00	50.00
39 Dan Costello *	60.00	30.00
40 Harry Coveleskie	60.00	30.00
41 Gavvy Cravath	60.00	30.00
42 Sam Crawford	100.00	50.00
43 Jean Dale	50.00	25.00
44 Jake Daubert	60.00	30.00
45 G.A. Davis Jr. *	60.00	30.00
46 Charles Deal	50.00	25.00
47 Al Demaree	50.00	25.00
48 Bill Doak	50.00	25.00
49 Bill Donovan	50.00	25.00
50 Red Dooin	50.00	25.00
51 Mike Doolan	50.00	25.00
52 Larry Doyle	60.00	30.00
53 Jean Dubuc	50.00	25.00
54 Oscar Dugey	50.00	25.00
55 John Evers	150.00	75.00
56 Red Faber	100.00	50.00
57 Happy Felsch	150.00	75.00
58 Bill Fischer	50.00	25.00
59 Ray Fisher	50.00	25.00
60 Max Flack	50.00	25.00
61 Art Fletcher	50.00	25.00
62 Eddie Foster	50.00	25.00
63 Jacques Fournier	50.00	25.00
64 Del Gainer	50.00	25.00
65 Larry Gardner	50.00	25.00
66 Joe Gedeon	50.00	25.00
67 Gus Getz	50.00	25.00
68 George Gibson	50.00	25.00
69 Wilbur Good	50.00	25.00
70 Hank Gowdy	60.00	30.00
71 Jack Graney	60.00	30.00
72 Tommy Griffith	50.00	25.00
73 Heinie Groh	60.00	30.00
74 Earl Hamilton	50.00	25.00
75 Bob Harmon	50.00	25.00
76 Roy Hartzell	50.00	25.00
77 Claude Hendrix	50.00	25.00
78 Olaf Henriksen	50.00	25.00
79 John Henry	50.00	25.00
80 Buck Herzog	50.00	25.00
81 Hugh High	50.00	25.00
82 Dick Hoblitzell	50.00	25.00
83 Harry Hooper	100.00	50.00
84 Ivan Howard	50.00	25.00
85 Miller Huggins	100.00	50.00
86 Joe Jackson	4000.00	2000.00
87 William James	50.00	25.00
88 Harold Janvrin	50.00	25.00
89 Hughie Jennings MG	100.00	50.00
90 Walter Johnson	600.00	300.00
91 Fielder Jones	50.00	25.00
92 Benny Kauff	50.00	25.00
93 Bill Killefer	50.00	25.00
94 Ed Konetchy	50.00	25.00
95 Napoleon Lajoie	300.00	150.00
96 Jack Lapp	50.00	25.00
97 John Lavan	50.00	25.00
98 Jimmy Lavender	50.00	25.00
99 Nemo Leibold	50.00	25.00
100 Hub Leonard	60.00	30.00
101 Duffy Lewis	60.00	30.00
102 Hans Lobert	50.00	25.00
103 Tom Long	50.00	25.00
104 Fred Luderus	50.00	25.00
105 Connie Mack MG	200.00	100.00
106 Lee Magee	50.00	25.00
107 Al Mamaux	50.00	25.00
108 Leslie Mann	50.00	25.00
109 Rabbit Maranville	100.00	50.00
110 Rube Marquard	100.00	50.00
111 Armando Marsans *	60.00	30.00
112 J.E.(Erskine) Mayer	50.00	25.00
113 George McBride	50.00	25.00
114 John McGraw	150.00	75.00
115 Jack McInnis	60.00	30.00
116 Fred Merkle	60.00	30.00
117 Chief Meyers	50.00	25.00
118 Clyde Milan	60.00	30.00
119 Otto Miller	50.00	25.00
120 Willie Mitchell	50.00	25.00
121 Fred Mollwitz	50.00	25.00
122 J.H.(Herbie) Moran *	60.00	30.00
123 Pat Moran MG	50.00	25.00
124 Ray Morgan	50.00	25.00
125 George Moriarty	50.00	25.00
126 Guy Morton	50.00	25.00
127 Eddie Murphy	60.00	30.00
128 Jack Murray *	60.00	30.00
129 Hy Myers	50.00	25.00
130 Bert Niehoff	50.00	25.00
131 Les Nunamaker *	60.00	30.00
132 Rube Oldring	50.00	25.00
133 Oliver O'Mara	50.00	25.00
134 Steve O'Neill	60.00	30.00
135 Dode Paskert	50.00	25.00
136 Roger Peckinpaugh	60.00	30.00
137 E.J.(Jeff) Pfeffer *	60.00	30.00
138 George Pierce *	60.00	30.00
139 Wally Pipp	60.00	30.00
140 Del Pratt	50.00	25.00
141 Bill Rariden	50.00	25.00
142 Eppa Rixey	100.00	50.00
143 Davey Robertson	50.00	25.00
144 Wilbert Robinson MG	150.00	75.00
145 Bob Roth	50.00	25.00
146 Eddie Roush	100.00	50.00
147 Clarence Rowland MG	50.00	25.00
148 Nap Rucker	60.00	30.00
149 Dick Rudolph	60.00	30.00
150 Reb Russell	50.00	25.00
151 Babe Ruth	6000.00	3000.00
152 Vic Saier	50.00	25.00
153 Slim Sallee	50.00	25.00
154 Germany Schaefer *	60.00	30.00
155 Ray Schalk	100.00	50.00
156 Wally Schang	60.00	30.00
157 Charles Schmidt *	60.00	30.00
158 Frank Schulte	50.00	25.00
159 Jim Scott	50.00	25.00
160 Everett Scott	60.00	30.00
161 Tom Seaton	50.00	25.00
162 Howard Shanks	50.00	25.00
163 Bob Shawkey	60.00	30.00
164 Ernie Shore	60.00	30.00
165 Burt Shotton	50.00	25.00
166 George Sisler	150.00	75.00
167 Red Smith	50.00	25.00
168 Fred Snodgrass	60.00	30.00
169 George Stallings MG	50.00	25.00
170 Oscar Stanage	50.00	25.00
171 Casey Stengel	600.00	300.00
172 Milton Stock	50.00	25.00
173 Amos Strunk	50.00	25.00
174 Billy Sullivan	60.00	30.00
175 Jeff Tesreau	50.00	25.00
176 Jim Thorpe *	4000.00	2000.00
177 Joe Tinker	150.00	75.00
178 Fred Toney	50.00	25.00
179 Terry Turner	50.00	25.00
180 Jim Vaughn	50.00	25.00
181 Bobby Veach	50.00	25.00
182 James Viox	50.00	25.00
183 Oscar Vitt	50.00	25.00
184 Honus Wagner	800.00	400.00
185 Clarence Walker	50.00	25.00
186 Zack Wheat	100.00	50.00
187 Ed Walsh	100.00	50.00
188 Buck Weaver	200.00	100.00
189 Carl Weilman	50.00	25.00
190 George Whitted	50.00	25.00
191 Fred Williams	50.00	25.00
192 Arthur Wilson	50.00	25.00
193 Chief Wilson	50.00	25.00
194 Ivy Wingo	50.00	25.00
195 Meldon Wolfgang	50.00	25.00
196 Joe Wood	100.00	50.00
197 Steve Yerkes	50.00	25.00
198 Rollie Zeider	50.00	25.00
199 Heinie Zimmerman	50.00	25.00
200 Dutch Zwilling	50.00	25.00

1915 Sporting News PC757

These postcards feature color, a rare commodity in early baseball postcards. The inscription "published by the Sporting News" appears on the front of the card along with the player's name and team. The postcards are believed to have been issued as premiums and mailed in one envelope, and the set is believed to be complete at six cards.

	Ex-Mt	VG
COMPLETE SET (6)	1500.00	750.00
1 Roger Bresnahan	200.00	100.00
2 Ty Cobb	800.00	400.00
3 Eddie Collins	200.00	100.00
4 Vean Gregg	100.00	50.00
5 Walter Johnson Gabby Street	300.00	150.00
6 Rube Marquard	200.00	100.00

1917 Sporting News M101-4

The cards in this 200-card set measure approximately 1 5/8" by 3". Issued in 1916 as a premium offer, the M101-4 set features black and white photos of current ballplayers. Each card is numbered and the reverse carries Sporting News advertising. The fronts are the same as D329, H801-9 and the unclassified Famous and Barr set. Most of the players in this also appear in the M101-5 set. Those cards which are asterisked in the checklist below are those cards which do not appear in the companion M101-5 set issued the year before. At least 10 different backs are known: they are Altoona Tribune, Block and Kuhl, Everybody's, Famous and Barr, Gimbels, Herposheimer, Indianapolis Brewing Co, Sporting News, Successful Farming and The Globe.

	Ex-Mt	VG
COMPLETE SET (200)	20000.00	10000.00
1 Babe Adams	50.00	25.00
2 Sam Agnew	50.00	25.00
3 Eddie Ainsmith	40.00	20.00
4 Grover C. Alexander	250.00	125.00
5 Leon Ames	50.00	25.00
6 Jimmy Archer	50.00	25.00
7 Jimmy Austin	50.00	25.00
8 H.D.(Doug) Baird *	50.00	25.00
9 Frank Baker	80.00	40.00
10 Dave Bancroft	60.00	30.00
11 Jack Barry	50.00	25.00
12 Zinn Beck	40.00	20.00
13 Chief Bender *	80.00	40.00
14 Joe Benz	40.00	20.00
15 Bob Bescher	40.00	20.00
16 Al Betzel	40.00	20.00
17 Mordecai Brown	60.00	30.00
18 Eddie Burns	40.00	20.00
19 George H. Burns *	50.00	25.00
20 George J. Burns	40.00	20.00
21 Joe Bush	50.00	25.00
22 Donie Bush	50.00	25.00
23 Art Butler	40.00	20.00
24 Bobbie Byrne	40.00	20.00
25 Forrest Cady *	50.00	25.00
26 Jim Callahan	40.00	20.00
27 Ray Caldwell	40.00	20.00
28 Max Carey	60.00	30.00
29 George Chalmers	40.00	20.00
30 Ray Chapman	50.00	25.00
31 Larry Cheney	40.00	20.00
32 Ed Cicotte	150.00	75.00
33 Tommy Clarke	40.00	20.00
34 Eddie Collins	80.00	40.00
35 Shano Collins	40.00	20.00
36 Chas. Comiskey OWN	80.00	40.00
37 Joe Connolly	40.00	20.00
38 Ty Cobb *	2000.00	1000.00
39 Harry Coveleskie	40.00	20.00
40 Gavvy Cravath	50.00	25.00
41 Sam Crawford	60.00	30.00
42 Jean Dale	40.00	20.00
43 Jake Daubert	50.00	25.00
44 Charles Deal	40.00	20.00
45 Al Demaree	40.00	20.00
46 Josh Devore *	50.00	25.00
47 William Doak	40.00	20.00
48 Bill Donovan	40.00	20.00
49 Red Dooin	40.00	20.00
50 Mike Doolan	40.00	20.00
51 Larry Doyle	50.00	25.00
52 Jean Dubuc	40.00	20.00
53 Oscar J. Dugey	40.00	20.00
54 John Evers	80.00	40.00
55 Red Faber	60.00	30.00
56 Happy Felsch	150.00	75.00
57 Bill Fischer	40.00	20.00
58 Ray Fisher	40.00	20.00
59 Max Flack	40.00	20.00
60 Art Fletcher	40.00	20.00
61 Eddie Foster	40.00	20.00
62 Jacques Fournier	40.00	20.00
63 Del Gainer	40.00	20.00
64 Chick Gandil *	200.00	100.00
65 Larry Gardner	50.00	25.00
66 Joe Gedeon	50.00	25.00
67 Gus Getz	50.00	25.00
68 George Gibson	50.00	25.00
69 Wilbur Good	50.00	25.00
70 Hank Gowdy	50.00	25.00
71 Jack Graney	50.00	25.00
72 Clark Griffith *	80.00	40.00
73 Tommy Griffith	40.00	20.00
74 Heinie Groh	50.00	25.00
75 Earl Hamilton	40.00	20.00
76 Bob Harmon	40.00	20.00
77 Topsy Hartzell	40.00	20.00
78 Claude Hendrix	40.00	20.00
79 Olaf Henriksen	40.00	20.00
80 John Henry	40.00	20.00
81 Buck Herzog	40.00	20.00
82 Hugh High	40.00	20.00
83 Dick Hoblitzell	40.00	20.00
84 Harry Hooper	60.00	30.00
85 Ivan Howard	40.00	20.00
86 Miller Huggins	60.00	30.00
87 Joe Jackson	5000.00	2500.00
88 William James	40.00	20.00
89 Harold Janvrin	40.00	20.00
90 Hughie Jennings MG	60.00	30.00
91 Walter Johnson	600.00	300.00
92 Fielder Jones	40.00	20.00
93 Joe Judge *	50.00	25.00
94 Benny Kauff	40.00	20.00
95 Bill Killifer	40.00	20.00
96 Ed Konetchy	40.00	20.00
97 Nap Lajoie	250.00	125.00
98 Jack Lapp	40.00	20.00
99 John Lavan	40.00	20.00
100 Jimmy Lavender	40.00	20.00
101 Nemo Leibold	40.00	20.00
102 Hub Leonard	50.00	25.00
103 Duffy Lewis	50.00	25.00
104 Hans Lobert	40.00	20.00
105 Tom Long	40.00	20.00
106 Fred Luderus	40.00	20.00
107 Connie Mack MG	200.00	100.00
108 Lee Magee	40.00	20.00
109 Sherry Magee *	50.00	25.00
110 Al Mamaux	40.00	20.00
111 Leslie Mann	40.00	20.00
112 Rabbit Maranville	60.00	30.00
113 Rube Marquard	60.00	30.00
114 J.E.(Erskine) Mayer	40.00	20.00
115 George McBride	40.00	20.00
116 John McGraw MG	150.00	75.00
117 Jack McInnis	50.00	25.00
118 Fred Merkle	50.00	25.00
119 Chief Meyers	50.00	25.00
120 Clyde Milan	40.00	20.00
121 John Miller *	50.00	25.00
122 Otto Miller	40.00	20.00
123 Willie Mitchell	40.00	20.00
124 Fred Mollwitz	40.00	20.00
125 Pat Moran MG	40.00	20.00
126 Ray Morgan	40.00	20.00
127 George Moriarty	40.00	20.00
128 Guy Morton	40.00	20.00
129 Mike Mowrey *	50.00	25.00
130 Eddie Murphy	40.00	20.00
131 Hy Myers	40.00	20.00
132 Bert Niehoff	40.00	20.00
133 Rube Oldring	40.00	20.00
134 Oliver O'Mara	40.00	20.00
135 Steve O'Neill	50.00	25.00
136 Dode Paskert	40.00	20.00
137 Roger Peckinpaugh	50.00	25.00
138 Wally Pipp	50.00	25.00
139 Del Pratt	40.00	20.00
140 Pat Ragan *	50.00	25.00
141 Bill Rariden	40.00	20.00
142 Eppa Rixey	60.00	30.00
143 Davey Robertson	40.00	20.00
144 Wilbert Robinson MG	150.00	75.00
145 Bob Roth	40.00	20.00
146 Eddie Roush	80.00	40.00
147 Clarence Rowland MG	40.00	20.00
148 Nap Rucker	50.00	25.00
149 Dick Rudolph	50.00	25.00
150 Reb Russell	40.00	20.00
151 Babe Ruth	6000.00	3000.00
152 Vic Saier	40.00	20.00
153 Slim Sallee	50.00	25.00
154 Ray Schalk	60.00	30.00
155 Wally Schang	50.00	25.00
156 Frank Schulte	40.00	20.00
157 Everett Scott	50.00	25.00
158 Jim Scott	40.00	20.00
159 Tom Seaton	40.00	20.00
160 Howard Shanks	40.00	20.00
161 Bob Shawkey	50.00	25.00
162 Ernie Shore	40.00	20.00
163 Burt Shotton	40.00	20.00
164 George Sisler	150.00	75.00
165 Red Smith	40.00	20.00
166 Fred Snodgrass	50.00	25.00
167 George Stallings MG	40.00	20.00
168 Oscar Stanage	40.00	20.00
169 Casey Stengel	600.00	300.00
170 Milton Stock	40.00	20.00
171 Amos Strunk	40.00	20.00
172 Billy Sullivan	50.00	25.00
173 Jeff Tesreau	40.00	20.00
174 Joe Tinker	80.00	40.00
175 Fred Toney	40.00	20.00
176 Terry Turner	40.00	20.00
177 George Tyler *	50.00	25.00
178 Jim Vaughn	40.00	20.00
179 Bobby Veach	40.00	20.00
180 James Viox	40.00	20.00
181 Oscar Vitt	40.00	20.00
182 Honus Wagner	600.00	300.00
183 Clarence Walker	40.00	20.00
184 Ed Walsh	60.00	30.00
185 Bill Wambsganss *	50.00	25.00
186 Buck Weaver	200.00	100.00
187 Carl Weilman	40.00	20.00
188 Zack Wheat	60.00	30.00
189 George Whitted	40.00	20.00
190 Fred Williams	40.00	20.00
191 Arthur Wilson	40.00	20.00
192 Chief Wilson	40.00	20.00
193 Ivy Wingo	40.00	20.00
194 Meldon Wolfgang	40.00	20.00
195 Joe Wood	60.00	30.00
196 Steve Yerkes	40.00	20.00
197 Pep Young *	40.00	20.00
198 Rollie Zeider	50.00	25.00
199 Heinie Zimmerman	50.00	25.00
200 Dutch Zwilling	50.00	25.00

1926-27 Sporting News Supplements M101-7

These 11 cards were included as inserts of the "Sporting News" publication. They are known to come in two sizes, 7" by 10" and 10" by 14 1/2". We have basically sequenced this set in alphabetical order.

	Ex-Mt	VG
COMPLETE SET (11)	1200.00	600.00
1 Kiki Cuyler December 16	120.00	60.00

2 Babe Ruth 500.00 250.00
December 30
3 Rogers Hornsby 250.00 125.00
December 2
4 Tony Lazzeri 120.00 60.00
5 Heinie Manush 120.00 60.00
November 11
6 John Mostil 80.00 40.00
7 Sam Rice 120.00 60.00
January 13,1927
8 Al Simmons 150.00 75.00
December 23
9 Pie Traynor 150.00 75.00
November 26
10 George Uhle 80.00 40.00
11 Glenn Wright 80.00 40.00
November 4

1932 Sporting News Supplement M101-8

These four supplements were issued in 1932 as an supplement to the popular Baseball weekly, the Sporting News. Unlike most of the other supplements, these photos have biographical information and stats on the back. Since these are unnumbered, we have sequenced them in alphabetical order.

	Ex-Mt	VG
COMPLETE SET (4)	500.00	250.00
1 Kiki Cuyler	150.00	75.00
2 Dizzy Dean	200.00	100.00
3 Charlie Grimm	100.00	50.00
4 Lon Warneke	80.00	40.00

1939 Sporting News Premiums

All of these premiums are blank-backed. The players premiums measure approximately 8" by 10" while the team premiums measure approximately 11" by 16". The catalog number on this set is M101-9.

	Ex-Mt	VG
1 New York Yankees Double Size Octoer 19	100.00	50.00
2 Joe DiMaggio October 26, 1939	150.00	75.00
3 Bob Feller November 9, 1939	120.00	60.00
4 Cincinnati Reds November 2, 1939 Double Size	50.00	25.00
5 St. Louis Cardinals November 16,1939	50.00	25.00

1888-89 Sporting Times M117

These 27 cards which measure 7 1/2" by 4 1/2" were included as premiums in the Sporting Times weekly newspaper. The cards are sequenced in alphabetical order and some of the other photos (most noticably) the Anson were used in other sets.

	Ex-Mt	VG
COMPLETE SET (27)	15000.00	7500.00
1 Cap Anson	1500.00	750.00
2 Jersey Bakely	400.00	200.00
3 Dan Brouthers	800.00	400.00
4 Doc Bushong	400.00	200.00
5 Jack Clements	400.00	200.00
6 Charles Comiskey	800.00	400.00
7 Hank O'Day	400.00	200.00
8 Jerry Denny	400.00	200.00
9 Buck Ewing	800.00	400.00
10 Dude Esterbrook	400.00	200.00
11 Jay Faatz	400.00	200.00
12 Pud Galvin	800.00	400.00
13 Jack Glasscock	500.00	250.00
14 Tim Keefe	800.00	400.00
15 King Kelly	800.00	400.00
16 Matt Kilroy	400.00	200.00
17 Arlie Latham	500.00	250.00
18 Doggie Miller	400.00	200.00
19 Fred Pfeffer	400.00	200.00
20 Henry Porter	400.00	200.00
21 Toad Ramsey	400.00	200.00
22 John Reilly	400.00	200.00
23 Elmer Smith	400.00	200.00
24 Harry Stovey	500.00	250.00
25 Sam Thompson	800.00	400.00
26 John Montgomery Ward	800.00	400.00
27 Curt Welch	500.00	250.00

1981 Sportrait Hall of Fame

This 25-card set measures approximately 3 5/8" by 5" and features a Hall of Fame player's sketch by Stan Sypulski inside a thin color frame on a white background. The player's name and card number are printed at the bottom in the frame color. The backs are blank.

	Nm-Mt	Ex-Mt
COMPLETE SET (25)	20.00	8.00
1 Honus Wagner	1.00	.40
2 Miller Huggins	.50	.20
3 Babe Ruth	4.00	1.60
4 Connie Mack	.50	.20
5 Ty Cobb	3.00	1.20
6 Lou Gehrig	3.00	1.20
7 Eddie Collins	.75	.30
8 Chuck Klein	.50	.20
9 Ted Williams	3.00	1.20
10 Jimmy Foxx	1.00	.40
11 Frank Baker	.50	.20
12 Nap Lajoie	.75	.30
13 Casey Stengel	.75	.30
14 Joe DiMaggio	3.00	1.20
15 Mickey Mantle	4.00	1.60
16 Frank Frisch	.50	.20
17 Bill Terry	.50	.20
18 Jackie Robinson	2.50	1.00
19 Sam Rice	.50	.20
20 Mickey Cochrane	.50	.20
21 George Sisler	.75	.30
22 Bob Feller	1.00	.40
23 Walter Johnson	1.00	.40
24 Tris Speaker	1.00	.40
NNO Checklist	.25	.10

1970 Sports Cards for Collectors Old-Timer Postcards

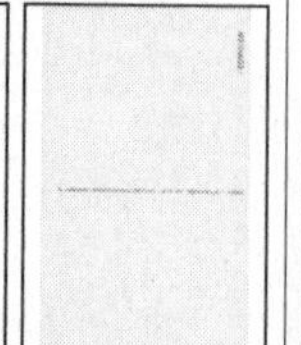

This 32-card set was issued by Sports Cards for Collectors of New York and features black-and-white portraits and action photos of some of baseball's old-timer great players in white borders. Some of the cards display facsimile player autographs. The backs carry a postcard format.

	NM	Ex
COMPLETE SET (32)	50.00	20.00
1 Babe Ruth Lou Gehrig	4.00	1.60
2 Larry Doby	1.00	.40
3 Mike Garcia	.50	.20
4 Bob Feller	1.50	.60
5 Gus Wynn	1.00	.40
6 Burleigh Grimes	1.00	.40
7 Rabbit Maranville	1.00	.40
8 Babe Ruth Batting	5.00	2.00
9 Lou Gehrig	4.00	1.60
10 Joe Dimaggio	4.00	1.60
11 Ty Cobb	4.00	1.60
12 Lou Boudreau	1.00	.40
13 Jimmy Foxx	3.00	1.20
14 Casey Stengel	1.50	.60
15 Kenesaw Landis	1.00	.40
16 Max Carey	1.00	.40
17 Wilbert Robinson	1.00	.40
18 Paul Richards	.50	.20
19 Zack Wheat	1.00	.40
20 Rube Marquard	1.00	.40
21 Dave Bancroft	.50	.20
22 Bobby Thomson	.50	.20
23 Melvin Ott	1.50	.60
24 Bobo Newsom	.50	.20
25 John Mize	1.00	.40
26 Walker Cooper	.50	.20
27 Dixie Walker	.50	.20
28 Augie Galan	.50	.20
29 George Stirnweiss	.50	.20
30 Floyd Herman	.50	.20
31 Babe Ruth Glove on knee	5.00	2.00
32 Babe Ruth Waist up	5.00	2.00

1984-85 Sports Design Products West

This 48-card standard-sized set was issued in two series and featured the drawings of sports artist Doug West. The set was produced and distributed by Sports Design Products (Charlie Mandel).

	Nm-Mt	Ex-Mt
COMPLETE SET (24)	15.00	6.00
1 Jackie Robinson	1.00	.40
2 Luis Aparicio	.20	.08
3 Roberto Clemente	1.00	.40
4 Mickey Mantle	1.50	.60
5 Joe DiMaggio	1.50	.60
6 Willie Stargell	.20	.08
7 Brooks Robinson	.30	.12
8 Ty Cobb	1.00	.40
9 Don Drysdale	.20	.08
10 Bob Feller	.30	.12
11 Stan Musial	.50	.20
12 Al Kaline	.20	.08
13 Willie Mays	.75	.30
14 Willie McCovey	.20	.08
15 Thurman Munson	.10	.04
16 Charlie Gehringer	.20	.08
17 Eddie Mathews	.20	.08
18 Carl Yastrzemski	.20	.08
19 Warren Spahn	.20	.08
20 Ted Williams	1.00	.40
21 Ernie Banks	.30	.12
22 Roy Campanella	.30	.12
23 Harmon Killebrew	.20	.08
24 Duke Snider	.20	.08
25 Lou Gehrig	1.00	.40
26 Hoyt Wilhelm	.20	.08
27 Enos Slaughter	.20	.08
28 Lou Brock	.20	.08
29 Mickey Cochrane	.20	.08
30 Gil Hodges	.20	.08
31 Yogi Berra	.50	.20
32 Carl Hubbell	.20	.08
33 Hank Greenberg	.20	.08
34 Pee Wee Reese	.50	.20
35 Casey Stengel MG	.50	.20
36 Ralph Kiner	.20	.08
37 Satchel Paige	.75	.30
38 Richie Ashburn UER Spelled Ritchie	.50	.20
39 Connie Mack MG	.20	.08
40 Dick Groat	.10	.04
41 Tony Oliva	.10	.04
42 Honus Wagner	.50	.20
43 Denny McLain	.10	.04
44 Johnny Mize	.20	.08
45 Bob Lemon	.20	.08
46 Ferguson Jenkins	.20	.08
47 Babe Ruth	1.50	.60
48 Ted Kluszewski	.20	.08

1986 Sports Design J.D. McCarthy

This 24-card standard-size set features the photography of J.D. McCarthy. The fronts have a similar design to the 1969 Topps issue, while the back identifies the player.

	Nm-Mt	Ex-Mt
COMPLETE SET (24)	8.00	3.20
1 J.D. McCarthy Ted Williams	.50	.20
2 Lou Brock	.30	.12
3 Carl Yastrzemski	.30	.12
4 Mickey Mantle	2.00	.80
5 Roger Maris	1.00	.40
6 Walter Alston	.10	.04
7 Ernie Banks	.50	.20
8 Billy Williams	.30	.12
9 Hank Aaron	1.50	.60
10 Brooks Robinson	.50	.20
11 Joe DiMaggio	1.50	.60
12 Casey Stengel	.30	.12
13 Juan Marichal	.50	.20
14 Jim Bunning	.30	.12
15 Matty Alou	.10	.04
16 Eddie Mathews	.20	.08
17 Sandy Koufax	1.00	.40
18 Roberto Clemente	1.50	.60
19 Gil Hodges Ernie Banks	.30	.12
20 Duke Snider	.30	.12
21 Robin Roberts	.20	.08
22 Willie Mays	1.50	.60
23 Willie Stargell	.20	.08
24 Whitey Ford	.30	.12

1946-49 Sports Exchange W603

These cards measuring approximately 7" by 10" were issued by Sports Exchange between 1946 and 1949. The cards are numbered but we have sequenced them alphabetically within series. This set is considered one of the first "collector-issued" sets as many copies were sold through what was then considered a small group of dedicated collectors.

	Ex-Mt	VG
COMPLETE SET (117)	2500.00	1250.00
1-1A Phil Cavaretta	12.00	6.00
1-1B Bill Dickey	40.00	20.00
1-2 John 'Al' Benton	10.00	5.00
1-3 Harry Brecheen	12.00	6.00
1-4 Jimmy Foxx	50.00	25.00
1-5 Edwin Dyer	10.00	5.00
1-6 Ewell Blackwell	12.00	6.00
1-7 Floyd Bevens	10.00	5.00
1-8 Nick Altrock	10.00	5.00
1-9 George Case	10.00	5.00
1-10 Lu Blue	10.00	5.00
1-11 Ralph Branca- Ken Keltner	12.00	6.00
1-12 Gene Bearden	10.00	5.00
2-1A Walker Cooper	10.00	5.00
2-1B Bob Doerr	15.00	7.50
2-2 Lou Boudreau	30.00	15.00
2-3 Dom DiMaggio	15.00	7.50
2-4 Frank Frisch	30.00	15.00
2-5 Charlie Grimm	12.00	6.00
2-6 Jimmy Outlaw	10.00	5.00
2-7 Hugh Casey	10.00	5.00
2-8 Mark Christman	10.00	5.00
2-9 Jake Early	10.00	5.00
2-10 Bruce Edwards	10.00	5.00
2-11 Mickey Cochrane- Bob Dillinger	15.00	7.50
2-12 Ben Chapman	10.00	5.00
3-1A Dave Ferriss	10.00	5.00
3-1B Bob Feller	30.00	15.00
3-2 Spud Chandler	12.00	6.00
3-3 Del Ennis	12.00	6.00
3-4 Lou Gehrig	200.00	100.00
3-5 William Herman	20.00	10.00
3-6 Andy Pafko	12.00	6.00
3-7 Sam Chapman	10.00	5.00
3-8 Earle Combs	20.00	10.00
3-9 Carl Furillo	15.00	7.50
3-10 Elbie Fletcher	10.00	5.00
3-11 Dizzy Dean- Edwin Joost	20.00	10.00
3-12 Steve Gromek	10.00	5.00
4-1A George Kurowski	10.00	5.00
4-1B Hank Greenberg	20.00	10.00
4-2 Jeff Heath	10.00	5.00
4-3 Al Evans	10.00	5.00
4-4 Lefty Grove	50.00	25.00
4-5 Ted Lyons	20.00	10.00
4-6 Pee Wee Reese	20.00	10.00
4-7 Joe DiMaggio	150.00	75.00
4-8 Travis Jackson	15.00	7.50
4-9 Augie Galan	10.00	5.00
4-10 Joe Gordon	12.00	6.00
4-11 Joe Jackson- Wally Westlake	120.00	60.00
4-12 Jim Hegan	10.00	5.00
5-1A Marty Marion	12.00	6.00
5-1B George McQuinn	10.00	5.00
5-2 Kirby Higbe	10.00	5.00
5-3 John Lindell	10.00	5.00
5-4 Bill Hallahan	10.00	5.00
5-5 Frank "Lefty" O'Doul	12.00	6.00
5-6 Phil Rizzuto	40.00	20.00
5-7 Tommy Henrich	12.00	6.00
5-8 Bob Muncrief	10.00	5.00
5-9 Berthold Haas	10.00	5.00
5-10 Tommy Holmes	12.00	6.00
5-11 Larry Jansen- Yogi Berra	20.00	10.00
5-12 Bob Lemon	20.00	10.00
6-1A Truett'Rip' Sewell	10.00	5.00
6-1B Ray Mueller	10.00	5.00
6-2 Tex Hughson	10.00	5.00
6-3 John Mize	20.00	10.00
6-4 Rogers Hornsby	50.00	25.00
6-5 Steve O'Neil	10.00	5.00
6-6 Buddy Rosar	10.00	5.00
6-7 Ralph Kiner	20.00	10.00
6-9 John Hopp	10.00	5.00
6-10 Bill Johnson	10.00	5.00
6-11 Harry Lowrey- Heinie Manush	12.00	6.00
6-12 Billy Meyer	10.00	5.00
7-1A Ed Stanky	12.00	6.00
7-1B Hal Newhouser	15.00	7.50
7-2 Stan Musial	80.00	40.00
7-3 Johnny Pesky	12.00	6.00
7-4 Carl Hubbell	20.00	10.00
7-5 Herb Pennock	20.00	10.00
7-6 Johnny Sain	12.00	6.00
7-7 Harry Lavagetto	12.00	6.00
7-8 Joe Page	12.00	6.00
7-9 John 'Buddy' Kelly	10.00	5.00
7-10 Phil Masi	10.00	5.00
7-12 Dale Mitchell	10.00	5.00
8-1A Fred'Dixie' Walker	10.00	5.00
8-1B Dick Wakefield	10.00	5.00
8-2 Howie Pollet	10.00	5.00
8-3 Harold Reiser	12.00	6.00
8-4 Babe Ruth	250.00	125.00
8-5 Luke Sewell	12.00	6.00
8-6 Dizzy Trout	10.00	5.00
8-7 Vic Lombardi	10.00	5.00
8-8 Honus Wagner	80.00	40.00
8-9 Ray Lamanno	10.00	5.00
8-10 George Munger	10.00	5.00
8-12 Red Rolfe	10.00	5.00
9-1B Ted Williams	120.00	60.00
9-2 Enos Slaughter	20.00	10.00
9-3 Aaron Robinson	10.00	5.00
9-4 Hack Wilson	20.00	10.00
9-5 William Southworth MG	10.00	5.00
9-6 Harry Walker	10.00	5.00
9-7 Cecil Travis	10.00	5.00
9-8 Mickey Witek	10.00	5.00
9-9 Warren Spahn	30.00	15.00
9-10 Vern Stephens	10.00	5.00
9-12 Sibbi Sisti	10.00	5.00
10-3 Bos. Red Sox-1946	12.00	6.00
10-12 Zach Taylor MG	10.00	5.00
11-3 St.L.Cardinals-1946	12.00	6.00
11-12 Earl Torgeson	10.00	5.00
12-12 Mickey Vernon	12.00	6.00

1997 Sports Illustrated

The 1997 Sports Illustrated set (created by Fleer) was issued in one series totalling 180 cards. Each pack contained six cards and

carried a $1.99 SRP. The fronts feature Sports Illustrated action player photos with player stories on the backs. The set contains the topical subsets: Fresh Faces (1-27), Season Highlights (28-36), Inside Baseball (37-54), S.I.BER Vision 55-72) and Classic Covers (169-180). An unnumbered Jose Cruz Jr. foldout checklist was also seeded in approximately 1:4 packs.

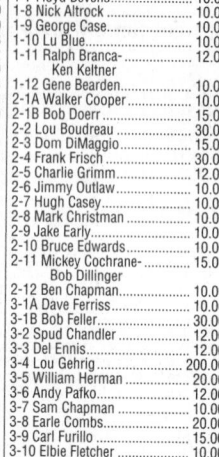

	Nm-Mt	Ex-Mt
COMPLETE SET (180)	40.00	12.00
1 Bob Abreu	.30	.09
2 Jaime Bluma	.30	.09
3 Emil Brown RC	.30	.09
4 Jose Cruz Jr. RC	1.25	.35
5 Jason Dickson	.30	.09
6 Nomar Garciaparra	1.25	.35
7 Todd Greene	.30	.09
8 Vladimir Guerrero	.75	.23
9 Wilton Guerrero	.30	.09
10 Jose Guillen	.30	.09
11 Hideki Irabu RC	.30	.09
12 Russ Johnson	.30	.09
13 Andruw Jones	.30	.09
14 Damon Mashore	.30	.09
15 Jason McDonald	.30	.09
16 Ryan McGuire	.30	.09
17 Matt Morris	.30	.09
18 Kevin Orie	.30	.09
19 Dante Powell	.30	.09
20 Pokey Reese	.30	.09
21 Joe Roa RC	.30	.09
22 Scott Rolen	.50	.15
23 Glendon Rusch	.30	.09
24 Scott Spiezio	.30	.09
25 Bubba Trammell RC	.30	.09
26 Todd Walker	.30	.09
27 Jamey Wright	.30	.09
28 Ken Griffey Jr. SH	.75	.23
29 Tino Martinez SH	.30	.09
30 Roger Clemens SH	.75	.23
31 Hideki Irabu SH	.30	.09
32 Kevin Brown SH	.30	.09
33 Chipper Jones SH Cal Ripken	1.00	.30
34 Sandy Alomar Jr. SH	.30	.09
35 Ken Caminiti SH	.30	.09
36 Randy Johnson SH	.50	.15
37 Andy Ashby IB	.30	.09
38 Jay Buhner IB	.30	.09
39 Joe Carter IB	.30	.09
40 Darren Daulton IB	.30	.09
41 Jeff Fassero IB	.30	.09
42 Andres Galarraga IB	.30	.09
43 Rusty Greer IB	.30	.09
44 Marquis Grissom IB	.30	.09
45 Joey Hamilton IB	.30	.09
46 Jimmy Key IB	.30	.09
47 Ryan Klesko IB	.30	.09
48 Eddie Murray IB	.50	.15
49 Charles Nagy IB	.30	.09
50 Dave Nilsson IB	.30	.09
51 Ricardo Rincon IB RC	.30	.09
52 Billy Wagner IB	.30	.09
53 Dan Wilson IB	.30	.09
54 Dmitri Young IB	.30	.09
55 Roberto Alomar SIV	.30	.09
56 Sandy Alomar Jr. SIV	.30	.09
57 Scott Brosius SIV	.30	.09
58 Tony Clark SIV	.30	.09
59 Carlos Delgado SIV	.30	.09
60 Jermaine Dye SIV	.30	.09
61 Darin Erstad SIV	.30	.09
62 Derek Jeter SIV	1.00	.30
63 Jason Kendall SIV	.30	.09
64 Hideo Nomo SIV	.30	.09
65 Rey Ordonez SIV	.30	.09
66 Andy Pettitte SIV	.30	.09
67 Manny Ramirez SIV	.30	.09
68 Edgar Renteria SIV	.30	.09
69 Shane Reynolds SIV	.30	.09
70 Alex Rodriguez SIV	.75	.23
71 Ivan Rodriguez SIV	.50	.15
72 Jose Rosado SIV	.30	.09
73 John Smoltz	.50	.15
74 Tom Glavine	.50	.15
75 Greg Maddux	1.25	.35
76 Chipper Jones	.75	.23
77 Kenny Lofton	.30	.09
78 Fred McGriff	.50	.15
79 Kevin Brown	.50	.15
80 Alex Fernandez	.30	.09
81 Al Leiter	.30	.09
82 Bobby Bonilla	.30	.09
83 Gary Sheffield	.30	.09
84 Moises Alou	.30	.09
85 Henry Rodriguez	.30	.09
86 Mark Grudzielanek	.30	.09
87 Pedro Martinez	.75	.23
88 Todd Hundley	.30	.09
89 Bernard Gilkey	.30	.09
90 Bobby Jones	.30	.09
91 Curt Schilling	.50	.15
92 Ricky Bottalico	.30	.09
93 Mike Lieberthal	.30	.09
94 Sammy Sosa	1.25	.35
95 Ryne Sandberg	1.25	.35
96 Mark Grace	.50	.15
97 Deion Sanders	.50	.15
98 Reggie Sanders	.30	.09
99 Barry Larkin	.75	.23
100 Craig Biggio	.50	.15
101 Jeff Bagwell	.50	.15
102 Derek Bell	.30	.09
103 Brian Jordan	.30	.09
104 Ray Lankford	.30	.09
105 Ron Gant	.30	.09

106 Al Martin .30 .09
107 Kevin Elster .30 .09
108 Jermaine Allensworth .30 .09
109 Vinny Castilla .30 .09
110 Dante Bichette .30 .09
111 Larry Walker .50 .15
112 Mike Piazza 1.25 .35
113 Eric Karros .30 .09
114 Todd Hollandsworth .30 .09
115 Raul Mondesi .30 .09
116 Hideo Nomo .75 .23
117 Ramon Martinez .30 .09
118 Ken Caminiti .30 .09
119 Tony Gwynn 1.00 .30
120 Steve Finley .30 .09
121 Barry Bonds 2.00 .60
122 J.T. Snow .30 .09
123 Rod Beck .30 .09
124 Cal Ripken 2.50 .75
125 Mike Mussina .75 .23
126 Brady Anderson .30 .09
127 Bernie Williams .50 .15
128 Derek Jeter 2.00 .60
129 Tino Martinez .50 .15
130 Andy Pettitte .50 .15
131 David Cone .30 .09
132 Mariano Rivera .50 .15
133 Roger Clemens 1.50 .45
134 Pat Hentgen .30 .09
135 Juan Guzman .30 .09
136 Bob Higginson .30 .09
137 Tony Clark .30 .09
138 Travis Fryman .30 .09
139 Mo Vaughn .30 .09
140 Tim Naehring .30 .09
141 John Valentin .30 .09
142 Matt Williams .30 .09
143 David Justice .30 .09
144 Jim Thome .75 .23
145 Chuck Knoblauch .30 .09
146 Paul Molitor .50 .15
147 Marty Cordova .30 .09
148 Frank Thomas .75 .23
149 Albert Belle .30 .09
150 Robin Ventura .30 .09
151 John Jaha .30 .09
152 Jeff Cirillo .30 .09
153 Jose Valentin .30 .09
154 Jay Bell .30 .09
155 Jeff King .30 .09
156 Kevin Appier .30 .09
157 Ken Griffey Jr. 1.25 .35
158 Alex Rodriguez 1.25 .35
159 Randy Johnson .75 .23
160 Juan Gonzalez .75 .23
161 Will Clark .75 .23
162 Dean Palmer .30 .09
163 Tim Salmon .50 .15
164 Jim Edmonds .30 .09
165 Jim Leyritz .30 .09
166 Jose Canseco .75 .23
167 Jason Giambi .75 .23
168 Mark McGwire 2.00 .60
169 Barry Bonds CC .75 .23
170 Alex Rodriguez CC .75 .23
171 Roger Clemens CC .75 .23
172 Ken Griffey Jr. CC .75 .23
173 Greg Maddux CC .75 .23
174 Mike Piazza CC .75 .23
175 Will Clark CC .75 .23
Mark McGwire
176 Hideo Nomo CC .30 .09
177 Cal Ripken CC 1.25 .35
178 Ken Griffey Jr. CC .75 .23
Frank Thomas
179 Alex Rodriguez CC 1.25 .35
Derek Jeter
180 John Wetteland CC .30 .09
P158 A.Rodriguez Promo 1.50 .45
NNO Jose Cruz Jr. CL .25 .07

1997 Sports Illustrated Extra Edition

Randomly inserted in packs, this 180-card set if parallel to the base set with etched holofoil accents. Only 500 of each card were produced and are sequentially numbered.

Nm-Mt Ex-Mt
*STARS: 6X TO 15X BASIC CARDS
*ROOKIES: 3X TO 8X BASIC CARDS

1997 Sports Illustrated Autographed Mini-Covers

Redemptions for these autographed cards were randomly inserted in packs. This six-card set features color photos of three current and three retired players on miniature SI covers. Only 250 of each card was produced and serially numbered and autographed.

Nm-Mt Ex-Mt
1 Alex Rodriguez 150.00 45.00
2 Cal Ripken 250.00 75.00
3 Kirby Puckett 80.00 24.00
4 Willie Mays 150.00 45.00
5 Frank Robinson 40.00 12.00
6 Hank Aaron 150.00 45.00

1997 Sports Illustrated Cooperstown Collection

Randomly inserted in packs at the rate of one in 12, this 12-card set features classic Sports Illustrated baseball covers with a description of the issue on the back.

Nm-Mt Ex-Mt
COMPLETE SET (12) 60.00 18.00
1 Hank Aaron 10.00 3.00
2 Yogi Berra 6.00 1.80
3 Lou Brock 5.00 1.50
4 Rod Carew 5.00 1.50
5 Juan Marichal 5.00 1.50
6 Al Kaline 6.00 1.80
7 Joe Morgan 5.00 1.50
8 Brooks Robinson 5.00 1.50
9 Willie Stargell 5.00 1.50
10 Kirby Puckett 5.00 1.50
11 Willie Mays 12.00 3.60
12 Frank Robinson 5.00 1.50

1997 Sports Illustrated Great Shots

Randomly inserted one per pack, this 25-card set showcases some of the greatest photography in Sports Illustrated history and features color player photos that unfold into mini posters. When unfolded the blank backed posters measure 5" by 7".

Nm-Mt Ex-Mt
COMPLETE SET (25) 8.00 2.40
1 Chipper Jones .50 .15
2 Ryan Klesko .20 .06
3 Kenny Lofton .20 .06
4 Greg Maddux .75 .23
5 John Smoltz .30 .09
6 Roberto Alomar .20 .06
7 Cal Ripken 1.50 .45
8 Mo Vaughn .20 .06
9 Albert Belle .20 .06
10 Frank Thomas .50 .15
11 Ryne Sandberg .75 .23
12 Deion Sanders .30 .09
13 Vinny Castilla .20 .06
Andres Galarraga
14 Eric Karros .20 .06
15 Mike Piazza .75 .23
16 Derek Jeter 1.25 .35
17 Mark McGwire 1.25 .35
18 Darren Daulton .20 .06
19 Andy Ashby .20 .06
20 Barry Bonds 1.25 .35
21 Jay Buhner .20 .06
22 Randy Johnson .50 .15
23 Alex Rodriguez .75 .23
24 Juan Gonzalez .50 .15
25 Ken Griffey Jr. .75 .23

1998 Sports Illustrated

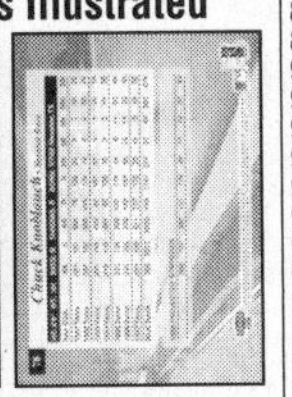

The 1998 Sports Illustrated set (created by Fleer) was issued in one series totalling 200 cards and was distributed in six-card packs with a suggested retail price of $1.99. The cards feature exclusive Sports Illustrated photography and commentary. The set contains the topical subsets: Baseball's Best (129-148), One to Watch (149-176/201), and 97 in Review (177-200). A Travis Lee One to Watch subset card (number 201) was inserted into the product just before going to press. Though official numbers were never released, it appears the card was seeded into approximately one in every four boxes, making it about two times tougher to pull than any of the other regular issue cards. Notable Rookie Cards include Maggio Ordonez. Also, a 3 1/2" by 5" Alex Rodriguez bonus card was randomly inserted one in every six packs displaying an action color player photo with the complete Sports Illustrated checklisted printed on the card. In addition a promotional card featuring Alex Rodriguez was distributed to dealers and hobby media severla weeks prior to the products release. The "Promotional Sample" text running diagonally across the front and back of the card makes it easy to distinguish.

Nm-Mt Ex-Mt
COMPLETE SET (200) 25.00 7.50
1 Edgardo Alfonzo .30 .09
2 Roberto Alomar .75 .23
3 Sandy Alomar Jr. .30 .09
4 Moises Alou .30 .09
5 Brady Anderson .30 .09
6 Garret Anderson .30 .09
7 Kevin Appier .30 .09
8 Jeff Bagwell .50 .15
9 Jay Bell .30 .09
10 Albert Belle .30 .09
11 Dante Bichette .30 .09
12 Craig Biggio .50 .15
13 Barry Bonds 2.00 .60
14 Bobby Bonilla .30 .09
15 Kevin Brown .50 .15
16 Jay Buhner .30 .09
17 Ellis Burks .30 .09
18 Mike Cameron .30 .09
19 Ken Caminiti .30 .09
20 Jose Canseco .75 .23
21 Joe Carter .30 .09
22 Vinny Castilla .30 .09
23 Jeff Cirillo .30 .09
24 Tony Clark .30 .09
25 Will Clark .75 .23
26 Roger Clemens 1.50 .45
27 David Cone .30 .09
28 Jose Cruz Jr. .30 .09
29 Carlos Delgado .30 .09
30 Jason Dickson .30 .09
31 Dennis Eckersley .30 .09
32 Jim Edmonds .30 .09
33 Scott Erickson .30 .09
34 Darin Erstad .30 .09
35 Shawn Estes .30 .09
36 Jeff Fassero .30 .09
37 Alex Fernandez .30 .09
38 Chuck Finley .30 .09
39 Steve Finley .30 .09
40 Travis Fryman .30 .09
41 Andres Galarraga .30 .09
42 Ron Gant .30 .09
43 Nomar Garciaparra 1.25 .35
44 Jason Giambi .75 .23
45 Tom Glavine .50 .15
46 Juan Gonzalez .75 .23
47 Mark Grace .50 .15
48 Willie Greene .30 .09
49 Rusty Greer .30 .09
50 Ben Grieve .30 .09
51 Ken Griffey Jr. 1.25 .35
52 Mark Grudzielanek .30 .09
53 Vladimir Guerrero .75 .23
54 Juan Guzman .30 .09
55 Tony Gwynn 1.00 .30
56 Joey Hamilton .30 .09
57 Rickey Henderson .75 .23
58 Pat Hentgen .30 .09
59 Livan Hernandez .30 .09
60 Bobby Higginson .30 .09
61 Todd Hundley .30 .09
62 Hideki Irabu .30 .09
63 John Jaha .30 .09
64 Derek Jeter 2.00 .60
65 Charles Johnson .30 .09
66 Randy Johnson .75 .23
67 Andruw Jones .30 .09
68 Bobby Jones .30 .09
69 Chipper Jones .75 .23
70 Brian Jordan .30 .09
71 David Justice .30 .09
72 Eric Karros .30 .09
73 Jeff Kent .30 .09
74 Jimmy Key .30 .09
75 Darryl Kile .30 .09
76 Jeff King .30 .09
77 Ryan Klesko .30 .09
78 Chuck Knoblauch .30 .09
79 Ray Lankford .30 .09
80 Barry Larkin .75 .23
81 Kenny Lofton .30 .09
82 Greg Maddux 1.25 .35
83 Al Martin .30 .09
84 Edgar Martinez .50 .15
85 Pedro Martinez .75 .23
86 Tino Martinez .50 .15
87 Mark McGwire 2.00 .60
88 Paul Molitor .50 .15
89 Raul Mondesi .30 .09
90 Jamie Moyer .30 .09
91 Mike Mussina .75 .23
92 Tim Naehring .30 .09
93 Charles Nagy .30 .09
94 Denny Neagle .30 .09
95 Dave Nilsson .30 .09
96 Hideo Nomo .75 .23
97 Rey Ordonez .30 .09
98 Dean Palmer .30 .09
99 Rafael Palmeiro .50 .15
100 Andy Pettitte .50 .15
101 Mike Piazza 1.25 .35
102 Brad Radke .30 .09
103 Manny Ramirez .30 .09
104 Edgar Renteria .30 .09
105 Cal Ripken 2.50 .75
106 Alex Rodriguez 1.25 .35
107 Henry Rodriguez .30 .09
108 Ivan Rodriguez .75 .23
109 Scott Rolen .50 .15
110 Tim Salmon .50 .15
111 Curt Schilling .50 .15
112 Gary Sheffield .30 .09
113 John Smoltz .50 .15
114 J.T. Snow .30 .09
115 Sammy Sosa 1.25 .35
116 Matt Stairs .30 .09
117 Shannon Stewart .30 .09
118 Frank Thomas .75 .23
119 Jim Thome .75 .23
120 Justin Thompson .30 .09
121 Mo Vaughn .30 .09
122 Robin Ventura .30 .09
123 Larry Walker .50 .15
124 Rondell White .30 .09
125 Bernie Williams .50 .15
126 Matt Williams .30 .09
127 Tony Womack .30 .09
128 Jaret Wright .30 .09
129 Edgar Renteria BB .30 .09
130 Kenny Lofton BB .30 .09
131 Tony Gwynn BB .50 .15
132 Mark McGwire BB 1.00 .30
133 Craig Biggio BB .30 .09
134 Charles Johnson BB .30 .09
135 J.T. Snow BB .30 .09
136 Ken Caminiti BB .30 .09
137 Vladimir Guerrero BB .50 .15
138 Jim Edmonds BB .30 .09
139 Randy Johnson BB .50 .15
140 Darryl Kile BB .30 .09
141 John Smoltz BB .30 .09
142 Greg Maddux BB .75 .23
143 Andy Pettitte BB .30 .09
144 Ken Griffey Jr. BB .75 .23
145 Mike Piazza BB .75 .23
146 Todd Greene BB .30 .09
147 Vinny Castilla BB .30 .09
148 Derek Jeter BB 1.00 .30
149 R.Machado OW RC .30 .09
150 Mike Gulan OW RC .30 .09
151 Randall Simon OW .30 .09
152 Michael Coleman OW .30 .09
153 Brian Rose OW .30 .09
154 Scott Eyre OW .30 .09
155 M.Ordonez OW RC 2.00 .60
156 Todd Helton OW .50 .15
157 Juan Encarnacion OW .30 .09
158 Mark Kotsay OW .30 .09
159 Josh Booty OW .30 .09
160 Melvin Rosario OW .30 .09
161 Shane Halter OW .30 .09
162 Paul Konerko OW .30 .09
163 Henry Blanco OW .30 .09
164 A.Williamson OW .30 .09
165 Brad Fullmer OW .30 .09
166 Ricky Ledee OW .30 .09
167 Ben Grieve OW .30 .09
168 F.Catalanotto OW RC .50 .15
169 Bobby Estalella OW .30 .09
170 Dennis Reyes OW .30 .09
171 Kevin Polcovich OW .30 .09
172 Jacob Cruz OW .30 .09
173 Ken Cloude OW .30 .09
174 Eli Marrero OW .30 .09
175 Fernando Tatis OW .30 .09
176 Tom Evans OW .30 .09
177 Rafael Palmeiro .50 .15
Chipper Jones '97
178 Eric Davis '97 .30 .09
179 Roger Clemens '97 .75 .23
180 Brett Butler .50 .15
Eddie Murray '97
181 Frank Thomas '97 .50 .15
182 Curt Schilling '97 .30 .09
183 Jeff Bagwell '97 .50 .15
184 Mark McGwire .75 .23
Ken Griffey Jr. '97
185 Kevin Brown '97 .30 .09
186 Francisco Cordova .30 .09
Ricardo Rincon '97
187 Charles Johnson '97 .30 .09
188 Hideki Irabu '97 .30 .09
189 Tony Gwynn '97 .50 .15
190 Sandy Alomar Jr. '97 .30 .09
191 Ken Griffey Jr. '97 .75 .23
192 Larry Walker '97 .30 .09
193 Roger Clemens '97 .75 .23
194 Pedro Martinez '97 .50 .15
195 Nomar Garciaparra '97 .75 .23
196 Scott Rolen '97 .30 .09
197 Brian Anderson '97 .30 .09
198 Tony Saunders '97 .30 .09
199 Florida Marlins '97 .30 .09
200 Livan Hernandez '97 .30 .09
201 Travis Lee OW SP 2.00 .60
P106 Alex Rodriguez PROMO 2.00 .60
NNO Alex Rodriguez CL .50 .15

1998 Sports Illustrated Extra Edition

Randomly inserted in packs, this 201-card set is a holofoil-stamped parallel version of the base set and is serially numbered to 250.

Nm-Mt Ex-Mt
*STARS: 6X TO 15X BASIC CARDS
*ROOKIES: 4X TO 10X BASIC CARDS

1998 Sports Illustrated Autographs

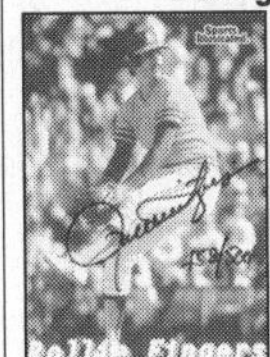

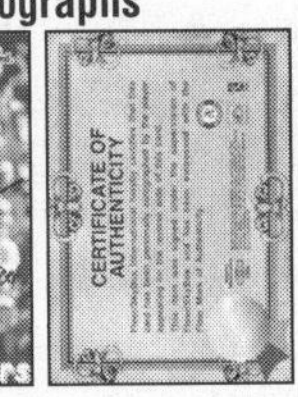

These six cards were randomly seeded into packs. The Grieve and Konerko cards are actually exchange cards with a deadline that expired on November 1st, 1999; but the other four are signed by the player. Only 500 serial numbered sets were made. The cards are unnumbered and listed in alphabetical order below.

Nm-Mt Ex-Mt
1 Lou Brock/500 40.00 12.00
2 Jose Cruz Jr./250 20.00 6.00
3 Rollie Fingers/500 25.00 7.50
4 Ben Grieve/250 20.00 6.00
5 Paul Konerko/250 20.00 6.00
6 Brooks Robinson/500 60.00 18.00

1998 Sports Illustrated Covers

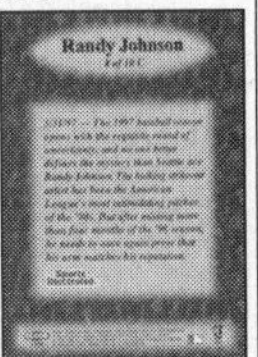

Randomly inserted in packs at the rate of one in nine, this 10-card set features trading-card sized versions of actual Sports Illustrated covers displaying photos of the listed active players.

Nm-Mt Ex-Mt
COMPLETE SET (10) 25.00 7.50
C1 Ken Griffey 4.00 1.20
Mike Piazza
C2 Derek Jeter 6.00 1.80
C3 Ken Griffey Jr. 4.00 1.20
C4 Cal Ripken 8.00 2.40
C5 Manny Ramirez 1.00 .30
C6 Jay Buhner 1.00 .30
C7 Matt Williams 1.00 .30
C8 Randy Johnson 2.50 .75
C9 Deion Sanders 1.00 .30
C10 Jose Canseco 2.50 .75

1998 Sports Illustrated Editor's Choice

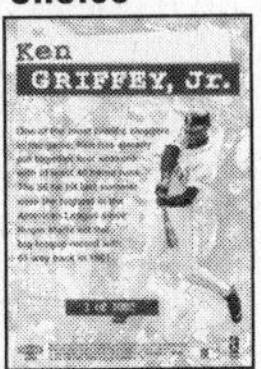

Randomly inserted in packs at the rate of one in 24, this 10-card set features color action photos of top stars for 1998 as profiled by the editors of Sports Illustrated.

Nm-Mt Ex-Mt
COMPLETE SET (10) 80.00 24.00
EC1 Ken Griffey Jr. 10.00 3.00
EC2 Alex Rodriguez 10.00 3.00
EC3 Frank Thomas 6.00 1.80
EC4 Mark McGwire 15.00 4.50
EC5 Greg Maddux 10.00 3.00
EC6 Derek Jeter 15.00 4.50
EC7 Cal Ripken 20.00 6.00
EC8 Nomar Garciaparra 10.00 3.00
EC9 Jeff Bagwell 4.00 1.20
EC10 Jose Cruz Jr. 2.50 .75

1998 Sports Illustrated Opening Day Mini Posters

Inserted at a rate of one per pack, this 30-card set features 5" by 7" blank-backed mini-posters with color photos of a top player from each team plus the team's 1998 schedule.

Nm-Mt Ex-Mt
COMPLETE SET (30) 10.00 3.00
OD1 Tim Salmon .30 .09
OD2 Matt Williams .20 .06
OD3 John Smoltz .75 .23
Greg Maddux
OD4 Cal Ripken 1.50 .45
OD5 Nomar Garciaparra .75 .23
OD6 Sammy Sosa .75 .23
OD7 Frank Thomas .50 .15
OD8 Barry Larkin .50 .15
OD9 David Justice .20 .06
OD10 Larry Walker .30 .09
OD11 Tony Clark .20 .06
OD12 Livan Hernandez .20 .06
OD13 Jeff Bagwell .30 .09
OD14 Kevin Appier .20 .06
OD15 Mike Piazza .75 .23
OD16 Fernando Vina .20 .06
OD17 Paul Molitor .30 .09
OD18 Vladimir Guerrero .50 .15
OD19 Rey Ordonez .20 .06
OD20 Bernie Williams .30 .09
OD21 Matt Stairs .20 .06
OD22 Curt Schilling .30 .09
OD23 Tony Womack .20 .06
OD24 Mark McGwire 1.25 .35
OD25 Tony Gwynn .60 .18
OD26 Barry Bonds 1.25 .35
OD27 Ken Griffey Jr. .75 .23
OD28 Fred McGriff .30 .09
OD29 Juan Gonzalez .50 .15
Ivan Rodriguez
OD30 Roger Clemens 1.00 .30

1999 Sports Illustrated

Released in mid-March, 1999, this set was produced by Fleer/SkyBox. Each pack contained six cards and carried an SRP of $1.99. The 180-card basic set features full-bleed action player photos printed on thick 20-pt. stock and contains the following subsets: Post-Season (1-9), Award Winners (10-20), Season Highlights (21-41), Prospects 2000 (42-71) and Checklists (179-180). In addition, a Kerry Wood sample card was distributed to dealers and hobby media a few months prior to the product's release. The card can be easily identified by the bold "SAMPLE" text running diagonally across the back.

Nm-Mt Ex-Mt
COMPLETE SET (180) 50.00 15.00
1 Yankees POST .30 .09
2 Scott Brosius POST .20 .06
3 David Wells POST .20 .06
4 Sterling Hitchcock POST .20 .06
5 David Justice POST .20 .06
6 David Cone POST .20 .06
7 Greg Maddux POST .75 .23
8 Jim Leyritz POST .20 .06

Card	Nm-Mt	Ex-Mt
9 Gary Gaetti POST	.20	.06
10 Mark McGwire	.75	.23
Ken Griffey Jr. AW		
11 Sammy Sosa	.75	.23
Juan Gonzalez AW		
12 Larry Walker	.30	.09
Bernie Williams AW		
13 Tony Womack	.50	.15
Rickey Henderson AW		
14 Tom Glavine	.30	.09
Roger Clemens		
David Cone		
Rick Helling AW		
15 Curt Schilling	.50	.15
Roger Clemens AW		
16 Greg Maddux	.75	.23
Roger Clemens AW		
17 Trevor Hoffman	.30	.09
Tom Gordon AW		
18 Kerry Wood	.50	.15
Ben Grieve AW		
19 Tom Glavine	.50	.15
Roger Clemens AW		
20 Sammy Sosa	.50	.15
Juan Gonzalez AW		
21 Travis Lee SH	.20	.06
22 Roberto Alomar SH	.50	.15
23 Roger Clemens SH	.75	.23
24 Barry Bonds SH	.75	.23
25 Paul Molitor SH	.30	.09
26 Todd Stottlemyre SH	.20	.06
27 Chris Hoiles SH	.20	.06
28 Albert Belle SH	.20	.06
29 Tony Clark SH	.20	.06
30 Kerry Wood SH	.50	.15
31 David Wells SH	.20	.06
32 Dennis Eckersley SH	.30	.09
33 Mark McGwire SH	1.00	.30
34 Cal Ripken SH	1.25	.35
35 Ken Griffey Jr. SH	.75	.23
36 Alex Rodriguez SH	.75	.23
37 Craig Biggio SH	.30	.09
38 Sammy Sosa SH	.75	.23
39 Dennis Martinez SH	.20	.06
40 Curt Schilling SH	.30	.09
41 Orlando Hernandez SH	.20	.06
42 Troy Glaus	.75	.23
Ben Molina RC		
Todd Greene		
43 Mitch Meluskey	.20	.06
Daryle Ward		
Mike Grzanich RC		
44 Eric Chavez	.30	.09
Blake Stein		
Mike Neill		
45 Roy Halladay	.30	.09
Tom Evans		
Kevin Witt		
46 George Lombard	.20	.06
Adam Butler		
Bruce Chen		
47 Rafael Roque RC	.20	.06
Ron Belliard		
Valerio de los Santos		
48 J.D.Drew	.30	.09
Placido Polanco		
Mark Little		
49 Jason Maxwell	.20	.06
Jose Nieves RC		
Jeremi Gonzalez		
50 Scott McClain	.20	.06
Kerry Robinson		
Mike Duvall RC		
51 Ben Ford	.20	.06
Bryan Corey RC		
Danny Klassen		
52 Angel Pena	.30	.09
Jeff Kubenka		
Paul LoDuca		
53 Fernando Seguignol	.20	.06
Kirk Bullinger		
Tim Young		
54 Ramon E. Martinez RC	.20	.06
Wilson Delgado		
Armando Rios		
55 Jolbert Cabrera RC	.20	.06
Russell Branyan		
Jason Rakers		
56 Carlos Guillen	.20	.06
Dave Holdridge RC		
Giomar Guevara		
57 Alex Gonzalez	.20	.06
Joe Fontenot		
Preston Wilson		
58 Mike Kinkade	.20	.06
Jay Payton		
Masato Yoshii		
59 Calvin Pickering	.20	.06
Ryan Minor		
Willis Otanez		
60 Ben Davis	.20	.06
Matt Clement		
Stan Spencer		
61 Marlon Anderson	.20	.06
Mike Welch		
Gary Bennett RC		
62 Abraham Nunez	.30	.09
Sean Lawrence		
Aramis Ramirez		
63 Jonathan Johnson	.20	.06
Robert Sasser RC		
Scott Sheldon		
64 Keith Glauber	.20	.06
Guillermo Garcia		
Eddie Priest		
65 Brian Barkley	.20	.06
Jin Ho Cho		
Donnie Sadler		
66 Derrick Gibson	.20	.06
Mark Strittmatter		
Edgard Clemente		
67 Jeremy Giambi	.20	.06
Dermal Brown		
Chris Hatcher		
68 Gabe Kapler	.20	.06
Robert Fick		
Marino Santana		
69 Corey Koskie	.30	.09
A.J.Pierzynski		
Benji Sampson		
70 Brian Simmons	.20	.06
Mark Johnson		
Craig Wilson		
71 Ryan Bradley	.30	.09
Mike Lowell		
Jay Tessmer		
72 Ben Grieve	.20	.06
73 Shawn Green	.30	.09
74 Rafael Palmeiro	.50	.15
75 Juan Gonzalez	.75	.23
76 Mike Piazza	1.25	.35
77 Devon White	.20	.06
78 Jim Thome	.75	.23
79 Barry Larkin	.75	.23
80 Scott Rolen	.50	.15
81 Raul Mondesi	.30	.09
82 Jason Giambi	.75	.23
83 Jose Canseco	.75	.23
84 Tony Gwynn	1.00	.30
85 Cal Ripken	2.50	.75
86 Andy Pettitte	.50	.15
87 Carlos Delgado	.30	.09
88 Jeff Cirillo	.20	.06
89 Bret Saberhagen	.30	.09
90 John Olerud	.30	.09
91 Ron Coomer	.20	.06
92 Todd Helton	.50	.15
93 Ray Lankford	.20	.06
94 Tim Salmon	.50	.15
95 Fred McGriff	.50	.15
96 Matt Stairs	.20	.06
97 Ken Griffey Jr.	1.25	.35
98 Chipper Jones	.75	.23
99 Mark Grace	.50	.15
100 Ivan Rodriguez	.75	.23
101 Jeromy Burnitz	.30	.09
102 Kenny Rogers	.30	.09
103 Kevin Millwood	.30	.09
104 Vinny Castilla	.30	.09
105 Jim Edmonds	.30	.09
106 Craig Biggio	.50	.15
107 Andres Galarraga	.30	.09
108 Sammy Sosa	1.25	.35
109 Juan Encarnacion	.20	.06
110 Larry Walker	.50	.15
111 John Smoltz	.50	.15
112 Randy Johnson	.75	.23
113 Bobby Higginson	.30	.09
114 Albert Belle	.30	.09
115 Jaret Wright	.30	.09
116 Edgar Renteria	.30	.09
117 Andruw Jones	.50	.15
118 Barry Bonds	2.00	.60
119 Rondell White	.30	.09
120 Jamie Moyer	.30	.09
121 Darin Erstad	.30	.09
122 Al Leiter	.30	.09
123 Mark McGwire	2.00	.60
124 Mo Vaughn	.30	.09
125 Livan Hernandez	.20	.06
126 Jason Kendall	.30	.09
127 Frank Thomas	.75	.23
128 Denny Neagle	.20	.06
129 Johnny Damon	.30	.09
130 Derek Bell	.20	.06
131 Jeff Kent	.30	.09
132 Tony Womack	.30	.09
133 Trevor Hoffman	.30	.09
134 Gary Sheffield	.30	.09
135 Tino Martinez	.50	.15
136 Travis Fryman	.30	.09
137 Rolando Arrojo	.20	.06
138 Dante Bichette	.30	.09
139 Nomar Garciaparra	1.25	.35
140 Moises Alou	.30	.09
141 Chuck Knoblauch	.30	.09
142 Robin Ventura	.30	.09
143 Scott Erickson	.20	.06
144 David Cone	.30	.09
145 Greg Vaughn	.30	.09
146 Wade Boggs	.50	.15
147 Mike Mussina	.75	.23
148 Tony Clark	.20	.06
149 Alex Rodriguez	1.25	.35
150 Javy Lopez	.30	.09
151 Bartolo Colon	.30	.09
152 Derek Jeter	2.00	.60
153 Greg Maddux	1.25	.35
154 Kevin Brown	.50	.15
155 Curt Schilling	.50	.15
156 Jeff King	.20	.06
157 Bernie Williams	.50	.15
158 Roberto Alomar	.75	.23
159 Travis Lee	.20	.06
160 Kerry Wood	.75	.23
161 Jeff Bagwell	.50	.15
162 Roger Clemens	1.50	.45
163 Matt Williams	.30	.09
164 Chan Ho Park	.30	.09
165 Damion Easley	.20	.06
166 Manny Ramirez	.30	.09
167 Quinton McCracken	.20	.06
168 Todd Walker	.30	.09
169 Eric Karros	.30	.09
170 Will Clark	.75	.23
171 Edgar Martinez	.50	.15
172 Cliff Floyd	.30	.09
173 Vladimir Guerrero	.75	.23
174 Tom Glavine	.50	.15
175 Pedro Martinez	.75	.23
176 Chuck Finley	.30	.09
177 Dean Palmer	.30	.09
178 Omar Vizquel	.30	.09
179 Checklist	.20	.06
180 Checklist	.20	.06
S160 Kerry Wood Sample	1.00	.30

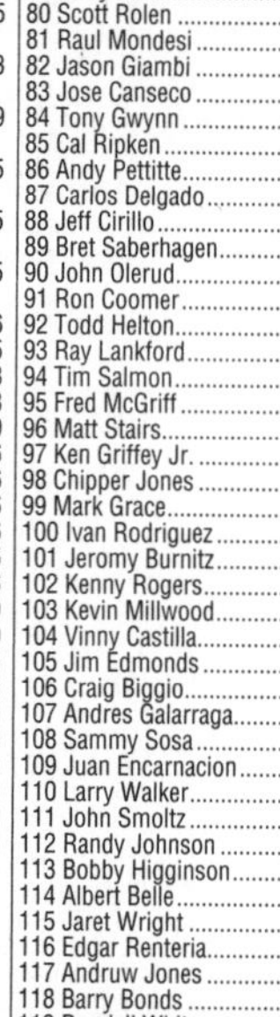

1999 Sports Illustrated Diamond Dominators

Randomly inserted in packs, this 10-card set features color action photos of star pitchers and hitters. The Pitchers (1-5) have an insertion rate of 1:90. The Hitters (6-10) are inserted 1:180.

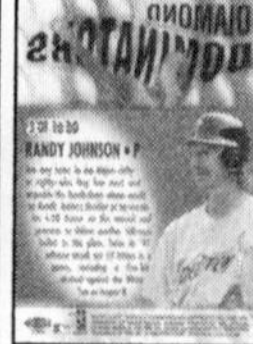

	Nm-Mt	Ex-Mt
COMPLETE SET (10)	250.00	75.00
1 Kerry Wood	12.00	3.60
2 Roger Clemens	25.00	7.50
3 Randy Johnson	12.00	3.60
4 Greg Maddux	20.00	6.00
5 Pedro Martinez	12.00	3.60
6 Ken Griffey Jr.	30.00	9.00
7 Sammy Sosa	30.00	9.00
8 Nomar Garciaparra	30.00	9.00
9 Mark McGwire	50.00	15.00
10 Alex Rodriguez	30.00	9.00

1999 Sports Illustrated Fabulous 40's

Randomly inserted in packs at the rate of one in 20, this 13-card set features color action photos of players who hit 40 or more home runs during the season and are printed on sculpture embossed foil-stamped cards showing the player's 1998 home run total.

	Nm-Mt	Ex-Mt
COMPLETE SET (13)	60.00	18.00
1 Mark McGwire	12.00	3.60
2 Sammy Sosa	8.00	2.40
3 Ken Griffey Jr.	8.00	2.40
4 Greg Vaughn	2.00	.60
5 Albert Belle	2.00	.60
6 Jose Canseco	5.00	1.50
7 Vinny Castilla	2.00	.60
8 Juan Gonzalez	5.00	1.50
9 Manny Ramirez	2.00	.60
10 Andres Galarraga	2.00	.60
11 Rafael Palmeiro	3.00	.90
12 Alex Rodriguez	8.00	2.40
13 Mo Vaughn	2.00	.60

1999 Sports Illustrated Fabulous 40's Extra

Randomly inserted in hobby packs only, this 13-card set is a silver patterned holo-foil stamped parallel version of the Sports Illustrated Fabulous 40's regular insert set. Each card is hand-numbered to the amount of home runs the pictured player hit during the season.

	Nm-Mt	Ex-Mt
1 Mark McGwire/70	60.00	18.00
2 Sammy Sosa/66	40.00	12.00
3 Ken Griffey Jr./56	40.00	12.00
4 Greg Vaughn/50	10.00	3.00
5 Albert Belle/49	10.00	3.00
6 Jose Canseco/46	25.00	7.50
7 Vinny Castilla/46	10.00	3.00
8 Juan Gonzalez/45	25.00	7.50
9 Manny Ramirez/45	10.00	3.00
10 Andres Galarraga/44	10.00	3.00
11 Rafael Palmeiro/43	15.00	4.50
12 Alex Rodriguez/42	40.00	12.00
13 Mo Vaughn/40	10.00	3.00

1999 Sports Illustrated Headliners

Randomly inserted in packs at the rate of one in four, this 25-card set features color action photos of leaders and star players printed on silver-foil stamped, team-color coded cards.

	Nm-Mt	Ex-Mt
COMPLETE SET (25)	40.00	12.00
1 Vladimir Guerrero	1.50	.45
2 Randy Johnson	1.50	.45
3 Mo Vaughn	.60	.18
4 Chipper Jones	1.50	.45
5 Jeff Bagwell	1.00	.30
6 Juan Gonzalez	1.50	.45
7 Mark McGwire	4.00	1.20
8 Cal Ripken	5.00	1.50
9 Frank Thomas	1.50	.45
10 Manny Ramirez	.60	.18
11 Ken Griffey Jr.	2.50	.75
12 Scott Rolen	1.00	.30
13 Alex Rodriguez	2.50	.75
14 Barry Bonds	4.00	1.20
15 Roger Clemens	3.00	.90
16 Darin Erstad	.60	.18
17 Nomar Garciaparra	2.50	.75
18 Mike Piazza	2.50	.75
19 Greg Maddux	2.50	.75
20 Ivan Rodriguez	1.50	.45
21 Derek Jeter	4.00	1.20
22 Sammy Sosa	2.50	.75
23 Andruw Jones	.60	.18
24 Pedro Martinez	1.50	.45
25 Kerry Wood	1.50	.45

1999 Sports Illustrated One's To Watch

Featuring a selection of the league's top young prospects, these silver board foil cards were seeded into packs at consumer friendly 1:12 rate. In addition, young slugger J.D. Drew signed 250 serial-numbered cards, of which were randomly seeded into packs.

	Nm-Mt	Ex-Mt
COMPLETE SET (15)	20.00	6.00
1 J.D. Drew	1.50	.45
2 Marlon Anderson	1.00	.30
3 Roy Halladay	1.50	.45
4 Ben Grieve	1.00	.30
5 Todd Helton	2.50	.75
6 Gabe Kapler	1.00	.30
7 Troy Glaus	4.00	1.20
8 Ben Davis	1.00	.30
9 Eric Chavez	1.50	.45
10 Richie Sexson	1.50	.45
11 Fernando Seguignol	1.00	.30
12 Kerry Wood	4.00	1.20
13 Bobby Smith	1.00	.30
14 Ryan Minor	1.00	.30
15 Jeremy Giambi	1.00	.30
NNO J.D. Drew AU/250	15.00	4.50

1999 Sports Illustrated Greats of the Game

The 1999 Sports Illustrated Greats of the Game (created by Fleer) was issued in one series totalling 90 cards and was distributed in seven-card packs with a suggested retail price of $15. The fronts feature color photos of some of Baseball's greatest players (including reproductions of numerous SI front covers). The backs carry player information.

	Nm-Mt	Ex-Mt
COMPLETE SET (90)	80.00	24.00
1 Jimmie Foxx	1.50	.45
2 Red Schoendienst	1.00	.30
3 Babe Ruth	5.00	1.50
4 Lou Gehrig	3.00	.90
5 Mel Ott	1.50	.45
6 Stan Musial	2.50	.75
7 Mickey Mantle	6.00	1.80
8 Carl Yastrzemski	2.50	.75
9 Enos Slaughter	.60	.18
10 Andre Dawson	.60	.18
11 Luis Aparicio	.60	.18
12 Ferguson Jenkins	.60	.18
13 Christy Mathewson	1.50	.45
14 Ernie Banks	1.50	.45
15 Johnny Podres	.60	.18
16 George Foster	.60	.18
17 Jerry Koosman	.60	.18
18 Curt Simmons	.40	.12
19 Bob Feller	1.00	.30
20 Frank Robinson	1.00	.30
21 Gary Carter	1.00	.30
22 Frank Thomas	.40	.12
23 Bill Lee	.60	.18
24 Willie Mays	3.00	.90
25 Tommie Agee	.60	.18
26 Boog Powell	.60	.18
27 Jim Wynn	.60	.18
28 Sparky Lyle	.60	.18
29 Bo Belinsky	.40	.12
30 Maury Wills	.60	.18
31 Bill Buckner	.60	.18
32 Steve Carlton	.60	.18
33 Harmon Killebrew	1.50	.45
34 Nolan Ryan	4.00	1.20
35 Randy Jones	.40	.12
36 Robin Roberts	.60	.18
37 Al Oliver	.60	.18
38 Rico Petrocelli	.40	.12
39 Dave Parker	.60	.18
40 Eddie Mathews	1.50	.45
41 Earl Weaver	.60	.18
42 Jackie Robinson	2.00	.60
43 Lou Brock	1.00	.30
44 Reggie Jackson	1.00	.30
45 Bob Gibson	1.00	.30
46 Jeff Burroughs	.40	.12
47 Jim Bouton	.60	.18
48 Bob Forsch	.40	.12
49 Ron Guidry	.60	.18
50 Ty Cobb	2.50	.75
51 Roy White	.60	.18
52 Joe Rudi	.60	.18
53 Moose Skowron	.60	.18
54 Goose Gossage	.60	.18
55 Ed Kranepool	.40	.12
56 Paul Blair	.40	.12
57 Kent Hrbek	.60	.18
58 Orlando Cepeda	.60	.18
59 Buck O'Neill	.60	.18
60 Al Kaline	1.50	.45
61 Vida Blue	.60	.18
62 Sam McDowell	.40	.12
63 Jesse Barfield	.40	.12
64 Dave Kingman	.60	.18
65 Ron Santo	1.00	.30
66 Steve Garvey	.60	.18
67 Gaylord Perry	.60	.18
68 Darrell Evans	.60	.18
69 Rollie Fingers	.60	.18
70 Walter Johnson	1.50	.45
71 Al Hrabosky	.60	.18
72 Mickey Rivers	.40	.12
73 Mike Torrez	.40	.12
74 Hank Bauer	.60	.18
75 Tug McGraw	.60	.18
76 David Clyde	.40	.12
77 Jim Lonborg	.40	.12
78 Clete Boyer	.60	.18
79 Harry Walker	.40	.12
80 Cy Young	1.50	.45
81 Bud Harrelson	.40	.12
82 Paul Splittorff	.40	.12
83 Bert Campaneris	.60	.18
84 Joe Niekro	.60	.18
85 Bob Horner	.60	.18
86 Jerry Royster	.40	.12
87 Tommy John	.60	.18
88 Mark Fidrych	.60	.18
89 Dick Williams	.60	.18
90 Graig Nettles	.60	.18

1999 Sports Illustrated Greats of the Game Autographs

Inserted one per pack, this 80-card set features color photos of top former big league players with their autograph in the white bar below the photo. The cards are unnumbered and checklisted below in alphabetical order.

	Nm-Mt	Ex-Mt
1 Tommie Agee	15.00	4.50
2 Luis Aparicio	15.00	4.50
3 Ernie Banks	40.00	12.00
4 Jesse Barfield	8.00	2.40
5 Hank Bauer	15.00	4.50
6 Bo Belinsky	15.00	4.50
7 Paul Blair	8.00	2.40
8 Vida Blue	15.00	4.50
9 Jim Bouton	15.00	4.50
10 Clete Boyer	15.00	4.50
11 Lou Brock	25.00	7.50
12 Bill Buckner	15.00	4.50
13 Jeff Burroughs	8.00	2.40
14 Bert Campaneris	15.00	4.50
15 Steve Carlton	25.00	7.50
16 Gary Carter	25.00	7.50
17 Orlando Cepeda	15.00	4.50
18 David Clyde	8.00	2.40
19 Andre Dawson	15.00	4.50
20 Darrell Evans	15.00	4.50
21 Bob Feller	25.00	7.50
22 Mark Fidrych	25.00	7.50
23 Rollie Fingers	15.00	4.50
24 Bob Forsch	8.00	2.40
25 George Foster	15.00	4.50
26 Steve Garvey	15.00	4.50
27 Bob Gibson	25.00	7.50
28 Goose Gossage	15.00	4.50
29 Ron Guidry	15.00	4.50
30 Bud Harrelson	15.00	4.50
31 Bob Horner	15.00	4.50
32 Al Hrabosky	15.00	4.50
33 Kent Hrbek	15.00	4.50
34A Reggie Jackson	120.00	36.00
34B Reggie Jackson	250.00	75.00
Mr. October		
34C Reggie Jackson	250.00	75.00
HOF 93		
35 Ferguson Jenkins	15.00	4.50
36 Tommy John	15.00	4.50
37 Randy Jones	8.00	2.40
38 Al Kaline	40.00	12.00
39 Harmon Killebrew	40.00	12.00
40 Dave Kingman	15.00	4.50
41 Jerry Koosman	15.00	4.50
42 Ed Kranepool	15.00	4.50
43 Bill Lee	15.00	4.50
44 Jim Lonborg	8.00	2.40
45 Sparky Lyle	15.00	4.50
46 Eddie Mathews	100.00	30.00
47 Willie Mays	150.00	45.00
48 Sam McDowell	15.00	4.50
49 Tug McGraw	40.00	12.00
50 Stan Musial	100.00	30.00
51 Graig Nettles	15.00	4.50
52 Joe Niekro	15.00	4.50
53 Buck O'Neill	25.00	7.50
54 Al Oliver	15.00	4.50
55 Dave Parker	15.00	4.50
56 Gaylord Perry	15.00	4.50
57 Rico Petrocelli	15.00	4.50
58 Johnny Podres	25.00	7.50
59 Boog Powell	25.00	7.50
60 Mickey Rivers	15.00	4.50
61 Robin Roberts	25.00	7.50
62 Frank Robinson	25.00	7.50
63 Jerry Royster	8.00	2.40
64 Joe Rudi	15.00	4.50
65 Nolan Ryan	150.00	45.00
66 Ron Santo	25.00	7.50
67 Red Schoendienst	15.00	4.50
68 Curt Simmons	8.00	2.40
69 Moose Skowron	25.00	7.50
70 Enos Slaughter	25.00	7.50
71 Paul Splittorff	8.00	2.40
72 Frank Thomas	8.00	2.40
73 Mike Torrez	8.00	2.40
74 Harry Walker	8.00	2.40
75 Earl Weaver	15.00	4.50
76 Roy White	15.00	4.50

77 Dick Williams 15.00 4.50
78 Maury Wills 15.00 4.50
79 Jim Wynn 15.00 4.50
80 Carl Yastrzemski 60.00 18.00

1999 Sports Illustrated Greats of the Game Cover Collection

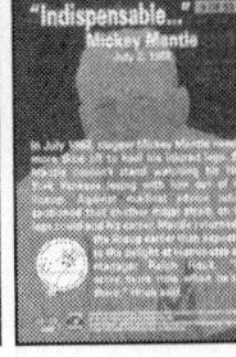

Randomly inserted one per pack, this 50-card set features reproductions of 50 classic Sports Illustrated covers covering over 40 years of baseball history.

	Nm-Mt	Ex-Mt
COMPLETE SET (50)	60.00	18.00
1 Johnny Podres	1.00	.30
2 Mickey Mantle	10.00	3.00
3 Stan Musial	4.00	1.20
4 Eddie Mathews	2.50	.75
5 Frank Thomas	.60	.18
6 Willie Mays	5.00	1.50
7 Red Schoendienst	1.50	.45
8 Luis Aparicio	1.00	.30
9 Mickey Mantle	10.00	3.00
10 Al Kaline	2.50	.75
11 Maury Wills	1.00	.30
12 Sam McDowell	.60	.18
13 Harry Walker	.60	.18
14 Carl Yastrzemski	4.00	1.20
15 Carl Yastrzemski	4.00	1.20
16 Lou Brock	1.50	.45
17 Ron Santo	1.50	.45
18 Reggie Jackson	1.50	.45
19 Frank Robinson	1.50	.45
20 Jerry Koosman	1.00	.30
21 Bud Harrelson	.60	.18
22 Vida Blue	1.00	.30
23 Ferguson Jenkins	1.00	.30
24 Sparky Lyle	1.00	.30
25 Steve Carlton	1.00	.30
26 Bert Campaneris	1.00	.30
27 Jim Wynn	1.00	.30
28 Steve Garvey	1.00	.30
29 Nolan Ryan	6.00	1.80
30 Randy Jones	.60	.18
31 Reggie Jackson	1.50	.45
32 Joe Rudi	1.00	.30
33 Reggie Jackson	1.50	.45
34 Dave Parker	1.00	.30
35 Mark Fidrych	1.00	.30
36 Earl Weaver	1.00	.30
37 Nolan Ryan	6.00	1.80
38 Steve Carlton	1.00	.30
39 Reggie Jackson	1.50	.45
40 Rollie Fingers	1.00	.30
41 Gary Carter	1.50	.45
42 Graig Nettles	1.00	.30
43 Gaylord Perry	1.00	.30
44 Kent Hrbek	1.00	.30
45 Gary Carter	1.50	.45
46 Steve Garvey	1.00	.30
47 Steve Carlton	1.00	.30
48 Nolan Ryan	6.00	1.80
49 Nolan Ryan	6.00	1.80
50 Mickey Mantle	10.00	3.00

1999 Sports Illustrated Greats of the Game Record Breakers

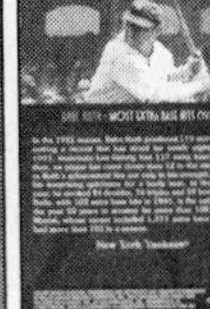

Randomly inserted in packs at the rate of one in 12, this 10-card set features action color photos of some of Baseball's record-setters printed on silver-foil stamped cards.

	Nm-Mt	Ex-Mt
COMPLETE SET (10)	120.00	36.00
*GOLD: 2X TO 5X BASIC RB'S		
GOLD STATED ODDS 1:120		
1 Mickey Mantle	30.00	9.00
2 Stan Musial	12.00	3.60
3 Babe Ruth	25.00	7.50
4 Christy Mathewson	8.00	2.40
5 Cy Young	8.00	2.40
6 Nolan Ryan	20.00	6.00
7 Jackie Robinson	10.00	3.00
8 Lou Gehrig	15.00	4.50
9 Ty Cobb	12.00	3.60
10 Walter Johnson	8.00	2.40

1998 Sports Illustrated Then and Now

The 1998 Sports Illustrated Then and Now set (created by Fleer) was issued in one series totalling 150 cards and was distributed in six-card packs containing five cards and one mini-poster with a suggested retail price of $1.99. The fronts feature color photos of active and retired players plus 1998 rookies and prospects. The backs carry ratings for each player in key skill areas. The set contains the topical subset: A Place in History (37-53) which displays statistical compairson between current players and retired greats. Notable Rookie Cards include Magglio Ordonez. An Alex Rodriguez checklist mini-poster was randomly seeded into 1:12 packs. In addition, an Alex Rodriguez promo card was distributed to dealers and hobby media several weeks to the product's release.

	Nm-Mt	Ex-Mt
COMPLETE SET (150)	25.00	7.50
1 Luis Aparicio	.30	.09
2 Richie Ashburn	.50	.15
3 Ernie Banks	.75	.23
4 Yogi Berra	.75	.23
5 Lou Boudreau	.30	.09
6 Lou Brock	.50	.15
7 Jim Bunning	.30	.09
8 Rod Carew	.50	.15
9 Bob Feller	.50	.15
10 Rollie Fingers	.30	.09
11 Bob Gibson	.50	.15
12 Ferguson Jenkins	.30	.09
13 Al Kaline	.75	.23
14 George Kell	.50	.15
15 Harmon Killebrew	.75	.23
16 Ralph Kiner	.30	.09
17 Tommy Lasorda	.30	.09
18 Juan Marichal	.30	.09
19 Eddie Mathews	.75	.23
20 Willie Mays	1.50	.45
21 Willie McCovey	.30	.09
22 Joe Morgan	.30	.09
23 Gaylord Perry	.30	.09
24 Kirby Puckett	.75	.23
25 Pee Wee Reese	.50	.15
26 Phil Rizzuto	.50	.15
27 Robin Roberts	.30	.09
28 Brooks Robinson	.75	.23
29 Frank Robinson	.50	.15
30 Red Schoendienst	.30	.09
31 Enos Slaughter	.30	.09
32 Warren Spahn	.50	.15
33 Willie Stargell	.50	.15
34 Earl Weaver	.30	.09
35 Billy Williams	.30	.09
36 Early Wynn	.30	.09
37 R. Henderson HIST	.50	.15
38 Greg Maddux HIST	.75	.23
39 Mike Mussina HIST	.50	.15
40 Cal Ripken HIST	1.25	.35
41 Albert Belle HIST	.30	.09
42 Frank Thomas HIST	.50	.15
43 Jeff Bagwell HIST	.30	.09
44 Paul Molitor HIST	.30	.09
45 Chuck Knoblauch HIST	.30	.09
46 Todd Hundley HIST	.30	.09
47 Bernie Williams HIST	.30	.09
48 Tony Gwynn HIST	.50	.15
49 Barry Bonds HIST	.75	.23
50 Ken Griffey Jr. HIST	.75	.23
51 Randy Johnson HIST	.50	.15
52 Mark McGwire HIST	1.00	.30
53 Roger Clemens HIST	.75	.23
54 Jose Cruz Jr. HIST	.30	.09
55 Roberto Alomar	.75	.23
56 Sandy Alomar Jr.	.30	.09
57 Brady Anderson	.30	.09
58 Kevin Appier	.30	.09
59 Jeff Bagwell	.50	.15
60 Albert Belle	.30	.09
61 Dante Bichette	.30	.09
62 Craig Biggio	.50	.15
63 Barry Bonds	2.00	.60
64 Kevin Brown	.50	.15
65 Jay Buhner	.30	.09
66 Ellis Burks	.30	.09
67 Ken Caminiti	.30	.09
68 Jose Canseco	.75	.23
69 Joe Carter	.30	.09
70 Vinny Castilla	.30	.09
71 Tony Clark	.30	.09
72 Roger Clemens	1.50	.45
73 David Cone	.30	.09
74 Jose Cruz Jr.	.30	.09
75 Jason Dickson	.30	.09
76 Jim Edmonds	.30	.09
77 Scott Erickson	.30	.09
78 Darin Erstad	.30	.09
79 Alex Fernandez	.30	.09
80 Steve Finley	.30	.09
81 Travis Fryman	.30	.09
82 Andres Galarraga	.30	.09
83 Nomar Garciaparra	1.25	.35
84 Tom Glavine	.50	.15
85 Juan Gonzalez	.75	.23
86 Mark Grace	.50	.15
87 Willie Greene	.30	.09
88 Ken Griffey Jr.	1.25	.35
89 Vladimir Guerrero	.75	.23
90 Tony Gwynn	1.00	.30
91 Livan Hernandez	.30	.09
92 Bobby Higginson	.30	.09
93 Derek Jeter	2.00	.60
94 Charles Johnson	.30	.09
95 Randy Johnson	.75	.23
96 Andruw Jones	.30	.09
97 Chipper Jones	.75	.23
98 David Justice	.30	.09
99 Eric Karros	.30	.09
100 Jason Kendall	.30	.09
101 Jimmy Key	.30	.09
102 Darryl Kile	.30	.09
103 Chuck Knoblauch	.30	.09
104 Ray Lankford	.30	.09
105 Barry Larkin	.75	.23
106 Kenny Lofton	.30	.09
107 Greg Maddux	1.25	.35
108 Al Martin	.30	.09
109 Edgar Martinez	.50	.15
110 Pedro Martinez	.75	.23
111 Ramon Martinez	.30	.09
112 Tino Martinez	.50	.15
113 Mark McGwire	2.00	.60
114 Raul Mondesi	.30	.09
115 Matt Morris	.30	.09
116 Charles Nagy	.30	.09
117 Denny Neagle	.30	.09
118 Hideo Nomo	.75	.23
119 Dean Palmer	.30	.09
120 Andy Pettitte	.50	.15
121 Mike Piazza	1.25	.35
122 Manny Ramirez	.30	.09
123 Edgar Renteria	.30	.09
124 Cal Ripken	2.50	.75
125 Alex Rodriguez	1.25	.35
126 Henry Rodriguez	.30	.09
127 Ivan Rodriguez	.75	.23
128 Scott Rolen	.50	.15
129 Tim Salmon	.50	.15
130 Curt Schilling	.50	.15
131 Gary Sheffield	.30	.09
132 John Smoltz	.50	.15
133 Sammy Sosa	1.25	.35
134 Frank Thomas	.75	.23
135 Jim Thome	.75	.23
136 Mo Vaughn	.30	.09
137 Robin Ventura	.30	.09
138 Larry Walker	.50	.15
139 Bernie Williams	.50	.15
140 Matt Williams	.30	.09
141 Jaret Wright	.30	.09
142 Michael Coleman	.30	.09
143 Juan Encarnacion	.30	.09
144 Brad Fullmer	.30	.09
145 Ben Grieve	.30	.09
146 Todd Helton	.50	.15
147 Paul Konerko	.30	.09
148 Derrek Lee	.30	.09
149 Magglio Ordonez RC	2.00	.60
150 Enrique Wilson	.30	.09
P125 A. Rodriguez PROMO	2.00	.60
NNO Alex Rodriguez CL	.50	.15

1998 Sports Illustrated Then and Now Extra Edition

Randomly inserted in packs, this 150-card set ia parallel to the base set and is distinguished by the "Extra Edition" stamp on the front. Only 500 sets were produced and each card is serial numbered on back.

	Nm-Mt	Ex-Mt
*STARS: 4X TO 10X BASIC CARDS		
*ROOKIES: 3X TO 8X BASIC CARDS		

1998 Sports Illustrated Then and Now Art of the Game

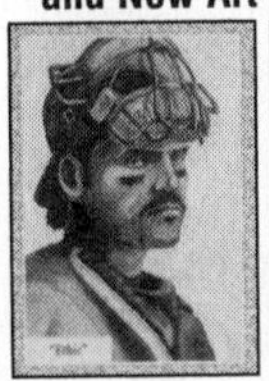
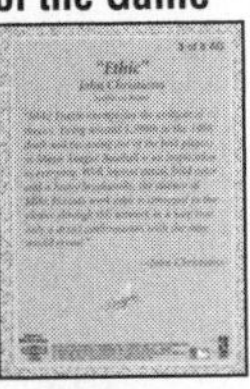

Randomly inserted in packs at the rate of one in nine, this eight-card set features reproductions of original artwork of past and present baseball heroes by eight popular sports artists.

	Nm-Mt	Ex-Mt
COMPLETE SET (8)	20.00	6.00
AG1 Ken Griffey Jr.	3.00	.90
AG2 Alex Rodriguez	3.00	.90
AG3 Mike Piazza	3.00	.90
AG4 Brooks Robinson	2.00	.60
AG5 David Justice	.75	.23
AG6 Cal Ripken	6.00	1.80
AG7 Prospect 'n Prospector	.75	.23
AG8 Barry Bonds	5.00	1.50

1998 Sports Illustrated Then and Now Autographs

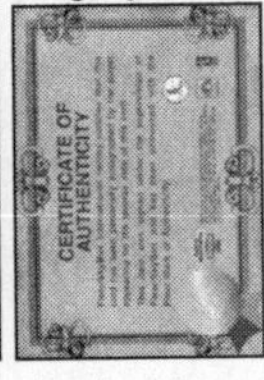

These six different signed cards were distributed via mail to lucky collectors that sent in an Autograph Redemption card prior to the November 1st, 1999 deadline. Each card is embossed with a Fleer logo for authenticity. Each player signed a total of 250 cards, except for Bob Gibson and Harmon Killebrew who each signed 500 cards.

	Nm-Mt	Ex-Mt
*EXCHANGE: .1X TO .25X BASIC AUTO		
1 Roger Clemens/250	120.00	36.00
2 Bob Gibson/500	40.00	12.00
3 Tony Gwynn/250	100.00	30.00
4 Harmon Killebrew/500	40.00	12.00
5 Willie Mays/250	150.00	45.00
6 Scott Rolen/250	40.00	12.00

1998 Sports Illustrated Then and Now Autograph Redemptions

Randomly inserted in packs, these six different redemption cards could be exchanged prior to the November 1st, 1999 deadline for special signed cards. Four of the six cards in the set (numbers 2, 3, 4 and 5) were serial numbered by hand to 250. The other two cards (numbers 1 and 6) were serial numbered by hand to 500. All of the cards except for Gibson and Rolen utilize the same card fronts as seen in the more common Covers insert set (featuring reproductions of classic SI covers). The Gibson and Rolen cards feature unique card fronts. All six card backs feature guidelines for the exchange program. The cards are unnumbered and checklisted below alphabetically.

	Nm-Mt	Ex-Mt
*EXCHANGE CARDS: .1X TO .25X BASIC AU'S		

1998 Sports Illustrated Then and Now Covers

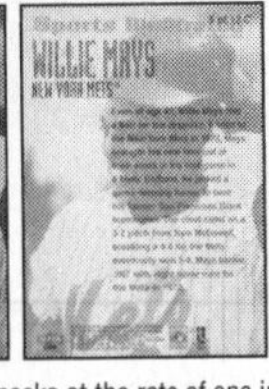

Randomly inserted in packs at the rate of one in 18, this 12-card set features color photos printed as Sports Illustrated Covers of six active and six retired players.

	Nm-Mt	Ex-Mt
COMPLETE SET (12)	80.00	24.00
C1 Lou Brock	3.00	.90
C2 Kirby Puckett	5.00	1.50
C3 Harmon Killebrew	5.00	1.50
C4 Eddie Mathews	5.00	1.50
C5 Willie Mays	10.00	3.00
C6 Frank Robinson	3.00	.90
C7 Cal Ripken	15.00	4.50
C8 Roger Clemens	10.00	3.00
C9 Ken Griffey Jr.	8.00	2.40
C10 Mark McGwire	12.00	3.60
C11 Tony Gwynn	6.00	1.80
C12 Ivan Rodriguez	5.00	1.50

1998 Sports Illustrated Then and Now Great Shots

Inserted one in every pack, this 25-card set features Sports Illustrated photos of top players on fold-out blank-backed mini-posters that measure approximately 5" by 7".

	Nm-Mt	Ex-Mt
COMPLETE SET (25)	10.00	3.00
1 Ken Griffey Jr.	.75	.23
2 Frank Thomas	.50	.15
3 Alex Rodriguez	.75	.23
4 Andruw Jones	.20	.06
5 Chipper Jones	.50	.15
6 Cal Ripken	1.50	.45
7 Mark McGwire	1.25	.35
8 Derek Jeter	1.25	.35
9 Greg Maddux	.75	.23
10 Jeff Bagwell	.30	.09
11 Mike Piazza	.75	.23
12 Scott Rolen	.30	.09
13 Nomar Garciaparra	.75	.23
14 Jose Cruz Jr.	.20	.06
15 Charles Johnson	.20	.06
16 Fergie Jenkins	.20	.06
17 Lou Brock	.30	.09
18 Bob Gibson	.30	.09
19 Harmon Killebrew	.50	.15
20 Juan Marichal	.20	.06
21 Brooks Robinson / Frank Robinson	.50	.15
22 Rod Carew	.30	.09
23 Yogi Berra	.50	.15
24 Willie Mays	1.00	.30
25 Kirby Puckett	.50	.15

1998 Sports Illustrated Then and Now Road to Cooperstown

Randomly inserted in packs at the rate of one in 24, this 10-card set features color photos of current players having Hall of Fame caliber careers.

	Nm-Mt	Ex-Mt
COMPLETE SET (10)	80.00	24.00
RC1 Barry Bonds	15.00	4.50
RC2 Roger Clemens	12.00	3.60
RC3 Ken Griffey Jr.	10.00	3.00
RC4 Tony Gwynn	8.00	2.40
RC5 Rickey Henderson	4.00	1.20
RC6 Greg Maddux	10.00	3.00
RC7 Paul Molitor	2.50	.75
RC8 Mike Piazza	10.00	3.00
RC9 Cal Ripken	20.00	6.00
RC10 Frank Thomas	6.00	1.80

1998 Sports Illustrated World Series Fever Postcard Promo

This one-card set was a promo postcard issued to advertise Fleer's Sports Illustrated World Series Fever '98 set that premiered on August 26, 1998. The front features a color action photo of Mark McGwire in a white border with a small head photo of Reggie Jackson in the bottom right. The white back advertises the Mr. October insert set of the World Series Fever '98 set. Only 3,500 of this set were produced and serially numbered.

	Nm-Mt	Ex-Mt
1 Mark McGwire	5.00	1.50

1998 Sports Illustrated World Series Fever

The 1998 Sports Illustrated World Series Fever set (created by Fleer) was issued in one series totalling 150 cards. The set contains the topical subsets: Covers (1-20), and Magnificent Moments (21-30). Notable Rookie Cards include Orlando Hernandez and Magglio Ordonez. A Cal Ripken promo card was distributed to dealers and hobby media to preview the brand a few month's before th product's national release. The promo is similar in design to the basic Ripken except for the text "PROMOTIONAL SAMPLE" running diagonally across the front and back of the card.

	Nm-Mt	Ex-Mt
COMPLETE SET (150)	25.00	7.50
1 Mickey Mantle COV	3.00	.90
2 W.S. Preview COV	.30	.09
3 W.S. Preview COV	.30	.09
4 Chicago (AL) COV	.30	.09
5 W.S. Preview COV	.30	.09
6 Lou Brock COV	.30	.09
7 Brooks Robinson COV	.50	.15
8 Frank Robinson COV	.30	.09
9 L.A. Oakland COV	.30	.09
10 Reggie Jackson COV	.30	.09
11 Kansas City COV	.30	.09
12 Minnesota COV	.30	.09
13 Orel Hershiser COV	.30	.09
14 Rickey Henderson COV	.50	.15
15 Minnesota COV	.30	.09
16 Toronto COV	.30	.09
17 Joe Carter COV	.30	.09
18 Atlanta COV	.30	.09
19 N.Y. Yankees COV	.30	.09
20 Edgar Renteria COV	.30	.09
21 Bill Mazeroski MM	.30	.09
22 Joe Carter MM	.30	.09
23 Carlton Fisk MM	.30	.09
24 Bucky Dent MM	.30	.09
25 Mookie Wilson MM	.30	.09
26 Enos Slaughter MM	.30	.09
27 Mickey Lolich MM	.30	.09
28 Bobby Richardson MM	.30	.09
29 Kirk Gibson MM	.30	.09
30 Edgar Renteria MM	.30	.09
31 Albert Belle	.30	.09
32 Kevin Brown	.50	.15
33 Brian Rose	.30	.09
34 Ron Gant	.30	.09
35 Jeromy Burnitz	.30	.09
36 Andres Galarraga	.30	.09
37 Jim Edmonds	.30	.09
38 Jose Cruz Jr.	.30	.09
39 Mark Grudzielanek	.30	.09
40 Shawn Estes	.30	.09
41 Mark Grace	.50	.15
42 Nomar Garciaparra	1.25	.35
43 Juan Gonzalez	.75	.23
44 Tom Glavine	.50	.15
45 Brady Anderson	.30	.09
46 Tony Clark	.30	.09
47 Jeff Cirillo	.30	.09
48 Dante Bichette	.30	.09
49 Ben Grieve	.30	.09
50 Ken Griffey Jr.	1.25	.35
51 Edgardo Alfonzo	.30	.09
52 Roger Clemens	1.50	.45
53 Pat Hentgen	.30	.09
54 Todd Helton	.50	.15
55 Andy Benes	.30	.09
56 Tony Gwynn	1.00	.30
57 Andruw Jones	.30	.09
58 Bobby Higginson	.30	.09
59 Bobby Jones	.30	.09
60 Darryl Kile	.30	.09
61 Chan Ho Park	.30	.09
62 Charles Johnson	.30	.09
63 Rusty Greer	.30	.09
64 Travis Fryman	.30	.09
65 Derek Jeter	2.00	.60
66 Jay Buhner	.30	.09
67 Chuck Knoblauch	.30	.09
68 David Justice	.30	.09

69 Brian Hunter .30 .09
70 Eric Karros .30 .09
71 Edgar Martinez .50 .15
72 Chipper Jones .75 .23
73 Barry Larkin .75 .23
74 Mike Lansing .30 .09
75 Craig Biggio .50 .15
76 Al Martin .30 .09
77 Barry Bonds 2.00 .60
78 Randy Johnson .75 .23
79 Ryan Klesko .30 .09
80 Mark McGwire 2.00 .60
81 Fred McGriff .50 .15
82 Javy Lopez .30 .09
83 Kenny Lofton .30 .09
84 Sandy Alomar Jr. .30 .09
85 Matt Morris .30 .09
86 Paul Konerko .30 .09
87 Ray Lankford .30 .09
88 Kerry Wood .75 .23
89 Roberto Alomar .75 .23
90 Greg Maddux 1.25 .35
91 Travis Lee .30 .09
92 Moises Alou .30 .09
93 Dean Palmer .30 .09
94 Hideo Nomo .75 .23
95 Ken Caminiti .30 .09
96 Pedro Martinez .75 .23
97 Raul Mondesi .30 .09
98 Denny Neagle .30 .09
99 Tino Martinez .50 .15
100 Mike Mussina .75 .23
101 Kevin Appier .30 .09
102 Vinny Castilla .30 .09
103 Jeff Bagwell .50 .15
104 Paul O'Neill .50 .15
105 Rey Ordonez .30 .09
106 Vladimir Guerrero .75 .23
107 Rafael Palmeiro .50 .15
108 Alex Rodriguez 1.25 .35
109 Andy Pettitte .50 .15
110 Carl Pavano .30 .09
111 Henry Rodriguez .30 .09
112 Gary Sheffield .30 .09
113 Curt Schilling .50 .15
114 John Smoltz .50 .15
115 Reggie Sanders .30 .09
116 Scott Rolen .50 .15
117 Mike Piazza 1.25 .35
118 Manny Ramirez .30 .09
119 Cal Ripken 2.50 .75
120 Brad Radke .30 .09
121 Tim Salmon .50 .15
122 Brett Tomko .30 .09
123 Robin Ventura .30 .09
124 Mo Vaughn .30 .09
125 A.J. Hinch .30 .09
126 Derrek Lee .30 .09
127 Orl. Hernandez RC .75 .23
128 Aramis Ramirez .30 .09
129 Frank Thomas .75 .23
130 J.T. Snow .30 .09
131 Maggio Ordonez RC 2.00 .60
132 Bobby Bonilla .30 .09
133 Marquis Grissom .30 .09
134 Jim Thome .75 .23
135 Justin Thompson .30 .09
136 Matt Williams .30 .09
137 Matt Stairs .30 .09
138 Wade Boggs .50 .15
139 Chuck Finley .30 .09
140 Jaret Wright .30 .09
141 Ivan Rodriguez .75 .23
142 Brad Fullmer .30 .09
143 Bernie Williams .50 .15
144 Jason Giambi .75 .23
145 Larry Walker .50 .15
146 Tony Womack .30 .09
147 Sammy Sosa 1.25 .35
148 Rondell White .30 .09
149 Todd Stottlemyre .30 .09
150 Shane Reynolds .30 .09
P8 Cal Ripken Promo 2.00 .60

1998 Sports Illustrated World Series Fever Extra Edition

This 150-card set is a parallel to the basic set. The cards are paralleled on gold holofoil and serially numbered to 98.

Nm-Mt Ex-Mt
*STARS: 10X TO 25X BASIC CARDS
*ROOKIES: 8X TO 20X BASIC CARDS

1998 Sports Illustrated World Series Fever Autumn Excellence

Randomly inserted in packs at a rate of 1:24, this set honors the great show Series records have stood the test of time.

Nm-Mt Ex-Mt
COMPLETE SET (10) 60.00 18.00
1 Willie Mays 8.00 2.40
2 Kirby Puckett 4.00 1.20
3 Babe Ruth 10.00 3.00
4 Reggie Jackson 2.50 .75
5 Whitey Ford 2.50 .75
6 Lou Brock 2.50 .75
7 Mickey Mantle 15.00 4.50
8 Yogi Berra 4.00 1.20
9 Bob Gibson 2.50 .75
10 Don Larsen 1.50 .45

1998 Sports Illustrated World Series Fever MVP Collection

Randomly inserted in packs at a rate of 1:4, this 10-card set profiles the Most Valuable Players from World Series history and how they achieved that status. The fronts feature color action photos with the player's name, team, and year he played in the World Series.

Nm-Mt Ex-Mt
COMPLETE SET (10) 8.00 2.40
1 Frank Robinson 1.25 .35
2 Brooks Robinson 2.00 .60
3 Willie Stargell 1.25 .35
4 Bret Saberhagen .75 .23
5 Rollie Fingers .75 .23
6 Orel Hershiser .75 .23
7 Paul Molitor 1.25 .35
8 Tom Glavine 1.25 .35
9 John Wetteland .75 .23
10 Livan Hernandez .75 .23

1998 Sports Illustrated World Series Fever Reggie Jackson's Picks

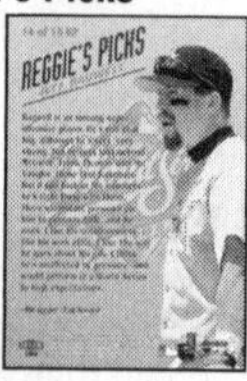

Randomly inserted in packs at a rate of 1:12, this 15-card set spotlights the World Series legend known as "Mr. October" as he gives his insight on current players he thinks can be World Series stars. The fronts feature an embossed player image and graphics.

Nm-Mt Ex-Mt
COMPLETE SET (15) 40.00 12.00
1 Paul O'Neill 1.50 .45
2 Barry Bonds 6.00 1.80
3 Ken Griffey Jr. 4.00 1.20
4 Juan Gonzalez 2.50 .75
5 Greg Maddux 4.00 1.20
6 Mike Piazza 4.00 1.20
7 Larry Walker 1.50 .45
8 Mo Vaughn 1.00 .30
9 Roger Clemens 5.00 1.50
10 John Smoltz 1.50 .45
11 Alex Rodriguez 4.00 1.20
12 Frank Thomas 2.50 .75
13 Mark McGwire 6.00 1.80
14 Jeff Bagwell 1.50 .45
15 Randy Johnson 2.50 .75

1968 Sports Memorabilia All-Time Greats

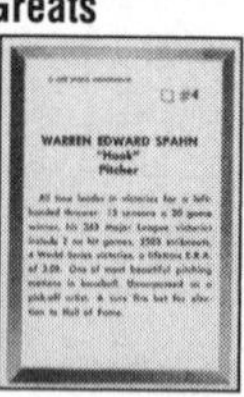

This 15-card standard-size set features some of the leading players of all-time. The fronts have crude drawings of the players, while the backs have a player biography. The drawings were done by sports artist Art Ouellette.

NM Ex
COMPLETE SET (15) 25.00 10.00
1 Checklist 1.00 .40
2 Connie Mack 1.50 .60
3 Walter Johnson 2.00 .80
4 Warren Spahn 1.50 .60
5 Christy Mathewson 2.00 .80
6 Lefty Grove 1.50 .60
7 Mickey Cochrane 1.00 .40
8 Bill Dickey 1.00 .40
9 Tris Speaker 1.50 .60
10 Ty Cobb 3.00 1.20
11 Babe Ruth 5.00 2.00
12 Lou Gehrig 3.00 1.20
13 Rogers Hornsby 2.00 .80
14 Honus Wagner 2.00 .80
15 Pie Traynor 1.00 .40

1987 Sports Reading

These 9" by 14" cards were issued to promote education and sports. They are part of of a reading series for schools. These cards all feature various fun facts about major leaguers. The cards have photos on both sides along with history about a specific event.

Nm-Mt Ex-Mt
COMPLETE SET 125.00 50.00
1 Carlos May .75 .30
2 Babe Ruth 15.00 6.00
3 Eddie Gaedel 2.00 .80
4 Cesar Gutierrez .75 .30
5 Ted Williams 12.00 4.80
6 Pete Gray 2.00 .80
7 Hank Aaron 10.00 4.00
8 Virgil Trucks .75 .30
9 Bob Gibson 4.00 1.60
10 Johnny Vander Meer .75 .30
11 Ron Hansen .75 .30
12 Roger Clemens 5.00 2.00
13 Dwight Gooden 1.00 .40
14 Jimmy Piersall .75 .30
15 Dale Long .75 .30
16 Herb Score .75 .30
17 Dizzy Dean 1.00 .40
Paul Dean
18 Stan Musial 8.00 3.20
19 Pete Rose 10.00 4.00
20 Cy Young 4.00 1.60
21 Don Mattingly 8.00 3.20
22 Pete Rose 10.00 4.00
Tom Seaver
Nolan Ryan
Phil Niekro
23 Minnie Minoso 1.00 .40
24 Walker Cooper .75 .30
Mort Cooper
25 Jim Thorpe 6.00 2.40
26 Robert Moses Grove 4.00 1.60
27 Roberto Clemente 12.00 4.80
28 Lou Gehrig 12.00 4.80
29 Shea Stadium, 1969 .75 .30
30 Yankee Stadium .75 .30
31 Carl Hubbell 3.00 1.20
32 Wade Boggs 3.00 1.20
33 Harvey Haddix .75 .30
34 Harold Reiser .75 .30
35 Jackie Robinson 12.00 4.80
36 Walter Johnson 4.00 1.60
37 The Hall of Fame .75 .30
38 Lou Boudreau 1.50 .60
39 Hank Greenberg 3.00 1.20
40 Fernando Valenzuela 1.00 .40

1973 Sports Scoop HOF Candidates

This 14-card set measures approximately 3 1/2" by 5 1/2" and features borderless black-and-white photos of National Baseball Hall of Fame Nominees according to Sports Scoop. The backs display the players name and why he might be considered for the Hall of Fame. The cards are unnumbered and checklisted below in alphabetical order.

NM Ex
COMPLETE SET (14) 12.00 4.80
1 Earl Averill 1.00 .40
2 Earl Averill 1.00 .40
3 Earl Averill 1.00 .40
4 George Burns .50 .20
5 Jack Fournier .50 .20
6 Jeff Heath .50 .20
7 Joe Jackson 4.00 1.60
8 Fred Lindstrom 1.00 .40
9 Fred Lindstrom 1.00 .40
10 Fred Lindstrom 1.00 .40
11 Barney McCoskey .50 .20
12 Johnny Mize 1.50 .60
13 Johnny Mize 1.50 .60
14 Johnny Mize 1.50 .60

1976 Sportstix

This set features color action photos of some of the favorite sport stars printed on various geometric shaped stickers with peel off backing. These are all that are known to date -- however, other groups may surface -- if so -- any additions to this checklist are appreciated.

NM Ex
COMPLETE SET (13) 125.00 50.00
1 Dave Kingman 10.00 4.00
2 Steve Busby 5.00 2.00
3 Bill Madlock 6.00 2.40
4 Jeff Burroughs 5.00 2.00
5 Ted Simmons 8.00 3.20
6 Randy Jones 5.00 2.00
7 Buddy Bell 6.00 2.40
8 Dave Cash 5.00 2.00
9 Jerry Grote 5.00 2.00
10 Dave Lopes 5.00 2.00
A Willie Mays 15.00 6.00
B Roberto Clemente 25.00 10.00
C Mickey Mantle 35.00 14.00

1986 Springhill Offset

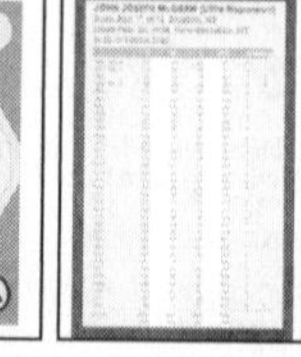

This five card set, which measures approximately 2 5/8" by 4 1/8" features a few retired players as well varying information about some information about what Springhill Offset could do. Since these cards are not numbered, we have sequenced them in alphabetical order

Nm-Mt Ex-Mt
COMPLETE SET (5) 8.00 2.40
1 Grover C. Alexander 1.50 .45
2 John McGraw 1.50 .45
3 Honus Wagner 2.50 .75
4 Cy Young 2.50 .75
5 Header Card .25 .07

1996 SPx

This 1996 SPx set (produced by Upper Deck) was issued in one series totalling 60 cards. The one-card packs had a suggested retail price of $3.49. Printed on 32 pt. card stock with Holoview technology and a perimeter diecut design, the set features color player photos with a Holography background on the fronts and decorative foil stamping on the back. Two special cards are included in the set: a Ken Griffey Jr. Commemorative card was inserted one in every 75 packs and a Mike Piazza Tribute card inserted one in every 95 packs. An autographed version of each of these cards was inserted at the rate of one in 2,000.

Nm-Mt Ex-Mt
COMPLETE SET (60) 50.00 15.00
1 Greg Maddux 3.00 .90
2 Chipper Jones 2.00 .60
3 Fred McGriff 1.25 .35
4 Tom Glavine 1.25 .35
5 Cal Ripken 6.00 1.80
6 Roberto Alomar 2.00 .60
7 Rafael Palmeiro 1.25 .35
8 Jose Canseco 2.00 .60
9 Roger Clemens 4.00 1.20
10 Mo Vaughn .75 .23
11 Jim Edmonds .75 .23
12 Tim Salmon 1.25 .35
13 Sammy Sosa 3.00 .90
14 Ryne Sandberg 3.00 .90
15 Mark Grace 1.25 .35
16 Frank Thomas 2.00 .60
17 Barry Larkin 2.00 .60
18 Kenny Lofton .75 .23
19 Albert Belle .75 .23
20 Eddie Murray 2.00 .60
21 Manny Ramirez .75 .23
22 Dante Bichette .75 .23
23 Larry Walker 1.25 .35
24 Vinny Castilla .75 .23
25 Andres Galarraga .75 .23
26 Cecil Fielder .75 .23
27 Gary Sheffield .75 .23
28 Craig Biggio 1.25 .35
29 Jeff Bagwell 1.25 .35
30 Derek Bell .75 .23
31 Johnny Damon .75 .23
32 Eric Karros .75 .23
33 Mike Piazza 3.00 .90
34 Raul Mondesi .75 .23
35 Hideo Nomo 2.00 .60
36 Kirby Puckett 2.00 .60
37 Paul Molitor 1.25 .35
38 Marty Cordova .75 .23
39 Rondell White .75 .23
40 Jason Isringhausen .75 .23
41 Paul Wilson .75 .23
42 Rey Ordonez .75 .23
43 Derek Jeter 5.00 1.50
44 Wade Boggs 1.25 .35
45 Mark McGwire 5.00 1.50
46 Jason Kendall .75 .23
47 Ron Gant .75 .23
48 Ozzie Smith 3.00 .90
49 Tony Gwynn 2.50 .75
50 Ken Caminiti .75 .23
51 Barry Bonds 5.00 1.50
52 Matt Williams .75 .23
53 Osvaldo Fernandez .75 .23
54 Jay Buhner .75 .23
55 Ken Griffey Jr. 3.00 .90
56 Randy Johnson 2.00 .60
57 Alex Rodriguez 4.00 1.20
58 Juan Gonzalez 2.00 .60
59 Joe Carter .75 .23
60 Carlos Delgado .75 .23
KG1 K.Griffey Jr. Comm. 5.00 1.50
MP1 Mike Piazza Trib. 5.00 1.50
KGA1 Ken Griffey Jr. Auto. 150.00 45.00
MPA1 Mike Piazza Auto. 300.00 90.00

1996 SPx Gold

Parallel to the regular version, this 60-card set was randomly inserted in hobby packs only at a rate of one in seven. The design is similar to the regular set with the exception being the gold foil borders on front.

Nm-Mt Ex-Mt
*STARS: 1.25X TO 3X BASIC CARDS

1996 SPx Bound for Glory

Randomly inserted in packs at a rate of one in 24, this 10-card set features players with a chance to be long remembered.

Nm-Mt Ex-Mt
COMPLETE SET (10) 80.00 24.00
1 Ken Griffey Jr. 8.00 2.40
2 Frank Thomas 5.00 1.50
3 Barry Bonds 12.00 3.60
4 Cal Ripken 15.00 4.50
5 Greg Maddux 8.00 2.40
6 Chipper Jones 5.00 1.50
7 Roberto Alomar 5.00 1.50
8 Manny Ramirez 2.00 .60
9 Tony Gwynn 6.00 1.80
10 Mike Piazza 8.00 2.40

1997 SPx

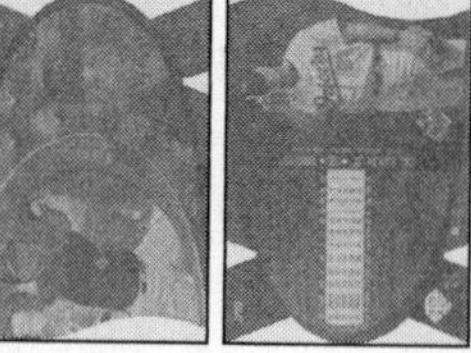

The 1997 SPx set (produced by Upper Deck) was issued in one series totalling 50 cards and was distributed in three-card hobby only packs with a suggested retail price of $5.99. The fronts feature color player images on a Holoview perimeter die cut design. The backs carry a player photo, player information, and career statistics. A sample card featuring Ken Griffey Jr. was distribued to dealers and hobby media several weeks prior to the products release.

Nm-Mt Ex-Mt
COMPLETE SET (50) 60.00 18.00
1 Eddie Murray 1.50 .45
2 Darin Erstad .60 .18
3 Tim Salmon 1.00 .30
4 Andruw Jones .60 .18
5 Chipper Jones 1.50 .45
6 John Smoltz 1.00 .30
7 Greg Maddux 2.50 .75
8 Kenny Lofton .60 .18
9 Roberto Alomar 1.50 .45
10 Rafael Palmeiro 1.00 .30
11 Brady Anderson .60 .18
12 Cal Ripken 5.00 1.50
13 Nomar Garciaparra 2.50 .75
14 Mo Vaughn .60 .18
15 Ryne Sandberg 2.50 .75
16 Sammy Sosa 2.50 .75
17 Frank Thomas 1.50 .45
18 Albert Belle .60 .18
19 Barry Larkin 1.50 .45
20 Deion Sanders 1.00 .30
21 Manny Ramirez .60 .18
22 Jim Thome 1.50 .45
23 Dante Bichette .60 .18
24 Andres Galarraga .60 .18
25 Larry Walker 1.00 .30
26 Gary Sheffield .60 .18
27 Jeff Bagwell 1.00 .30
28 Raul Mondesi .60 .18
29 Hideo Nomo 1.50 .45
30 Mike Piazza 2.50 .75
31 Paul Molitor 1.00 .30
32 Todd Walker .60 .18
33 Vladimir Guerrero 1.50 .45
34 Todd Hundley .60 .18
35 Andy Pettitte 1.00 .30
36 Derek Jeter 4.00 1.20
37 Jose Canseco 1.50 .45
38 Mark McGwire 4.00 1.20
39 Scott Rolen 1.00 .30
40 Ron Gant .60 .18
41 Ken Caminiti .60 .18
42 Tony Gwynn 2.00 .60
43 Barry Bonds 4.00 1.20
44 Jay Buhner .60 .18
45 Ken Griffey Jr. 2.50 .75
46 Alex Rodriguez 2.50 .75
47 Jose Cruz Jr. RC 2.50 .75
48 Juan Gonzalez 1.50 .45
49 Ivan Rodriguez 1.50 .45
50 Roger Clemens 3.00 .90
S45 Ken Griffey Jr. Sample 2.00 .60

1997 SPx Bronze

Randomly inserted in packs at the approximate rate of one in three, cards from this 50-card set are a parallel version of the base set with bronze etched foil enhancements.

Nm-Mt Ex-Mt
*STARS: 1X TO 2.5X BASIC CARDS
*ROOKIES: .6X TO 1.5X BASIC CARDS

1997 SPx Gold

Randomly inserted in packs at the rate of one in 17, This 50-card set is parallel to the base set and features etched gold foil enhancements.

Nm-Mt Ex-Mt
*STARS: 2.5X TO 6X BASIC CARDS
*ROOKIES: 1.5X TO 4X BASIC CARDS

1997 SPx Grand Finale

Randomly inserted in packs, cards from this 50-card set are an extremely limited edition parallel version of the base set and features an all gold holoview image. Only 50 of each card was produced. The set was entitled Grand Finale to signify the fact that this would be the last baseball product Upper Deck would ever use the holoview technology on.

Nm-Mt Ex-Mt
*STARS: 12.5X TO 30X BASIC CARDS
*ROOKIES: 5X TO 12X BASIC CARDS

1997 SPx Silver

Randomly inserted in packs at an approximate rate of one in six, cards from this 50-card set are a parallel version of the base set with etched silver foil enhancements.

Nm-Mt Ex-Mt
*STARS: 1.5X TO 4X BASIC CARDS
*ROOKIES: 1X TO 2.5X BASIC CARDS

1997 SPx Steel

Randomly inserted one in approximately one in every two packs, cards from this 50-card set are a parallel version of the base set. Many dealers and collectors believe that cards numbered 25-50 were printed in shorter supply. These cards can be distinguished from the similar looking silver cards by the holographic background behind the SPx logo and the player's number. Silvers lack the holographic background behind the SPx logo.

Nm-Mt Ex-Mt
*STARS: .6X TO 1.5X BASIC CARDS ..
*ROOKIES: .5X TO 1.2X BASIC CARDS

1997 SPx Bound for Glory

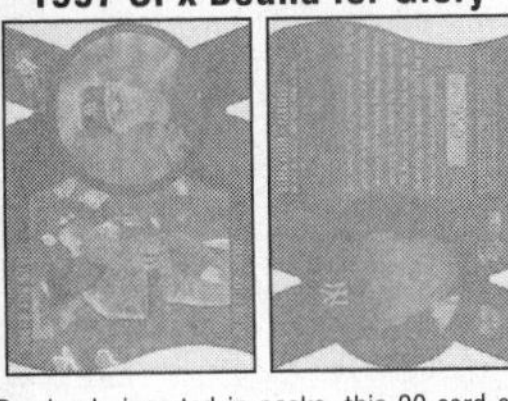

Randomly inserted in packs, this 20-card set features color photos of promising great players on a Holoview die cut card design. Only 1,500 of each card was produced and are sequentially numbered.

	Nm-Mt	Ex-Mt
COMPLETE SET (20)	250.00	75.00
1 Andruw Jones	4.00	1.20
2 Chipper Jones	10.00	3.00
3 Greg Maddux	15.00	4.50
4 Kenny Lofton	4.00	1.20
5 Cal Ripken	30.00	9.00
6 Mo Vaughn	4.00	1.20
7 Frank Thomas	10.00	3.00
8 Albert Belle	4.00	1.20
9 Manny Ramirez	4.00	1.20
10 Gary Sheffield	4.00	1.20
11 Jeff Bagwell	6.00	1.80
12 Mike Piazza	15.00	4.50
13 Derek Jeter	25.00	7.50
14 Mark McGwire	25.00	7.50
15 Tony Gwynn	12.00	3.60
16 Ken Caminiti	4.00	1.20
17 Barry Bonds	25.00	7.50
18 Alex Rodriguez	15.00	4.50
19 Ken Griffey Jr.	15.00	4.50
20 Juan Gonzalez	10.00	3.00

1997 SPx Bound for Glory Supreme Signatures

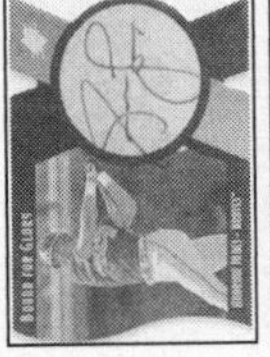

Randomly inserted in packs, this five-card set features unnumbered autographed Bound for Glory cards. Only 250 of each card was produced and signed and are sequentially numbered. The cards are checklisted below in alphabetical order.

	Nm-Mt	Ex-Mt
1 Jeff Bagwell	80.00	24.00
2 Ken Griffey Jr.	200.00	60.00
3 Andruw Jones	60.00	18.00
4 Alex Rodriguez	200.00	60.00
5 Gary Sheffield	60.00	18.00

1997 SPx Cornerstones of the Game

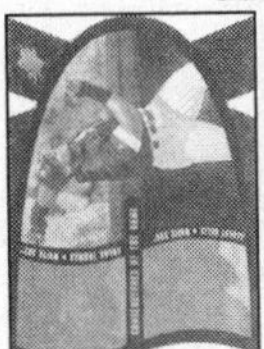

Randomly inserted in packs, cards from this 10-card set display color photos of 20 top players. Two players are featured on each card using double Holoview technology. Only 500 of each card was produced and each is sequentially numbered on back.

	Nm-Mt	Ex-Mt
COMPLETE SET (10)	250.00	75.00
1 Ken Griffey Jr. / Barry Bonds	25.00	7.50
2 Frank Thomas / Albert Belle	15.00	4.50
3 Chipper Jones / Greg Maddux	25.00	7.50
4 Tony Gwynn / Paul Molitor	20.00	6.00
5 Andruw Jones / Vladimir Guerrero	15.00	4.50
6 Jeff Bagwell / Ryne Sandberg	25.00	7.50
7 Mike Piazza / Ivan Rodriguez	25.00	7.50
8 Cal Ripken / Eddie Murray	50.00	15.00
9 Mo Vaughn / Mark McGwire	40.00	12.00
10 Alex Rodriguez / Derek Jeter	40.00	12.00

1998 SPx Finite Sample

A special Ken Griffey Jr. card serial numbered of 10,000 was issued as a promotional card and distributed within a silver foil wrapper along with a black and white information card to dealers with their first series order forms and at major industry events. The card is similar to Griffey's basic issue first series SPx Finite card (number 130) except for the lack of a card number on back, serial numbering to 10,000 coupled with the word "FINITE" running boldly across the back of the card in a diagonal manner.

	Nm-Mt	Ex-Mt
NNO Ken Griffey Jr.	5.00	1.50

1998 SPx Finite

The 1998 SPx Finite set contains a total of 180 cards, all serial numbered based upon specific subsets. The three-card packs retailed for $5.99 each and hit the market in June, 1998. The subsets and serial numbering are as follows: Youth Movement (1-30) - 5000 of each card, Power Explosion (31-50) - 4000 of each card, Basic Cards (51-140) - 9000 of each card, Star Focus (141-170) - 7000 of each card, Heroes of the Game (171-180) - 2000 of each card, Youth Movement (181-210) - 5000 of each card, Power Passion (211-240) - 7000 of each card, Basic Cards (241-330) - 9000 of each card, Tradewinds (331-350) - 4000 of each card and Cornerstones of the Game (351-360) -2000 of each card. Notable Rookie Cards include Kevin Millwood and Magglio Ordonez.

	Nm-Mt	Ex-Mt
COMP.YM SER.1 (30)	40.00	12.00
COMMON YM (1-30)	1.50	.45
COMP.PE SER.1 (20)	120.00	36.00
COMMON PE (31-50)	2.50	.75
COMP.BASIC SER.1 (90)	80.00	24.00
COMMON CARD (51-140)	1.00	.30
COMP.SF SER.1 (30)	100.00	30.00
COMMON SF (141-170)	1.25	.35
COMP.HG SER.1 (10)	150.00	45.00
COMMON HG (171-180)	10.00	3.00
COMP.YM SER.2 (30)	60.00	18.00
COMMON YM (181-210)	1.50	.45
COMP.PP SER.2 (30)	80.00	24.00
COMMON PP (211-240)	1.25	.35
COMP.BASIC SER.2 (90)	50.00	15.00
COMMON (241-330)	1.00	.30
COMP.TW SER.2 (20)	30.00	9.00
COMMON TW (331-350)	2.50	.75
COMP.CG SER.2 (10)	150.00	45.00
COMMON CG (351-360)	4.00	1.20
1 Nomar Garciaparra YM	6.00	1.80
2 Miguel Tejada YM	2.50	.75
3 Mike Cameron YM	1.50	.45
4 Ken Cloude YM	1.50	.45
5 Jaret Wright YM	1.50	.45
6 Mark Kotsay YM	1.50	.45
7 Craig Counsell YM	1.50	.45
8 Jose Guillen YM	1.50	.45
9 Neifi Perez YM	1.50	.45
10 Jose Cruz Jr. YM	1.50	.45
11 Brett Tomko YM	1.50	.45
12 Matt Morris YM	1.50	.45
13 Justin Thompson YM	1.50	.45
14 Jeremi Gonzalez YM	1.50	.45
15 Scott Rolen YM	2.50	.75
16 Vladimir Guerrero YM	4.00	1.20
17 Brad Fullmer YM	1.50	.45
18 Brian Giles YM	1.50	.45
19 Todd Dunwoody YM	1.50	.45
20 Ben Grieve YM	1.50	.45
21 Juan Encarnacion YM	1.50	.45
22 Aaron Boone YM	1.50	.45
23 Richie Sexson YM	1.50	.45
24 Richard Hidalgo YM	1.50	.45
25 Andruw Jones YM	1.50	.45
26 Todd Helton YM	2.50	.75
27 Paul Konerko YM	1.50	.45
28 Dante Powell YM	1.50	.45
29 Eli Marrero YM	1.50	.45
30 Derek Jeter YM	10.00	3.00
31 Mike Piazza PE	10.00	3.00
32 Tony Clark PE	2.50	.75
33 Larry Walker PE	4.00	1.20
34 Jim Thome PE	6.00	1.80
35 Juan Gonzalez PE	5.00	1.50
36 Jeff Bagwell PE	4.00	1.20
37 Jay Buhner PE	2.50	.75
38 Tim Salmon PE	4.00	1.20
39 Albert Belle PE	2.50	.75
40 Mark McGwire PE	15.00	4.50
41 Sammy Sosa PE	10.00	3.00
42 Mo Vaughn PE	2.50	.75
43 Manny Ramirez PE	2.50	.75
44 Tino Martinez PE	4.00	1.20
45 Frank Thomas PE	6.00	1.80
46 Nomar Garciaparra PE	10.00	3.00
47 Alex Rodriguez PE	10.00	3.00
48 Chipper Jones PE	6.00	1.80
49 Barry Bonds PE	15.00	4.50
50 Ken Griffey Jr. PE	10.00	3.00
51 Jason Dickson	1.00	.30
52 Jim Edmonds	1.00	.30
53 Darin Erstad	1.00	.30
54 Tim Salmon	1.00	.30
55 Chipper Jones	2.50	.75
56 Ryan Klesko	1.00	.30
57 Tom Glavine	1.50	.45
58 Denny Neagle	1.00	.30
59 John Smoltz	1.50	.45
60 Javy Lopez	1.00	.30
61 Roberto Alomar	2.50	.75
62 Rafael Palmeiro	1.50	.45
63 Mike Mussina	2.50	.75
64 Cal Ripken	8.00	2.40
65 Mo Vaughn	1.00	.30
66 Tim Naehring	1.00	.30
67 John Valentin	1.00	.30
68 Mark Grace	1.50	.45
69 Kevin Orie	1.00	.30
70 Sammy Sosa	4.00	1.20
71 Albert Belle	1.00	.30
72 Frank Thomas	2.50	.75
73 Robin Ventura	1.00	.30
74 David Justice	1.00	.30
75 Kenny Lofton	1.00	.30
76 Omar Vizquel	1.00	.30
77 Manny Ramirez	1.00	.30
78 Jim Thome	2.50	.75
79 Dante Bichette	1.00	.30
80 Larry Walker	1.50	.45
81 Vinny Castilla	1.00	.30
82 Ellis Burks	1.00	.30
83 Bobby Higginson	1.00	.30
84 Brian Hunter	1.00	.30
85 Tony Clark	1.00	.30
86 Mike Hampton	1.00	.30
87 Jeff Bagwell	1.50	.45
88 Craig Biggio	1.50	.45
89 Derek Bell	1.00	.30
90 Mike Piazza	4.00	1.20
91 Ramon Martinez	1.00	.30
92 Raul Mondesi	1.00	.30
93 Hideo Nomo	2.50	.75
94 Eric Karros	1.00	.30
95 Paul Molitor	1.50	.45
96 Marty Cordova	1.00	.30
97 Brad Radke	1.00	.30
98 Mark Grudzielanek	1.00	.30
99 Carlos Perez	1.00	.30
100 Rondell White	1.00	.30
101 Todd Hundley	1.00	.30
102 Edgardo Alfonzo	1.00	.30
103 John Franco	1.00	.30
104 John Olerud	1.00	.30
105 Tino Martinez	1.50	.45
106 David Cone	1.00	.30
107 Paul O'Neill	1.50	.45
108 Andy Pettitte	1.50	.45
109 Bernie Williams	1.50	.45
110 Rickey Henderson	4.00	1.20
111 Jason Giambi	2.50	.75
112 Matt Stairs	1.00	.30
113 Gregg Jefferies	1.00	.30
114 Rico Brogna	1.00	.30
115 Curt Schilling	1.50	.45
116 Jason Schmidt	1.00	.30
117 Jose Guillen	1.00	.30
118 Kevin Young	1.00	.30
119 Ray Lankford	1.00	.30
120 Mark McGwire	6.00	1.80
121 Delino DeShields	1.00	.30
122 Ken Caminiti	1.00	.30
123 Tony Gwynn	3.00	.90
124 Trevor Hoffman	1.00	.30
125 Barry Bonds	6.00	1.80
126 Jeff Kent	1.00	.30
127 Shawn Estes	1.00	.30
128 J.T. Snow	1.00	.30
129 Jay Buhner	1.00	.30
130 Ken Griffey Jr.	4.00	1.20
131 Dan Wilson	1.00	.30
132 Edgar Martinez	1.50	.45
133 Alex Rodriguez	4.00	1.20
134 Rusty Greer	1.00	.30
135 Juan Gonzalez	2.50	.75
136 Fernando Tatis	1.00	.30
137 Ivan Rodriguez	2.50	.75
138 Carlos Delgado	1.00	.30
139 Pat Hentgen	1.00	.30
140 Roger Clemens	5.00	1.50
141 Chipper Jones SF	3.00	.90
142 Greg Maddux SF	5.00	1.50
143 Rafael Palmeiro SF	2.00	.60
144 Mike Mussina SF	3.00	.90
145 Cal Ripken SF	10.00	3.00
146 Nomar Garciaparra SF	5.00	1.50
147 Mo Vaughn SF	1.25	.35
148 Sammy Sosa SF	5.00	1.50
149 Albert Belle SF	1.25	.35
150 Frank Thomas SF	3.00	.90
151 Jim Thome SF	3.00	.90
152 Kenny Lofton SF	1.25	.35
153 Manny Ramirez SF	1.25	.35
154 Larry Walker SF	2.00	.60
155 Jeff Bagwell SF	2.00	.60
156 Craig Biggio SF	2.00	.60
157 Mike Piazza SF	5.00	1.50
158 Paul Molitor SF	2.00	.60
159 Derek Jeter SF	8.00	2.40
160 Tino Martinez SF	2.00	.60
161 Curt Schilling SF	2.00	.60
162 Mark McGwire SF	8.00	2.40
163 Tony Gwynn SF	4.00	1.20
164 Barry Bonds SF	8.00	2.40
165 Ken Griffey Jr. SF	5.00	1.50
166 Randy Johnson SF	3.00	.90
167 Alex Rodriguez SF	5.00	1.50
168 Juan Gonzalez SF	3.00	.90
169 Ivan Rodriguez SF	3.00	.90
170 Roger Clemens SF	6.00	1.80
171 Greg Maddux HG	15.00	4.50
172 Cal Ripken HG	30.00	9.00
173 Frank Thomas HG	10.00	3.00
174 Jeff Bagwell HG	10.00	3.00
175 Mike Piazza HG	15.00	4.50
176 Mark McGwire HG	25.00	7.50
177 Barry Bonds HG	25.00	7.50
178 Ken Griffey Jr. HG	15.00	4.50
179 Alex Rodriguez HG	15.00	4.50
180 Roger Clemens HG	20.00	6.00
181 Mike Caruso YM	1.50	.45
182 David Ortiz YM	1.50	.45
183 Gabe Alvarez YM	1.50	.45
184 G.Matthews Jr. YM RC	1.50	.45
185 Kerry Wood YM	4.00	1.20
186 Carl Pavano YM	1.50	.45
187 Alex Gonzalez YM	1.50	.45
188 Masato Yoshii YM RC	2.50	.75
189 Larry Sutton YM	1.50	.45
190 Russell Branyan YM	1.50	.45
191 Bruce Chen YM	1.50	.45
192 R. Arrojo YM RC	1.50	.45
193 R.Christenson YM RC	1.50	.45
194 Cliff Politte YM	1.50	.45
195 A.J. Hinch YM	1.50	.45
196 Kevin Witt YM	1.50	.45
197 Daryle Ward YM	1.50	.45
198 Corey Koskie YM RC	5.00	1.50
199 Mike Lowell YM RC	8.00	2.40
200 Travis Lee YM	1.50	.45
201 K.Millwood YM RC	6.00	1.80
202 Robert Smith YM	1.50	.45
203 M.Ordonez YM RC	10.00	3.00
204 Eric Milton YM	1.50	.45
205 Geoff Jenkins YM	1.50	.45
206 Rich Butler YM RC	1.50	.45
207 Mike Kinkade YM RC	1.50	.45
208 Braden Looper YM	1.50	.45
209 Matt Clement YM	1.50	.45
210 Derrek Lee YM	1.50	.45
211 Randy Johnson PP	3.00	.90
212 John Smoltz PP	2.00	.60
213 Roger Clemens PP	6.00	1.80
214 Curt Schilling PP	2.00	.60
215 Pedro Martinez PP	3.00	.90
216 Vinny Castilla PP	1.25	.35
217 Jose Cruz Jr. PP	1.25	.35
218 Jim Thome PP	3.00	.90
219 Alex Rodriguez PP	5.00	1.50
220 Frank Thomas PP	3.00	.90
221 Tim Salmon PP	2.00	.60
222 Larry Walker PP	2.00	.60
223 Albert Belle PP	1.25	.35
224 Manny Ramirez PP	1.25	.35
225 Mark McGwire PP	8.00	2.40
226 Mo Vaughn PP	1.25	.35
227 Andres Galarraga PP	1.25	.35
228 Scott Rolen PP	2.00	.60
229 Travis Lee PP	1.25	.35
230 Mike Piazza PP	5.00	1.50
231 N.Garciaparra PP	5.00	1.50
232 Andruw Jones PP	1.25	.35
233 Barry Bonds PP	8.00	2.40
234 Jeff Bagwell PP	2.00	.60
235 Juan Gonzalez PP	3.00	.90
236 Tino Martinez PP	2.00	.60
237 Vladimir Guerrero PP	3.00	.90
238 Rafael Palmeiro PP	2.00	.60
239 Russell Branyan PP	1.25	.35
240 Ken Griffey Jr. PP	5.00	1.50
241 Cecil Fielder	1.00	.30
242 Chuck Finley	1.00	.30
243 Jay Bell	1.00	.30
244 Andy Benes	1.00	.30
245 Matt Williams	1.00	.30
246 Brian Anderson	1.00	.30
247 Dave Dellucci RC	1.00	.30
248 Andres Galarraga	1.00	.30
249 Andruw Jones	1.00	.30
250 Greg Maddux	4.00	1.20
251 Brady Anderson	1.00	.30
252 Joe Carter	1.00	.30
253 Eric Davis	1.00	.30
254 Pedro Martinez	2.50	.75
255 Nomar Garciaparra	4.00	1.20
256 Dennis Eckersley	1.00	.30
257 Henry Rodriguez	1.00	.30
258 Jeff Blauser	1.00	.30
259 Jaime Navarro	1.00	.30
260 Ray Durham	1.00	.30
261 Chris Stynes	1.00	.30
262 Willie Greene	1.00	.30
263 Reggie Sanders	1.00	.30
264 Bret Boone	1.00	.30
265 Barry Larkin	2.50	.75
266 Travis Fryman	1.00	.30
267 Charles Nagy	1.00	.30
268 Sandy Alomar Jr.	1.00	.30
269 Darryl Kile	1.00	.30
270 Mike Lansing	1.00	.30
271 Pedro Astacio	1.00	.30
272 Damion Easley	1.00	.30
273 Joe Randa	1.00	.30
274 Luis Gonzalez	1.00	.30
275 Mike Piazza	4.00	1.20
276 Todd Zeile	1.00	.30
277 Edgar Renteria	1.00	.30
278 Livan Hernandez	1.00	.30
279 Cliff Floyd	1.00	.30
280 Moises Alou	1.00	.30
281 Billy Wagner	1.00	.30
282 Jeff King	1.00	.30
283 Hal Morris	1.00	.30
284 Johnny Damon	1.00	.30
285 Dean Palmer	1.00	.30
286 Tim Belcher	1.00	.30
287 Eric Young	1.00	.30
288 Bobby Bonilla	1.00	.30
289 Gary Sheffield	1.00	.30
290 Chan Ho Park	1.00	.30
291 Charles Johnson	1.00	.30
292 Jeff Cirillo	1.00	.30
293 Jeromy Burnitz	1.00	.30
294 Jose Valentin	1.00	.30
295 Marquis Grissom	1.00	.30
296 Todd Walker	1.00	.30
297 Terry Steinbach	1.00	.30
298 Rick Aguilera	1.00	.30
299 Vladimir Guerrero	2.50	.75
300 Rey Ordonez	1.00	.30
301 Butch Huskey	1.00	.30
302 Bernard Gilkey	1.00	.30
303 Mariano Rivera	1.50	.45
304 Chuck Knoblauch	1.00	.30
305 Derek Jeter	6.00	1.80
306 Ricky Bottalico	1.00	.30
307 Bob Abreu	1.00	.30
308 Scott Rolen	1.50	.45
309 Al Martin	1.00	.30
310 Jason Kendall	1.00	.30
311 Brian Jordan	1.00	.30
312 Ron Gant	1.00	.30
313 Todd Stottlemyre	1.00	.30
314 Greg Vaughn	1.00	.30
315 Kevin Brown	1.50	.45
316 Wally Joyner	1.00	.30
317 Robb Nen	1.00	.30
318 Orel Hershiser	1.00	.30
319 Russ Davis	1.00	.30
320 Randy Johnson	2.50	.75
321 Quinton McCracken	1.00	.30
322 Tony Saunders	1.00	.30
323 Wilson Alvarez	1.00	.30
324 Wade Boggs	1.50	.45
325 Fred McGriff	1.50	.45
326 Lee Stevens	1.00	.30
327 John Wetteland	1.00	.30
328 Jose Canseco	2.50	.75
329 Randy Myers	1.00	.30
330 Jose Cruz Jr.	1.00	.30
331 Matt Williams TW	2.50	.75
332 Andres Galarraga TW	2.50	.75
333 Walt Weiss TW	2.50	.75
334 Joe Carter TW	2.50	.75
335 Pedro Martinez TW	6.00	1.80
336 Henry Rodriguez TW	2.50	.75
337 Travis Fryman TW	2.50	.75
338 Darryl Kile TW	2.50	.75
339 Mike Lansing TW	2.50	.75
340 Mike Piazza TW	10.00	3.00
341 Moises Alou TW	2.50	.75
342 Charles Johnson TW	2.50	.75
343 Chuck Knoblauch TW	2.50	.75
344 Rickey Henderson TW	6.00	1.80
345 Kevin Brown TW	4.00	1.20
346 Orel Hershiser TW	2.50	.75
347 Wade Boggs TW	4.00	1.20
348 Fred McGriff TW	4.00	1.20
349 Jose Canseco TW	6.00	1.80
350 Gary Sheffield TW	2.50	.75
351 Travis Lee CG	4.00	1.20
352 N.Garciaparra CG	15.00	4.50
353 Frank Thomas CG	10.00	3.00
354 Cal Ripken CG	30.00	9.00
355 Mark McGwire CG	25.00	7.50
356 Mike Piazza CG	15.00	4.50
357 Alex Rodriguez CG	15.00	4.50
358 Barry Bonds CG	25.00	7.50
359 Tony Gwynn CG	12.00	3.60
360 Ken Griffey Jr. CG	15.00	4.50

1998 SPx Finite Radiance

Randomly inserted in packs, this 360-card set is a parallel to the SPx Finite base set. Due to problems in the manufacturing process, exchange cards had to be inserted into packs for Power Explosion cards 40, 41 and 45. The deadline to redeem these exchange cards was June 2nd, 1999. Serial numbering of the various subsets is as follows: Youth Movement (1-30) - 2500 of each card, Power Explosion (31-50) - 1000 of each card, Basic Cards (51-140) - 4500 of each card, Star Focus (141-170) - 3500 of each card, Heroes of the Game (171-180) - 100 of each card, Youth Movement (181-210) - 2500 of each card, Power Passion (211-240) - 3500 of each card, Basic Cards (241-330) - 4500 of each card, Tradewinds (331-350) -1000 of each card, Cornerstones of the Game (351-360) -100 of each card.

Nm-Mt Ex-Mt
*YOUTH: .6X TO 1.5X BASIC YOUTH..
*PE RADIANCE: 1.25X TO 3X BASIC POW.EXP.
*BASIC RADIANCE: .75X TO 2X BASIC CARDS
*SF RADIANCE: .75X TO 2X BASIC SF
*HG RADIANCE: 1.5X TO 4X BASIC HG
*YM RADIANCE: .6X TO 1.5X BASIC YM
*YM RADIANCE RC's: .3X TO .8X BASIC YM
*PP RADIANCE: .6X TO 1.5X BASIC PP
*BASIC RADIANCE: .75X TO 2X BASIC CARDS
*TW RADIANCE: 1.25X TO 3X BASIC TW
*CG RADIANCE: 1.5X TO 4X BASIC CG

1998 SPx Finite Spectrum

Randomly inserted in packs, this 360-card set is a parallel to the SPx Finite base set. Due to problems in the manufacturing process, exchange cards had to be inserted into packs for Power Explosion cards 40, 41 and 45. The deadline to redeem these exchange cards was June 2nd, 1999. This version is the most difficult to obtain of the three varieties of SPx Finite. Serial numbering for the various subsets is as follows: Youth Movement (1-30) - 1250 of each card, Power Explosion (31-50) - 50 of each card, Basic Cards (51-140) - 2250 of each card, Star Focus (141-170) - 1750 of each card, Heroes of the Game (171-180) - 1 of each card, Youth Movement (181-210) - 1250 of each card, Power Passion (211-240) -1750 of each card, Basic Cards (241-330) - 2250 of each card, Tradewinds (331-350) - 50 of each card and Cornerstones of the Game (351-360) - 1 of each card. Neither the Heroes of the Game nor the Cornerstones of the Game subsets are priced due to scarcity.

Nm-Mt Ex-Mt
*YM SPECTRUM: 1X TO 2.5X BASIC YM
*PE SPECTRUM: 4X TO 10X BASIC PE
*BASIC SPECTRUM: 1.25X TO 3X BASIC
*SF SPECTRUM: 1.25X TO 3X BASIC SF
*YM SPECTRUM: .75X TO 2X BASIC YM
*YM SPECTRUM RC's: .5X TO 1.2X BASIC YM
*PP SPECTRUM: 1.25X TO 3X BASIC PP
*BASIC SPECTRUM: 1.25X TO 3X BASIC
*TW SPECTRUM: 4X TO 10X BASIC TW

1998 SPx Finite Home Run Hysteria

Randomly seeded exclusively into second series packs, these ten different inserts chronicle the epic home run race of the 1998 season. Each card is serial numbered to 62 on back.

	Nm-Mt	Ex-Mt
COMPLETE SET (10)	500.00	150.00
HR1 Ken Griffey Jr.	80.00	24.00
HR2 Mark McGwire	120.00	36.00
HR3 Sammy Sosa	80.00	24.00
HR4 Albert Belle	20.00	6.00

HR5 Alex Rodriguez 80.00 24.00
HR6 Greg Vaughn 20.00 6.00
HR7 Andres Galarraga 20.00 6.00
HR8 Vinny Castilla 20.00 6.00
HR9 Juan Gonzalez 50.00 15.00
HR10 Chipper Jones 50.00 15.00

1999 SPx

The 1999 SPx set (produced by Upper Deck) was issued in one series for a total of 120 cards and distributed in thee-card packs with a suggested retail price of $5.99. The set features color photos of 80 MLB verteran players (1-80) with 40 top rookies on subset cards (81-120) numbered to 1,999. J.D. Drew and Gabe Kapler autographed all 1,999 of their respective rookie cards. A Ken Griffey Jr. Sample card was distributed to dealers and hobby media several weeks prior to the product's release. This card is serial numbered "0000/0000" on front, has the word "SAMPLE" pasted across the back in red ink and is oddly numbered "24 East" on back (even though the basic cards have no regional references). Also, 350 Willie Mays A Piece of History 500 Home Run bat cards were randomly seeded into packs. Mays personally signed an additional 24 cards (matching his jersey number) - all of which were then serial numbered by hand and randomly seeded into packs. Pricing for these bat cards can be referenced under 1999 Upper Deck A Piece of History 500 Club.

	Nm-Mt	Ex-Mt
COMP.SET w/o SP's (80)	25.00	7.50
COMMON (1-10)	1.50	.45
COMMON CARD (11-80)	.50	.15
COMMON SP (81-120)	10.00	3.00
1 Mark McGwire 61	3.00	.90
2 Mark McGwire 62	3.00	.90
3 Mark McGwire 63	1.50	.45
4 Mark McGwire 64	1.50	.45
5 Mark McGwire 65	1.50	.45
6 Mark McGwire 66	1.50	.45
7 Mark McGwire 67	1.50	.45
8 Mark McGwire 68	1.50	.45
9 Mark McGwire 69	1.50	.45
10 Mark McGwire 70	4.00	1.20
11 Mo Vaughn	.50	.15
12 Darin Erstad	.50	.15
13 Travis Lee	.50	.15
14 Randy Johnson	1.25	.35
15 Matt Williams	.50	.15
16 Chipper Jones	1.25	.35
17 Greg Maddux	2.00	.60
18 Andruw Jones	.50	.15
19 Andres Galarraga	.50	.15
20 Cal Ripken	4.00	1.20
21 Albert Belle	.50	.15
22 Mike Mussina	1.25	.35
23 Nomar Garciaparra	2.00	.60
24 Pedro Martinez	1.25	.35
25 John Valentin	.50	.15
26 Kerry Wood	1.25	.35
27 Sammy Sosa	2.00	.60
28 Mark Grace	.75	.23
29 Frank Thomas	1.25	.35
30 Mike Caruso	.50	.15
31 Barry Larkin	1.25	.35
32 Sean Casey	.50	.15
33 Jim Thome	1.25	.35
34 Kenny Lofton	.50	.15
35 Manny Ramirez	.50	.15
36 Larry Walker	.75	.23
37 Todd Helton	.75	.23
38 Vinny Castilla	.50	.15
39 Tony Clark	.50	.15
40 Derrek Lee	.50	.15
41 Mark Kotsay	.50	.15
42 Jeff Bagwell	.75	.23
43 Craig Biggio	.75	.23
44 Moises Alou	.50	.15
45 Larry Sutton	.50	.15
46 Johnny Damon	.50	.15
47 Gary Sheffield	.50	.15
48 Raul Mondesi	.50	.15
49 Jeromy Burnitz	.50	.15
50 Todd Walker	.50	.15
51 David Ortiz	.50	.15
52 Vladimir Guerrero	1.25	.35
53 Rondell White	.50	.15
54 Mike Piazza	2.00	.60
55 Derek Jeter	3.00	.90
56 Tino Martinez	.75	.23
57 Roger Clemens	2.50	.75
58 Ben Grieve	.50	.15
59 A.J. Hinch	.50	.15
60 Scott Rolen	.75	.23
61 Doug Glanville	.50	.15
62 Aramis Ramirez	.50	.15
63 Jose Guillen	.50	.15
64 Tony Gwynn	1.50	.45
65 Greg Vaughn	.50	.15
66 Ruben Rivera	.50	.15
67 Barry Bonds	3.00	.90
68 J.T. Snow	.50	.15
69 Alex Rodriguez	2.00	.60
70 Ken Griffey Jr.	2.00	.60
71 Jay Buhner	.50	.15
72 Mark McGwire	3.00	.90
73 Fernando Tatis	.50	.15
74 Quinton McCracken	.50	.15
75 Wade Boggs	.75	.23
76 Ivan Rodriguez	1.25	.35
77 Juan Gonzalez	1.25	.35
78 Rafael Palmeiro	.75	.23
79 Jose Cruz Jr.	.50	.15
80 Carlos Delgado	.50	.15
81 Troy Glaus SP	15.00	4.50
82 Vladimir Nunez SP	10.00	3.00
83 George Lombard SP	10.00	3.00
84 Bruce Chen SP	10.00	3.00
85 Ryan Minor SP	10.00	3.00
86 Calvin Pickering SP	10.00	3.00
87 Jin Ho Cho SP	10.00	3.00
88 Russ Branyan SP	10.00	3.00
89 Derrick Gibson SP	10.00	3.00
90 Gabe Kapler SP AU	25.00	7.50
91 Matt Anderson SP	10.00	3.00
92 Robert Fick SP	10.00	3.00
93 Juan Encarnacion SP	10.00	3.00
94 Preston Wilson SP	10.00	3.00
95 Alex Gonzalez SP	10.00	3.00
96 Carlos Beltran SP	10.00	3.00
97 Jeremy Giambi SP	10.00	3.00
98 Dee Brown SP	10.00	3.00
99 Adrian Beltre SP	10.00	3.00
100 Alex Cora SP	10.00	3.00
101 Angel Pena SP	10.00	3.00
102 Geoff Jenkins SP	10.00	3.00
103 Ronnie Belliard SP	10.00	3.00
104 Corey Koskie SP	10.00	3.00
105 A.J. Pierzynski SP	10.00	3.00
106 Michael Barrett SP	10.00	3.00
107 Fern.Seguignol SP	10.00	3.00
108 Mike Kinkade SP	10.00	3.00
109 Mike Lowell SP	10.00	3.00
110 Ricky Ledee SP	10.00	3.00
111 Eric Chavez SP	10.00	3.00
112 Abraham Nunez SP	10.00	3.00
113 Matt Clement SP	10.00	3.00
114 Ben Davis SP	10.00	3.00
115 Mike Darr SP	10.00	3.00
116 Ramon E.Martinez SP RC	10.00	3.00
117 Carlos Guillen SP	10.00	3.00
118 Shane Monahan SP	10.00	3.00
119 J.D. Drew SP AU	25.00	7.50
120 Kevin Witt SP	10.00	3.00
24EAST K.Griffey Jr. SAMP	2.00	.60

1999 SPx Finite Radiance

Randomly inserted in Finite Radiance Hot Packs only, this 120-card set is parallel to the SPx base set. Only 100 serial-numbered sets were produced.

	Nm-Mt	Ex-Mt
*RADIANCE 1-10: 5X TO 12X BASIC 1-10		
*RADIANCE 11-80: 8X TO 20X BASIC 11-80		
*RADIANCE 81-120: .75X TO 2X BASIC 81-120		
90 Gabe Kapler AU	25.00	7.50
119 J.D. Drew AU	40.00	12.00

1999 SPx Dominance

Randomly inserted into packs at the rate of one in 17, this 20-card set features color photos of some of the most dominant MLB superstars.

	Nm-Mt	Ex-Mt
COMPLETE SET (20)	120.00	36.00
FB1 Chipper Jones	6.00	1.80
FB2 Greg Maddux	10.00	3.00
FB3 Cal Ripken	20.00	6.00
FB4 Nomar Garciaparra	10.00	3.00
FB5 Mo Vaughn	2.50	.75
FB6 Sammy Sosa	10.00	3.00
FB7 Albert Belle	2.50	.75
FB8 Frank Thomas	6.00	1.80
FB9 Jim Thome	6.00	1.80
FB10 Jeff Bagwell	4.00	1.20
FB11 Vladimir Guerrero	6.00	1.80
FB12 Mike Piazza	10.00	3.00
FB13 Derek Jeter	15.00	4.50
FB14 Tony Gwynn	120.00	36.00
FB15 Barry Bonds	15.00	4.50
FB16 Ken Griffey Jr.	10.00	3.00
FB17 Alex Rodriguez	10.00	3.00
FB18 Mark McGwire	15.00	4.50
FB19 J.D. Drew	4.00	1.20
FB20 Juan Gonzalez	6.00	1.80

1999 SPx Power Explosion

Randomly inserted in packs at the rate of one in three, this 30-card set features color action photos of some of the top power hitters of the game.

	Nm-Mt	Ex-Mt
COMPLETE SET (30)	40.00	12.00
PE1 Troy Glaus	1.50	.45
PE2 Mo Vaughn	.75	.23
PE3 Travis Lee	.75	.23
PE4 Chipper Jones	2.00	.60
PE5 Andres Galarraga	.75	.23
PE6 Brady Anderson	.75	.23
PE7 Albert Belle	.75	.23
PE8 Nomar Garciaparra	3.00	.90
PE9 Sammy Sosa	3.00	.90
PE10 Frank Thomas	2.00	.60
PE11 Jim Thome	2.00	.60
PE12 Manny Ramirez	.75	.23
PE13 Larry Walker	1.25	.35
PE14 Tony Clark	.75	.23
PE15 Jeff Bagwell	1.25	.35
PE16 Moises Alou	.75	.23
PE17 Ken Caminiti	.75	.23
PE18 Vladimir Guerrero	2.00	.60
PE19 Mike Piazza	3.00	.90
PE20 Tino Martinez	1.25	.35
PE21 Ben Grieve	.75	.23
PE22 Scott Rolen	1.25	.35
PE23 Greg Vaughn	.75	.23
PE24 Barry Bonds	5.00	1.50
PE25 Ken Griffey Jr.	3.00	.90
PE26 Alex Rodriguez	3.00	.90
PE27 Mark McGwire	5.00	1.50
PE28 J.D. Drew	1.50	.45
PE29 Juan Gonzalez	2.00	.60
PE30 Ivan Rodriguez	2.00	.60

1999 SPx Premier Stars

Randomly inserted in packs at the rate of one in 17, this 30-card set features color action photos of some of the game's most powerful players captured on cards with a unique rainbow-foil design.

	Nm-Mt	Ex-Mt
PS1 Mark McGwire	20.00	6.00
PS2 Sammy Sosa	12.00	3.60
PS3 Frank Thomas	8.00	2.40
PS4 J.D. Drew	2.50	.75
PS5 Kerry Wood	8.00	2.40
PS6 Moises Alou	3.00	.90
PS7 Kenny Lofton	3.00	.90
PS8 Jeff Bagwell	5.00	1.50
PS9 Tony Clark	3.00	.90
PS10 Roberto Alomar	8.00	2.40
PS11 Cal Ripken	25.00	7.50
PS12 Derek Jeter	20.00	6.00
PS13 Mike Piazza	12.00	3.60
PS14 Jose Cruz Jr.	3.00	.90
PS15 Chipper Jones	8.00	2.40
PS16 Nomar Garciaparra	12.00	3.60
PS17 Greg Maddux	12.00	3.60
PS18 Scott Rolen	5.00	1.50
PS19 Vladimir Guerrero	8.00	2.40
PS20 Albert Belle	3.00	.90
PS21 Ken Griffey Jr.	12.00	3.60
PS22 Alex Rodriguez	12.00	3.60
PS23 Ben Grieve	3.00	.90
PS24 Juan Gonzalez	8.00	2.40
PS25 Barry Bonds	20.00	6.00
PS26 Roger Clemens	15.00	4.50
PS27 Tony Gwynn	10.00	3.00
PS28 Randy Johnson	8.00	2.40
PS29 Travis Lee	3.00	.90
PS30 Mo Vaughn	3.00	.90

1999 SPx Star Focus

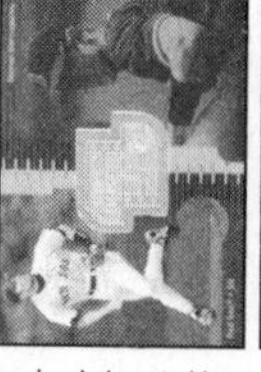

Randomly inserted in packs at the rate of one in eight, this 30-card set features action color photos of some of the brightest stars in the game beside a black-and-white portrait of the player.

	Nm-Mt	Ex-Mt
COMPLETE SET (30)	120.00	36.00
SF1 Chipper Jones	5.00	1.50
SF2 Greg Maddux	8.00	2.40
SF3 Cal Ripken	15.00	4.50
SF4 Nomar Garciaparra	8.00	2.40
SF5 Mo Vaughn	2.00	.60
SF6 Sammy Sosa	8.00	2.40
SF7 Albert Belle	2.00	.60
SF8 Frank Thomas	5.00	1.50
SF9 Jim Thome	5.00	1.50
SF10 Kenny Lofton	2.00	.60
SF11 Manny Ramirez	2.00	.60
SF12 Larry Walker	3.00	.90
SF13 Jeff Bagwell	3.00	.90
SF14 Craig Biggio	3.00	.90
SF15 Randy Johnson	5.00	1.50
SF16 Vladimir Guerrero	5.00	1.50
SF17 Mike Piazza	8.00	2.40
SF18 Derek Jeter	12.00	3.60
SF19 Tino Martinez	3.00	.90
SF20 Bernie Williams	5.00	1.50
SF21 Curt Schilling	2.00	.60
SF22 Tony Gwynn	6.00	1.80
SF23 Barry Bonds	12.00	3.60
SF24 Ken Griffey Jr.	8.00	2.40
SF25 Alex Rodriguez	8.00	2.40
SF26 Mark McGwire	12.00	3.60
SF27 J.D. Drew	3.00	.90
SF28 Juan Gonzalez	5.00	1.50
SF29 Ivan Rodriguez	5.00	1.50
SF30 Ben Grieve	2.00	.60

1999 SPx Winning Materials

Randomly inserted into packs at the rate of one in 251, this eight-card set features color photos of top players with a piece of the player's game-worn jersey and game-used bat embedded in the card.

	Nm-Mt	Ex-Mt
IR Ivan Rodriguez	25.00	7.50
JD J.D. Drew	15.00	4.50
JR Ken Griffey Jr.	50.00	15.00

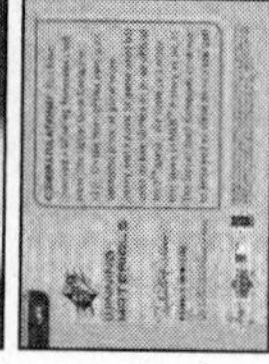

	Nm-Mt	Ex-Mt
TG Tony Gwynn	40.00	12.00
TH Todd Helton	25.00	7.50
TL Travis Lee	10.00	3.00
VC Vinny Castilla	15.00	4.50
VG Vladimir Guerrero	25.00	7.50

2000 SPx

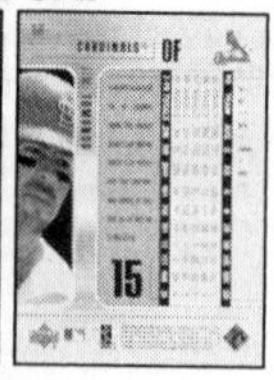

The 2000 SPx (produced by Upper Deck) was initially released in May, 2000 as a 120-card set. Each pack contained four cards and carried a suggested retail price of $5.99. The set featured 90-player cards, and a 30-card "Young Stars" subset. There are three tiers within the Young Stars subset. Tier one cards are serial numbered to 1000, Tier two cards are serial numbered to 1500 and autographed by the player and Tier three cards are serial numbered to 500 and autographed by the player. Redemption cards were issued for several of the autograph cards and they were to be postmarked by 1/24/01 to be valid for exchange. In late December, 2000, Upper Deck issued a new product called Rookie Update which contained a selection of new cards for SP Authentic, SPx and UD Pros and Prospects. Rookie Update packs contained four cards and the collector was guaranteed one card from each featured brand, plus a fourth card. For SPx, these "high series" cards were numbered 121-196. The Young Stars subset was extended with cards 121-151 and cards 182-196. Cards 121-135 and 182-196 featured a selection of prospects each serial numbered to 1600. Cards 136-151 featured a selection of prospect cards signed by the player and each serial numbered to 1500. Cards 152-181 contained a selection of veteran players that were either initially not included in the basic 120-card "first series" set or traded to new teams. Notable Rookie Cards include Xavier Nady, Kazuhiro Sasaki, Ben Sheets and Barry Zito. Also, a selection of A Piece of History 3000 Club Ty Cobb memorabilia cards were randomly seeded into packs. 350 bat cards, three hand-numbered autograph cut cards and one hand-numbered, combination bat chip and autograph cut card were produced. Pricing for these memorabilia cards can be referenced under 2000 Upper Deck A Piece of History 3000 Club.

	Nm-Mt	Ex-Mt
COMP.BASIC w/o SP's (90)	25.00	7.50
COMP.UPDATE w/o SP's (30)	10.00	3.00
COMMON CARD (1-90)	.50	.15
COMMON AU/1500 (91-120)	15.00	4.50
COMMON (121-135/182-196)	10.00	3.00
COMMON (136-151)	15.00	4.50
COMMON (152-181)	.75	.23
1 Troy Glaus	.75	.23
2 Mo Vaughn	.50	.15
3 Ramon Ortiz	.50	.15
4 Jeff Bagwell	.75	.23
5 Moises Alou	.50	.15
6 Craig Biggio	.75	.23
7 Jose Lima	.50	.15
8 Jason Giambi	1.25	.35
9 John Jaha	.50	.15
10 Matt Stairs	.50	.15
11 Chipper Jones	1.25	.35
12 Greg Maddux	2.00	.60
13 Andres Galarraga	.50	.15
14 Andruw Jones	.50	.15
15 Jeromy Burnitz	.50	.15
16 Ron Belliard	.50	.15
17 Carlos Delgado	.50	.15
18 David Wells	.50	.15
19 Tony Batista	.50	.15
20 Shannon Stewart	.50	.15
21 Sammy Sosa	2.00	.60
22 Mark Grace	.75	.23
23 Henry Rodriguez	.50	.15
24 Mark McGwire	3.00	.90
25 J.D. Drew	.50	.15
26 Luis Gonzalez	.50	.15
27 Randy Johnson	1.25	.35
28 Matt Williams	.50	.15
29 Steve Finley	.50	.15
30 Shawn Green	.50	.15
31 Kevin Brown	.75	.23
32 Gary Sheffield	.50	.15
33 Jose Canseco	1.25	.35
34 Greg Vaughn	.50	.15
35 Vladimir Guerrero	1.25	.35
36 Michael Barrett	.50	.15
37 Russ Ortiz	.50	.15
38 Barry Bonds	3.00	.90
39 Jeff Kent	.50	.15
40 Richie Sexson	.50	.15
41 Manny Ramirez	.50	.15
42 Jim Thome	1.25	.35
43 Roberto Alomar	1.25	.35
44 Edgar Martinez	.75	.23
45 Alex Rodriguez	2.00	.60
46 John Olerud	.50	.15
47 Alex Gonzalez	.50	.15
48 Cliff Floyd	.50	.15
49 Mike Piazza	2.00	.60
50 Al Leiter	.50	.15
51 Robin Ventura	.75	.23
52 Edgardo Alfonzo	.50	.15
53 Albert Belle	.50	.15
54 Cal Ripken	4.00	1.20
55 B.J. Surhoff	.50	.15
56 Tony Gwynn	1.50	.45
57 Trevor Hoffman	.50	.15
58 Brian Giles	.50	.15
59 Jason Kendall	.50	.15
60 Kris Benson	.50	.15
61 Bob Abreu	.50	.15
62 Scott Rolen	.75	.23
63 Curt Schilling	.75	.23
64 Mike Lieberthal	.50	.15
65 Sean Casey	.50	.15
66 Dante Bichette	.50	.15
67 Ken Griffey Jr.	2.00	.60
68 Pokey Reese	.50	.15
69 Mike Sweeney	.50	.15
70 Carlos Febles	.50	.15
71 Ivan Rodriguez	1.25	.35
72 Ruben Mateo	.50	.15
73 Rafael Palmeiro	.75	.23
74 Larry Walker	.75	.23
75 Todd Helton	.75	.23
76 Nomar Garciaparra	2.00	.60
77 Pedro Martinez	1.25	.35
78 Troy O'Leary	.50	.15
79 Jacque Jones	.50	.15
80 Corey Koskie	.50	.15
81 Juan Gonzalez	1.25	.35
82 Dean Palmer	.50	.15
83 Juan Encarnacion	.50	.15
84 Frank Thomas	1.25	.35
85 Magglio Ordonez	.50	.15
86 Paul Konerko	.50	.15
87 Bernie Williams	.75	.23
88 Derek Jeter	3.00	.90
89 Roger Clemens	2.50	.75
90 Orlando Hernandez	.50	.15
91 Vernon Wells/1500 AU	25.00	7.50
92 Rick Ankiel/1500 AU	25.00	7.50
93 Eric Chavez/1500 AU	25.00	7.50
94 A.Soriano/1500 AU	50.00	15.00
95 Eric Gagne/1500 AU	60.00	18.00
96 Rob Bell/1500 AU	15.00	4.50
97 Matt Riley/1500 AU	25.00	7.50
98 Josh Beckett/1500 AU	80.00	24.00
99 Ben Petrick/1500 AU	15.00	4.50
100 Rob Ramsay/1500 AU	15.00	4.50
101 Scott Williamson 1500 AU	15.00	4.50
102 Doug Davis/1500 AU	15.00	4.50
103 E.Munson/1500 AU*	25.00	7.50
104 Pat Burrell/500 AU	60.00	18.00
105 Jim Morris/1500 AU	40.00	12.00
106 Gabe Kapler/500 AU	25.00	7.50
107 Lance Berkman/1000	10.00	3.00
108 E.Durazo/1500 AU	25.00	7.50
109 Tim Hudson/1500 AU	40.00	12.00
110 Ben Davis/1500 AU*	15.00	4.50
111 N.Johnson/1500 AU	25.00	7.50
112 O.Dotel/1500 AU	15.00	4.50
113 Jerry Hairston/1000	10.00	3.00
114 Ruben Mateo/1000	10.00	3.00
115 Chris Singleton/1000	10.00	3.00
116 Bruce Chen/1500 AU	15.00	4.50
117 Derrick Gibson/1000	10.00	3.00
118 Carlos Beltran/500 AU	40.00	12.00
119 F.Garcia/1500 AU	25.00	7.50
120 P.Wilson/1500 AU	25.00	7.50
121 B.Wilkerson/1600 RC	15.00	4.50
122 Roy Oswalt/1600 RC	60.00	18.00
123 W.Serrano/1600 RC	10.00	3.00
124 Sean Burnett/1600 RC	15.00	4.50
125 Alex Cabrera/1600 RC	10.00	3.00
126 Timo Perez/1600 RC	10.00	3.00
127 Juan Pierre/1600 RC	15.00	4.50
128 Daylan Holt/1600 RC	10.00	3.00
129 T.Ohka/1600 RC	10.00	3.00
130 K.Sasaki/1600 RC	15.00	4.50
131 K.Ainsworth/1600 RC	15.00	4.50
132 B.Abernathy/1600 RC	10.00	3.00
133 Danys Baez/1600 RC	15.00	4.50
134 Brad Cresse/1600 RC	10.00	3.00
135 R.Franklin/1600 RC	10.00	3.00
136 M.Lamb/1500 AU RC	15.00	4.50
137 David Espinosa 1500 AU RC	15.00	4.50
138 Matt Wheatland 1500 AU RC	15.00	4.50
139 X.Nady/1500 AU RC	40.00	12.00
140 S.Heard/1500 AU RC	15.00	4.50
141 P.Coco/1500 AU RC (Card erroneously numbered 54 instead of 141)	15.00	4.50
142 J.Miller/1500 AU RC	15.00	4.50
143 Dave Krynzel 1500 AU RC	15.00	4.50
144 Dane Sardinha 1500 AU RC	15.00	4.50
145 B.Sheets/1500 AU RC	25.00	7.50
146 L.Estrella/1500 AU RC	15.00	4.50
147 Ben Diggins 1500 AU RC	15.00	4.50
148 B.Zito/1500 AU RC	100.00	30.00
149 J.Torres/1500 AU RC	15.00	4.50
150 Mike Meyers 1500 AU RC	15.00	4.50
151 K.Wilson/1500 AU RC	15.00	4.50
152 Darin Erstad	.75	.23
153 Richard Hidalgo	.75	.23
154 Eric Chavez	.75	.23
155 B.J. Surhoff	.75	.23
156 Richie Sexson	.75	.23
157 Raul Mondesi	.75	.23
158 Rondell White	.75	.23
159 Jim Edmonds	.75	.23
160 Curt Schilling	1.25	.35
161 Tom Goodwin	.75	.23
162 Fred McGriff	1.25	.35
163 Jose Vidro	.75	.23
164 Ellis Burks	.75	.23
165 David Segui	.75	.23
166 Aaron Sele	.75	.23
167 Henry Rodriguez	.75	.23
168 Mike Bordick	.75	.23

Card	Nm-Mt	Ex-Mt
169 Mike Mussina	2.00	.60
170 Ryan Klesko	.75	.23
171 Kevin Young	.75	.23
172 Travis Lee	.75	.23
173 Aaron Boone	.75	.23
174 Jermaine Dye	.75	.23
175 Ricky Ledee	.75	.23
176 Jeffrey Hammonds	.75	.23
177 Carl Everett	.75	.23
178 Matt Lawton	.75	.23
179 Bobby Higginson	.75	.23
180 Charles Johnson	.75	.23
181 David Justice	.75	.23
182 Joey Nation/1600 RC	10.00	3.00
183 Rico Washington/ 1600 RC	10.00	3.00
184 Luis Matos/1600 RC	15.00	4.50
185 C.Wakeland/1600 RC	10.00	3.00
186 SW Kim/1600 RC	10.00	3.00
187 Keith Ginter/1600 RC	10.00	3.00
188 G.Guzman/1600 RC	10.00	3.00
189 J.Spurgeon/1600 RC	10.00	3.00
190 Jace Brewer/1600 RC	10.00	3.00
191 J.Guzman/1600 RC	10.00	3.00
192 Ross Gload/1600 RC	10.00	3.00
193 P.Crawford/1600 RC	10.00	3.00
194 R.Kohlmeier/1600 RC	10.00	3.00
195 Julio Zuleta/1600 RC	10.00	3.00
196 Matt Ginter/1600 RC	10.00	3.00

2000 SPx Radiance

Randomly inserted into packs, this 135-card insert is a parallel of the SPx base set. Each card in the set is individually serial numbered to 100. Please note the cards with asterisks next to their name were not issued in the basic set but were prepared and accidentally issued in the 2000 SPx packs. They are numbered and packed out to 100 just like the other Radiance cards.

Card	Nm-Mt	Ex-Mt
COMMON CARD (1-90)	4.00	1.20
*STARS 1-90: 6X TO 15X BASIC CARDS		
COMMON CARD (91-120)	8.00	2.40
91 Vernon Wells	8.00	2.40
92 Rick Ankiel	8.00	2.40
93 Eric Chavez	8.00	2.40
94 Alfonso Soriano	15.00	4.50
95 Eric Gagne	15.00	4.50
96 Rob Bell	8.00	2.40
97 Matt Riley	8.00	2.40
98 John Bale *	8.00	2.40
98 Josh Beckett	25.00	7.50
98 Alex Escobar *	8.00	2.40
98 Joe Mays *	8.00	2.40
98 Calvin Pickering *	8.00	2.40
98 Dave Roberts *	8.00	2.40
98 Jared Sandberg *	8.00	2.40
98 Dernell Stenson *	8.00	2.40
98 Reggie Taylor *	8.00	2.40
98 Ed Yarnall *	8.00	2.40
99 Ben Petrick	8.00	2.40
100 Rob Ramsay	8.00	2.40
101 Scott Williamson	8.00	2.40
102 Doug Davis	8.00	2.40
103 Tony Armas Jr. *	8.00	2.40
103 Travis Dawkins *	8.00	2.40
103 Mike Lamb *	8.00	2.40
103 Eric Munson	8.00	2.40
103 Rico Washington *	8.00	2.40
104 Pat Burrell	10.00	3.00
105 Jim Morris	10.00	3.00
106 Gabe Kapler	8.00	2.40
106 Adam Piatt *	8.00	2.40
106 Mark Quinn *	8.00	2.40
107 Lance Berkman	8.00	2.40
108 Erubiel Durazo	8.00	2.40
109 Tim Hudson	10.00	3.00
110 Ben Davis	8.00	2.40
111 Nick Johnson	8.00	2.40
112 Octavio Dotel	8.00	2.40
113 Jerry Hairston	8.00	2.40
114 Ruben Mateo	8.00	2.40
115 Chris Singleton	8.00	2.40
116 Bruce Chen	8.00	2.40
117 Derrick Gibson	8.00	2.40
118 Carlos Beltran	8.00	2.40
119 Freddy Garcia	8.00	2.40
120 Preston Wilson	8.00	2.40

2000 SPx Foundations

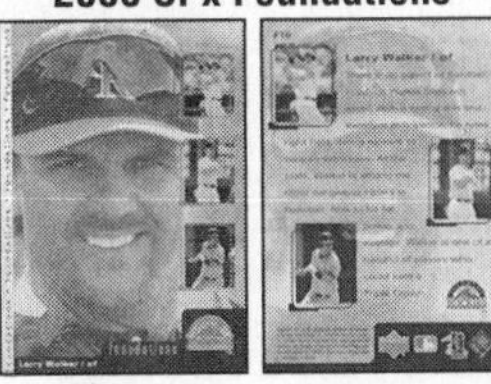

Randomly inserted into packs at one 32, this 10-card insert features players that are the cornerstones teams build around. Card backs carry a "F" prefix.

Card	Nm-Mt	Ex-Mt
COMPLETE SET (10)	100.00	30.00
F1 Ken Griffey Jr.	10.00	3.00
F2 Nomar Garciaparra	10.00	3.00
F3 Cal Ripken	20.00	6.00
F4 Chipper Jones	6.00	1.80
F5 Mike Piazza	10.00	3.00
F6 Derek Jeter	15.00	4.50
F7 Manny Ramirez	2.50	.75
F8 Jeff Bagwell	4.00	1.20
F9 Tony Gwynn	8.00	2.40
F10 Larry Walker	4.00	1.20

2000 SPx Heart of the Order

Randomly inserted into packs at one in eight, this 20-card insert features players that can lift their teams to victory with one swing of the bat. Card backs carry a "H" prefix.

Card	Nm-Mt	Ex-Mt
COMPLETE SET (20)	60.00	18.00
H1 Bernie Williams	2.00	.60
H2 Mike Piazza	5.00	1.50
H3 Ivan Rodriguez	3.00	.90
H4 Mark McGwire	8.00	2.40
H5 Manny Ramirez	1.25	.35
H6 Ken Griffey Jr.	5.00	1.50
H7 Matt Williams	1.25	.35
H8 Sammy Sosa	5.00	1.50
H9 Mo Vaughn	1.25	.35
H10 Carlos Delgado	1.25	.35
H11 Brian Giles	1.25	.35
H12 Chipper Jones	3.00	.90
H13 Sean Casey	1.25	.35
H14 Tony Gwynn	4.00	1.20
H15 Barry Bonds	8.00	2.40
H16 Carlos Beltran	1.00	.30
H17 Scott Rolen	2.00	.60
H18 Juan Gonzalez	3.00	.90
H19 Larry Walker	2.00	.60
H20 Vladimir Guerrero	3.00	.90

2000 SPx Highlight Heroes

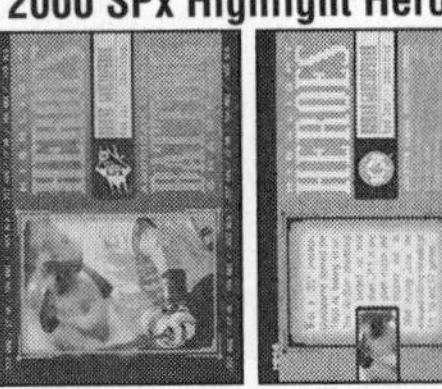

Randomly inserted into packs at one in 16, this 10-card insert features players that have a flair for heroics. Card backs carry a "HH" prefix.

Card	Nm-Mt	Ex-Mt
COMPLETE SET (10)	30.00	9.00
HH1 Pedro Martinez	3.00	.90
HH2 Ivan Rodriguez	3.00	.90
HH3 Carlos Beltran	1.00	.30
HH4 Nomar Garciaparra	5.00	1.50
HH5 Ken Griffey Jr.	5.00	1.50
HH6 Randy Johnson	3.00	.90
HH7 Chipper Jones	3.00	.90
HH8 Scott Williamson	1.00	.30
HH9 Larry Walker	2.00	.60
HH10 Mark McGwire	8.00	2.40

2000 SPx Power Brokers

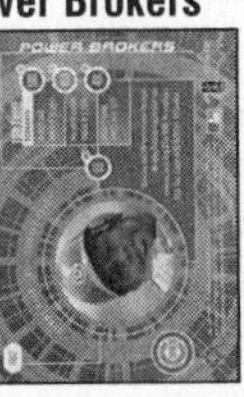

Randomly inserted into packs at one in eight, this 20-card insert features some of the greatest power hitters of all time. Card backs carry a "PB" prefix.

Card	Nm-Mt	Ex-Mt
COMPLETE SET (20)	60.00	18.00
PB1 Rafael Palmeiro	2.00	.60
PB2 Carlos Delgado	1.25	.35
PB3 Ken Griffey Jr.	5.00	1.50
PB4 Matt Stairs	1.25	.35
PB5 Mike Piazza	5.00	1.50
PB6 Vladimir Guerrero	3.00	.90
PB7 Chipper Jones	3.00	.90
PB8 Mark McGwire	8.00	2.40
PB9 Matt Williams	1.25	.35
PB10 Juan Gonzalez	3.00	.90
PB11 Shawn Green	1.25	.35
PB12 Sammy Sosa	5.00	1.50
PB13 Brian Giles	1.25	.35
PB14 Jeff Bagwell	2.00	.60
PB15 Alex Rodriguez	5.00	1.50
PB16 Frank Thomas	3.00	.90
PB17 Larry Walker	2.00	.60
PB18 Albert Belle	1.25	.35
PB19 Dean Palmer	1.25	.35
PB20 Mo Vaughn	1.25	.35

2000 SPx Signatures

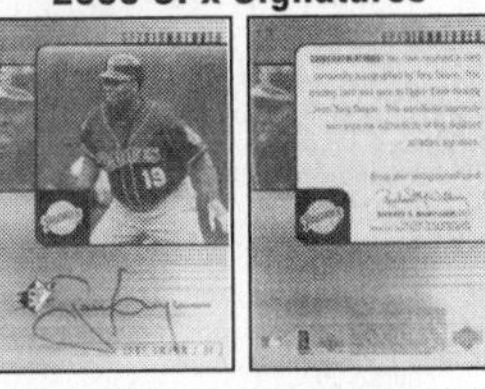

Randomly inserted into packs at one in 179, this 15-card insert features autographed cards of some of the hottest players in major league baseball. The following players went out as stickered exchange cards: Jeff Bagwell (100 percent), Ken Griffey Jr. (100 percent), Tony Gwynn (25 percent), Vladimir Guerrero (50 percent), Manny Ramirez (100 percent) and Ivan Rodriguez (25 percent). The exchange deadline for the stickered cards was February 3rd, 2001. Card backs carry a "X" prefix followed by the players initials.

Card	Nm-Mt	Ex-Mt
XBB Barry Bonds	200.00	60.00
XCJ Chipper Jones	40.00	12.00
XCR Cal Ripken	150.00	45.00
XDJ Derek Jeter	150.00	45.00
XIR I.Rodriguez EXCH *	40.00	12.00
XJB Jeff Bagwell	40.00	12.00
XJC Jose Canseco	40.00	12.00
XKG Ken Griffey Jr.	100.00	30.00
XMR M.Ramirez EXCH	25.00	7.50
XOH Orlando Hernandez	50.00	15.00
XRC Roger Clemens	120.00	36.00
XSC Sean Casey	15.00	4.50
XSR Scott Rolen	25.00	7.50
XTG Tony Gwynn	50.00	15.00
XVG V.Guerrero EXCH *	40.00	12.00

2000 SPx SPXcitement

Randomly inserted into packs at one in four, this 20-card insert features some of the most exciting players in the major leagues. Card backs carry a "XC" prefix.

Card	Nm-Mt	Ex-Mt
COMPLETE SET (20)	30.00	9.00
XC1 Nomar Garciaparra	2.50	.75
XC2 Mark McGwire	4.00	1.20
XC3 Derek Jeter	4.00	1.20
XC4 Cal Ripken	5.00	1.50
XC5 Barry Bonds	4.00	1.20
XC6 Alex Rodriguez	2.50	.75
XC7 Scott Rolen	1.00	.30
XC8 Pedro Martinez	1.50	.45
XC9 Sean Casey	.60	.18
XC10 Sammy Sosa	2.50	.75
XC11 Randy Johnson	1.50	.45
XC12 Ivan Rodriguez	1.50	.45
XC13 Frank Thomas	1.50	.45
XC14 Greg Maddux	2.50	.75
XC15 Tony Gwynn	2.00	.60
XC16 Ken Griffey Jr.	2.50	.75
XC17 Carlos Beltran	.60	.18
XC18 Mike Piazza	2.50	.75
XC19 Chipper Jones	1.50	.45
XC20 Craig Biggio	1.00	.30

2000 SPx Untouchable Talents

Randomly inserted into packs at one in 96, this 10-card insert features players that have skills that are unmatched. Card backs carry a "UT" prefix.

Card	Nm-Mt	Ex-Mt
COMPLETE SET (10)	200.00	60.00
UT1 Mark McGwire	40.00	12.00
UT2 Ken Griffey Jr.	25.00	7.50
UT3 Shawn Green	6.00	1.80
UT4 Ivan Rodriguez	15.00	4.50
UT5 Sammy Sosa	25.00	7.50
UT6 Derek Jeter	40.00	12.00
UT7 Sean Casey	6.00	1.80
UT8 Chipper Jones	15.00	4.50
UT9 Pedro Martinez	15.00	4.50
UT10 Vladimir Guerrero	15.00	4.50

2000 SPx Winning Materials

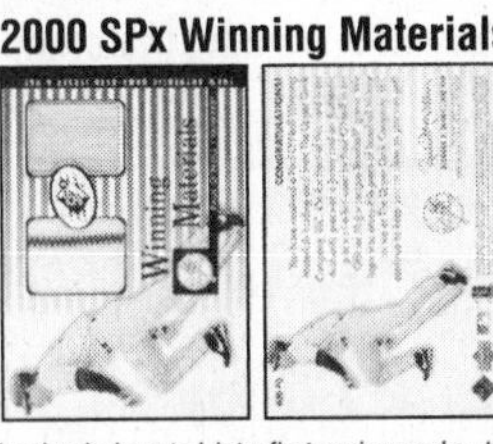

Randomly inserted into first series packs, this 30-card insert features game-used memorabilia cards from some of the top names in baseball. The set includes Bat/Jersey cards, Cap/Jersey cards, Ball/Jersey cards, and autographed Bat/Jersey cards. Card backs carry the players initals. Please note that the Ken Griffey Jr. autographed Bat/Jersey cards, and the Manny Ramirez autographed Bat/Jersey cards were both redemptions with an exchang deadline of 12/31/2000.

Card	Nm-Mt	Ex-Mt
AR1 Alex Rodriguez Bat-Jsy	25.00	7.50
AR2 Alex Rodriguez Cap-Jsy/100	50.00	15.00
AR3 Alex Rodriguez Ball-Jsy/50	60.00	18.00
BB1 Barry Bonds Bat-Jsy	40.00	12.00
BB2 Barry Bonds Cap-Jsy/100	60.00	18.00
BB3 Barry Bonds Bat-Jsy AU/25		
BW Bernie Williams Bat-Jsy	15.00	4.50
DJ1 Derek Jeter Bat-Jsy	50.00	15.00
DJ2 Derek Jeter Ball-Jsy/50	100.00	30.00
DJ3 Derek Jeter Bat-Jsy AU/2		
EC1 Eric Chavez Bat-Jsy	10.00	3.00
EC2 Eric Chavez Cap-Jsy/100	15.00	4.50
GM Greg Maddux Bat-Jsy	25.00	7.50
IR Ivan Rodriguez Bat-Jsy	15.00	4.50
JB1 Jeff Bagwell Bat-Jsy	15.00	4.50
JB2 Jeff Bagwell Ball-Jsy/50	40.00	12.00
JC Jose Canseco Bat-Jsy	15.00	4.50
JL1 Javy Lopez Bat-Jsy	10.00	3.00
JL2 Javy Lopez Cap-Jsy	15.00	4.50
KG1 Ken Griffey Jr. Bat-Jsy	25.00	7.50
KG2 Ken Griffey Jr. Ball-Jsy/50	60.00	18.00
KG3 Ken Griffey Jr. Bat-Jsy AU/24		
MM1 Mark McGwire Ball-Base/250	50.00	15.00
MM2 Mark McGwire Ball-Base/250	50.00	15.00
MR1 Manny Ramirez Bat-Jsy	10.00	3.00
MR2 Manny Ramirez Bat-Jsy AU/24		
MW Matt Williams Bat-Jsy	10.00	3.00
PM Pedro Martinez Cap-Jsy/100	25.00	7.50
PO Paul O'Neill Bat-Jsy	15.00	4.50
VG1 Vladimir Guerrero Bat-Jsy	15.00	4.50
VG2 Vladimir Guerrero Cap-Jsy/100	25.00	7.50
VG3 Vladimir Guerrero Ball-Jsy/50	40.00	12.00
TGL Troy Glaus Bat-Jsy	15.00	4.50
TGW1 Tony Gwynn Bat-Jsy	15.00	4.50
TGW2 Tony Gwynn Ball-Jsy/50	50.00	15.00
TGW3 Tony Gwynn Cap-Jsy/100	30.00	9.00

2000 SPx Winning Materials Update

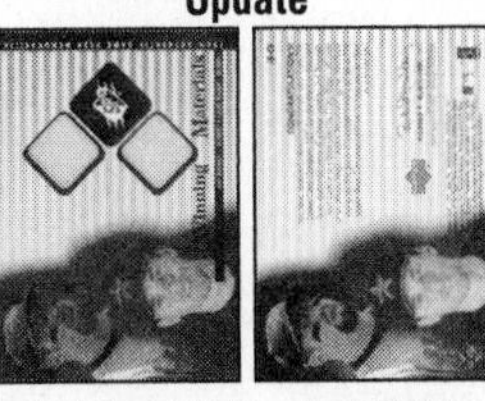

Randomly inserted into packs of 2000 Upper Deck Rookie Update (at an approximate rate of one per box), this 28-card insert features game-used memorabilia cards from some of baseball's top athletes. The set also includes a few members of the 2000 USA Olympic Baseball team. Card backs carry the player's initials as numbering.

Card	Nm-Mt	Ex-Mt
BA-AE Brent Abernathy / Adam Everett Bat-Bat	8.00	2.40
BW-EY Brad Wilkerson / Ernie Young Bat-Bat	10.00	3.00
CR-TG Cal Ripken / Tony Gwynn Base-Base	40.00	12.00
DJ-AR Derek Jeter / Alex Rodriguez Base-Bat	40.00	12.00
DJ-NG Derek Jeter / Nomar Garciaparra Base-Bat	50.00	15.00
FT-MO Frank Thomas / Magglio Ordonez Base-Base	15.00	4.50
G-S-R Ken Griffey Jr. / Sammy Sosa / Alex Rodriguez Jsy-Jsy-Jsy	50.00	15.00
GW-BS Ben Sheets Ball-Jsy	10.00	3.00
GW-DM D.Mientkiewicz Bat-Base	8.00	2.40
GW-EY Ernie Young Bat-Base	8.00	2.40
GW-GD Travis Dawkins / Mike Kinkade Bat-Bat	8.00	2.40
GW-JC John Cotton Bat-Jsy	8.00	2.40
GW-MN Mike Neill Bat-Jsy	8.00	2.40
GW-SB Sean Burroughs Bat-Jsy	10.00	3.00
IR-RP Ivan Rodriguez / Rafael Palmeiro Ball-Ball	15.00	4.50
J-G-R Derek Jeter / Nomar Garciaparra / Alex Rodriguez Base-Ball-Bat	120.00	36.00
JB-CB Jeff Bagwell / Craig Biggio Base-Base	15.00	4.50
JC-BB Jose Canseco / Barry Bonds Ball-Ball	30.00	9.00
KG-SS Ken Griffey Jr. / Sammy Sosa Bat-Bat	30.00	9.00
MM-KG Mark McGwire / Ken Griffey Jr. Ball-Bat	50.00	15.00
MM-RA Mark McGwire / Rick Ankiel Base-Base	40.00	12.00
MM-SS Mark McGwire / Sammy Sosa Ball-Ball	50.00	15.00
MP-RV Mike Piazza / Robin Ventura Ball-Ball	25.00	7.50
NG-PM N.Garciaparra / Pedro Martinez Ball-Ball	30.00	9.00
RC-PM Roger Clemens / Pedro Martinez Ball-Ball	40.00	12.00
SB-BS Sean Burroughs / Ben Sheets Bat-Base	15.00	4.50

2000 SPx Winning Materials Update Numbered

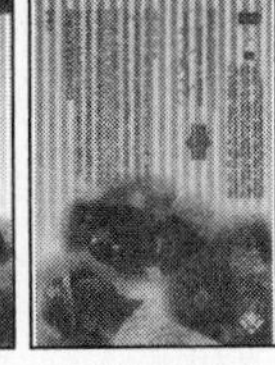

Randomly inserted into 2001 Rookie Update packs, this 3-card insert features game-used memorabilia from three different major leaguers on the same card. These rare gems are individually serial numbered to 50. Card backs carry the players initials as numbering

Card	Nm-Mt	Ex-Mt
C-B-G Jose Canseco / Barry Bonds / Ken Griffey Jr / Ball-Ball-Bat	120.00	36.00
G-S-M Ken Griffey Jr. / Sammy Sosa / Mark McGwire / Bat-Ball-Base	150.00	45.00
J-G-R Derek Jeter / Nomar Garciaparra / Alex Rodriguez / Base-Ball-Bat	100.00	30.00

2001 SPx

The 2001 SPx product was initially released in early May, 2001, and featured a 150-card base set. 60 additional update cards (151-210) were distributed within Upper Deck Rookie Update packs in late December, 2001. The base set is broken into tiers as follows: Base Veterans (1-90), Young Stars (91-120) serial numbered to 2000, Rookie Jerseys (121-135), and Jersey Autographs (136-150). The Rookie Update SPx cards were broken into tiers as follows: base veterans (151-180) and Young Stars (181-210) serial numbered to 1500. Each basic pack contained four cards and carried a suggested retail price of $6.99. Rookie Update packs contained four cards with an SRP of $4.99.

Card	Nm-Mt	Ex-Mt
COMP.BASIC w/o SP's (90)	25.00	7.50
COMP.UPDATE w/o SP's (30)	10.00	3.00
COMMON CARD (1-90)	.50	.15
COMMON YS (91-120)	8.00	2.40
COMMON JSY (121-135)	10.00	3.00
COMMON (136-150)	15.00	4.50
COMMON (151-180)	.75	.23
COMMON (181-210)	5.00	1.50
1 Darin Erstad	.50	.15
2 Troy Glaus	.75	.23
3 Mo Vaughn	.50	.15
4 Johnny Damon	.50	.15
5 Jason Giambi	1.25	.35
6 Tim Hudson	.50	.15
7 Miguel Tejada	.50	.15
8 Carlos Delgado	.50	.15
9 Raul Mondesi	.50	.15
10 Tony Batista	.50	.15
11 Ben Grieve	.50	.15
12 Greg Vaughn	.50	.15
13 Juan Gonzalez	1.25	.35
14 Jim Thome	1.25	.35
15 Roberto Alomar	1.25	.35
16 John Olerud	.50	.15
17 Edgar Martinez	.75	.23
18 Albert Belle	.50	.15
19 Cal Ripken	4.00	1.20
20 Ivan Rodriguez	1.25	.35
21 Rafael Palmeiro	.75	.23
22 Alex Rodriguez	2.00	.60
23 Nomar Garciaparra	2.00	.60
24 Pedro Martinez	1.25	.35
25 Manny Ramirez	.50	.15
26 Jermaine Dye	.50	.15
27 Mark Quinn	.50	.15
28 Carlos Beltran	.50	.15
29 Tony Clark	.50	.15
30 Bobby Higginson	.50	.15
31 Eric Milton	.50	.15
32 Matt Lawton	.50	.15
33 Frank Thomas	1.25	.35
34 Magglio Ordonez	.50	.15
35 Ray Durham	.50	.15
36 David Wells	.50	.15
37 Derek Jeter	3.00	.90
38 Bernie Williams	.75	.23
39 Roger Clemens UER Wrong uniform number on card	2.50	.75
40 David Justice	.50	.15
41 Jeff Bagwell	.75	.23
42 Richard Hidalgo	.50	.15
43 Moises Alou	.50	.15
44 Chipper Jones	1.25	.35

45 Andruw Jones .50 .15
46 Greg Maddux 2.00 .60
47 Rafael Furcal .50 .15
48 Jeromy Burnitz .50 .15
49 Geoff Jenkins .50 .15
50 Mark McGwire 3.00 .90
51 Jim Edmonds .50 .15
52 Rick Ankiel .50 .15
53 Edgar Renteria .50 .15
54 Sammy Sosa 2.00 .60
55 Kerry Wood 1.25 .35
56 Rondell White .50 .15
57 Randy Johnson 1.25 .35
58 Steve Finley .50 .15
59 Matt Williams .50 .15
60 Luis Gonzalez .50 .15
61 Kevin Brown .50 .15
62 Gary Sheffield .50 .15
63 Shawn Green .50 .15
64 Vladimir Guerrero 1.25 .35
65 Jose Vidro .50 .15
66 Barry Bonds 3.00 .90
67 Jeff Kent .50 .15
68 Livan Hernandez .50 .15
69 Preston Wilson .50 .15
70 Charles Johnson .50 .15
71 Cliff Floyd .50 .15
72 Mike Piazza 2.00 .60
73 Edgardo Alfonzo .50 .15
74 Jay Payton .50 .15
75 Robin Ventura .50 .15
76 Tony Gwynn 1.50 .45
77 Phil Nevin .50 .15
78 Ryan Klesko .50 .15
79 Scott Rolen .75 .23
80 Pat Burrell .50 .15
81 Bob Abreu .50 .15
82 Brian Giles .50 .15
83 Kris Benson .50 .15
84 Jason Kendall .50 .15
85 Ken Griffey Jr. 2.00 .60
86 Barry Larkin 1.25 .35
87 Sean Casey .50 .15
88 Todd Helton .75 .23
89 Larry Walker .75 .23
90 Mike Hampton .50 .15
91 Billy Sylvester YS RC 8.00 2.40
92 Josh Towers YS RC 8.00 2.40
93 Zach Day YS RC 8.00 2.40
94 Martin Vargas YS RC 8.00 2.40
95 Adam Pettyjohn YS RC 8.00 2.40
96 Andres Torres YS RC 8.00 2.40
97 Kris Keller YS RC 8.00 2.40
98 Blaine Neal YS RC 8.00 2.40
99 Kyle Kessel YS RC 8.00 2.40
100 Greg Miller YS RC 8.00 2.40
101 Shawn Sonnier YS 8.00 2.40
102 Alexis Gomez YS RC 8.00 2.40
103 Grant Balfour YS RC 8.00 2.40
104 Henry Mateo YS RC 8.00 2.40
105 Wilken Ruan YS RC 8.00 2.40
106 Nick Maness YS RC 8.00 2.40
107 J. Michaels YS RC 8.00 2.40
108 Esix Snead YS RC 8.00 2.40
109 William Ortega YS RC 8.00 2.40
110 David Elder YS RC 8.00 2.40
111 J. Melian YS RC 8.00 2.40
112 Nate Teut YS RC 8.00 2.40
113 Jason Smith YS RC 8.00 2.40
114 Mike Penney YS RC 8.00 2.40
115 Jose Mieses YS RC 8.00 2.40
116 Juan Pena YS 8.00 2.40
117 B. Lawrence YS RC 8.00 2.40
118 Jeremy Owens YS RC 8.00 2.40
119 C. Valderrama YS RC 8.00 2.40
120 Rafael Soriano YS RC 15.00 4.50
121 H. Ramirez JSY RC 15.00 4.50
122 R. Rodriguez JSY RC 10.00 3.00
123 Juan Diaz JSY RC 10.00 3.00
124 Donnie Bridges JSY 10.00 3.00
125 Tyler Walker JSY RC 10.00 3.00
126 Erick Almonte JSY RC 10.00 3.00
127 Jesus Colome JSY 10.00 3.00
128 Ryan Freel JSY RC 10.00 3.00
129 Elpidio Guzman JSY RC 10.00 3.00
130 Jack Cust JSY 10.00 3.00
131 Eric Hinske JSY RC 15.00 4.50
132 Josh Fogg JSY RC 10.00 3.00
133 Juan Uribe JSY RC 10.00 3.00
134 Bert Snow JSY RC 10.00 3.00
135 Pedro Feliz JSY 10.00 3.00
136 W. Betemit JSY AU RC 15.00 4.50
137 S. Douglass JSY AU RC 15.00 4.50
138 D. Stenson JSY AU 15.00 4.50
139 Brandon Inge JSY AU 15.00 4.50
140 M. Ensberg JSY AU RC 30.00 9.00
141 Brian Cole JSY AU 15.00 4.50
142 A. Hernandez JSY AU RC 15.00 4.50
143 Brandon Duckworth JSY AU RC 15.00 4.50
144 J. Wilson JSY AU RC 15.00 4.50
145 T. Hafner JSY AU RC 40.00 12.00
146 Carlos Pena JSY AU 15.00 4.50
147 C. Patterson JSY AU 25.00 7.50
148 Xavier Nady JSY AU 15.00 4.50
149 Jason Hart JSY AU 15.00 4.50
150 I. Suzuki JSY AU RC 600.00 180.00
151 Garret Anderson .75 .23
152 Jermaine Dye .75 .23
153 Shannon Stewart .75 .23
154 Toby Hall .75 .23
155 C.C. Sabathia .75 .23
156 Bret Boone .75 .23
157 Tony Batista .75 .23
158 Gabe Kapler .75 .23
159 Carl Everett .75 .23
160 Mike Sweeney .75 .23
161 Dean Palmer .75 .23
162 Doug Mientkiewicz .75 .23
163 Carlos Lee .75 .23
164 Mike Mussina 2.00 .60
165 Lance Berkman .75 .23
166 Ken Caminiti .75 .23
167 Ben Sheets .75 .23
168 Matt Morris .75 .23
169 Fred McGriff 1.25 .35
170 Curt Schilling 1.25 .35
171 Paul LoDuca .75 .23
172 Javier Vazquez .75 .23
173 Rich Aurilia .75 .23
174 A.J. Burnett .75 .23
175 Al Leiter .75 .23
176 Mark Kotsay .75 .23
177 Jimmy Rollins .75 .23
178 Aramis Ramirez .75 .23
179 Aaron Boone .75 .23
180 Jeff Cirillo .75 .23
181 J.Estrada YS RC 6.00 1.80
182 Dave Williams YS RC 5.00 1.50
183 D.Mendez YS RC 5.00 1.50
184 Junior Spivey YS RC 10.00 3.00
185 Jay Gibbons YS RC 12.00 3.60
186 Kyle Lohse YS RC 10.00 3.00
187 Willie Harris YS RC 5.00 1.50
188 Juan Cruz YS RC 5.00 1.50
189 Joe Kennedy YS RC 5.00 1.50
190 D.Sanchez YS RC 5.00 1.50
191 Jorge Julio YS RC 5.00 1.50
192 Cesar Crespo YS RC 5.00 1.50
193 Casey Fossum YS RC 5.00 1.50
194 Brian Roberts YS RC 5.00 1.50
195 Troy Mattes YS RC 5.00 1.50
196 R.Mackowiak YS RC 5.00 1.50
197 T.Shinjo YS RC 12.00 3.60
198 Nick Punto YS RC 5.00 1.50
199 Wilmy Caceres YS RC 5.00 1.50
200 Jeremy Affeldt YS RC 10.00 3.00
201 Bret Prinz YS RC 5.00 1.50
202 Delvin James YS RC 5.00 1.50
203 Luis Pineda YS RC 5.00 1.50
204 Matt White YS RC 5.00 1.50
205 B.Knight YS RC 5.00 1.50
206 Albert Pujols YS AU RC 350.00 105.00
207 M.Teixeira YS AU RC 100.00 30.00
208 Mark Prior YS AU RC 300.00 90.00
209 D.Brazelton YS AU RC 25.00 7.50
210 Bud Smith YS AU RC 15.00 4.50

2001 SPx Spectrum

Randomly inserted into packs, this 120-card insert is a partial parallel of the 2001 SPx base set. Please note that each card is individually serial numbered to 50.

Nm-Mt Ex-Mt
*STARS 1-90: 12.5X TO 30X BASIC CARDS
*YS 91-120: 1X TO 2.5X BASIC CARDS

2001 SPx Foundations

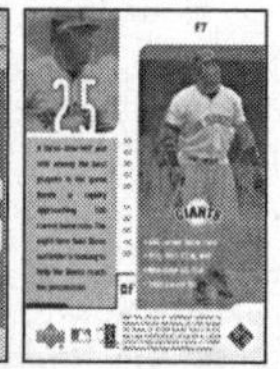

Randomly inserted into packs at one in eight, this 12-card insert features players that are the major foundation that keeps their respective ballclubs together. Card backs carry a "F" prefix.

Nm-Mt Ex-Mt
COMPLETE SET (12) 50.00 15.00
F1 Mark McGwire 8.00 2.40
F2 Jeff Bagwell 2.00 .60
F3 Alex Rodriguez 5.00 1.50
F4 Ken Griffey Jr. 5.00 1.50
F5 Andruw Jones 2.00 .60
F6 Cal Ripken 10.00 3.00
F7 Barry Bonds 8.00 2.40
F8 Derek Jeter 8.00 2.40
F9 Frank Thomas 3.00 .90
F10 Sammy Sosa 5.00 1.50
F11 Tony Gwynn 4.00 1.20
F12 Vladimir Guerrero 3.00 .90

2001 SPx SPXcitement

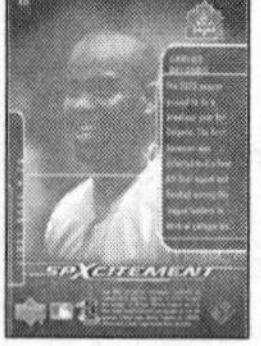

Randomly inserted into packs at one in eight, this 12-card insert features players that are known for bringing excitement to the game. Card backs carry an "X" prefix.

Nm-Mt Ex-Mt
COMPLETE SET (12) 50.00 15.00
X1 Alex Rodriguez 5.00 1.50
X2 Jason Giambi 3.00 .90
X3 Ken Griffey Jr. 5.00 1.50
X4 Sammy Sosa 5.00 1.50
X5 Frank Thomas 3.00 .90
X6 Todd Helton 2.00 .60
X7 Mark McGwire 8.00 2.40
X8 Mike Piazza 5.00 1.50
X9 Derek Jeter 8.00 2.40
X10 Vladimir Guerrero 3.00 .90
X11 Carlos Delgado 2.00 .60
X12 Chipper Jones 3.00 .90

2001 SPx Untouchable Talents

Randomly inserted into packs at one in 15, this six-card insert features players whose skills are unmatched. Card backs carry a "UT" prefix.

Nm-Mt Ex-Mt
COMPLETE SET (6) 40.00 12.00
UT1 Ken Griffey Jr. 5.00 1.50
UT2 Mike Piazza 5.00 1.50
UT3 Mark McGwire 8.00 2.40
UT4 Alex Rodriguez 5.00 1.50
UT5 Sammy Sosa 5.00 1.50
UT6 Derek Jeter 8.00 2.40

2001 SPx Winning Materials Ball-Base

Randomly inserted into packs, this 13-card insert features actual swatches of both game-used baseball and base. Card backs carry a "B" prefix followed by the player's initials. Each card is individually serial numbered to 250.

Nm-Mt Ex-Mt
B-AJ Andruw Jones 15.00 4.50
B-AR Alex Rodriguez 50.00 15.00
B-BB Barry Bonds 80.00 24.00
B-CJ Chipper Jones 25.00 7.50
B-DJ Derek Jeter 80.00 24.00
B-FT Frank Thomas 25.00 7.50
B-KG Ken Griffey Jr. 50.00 15.00
B-MM Mark McGwire 120.00 36.00
B-MP Mike Piazza 50.00 15.00
B-NG Nomar Garciaparra 50.00 15.00
B-PM Pedro Martinez 25.00 7.50
B-SS Sammy Sosa 50.00 15.00
B-VG Vladimir Guerrero 25.00 7.50

2001 SPx Winning Materials Base Duos

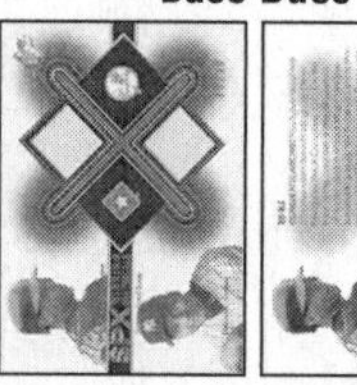

Randomly inserted into packs, this 10-card insert features actual swatches of game-used bases. Card backs carry a "B2" prefix followed by the player's initials. Each card is individually serial numbered to 50.

Nm-Mt Ex-Mt
B2-GJ Nomar Garciaparra / Derek Jeter 120.00 36.00
B2-JG Derek Jeter / Jason Giambi 120.00 36.00
B2-JP Derek Jeter / Mike Piazza 120.00 36.00
B2-MG Mark McGwire / Ken Griffey Jr. 150.00 45.00
B2-MR Mark McGwire / Alex Rodriguez 200.00 60.00
B2-MS Mark McGwire / Sammy Sosa 150.00 45.00
B2-PB Mike Piazza / Barry Bonds 120.00 36.00
B2-PM Mike Piazza / Mark McGwire 200.00 60.00
B2-RJ Alex Rodriguez / Derek Jeter 150.00 45.00
B2-TR Frank Thomas / Alex Rodriguez 100.00 30.00

2001 SPx Winning Materials Base Trios

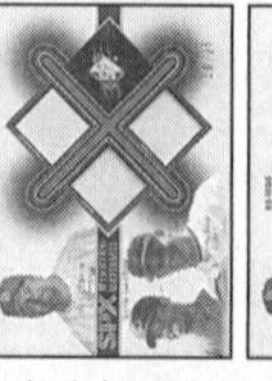

Randomly inserted into packs, this five-card insert set features actual swatches of game-used bases. Card backs carry a "B3" prefix followed by the player's initials. Each card is individually serial numbered to 25. Due to market scarcity, no pricing is provided.

Nm-Mt Ex-Mt
B3-BMS Barry Bonds / Mark McGwire / Sammy Sosa
B3-GJR Ken Griffey Jr. / Derek Jeter / Alex Rodriguez
B3-JRG Derek Jeter / Alex Rodriguez / Nomar Garciaparra
B3-MGS Mark McGwire / Ken Griffey Jr. / Sammy Sosa
B3-PJW Mike Piazza / Derek Jeter / Bernie Williams

2001 SPx Winning Materials Bat-Jersey

Randomly inserted into packs, this 21-card insert features actual swatches of both game-used bats and jerseys. Card backs carry the player's initials as numbering.

Nm-Mt Ex-Mt
AJ1 Andruw Jones AS 15.00 4.50
AJ2 Andruw Jones 15.00 4.50
AR1 Alex Rodriguez AS 25.00 7.50
AR2 Alex Rodriguez 25.00 7.50
BB1 Barry Bonds AS 40.00 12.00
BB2 Barry Bonds 40.00 12.00
CD Carlos Delgado AS * 15.00 4.50
CJ1 Chipper Jones AS 20.00 6.00
CJ2 Chipper Jones 20.00 6.00
CR Cal Ripken 50.00 15.00
FT Frank Thomas 20.00 6.00
IR1 Ivan Rodriguez AS 20.00 6.00
IR2 Ivan Rodriguez 20.00 6.00
JD Joe DiMaggio 150.00 45.00
JE Jim Edmonds * 15.00 4.50
KG1 Ken Griffey Jr. AS 25.00 7.50
KG2 Ken Griffey Jr. 25.00 7.50
RA Rick Ankiel * 15.00 4.50
RJ1 Randy Johnson AS 20.00 6.00
RJ2 Randy Johnson 20.00 6.00
SS Sammy Sosa 25.00 7.50

2001 SPx Winning Materials Jersey Duos

Randomly inserted into packs, this 13-card insert features actual swatches of game-used jerseys. Card backs carry both player's initials as numbering. Each card is individually serial numbered to 50.

Nm-Mt Ex-Mt
AJCJ Andruw Jones / Chipper Jones 40.00 12.00
ARCR Alex Rodriguez / Cal Ripken 150.00 45.00
BBSS Barry Bonds / Sammy Sosa 100.00 30.00
CJDW Chipper Jones / David Wells 40.00 12.00
IRAR Ivan Rodriguez / Alex Rodriguez 80.00 24.00
KGAR Ken Griffey Jr. / Alex Rodriguez AS 100.00 30.00
KGBB Ken Griffey Jr. / Barry Bonds AS 150.00 45.00
KGJD Ken Griffey Jr. / Joe DiMaggio 200.00 60.00
KGKG Ken Griffey Jr. / Ken Griffey Jr. AS 100.00 30.00
KGRJ Ken Griffey Jr. / Randy Johnson AS 100.00 30.00
KGSS Ken Griffey Jr. / Sammy Sosa 100.00 30.00
SSCD Sammy Sosa / Carlos Delgado 50.00 15.00
SSFT Sammy Sosa / Frank Thomas 50.00 15.00

2001 SPx Winning Materials Jersey Trios

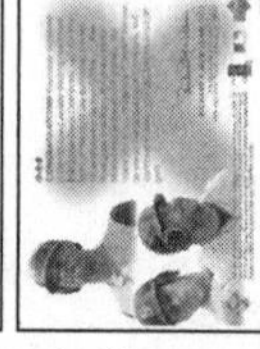

Randomly inserted into packs, this seven-card insert set features actual swatches of game-used jerseys. Card backs carry the first letter of each player's last name as numbering. Each card is individually serial numbered to 25. Due to market scarcity, no pricing is provided for these cards.

Nm-Mt Ex-Mt
B-G-J Barry Bonds / Ken Griffey Jr. / Andruw Jones
D-B-S Carlos Delgado / Barry Bonds / Sammy Sosa
D-G-J Joe DiMaggio / Ken Griffey Jr. / Andruw Jones
G-R-B Ken Griffey Jr. / Alex Rodriguez / Barry Bonds
R-J-D Cal Ripken / Chipper Jones / Carlos Delgado
R-R-D Alex Rodriguez / Ivan Rodriguez / Carlos Delgado
S-G-C Sammy Sosa / Ken Griffey Jr. / Chipper Jones

2001 SPx Winning Materials Update Duos

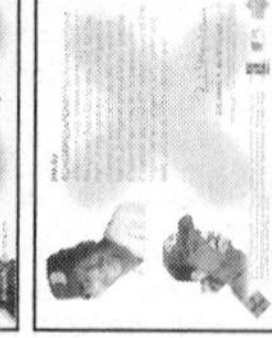

Inserted into 2001 Upper Deck Rookie Update packs at a rate of one in 15, these cards feature two players and a memorabilia piece from each of them.

Nm-Mt Ex-Mt
AP-JE Albert Pujols / Jim Edmonds 50.00 15.00
AS-KS Aaron Sele / Kazuhiro Sasaki 10.00 3.00
BB-LG Barry Bonds / Luis Gonzalez 25.00 7.50
BW-MR Bernie Williams / Mariano Rivera 15.00 4.50
BW-RJ Bernie Williams / Reggie Jackson 15.00 4.50
CP-BK Chan Ho Park / Byung-Hyun Kim 10.00 3.00
CP-FV Chan Ho Park / Fernando Valenzuela 15.00 4.50
CR-EM Cal Ripken / Eddie Murray 40.00 12.00
CR-X2 Cal Ripken / Cal Ripken 50.00 15.00
CS-RJ Curt Schilling / Randy Johnson 15.00 4.50
EM-JM Eric Milton / Joe Mays 10.00 3.00
FT-MO Frank Thomas / Magglio Ordonez 15.00 4.50
GS-SG Gary Sheffield / Shawn Green 10.00 3.00
HN-MY Hideo Nomo / Masato Yoshii 20.00 6.00
IR-AR Ivan Rodriguez / Alex Rodriguez 20.00 6.00
JB-CB Jeff Bagwell / Craig Biggio 15.00 4.50
JB-RY Jeromy Burnitz / Robin Yount 15.00 4.50
JG-BB Jason Giambi / Barry Bonds 25.00 7.50
KG-SC Ken Griffey Jr. / Sean Casey 20.00 6.00
LW-TH Larry Walker / Todd Helton 15.00 4.50
MP-EA Mike Piazza / Edgardo Alfonzo 15.00 4.50
MR-JG Manny Ramirez / Juan Gonzalez 15.00 4.50
PM-GM Pedro Martinez / Greg Maddux 15.00 4.50
PM-RJ Pedro Martinez / Randy Johnson 15.00 4.50
SR-BA Scott Rolen / Bobby Abreu 15.00 4.50
SS-EB Sammy Sosa / Ernie Banks 20.00 6.00
SS-JG Sammy Sosa / Jason Giambi 20.00 6.00
TG-CR Tony Gwynn / Cal Ripken 40.00 12.00
TG-DW Tony Gwynn / Dave Winfield 15.00 4.50
TG-X2 Tony Gwynn / Tony Gwynn 20.00 6.00
TS-HN Tsuyoshi Shinjo / Hideo Nomo 20.00 6.00

2001 SPx Winning Materials Update Trios

Inserted into 2001 Upper Deck Rookie Update Packs at a rate of one in 15, these 22 cards feature three players as well as a piece of memorabilia from each one.

Nm-Mt Ex-Mt
BGG Barry Bonds / Luis Gonzalez / Ken Griffey Jr. 40.00 12.00
BTD Jeff Bagwell / Frank Thomas / Carlos Delgado 25.00 7.50
CHN Roger Clemens / Tim Hudson / Hideo Nomo 25.00 7.50
DEA J.D. Drew / Jim Edmonds / Bobby Abreu 10.00 3.00
DOP Carlos Delgado / Magglio Ordonez / Albert Pujols 50.00 15.00
GWS Luis Gonzalez / Matt Williams / Curt Schilling 15.00 4.50
GZH Jason Giambi 25.00 7.50

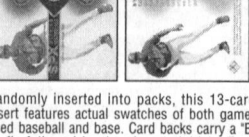

Barry Zito
Tim Hudson
HDG Todd Helton 25.00 7.50
Carlos Delgado
Jason Giambi
JAF Chipper Jones 25.00 7.50
Andruw Jones
Rafael Furcal
KBA Jeff Kent 25.00 7.50
Barry Bonds
Rich Aurilia
MGJ Greg Maddux 25.00 7.50
Tom Glavine
Andruw Jones
PPV Jay Payton 20.00 6.00
Mike Piazza
Robin Ventura
PWO Andy Pettitte 15.00 4.50
Bernie Williams
Paul O'Neill
RPK Ivan Rodriguez 20.00 6.00
Mike Piazza
Jason Kendall
RRK Alex Rodriguez 20.00 6.00
Ivan Rodriguez
Gabe Kapler
SJC Curt Schilling 40.00 12.00
Randy Johnson
Roger Clemens
SKB Gary Sheffield 10.00 3.00
Eric Karros
Kevin Brown
SSM Aaron Sele 50.00 15.00
Ichiro Suzuki
Edgar Martinez
SYN Kazuhiro Sasaki 25.00 7.50
Masato Yoshii
Hideo Nomo
TDK Frank Thomas 25.00 7.50
Ray Durham
Paul Konerko
TGA Jim Thome 25.00 7.50
Juan Gonzalez
Roberto Alomar
VRF Omar Vizquel 20.00 6.00
Alex Rodriguez
Rafael Furcal

2002 SPx

This 280-card set was issued in two separate brands. The SPx product itself was released in late April, 2002 and contained cards 1-250. These cards were issued in four card packs of which were distributed at a rate of 18 packs per box and 14 boxes per case. Cards numbered from 91 through 120 feature either a portrait or an action shot of a prospect. Both the portrait and the action shot were issued with separate stated print runs of 1800 serial numbered cards (for a total of 3,600 of each player in the subset). Cards 121-150 were not serial-numbered but instead feature autographs and were seeded into packs at a rate of 1:18. Cards numbered 151 through 190 were issued and featured jersey swatches of leading major league players. These cards had a stated print run of either 700 or 800 serial numbered cards. High series cards 191-250 were distributed in mid-December, 2002 within packs of 2002 Upper Deck Rookie Update. Cards 191-220 feature veterans on new teams and were commonly distributed in all packs. Cards 221-250 feature prospects and were signed by the player. In addition, the card were serial numbered to 825 copies. Though stated pack odds were not released by the manufacturer, we believe these signed cards were seeded at an approximate rate of 1:16 Upper Deck Rookie Update packs.

	Nm-Mt	Ex-Mt
COMP.LOW w/o SP's (90)	25.00	7.50
COMP.UPDATE w/o SP's (30)	10.00	3.00
COMMON CARD (1-90)	.50	.15
COMMON ROOKIE (91A-	10.00	3.00
COMMON CARD (121-150)	15.00	4.50
COMMON CARD (151-190)	10.00	3.00
COMMON CARD (191-220)	.75	.23
COMMON CARD (221-250)	15.00	4.50
1 Troy Glaus	.75	.23
2 Darin Erstad	.50	.15
3 David Justice	.50	.15
4 Tim Hudson	.50	.15
5 Miguel Tejada	.50	.15
6 Barry Zito	.75	.23
7 Carlos Delgado	.50	.15
8 Shannon Stewart	.50	.15
9 Greg Vaughn	.75	.23
10 Toby Hall	.50	.15
11 Jim Thome	1.25	.35
12 C.C. Sabathia	.50	.15
13 Ichiro Suzuki	2.00	.60
14 Edgar Martinez	.75	.23
15 Freddy Garcia	.50	.15
16 Mike Cameron	.50	.15
17 Jeff Conine	.50	.15
18 Tony Batista	.50	.15
19 Alex Rodriguez	2.00	.60
20 Rafael Palmeiro	.75	.23
21 Ivan Rodriguez	1.25	.35
22 Carl Everett	.50	.15
23 Pedro Martinez	1.25	.35
24 Manny Ramirez	.50	.15
25 Nomar Garciaparra	2.00	.60
26 Johnny Damon	.50	.15
27 Mike Sweeney	.50	.15
28 Carlos Beltran	.50	.15
29 Dmitri Young	.50	.15
30 Joe Mays	.50	.15
31 Doug Mientkiewicz	.50	.15
32 Cristian Guzman	.50	.15
33 Corey Koskie	.50	.15
34 Frank Thomas	1.25	.35
35 Magglio Ordonez	.50	.15
36 Mark Buehrle	.50	.15
37 Bernie Williams	.75	.23
38 Roger Clemens	2.50	.75
39 Derek Jeter	3.00	.90
40 Jason Giambi	1.25	.35
41 Mike Mussina	1.25	.35
42 Lance Berkman	.50	.15
43 Jeff Bagwell	.75	.23
44 Roy Oswalt	.50	.15
45 Greg Maddux	2.00	.60
46 Chipper Jones	1.25	.35
47 Andruw Jones	.50	.15
48 Gary Sheffield	.50	.15
49 Geoff Jenkins	.50	.15
50 Richie Sexson	.50	.15
51 Ben Sheets	.50	.15
52 Albert Pujols	2.50	.75
53 J.D. Drew	.50	.15
54 Jim Edmonds	.50	.15
55 Sammy Sosa	2.00	.60
56 Moises Alou	.50	.15
57 Kerry Wood	1.25	.35
58 Jon Lieber	.50	.15
59 Fred McGriff	.75	.23
60 Randy Johnson	1.25	.35
61 Luis Gonzalez	.50	.15
62 Curt Schilling	.75	.23
63 Kevin Brown	.50	.15
64 Hideo Nomo	1.25	.35
65 Shawn Green	.50	.15
66 Vladimir Guerrero	1.25	.35
67 Jose Vidro	.50	.15
68 Barry Bonds	3.00	.90
69 Jeff Kent	.50	.15
70 Rich Aurilia	.50	.15
71 Cliff Floyd	.50	.15
72 Josh Beckett	.75	.23
73 Preston Wilson	.50	.15
74 Mike Piazza	2.00	.60
75 Mo Vaughn	.50	.15
76 Jeromy Burnitz	.50	.15
77 Roberto Alomar	1.25	.35
78 Phil Nevin	.50	.15
79 Ryan Klesko	.50	.15
80 Scott Rolen	.75	.23
81 Bobby Abreu	.50	.15
82 Jimmy Rollins	.50	.15
83 Brian Giles	.50	.15
84 Aramis Ramirez	.50	.15
85 Ken Griffey Jr.	2.00	.60
86 Sean Casey	.50	.15
87 Barry Larkin	1.25	.35
88 Mike Hampton	.50	.15
89 Larry Walker	.75	.23
90 Todd Helton	.75	.23
91A Ron Calloway YS RC	10.00	3.00
91P Ron Calloway YS RC	10.00	3.00
92A Joe Orloski YS RC	10.00	3.00
92P Joe Orloski YS RC	10.00	3.00
93A An. Machado YS RC	10.00	3.00
93P An. Machado YS RC	10.00	3.00
94A Eric Good YS RC	10.00	3.00
94P Eric Good YS RC	10.00	3.00
95A Reed Johnson YS RC	10.00	3.00
95P Reed Johnson YS RC	10.00	3.00
96A Brendan Donnelly YS RC	10.00	3.00
96P Brendan Donnelly YS RC	10.00	3.00
97A Chris Baker YS RC	10.00	3.00
97P Chris Baker YS RC	10.00	3.00
98A Wilson Valdez YS RC	10.00	3.00
98P Wilson Valdez YS RC	10.00	3.00
99A Scotty Layfield YS RC	10.00	3.00
99P Scotty Layfield YS RC	10.00	3.00
100A P.J. Bevis YS RC	10.00	3.00
100P P.J. Bevis YS RC	10.00	3.00
101A Edwin Almonte YS RC	10.00	3.00
101P Edwin Almonte YS RC	10.00	3.00
102A Francis Beltran YS RC	10.00	3.00
102P Francis Beltran YS RC	10.00	3.00
103A Val Pascucci YS	10.00	3.00
103P Val Pascucci YS	10.00	3.00
104A Nelson Castro YS RC	10.00	3.00
104P Nelson Castro YS RC	10.00	3.00
105A Michael Crudale YS RC	10.00	3.00
105P Michael Crudale YS RC	10.00	3.00
106A Colin Young YS RC	10.00	3.00
106P Colin Young YS RC	10.00	3.00
107A Todd Donovan YS RC	10.00	3.00
107P Todd Donovan YS RC	10.00	3.00
108A Felix Escalona YS RC	10.00	3.00
108P Felix Escalona YS RC	10.00	3.00
109A Brandon Backe YS RC	10.00	3.00
109P Brandon Backe YS RC	10.00	3.00
110A Corey Thurman YS RC	10.00	3.00
110P Corey Thurman YS RC	10.00	3.00
111A Kyle Kane YS RC	10.00	3.00
111P Kyle Kane YS RC	10.00	3.00
112A Allan Simpson YS RC	10.00	3.00
112P Allan Simpson YS RC	10.00	3.00
113A Jose Valverde YS RC	10.00	3.00
113P Jose Valverde YS RC	10.00	3.00
114A Chris Booker YS RC	10.00	3.00
114P Chris Booker YS RC	10.00	3.00
115A Brandon Puffer YS RC	10.00	3.00
115P Brandon Puffer YS RC	10.00	3.00
116A John Foster YS RC	10.00	3.00
116P John Foster YS RC	10.00	3.00
117A Cliff Bartosh YS RC	10.00	3.00
117P Cliff Bartosh YS RC	10.00	3.00
118A Gustavo Chacin YS RC	10.00	3.00
118P Gustavo Chacin YS RC	10.00	3.00
119A Steve Kent YS RC	10.00	3.00
119P Steve Kent YS RC	10.00	3.00
120A Nate Field YS RC	10.00	3.00
120P Nate Field YS RC	10.00	3.00
121 Victor Alvarez AU RC	15.00	4.50
122 Steve Bechler AU RC	15.00	4.50
123 Adrian Burnside AU RC	15.00	4.50
124 Marlon Byrd AU	15.00	4.50
125 Jaime Cerda AU RC	15.00	4.50
126 Brandon Claussen AU	25.00	7.50
127 Mark Corey AU RC	15.00	4.50
128 Doug Devore AU RC	15.00	4.50
129 Kazuhisa Ishii AU SP RC	100.00	30.00
130 John Ennis AU RC	15.00	4.50
131 Kevin Frederick AU RC	15.00	4.50
132 Josh Hancock AU RC	15.00	4.50
133 Ben Howard AU RC	15.00	4.50
134 Orlando Hudson AU	15.00	4.50
135 Hansel Izquierdo AU RC	15.00	4.50
136 Eric Junge AU RC	15.00	4.50
137 Austin Kearns AU	15.00	4.50
138 Victor Martinez AU	15.00	4.50
139 Luis Martinez AU RC	15.00	4.50
140 Danny Mota AU RC	15.00	4.50
141 Jorge Padilla AU RC	15.00	4.50
142 Andy Pratt AU RC	15.00	4.50
143 Rene Reyes AU RC	15.00	4.50
144 Rodrigo Rosario AU RC	15.00	4.50
145 Tom Shearn AU RC	15.00	4.50
146 So Taguchi AU SP RC	40.00	12.00
147 Dennis Tankersley AU	15.00	4.50
148 Matt Thornton AU RC	15.00	4.50
149 Jeremy Ward AU RC	15.00	4.50
150 Mitch Wylie AU RC	15.00	4.50
151 Pedro Martinez JSY/800	15.00	4.50
152 Cal Ripken JSY/800	40.00	12.00
153 Roger Clemens JSY/800	25.00	7.50
154 Bernie Williams JSY/800	15.00	4.50
155 Jason Giambi JSY/700	25.00	7.50
156 Robin Ventura JSY/800	10.00	3.00
157 Carlos Delgado JSY/800	10.00	3.00
158 Frank Thomas JSY/800	15.00	4.50
159 Mag. Ordonez JSY/800	10.00	3.00
160 Jim Thome JSY/800	15.00	4.50
161 Darin Erstad JSY/800	10.00	3.00
162 Tim Salmon JSY/800	15.00	4.50
163 Tim Hudson JSY/800	10.00	3.00
164 Barry Zito JSY/800	15.00	4.50
165 Ichiro Suzuki JSY/800	40.00	12.00
166 Edgar Martinez JSY/800	15.00	4.50
167 Alex Rodriguez JSY/800	20.00	6.00
168 Ivan Rodriguez JSY/800	15.00	4.50
169 Juan Gonzalez JSY/800	15.00	4.50
170 Greg Maddux JSY/800	15.00	4.50
171 Chipper Jones JSY/800	15.00	4.50
172 Andruw Jones JSY/800	10.00	3.00
173 Tom Glavine JSY/800	15.00	4.50
174 Mike Piazza JSY/800	15.00	4.50
175 Roberto Alomar JSY/800	15.00	4.50
176 Scott Rolen JSY/800	15.00	4.50
177 Sammy Sosa JSY/800	20.00	6.00
178 Moises Alou JSY/800	10.00	3.00
179 Ken Griffey Jr. JSY/700	20.00	6.00
180 Jeff Bagwell JSY/800	15.00	4.50
181 Jim Edmonds JSY/800	10.00	3.00
182 J.D. Drew JSY/800	10.00	3.00
183 Brian Giles JSY/800	10.00	3.00
184 Randy Johnson JSY/800	15.00	4.50
185 Curt Schilling JSY/800	15.00	4.50
186 Luis Gonzalez JSY/800	10.00	3.00
187 Todd Helton JSY/800	15.00	4.50
188 Shawn Green JSY/800	10.00	3.00
189 David Wells JSY/800	10.00	3.00
190 Jeff Kent JSY/800	10.00	3.00
191 Tom Glavine	1.25	.35
192 Cliff Floyd	.75	.23
193 Mark Prior	4.00	1.20
194 Corey Patterson	.75	.23
195 Paul Konerko	.75	.23
196 Adam Dunn	.75	.23
197 Joe Borchard	.75	.23
198 Carlos Pena	.75	.23
199 Juan Encarnacion	.75	.23
200 Luis Castillo	.75	.23
201 Torii Hunter	.75	.23
202 Hee Seop Choi	1.25	.35
203 Bartolo Colon	.75	.23
204 Raul Mondesi	.75	.23
205 Jeff Weaver	.75	.23
206 Eric Munson	.75	.23
207 Alfonso Soriano	1.25	.35
208 Ray Durham	.75	.23
209 Eric Chavez	.75	.23
210 Brett Myers	.75	.23
211 Jeremy Giambi	.75	.23
212 Vicente Padilla	.75	.23
213 Felipe Lopez	.75	.23
214 Sean Burroughs	.75	.23
215 Kenny Lofton	.75	.23
216 Scott Rolen	1.25	.35
217 Carl Crawford	.75	.23
218 Juan Gonzalez	2.00	.60
219 Orlando Hudson	.75	.23
220 Eric Hinske	.75	.23
221 Adam Walker AU RC	15.00	4.50
222 Aaron Cook AU RC	15.00	4.50
223 Cam Esslinger AU RC	15.00	4.50
224 Kirk Saarloos AU RC	15.00	4.50
225 Jose Diaz AU RC	15.00	4.50
226 David Ross AU RC	15.00	4.50
227 Jayson Durocher AU RC	15.00	4.50
228 Brian Mallette AU RC	15.00	4.50
229 Aaron Guiel AU RC	15.00	4.50
230 Jorge Nunez AU RC	15.00	4.50
231 Satoru Komiyama AU RC	25.00	7.50
232 Tyler Yates AU RC	25.00	7.50
233 Pete Zamora AU RC	15.00	4.50
234 Mike Gonzalez AU RC	15.00	4.50
235 Oliver Perez AU RC	25.00	7.50
236 Julius Matos AU RC	15.00	4.50
237 Andy Shibilo AU RC	15.00	4.50
238 J.Simontacchi AU RC	15.00	4.50
239 Ron Chiavacci AU	15.00	4.50
240 Deivis Santos AU	15.00	4.50
241 Travis Driskill AU RC	15.00	4.50
242 Jorge De La Rosa AU RC	15.00	4.50
243 An. Martinez AU RC	15.00	4.50
244 Earl Snyder AU RC	15.00	4.50
245 Freddy Sanchez AU RC	15.00	4.50
246 Miguel Asencio AU RC	15.00	4.50
247 Juan Brito AU RC	15.00	4.50
248 Franklyn German AU RC	15.00	4.50
249 Chris Snelling AU RC	25.00	7.50
250 Ken Huckaby AU RC	15.00	4.50

2002 SPx SuperStar Swatch Gold

Randomly inserted in packs, these cards parallel the final forty cards of the base set. These cards were printed to a stated print run of 150 serial numbered sets.

Nm-Mt Ex-Mt
*GOLD JSY: .6X TO 1.5X BASIC JSY..

2002 SPx SuperStar Swatch Silver

Randomly inserted in packs, these cards parallel the final forty cards of the base set. These cards were printed to a stated print run of 400 serial numbered sets.

Nm-Mt Ex-Mt
*SILVER JSY: .4X TO 1X BASIC JSY ..

2002 SPx Sweet Spot Preview Bat Barrel

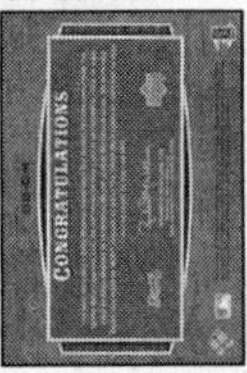

Randomly inserted in packs, these cards feature bat "barrel" cards of leading players. Each card was printed to a different amount and we have notated that information next to their name in our checklist. Due to market scarcity, no pricing is provided for these cards.

Nm-Mt Ex-Mt
BB-AJ Andruw Jones/5
BB-AR Alex Rodriguez/5
BB-CB Carlos Beltran/1
BB-CD Carlos Delgado/1
BB-CJ Chipper Jones/5
BB-EC Eric Chavez/1
BB-EM Edgar Martinez/2
BB-FT Frank Thomas/8
BB-GM Greg Maddux/5
BB-GS Gary Sheffield/5
BB-IR Ivan Rodriguez/7
BB-IS Ichiro Suzuki/2
BB-JD J.D. Drew/1
BB-JE Jim Edmonds/1
BB-JG Jason Giambi/1
BB-JT Jim Thome/1
BB-KG Ken Griffey Jr./6
BB-KW Kerry Wood/1
BB-MP Mike Piazza/7
BB-MR Manny Ramirez/4
BB-MW Matt Williams/5
BB-PW Preston Wilson/1
BB-RA Roberto Alomar/3
BB-RC Roger Clemens/1
BB-RP Rafael Palmeiro/1
BB-SG Shawn Green/7
BB-SS Sammy Sosa/5
BB-TG Tom Glavine/5
BB-TH Todd Helton/3

2002 SPx Winning Materials 2-Player Base Combos

Randomly inserted into packs, these cards include bases used by both players featured on the card. These cards were issued to a stated print run of 200 serial numbered sets.

	Nm-Mt	Ex-Mt
B-BG Barry Bonds	40.00	12.00
Shawn Green		
B-GR Troy Glaus	30.00	9.00
Alex Rodriguez		
B-GS Ken Griffey Jr.	40.00	12.00
Sammy Sosa		
B-IM Ichiro Suzuki	60.00	18.00
Edgar Martinez		
B-PE Mike Piazza	25.00	7.50
Jim Edmonds		
B-PI Albert Pujols	100.00	30.00
Ichiro Suzuki		
B-RJ Alex Rodriguez	60.00	18.00
Derek Jeter		
B-SG Sammy Sosa	30.00	9.00
Luis Gonzalez		
B-SR Kazuhiro Sasaki	25.00	7.50
Mariano Rivera		
B-WJ Bernie Williams	50.00	15.00
Derek Jeter		

2002 SPx Winning Materials 2-Player Jersey Combos

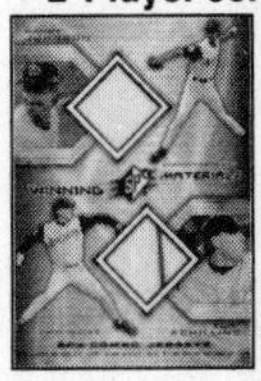

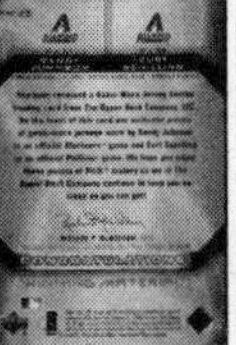

Inserted at stated odds of one in 18, these 29 cards feature not only the players but a jersey swatch from each player. A few players were issued in lesser quantities and we have notated that with an SP in our checklist. Other players were issued in larger quantities and we have notated that with an asterisk next to the player's name.

	Nm-Mt	Ex-Mt
WM-AR Alex Rodriguez	20.00	6.00
Ivan Rodriguez		
WM-BA Jeromy Burnitz	15.00	4.50
Edgardo Alfonzo		
WM-BG Jeff Bagwell	15.00	4.50
Juan Gonzalez		
WM-BR Jeff Bagwell	15.00	4.50
Alex Rodriguez*		
WM-DH Jermaine Dye	15.00	4.50
Tim Hudson		
WM-DS Carlos Delgado	15.00	4.50
Shannon Stewart		
WM-ED Jim Edmonds	15.00	4.50
J.D. Drew		
WM-GC Ken Griffey Jr.	20.00	6.00
Sean Casey SP		
WM-GK Shawn Green	15.00	4.50
Eric Karros		
WM-GR Juan Gonzalez	15.00	4.50
Ivan Rodriguez		
WM-HW Mike Hampton	15.00	4.50
Larry Walker		
WM-JJ Chipper Jones	15.00	4.50
Andruw Jones		
WM-JS Randy Johnson	15.00	4.50
Curt Schilling		
WM-KG Jason Kendall	15.00	4.50
Brian Giles		
WM-LH Al Leiter	15.00	4.50
Mike Hampton		
WM-MC Edgar Martinez	15.00	4.50
Mike Cameron		
WM-MJ Greg Maddux	25.00	7.50
Chipper Jones		
WM-NM Hideo Nomo	25.00	7.50
Pedro Martinez SP		
WM-PA Mike Piazza	15.00	4.50
Roberto Alomar *		
WM-RA Scott Rolen	15.00	4.50
Bob Abreu		
WM-RP Ivan Rodriguez	15.00	4.50
Chan Ho Park		
WM-SE Aaron Sele	15.00	4.50
Darin Erstad		
WM-SH Kazuhiro Sasaki	15.00	4.50
Shigetoshi Hasegawa		
WM-SP Sammy Sosa	25.00	7.50
Corey Patterson		
WM-TO Frank Thomas	15.00	4.50
Magglio Ordonez		
WM-TS Jim Thome	15.00	4.50
C.C. Sabathia*		
WM-VR Omar Vizquel	20.00	6.00
Alex Rodriguez		
WM-WG Bernie Williams	15.00	4.50
Jason Giambi*		
WM-WP David Wells	15.00	4.50
Jorge Posada*		

2002 SPx Winning Materials Ball Patch Combos

Randomly inserted into packs, these nine cards feature both a ball piece along with a jersey patch of the featured players. Each of these cards were issued to a stated print run of 25 serial numbered sets and we are not pricing these cards due to market scarcity.

Nm-Mt Ex-Mt
PC-AR Alex Rodriguez
PC-CJ Chipper Jones
PC-IS Ichiro Suzuki
PC-KG Ken Griffey Jr.
PC-MP Mike Piazza
PC-RC Roger Clemens
PC-SG Shawn Green
PC-SS Sammy Sosa
PC-TH Todd Helton

2002 SPx Winning Materials Base Patch Combos

Randomly inserted into packs, these eight cards feature both a base piece along with a jersey patch of the featured players. Each of these cards were issued to a stated print run of 25 serial numbered sets and we are not pricing these cards due to market scarcity.

Nm-Mt Ex-Mt
BP-AR Alex Rodriguez
BP-BW Bernie Williams
BP-IS Ichiro Suzuki
BP-JG Jason Giambi
BP-KG Ken Griffey Jr.
BP-LG Luis Gonzalez
BP-MP Mike Piazza
BP-SS Sammy Sosa

2002 SPx Winning Materials USA Jersey Combos

Randomly inserted into packs, these 23 cards feature two uniform swatches from players who played for the USA National team. These cards had a stated print run of 150 serial numbered sets.

Nm-Mt Ex-Mt
USA-AH Brent Abernathy 15.00 4.50
Orlando Hudson
USA-AW Matt Anderson 15.00 4.50
Jeff Weaver
USA-BT Sean Burroughs 25.00 7.50
MarkTeixeira
USA-GB Jason Giambi 25.00 7.50
Sean Burroughs
USA-GT Jason Giambi 25.00 7.50
Mark Teixeira
USA-HD Orlando Hudson 15.00 4.50
Jeff Deardorff
USA-HP Dustin Hermanson 50.00 15.00
Mark Prior
USA-JC Jacques Jones 15.00 4.50
Michael Cuddyer
USA-KB Austin Kearns 15.00 4.50
Sean Burroughs
USA-KC Aaron Kearns 15.00 4.50
Michael Cuddyer
USA-MG Doug Mientkiewicz 25.00 7.50
Jason Giambi
USA-MO Matt Morris 15.00 4.50
Roy Oswalt
USA-MP Matt Morris 50.00 15.00
Mark Prior
USA-MW Matt Morris 15.00 4.50
Jeff Weaver
USA-PB Mark Prior 50.00 15.00
Dewon Brazelton
USA-RE Brian Roberts 15.00 4.50
Adam Everett
USA-SD Mark Kotsay 15.00 4.50
Sean Burroughs
USA-TB Brent Abernathy 15.00 4.50
Dewon Brazelton
USA-TP Mark Teixeira 60.00 18.00
Mark Prior
USA-WB Jeff Weaver 15.00 4.50
Dewon Brazelton
USA-WH Jeff Weaver 15.00 4.50
Dustin Hermanson
USA-HOU Roy Oswalt 15.00 4.50
Adam Everett
USA-MIN Doug Mientkiewicz 15.00 4.50
Michael Cuddyer

2003 SPx

This 199 card set was released in two series. The primary 178-card set was issued in August, 2003 followed up with 21 Update cards randomly seeded within a special rookie pack within sealed boxes of 2003 Upper Deck Finite baseball (of which was released in December, 2003). The primary SPx product was distributed in four card packs carrying an SRP of $7. Each sealed box contained 18 packs and each sealed case contained 14 boxes. Cards numbered 1 to 125 featured veterans with 25 short print cards inserted. Cards numbered 126 through 160 featured rookie cards which were issued to a stated print run of 999 serial numbered sets. Cards 161 and 162 featured New York Yankees rookies Hideki Matsui and Jose Contreras. The Matsui card was issued to a serial numbered print run of 864 copies while the Contreras was issued to a serial numbered print run of 800 copies. Both cards were signed while the Matsui also included a game-used jersey swatch. Cards numbered 163 through 178 featured both autographs and jersey swatches of the featured player and those cards were issued to a stated print run of 1224 cards. The Update cards 179-193 featured a selection of prospects and each card was serial numbered to 150 copies. For reasons unknown to us, the set then skipped to cards 381-387, of which featured additional prospects on cards enriched with both certified autographs and game jersey swatches. These "high number" cards were printed to a serial numbered quantity of 355 copies each.

MINT NRMT
COMP.LO SET w/o SP's (100) 25.00 11.00
COMP.LO SET w/ SP's (125) 100.00 45.00
COMMON CARD (1-125) .50 .23
COMMON SP (1-125) 4.00 1.80
COMMON CARD (126-160) 8.00 3.60
COMMON CARD (163-178) 15.00 6.75
163-178 PRINT RUN 1224 SERIAL #'d SETS
126-178 RANDOM INSERTS IN SPx PACKS
COMMON CARD (179-193) 15.00 6.75
COMMON CARD (381-387) 20.00 9.00
1 Darin Erstad .50 .23
2 Garret Anderson .50 .23
3 Tim Salmon .75 .35
4 Troy Glaus SP 4.00 1.80
5 Luis Gonzalez .50 .23
6 Randy Johnson 1.25 .55
7 Curt Schilling .75 .35
8 Lyle Overbay .50 .23
9 Andruw Jones SP 4.00 1.80
10 Gary Sheffield .50 .23
11 Rafael Furcal .50 .23
12 Greg Maddux 2.00 .90
13 Chipper Jones SP 5.00 2.20
14 Tony Batista .50 .23
15 Rodrigo Lopez .50 .23
16 Jay Gibbons .50 .23
17 Byung-Hyun Kim .50 .23
18 Johnny Damon .50 .23
19 Derek Lowe .50 .23
20 Nomar Garciaparra SP 8.00 3.60
21 Pedro Martinez 1.25 .55
22 Manny Ramirez SP 4.00 1.80
23 Mark Prior 2.50 1.10
24 Kerry Wood 1.25 .55
25 Corey Patterson .50 .23
26 Sammy Sosa SP 8.00 3.60
27 Moises Alou .50 .23
28 Magglio Ordonez .50 .23
29 Frank Thomas 1.25 .55
30 Paul Konerko .50 .23
31 Bartolo Colon .50 .23
32 Adam Dunn .50 .23
33 Austin Kearns .50 .23
34 Aaron Boone .50 .23
35 Ken Griffey Jr. SP 8.00 3.60
36 Omar Vizquel .50 .23
37 C.C. Sabathia .50 .23
38 Jason Davis .50 .23
39 Travis Hafner .50 .23
40 Brandon Phillips .50 .23
41 Larry Walker .75 .35
42 Preston Wilson .50 .23
43 Jay Payton .50 .23
44 Todd Helton .75 .35
45 Carlos Pena .50 .23
46 Eric Munson .50 .23
47 Ivan Rodriguez 1.25 .55
48 Josh Beckett .75 .35
49 Alex Gonzalez .50 .23
50 Roy Oswalt .50 .23
51 Craig Biggio .75 .35
52 Jeff Bagwell .75 .35
53 Dontrelle Willis SP 5.00 2.20
54 Mike Sweeney .50 .23
55 Carlos Beltran .50 .23
56 Brent Mayne .50 .23
57 Hideo Nomo 1.25 .55
58 Rickey Henderson 1.25 .55
59 Adrian Beltre .50 .23
60 Miguel Cabrera SP 10.00 4.50
61 Kazuhisa Ishii .50 .23
62 Ben Sheets .50 .23
63 Richie Sexson .50 .23
64 Torii Hunter SP 4.00 1.80
65 Jacque Jones .50 .23
66 Joe Mays .50 .23
67 Corey Koskie .50 .23
68 A.J. Pierzynski .50 .23
69 Jose Vidro .50 .23
70 Vladimir Guerrero SP 5.00 2.20
71 Tom Glavine .75 .35
72 Jose Reyes SP 4.00 1.80
73 Aaron Heilman .50 .23
74 Mike Piazza 2.00 .90
75 Jorge Posada .75 .35
76 Mike Mussina 1.25 .55
77 Robin Ventura .50 .23
78 Mariano Rivera .75 .35
79 Roger Clemens SP 10.00 4.50
80 Jason Giambi 1.25 .55
81 Bernie Williams .75 .35
82 Alfonso Soriano SP 4.00 1.80
83 Derek Jeter SP 12.00 5.50
84 Miguel Tejada SP 4.00 1.80
85 Eric Chavez .50 .23
86 Tim Hudson .50 .23
87 Barry Zito .75 .35
88 Mark Mulder .50 .23
89 Erubiel Durazo .50 .23
90 Pat Burrell .50 .23
91 Jim Thome SP 5.00 2.20
92 Bobby Abreu .50 .23
93 Brian Giles .50 .23
94 Reggie Sanders SP 4.00 1.80
95 Kenny Lofton .50 .23
96 Ryan Klesko .50 .23
97 Sean Burroughs .50 .23
98 Edgardo Alfonzo .50 .23
99 Rich Aurilia .50 .23
100 Jose Cruz Jr. .50 .23
101 Barry Bonds SP 12.00 5.50
102 Mike Cameron .50 .23
103 Kazuhiro Sasaki .50 .23
104 Bret Boone .50 .23
105 Ichiro Suzuki SP 8.00 3.60
106 J.D. Drew .50 .23
107 Jim Edmonds .50 .23
108 Scott Rolen SP 4.00 1.80
109 Matt Morris .50 .23
110 Tino Martinez .75 .35
111 Albert Pujols SP 10.00 4.50
112 Damian Rolls .50 .23
113 Carl Crawford .50 .23
114 Rocco Baldelli SP 10.00 4.50
115 Hank Blalock .75 .35
116 Alex Rodriguez SP 8.00 3.60
117 Kevin Mench .50 .23
118 Rafael Palmeiro .75 .35
119 Mark Teixeira .75 .35
120 Shannon Stewart .50 .23
121 Vernon Wells .50 .23
122 Josh Phelps .50 .23
123 Eric Hinske .50 .23
124 Orlando Hudson .50 .23
125 Carlos Delgado SP 4.00 1.80
126 Jason Roach ROO RC 8.00 3.60
127 Dan Haren ROO RC 10.00 4.50
128 Luis Ayala ROO RC 8.00 3.60
129 Bo Hart ROO RC 25.00 11.00
130 Wil. Ledezma ROO RC 8.00 3.60
131 Rick Roberts ROO RC 8.00 3.60
132 Miguel Ojeda ROO RC 8.00 3.60
133 Aquilino Lopez ROO RC 8.00 3.60
134 Roger Deago ROO RC 8.00 3.60
135 Arnie Munoz ROO RC 8.00 3.60
136 Brent Hoard ROO RC 8.00 3.60
137 Terrmel Sledge ROO RC 10.00 4.50
138 Ryan Cameron ROO RC 8.00 3.60
139 Pr. Redman ROO RC 8.00 3.60
140 Clint Barmes ROO RC 10.00 4.50
141 Jeremy Griffiths ROO RC 10.00 4.50
142 Jon Leicester ROO RC 8.00 3.60
143 Brandon Webb ROO RC 20.00 9.00
144 T.Wellemeyer ROO RC 10.00 4.50
145 Felix Sanchez ROO RC 8.00 3.60
146 Anthony Ferrari ROO RC 8.00 3.60
147 Ian Ferguson ROO RC 8.00 3.60
148 Mi. Nakamura ROO RC 8.00 3.60
149 Lew Ford ROO RC 10.00 4.50
150 Nate Bland ROO RC 8.00 3.60
151 David Matranga ROO RC 8.00 3.60
152 Edgar Gonzalez ROO RC 8.00 3.60
153 Carlos Mendez ROO RC 8.00 3.60
154 Jason Gilfillan ROO RC 8.00 3.60
155 Mike Neu ROO RC 8.00 3.60
156 Jason Shiell ROO RC 8.00 3.60
157 Jeff Duncan ROO RC 10.00 4.50
158 Oscar Villarreal ROO RC 8.00 3.60
159 D.Markwell ROO RC 8.00 3.60
160 Joe Valentine ROO RC 8.00 3.60
161 H.Matsui AU JSY RC 300.00 135.00
162 Jose Contreras AU RC 40.00 18.00
163 Willie Eyre AU JSY RC 15.00 6.75
164 Matt Bruback AU JSY RC 15.00 6.75
165 Rett Johnson AU JSY RC 15.00 6.75
166 Jeremy Griffiths AU JSY 15.00 6.75
167 Fran Cruceta AU JSY RC 15.00 6.75
168 Fern Cabrera AU JSY RC 15.00 6.75
169 J.Peralta AU JSY RC 15.00 6.75
170 S.Bazzell AU JSY RC 15.00 6.75
171 B.Madritsch AU JSY RC 15.00 6.75
172 Phil Seibel AU JSY RC 15.00 6.75
173 J.Willingham AU JSY RC 30.00 13.50
174 R.Hammock AU JSY RC 15.00 6.75
175 A.Machado AU JSY RC 15.00 6.75
176 D.Sanders AU JSY RC 15.00 6.75
177 Matt Kata AU JSY RC 20.00 9.00
178 Heath Bell AU JSY RC 15.00 6.75
179 Chad Gaudin ROO RC 15.00 6.75
180 Chris Capuano ROO RC 15.00 6.75
181 Danny Garcia ROO RC 15.00 6.75
182 Delmon Young ROO 60.00 27.00
183 Edwin Jackson ROO RC 80.00 36.00
184 Greg Jones ROO RC 15.00 6.75
185 Jeremy Bonderman ROO RC 25.00 11.00
186 Jorge DePaula ROO 15.00 6.75
187 Khalil Greene ROO 15.00 6.75
188 Chad Cordero ROO RC 15.00 6.75
189 Miguel Cabrera ROO 25.00 11.00
190 Rich Harden ROO 15.00 6.75
191 Rickie Weeks ROO 50.00 22.00
192 Rosman Garcia ROO RC 15.00 6.75
193 Tom Gregorio ROO RC 15.00 6.75
381 Andrew Brown AU JSY RC 20.00 9.00
382 Delm Young AU JSY RC 200.00 90.00
383 Colin Porter AU JSY RC 20.00 9.00
385 Rickie Weeks AU JSY RC 200.00 90.00
386 David Matranga AU JSY RC 20.00 9.00
387 Bo Hart AU JSY 40.00 18.00

2003 SPx Spectrum

MINT NRMT
*SPECTRUM 1-125 p/r 51-75: 5X TO 12X
*SPECTRUM 1-125 p/r 36-50: 6X TO 15X
*SPECTRUM 1-125 p/r 26-35: 8X TO 20X
*SPECTRUM 1-125 p/r 51-75: 1.25X TO 3X SP
*SPECTRUM 1-125 p/r 36-50: 1.5X TO 4X SP
*SPECTRUM 1-125 p/r 26-35: 2X TO 5X SP
1-125 PRINT RUNS B/WN 1-75 COPIES PER
*SPECTRUM 126-160: .6X TO 1.5X BASIC
126-160 PRINT RUN 125 SERIAL #'d SETS
161-178 PRINT RUN 25 SERIAL #'d SETS
161-178 NO PRICING DUE TO SCARCITY
RANDOM INSERTS IN PACKS

2003 SPx Game Used Combos

Randomly inserted into packs, these 42 cards feature two players along with game-used memorabilia of each player. Since these cards were issued in varying quantities, we have notated the print run next to the card in our checklist. Please note that if a card was issued to a print run of 25 or fewer copies, no pricing is provided due to market scarcity.

MINT NRMT
BK Jeff Bagwell Patch 40.00 18.00
Jeff Kent Patch/90
BM Barry Bonds Base 120.00 55.00
Roger Maris Jsy/50
BT Barry Bonds Base 200.00 90.00
Ted Williams Patch/50
CA Cal Ripken Patch 200.00 90.00
Alex Rodriguez Patch/50
CC Jose Contreras Base 50.00 22.00
Roger Clemens Patch/50
CL Cal Ripken Patch 400.00 180.00
Lou Gehrig Pants/90
CM Jose Contreras Base 40.00 18.00
Pedro Martinez Patch/90
EG Darin Erstad Patch 40.00 18.00
Troy Glaus Patch/90
FC Carlton Fisk Patch 40.00 18.00
Gary Carter Patch/90
GC Greg Maddux Patch 60.00 27.00
Chipper Jones Patch/90
GD Ken Griffey Jr. Patch 100.00 45.00
Adam Dunn Patch/90
GR Ken Griffey Jr. Patch 80.00 36.00
Sammy Sosa Patch/90
GS Jason Giambi Patch 40.00 18.00
Alfonso Soriano Patch/90
HJ Hideki Matsui Patch 150.00 70.00
Jason Giambi Patch/50
HM Hideki Matsui Patch
Mickey Mantle Bat/10
IA Ichiro Suzuki Patch 250.00 110.00
Albert Pujols Patch/50
JJ Chipper Jones Patch 40.00 18.00
Andruw Jones Patch/90
MB Mickey Mantle Bat 150.00 70.00
Barry Bonds Base/50
MC Hideki Matsui Patch
Jose Contreras Base/10
MD Mickey Mantle Bat 250.00 110.00
Derek Jeter Base/50
MG Pedro Martinez Patch 60.00 27.00
Nomar Garciaparra Base/90
MJ Hideki Matsui Patch 200.00 90.00
Derek Jeter Base/90
MR Mickey Mantle Bat
Roger Maris Jsy/10
MS Hideki Matsui Patch 500.00 220.00
Ichiro Suzuki Patch/50
MW Mickey Mantle Bat 400.00 180.00
Ted Williams Jsy/50
NI Hideo Nomo Patch 80.00 36.00
Kazuhisa Ishii Patch/50
PM Rafael Palmeiro Patch 40.00 18.00
Fred McGriff Patch/90
PS Rafael Palmeiro Patch 80.00 36.00
Sammy Sosa Patch/10
RC Nolan Ryan Patch 150.00 70.00
Roger Clemens Patch/90
RG Alex Rodriguez Patch 80.00 36.00
Nomar Garciaparra Base/90
RM Babe Ruth Bat
Hideki Matsui Patch/10
RR Cal Ripken Patch 100.00 45.00
Scott Rolen Patch/90
RS Nolan Ryan Patch 150.00 70.00
Tom Seaver Patch/90
RT Alex Rodriguez Patch 60.00 27.00
Miguel Tejada Patch/90
RY Nolan Ryan Patch
Pedro Martinez Patch/10
SB Sammy Sosa Patch 60.00 27.00
Barry Bonds Base/90
SJ Curt Schilling Patch 40.00 18.00
Randy Johnson Patch/90
SN Ichiro Suzuki Patch 200.00 90.00
Hideo Nomo Patch/90
SP Sammy Sosa Patch 80.00 36.00
Rafael Palmeiro Patch/90
TB Thurman Munson Patch
Yogi Berra Bat/10
WG Ted Williams Patch
Nomar Garciaparra Base/10
WM Ted Williams Patch
Pedro Martinez Patch/10

2003 SPx Stars Autograph Jersey

Randomly inserted in packs, these cards feature both a game-used jersey swatch as well as an authentic signature. Since these cards were issued in varying print runs, we have notated the stated print run next to their name in our checklist.

MINT NRMT
SPECTRUM PRINT RUN 1 SERIAL #'d SET
NO SPECTRUM PRICING DUE TO SCARCITY
RANDOM INSERTS IN PACKS
CJO Chipper Jones/195 60.00 27.00
CS Curt Schilling/490 40.00 18.00
JG Jason Giambi/315 50.00 22.00
KG Ken Griffey Jr./690 120.00 55.00
LB Lance Berkman/590 25.00 11.00
LG Luis Gonzalez/790 25.00 11.00
MP Mark Prior/490 100.00 45.00
NM Nomar Garciaparra/195 150.00 70.00
PB Pat Burrell/590 25.00 11.00
TG Troy Glaus/490 40.00 18.00
VG Vladimir Guerrero/390 50.00 22.00

2003 SPx Stars Autograph Jersey Spectrum

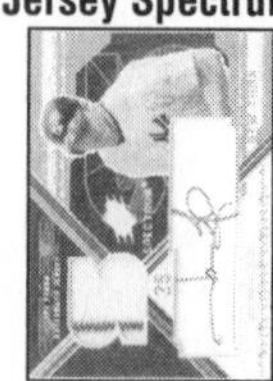

MINT NRMT
RANDOM INSERTS IN PACKS
STATED PRINT RUN 1 SERIAL #'d SET
NO PRICING DUE TO SCARCITY

2003 SPx Winning Materials 375

MINT NRMT
LOGO'S CONSECUTIVELY #'d FROM 41-375
NUMBERS CONSECUTIVELY #'d FROM 1-40
CARDS CUMULATIVELY SERIAL #'d TO 375
*WIN.MAT.250: .5X TO 1.2X WIN.MAT.375
NUMBERS CONSECUTIVELY #'d FROM 1-28

LOGOS CONSECUTIVELY #'d FROM 29-250
WM 250 CUMULATIVELY SERIAL #'d TO 250
LOGO/NUMBER PRINTS PROVIDED BY UD
RANDOM INSERTS IN PACKS
AJ1A Andruw Jones Logo 8.00 3.60
AJ1B Andruw Jones Num 15.00 6.75
AP1A Albert Pujols Logo 25.00 11.00
AP1B Albert Pujols Num 50.00 22.00
AR1A Alex Rodriguez Logo 15.00 6.75
AR1B Alex Rodriguez Num 30.00 13.50
AS1A Alfonso Soriano Logo 10.00 4.50
AS1B Alfonso Soriano Num 20.00 9.00
BW1A Bernie Williams Logo 10.00 4.50
BW1B Bernie Williams Num 20.00 9.00
BZ1A Barry Zito Logo 10.00 4.50
BZ1B Barry Zito Num 20.00 9.00
CD1A Carlos Delgado Logo 8.00 3.60
CD1B Carlos Delgado Num 15.00 6.75
CJ1A Chipper Jones Logo 10.00 4.50
CJ1B Chipper Jones Num 20.00 9.00
CS1A Curt Schilling Logo 10.00 4.50
CS1B Curt Schilling Num 20.00 9.00
FT1A Frank Thomas Logo 10.00 4.50
FT1B Frank Thomas Num 20.00 9.00
GM1A Greg Maddux Logo 15.00 6.75
GM1B Greg Maddux Num 30.00 13.50
GS1A Gary Sheffield Logo 8.00 3.60
GS1B Gary Sheffield Num 15.00 6.75
HM1A Hideki Matsui Logo 30.00 13.50
HM1B Hideki Matsui Num 50.00 22.00
HN1A Hideo Nomo Logo 25.00 11.00
HN1B Hideo Nomo Num 50.00 22.00
IR1A Ivan Rodriguez Logo 10.00 4.50
IR1B Ivan Rodriguez Num 20.00 9.00
IS1A Ichiro Suzuki Logo 40.00 18.00
IS1B Ichiro Suzuki Num 80.00 36.00
JB1A Jeff Bagwell Logo 10.00 4.50
JB1B Jeff Bagwell Num 20.00 9.00
JG1A Jason Giambi Logo 10.00 4.50
JG1B Jason Giambi Num 20.00 9.00
JK1A Jeff Kent Logo 8.00 3.60
JK1B Jeff Kent Num 15.00 6.75
JT1A Jim Thome Logo 10.00 4.50
JT1B Jim Thome Num 20.00 9.00
KG1A Ken Griffey Jr. Logo 20.00 9.00
KG1B Ken Griffey Jr. Num 40.00 18.00
LB1A Lance Berkman Logo 8.00 3.60
LB1B Lance Berkman Num 15.00 6.75
LG1A Luis Gonzalez Logo 8.00 3.60
LG1B Luis Gonzalez Num 15.00 6.75
MA1A Mark Prior Logo 20.00 9.00
MA1B Mark Prior Num 40.00 18.00
MP1A Mike Piazza Logo 15.00 6.75
MP1B Mike Piazza Num 30.00 13.50
MR1A Manny Ramirez Logo 8.00 3.60
MR1B Manny Ramirez Num 15.00 6.75
MT1A Miguel Tejada Logo 8.00 3.60
MT1B Miguel Tejada Num 15.00 6.75
PB1A Pat Burrell Logo 8.00 3.60
PB1B Pat Burrell Num 15.00 6.75
PM1A Pedro Martinez Logo 10.00 4.50
PM1B Pedro Martinez Num 20.00 9.00
RA1A Roberto Alomar Logo 10.00 4.50
RA1B Roberto Alomar Num 20.00 9.00
RC1A Roger Clemens Logo 20.00 9.00
RC1B Roger Clemens Num 40.00 18.00
RF1A Rafael Furcal Logo 8.00 3.60
RF1B Rafael Furcal Num 15.00 6.75
RJ1A Randy Johnson Logo 10.00 4.50
RJ1B Randy Johnson Num 20.00 9.00
SG1A Shawn Green Logo 8.00 3.60
SG1B Shawn Green Num 15.00 6.75
SS1A Sammy Sosa Logo 20.00 9.00
SS1B Sammy Sosa Num 40.00 18.00
TG1A Tom Glavine Logo 10.00 4.50
TG1B Tom Glavine Num 20.00 9.00
TH1A Torii Hunter Logo 8.00 3.60
TH1B Torii Hunter Num 15.00 6.75
TO1A Todd Helton Logo 10.00 4.50
TO1B Todd Helton Num 20.00 9.00
TR1A Troy Glaus Logo 10.00 4.50
TR1B Troy Glaus Num 20.00 9.00
VG1A Vladimir Guerrero Logo 10.00 4.50
VG1B Vladimir Guerrero Num 20.00 9.00

2003 SPx Winning Materials 175

MINT NRMT
NUMBERS CONSECUTIVELY #'d FROM 1-20
LOGOS CONSECUTIVELY #'d FROM 21-175
CARDS CUMULATIVELY SERIAL #'d TO 175
*WM LOGO 50: .75X TO 2X WM LOGO 175
WM 50 NUMBERS CONSECUTIVELY #'d 1-10
WM 50 LOGOS CONSECUTIVELY #'d 11-50
WM 50 CUMULATIVELY SERIAL #'d TO 50
NO NUMBER PRICING DUE TO SCARCITY
LOGO/NUMBER PRINTS PROVIDED BY UD
AJ2A Andruw Jones Logo 10.00 4.50
AP2A Albert Pujols Logo 30.00 13.50
AR2A Alex Rodriguez Logo 20.00 9.00
AS2A Alfonso Soriano Logo 12.00 5.50
BW2A Bernie Williams Logo 12.00 5.50
BZ2A Barry Zito Logo 12.00 5.50
CD2A Carlos Delgado Logo 10.00 4.50
CJ2A Chipper Jones Logo 12.00 5.50
CS2A Curt Schilling Logo 12.00 5.50
FT2A Frank Thomas Logo 12.00 5.50
GM2A Greg Maddux Logo 20.00 9.00
GS2A Gary Sheffield Logo 10.00 4.50
HM2A Hideki Matsui Logo 40.00 18.00
HN2A Hideo Nomo Logo 30.00 13.50
IR2A Ivan Rodriguez Logo 12.00 5.50
IS2A Ichiro Suzuki Logo 50.00 22.00
JB2A Jeff Bagwell Logo 12.00 5.50
JG2A Jason Giambi Logo 12.00 5.50
JK2A Jeff Kent Logo 10.00 4.50

JT2A Jim Thome Logo 12.00 5.50
KG2A Ken Griffey Jr. Logo 25.00 11.00
LB2A Lance Berkman Logo 10.00 4.50
LG2A Luis Gonzalez Logo 10.00 4.50
MM2A M.Mantle Pants Logo... 150.00 70.00
MP2RA Mark Prior Logo 25.00 11.00
MP2A Mike Piazza Logo 20.00 9.00
MR2A Manny Ramirez Logo 10.00 4.50
MT2A Miguel Tejada Logo......... 10.00 4.50
PB2A Pat Burrell Logo............. 10.00 4.50
PM2A Pedro Martinez Logo 12.00 5.50
RA2A Roberto Alomar Logo 12.00 5.50
RC2A Roger Clemens Logo....... 25.00 11.00
RF2A Rafael Furcal Logo.......... 10.00 4.50
RJ2A Randy Johnson Logo 12.00 5.50
SG2A Shawn Green Logo 10.00 4.50
SS2A Sammy Sosa Logo 25.00 11.00
TGL2A Troy Glaus Logo 12.00 5.50
TG2A Tom Glavine Logo 12.00 5.50
THE2A Todd Helton Logo.......... 12.00 5.50
TH2A Torii Hunter Logo 10.00 4.50
TW2A T.Williams Pants Logo.... 80.00 36.00
VG2A Vladimir Guerrero Logo.... 12.00 5.50

2003 SPx Young Stars Autograph Jersey

20 of the 23 cards within this set were randomly inserted in 2003 SPx packs (released in August, 2003). Serial #'d print runs for the 20 low series cards range between 964-1460 copies each. An additional three cards (all of which are much scarcer with serial #'d print runs of only 355 copies per), were randomly seeded in packs of 2003 Upper Deck Finite of which was released in December, 2003. These cards feature game-used jersey swatches and authentic autographs from each player. Since these cards were issued in varying quantities, we have noted the stated print run next to the player's name in our checklist. Rocco Baldelli did not return his autographs prior to packout thus an exchange card with a redemption deadline of August 15th, 2006 was placed into packs.

MINT NRMT
SPECTRUM PRINT RUN 25 SERIAL #'d SETS
NO SPECTRUM PRICING DUE TO SCARCITY
AD Adam Dunn/1295 .... 25.00 11.00
AK Austin Kearns/964 .... 15.00 6.75
BM Brett Myers/1295 .... 15.00 6.75
BP Brandon Phillips/1295 .... 15.00 6.75
CG Chris George/1260 .... 15.00 6.75
DW Dontrelle Willis/355 .... 50.00 22.00
EH Eric Hinske/1295................. 15.00 6.75
HB Hank Blalock/1295.............. 25.00 11.00
JA Jason Jennings/1295 .... 15.00 6.75
JBA Josh Bard/1295.................. 15.00 6.75
JJ Jacque Jones/1260............... 15.00 6.75
JP Josh Phelps/1295 .... 15.00 6.75
KA Kurt Ainsworth/1460 .... 15.00 6.75
KG Khalil Greene/355 .... 50.00 22.00
KS Kirk Saarloos/1295 .... 15.00 6.75
MD Michael Cuddyer/1156.......... 15.00 6.75
MK Mike Kinkade/1295 .... 15.00 6.75
MT Mark Teixeira/1295 .... 25.00 11.00
NJ Nick Johnson/1295 .... 25.00 11.00
RB Rocco Baldelli/1295 EXCH... 50.00 22.00
RH Rich Harden/355 .... 50.00 22.00
RO Roy Oswalt/1295.................. 15.00 6.75
SB Sean Burroughs/1295........... 15.00 6.75

2003 SPx Young Stars Autograph Jersey Spectrum

MINT NRMT
STATED PRINT RUN 25 SERIAL #'d SETS
NO PRICING DUE TO SCARCITY........
EXCHANGE DEADLINE 08/15/06.........

1981 Squirt

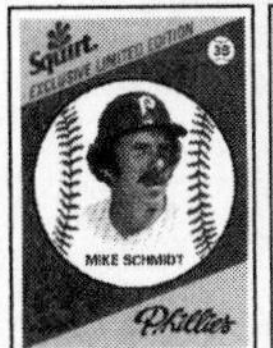

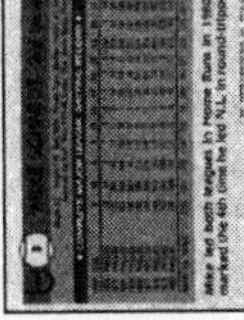

The cards in this 22-panel set consist of 33 different individual cards, each measuring the standard-size. The set was also available as two-card panels measuring approximately 2 1/2" by 10 1/2". Cards numbered 1-11 appear twice, whereas cards 12-33 appear only once in the 22-panel set. The pattern for pairings was 1/12 and 1/23, 2/13 and 2/24, 3/14 and 3/25, and so forth on up to 11/22 and 11/33. Two card panels have a value equal to the sum of the individual cards on the panel. Supposedly panels 4/15, 4/26, 5/27, and 6/28 are more difficult to find than the other panels and are marked as SP in the checklist below.

Nm-Mt Ex-Mt
COMPLETE PANEL SET............ 25.00 10.00
COMPLETE IND. SET 15.00 6.00
COMMON PANEL........................ .50 .20
COMMON DP (1-11) .... .25 .10
COMMON CARD (12-33)............ .25 .10
COMMON SP .... 1.00 .40
COMMON DP .... .25 .10
1 George Brett DP 3.00 1.20
2 George Foster DP .... .50 .20
3 Ben Oglivie DP .... .25 .10
4 Steve Garvey DP .... .75 .30
5 Reggie Jackson DP .... 1.00 .40
6 Bill Buckner DP .... .50 .20
7 Jim Rice DP .... .50 .20
8 Mike Schmidt DP .... 2.00 .80
9 Rod Carew DP......................... 1.00 .40
10 Dave Parker DP .... .50 .20
11 Pete Rose DP .... 2.00 .80
12 Garry Templeton .... .25 .10
13 Rick Burleson........................... .25 .10
14 Dave Kingman .... .50 .20
15 Eddie Murray SP 8.00 3.20
16 Don Sutton .... 1.00 .40
17 Dusty Baker.............................. .50 .20
18 Jack Clark................................. .25 .10
19 Dave Winfield .... 1.25 .50
20 Johnny Bench .... 1.50 .60
21 Lee Mazzilli.............................. .25 .10
22 Al Oliver.................................... .50 .20
23 Jerry Mumphrey........................ .25 .10
24 Tony Armas............................... .25 .10
25 Fred Lynn .... .50 .20
26 Ron LeFlore SP .... 1.00 .40
27 Steve Kemp SP .... 1.00 .40
28 Rickey Henderson SP........... 12.00 4.80
29 John Castino .... .25 .10
30 Cecil Cooper............................. .25 .10
31 Bruce Bochte............................ .25 .10
32 Joe Charboneau .... .50 .20
33 Chet Lemon.............................. .25 .10

1982 Squirt

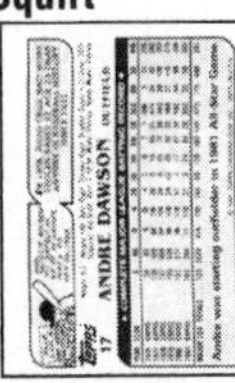

The cards in this 22-card set measure the standard size. Although the 1982 "Exclusive Limited Edition" was prepared for Squirt by Topps, the format and pictures are completely different from the regular Topps cards of this year. Each color picture is obliquely cut and the word Squirt is printed in red in the top left corner. The cards are numbered 1 through 22 and the reverses are yellow and black on white. The cards were issued on four types of panels: (1) yellow attachment card at top with picture card in center and scratch-off game at bottom; (2) yellow attachment card at top with scratch-off game in center and picture card at bottom; (3) white attachment card at top with "Collect all 22" panel in center and picture card at bottom; (4) two card panel with attachment card at top. The two card panels have parallel cards; that is, numbers 1 and 12 together, numbers 2 and 13 together, etc. Two card panels have a value equal to the sum of the individual cards on the panel. The two types (1 and 2) with the scratch-off games are more slightly difficult to obtain than the other two types and hence command prices double those below.

Nm-Mt Ex-Mt
COMPLETE SET (22)................ 10.00 4.00
1 Cecil Cooper............................ .50 .20
2 Jerry Remy............................... .25 .10
3 George Brett 3.00 1.20
4 Alan Trammell .... .75 .30
5 Reggie Jackson .... 1.25 .50
6 Kirk Gibson .... .75 .30
7 Dave Winfield .... 1.25 .50
8 Carlton Fisk .... 1.50 .60
9 Ron Guidry................................ .50 .20
10 Dennis Leonard........................ .25 .10
11 Rollie Fingers .... 1.25 .50
12 Pete Rose............................... 1.50 .60
13 Phil Garner .... .25 .10
14 Mike Schmidt......................... 1.50 .60
15 Dave Concepcion..................... .50 .20
16 George Hendrick .... .25 .10
17 Andre Dawson........................ 1.00 .40
18 George Foster........................... .50 .20
19 Gary Carter............................. 1.25 .50
20 Fernando Valenzuela .... .50 .20
21 Tom Seaver............................ 1.25 .50
22 Bruce Sutter .... .50 .20

1975 SSPC 18

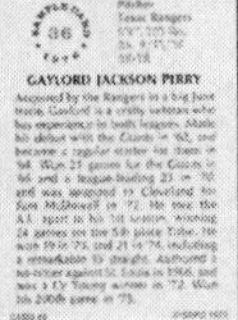

This 18-card promo standard-size set was released the year before the 1976 SSPC 630-card set. Like the 1976 "Pure Card" set, the cards feature white-bordered color player photos on their otherwise plain fronts. The back carries the player's position, team, and biography in red lettering at the upper right. The player's uniform number appears in red within a black-lettered circle formed by the words "Sample Card 1976" at the upper left. Shown below are the player's full name and his career highlights in black lettering. The card number appears on the back at the bottom, as does the copyright date, 1975. These cards were also included as inserts in the Winter 1975 issue of Collectors Quarterly.

NM Ex
COMPLETE SET (18)................ 18.00 7.25
1 Harry Parker............................. .50 .20
2 Jim Bibby .... .50 .20
3 Mike Wallace .... .50 .20
4 Tony Muser .... .50 .20
5 Yogi Berra MG....................... 6.00 2.40
6 Preston Gomez MG .... .50 .20
7 Jack McKeon MG .... .50 .20
8 Sam McDowell .... 1.00 .40
9 Gaylord Perry 5.00 2.00
10 Fred Scherman........................ .50 .20
11 Willie Davis .... .50 .20
12 Don Hopkins .... .50 .20
13 Whitey Herzog MG .... 1.00 .40
14 Ray Sadecki............................. .50 .20
15 Stan Bahnsen .... .50 .20
16 Bob Oliver .... .50 .20
17 Denny Doyle............................ .50 .20
18 Deron Johnson......................... .50 .20

1975 SSPC 42

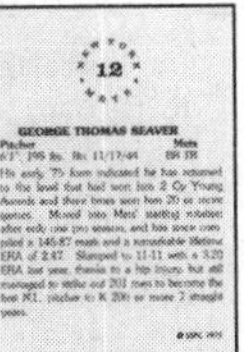

This 42-card standard-size set features posed color player photos with white borders. The horizontal backs are plain white card stock and carry the player's name, biographical information, career highlights, and statistics.

NM Ex
COMPLETE SET (42)................ 75.00 30.00
1 Wilbur Wood .... .50 .20
2 Johnny Sain CO...................... 1.00 .40
3 Bill Melton .... .50 .20
4 Dick Allen .... 1.50 .60
5 Jim Palmer 5.00 2.00
6 Brooks Robinson..................... 6.00 2.40
7 Tommy Davis .... 1.00 .40
8 Frank Robinson MG 5.00 2.00
9 Vada Pinson .... 1.00 .40
10 Nolan Ryan........................... 25.00 10.00
11 Reggie Jackson 8.00 3.20
12 Vida Blue............................... 1.00 .40
13 Sal Bando.............................. 1.00 .40
14 Bert Campaneris.................... 1.00 .40
15 Tom Seaver............................ 6.00 2.40
16 Bud Harrelson .... 1.00 .40
17 Jerry Koosman....................... 1.00 .40
18 David Nelson........................... .50 .20
19 Ted Williams 10.00 4.00
20 Tony Oliva .... 1.50 .60
21 Mickey Lolich .... 1.00 .40
22 Amos Otis .... .50 .20
23 Carl Yastrzemski 5.00 2.00
24 Mike Cuellar .... 1.00 .40
25 Doc Medich.............................. .50 .20
26 Cesar Cedeno .... .50 .20
27 Jeff Burroughs .... 1.00 .40
28 Sparky Lyle and..................... 5.00 2.00
Ted Williams
29 Johnny Bench 6.00 2.40
30 Gaylord Perry 4.00 1.60
31 John Mayberry .... .50 .20
32 Rod Carew.............................. 5.00 2.00
33 Whitey Ford CO 5.00 2.00
34 Al Kaline 5.00 2.00
35 Willie Mays CO..................... 10.00 4.00
36 Warren Spahn 5.00 2.00
37 Mickey Mantle...................... 20.00 8.00
38 Norm Cash .... 1.50 .60
39 Steve Busby .... .50 .20
40 Yogi Berra MG........................ 5.00 2.00
41 Harvey Kuenn CO .... .50 .20
42 Felipe Alou.............................. 1.00 .40
Matty Alou
Jesus Alou

1975 SSPC Puzzle Back

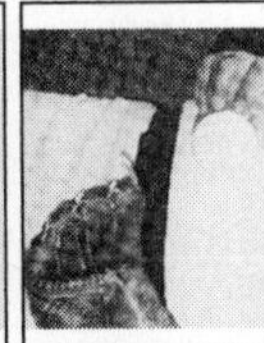

The 24 cards in this set measure approximately 3 1/2" by 4 1/4" and feature posed color player photos with white borders on the front. The player's name, position, and team are printed at the bottom. The backs are the pieces of a puzzle that shows a 17" by 21" black-and-white photo of Nolan Ryan and Catfish Hunter. When the puzzle is assembled, the player's names appear at the bottom. The name and address of Sports Stars Publishing Company is printed around the left, top, and right edges. The cards are unnumbered and checklisted below in alphabetical order.

NM Ex
COMPLETE SET (24)................ 35.00 14.00
1 Hank Aaron 6.00 2.40
2 Johnny Bench 3.00 1.20
3 Bobby Bonds.......................... 1.00 .40
4 Jeff Burroughs .... .25 .10
5 Rod Carew.............................. 2.00 .80
6 Dave Cash .... .25 .10
7 Cesar Cedeno UER .... .25 .10
Spelled as Cedano
8 Bucky Dent............................. 1.00 .40
9 Rollie Fingers .... 1.50 .60
10 Steve Garvey .... 1.00 .40
11 John Grubb .... .25 .10
12 Reggie Jackson 5.00 2.00
13 Jim Kaat UER .... 1.00 .40
Spelled as Katt
14 Greg Luzinski .... .50 .20
15 Fred Lynn .... 1.00 .40
16 Bill Madlock............................... .50 .20
17 Andy Messersmith .... .25 .10
18 Thurman Munson.................... 2.00 .80
19 Jim Palmer.............................. 2.50 1.00
20 Dave Parker............................ 1.50 .60
21 Jim Rice .... 1.00 .40
22 Pete Rose............................... 3.00 1.20
23 Tom Seaver............................ 3.00 1.20
24 Chris Speier............................... .25 .10

1975 SSPC Samples

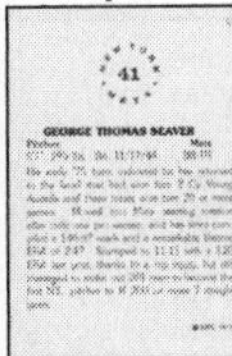

This six-card standard-size set features posed color player photos with white borders. The backs are white card stock and have either a horizontal or vertical format. Each card carries the player's name, biographical information, and career highlights. The horizontal backs also carry statistics. The cards are unnumbered, and checklisted below in alphabetical order.

NM Ex
COMPLETE SET (6)................. 30.00 12.00
1 Hank Aaron 8.00 3.20
2 Catfish Hunter 2.50 1.00
3 Dave Kingman .... 1.00 .40
4 Mickey Mantle....................... 15.00 6.00
5 Willie Mays.............................. 8.00 3.20
6 Tom Seaver............................. 5.00 2.00

1976 SSPC Promos

These standard-size cards were issued by SSPC/TCMA to promote their first (and would prove to be their only) major set. These cards feature the photos used in the 1975 SSPC 42 set on the front with a description about the set (how many cards, suggested retail price) and some details about what the cards would contain on them. There might be additions to this checklist so any additional information would be appreciated. These cards are not numbered, so we have sequenced them in alphabetical order.

NM Ex
COMPLETE SET 30.00 12.00
1 Mickey Mantle........................ 15.00 6.00
2 Willie Mays............................ 12.00 4.80
3 Tom Seaver............................ 12.00 4.80

1976 SSPC

The cards in this 630-card set measure 2 1/2" by 3 1/2". The 1976 "Pure Card" set issued by TCMA derives its name from the lack of borders, logos, signatures, etc., which often clutter up the picture areas of some baseball sets. It differs from other sets produced by this company in that it cannot be re-issued due to an agreement entered into by the manufacturer. Thus, while not technically a legitimate issue, it is significant because it cannot be reprinted, unlike other collector issues. The cards are numbered in team groups, i.e., Atlanta (1-21), Cincinnati (22-46), Houston (47-65), Los Angeles (66-91), San Francisco (92-113), San Diego (114-133), Chicago White Sox (134-158), Kansas City (159-185), California (186-204), Minnesota (205-225), Milwaukee (226-251), Texas (252-273), St. Louis (274-300), Chicago Cubs (301-321), Montreal (322-351), Detroit (352-373), Baltimore (374-401), Boston (402-424), New York Yankees (425-455), Philadelphia (456-477), Oakland (478-503), Cleveland (504-532), New York Mets (533-560), and Pittsburgh (561-586). The rest of the numbers are filled in with checklists (589-595), miscellaneous players, and a heavy dose of coaches. There are a few instances in the set where the team identified on the back is different from the team shown on the front due to trades made after the completion of the 1975 season. The set features rookie year cards of Dennis Eckersley and Willie Randolph as well as early cards of George Brett, Gary Carter, and Robin Yount. The card backs were edited by Keith Olbermann, prior to his network broadcasting days. Although some of these cards were copyrighted in 1975, they were not released until spring of 1976 and have always been considered cards from 1976 within the hobby. These cards were originally available directly from SSPC for $10.99 per set.

NM Ex
COMPLETE SET (630)............ 80.00 32.00
1 Buzz Capra .... .10 .04
2 Tom House................................ .10 .04
3 Max Leon .... .10 .04
4 Carl Morton............................... .10 .04
5 Phil Niekro.............................. 4.00 1.60
6 Mike Thompson .... .10 .04
7 Elias Sosa.................................. .10 .04
8 Larvell Blanks............................ .10 .04
9 Darrell Evans .... .20 .08
10 Rod Gilbreath .... .10 .04
11 Mike Lum................................. .10 .04
12 Craig Robinson .... .10 .04
13 Earl Williams .... .10 .04
14 Vic Correll .... .10 .04
15 Biff Pocoroba .... .10 .04
16 Dusty Baker.............................. .30 .12
17 Ralph Garr................................ .15 .06
18 Cito Gaston .... .15 .06
19 Dave May .... .10 .04
20 Rowland Office .... .10 .04
21 Bob Beall .... .10 .04
22 Sparky Anderson MG .... .75 .30
23 Jack Billingham......................... .10 .04
24 Pedro Borbon............................ .10 .04
25 Clay Carroll............................... .10 .04
26 Pat Darcy.................................. .10 .04
27 Don Gullett .... .15 .06
28 Clay Kirby .... .10 .04
29 Gary Nolan .... .10 .04
30 Fred Norman .... .10 .04
31 Johnny Bench 6.00 2.40
32 Bill Plummer .... .10 .04
33 Darrel Chaney........................... .10 .04
34 Dave Concepcion...................... .30 .12
35 Terry Crowley............................ .10 .04
36 Dan Driessen .... .15 .06
37 Doug Flynn................................ .10 .04
38 Joe Morgan............................. 3.00 1.20
39 Tony Perez 2.50 1.00
40 Ken Griffey .... 1.00 .40
41 Pete Rose................................ 8.00 3.20
42 Ed Armbrister............................ .10 .04
43 John Vukovich........................... .10 .04
44 George Foster........................... .50 .20
45 Cesar Geronimo .... .10 .04
46 Merv Rettenmund .... .10 .04
47 Jim Crawford............................. .10 .04
48 Ken Forsch .... .10 .04
49 Doug Konieczny .... .10 .04
50 Joe Niekro .... .20 .08
51 Cliff Johnson .... .10 .04
52 Skip Jutze.................................. .10 .04
53 Milt May .... .10 .04
54 Rob Andrews............................. .10 .04
55 Ken Boswell............................... .10 .04
56 Tommy Helms............................ .10 .04
57 Roger Metzger........................... .10 .04
58 Larry Milbourne......................... .10 .04
59 Doug Rader .... .15 .06
60 Bob Watson............................... .30 .12
61 Enos Cabell .... .10 .04
62 Jose Cruz .... .20 .08
63 Cesar Cedeno .... .20 .08
64 Greg Gross................................ .10 .04
65 Wilbur Howard .... .10 .04
66 Al Downing................................ .10 .04
67 Burt Hooton .... .10 .04
68 Charlie Hough .... .30 .12
69 Tommy John.............................. .75 .30
70 Andy Messersmith .... .15 .06
71 Doug Rau.................................. .10 .04
72 Rick Rhoden.............................. .15 .06
73 Don Sutton.............................. 2.50 1.00
74 Rick Auerbach........................... .10 .04
75 Ron Cey.................................... .30 .12
76 Ivan DeJesus............................. .10 .04
77 Steve Garvey .... 1.50 .60
78 Lee Lacy.................................... .10 .04
79 Dave Lopes .... .15 .06
80 Ken McMullen .... .10 .04
81 Joe Ferguson............................. .10 .04
82 Paul Powell .... .10 .04
83 Steve Yeager .... .10 .04
84 Willie Crawford.......................... .10 .04
85 Henry Cruz .... .10 .04
86 Charlie Manuel .... .10 .04
87 Manny Mota............................... .15 .06
88 Tom Paciorek .... .15 .06
89 Jim Wynn................................... .15 .06
90 Walt Alston MG.......................... .75 .30
91 Bill Buckner .... .30 .12
92 Jim Barr .... .10 .04
93 Mike Caldwell .... .10 .04
94 John D'Acquisto.......................... .10 .04
95 Dave Heaverlo .... .10 .04
96 Gary Lavelle................................ .10 .04
97 John Montefusco .... .15 .06
98 Charlie Williams .... .10 .04
99 Chris Arnold .... .10 .04
100 Marc Hill.................................... .10 .04
101 Dave Rader .... .10 .04
102 Bruce Miller................................ .10 .04
103 Willie Montanez......................... .10 .04
104 Steve Ontiveros .... .10 .04
105 Chris Speier................................ .10 .04
106 Derrel Thomas............................ .10 .04
107 Gary Thomasson .... .10 .04
108 Glenn Adams.............................. .10 .04
109 Von Joshua .... .10 .04
110 Gary Matthews .... .15 .06
111 Bobby Murcer .... .30 .12
112 Horace Speed............................. .10 .04
113 Wes Westrum MG....................... .10 .04
114 Rich Folkers .... .10 .04
115 Alan Foster .... .10 .04
116 Dave Freisleben.......................... .10 .04
117 Dan Frisella .... .10 .04
118 Randy Jones .... .15 .06
119 Dan Spillner................................ .10 .04
120 Larry Hardy .... .10 .04
121 Randy Hundley .... .15 .06
122 Fred Kendall .... .10 .04
123 John McNamara MG................... .10 .04
124 Tito Fuentes................................ .10 .04
125 Enzo Hernandez.......................... .10 .04
126 Steve Huntz .... .10 .04
127 Mike Ivie..................................... .10 .04

128 Hector Torres .10 .04
129 Ted Kubiak .10 .04
130 John Grubb .10 .04
131 John Scott .10 .04
132 Bob Tolan .15 .06
133 Dave Winfield 12.00 4.80
134 Bill Gogolewski .10 .04
135 Dan Osborn .10 .04
136 Jim Kaat .75 .30
137 Claude Osteen .15 .06
138 Cecil Upshaw .10 .04
139 Wilbur Wood .15 .06
140 Lloyd Allen .10 .04
141 Brian Downing .20 .08
142 Jim Essian .10 .04
143 Bucky Dent .15 .06
144 Jorge Orta .10 .04
145 Lee Richard .10 .04
146 Bill Stein .10 .04
147 Ken Henderson .10 .04
148 Carlos May .10 .04
149 Nyls Nyman .10 .04
150 Bob Coluccio .10 .04
151 Chuck Tanner MG .15 .06
152 Pat Kelly .10 .04
153 Jerry Hairston .10 .04
154 Pete Varney .10 .04
155 Bill Melton .10 .04
156 Goose Gossage 1.25 .50
157 Terry Forster .15 .06
158 Rich Hinton .10 .04
159 Nelson Briles .10 .04
160 Al Fitzmorris .10 .04
161 Steve Mingori .10 .04
162 Marty Pattin .10 .04
163 Paul Splittorff .10 .04
164 Dennis Leonard .15 .06
165 Buck Martinez .10 .04
166 Bob Stinson .10 .04
167 George Brett 20.00 8.00
168 Harmon Killebrew 3.00 1.20
169 John Mayberry .15 .06
170 Fred Patek .15 .06
171 Cookie Rojas .15 .06
172 Rodney Scott .10 .04
173 Tony Solaita .10 .04
174 Frank White .30 .12
175 Al Cowens .10 .04
176 Hal McRae .30 .12
177 Amos Otis .20 .08
178 Vada Pinson .30 .12
179 Jim Wohlford .10 .04
180 Doug Bird .10 .04
181 Mark Littell .10 .04
182 Bob McClure .10 .04
183 Steve Busby .15 .06
184 Fran Healy .10 .04
185 Whitey Herzog MG .20 .08
186 Andy Hassler .10 .04
187 Nolan Ryan 25.00 10.00
188 Bill Singer .10 .04
189 Frank Tanana .30 .12
190 Ed Figueroa .10 .04
191 Dave Collins .15 .06
192 Dick Williams MG .15 .06
193 Ellie Rodriguez .10 .04
194 Dave Chalk .10 .04
195 Winston Llenas .10 .04
196 Rudy Meoli .10 .04
197 Orlando Ramirez .10 .04
198 Jerry Remy .10 .04
199 Billy Smith .10 .04
200 Bruce Bochte .10 .04
201 Joe Lahoud .10 .04
202 Morris Nettles .10 .04
203 Mickey Rivers .15 .06
204 Leroy Stanton .10 .04
205 Vic Albury .10 .04
206 Tom Burgmeier .10 .04
207 Bill Butler .10 .04
208 Bill Campbell .10 .04
209 Ray Corbin .10 .04
210 Joe Decker .10 .04
211 Jim Hughes .10 .04
212 Ed Bane UER .10 .04
(Photo actually
Mike Pazik)
213 Glenn Borgmann .10 .04
214 Rod Carew 5.00 2.00
215 Steve Brye .10 .04
216 Dan Ford .10 .04
217 Tony Oliva .75 .30
218 Dave Goltz .10 .04
219 Bert Blyleven .50 .20
220 Larry Hisle .15 .06
221 Steve Braun .10 .04
222 Jerry Terrell .10 .04
223 Eric Soderholm .10 .04
224 Phil Roof .10 .04
225 Danny Thompson .10 .04
226 Jim Colborn .10 .04
227 Tom Murphy .10 .04
228 Ed Rodriguez .10 .04
229 Jim Slaton .10 .04
230 Ed Sprague .10 .04
231 Charlie Moore .10 .04
232 Darrell Porter .15 .06
233 Kurt Bevacqua .15 .06
234 Pedro Garcia .10 .04
235 Mike Hegan .10 .04
236 Don Money .15 .06
237 George Scott .15 .06
238 Robin Yount UER 12.00 4.80
1st mention of career triples should be doubles
239 Hank Aaron 10.00 4.00
240 Rob Ellis .10 .04
241 Sixto Lezcano .15 .06
242 Bob Mitchell .10 .04
243 Gorman Thomas .15 .06
244 Bill Travers .10 .04
245 Pete Broberg .10 .04
246 Bill Sharp .10 .04
247 Bobby Darwin .10 .04
248 Rick Austin UER .10 .04
(Photo actually
Larry Anderson)
249 Larry Anderson UER .10 .04
(Photo actually
Rick Austin)
250 Tom Bianco .10 .04
251 Lafayette Currence .10 .04
252 Steve Foucault .10 .04
253 Bill Hands .10 .04
254 Steve Hargan .10 .04
255 Fergie Jenkins 3.00 1.20
256 Bob Sheldon .10 .04
257 Jim Umbarger .10 .04
258 Clyde Wright .10 .04
259 Bill Fahey .10 .04
260 Jim Sundberg .20 .08
261 Leo Cardenas .10 .04
262 Jim Fregosi .20 .08
263 Mike Hargrove .20 .08
264 Toby Harrah .15 .06
265 Roy Howell .10 .04
266 Lenny Randle .10 .04
267 Roy Smalley .15 .06
268 Jim Spencer .10 .04
269 Jeff Burroughs .15 .06
270 Tom Grieve .15 .06
271 Joe Lovitto .10 .04
272 Frank Lucchesi MG .10 .04
273 Dave Nelson .10 .04
274 Ted Simmons .75 .30
275 Lou Brock 4.00 1.60
276 Ron Fairly .15 .06
277 Bake McBride .10 .04
278 Reggie Smith .20 .08
279 Willie Davis .15 .06
280 Ken Reitz .10 .04
281 Buddy Bradford .10 .04
282 Luis Melendez .10 .04
283 Mike Tyson .10 .04
284 Ted Sizemore .10 .04
285 Mario Guerrero .10 .04
286 Larry Lintz .10 .04
287 Ken Rudolph .10 .04
288 Dick Billings .10 .04
289 Jerry Mumphrey .15 .06
290 Mike Wallace .10 .04
291 Al Hrabosky .15 .06
292 Ken Reynolds .10 .04
293 Mike Garman .10 .04
294 Bob Forsch .15 .06
295 John Denny .15 .06
296 Harry Rasmussen .10 .04
297 Lynn McGlothen .10 .04
298 Mike Barlow .10 .04
299 Greg Terlecky .10 .04
300 Red Schoendienst MG .50 .20
301 Rick Reuschel .20 .08
302 Steve Stone .15 .06
303 Bill Bonham .10 .04
304 Oscar Zamora .10 .04
305 Ken Frailing .10 .04
306 Milt Wilcox .10 .04
307 Darold Knowles .10 .04
308 Jim Marshall MG .10 .04
309 Bill Madlock .50 .20
310 Jose Cardenal .15 .06
311 Rick Monday .15 .06
312 Jerry Morales .10 .04
313 Tim Hosley .10 .04
314 Gene Hiser .10 .04
315 Don Kessinger .15 .06
316 Manny Trillo .15 .06
317 Pete LaCock .10 .04
318 George Mitterwald .10 .04
319 Steve Swisher .10 .04
320 Rob Sperring .10 .04
321 Vic Harris .10 .04
322 Ron Dunn .10 .04
323 Jose Morales .10 .04
324 Pete Mackanin .10 .04
325 Jim Cox .10 .04
326 Larry Parrish .15 .06
327 Mike Jorgensen .10 .04
328 Tim Foli .10 .04
329 Hal Breeden .10 .04
330 Nate Colbert .10 .04
331 Pepe Frias .10 .04
332 Pat Scanlon .10 .04
333 Bob Bailey .10 .04
334 Gary Carter 5.00 2.00
335 Pepe Mangual .10 .04
336 Larry Biittner .10 .04
337 Jim Lyttle .10 .04
338 Gary Roenicke .20 .08
339 Tony Scott .10 .04
340 Jerry White .10 .04
341 Jim Dwyer .10 .04
342 Ellis Valentine .15 .06
343 Fred Scherman .10 .04
344 Dennis Blair .10 .04
345 Woodie Fryman .10 .04
346 Chuck Taylor .10 .04
347 Dan Warthen .10 .04
348 Dan Carrithers .10 .04
349 Steve Rogers .15 .06
350 Dale Murray .10 .04
351 Duke Snider CO 2.00 .80
352 Ralph Houk MG .15 .06
353 John Hiller .10 .04
354 Mickey Lolich .30 .12
355 Dave Lemancyzk .10 .04
356 Lerrin LaGrow .10 .04
357 Fred Arroyo .10 .04
358 Joe Coleman .10 .04
359 Ben Oglivie .15 .06
360 Willie Horton .15 .06
361 John Knox .10 .04
362 Leon Roberts .10 .04
363 Ron LeFlore .15 .06
364 Gary Sutherland .10 .04
365 Dan Meyer .10 .04
366 Aurelio Rodriguez .10 .04
367 Tom Veryzer .10 .04
368 Jack Pierce .10 .04
369 Gene Michael .15 .06
370 Billy Baldwin .10 .04
371 Gates Brown .15 .06
372 Mickey Stanley .15 .06
373 Terry Humphrey .10 .04
374 Doyle Alexander .10 .04
375 Mike Cuellar .20 .08
376 Wayne Garland .10 .04
377 Ross Grimsley .10 .04
378 Grant Jackson .10 .04
379 Dyar Miller .10 .04
380 Jim Palmer 4.00 1.60
381 Mike Torrez .15 .06
382 Mike Willis .10 .04
383 Dave Duncan .15 .06
384 Ellie Hendricks .10 .04
385 Jim Hutto .10 .04
386 Bob Bailor .10 .04
387 Doug DeCinces .20 .08
388 Bob Grich .20 .08
389 Lee May .20 .08
390 Tony Muser .10 .04
391 Tim Nordbrook .10 .04
392 Brooks Robinson 4.00 1.60
393 Royle Stillman .10 .04
394 Don Baylor .75 .30
395 Paul Blair .15 .06
396 Al Bumbry .10 .04
397 Larry Harlow .10 .04
398 Tommy Davis .15 .06
399 Jim Northrup .15 .06
400 Ken Singleton .15 .06
401 Tom Shopay .10 .04
402 Fred Lynn .75 .30
403 Carlton Fisk 5.00 2.00
404 Cecil Cooper .30 .12
405 Jim Rice 2.00 .80
406 Juan Beniquez .10 .04
407 Denny Doyle .10 .04
408 Dwight Evans 1.00 .40
409 Carl Yastrzemski 5.00 2.00
410 Rick Burleson .10 .04
411 Bernie Carbo .10 .04
412 Doug Griffin .10 .04
413 Rico Petrocelli .15 .06
414 Bob Montgomery .10 .04
415 Tim Blackwell .10 .04
416 Rick Miller .10 .04
417 Darrell Johnson MG .10 .04
418 Jim Burton .10 .04
419 Jim Willoughby .10 .04
420 Rogelio Moret .10 .04
421 Bill Lee .15 .06
422 Dick Drago .10 .04
423 Diego Segui .10 .04
424 Luis Tiant .30 .12
425 Jim Hunter 3.00 1.20
426 Rick Sawyer .10 .04
427 Rudy May .10 .04
428 Dick Tidrow .10 .04
429 Sparky Lyle .30 .12
430 Doc Medich .10 .04
431 Pat Dobson .10 .04
432 Dave Pagan .10 .04
433 Thurman Munson 3.00 1.20
434 Chris Chambliss .30 .12
435 Roy White .15 .06
436 Walt Williams .10 .04
437 Graig Nettles .50 .20
438 Rick Dempsey .15 .06
439 Bobby Bonds .75 .30
440 Ed Herrmann .10 .04
441 Sandy Alomar .15 .06
442 Fred Stanley .10 .04
443 Terry Whitfield .10 .04
444 Rich Bladt .10 .04
445 Lou Piniella .50 .20
446 Rich Coggins .10 .04
447 Ed Brinkman .10 .04
448 Jim Mason .10 .04
449 Larry Murray .10 .04
450 Ron Blomberg .10 .04
451 Elliott Maddox .10 .04
452 Kerry Dineen .10 .04
453 Billy Martin MG .75 .30
454 Dave Bergman .10 .04
455 Otto Velez .10 .04
456 Joe Hoerner .10 .04
457 Tug McGraw .30 .12
458 Gene Garber .15 .06
459 Steve Carlton 5.00 2.00
460 Larry Christenson .10 .04
461 Tom Underwood .10 .04
462 Jim Lonborg .15 .06
463 Jay Johnstone .20 .08
464 Larry Bowa .20 .08
465 Dave Cash .10 .04
466 Ollie Brown .10 .04
467 Greg Luzinski .30 .12
468 Johnny Oates .10 .04
469 Mike Anderson .10 .04
470 Mike Schmidt 15.00 6.00
471 Bob Boone .50 .20
472 Tom Hutton .10 .04
473 Rich Allen .75 .30
474 Tony Taylor .15 .06
475 Jerry Martin .10 .04
476 Danny Ozark MG .10 .04
477 Dick Ruthven .10 .04
478 Jim Todd .10 .04
479 Paul Lindblad .10 .04
480 Rollie Fingers 3.00 1.20
481 Vida Blue .20 .08
482 Ken Holtzman .15 .06
483 Dick Bosman .10 .04
484 Sonny Siebert .10 .04
485 Glenn Abbott .10 .04
486 Stan Bahnsen .10 .04
487 Mike Norris .15 .06
488 Alvin Dark MG .15 .06
489 Claudell Washington .15 .06
490 Joe Rudi .15 .06
491 Bill North .10 .04
492 Bert Campaneris .15 .06
493 Gene Tenace .15 .06
494 Reggie Jackson 8.00 3.20
495 Phil Garner .10 .04
496 Billy Williams 3.00 1.20
497 Sal Bando .15 .06
498 Jim Holt .10 .04
499 Ted Martinez .10 .04
500 Ray Fosse .10 .04
501 Matt Alexander .10 .04
502 Larry Haney .10 .04
503 Angel Mangual .10 .04
504 Fred Beene .10 .04
505 Tom Buskey .10 .04
506 Dennis Eckersley 12.00 4.80
507 Roric Harrison .10 .04
508 Don Hood .10 .04
509 Jim Kern .10 .04
510 Dave LaRoche .10 .04
511 Fritz Peterson .10 .04
512 Jim Strickland .10 .04
513 Rick Waits .10 .04
514 Alan Ashby .20 .08
515 John Ellis .10 .04
516 Rick Cerone .20 .08
517 Buddy Bell .20 .08
518 Jack Brohamer .10 .04
519 Rico Carty .15 .06
520 Ed Crosby .10 .04
521 Frank Duffy .10 .04
522 Duane Kuiper UER .10 .04
(Photo actually
Rick Manning)
523 Joe Lis .10 .04
524 Boog Powell 1.00 .40
525 Frank Robinson 4.00 1.60
526 Oscar Gamble .15 .06
527 George Hendrick .15 .06
528 John Lowenstein .10 .04
529 Rick Manning UER .15 .06
(Photo actually
Duane Kuiper)
530 Tommy Smith .10 .04
531 Charlie Spikes .10 .04
532 Steve Kline .10 .04
533 Ed Kranepool .15 .06
534 Mike Vail .10 .04
535 Del Unser .10 .04
536 Felix Millan .10 .04
537 Rusty Staub .30 .12
538 Jesus Alou .10 .04
539 Wayne Garrett .10 .04
540 Mike Phillips .10 .04
541 Joe Torre .50 .20
542 Dave Kingman .50 .20
543 Gene Clines .10 .04
544 Jack Heidemann .10 .04
545 Bud Harrelson .15 .06
546 John Stearns .15 .06
547 John Milner .10 .04
548 Bob Apodaca .10 .04
549 Skip Lockwood .10 .04
550 Ken Sanders .10 .04
551 Tom Seaver 6.00 2.40
552 Rick Baldwin .10 .04
553 Hank Webb .10 .04
554 Jon Matlack .10 .04
555 Randy Tate .10 .04
556 Tom Hall .10 .04
557 George Stone .10 .04
558 Craig Swan .10 .04
559 Jerry Cram .10 .04
560 Roy Staiger .10 .04
561 Kent Tekulve .30 .12
562 Jerry Reuss .15 .06
563 John Candelaria .20 .08
564 Larry Demery .10 .04
565 Dave Giusti .10 .04
566 Jim Rooker .10 .04
567 Ramon Hernandez .10 .04
568 Bruce Kison .10 .04
569 Ken Brett .10 .04
570 Bob Moose .10 .04
571 Manny Sanguillen .15 .06
572 Dave Parker 2.50 1.00
573 Willie Stargell 3.00 1.20
574 Richie Zisk .15 .06
575 Rennie Stennett .10 .04
576 Al Oliver .50 .20
577 Bill Robinson .15 .06
578 Bob Robertson .10 .04
579 Rich Hebner .15 .06
580 Ed Kirkpatrick .10 .04
581 Duffy Dyer .10 .04
582 Craig Reynolds .10 .04
583 Frank Taveras .10 .04
584 Willie Randolph 3.00 1.20
585 Art Howe .30 .12
586 Danny Murtaugh MG .15 .06
587 Rick McKinney .10 .04
588 Ed Goodson .10 .04
589 George Brett 4.00 1.60
Al Cowens CL
590 Keith Hernandez 1.00 .40
Lou Brock CL
591 Jerry Koosman 1.00 .40
Duke Snider CL
592 Maury Wills .15 .06
John Knox CL
593A Jim Hunter 15.00 6.00
Nolan Ryan CL ERR
(Noland on front)
593B Jim Hunter 5.00 2.00
Nolan Ryan CL COR
594 Ralph Branca .20 .08
Carl Erskine
Pee Wee Reese CL
595 Willie Mays 1.50 .60
Herb Score CL
596 Larry Cox .10 .04
597 Gene Mauch MG .15 .06
598 W. Wietelmann CO .15 .06
599 Wayne Simpson .10 .04
600 Mel Thomason .10 .04
601 Ike Hampton .10 .04
602 Ken Crosby .10 .04
603 Ralph Rowe .15 .06
604 Jim Tyrone .10 .04
605 Mick Kelleher .15 .06
606 Mario Mendoza .15 .06
607 Mike Rogodzinski .10 .04
608 Bob Gallagher .10 .04
609 Jerry Koosman .20 .08
610 Joe Frazier MG .10 .04
611 Karl Kuehl MG .10 .04
612 Frank LaCorte .10 .04
613 Ray Bare .10 .04
614 Billy Muffett CO .10 .04
615 Bill Laxton .10 .04
616 Willie Mays CO 8.00 3.20
617 Phil Cavarretta CO .15 .06
618 Ted Kluszewski CO .30 .12
619 Elston Howard CO .20 .08
620 Alex Grammas CO .10 .04
621 Mickey Vernon CO .15 .06
622 Dick Sisler CO .10 .04
623 Harvey Haddix CO .10 .04
624 Bobby Winkles CO .10 .04
625 John Pesky CO .15 .06
626 Jim Davenport CO .10 .04
627 Dave Tomlin .10 .04
628 Roger Craig CO .15 .06
629 Joe Amalfitano CO .10 .04
630 Jim Reese CO .30 .12

1976 SSPC 1887 World Series

This 18-card standard-size set was inserted into the Fall 1976 Collectors Quarterly issue. Many of the players featured have few cards issued of them during their career. The fronts feature drawings while the backs talk about the 1887 World Series.

	NM	Ex
COMPLETE SET (18)	12.00	4.80
1 Bob Caruthers	.75	.30
2 Dave Foutz	.50	.20
3 Arlie Latham	.75	.30
4 Charlie Getzein	.50	.20
5 Jack Rowe	.50	.20
6 Fred Dunlap	.50	.20
7 Tip O'Neill	.75	.30
8 Curt Welch	.75	.30
9 Kid Gleason	1.00	.40
10 Sam Thompson	1.50	.60
11 Ned Hanlon	1.50	.60
12 Dan Brouthers	1.50	.60
13 Doc Bushong	.50	.20
14 Charles Comiskey	3.00	1.20
15 Yank Robinson	.50	.20
16 Charlie Bennett	.75	.30
17 Hardy Richardson	.50	.20
18 Deacon White	.75	.30

1976 SSPC Yankees Old-Timers Day

These nine standard-size cards were inserted in the Collectors Quarterly Spring 1976 edition. The cards feature the player's photo and his name on the bottom. The backs form a puzzle of four Yankee greats: Billy Martin, Joe DiMaggio, Whitey Ford and Mickey Mantle. The cards are unnummbered and thus sequenced in alphabetical order.

	NM	Ex
COMPLETE SET (9)	8.00	3.20
1 Earl Averill	.75	.30
2 Joe DiMaggio	3.00	1.20
3 Tommy Henrich	.50	.20
4 Billy Herman	.75	.30
5 Monte Irvin	.75	.30
6 Jim Konstanty	.25	.10
7 Mickey Mantle	3.00	1.20
8 Pee Wee Reese	1.00	.40
9 Bobby Thomson	.50	.20

1978 SSPC 270

This 270-card set was issued as magazine (All-Star Gallery) inserts in sets of three panels, with each panel measuring approximately 7 1/4" by 10 3/4". Each of the three panels contains nine cards. If cut, the individual cards would measure the standard size (2 1/2" by 3 1/2"). The fronts display color posed and action player photos with thin black inner borders and white outer borders. The backs carry the player's name, biographical information, and career summary. The cards are checklisted below alphabetically according to teams as follows: New York Yankees (1-27)), Philadelphia Phillie (28-54), Los Angeles Dodgers (55-81), Texas Rangers (82-108), Cincinnati Reds (109-135), Chicago White Sox (136-162), Boston Red Sox (163-189), California Angels (190-216), Kansas City Royals (217-243), and Chicago Cubs (244-270). The pricing below is for individual cards.

	NM	Ex
COMPLETE SET (270)	100.00	40.00
1 Thurman Munson	2.00	.80
2 Cliff Johnson	.10	.04
3 Lou Piniella	.40	.16
4 Dell Alston	.10	.04
5 Yankee Stadium	.10	.04
6 Ken Holtzman	.20	.08
7 Chris Chambliss	.30	.12
8 Roy White	.20	.08
9 Ed Figueroa	.10	.04
10 Dick Tidrow	.10	.04
11 Sparky Lyle	.30	.12
12 Fred Stanley	.10	.04
13 Mickey Rivers	.20	.08
14 Billy Martin MG	.40	.16
15 George Zeber	.10	.04
16 Ken Clay	.10	.04
17 Ron Guidry	.30	.12
18 Don Gullett	.20	.08
19 Fran Healy	.10	.04
20 Paul Blair	.10	.04
21 Mickey Klutts	.10	.04
22 Yankees Team Photo	.20	.08
23 Catfish Hunter	2.00	.80
24 Bucky Dent	.20	.08
25 Graig Nettles	.40	.16

26 Reggie Jackson 4.00 1.60
27 Willie Randolph .30 .12
28 Garry Maddox .20 .08
29 Steve Carlton 3.00 1.20
30 Ron Reed .10 .04
31 Greg Luzinski .30 .12
32 Bobby Wine CO .10 .04
33 Bob Boone .30 .12
34 Carroll Beringer CO .10 .04
35 Richie Hebner .20 .08
36 Ray Rippelmeyer CO .10 .04
37 Terry Harmon .10 .04
38 Gene Garber .20 .08
39 Ted Sizemore .10 .04
40 Barry Foote .10 .04
41 Tony Taylor CO .10 .04
42 Tug McGraw .40 .16
43 Jay Johnstone .30 .12
44 Randy Lerch .10 .04
45 Billy DeMars CO .10 .04
46 Mike Schmidt 5.00 2.00
47 Larry Christenson .10 .04
48 Tim McCarver .40 .16
49 Larry Bowa .30 .12
50 Danny Ozark MG .10 .04
51 Jerry Martin .10 .04
52 Jim Lonborg .20 .08
53 Bake McBride .10 .04
54 Warren Brusstar .10 .04
55 Burt Hooton .20 .08
56 Bill Russell .10 .04
57 Dusty Baker .30 .12
58 Reggie Smith .30 .12
59 Rick Rhoden .10 .04
60 Jerry Grote .20 .08
61 Bill Butler .10 .04
62 Ron Cey .30 .12
63 Tom Lasorda MG .75 .30
64 Teddy Martinez .10 .04
65 Ed Goodson .10 .04
66 Vic Davalillo .10 .04
67 Davey Lopes .20 .08
68 Terry Forster .10 .04
69 Lee Lacy .10 .04
70 Mike Garman .10 .04
71 Steve Garvey .75 .30
72 Johnny Oates .10 .04
73 Steve Yeager .10 .04
74 Rafael Landestoy .10 .04
75 Tommy John .40 .16
76 Glenn Burke .10 .04
77 Rick Monday .20 .08
78 Doug Rau .10 .04
79 Manny Mota .20 .08
80 Don Sutton 1.00 .40
81 Charlie Hough .30 .12
82 Mike Hargrove .20 .08
83 Jim Sundberg .20 .08
84 Fergie Jenkins 1.50 .60
85 Paul Lindblad .10 .04
86 Sandy Alomar .10 .04
87 John Lowenstein .10 .04
88 Claudell Washington .20 .08
89 Toby Harrah .20 .08
90 Jim Umbarger .10 .04
91 Len Barker .10 .04
92 Dave May .10 .04
93 Kurt Bevacqua .10 .04
94 Jim Mason .10 .04
95 Bump Wills .10 .04
96 Dock Ellis .10 .04
97 Bill Fahey .10 .04
98 Richie Zisk .10 .04
99 Jon Matlack .10 .04
100 John Ellis .10 .04
101 Bert Campaneris .20 .08
102 Doc Medich .10 .04
103 Juan Beniquez .10 .04
104 Billy Hunter MG .10 .04
105 Doyle Alexander .20 .08
106 Roger Moret .10 .04
107 Mike Jorgensen .10 .04
108 Al Oliver .30 .12
109 Fred Norman .10 .04
110 Ray Knight .40 .16
111 Pedro Borbon .10 .04
112 Bill Bonham .10 .04
113 George Foster .40 .16
114 Doug Bair .10 .04
115 Cesar Geronimo .10 .04
116 Tom Seaver 2.50 1.00
117 Mario Soto .20 .08
118 Ken Griffey .30 .12
119 Mike Lum .10 .04
120 Tom Hume .10 .04
121 Joe Morgan 2.00 .80
122 Manny Sarmiento .10 .04
123 Dan Driessen .20 .08
124 Ed Armbrister .10 .04
125 Champ Summers .10 .04
126 Rick Auerbach .10 .04
127 Doug Capilla .10 .04
128 Johnny Bench 2.50 1.00
129 Sparky Anderson MG .40 .16
130 Raul Ferreyra .10 .04
131 Dale Murray .10 .04
132 Pete Rose 3.00 1.20
133 Dave Concepcion .30 .12
134 Junior Kennedy .10 .04
135 Dave Collins .20 .08
136 Mike Eden .10 .04
137 Lamar Johnson .10 .04
138 Ron Schueler .10 .04
139 Bob Lemon MG .40 .16
140 Bobby Bonds .40 .16
141 Thad Bosley .10 .04
142 Jorge Orta .10 .04
143 Wilbur Wood .10 .04
144 Francisco Barrios .10 .04
145 Greg Prior .10 .04
146 Chet Lemon .20 .08
147 Mike Squires .10 .04
148 Eric Soderholm .10 .04
149 Reggie Sanders .10 .04
150 Kevin Bell .10 .04
151 Alan Bannister .10 .04
152 Henry Cruz .10 .04
153 Larry Doby CO .40 .16
154 Don Kessinger .20 .08
155 Ralph Garr .20 .08
156 Bill Nahorodny .10 .04
157 Ron Blomberg .10 .04
158 Bob Molinaro .10 .04
159 Junior Moore .10 .04
160 Minnie Minoso CO .30 .12
161 Lerrin LaGrow .10 .04
162 Wayne Nordhagen .10 .04
163 Ramon Aviles .10 .04
164 Bob Stanley .30 .12
165 Reggie Cleveland .10 .04
166 Jack Brohamer .10 .04
167 Bill Lee .20 .08
168 Jim Burton .10 .04
169 Bill Campbell .10 .04
170 Mike Torrez .10 .04
171 Dick Drago .10 .04
172 Butch Hobson .10 .04
173 Bob Bailey .10 .04
174 Fred Lynn .20 .08
175 Rick Burleson .20 .08
176 Luis Tiant .30 .12
177 Ted Williams CO 8.00 3.20
178 Dennis Eckersley 4.00 1.60
179 Don Zimmer MG .10 .04
180 Carlton Fisk 4.00 1.60
181 Dwight Evans .40 .16
182 Fred Kendall .10 .04
183 George Scott .20 .08
184 Frank Duffy .10 .04
185 Bernie Carbo .10 .04
186 Jerry Remy .10 .04
187 Carl Yastrzemski 4.00 1.60
188 Allen Ripley .10 .04
189 Jim Rice 1.00 .40
190 Ken Landreaux .10 .04
191 Paul Hartzell .10 .04
192 Ken Brett .10 .04
193 Dave Garcia MG .10 .04
194 Bobby Grich .30 .12
195 Lyman Bostock Jr. .30 .12
196 Ike Hampton .10 .04
197 Dave LaRoche .10 .04
198 Dave Chalk .10 .04
199 Rick Miller .10 .04
200 Floyd Rayford .10 .04
201 Willie Aikens .20 .08
202 Balor Moore .10 .04
203 Nolan Ryan 20.00 8.00
204 Danny Goodwin .10 .04
205 Ron Fairly .20 .08
206 Dyar Miller .10 .04
207 Carney Lansford .40 .16
208 Don Baylor .40 .16
209 Gil Flores .10 .04
210 Terry Humphrey .10 .04
211 Frank Tanana .40 .16
212 Chris Knapp .10 .04
213 Ron Jackson .10 .04
214 Joe Rudi .20 .08
215 Tony Solaita .10 .04
216 Rance Mulliniks .10 .04
217 George Brett 15.00 6.00
218 Doug Bird .10 .04
219 Hal McRae .40 .16
220 Dennis Leonard .20 .08
221 Darrell Porter .20 .08
222 Randy McGilberry .10 .04
223 Pete LaCock .10 .04
224 Whitey Herzog MG .30 .12
225 Andy Hassler .10 .04
226 Joe Lahoud .10 .04
227 Amos Otis .20 .08
228 Al Hrabosky .20 .08
229 Clint Hurdle .40 .16
230 Paul Splittorff .10 .04
231 Marty Pattin .20 .08
232 Frank White .30 .12
233 John Wathan .10 .04
234 Freddie Patek .20 .08
235 Rich Gale .10 .04
236 U.L. Washington .10 .04
237 Larry Gura .10 .04
238 Jim Colborn .10 .04
239 Tom Poquette .10 .04
240 Al Cowens .10 .04
241 Willie Wilson .40 .16
242 Steve Mingori .10 .04
243 Jerry Terrell .10 .04
244 Larry Biittner .10 .04
245 Rick Reuschel .20 .08
246 Dave Rader .10 .04
247 Paul Reuschel .10 .04
248 Heity Cruz .10 .04
249 Woodie Fryman .10 .04
250 Steve Ontiveros .10 .04
251 Mike Gordon .10 .04
252 Dave Kingman .40 .16
253 Gene Clines .10 .04
254 Bruce Sutter .30 .12
255 Willie Hernandez .20 .08
256 Ivan DeJesus .10 .04
257 Greg Gross .10 .04
258 Larry Cox .10 .04
259 Joe Wallis .10 .04
260 Dennis Lamp .10 .04
261 Ray Burris .10 .04
262 Bill Caudill .10 .04
263 Donnie Moore .10 .04
264 Bill Buckner .30 .12
265 Bobby Murcer .30 .12
266 Dave Roberts .10 .04
267 Mike Krukow .10 .04
268 Herman Franks MG .10 .04
269 Mick Kelleher .10 .04
270 Rudy Meoli .10 .04

1980-87 SSPC HOF

The 1980 SSPC set was commonly known as the Baseball Immortals set. This standard-size set honored all of the members of the Hall of Fame. When the set was first issued the first 10,000 sets made indicated first printing on the back. This set continued to be issued as new additions were inducted into the Hall of Fame.

NRMT VG-E
COMPLETE SET (199) 30.00 13.50
1 Babe Ruth 2.00 .90
2 Ty Cobb 1.50 .70
3 Walter Johnson .75 .35
4 Christy Mathewson .75 .35
5 Honus Wagner 1.00 .45
6 Morgan Bulkeley .05 .02
7 Ban Johnson .05 .02
8 Larry Lajoie .50 .23
9 Connie Mack .25 .11
10 John McGraw .25 .11
11 Tris Speaker .25 .11
12 George Wright .05 .02
13 Cy Young .75 .35
14 Grover Alexander .75 .35
15 Alexander Cartwright .05 .02
16 Henry Chadwick .05 .02
17 Cap Anson .25 .11
18 Eddie Collins .15 .07
19 Charles Comiskey .05 .02
20 Candy Cummings .05 .02
21 Buck Ewing .05 .02
22 Lou Gehrig 1.50 .70
23 Willie Keeler .05 .02
24 Hoss Radbourne .05 .02
25 George Sisler .15 .07
26 Albert Spalding .05 .02
27 Rogers Hornsby .75 .35
28 Judge Landis .05 .02
29 Roger Bresnahan .05 .02
30 Dan Brouthers .05 .02
31 Fred Clarke .05 .02
32 James Collins .05 .02
33 Ed Delahanty .05 .02
34 Hugh Duffy .05 .02
35 Hughie Jennings .05 .02
36 Mike(King) Kelly .15 .07
37 James O'Rourke .05 .02
38 Wilbert Robinson .05 .02
39 Jesse Burkett .05 .02
40 Frank Chance .15 .07
41 Jack Chesbro .05 .02
42 John Evers .15 .07
43 Clark Griffith .05 .02
44 Thomas McCarthy .05 .02
45 Joe McGinnity .05 .02
46 Eddie Plank .05 .02
47 Joe Tinker .15 .07
48 Rube Waddell .05 .02
49 Ed Walsh .05 .02
50 Mickey Cochrane .15 .07
51 Frankie Frisch .15 .07
52 Lefty Grove .15 .07
53 Carl Hubbell .25 .11
54 Herb Pennock .05 .02
55 Pie Traynor .15 .07
56 Three Finger Brown .05 .02
57 Charlie Gehringer .15 .07
58 Kid Nichols .05 .02
59 Jimmie Foxx .75 .35
60 Mel Ott .50 .23
61 Harry Heilmann .05 .02
62 Paul Waner .15 .07
63 Ed Barrow .05 .02
64 Chief Bender .05 .02
65 Tom Connolly .05 .02
66 Dizzy Dean .75 .35
67 Bill Klem .05 .02
68 Al Simmons .15 .07
69 Bobby Wallace .05 .02
70 Harry Wright .05 .02
71 Bill Dickey .25 .11
72 Rabbit Maranville .05 .02
73 Bill Terry .15 .07
74 Home Run Baker .15 .07
75 Joe DiMaggio 1.50 .70
76 Gabby Hartnett .05 .02
77 Ted Lyons .05 .02
78 Ray Schalk .05 .02
79 Dazzy Vance .05 .02
80 Joe Cronin .15 .07
81 Hank Greenberg .15 .07
82 Sam Crawford .05 .02
83 Joe McCarthy .05 .02
84 Zack Wheat .05 .02
85 Max Carey .05 .02
86 Billy Hamilton .05 .02
87 Bob Feller .75 .35
88 Bill McKechnie .05 .02
89 Jackie Robinson 1.00 .45
90 Ed Roush .05 .02
91 John Clarkson .05 .02
92 Elmer Flick .05 .02
93 Sam Rice .05 .02
94 Eppa Rixey .05 .02
95 Luke Appling .05 .02
96 Red Faber .05 .02
97 Burleigh Grimes .05 .02
98 Miller Huggins .05 .02
99 Tim Keefe .05 .02
100 Heinie Manush .05 .02
101 John Ward .05 .02
102 Pud Galvin .05 .02
103 Casey Stengel .25 .11
104 Ted Williams 1.00 .45
105 Branch Rickey .15 .07
106 Red Ruffing .05 .02
107 Lloyd Waner .05 .02
108 Kiki Cuyler .05 .02
109 Goose Goslin .05 .02
110 Joe Medwick .05 .02
111 Roy Campanella .50 .23
112 Stan Coveleski .05 .02
113 Waite Hoyt .05 .02
114 Stan Musial .75 .35
115 Lou Boudreau .05 .02
116 Earle Combs .05 .02
117 Ford Frick .05 .02
118 Jesse Haines .05 .02
119 Dave Bancroft .05 .02
120 Jake Beckley .05 .02
121 Chick Hafey .05 .02
122 Harry Hooper .05 .02
123 Joe Kelley .05 .02
124 Rube Marquard .05 .02
125 Satchel Paige .50 .23
126 George Weiss .05 .02
127 Yogi Berra .50 .23
128 Josh Gibson .50 .23
129 Lefty Gomez .15 .07
130 Will Harridge .05 .02
131 Sandy Koufax .75 .35
132 Buck Leonard .15 .07
133 Early Wynn .15 .07
134 Ross Youngs .05 .02
135 Roberto Clemente 1.00 .45
136 Billy Evans .05 .02
137 Monte Irvin .15 .07
138 George Kelly .05 .02
139 Warren Spahn .15 .07
140 Mickey Welch .05 .02
141 Cool Papa Bell .15 .07
142 Jim Bottomley .05 .02
143 Jocko Conlan .05 .02
144 Whitey Ford .25 .11
145 Mickey Mantle 1.50 .70
146 Sam Thompson .05 .02
147 Earl Averill .05 .02
148 Bucky Harris .05 .02
149 Billy Herman .05 .02
150 Judy Johnson .05 .02
151 Ralph Kiner .15 .07
152 Oscar Charleston .05 .02
153 Roger Connor .05 .02
154 Cal Hubbard .05 .02
155 Bob Lemon .05 .02
156 Fred Lindstrom .05 .02
157 Robin Roberts .15 .07
158 Ernie Banks .50 .23
159 Martin Dihigo .05 .02
160 John Henry Lloyd .05 .02
161 Al Lopez .05 .02
162 Amos Rusie .05 .02
163 Joe Sewell .05 .02
164 Addie Joss .05 .02
165 Larry McPhail .05 .02
166 Eddie Mathews .50 .23
167 Warren Giles .05 .02
168 Willie Mays 1.00 .45
169 Hack Wilson .05 .02
170 Duke Snider .75 .35
171 Al Kaline .75 .35
172 Chuck Klein .05 .02
173 Tom Yawkey .05 .02
174 Bob Gibson .50 .23
175 Rube Foster .05 .02
176 Johnny Mize .05 .02
177 Hank Aaron 1.00 .45
178 Frank Robinson .50 .23
179 Happy Chandler .05 .02
180 Travis Jackson .05 .02
181 Brooks Robinson .25 .11
182 Juan Marichal .25 .11
183 George Kell .15 .07
184 Walter Alston .05 .02
185 Harmon Killebrew .25 .11
186 Luis Aparicio .15 .07
187 Don Drysdale .15 .07
188 Pee Wee Reese .25 .11
189 Rick Ferrell .05 .02
190 Willie McCovey .25 .11
191 Ernie Lombardi .05 .02
192 Bobby Doerr .15 .07
193 Arky Vaughan .05 .02
194 Enos Slaughter .50 .23
195 Lou Brock .50 .23
196 Hoyt Wilhelm .50 .23
197 Billy Williams .50 .23
198 Jim Hunter .50 .23
199 Ray Dandridge .15 .07

1992 St. Vincent HOF Heroes Stamps

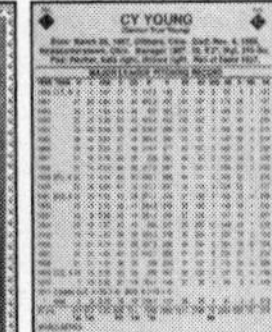

This 12-card standard-size set was issued by the St. Vincent Philatelic Services, Ltd. The peel-away stamps are official legal postage in St. Vincent and the Grenadines. The fronts have a head shot of various HOFers in sepia tones on a gold background that fades to red. The borders have a stamp edge design with an inner border of green. A blue banner across the top carries the words Baseball Hall of Fame Heroes and is placed over a baseball. The card's stamp value of $4.00 is shown in the top right. The lower margin carries the year the player entered the major leagues, his name and final year in the majors. The backs carry the player's name, biography and career statistics.

Nm-Mt Ex-Mt
COMPLETE SET (12) 10.00 3.00
1 Ty Cobb 1.50 .45
2 Dizzy Dean .50 .15
3 Bob Feller .50 .15
4 Whitey Ford .50 .15
5 Lou Gehrig 3.00 .90
6 Rogers Hornsby .50 .15
7 Mel Ott .50 .15
8 Satchel Paige .75 .23
9 Babe Ruth 3.00 .90
10 Casey Stengel .50 .15
11 Honus Wagner 1.00 .30
12 Cy Young .75 .23

1997 St. Vincent HOF Heroes Stamps

This 17-card set commemorates the 50th anniversary of Jackie Robinson breaking

Baseball's color barrier. The set features color head portraits of 16 different Black Hall of Famers on 1 3/16" by 1 9/16" $1 stamps. The player's name and year he entered the Hall of Fame are printed down the left. The last stamp listed in the checklist is a $6 stamp and honors Jackie Robinson. It measures approximately 2 3/4" by 4 1/8". The stamps were designed to be placed in a 9" by 8" album with a black-and-white picture of Jackie Robinson in action on the cover. The stamps are unnumbered and checklisted below in alphabetical order.

Nm-Mt Ex-Mt
COMPLETE SET (17) 12.00 3.60
1 Hank Aaron 1.50 .45
2 Ernie Banks .75 .23
3 Lou Brock .50 .15
4 Roy Campanella .75 .23
5 Rod Carew .50 .15
6 Roberto Clemente 3.00 .90
7 Bob Gibson .50 .15
8 Monte Irvin .50 .15
9 Reggie Jackson .75 .23
10 Ferguson Jenkins .50 .15
11 Willie McCovey .50 .15
12 Joe Morgan .50 .15
13 Satchel Paige .75 .23
14 Frank Robinson .75 .23
15 Willie Stargell .50 .15
16 Billy Williams .50 .15
17 Jackie Robinson 5.00 1.50

1991 Stadium Club Pre-Production

The exact origins of this scarce 50-card set is unclear, but speculation is that Topps distributed single cards or uncut strips to its employees and/or major candy wholesale accounts. The card fronts are very similar to the player's corresponding regular Stadium Club cards with the addition of an extra horizontal gold foil stripe at the bottom. The backs of all 50 cards are identical -- unnumbered with a reproduction of Jose Canseco's 1986 Topps Traded card.

Nm-Mt Ex-Mt
COMPLETE SET (50) 1200.00 350.00
1 Allan Anderson 15.00 4.50
2 Steve Balboni 15.00 4.50
3 Jeff Ballard 15.00 4.50
4 Jesse Barfield 15.00 4.50
5 Andy Benes 15.00 4.50
6 Bobby Bonilla 20.00 6.00
7 Chris Bosio 15.00 4.50
8 Daryl Boston 15.00 4.50
9 Chuck Cary 15.00 4.50
10 Pat Combs 15.00 4.50
11 Delino DeShields 20.00 6.00
12 Shawon Dunston 20.00 6.00
13 Alvaro Espinoza 15.00 4.50
14 Sid Fernandez 15.00 4.50
15 Bob Geren 15.00 4.50
16 Brian Holman 15.00 4.50
17 Jay Howell 15.00 4.50
18 Stan Javier 15.00 4.50
19 Dave Johnson 15.00 4.50
20 Howard Johnson 15.00 4.50
21 Kevin Maas 15.00 4.50
22 Shane Mack 15.00 4.50
23 Joe Magrane 15.00 4.50
24 Denny Martinez 15.00 4.50
25 Don Mattingly 150.00 45.00
26 Ben McDonald 15.00 4.50
27 Eddie Murray 80.00 24.00
28 Matt Nokes 15.00 4.50
29 Greg Olson 15.00 4.50
30 Gregg Olson 15.00 4.50
31 Jose Oquendo 15.00 4.50
32 Tony Phillips 15.00 4.50
33 Rafael Ramirez 15.00 4.50
34 Dennis Rasmussen 15.00 4.50
35 Billy Ripken 15.00 4.50
36 Nolan Ryan 300.00 90.00
37 Bill Sampen 15.00 4.50
38 Steve Sax 15.00 4.50
39 Mike Scioscia 30.00 9.00
40 David Segui 15.00 4.50
41 Zane Smith 15.00 4.50
42 B.J. Surhoff 20.00 6.00
43 Bobby Thigpen 15.00 4.50
44 Alan Trammell 40.00 12.00
45 Fernando Valenzuela 30.00 9.00
46 Andy Van Slyke 20.00 6.00
47 Hector Villanueva 15.00 4.50
48 Larry Walker 40.00 12.00
49 Walt Weiss 15.00 4.50
50 Bob Walk 15.00 4.50

1991 Stadium Club

This 600-card standard size set marked Topps first premium quality set. The set was issued in two separate series of 300 cards each. Cards were distributed in plastic wrapped packs.

Series II cards were also available at McDonald's restaurants in the Northeast at three cards per pack. The set created a stir in the hobby upon release with dazzling full-color borderless photos and slick, glossy card stock. The back of each card has the basic biographical information as well as making use of the Fastball BARS system and an inset photo of the player's Topps rookie card. Notable Rookie Cards include Jeff Bagwell.

	Nm-Mt	Ex-Mt
COMPLETE SET (600)	60.00	18.00
COMP.SERIES 1 (300)	40.00	12.00
COMP.SERIES 2 (300)	20.00	6.00
1 Dave Stewart TUX	.50	.15
2 Wally Joyner	.50	.15
3 Shawon Dunston	.25	.07
4 Darren Daulton	.50	.15
5 Will Clark	1.25	.35
6 Sammy Sosa	2.50	.75
7 Dan Plesac	.25	.07
8 Marquis Grissom	.25	.07
9 Erik Hanson	.25	.07
10 Geno Petralli	.25	.07
11 Jose Rijo	.25	.07
12 Carlos Quintana	.25	.07
13 Junior Ortiz	.25	.07
14 Bob Walk	.25	.07
15 Mike Macfarlane	.25	.07
16 Eric Yelding	.25	.07
17 Bryn Smith	.25	.07
18 Bip Roberts	.25	.07
19 Mike Scioscia	.25	.07
20 Mark Williamson	.25	.07
21 Don Mattingly	3.00	.90
22 John Franco	.50	.15
23 Chet Lemon	.25	.07
24 Tom Henke	.25	.07
25 Jerry Browne	.25	.07
26 Dave Justice	.50	.15
27 Mark Langston	.25	.07
28 Damon Berryhill	.25	.07
29 Kevin Bass	.25	.07
30 Scott Fletcher	.25	.07
31 Moises Alou	.50	.15
32 Dave Valle	.25	.07
33 Jody Reed	.25	.07
34 Dave West	.25	.07
35 Kevin McReynolds	.25	.07
36 Pat Combs	.25	.07
37 Eric Davis	.50	.15
38 Bret Saberhagen	.50	.15
39 Stan Javier	.25	.07
40 Chuck Cary	.25	.07
41 Tony Phillips	.25	.07
42 Lee Smith	.50	.15
43 Tim Teufel	.25	.07
44 Lance Dickson RC	.25	.07
45 Greg Litton	.25	.07
46 Ted Higuera	.25	.07
47 Edgar Martinez	.75	.23
48 Steve Avery	.25	.07
49 Walt Weiss	.25	.07
50 David Segui	.25	.07
51 Andy Benes	.25	.07
52 Karl Rhodes	.25	.07
53 Neal Heaton	.25	.07
54 Danny Gladden	.25	.07
55 Luis Rivera	.25	.07
56 Kevin Brown	.50	.15
57 Frank Thomas	1.25	.35
58 Terry Mulholland	.25	.07
59 Dick Schofield	.25	.07
60 Ron Darling	.25	.07
61 Sandy Alomar Jr.	.25	.07
62 Dave Stieb	.25	.07
63 Alan Trammell	.75	.23
64 Matt Nokes	.25	.07
65 Lenny Harris	.25	.07
66 Milt Thompson	.25	.07
67 Storm Davis	.25	.07
68 Joe Oliver	.25	.07
69 Andres Galarraga	.50	.15
70 Ozzie Guillen	.25	.07
71 Ken Howell	.25	.07
72 Garry Templeton	.25	.07
73 Derrick May	.25	.07
74 Xavier Hernandez	.25	.07
75 Dave Parker	.50	.15
76 Rick Aguilera	.50	.15
77 Robby Thompson	.25	.07
78 Pete Incaviglia	.25	.07
79 Bob Welch	.25	.07
80 Randy Milligan	.25	.07
81 Chuck Finley	.50	.15
82 Alvin Davis	.25	.07
83 Tim Naehring	.25	.07
84 Jay Bell	.50	.15
85 Joe Magrane	.25	.07
86 Howard Johnson	.25	.07
87 Jack McDowell	.25	.07
88 Kevin Seitzer	.25	.07
89 Bruce Ruffin	.25	.07
90 Fernando Valenzuela	.50	.15
91 Terry Kennedy	.25	.07
92 Barry Larkin	1.25	.35
93 Larry Walker	1.25	.35
94 Luis Salazar	.25	.07
95 Gary Sheffield	.50	.15
96 Bobby Witt	.25	.07
97 Lonnie Smith	.25	.07
98 Bryan Harvey	.25	.07
99 Mookie Wilson	.50	.15
100 Dwight Gooden	.75	.23
101 Lou Whitaker	.50	.15
102 Ron Karkovice	.25	.07
103 Jesse Barfield	.25	.07
104 Jose DeJesus	.25	.07
105 Benito Santiago	.50	.15
106 Brian Holman	.25	.07
107 Rafael Ramirez	.25	.07
108 Ellis Burks	.50	.15
109 Mike Bielecki	.25	.07
110 Kirby Puckett	1.25	.35
111 Terry Shumpert	.25	.07
112 Chuck Crim	.25	.07
113 Todd Benzinger	.25	.07
114 Brian Barnes RC	.25	.07
115 Carlos Baerga	.25	.07
116 Kal Daniels	.25	.07
117 Dave Johnson	.25	.07
118 Andy Van Slyke	.50	.15
119 John Burkett	.25	.07
120 Rickey Henderson	1.25	.35
121 Tim Jones	.25	.07
122 Daryl Irvine	.25	.07
123 Ruben Sierra	.25	.07
124 Jim Abbott	.75	.23
125 Daryl Boston	.25	.07
126 Greg Maddux	2.00	.60
127 Von Hayes	.25	.07
128 Mike Fitzgerald	.25	.07
129 Wayne Edwards	.25	.07
130 Greg Briley	.25	.07
131 Rob Dibble	.50	.15
132 Gene Larkin	.25	.07
133 David Wells	.50	.15
134 Steve Balboni	.25	.07
135 Greg Vaughn	.50	.15
136 Mark Davis	.25	.07
137 Dave Rhode	.25	.07
138 Eric Show	.25	.07
139 Bobby Bonilla	.50	.15
140 Dana Kiecker	.25	.07
141 Gary Pettis	.25	.07
142 Dennis Boyd	.25	.07
143 Mike Benjamin	.25	.07
144 Luis Polonia	.25	.07
145 Doug Jones	.25	.07
146 Al Newman	.25	.07
147 Alex Fernandez	.25	.07
148 Bill Doran	.25	.07
149 Kevin Elster	.25	.07
150 Len Dykstra	.50	.15
151 Mike Gallego	.25	.07
152 Tim Belcher	.25	.07
153 Jay Buhner	.50	.15
154 Ozzie Smith UER	2.00	.60
(Rookie card is 1979, but card back says '78)		
155 Jose Canseco	1.25	.35
156 Gregg Olson	.25	.07
157 Charlie O'Brien	.25	.07
158 Frank Tanana	.25	.07
159 George Brett	3.00	.90
160 Jeff Huson	.25	.07
161 Kevin Tapani	.25	.07
162 Jerome Walton	.25	.07
163 Charlie Hayes	.25	.07
164 Chris Bosio	.25	.07
165 Chris Sabo	.25	.07
166 Lance Parrish	.50	.15
167 Don Robinson	.25	.07
168 Manny Lee	.25	.07
169 Dennis Rasmussen	.25	.07
170 Wade Boggs	.75	.23
171 Bob Geren	.25	.07
172 Mackey Sasser	.25	.07
173 Julio Franco	.50	.15
174 Otis Nixon	.50	.15
175 Bert Blyleven	.50	.15
176 Craig Biggio	.75	.23
177 Eddie Murray	1.25	.35
178 Randy Tomlin RC	.25	.07
179 Tino Martinez	.75	.23
180 Carlton Fisk	.75	.23
181 Dwight Smith	.25	.07
182 Scott Garrelts	.25	.07
183 Jim Gantner	.25	.07
184 Dickie Thon	.25	.07
185 John Farrell	.25	.07
186 Cecil Fielder	.50	.15
187 Glenn Braggs	.25	.07
188 Allan Anderson	.25	.07
189 Kurt Stillwell	.25	.07
190 Jose Oquendo	.25	.07
191 Joe Orsulak	.25	.07
192 Ricky Jordan	.25	.07
193 Kelly Downs	.25	.07
194 Delino DeShields	.50	.15
195 Omar Vizquel	.50	.15
196 Mark Carreon	.25	.07
197 Mike Harkey	.25	.07
198 Jack Howell	.25	.07
199 Lance Johnson	.25	.07
200 Nolan Ryan TUX	5.00	1.50
201 John Marzano	.25	.07
202 Doug Drabek	.25	.07
203 Mark Lemke	.25	.07
204 Steve Sax	.50	.15
205 Greg Harris	.25	.07
206 B.J. Surhoff	.50	.15
207 Todd Burns	.25	.07
208 Jose Gonzalez	.25	.07
209 Mike Scott	.25	.07
210 Dave Magadan	.25	.07
211 Dante Bichette	.50	.15
212 Trevor Wilson	.25	.07
213 Hector Villanueva	.25	.07
214 Dan Pasqua	.25	.07
215 Greg Colbrunn RC	.50	.15
216 Mike Jeffcoat	.25	.07
217 Harold Reynolds	.50	.15
218 Paul O'Neill	.75	.23
219 Mark Guthrie	.25	.07
220 Barry Bonds	3.00	.90
221 Jimmy Key	.50	.15
222 Billy Ripken	.25	.07
223 Tom Pagnozzi	.25	.07
224 Bo Jackson	1.25	.35
225 Sid Fernandez	.25	.07
226 Mike Marshall	.25	.07
227 John Kruk	.50	.15
228 Mike Fetters	.25	.07
229 Eric Anthony	.25	.07
230 Ryne Sandberg	2.00	.60
231 Carney Lansford	.50	.15
232 Melido Perez	.25	.07
233 Jose Lind	.25	.07
234 Darryl Hamilton	.25	.07
235 Tom Browning	.25	.07
236 Spike Owen	.25	.07
237 Juan Gonzalez	1.25	.35
238 Felix Fermin	.25	.07
239 Keith Miller	.25	.07
240 Mark Gubicza	.25	.07
241 Kent Anderson	.25	.07
242 Alvaro Espinoza	.25	.07
243 Dale Murphy	1.25	.35
244 Orel Hershiser	.50	.15
245 Paul Molitor	.75	.23
246 Eddie Whitson	.25	.07
247 Joe Girardi	.25	.07
248 Kent Hrbek	.50	.15
249 Bill Sampen	.25	.07
250 Kevin Mitchell	.25	.07
251 Mariano Duncan	.25	.07
252 Scott Bradley	.25	.07
253 Mike Greenwell	.25	.07
254 Tom Gordon	.25	.07
255 Todd Zeile	.25	.07
256 Bobby Thigpen	.25	.07
257 Gregg Jefferies	.25	.07
258 Kenny Rogers	.50	.15
259 Shane Mack	.25	.07
260 Zane Smith	.25	.07
261 Mitch Williams	.25	.07
262 Jim Deshaies	.25	.07
263 Dave Winfield	.50	.15
264 Ben McDonald	.25	.07
265 Randy Ready	.25	.07
266 Pat Borders	.25	.07
267 Jose Uribe	.25	.07
268 Derek Lilliquist	.25	.07
269 Greg Brock	.25	.07
270 Ken Griffey Jr.	2.50	.75
271 Jeff Gray	.25	.07
272 Danny Tartabull	.25	.07
273 Dennis Martinez	.50	.15
274 Robin Ventura	.50	.15
275 Randy Myers	.25	.07
276 Jack Daugherty	.25	.07
277 Greg Gagne	.25	.07
278 Jay Howell	.25	.07
279 Mike LaValliere	.25	.07
280 Rex Hudler	.25	.07
281 Mike Simms	.25	.07
282 Kevin Maas	.25	.07
283 Jeff Ballard	.25	.07
284 Dave Henderson	.25	.07
285 Pete O'Brien	.25	.07
286 Brook Jacoby	.25	.07
287 Mike Henneman	.25	.07
288 Greg Olson	.25	.07
289 Greg Myers	.25	.07
290 Mark Grace	.75	.23
291 Shawn Abner	.25	.07
292 Frank Viola	.50	.15
293 Lee Stevens	.25	.07
294 Jason Grimsley	.25	.07
295 Matt Williams	.50	.15
296 Ron Robinson	.25	.07
297 Tom Brunansky	.25	.07
298 Checklist 1-100	.25	.07
299 Checklist 101-200	.25	.07
300 Checklist 201-300	.25	.07
301 Darryl Strawberry	.75	.23
302 Bud Black	.25	.07
303 Harold Baines	.50	.15
304 Roberto Alomar	1.25	.35
305 Norm Charlton	.25	.07
306 Gary Thurman	.25	.07
307 Mike Felder	.25	.07
308 Tony Gwynn	1.50	.45
309 Roger Clemens	2.50	.75
310 Andre Dawson	.50	.15
311 Scott Radinsky	.25	.07
312 Bob Melvin	.25	.07
313 Kirk McCaskill	.25	.07
314 Pedro Guerrero	.50	.15
315 Walt Terrell	.25	.07
316 Sam Horn	.25	.07
317 W.Chamberlain RC UER	.25	.07
Card listed as 1989 Debut card, should be 1990		
318 Pedro Munoz RC	.25	.07
319 Roberto Kelly	.25	.07
320 Mark Portugal	.25	.07
321 Tim McIntosh	.25	.07
322 Jesse Orosco	.25	.07
323 Gary Green	.25	.07
324 Greg Harris	.25	.07
325 Hubie Brooks	.25	.07
326 Chris Nabholz	.25	.07
327 Terry Pendleton	.50	.15
328 Eric King	.25	.07
329 Chili Davis	.50	.15
330 Anthony Telford	.25	.07
331 Kelly Gruber	.25	.07
332 Dennis Eckersley	.50	.15
333 Mel Hall	.25	.07
334 Bob Kipper	.25	.07
335 Willie McGee	.50	.15
336 Steve Olin	.25	.07
337 Steve Buechele	.25	.07
338 Scott Leius	.25	.07
339 Hal Morris	.25	.07
340 Jose Offerman	.25	.07
341 Kent Mercker	.25	.07
342 Ken Griffey Sr.	.50	.15
343 Pete Harnisch	.25	.07
344 Kirk Gibson	.50	.15
345 Dave Smith	.25	.07
346 Dave Martinez	.25	.07
347 Atlee Hammaker	.25	.07
348 Brian Downing	.25	.07
349 Todd Hundley	.50	.15
350 Candy Maldonado	.25	.07
351 Dwight Evans	.50	.15
352 Steve Searcy	.25	.07
353 Gary Gaetti	.50	.15
354 Jeff Reardon	.50	.15
355 Travis Fryman	.50	.15
356 Dave Righetti	.50	.15
357 Fred McGriff	.75	.23
358 Don Slaught	.25	.07
359 Gene Nelson	.25	.07
360 Billy Spiers	.25	.07
361 Lee Guetterman	.25	.07
362 Darren Lewis	.25	.07
363 Duane Ward	.25	.07
364 Lloyd Moseby	.25	.07
365 John Smoltz	.75	.23
366 Felix Jose	.25	.07
367 David Cone	.50	.15
368 Wally Backman	.25	.07
369 Jeff Montgomery	.25	.07
370 Rich Garces RC	.25	.07
371 Billy Hatcher	.25	.07
372 Bill Swift	.25	.07
373 Jim Eisenreich	.25	.07
374 Rob Ducey	.25	.07
375 Tim Crews	.25	.07
376 Steve Finley	.50	.15
377 Jeff Blauser	.25	.07
378 Willie Wilson	.25	.07
379 Gerald Perry	.25	.07
380 Jose Mesa	.25	.07
381 Pat Kelly RC	.25	.07
382 Matt Merullo	.25	.07
383 Ivan Calderon	.25	.07
384 Scott Chiamparino	.25	.07
385 Lloyd McClendon	.25	.07
386 Dave Bergman	.25	.07
387 Ed Sprague	.25	.07
388 Jeff Bagwell RC	3.00	.90
389 Brett Butler	.50	.15
390 Larry Andersen	.25	.07
391 Glenn Davis	.25	.07
392 Alex Cole UER	.25	.07
(Front photo actually Otis Nixon)		
393 Mike Heath	.25	.07
394 Danny Darwin	.25	.07
395 Steve Lake	.25	.07
396 Tim Layana	.25	.07
397 Terry Leach	.25	.07
398 Bill Wegman	.25	.07
399 Mark McGwire	3.00	.90
400 Mike Boddicker	.25	.07
401 Steve Howe	.25	.07
402 Bernard Gilkey	.25	.07
403 Thomas Howard	.25	.07
404 Rafael Belliard	.25	.07
405 Tom Candiotti	.25	.07
406 Rene Gonzales	.25	.07
407 Chuck McElroy	.25	.07
408 Paul Sorrento	.25	.07
409 Randy Johnson	1.50	.45
410 Brady Anderson	.50	.15
411 Dennis Cook	.25	.07
412 Mickey Tettleton	.25	.07
413 Mike Stanton	.25	.07
414 Ken Oberkfell	.25	.07
415 Rick Honeycutt	.25	.07
416 Nelson Santovenia	.25	.07
417 Bob Tewksbury	.25	.07
418 Brent Mayne	.25	.07
419 Steve Farr	.25	.07
420 Phil Stephenson	.25	.07
421 Jeff Russell	.25	.07
422 Chris James	.25	.07
423 Tim Leary	.25	.07
424 Gary Carter	.75	.23
425 Glenallen Hill	.25	.07
426 Matt Young UER	.25	.07
Card mentions 83T/Tr as RC, but 84T shown		
427 Sid Bream	.25	.07
428 Greg Swindell	.25	.07
429 Scott Aldred	.25	.07
430 Cal Ripken	4.00	1.20
431 Bill Landrum	.25	.07
432 Earnest Riles	.25	.07
433 Danny Jackson	.25	.07
434 Casey Candaele	.25	.07
435 Ken Hill	.25	.07
436 Jaime Navarro	.25	.07
437 Lance Blankenship	.25	.07
438 Randy Velarde	.25	.07
439 Frank DiPino	.25	.07
440 Carl Nichols	.25	.07
441 Jeff M. Robinson	.25	.07
442 Deion Sanders	.75	.23
443 Vicente Palacios	.25	.07
444 Devon White	.25	.07
445 John Cerutti	.25	.07
446 Tracy Jones	.25	.07
447 Jack Morris	.50	.15
448 Mitch Webster	.25	.07
449 Bob Ojeda	.25	.07
450 Oscar Azocar	.25	.07
451 Luis Aquino	.25	.07
452 Mark Whiten	.25	.07
453 Stan Belinda	.25	.07
454 Ron Gant	.50	.15
455 Jose DeLeon	.25	.07
456 Mark Salas UER	.25	.07
Back has 85T photo, but calls it 86T		
457 Junior Felix	.25	.07
458 Wally Whitehurst	.25	.07
459 Phil Plantier RC	.25	.07
460 Juan Berenguer	.25	.07
461 Franklin Stubbs	.25	.07
462 Joe Boever	.25	.07
463 Tim Wallach	.25	.07
464 Mike Moore	.25	.07
465 Albert Belle	.50	.15
466 Mike Witt	.25	.07
467 Craig Worthington	.25	.07
468 Jerald Clark	.25	.07
469 Scott Terry	.25	.07
470 Milt Cuyler	.25	.07
471 John Smiley	.25	.07
472 Charles Nagy	.25	.07
473 Alan Mills	.25	.07
474 John Russell	.25	.07
475 Bruce Hurst	.25	.07
476 Andujar Cedeno	.25	.07
477 Dave Eiland	.25	.07
478 Brian McRae RC	.50	.15
479 Mike LaCoss	.25	.07
480 Chris Gwynn	.25	.07
481 Jamie Moyer	.50	.15
482 John Olerud	.50	.15
483 Efrain Valdez	.25	.07
484 Sil Campusano	.25	.07
485 Pascual Perez	.25	.07
486 Gary Redus	.25	.07
487 Andy Hawkins	.25	.07
488 Cory Snyder	.25	.07
489 Chris Hoiles	.25	.07
490 Ron Hassey	.25	.07
491 Gary Wayne	.25	.07
492 Mark Lewis	.25	.07
493 Scott Coolbaugh	.25	.07
494 Gerald Young	.25	.07
495 Juan Samuel	.25	.07
496 Willie Fraser	.25	.07
497 Jeff Treadway	.25	.07
498 Vince Coleman	.25	.07
499 Cris Carpenter	.25	.07
500 Jack Clark	.50	.15
501 Kevin Appier	.50	.15
502 Rafael Palmeiro	.75	.23
503 Hensley Meulens	.25	.07
504 George Bell	.25	.07
505 Tony Pena	.25	.07
506 Roger McDowell	.25	.07
507 Luis Sojo	.25	.07
508 Mike Schooler	.25	.07
509 Robin Yount	2.00	.60
510 Jack Armstrong	.25	.07
511 Rick Cerone	.25	.07
512 Curt Wilkerson	.25	.07
513 Joe Carter	.50	.15
514 Tim Burke	.25	.07
515 Tony Fernandez	.25	.07
516 Ramon Martinez	.25	.07
517 Tim Hulett	.25	.07
518 Terry Steinbach	.25	.07
519 Pete Smith	.25	.07
520 Ken Caminiti	.50	.15
521 Shawn Boskie	.25	.07
522 Mike Pagliarulo	.25	.07
523 Tim Raines	.50	.15
524 Alfredo Griffin	.25	.07
525 Henry Cotto	.25	.07
526 Mike Stanley	.25	.07
527 Charlie Leibrandt	.25	.07
528 Jeff King	.25	.07
529 Eric Plunk	.25	.07
530 Tom Lampkin	.25	.07
531 Steve Bedrosian	.25	.07
532 Tom Herr	.25	.07
533 Craig Lefferts	.25	.07
534 Jeff Reed	.25	.07
535 Mickey Morandini	.25	.07
536 Greg Cadaret	.25	.07
537 Ray Lankford	.25	.07
538 John Candelaria	.25	.07
539 Rob Deer	.25	.07
540 Brad Arnsberg	.25	.07
541 Mike Sharperson	.25	.07
542 Jeff D. Robinson	.25	.07
543 Mo Vaughn	.50	.15
544 Jeff Parrett	.25	.07
545 Willie Randolph	.50	.15
546 Herm Winningham	.25	.07
547 Jeff Innis	.25	.07
548 Chuck Knoblauch	.50	.15
549 Tommy Greene UER	.25	.07
(Born in North Carolina, not South Carolina)		
550 Jeff Hamilton	.25	.07
551 Barry Jones	.25	.07
552 Ken Dayley	.25	.07
553 Rick Dempsey	.25	.07
554 Greg Smith	.25	.07
555 Mike Devereaux	.25	.07
556 Keith Comstock	.25	.07
557 Paul Faries	.25	.07
558 Tom Glavine	.75	.23
559 Craig Grebeck	.25	.07
560 Scott Erickson	.25	.07
561 Joel Skinner	.25	.07
562 Mike Morgan	.25	.07
563 Dave Gallagher	.25	.07
564 Todd Stottlemyre	.25	.07
565 Rich Rodriguez	.25	.07
566 Craig Wilson	.25	.07
567 Jeff Brantley	.25	.07
568 Scott Kamieniecki RC	.25	.07
569 Steve Decker RC	.25	.07
570 Juan Agosto	.25	.07
571 Tommy Gregg	.25	.07
572 Kevin Wickander	.25	.07
573 Jamie Quirk UER	.25	.07
(Rookie card is 1976, but card back is 1990)		
574 Jerry Don Gleaton	.25	.07
575 Chris Hammond	.25	.07
576 Luis Gonzalez RC	2.50	.75
577 Russ Swan	.25	.07
578 Jeff Conine RC	1.50	.45
579 Charlie Hough	.50	.15
580 Jeff Kunkel	.25	.07
581 Darrel Akerfelds	.25	.07
582 Jeff Manto	.25	.07
583 Alejandro Pena	.25	.07
584 Mark Davidson	.25	.07
585 Bob MacDonald RC	.25	.07
586 Paul Assenmacher	.25	.07
587 Dan Wilson RC	.50	.15
588 Tom Bolton	.25	.07
589 Brian Harper	.25	.07
590 John Habyan	.25	.07
591 John Orton	.25	.07
592 Mark Gardner	.25	.07
593 Turner Ward RC	.50	.15
594 Bob Patterson	.25	.07
595 Ed Nunez	.25	.07
596 Gary Scott RC UER	.25	.07
(Major League Batting Record should be Minor League)		
597 Scott Bankhead	.25	.07
598 Checklist 301-400	.25	.07
599 Checklist 401-500	.25	.07
600 Checklist 501-600	.25	.07

1992 Stadium Club Dome

The 1992 Stadium Club Dome set (issued by Topps) features 100 top draft picks, 56 1991 All-Star Game cards, 25 1991 Team U.S.A. cards, and 19 1991 Championship and World Series cards, all packaged in a factory set box inside a molded-plastic SkyDome display. Topps actually references this set as a 1991 set and the copyright lines on the card backs say

1991, but the set was released well into 1992. Rookie Cards in this set include Shawn Green and Manny Ramirez.

	Nm-Mt	Ex-Mt
COMP.FACT.SET (200)	15.00	4.50
1 Terry Adams RC	.50	.15
2 Tommy Adams RC	.25	.07
3 Rick Aguilera	.15	.04
4 Ron Allen RC	.25	.07
5 Roberto Alomar	.50	.15
6 Sandy Alomar Jr.	.10	.03
7 Greg Anthony RC	.25	.07
8 James Austin RC	.25	.07
9 Steve Avery	.10	.03
10 Harold Baines	.15	.04
11 Brian Barber RC	.25	.07
12 Jon Barnes RC	.25	.07
13 George Bell	.10	.03
14 Doug Bennett RC	.25	.07
15 Sean Bergman RC	.50	.15
16 Craig Biggio	.25	.07
17 Bill Bliss RC	.25	.07
18 Wade Boggs	.25	.07
19 Bobby Bonilla	.15	.04
20 Russell Brock RC	.25	.07
21 Tarrik Brock RC	.25	.07
22 Tom Browning	.10	.03
23 Brett Butler	.15	.04
24 Ivan Calderon	.10	.03
25 Joe Carter	.15	.04
26 Joe Caruso RC	.25	.07
27 Dan Cholowsky RC	.25	.07
28 Will Clark	.50	.15
29 Roger Clemens	1.00	.30
30 Shawn Curran RC	.25	.07
31 Chris Curtis RC	.25	.07
32 Chili Davis	.15	.04
33 Andre Dawson	.15	.04
34 Joe DeBerry RC	.25	.07
35 John Dettmer	.10	.03
36 Rob Dibble	.15	.04
37 John Donati RC	.25	.07
38 Dave Doorneweerd RC	.25	.07
39 Darren Dreifort	.15	.04
40 Mike Durant RC	.25	.07
41 Chris Durkin RC	.25	.07
42 Dennis Eckersley	.15	.04
43 Brian Edmondson RC	.25	.07
44 Vaughn Eshelman RC	.25	.07
45 Shawn Estes RC	.50	.15
46 Jorge Fabregas RC	.50	.15
47 Jon Farrell RC	.25	.07
48 Cecil Fielder	.15	.04
49 Carlton Fisk	.25	.07
50 Tim Flannelly RC	.25	.07
51 Cliff Floyd RC	1.25	.35
52 Julio Franco	.15	.04
53 Greg Gagne	.10	.03
54 Chris Gambs RC	.25	.07
55 Ron Gant	.15	.04
56 Brent Gates RC	.25	.07
57 Dwayne Gerald RC	.25	.07
58 Jason Giambi	4.00	1.20
59 Benji Gil RC	.50	.15
60 Mark Gipner RC	.25	.07
61 Danny Gladden	.10	.03
62 Tom Glavine	.25	.07
63 Jimmy Gonzalez RC	.25	.07
64 Jeff Granger	.10	.03
65 Dan Grapenthien RC	.25	.07
66 Dennis Gray RC	.25	.07
67 Shawn Green RC	4.00	1.20
68 Tyler Green RC	.25	.07
69 Todd Greene	.10	.03
70 Ken Griffey Jr.	.75	.23
71 Kelly Gruber	.10	.03
72 Ozzie Guillen	.10	.03
73 Tony Gwynn	.60	.18
74 Shane Halter RC	.25	.07
75 Jeffrey Hammonds	.15	.04
76 Larry Hanlon RC	.25	.07
77 Pete Harnisch	.10	.03
78 Mike Harrison RC	.25	.07
79 Bryan Harvey	.10	.03
80 Scott Hatteberg RC	.50	.15
81 Rick Helling	.10	.03
82 Dave Henderson	.10	.03
83 Rickey Henderson	.50	.15
84 Tyrone Hill RC	.25	.07
85 T.Hollandsworth RC	.50	.15
86 Brian Holliday RC	.25	.07
87 Terry Horn RC	.25	.07
88 Jeff Hostetler RC	.25	.07
89 Kent Hrbek	.15	.04
90 Mark Hubbard RC	.25	.07
91 Charles Johnson	.15	.04
92 Howard Johnson	.10	.03
93 Todd Johnson	.10	.03
94 Bobby Jones RC	.50	.15
95 Dan Jones RC	.25	.07
96 Felix Jose	.10	.03
97 David Justice	.15	.04
98 Jimmy Key	.15	.04
99 Marc Kroon RC	.25	.07
100 John Kruk	.15	.04
101 Mark Langston	.10	.03
102 Barry Larkin	.50	.15
103 Mike LaValliere	.10	.03
104 Scott Leius	.10	.03
105 Mark Lemke	.10	.03
106 Donnie Leshnock	.10	.03
107 Jimmy Lewis RC	.25	.07
108 Shane Livesy RC	.25	.07
109 Ryan Long RC	.25	.07
110 Trevor Mallory RC	.25	.07
111 Dennis Martinez	.15	.04
112 Justin Mashore RC	.25	.07
113 Jason McDonald	.10	.03
114 Jack McDowell	.10	.03
115 Tom McKinnon RC	.25	.07
116 Billy McMillon	.10	.03
117 Buck McNabb RC	.25	.07
118 Jim Mecir RC	.25	.07
119 Dan Melendez	.25	.07
120 Shawn Miller RC	.25	.07
121 Trever Miller RC	.25	.07
122 Paul Molitor	.25	.07
123 Vincent Moore RC	.25	.07
124 Mike Morgan	.10	.03
125 Jack Morris WS	.10	.03
126 Jack Morris AS	.10	.03
127 Sean Mulligan RC	.25	.07
128 Eddie Murray AS	.50	.15
129 Mike Neill RC	.50	.15
130 Phil Nevin	1.00	.30
131 Mark O'Brien RC	.25	.07
132 Alex Ochoa RC	.50	.15
133 Chad Ogea RC	.25	.07
134 Greg Olson	.10	.03
135 Paul O'Neill	.25	.07
136 Jared Osentowski RC	.25	.07
137 Mike Pagliarulo	.10	.03
138 Rafael Palmeiro	.25	.07
139 Rodney Pedraza RC	.25	.07
140 Tony Phillips (P)	.10	.03
141 Scott Pisciotta RC	.25	.07
142 C.Pritchett RC	.25	.07
143 Jason Pruitt RC	.25	.07
144 K.Puckett WS UER	.50	.15
Championship series AB and BA is wrong		
145 Kirby Puckett AS	.50	.15
146 Manny Ramirez RC	4.00	1.20
147 Eddie Ramos RC	.25	.07
148 Mark Ratekin RC	.25	.07
149 Jeff Reardon	.15	.04
150 Sean Rees RC	.25	.07
151 Pokey Reese RC	.50	.15
152 Desmond Relaford RC	.50	.15
153 Eric Richardson RC	.25	.07
154 Cal Ripken	1.50	.45
155 Chris Roberts	.10	.03
156 Mike Robertson RC	.25	.07
157 Steve Rodriguez	.10	.03
158 Mike Rossiter RC	.25	.07
159 Scott Ruffcorn RC	.25	.07
160 Chris Sabo	.10	.03
161 Juan Samuel	.10	.03
162 Ryne Sandberg UER	.75	.23
(On 5th line, prior misspelled as prilor)		
163 Scott Sanderson	.10	.03
164 Benny Santiago	.15	.04
165 Gene Schall RC	.25	.07
166 Chad Schoenvogel RC	.25	.07
167 Chris Seelbach RC	.25	.07
168 Aaron Sele RC	.75	.23
169 Basil Shabazz RC	.25	.07
170 Al Shirley RC	.25	.07
171 Paul Shuey	.10	.03
172 Ruben Sierra	.10	.03
173 John Smiley	.10	.03
174 Lee Smith	.15	.04
175 Ozzie Smith	.75	.23
176 Tim Smith RC	.25	.07
177 Zane Smith	.10	.03
178 John Smoltz	.25	.07
179 Scott Stahoviak RC	.25	.07
180 Kennie Steenstra	.10	.03
181 Kevin Stocker RC	.25	.07
182 Chris Stynes RC	.50	.15
183 Danny Tartabull	.10	.03
184 Brien Taylor RC	.50	.15
185 Todd Taylor	.10	.03
186 Larry Thomas RC	.25	.07
187 Ozzie Timmons RC	.25	.07
(See also 188)		
188 David Tuttle UER	.10	.03
(Mistakenly numbered as 187 on card)		
189 Andy Van Slyke	.15	.04
190 Frank Viola	.15	.04
191 Michael Walkden RC	.25	.07
192 Jeff Ware	.10	.03
193 Allen Watson RC	.25	.07
194 Steve Whitaker RC	.25	.07
195 Jerry Willard	.10	.03
196 Craig Wilson	.10	.03
197 Chris Wimmer	.10	.03
198 S.Wojciechowski RC	.25	.07
199 Joel Wolfe RC	.25	.07
200 Ivan Zweig	.10	.03

1992 Stadium Club

The 1992 Stadium Club baseball card set consists of 900 standard-size cards issued in three series of 300 cards each. Cards were issued in plastic wrapped packs. A card-like application form for membership in Topps Stadium Club was inserted in each pack. Card numbers 591-610 form a "Members Choice" subset.

	Nm-Mt	Ex-Mt
COMPLETE SET (900)	45.00	13.50
COMP.SERIES 1 (300)	15.00	4.50
COMP.SERIES 2 (300)	15.00	4.50
COMP.SERIES 3 (300)	15.00	4.50
1 Cal Ripken UER	1.50	.45
(Misspelled Ripkin on card back)		
2 Eric Yelding	.10	.03
3 Geno Petralli	.10	.03
4 Wally Backman	.10	.03
5 Milt Cuyler	.10	.03
6 Kevin Bass	.10	.03
7 Dante Bichette	.15	.04
8 Ray Lankford	.10	.03
9 Mel Hall	.10	.03
10 Joe Carter	.15	.04
11 Juan Samuel	.10	.03
12 Jeff Montgomery	.10	.03
13 Glenn Braggs	.10	.03
14 Henry Cotto	.10	.03
15 Deion Sanders	.25	.07
16 Dick Schofield	.10	.03
17 David Cone	.15	.04
18 Chili Davis	.15	.04
19 Tom Foley	.10	.03
20 Ozzie Guillen	.10	.03
21 Luis Salazar	.10	.03
22 Terry Steinbach	.10	.03
23 Chris James	.10	.03
24 Jeff King	.10	.03
25 Carlos Quintana	.10	.03
26 Mike Maddux	.10	.03
27 Tommy Greene	.10	.03
28 Jeff Russell	.10	.03
29 Steve Finley	.15	.04
30 Mike Flanagan	.10	.03
31 Darren Lewis	.10	.03
32 Mark Lee	.10	.03
33 Willie Fraser	.10	.03
34 Mike Henneman	.10	.03
35 Kevin Maas	.10	.03
36 Dave Hansen	.10	.03
37 Erik Hanson	.10	.03
38 Bill Doran	.10	.03
39 Mike Boddicker	.10	.03
40 Vince Coleman	.10	.03
41 Devon White	.10	.03
42 Mark Gardner	.10	.03
43 Scott Lewis	.10	.03
44 Juan Berenguer	.10	.03
45 Carney Lansford	.15	.04
46 Curt Wilkerson	.10	.03
47 Shane Mack	.10	.03
48 Bip Roberts	.10	.03
49 Greg A. Harris	.10	.03
50 Ryne Sandberg	.75	.23
51 Mark Whiten	.10	.03
52 Jack McDowell	.10	.03
53 Jimmy Jones	.10	.03
54 Steve Lake	.10	.03
55 Bud Black	.10	.03
56 Dave Valle	.10	.03
57 Kevin Reimer	.10	.03
58 Rich Gedman UER	.10	.03
(Wrong BARS chart used)		
59 Travis Fryman	.15	.04
60 Steve Avery	.10	.03
61 Francisco de la Rosa	.10	.03
62 Scott Hemond	.10	.03
63 Hal Morris	.10	.03
64 Hensley Meulens	.10	.03
65 Frank Castillo	.10	.03
66 Gene Larkin	.10	.03
67 Jose DeLeon	.10	.03
68 Al Osuna	.10	.03
69 Dave Cochrane	.10	.03
70 Robin Ventura	.15	.04
71 John Cerutti	.10	.03
72 Kevin Gross	.10	.03
73 Ivan Calderon	.10	.03
74 Mike Macfarlane	.10	.03
75 Stan Belinda	.10	.03
76 Shawn Hillegas	.10	.03
77 Pat Borders	.10	.03
78 Jim Vatcher	.10	.03
79 Bobby Rose	.10	.03
80 Roger Clemens	1.00	.30
81 Craig Worthington	.10	.03
82 Jeff Treadway	.10	.03
83 Jamie Quirk	.10	.03
84 Randy Bush	.10	.03
85 Anthony Young	.10	.03
86 Trevor Wilson	.10	.03
87 Jaime Navarro	.10	.03
88 Les Lancaster	.10	.03
89 Pat Kelly	.10	.03
90 Alvin Davis	.10	.03
91 Larry Andersen	.10	.03
92 Rob Deer	.10	.03
93 Mike Sharperson	.10	.03
94 Lance Parrish	.15	.04
95 Cecil Espy	.10	.03
96 Tim Spehr	.10	.03
97 Dave Stieb	.10	.03
98 Terry Mulholland	.10	.03
99 Dennis Boyd	.10	.03
100 Barry Larkin	.50	.15
101 Ryan Bowen	.10	.03
102 Felix Fermin	.10	.03
103 Luis Alicea	.10	.03
104 Tim Hulett	.10	.03
105 Rafael Belliard	.10	.03
106 Mike Gallego	.10	.03
107 Dave Righetti	.15	.04
108 Jeff Schaefer	.10	.03
109 Ricky Bones	.10	.03
110 Scott Erickson	.10	.03
111 Matt Nokes	.10	.03
112 Bob Scanlan	.10	.03
113 Tom Candiotti	.10	.03
114 Sean Berry	.10	.03
115 Kevin Morton	.10	.03
116 Scott Fletcher	.10	.03
117 B.J. Surhoff	.15	.04
118 Dave Magadan UER	.10	.03
(Born Tampa, not Tamps)		
119 Bill Gullickson	.10	.03
120 Marquis Grissom	.10	.03
121 Lenny Harris	.10	.03
122 Wally Joyner	.15	.04
123 Kevin Brown	.10	.03
124 Braulio Castillo	.10	.03
125 Eric King	.10	.03
126 Mark Portugal	.10	.03
127 Calvin Jones	.10	.03
128 Mike Heath	.10	.03
129 Todd Van Poppel	.10	.03
130 Benny Santiago	.15	.04
131 Gary Thurman	.10	.03
132 Joe Girardi	.10	.03
133 Dave Eiland	.10	.03
134 Orlando Merced	.10	.03
135 Joe Orsulak	.10	.03
136 John Burkett	.10	.03
137 Ken Dayley	.10	.03
138 Ken Hill	.10	.03
139 Walt Terrell	.10	.03
140 Mike Scioscia	.10	.03
141 Junior Felix	.10	.03
142 Ken Caminiti	.15	.04
143 Carlos Baerga	.10	.03
144 Tony Fossas	.10	.03
145 Craig Grebeck	.10	.03
146 Scott Bradley	.10	.03
147 Kent Mercker	.10	.03
148 Derrick May	.10	.03
149 Jerald Clark	.10	.03
150 George Brett	1.25	.35
151 Luis Quinones	.10	.03
152 Mike Pagliarulo	.10	.03
153 Jose Guzman	.10	.03
154 Charlie O'Brien	.10	.03
155 Darren Holmes	.10	.03
156 Joe Boever	.10	.03
157 Rich Monteleone	.10	.03
158 Reggie Harris	.10	.03
159 Roberto Alomar	.50	.15
160 Robby Thompson	.10	.03
161 Chris Hoiles	.10	.03
162 Tom Pagnozzi	.10	.03
163 Omar Vizquel	.15	.04
164 John Candelaria	.10	.03
165 Terry Shumpert	.10	.03
166 Andy Mota	.10	.03
167 Scott Bailes	.10	.03
168 Jeff Blauser	.10	.03
169 Steve Olin	.10	.03
170 Doug Drabek	.10	.03
171 Dave Bergman	.10	.03
172 Eddie Whitson	.10	.03
173 Gilberto Reyes	.10	.03
174 Mark Grace	.25	.07
175 Paul O'Neill	.25	.07
176 Greg Cadaret	.10	.03
177 Mark Williamson	.10	.03
178 Casey Candaele	.10	.03
179 Candy Maldonado	.10	.03
180 Lee Smith	.15	.04
181 Harold Reynolds	.15	.04
182 David Justice	.15	.04
183 Lenny Webster	.10	.03
184 Donn Pall	.10	.03
185 Gerald Alexander	.10	.03
186 Jack Clark	.15	.04
187 Stan Javier	.10	.03
188 Ricky Jordan	.10	.03
189 Franklin Stubbs	.10	.03
190 Dennis Eckersley	.15	.04
191 Danny Tartabull	.10	.03
192 Pete O'Brien	.10	.03
193 Mark Lewis	.10	.03
194 Mike Felder	.10	.03
195 Mickey Tettleton	.10	.03
196 Dwight Smith	.10	.03
197 Shawn Abner	.10	.03
198 Jim Leyritz UER	.10	.03
(Career totals less than 1991 totals)		
199 Mike Devereaux	.10	.03
200 Craig Biggio	.25	.07
201 Kevin Elster	.10	.03
202 Rance Mulliniks	.10	.03
203 Tony Fernandez	.10	.03
204 Allan Anderson	.10	.03
205 Herm Winningham	.10	.03
206 Tim Jones	.10	.03
207 Ramon Martinez	.10	.03
208 Teddy Higuera	.10	.03
209 John Kruk	.15	.04
210 Jim Abbott	.25	.07
211 Dean Palmer	.15	.04
212 Mark Davis	.10	.03
213 Jay Buhner	.15	.04
214 Jesse Barfield	.10	.03
215 Kevin Mitchell	.10	.03
216 Mike LaValliere	.10	.03
217 Mark Wohlers	.10	.03
218 Dave Henderson	.10	.03
219 Dave Smith	.10	.03
220 Albert Belle	.15	.04
221 Spike Owen	.10	.03
222 Jeff Gray	.10	.03
223 Paul Gibson	.10	.03
224 Bobby Thigpen	.10	.03
225 Mike Mussina	.50	.15
226 Darrin Jackson	.10	.03
227 Luis Gonzalez	.25	.07
228 Greg Briley	.10	.03
229 Brent Mayne	.10	.03
230 Paul Molitor	.25	.07
231 Al Leiter	.15	.04
232 Andy Van Slyke	.15	.04
233 Ron Tingley	.10	.03
234 Bernard Gilkey	.10	.03
235 Kent Hrbek	.15	.04
236 Eric Karros	.15	.04
237 Randy Velarde	.10	.03
238 Andy Allanson	.10	.03
239 Willie McGee	.15	.04
240 Juan Gonzalez	.50	.15
241 Karl Rhodes	.10	.03
242 Luis Mercedes	.10	.03
243 Bill Swift	.10	.03
244 Tommy Gregg	.10	.03
245 David Howard	.10	.03
246 Dave Hollins	.10	.03
247 Kip Gross	.10	.03
248 Walt Weiss	.10	.03
249 Mackey Sasser	.10	.03
250 Cecil Fielder	.15	.04
251 Jerry Browne	.10	.03
252 Doug Dascenzo	.10	.03
253 Darryl Hamilton	.10	.03
254 Dann Bilardello	.10	.03
255 Luis Rivera	.10	.03
256 Larry Walker	.25	.07
257 Ron Karkovice	.10	.03
258 Bob Tewksbury	.10	.03
259 Jimmy Key	.15	.04
260 Bernie Williams	.25	.07
261 Gary Wayne	.10	.03
262 Mike Simms UER	.10	.03
(Reversed negative)		
263 John Orton	.10	.03
264 Marvin Freeman	.10	.03
265 Mike Jeffcoat	.10	.03
266 Roger Mason	.10	.03
267 Edgar Martinez	.25	.07
268 Henry Rodriguez	.10	.03
269 Sam Horn	.10	.03
270 Brian McRae	.10	.03
271 Kirt Manwaring	.10	.03
272 Mike Bordick	.10	.03
273 Chris Sabo	.10	.03
274 Jim Olander	.10	.03
275 Greg W. Harris	.10	.03
276 Dan Gakeler	.10	.03
277 Bill Sampen	.10	.03
278 Joel Skinner	.10	.03
279 Curt Schilling	.25	.07
280 Dale Murphy	.50	.15
281 Lee Stevens	.10	.03
282 Lonnie Smith	.10	.03
283 Manuel Lee	.10	.03
284 Shawn Boskie	.10	.03
285 Kevin Seitzer	.10	.03
286 Stan Royer	.10	.03
287 John Dopson	.10	.03
288 Scott Bullett RC	.10	.03
289 Ken Patterson	.10	.03
290 Todd Hundley	.10	.03
291 Tim Leary	.10	.03
292 Brett Butler	.15	.04
293 Gregg Olson	.10	.03
294 Jeff Brantley	.10	.03
295 Brian Holman	.10	.03
296 Brian Harper	.10	.03
297 Brian Bohanon	.10	.03
298 Checklist 1-100	.10	.03
299 Checklist 101-200	.10	.03
300 Checklist 201-300	.10	.03
301 Frank Thomas	.50	.15
302 Lloyd McClendon	.10	.03
303 Brady Anderson	.15	.04
304 Julio Valera	.10	.03
305 Mike Aldrete	.10	.03
306 Joe Oliver	.10	.03
307 Todd Stottlemyre	.10	.03
308 Rey Sanchez RC	.15	.04
309 Gary Sheffield UER	.15	.04
(Listed as 5'1", should be 5'11")		
310 Andujar Cedeno	.10	.03
311 Kenny Rogers	.15	.04
312 Bruce Hurst	.10	.03
313 Mike Schooler	.10	.03
314 Mike Benjamin	.10	.03
315 Chuck Finley	.15	.04
316 Mark Lemke	.10	.03
317 Scott Livingstone	.10	.03
318 Chris Nabholz	.10	.03
319 Mike Humphreys	.10	.03
320 Pedro Guerrero	.15	.04
321 Willie Banks	.10	.03
322 Tom Goodwin	.10	.03
323 Hector Wagner	.10	.03
324 Wally Ritchie	.10	.03
325 Mo Vaughn	.15	.04
326 Joe Klink	.10	.03
327 Cal Eldred	.10	.03
328 Daryl Boston	.10	.03
329 Mike Huff	.10	.03
330 Jeff Bagwell	.50	.15
331 Bob Milacki	.10	.03
332 Tom Prince	.10	.03
333 Pat Tabler	.10	.03
334 Ced Landrum	.10	.03
335 Reggie Jefferson	.10	.03
336 Mo Sanford	.10	.03
337 Kevin Ritz	.10	.03
338 Gerald Perry	.10	.03
339 Jeff Hamilton	.10	.03
340 Tim Wallach	.10	.03
341 Jeff Huson	.10	.03
342 Jose Melendez	.10	.03
343 Willie Wilson	.10	.03
344 Mike Stanton	.10	.03
345 Joel Johnston	.10	.03
346 Lee Guetterman	.10	.03
347 Francisco Oliveras	.10	.03
348 Dave Burba	.10	.03
349 Tim Crews	.10	.03
350 Scott Leius	.10	.03
351 Danny Cox	.10	.03
352 Wayne Housie	.10	.03
353 Chris Donnels	.10	.03
354 Chris George	.10	.03
355 Gerald Young	.10	.03
356 Roberto Hernandez	.10	.03
357 Neal Heaton	.10	.03
358 Todd Frohwirth	.10	.03
359 Jose Vizcaino	.10	.03
360 Jim Thome	.50	.15
361 Craig Wilson	.10	.03
362 Dave Haas	.10	.03
363 Billy Hatcher	.10	.03
364 John Barfield	.10	.03
365 Luis Aquino	.10	.03
366 Charlie Leibrandt	.10	.03
367 Howard Farmer	.10	.03
368 Bryn Smith	.10	.03
369 Mickey Morandini	.10	.03
370 Jose Canseco	.50	.15
(See also 597)		
371 Jose Uribe	.10	.03
372 Bob MacDonald	.10	.03
373 Luis Sojo	.10	.03
374 Craig Shipley	.10	.03
375 Scott Bankhead	.10	.03
376 Greg Gagne	.10	.03
377 Scott Cooper	.10	.03
378 Jose Offerman	.10	.03
379 Bill Spiers	.10	.03
380 John Smiley	.10	.03
381 Jeff Carter	.10	.03
382 Heathcliff Slocumb	.10	.03
383 Jeff Tackett	.10	.03
384 John Kiely	.10	.03
385 John Vander Wal	.10	.03
386 Omar Olivares	.10	.03
387 Ruben Sierra	.10	.03
388 Tom Gordon	.10	.03
389 Charles Nagy	.10	.03
390 Dave Stewart	.15	.04
391 Pete Harnisch	.10	.03
392 Tim Burke	.10	.03
393 Roberto Kelly	.10	.03
394 Freddie Benavides	.10	.03
395 Tom Glavine	.25	.07
396 Wes Chamberlain	.10	.03
397 Eric Gunderson	.10	.03
398 Dave West	.10	.03
399 Ellis Burks	.15	.04
400 Ken Griffey Jr.	.75	.23

401 Thomas Howard .10 .03
402 Juan Guzman .10 .03
403 Mitch Webster .10 .03
404 Matt Merullo .10 .03
405 Steve Buechele .10 .03
406 Danny Jackson .10 .03
407 Felix Jose .10 .03
408 Doug Piatt .10 .03
409 Jim Eisenreich .10 .03
410 Bryan Harvey .10 .03
411 Jim Austin .10 .03
412 Jim Poole .10 .03
413 Glenallen Hill .10 .03
414 Gene Nelson .10 .03
415 Ivan Rodriguez .50 .15
416 Frank Tanana .10 .03
417 Steve Decker .10 .03
418 Jason Grimsley .10 .03
419 Tim Layana .10 .03
420 Don Mattingly 1.25 .35
421 Jerome Walton .10 .03
422 Rob Ducey .10 .03
423 Andy Benes .10 .03
424 John Marzano .10 .03
425 Gene Harris .10 .03
426 Tim Raines .15 .04
427 Bret Barberie .10 .03
428 Harvey Pulliam .10 .03
429 Cris Carpenter .10 .03
430 Howard Johnson .10 .03
431 Orel Hershiser .15 .04
432 Brian Hunter .10 .03
433 Kevin Tapani .10 .03
434 Rick Reed .10 .03
435 Ron Witmeyer RC .10 .03
436 Gary Gaetti .15 .04
437 Alex Cole .10 .03
438 Chito Martinez .10 .03
439 Greg Litton .10 .03
440 Julio Franco .15 .04
441 Mike Munoz .10 .03
442 Erik Pappas .10 .03
443 Pat Combs .10 .03
444 Lance Johnson .10 .03
445 Ed Sprague .10 .03
446 Mike Greenwell .10 .03
447 Milt Thompson .10 .03
448 Mike Magnante RC .10 .03
449 Chris Haney .10 .03
450 Robin Yount .75 .23
451 Rafael Ramirez .10 .03
452 Gino Minutelli .10 .03
453 Tom Lampkin .10 .03
454 Tony Perezchica .10 .03
455 Dwight Gooden .25 .07
456 Mark Guthrie .10 .03
457 Jay Howell .10 .03
458 Gary DiSarcina .10 .03
459 John Smoltz .25 .07
460 Will Clark .50 .15
461 Dave Otto .10 .03
462 Rob Maurer .10 .03
463 Dwight Evans .15 .04
464 Tom Brunansky .10 .03
465 Shawn Hare RC .10 .03
466 Geronimo Pena .10 .03
467 Alex Fernandez .10 .03
468 Greg Myers .10 .03
469 Jeff Fassero .10 .03
470 Len Dykstra .15 .04
471 Jeff Johnson .10 .03
472 Russ Swan .10 .03
473 Archie Corbin .10 .03
474 Chuck McElroy .10 .03
475 Mark McGwire 1.25 .35
476 Wally Whitehurst .10 .03
477 Tim McIntosh .10 .03
478 Sid Bream .10 .03
479 Jeff Juden .10 .03
480 Carlton Fisk .25 .07
481 Jeff Plympton .10 .03
482 Carlos Martinez .10 .03
483 Jim Gott .10 .03
484 Bob McClure .10 .03
485 Tim Teufel .10 .03
486 Vicente Palacios .10 .03
487 Jeff Reed .10 .03
488 Tony Phillips .10 .03
489 Mel Rojas .10 .03
490 Ben McDonald .10 .03
491 Andres Santana .10 .03
492 Chris Beasley .10 .03
493 Mike Timlin .10 .03
494 Brian Downing .10 .03
495 Kirk Gibson .15 .04
496 Scott Sanderson .10 .03
497 Nick Esasky .10 .03
498 Johnny Guzman RC .10 .03
499 Mitch Williams .10 .03
500 Kirby Puckett .50 .15
501 Mike Harkey .10 .03
502 Jim Gantner .10 .03
503 Bruce Egloff .10 .03
504 Josias Manzanillo RC .10 .03
505 Delino DeShields .10 .03
506 Rheal Cormier .10 .03
507 Jay Bell .15 .04
508 Rich Rowland RC .10 .03
509 Scott Servais .10 .03
510 Terry Pendleton .15 .04
511 Rich DeLucia .10 .03
512 Warren Newson .10 .03
513 Paul Faries .10 .03
514 Kal Daniels .10 .03
515 Jarvis Brown .10 .03
516 Rafael Palmeiro .25 .07
517 Kelly Downs .10 .03
518 Steve Chitren .10 .03
519 Moises Alou .15 .04
520 Wade Boggs .25 .07
521 Pete Schourek .10 .03
522 Scott Terry .10 .03
523 Kevin Appier .15 .04
524 Gary Redus .10 .03
525 George Bell .10 .03
526 Jeff Kaiser .10 .03
527 Alvaro Espinoza .10 .03
528 Luis Polonia .10 .03
529 Darren Daulton .15 .04
530 Norm Charlton .10 .03
531 John Olerud .15 .04
532 Dan Plesac .10 .03
533 Billy Ripken .10 .03
534 Rod Nichols .10 .03
535 Joey Cora .10 .03
536 Harold Baines .15 .04
537 Bob Ojeda .10 .03
538 Mark Leonard .10 .03
539 Danny Darwin .10 .03
540 Shawon Dunston .10 .03
541 Pedro Munoz .10 .03
542 Mark Gubicza .10 .03
543 Kevin Baez .10 .03
544 Todd Zeile .10 .03
545 Don Slaught .10 .03
546 Tony Eusebio .15 .04
547 Alonzo Powell .10 .03
548 Gary Pettis .10 .03
549 Brian Barnes .10 .03
550 Lou Whitaker .15 .04
551 Keith Mitchell .10 .03
552 Oscar Azocar .10 .03
553 Stu Cole RC .10 .03
554 Steve Wapnick .10 .03
555 Derek Bell .15 .04
556 Luis Lopez .10 .03
557 Anthony Telford .10 .03
558 Tim Mauser .10 .03
559 Glen Sutko .10 .03
560 Darryl Strawberry .25 .07
561 Tom Bolton .10 .03
562 Cliff Young .10 .03
563 Bruce Walton .10 .03
564 Chico Walker .10 .03
565 John Franco .15 .04
566 Paul McClellan .10 .03
567 Paul Abbott .10 .03
568 Gary Varsho .10 .03
569 Carlos Maldonado RC .10 .03
570 Kelly Gruber .10 .03
571 Jose Oquendo .10 .03
572 Steve Frey .10 .03
573 Tino Martinez .25 .07
574 Bill Haselman .10 .03
575 Eric Anthony .10 .03
576 John Habyan .10 .03
577 Jeff McNeely .10 .03
578 Chris Bosio .10 .03
579 Joe Grahe .10 .03
580 Fred McGriff .25 .07
581 Rick Honeycutt .10 .03
582 Matt Williams .15 .04
583 Cliff Brantley .10 .03
584 Rob Dibble .15 .04
585 Skeeter Barnes .10 .03
586 Greg Hibbard .10 .03
587 Randy Milligan .10 .03
588 Checklist 301-400 .10 .03
589 Checklist 401-500 .10 .03
590 Checklist 501-600 .10 .03
591 Frank Thomas MC .25 .07
592 David Justice MC .10 .03
593 Roger Clemens MC .50 .15
594 Steve Avery MC .10 .03
595 Cal Ripken MC .75 .23
596 Barry Larkin MC UER .15 .04
(Ranked in AL,
should be NL)
597 J.Canseco MC UER .15 .04
Mistakenly numbered
370 on card back
598 Will Clark MC .15 .04
599 Cecil Fielder MC .10 .03
600 Ryne Sandberg MC .50 .15
601 Chuck Knoblauch MC .10 .03
602 Dwight Gooden MC .15 .04
603 Ken Griffey Jr. MC .50 .15
604 Barry Bonds MC .60 .18
605 Nolan Ryan MC .75 .23
606 Jeff Bagwell MC .25 .07
607 Robin Yount MC .50 .15
608 Bobby Bonilla MC .10 .03
609 George Brett MC .60 .18
610 Howard Johnson MC .10 .03
611 Esteban Beltre .10 .03
612 Mike Christopher .10 .03
613 Troy Afenir .10 .03
614 Mariano Duncan .10 .03
615 Doug Henry RC .10 .03
616 Doug Jones .10 .03
617 Alvin Davis .10 .03
618 Craig Lefferts .10 .03
619 Kevin McReynolds .10 .03
620 Barry Bonds 1.25 .35
621 Turner Ward .10 .03
622 Joe Magrane .10 .03
623 Mark Parent .10 .03
624 Tom Browning .10 .03
625 John Smiley .10 .03
626 Steve Wilson .10 .03
627 Mike Gallego .10 .03
628 Sammy Sosa .75 .23
629 Rico Rossy .10 .03
630 Royce Clayton .10 .03
631 Clay Parker .10 .03
632 Pete Smith .10 .03
633 Jeff McKnight .10 .03
634 Jack Daugherty .10 .03
635 Steve Sax .10 .03
636 Joe Hesketh .10 .03
637 Vince Horsman .10 .03
638 Eric King .10 .03
639 Joe Boever .10 .03
640 Jack Morris .15 .04
641 Arthur Rhodes .10 .03
642 Bob Melvin .10 .03
643 Rick Wilkins .10 .03
644 Scott Scudder .10 .03
645 Bip Roberts .10 .03
646 Julio Valera .10 .03
647 Kevin Campbell .10 .03
648 Steve Searcy .10 .03
649 Scott Kamieniecki .10 .03
650 Kurt Stillwell .10 .03
651 Bob Welch .10 .03
652 Andres Galarraga .15 .04
653 Mike Jackson .10 .03
654 Bo Jackson .50 .15
655 Sid Fernandez .10 .03
656 Mike Bielecki .10 .03
657 Jeff Reardon .15 .04
658 Wayne Rosenthal .10 .03
659 Eric Bullock .10 .03
660 Eric Davis .15 .04
661 Randy Tomlin .10 .03
662 Tom Edens .10 .03
663 Rob Murphy .10 .03
664 Leo Gomez .10 .03
665 Greg Maddux .75 .23
666 Greg Vaughn .15 .04
667 Wade Taylor .10 .03
668 Brad Arnsberg .10 .03
669 Mike Moore .10 .03
670 Mark Langston .10 .03
671 Barry Jones .10 .03
672 Bill Landrum .10 .03
673 Greg Swindell .10 .03
674 Wayne Edwards .10 .03
675 Greg Olson .10 .03
676 Bill Pulsipher RC .10 .03
677 Bobby Witt .10 .03
678 Mark Carreon .10 .03
679 Patrick Lennon .10 .03
680 Ozzie Smith .75 .23
681 John Briscoe .10 .03
682 Matt Young .10 .03
683 Jeff Conine .15 .04
684 Phil Stephenson .10 .03
685 Ron Darling .10 .03
686 Bryan Hickerson RC .10 .03
687 Dale Sveum .10 .03
688 Kirk McCaskill .10 .03
689 Rich Amaral .10 .03
690 Danny Tartabull .10 .03
691 Donald Harris .10 .03
692 Doug Davis .10 .03
693 John Farrell .10 .03
694 Paul Gibson .10 .03
695 Kenny Lofton .50 .15
696 Mike Fetters .10 .03
697 Rosario Rodriguez .10 .03
698 Chris Jones .10 .03
699 Jeff Manto .10 .03
700 Rick Sutcliffe .15 .04
701 Scott Bankhead .10 .03
702 Donnie Hill .10 .03
703 Todd Worrell .10 .03
704 Rene Gonzales .10 .03
705 Rick Cerone .10 .03
706 Tony Pena .10 .03
707 Paul Sorrento .10 .03
708 Gary Scott .10 .03
709 Junior Noboa .10 .03
710 Wally Joyner .15 .04
711 Charlie Hayes .10 .03
712 Rich Rodriguez .10 .03
713 Rudy Seanez .10 .03
714 Jim Bullinger .10 .03
715 Jeff M. Robinson .10 .03
716 Jeff Branson .10 .03
717 Andy Ashby .10 .03
718 Dave Burba .10 .03
719 Rich Gossage .15 .04
720 Randy Johnson .50 .15
721 David Wells .15 .04
722 Paul Kilgus .10 .03
723 Dave Martinez .10 .03
724 Denny Neagle .15 .04
725 Andy Stankiewicz .10 .03
726 Rick Aguilera .15 .04
727 Junior Ortiz .10 .03
728 Storm Davis .10 .03
729 Don Robinson .10 .03
730 Ron Gant .15 .04
731 Paul Assenmacher .10 .03
732 Mike Gardiner .10 .03
733 Milt Hill .10 .03
734 Jeremy Hernandez RC .10 .03
735 Ken Hill .10 .03
736 Xavier Hernandez .10 .03
737 Gregg Jefferies .10 .03
738 Dick Schofield .10 .03
739 Ron Robinson .10 .03
740 Sandy Alomar Jr. .10 .03
741 Mike Stanley .10 .03
742 Butch Henry RC .10 .03
743 Floyd Bannister .10 .03
744 Brian Drahman .10 .03
745 Dave Winfield .15 .04
746 Bob Walk .10 .03
747 Chris James .10 .03
748 Don Prybylinski RC .10 .03
749 Dennis Rasmussen .10 .03
750 Rickey Henderson .50 .15
751 Chris Hammond .10 .03
752 Bob Kipper .10 .03
753 Dave Rohde .10 .03
754 Hubie Brooks .10 .03
755 Bret Saberhagen .15 .04
756 Jeff D. Robinson .10 .03
757 Pat Listach RC .15 .04
758 Bill Wegman .10 .03
759 John Wetteland .15 .04
760 Phil Plantier .10 .03
761 Wilson Alvarez .10 .03
762 Scott Aldred .10 .03
763 Armando Reynoso RC .15 .04
764 Todd Benzinger .10 .03
765 Kevin Mitchell .10 .03
766 Gary Sheffield .15 .04
767 Allan Anderson .10 .03
768 Rusty Meacham .10 .03
769 Rick Parker .10 .03
770 Nolan Ryan 2.00 .60
771 Jeff Ballard .10 .03
772 Cory Snyder .10 .03
773 Denis Boucher .10 .03
774 Jose Gonzalez .10 .03
775 Juan Guerrero .10 .03
776 Ed Nunez .10 .03
777 Scott Ruskin .10 .03
778 Terry Leach .10 .03
779 Carl Willis .10 .03
780 Bobby Bonilla .15 .04
781 Duane Ward .10 .03
782 Joe Slusarski .10 .03
783 David Segui .10 .03
784 Kirk Gibson .15 .04
785 Frank Viola .15 .04
786 Keith Miller .10 .03
787 Mike Morgan .10 .03
788 Kim Batiste .10 .03
789 Sergio Valdez .10 .03
790 Eddie Taubensee RC .15 .04
791 Jack Armstrong .10 .03
792 Scott Fletcher .10 .03
793 Steve Farr .10 .03
794 Dan Pasqua .10 .03
795 Eddie Murray .50 .15
796 John Morris .10 .03
797 Francisco Cabrera .10 .03
798 Mike Perez .10 .03
799 Ted Wood .10 .03
800 Jose Rijo .10 .03
801 Danny Gladden .10 .03
802 Archi Cianfrocco RC .10 .03
803 Monty Fariss .10 .03
804 Roger McDowell .10 .03
805 Randy Myers .10 .03
806 Kirk Dressendorfer .10 .03
807 Zane Smith .10 .03
808 Glenn Davis .10 .03
809 Torey Lovullo .10 .03
810 Andre Dawson .15 .04
811 Bill Pecota .10 .03
812 Ted Power .10 .03
813 Willie Blair .10 .03
814 Dave Fleming .10 .03
815 Chris Gwynn .10 .03
816 Jody Reed .10 .03
817 Mark Dewey .10 .03
818 Kyle Abbott .10 .03
819 Tom Henke .10 .03
820 Kevin Seitzer .10 .03
821 Al Newman .10 .03
822 Tim Sherrill .10 .03
823 Chuck Crim .10 .03
824 Darren Reed .10 .03
825 Tony Gwynn .60 .18
826 Steve Foster .10 .03
827 Steve Howe .10 .03
828 Brook Jacoby .10 .03
829 Rodney McCray .10 .03
830 Chuck Knoblauch .15 .04
831 John Wehner .10 .03
832 Scott Garrelts .10 .03
833 Alejandro Pena .10 .03
834 Jeff Parrett UER .10 .03
(Kentucy)
835 Juan Bell .10 .03
836 Lance Dickson .10 .03
837 Darryl Kile .15 .04
838 Efrain Valdez .10 .03
839 Bob Zupcic RC .10 .03
840 George Bell .10 .03
841 Dave Gallagher .10 .03
842 Tim Belcher .10 .03
843 Jeff Shaw .10 .03
844 Mike Fitzgerald .10 .03
845 Gary Carter .25 .07
846 John Russell .10 .03
847 Eric Hillman RC .10 .03
848 Mike Witt .10 .03
849 Curt Wilkerson .10 .03
850 Alan Trammell .25 .07
851 Rex Hudler .10 .03
852 Mike Walkden RC .10 .03
853 Kevin Ward .10 .03
854 Tim Naehring .10 .03
855 Bill Swift .10 .03
856 Damon Berryhill .10 .03
857 Mark Eichhorn .10 .03
858 Hector Villanueva .10 .03
859 Jose Lind .10 .03
860 Dennis Martinez .15 .04
861 Bill Krueger .10 .03
862 Mike Kingery .10 .03
863 Jeff Innis .10 .03
864 Derek Lilliquist .10 .03
865 Reggie Sanders .15 .04
866 Ramon Garcia .10 .03
867 Bruce Ruffin .10 .03
868 Dickie Thon .10 .03
869 Melido Perez .10 .03
870 Ruben Amaro .10 .03
871 Alan Mills .10 .03
872 Matt Sinatro .10 .03
873 Eddie Zosky .10 .03
874 Pete Incaviglia .10 .03
875 Tom Candiotti .10 .03
876 Bob Patterson .10 .03
877 Neal Heaton .10 .03
878 Terrel Hansen RC .10 .03
879 Dave Eiland .10 .03
880 Von Hayes .10 .03
881 Tim Scott .10 .03
882 Otis Nixon .10 .03
883 Herm Winningham .10 .03
884 Dion James .10 .03
885 Dave Wainhouse .10 .03
886 Frank DiPino .10 .03
887 Dennis Cook .10 .03
888 Jose Mesa .10 .03
889 Mark Leiter .10 .03
890 Willie Randolph .15 .04
891 Craig Colbert .10 .03
892 Dwayne Henry .10 .03
893 Jim Lindeman .10 .03
894 Charlie Hough .15 .04
895 Gil Heredia RC .15 .04
896 Scott Chiamparino .10 .03
897 Lance Blankenship .10 .03
898 Checklist 601-700 .10 .03
899 Checklist 701-800 .10 .03
900 Checklist 801-900 .10 .03

1992 Stadium Club First Draft Picks

This three-card standard-size set, featuring Major League Baseball's Number 1 draft pick for 1990, 1991, and 1992, was randomly inserted into 1992 Stadium Club Series III packs at an approximate rate of 1:72. One card also was mailed to each member of Topps Stadium Club.

Nm-Mt Ex-Mt
1 Chipper Jones 5.00 1.50
2 Brien Taylor 2.00 .60
3 Phil Nevin 2.00 .60

1992 Stadium Club Master Photos

In the first package of materials sent to 1992 Topps Stadium Club members, along with an 11-card boxed set, members received a randomly chosen "Master Photo" printed on (approximately) 5" by 7" white card stock to demonstrate how the photos are cropped to create a borderless design. Each master photo has the Topps Stadium Club logo and the words "Master Photo" above a gold foil picture frame enclosing the color player photo. The backs are blank. The cards are unnumbered and checklisted below alphabetically. Master photos were also available through a special promotion at Walmart as an insert one-per-box in specially marked wax boxes of regular Topps Stadium Club cards.

Nm-Mt Ex-Mt
COMPLETE SET (15) 20.00 6.00
1 Wade Boggs 1.25 .35
2 Barry Bonds 2.50 .75
3 Jose Canseco 1.25 .35
4 Will Clark 1.00 .30
5 Cecil Fielder .50 .15
6 Dwight Gooden .50 .15
7 Ken Griffey Jr. 3.00 .90
8 Rickey Henderson 1.50 .45
9 Lance Johnson .25 .07
10 Cal Ripken 5.00 1.50
11 Nolan Ryan 5.00 1.50
12 Deion Sanders 1.00 .30
13 Darryl Strawberry .50 .15
14 Danny Tartabull .25 .07
15 Frank Thomas 1.50 .45

1992 Stadium Club East Coast National

These cards were selected from the regular Stadium Club series and were printed for the Gloria Rothstein's East Coast National Convention. The fronts feature borderless color player photos with the East Coast National Convention logo printed in gold foil in a top corner while the backs display a mini reprint of the player's rookie card and "BARS" (Baseball Analysis and Reporting System) statistics. The cards are checklisted below according to their numbers in the regular series.

Nm-Mt Ex-Mt
COMPLETE SET (100) 200.00 60.00
601 Chuck Knoblauch MC 5.00 1.50
602 Doc Gooden MC 2.00 .60
603 Ken Griffey Jr. MC 30.00 9.00
604 Barry Bonds MC 25.00 7.50
605 Nolan Ryan MC 50.00 15.00
606 Jeff Bagwell MC 15.00 4.50
607 Robin Yount MC 6.00 1.80
608 Bobby Bonilla MC 1.00 .30
609 George Brett MC 25.00 7.50
610 Howard Johnson MC 1.00 .30
611 Esteban Beltre 1.00 .30
612 Mike Christopher 1.00 .30
613 Troy Afenir 1.00 .30
619 Kevin McReynolds 1.00 .30
620 Barry Bonds 25.00 7.50
622 Joe Magrane 1.00 .30
623 Mark Parent 1.00 .30
626 Steve Wilson 1.00 .30
629 Rico Rossy 1.00 .30
631 Clay Parker 1.00 .30
633 Jeff McKnight 1.00 .30
637 Vince Horsman 1.00 .30
638 Eric King 1.00 .30
639 Joe Boever 1.00 .30
641 Arthur Rhodes 1.00 .30
647 Kevin Campbell 1.00 .30
653 Mike Jackson 1.00 .30
661 Randy Tomlin 1.00 .30
665 Greg Maddux 30.00 9.00
668 Brad Arnsberg 1.00 .30
671 Barry Jones 1.00 .30
672 Bill Landrum 1.00 .30
673 Greg Swindell 1.00 .30
676 Bill Pulsipher 1.00 .30
679 Patrick Lennon 1.00 .30
681 John Briscoe 1.00 .30
684 Phil Stephenson 1.00 .30
685 Ron Darling 1.00 .30
686 Bryan Hickerson 1.00 .30
688 Kirk McCaskill 1.00 .30
689 Rich Amaral 1.00 .30
692 Doug Davis 1.00 .30
693 John Farrell 1.00 .30
700 Rick Sutcliffe 2.00 .60
704 Rene Gonzalez 1.00 .30
713 Rudy Seanez 1.00 .30
714 Jim Bullinger 1.00 .30
716 Jeff Branson 1.00 .30
717 Andy Ashby 1.00 .30
725 Andy Stankiewicz 1.00 .30
733 Milt Hill 1.00 .30
739 Ron Robinson 1.00 .30
742 Butch Henry 1.00 .30
747 Chris James 1.00 .30
749 Dennis Rasmussen 1.00 .30

753 Dave Rohde 1.00 .30
757 Pat Listach 1.00 .30
758 Bill Wegman 1.00 .30
763 Armando Reynoso 1.00 .30
765 Kevin Mitchell 1.00 .30
766 Gary Sheffield 6.00 1.80
769 Rick Parker 1.00 .30
771 Jeff Ballard 1.00 .30
772 Cory Snyder 1.00 .30
774 Jose Gonzalez 1.00 .30
775 Juan Guerrero 1.00 .30
776 Ed Nunez 1.00 .30
778 Terry Leach 1.00 .30
782 Joe Slusarski 1.00 .30
784 Kirk Gibson 2.00 .60
788 Kim Batiste 1.00 .30
802 Archi Cianfrocco 1.00 .30
806 Kirk Dressendorfer 1.00 .30
807 Zane Smith 1.00 .30
814 Dave Fleming 1.00 .30
815 Chris Gwynn 1.00 .30
817 Mark Dewey 1.00 .30
819 Tom Henke 2.00 .60
822 Tim Sherrill 1.00 .30
826 Steve Foster 1.00 .30
831 John Wehner 1.00 .30
832 Scott Garrelts 1.00 .30
840 George Bell 1.00 .30
841 Dave Gallagher 1.00 .30
846 John Russell 1.00 .30
847 Eric Hillman 1.00 .30
852 Mike Walkden 1.00 .30
855 Bill Swift 1.00 .30
864 Derek Lilliquist 1.00 .30
876 Bob Patterson 1.00 .30
878 Terrel Hansen 1.00 .30
881 Tim Scott 1.00 .30
886 Frank DiPino 1.00 .30
891 Craig Colbert 1.00 .30
892 Dwayne Henry 1.00 .30
893 Jim Lindeman 1.00 .30
895 Gil Heredia 1.00 .30
898 Checklist 1.00 .30
899 Checklist 1.00 .30
900 Checklist 1.00 .30

1992 Stadium Club National Convention

These cards were selected from the regular Stadium Club series and were printed for the National Convention in Atlanta. The fronts feature borderless color player photos with the National Convention logo printed in gold foil in a top corner while the backs display a mini reprint of the player's rookie card and "BARS" (Baseball Analysis and Reporting System) statistics. The cards are checklisted below according to their numbers in the regular series.

Nm-Mt Ex-Mt
COMPLETE SET (100) 150.00 45.00
616 Doug Jones 2.00 .60
617 Alvin Davis 1.00 .30
618 Craig Lefferts 1.00 .30
621 Turner Ward 1.00 .30
625 John Smiley 1.00 .30
627 Mike Gallego 1.00 .30
630 Royce Clayton 1.00 .30
634 Jack Daugherty 1.00 .30
635 Steve Sax 1.00 .30
636 Joe Hesketh 1.00 .30
643 Rick Wilkins 1.00 .30
644 Scott Scudder 1.00 .30
645 Bip Roberts 1.00 .30
650 Kurt Stillwell 1.00 .30
652 Andres Galarraga 5.00 1.50
657 Jeff Reardon 2.00 .60
660 Eric Davis 2.00 .60
662 Tom Edens 1.00 .30
675 Greg Olson 1.00 .30
678 Mark Carreon 1.00 .30
680 Ozzie Smith 20.00 6.00
682 Matt Young 1.00 .30
690 Danny Tartabull 1.00 .30
691 Donald Harris 1.00 .30
695 Kenny Lofton 8.00 2.40
697 Rosario Rodriguez 1.00 .30
701 Scott Bankhead 1.00 .30
705 Rick Cerone 1.00 .30
706 Tony Pena 2.00 .60
709 Junior Noboa 1.00 .30
710 Wally Joyner 2.00 .60
711 Charlie Hayes 1.00 .30
712 Rich Rodriguez 1.00 .30
721 David Wells 3.00 .90
723 Dave Martinez 1.00 .30
726 Rick Aguilera 2.00 .60
727 Junior Ortiz 1.00 .30
729 Don Robinson 1.00 .30
730 Ron Gant 2.00 .60
731 Paul Assenmacher 1.00 .30
732 Mark Gardiner 1.00 .30
735 Ken Hill 1.00 .30
736 Xavier Hernandez 1.00 .30
737 Gregg Jefferies 1.00 .30
740 Sandy Alomar 2.00 .60
741 Mike Stanley 1.00 .30
744 Brian Drahman 1.00 .30
746 Bob Walk 1.00 .30
751 Chris Hammond 1.00 .30
759 John Wetteland 2.00 .60
760 Phil Plantier 2.00 .60
761 Wilson Alvarez 2.00 .60
773 Dennis Boucher 1.00 .30
777 Scott Ruskin 1.00 .30
779 Carl Willis 1.00 .30
783 David Segui 2.00 .60
786 Keith Miller 1.00 .30
790 Eddie Taubensee 1.00 .30
791 Jack Armstrong 1.00 .30
792 Scott Fletcher 1.00 .30
793 Steve Farr 1.00 .30
794 Dan Pasqua 1.00 .30
797 Francisco Cabrera 1.00 .30
798 Mike Perez 1.00 .30
801 Danny Gladden 1.00 .30
803 Monty Fariss 1.00 .30
804 Roger McDowell 1.00 .30
805 Randy Myers 2.00 .60
808 Glenn Davis 1.00 .30
809 Torey Lovullo 1.00 .30
816 Jody Reed 1.00 .30
825 Tony Gwynn 25.00 7.50
827 Steve Howe 1.00 .30
828 Brook Jacoby 1.00 .30
829 Rodney McCray 1.00 .30
830 Chuck Knoblauch 8.00 2.40
835 Juan Bell 1.00 .30
836 Lance Dickson 1.00 .30
837 Darryl Kile 1.00 .30
842 Tim Belcher 1.00 .30
843 Jeff Shaw 1.00 .30
844 Mike Fitzgerald 1.00 .30
845 Gary Carter 12.00 3.60
850 Alan Trammell 3.00 .90
851 Rex Hudler 2.00 .60
856 Damon Berryhill 1.00 .30
857 Mark Eichhorn 1.00 .30
858 Hector Villanueva 1.00 .30
860 Denny Martinez 2.00 .60
865 Reggie Sanders 2.00 .60
869 Melido Perez 1.00 .30
874 Pete Incaviglia 1.00 .30
875 Tom Candiotti 1.00 .30
877 Neal Heaton 1.00 .30
879 Dave Eiland 1.00 .30
882 Otis Nixon 1.00 .30
883 Herm Winningham 1.00 .30
884 Dion James 1.00 .30
887 Dennis Cook 1.00 .30
894 Charlie Hough 2.00 .60

1993 Stadium Club Murphy

This 200-card boxed set features 1992 All-Star Game cards, 1992 Team USA cards, and 1992 Championship and World Series cards. Topps actually refers to this set as a 1992 issue, but the set was released in 1993. This set is housed in a replica of San Diego's Jack Murphy Stadium, site of the 1992 All-Star Game. Production was limited to 8,000 cases, with 16 boxes per case. The set includes 100 Draft Pick cards, 56 All-Star cards, 25 Team USA cards, and 19 cards commemorating the 1992 National and American League Championship Series and the World Series. Notable Rookie Cards in this set include Derek Jeter, Jason Kendall, Shannon Stewart and Preston Wilson. A second year Team USA Nomar Garciaparra is featured in this set as well.

Nm-Mt Ex-Mt
COMP.FACT.SET (212) 40.00 12.00
COMPLETE SET (200) 25.00 7.50
COMMON CARD (1-200) .15 .04
COMMON RC .15 .04
1 Dave Winfield .15 .04
2 Juan Guzman .15 .04
3 Tony Gwynn 1.00 .30
4 Chris Roberts .15 .04
5 Benny Santiago .30 .09
6 Sherard Clinkscales RC .15 .04
7 Jon Nunnally RC .50 .15
8 Chuck Knoblauch .30 .09
9 Bob Wolcott RC .15 .04
10 Steve Rodriguez .15 .04
11 Mark Williams RC .15 .04
12 Danny Clyburn RC .15 .04
13 Darren Dreifort .30 .09
14 Andy Van Slyke .30 .09
15 Wade Boggs .50 .15
16 Scott Patton RC .15 .04
17 Gary Sheffield .30 .09
18 Ron Villone .15 .04
19 Roberto Alomar .75 .23
20 Marc Valdes .15 .04
21 Daron Kirkreit .15 .04
22 Jeff Granger .15 .04
23 Levon Largusa RC .15 .04
24 Jimmy Key .30 .09
25 Kevin Pearson RC .15 .04
26 Michael Moore RC .15 .04
27 Preston Wilson RC 5.00 1.50
28 Kirby Puckett .75 .23
29 Tim Crabtree RC .15 .04
30 Bip Roberts .15 .04
31 Kelly Gruber .15 .04
32 Tony Fernandez .15 .04
33 Jason Angel RC .15 .04
34 Calvin Murray .15 .04
35 Chad McConnell .15 .04
36 Jason Moler .15 .04
37 Mark Lemke .15 .04
38 Tom Knauss RC .15 .04
39 Larry Mitchell RC .15 .04
40 Doug Mirabelli RC .15 .04
41 Everett Stull II RC .15 .04
42 Chris Wimmer .15 .04
43 Dan Serafini RC .15 .04
44 Ryne Sandberg 1.25 .35
45 Steve Lyons RC .15 .04
46 Ryan Freeburg RC .15 .04
47 Ruben Sierra .15 .04
48 David Mysel RC .15 .04
49 Joe Hamilton RC .15 .04
50 Steve Rodriguez .15 .04
51 Tim Wakefield .30 .09
52 Scott Gentile RC .15 .04
53 Doug Jones .15 .04
54 Willie Brown RC .15 .04
55 Chad Mottola RC .50 .15
56 Ken Griffey Jr. 1.25 .35
57 Jon Lieber RC .50 .15
58 Dennis Martinez .30 .09
59 Joe Petcka RC .15 .04
60 Benji Simonton RC .15 .04
61 Brett Backlund RC .15 .04
62 Damon Berryhill .15 .04
63 Juan Guzman .15 .04
64 Doug Hecker RC .15 .04
65 Jamie Arnold RC .15 .04
66 Bob Tewksbury .15 .04
67 Tim Leger RC .15 .04
68 Todd Etler RC .15 .04
69 Lloyd McClendon .15 .04
70 Kurt Ehmann RC .15 .04
71 Rick Magdaleno RC .15 .04
72 Tom Pagnozzi .15 .04
73 Jeffrey Hammonds .15 .04
74 Joe Carter .30 .09
75 Chris Holt RC .30 .09
76 Charles Johnson .30 .09
77 Bob Walk .15 .04
78 Fred McGriff .50 .15
79 Tom Evans RC .15 .04
80 Scott Klingenbeck RC .15 .04
81 Chad McConnell .15 .04
82 Chris Eddy RC .15 .04
83 Phil Nevin .30 .09
84 John Kruk .30 .09
85 Tony Sheffield RC .15 .04
86 John Smoltz .50 .15
87 Trevor Humphry RC .15 .04
88 Charles Nagy .15 .04
89 Sean Runyan RC .15 .04
90 Mike Gulan RC .15 .04
91 Darren Daulton .30 .09
92 Otis Nixon .15 .04
93 Nomar Garciaparra 15.00 4.50
94 Larry Walker .50 .15
95 Hut Smith RC .15 .04
96 Rick Helling .15 .04
97 Roger Clemens 1.50 .45
98 Ron Gant .30 .09
99 Kenny Felder RC .15 .04
100 Steve Murphy RC .15 .04
101 Mike Smith RC .15 .04
102 Terry Pendleton .30 .09
103 Tim Davis .15 .04
104 Jeff Patzke RC .15 .04
105 Craig Wilson .15 .04
106 Tom Glavine .50 .15
107 Mark Langston .15 .04
108 Mark Thompson RC .15 .04
109 Eric Owens RC 1.00 .30
110 Keith Johnson RC .15 .04
111 Robin Ventura .30 .09
112 Ed Sprague .15 .04
113 Jeff Schmidt RC .15 .04
114 Don Wengert RC .15 .04
115 Craig Biggio .50 .15
116 Kenny Carlyle RC .15 .04
117 Derek Jeter RC 25.00 7.50
118 Manuel Lee .15 .04
119 Jeff Haas RC .15 .04
120 Roger Bailey RC .15 .04
121 Sean Lowe RC .15 .04
122 Rick Aguilera .15 .04
123 Sandy Alomar Jr. .15 .04
124 Derek Wallace RC .15 .04
125 B.J. Wallace .15 .04
126 Greg Maddux 1.25 .35
127 Tim Moore RC .15 .04
128 Lee Smith .30 .09
129 Todd Steverson RC .15 .04
130 Chris Widger RC .50 .15
131 Paul Molitor .50 .15
132 Chris Smith RC .15 .04
133 Chris Gomez RC .50 .15
134 Jimmy Baron RC .15 .04
135 John Smoltz .50 .15
136 Pat Borders .15 .04
137 Donnie Leshnock .15 .04
138 Gus Gandarillos RC .15 .04
139 Will Clark .75 .23
140 Ryan Luzinski RC .15 .04
141 Cal Ripken 2.50 .75
142 B.J. Wallace .15 .04
143 Trey Beamon RC .50 .15
144 Norm Charlton .15 .04
145 Mike Mussina .75 .23
146 Billy Owens RC .15 .04
147 Ozzie Smith 1.25 .35
148 Jason Kendall RC 2.00 .60
149 Mike Matthews RC .15 .04
150 David Spykstra RC .15 .04
151 Benji Grigsby RC .15 .04
152 Sean Smith RC .15 .04
153 Mark McGwire 2.00 .60
154 David Cone .30 .09
155 Shon Walker RC .15 .04
156 Jason Giambi 1.50 .45
157 Jack McDowell .15 .04
158 Paxton Briley RC .15 .04
159 Edgar Martinez .50 .15
160 Brian Sackinsky RC .15 .04
161 Barry Bonds 2.00 .60
162 Roberto Kelly .15 .04
163 Jeff Alkire .15 .04
164 Mike Sharperson .15 .04
165 Jamie Taylor RC .15 .04
166 John Saffer UER RC .15 .04
167 Jerry Browne .15 .04
168 Travis Fryman .30 .09
169 Brady Anderson .30 .09
170 Chris Roberts .15 .04
171 Lloyd Peever RC .15 .04
172 Francisco Cabrera .15 .04
173 Ramiro Martinez RC .15 .04
174 Jeff Alkire .15 .04
175 Ivan Rodriguez .75 .23
176 Kevin Brown .30 .09
177 Chad Roper RC .15 .04
178 Rod Henderson RC .15 .04
179 Dennis Eckersley .30 .09
180 Shannon Stewart RC 2.00 .60
181 DeShawn Warren RC .15 .04
182 Lonnie Smith .15 .04
183 Willie Adams .15 .04
184 Jeff Montgomery .15 .04
185 Damon Hollins RC .50 .15
186 Byron Mathews RC .15 .04
187 Harold Baines .30 .09
188 Rick Greene .15 .04
189 Carlos Baerga .15 .04
190 Brandon Cromer RC .15 .04
191 Roberto Alomar .75 .23
192 Rich Ireland RC .15 .04
193 S.Montgomery RC .15 .04
194 Brant Brown RC .15 .04
195 Ritchie Moody RC .15 .04
196 Michael Tucker .15 .04
197 Jason Varitek .50 .15
198 David Manning RC .15 .04
199 Marquis Riley RC .15 .04
200 Jason Giambi 2.00 .60

1993 Stadium Club Murphy Master Photos

One Murphy Master Photo was included in each 1993 Stadium Club Murphy Special factory set. Each of these twelve uncropped Murphy Master Photos is inlaid in a 5" by 7" white frame and bordered with a prismatic foil trim. The photo within parallels the corresponding player's regular issue Murphy card. The cards are unnumbered and checklisted below in alphabetical order.

Nm-Mt Ex-Mt
COMPLETE SET (12) 5.00 1.50
1 Sandy Alomar Jr. AS .15 .04
2 Tom Glavine AS .50 .15
3 Ken Griffey Jr. AS 1.25 .35
4 Tony Gwynn AS 1.00 .30
5 Chuck Knoblauch AS .30 .09
6 Chad Mottola '92 .50 .15
7 Kirby Puckett AS .75 .23
8 Chris Roberts USA .15 .04
9 Ryne Sandberg AS 1.25 .35
10 Gary Sheffield AS .30 .09
11 Larry Walker AS .50 .15
12 Preston Wilson '92 2.00 .60

1993 Stadium Club

The 1993 Stadium Club baseball set consists of 750 standard-size cards issued in three series of 300, 300, and 150 cards respectively. Each series closes with a Members Choice subset (291-300, 591-600, and 746-750.

Nm-Mt Ex-Mt
COMPLETE SET (750) 50.00 15.00
COMP.SERIES 1 (300) 15.00 4.50
COMP.SERIES 2 (300) 20.00 6.00
COMP.SERIES 3 (150) 15.00 4.50
1 Pat Borders .15 .04
2 Greg Maddux 1.25 .35
3 Daryl Boston .15 .04
4 Bob Ayrault .15 .04
5 Tony Phillips IF .15 .04
6 Damion Easley .15 .04
7 Kip Gross .15 .04
8 Jim Thome .75 .23
9 Tim Belcher .15 .04
10 Gary Wayne .15 .04
11 Sam Militello .15 .04
12 Mike Magnante .15 .04
13 Tim Wakefield .30 .09
14 Tim Hulett .15 .04
15 Rheal Cormier .15 .04
16 Juan Guerrero .15 .04
17 Rich Gossage .30 .09
18 Tim Laker RC .15 .04
19 Darrin Jackson .15 .04
20 Jack Clark .30 .09
21 Roberto Hernandez .15 .04
22 Dean Palmer .30 .09
23 Harold Reynolds .30 .09
24 Dan Plesac .15 .04
25 Brent Mayne .15 .04
26 Pat Hentgen .15 .04
27 Luis Sojo .15 .04
28 Ron Gant .30 .09
29 Paul Gibson .15 .04
30 Bip Roberts .15 .04
31 Mickey Tettleton .15 .04
32 Randy Velarde .15 .04
33 Brian McRae .15 .04
34 Wes Chamberlain .15 .04
35 Wayne Kirby .15 .04
36 Rey Sanchez .15 .04
37 Jesse Orosco .15 .04
38 Mike Stanton .15 .04
39 Royce Clayton .15 .04
40 Cal Ripken UER 2.50 .75
(Place of birth Havre de Grave; should be Havre de Grace)
41 John Dopson .15 .04
42 Gene Larkin .15 .04
43 Tim Raines .30 .09
44 Randy Myers .15 .04
45 Clay Parker .15 .04
46 Mike Scioscia .15 .04
47 Pete Incaviglia .15 .04
48 Todd Van Poppel .15 .04
49 Ray Lankford .15 .04
50 Eddie Murray .75 .23
51 Barry Bonds COR 2.00 .60
51A Barry Bonds ERR 2.00 .60
(Missing four stars over name to indicate NL MVP)
52 Gary Thurman .15 .04
53 Bob Wickman .15 .04
54 Joey Cora .15 .04
55 Kenny Rogers .30 .09
56 Mike Devereaux .15 .04
57 Kevin Seitzer .15 .04
58 Rafael Belliard .15 .04
59 David Wells .30 .09
60 Mark Clark .15 .04
61 Carlos Baerga .15 .04
62 Scott Brosius .30 .09
63 Jeff Grotewold .15 .04
64 Rick Wrona .15 .04
65 Kurt Knudsen .15 .04
66 Lloyd McClendon .15 .04
67 Omar Vizquel .30 .09
68 Jose Vizcaino .15 .04
69 Rob Ducey .15 .04
70 Casey Candaele .15 .04
71 Ramon Martinez .15 .04
72 Todd Hundley .15 .04
73 John Marzano .15 .04
74 Derek Parks .15 .04
75 Jack McDowell .15 .04
76 Tim Scott .15 .04
77 Mike Mussina .75 .23
78 Delino DeShields .15 .04
79 Chris Bosio .15 .04
80 Mike Bordick .15 .04
81 Rod Beck .15 .04
82 Ted Power .15 .04
83 John Kruk .30 .09
84 Steve Shifflett .15 .04
85 Danny Tartabull .15 .04
86 Mike Greenwell .15 .04
87 Jose Melendez .15 .04
88 Craig Wilson .15 .04
89 Melvin Nieves .15 .04
90 Ed Sprague .15 .04
91 Willie McGee .30 .09
92 Joe Orsulak .15 .04
93 Jeff King .15 .04
94 Dan Pasqua .15 .04
95 Brian Harper .15 .04
96 Joe Oliver .15 .04
97 Shane Turner .15 .04
98 Lenny Harris .15 .04
99 Jeff Parrett .15 .04
100 Luis Polonia .15 .04
101 Kent Bottenfield .15 .04
102 Albert Belle .30 .09
103 Mike Maddux .15 .04
104 Randy Tomlin .15 .04
105 Andy Stankiewicz .15 .04
106 Rico Rossy .15 .04
107 Joe Hesketh .15 .04
108 Dennis Powell .15 .04
109 Derrick May .15 .04
110 Pete Harnisch .15 .04
111 Kent Mercker .15 .04
112 Scott Fletcher .15 .04
113 Rex Hudler .15 .04
114 Chico Walker .15 .04
115 Rafael Palmeiro .50 .15
116 Mark Leiter .15 .04
117 Pedro Munoz .15 .04
118 Jim Bullinger .15 .04
119 Ivan Calderon .15 .04
120 Mike Timlin .15 .04
121 Rene Gonzales .15 .04
122 Greg Vaughn .30 .09
123 Mike Flanagan .15 .04
124 Mike Hartley .15 .04
125 Jeff Montgomery .15 .04
126 Mike Gallego .15 .04
127 Don Slaught .15 .04
128 Charlie O'Brien .15 .04
129 Jose Offerman .15 .04
(Can be found with home town missing on back)
130 Mark Wohlers .15 .04
131 Eric Fox .15 .04
132 Doug Strange .15 .04
133 Jeff Frye .15 .04
134 Wade Boggs UER .50 .15
(Redundantly lists lefty breakdown)
135 Lou Whitaker .30 .09
136 Craig Grebeck .15 .04
137 Rich Rodriguez .15 .04
138 Jay Bell .30 .09
139 Felix Fermin .15 .04
140 Dennis Martinez .30 .09
141 Eric Anthony .15 .04
142 Roberto Alomar .75 .23
143 Darren Lewis .15 .04
144 Mike Blowers .15 .04
145 Scott Bankhead .15 .04
146 Jeff Reboulet .15 .04
147 Frank Viola .30 .09
148 Bill Pecota .15 .04
149 Carlos Hernandez .15 .04
150 Bobby Witt .15 .04
151 Sid Bream .15 .04
152 Todd Zeile .15 .04
153 Dennis Cook .15 .04
154 Brian Bohanon .15 .04
155 Pat Kelly .15 .04
156 Milt Cuyler .15 .04
157 Juan Bell .15 .04
158 Randy Milligan .15 .04
159 Mark Gardner .15 .04
160 Pat Tabler .15 .04
161 Jeff Reardon .30 .09
162 Ken Patterson .15 .04
163 Bobby Bonilla .30 .09
164 Tony Pena .15 .04
165 Greg Swindell .15 .04
166 Kirk McCaskill .15 .04
167 Doug Drabek .15 .04
168 Franklin Stubbs .15 .04
169 Ron Tingley .15 .04
170 Willie Banks .15 .04
171 Sergio Valdez .15 .04
172 Mark Lemke .15 .04
173 Robin Yount 1.25 .35
174 Storm Davis .15 .04
175 Dan Walters .15 .04
176 Steve Farr .15 .04
177 Curt Wilkerson .15 .04

178 Luis Alicea .15 .04
179 Russ Swan .15 .04
180 Mitch Williams .15 .04
181 Wilson Alvarez .15 .04
182 Carl Willis .15 .04
183 Craig Biggio .50 .15
184 Sean Berry .15 .04
185 Trevor Wilson .15 .04
186 Jeff Tackett .15 .04
187 Ellis Burks .30 .09
188 Jeff Branson .15 .04
189 Matt Nokes .15 .04
190 John Smiley .15 .04
191 Danny Gladden .15 .04
192 Mike Boddicker .15 .04
193 Roger Pavlik .15 .04
194 Paul Sorrento .15 .04
195 Vince Coleman .15 .04
196 Gary DiSarcina .15 .04
197 Rafael Bournigal .15 .04
198 Mike Schooler .15 .04
199 Scott Ruskin .15 .04
200 Frank Thomas .75 .23
201 Kyle Abbott .15 .04
202 Mike Perez .15 .04
203 Andre Dawson .30 .09
204 Bill Swift .15 .04
205 Alejandro Pena .15 .04
206 Dave Winfield .30 .09
207 Andujar Cedeno .15 .04
208 Terry Steinbach .15 .04
209 Chris Hammond .15 .04
210 Todd Burns .15 .04
211 Hipolito Pichardo .15 .04
212 John Kiely .15 .04
213 Tim Teufel .15 .04
214 Lee Guetterman .15 .04
215 Geronimo Pena .15 .04
216 Brett Butler .30 .09
217 Bryan Hickerson .15 .04
218 Rick Trlicek .15 .04
219 Lee Stevens .15 .04
220 Roger Clemens 1.50 .45
221 Carlton Fisk .50 .15
222 Chili Davis .30 .09
223 Walt Terrell .15 .04
224 Jim Eisenreich .15 .04
225 Ricky Bones .15 .04
226 Henry Rodriguez .15 .04
227 Ken Hill .15 .04
228 Rick Wilkins .15 .04
229 Ricky Jordan .15 .04
230 Bernard Gilkey .15 .04
231 Tim Fortugno .15 .04
232 Geno Petralli .15 .04
233 Jose Rijo .15 .04
234 Jim Leyritz .15 .04
235 Kevin Campbell .15 .04
236 Al Osuna .15 .04
237 Pete Smith .15 .04
238 Pete Schourek .15 .04
239 Moises Alou .30 .09
240 Donn Pall .15 .04
241 Denny Neagle .30 .09
242 Dan Peltier .15 .04
243 Scott Scudder .15 .04
244 Juan Guzman .15 .04
245 Dave Burba .15 .04
246 Rick Sutcliffe .30 .09
247 Tony Fossas .15 .04
248 Mike Munoz .15 .04
249 Tim Salmon .50 .15
250 Rob Murphy .15 .04
251 Roger McDowell .15 .04
252 Lance Parrish .30 .09
253 Cliff Brantley .15 .04
254 Scott Leius .15 .04
255 Carlos Martinez .15 .04
256 Vince Horsman .15 .04
257 Oscar Azocar .15 .04
258 Craig Shipley .15 .04
259 Ben McDonald .15 .04
260 Jeff Brantley .15 .04
261 Damon Berryhill .15 .04
262 Joe Grahe .15 .04
263 Dave Hansen .15 .04
264 Rich Amaral .15 .04
265 Tim Pugh RC .15 .04
266 Dion James .15 .04
267 Frank Tanana .15 .04
268 Stan Belinda .15 .04
269 Jeff Kent .75 .23
270 Bruce Ruffin .15 .04
271 Xavier Hernandez .15 .04
272 Darrin Fletcher .15 .04
273 Tino Martinez .50 .15
274 Benny Santiago .30 .09
275 Scott Radinsky .15 .04
276 Mariano Duncan .15 .04
277 Kenny Lofton .30 .09
278 Dwight Smith .15 .04
279 Joe Carter .30 .09
280 Tim Jones .15 .04
281 Jeff Huson .15 .04
282 Phil Plantier .15 .04
283 Kirby Puckett .75 .23
284 Johnny Guzman .15 .04
285 Mike Morgan .15 .04
286 Chris Sabo .15 .04
287 Matt Williams .30 .09
288 Checklist 1-100 .15 .04
289 Checklist 101-200 .15 .04
290 Checklist 201-300 .15 .04
291 Dennis Eckersley MC .30 .09
292 Eric Karros MC .15 .04
293 Pat Listach MC .15 .04
294 Andy Van Slyke MC .15 .04
295 Robin Ventura MC .15 .04
296 Tom Glavine MC .30 .09
297 J.Gonzalez MC UER .50 .15
Misspelled Gonzales
298 Travis Fryman MC .15 .04
299 Larry Walker MC .50 .15
300 Gary Sheffield MC .15 .04
301 Chuck Finley .30 .09
302 Luis Gonzalez .30 .09
303 Darryl Hamilton .15 .04
304 Bien Figueroa .15 .04
305 Ron Darling .15 .04
306 Jonathan Hurst .15 .04
307 Mike Sharperson .15 .04
308 Mike Christopher .15 .04
309 Marvin Freeman .15 .04
310 Jay Buhner .30 .09
311 Butch Henry .15 .04
312 Greg W. Harris .15 .04
313 Darren Daulton .30 .09
314 Chuck Knoblauch .30 .09
315 Greg A. Harris .15 .04
316 John Franco .30 .09
317 John Wehner .15 .04
318 Donald Harris .15 .04
319 Benny Santiago .30 .09
320 Larry Walker .50 .15
321 Randy Knorr .15 .04
322 Ramon Martinez RC .15 .04
323 Mike Stanley .15 .04
324 Bill Wegman .15 .04
325 Tom Candiotti .15 .04
326 Glenn Davis .15 .04
327 Chuck Crim .15 .04
328 Scott Livingstone .15 .04
329 Eddie Taubensee .15 .04
330 George Bell .15 .04
331 Edgar Martinez .50 .15
332 Paul Assenmacher .15 .04
333 Steve Hosey .15 .04
334 Mo Vaughn .30 .09
335 Bret Saberhagen .30 .09
336 Mike Trombley .15 .04
337 Mark Lewis .15 .04
338 Terry Pendleton .30 .09
339 Dave Hollins .15 .04
340 Jeff Conine .30 .09
341 Bob Tewksbury .15 .04
342 Billy Ashley .15 .04
343 Zane Smith .15 .04
344 John Wetteland .30 .09
345 Chris Hoiles .15 .04
346 Frank Castillo .15 .04
347 Bruce Hurst .15 .04
348 Kevin McReynolds .15 .04
349 Dave Henderson .15 .04
350 Ryan Bowen .15 .04
351 Sid Fernandez .15 .04
352 Mark Whiten .15 .04
353 Nolan Ryan 3.00 .90
354 Rick Aguilera .15 .04
355 Mark Langston .15 .04
356 Jack Morris .30 .09
357 Rob Deer .15 .04
358 Dave Fleming .15 .04
359 Lance Johnson .15 .04
360 Joe Millette .15 .04
361 Wil Cordero .15 .04
362 Chito Martinez .15 .04
363 Scott Servais .15 .04
364 Bernie Williams .50 .15
365 Pedro Martinez 1.50 .45
366 Ryne Sandberg 1.25 .35
367 Brad Ausmus .15 .04
368 Scott Cooper .15 .04
369 Rob Dibble .30 .09
370 Walt Weiss .15 .04
371 Mark Davis .15 .04
372 Orlando Merced .15 .04
373 Mike Jackson .15 .04
374 Kevin Appier .30 .09
375 Esteban Beltre .15 .04
376 Joe Slusarski .15 .04
377 William Suero .15 .04
378 Pete O'Brien .15 .04
379 Alan Embree .15 .04
380 Lenny Webster .15 .04
381 Eric Davis .30 .09
382 Duane Ward .15 .04
383 John Habyan .15 .04
384 Jeff Bagwell .50 .15
385 Ruben Amaro .15 .04
386 Julio Valera .15 .04
387 Robin Ventura .30 .09
388 Archi Cianfrocco .15 .04
389 Skeeter Barnes .15 .04
390 Tim Costo .15 .04
391 Luis Mercedes .15 .04
392 Jeremy Hernandez .15 .04
393 Shawon Dunston .15 .04
394 Andy Van Slyke .30 .09
395 Kevin Maas .15 .04
396 Kevin Brown .30 .09
397 J.T. Bruett .15 .04
398 Darryl Strawberry .50 .15
399 Tom Pagnozzi .15 .04
400 Sandy Alomar Jr. .15 .04
401 Keith Miller .15 .04
402 Rich DeLucia .15 .04
403 Shawn Abner .15 .04
404 Howard Johnson .15 .04
405 Mike Benjamin .15 .04
406 Roberto Mejia RC .15 .04
407 Mike Butcher .15 .04
408 Deion Sanders UER .50 .15
(Braves on front and Yankees on back)
409 Todd Stottlemyre .15 .04
410 Scott Kamieniecki .15 .04
411 Doug Jones .15 .04
412 John Burkett .15 .04
413 Lance Blankenship .15 .04
414 Jeff Parrett .15 .04
415 Barry Larkin .75 .23
416 Alan Trammell .50 .15
417 Mark Kiefer .15 .04
418 Gregg Olson .15 .04
419 Mark Grace .50 .15
420 Shane Mack .15 .04
421 Bob Walk .15 .04
422 Curt Schilling .50 .15
423 Erik Hanson .15 .04
424 George Brett 2.00 .60
425 Reggie Jefferson .15 .04
426 Mark Portugal .15 .04
427 Ron Karkovice .15 .04
428 Matt Young .15 .04
429 Troy Neel .15 .04
430 Hector Fajardo .15 .04
431 Dave Righetti .30 .09
432 Pat Listach .15 .04
433 Jeff Innis .15 .04
434 Bob MacDonald .15 .04
435 Brian Jordan .30 .09
436 Jeff Blauser .15 .04
437 Mike Myers RC .15 .04
438 Frank Seminara .15 .04
439 Rusty Meacham .15 .04
440 Greg Briley .15 .04
441 Derek Lilliquist .15 .04
442 John Vander Wal .15 .04
443 Scott Erickson .15 .04
444 Bob Scanlan .15 .04
445 Todd Frohwirth .15 .04
446 Tom Goodwin .15 .04
447 William Pennyfeather .15 .04
448 Travis Fryman .30 .09
449 Mickey Morandini .15 .04
450 Greg Olson .15 .04
451 Trevor Hoffman .30 .09
452 Dave Magadan .15 .04
453 Shawn Jeter .15 .04
454 Andres Galarraga .30 .09
455 Ted Wood .15 .04
456 Freddie Benavides .15 .04
457 Junior Felix .15 .04
458 Alex Cole .15 .04
459 John Orton .15 .04
460 Eddie Zosky .15 .04
461 Dennis Eckersley .30 .09
462 Lee Smith .30 .09
463 John Smoltz .50 .15
464 Ken Caminiti .30 .09
465 Melido Perez .15 .04
466 Tom Marsh .15 .04
467 Jeff Nelson .15 .04
468 Jesse Levis .15 .04
469 Chris Nabholz .15 .04
470 Mike Macfarlane .15 .04
471 Reggie Sanders .30 .09
472 Chuck McElroy .15 .04
473 Kevin Gross .15 .04
474 Matt Whiteside RC .15 .04
475 Cal Eldred .15 .04
476 Dave Gallagher .15 .04
477 Len Dykstra .30 .09
478 Mark McGwire 2.00 .60
479 David Segui .15 .04
480 Mike Henneman .15 .04
481 Bret Barberie .15 .04
482 Steve Sax .15 .04
483 Dave Valle .15 .04
484 Danny Darwin .15 .04
485 Devon White .15 .04
486 Eric Plunk .15 .04
487 Jim Gott .15 .04
488 Scooter Tucker .15 .04
489 Omar Olivares .15 .04
490 Greg Myers .15 .04
491 Brian Hunter .15 .04
492 Kevin Tapani .15 .04
493 Rich Monteleone .15 .04
494 Steve Buechele .15 .04
495 Bo Jackson .75 .23
496 Mike LaValliere .15 .04
497 Mark Leonard .15 .04
498 Daryl Boston .15 .04
499 Jose Canseco .75 .23
500 Brian Barnes .15 .04
501 Randy Johnson .75 .23
502 Tim McIntosh .15 .04
503 Cecil Fielder .30 .09
504 Derek Bell .15 .04
505 Kevin Koslofski .15 .04
506 Darren Holmes .15 .04
507 Brady Anderson .30 .09
508 John Valentin .15 .04
509 Jerry Browne .15 .04
510 Fred McGriff .50 .15
511 Pedro Astacio .15 .04
512 Gary Gaetti .30 .09
513 John Burke RC .15 .04
514 Dwight Gooden .50 .15
515 Thomas Howard .15 .04
516 D.Whitmore RC UER .15 .04
11 games played in 1992; should be 121
517 Ozzie Guillen .15 .04
518 Darryl Kile .30 .09
519 Rich Rowland .15 .04
520 Carlos Delgado .75 .23
521 Doug Henry .15 .04
522 Greg Colbrunn .15 .04
523 Tom Gordon .15 .04
524 Ivan Rodriguez .75 .23
525 Kent Hrbek .30 .09
526 Eric Young .15 .04
527 Rod Brewer .15 .04
528 Eric Karros .30 .09
529 Marquis Grissom .15 .04
530 Rico Brogna .15 .04
531 Sammy Sosa 1.25 .35
532 Bret Boone .50 .15
533 Luis Rivera .15 .04
534 Hal Morris .15 .04
535 Monty Fariss .15 .04
536 Leo Gomez .15 .04
537 Wally Joyner .30 .09
538 Tony Gwynn 1.00 .30
539 Mike Williams .15 .04
540 Juan Gonzalez .75 .23
541 Ryan Klesko .30 .09
542 Ryan Thompson .15 .04
543 Chad Curtis .15 .04
544 Orel Hershiser .30 .09
545 Carlos Garcia .15 .04
546 Bob Welch .15 .04
547 Vinny Castilla .30 .09
548 Ozzie Smith 1.25 .35
549 Luis Salazar .15 .04
550 Mark Guthrie .15 .04
551 Charles Nagy .15 .04
552 Alex Fernandez .15 .04
553 Mel Rojas .15 .04
554 Orestes Destrade .15 .04
555 Mark Gubicza .15 .04
556 Steve Finley .30 .09
557 Don Mattingly 2.00 .60
558 Rickey Henderson .75 .23
559 Tommy Greene .15 .04
560 Arthur Rhodes .15 .04
561 Alfredo Griffin .15 .04
562 Will Clark .75 .23
563 Bob Zupcic .15 .04
564 Chuck Carr .15 .04
565 Henry Cotto .15 .04
566 Billy Spiers .15 .04
567 Jack Armstrong .15 .04
568 Kurt Stillwell .15 .04
569 David McCarty .15 .04
570 Joe Vitiello .15 .04
571 Gerald Williams .15 .04
572 Dale Murphy .75 .23
573 Scott Aldred .15 .04
574 Bill Gullickson .15 .04
575 Bobby Thigpen .15 .04
576 Glenallen Hill .15 .04
577 Dwayne Henry .15 .04
578 Calvin Jones .15 .04
579 Al Martin .15 .04
580 Ruben Sierra .15 .04
581 Andy Benes .15 .04
582 Anthony Young .15 .04
583 Shawn Boskie .15 .04
584 Scott Pose RC .15 .04
585 Mike Piazza 2.00 .60
586 Donovan Osborne .15 .04
587 Jim Austin .15 .04
588 Checklist 301-400 .15 .04
589 Checklist 401-500 .15 .04
590 Checklist 501-600 .15 .04
591 Ken Griffey Jr. MC .75 .23
592 Ivan Rodriguez MC .50 .15
593 Carlos Baerga MC .15 .04
594 Fred McGriff MC .30 .09
595 Mark McGwire MC 1.00 .30
596 Roberto Alomar MC .30 .09
597 Kirby Puckett MC .50 .15
598 Marquis Grissom MC .15 .04
599 John Smoltz MC .30 .09
600 Ryne Sandberg MC .75 .23
601 Wade Boggs .50 .15
602 Jeff Reardon .30 .09
603 Billy Ripken .15 .04
604 Bryan Harvey .15 .04
605 Carlos Quintana .15 .04
606 Greg Hibbard .15 .04
607 Ellis Burks .30 .09
608 Greg Swindell .15 .04
609 Dave Winfield .30 .09
610 Charlie Hough .30 .09
611 Chili Davis .30 .09
612 Jody Reed .15 .04
613 Mark Williamson .15 .04
614 Phil Plantier .15 .04
615 Jim Abbott .50 .15
616 Dante Bichette .30 .09
617 Mark Eichhorn .15 .04
618 Gary Sheffield .30 .09
619 Richie Lewis RC .15 .04
620 Joe Girardi .15 .04
621 Jaime Navarro .15 .04
622 Willie Wilson .15 .04
623 Scott Fletcher .15 .04
624 Bud Black .15 .04
625 Tom Brunansky .15 .04
626 Steve Avery .15 .04
627 Paul Molitor .50 .15
628 Gregg Jefferies .15 .04
629 Dave Stewart .30 .09
630 Javier Lopez .50 .15
631 Greg Gagne .15 .04
632 Roberto Kelly .15 .04
633 Mike Fetters .15 .04
634 Ozzie Canseco .15 .04
635 Jeff Russell .15 .04
636 Pete Incaviglia .15 .04
637 Tom Henke .15 .04
638 Chipper Jones .75 .23
639 Jimmy Key .30 .09
640 Dave Martinez .15 .04
641 Dave Stieb .15 .04
642 Milt Thompson .15 .04
643 Alan Mills .15 .04
644 Tony Fernandez .15 .04
645 Randy Bush .15 .04
646 Joe Magrane .15 .04
647 Ivan Calderon .15 .04
648 Jose Guzman .15 .04
649 John Olerud .30 .09
650 Tom Glavine .50 .15
651 Julio Franco .30 .09
652 Armando Reynoso .15 .04
653 Felix Jose .15 .04
654 Ben Rivera .15 .04
655 Andre Dawson .30 .09
656 Mike Harkey .15 .04
657 Kevin Seitzer .15 .04
658 Lonnie Smith .15 .04
659 Norm Charlton .15 .04
660 David Justice .30 .09
661 Fernando Valenzuela .30 .09
662 Dan Wilson .30 .09
663 Mark Gardner .15 .04
664 Doug Dascenzo .15 .04
665 Greg Maddux 1.25 .35
666 Harold Baines .30 .09
667 Randy Myers .15 .04
668 Harold Reynolds .30 .09
669 Candy Maldonado .15 .04
670 Al Leiter .30 .09
671 Jerald Clark .15 .04
672 Doug Drabek .15 .04
673 Kirk Gibson .30 .09
674 Steve Reed RC .15 .04
675 Mike Felder .15 .04
676 Ricky Gutierrez .15 .04
677 Spike Owen .15 .04
678 Otis Nixon .15 .04
679 Scott Sanderson .15 .04
680 Mark Carreon .15 .04
681 Troy Percival .50 .15
682 Kevin Stocker .15 .04
683 Jim Converse RC .15 .04
684 Barry Bonds 2.00 .60
685 Greg Gohr .15 .04
686 Tim Wallach .15 .04
687 Matt Mieske .15 .04
688 Robby Thompson .15 .04
689 Brien Taylor .15 .04
690 Kirt Manwaring .15 .04
691 Mike Lansing RC .30 .09
692 Steve Decker .15 .04
693 Mike Moore .15 .04
694 Kevin Mitchell .15 .04
695 Phil Hiatt .15 .04
696 Tony Tarasco RC .15 .04
697 Benji Gil .15 .04
698 Jeff Juden .15 .04
699 Kevin Reimer .15 .04
700 Andy Ashby .15 .04
701 John Jaha .15 .04
702 Tim Bogar RC .15 .04
703 David Cone .30 .09
704 Willie Greene .15 .04
705 David Hulse RC .15 .04
706 Cris Carpenter .15 .04
707 Ken Griffey Jr. 1.25 .35
708 Steve Bedrosian .15 .04
709 Dave Nilsson .15 .04
710 Paul Wagner .15 .04
711 B.J. Surhoff .30 .09
712 Rene Arocha RC .30 .09
713 Manuel Lee .15 .04
714 Brian Williams .15 .04
715 Sherman Obando RC .15 .04
716 Terry Mulholland .15 .04
717 Paul O'Neill .50 .15
718 David Nied .15 .04
719 J.T. Snow RC .75 .23
720 Nigel Wilson .15 .04
721 Mike Bielecki .15 .04
722 Kevin Young .30 .09
723 Charlie Leibrandt .15 .04
724 Frank Bolick .15 .04
725 Jon Shave RC .15 .04
726 Steve Cooke .15 .04
727 Domingo Martinez RC .15 .04
728 Todd Worrell .15 .04
729 Jose Lind .15 .04
730 Jim Tatum RC .15 .04
731 Mike Hampton .30 .09
732 Mike Draper .15 .04
733 Henry Mercedes .15 .04
734 John Johnstone RC .15 .04
735 Mitch Webster .15 .04
736 Russ Springer .15 .04
737 Rob Natal .15 .04
738 Steve Howe .15 .04
739 Darrell Sherman RC .15 .04
740 Pat Mahomes .15 .04
741 Alex Arias .15 .04
742 Damon Buford .15 .04
743 Charlie Hayes .15 .04
744 Guillermo Velasquez .15 .04
745 CL 601-750 UER .15 .04
650 Tom Glavine
746 Frank Thomas MC .50 .15
747 Barry Bonds MC 1.00 .30
748 Roger Clemens MC .75 .23
749 Joe Carter MC .15 .04
750 Greg Maddux MC .75 .23

1993 Stadium Club First Day Issue

Two thousand of each 1993 Stadium Club baseball card were produced on the first day and then randomly inserted in packs at a rate of 1:24. These standard-size cards are identical to the regular-issue 1993 Stadium Club cards, except for the embossed prismatic-foil "1st Day Production" logo stamped in an upper corner. Some of the logos have been transferred from "common" 1st day cards to the fronts of better players.

Nm-Mt Ex-Mt
*STARS: 8X TO 20X BASIC CARDS ....

1993 Stadium Club Members Only Parallel

These standard-sized cards were issued in complete set form only through Topps' Stadium Club. These cards are the same as the regular Stadium Club cards except they are imprinted with the Stadium Club logo on the front. The set includes parallel versions of both the basic cards and the insert cards. Only the inserts cards have been priced below. Please use the multiplier for values on the basic cards. These sets were issued at an approximate cost of $200 to Stadium Club members. Even though, the set was issued at $200, the current market conditions makes this set available at less than original issue cost.

Nm-Mt Ex-Mt
COMP.FACT.SET (760) 150.00 45.00
COMMON CARD (1-750) .25 .07
*STARS: 2X TO 4X BASIC CARDS ....
*ROOKIES: 1.5X TO 3X BASIC CARDS.
MA1 Robin Yount 4.00 1.20
MA2 George Brett 8.00 2.40
MA3 David Nied 1.00 .30
MA4 Nigel Wilson 1.00 .30
MB1 Will Clark 8.00 2.40
Mark McGwire
MB2 Dwight Gooden 4.00 1.20
Don Mattingly
MB3 Ryne Sandberg 5.00 1.50
Frank Thomas
MB4 Darryl Strawberry 5.00 1.50
Ken Griffey
MC1 David Nied 1.00 .30
MC2 Charlie Hough 1.50 .45

1993 Stadium Club Inserts

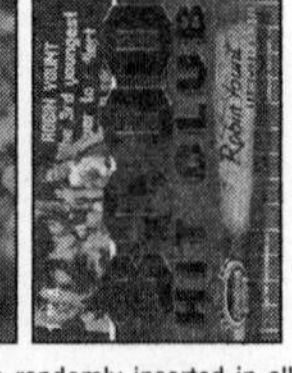

This 10-card set was randomly inserted in all series of Stadium Club packs, the first four in series 1, the second four in series 2 and the last two in series 3. The themes of the standard-size cards differ from series to series, but the basic design -- borderless color action shots on the fronts -- remains the same throughout. The series 1 and 3 cards are numbered on the back, the series 2 cards are unnumbered. No matter what series, all of these inserts were included one every 15 packs.

	Nm-Mt	Ex-Mt
COMPLETE SERIES 1 (4)	2.00	.60
COMPLETE SERIES 2 (4)	10.00	3.00
COMPLETE SERIES 3 (2)	.50	.15
COMMON SER.1 (A1-A4)	.30	.09
COMMON SER.2 (B1-B4)	2.50	.75
COMMON SER.3 (C1-C2)	.30	.09
A1 Robin Yount	2.50	.75
A2 George Brett	4.00	1.20
A3 David Nied FDP	.30	.09
A4 Nigel Wilson FDP	.30	.09
B1 Will Clark Mark McGwire	4.00	1.20
B2 Dwight Gooden Don Mattingly	4.00	1.20
B3 Ryne Sandberg Frank Thomas	1.50	.45
B4 Darryl Strawberry Ken Griffey Jr.	2.50	.75
C1 David Nied UER Colorado Rockies Firsts (Misspelled pitch-hitter on back)	.30	.09
C2 Charlie Hough	.60	.18

1993 Stadium Club Master Photos

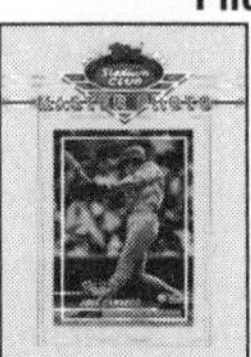
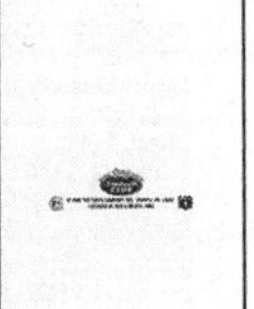

Each of the three Stadium Club series features Master Photos, uncropped versions of the regular Stadium Club cards. Each Master Photo is inlaid in a 5" by 7" white frame and bordered with a prismatic foil trim. The Master Photos were made available to the public in two ways. First, one in every 24 packs included a Master Photo winner card redeemable for a group of three Master Photos until Jan. 31, 1994. Second, each hobby box contained one Master Photo. The cards are unnumbered and checklisted below in alphabetical order within series I (1-12), II (13-24), and III (25-30). Two different versions of these master photos were issued, one with and one without the "Members Only" gold foil seal at the upper right corner. The "Members Only" Master Photos were only available with the direct-mail solicited 750-card Stadium Club Members Only set.

	Nm-Mt	Ex-Mt
COMPLETE SERIES 1 (12)	6.00	1.80
COMPLETE SERIES 2 (12)	8.00	2.40
COMPLETE SERIES 3 (6)	10.00	3.00
1 Carlos Baerga	.25	.07
2 Delino DeShields	.25	.07
3 Brian McRae	.25	.07
4 Sam Militello	.25	.07
5 Joe Oliver	.25	.07
6 Kirby Puckett	1.25	.35
7 Cal Ripken	4.00	1.20
8 Bip Roberts	.25	.07
9 Mike Scioscia	.25	.07
10 Rick Sutcliffe	.50	.15
11 Danny Tartabull	.25	.07
12 Tim Wakefield	.50	.15
13 George Brett	3.00	.90
14 Jose Canseco	1.25	.35
15 Will Clark	1.25	.35
16 Travis Fryman	.50	.15
17 Dwight Gooden	.75	.23
18 Mark Grace	.75	.23
19 Rickey Henderson	1.25	.35
20 Mark McGwire MC	3.00	.90
21 Nolan Ryan	5.00	1.50
22 Ruben Sierra	.25	.07
23 Darryl Strawberry	.75	.23
24 Larry Walker	.75	.23
25 Barry Bonds	3.00	.90
26 Ken Griffey Jr.	2.00	.60
27 Greg Maddux	2.00	.60
28 David Nied	.25	.07
29 J.T. Snow	1.25	.35
30 Brien Taylor	.25	.07

1993 Stadium Club Ultra-Pro

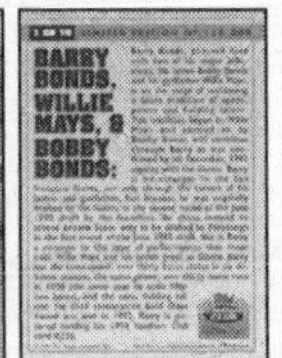

The ten cards in this set measure the standard size and were available singly as limited edition random inserts in the Topps Stadium Club Ultra-Pro Platinum collector pages refill packs (1-6) and individual semi-rigid card protector packs (7-10). In light of a marketing partnership with the Rembrandt Company, this ten-card set was produced by Stadium Club to mark the launch of a new accessory line of premium card storage accessory products. Reportedly no more than 150,000 sets were produced. Willie Mays is Barry Bonds' godfather.

	Nm-Mt	Ex-Mt
COMPLETE SET (10)	20.00	6.00
1 Barry Bonds Willie Mays Bobby Bonds	2.50	.75
2 Willie Mays	3.00	.90
3 Bobby Bonds	1.00	.30
4 Barry Bonds	2.00	.60
5 Barry Bonds Bobby Bonds	2.00	.60
6 Willie Mays	3.00	.90
7 Barry Bonds	2.00	.60
8 Bobby Bonds Willie Mays	2.00	.60
9 Willie Mays	3.00	.90
10 Barry Bonds	2.00	.60

1994 Stadium Club Pre-Production

Issued to herald the release of 1994 Stadium Club Series I, the nine standard-size cards comprising this promo set feature on their fronts borderless color player action shots. The cards have the disclaimer "Pre-Production Sample" printed vertically running down the left edge of the back.

	Nm-Mt	Ex-Mt
COMPLETE SET (9)	6.00	1.80
6 Al Martin	.50	.15
15 Junior Ortiz	.50	.15
36 Tim Salmon	1.25	.35
56 Jerry Spradlin	.50	.15
122 Tom Pagnozzi	.50	.15
123 Ron Gant	.75	.23
125 Dennis Eckersley	1.50	.45
135 Jose Lind	.50	.15
238 Barry Bonds	2.50	.75

1994 Stadium Club

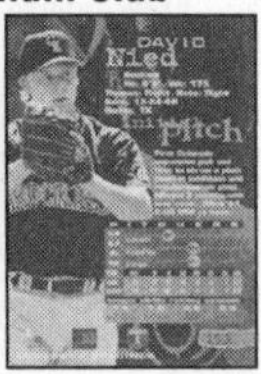

The 720 standard-size cards comprising this set were issued two series of 270 and a third series of 180. There are a number of subsets including Home Run Club (258-268), Tale of Two Players (525/526), Division Leaders (527-532), Quick Starts (533-538), Career Contributors (541-543), Rookie Rocker (626-630), Rookie Rocket (631-634) and Fantastic Finishes (714-719). Rookie Cards include Jeff Cirillo and Chan Ho Park.

	Nm-Mt	Ex-Mt
COMPLETE SET (720)	55.00	16.50
COMP.SERIES 1 (270)	20.00	6.00
COMP.SERIES 2 (270)	20.00	6.00
COMP.SERIES 3 (180)	15.00	4.50
1 Robin Yount	1.25	.35
2 Rick Wilkins	.15	.04
3 Steve Scarsone	.15	.04
4 Gary Sheffield	.30	.09
5 George Brett UER (birthdate listed as 1963; should be 1953)	2.00	.60
6 Al Martin	.15	.04
7 Joe Oliver	.15	.04
8 Stan Belinda	.15	.04
9 Denny Hocking	.15	.04
10 Roberto Alomar	.75	.23
11 Luis Polonia	.15	.04
12 Scott Hemond	.15	.04
13 Jody Reed	.15	.04
14 Mel Rojas	.15	.04
15 Junior Ortiz	.15	.04
16 Harold Baines	.30	.09
17 Brad Pennington	.15	.04
18 Jay Bell	.30	.09
19 Tom Henke	.15	.04
20 Jeff Branson	.15	.04
21 Roberto Mejia	.15	.04
22 Pedro Munoz	.15	.04
23 Matt Nokes	.15	.04
24 Jack McDowell	.15	.04
25 Cecil Fielder	.30	.09
26 Tony Fossas	.15	.04
27 Jim Eisenreich	.15	.04
28 Anthony Young	.15	.04
29 Chuck Carr	.15	.04
30 Jeff Treadway	.15	.04
31 Chris Nabholz	.15	.04
32 Tom Candiotti	.15	.04
33 Mike Maddux	.15	.04
34 Nolan Ryan	3.00	.90
35 Luis Gonzalez	.30	.09
36 Tim Salmon	.50	.15
37 Mark Whiten	.15	.04
38 Roger McDowell	.15	.04
39 Royce Clayton	.15	.04
40 Troy Neel	.15	.04
41 Mike Harkey	.15	.04
42 Darrin Fletcher	.15	.04
43 Wayne Kirby	.15	.04
44 Rich Amaral	.15	.04
45 Robb Nen UER (Nenn on back)	.30	.09
46 Tim Teufel	.15	.04
47 Steve Cooke	.15	.04
48 Jeff McNeely	.15	.04
49 Jeff Montgomery	.15	.04
50 Skeeter Barnes	.15	.04
51 Scott Stahoviak	.15	.04
52 Pat Kelly	.15	.04
53 Brady Anderson	.30	.09
54 Mariano Duncan	.15	.04
55 Brian Bohanon	.15	.04
56 Jerry Spradlin	.15	.04
57 Ron Karkovice	.15	.04
58 Jeff Gardner	.15	.04
59 Bobby Bonilla	.30	.09
60 Tino Martinez	.50	.15
61 Todd Benzinger	.15	.04
62 Steve Trachsel	.15	.04
63 Brian Jordan	.30	.09
64 Steve Bedrosian	.15	.04
65 Brent Gates	.15	.04
66 Shawn Green	.75	.23
67 Sean Berry	.15	.04
68 Joe Klink	.15	.04
69 Fernando Valenzuela	.30	.09
70 Andy Tomberlin	.15	.04
71 Tony Pena	.15	.04
72 Eric Young	.15	.04
73 Chris Gomez	.15	.04
74 Paul O'Neill	.50	.15
75 Ricky Gutierrez	.15	.04
76 Brad Holman	.15	.04
77 Lance Painter	.15	.04
78 Mike Butcher	.15	.04
79 Sid Bream	.15	.04
80 Sammy Sosa	1.25	.35
81 Felix Fermin	.15	.04
82 Todd Hundley	.15	.04
83 Kevin Higgins	.15	.04
84 Todd Pratt	.15	.04
85 Ken Griffey Jr.	1.25	.35
86 John O'Donoghue	.15	.04
87 Rick Renteria	.15	.04
88 John Burkett	.15	.04
89 Jose Vizcaino	.15	.04
90 Kevin Seitzer	.15	.04
91 Bobby Witt	.15	.04
92 Chris Turner	.15	.04
93 Omar Vizquel	.30	.09
94 David Justice	.30	.09
95 David Segui	.15	.04
96 Dave Hollins	.15	.04
97 Doug Strange	.15	.04
98 Jerald Clark	.15	.04
99 Mike Moore	.15	.04
100 Joey Cora	.15	.04
101 Scott Kamieniecki	.15	.04
102 Andy Benes	.15	.04
103 Chris Bosio	.15	.04
104 Rey Sanchez	.15	.04
105 John Jaha	.15	.04
106 Otis Nixon	.15	.04
107 Rickey Henderson	.75	.23
108 Jeff Bagwell	.50	.15
109 Gregg Jefferies	.15	.04
110 Roberto Alomar Paul Molitor John Olerud	.30	.09
111 Ron Gant David Justice Fred McGriff	.30	.09
112 Juan Gonzalez Rafael Palmeiro Dean Palmer	.50	.15
113 Greg Swindell	.15	.04
114 Bill Haselman	.15	.04
115 Phil Plantier	.15	.04
116 Ivan Rodriguez	.75	.23
117 Kevin Tapani	.15	.04
118 Mike LaValliere	.15	.04
119 Tim Costo	.15	.04
120 Mickey Morandini	.15	.04
121 Brett Butler	.30	.09
122 Tom Pagnozzi	.15	.04
123 Ron Gant	.30	.09
124 Damion Easley	.15	.04
125 Dennis Eckersley	.30	.09
126 Matt Mieske	.15	.04
127 Cliff Floyd	.30	.09
128 Julian Tavarez RC	.30	.09
129 Arthur Rhodes	.15	.04
130 Dave West	.15	.04
131 Tim Naehring	.15	.04
132 Freddie Benavides	.15	.04
133 Paul Assenmacher	.15	.04
134 David McCarty	.15	.04
135 Jose Lind	.15	.04
136 Reggie Sanders	.30	.09
137 Don Slaught	.15	.04
138 Andujar Cedeno	.15	.04
139 Rob Deer	.15	.04
140 Mike Piazza UER (listed as outfielder)	1.50	.45
141 Moises Alou	.30	.09
142 Tom Foley	.15	.04
143 Benito Santiago	.30	.09
144 Sandy Alomar Jr.	.15	.04
145 Carlos Hernandez	.15	.04
146 Luis Alicea	.15	.04
147 Tom Lampkin	.15	.04
148 Ryan Klesko	.30	.09
149 Juan Guzman	.15	.04
150 Scott Servais	.15	.04
151 Tony Gwynn	1.00	.30
152 Tim Wakefield	.30	.09
153 David Nied	.15	.04
154 Chris Haney	.15	.04
155 Danny Bautista	.15	.04
156 Randy Velarde	.15	.04
157 Darrin Jackson	.15	.04
158 J.R. Phillips	.15	.04
159 Greg Gagne	.15	.04
160 Luis Aquino	.15	.04
161 John Vander Wal	.15	.04
162 Randy Myers	.15	.04
163 Ted Power	.15	.04
164 Scott Brosius	.30	.09
165 Len Dykstra	.30	.09
166 Jacob Brumfield	.15	.04
167 Bo Jackson	.75	.23
168 Eddie Taubensee	.15	.04
169 Carlos Baerga	.15	.04
170 Tim Bogar	.15	.04
171 Jose Canseco	.75	.23
172 Greg Blosser UER (Gregg on front)	.15	.04
173 Chili Davis	.30	.09
174 Randy Knorr	.15	.04
175 Mike Perez	.15	.04
176 Henry Rodriguez	.15	.04
177 Brian Turang RC	.15	.04
178 Roger Pavlik	.15	.04
179 Aaron Sele	.15	.04
180 Fred McGriff Gary Sheffield	.50	.15
181 J.T. Snow Tim Salmon	.50	.15
182 Roberto Hernandez	.15	.04
183 Jeff Reboulet	.15	.04
184 John Doherty	.15	.04
185 Danny Sheaffer	.15	.04
186 Bip Roberts	.15	.04
187 Dennis Martinez	.30	.09
188 Darryl Hamilton	.15	.04
189 Eduardo Perez	.15	.04
190 Pete Harnisch	.15	.04
191 Rich Gossage	.30	.09
192 Mickey Tettleton	.15	.04
193 Lenny Webster	.15	.04
194 Lance Johnson	.15	.04
195 Don Mattingly	2.00	.60
196 Gregg Olson	.15	.04
197 Mark Gubicza	.15	.04
198 Scott Fletcher	.15	.04
199 Jon Shave	.15	.04
200 Tim Mauser	.15	.04
201 Jeromy Burnitz	.30	.09
202 Rob Dibble	.30	.09
203 Will Clark	.75	.23
204 Steve Buechele	.15	.04
205 Brian Williams	.15	.04
206 Carlos Garcia	.15	.04
207 Mark Clark	.15	.04
208 Rafael Palmeiro	.50	.15
209 Eric Davis	.30	.09
210 Pat Meares	.15	.04
211 Chuck Finley	.30	.09
212 Jason Bere	.15	.04
213 Gary DiSarcina	.15	.04
214 Tony Fernandez	.15	.04
215 B.J. Surhoff	.30	.09
216 Lee Guetterman	.15	.04
217 Tim Wallach	.15	.04
218 Kirt Manwaring	.15	.04
219 Albert Belle	.30	.09
220 Dwight Gooden	.50	.15
221 Archi Cianfrocco	.15	.04
222 Terry Mulholland	.15	.04
223 Hipolito Pichardo	.15	.04
224 Kent Hrbek	.30	.09
225 Craig Grebeck	.15	.04
226 Todd Jones	.15	.04
227 Mike Bordick	.15	.04
228 John Olerud	.30	.09
229 Jeff Blauser	.15	.04
230 Alex Arias	.15	.04
231 Bernard Gilkey	.15	.04
232 Denny Neagle	.30	.09
233 Pedro Borbon	.15	.04
234 Dick Schofield	.15	.04
235 Matias Carrillo	.15	.04
236 Juan Bell	.15	.04
237 Mike Hampton	.30	.09
238 Barry Bonds	2.00	.60
239 Cris Carpenter	.15	.04
240 Eric Karros	.30	.09
241 Greg McMichael	.15	.04
242 Pat Hentgen	.15	.04
243 Tim Pugh	.15	.04
244 Vinny Castilla	.30	.09
245 Charlie Hough	.30	.09
246 Bobby Munoz	.15	.04
247 Kevin Baez	.15	.04
248 Todd Frohwirth	.15	.04
249 Charlie Hayes	.15	.04
250 Mike Macfarlane	.15	.04
251 Danny Darwin	.15	.04
252 Ben Rivera	.15	.04
253 Dave Henderson	.15	.04
254 Steve Avery	.15	.04
255 Tim Belcher	.15	.04
256 Dan Plesac	.15	.04
257 Jim Thome	.75	.23
258 Albert Belle HR	.30	.09
259 Barry Bonds HR	1.00	.30
260 Ron Gant HR	.15	.04
261 Juan Gonzalez HR	.50	.15
262 Ken Griffey Jr. HR	.75	.23
263 David Justice HR	.15	.04
264 Fred McGriff HR	.30	.09
265 Rafael Palmeiro HR	.30	.09
266 Mike Piazza HR	.75	.23
267 Frank Thomas HR	.50	.15
268 Matt Williams HR	.15	.04
269 Checklist 1-135	.15	.04
270 Checklist 136-270	.15	.04
271 Mike Stanley	.15	.04
272 Tony Tarasco	.15	.04
273 Teddy Higuera	.15	.04
274 Ryan Thompson	.15	.04
275 Rick Aguilera	.15	.04
276 Ramon Martinez	.15	.04
277 Orlando Merced	.15	.04
278 Guillermo Velasquez	.15	.04
279 Mark Hutton	.15	.04
280 Larry Walker	.50	.15
281 Kevin Gross	.15	.04
282 Jose Offerman	.15	.04
283 Jim Leyritz	.15	.04
284 Jamie Moyer	.30	.09
285 Frank Thomas	.75	.23
286 Derek Bell	.15	.04
287 Derrick May	.15	.04
288 Dave Winfield	.30	.09
289 Curt Schilling	.50	.15
290 Carlos Quintana	.15	.04
291 Bob Natal	.15	.04
292 David Cone	.30	.09
293 Al Osuna	.15	.04
294 Bob Hamelin	.15	.04
295 Chad Curtis	.15	.04
296 Danny Jackson	.15	.04
297 Bob Welch	.15	.04
298 Felix Jose	.15	.04
299 Jay Buhner	.30	.09
300 Joe Carter	.30	.09
301 Kenny Lofton	.30	.09
302 Kirk Rueter	.30	.09
303 Kim Batiste	.15	.04
304 Mike Morgan	.15	.04
305 Pat Borders	.15	.04
306 Rene Arocha	.15	.04
307 Ruben Sierra	.15	.04
308 Steve Finley	.30	.09
309 Travis Fryman	.30	.09
310 Zane Smith	.15	.04
311 Willie Wilson	.15	.04
312 Trevor Hoffman	.30	.09
313 Terry Pendleton	.30	.09
314 Salomon Torres	.15	.04
315 Robin Ventura	.30	.09
316 Randy Tomlin	.15	.04
317 Dave Stewart	.30	.09
318 Mike Benjamin	.15	.04
319 Matt Turner	.15	.04
320 Manny Ramirez	.50	.15
321 Kevin Young	.15	.04
322 Ken Caminiti	.30	.09
323 Joe Girardi	.15	.04
324 Jeff McKnight	.15	.04
325 Gene Harris	.15	.04
326 Devon White	.15	.04
327 Darryl Kile	.30	.09
328 Craig Paquette	.15	.04
329 Cal Eldred	.15	.04
330 Bill Swift	.15	.04
331 Alan Trammell	.50	.15
332 Armando Reynoso	.15	.04
333 Brent Mayne	.15	.04
334 Chris Donnels	.15	.04
335 Darryl Strawberry	.50	.15
336 Dean Palmer	.30	.09
337 Frank Castillo	.15	.04
338 Jeff King	.15	.04
339 John Franco	.30	.09
340 Kevin Appier	.30	.09
341 Lance Blankenship	.15	.04
342 Mark McLemore	.15	.04
343 Pedro Astacio	.15	.04
344 Rich Batchelor	.15	.04
345 Ryan Bowen	.15	.04
346 Terry Steinbach	.15	.04
347 Troy O'Leary	.15	.04
348 Willie Blair	.15	.04
349 Wade Boggs	.50	.15
350 Tim Raines	.30	.09
351 Scott Livingstone	.15	.04
352 Rod Correia	.15	.04
353 Ray Lankford	.15	.04
354 Pat Listach	.15	.04
355 Milt Thompson	.15	.04
356 Miguel Jimenez	.15	.04
357 Marc Newfield	.15	.04
358 Mark McGwire	2.00	.60
359 Kirby Puckett	.75	.23
360 Kent Mercker	.15	.04
361 John Kruk	.30	.09
362 Jeff Kent	.30	.09
363 Hal Morris	.15	.04
364 Edgar Martinez	.50	.15
365 Dave Magadan	.15	.04
366 Dante Bichette	.30	.09
367 Chris Hammond	.15	.04
368 Bret Saberhagen	.30	.09
369 Billy Ripken	.15	.04
370 Bill Gullickson	.15	.04
371 Andre Dawson	.30	.09
372 Roberto Kelly	.15	.04
373 Cal Ripken	2.50	.75
374 Craig Biggio	.50	.15
375 Dan Pasqua	.15	.04
376 Dave Nilsson	.15	.04
377 Duane Ward	.15	.04
378 Greg Vaughn	.30	.09
379 Jeff Fassero	.15	.04
380 Jerry DiPoto	.15	.04
381 John Patterson	.15	.04
382 Kevin Brown	.30	.09
383 Kevin Roberson	.15	.04
384 Joe Orsulak	.15	.04
385 Hilly Hathaway	.15	.04
386 Mike Greenwell	.15	.04
387 Orestes Destrade	.15	.04
388 Mike Gallego	.15	.04
389 Ozzie Guillen	.15	.04
390 Raul Mondesi	.30	.09
391 Scott Lydy	.15	.04
392 Tom Urbani	.15	.04
393 Wil Cordero	.15	.04
394 Tony Longmire	.15	.04
395 Todd Zeile	.15	.04
396 Scott Cooper	.15	.04
397 Ryne Sandberg	1.25	.35
398 Ricky Bones	.15	.04
399 Phil Clark	.15	.04
400 Orel Hershiser	.30	.09
401 Mike Henneman	.15	.04
402 Mark Lemke	.15	.04
403 Mark Grace	.50	.15
404 Ken Ryan	.15	.04
405 John Smoltz	.50	.15
406 Jeff Conine	.30	.09
407 Greg Harris	.15	.04
408 Doug Drabek	.15	.04
409 Dave Fleming	.15	.04
410 Danny Tartabull	.15	.04
411 Chad Kreuter	.15	.04
412 Brad Ausmus	.15	.04
413 Ben McDonald	.15	.04
414 Barry Larkin	.75	.23
415 Bret Barberie	.15	.04
416 Chuck Knoblauch	.30	.09
417 Ozzie Smith	1.25	.35
418 Ed Sprague	.15	.04
419 Matt Williams	.30	.09
420 Jeremy Hernandez	.15	.04
421 Jose Bautista	.15	.04
422 Kevin Mitchell	.15	.04
423 Manuel Lee	.15	.04
424 Mike Devereaux	.15	.04
425 Omar Olivares	.15	.04
426 Rafael Belliard	.15	.04
427 Richie Lewis	.15	.04
428 Ron Darling	.15	.04
429 Shane Mack	.15	.04
430 Tim Hulett	.15	.04
431 Wally Joyner	.30	.09
432 Wes Chamberlain	.15	.04
433 Tom Browning	.15	.04
434 Scott Radinsky	.15	.04
435 Rondell White	.30	.09
436 Rod Beck	.15	.04
437 Rheal Cormier	.15	.04
438 Randy Johnson	.75	.23
439 Pete Schourek	.15	.04
440 Mo Vaughn	.30	.09
441 Mike Timlin	.15	.04
442 Mark Langston	.15	.04
443 Lou Whitaker	.30	.09

444 Kevin Stocker .15 .04
445 Ken Hill .15 .04
446 John Wetteland .30 .09
447 J.T. Snow .30 .09
448 Erik Pappas .15 .04
449 David Hulse .15 .04
450 Darren Daulton .30 .09
451 Chris Hoiles .15 .04
452 Bryan Harvey .15 .04
453 Darren Lewis .15 .04
454 Andres Galarraga .30 .09
455 Joe Hesketh .15 .04
456 Jose Valentin .15 .04
457 Dan Peltier .15 .04
458 Joe Boever .15 .04
459 Kevin Rogers .15 .04
460 Craig Shipley .15 .04
461 Alvaro Espinoza .15 .04
462 Wilson Alvarez .15 .04
463 Cory Snyder .15 .04
464 Candy Maldonado .15 .04
465 Blas Minor .15 .04
466 Rod Bolton .15 .04
467 Kenny Rogers .30 .09
468 Greg Myers .15 .04
469 Jimmy Key .30 .09
470 Tony Castillo .15 .04
471 Mike Stanton .15 .04
472 Deion Sanders .50 .15
473 Tito Navarro .15 .04
474 Mike Gardiner .15 .04
475 Steve Reed .15 .04
476 John Roper .15 .04
477 Mike Trombley .15 .04
478 Charles Nagy .15 .04
479 Larry Casian .15 .04
480 Eric Hillman .15 .04
481 Bill Wertz .15 .04
482 Jeff Schwarz .15 .04
483 John Valentin .15 .04
484 Carl Willis .15 .04
485 Gary Gaetti .30 .09
486 Bill Pecota .15 .04
487 John Smiley .15 .04
488 Mike Mussina .75 .23
489 Mike Ignasiak .15 .04
490 Billy Brewer .15 .04
491 Jack Voigt .15 .04
492 Mike Munoz .15 .04
493 Lee Tinsley .15 .04
494 Bob Wickman .15 .04
495 Roger Salkeld .15 .04
496 Thomas Howard .15 .04
497 Mark Davis .15 .04
498 Dave Clark .15 .04
499 Turk Wendell .15 .04
500 Rafael Bournigal .15 .04
501 Chip Hale .15 .04
502 Matt Whiteside .15 .04
503 Brian Koelling .15 .04
504 Jeff Reed .15 .04
505 Paul Wagner .15 .04
506 Torey Lovullo .15 .04
507 Curt Leskanic .15 .04
508 Derek Lilliquist .15 .04
509 Joe Magrane .15 .04
510 Mackey Sasser .15 .04
511 Lloyd McClendon .15 .04
512 Jayhawk Owens .15 .04
513 Woody Williams .15 .04
514 Gary Redus .15 .04
515 Tim Spehr .15 .04
516 Jim Abbott .50 .15
517 Lou Frazier .15 .04
518 Erik Plantenberg RC .15 .04
519 Tim Worrell .15 .04
520 Brian McRae .15 .04
521 Chan Ho Park RC .75 .23
522 Mark Wohlers .15 .04
523 Geronimo Pena .15 .04
524 Andy Ashby .15 .04
525 Tim Raines .15 .04
Andre Dawson TALE
526 Paul Molitor TALE .30 .09
527 Joe Carter DL .15 .04
528 F.Thomas DL UER .50 .15
listed as third in RBI in 1993; was actually second
529 Ken Griffey Jr. DL .75 .23
530 David Justice DL .15 .04
531 Gregg Jefferies DL .15 .04
532 Barry Bonds DL 1.00 .30
533 John Kruk QS .15 .04
534 Roger Clemens QS .75 .23
535 Cecil Fielder QS .15 .04
536 Ruben Sierra QS .15 .04
537 Tony Gwynn QS .50 .15
538 Tom Glavine QS .30 .09
539 CL 271-405 UER .15 .04
number on back is 269
540 CL 406-540 UER .15 .04
numbered 270 on back
541 Ozzie Smith ATL .75 .23
542 Eddie Murray ATL .50 .15
543 Lee Smith ATL .15 .04
544 Greg Maddux 1.25 .35
545 Denis Boucher .15 .04
546 Mark Gardner .15 .04
547 Bo Jackson .75 .23
548 Eric Anthony .15 .04
549 Delino DeShields .15 .04
550 Turner Ward .15 .04
551 Scott Sanderson .15 .04
552 Hector Carrasco .15 .04
553 Tony Phillips .15 .04
554 Melido Perez .15 .04
555 Mike Felder .15 .04
556 Jack Morris .30 .09
557 Rafael Palmeiro .50 .15
558 Shane Reynolds .15 .04
559 Pete Incaviglia .15 .04
560 Greg Harris .15 .04
561 Matt Walbeck .15 .04
562 Todd Van Poppel .15 .04
563 Todd Stottlemyre .15 .04
564 Ricky Bones .15 .04
565 Mike Jackson .15 .04
566 Kevin McReynolds .15 .04
567 Melvin Nieves .15 .04
568 Juan Gonzalez .75 .23
569 Frank Viola .30 .09
570 Vince Coleman .15 .04
571 Brian Anderson RC .30 .09
572 Omar Vizquel .30 .09
573 Bernie Williams .50 .15
574 Tom Glavine .50 .15
575 Mitch Williams .15 .04
576 Shawon Dunston .15 .04
577 Mike Lansing .15 .04
578 Greg Pirkl .15 .04
579 Sid Fernandez .15 .04
580 Doug Jones .15 .04
581 Walt Weiss .15 .04
582 Tim Belcher .15 .04
583 Alex Fernandez .15 .04
584 Alex Cole .15 .04
585 Greg Cadaret .15 .04
586 Bob Tewksbury .15 .04
587 Dave Hansen .15 .04
588 Kurt Abbott RC .30 .09
589 Rick White RC .15 .04
590 Kevin Bass .15 .04
591 Geronimo Berroa .15 .04
592 Jaime Navarro .15 .04
593 Steve Farr .15 .04
594 Jack Armstrong .15 .04
595 Steve Howe .15 .04
596 Jose Rijo .15 .04
597 Otis Nixon .15 .04
598 Robby Thompson .15 .04
599 Kelly Stinnett RC .30 .09
600 Carlos Delgado .50 .15
601 Brian Johnson RC .15 .04
602 Gregg Olson .15 .04
603 Jim Edmonds .50 .15
604 Mike Blowers .15 .04
605 Lee Smith .30 .09
606 Pat Rapp .15 .04
607 Mike Magnante .15 .04
608 Karl Rhodes .15 .04
609 Jeff Juden .15 .04
610 Rusty Meacham .15 .04
611 Pedro Martinez .75 .23
612 Todd Worrell .15 .04
613 Stan Javier .15 .04
614 Mike Hampton .30 .09
615 Jose Guzman .15 .04
616 Xavier Hernandez .15 .04
617 David Wells .30 .09
618 John Habyan .15 .04
619 Chris Nabholz .15 .04
620 Bobby Jones .15 .04
621 Chris James .15 .04
622 Ellis Burks .30 .09
623 Erik Hanson .15 .04
624 Pat Meares .15 .04
625 Harold Reynolds .30 .09
626 Bob Hamelin RR .15 .04
627 Manny Ramirez RR .30 .09
628 Ryan Klesko RR .30 .09
629 Carlos Delgado RR .30 .09
630 Javier Lopez RR .30 .09
631 Steve Karsay RR .15 .04
632 Rick Helling RR .15 .04
633 Steve Trachsel RR .15 .04
634 Hector Carrasco RR .15 .04
635 Andy Stankiewicz .15 .04
636 Paul Sorrento .15 .04
637 Scott Erickson .15 .04
638 Chipper Jones .75 .23
639 Luis Polonia .15 .04
640 Howard Johnson .15 .04
641 John Dopson .15 .04
642 Jody Reed .15 .04
643 Lonnie Smith UER .15 .04
Card numbered 543
644 Mark Portugal .15 .04
645 Paul Molitor .50 .15
646 Paul Assenmacher .15 .04
647 Hubie Brooks .15 .04
648 Gary Wayne .15 .04
649 Sean Berry .15 .04
650 Roger Clemens 1.50 .45
651 Brian R. Hunter .15 .04
652 Wally Whitehurst .15 .04
653 Allen Watson .15 .04
654 Rickey Henderson .75 .23
655 Sid Bream .15 .04
656 Dan Wilson .15 .04
657 Ricky Jordan .15 .04
658 Sterling Hitchcock .15 .04
659 Darrin Jackson .15 .04
660 Junior Felix .15 .04
661 Tom Brunansky .15 .04
662 Jose Vizcaino .15 .04
663 Mark Leiter .15 .04
664 Gil Heredia .15 .04
665 Fred McGriff .50 .15
666 Will Clark .75 .23
667 Al Leiter .30 .09
668 James Mouton .15 .04
669 Billy Bean .15 .04
670 Scott Leius .15 .04
671 Bret Boone .30 .09
672 Darren Holmes .15 .04
673 Dave Weathers .15 .04
674 Eddie Murray .75 .23
675 Felix Fermin .15 .04
676 Chris Sabo .15 .04
677 Billy Spiers .15 .04
678 Aaron Sele .15 .04
679 Juan Samuel .15 .04
680 Julio Franco .30 .09
681 Heathcliff Slocumb .15 .04
682 Dennis Martinez .30 .09
683 Jerry Browne .15 .04
684 Pedro Martinez RC .15 .04
685 Rex Hudler .15 .04
686 Willie McGee .30 .09
687 Andy Van Slyke .30 .09
688 Pat Mahomes .15 .04
689 Dave Henderson .15 .04
690 Tony Eusebio .15 .04
691 Rick Sutcliffe .30 .09
692 Willie Banks .15 .04
693 Alan Mills .15 .04
694 Jeff Treadway .15 .04
695 Alex Gonzalez .15 .04
696 David Segui .15 .04
697 Rick Helling .15 .04
698 Bip Roberts .15 .04
699 Jeff Cirillo RC .75 .23
700 Terry Mulholland .15 .04
701 Marvin Freeman .15 .04
702 Jason Bere .15 .04
703 Javier Lopez .30 .09
704 Greg Hibbard .15 .04
705 Tommy Greene .15 .04
706 Marquis Grissom .15 .04
707 Brian Harper .15 .04
708 Steve Karsay .15 .04
709 Jeff Brantley .15 .04
710 Jeff Russell .15 .04
711 Bryan Hickerson .15 .04
712 Jim Pittsley RC .15 .04
713 Bobby Ayala .15 .04
714 John Smoltz .50 .15
715 Jose Rijo .15 .04
716 Greg Maddux .75 .23
717 Matt Williams .15 .04
718 Frank Thomas .50 .15
719 Ryne Sandberg .75 .23
720 Checklist .15 .04

1994 Stadium Club First Day Issue

Randomly inserted in one of every 24 packs, these First Day Production cards are identical to the regular issues except for a special 1st Day foil stamp engraved on the front of each card. No more than 2,000 of each Stadium Club card was issued as First Day Issue. Some FDI logos have been transferred from "common" players to the front of "star" players.

Nm-Mt Ex-Mt
*STARS: 8X TO 20X BASIC CARDS
*ROOKIES: 6X to 15X BASIC CARDS

1994 Stadium Club Golden Rainbow

Parallel to the basic Stadium Club set, Golden Rainbows differ in that the player's last name on front has gold refracting foil over it. The cards were inserted one per Stadium Club foil pack and two per jumbo.

	Nm-Mt	Ex-Mt
COMPLETE SET (720)	160.00	47.50
COMP.SERIES 1 (270)	60.00	18.00
COMP.SERIES 2 (270)	60.00	18.00
COMP.SERIES 3 (180)	40.00	12.00

*STARS: 1.25X TO 3X BASIC CARDS
*ROOKIES: 1X TO 2.5X BASIC CARDS

1994 Stadium Club Members Only Parallel

This set, issued only to Topps Stadium Club Members, is a parallel of the regular Stadium Club set. This set was issued in factory set form only and includes parallel versions of both the basic issue and insert cards from the 1994 Stadium Club set. According to Topps, 5,000 sets were produced. However, some dealers believe less cards than that were actually produced. Only the insert cards have been listed below. Please use the multiplier for values on the basic issue cards.

Nm-Mt Ex-Mt
COMP.FACT.SET (770) 200.00 60.00
*1ST SERIES MEMBERS ONLY: 4X BASIC CARDS
2ND AND 3RD SERIES MEMBERS ONLY STARS: 6X BASIC CARDS
F1 Jeff Bagwell 4.00 1.20
F2 Albert Belle 1.50 .45
F3 Barry Bonds 8.00 2.40
F4 Juan Gonzalez 3.00 .90
F5 Ken Griffey Jr. 12.00 3.60
F6 Marquis Grissom 1.00 .30
F7 David Justice 3.00 .90
F8 Mike Piazza 8.00 2.40
F9 Tim Salmon 3.00 .90
F10 Frank Thomas 6.00 1.80
DD1 Mike Piazza 8.00 2.40
DD2 Dave Winfield 3.00 .90
DD3 John Kruk 1.50 .45
DD4 Cal Ripken 15.00 4.50
DD5 Jack McDowell 6.00 1.80
DD6 Barry Bonds 8.00 2.40
DD7 Ken Griffey Jr. 12.00 3.60
DD8 Tim Salmon 3.00 .90
DD9 Frank Thomas 5.00 1.50
DD10 Jeff Kent 3.00 .90
DD11 Randy Johnson 4.00 1.20
DD12 Darren Daulton 1.50 .45
ST1 Jeff Blauser .75 .23
Terry Pendleton
ST2 Sammy Sosa 1.50 .45
Derrick May
ST3 Reggie Sanders 1.00 .30
Barry Larkin
ST4 Vinny Castilla .50 .15
Eric Young
ST5 Alex Arias .50 .15
ST6 Eric Anthony .75 .23
Steve Finley
ST7 Mike Piazza 5.00 1.50
ST8 Marquis Grissom .75 .23
ST9 Bobby Bonilla .50 .15
ST10 Mickey Morandini .50 .15
ST11 Andy Van Slyke .75 .23
Jay Bell
ST12 Todd Zeile .50 .15
Gregg Jefferies
ST13 Ricky Gutierrez .50 .15
ST14 Matt Williams 1.00 .30
Kirt Manwaring
ST15 Cal Ripken 6.00 1.80
ST16 Luis Rivera .50 .15
John Valentin
ST17 Tim Salmon 1.50 .45
ST18 Ozzie Guillen .50 .15
ST19 Kenny Lofton 1.00 .30
Carlos Baerga
Albert Belle
ST20 Alan Trammell .75 .23
Tony Phillips
ST21 Jose Lind .50 .15
Curt Wilkerson
ST22 Pat Listach .50 .15
John Jaha
Cal Eldred
ST23 Kirby Puckett 3.00 .90
Kent Hrbek
ST24 Don Mattingly 3.00 .90
Bernie Williams
ST25 Mike Bordick .50 .15
Brent Gates
ST26 Jay Buhner 1.00 .30
Mike Blowers
ST27 Ivan Rodriguez 1.50 .45
Dean Palmer
Jose Canseco
Juan Gonzalez
ST28 John Olerud .50 .15

1994 Stadium Club Dugout Dirt

Randomly inserted at a rate of one per six packs, these standard-size cards feature some of baseball's most popular and colorful players by sports cartoonists Daniel Guidera and Steve Benson. The cards resemble basic Stadium Club cards except for a Dugout Dirt logo at the bottom. Backs contain a cartoon. Cards 1-4 were found in first series packs with cards 5-8 and 9-12 were inserted in second series and third series packs respectively.

	Nm-Mt	Ex-Mt
COMPLETE SERIES 1 (4)	5.00	1.50
COMPLETE SERIES 2 (4)	3.00	.90
COMPLETE SERIES 3 (4)	3.00	.90
DD1 Mike Piazza	1.50	.45
DD2 Dave Winfield	.30	.09
DD3 John Kruk	.30	.09
DD4 Cal Ripken	2.50	.75
DD5 Jack McDowell	.15	.04
DD6 Barry Bonds	2.00	.60
DD7 Ken Griffey Jr.	1.25	.35
DD8 Tim Salmon	.50	.15
DD9 Frank Thomas	.75	.23
DD10 Jeff Kent	.30	.09
DD11 Randy Johnson	.75	.23
DD12 Darren Daulton	.30	.09

1994 Stadium Club Finest

This set contains 10 standard-size metallic cards of top players. They were randomly inserted one in six third series packs. Jumbo versions measuring approximately five inches by seven inches were issued for retail repacks.

Nm-Mt Ex-Mt
COMPLETE SET (10) 25.00 7.50
*JUMBOS: .6X TO 1.5X BASIC SC FINEST
JUMBOS DISTRIBUTED IN RETAIL PACKS
F1 Jeff Bagwell 1.50 .45
F2 Albert Belle 1.00 .30
F3 Barry Bonds 6.00 1.80
F4 Juan Gonzalez 2.50 .75
F5 Ken Griffey Jr. 4.00 1.20
F6 Marquis Grissom .50 .15
F7 David Justice 1.00 .30
F8 Mike Piazza 5.00 1.50
F9 Tim Salmon 1.50 .45
F10 Frank Thomas 2.50 .75

1994 Stadium Club Super Teams

Randomly inserted at a rate of one per 24 first series packs only, this 28-card standard-size features one card for each of the 28 MLB teams. Collectors holding team cards could redeem them for special prizes if those teams won a division title, a league championship, or the World Series. But, since the strike affected the 1994 season, Topps postponed the promotion until the 1995 season. The expiration was pushed back to January 31, 1996.

Nm-Mt Ex-Mt
COMPLETE SET (28) 50.00 15.00
ST1 Jeff Blauser 2.50 .75
Terry Pendleton
ST2 Sammy Sosa 1.00 .30
Derrick May
ST3 Reggie Sanders 2.50 .75
Barry Larkin
ST4 Vinny Castilla 1.00 .30
Eric Young
ST5 Alex Arias 1.00 .30
ST6 Eric Anthony 1.00 .30
Steve Finley
ST7 Mike Piazza 5.00 1.50
ST8 Marquis Grissom 1.00 .30
ST9 Bobby Bonilla 1.00 .30
ST10 Mickey Morandini 1.00 .30
ST11 Andy Van Slyke 1.00 .30
Jay Bell
ST12 Todd Zeile 1.00 .30
Gregg Jefferies
ST13 Ricky Gutierrez 1.00 .30
ST14 Matt Williams 1.00 .30
Kirt Manwaring
ST15 Cal Ripken 8.00 2.40
ST16 Luis Rivera 1.00 .30
John Valentin
ST17 Tim Salmon 1.00 .30
ST18 Joey Cora 1.00 .30
ST19 Kenny Lofton 1.00 .30
Carlos Baerga
Albert Belle
ST20 (Alan Trammell 1.00 .30
Tony Phillips
ST21 Jose Lind 1.00 .30
Curt Wilkerson
ST22 Pat Listach 1.00 .30
John Jaha
Cal Eldred
ST23 Kirby Puckett 2.50 .75
Kent Hrbek
ST24 Don Mattingly 6.00 1.80
Bernie Williams
ST25 Mike Bordick 1.00 .30
Brent Gates
ST26 Jay Buhner 1.00 .30
Mike Blowers
ST27 Ivan Rodriguez 2.50 .75
Dean Palmer
Jose Canseco
Juan Gonzalez
ST28 John Olerud 1.00 .30

1994 Stadium Club Members Only

Issued to Stadium Club members, this 50-card standard-size set features 45 regular Stadium Club cards as well as five Stadium Club Finest cards.

	Nm-Mt	Ex-Mt
COMP. FACT SET (50)	20.00	6.00
1 Juan Gonzalez	.75	.23
2 Tom Henke	.10	.03
3 John Kruk	.25	.07
4 Paul Molitor	.75	.23
5 David Justice	.25	.07
6 Rafael Palmeiro	.60	.18
7 John Smoltz	.60	.18
8 Matt Williams	.40	.12
9 John Olerud	.25	.07
10 Mark Grace	.40	.12
11 Joe Carter	.25	.07
12 Wilson Alvarez	.25	.07
13 Len Dykstra	.25	.07
14 Kevin Appier	.25	.07
15 Andres Galarraga	.60	.18
16 Mark Langston	.10	.03
17 Ken Griffey Jr.	2.00	.60
18 Albert Belle	.25	.07
19 Gregg Jefferies	.10	.03
20 Duane Ward	.10	.03
21 Jack McDowell	.10	.03
22 Randy Johnson	.75	.23
23 Tom Glavine	.60	.18
24 Barry Bonds	1.50	.45
25 Chuck Carr	.10	.03
26 Ron Gant	.25	.07
27 Kenny Lofton	.40	.12
28 Mike Piazza	1.50	.45
29 Frank Thomas	1.00	.30
30 Fred McGriff	.40	.12
31 Bryan Harvey	.10	.03
32 John Burkett	.10	.03
33 Roberto Alomar	.60	.18
34 Cecil Fielder	.25	.07
35 Marquis Grissom	.25	.07
36 Randy Myers	.10	.03
37 Tony Phillips	.10	.03
38 Rickey Henderson	.75	.23
39 Luis Polonia	.10	.03
40 Jose Rijo	.10	.03
41 Jeff Montgomery	.10	.03
42 Greg Maddux	2.00	.60
43 Tony Gwynn	1.50	.45
44 Rod Beck	.10	.03
45 Carlos Baerga	.25	.07
46 Wil Cordero FIN	.50	.15
47 Tim Salmon FIN	2.00	.60
48 Mike Lansing FIN	.50	.15
49 J.T. Snow FIN	.50	.15
50 Jeff Conine FIN	.75	.23

1994 Stadium Club Members Only Finest Bronze

Available only to members who purchase the Members Only baseball set, this three-card set is the first edition of Topps Finest Bronze cards. Measuring 2 3/4" by 3 3/4", the cards are mounted on bronze and factory sealed in clear resin. On a colorful reflective background, the fronts display a player cutout that is highlighted by a circle design. In black lettering, the horizontal backs present biography as well as major and minor league batting record.

Nm-Mt Ex-Mt
COMPLETE SET (3) 30.00 9.00
1 Barry Bonds 12.00 3.60
2 Ken Griffey Jr. 15.00 4.50
3 Frank Thomas 10.00 3.00

1994 Stadium Club Team

This 360-card standard-size set features 30 players from 12 teams. The cards are checklisted alphabetically according to teams.

Nm-Mt Ex-Mt
COMPLETE SET (360) 40.00 12.00
1 Barry Bonds 1.50 .45
2 Royce Clayton .10 .03
3 Kirt Manwaring .10 .03
4 J.R. Phillips .10 .03
5 Robby Thompson .10 .03
6 Willie McGee .20 .06
7 Steve Hosey .10 .03
8 Dave Burba .10 .03
9 Steve Scarsone .10 .03
10 Salomon Torres .10 .03
11 Bryan Hickerson .10 .03
12 Mike Benjamin .10 .03
13 Mark Carreon .10 .03
14 Rich Monteleone .10 .03
15 Dave Martinez .10 .03
16 Bill Swift .10 .03
17 Jeff Reed .10 .03
18 John Patterson .10 .03
19 Darren Lewis .10 .03
20 Mark Portugal .10 .03
21 Trevor Wilson .10 .03
22 Matt Williams .40 .12
23 Kevin Rogers .10 .03
24 Luis Mercedes .10 .03
25 Mike Jackson .10 .03
26 Steve Frey .10 .03
27 Tony Menendez .10 .03
28 John Burkett .10 .03
29 Todd Benzinger .10 .03
30 Rod Beck .10 .03
31 Greg Maddux 2.00 .60
32 Steve Avery .10 .03
33 Milt Hill .10 .03
34 Charlie O'Brien .10 .03
35 John Smoltz .20 .06
36 Jarvis Brown .10 .03
37 Dave Gallagher .10 .03
Wearing Mets Uniform
38 Ryan Klesko .40 .12
39 Kent Mercker .10 .03
40 Terry Pendleton .10 .03
41 Ron Gant .20 .06
42 Pedro Borbon Jr. .10 .03
43 Steve Bedrosian .10 .03
44 Ramon Caraballo .10 .03
45 Tyler Houston .10 .03
46 Mark Lemke .10 .03
47 Fred McGriff .40 .12
48 Jose Oliva .10 .03
49 David Justice .60 .18
50 Chipper Jones 1.50 .45
51 Tony Tarasco .10 .03
52 Javier Lopez .40 .12
53 Mark Wohlers .10 .03
54 Deion Sanders .60 .18
55 Greg McMichael .10 .03
56 Tom Glavine .75 .23
57 Bill Pecota .10 .03
58 Mike Stanton .10 .03
59 Rafael Belliard .10 .03
60 Jeff Blauser .10 .03
61 Bryan Harvey .10 .03
62 Bret Barberie .10 .03
63 Rick Renteria .10 .03
64 Chris Hammond .10 .03
65 Pat Rapp .10 .03
66 Nigel Wilson .10 .03
67 Gary Sheffield .75 .23
68 Jerry Browne .10 .03
69 Charlie Hough .20 .06
70 Orestes Destrade .10 .03
71 Mario Diaz .10 .03
72 Ryan Bowen .10 .03
73 Carl Everett .20 .06
74 Richie Lewis .10 .03
75 Bob Natal .10 .03
76 Rich Rodriguez .10 .03
77 Darrell Whitmore .10 .03
78 Matt Turner .10 .03
79 Benito Santiago .20 .06
80 Robb Nen .20 .06
81 Dave Magadan .10 .03
82 Brian Drahman .10 .03
83 Mark Gardner .10 .03
84 Chuck Carr .10 .03
85 Alex Arias .10 .03
86 Kurt Abbott .10 .03
87 Joe Klink .10 .03
88 Jeff Mutis .10 .03
89 Dave Weathers .10 .03
90 Jeff Conine .20 .06
91 Andres Galarraga .60 .18
92 Vinny Castilla .20 .06
93 Roberto Mejia .10 .03
94 Darrell Sherman .10 .03
95 Mike Harkey .10 .03
96 Danny Sheaffer .10 .03
97 Pedro Castellano .10 .03
98 Walt Weiss .10 .03
99 Greg W. Harris .10 .03
100 Jayhawk Owens .10 .03
101 Bruce Ruffin .10 .03
102 Mike Munoz .10 .03
103 Armando Reynoso .10 .03
104 Eric Young .20 .06
105 Dante Bichette .20 .06
106 Marvin Freeman .10 .03
107 Joe Girardi .10 .03
108 Kent Bottenfield .10 .03
109 Howard Johnson .10 .03
110 Nelson Liriano .10 .03
111 David Nied .10 .03
112 Steve Reed .10 .03
113 Eric Wedge .20 .06
114 Charlie Hayes .10 .03
115 Ellis Burks .40 .12
116 Willie Blair .10 .03
117 Darren Holmes .10 .03
118 Curtis Leskanic .10 .03
119 Lance Painter .10 .03
120 Jim Tatum .10 .03
121 Frank Thomas 1.25 .35
122 Jack McDowell .10 .03
123 Ron Karkovice .10 .03
124 Mike LaValliere .10 .03
125 Scott Radinsky .10 .03
126 Robin Ventura .40 .12
127 Scott Ruffcorn .10 .03
128 Steve Sax .10 .03
129 Roberto Hernandez .20 .06
130 Jose DeLeon .10 .03
131 Rod Bolton .10 .03
132 Wilson Alvarez .10 .03
133 Craig Grebeck .10 .03
134 Lance Johnson .10 .03
135 Kirk McCaskill .10 .03
136 Tim Raines .20 .06
137 Jeff Schwarz .10 .03
138 Warren Newson .10 .03
139 Norberto Martin .10 .03
140 Mike Huff .10 .03
141 Ozzie Guillen .20 .06
142 Alex Fernandez .10 .03
143 Joey Cora .10 .03
144 Jason Bere .10 .03
145 James Baldwin .20 .06
146 Esteban Beltre .10 .03
147 Julio Franco .20 .06
148 Matt Merullo .10 .03
149 Dan Pasqua .10 .03
150 Darrin Jackson .10 .03
151 Joe Carter .20 .06
152 Danny Cox .10 .03
153 Roberto Alomar .60 .18
154 Woody Williams .20 .06
155 Duane Ward .10 .03
156 Ed Sprague .10 .03
157 Domingo Martinez .10 .03
158 Pat Hentgen .20 .06
159 Shawn Green .75 .23
160 Dick Schofield .10 .03
161 Paul Molitor .75 .23
162 Darnell Coles .10 .03
163 Willie Canate .10 .03
164 Domingo Cedeno .10 .03
165 Pat Borders .10 .03
166 Greg Cadaret .10 .03
167 Tony Castillo .10 .03
168 Carlos Delgado .75 .23
169 Scott Brow .10 .03
170 Juan Guzman .10 .03
171 Al Leiter .20 .06
172 John Olerud .40 .12
173 Todd Stottlemyre .10 .03
174 Devon White .20 .06
175 Paul Spoljaric .10 .03
176 Randy Knorr .10 .03
177 Huck Flener .10 .03
178 Rob Butler .10 .03
179 Dave Stewart .20 .06
180 Mike Timlin .10 .03
181 Don Mattingly 1.50 .45
182 Mark Hutton .10 .03
183 Mike Gallego .10 .03
184 Jim Abbott .20 .06
185 Paul Gibson .10 .03
186 Scott Kamieniecki .10 .03
187 Sam Horn .10 .03
188 Melido Perez .10 .03
189 Randy Velarde .10 .03
190 Gerald Williams .10 .03
191 Dave Silvestri .10 .03
192 Jim Leyritz .10 .03
193 Steve Howe .10 .03
194 Russ Davis .10 .03
195 Paul Assenmacher .10 .03
196 Pat Kelly .10 .03
197 Mike Stanley .10 .03
198 Bernie Williams .60 .18
199 Paul O'Neill .60 .18
200 Donn Pall .10 .03
201 Xavier Hernandez .10 .03
202 Jim Austin .10 .03
203 Sterling Hitchcock .20 .06
204 Wade Boggs .75 .23
205 Jimmy Key .20 .06
206 Matt Nokes .10 .03
207 Terry Mulholland .10 .03
208 Luis Polonia .10 .03
209 Danny Tartabull .20 .06
210 Bob Wickman .10 .03
211 Len Dykstra .20 .06
212 Kim Batiste .10 .03
213 Tony Longmire .10 .03
214 Bobby Munoz .10 .03
215 Pete Incaviglia .10 .03
216 Doug Jones .20 .06
217 Mariano Duncan .10 .03
218 Jeff Juden .10 .03
219 Milt Thompson .10 .03
220 Dave West .10 .03
221 Roger Mason .10 .03
222 Tommy Greene .10 .03
223 Larry Andersen .10 .03
224 Jim Eisenreich .10 .03
225 Dave Hollins .10 .03
226 John Kruk .20 .06
227 Todd Pratt .10 .03
228 Ricky Jordan .10 .03
229 Curt Schilling 1.00 .30
230 Mike Williams .10 .03
231 Heathcliff Slocumb .10 .03
232 Ben Rivera .10 .03
233 Mike Lieberthal .20 .06
234 Mickey Morandini .10 .03
235 Danny Jackson .10 .03
236 Kevin Foster .10 .03
237 Darren Daulton .20 .06
238 Wes Chamberlain .10 .03
239 Tyler Green .10 .03
240 Kevin Stocker .10 .03
241 Juan Gonzalez .75 .23
242 Rick Honeycutt .10 .03
243 Bruce Hurst .10 .03
244 Steve Dreyer .10 .03
245 Brian Bohanon .10 .03
246 Benji Gil .10 .03
247 Jon Shave .10 .03
248 Manuel Lee .10 .03
249 Donald Harris .10 .03
250 Jose Canseco .60 .18
251 David Hulse .10 .03
252 Kenny Rogers .10 .03
253 Jeff Huson .10 .03
254 Dan Peltier .10 .03
255 Mike Scioscia .20 .06
256 Jack Armstrong .10 .03
257 Rob Ducey .10 .03
258 Will Clark .60 .18
259 Cris Carpenter .10 .03
260 Kevin Brown .40 .12
261 Jeff Frye .10 .03
262 Jay Howell .10 .03
263 Roger Pavlik .10 .03
264 Gary Redus .10 .03
265 Ivan Rodriguez .75 .23
266 Matt Whiteside .10 .03
267 Doug Strange .10 .03
268 Billy Ripken .10 .03
269 Dean Palmer .20 .06
270 Tom Henke .10 .03
271 Cal Ripken 3.00 .90
272 Mark McLemore .20 .06
273 Sid Fernandez .20 .06
274 Sherman Obando .10 .03
275 Paul Carey .10 .03
276 Mike Oquist .10 .03
277 Alan Mills .10 .03
278 Harold Baines .20 .06
279 Mike Mussina .75 .23
280 Arthur Rhodes .10 .03
281 Kevin McGehee .10 .03
282 Mark Eichhorn .10 .03
283 Damon Buford .10 .03
284 Ben McDonald .10 .03
285 David Segui .20 .06
286 Brad Pennington .10 .03
287 Jamie Moyer .40 .12
288 Chris Hoiles .10 .03
289 Mike Cook .10 .03
290 Brady Anderson .20 .06
291 Chris Sabo .10 .03
292 Jack Voigt .10 .03
293 Jim Poole .10 .03
294 Jeff Tackett .10 .03
295 Rafael Palmeiro .60 .18
296 Alex Ochoa .10 .03
297 John O'Donoghue .10 .03
298 Tim Hulett .10 .03
299 Mike Devereaux .10 .03
300 Manny Alexander .10 .03
301 Ozzie Smith .75 .23
302 Omar Olivares .10 .03
303 Rheal Cormier .10 .03
304 Donovan Osborne .10 .03
305 Mark Whiten .10 .03
306 Todd Zeile .20 .06
307 Geronimo Pena .10 .03
308 Brian Jordan .20 .06
309 Luis Alicea .10 .03
310 Ray Lankford .20 .06
311 Stan Royer .10 .03
312 Bob Tewksbury .10 .03
313 Jose Oquendo .10 .03
314 Steve Dixon .10 .03
315 Rene Arocha .10 .03
316 Bernard Gilkey .10 .03
317 Gregg Jefferies .10 .03
318 Rob Murphy .10 .03
319 Tom Pagnozzi .10 .03
320 Mike Perez .10 .03
321 Tom Urbani .10 .03
322 Allen Watson .10 .03
323 Erik Pappas .10 .03
324 Paul Kilgus .10 .03
325 John Habyan .10 .03
326 Rod Brewer .10 .03
327 Rich Batchelor .10 .03
328 Tripp Cromer .10 .03
329 Gerald Perry .10 .03
330 Les Lancaster .10 .03
331 Ryne Sandberg 1.50 .45
332 Derrick May .10 .03
333 Steve Buechele .10 .03
334 Willie Banks .10 .03
335 Larry Luebbers .10 .03
336 Tommy Shields .10 .03
337 Eric Yelding .10 .03
338 Rey Sanchez .10 .03
339 Mark Grace .40 .12
340 Jose Bautista .10 .03
341 Frank Castillo .10 .03
342 Jose Guzman .10 .03
343 Rafael Novoa .10 .03
Wearing Milwaukee Brewer uniform
344 Karl Rhodes .10 .03
345 Steve Trachsel .10 .03
346 Rick Wilkins .10 .03
347 Sammy Sosa 1.50 .45
348 Kevin Roberson .10 .03
349 Mark Parent .10 .03
350 Randy Myers .20 .06
351 Glenallen Hill .10 .03
352 Lance Dickson .10 .03
353 Shawn Boskie .10 .03
354 Shawon Dunston .20 .06
355 Dan Plesac .10 .03
356 Jose Vizcaino .10 .03
357 Willie Wilson .10 .03
358 Turk Wendell .10 .03
359 Mike Morgan .10 .03
360 Jim Bullinger .10 .03

1994 Stadium Club Team First Day Issue

This 360-card standard-size set features 30 players from 12 teams. First Day Issue cards were randomly packed one in every six 12-card packs; the odds of finding these insert cards in 20-card jumbo packs are one in three. Also one 1st Day Issue card was included in the 30-card team sets sold in blister packs. They are identical in design with the regular Stadium Club Team cards except for a holographic "1st Day Issue" emblem on the fronts.

Nm-Mt Ex-Mt
*STARS: 10X to 20X BASIC CARDS ...

1994 Stadium Club Team Finest

This 12-card standard-size set consists of one player from each of the 12 teams featured in the 1994 Stadium Club team series. The cards were randomly inserted in 12-card foil packs. Also one card was included in the 30-card team sets sold in blister packs. The cards are identical in design with the regular series, except for the metallic sheen characteristic of the Finest series.

Nm-Mt Ex-Mt
COMPLETE SET (12) 30.00 9.00
1 Roberto Alomar 2.00 .60
2 Barry Bonds 5.00 1.50
3 Len Dykstra 1.00 .30
4 Andres Galarraga 2.00 .60
5 Juan Gonzalez 2.50 .75
6 David Justice 2.00 .60
7 Don Mattingly 4.00 1.20
8 Cal Ripken 10.00 3.00
9 Ryne Sandberg 5.00 1.50
10 Gary Sheffield 2.50 .75
11 Ozzie Smith 4.00 1.20
12 Frank Thomas 2.50 .75

1994 Stadium Club Draft Picks

This 90-card standard-size set features players chosen in the June 1994 MLB draft and photographed in their major league uniforms. Each 24-pack box included four First Day Issue Draft Pick cards randomly packed, one in every six packs. Early cards of Nomar Garciaparra, Ben Grieve and Terrence Long are featured in this set.

Nm-Mt Ex-Mt
COMPLETE SET (90) 15.00 4.50
1 Jacob Shumate XRC .25 .07
2 C.J. Nitkowski XRC .25 .07
3 Doug Million XRC .25 .07
4 Matt Smith XRC .25 .07
5 Kevin Lovinger XRC .25 .07
6 Alberto Castillo XRC .25 .07
7 Mike Russell XRC .25 .07
8 Dan Lock XRC .25 .07
9 Tom Szimanski XRC .25 .07
10 Aaron Boone XRC 2.50 .75
11 Jayson Peterson XRC .25 .07
12 Mark Johnson XRC .25 .07
13 Cade Gaspar XRC .25 .07
14 George Lombard XRC .40 .12
15 Russ Johnson .25 .07
16 Travis Miller XRC .25 .07
17 Jay Payton XRC .50 .15
18 Brian Buchanan XRC .25 .07
19 Jacob Cruz XRC .40 .12
20 Gary Rath XRC .25 .07
21 Ramon Castro XRC .25 .07
22 Tommy Davis XRC .25 .07
23 Tony Terry XRC .25 .07
24 Jerry Whittaker XRC .25 .07
25 Mike Darr XRC .40 .12
26 Doug Webb XRC .25 .07
27 Jason Camilli XRC .25 .07
28 Brad Rigby XRC .25 .07
29 Ryan Nye XRC .25 .07
30 Carl Dale XRC .25 .07
31 Andy Taulbee XRC .25 .07
32 Trey Moore XRC .25 .07
33 John Crowther XRC .25 .07
34 Joe Giuliano XRC .25 .07
35 Brian Rose XRC .25 .07
36 Paul Failla XRC .25 .07
37 Brian Meadows XRC .25 .07
38 Oscar Robles XRC .25 .07
39 Mike Metcalfe XRC .25 .07
40 Larry Barnes XRC .25 .07
41 Paul Ottavinia XRC .25 .07
42 Chris McBride XRC .25 .07
43 Ricky Stone XRC .25 .07
44 Billy Blythe XRC .25 .07
45 Eddie Priest XRC .25 .07
46 Scott Forster XRC .25 .07
47 Eric Pickett XRC .25 .07
48 Matt Beaumont .25 .07
49 Darrell Nicholas XRC .25 .07
50 Mike A. Hampton XRC .25 .07
51 Paul O'Malley XRC .25 .07
52 Steve Shoemaker XRC .25 .07
53 Jason Sikes XRC .25 .07
54 Bryan Farson XRC .25 .07
55 Yates Hall XRC .25 .07
56 Troy Brohawn XRC .25 .07
57 Dan Hower XRC .25 .07
58 Clay Caruthers XRC .25 .07
59 Pepe McNeal XRC .25 .07
60 Ray Ricken XRC .25 .07
61 Scott Shores XRC .25 .07
62 Eddie Brooks XRC .25 .07
63 Dave Kauflin XRC .25 .07
64 David Meyer XRC .25 .07
65 Geoff Blum XRC .40 .12
66 Roy Marsh XRC .25 .07
67 Ryan Beeney XRC .25 .07
68 Derek Dukart XRC .25 .07
69 Nomar Garciaparra 4.00 1.20
70 Jason Kelly XRC .25 .07
71 Jesse Ibarra XRC .25 .07
72 Bucky Buckles XRC .25 .07
73 Mark Little XRC .25 .07
74 Heath Murray XRC .25 .07
75 Greg Morris XRC .25 .07
76 Mike Halperlin XRC .25 .07
77 Wes Helms XRC .50 .15
78 Ray Brown XRC .25 .07
79 Kevin L.Brown XRC .40 .12
80 Paul Konerko XRC 1.50 .45
81 Mike Thurman XRC .25 .07
82 Paul Wilson .25 .07
83 Terrence Long XRC 1.00 .30
84 Ben Grieve XRC .50 .15
85 Mark Farris XRC .25 .07
86 Bret Wagner .25 .07
87 Dustin Hermanson .40 .12
88 Kevin Witt XRC .40 .12
89 Corey Pointer XRC .25 .07
90 Tim Grieve XRC .25 .07

1994 Stadium Club Draft Picks First Day Issue

Randomly inserted in packs, this 90-card standard-size set is identical in design with the regular Stadium Club Draft Picks cards except for a holographic "1st Day Issue" emblem on the fronts.

Nm-Mt Ex-Mt
*FIRST DAY: 1.5X TO 4X BASIC CARDS

1994 Stadium Club Draft Picks Members Only

This parallel to the Stadium Club Draft Pick set was issued only in Factory set form and features a special "Members Only" logo on the card.

*MEMBERS ONLY: 1.25X TO 3X BASIC CARD

1995 Stadium Club

The 1995 Stadium Club baseball card set was issued in three series of 270, 225 and 135 standard-size cards for a total of 630. The cards were distributed in 14-card packs at a suggested retail price of $2.50 and contained 24 packs per box. Notable Rookie Cards include Mark Grudzielanek, Bobby Higginson and Hideo Nomo.

Nm-Mt Ex-Mt
COMPLETE SET (630) 60.00 18.00
COMP.SERIES 1 (270) 25.00 7.50
COMP.SERIES 2 (225) 20.00 6.00
COMP.SERIES 3 (135) 15.00 4.50
1 Cal Ripken 2.50 .75
2 Bo Jackson .75 .23
3 Bryan Harvey .15 .04
4 Curt Schilling .50 .15
5 Bruce Ruffin .15 .04
6 Travis Fryman .30 .09
7 Jim Abbott .50 .15
8 David McCarty .15 .04
9 Gary Gaetti .30 .09
10 Roger Clemens 1.50 .45
11 Carlos Garcia .15 .04
12 Lee Smith .30 .09
13 Bobby Ayala .15 .04
14 Charles Nagy .15 .04
15 Lou Frazier .15 .04
16 Rene Arocha .15 .04
17 Carlos Delgado .30 .09
18 Steve Finley .30 .09
19 Ryan Klesko .30 .09
20 Cal Eldred .15 .04
21 Rey Sanchez .15 .04
22 Ken Hill .15 .04
23 Benito Santiago .30 .09
24 Julian Tavarez .15 .04
25 Jose Vizcaino .15 .04
26 Andy Benes .15 .04
27 Mariano Duncan .15 .04
28 Checklist A .15 .04
29 Shawon Dunston .15 .04
30 Rafael Palmeiro .50 .15
31 Dean Palmer .30 .09

32 Andres Galarraga .30 .09
33 Joey Cora .15 .04
34 Mickey Tettleton .15 .04
35 Barry Larkin .75 .23
36 Carlos Baerga .15 .04
37 Orel Hershiser .30 .09
38 Jody Reed .15 .04
39 Paul Molitor .50 .15
40 Jim Edmonds .30 .09
41 Bob Tewksbury .15 .04
42 John Patterson .15 .04
43 Ray McDavid .15 .04
44 Zane Smith .15 .04
45 Bret Saberhagen SE .15 .04
46 Greg Maddux SE .75 .23
47 Frank Thomas SE .50 .15
48 Carlos Baerga SE .15 .04
49 Billy Spiers .15 .04
50 Stan Javier .15 .04
51 Rex Hudler .15 .04
52 Denny Hocking .15 .04
53 Todd Worrell .15 .04
54 Mark Clark .15 .04
55 Hipolito Pichardo .15 .04
56 Bob Wickman .15 .04
57 Raul Mondesi .30 .09
58 Steve Cooke .15 .04
59 Rod Beck .15 .04
60 Tim Davis .15 .04
61 Jeff Kent .30 .09
62 John Valentin .15 .04
63 Alex Arias .15 .04
64 Steve Reed .15 .04
65 Ozzie Smith 1.25 .35
66 Terry Pendleton .30 .09
67 Kenny Rogers .30 .09
68 Vince Coleman .15 .04
69 Tom Pagnozzi .15 .04
70 Roberto Alomar .75 .23
71 Darrin Jackson .15 .04
72 Dennis Eckersley .30 .09
73 Jay Buhner .30 .09
74 Darren Lewis .15 .04
75 Dave Weathers .15 .04
76 Matt Walbeck .15 .04
77 Brad Ausmus .15 .04
78 Danny Bautista .15 .04
79 Bob Hamelin .15 .04
80 Steve Trachsel .15 .04
81 Ken Ryan .15 .04
82 Chris Turner .15 .04
83 David Segui .15 .04
84 Ben McDonald .15 .04
85 Wade Boggs .50 .15
86 John Vander Wal .15 .04
87 Sandy Alomar Jr. .15 .04
88 Ron Karkovice .15 .04
89 Doug Jones .15 .04
90 Gary Sheffield .30 .09
91 Ken Caminiti .30 .09
92 Chris Bosio .15 .04
93 Kevin Tapani .15 .04
94 Walt Weiss .15 .04
95 Erik Hanson .15 .04
96 Ruben Sierra .15 .04
97 Nomar Garciaparra 2.50 .75
98 Terrence Long .30 .09
99 Jacob Shumate .15 .04
100 Paul Wilson .15 .04
101 Kevin Witt .15 .04
102 Paul Konerko .30 .09
103 Ben Grieve .30 .09
104 Mark Johnson RC .30 .09
105 Cade Gaspar RC .15 .04
106 Mark Farris RC .15 .04
107 Dustin Hermanson .15 .04
108 Scott Elarton RC .75 .23
109 Doug Million .15 .04
110 Matt Smith RC .15 .04
111 Brian Buchanan RC .15 .04
112 Jayson Peterson RC .15 .04
113 Bret Wagner RC .15 .04
114 C.J. Nitkowski RC .15 .04
115 Ramon Castro RC .30 .09
116 Rafael Bournigal .15 .04
117 Jeff Fassero .15 .04
118 Bobby Bonilla .30 .09
119 Ricky Gutierrez .15 .04
120 Roger Pavlik .15 .04
121 Mike Greenwell .15 .04
122 Deion Sanders .50 .15
123 Charlie Hayes .15 .04
124 Paul O'Neill .50 .15
125 Jay Bell .30 .09
126 Royce Clayton .15 .04
127 Willie Banks .15 .04
128 Mark Wohlers .15 .04
129 Todd Jones .15 .04
130 Todd Stottlemyre .15 .04
131 Will Clark .75 .23
132 Wilson Alvarez .15 .04
133 Chili Davis .30 .09
134 Dave Burba .15 .04
135 Chris Hoiles .15 .04
136 Jeff Blauser .15 .04
137 Jeff Reboulet .15 .04
138 Bret Saberhagen .30 .09
139 Kirk Rueter .15 .04
140 Dave Nilsson .15 .04
141 Pat Borders .15 .04
142 Ron Darling .15 .04
143 Derek Bell .15 .04
144 Dave Hollins .15 .04
145 Juan Gonzalez .75 .23
146 Andre Dawson .30 .09
147 Jim Thome .75 .23
148 Larry Walker .50 .15
149 Mike Piazza 1.25 .35
150 Mike Perez .15 .04
151 Steve Avery .15 .04
152 Dan Wilson .15 .04
153 Andy Van Slyke .30 .09
154 Junior Felix .15 .04
155 Jack McDowell .15 .04
156 Danny Tartabull .15 .04
157 Willie Blair .15 .04
158 Wm.VanLandingham .15 .04
159 Robb Nen .30 .09
160 Lee Tinsley .15 .04
161 Ismael Valdes .15 .04
162 Juan Guzman .15 .04
163 Scott Servais .15 .04
164 Cliff Floyd .30 .09
165 Allen Watson .15 .04
166 Eddie Taubensee .15 .04
167 Scott Hemond .15 .04
168 Jeff Tackett .15 .04
169 Chad Curtis .15 .04
170 Rico Brogna .15 .04
171 Luis Polonia .15 .04
172 Checklist B .15 .04
173 Lance Johnson .15 .04
174 Sammy Sosa 1.25 .35
175 Mike Macfarlane .15 .04
176 Darryl Hamilton .15 .04
177 Rick Aguilera .15 .04
178 Dave West .15 .04
179 Mike Gallego .15 .04
180 Marc Newfield .15 .04
181 Steve Buechele .15 .04
182 David Wells .30 .09
183 Tom Glavine .50 .15
184 Joe Girardi .15 .04
185 Craig Biggio .50 .15
186 Eddie Murray .75 .23
187 Kevin Gross .15 .04
188 Sid Fernandez .15 .04
189 John Franco .30 .09
190 Bernard Gilkey .15 .04
191 Matt Williams .30 .09
192 Darrin Fletcher .15 .04
193 Jeff Conine .30 .09
194 Ed Sprague .15 .04
195 Eduardo Perez .15 .04
196 Scott Livingstone .15 .04
197 Ivan Rodriguez .75 .23
198 Orlando Merced .15 .04
199 Ricky Bones .15 .04
200 Javier Lopez .30 .09
201 Miguel Jimenez .15 .04
202 Terry McGriff .15 .04
203 Mike Lieberthal .30 .09
204 David Cone .30 .09
205 Todd Hundley .15 .04
206 Ozzie Guillen .15 .04
207 Alex Cole .15 .04
208 Tony Phillips .15 .04
209 Jim Eisenreich .15 .04
210 Greg Vaughn BES .15 .04
211 Barry Larkin BES .30 .09
212 Don Mattingly BES 1.00 .30
213 Mark Grace BES .30 .09
214 Jose Canseco BES .30 .09
215 Joe Carter BES .15 .04
216 David Cone BES .15 .04
217 Sandy Alomar Jr. BES .15 .04
218 Al Martin BES .15 .04
219 Roberto Kelly BES .15 .04
220 Paul Sorrento .15 .04
221 Tony Fernandez .15 .04
222 Stan Belinda .15 .04
223 Mike Stanley .15 .04
224 Doug Drabek .15 .04
225 Todd Van Poppel .15 .04
226 Matt Mieske .15 .04
227 Tino Martinez .50 .15
228 Andy Ashby .15 .04
229 Midre Cummings .15 .04
230 Jeff Frye .15 .04
231 Hal Morris .15 .04
232 Jose Lind .15 .04
233 Shawn Green .30 .09
234 Rafael Belliard .15 .04
235 Randy Myers .15 .04
236 Frank Thomas CE .50 .15
237 Darren Daulton CE .15 .04
238 Sammy Sosa CE .75 .23
239 Cal Ripken CE 1.25 .35
240 Jeff Bagwell CE .30 .09
241 Ken Griffey Jr. 1.25 .35
242 Brett Butler .30 .09
243 Derrick May .15 .04
244 Pat Listach .15 .04
245 Mike Bordick .15 .04
246 Mark Langston .15 .04
247 Randy Velarde .15 .04
248 Julio Franco .30 .09
249 Chuck Knoblauch .30 .09
250 Bill Gullickson .15 .04
251 Dave Henderson .15 .04
252 Bret Boone .30 .09
253 Al Martin .15 .04
254 Armando Benitez .30 .09
255 Wil Cordero .15 .04
256 Al Leiter .30 .09
257 Luis Gonzalez .30 .09
258 Charlie O'Brien .15 .04
259 Tim Wallach .15 .04
260 Scott Sanders .15 .04
261 Tom Henke .15 .04
262 Otis Nixon .15 .04
263 Darren Daulton .30 .09
264 Manny Ramirez .30 .09
265 Bret Barberie .15 .04
266 Mel Rojas .15 .04
267 John Burkett .15 .04
268 Brady Anderson .30 .09
269 John Roper .15 .04
270 Shane Reynolds .15 .04
271 Barry Bonds 2.00 .60
272 Alex Fernandez .15 .04
273 Brian McRae .15 .04
274 Todd Zeile .15 .04
275 Greg Swindell .15 .04
276 Johnny Ruffin .15 .04
277 Troy Neel .15 .04
278 Eric Karros .30 .09
279 John Hudek .15 .04
280 Thomas Howard .15 .04
281 Joe Carter .30 .09
282 Mike Devereaux .15 .04
283 Butch Henry .15 .04
284 Reggie Jefferson .15 .04
285 Mark Lemke .15 .04
286 Jeff Montgomery .15 .04
287 Ryan Thompson .15 .04
288 Paul Shuey .15 .04
289 Mark McGwire 2.00 .60
290 Bernie Williams .50 .15
291 Mickey Morandini .15 .04
292 Scott Leius .15 .04
293 David Hulse .15 .04
294 Greg Gagne .15 .04
295 Moises Alou .30 .09
296 Geronimo Berroa .15 .04
297 Eddie Zambrano .15 .04
298 Alan Trammell .50 .15
299 Don Slaught .15 .04
300 Jose Rijo .15 .04
301 Joe Ausanio .15 .04
302 Tim Raines .30 .09
303 Melido Perez .15 .04
304 Kent Mercker .15 .04
305 James Mouton .15 .04
306 Luis Lopez .15 .04
307 Mike Kingery .15 .04
308 Willie Greene .15 .04
309 Cecil Fielder .30 .09
310 Scott Kamieniecki .15 .04
311 Mike Greenwell BES .15 .04
312 Bobby Bonilla BES .15 .04
313 A.Galarraga BES .15 .04
314 Cal Ripken BES 1.25 .35
315 Matt Williams BES .15 .04
316 Tom Pagnozzi BES .15 .04
317 Len Dykstra BES .15 .04
318 Frank Thomas BES .50 .15
319 Kirby Puckett BES .75 .23
320 Mike Piazza BES .75 .23
321 Jason Jacome .15 .04
322 Brian Hunter .15 .04
323 Brent Gates .15 .04
324 Jim Converse .15 .04
325 Damion Easley .15 .04
326 Dante Bichette .30 .09
327 Kurt Abbott .15 .04
328 Scott Cooper .15 .04
329 Mike Henneman .15 .04
330 Orlando Miller .15 .04
331 John Kruk .30 .09
332 Jose Oliva .15 .04
333 Reggie Sanders .30 .09
334 Omar Vizquel .30 .09
335 Devon White .30 .09
336 Mike Morgan .15 .04
337 J.R. Phillips .15 .04
338 Gary DiSarcina .15 .04
339 Joey Hamilton .15 .04
340 Randy Johnson .75 .23
341 Jim Leyritz .15 .04
342 Bobby Jones .15 .04
343 Jaime Navarro .15 .04
344 Bip Roberts .15 .04
345 Steve Karsay .15 .04
346 Kevin Stocker .15 .04
347 Jose Canseco .75 .23
348 Bill Wegman .15 .04
349 Rondell White .30 .09
350 Mo Vaughn .30 .09
351 Joe Orsulak .15 .04
352 Pat Meares .15 .04
353 Albie Lopez .15 .04
354 Edgar Martinez .50 .15
355 Brian Jordan .30 .09
356 Tommy Greene .15 .04
357 Chuck Carr .15 .04
358 Pedro Astacio .15 .04
359 Russ Davis .15 .04
360 Chris Hammond .15 .04
361 Gregg Jefferies .15 .04
362 Shane Mack .15 .04
363 Fred McGriff .50 .15
364 Pat Rapp .15 .04
365 Bill Swift .15 .04
366 Checklist .15 .04
367 Robin Ventura .30 .09
368 Bobby Witt .15 .04
369 Karl Rhodes .15 .04
370 Eddie Williams .15 .04
371 John Jaha .15 .04
372 Steve Howe .15 .04
373 Leo Gomez .15 .04
374 Hector Fajardo .15 .04
375 Jeff Bagwell .50 .15
376 Mark Acre .15 .04
377 Wayne Kirby .15 .04
378 Mark Portugal .15 .04
379 Jesus Tavarez .15 .04
380 Jim Lindeman .15 .04
381 Don Mattingly 2.00 .60
382 Trevor Hoffman .30 .09
383 Chris Gomez .15 .04
384 Garret Anderson .30 .09
385 Bobby Munoz .15 .04
386 Jon Lieber .15 .04
387 Rick Helling .15 .04
388 Marvin Freeman .15 .04
389 Juan Castillo .15 .04
390 Jeff Cirillo .15 .04
391 Sean Berry .15 .04
392 Hector Carrasco .15 .04
393 Mark Grace .50 .15
394 Pat Kelly .15 .04
395 Tim Naehring .15 .04
396 Greg Pirkl .15 .04
397 John Smoltz .50 .15
398 Robby Thompson .15 .04
399 Rick White .15 .04
400 Frank Thomas .75 .23
401 Jeff Conine CS .15 .04
402 Jose Valentin CS .15 .04
403 Carlos Baerga CS .15 .04
404 Rick Aguilera CS .15 .04
405 Wilson Alvarez CS .15 .04
406 Juan Gonzalez CS .50 .15
407 Barry Larkin CS .30 .09
408 Ken Hill CS .15 .04
409 Chuck Carr CS .15 .04
410 Tim Raines CS .15 .04
411 Bryan Eversgerd .15 .04
412 Phil Plantier .15 .04
413 Josias Manzanillo .15 .04
414 Roberto Kelly .15 .04
415 Rickey Henderson .75 .23
416 John Smiley .15 .04
417 Kevin Brown .30 .09
418 Jimmy Key .30 .09
419 Wally Joyner .30 .09
420 Roberto Hernandez .15 .04
421 Felix Fermin .15 .04
422 Checklist .15 .04
423 Greg Vaughn .30 .09
424 Ray Lankford .15 .04
425 Greg Maddux 1.25 .35
426 Mike Mussina .75 .23
427 Geronimo Pena .15 .04
428 David Nied .15 .04
429 Scott Erickson .15 .04
430 Kevin Mitchell .15 .04
431 Mike Lansing .15 .04
432 Brian Anderson .15 .04
433 Jeff King .15 .04
434 Ramon Martinez .15 .04
435 Kevin Seitzer .15 .04
436 Salomon Torres .15 .04
437 Brian L.Hunter .15 .04
438 Melvin Nieves .15 .04
439 Mike Kelly .15 .04
440 Marquis Grissom .15 .04
441 Chuck Finley .30 .09
442 Len Dykstra .30 .09
443 Ellis Burks .30 .09
444 Harold Baines .30 .09
445 Kevin Appier .30 .09
446 David Justice .30 .09
447 Darryl Kile .30 .09
448 John Olerud .30 .09
449 Greg McMichael .15 .04
450 Kirby Puckett .75 .23
451 Jose Valentin .15 .04
452 Rick Wilkins .15 .04
453 Arthur Rhodes .15 .04
454 Pat Hentgen .15 .04
455 Tom Gordon .15 .04
456 Tom Candiotti .15 .04
457 Jason Bere .15 .04
458 Wes Chamberlain .15 .04
459 Greg Colbrunn .15 .04
460 John Doherty .15 .04
461 Kevin Foster .15 .04
462 Mark Whiten .15 .04
463 Terry Steinbach .15 .04
464 Aaron Sele .15 .04
465 Kirt Manwaring .15 .04
466 Darren Hall .15 .04
467 Delino DeShields .15 .04
468 Andujar Cedeno .15 .04
469 Billy Ashley .15 .04
470 Kenny Lofton .30 .09
471 Pedro Munoz .15 .04
472 John Wetteland .30 .09
473 Tim Salmon .50 .15
474 Denny Neagle .30 .09
475 Tony Gwynn 1.00 .30
476 Vinny Castilla .30 .09
477 Steve Dreyer .15 .04
478 Jeff Shaw .15 .04
479 Chad Ogea .15 .04
480 Scott Ruffcorn .15 .04
481 Lou Whitaker .30 .09
482 J.T. Snow .30 .09
483 Rich Rowland .15 .04
484 Denny Martinez .30 .09
485 Pedro Martinez .75 .23
486 Rusty Greer .30 .09
487 Dave Fleming .15 .04
488 John Dettmer .15 .04
489 Albert Belle .30 .09
490 Ravelo Manzanillo .15 .04
491 Henry Rodriguez .15 .04
492 Andrew Lorraine .15 .04
493 Dwayne Hosey .15 .04
494 Mike Blowers .15 .04
495 Turner Ward .15 .04
496 Fred McGriff EC .30 .09
497 Sammy Sosa EC .75 .23
498 Barry Larkin EC .30 .09
499 Andres Galarraga EC .15 .04
500 Gary Sheffield EC .15 .04
501 Jeff Bagwell EC .30 .09
502 Mike Piazza EC .75 .23
503 Moises Alou EC .15 .04
504 Bobby Bonilla EC .15 .04
505 Darren Daulton EC .15 .04
506 Jeff King EC .15 .04
507 Ray Lankford EC .15 .04
508 Tony Gwynn EC .50 .15
509 Barry Bonds EC 1.00 .30
510 Cal Ripken EC 1.25 .35
511 Mo Vaughn EC .15 .04
512 Tim Salmon EC .30 .09
513 Frank Thomas EC .50 .15
514 Albert Belle EC .15 .04
515 Cecil Fielder EC .15 .04
516 Kevin Appier EC .15 .04
517 Greg Vaughn EC .15 .04
518 Kirby Puckett EC .50 .15
519 Paul O'Neill EC .30 .09
520 Ruben Sierra EC .15 .04
521 Ken Griffey Jr. EC .75 .23
522 Will Clark EC .30 .09
523 Joe Carter EC .15 .04
524 Antonio Osuna .15 .04
525 Glenallen Hill .15 .04
526 Alex Gonzalez .15 .04
527 Dave Stewart .30 .09
528 Ron Gant .30 .09
529 Jason Bates .15 .04
530 Mike Macfarlane .15 .04
531 Esteban Loaiza .30 .09
532 Joe Randa .15 .04
533 Dave Winfield .30 .09
534 Danny Darwin .15 .04
535 Pete Harnisch .15 .04
536 Joey Cora .15 .04
537 Jaime Navarro .15 .04
538 Marty Cordova .15 .04
539 Andujar Cedeno .15 .04
540 Mickey Tettleton .15 .04
541 Andy Van Slyke .30 .09
542 Carlos Perez RC .30 .09
543 Chipper Jones .75 .23
544 Tony Fernandez .15 .04
545 Tom Henke .15 .04
546 Pat Borders .15 .04
547 Chad Curtis .15 .04
548 Ray Durham .30 .09
549 Joe Oliver .15 .04
550 Jose Mesa .15 .04
551 Steve Finley .30 .09
552 Otis Nixon .15 .04
553 Jacob Brumfield .15 .04
554 Bill Swift .15 .04
555 Quilvio Veras .15 .04
556 Hideo Nomo RC UER 2.00 .60
Wins and IP totals reversed
557 Joe Vitiello .15 .04
558 Mike Perez .15 .04
559 Charlie Hayes .15 .04
560 Brad Radke RC 1.25 .35
561 Darren Bragg .15 .04
562 Orel Hershiser .30 .09
563 Edgardo Alfonzo .30 .09
564 Doug Jones .15 .04
565 Andy Pettitte .50 .15
566 Benito Santiago .30 .09
567 John Burkett .15 .04
568 Brad Clontz .15 .04
569 Jim Abbott .50 .15
570 Joe Rosselli .15 .04
571 Mark Grudzielanek RC .50 .15
572 Dustin Hermanson .15 .04
573 Benji Gil .15 .04
574 Mark Whiten .15 .04
575 Mike Ignasiak .15 .04
576 Kevin Ritz .15 .04
577 Paul Quantrill .15 .04
578 Andre Dawson .30 .09
579 Jerald Clark .15 .04
580 Frank Rodriguez .15 .04
581 Mark Kiefer .15 .04
582 Trevor Wilson .15 .04
583 Gary Wilson RC .15 .04
584 Andy Stankiewicz .15 .04
585 Felipe Lira .15 .04
586 Mike Mimbs RC .15 .04
587 Jon Nunnally .15 .04
588 Tomas Perez RC .15 .04
589 Chad Fonville .15 .04
590 Todd Hollandsworth .15 .04
591 Roberto Petagine .15 .04
592 Mariano Rivera .50 .15
593 Mark McLemore .15 .04
594 Bobby Witt .15 .04
595 Jose Offerman .15 .04
596 J.Christiansen RC .15 .04
597 Jeff Manto .15 .04
598 Jim Dougherty RC .15 .04
599 Juan Acevedo RC .15 .04
600 Troy O'Leary .15 .04
601 Ron Villone .15 .04
602 Tripp Cromer .15 .04
603 Steve Scarsone .15 .04
604 Lance Parrish .30 .09
605 Ozzie Timmons .15 .04
606 Ray Holbert .15 .04
607 Tony Phillips .15 .04
608 Phil Plantier .15 .04
609 Shane Andrews .15 .04
610 Heathcliff Slocumb .15 .04
611 Bobby Higginson RC .75 .23
612 Bob Tewksbury .15 .04
613 Terry Pendleton .30 .09
614 Scott Cooper TA .15 .04
615 John Wetteland TA .15 .04
616 Ken Hill TA .15 .04
617 Marquis Grissom TA .15 .04
618 Larry Walker TA .15 .04
619 Derek Bell TA .15 .04
620 David Cone TA .15 .04
621 Ken Caminiti TA .15 .04
622 Jack McDowell TA .15 .04
623 Vaughn Eshelman TA .15 .04
624 Brian McRae TA .15 .04
625 Gregg Jefferies TA .15 .04
626 Kevin Brown TA .15 .04
627 Lee Smith TA .15 .04
628 Tony Tarasco TA .15 .04
629 Brett Butler TA .15 .04
630 Jose Canseco TA .30 .09

1995 Stadium Club First Day Issue

Parallel to the basic first series Stadium Club issue, these cards, were primarily inserted in second series Topps packs. They were also inserted at a rate of ten per Topps factory set. Nine double printed cards were issued in both first and second series Topps packs. Those cards are as follows: 29, 39, 79, 96, 131, 149, 153, 168 and 197. Limited instances of duplicitous parties transferring the FDI foil logos from "common" players to the fronts of "star" players were chronicled shortly after release - thus it's recommended for collectors to take a close look at the logo on front before purchasing these cards.

	Nm-Mt	Ex-Mt
COMPLETE SET (270)	250.00	75.00
COMMON CARD (1-270)	2.00	.60

*STARS: 5X TO 12X BASIC CARDS ....
*ROOKIES: 3X TO 8X BASIC CARDS ..
*DP STARS: 1.25X TO 3X BASIC CARDS

1995 Stadium Club Members Only Parallel

This set is a parallel to the regular 1995 Stadium Club set.These cards are identical to their regular issue counterparts except for the distinctive "Members Only" logo. According to Topps, only 4,000 factory sets were issued through the Topps Stadium Club at a price of $200 each. A certificate of authenticity carrying the serial number accompanied each set. In addition to the 630 regular cards, the factory set includes Members Only versions of the following inserts: Crystal Ball, Clear Cut, Power Zone, Ring Leaders, Super Skills, Virtual Extremists and Virtual Reality (listed separately). Only the insert cards are listed below. Please use the multipliers for values on the basic cards.

	Nm-Mt	Ex-Mt
COMP.SET w/o VR (755)	250.00	75.00

*MEM.ONLY 1-630: 1.5X TO 4X BASIC CARDS

CB1 Chipper Jones 8.00 2.40
CB2 Dustin Hermanson .75 .23
CB3 Ray Durham 1.50 .45
CB4 Phil Nevin .75 .23
CB5 Billy Ashley .25 .07
CB6 Shawn Green 2.00 .60

CB7 Jason Bates .25 .07
CB8 Benji Gil .25 .07
CB9 Marty Cordova .25 .07
CB10 Quilvio Veras .75 .23
CB11 Mark Grudzielanek .75 .23
CB12 Ruben Rivera .25 .07
CB13 Bill Pulsipher .25 .07
CB14 Derek Jeter 15.00 4.50
CB15 LaTroy Hawkins .25 .07
CC1 Mike Piazza 8.00 2.40
CC2 Ruben Sierra .25 .07
CC3 Tony Gwynn 8.00 2.40
CC4 Frank Thomas 6.00 1.80
CC5 Fred McGriff 1.50 .45
CC6 Rafael Palmeiro 2.00 .60
CC7 Bobby Bonilla .25 .07
CC8 Chili Davis .75 .23
CC9 Hal Morris .25 .07
CC10 Jose Canseco 3.00 .90
CC11 Jay Bell .75 .23
CC12 Kirby Puckett 6.00 1.80
CC13 Gary Sheffield 2.00 .60
CC14 Bob Hamelin .25 .07
CC15 Jeff Bagwell 3.00 .90
CC16 Albert Belle .75 .23
CC17 Sammy Sosa 8.00 2.40
CC18 Ken Griffey Jr. 12.00 3.60
CC19 Todd Zeile .75 .23
CC20 Mo Vaughn .75 .23
CC21 Moises Alou .75 .23
CC22 Paul O'Neill .75 .23
CC23 Andres Galarraga 2.00 .60
CC24 Greg Vaughn .75 .23
CC25 Len Dykstra .75 .23
CC26 Joe Carter .75 .23
CC27 Barry Bonds 8.00 2.40
CC28 Cecil Fielder .75 .23
PZ1 Jeff Bagwell 3.00 .90
PZ2 Albert Belle .75 .23
PZ3 Barry Bonds 8.00 2.40
PZ4 Joe Carter .75 .23
PZ5 Cecil Fielder .75 .23
PZ6 Andres Galarraga 2.00 .60
PZ7 Ken Griffey Jr. 12.00 3.60
PZ8 Paul Molitor 2.00 .60
PZ9 Fred McGriff 1.50 .45
PZ10 Rafael Palmeiro 2.00 .60
PZ11 Frank Thomas 6.00 1.80
PZ12 Matt Williams 1.50 .45
RL1 Jeff Bagwell 3.00 .90
RL2 Mark McGwire 12.00 3.60
RL3 Ozzie Smith 6.00 1.80
RL4 Paul Molitor 2.00 .60
RL5 Darryl Strawberry .25 .07
RL6 Eddie Murray 2.00 .60
RL7 Tony Gwynn 8.00 2.40
RL8 Jose Canseco 3.00 .90
RL9 Howard Johnson .25 .07
RL10 Andre Dawson 1.50 .45
RL11 Matt Williams 1.50 .45
RL12 Tim Raines .75 .23
RL13 Fred McGriff 1.50 .45
RL14 Ken Griffey Jr. 12.00 3.60
RL15 Gary Sheffield 2.00 .60
RL16 Dennis Eckersley .75 .23
RL17 Kevin Mitchell .25 .07
RL18 Will Clark 2.00 .60
RL19 Darren Daulton .75 .23
RL20 Paul O'Neill 2.00 .60
RL21 Julio Franco .25 .07
RL22 Albert Belle .75 .23
RL23 Juan Gonzalez 3.00 .90
RL24 Kirby Puckett 6.00 1.80
RL25 Joe Carter .75 .23
RL26 Frank Thomas 6.00 1.80
RL27 Cal Ripken 15.00 4.50
RL28 John Olerud .75 .23
RL29 Ruben Sierra .75 .23
RL30 Barry Bonds 8.00 2.40
RL31 Cecil Fielder .75 .23
RL32 Roger Clemens 8.00 2.40
RL33 Don Mattingly 8.00 2.40
RL34 Terry Pendleton .25 .07
RL35 Rickey Henderson 3.00 .90
RL36 Dave Winfield 3.00 .90
RL37 Edgar Martinez 1.50 .45
RL38 Wade Boggs 3.00 .90
RL39 Willie McGee .75 .23
RL40 Andres Galarraga 2.00 .60
SS1 Roberto Alomar 2.00 .60
SS2 Barry Bonds 8.00 2.40
SS3 Jay Buhner .75 .23
SS4 Chuck Carr .25 .07
SS5 Don Mattingly 8.00 2.40
SS6 Raul Mondesi 1.50 .45
SS7 Tim Salmon 2.00 .60
SS8 Deion Sanders .75 .23
SS9 Devon White .25 .07
SS10 Mark Whiten .25 .07
SS11 Ken Griffey Jr. 12.00 3.60
SS12 Marquis Grissom .25 .07
SS13 Paul O'Neill .75 .23
SS14 Kenny Lofton .25 .07
SS15 Larry Walker 2.00 .60
SS16 Scott Cooper .25 .07
SS17 Barry Larkin 2.00 .60
SS18 Matt Williams 1.50 .45
SS19 John Wetteland .75 .23
SS20 Randy Johnson 3.00 .90
VRE1 Barry Bonds 8.00 2.40
VRE2 Ken Griffey Jr. 12.00 3.60
VRE3 Jeff Bagwell 3.00 .90
VRE4 Albert Belle .75 .23
VRE5 Frank Thomas 6.00 1.80
VRE6 Tony Gwynn 8.00 2.40
VRE7 Kenny Lofton .75 .23
VRE8 Deion Sanders 2.00 .60
VRE9 Ken Hill .25 .07
VRE10 Jimmy Key .75 .23

1995 Stadium Club Super Team Division Winners

Each of these six team sets was available exclusively by mailing in the corresponding winning 1994 Super Team card. Each team set was distributed in a clear plastic sealed wrapper and included ten player cards and a Super Team card (of which was stamped "REDEEMED" on back). The card design and numbering for the player cards parallels regular issue 1995 Stadium Club cards. In fact, the only way to tell these cards apart is by the gold foil "Division Winner" logo on each card front. The cards are listed below alphabetically by team; the prefixes B, D, I, M, R and RS have been added to denote Braves, Dodgers, Indians, Mariners, Reds and Red Sox.

Nm-Mt Ex-Mt
COMP.BRAVES SET (11) 8.00 2.40
COMP.DODGERS (11) 8.00 2.40
COMP.INDIANS SET (11) 6.00 1.80
COMP.MARINERS (11) 8.00 2.40
COMP.REDS SET (11) 3.00 .90
COMP.RED SOX SET (11) 6.00 1.80
COMMON CARD .30 .09
COMMON SUPER TEAM 1.00 .30
B1T Braves DW 1.00 .30
Super Team
Jeff Blauser
Terry Pendleton
B19 Ryan Klesko .60 .18
B128 Mark Wohlers .30 .09
B151 Steve Avery .30 .09
B183 Tom Glavine 1.00 .30
B200 Javy Lopez .60 .18
B393 Fred McGriff 1.00 .30
B397 John Smoltz 1.00 .30
B425 Greg Maddux 2.50 .75
B446 Dave Justice .60 .18
B543 Chipper Jones 1.50 .45
D7T Dodgers DW 1.00 .30
Super Team
Mike Piazza
D57 Raul Mondesi .60 .18
D149 Mike Piazza 2.50 .75
D161 Ismael Valdes .30 .09
D242 Brett Butler .60 .18
D259 Tim Wallach .30 .09
D278 Eric Karros .60 .18
D434 Ramon Martinez .30 .09
D456 Tom Candiotti .30 .09
D467 Delino DeShields .30 .09
D556 Hideo Nomo 4.00 1.20
I19T Indians DW 1.00 .30
Super Team
Carlos Baerga
Albert Belle
Kenny Lofton
I36 Carlos Baerga .30 .09
I147 Jim Thome 1.50 .45
I186 Eddie Murray 1.50 .45
I264 Manny Ramirez .60 .18
I334 Omar Vizquel .60 .18
I470 Kenny Lofton .60 .18
I484 Dennis Martinez .60 .18
I489 Albert Belle .60 .18
I550 Jose Mesa .30 .09
I562 Orel Hershiser .60 .18
M26T Mariners DW 1.00 .16
Super Team
Mike Blowers
Jay Buhner
M73 Jay Buhner .60 .18
M92 Chris Bosio .30 .09
M152 Dan Wilson .30 .09
M227 Tino Martinez 1.00 .30
M241 Ken Griffey Jr. 2.50 .75
M340 Randy Johnson 1.50 .45
M354 Edgar Martinez 1.00 .30
M421 Felix Fermin .30 .09
M494 Mike Blowers .30 .09
M536 Joey Cora .30 .09
RE3T Reds DW
Super Team
Barry Larkin
Reggie Sanders
RE35 Barry Larkin 1.50 .45
RE231 Hal Morris .30 .09
RE252 Bret Boone .60 .18
RE280 Thomas Howard .30 .09
RE300 Jose Rijo .30 .09
RE333 Reggie Sanders .60 .18
RE392 Hector Carrasco .30 .09
RE416 John Smiley .30 .09
RE528 Ron Gant .60 .18
RE566 Benito Santiago .60 .18
RS1T Red Sox DW 1.00 .30
Super Team
Luis Rivera
John Valentin
RS10 Roger Clemens 3.00 .90
RS62 John Valentin .30 .09
RS121 Mike Greenwell .30 .09
RS160 Lee Tinsley .30 .09
RS347 Jose Canseco 1.50 .45
RS350 Mo Vaughn .60 .18
RS395 Tim Naehring .30 .09
RS464 Aaron Sele .30 .09
RS530 Mike Macfarlane .30 .09
RS600 Troy O'Leary .30 .09

1995 Stadium Club Super Team Master Photos

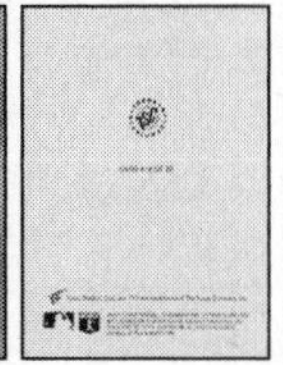

This 20-card set was distributed in two separate 10-card sealed team bags. The cards were available exclusively by mailing in a Braves or Indians 1994 Super Team card. These oversized cards (5" by 7") feature a reproduction of the player's standard 1995 Stadium Club card enframed around a shining blue background. Unlike the standard issue cards they parallel, these are numbered X of 20.

Nm-Mt Ex-Mt
COMP.BRAVES SET (10) 10.00 3.00
COMP.INDIANS SET (10) 8.00 2.40
1 Steve Avery .40 .12
2 Tom Glavine 1.25 .35
3 Chipper Jones 2.00 .60
4 Dave Justice .75 .23
5 Ryan Klesko .75 .23
6 Javy Lopez .75 .23
7 Greg Maddux 3.00 .90
8 Fred McGriff 1.25 .35
9 John Smoltz 1.25 .35
10 Mark Wohlers .40 .12
11 Carlos Baerga .40 .12
12 Albert Belle .75 .23
13 Orel Hershiser .75 .23
14 Kenny Lofton .75 .23
15 Dennis Martinez .75 .23
16 Jose Mesa .40 .12
17 Eddie Murray 2.00 .60
18 Manny Ramirez .75 .23
19 Jim Thome 2.00 .60
20 Omar Vizquel .75 .23

1995 Stadium Club Super Team World Series

Because of the strike-interrupted season, the 1994 Stadium Club Super Team insert program had to be finished up with the 1995 product. Collectors who redeemed the 1994 Atlanta Braves Super Team card received: 1) a complete 630-card 1995 Stadium Club parallel set stamped with a special gold foil World Series logo (of which was mailed in two separate series of 585 and 45 cards) 2) a Division Winner parallel Braves team set along with the winner card stamped "redeemed" on its back 3) a jumbo-sized (3" by 5") parallel Master Photo Braves team set. Collectors who redeemed the 1994 Cleveland Indians Super Team card got parallel Indians Division Winner and Master Photo team sets. Collectors who redeemed the 1994 Super Team card of a division winner (Dodgers, Mariners, Red Sox and Reds) received a Division Winner parallel team set of the respective team that they sent in. All of these winner cards parallel the 1995 Stadium Club regular series cards.

Nm-Mt Ex-Mt
COMP.WS SET (585) 80.00 24.00
COMP.EC/TA SET (45) 15.00 4.50
*STARS: .6X TO 1.5X BASIC CARDS..
*ROOKIES: .6X TO 1.5X BASIC CARDS

1995 Stadium Club Virtual Reality

This 270-card standard-size set parallels a selection of cards from the regular 1995 Stadium Club set. Differences include the words "Virtual Reality" printed above the player's name and the numbering on the back. These cards were inserted in the first two Stadium Club series on a one per pack, two per rack pack basis.

Nm-Mt Ex-Mt
COMPLETE SET (270) 100.00 30.00
COMP.SERIES 1 (135) 50.00 15.00
COMP.SERIES 2 (135) 50.00 15.00
*STARS: .75X TO 2X BASIC CARDS...

1995 Stadium Club Virtual Reality Members Only

These cards parallel the regular 1995 Stadium Club Stadium Club Virtual Reality cards. The only difference is that they all have a Stadium Club Members Only logo imprinted on the front. These cards were distributed as part of the package of material that members of the "Stadium Club Members Only" club received when they ordered the 1995 parallel master set.

Nm-Mt Ex-Mt
COMP.FACT.SET (270) 100.00 30.00
*MEMBERS ONLY: 2X BASIC VIRTUAL REALITY

1995 Stadium Club Clear Cut

Randomly inserted at a rate of one in 24 hobby and retail packs, this 28-card set features a full color action photo of the player against a clear acetate background with the player's name printed vertically.

Nm-Mt Ex-Mt
COMPLETE SET (28) 80.00 24.00
COMPLETE SERIES 1 (14) 40.00 12.00
COMP.SERIES 2 (14) 40.00 12.00
CC1 Mike Piazza 10.00 3.00
CC2 Ruben Sierra 1.25 .35
CC3 Tony Gwynn 8.00 2.40
CC4 Frank Thomas 6.00 1.80
CC5 Fred McGriff 4.00 1.20
CC6 Rafael Palmeiro 4.00 1.20
CC7 Bobby Bonilla 2.50 .75
CC8 Chili Davis 2.50 .75
CC9 Hal Morris 1.25 .35
CC10 Jose Canseco 6.00 1.80
CC11 Jay Bell 2.50 .75
CC12 Kirby Puckett 6.00 1.80
CC13 Gary Sheffield 2.50 .75
CC14 Bob Hamelin 1.25 .35
CC15 Jeff Bagwell 4.00 1.20
CC16 Albert Belle 2.50 .75
CC17 Sammy Sosa 10.00 3.00
CC18 Ken Griffey Jr. 10.00 3.00
CC19 Todd Zeile 1.25 .35
CC20 Mo Vaughn 2.50 .75
CC21 Moises Alou 2.50 .75
CC22 Paul O'Neill 4.00 1.20
CC23 Andres Galarraga 2.50 .75
CC24 Greg Vaughn 2.50 .75
CC25 Len Dykstra 2.50 .75
CC26 Joe Carter 2.50 .75
CC27 Barry Bonds 15.00 4.50
CC28 Cecil Fielder 2.50 .75

1995 Stadium Club Crunch Time

This 20-card standard-size set features home run hitters and was randomly inserted in first series rack packs. The cards are numbered as "X" of 20 in the upper right corner.

Nm-Mt Ex-Mt
COMPLETE SET (20) 50.00 15.00
1 Jeff Bagwell 2.00 .60
2 Kirby Puckett 3.00 .90
3 Frank Thomas 3.00 .90
4 Albert Belle 1.25 .35
5 Julio Franco 1.25 .35
6 Jose Canseco 3.00 .90
7 Paul Molitor 2.00 .60
8 Joe Carter 1.25 .35
9 Ken Griffey Jr. 5.00 1.50
10 Larry Walker 2.00 .60
11 Dante Bichette 1.25 .35
12 Carlos Baerga .60 .18
13 Fred McGriff 2.00 .60
14 Ruben Sierra .60 .18
15 Will Clark 3.00 .90
16 Moises Alou 1.25 .35
17 Rafael Palmeiro 2.00 .60
18 Travis Fryman 1.25 .35
19 Barry Bonds 8.00 2.40
20 Cal Ripken 10.00 3.00

1995 Stadium Club Crystal Ball

This 15-card standard-size set was inserted into series three packs at a rate of one in 24. Fifteen leading 1995 rookies and prospects were featured in this set. The player is identified on the top and the cards are numbered with a "CB" prefix in the upper left corner.

Nm-Mt Ex-Mt
COMPLETE SET (15) 80.00 24.00
CB1 Chipper Jones 10.00 3.00
CB2 Dustin Hermanson 2.00 .60
CB3 Ray Durham 4.00 1.20
CB4 Phil Nevin 4.00 1.20
CB5 Billy Ashley 2.00 .60
CB6 Shawn Green 4.00 1.20
CB7 Jason Bates 2.00 .60
CB8 Benji Gil 2.00 .60
CB9 Marty Cordova 2.00 .60
CB10 Quilvio Veras 2.00 .60
CB11 Mark Grudzielanek 6.00 1.80
CB12 Ruben Rivera 2.00 .60
CB13 Bill Pulsipher 2.00 .60
CB14 Derek Jeter 20.00 6.00
CB15 LaTroy Hawkins 2.00 .60

1995 Stadium Club Phone Cards

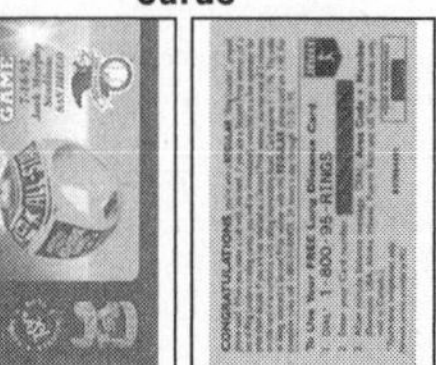

These phone cards were randomly inserted into packs. The prizes for these cards were as follows. The Gold Winner card was redeemable for the ring depicted on the front of the card. The silver winner card was redeemable for a set of all 39 phone cards. The regular winner card was redeemable for a Ring Leaders set. The fronts feature a photo of a specific ring while the backs have game information. If the card was not a winner for any of the prizes, it was still good for three minutes of time. The phone cards expired on January 1, 1996. If the PIN number is revealed the value is a percentage of an untouched card.

Nm-Mt Ex-Mt
COMP.REGULAR (13) 20.00 6.00
COMMON REGULAR 2.00 .60
COMP.SILVER SET (13) 30.00 9.00
COMMON SILVER CARD 4.00 1.20
COMP.GOLD SET (13) 75.00 22.00
COMMON GOLD CARD 8.00 2.40
*PIN NUMBER REVEALED: .25X to .50X BASIC CARDS

1995 Stadium Club Power Zone

This 12-card standard-size set was inserted into series three packs at a rate of one in 24. The cards are numbered in the upper right corner with a "PZ" prefix.

Nm-Mt Ex-Mt
COMPLETE SET (12) 50.00 15.00
PZ1 Jeff Bagwell 4.00 1.20
PZ2 Albert Belle 2.50 .75
PZ3 Barry Bonds 15.00 4.50
PZ4 Joe Carter 2.50 .75
PZ5 Cecil Fielder 2.50 .75
PZ6 Andres Galarraga 2.50 .75
PZ7 Ken Griffey Jr. 10.00 3.00
PZ8 Paul Molitor 4.00 1.20
PZ9 Fred McGriff 4.00 1.20
PZ10 Rafael Palmeiro 4.00 1.20
PZ11 Frank Thomas 6.00 1.80
PZ12 Matt Williams 2.50 .75

1995 Stadium Club Ring Leaders

Randomly inserted in packs, this set features players who have won various awards or titles. This set was also redeemable as a prize with winning regular phone cards. This set features Stadium Club's "Power Matrix Technology," which makes the cards shine and glow. The horizontal fronts feature a player photo, rings in both upper corners as well as other designs that make for a very busy front. The backs have information on how the player earned his rings, along with a player photo and some other pertinent information.

Nm-Mt Ex-Mt
COMPLETE SET (40) 100.00 30.00
COMPLETE SERIES 1 (20) 50.00 15.00
COMP.SERIES 2 (20) 50.00 15.00
RL1 Jeff Bagwell 5.00 1.50
RL2 Mark McGwire 20.00 6.00
RL3 Ozzie Smith 12.00 3.60
RL4 Paul Molitor 5.00 1.50
RL5 Darryl Strawberry 1.50 .45
RL6 Eddie Murray 8.00 2.40
RL7 Tony Gwynn 10.00 3.00
RL8 Jose Canseco 8.00 2.40
RL9 Howard Johnson 1.50 .45
RL10 Andre Dawson 3.00 .90
RL11 Matt Williams 3.00 .90
RL12 Tim Raines 3.00 .90
RL13 Fred McGriff 5.00 1.50
RL14 Ken Griffey Jr. 12.00 3.60
RL15 Gary Sheffield 3.00 .90
RL16 Dennis Eckersley 3.00 .90
RL17 Kevin Mitchell 1.50 .45
RL18 Will Clark 8.00 2.40
RL19 Darren Daulton 3.00 .90
RL20 Paul O'Neill 5.00 1.50
RL21 Julio Franco 3.00 .90
RL22 Albert Belle 3.00 .90
RL23 Juan Gonzalez 8.00 2.40
RL24 Kirby Puckett 8.00 2.40
RL25 Joe Carter 3.00 .90
RL26 Frank Thomas 8.00 2.40
RL27 Cal Ripken 25.00 7.50
RL28 John Olerud 3.00 .90
RL29 Ruben Sierra 1.50 .45
RL30 Barry Bonds 20.00 6.00
RL31 Cecil Fielder 3.00 .90
RL32 Roger Clemens 15.00 4.50
RL33 Don Mattingly 20.00 6.00
RL34 Terry Pendleton 3.00 .90
RL35 Rickey Henderson 8.00 2.40
RL36 Dave Winfield 3.00 .90
RL37 Edgar Martinez 5.00 1.50
RL38 Wade Boggs 5.00 1.50
RL39 Willie McGee 3.00 .90
RL40 Andres Galarraga 3.00 .90

1995 Stadium Club Super Skills

This 20-card set was randomly inserted into hobby packs. The cards are numbered in the upper left as "X" of 9.

Nm-Mt Ex-Mt
COMPLETE SERIES 1 (9) 30.00 9.00
COMP.SERIES 2 (11) 40.00 12.00
SS1 Roberto Alomar 6.00 1.80

SS2 Barry Bonds 15.00 4.50
SS3 Jay Buhner 2.50 .75
SS4 Chuck Carr 1.25 .35
SS5 Don Mattingly 15.00 4.50
SS6 Raul Mondesi 2.50 .75
SS7 Tim Salmon 4.00 1.20
SS8 Deion Sanders 4.00 1.20
SS9 Devon White 2.50 .75
SS10 Mark Whiten 1.25 .35
SS11 Ken Griffey Jr. 10.00 3.00
SS12 Marquis Grissom 1.25 .35
SS13 Paul O'Neill 4.00 1.20
SS14 Kenny Lofton 2.50 .75
SS15 Larry Walker 4.00 1.20
SS16 Scott Cooper 1.25 .35
SS17 Barry Larkin 6.00 1.80
SS18 Matt Williams 2.50 .75
SS19 John Wetteland 2.50 .75
SS20 Randy Johnson 6.00 1.80

1995 Stadium Club Virtual Extremists

This 10-card set was inserted randomly into second series rack packs. The fronts feature a player photo against a baseball backdrop. The words "VR Extremist" are spelled vertically down the right side while the player name is in silver foil on the bottom. All of this is surrounded by blue and purple borders. The horizontal backs feature projected full-season 1994 stats. The cards are numbered with a "VRE" prefix in the upper right corner.

Nm-Mt Ex-Mt
COMPLETE SET (10) 80.00 24.00
VRE1 Barry Bonds 25.00 7.50
VRE2 Ken Griffey Jr. 15.00 4.50
VRE3 Jeff Bagwell 6.00 1.80
VRE4 Albert Belle 4.00 1.20
VRE5 Frank Thomas 10.00 3.00
VRE6 Tony Gwynn 12.00 3.60
VRE7 Kenny Lofton 4.00 1.20
VRE8 Deion Sanders 6.00 1.80
VRE9 Ken Hill 2.00 .60
VRE10 Jimmy Key 4.00 1.20

1995 Stadium Club Members Only

Topps produced a 50-card boxed set for each of the four major sports. With their club membership, members received one set of their choice and had the option of purchasing additional sets for $10.00 each. Player section was based on 1994 leaders from both leagues in various statistical categories. The five Finest cards (46-50) represent Topps' selection of the top rookies of 1994. The color action photos on the fronts have brightly-colored backgrounds and carry the distinctive Topps Stadium Club Members Only gold foil seal. The backs present a second color photo and player profile.

Nm-Mt Ex-Mt
COMP. FACT SET (50) 20.00 6.00
1 Moises Alou .25 .07
2 Jeff Bagwell 1.00 .30
3 Albert Belle .25 .07
4 Andy Benes .10 .03
5 Dante Bichette .25 .07
6 Craig Biggio .50 .15
7 Wade Boggs 1.00 .30
8 Barry Bonds 2.00 .60
9 Brett Butler .25 .07
10 Jose Canseco 1.00 .30
11 Joe Carter .25 .07
12 Vince Coleman .10 .03
13 Jeff Conine .10 .03
14 Cecil Fielder .25 .07
15 John Franco .25 .07
16 Julio Franco .25 .07
17 Travis Fryman .25 .07
18 Andres Galarraga .75 .23
19 Ken Griffey Jr. 2.50 .75
20 Marquis Grissom .10 .03
21 Tony Gwynn 2.00 .60
22 Ken Hill .10 .03
23 Randy Johnson 1.25 .35
24 Lance Johnson .10 .03
25 Jimmy Key .25 .07
26 Chuck Knoblauch .50 .15
27 Ray Lankford .25 .07
28 Darren Lewis .10 .03
29 Kenny Lofton .50 .15
30 Greg Maddux 2.50 .75
31 Fred McGriff .50 .15
32 Kevin Mitchell .10 .03
33 Paul Molitor 1.00 .30
34 Hal Morris .10 .03
35 Paul O'Neill .25 .07
36 Rafael Palmeiro .75 .23
37 Tony Phillips .10 .03
38 Mike Piazza 2.50 .75
39 Kirby Puckett 1.00 .30
40 Cal Ripken 4.00 1.20
41 Deion Sanders .75 .23
42 Lee Smith .25 .07
43 Frank Thomas 1.25 .35
44 Larry Walker .25 .07
45 Matt Williams .50 .15
46 Manny Ramirez 1.00 .30
47 Joey Hamilton .10 .03
48 Raul Mondesi .50 .15
49 Bob Hamelin .10 .03
50 Ryan Klesko .25 .07

1995 Stadium Club Members Only Finest Bronze

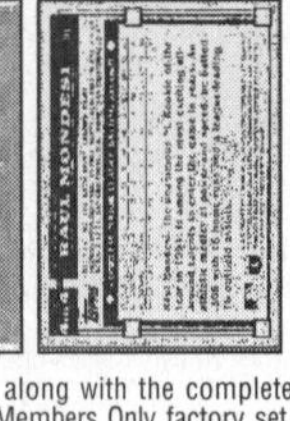

As a special bonus along with the complete 1995 Stadium Club Members Only factory set, members received these four cards featuring the 1994 Rookie of the Year and Cy Young Award Winners. The first shipment included series 1 and 2 cards as well as two of the Finest Bronze cards. The second shipment included series 3 cards and the remaining two Finest Bronze cards. The cards feature chromium metallized graphics, mounted on bronze and factory sealed in clear resin. Also, collectors got one of thsese cards if they only ordered one series. Bob Hamelin (series 1), Greg Maddux (Series 2) and David Cone (series 3). Mondesi was only available if one bought a complete set.

Nm-Mt Ex-Mt
COMPLETE SET (4) 50.00 15.00
1 Bob Hamelin 3.00 .90
2 Greg Maddux 40.00 12.00
3 David Cone 5.00 1.50
4 Raul Mondesi 5.00 1.50

1996 Stadium Club

The 1996 Stadium Club set consists of 450 cards with cards 1-225 in first series packs and 226-450 in second series packs. The product was primarily distributed in first and second series foil-wrapped packs.There was also a factory set, which included the Mantle insert cards, packaged in mini-cereal box type cartons and made available through retail outlets. The set includes a Team TSC subset (181-270). These subset cards were slightly shortprinted in comparison to the other cards in the set. Though not confirmed by the manufacturer, it is believed that card number 22 (Roberto Hernandez) is a short-print.

Nm-Mt Ex-Mt
COMPLETE SET (450) 80.00 24.00
COMP.CEREAL SET (454) 80.00 24.00
COMP.SERIES 1 (225) 40.00 12.00
COMP.SERIES 2 (225) 40.00 12.00
COMMON (1-180/271-450) .30 .09
COMMON SP (181-270) .50 .15
1 Hideo Nomo .75 .23
2 Paul Molitor .50 .15
3 Garret Anderson .30 .09
4 Jose Mesa .30 .09
5 Vinny Castilla .30 .09
6 Mike Mussina .75 .23
7 Ray Durham .30 .09
8 Jack McDowell .30 .09
9 Juan Gonzalez .75 .23
10 Chipper Jones .75 .23
11 Deion Sanders .50 .15
12 Rondell White .30 .09
13 Tom Henke .30 .09
14 Derek Bell .30 .09
15 Randy Myers .30 .09
16 Randy Johnson .75 .23
17 Len Dykstra .30 .09
18 Bill Pulsipher .30 .09
19 Greg Colbrunn .30 .09
20 David Wells .30 .09
21 Chad Curtis .30 .09
22 Roberto Hernandez SP 5.00 1.50
23 Kirby Puckett .75 .23
24 Joe Vitiello .30 .09
25 Roger Clemens 1.50 .45
26 Al Martin .30 .09
27 Chad Ogea .30 .09
28 David Segui .30 .09
29 Joey Hamilton .30 .09
30 Dan Wilson .30 .09
31 Chad Fonville .30 .09
32 Bernard Gilkey .30 .09
33 Kevin Seitzer .30 .09
34 Shawn Green .30 .09
35 Rick Aguilera .30 .09
36 Gary DiSarcina .30 .09
37 Jaime Navarro .30 .09
38 Doug Jones .30 .09
39 Brent Gates .30 .09
40 Dean Palmer .30 .09
41 Pat Rapp .30 .09
42 Tony Clark .30 .09
43 Bill Swift .30 .09
44 Randy Velarde .30 .09
45 Matt Williams .30 .09
46 John Mabry .30 .09
47 Mike Fetters .30 .09
48 Orlando Miller .30 .09
49 Tom Glavine .50 .15
50 Delino DeShields .30 .09
51 Scott Erickson .30 .09
52 Andy Van Slyke .30 .09
53 Jim Bullinger .30 .09
54 Lyle Mouton .30 .09
55 Bret Saberhagen .30 .09
56 Benito Santiago .30 .09
57 Dan Miceli .30 .09
58 Carl Everett .30 .09
59 Rod Beck .30 .09
60 Phil Nevin .30 .09
61 Jason Giambi .75 .23
62 Paul Menhart .30 .09
63 Eric Karros .30 .09
64 Allen Watson .30 .09
65 Jeff Cirillo .30 .09
66 Lee Smith .30 .09
67 Sean Berry .30 .09
68 Luis Sojo .30 .09
69 Jeff Montgomery .30 .09
70 Todd Hundley .30 .09
71 John Burkett .30 .09
72 Mark Gubicza .30 .09
73 Don Mattingly 2.00 .60
74 Jeff Brantley .30 .09
75 Matt Walbeck .30 .09
76 Steve Parris .30 .09
77 Ken Caminiti .30 .09
78 Kirt Manwaring .30 .09
79 Greg Vaughn .30 .09
80 Pedro Martinez .75 .23
81 Benji Gil .30 .09
82 Heathcliff Slocumb .30 .09
83 Joe Girardi .30 .09
84 Sean Bergman .30 .09
85 Matt Karchner .30 .09
86 Butch Huskey .30 .09
87 Mike Morgan .30 .09
88 Todd Worrell .30 .09
89 Mike Bordick .30 .09
90 Bip Roberts .30 .09
91 Mike Hampton .30 .09
92 Troy O'Leary .30 .09
93 Wally Joyner .30 .09
94 Dave Stevens .30 .09
95 Cecil Fielder .30 .09
96 Wade Boggs .50 .15
97 Hal Morris .30 .09
98 Mickey Tettleton .30 .09
99 Jeff Kent .30 .09
100 Denny Martinez .30 .09
101 Luis Gonzalez .30 .09
102 John Jaha .30 .09
103 Javier Lopez .30 .09
104 Mark McGwire 2.00 .60
105 Ken Griffey Jr. 1.25 .35
106 Darren Daulton .30 .09
107 Bryan Rekar .30 .09
108 Mike Macfarlane .30 .09
109 Gary Gaetti .30 .09
110 Shane Reynolds .30 .09
111 Pat Meares .30 .09
112 Jason Schmidt .30 .09
113 Otis Nixon .30 .09
114 John Franco .30 .09
115 Marc Newfield .30 .09
116 Andy Benes .30 .09
117 Ozzie Guillen .30 .09
118 Brian Jordan .30 .09
119 Terry Pendleton .30 .09
120 Chuck Finley .30 .09
121 Scott Stahoviak .30 .09
122 Sid Fernandez .30 .09
123 Derek Jeter 2.00 .60
124 John Smiley .30 .09
125 David Bell .30 .09
126 Brett Butler .30 .09
127 Doug Drabek .30 .09
128 J.T. Snow .30 .09
129 Joe Carter .30 .09
130 Dennis Eckersley .30 .09
131 Marty Cordova .30 .09
132 Greg Maddux 1.25 .35
133 Tom Goodwin .30 .09
134 Andy Ashby .30 .09
135 Paul Sorrento .30 .09
136 Ricky Bones .30 .09
137 Shawon Dunston .30 .09
138 Moises Alou .30 .09
139 Mickey Morandini .30 .09
140 Ramon Martinez .30 .09
141 Royce Clayton .30 .09
142 Brad Ausmus .30 .09
143 Kenny Rogers .30 .09
144 Tim Naehring .30 .09
145 Chris Gomez .30 .09
146 Bobby Bonilla .30 .09
147 Wilson Alvarez .30 .09
148 Johnny Damon .30 .09
149 Pat Hentgen .30 .09
150 Andres Galarraga .30 .09
151 David Cone .30 .09
152 Lance Johnson .30 .09
153 Carlos Garcia .30 .09
154 Doug Johns .30 .09
155 Midre Cummings .30 .09
156 Steve Sparks .30 .09
157 Sandy Martinez .30 .09
158 Wm. Van Landingham .30 .09
159 David Justice .30 .09
160 Mark Grace .50 .15
161 Robb Nen .30 .09
162 Mike Greenwell .30 .09
163 Brad Radke .30 .09
164 Edgardo Alfonzo .30 .09
165 Mark Leiter .30 .09
166 Walt Weiss .30 .09
167 Mel Rojas .30 .09
168 Bret Boone .30 .09
169 Ricky Bottalico .30 .09
170 Bobby Higginson .30 .09
171 Trevor Hoffman .30 .09
172 Jay Bell .30 .09
173 Gabe White .30 .09
174 Curtis Goodwin .30 .09
175 Tyler Green .30 .09
176 Roberto Alomar .75 .23
177 Sterling Hitchcock .30 .09
178 Ryan Klesko .30 .09
179 Donne Wall .30 .09
180 Brian McRae .30 .09
181 Will Clark TSC SP 1.00 .30
182 F.Thomas TSC SP 1.00 .30
183 Jeff Bagwell TSC SP .50 .15
184 Mo Vaughn TSC SP .50 .15
185 Tino Martinez TSC SP .75 .23
186 Craig Biggio TSC SP .75 .23
187 C. Knoblauch TSC SP .50 .15
188 Carlos Baerga TSC SP .50 .15
189 Quilvio Veras TSC SP .50 .15
190 Luis Alicea TSC SP .50 .15
191 Jim Thome TSC SP 1.00 .30
192 Mike Blowers TSC SP .50 .15
193 R.Ventura TSC SP .50 .15
194 Jeff King TSC SP .50 .15
195 Tony Phillips TSC SP .50 .15
196 John Valentin TSC SP .50 .15
197 Barry Larkin TSC SP 1.00 .30
198 Cal Ripken TSC SP 3.00 .90
199 Omar Vizquel TSC SP .50 .15
200 Kurt Abbott TSC SP .50 .15
201 Albert Belle TSC SP .50 .15
202 Barry Bonds TSC SP 2.50 .75
203 Ron Gant TSC SP .50 .15
204 D.Bichette TSC SP .50 .15
205 Jeff Conine TSC SP .50 .15
206 Jim Edmonds TSC .50 .15
SP UER
Greg Myers pictured on front
207 Stan Javier TSC SP .50 .15
208 Kenny Lofton TSC SP .50 .15
209 Ray Lankford TSC SP .50 .15
210 B.Williams TSC SP .75 .23
211 Jay Buhner TSC SP .50 .15
212 Paul O'Neill TSC SP .75 .23
213 Tim Salmon TSC SP .75 .23
214 R.Sanders TSC SP .50 .15
215 M.Ramirez TSC SP .50 .15
216 Mike Piazza TSC SP 1.50 .45
217 Mike Stanley TSC SP .50 .15
218 Tony Eusebio TSC SP .50 .15
219 Chris Hoiles TSC SP .50 .15
220 R.Karkovice TSC SP .50 .15
221 E.Martinez TSC SP .75 .23
222 Chili Davis TSC SP .50 .15
223 Jose Canseco TSC SP .75 .23
224 Eddie Murray TSC SP 1.00 .30
225 G.Berroa TSC SP .50 .15
226 C.Jones TSC SP 1.00 .30
227 G.Anderson TSC SP .50 .15
228 M.Cordova TSC SP .50 .15
229 Jon Nunnally TSC SP .50 .15
230 Brian L.Hunter TSC SP .50 .15
231 Shawn Green TSC SP .50 .15
232 Ray Durham TSC SP .50 .15
233 Alex Gonzalez TSC SP .50 .15
234 B.Higginson TSC SP .50 .15
235 R.Johnson TSC SP 1.00 .30
236 Al Leiter TSC SP .50 .15
237 Tom Glavine TSC SP .75 .23
238 Kenny Rogers TSC SP .50 .15
239 M.Hampton TSC SP .50 .15
240 David Wells TSC SP .50 .15
241 Jim Abbott TSC SP .75 .23
242 Denny Neagle TSC SP .50 .15
243 W.Alvarez TSC SP .50 .15
244 John Smiley TSC SP .50 .15
245 Greg Maddux TSC SP .75 .23
246 Andy Ashby TSC SP .50 .15
247 Hideo Nomo TSC SP 1.00 .30
248 Pat Rapp TSC SP .50 .15
249 T.Wakefield TSC SP .50 .15
250 John Smoltz TSC SP .75 .23
251 J.Hamilton TSC SP .50 .15
252 Frank Castillo TSC SP .50 .15
253 D.Martinez TSC SP .50 .15
254 J.Navarro TSC SP .50 .15
255 Karim Garcia TSC SP .50 .15
256 Bob Abreu TSC SP .50 .15
257 Butch Huskey TSC SP .50 .15
258 Ruben Rivera TSC SP .50 .15
259 J.Damon TSC SP .50 .15
260 Derek Jeter TSC SP 2.50 .75
261 D. Eckersley TSC SP .50 .15
262 Jose Mesa TSC SP .50 .15
263 Tom Henke TSC SP .50 .15
264 Rick Aguilera TSC SP .50 .15
265 Randy Myers TSC SP .50 .15
266 John Franco TSC SP .50 .15
267 Jeff Brantley TSC SP .50 .15
268 J.Wetteland TSC SP .50 .15
269 Mark Wohlers TSC SP .50 .15
270 Rod Beck TSC SP .50 .15
271 Barry Larkin .75 .23
272 Paul O'Neill .50 .15
273 Bobby Jones .30 .09
274 Will Clark .75 .23
275 Steve Avery .30 .09
276 Jim Edmonds .30 .09
277 John Olerud .30 .09
278 Carlos Perez .30 .09
279 Chris Hoiles .30 .09
280 Jeff Conine .30 .09
281 Jim Eisenreich .30 .09
282 Jason Jacome .30 .09
283 Ray Lankford .30 .09
284 John Wasdin .30 .09
285 Frank Thomas .75 .23
286 Jason Isringhausen .30 .09
287 Glenallen Hill .30 .09
288 Esteban Loaiza .30 .09
289 Bernie Williams .50 .15
290 Curtis Leskanic .30 .09
291 Scott Cooper .30 .09
292 Curt Schilling .50 .15
293 Eddie Murray .75 .23
294 Rick Krivda .30 .09
295 Domingo Cedeno .30 .09
296 Jeff Fassero .30 .09
297 Albert Belle .30 .09
298 Craig Biggio .50 .15
299 Fernando Vina .30 .09
300 Edgar Martinez .50 .15
301 Tony Gwynn 1.00 .30
302 Felipe Lira .30 .09
303 Mo Vaughn .30 .09
304 Alex Fernandez .30 .09
305 Keith Lockhart .30 .09
306 Roger Pavlik .30 .09
307 Lee Tinsley .30 .09
308 Omar Vizquel .30 .09
309 Scott Servais .30 .09
310 Danny Tartabull .30 .09
311 Chili Davis .30 .09
312 Cal Eldred .30 .09
313 Roger Cedeno .30 .09
314 Chris Hammond .30 .09
315 Rusty Greer .30 .09
316 Brady Anderson .30 .09
317 Ron Villone .30 .09
318 Mark Carreon .30 .09
319 Larry Walker .50 .15
320 Pete Harnisch .30 .09
321 Robin Ventura .30 .09
322 Tim Belcher .30 .09
323 Tony Tarasco .30 .09
324 Juan Guzman .30 .09
325 Kenny Lofton .30 .09
326 Kevin Foster .30 .09
327 Wil Cordero .30 .09
328 Troy Percival .30 .09
329 Turk Wendell .30 .09
330 Thomas Howard .30 .09
331 Carlos Baerga .30 .09
332 B.J. Surhoff .30 .09
333 Jay Buhner .30 .09
334 Andujar Cedeno .30 .09
335 Jeff King .30 .09
336 Dante Bichette .30 .09
337 Alan Trammell .50 .15
338 Scott Leius .30 .09
339 Chris Snopek .30 .09
340 Roger Bailey .30 .09
341 Jacob Brumfield .30 .09
342 Jose Canseco .75 .23
343 Rafael Palmeiro .50 .15
344 Quilvio Veras .30 .09
345 Darrin Fletcher .30 .09
346 Carlos Delgado .30 .09
347 Tony Eusebio .30 .09
348 Ismael Valdes .30 .09
349 Terry Steinbach .30 .09
350 Orel Hershiser .30 .09
351 Kurt Abbott .30 .09
352 Jody Reed .30 .09
353 David Howard .30 .09
354 Ruben Sierra .30 .09
355 John Ericks .30 .09
356 Buck Showalter MG .30 .09
357 Jim Thome .75 .23
358 Geronimo Berroa .30 .09
359 Robby Thompson .30 .09
360 Jose Vizcaino .30 .09
361 Jeff Frye .30 .09
362 Kevin Appier .30 .09
363 Pat Kelly .30 .09
364 Ron Gant .30 .09
365 Luis Alicea .30 .09
366 Armando Benitez .30 .09
367 Rico Brogna .30 .09
368 Manny Ramirez .30 .09
369 Mike Lansing .30 .09
370 Sammy Sosa 1.25 .35
371 Don Wengert .30 .09
372 Dave Nilsson .30 .09
373 Sandy Alomar Jr. .30 .09
374 Joey Cora .30 .09
375 Larry Thomas .30 .09
376 John Valentin .30 .09
377 Kevin Ritz .30 .09
378 Steve Finley .30 .09
379 Frank Rodriguez .30 .09
380 Ivan Rodriguez .75 .23
381 Alex Ochoa .30 .09
382 Mark Lemke .30 .09
383 Scott Brosius .30 .09
384 James Mouton .30 .09
385 Mark Langston .30 .09
386 Ed Sprague .30 .09
387 Joe Oliver .30 .09
388 Steve Ontiveros .30 .09
389 Rey Sanchez .30 .09
390 Mike Henneman .30 .09
391 Jose Valentin .30 .09
392 Tom Candiotti .30 .09
393 Damon Buford .30 .09
394 Erik Hanson .30 .09
395 Mark Smith .30 .09
396 Pete Schourek .30 .09
397 John Flaherty .30 .09
398 Dave Martinez .30 .09
399 Tommy Greene .30 .09
400 Gary Sheffield .30 .09
401 Glenn Dishman .30 .09
402 Barry Bonds 2.00 .60
403 Tom Pagnozzi .30 .09
404 Todd Stottlemyre .30 .09
405 Tim Salmon .50 .15
406 John Hudek .30 .09
407 Fred McGriff .50 .15
408 Orlando Merced .30 .09
409 Brian Barber .30 .09
410 Ryan Thompson .30 .09
411 Mariano Rivera .50 .15
412 Eric Young .30 .09
413 Chris Bosio .30 .09
414 Chuck Knoblauch .30 .09
415 Jamie Moyer .30 .09
416 Chan Ho Park .30 .09
417 Mark Portugal .30 .09
418 Tim Raines .30 .09
419 Antonio Osuna .30 .09
420 Todd Zeile .30 .09
421 Steve Wojciechowski .30 .09
422 Marquis Grissom .30 .09
423 Norm Charlton .30 .09
424 Cal Ripken 2.50 .75
425 Gregg Jefferies .30 .09
426 Mike Stanton .30 .09
427 Tony Fernandez .30 .09
428 Jose Rijo .30 .09
429 Jeff Bagwell .50 .15
430 Raul Mondesi .30 .09
431 Travis Fryman .30 .09
432 Ron Karkovice .30 .09
433 Alan Benes .30 .09
434 Tony Phillips .30 .09
435 Reggie Sanders .30 .09
436 Andy Pettitte .50 .15
437 Matt Lawton RC .30 .09
438 Jeff Blauser .30 .09
439 Michael Tucker .30 .09

440 Mark Loretta .30 .09
441 Charlie Hayes .30 .09
442 Mike Piazza 1.25 .35
443 Shane Andrews .30 .09
444 Jeff Suppan .30 .09
445 Steve Rodriguez .30 .09
446 Mike Matheny .30 .09
447 Trenidad Hubbard .30 .09
448 Denny Hocking .30 .09
449 Mark Grudzielanek .30 .09
450 Joe Randa .30 .09

1996 Stadium Club Members Only Parallel

This set, of which only 750 were produced is a parallel to the regular 1996 Stadium Club set. The cards are embossed with a "Members Only" logo and were available only to members of Topps' Stadium Club. The set includes a parallel of the complete 450-card basic set plus the following inserts: Bash and Burn, Mickey Mantle Heroes, Megaheroes, Metalists, Midsummer Matchups, Power Packed, Power Streak, Prime Cuts and TSC Awards. Only the inserts cards are priced below. Please refer to the multiplier for value on parallels to the basic issue cards.

Nm-Mt Ex-Mt
COMP.SET W/INSERTS (555) 500.00 150.00
COMP.BASE SET (450) 200.00 60.00
COMMON CARD (1-450) .25 .07
COMMON (M1-M19) 5.00 1.50
*MEMBERS ONLY: 6X BASIC CARDS.
M1 Jeff Bagwell 4.00 1.20
M2 Barry Bonds 10.00 3.00
M3 Jose Canseco 4.00 1.20
M4 Roger Clemens 10.00 3.00
M5 Dennis Eckersley 1.50 .45
M6 Greg Maddux 12.00 3.60
M7 Cal Ripken 20.00 6.00
M8 Frank Thomas 8.00 2.40
BB1 Sammy Sosa 10.00 3.00
BB2 Barry Bonds 10.00 3.00
BB3 Reggie Sanders 1.00 .30
BB4 Craig Biggio 2.00 .60
BB5 Raul Mondesi 2.00 .60
BB6 Ron Gant 1.00 .30
BB7 Ray Lankford 1.50 .45
BB8 Glenallen Hill 1.00 .30
BB9 Chad Curtis 1.00 .30
BB10 John Valentin 1.50 .45
MH1 Frank Thomas 8.00 2.40
MH2 Ken Griffey Jr. 15.00 4.50
MH3 Hideo Nomo 4.00 1.20
MH4 Ozzie Smith 4.00 1.20
MH5 Will Clark 3.00 .90
MH6 Jack McDowell 1.00 .30
MH7 Andres Galarraga 3.00 .90
MH8 Roger Clemens 10.00 3.00
MH9 Deion Sanders 1.50 .45
MH10 Mo Vaughn 1.50 .45
MM1 Hideo Nomo 5.00 1.50
Randy Johnson
MM2 Mike Piazza 12.00 3.60
Ivan Rodriguez
MM3 Fred McGriff 8.00 2.40
Frank Thomas
MM4 Craig Biggio 2.00 .60
Carlos Baerga
MM5 Vinny Castilla 4.00 1.20
Wade Boggs
MM6 Barry Larkin 20.00 6.00
Cal Ripken
MM7 Barry Bonds 8.00 2.40
Albert Belle
MM8 Len Dykstra 1.50 .45
Kenny Lofton
MM9 Tony Gwynn 10.00 3.00
Kirby Puckett
MM10 Ron Gant 2.00 .60
Edgar Martinez
PC1 Albert Belle 1.50 .45
PC2 Barry Bonds 4.00 1.20
PC3 Ken Griffey Jr. 15.00 4.50
PC4 Tony Gwynn 10.00 3.00
PC5 Edgar Martinez 2.00 .60
PC6 Rafael Palmeiro 3.00 .90
PC7 Mike Piazza 10.00 3.00
PC8 Frank Thomas 8.00 2.40
PP1 Albert Belle 1.50 .45
PP2 Mark McGwire 15.00 4.50
PP3 Jose Canseco 4.00 1.20
PP4 Mike Piazza 10.00 3.00
PP5 Ron Gant 1.50 .45
PP6 Ken Griffey Jr. 15.00 4.50
PP7 Mo Vaughn 1.50 .45
PP8 Cecil Fielder 1.50 .45
PP9 Tim Salmon 3.00 .90
PP10 Frank Thomas 8.00 2.40
PP11 Juan Gonzalez 4.00 1.20
PP12 Andres Galarraga 3.00 .90
PP13 Fred McGriff 2.00 .60
PP14 Jay Buhner 1.50 .45
PP15 Dante Bichette 1.50 .45
PS1 Randy Johnson 4.00 1.20
PS2 Hideo Nomo 5.00 1.50
PS3 Albert Belle 1.50 .45
PS4 Dante Bichette 1.50 .45
PS5 Jay Buhner 1.50 .45
PS6 Frank Thomas 8.00 2.40
PS7 Mark McGwire 15.00 4.50
PS8 Rafael Palmeiro 3.00 .90
PS9 Mo Vaughn 1.50 .45
PS10 Sammy Sosa 10.00 3.00
PS11 Larry Walker 3.00 .90
PS12 Gary Gaetti 1.50 .45
PS13 Tim Salmon 3.00 .90
PS14 Barry Bonds 10.00 3.00
PS15 Jim Edmonds 3.00 .90
TSCA1 Cal Ripken 20.00 6.00
TSCA2 Albert Belle 1.50 .45
TSCA3 Tom Glavine 3.00 .90
TSCA4 Jeff Conine 1.00 .30
TSCA5 Ken Griffey Jr. 15.00 4.50
TSCA6 Hideo Nomo 4.00 1.20
TSCA7 Greg Maddux 10.00 3.00
TSCA8 Chipper Jones 10.00 3.00
TSCA9 Randy Johnson 4.00 1.20
TSCA10 Jose Mesa 1.00 .30

1996 Stadium Club Bash and Burn

Randomly inserted in packs at a rate of one in 24 (retail) and one in 48 (hobby), this ten card set features power/speed players.

Nm-Mt Ex-Mt
COMPLETE SET (10) 40.00 12.00
BB1 Sammy Sosa 15.00 4.50
BB2 Barry Bonds 25.00 7.50
BB3 Reggie Sanders 4.00 1.20
BB4 Craig Biggio 6.00 1.80
BB5 Raul Mondesi 4.00 1.20
BB6 Ron Gant 4.00 1.20
BB7 Ray Lankford 4.00 1.20
BB8 Glenallen Hill 4.00 1.20
BB9 Chad Curtis 4.00 1.20
BB10 John Valentin 4.00 1.20

1996 Stadium Club Extreme Players Bronze

One hundred and seventy nine different players were featured on Extreme Player game cards randomly issued in 1996 Stadium Club first and second series packs. Each player has three versions: Bronze, Silver and Gold. All of these cards parallel their corresponding regular issue card except for the Bronze foil "Extreme Players" logo on each card front and the "EP" suffix on the card number, thus creating a skip-numbered set. The Bronze cards listed below were seeded at a rate of 1:12 packs. At the conclusion of the 1996 regular season, an Extreme Player from each of ten positions was identified as a winner based on scores calculated from their actual playing statistics. The 10 winning players are noted with a "W" below. Prior to the December 31st, 1996 deadline, each of the ten winning Extreme Players Bronze cards was redeemable for a 10-card set of Extreme Winners Bronze. Unreedemed winners are now in much shorter supply than other cards in this set and carry premium values.

Nm-Mt Ex-Mt
COMP.BRONZE SER.1 (90) 120.00 36.00
COMP.BRONZE SER.2 (90) 120.00 36.00
*BRONZE: 2X TO 5X BASE CARD HI...
*SILVER SINGLES: .6X TO 1.5X BRONZE
*SILVER WIN: .6X TO 1.5X BRONZE WIN
*GOLD SINGLES: 1.25X TO 3X BRONZE
*GOLD WIN: 1.25X TO 3X BRONZE WIN
GOLD STATED ODDS 1:48
SKIP-NUMBERED 179-CARD SET
77 Ken Caminiti W 4.00 1.20
88 Todd Worrell W 1.50 .45
105 Ken Griffey Jr. W 12.00 3.60
132 Greg Maddux W 12.00 3.60
150 Andres Galarraga W 4.00 1.20
271 Barry Larkin W 4.00 1.20
400 Gary Sheffield W 5.00 1.50
402 Barry Bonds W 20.00 6.00
414 Chuck Knoblauch W 3.00 .90
442 Mike Piazza W 12.00 3.60

1996 Stadium Club Extreme Winners Bronze

This 10-card skip-numbered set was only available to collectors who redeemed one of the ten winning Bronze Extreme Players cards before the December 31st, 1996 deadline. The cards parallel the Extreme Players cards inserted in Stadium Club packs except for their distinctive diffraction foil fronts.

Nm-Mt Ex-Mt
COMPLETE SET (10) 25.00 7.50
*SILVER: 1.25X TO 3X BRONZE WINNERS
ONE SILV.SET VIA MAIL PER SILV.WINNER
*GOLD: 5X TO 12X BRONZE WINNERS
ONE GOLD CARD VIA MAIL PER GOLD WNR.
EW1 Greg Maddux 4.00 1.20
EW2 Mike Piazza 4.00 1.20
EW3 Andres Galarraga 1.00 .30
EW4 Chuck Knoblauch 1.00 .30
EW5 Ken Caminiti 1.00 .30
EW6 Barry Larkin 2.50 .75
EW7 Barry Bonds 6.00 1.80
EW8 Ken Griffey Jr. 4.00 1.20
EW9 Gary Sheffield 1.00 .30
EW10 Todd Worrell 1.00 .30

1996 Stadium Club Mantle

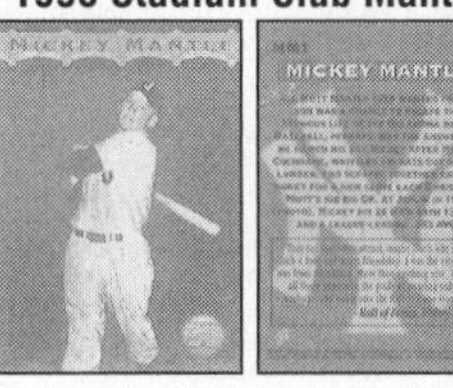

Randomly inserted at a rate of one card in every 24 packs in series one, one in 12 packs in series two, this 19-card retrospective set chronicles Mantle's career with classic photography, celebrity quotes and highlights from each year. The cards are double foil-stamped. The series one cards feature black-and-white photos, series two color photos. Mantle's name is printed across a silver foil facade of Yankee Stadium on each card top. Cereal Box factory sets include these cards with gold foil. They are valued the same as the pack inserts.

Nm-Mt Ex-Mt
COMPLETE SET (19) 120.00 36.00
COMMON (MM1-MM9) 10.00 3.00
COMMON (MM10-MM19) 6.00 1.80

1996 Stadium Club Megaheroes

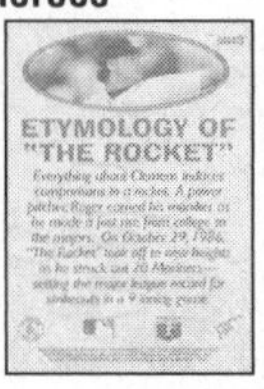

Randomly inserted at a rate of one in every 48 hobby and 24 retail packs, this 10-card set features super-heroic players matched with a comic book-style illustration depicting their nicknames.

Nm-Mt Ex-Mt
COMPLETE SET (10) 40.00 12.00
MH1 Frank Thomas 5.00 1.50
MH2 Ken Griffey Jr. 8.00 2.40
MH3 Hideo Nomo 5.00 1.50
MH4 Ozzie Smith 5.00 1.50
MH5 Will Clark 5.00 1.50
MH6 Jack McDowell 2.00 .60
MH7 Andres Galarraga 2.00 .60
MH8 Roger Clemens 10.00 3.00
MH9 Deion Sanders 3.00 .90
MH10 Mo Vaughn 2.00 .60

1996 Stadium Club Metalists

Randomly inserted in packs at a rate of one in 96 (retail) and one in 48 (hobby), this eight-card set features players with two or more MLB awards and is printed on laser-cut foil board.

Nm-Mt Ex-Mt
COMPLETE SET (8) 40.00 12.00
M1 Jeff Bagwell 2.50 .75
M2 Barry Bonds 10.00 3.00
M3 Jose Canseco 4.00 1.20
M4 Roger Clemens 8.00 2.40
M5 Dennis Eckersley 1.50 .45
M6 Greg Maddux 6.00 1.80
M7 Cal Ripken 12.00 3.60
M8 Frank Thomas 4.00 1.20

1996 Stadium Club Midsummer Matchups

Randomly inserted at a rate of one in every 48 hobby and 24 retail packs, this 10-card set salutes 1995 National League and American League All-Stars as they are matched back-to-back by position on these two-sided etched foil cards.

Nm-Mt Ex-Mt
COMPLETE SET (10) 60.00 18.00
M1 Hideo Nomo 5.00 1.50
Randy Johnson
M2 Mike Piazza 8.00 2.40
Ivan Rodriguez
M3 Fred McGriff 5.00 1.50
Frank Thomas
M4 Craig Biggio 3.00 .90
Carlos Baerga
M5 Vinny Castilla 3.00 .90
Wade Boggs
M6 Barry Larkin 15.00 4.50
Cal Ripken
M7 Barry Bonds 12.00 3.60
Albert Belle
M8 Len Dykstra 2.00 .60
Kenny Lofton
M9 Tony Gwynn 6.00 1.80
Kirby Puckett
M10 Ron Gant 3.00 .90
Edgar Martinez

1996 Stadium Club Power Packed

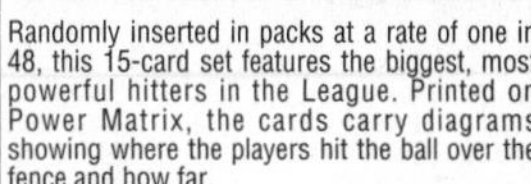

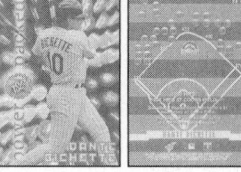

Randomly inserted in packs at a rate of one in 48, this 15-card set features the biggest, most powerful hitters in the League. Printed on Power Matrix, the cards carry diagrams showing where the players hit the ball over the fence and how far.

Nm-Mt Ex-Mt
COMPLETE SET (15) 60.00 18.00
PP1 Albert Belle 2.50 .75
PP2 Mark McGwire 15.00 4.50
PP3 Jose Canseco 6.00 1.80
PP4 Mike Piazza 10.00 3.00
PP5 Ron Gant 2.50 .75
PP6 Ken Griffey Jr. 10.00 3.00
PP7 Mo Vaughn 2.50 .75
PP8 Cecil Fielder 2.50 .75
PP9 Tim Salmon 4.00 1.20
PP10 Frank Thomas 6.00 1.80
PP11 Juan Gonzalez 6.00 1.80
PP12 Andres Galarraga 2.50 .75
PP13 Fred McGriff 4.00 1.20
PP14 Jay Buhner 2.50 .75
PP15 Dante Bichette 2.50 .75

1996 Stadium Club Power Streak

Randomly inserted at a rate of one in every 24 hobby packs and 48 retail packs, this 15-card set spotlights baseball's most awesome power hitters and strikeout artists.

Nm-Mt Ex-Mt
COMPLETE SET (15) 60.00 18.00
PS1 Randy Johnson 6.00 1.80
PS2 Hideo Nomo 6.00 1.80
PS3 Albert Belle 2.50 .75
PS4 Dante Bichette 2.50 .75
PS5 Jay Buhner 2.50 .75
PS6 Frank Thomas 6.00 1.80
PS7 Mark McGwire 15.00 4.50
PS8 Rafael Palmeiro 4.00 1.20
PS9 Mo Vaughn 2.50 .75
PS10 Sammy Sosa 10.00 3.00
PS11 Larry Walker 4.00 1.20
PS12 Gary Gaetti 2.50 .75
PS13 Tim Salmon 4.00 1.20
PS14 Barry Bonds 15.00 4.50
PS15 Jim Edmonds 2.50 .75

1996 Stadium Club Prime Cuts

Randomly inserted at a rate of one in every 36 hobby and 72 retail packs, this eight card set this set highlights hitters with the purest swings. The cards are numbered on the back with a "PC" prefix.

Nm-Mt Ex-Mt
COMPLETE SET (8) 50.00 15.00
PC1 Albert Belle 2.00 .60
PC2 Barry Bonds 12.00 3.60
PC3 Ken Griffey Jr. 8.00 2.40
PC4 Tony Gwynn 6.00 1.80
PC5 Edgar Martinez 3.00 .90
PC6 Rafael Palmeiro 3.00 .90
PC7 Mike Piazza 8.00 2.40
PC8 Frank Thomas 5.00 1.50

1996 Stadium Club TSC Awards

Randomly inserted in packs at a rate of one in 24 (retail) and one in 48 (hobby), this ten-card set features players whom TSC baseball experts voted to win various awards and is printed on diffraction foil.

Nm-Mt Ex-Mt
COMPLETE SET (10) 40.00 12.00
1 Cal Ripken 12.00 3.60

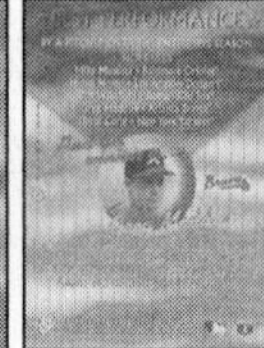

2 Albert Belle 1.50 .45
3 Tom Glavine 2.50 .75
4 Jeff Conine 1.50 .45
5 Ken Griffey Jr. 6.00 1.80
6 Hideo Nomo 4.00 1.20
7 Greg Maddux 6.00 1.80
8 Chipper Jones 4.00 1.20
9 Randy Johnson 4.00 1.20
10 Jose Mesa 1.50 .45

1996 Stadium Club Members Only

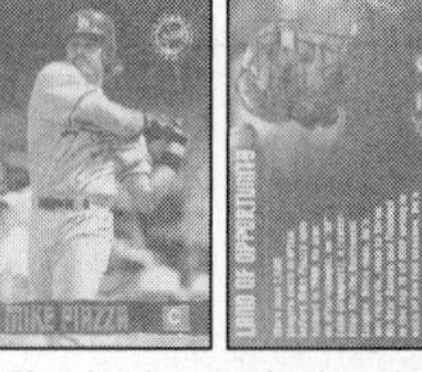

This 50-card set features color player photos of Topps' selection of 45 (numbers 1-45) of the top 1995 American and National League players. The set includes five Finest Cards (numbers 46-50) which represent Topps' selection of the top rookies from 1995. The backs carry information about the player.

Nm-Mt Ex-Mt
COMP. FACT SET (50) 20.00 6.00
1 Carlos Baerga .25 .07
2 Derek Bell .10 .03
3 Albert Belle .25 .07
4 Dante Bichette .25 .07
5 Craig Biggio .40 .12
6 Wade Boggs .75 .23
7 Barry Bonds 1.50 .45
8 Jay Buhner .25 .07
9 Vinny Castilla .25 .07
10 Jeff Conine .10 .03
11 Jim Edmonds .60 .18
12 Steve Finley .25 .07
13 Andres Galarraga .60 .18
14 Mark Grace .40 .12
15 Tony Gwynn 1.50 .45
16 Lance Johnson .10 .03
17 Randy Johnson .75 .23
18 Eric Karros .25 .07
19 Chuck Knoblauch .40 .12
20 Barry Larkin .60 .18
21 Kenny Lofton .40 .12
22 Greg Maddux 2.00 .60
23 Edgar Martinez .40 .12
24 Tino Martinez .25 .07
25 Mark McGwire 2.50 .75
26 Brian McRae .10 .03
27 Jose Mesa .10 .03
28 Eddie Murray .75 .23
29 Mike Mussina .60 .18
30 Randy Myers .10 .03
31 Hideo Nomo .75 .23
32 Rafael Palmeiro .60 .18
33 Tony Phillips .10 .03
34 Mike Piazza 2.00 .60
35 Kirby Puckett .75 .23
36 Manny Ramirez .75 .23
37 Tim Salmon .40 .12
38 Reggie Sanders .10 .03
39 Sammy Sosa 1.50 .45
40 Frank Thomas 1.00 .30
41 Jim Thome .75 .23
42 John Valentin .10 .03
43 Mo Vaughn .25 .07
44 Quilvio Veras .10 .03
45 Larry Walker .60 .18
46 Hideo Nomo FIN 1.50 .45
47 Marty Cordova FIN .25 .07
48 Chipper Jones FIN 3.00 .90
49 Garret Anderson FIN 1.00 .30
50 Andy Pettitte FIN .60 .18

1997 Stadium Club Pre-Production

Each Topps wholesale account received one of these three Pre-Production sample cards along with their order forms for 1997 Stadium Club Series 1 baseball. The cards were designed to provide wholesale customers with a sneak preview of the upcoming Stadium Club release. The design parallels the regular issue cards excpt for the PP-prefixed numbering. In addition, the term "Pre-Production Sample" replaces the line of 1996 statistics on back.

Nm-Mt Ex-Mt
COMPLETE SET (3) 5.00 1.50
PP1 Chipper Jones 3.00 .90
PP2 Kenny Lofton 1.00 .30
PP3 Gary Sheffield 2.50 .75

1997 Stadium Club

Cards from this 390 card set were distributed in eight-card hobby and retail packs (SRP $3) and 13-card hobby collector packs (SRP $5). Card fronts feature color action player photos printed on 20 pt. card stock with Topps Super Color processing, Hi-gloss laminating, embossing and double foil stamping. The backs carry player information and statistics. In addition to the standard selection of major leaguers, the set contains a 15-card TSC 2000 subset (181-195) featuring a selection of top

young prospects. These subset cards were inserted one in every two eight-card first series packs and one per 13-card first series pack. First series cards were released in February, 1997. The 195-card Series two set was issued in six-card retail packs with a suggested retail price of $2 and in nine-card hobby packs with a suggested retail price of $3. The second series set features a 15-card Stadium Sluggers subset (376-390) with an insertion rate of one in every two hobby and three retail Series 2 packs. Second series cards were released in April, 1997. Please note that cards 361 and 374 do not exist. Due to an error at the manufacturer both Mike Sweeney and Tom Pagnozzi had their cards numbered as 274. In addition, Jermaine Dye and Brant Brown both had their cards numbered as 351. These numbering errors were never corrected and no premiums in value are associated.

	Nm-Mt	Ex-Mt
COMPLETE SET (390)	80.00	24.00
COMP.SERIES 1 (195)	40.00	12.00
COMP.SERIES 2 (195)	40.00	12.00
COMMON (1-180/196-375)	.30	.09
COM.SP (181-195/376-390)	.75	.23
1 Chipper Jones	.75	.23
2 Gary Sheffield	.30	.09
3 Kenny Lofton	.30	.09
4 Brian Jordan	.30	.09
5 Mark McGwire	2.00	.60
6 Charles Nagy	.30	.09
7 Tim Salmon	.50	.15
8 Cal Ripken	2.50	.75
9 Jeff Conine	.30	.09
10 Paul Molitor	.50	.15
11 Mariano Rivera	.50	.15
12 Pedro Martinez	.75	.23
13 Jeff Bagwell	.50	.15
14 Bobby Bonilla	.30	.09
15 Barry Bonds	2.00	.60
16 Ryan Klesko	.30	.09
17 Barry Larkin	.75	.23
18 Jim Thome	.75	.23
19 Jay Buhner	.30	.09
20 Juan Gonzalez	.75	.23
21 Mike Mussina	.75	.23
22 Kevin Appier	.30	.09
23 Eric Karros	.30	.09
24 Steve Finley	.30	.09
25 Ed Sprague	.30	.09
26 Bernard Gilkey	.30	.09
27 Tony Phillips	.30	.09
28 Henry Rodriguez	.30	.09
29 John Smoltz	.50	.15
30 Dante Bichette	.30	.09
31 Mike Piazza	1.25	.35
32 Paul O'Neill	.50	.15
33 Billy Wagner	.30	.09
34 Reggie Sanders	.30	.09
35 John Jaha	.30	.09
36 Eddie Murray	.75	.23
37 Eric Young	.30	.09
38 Roberto Hernandez	.30	.09
39 Pat Hentgen	.30	.09
40 Sammy Sosa	1.25	.35
41 Todd Hundley	.30	.09
42 Mo Vaughn	.30	.09
43 Robin Ventura	.30	.09
44 Mark Grudzielanek	.30	.09
45 Shane Reynolds	.30	.09
46 Andy Pettitte	.50	.15
47 Fred McGriff	.50	.15
48 Rey Ordonez	.30	.09
49 Will Clark	.75	.23
50 Ken Griffey Jr.	1.25	.35
51 Todd Worrell	.30	.09
52 Rusty Greer	.30	.09
53 Mark Grace	.50	.15
54 Tom Glavine	.50	.15
55 Derek Jeter	2.00	.60
56 Rafael Palmeiro	.50	.15
57 Bernie Williams	.50	.15
58 Marty Cordova	.30	.09
59 Andres Galarraga	.30	.09
60 Ken Caminiti	.30	.09
61 Garret Anderson	.30	.09
62 Denny Martinez	.30	.09
63 Mike Greenwell	.30	.09
64 David Segui	.30	.09
65 Julio Franco	.30	.09
66 Rickey Henderson	.75	.23
67 Ozzie Guillen	.30	.09
68 Pete Harnisch	.30	.09
69 Chan Ho Park	.30	.09
70 Harold Baines	.30	.09
71 Mark Clark	.30	.09
72 Steve Avery	.30	.09
73 Brian Hunter	.30	.09
74 Pedro Astacio	.30	.09
75 Jack McDowell	.30	.09
76 Gregg Jefferies	.30	.09
77 Jason Kendall	.30	.09
78 Todd Walker	.30	.09
79 B.J. Surhoff	.30	.09
80 Moises Alou	.30	.09
81 Fernando Vina	.30	.09
82 Darryl Strawberry	.50	.15
83 Jose Rosado	.30	.09
84 Chris Gomez	.30	.09
85 Chili Davis	.30	.09
86 Alan Benes	.30	.09
87 Todd Hollandsworth	.30	.09
88 Jose Vizcaino	.30	.09
89 Edgardo Alfonzo	.30	.09
90 Ruben Rivera	.30	.09
91 Donovan Osborne	.30	.09
92 Doug Glanville	.30	.09
93 Gary DiSarcina	.30	.09
94 Brooks Kieschnick	.30	.09
95 Bobby Jones	.30	.09
96 Raul Casanova	.30	.09
97 Jermaine Allensworth	.30	.09
98 Kenny Rogers	.30	.09
99 Mark McLemore	.30	.09
100 Jeff Fassero	.30	.09
101 Sandy Alomar Jr.	.30	.09
102 Chuck Finley	.30	.09
103 Eric Owens	.30	.09
104 Billy McMillon	.30	.09
105 Dwight Gooden	.50	.15
106 Sterling Hitchcock	.30	.09
107 Doug Drabek	.30	.09
108 Paul Wilson	.30	.09
109 Chris Snopek	.30	.09
110 Al Leiter	.30	.09
111 Bob Tewksbury	.30	.09
112 Todd Greene	.30	.09
113 Jose Valentin	.30	.09
114 Delino DeShields	.30	.09
115 Mike Bordick	.30	.09
116 Pat Meares	.30	.09
117 Mariano Duncan	.30	.09
118 Steve Trachsel	.30	.09
119 Luis Castillo	.30	.09
120 Andy Benes	.30	.09
121 Donne Wall	.30	.09
122 Alex Gonzalez	.30	.09
123 Dan Wilson	.30	.09
124 Omar Vizquel	.50	.15
125 Devon White	.30	.09
126 Darryl Hamilton	.30	.09
127 Orlando Merced	.30	.09
128 Royce Clayton	.30	.09
129 W.VanLandingham	.30	.09
130 Terry Steinbach	.30	.09
131 Jeff Blauser	.30	.09
132 Jeff Cirillo	.30	.09
133 Roger Pavlik	.30	.09
134 Danny Tartabull	.30	.09
135 Jeff Montgomery	.30	.09
136 Bobby Higginson	.30	.09
137 Mike Grace	.30	.09
138 Kevin Elster	.30	.09
139 Brian Giles RC	1.50	.45
140 Rod Beck	.30	.09
141 Ismael Valdes	.30	.09
142 Scott Brosius	.30	.09
143 Mike Fetters	.30	.09
144 Gary Gaetti	.30	.09
145 Mike Lansing	.30	.09
146 Glenallen Hill	.30	.09
147 Shawn Green	.30	.09
148 Mel Rojas	.30	.09
149 Joey Cora	.30	.09
150 John Smiley	.30	.09
151 Marvin Benard	.30	.09
152 Curt Schilling	.50	.15
153 Dave Nilsson	.30	.09
154 Edgar Renteria	.30	.09
155 Joey Hamilton	.30	.09
156 Carlos Garcia	.30	.09
157 Nomar Garciaparra	1.25	.35
158 Kevin Ritz	.30	.09
159 Keith Lockhart	.30	.09
160 Justin Thompson	.30	.09
161 Terry Adams	.30	.09
162 Jamey Wright	.30	.09
163 Otis Nixon	.30	.09
164 Michael Tucker	.30	.09
165 Mike Stanley	.30	.09
166 Ben McDonald	.30	.09
167 John Mabry	.30	.09
168 Troy O'Leary	.30	.09
169 Mel Nieves	.30	.09
170 Bret Boone	.30	.09
171 Mike Timlin	.30	.09
172 Scott Rolen	.50	.15
173 Reggie Jefferson	.30	.09
174 Neifi Perez	.30	.09
175 Brian McRae	.30	.09
176 Tom Goodwin	.30	.09
177 Aaron Sele	.30	.09
178 Benito Santiago	.30	.09
179 Frank Rodriguez	.30	.09
180 Eric Davis	.30	.09
181 A.Jones 2000 SP	.75	.23
182 Todd Walker 2000 SP	.75	.23
183 Wes Helms 2000 SP	.75	.23
184 Nelson Figueroa 2000 SP RC	.75	.23
185 V. Guerrero 2000 SP	1.25	.35
186 B.McMillon 2000 SP	.75	.23
187 Todd Helton 2000 SP	1.25	.35
188 Nomar Garciaparra 2000 SP	2.50	.75
189 K. Maeda 2000 SP	.75	.23
190 R.Branyan 2000 SP	.75	.23
191 G.Rusch 2000 SP	.75	.23
192 B.Colon 2000 SP	.75	.23
193 Scott Rolen 2000 SP	.75	.23
194 A. Echevarria 2000 SP	.75	.23
195 Bob Abreu 2000 SP	.75	.23
196 Greg Maddux	1.25	.35
197 Joe Carter	.30	.09
198 Alex Ochoa	.30	.09
199 Ellis Burks	.30	.09
200 Ivan Rodriguez	.75	.23
201 Marquis Grissom	.30	.09
202 Trevor Hoffman	.30	.09
203 Matt Williams	.30	.09
204 Carlos Delgado	.30	.09
205 Ramon Martinez	.30	.09
206 Chuck Knoblauch	.30	.09
207 Juan Guzman	.30	.09
208 Derek Bell	.30	.09
209 Roger Clemens	1.50	.45
210 Vladimir Guerrero	.75	.23
211 Cecil Fielder	.30	.09
212 Hideo Nomo	.75	.23
213 Frank Thomas	.75	.23
214 Greg Vaughn	.30	.09
215 Javy Lopez	.30	.09
216 Raul Mondesi	.30	.09
217 Wade Boggs	.50	.15
218 Carlos Baerga	.30	.09
219 Tony Gwynn	1.00	.30
220 Tino Martinez	.50	.15
221 Vinny Castilla	.30	.09
222 Lance Johnson	.30	.09
223 David Justice	.30	.09
224 Rondell White	.30	.09
225 Dean Palmer	.30	.09
226 Jim Edmonds	.30	.09
227 Albert Belle	.30	.09
228 Alex Fernandez	.30	.09
229 Ryne Sandberg	1.25	.35
230 Jose Mesa	.30	.09
231 David Cone	.30	.09
232 Troy Percival	.30	.09
233 Edgar Martinez	.50	.15
234 Jose Canseco	.75	.23
235 Kevin Brown	.30	.09
236 Ray Lankford	.30	.09
237 Karim Garcia	.30	.09
238 J.T. Snow	.30	.09
239 Dennis Eckersley	.30	.09
240 Roberto Alomar	.75	.23
241 John Valentin	.30	.09
242 Ron Gant	.30	.09
243 Geronimo Berroa	.30	.09
244 Manny Ramirez	.30	.09
245 Travis Fryman	.30	.09
246 Denny Neagle	.30	.09
247 Randy Johnson	.75	.23
248 Darin Erstad	.30	.09
249 Mark Wohlers	.30	.09
250 Ken Hill	.30	.09
251 Larry Walker	.50	.15
252 Craig Biggio	.50	.15
253 Brady Anderson	.30	.09
254 John Wetteland	.30	.09
255 Andruw Jones	.30	.09
256 Turk Wendell	.30	.09
257 Jason Isringhausen	.30	.09
258 Jaime Navarro	.30	.09
259 Sean Berry	.30	.09
260 Albie Lopez	.30	.09
261 Jay Bell	.30	.09
262 Bobby Witt	.30	.09
263 Tony Clark	.30	.09
264 Tim Wakefield	.30	.09
265 Brad Radke	.30	.09
266 Tim Belcher	.30	.09
267 Nerio Rodriguez RC	.30	.09
268 Roger Cedeno	.30	.09
269 Tim Naehring	.30	.09
270 Kevin Tapani	.30	.09
271 Joe Randa	.30	.09
272 Randy Myers	.30	.09
273 Dave Burba	.30	.09
274 Mike Sweeney	.30	.09
275 Danny Graves	.30	.09
276 Chad Mottola	.30	.09
277 Ruben Sierra	.30	.09
278 Norm Charlton	.30	.09
279 Scott Servais	.30	.09
280 Jacob Cruz	.30	.09
281 Mike Macfarlane	.30	.09
282 Rich Becker	.30	.09
283 Shannon Stewart	.30	.09
284 Gerald Williams	.30	.09
285 Jody Reed	.30	.09
286 Jeff D'Amico	.30	.09
287 Walt Weiss	.30	.09
288 Jim Leyritz	.30	.09
289 Francisco Cordova	.30	.09
290 F.P. Santangelo	.30	.09
291 Scott Erickson	.30	.09
292 Hal Morris	.30	.09
293 Ray Durham	.30	.09
294 Andy Ashby	.30	.09
295 Darryl Kile	.30	.09
296 Jose Paniagua	.30	.09
297 Mickey Tettleton	.30	.09
298 Joe Girardi	.30	.09
299 Rocky Coppinger	.30	.09
300 Bob Abreu	.30	.09
301 John Olerud	.30	.09
302 Paul Shuey	.30	.09
303 Jeff Brantley	.30	.09
304 Bob Wells	.30	.09
305 Kevin Seitzer	.30	.09
306 Shawon Dunston	.30	.09
307 Jose Herrera	.30	.09
308 Butch Huskey	.30	.09
309 Jose Offerman	.30	.09
310 Rick Aguilera	.30	.09
311 Greg Gagne	.30	.09
312 John Burkett	.30	.09
313 Mark Thompson	.30	.09
314 Alvaro Espinoza	.30	.09
315 Todd Stottlemyre	.30	.09
316 Al Martin	.30	.09
317 James Baldwin	.30	.09
318 Cal Eldred	.30	.09
319 Sid Fernandez	.30	.09
320 Mickey Morandini	.30	.09
321 Robb Nen	.30	.09
322 Mark Lemke	.30	.09
323 Pete Schourek	.30	.09
324 Marcus Jensen	.30	.09
325 Rich Aurilia	.30	.09
326 Jeff King	.30	.09
327 Scott Stahoviak	.30	.09
328 Ricky Otero	.30	.09
329 Antonio Osuna	.30	.09
330 Chris Hoiles	.30	.09
331 Luis Gonzalez	.30	.09
332 Wil Cordero	.30	.09
333 Johnny Damon	.30	.09
334 Mark Langston	.30	.09
335 Orlando Miller	.30	.09
336 Jason Giambi	.75	.23
337 Damian Jackson	.30	.09
338 David Wells	.30	.09
339 Bip Roberts	.30	.09
340 Matt Ruebel	.30	.09
341 Tom Candiotti	.30	.09
342 Wally Joyner	.30	.09
343 Jimmy Key	.30	.09
344 Tony Batista	.30	.09
345 Paul Sorrento	.30	.09
346 Ron Karkovice	.30	.09
347 Wilson Alvarez	.30	.09
348 John Flaherty	.30	.09
349 Rey Sanchez	.30	.09
350 John Vander Wal	.30	.09
351 Jermaine Dye	.30	.09
352 Mike Hampton	.30	.09
353 Greg Colbrunn	.30	.09
354 Heathcliff Slocumb	.30	.09
355 Ricky Bottalico	.30	.09
356 Marty Janzen	.30	.09
357 Orel Hershiser	.30	.09
358 Rex Hudler	.30	.09
359 Amaury Telemaco	.30	.09
360 Darrin Fletcher	.30	.09
361 Brant Brown UER Card numbered 351	.30	.09
362 Russ Davis	.30	.09
363 Allen Watson	.30	.09
364 Mike Lieberthal	.30	.09
365 Dave Stevens	.30	.09
366 Jay Powell	.30	.09
367 Tony Fossas	.30	.09
368 Bob Wolcott	.30	.09
369 Mark Loretta	.30	.09
370 Shawn Estes	.30	.09
371 Sandy Martinez	.30	.09
372 Wendell Magee Jr.	.30	.09
373 John Franco	.30	.09
374 Tom Pagnozzi UER misnumbered as 274	.30	.09
375 Willie Adams	.30	.09
376 Chipper Jones SS SP	1.25	.35
377 Mo Vaughn SS SP	.75	.23
378 Frank Thomas SS SP	1.25	.35
379 Albert Belle SS SP	.75	.23
380 A.Galarraga SS SP	.75	.23
381 Gary Sheffield SS SP	.75	.23
382 Jeff Bagwell SS SP	.75	.23
383 Mike Piazza SS SP	2.50	.75
384 Mark McGwire SS SP	4.00	1.20
385 Ken Griffey Jr. SS SP	2.50	.75
386 Barry Bonds SS SP	4.00	1.20
387 Juan Gonzalez SS SP	1.25	.35
388 B.Anderson SS SP	.75	.23
389 Ken Caminiti SS SP	.75	.23
390 Jay Buhner SS SP	.75	.23

1997 Stadium Club Matrix

Randomly inserted in first and second series eight-card packs at a rate of one in 12 and in 13-card packs at a rate of one in six, this 120-card set is parallel to the first 60 cards of both the series one and series two of the regular set. Each Matrix card was reproduced with Power Matrix technology, giving the card fronts a glittering effect.

	Nm-Mt	Ex-Mt
*STARS: 4X TO 10X BASIC CARDS		

1997 Stadium Club Members Only Parallel

These cards are a parallel issue to the 1997 Stadium Club Series one and Series two sets and the following insert sets: Millennium, Instavision, Firebrand, and Pure Gold. No first series Co-Signers insert cards are in this set, but it does contain the second series Patent Leather insert set. The only difference between the regular issue cards and these parallels are the words "TSC Members Only" printed lightly in the background. The cards all come together in factory set form and one must be a member of Topps Stadium Club to order these cards.

	Nm-Mt	Ex-Mt
COMPLETE SET (497)	400.00	120.00
COMP.SERIES 1 (235)	200.00	60.00
COMP.SERIES 2 (242)	200.00	60.00
COMMON CARD (1-390)	.25	.07
*MEMBERS ONLY: 6X BASIC CARDS.		
I1 Eddie Murray	4.00	1.20
I2 Paul Molitor	4.00	1.20
I3 Todd Hundley	2.00	.60
I4 Roger Clemens	10.00	3.00
I5 Barry Bonds	5.00	1.50
I6 Mark McGwire	25.00	7.50
I7 Brady Anderson	2.00	.60
I8 Barry Larkin	4.00	1.20
I9 Ken Caminiti	3.00	.90
I10 Hideo Nomo	4.00	1.20
I11 Bernie Williams	4.00	1.20
I12 Juan Gonzalez	4.00	1.20
I13 Andy Pettitte	3.00	.90
I14 Albert Belle	2.00	.60
I15 John Smoltz	2.00	.60
I16 Brian Jordan	1.00	.30
I17 Derek Jeter	25.00	7.50
I18 Ken Caminiti	2.00	.60
I19 John Wetteland	2.00	.60
I20 Brady Anderson	2.00	.60
I21 Andruw Jones	5.00	1.50
I22 Jim Leyritz	1.00	.30
M1 Derek Jeter	25.00	7.50
M2 Mark Grudzielanek	2.00	.60
M3 Jacob Cruz	1.00	.30
M4 Ray Durham	3.00	.90
M5 Tony Clark	2.00	.60
M6 Chipper Jones	12.00	3.60
M7 Luis Castillo	2.00	.60
M8 Carlos Delgado	5.00	1.50
M9 Brant Brown	1.00	.30
M10 Jason Kendall	3.00	.90
M11 Alan Benes	1.00	.30
M12 Rey Ordonez	1.00	.30
M13 Justin Thompson	1.00	.30
M14 J.Allensworth	1.00	.30
M15 Brian L. Hunter	1.00	.30
M16 Marty Cordova	1.00	.30
M17 Edgar Renteria	1.00	.30
M18 Karim Garcia	1.00	.30
M19 Todd Greene	1.00	.30
M20 Paul Wilson	1.00	.30
M21 Andruw Jones	5.00	1.50
M22 Todd Walker	1.00	.30
M23 Alex Ochoa	1.00	.30
M24 Bartolo Colon	4.00	1.20
M25 Wendell Magee Jr.	1.00	.30
M26 Jose Rosado	1.00	.30
M27 Katsuhiro Maeda	1.00	.30
M28 Bob Abreu	4.00	1.20
M29 Brooks Kieschnick	1.00	.30
M30 Derrick Gibson	1.00	.30
M31 Mike Sweeney	5.00	1.50
M32 Jeff D'Amico	1.00	.30
M33 Chad Mottola	1.00	.30
M34 Chris Snopek	1.00	.30
M35 Jaime Bluma	1.00	.30
M36 Vladimir Guerrero	8.00	2.40
M37 Nomar Garciaparra	15.00	4.50
M38 Scott Rolen	4.00	1.20
M39 Dmitri Young	2.00	.60
M40 Neifi Perez	1.00	.30
FB1 Jeff Bagwell	5.00	1.50
FB2 Albert Belle	2.00	.60
FB3 Barry Bonds	12.00	3.60
FB4 Andres Galarraga	4.00	1.20
FB5 Ken Griffey Jr.	20.00	6.00
FB6 Brady Anderson	2.00	.60
FB7 Mark McGwire	20.00	6.00
FB8 Chipper Jones	12.00	3.60
FB9 Frank Thomas	8.00	2.40
FB10 Mike Piazza	15.00	4.50
FB11 Mo Vaughn	2.00	.60
FB12 Juan Gonzalez	5.00	1.50
PG1 Brady Anderson	2.00	.60
PG2 Albert Belle	2.00	.60
PG3 Dante Bichette	2.00	.60
PG4 Barry Bonds	12.00	3.60
PG5 Jay Buhner	2.00	.60
PG6 Tony Gwynn	12.00	3.60
PG7 Chipper Jones	12.00	3.60
PG8 Mark McGwire	20.00	6.00
PG9 Gary Sheffield	4.00	1.20
PG10 Frank Thomas	10.00	3.00
PG11 Juan Gonzalez	5.00	1.50
PG12 Ken Caminiti	2.00	.60
PG13 Kenny Lofton	2.00	.60
PG14 Jeff Bagwell	5.00	1.50
PG15 Ken Griffey Jr	20.00	6.00
PG16 Cal Ripken	25.00	7.50
PG17 Mo Vaughn	2.00	.60
PG18 Mike Piazza	12.00	3.60
PG19 Derek Jeter	25.00	7.50
PG20 Andres Galarraga	4.00	1.20
PL1 Ivan Rodriguez	5.00	1.50
PL2 Ken Caminiti	2.00	.60
PL3 Barry Bonds	12.00	3.60
PL4 Ken Griffey Jr.	20.00	6.00
PL5 Greg Maddux	15.00	4.50
PL6 Craig Biggio	3.00	.90
PL7 Andres Galarraga	4.00	1.20
PL8 Kenny Lofton	2.00	.60
PL9 Barry Larkin	4.00	1.20
PL10 Mark Grace	4.00	1.20
PL11 Rey Ordonez	1.00	.30
PL12 Roberto Alomar	4.00	1.20
PL13 Derek Jeter	25.00	7.50

1997 Stadium Club Co-Signers

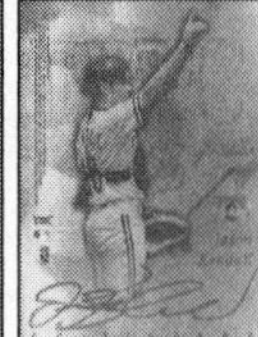

Randomly inserted in first series eight-card hobby packs at a rate of one in 168 and first series 13-card hobby collector packs at a rate of one in 96, cards (CO1-CO5) from this dual-sided, dual-player set feature color action player photos printed on 20pt. card stock with authentic signatures of two major league standouts per card. The last five cards (CO6-CO10) were randomly inserted in second series 10-card hobby packs with a rate of one in 168 and inserted with a rate of one in 96 Hobby Collector packs.

	Nm-Mt	Ex-Mt
CO1 Andy Pettitte / Derek Jeter	150.00	45.00
CO2 Paul Wilson / Todd Hundley	10.00	3.00
CO3 Jermaine Dye / Mark Wohlers	15.00	4.50
CO4 Scott Rolen / Gregg Jefferies	25.00	7.50
CO5 Todd Hollandsworth / Jason Kendall	15.00	4.50
CO6 Alan Benes / Robin Ventura	15.00	4.50
CO7 Eric Karros / Raul Mondesi	15.00	4.50
CO8 Rey Ordonez / Nomar Garciaparra	100.00	30.00
CO9 Rondell White / Marty Cordova	15.00	4.50
CO10 Tony Gwynn / Karim Garcia	40.00	12.00

1997 Stadium Club Firebrand Wood

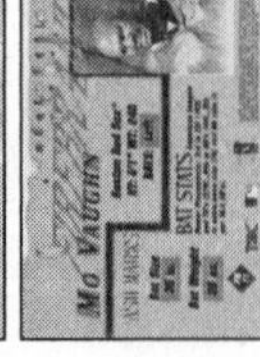

These wood cards were returned on a one for one basis for each Stadium Club Firebrand Redemption Card issued. They are valued as a multiple of the redemption cards; please see values below for these cards. The cards, although they measure the standard size have the word "Firebrand" as a die cut etching on the top and other than the Stadium Club words in the background, all lettering is in gold foil on the front. The card does feel like a bat would and the back has the bat size and weight along with some batting stats and a photo of the player.

Nm-Mt Ex-Mt
*WOOD: .4X TO 1X REDEMPTION......

1997 Stadium Club Instavision

The first ten cards of this 22-card set were randomly inserted in first series eight-card packs at a rate of one in 24 and first series 13-card packs at a rate of 1:12. The last 12 cards were inserted in series two packs at the rate of one in 24 and one in 12 in hobby collector packs. The set highlights some of the 1996 season's most exciting moments through exclusive holographic video action.

	Nm-Mt	Ex-Mt
COMPLETE SET (22)	50.00	15.00
COMPLETE SERIES 1 (10)	25.00	7.50
COMPLETE SERIES 2 (12)	25.00	7.50
I1 Eddie Murray	4.00	1.20
I2 Paul Molitor	2.50	.75
I3 Todd Hundley	1.50	.45
I4 Roger Clemens	8.00	2.40
I5 Barry Bonds	10.00	3.00
I6 Mark McGwire	10.00	3.00
I7 Brady Anderson	1.50	.45
I8 Barry Larkin	4.00	1.20
I9 Ken Caminiti	1.50	.45
I10 Hideo Nomo	4.00	1.20
I11 Bernie Williams	2.50	.75
I12 Juan Gonzalez	4.00	1.20
I13 Andy Pettitte	2.50	.75
I14 Albert Belle	1.50	.45
I15 John Smoltz	2.50	.75
I16 Brian Jordan	1.50	.45
I17 Derek Jeter	10.00	3.00
I18 Ken Caminiti	1.50	.45
I19 John Wetteland	1.50	.45
I20 Brady Anderson	1.50	.45
I21 Andruw Jones	1.50	.45
I22 Jim Leyritz	1.50	.45

1997 Stadium Club Millennium

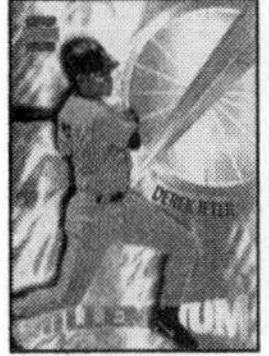

Randomly inserted in first and second series eight-card packs at a rate of one in 24 and 13-card packs at a rate of 1:12, this 40-card set features color player photos of breakthrough stars of Major League Baseball reproduced using state-of-the-art advanced embossed holographic technology.

	Nm-Mt	Ex-Mt
COMPLETE SET (40)	130.00	39.00
COMPLETE SERIES 1 (20)	50.00	15.00
COMPLETE SERIES 2 (20)	80.00	24.00
M1 Derek Jeter	20.00	6.00
M2 Mark Grudzielanek	1.50	.45
M3 Jacob Cruz	1.50	.45
M4 Ray Durham	2.50	.75
M5 Tony Clark	1.50	.45
M6 Chipper Jones	6.00	1.80
M7 Luis Castillo	2.50	.75
M8 Carlos Delgado	2.50	.75
M9 Brant Brown	1.50	.45
M10 Jason Kendall	2.50	.75
M11 Alan Benes	1.50	.45
M12 Rey Ordonez	1.50	.45
M13 Justin Thompson	1.50	.45
M14 J.Allensworth	1.50	.45
M15 Brian Hunter	1.50	.45
M16 Marty Cordova	1.50	.45
M17 Edgar Renteria	2.50	.75
M18 Karim Garcia	1.50	.45
M19 Todd Greene	1.50	.45
M20 Paul Wilson	1.50	.45

1997 Stadium Club Patent Leather

Randomly inserted in second series retail packs only at a rate of one in 36, this 13-card set features action player images standing in a baseball glove and with an inner die-cut glove background printed on leather card stock.

	Nm-Mt	Ex-Mt
COMPLETE SET (13)	120.00	36.00
PL1 Ivan Rodriguez	10.00	3.00
PL2 Ken Caminiti	4.00	1.20
PL3 Barry Bonds	25.00	7.50
PL4 Ken Griffey Jr.	15.00	4.50
PL5 Greg Maddux	15.00	4.50
PL6 Craig Biggio	6.00	1.80
PL7 Andres Galarraga	4.00	1.20
PL8 Kenny Lofton	4.00	1.20
PL9 Barry Larkin	10.00	3.00
PL10 Mark Grace	6.00	1.80
PL11 Rey Ordonez	4.00	1.20
PL12 Roberto Alomar	10.00	3.00
PL13 Derek Jeter	25.00	7.50

1997 Stadium Club Pure Gold

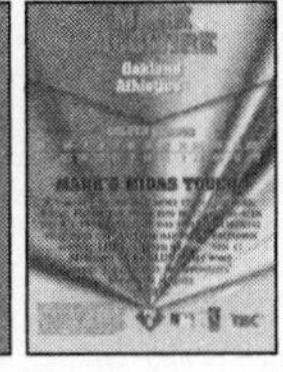

Randomly inserted in first and second series eight-card packs at a rate of one in 72 and 13-card packs at a rate of one in 36, this 20-card set features color action star player photos reproduced on 20 pt. embossed gold mirror foilboard.

	Nm-Mt	Ex-Mt
COMPLETE SERIES 1 (10)	120.00	36.00
COMPLETE SERIES 2 (10)	200.00	60.00
PG1 Brady Anderson	3.00	.90
PG2 Albert Belle	3.00	.90
PG3 Dante Bichette	3.00	.90
PG4 Barry Bonds	20.00	6.00
PG5 Jay Buhner	3.00	.90
PG6 Tony Gwynn	10.00	3.00
PG7 Chipper Jones	8.00	2.40
PG8 Mark McGwire	20.00	6.00
PG9 Gary Sheffield	3.00	.90
PG10 Frank Thomas	8.00	2.40
PG11 Juan Gonzalez	8.00	2.40
PG12 Ken Caminiti	3.00	.90
PG13 Kenny Lofton	3.00	.90
PG14 Jeff Bagwell	5.00	1.50
PG15 Ken Griffey Jr.	12.00	3.60
PG16 Cal Ripken	25.00	7.50
PG17 Mo Vaughn	3.00	.90
PG18 Mike Piazza	12.00	3.60
PG19 Derek Jeter	20.00	6.00
PG20 Andres Galarraga	3.00	.90

1998 Stadium Club

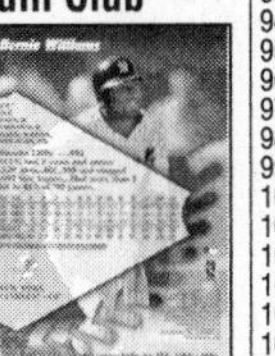

The 1998 Stadium Club set was issued in two separate 200-card series and distributed in six-card retail packs for $2, nine-card hobby packs for $3, and 15-card Home Team Advantage packs for $5. The card fronts feature action color player photos with player information displayed on the backs. The series one set included odd numbered cards only and series two included even numbered cards only. The set contains the topical subsets: Future Stars (odd-numbered 361-379), Draft Picks (odd-numbered 381-399) and Traded (even-numbered 356-400). Two separate Cal Ripken Sound Chip cards were distributed as chiptoppers in Home Team Advantage boxes. The second series features a 23-card Transaction subset (356-400). Second series cards were released in April, 1998. Rookie Cards include Kevin Millwood and Magglio Ordonez.

	Nm-Mt	Ex-Mt
COMPLETE SET (400)	80.00	24.00
COMP.SERIES 1 (200)	40.00	12.00
COMP.SERIES 2 (200)	40.00	12.00
1 Chipper Jones	.75	.23
2 Frank Thomas	.75	.23
3 Vladimir Guerrero	.75	.23
4 Ellis Burks	.30	.09
5 John Franco	.30	.09
6 Paul Molitor	.50	.15
7 Rusty Greer	.30	.09
8 Todd Hundley	.30	.09
9 Brett Tomko	.30	.09
10 Eric Karros	.30	.09
11 Mike Cameron	.30	.09
12 Jim Edmonds	.30	.09
13 Bernie Williams	.50	.15
14 Denny Neagle	.30	.09
15 Jason Dickson	.30	.09
16 Sammy Sosa	1.25	.35
17 Brian Jordan	.30	.09
18 Jose Vidro	.30	.09
19 Scott Spiezio	.30	.09
20 Jay Buhner	.30	.09
21 Jim Thome	.75	.23
22 Sandy Alomar Jr.	.30	.09
23 Livan Hernandez	.30	.09
24 Roberto Alomar	.75	.23
25 Chris Gomez	.30	.09
26 John Wetteland	.30	.09
27 Willie Greene	.30	.09
28 Gregg Jefferies	.30	.09
29 Johnny Damon	.30	.09
30 Barry Larkin	.75	.23
31 Chuck Knoblauch	.30	.09
32 Mo Vaughn	.30	.09
33 Tony Clark	.30	.09
34 Marty Cordova	.30	.09
35 Vinny Castilla	.30	.09
36 Jeff King	.30	.09
37 Reggie Jefferson	.30	.09
38 Mariano Rivera	.50	.15
39 Jermaine Allensworth	.30	.09
40 Livan Hernandez	.30	.09
41 Heathcliff Slocumb	.30	.09
42 Jacob Cruz	.30	.09
43 Barry Bonds	2.00	.60
44 Dave Magadan	.30	.09
45 Chan Ho Park	.30	.09
46 Jeremi Gonzalez	.30	.09
47 Jeff Cirillo	.30	.09
48 Delino DeShields	.30	.09
49 Craig Biggio	.50	.15
50 Benito Santiago	.30	.09
51 Mark Clark	.30	.09
52 Fernando Vina	.30	.09
53 F.P. Santangelo	.30	.09
54 Pep Harris	.30	.09
55 Edgar Renteria	.30	.09
56 Jeff Bagwell	.50	.15
57 Jimmy Key	.30	.09
58 Bartolo Colon	.30	.09
59 Curt Schilling	.50	.15
60 Steve Finley	.30	.09
61 Andy Ashby	.30	.09
62 John Burkett	.30	.09
63 Orel Hershiser	.30	.09
64 Pokey Reese	.30	.09
65 Scott Servais	.30	.09
66 Todd Jones	.30	.09
67 Javy Lopez	.30	.09
68 Robin Ventura	.30	.09
69 Miguel Tejada	.50	.15
70 Raul Casanova	.30	.09
71 Reggie Sanders	.30	.09
72 Edgardo Alfonzo	.30	.09
73 Dean Palmer	.30	.09
74 Todd Stottlemyre	.30	.09
75 David Wells	.30	.09
76 Troy Percival	.30	.09
77 Albert Belle	.30	.09
78 Pat Hentgen	.30	.09
79 Brian Hunter	.30	.09
80 Richard Hidalgo	.30	.09
81 Darren Oliver	.30	.09
82 Mark Wohlers	.30	.09
83 Cal Ripken	2.50	.75
84 Hideo Nomo	.75	.23
85 Derrek Lee	.30	.09
86 Stan Javier	.30	.09
87 Rey Ordonez	.30	.09
88 Randy Johnson	.75	.23
89 Jeff Kent	.30	.09
90 Brian McRae	.30	.09
91 Manny Ramirez	.30	.09
92 Trevor Hoffman	.30	.09
93 Doug Glanville	.30	.09
94 Todd Walker	.30	.09
95 Andy Benes	.30	.09
96 Jason Schmidt	.30	.09
97 Mike Matheny	.30	.09
98 Tim Naehring	.30	.09
99 Keith Lockhart	.30	.09
100 Jose Rosado	.30	.09
101 Roger Clemens	1.50	.45
102 Pedro Astacio	.30	.09
103 Mark Bellhorn	.30	.09
104 Paul O'Neill	.50	.15
105 Darin Erstad	.30	.09
106 Mike Lieberthal	.30	.09
107 Wilson Alvarez	.30	.09
108 Mike Mussina	.75	.23
109 George Williams	.30	.09
110 Cliff Floyd	.30	.09
111 Shawn Estes	.30	.09
112 Mark Grudzielanek	.30	.09
113 Tony Gwynn	1.00	.30
114 Alan Benes	.30	.09
115 Terry Steinbach	.30	.09
116 Greg Maddux	1.25	.35
117 Andy Pettitte	.50	.15
118 Dave Nilsson	.30	.09
119 Deivi Cruz	.30	.09
120 Carlos Delgado	.30	.09
121 Scott Hatteberg	.30	.09
122 John Olerud	.30	.09
123 Todd Dunwoody	.30	.09
124 Garret Anderson	.30	.09
125 Royce Clayton	.30	.09
126 Dante Powell	.30	.09
127 Tom Glavine	.50	.15
128 Gary DiSarcina	.30	.09
129 Terry Adams	.30	.09
130 Raul Mondesi	.30	.09
131 Dan Wilson	.30	.09
132 Al Martin	.30	.09
133 Mickey Morandini	.30	.09
134 Rafael Palmeiro	.50	.15
135 Juan Encarnacion	.30	.09
136 Jim Pittsley	.30	.09
137 Magglio Ordonez RC	2.00	.60
138 Will Clark	.75	.23
139 Todd Helton	.50	.15
140 Kelvim Escobar	.30	.09
141 Esteban Loaiza	.30	.09
142 John Jaha	.30	.09
143 Jeff Fassero	.30	.09
144 Harold Baines	.30	.09
145 Butch Huskey	.30	.09
146 Pat Meares	.30	.09
147 Brian Giles	.30	.09
148 Ramiro Mendoza	.30	.09
149 John Smoltz	.50	.15
150 Felix Martinez	.30	.09
151 Jose Valentin	.30	.09
152 Brad Rigby	.30	.09
153 Ed Sprague	.30	.09
154 Mike Hampton	.30	.09
155 Carlos Perez	.30	.09
156 Ray Lankford	.30	.09
157 Bobby Bonilla	.30	.09
158 Bill Mueller	.30	.09
159 Jeffrey Hammonds	.30	.09
160 Charles Nagy	.30	.09
161 Rich Loiselle RC	.30	.09
162 Al Leiter	.30	.09
163 Larry Walker	.50	.15
164 Chris Hoiles	.30	.09
165 Jeff Montgomery	.30	.09
166 Francisco Cordova	.30	.09
167 James Baldwin	.30	.09
168 Mark McLemore	.30	.09
169 Kevin Appier	.30	.09
170 Jamey Wright	.30	.09
171 Nomar Garciaparra	1.25	.35
172 Matt Franco	.30	.09
173 Armando Benitez	.30	.09
174 Jeromy Burnitz	.30	.09
175 Ismael Valdes	.30	.09
176 Lance Johnson	.30	.09
177 Paul Sorrento	.30	.09
178 Rondell White	.30	.09
179 Kevin Elster	.30	.09
180 Jason Giambi	.75	.23
181 Carlos Baerga	.30	.09
182 Russ Davis	.30	.09
183 Ryan McGuire	.30	.09
184 Eric Young	.30	.09
185 Ron Gant	.30	.09
186 Manny Alexander	.30	.09
187 Scott Karl	.30	.09
188 Brady Anderson	.30	.09
189 Randall Simon	.30	.09
190 Tim Belcher	.30	.09
191 Jaret Wright	.30	.09
192 Dante Bichette	.30	.09
193 John Valentin	.30	.09
194 Darren Bragg	.30	.09
195 Mike Sweeney	.30	.09
196 Craig Counsell	.30	.09
197 Jaime Navarro	.30	.09
198 Todd Dunn	.30	.09
199 Ken Griffey Jr.	1.25	.35
200 Juan Gonzalez	.75	.23
201 Billy Wagner	.30	.09
202 Tino Martinez	.50	.15
203 Mark McGwire	2.00	.60
204 Jeff D'Amico	.30	.09
205 Rico Brogna	.30	.09
206 Todd Hollandsworth	.30	.09
207 Chad Curtis	.30	.09
208 Tom Goodwin	.30	.09
209 Neifi Perez	.30	.09
210 Derek Bell	.30	.09
211 Quilvio Veras	.30	.09
212 Greg Vaughn	.30	.09
213 Kirk Rueter	.30	.09
214 Arthur Rhodes	.30	.09
215 Cal Eldred	.30	.09
216 Bill Taylor	.30	.09
217 Todd Greene	.30	.09
218 Mario Valdez	.30	.09
219 Ricky Bottalico	.30	.09
220 Frank Rodriguez	.30	.09
221 Rich Becker	.30	.09
222 Roberto Duran RC	.30	.09
223 Ivan Rodriguez	.75	.23
224 Mike Jackson	.30	.09
225 Deion Sanders	.50	.15
226 Tony Womack	.30	.09
227 Mark Kotsay	.30	.09
228 Steve Trachsel	.30	.09
229 Ryan Klesko	.30	.09
230 Ken Cloude	.30	.09
231 Luis Gonzalez	.30	.09
232 Gary Gaetti	.30	.09
233 Michael Tucker	.30	.09
234 Shawn Green	.30	.09
235 Ariel Prieto	.30	.09
236 Kirt Manwaring	.30	.09
237 Omar Vizquel	.30	.09
238 Matt Beech	.30	.09
239 Justin Thompson	.30	.09
240 Bret Boone	.30	.09
241 Derek Jeter	2.00	.60
242 Ken Caminiti	.30	.09
243 Jose Offerman	.30	.09
244 Kevin Tapani	.30	.09
245 Jason Kendall	.30	.09
246 Jose Guillen	.30	.09
247 Mike Bordick	.30	.09
248 Dustin Hermanson	.30	.09
249 Darrin Fletcher	.30	.09
250 Dave Hollins	.30	.09
251 Ramon Martinez	.30	.09
252 Hideki Irabu	.30	.09
253 Mark Grace	.50	.15
254 Jason Isringhausen	.30	.09
255 Jose Cruz Jr.	.30	.09
256 Brian Johnson	.30	.09
257 Brad Ausmus	.30	.09
258 Andruw Jones	.30	.09
259 Doug Jones	.30	.09
260 Jeff Shaw	.30	.09
261 Chuck Finley	.30	.09
262 Gary Sheffield	.30	.09
263 David Segui	.30	.09
264 John Smiley	.30	.09
265 Tim Salmon	.50	.15
266 J.T. Snow	.30	.09
267 Alex Fernandez	.30	.09
268 Matt Stairs	.30	.09
269 B.J. Surhoff	.30	.09
270 Keith Foulke	.30	.09
271 Edgar Martinez	.50	.15
272 Shannon Stewart	.30	.09
273 Eduardo Perez	.30	.09
274 Wally Joyner	.30	.09
275 Kevin Young	.30	.09
276 Eli Marrero	.30	.09
277 Brad Radke	.30	.09
278 Jamie Moyer	.30	.09
279 Joe Girardi	.30	.09
280 Troy O'Leary	.30	.09
281 Jeff Frye	.30	.09
282 Jose Offerman	.30	.09
283 Scott Erickson	.30	.09
284 Sean Berry	.30	.09
285 Shigetoshi Hasegawa	.30	.09
286 Felix Heredia	.30	.09
287 Willie McGee	.30	.09
288 Alex Rodriguez	1.25	.35
289 Ugueth Urbina	.30	.09
290 Jon Lieber	.30	.09
291 Fernando Tatis	.30	.09
292 Chris Stynes	.30	.09
293 Bernard Gilkey	.30	.09
294 Joey Hamilton	.30	.09
295 Matt Karchner	.30	.09
296 Paul Wilson	.30	.09
297 Damion Easley	.30	.09
298 Kevin Millwood RC	1.25	.35
299 Ellis Burks	.30	.09
300 Jerry DiPoto	.30	.09
301 Jermaine Dye	.30	.09
302 Travis Lee	.30	.09
303 Ron Coomer	.30	.09
304 Matt Williams	.30	.09
305 Bobby Higginson	.30	.09
306 Jorge Fabregas	.30	.09
307 Jon Nunnally	.30	.09
308 Jay Bell	.30	.09
309 Jason Schmidt	.30	.09
310 Andy Benes	.30	.09
311 Sterling Hitchcock	.30	.09
312 Jeff Suppan	.30	.09
313 Shane Reynolds	.30	.09
314 Willie Blair	.30	.09
315 Scott Rolen	.50	.15
316 Wilson Alvarez	.30	.09
317 David Justice	.30	.09
318 Fred McGriff	.50	.15
319 Bobby Jones	.30	.09
320 Wade Boggs	.50	.15
321 Tim Wakefield	.30	.09
322 Tony Saunders	.30	.09
323 David Cone	.30	.09
324 Roberto Hernandez	.30	.09
325 Jose Canseco	.75	.23
326 Kevin Stocker	.30	.09
327 Gerald Williams	.30	.09
328 Quinton McCracken	.30	.09
329 Mark Gardner	.30	.09
330 Ben Grieve	.30	.09
331 Kevin Brown	.50	.15
332 Mike Lowell RC	1.50	.45
333 Jed Hansen	.30	.09
334 Abraham Nunez	.30	.09
335 John Thomson	.30	.09
336 Masato Yoshii RC	.75	.23
337 Mike Piazza	1.25	.35
338 Brad Fullmer	.30	.09
339 Ray Durham	.30	.09
340 Kerry Wood	.75	.23
341 Kevin Polcovich	.30	.09
342 Russ Johnson	.30	.09
343 Darryl Hamilton	.30	.09
344 David Ortiz	.30	.09
345 Kevin Orie	.30	.09
346 Mike Caruso	.30	.09
347 Juan Guzman	.30	.09
348 Ruben Rivera	.30	.09
349 Rick Aguilera	.30	.09
350 Bobby Estalella	.30	.09
351 Bobby Witt	.30	.09
352 Paul Konerko	.30	.09
353 Matt Morris	.30	.09
354 Carl Pavano	.30	.09
355 Todd Zeile	.30	.09
356 Kevin Brown TR	.50	.15
357 Alex Gonzalez	.30	.09
358 Chuck Knoblauch TR	.30	.09
359 Joey Cora	.30	.09
360 Mike Lansing TR	.30	.09
361 Adrian Beltre	.30	.09
362 Dennis Eckersley TR	.30	.09
363 A.J. Hinch	.30	.09
364 Kenny Lofton TR	.30	.09
365 Alex Gonzalez	.30	.09
366 Henry Rodriguez TR	.30	.09
367 Mike Stoner RC	.30	.09
368 Darryl Kile TR	.30	.09
369 Kevin McGlinchy	.30	.09
370 Walt Weiss TR	.30	.09
371 Kris Benson	.30	.09
372 Cecil Fielder TR	.30	.09
373 Dermal Brown	.30	.09
374 Rod Beck TR	.30	.09
375 Eric Milton	.30	.09
376 Travis Fryman TR	.30	.09
377 Preston Wilson	.30	.09
378 Chili Davis TR	.30	.09
379 Travis Lee	.30	.09
380 Jim Leyritz TR	.30	.09
381 Vernon Wells	.50	.15
382 Joe Carter TR	.30	.09
383 J.J. Davis	.30	.09
384 Marquis Grissom TR	.30	.09
385 Mike Cuddyer RC	1.00	.30
386 Rickey Henderson TR	.75	.23
387 Chris Enochs RC	.30	.09
388 Andres Galarraga TR	.30	.09
389 Jason Dellaero	.30	.09
390 Robb Nen TR	.30	.09
391 Mark Mangum	.30	.09
392 Jeff Blauser TR	.30	.09
393 Adam Kennedy	.30	.09
394 Bob Abreu TR	.30	.09
395 Jack Cust RC	.50	.15
396 Jose Vizcaino TR	.30	.09
397 Jon Garland	.30	.09
398 Pedro Martinez TR	.75	.23
399 Aaron Akin	.30	.09
400 Jeff Conine TR	.30	.09
NNO Cal Ripken Sound Chip 1	15.00	4.50
NNO Cal Ripken Sound Chip 2	15.00	4.50

1998 Stadium Club First Day Issue

Randomly inserted in first series retail packs at the rate of one in 42 and second series retail packs at the rate of one in 47, this 400-card set parallels the 1998 Stadium Club base set and features a "First Day Issue" foil stamp on the front. Each card is serial numbered out of 200 on back.

Nm-Mt Ex-Mt
*STARS: 6X TO 15X BASIC CARDS....
*ROOKIES: 6X TO 15X BASIC CARDS

1998 Stadium Club One Of A Kind

Randomly inserted in first and second series hobby and Home Team Advantage packs this 400-card set parallels the 1998 Stadium Club base set. First series cards were seeded at 1:21 hobby and 1:13 HTA packs. Series 2 cards were seeded at 1:24 hobby and 1:14 HTA packs. Each card front features a special metalized foil treatment coupled with a "One of a Kind" logo. In addition, each card is serial numbered out of 150 on back.

	Nm-Mt	Ex-Mt
*STARS: 8X TO 20X BASIC CARDS		
*ROOKIES: 8X TO 20X BASIC CARDS		

1998 Stadium Club Co-Signers

Randomly inserted exclusively in first and second series hobby and Home Team Advantage packs, this 36-card set features color photos of two top players on each card along with their autographs. These cards were released in three different levels of scarcity: A, B and C. Seeding rates are as follows: Series 1 Group A 1:4372 hobby and 1:2623 HTA, Series 1 Group B 1:1457 hobby and 1:874 HTA, Series 1 Group C 1:121 hobby and 1:73 HTA, Series 2 Group A 1:4702 hobby and 1:2821 HTA, Series 2 Group B 1:1567 hobby and 1:940 HTA and Series 2 Group C 1:131 hobby and 1:78 HTA. The scarce group A cards (rumored to be only 25 of each made) are the most difficult to obtain.

	Nm-Mt	Ex-Mt
CS1 Nomar Garciaparra A Scott Rolen	200.00	60.00
CS2 Nomar Garciaparra B Derek Jeter	500.00	150.00
CS3 Nomar Garciaparra C Eric Karros	80.00	24.00
CS4 Scott Rolen C Derek Jeter	120.00	36.00
CS5 Scott Rolen B Eric Karros	50.00	15.00
CS6 Derek Jeter A Eric Karros	250.00	75.00
CS7 Travis Lee B Jose Cruz Jr.	40.00	12.00
CS8 Travis Lee C Mark Kotsay	15.00	4.50
CS9 Travis Lee A Paul Konerko	80.00	24.00
CS10 Jose Cruz Jr. A Mark Kotsay	80.00	24.00
CS11 Jose Cruz Jr. C Paul Konerko	15.00	4.50
CS12 Mark Kotsay B Paul Konerko	40.00	12.00
CS13 Tony Gwynn A Larry Walker	120.00	36.00
CS14 Tony Gwynn C Mark Grudzielanek	40.00	12.00
CS15 Tony Gwynn B Andres Galarraga	100.00	30.00
CS16 Larry Walker B Mark Grudzielanek	60.00	18.00
CS17 Larry Walker C Andres Galarraga	40.00	12.00
CS18 Mark Grudzielanek A Andres Galarraga	80.00	24.00
CS19 Sandy Alomar A Roberto Alomar	150.00	45.00
CS20 Sandy Alomar C Andy Pettitte	25.00	7.50
CS21 Sandy Alomar B Tino Martinez	50.00	15.00
CS22 Roberto Alomar B Andy Pettitte	80.00	24.00
CS23 Roberto Alomar C Tino Martinez	40.00	12.00
CS24 Andy Pettitte A Tino Martinez	120.00	36.00
CS25 Tony Clark A Todd Hundley	50.00	15.00
CS26 Tony Clark B Tim Salmon	50.00	15.00
CS27 Tony Clark C Robin Ventura	15.00	4.50
CS28 Todd Hundley C Tim Salmon	25.00	7.50
CS29 Todd Hundley B Robin Ventura	40.00	12.00
CS30 Tim Salmon A Robin Ventura	100.00	30.00
CS31 Roger Clemens B Randy Johnson	300.00	90.00
CS32 Roger Clemens A Jaret Wright	200.00	60.00
CS33 Roger Clemens C Matt Morris	60.00	18.00
CS34 Randy Johnson C Jaret Wright	50.00	15.00
CS35 Randy Johnson A Matt Morris	120.00	36.00
CS36 Jaret Wright B Matt Morris	40.00	12.00

1998 Stadium Club In The Wings

Randomly inserted in first series hobby and retail packs at the rate of one in 36 and first series Home Team Advantage packs at a rate of one in 12, this 15-card set features color photos of some of the top young players in the league.

	Nm-Mt	Ex-Mt
COMPLETE SET (15)	40.00	12.00
W1 Juan Encarnacion	4.00	1.20
W2 Brad Fullmer	4.00	1.20
W3 Ben Grieve	4.00	1.20
W4 Todd Helton	6.00	1.80
W5 Richard Hidalgo	4.00	1.20
W6 Russ Johnson	4.00	1.20
W7 Paul Konerko	4.00	1.20
W8 Mark Kotsay	4.00	1.20
W9 Derrek Lee	4.00	1.20
W10 Travis Lee	4.00	1.20
W11 Eli Marrero	4.00	1.20
W12 David Ortiz	4.00	1.20
W13 Randall Simon	4.00	1.20
W14 Shannon Stewart	4.00	1.20
W15 Fernando Tatis	4.00	1.20

1998 Stadium Club Never Compromise

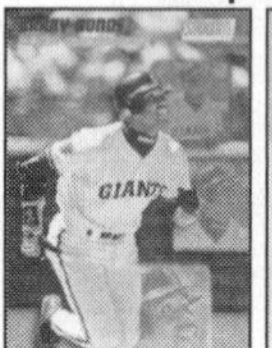

Randomly inserted in first series hobby and retail packs at the rate of one in 12 and first series HTA packs at the rate of one in four, this 20-card set features color photos of top players who never compromise in their game play.

	Nm-Mt	Ex-Mt
COMPLETE SET (20)	80.00	24.00
NC1 Cal Ripken	10.00	3.00
NC2 Ivan Rodriguez	3.00	.90
NC3 Ken Griffey Jr.	5.00	1.50
NC4 Frank Thomas	3.00	.90
NC5 Tony Gwynn	4.00	1.20
NC6 Mike Piazza	5.00	1.50
NC7 Randy Johnson	3.00	.90
NC8 Greg Maddux	5.00	1.50
NC9 Roger Clemens	6.00	1.80
NC10 Derek Jeter	8.00	2.40
NC11 Chipper Jones	3.00	.90
NC12 Barry Bonds	8.00	2.40
NC13 Larry Walker	2.00	.60
NC14 Jeff Bagwell	2.00	.60
NC15 Barry Larkin	3.00	.90
NC16 Ken Caminiti	1.25	.35
NC17 Mark McGwire	8.00	2.40
NC18 Manny Ramirez	1.25	.35
NC19 Tim Salmon	2.00	.60
NC20 Paul Molitor	2.00	.60

1998 Stadium Club Playing With Passion

Randomly seeded into second series hobby and retail packs at a rate of one in 12 and second series Home Team Advantage packs at a rate of one in four, cards from this 10-card set feature a selection of players who've got true fire in their hearts and the burning desire to win.

	Nm-Mt	Ex-Mt
COMPLETE SET (10)	25.00	7.50
P1 Bernie Williams	1.50	.45
P2 Jim Edmonds	1.00	.30
P3 Chipper Jones	2.50	.75
P4 Cal Ripken	8.00	2.40
P5 Craig Biggio	1.50	.45
P6 Juan Gonzalez	2.50	.75
P7 Alex Rodriguez	4.00	1.20
P8 Tino Martinez	1.50	.45
P9 Mike Piazza	4.00	1.20
P10 Ken Griffey Jr.	4.00	1.20

1998 Stadium Club Royal Court

Randomly seeded into second series hobby and retail packs at a rate of one in 36 and second series Home Team Advantage packs at a rate of one in 12, cards from this 15-card set feature a selection of players that have proven their talent and dedication that they've got what it takes to achieve royalty. Players are broken into groups of ten Kings (veterans) and five Princes (rookies). Each card features a special Uniluster technology on front.

	Nm-Mt	Ex-Mt
COMPLETE SET (15)	120.00	36.00
RC1 Ken Griffey Jr.	12.00	3.60
RC2 Frank Thomas	8.00	2.40
RC3 Mike Piazza	12.00	3.60
RC4 Chipper Jones	8.00	2.40
RC5 Mark McGwire	20.00	6.00
RC6 Cal Ripken	25.00	7.50
RC7 Jeff Bagwell	5.00	1.50
RC8 Barry Bonds	20.00	6.00
RC9 Juan Gonzalez	8.00	2.40
RC10 Alex Rodriguez	12.00	3.60
RC11 Travis Lee	3.00	.90
RC12 Paul Konerko	3.00	.90
RC13 Todd Helton	5.00	1.50
RC14 Ben Grieve	3.00	.90
RC15 Mark Kotsay	3.00	.90

1998 Stadium Club Triumvirate Luminous

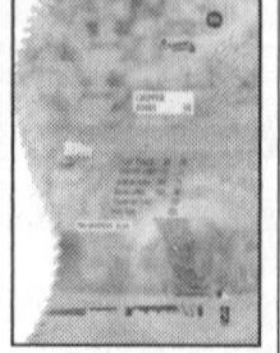

Randomly inserted in first and second series retail packs at the rate of one in 48, the cards of this 54-card set feature color photos of three teammates that can be fused together to make one big card. These laser cut cards use Luminous technology.

	Nm-Mt	Ex-Mt
*LUMINESCENT: 1.25X TO 3X LUMINOUS		
LUMINESCENT STATED ODDS 1:192 RETAIL		
*ILLUMINATOR: 2X TO 5X LUMINOUS		
ILLUMINATOR STATED ODDS 1:384 RETAIL		
T1A Chipper Jones	6.00	1.80
T1B Andruw Jones	2.50	.75
T1C Kenny Lofton	2.50	.75
T2A Derek Jeter	15.00	4.50
T2B Bernie Williams	4.00	1.20
T2C Tino Martinez	4.00	1.20
T3A Jay Buhner	2.50	.75
T3B Edgar Martinez	4.00	1.20
T3C Ken Griffey Jr.	10.00	3.00
T4A Albert Belle	2.50	.75
T4B Robin Ventura	2.50	.75
T4C Frank Thomas	6.00	1.80
T5A Brady Anderson	2.50	.75
T5B Cal Ripken	20.00	6.00
T5C Rafael Palmeiro	4.00	1.20
T6A Mike Piazza	10.00	3.00
T6B Raul Mondesi	2.50	.75
T6C Eric Karros	2.50	.75
T7A Vinny Castilla	2.50	.75
T7B Andres Galarraga	2.50	.75
T7C Larry Walker	4.00	1.20
T8A Jim Thome	6.00	1.80
T8B Manny Ramirez	2.50	.75
T8C David Justice	2.50	.75
T9A Mike Mussina	6.00	1.80
T9B Greg Maddux	10.00	3.00
T9C Randy Johnson	6.00	1.80
T10A Mike Piazza	10.00	3.00
T10B Sandy Alomar Jr.	2.50	.75
T10C Ivan Rodriguez	6.00	1.80
T11A Mark McGwire	15.00	4.50
T11B Tino Martinez	4.00	1.20
T11C Frank Thomas	6.00	1.80
T12A Roberto Alomar	6.00	1.80
T12B Chuck Knoblauch	2.50	.75
T12C Craig Biggio	4.00	1.20
T13A Cal Ripken	20.00	6.00
T13B Chipper Jones	6.00	1.80
T13C Ken Caminiti	2.50	.75
T14A Derek Jeter	15.00	4.50
T14B Nomar Garciaparra	10.00	3.00
T14C Alex Rodriguez	10.00	3.00
T15A Barry Bonds	15.00	4.50
T15B David Justice	2.50	.75
T15C Albert Belle	2.50	.75
T16A Bernie Williams	4.00	1.20
T16B Ken Griffey Jr.	10.00	3.00
T16C Ray Lankford	2.50	.75
T17A Tim Salmon	4.00	1.20
T17B Larry Walker	4.00	1.20
T17C Tony Gwynn	8.00	2.40
T18A Paul Molitor	4.00	1.20
T18B Edgar Martinez	4.00	1.20
T18C Juan Gonzalez	6.00	1.80

1999 Stadium Club

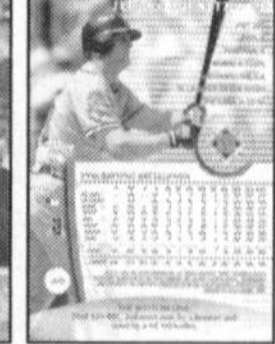

This 355-card set of 1999 Stadium Club cards was distributed in two separate series of 170 and 185 cards respectively. Six-card hobby and six-card retail packs each carried a suggested retail price of $2. 15-card Home Team Advantage packs (SRP of $5) were also distributed. All pack types contained a trifold/checklist info card. The card fronts feature color action player photos printed on 20 pt. card stock. The backs carry player information and career statistics. Draft Pick and Future Stars cards at 141-160 and 336-355 were shortprinted at the following rates: 1:3 hobby/retail packs, one per HTA pack. Key Rookie Cards include Pat Burrell, Nick Johnson and Austin Kearns.

	Nm-Mt	Ex-Mt
COMPLETE SET (355)	100.00	30.00
COMP.SERIES 1 (170)	50.00	15.00
COMP.SER.1 w/o SP's (150)	25.00	7.50
COMP.SERIES 2 (185)	50.00	15.00
COMP.SER.2 w/o SP's (165)	25.00	7.50
COMMON (1-140/161-170)	.30	.09
COMMON (171-335)	.30	.09
COMMON (141-160/336-355)	1.00	.30
1 Alex Rodriguez	1.25	.35
2 Chipper Jones	.75	.23
3 Rusty Greer	.30	.09
4 Jim Edmonds	.30	.09
5 Ron Gant	.30	.09
6 Kevin Polcovich	.30	.09
7 Darryl Strawberry	.50	.15
8 Bill Mueller	.30	.09
9 Vinny Castilla	.30	.09
10 Wade Boggs	.50	.15
11 Jose Lima	.30	.09
12 Darren Dreifort	.30	.09
13 Jay Bell	.30	.09
14 Ben Grieve	.30	.09
15 Shawn Green	.30	.09
16 Andres Galarraga	.30	.09
17 Bartolo Colon	.30	.09
18 Francisco Cordova	.30	.09
19 Paul O'Neill	.50	.15
20 Trevor Hoffman	.30	.09
21 Darren Oliver	.30	.09
22 John Franco	.30	.09
23 Eli Marrero	.30	.09
24 Roberto Hernandez	.30	.09
25 Craig Biggio	.50	.15
26 Brad Fullmer	.30	.09
27 Scott Erickson	.30	.09
28 Tom Gordon	.30	.09
29 Brian Hunter	.30	.09
30 Raul Mondesi	.30	.09
31 Rick Reed	.30	.09
32 Jose Canseco	.75	.23
33 Robb Nen	.30	.09
34 Turner Ward	.30	.09
35 Orlando Hernandez	.30	.09
36 Jeff Shaw	.30	.09
37 Matt Lawton	.30	.09
38 David Wells	.30	.09
39 Bob Abreu	.30	.09
40 Jeromy Burnitz	.30	.09
41 Deivi Cruz	.30	.09
42 Derek Bell	.30	.09
43 Rico Brogna	.30	.09
44 Dmitri Young	.30	.09
45 Chuck Knoblauch	.30	.09
46 Johnny Damon	.30	.09
47 Brian Meadows	.30	.09
48 Jeremi Gonzalez	.30	.09
49 Gary DiSarcina	.30	.09
50 Frank Thomas	.75	.23
51 F.P. Santangelo	.30	.09
52 Tom Candiotti	.30	.09
53 Shane Reynolds	.30	.09
54 Rod Beck	.30	.09
55 Rey Ordonez	.30	.09
56 Todd Helton	.50	.15
57 Mickey Morandini	.30	.09
58 Jorge Posada	.50	.15
59 Mike Mussina	.75	.23
60 Al Leiter	.30	.09
61 David Segui	.30	.09
62 Brian McRae	.30	.09
63 Fred McGriff	.50	.15
64 Brett Tomko	.30	.09
65 Derek Jeter	2.00	.60
66 Sammy Sosa	1.25	.35
67 Kenny Rogers	.30	.09
68 Dave Nilsson	.30	.09
69 Eric Young	.30	.09
70 Mark McGwire	2.00	.60
71 Kenny Lofton	.30	.09
72 Tom Glavine	.50	.15
73 Joey Hamilton	.30	.09
74 John Valentin	.30	.09
75 Mariano Rivera	.50	.15
76 Ray Durham	.30	.09
77 Tony Clark	.30	.09
78 Livan Hernandez	.30	.09
79 Rickey Henderson	.75	.23
80 Vladimir Guerrero	.75	.23
81 J.T. Snow	.30	.09
82 Juan Guzman	.30	.09
83 Darryl Hamilton	.30	.09
84 Matt Anderson	.30	.09
85 Travis Lee	.30	.09
86 Joe Randa	.30	.09
87 Dave Dellucci	.30	.09
88 Moises Alou	.30	.09
89 Alex Gonzalez	.30	.09
90 Tony Womack	.30	.09
91 Neifi Perez	.30	.09
92 Travis Fryman	.30	.09
93 Masato Yoshii	.30	.09
94 Woody Williams	.30	.09
95 Ray Lankford	.30	.09
96 Roger Clemens	1.50	.45
97 Dustin Hermanson	.30	.09
98 Joe Carter	.30	.09
99 Jason Schmidt	.30	.09
100 Greg Maddux	1.25	.35
101 Kevin Tapani	.30	.09
102 Charles Johnson	.30	.09
103 Derrek Lee	.30	.09
104 Pete Harnisch	.30	.09
105 Dante Bichette	.30	.09
106 Scott Brosius	.30	.09
107 Mike Caruso	.30	.09
108 Eddie Taubensee	.30	.09
109 Jeff Fassero	.30	.09
110 Marquis Grissom	.30	.09
111 Jose Hernandez	.30	.09
112 Chan Ho Park	.30	.09
113 Wally Joyner	.30	.09
114 Bobby Estalella	.30	.09
115 Pedro Martinez	.75	.23
116 Shawn Estes	.30	.09
117 Walt Weiss	.30	.09
118 John Mabry	.30	.09
119 Brian Johnson	.30	.09
120 Jim Thome	.75	.23
121 Bill Spiers	.30	.09
122 John Olerud	.30	.09
123 Jeff King	.30	.09
124 Tim Belcher	.30	.09
125 John Wetteland	.30	.09
126 Tony Gwynn	1.00	.30
127 Brady Anderson	.30	.09
128 Randy Winn	.30	.09
129 Andy Fox	.30	.09
130 Eric Karros	.30	.09
131 Kevin Millwood	.30	.09
132 Andy Benes	.30	.09
133 Andy Ashby	.30	.09
134 Ron Coomer	.30	.09
135 Juan Gonzalez	.75	.23
136 Randy Johnson	.75	.23
137 Aaron Sele	.30	.09
138 Edgardo Alfonzo	.30	.09
139 B.J. Surhoff	.30	.09
140 Jose Vizcaino	.30	.09
141 Chad Moeller SP RC	1.00	.30
142 Mike Zywica SP RC	1.00	.30
143 Angel Pena SP	1.00	.30
144 Nick Johnson SP RC	2.50	.75
145 G. Chiaramonte SP RC	1.00	.30
146 Kit Pellow SP RC	1.00	.30
147 C.Andrews SP RC	1.00	.30
148 Jerry Hairston Jr. SP	1.00	.30
149 Jason Tyner SP RC	1.00	.30
150 Chip Ambres SP RC	1.00	.30
151 Pat Burrell SP RC	5.00	1.50
152 Josh McKinley SP RC	1.00	.30
153 Choo Freeman SP RC	1.00	.30
154 Rick Elder SP RC	1.00	.30
155 Eric Valent SP RC	1.00	.30
156 J.Winchester SP RC	1.00	.30
157 Mike Nannini SP RC	1.00	.30
158 Mamon Tucker SP RC	1.00	.30
159 Nate Bump SP RC	1.00	.30
160 Andy Brown SP RC	1.00	.30
161 Troy Glaus	.50	.15
162 Adrian Beltre	.30	.09
163 Mitch Meluskey	.30	.09
164 Alex Gonzalez	.30	.09
165 George Lombard	.30	.09
166 Eric Chavez	.30	.09
167 Ruben Mateo	.30	.09
168 Calvin Pickering	.30	.09
169 Gabe Kapler	.30	.09
170 Bruce Chen	.30	.09
171 Darin Erstad	.30	.09
172 Sandy Alomar Jr.	.30	.09
173 Miguel Cairo	.30	.09
174 Jason Kendall	.30	.09
175 Cal Ripken	2.50	.75
176 Darryl Kile	.30	.09
177 David Cone	.30	.09
178 Mike Sweeney	.30	.09
179 Royce Clayton	.30	.09
180 Curt Schilling	.50	.15
181 Barry Larkin	.75	.23
182 Eric Milton	.30	.09
183 Ellis Burks	.30	.09
184 A.J. Hinch	.30	.09
185 Garret Anderson	.30	.09
186 Sean Bergman	.30	.09
187 Shannon Stewart	.30	.09
188 Bernard Gilkey	.30	.09
189 Jeff Blauser	.30	.09
190 Andruw Jones	.30	.09
191 Omar Daal	.30	.09
192 Jeff Kent	.30	.09
193 Mark Kotsay	.30	.09
194 Dave Burba	.30	.09
195 Bobby Higginson	.30	.09
196 Hideki Irabu	.30	.09
197 Jamie Moyer	.30	.09
198 Doug Glanville	.30	.09
199 Quinton McCracken	.30	.09
200 Ken Griffey Jr.	1.25	.35
201 Mike Lieberthal	.30	.09
202 Carl Everett	.30	.09
203 Omar Vizquel	.30	.09
204 Mike Lansing	.30	.09
205 Manny Ramirez	.30	.09
206 Ryan Klesko	.30	.09
207 Jeff Montgomery	.30	.09
208 Chad Curtis	.30	.09
209 Rick Helling	.30	.09
210 Justin Thompson	.30	.09
211 Tom Goodwin	.30	.09
212 Todd Dunwoody	.30	.09
213 Kevin Young	.30	.09
214 Tony Saunders	.30	.09
215 Gary Sheffield	.30	.09
216 Jaret Wright	.30	.09
217 Quilvio Veras	.30	.09
218 Marty Cordova	.30	.09
219 Tino Martinez	.50	.15
220 Scott Rolen	.50	.15
221 Fernando Tatis	.30	.95
222 Damion Easley	.30	.09
223 Aramis Ramirez	.30	.09
224 Brad Radke	.30	.09
225 Nomar Garciaparra	1.25	.35
226 Magglio Ordonez	.30	.09
227 Andy Pettitte	.50	.15
228 David Ortiz	.30	.09
229 Todd Jones	.30	.09
230 Larry Walker	.50	.15
231 Tim Wakefield	.30	.09
232 Jose Guillen	.30	.09
233 Gregg Olson	.30	.09
234 Ricky Gutierrez	.30	.09
235 Todd Walker	.30	.09
236 Abraham Nunez	.30	.09
237 Sean Casey	.30	.09
238 Greg Norton	.30	.09
239 Bret Saberhagen	.30	.09
240 Bernie Williams	.50	.15
241 Tim Salmon	.50	.15
242 Jason Giambi	.75	.23
243 Fernando Vina	.30	.09
244 Darrin Fletcher	.30	.09
245 Mike Bordick	.30	.09
246 Dennis Reyes	.30	.09
247 Hideo Nomo	.75	.23
248 Kevin Stocker	.30	.09
249 Mike Hampton	.30	.09
250 Kerry Wood	.75	.23
251 Ismael Valdes	.30	.09
252 Pat Hentgen	.30	.09
253 Scott Spiezio	.30	.09
254 Chuck Finley	.30	.09
255 Troy Glaus	.50	.15
256 Bobby Jones	.30	.09
257 Wayne Gomes	.30	.09

258 Rondell White .30 .09
259 Todd Zeile .30 .09
260 Matt Williams .30 .09
261 Henry Rodriguez .30 .09
262 Matt Stairs .30 .09
263 Jose Valentin .30 .09
264 David Justice .30 .09
265 Javy Lopez .30 .09
266 Matt Morris .30 .09
267 Steve Trachsel .30 .09
268 Edgar Martinez .50 .15
269 Al Martin .30 .09
270 Ivan Rodriguez .75 .23
271 Carlos Delgado .30 .09
272 Mark Grace .50 .15
273 Ugueth Urbina .30 .09
274 Jay Buhner .30 .09
275 Mike Piazza 1.25 .35
276 Rick Aguilera .30 .09
277 Javier Valentin .30 .09
278 Brian Anderson .30 .09
279 Cliff Floyd .30 .09
280 Barry Bonds 2.00 .60
281 Troy O'Leary .30 .09
282 Seth Greisinger .30 .09
283 Mark Grudzielanek .30 .09
284 Jose Cruz Jr. .30 .09
285 Jeff Bagwell .50 .15
286 John Smoltz .50 .15
287 Jeff Cirillo .30 .09
288 Richie Sexson .30 .09
289 Charles Nagy .30 .09
290 Pedro Martinez .75 .23
291 Juan Encarnacion .30 .09
292 Phil Nevin .30 .09
293 Terry Steinbach .30 .09
294 Miguel Tejada .30 .09
295 Dan Wilson .30 .09
296 Chris Peters .30 .09
297 Brian Moehler .30 .09
298 Jason Christiansen .30 .09
299 Kelly Stinnett .30 .09
300 Dwight Gooden .50 .15
301 Randy Velarde .30 .09
302 Kirt Manwaring .30 .09
303 Jeff Abbott .30 .09
304 Dave Hollins .30 .09
305 Kerry Ligtenberg .30 .09
306 Aaron Boone .30 .09
307 Carlos Hernandez .30 .09
308 Mike Difelice .30 .09
309 Brian Meadows .30 .09
310 Tim Bogar .30 .09
311 Greg Vaughn TR .30 .09
312 Brant Brown TR .30 .09
313 Steve Finley TR .30 .09
314 Bret Boone TR .30 .09
315 Albert Belle TR .30 .09
316 Robin Ventura TR .30 .09
317 Eric Davis TR .30 .09
318 Todd Hundley TR .30 .09
319 Roger Clemens TR 1.50 .45
320 Kevin Brown TR .30 .09
321 Jose Offerman TR .30 .09
322 Brian Jordan TR .30 .09
323 Mike Cameron TR .30 .09
324 Bobby Bonilla TR .30 .09
325 Roberto Alomar TR .75 .23
326 Ken Caminiti TR .30 .09
327 Todd Stottlemyre TR .30 .09
328 Randy Johnson TR .75 .23
329 Luis Gonzalez TR .30 .09
330 Rafael Palmeiro TR .50 .15
331 Devon White TR .30 .09
332 Will Clark TR .75 .23
333 Dean Palmer TR .30 .09
334 Gregg Jefferies TR .30 .09
335 Mo Vaughn TR .30 .09
336 Brad Lidge SP RC 1.00 .30
337 Chris George SP RC 1.00 .30
338 Austin Kearns SP RC 6.00 1.80
339 Matt Belisle SP RC 1.00 .30
340 Nate Cornejo SP RC 1.50 .45
341 Matt Holliday SP RC 1.00 .30
342 J.M. Gold SP RC 1.00 .30
343 Matt Roney SP RC 1.00 .55
344 Seth Etherton SP RC 1.00 .30
345 Adam Everett SP RC 1.00 .30
346 Marlon Anderson SP 1.00 .30
347 Ron Belliard SP 1.00 .30
348 F.Seguignol SP 1.00 .30
349 Michael Barrett SP 1.00 .30
350 Dernell Stenson SP 1.00 .30
351 Ryan Anderson SP 1.00 .30
352 Ramon Hernandez SP 1.00 .30
353 Jeremy Giambi SP 1.00 .30
354 Ricky Ledee SP 1.00 .30
355 Carlos Lee SP 1.00 .30

1999 Stadium Club First Day Issue

Randomly inserted in retail packs only at the rate of 1:75 series one packs and 1:60 series two packs, this 355-card set is parallel to Stadium Club Series one base set. Only 170 serially numbered series one sets were produced and 200 serial numbered series two sets were produced.

Nm-Mt Ex-Mt
*STARS: 6X TO 15X BASIC CARDS ....
*SP 141-160/336-355: 2X TO 5X BASIC SP

1999 Stadium Club One of a Kind

This set is a parallel version of the regular issue printed on mirrorboard and sequentially numbered to 150. The cards were randomly inserted packs at the rate of 1:53 first series hobby packs, 1:21 first series HTA packs, 1:48 second series retail packs and 1:19 second series HTA packs.

Nm-Mt Ex-Mt
*STARS: 6X TO 15X BASIC CARDS ....
*SP'S 141-160/336-355: 2X TO 5X BASIC

1999 Stadium Club Autographs

This 10-card set features color player photos with the pictured player's autograph and a gold-foil Topps Certified Autograph Issue stamp on the card front. They were inserted exclusively into retail packs as follows: series 1 1:1107, series 2 1:877.

Nm-Mt Ex-Mt
SCA1 Alex Rodriguez 100.00 30.00
SCA2 Chipper Jones 50.00 15.00
SCA3 Barry Bonds 175.00 52.50
SCA4 Tino Martinez 25.00 7.50
SCA5 Ben Grieve 15.00 4.50
SCA6 Juan Gonzalez 40.00 12.00
SCA7 Vladimir Guerrero 40.00 12.00
SCA8 Albert Belle 15.00 4.50
SCA9 Kerry Wood 40.00 12.00
SCA10 Todd Helton 25.00 7.50

1999 Stadium Club Chrome

Randomly inserted in packs at the rate of one in 24 hobby and retail packs and one in six HTA packs, this 40-card set features color player photos printed using chromium technology which gives the cards the shimmering metallic light of fresh steel.

Nm-Mt Ex-Mt
COMPLETE SERIES 1 (20) 60.00 18.00
COMPLETE SERIES 2 (20) 60.00 18.00
*REFRACTORS: 1X TO 2.5X BASIC CHROME
REFRACTOR ODDS 1:96 HOB/RET, 1:24 HTA
SCC1 Nomar Garciaparra 6.00 1.80
SCC2 Kerry Wood 4.00 1.20
SCC3 Jeff Bagwell 2.50 .75
SCC4 Ivan Rodriguez 4.00 1.20
SCC5 Albert Belle 1.50 .45
SCC6 Gary Sheffield 1.50 .45
SCC7 Andruw Jones 1.50 .45
SCC8 Kevin Brown 1.50 .45
SCC9 David Cone 1.50 .45
SCC10 Darin Erstad 1.50 .45
SCC11 Manny Ramirez 1.50 .45
SCC12 Larry Walker 2.50 .75
SCC13 Mike Piazza 6.00 1.80
SCC14 Cal Ripken 12.00 3.60
SCC15 Pedro Martinez 4.00 1.20
SCC16 Greg Vaughn 1.50 .45
SCC17 Barry Bonds 10.00 3.00
SCC18 Mo Vaughn 1.50 .45
SCC19 Bernie Williams 2.50 .75
SCC20 Ken Griffey Jr. 6.00 1.80
SCC21 Alex Rodriguez 6.00 1.80
SCC22 Chipper Jones 6.00 1.80
SCC23 Ben Grieve 1.50 .45
SCC24 Frank Thomas 4.00 1.20
SCC25 Derek Jeter 10.00 3.00
SCC26 Sammy Sosa 6.00 1.80
SCC27 Mark McGwire 10.00 3.00
SCC28 Vladimir Guerrero 4.00 1.20
SCC29 Greg Maddux 6.00 1.80
SCC30 Juan Gonzalez 4.00 1.20
SCC31 Troy Glaus 2.50 .75
SCC32 Adrian Beltre 1.50 .45
SCC33 Mitch Meluskey 1.50 .45
SCC34 Alex Gonzalez 1.50 .45
SCC35 George Lombard 1.50 .45
SCC36 Eric Chavez 1.50 .45
SCC37 Ruben Mateo 1.50 .45
SCC38 Calvin Pickering 1.50 .45
SCC39 Gabe Kapler 1.50 .45
SCC40 Bruce Chen 1.50 .45

1999 Stadium Club Co-Signers

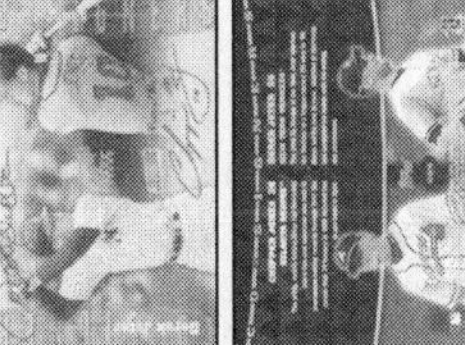

Randomly inserted in hobby packs only, this 42-card set features color player photos with their autographs and Topps "Certified Autograph Issue" stamp. Cards 1-21 were seeded in first series packs and 22-42 in second series. The cards are divided into four groups. Group A was signed by all four players appearing on the cards. Groups B-D are dual player cards featuring two autographs. Series 1 hobby pack insertion rates are as follows: Group A 1:45,213, Group B 1:3617, Group C 1:1006, and Group D 1:102. Series 2 hobby pack insertion rates are as follows: Group A 1:43,369, Group B 1:8984, Group C 1:2975 and Group D 1:251. Series 2 HTA pack insertion rates are as follows: Group A 1:18,171, Group B 1:3533, Group C 1:1189 and Group D 1:100. Pricing is available for all cards where possible.

Nm-Mt Ex-Mt
NO GROUP A PRICING DUE TO SCARCITY
NO SER.2 GROUP B PRICING AVAILABLE
CS1 Ben Grieve 15.00 4.50
Richie Sexson D
CS2 Todd Helton 60.00 18.00
Troy Glaus D
CS3 Alex Rodriguez 150.00 45.00
Scott Rolen D
CS4 Derek Jeter 200.00 60.00
Chipper Jones D
CS5 Cliff Floyd 15.00 4.50
Eli Marrero D
CS6 Jay Buhner 15.00 4.50
Kevin Young D
CS7 Ben Grieve 50.00 15.00
Troy Glaus C
CS8 Todd Helton 80.00 24.00
Richie Sexson C
CS9 Alex Rodriguez 200.00 60.00
Chipper Jones C
CS10 Derek Jeter 150.00 45.00
Scott Rolen C
CS11 Cliff Floyd 15.00 4.50
Kevin Young C
CS12 Jay Buhner 40.00 12.00
Eli Marrero B
CS13 Ben Grieve 100.00 30.00
Todd Helton B
CS14 Richie Sexson 50.00 15.00
Troy Glaus B
CS15 Alex Rodriguez 500.00 150.00
Derek Jeter B
CS16 Chipper Jones 150.00 45.00
Scott Rolen B
CS17 Cliff Floyd 40.00 12.00
Jay Buhner B
CS18 Eli Marrero 25.00 7.50
Kevin Young B
CS19 Ben Grieve
Todd Helton
Richie Sexson
Troy Glaus A
CS20 Alex Rodriguez
Derek Jeter
Chipper Jones
Scott Rolen A
CS21 Cliff Floyd
Jay Buhner
Eli Marrero
Kevin Young A
CS22 Edgardo Alfonzo 15.00 4.50
Jose Guillen D
CS23 Mike Lowell 15.00 4.50
Ricardo Rincon D
CS24 Juan Gonzalez 40.00 12.00
Vinny Castilla D
CS25 Moises Alou 80.00 24.00
Roger Clemens D
CS26 Scott Spiezio 15.00 4.50
Tony Womack D
CS27 Fernando Vina 15.00 4.50
Quilvio Veras D
CS28 Edgardo Alfonzo 15.00 4.50
Ricardo Rincon C
CS29 Jose Guillen 15.00 4.50
Mike Lowell C
CS30 Juan Gonzalez 60.00 18.00
Moises Alou C
CS31 Roger Clemens 120.00 36.00
Vinny Castilla C
CS32 Scott Spiezio 15.00 4.50
Fernando Vina C
CS33 Tony Womack
Quilvio Veras B
CS34 Edgardo Alfonzo
Mike Lowell B
CS35 Jose Guillen
Ricardo Rincon B
CS36 Juan Gonzalez
Roger Clemens B
CS37 Moises Alou
Vinny Castilla B
CS38 Scott Spiezio
Quilvio Veras B
CS39 Tony Womack
Fernando Vina B
CS40 Edgardo Alfonzo
Jose Guillen
Mike Lowell
Ricardo Rincon A
CS41 Juan Gonzalez
Moises Alou
Roger Clemens
Vinny Castilla A
CS42 Scott Spiezio
Tony Womack
Fernando Vina
Quilvio Veras A

1999 Stadium Club Never Compromise

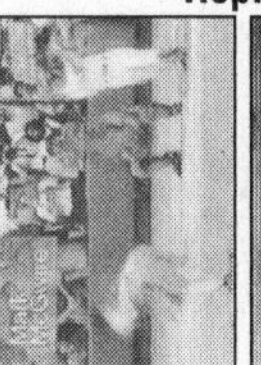

Randomly inserted in packs at the rate of one in 12 hobby and retail packs and one in four HTA packs, this 10-card set features color action photos of top players.

Nm-Mt Ex-Mt
COMPLETE SET (20) 50.00 15.00
COMPLETE SERIES 1 (10) 30.00 9.00
COMPLETE SERIES 2 (10) 20.00 6.00
NC1 Mark McGwire 5.00 1.50
NC2 Sammy Sosa 3.00 .90
NC3 Ken Griffey Jr. 3.00 .90
NC4 Greg Maddux 3.00 .90
NC5 Barry Bonds 5.00 1.50
NC6 Alex Rodriguez 3.00 .90
NC7 Darin Erstad .75 .23
NC8 Roger Clemens 4.00 1.20
NC9 Nomar Garciaparra 3.00 .90
NC10 Derek Jeter 5.00 1.50
NC11 Cal Ripken 6.00 1.80
NC12 Mike Piazza 3.00 .90
NC13 Kerry Wood 2.00 .60
NC14 Andres Galarraga .75 .23
NC15 Vinny Castilla .75 .23
NC16 Jeff Bagwell 1.25 .35
NC17 Chipper Jones 2.00 .60
NC18 Eric Chavez .75 .23
NC19 Orlando Hernandez .75 .23
NC20 Troy Glaus 1.25 .35

1999 Stadium Club Triumvirate Luminous

Randomly inserted in hobby packs at the rate of one in 36 and in retail packs at the rate of one in 48, this 24-card set features color player photos printed on cards made to fit together to form eight different long cards.

Nm-Mt Ex-Mt
COMPLETE SERIES 1 (24) 120.00 36.00
COMPLETE SERIES 2 (24) 150.00 45.00
*ILLUMINATOR: 2X TO 5X LUMINOUS
ILLUM.ODDS 1:288 H, 1:384 R, 1:144 HTA
*LUMINESCENT: 1X TO 2.5X LUMINOUS
L'SCENT.ODDS 1:144 H, 1:192 R, 1:72 HTA
T1A Greg Vaughn 2.00 .60
T1B Ken Caminiti 2.00 .60
T1C Tony Gwynn 6.00 1.80
T2A Andruw Jones 2.00 .60
T2B Chipper Jones 5.00 1.50
T2C Andres Galarraga 2.00 .60
T3A Jay Buhner 2.00 .60
T3B Ken Griffey Jr. 8.00 2.40
T3C Alex Rodriguez 8.00 2.40
T4A Derek Jeter 12.00 3.60
T4B Tino Martinez 3.00 .90
T4C Bernie Williams 3.00 .90
T5A Brian Jordan 2.00 .60
T5B Ray Lankford 2.00 .60
T5C Mark McGwire 12.00 3.60
T6A Jeff Bagwell 3.00 .90
T6B Craig Biggio 3.00 .90
T6C Randy Johnson 5.00 1.50
T7A Nomar Garciaparra 8.00 2.40
T7B Pedro Martinez 5.00 1.50
T7C Mo Vaughn 2.00 .60
T8A Sammy Sosa 8.00 2.40
T8B Mark Grace 3.00 .90
T8C Kerry Wood 5.00 1.50
T9A Alex Rodriguez 8.00 2.40
T9B Nomar Garciaparra 8.00 2.40
T9C Derek Jeter 12.00 3.60
T10A Todd Helton 3.00 .90
T10B Travis Lee 2.00 .60
T10C Pat Burrell 5.00 1.50
T11A Greg Maddux 8.00 2.40
T11B Kerry Wood 5.00 1.50
T11C Tom Glavine 3.00 .90
T12A Chipper Jones 5.00 1.50
T12B Vinny Castilla 2.00 .60
T12C Scott Rolen 3.00 .90
T13A Juan Gonzalez 5.00 1.50
T13B Ken Griffey Jr. 8.00 2.40
T13C Ben Grieve 2.00 .60
T14A Sammy Sosa 8.00 2.40
T14B Vladimir Guerrero 5.00 1.50
T14C Barry Bonds 12.00 3.60
T15A Frank Thomas 5.00 1.50
T15B Jim Thome 5.00 1.50
T15C Tino Martinez 3.00 .90
T16A Mark McGwire 12.00 3.60
T16B Andres Galarraga 2.00 .60
T16C Jeff Bagwell 3.00 .90

1999 Stadium Club Video Replay

Randomly inserted in Series two hobby and retail packs at the rate of one in 12 and HTA packs at the rate of one in four, this five-card set features live-action video images of top players on lenticular cards.

Nm-Mt Ex-Mt
COMPLETE SET (5) 12.00 3.60
VR1 Mark McGwire 4.00 1.20
VR2 Sammy Sosa 2.50 .75
VR3 Ken Griffey Jr. 2.50 .75
VR4 Kerry Wood 1.50 .45
VR5 Alex Rodriguez 2.50 .75

2000 Stadium Club Pre-Production

These three cards were issued by Topps to preview their 2000 Stadium Club set. The cards were distributed as a set within a sealed cello wrapper to dealers and hobby media several weeks before the product's release. The cards, while they are in the style of the 2000 set, are differentiated by having a "PP" prefix.

Nm-Mt Ex-Mt
COMPLETE SET (3) 6.00 1.80
PP1 Ivan Rodriguez 3.00 .90
PP2 Magglio Ordonez 2.00 .60
PP3 Craig Biggio 2.50 .75

2000 Stadium Club

This 250-card single series set was released in February, 2000. Six-card hobby and retail packs carried an SRP of $2.00. There was also a HTC (Home Team Collector) fourteen card pack issued with a SRP of $5.00. The last 50 cards were printed in shorter supply the first 200 cards. These cards were inserted one in five packs and one per HTC pack. This was the first time the Stadium Club set was issued in a single series. Notable Rookie Cards include Rick Asadoorian and Bobby Bradley.

Nm-Mt Ex-Mt
COMPLETE SET (250) 120.00 36.00
COMP.SET w/o SP'S (200) 30.00 9.00
COMMON CARD (1-200) .30 .09
COMMON SP (201-250) 3.00 .90
1 Nomar Garciaparra 1.25 .35
2 Brian Jordan .30 .09
3 Mark Grace .50 .15
4 Jeromy Burnitz .30 .09
5 Shane Reynolds .30 .09
6 Alex Gonzalez .30 .09
7 Jose Offerman .30 .09
8 Orlando Hernandez .30 .09
9 Mike Caruso .30 .09
10 Tony Clark .30 .09
11 Sean Casey .30 .09
12 Johnny Damon .30 .09
13 Dante Bichette .30 .09
14 Kevin Young .30 .09
15 Juan Gonzalez .75 .23
16 Chipper Jones .75 .23
17 Quilvio Veras .30 .09
18 Trevor Hoffman .30 .09
19 Roger Cedeno .30 .09
20 Ellis Burks .30 .09
21 Richie Sexson .30 .09
22 Gary Sheffield .30 .09
23 Delino DeShields .30 .09
24 Wade Boggs .50 .15
25 Ray Lankford .30 .09
26 Kevin Appier .30 .09
27 Roy Halladay .30 .09
28 Harold Baines .30 .09
29 Todd Zeile .30 .09
30 Barry Larkin .75 .23
31 Ron Coomer .30 .09
32 Jorge Posada .50 .15
33 Magglio Ordonez .30 .09
34 Brian Giles .30 .09
35 Jeff Kent .30 .09
36 Henry Rodriguez .30 .09
37 Fred McGriff .50 .15
38 Shawn Green .30 .09
39 Derek Bell .30 .09
40 Ben Grieve .30 .09
41 Dave Nilsson .30 .09
42 Mo Vaughn .30 .09
43 Rondell White .30 .09
44 Doug Glanville .30 .09
45 Paul O'Neill .50 .15
46 Carlos Lee .30 .09
47 Vinny Castilla .30 .09
48 Mike Sweeney .30 .09
49 Rico Brogna .30 .09
50 Alex Rodriguez 1.25 .35
51 Luis Castillo .30 .09
52 Kevin Brown .50 .15
53 Jose Vidro .30 .09
54 John Smoltz .50 .15
55 Garret Anderson .30 .09
56 Matt Stairs .30 .09
57 Omar Vizquel .30 .09
58 Tom Goodwin .30 .09
59 Scott Brosius .30 .09
60 Robin Ventura .50 .15
61 B.J. Surhoff .30 .09
62 Andy Ashby .30 .09
63 Chris Widger .30 .09
64 Tim Hudson .50 .15
65 Javy Lopez .30 .09
66 Tim Salmon .50 .15
67 Warren Morris .30 .09
68 John Wetteland .30 .09
69 Gabe Kapler .30 .09
70 Bernie Williams .50 .15
71 Rickey Henderson .75 .23
72 Andruw Jones .30 .09
73 Eric Young .30 .09
74 Bob Abreu .30 .09
75 David Cone .30 .09
76 Rusty Greer .30 .09
77 Ron Belliard .30 .09
78 Troy Glaus .50 .15
79 Mike Hampton .30 .09
80 Miguel Tejada .30 .09
81 Jeff Cirillo .30 .09
82 Todd Hundley .30 .09
83 Roberto Alomar .75 .23
84 Charles Johnson .30 .09
85 Rafael Palmeiro .50 .15
86 Doug Mientkiewicz .30 .09
87 Mariano Rivera .50 .15
88 Neifi Perez .30 .09
89 Jermaine Dye .30 .09

2000 Stadium Club

90 Ivan Rodriguez .75 .23
91 Jay Buhner .30 .09
92 Pokey Reese .30 .09
93 John Olerud .30 .09
94 Brady Anderson .30 .09
95 Manny Ramirez .30 .09
96 Keith Osik RC .30 .09
97 Mickey Morandini .30 .09
98 Matt Williams .30 .09
99 Eric Karros .30 .09
100 Ken Griffey Jr. 1.25 .35
101 Bret Boone .30 .09
102 Ryan Klesko .30 .09
103 Craig Biggio .50 .15
104 John Jaha .30 .09
105 Vladimir Guerrero .75 .23
106 Devon White .30 .09
107 Tony Womack .30 .09
108 Marvin Benard .30 .09
109 Kenny Lofton .30 .09
110 Preston Wilson .30 .09
111 Al Leiter .30 .09
112 Reggie Sanders .30 .09
113 Scott Williamson .30 .09
114 Deivi Cruz .30 .09
115 Carlos Beltran .30 .09
116 Ray Durham .30 .09
117 Ricky Ledee .30 .09
118 Torii Hunter .30 .09
119 John Valentin .30 .09
120 Scott Rolen .50 .15
121 Jason Kendall .30 .09
122 Dave Martinez .30 .09
123 Jim Thome .75 .23
124 David Bell .30 .09
125 Jose Canseco .75 .23
126 Jose Lima .30 .09
127 Carl Everett .30 .09
128 Kevin Millwood .30 .09
129 Bill Spiers .30 .09
130 Omar Daal .30 .09
131 Miguel Cairo .30 .09
132 Mark Grudzielanek .30 .09
133 David Justice .30 .09
134 Russ Ortiz .30 .09
135 Mike Piazza 1.25 .35
136 Brian Meadows .30 .09
137 Tony Gwynn 1.00 .30
138 Cal Ripken 2.50 .75
139 Kris Benson .30 .09
140 Larry Walker .50 .15
141 Cristian Guzman .30 .09
142 Tino Martinez .50 .15
143 Chris Singleton .30 .09
144 Lee Stevens .30 .09
145 Rey Ordonez .30 .09
146 Russ Davis .30 .09
147 J.T. Snow .30 .09
148 Luis Gonzalez .30 .09
149 Marquis Grissom .30 .09
150 Greg Maddux 1.25 .35
151 Fernando Tatis .30 .09
152 Jason Giambi .75 .23
153 Carlos Delgado .30 .09
154 Joe McEwing .30 .09
155 Raul Mondesi .30 .09
156 Rich Aurilia .30 .09
157 Alex Fernandez .30 .09
158 Albert Belle .30 .09
159 Pat Meares .30 .09
160 Mike Lieberthal .30 .09
161 Mike Cameron .30 .09
162 Juan Encarnacion .30 .09
163 Chuck Knoblauch .30 .09
164 Pedro Martinez .75 .23
165 Randy Johnson .75 .23
166 Shannon Stewart .30 .09
167 Jeff Bagwell .50 .15
168 Edgar Renteria .30 .09
169 Barry Bonds 2.00 .60
170 Steve Finley .30 .09
171 Brian Hunter .30 .09
172 Tom Glavine .50 .15
173 Mark Kotsay .30 .09
174 Tony Fernandez .30 .09
175 Sammy Sosa 1.25 .35
176 Geoff Jenkins .30 .09
177 Adrian Beltre .30 .09
178 Jay Bell .30 .09
179 Mike Bordick .30 .09
180 Ed Sprague .30 .09
181 Dave Roberts .30 .09
182 Greg Vaughn .30 .09
183 Brian Daubach .30 .09
184 Damion Easley .30 .09
185 Carlos Febles .30 .09
186 Kevin Tapani .30 .09
187 Frank Thomas .75 .23
188 Roger Clemens 1.50 .45
189 Mike Benjamin .30 .09
190 Curt Schilling .50 .15
191 Edgardo Alfonzo .30 .09
192 Mike Mussina .75 .23
193 Todd Helton .50 .15
194 Todd Jones .30 .09
195 Dean Palmer .30 .09
196 John Flaherty .30 .09
197 Derek Jeter 2.00 .60
198 Todd Walker .30 .09
199 Brad Ausmus .30 .09
200 Mark McGwire 2.00 .60
201 Erubiel Durazo SP 3.00 .90
202 Nick Johnson SP 3.00 .90
203 Ruben Mateo SP 3.00 .90
204 Lance Berkman SP 3.00 .90
205 Pat Burrell SP 4.00 1.20
206 Pablo Ozuna SP 3.00 .90
207 Roosevelt Brown SP 3.00 .90
208 Alfonso Soriano SP 4.00 1.20
209 A.J. Burnett SP 3.00 .90
210 Rafael Furcal SP 3.00 .90
211 Scott Morgan SP 3.00 .90
212 Adam Piatt SP 3.00 .90
213 Dee Brown SP 3.00 .90
214 Corey Patterson SP 4.00 1.20
215 Mickey Lopez SP 3.00 .90
216 Rob Ryan SP 3.00 .90
217 Sean Burroughs SP 4.00 1.20
218 Jack Cust SP 3.00 .90
219 John Patterson SP 3.00 .90
220 Kit Pellow SP 3.00 .90
221 Chad Hermansen SP 3.00 .90
222 Daryle Ward SP 3.00 .90
223 Jayson Werth SP 3.00 .90
224 Jason Standridge SP 3.00 .90
225 Mark Mulder SP 4.00 1.20
226 Peter Bergeron SP 3.00 .90
227 Willi Mo Pena SP 3.00 .90
228 Aramis Ramirez SP 3.00 .90
229 John Sneed SP RC 3.00 .90
230 Wilton Veras SP 3.00 .90
231 Josh Hamilton SP 3.00 .90
232 Eric Munson SP 3.00 .90
233 Bobby Bradley SP RC 3.00 .90
234 Larry Bigbie SP RC 4.00 1.20
235 B.J. Garbe SP RC 3.00 .90
236 Brett Myers SP RC 8.00 2.40
237 Jason Stumm SP RC 3.00 .90
238 Corey Myers SP RC 3.00 .90
239 R.Christianson SP RC 3.00 .90
240 David Walling SP 3.00 .90
241 Josh Girdley SP 3.00 .90
242 Omar Ortiz SP 3.00 .90
243 Jason Jennings SP 3.00 .90
244 Kyle Snyder SP 3.00 .90
245 Jay Gehrke SP 3.00 .90
246 Mike Paradis SP 3.00 .90
247 Chance Caple SP RC 3.00 .90
248 B.Christensen SP RC 3.00 .90
249 Brad Baker SP RC 3.00 .90
250 R.Asadoorian SP RC 3.00 .90

2000 Stadium Club First Day Issue

This parallel to the Stadium Club set was inserted at a rate of one in 36 retail packs and were serial numbered to 150. These cards can be identified by the first day issue stamp on the front.

Nm-Mt Ex-Mt
*STARS: 10X TO 25X BASIC CARDS ..
*SP'S 201-250: 1X TO 2.5X BASIC.....
*SP RC'S 201-250: 1.25X TO 3X BASIC

2000 Stadium Club One of a Kind

This parallel set was issued at a rate of one in 27 hobby and one in 11 HTC packs. The cards are serial numbered to 150 as well. These cards are differentiated from the regular cards by the mirrorboard technology.

Nm-Mt Ex-Mt
*STARS 1-250: 10X TO 25X BASIC CARDS
*SP'S 201-250: 1X TO 2.5X BASIC....
*SP RC'S 201-250: 1.25X TO 3X BASIC

2000 Stadium Club Bats of Brilliance

Issued at a rate of one in 12 hobby packs, one in 15 retail packs and one in six HTC packs these 10 cards feature some of the best clutch hitters in the game.

Nm-Mt Ex-Mt
COMPLETE SET (10) 20.00 6.00
*DIE CUTS: 1.25X TO 3X BASIC BATS
DIE CUT ODDS 1:60 HOB, 1:75 RET, 1:30 HTC
BB1 Mark McGwire 4.00 1.20
BB2 Sammy Sosa 2.50 .75
BB3 Jose Canseco 1.50 .45
BB4 Jeff Bagwell 1.00 .30
BB5 Ken Griffey Jr. 2.50 .75
BB6 Nomar Garciaparra 2.50 .75
BB7 Mike Piazza 2.50 .75
BB8 Alex Rodriguez 2.50 .75
BB9 Vladimir Guerrero 1.50 .45
BB10 Chipper Jones 1.50 .45

2000 Stadium Club Capture the Action

Inserted one in 12 hobby and retail packs and one in six HTC packs, these 20 cards feature players who continually hustle when on the field. This set is broken up into three groups: Rookies (CA1 through CA5); Stars (CA6 through CA14) and Legends (CA15 through CA20).

Nm-Mt Ex-Mt
COMPLETE SET (20) 60.00 18.00
*GAME VIEW 1-5: 5X TO 12X BASIC CAPT
*GAME VIEW: 5X TO 12X BASIC CAPTURE
GAME VIEW ODDS 1:508 HOB, 1:203 HTC
GAME VIEW PRINT RUN 100 SERIAL #'d SETS
CA1 Josh Hamilton 1.00 .30
CA2 Pat Burrell 1.25 .35
CA3 Erubiel Durazo 1.00 .30
CA4 Alfonso Soriano 1.25 .35
CA5 A.J. Burnett 1.00 .30
CA6 Alex Rodriguez 4.00 1.20
CA7 Sean Casey 1.00 .30
CA8 Derek Jeter 6.00 1.80
CA9 Vladimir Guerrero 2.50 .75
CA10 Nomar Garciaparra 4.00 1.20
CA11 Mike Piazza 4.00 1.20
CA12 Ken Griffey Jr. 4.00 1.20
CA13 Sammy Sosa 4.00 1.20
CA14 Juan Gonzalez 2.50 .75
CA15 Mark McGwire 6.00 1.80
CA16 Ivan Rodriguez 2.50 .75
CA17 Barry Bonds 6.00 1.80
CA18 Wade Boggs 1.50 .45
CA19 Tony Gwynn 3.00 .90
CA20 Cal Ripken 8.00 2.40

2000 Stadium Club Capture the Action Game View

Inserted at a rate of one in 508 hobby packs, these cards parallel the regular Capture the Action insert set. These cards, issued only through hobby packs, feature a replica of the actual photo slide used to create the card and is viewable from both sides. Each card back has a "Topps3M" sticker to ensure the autenticity.

Nm-Mt Ex-Mt
*GAME VIEW: 5X TO 12X BASIC CAPTURE

2000 Stadium Club Chrome Preview

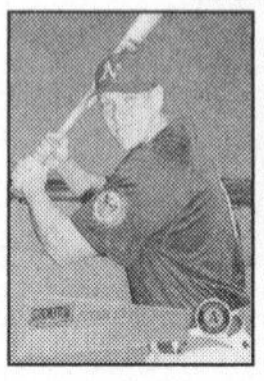

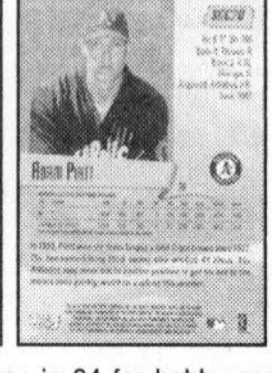

Inserted at a rate of one in 24 for hobby and retail and one in 12 HTC packs, these 20 cards preview the "Chrome" set. These cards carry a "SCC" prefix.

Nm-Mt Ex-Mt
COMPLETE SET (20) 100.00 30.00
*REFRACTOR: 1.25X TO 3X BASIC CHR.PREV.
REFRACTOR ODDS 1:120 HOB/RET, 1:60 HTC
SCC1 Nomar Garciaparra 6.00 1.80
SCC2 Juan Gonzalez 4.00 1.20
SCC3 Chipper Jones 4.00 1.20
SCC4 Alex Rodriguez 6.00 1.80
SCC5 Ivan Rodriguez 4.00 1.20
SCC6 Manny Ramirez 1.50 .45
SCC7 Ken Griffey Jr. 6.00 1.80
SCC8 Vladimir Guerrero 4.00 1.20
SCC9 Mike Piazza 6.00 1.80
SCC10 Pedro Martinez 4.00 1.20
SCC11 Jeff Bagwell 2.50 .75
SCC12 Barry Bonds 10.00 3.00
SCC13 Sammy Sosa 6.00 1.80
SCC14 Derek Jeter 10.00 3.00
SCC15 Mark McGwire 10.00 3.00
SCC16 Erubiel Durazo 1.50 .45
SCC17 Nick Johnson 1.50 .45
SCC18 Pat Burrell 2.50 .75
SCC19 Alfonso Soriano 4.00 1.20
SCC20 Adam Piatt 1.50 .45

2000 Stadium Club Co-Signers

Inserted in hobby packs only at different rates, these 15 cards feature a pair of players who have signed these cards. The odds are broken down like this: Group A was issued one every 10,184 hobby packs and one every 4060 HTC packs. Group B was issued one every 5092 hobby packs and one every 2032 HTC packs. Group C was issued one every 508 hobby packs and one every 203 HTC packs.

Nm-Mt Ex-Mt
CO1 Alex Rodriguez 600.00 180.00
Derek Jeter A
CO2 Derek Jeter 150.00 45.00
Omar Vizquel B
CO3 Alex Rodriguez 150.00 45.00
Rey Ordonez B
CO4 Derek Jeter 150.00 45.00
Rey Ordonez B
CO5 Omar Vizquel 150.00 45.00
Alex Rodriguez B
CO6 Rey Ordonez 25.00 7.50
Omar Vizquel C
CO7 Wade Boggs 40.00 12.00
Robin Ventura C
CO8 Randy Johnson 120.00 36.00
Mike Mussina C
CO9 Pat Burrell 40.00 12.00
Magglio Ordonez C
CO10 Chad Hermansen 25.00 7.50
Pat Burrell C
CO11 Magglio Ordonez 25.00 7.50
Chad Hermansen C
CO12 Josh Hamilton 15.00 4.50
Corey Myers C
CO13 B.J.Garbe 15.00 4.50
Josh Hamilton C
CO14 Corey Myers 15.00 4.50
B.J. Garbe C
CO15 Tino Martinez 40.00 12.00
Fred McGriff C

2000 Stadium Club Lone Star Signatures

Issued at different rates throughout the various packaging, these 16 cards feature signed cards

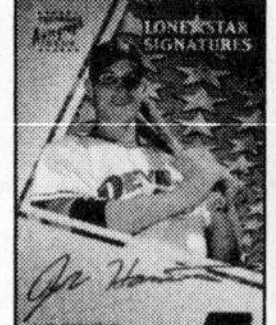

of various stars. The cards were inserted at these rates: Group 1 was inserted at a rate of one in 1981 retail packs, one in 1979 hobby packs and one in 792 HTC packs. Group 2 was inserted at a rate of one in 2421 retail packs, one in 2374 hobby packs and one in 946 HTC packs. Group 3 was issued at the same rate as Group 1 (1:1979 hobby, 1:1981 retail; 1:792 HTC packs). Group 4 were issued at a rate of one in 424 hobby packs, one in 423 retail packs and one in 169 HTC packs. These cards are authenticated with a "Topps Certified Autograph" stamp as well as a "Topps3M" sticker.

Nm-Mt Ex-Mt
LS1 Derek Jeter G1 120.00 36.00
LS2 Alex Rodriguez G1 150.00 45.00
LS3 Wade Boggs G1 40.00 12.00
LS4 Robin Ventura G1 15.00 4.50
LS5 Randy Johnson G2 80.00 24.00
LS6 Mike Mussina G2 40.00 12.00
LS7 Tino Martinez G3 50.00 15.00
LS8 Fred McGriff G3 50.00 15.00
LS9 Omar Vizquel G4 25.00 7.50
LS10 Rey Ordonez G4 10.00 3.00
LS11 Pat Burrell G4 25.00 7.50
LS12 Chad Hermansen G4 10.00 3.00
LS13 Magglio Ordonez G4 15.00 4.50
LS14 Josh Hamilton G4 10.00 3.00
LS15 Corey Myers G4 10.00 3.00
LS16 B.J. Garbe G4 10.00 3.00

2000 Stadium Club Onyx Extreme

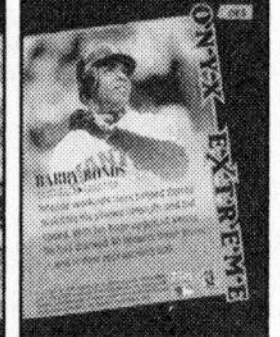

Inserted at a rate of one in 12 hobby, one in 15 retail and one in six HTC packs, these 10 cards feature 10 cards printed using black styrene technology with silver foil stamping.

Nm-Mt Ex-Mt
COMPLETE SET (10) 25.00 7.50
*DIE CUTS: 1.25X TO 3X BASIC ONYX
DIE CUT ODDS 1:60 HOB, 1:75 RET, 1:30 HTC
OE1 Ken Griffey Jr. 2.50 .75
OE2 Derek Jeter 4.00 1.20
OE3 Vladimir Guerrero 1.50 .45
OE4 Nomar Garciaparra 2.50 .75
OE5 Barry Bonds 4.00 1.20
OE6 Alex Rodriguez 2.50 .75
OE7 Sammy Sosa 2.50 .75
OE8 Ivan Rodriguez 1.50 .45
OE9 Larry Walker 1.00 .30
OE10 Andruw Jones .60 .18

2000 Stadium Club Scenes

Inserted as a box-topper in hobby and HTC boxes, these eight cards which measure 2 1/2" by 4 11/16" feature superstar players in a special "widevision" format.

Nm-Mt Ex-Mt
COMPLETE SET (8) 25.00 7.50
SCS1 Mark McGwire 5.00 1.50
SCS2 Alex Rodriguez 3.00 .90
SCS3 Cal Ripken 6.00 1.80
SCS4 Sammy Sosa 3.00 .90
SCS5 Derek Jeter 5.00 1.50
SCS6 Ken Griffey Jr. 3.00 .90
SCS7 Nomar Garciaparra 3.00 .90
SCS8 Chipper Jones 2.00 .60

2000 Stadium Club Souvenir

Inserted exclusively into hobby packs at a rate of one in 339 hobby packs and one in 136 HTC packs, these cards feature die-cut technology which incorporates an actual piece of a game-used uniform.

Nm-Mt Ex-Mt
S1 Wade Boggs 25.00 7.50
S2 Edgardo Alfonzo 15.00 4.50
S3 Robin Ventura 15.00 4.50

2000 Stadium Club 3 X 3 Luminous

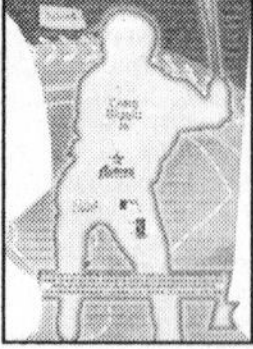

Inserted at a rate of one in 18 hobby, one in 24 retail and one in nine HTC packs, these 30 cards can be fused together to form one very oversized card. The luminous variety is the most common of the three forms used (Luminous, Luminescent and Illuminator).

Nm-Mt Ex-Mt
COMPLETE SET (30) 120.00 36.00
*ILLUMINATOR: 1.5X TO 4X LUMINOUS
ILLUM ODDS 1:144 HOB, 1:192 RET, 1:72 HTC
*L'SCENT: .75X TO 2X LUMINOUS.....
L'SCENT ODDS 1:72 HOB, 1:96 RET, 1:36 HTC
1A Randy Johnson 4.00 1.20
1B Pedro Martinez 4.00 1.20
1C Greg Maddux 6.00 1.80
2A Mike Piazza 6.00 1.80
2B Ivan Rodriguez 4.00 1.20
2C Mike Lieberthal 1.50 .45
3A Mark McGwire 10.00 3.00
3B Jeff Bagwell 2.50 .75
3C Sean Casey 1.50 .45
4A Craig Biggio 2.50 .75
4B Roberto Alomar 4.00 1.20
4C Jay Bell 1.50 .45
5A Chipper Jones 4.00 1.20
5B Matt Williams 1.50 .45
5C Robin Ventura 2.50 .75
6A Alex Rodriguez 6.00 1.80
6B Derek Jeter 10.00 3.00
6C Nomar Garciaparra 6.00 1.80
7A Barry Bonds 10.00 3.00
7B Luis Gonzalez 1.50 .45
7C Dante Bichette 1.50 .45
8A Ken Griffey Jr. 6.00 1.80
8B Bernie Williams 2.50 .75
8C Andruw Jones 1.50 .45
9A Manny Ramirez 1.50 .45
9B Sammy Sosa 6.00 1.80
9C Juan Gonzalez 4.00 1.20
10A Jose Canseco 4.00 1.20
10B Frank Thomas 4.00 1.20
10C Rafael Palmeiro 2.50 .75

2001 Stadium Club Pre-Production

This three-card set was distributed to dealers and hobby media in a sealed cello wrap bag several weeks prior to the release of 2001 Stadium Club. The cards can be distinguished from their basic issue counterparts by their "PP" prefixed numbering.

Nm-Mt Ex-Mt
COMPLETE SET (3) 3.00 .90
PP1 Andruw Jones 1.50 .45
PP2 Jorge Posada .75 .23
PP3 Jeff Bagwell 1.50 .45

2001 Stadium Club

The 2001 Stadium Club product was released in late December, 2000 and features a 200-card base set. The set is broken into tiers as follows: 175 Base Veterans and 25 Prospects (1:6). Each pack contained seven cards and carried a suggested retail price of $1.99.

Nm-Mt Ex-Mt
COMPLETE SET (200) 120.00 36.00
COMP.SET w/o SP's (175) 25.00 7.50
COMMON CARD (1-150) .30 .09
COMMON SP (151-200) 3.00 .90
1 Nomar Garciaparra 1.25 .35
2 Chipper Jones .75 .23
3 Jeff Bagwell .50 .15
4 Chad Kreuter .30 .09
5 Randy Johnson .75 .23
6 Mike Hampton .30 .09
7 Barry Larkin .75 .23
8 Bernie Williams .50 .15
9 Chris Singleton .30 .09
10 Larry Walker .50 .15
11 Brad Ausmus .30 .09
12 Ron Coomer .30 .09
13 Edgardo Alfonzo .30 .09
14 Delino DeShields .30 .09
15 Tony Gwynn 1.00 .30
16 Andruw Jones .30 .09

17 Raul Mondesi .30 .09
18 Troy Glaus .50 .15
19 Ben Grieve .30 .09
20 Sammy Sosa 1.25 .35
21 Fernando Vina .30 .09
22 Jeromy Burnitz .30 .09
23 Jay Bell .30 .09
24 Pete Harnisch .30 .09
25 Barry Bonds 2.00 .60
26 Eric Karros .30 .09
27 Alex Gonzalez .30 .09
28 Mike Lieberthal .30 .09
29 Juan Encarnacion .30 .09
30 Derek Jeter 2.00 .60
31 Luis Sojo .30 .09
32 Eric Milton .30 .09
33 Aaron Boone .30 .09
34 Roberto Alomar .75 .23
35 John Olerud .30 .09
36 Orlando Cabrera .30 .09
37 Shawn Green .30 .09
38 Roger Cedeno .30 .09
39 Garret Anderson .30 .09
40 Jim Thome .75 .23
41 Gabe Kapler .30 .09
42 Mo Vaughn .30 .09
43 Sean Casey .30 .09
44 Preston Wilson .30 .09
45 Javy Lopez .30 .09
46 Ryan Klesko .30 .09
47 Ray Durham .30 .09
48 Dean Palmer .30 .09
49 Jorge Posada .50 .15
50 Alex Rodriguez 1.25 .35
51 Tom Glavine .50 .15
52 Ray Lankford .30 .09
53 Jose Canseco .75 .23
54 Tim Salmon .50 .15
55 Cal Ripken 2.50 .75
56 Bob Abreu .30 .09
57 Robin Ventura .30 .09
58 Damion Easley .30 .09
59 Paul O'Neill .50 .15
60 Ivan Rodriguez .75 .23
61 Carl Everett .30 .09
62 Doug Glanville .30 .09
63 Jeff Kent .30 .09
64 Jay Buhner .30 .09
65 Cliff Floyd .30 .09
66 Rick Ankiel .30 .09
67 Mark Grace .50 .15
68 Brian Jordan .30 .09
69 Craig Biggio .50 .15
70 Carlos Delgado .30 .09
71 Brad Radke .30 .09
72 Greg Maddux 1.25 .35
73 Al Leiter .30 .09
74 Pokey Reese .30 .09
75 Todd Helton .50 .15
76 Mariano Rivera .50 .15
77 Shane Spencer .30 .09
78 Jason Kendall .30 .09
79 Chuck Knoblauch .30 .09
80 Scott Rolen .50 .15
81 Jose Offerman .30 .09
82 J.T. Snow .30 .09
83 Pat Meares .30 .09
84 Quilvio Veras .30 .09
85 Edgar Renteria .30 .09
86 Luis Matos .30 .09
87 Adrian Beltre .30 .09
88 Luis Gonzalez .30 .09
89 Rickey Henderson .75 .23
90 Brian Giles .30 .09
91 Carlos Febles .30 .09
92 Tino Martinez .50 .15
93 Maggio Ordonez .30 .09
94 Rafael Furcal .30 .09
95 Mike Mussina .75 .23
96 Gary Sheffield .30 .09
97 Kenny Lofton .30 .09
98 Fred McGriff .50 .15
99 Ken Caminiti .30 .09
100 Mark McGwire 2.00 .60
101 Tom Goodwin .30 .09
102 Mark Grudzielanek .30 .09
103 Derek Bell .30 .09
104 Mike Lowell .30 .09
105 Jeff Cirillo .30 .09
106 Orlando Hernandez .30 .09
107 Jose Valentin .30 .09
108 Warren Morris .30 .09
109 Mike Williams .30 .09
110 Greg Zaun .30 .09
111 Jose Vidro .30 .09
112 Omar Vizquel .30 .09
113 Vinny Castilla .30 .09
114 Gregg Jefferies .30 .09
115 Kevin Brown .30 .09
116 Shannon Stewart .30 .09
117 Marquis Grissom .30 .09
118 Manny Ramirez .30 .09
119 Albert Belle .30 .09
120 Bret Boone .30 .09
121 Johnny Damon .30 .09
122 Juan Gonzalez .75 .23
123 David Justice .30 .09
124 Jeffrey Hammonds .30 .09
125 Ken Griffey Jr. 1.25 .35
126 Mike Sweeney .30 .09
127 Tony Clark .30 .09
128 Todd Zeile .30 .09
129 Mark Johnson .30 .09
130 Matt Williams .30 .09
131 Geoff Jenkins .30 .09
132 Jason Giambi .75 .23
133 Steve Finley .30 .09
134 Derek Lee .30 .09
135 Royce Clayton .30 .09
136 Joe Randa .30 .09
137 Rafael Palmeiro .50 .15
138 Kevin Young .30 .09
139 Mike Redmond .30 .09
140 Vladimir Guerrero .75 .23
141 Greg Vaughn .30 .09
142 Jermaine Dye .30 .09
143 Roger Clemens 1.50 .45
144 Denny Hocking .30 .09
145 Frank Thomas .75 .23
146 Carlos Beltran .30 .09
147 Eric Young .30 .09
148 Pat Burrell .30 .09
149 Pedro Martinez .75 .23
150 Mike Piazza 1.25 .35
151 Adrian Gonzalez .50 .15
152 Adam Johnson .50 .15
153 Luis Montanez SP RC 3.00 .90
154 Mike Stodolka .50 .15
155 Phil Dumatrait .50 .15
156 Sean Burnett SP 3.00 .90
157 Dominic Rich SP RC 3.00 .90
158 Adam Wainwright .50 .15
159 Scott Thorman .50 .15
160 Scott Heard SP 3.00 .90
161 Chad Petty SP RC 3.00 .90
162 Matt Wheatland .50 .15
163 Bryan Digby .50 .15
164 Rocco Baldelli 3.00 .90
165 Grady Sizemore 1.25 .35
166 Brian Sellier SP RC 3.00 .90
167 Rick Brosseau SP RC 3.00 .90
168 Shawn Fagan SP RC 3.00 .90
169 Sean Smith SP 3.00 .90
170 Chris Bass SP RC 3.00 .90
171 Corey Patterson .50 .15
172 Sean Burroughs .50 .15
173 Ben Petrick .50 .15
174 Mike Glendenning .50 .15
175 Barry Zito 1.00 .30
176 Milton Bradley .50 .15
177 Bobby Bradley .50 .15
178 Jason Hart .50 .15
179 Ryan Anderson .50 .15
180 Ben Sheets .50 .15
181 Adam Everett .50 .15
182 Alfonso Soriano .50 .15
183 Josh Hamilton .50 .15
184 Eric Munson .50 .15
185 Chin-Feng Chen .50 .15
186 Tim Christman SP RC 3.00 .90
187 J.R. House SP 3.00 .90
188 B.Parker SP RC 3.00 .90
189 Sean Fesh SP RC 3.00 .90
190 Joel Pineiro SP 4.00 1.20
191 Oscar Ramirez SP RC 3.00 .90
192 Alex Santos SP RC 3.00 .90
193 Eddy Reyes SP RC 3.00 .90
194 Mike Jacobs SP RC 3.00 .90
195 Erick Almonte SP RC 3.00 .90
196 B.Claussen SP RC 15.00 4.50
197 Kris Keller SP RC 3.00 .90
198 Wilson Betemit SP RC 3.00 .90
199 Andy Phillips SP RC 3.00 .90
200 A.Pettyjohn SP RC 3.00 .90

2001 Stadium Club Beam Team

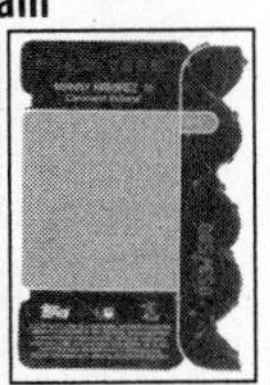

Randomly inserted into packs at one in 175 Hobby, and one in 68 HTA, this 30-card die-cut insert set features players who possess unparalleled style to accompany their world-class talent. Please note that these cards are individually serial numbered to 500, and that the card backs carry a "BT" prefix.

	Nm-Mt	Ex-Mt
COMPLETE SET (30)	500.00	150.00
BT1 Sammy Sosa	20.00	6.00
BT2 Mark McGwire	30.00	9.00
BT3 Vladimir Guerrero	12.00	3.60
BT4 Chipper Jones	12.00	3.60
BT5 Manny Ramirez	5.00	1.50
BT6 Derek Jeter	30.00	9.00
BT7 Alex Rodriguez	20.00	6.00
BT8 Cal Ripken	40.00	12.00
BT9 Ken Griffey Jr.	20.00	6.00
BT10 Greg Maddux	20.00	6.00
BT11 Barry Bonds	30.00	9.00
BT12 Pedro Martinez	12.00	3.60
BT13 Nomar Garciaparra	20.00	6.00
BT14 Randy Johnson	12.00	3.60
BT15 Frank Thomas	12.00	3.60
BT16 Ivan Rodriguez	12.00	3.60
BT17 Jeff Bagwell	8.00	2.40
BT18 Mike Piazza	20.00	6.00
BT19 Todd Helton	8.00	2.40
BT20 Shawn Green	5.00	1.50
BT21 Juan Gonzalez	12.00	3.60
BT22 Larry Walker	8.00	2.40
BT23 Tony Gwynn	20.00	6.00
BT24 Pat Burrell	5.00	1.50
BT25 Rafael Furcal	5.00	1.50
BT26 Corey Patterson	5.00	1.50
BT27 Chin-Feng Chen	5.00	1.50
BT28 Sean Burroughs	5.00	1.50
BT29 Ryan Anderson	5.00	1.50
BT30 Josh Hamilton	5.00	1.50

2001 Stadium Club Capture the Action

Randomly inserted into packs at one in eight HOB/RET and one in two HTA, this 15-card insert features transformer technology that open up to enlarged action photos of ballplayers at the top of their game. Card backs carry a "CA" prefix.

	Nm-Mt	Ex-Mt
COMPLETE SET (15)	30.00	9.00
*GAME VIEW: 10X TO 25X BASIC CAPTURE		
GAME VIEW ODDS 1:577 HOBBY, 1:224 HTA		
GAME VIEW PRINT RUN 100 SERIAL #'d SETS		
CA1 Cal Ripken	4.00	1.20
CA2 Alex Rodriguez	2.00	.60
CA3 Mike Piazza	2.00	.60
CA4 Mark McGwire	3.00	.90
CA5 Greg Maddux	2.00	.60
CA6 Derek Jeter	3.00	.90
CA7 Chipper Jones	1.25	.35
CA8 Pedro Martinez	1.25	.35
CA9 Ken Griffey Jr.	2.00	.60
CA10 Nomar Garciaparra	2.00	.60
CA11 Randy Johnson	1.25	.35
CA12 Sammy Sosa	2.00	.60
CA13 Vladimir Guerrero	1.25	.35
CA14 Barry Bonds	3.00	.90
CA15 Ivan Rodriguez	1.25	.35

2001 Stadium Club Co-Signers

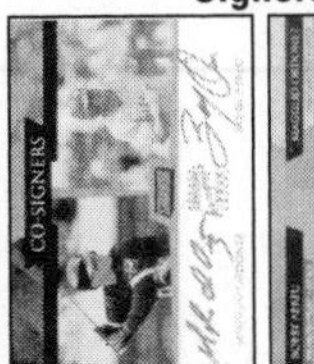

Randomly inserted into packs at one in 962 Hobby and one in 374 HTA packs, this nine-card insert features authenticated autographs of two players on the same card. Please note that the Chipper Jones/Troy Glaus and the Corey Patterson/Nick Johnson cards packed out as exchange cards, and must be redeemed by 11/30/01.

	Nm-Mt	Ex-Mt
CO1 Nomar Garciaparra Derek Jeter	500.00	150.00
CO2 Roberto Alomar Edgardo Alfonzo	100.00	30.00
CO3 Rick Ankiel Kevin Millwood	25.00	7.50
CO4 Chipper Jones Troy Glaus	100.00	30.00
CO5 Magglio Ordonez Bob Abreu	50.00	15.00
CO6 Adam Piatt Sean Burroughs	25.00	7.50
CO7 Corey Patterson Nick Johnson	80.00	24.00
CO8 Adrian Gonzalez Rocco Baldelli	80.00	24.00
CO9 Adam Johnson Mike Stodolka	25.00	7.50

2001 Stadium Club Diamond Pearls

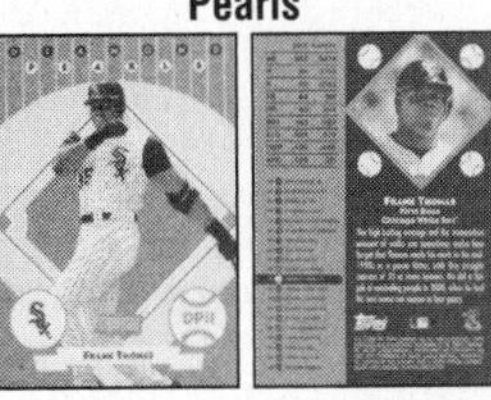

Randomly inserted into packs at one in eight HOB/RET packs, and one in 3 HTA packs; this 20-card insert features players that are the most sought after treasures in the game today. Card backs carry a "DP" prefix.

	Nm-Mt	Ex-Mt
COMPLETE SET (20)	50.00	15.00
DP1 Ken Griffey Jr.	3.00	.90
DP2 Alex Rodriguez	3.00	.90
DP3 Derek Jeter	5.00	1.50
DP4 Chipper Jones	2.00	.60
DP5 Nomar Garciaparra	3.00	.90
DP6 Vladimir Guerrero	2.00	.60
DP7 Jeff Bagwell	1.50	.45
DP8 Cal Ripken	6.00	1.80
DP9 Sammy Sosa	3.00	.90
DP10 Mark McGwire	5.00	1.50
DP11 Frank Thomas	2.00	.60
DP12 Pedro Martinez	2.00	.60
DP13 Manny Ramirez	1.50	.45
DP14 Randy Johnson	2.00	.60
DP15 Barry Bonds	5.00	1.50
DP16 Ivan Rodriguez	2.00	.60
DP17 Greg Maddux	3.00	.90
DP18 Mike Piazza	3.00	.90
DP19 Todd Helton	1.50	.45
DP20 Shawn Green	1.50	.45

2001 Stadium Club King of the Hill Dirt Relic

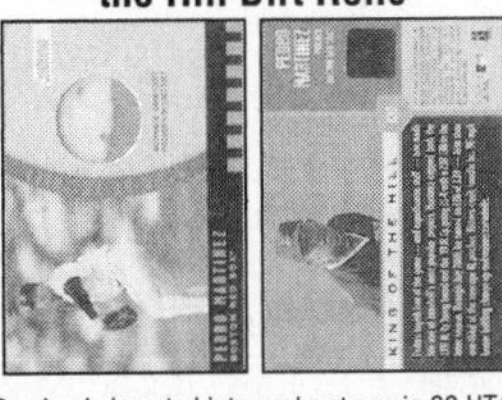

Randomly inserted into packs at one in 20 HTA, this five-card insert features game-used dirt cards from the pitchers mound of today's top pitchers. The Topps Company announced that the ten exchange subjects from Stadium Club Play at the Plate, King of the Hill, and Souvenirs contain the wrong card back stating that they were autographed. None of these cards are actually autographed. Also note that these cards were inserted into packs with a white "waxpaper" covering to protect the cards. Card backs carry a "KH" prefix. Please note that Greg Maddux and Rick Ankiel both packed out as exchange cards and must be returned to Topps by 11/30/01.

	Nm-Mt	Ex-Mt
KH1 Pedro Martinez	10.00	3.00
KH2 Randy Johnson	10.00	3.00
KH3 G.Maddux ERR	10.00	3.00
KH4 R.Ankiel ERR	8.00	2.40
KH5 Kevin Brown	8.00	2.40

2001 Stadium Club Lone Star Signatures

Randomly inserted into packs, this 18-card inserrt features authentic autographs from some of the Major Leagues most prolific players. Please note that this insert was broken into four tiers as follows: Group A (1:937 HOB/RET, 1:364 HTA), Group B (1:1010 HOB/RET, 1:392 HTA), Group C (1:1541 HOB/RET, 1:600 HTA), and Group D (1:354 HOB/RET, 1:138 HTA). The overall odds for pulling an autograph was one in 181 HOB/RET and one in 70 HTA.

	Nm-Mt	Ex-Mt
LS1 Nomar Garciaparra A	150.00	45.00
LS2 Derek Jeter A	150.00	45.00
LS3 Edgardo Alfonzo A	40.00	12.00
LS4 Roberto Alomar A	60.00	18.00
LS5 Magglio Ordonez A	25.00	7.50
LS6 Bobby Abreu A	40.00	12.00
LS7 Chipper Jones A	50.00	15.00
LS8 Troy Glaus A	50.00	15.00
LS9 Nick Johnson B	15.00	4.50
LS10 Adam Piatt B	15.00	4.50
LS11 Sean Burroughs B	15.00	4.50
LS12 Corey Patterson B	15.00	4.50
LS13 Rick Ankiel C	10.00	3.00
LS14 Kevin Millwood C	15.00	4.50
LS15 Adrian Gonzalez D	15.00	4.50
LS16 Adam Johnson D	10.00	3.00
LS17 Rocco Baldelli D	50.00	15.00
LS18 Mike Stodolka D	10.00	3.00

2001 Stadium Club Play at the Plate Dirt Relic

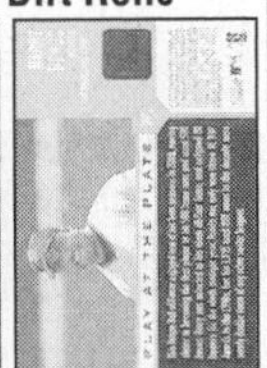

Randomly inserted into packs at one in 10 HTA, this 11-card insert features game-used dirt from the batter's box in which these top players played in. The Topps Company announced that the ten exchange subjects from Stadium Club Play at the Plate, King of the Hill, and Souvenirs contain the wrong card back stating that they were autographed. None of these cards are actually autographed. Please note that both Chipper Jones and Jeff Bagwell are number PP6. Also note that these cards were inserted into packs with a white "waxpaper" covering to protect the cards. The exchange deadline for these cards was 11/30/01.

	Nm-Mt	Ex-Mt
PP1 Mark McGwire ERR	40.00	12.00
PP2 S.Sosa ERR	15.00	4.50
PP3 Vladimir Guerrero	10.00	3.00
PP4 Ken Griffey Jr. ERR	15.00	4.50
PP5 Mike Piazza	10.00	3.00
PP6 J.Bagwell ERR	10.00	3.00
PP7 Barry Bonds	25.00	7.50
PP8 Alex Rodriguez	15.00	4.50
PP10 Nomar Garciaparra ERR	15.00	4.50

2001 Stadium Club Prospect Performance

Randomly inserted into packs at one in 262 HOB/RET and one in 102 HTA, this 20-card insert features game-used jersey cards from some of the hottest young players in the Major Leagues. Card backs carry a "PRP" prefix.

	Nm-Mt	Ex-Mt
PRP1 Chin-Feng Chen	50.00	15.00
PRP2 Bobby Bradley	8.00	2.40
PRP3 Tomokazu Ohka	10.00	3.00
PRP4 Kurt Ainsworth	8.00	2.40
PRP5 Craig Anderson	8.00	2.40
PRP6 Josh Hamilton	8.00	2.40
PRP7 Felipe Lopez	8.00	2.40
PRP8 Ryan Anderson	8.00	2.40
PRP9 Alex Escobar	8.00	2.40
PRP10 Ben Sheets	10.00	3.00
PRP11 Ntema Ndungidi	8.00	2.40
PRP12 Eric Munson	8.00	2.40
PRP13 Aaron Myette	8.00	2.40
PRP14 Jack Cust	8.00	2.40
PRP15 Julio Zuleta	8.00	2.40
PRP16 Corey Patterson	10.00	3.00
PRP17 Carlos Pena	8.00	2.40
PRP18 Marcus Giles	10.00	3.00
PRP19 Travis Wilson	8.00	2.40
PRP20 Barry Zito	25.00	7.50

2001 Stadium Club Souvenirs

Randomly inserted into HTA packs, this eight-card insert features game-used bat cards and game-used jersey cards of modern superstars. Card backs carry a "SCS" prefix. Please note that the Topps Company announced that the ten exchange subjects from Stadium Club Play at the Plate, King of the Hill, and Souvenirs contain the wrong card back stating that they were autographed. None of these cards are actually autographed. Also note that cards of Scott Rolen, Matt Lawton, Jose Vidro, and Pat Burrell all packed out as exchange cards. These cards needed to have been returned to Topps by 11/30/01.

	Nm-Mt	Ex-Mt
SCS1 Scott Rolen Bat A ERR	15.00	4.50
SCS2 Larry Walker Bat B	15.00	4.50
SCS3 Rafael Furcal Bat A	15.00	4.50
SCS4 Darin Erstad Bat A	15.00	4.50
SCS5 Mike Sweeney Jsy	10.00	3.00
SCS6 Matt Lawton Jsy ERR	10.00	3.00
SCS7 Jose Vidro Jsy ERR	10.00	3.00
SCS8 Pat Burrell Jsy ERR	10.00	3.00

2002 Stadium Club

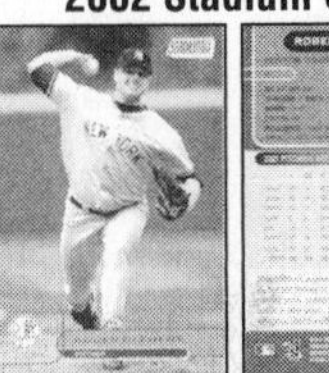

This 125 card set was issued in late 2001. The set was issued in either six card regular packs or 15 card HTA packs. Cards numbered 101-125 were short printed and are serial numbered to 2999.

	Nm-Mt	Ex-Mt
COMP.SET w/o SP's (100)	25.00	7.50
COMMON CARD (1-100)	.30	.09
COMMON (101-125)	20.00	6.00
1 Pedro Martinez	.75	.23
2 Derek Jeter	2.00	.60
3 Chipper Jones	.75	.23
4 Roberto Alomar	.75	.23
5 Albert Pujols	1.50	.45
6 Bret Boone	.30	.09
7 Alex Rodriguez	1.25	.35
8 Jose Cruz Jr.	.30	.09
9 Mike Hampton	.30	.09
10 Vladimir Guerrero	.75	.23
11 Jim Edmonds	.30	.09
12 Luis Gonzalez	.30	.09
13 Jeff Kent	.30	.09
14 Mike Piazza	1.25	.35
15 Ben Sheets	.30	.09
16 Tsuyoshi Shinjo	.30	.09
17 Pat Burrell UER Card has a photo of Scott Rolen	.30	.09
18 Jermaine Dye	.30	.09
19 Rafael Furcal	.30	.09
20 Randy Johnson	.75	.23
21 Carlos Delgado	.30	.09
22 Roger Clemens	1.50	.45
23 Eric Chavez	.30	.09
24 Nomar Garciaparra	1.25	.35
25 Ivan Rodriguez	.75	.23
26 Juan Gonzalez	.75	.23
27 Reggie Sanders	.30	.09
28 Jeff Bagwell	.50	.15
29 Kazuhiro Sasaki	.30	.09
30 Larry Walker	.50	.15
31 Ben Grieve	.30	.09
32 David Justice	.30	.09
33 David Wells	.30	.09
34 Kevin Brown	.30	.09
35 Miguel Tejada	.30	.09
36 Jorge Posada	.50	.15
37 Javy Lopez	.30	.09
38 Cliff Floyd	.30	.09
39 Carlos Lee	.30	.09
40 Manny Ramirez	.30	.09
41 Jim Thome	.75	.23
42 Pokey Reese	.30	.09
43 Scott Rolen	.50	.15

44 Richie Sexson .30 .09
45 Dean Palmer .30 .09
46 Rafael Palmeiro .50 .15
47 Alfonso Soriano .50 .15
48 Craig Biggio .50 .15
49 Troy Glaus .50 .15
50 Andruw Jones .30 .09
51 Ichiro Suzuki 1.25 .35
52 Kenny Lofton .30 .09
53 Hideo Nomo .75 .23
54 Magglio Ordonez .30 .09
55 Brad Penny .30 .09
56 Omar Vizquel .30 .09
57 Mike Sweeney .30 .09
58 Gary Sheffield .30 .09
59 Ken Griffey Jr. 1.25 .35
60 Curt Schilling .50 .15
61 Bobby Higginson .30 .09
62 Terrence Long .30 .09
63 Moises Alou .30 .09
64 Sandy Alomar Jr. .30 .09
65 Cristian Guzman .30 .09
66 Sammy Sosa 1.25 .35
67 Jose Vidro .30 .09
68 Edgar Martinez .50 .15
69 Jason Giambi .75 .23
70 Mark McGwire 2.00 .60
71 Barry Bonds 2.00 .60
72 Greg Vaughn .30 .09
73 Phil Nevin .30 .09
74 Jason Kendall .30 .09
75 Greg Maddux 1.25 .35
76 Jeromy Burnitz .30 .09
77 Mike Mussina .75 .23
78 Johnny Damon .30 .09
79 Shawn Green .30 .09
80 Jimmy Rollins .30 .09
81 Edgardo Alfonzo .30 .09
82 Barry Larkin .75 .23
83 Raul Mondesi .30 .09
84 Preston Wilson .30 .09
85 Mike Lieberthal .30 .09
86 J.D. Drew .30 .09
87 Ryan Klesko .30 .09
88 David Segui .30 .09
89 Derek Bell .30 .09
90 Bernie Williams .50 .15
91 Doug Mientkiewicz .30 .09
92 Rich Aurilia .30 .09
93 Ellis Burks .30 .09
94 Placido Polanco .30 .09
95 Darin Erstad .30 .09
96 Brian Giles .30 .09
97 Geoff Jenkins .30 .09
98 Kerry Wood .75 .23
99 Mariano Rivera .50 .15
100 Todd Helton .50 .15
101 Adam Dunn FS 20.00 6.00
102 Grant Balfour FS 20.00 6.00
103 Jae Seo FS 20.00 6.00
104 Hank Blalock FS 25.00 7.50
105 Chris George FS 20.00 6.00
106 Jack Cust FS 20.00 6.00
107 Juan Cruz FS 20.00 6.00
108 Adrian Gonzalez FS 20.00 6.00
109 Nick Johnson FS 20.00 6.00
110 Jeff DaVanon FS 20.00 6.00
111 Juan Diaz FS 20.00 6.00
112 B. Duckworth FS 20.00 6.00
113 Jason Lane FS 20.00 6.00
114 Seung Song FS 20.00 6.00
115 Morgan Ensberg FS 20.00 6.00
116 Marlyn Tisdale FY RC 20.00 6.00
117 Jason Botts FY RC 20.00 6.00
118 Henry Pichardo FY RC 20.00 6.00
119 J. Rodriguez FY RC 20.00 6.00
120 Mike Peeples FY RC 20.00 6.00
121 Rob Bowen EFY RC 20.00 6.00
122 Jeremy Affeldt EFY 20.00 6.00
123 Jorge Buret EFY RC 20.00 6.00
124 Manny Ravelo EFY RC 20.00 6.00
125 Eudy Lajara EFY RC 20.00 6.00
NNO B.Bonds AU Ball EXCH 200.00 60.00

2002 Stadium Club All-Star Relics

Randomly inserted in packs, these 28 cards feature relics of players who participated in the All-Star game. Depending on which group the player belonged to there could be between 400 and 4800 of each card printed.

Nm-Mt Ex-Mt
GROUP 1 ODDS 1:477 H, 1:548 R, 1:80 HTA
GROUP 1 PRINT RUN 400 SERIAL #'d SETS
GROUP 2 ODDS 1:795 H, 1:915 R, 1:133 HTA
GROUP 2 PRINT RUN 800 SERIAL #'d SETS
GROUP 3 ODDS 1:199 H, 1:247 R, 1:33 HTA
GROUP 3 PRINT RUN 1200 SERIAL #'d SETS
GROUP 4 ODDS 1:199 H, 1:247 R, 1:33 HTA
GROUP 4 PRINT RUN 2400 SERIAL #'d SETS
GROUP 5 ODDS 1:265 H, 1:305 R, 1:44 HTA
GROUP 5 PRINT RUN 3600 SERIAL #'d SETS
GROUP 6 ODDS 1:397 H, 1:457 R, 1:67 HTA
GROUP 6 PRINT RUN 4800 SERIAL #'d SETS
SCAS-AP Albert Pujols 40.00 12.00
Bat/800 G2
SCAS-BB Barry Bonds 30.00 9.00
Uni/4800 G6
SCAS-BG Brian Giles 10.00 3.00
Bat/800 G2
SCAS-CF Cliff Floyd 10.00 3.00
Bat/400 G1
SCAS-CG C.Guzman 10.00 3.00
Bat/400 G1
SCAS-CJ Chipper Jones 15.00 4.50
Jsy/1200 G3
SCAS-EM Edgar Martinez 15.00 4.50
Jsy/1200 G3
SCAS-IR Ivan Rodriguez 15.00 4.50
Uni/2400 G4
SCAS-JG Juan Gonzalez 15.00 4.50
Bat/400 G1
SCAS-JK Jeff Kent 10.00 3.00
Bat/400 G1
SCAS-JO John Olerud 10.00 3.00
Jsy/1200 G3
SCAS-JP Jorge Posada 15.00 4.50
Bat/400 G1
SCAS-KS Kaz Sasaki 10.00 3.00
Jsy/1200 G3
SCAS-LW Larry Walker 15.00 4.50
Jsy/2400 G4
SCAS-MA Moises Alou 10.00 3.00
Bat/400 G1
SCAS-MC Mike Cameron 10.00 3.00
Bat/400 G1
SCAS-MO M. Ordonez 10.00 3.00
Bat/400 G1
SCAS-MP Mike Piazza 40.00 12.00
Uni/1200 G3
SCAS-MR Manny Ramirez 10.00 3.00
Uni/3600 G5
SCAS-MS Mike Sweeney 10.00 3.00
Bat/400 G1
SCAS-RA Roberto Alomar 15.00 4.50
Uni/3600 G5
SCAS-RJ Randy Johnson 15.00 4.50
Jsy/2400 G4
SCAS-RK Ryan Klesko 10.00 3.00
Jsy/1200 G3
SCAS-SC Sean Casey 10.00 3.00
Bat/400 G1
SCAS-TG Tony Gwynn 20.00 6.00
Jsy/2400 G4
SCAS-TH Todd Helton 15.00 4.50
Jsy/1200 G3
SCAS-BRB Bret Boone 10.00 3.00
Bat/1200 G3
SCAS-LG3 Luis Gonzalez 10.00 3.00
Bat/800 G2

2002 Stadium Club Chasing 500-500

Randomly inserted in packs, these three cards feature memorabilia from Barry Bonds as he chases becoming the first member of the 500 homer, 500 stolen base club.

Nm-Mt Ex-Mt
C55-BB1 Barry Bonds 50.00 15.00
Dual
C55-BB2 Barry Bonds 40.00 12.00
Jsy/600
C55-BB3 Barry Bonds 100.00 30.00
Multiple/200

2002 Stadium Club Passport to the Majors

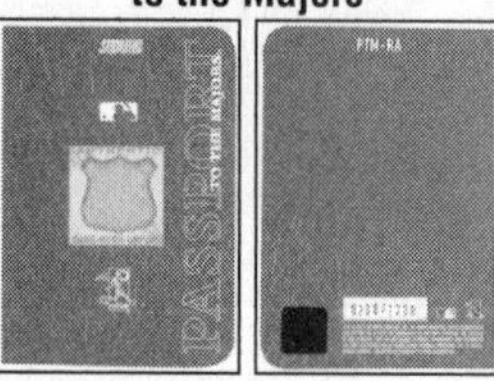

Randomly inserted in packs, these cards feature foreign players as well as a game-used relic. The jersey relics are serial numbered to 1200 while the bats are printed to differing amounts. The specific print information is notated in our checklist.

Nm-Mt Ex-Mt
PTM-AG Andres Galarraga 10.00 3.00
Jsy
PTM-AJ Andruw Jones 10.00 3.00
Jsy
PTM-AP Albert Pujols 50.00 15.00
Bat/450
PTM-AS Alfonso Soriano 15.00 4.50
Bat/400
PTM-BA Bob Abreu 10.00 3.00
Bat/450
PTM-BC Bartolo Colon Uni 10.00 3.00
PTM-CL Carlos Lee Jsy 10.00 3.00
PTM-CP Chan Ho Park Jsy 10.00 3.00
PTM-EA Edgardo Alfonzo 10.00 3.00
Jsy
PTM-IR Ivan Rodriguez 15.00 4.50
Uni
PTM-JG Juan Gonzalez 15.00 4.50
Jsy
PTM-JL Javier Lopez Jsy 10.00 3.00
PTM-KS Kazuhiro Sasaki 10.00 3.00
Jsy
PTM-LW Larry Walker Jsy 15.00 4.50
PTM-MO Magglio Ordonez 10.00 3.00
Jsy
PTM-MR Manny Ramirez 10.00 3.00
Jsy
PTM-MT Miguel Tejada 10.00 3.00
Bat/375
PTM-PM Pedro Martinez 15.00 4.50
Jsy
PTM-RA Roberto Alomar 15.00 4.50
Uni
PTM-RF Rafael Furcal Jsy 10.00 3.00
PTM-RM Raul Mondesi 10.00 3.00
Jsy
PTM-RP Rafael Palmeiro 15.00 4.50
Jsy
PTM-SH Sh. Hasegawa 10.00 3.00
Jsy
PTM-TS Tsuyoshi Shinjo 10.00 3.00
Bat/400
PTM-WB Wilson Betemit 10.00 3.00
Bat/325

2002 Stadium Club Reel Time

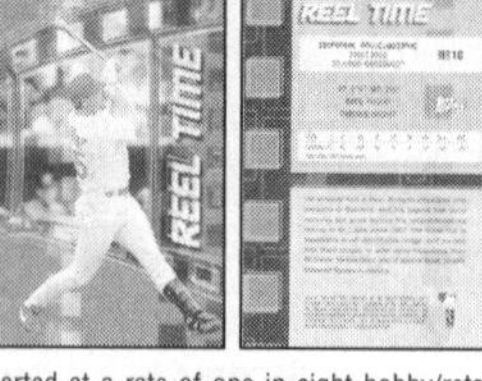

Inserted at a rate of one in eight hobby/retail packs and one in four HTA packs this 20 card set features players who constantly make the highlight reel.

Nm-Mt Ex-Mt
COMPLETE SET (20) 60.00 18.00
RT1 Luis Gonzalez 2.00 .60
RT2 Derek Jeter 6.00 1.80
RT3 Ken Griffey Jr. 4.00 1.20
RT4 Alex Rodriguez 4.00 1.20
RT5 Barry Bonds 6.00 1.80
RT6 Ichiro Suzuki 4.00 1.20
RT7 Carlos Delgado 2.00 .60
RT8 Manny Ramirez 2.00 .60
RT9 Mike Piazza 4.00 1.20
RT10 Mark McGwire 6.00 1.80
RT11 Todd Helton 2.00 .60
RT12 Vladimir Guerrero 2.50 .75
RT13 Jim Thome 2.50 .75
RT14 Rich Aurilia 2.00 .60
RT15 Bret Boone 2.00 .60
RT16 Roberto Alomar 2.50 .75
RT17 Jason Giambi 2.50 .75
RT18 Chipper Jones 2.50 .75
RT19 Albert Pujols 5.00 1.50
RT20 Sammy Sosa 4.00 1.20

2002 Stadium Club Stadium Shots

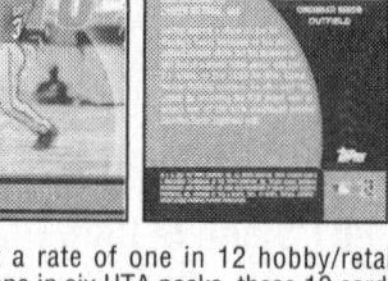

Inserted at a rate of one in 12 hobby/retail packs and one in six HTA packs, these 10 cards feature 10 sluggers known for their long homers.

Nm-Mt Ex-Mt
COMPLETE SET (10) 25.00 7.50
SS1 Sammy Sosa 4.00 1.20
SS2 Manny Ramirez 2.50 .75
SS3 Jason Giambi 2.50 .75
SS4 Mike Piazza 4.00 1.20
SS5 Barry Bonds 6.00 1.80
SS6 Ken Griffey Jr. 4.00 1.20
SS7 Juan Gonzalez 2.50 .75
SS8 Jeff Bagwell 2.50 .75
SS9 Jim Thome 2.50 .75
SS10 Mark McGwire 6.00 1.80

2002 Stadium Club Stadium Slices Barrel Relics

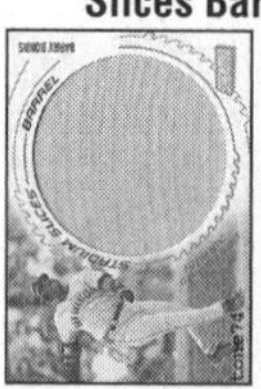

These five cards were inserted in packs and feature bat slices cut from the barrel of the bat. Each card is printed to a different amount and that information is notated in our checklist.

Nm-Mt Ex-Mt
GROUP A ODDS 1:4289 HOBBY, 1:1700 HTA
GROUP B ODDS 1:6768 HOBBY, 1:2680 HTA
GROUP C ODDS 1:6465 HOBBY, 1:2581 HTA
GROUP D ODDS 1:6101 HOBBY, 1:2489 HTA
SCSS-AP A.Pujols/95 B 100.00 30.00
SCSS-BB B.Bonds/100 C 100.00 30.00
SCSS-BW Bernie Williams 30.00 9.00
100 A
SCSS-IR Ivan Rodriguez 50.00 15.00
105 D
SCSS-LG Luis Gonzalez 30.00 9.00
75 A

2002 Stadium Club Stadium Slices Handle Relics

These five cards were inserted in packs and feature bat slices cut from the handle of the bat. Each card is printed to a different amount and that information is notated in our checklist.

Nm-Mt Ex-Mt
GROUP A ODDS 1:3671 HOBBY, 1:1483 HTA
GROUP B ODDS 1:3580 HOBBY, 1:1422 HTA
GROUP C ODDS 1:3384 HOBBY, 1:1366 HTA
GROUP D ODDS 1:3209 HOBBY, 1:1290 HTA

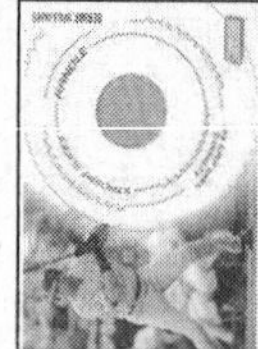

GROUP E ODDS 1:3050 HOBBY, 1:1222 HTA
SCSS-AP A.Pujols/190 C 60.00 18.00
SCSS-BB B.Bonds/175 A 60.00 18.00
SCSS-BW B.Williams/210 E 20.00 6.00
SCSS-IR I.Rodriguez/180 B 30.00 9.00
SCSS-LG L.Gonzalez/200 D 20.00 6.00

2002 Stadium Club Stadium Slices Trademark Relics

These five cards were inserted in packs and feature bat slices cut from the middle of the bat. Each card is printed to a different amount and that information is notated in our checklist.

Nm-Mt Ex-Mt
SCSS-AP A.Pujols/130 C 80.00 24.00
SCSS-BB B.Bonds/105 A 80.00 24.00
SCSS-BW Bernie Williams 25.00 7.50
110 B
SCSS-IR Ivan Rodriguez 25.00 7.50
170 E
SCSS-LG Luis Gonzalez 25.00 7.50
140 D

2002 Stadium Club World Champion Relics

Inserted at different odds depending on what type of relic, these 69 cards feature game-used relics from World Series ring holders. The Rickey Henderson card was short printed and we have notated this information in our checklist.

Nm-Mt Ex-Mt
BAT ODDS 1:94 H, 1:108 R, 1:16 HTA
JERSEY ODDS 1:106 H, 1:122 R, 1:18 HTA
PANTS ODDS 1:795 H, 1:1022 R, 1:133 HTA
SPIKES 1:38,400 H, 1:51,696 R, 1:6335 HTA
WC-AB Al Bumbry Bat 10.00 3.00
WC-AL Al Leiter Jsy 15.00 4.50
WC-AT Alan Trammell Bat 20.00 6.00
WC-BB Bert Blyleven Jsy 15.00 4.50
WC-BD Bucky Dent Bat 15.00 4.50
WC-BM Bill Madlock Bat 15.00 4.50
WC-BW B.Williams Bat 20.00 6.00
WC-BRB Bob Boone Jsy 15.00 4.50
WC-CC C.Chambliss Bat 15.00 4.50
WC-CJ Chipper Jones Bat 25.00 7.50
WC-CK C.Knoblauch Bat 15.00 4.50
WC-DB Don Baylor Bat 15.00 4.50
WC-DC D.Concepcion Bat 15.00 4.50
WC-DJ David Justice Bat 15.00 4.50
WC-DL Dave Lopes Bat 15.00 4.50
WC-DP Dave Parker Bat 15.00 4.50
WC-DW Dave Winfield Bat 15.00 4.50
WC-ED Eric Davis Bat 15.00 4.50
WC-ES Ed Sprague Jsy 10.00 3.00
WC-EM1 Eddie Murray Bat 25.00 7.50
WC-EM2 Ed. Murray Jsy 25.00 7.50
WC-FM Fred McGriff Bat 20.00 6.00
WC-FV F. Valenzuela Bat 15.00 4.50
WC-GB George Brett Bat 60.00 18.00
WC-GF George Foster Bat 15.00 4.50
WC-GH G. Hendrick Bat 15.00 4.50
WC-GL Greg Luzinski Bat 15.00 4.50
WC-GM Greg Maddux Jsy 40.00 12.00
WC-GC1 Gary Carter Bat 20.00 6.00
WC-GC2 Gary Carter Jsy 20.00 6.00
WC-HM Hal McRae Bat 15.00 4.50
WC-JB Johnny Bench Bat 25.00 7.50
WC-JC Joe Carter Jsy 15.00 4.50
WC-JL Javy Lopez Bat 15.00 4.50
WC-JO John Olerud Jsy 15.00 4.50
WC-JP Jorge Posada Bat 20.00 6.00
WC-JS John Smoltz Jsy 20.00 6.00
WC-JV Jose Vizcaino Bat 10.00 3.00
WC-JC1 Jose Canseco 25.00 7.50
Yankees Bat
WC-JC2 Jose Canseco 25.00 7.50
A's Bat
WC-KG Ken Griffey Sr. Bat 20.00 6.00
WC-KH K. Hernandez Bat 20.00 6.00
WC-KP Kirby Puckett Bat 25.00 7.50
WC-KG1 Kirk Gibson Bat 20.00 6.00
WC-KG2 Kirk Gibson Jsy 20.00 6.00
WC-LW Lou Whitaker Bat 15.00 4.50
WC-LVP Lou Piniella Bat 15.00 4.50
WC-MA Moises Alou Bat 15.00 4.50
WC-MS Mike Scioscia Bat 15.00 4.50
WC-MW M. Wilson Bat 15.00 4.50
WC-MJS M. Schmidt Bat 60.00 18.00
WC-OH Orel Hershiser Jsy 15.00 4.50
WC-OS Ozzie Smith Bat 40.00 12.00
WC-PG Phil Garner Bat 10.00 3.00
WC-PM Paul Molitor Bat 20.00 6.00
WC-PO Paul O'Neill Pants 20.00 6.00
WC-RA R. Alomar Pants 25.00 7.50
WC-RC Ron Cey Bat 15.00 4.50
WC-RH R.Henderson Spikes SP/50
WC-RJ R. Jackson Bat 20.00 6.00
WC-SB Scott Brosius Bat 15.00 4.50
WC-TG Tom Glavine Jsy 20.00 6.00
WC-TM T. Munson Bat 60.00 18.00
WC-TP Tony Perez Bat 15.00 4.50
WC-TLM T. Martinez Bat 20.00 6.00
WC-WB Wade Boggs Bat 20.00 6.00
WC-WH W. Hernandez Jsy 15.00 4.50
WC-WR W. Randolph Bat 15.00 4.50
WC-WS Willie Stargell Bat 20.00 6.00

2003 Stadium Club

This 125 card set was released in November, 2002. This set marked the conclusion of the 13 year run of Stadium Club product being released as a baseball brand by Topps. This set was issued in either 10 card packs or 20 card HTA packs. The 10-card packs were issued 10 cards to a pack with 24 packs to a box and 12 boxes to a case with an SRP of $3 per pack. The 20-card HTA packs were issued 10 packs to a box and eight boxes to a case with an SRP of $10 per pack. Cards numbered from 101 through 113 featured future stars while cards numbered 114 through 125 feature players in their first year on a Stadium Club card. Cards numbered 101 through 125 were issued with different photos depending on whether or not they came from hobby or retail packs. These cards have two different varieties in all the parallel sets as well. Sets are considered complete at 125 cards - with one copy of either the hobby or retail versions of cards 101-125.

Nm-Mt Ex-Mt
COMP.MASTER SET (150) 60.00 18.00
COMPLETE SET (125) 40.00 12.00
COMMON CARD (1-100) .30 .09
COMMON CARD (101-115) .50 .15
COMMON CARD (116-125) 1.00 .30
1 Rafael Furcal .30 .09
2 Randy Winn .30 .09
3 Eric Chavez .30 .09
4 Fernando Vina .30 .09
5 Pat Burrell .30 .09
6 Derek Jeter 2.00 .60
7 Ivan Rodriguez .75 .23
8 Eric Hinske .30 .09
9 Roberto Alomar .75 .23
10 Tony Batista .30 .09
11 Jacque Jones .30 .09
12 Alfonso Soriano .50 .15
13 Omar Vizquel .30 .09
14 Paul Konerko .30 .09
15 Shawn Green .30 .09
16 Garret Anderson .30 .09
17 Darin Erstad .30 .09
18 Johnny Damon .30 .09
19 Juan Gonzalez .75 .23
20 Luis Gonzalez .30 .09
21 Sean Burroughs .30 .09
22 Mark Prior 1.50 .45
23 Javier Vazquez .30 .09
24 Shannon Stewart .30 .09
25 Jay Gibbons .30 .09
26 A.J. Pierzynski .30 .09
27 Vladimir Guerrero .75 .23
28 Austin Kearns .30 .09
29 Shea Hillenbrand .30 .09
30 Magglio Ordonez .30 .09
31 Mike Cameron .30 .09
32 Tim Salmon .50 .15
33 Brian Jordan .30 .09
34 Moises Alou .30 .09
35 Rich Aurilia .30 .09
36 Nick Johnson .30 .09
37 Junior Spivey .30 .09
38 Curt Schilling .50 .15
39 Jose Vidro .30 .09
40 Orlando Cabrera .30 .09
41 Jeff Bagwell .50 .15
42 Mo Vaughn .30 .09
43 Luis Castillo .30 .09
44 Vicente Padilla .30 .09
45 Pedro Martinez .75 .23
46 John Olerud .30 .09
47 Tom Glavine .50 .15
48 Torii Hunter .30 .09
49 J.D. Drew .30 .09
50 Alex Rodriguez 1.25 .35
51 Randy Johnson .75 .23
52 Richie Sexson .30 .09
53 Jimmy Rollins .30 .09
54 Cristian Guzman .30 .09
55 Tim Hudson .30 .09
56 Mark Buehrle .30 .09
57 Paul Lo Duca .30 .09
58 Aramis Ramirez .30 .09
59 Todd Helton .50 .15
60 Lance Berkman .30 .09
61 Josh Beckett .50 .15
62 Bret Boone .30 .09
63 Miguel Tejada .30 .09
64 Nomar Garciaparra 1.25 .35
65 Albert Pujols 1.50 .45
66 Chipper Jones .75 .23
67 Scott Rolen .50 .15
68 Kerry Wood .75 .23
69 Jorge Posada .50 .15
70 Ichiro Suzuki 1.25 .35
71 Jeff Kent .30 .09

72 David Eckstein .30 .09
73 Phil Nevin .30 .09
74 Brian Giles .30 .09
75 Barry Zito .50 .15
76 Andruw Jones .30 .09
77 Jim Thome .75 .23
78 Robert Fick .30 .09
79 Rafael Palmeiro .50 .15
80 Barry Bonds 2.00 .60
81 Gary Sheffield .30 .09
82 Jim Edmonds .30 .09
83 Kazuhisa Ishii .30 .09
84 Jose Hernandez .30 .09
85 Jason Giambi .75 .23
86 Mark Mulder .30 .09
87 Roger Clemens 1.50 .45
88 Troy Glaus .50 .15
89 Carlos Delgado .30 .09
90 Mike Sweeney .30 .09
91 Ken Griffey Jr. 1.25 .35
92 Manny Ramirez .30 .09
93 Ryan Klesko .30 .09
94 Larry Walker .50 .15
95 Adam Dunn .30 .09
96 Raul Ibanez .30 .09
97 Preston Wilson .30 .09
98 Roy Oswalt .30 .09
99 Sammy Sosa 1.25 .35
100 Mike Piazza 1.25 .35
101H Jose Reyes FS 1.00 .30
101R Jose Reyes FS 1.00 .30
102H Ed Rogers FS .50 .15
102R Ed Rogers FS .50 .15
103H Hank Blalock FS 1.00 .30
103R Hank Blalock FS 1.00 .30
104H Mark Teixeira FS 1.00 .30
104R Mark Teixeira FS 1.00 .30
105H Orlando Hudson FS .50 .15
105R Orlando Hudson FS .50 .15
106H Drew Henson FS .75 .23
106R Drew Henson FS .75 .23
107H Joe Mauer FS 1.50 .45
107R Joe Mauer FS 1.50 .45
108H Carl Crawford FS .75 .23
108R Carl Crawford FS .75 .23
109H Marlon Byrd FS .75 .23
109R Marlon Byrd FS .75 .23
110H Jason Stokes FS 1.50 .45
110R Jason Stokes FS 1.50 .45
111H Miguel Cabrera FS 3.00 .90
111R Miguel Cabrera FS 3.00 .90
112H Wilson Betemit FS .50 .15
112R Wilson Betemit FS .50 .15
113H Jerome Williams FS .75 .23
113R Jerome Williams FS .75 .23
114H Walter Young FYP 1.00 .30
114R Walter Young FYP 1.00 .30
115H Juan Camacho FYP RC 1.00 .30
115R Juan Camacho FYP RC 1.00 .30
116H Chris Duncan FYP RC 1.00 .30
116R Chris Duncan FYP RC 1.00 .30
117H F.Gutierrez FYP RC 5.00 1.50
117R F.Gutierrez FYP RC 5.00 1.50
118H Adam LaRoche FYP 1.50 .45
118R Adam LaRoche FYP 1.50 .45
119H M.Ramirez FYP RC 1.50 .45
119R M.Ramirez FYP RC 1.50 .45
120H Il Kim FYP RC 1.00 .30
120R Il Kim FYP RC 1.00 .30
121H Wayne Lydon FYP RC 1.00 .30
121R Wayne Lydon FYP RC 1.00 .30
122H Daryl Clark FYP RC 1.50 .45
122R Daryl Clark FYP RC 1.50 .45
123H Sean Pierce FYP 1.00 .30
123R Sean Pierce FYP 1.00 .30
124H Andy Marte FYP RC 6.00 1.80
124R Andy Marte FYP RC 6.00 1.80
125H Mat.Peterson FYP RC 1.00 .30
125R Mat.Peterson FYP RC 1.00 .30

2003 Stadium Club Photographer's Proof

Randomly inserted into packs:, this is a parallel to the Stadium Club set. These cards were issued to a stated print run of 299 serial numbered sets.

Nm-Mt Ex-Mt
*PROOF 1-100: 4X TO 10X BASIC
*PROOF 101-115: 2X TO 5X BASIC
*PROOF 116-125: 1.5X TO 4X BASIC
1-100 ODDS 1:39 H, 1:23 HTA, 1:34 R
101-125 ODDS 1:61 H, 1:17 HTA, 1:92 R

2003 Stadium Club Royal Gold

Inserted one per pack, this is a parallel to the Stadium Club set. These cards can be differentiated by their thickness compared to the regular cards. Photo variations were created for cards 101-125 whereby hobby and retail packs each had exclusive distribution on one image per player.

Nm-Mt Ex-Mt
*GOLD 1-100: 1X TO 2.5X BASIC
*GOLD 101-115: 1X TO 2.5X BASIC
*GOLD 116-125: .75X TO 2X BASIC

2003 Stadium Club Beam Team

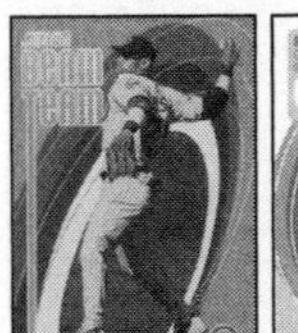

Inserted into packs at a stated rate of one in 12 hobby, one in 12 retail and one in two HTA, these 20 cards feature some of the hottest talents in baseball.

Nm-Mt Ex-Mt
BT1 Lance Berkman 2.00 .60
BT2 Barry Bonds 8.00 2.40
BT3 Carlos Delgado 2.00 .60
BT4 Adam Dunn 2.00 .60
BT5 Nomar Garciaparra 5.00 1.50
BT6 Jason Giambi 3.00 .90
BT7 Brian Giles 2.00 .60
BT8 Shawn Green 2.00 .60
BT9 Vladimir Guerrero 3.00 .90
BT10 Todd Helton 3.00 .90
BT11 Derek Jeter 8.00 2.40
BT12 Chipper Jones 3.00 .90
BT13 Jeff Kent 2.00 .60
BT14 Mike Piazza 5.00 1.50
BT15 Alex Rodriguez 5.00 1.50
BT16 Ivan Rodriguez 3.00 .90
BT17 Sammy Sosa 5.00 1.50
BT18 Ichiro Suzuki 5.00 1.50
BT19 Miguel Tejada 2.00 .60
BT20 Larry Walker 3.00 .90

2003 Stadium Club Born in the USA Relics

Inserted into packs at different odds depending on what type of game-used memorabilia piece was used, these 50 cards feature those memorabilia pieces cut into the shape of the player's home state.

Nm-Mt Ex-Mt
BAT ODDS 1:76 H, 1:23 HTA, 1:89 R
JERSEY ODDS 1:52 H, 1:15 HTA, 1:61 R
UNIFORM ODDS 1:413 H, 1:126 HTA, 1:484 R
AB A.J. Burnett Jsy 10.00 3.00
AD Adam Dunn Bat 10.00 3.00
AR Alex Rodriguez Bat 25.00 7.50
BB Bret Boone Jsy 10.00 3.00
BF Brad Fullmer Bat 10.00 3.00
BL Barry Larkin Jsy 15.00 4.50
CB Craig Biggio Jsy 15.00 4.50
CF Cliff Floyd Bat 10.00 3.00
CJ Chipper Jones Jsy 15.00 4.50
CP Corey Patterson Bat 10.00 3.00
EC Eric Chavez Uni 10.00 3.00
EM Eric Milton Jsy 10.00 3.00
FT Frank Thomas Bat 15.00 4.50
GM Greg Maddux Jsy 15.00 4.50
GS Gary Sheffield Bat 10.00 3.00
JB Jeff Bagwell Jsy 15.00 4.50
JD Johnny Damon Bat 10.00 3.00
JDD J.D. Drew Bat 10.00 3.00
JE Jim Edmonds Jsy 10.00 3.00
JH Josh Hamilton Bat 10.00 3.00
JNB Jeromy Burnitz Bat 10.00 3.00
JO John Olerud Jsy 10.00 3.00
JS John Smoltz Jsy 15.00 4.50
JT Jim Thome Jsy 15.00 4.50
KW Kerry Wood Bat 15.00 4.50
LG Luis Gonzalez Bat 10.00 3.00
MG Mark Grace Jsy 15.00 4.50
MP Mike Piazza Jsy 15.00 4.50
MV Mo Vaughn Bat 10.00 3.00
MW Matt Williams Bat 10.00 3.00
NG Nomar Garciaparra Bat 25.00 7.50
PB Pat Burrell Bat 10.00 3.00
PK Paul Konerko Bat 10.00 3.00
PW Preston Wilson Jsy 10.00 3.00
RA Rich Aurilia Jsy 10.00 3.00
RH Rickey Henderson Bat 15.00 4.50
RJ Randy Johnson Bat 15.00 4.50
RK Ryan Klesko Bat 10.00 3.00
RS Richie Sexson Bat 10.00 3.00
RV Robin Ventura Bat 10.00 3.00
SB Sean Burroughs Bat 10.00 3.00
SG Shawn Green Bat 10.00 3.00
SR Scott Rolen Bat 15.00 4.50
TC Tony Clark Bat 10.00 3.00
TH Todd Helton Bat 15.00 4.50
TJH Toby Hall Bat 10.00 3.00
TL Terrence Long Uni 10.00 3.00
TM Tino Martinez Bat 15.00 4.50
TRL Travis Lee Bat 10.00 3.00
WM Willie Mays Bat 60.00 18.00

2003 Stadium Club Clubhouse Exclusive

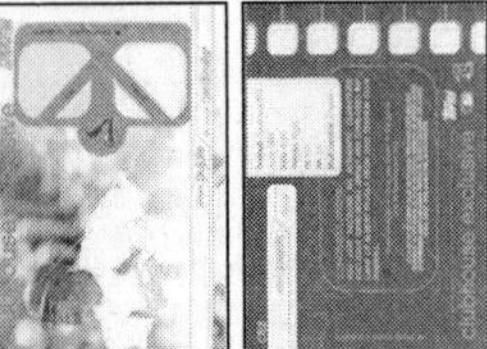

Inserted into packs at a different rate depending on how many memorabilia pieces are used, these four cards feature game-worn memorabilia pieces of Cardinals star Albert Pujols.

Nm-Mt Ex-Mt
JSY ODDS 1:488 H, 1:178 HTA
BAT-JSY ODDS 1:2073 H, 1:758 HTA
BAT-JSY-SPK ODDS 1:2750 H, 1:1016 HTA
BAT-HAT-JSY-SPK ODDS 1:1016 HTA
CE1 Albert Pujols Jsy 20.00 6.00
CE2 Albert Pujols Bat-Jsy 40.00 12.00
CE3 Albert Pujols Bat-Jsy-Spike 100.00 30.00
CE4 Albert Pujols Bat-Hat-Jsy-Spike

2003 Stadium Club Co-Signers

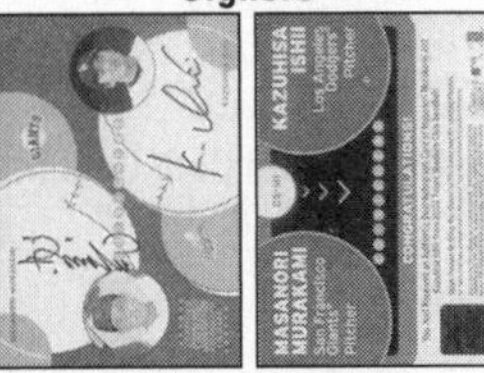

Randomly inserted into packs, these two cards featue a pair of important baseball players who each signed cards for this set. This set features the first Masanori Murakami (the first Japanese player to play in the majors) certified signed cards. Murakami, to honor his heritage, signed an equivalent amount of cards in English and Japanese.

Nm-Mt Ex-Mt
GROUP A STATED ODDS 1: 339 HTA .
GROUP B STATED ODDS 1:1016 HTA
AM Hank Aaron 500.00 150.00
Willie Mays A
MI Masanori Murakami 300.00 90.00
Kazuhisa Ishii B

2003 Stadium Club License to Drive Bat Relics

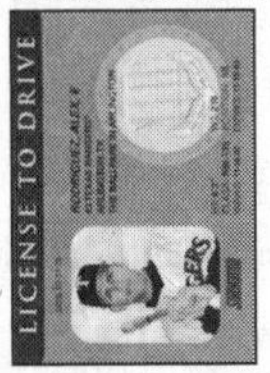

Inserted into packs at a stated rate of one in 98 hobby, one in 114 retail and one in 29 HTA, these 25 cards feature game-used bat relics of players who have driven in 100 runs in a season.

Nm-Mt Ex-Mt
AB Adrian Beltre 10.00 3.00
AD Adam Dunn 10.00 3.00
AJ Andruw Jones 10.00 3.00
ANR Aramis Ramirez 10.00 3.00
AP Albert Pujols 20.00 6.00
AR Alex Rodriguez 25.00 7.50
BW Bernie Williams 15.00 4.50
CJ Chipper Jones 15.00 4.50
EC Eric Chavez 10.00 3.00
FT Frank Thomas 15.00 4.50
GS Gary Sheffield 10.00 3.00
IR Ivan Rodriguez 15.00 4.50
JG Juan Gonzalez 15.00 4.50
LB Lance Berkman 10.00 3.00
LG Luis Gonzalez 10.00 3.00
LW Larry Walker 15.00 4.50
MA Moises Alou 10.00 3.00
MP Mike Piazza 25.00 7.50
NG Nomar Garciaparra 25.00 7.50
RA Roberto Alomar 15.00 4.50
RP Rafael Palmeiro 15.00 4.50
SG Shawn Green 10.00 3.00
SR Scott Rolen 15.00 4.50
TH Todd Helton 15.00 4.50
TM Tino Martinez 15.00 4.50

2003 Stadium Club MLB Match-Up Dual Relics

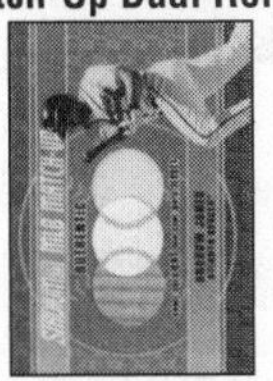

Inserted into hobby packs at a stated rate of one in 485, one in 570 retail and HTA packs at one in 148, these five cards feature both a game-worn jersey swatch as well as a game-used bat relic of the featured players.

Nm-Mt Ex-Mt
AJ Andruw Jones 20.00 6.00
AP Albert Pujols 40.00 12.00
BB Bret Boone 20.00 6.00
GM Greg Maddux 30.00 9.00
TH Todd Helton 25.00 7.50

2003 Stadium Club Shots

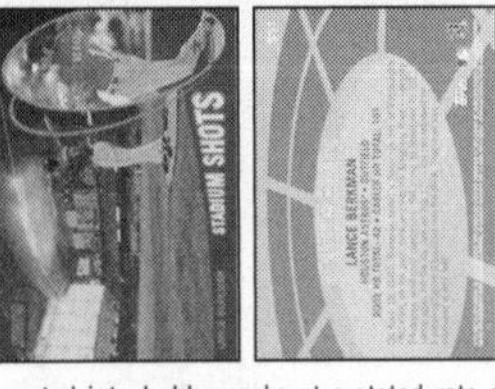

Inserted into hobby packs at a stated rate of one in 24, retail packs at one in 24 and HTA packs at a stated rate of one in four, these 10 cards feature players who are known for their long distance slugging.

Nm-Mt Ex-Mt
SS1 Lance Berkman 2.00 .60
SS2 Barry Bonds 8.00 2.40
SS3 Jason Giambi 3.00 .90
SS4 Shawn Green 2.00 .60
SS5 Miguel Tejada 2.00 .60
SS6 Paul Konerko 2.00 .60
SS7 Mike Piazza 5.00 1.50
SS8 Alex Rodriguez 5.00 1.50
SS9 Sammy Sosa 5.00 1.50
SS10 Gary Sheffield 2.00 .60

2003 Stadium Club Stadium Slices Barrel Relics

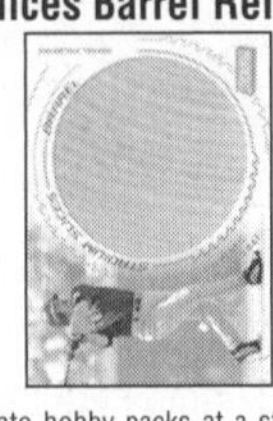

Inserted into hobby packs at a stated rate of one in 550 and HTA packs at a stated rate of one in 204, these 10 cards feature game-used bat pieces taken from the barrel.

Nm-Mt Ex-Mt
AJ Andruw Jones 25.00 7.50
AP Albert Pujols 50.00 15.00
AR Alex Rodriguez 60.00 18.00
CD Carlos Delgado 25.00 7.50
GS Gary Sheffield 25.00 7.50
MP Mike Piazza 60.00 18.00
NG Nomar Garciaparra 80.00 24.00
RA Roberto Alomar 40.00 12.00
RP Rafael Palmeiro 40.00 12.00
TH Todd Helton 40.00 12.00

2003 Stadium Club Stadium Slices Handle Relics

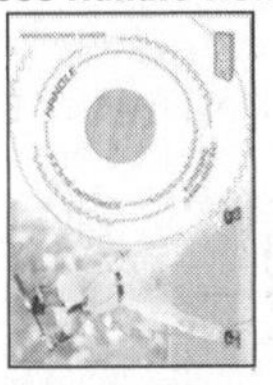

Inserted into hobby packs at a stated rate of one in 237 and HTA packs at a stated rate of one in 86, these 10 cards feature game-used bat pieces taken from the handle.

Nm-Mt Ex-Mt
AJ Andruw Jones 12.00 3.60
AP Albert Pujols 25.00 7.50
AR Alex Rodriguez 30.00 9.00
CD Carlos Delgado 12.00 3.60
GS Gary Sheffield 12.00 3.60
MP Mike Piazza 30.00 9.00
NG Nomar Garciaparra 40.00 12.00
RA Roberto Alomar 20.00 6.00
RP Rafael Palmeiro 20.00 6.00
TH Todd Helton 20.00 6.00

2003 Stadium Club Stadium Slices Trademark Relics

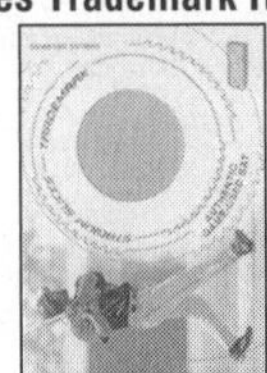

Inserted into hobby packs at a stated rate of one in 415 and HTA packs at a stated rate of one in 151, these 10 cards feature game-used bat pieces taken from the middle of the bat.

Nm-Mt Ex-Mt
AJ Andruw Jones 15.00 4.50
AP Albert Pujols 30.00 9.00
AR Alex Rodriguez 40.00 12.00
CD Carlos Delgado 15.00 4.50
GS Gary Sheffield 15.00 4.50
MP Mike Piazza 40.00 12.00
NG Nomar Garciaparra 50.00 15.00
RA Roberto Alomar 25.00 7.50
RP Rafael Palmeiro 25.00 7.50
TH Todd Helton 25.00 7.50

2003 Stadium Club World Stage Relics

Inserted into packs at a different rate depending on whether or not it is a bat or a jersey, these 10 cards feature game-used memorabilia pieces of players born outside the continental U.S.

Nm-Mt Ex-Mt
BAT ODDS 1:809 H, 1:246 HTA, 1:950 R
JSY ODDS 1:118 H, 1:36 HTA, 1:138 R
AB Adrian Beltre Jsy 8.00 2.40
AP Albert Pujols Jsy 20.00 6.00
AS Alfonso Soriano Bat 15.00 4.50
BK Byung-Hyun Kim Jsy 10.00 3.00
HN Hideo Nomo Bat 25.00 7.50
IR Ivan Rodriguez Jsy 10.00 3.00
KI Kazuhisa Ishii Jsy 8.00 2.40
KS Kazuhiro Sasaki Jsy 8.00 2.40
MT Miguel Tejada Jsy 8.00 2.40
TS Tsuyoshi Shinjo Bat 10.00 3.00

2000 Stadium Club Chrome

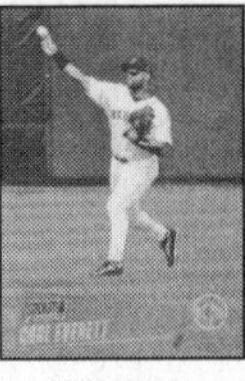

The 2000 Stadium Club Chrome set was released in May, 2000 as a 250-card set. The set features 200 Player cards, 30 Future Star cards, and 20 Draft Pick cards. Each pack contained five cards and carried a suggested retail price of $4.00. Notable Rookie Cards include Rick Asadoorian and Bobby Bradley.

Nm-Mt Ex-Mt
COMPLETE SET (250) 50.00 15.00
COMMON CARD (1-250) .50 .15
COMMON RC .75 .23
1 Nomar Garciaparra 2.00 .60
2 Brian Jordan .50 .15
3 Mark Grace .75 .23
4 Jeromy Burnitz .50 .15
5 Shane Reynolds .50 .15
6 Alex Gonzalez .50 .15
7 Jose Offerman .50 .15
8 Orlando Hernandez .50 .15
9 Mike Caruso .50 .15
10 Tony Clark .50 .15
11 Sean Casey .50 .15
12 Johnny Damon .50 .15
13 Dante Bichette .50 .15
14 Kevin Young .50 .15
15 Juan Gonzalez 1.25 .35
16 Chipper Jones 1.25 .35
17 Quilvio Veras .50 .15
18 Trevor Hoffman .50 .15
19 Roger Cedeno .50 .15
20 Ellis Burks .50 .15
21 Richie Sexson .50 .15
22 Gary Sheffield .50 .15
23 Delino DeShields .50 .15
24 Wade Boggs .75 .23
25 Ray Lankford .50 .15
26 Kevin Appier .50 .15
27 Roy Halladay .50 .15
28 Harold Baines .50 .15
29 Todd Zeile .50 .15
30 Barry Larkin 1.25 .35
31 Ron Coomer .50 .15
32 Jorge Posada .75 .23
33 Magglio Ordonez .50 .15
34 Brian Giles .50 .15
35 Jeff Kent .50 .15
36 Henry Rodriguez .50 .15
37 Fred McGriff .75 .23
38 Shawn Green .50 .15
39 Derek Bell .50 .15
40 Ben Grieve .50 .15
41 Dave Nilsson .50 .15
42 Mo Vaughn .50 .15
43 Rondell White .50 .15
44 Doug Glanville .50 .15
45 Paul O'Neill .75 .23
46 Carlos Lee .50 .15
47 Vinny Castilla .50 .15
48 Mike Sweeney .50 .15
49 Rico Brogna .50 .15
50 Alex Rodriguez 2.00 .60
51 Luis Castillo .50 .15
52 Kevin Brown .75 .23
53 Jose Vidro .50 .15
54 John Smoltz .75 .23
55 Garret Anderson .50 .15
56 Matt Stairs .50 .15
57 Omar Vizquel .50 .15
58 Tom Goodwin .50 .15
59 Scott Brosius .50 .15
60 Robin Ventura .75 .23
61 B.J. Surhoff .50 .15
62 Andy Ashby .50 .15
63 Chris Widger .50 .15
64 Tim Hudson .75 .23
65 Javy Lopez .50 .15
66 Tim Salmon .75 .23
67 Warren Morris .50 .15
68 John Wetteland .50 .15
69 Gabe Kapler .50 .15
70 Bernie Williams .75 .23
71 Rickey Henderson 1.25 .35
72 Andruw Jones .50 .15
73 Eric Young .50 .15
74 Bob Abreu .50 .15
75 David Cone .50 .15
76 Rusty Greer .50 .15
77 Ron Belliard .50 .15
78 Troy Glaus .75 .23
79 Mike Hampton .50 .15
80 Miguel Tejada .50 .15
81 Jeff Cirillo .50 .15
82 Todd Hundley .50 .15
83 Roberto Alomar 1.25 .35
84 Charles Johnson .50 .15
85 Rafael Palmeiro .75 .23
86 Doug Mientkiewicz .50 .15
87 Mariano Rivera .75 .23
88 Neifi Perez .50 .15
89 Jermaine Dye .50 .15
90 Ivan Rodriguez 1.25 .35
91 Jay Buhner .50 .15
92 Pokey Reese .50 .15
93 John Olerud .50 .15
94 Brady Anderson .50 .15
95 Manny Ramirez .50 .15
96 Keith Osik RC .75 .23

97 Mickey Morandini .50 .15
98 Matt Williams .50 .15
99 Eric Karros .50 .15
100 Ken Griffey Jr. 2.00 .60
101 Bret Boone .50 .15
102 Ryan Klesko .50 .15
103 Craig Biggio .75 .23
104 John Jaha .50 .15
105 Vladimir Guerrero 1.25 .35
106 Devon White .50 .15
107 Tony Womack .50 .15
108 Marvin Benard .50 .15
109 Kenny Lofton .50 .15
110 Preston Wilson .50 .15
111 Al Leiter .50 .15
112 Reggie Sanders .50 .15
113 Scott Williamson .50 .15
114 Deivi Cruz .50 .15
115 Carlos Beltran .50 .15
116 Ray Durham .50 .15
117 Ricky Ledee .50 .15
118 Torii Hunter .50 .15
119 John Valentin .50 .15
120 Scott Rolen .75 .23
121 Jason Kendall .50 .15
122 Dave Martinez .50 .15
123 Jim Thome 1.25 .35
124 David Bell .50 .15
125 Jose Canseco 1.25 .35
126 Jose Lima .50 .15
127 Carl Everett .50 .15
128 Kevin Millwood .50 .15
129 Bill Spiers .50 .15
130 Omar Daal .50 .15
131 Miguel Cairo .50 .15
132 Mark Grudzielanek .50 .15
133 David Justice .50 .15
134 Russ Ortiz .50 .15
135 Mike Piazza 2.00 .60
136 Brian Meadows .50 .15
137 Tony Gwynn 1.50 .45
138 Cal Ripken 4.00 1.20
139 Kris Benson .50 .15
140 Larry Walker .75 .23
141 Cristian Guzman .50 .15
142 Tino Martinez .75 .23
143 Chris Singleton .50 .15
144 Lee Stevens .50 .15
145 Rey Ordonez .50 .15
146 Russ Davis .50 .15
147 J.T. Snow .50 .15
148 Luis Gonzalez .50 .15
149 Marquis Grissom .50 .15
150 Greg Maddux 2.00 .60
151 Fernando Tatis .50 .15
152 Jason Giambi 1.25 .35
153 Carlos Delgado .50 .15
154 Joe McEwing .50 .15
155 Raul Mondesi .50 .15
156 Rich Aurilia .50 .15
157 Alex Fernandez .50 .15
158 Albert Belle .50 .15
159 Pat Meares .50 .15
160 Mike Lieberthal .50 .15
161 Mike Cameron .50 .15
162 Juan Encarnacion .50 .15
163 Chuck Knoblauch .50 .15
164 Pedro Martinez 1.25 .35
165 Randy Johnson 1.25 .35
166 Shannon Stewart .50 .15
167 Jeff Bagwell .75 .23
168 Edgar Renteria .50 .15
169 Barry Bonds 3.00 .90
170 Steve Finley .50 .15
171 Brian Hunter .50 .15
172 Tom Glavine .75 .23
173 Mark Kotsay .50 .15
174 Tony Fernandez .50 .15
175 Sammy Sosa 2.00 .60
176 Geoff Jenkins .50 .15
177 Adrian Beltre .50 .15
178 Jay Bell .50 .15
179 Mike Bordick .50 .15
180 Ed Sprague .50 .15
181 Dave Roberts .50 .15
182 Greg Vaughn .50 .15
183 Brian Daubach .50 .15
184 Damion Easley .50 .15
185 Carlos Febles .50 .15
186 Kevin Tapani .50 .15
187 Frank Thomas 1.25 .35
188 Roger Clemens 2.50 .75
189 Mike Benjamin .50 .15
190 Curt Schilling .75 .23
191 Edgardo Alfonzo .50 .15
192 Mike Mussina 1.25 .35
193 Todd Helton .75 .23
194 Todd Jones .50 .15
195 Dean Palmer .50 .15
196 John Flaherty .50 .15
197 Derek Jeter 3.00 .90
198 Todd Walker .50 .15
199 Brad Ausmus .50 .15
200 Mark McGwire 3.00 .90
201 Erubiel Durazo .50 .15
202 Nick Johnson .50 .15
203 Ruben Mateo .50 .15
204 Lance Berkman .50 .15
205 Pat Burrell .75 .23
206 Pablo Ozuna .50 .15
207 Roosevelt Brown .50 .15
208 Alfonso Soriano 1.25 .35
209 A.J. Burnett .50 .15
210 Rafael Furcal .50 .15
211 Scott Morgan .50 .15
212 Adam Piatt .50 .15
213 Dee Brown .50 .15
214 Corey Patterson .75 .23
215 Mickey Lopez .50 .15
216 Rob Ryan .50 .15
217 Sean Burroughs .75 .23
218 Jack Cust .50 .15
219 John Patterson .50 .15
220 Kit Pellow .50 .15
221 Chad Hermansen .50 .15
222 Daryle Ward .50 .15
223 Jayson Werth .50 .15
224 Jason Standridge .50 .15
225 Mark Mulder .75 .23
226 Peter Bergeron .50 .15
227 Willi Mo Pena .50 .15
228 Aramis Ramirez .50 .15
229 John Sneed RC .75 .23
230 Wilton Veras .50 .15
231 Josh Hamilton .50 .15
232 Eric Munson .50 .15
233 Bobby Bradley RC .75 .23
234 Larry Bigbie RC 1.25 .35
235 B.J. Garbe RC .75 .23
236 Brett Myers RC 4.00 1.20
237 Jason Stumm RC .75 .23
238 Corey Myers RC .75 .23
239 Ryan Christianson RC .75 .23
240 David Walling .50 .15
241 Josh Girdley .50 .15
242 Omar Ortiz .50 .15
243 Jason Jennings .50 .15
244 Kyle Snyder .50 .15
245 Jay Gehrke .50 .15
246 Mike Paradis .50 .15
247 Chance Caple RC .75 .23
248 Ben Christensen RC .75 .23
249 Brad Baker RC .75 .23
250 Rick Asadoorian RC .75 .23

2000 Stadium Club Chrome First Day Issue

Randomly inserted into packs at one in 33, this 250-card insert is a complete parallel of the Stadium Club Chrome base set. Each card is individually serial numbered to 100.

Nm-Mt Ex-Mt
*STARS: 6X TO 15X BASIC CARDS ....
*ROOKIES: 2.5X TO 6X BASIC CARDS

2000 Stadium Club Chrome First Day Issue Refractors

Randomly inserted into packs at one in 131, this 250-card insert is a complete parallel of the Stadium Club Chrome base set. Each card features Topps' 'refractor' technology. Each card is also individually serial numbered to 25.

Nm-Mt Ex-Mt
*STARS: 15X TO 40X BASIC CARDS ..

2000 Stadium Club Chrome Refractors

Randomly inserted into packs at one in 12, this 250-card insert is a complete parallel of the Stadium Club Chrome base set. Each card features Topps' 'refractor' technology.

Nm-Mt Ex-Mt
*STARS: 4X TO 10X BASIC CARDS ....
*ROOKIES: 1.5X TO 4X BASIC CARDS

2000 Stadium Club Chrome Capture the Action

Randomly inserted into packs at one in 18, this 20-card insert features some of the major league's top prospects and veteran players. Card backs carry a "CA" prefix.

Nm-Mt Ex-Mt
COMPLETE SET (20) 150.00 45.00
*REFRACTORS: 1X TO 2.5X BASIC CAPTURE
REFRACTOR STATED ODDS 1:90
CA1 Josh Hamilton 1.25 .35
CA2 Pat Burrell 2.00 .60
CA3 Erubiel Durazo 1.25 .35
CA4 Alfonso Soriano 3.00 .90
CA5 A.J. Burnett 1.25 .35
CA6 Alex Rodriguez 5.00 1.50
CA7 Sean Casey 1.25 .35
CA8 Derek Jeter 8.00 2.40
CA9 Vladimir Guerrero 3.00 .90
CA10 Nomar Garciaparra 5.00 1.50
CA11 Mike Piazza 5.00 1.50
CA12 Ken Griffey Jr. 5.00 1.50
CA13 Sammy Sosa 5.00 1.50
CA14 Juan Gonzalez 3.00 .90
CA15 Mark McGwire 8.00 2.40
CA16 Ivan Rodriguez 3.00 .90
CA17 Barry Bonds 8.00 2.40
CA18 Wade Boggs 2.00 .60
CA19 Tony Gwynn 4.00 1.20
CA20 Cal Ripken 10.00 3.00

2000 Stadium Club Chrome Clear Shots

Randomly inserted into packs at one in 24, this insert features ten of the major leagues most famous stars from both front and back angles at the same time. Card backs carry a "CS" prefix.

Nm-Mt Ex-Mt
COMPLETE SET (10) 30.00 9.00
*REFRACTORS: 1X TO 2.5X BASIC CLEAR
REFRACTOR ODDS 1:120
CS1 Derek Jeter 6.00 1.80
CS2 Bernie Williams 1.50 .45
CS3 Roger Clemens 5.00 1.50
CS4 Chipper Jones 2.50 .75
CS5 Greg Maddux 4.00 1.20
CS6 Andruw Jones 1.00 .30
CS7 Juan Gonzalez 2.50 .75
CS8 Manny Ramirez 1.00 .30
CS9 Ken Griffey Jr. 4.00 1.20
CS10 Josh Hamilton 1.00 .30

2000 Stadium Club Chrome Eyes of the Game

Randomly inserted into packs at one in 16, this 10-card insert features players who have an "eye" for the game. Card backs carry an "EG" prefix.

Nm-Mt Ex-Mt
COMPLETE SET (10) 30.00 9.00
*REFRACTORS: 1X TO 2.5X BASIC EYES
REFRACTOR ODDS 1:80
EG1 Randy Johnson 2.00 .60
EG2 Mike Piazza 3.00 .90
EG3 Nomar Garciaparra 3.00 .90
EG4 Mark McGwire 5.00 1.50
EG5 Alex Rodriguez 3.00 .90
EG6 Derek Jeter 5.00 1.50
EG7 Tony Gwynn 2.50 .75
EG8 Sammy Sosa 3.00 .90
EG9 Larry Walker 1.25 .35
EG10 Ken Griffey Jr. 3.00 .90

2000 Stadium Club Chrome True Colors

Randomly inserted into packs at one in 32, this 10-card insert features players that rise to the occasion when the game's on the line. Card backs carry a "TC" prefix.

Nm-Mt Ex-Mt
COMPLETE SET (10) 50.00 15.00
*REFRACTORS: 1X TO 2.5X BASIC TRUE
REFRACTOR ODDS 1:160
TC1 Sammy Sosa 5.00 1.50
TC2 Nomar Garciaparra 5.00 1.50
TC3 Alex Rodriguez 5.00 1.50
TC4 Derek Jeter 8.00 2.40
TC5 Mark McGwire 8.00 2.40
TC6 Chipper Jones 3.00 .90
TC7 Mike Piazza 5.00 1.50
TC8 Ken Griffey Jr. 5.00 1.50
TC9 Manny Ramirez 1.25 .35
TC10 Vladimir Guerrero 3.00 .90

2000 Stadium Club Chrome Visionaries

Randomly inserted into packs at one in 18, this 20-card insert features some of the major league's most talented prospects. Card backs carry a "V" prefix.

Nm-Mt Ex-Mt
COMPLETE SET (20) 60.00 18.00
*REF: .75X TO 2X BASIC VISIONARIES
REFRACTOR ODDS 1:90
V1 Alfonso Soriano 3.00 .90
V2 Josh Hamilton 1.25 .35
V3 A.J. Burnett 1.25 .35
V4 Pat Burrell 2.00 .60
V5 Ruben Salazar 2.00 .60
V6 Aaron Rowand 2.00 .60
V7 Adam Piatt 1.25 .35
V8 Nick Johnson 1.25 .35
V9 Brett Myers 5.00 1.50
V10 Jack Cust 1.25 .35
V11 Corey Patterson 2.00 .60
V12 Sean Burroughs 2.00 .60
V13 Pablo Ozuna 1.25 .35
V14 Dee Brown 1.25 .35
V15 John Patterson 1.25 .35
V16 Willi Mo Pena 1.25 .35
V17 Mark Mulder 2.00 .60
V18 Eric Munson 1.25 .35
V19 Alex Escobar 3.00 .90
V20 Rick Asadoorian 2.00 .60

1996 Stadum Club Porcelain

These six cards were available through the Topps catalog at an issue price of $79. The six players in the set each represent a key player from each year of the Stadium Club brand history. A special display which cost an additional $19.95 was also available for this set.

Nm-Mt Ex-Mt
1 Ken Griffey Jr 25.00 7.50
2 Frank Thomas 25.00 7.50
3 Kenny Lofton 20.00 6.00
4 Barry Bonds 30.00 9.00
5 Paul Molitor 20.00 6.00
6 Randy Johnson 25.00 7.50

1953 Stahl Meyer

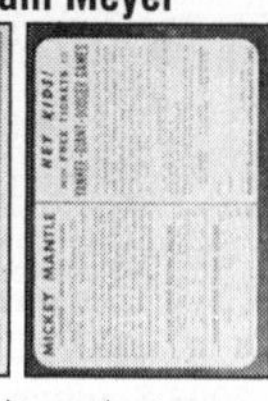

The cards in this nine-card set measure approximately 3 1/4" by 4 1/2". The 1953 Stahl Meyer set of full color, unnumbered cards includes three players from each of the three New York teams. The cards have white borders. The Lockman card is the most plentiful of any card in the set. Some batting and fielding statistics and short biography are included on the back. The cards are ordered in the checklist below by alphabetical order without regard to team affiliation. A promotional kit, titled a "Baseball Kit" was also issued and sent to stores to promote this set. Information about the cards and a checklist was included in that kit.

NM Ex
COMPLETE SET 5000.00 2500.00
1 Hank Bauer 200.00 100.00
2 Roy Campanella 800.00 400.00
3 Gil Hodges 400.00 200.00
4 Monte Irvin 250.00 125.00
5 Whitey Lockman 150.00 75.00
6 Mickey Mantle 3000.00 1500.00
7 Phil Rizzuto 400.00 200.00
8 Duke Snider 800.00 400.00
9 Bobby Thomson 200.00 100.00

1954 Stahl Meyer

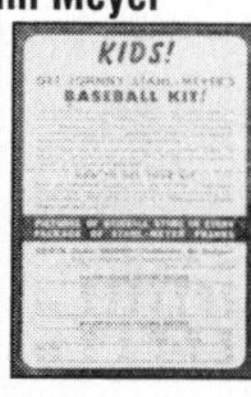

The cards in this 12-card set measure approximately 3 1/4" by 4 1/2". The 1954 Stahl Meyer set of full color, unnumbered cards includes four players from each of the three New York teams. The cards have yellow borders and the backs, oriented horizontally, include an ad for a baseball kit and the player's statistics. No player biography is included on the back. The cards are ordered in the checklist below by alphabetical order without regard to team affiliation.

NM Ex
COMPLETE SET (12) 7000.00 3500.00
1 Hank Bauer 200.00 100.00
2 Carl Erskine 200.00 100.00
3 Gil Hodges 300.00 150.00
4 Monte Irvin 250.00 125.00
5 Whitey Lockman 150.00 75.00
6 Mickey Mantle 3000.00 1500.00
7 Willie Mays 1500.00 750.00
8 Gil McDougald 200.00 100.00
9 Don Mueller 150.00 75.00
10 Don Newcombe 200.00 100.00
11 Phil Rizzuto 300.00 150.00
12 Duke Snider 600.00 300.00

1955 Stahl Meyer

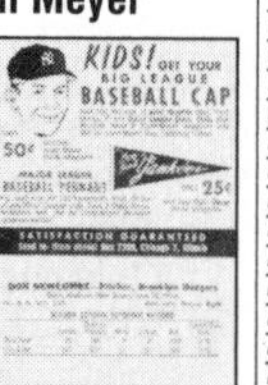

The cards in this 12-card set measure approximately 3 1/4" by 4 1/2". The 1955 Stahl Meyer set of full color, unnumbered cards contains four players each from the three New York teams. As in the 1954 set, the cards have yellow borders; however, the back of the cards contain a sketch of Mickey Mantle with an ad for a baseball cap or a pennant. The cards are ordered in the checklist below by alphabetical order without regard to team affiliation.

NM Ex
COMPLETE SET (12) 5500.00 2800.00
1 Hank Bauer 200.00 100.00
2 Carl Erskine 200.00 100.00
3 Gil Hodges 300.00 150.00
4 Monte Irvin 250.00 125.00
5 Whitey Lockman 150.00 75.00
6 Mickey Mantle 3000.00 1500.00
7 Gil McDougald 200.00 100.00
8 Don Mueller 150.00 75.00
9 Don Newcombe 200.00 100.00
10 Dusty Rhodes 150.00 75.00
11 Phil Rizzuto 300.00 150.00
12 Duke Snider 600.00 300.00

1910 Standard Caramel E93

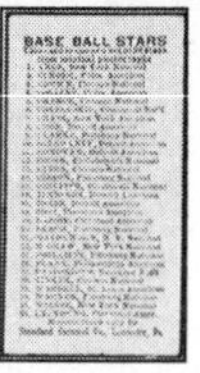

The cards in this 30-card set measure 1 1/2" by 2 3/4". The E93 set was distributed by Standard Caramel in 1910. It consists of black and white player photos which were tinted and placed against solid color backgrounds. A checklist, starting with Ames, is printed in brown ink on the reverse. Some blank backs are known and all poses also appear in W555.

Ex-Mt VG
COMPLETE SET (30) 10000.00 5000.00
1 Red Ames 120.00 60.00
2 Chief Bender 250.00 125.00
3 Mordecai Brown 250.00 125.00
4 Frank Chance 400.00 200.00
5 Hal Chase 200.00 100.00
6 Ty Cobb 1500.00 750.00
7 Eddie Collins 400.00 200.00
8 Stan Coveleskie 250.00 125.00
9 Fred Clarke 250.00 125.00
10 Jim Delehanty 120.00 60.00
11 Bill Donovan 120.00 60.00
12 Red Dooin 120.00 60.00
13 Johnny Evers 400.00 200.00
14 George Gibson 120.00 60.00
15 Clark Griffith 250.00 125.00
16 Hugh Jennings 250.00 125.00
17 Davy Jones 120.00 60.00
18 Addie Joss 250.00 125.00
19 Napoleon Lajoie 500.00 250.00
20 Tommy Leach 150.00 75.00
21 Christy Mathewson 800.00 400.00
22 John McGraw 500.00 250.00
23 Jim Pastorius 120.00 60.00
24 Deacon Phillippe 150.00 75.00
25 Eddie Plank 400.00 200.00
26 Joe Tinker 400.00 200.00
27 Rube Waddell 250.00 125.00
28 Honus Wagner 800.00 400.00
29 Hooks Wiltse 120.00 60.00
30 Cy Young 500.00 250.00

1952 Star Cal Large

Type One of the Star Cal Decal set, issued in 1952, contains the cards listed in the checklist below. Each decal sheet measures 4 1/8" by 6 1/8". When the decal is taken from the paper wrapper, a checklist of existing decals is revealed on the wrapper. The set was issued by the Meyercord Company of Chicago and carries a catalog designation of W625-1.

NM Ex
COMPLETE SET 4000.00 2000.00
70A Allie Reynolds 25.00 12.50
70B Ed Lopat 25.00 12.50
70C Yogi Berra 80.00 40.00
70D Vic Raschi 20.00 10.00
70E Jerry Coleman 20.00 10.00
70F Phil Rizzuto 50.00 25.00
70G Mickey Mantle 1000.00 500.00
71A Mel Parnell 20.00 10.00
71B Ted Williams 200.00 100.00
71C Ted Williams 200.00 100.00
71D Vern Stephens 20.00 10.00
71E Billy Goodman 20.00 10.00
71F Dom DiMaggio 25.00 12.50
71G Dick Gernert 15.00 7.50
71H Hoot Evers 80.00 40.00
72A George Kell 50.00 25.00
72B Hal Newhouser 40.00 20.00
72C Hoot Evers 15.00 7.50
72D Vic Wertz 15.00 7.50
72E Fred Hutchinson 20.00 10.00
72F Johnny Groth 15.00 7.50
73A Al Zarilla 15.00 7.50
73B Billy Pierce 25.00 12.50
73C Eddie Robinson 15.00 7.50
73D Chico Carrasquel 20.00 10.00
73E Minnie Minoso 30.00 15.00
73F Jim Busby 15.00 7.50
73G Nellie Fox 40.00 20.00
73H Sam Mele 80.00 40.00
74A Larry Doby 40.00 20.00
74B Al Rosen 25.00 12.50
74C Bob Lemon 40.00 20.00
74D Jim Hegan 15.00 7.50
74E Bob Feller 80.00 40.00
74F Dale Mitchell 20.00 10.00
75A Ned Garver 15.00 7.50
76A Gus Zernial 20.00 10.00
76B Ferris Fain 15.00 7.50
76C Bobby Shantz 80.00 40.00
77A Richie Ashburn 40.00 20.00
77B Ralph Kiner 50.00 25.00
77C Curt Simmons 80.00 40.00
78A Bobby Thomson 20.00 10.00
78B Alvin Dark 20.00 10.00
78C Sal Maglie 20.00 10.00
78D Larry Jansen 15.00 7.50
78E Willie Mays 300.00 150.00
78F Monte Irvin 50.00 25.00
78G Whitey Lockman 15.00 7.50
79A Gil Hodges 50.00 25.00
79B Pee Wee Reese 60.00 30.00

79C Roy Campanella 150.00 75.00
79D Don Newcombe 30.00 15.00
79E Duke Snider.................. 100.00 50.00
79F Preacher Roe................. 25.00 12.50
79G Jackie Robinson 200.00 100.00
80A Eddie Miksis................. 15.00 7.50
80B Dutch Leonard 15.00 7.50
80C Randy Jackson................ 15.00 7.50
80D Bob Rush..................... 15.00 7.50
80E Hank Sauer................... 15.00 7.50
80F Phil Cavarretta.............. 20.00 10.00
80G Warren Hacker................ 15.00 7.50
81A Red Schoendienst............. 40.00 20.00
81B Wally Westlake............... 15.00 7.50
81C Cliff Chambers............... 15.00 7.50
81D Enos Slaughter............... 40.00 20.00
81E Stan Musial.................. 120.00 60.00
81F Stan Musial.................. 120.00 60.00
81G Gerry Staley................. 15.00 7.50

1952 Star Cal Small

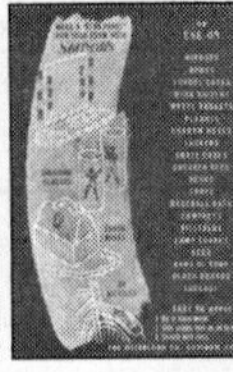

Type Two of the Star Cal Decal set features a decal package half the size of the W625-1 set, each sheet contains two decals, each of which is approximately half the size of the large decal found in the W625-1 set. Each decal package (sheet) measures 3 1/16" by 4 1/8". The set was issued by the Meyercord Company of Chicago and carries a catalog designation of W625-2. The checklist below features two players per "card".

	NM	Ex
COMPLETE SET	1300.00	650.00
84A Allie Reynolds and Vic Raschi	25.00	12.50
84B Ed Lopat and Yogi Berra	40.00	20.00
84C Phil Rizzuto and Jerry Coleman	30.00	15.00
85A Ted Williams and Ted Williams	200.00	100.00
85B Dom DiMaggio Mel Parnell	25.00	12.50
85C Vern Stephens and Billy Goodman	20.00	10.00
86A George Kell and Hal Newhouser	40.00	20.00
86B Hoot Evers and Vic Wertz	20.00	10.00
86C Johnny Groth and Fred Hutchinson	20.00	10.00
87A Eddie Robinson and Eddie Robinson	20.00	10.00
87B Chico Carrasquel and Minnie Minoso	25.00	12.50
87C Billy Pierce and Nellie Fox	40.00	20.00
87D Al Zarilla and Jim Busby	20.00	10.00
88A Bob Lemon and Jim Hegan	25.00	12.50
88B Larry Doby and Bob Feller	50.00	25.00
88C Dale Mitchell and Al Rosen	25.00	12.50
89A Ned Garver and Ned Garver	20.00	10.00
89B Ferris Fain and Gus Zernial	20.00	10.00
89C Richie Ashburn and Richie Ashburn	40.00	20.00
89D Ralph Kiner and Ralph Kiner	50.00	25.00
90A Willie Mays and Monte Irvin	150.00	75.00
90B Larry Jansen and Sal Maglie	25.00	12.50
90C Bobby Thomson and Al Dark	25.00	12.50
91A Gil Hodges and Pee Wee Reese	50.00	25.00
91B Roy Campanella and Jackie Robinson	150.00	75.00
91C Duke Snider and Preacher Roe	50.00	25.00
92A Phil Cavarretta and Dutch Leonard	20.00	10.00
92B Randy Jackson and Eddie Miksis	20.00	10.00
92C Bob Rush and Hank Sauer	20.00	10.00
93A Stan Musial and Stan Musial	150.00	75.00
93B Red Schoendienst and Enos Slaughter	30.00	15.00
93C Cliff Chambers and Wally Westlake	20.00	10.00

1983 Star Schmidt

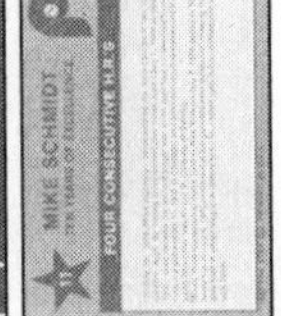

This 15-card standard-size set features Phillies great Mike Schmidt. This was the first baseball set issued by the Star Company, who had the NBA contract in the mid-1980's. Star company products are usually sold in complete set form.

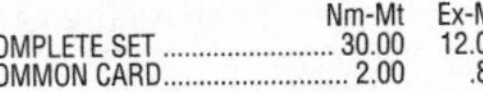

	Nm-Mt	Ex-Mt
COMPLETE SET	30.00	12.00
COMMON CARD	2.00	.80

1984 Star Brett

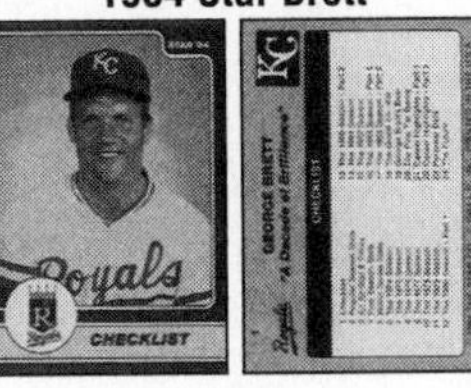

This 24 card standard-size set features long time Kansas City Royals star George Brett. This set was issued in complete set form.

	Nm-Mt	Ex-Mt
COMPLETE SET (24)	20.00	8.00
COMMON CARD (1-24)	1.00	.40

1984 Star Carlton

This 24-card standard-size set features another Philly great, Steve Carlton. The set was issued in complete form and can be dated by the "Star 84" notation.

	Nm-Mt	Ex-Mt
COMPLETE SET	20.00	8.00
COMMON CARD	1.00	.40

1984 Star Garvey

This 36 card standard-size set features San Diego and Los Angeles star Steve Garvey. Garvey, who established a consecutive game streak in the National League, led the Padres to the 1984 National League Pennant. These card trace his career.

	Nm-Mt	Ex-Mt
COMPLETE SET (36)	20.00	8.00
COMMON CARD (1-36)	.60	.24

1984 Star Strawberry

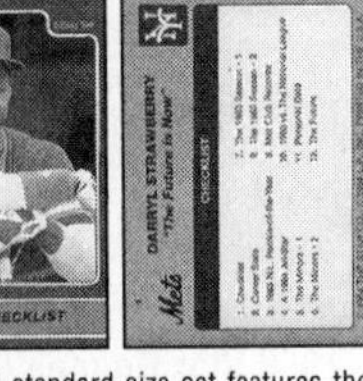

This 12-card standard-size set features then Met phenom Darryl Strawberry. This set was issued by the Star company and takes the collector through the early part of Strawberry's career. The set is dated with the "Star 84" logo in the upper right corner.

	Nm-Mt	Ex-Mt
COMPLETE SET (12)	8.00	3.20
COMMON CARD (1-12)	.75	.30

1984 Star Yastrzemski

This 24 card standard-size set feature the long career of Red Sox star Carl Yastrzemski. These cards which have pictures of Yaz career surrounded by red borders traces his career from the beginning through the end in 1983.

	Nm-Mt	Ex-Mt
COMPLETE SET (24)	20.00	8.00
COMMON CARD (1-24)	1.00	.40
4 Carl Yastrzemski George Brett World Series Stats	1.00	.40
9 Carl Yastrzemski Joe Cronin Seven Times Gold Glove	1.00	.40
13 Carl Yastrzemski Gaylord Perry Milestone Hits	1.00	.40
19 Carl Yastrzemski Johnny Bench Red Sox Club Records III	1.00	.40

1985 Star Carew

This 24 card standard-size set features all time great hitter Rod Carew from his early days with the Minnesota Twins until near the end of his career.

	Nm-Mt	Ex-Mt
COMPLETE SET	20.00	8.00
COMMON CARD	.75	.30

1985 Star Reggie Jackson

This 24-card standard-size set features California Angels star, Reggie Jackson. These cards trace Reggie's career beginning with his early days. The set is dated by the "Star 85" logo in the top right.

	Nm-Mt	Ex-Mt
COMPLETE SET (24)	20.00	8.00
COMMON CARD (1-24)	1.00	.40

1986 Star Boggs

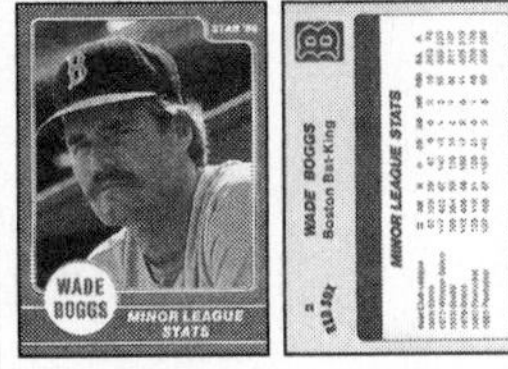

This 12-card standard-size set features then Boston Red Sox hitting star Wade Boggs. The set traces Boggs through the early part of his career. There was also a yellow sticker set issued which has the same value as these red bordered cards. This set was originally issued as eight 3 card panels. The backs of the not listed four panels form an action picture of Boggs.

	Nm-Mt	Ex-Mt
COMPLETE SET (12)	5.00	2.00
COMMON CARD (1-12)	.50	.20

1986 Star Canseco

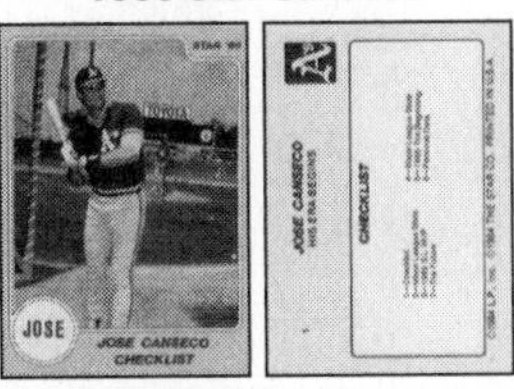

This 15-card standard-size set was issued by the Star Company to honor young star Jose Canseco. Since many of the cards are titled "His Era Begins," we have given pose descriptions to those cards.

	Nm-Mt	Ex-Mt
COMPLETE SET (15)	6.00	2.40
COMMON CARD (1-15)	.50	.20

1986 Star Joyner Red

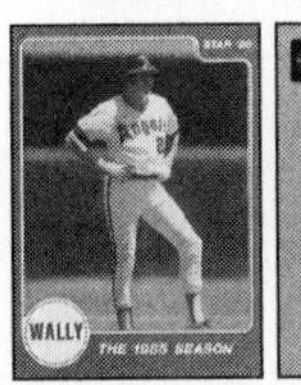
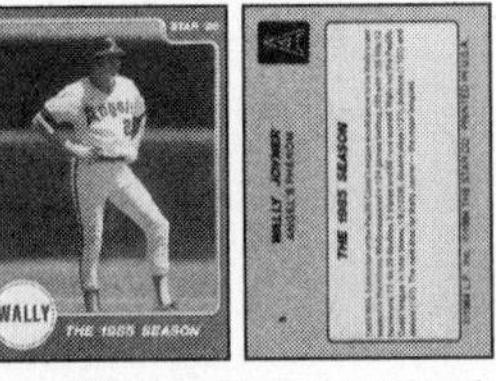

The year 1986 was a big year for young major league players. Wally Joyner, another star rookie in this class is featured in this 15-card standard-size set issued by the Star Company. We have called this the "red" set since the borders are red in color.

	Nm-Mt	Ex-Mt
COMPLETE SET (15)	6.00	2.40
COMMON CARD (1-15)	.50	.20

1986 Star Murphy

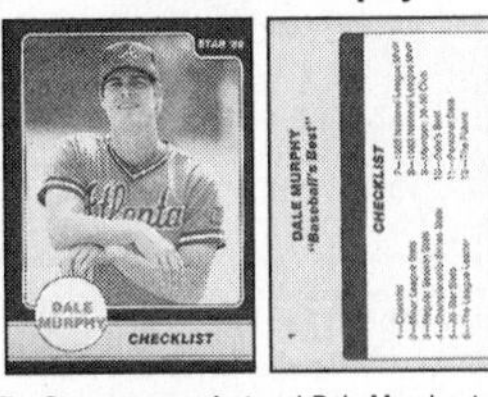

The Star company featured Dale Murphy, twice the National League MVP in this 12-card standard-size set. These cards trace the career of Murphy from his early days to the middle of his career.

	Nm-Mt	Ex-Mt
COMPLETE SET (12)	5.00	2.00
COMMON CARD (1-12)	.50	.20

1986 Star Rice

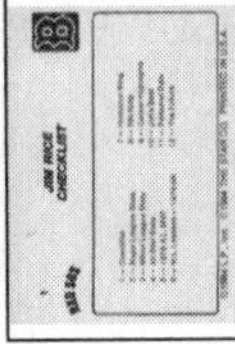

This 12-card standard-size set features Red Sox slugger Jim Rice. The set was issued by the Star company and has the traditional "Star 86" logo in the upper right corner.

	Nm-Mt	Ex-Mt
COMPLETE SET (12)	5.00	2.00
COMMON CARD (1-12)	.50	.20

1986 Star Ryan

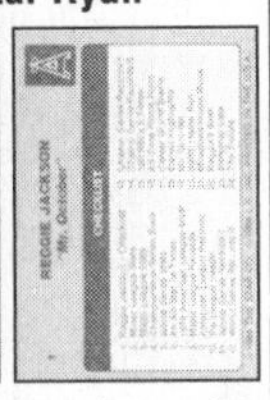

This 12-card standard-size set features photos of pitching great, Nolan Ryan. These cards trace Ryan's career beginning with his early days to the present. Twelve Puzzle Back cards were also issued for this set

	Nm-Mt	Ex-Mt
COMPLETE SET (24)	40.00	16.00
COMMON CARD (1-24)	2.00	.80

1986 Star Seaver

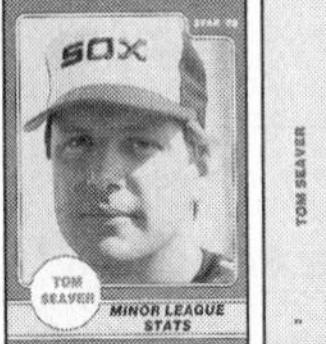
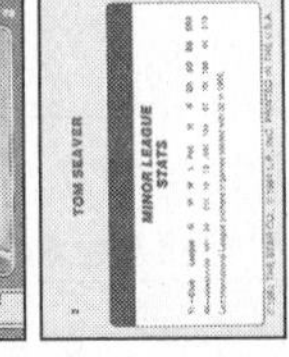

This 12-card standard-size set features Hall of Fame pitcher to be Tom Seaver. These cards trace Seaver's career from his early days in the Mets organization through the end of his career. This set, similar to the Boggs set was originally issued as eight panels. The backs form an action picture of Seaver when properly arranged.

	Nm-Mt	Ex-Mt
COMPLETE SET (12)	5.00	2.00
COMMON CARD (1-12)	.50	.20

1986 Star Stickers Canseco

This 15-card standard-size set features young star Jose Canseco. This set displays the same photos as the regular Star set but these items are blank-backed.

	Nm-Mt	Ex-Mt
COMPLETE SET (15)	6.00	2.40
COMMON CARD (1-15)	.40	.16

1986 Star Stickers Joyner Blue

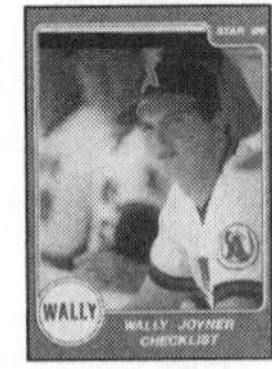

The same photos as in the 1986 Star Joyner Red set are featured. The difference between this set and the cards are the blank backed stickers and the blue borders for these cards.

	Nm-Mt	Ex-Mt
COMPLETE SET (15)	6.00	2.40
COMMON CARD (1-15)	.40	.16

1987 Star Award Winners

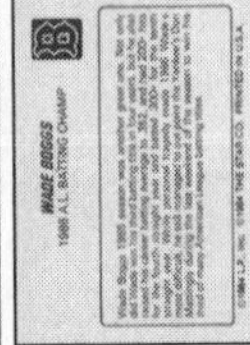

These five standard-size cards feature Jose Canseco and Wade Boggs who won various honors during the 1986 season.

	Nm-Mt	Ex-Mt
COMPLETE SET (5)	2.00	.80
1 Jose Canseco	.50	.20
2 Jose Canseco	.50	.20
3 Jose Canseco	.50	.20
4 Wade Boggs	.50	.20
5 Wade Boggs	.50	.20

1987 Star Gary Carter

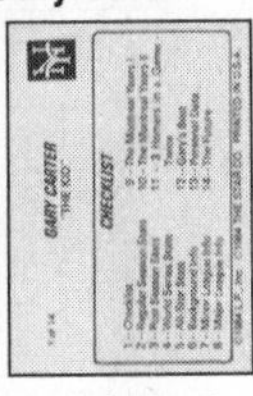

This 14-card standard-size set features long-time star catcher Gary Carter. These cards have a "Star 87" logo in the upper right corner.

	Nm-Mt	Ex-Mt
COMPLETE SET (14)	5.00	2.00
COMMON CARD (1-14)	.40	.16

1987 Star Clemens

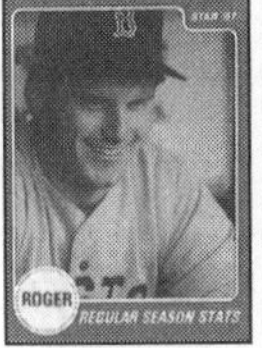
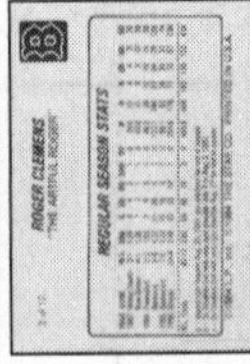

This 12-card standard-size set features Roger Clemens, who was in the process of winning consecutive Cy Young Awards. Clemens' career is traced from the beginning to his sensational 1986 season.

	Nm-Mt	Ex-Mt
COMPLETE SET (12)	6.00	2.40
COMMON CARD (1-12)	.75	.30

1987 Star Clemens II

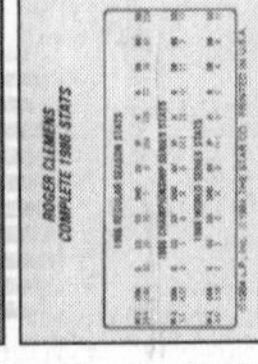

These five standard-size cards update the first Roger Clemens set issued earlier in 1987. These cards have a pink border as compared to the red border in the regular issue.

	Nm-Mt	Ex-Mt
COMPLETE SET (5)	2.00	.80
COMMON CARD (1-5)	.50	.20

1987 Star Hernandez

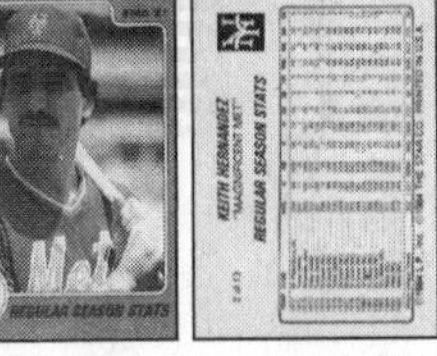

This 13-card standard-size set features Keith Hernandez. These cards trace Hernandez' career from its beginnings to the time of issue.

	Nm-Mt	Ex-Mt
COMPLETE SET (13)	5.00	2.00
COMMON CARD (1-13)	.40	.16

1987 Star Mattingly

This 12-card standard-size set features Yankee great, Don Mattingly. These cards trace Mattingly's career beginning with his early days to the present. The set is dated by the "Star 87" logo in the top right.

	Nm-Mt	Ex-Mt
COMPLETE SET (12)	10.00	4.00
COMMON CARD (1-12)	1.00	.40

1987 Star Mattingly Blankback

These six cards feature Yankee great Don Mattingly. These cards are differentiated from the other Mattingly cards because of the blank back

	Nm-Mt	Ex-Mt
COMPLETE SET (6)	2.50	1.00
COMMON CARD (1-6)	.50	.20

1987 Star Raines

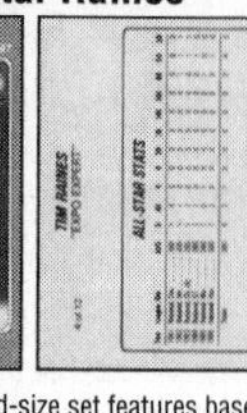

This 12-card standard-size set features baseball star Tim Raines. The "Star '87" logo in the upper right dates the set which traces his career from its beginnings to the present day.

	Nm-Mt	Ex-Mt
COMPLETE SET (12)	4.00	1.60
COMMON CARD (1-12)	.40	.16

1987 Star Valenzuela

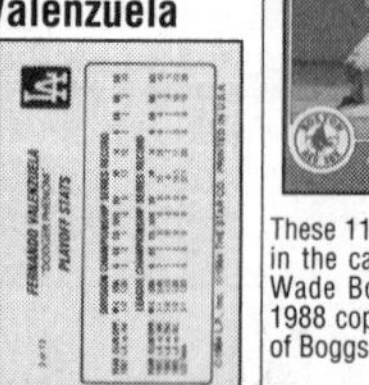

These 13 standard-size cards feature highlights in the career of Fernando Valuenzuela. These cards trace his career from its beginnings to the present day.

	Nm-Mt	Ex-Mt
COMPLETE SET (13)	5.00	2.00
COMMON CARD (1-13)	.40	.16

1987 Star Sticker Mattingly

These 24 standard-size stickers feature Yankee great Don Mattingly. These stickers are blank backed and trace his career from the minors to the present day.

	Nm-Mt	Ex-Mt
COMPLETE SET (24)	10.00	4.00
COMMON CARD (1-24)	.50	.20

1987 Star Sticker Valenzuela

These 10 standard-size sticker set is different from the regular cards issued by Star about Valenzuela. These cards have blank backs and also feature highlights in Valenzuela's career.

	Nm-Mt	Ex-Mt
COMPLETE SET (10)	3.50	1.40
COMMON CARD (1-10)	.40	.16

1988 Star Bell

These 11 standard-size cards feature highlights in the career of George Bell, 1987 American League MVP. The cards are dated by the 1988 copyright on the back..

	Nm-Mt	Ex-Mt
COMPLETE SET (11)	4.00	1.60
COMMON CARD (1-11)	.40	.16

1988 Star Boggs

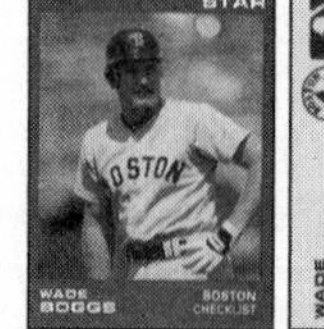
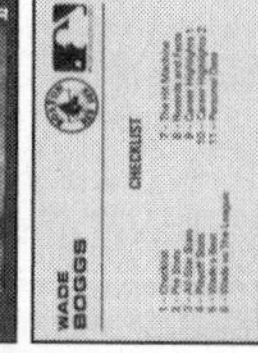

This 11-card set of Wade Boggs features color player photos in a red border. The player's name, team, and card title are printed in the bottom margin while the top contains the word, "Star," in the upper right margin. The backs carry the information indicated by the card title.

	Nm-Mt	Ex-Mt
COMPLETE SET (11)	5.00	2.00
COMMON CARD (1-11)	.50	.20

1988 Star Boggs Glossy

This 10 card standard-size set features the career of then Red Sox hitting star Wade Boggs from the beginning of his career through the 1987 season. These cards feature shots of Wade Boggs surrounded by a yellow border.

	Nm-Mt	Ex-Mt
COMPLETE SET (10)	10.00	4.00
COMMON CARD (1-10)	1.00	.40

1988 Star Boggs Hitman

These 11 standard-size cards feature highlights in the career of Boston Red Sox hitting star, Wade Boggs. These cards are dated by the 1988 copyright on the back. Various highlights of Boggs' career are noted.

	Nm-Mt	Ex-Mt
COMPLETE SET (11)	5.00	2.00
COMMON CARD (1-11)	.50	.20

1988 Star Boggs/Gwynn

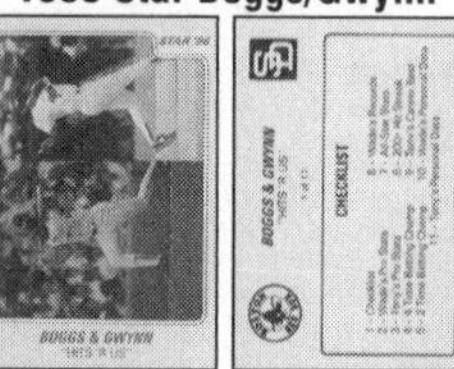

Two of baseball's best hitters: Wade Boggs and Tony Gwynn are featured in this 11-card standard-size set. Other than the checklist card on which both players are pictured, the set alternates between Boggs and Gwynn cards.

	Nm-Mt	Ex-Mt
COMPLETE SET (11)	5.00	2.00
COMMON BOGGS (1-11)	.50	.20
COMMON GWYNN	.75	.30
1 Wade Boggs Tony Gwynn CL	.75	.30

1988 Star Brett Platinum

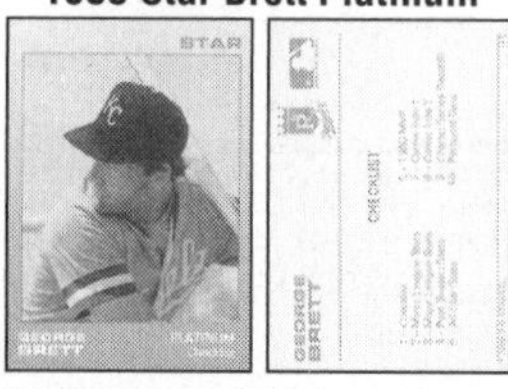

This 10 card standard-size set features highlights from the career of long time Kansas City Royal superstar George Brett. These cards have a glossy front and came with a note that there were 1,000 sets produced.

	Nm-Mt	Ex-Mt
COMPLETE SET	10.00	4.00
COMMON CARD	1.00	.40

1988 Star Canseco

This 11-card standard-size set features highlights in the career of Jose Canseco. The set is dated to 1988 with the 1988 copyright on the back.

	Nm-Mt	Ex-Mt
COMPLETE SET (11)	5.00	2.00
COMMON CARD (1-11)	.50	.20

1988 Star Gary Carter

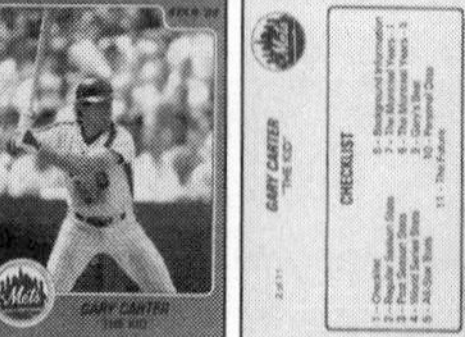

These 11 standard-size set, features yet again, Mets catcher Gary Carter. These cards trace his career from the beginning to the present day. The set is dated by the 1988 copyright on the back.

	Nm-Mt	Ex-Mt
COMPLETE SET (11)	5.00	2.00
COMMON CARD (1-11)	.50	.20

1988 Star Will Clark

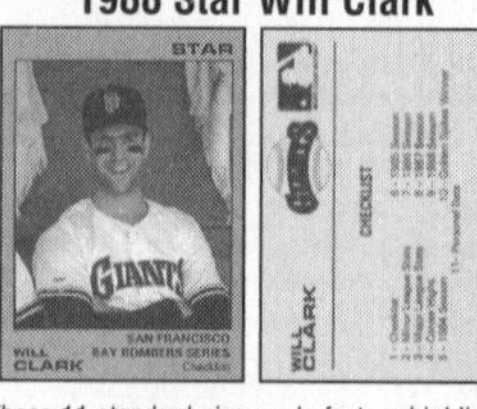

These 11 standard-size cards feature highlights in the career of former Olympian and current star, Will Clark. These cards are dated by the1988 copyright on the back.

	Nm-Mt	Ex-Mt
COMPLETE SET (11)	5.00	2.00
COMMON CARD (1-11)	.50	.20

1988 Star Clemens

This 10 card standard-size set features the career of then Red Sox fireballer Roger Clemens. This set traces his career from the beginning through the 1987 season.

	Nm-Mt	Ex-Mt
COMPLETE SET (10)	10.00	4.00
COMMON CARD	1.00	.40

1988 Star Clemens/Gooden

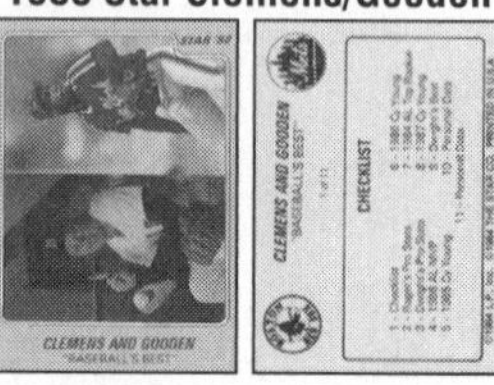

Two pitchers with very parallel careers: Dwight Gooden and Roger Clemens are featured in this set. Other than the checklist card in which pictures of both players are found, the set alternates between cards of Clemens and Gooden.

	Nm-Mt	Ex-Mt
COMPLETE SET (11)	5.00	2.00
COMMON GOODEN (1-11)	.50	.20
COMMON CLEMENS	1.00	.40
1 Roger Clemens Dwight Gooden CL	1.00	.40

1988 Star Cone

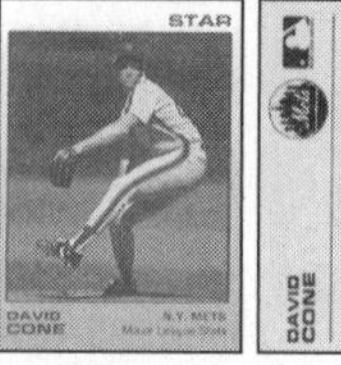

These 11 standard-size cards feature New York Mets star pitcher David Cone. These cards trace his career from the beginning through his breakthrough season in 1988.

	Nm-Mt	Ex-Mt
COMPLETE SET (11)	4.00	1.60
COMMON CARD (1-11)	.40	.16

1988 Star Eric Davis

Eric Daivs is featured in this 12-card standard-size set. The cards trace his career from the minors through the present day. The set is dated by the 1988 copyright on the back.

	Nm-Mt	Ex-Mt
COMPLETE SET (12)	4.00	1.60
COMMON CARD (1-12)	.40	.16

1988 Star Eric Davis Gold

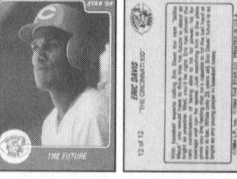

This 10 card standard-size set, which had a print run to 1,500 featured then up and coming Reds star Eric Davis. One can tell the set is the "gold" variety by the lettering on the front.

	Nm-Mt	Ex-Mt
COMPLETE SET	20.00	8.00
COMMON CARD	2.00	.80

1988 Star Davis/McGwire

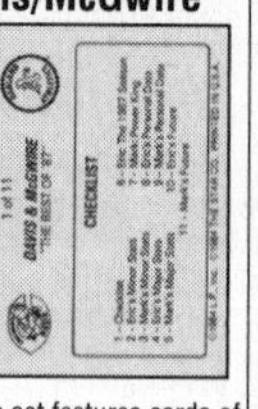

This 11-card standard-size set features cards of Eric Davis and Mark McGwire. Other than the checklist card, the set features a picture of either Davis or McGwire.

	Nm-Mt	Ex-Mt
COMPLETE SET (11)	6.00	2.40
COMMON DAVIS (1-11)	.40	.16
COMMON MCGWIRE	1.00	.40
1 Eric Davis Mark McGwire CL	1.00	.40

1988 Star Dawson

This 11-card standard-size set feature 1987 NL MVP Andre Dawson. Dawson's career is traced from its start to the time of issue. The set is dated with a 1988 copyright on the back.

	Nm-Mt	Ex-Mt
COMPLETE SET (11)	4.00	1.60
COMMON CARD (1-11)	.40	.16

1988 Star Gooden Blue

This 12-card set features color photos of Dwight Gooden inside a thin white and red border surrounded by a wider blue border. The card title is printed in the bottom margin with "Star '88" in the top margin. The backs carry the information as indicated by the card title on the front.

	Nm-Mt	Ex-Mt
COMPLETE SET (12)	5.00	2.00
COMMON CARD (1-12)	.50	.20

1988 Star Gooden Orange

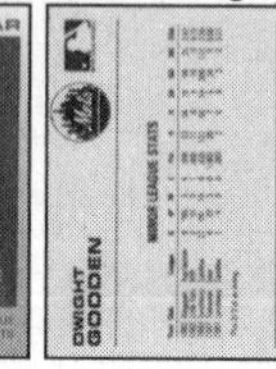

This 11-card standard-size set traces Dwight Gooden's career. These cards are dated by the 1988 copyright on the back. These cards are usually sold as a complete set but we have identified each card from this issue. The fronts feature orange-bordered color phots of Dwight Gooden with his name and card name printed in the bottom margin. The word, "Star," is printed in the top margin. The backs lists the information that identifies the card on the front.

	Nm-Mt	Ex-Mt
COMPLETE SET (11)	5.00	2.00
COMMON CARD (1-11)	.50	.20

1988 Star Grace

This 11 card standard-size set features then Cub rookie star, Mark Grace. This set takes the collector from the beginning of his professional career through 1988.

	Nm-Mt	Ex-Mt
COMPLETE SET (11)	10.00	4.00
COMMON CARD (1-11)	1.00	.40

1988 Star Grace Gold

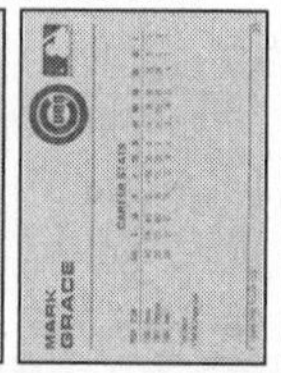

This 10 card standard-size set features then Cub Rookie Mark Grace. This set features Grace at the beginning of his career. And according to the set information, the print run was limited to 1,500 sets.

	Nm-Mt	Ex-Mt
COMPLETE SET	50.00	20.00
COMMON CARD	5.00	2.00

1988 Star Greenwell Purple

Mike Greenwell, Boston Red Sox outfielder, is the focus of this 11-card standard-size set. This set traces Greenwell's career from its beginnings to his breakthrough as a major leaguer. The set is dated by the 1988 copyright on the back. The fronts feature color player phots in a border of various shades of purple. The backs carry the information that the front card title indicates.

	Nm-Mt	Ex-Mt
COMPLETE SET (11)	4.00	1.60
COMMON CARD (1-11)	.40	.16

1988 Star Greenwell Red

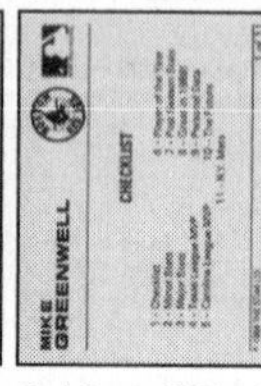

Mike Greenwell, Boston Red Sox outfielder, is the focus of this 11-card standard-size set. This set traces Greenwell's career from its beginnings to his breakthrough as a major leaguer. The set is dated by the 1988 copyright on the back. The fronts feature color player phots in a border of various shades of red. The backs carry the information that the front card title indicates.

	Nm-Mt	Ex-Mt
COMPLETE SET (11)	4.00	1.60
COMMON CARD (1-11)	.40	.16

1988 Star Gwynn

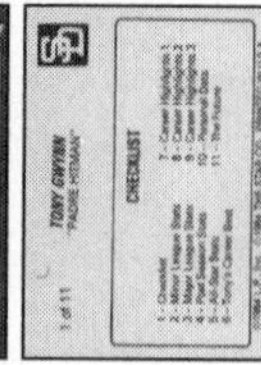

This 11-card standard-size set features highlights of Tony Gwynn's career. The set is dated with a 1988 copyright on the back.

	Nm-Mt	Ex-Mt
COMPLETE SET (11)	5.00	2.00
COMMON CARD (1-11)	.50	.20

1988 Star Hershiser

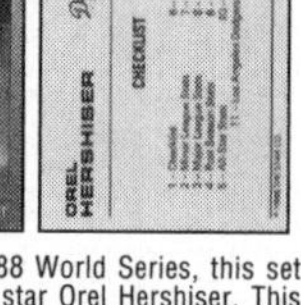

Issued after the 1988 World Series, this set focuses on Dodger star Orel Hershiser. This 11-card standard-size set includes career highlights such as his consecutive scoreless inning streak and his dominant 1988 post season.

	Nm-Mt	Ex-Mt
COMPLETE SET (11)	4.00	1.60
COMMON CARD (1-11)	.40	.16

1988 Star Horn

Soon to be failed Red Sox prospect, Sam Horn is featured in this set. These cards were issued after Horn tore up the American League in a late season call up in 1987. These 11 standard-size cards take the collectors through Horn's career highlights.

	Nm-Mt	Ex-Mt
COMPLETE SET (11)	2.00	.80
COMMON CARD (1-11)	.25	.10

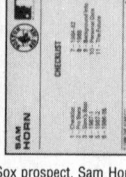

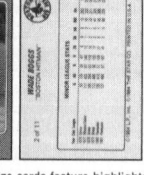

1988 Star Bo Jackson

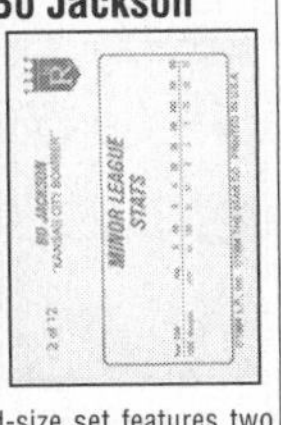

This 16-card standard-size set features two sport star Bo Jackson. The first 12 cards of the set feature him playing baseball while the final four cards feature him in an Auburn uniform, playing football and are blank-backed.

	Nm-Mt	Ex-Mt
COMPLETE SET (16)	15.00	6.00
COMMON CARD (1-16_	1.00	.40

1988 Star Jefferies

Two time minor league player of the year, Gregg Jefferies is feature in this set. As the hottest prospect entering the 1988 season, this set took a person through Jefferies' minor league career. These 11 standard-size cards were issued with the 1988 copyright on the back.

	Nm-Mt	Ex-Mt
COMPLETE SET (11)	5.00	2.00
COMMON CARD (1-11)	.50	.20

1988 Star Jordan

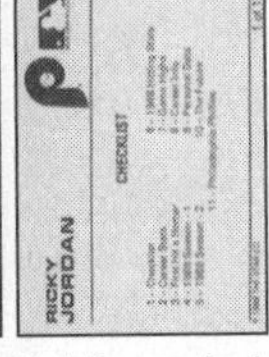

After having a great rookie half season for the Philadelphia Phillies, Ricky Jordan is featured in this 11-card standard-size set. Sold in complete set form, we have described all of these cards individually.

	Nm-Mt	Ex-Mt
COMPLETE SET (11)	2.00	.80
COMMON CARD (1-11)	.25	.10

1988 Star Mattingly

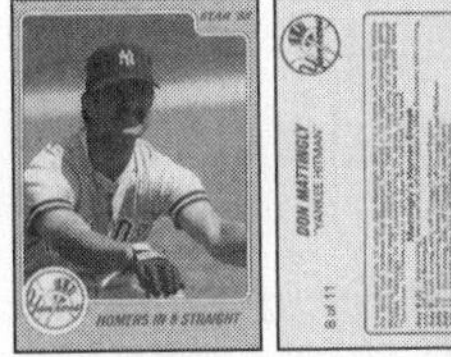

Yankee superstar Don Mattingly is featured in this 11-card standard-size set. The 1988 copyright date is located on the back. That is how this set can be differentiated from other Mattingly Star sets. Numbered to 1000.

	Nm-Mt	Ex-Mt
COMPLETE SET (11)	5.00	2.00
COMMON CARD (1-11)	.50	.20

1988 Star Mattingly/Schmidt

This 11-card standard-size set features East Coast stars: Don Mattingly and Mike Schmidt. Other than the first card in the set, either Mattingly or Schmidt is featured.

	Nm-Mt	Ex-Mt
COMPLETE SET (11)	5.00	2.00
COMMON CARD (1-11)	.50	.20
1 Don Mattingly Mike Schmidt	.50	.20

1988 Star McGwire

This 11-card standard-size set feature Oakland A's slugger Mark McGwire. This set is differentiated from the other Star McGwire issues by the 1988 copyright on the back.

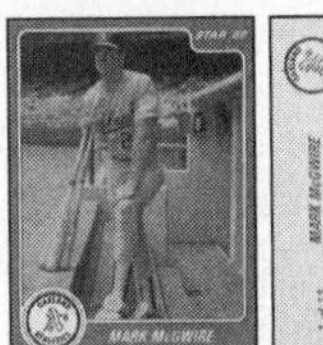

	Nm-Mt	Ex-Mt
COMPLETE SET (11)	20.00	8.00
COMMON CARD (1-11)	2.00	.80

1988 Star McGwire Green

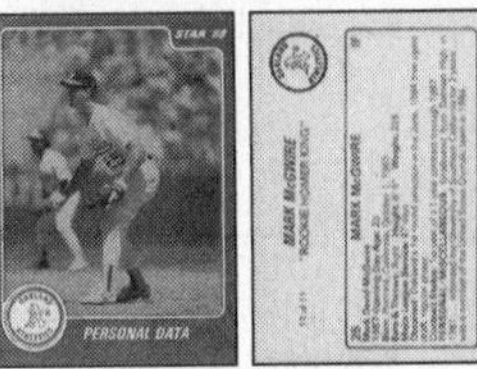

This 11-card standard-size set features Oakland A's slugger Mark McGwire. This set is differentiated from the other McGwire sets by the green borders.

	Nm-Mt	Ex-Mt
COMPLETE SET (11)	20.00	8.00
COMMON CARD (1-11)	2.00	.80

1988 Star McGwire Yellow

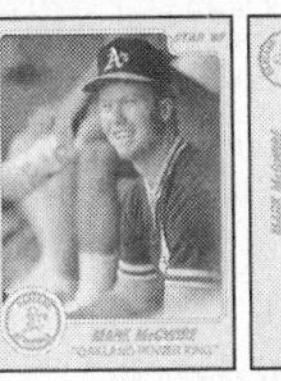

This 12-card standard-size set features slugger Mark McGwire at the beginning of his career. The cards have yellow borders.

	Nm-Mt	Ex-Mt
COMPLETE SET (12)	20.00	8.00
COMMON CARD (1-12)	2.00	.80
10 Mark McGuire Jose Canseco Carney Lansford Career Highlights 2	2.00	.80

1988 Star McReynolds

These 11 standard-size cards feature New York Mets outfielder Kevin McReynolds. These cards take McReynolds from his beginnings to the present day.

	Nm-Mt	Ex-Mt
COMPLETE SET (11)	3.00	1.20
COMMON CARD (1-11)	.30	.12

1988 Star Murphy Platinum

This 10-card standard-size set was issued by Star to honor the career of two-time NL MVP Dale Murphy. Unlike the regular sets issued by Star, these sets clearly say platinum on the front.

	Nm-Mt	Ex-Mt
COMPLETE SET (10)	30.00	12.00
COMMON CARD (1-10)	3.00	1.20

1988 Star Nokes

This 11-card standard-size set features Matt Nokes. These cards were printed after Nokes' 30 homer rookie season. They were designed to take advantage of Nokes' popularity.

	Nm-Mt	Ex-Mt
COMPLETE SET (11)	3.00	1.20
COMMON CARD (1-11)	.30	.12

1988 Star Puckett

This 11-card standard-size set features Minnesota Twins superstar Kirby Puckett. The cards trace Puckett's career from the beginning through the present day.

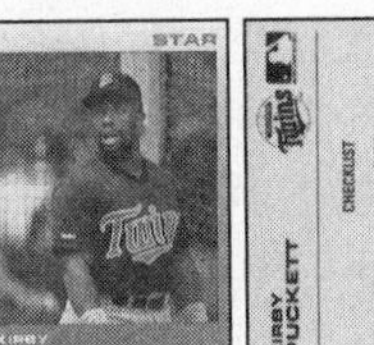

	Nm-Mt	Ex-Mt
COMPLETE SET (11)	5.00	2.00
COMMON CARD (1-11)	.50	.20

1988 Star Puckett Ad Card

This one card standard-size red bordered set featured a photo of Kirby Puckett on the front along with ad information about Star Company products on the back.

	Nm-Mt	Ex-Mt
1 Kirby Puckett	3.00	1.20

1988 Star Scott

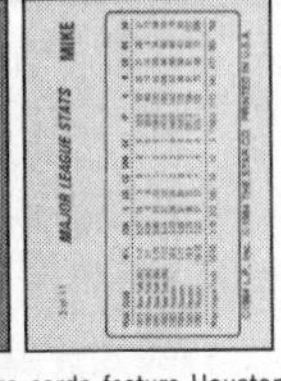

These 11 standard-size cards feature Houston Astros star pitcher Mike Scott. These cards trace Scott's career from the beginning through the present day. The cards are dated in the back by a 1988 copyright.

	Nm-Mt	Ex-Mt
COMPLETE SET (11)	3.00	1.20
COMMON CARD (1-11)	.30	.12

1988 Star Seitzer

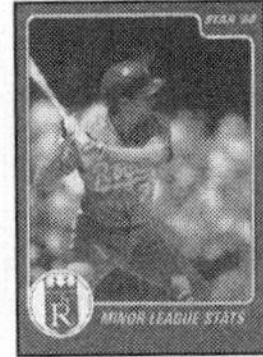
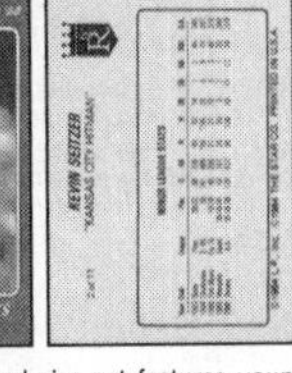

This 11-card standard-size set features young Royals player Kevin Seitzer. These cards take Seitzer's career from its beginning through the present day. The cards are notated on the back with a 1988 copyright.

	Nm-Mt	Ex-Mt
COMPLETE SET (11)	4.00	1.60
COMMON CARD (1-11)	.40	.16

1988 Star Snyder

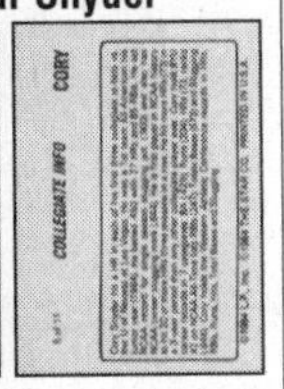

Former Olympian Cory Snyder is featured in this 11-card standard-size set. These cards trace Snyder's career from its beginnings through 1988. The cards are dated on the back with a 1988 copyright date.

	Nm-Mt	Ex-Mt
COMPLETE SET (11)	3.00	1.20
COMMON CARD (1-11)	.30	.12

1988 Star Strawberry

This 11-card standard-size set again features Mets player Darryl Strawberry. This set is differentiated from other Strawberry sets by the 1988 copyright date on the back and was issued with two different color borders--one violet and the other blue. The corresponding fronts of each set display different color photos of Darryl Strawberry while the backs carry the same information on the corresponding violet and blue bordered cards.

	Nm-Mt	Ex-Mt
COMPLETE SET (11)	4.00	1.60
COMMON CARD (1-11)	.40	.16

1988 Star Trammell

Long term Detroit Tiger star Alan Trammell is featured in this set. These 11 standard-sized cards trace his career from the minors through his major league career. These cards are dated by the 1988 copyright date on the back.

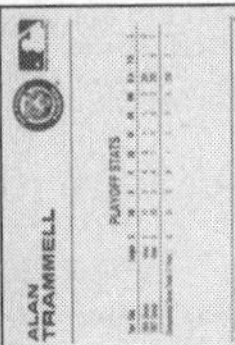

	Nm-Mt	Ex-Mt
COMPLETE SET (11)	4.00	1.60
COMMON CARD (1-11)	.40	.16

1988 Star Trammell Platinum

This 10 card standard-size set features Detroit Tiger star Alan Trammell. The set has a glossy feel to it and production was limited to 1,000 sets.

	Nm-Mt	Ex-Mt
COMPLETE SET	30.00	12.00
COMMON CARD	3.00	1.20

1988 Star Ventura

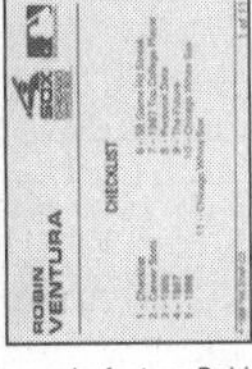

These 11 standard-size cards feature Robin Ventura. Ventura, who had established a consecutive-game hitting streak at Oklahoma State, was a highly regarded prospect. These cards feature highlights of his pre-White Sox career.

	Nm-Mt	Ex-Mt
COMPLETE SET (11)	5.00	2.00
COMMON CARD (1-11)	.50	.20

1988 Star Winfield

These 12 standard-size cards feature highlights in the career of Dave Winfield. These cards are dated by the 1988 copyright date on the back. Even though these issues are usually sold in complete set form we have noted all the individual cards.

	Nm-Mt	Ex-Mt
COMPLETE SET (12)	5.00	2.00
COMMON CARD (1-12)	.50	.20

1988 Star Stickers George Bell

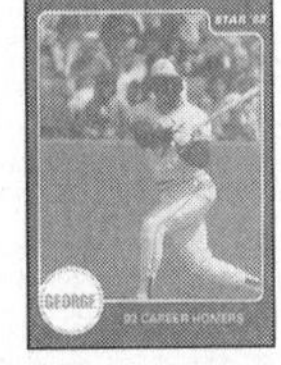

These 10 standard-size stickers feature Toronto slugging outfielder, George Bell. These stickers are blank backed and the fronts describe various career highlights.

	Nm-Mt	Ex-Mt
COMPLETE SET (10)	2.50	1.00
COMMON CARD (1-10)	.25	.10

1988 Star Stickers Snyder

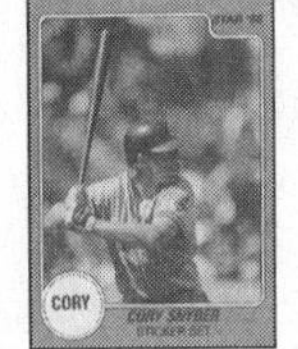

These stickers, which are not the same as the regular card issue, feature Cleveland Indians outfielder Cory Snyder. These standard-sized stickers are blank backed and have various career highlights.

	Nm-Mt	Ex-Mt
COMPLETE SET (8)	2.00	.80
COMMON CARD (1-8)	.25	.10

1988 Star Stickers Winfield

These 10 standard-sized stickers feature Yankee outfielder Dave Winfield. Various highlights from Winfield's career are featured in this set.

	Nm-Mt	Ex-Mt
COMPLETE SET (10)	5.00	2.00
COMMON CARD (1-10)	.50	.20

1989 Star Canseco Platinum

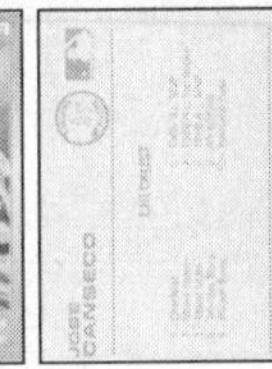

This 10 card standard-size set was issued to honor the career of the first 40 homer/40 stolen base player, Jose Canseco. The set was limited to a production run of 1,000 sets.

	Nm-Mt	Ex-Mt
COMPLETE SET	40.00	16.00
COMMON CARD	4.00	1.60

1989 Star Gordon

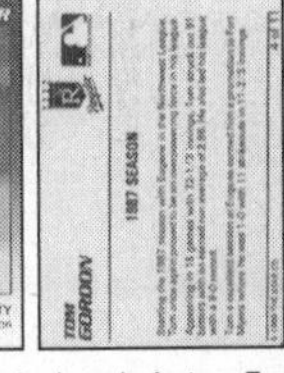

These 11 standard-sized cards feature Tom "Flash" Gordon, rookie pitcher for the Kansas City Royals. This set was issued as Gordon had an excellent rookie season and became very popular in the hobby.

	Nm-Mt	Ex-Mt
COMPLETE SET (11)	4.00	1.60
COMMON CARD (1-11)	.40	.16

1989 Star Greenwell Gold

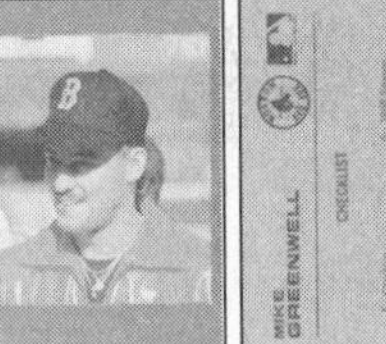

This 10 card standard-size set features highlights from the career of Red Sox slugger Mike Greenwell. Fifteen hundred of these sets were produced.

	Nm-Mt	Ex-Mt
COMPLETE SET	15.00	6.00
COMMON CARD	1.50	.60

1989 Star Greenwell Platinum

This set has the same checklist as the Star Greenwell Gold set but uses different photos and is limited to 1,000 sets produced.

	Nm-Mt	Ex-Mt
COMPLETE SET	20.00	8.00
COMMON CARD	2.00	.80

1989 Star Griffey Jr.

This 11 card standard-size set details Ken Griffey Jr.'s career as it was beginning on the major league level. Like the other Star sets, it was issued in its own individual bag.

	Nm-Mt	Ex-Mt
COMPLETE SET (11)	20.00	8.00
COMMON CARD (1-11)	2.00	.80
7 Ken Griffey Jr. Ken Griffey Sr.	2.00	.80

1989 Star Hershiser Gold

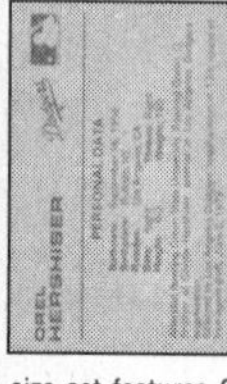

This 10 card standard-size set features Orel Hershisher just after the end of his greatest major league season. These cards, which feature highlights of his career, was limited to 1,000 sets produced

	Nm-Mt	Ex-Mt
COMPLETE SET (10)	20.00	8.00
COMMON CARD	2.00	.80

1989 Star Mitchell

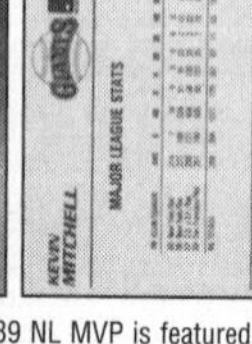

Kevin Mitchell, the 1989 NL MVP is featured in this 11 card standard-sized set. These cards trace Mitchell's career from his earliest days to the present. These cards are dated on the back and are arranged that way.

	Nm-Mt	Ex-Mt
COMPLETE SET (11)	4.00	1.60
COMMON CARD (1-11)	.40	.16

1989 Star Mitchell/Clark

This 11 card standard-sized set features San Francisco Giant sluggers: Kevin Mitchell and Will Clark. Other than the first card, either Mitchell or Clark is pictured seperately.

	Nm-Mt	Ex-Mt
COMPLETE SET (11)	4.00	1.60
COMMON MITCHELL (1-11)	.30	.12
COMMON CLARK	.75	.30
1 Kevin Mitchell Will Clark CL	.75	.30

1989 Star Puckett Platinum

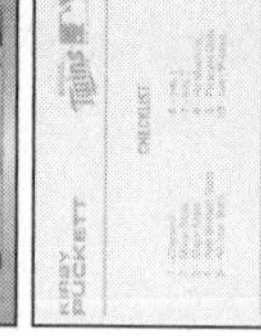

This 10 card standard-size set features highlights from the career of the Minnesota Twins superstar Kirby Puckett. The set was limited to 1,000 sets produced

	Nm-Mt	Ex-Mt
COMPLETE SET	50.00	20.00
COMMON CARD	5.00	2.00

1989 Star Strawberry Platinum

This 10 card standard-size set features highlights from the career of Darryl Strawberry. The set was limited to 1,000 sets produced.

	Nm-Mt	Ex-Mt
COMPLETE SET	20.00	8.00
COMMON CARD	2.00	.80

1989 Star Santiago

This 11 card standard-sized set features Benito Santiago. The set can be dated thanks to the 1989 copyright date on the back. This set traces Santiago's career from the earliest days through the 1988 season.

	Nm-Mt	Ex-Mt
COMPLETE SET (11)	3.00	1.20
COMMON CARD (1-11)	.30	.12

1989 Star Walton

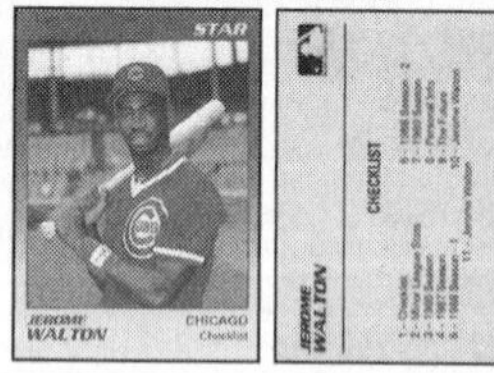

Jerome Walton is featured in this 11-card standard-size set. Walton, the 1989 NL Rookie of the Year, has his career highlighted in this set. The set is dated by the 1989 copyright on the back.

	Nm-Mt	Ex-Mt
COMPLETE SET (11)	2.50	1.00
COMMON CARD (1-11)	.25	.10

1989 Star Walton/Olson

This 11 card standard-sized set features Gregg Olson and Jerome Walton, the 1989 Rookies of the Year. Other than the 1st checklist card, either Walton or Olson are only featured in this set.

	Nm-Mt	Ex-Mt
COMPLETE SET (11)	2.50	1.00
1 Jerome Walton Gregg Olson CL	.25	.10

1990 Star Abbott

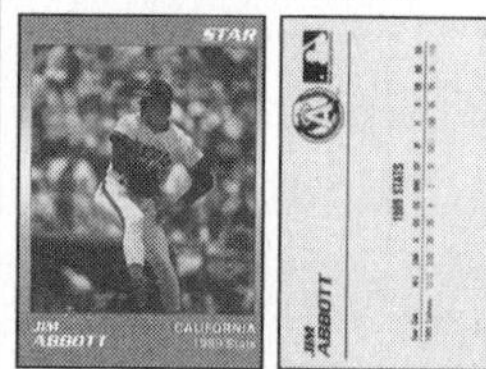

This 11-card standard-size set features highlights in the career of inspirational player, Jim Abbott. Abbott, who only has one hand, became a sucsessful major league pitcher. These cards are dated by the 1990 copyright on the back.

	Nm-Mt	Ex-Mt
COMPLETE SET (11)	4.00	1.20
COMMON CARD (1-11)	.40	.12

1990 Star Sandy Alomar

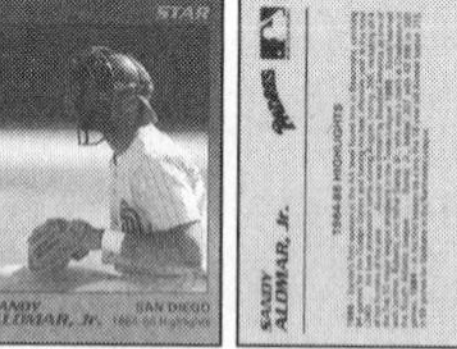

This 11-card standard-size set features Sandy Alomar Jr. While this set (as well as all Star products) are usually sold in complete set form, we have broken down this set into its individual components. The set is dated by the 1990 copyright on the back.

	Nm-Mt	Ex-Mt
COMPLETE SET (11)	5.00	1.50
COMMON CARD (1-11)	.50	.15

1990 Star Alomar Brothers

This 11-card standard-size set features the Alomar Brothers. These players, sons of former major league second basemall Sandy Alomar, each came up with the San Diego Padres. The brothers are only pictured together on card number 1.

	Nm-Mt	Ex-Mt
COMPLETE SET (11)	4.00	1.20
COMMON S. ALOMAR (1-11)	.30	.09
COMMON R. ALOMAR (1-11)	.75	.23
1 Roberto Alomar CL Sandy Alomar Jr.	.75	.23

1990 Star Benes

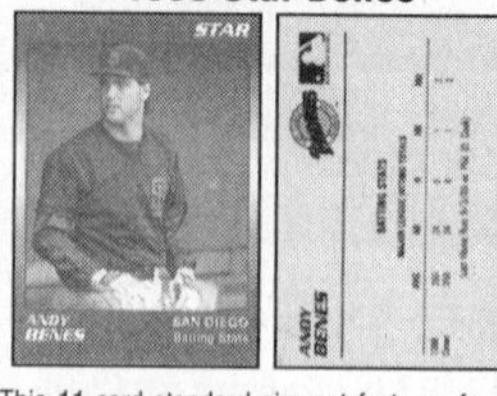

This 11-card standard-size set features former number one overall draft pick Andy Benes. These cards have highlights of Benes' career and is dated by the 1990 copyright date on the back.

	Nm-Mt	Ex-Mt
COMPLETE SET (11)	4.00	1.20
COMMON CARD (1-11)	.40	.12

1990 Star Bonds

This 11-card standard-size set was issued by Star Co. in honor of Pittsburgh Pirates superstar Barry Bonds. The cards have on the fronts a mix of action and non-action color shots, with purple borders and white lettering. The horizontally oriented backs are also in purple print and have player information.

	Nm-Mt	Ex-Mt
COMPLETE SET (11)	10.00	3.00
COMMON CARD	1.00	.30

1990 Star Clark/Grace

The two competing first baseman in the 1989 NL Championship series are featured in this set. These 11 standard-sized cards, other than the first card, feature either Will Clark or Mark Grace and we have identified which player is pictured.

	Nm-Mt	Ex-Mt
COMPLETE SET (11)	5.00	1.50
COMMON CARD (1-11)	.50	.15
1 Will Clark Mark Grace CL	.50	.15

1990 Star Fielder

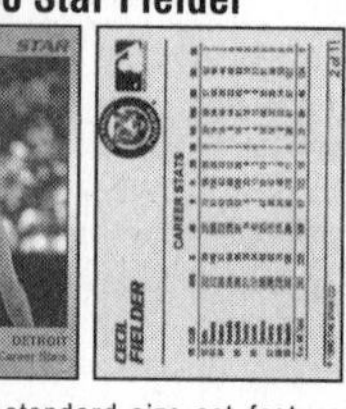

This 11-card standard-size set features homerun specialist Cecil Fielder. After playing in Japan, Fielder came back to the American League and hit 50 homers in the 1990 season. This set was issued soon after that season to take advantage of Fielder's popularity.

	Nm-Mt	Ex-Mt
COMPLETE SET (11)	5.00	1.50
COMMON CARD (1-11)	.50	.15

1990 Star Griffey Jr.

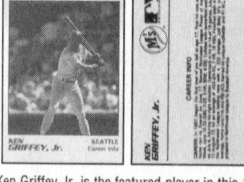

Ken Griffey Jr. is the featured player in this 11-card standard-sized set. These cards, dated by the copyright date on the back, feature highlights from the early part of his career.

	Nm-Mt	Ex-Mt
COMPLETE SET (11)	15.00	4.50
COMMON CARD (1-11)	1.50	.45
9 Ken Griffey, Jr. Ken Griffey Sr.	1.50	.45

1990 Star Rickey Henderson

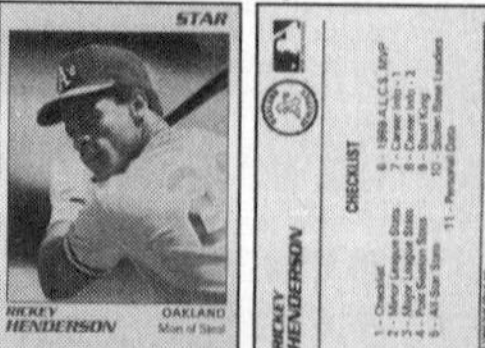

Rickey Henderson, perhaps the finest lead-off hitter ever, is featured in this 11-card standard-size set. These cards take the collector from the beginnings of Henderson's career to the present day.

	Nm-Mt	Ex-Mt
COMPLETE SET (11)	6.00	1.80
COMMON CARD (1-11)	.75	.23

1990 Star Justice

After the Atlanta Braves traded Dale Murphy, David Justice got a chance to play every day. By responding in fine fashion, collectors took notice of this young right fielder. After his rookie season, the Star Company issued this set to honor Justice.

	Nm-Mt	Ex-Mt
COMPLETE SET (11)	5.00	1.50
COMMON CARD (1-11)	.50	.15

1990 Star Larkin

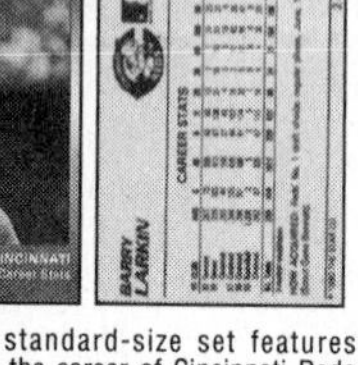

This 11-card standard-size set features highlights from the career of Cincinnati Reds shortstop Barry Larkin. These cards take the collector from the beginnings of Larkin's career to the present day.

	Nm-Mt	Ex-Mt
COMPLETE SET (11)	5.00	1.50
COMMON CARD (1-11)	.50	.15

1990 Star Maas

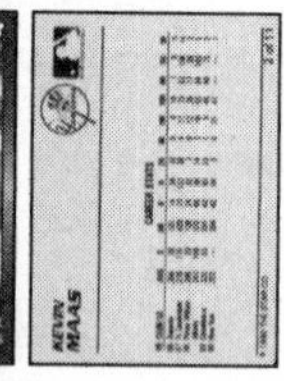

This 11-card standard-size set features highlights from the meteoric career of Yankee first baseman, Kevin Maas. Maas, who established a record for hitting his first 20 homers in the shortest number of at bats became very popular in the hobby. The Star Company issued this set to capitialize on that popularity.

	Nm-Mt	Ex-Mt
COMPLETE SET (11)	2.50	.75
COMMON CARD (1-11)	.25	.07

1990 Star Matt Williams

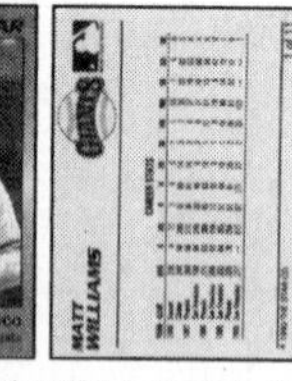

Matt Williams, slugging third baseman for the San Francisco Giants, is featured in this 11-card standard-size set. These card display various highlights (noted explicitly below) from his career.

	Nm-Mt	Ex-Mt
COMPLETE SET (11)	5.00	1.50
COMMON CARD (1-11)	.50	.15

1990 Star McDonald

This 11-card standard-size set features young Baltimore Oriole pitcher Ben McDonald. McDonald, who was drafted first overall in 1989, has his career traced from its earliest days to the present.

	Nm-Mt	Ex-Mt
COMPLETE SET (11)	4.00	1.20
COMMON CARD (1-11)	.40	.12

1990 Star Mitchell/Yount

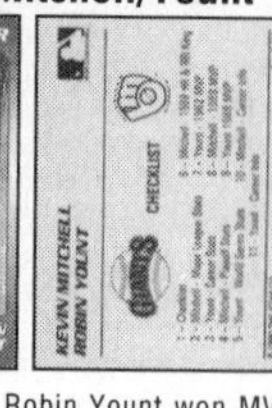

Kevin Mitchell and Robin Yount won MVP awards in 1989. This set features Mitchell and Yount on various cards. Other than the first card in the set, only one of the players is pictured.

	Nm-Mt	Ex-Mt
COMPLETE SET (11)	4.00	1.20
COMMON MITCHELL (1-11)	.30	.09
COMMON YOUNT	.75	.23
1 Kevin Mitchell Robin Yount CL	.50	.15

1990 Star Ripken

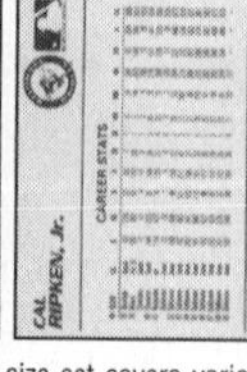

This 11-card standard-size set covers various highlights of Cal Ripken's Jr. career.

	Nm-Mt	Ex-Mt
COMPLETE SET (11)	10.00	3.00
COMMON CARD (1-11)	1.00	.30

1990 Star Ryan

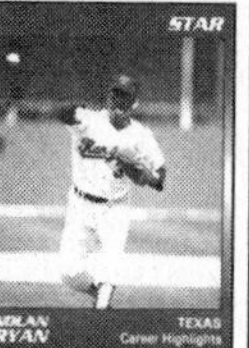

This 12-card standard-size set was issued by Star Co. in honor of Texas Rangers' pitching ace Nolan Ryan. The cards have on the fronts a mix of action and non-action color shots, with blue borders and white lettering. The horizontally oriented backs are in blue print and have player information.

	Nm-Mt	Ex-Mt
COMPLETE SET (11)	10.00	3.00
COMMON CARD (1-11)	1.00	.30

1990 Star Saberhagen/Davis

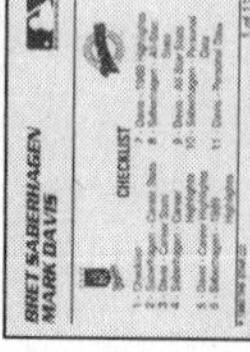

Bret Saberhagen and Mark Davis won their respective leagues Cy Young award in 1989. The Star Company than issued an 11-card standard-size set to honor these pitcher. Other than the first card, either Davis or Saberhagen appears on the card and we have noted who is portrayed on the card.

	Nm-Mt	Ex-Mt
COMPLETE SET (11)	3.00	.90
COMMON DAVIS (1-11)	.25	.07
COMMON SABERHAGEN	.50	.15
1 Bret Saberhagen Mark Davis CL	.30	.09

1990 Star Sandberg

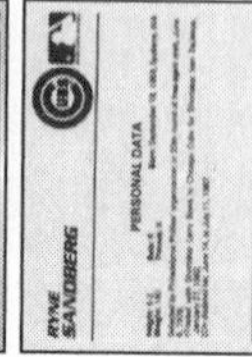

This 11-card standard-size set features highlights from the career of Chicago Cub second baseman Ryne Sandberg. These cards trace Sandberg's career from its earliest days through major league stardom.

	Nm-Mt	Ex-Mt
COMPLETE SET (11)	5.00	1.50
COMMON CARD (1-11)	.50	.15

1990 Star Yount

This 11-card standard-size set features highlights from the career of long-time Milwaukee Brewers star Robin Yount. These cards cover some of the best moments from

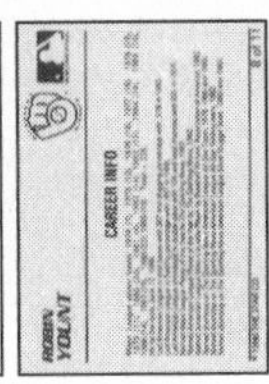

his major league career. The set is dated by the 1990 copyright on the back.

Nm-Mt Ex-Mt
COMPLETE SET (11)................. 5.00 1.50
COMMON CARD (1-11)................ .50 .15

1991 Star Belle Rookie Guild

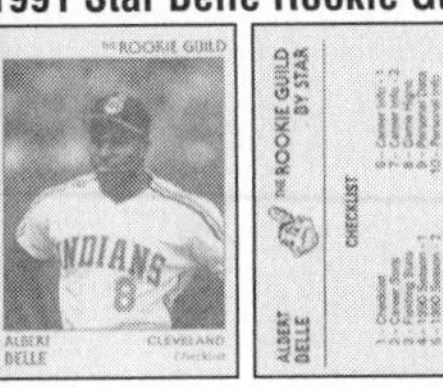
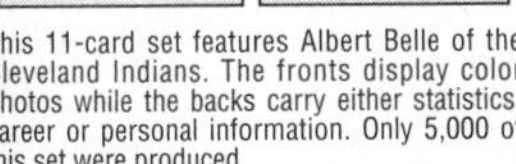

This 11-card set features Albert Belle of the Cleveland Indians. The fronts display color photos while the backs carry either statistics, career or personal information. Only 5,000 of this set were produced.

Nm-Mt Ex-Mt
COMPLETE SET (11)................. 5.00 1.50
COMMON CARD (1-11)................ .50 .15

1991 Star Gonzalez Rookie Guild

This 11-card set features Juan Gonzalez of the Texas Rangers. The fronts display color photos while the backs carry either statistics, career or personal information. Only 5,000 of this set were produced.

Nm-Mt Ex-Mt
COMPLETE SET (11)................. 5.00 1.50
COMMON CARD (1-11)................ .50 .15

1991 Star Griffeys

Both Ken Griffey Sr. and Ken Griffey Jr. are featured in this set. Only the first card in the set features both Griffeys. Otherwise, we have listed only which Griffey is pictured on the card.

Nm-Mt Ex-Mt
COMPLETE SET (11)................. 8.00 2.40
COMMON GRIFFEY SR (1-11)....... .40 .12
COMMON GRIFFEY JR............... 1.50 .45
1 Ken Griffey Jr......................... 1.00 .30
Ken Griffey Sr. CL

1991 Star Rickey Henderson

The only difference with this set as opposed to the 1990 Star Rickey Henderson set is the copyright date on the back. These cards are dated with a 1991 copyright.

Nm-Mt Ex-Mt
COMPLETE SET (11)................. 6.00 1.80
COMMON CARD (1-11)................ .75 .23

1991 Star Lewis Rookie Guild

This 11-card set features Mark Lewis of the Cleveland Indians. The fronts display color photos while the backs carry either statistics, career or personal information. Only 5,000 of this set were produced.

Nm-Mt Ex-Mt
COMPLETE SET (11)................. 4.00 1.20
COMMON CARD (1-11)................ .40 .12

1991 Star Ryan

This 11-card set was issued by Star Co. in honor of Texas Rangers' pitching ace Nolan Ryan. The fronts feature a mix of action and non-action color photos, with red-and-gray borders. The backs carry player information printed in red.

Nm-Mt Ex-Mt
COMPLETE SET (11)................. 8.00 2.40
COMMON CARD (1-11)................ .75 .23

1991 Star Strawberry

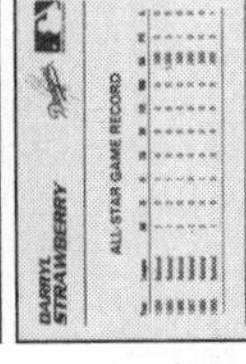

This 11-card standard-size set features outfielder Darryl Strawberry. This set can be dated to 1991 by his appearence as an Los Angeles Dodger.

Nm-Mt Ex-Mt
COMPLETE SET (11)................. 4.00 1.20
COMMON CARD (1-11)................ .40 .12

1991 Star Thomas Rookie Guild

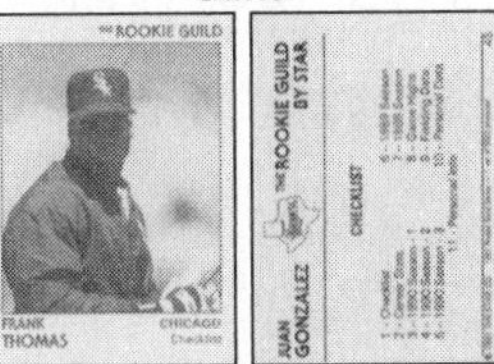

This 11-card set features Frank Thomas of the Chicago White Sox. The fronts display color photos while the backs carry either statistics, career or personal information. Only 5,000 of this set were produced.

Nm-Mt Ex-Mt
COMPLETE SET (11)................. 8.00 2.40
COMMON CARD (1-11)................ .75 .23

1992 Star Promos

These 11 standard-size cards were issued separately. The purpose of these cards was to promote some upcoming 1992 Star Company issues.

Nm-Mt Ex-Mt
COMPLETE SET (11)................ 20.00 6.00
1 Roberto Alomar...................... 2.50 .75
2 Steve Avery .... 1.00 .30
3 Jeff Bagwell............................ 3.00 .90
4 Rickey Henderson .... 3.00 .90
5 Eric Karros.............................. 2.00 .60
6 Kevin Maas............................. 1.00 .30
7 Don Mattingly.......................... 5.00 1.50
8 Benito Santiago .... 1.50 .45
9 Darryl Strawberry.................... 1.50 .45
10 Frank Thomas 4.00 1.20
11 Jerome Walton...................... 1.00 .30

1992 Star Avery

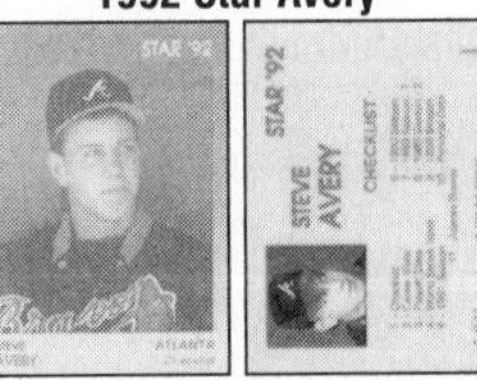

This 11-card standard-size set features Atlanta Braves pitcher Steve Avery. These cards were issued after Avery's sensational post season pitching efforts. These cards trace Avery's career from its beginnings to major league stardom.

Nm-Mt Ex-Mt
COMPLETE SET (11)................. 4.00 1.20
COMMON CARD (1-11)................ .40 .12

1992 Star Bagwell

These 11 standard-size cards feature Houston Astros star player Jeff Bagwell. These cards trace Bagwell's career from his minor league days through his rookie season.

Nm-Mt Ex-Mt
COMPLETE SET (11)................. 5.00 1.50
COMMON CARD (1-11)................ .50 .15

1992 Star Belle

Cleveland Indians outfielder Albert Belle is featured in this 11-card standard-size set. These cards take Belle's career from his earliest days to the present day.

Nm-Mt Ex-Mt
COMPLETE SET (11)................. 5.00 1.50
COMMON CARD (1-11)................ .50 .15

1992 Star Will Clark

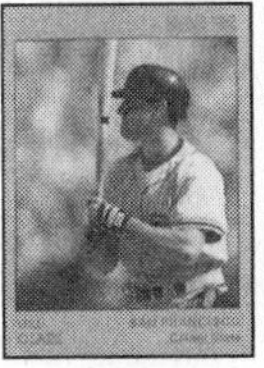
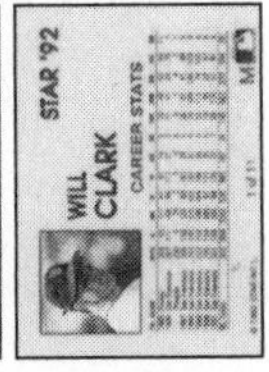

These 11 standard-size cards feature San Francisco Giants first baseman Will Clark. Clark's career is traced from its earliest days through the present day. These cards are dated by the 1992 copyright on the back.

Nm-Mt Ex-Mt
COMPLETE SET (11)................. 5.00 1.50
COMMON CARD (1-11)................ .50 .15

1992 Star Gant

These 11 standard-sized cards feature outfielder Ron Gant. These cards are dated by the 1992 copyright on the back. These cards trace Gant's career from his minor league days to the present.

Nm-Mt Ex-Mt
COMPLETE SET (11)................. 4.00 1.20
COMMON CARD (1-11)................ .40 .12

1992 Star Griffey Jr.

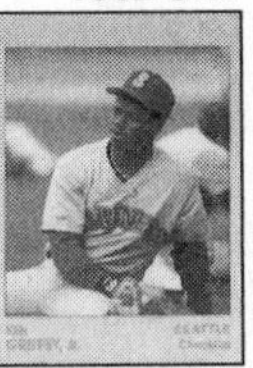
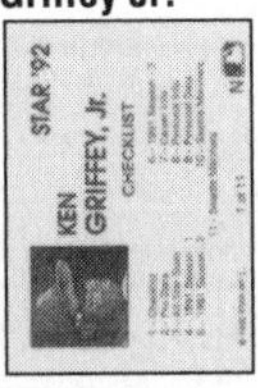

This set, like many others issued, feature Ken Griffey Jr. These 11 standard-sized cards take the collector through various highlights of Griffey's career.

Nm-Mt Ex-Mt
COMPLETE SET (11)................ 10.00 3.00
COMMON CARD (1-11)................ 1.00 .30

1992 Star Bo Jackson

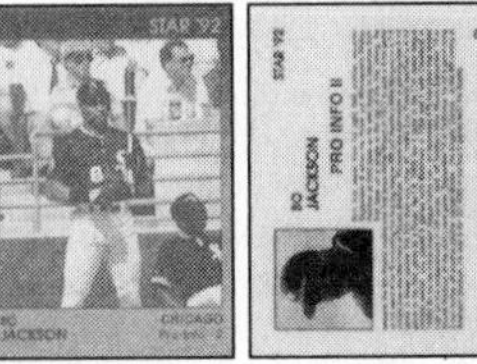

These 11 standard-size cards feature two sport star Bo Jackson. These cards basically cover only Bo's baseball career.

Nm-Mt Ex-Mt
COMPLETE SET (11)................. 4.00 1.20
COMMON CARD (1-11)................ .40 .12

1992 Star Justice

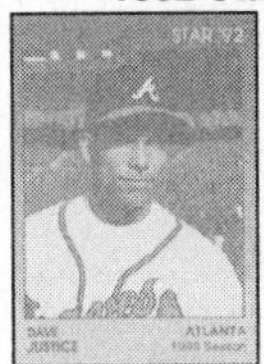

This is another set issued by Star Company about David Justice. These cards are differentiated from the first set as it had different cards as well as a 1992 copyright date.

Nm-Mt Ex-Mt
COMPLETE SET (11)................. 4.00 1.20
COMMON CARD (1-11)................ .40 .12

1992 Star Knoblauch

Chuck Knoblauch, second baseman for the Minnesota Twins is featured in this set. These 11 standard-size cards take the collector from his earliest playing days to the present day.

Nm-Mt Ex-Mt
COMPLETE SET (11)................. 5.00 1.50
COMMON CARD (1-11)................ .50 .15

1992 Star Palmer

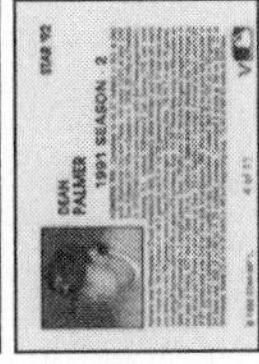

Dean Palmer, young third baseman for the Texas Rangers is featured in this set. These 11 standard-size cards take Palmer's career from its beginning to the present day.

Nm-Mt Ex-Mt
COMPLETE SET (11)................. 4.00 1.20
COMMON CARD (1-11)................ .40 .12

1992 Star Plantier

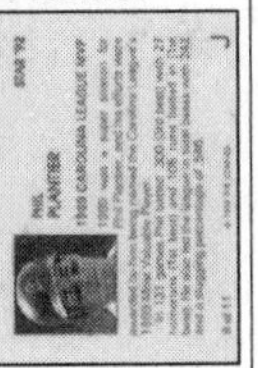

As the 1991 season ended Phil Plantier was one of the hottest players in the game. To take advantage of his popularity, Star Company issued this 11 card standard-size set featuring highlights from Plantier's career.

Nm-Mt Ex-Mt
COMPLETE SET (11)................. 3.00 .90
COMMON CARD (1-11)................ .30 .09

1992 Star Puckett

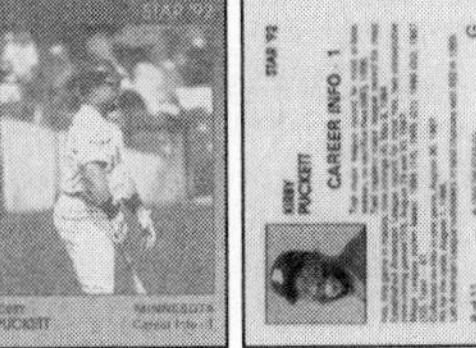

This 1992 Star Kirby Puckett set consists of 11 standard-sized cards. These cards are broken down by subject and pertain to various highlights in his career. The set is dated by the 1992 copyright on the back.

Nm-Mt Ex-Mt
COMPLETE SET (11)................. 5.00 1.50
COMMON CARD (1-11)................ .50 .15

1992 Star Sandberg

These 11 standard-size cards feature highlights in the career of Cubs second baseman Ryne Sandberg. These cards trace his career from his earliest days through the present.

Nm-Mt Ex-Mt
COMPLETE SET (11)................. 5.00 1.50
COMMON CARD (1-11)................ .50 .15

1992 Star Tartabull

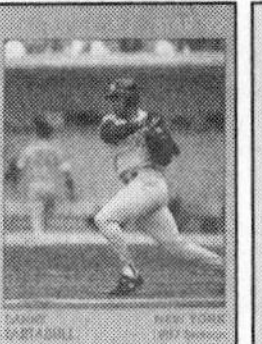
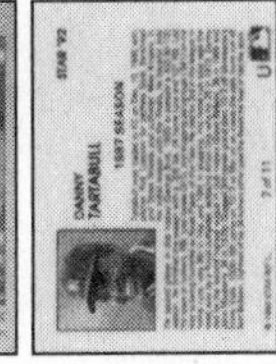

Danny Tartabull is featured in this 11-card standard-size set. These cards trace Tartabull's career from its beginnings to the present day. The set is dated by the 1992 copyright on the back. Also, Star Company sets are usually sold in complete set form.

Nm-Mt Ex-Mt
COMPLETE SET (11)................. 3.00 .90
COMMON CARD (1-11)................ .30 .09

1992 Star Van Poppel

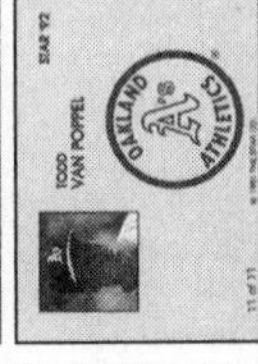

The 1992 Star Todd Van Poppel card set consists of 11 standard-size cards. The fronts display color action shots of Van Poppel with a border that fades from green to gray. The card title is printed in green lettering at the lower right corner. The horizontal backs are yellow with green lettering. In the upper left corner is a color head shot photo of Van Poppel. The backs also contain career statistics, 1990 highlights and biography.

Nm-Mt Ex-Mt
COMPLETE SET (10)................. 2.00 .60
COMMON CARD (1-10)................ .25 .07

1993 Star Autographs

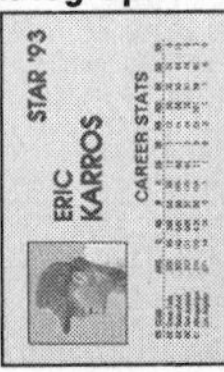

These cards features players on 1993 Star cards which have been autographed. The card features a Certificate of Authenticity issued by Star.

Nm-Mt Ex-Mt
COMPLETE SET 8.00 2.40
1 Andy Benes 4.00 1.20
2 Eric Karros 5.00 1.50

1995 Star Ripken 80

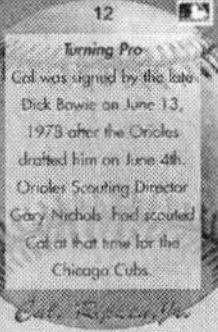

This 80-card set commemorates the 2,131 Consecutive Games Played Record set by Cal Ripken Jr. The fronts feature color action pictures of Ripken while the backs carry facts about his career.

Nm-Mt Ex-Mt
COMPLETE SET (80)................ 10.00 3.00
COMMON CARD (1-80)................ .15 .04

1995 Star Ripken 110

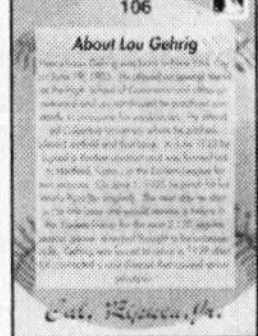

This 110-card standard-size set came in its own special box. These cards are basically an update of the previously issued 80-card set issued earlier in the year. Please note that these cards have glossy fronts and discuss highlights of Cal's career. The backs provide either statistical or factual information.

Nm-Mt Ex-Mt
COMPLETE SET 25.00 7.50
COMMON CARD.......................... .25 .07

1928 Star Player Candy E-Unc.

This 72-card set is presumed to have been inserts to a candy box named "Star Player Candy." The cards are sepia colored and measure approximately 1 7/8" by 2 7/8" with blank backs. The fronts feature full length action shots except for Card number 1 which is a portrait. The player's name is printed in brown capital letters in the bottom border. The pictures used appear to be unique and cannot be found on other sets.

	Ex-Mt	VG
COMPLETE SET (72)	10000.00	5000.00
1 Dave Bancroft	120.00	60.00
2 Emile Barnes	60.00	30.00
3 Lu Blue	60.00	30.00
4 Garland Buckeye	60.00	30.00
5 George Burns	60.00	30.00
6 Guy Bush	60.00	30.00
7 Owen Carroll	60.00	30.00
8 Bud Cissell	60.00	30.00
9 Ty Cobb	1500.00	750.00
10 Mickey Cochrane	120.00	60.00
11 Richard Coffman	60.00	30.00
12 Eddie Collins	200.00	100.00
13 Stan Coveleskie	120.00	60.00
14 Hugh Critz	60.00	30.00
15 Kiki Cuyler	120.00	60.00
16 Chuck Dressen	80.00	40.00
17 Joe Dugan	80.00	40.00
18 Woody English	60.00	30.00
19 Bibb Falk	60.00	30.00
20 Ira Flagstead	60.00	30.00
21 Bob Fothergill	60.00	30.00
22 Frank Frisch	120.00	60.00
23 Foster Ganzel	60.00	30.00
24 Lou Gehrig	1500.00	750.00
25 Charley Gehringer	120.00	60.00
26 George Gerken	60.00	30.00
27 Grant Gillis	60.00	30.00
28 Mike Gonzales	60.00	30.00
29 Sam Gray	60.00	30.00
30 Charlie Grimm	100.00	50.00
31 Lefty Grove	250.00	125.00
32 Chick Hafey	120.00	60.00
33 Jesse Haines	120.00	60.00
34 Gabby Hartnett	120.00	60.00
35 Clifton Heathcote	60.00	30.00
36 Harry Heilmann	120.00	60.00
37 John Heving	60.00	30.00
38 Waite Hoyt	120.00	60.00
39 Charles Jamieson	60.00	30.00
40 Joe Judge	60.00	30.00
41 Willie Kamm	60.00	30.00
42 George Kelly	120.00	60.00
43 Tony Lazzeri	120.00	60.00
44 Adolfo Luque	100.00	50.00
45 Ted Lyons	120.00	60.00
46 Hugh McMullen	60.00	30.00
47 Bob Meusel	100.00	50.00
48 Wilcy Moore	60.00	30.00
49 Ed Morgan	60.00	30.00
50 Herb Pennock	120.00	60.00
51 Everett Purdy	60.00	30.00
52 William Regan	60.00	30.00
53 Eppa Rixey	120.00	60.00
54 Charles Root	60.00	30.00
55 Jack Rothrock	60.00	30.00
56 Muddy Ruel	60.00	30.00
57 Babe Ruth	2000.00	1000.00
58 Wally Schang	60.00	30.00
59 Joe Sewell	120.00	60.00
60 Luke Sewell	60.00	30.00
61 Joe Shaute	60.00	30.00
62 George Sisler	200.00	100.00
63 Tris Speaker	250.00	125.00
64 Riggs Stephenson	100.00	50.00
65 Jack Tavener	60.00	30.00
66 Al Thomas	60.00	30.00
67 Pie Traynor	120.00	60.00
68 George Uhle	60.00	30.00
69 Dazzy Vance	120.00	60.00
70 Cy Williams	80.00	40.00
71 Ken Williams	80.00	40.00
72 Hack Wilson	120.00	60.00

1983 Stargell Junior Watson Dinner

This one card set featured retired Pirate great Willie Stargell and was handed out at the Junior Watson dinner. The front has black borders and features a head shot of Stargell. The horizontal back has career statistics.

	Nm-Mt	Ex-Mt
1 Willie Stargell	5.00	2.00

1990 Starline Long John Silver

The 1990 Starline Long John Silver set was issued over an eight-week promotion, five cards at a time within a cello pack. The set was initially available only through the Long John Silver seafood fast-food chain with one pack being given to each customer who ordered a meal with a 32-ounce Coke. This 40-card, standard-size set featured the best of today's players. There are several cards for some of the players in the set. After the promotion at Long John Silver had been completed, there were reportedly more than 100,000 sets left over that were released into the organized hobby.

	Nm-Mt	Ex-Mt
COMPLETE SET (40)	6.00	1.80
1 Don Mattingly	.75	.23
2 Mark Grace	.30	.09
3 Eric Davis	.10	.03
4 Tony Gwynn	.75	.23
5 Bobby Bonilla	.05	.02
6 Wade Boggs	.40	.12
7 Frank Viola	.05	.02
8 Ruben Sierra	.10	.03
9 Mark McGwire	1.25	.35
10 Alan Trammell	.20	.06
11 Mark McGwire	1.25	.35
12 Gregg Jefferies	.05	.02
13 Nolan Ryan	1.50	.45
14 John Smoltz	.10	.03
15 Glenn Davis	.05	.02
16 Mark Grace	.30	.09
17 Wade Boggs	.40	.12
18 Frank Viola	.05	.02
19 Bret Saberhagen	.10	.03
20 Chris Sabo	.05	.02
21 Darryl Strawberry	.10	.03
22 Wade Boggs	.40	.12
23 Tim Raines	.10	.03
24 Alan Trammell	.20	.06
25 Chris Sabo	.05	.02
26 Nolan Ryan	1.50	.45
27 Mark McGwire	1.25	.35
28 Don Mattingly	.75	.23
29 Tony Gwynn	.75	.23
30 Glenn Davis	.05	.02
31 Bobby Bonilla	.05	.02
32 Gregg Jefferies	.05	.02
33 Ruben Sierra	.10	.03
34 John Smoltz	.10	.03
35 Don Mattingly	.75	.23
36 Bret Saberhagen	.10	.03
37 Darryl Strawberry	.10	.03
38 Eric Davis	.10	.03
39 Tim Raines	.10	.03
40 Mark Grace	.30	.09

1991 Starline Prototypes

This five-card set measures approximately 2 11/16" by 3 11/16". Sixty of each card were produced and submitted to Major League Baseball for approval to be offered to prospective sponsors.The cards are unnumbered and checklisted below in alphabetical order.

	Nm-Mt	Ex-Mt
COMPLETE SET (5)	200.00	60.00
1 George Bell	25.00	7.50
2 Bobby Bonilla	25.00	7.50
3 Roger Clemens	100.00	30.00
4 Tim Raines	30.00	9.00
5 Darryl Strawberry	30.00	9.00

1988 Starting Lineup All-Stars

This set measures approximately 2 5/8" by 3" and were included in the Starting Lineup game. The fronts have a player photo while the back has recent seasonal stats and some personal information.

	Nm-Mt	Ex-Mt
COMPLETE SET (39)	25.00	10.00
1 Buddy Bell	.30	.12
2 George Bell	.20	.08
3 Wade Boggs	.75	.30
4 George Brett	2.00	.80
5 Gary Carter	.75	.30
6 Jack Clark	.30	.12
7 Roger Clemens	2.00	.80
8 Eric Davis	.30	.12
9 Jody Davis	.20	.08
10 Andre Dawson	.50	.20
11 Carlton Fisk	.75	.30
12 Dwight Gooden	.30	.12
13 Tony Gwynn	2.00	.80
14 Rickey Henderson	1.00	.40
15 Keith Hernandez	.30	.12
16 Terry Kennedy	.20	.08
17 Don Mattingly	3.00	1.20
18 Jack Morris	.30	.12
19 Dale Murphy	.40	.16
20 Eddie Murray	.75	.30
21 Kirby Puckett	1.00	.40
22 Dan Quisenberry	.20	.08
23 Tim Raines	.30	.12
24 Willie Randolph	.20	.08
25 Dave Righetti	.20	.08
26 Cal Ripken	4.00	1.60
27 Nolan Ryan	4.00	1.60
28 Ryne Sandberg	1.50	.60
29 Steve Sax	.20	.08
30 Mike Schmidt	1.00	.40
31 Mike Scott	.20	.08
32 Ozzie Smith	1.00	.40
33 Darryl Strawberry	.30	.12
34 Fernando Valenzuela	.30	.12
35 Lou Whitaker	.30	.12
36 Dave Winfield	.75	.30
37 Todd Worrell	.20	.08
38 Robin Yount	.75	.30
39 Game card and Help 2	.20	.08

1988 Starting Lineup Angels

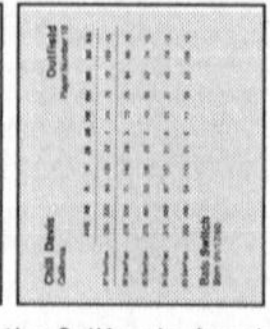

This 21-card set of the California Angels measures approximately 2 5/8" by 3" and features colored drawings of the players on the fronts while the backs carry the player's statistics. The cards are unnumbered and checklisted below in alphabetical order.

	Nm-Mt	Ex-Mt
COMPLETE SET (21)	5.00	2.00
1 Bob Boone	.40	.16
2 Bill Buckner	.30	.12
3 DeWayne Buice	.20	.08
4 Chili Davis	.40	.16
5 Brian Downing	.20	.08
6 Chuck Finley	.50	.20
7 Willie Frasier	.20	.08
8 George Hendrick	.20	.08
9 Jack Howell	.20	.08
10 Ruppert Jones	.20	.08
11 Wally Joyner	.50	.20
12 Kirk McCaskill	.20	.08
13 Mark McLemore	.30	.12
14 Darrell Miller	.20	.08
15 Greg Minton	.20	.08
16 Gary Pettis	.20	.08
17 Johnny Ray	.20	.08
18 Dick Schofield	.20	.08
19 Devon White	.50	.20
20 Mike Witt	.20	.08
21 Team Checklist	.20	.08

1988 Starting Lineup A's

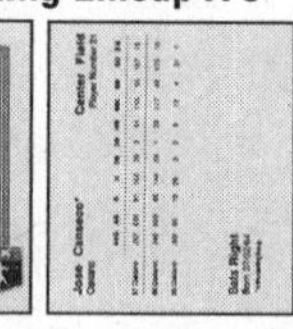

This 21-card set of the Oakland A's measures approximately 2 5/8" by 3" and features colored drawings of the players on the fronts while the backs carry the player's statistics. The cards are unnumbered and checklisted below in alphabetical order.

	Nm-Mt	Ex-Mt
COMPLETE SET (21)	8.00	3.20
1 Tony Bernazard	.20	.08
2 Jose Canseco	1.50	.60
3 Mike Davis	.20	.08
4 Dennis Eckersley	.75	.30
5 Mike Gallego	.20	.08
6 Alfredo Griffin	.20	.08
7 Dave Henderson	.20	.08
8 Reggie Jackson	.75	.30
9 Carney Lansford	.30	.12
10 Mark McGwire	4.00	1.60
11 Steve Ontiveros	.20	.08
12 Dave Parker	.40	.16
13 Tony Phillips	.20	.08
14 Luis Polonia	.20	.08
15 Terry Steinbach	.30	.12
16 Dave Stewart	.40	.16
17 Mickey Tettleton	.30	.12
18 Bob Welch	.30	.12
19 Curt Young	.20	.08
20 Matt Young	.20	.08
21 Team Checklist	.20	.08

1988 Starting Lineup Astros

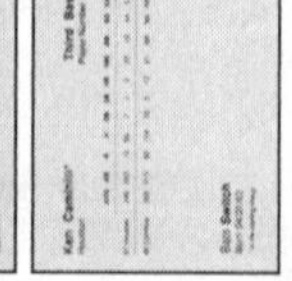

These cards feature members of the 1988 Houston Astros. These cards measure approximately 2 5/8" by 3" and have player photos on the front. The backs have recent seasonal statistics and some personal information. Ken Caminiti is featured in his Rookie Card season.

	Nm-Mt	Ex-Mt
COMPLETE SET (21)	10.00	4.00
1 Juan Agosto	.20	.08
2 Larry Andersen	.20	.08
3 Alan Ashby	.20	.08
4 Kevin Bass	.20	.08
5 Ken Caminiti	.75	.30
6 Jose Cruz	.30	.12
7 Danny Darwin	.20	.08
8 Glenn Davis	.20	.08
9 Bill Doran	.20	.08
10 Billy Hatcher	.20	.08
11 Jim Pankovitz	.20	.08
12 Terry Puhl	.20	.08
13 Rafael Ramirez	.20	.08
14 Craig Reynolds	.20	.08
15 Nolan Ryan	6.00	2.40
16 Mike Scott	.40	.16
17 Dave Smith	.20	.08
18 Marc Sullivan	.20	.08
19 Denny Walling	.20	.08
20 Gerald Young	.20	.08
21 Team Checklist	.20	.08

1988 Starting Lineup Blue Jays

These cards feature members of the 1988 Toronto Blue Jays. These cards measure approximately 2 5/8" by 3" and have player photos on the front. The backs have recent seasonal statistics and some personal information.

	Nm-Mt	Ex-Mt
COMPLETE SET (21)	5.00	2.00
1 Jesse Barfield	.30	.12
2 George Bell	.30	.12
3 Juan Beniquez	.20	.08
4 Jim Clancy	.20	.08
5 Mark Eichhorn	.20	.08
6 Tony Fernandez	.40	.16
7 Cecil Fielder	.50	.20
8 Tom Henke	.20	.08
9 Garth Iorg	.20	.08
10 Jimmy Key	.50	.20
11 Rick Leach	.20	.08
12 Manuel Lee	.20	.08
13 Nelson Liriano	.20	.08
14 Fred McGriff	1.50	.60
15 Lloyd Moseby	.20	.08
16 Rance Mulliniks	.20	.08
17 Jeff Musselman	.20	.08
18 Dave Stieb	.30	.12
19 Willie Upshaw	.20	.08
20 Ernie Whitt	.20	.08
21 Team Checklist	.20	.08

1988 Starting Lineup Braves

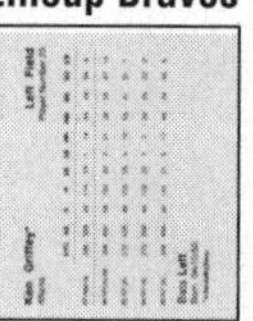

These cards feature members of the 1988 Atlanta Braves. These cards measure approximately 2 5/8" by 3" and have player photos on the front. The backs have recent seasonal statistics and some personal information. Jeff Blauser, Ron Gant and Tom Glavine are all featured in their Rookie Card season.

	Nm-Mt	Ex-Mt
COMPLETE SET (21)	8.00	3.20
1 Jim Acker	.20	.08
2 Paul Assenmacher	.20	.08
3 Jeff Blauser	.50	.20
4 Jeff Dedman	.20	.08
5 Ron Gant	.75	.30
6 Tom Glavine	3.00	1.20
7 Ken Griffey	.30	.12
8 Albert Hall	.20	.08
9 Glenn Hubbard	.20	.08
10 Dion James	.20	.08
11 Rick Mahler	.20	.08
12 Dale Murphy	.75	.30
13 Ken Oberkfell	.20	.08
14 Gerald Perry	.20	.08
15 Gary Roenicke	.20	.08
16 Paul Runge	.20	.08
17 Ted Simmons	.30	.12
18 Zane Smith	.20	.08
19 Andres Thomas	.20	.08
20 Ozzie Virgil	.20	.08
21 Team Checklist	.20	.08

1988 Starting Lineup Brewers

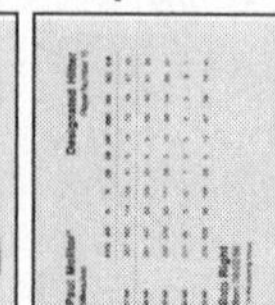

These cards feature members of the 1988 Milwaukee Brewers. These cards measure approximately 2 5/8" by 3" and have player photos on the front. The backs have recent seasonal statistics and some personal information.

	Nm-Mt	Ex-Mt
COMPLETE SET (21)	5.00	2.00
1 Chris Bosio	.20	.08
2 Glenn Braggs	.20	.08
3 Greg Brock	.20	.08
4 Juan Castillo	.20	.08
5 Chuck Crim	.20	.08
6 Rob Deer	.20	.08
7 Mike Felder	.20	.08
8 Jim Gantner	.20	.08
9 Ted Higuera	.20	.08
10 Steve Kiefer	.20	.08
11 Paul Molitor	1.00	.40
12 Juan Nieves	.20	.08
13 Dan Plesac	.20	.08
14 Ernest Riles	.20	.08
15 Billy Jo Robidoux	.20	.08
16 Bill Schroeder	.20	.08
17 B. J. Surhoff	.40	.16
18 Dale Sveum	.20	.08
19 Bill Wegman	.20	.08
20 Robin Yount	.75	.30
21 Team Checklist	.20	.08

1988 Starting Lineup Cardinals

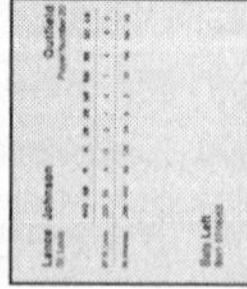

These cards feature members of the 1988 St. Louis Cardinals. These cards measure approximately 2 5/8" by 3" and have player photos on the front. The backs have recent seasonal statistics and some personal information.

	Nm-Mt	Ex-Mt
COMPLETE SET (21)	6.00	2.40
1 Rob Booker	.20	.08
2 Jack Clark	.30	.12
3 Vince Coleman	.30	.12
4 Danny Cox	.20	.08
5 Ken Dayley	.20	.08
6 Curt Ford	.20	.08
7 Tommy Herr	.20	.08
8 Bob Horner	.30	.12
9 Ricky Horton	.20	.08
10 Lance Johnson	.50	.20
11 Steve Lake	.20	.08
12 Jim Lindeman	.20	.08
13 Greg Mathews	.20	.08
14 Willie McGee	.50	.20
15 Jose Oquendo	.20	.08
16 Tony Pena	.30	.12
17 Terry Pendleton	.40	.16
18 Ozzie Smith	3.00	1.20
19 John Tudor	.20	.08
20 Todd Worrell	.30	.12
21 Team Checklist	.20	.08

1988 Starting Lineup Cubs

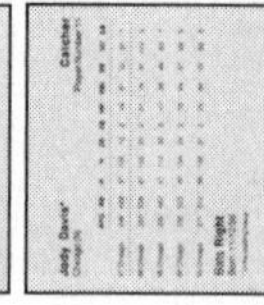

These cards feature members of the 1988 Chicago Cubs. These cards measure approximately 2 5/8" by 3" and have player photos on the front. The backs have recent seasonal statistics and some personal information.

	Nm-Mt	Ex-Mt
COMPLETE SET (14)	6.00	2.40
1 Jody Davis	.20	.08
2 Andre Dawson	.75	.30
3 Bob Dernier	.20	.08
4 Frank DiPino	.20	.08
5 Leon Durham	.20	.08
6 Dave Martinez	.20	.08
7 Keith Moreland	.20	.08
8 Jamie Moyer	.50	.20
9 Jerry Mumphrey	.20	.08
10 Ryne Sandberg	2.00	.80
11 Scott Sanderson	.20	.08
12 Calvin Schiraldi	.20	.08
13 Lee Smith	.40	.16
14 Jim Sundberg	.20	.08
15 Rick Sutcliffe	.30	.12
16 Manny Trillo	.20	.08

1988 Starting Lineup Dodgers

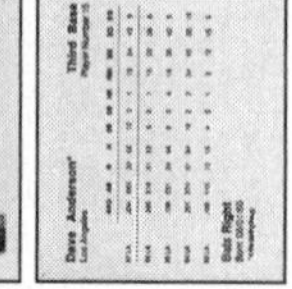

This 21-card set of the Los Angeles Dodgers measures approximately 2 5/8" by 3" and features colored drawings of the players on the fronts while the backs carry the player's statistics. The cards are unnumbered and checklisted below in alphabetical order.

	Nm-Mt	Ex-Mt
COMPLETE SET (21)	4.00	1.60
1 Dave Anderson	.20	.08
2 Mike Davis	.20	.08
3 Mariano Duncan	.20	.08
4 Kirk Gibson	.50	.20
5 Alfredo Griffin	.20	.08
6 Pedro Guerrero	.40	.16
7 Mickey Hatcher	.20	.08
8 Orel Hershiser	.50	.20
9 Glenn Hoffman	.20	.08
10 Brian Holton	.20	.08
11 Mike Marshall	.20	.08
12 Jesse Orosco	.30	.12
13 Alejandro Pena	.20	.08
14 Steve Sax	.40	.16
15 Mike Scioscia	.40	.16
16 John Shelby	.20	.08

17 Franklin Stubbs	.20	.08
18 Don Sutton	.50	.20
19 Alex Trevino	.20	.08
20 Fernando Valenzuela	.40	.16
21 Team Checklist	.20	.08

1988 Starting Lineup Expos

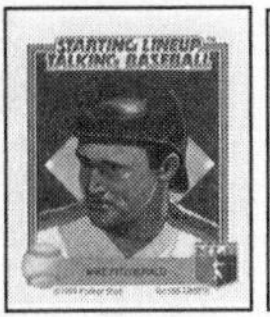
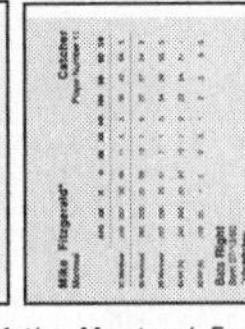

This 21-card set of the Montreal Expos measures approximately 2 5/8" by 3" and features colored drawings of the players on the fronts while the backs carry the player's statistics. The cards are unnumbered and checklisted below in alphabetical order.

	Nm-Mt	Ex-Mt
COMPLETE SET (21)	5.00	2.00
1 Hubie Brooks	.20	.08
2 Tim Burke	.20	.08
3 Casey Candaele	.20	.08
4 Mike Fitzgerald	.20	.08
5 Tom Foley	.20	.08
6 Andres Galarraga	.75	.30
7 Neal Heaton	.20	.08
8 Wallace Johnson	.20	.08
9 Vance Law	.20	.08
10 Bob McClure	.20	.08
11 Andy McGaffigan	.20	.08
12 Alonzo Powell	.20	.08
13 Tim Raines	.50	.20
14 Jeff Reed	.20	.08
15 Luis Rivera	.20	.08
16 Bryn Smith	.20	.08
17 Tim Wallach	.30	.12
18 Mitch Webster	.20	.08
19 Herm Winningham	.20	.08
20 Floyd Youmans	.20	.08
21 Team Checklist	.20	.08

1988 Starting Lineup Giants

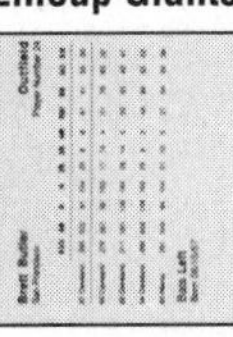

These cards feature members of the 1988 San Francisco Giants. These cards measure approximately 2 5/8" by 3" and have player photos on the front. The backs have recent seasonal statistics and some personal information. An early card of Matt Williams is included in this set.

	Nm-Mt	Ex-Mt
COMPLETE SET (21)	8.00	3.20
1 Mike Aldrete	.20	.08
2 Bob Brenly	.30	.12
3 Brett Butler	.30	.12
4 Will Clark	1.50	.60
5 Chili Davis	.40	.16
6 Dave Dravecky	.30	.12
7 Scott Garrelts	.20	.08
8 Atlee Hammaker	.20	.08
9 Craig Lefferts	.20	.08
10 Jeffrey Leonard	.20	.08
11 Candy Maldonado	.20	.08
12 Bob Melvin	.30	.12
13 Kevin Mitchell	.30	.12
14 Rick Reuschel	.30	.12
15 Don Robinson	.20	.08
16 Chris Speier	.20	.08
17 Harry Spilman	.20	.08
18 Robby Thompson	.20	.08
19 Jose Uribe	.20	.08
20 Matt Williams	2.00	.80
21 Team Checklist	.20	.08

1988 Starting Lineup Indians

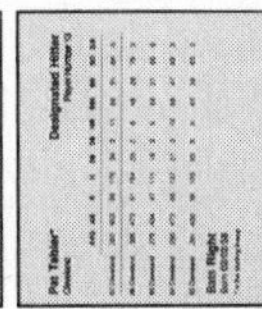

This 21-card set of the Cleveland Indians measures approximately 2 5/8" by 3" and features colored drawings of the players on the fronts while the backs carry the player's statistics. The cards are unnumbered and checklisted below in alphabetical order.

	Nm-Mt	Ex-Mt
COMPLETE SET (21)	5.00	2.00
1 Andy Allanson	.20	.08
2 Scott Bailes	.20	.08
3 Chris Bando	.20	.08
4 Jay Bell	.50	.20
5 Brett Butler	.30	.12
6 Tom Candiotti	.20	.08
7 Joe Carter	.75	.30
8 Carmen Castillo	.20	.08
9 Dave Clark	.20	.08
10 John Farrell	.20	.08
11 Julio Franco	.30	.12
12 Mel Hall	.20	.08
13 Tommy Hinzo	.20	.08
14 Brook Jacoby	.20	.08
15 Doug Jones	.20	.08
16 Junior Noboa	.20	.08
17 Ken Schrom	.20	.08
18 Cory Snyder	.20	.08
19 Greg Swindell	.20	.08
20 Pat Tabler	.20	.08
21 Team Checklist	.20	.08

1988 Starting Lineup Mariners

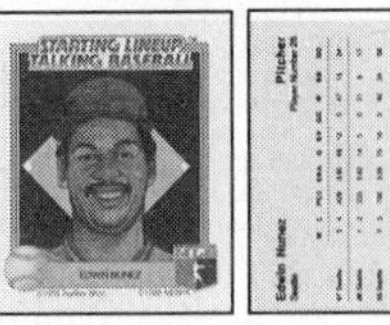

This 21-card set of the Seattle Mariners measures approximately 2 5/8" by 3" and features colored drawings of the players on the fronts while the backs carry the player's statistics. The cards are unnumbered and checklisted below in alphabetical order.

	Nm-Mt	Ex-Mt
COMPLETE SET (21)	4.00	1.60
1 Phil Bradley	.20	.08
2 Scott Bradley	.20	.08
3 Mickey Brantley	.20	.08
4 Mike Campbell	.20	.08
5 Henry Cotto	.20	.08
6 Alvin Davis	.30	.12
7 Mike Kingery	.20	.08
8 Mark Langston	.40	.16
9 Mike Moore	.20	.08
10 John Moses	.20	.08
11 Otis Nixon	.20	.08
12 Edwin Nunez	.20	.08
13 Ken Phelps	.20	.08
14 Jim Presley	.20	.08
15 Rey Quinones	.20	.08
16 Jerry Reed	.20	.08
17 Harold Reynolds	.30	.12
18 Dave Valle	.20	.08
19 Bill Wilkinson	.20	.08
20 Glenn Wilson	.20	.08
21 Team Checklist	.20	.08

1988 Starting Lineup Mets

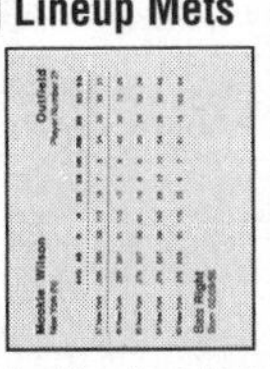

This 21-card set of the New York Mets measures approximately 2 5/8" by 3" and features colored drawings of the players on the fronts while the backs carry the player's statistics. The cards are unnumbered and checklisted below in alphabetical order.

	Nm-Mt	Ex-Mt
COMPLETE SET (21)	5.00	2.00
1 Bill Almon	.20	.08
2 Wally Backman	.20	.08
3 Gary Carter	.75	.30
4 Dave Cone	1.00	.40
5 Ron Darling	.30	.12
6 Len Dykstra	.40	.16
7 Sid Fernandez	.30	.12
8 Dwight Gooden	.50	.20
9 Keith Hernandez	.40	.16
10 Howard Johnson	.30	.12
11 Barry Lyons	.20	.08
12 Dave Magadan	.20	.08
13 Lee Mazzilli	.30	.12
14 Roger McDowell	.20	.08
15 Kevin McReynolds	.30	.12
16 Jesse Orosco	.30	.12
17 Rafael Santana	.20	.08
18 Darryl Strawberry	.50	.20
19 Tim Teufel	.20	.08
20 Mookie Wilson	.30	.12
21 Team Checklist	.20	.08

1988 Starting Lineup Orioles

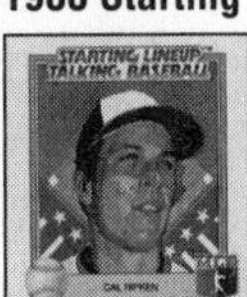

This 21-card set of the Baltimore Orioles measures approximately 2 5/8" by 3" and features colored drawings of the players on the fronts while the backs carry the player's statistics. The cards are unnumbered and checklisted below in alphabetical order.

	Nm-Mt	Ex-Mt
COMPLETE SET (21)	8.00	3.20
1 Eric Bell	.20	.08
2 Mike Boddicker	.20	.08
3 Jim Dwyer	.20	.08
4 Ken Gerhart	.20	.08
5 Rene Gonzales	.20	.08
6 Terry Kennedy	.20	.08
7 Ray Knight	.20	.08
8 Lee Lacy	.20	.08
9 Fred Lynn	.40	.16
10 Eddie Murray	1.00	.40
11 Tom Niedenfuer	.20	.08
12 Billy Ripken	.20	.08
13 Cal Ripken	5.00	2.00
14 Dave Schmidt	.20	.08
15 Larry Sheets	.20	.08
16 Steve Stanicek	.20	.08
17 Mark Thurmond	.20	.08
18 Ron Washington	.20	.08
19 Mark Williamson	.20	.08
20 Mike Young	.20	.08
21 Team Checklist	.20	.08

1988 Starting Lineup Padres

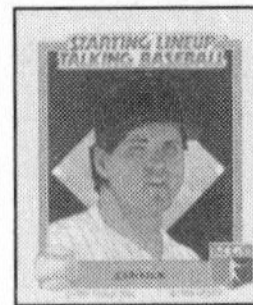
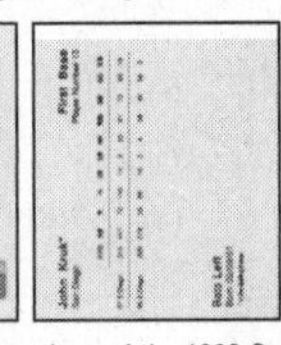

These cards feature members of the 1988 San Diego Padres. These cards measure approximately 2 5/8" by 3" and have player photos on the front. The backs have recent seasonal statistics and some personal information. Roberto Alomar has a card in his rookie season in this set.

	Nm-Mt	Ex-Mt
COMPLETE SET	8.00	3.20
1 Shawn Abner	.20	.08
2 Roberto Alomar	3.00	1.20
3 Chris Brown	.20	.08
4 Joey Cora	.20	.08
5 Mark Davis	.20	.08
6 Tim Flannery	.20	.08
7 Goose Gossage	.40	.16
8 Mark Grant	.20	.08
9 Tony Gwynn	3.00	1.20
10 Stan Jefferson	.20	.08
11 John Kruk	.50	.20
12 Shane Mack	.20	.08
13 Carmelo Martinez	.20	.08
14 Lance McCullers	.20	.08
15 Randy Ready	.20	.08
16 Benito Santiago	.30	.12
17 Eric Show	.20	.08
18 Ed Whitson	.20	.08
19 Marvell Wynne	.20	.08

1988 Starting Lineup Phillies

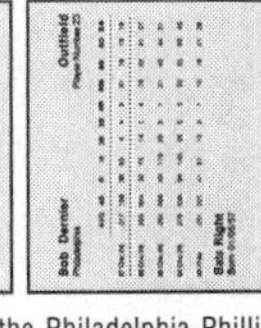

This 21-card set of the Philadelphia Phillies measures approximately 2 5/8" by 3" and features colored drawings of the players on the fronts while the backs carry the player's statistics. The cards are unnumbered and checklisted below in alphabetical order.

	Nm-Mt	Ex-Mt
COMPLETE SET (21)	5.00	2.00
1 Luis Aguayo	.20	.08
2 Steve Bedrosian	.20	.08
3 Phil Bradley	.20	.08
4 Jeff Calhoun	.20	.08
5 Don Carman	.20	.08
6 Darren Daulton	.50	.20
7 Bob Dernier	.20	.08
8 Greg Gross	.20	.08
9 Von Hayes	.20	.08
10 Chris James	.20	.08
11 Steve Jeltz	.20	.08
12 Lance Parrish	.30	.12
13 Shane Rawley	.20	.08
14 Bruce Ruffin	.20	.08
15 Juan Samuel	.20	.08
16 Mike Schmidt	1.50	.60
17 Rick Schu	.20	.08
18 Kent Tekulve	.30	.12
19 Milt Thompson	.20	.08
20 Glenn Wilson	.20	.08
21 Team Checklist	.20	.08

1988 Starting Lineup Pirates

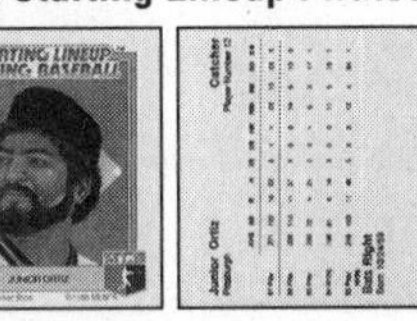

This 21-card set of the Pittsburgh Pirates measures approximately 2 5/8" by 3" and features colored drawings of the players on the fronts while the backs carry the player's statistics. The cards are unnumbered and checklisted below in alphabetical order.

	Nm-Mt	Ex-Mt
COMPLETE SET (21)	6.00	2.40
1 Rafael Belliard	.20	.08
2 Barry Bonds	3.00	1.20
3 Bobby Bonilla	.30	.12
4 Sid Bream	.20	.08
5 John Cangelosi	.20	.08
6 Darnell Coles	.20	.08
7 Mike Diaz	.20	.08
8 Doug Drabek	.30	.12
9 Mike Dunne	.20	.08
10 Felix Fermin	.20	.08
11 Brian Fisher	.20	.08
12 Jim Gott	.20	.08
13 Mike LaValliere	.20	.08
14 Jose Lind	.20	.08
15 Junior Ortiz	.20	.08
16 Al Pedrique	.20	.08
17 R.J. Reynolds	.20	.08
18 Jeff Robinson	.20	.08
19 John Smiley	.30	.12
20 Andy Van Slyke	.40	.16
21 Team Checklist	.20	.08

1988 Starting Lineup Rangers

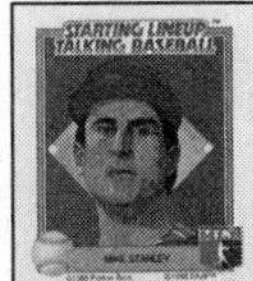
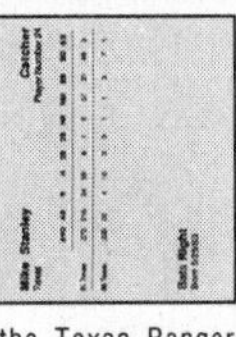

This 21-card set of the Texas Rangers measures approximately 2 5/8" by 3" and features colored drawings of the players on the fronts while the backs carry the player's statistics. The cards are unnumbered and checklisted below in alphabetical order.

	Nm-Mt	Ex-Mt
COMPLETE SET (21)	4.00	1.60
1 Bob Brower	.20	.08
2 Jerry Browne	.20	.08
3 Steve Buechele	.20	.08
4 Scott Fletcher	.20	.08
5 Jose Guzman	.20	.08
6 Charlie Hough	.30	.12
7 Pete Incaviglia	.30	.12
8 Oddibe McDowell	.20	.08
9 Dale Mohorcic	.20	.08
10 Pete O'Brien	.20	.08
11 Tom O'Malley	.20	.08
12 Larry Parrish	.20	.08
13 Geno Petralli	.20	.08
14 Jeff Russell	.20	.08
15 Ruben Sierra	.30	.12
16 Don Slaught	.20	.08
17 Mike Stanley	.20	.08
18 Curt Wilkerson	.20	.08
19 Mitch Williams	.30	.12
20 Bobby Witt	.30	.12
21 Title Card Batting Order	.20	.08

1988 Starting Lineup Red Sox

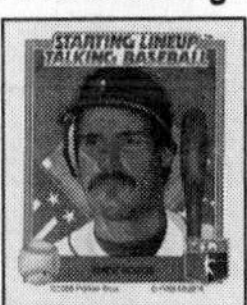
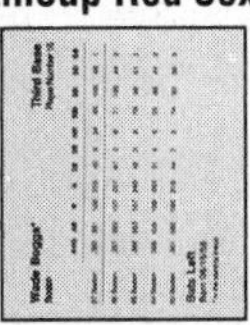

This 21-card set of the Boston Red Sox measures approximately 2 5/8" by 3" and features colored drawings of the players on the fronts while the backs carry the player's statistics. The cards are unnumbered and checklisted below in alphabetical order.

	Nm-Mt	Ex-Mt
COMPLETE SET (21)	6.00	2.40
1 Marty Barrett	.20	.08
2 Todd Benzinger	.20	.08
3 Wade Boggs	1.00	.40
4 Oil Can Boyd	.20	.08
5 Ellis Burks	.75	.30
6 Roger Clemens	3.00	1.20
7 Dwight Evans	.50	.20
8 Wes Gardner	.20	.08
9 Rich Gedman	.20	.08
10 Mike Greenwell	.30	.12
11 Sam Horn	.20	.08
12 Bruce Hurst	.20	.08
13 John Marzano	.20	.08
14 Spike Owen	.20	.08
15 Jody Reed	.20	.08
16 Jim Rice	.40	.16
17 Ed Romero	.20	.08
18 Kevin Romine	.20	.08
19 Lee Smith	.30	.12
20 Bob Stanley	.20	.08
21 Team Checklist	.20	.08

1988 Starting Lineup Reds

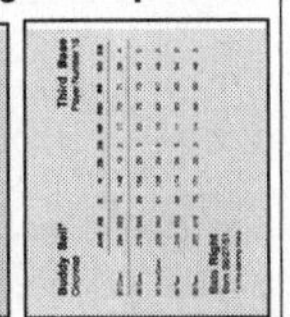

This 21-card set of the Cincinnati Reds measures approximately 2 5/8" by 3" and features colored drawings of the players on the fronts while the backs carry the player's statistics. The cards are unnumbered and checklisted below in alphabetical order.

	Nm-Mt	Ex-Mt
COMPLETE SET (21)	5.00	2.00
1 Buddy Bell	.30	.12
2 Tom Browning	.20	.08
3 Dave Collins	.20	.08
4 Dave Concepcion	.40	.16
5 Kal Daniels	.20	.08
6 Eric Davis	.50	.20
7 Bo Diaz	.20	.08
8 Nick Esasky	.20	.08
9 John Franco	.50	.20
10 Terry Francona	.30	.12
11 Tracy Jones	.20	.08
12 Barry Larkin	1.00	.40
13 Rob Murphy	.20	.08
14 Paul O'Neill	.50	.20
15 Dave Parker	.40	.16
16 Ted Power	.20	.08
17 Dennis Rasmussen	.20	.08
18 Kurt Stillwell	.20	.08
19 Jeff Treadway	.20	.08
20 Frank Williams	.20	.08
21 Team Checklist	.20	.08

1988 Starting Lineup Royals

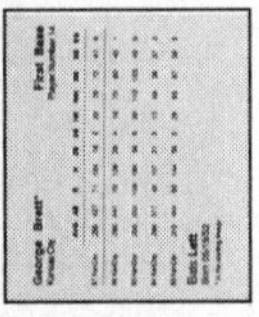

This 21-card set of the Kansas City Royals measures approximately 2 5/8" by 3" and features colored drawings of the players on the fronts while the backs carry the player's statistics. The cards are unnumbered and checklisted below in alphabetical order.

	Nm-Mt	Ex-Mt
COMPLETE SET (21)	6.00	2.40
1 Steve Balboni	.20	.08
2 George Brett	2.00	.80
3 Jim Eisenreich	.30	.12
4 Gene Garber	.30	.12
5 Jerry Don Gleaton	.20	.08
6 Mark Gubicza	.20	.08
7 Bo Jackson	.50	.20
8 Charlie Leibrandt	.20	.08
9 Mike MacFarlane	.20	.08
10 Larry Owen	.20	.08
11 Bill Pecota	.20	.08
12 Jamie Quirk	.20	.08
13 Dan Quisenberry	.30	.12
14 Bret Saberhagen	.40	.16
15 Kevin Seitzer	.30	.12
16 Kurt Stillwell	.20	.08
17 Danny Tartabull	.30	.12
18 Gary Thurman	.20	.08
19 Frank White	.30	.12
20 Willie Wilson	.30	.12
21 Team Checklist	.20	.08

1988 Starting Lineup Tigers

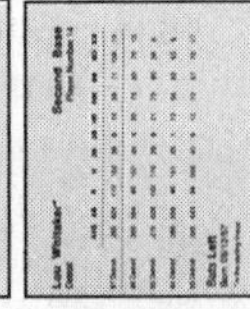

This 21-card set of the Detroit Tigers measures approximately 2 5/8" by 3" and features colored drawings of the players on the fronts while the backs carry the player's statistics. The cards are unnumbered and checklisted below in alphabetical order.

	Nm-Mt	Ex-Mt
COMPLETE SET (21)	5.00	2.00
1 Doyle Alexander	.20	.08
2 Dave Bergman	.20	.08
3 Tom Brookens	.20	.08
4 Darrell Evans	.30	.12
5 Kirk Gibson	.50	.20
6 Mike Heath	.20	.08
7 Mike Henneman	.40	.16
8 Guillermo"Willie" Hernandez	.20	.08
9 Larry Herndon	.20	.08
10 Eric King	.20	.08
11 Ray Knight	.20	.08
12 Chet Lemon	.20	.08
13 Bill Madlock	.30	.12
14 Jack Morris	.50	.20
15 Jim Morrison	.20	.08
16 Matt Nokes	.30	.12
17 Pat Sheridan	.20	.08
18 Frank Tanana	.30	.12
19 Alan Trammell	.75	.30
20 Lou Whitaker	.50	.20
21 Team Checklist	.20	.08

1988 Starting Lineup Twins

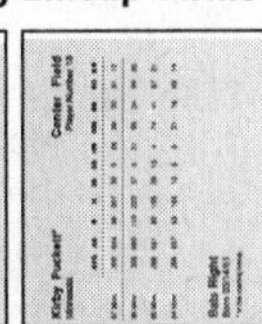

This 21-card set of the Minnesota Twins measures approximately 2 5/8" by 3" and features colored drawings of the players on the fronts while the backs carry the player's statistics. The cards are unnumbered and checklisted below in alphabetical order.

	Nm-Mt	Ex-Mt
COMPLETE SET (21)	5.00	2.00
1 Don Baylor	.30	.12
2 Juan Berenguer	.20	.08
3 Bert Blyleven	.40	.16
4 Tom Brunansky	.20	.08
5 Randy Bush	.20	.08
6 Mark Davidson	.20	.08
7 Gary Gaetti	.40	.16
8 Greg Gagne	.20	.08
9 Dan Gladden	.20	.08
10 Kent Hrbek	.50	.20
11 Gene Larkin	.30	.12
12 Tim Laudner	.20	.08
13 Steve Lombardozzi	.20	.08
14 Al Newman	.20	.08
15 Kirby Puckett	1.00	.40
16 Jeff Reardon	.30	.12
17 Dan Schatzeder	.20	.08
18 Roy Smalley	.20	.08
19 Les Straker	.20	.08
20 Frank Viola	.40	.16
21 Team Checklist	.20	.08

1988 Starting Lineup White Sox

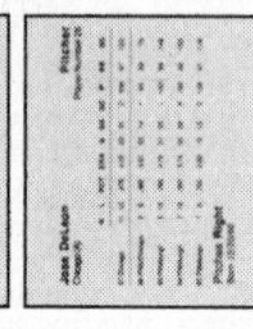

These cards feature members of the 1988 San Diego Padres. These cards measure approximately 2 5/8" by 3" and have player photos on the front. The backs have recent seasonal statistics and some personal information. The cards are unnumbered and checklisted below in alphabetical order.

	Nm-Mt	Ex-Mt
COMPLETE SET (21)	4.00	1.60
1 Harold Baines	.40	.16
2 Floyd Bannister	.20	.08
3 Daryl Boston	.20	.08
4 Ivan Calderon	.20	.08
5 Jose DeLeon	.20	.08
6 Rich Dotson	.20	.08
7 Carlton Fisk	1.00	.40
8 Ozzie Guillen	.40	.16
9 Jerry Hairston	.20	.08
10 Donnie Hill	.20	.08
11 Dave LaPoint	.20	.08
12 Steve Lyons	.30	.12
13 Fred Manrique	.20	.08
14 Dan Pasqua	.20	.08
15 Gary Redus	.20	.08
16 Mark Salas	.20	.08
17 Ray Searage	.20	.08
18 Bobby Thigpen	.20	.08
19 Greg Walker	.20	.08
20 Ken Williams	.40	.16
21 Team Checklist	.20	.08

1988 Starting Lineup Yankees

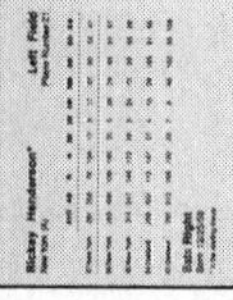

This 21-card set of the New York Yankees measures approximately 2 5/8" by 3" and features colored drawings of the players on the fronts while the backs carry the player's statistics. The cards are unnumbered and checklisted below in alphabetical order.

	Nm-Mt	Ex-Mt
COMPLETE SET (21)	6.00	2.40
1 Rick Cerone	.20	.08
2 Jack Clark	.30	.12
3 Pat Clements	.20	.08
4 Mike Easler	.20	.08
5 Ron Guidry	.40	.16
6 Rickey Henderson	1.50	.60
7 Tommy John	.40	.16
8 Don Mattingly	3.00	1.20
9 Bobby Meacham	.20	.08
10 Mike Pagliarulo	.20	.08
11 Willie Randolph	.30	.12
12 Rick Rhoden	.20	.08
13 Dave Righetti	.30	.12
14 Jerry Royster	.20	.08
15 Don Slaught	.20	.08
16 Tim Stoddard	.20	.08
17 Wayne Tolleson	.20	.08
18 Gary Ward	.20	.08
19 Claudell Washington	.20	.08
20 Dave Winfield	.75	.30
21 Team Checklist	.20	.08

1985 George Steinbrenner Menu

Issued in the mid 1980's these cards honored some all-time Yankee greats. These cards were issued to promote George Steinbrenner's restaurant in Tampa, Florida, spring training home of the New York Yankees. Steinbrenner has also been the Yankees owner for more than two decades.

	Nm-Mt	Ex-Mt
COMPLETE SET (8)	30.00	12.00
1 Yogi Berra	2.50	1.00
2 Lou Gehrig	5.00	2.00
3 Whitey Ford	2.50	1.00
4 Elston Howard	1.00	.40
5 Mickey Mantle	8.00	3.20
6 Roger Maris	4.00	1.60
7 Thurman Munson	2.00	.80
8 Babe Ruth	8.00	3.20

1965 Stengel Dugan Brothers

This one card set was issued to commemorate the retirement of Casey Stengel from baseball. The black and white front features him in a Mets uniform while the back contains biographical information.

	NM	Ex
1 Casey Stengel	150.00	60.00

1992 Sterling Dravecky

This Heroes of Life set measures the standard size. According to serious Dravecky collectors, so far only cards numbered 2 and 12 are known. If other cards are discovered, please let us know.

	Nm-Mt	Ex-Mt
COMPLETE SET (2)	10.00	3.00
COMMON CARD (2/12)	5.00	1.50

1995 Stouffer Pop-ups

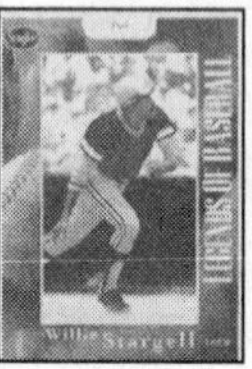

This five-card set was distributed by Stouffer's Frozen Foods and features small color photos of great baseball players set on a ball and glove background. When the tab at the top of the card is pulled, the player's image "pops" out. The backs carry another player photo with player information.

	Nm-Mt	Ex-Mt
COMPLETE SET (5)	15.00	4.50
1 Yogi Berra	4.00	1.20
1A Yogi Berra AU	100.00	30.00
2 Gary Carter	2.00	.60
3 Don Drysdale	4.00	1.20
4 Bob Feller	4.00	1.20
5 Willie Stargell	3.00	.90

1997 Strat-O-Matic All-Stars

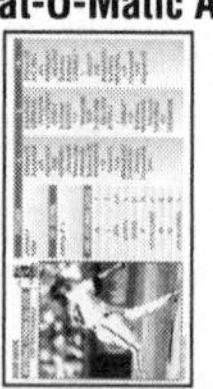

This 62-card set features small color action photos of all the players from the 1997 All-Star Game with player statistics printed on perforated cards measuring approximately 3" by 5 1/2". The backs are blank. The cards are unnumbered and checklisted below in alphabetical order.

	Nm-Mt	Ex-Mt
COMPLETE SET (62)	30.00	9.00
1 Roberto Alomar	1.00	.30
2 Sandy Alomar	.50	.15
3 Moises Alou	.75	.23
4 Brady Anderson	.50	.15
5 Jeff Bagwell	1.25	.35
6 Rod Beck	.25	.07
7 Albert Belle	.50	.15
8 Craig Biggio	.75	.23
9 Jeff Blauser	.25	.07
10 Barry Bonds	2.50	.75
11 Kevin Brown	.75	.23
12 Ken Caminiti	.50	.15
13 Jeff Cirillo	.50	.15
14 Royce Clayton	.25	.07
15 Roger Clemens	2.50	.75
16 David Cone	.75	.23
17 Joey Cora	.25	.07
18 Jason Dickson	.25	.07
19 Shawn Estes	.25	.07
20 Steve Finley	.50	.15
21 Andres Galarraga	1.00	.30
22 Nomar Garciaparra	3.00	.90
23 Tom Glavine	1.25	.35
24 Mark Grace	.75	.23
25 Ken Griffey Jr.	3.00	.90
26 Tony Gwynn	2.50	.75
27 Pat Hentgen	.50	.15
28 Todd Hundley	.50	.15
29 Charles Johnson	.25	.07
30 Randy Johnson	1.50	.45
31 Bobby Jones	.25	.07
32 Chipper Jones	2.50	.75
33 Dave Justice	1.00	.30
34 Jimmy Key	.50	.15
35 Darryl Kile	.25	.07
36 Chuck Knoblauch	1.00	.30
37 Ray Lankford	.50	.15
38 Barry Larkin	1.00	.30
39 Kenny Lofton	.75	.23
40 Javy Lopez	.50	.15
41 Greg Maddux	3.00	.90
42 Edgar Martinez	.75	.23
43 Pedro Martinez	1.25	.35
44 Tino Martinez	1.00	.30
45 Mark McGwire	4.00	1.20
46 Mike Mussina	1.00	.30
47 Randy Myers	.25	.07
48 Denny Neagle	.50	.15
49 Paul O'Neill	.50	.15
50 Mike Piazza	3.00	.90
51 Cal Ripken	5.00	1.50
52 Mariano Rivera	1.00	.30
53 Alex Rodriguez	3.00	.90
54 Ivan Rodriguez	1.25	.35
55 Jose Rosado	.25	.07
56 Curt Schilling	1.25	.35
57 Frank Thomas	1.25	.35
58 Jim Thome	1.25	.35
59 Justin Thompson	.25	.07
60 Larry Walker	1.00	.30
61 Bernie Williams	1.00	.30
62 Tony Womack	.25	.07

1987 Stuart Panels

Subtitled "Super Stars" in English and French, this set consists of 28 four-part perforated panels each featuring three players from the same team and a contest entry card. All 26 teams are included at least once; the Montreal Expos and Toronto Blue Jays each have two panels. Printed on white stock, the four-part panels measure 10 1/8" by 3 7/16"; each card measures 2 1/2" by 3 7/16". The fronts feature color player headshots with white stars on a blue field on each side of the photo. The player's name, along with bilingual team name and position, appear at the bottom, below a crossed bats and baseballs icon. The plain white back carries the player's bilingual biography and 1986 statistics. Team insignias are not shown on the cards because the set was licensed only by the Major League Baseball Players Association. The set is priced below as panels because that is the way the cards are typically found and because the three player cards on each panel carry the same number (No. X de/of 28) on the back.

	Nm-Mt	Ex-Mt
COMPLETE SET (28)	100.00	40.00
1 Darryl Strawberry Keith Hernandez Gary Carter	5.00	2.00
2 Bruce Benedict Ken Griffey Sr. Dale Murphy	3.00	1.20
3 Leon Durham Jody Davis Andre Dawson	3.00	1.20
4 Buddy Bell Dave Parker Eric Davis	3.00	1.20
5 Mike Scott Nolan Ryan Glenn Davis	10.00	4.00
6 Mike Marshall Fernando Valenzuela Pedro Guerrero	2.00	.80
7 Mitch Webster Tim Wallach Tim Raines	3.00	1.20
8 Bryn Smith Hubie Brooks Floyd Youmans	2.00	.80
9 Juan Samuel Shane Rawley Mike Schmidt	4.00	1.60
10 Jim Morrison R.J. Reynolds Johnny Ray	2.00	.80
11 Ozzie Smith Vince Coleman Jack Clark	8.00	3.20
12 John Kruk Tony Gwynn Steve Garvey	8.00	3.20
13 Robby Thompson Jeffrey Leonard Chili Davis	3.00	1.20
14 Fred Lynn Eddie Murray Cal Ripken	10.00	4.00
15 Roger Clemens Wade Boggs Don Baylor	8.00	3.20
16 Mike Witt Wally Joyner Doug DeCinces	2.00	.80
17 Ozzie Guillen Carlton Fisk Harold Baines	4.00	1.60
18 Joe Carter Julio Franco Pat Tabler	2.00	.80
19 Kirk Gibson Alan Trammell Jack Morris	4.00	1.60
20 Willie Wilson Bret Saberhagen George Brett	8.00	3.20
21 Paul Molitor Robin Yount Cecil Cooper	8.00	3.20
22 Kirby Puckett Kent Hrbek Tom Brunansky	8.00	3.20
23 Dave Winfield Don Mattingly Rickey Henderson	10.00	4.00
24 Alfredo Griffin Carney Lansford Jose Canseco	3.00	1.20
25 Mark Langston Phil Bradley Alvin Davis	2.00	.80
26 Larry Parrish Pete O'Brien Pete Incaviglia	2.00	.80
27 George Bell Tony Fernandez Jesse Barfield	3.00	1.20
28 Ernie Whitt Lloyd Moseby Dave Stieb	3.00	1.20

1991 Studio Previews

This 18-card preview set was issued four at a time within 1991 Donruss retail factory sets in order to show dealers and collectors the look of their new Studio cards. The standard-size cards are exactly the same style as those in the Studio series, with black and white player photos bordered in mauve and player information on the backs.

	Nm-Mt	Ex-Mt
COMPLETE SET (18)	30.00	9.00
1 Juan Bell	1.00	.30
2 Roger Clemens	12.00	3.60
3 Dave Parker	2.00	.60
4 Tim Raines	2.00	.60
5 Kevin Seitzer	1.00	.30
6 Ted Higuera	1.00	.30
7 Bernie Williams	6.00	1.80
8 Harold Baines	2.00	.60
9 Gary Pettis	1.00	.30
10 Dave Justice	2.00	.60
11 Eric Davis	2.00	.60
12 Andujar Cedeno	1.00	.30
13 Tom Foley	1.00	.30
14 Dwight Gooden	4.00	1.20
15 Doug Drabek	1.00	.30
16 Steve Decker	1.00	.30
17 Joe Torre MG	2.00	.60
NNO0 Title Card	1.00	.30

1991 Studio

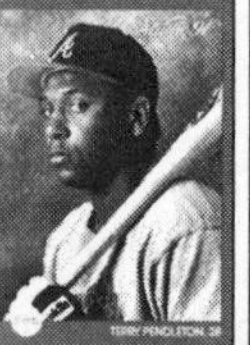

The 1991 Studio set, issued by Donruss/Leaf, contains 264 standard-size cards issued in one series. Cards were distributed in foil packs each of which contained one of 21 different Rod Carew puzzle panels. The Studio card fronts feature posed black and white head-and-shoulders player photos with mauve borders. The team logo, player's name, and position appear along the bottom of the card face. The cards are ordered alphabetically within and according to teams for each league with American League teams preceding National League. Rookie Cards in the set include Jeff Bagwell, Jeff Conine and Brian McRae.

	Nm-Mt	Ex-Mt
COMPLETE SET (264)	15.00	4.50
1 Glenn Davis	.10	.03
2 Dwight Evans	.15	.04
3 Leo Gomez	.10	.03
4 Chris Hoiles	.10	.03
5 Sam Horn	.10	.03
6 Ben McDonald	.10	.03
7 Randy Milligan	.10	.03
8 Gregg Olson	.10	.03
9 Cal Ripken	1.50	.45
10 David Segui	.10	.03
11 Wade Boggs	.25	.07
12 Ellis Burks	.15	.04
13 Jack Clark	.15	.04
14 Roger Clemens	1.00	.30
15 Mike Greenwell	.10	.03
16 Tim Naehring	.10	.03
17 Tony Pena	.10	.03
18 Phil Plantier RC	.10	.03
19 Jeff Reardon	.15	.04
20 Mo Vaughn	.15	.04
21 Jimmie Reese CO	.15	.04
22 Jim Abbott UER (Born in 1967, not 1969)	.25	.07
23 Bert Blyleven	.15	.04
24 Chuck Finley	.15	.04
25 Gary Gaetti	.15	.04
26 Wally Joyner	.15	.04
27 Mark Langston	.10	.03
28 Kirk McCaskill	.10	.03
29 Lance Parrish	.15	.04
30 Dave Winfield	.15	.04
31 Alex Fernandez	.10	.03
32 Carlton Fisk	.25	.07
33 Scott Fletcher	.10	.03
34 Greg Hibbard	.10	.03
35 Charlie Hough	.15	.04
36 Jack McDowell	.10	.03
37 Tim Raines	.15	.04
38 Sammy Sosa	1.00	.30
39 Bobby Thigpen	.10	.03
40 Frank Thomas	.50	.15
41 Sandy Alomar Jr.	.10	.03
42 John Farrell	.10	.03
43 Glenallen Hill	.10	.03
44 Brook Jacoby	.10	.03
45 Chris James	.10	.03
46 Doug Jones	.10	.03
47 Eric King	.10	.03
48 Mark Lewis	.10	.03
49 Greg Swindell UER (Photo actually Turner Ward)	.10	.03
50 Mark Whiten	.10	.03
51 Milt Cuyler	.10	.03
52 Rob Deer	.10	.03
53 Cecil Fielder	.15	.04
54 Travis Fryman	.15	.04
55 Bill Gullickson	.10	.03
56 Lloyd Moseby	.10	.03
57 Frank Tanana	.10	.03
58 Mickey Tettleton	.10	.03
59 Alan Trammell	.25	.07
60 Lou Whitaker	.15	.04
61 Mike Boddicker	.10	.03
62 George Brett	1.25	.35
63 Jeff Conine RC	.50	.15
64 Warren Cromartie	.10	.03
65 Storm Davis	.10	.03
66 Kirk Gibson	.15	.04
67 Mark Gubicza	.10	.03
68 Brian McRae RC	.15	.04
69 Bret Saberhagen	.15	.04
70 Kurt Stillwell	.10	.03
71 Tim McIntosh	.10	.03
72 Candy Maldonado	.10	.03
73 Paul Molitor	.25	.07
74 Willie Randolph	.15	.04
75 Ron Robinson	.10	.03
76 Gary Sheffield	.15	.04
77 Franklin Stubbs	.10	.03
78 B.J. Surhoff	.15	.04
79 Greg Vaughn	.15	.04
80 Robin Yount	.75	.23
81 Rick Aguilera	.15	.04
82 Steve Bedrosian	.10	.03
83 Scott Erickson	.10	.03
84 Greg Gagne	.10	.03
85 Dan Gladden	.10	.03
86 Brian Harper	.10	.03
87 Kent Hrbek	.15	.04
88 Shane Mack	.10	.03
89 Jack Morris	.15	.04
90 Kirby Puckett	.50	.15
91 Jesse Barfield	.10	.03
92 Steve Farr	.10	.03
93 Steve Howe	.10	.03
94 Roberto Kelly	.10	.03
95 Tim Leary	.10	.03
96 Kevin Maas	.10	.03
97 Don Mattingly	1.25	.35
98 Hensley Meulens	.10	.03
99 Scott Sanderson	.10	.03
100 Steve Sax	.10	.03
101 Jose Canseco	.50	.15
102 Dennis Eckersley	.15	.04
103 Dave Henderson	.10	.03
104 Rickey Henderson	.50	.15
105 Rick Honeycutt	.10	.03
106 Mark McGwire	1.25	.35
107 Dave Stewart UER (No-hitter against Toronto& not Texas)	.15	.04
108 Eric Show	.10	.03
109 Todd Van Poppel RC	.10	.03
110 Bob Welch	.10	.03
111 Alvin Davis	.10	.03
112 Ken Griffey Jr.	1.00	.30
113 Ken Griffey Sr.	.15	.04
114 Erik Hanson UER (Misspelled Eric)	.10	.03
115 Brian Holman	.10	.03
116 Randy Johnson	.60	.18
117 Edgar Martinez	.25	.07
118 Tino Martinez	.25	.07
119 Harold Reynolds	.15	.04
120 David Valle	.10	.03
121 Kevin Belcher	.10	.03
122 Scott Chiamparino	.10	.03
123 Julio Franco	.15	.04
124 Juan Gonzalez	.50	.15
125 Rich Gossage	.15	.04
126 Jeff Kunkel	.10	.03
127 Rafael Palmeiro	.25	.07
128 Nolan Ryan	2.00	.60
129 Ruben Sierra	.10	.03
130 Bobby Witt	.10	.03
131 Roberto Alomar	.50	.15
132 Tom Candiotti	.10	.03
133 Joe Carter	.15	.04
134 Ken Dayley	.10	.03
135 Kelly Gruber	.10	.03
136 John Olerud	.15	.04
137 Dave Stieb	.10	.03
138 Turner Ward RC	.15	.04
139 Devon White	.10	.03
140 Mookie Wilson	.15	.04
141 Steve Avery	.10	.03
142 Sid Bream	.10	.03
143 Nick Esasky UER (Homers abbreviated RH)	.10	.03
144 Ron Gant	.15	.04
145 Tom Glavine	.25	.07
146 David Justice	.15	.04
147 Kelly Mann	.10	.03
148 Terry Pendleton	.15	.04
149 John Smoltz	.25	.07
150 Jeff Treadway	.10	.03
151 George Bell	.10	.03
152 Shawn Boskie	.10	.03
153 Andre Dawson	.15	.04
154 Lance Dickson RC	.10	.03
155 Shawon Dunston	.10	.03
156 Joe Girardi	.10	.03
157 Mark Grace	.25	.07
158 Ryne Sandberg	.75	.23
159 Gary Scott RC	.10	.03
160 Dave Smith	.10	.03
161 Tom Browning	.10	.03
162 Eric Davis	.15	.04
163 Rob Dibble	.15	.04
164 Mariano Duncan	.10	.03
165 Chris Hammond	.10	.03
166 Billy Hatcher	.10	.03
167 Barry Larkin	.50	.15
168 Hal Morris	.10	.03
169 Paul O'Neill	.25	.07
170 Chris Sabo	.10	.03
171 Eric Anthony	.10	.03
172 Jeff Bagwell RC	2.00	.60
173 Craig Biggio	.25	.07
174 Ken Caminiti	.15	.04
175 Jim Deshaies	.10	.03
176 Steve Finley	.15	.04
177 Pete Harnisch	.10	.03
178 Darryl Kile	.15	.04
179 Curt Schilling	.25	.07
180 Mike Scott	.10	.03
181 Brett Butler	.15	.04
182 Gary Carter	.25	.07
183 Orel Hershiser	.15	.04
184 Ramon Martinez	.10	.03
185 Eddie Murray	.50	.15
186 Jose Offerman	.10	.03
187 Bob Ojeda	.10	.03
188 Juan Samuel	.10	.03

189 Mike Scioscia .10 .03
190 Darryl Strawberry .25 .07
191 Moises Alou .15 .04
192 Brian Barnes RC .10 .03
193 Oil Can Boyd .10 .03
194 Ivan Calderon .10 .03
195 Delino DeShields .15 .04
196 Mike Fitzgerald .10 .03
197 Andres Galarraga .15 .04
198 Marquis Grissom .10 .03
199 Bill Sampen .10 .03
200 Tim Wallach .10 .03
201 Daryl Boston .10 .03
202 Vince Coleman .10 .03
203 John Franco .15 .04
204 Dwight Gooden .25 .07
205 Tom Herr .10 .03
206 Gregg Jefferies .10 .03
207 Howard Johnson .10 .03
208 Dave Magadan UER .10 .03
(Born 1862& should be 1962)
209 Kevin McReynolds .10 .03
210 Frank Viola .15 .04
211 Wes Chamberlain RC .10 .03
212 Darren Daulton .15 .04
213 Len Dykstra .15 .04
214 Charlie Hayes .10 .03
215 Ricky Jordan .10 .03
216 Steve Lake .10 .03
(Pictured with parrot on his shoulder)
217 Roger McDowell .10 .03
218 Mickey Morandini .10 .03
219 Terry Mulholland .10 .03
220 Dale Murphy .50 .15
221 Jay Bell .15 .04
222 Barry Bonds 1.25 .35
223 Bobby Bonilla .15 .04
224 Doug Drabek .10 .03
225 Bill Landrum .10 .03
226 Mike LaValliere .10 .03
227 Jose Lind .10 .03
228 Don Slaught .10 .03
229 John Smiley .10 .03
230 Andy Van Slyke .15 .04
231 Bernard Gilkey .10 .03
232 Pedro Guerrero .15 .04
233 Rex Hudler .10 .03
234 Ray Lankford .10 .03
235 Joe Magrane .10 .03
236 Jose Oquendo .10 .03
237 Lee Smith .15 .04
238 Ozzie Smith .75 .23
239 Milt Thompson .10 .03
240 Todd Zeile .10 .03
241 Larry Andersen .10 .03
242 Andy Benes .10 .03
243 Paul Faries .10 .03
244 Tony Fernandez .10 .03
245 Tony Gwynn .60 .18
246 Atlee Hammaker .10 .03
247 Fred McGriff .25 .07
248 Bip Roberts .10 .03
249 Bentio Santiago .15 .04
250 Ed Whitson .10 .03
251 Dave Anderson .10 .03
252 Mike Benjamin .10 .03
253 John Burkett UER .10 .03
(Front photo actually Trevor Wilson)
254 Will Clark .50 .15
255 Scott Garrelts .10 .03
256 Willie McGee .15 .04
257 Kevin Mitchell .10 .03
258 Dave Righetti .15 .04
259 Matt Williams .15 .04
260 Bud Black .10 .03
Steve Decker
261 S.Anderson MG CL .15 .04
262 Tom Lasorda MG CL .25 .07
263 Tony LaRussa MG CL .15 .04
NNO Title Card .10 .03

1992 Studio Previews

This 22-card standard-sized set was issued by Leaf to preview the design of the 1992 Leaf Studio series. A color posed player photo has been cut out and superimposed against the background of a black and white action shot of the player. These pictures are framed in black on a gold card face. The player's name and team name appear in the bottom gold border. On a white panel bordered in gold, the backs feature player information under five headings (Personal, Career, Loves to face, Hates to face, and Up Close). The cards are numbered on the back. These Preview cards were distributed on a limited basis to members of the Donruss Dealer Network to show them the new Studio design, and are among the tougher promos to obtain from the 1990s. Unlike the 1991 set of the same name, the 1992 set was not inserted in 1992 Donruss factory sets. It appears that Roberto Alomar and Ozzie Smith are a little more difficult to find than the other 20 cards; they are designated SP in the checklist below.

Nm-Mt Ex-Mt
COMPLETE SET (22) 200.00 60.00
COMMON CARD (1-22) 2.00 .60
COMMON SP
1 Ruben Sierra 3.00 .90
2 Kirby Puckett 8.00 2.40
3 Ryne Sandberg 12.00 3.60
4 John Kruk 3.00 .90
5 Cal Ripken 30.00 9.00
6 Robin Yount 5.00 1.50
7 Dwight Gooden 3.00 .90
8 David Justice 5.00 1.50
9 Don Mattingly 15.00 4.50
10 Wally Joyner 3.00 .90
11 Will Clark 5.00 1.50
12 Rob Dibble 3.00 .90
13 Roberto Alomar SP 20.00
14 Wade Boggs 8.00 2.40
15 Barry Bonds 15.00 4.50
16 Jeff Bagwell 8.00 2.40
17 Mark McGwire 25.00 7.50
18 Frank Thomas 10.00 3.00
19 Brett Butler 3.00 .90
20 Ozzie Smith SP 25.00
21 Jim Abbott 3.00 .90
22 Tony Gwynn 15.00 4.50

1992 Studio

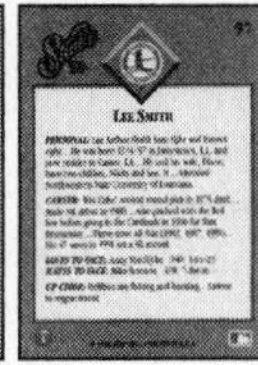

The 1992 Studio set consists of ten players from each of the 26 major league teams, three checklists, and an introduction card for a total of 264 standard-size cards. The key Rookie Cards in this set are Chad Curtis and Brian Jordan.

Nm-Mt Ex-Mt
COMPLETE SET (264) 15.00 4.50
1 Steve Avery .10 .03
2 Sid Bream .10 .03
3 Ron Gant .15 .04
4 Tom Glavine .25 .07
5 David Justice .15 .04
6 Mark Lemke .10 .03
7 Greg Olson .10 .03
8 Terry Pendleton .15 .04
9 Deion Sanders .25 .07
10 John Smoltz .25 .07
11 Doug Dascenzo .10 .03
12 Andre Dawson .15 .04
13 Joe Girardi .10 .03
14 Mark Grace .25 .07
15 Greg Maddux .60 .18
16 Chuck McElroy .10 .03
17 Mike Morgan .10 .03
18 Ryne Sandberg .60 .18
19 Gary Scott .10 .03
20 Sammy Sosa .60 .18
21 Norm Charlton .10 .03
22 Rob Dibble .15 .04
23 Barry Larkin .40 .12
24 Hal Morris .10 .03
25 Paul O'Neill .25 .07
26 Jose Rijo .10 .03
27 Bip Roberts .10 .03
28 Chris Sabo .10 .03
29 Reggie Sanders .15 .04
30 Greg Swindell .10 .03
31 Jeff Bagwell .40 .12
32 Craig Biggio .25 .07
33 Ken Caminiti .15 .04
34 Andujar Cedeno .10 .03
35 Steve Finley .15 .04
36 Pete Harnisch .10 .03
37 Butch Henry RC .15 .04
38 Doug Jones .10 .03
39 Darryl Kile .15 .04
40 Eddie Taubensee RC .25 .07
41 Brett Butler .15 .04
42 Tom Candiotti .10 .03
43 Eric Davis .15 .04
44 Orel Hershiser .15 .04
45 Eric Karros .15 .04
46 Ramon Martinez .10 .03
47 Jose Offerman .10 .03
48 Mike Scioscia .10 .03
49 Mike Sharperson .10 .03
50 Darryl Strawberry .25 .07
51 Bret Barberie .10 .03
52 Ivan Calderon .10 .03
53 Gary Carter .25 .07
54 Delino DeShields .10 .03
55 Marquis Grissom .10 .03
56 Ken Hill .10 .03
57 Dennis Martinez .15 .04
58 Spike Owen .10 .03
59 Larry Walker .25 .07
60 Tim Wallach .10 .03
61 Bobby Bonilla .15 .04
62 Tim Burke .10 .03
63 Vince Coleman .10 .03
64 John Franco .15 .04
65 Dwight Gooden .25 .07
66 Todd Hundley .10 .03
67 Howard Johnson .10 .03
68 Eddie Murray UER .40 .12
(He's not all-time switch homer leader, but he has most games with homers from both sides)
69 Bret Saberhagen .15 .04
70 Anthony Young .10 .03
71 Kim Batiste .10 .03
72 Wes Chamberlain .10 .03
73 Darren Daulton .15 .04
74 Mariano Duncan .10 .03
75 Len Dykstra .15 .04
76 John Kruk .15 .04
77 Mickey Morandini .10 .03
78 Terry Mulholland .10 .03
79 Dale Murphy .40 .12
80 Mitch Williams .10 .03
81 Jay Bell .15 .04
82 Barry Bonds 1.00 .30
83 Steve Buechele .10 .03
84 Doug Drabek .10 .03
85 Mike LaValliere .10 .03
86 Jose Lind .10 .03
87 Denny Neagle .15 .04
88 Randy Tomlin .10 .03
89 Andy Van Slyke .15 .04
90 Gary Varsho .10 .03
91 Pedro Guerrero .15 .04
92 Rex Hudler .10 .03
93 Brian Jordan RC .75 .23
94 Felix Jose .10 .03
95 Donovan Osborne .10 .03
96 Tom Pagnozzi .10 .03
97 Lee Smith .15 .04
98 Ozzie Smith .60 .18
99 Todd Worrell .10 .03
100 Todd Zeile .10 .03
101 Andy Benes .10 .03
102 Jerald Clark .10 .03
103 Tony Fernandez .10 .03
104 Tony Gwynn .50 .15
105 Greg W. Harris .10 .03
106 Fred McGriff .25 .07
107 Benito Santiago .15 .04
108 Gary Sheffield .15 .04
109 Kurt Stillwell .10 .03
110 Tim Teufel .10 .03
111 Kevin Bass .10 .03
112 Jeff Brantley .10 .03
113 John Burkett .10 .03
114 Will Clark .40 .12
115 Royce Clayton .10 .03
116 Mike Jackson .10 .03
117 Darren Lewis .10 .03
118 Bill Swift .10 .03
119 Robby Thompson .10 .03
120 Matt Williams .15 .04
121 Brady Anderson .15 .04
122 Glenn Davis .10 .03
123 Mike Devereaux .10 .03
124 Chris Hoiles .10 .03
125 Sam Horn .10 .03
126 Ben McDonald .10 .03
127 Mike Mussina .40 .12
128 Gregg Olson .10 .03
129 Cal Ripken Jr. 1.25 .35
130 Rick Sutcliffe .15 .04
131 Wade Boggs .25 .07
132 Roger Clemens .75 .23
133 Greg A. Harris .10 .03
134 Tim Naehring .10 .03
135 Tony Pena .10 .03
136 Phil Plantier .10 .03
137 Jeff Reardon .15 .04
138 Jody Reed .10 .03
139 Mo Vaughn .15 .04
140 Frank Viola .15 .04
141 Jim Abbott .25 .07
142 Hubie Brooks .10 .03
143 Chad Curtis RC .25 .07
144 Gary DiSarcina .10 .03
145 Chuck Finley .15 .04
146 Bryan Harvey .10 .03
147 Von Hayes .10 .03
148 Mark Langston .10 .03
149 Lance Parrish .15 .04
150 Lee Stevens .10 .03
151 George Bell .10 .03
152 Alex Fernandez .10 .03
153 Greg Hibbard .10 .03
154 Lance Johnson .10 .03
155 Kirk McCaskill .10 .03
156 Tim Raines .15 .04
157 Steve Sax .10 .03
158 Bobby Thigpen .10 .03
159 Frank Thomas .40 .12
160 Robin Ventura .15 .04
161 Sandy Alomar Jr. .10 .03
162 Jack Armstrong .10 .03
163 Carlos Baerga .10 .03
164 Albert Belle .15 .04
165 Alex Cole .10 .03
166 Glenallen Hill .10 .03
167 Mark Lewis .10 .03
168 Kenny Lofton .40 .12
169 Paul Sorrento .10 .03
170 Mark Whiten .10 .03
171 Milt Cuyler .10 .03
172 Rob Deer .10 .03
173 Cecil Fielder .15 .04
174 Travis Fryman .15 .04
175 Mike Henneman .10 .03
176 Tony Phillips .10 .03
177 Frank Tanana .10 .03
178 Mickey Tettleton .10 .03
179 Alan Trammell .25 .07
180 Lou Whitaker .15 .04
181 George Brett 1.00 .30
182 Tom Gordon .10 .03
183 Mark Gubicza .10 .03
184 Gregg Jefferies .10 .03
185 Wally Joyner .15 .04
186 Brent Mayne .10 .03
187 Brian McRae .10 .03
188 Kevin McReynolds .10 .03
189 Keith Miller .10 .03
190 Jeff Montgomery .15 .04
191 Dante Bichette .15 .04
192 Ricky Bones .10 .03
193 Scott Fletcher .10 .03
194 Paul Molitor .25 .07
195 Jaime Navarro .10 .03
196 Franklin Stubbs .10 .03
197 B.J. Surhoff .15 .04
198 Greg Vaughn .15 .04
199 Bill Wegman .10 .03
200 Robin Yount .60 .18
201 Rick Aguilera .15 .04
202 Scott Erickson .10 .03
203 Greg Gagne .10 .03
204 Brian Harper .10 .03
205 Kent Hrbek .15 .04
206 Scott Leius .10 .03
207 Shane Mack .10 .03
208 Pat Mahomes RC .25 .07
209 Kirby Puckett .40 .12
210 John Smiley .10 .03
211 Mike Gallego .10 .03
212 Charlie Hayes .10 .03
213 Pat Kelly .10 .03
214 Roberto Kelly .10 .03
215 Kevin Maas .10 .03
216 Don Mattingly 1.00 .30
217 Matt Nokes .10 .03
218 Melido Perez .10 .03
219 Scott Sanderson .10 .03
220 Danny Tartabull .10 .03
221 Harold Baines .15 .04
222 Jose Canseco .40 .12
223 Dennis Eckersley .15 .04
224 Dave Henderson .10 .03
225 Carney Lansford .15 .04
226 Mark McGwire 1.00 .30
227 Mike Moore .10 .03
228 Randy Ready .10 .03
229 Terry Steinbach .10 .03
230 Dave Stewart .15 .04
231 Jay Buhner .15 .04
232 Ken Griffey Jr. .60 .18
233 Erik Hanson .10 .03
234 Randy Johnson .40 .12
235 Edgar Martinez .25 .07
236 Tino Martinez .25 .07
237 Kevin Mitchell .10 .03
238 Pete O'Brien .10 .03
239 Harold Reynolds .15 .04
240 David Valle .10 .03
241 Julio Franco .15 .04
242 Juan Gonzalez .40 .12
243 Jose Guzman .10 .03
244 Rafael Palmeiro .25 .07
245 Dean Palmer .15 .04
246 Ivan Rodriguez .40 .12
247 Jeff Russell .10 .03
248 Nolan Ryan 1.50 .45
249 Ruben Sierra .10 .03
250 Dickie Thon .10 .03
251 Roberto Alomar .40 .12
252 Derek Bell .15 .04
253 Pat Borders .10 .03
254 Joe Carter .15 .04
255 Kelly Gruber .10 .03
256 Juan Guzman .10 .03
257 Jack Morris .15 .04
258 John Olerud .15 .04
259 Devon White .10 .03
260 Dave Winfield .15 .04
261 Checklist .10 .03
262 Checklist .10 .03
263 Checklist .10 .03
264 History Card .10 .03

1992 Studio Heritage

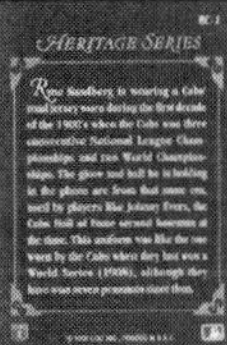

The 1992 Studio Heritage standard-size insert set presents today's star players dressed in vintage uniforms. Cards numbered 1-8 were randomly inserted in 12-card foil packs while cards numbered 9-14 were inserted one per pack in 28-card jumbo packs. The fronts display sepia-toned portraits of the players dressed in vintage uniforms of their current teams. The cards are numbered on the back with a "BC" prefix.

Nm-Mt Ex-Mt
COMPLETE SET (14) 25.00 7.50
COMP.FOIL SET (8) 15.00 4.50
COMP.JUMBO SET (6) 10.00 3.00
BC1 Ryne Sandberg 3.00 .90
BC2 Carlton Fisk 2.00 .60
BC3 Wade Boggs 1.25 .35
BC4 Jose Canseco 2.00 .60
BC5 Don Mattingly 5.00 1.50
BC6 Darryl Strawberry 1.25 .35
BC7 Cal Ripken 6.00 1.80
BC8 Will Clark 2.00 .60
BC9 Andre Dawson .75 .23
BC10 Andy Van Slyke .75 .23
BC11 Paul Molitor 1.25 .35
BC12 Jeff Bagwell 2.00 .60
BC13 Darren Daulton .75 .23
BC14 Kirby Puckett 2.00 .60

1993 Studio Promo

It is unknown how many different cards were issued to preview the 1993 Studio set. This Ryne Sandberg card is similar to the regular issue card but has subtle differences in the biography spacing that makes it different from the regular issue card. There might be more promos,so any additional information is appreciated.

Nm-Mt Ex-Mt
COMPLETE SET 5.00 1.50
176 Ryne Sandberg 5.00 1.50

1993 Studio

The 220 standard-size cards comprising this set feature borderless fronts with posed color player photos that are cut out and superposed upon a closeup of an embroidered team logo. The key Rookie Card in this set is J.T. Snow.

Nm-Mt Ex-Mt
COMPLETE SET (220) 20.00 6.00
1 Dennis Eckersley .25 .07
2 Chad Curtis .15 .04
3 Eric Anthony .15 .04
4 Roberto Alomar .60 .18
5 Steve Avery .15 .04
6 Cal Eldred .15 .04
7 Bernard Gilkey .15 .04
8 Steve Buechele .15 .04
9 Brett Butler .25 .07
10 Terry Mulholland .15 .04
11 Moises Alou .25 .07
12 Barry Bonds 1.50 .45
13 Sandy Alomar Jr. .15 .04
14 Chris Bosio .15 .04
15 Scott Sanderson .15 .04
16 Bobby Bonilla .25 .07
17 Brady Anderson .25 .07
18 Derek Bell .15 .04
19 Wes Chamberlain .15 .04
20 Jay Bell .25 .07
21 Kevin Brown .25 .07
22 Roger Clemens 1.25 .35
23 Roberto Kelly .15 .04
24 Dante Bichette .25 .07
25 George Brett 1.50 .45
26 Rob Deer .15 .04
27 Brian Harper .15 .04
28 George Bell .15 .04
29 Jim Abbott .40 .12
30 Dave Henderson .15 .04
31 Wade Boggs .40 .12
32 Chili Davis .25 .07
33 Ellis Burks .25 .07
34 Jeff Bagwell .40 .12
35 Kent Hrbek .25 .07
36 Pat Borders .15 .04
37 Cecil Fielder .25 .07
38 Sid Bream .15 .04
39 Greg Gagne .15 .04
40 Darryl Hamilton .15 .04
41 Jerald Clark .15 .04
42 Mark Grace .40 .12
43 Barry Larkin .60 .18
44 John Burkett .15 .04
45 Scott Cooper .15 .04
46 Mike Lansing RC .25 .07
47 Jose Canseco .60 .18
48 Will Clark .60 .18
49 Carlos Garcia .15 .04
50 Carlos Baerga .15 .04
51 Darren Daulton .25 .07
52 Jay Buhner .25 .07
53 Andy Benes .15 .04
54 Jeff Conine .25 .07
55 Mike Devereaux .15 .04
56 Vince Coleman .15 .04
57 Terry Steinbach .15 .04
58 J.T. Snow RC .60 .18
59 Greg Swindell .15 .04
60 Devon White .15 .04
61 John Smoltz .40 .12
62 Todd Zeile .15 .04
63 Rick Wilkins .15 .04
64 Tim Wallach .15 .04
65 John Wetteland .25 .07
66 Matt Williams .25 .07
67 Paul Sorrento .15 .04
68 David Valle .15 .04
69 Walt Weiss .15 .04
70 John Franco .25 .07
71 Nolan Ryan 2.50 .75
72 Frank Viola .25 .07
73 Chris Sabo .15 .04
74 David Nied .15 .04
75 Kevin McReynolds .15 .04
76 Lou Whitaker .25 .07
77 Dave Winfield .25 .07
78 Robin Ventura .25 .07
79 Spike Owen .15 .04
80 Cal Ripken Jr. 2.00 .60
81 Dan Walters .15 .04
82 Mitch Williams .15 .04
83 Tim Wakefield .25 .07
84 Rickey Henderson .60 .18
85 Gary DiSarcina .15 .04
86 Craig Biggio .40 .12
87 Joe Carter .25 .07
88 Ron Gant .25 .07
89 John Jaha .15 .04
90 Gregg Jefferies .15 .04
91 Jose Guzman .15 .04
92 Eric Karros .25 .07
93 Wil Cordero .15 .04
94 Royce Clayton .15 .04
95 Albert Belle .25 .07
96 Ken Griffey Jr. 1.00 .30
97 Orestes Destrade .15 .04
98 Tony Fernandez .15 .04
99 Leo Gomez .15 .04
100 Tony Gwynn .75 .23
101 Len Dykstra .25 .07
102 Jeff King .15 .04
103 Julio Franco .25 .07
104 Andre Dawson .25 .07
105 Randy Milligan .15 .04
106 Alex Cole .15 .04
107 Phil Hiatt .15 .04
108 Travis Fryman .25 .07
109 Chuck Knoblauch .25 .07
110 Bo Jackson .60 .18
111 Pat Kelly .15 .04
112 Bret Saberhagen .25 .07
113 Ruben Sierra .15 .04
114 Tim Salmon .40 .12
115 Doug Jones .15 .04
116 Ed Sprague .15 .04
117 Terry Pendleton .25 .07
118 Robin Yount 1.00 .30
119 Mark Whiten .15 .04
120 Checklist 1-110 .15 .04
121 Sammy Sosa 1.00 .30
122 Darryl Strawberry .40 .12
123 Larry Walker .40 .12
124 Robby Thompson .15 .04
125 Carlos Martinez .15 .04
126 Edgar Martinez .40 .12
127 Benito Santiago .25 .07
128 Howard Johnson .15 .04
129 Harold Reynolds .25 .07
130 Craig Shipley .15 .04
131 Curt Schilling .40 .12
132 Andy Van Slyke .25 .07
133 Ivan Rodriguez .60 .18
134 Mo Vaughn .25 .07
135 Bip Roberts .15 .04
136 Charlie Hayes .15 .04
137 Brian McRae .15 .04
138 Mickey Tettleton .15 .04
139 Frank Thomas .60 .18
140 Paul O'Neill .40 .12
141 Mark McGwire 1.50 .45
142 Damion Easley .15 .04
143 Ken Caminiti .25 .07
144 Juan Guzman .15 .04
145 Tom Glavine .40 .12
146 Pat Listach .15 .04

147 Lee Smith .25 .07
148 Derrick May .15 .04
149 Ramon Martinez .15 .04
150 Delino DeShields .15 .04
151 Kirt Manwaring .15 .04
152 Reggie Jefferson .15 .04
153 Randy Johnson .60 .18
154 Dave Magadan .15 .04
155 Dwight Gooden .40 .12
156 Chris Hoiles .15 .04
157 Fred McGriff .40 .12
158 Dave Hollins .15 .04
159 Al Martin .15 .04
160 Juan Gonzalez .60 .18
161 Mike Greenwell .15 .04
162 Kevin Mitchell .15 .04
163 Andres Galarraga .25 .07
164 Wally Joyner .25 .07
165 Kirk Gibson .25 .07
166 Pedro Munoz .15 .04
167 Ozzie Guillen .15 .04
168 Jimmy Key .25 .07
169 Kevin Seitzer .15 .04
170 Luis Polonia .15 .04
171 Luis Gonzalez .25 .07
172 Paul Molitor .40 .12
173 David Justice .25 .07
174 B.J. Surhoff .25 .07
175 Ray Lankford .15 .04
176 Ryne Sandberg 1.00 .30
177 Jody Reed .15 .04
178 Marquis Grissom .15 .04
179 Willie McGee .25 .07
180 Kenny Lofton .25 .07
181 Junior Felix .15 .04
182 Jose Offerman .15 .04
183 John Kruk .25 .07
184 Orlando Merced .15 .04
185 Rafael Palmeiro .40 .12
186 Billy Hatcher .15 .04
187 Joe Oliver .15 .04
188 Joe Girardi .15 .04
189 Jose Lind .15 .04
190 Harold Baines .25 .07
191 Mike Pagliarulo .15 .04
192 Lance Johnson .15 .04
193 Don Mattingly 1.50 .45
194 Doug Drabek .15 .04
195 John Olerud .25 .07
196 Greg Maddux 1.00 .30
197 Greg Vaughn .25 .07
198 Tom Pagnozzi .15 .04
199 Willie Wilson .15 .04
200 Jack McDowell .15 .04
201 Mike Piazza 1.50 .45
202 Mike Mussina .60 .18
203 Charles Nagy .15 .04
204 Tino Martinez .40 .12
205 Charlie Hough .25 .07
206 Todd Hundley .15 .04
207 Gary Sheffield .25 .07
208 Mickey Morandini .15 .04
209 Don Slaught .15 .04
210 Dean Palmer .25 .07
211 Jose Rijo .15 .04
212 Vinny Castilla .25 .07
213 Tony Phillips .15 .04
214 Kirby Puckett .60 .18
215 Tim Raines .25 .07
216 Otis Nixon .15 .04
217 Ozzie Smith 1.00 .30
218 Jose Vizcaino .15 .04
219 Randy Tomlin .15 .04
220 Checklist 111-220 .15 .04

1993 Studio Heritage

This 12-card standard-size set was randomly inserted in all 1993 Leaf Studio foil packs, and features sepia-toned portraits of current players in vintage team uniforms.

Nm-Mt Ex-Mt
COMPLETE SET (12) 30.00 9.00
1 George Brett 10.00 3.00
2 Juan Gonzalez 4.00 1.20
3 Roger Clemens 8.00 2.40
4 Mark McGwire 10.00 3.00
5 Mark Grace 2.50 .75
6 Ozzie Smith 6.00 1.80
7 Barry Larkin 4.00 1.20
8 Frank Thomas 4.00 1.20
9 Carlos Baerga 1.00 .30
10 Eric Karros 1.50 .45
11 J.T. Snow 4.00 1.20
12 John Kruk 1.50 .45

1993 Studio Silhouettes

The 1993 Studio Silhouettes 10-card standard-size set was inserted one per 20-card Studio jumbo pack.

Nm-Mt Ex-Mt
COMPLETE SET (10) 25.00 7.50
1 Frank Thomas 2.00 .60
2 Barry Bonds 5.00 1.50
3 Jeff Bagwell 1.25 .35
4 Juan Gonzalez 2.00 .60
5 Travis Fryman .75 .23
6 J.T. Snow 2.00 .60
7 John Kruk .75 .23
8 Jeff Blauser .50 .15
9 Mike Piazza 5.00 1.50
10 Nolan Ryan 8.00 2.40

1993 Studio Superstars on Canvas

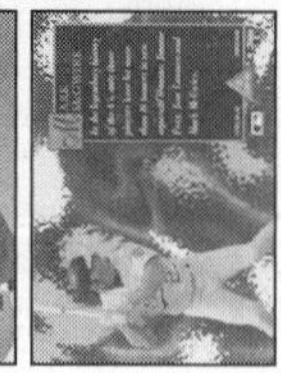

This ten-card standard-size set was randomly inserted in 1993 Studio hobby and retail foil packs.

Nm-Mt Ex-Mt
COMPLETE SET (10) 40.00 12.00
1 Ken Griffey Jr. 6.00 1.80
2 Jose Canseco 4.00 1.20
3 Mark McGwire 10.00 3.00
4 Mike Mussina 4.00 1.20
5 Joe Carter 1.50 .45
6 Frank Thomas 4.00 1.20
7 Darren Daulton 1.50 .45
8 Mark Grace 2.50 .75
9 Andres Galarraga 1.50 .45
10 Barry Bonds 10.00 3.00

1993 Studio Thomas

The 1993 Studio Frank Thomas five-card standard-size set was randomly inserted in all 1993 Studio packs. The cards feature borderless posed black-and-white portraits of the Chicago White Sox slugging first baseman.

Nm-Mt Ex-Mt
COMPLETE SET (5) 8.00 2.40
COMMON THOMAS (1-5) 2.00 .60

1994 Studio Promos

These three cards were distributed to hobby media and dealers several weeks prior to the national release of 1994 Studio. They parallel their basic brethren except, of course, for the text "PROMOTIONAL SAMPLE" running diagonally across the front and back.

Nm-Mt Ex-Mt
COMPLETE SET (3) 6.00 1.80
83 Barry Bonds 4.00 1.20
154 Juan Gonzalez 3.00 .90
209 Frank Thomas 3.00 .90

1994 Studio

The 1994 Studio set consists of 220 full-bleed, standard-size cards. Card fronts offer a player photo with his jersey hanging in a locker room setting in the background. The set is grouped alphabetically within teams.

Nm-Mt Ex-Mt
COMPLETE SET (220) 15.00 4.50
1 Dennis Eckersley .30 .09
2 Brent Gates .15 .04
3 Rickey Henderson .75 .23
4 Mark McGwire 2.00 .60
5 Troy Neel .15 .04
6 Ruben Sierra .15 .04
7 Terry Steinbach .15 .04
8 Chad Curtis .15 .04
9 Chili Davis .30 .09
10 Gary DiSarcina .15 .04
11 Damion Easley .15 .04
12 Bo Jackson .75 .23
13 Mark Langston .15 .04
14 Eduardo Perez .15 .04
15 Tim Salmon .50 .15
16 Jeff Bagwell .50 .15
17 Craig Biggio .50 .15
18 Ken Caminiti .30 .09
19 Andujar Cedeno .15 .04
20 Doug Drabek .15 .04
21 Steve Finley .30 .09
22 Luis Gonzalez .30 .09
23 Darryl Kile .30 .09
24 Roberto Alomar .75 .23
25 Pat Borders .15 .04
26 Joe Carter .30 .09
27 Carlos Delgado .50 .15
28 Pat Hentgen .15 .04
29 Paul Molitor .50 .15
30 John Olerud .30 .09
31 Ed Sprague .15 .04
32 Devon White .15 .04
33 Steve Avery .15 .04
34 Tom Glavine .50 .15
35 David Justice .30 .09
36 Roberto Kelly .15 .04
37 Ryan Klesko .30 .09
38 Javier Lopez .30 .09
39 Greg Maddux 1.25 .35
40 Fred McGriff .50 .15
41 Terry Pendleton .30 .09
42 Ricky Bones .15 .04
43 Darryl Hamilton .15 .04
44 Brian Harper .15 .04
45 John Jaha .15 .04
46 Dave Nilsson .15 .04
47 Kevin Seitzer .15 .04
48 Greg Vaughn .30 .09
49 Turner Ward .15 .04
50 Bernard Gilkey .15 .04
51 Gregg Jefferies .15 .04
52 Ray Lankford .15 .04
53 Tom Pagnozzi .15 .04
54 Ozzie Smith 1.25 .35
55 Bob Tewksbury .15 .04
56 Mark Whiten .15 .04
57 Todd Zeile .15 .04
58 Steve Buechele .15 .04
59 Shawon Dunston .15 .04
60 Mark Grace .50 .15
61 Derrick May .15 .04
62 Karl Rhodes .15 .04
63 Ryne Sandberg 1.25 .35
64 Sammy Sosa 1.25 .35
65 Rick Wilkins .15 .04
66 Brett Butler .30 .09
67 Delino DeShields .15 .04
68 Orel Hershiser .30 .09
69 Eric Karros .30 .09
70 Raul Mondesi .30 .09
71 Jose Offerman .15 .04
72 Mike Piazza 1.50 .45
73 Tim Wallach .15 .04
74 Moises Alou .30 .09
75 Sean Berry .15 .04
76 Wil Cordero .15 .04
77 Cliff Floyd .30 .09
78 Marquis Grissom .15 .04
79 Ken Hill .15 .04
80 Larry Walker .50 .15
81 John Wetteland .30 .09
82 Rod Beck .15 .04
83 Barry Bonds 2.00 .60
84 Royce Clayton .15 .04
85 Darren Lewis .15 .04
86 Willie McGee .30 .09
87 Bill Swift .15 .04
88 Robby Thompson .15 .04
89 Matt Williams .30 .09
90 Sandy Alomar Jr. .15 .04
91 Carlos Baerga .15 .04
92 Albert Belle .30 .09
93 Kenny Lofton .30 .09
94 Eddie Murray .75 .23
95 Manny Ramirez .50 .15
96 Paul Sorrento .15 .04
97 Jim Thome .75 .23
98 Rich Amaral .15 .04
99 Eric Anthony .15 .04
100 Jay Buhner .30 .09
101 Ken Griffey Jr. 1.25 .35
102 Randy Johnson .75 .23
103 Edgar Martinez .50 .15
104 Tino Martinez .50 .15
105 Kurt Abbott RC .30 .09
106 Bret Barberie .15 .04
107 Chuck Carr .15 .04
108 Jeff Conine .30 .09
109 Chris Hammond .15 .04
110 Bryan Harvey .15 .04
111 Benito Santiago .30 .09
112 Gary Sheffield .30 .09
113 Bobby Bonilla .30 .09
114 Dwight Gooden .50 .15
115 Todd Hundley .15 .04
116 Bobby Jones .15 .04
117 Jeff Kent .30 .09
118 Kevin McReynolds .15 .04
119 Bret Saberhagen .30 .09
120 Ryan Thompson .15 .04
121 Harold Baines .30 .09
122 Mike Devereaux .15 .04
123 Jeffrey Hammonds .15 .04
124 Ben McDonald .15 .04
125 Mike Mussina .75 .23
126 Rafael Palmeiro .50 .15
127 Cal Ripken Jr. 2.50 .75
128 Lee Smith .30 .09
129 Brad Ausmus .15 .04
130 Derek Bell .15 .04
131 Andy Benes .15 .04
132 Tony Gwynn 1.00 .30
133 Trevor Hoffman .30 .09
134 Scott Livingstone .15 .04
135 Phil Plantier .15 .04
136 Darren Daulton .30 .09
137 Mariano Duncan .15 .04
138 Lenny Dykstra .30 .09
139 Dave Hollins .15 .04
140 Pete Incaviglia .15 .04
141 Danny Jackson .15 .04
142 John Kruk .30 .09
143 Kevin Stocker .15 .04
144 Jay Bell .30 .09
145 Carlos Garcia .15 .04
146 Jeff King .15 .04
147 Al Martin .15 .04
148 Orlando Merced .15 .04
149 Don Slaught .15 .04
150 Andy Van Slyke .30 .09
151 Kevin Brown .30 .09
152 Jose Canseco .75 .23
153 Will Clark .75 .23
154 Juan Gonzalez .75 .23
155 David Hulse .15 .04
156 Dean Palmer .30 .09
157 Ivan Rodriguez .75 .23
158 Kenny Rogers .30 .09
159 Roger Clemens 1.50 .45
160 Scott Cooper .15 .04
161 Andre Dawson .30 .09
162 Mike Greenwell .15 .04
163 Otis Nixon .15 .04
164 Aaron Sele .15 .04
165 John Valentin .15 .04
166 Mo Vaughn .30 .09
167 Bret Boone .30 .09
168 Barry Larkin .75 .23
169 Kevin Mitchell .15 .04
170 Hal Morris .15 .04
171 Jose Rijo .15 .04
172 Deion Sanders .50 .15
173 Reggie Sanders .30 .09
174 John Smiley .15 .04
175 Dante Bichette .30 .09
176 Ellis Burks .30 .09
177 Andres Galarraga .30 .09
178 Joe Girardi .15 .04
179 Charlie Hayes .15 .04
180 Roberto Mejia .15 .04
181 Walt Weiss .15 .04
182 David Cone .30 .09
183 Gary Gaetti .30 .09
184 Greg Gagne .15 .04
185 Felix Jose .15 .04
186 Wally Joyner .30 .09
187 Mike Macfarlane .15 .04
188 Brian McRae .15 .04
189 Eric Davis .30 .09
190 Cecil Fielder .30 .09
191 Travis Fryman .30 .09
192 Tony Phillips .15 .04
193 Mickey Tettleton .15 .04
194 Alan Trammell .50 .15
195 Lou Whitaker .30 .09
196 Kent Hrbek .30 .09
197 Chuck Knoblauch .30 .09
198 Shane Mack .15 .04
199 Pat Meares .15 .04
200 Kirby Puckett .75 .23
201 Matt Walbeck .15 .04
202 Dave Winfield .30 .09
203 Wilson Alvarez .15 .04
204 Alex Fernandez .15 .04
205 Julio Franco .30 .09
206 Ozzie Guillen .15 .04
207 Jack McDowell .15 .04
208 Tim Raines .30 .09
209 Frank Thomas .75 .23
210 Robin Ventura .30 .09
211 Jim Abbott .50 .15
212 Wade Boggs .50 .15
213 Pat Kelly .15 .04
214 Jimmy Key .30 .09
215 Don Mattingly 2.00 .60
216 Paul O'Neill .50 .15
217 Mike Stanley .15 .04
218 Danny Tartabull .15 .04
219 Checklist .15 .04
220 Checklist .15 .04

1994 Studio Editor's Choice

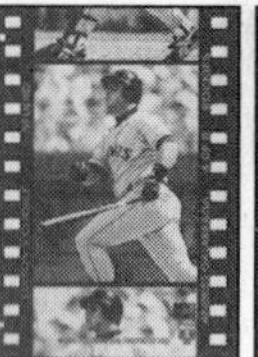
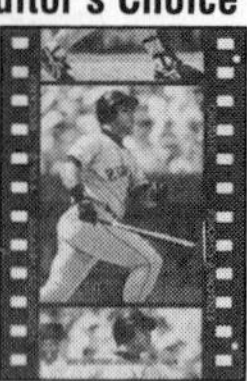

This eight-card standard-sized set was randomly inserted in foil packs at a rate of one in 36. These cards are acetate and were designed much like a film strip with black borders.

Nm-Mt Ex-Mt
COMPLETE SET (8) 30.00 9.00
1 Barry Bonds 10.00 3.00
2 Frank Thomas 4.00 1.20
3 Ken Griffey Jr. 6.00 1.80
4 Andres Galarraga 1.50 .45
5 Juan Gonzalez 4.00 1.20
6 Tim Salmon 2.50 .75
7 Paul O'Neill 2.50 .75
8 Mike Piazza 8.00 2.40

1994 Studio Heritage

Each player in this eight-card insert set (randomly inserted in foil packs at a rate of one in nine) is modelling a vintage uniform of his team. The year of the uniform is noted in gold lettering at the top with a gold Heritage Collection logo at the bottom.

Nm-Mt Ex-Mt
COMPLETE SET (8) 12.00 3.60
1 Barry Bonds 5.00 1.50
2 Frank Thomas 2.00 .60
3 Joe Carter .75 .23
4 Don Mattingly 5.00 1.50
5 Ryne Sandberg 3.00 .90
6 Javier Lopez .75 .23
7 Gregg Jefferies .40 .12
8 Mike Mussina 2.00 .60

1994 Studio Series Stars

This 10-card acetate set showcases top stars and was limited to 10,000 of each card. They were randomly inserted in foil packs at a rate of one in 60. The player cutout is surrounded by a small circle of stars with the player's name at the top. The team name, limited edition notation and the Series Stars logo are at the bottom. The back of the cutout contains a photo. Gold versions of this set were more difficult to obtain in packs (one in 120, 5,000 total).

Nm-Mt Ex-Mt
COMPLETE SET (10) 120.00 36.00
*GOLD: .75X TO 2X BASIC SERIES STARS
GOLD STATED ODDS 1:120
GOLD PRINT RUN 5000 SERIAL #'d SETS
1 Tony Gwynn 10.00 3.00
2 Barry Bonds 20.00 6.00
3 Frank Thomas 8.00 2.40
4 Ken Griffey Jr. 12.00 3.60
5 Joe Carter 3.00 .90
6 Mike Piazza 15.00 4.50
7 Cal Ripken Jr. 25.00 7.50
8 Greg Maddux 12.00 3.60
9 Juan Gonzalez 8.00 2.40
10 Don Mattingly 20.00 6.00

1995 Studio

This 200-card horizontal set was issued by Donruss for the fifth consecutive year. Using a different design than past Studio issues, these cards were designed similarly to credit cards. The cards were issued in five-card packs with a suggested retail price of $1.49. There are no Rookie Cards in this set.

Nm-Mt Ex-Mt
COMPLETE SET (200) 50.00 15.00
1 Frank Thomas 1.00 .30
2 Jeff Bagwell .60 .18
3 Don Mattingly 2.50 .75
4 Mike Piazza 1.50 .45
5 Ken Griffey Jr. 1.50 .45
6 Greg Maddux 1.50 .45
7 Barry Bonds 2.50 .75
8 Cal Ripken Jr. 3.00 .90
9 Jose Canseco 1.00 .30
10 Paul Molitor .60 .18
11 Kenny Lofton .40 .12
12 Will Clark 1.00 .30
13 Tim Salmon .60 .18
14 Joe Carter .40 .12
15 Albert Belle .40 .12
16 Roger Clemens 2.00 .60
17 Roberto Alomar 1.00 .30
18 Alex Rodriguez 2.50 .75
19 Raul Mondesi .40 .12
20 Deion Sanders .60 .18
21 Juan Gonzalez 1.00 .30
22 Kirby Puckett 1.00 .30
23 Fred McGriff .60 .18
24 Matt Williams .40 .12
25 Tony Gwynn 1.25 .35
26 Cliff Floyd .40 .12
27 Travis Fryman .40 .12
28 Shawn Green .40 .12
29 Mike Mussina 1.00 .30
30 Bob Hamelin .20 .06
31 David Justice .40 .12
32 Manny Ramirez .40 .12
33 David Cone .40 .12
34 Marquis Grissom .20 .06
35 Moises Alou .40 .12
36 Carlos Baerga .20 .06
37 Barry Larkin 1.00 .30
38 Robin Ventura .40 .12
39 Mo Vaughn .40 .12
40 Jeffrey Hammonds .20 .06
41 Ozzie Smith 1.50 .45
42 Andres Galarraga .40 .12
43 Carlos Delgado .40 .12
44 Lenny Dykstra .40 .12
45 Cecil Fielder .40 .12
46 Wade Boggs .60 .18
47 Gregg Jefferies .20 .06
48 Randy Johnson 1.00 .30
49 Rafael Palmeiro .60 .18
50 Craig Biggio .60 .18
51 Steve Avery .20 .06
52 Ricky Bottalico .20 .06
53 Chris Gomez .20 .06
54 Carlos Garcia .20 .06
55 Brian Anderson .20 .06
56 Wilson Alvarez .20 .06
57 Roberto Kelly .20 .06
58 Larry Walker .60 .18
59 Dean Palmer .40 .12
60 Rick Aguilera .20 .06
61 Javier Lopez .40 .12
62 Shawon Dunston .20 .06
63 Wm. VanLandingham .20 .06
64 Jeff Kent .40 .12
65 David McCarty .20 .06
66 Armando Benitez .40 .12
67 Brett Butler .40 .12
68 Bernard Gilkey .20 .06
69 Joey Hamilton .20 .06
70 Chad Curtis .20 .06
71 Dante Bichette .40 .12
72 Chuck Carr .20 .06
73 Pedro Martinez 1.00 .30
74 Ramon Martinez .20 .06
75 Rondell White .40 .12
76 Alex Fernandez .20 .06
77 Dennis Martinez .40 .12
78 Sammy Sosa 1.50 .45

79 Bernie Williams .60 .18
80 Lou Whitaker .40 .12
81 Kurt Abbott .20 .06
82 Tino Martinez .60 .18
83 Willie Greene .20 .06
84 Garret Anderson .40 .12
85 Jose Rijo .20 .06
86 Jeff Montgomery .20 .06
87 Mark Langston .20 .06
88 Reggie Sanders .40 .12
89 Rusty Greer .40 .12
90 Delino DeShields .20 .06
91 Jason Bere .20 .06
92 Lee Smith .40 .12
93 Devon White .40 .12
94 John Wetteland .40 .12
95 Luis Gonzalez .40 .12
96 Greg Vaughn .40 .12
97 Lance Johnson .20 .06
98 Alan Trammell .60 .18
99 Bret Saberhagen .40 .12
100 Jack McDowell .20 .06
101 Trevor Hoffman .40 .12
102 Dave Nilsson .20 .06
103 Bryan Harvey .20 .06
104 Chuck Knoblauch .40 .12
105 Bobby Bonilla .40 .12
106 Hal Morris .20 .06
107 Mark Whiten .20 .06
108 Phil Plantier .20 .06
109 Ryan Klesko .40 .12
110 Greg Gagne .20 .06
111 Ruben Sierra .20 .06
112 J.R. Phillips .20 .06
113 Terry Steinbach .20 .06
114 Jay Buhner .40 .12
115 Ken Caminiti .40 .12
116 Gary DiSarcina .20 .06
117 Ivan Rodriguez 1.00 .30
118 Bip Roberts .20 .06
119 Jay Bell .40 .12
120 Ken Hill .20 .06
121 Mike Greenwell .20 .06
122 Rick Wilkins .20 .06
123 Rickey Henderson 1.00 .30
124 Dave Hollins .20 .06
125 Terry Pendleton .40 .12
126 Rich Becker .20 .06
127 Billy Ashley .20 .06
128 Derek Bell .20 .06
129 Dennis Eckersley .40 .12
130 Andujar Cedeno .20 .06
131 John Jaha .20 .06
132 Chuck Finley .40 .12
133 Steve Finley .40 .12
134 Danny Tartabull .20 .06
135 Jeff Conine .40 .12
136 Jon Lieber .20 .06
137 Jim Abbott .60 .18
138 Steve Trachsel .20 .06
139 Bret Boone .40 .12
140 Charles Johnson .40 .12
141 Mark McGwire 2.50 .75
142 Eddie Murray 1.00 .30
143 Doug Drabek .20 .06
144 Steve Cooke .20 .06
145 Kevin Seitzer .20 .06
146 Rod Beck .20 .06
147 Eric Karros .40 .12
148 Tim Raines .40 .12
149 Joe Girardi .20 .06
150 Aaron Sele .20 .06
151 Robby Thompson .20 .06
152 Chan Ho Park .40 .12
153 Ellis Burks .40 .12
154 Brian McRae .20 .06
155 Jimmy Key .40 .12
156 Rico Brogna .20 .06
157 Ozzie Guillen .20 .06
158 Chili Davis .40 .12
159 Darren Daulton .40 .12
160 Chipper Jones 1.00 .30
161 Walt Weiss .20 .06
162 Paul O'Neill .60 .18
163 Al Martin .20 .06
164 John Valentin .20 .06
165 Tim Wallach .20 .06
166 Scott Erickson .20 .06
167 Ryan Thompson .20 .06
168 Todd Zeile .20 .06
169 Scott Cooper .20 .06
170 Matt Mieske .20 .06
171 Allen Watson .20 .06
172 Brian L.Hunter .20 .06
173 Kevin Stocker .20 .06
174 Cal Eldred .20 .06
175 Tony Phillips .20 .06
176 Ben McDonald .20 .06
177 Mark Grace .60 .18
178 Midre Cummings .20 .06
179 Orlando Merced .20 .06
180 Jeff King .20 .06
181 Gary Sheffield .40 .12
182 Tom Glavine .60 .18
183 Edgar Martinez .60 .18
184 Steve Karsay .20 .06
185 Pat Listach .20 .06
186 Wil Cordero .20 .06
187 Brady Anderson .40 .12
188 Bobby Jones .20 .06
189 Andy Benes .20 .06
190 Ray Lankford .20 .06
191 John Doherty .20 .06
192 Wally Joyner .40 .12
193 Jim Thome 1.00 .30
194 Royce Clayton .20 .06
195 John Olerud .40 .12
196 Steve Buechele .20 .06
197 Harold Baines .40 .12
198 Geronimo Berroa .20 .06
199 Checklist .20 .06
200 Checklist .20 .06

1995 Studio Gold Series

This 50-card set was inserted one per packs. This set parallels the first 50 cards of the regular studio set. The only differences between these cards and the regular issue are they were printed with a gold background and are numbered in the right corner as "X" of 50. Also the words "Studio Gold" are printed in the upper front left corner.

Nm-Mt Ex-Mt
COMPLETE SET (50) 30.00 9.00
*GOLD: .5X TO 1.2X BASIC CARDS

1995 Studio Platinum Series

This 25-card set was randomly inserted into packs at a rate of one in 10 packs. This set parallels the first 25 cards of the regular issue. These cards are different from the regular issue in that they have a platinum background, the words "Studio Platinum" in the upper left corner and are numbered on the back as "X" of 25.

Nm-Mt Ex-Mt
*PLATINUM: 2.5X TO 6X BASIC CARDS

1996 Studio

The 1996 Studio set was issued in one series totalling 150 cards and was distributed in seven-card packs. The fronts feature color action player photos with a player portrait in the background.

Nm-Mt Ex-Mt
COMPLETE SET (150) 15.00 4.50
1 Cal Ripken 2.00 .60
2 Alex Gonzalez .25 .07
3 Roger Cedeno .25 .07
4 Todd Hollandsworth .25 .07
5 Gregg Jefferies .25 .07
6 Ryne Sandberg 1.00 .30
7 Eric Karros .25 .07
8 Jeff Conine .25 .07
9 Rafael Palmeiro .40 .12
10 Bip Roberts .25 .07
11 Roger Clemens 1.25 .35
12 Tom Glavine .40 .12
13 Jason Giambi .60 .18
14 Rey Ordonez .25 .07
15 Chan Ho Park .25 .07
16 Vinny Castilla .25 .07
17 Butch Huskey .25 .07
18 Greg Maddux 1.00 .30
19 Bernard Gilkey .25 .07
20 Marquis Grissom .25 .07
21 Chuck Knoblauch .25 .07
22 Ozzie Smith 1.00 .30
23 Garret Anderson .25 .07
24 J.T. Snow .25 .07
25 John Valentin .25 .07
26 Barry Larkin .60 .18
27 Bobby Bonilla .25 .07
28 Todd Zeile .25 .07
29 Roberto Alomar .60 .18
30 Ramon Martinez .25 .07
31 Jeff King .25 .07
32 Dennis Eckersley .25 .07
33 Derek Jeter 1.50 .45
34 Edgar Martinez .40 .12
35 Geronimo Berroa .25 .07
36 Hal Morris .25 .07
37 Troy Percival .25 .07
38 Jason Isringhausen .25 .07
39 Greg Vaughn .25 .07
40 Robin Ventura .25 .07
41 Craig Biggio .40 .12
42 Will Clark .60 .18
43 Sammy Sosa 1.00 .30
44 Bernie Williams .40 .12
45 Kenny Lofton .25 .07
46 Wade Boggs .40 .12
47 Javy Lopez .25 .07
48 Reggie Sanders .25 .07
49 Jeff Bagwell .40 .12
50 Fred McGriff .40 .12
51 Charles Johnson .25 .07
52 Darren Daulton .25 .07
53 Jose Canseco .60 .18
54 Cecil Fielder .25 .07
55 Hideo Nomo .60 .18
56 Tim Salmon .40 .12
57 Carlos Delgado .25 .07
58 David Cone .25 .07
59 Tim Raines .25 .07
60 Lyle Mouton .25 .07
61 Wally Joyner .25 .07
62 Bret Boone .25 .07
63 Raul Mondesi .25 .07
64 Gary Sheffield .25 .07
65 Alex Rodriguez 1.25 .35
66 Russ Davis .25 .07
67 Checklist .25 .07
68 Marty Cordova .25 .07
69 Ruben Sierra .25 .07
70 Jose Mesa .25 .07
71 Matt Williams .25 .07
72 Chipper Jones .60 .18
73 Randy Johnson .60 .18
74 Kirby Puckett .60 .18
75 Jim Edmonds .25 .07
76 Barry Bonds 1.50 .45
77 David Segui .25 .07
78 Larry Walker .40 .12
79 Jason Kendall .25 .07
80 Mike Piazza 1.00 .30
81 Brian L.Hunter .25 .07
82 Julio Franco .25 .07
83 Jay Bell .25 .07
84 Kevin Seitzer .25 .07
85 John Smoltz .40 .12
86 Joe Carter .25 .07
87 Ray Durham .25 .07
88 Carlos Baerga .25 .07
89 Ron Gant .25 .07
90 Orlando Merced .25 .07
91 Lee Smith .25 .07
92 Pedro Martinez .60 .18
93 Frank Thomas .60 .18
94 Al Martin .25 .07
95 Chad Curtis .25 .07
96 Eddie Murray .60 .18
97 Rusty Greer .25 .07
98 Jay Buhner .25 .07
99 Rico Brogna .25 .07
100 Todd Hundley .25 .07
101 Moises Alou .25 .07
102 Chili Davis .25 .07
103 Ismael Valdes .25 .07
104 Mo Vaughn .25 .07
105 Juan Gonzalez .60 .18
106 Mark Grudzielanek .25 .07
107 Derek Bell .25 .07
108 Shawn Green .25 .07
109 David Justice .25 .07
110 Paul O'Neill .40 .12
111 Kevin Appier .25 .07
112 Ray Lankford .25 .07
113 Travis Fryman .25 .07
114 Manny Ramirez .25 .07
115 Brooks Kieschnick .25 .07
116 Ken Griffey Jr. 1.00 .30
117 Jeffrey Hammonds .25 .07
118 Mark McGwire 1.50 .45
119 Denny Neagle .25 .07
120 Quilvio Veras .25 .07
121 Alan Benes .25 .07
122 Rondell White .25 .07
123 Osvaldo Fernandez RC .25 .07
124 Andres Galarraga .25 .07
125 Johnny Damon .25 .07
126 Lenny Dykstra .25 .07
127 Jason Schmidt .25 .07
128 Mike Mussina .60 .18
129 Ken Caminiti .25 .07
130 Michael Tucker .25 .07
131 LaTroy Hawkins .25 .07
132 Checklist .25 .07
133 Delino DeShields .25 .07
134 Dave Nilsson .25 .07
135 Jack McDowell .25 .07
136 Joey Hamilton .25 .07
137 Dante Bichette .25 .07
138 Paul Molitor .40 .12
139 Ivan Rodriguez .60 .18
140 Mark Grace .40 .12
141 Paul Wilson .25 .07
142 Orel Hershiser .25 .07
143 Albert Belle .25 .07
144 Tino Martinez .40 .12
145 Tony Gwynn .75 .23
146 George Arias .25 .07
147 Brian Jordan .25 .07
148 Brian McRae .25 .07
149 Rickey Henderson .60 .18
150 Ryan Klesko .25 .07

1996 Studio Bronze Press Proofs

Randomly inserted in packs, this 150-card Bronze set is parallel to the regular set and is similar in design with bronze foil stamping. Only 2,000 sets were produced. Prices below refer to Bronze cards.

Nm-Mt Ex-Mt
*STARS: 5X TO 12X BASIC CARDS

1996 Studio Gold Press Proofs

Randomly inserted in packs at a rate of 1:24, this 150-card set is parallel to the regular set and is similar in design with gold foil stamping. Only 500 sets were produced.

Nm-Mt Ex-Mt
*STARS: 12.5X TO 30X BASIC CARDS

1996 Studio Silver Press Proofs

Randomly inserted in magazine packs, this 150-card set is parallel to the regular set and is similar in design with silver foil stamping. Only 100 sets were produced.

Nm-Mt Ex-Mt
*STARS: 30X TO 80X BASIC CARDS

1996 Studio Hit Parade

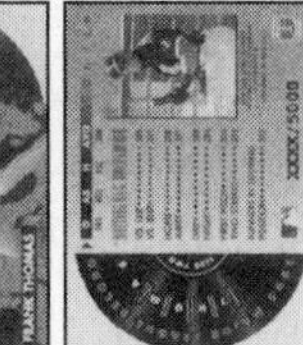

Randomly inserted in packs at a rate of 1:48, cards from this ten-card set feature some of the League's top long-ball hitters. Each card is serial numbered of 5,000 on back.

Nm-Mt Ex-Mt
COMPLETE SET (10) 60.00 18.00
1 Tony Gwynn 8.00 2.40
2 Ken Griffey Jr. 10.00 3.00
3 Frank Thomas 6.00 1.80
4 Jeff Bagwell 4.00 1.20
5 Kirby Puckett 6.00 1.80
6 Mike Piazza 10.00 3.00
7 Barry Bonds 15.00 4.50
8 Albert Belle 2.50 .75
9 Tim Salmon 4.00 1.20
10 Mo Vaughn 2.50 .75

1996 Studio Masterstrokes Samples

These cards were released early to dealers and hobby media to preview what the 1996 Studio Masterstroke insert set would look like.

Nm-Mt Ex-Mt
COMPLETE SET (8) 40.00 12.00
1 Tony Gwynn 5.00 1.50
2 Mike Piazza 6.00 1.80
3 Jeff Bagwell 4.00 1.20
4 Manny Ramirez 3.00 .90
5 Cal Ripken 10.00 3.00
6 Frank Thomas 3.00 .90
7 Ken Griffey Jr. 6.00 1.80
8 Greg Maddux 5.00 1.50

1996 Studio Masterstrokes

Randomly inserted in packs, this eight-card set features some of the League's most popular stars. Each card from this set was also produced in a promo form.

Nm-Mt Ex-Mt
COMPLETE SET (8) 100.00 30.00
1 Tony Gwynn 12.00 3.60
2 Mike Piazza 15.00 4.50
3 Jeff Bagwell 6.00 1.80
4 Manny Ramirez 4.00 1.20
5 Cal Ripken 30.00 9.00
6 Frank Thomas 10.00 3.00
7 Ken Griffey Jr. 15.00 4.50
8 Greg Maddux 15.00 4.50

1996 Studio Stained Glass Stars

Randomly inserted in packs, this 12-card set honors some of the league's hottest superstars. The cards feature color player images on a genuine-look stained glass background and were printed with a clear plastic, die-cut technology.

Nm-Mt Ex-Mt
COMPLETE SET (12) 60.00 18.00
1 Cal Ripken 12.00 3.60
2 Ken Griffey Jr. 6.00 1.80
3 Frank Thomas 4.00 1.20
4 Greg Maddux 6.00 1.80
5 Chipper Jones 4.00 1.20
6 Mike Piazza 6.00 1.80
7 Albert Belle 1.50 .45
8 Jeff Bagwell 2.50 .75
9 Hideo Nomo 4.00 1.20
10 Barry Bonds 10.00 3.00
11 Manny Ramirez 1.50 .45
12 Kenny Lofton 1.50 .45

1997 Studio

The 1997 Studio set was issued in one series totalling 165 cards and was distributed in five-card packs with an 8x10 Studio Portrait for a suggested retail price of $2.49. The fronts feature color player portraits, while the backs carry player information. It is believed that the following cards: 112, 133, 137, 147 and 161 were short printed.

Nm-Mt Ex-Mt
COMPLETE SET (165) 60.00 18.00
1 Frank Thomas .75 .23
2 Gary Sheffield .30 .09
3 Jason Isringhausen .30 .09
4 Ron Gant .30 .09
5 Andy Pettitte .50 .15
6 Todd Hollandsworth .30 .09
7 Troy Percival .30 .09
8 Mark McGwire 2.00 .60
9 Barry Larkin .75 .23
10 Ken Caminiti .30 .09
11 Paul Molitor .50 .15
12 Travis Fryman .30 .09
13 Kevin Brown .30 .09
14 Robin Ventura .30 .09
15 Andres Galarraga .30 .09
16 Ken Griffey Jr. 1.25 .35
17 Roger Clemens 1.50 .45
18 Alan Benes .30 .09
19 Dave Justice .30 .09
20 Damon Buford .30 .09
21 Mike Piazza 1.25 .35
22 Ray Durham .30 .09
23 Billy Wagner .30 .09
24 Dean Palmer .30 .09
25 David Cone .30 .09
26 Ruben Sierra .30 .09
27 Henry Rodriguez .30 .09
28 Ray Lankford .30 .09
29 Jamey Wright .30 .09
30 Brady Anderson .30 .09
31 Tino Martinez .50 .15
32 Manny Ramirez .30 .09
33 Jeff Conine .30 .09
34 Dante Bichette .30 .09
35 Jose Canseco .75 .23
36 Mo Vaughn .30 .09
37 Sammy Sosa 1.25 .35
38 Mark Grudzielanek .30 .09
39 Mike Mussina .75 .23
40 Bill Pulsipher .30 .09
41 Ryne Sandberg 1.25 .35
42 Rickey Henderson .75 .23
43 Alex Rodriguez 1.25 .35
44 Eddie Murray .75 .23
45 Ernie Young .30 .09
46 Joey Hamilton .30 .09
47 Wade Boggs .50 .15
48 Rusty Greer .30 .09
49 Carlos Delgado .30 .09
50 Ellis Burks .30 .09
51 Cal Ripken 2.50 .75
52 Alex Fernandez .30 .09
53 Wally Joyner .30 .09
54 James Baldwin .30 .09
55 Juan Gonzalez .75 .23
56 John Smoltz .50 .15
57 Omar Vizquel .30 .09
58 Shane Reynolds .30 .09
59 Barry Bonds 2.00 .60
60 Jason Kendall .30 .09
61 Marty Cordova .30 .09
62 Charles Johnson .30 .09
63 John Jaha .30 .09
64 Chan Ho Park .30 .09
65 Jermaine Allensworth .30 .09
66 Mark Grace .50 .15
67 Tim Salmon .50 .15
68 Edgar Martinez .50 .15
69 Marquis Grissom .30 .09
70 Craig Biggio .50 .15
71 Bobby Higginson .30 .09
72 Kevin Seitzer .30 .09
73 Hideo Nomo .75 .23
74 Dennis Eckersley .30 .09
75 Bobby Bonilla .30 .09
76 Dwight Gooden .50 .15
77 Jeff Cirillo .30 .09
78 Brian McRae .30 .09
79 Chipper Jones .75 .23
80 Jeff Fassero .30 .09
81 Fred McGriff .50 .15
82 Garret Anderson .30 .09
83 Eric Karros .30 .09
84 Derek Bell .30 .09
85 Kenny Lofton .30 .09
86 John Mabry .30 .09
87 Pat Hentgen .30 .09
88 Greg Maddux 1.25 .35
89 Jason Giambi .75 .23
90 Al Martin .30 .09
91 Derek Jeter 2.00 .60
92 Rey Ordonez .30 .09
93 Will Clark .75 .23
94 Kevin Appier .30 .09
95 Roberto Alomar .75 .23
96 Joe Carter .30 .09
97 Bernie Williams .50 .15
98 Albert Belle .30 .09
99 Greg Vaughn .30 .09
100 Tony Clark .30 .09
101 Matt Williams .30 .09
102 Jeff Bagwell .50 .15
103 Reggie Sanders .30 .09
104 Mariano Rivera .50 .15
105 Larry Walker .50 .15
106 Shawn Green .30 .09
107 Alex Ochoa .30 .09
108 Ivan Rodriguez .75 .23
109 Eric Young .30 .09
110 Javier Lopez .30 .09
111 Brian Hunter .30 .09
112 Raul Mondesi SP 4.00 1.20
113 Randy Johnson .75 .23
114 Tony Phillips .30 .09
115 Carlos Garcia .30 .09
116 Moises Alou .30 .09
117 Paul O'Neill .50 .15
118 Jim Thome .75 .23
119 Jermaine Dye .30 .09
120 Wilson Alvarez .30 .09
121 Rondell White .30 .09
122 Michael Tucker .30 .09
123 Mike Lansing .30 .09
124 Tony Gwynn 1.00 .30
125 Ryan Klesko .30 .09
126 Jim Edmonds .30 .09
127 Chuck Knoblauch .30 .09
128 Rafael Palmeiro .50 .15
129 Jay Buhner .30 .09
130 Tom Glavine .50 .15
131 Julio Franco .30 .09
132 Cecil Fielder .30 .09
133 Paul Wilson SP 4.00 1.20
134 Deion Sanders .50 .15
135 Alex Gonzalez .30 .09
136 Charles Nagy .30 .09
137 Andy Ashby SP 4.00 1.20
138 Edgar Renteria .30 .09
139 Pedro Martinez .75 .23
140 Brian Jordan .30 .09
141 Todd Hundley .30 .09
142 Marc Newfield .30 .09
143 Darryl Strawberry .50 .15
144 Dan Wilson .30 .09
145 Brian Giles RC 1.50 .45
146 F.P. Santangelo .30 .09
147 Shannon Stewart SP 4.00 1.20
148 Scott Spiezio .30 .09
149 Andruw Jones .30 .09
150 Karim Garcia .30 .09
151 Vladimir Guerrero .75 .23
152 George Arias .30 .09
153 Brooks Kieschnick .30 .09
154 Todd Walker .30 .09
155 Scott Rolen .50 .15
156 Todd Greene .30 .09
157 Dmitri Young .30 .09
158 Ruben Rivera .30 .09
159 Bartolo Colon .30 .09

160 Nomar Garciaparra 1.25 .35
161 Bob Abreu SP 4.00 1.20
162 Darin Erstad .30 .09
163 Ken Griffey Jr. CL .75 .23
164 Frank Thomas CL .50 .15
165 Alex Rodriguez CL .75 .23

1997 Studio Gold Press Proofs

Randomly inserted in packs, this 165-card set is parallel to the regular Studio set. The difference is found in the special micro-etched border with gold holographic foil stamping. Only 500 of each card was produced.

Nm-Mt Ex-Mt
*STARS: 8X TO 20X BASIC CARDS ....
*SP'S: .6X TO 1.5X BASIC CARDS.....
*ROOKIES: 2.5X TO 6X BASIC CARDS

1997 Studio Silver Press Proofs

Randomly inserted in packs, this 165-card set is parallel to the regular Studio set. The difference is found in the special micro-etched border with silver holographic foil stamping. Only 1500 of each card was produced.

Nm-Mt Ex-Mt
*STARS: 4X TO 10X BASIC CARDS ....
*SP's: .3X TO .8X BASIC CARDS.......
*ROOKIES: 1.25X TO 3X BASIC CARDS

1997 Studio Autographs

Randomly inserted in packs at an approximate rate of 1 in every 30 or more boxes, each of these three different cards feature an autographed and serial-numbered parallel version of the 8x10 Studio Portraits insert. Cards are distinguished by a silver "Autographed Signature" stamp on the front. Only a limited number of portraits were signed by each player. The amount each player signed is listed next to his name. Each player signed the first 100 serial #'d cards in blue ink and all the preceding cards in black ink.

Nm-Mt Ex-Mt
12 Todd Walker/1250 15.00 4.50
21 Vladimir Guerrero/500 50.00 15.00
24 Scott Rolen/1000 25.00 7.50

1997 Studio Hard Hats Samples

Issued to promote the 1997 Studio Hard Hat insert set, these cards can be differenentiated from the regular Hard Hat cards as they are numbered XXXX/5000.

Nm-Mt Ex-Mt
COMPLETE SET (24) 60.00 18.00
1 Ivan Rodriguez 2.50 .75
2 Albert Belle 1.00 .30
3 Ken Griffey Jr. 6.00 1.80
4 Chuck Knoblauch 1.25 .35
5 Frank Thomas 3.00 .90
6 Cal Ripken 10.00 3.00
7 Todd Walker 1.25 .35
8 Alex Rodriguez 5.00 1.50
9 Jim Thome 2.50 .75
10 Mike Piazza 6.00 1.80
11 Barry Larkin 2.00 .60
12 Chipper Jones 5.00 1.50
13 Derek Jeter 10.00 3.00
14 Matt Williams 1.50 .45
15 Jason Giambi 3.00 .90
16 Tim Salmon 1.25 .35
17 Brady Anderson 1.25 .35
18 Rondell White 1.25 .35
19 Bernie Williams 2.00 .60
20 Juan Gonzalez 2.50 .75
21 Karim Garcia 1.25 .35
22 Scott Rolen 3.00 .90
23 Darin Erstad 3.00 .90
24 Brian Jordan 1.25 .35

1997 Studio Hard Hats

Randomly inserted in packs, this 24-card set features color player images of 24 major league superstars on a unique clear plastic, foil-stamped, die cut batting helmet design. Only 5000 of each card was produced and are sequentially numbered.

Nm-Mt Ex-Mt
COMPLETE SET (24) 150.00 45.00
1 Ivan Rodriguez 6.00 1.80
2 Albert Belle 2.50 .75
3 Ken Griffey Jr. 10.00 3.00
4 Chuck Knoblauch 2.50 .75
5 Frank Thomas 6.00 1.80
6 Cal Ripken 20.00 6.00
7 Todd Walker 2.50 .75
8 Alex Rodriguez 10.00 3.00
9 Jim Thome 6.00 1.80
10 Mike Piazza 10.00 3.00
11 Barry Larkin 6.00 1.80
12 Chipper Jones 6.00 1.80
13 Derek Jeter 15.00 4.50
14 Matt Williams 2.50 .75
15 Jason Giambi 6.00 1.80
16 Tim Salmon 4.00 1.20
17 Brady Anderson 2.50 .75
18 Rondell White 2.50 .75
19 Bernie Williams 4.00 1.20
20 Juan Gonzalez 6.00 1.80
21 Karim Garcia 2.50 .75
22 Scott Rolen 4.00 1.20
23 Darin Erstad 2.50 .75
24 Brian Jordan 2.50 .75

1997 Studio Master Strokes

Randomly inserted in packs, this 24-card set features color photos of superstar players on all canvas card stock with gold foil stamping. Only 2,000 of each card was produced and is sequentially numbered.

Nm-Mt Ex-Mt
COMPLETE SET (24) 300.00 90.00
8 X 10: RANDOM INSERTS IN PACKS
8 X 10 PRINT RUN 5000 SERIAL #'d SETS
1 Derek Jeter 30.00 9.00
2 Jeff Bagwell 8.00 2.40
3 Ken Griffey Jr. 20.00 6.00
4 Barry Bonds 30.00 9.00
5 Frank Thomas 12.00 3.60
6 Andy Pettitte 8.00 2.40
7 Mo Vaughn 5.00 1.50
8 Alex Rodriguez 20.00 6.00
9 Andruw Jones 5.00 1.50
10 Kenny Lofton 5.00 1.50
11 Cal Ripken 40.00 12.00
12 Greg Maddux 20.00 6.00
13 Manny Ramirez 5.00 1.50
14 Mike Piazza 20.00 6.00
15 Vladimir Guerrero 12.00 3.60
16 Albert Belle 5.00 1.50
17 Chipper Jones 12.00 3.60
18 Hideo Nomo 12.00 3.60
19 Sammy Sosa 20.00 6.00
20 Tony Gwynn 15.00 4.50
21 Gary Sheffield 5.00 1.50
22 Mark McGwire 30.00 9.00
23 Juan Gonzalez 12.00 3.60
24 Paul Molitor 8.00 2.40

1997 Studio Portraits 8 x 10

Inserted one per pack, this 24-card set is a partial parallel version of the base set and features full-color portraits of star players measuring approximately 8" by 10" with a signable UV coating.

Nm-Mt Ex-Mt
COMPLETE SET (24) 25.00 7.50
1 Ken Griffey Jr. 2.50 .75
2 Frank Thomas 1.50 .45
3 Alex Rodriguez 2.50 .75
4 Andruw Jones .60 .18
5 Cal Ripken 5.00 1.50
6 Greg Maddux 2.50 .75
7 Mike Piazza 2.50 .75
8 Chipper Jones 1.50 .45
9 Albert Belle .60 .18
10 Derek Jeter 4.00 1.20
11 Juan Gonzalez 1.50 .45
12 Todd Walker .60 .18
13 Mark McGwire 4.00 1.20
14 Barry Bonds 4.00 1.20
15 Jeff Bagwell 1.00 .30
16 Manny Ramirez .60 .18
17 Kenny Lofton .60 .18
18 Mo Vaughn .60 .18
19 Hideo Nomo 1.50 .45
20 Tony Gwynn 2.00 .60
21 Vladimir Guerrero 1.50 .45
22 Gary Sheffield .60 .18
23 Ryne Sandberg 2.50 .75
24 Scott Rolen 1.00 .30

1998 Studio 8 x 10 Samples

One of these three different sample cards was distributed along with dealer order forms to preview the upcoming 1998 Studio baseball release. The cards are identical to the 1998 Studio 8 x 10 Autograph's except of course for the lack of an autograph on the front of the card and the addition of the bold "SAMPLE" text running diagonally across the card back. These samples were distributed around April, 1998.

Nm-Mt Ex-Mt
COMPLETE SET (3) 5.00 1.50
1 Travis Lee 1.00 .30
2 Todd Helton 3.00 .90
3 Ben Grieve 1.50 .45

1998 Studio

The 1998 Studio set consists of 220 cards. The eight-card packs retailed for $2.99 each. Each pack contains 1-8"x10" card and seven standard size cards. The fronts feature candid head/shoulder player photos with game action photography in the background. The player's name lines the bottom border and the Donruss logo sits in the upper left corner. The release date was June, 1998.

Nm-Mt Ex-Mt
COMPLETE SET (220) 50.00 15.00
1 Tony Clark .30 .09
2 Jose Cruz Jr. .30 .09
3 Ivan Rodriguez .75 .23
4 Mo Vaughn .30 .09
5 Kenny Lofton .30 .09
6 Will Clark .75 .23
7 Barry Larkin .75 .23
8 Jay Bell .30 .09
9 Kevin Young .30 .09
10 Francisco Cordova .30 .09
11 Justin Thompson .30 .09
12 Paul Molitor .50 .15
13 Jeff Bagwell .50 .15
14 Jose Canseco .75 .23
15 Scott Rolen .50 .15
16 Wilton Guerrero .30 .09
17 Shannon Stewart .30 .09
18 Hideki Irabu .30 .09
19 Michael Tucker .30 .09
20 Joe Carter .30 .09
21 Gabe Alvarez .30 .09
22 Ricky Ledee .30 .09
23 Karim Garcia .30 .09
24 Eli Marrero .30 .09
25 Scott Elarton .30 .09
26 Mario Valdez .30 .09
27 Ben Grieve .30 .09
28 Paul Konerko .30 .09
29 Esteban Yan RC .30 .09
30 Esteban Loaiza .30 .09
31 Delino DeShields .30 .09
32 Bernie Williams .50 .15
33 Joe Randa .30 .09
34 Randy Johnson .75 .23
35 Brett Tomko .30 .09
36 Todd Erdos RC .30 .09
37 Bobby Higginson .30 .09
38 Jason Kendall .30 .09
39 Ray Lankford .30 .09
40 Mark Grace .50 .15
41 Andy Pettitte .50 .15
42 Alex Rodriguez 1.25 .35
43 Hideo Nomo .75 .23
44 Sammy Sosa 1.25 .35
45 J.T. Snow .30 .09
46 Jason Varitek .30 .09
47 Vinny Castilla .30 .09
48 Neifi Perez .30 .09
49 Todd Walker .50 .15
50 Mike Cameron .30 .09
51 Jeffrey Hammonds .30 .09
52 Deivi Cruz .30 .09
53 Brian Hunter .30 .09
54 Al Martin .30 .09
55 Ron Coomer .30 .09
56 Chan Ho Park .30 .09
57 Pedro Martinez .75 .23
58 Darin Erstad .30 .09
59 Albert Belle .30 .09
60 Nomar Garciaparra 1.25 .35
61 Tony Gwynn 1.00 .30
62 Mike Piazza 1.25 .35
63 Todd Helton .50 .15
64 David Ortiz .30 .09
65 Todd Dunwoody .30 .09
66 Orlando Cabrera .30 .09
67 Ken Cloude .30 .09
68 Andy Benes .30 .09
69 Mariano Rivera .50 .15
70 Cecil Fielder .30 .09
71 Brian Jordan .30 .09
72 Darryl Kile .30 .09
73 Reggie Jefferson .30 .09
74 Shawn Estes .30 .09
75 Bobby Bonilla .30 .09
76 Denny Neagle .30 .09
77 Robin Ventura .30 .09
78 Omar Vizquel .30 .09
79 Craig Biggio .50 .15
80 Moises Alou .30 .09
81 Garret Anderson .30 .09
82 Eric Karros .30 .09
83 Dante Bichette .30 .09
84 Charles Johnson .30 .09
85 Rusty Greer .30 .09
86 Travis Fryman .30 .09
87 Fernando Tatis .30 .09
88 Wilson Alvarez .30 .09
89 Carl Pavano .30 .09
90 Brian Rose .30 .09
91 Geoff Jenkins .30 .09
92 Magglio Ordonez RC 2.00 .60
93 David Segui .30 .09
94 David Cone .30 .09
95 John Smoltz .50 .15
96 Jim Thome .75 .23
97 Gary Sheffield .30 .09
98 Barry Bonds 2.00 .60
99 Andres Galarraga .30 .09
100 Brad Fullmer .30 .09
101 Bobby Estalella .30 .09
102 Enrique Wilson .30 .09
103 Frank Catalanotto RC .50 .15
104 Mike Lowell RC 1.50 .45
105 Kevin Orie .30 .09
106 Matt Morris .30 .09
107 Pokey Reese .30 .09
108 Shawn Green .30 .09
109 Tony Womack .30 .09
110 Ken Caminiti .30 .09
111 Roberto Alomar .75 .23
112 Ken Griffey Jr. 1.25 .35
113 Cal Ripken 2.50 .75
114 Lou Collier .30 .09
115 Larry Walker .50 .15
116 Fred McGriff .50 .15
117 Jim Edmonds .30 .09
118 Edgar Martinez .50 .15
119 Matt Williams .30 .09
120 Ismael Valdes .30 .09
121 Bartolo Colon .30 .09
122 Jeff Cirillo .30 .09
123 Steve Woodard .30 .09
124 Kevin Millwood RC 1.25 .35
125 Derrick Gibson .30 .09
126 Jacob Cruz .30 .09
127 Russell Branyan .30 .09
128 Sean Casey .30 .09
129 Derrek Lee .30 .09
130 Paul O'Neill .50 .15
131 Brad Radke .30 .09
132 Kevin Appier .30 .09
133 John Olerud .30 .09
134 Alan Benes .30 .09
135 Todd Greene .30 .09
136 Carlos Mendoza RC .30 .09
137 Wade Boggs .50 .15
138 Jose Guillen .30 .09
139 Tino Martinez .50 .15
140 Aaron Boone .30 .09
141 Abraham Nunez .30 .09
142 Preston Wilson .30 .09
143 Randall Simon .30 .09
144 Dennis Reyes .30 .09
145 Mark Kotsay .30 .09
146 Richard Hidalgo .30 .09
147 Travis Lee .30 .09
148 Hanley Frias RC .30 .09
149 Ruben Rivera .30 .09
150 Rafael Medina .30 .09
151 Dave Nilsson .30 .09
152 Curt Schilling .50 .15
153 Brady Anderson .30 .09
154 Carlos Delgado .30 .09
155 Jason Giambi .75 .23
156 Pat Hentgen .30 .09
157 Tom Glavine .50 .15
158 Ryan Klesko .30 .09
159 Chipper Jones .75 .23
160 Juan Gonzalez .75 .23
161 Mark McGwire 2.00 .60
162 Vladimir Guerrero .75 .23
163 Derek Jeter 2.00 .60
164 Manny Ramirez .30 .09
165 Mike Mussina .75 .23
166 Rafael Palmeiro .50 .15
167 Henry Rodriguez .30 .09
168 Jeff Suppan .30 .09
169 Eric Milton .30 .09
170 Scott Spiezio .30 .09
171 Wilson Delgado .30 .09
172 Bubba Trammell .30 .09
173 Ellis Burks .30 .09
174 Jason Dickson .30 .09
175 Butch Huskey .30 .09
176 Edgardo Alfonzo .30 .09
177 Eric Young .30 .09
178 Marquis Grissom .30 .09
179 Lance Johnson .30 .09
180 Kevin Brown .50 .15
181 Sandy Alomar Jr. .30 .09
182 Todd Hundley .30 .09
183 Rondell White .30 .09
184 Javier Lopez .30 .09
185 Damian Jackson .30 .09
186 Raul Mondesi .30 .09
187 Rickey Henderson .75 .23
188 David Justice .30 .09
189 Jay Buhner .30 .09
190 Jaret Wright .30 .09
191 Miguel Tejada .50 .15
192 Ron Wright .30 .09
193 Livan Hernandez .30 .09
194 A.J. Hinch .30 .09
195 Richie Sexson .30 .09
196 Bob Abreu .30 .09
197 Louis Castillo .30 .09
198 Michael Coleman .30 .09
199 Greg Maddux 1.25 .35
200 Frank Thomas .75 .23
201 Andruw Jones .30 .09
202 Roger Clemens 1.50 .45
203 Tim Salmon .50 .15
204 Chuck Knoblauch .30 .09
205 Wes Helms .30 .09
206 Juan Encarnacion .30 .09
207 Russ Davis .30 .09
208 John Valentin .30 .09
209 Tony Saunders .30 .09
210 Mike Sweeney .50 .15
211 Steve Finley .30 .09
212 Dave Dellucci RC .30 .09
213 Edgar Renteria .30 .09
214 Jeremi Gonzalez .30 .09
CL1 Jeff Bagwell CL .30 .09
CL2 Mike Piazza CL .75 .23
CL3 Greg Maddux CL .75 .23
CL4 Cal Ripken CL 1.25 .35
CL5 Frank Thomas CL .50 .15
CL6 Ken Griffey Jr. CL .75 .23

1998 Studio Gold Press Proofs

Randomly inserted in packs, this 220-card set is a parallel to the Studio base set. Each card features striking gold foil borders and is sequentially serial numbered to 300 on back.

Nm-Mt Ex-Mt
*STARS: 4X TO 10X BASIC CARDS ....
*ROOKIES: 4X TO 10X BASIC CARDS

1998 Studio Silver Press Proofs

Randomly inserted in packs, this 220-card set is a parallel to the Studio base set. Each card features silver foil borders on front. Though they are not serial numbered, each card states "1 of 1,000" on back.

Nm-Mt Ex-Mt
COMMON CARD 2.00 .60
*STARS: 2X TO 5X BASIC CARDS .....
*ROOKIES: 2X TO 5X BASIC CARDS ..

1998 Studio Autographs 8 x 10

Three of the games youngest and brightest stars signed these 8" by 10" photos . Each player signed a limited amount of autographs and the amount they signed is notated next to their names

Nm-Mt Ex-Mt
1 Travis Lee/500 10.00 3.00
2 Todd Helton/1000 25.00 7.50
3 Ben Grieve/1000 10.00 3.00

1998 Studio Freeze Frame

Randomly inserted in packs, this 30-card set features a selection of top stars in a design mimicking a roll of film. The set is sequentially numbered to 4,000, and the first 500 cards in this set are die cut.

Nm-Mt Ex-Mt
COMPLETE SET (30) 150.00 45.00
DIE CUT PRINT RUN 500 SERIAL #'d SETS
RANDOM INSERTS IN PACKS
1 Ken Griffey Jr. 10.00 3.00
2 Derek Jeter 15.00 4.50
3 Ben Grieve 2.50 .75
4 Cal Ripken 20.00 6.00
5 Alex Rodriguez 10.00 3.00
6 Greg Maddux 10.00 3.00
7 David Justice 2.50 .75
8 Mike Piazza 10.00 3.00
9 Chipper Jones 6.00 1.80
10 Randy Johnson 6.00 1.80
11 Jeff Bagwell 4.00 1.20
12 Nomar Garciaparra 10.00 3.00
13 Andruw Jones 2.50 .75
14 Frank Thomas 6.00 1.80
15 Scott Rolen 4.00 1.20
16 Barry Bonds 15.00 4.50
17 Kenny Lofton 2.50 .75
18 Ivan Rodriguez 6.00 1.80
19 Chuck Knoblauch 2.50 .75
20 Jose Cruz Jr. 2.50 .75
21 Bernie Williams 4.00 1.20
22 Tony Gwynn 8.00 2.40
23 Juan Gonzalez 6.00 1.80
24 Gary Sheffield 2.50 .75
25 Roger Clemens 12.00 3.60
26 Travis Lee 2.50 .75
27 Brad Fullmer 2.50 .75
28 Tim Salmon 4.00 1.20
29 Raul Mondesi 2.50 .75
30 Roberto Alomar 6.00 1.80

1998 Studio Hit Parade

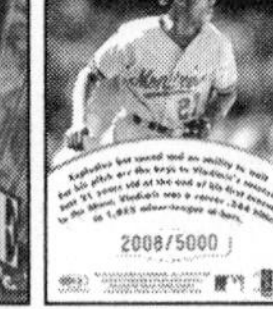

Randomly inserted in packs, this 20-card set is an insert to the Studio base set. The set is sequentially numbered to 5000. The fronts feature 20 of the game's most accomplished batsmen in color action photography. The backgrounds help showcase the players with a sunburst design. The player's name and team logo are found below the photo and the Donruss logo is in the upper left corner.

Nm-Mt Ex-Mt
COMPLETE SET (20) 100.00 30.00
1 Tony Gwynn 8.00 2.40
2 Larry Walker 4.00 1.20
3 Mike Piazza 10.00 3.00
4 Frank Thomas 6.00 1.80
5 Manny Ramirez 2.50 .75
6 Ken Griffey Jr. 10.00 3.00
7 Todd Helton 4.00 1.20
8 Vladimir Guerrero 6.00 1.80
9 Albert Belle 2.50 .75
10 Jeff Bagwell 4.00 1.20
11 Juan Gonzalez 6.00 1.80
12 Jim Thome 6.00 1.80
13 Scott Rolen 4.00 1.20
14 Tino Martinez 4.00 1.20
15 Mark McGwire 15.00 4.50
16 Barry Bonds 15.00 4.50
17 Tony Clark 2.50 .75
18 Mo Vaughn 2.50 .75
19 Darin Erstad 2.50 .75
20 Paul Konerko 2.50 .75

1998 Studio Masterstrokes

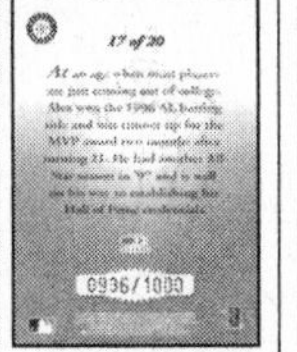

Randomly inserted in packs, this 20-card set is an insert to the Studio base set. The set is sequentially numbered to 1000. Each card resembles an artist's canvas on which a color player photo is featured. An artist's paintbrush sits at the bottom border of the card with the word "Masterstrokes" written in italics above it.

	Nm-Mt	Ex-Mt
COMPLETE SET (20)	250.00	75.00
1 Travis Lee	5.00	1.50
2 Kenny Lofton	5.00	1.50
3 Mo Vaughn	5.00	1.50
4 Ivan Rodriguez	12.00	3.60
5 Roger Clemens	25.00	7.50
6 Mark McGwire	30.00	9.00
7 Hideo Nomo	12.00	3.60
8 Andruw Jones	5.00	1.50
9 Nomar Garciaparra	20.00	6.00
10 Juan Gonzalez	12.00	3.60
11 Jeff Bagwell	8.00	2.40
12 Derek Jeter	30.00	9.00
13 Tony Gwynn	15.00	4.50
14 Chipper Jones	12.00	3.60
15 Mike Piazza	20.00	6.00
16 Greg Maddux	20.00	6.00
17 Alex Rodriguez	20.00	6.00
18 Cal Ripken	40.00	12.00
19 Frank Thomas	12.00	3.60
20 Ken Griffey Jr.	20.00	6.00

1998 Studio Portraits 8 x 10

Inserted one per Studio pack, this 36-card set is an insert to the Studio base set. Twelve of the Studio Portraits are exclusive to the retail/hobby configuration of the product.

	Nm-Mt	Ex-Mt
COMPLETE SET (36)	40.00	12.00
GOLD: RANDOM INSERTS IN PACKS		
GOLD PRINT RUN 300 SERIAL #'d SETS		
1 Travis Lee	.50	.15
2 Todd Helton	.75	.23
3 Ben Grieve	.50	.15
4 Paul Konerko	.50	.15
5 Jeff Bagwell	.75	.23
6 Derek Jeter	3.00	.90
7 Ivan Rodriguez	1.25	.35
8 Cal Ripken	4.00	1.20
9 Mike Piazza	2.00	.60
10 Chipper Jones	1.25	.35
11 Frank Thomas	1.25	.35
12 Tony Gwynn	1.50	.45
13 Nomar Garciaparra	2.00	.60
14 Juan Gonzalez	1.25	.35
15 Greg Maddux	2.00	.60
16 Hideo Nomo	1.25	.35
17 Scott Rolen	.75	.23
18 Barry Bonds	3.00	.90
19 Ken Griffey Jr.	2.00	.60
20 Alex Rodriguez	2.00	.60
21 Roger Clemens	2.50	.75
22 Mark McGwire	3.00	.90
23 Jose Cruz Jr.	.50	.15
24 Andruw Jones	.50	.15
25 Tino Martinez	.75	.23
26 Mo Vaughn	.50	.15
27 Vladimir Guerrero	1.25	.35
28 Tony Clark	.50	.15
29 Andy Pettitte	.75	.23
30 Jaret Wright	.50	.15
31 Paul Molitor	.75	.23
32 Darin Erstad	.50	.15
33 Larry Walker	.75	.23
34 Chuck Knoblauch	.50	.15
35 Barry Larkin	1.25	.35
36 Kenny Lofton	.50	.15

1998 Studio MLB 99

This 20 card set was inserted into both Donruss Update and Studio packs. These cards feature 20 of the leading Baseball players and were widely available because of the insertion into both of the aforementioned brands. Please see 1998 Donruss MLB 99 for pricing.

	Nm-Mt	Ex-Mt
PLEASE SEE 1998 DONRUSS MLB 99		

2001 Studio

This 200 card set was issued in six-card packs with 18 packs per box. Cards numbered 151-200 were shorter printed than cards 1-150. Each of the cards from 151-200 were serial numbered to 700.

	Nm-Mt	Ex-Mt
COMP.SET w/o SP's (150)	40.00	12.00
COMMON CARD (1-150)	.50	.15
COMMON (151-200)	8.00	2.40
1 Alex Rodriguez	2.00	.60
2 Barry Bonds	3.00	.90
3 Cal Ripken	4.00	1.20
4 Chipper Jones	1.25	.35
5 Derek Jeter	3.00	.90
6 Troy Glaus	.75	.23
7 Frank Thomas	1.25	.35
8 Greg Maddux	2.00	.60
9 Ivan Rodriguez	1.25	.35
10 Jeff Bagwell	.75	.23
11 Mark Quinn	.50	.15
12 Todd Helton	.75	.23
13 Ken Griffey Jr.	2.00	.60
14 Manny Ramirez	.50	.15
15 Mark McGwire	3.00	.90
16 Mike Piazza	2.00	.60
17 Nomar Garciaparra	2.00	.60
18 Robin Ventura	.50	.15
19 Aramis Ramirez	.50	.15
20 J.T. Snow	.50	.15
21 Pat Burrell	.50	.15
22 Curt Schilling	.75	.23
23 Carlos Delgado	.50	.15
24 J.D. Drew	.50	.15
25 Cliff Floyd	.50	.15
26 Brian Jordan	.50	.15
27 Roberto Alomar	1.25	.35
28 Barry Zito	1.25	.35
29 Harold Baines	.50	.15
30 Brad Penny	.50	.15
31 Jose Cruz Jr.	.50	.15
32 Andy Pettitte	.75	.23
33 Jim Edmonds	.50	.15
34 Darin Erstad	.50	.15
35 Jason Giambi	1.25	.35
36 Tom Glavine	.75	.23
37 Juan Gonzalez	1.25	.35
38 Mark Grace	.75	.23
39 Shawn Green	.50	.15
40 Tim Hudson	.50	.15
41 Andruw Jones	.50	.15
42 Jeff Kent	.50	.15
43 Barry Larkin	1.25	.35
44 Rafael Furcal	.50	.15
45 Mike Mussina	1.25	.35
46 Hideo Nomo	1.25	.35
47 Rafael Palmeiro	.75	.23
48 Scott Rolen	.75	.23
49 Gary Sheffield	.50	.15
50 Bernie Williams	.75	.23
51 Bob Abreu	.50	.15
52 Edgardo Alfonzo	.50	.15
53 Edgar Martinez	.75	.23
54 Magglio Ordonez	.50	.15
55 Kerry Wood	1.25	.35
56 Matt Morris	.50	.15
57 Lance Berkman	.50	.15
58 Kevin Brown	.50	.15
59 Sean Casey	.50	.15
60 Eric Chavez	.50	.15
61 Bartolo Colon	.50	.15
62 Johnny Damon	.50	.15
63 Jermaine Dye	.50	.15
64 Juan Encarnacion	.50	.15
65 Carl Everett	.50	.15
66 Brian Giles	.50	.15
67 Mike Hampton	.50	.15
68 Richard Hidalgo	.50	.15
69 Geoff Jenkins	.50	.15
70 Jacque Jones	.50	.15
71 Jason Kendall	.50	.15
72 Ryan Klesko	.50	.15
73 Chan Ho Park	.50	.15
74 Richie Sexson	.50	.15
75 Mike Sweeney	.50	.15
76 Fernando Tatis	.50	.15
77 Miguel Tejada	.50	.15
78 Jose Vidro	.50	.15
79 Larry Walker	2.00	.60
80 Preston Wilson	.50	.15
81 Craig Biggio	.75	.23
82 Fred McGriff	.75	.23
83 Jim Thome	1.25	.35
84 Garret Anderson	.50	.15
85 Mark Mulder	.50	.15
86 Tony Batista	.50	.15
87 Terrence Long	.50	.15
88 Brad Fullmer	.50	.15
89 Rusty Greer	.50	.15
90 Orlando Hernandez	.50	.15
91 Gabe Kapler	.50	.15
92 Paul Konerko	.50	.15
93 Carlos Lee	.50	.15
94 Kenny Lofton	.50	.15
95 Raul Mondesi	.50	.15
96 Jorge Posada	.75	.23
97 Tim Salmon	.75	.23
98 Greg Vaughn	.50	.15
99 Mo Vaughn	.50	.15
100 Omar Vizquel	.50	.15
101 Ben Grieve	.50	.15
102 Luis Gonzalez	.50	.15
103 Ray Durham	.50	.15
104 Ryan Dempster	.50	.15
105 Eric Karros	.50	.15
106 David Justice	.50	.15
107 Pedro Martinez	1.25	.35
108 Randy Johnson	1.25	.35
109 Rick Ankiel	.50	.15
110 Rickey Henderson	1.25	.35
111 Roger Clemens	2.50	.75
112 Sammy Sosa	2.00	.60
113 Tony Gwynn	1.50	.45
114 Vladimir Guerrero	1.25	.35
115 Kazuhiro Sasaki	.50	.15
116 Phil Nevin	.50	.15
117 Ruben Mateo	.50	.15
118 Shannon Stewart	.50	.15
119 Matt Williams	.50	.15
120 Tino Martinez	.75	.23
121 Ken Caminiti	.50	.15
122 Edgar Renteria	.50	.15
123 Charles Johnson	.50	.15
124 Aaron Sele	.50	.15
125 Javy Lopez	.50	.15
126 Mariano Rivera	.75	.23
127 Shea Hillenbrand	.50	.15
128 Jeff D'Amico	.50	.15
129 Brady Anderson	.50	.15
130 Kevin Millwood	.50	.15
131 Trot Nixon	.75	.23
132 Mike Lieberthal	.50	.15
133 Juan Pierre	.50	.15
134 Russ Ortiz	.50	.15
135 Jose Macias	.50	.15
136 John Smoltz	.75	.23
137 Jason Varitek	.50	.15
138 Dean Palmer	.50	.15
139 Jeff Cirillo	.50	.15
140 Paul O'Neill	.75	.23
141 Andres Galarraga	.50	.15
142 David Wells	.50	.15
143 Brad Radke	.50	.15
144 Wade Miller	.50	.15
145 John Olerud	.50	.15
146 Moises Alou	.50	.15
147 Carlos Beltran	.50	.15
148 Jeromy Burnitz	.50	.15
149 Steve Finley	.50	.15
150 Joe Mays	.50	.15
151 Alex Escobar ROO	8.00	2.40
152 J. Estrada ROO RC	10.00	3.00
153 Pedro Feliz ROO	8.00	2.40
154 Nate Frese ROO RC	8.00	2.40
155 Dee Brown ROO	8.00	2.40
156 B. Larson ROO RC	8.00	2.40
157 A. Gomez ROO RC	8.00	2.40
158 Jason Hart ROO	8.00	2.40
159 C.C. Sabathia ROO	8.00	2.40
160 Josh Towers ROO RC	8.00	2.40
161 C. Parker ROO RC	8.00	2.40
162 J. Melian ROO RC	8.00	2.40
163 Joe Kennedy ROO RC	8.00	2.40
164 A. Hernandez ROO RC	8.00	2.40
165 Jimmy Rollins ROO	8.00	2.40
166 Jose Mieses ROO RC	8.00	2.40
167 Roy Oswalt ROO	10.00	3.00
168 Eric Munson ROO	8.00	2.40
169 Xavier Nady ROO	8.00	2.40
170 H. Ramirez ROO RC	10.00	3.00
171 Abraham Nunez ROO	8.00	2.40
172 Jose Ortiz ROO	8.00	2.40
173 Jeremy Owens ROO RC UER Eric Owens pictured on front	8.00	2.40
174 C. Vargas ROO RC	8.00	2.40
175 Corey Patterson ROO	8.00	2.40
176 Carlos Pena ROO	8.00	2.40
177 Bud Smith ROO RC	8.00	2.40
178 Adam Dunn ROO	8.00	2.40
179 A. Pettyjohn ROO RC	8.00	2.40
180 E. Guzman ROO RC	8.00	2.40
181 Jay Gibbons ROO RC	10.00	3.00
182 Wilkin Ruan ROO RC	8.00	2.40
183 T. Shinjo ROO RC	10.00	3.00
184 Alfonso Soriano ROO	10.00	3.00
185 Marcus Giles ROO	8.00	2.40
186 Ichiro Suzuki ROO RC	50.00	15.00
187 Juan Uribe ROO RC	8.00	2.40
188 D. Williams ROO RC	8.00	2.40
189 Carlos Valderrama ROO RC	8.00	2.40
190 Matt White ROO RC	8.00	2.40
191 Albert Pujols ROO RC	100.00	30.00
192 D. Mendez ROO RC	8.00	2.40
193 C. Aldridge ROO RC	8.00	2.40
194 Endy Chavez ROO RC	8.00	2.40
195 Josh Beckett ROO	10.00	3.00
196 W. Betemit ROO RC	8.00	2.40
197 Ben Sheets ROO	8.00	2.40
198 A. Torres ROO RC	8.00	2.40
199 Aubrey Huff ROO	8.00	2.40
200 Jack Wilson ROO RC	8.00	2.40

2001 Studio Diamond Collection

Randomly inserted in packs, these 47 cards feature each of these players along with a game-worn jersey swatch. Cards numbered 24, 35 and 44 were not printed for this set.

	Nm-Mt	Ex-Mt
DC-1 Vladimir Guerrero	15.00	4.50
DC-2 Barry Bonds	40.00	12.00
DC-3 Cal Ripken	50.00	15.00
DC-4 Nomar Garciaparra	25.00	7.50
DC-5 Greg Maddux	15.00	4.50
DC-6 Frank Thomas	15.00	4.50
DC-7 Roger Clemens	30.00	9.00
DC-8 Luis Gonzalez SP	15.00	4.50
DC-9 Tony Gwynn	20.00	6.00
DC-10 Carlos Lee SP	15.00	4.50
DC-11 Troy Glaus	15.00	4.50
DC-12 Randy Johnson	15.00	4.50
DC-13 Manny Ramirez SP	15.00	4.50
DC-14 Pedro Martinez	15.00	4.50
DC-15 Todd Helton	15.00	4.50
DC-16 Jeff Bagwell	15.00	4.50
DC-17 Rickey Henderson	15.00	4.50
DC-18 Kazuhiro Sasaki	10.00	3.00
DC-19 Albert Pujols SP	50.00	15.00
DC-20 Ivan Rodriguez	15.00	4.50
DC-21 Darin Erstad	10.00	3.00
DC-22 Andruw Jones	10.00	3.00
DC-23 Roberto Alomar	15.00	4.50
DC-24 Does Not Exist		
DC-25 Juan Gonzalez	15.00	4.50
DC-26 Shawn Green	10.00	3.00
DC-27 Lance Berkman	10.00	3.00
DC-28 Scott Rolen	15.00	4.50
DC-29 Rafael Palmeiro	15.00	4.50
DC-30 J.D. Drew	10.00	3.00
DC-31 Kerry Wood	15.00	4.50
DC-32 Jim Edmonds	10.00	3.00
DC-33 Tom Glavine SP	25.00	7.50
DC-34 Hideo Nomo SP	50.00	15.00
DC-35 Does Not Exist		
DC-36 Tim Hudson	10.00	3.00
DC-37 Miguel Tejada	10.00	3.00
DC-38 Chipper Jones	15.00	4.50
DC-39 Edgar Martinez SP	25.00	7.50
DC-40 Chan Ho Park	10.00	3.00
DC-41 Magglio Ordonez	10.00	3.00
DC-42 Sean Casey	10.00	3.00
DC-43 Larry Walker	15.00	4.50
DC-44 Does Not Exist		
DC-45 Cliff Floyd	10.00	3.00
DC-46 Mike Sweeney	10.00	3.00
DC-47 Kevin Brown	10.00	3.00
DC-48 Richie Sexson	10.00	3.00
DC-49 Jermaine Dye	10.00	3.00
DC-50 Craig Biggio	15.00	4.50

2001 Studio Diamond Cut Collection

This parallel to the Diamond Cut insert set was randomly inserted in packs. Each card was serial numbered to 75 except for six players for whom only 50 cards were issued. We have notated those cards with an SP/50 in our checklist. Those players signed 25 of these cards for inclusion in this product.

	Nm-Mt	Ex-Mt
DC-1 Vladimir Guerrero SP/50		
DC-8 Luis Gonzalez SP/50		
DC-19 Albert Pujols SP/50		
DC-26 Shawn Green SP/50		
DC-27 Lance Berkman SP/50		
DC-28 Scott Rolen SP/50		

2001 Studio Leather and Lumber

Randomly inserted in packs, these 47 cards feature player cards along with one swatch of a game-used bat. A few players were printed in lesser quantity and we have notated those players with an SP. Also, cards numbered 4,22 and 39 do not exist.

	Nm-Mt	Ex-Mt
LL-1 Barry Bonds	30.00	9.00
LL-2 Cal Ripken	40.00	12.00
LL-3 Miguel Tejada	10.00	3.00
LL-4 Does Not Exist		
LL-5 Frank Thomas	15.00	4.50
LL-6 Greg Maddux	15.00	4.50
LL-7 Ivan Rodriguez	15.00	4.50
LL-8 Jeff Bagwell SP	25.00	7.50
LL-9 Sean Casey SP	15.00	4.50
LL-10 Todd Helton	15.00	4.50
LL-11 Cliff Floyd	10.00	3.00
LL-12 Hideo Nomo	25.00	7.50
LL-13 Chipper Jones	15.00	4.50
LL-14 Rickey Henderson	15.00	4.50
LL-15 Richard Hidalgo	10.00	3.00
LL-16 Mike Piazza	15.00	4.50
LL-17 Larry Walker	15.00	4.50
LL-18 Tony Gwynn	15.00	4.50
LL-19 Vladimir Guerrero	15.00	4.50
LL-20 Rafael Furcal	10.00	3.00
LL-21 Roberto Alomar SP	25.00	7.50
LL-22 Does Not Exist		
LL-23 Albert Pujols	50.00	15.00
LL-24 Raul Mondesi	10.00	3.00
LL-25 J.D. Drew	10.00	3.00
LL-26 Jim Edmonds	10.00	3.00
LL-27 Darin Erstad SP	15.00	4.50
LL-28 Craig Biggio	15.00	4.50
LL-29 Kenny Lofton	10.00	3.00
LL-30 Juan Gonzalez	15.00	4.50
LL-31 John Olerud	10.00	3.00
LL-32 Shawn Green	10.00	3.00
LL-33 Andruw Jones SP	15.00	4.50
LL-34 Moises Alou	10.00	3.00
LL-35 Jeff Kent	10.00	3.00
LL-36 Ryan Klesko	10.00	3.00
LL-37 Luis Gonzalez	10.00	3.00
LL-38 Rafael Palmeiro	15.00	4.50
LL-39 Does Not Exist		
LL-40 Scott Rolen	15.00	4.50
LL-41 Carlos Lee	10.00	3.00
LL-42 Bob Abreu	10.00	3.00
LL-43 Edgardo Alfonzo	10.00	3.00
LL-44 Bernie Williams	15.00	4.50
LL-45 Brian Giles	10.00	3.00
LL-46 Jermaine Dye	10.00	3.00
LL-47 Lance Berkman	10.00	3.00
LL-48 Edgar Martinez	15.00	4.50
LL-49 Richie Sexson	10.00	3.00
LL-50 Magglio Ordonez	10.00	3.00

2001 Studio Masterstrokes

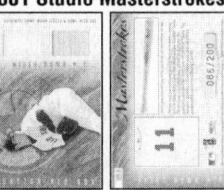

Randomly inserted in packs, these 30 cards feature the player along with both a swatch of game-used bat and a game-used jersey. These cards are serial numbered to 200 and cards numbered 13 and 15 were not issued.

	Nm-Mt	Ex-Mt
MS-1 Tony Gwynn	40.00	12.00
MS-2 Ivan Rodriguez	25.00	7.50
MS-3 J.D. Drew	15.00	4.50
MS-4 Cal Ripken	100.00	30.00
MS-5 Hideo Nomo	50.00	15.00
MS-6 Darin Erstad	15.00	4.50
MS-7 Frank Thomas	25.00	7.50
MS-8 Andruw Jones	15.00	4.50
MS-9 Roberto Alomar	25.00	7.50
MS-10 Larry Walker	25.00	7.50
MS-11 Vladimir Guerrero	25.00	7.50
MS-12 Barry Bonds	80.00	24.00
MS-13 Does Not Exist		
MS-14 Luis Gonzalez	15.00	4.50
MS-15 Does Not Exist		
MS-16 Juan Gonzalez	25.00	7.50
MS-17 Todd Helton	25.00	7.50
MS-18 Jeff Bagwell	25.00	7.50
MS-19 Albert Pujols	80.00	24.00
MS-20 Shawn Green	15.00	4.50
MS-21 Magglio Ordonez	15.00	4.50
MS-22 Scott Rolen	25.00	7.50
MS-23 Rafael Palmeiro	25.00	7.50
MS-24 Sean Casey	15.00	4.50
MS-25 Jim Edmonds	15.00	4.50
MS-26 Chipper Jones	25.00	7.50
MS-27 Cliff Floyd	15.00	4.50
MS-28 Carlos Lee	15.00	4.50
MS-29 Edgar Martinez	25.00	7.50
MS-30 Lance Berkman		

2001 Studio Masterstrokes Artist's Proofs

This parallel to the Studio Masterstroke set was issued to a print run of 25 sets. A few of the players signed their cards for inclusion in the set.

	Nm-Mt	Ex-Mt
MS-2 Ivan Rodriguez AU		
MS-11 Vladimir Guerrero AU		
MS-14 Luis Gonzalez AU		
MS-19 Albert Pujols AU		
MS-20 Shawn Green AU		
MS-24 Sean Casey AU		

2001 Studio Private Signings 5 x 7

Issued one per sealed box, these cards measure 5" by 7" and were signed by the players. A few cards were issued in shorter supply and we have notated them with an SP and print run information supplied by Donruss/Playoff.

	Nm-Mt	Ex-Mt
1 Bob Abreu	15.00	4.50
2 Roberto Alomar SP/200	40.00	12.00
3 Rick Ankiel	10.00	3.00
4 Josh Beckett	40.00	12.00
5 Lance Berkman	15.00	4.50
6 Wilson Betemit	15.00	4.50
7 Barry Bonds SP/95	200.00	60.00
8 Sean Casey	15.00	4.50
9 Roger Clemens SP/200	100.00	30.00
10 Adam Dunn	25.00	7.50
11 Darin Erstad SP/25		
12 Alex Escobar	10.00	3.00
13 Cliff Floyd	15.00	4.50
14 Jason Giambi SP/250	40.00	12.00
15 Brian Giles	15.00	4.50
16 Troy Glaus	25.00	7.50
17 Tom Glavine	40.00	12.00
18 Luis Gonzalez	15.00	4.50
19 Shawn Green SP/190	25.00	7.50
20 Vladimir Guerrero	40.00	12.00
21 Tony Gwynn SP/190	80.00	24.00
22 Todd Helton SP/125	25.00	7.50
23 Andruw Jones SP/250	25.00	7.50
24 Gabe Kapler	10.00	3.00
25 Ryan Klesko	15.00	4.50
26 Carlos Lee	15.00	4.50
27 Greg Maddux SP/200	80.00	24.00
28 Edgar Martinez	40.00	12.00
29 Mike Mussina SP/144	50.00	15.00
30 Magglio Ordonez	15.00	4.50
31 R. Palmeiro SP/250	40.00	12.00
32 Corey Patterson	15.00	4.50
33 Brad Penny	10.00	3.00
34 Albert Pujols SP/50		
35 Manny Ramirez SP/115	50.00	15.00
36 Cal Ripken SP/50		
37 Alex Rodriguez	100.00	30.00
38 Ivan Rodriguez SP/150	40.00	12.00
39 Scott Rolen	25.00	7.50
40 C.C. Sabathia	15.00	4.50
41 Curt Schilling	25.00	7.50

42 Ben Sheets 15.00 4.50
43 Alfonso Soriano 50.00 15.00
44 Mike Sweeney 15.00 4.50
45 Miguel Tejada 15.00 4.50
46 Frank Thomas 40.00 12.00
47 Kerry Wood 40.00 12.00
48 Barry Zito 40.00 12.00

2001 Studio Warning Track

Randomly inserted in packs, these 35 cards feature the player along with a swatch from an outfield-wall. Card number 26 does not exist in this set.

Nm-Mt Ex-Mt
*OFF THE WALL: RANDOM INSERTS IN PACKS
OFF THE WALL 25 SERIAL #'D SETS..
OFF THE WALL: NO PRICING DUE TO SCARCITY
OTW: RANDOM INSERTS IN PACKS...
WT-1 Andruw Jones 8.00 2.40
WT-2 Rafael Palmeiro 10.00 3.00
WT-3 Gary Sheffield 8.00 2.40
WT-4 Larry Walker 10.00 3.00
WT-5 Shawn Green 8.00 2.40
WT-6 Mike Piazza 15.00 4.50
WT-7 Barry Bonds 25.00 7.50
WT-8 J.D. Drew 8.00 2.40
WT-9 Magglio Ordonez 8.00 2.40
WT-10 Todd Helton 10.00 3.00
WT-11 Juan Gonzalez 10.00 3.00
WT-12 Pat Burrell 8.00 2.40
WT-13 Mark McGwire 30.00 9.00
WT-14 Frank Robinson 10.00 3.00
WT-15 Manny Ramirez 8.00 2.40
WT-16 Lance Berkman 8.00 2.40
WT-17 Kirby Puckett 10.00 3.00
WT-18 Johnny Bench 10.00 3.00
WT-19 Chipper Jones 10.00 3.00
WT-20 Mike Schmidt 20.00 6.00
WT-21 Vladimir Guerrero 10.00 3.00
WT-22 Sammy Sosa 20.00 6.00
WT-23 Cal Ripken 30.00 9.00
WT-24 Roberto Alomar 10.00 3.00
WT-25 Willie Stargell 10.00 3.00
WT-26 Does Not Exist
WT-27 Scott Rolen 10.00 3.00
WT-28 R. Clemente SP 60.00 18.00
WT-29 Tony Gwynn 15.00 4.50
WT-30 Ivan Rodriguez 10.00 3.00
WT-31 Sean Casey 8.00 2.40
WT-32 Frank Thomas 10.00 3.00
WT-33 Jeff Bagwell 10.00 3.00
WT-34 Jeff Kent 8.00 2.40
WT-35 Reggie Jackson 10.00 3.00

2001-02 Studio Chicago Collection

These cards were among the first in a project in which Donruss/Playoff unveiled a show-exclusive program. At the March 2002 Chicago Sun-Times Show, if a collector opened a box at the Donruss/Playoff booth -- they received a card from what Donruss/Playoff called the "Chicago Collection". Donruss/Playoff created a limited amount of singles from selected products and sequentially numbered each card to 5. The cards were distributed on a strict product-specific basis. For example, collectors who opened 2001 Donruss packs or boxes in front of a Donruss representative were be rewarded with the appropriate number of 2001 Playoff Contenders Chicago Collection cards. Due to scarcity, no pricing is provided for these cards.

Nm-Mt Ex-Mt

2002 Studio Samples

This 200 card set, which previewed the veteran players from the Studio set, was issued one per Beckett Baseball Card Monthly issue number 210. These cards are valued at a multiple of the regular Studio cards. These cards can be differentiated from the regular cards with the "Sample" verbiage in the back.

Nm-Mt Ex-Mt
*SAMPLES: 1.5X TO 4X BASIC CARDS
ONE PER ICHIRO BBCM 210
*GOLD: 1.5X TO 4X BASIC SAMPLES
GOLD: ISSUED IN 10% OF TOTAL RUN

2002 Studio

This 275 card set was issued in two separate series. The Studio product, containing cards 1-250, was released in July, 2002. The product was issued in five card packs which came 18 packs to a box and 16 boxes to a case. Cards numbered 1 through 200 feature veterans while cards 201 through 250 feature rookies and prospects and have a stated print run of 1500 serial numbered sets. Cards 251-275 were distributed in 2002 Donruss the Rookies packs in mid-December 2002. Like cards 201-250, these update cards featured a selection of prospects and were each serial-numbered to 1500 copies.

Nm-Mt Ex-Mt
COMP.LOW SET w/o SP's (200) 50.00 15.00
COMMON CARD (1-200) .50 .15
COMMON ROOKIE (1-200) .50 .15
COMMON CARD (201-275) 5.00 1.50
1 Vladimir Guerrero 1.25 .35
2 Chipper Jones 1.25 .35
3 Bob Abreu .50 .15
4 Barry Zito .75 .23
5 Larry Walker .75 .23
6 Miguel Tejada .50 .15
7 Mike Sweeney .50 .15
8 Shannon Stewart .50 .15
9 Sammy Sosa 2.00 .60
10 Bud Smith .50 .15
11 Wilson Betemit .50 .15
12 Kevin Brown .50 .15
13 Ellis Burks .50 .15
14 Pat Burrell .50 .15
15 Cliff Floyd .50 .15
16 Marcus Giles .50 .15
17 Troy Glaus .75 .23
18 Barry Larkin 1.25 .35
19 Carlos Lee .50 .15
20 Brian Lawrence .50 .15
21 Paul Lo Duca .50 .15
22 Ben Grieve .50 .15
23 Shawn Green .50 .15
24 Mike Cameron .50 .15
25 Roger Clemens 2.50 .75
26 Joe Crede .50 .15
27 Jose Cruz Jr. .50 .15
28 Jeremy Affeldt .50 .15
29 Adrian Beltre .50 .15
30 Josh Beckett .75 .23
31 Roberto Alomar 1.25 .35
32 Toby Hall .50 .15
33 Mike Hampton .50 .15
34 Eric Milton .50 .15
35 Eric Munson .50 .15
36 Trot Nixon .75 .23
37 Roy Oswalt .50 .15
38 Chan Ho Park .50 .15
39 Charles Johnson .50 .15
40 Nick Johnson .50 .15
41 Tim Hudson .50 .15
42 Cristian Guzman .50 .15
43 Drew Henson .50 .15
44 Mark Grace .75 .23
45 Luis Gonzalez .50 .15
46 Pedro Martinez 1.25 .35
47 Joe Mays .50 .15
48 Jorge Posada .75 .23
49 Aramis Ramirez .50 .15
50 Kip Wells .50 .15
51 Moises Alou .50 .15
52 Omar Vizquel .50 .15
53 Ichiro Suzuki 2.00 .60
54 Jimmy Rollins .50 .15
55 Freddy Garcia .50 .15
56 Steve Green .50 .15
57 Brian Jordan .50 .15
58 Paul Konerko .50 .15
59 Jack Cust .50 .15
60 Sean Casey .50 .15
61 Bret Boone .50 .15
62 Hideo Nomo 1.25 .35
63 Magglio Ordonez .50 .15
64 Frank Thomas 1.25 .35
65 Josh Towers .50 .15
66 Javier Vazquez .50 .15
67 Robin Ventura .50 .15
68 Aubrey Huff .50 .15
69 Richard Hidalgo .50 .15
70 Brandon Claussen 1.25 .35
71 Bartolo Colon .50 .15
72 John Buck .50 .15
73 Dee Brown .50 .15
74 Barry Bonds 3.00 .90
75 Jason Giambi 1.25 .35
76 Erick Almonte .50 .15
77 Ryan Dempster .50 .15
78 Jim Edmonds .50 .15
79 Jay Gibbons .50 .15
80 Shigetoshi Hasegawa .50 .15
81 Todd Helton .75 .23
82 Erik Bedard .50 .15
83 Carlos Beltran .50 .15
84 Rafael Soriano .50 .15
85 Gary Sheffield .50 .15
86 Richie Sexson .50 .15
87 Mike Rivera .50 .15
88 Jose Ortiz .50 .15
89 Abraham Nunez .50 .15
90 Dave Williams .50 .15
91 Preston Wilson .50 .15
92 Jason Jennings .50 .15
93 Juan Diaz .50 .15
94 Steve Smyth .50 .15
95 Phil Nevin .50 .15
96 John Olerud .50 .15
97 Brad Penny .50 .15
98 Andy Pettitte .75 .23
99 Juan Pierre .50 .15
100 Manny Ramirez .50 .15
101 Edgardo Alfonzo .50 .15
102 Michael Cuddyer .50 .15
103 Johnny Damon .50 .15
104 Carlos Zambrano .50 .15
105 Jose Vidro .50 .15
106 Tsuyoshi Shinjo .50 .15
107 Ed Rogers .50 .15
108 Scott Rolen .75 .23
109 Mariano Rivera .75 .23
110 Tim Redding .50 .15
111 Josh Phelps .50 .15
112 Gabe Kapler .50 .15
113 Edgar Martinez .75 .23
114 Fred McGriff .75 .23
115 Raul Mondesi .50 .15
116 Wade Miller .50 .15
117 Mike Mussina 1.25 .35
118 Rafael Palmeiro .75 .23
119 Adam Johnson .50 .15
120 Rickey Henderson 1.25 .35
121 Bill Hall .50 .15
122 Ken Griffey Jr. 2.00 .60
123 Geronimo Gil .50 .15
124 Robert Fick .50 .15
125 Darin Erstad .50 .15
126 Brandon Duckworth .50 .15
127 Garret Anderson .50 .15
128 Pedro Feliz .50 .15
129 Jeff Cirillo .50 .15
130 Brian Giles .50 .15
131 Craig Biggio .75 .23
132 Willie Harris .50 .15
133 Doug Davis .50 .15
134 Jeff Kent .50 .15
135 Terrence Long .50 .15
136 Carlos Delgado .50 .15
137 Tino Martinez .75 .23
138 Donaldo Mendez .50 .15
139 Sean Douglass .50 .15
140 Eric Chavez .50 .15
141 Rick Ankiel .50 .15
142 Jeremy Giambi .50 .15
143 Juan Pena .50 .15
144 Bernie Williams .75 .23
145 Craig Wilson .50 .15
146 Ricardo Rodriguez .50 .15
147 Albert Pujols 2.50 .75
148 Antonio Perez .50 .15
149 Russ Ortiz .50 .15
150 Corky Miller .50 .15
151 Rich Aurilia .50 .15
152 Kerry Wood 1.25 .35
153 Joe Thurston .50 .15
154 Jeff Deardorff .50 .15
155 Jermaine Dye .50 .15
156 Andruw Jones .50 .15
157 Victor Martinez .50 .15
158 Nick Neugebauer .50 .15
159 Matt Morris .50 .15
160 Casey Fossum .50 .15
161 J.D. Drew .50 .15
162 Matt Childers .50 .15
163 Mark Buehrle .50 .15
164 Jeff Bagwell .75 .23
165 Kazuhiro Sasaki .50 .15
166 Ben Sheets .50 .15
167 Alex Rodriguez 2.00 .60
168 Adam Pettyjohn .50 .15
169 Chris Snelling RC 1.50 .45
170 Robert Person .50 .15
171 Juan Uribe .50 .15
172 Mo Vaughn .50 .15
173 Alfredo Amezaga .50 .15
174 Ryan Drese .50 .15
175 Corey Thurman RC .50 .15
176 Jim Thome 1.25 .35
177 Orlando Cabrera .50 .15
178 Eric Cyr .50 .15
179 Greg Maddux 2.00 .60
180 Earl Snyder RC .50 .15
181 C.C. Sabathia .50 .15
182 Mark Mulder .50 .15
183 Jose Mieses .50 .15
184 Joe Kennedy .50 .15
185 Randy Johnson 1.25 .35
186 Tom Glavine .75 .23
187 Eric Junge RC .50 .15
188 Mike Piazza 2.00 .60
189 Corey Patterson .50 .15
190 Carlos Pena .50 .15
191 Curt Schilling .75 .23
192 Nomar Garciaparra 2.00 .60
193 Lance Berkman .50 .15
194 Ryan Klesko .50 .15
195 Ivan Rodriguez 1.25 .35
196 Alfonso Soriano .75 .23
197 Derek Jeter 3.00 .90
198 David Justice .50 .15
199 Juan Gonzalez 1.25 .35
200 Adam Dunn .50 .15
201 Victor Alvarez ROO RC 5.00 1.50
202 Miguel Asencio ROO RC 5.00 1.50
203 Brandon Backe ROO RC 5.00 1.50
204 Chris Baker ROO RC 5.00 1.50
205 Steve Bechler ROO RC 5.00 1.50
206 Francis Beltran ROO RC 5.00 1.50
207 Angel Berroa ROO 5.00 1.50
208 Hank Blalock ROO 8.00 2.40
209 Dewon Brazelton ROO 5.00 1.50
210 Sean Burroughs ROO 5.00 1.50
211 Marlon Byrd ROO 5.00 1.50
212 Raul Chavez ROO RC 5.00 1.50
213 Juan Cruz ROO 5.00 1.50
214 J.De La Rosa ROO RC 5.00 1.50
215 Doug Devore ROO RC 5.00 1.50
216 John Ennis ROO RC 5.00 1.50
217 Felix Escalona ROO RC 5.00 1.50
218 Morgan Ensberg ROO 5.00 1.50
219 Cam Esslinger ROO RC 5.00 1.50
220 Kevin Frederick ROO RC 5.00 1.50
221 Fr.German ROO RC 5.00 1.50
222 Eric Hinske ROO 5.00 1.50
223 Ben Howard ROO RC 5.00 1.50
224 Orlando Hudson ROO 5.00 1.50
225 Travis Hughes ROO RC 5.00 1.50
226 Kazuhisa Ishii ROO RC 10.00 3.00
227 Ryan Jamison ROO 5.00 1.50
228 Reed Johnson ROO RC 8.00 2.40
229 Kyle Kane ROO RC 5.00 1.50
230 Austin Kearns ROO 5.00 1.50
231 Sat.Komiyama ROO RC 5.00 1.50
232 Jason Lane ROO 5.00 1.50
233 Jeremy Lambert ROO RC 5.00 1.50
234 And. Machado ROO RC 5.00 1.50
235 Brian Mallette ROO RC 5.00 1.50
236 Tak. Nomura ROO RC 5.00 1.50
237 Jorge Padilla ROO RC 5.00 1.50
238 Luis Ugueto ROO RC 5.00 1.50
239 Mark Prior ROO 15.00 4.50
240 Rene Reyes ROO RC 5.00 1.50
241 Deivis Santos ROO RC 5.00 1.50
242 Elio Serrano ROO RC 5.00 1.50
243 Tom Shearn ROO RC 5.00 1.50
244 Allan Simpson ROO RC 5.00 1.50
245 So Taguchi ROO RC 8.00 2.40
246 Dennis Tankersley ROO 5.00 1.50
247 Mark Teixeira ROO 8.00 2.40
248 Matt Thornton ROO RC 5.00 1.50
249 Bobby Hill ROO 5.00 1.50
250 Ramon Vazquez ROO 5.00 1.50
251 Freddy Sanchez ROO RC 5.00 1.50
252 Josh Bard ROO RC 5.00 1.50
253 Trey Hodges ROO RC 5.00 1.50
254 Jorge Sosa ROO RC 5.00 1.50
255 Ben Kozlowski ROO RC 5.00 1.50
256 Eric Good ROO RC 5.00 1.50
257 Brian Tallet ROO RC 8.00 2.40
258 P.J. Bevis ROO RC 5.00 1.50
259 Rodrigo Rosario ROO RC 5.00 1.50
260 Kirk Saarloos ROO RC 5.00 1.50
261 Run. Hernandez ROO RC 5.00 1.50
262 Josh Hancock ROO RC 5.00 1.50
263 Tim Kalita ROO RC 5.00 1.50
264 J.Simontacchi ROO RC 5.00 1.50
265 Clay Condrey ROO RC 5.00 1.50
266 Cliff Lee ROO RC 8.00 2.40
267 Aaron Guiel ROO RC 5.00 1.50
268 Andy Pratt ROO RC 5.00 1.50
269 Wilson Valdez ROO RC 5.00 1.50
270 Oliver Perez ROO RC .75 .23
271 Joe Borchard ROO 5.00 1.50
272 J.Robertson ROO RC 5.00 1.50
273 Aaron Cook ROO RC 5.00 1.50
274 Kevin Cash ROO RC 5.00 1.50
275 Chone Figgins ROO RC 5.00 1.50

2002 Studio Private Signings

Randomly inserted in packs of Studio and Donruss the Rookies, these 210 cards partially parallel the 2002 Studio set. Since these cards are signed to a variable amount of cards, we have listed the print run next to the player's name. Those players who signed 25 or fewer cards are not priced due to market scarcity.

Nm-Mt Ex-Mt
1 Vladimir Guerrero/25
2 Chipper Jones/15
3 Bob Abreu/50 25.00 7.50
4 Barry Zito/25
6 Miguel Tejada/50 25.00 7.50
7 Mike Sweeney/50 25.00 7.50
8 Shannon Stewart/50 25.00 7.50
10 Bud Smith/100 15.00 4.50
11 Wilson Betemit/250 10.00 3.00
12 Kevin Brown/25
15 Cliff Floyd/50 25.00 7.50
16 Marcus Giles/250 15.00 4.50
17 Troy Glaus/50 40.00 12.00
18 Barry Larkin/25
19 Carlos Lee/25
20 Brian Lawrence/250 10.00 3.00
21 Paul Lo Duca/50 25.00 7.50
25 Roger Clemens/15
26 Joe Crede/250 10.00 3.00
28 Jeremy Affeldt/250 10.00 3.00
29 Adrian Beltre/25
30 Josh Beckett/25
31 Roberto Alomar/25
32 Toby Hall/250 10.00 3.00
35 Eric Munson/25
37 Roy Oswalt/50 25.00 7.50
40 Nick Johnson/250 15.00 4.50
41 Tim Hudson/25
43 Drew Henson/150 25.00 7.50
45 Luis Gonzalez/15
46 Pedro Martinez/15
47 Joe Mays/100 15.00 4.50
49 Aramis Ramirez/50 25.00 7.50
50 Kip Wells/250 10.00 3.00
51 Moises Alou/15
55 Freddy Garcia/50 25.00 7.50
56 Steve Green/250 10.00 3.00
59 Jack Cust/250 10.00 3.00
60 Sean Casey/50 25.00 7.50
63 Magglio Ordonez/15
64 Frank Thomas/15
65 Josh Towers/250 10.00 3.00
66 Javier Vazquez/100 20.00 6.00
68 Aubrey Huff/250 15.00 4.50
69 Richard Hidalgo/25
70 Brandon Claussen/250 25.00 7.50
72 John Buck/250 10.00 3.00
73 Dee Brown/250 10.00 3.00
75 Jason Giambi/25
76 Erick Almonte/250 10.00 3.00
79 Jay Gibbons/250 15.00 4.50
81 Todd Helton/15
82 Erik Bedard/250 10.00 3.00
83 Carlos Beltran/15
84 Rafael Soriano/250 15.00 4.50
85 Gary Sheffield/15
86 Richie Sexson/50 25.00 7.50
87 Mike Rivera/250 10.00 3.00
88 Jose Ortiz/250 10.00 3.00
89 Abraham Nunez/250 10.00 3.00
90 Dave Williams/250 10.00 3.00
92 Jason Jennings/250 10.00 3.00
93 Juan Diaz/250 10.00 3.00
94 Steve Smyth/250 10.00 3.00
97 Brad Penny/80 15.00 4.50
99 Juan Pierre/100 20.00 6.00
100 Manny Ramirez/15
102 Michael Cuddyer/250 10.00 3.00
104 Carlos Zambrano/250 25.00 7.50
105 Jose Vidro/100 20.00 6.00
107 Ed Rogers/250 10.00 3.00
108 Scott Rolen/15
110 Tim Redding/250 10.00 3.00
111 Josh Phelps/250 10.00 3.00
112 Gabe Kapler/100 15.00 4.50
113 Edgar Martinez/50 50.00 15.00
116 Wade Miller/250 15.00 4.50
117 Mike Mussina/15
118 Rafael Palmeiro/25
120 Rickey Henderson/15
121 Bill Hall/250 10.00 3.00
123 Geronimo Gil/250 10.00 3.00
124 Robert Fick/150 15.00 4.50
125 Darin Erstad/15
126 Brandon Duckworth/250 10.00 3.00
128 Pedro Feliz/250 10.00 3.00
130 Brian Giles/15
131 Craig Biggio/15
132 Willie Harris/250 10.00 3.00
133 Doug Davis/250 10.00 3.00
135 Terrence Long/50 25.00 7.50
138 Donaldo Mendez/250 10.00 3.00
139 Sean Douglass/250 10.00 3.00
140 Eric Chavez/15
141 Rick Ankiel/250 10.00 3.00
142 Jeremy Giambi/100 15.00 4.50
143 Juan Pena/250 10.00 3.00
144 Bernie Williams/15
145 Craig Wilson/250 10.00 3.00
146 Ricardo Rodriguez/250 10.00 3.00
147 Albert Pujols/25
148 Antonio Perez/250 10.00 3.00
150 Corky Miller/250 10.00 3.00
151 Rich Aurilia/25
152 Kerry Wood/15
153 Joe Thurston/250 10.00 3.00
154 Jeff Deardorff/250 10.00 3.00
155 Jermaine Dye/15
156 Andruw Jones/15
157 Victor Martinez/250 15.00 4.50
158 Nick Neugebauer/150 10.00 3.00
160 Casey Fossum/250 10.00 3.00
161 J.D. Drew/25
162 Matt Childers/250 10.00 3.00
163 Mark Buehrle/150 15.00 4.50
164 Jeff Bagwell/15
166 Ben Sheets/100 20.00 6.00
167 Alex Rodriguez/15
168 Adam Pettyjohn/250 10.00 3.00
169 Chris Snelling/250 25.00 7.50
170 Robert Person/250 10.00 3.00
171 Juan Uribe/250 10.00 3.00
173 Alfredo Amezaga/250 10.00 3.00
175 Corey Thurman/250 10.00 3.00
176 Jim Thome/15
178 Eric Cyr/250 10.00 3.00
179 Greg Maddux/15
180 Earl Snyder/250 10.00 3.00
181 C.C. Sabathia/50 25.00 7.50
182 Mark Mulder/50 40.00 12.00
183 Jose Mieses/250 10.00 3.00
184 Joe Kennedy/250 10.00 3.00
186 Tom Glavine/15
187 Eric Junge/250 10.00 3.00
189 Corey Patterson/205 15.00 4.50
190 Carlos Pena/200 10.00 3.00
191 Curt Schilling/15
192 Nomar Garciaparra/15
193 Lance Berkman/15
194 Ryan Klesko/15
195 Ivan Rodriguez/15
196 Alfonso Soriano/50 50.00 15.00
198 David Justice/15
199 Juan Gonzalez/15
200 Adam Dunn/25
201 Victor Alvarez ROO/250 10.00 3.00
203 Brandon Backe ROO/250 10.00 3.00
204 Chris Baker ROO/250 10.00 3.00
205 Steve Bechler ROO/250 10.00 3.00
206 Francis Beltran ROO/250 10.00 3.00
207 Angel Berroa ROO/250 15.00 4.50
208 Hank Blalock ROO/100 25.00 7.50
209 Dewon Brazelton ROO/200 10.00 3.00
210 Sean Burroughs ROO/50 25.00 7.50
211 Marlon Byrd ROO/200 15.00 4.50
212 Raul Chavez ROO/250 10.00 3.00
213 Juan Cruz ROO/50 25.00 7.50
214 Jorge De La Rosa ROO/250 10.00 3.00
215 Doug Devore ROO/250 10.00 3.00
216 John Ennis ROO/250 10.00 3.00
217 Felix Escalona ROO/250 10.00 3.00
218 Morgan Ensberg ROO/250 15.00 4.50
219 Cam Esslinger ROO/250 10.00 3.00
220 Kevin Frederick ROO/250 10.00 3.00
221 Franklyn German ROO/250 10.00 3.00
222 Eric Hinske ROO/250 10.00 3.00
223 Ben Howard ROO/250 10.00 3.00
224 Orlando Hudson ROO/250 10.00 3.00
225 Travis Hughes ROO/250 10.00 3.00
226 Kazuhisa Ishii ROO/50 50.00 15.00
227 Ryan Jamison ROO/250 10.00 3.00
228 Reed Johnson ROO/250 15.00 4.50
229 Kyle Kane ROO/250 10.00 3.00
230 Austin Kearns ROO/250 15.00 4.50
231 Satoru Komiyama ROO/50 15.00 4.50
232 Jason Lane ROO/200 10.00 3.00
233 Jeremy Lambert ROO/250 10.00 3.00
234 And Machado ROO/200 10.00 3.00
235 Brian Mallette ROO/250 10.00 3.00
236 Takahito Nomura ROO/100 25.00 7.50
237 Jorge Padilla ROO/200 10.00 3.00
238 Luis Ugueto ROO/250 10.00 3.00
239 Mark Prior ROO/100 80.00 24.00
240 Rene Reyes ROO/250 10.00 3.00
241 Deivis Santos ROO/250 10.00 3.00
242 Elio Serrano ROO/250 10.00 3.00
243 Tom Shearn ROO/250 10.00 3.00
244 Allan Simpson ROO/250 10.00 3.00
245 So Taguchi ROO/100 20.00 6.00
246 Dennis Tankersley ROO/100 15.00 4.50
247 Mark Teixeira ROO/50 40.00 12.00
248 Matt Thornton ROO/250 10.00 3.00
249 Bobby Hill ROO/100 15.00 4.50
250 Ramon Vazquez ROO/250 10.00 3.00
252 Josh Bard ROO/100 15.00 4.50
253 Trey Hodges ROO/250 10.00 3.00
255 Ben Kozlowski ROO/200 10.00 3.00
256 Eric Good ROO/200 10.00 3.00
257 Brian Tallet ROO/100 20.00 6.00
258 P.J. Bevis ROO/50 25.00 7.50
259 Rodrigo Rosario ROO/250 10.00 3.00
260 Kirk Saarloos ROO/100 15.00 4.50
263 Tim Kalita ROO/50 15.00 4.50
266 Cliff Lee ROO/100 25.00 7.50
268 Andy Pratt ROO/250 10.00 3.00
269 Wilson Valdez ROO/200 10.00 3.00
270 Oliver Perez ROO/25
271 Joe Borchard ROO/100 20.00 6.00
274 Kevin Cash ROO/100 15.00 4.50
275 Chone Figgins ROO/100 15.00 4.50

2002 Studio Proofs

Randomly issued in Studio and Donruss the Rookies packs, this is a complete parallel of the 2002 Studio set. Cards 1-250 were distributed in Studio packs and 251-275 in Donruss the Rookies. These cards were printed to a stated print run of 100 serial numbered sets.

Nm-Mt Ex-Mt
*PROOFS 1-200: 4X TO 10X BASIC....
*PROOFS RC'S 1-200: 3X TO 8X BASIC
201 Victor Alvarez ROO.............. 5.00 1.50
202 Miguel Asencio ROO............ 5.00 1.50
203 Brandon Backe ROO............ 5.00 1.50
204 Chris Baker ROO.................. 5.00 1.50
205 Steve Bechler ROO.............. 5.00 1.50
206 Francis Beltran ROO............ 5.00 1.50
207 Angel Berroa ROO................ 5.00 1.50
208 Hank Blalock ROO.............. 12.00 3.60
209 Dewon Brazelton ROO......... 5.00 1.50
210 Sean Burroughs ROO.......... 5.00 1.50
211 Marlon Byrd ROO................ 5.00 1.50
212 Raul Chavez ROO................ 5.00 1.50
213 Juan Cruz ROO.................... 5.00 1.50
214 Jorge De La Rosa ROO........ 5.00 1.50
215 Doug Devore ROO............... 5.00 1.50
216 John Ennis ROO.................. 5.00 1.50
217 Felix Escalona ROO............ 5.00 1.50
218 Morgan Ensberg ROO.......... 5.00 1.50
219 Cam Esslinger ROO............ 5.00 1.50
220 Kevin Frederick ROO.......... 5.00 1.50
221 Franklyn German ROO......... 5.00 1.50
222 Eric Hinske ROO................. 5.00 1.50
223 Ben Howard ROO................. 5.00 1.50
224 Orlando Hudson ROO.......... 5.00 1.50
225 Travis Hughes ROO............. 5.00 1.50
226 Kazuhisa Ishii ROO............ 20.00 6.00
227 Ryan Jamison ROO.............. 5.00 1.50
228 Reed Johnson ROO.............. 8.00 2.40
229 Kyle Kane ROO.................... 5.00 1.50
230 Austin Kearns ROO............. 5.00 1.50
231 Satoru Komiyama ROO........ 5.00 1.50
232 Jason Lane ROO.................. 5.00 1.50
233 Jeremy Lambert ROO.......... 5.00 1.50
234 Anderson Machado ROO...... 5.00 1.50
235 Brian Mallette ROO............. 5.00 1.50
236 Takahito Nomura ROO......... 5.00 1.50
237 Jorge Padilla ROO.............. 5.00 1.50
238 Luis Ugueto ROO................ 5.00 1.50
239 Mark Prior ROO.................. 25.00 7.50
240 Rene Reyes ROO................. 5.00 1.50
241 Deivis Santos ROO.............. 5.00 1.50
242 Elio Serrano ROO................ 5.00 1.50
243 Tom Shearn ROO................. 5.00 1.50
244 Allan Simpson ROO.............. 5.00 1.50
245 So Taguchi ROO.................. 8.00 2.40
246 Dennis Tankersley ROO........ 5.00 1.50
247 Mark Teixeira ROO.............. 12.00 3.60
248 Matt Thornton ROO.............. 5.00 1.50
249 Bobby Hill ROO.................... 5.00 1.50
250 Ramon Vazquez ROO........... 5.00 1.50
251 Freddy Sanchez ROO........... 5.00 1.50
252 Josh Bard ROO.................... 5.00 1.50
253 Trey Hodges ROO................ 5.00 1.50
254 Jorge Sosa ROO................... 5.00 1.50
255 Ben Kozlowski ROO.............. 5.00 1.50
256 Eric Good ROO..................... 5.00 1.50
257 Brian Tallet ROO.................. 8.00 2.40
258 P.J. Bevis ROO..................... 5.00 1.50
259 Rodrigo Rosario ROO........... 5.00 1.50
260 Kirk Saarloos ROO............... 5.00 1.50
261 Runelvys Hernandez ROO 5.00 1.50
262 Josh Hancock ROO............... 5.00 1.50
263 Tim Kalita ROO.................... 5.00 1.50
264 Jason Simontacchi ROO....... 5.00 1.50
265 Clay Condrey ROO............... 5.00 1.50
266 Cliff Lee ROO...................... 12.00 3.60
267 Aaron Guiel ROO.................. 5.00 1.50
268 Andy Pratt ROO.................... 5.00 1.50
269 Wilson Valdez ROO.............. 5.00 1.50
270 Oliver Perez ROO................. 8.00 2.40
271 Joe Borchard ROO................ 5.00 1.50
272 Jeriome Robertson ROO....... 5.00 1.50
273 Aaron Cook ROO.................. 5.00 1.50
274 Kevin Cash ROO................... 5.00 1.50
275 Chone Figgins ROO.............. 5.00 1.50

2002 Studio Classic

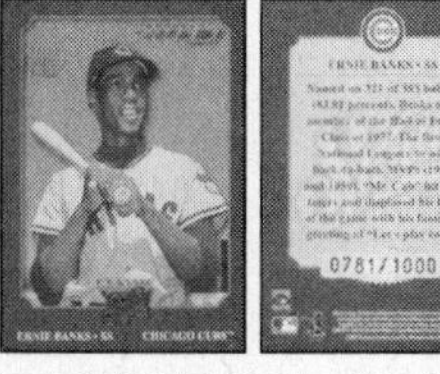

Randomly inserted in packs, these 25 card feature players elected to the Hall of Fame on the first ballot and have a stated print run of 1,000 serial numbered sets.

Nm-Mt Ex-Mt
COMPLETE SET (25).............. 150.00 45.00
*1ST BALLOT: 2X TO 5X BASIC CLASSIC
1ST BALLOT RANDOM IN PACKS........
1ST BALLOT PRINT RUN BASED ON HOF YR
1 Kirby Puckett........................ 8.00 2.40
2 George Brett........................ 15.00 4.50
3 Nolan Ryan........................... 15.00 4.50
4 Mike Schmidt........................ 12.00 3.60
5 Steve Carlton........................ 5.00 1.50
6 Reggie Jackson...................... 5.00 1.50
7 Tom Seaver............................ 5.00 1.50
8 Joe Morgan............................ 5.00 1.50
9 Jim Palmer............................. 5.00 1.50
10 Johnny Bench....................... 8.00 2.40
11 Willie McCovey.................... 5.00 1.50
12 Brooks Robinson.................. 8.00 2.40
13 Al Kaline............................... 8.00 2.40
14 Stan Musial.......................... 10.00 3.00
15 Ozzie Smith......................... 10.00 3.00
16 Dave Winfield....................... 5.00 1.50
17 Robin Yount......................... 10.00 3.00
18 Rod Carew............................. 5.00 1.50
19 Willie Stargell....................... 5.00 1.50
20 Lou Brock............................. 5.00 1.50
21 Ernie Banks.......................... 8.00 2.40
22 Ted Williams........................ 15.00 4.50
23 Jackie Robinson.................... 8.00 2.40
24 Roberto Clemente................ 15.00 4.50
25 Lou Gehrig.......................... 15.00 4.50

2002 Studio Classic Autographs

Randomly inserted in packs, these 19 cards partially parallel the Studio Classic insert set. We have listed the stated print runs next to the player's name and since no player signed more than 20 cards there is no pricing due to market scarcity.

Nm-Mt Ex-Mt
1 Kirby Puckett/15..............................
2 George Brett/15...............................
3 Nolan Ryan/15..................................
4 Mike Schmidt/20...............................
5 Steve Carlton/20..............................
6 Reggie Jackson/15............................
7 Tom Seaver/15..................................
8 Joe Morgan/20..................................
10 Johnny Bench/20.............................
11 Willie McCovey/15..........................
12 Brooks Robinson/20........................
13 Al Kaline/20...................................
14 Stan Musial/15................................
15 Ozzie Smith/15...............................
16 Dave Winfield/15............................
17 Robin Yount/15...............................
18 Rod Carew/25..................................
20 Lou Brock/20..................................
21 Ernie Banks/20................................

2002 Studio Classic First Ballot Autographs

Another parallel to the Studio Classic insert set, these 20 cards feature autographs on the First Ballot insert set. These cards have a stated print run of one and due to market scarcity, no pricing is provided.

Nm-Mt Ex-Mt
1 Kirby Puckett..................................
2 George Brett...................................
3 Nolan Ryan.....................................
4 Mike Schmidt..................................
5 Steve Carlton..................................
6 Reggie Jackson................................
7 Tom Seaver......................................
8 Joe Morgan......................................
9 Jim Palmer.......................................
10 Johnny Bench.................................
11 Willie McCovey..............................
12 Brooks Robinson............................
13 Al Kaline...
14 Stan Musial....................................
15 Ozzie Smith....................................
16 Dave Winfield.................................
17 Robin Yount...................................
18 Rod Carew......................................
20 Lou Brock.......................................
21 Ernie Banks....................................

2002 Studio Diamond Collection

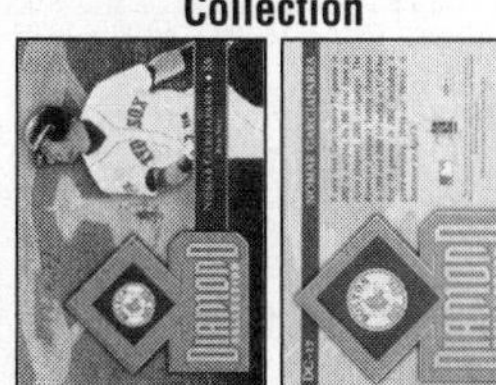

Inserted in packs at stated odds of one in 17, these 25 cards feature some of the most popular players in baseball.

Nm-Mt Ex-Mt
COMPLETE SET (25).............. 120.00 36.00
1 Todd Helton........................... 4.00 1.20
2 Chipper Jones........................ 4.00 1.20
3 Lance Berkman...................... 4.00 1.20
4 Derek Jeter.......................... 10.00 3.00
5 Hideo Nomo.......................... 4.00 1.20
6 Kazuhisa Ishii........................ 5.00 1.50
7 Barry Bonds........................ 10.00 3.00
8 Alex Rodriguez...................... 6.00 1.80
9 Ichiro Suzuki......................... 6.00 1.80
10 Mike Piazza......................... 6.00 1.80
11 Jim Thome........................... 4.00 1.20
12 Greg Maddux....................... 6.00 1.80
13 Jeff Bagwell......................... 4.00 1.20
14 Vladimir Guerrero................ 4.00 1.20
15 Ken Griffey Jr...................... 6.00 1.80
16 Jason Giambi....................... 4.00 1.20
17 Nomar Garciaparra.............. 6.00 1.80
18 Albert Pujols........................ 8.00 2.40
19 Manny Ramirez................... 4.00 1.20
20 Pedro Martinez.................... 4.00 1.20
21 Roger Clemens..................... 8.00 2.40
22 Randy Johnson..................... 4.00 1.20
23 Mark Prior............................ 8.00 2.40
24 So Taguchi........................... 4.00 1.20
25 Sammy Sosa......................... 6.00 1.80

2002 Studio Diamond Collection Artist's Proofs

Randomly inserted in packs, these cards partially parallel the Diamond Collection insert set. Each card features a memorabilia piece and we have notated both the information as to what type of piece along with the stated print run next to the player's name in our checklist.

Nm-Mt Ex-Mt
1 Todd Helton Jsy/200............. 15.00 4.50
2 Chipper Jones Jsy/150........... 15.00 4.50
3 Lance Berkman Jsy/200......... 15.00 4.50
4 Derek Jeter Base/200............ 25.00 7.50
5 Hideo Nomo Jsy/150............. 80.00 24.00
6 Kazuhisa Ishii Jsy/150........... 20.00 6.00
7 Barry Bonds Base/200........... 25.00 7.50
8 Alex Rodriguez Jsy/150......... 20.00 6.00
9 Ichiro Suzuki Base/200.......... 25.00 7.50
10 Mike Piazza Jsy/150............ 15.00 4.50
11 Jim Thome Jsy/150.............. 15.00 4.50
12 Greg Maddux Jsy/150.......... 15.00 4.50
13 Jeff Bagwell Jsy/150............ 15.00 4.50
14 Vladimir Guerrero Jsy/200 ... 15.00 4.50
15 Ken Griffey Jr. Base/200....... 15.00 4.50
16 Jason Giambi Base/200......... 15.00 4.50
17 Nomar Garciaparra Jsy/150 . 20.00 6.00
18 Albert Pujols Base/200......... 15.00 4.50
19 Manny Ramirez Jsy/150........ 15.00 4.50
20 Pedro Martinez Jsy/150........ 15.00 4.50
21 Roger Clemens Jsy/150........ 25.00 7.50
22 Randy Johnson Jsy/150........ 15.00 4.50
24 So Taguchi Jsy/200.............. 15.00 4.50
25 Sammy Sosa Base/200......... 15.00 4.50

2002 Studio Heroes Icons Texans

Randomly inserted in packs, these four cards honor that Texas sports legend, Nolan Ryan. There are four stated print runs with the highlight being an autograph card numbered to a stated print run of 32 serial numbered cards.

Nm-Mt Ex-Mt
HIT-2 Nolan Ryan...................... 10.00 3.00
HIT-2 Nolan Ryan/500............... 15.00 4.50
HIT-2 Nolan Ryan/100............... 50.00 15.00
HIT-2 Nolan Ryan AU/32......... 250.00 75.00

2002 Studio Leather and Lumber

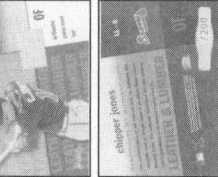

Randomly inserted in packs, these 25 cards feature some of the game's most dominating batsmen. Each card contains one game-used bat piece. And since there are different print runs, we have put that information next to the player's name in our checklist.

Nm-Mt Ex-Mt
1 Nomar Garciaparra/200.......... 25.00 7.50
2 Jeff Bagwell/150................... 15.00 4.50
3 Alex Rodriguez/200.............. 20.00 6.00
4 Vladimir Guerrero/100........... 20.00 6.00
5 Luis Gonzalez/200................ 10.00 3.00
6 Chipper Jones/200................ 15.00 4.50
7 Shawn Green/200.................. 10.00 3.00
8 Kirby Puckett/100................. 20.00 6.00
9 Juan Gonzalez/200................ 15.00 4.50
10 Troy Glaus/200................... 15.00 4.50
11 Don Mattingly/100.............. 40.00 12.00
12 Todd Helton/200................. 15.00 4.50
13 Jim Thome/200................... 15.00 4.50
14 Rickey Henderson/200......... 15.00 4.50
15 Mike Schmidt/100............... 60.00 18.00
16 Adam Dunn/100.................. 15.00 4.50
17 Ivan Rodriguez/200............. 15.00 4.50
18 Manny Ramirez/150............ 10.00 3.00
19 Tsuyoshi Shinjo/200........... 10.00 3.00
20 Andruw Jones/150............... 10.00 3.00
21 Roberto Alomar/200............ 15.00 4.50
22 Lance Berkman/200............. 10.00 3.00
23 Derek Jeter Ball/50............. 80.00 24.00
24 Ichiro Suzuki Ball/50........... 80.00 24.00
25 Mike Piazza/200.................. 15.00 4.50

2002 Studio Leather and Lumber Artist's Proofs

Randomly inserted in packs, these cards parallel the Leather and Lumber insert set. These cards have a stated print run of 50 serial numbered sets which included not only the bat piece but also either a ball or batting glove piece.

Nm-Mt Ex-Mt
5 Luis Gonzalez SP/25..............................

2002 Studio Masterstrokes

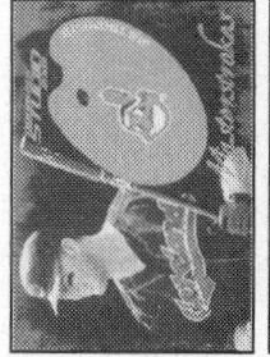

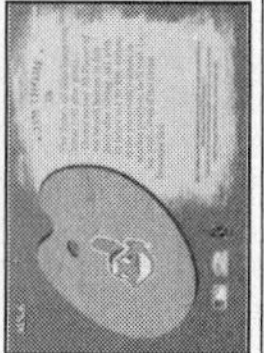

Inserted in packs at stated odds of one in 17, these 25 cards feature baseball's most skilled hitters.

Nm-Mt Ex-Mt
COMPLETE SET (25).............. 100.00 30.00
1 Vladimir Guerrero.................. 4.00 1.20
2 Frank Thomas........................ 4.00 1.20
3 Alex Rodriguez...................... 6.00 1.80
4 Manny Ramirez..................... 4.00 1.20
5 Jeff Bagwell........................... 4.00 1.20
6 Jim Thome............................. 4.00 1.20
7 Ichiro Suzuki......................... 6.00 1.80
8 Andruw Jones........................ 4.00 1.20
9 Troy Glaus............................. 4.00 1.20
10 Chipper Jones...................... 4.00 1.20
11 Juan Gonzalez...................... 4.00 1.20
12 Lance Berkman..................... 4.00 1.20
13 Mike Piazza.......................... 6.00 1.80
14 Darin Erstad......................... 4.00 1.20
15 Albert Pujols........................ 8.00 2.40
16 Kazuhisa Ishii....................... 5.00 1.50
17 Shawn Green........................ 4.00 1.20
18 Rafael Palmeiro.................... 4.00 1.20
19 Todd Helton.......................... 4.00 1.20
20 Carlos Delgado..................... 4.00 1.20
21 Ivan Rodriguez..................... 4.00 1.20
22 Luis Gonzalez....................... 4.00 1.20
23 Derek Jeter......................... 10.00 3.00
24 Nomar Garciaparra................ 6.00 1.80
25 J.D. Drew............................. 4.00 1.20

2002 Studio Masterstrokes Artist's Proofs

Randomly inserted in packs, these 25 cards are a parallel to the Masterstrokes insert set and most of them feature a bat-jersey combo. The Ichiro Suzuki, Derek Jeter and J.D. Drew cards feature a ball-base combo.

Nm-Mt Ex-Mt
1 Vladimir Guerrero/200........... 20.00 6.00
2 Frank Thomas/200................. 20.00 6.00
3 Alex Rodriguez/100............... 40.00 12.00
4 Manny Ramirez/200............... 15.00 4.50
5 Jeff Bagwell/150.................... 20.00 6.00
6 Jim Thome/200...................... 20.00 6.00
7 Ichiro Suzuki/100.................. 60.00 18.00
8 Andruw Jones/200................. 15.00 4.50
9 Troy Glaus/200...................... 20.00 6.00
10 Chipper Jones/200............... 20.00 6.00
11 Juan Gonzalez/200............... 20.00 6.00
12 Lance Berkman/200.............. 15.00 4.50
13 Mike Piazza/200.................. 40.00 12.00
14 Darin Erstad/200................. 15.00 4.50
15 Albert Pujols/100................. 40.00 12.00
16 Kazuhisa Ishii/150............... 25.00 7.50
17 Shawn Green/200................. 15.00 4.50
18 Rafael Palmeiro/200............. 20.00 6.00
19 Todd Helton/200.................. 20.00 6.00
20 Carlos Delgado/200............. 15.00 4.50
21 Ivan Rodriguez/200.............. 20.00 6.00
22 Luis Gonzalez/200............... 15.00 4.50
23 Derek Jeter/100................... 60.00 18.00
24 Nomar Garciaparra/150........ 40.00 12.00
25 J.D. Drew/150..................... 15.00 4.50

2002 Studio Spirit of the Game

Inserted in packs at a stated odds of one in nine, these 50 cards highlight players who play the game with a real passion.

Nm-Mt Ex-Mt
COMPLETE SET (50).............. 120.00 36.00
1 Alex Rodriguez...................... 6.00 1.80
2 Curt Schilling........................ 2.50 .75
3 Hideo Nomo.......................... 4.00 1.20
4 Derek Jeter.......................... 10.00 3.00
5 Mike Sweeney....................... 2.50 .75
6 Mike Piazza.......................... 6.00 1.80
7 Roger Clemens...................... 8.00 2.40
8 Shawn Green........................ 2.50 .75
9 Vladimir Guerrero.................. 4.00 1.20
10 Carlos Lee.......................... 2.50 .75
11 Edgar Martinez.................... 2.50 .75
12 Albert Pujols........................ 8.00 2.40
13 Mark Prior........................... 8.00 2.40
14 Mark Buehrle....................... 2.50 .75
15 Chipper Jones...................... 4.00 1.20
16 Paul Lo Duca....................... 2.50 .75
17 Frank Thomas...................... 4.00 1.20
18 Randy Johnson.................... 4.00 1.20
19 Cliff Floyd........................... 2.50 .75
20 Todd Helton........................ 2.50 .75
21 Luis Gonzalez...................... 2.50 .75
22 Brandon Duckworth.............. 2.50 .75
23 Jason Giambi...................... 4.00 1.20
24 Juan Uribe........................... 2.50 .75
25 Dewon Brazelton.................. 2.50 .75
26 J.D. Drew............................ 2.50 .75
27 Troy Glaus.......................... 2.50 .75
28 Wade Miller......................... 2.50 .75
29 Darin Erstad........................ 2.50 .75
30 Brian Giles.......................... 2.50 .75
31 Lance Berkman.................... 2.50 .75
32 Shannon Stewart.................. 2.50 .75
33 Kazuhisa Ishii...................... 5.00 1.50
34 Corey Patterson................... 2.50 .75
35 Rafael Palmeiro................... 2.50 .75
36 Roy Oswalt.......................... 2.50 .75
37 Jason Lane.......................... 2.50 .75
38 Andruw Jones...................... 2.50 .75
39 Brad Penny.......................... 2.50 .75
40 Bud Smith........................... 2.50 .75
41 Carlos Beltran...................... 2.50 .75
42 Magglio Ordonez.................. 2.50 .75
43 Craig Biggio........................ 2.50 .75
44 Hank Blalock....................... 4.00 1.20
45 Jeff Bagwell......................... 2.50 .75
46 Josh Beckett........................ 2.50 .75
47 Juan Cruz........................... 2.50 .75
48 Kerry Wood......................... 4.00 1.20
49 Brandon Berger.................... 2.50 .75
50 Juan Pierre.......................... 2.50 .75

2002 Studio Spirit of the Game Hats Off

Randomly inserted in packs, these 24 cards form a partial parallel to the Spirit of the Game insert set. These cards feature pieces of game-used hats and most are serial numbered to 100. The Kazuishi Ishii card has a stated print run of 50 serial numbered sets.

Nm-Mt Ex-Mt
10 Carlos Lee......................... 25.00 7.50
14 Mark Buehrle...................... 25.00 7.50
16 Paul Lo Duca...................... 25.00 7.50
22 Brandon Duckworth............. 15.00 4.50
26 J.D. Drew........................... 25.00 7.50
28 Wade Miller........................ 25.00 7.50
30 Brian Giles......................... 25.00 7.50
31 Lance Berkman.................... 25.00 7.50
32 Shannon Stewart................. 25.00 7.50
33 Kazuhisa Ishii SP/50............ 50.00 15.00
35 Rafael Palmeiro.................. 40.00 12.00
36 Roy Oswalt......................... 25.00 7.50
37 Jason Lane......................... 15.00 4.50
38 Andruw Jones..................... 25.00 7.50
39 Brad Penny......................... 15.00 4.50
40 Bud Smith.......................... 15.00 4.50
41 Carlos Beltran..................... 25.00 7.50
42 Magglio Ordonez................. 25.00 7.50
43 Craig Biggio....................... 40.00 12.00
45 Jeff Bagwell........................ 40.00 12.00
47 Juan Cruz.......................... 15.00 4.50
48 Kerry Wood........................ 40.00 12.00
49 Brandon Berger................... 15.00 4.50
50 Juan Pierre......................... 25.00 7.50

2002 Studio Spirit of the Game Hats Off MLB Logo

Randomly inserted in packs, these 17 cards are also a partial parallel the the Spirit of the Game insert set. These cards feature the MLB logo on them and have a state print run of one serial numbered sets. Due to market scarcity, no pricing is provided for these cards.

Nm-Mt Ex-Mt
10 Carlos Lee...
14 Mark Buehrle......................................
16 Paul Lo Duca......................................
22 Brandon Duckworth.............................
28 Wade Miller..
30 Brian Giles..
33 Kazuhisa Ishii.....................................
35 Rafael Palmeiro..................................
36 Roy Oswalt...
37 Jason Lane...
39 Brad Penny...
40 Bud Smith..
41 Carlos Beltran.....................................
43 Craig Biggio.......................................
47 Juan Cruz..
48 Kerry Wood..
49 Brandon Berger...................................

2002 Studio Spirit of the Game Hats Off USA Flag

Randomly inserted in packs, these 17 cards are also a partial parallel the the Spirit of the Game insert set. These cards feature the USA Flag logo on them and have a stated print run of one serial numbered sets. Due to market scarcity, no pricing is provided for these cards.

Nm-Mt Ex-Mt
16 Paul Lo Duca......................................
22 Brandon Duckworth.............................
26 J.D. Drew...
28 Wade Miller..
48 Kerry Wood..
49 Brandon Berger...................................

2002 Studio Spirit of the USA

Randomly inserted into packs, these 15 cards feature the part of the uniform that included the American Flag addition to the jersey. These cards have a stated print run of one serial numbered set and due to market scarcity no pricing is provided.

Card	Nm-Mt	Ex-Mt
1 Alex Rodriguez		
2 Curt Schilling		
3 Hideo Nomo		
5 Mike Sweeney		
7 Roger Clemens		
8 Shawn Green		
9 Vladimir Guerrero		
10 Carlos Lee		
11 Edgar Martinez		
14 Mark Buehrle		
16 Paul Lo Duca		
19 Cliff Floyd		
22 Brandon Duckworth		
24 Juan Uribe		
25 Dewon Brazelton		

2002 Studio Stars

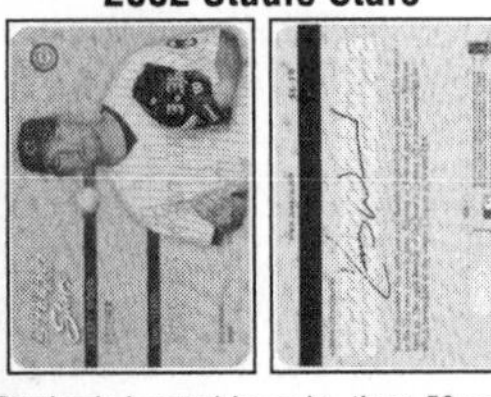

Randomly inserted in packs, these 50 cards feature leading players in a credit charge design. These cards have some key statistics for the players listed across the front of their cards.

Card	Nm-Mt	Ex-Mt
COMPLETE SET (50)	100.00	30.00
1 Mike Piazza	4.00	1.20
2 Ivan Rodriguez	2.00	.60
3 Albert Pujols	5.00	1.50
4 Scott Rolen	2.00	.60
5 Alex Rodriguez	4.00	1.20
6 Curt Schilling	2.00	.60
7 Vladimir Guerrero	2.00	.60
8 Jim Thome	2.00	.60
9 Derek Jeter	6.00	1.80
10 C.C. Sabathia	2.00	.60
11 Sammy Sosa	4.00	1.20
12 Adam Dunn	2.00	.60
13 Bernie Williams	2.00	.60
14 Ichiro Suzuki	4.00	1.20
15 Barry Bonds	6.00	1.80
16 Rickey Henderson	2.00	.60
17 Ken Griffey Jr.	4.00	1.20
18 Kazuhisa Ishii	2.50	.75
19 Kerry Wood	2.00	.60
20 Todd Helton	2.00	.60
21 Hideo Nomo	2.00	.60
22 Frank Thomas	2.00	.60
23 Manny Ramirez	2.00	.60
24 Luis Gonzalez	2.00	.60
25 Rafael Palmeiro	2.00	.60
26 Mike Mussina	2.00	.60
27 Roy Oswalt	2.00	.60
28 Darin Erstad	2.00	.60
29 Barry Larkin	2.00	.60
30 Randy Johnson	2.00	.60
31 Tom Glavine	2.00	.60
32 Lance Berkman	2.00	.60
33 Juan Gonzalez	2.00	.60
34 Shawn Green	2.00	.60
35 Nomar Garciaparra	4.00	1.20
36 Troy Glaus	2.00	.60
37 Tim Hudson	2.00	.60
38 Carlos Delgado	2.00	.60
39 Jason Giambi	2.00	.60
40 Andruw Jones	2.00	.60
41 Roberto Alomar	2.00	.60
42 Greg Maddux	4.00	1.20
43 Pedro Martinez	2.00	.60
44 Tony Gwynn	3.00	.90
45 Alfonso Soriano	2.00	.60
46 Chipper Jones	2.00	.60
47 J.D. Drew	2.00	.60
48 Roger Clemens	5.00	1.50
49 Barry Zito	2.00	.60
50 Jeff Bagwell	2.00	.60

2003 Studio

This 210-card set was issued in two separate series. The primary Studio product - containing cards 1-200 from the basic set - was released in June, 2003. The set was issued in six card packs with an $4 SRP which came packed 20 packs to a box and 16 boxes to a case. The first 190 cards feature just one player while the final 10 cards portray two teammates. Cards 201-211 were randomly seeded into packs of DLP Rookies and Traded of which was distributed in December, 2003. Each of these update cards featured a top prospect and was serial numbered to 1500 copies.

Card	Nm-Mt	Ex-Mt
COMP.LO SET (200)	50.00	15.00
COMMON CARD (1-190)	.50	.15
COMMON RC (1-190)	.60	.18
COMMON CARD (191-200)	1.00	.30
COMMON CARD (201-211)	4.00	1.20
1 Darin Erstad	.50	.15
2 David Eckstein	.50	.15
3 Garret Anderson	.50	.15
4 Jarrod Washburn	.50	.15
5 Tim Salmon	.75	.23
6 Troy Glaus	.75	.23
7 Jay Gibbons	.50	.15
8 Melvin Mora	.50	.15
9 Rodrigo Lopez	.50	.15
10 Tony Batista	.50	.15
11 Freddy Sanchez	.50	.15
12 Derek Lowe	.50	.15
13 Johnny Damon	.50	.15
14 Manny Ramirez	.50	.15
15 Nomar Garciaparra	2.00	.60
16 Pedro Martinez	1.25	.35
17 Rickey Henderson	1.25	.35
18 Shea Hillenbrand	.50	.15
19 Carlos Lee	.50	.15
20 Frank Thomas	1.25	.35
21 Magglio Ordonez	.50	.15
22 Bartolo Colon	.50	.15
23 Paul Konerko	.50	.15
24 Josh Stewart RC	.60	.18
25 C.C. Sabathia	.50	.15
26 Jeremy Guthrie	.50	.15
27 Ellis Burks	.50	.15
28 Omar Vizquel	.50	.15
29 Victor Martinez	.50	.15
30 Cliff Lee	.50	.15
31 Jhonny Peralta RC	.60	.18
32 Brian Tallet	.50	.15
33 Bobby Higginson	.50	.15
34 Carlos Pena	.50	.15
35 Nook Logan RC	.60	.18
36 Steve Sparks	.50	.15
37 Travis Chapman	.50	.15
38 Carlos Beltran	.50	.15
39 Joe Randa	.50	.15
40 Mike Sweeney	.50	.15
41 Jimmy Gobble	.50	.15
42 Michael Tucker	.50	.15
43 Runelvys Hernandez	.50	.15
44 Brad Radke	.50	.15
45 Corey Koskie	.50	.15
46 Cristian Guzman	.50	.15
47 J.C. Romero	.50	.15
48 Doug Mientkiewicz	.50	.15
49 Lew Ford RC	1.00	.30
50 Jacque Jones	.50	.15
51 Torii Hunter	.50	.15
52 Alfonso Soriano	.75	.23
53 Nick Johnson	.50	.15
54 Bernie Williams	.75	.23
55 Jose Contreras RC	3.00	.90
56 Derek Jeter	3.00	.90
57 Jason Giambi	1.25	.35
58 Brandon Claussen	.50	.15
59 Jorge Posada	.75	.23
60 Mike Mussina	1.25	.35
61 Roger Clemens	2.50	.75
62 Hideki Matsui RC	6.00	1.80
63 Barry Zito	.75	.23
64 Adam Morrissey	.50	.15
65 Eric Chavez	.50	.15
66 Jermaine Dye	.50	.15
67 Mark Mulder	.50	.15
68 Miguel Tejada	.50	.15
69 Joe Valentine RC	.60	.18
70 Tim Hudson	.50	.15
71 Bret Boone	.50	.15
72 Chris Snelling	.50	.15
73 Edgar Martinez	.75	.23
74 Freddy Garcia	.50	.15
75 Ichiro Suzuki	2.00	.60
76 Jamie Moyer	.50	.15
77 John Olerud	.50	.15
78 Kazuhiro Sasaki	.50	.15
79 Aubrey Huff	.50	.15
80 Joe Kennedy	.50	.15
81 Dewon Brazelton	.50	.15
82 Pete LaForest RC	1.00	.30
83 Alex Rodriguez	2.00	.60
84 Chan Ho Park	.50	.15
85 Hank Blalock	.75	.23
86 Juan Gonzalez	1.25	.35
87 Kevin Mench	.50	.15
88 Rafael Palmeiro	.75	.23
89 Carlos Delgado	.50	.15
90 Eric Hinske	.50	.15
91 Josh Phelps	.50	.15
92 Roy Halladay	.50	.15
93 Shannon Stewart	.50	.15
94 Vernon Wells	.50	.15
95 Vinny Chulk	.50	.15
96 Curt Schilling	.75	.23
97 Junior Spivey	.50	.15
98 Luis Gonzalez	.50	.15
99 Mark Grace	.75	.23
100 Randy Johnson	1.25	.35
101 Andruw Jones	.50	.15
102 Chipper Jones	1.25	.35
103 Gary Sheffield	.50	.15
104 Greg Maddux	2.00	.60
105 John Smoltz	.75	.23
106 Mike Hampton	.50	.15
107 Adam LaRoche	.75	.23
108 Michael Hessman RC	.60	.18
109 Corey Patterson	.50	.15
110 Kerry Wood	1.25	.35
111 Mark Prior	2.50	.75
112 Moises Alou	.50	.15
113 Sammy Sosa	2.00	.60
114 Adam Dunn	.50	.15
115 Austin Kearns	.50	.15
116 Barry Larkin	1.25	.35
117 Ken Griffey Jr.	2.00	.60
118 Sean Casey	.50	.15
119 Jason Jennings	.50	.15
120 Jay Payton	.50	.15
121 Larry Walker	.75	.23
122 Todd Helton	.75	.23
123 Jeff Baker	.50	.15
124 Clint Barmes RC	1.00	.30
125 Ivan Rodriguez	1.25	.35
126 Josh Beckett	.75	.23
127 Juan Encarnacion	.50	.15
128 Mike Lowell	.50	.15
129 Craig Biggio	.75	.23
130 Jason Lane	.50	.15
131 Jeff Bagwell	.75	.23
132 Lance Berkman	.50	.15
133 Roy Oswalt	.50	.15
134 Jeff Kent	.50	.15
135 Hideo Nomo	1.25	.35
136 Kazuhisa Ishii	.50	.15
137 Kevin Brown	.50	.15
138 Odalis Perez	.50	.15
139 Paul Lo Duca	.50	.15
140 Shawn Green	.50	.15
141 Adrian Beltre	.50	.15
142 Ben Sheets	.50	.15
143 Bill Hall	.50	.15
144 Jeffrey Hammonds	.50	.15
145 Richie Sexson	.50	.15
146 Terrmel Sledge RC	1.00	.30
147 Brad Wilkerson	.50	.15
148 Javier Vazquez	.50	.15
149 Jose Vidro	.50	.15
150 Michael Barrett	.50	.15
151 Vladimir Guerrero	1.25	.35
152 Al Leiter	.50	.15
153 Mike Piazza	2.00	.60
154 Mo Vaughn	.50	.15
155 Cliff Floyd	.50	.15
156 Roberto Alomar	1.25	.35
157 Roger Cedeno	.50	.15
158 Tom Glavine	.75	.23
159 Prentice Redman RC	.60	.18
160 Bobby Abreu	.50	.15
161 Jimmy Rollins	.50	.15
162 Mike Lieberthal	.50	.15
163 Pat Burrell	.50	.15
164 Vicente Padilla	.50	.15
165 Jim Thome	1.25	.35
166 Kevin Millwood	.50	.15
167 Aramis Ramirez	.50	.15
168 Brian Giles	.50	.15
169 Jason Kendall	.50	.15
170 Josh Fogg	.50	.15
171 Kip Wells	.50	.15
172 Jose Castillo	.50	.15
173 Mark Kotsay	.50	.15
174 Oliver Perez	.50	.15
175 Phil Nevin	.50	.15
176 Ryan Klesko	.50	.15
177 Sean Burroughs	.50	.15
178 Brian Lawrence	.50	.15
179 Shane Victorino RC	.60	.18
180 Barry Bonds	3.00	.90
181 Benito Santiago	.50	.15
182 Ray Durham	.50	.15
183 Rich Aurilla	.50	.15
184 Damian Moss	.50	.15
185 Albert Pujols	2.50	.75
186 J.D. Drew	.50	.15
187 Jim Edmonds	.50	.15
188 Matt Morris	.50	.15
189 Tino Martinez	.75	.23
190 Scott Rolen	.75	.23
191 Troy Glaus Tim Salmon	1.50	.45
192 Sean Casey Corky Miller	1.00	.30
193 Carlos Lee Frank Thomas	1.50	.45
194 Lance Berkman Jeff Kent	1.00	.30
195 Jose Contreras Mariano Rivera	1.50	.45
196 Alex Rodriguez Juan Gonzalez	1.50	.45
197 Andy Pettitte David Wells	1.50	.45
198 Shawn Green Dave Roberts	1.00	.30
199 Mike Lieberthal Jimmy Rollins	1.00	.30
200 Mike Mussina Hideki Matsui	3.00	.90
201 Adam Loewen ROO RC	8.00	2.40
202 Jeremy Bonderman ROO RC	5.00	1.50
203 Brandon Webb ROO RC	8.00	2.40
204 Chien-Ming Wang ROO RC	6.00	1.80
205 Chad Gaudin ROO RC	4.00	1.20
206 Ryan Wagner ROO RC	5.00	1.50
207 Hong-Chih Kuo ROO RC	5.00	1.50
208 Dan Haren ROO RC	5.00	1.50
209 Rickie Weeks ROO RC	12.00	3.60
210 Ramon Nivar ROO RC	5.00	1.50
211 Delmon Young ROO RC	15.00	4.50

2003 Studio Private Signings

1-200 RANDOM INSERTS IN PACKS
201-211 RANDOM IN DLP R/T PACKS
PRINT RUNS B/WN 5-200 COPIES PER
NO PRICING ON QTY OF 35 OR LESS.

Card	Nm-Mt	Ex-Mt
1 Darin Erstad/5		
6 Troy Glaus/15		
7 Jay Gibbons/100	20.00	6.00
11 Freddy Sanchez/150	10.00	3.00
16 Pedro Martinez/5		
17 Rickey Henderson/10		
19 Carlos Lee/25		
20 Frank Thomas/5		
22 Mark Buehrle/50		
24 Josh Stewart/200	10.00	3.00
25 C.C. Sabathia/10		
26 Jeremy Guthrie/125	10.00	3.00
29 Victor Martinez/200	15.00	4.50
30 Cliff Lee/150	10.00	3.00
31 Jhonny Peralta/200	10.00	3.00
32 Brian Tallet/35		
35 Nook Logan/100	10.00	3.00
37 Travis Chapman/150	10.00	3.00
38 Carlos Beltran/25		
40 Mike Sweeney/25		
41 Jimmy Gobble/200	15.00	4.50
47 J.C. Romero/200	10.00	3.00
49 Lew Ford/200	15.00	4.50
51 Torii Hunter/50	25.00	7.50
52 Alfonso Soriano/5		
53 Nick Johnson/100	20.00	6.00
54 Bernie Williams/5		
55 Jose Contreras/100	40.00	12.00
58 Brandon Claussen/200	15.00	4.50
60 Mike Mussina/5		
61 Roger Clemens/10		
63 Barry Zito/25		
64 Adam Morrissey/100		
66 Jermaine Dye/25		
67 Mark Mulder/15		
69 Joe Valentine/200	10.00	3.00
70 Tim Hudson/15		
72 Chris Snelling/25		
73 Edgar Martinez/15		
74 Freddy Garcia/5		
79 Aubrey Huff/50	25.00	7.50
80 Joe Kennedy/25		
81 Dewon Brazelton/75	15.00	4.50
82 Pete LaForest/200	15.00	4.50
83 Alex Rodriguez/5		
85 Hank Blalock/50	40.00	12.00
87 Kevin Mench/200	10.00	3.00
90 Eric Hinske/125	10.00	3.00
95 Vinny Chulk/100	15.00	4.50
97 Junior Spivey/50	15.00	4.50
98 Luis Gonzalez/5		
101 Andruw Jones/15		
102 Chipper Jones/5		
103 Gary Sheffield/10		
104 Greg Maddux/10		
107 Adam LaRoche/200	25.00	7.50
108 Michael Hessman/200	10.00	3.00
109 Corey Patterson/20		
110 Kerry Wood/15		
111 Mark Prior/50	100.00	30.00
114 Adam Dunn/25		
115 Austin Kearns/25		
116 Barry Larkin/15		
119 Jason Jennings/50	15.00	4.50
123 Jeff Baker/75	15.00	4.50
124 Clint Barmes/200	15.00	4.50
125 Ivan Rodriguez/5		
126 Josh Beckett/10		
129 Craig Biggio/10		
130 Jason Lane/100	15.00	4.50
132 Lance Berkman/10		
133 Roy Oswalt/25		
136 Kazuhisa Ishii/10		
139 Paul Lo Duca/75	20.00	6.00
140 Shawn Green/5		
143 Bill Hall/50	15.00	4.50
145 Richie Sexson/15		
146 Terrmel Sledge/125	15.00	4.50
148 Javier Vazquez/25		
149 Jose Vidro/50	25.00	7.50
151 Vladimir Guerrero/15		
156 Roberto Alomar/20		
158 Tom Glavine/15		
159 Prentice Redman/200	10.00	3.00
160 Bobby Abreu/50	25.00	7.50
163 Pat Burrell/10		
165 Jim Thome/10		
167 Aramis Ramirez/15		
168 Brian Giles/25		
171 Kip Wells/100	15.00	4.50
172 Jose Castillo/175	15.00	4.50
176 Ryan Klesko/20		
178 Brian Lawrence/100	15.00	4.50
179 Shane Victorino/200	10.00	3.00
185 Albert Pujols/15		
187 Jim Edmonds/5		
201 Adam Loewen ROO/100	40.00	12.00
202 Jeremy Bonderman ROO/100	30.00	9.00
203 Brandon Webb ROO/100	40.00	12.00
204 Chien-Ming Wang ROO/50	60.00	18.00
205 Chad Gaudin ROO/25		
206 Ryan Wagner ROO/100	25.00	7.50
207 Hong-Chih Kuo ROO/25		
208 Dan Haren ROO/100	20.00	6.00
209 Rickie Weeks ROO/10		
210 Ramon Nivar ROO/100	20.00	6.00
211 Delmon Young ROO/25		

2003 Studio Proofs

Nm-Mt Ex-Mt

*PROOFS 1-190: 4X TO 10X BASIC
*PROOFS RC's 1-190: 2X TO 5X BASIC
*PROOFS 191-200: 1.5X TO 4X BASIC
*PROOFS 201-211: .6X TO 1.5X BASIC
1-200 RANDOM INSERTS IN PACKS
201-211 RANDOM IN DLP R/T PACKS
STATED PRINT RUN 100 SERIAL #'d SETS

2003 Studio Big League Challenge

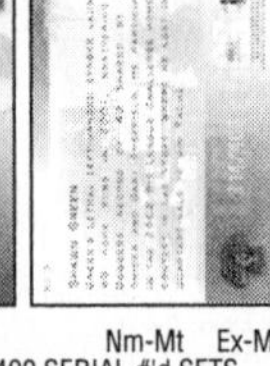

STATED PRINT RUN 400 SERIAL #'d SETS
*PROOFS: 1.5X TO 4X BASIC BLC
PROOFS PRINT RUN 25 SERIAL #'d SETS
NO PROOFS PRICING DUE TO SCARCITY

Card	Nm-Mt	Ex-Mt
1 Jose Canseco 00 WIN	8.00	2.40
2 Magglio Ordonez 03 WIN	5.00	1.50
3 Alex Rodriguez 03	10.00	3.00
4 Lance Berkman 03	5.00	1.50
5 Rafael Palmeiro 03	8.00	2.40
6 Nomar Garciaparra 00	10.00	3.00
7 Nomar Garciaparra 00	10.00	3.00
8 Nomar Garciaparra 00	10.00	3.00
9 Troy Glaus 02 WIN	8.00	2.40
10 Mark McGwire 00	15.00	4.50
11 Mark McGwire 00	15.00	4.50
12 Mark McGwire 00	15.00	4.50
13 Jim Thome 02	8.00	2.40
14 Chipper Jones 00	8.00	2.40
15 Shawn Green 02	5.00	1.50
16 Alex Rodriguez 00	10.00	3.00
17 Alex Rodriguez 00	10.00	3.00
18 Alex Rodriguez 00	10.00	3.00
19 Alex Rodriguez 01	10.00	3.00
20 Jason Giambi 01	8.00	2.40
21 Pat Burrell 03	5.00	1.50
22 Mike Piazza 01	10.00	3.00
23 Mike Piazza 01	10.00	3.00
24 Mike Piazza 01	10.00	3.00
25 Frank Thomas 01	8.00	2.40
26 Rafael Palmeiro 01 WIN	8.00	2.40
27 Todd Helton 01	8.00	2.40
28 Jose Canseco 01	8.00	2.40
29 Albert Pujols 03	10.00	3.00
30 Troy Glaus 01	8.00	2.40
31 Barry Bonds 01	10.00	3.00
32 Barry Bonds 01	10.00	3.00
33 Barry Bonds 01	10.00	3.00
34 Todd Helton 02	8.00	2.40
35 Rafael Palmeiro 02	8.00	2.40
36 Jim Thome 02	8.00	2.40
37 Ozzie Smith 02	15.00	4.50
38 Troy Glaus 02 WIN	8.00	2.40
39 Shawn Green 02	5.00	1.50
40 Barry Bonds 02	10.00	3.00
41 Barry Bonds 02	10.00	3.00
42 Barry Bonds 02	10.00	3.00
43 Magglio Ordonez 03 WIN	5.00	1.50
44 Alex Rodriguez 03	10.00	3.00
45 Alex Rodriguez 03	10.00	3.00
46 Alex Rodriguez 03	10.00	3.00
47 Lance Berkman 03	5.00	1.50
48 Rafael Palmeiro 03	8.00	2.40
49 Pat Burrell 03	5.00	1.50
50 Albert Pujols 03	10.00	3.00

2003 Studio Big League Challenge Materials

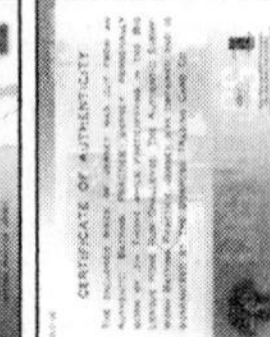

STATED ODDS 1:20
*PRIME 100: 1X TO 2.5X BASIC MATERIAL
*PRIME 50: 1.5X TO 4X BASIC MATERIAL
PRIME RANDOM INSERTS IN PACKS.
PRIME PRINT RUN B/WN 50-100 COPIES PER

Card	Nm-Mt	Ex-Mt
2 Magglio Ordonez 03 BP Jsy	8.00	2.40
3 Alex Rodriguez 03 BP Jsy	15.00	4.50
4 Lance Berkman 03 Jsy	8.00	2.40
15 Shawn Green 02 BP Jsy	8.00	2.40
29 Albert Pujols 03 Jsy	25.00	7.50
36 Jim Thome 02 BP Jsy	8.00	2.40
39 Shawn Green 02 Pants	8.00	2.40
40 Barry Bonds 02 Base	15.00	4.50
41 Barry Bonds 02 Base	15.00	4.50
42 Barry Bonds 02 Plate	15.00	4.50
43 Magglio Ordonez 03 Jsy	8.00	2.40
45 Alex Rodriguez 03 Jsy	15.00	4.50
46 Alex Rodriguez 03 Pants	15.00	4.50
47 Lance Berkman 03 BP Jsy	8.00	2.40
48 Rafael Palmeiro 03 BP Jsy	8.00	2.40
50 Albert Pujols 03 Pants	15.00	4.50

2003 Studio Enshrinement

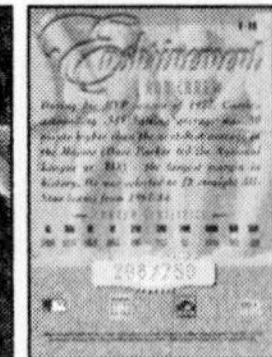

STATED PRINT RUN 750 SERIAL #'d SETS
PROOFS PRINT RUN B/WN 20-21 COPIES PER
NO PROOFS PRICING DUE TO SCARCITY
RANDOM INSERTS IN PACKS

Card	Nm-Mt	Ex-Mt
1 Gary Carter	8.00	2.40
2 Ozzie Smith	10.00	3.00
3 Kirby Puckett	8.00	2.40
4 Carlton Fisk	8.00	2.40
5 Tony Perez	5.00	1.50
6 Nolan Ryan	15.00	4.50
7 George Brett	15.00	4.50
8 Robin Yount	10.00	3.00
9 Orlando Cepeda	5.00	1.50
10 Phil Niekro	5.00	1.50
11 Mike Schmidt	12.00	3.60
12 Richie Ashburn	8.00	2.40
13 Steve Carlton	5.00	1.50
14 Phil Rizzuto	8.00	2.40
15 Reggie Jackson	8.00	2.40
16 Tom Seaver	8.00	2.40
17 Rollie Fingers	5.00	1.50
18 Rod Carew	8.00	2.40
19 Gaylord Perry	5.00	1.50
20 Fergie Jenkins	5.00	1.50
21 Jim Palmer	5.00	1.50
22 Joe Morgan	5.00	1.50
23 Johnny Bench	8.00	2.40
24 Willie Stargell	8.00	2.40
25 Billy Williams	5.00	1.50
26 Catfish Hunter	8.00	2.40
27 Willie McCovey	5.00	1.50

28 Bobby Doerr 5.00 1.50
29 Lou Brock 8.00 2.40
30 Enos Slaughter 5.00 1.50
31 Hoyt Wilhelm 5.00 1.50
32 Harmon Killebrew 8.00 2.40
33 Pee Wee Reese 8.00 2.40
34 Luis Aparicio 5.00 1.50
35 Brooks Robinson 8.00 2.40
36 Juan Marichal 5.00 1.50
37 Frank Robinson 8.00 2.40
38 Bob Gibson 8.00 2.40
39 Al Kaline 8.00 2.40
40 Duke Snider 8.00 2.40
41 Eddie Mathews 8.00 2.40
42 Robin Roberts 5.00 1.50
43 Ralph Kiner 5.00 1.50
44 Whitey Ford 8.00 2.40
45 Roberto Clemente 15.00 4.50
46 Warren Spahn 8.00 2.40
47 Yogi Berra 8.00 2.40
48 Early Wynn 5.00 1.50
49 Stan Musial 10.00 3.00
50 Bob Feller 8.00 2.40

2003 Studio Enshrinement Autographs

Randomly inserted into packs, this is a partial parallel to the Enshriement insert set. Each of these cards is signed to beween one and 100 copies and we have notated the print run in our checklist. If a card was printed to 25 or fewer copies there is no pricing available due to market scarcity.

Nm-Mt Ex-Mt
1 Gary Carter/50 50.00 15.00
2 Ozzie Smith/5
3 Kirby Puckett/5
4 Carlton Fisk/5
5 Tony Perez/50 50.00 15.00
6 Nolan Ryan/5
7 George Brett/5
8 Robin Yount/5
9 Orlando Cepeda/50 30.00 9.00
10 Phil Niekro/50 30.00 9.00
11 Mike Schmidt/5
13 Steve Carlton/50 50.00 15.00
14 Phil Rizzuto/15
15 Reggie Jackson/5
16 Tom Seaver/5
20 Fergie Jenkins/50 30.00 9.00
21 Jim Palmer/25
22 Joe Morgan/10
23 Johnny Bench/10
27 Willie McCovey/10
28 Bobby Doerr/100 25.00 7.50
29 Lou Brock/25
31 Hoyt Wilhelm/50 30.00 9.00
32 Harmon Killebrew/10
34 Luis Aparicio/100 25.00 7.50
35 Brooks Robinson/25
37 Frank Robinson/25
39 Al Kaline/25
40 Duke Snider/10
43 Ralph Kiner/25
46 Warren Spahn/1
47 Yogi Berra/10
49 Stan Musial/5
50 Bob Feller/100 40.00 12.00

2003 Studio Leather and Lumber

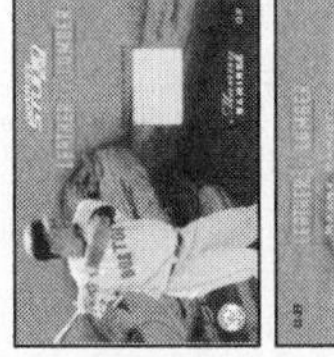
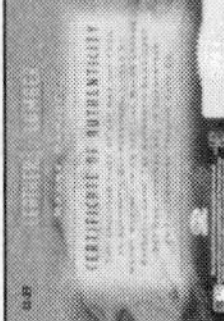

Nm-Mt Ex-Mt
COMMON CARD p/r 300-400 8.00 2.40
RANDOM INSERTS IN PACKS
PRINT RUNS B/WN 100-400 COPIES PER
1 Adam Dunn Bat/400 8.00 2.40
2 Alex Rodriguez Bat/250 20.00 6.00
3 Alfonso Soriano Bat/250 15.00 4.50
4 Andruw Jones Bat/400 8.00 2.40
5 Austin Kearns Bat/400 8.00 2.40
6 Chipper Jones Bat/400 10.00 3.00
7 Derek Jeter Ball/100 40.00 12.00
8 Don Mattingly Bat/100 40.00 12.00
9 Edgar Martinez Bat/400 10.00 3.00
10 Frank Thomas Bat/400 10.00 3.00
11 Fred McGriff Bat/400 10.00 3.00
12 Garret Anderson Bat/400
13 Greg Maddux Bat/150 15.00 4.50
14 Hideki Matsui Ball/100 50.00 15.00
15 Hideo Nomo Bat/150 20.00 6.00
16 Ichiro Suzuki Ball/100 40.00 12.00
17 Ivan Rodriguez Bat/250 15.00 4.50
18 Jason Giambi Bat/400 10.00 3.00
19 Jeff Bagwell Bat/400 10.00 3.00
20 Jim Edmonds Bat/150 10.00 3.00
21 Jim Thome Bat/400 10.00 3.00
22 Juan Gonzalez Bat/400 10.00 3.00
23 Kerry Wood Bat/250 15.00 4.50
24 Kirby Puckett Bat/100 25.00 7.50
25 Lance Berkman Bat/400 8.00 2.40
26 Magglio Ordonez Bat/400 8.00 2.40
27 Manny Ramirez Bat/250 10.00 3.00
28 Mark Prior Bat/400 20.00 6.00
29 Miguel Tejada Bat/200 10.00 3.00
30 Mike Piazza Bat/400 10.00 3.00
31 Mike Schmidt Bat/200 40.00 12.00
32 Nomar Garciaparra Bat/400 15.00 4.50
33 Pat Burrell Bat/400 8.00 2.40
34 Pedro Martinez Bat/150 15.00 4.50
35 Rafael Palmeiro Bat/400
36 Randy Johnson Bat/250 15.00 4.50
37 Rickey Henderson Bat/175 15.00 4.50
38 Sammy Sosa Bat/300 15.00 4.50
39 Shawn Green Bat/400 8.00 2.40
40 Vladimir Guerrero Bat/400 10.00 3.00

2003 Studio Leather and Lumber Combos

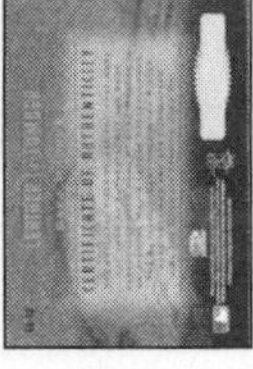

Nm-Mt Ex-Mt
RANDOM INSERTS IN PACKS
PRINT RUNS B/WN 25-50 COPIES PER
NO PRICING ON QTY OF 25 OR LESS.
1 Adam Dunn Bat-Btg Glv/50 25.00 7.50
2 Alex Rodriguez Bat-Fld Glv/50 50.00 15.00
3 Alfonso Soriano Bat-Ball/25
4 Andruw Jones Bat-Fld Glv/50 25.00 7.50
5 Austin Kearns Bat-Shoe/50 25.00 7.50
6 Chipper Jones Bat-Ball/25
7 Derek Jeter Ball-Ball/25
8 Don Mattingly Bat-Btg Glv/25
9 Edgar Martinez Bat-Ball/25
10 Frank Thomas Bat-Btg Glv/50 40.00 12.00
11 Fred McGriff Bat-Ball/25
12 Garret Anderson Bat-Ball/25
13 Greg Maddux Bat-Shoe/50 40.00 12.00
14 Hideki Matsui Ball-Ball/25
15 Hideo Nomo Bat-Ball/25
16 Ichiro Suzuki Ball-Ball/25
17 Ivan Rodriguez Bat-Btg Glv/50 40.00 12.00
18 Jason Giambi Bat-Ball/25
19 Jeff Bagwell Bat-Ball/25
20 Jim Edmonds Bat-Shoe/50 25.00 7.50
21 Jim Thome Bat-Ball/25
22 Juan Gonzalez Bat-Ball/25
23 Kerry Wood Bat-Fld Glv/50 40.00 12.00
24 Kirby Puckett Bat-Btg Glv/25
25 Lance Berkman Bat-Fld Glv/50 25.00 7.50
26 Magglio Ordonez Bat-Shoe/25
27 Manny Ramirez Bat-Ball/25
28 Mark Prior Bat-Shoe/25
29 Miguel Tejada Bat-Ball/25
30 Mike Piazza Bat-Shoe/25
31 Mike Schmidt Bat-Btg Glv/25
32 Nomar Garciaparra Bat-Ball/25
33 Pat Burrell Bat-Ball/25
34 Pedro Martinez Bat-Ball/25
35 Rafael Palmeiro Bat-Fld Glv/25
36 Randy Johnson Bat-Ball/25
37 Rickey Henderson Bat-Ball/25
38 Sammy Sosa Bat-Shoe/25
39 Shawn Green Bat-Ball/25
40 Vladimir Guerrero Bat-Ball/25

2003 Studio Masterstrokes

Nm-Mt Ex-Mt
RANDOM INSERTS IN PACKS
STATED PRINT RUN 1000 SERIAL #'d SETS
1 Adam Dunn 3.00 .90
2 Albert Pujols 10.00 3.00
3 Alex Rodriguez 8.00 2.40
4 Alfonso Soriano 5.00 1.50
5 Andruw Jones 3.00 .90
6 Chipper Jones 5.00 1.50
7 Derek Jeter 12.00 3.60
8 Greg Maddux 8.00 2.40
9 Hideki Matsui 15.00 4.50
10 Hideo Nomo 5.00 1.50
11 Ivan Rodriguez 5.00 1.50
12 Jason Giambi 5.00 1.50
13 Jeff Bagwell 5.00 1.50
14 Juan Gonzalez 5.00 1.50
15 Ken Griffey Jr. 8.00 2.40
16 Lance Berkman 3.00 .90
17 Magglio Ordonez 3.00 .90
18 Manny Ramirez 3.00 .90
19 Mark Prior 10.00 3.00
20 Miguel Tejada 3.00 .90
21 Mike Piazza 8.00 2.40
22 Nomar Garciaparra 8.00 2.40
23 Pat Burrell 3.00 .90
24 Sammy Sosa 8.00 2.40
25 Vladimir Guerrero 5.00 1.50

2003 Studio Masterstrokes Proofs

Nm-Mt Ex-Mt
RANDOM INSERTS IN PACKS
STATED PRINT RUN 50 SERIAL #'d SETS
1 Adam Dunn Bat-Jsy 25.00 7.50
2 Albert Pujols Bat-Jsy 60.00 18.00
3 Alex Rodriguez Bat-Jsy 60.00 18.00
4 Alfonso Soriano Bat-Jsy 30.00 9.00
5 Andruw Jones Bat-Jsy 25.00 7.50
6 Chipper Jones Bat-Jsy 30.00 9.00
7 Derek Jeter Base-Ball 80.00 24.00

8 Greg Maddux Bat-Jsy 40.00 12.00
9 Hideki Matsui Base-Ball 150.00 45.00
10 Hideo Nomo Bat-Jsy 120.00 36.00
11 Ivan Rodriguez Bat-Jsy 30.00 9.00
12 Jason Giambi Bat-Jsy 30.00 9.00
13 Jeff Bagwell Bat-Jsy 30.00 9.00
14 Juan Gonzalez Bat-Jsy 30.00 9.00
15 Ken Griffey Jr. Base-Base 50.00 15.00
16 Lance Berkman Bat-Jsy 25.00 7.50
17 Magglio Ordonez Bat-Jsy 25.00 7.50
18 Manny Ramirez Bat-Jsy 25.00 7.50
19 Mark Prior Bat-Jsy 50.00 15.00
20 Miguel Tejada Bat-Jsy 25.00 7.50
21 Mike Piazza Bat-Jsy 40.00 12.00
22 Nomar Garciaparra Bat-Jsy 50.00 15.00
23 Pat Burrell Bat-Jsy 25.00 7.50
24 Sammy Sosa Bat-Jsy 50.00 15.00
25 Vladimir Guerrero Bat-Jsy 30.00 9.00

2003 Studio Player Collection

*PLAY.COLL: .4X TO 1X PRESTIGE PLAY.COLL
RANDOM INSERTS IN PACKS
STATED PRINT RUN 300 SERIAL #'d SETS
SEE 2003 PRESTIGE PLAY.COLL FOR PRICING

2003 Studio Recollection Autographs 5 x 7

Inserted at a stated rate of one per sealed hobby case, these 27 cards feature authentic autographs of the featured players. Please note that these cards are alll 2001 Studio buybacks and we have put the stated print run next to the player's name in our checklist. In addition, if a card has a print run of 25 or fewer copies, there is no pricing due to market scarcity.

Nm-Mt Ex-Mt
1 Josh Beckett/3
2 Lance Berkman/13
3 Sean Casey/125 20.00 6.00
4 Adam Dunn/12
5 Troy Glaus/82 30.00 9.00
6 Tom Glavine/3
7 Shawn Green/3
8 Vladimir Guerrero/125 40.00 12.00
9 Tony Gwynn/13
10 Todd Helton/55 40.00 12.00
11 Andruw Jones/3
12 Ryan Klesko/75 20.00 6.00
13 Greg Maddux/25
14 Edgar Martinez/11
15 Magglio Ordonez/6
16 Cal Ripken/4
17 Alex Rodriguez/3
18 Ivan Rodriguez/50 50.00 15.00
19 C.C. Sabathia/50 25.00 7.50
20 Curt Schilling/75 30.00 9.00
21 Ben Sheets/1
22 Alfonso Soriano/8
23 Mike Sweeney/42 25.00 7.50
24 Miguel Tejada/44 25.00 7.50
25 Frank Thomas/11
26 Kerry Wood/200 25.00 7.50
27 Barry Zito/200 25.00 7.50

2003 Studio Spirit of the Game

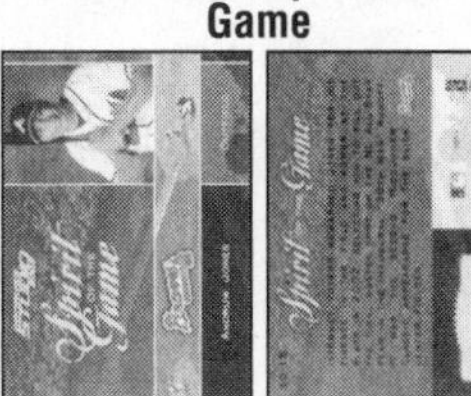

Nm-Mt Ex-Mt
RANDOM INSERTS IN PACKS
STATED PRINT RUN 1250 SERIAL #'d SETS
1 Garret Anderson 2.50 .75
2 Nomar Garciaparra 6.00 1.80
3 Pedro Martinez 4.00 1.20
4 Rickey Henderson 4.00 1.20
5 Magglio Ordonez 2.50 .75
6 Torii Hunter 2.50 .75
7 Alfonso Soriano 4.00 1.20
8 Jose Contreras 5.00 1.50
9 Derek Jeter 10.00 3.00
10 Jason Giambi 4.00 1.20
11 Roger Clemens 8.00 2.40
12 Hideki Matsui 10.00 3.00
13 Barry Zito 4.00 1.20
14 Ichiro Suzuki 6.00 1.80
15 Alex Rodriguez 6.00 1.80
16 Curt Schilling 4.00 1.20
17 Randy Johnson 4.00 1.20
18 Andruw Jones 2.50 .75
19 Chipper Jones 4.00 1.20
20 Greg Maddux 6.00 1.80
21 Sammy Sosa 6.00 1.80
22 Adam Dunn 2.50 .75
23 Ken Griffey Jr. 6.00 1.80
24 Todd Helton 4.00 1.20
25 Ivan Rodriguez 4.00 1.20
26 Lance Berkman 2.50 .75
27 Hideo Nomo 4.00 1.20
28 Shawn Green 2.50 .75
29 Vladimir Guerrero 4.00 1.20
30 Mike Piazza 6.00 1.80
31 Roberto Alomar 4.00 1.20
32 Jim Thome 4.00 1.20
33 Barry Bonds 10.00 3.00
34 Albert Pujols 8.00 2.40
35 Scott Rolen 4.00 1.20

2003 Studio Spirit of MLB

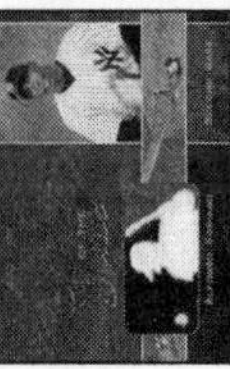

Nm-Mt Ex-Mt
RANDOM INSERTS IN PACKS
STATED PRINT RUN 1 SERIAL #'d SET

2003 Studio Stars

Nm-Mt Ex-Mt
STATED ODDS 1:5
*GOLD: 1X TO 2.5X BASIC STARS
GOLD PRINT RUN 100 SERIAL #'d SETS
PLATINUM PRINT RUN 25 SERIAL #'d SETS
NO PLATINUM PRICING DUE TO SCARCITY
GOLD/PLATINUM RANDOM IN PACKS
1 Troy Glaus 2.00 .60
2 Manny Ramirez 2.00 .60
3 Nomar Garciaparra 5.00 1.50
4 Pedro Martinez 3.00 .90
5 Rickey Henderson 3.00 .90
6 Torii Hunter 2.00 .60
7 Frank Thomas 3.00 .90
8 Magglio Ordonez 2.00 .60
9 Alfonso Soriano 2.00 .60
10 Jose Contreras 4.00 1.20
11 Derek Jeter 8.00 2.40
12 Jason Giambi 3.00 .90
13 Roger Clemens 6.00 1.80
14 Mike Mussina 3.00 .90
15 Barry Zito 2.00 .60
16 Miguel Tejada 2.00 .60
17 Ichiro Suzuki 5.00 1.50
18 Alex Rodriguez 5.00 1.50
19 Juan Gonzalez 3.00 .90
20 Rafael Palmeiro 2.00 .60
21 Hank Blalock 2.00 .60
22 Curt Schilling 2.00 .60
23 Randy Johnson 3.00 .90
24 Junior Spivey 2.00 .60
25 Andruw Jones 2.00 .60
26 Chipper Jones 3.00 .90
27 Greg Maddux 5.00 1.50
28 Kerry Wood 3.00 .90
29 Mark Prior 6.00 1.80
30 Sammy Sosa 5.00 1.50
31 Adam Dunn 2.00 .60
32 Ken Griffey Jr. 5.00 1.50
33 Austin Kearns 2.00 .60
34 Larry Walker 2.00 .60
35 Todd Helton 2.00 .60
36 Ivan Rodriguez 3.00 .90
37 Jeff Bagwell 2.00 .60
38 Lance Berkman 2.00 .60
39 Craig Biggio 2.00 .60
40 Hideo Nomo 3.00 .90
41 Shawn Green 2.00 .60
42 Vladimir Guerrero 3.00 .90
43 Mike Piazza 5.00 1.50
44 Tom Glavine 2.00 .60
45 Roberto Alomar 3.00 .90
46 Pat Burrell 2.00 .60
47 Jim Thome 3.00 .90
48 Barry Bonds 8.00 2.40
49 Albert Pujols 6.00 1.80
50 Scott Rolen 2.00 .60

2003 Studio Atlantic City National

Collectors who opened a speficied number of Donruss/Playoff packs at the 2003 Atlantic City National Convention were able to receive one of these cards which had a special Atlantic City Logo stamped on the front and were serial numbered to five on the back. Please note that due to market scarcity, no pricing is provided

MINT NRMT
PRINT RUN 5 SERIAL #'d SETS

1985 Subway Discs

This set is parallel to the 1985 Thom McAn discs. While the same design was used, it was distributed in outlets of the sandwhich chain. Thi s set is much easier than the Thom McAn set.

Nm-Mt Ex-Mt
COMPLETE SET (46) 100.00 40.00
1 Benny Ayala .25 .10
2 Buddy Bell .50 .20
3 Juan Beniquez .25 .10
4 Tony Bernazard .25 .10
5 Mike Boddicker .25 .10
6 Bill Buckner .25 .10
7 Rod Carew 10.00 4.00
8 Onix Concepcion .25 .10
9 Cecil Cooper .50 .20
10 Al Cowens .25 .10
11 Ron Guidry .50 .20
12 Mike Hargrove .50 .20
13 Kent Hrbek .50 .20
14 Rick Langford .25 .10
15 Jack Morris .50 .20
16 Dan Quisenberry .25 .10
17 Cal Ripken 30.00 12.00
18 Ed Romero .25 .10
19 Tom Seaver 10.00 4.00
20 Alan Trammell 1.00 .40
21 Greg Walker .25 .10
22 Willie Wilson .25 .10
23 Dave Winfield 10.00 4.00
24 Geoff Zahn .25 .10
25 Steve Carlton 10.00 4.00
26 Cesar Cedeno .25 .10
27 Jose Cruz .25 .10
28 Ivan DeJesus .25 .10
29 Luis DeLeon .25 .10
30 Rich Gossage .50 .20
31 Pedro Guerrero .25 .10
32 Tony Gwynn 25.00 10.00
33 Keith Hernandez .50 .20
34 Bob Horner .25 .10
35 Jeff Leonard .25 .10
36 Willie McGee .50 .20
37 Jesse Orosco .50 .20
38 Junior Ortiz .25 .10
39 Terry Puhl .25 .10
40 Johnny Ray .25 .10
41 Ryne Sandberg 15.00 6.00
42 Mike Schmidt 10.00 4.00
43 Rick Sutcliffe .50 .20
44 Bruce Sutter .50 .20
45 Fernando Valenzuela .50 .20
46 Ozzie Virgil .25 .10

1994 Sucker Saver

These sucker saver lollipops were produced by Innovative Confections. The actual discs were issued by Michael Schechter Associates, and one disc was included with each sucker. It is reported that sales of this confectionary product were so poor that it was discontinued. Each disc measures 2 5/8" in diameter. Inside a red ring, the fronts display a color player headshot within a diamond design. The player's name appears in black lettering on a yellow stripe across the top of the disc. The backs of the discs are printed in blue and are numbered "X of 20."

Nm-Mt Ex-Mt
COMPLETE SET (20) 50.00 15.00
1 Rickey Henderson 4.00 1.20
2 Ken Caminiti 1.00 .30
3 Terry Pendleton .50 .15
4 Tim Raines 1.00 .30
5 Joe Carter 1.00 .30
6 Benito Santiago 1.00 .30
7 Jim Abbott 1.00 .30
8 Ozzie Smith 8.00 2.40
9 Don Slaught .50 .15
10 Tony Gwynn 8.00 2.40
11 Mark Langston .50 .15
12 Darryl Strawberry 1.00 .30
13 Dave Justice 2.00 .60
14 Cecil Fielder 1.00 .30
15 Cal Ripken 15.00 4.50
16 Jeff Bagwell 4.00 1.20
17 Mike Piazza 10.00 3.00
18 Bobby Bonilla .50 .15
19 Barry Bonds 8.00 2.40
20 Roger Clemens 8.00 2.40

1995 Summit Samples

This nine-card standard-sized set was issued in an 8 1/2" by 14 1/2" black portfolio in complete set form. The fronts freature color action cut-out player photos on a background that is partly white and partly game action. The player's name and team logo are gold-foil stamped on a black bar below. The backs carry a color closeup photo that partially overlays a baseball diamond containing 1994 monthly statistics. The player's name, sponsors' logos and card number round out the back. The disclaimer "sample" is printed diagonally across both sides of the card.

Nm-Mt Ex-Mt
COMPLETE SET (9) 8.00 2.40
10 Barry Larkin 1.00 .30
11 Albert Belle .50 .15
79 Cal Ripken 5.00 1.50
80 David Cone .50 .15
125 Alex Gonzalez .25 .07
130 Charles Johnson .25 .07
BB12 Jose Canseco 1.25 .35
BB17 Fred McGriff .75 .23
NNO Title Card .25 .07

1995 Summit

This set contains 200 standard-size cards and was sold in seven-card retail packs for a suggested price of $1.99. This set is a premium product issued by Pinnacle Brands and produced on thicker paper than the regular set. Subsets featured are Rookies (112-173), Bat

Speed (174-188) and Special Delivery (189-193). Notable Rookie Cards in this set include Bobby Higginson and Hideo Nomo.

Nm-Mt Ex-Mt
COMPLETE SET (200) 20.00 6.00
1 Ken Griffey Jr. 1.00 .30
2 Alex Fernandez .15 .04
3 Fred McGriff .40 .12
4 Ben McDonald .15 .04
5 Rafael Palmeiro .40 .12
6 Tony Gwynn .75 .23
7 Jim Thome .60 .18
8 Ken Hill .15 .04
9 Barry Bonds 1.50 .45
10 Barry Larkin .60 .18
11 Albert Belle .25 .07
12 Billy Ashley .15 .04
13 Matt Williams .25 .07
14 Andy Benes .15 .04
15 Midre Cummings .15 .04
16 J.R. Phillips .15 .04
17 Edgar Martinez .40 .12
18 Manny Ramirez .25 .07
19 Jose Canseco .60 .18
20 Chili Davis .25 .07
21 Don Mattingly 1.50 .45
22 Bernie Williams .40 .12
23 Tom Glavine .40 .12
24 Robin Ventura .25 .07
25 Jeff Conine .25 .07
26 Mark Grace .40 .12
27 Mark McGwire 1.50 .45
28 Carlos Delgado .25 .07
29 Greg Colbrunn .15 .04
30 Greg Maddux 1.00 .30
31 Craig Biggio .40 .12
32 Kirby Puckett .60 .18
33 Derek Bell .15 .04
34 Lenny Dykstra .25 .07
35 Tim Salmon .40 .12
36 Deion Sanders .40 .12
37 Moises Alou .25 .07
38 Ray Lankford .15 .04
39 Willie Greene .15 .04
40 Ozzie Smith 1.00 .30
41 Roger Clemens 1.25 .35
42 Andres Galarraga .25 .07
43 Gary Sheffield .25 .07
44 Sammy Sosa 1.00 .30
45 Larry Walker .40 .12
46 Kevin Appier .25 .07
47 Raul Mondesi .25 .07
48 Kenny Lofton .25 .07
49 Darryl Hamilton .15 .04
50 Roberto Alomar .60 .18
51 Hal Morris .15 .04
52 Cliff Floyd .25 .07
53 Brent Gates .15 .04
54 Rickey Henderson .60 .18
55 John Olerud .25 .07
56 Gregg Jefferies .15 .04
57 Cecil Fielder .25 .07
58 Paul Molitor .40 .12
59 Bret Boone .25 .07
60 Greg Vaughn .25 .07
61 Wally Joyner .25 .07
62 Jeffrey Hammonds .15 .04
63 James Mouton .15 .04
64 Omar Vizquel .25 .07
65 Wade Boggs .40 .12
66 Terry Steinbach .15 .04
67 Wil Cordero .15 .04
68 Joey Hamilton .15 .04
69 Rico Brogna .15 .04
70 Darren Daulton .25 .07
71 Chuck Knoblauch .25 .07
72 Bob Hamelin .15 .04
73 Carl Everett .25 .07
74 Joe Carter .25 .07
75 Dave Winfield .25 .07
76 Bobby Bonilla .25 .07
77 Paul O'Neill .40 .12
78 Javier Lopez .25 .07
79 Cal Ripken 2.00 .60
80 David Cone .25 .07
81 Bernard Gilkey .15 .04
82 Ivan Rodriguez .60 .18
83 Dean Palmer .25 .07
84 Jason Bere .15 .04
85 Will Clark .60 .18
86 Scott Cooper .15 .04
87 Royce Clayton .15 .04
88 Mike Piazza 1.00 .30
89 Ryan Klesko .25 .07
90 Juan Gonzalez .60 .18
91 Travis Fryman .25 .07
92 Frank Thomas .60 .18
93 Eduardo Perez .15 .04
94 Mo Vaughn .25 .07
95 Jay Bell .25 .07
96 Jeff Bagwell .40 .12
97 Randy Johnson .60 .18
98 Jimmy Key .25 .07
99 Dennis Eckersley .25 .07
100 Carlos Baerga .15 .04
101 Eddie Murray .60 .18
102 Mike Mussina .60 .18
103 Brian Anderson .15 .04
104 Jeff Cirillo .15 .04
105 Dante Bichette .25 .07
106 Bret Saberhagen .25 .07
107 Jeff Kent .25 .07
108 Ruben Sierra .15 .04
109 Kirk Gibson .25 .07
110 Steve Karsay .15 .04
111 David Justice .25 .07
112 Benji Gil .15 .04
113 Vaughn Eshelman .15 .04
114 Carlos Perez RC .25 .07
115 Chipper Jones .60 .18
116 Shane Andrews .15 .04
117 Orlando Miller .15 .04
118 Scott Ruffcorn .15 .04
119 Jose Oliva .15 .04
120 Joe Vitiello .15 .04
121 Jon Nunnally .15 .04
122 Garret Anderson .25 .07
123 Curtis Goodwin .15 .04
124 Mark Grudzielanek RC .40 .12
125 Alex Gonzalez .15 .04
126 David Bell .15 .04
127 Dustin Hermanson .15 .04
128 Dave Nilsson .15 .04
129 Wilson Heredia .15 .04
130 Charles Johnson .25 .07
131 Frank Rodriguez .15 .04
132 Alex Ochoa .15 .04
133 Alex Rodriguez 1.50 .45
134 Bobby Higginson RC .60 .18
135 Edgardo Alfonzo .25 .07
136 Armando Benitez .25 .07
137 Rich Aude .15 .04
138 Tim Naehring .15 .04
139 Joe Randa .15 .04
140 Quilvio Veras .15 .04
141 Hideo Nomo RC 1.50 .45
142 Ray Holbert .15 .04
143 Michael Tucker .15 .04
144 Chad Mottola .15 .04
145 John Valentin .15 .04
146 James Baldwin .15 .04
147 Esteban Loaiza .25 .07
148 Marty Cordova .15 .04
149 Juan Acevedo RC .15 .04
150 Tim Unroe RC UER .15 .04
Cardinals logo
151 Brad Clontz UER .15 .04
A's logo
152 Steve Rodriguez UER .15 .04
Yankees logo
153 Rudy Pemberton UER .15 .04
Dodgers logo
154 Ozzie Timmons UER .15 .04
Tigers logo
155 Ricky Otero .15 .04
156 Allen Battle .15 .04
157 Joe Rosselli .15 .04
158 Roberto Petagine .15 .04
159 Todd Hollandsworth .15 .04
160 Shannon Penn UER .15 .04
Cubs logo
161 Antonio Osuna UER .15 .04
Tigers logo
162 Russ Davis UER .15 .04
Red Sox logo
163 Jason Giambi UER .60 .18
two errors: front photo actually Brent Gates
also Braves logo
164 Terry Bradshaw UER .15 .04
Brewers logo
165 Ray Durham .25 .07
166 Todd Steverson .15 .04
167 Tim Belk .15 .04
168 Andy Pettitte .40 .12
169 Roger Cedeno .15 .04
170 Jose Parra .15 .04
171 Scott Sullivan .15 .04
172 LaTroy Hawkins .15 .04
173 Jeff McCurry .15 .04
174 Ken Griffey Jr. BS .60 .18
175 Frank Thomas BS .40 .12
176 Cal Ripken Jr. BS 1.00 .30
177 Jeff Bagwell BS .25 .07
178 Mike Piazza BS .60 .18
179 Barry Bonds BS .75 .23
180 Matt Williams BS .15 .04
181 Don Mattingly BS 1.00 .30
182 Will Clark BS .25 .07
183 Tony Gwynn BS .40 .12
184 Kirby Puckett BS .40 .12
185 Jose Canseco BS .25 .07
186 Paul Molitor BS .25 .07
187 Albert Belle BS .15 .04
188 Joe Carter BS .15 .04
189 Greg Maddux SD .60 .18
190 Roger Clemens SD .60 .18
191 David Cone SD .15 .04
192 Mike Mussina SD .40 .12
193 Randy Johnson SD .40 .12
194 Frank Thomas CL .40 .12
195 Ken Griffey Jr. CL .60 .18
196 Cal Ripken CL 1.00 .30
197 Jeff Bagwell CL .25 .07
198 Mike Piazza CL .60 .18
199 Barry Bonds CL .75 .23
200 Mo Vaughn CL .15 .04
Matt Williams

1995 Summit Nth Degree

This set is a parallel of the 200 regular cards from the Summit set and inserted one per four packs. The only difference between these cards and the regular set is that "Nth degree" card fronts have a prismatic foil background.

Nm-Mt Ex-Mt
*STARS: 3X TO 8X BASIC CARDS
*ROOKIES: 2.5X TO 6X BASIC CARDS

1995 Summit Big Bang

This 20-card set was randomly inserted in packs at a rate of one in 72. The set is comprised of the best home run hitters in the game. The set uses a process called "Spectrotech" which allows the card to be made of foil and have a holographic image. The fronts have an action photo with a game background which also shows the player. The backs have a player photo and information on his power exploits.

Nm-Mt Ex-Mt
COMPLETE SET (20) 250.00 75.00
BB1 Ken Griffey Jr. 20.00 6.00
BB2 Frank Thomas 12.00 3.60
BB3 Cal Ripken 40.00 12.00
BB4 Jeff Bagwell 8.00 2.40
BB5 Mike Piazza 20.00 6.00
BB6 Barry Bonds 30.00 9.00
BB7 Matt Williams 5.00 1.50
BB8 Don Mattingly 30.00 9.00
BB9 Will Clark 12.00 3.60
BB10 Tony Gwynn 15.00 4.50
BB11 Kirby Puckett 12.00 3.60
BB12 Jose Canseco 12.00 3.60
BB13 Paul Molitor 8.00 2.40
BB14 Albert Belle 5.00 1.50
BB15 Joe Carter 5.00 1.50
BB16 Rafael Palmeiro 8.00 2.40
BB17 Fred McGriff 8.00 2.40
BB18 David Justice 5.00 1.50
BB19 Tim Salmon 8.00 2.40
BB20 Mo Vaughn 5.00 1.50

1995 Summit New Age

This 15-card set was randomly inserted in packs at a rate of one in 18. The set is comprised of 15 of the best young players in baseball. The fronts are horizontally designed and have a color-action photo with a background of a baseball stadium with a red and gray background. The backs have a photo with player information and the words "New Age" at the bottom in red and white.

Nm-Mt Ex-Mt
COMPLETE SET (15) 40.00 12.00
NA1 Cliff Floyd 2.00 .60
NA2 Manny Ramirez 2.00 .60
NA3 Raul Mondesi 2.00 .60
NA4 Alex Rodriguez 12.00 3.60
NA5 Billy Ashley 1.00 .30
NA6 Alex Gonzalez 1.00 .30
NA7 Michael Tucker 1.00 .30
NA8 Charles Johnson 2.00 .60
NA9 Carlos Delgado 2.00 .60
NA10 Benji Gil 1.00 .30
NA11 Chipper Jones 5.00 1.50
NA12 Todd Hollandsworth 1.00 .30
NA13 Frankie Rodriguez 1.00 .30
NA14 Shawn Green 2.00 .60
NA15 Ray Durham 2.00 .60

1995 Summit 21 Club

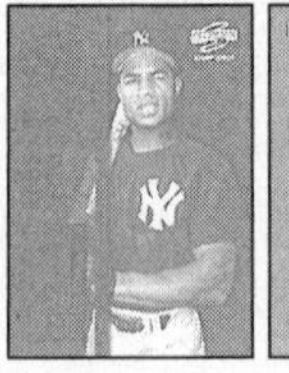
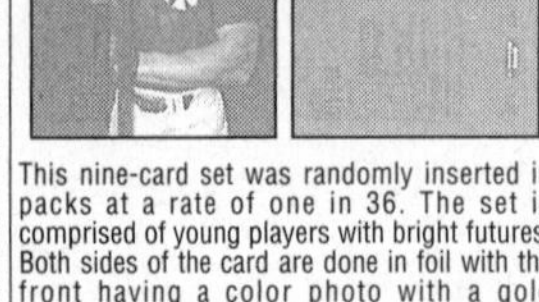

This nine-card set was randomly inserted in packs at a rate of one in 36. The set is comprised of young players with bright futures. Both sides of the card are done in foil with the front having a color photo with a gold background with "21 Club" in gray and red in the bottom right hand corner. The backs are laid out horizontally with a player head shot and information done in foil.

Nm-Mt Ex-Mt
COMPLETE SET (9) 25.00 7.50
TC1 Bob Abreu 5.00 1.50
TC2 Pokey Reese 2.00 .60
TC3 Edgardo Alfonzo 3.00 .90
TC4 Jim Pittsley 2.00 .60
TC5 Ruben Rivera 2.00 .60
TC6 Chan Ho Park 3.00 .90
TC7 Julian Tavarez 2.00 .60
TC8 Ismael Valdes 2.00 .60
TC9 Dmitri Young 3.00 .90

1996 Summit

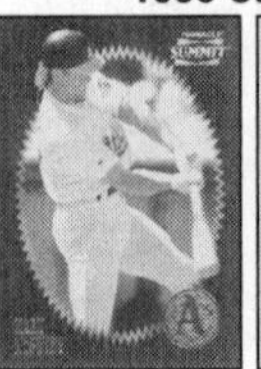
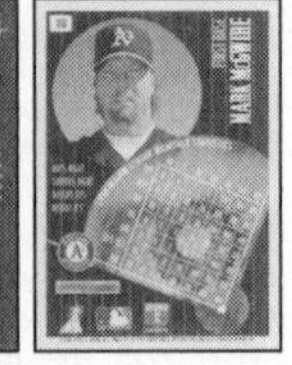

The 1996 Summit set was issued in one series totalling 200 cards. The seven-card packs had a suggested retail of $2.99 each. The fronts feature color player photos on a gold striped black background. The backs carry another player photo with player information and statistics.

Nm-Mt Ex-Mt
COMPLETE SET (200) 25.00 7.50
1 Mike Piazza 1.25 .35
2 Matt Williams .30 .09
3 Tino Martinez .50 .15
4 Reggie Sanders .30 .09
5 Ray Durham .30 .09
6 Brad Radke .30 .09
7 Jeff Bagwell .50 .15
8 Ron Gant .30 .09
9 Lance Johnson .30 .09
10 Kevin Seitzer .30 .09
11 Dante Bichette .30 .09
12 Ivan Rodriguez .75 .23
13 Jim Abbott .50 .15
14 Greg Colbrunn .30 .09
15 Rondell White .30 .09
16 Shawn Green .30 .09
17 Gregg Jefferies .30 .09
18 Omar Vizquel .30 .09
19 Cal Ripken 2.50 .75
20 Mark McGwire 2.00 .60
21 Wally Joyner .30 .09
22 Chili Davis .30 .09
23 Jose Canseco .75 .23
24 Royce Clayton .30 .09
25 Jay Bell .30 .09
26 Travis Fryman .30 .09
27 Jeff King .30 .09
28 Todd Hundley .30 .09
29 Joe Vitiello .30 .09
30 Russ Davis .30 .09
31 Mo Vaughn .30 .09
32 Raul Mondesi .30 .09
33 Ray Lankford .30 .09
34 Mike Stanley .30 .09
35 B.J. Surhoff .30 .09
36 Greg Vaughn .30 .09
37 Todd Stottlemyre .30 .09
38 Carlos Delgado .30 .09
39 Kenny Lofton .30 .09
40 Hideo Nomo .75 .23
41 Sterling Hitchcock .30 .09
42 Pete Schourek .30 .09
43 Edgardo Alfonzo .30 .09
44 Ken Hill .30 .09
45 Ken Caminiti .30 .09
46 Bobby Higginson .30 .09
47 Michael Tucker .30 .09
48 David Cone .30 .09
49 Cecil Fielder .30 .09
50 Brian L. Hunter .30 .09
51 Charles Johnson .30 .09
52 Bobby Bonilla .30 .09
53 Eddie Murray .75 .23
54 Kenny Rogers .30 .09
55 Jim Edmonds .30 .09
56 Trevor Hoffman .30 .09
57 Kevin Mitchell UER .30 .09
58 Ruben Sierra .30 .09
59 Benji Gil .30 .09
60 Juan Gonzalez .75 .23
61 Larry Walker .50 .15
62 Jack McDowell .30 .09
63 Shawon Dunston .30 .09
64 Andy Benes .30 .09
65 Jay Buhner .30 .09
66 Rickey Henderson .75 .23
67 Alex Gonzalez .30 .09
68 Mike Kelly .30 .09
69 Fred McGriff .50 .15
70 Ryne Sandberg 1.25 .35
71 Ernie Young .30 .09
72 Kevin Appier .30 .09
73 Moises Alou .30 .09
74 John Jaha .30 .09
75 J.T. Snow .30 .09
76 Jim Thome .75 .23
77 Kirby Puckett .75 .23
78 Hal Morris .30 .09
79 Robin Ventura .30 .09
80 Ben McDonald .30 .09
81 Tim Salmon .50 .15
82 Albert Belle .30 .09
83 Marquis Grissom .30 .09
84 Alex Rodriguez 1.50 .45
85 Manny Ramirez .30 .09
86 Ken Griffey Jr. 1.25 .35
87 Sammy Sosa 1.25 .35
88 Frank Thomas .75 .23
89 Lee Smith .30 .09
90 Marty Cordova .30 .09
91 Greg Maddux 1.25 .35
92 Lenny Dykstra .30 .09
93 Butch Huskey .30 .09
94 Garret Anderson .30 .09
95 Mike Bordick .30 .09
96 Dave Justice .30 .09
97 Chad Curtis .30 .09
98 Carlos Baerga .30 .09
99 Jason Isringhausen .30 .09
100 Gary Sheffield .30 .09
101 Roger Clemens 1.50 .45
102 Ozzie Smith 1.25 .35
103 Ramon Martinez .30 .09
104 Paul O'Neill .50 .15
105 Will Clark .75 .23
106 Tom Glavine .50 .15
107 Barry Bonds 2.00 .60
108 Barry Larkin .75 .23
109 Derek Bell .30 .09
110 Randy Johnson .75 .23
111 Jeff Conine .30 .09
112 John Mabry .30 .09
113 Julian Tavarez .30 .09
114 Gary DiSarcina .30 .09
115 Andres Galarraga .30 .09
116 Marc Newfield .30 .09
117 Frank Rodriguez .30 .09
118 Brady Anderson .30 .09
119 Mike Mussina .75 .23
120 Orlando Merced .30 .09
121 Melvin Nieves .30 .09
122 Brian Jordan .30 .09
123 Rafael Palmeiro .50 .15
124 Johnny Damon .30 .09
125 Wil Cordero .30 .09
126 Chipper Jones .75 .23
127 Eric Karros .30 .09
128 Darren Daulton .30 .09
129 Vinny Castilla .30 .09
130 Joe Carter .30 .09
131 Bernie Williams .50 .15
132 Bernard Gilkey .30 .09
133 Bret Boone .30 .09
134 Tony Gwynn 1.00 .30
135 Dave Nilsson .30 .09
136 Ryan Klesko .30 .09
137 Paul Molitor .50 .15
138 John Olerud .30 .09
139 Craig Biggio .50 .15
140 John Valentin .30 .09
141 Chuck Knoblauch .30 .09
142 Edgar Martinez .50 .15
143 Rico Brogna .30 .09
144 Dean Palmer .30 .09
145 Mark Grace .50 .15
146 Roberto Alomar .75 .23
147 Alex Fernandez .30 .09
148 Andre Dawson .30 .09
149 Wade Boggs .50 .15
150 Mark Lewis .30 .09
151 Gary Gaetti .30 .09
152 Paul Wilson .75 .23
Roger Clemens
153 Rey Ordonez .50 .15
Ozzie Smith
154 Derek Jeter 1.00 .30
Cal Ripken
155 Andy Benes .30 .09
Alan Benes
156 Jason Kendall .75 .23
Mike Piazza
157 Ryan Klesko .50 .15
Frank Thomas
158 Johnny Damon .75 .23
Ken Griffey Jr.
159 Karim Garcia .75 .23
Sammy Sosa
160 Raul Mondesi .50 .15
Tim Salmon
161 Chipper Jones .50 .15
Matt Williams
162 Rey Ordonez .30 .09
163 Bob Wolcott .30 .09
164 Brooks Kieschnick .30 .09
165 Steve Gibralter .30 .09
166 Rob Abreu .30 .09
167 Greg Zaun .30 .09
168 Tavo Alvarez .30 .09
169 Sal Fasano .30 .09
170 George Arias .30 .09
171 Derek Jeter 2.00 .60
172 Livan Hernandez RC .60 .18
173 Alan Benes .30 .09
174 George Williams .30 .09
175 John Wasdin .30 .09
176 Chan Ho Park .30 .09
177 Paul Wilson .30 .09
178 Jeff Suppan .30 .09
179 Quinton McCracken .30 .09
180 Wilton Guerrero RC .30 .09
181 Eric Owens .30 .09
182 Felipe Crespo .30 .09
183 LaTroy Hawkins .30 .09
184 Jason Schmidt .30 .09
185 Terrell Wade .30 .09
186 Mike Grace RC .30 .09
187 Chris Snopek .30 .09
188 Jason Kendall .30 .09
189 Todd Hollandsworth .30 .09
190 Jim Pittsley .30 .09
191 Jermaine Dye .30 .09
192 Mike Busby RC .30 .09
193 Richard Hidalgo .30 .09
194 Tyler Houston .30 .09
195 Jimmy Haynes .30 .09
196 Karim Garcia .30 .09
197 Ken Griffey Jr. CL .75 .23
198 Frank Thomas CL .50 .15
199 Greg Maddux CL .75 .23
200 Cal Ripken CL 1.25 .35

1996 Summit Above and Beyond

Randomly inserted in packs at a rate of one in four, this 200-card set is parallel to the regular set and is similar in design. The prismatic foil background distinguishes it from the regular set.

Nm-Mt Ex-Mt
*STARS: 4X TO 10X BASIC CARDS
*ROOKIES: 2.5X TO 6X BASIC CARDS

1996 Summit Artist's Proofs

Randomly inserted in packs at a rate of one in 36, this 200-card set is parallel to the regular set and is similar in design with the foil stamped Artist's Proof logo on the front.

Nm-Mt Ex-Mt
*STARS: 10X TO 25X BASIC CARDS
*ROOKIES: 6X TO 15X BASIC CARDS

1996 Summit Foil

Available exclusively through seven-card retail Super Packs (SRP $2.99), these foil cards parallel the basic 200-card Summit set. The micro-etched foil card fronts distinguishes them from basic cards.

Nm-Mt Ex-Mt
COMPLETE SET (200) 50.00 15.00
*STARS: .6X TO 1.5X BASIC CARDS

1996 Summit Ballparks

Randomly inserted in packs at a rate of one in seven, this 18-card set features color action player photos on picture backgrounds of their home ballparks. The backs carry the name of the ballparks and players statistics. Eight thousand of these sets were produced and each card was serial numbered on the back.

Nm-Mt Ex-Mt
COMPLETE SET (18) 100.00 30.00
1 Cal Ripken 20.00 6.00
2 Albert Belle 2.50 .75
3 Dante Bichette 2.50 .75
4 Mo Vaughn 2.50 .75
5 Ken Griffey Jr. 10.00 3.00
6 Derek Jeter 15.00 4.50
7 Juan Gonzalez 6.00 1.80
8 Greg Maddux 10.00 3.00
9 Frank Thomas 6.00 1.80
10 Ryne Sandberg 10.00 3.00
11 Mike Piazza 10.00 3.00

12 Johnny Damon 2.50 .75
13 Barry Bonds 15.00 4.50
14 Jeff Bagwell 4.00 1.20
15 Paul Wilson 2.50 .75
16 Tim Salmon 4.00 1.20
17 Kirby Puckett 6.00 1.80
18 Tony Gwynn 8.00 2.40

1996 Summit Big Bang

Randomly inserted in packs at a rate of one in 72, this 16-card set features the League's big hitters on Spectroetched backgrounds with etched foil highlights. Only 600 sets were produced and each card is individually numbered of 600 on back.The backs carry a player portrait in a diamond with a faded version of the front as a background and information about the player.

	Nm-Mt	Ex-Mt
COMPLETE SET (16)	400.00	120.00
MIRAGE STATED ODDS 1:72		
MIRAGE PRINT RUN 600 SERIAL #'d SETS		
1 Frank Thomas	25.00	7.50
2 Ken Griffey Jr.	40.00	12.00
3 Albert Belle	10.00	3.00
4 Mo Vaughn	10.00	3.00
5 Barry Bonds	60.00	18.00
6 Cal Ripken	80.00	24.00
7 Jeff Bagwell	15.00	4.50
8 Mike Piazza	40.00	12.00
9 Ryan Klesko	10.00	3.00
10 Manny Ramirez	10.00	3.00
11 Tim Salmon	15.00	4.50
12 Dante Bichette	10.00	3.00
13 Sammy Sosa	40.00	12.00
14 Raul Mondesi	10.00	3.00
15 Chipper Jones	25.00	7.50
16 Garret Anderson	10.00	3.00

1996 Summit Hitters Inc.

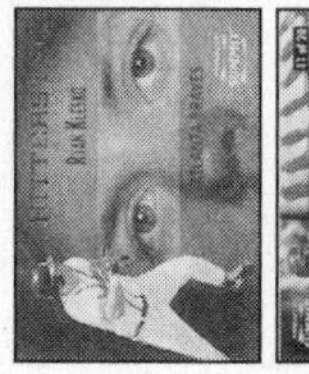

Randomly inserted in packs at a rate of one in 36, this 16-card set features color action player images with embossed highlights on an enlarged photo of the player's eyes for background. The backs carry information about the player's batting ability. Four thousand of these sets were produced and individually serially numbered on the back.

	Nm-Mt	Ex-Mt
COMPLETE SET (16)	150.00	45.00
1 Tony Gwynn	12.00	3.60
2 Mo Vaughn	4.00	1.20
3 Tim Salmon	6.00	1.80
4 Ken Griffey Jr.	15.00	4.50
5 Sammy Sosa	15.00	4.50
6 Frank Thomas	10.00	3.00
7 Wade Boggs	6.00	1.80
8 Albert Belle	4.00	1.20
9 Cal Ripken	30.00	9.00
10 Manny Ramirez	4.00	1.20
11 Ryan Klesko	4.00	1.20
12 Dante Bichette	4.00	1.20
13 Mike Piazza	15.00	4.50
14 Chipper Jones	10.00	3.00
15 Ryne Sandberg	15.00	4.50
16 Matt Williams	4.00	1.20
S11 Ryan Klesko Sample		

1996 Summit Positions

Randomly inserted in Magazine packs only at the rate of one in 50, this nine-card set honors the best players at each playing position. The fronts feature color action player images on a baseball diamond background with head photos of the players at the bottom. The backs carry information about how well the players perform at their position.

	Nm-Mt	Ex-Mt
COMPLETE SET (9)	300.00	90.00
1 Jeff Bagwell Mo Vaughn Frank Thomas	12.00	3.60
2 Roberto Alomar Craig Biggio Chuck Knoblauch	10.00	3.00
3 Matt Williams Jim Thome Chipper Jones	12.00	3.60
4 Barry Larkin Cal Ripken Alex Rodriguez	60.00	18.00
5 Mike Piazza Ivan Rodriguez Charles Johnson	25.00	7.50
6 Hideo Nomo Greg Maddux Randy Johnson	25.00	7.50
7 Barry Bonds Albert Belle Ryan Klesko	40.00	12.00
8 Johnny Damon Jim Edmonds Ken Griffey Jr.	25.00	7.50
9 Manny Ramirez Gary Sheffield Sammy Sosa	30.00	9.00

1990 Sunflower Seeds

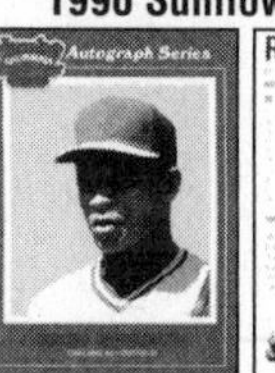
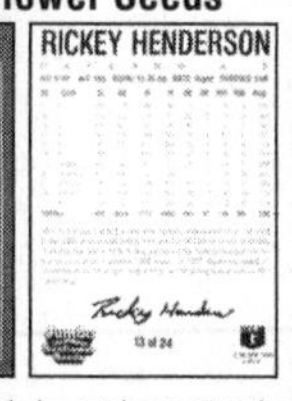

This 24-card, standard-size set is an attractive set which frames the players photo by solid blue borders. This set was issued by Stagi and Scriven Farms Inc. with the cooperation of Michael Schechter Associates (MSA) and features some of the big-name stars in baseball at the time of printing of the set. The set was an attempt by the company to promote sunflower seeds as an alternative to chewing tobacco in the dugout. Three cards were available as an insert in each specially marked bag of Jumbo California Sunflower Seeds.

	Nm-Mt	Ex-Mt
COMPLETE SET (24)	15.00	4.50
1 Kevin Mitchell	.10	.03
2 Ken Griffey Jr.	3.00	.90
3 Howard Johnson	.10	.03
4 Bo Jackson	.75	.23
5 Kirby Puckett	1.00	.30
6 Robin Yount	1.25	.35
7 Dave Stieb	.25	.07
8 Don Mattingly	2.50	.75
9 Barry Bonds	2.50	.75
10 Pedro Guerrero	.10	.03
11 Tony Gwynn	2.50	.75
12 Von Hayes	.10	.03
13 Rickey Henderson	1.25	.35
14 Tim Raines	.25	.07
15 Alan Trammell	.50	.15
16 Dave Stewart	.25	.07
17 Will Clark	.75	.23
18 Roger Clemens	2.50	.75
19 Wally Joyner	.25	.07
20 Ryne Sandberg	2.00	.60
21 Eric Davis	.25	.07
22 Mike Scott	.10	.03
23 Cal Ripken	5.00	1.50
24 Eddie Murray	1.25	.35

1991 Sunflower Seeds

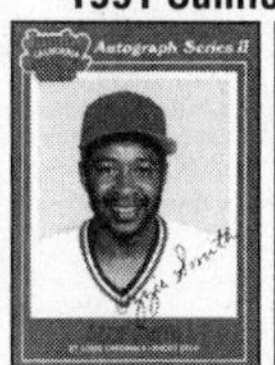
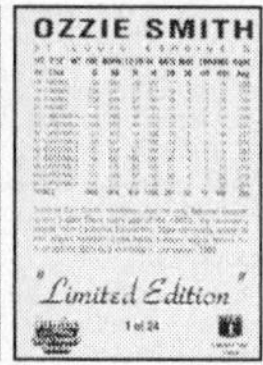

This 24-card, standard-size set was sponsored by Jumbo California Sunflower Seeds. The set was again issued by Stagi and Scriven Farms Inc. with the cooperation of Michael Schechter Associates (MSA). The set was another attempt by the company to promote sunflower seeds as an alternative to chewing tobacco in the dugout. Two cards were available as an insert in each specially marked bag of Jumbo California Sunflower Seeds.

	Nm-Mt	Ex-Mt
COMPLETE SET (24)	10.00	3.00
1 Ozzie Smith	1.50	.45
2 Wade Boggs	1.00	.30
3 Bobby Bonilla	.25	.07
4 George Brett	2.00	.60
5 Kal Daniels	.10	.03
6 Glenn Davis	.10	.03
7 Chuck Finley	.25	.07
8 Cecil Fielder	.25	.07
9 Len Dykstra	.25	.07
10 Dwight Gooden	.25	.07
11 Ken Griffey Jr.	2.50	.75
12 Kelly Gruber	.10	.03
13 Kent Hrbek	.25	.07
14 Andre Dawson	.75	.23
15 Dave Justice	.75	.23
16 Barry Larkin	.75	.23
17 Ben McDonald	.10	.03
18 Mark McGwire	3.00	.90
19 Roberto Alomar	.75	.23
20 Nolan Ryan	4.00	1.20
21 Sandy Alomar Jr.	.25	.07
22 Bobby Thigpen	.10	.03
23 Tim Wallach	.10	.03
24 Matt Williams	.50	.15

1992 Sunflower Seeds

This 24-card, standard-size set was sponsored by Jumbo California Sunflower Seeds and produced by Michael Schechter Associates (MSA). The posed color player photos are framed in white and bright blue on a white background. The company log appears in the upper left corner. The words "Autograph Series III" are printed in red at the top.

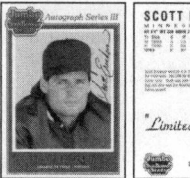

	Nm-Mt	Ex-Mt
COMPLETE SET (24)	10.00	3.00
1 Jeff Reardon	.25	.07
2 Bill Gullickson	.10	.03
3 Todd Zeile	.25	.07
4 Terry Mulholland	.10	.03
5 Kirby Puckett	1.00	.30
6 Howard Johnson	.10	.03
7 Terry Pendleton	.10	.03
8 Will Clark	.75	.23
9 Cal Ripken	4.00	1.20
10 Chris Sabo	.10	.03
11 Jim Abbott	.25	.07
12 Joe Carter	.25	.07
13 Paul Molitor	1.00	.30
14 Ken Griffey Jr.	2.50	.75
15 Randy Johnson	1.25	.35
16 Bobby Bonilla	.10	.03
17 John Smiley	.10	.03
18 Jose Canseco	1.00	.30
19 Tom Glavine	1.00	.30
20 Darryl Strawberry	.25	.07
21 Brett Butler	.25	.07
22 Devon White	.10	.03
23 Scott Erickson	.10	.03
24 Willie McGee	.25	.07

2001 Sunoco Dream Team

The Major League Baseball Players Alumni Association (MLBPAA), in association with Sunoco, Inc. (R and M) and Coca-Cola teamed up to create this exclusive trading card set. Twenty-four Major League Baseball greats featuring seventeen Hall of Famers have been brought together to create a Limited Edition twelve-card set "The Sunoco Dream Team". These gold-foil embossed cards were distributed throughout Sunoco's market area in their gasoline stations located in the following states: Connecticut, Delaware, Illinois, Indiana, Kentucky, Maine, Maryland, Massachusetts, Michigan, New Hampshire, New Jersey, New York, Ohio, Pennsylvania, Rhode Island, Vermont, Virginia, Washington, D.C. and West Virginia. The packs retailed for $.49 each and were available with either a gasoline fill-up or a purchase of (2) 20 oz. bottles of Coca-Cola.

	Nm-Mt	Ex-Mt
COMPLETE SET (12)	8.00	2.40
1 Willie Stargell Bill Mazeroski	1.00	.30
2 Mike Schmidt Steve Carlton	1.50	.45
3 Tony Perez Joe Morgan	1.00	.30
4 Don Mattingly Yogi Berra	1.50	.45
5 Jim Palmer Frank Robinson	1.00	.30
6 Luis Tiant Carlton Fisk	.75	.23
7 Fred Lynn Jim Rice	.50	.15
8 Sparky Anderson MG Al Kaline	1.00	.30
9 Robin Roberts Richie Ashburn	1.25	.35
10 Tug McGraw Gary Carter	.25	.07
11 Lou Boudreau Bob Feller	.50	.15
12 Roger Maris Catfish Hunter	1.00	.30

1994 SuperSlam McDowell Promos

Gold and silver-bordered versions of 3 1/2 by 5 color cutouts of Jack McDowell beginning his pitching delivery. Measure 5 1/2 by 7 1/2 outside dimensions. Can be unfolded and stood up. The creator of this concept was also one of the founders of the Upper Deck company.

	Nm-Mt	Ex-Mt
COMPLETE SET (2)	10.00	3.00
COMMON CARD (1-2)	5.00	1.50

1962 Sugardale

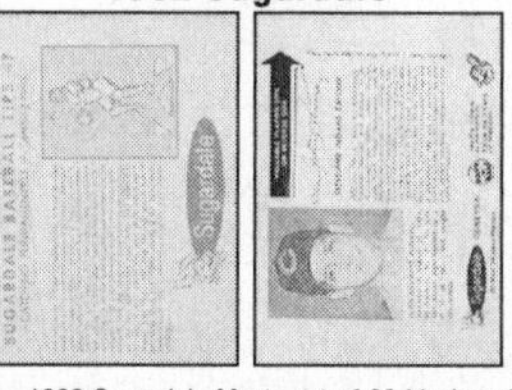

The 1962 Sugardale Meats set of 22 black and white, numbered and lettered cards featuring the Cleveland Indians and Pittsburgh Pirates. The Indians are numbered while the Pirates are lettered. The backs, in red print, give player tips. The Bob Nieman card is considered to be scarce. The catalog numbering for this set is F174-1.

	NM	Ex
COMPLETE SET (22)	1800.00	700.00
COMMON CARD (1-22)	40.00	16.00
COMMON SP	300.00	120.00
1 Barry Latman	40.00	16.00
2 Gary Bell	40.00	16.00
3 Dick Donovan	40.00	16.00
4 Frank Funk	40.00	16.00
5 Jim Perry	50.00	20.00
7 John Romano	40.00	16.00
8 Ty Cline	40.00	16.00
9 Tito Francona	40.00	16.00
10 Bob Nieman SP	300.00	120.00
11 Willie Kirkland	40.00	16.00
12 Woody Held	40.00	16.00
13 Jerry Kindall	40.00	16.00
14 Bubba Phillips	40.00	16.00
15 Mel Harder CO	50.00	20.00
16 Salty Parker CO	40.00	16.00
17 Ray Katt CO	40.00	16.00
18 Mel McGaha MG	40.00	16.00
19 Pedro Ramos	40.00	16.00
A Dick Groat	60.00	24.00
B Roberto Clemente	800.00	325.00
C Don Hoak	40.00	16.00
D Dick Stuart	40.00	16.00

1963 Sugardale

The 1963 Sugardale Meats set of 31 black and white, numbered and lettered cards, features the Cleveland Indians and Pittsburgh Pirates. The Indians cards are numbered while the Pirates cards are lettered. The backs are printed in red and give player tips. The 1963 Sugardale set can be distinguished from the 1962 set by examing the biographies on the card for mentions of the 1962 season. The Perry and Skinner cards were withdrawn after June trades and are quite scarce

	NM	Ex
COMPLETE SET (31)	1500.00	600.00
COMMON CARD	40.00	16.00
COMMON SP	200.00	80.00
1 Barry Latman	40.00	16.00
2 Gary Bell	40.00	16.00
3 Dick Donovan	40.00	16.00
4 Joe Adcock	60.00	24.00
5 Jim Perry SP	200.00	80.00
7 John Romano	40.00	16.00
8 Mike de la Hoz	40.00	16.00
9 Tito Francona	40.00	16.00
10 Gene Green	40.00	16.00
11 Willie Kirkland	40.00	16.00
12 Woody Held	40.00	16.00
13 Jerry Kindall	40.00	16.00
14 Max Alvis	40.00	16.00
15 Mel Harder CO	50.00	20.00
16 George Strickland CO	40.00	16.00
17 Elmer Valo CO	40.00	16.00
18 Birdie Tebbetts MG	40.00	16.00
19 Pedro Ramos	40.00	16.00
20 Al Luplow	40.00	16.00
23 Jim Grant	40.00	16.00
24 Vic Davalillo	40.00	16.00
25 Jerry Walker	40.00	16.00
26 Sam McDowell	80.00	32.00
27 Fred Whitfield	40.00	16.00
28 Jack Kralick	40.00	16.00
33 Bob Allen	40.00	16.00
A Don Cardwell	40.00	16.00
B Bob Skinner SP	200.00	80.00
C Don Schwall	40.00	16.00
D Jim Pagliaroni	40.00	16.00
E Dick Schofield	40.00	16.00

2001 Sweet Spot

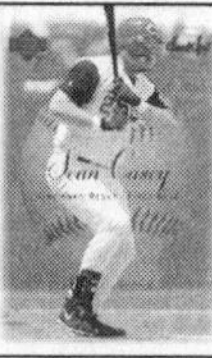

The 2001 Upper Deck Sweet Spot product was initially released in February, 2001 and offered a 90-card base set. An additional 60-card Update set was distributed within Upper Deck Rookie Update packs in late December, 2001. The basic 90-card set is broken into tiers as follows: 60 basic veterans (1-60), and 30 Sweet Beginnings subset cards (each individually serial numbered to 1000). The Update set was composed of 30 basic veterans (91-120) and 30 Sweet Beginnings subset cards (121-150) each serial numbered to 1500. Basic packs contained four cards and carried a suggested retail price of $2.99. Rookie Update packs contained four cards and carried a suggested retail price of $4.99.

	Nm-Mt	Ex-Mt
COMP.BASIC w/o SP's (60)	25.00	7.50
COMP.UPDATE w/o SP's (30)	10.00	3.00
COMMON CARD (1-60)	.40	.12
COMMON CARD (61-90)	10.00	3.00
COMMON CARD (91-120)	.60	.18
COMMON (121-150)	5.00	1.50
1 Troy Glaus	.60	.18
2 Darin Erstad	.40	.12
3 Jason Giambi	1.00	.30
4 Tim Hudson	.40	.12
5 Ben Grieve	.40	.12
6 Carlos Delgado	.40	.12
7 David Wells	.40	.12
8 Greg Vaughn	.40	.12
9 Roberto Alomar	1.00	.30
10 Jim Thome	1.00	.30
11 John Olerud	.40	.12
12 Edgar Martinez	.60	.18
13 Cal Ripken	3.00	.90
14 Albert Belle	.40	.12
15 Ivan Rodriguez	1.00	.30
16 Alex Rodriguez Rangers	3.00	.90
17 Pedro Martinez	1.00	.30
18 Nomar Garciaparra	1.50	.45
19 Manny Ramirez	.40	.12
20 Jermaine Dye	.40	.12
21 Juan Gonzalez	1.00	.30
22 Dean Palmer	.40	.12
23 Matt Lawton	.40	.12
24 Eric Milton	.40	.12
25 Frank Thomas	1.00	.30
26 Magglio Ordonez	.40	.12
27 Derek Jeter	2.50	.75
28 Bernie Williams	.60	.18
29 Roger Clemens	2.00	.60
30 Jeff Bagwell	.60	.18
31 Richard Hidalgo	.40	.12
32 Chipper Jones	1.00	.30
33 Greg Maddux	1.50	.45
34 Richie Sexson	.40	.12
35 Jeromy Burnitz	.40	.12
36 Mark McGwire	2.50	.75
37 Jim Edmonds	.40	.12
38 Sammy Sosa	1.50	.45
39 Randy Johnson	1.00	.30
40 Steve Finley	.40	.12
41 Gary Sheffield	.40	.12
42 Shawn Green	.40	.12
43 Vladimir Guerrero	1.00	.30
44 Jose Vidro	.40	.12
45 Barry Bonds	2.50	.75
46 Jeff Kent	.40	.12
47 Preston Wilson	.40	.12
48 Luis Castillo	.40	.12
49 Mike Piazza	1.50	.45
50 Edgardo Alfonzo	.40	.12
51 Tony Gwynn	1.25	.35
52 Ryan Klesko	.40	.12
53 Scott Rolen	.60	.18
54 Bob Abreu	.40	.12
55 Jason Kendall	.40	.12
56 Brian Giles	.40	.12
57 Ken Griffey Jr.	1.50	.45
58 Barry Larkin	1.00	.30
59 Todd Helton	.60	.18
60 Mike Hampton Card back has batting header lines UER	.40	.12
61 Corey Patterson SB	10.00	3.00
62 Ichiro Suzuki SB RC	150.00	45.00
63 Jason Grilli SB	10.00	3.00
64 Brian Cole SB	10.00	3.00
65 Juan Pierre SB	10.00	3.00
66 Matt Ginter SB	10.00	3.00
67 Jimmy Rollins SB	10.00	3.00
68 Jason Smith SB RC	10.00	3.00
69 Israel Alcantara SB	10.00	3.00
70 Adam Pettyjohn SB RC	10.00	3.00
71 Luke Prokopec SB	10.00	3.00
72 Barry Zito SB	12.00	3.60
73 Keith Ginter SB	10.00	3.00
74 Sun Woo Kim SB	10.00	3.00
75 Ross Gload SB	10.00	3.00
76 Matt Wise SB	10.00	3.00
77 Aubrey Huff SB	10.00	3.00
78 Ryan Franklin SB	10.00	3.00
79 Brandon Inge SB	10.00	3.00
80 Wes Helms SB	10.00	3.00
81 Junior Spivey SB RC	12.00	3.60
82 Ryan Vogelsong SB	10.00	3.00
83 John Parrish SB	10.00	3.00
84 Joe Crede SB	10.00	3.00
85 Damian Rolls SB	10.00	3.00
86 Esix Snead SB RC	10.00	3.00
87 Rocky Biddle SB	10.00	3.00
88 Brady Clark SB	10.00	3.00
89 Timo Perez SB	10.00	3.00
90 Jay Spurgeon SB	10.00	3.00
91 Garret Anderson	.60	.18
92 Jermaine Dye	.60	.18
93 Shannon Stewart	.60	.18
94 Ben Grieve	.60	.18
95 Juan Gonzalez	1.50	.45
96 Brett Boone	.60	.18
97 Tony Batista	.60	.18
98 Rafael Palmeiro	1.00	.30
99 Carl Everett	.60	.18
100 Mike Sweeney	.60	.18
101 Tony Clark	.60	.18
102 Doug Mientkiewicz	.60	.18
103 Jose Canseco	1.50	.45
104 Mike Mussina	1.50	.45
105 Lance Berkman	.60	.18
106 Andruw Jones	.60	.18
107 Geoff Jenkins	.60	.18
108 Matt Morris	.60	.18
109 Fred McGriff	1.00	.30
110 Luis Gonzalez	.60	.18
111 Kevin Brown	.60	.18
112 Tony Armas Jr.	.60	.18
113 John Vander Wal	.60	.18
114 Cliff Floyd	.60	.18
115 Matt Lawton	.60	.18
116 Phil Nevin	.60	.18
117 Pat Burrell	.60	.18
118 Aramis Ramirez	.60	.18
119 Sean Casey	.60	.18
120 Larry Walker	1.00	.30
121 Albert Pujols SB RC	100.00	30.00
122 J.Estrada SB RC	5.00	1.50
123 Wilson Betemit SB RC	5.00	1.50
124 A.Hernandez SB RC	5.00	1.50
125 M.Ensberg SB RC	10.00	3.00
126 H.Ramirez SB RC	8.00	2.40
127 Josh Towers SB RC	5.00	1.50
128 Juan Uribe SB RC	5.00	1.50
129 Wilken Ruan SB RC	5.00	1.50
130 Andres Torres SB RC	5.00	1.50
131 B.Lawrence SB RC	5.00	1.50
132 Ryan Freel SB RC	5.00	1.50
133 B.Duckworth SB RC	5.00	1.50
134 Juan Diaz SB RC	5.00	1.50
135 Rafael Soriano SB RC	10.00	3.00
136 R.Rodriguez SB RC	5.00	1.50
137 Bud Smith SB RC	5.00	1.50
138 Mark Teixeira SB RC	50.00	15.00
139 Mark Prior SB RC	100.00	30.00
140 J.Melian SB RC	5.00	1.50
141 D.Brazelton SB RC	5.00	1.50

142 Greg Miller SB RC 5.00 1.50
143 Billy Sylvester SB RC 5.00 1.50
144 E.Guzman SB RC 5.00 1.50
145 Jack Wilson SB RC 5.00 1.50
146 Jose Mieses SB RC 5.00 1.50
147 Brandon Lyon SB RC 5.00 1.50
148 T.Shinjo SB RC 10.00 3.00
149 Juan Cruz SB RC 5.00 1.50
150 Jay Gibbons SB RC 10.00 3.00

2001 Sweet Spot Big League Challenge

Randomly inserted into packs at one in six, this 20-card insert features the top power-hitting players in the league. Card backs carry a "BL" prefix.

Nm-Mt Ex-Mt
COMPLETE SET (20) 60.00 18.00
BL1 Mark McGwire 8.00 2.40
BL2 Richard Hidalgo 2.00 .60
BL3 Alex Rodriguez 5.00 1.50
BL4 Shawn Green 2.00 .60
BL5 Frank Thomas 3.00 .90
BL6 Chipper Jones 3.00 .90
BL7 Rafael Palmeiro 2.00 .60
BL8 Troy Glaus 2.00 .60
BL9 Mike Piazza 5.00 1.50
BL10 Andruw Jones 2.00 .60
BL11 Todd Helton 2.00 .60
BL12 Jason Giambi 3.00 .90
BL13 Sammy Sosa 5.00 1.50
BL14 Carlos Delgado 2.00 .60
BL15 Barry Bonds 8.00 2.40
BL16 Jose Canseco 3.00 .90
BL17 Jim Edmonds 2.00 .60
BL18 Manny Ramirez 2.00 .60
BL19 Gary Sheffield 2.00 .60
BL20 Nomar Garciaparra 5.00 1.50

2001 Sweet Spot Game Base Duos

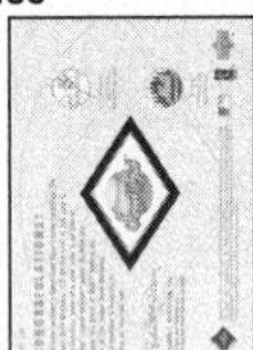

Randomly inserted into packs at one in 18, this 16-card insert set features dual-player cards with a swatch of an actual game-used base. Card backs carry a "B1" prefix followed by the player's initials.

Nm-Mt Ex-Mt
B1-BD Jeff Bagwell 15.00 4.50
Jermaine Dye
B1-BH Barry Bonds 30.00 9.00
Todd Helton
B1-CP Roger Clemens 25.00 7.50
Mike Piazza
B1-GD Vladimir Guerrero 15.00 4.50
Carlos Delgado
B1-HG Jeffrey Hammonds 15.00 4.50
Troy Glaus
B1-JG Chipper Jones 25.00 7.50
Nomar Garciaparra
B1-JP Mike Piazza 40.00 12.00
Derek Jeter
B1-MG Mark McGwire 80.00 24.00
Ken Griffey Jr.
B1-MP Mark McGwire 50.00 15.00
Timo Perez
B1-RJ Alex Rodriguez 50.00 15.00
Derek Jeter
B1-RR Scott Rolen 30.00 9.00
Cal Ripken
B1-SR Gary Sheffield 15.00 4.50
Alex Rodriguez
B1-ST Sammy Sosa 25.00 7.50
Frank Thomas
B1-GRA Ken Griffey Jr. 25.00 7.50
Manny Ramirez
B1-GRO Tony Gwynn 15.00 4.50
Ivan Rodriguez
B1-JGI Randy Johnson 15.00 4.50
Jason Giambi

2001 Sweet Spot Game Base Trios

Randomly inserted into packs, this 13-card insert set features three players on one card with a swatch of an actual game-used base. Card backs carry a "B2" prefix followed by the player's initials. Please note that there were only 50 serial numbered sets produced.

Nm-Mt Ex-Mt
BDH Jef Bagwell 40.00 12.00
Jermaine Dye
Richard Hidalgo
BHK Barry Bonds 100.00 30.00
Todd Helton
Jeff Kent
GDM V. Guerrero 40.00 12.00
Carlos Delgado
Raul Mondesi
GRP Tony Gwynn 50.00 15.00
Ivan Rodriguez
Rafael Palmeiro
GRT Ken Griffey Jr. 50.00 15.00
Manny Ramirez
Jim Thome
HGH Jeffrey Hammonds 40.00 12.00
Troy Glaus
Todd Helton
JGC Randy Johnson 40.00 12.00
Jason Giambi
Eric Chavez
JGJ Chipper Jones 60.00 18.00
Nomar Garciaparra
Andruw Jones
MGE Mark McGwire 120.00 36.00
Ken Griffey Jr.
Jim Edmonds
PJW Mike Piazza 100.00 30.00
Derek Jeter
Bernie Williams
RRB Scott Rolen 100.00 30.00
Cal Ripken
Albert Belle
SRM Gary Sheffield 50.00 15.00
Alex Rodriguez
Edgar Martinez
STO Sammy Sosa 60.00 18.00
Frank Thomas
Magglio Ordonez

2001 Sweet Spot Game Bat

Randomly inserted into packs at one in 18, this 19-card insert set features a swatch of actual game-used bat. Card backs carry a "B" prefix followed by the player's initials.

Nm-Mt Ex-Mt
B-AJ Andruw Jones 10.00 3.00
B-AR Alex Rodriguez 15.00 4.50
B-BB Barry Bonds 25.00 7.50
B-CR Cal Ripken 40.00 12.00
B-FT Frank Thomas 15.00 4.50
B-GS Gary Sheffield 10.00 3.00
B-HA Hank Aaron 60.00 18.00
B-IR Ivan Rodriguez 15.00 4.50
B-JC Jose Canseco 15.00 4.50
B-JD Joe DiMaggio 100.00 30.00
B-KG Ken Griffey Jr. 15.00 4.50
B-MM Mickey Mantle 150.00 45.00
B-NR Nolan Ryan 50.00 15.00
B-RA Rick Ankiel 10.00 3.00
B-RJ Reggie Jackson 15.00 4.50
B-SM Stan Musial 50.00 15.00
B-SS Sammy Sosa 15.00 4.50
B-TC Ty Cobb 175.00 52.50
B-WM Willie Mays 60.00 18.00

2001 Sweet Spot Game Jersey

Randomly inserted into packs at one in 18, this 20-card insert set features a swatch from an actual game-used jersey. Card backs carry a "J" prefix followed by the player's initials. The Ichiro jersey actually was not major league regular-season game worn, but was worn in an spring training game in 1999.

Nm-Mt Ex-Mt
J-AJ Andruw Jones 10.00 3.00
J-AR Alex Rodriguez 15.00 4.50
J-BB Barry Bonds 25.00 7.50
J-CJ Chipper Jones 15.00 4.50
J-CR Cal Ripken 40.00 12.00
J-DS Duke Snider 15.00 4.50
J-FT Frank Thomas 15.00 4.50
J-IR Ivan Rodriguez 15.00 4.50
J-IS Ichiro Suzuki 100.00 30.00
J-JC Jose Canseco 15.00 4.50
J-JD Joe DiMaggio 100.00 30.00
J-KG Ken Griffey Jr. 15.00 4.50
J-MM Mickey Mantle 150.00 45.00
J-NR Nolan Ryan 50.00 15.00
J-RC Roberto Clemente 120.00 36.00
J-RC Roger Clemens 15.00 4.50
J-RJ Randy Johnson 15.00 4.50
J-SM Stan Musial 50.00 15.00
J-SS Sammy Sosa 15.00 4.50
J-WM Willie Mays 80.00 24.00

2001 Sweet Spot Players Party

Inserted at a rate of one in 12 packs, these 10 cards feature some of Baseball's leading players. These cards have a "PP" prefix.

Nm-Mt Ex-Mt
COMPLETE SET (10) 50.00 15.00
PP1 Derek Jeter 8.00 2.40
PP2 Randy Johnson 3.00 .90
PP3 Frank Thomas 3.00 .90
PP4 Nomar Garciaparra 5.00 1.50
PP5 Ken Griffey Jr. 5.00 1.50
PP6 Carlos Delgado 2.00 .60
PP7 Mike Piazza 5.00 1.50
PP8 Barry Bonds 8.00 2.40
PP9 Sammy Sosa 5.00 1.50
PP10 Pedro Martinez 3.00 .90

2001 Sweet Spot Signatures

This 52-card insert set features authentic autographs from some of the Major League's top active and retired players. These cards incorporate the leather sweet spots from actual baseballs, whereby the featured athlete signed the leather swatch. The stunning design of these cards made them one of the most popular autograph inserts of the modern era. One in every eighteen packs of Sweet Spot contained either a Game Base insert or one of these Signatures inserts. Please note the following players packed out as exchange cards with a redemption deadline of November 8th, 2001: Roger Clemens and Willie Mays. In addition, the following players packed out as 50% exchange cards and 50% actual signed cards: Albert Belle, Pat Burrell and Rafael Furcal. Though the cards lack actual serial-numbering, representatives at Upper Deck publicly announced specific print runs on several short-printed cards within this set. That information is listed within our checklist. Forty of the 150 serial numbered Joe DiMaggio cards were actually inscribed by DiMaggio as "Joe DiMaggio - Yankee Clipper".Card backs carry a "S" prefix followed by the player's initials.

Nm-Mt Ex-Mt
S-AB Albert Belle 40.00 12.00
S-AH Art Howe 25.00 7.50
S-AJ Andruw Jones 50.00 15.00
S-AR A. Rodriguez SP/154 250.00 75.00
S-AT Alan Trammell 50.00 15.00
S-BB Buddy Bell 40.00 12.00
S-BM Bill Madlock 40.00 12.00
S-BR Babe Ruth SP/1
S-BV Bobby Valentine 40.00 12.00
S-CB Chris Chambliss 40.00 12.00
S-CD Carlos Delgado 40.00 12.00
S-CJ Chipper Jones 100.00 30.00
S-DB Dusty Baker 50.00 15.00
S-DB Don Baylor 40.00 12.00
S-DE Darin Erstad 40.00 12.00
S-DJ Davey Johnson 40.00 12.00
S-DL Davey Lopes 40.00 12.00
S-FT Frank Thomas 80.00 24.00
S-GS Gary Sheffield 50.00 15.00
S-HM Hal McRae 40.00 12.00
S-IR I. Rodriguez SP/150 150.00 45.00
S-JB Jeff Bagwell SP/214 150.00 45.00
S-JC Jose Canseco 80.00 24.00
S-JD J.DiMaggio SP/110 600.00 180.00
S-JDa Joe DiMaggio Clipper SP/40
S-JG Joe Garagiola 60.00 18.00
S-JG Jason Giambi 80.00 24.00
S-JR Jim Rice 40.00 12.00
S-KG Ken Griffey Jr. SP/100 500.00 150.00
S-LP Lou Piniella 40.00 12.00
S-MB Milton Bradley 40.00 12.00
S-ML Mike Lamb 25.00 7.50
S-MM Mickey Mantle SP/10
S-MW Matt Williams 40.00 12.00
S-NR Nolan Ryan 250.00 75.00
S-PB Pat Burrell 40.00 12.00
S-PO Paul O'Neill 50.00 15.00
S-RAI Roberto Alomar 80.00 24.00
S-RAN Rick Ankiel 25.00 7.50
S-RC R. Clemens EXCH 175.00 52.50
S-RF Rafael Furcal 40.00 12.00
S-RJ Randy Johnson 120.00 36.00
S-RV Robin Ventura 40.00 12.00
S-SG Shawn Green 40.00 12.00
S-SM Stan Musial 150.00 45.00
S-SS S. Sosa SP/148 350.00 105.00
S-TC Ty Cobb SP/1
S-TGL Troy Glaus 50.00 15.00
S-TGW Tony Gwynn 150.00 45.00
S-TH Tim Hudson 50.00 15.00
S-TL Tony LaRussa 40.00 12.00
S-WM Willie Mays 250.00 75.00

2002 Sweet Spot

This 175 card set was released in October, 2002. The four card packs were issued 12 packs to a box and 16 boxes to a case with an $10 SRP per pack. Cards numbered 1 through 90 feature veterans while cards numbered 91 through 145 feature rookies and cards numbered 146-175 feature veterans as part of the "Game Face" subset. Cards numbered 91 through 130 were issued to a stated print run of 1300 serial numbered sets while cards 131 through 145 were issued to either a stated print run of 750 or 100 serial numbered sets. Cards numbered 146 through 175 were issued at stated odds of one in 24. Also randomly inserted in packs were redemptions for Mark McGwire autographs which had an exchange deadline of September 12, 2003.

Nm-Mt Ex-Mt
COMP.SET w/o SP's (90) 25.00 7.50
COMMON CARD (1-90) .40 .12
COMMON CARD (91-130) 5.00 1.50
COMMON TIER 1 AU (131-145) 15.00 4.50
COMMON TIER 2 AU (131-145) 25.00 7.50
COMMON CARD (146-175) 10.00 3.00
1 Troy Glaus .60 .18
2 Darin Erstad .40 .12
3 Tim Hudson .40 .12
4 Eric Chavez .40 .12
5 Barry Zito .60 .18
6 Miguel Tejada .40 .12
7 Carlos Delgado .40 .12
8 Eric Hinske .40 .12
9 Ben Grieve .40 .12
10 Jim Thome 1.00 .30
11 C.C. Sabathia .40 .12
12 Omar Vizquel .40 .12
13 Ichiro Suzuki 1.50 .45
14 Edgar Martinez .60 .18
15 Bret Boone .40 .12
16 Freddy Garcia .40 .12
17 Tony Batista .40 .12
18 Geronimo Gil .40 .12
19 Alex Rodriguez 1.50 .45
20 Rafael Palmeiro .60 .18
21 Ivan Rodriguez 1.00 .30
22 Hank Blalock 1.00 .30
23 Juan Gonzalez 1.00 .30
24 Nomar Garciaparra 1.50 .45
25 Pedro Martinez 1.00 .30
26 Manny Ramirez .40 .12
27 Mike Sweeney .40 .12
28 Carlos Beltran .40 .12
29 Dmitri Young .40 .12
30 Torii Hunter .40 .12
31 Eric Milton .40 .12
32 Corey Koskie .40 .12
33 Frank Thomas 1.00 .30
34 Mark Buehrle .40 .12
35 Magglio Ordonez .40 .12
36 Roger Clemens 2.00 .60
37 Derek Jeter 2.50 .75
38 Jason Giambi 1.00 .30
39 Alfonso Soriano .60 .18
40 Bernie Williams .60 .18
41 Jeff Bagwell .60 .18
42 Roy Oswalt .40 .12
43 Lance Berkman .40 .12
44 Greg Maddux 1.50 .45
45 Chipper Jones 1.00 .30
46 Gary Sheffield .40 .12
47 Andruw Jones .40 .12
48 Richie Sexson .40 .12
49 Ben Sheets .40 .12
50 Albert Pujols 2.00 .60
51 Matt Morris .40 .12
52 J.D. Drew .40 .12
53 Sammy Sosa 1.50 .45
54 Kerry Wood 1.00 .30
55 Mark Prior 2.00 .60
56 Moises Alou .40 .12
57 Corey Patterson .40 .12
58 Randy Johnson 1.00 .30
59 Luis Gonzalez .40 .12
60 Curt Schilling .60 .18
61 Shawn Green .40 .12
62 Kevin Brown .40 .12
63 Paul Lo Duca .40 .12
64 Adrian Beltre .40 .12
65 Vladimir Guerrero 1.00 .30
66 Jose Vidro .40 .12
67 Javier Vazquez .40 .12
68 Barry Bonds 2.50 .75
69 Jeff Kent .40 .12
70 Rich Aurilia .40 .12
71 Mike Lowell .40 .12
72 Josh Beckett .60 .18
73 Brad Penny .40 .12
74 Roberto Alomar 1.00 .30
75 Mike Piazza 1.50 .45
76 Jeromy Burnitz .40 .12
77 Mo Vaughn .40 .12
78 Phil Nevin .40 .12
79 Sean Burroughs .40 .12
80 Jeremy Giambi .40 .12
81 Bobby Abreu .40 .12
82 Jimmy Rollins .40 .12
83 Pat Burrell .40 .12
84 Brian Giles .40 .12
85 Aramis Ramirez .40 .12
86 Ken Griffey Jr. 1.50 .45
87 Adam Dunn .40 .12
88 Austin Kearns .40 .12
89 Todd Helton .60 .18
90 Larry Walker .60 .18
91 Earl Snyder SB RC 5.00 1.50
92 Jorge Padilla SB RC 5.00 1.50
93 Felix Escalona SB RC 5.00 1.50
94 John Foster SB RC 5.00 1.50
95 Brandon Puffer SB RC 5.00 1.50
96 Steve Bechler SB RC 5.00 1.50
97 Hansel Izquierdo SB RC 5.00 1.50
98 Chris Baker SB RC 5.00 1.50
99 Jeremy Ward SB RC 5.00 1.50
100 Kevin Frederick SB RC 5.00 1.50
101 Josh Hancock SB RC 5.00 1.50
102 Allan Simpson SB RC 5.00 1.50
103 Mitch Wylie SB RC 5.00 1.50
104 Mark Corey SB RC 5.00 1.50
105 Victor Alvarez SB RC 5.00 1.50
106 Todd Donovan SB RC 5.00 1.50
107 Nelson Castro SB RC 5.00 1.50
108 Chris Booker SB RC 5.00 1.50
109 Corey Thurman SB RC 5.00 1.50
110 Kirk Saarloos SB RC 5.00 1.50
111 Michael Crudale SB RC 5.00 1.50
112 J.Simontacchi SB RC 5.00 1.50
113 Ron Calloway SB RC 5.00 1.50
114 Brandon Backe SB RC 5.00 1.50
115 Tom Shearn SB RC 5.00 1.50
116 Oliver Perez SB RC 8.00 2.40
117 Kyle Kane SB RC 5.00 1.50
118 Francis Beltran SB RC 5.00 1.50
119 So Taguchi SB RC 8.00 2.40
120 Doug Devore SB RC 5.00 1.50
121 Juan Brito SB RC 5.00 1.50
122 Cliff Bartosh SB RC 5.00 1.50
123 Eric Junge SB RC 5.00 1.50
124 Joe Orloski SB RC 5.00 1.50
125 Scotty Layfield SB RC 5.00 1.50
126 Jorge Sosa SB RC 5.00 1.50
127 Satoru Komiyama SB RC 5.00 1.50
128 Edwin Almonte SB RC 5.00 1.50
129 Takahito Nomura SB RC 5.00 1.50
130 John Ennis SB RC 5.00 1.50
131 Kazuhisa Ishii T2 AU RC 120.00 36.00
132 Ben Howard T2 AU RC 25.00 7.50
133 Aaron Cook T1 AU RC 15.00 4.50
134 Andy Machado T1 AU RC 15.00 4.50
135 Luis Ugueto T1 AU RC 15.00 4.50
136 Tyler Yates T1 AU RC 25.00 7.50
137 Rod. Rosario T1 AU RC 15.00 4.50
138 Jaime Cerda T1 AU RC 15.00 4.50
139 Luis Martinez T1 AU RC 15.00 4.50
140 Rene Reyes T1 AU RC 15.00 4.50
141 Eric Good T1 AU RC 15.00 4.50
142 Matt Thornton T2 AU RC 25.00 7.50
143 Steve Kent T1 AU RC 15.00 4.50
144 Jose Valverde T1 AU RC 25.00 7.50
145 A.Burnside T1 AU RC 15.00 4.50
146 Barry Bonds GF 25.00 7.50
147 Ken Griffey Jr. GF 15.00 4.50
148 Alex Rodriguez GF 15.00 4.50
149 Jason Giambi GF 8.00 2.40
150 Chipper Jones GF 10.00 3.00
151 Nomar Garciaparra GF 15.00 4.50
152 Mike Piazza GF 15.00 4.50
153 Sammy Sosa GF 15.00 4.50
154 Derek Jeter GF 25.00 7.50
155 Jeff Bagwell GF 10.00 3.00
156 Albert Pujols GF 20.00 6.00
157 Ichiro Suzuki GF 15.00 4.50
158 Randy Johnson GF 10.00 3.00
159 Frank Thomas GF 10.00 3.00
160 Greg Maddux GF 15.00 4.50
161 Jim Thome GF 10.00 3.00
162 Scott Rolen GF 10.00 3.00
163 Shawn Green GF 10.00 3.00
164 Vladimir Guerrero GF 10.00 3.00
165 Troy Glaus GF 10.00 3.00
166 Carlos Delgado GF 10.00 3.00
167 Luis Gonzalez GF 10.00 3.00
168 Roger Clemens GF 20.00 6.00
169 Todd Helton GF 10.00 3.00
170 Eric Chavez GF 10.00 3.00
171 Rafael Palmeiro GF 10.00 3.00
172 Pedro Martinez GF 10.00 3.00
173 Lance Berkman GF 10.00 3.00
174 Josh Beckett GF 10.00 3.00
175 Sean Burroughs GF 10.00 3.00
MM Mark McGwire 600.00 180.00
AU EXCH/100

2002 Sweet Spot Game Face Blue Portraits

Randomly inserted in packs, this is a parallel to the Game Face subset. These cards can be differentiated from the regular card by their "blue" tint and were issued to a stated print run of 100 serial numbered sets.

Nm-Mt Ex-Mt
*GAME FACE: .6X TO 1.5X BASIC CARDS

2002 Sweet Spot Bat Barrels

Randomly inserted in packs, these cards feature game-used "barrel" pieces of the featured players. We have included the stated print run information next to the player's name and since each card has a print run of 25 or fewer copies, there is no pricing available due to market scarcity.

Nm-Mt Ex-Mt
AJ Andruw Jones/7
AR Alex Rodriguez/6
BG Brian Giles/4
BW Bernie Williams/6
CJ Chipper Jones/5
FT Frank Thomas/6
GM Greg Maddux/3
GS Gary Sheffield/6
IR Ivan Rodriguez/7
IS Ichiro Suzuki/2
JD J.D. Drew/2
JGo Juan Gonzalez/1
JT Jim Thome/3
KG Ken Griffey Jr./7
LG Luis Gonzalez/3
LW Larry Walker/2
MA Moises Alou/2
MC Mark McGwire/1
MO Magglio Ordonez/2
PW Preston Wilson/1
RA Roberto Alomar/4
RAn Rick Ankiel/2

RC Roger Clemens/1		
RP Rafael Palmeiro/1		
SG Shawn Green/4		
SS Sammy Sosa/5		
TG Tom Glavine/4		
TH Todd Helton/3		

2002 Sweet Spot Legendary Signatures

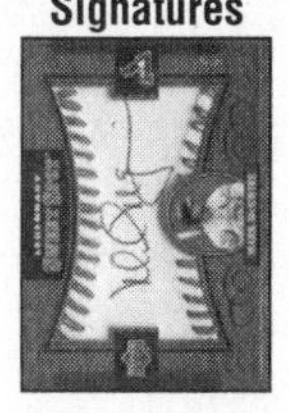

Inserted at stated odds of one in 72, these 16 cards feature signatures of retired greats. Since each player signed a different amount of cards we have notated that stated print run information next to their name in our checklist.

	Nm-Mt	Ex-Mt
AK Al Kaline/835	50.00	15.00
AT Alan Trammell/843	30.00	9.00
BP Boog Powell/944	30.00	9.00
BR Brooks Robinson/TBD	30.00	9.00
CR Cal Ripken/194	200.00	60.00
FJ Ferguson Jenkins/857	25.00	7.50
FL Fred Lynn/853	25.00	7.50
GP Gaylord Perry/921	25.00	7.50
JD Joe DiMaggio/50		
KH Keith Hernandez/906	30.00	9.00
LA Luis Aparicio/485	25.00	7.50
MM Mark McGwire/90	600.00	180.00
PM Paul Molitor/852	30.00	9.00
RF Rollie Fingers/866	25.00	7.50
SG Steve Garvey/871	25.00	7.50
SK Sandy Koufax/485	300.00	90.00

2002 Sweet Spot Signatures

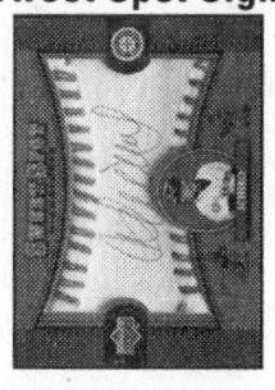

Inserted at stated odds of one in 72, these 25 cards feature signatures of some of today's leading players. Since each player signed a different amount of cards we have notated that stated print run information next to their name in our checklist. The Barry Bonds cards were not returned in time for inclusion in packs and those cards could be redeemed until October 23, 2005.

	Nm-Mt	Ex-Mt
AD Adam Dunn/291	50.00	15.00
AJ Andruw Jones/291	50.00	15.00
AR Alex Rodriguez/291	200.00	60.00
BB Barry Bonds/380 EXCH	300.00	90.00
BG Brian Giles/291	30.00	9.00
BZ Barry Zito/291	60.00	18.00
CD Carlos Delgado/291	30.00	9.00
FG Freddy Garcia/145	30.00	9.00
FT Frank Thomas/291	80.00	24.00
HB Hank Blalock/291	50.00	15.00
IS Ichiro Suzuki/145	400.00	120.00
JB Jeromy Burnitz/291	30.00	9.00
JG Jason Giambi/291	60.00	18.00
JT Jim Thome/291	60.00	18.00
KG Ken Griffey Jr./291	200.00	60.00
LB Lance Berkman/291	50.00	15.00
LG Luis Gonzalez/291	30.00	9.00
MPr Mark Prior/291	150.00	45.00
MS Mike Sweeney/291	30.00	9.00
RC Roger Clemens/194	200.00	60.00
RO Roy Oswalt/291	50.00	15.00
SB Sean Burroughs/291	30.00	9.00
SR Scott Rolen/291	50.00	15.00
SS Sammy Sosa/145	200.00	60.00
TG Tom Glavine/291	60.00	18.00

2002 Sweet Spot Swatches

Inserted at stated odds of one in 12, these 25 cards feature game-used swatches of the featured players.

	Nm-Mt	Ex-Mt
AR Alex Rodriguez	15.00	4.50
BG Brian Giles	10.00	3.00
BW Bernie Williams	10.00	3.00
CJ Chipper Jones	10.00	3.00
DE Darin Erstad	10.00	3.00
EC Eric Chavez	10.00	3.00
FT Frank Thomas	10.00	3.00
GM Greg Maddux	15.00	4.50
IR Ivan Rodriguez	10.00	3.00
IS Ichiro Suzuki	50.00	15.00
JBa Jeff Bagwell	10.00	3.00
JBe Josh Beckett	10.00	3.00
JE Jim Edmonds	10.00	3.00
JGI Jason Giambi	10.00	3.00
JGo Juan Gonzalez	10.00	3.00
KG Ken Griffey Jr	15.00	4.50
KI Kazuhisa Ishii	15.00	4.50
LG Luis Gonzalez	10.00	3.00
MP Mike Piazza	15.00	4.50
OV Omar Vizquel	10.00	3.00
PM Pedro Martinez	10.00	3.00
SB Sean Burroughs	10.00	3.00
SG Shawn Green	10.00	3.00
SR Scott Rolen	10.00	3.00
SS Sammy Sosa	15.00	4.50

2002 Sweet Spot USA Jerseys

Issued at a stated rate of one in 12, these 17 cards feature jersey swatches from players who represented the USA team in International competition.

	Nm-Mt	Ex-Mt
AE Adam Everett	10.00	3.00
AK Adam Kennedy	10.00	3.00
BA Brent Abernathy	10.00	3.00
DB Dewon Brazelton	10.00	3.00
DG Danny Graves	10.00	3.00
DM Doug Mientkiewicz	10.00	3.00
EM Eric Munson	10.00	3.00
JG Jake Gautreau	10.00	3.00
JK Josh Karp	10.00	3.00
JM Joe Mauer	25.00	7.50
JR Jon Rauch	10.00	3.00
JW Justin Wayne	10.00	3.00
MP Mark Prior	20.00	6.00
MT Mark Teixeira	15.00	4.50
RO Roy Oswalt	10.00	3.00
TB Tagg Bozied	15.00	4.50
XN Xavier Nady	10.00	3.00

2003 Sweet Spot

This 231 card set was released in September, 2003. The set was issued in four card packs with an $10 SRP which were issued in 12 pack boxes which came 16 boxes to a case. Thirty of the first 130 cards were issued at a stated rate of one in four packs and we have notated those cards with an SP in our checklist. Cards number 131 through 190 are part of the Sweet Beginning subset and those cards were issued at a stated rate of one in three. Cards numbered 191 through 232 were issued at an overall stated rate of one in nine and those cards were issued in three different tiers. Card number 217 was not issued.

	MINT	NRMT
COMP.SET w/o SP's (100)	25.00	11.00
COMP.SET w/SP's (130)	120.00	55.00
COMMON CARD (1-130)	.50	.23
COMMON SP (1-130)	3.00	1.35
COMMON CARD (131-190)	5.00	2.20
131-190 PRINT RUN 2003 SERIAL #'d SETS		
COMMON P1 (191-232)	8.00	3.60
P1 191-232 PRINT RUN 500 SERIAL #'d SETS		
COMMON P2-P3 (191-232)	5.00	2.20
P2 191-232 PRINT RUN 1200 SERIAL #'d SETS		
P3 191-232 PRINT RUN 1430 SERIAL #'d SETS		
1 Darin Erstad	.50	.23
2 Garret Anderson	.50	.23
3 Tim Salmon	.75	.35
4 Troy Glaus	.75	.35
5 Luis Gonzalez	.50	.23
6 Randy Johnson	1.25	.55
7 Curt Schilling	.75	.35
8 Lyle Overbay	.50	.23
9 Andruw Jones SP	3.00	1.35
10 Gary Sheffield SP	3.00	1.35
11 Rafael Furcal SP	3.00	1.35
12 Greg Maddux SP	6.00	2.70
13 Chipper Jones SP	5.00	2.20
14 Tony Batista	.50	.23
15 Rodrigo Lopez	.50	.23
16 Jay Gibbons	.50	.23
17 Jason Johnson	.50	.23
18 Byung-Hyun Kim SP	3.00	1.35
19 Johnny Damon SP	3.00	1.35
20 Derek Lowe SP	3.00	1.35
21 Nomar Garciaparra SP	6.00	2.70
22 Pedro Martinez SP	5.00	2.20
23 Manny Ramirez SP	3.00	1.35
24 Mark Prior	2.50	1.10
25 Kerry Wood	1.25	.55
26 Corey Patterson	.50	.23
27 Sammy Sosa	2.00	.90
28 Moises Alou	.50	.23
29 Magglio Ordonez	.50	.23
30 Frank Thomas	1.25	.55
31 Paul Konerko	.50	.23
32 Roberto Alomar	1.25	.55
33 Adam Dunn	.50	.23
34 Austin Kearns	.50	.23
35 Ryan Wagner RC	3.00	1.35
36 Ken Griffey Jr.	2.00	.90
37 Sean Casey	.50	.23
38 Omar Vizquel	.50	.23
39 C.C. Sabathia	.50	.23
40 Jason Davis	.50	.23
41 Travis Hafner	.50	.23
42 Brandon Phillips	.50	.23
43 Larry Walker	.75	.35
44 Preston Wilson	.50	.23
45 Jay Payton	.50	.23
46 Todd Helton	.75	.35
47 Carlos Pena	.50	.23
48 Eric Munson	.50	.23
49 Ivan Rodriguez	1.25	.55
50 Josh Beckett	.75	.35
51 Alex Gonzalez	.50	.23
52 Roy Oswalt	.50	.23
53 Craig Biggio	.75	.35
54 Jeff Bagwell	.75	.35
55 Lance Berkman	.50	.23
56 Mike Sweeney	.50	.23
57 Carlos Beltran	.50	.23
58 Brent Mayne	.50	.23
59 Mike MacDougal	.50	.23
60 Hideo Nomo	1.25	.55
61 Dave Roberts	.50	.23
62 Adrian Beltre	.50	.23
63 Shawn Green	.50	.23
64 Kazuhisa Ishii	.50	.23
65 Rickey Henderson	1.25	.55
66 Richie Sexson	.50	.23
67 Torii Hunter	.50	.23
68 Jacque Jones	.50	.23
69 Joe Mays	.50	.23
70 Corey Koskie	.50	.23
71 A.J. Pierzynski	.50	.23
72 Jose Vidro	.50	.23
73 Vladimir Guerrero	1.25	.55
74 Tom Glavine	.75	.35
75 Mike Piazza	2.00	.90
76 Jose Reyes	.75	.35
77 Jae Weong Seo	.50	.23
78 Jorge Posada SP	5.00	2.20
79 Mike Mussina SP	5.00	2.20
80 Robin Ventura SP	3.00	1.35
81 Mariano Rivera SP	5.00	2.20
82 Roger Clemens SP	8.00	3.60
83 Jason Giambi SP	5.00	2.20
84 Bernie Williams SP	5.00	2.20
85 Alfonso Soriano SP	5.00	2.20
86 Derek Jeter	3.00	1.35
87 Miguel Tejada	.50	.23
88 Eric Chavez	.50	.23
89 Tim Hudson	.50	.23
90 Barry Zito	.75	.35
91 Mark Mulder	.50	.23
92 Erubiel Durazo	.50	.23
93 Pat Burrell	.50	.23
94 Jim Thome	1.25	.55
95 Bobby Abreu	.50	.23
96 Brian Giles	.50	.23
97 Reggie Sanders	.50	.23
98 Jose Hernandez	.50	.23
99 Ryan Klesko	.50	.23
100 Sean Burroughs	.50	.23
101 Edgardo Alfonzo SP	3.00	1.35
102 Rich Aurilia SP	3.00	1.35
103 Jose Cruz Jr. SP	3.00	1.35
104 Barry Bonds SP	10.00	4.50
105 Andres Galarraga SP	3.00	1.35
106 Mike Cameron	.50	.23
107 Kazuhiro Sasaki	.50	.23
108 Bret Boone	.50	.23
109 Ichiro Suzuki	2.00	.90
110 John Olerud	.50	.23
111 J.D. Drew SP	3.00	1.35
112 Jim Edmonds SP	3.00	1.35
113 Scott Rolen SP	5.00	2.20
114 Matt Morris SP	3.00	1.35
115 Tino Martinez SP	5.00	2.20
116 Albert Pujols SP	8.00	3.60
117 Jared Sandberg	.50	.23
118 Carl Crawford	.50	.23
119 Rafael Palmeiro	.75	.35
120 Hank Blalock	.75	.35
121 Alex Rodriguez SP	6.00	2.70
122 Kevin Mench	.50	.23
123 Juan Gonzalez	1.25	.55
124 Mark Teixeira	.75	.35
125 Shannon Stewart	.50	.23
126 Vernon Wells	.50	.23
127 Josh Phelps	.50	.23
128 Eric Hinske	.50	.23
129 Orlando Hudson	.50	.23
130 Carlos Delgado	.50	.23
131 Jason Shiell SB RC	5.00	2.20
132 Kevin Tolar SB RC	5.00	2.20
133 Nathan Bland SB RC	5.00	2.20
134 Brent Hoard SB RC	5.00	2.20
135 Jon Pridie SB RC	5.00	2.20
136 Mike Ryan SB RC	8.00	3.60
137 Francisco Rosario SB RC	5.00	2.20
138 Runelvys Hernandez SB	5.00	2.20
139 Guillermo Quiroz SB RC	8.00	3.60
140 Chin-Hui Tsao SB	5.00	2.20
141 Rett Johnson SB RC	8.00	3.60
142 Colin Porter SB RC	5.00	2.20
143 Jose Castillo SB	5.00	2.20
144 Chris Waters SB RC	5.00	2.20
145 Jeremy Guthrie SB	5.00	2.20
146 Pedro Liriano SB	5.00	2.20
147 Joe Borowski SB	5.00	2.20
148 Felix Sanchez SB RC	5.00	2.20
149 Todd Wellemeyer SB RC	8.00	3.60
150 Gerald Laird SB	5.00	2.20
151 Brandon Webb SB RC	10.00	4.50
152 Tommy Whiteman SB	5.00	2.20
153 Carlos Rivera SB	5.00	2.20
154 Rick Roberts SB RC	5.00	2.20
155 Terrmel Sledge SB RC	8.00	3.60
156 Jeff Duncan SB RC	8.00	3.60
157 Craig Brazell SB RC	8.00	3.60
158 Bernie Castro SB RC	5.00	2.20
159 Cory Stewart SB RC	5.00	2.20
160 Brandon Villafuerte SB	5.00	2.20
161 Tommy Phelps SB	5.00	2.20
162 Josh Hall SB RC	8.00	3.60
163 Ryan Cameron SB RC	5.00	2.20
164 Garret Atkins SB	5.00	2.20
165 Brian Stokes SB RC	5.00	2.20
166 Rafael Betancourt SB RC	8.00	3.60
167 Jaime Cerda SB	5.00	2.20
168 D.J. Carrasco SB RC	5.00	2.20
169 Ian Ferguson SB RC	5.00	2.20
170 Jorge Cordova SB RC	5.00	2.20
171 Eric Munson SB	5.00	2.20
172 Nook Logan SB RC	5.00	2.20
173 Jeremy Bonderman SB RC	8.00	3.60
174 Kyle Snyder SB	5.00	2.20
175 Rich Harden SB	8.00	3.60
176 Kevin Ohme SB RC	5.00	2.20
177 Roger Deago SB RC	5.00	2.20
178 Marlon Byrd SB	5.00	2.20
179 Dontrelle Willis SB	8.00	3.60
180 Bobby Hill SB	5.00	2.20
181 Jesse Foppert SB	5.00	2.20
182 Andrew Good SB	5.00	2.20
183 Chase Utley SB	5.00	2.20
184 Bo Hart SB RC	10.00	4.50
185 Dan Haren SB RC	8.00	3.60
186 Tim Olson SB RC	8.00	3.60
187 Joe Thurston SB	5.00	2.20
188 Jason Anderson SB	5.00	2.20
189 Jason Gilfillan SB RC	5.00	2.20
190 Rickie Weeks SB RC	15.00	6.75
191 Hideki Matsui SB P1 RC	40.00	18.00
192 J.Contreras SB P3 RC	10.00	4.50
193 Willie Eyre SB P3 RC	5.00	2.20
194 Matt Bruback SB P3 RC	5.00	2.20
195 Heath Bell SB P3 RC	5.00	2.20
196 Lew Ford SB P3 RC	8.00	3.60
197 J.Griffiths SB P3 RC	8.00	3.60
198 O.Villarreal SB P1 RC	8.00	3.60
199 Fr. Cruceta SB P3 RC	5.00	2.20
200 Fern Cabrera SB P3 RC	5.00	2.20
201 Jhonny Peralta SB P3 RC	5.00	2.20
202 Shane Bazzell SB P3 RC	5.00	2.20
203 B.Madritsch SB P1 RC	8.00	3.60
204 Phil Seibel SB P3 RC	5.00	2.20
205 J.Willingham SB P3 RC	10.00	4.50
206 Rob Hammock SB P1 RC	10.00	4.50
207 Al. Machado SB P3 RC	5.00	2.20
208 David Sanders SB P3 RC	5.00	2.20
209 Mike Neu SB P1 RC	8.00	3.60
210 Andrew Brown SB P3 RC	5.00	2.20
211 N. Robertson SB P3 RC	8.00	3.60
212 Miguel Ojeda SB P3 RC	5.00	2.20
213 Beau Kemp SB P3 RC	5.00	2.20
214 Aaron Looper SB P3 RC	5.00	2.20
215 Alf.Gonzalez SB P3 RC	5.00	2.20
216 Rich Fischer SB P1 RC	8.00	3.60
218 Jeremy Wedel SB P3 RC	5.00	2.20
219 Pr.Redman SB P3 RC	5.00	2.20
220 Mi.Hernandez SB P3 RC	5.00	2.20
221 Rocco Baldelli SB P1	20.00	9.00
222 Luis Ayala SB P3 RC	5.00	2.20
223 Arnaldo Munoz SB P3 RC	5.00	2.20
224 Wil.Ledezma SB P3 RC	5.00	2.20
225 Chris Capuano SB P3 RC	5.00	2.20
226 Aquilino Lopez SB P3 RC	5.00	2.20
227 Joe Valentine SB P1 RC	8.00	3.60
228 Matt Kata SB P2 RC	8.00	3.60
229 D.Markwell SB P2 RC	5.00	2.20
230 Clint Barmes SB P2 RC	8.00	3.60
231 Mike Nicolas SB P1 RC	8.00	3.60
232 Jon Leicester SB P2 RC	5.00	2.20

2003 Sweet Spot Sweet Beginnings 75

	MINT	NRMT
*SB 75: .5X TO 1.2X BASIC P1		
*SB 75 MATSUI: .75X TO 1.5X BASIC MATSUI		
*SB 75: .6X TO 1.5X BASIC P2-P3		
RANDOM INSERTS IN PACKS		
STATED PRINT RUN 75 SERIAL #'d SETS		
CARDS ARE NOT GAME-USED MATERIAL		

2003 Sweet Spot Sweet Beginnings Game Used 25

	MINT	NRMT
RANDOM INSERTS IN PACKS		
STATED PRINT RUN 25 SERIAL #'d SETS		
NO PRICING DUE TO SCARCITY		
191 Hideki Matsui		
193 Willie Eyre		
194 Matt Bruback		
195 Heath Bell		
197 Jeremy Griffiths		

2003 Sweet Spot Sweet Beginnings Game Used 10

	MINT	NRMT
RANDOM INSERTS IN PACKS		
STATED PRINT RUN 10 SERIAL #'d SETS		
NO PRICING DUE TO SCARCITY		
191 Hideki Matsui		
202 Shane Bazzell		
203 Bobby Madritsch		
204 Phil Seibel		
206 Robby Hammock		
207 Alejandro Machado		

2003 Sweet Spot Barrel Signatures

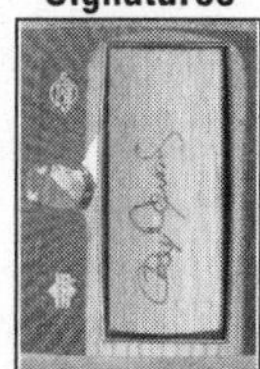

	MINT	NRMT
CUMULATIVE AUTO ODDS 1:24		
PRINT RUNS B/WN 49-445 COPIES PER		
CARDS ARE NOT GAME-USED MATERIAL		
AD Adam Dunn/345	50.00	22.00
CR Cal Ripken/149	250.00	110.00
HB Hank Blalock/420	50.00	22.00
HM Hideki Matsui/124	400.00	180.00
JT Jim Thome/345	100.00	45.00
KG Ken Griffey Jr./295	150.00	70.00
NR Nolan Ryan/445	150.00	70.00
PB Pat Burrell/345	40.00	18.00
RC Roger Clemens/49	250.00	110.00
TG Tom Glavine/345	50.00	22.00
TR Troy Glaus/345	50.00	22.00

2003 Sweet Spot Game Used Bat Barrels

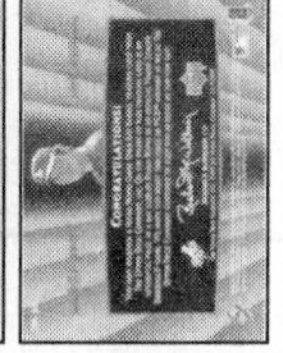

	MINT	NRMT
STATED ODDS 1:6000		
NO PRICING DUE TO SCARCITY		
AJ Andruw Jones/7		
AR Alex Rodriguez/4		
AS Alfonso Soriano/1		
BA Bobby Abreu/4		
BW Bernie Williams/4		
CJ Chipper Jones/1		
CS Curt Schilling/1		
DE Darin Erstad/4		
GM Greg Maddux/2		
GS Gary Sheffield/6		
HN Hideo Nomo/3		
IS Ichiro Suzuki/1		
JD Jermaine Dye/3		
JE Jeff Kent/4		
JT Jim Thome/3		
KG Ken Griffey Jr./6		
KW Kerry Wood/2		
LB Lance Berkman/2		
LW Larry Walker/6		
MP Mike Piazza/3		
MR Manny Ramirez/1		
MT Miguel Tejada/2		
MW Matt Williams/5		
OV Omar Vizquel/5		
RA Roberto Alomar/7		
RJ Randy Johnson/2		
RP Rafael Palmeiro/2		
SG Shawn Green/2		
SS Sammy Sosa/7		
TG Troy Glaus/1		

2003 Sweet Spot Instant Win Redemptions

Randomly inserted into packs, these cards enabled a lucky collector to receive a prize from the Upper Deck Company.

	MINT	NRMT
ONE OR MORE CARDS PER CASE		
PRINT RUNS B/WN 1-350 COPIES PER		
NO PRICING ON QTY OF 28 OR LESS.		
EXCHANGE DEADLINE 09/16/06		

2003 Sweet Spot Patches

	MINT	NRMT
*PATCH 75: 1X TO 2.5X BASIC		
PATCH 75 PRINT RUN 75 SERIAL #'d SETS		
CUMULATIVE PATCHES ODDS 1:8		
CARDS ARE NOT GAME-USED MATERIAL		
AD1 Adam Dunn	8.00	3.60
AJ1 Andruw Jones	8.00	3.60
AP1 Albert Pujols	15.00	6.75
AR1 Alex Rodriguez	15.00	6.75
AS1 Alfonso Soriano	10.00	4.50
BB1 Barry Bonds	20.00	9.00
BW1 Bernie Williams	10.00	4.50
BZ1 Barry Zito	10.00	4.50
CD1 Carlos Delgado	8.00	3.60
CJ1 Chipper Jones	10.00	4.50
CP1 Corey Patterson	8.00	3.60
CS1 Curt Schilling	10.00	4.50
DE1 Darin Erstad	8.00	3.60
DJ1 Derek Jeter	20.00	9.00
GM1 Greg Maddux	15.00	6.75
GS1 Gary Sheffield	8.00	3.60
HN1 Hideo Nomo	10.00	4.50
IS1 Ichiro Suzuki	15.00	6.75
JB1 Jeff Bagwell	10.00	4.50
JE1 Jim Edmonds	8.00	3.60

JG1 Jason Giambi 10.00 4.50
JK1 Jeff Kent 8.00 3.60
JT1 Jim Thome 10.00 4.50
KG1 Ken Griffey Jr. 15.00 6.75
KI1 Kazuhisa Ishii 8.00 3.60
LB1 Lance Berkman 8.00 3.60
LG1 Luis Gonzalez 8.00 3.60
MA1 Mark Prior 15.00 6.75
MO1 Magglio Ordonez 8.00 3.60
MP1 Mike Piazza 15.00 6.75
MT1 Miguel Tejada 8.00 3.60
NG1 Nomar Garciaparra 15.00 6.75
PB1 Pat Burrell 8.00 3.60
PM1 Pedro Martinez 10.00 4.50
RC1 Roger Clemens 15.00 6.75
RJ1 Randy Johnson 10.00 4.50
SG1 Shawn Green 8.00 3.60
SS1 Sammy Sosa 15.00 6.75
TG1 Troy Glaus 10.00 4.50
TH1 Torii Hunter 8.00 3.60
TO1 Tom Glavine 10.00 4.50
VG1 Vladimir Guerrero 10.00 4.50

2003 Sweet Spot Patches Game Used 25

MINT NRMT
RANDOM INSERTS IN PACKS
STATED PRINT RUN 25 SERIAL #'d SETS
NO PRICING DUE TO SCARCITY
AS3 Alfonso Soriano
KG3 Ken Griffey Jr.
MP3 Mike Piazza
NG3 Nomar Garciaparra
SS3 Sammy Sosa
TG3 Troy Glaus

2003 Sweet Spot Patches Game Used 10

MINT NRMT
RANDOM INSERTS IN PACKS
STATED PRINT RUN 10 SERIAL #'d SETS
NO PRICING DUE TO SCARCITY
AP3 Albert Pujols
AR3 Alex Rodriguez
IS3 Ichiro Suzuki
JG3 Jason Giambi
JT3 Jim Thome
RC3 Roger Clemens

2003 Sweet Spot Signatures Black Ink

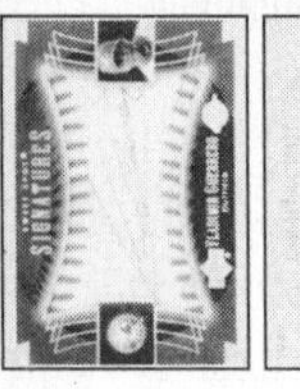
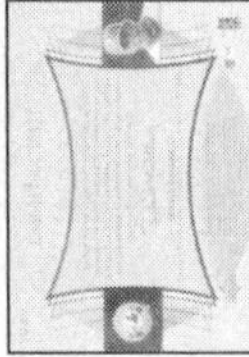

MINT NRMT
CUMULATIVE AUTO ODDS 1:24
SP PRINT RUNS PROVIDED BY UPPER DECK
SP'S ARE NOT SERIAL-NUMBERED
AD Adam Dunn 40.00 18.00
AK Austin Kearns 25.00 11.00
BH Bo Hart 50.00 22.00
BP Brandon Phillips 15.00 6.75
BW Brandon Webb 50.00 22.00
CR Cal Ripken SP/122 250.00 110.00
CS Curt Schilling 40.00 18.00
DH Drew Henson 40.00 18.00
DW Dontrelle Willis 50.00 22.00
GL Tom Glavine 50.00 22.00
GS Gary Sheffield 40.00 18.00
HA Travis Hafner 25.00 11.00
HB Hank Blalock 40.00 18.00
HM Hideki Matsui SP/147 350.00 160.00
JC Jose Contreras 50.00 22.00
JG Jason Giambi SP 60.00 27.00
JR Jose Reyes 40.00 18.00
JT Jim Thome 50.00 22.00
JW Jerome Williams 25.00 11.00
KGJ Ken Griffey Jr. 120.00 55.00
KGS Ken Griffey Sr. 25.00 11.00
KI Kazuhisa Ishii SP 50.00 22.00
LO Lyle Overbay 15.00 6.75
MP Mark Prior 150.00 70.00
MT Mark Teixeira 40.00 18.00
NG Nomar Garciaparra 120.00 55.00
NR Nolan Ryan SP 150.00 70.00
PB Pat Burrell 25.00 11.00
RC Roger Clemens SP/73 150.00 70.00
RO Roy Oswalt 25.00 11.00
TH Todd Helton SP/45 80.00 36.00
TR Troy Glaus 40.00 18.00
TS Tim Salmon 40.00 18.00
VG Vladimir Guerrero 50.00 22.00

2003 Sweet Spot Signatures Black Ink Holo-Foil

MINT NRMT
CUMULATIVE AUTO ODDS 1:24
STATED PRINT RUN 25 SERIAL #'d SETS
SOSA PRINT RUN 7 SERIAL #'d CARDS
NO PRICING DUE TO SCARCITY

2003 Sweet Spot Signatures Blue Ink

Rickie Weeks did not return his cards in time for inclusion in this product. Those cards were issued as exchange cards and were redeemable until September 16, 2006.

MINT NRMT
CUMULATIVE AUTO ODDS 1:24
STATED PRINT RUN 40 SERIAL #'d SETS
T.GWYNN CARD NOT SERIAL-NUMBERED
T.GWYNN AU IN FAR GREATER SUPPLY
AD Adam Dunn 60.00 27.00
AK Austin Kearns 40.00 18.00
BH Bo Hart 80.00 36.00
BP Brandon Phillips 25.00 11.00
BW Brandon Webb 80.00 36.00
CR Cal Ripken 250.00 110.00
CS Curt Schilling 60.00 27.00
DH Drew Henson 60.00 27.00
DW Dontrelle Willis 80.00 36.00
GL Tom Glavine 80.00 36.00
GS Gary Sheffield 60.00 27.00
HA Travis Hafner 40.00 18.00
HB Hank Blalock 60.00 27.00
HM Hideki Matsui 400.00 180.00
IS Ichiro Suzuki 500.00 220.00
JC Jose Contreras 80.00 36.00
JG Jason Giambi 100.00 45.00
JR Jose Reyes 60.00 27.00
JT Jim Thome 80.00 36.00
JW Jerome Williams 40.00 18.00
KGJ Ken Griffey Jr. 200.00 90.00
KGS Ken Griffey Sr. 40.00 18.00
KI Kazuhisa Ishii 60.00 27.00
LO Lyle Overbay 25.00 11.00
MM Mickey Mantle/7
MP Mark Prior 200.00 90.00
MT Mark Teixeira 60.00 27.00
NG Nomar Garciaparra 200.00 90.00
NR Nolan Ryan 200.00 90.00
PB Pat Burrell 40.00 18.00
RC Roger Clemens 200.00 90.00
RO Roy Oswalt 40.00 18.00
RW Rickie Weeks/100 EXCH 120.00 55.00
SS Sammy Sosa 200.00 90.00
TG Tony Gwynn NNO 50.00 22.00
TH Todd Helton 80.00 36.00
TR Troy Glaus 60.00 27.00
TS Tim Salmon 40.00 18.00
TW Ted Williams/9
VG Vladimir Guerrero 80.00 36.00

2003 Sweet Spot Signatures Red Ink

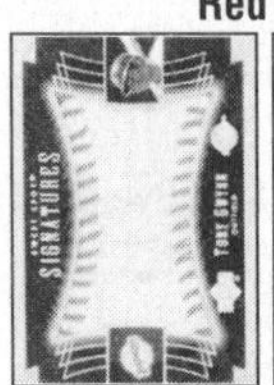
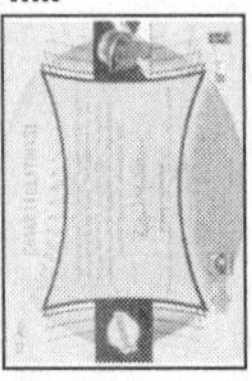

MINT NRMT
CUMULATIVE AUTO ODDS 1:24
PRINT RUNS B/WN 9-35 COPIES PER
GWYNN CARD NOT SERIAL-NUMBERED
NO PRICING ON QTY OF 10 OR LESS.

2003 Sweet Spot Swatches

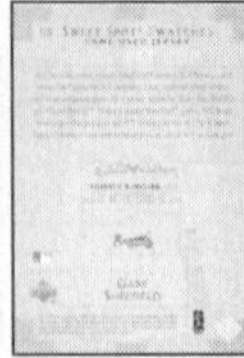

MINT NRMT
SP INFO PROVIDED BY UPPER DECK
SP'S ARE NOT SERIAL-NUMBERED
CUMULATIVE SWATCHES ODDS 1:20
AJ Andruw Jones 8.00 3.60
AK Austin Kearns 8.00 3.60
AP Albert Pujols 20.00 9.00
AR Alex Rodriguez 10.00 4.50
AS Alfonso Soriano SP/81 15.00 6.75
BW Bernie Williams SP 15.00 6.75
BZ Barry Zito SP 15.00 6.75
CJ Chipper Jones 8.00 3.60
CS Curt Schilling 8.00 3.60
FT Frank Thomas 8.00 3.60
GM Greg Maddux 10.00 4.50
GS Gary Sheffield SP 10.00 4.50
HM Hideki Matsui SP/150 60.00 27.00
IS Ichiro Suzuki 25.00 11.00
JG Jason Giambi 8.00 3.60
JT Jim Thome 8.00 3.60
KG Ken Griffey Jr. 15.00 6.75
LG Luis Gonzalez 8.00 3.60
MM M.Mantle Pants UER SP/100 150.00 70.00
Card erroneously states Game Used Jersey
MP Mark Prior SP 20.00 9.00
MP Mike Piazza 10.00 4.50
MT Miguel Tejada 8.00 3.60
NG Nomar Garciaparra SP/75
PB Pat Burrell 8.00 3.60
RA Roberto Alomar SP 15.00 6.75
RC Roger Clemens 10.00 4.50
RJ Randy Johnson SP 15.00 6.75
RO Roy Oswalt 8.00 3.60
SS Sammy Sosa 10.00 4.50
TG Troy Glaus 8.00 3.60
TG Tom Glavine SP 15.00 6.75
TH Torii Hunter 8.00 3.60
TW Ted Williams Pants SP/100 100.00 45.00
VG Vladimir Guerrero 8.00 3.60

2003 Sweet Spot Swatches 75

MINT NRMT
CUMULATIVE SWATCHES ODDS 1:20
STATED PRINT RUN 75 SERIAL #'d SETS
AJ1 Andruw Jones
AK1 Austin Kearns
AP1 Albert Pujols
AR1 Alex Rodriguez
AS1 Alfonso Soriano 15.00 6.75
CJ1 Chipper Jones
CS1 Curt Schilling
FT1 Frank Thomas
GM1 Greg Maddux
HM1 Hideki Matsui 100.00 45.00
IS1 Ichiro Suzuki
JG1 Jason Giambi
JT1 Jim Thome
KG1 Ken Griffey Jr.
LG1 Luis Gonzalez
MM1 Mickey Mantle Pants UER
Card erroneously states Game Used Jersey
MP1 Mike Piazza
MT1 Miguel Tejada
NM1 Nomar Garciaparra 40.00 18.00
PB1 Pat Burrell
RC1 Roger Clemens
RJ1 Randy Johnson
RO1 Roy Oswalt 15.00 6.75
SS1 Sammy Sosa
TG1 Troy Glaus 15.00 6.75
TH1 Torii Hunter
TW1 Ted Williams
VG1 Vladimir Guerrero

2002 Sweet Spot Classics

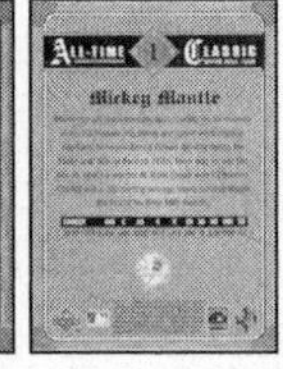

This 90 card set was issued in February, 2002. These cards were issued in four card packs which came 12 packs to a box and eight boxes to a case.

Nm-Mt Ex-Mt
COMPLETE SET (90) 40.00 12.00
1 Mickey Mantle 6.00 1.80
2 Joe DiMaggio 3.00 .90
3 Babe Ruth 5.00 1.50
4 Ty Cobb 2.50 .75
5 Nolan Ryan 4.00 1.20
6 Sandy Koufax 3.00 .90
7 Cy Young 1.50 .45
8 Roberto Clemente 4.00 1.20
9 Lefty Grove 1.00 .30
10 Lou Gehrig 3.00 .90
11 Walter Johnson 1.50 .45
12 Honus Wagner 2.00 .60
13 Christy Mathewson 1.50 .45
14 Jackie Robinson 2.00 .60
15 Joe Morgan 1.00 .30
16 Reggie Jackson 1.00 .30
17 Eddie Collins 1.00 .30
18 Cal Ripken 5.00 1.50
19 Hank Greenberg 1.50 .45
20 Harmon Killebrew 1.50 .45
21 Johnny Bench 1.50 .45
22 Ernie Banks 1.50 .45
23 Willie McCovey 1.00 .30
24 Mel Ott 1.50 .45
25 Tom Seaver 1.00 .30
26 Tony Gwynn 2.00 .60
27 Dave Winfield 1.00 .30
28 Willie Stargell 1.00 .30
29 Mark McGwire 4.00 1.20
30 Al Kaline 1.50 .45
31 Jimmie Foxx 1.50 .45
32 Satchel Paige 1.50 .45
33 Eddie Murray 1.50 .45
34 Lou Boudreau 1.00 .30
35 Joe Jackson 3.00 .90
36 Luke Appling 1.00 .30
37 Ralph Kiner 1.00 .30
38 Robin Yount 2.50 .75
39 Paul Molitor 1.00 .30
40 Juan Marichal 1.00 .30
41 Brooks Robinson 1.50 .45
42 Wade Boggs 1.00 .30
43 Kirby Puckett 1.50 .45
44 Yogi Berra 1.50 .45
45 George Sisler 1.00 .30
46 Buck Leonard 1.00 .30
47 Billy Williams 1.00 .30
48 Duke Snider 1.50 .45
49 Don Drysdale 1.50 .45
50 Bill Mazeroski 1.00 .30
51 Tony Oliva 1.00 .30
52 Luis Aparicio 1.00 .30
53 Carlton Fisk 1.00 .30
54 Kirk Gibson 1.00 .30
55 Catfish Hunter 1.00 .30
56 Joe Carter 1.00 .30
57 Gaylord Perry 1.00 .30
58 Don Mattingly 4.00 1.20
59 Eddie Mathews 1.50 .45
60 Fergie Jenkins 1.00 .30
61 Roy Campanella 1.50 .45
62 Orlando Cepeda 1.00 .30
63 Tony Perez 1.00 .30
64 Dave Parker 1.00 .30
65 Richie Ashburn 1.00 .30
66 Andre Dawson 1.00 .30
67 Dwight Evans 1.00 .30
68 Rollie Fingers 1.00 .30
69 Dale Murphy 1.50 .45
70 Ron Santo 1.00 .30
71 Steve Garvey 1.00 .30
72 Monte Irvin 1.00 .30
73 Alan Trammell 1.00 .30
74 Ryne Sandberg 2.50 .75
75 Gary Carter 1.00 .30
76 Fred Lynn 1.00 .30
77 Maury Wills 1.00 .30
78 Ozzie Smith 2.50 .75
79 Bobby Bonds 1.00 .30
80 Mickey Cochrane 1.00 .30
81 Dizzy Dean 1.50 .45
82 Graig Nettles 1.00 .30
83 Keith Hernandez 1.00 .30
84 Boog Powell 1.00 .30
85 Jack Clark 1.00 .30
86 Dave Stewart 1.00 .30
87 Tommy Lasorda 1.00 .30
88 Dennis Eckersley 1.00 .30
89 Ken Griffey Sr. 1.00 .30
90 Bucky Dent 1.00 .30

2002 Sweet Spot Classics Bat Barrels

Randomly inserted in packs, these cards feature pieces of bat barrels from bats that Upper Deck has already cut up for inclusion in this or other products. These bat slivers include the nameplate and player facsimile signature. Each card has a very small print run which we have notated in our checklist. Please note that due to scarcity, no pricing is provided.

Nm-Mt Ex-Mt
BB-AK Al Kaline/4
BB-BM Bill Madlock/1
BB-BR Brooks Robinson/2
BB-BW Billy Williams/2
BB-BAR Babe Ruth/1
BB-BBO Bob Boone/2
BB-CR Cal Ripken/5
BB-DE Dwight Evans/1
BB-DM Don Mattingly/1
BB-DP Dave Parker/4
BB-DW Dave Winfield/1
BB-FJ Ferguson Jenkins/1
BB-FL Fred Lynn/2
BB-GC Gary Carter/1
BB-GN Graig Nettles/2
BB-HG Hank Greenberg/1
BB-JB Johnny Bench/5
BB-JD Joe DiMaggio/5
BB-KG Ken Griffey Sr./3
BB-KP Kirby Puckett/4
BB-NR Nolan Ryan/4
BB-PM Paul Molitor/4
BB-RC Roberto Clemente/1
BB-RJ Reggie Jackson/13
BB-SG Steve Garvey/1
BB-TG Tony Gwynn/12
BB-TM Thurman Munson/1
BB-WB Wade Boggs/2
BB-YB Yogi Berra/3

2002 Sweet Spot Classics Game Bat

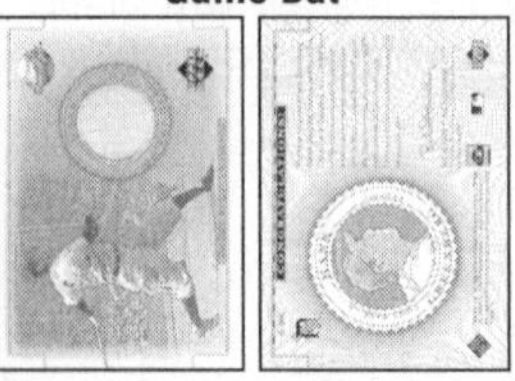

Inserted at stated odds of one in eight, these cards feature the most notable tools of the trade. Please note that if the player has an asterisk next to their name than that card is perceived to be in larger supply. Also note that some player have shorter print runs and that information is notated in our checklist along with a stated print run from the company.

Nm-Mt Ex-Mt
GOLD RANDOM INSERTS IN PACKS
GOLD PRINT RUN 25 SERIAL #'d SETS
GOLD NO PRICING DUE TO SCARCITY
B-AK Al Kaline 15.00 4.50
B-BBO Bob Boone 10.00 3.00
B-BBU Bill Buckner 10.00 3.00
B-BD Bucky Dent 10.00 3.00
B-BM Bill Madlock 10.00 3.00
B-BR Brooks Robinson 15.00 4.50
B-BW Billy Williams 10.00 3.00
B-CR Cal Ripken * 25.00 7.50
B-DE Dwight Evans 10.00 3.00
B-DM Don Mattingly 40.00 12.00
B-DP Dave Parker 10.00 3.00
B-DW Dave Winfield * 10.00 3.00
B-FJ Fergie Jenkins 10.00 3.00
B-FL Fred Lynn 10.00 3.00
B-GC Gary Carter 15.00 4.50
B-GN Graig Nettles 10.00 3.00
B-HG Hank Greenberg SP 60.00 18.00
B-JB Johnny Bench 15.00 4.50
B-JD Joe DiMaggio SP/40
B-KG Ken Griffey Sr. * 10.00 3.00
B-KP Kirby Puckett * 15.00 4.50
B-NR Nolan Ryan 50.00 15.00
B-PM Paul Molitor 15.00 4.50
B-RC Roberto Clemente 60.00 18.00
B-RJ Reggie Jackson 15.00 4.50
B-SG Steve Garvey 10.00 3.00
B-TG Tony Gwynn * 15.00 4.50
B-TM Thurman Munson 50.00 15.00
B-WB Wade Boggs * 15.00 4.50
B-YB Yogi Berra 15.00 4.50

2002 Sweet Spot Classics Game Jersey

Inserted at stated odds of one in eight, these cards feature memorabilia from the featured player. Please note that if the player has an asterisk next to their name than that card is perceived to be in larger supply. Also note that some player have shorter print runs and that information is notated in our checklist along with a stated print run from the company.

Nm-Mt Ex-Mt
GOLD RANDOM INSERTS IN PACKS
GOLD PRINT RUN 25 SERIAL #'d SETS
GOLD NO PRICING DUE TO SCARCITY
J-BM Bill Madlock 10.00 3.00
J-BW Billy Williams 10.00 3.00
J-CR Cal Ripken * 30.00 9.00
J-DM Don Mattingly * 25.00 7.50
J-DP Dave Parker 10.00 3.00
J-DSN Duke Snider SP/53 100.00 30.00
J-DST Dave Stewart 10.00 3.00
J-EM Eddie Murray 15.00 4.50
J-GC Gary Carter 15.00 4.50
J-GN Graig Nettles 10.00 3.00
J-JC Joe Carter 10.00 3.00
J-JD Joe DiMaggio SP/53 250.00 75.00
J-JMA Juan Marichal 10.00 3.00
J-MM Mickey Mantle SP/53 350.00 105.00
J-NR Nolan Ryan * 40.00 12.00
J-OS Ozzie Smith 15.00 4.50
J-PM Paul Molitor * 15.00 4.50
J-RF Rollie Fingers 10.00 3.00
J-RJ Reggie Jackson 15.00 4.50
J-RS Ryne Sandberg 20.00 6.00
J-RY Robin Yount * 15.00 4.50
J-SG Steve Garvey 10.00 3.00
J-SK Sandy Koufax SP 150.00 45.00
J-TG Tony Gwynn * 15.00 4.50
J-TS Tom Seaver 15.00 4.50
J-WB Wade Boggs 15.00 4.50
J-WS Willie Stargell 15.00 4.50

2002 Sweet Spot Classics Signatures

Inserted at stated odds of one in 24, these cards feature the top stars of yesterday with their signature on a "sweet spot". Please note that if the player has an asterisk next to their name than that card is perceived to be in larger supply. Also note that some player have shorter print runs and that information is notated in our checklist along with a stated print run from the company.

Nm-Mt Ex-Mt
GOLD RANDOM INSERTS IN PACKS
GOLD PRINT RUN 25 SERIAL #'d SETS
GOLD NO PRICING DUE TO SCARCITY
S-AD Andre Dawson SP/100 120.00 36.00
S-AK Al Kaline 50.00 15.00
S-AT Alan Trammell 40.00 12.00
S-BD Bucky Dent 30.00 9.00
S-BM Bill Mazeroski 50.00 15.00
S-BP Boog Powell 30.00 9.00
S-BR Brooks Robinson 50.00 15.00
S-CF Carlton Fisk SP/100 150.00 45.00
S-CR Cal Ripken 175.00 52.50
S-DAM Dale Murphy 50.00 15.00
S-DAS Dave Stewart 30.00 9.00
S-DEE Dennis Eckersley 40.00 12.00
S-DOM Don Mattingly * 100.00 30.00
S-DW Dave Winfield SP/70 150.00 45.00
S-EB Ernie Banks 80.00 24.00
S-FJ Fergie Jenkins 30.00 9.00
S-FL Fred Lynn 30.00 9.00
S-GP Gaylord Perry 30.00 9.00
S-JB Johnny Bench 80.00 24.00
S-JM Joe Morgan 30.00 9.00
S-KG Kirk Gibson/SP 60.00 18.00
S-KH Keith Hernandez 40.00 12.00
S-KP Kirby Puckett SP/74 200.00 60.00
S-NR Nolan Ryan SP/74 350.00 105.00
S-OS Ozzie Smith SP/137 200.00 60.00
S-PM Paul Molitor 40.00 12.00
S-RF Rollie Fingers 30.00 9.00
S-RJ Reggie Jackson SP 120.00 36.00
S-SG Steve Garvey 30.00 9.00
S-SK Sandy Koufax SP 250.00 75.00
S-TL Tommy Lasorda 40.00 12.00
S-TS Tom Seaver 60.00 18.00

	Nm-Mt	Ex-Mt
S-WM Willie McCovey SP	100.00	30.00
S-YB Yogi Berra SP/100	200.00	60.00

2002 Sweet Spot Classics Hawaii Signatures

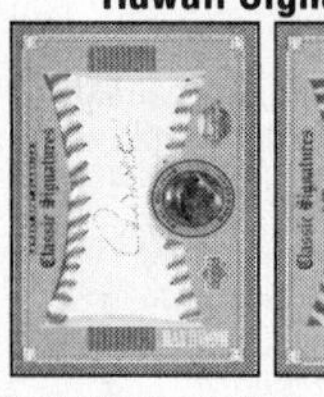

These attractive cards were distributed in a sealed silver foil wrapper one per attendee at the 2002 Hawaii Trade Conference. The cards are similar in design to the mainstream Sweet Spot Classics Signatures except for the "Hawaii XVII" logo running vertically up the left hand, side border of the card front. Each of these cards is about as thick as six standard issue trading cards. Their extraordinary width allows for the use of a real leather baseball sweet spot, cut out with the red stitches and incorporated directly into the center of the card. Though the cards are not serial-numbered in any manner, representatives at Upper Deck provided print runs of which run after each player's name in our checklist. Due to market scarcity, no pricing is provided.

	Nm-Mt	Ex-Mt
S-AD Andre Dawson/10		
S-AK Al Kaline/25		
S-AT Alan Trammell/25		
S-BD Bucky Dent/25		
S-BP Boog Powell/25		
S-BR Brooks Robinson/25		
S-CF Carlton Fisk/10		
S-CR Cal Ripken/10		
S-DE Dennis Eckersley/25		
S-DM Dale Murphy/10		
S-DS Dave Stewart/25		
S-EB Ernie Banks/10		
S-FJ Ferguson Jenkins/25		
S-FL Fred Lynn/25		
S-GP Gaylord Perry/25		
S-KH Keith Hernandez/20		
S-PM Paul Molitor/25		
S-RF Rollie Fingers/25		
S-SG Steve Garvey/25		
S-SK Sandy Koufax/5		

2003 Sweet Spot Classics

This 150 card set was issued in March, 2003. It was issued in five-card packs with an $10 SRP. The packs were issued in 12 pack boxes which came 16 boxes to a case. The following subsets are included: Ted Williams Ball Game (91-120) and Yankee Heritage (121-150). The Williams's cards were printed to a stated print run of 1941 and the Yankee Heritage cards were printed to a stated print run of 1500 serial numbered sets. While this set features mainly retired players, a special Hideki Matsui card (75) was issued. That card was issued to a stated print run of 1999 serial numbered sets. Originally that card was supposed to be Rod Carew and a few Carew cards made it through the production process. However, at this time no pricing information is available on the Carew card which was supposed to be card number 75 originally.

	Nm-Mt	Ex-Mt
COMP.SET w/o SP's (89)	40.00	12.00
COMMON (1-74/76-90)	.75	.23
COMMON CARD (91-120)	8.00	2.40
COMMON CARD (121-150)	5.00	1.50
1 Al Hrabosky	.75	.23
2 Al Lopez	.75	.23
3 Andre Dawson	.75	.23
4 Bill Buckner	.75	.23
5 Billy Williams	.75	.23
6 Bob Feller	.75	.23
7 Bob Lemon	.75	.23
8 Bobby Doerr	.75	.23
9 Cecil Cooper	.75	.23
10 Cal Ripken	6.00	1.80
11 Carlton Fisk	1.25	.35
12 Catfish Hunter	1.25	.35
13 Chris Chambliss	.75	.23
14 Dale Murphy	2.00	.60
15 Gaylord Perry	.75	.23
16 Dave Kingman	.75	.23
17 Dave Parker	.75	.23
18 Dave Stewart	.75	.23
19 David Cone	.75	.23
20 Dennis Eckersley	.75	.23
21 Don Baylor	.75	.23
22 Don Sutton	.75	.23
23 Duke Snider	1.25	.35
24 Dwight Evans	.75	.23
25 Dwight Gooden	1.25	.35
26 Earl Weaver MG	.75	.23
27 Early Wynn	.75	.23
28 Eddie Mathews	2.00	.60
29 Enos Slaughter	1.25	.35
30 Ernie Banks	2.00	.60
31 Fred Lynn	.75	.23
32 Fred Stanley	.75	.23
33 Gary Carter	1.25	.35
34 George Foster	.75	.23
35 Hal Newhouser	.75	.23
36 George Kell	.75	.23
37 Harmon Killebrew	2.00	.60
38 Hoyt Wilhelm	.75	.23
39 Jack Morris	.75	.23
40 Jim Bunning	.75	.23
41 Jim Gilliam	.75	.23
42 Jim Leyritz	.75	.23
43 Jimmy Key	.75	.23
44 Joe Carter	.75	.23
45 Joe Morgan	.75	.23
46 John Montefusco	.75	.23
47 Johnny Bench	2.00	.60
48 Johnny Podres	.75	.23
49 Jose Canseco	2.00	.60
50 Juan Marichal	.75	.23
51 Keith Hernandez	.75	.23
52 Ken Griffey Sr.	.75	.23
53 Kirby Puckett	2.00	.60
54 Kirk Gibson	.75	.23
55 Larry Doby	.75	.23
56 Lee May	.75	.23
57 Lee Mazzilli	.75	.23
58 Lou Boudreau	.75	.23
59 Mark McGwire	5.00	1.50
60 Maury Wills	.75	.23
61 Mike Pagliarulo	.75	.23
62 Monte Irvin	.75	.23
63 Nolan Ryan	5.00	1.50
64 Orlando Cepeda	.75	.23
65 Ozzie Smith	3.00	.90
66 Paul O'Neill	1.25	.35
67 Pee Wee Reese	1.25	.35
68 Phil Niekro	.75	.23
69 Ralph Kiner	.75	.23
70 Red Schoendienst	.75	.23
71 Richie Ashburn	1.25	.35
72 Rick Ferrell	.75	.23
73 Robin Roberts	.75	.23
74 Robin Yount	3.00	.90
75 Hideki Matsui/1999 XRC	25.00	7.50
75B Rod Carew ERR Not Intended for Public Release		
76 Rollie Fingers	.75	.23
77 Ron Cey	.75	.23
78 Tom Seaver	1.25	.35
79 Sparky Anderson MG	.75	.23
80 Stan Musial	3.00	.90
81 Steve Garvey	.75	.23
82 Ted Williams	5.00	1.50
83 Tommy Lasorda	.75	.23
84 Tony Gwynn	2.50	.75
85 Tony Perez	.75	.23
86 Vida Blue	.75	.23
87 Warren Spahn	1.25	.35
88 Bob Gibson	1.25	.35
89 Willie McCovey	.75	.23
90 Willie Stargell	1.25	.35
91 Ted Williams TB	8.00	2.40
92 Ted Williams TB	8.00	2.40
93 Ted Williams TB	8.00	2.40
94 Ted Williams TB	8.00	2.40
95 Ted Williams TB	8.00	2.40
96 Ted Williams TB	8.00	2.40
97 Ted Williams TB	8.00	2.40
98 Ted Williams TB	8.00	2.40
99 Ted Williams TB	8.00	2.40
100 Ted Williams TB	8.00	2.40
101 Ted Williams TB	8.00	2.40
102 Ted Williams TB	8.00	2.40
103 Ted Williams TB	8.00	2.40
104 Ted Williams TB	8.00	2.40
105 Ted Williams TB	8.00	2.40
106 Ted Williams TB	8.00	2.40
107 Ted Williams TB	8.00	2.40
108 Ted Williams TB	8.00	2.40
109 Ted Williams TB	8.00	2.40
110 Ted Williams TB	8.00	2.40
111 Ted Williams TB	8.00	2.40
112 Ted Williams TB	8.00	2.40
113 Ted Williams TB	8.00	2.40
114 Ted Williams TB	8.00	2.40
115 Ted Williams TB	8.00	2.40
116 Ted Williams TB	8.00	2.40
117 Ted Williams TB	8.00	2.40
118 Ted Williams TB	8.00	2.40
119 Ted Williams TB	8.00	2.40
120 Ted Williams TB	8.00	2.40
121 Babe Ruth YH	15.00	4.50
122 Bucky Dent YH	5.00	1.50
123 Casey Stengel YH	5.00	1.50
124 Dave Righetti YH	5.00	1.50
125 Dave Winfield YH	5.00	1.50
126 Dick Tidrow YH	5.00	1.50
127 Dock Ellis YH	5.00	1.50
128 Don Mattingly YH	15.00	4.50
129 Hank Bauer YH	5.00	1.50
130 Jim Bouton YH	5.00	1.50
131 Jim Kaat YH	5.00	1.50
132 Joe DiMaggio YH	10.00	3.00
133 Joe Torre YH	8.00	2.40
134 Lou Piniella YH	5.00	1.50
135 Mel Stottlemyre YH	5.00	1.50
136 Mickey Mantle YH	20.00	6.00
137 Mickey Rivers YH	5.00	1.50
138 Phil Rizzuto YH	5.00	1.50
139 Ralph Branca YH	5.00	1.50
140 Ralph Houk YH	5.00	1.50
141 Roger Maris YH	10.00	3.00
142 Ron Guidry YH	5.00	1.50
143 Ruben Amaro Sr. YH	5.00	1.50
144 Sparky Lyle YH	5.00	1.50
145 Thurman Munson YH	10.00	3.00
146 Tommy Henrich YH	5.00	1.50
147 Tommy John YH	5.00	1.50
148 Tony Kubek YH	5.00	1.50
149 Whitey Ford YH	5.00	1.50
150 Yogi Berra YH	8.00	2.40

2003 Sweet Spot Classics Matsui Parallel

Randomly inserted into packs, these cards parallel the Hideki Matsui base card. There are three different versions of this card and they were all issued to different stated print runs. Please note the silver version (75C) was issued to a stated print run of 25 serial numbered sets and there is no pricing due to market scarcity.

	Nm-Mt	Ex-Mt
75A Hideki Matsui Red/500	25.00	7.50
75B Hideki Matsui Blue/250	30.00	9.00
75C Hideki Matsui Silver/25		

2003 Sweet Spot Classics Autographs Black Ink

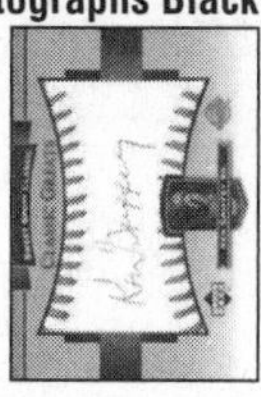

Randomly inserted into packs, these cards feature the players signing in black ink. These autograph cards were in packs at overall rate of one in 24. Each card was printed to a different amount and we have noted that information next to the player's name in our checklist. All the Mark McGwire autos are inscribed "Maris '61"

	Nm-Mt	Ex-Mt
AD Andre Dawson/75	50.00	15.00
AH Al Hrabosky/100	40.00	12.00
AT Alan Trammell/173	40.00	12.00
BB Bill Buckner/85	40.00	12.00
BW Billy Williams/173	40.00	12.00
CR Cal Ripken/38		
DB Don Baylor/50	50.00	15.00
DE Dwight Evans/100	50.00	15.00
DP Dave Parker/113	40.00	12.00
DS Don Sutton/123	40.00	12.00
EB Ernie Banks/73	120.00	36.00
GC Gary Carter/173	50.00	15.00
GF George Foster/173	40.00	12.00
GI Kirk Gibson/173	40.00	12.00
HK Harmon Killebrew/73	120.00	36.00
JB Johnny Bench/73	150.00	45.00
JC Joe Carter/123	40.00	12.00
JM Joe Morgan/169	40.00	12.00
JM Jack Morris/123	40.00	12.00
JP Johnny Podres/173	40.00	12.00
KG Ken Griffey Sr./100	50.00	15.00
KH Keith Hernandez/173	50.00	15.00
KP Kirby Puckett/174	60.00	18.00
MM Mark McGwire/73	700.00	210.00
MW Maury Wills/173	40.00	12.00
OC Orlando Cepeda/34		
PN Phil Niekro/173	40.00	12.00
RF Rollie Fingers/73	50.00	15.00
RR Robin Roberts/173	50.00	15.00
RY Robin Yount/73	150.00	45.00
SG Steve Garvey/173	40.00	12.00
SN Duke Snider/100	80.00	24.00
TG Tony Gwynn/101	80.00	24.00
TP Tony Perez/51	80.00	24.00
TS Tom Seaver/74	80.00	24.00

2003 Sweet Spot Classics Autographs Blue Ink

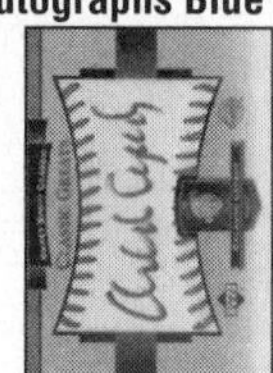

Randomly inserted in packs, these cards feature the players signing their cards in black ink. A few players were issued in shorter quantity and we have notated that information with an SP next to their name in our checklist. In addition, Upper Deck purchased nine Ted Williams cuts and issued nine of these cards to match his uniform number.

	Nm-Mt	Ex-Mt
AD Andre Dawson	25.00	7.50
AH Al Hrabosky SP	25.00	7.50
BB Bill Buckner SP	25.00	7.50
CF Carlton Fisk	60.00	18.00
CR Cal Ripken	200.00	60.00
DB Don Baylor SP	25.00	7.50
DE Dennis Eckersley	25.00	7.50
DE Dwight Evans *	25.00	7.50
DM Dale Murphy	40.00	12.00
DS Dave Stewart	25.00	7.50
KG Ken Griffey Sr.	25.00	7.50
KP Kirby Puckett	40.00	12.00
OC Orlando Cepeda *	25.00	7.50
SN Duke Snider	50.00	15.00
TG Tony Gwynn	50.00	15.00
TW Ted Williams/9		

2003 Sweet Spot Classics Autographs Yankee Greats Black Ink

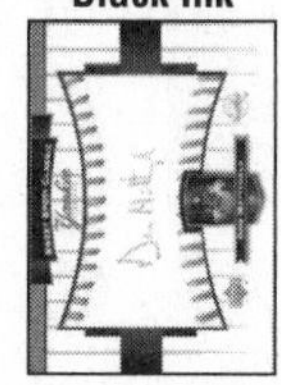

Randomly inserted in packs, these cards feature former New York Yankees who signed their card in black ink. We have notated the stated print run information next to the player's name in our checklist. Please note that the Hideki Matsui card was issued as an exchange card and has an exchange deadline of March 13, 2006.

	Nm-Mt	Ex-Mt
CC Chris Chambliss/101	60.00	18.00
DC David Cone/74	80.00	24.00
DE Dock Ellis/174	40.00	12.00
DG Dwight Gooden/74	80.00	24.00
DK Dave Kingman/100	60.00	18.00
DM Don Mattingly/74	150.00	45.00
DR Dave Righetti/173	60.00	18.00
DT Dick Tidrow/101	40.00	12.00
DW Dave Winfield/25		
FS Fred Stanley/101	40.00	12.00
GU Ron Guidry/100	60.00	18.00
HB Hank Bauer/75	60.00	18.00
HM Hideki Matsui/25 EXCH		
JB Jim Bouton/100	40.00	12.00
JC Jose Canseco/73	100.00	30.00
JD Joe DiMaggio/5		
JK Jim Kaat/100	40.00	12.00
JK Jimmy Key/100	40.00	12.00
JL Jim Leyritz/100	40.00	12.00
JM John Montefusco/100	40.00	12.00
JT Joe Torre/73	100.00	30.00
LM Lee Mazzilli/100	40.00	12.00
LP Lou Piniella/100	40.00	12.00
MP Mike Pagliarulo/99	40.00	12.00
MR Mickey Rivers/73	60.00	18.00
MS Mel Stottlemyre/73	60.00	18.00
PO Paul O'Neill/100	80.00	24.00
PR Phil Rizzuto/173	80.00	24.00
RA Ruben Amaro Sr./100	40.00	12.00
RB Ralph Branca/100	40.00	12.00
RH Ralph Houk/100	40.00	12.00
SL Sparky Lyle/100	40.00	12.00
TH Tommy Henrich/100	40.00	12.00
TJ Tommy John/100	40.00	12.00
TK Tony Kubek/123	60.00	18.00
YB Yogi Berra/73	120.00	36.00

2003 Sweet Spot Classics Autographs Yankee Greats Blue Ink

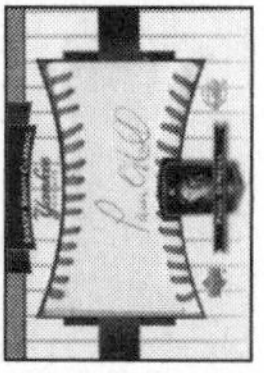

Randomly inserted in packs, these cards feature former New York Yankees who signed their card in blue ink. A few cards were issued in lesser quantity and we have notated those cards with an SP in our checklist. In addition, the Bucky Dent card seems to be in larger supply and we have notated that with an asterisk in our checklist. Also, Upper Deck purchased seven Mickey Mantle autographs and used those as scarce cuts in this product.

	Nm-Mt	Ex-Mt
BD Bucky Dent *	25.00	7.50
CC Chris Chambliss SP	40.00	12.00
DK Dave Kingman	40.00	12.00
DT Dick Tidrow	25.00	7.50
FS Fred Stanley	25.00	7.50
GU Ron Guidry	50.00	15.00
HB Hank Bauer SP	40.00	12.00
JB Jim Bouton	25.00	7.50
JK Jim Kaat	25.00	7.50
JK Jimmy Key	40.00	12.00
JL Jim Leyritz	25.00	7.50
JM John Montefusco	25.00	7.50
LM Lee Mazzilli	25.00	7.50
LP Lou Piniella SP	40.00	12.00
MM Mickey Mantle/7		
MP Mike Pagliarulo	25.00	7.50
PO Paul O'Neill	50.00	15.00
RA Ruben Amaro Sr.	25.00	7.50
RB Ralph Branca	25.00	7.50
RH Ralph Houk	25.00	7.50
SL Sparky Lyle SP	40.00	12.00
TH Tommy Henrich SP	40.00	12.00
TJ Tommy John	25.00	7.50

2003 Sweet Spot Classics Autographs Yankee Greats Matsui Exchange

Randomly inserted in packs, this was a card issued as an exchange card for a collector to obtain an Hideki Matsui signed card. This card was issued to a stated print run of 50 sets of which Matsui signed 25 cards in black and 25 cards in red. This card could be exchanged until March 13, 2006.

	Nm-Mt	Ex-Mt
HM Hideki Matsui EXCH		

2003 Sweet Spot Classics Game Jersey

Issued at a stated rate of one in 16, these 30 cards feature game-worn jersey swatches on the card. A few cards were issued in smaller quantities and we have notated those cards with an SP in our checklist.

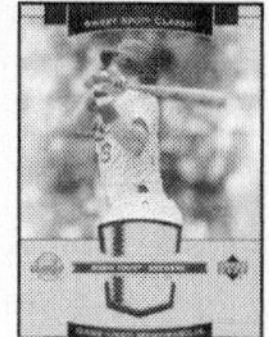
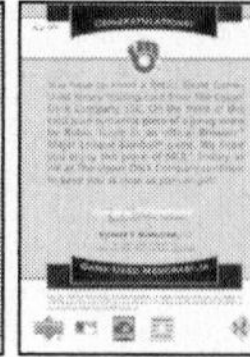

	Nm-Mt	Ex-Mt
AD Andre Dawson SP	10.00	3.00
CC Cecil Cooper	10.00	3.00
CF Carlton Fisk	15.00	4.50
CR Cal Ripken	25.00	7.50
DM Dale Murphy	15.00	4.50
DP0 Dave Parker Pants	10.00	3.00
DS Duke Snider SP	15.00	4.50
EB Ernie Banks SP	15.00	4.50
FL Fred Lynn	10.00	3.00
GC Gary Carter SP	15.00	4.50
GF George Foster	10.00	3.00
HK Harmon Killebrew	15.00	4.50
JB Johnny Bench	15.00	4.50
JC Jose Canseco	15.00	4.50
JG Jim Gilliam	10.00	3.00
JM0 Joe Morgan Pants	10.00	3.00
JP Johnny Podres	10.00	3.00
KP Kirby Puckett	15.00	4.50
LM Lee May	10.00	3.00
MM Mark McGwire	40.00	12.00
NR Nolan Ryan	40.00	12.00
OS Ozzie Smith	15.00	4.50
RC Ron Cey	10.00	3.00
RF Rollie Fingers	10.00	3.00
RY Robin Yount	15.00	4.50
SG Steve Garvey	10.00	3.00
SM Stan Musial SP	40.00	12.00
TG Tony Gwynn	15.00	4.50
TW Ted Williams SP	100.00	30.00
WS Willie Stargell SP	15.00	4.50

2003 Sweet Spot Classics Patch Cards

Inserted at a stated rate of one in six, these 83 cards feature special patch-type pieces. These cards honor different highlights in many player's career and we have notated that information next to their name in our checklist.

	Nm-Mt	Ex-Mt
BR1 Babe Ruth Red Sox/350	50.00	15.00
BR2 Babe Ruth Yankees	40.00	12.00
BR3 Babe Ruth 27 WS/150	60.00	18.00
BW1 Billy Williams	10.00	3.00
CF1 Carlton Fisk Red Sox	15.00	4.50
CF2 Carlton Fisk White Sox/150	25.00	7.50
CH1 Catfish Hunter A's/350	15.00	4.50
CH2 Catfish Hunter Yankees	15.00	4.50
CH3 Catfish Hunter A's GU/39	60.00	18.00
CH4 Catfish Hunter 72 WS/50	40.00	12.00
CR1 Cal Ripken	25.00	7.50
CR2 Cal Ripken GU/75	150.00	45.00
CR3 Cal Ripken 83 WS/150	60.00	18.00
DS1 Duke Snider	15.00	4.50
DS2 Duke Snider LA/150	25.00	7.50
DS3 Duke Snider Mets/350	15.00	4.50
DS4 Duke Snider Dodgers GU/25		
DS5 Duke Snider Brooklyn/150	25.00	7.50
DS6 Duke Snider 59 WS/150	25.00	7.50
EB1 Ernie Banks	15.00	4.50
FL1 Fred Lynn Red Sox	10.00	3.00
FL2 Fred Lynn Angels/350	10.00	3.00
FL3 Fred Lynn O's/150	15.00	4.50
FL4 Fred Lynn Tigers/50	25.00	7.50
GF1 George Foster Mets/350	10.00	3.00
GF2 George Foster Reds	10.00	3.00
HM1 Hideki Matsui	25.00	7.50
JB1 Johnny Bench	15.00	4.50
JB2 Johnny Bench GU/150	60.00	18.00
JB3 Johnny Bench 76 WS/150	40.00	12.00
JD1 Joe DiMaggio	15.00	4.50
JD2 Joe DiMaggio 47 WS/50	100.00	30.00
JD3 Joe DiMaggio 37 WS/350	30.00	9.00
JD4 Joe DiMaggio 39 WS/150	40.00	12.00
JM1 Joe Morgan Reds	10.00	3.00
JM2 Joe Morgan Astros/350	10.00	3.00
JM3 Joe Morgan Giants/150	15.00	4.50
JM4 Joe Morgan Reds GU/150	40.00	12.00
JM5 Joe Morgan 76 WS/100	15.00	4.50
KG1 Kirk Gibson Dodgers	10.00	3.00
KG2 Kirk Gibson Tigers/350	10.00	3.00
KP1 Kirby Puckett	15.00	4.50
KP2 Kirby Puckett GU/40	100.00	30.00
MC1 Mark McGwire A's	25.00	7.50
MC2 Mark McGwire Cards/350	50.00	15.00
MC3 Mark McGwire Cards GU/9		
MM1 Mickey Mantle	40.00	12.00
MM2 M.Mantle 52 WS/150	120.00	36.00
MM3 M.Mantle 56 WS/150	120.00	36.00
MM4 M.Mantle 60 WS/150	120.00	36.00
MM5 Mickey Mantle Logo/7		
NR1 Nolan Ryan Astros	25.00	7.50
NR2 Nolan Ryan Rangers/350	50.00	15.00
NR3 Nolan Ryan Angels/150	60.00	18.00
NR4 N.Ryan Astros GU/105	120.00	36.00
OS1 Ozzie Smith Cards	15.00	4.50
OS2 Ozzie Smith Padres/350	25.00	7.50
OS3 Ozzie Smith Cards GU/150	60.00	18.00
OS4 Ozzie Smith 82 WS/100	40.00	12.00
OS5 Ozzie Smith 85 WS/100	40.00	12.00
RM1 Roger Maris Yankees	20.00	6.00
RM2 Roger Maris Cards/350	30.00	9.00
RM3 Roger Maris 62 WS/150	40.00	12.00

Card	Nm-Mt	Ex-Mt
RM4 Roger Maris 67 WS/50	100.00	30.00
RY1 Robin Yount	15.00	4.50
RY2 Robin Yount GU/150	60.00	18.00
RY3 Robin Yount 82 WS/350	25.00	7.50
SG1 Steve Garvey Dodgers	10.00	3.00
SG2 Steve Garvey Padres/350	10.00	3.00
SG3 S.Garvey Dodgers GU/150	40.00	12.00
SG4 Steve Garvey 77 WS/50	25.00	7.50
SG5 Steve Garvey 81 WS/50	25.00	7.50
TG1 Tony Gwynn	15.00	4.50
TG2 Tony Gwynn GU/150	80.00	24.00
TG3 Tony Gwynn 84 WS/350	25.00	7.50
TW1 Ted Williams	25.00	7.50
TW2 Ted Williams 46 WS/350	50.00	15.00
WS1 Willie Stargell	15.00	4.50
WS2 Willie Stargell GU/137	50.00	15.00
WS3 Willie Stargell 71 WS/150	25.00	7.50
WS4 Willie Stargell 79 WS/50	40.00	12.00
YB1 Yogi Berra	15.00	4.50
YB2 Yogi Berra 53 WS/350	25.00	7.50
YB3 Yogi Berra 56 WS/150	40.00	12.00

2003 Sweet Spot Classics Pinstripes

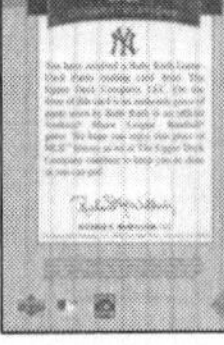

Inserted at a stated rate of one in 40, these 12 cards feature authentic game-used pieces of New York Yankee uniforms. Please note that a few cards were issued in shorter supply and we have notated that information with an SP notation in our checklist.

Card	Nm-Mt	Ex-Mt
BR0 Babe Ruth Pants SP	350.00	105.00
CS Casey Stengel	15.00	4.50
DE Bucky Dent	10.00	3.00
DG0 Dwight Gooden Pants	15.00	4.50
DM0 Don Mattingly Pants	40.00	12.00
DR Dave Righetti	10.00	3.00
JB Jim Bouton	10.00	3.00
JD Joe DiMaggio SP	120.00	36.00
MM Mickey Mantle SP	180.00	55.00
PR Phil Rizzuto	15.00	4.50
TM Thurman Munson SP	40.00	12.00
YB Yogi Berra	20.00	6.00

2004 Sweet Spot Classic

This 159 card standard-size set was released in February, 2004. The set was issued in four card packs which came 12 packs to a box and 8 boxes to a case. Cards numbered 1-90 were issued in higher quantity than cards 91-161. The cards 91 through 161 feature "famous firsts" in players careers. Each of these cards are numbered to that year in issue. Cards numbered 143 and 148 which were supposed to feature Roger Clemens were removed from the set when Clemens came out of a very short retirement to sign with the Houston Astros.

Card	Nm-Mt	Ex-Mt
COMP.SET w/o SP'S (90)	40.00	12.00
COMMON CARD (1-90)	.75	.23
COMMON CARD (91-161)	5.00	1.50
91-161 STATED ODDS 1:3		
1 Al Kaline	2.00	.60
2 Andre Dawson	.75	.23
3 Bert Blyleven	.75	.23
4 Bill Dickey	1.25	.35
5 Bill Mazeroski	1.25	.35
6 Billy Martin	1.25	.35
7 Bob Feller	1.25	.35
8 Bob Gibson	1.25	.35
9 Bob Lemon	.75	.23
10 George Kell	.75	.23
11 Bobby Doerr	.75	.23
12 Brooks Robinson	2.00	.60
13 Cal Ripken	6.00	1.80
14 Carl Hubbell	1.25	.35
15 Carl Yastrzemski	3.00	.90
16 Charlie Keller	.75	.23
17 Chuck Dressen	.75	.23
18 Cy Young	2.00	.60
19 Dave Winfield	.75	.23
20 Dizzy Dean	1.25	.35
21 Don Drysdale	2.00	.60
22 Don Larsen	.75	.23
23 Don Mattingly	5.00	1.50
24 Don Newcombe	.75	.23
25 Duke Snider	1.25	.35
26 Early Wynn	.75	.23
27 Eddie Mathews	2.00	.60
28 Elston Howard	.75	.23
29 Frank Robinson	.75	.23
30 Gary Carter	1.25	.35
31 Gil Hodges	1.25	.35
32 Gil McDougald	1.25	.35
33 Hank Greenberg	2.00	.60
34 Harmon Killebrew	2.00	.60
35 Harry Caray	.75	.23
36 Honus Wagner	2.00	.60
37 Hoyt Wilhelm	.75	.23
38 Jackie Robinson	2.50	.75
39 Jim Bunning	.75	.23
40 Jim Palmer	.75	.23
41 Jimmie Foxx	2.00	.60
42 Jimmy Wynn	.75	.23
43 Joe DiMaggio	4.00	1.20
44 Joe Torre	1.25	.35
45 Johnny Mize	.75	.23
46 Juan Marichal	.75	.23
47 Larry Doby	.75	.23
48 Lefty Gomez	1.25	.35
49 Lefty Grove	1.25	.35
50 Leo Durocher	.75	.23
51 Lou Boudreau	.75	.23
52 Lou Brock	1.25	.35
53 Lou Gehrig	4.00	1.20
54 Luis Aparicio	.75	.23
55 Maury Wills	.75	.23
56 Mel Allen	.75	.23
57 Mel Ott	2.00	.60
58 Mickey Cochrane	.75	.23
59 Mickey Mantle	8.00	2.40
60 Mike Schmidt	4.00	1.20
61 Monte Irvin	.75	.23
62 Nolan Ryan	5.00	1.50
63 Pee Wee Reese	1.25	.35
64 Phil Rizzuto	1.25	.35
65 Ralph Kiner	.75	.23
66 Richie Ashburn	1.25	.35
67 Rick Ferrell	.75	.23
68 Roberto Clemente	5.00	1.50
69 Robin Roberts	.75	.23
70 Robin Yount	3.00	.90
71 Rogers Hornsby	2.00	.60
72 Rollie Fingers	.75	.23
73 Roy Campanella	2.00	.60
74 Ryne Sandberg	4.00	1.20
75 Tony Gwynn	2.50	.75
76 Satchel Paige	2.00	.60
77 Shoeless Joe Jackson	3.00	.90
78 Stan Musial	3.00	.90
79 Ted Williams	5.00	1.50
80 Thurman Munson	2.50	.75
81 Tom Seaver	1.25	.35
82 Tommy Henrich	.75	.23
83 Tony Perez	.75	.23
84 Tris Speaker	1.25	.35
85 Vida Blue	.75	.23
86 Wade Boggs	1.25	.35
87 Walter Johnson	2.00	.60
88 Warren Spahn	1.25	.35
89 Whitey Ford	1.25	.35
90 Willie McCovey	1.25	.35
91 Andre Dawson FF/1987	5.00	1.50
92 Andre Dawson FF/1990	5.00	1.50
93 Ernie Banks FF/1958	8.00	2.40
94 Bob Lemon FF/1948	5.00	1.50
95 Cal Ripken FF/1982	15.00	4.50
96 Cal Ripken FF/1995	15.00	4.50
97 Carl Yastrzemski FF/1979	8.00	2.40
98 Carlton Fisk FF/1972	8.00	2.40
99 Cy Young FF/1910	8.00	2.40
100 Don Larsen FF/1956	5.00	1.50
101 Don Newcombe FF/1949	5.00	1.50
102 Don Newcombe FF/1956	5.00	1.50
103 Dwight Evans FF/1986	8.00	2.40
104 Elston Howard FF/1955	5.00	1.50
105 Frank Robinson FF/1956	5.00	1.50
106 Frank Robinson FF/1966	5.00	1.50
107 Frank Robinson FF/1973	5.00	1.50
108 Gil McDougald FF/1951	8.00	2.40
109 Hank Greenberg FF/1941	8.00	2.40
110 Harmon Killebrew FF/1964	8.00	2.40
111 Hoyt Wilhelm FF/1952	5.00	1.50
112 Hoyt Wilhelm FF/1958	5.00	1.50
113 Jackie Robinson FF/1946	8.00	2.40
114 J.Robinson FF Black/1947	8.00	2.40
115 J.Robinson FF ROY/1947	8.00	2.40
116 Jackie Robinson FF/1997	8.00	2.40
117 Jim Bunning FF/1964	5.00	1.50
118 J.DiMaggio FF Bench/1950	10.00	3.00
119 Joe Morgan FF/1976	5.00	1.50
120 Johnny Mize FF/1939	5.00	1.50
121 Johnny Mize FF/1947	5.00	1.50
122 Juan Marichal FF/1968	5.00	1.50
123 Ken Griffey Sr. FF/1990	5.00	1.50
124 Larry Doby FF/1947	5.00	1.50
125 Lefty Gomez FF/1933	8.00	2.40
126 Lou Boudreau FF/1946	5.00	1.50
127 Lou Gehrig FF Lineup/1939	10.00	3.00
128 Lou Gehrig FF Number/1939	10.00	3.00
129 Mark McGwire FF/1989	12.00	3.60
130 Mark McGwire FF/1998	12.00	3.60
131 Maury Wills FF/1962	5.00	1.50
132 Mel Ott FF/1946	8.00	2.40
133 Mike Schmidt FF/1980	10.00	3.00
134 Nolan Ryan FF/1973	12.00	3.60
135 Nolan Ryan FF/1989	12.00	3.60
136 Pee Wee Reese FF/1955	8.00	2.40
137 Nolan Ryan FF/1979	12.00	3.60
138 Richie Ashburn FF/1962	8.00	2.40
139 Roberto Clemente FF/1971	12.00	3.60
140 Roberto Clemente FF/1973	12.00	3.60
141 Robin Roberts FF/1956	5.00	1.50
142 Robin Yount FF/1982	8.00	2.40
143 Does Not Exist		
144 Rollie Fingers FF/1975	5.00	1.50
145 Rollie Fingers FF/1981	5.00	1.50
146 Roy Campanella FF/1953	8.00	2.40
147 Ryne Sandberg FF/1990	10.00	3.00
148 Does Not Exist		
149 Satchel Paige FF/1948	8.00	2.40
150 Stan Musial FF/1952	8.00	2.40
151 Stan Musial FF/1954	8.00	2.40
152 Stan Musial FF/1963	8.00	2.40
153 Ted Williams FF/1947	12.00	3.60
154 Ted Williams FF/1957	12.00	3.60
155 Tom Seaver FF/1970	8.00	2.40
156 Tom Seaver FF/1975	8.00	2.40
157 Wade Boggs FF/1999	8.00	2.40
158 Warren Spahn FF/1957	8.00	2.40
159 Warren Spahn FF/1958	8.00	2.40
160 Joe DiMaggio FF AS/1950	10.00	3.00
161 Yogi Berra FF/1947	8.00	2.40

2004 Sweet Spot Classic Barrel Signatures

Lou Brock did not return his cards in time for inclusion in this product. Those cards could be redeemed until January 27, 2004. A few cards have been seen on the secondary market with Duke Snider's photo used on Wade Boggs' card.

Card	Nm-Mt	Ex-Mt
OVERALL AUTO ODDS 1:24		
PRINT RUNS B/WN 24-203 COPIES PER		
NO PRICING ON QTY OF 25 OR LESS.		
BM Bill Mazeroski/24		
BW Billy Williams/200	50.00	15.00
CR Cal Ripken/25		
HB Harold Baines/200	50.00	15.00
JB Johnny Bench/50		
LB Lou Brock/50 EXCH		
NR Nolan Ryan/25		
RS Ron Santo/203	50.00	15.00
SM Stan Musial/25		
TS Tom Seaver/25		
WB Wade Boggs/200	80.00	24.00

2004 Sweet Spot Classic Game Used Memorabilia

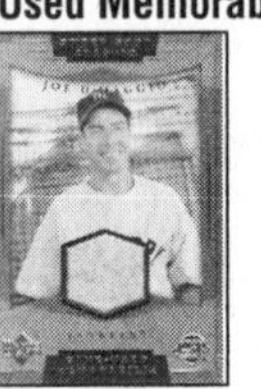

Card	Nm-Mt	Ex-Mt
OVERALL GU MEMORABILIA ODDS 1:24		
STATED PRINT RUN 275 SERIAL #'d SETS		
AD Andre Dawson Expos Jsy	10.00	3.00
AD1 Andre Dawson Cubs Jsy	10.00	3.00
BB Bert Blyleven Jsy	10.00	3.00
BM Billy Martin Pants	15.00	4.50
CD Chuck Dressen Pants	10.00	3.00
CK Charlie Keller Jsy	10.00	3.00
CR Cal Ripken Jsy	40.00	12.00
CY Carl Yastrzemski Jsy	25.00	7.50
DM Don Mattingly Jsy	25.00	7.50
EH Elston Howard Jsy	15.00	4.50
EM Eddie Mathews Jsy	15.00	4.50
FR Frank Robinson Jsy	10.00	3.00
GC Gary Carter Pants	15.00	4.50
GM Gil McDougald Jsy	15.00	4.50
JB Jim Bunning Pants	15.00	4.50
JD Joe DiMaggio Pants	80.00	24.00
JM Juan Marichal Pants	10.00	3.00
JO Johnny Mize Pants	15.00	4.50
JP Jim Palmer Jsy	10.00	3.00
JR Jackie Robinson Pants	40.00	12.00
JT Joe Torre Jsy	15.00	4.50
KG Ken Griffey Sr. Jsy	10.00	3.00
ML Mickey Lolich Jsy	10.00	3.00
MM Mickey Mantle Pants	150.00	45.00
MW Maury Wills Pants	10.00	3.00
NR Nolan Ryan Jsy	40.00	12.00
OS Ozzie Smith Jsy	15.00	4.50
PR Phil Rizzuto Pants	15.00	4.50
RB Ron Blomberg Jsy	10.00	3.00
RC Roberto Clemente Pants	80.00	24.00
RM Roger Maris Pants	60.00	18.00
RY Robin Yount Jsy	15.00	4.50
SA Sparky Anderson Jsy	10.00	3.00
SB Sal Bando Jsy	10.00	3.00
SM Stan Musial Pants	40.00	12.00
TG Tony Gwynn Pants	15.00	4.50
TM Thurman Munson Jsy	30.00	9.00
TS Tom Seaver Pants	15.00	4.50
TW Ted Williams Pants	80.00	24.00
WB Wade Boggs Sox Pants	15.00	4.50
WB1 Wade Boggs Yanks Pants	15.00	4.50

2004 Sweet Spot Classic Game Used Memorabilia Silver Rainbow

Card	Nm-Mt	Ex-Mt
*SILVER RBW: .75X TO 2X BASIC SWATCH		
OVERALL GU MEMORABILIA ODDS 1:24		
STATED PRINT RUN 50 SERIAL #'d SETS		
JD Joe DiMaggio Pants	120.00	36.00
MM Mickey Mantle Pants	250.00	75.00
RC Roberto Clemente Pants	120.00	36.00
TW Ted Williams Pants	120.00	36.00

2004 Sweet Spot Classic Game Used Patch

Card	Nm-Mt	Ex-Mt
PRINT RUNS B/WN 17-176 COPIES PER		
NO PRICING ON QTY OF 31 OR LESS.		
SILVER RAINBOW PRINT RUN 10 #'d SETS		
NO SILV.RAIN.PRICING DUE TO SCARCITY		
RANDOM INSERTS IN PACKS		
AD Andre Dawson/100	25.00	7.50
BB Bert Blyleven/113	25.00	7.50
CK Charlie Keller/55		
CR Cal Ripken/17		
CY Carl Yastrzemski/20		
DM Don Mattingly/176	60.00	18.00
EH Elston Howard/23		
FR Frank Robinson/50		
GM Gil McDougald/31		
ML Mickey Lolich/115	25.00	7.50
MW Maury Wills/78	25.00	7.50
NR Nolan Ryan/96	100.00	30.00
RY Robin Yount/100	60.00	18.00
TG Tony Gwynn/100	60.00	18.00
TM Thurman Munson/100	60.00	18.00
TS Tom Seaver/94	40.00	12.00
WB Wade Boggs/90	40.00	12.00

2004 Sweet Spot Classic Patch 300

Card	Nm-Mt	Ex-Mt
STATED PRINT RUN 300 SERIAL #'d SETS		
*PATCH 230: .4X TO 1X BASIC		
PATCH 230 PRINT RUN 230 SERIAL #'d SETS		
*PATCH 200: .4X TO 1X BASIC		
PATCH 200 PRINT RUN 200 SERIAL #'d SETS		
*PATCH 150: .5X TO 1.2X BASIC		
PATCH 150 PRINT RUN 150 SERIAL #'d SETS		
*PATCH 125: .5X TO 1.2X BASIC		
PATCH 125 PRINT RUN 125 SERIAL #'d SETS		
*PATCH 75: .6X TO 1.5X BASIC		
PATCH 75 PRINT RUN 75 SERIAL #'d SETS		
*PATCH 50: .75X TO 2X BASIC		
PATCH 50 PRINT RUN 50 SERIAL #'d SETS		
PATCH 25 PRINT RUN 25 SERIAL #'d SETS		
NO PATCH 25 PRICING DUE TO SCARCITY		
PATCH 10 PRINT RUN 10 SERIAL #'d SETS		
NO PATCH 10 PRICING DUE TO SCARCITY		
OVERALL PATCH ODDS 1:3		
AD Andre Dawson Cubs	10.00	3.00
AK Al Kaline Tigers	20.00	6.00
AL Mel Allen Yanks	10.00	3.00
BD Bill Dickey Yanks	15.00	4.50
BF Bob Feller Indians	15.00	4.50
BG Bob Gibson Cards	15.00	4.50
BL Bob Lemon Indians	10.00	3.00
BM Billy Martin Yanks	15.00	4.50
BR Lou Brock Cards	15.00	4.50
CA Roy Campanella Dodgers	15.00	4.50
CG Charlie Gehringer Tigers	10.00	3.00
CH Carl Hubbell Giants	15.00	4.50
CM Christy Mathewson Giants	15.00	4.50
CO Mickey Cochrane Tigers	10.00	3.00
CR Cal Ripken AS	40.00	12.00
CY Cy Young Indians	15.00	4.50
DD Dizzy Dean Cards	15.00	4.50
DL Don Larsen Yanks	10.00	3.00
DM Don Mattingly Yanks	30.00	9.00
DN Don Newcombe Dodgers	10.00	3.00
DO Bobby Doerr Red Sox	10.00	3.00
DR Don Drysdale Dodgers	15.00	4.50
DS Duke Snider AS	15.00	4.50
DU Leo Durocher Dodgers	10.00	3.00
DW Dave Winfield Yanks	10.00	3.00
EM Eddie Mathews Braves	15.00	4.50
ES Enos Slaughter Cards	10.00	3.00
EW Early Wynn Indians	10.00	3.00
FF Frankie Frisch Cards	10.00	3.00
FI Rollie Fingers A's	10.00	3.00
FJ Ferguson Jenkins Cubs	10.00	3.00
FR Frank Robinson Reds	10.00	3.00
GC Gary Carter Mets	15.00	4.50
GE Lou Gehrig Yanks	20.00	6.00
GH Gil Hodges Dodgers	15.00	4.50
GP Gaylord Perry Giants	10.00	3.00
GR Lefty Grove A's	15.00	4.50
HC Harry Caray Cubs	10.00	3.00
HG Hank Greenberg Tigers	15.00	4.50
HK Harmon Killebrew Twins	20.00	6.00
HW Honus Wagner Pirates	15.00	4.50
IR Monte Irvin Giants	10.00	3.00
JB Jim Bunning Phils	15.00	4.50
JD Joe DiMaggio AS	20.00	6.00
JF Jimmie Foxx A's	15.00	4.50
JJ Shoeless Joe Jackson Sox	20.00	6.00
JM Johnny Mize Cards	10.00	3.00
JP Jim Palmer O's	10.00	3.00
JR Jackie Robinson Dodgers	15.00	4.50
JT Joe Torre Braves	15.00	4.50
LA Luis Aparicio White Sox	10.00	3.00
LB Lou Boudreau Indians	10.00	3.00
LD Larry Doby Indians	10.00	3.00
LG Lefty Gomez Yanks	15.00	4.50
MA Juan Marichal Giants	10.00	3.00
MI Mickey Mantle AS	50.00	15.00
ML Mickey Lolich Tigers	10.00	3.00
MO Mel Ott Giants	15.00	4.50
MS Mike Schmidt Phils	25.00	7.50
MW Maury Wills Dodgers	10.00	3.00
NR Nolan Ryan Mets	30.00	9.00
PR Pee Wee Reese Dodgers	15.00	4.50
RA Richie Ashburn Phils	15.00	4.50
RC Roberto Clemente Pirates	30.00	9.00
RF Rick Ferrell Red Sox	10.00	3.00
RH Rogers Hornsby Cards	15.00	4.50
RI Phil Rizzuto Yanks	15.00	4.50
RK Ralph Kiner Pirates	10.00	3.00
RO Brooks Robinson O's	20.00	6.00
RR Robin Roberts Phils	10.00	3.00
RS Ryne Sandberg Cubs	25.00	7.50
RU Babe Ruth AS	30.00	9.00
SK Bill Skowron Yanks	10.00	3.00
SM Stan Musial Cards	20.00	6.00
SP Satchel Paige Indians	15.00	4.50
TC Ty Cobb Tigers	20.00	6.00
TH Tommy Henrich Yanks	10.00	3.00
TL Tommy Lasorda Dodgers	10.00	3.00
TM Thurman Munson Yanks	20.00	6.00
TP Tony Perez Reds	10.00	3.00
TR Tris Speaker Red Sox	15.00	4.50
TS Tom Seaver Mets	15.00	4.50
TW Ted Williams AS	30.00	9.00
WB Wade Boggs Red Sox	15.00	4.50
WF Whitey Ford Yanks	15.00	4.50
WI Hoyt Wilhelm White Sox	10.00	3.00
WJ Walter Johnson Senators	15.00	4.50
WM Willie McCovey Giants	15.00	4.50
WS Warren Spahn Braves	15.00	4.50
YA Carl Yastrzemski Red Sox	25.00	7.50

2004 Sweet Spot Classic Signatures Black

Randomly inserted in packs, these cards feature signatures from the noted personages in black ink. Several people including long-time Phillies announcer Harry Kalas and one time NL consecutive-games played leader Gus Suhr have their 1st certified autograph card in this set. Please note that several people did not return their cards in time for inclusion in pack out and those cards could be redeemed until January 27, 2004. Please note that for players with 25 or fewer signatures that no pricing is provided due to market scarcity.

Card	Nm-Mt	Ex-Mt
OVERALL AUTO ODDS 1:24		
PRINT RUNS B/WN 25-275 COPIES PER		
2 Preacher Roe/225	40.00	12.00
4 Bob Feller/65	80.00	24.00
5 Bob Gibson/50	80.00	24.00
6 Harry Kalas/100	60.00	18.00
7 Bobby Doerr/100	40.00	12.00
8 Cal Ripken/50	175.00	52.50
9 Carl Yastrzemski/35		
10 Carlton Fisk/100	60.00	18.00
11 Chuck Tanner/150	25.00	7.50
12 Cito Gaston/150	25.00	7.50
13 Danny Ozark/150	25.00	7.50
14 Dave Winfield/80	80.00	24.00
15 Davey Johnson/175	40.00	12.00
16 Ernie Harwell/100 EXCH	60.00	18.00
17 Dick Williams/150	25.00	7.50
18 Don Mattingly/40		
19 Don Newcombe/40	50.00	15.00
20 Duke Snider/35	80.00	24.00
21 Steve Carlton/150	60.00	18.00
22 Felipe Alou/175	25.00	7.50
23 Frank Robinson/65	80.00	24.00
24 Gary Carter/100	60.00	18.00
25 Gene Mauch/225	25.00	7.50
26 George Bamberger/225	25.00	7.50
28 Gus Suhr/100	40.00	12.00
30 Harmon Killebrew/50	100.00	30.00
31 Jack McKeon/225	40.00	12.00
32 Jim Bunning/100	60.00	18.00
33 Jimmy Piersall/212	40.00	12.00
35 Johnny Bench/50	100.00	30.00
36 Juan Marichal/50	50.00	15.00
37 Lou Brock/50 EXCH	80.00	24.00
38 George Kell/40	50.00	15.00
39 Maury Wills/40	50.00	15.00
41 Mike Schmidt/40 EXCH		
42 Nolan Ryan/50		
43 Ozzie Smith/65	100.00	30.00
44 Eddie Mayo/140	25.00	7.50
45 Phil Rizzuto/50	80.00	24.00
46 Ralph Kiner/40 EXCH	50.00	15.00
47 Lonny Frey/114	25.00	7.50
48 Bill Mazeroski/50	80.00	24.00
49 Robin Roberts/40	80.00	24.00
50 Robin Yount/40	100.00	30.00
52 Roger Craig/175	40.00	12.00
55 Tony Perez/40	50.00	15.00
56 Sparky Anderson/175	40.00	12.00
57 Stan Musial/40		
58 Ted Radcliffe/225	40.00	12.00
60 Tom Seaver/25		
61 Tony Gwynn/65		
62 Tony LaRussa/275	25.00	7.50
63 Tony Oliva/150	40.00	12.00
64 Tony Pena/150	25.00	7.50
66 Whitey Ford/45	80.00	24.00
67 Yogi Berra/65	100.00	30.00

2004 Sweet Spot Classic Signatures Black Holo-Foil

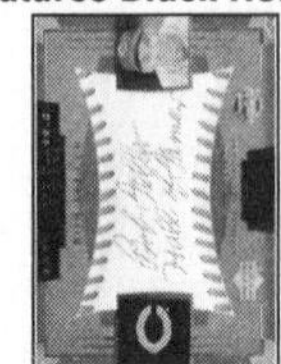

For those people who did not return their cards in time for inclusion in this product, those exchange cards could be returned until January 27, 2007.

Card	Nm-Mt	Ex-Mt
OVERALL AUTO ODDS 1:24		
PRINT RUNS B/WN 10-100 COPIES PER		
NO PRICING ON QTY OF 25 OR LESS.		
MOST CARDS FEATURE INSCRIPTIONS		
11 Chuck Tanner/100	25.00	7.50
12 Cito Gaston/100	25.00	7.50
13 Danny Ozark/100	25.00	7.50
15 Davey Johnson/50	50.00	15.00
17 Dick Williams/100	25.00	7.50
22 Felipe Alou/50	30.00	9.00
24 Gary Carter/50	80.00	24.00
52 Roger Craig/50	50.00	15.00
56 Sparky Anderson/50	50.00	15.00
62 Tony LaRussa/50	30.00	9.00

	Nm-Mt	Ex-Mt
63 Tony Oliva/100	40.00	12.00
64 Tony Pena/100	25.00	7.50

2004 Sweet Spot Classic Signatures Blue

A few people did not return their cards in time for inclusion in packs, those signed cards could be redeemed until January 27, 2004.

	Nm-Mt	Ex-Mt
OVERALL AUTO ODDS 1:24		
PRINT RUNS B/WN 15-150 COPIES PER		
NO PRICING ON QTY OF 25 OR LESS.		
2 Preacher Roe/150	40.00	12.00
4 Bob Feller/50	80.00	24.00
5 Bob Gibson/25		
6 Harry Kalas/50	80.00	24.00
7 Bobby Doerr/50	50.00	15.00
8 Cal Ripken/25		
9 Carl Yastrzemski/15		
10 Carlton Fisk/50	80.00	24.00
11 Chuck Tanner/125	25.00	7.50
12 Cito Gaston/125	25.00	7.50
13 Danny Ozark/125	25.00	7.50
14 Dave Winfield/35	80.00	24.00
15 Davey Johnson/150	40.00	12.00
16 Ernie Harwell/50 EXCH	80.00	24.00
17 Dick Williams/125	25.00	7.50
18 Don Mattingly/25		
19 Don Newcombe/25		
20 Duke Snider/25		
21 Steve Carlton/100	60.00	18.00
22 Felipe Alou/150	25.00	7.50
23 Frank Robinson/50	80.00	24.00
24 Gary Carter/75	80.00	24.00
25 Gene Mauch/150	25.00	7.50
26 George Bamberger/150	25.00	7.50
28 Gus Suhr/85	50.00	15.00
30 Harmon Killebrew/25		
31 Jack McKeon/150	40.00	12.00
32 Jim Bunning/65	80.00	24.00
33 Jimmy Piersall/150	40.00	12.00
35 Johnny Bench/20		
36 Juan Marichal/25		
37 Lou Brock/20 EXCH		
38 George Kell/25		
39 Maury Wills/25		
41 Mike Schmidt/25 EXCH		
42 Nolan Ryan/25		
43 Ozzie Smith/50	100.00	30.00
44 Eddie Mayo/50	30.00	9.00
45 Phil Rizzuto/25		
46 Ralph Kiner/25 EXCH		
47 Lonny Frey/75	30.00	9.00
48 Bill Mazeroski/25		
49 Robin Roberts/25		
50 Robin Yount/25		
52 Roger Craig/150	40.00	12.00
55 Tony Perez/25		
56 Sparky Anderson/150	40.00	12.00
57 Stan Musial/25		
58 Ted Radcliffe/150	40.00	12.00
60 Tom Seaver/15		
61 Tony Gwynn/25		
62 Tony LaRussa/145	25.00	7.50
63 Tony Oliva/125	40.00	12.00
64 Tony Pena/115	25.00	7.50
66 Whitey Ford/20		
67 Yogi Berra/50	100.00	30.00

2004 Sweet Spot Classic Signatures Red

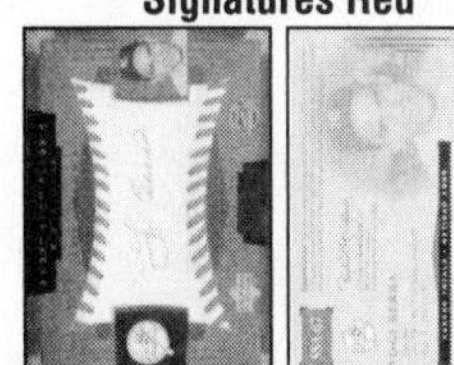

Ernie Harwell, Lou Brock, Mike Schmidt and Ralph Kiner did not return their cards in time for inclusion in packs. Redemption cards with an expiration date of January 27th, 2007 were seeded into packs for these aforementioned athletes. The Joe DiMaggio and Ted Williams cards from this set feature blue ink signed leather baseball patches (as averse to the red ink featured on the other cards). Representatives at Upper Deck have confirmed that they estimate approximately 25% of the Joe DiMaggio cards actually feature the added notation "Yankee Clipper".

	Nm-Mt	Ex-Mt
OVERALL AUTO ODDS 1:24		
PRINT RUNS B/WN 2-86 COPIES PER		
NO PRICING ON QTY OF 25 OR LESS.		
34 Joe DiMaggio/86	600.00	180.00

1948 Swell Sport Thrills

The cards in this 20-card set measure approximately 2 7/16" by 3". The 1948 Swell Gum Sports Thrills set of black and white, numbered cards highlights events from baseball history. The cards have picture framed borders with the title "Sports Thrills Highlights in the World of Sport" on the front. The backs of the cards give the story of the event pictured on the front. Cards numbered 9, 11, 16, and 20 are more difficult to obtain than the other cards in this set. The catalog designation is R448.

	NM	Ex
COMPLETE SET (20)	1000.00	500.00
1 Greatest Single Inning	35.00	17.50
Athletics' 10		
Run Rally		
2 Pete Reiser	25.00	12.50
Amazing Record		
Debut With Dodgers		
3 Jackie Robinson	150.00	75.00
Dramatic Debut ROY		
4 Walter Johnson	60.00	30.00
Greatest Pitcher of		
Them All		
5 Tommy Henrich	25.00	12.50
Mickey Owen		
Three Strikes Not Out:		
Lost Third Strike		
Changes Tide of 1941		
World Series		
6 Bill Dickey	40.00	20.00
Last Home Run		
Wins Series		
7 Hal Schumacher	25.00	12.50
Never Say Die Pitcher		
8 Carl Hubbell	40.00	20.00
Five Strikeouts		
Nationals Lose		
All-Star Game		
9 Al Gionfriddo	30.00	15.00
Greatest Catch		
10 Johnny VanderMeer	30.00	15.00
No Hits No Runs		
11 Tony Lazzeri	40.00	20.00
Bob O'Farrell		
Bases Loaded		
Grover C. Alexander's pitching described on back		
12 Babe Ruth	200.00	100.00
Crossing the Plate		
Most Dramatic Homer		
13 Tommy Bridges	25.00	12.50
Goose Goslin		
Mickey Cochrane		
Winning Run: 1935 World Series		
14 Lou Gehrig	120.00	60.00
Four Homers		
15 Jim Bagby Jr.	35.00	17.50
Al Smith		
Four Men To Stop Him		
Joe DiMaggio's Bat Streak		
16 Ted Williams	200.00	100.00
Three Run Homer in		
Ninth		
17 Johnny Lindell	25.00	12.50
Whitey Kurowski		
Football Block		
Paves Way For		
Yank's Series Victory		
18 Pee Wee Reese	40.00	20.00
Home Run To Fame		
Grand Slam		
19 Bob Feller	40.00	20.00
Strikeout Record		
Whiffs Five		
20 Carl Furillo	35.00	17.50
Rifle Arm		

1989 Swell Baseball Greats

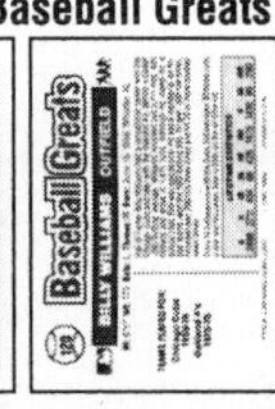

The 1989 Swell Baseball Greats set contains 135 standard-size cards. The fronts have vintage color photos with beige, red and white borders. The horizontally oriented backs are white and scarlet, and feature career highlights and lifetime stats. The set was produced by Philadelphia Chewing Gum Corporation.

	Nm-Mt	Ex-Mt
COMPLETE SET (135)	12.00	4.80
1 Babe Ruth	2.50	1.00
2 Ty Cobb	2.00	.80
3 Walter Johnson	.50	.20
4 Honus Wagner	.50	.20
5 Cy Young	.50	.20
6 Joe Adcock	.05	.02
7 Jim Bunning	.25	.10
8 Orlando Cepeda	.15	.06
9 Harvey Kuenn	.15	.06
10 Jim Hunter	.25	.10
11 Johnny VanderMeer	.10	.04
12 Tony Oliva	.15	.06
13 Harvey Haddix UER	.05	.02
(Reverse negative)		
14 Dick McAuliffe	.05	.02
15 Lefty Grove	.25	.10
16 Bo Belinsky	.10	.04
17 Claude Osteen	.05	.02
18 Doc Medich	.05	.02
19 Del Ennis	.05	.02
20 Rogers Hornsby	.50	.20
21 Bob Buhl	.05	.02
22 Phil Niekro	.25	.10
23 Don Zimmer	.05	.02
24 Greg Luzinski	.10	.04
25 Lou Gehrig	2.00	.80
26 Ken Singleton	.05	.02
27 Bob Allison	.05	.02
28 Ed Kranepool	.05	.02
29 Manny Sanguillen	.05	.02
30 Luke Appling	.25	.10
31 Ralph Terry	.05	.02
32 Smoky Burgess	.05	.02
33 Gil Hodges	.25	.10
34 Harry Walker	.05	.02
35 Edd Roush	.25	.10
36 Ron Santo	.15	.06
37 Jim Perry	.05	.02
38 Jose Morales	.05	.02
39 Stan Bahnsen	.05	.02
40 Al Kaline	.50	.20
41 Mel Harder	.05	.02
42 Ralph Houk	.05	.02
43 Jack Billingham	.05	.02
44 Carl Erskine	.10	.04
45 Hoyt Wilhelm	.25	.10
46 Dick Radatz	.05	.02
47 Roy Sievers	.05	.02
48 Jim Lonborg	.05	.02
49 Bobby Richardson	.10	.04
50 Whitey Ford	.50	.20
51 Roy Face	.05	.02
52 Tom Tresh	.05	.02
53 Joe Nuxhall	.05	.02
54 Mickey Vernon	.05	.02
55 Johnny Mize	.25	.10
56 Scott McGregor	.05	.02
57 Billy Pierce	.10	.04
58 Dave Giusti	.05	.02
59 Minnie Minoso	.15	.06
60 Early Wynn	.25	.10
61 Jose Cardenal	.05	.02
62 Sam Jethroe	.10	.04
63 Sal Bando	.05	.02
64 Elrod Hendricks	.05	.02
65 Enos Slaughter	.25	.10
66 Jim Bouton	.10	.04
67 Bill Mazeroski	.15	.06
68 Tony Kubek	.10	.04
69 Joe Black	.05	.02
70 Harmon Killebrew	.25	.10
71 Sam McDowell	.05	.02
72 Bucky Dent	.05	.02
73 Virgil Trucks	.05	.02
74 Andy Pafko	.05	.02
75 Bob Feller	.50	.20
76 Tito Francona	.05	.02
77 Al Dark	.05	.02
78 Larry Dierker	.10	.04
79 Nellie Briles	.05	.02
80 Lou Boudreau	.25	.10
81 Wally Moon	.05	.02
82 Hank Bauer	.10	.04
83 Jim Piersall	.10	.04
84 Jim Grant	.05	.02
85 Richie Ashburn	.25	.10
86 Bob Friend	.05	.02
87 Ken Keltner	.05	.02
88 Jim Kaat	.10	.04
89 Dean Chance	.05	.02
90 Al Lopez	.25	.10
91 Dick Groat	.10	.04
92 Johnny Blanchard	.05	.02
93 Chuck Hinton	.05	.02
94 Clete Boyer	.10	.04
95 Steve Carlton	.50	.20
96 Tug McGraw	.10	.04
97 Mickey Lolich	.10	.04
98 Earl Weaver MG	.25	.10
99 Sal Maglie	.05	.02
100 Ted Williams	2.00	.80
101 Allie Reynolds UER	.10	.04
(Photo actually		
Marius Russo)		
102 Gene Woodling UER	.05	.02
(Photo actually		
Irv Noren)		
103 Moe Drabowsky	.05	.02
104 Mickey Stanley	.05	.02
105 Jim Palmer	.50	.20
106 Bill Freehan	.10	.04
107 Bob Robertson	.05	.02
108 Walt Dropo	.05	.02
109 Jerry Koosman	.10	.04
110 Bobby Doerr	.25	.10
111 Phil Rizzuto	.50	.20
112 Don Kessinger	.05	.02
113 Milt Pappas	.05	.02
114 Herb Score	.10	.04
115 Larry Doby	.25	.10
116 Glenn Beckert	.05	.02
117 Andre Thornton	.05	.02
118 Gary Matthews	.05	.02
119 Bill Virdon	.05	.02
120 Billy Williams	.25	.10
121 Johnny Sain	.05	.02
122 Don Newcombe	.10	.04
123 Rico Petrocelli	.10	.04
124 Dick Bosman	.05	.02
125 Roberto Clemente	2.00	.80
126 Rocky Colavito	.15	.06
127 Wilbur Wood	.05	.02
128 Duke Sims	.05	.02
129 Ken Holtzman	.05	.02
130 Casey Stengel	.25	.10
131 Bobby Shantz	.05	.02
132 Del Crandall	.05	.02
133 Bobby Thomson	.10	.04
134 Brooks Robinson	.50	.20
135 Checklist Card	.05	.02

1990 Swell Baseball Greats

The 1990 Swell Baseball Greats set is a standard-size 135-card set. The words Baseball Greats is boldly proclaimed on the top of the card. This set was issued by Swell in both complete set form and in 10-card wax packs.

	Nm-Mt	Ex-Mt
COMPLETE SET (135)	12.00	3.60
1 Tom Seaver	.50	.15
2 Hank Aaron	2.00	.60
3 Mickey Cochrane	.25	.07
4 Rod Carew	.50	.15
5 Carl Yastrzemski	.50	.15
6 Dizzy Dean	.50	.15
7 Sal Bando	.05	.02
8 Whitey Ford	.50	.15
9 Bill White	.10	.03
10 Babe Ruth	2.50	.75
11 Robin Roberts	.25	.07
12 Warren Spahn	.25	.07
13 Billy Williams	.25	.07
14 Joe Garagiola	.10	.03
15 Ty Cobb	2.00	.60
16 Boog Powell	.15	.04
17 Tom Tresh	.05	.02
18 Luke Appling	.25	.07
19 Tommie Agee	.05	.02
20 Roberto Clemente	2.00	.60
21 Bobby Thomson	.10	.03
22 Charlie Keller	.05	.02
23 George Bamberger	.05	.02
24 Eddie Lopat	.10	.03
25 Lou Gehrig	2.00	.60
26 Manny Mota	.05	.02
27 Steve Stone	.05	.02
28 Orlando Cepeda	.15	.04
29 Al Bumbry	.05	.02
30 Grover Alexander	.25	.07
31 Lou Boudreau	.25	.07
32 Herb Score	.10	.03
33 Harry Walker	.05	.02
34 Deron Johnson	.05	.02
35 Edd Roush	.25	.07
36 Carl Erskine	.10	.03
37 Ken Forsch	.05	.02
38 Sal Maglie	.05	.02
39 Al Rosen	.10	.03
40 Casey Stengel	.25	.07
41 Cesar Cedeno	.05	.02
42 Roy White	.05	.02
43 Larry Doby	.25	.07
44 Rod Kanehl	.05	.02
45 Tris Speaker	.25	.07
46 Ralph Garr	.05	.02
47 Andre Thornton	.05	.02
48 Frankie Crosetti	.10	.03
49 Dick Groat	.10	.03
50 Honus Wagner	.50	.15
51 Rogers Hornsby	.50	.15
52 Ken Brett	.05	.02
53 Lenny Randle	.05	.02
54 Enos Slaughter	.25	.07
55 Mel Ott	.25	.07
56 Rico Petrocelli	.10	.03
57 Walt Dropo	.05	.02
58 Bob Grich	.05	.02
59 Billy Herman	.25	.07
60 Bob Feller	.50	.15
61 Davey Johnson	.10	.03
62 Don Drysdale	.25	.07
63 Lary Sorensen	.05	.02
64 Ron Santo	.15	.04
65 Eddie Mathews	.25	.07
66 Gaylord Perry	.25	.07
67 Lee May	.05	.02
68 Johnnie LeMaster	.05	.02
69 Don Kessinger	.05	.02
70 Lefty Grove	.25	.07
71 Lou Brock	.25	.07
72 Don Cardwell	.05	.02
73 Harvey Haddix	.05	.02
74 Frank Torre	.05	.02
75 Walter Johnson	.50	.15
76 Don Newcombe	.10	.03
77 Marv Throneberry	.10	.03
78 Jim Northrup	.05	.02
79 Fritz Peterson	.05	.02
80 Ralph Kiner	.25	.07
81 Mickey Lolich	.10	.03
82 Donn Clendenon	.05	.02
83 Pete Vuckovich	.05	.02
84 Lefty Gomez	.25	.07
85 Monte Irvin	.25	.07
86 Rick Ferrell	.25	.07
87 Tommy Hutton	.05	.02
88 Julio Cruz	.05	.02
89 Vida Blue	.10	.03
90 Johnny Mize	.25	.07
91 Rusty Staub	.10	.03
92 Jimmy Piersall	.10	.03
93 Bill Mazeroski	.15	.04
94 Lee Lacy	.05	.02
95 Ernie Banks	.50	.15
96 Bobby Doerr	.25	.07
97 George Foster	.10	.03
98 Eric Soderholm	.05	.02
99 Johnny Vander Meer	.10	.03
100 Cy Young	.50	.15
101 Jimmie Foxx	.50	.15
102 Clete Boyer	.10	.03
103 Steve Garvey	.15	.04
104 Johnny Podres	.10	.03
105 Yogi Berra	.50	.15
106 Bill Monbouquette	.05	.02
107 Milt Pappas	.05	.02
108 Dave LaRoche	.05	.02
109 Elliott Maddox	.05	.02
110 Steve Carlton	.50	.15
111 Bud Harrelson	.05	.02
112 Mark Littell	.05	.02
113 Frank Thomas	.05	.02
114 Bill Robinson	.05	.02
115 Satchel Paige	1.25	.35
116 John Denny	.05	.02
117 Clyde King	.05	.02
118 Billy Sample	.05	.02
119 Rocky Colavito	.15	.04
120 Bob Gibson	.50	.15
121 Bert Campaneris	.10	.03
122 Mark Fidrych	.15	.04
123 Ed Charles	.05	.02
124 Jim Lonborg	.05	.02
125 Ted Williams	2.00	.60
126 Manny Sanguillen	.05	.02
127 Matt Keough	.05	.02
128 Vern Ruhle	.05	.02
129 Bob Skinner	.05	.02
130 Joe Torre	.15	.04
131 Ralph Houk	.05	.02
132 Gil Hodges	.25	.07
133 Ralph Branca	.10	.03
134 Christy Mathewson	.50	.15
135 Checklist Card	.05	.02

1991 Swell Baseball Greats

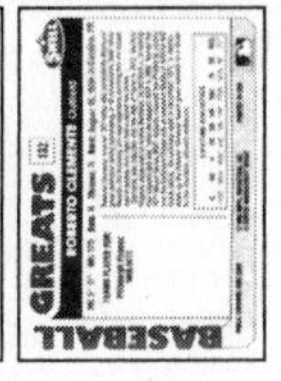

This set marks the third year Philadelphia Chewing Gum (using the Swell trade name) issued a set honoring retired players. The front of the cards feature yellow and red borders framing the full-color photo of the player(where full color was available) The cards were issued with cooperation from Impel Marketing. This 150-card standard-size set is sequenced in alphabetical orders within several seperate categories.

	Nm-Mt	Ex-Mt
COMPLETE SET (150)	12.00	3.60
1 Tommie Agee	.05	.02
2 Matty Alou	.05	.02
3 Luke Appling	.25	.07
4 Richie Ashburn	.25	.07
5 Ernie Banks	.50	.15
6 Don Baylor	.15	.04
7 Buddy Bell	.10	.03
8 Yogi Berra	.50	.15
9 Joe Black	.10	.03
10 Vida Blue	.10	.03
11 Bobby Bonds	.10	.03
12 Lou Boudreau	.25	.07
13 Lou Brock	.25	.07
14 Ralph Branca	.10	.03
15 Bobby Brown	.10	.03
16 Lou Burdette	.10	.03
17 Steve Carlton	.50	.15
18 Rico Carty	.10	.03
19 Jerry Coleman	.10	.03
20 Frankie Crosetti	.10	.03
21 Julio Cruz	.05	.02
22 Alvin Dark	.10	.03
23 Doug DeCinces	.05	.02
24 Larry Doby	.25	.07
25 Bobby Doerr	.25	.07
26 Don Drysdale	.25	.07
27 Carl Erskine	.10	.03
28 Roy Face	.05	.02
29 Rick Ferrell	.25	.07
30 Rollie Fingers	.25	.07
31 Joe Garagiola	.10	.03
32 Steve Garvey	.15	.04
33 Bob Gibson	.50	.15
34 Mudcat Grant	.05	.02
35 Dick Groat	.10	.03
36 Jerry Grote	.05	.02
37 Toby Harrah	.05	.02
38 Bud Harrelson	.05	.02
39 Billy Herman	.25	.07
40 Ken Holtzman	.05	.02
41 Willie Horton	.05	.02
42 Ralph Houk	.05	.02
43 Al Hrabosky	.05	.02
44 Monte Irvin	.25	.07
45 Fergie Jenkins	.25	.07
46 Davey Johnson	.05	.02
47 George Kell	.25	.07
48 Charlie Keller	.05	.02
49 Harmon Killebrew	.25	.07
50 Ralph Kiner	.25	.07
51 Clyde King	.05	.02
52 Dave Kingman	.10	.03
53 Al Kaline	.50	.15
54 Clem Labine	.05	.02
55 Vern Law	.05	.02
56 Mickey Lolich	.10	.03
57 Jim Lonborg	.05	.02
58 Eddie Lopat	.10	.03
59 Sal Maglie	.05	.02
60 Bill Mazeroski	.15	.04
61 Johnny VanderMeer	.10	.03
62 Johnny Mize	.25	.07
63 Manny Mota	.05	.02
64 Wally Moon	.05	.02
65 Rick Monday	.05	.02
66 Tom Tresh	.05	.02
67 Graig Nettles	.15	.04
68 Don Newcombe	.10	.03
69 Milt Pappas	.05	.02
70 Gaylord Perry	.25	.07
71 Rico Petrocelli	.10	.03
72 Jimmy Piersall	.10	.03
73 Johnny Podres	.10	.03
74 Boog Powell	.15	.04
75 Bobby Richardson	.10	.03
76 Vern Ruhle	.05	.02
77 Robin Roberts	.25	.07
78 Al Rosen	.10	.03
79 Billy Sample	.05	.02
80 Manny Sanguillen	.05	.02
81 Ron Santo	.15	.04
82 Herb Score	.10	.03
83 Bobby Shantz	.05	.02
84 Enos Slaughter	.25	.07
85 Eric Soderholm	.05	.02
86 Warren Spahn	.25	.07
87 Rusty Staub	.10	.03
88 Bobby Thomson	.10	.03
89 Marv Throneberry	.10	.03
90 Luis Tiant	.10	.03
91 Frank Torre	.05	.02
92 Joe Torre	.15	.04
93 Bill Virdon	.05	.02
94 Harry Walker MG	.05	.02

95 Earl Weaver .25 .07
96 Bill White .10 .03
97 Roy White .05 .02
98 Billy Williams .25 .07
99 Dick Williams .05 .02
100 Ted Williams 2.00 .60
101 Gene Woodling .05 .02
102 Hank Aaron 2.00 .60
103 Rod Carew .50 .15
104 Cesar Cedeno .05 .02
105 Orlando Cepeda .15 .04
106 Willie Mays 2.00 .60
107 Tom Seaver .50 .15
108 Carl Yastrzemski .50 .15
109 Clete Boyer .10 .03
110 Bert Campaneris .10 .03
111 Walt Dropo .05 .02
112 George Foster .10 .03
113 Phil Garner .05 .02
114 Harvey Haddix
115 Don Kessinger .05 .02
116 Rocky Colavito .15 .04
117 Bobby Murcer .10 .03
118 Mel Parnell .05 .02
119 Ken Reitz .05 .02
120 Earl Wilson .05 .02
121 Wilbur Wood .05 .02
122 Ed Yost .05 .02
123 Jim Bouton .10 .03
124 Babe Ruth 2.50 .75
125 Lou Gehrig 2.00 .60
126 Honus Wagner .50 .15
127 Ty Cobb 2.00 .60
128 Grover C. Alexander .50 .15
129 Lefty Gomez .25 .07
130 Walter Johnson .50 .15
131 Gil Hodges .25 .07
132 Roberto Clemente 2.00 .60
133 Satchel Paige 1.25 .35
134 Edd Roush .25 .07
135 Cy Young .50 .15
136 Casey Stengel .25 .07
137 Rogers Hornsby .50 .15
138 Dizzy Dean .50 .15
139 Lefty Grove .25 .07
140 Tris Speaker .25 .07
141 Christy Mathewson .50 .15
142 Mickey Cochrane .25 .07
143 Jimmie Foxx .50 .15
144 Mel Ott .25 .07
145 Bob Feller .50 .15
146 Brooks Robinson .50 .15
147 Eddie Mathews .25 .07
148 Pie Traynor .25 .07
149 Thurman Munson .15 .04
150 Checklist Card .05 .02

1957 Swifts Franks

The cards in this 18-card set measure approximately 3 1/2" by 4". These full color, numbered cards issued in 1957 by the Swift Company are die-cut and have rounded corners. Each card consists of several pieces which can be punched out and assembled to form a stand-up model of the player. The cards and a game board were available directly from the company. The company-direct set consisted of three panels each containing six cards; sets found in this "uncut~ state carry a value 25 percent higher than the values listed below. The catalog designation for this set is F162. Rocky Colavito appears in his Rookie Card year.

NM Ex
COMPLETE SET (18) 1200.00 600.00
1 John Podres 50.00 25.00
2 Gus Triandos 40.00 20.00
3 Dale Long 40.00 20.00
4 Billy Pierce 50.00 25.00
5 Ed Bailey 40.00 20.00
6 Vic Wertz 40.00 20.00
7 Nelson Fox 40.00 20.00
8 Ken Boyer 60.00 30.00
9 Gil McDougald 50.00 25.00
10 Junior Gilliam 50.00 25.00
11 Eddie Yost 40.00 20.00
12 Johnny Logan 40.00 20.00
13 Hank Aaron 300.00 150.00
14 Bill Tuttle 40.00 20.00
15 Jackie Jensen 60.00 30.00
16 Frank Robinson 200.00 100.00
17 Richie Ashburn 120.00 60.00
18 Rocky Colavito 80.00 40.00

1988 T/M Umpires

This set of 64 standard-size color cards was distributed as a small boxed set featuring Major League umpires exclusively. The box itself is blank, white, and silver. The set was produced by T and M Sports under licenses from Major League Baseball and the Major League Umpires Association. Card backs are printed in black on light blue. All the cards are black bordered, but the American Leaguers have a red thin inner border, whereas the National Leaguers have a green thin inner border. A short biographical sketch is given on the back for each umpire. The cards are numbered on the back; the number on the front of each card refers to the umpire's uniform number.

Nm-Mt Ex-Mt
COMP. FACT SET (64) 10.00 4.00
1 Doug Harvey .60 .24
2 Lee Weyer .25 .10
3 Billy Williams .25 .10
4 John Kibler .25 .10
5 Bob Engel .60 .24
6 Harry Wendelstedt .40 .16
7 Larry Barnett .25 .10
8 Don Denkinger .40 .16
9 Dave Phillips .40 .16
10 Larry McCoy .25 .10
11 Bruce Froemming .40 .16
12 John McSherry .75 .30
13 Jim Evans .25 .10
14 Frank Pulli .25 .10
15 Joe Brinkman .25 .10
16 Terry Tata .25 .10
17 Paul Runge .25 .10
18 Dutch Rennert .25 .10
19 Nick Bremigan .25 .10
20 Jim McKean .25 .10
21 Terry Cooney .25 .10
22 Rich Garcia .25 .10
23 Dale Ford .25 .10
24 Al Clark .25 .10
25 Greg Kosc .25 .10
26 Jim Quick .25 .10
27 Eddie Montague .25 .10
28 Jerry Crawford .25 .10
29 Steve Palermo .75 .30
30 Durwood Merrill .25 .10
31 Ken Kaiser .40 .16
32 Vic Voltaggio .25 .10
33 Mike Reilly .25 .10
34 Eric Gregg .60 .24
35 Ted Hendry .25 .10
36 Joe West .25 .10
37 Dave Pallone .40 .16
38 Fred Brocklander .25 .10
39 John Shulock .25 .10
40 Derryl Cousins .25 .10
41 Charlie Williams .25 .10
42 Rocky Roe .25 .10
43 Randy Marsh .25 .10
44 Bob Davidson .25 .10
45 Drew Coble .25 .10
46 Tim McClelland .25 .10
47 Dan Morrison .25 .10
48 Rick Reed .25 .10
49 Steve Rippley .25 .10
50 John Hirschbeck .60 .24
51 Mark Johnson .25 .10
52 Gerry Davis .25 .10
53 Dana DeMuth .25 .10
54 Larry Young .25 .10
55 Tim Welke .25 .10
56 Greg Bonin .25 .10
57 Tom Hallion .25 .10
58 Dale Scott .25 .10
59 Tim Tschida .25 .10
60 Dick Stello MEM .25 .10
61 All-Star Game .25 .10
62 World Series .25 .10
63 Jocko Conlan HOF .75 .30
64 Checklist Card .25 .10

1989 T/M Umpires

The 1989 Umpires set contains 63 standard-size cards. The fronts have borderless color photos with AL or NL logos. The backs are grey and include biographical information. The cards were distributed as a boxed set along with a custom album.

Nm-Mt Ex-Mt
COMP. FACT SET (63) 8.00 3.20
1 Doug Harvey .60 .24
2 John Kibler .25 .10
3 Bob Engel .60 .24
4 Harry Wendelstedt .40 .16
5 Larry Barnett .25 .10
6 Don Denkinger .40 .16
7 Dave Phillips .40 .16
8 Larry McCoy .25 .10
9 Bruce Froemming .40 .16
10 John McSherry .75 .30
11 Jim Evans .25 .10
12 Frank Pulli .25 .10
13 Joe Brinkman .25 .10
14 Terry Tata .25 .10
15 Nick Bremigan .25 .10
16 Jim McKean .25 .10
17 Paul Runge .25 .10
18 Dutch Rennert .25 .10
19 Terry Cooney .25 .10
20 Rich Garcia .25 .10
21 Dale Ford .25 .10
22 Al Clark .25 .10
23 Greg Kosc .25 .10
24 Jim Quick .25 .10
25 Eddie Montague .25 .10
26 Jerry Crawford .25 .10
27 Steve Palermo .75 .30
28 Durwood Merrill .25 .10
29 Ken Kaiser .40 .16
30 Vic Voltaggio .25 .10
31 Mike Reilly .25 .10
32 Eric Gregg .60 .24
33 Ted Hendry .25 .10
34 Joe West .25 .10
35 Dave Pallone .40 .16
36 Fred Brocklander .25 .10
37 John Shulock .25 .10
38 Derryl Cousins .25 .10
39 Charlie Williams .25 .10
40 Rocky Roe .25 .10
41 Randy Marsh .25 .10
42 Bob Davidson .25 .10
43 Drew Coble .25 .10
44 Tim McClelland .25 .10
45 Dan Morrison .25 .10
46 Rick Reed .25 .10
47 Steve Rippley .25 .10
48 John Hirschbeck .60 .24
49 Mark Johnson .25 .10
50 Gerry Davis .25 .10
51 Dana DeMuth .25 .10
52 Larry Young .25 .10
53 Tim Welke .25 .10
54 Greg Bonin .25 .10
55 Tom Hallion .25 .10
56 Dale Scott .25 .10
57 Tim Tschida .25 .10
58 Gary Darling .25 .10
59 Mark Hirschbeck .25 .10
60 Randy Marsh .25 .10
Terry Tata
Frank Pulli
Dan Morrison
Dale Ford
Larry Barnett
61 World Series .25 .10
62 Lee Weyer .25 .10
63 Tommy Connolly and .75 .30
Bill Klem

1989-90 T/M Senior League

The 1989-90 T/M Senior League set contains 120 standard-size cards depicting members of the Senior League. The fronts are borderless, with full color photos and black bands at the bottom with player names and positions. The vertically oriented backs are gray and red, and show career major league totals and highlights. The cards were distributed as a boxed set with a checklist card and eight card-sized puzzle pieces. The set ordering is essentially alphabetical according to the player's name.

NRMT-MT NM
COMP. FACT SET (121) 10.00 4.50
1 Curt Flood COMM .25 .11
2 Willie Aikens .05 .02
3 Gary Allenson .05 .02
4 Stan Bahnsen .05 .02
5 Alan Bannister .05 .02
6 Juan Beniquez .05 .02
7 Jim Bibby .05 .02
8 Paul Blair .05 .02
9 Vida Blue .10 .05
10 Bobby Bonds .25 .11
11 Pedro Borbon .05 .02
12 Clete Boyer .10 .05
13 Gates Brown .05 .02
14 Al Bumbry .05 .02
15 Sal Butera .05 .02
16 Bert Campaneris .10 .05
17 Bill Campbell .05 .02
18 Bernie Carbo .05 .02
19 Dave Cash .05 .02
20 Cesar Cedeno .10 .05
21 Gene Clines .05 .02
22 Dave Collins .05 .02
23 Cecil Cooper .10 .05
24 Doug Corbett .05 .02
25 Al Cowens .05 .02
26 Jose Cruz .10 .05
27 Mike Cuellar .10 .05
28 Pat Dobson .05 .02
29 Dick Drago .05 .02
30 Dan Driessen .05 .02
31 Jamie Easterly .05 .02
32 Juan Eichelberger .05 .02
33 Dock Ellis .05 .02
34 Ed Figueroa .05 .02
35 Rollie Fingers .50 .23
36 George Foster .25 .11
37 Oscar Gamble .10 .05
38 Wayne Garland .05 .02
39 Wayne Garrett .05 .02
40 Ross Grimsley .05 .02
41 Jerry Grote .10 .05
42 Johnny Grubb .05 .02
43 Mario Guerrero .05 .02
44 Toby Harrah .10 .05
45 Steve Henderson .05 .02
46 George Hendrick .10 .05
47 Butch Hobson .05 .02
48 Roy Howell .05 .02
49 Al Hrabosky .10 .05
50 Clint Hurdle .10 .05
51 Garth Iorg .05 .02
52 Tim Ireland .05 .02
53 Grant Jackson .05 .02
54 Ron Jackson .05 .02
55 Ferguson Jenkins .50 .23
56 Odell Jones .05 .02
57 Mike Kekich .05 .02
58 Steve Kemp .05 .02
59 Dave Kingman .25 .11
60 Bruce Kison .05 .02
61 Lee Lacy .05 .02
62 Rafael Landestoy .05 .02
63 Ken Landreaux .05 .02
64 Tito Landrum .05 .02
65 Dave LaRoche .05 .02
66 Bill Lee .10 .05
67 Ron LeFlore .10 .05
68 Dennis Leonard .05 .02
69 Bill Madlock .15 .07
70 Mickey Mahler .05 .02
71 Rich Manning .05 .02
72 Tippy Martinez .05 .02
73 Jon Matlack .05 .02
74 Bake McBride .05 .02
75 Steve McCatty .05 .02
76 Hal McRae .10 .05
77 Dan Meyer .05 .02
78 Felix Millan .05 .02
79 Paul Mirabella .05 .02
80 Omar Moreno .05 .02
81 Jim Morrison .05 .02
82 Graig Nettles .15 .07
83 Al Oliver .15 .07
84 Amos Otis .10 .05
85 Tom Paciorek .05 .02
86 Lowell Palmer .05 .02
87 Pat Putnam .05 .02
88 Lenny Randle .05 .02
89 Ken Reitz .05 .02
90 Gene Richards .05 .02
91 Mickey Rivers .10 .05
92 Leon Roberts .05 .02
93 Joe Sambito .05 .02
94 Rodney Scott .05 .02
95 Bob Shirley .05 .02
96 Jim Slaton .05 .02
97 Elias Sosa .05 .02
98 Fred Stanley .05 .02
99 Bill Stein .05 .02
100 Rennie Stennett .05 .02
101 Sammy Stewart .05 .02
102 Tim Stoddard .05 .02
103 Champ Summers .05 .02
104 Derrel Thomas .05 .02
105 Luis Tiant .15 .07
106 Bobby Tolan MG .05 .02
107 Bill Travers .05 .02
108 Tom Underwood .05 .02
109 Rick Waits .05 .02
110 Ron Washington .05 .02
111 U.L. Washington .05 .02
112 Earl Weaver MG .50 .23
113 Jerry White .05 .02
114 Milt Wilcox .05 .02
115 Dick Williams MG .10 .05
116 Walt Williams .05 .02
117 Rick Wise .05 .02
118 Luis Tiant .10 .05
Cesar Cedeno
119 George Foster .25 .11
Bobby Bonds
120 Earl Weaver MG .15 .07
Dick Williams MG
NNO Checklist 1-120 .05 .02

1990 T/M Umpires

The 1990 T/M Umpires set is a standard-size set which features a picture of each umpire on the front of the card with a baseball rules question on the back of the card. The set was issued as a boxed set as well as in packs.

Nm-Mt Ex-Mt
COMP. FACT SET (70) 8.00 2.40
1 Doug Harvey .40 .12
2 John Kibler .20 .06
3 Bob Engel .40 .12
4 Harry Wendelstedt .30 .09
5 Larry Barnett .20 .06
6 Don Denkinger .30 .09
7 Dave Phillips .30 .09
8 Larry McCoy .20 .06
9 Bruce Froemming .30 .09
10 John McSherry .50 .15
11 Jim Evans .20 .06
12 Frank Pulli .20 .06
13 Joe Brinkman .20 .06
14 Terry Tata .20 .06
15 Jim McKean .20 .06
16 Dutch Rennert .20 .06
17 Paul Runge .20 .06
18 Terry Cooney .20 .06
19 Rich Garcia .20 .06
20 Dale Ford .20 .06
21 Al Clark .20 .06
22 Greg Kosc .20 .06
23 Jim Quick .20 .06
24 Eddie Montague .20 .06
25 Jerry Crawford .20 .06
26 Steve Palermo .50 .15
27 Durwood Merrill .20 .06
28 Ken Kaiser .30 .09
29 Vic Voltaggio .20 .06
30 Mike Reilly .20 .06
31 Eric Gregg .40 .12
32 Ted Hendry .20 .06
33 Joe West .20 .06
34 Fred Brocklander .20 .06
35 John Shulock .20 .06
36 Derryl Cousins .20 .06
37 Charlie Williams .20 .06
38 Rocky Roe .20 .06
39 Randy Marsh .20 .06
40 Bob Davidson .20 .06
41 Drew Coble .20 .06
42 Tim McClelland .20 .06
43 Dan Morrison .20 .06
44 Rick Reed .20 .06
45 Steve Rippley .20 .06
46 John Hirschbeck .40 .12
47 Mark Johnson .20 .06
48 Gerry Davis .20 .06
49 Dana DeMuth .20 .06
50 Larry Young .20 .06
51 Tim Welke .20 .06
52 Greg Bonin .20 .06
53 Tom Hallion .20 .06
54 Dale Scott .20 .06
55 Tim Tschida .20 .06
56 Gary Darling .20 .06
57 Mark Hirschbeck .20 .06
58 Jerry Layne .20 .06
59 Jim Joyce .20 .06
60 Bill Hohn .20 .06
61 All-Star Game .20 .06
62 World Series .20 .06
63 Nick Bremigan .20 .06
64 Ed Runge .30 .09
Paul Runge
The Runges
65 Bart Giamatti MEM .50 .15
66 Puzzle Piece 1 .20 .06
67 Puzzle Piece 2 .20 .06
68 Puzzle Piece 3 .20 .06
69 Puzzle Piece 4 .20 .06
70 Checklist Card .20 .06
71 Al Barlick HOF .50 .15

1911 T205 Gold Border

The cards in this 218-card set measure approximately 1 1/2" by 2 5/8". The T205 set (catalog designation), also known as the "Gold Border" set, was issued in 1911 in packages of the following cigarette brands: American Beauty, Broadleaf, Cycle, Drum, Hassan, Honest Long Cut, Piedmont, Polar Bear, Sovereign and Sweet Caporal. All the above were products of the American Tobacco Company, and the ads for the various brands appear below the biographical section on the back of each card. There are pose variations noted in the checklist (which is alphabetized and numbered for reference) and there are 12 minor league cards of a more ornate design which are somewhat scarce. The numbers below correspond to alphabetical order within category, i.e., major leaguers and minor leaguers are alphabetized separately. The gold borders of T205 cards chip easily and they are hard to find in "Mint" or even "Near Mint" condition, due to this there is a high premium on these high condition cards.

Ex-Mt VG
COMPLETE SET (218) 35000.00 17500.00
COMMON (1-186) 100.00 50.00
COMMON (187-198) 200.00 100.00
1 Ed Abbaticchio 100.00 50.00
2 Red Ames 100.00 50.00
3 Jimmy Archer 100.00 50.00
4 Jimmy Austin 100.00 50.00
5 Bill Bailey 100.00 50.00
6 Frank "Homerun" Baker 400.00 200.00
7 Neal Ball 100.00 50.00
8A Cy Barger 100.00 50.00
(Full B)
8B Cy Barger 300.00 150.00
Part B
9 Jack Barry 100.00 50.00
10 Johnny Bates 100.00 50.00
11 Fred Beck 100.00 50.00
12 Beals Becker 100.00 50.00
13 George Bell 100.00 50.00
14 Chief Bender 250.00 125.00
15 Bill Bergen 100.00 50.00
16 Bob Bescher 100.00 50.00
17 Joe Birmingham 100.00 50.00
18 Russ Blackburne 100.00 50.00
19 Kitty Bransfield 100.00 50.00
20A Roger Bresnahan 250.00 125.00
(Mouth closed)
20B Roger Bresnahan 400.00 200.00
(Mouth open)
21 Al Bridwell 100.00 50.00
22 Mordecai Brown 400.00 200.00
23 Bobby Byrne 100.00 50.00
24 Howie Camnitz 100.00 50.00
25 Bill Carrigan 100.00 50.00
26 Frank Chance 300.00 150.00
27A Hal Chase 300.00 150.00
(Chase only)
27B Hal Chase 150.00 75.00
(Hal Chase)
28 Eddie Cicotte 200.00 100.00
29 Fred Clarke 400.00 200.00
30 Ty Cobb 5000.00 2500.00
31A Edward T. Collins 300.00 150.00
(Mouth closed)
31B Edward T. Collins 500.00 250.00
(Mouth open)
32 Frank Corridon 100.00 50.00
33A Otis Crandall 100.00 50.00
T Crossed in name
33B Otis Crandall 100.00 50.00
T Not Crossed in Name
34 Lou Criger 100.00 50.00
35 Bill Dahlen 150.00 75.00
36 Jake Daubert 100.00 50.00
37 Jim Delahanty 100.00 50.00
38 Art Devlin 100.00 50.00
39 Josh Devore 100.00 50.00
40 Walt Dickson 100.00 50.00
41 Jiggs Donahue UER 150.00 75.00
(Misspelled Donohue
on card)
42 Red Dooin 100.00 50.00
43 Mickey Doolan 100.00 50.00
44A Patsy Dougherty 150.00 75.00
(White stocking)
44B Patsy Dougherty 100.00 50.00
(Red stocking)
45 Tom Downey 100.00 50.00
46 Larry Doyle 100.00 50.00
47 Hugh Duffy 300.00 150.00
48 Jimmy Dygert 100.00 50.00
49 Dick Egan 100.00 50.00

50 Kid Elberfeld 100.00 50.00
51 Clyde Engle 100.00 50.00
52 Steve Evans 100.00 50.00
53 Johnny Evers 250.00 125.00
54 Bob Ewing 100.00 50.00
55 George Ferguson 100.00 50.00
56 Ray Fisher 150.00 75.00
57 Art Fletcher 100.00 50.00
58 John Flynn 100.00 50.00
59A Russell Ford 100.00 50.00
(Dark cap)
59B Russell Ford 150.00 75.00
(Light cap)
60 Bill Foxen 100.00 50.00
61 Art Fromme 100.00 50.00
62 Earl Gardner 100.00 50.00
63 Harry Gaspar 100.00 50.00
64 George Gibson 100.00 50.00
65 Wilbur Good 100.00 50.00
66A George F. Graham 100.00 50.00
(Boston Rustlers)
66B George F. Graham 400.00 200.00
(Chicago Cubs)
67 Eddie Grant 150.00 75.00
68A Dolly Gray 100.00 50.00
No stats on back
68B Dolly Gray 400.00 200.00
Stats on Back
69 Clark Griffith 300.00 150.00
70 Bob Groom 100.00 50.00
71A Robert Harmon 100.00 50.00
(Both ears)
71B Robert Harmon 300.00 150.00
(Left ear only)
72 Topsy Hartsel 100.00 50.00
73 Arnold Hauser 100.00 50.00
74 Charlie Hemphill 100.00 50.00
75 Buck Herzog 100.00 50.00
76A Dick Hoblitzell 10000.00 5000.00
No Stats
76B Dick Hoblitzell 100.00 50.00
No CIN after second 1908
76C Dick Hoblitzell 150.00 75.00
CIN after second 1908
76D Dick Hoblitzell 100.00 50.00
sic.Hoblitzel
77 Danny Hoffman 100.00 50.00
78 Miller Huggins 400.00 200.00
79 John Hummell 100.00 50.00
80 Fred Jacklitsch 100.00 50.00
81 Hughie Jennings 300.00 150.00
82 Walter Johnson 2000.00 1000.00
83 Davy Jones 100.00 50.00
84 Tom Jones 100.00 50.00
85 Addie Joss 700.00 350.00
86 Ed Karger 150.00 75.00
87 Ed Killian 100.00 50.00
88 Red Kleinow 150.00 75.00
89 John Kling 100.00 50.00
90 John Knight 100.00 50.00
91 Ed Konetchy 100.00 50.00
92 Harry Krause 100.00 50.00
93 Rube Kroh 100.00 50.00
94 Frank Lang 100.00 50.00
95 Frank LaPorte 100.00 50.00
96A Arlie Latham 100.00 50.00
Back says W.A. Latham
96B Arlie Latham 100.00 50.00
A. Latham on back
97 Tommy Leach 100.00 50.00
98 Sam Leever 100.00 50.00
99A Lefty Leifield 100.00 50.00
A.Leifield on front
99B Lefty Leifield 100.00 50.00
A.P.Leifield on front
100 Ed Lennox 100.00 50.00
101 Paddy Livingston 100.00 50.00
102 Hans Lobert 100.00 50.00
103 Bris Lord 100.00 50.00
104 Harry Lord 100.00 50.00
105 John Lush 100.00 50.00
106 Nick Maddox 100.00 50.00
107 Sherry Magee 100.00 50.00
108 Rube Marquard 400.00 200.00
109 Christy Mathewson 2000.00 1000.00
110 Al Mattern 100.00 50.00
111 George McBride 100.00 50.00
112 Amby McConnell 100.00 50.00
113 Pryor McElveen 100.00 50.00
114 John McGraw MG 400.00 200.00
115 Harry McIntire 100.00 50.00
116 Matty McIntyre 100.00 50.00
117 Larry McLean 100.00 50.00
118 Fred Merkle 100.00 50.00
119 Chief Meyers 100.00 50.00
120 Clyde Milan 100.00 50.00
121 Dots Miller 100.00 50.00
122 Mike Mitchell 100.00 50.00
123A Pat Moran 300.00 150.00
Extra Stat Line on Card
123B Pat Moran 100.00 50.00
124 George Moriarity 100.00 50.00
125 George Mullin 100.00 50.00
126 Danny Murphy 100.00 50.00
127 Red Murray 100.00 50.00
128 Tom Needham 100.00 50.00
129 Rebel Oakes 100.00 50.00
130 Rube Oldring 100.00 50.00
131 Charley O'Leary 100.00 50.00
132 Fred Olmstead 100.00 50.00
133 Orval Overall 100.00 50.00
134 Freddy Parent 100.00 50.00
135 Dode Paskert 100.00 50.00
136 Fred Payne 100.00 50.00
137 Barney Pelty 100.00 50.00
138 Jack Pfiester 100.00 50.00
139 Ed Phelps 100.00 50.00
140 Decon Phillippe 100.00 50.00
141 Jack Quinn 100.00 50.00
142 Bugs Raymond 150.00 75.00
143 Ed Reulbach 100.00 50.00
144 Lewis Richie 100.00 50.00
145 Jack Rowan 150.00 75.00
146 Nap Rucker 100.00 50.00
147 Doc Scanlan 150.00 75.00
148 Germany Schaefer 100.00 50.00
149 Admiral Schlei 100.00 50.00
150 Boss Schmidt 100.00 50.00
151 Wildfire Schulte 100.00 50.00
152 Jim Scott 100.00 50.00
153 Bayard Sharpe 100.00 50.00
154A David Shean 100.00 50.00
(Boston Rustlers)
154B David Shean 400.00 200.00
(Chicago Cubs)
155 Jimmy Sheckard 100.00 50.00
156 Hack Simmons 100.00 50.00
157 Tony Smith 100.00 50.00
158 Fred Snodgrass 100.00 50.00
159 Tris Speaker 1000.00 500.00
160 Jake Stahl 100.00 50.00
161 Oscar Stanage 100.00 50.00
162 Harry Steinfeldt 100.00 50.00
163 George Stone 100.00 50.00
164 George Stovall 100.00 50.00
165 Gabby Street 100.00 50.00
166 George Suggs 150.00 75.00
167 Ed Summers 100.00 50.00
168 Jeff Sweeney 150.00 75.00
169 Lee Tannehill 100.00 50.00
170 Ira Thomas 100.00 50.00
171 Joe Tinker 600.00 300.00
172 John Titus 100.00 50.00
173 Terry Turner 300.00 150.00
174 Hippo Vaughn 150.00 75.00
175 Heinie Wagner 150.00 75.00
176A Bobby Wallace 250.00 125.00
(With cap)
176B Bobby Wallace 500.00 250.00
(Without cap)
176C Bobby Wallace 300.00 150.00
no cap 2/1910
177 Ed Walsh 500.00 250.00
178 Zach Wheat 300.00 150.00
179 Doc White 100.00 50.00
180 Kirby White 150.00 75.00
181 Kaiser Wilhelm 150.00 75.00
182 Ed Willett 100.00 50.00
183A Hooks Wiltse 100.00 50.00
(Both ears)
183B Hooks Wiltse 300.00 150.00
(Right ear only)
184 Owen Wilson 100.00 50.00
185 Harry Wolter 100.00 50.00
186 Cy Young 2000.00 1000.00
187 Dr.Merle T. Adkins: 200.00 100.00
Baltimore
188 Jack Dunn 250.00 125.00
189 George Merritt 200.00 100.00
190 Charles Hanford 200.00 100.00
191 Hick Cady 200.00 100.00
192 James Frick 200.00 100.00
193 Wyatt Lee 200.00 100.00
194 Lewis McAllister 200.00 100.00
195 John Nee 200.00 100.00
196 Jimmy Collins 500.00 250.00
197 James Phelan 200.00 100.00
198 Emil Batch 200.00 100.00

1909 T206 White Border

The T206 set was and is the most popular of all the tobacco issues. The set was issued from 1909 to 1911 with sixteen different brands of cigarettes: American Beauty, Broadleaf, Cycle, Carolina Brights, Drum, El Principe de Gales, Hindu, Lenox, Old Mill, Piedmont, Polar Bear, Sovereign, Sweet Caporal, Tolstoi, and Uzit. There was also a Ty Cobb back version that was a promotional issue and is very scarce. Only Cobb appears on cards with Ty Cobb backs. The minor league cards are supposedly slightly more difficult to obtain than the cards of the major leaguers, with the Southern League player cards being the most difficult. Minor League players were obtained from the American Association and the Eastern league. Southern League players were obtained from a variety of leagues including the following: South Atlantic League, Southern League, Texas League, and Virginia League. Series 150 was issued between February 1909 thru the end of May, 1909. Series 350 was issued from the end of May, 1909 thru April, 1910. The last series 350-to-406 was issued in late December 1910 through early 1911. The set price below does not include ultra-expensive Wagner, Plank, Magie error, or Doyle variation. The Wagner card is one of the most sought after cards in the hobby. This card (number 366 in the checklist below) was pulled from circulation almost immediately after being issued. While estimates of how many Wagners are in existence vary, the card is considered by many collectors the ultimate card to own. Perhaps the best conditioned example of this card was sold in a public auction in 1991 for $451,000 to hockey great Wayne Gretzky and Bruce McNall. That same card was later used in a major giveaway sponsored by most of the card companies, Treat products and Wal-Mart. That card sold for more than $640,500 in 1996. The next recorded sale of that Wagner card was for more than $1 million dollars. The backs are scarce in the following order: Exceedingly Rare: Ty Cobb; Rare: Drum, Uzit, Lenox, Broadleaf 460 and Hindu; Scarce: Broadleaf 350, Carolina Brights, Hindu (Red); Less Common: American Beauty, Cycle and Tolstoi; Readily Available: El Principe De Gates, Old Mill, Polar Bear and Soverign and Common: Piedmont and Sweet Caporal.

	Ex-Mt	VG
COMPLETE SET (520)	55000.00	27500.00
COMMON (1-389)	60.00	30.00
COMMON (390-475)	50.00	25.00
COMMON (476-523)	125.00	60.00

1 Ed Abbaticchio: 60.00 30.00
Pitt
Batting follow thru
2 Ed Abbaticchio: 75.00 38.00
Pitt.
Batting waiting pitch
3 Bill Abstein 60.00 30.00
4 Whitey Alperman 75.00 38.00
5 Red Ames: N.Y. NL 75.00 38.00
Portrait
6 Red Ames: N.Y. NL 60.00 30.00
Hands over head
7 Red Ames: N.Y. NL 75.00 38.00
Hands in front of chest
8 Frank Arellanes 60.00 30.00
9 Jake Atz 60.00 30.00
10 Frank Baker 300.00 150.00
11 Neal Ball: N.Y. AL 75.00 38.00
12 Neal Ball: Cleveland 60.00 30.00
13 Jap Barbeau 60.00 30.00
14 Jack Barry 60.00 30.00
15 Johnny Bates 75.00 38.00
16 Ginger Beaumont 75.00 38.00
17 Fred Beck 60.00 30.00
18 Beals Becker 60.00 30.00
19 George Bell: 60.00 30.00
Brooklyn
pitching follow thru
20 George Bell: 75.00 38.00
Brooklyn
Hands
over head
21 Chief Bender 400.00 200.00
Phila. AL
Portrait
22 Chief Bender 500.00 250.00
Phila. AL
pitching, trees
23 Chief Bender 400.00 200.00
Phila AL
pitching, no trees
24 Bill Bergen: 60.00 30.00
Brooklyn
Catching
25 Bill Bergen: 75.00 38.00
Brooklyn
Batting
26 Heinie Berger 60.00 30.00
27 Bob Bescher: Cinc. 60.00 30.00
Catching fly ball
28 Bob Bescher: Cinc. 60.00 30.00
Portrait
29 Joe Birmingham 75.00 38.00
30 Jack Bliss 60.00 30.00
31 Frank Bowerman 75.00 38.00
32 Bill Bradley: 75.00 38.00
Cleveland
Portrait
33 Bill Bradley: 60.00 30.00
Cleveland
Batting
34 Kitty Bransfield 75.00 38.00
35 Roger Bresnahan: 250.00 125.00
St.L. NL
Portrait
36 Roger Bresnahan: 200.00 100.00
St.L. NL
Batting
37 Al Bridwell 75.00 38.00
N.Y. NL
Portrait
38 Al Bridwell 60.00 30.00
N.Y. NL
Wearing sweater
39 George Brown: 125.00 60.00
Chicago NL
Sic, Browne
40 George Brown: 400.00 200.00
Washington
Sic, Browne
41 Mordecai Brown: 500.00 250.00
Chicago NL
Portrait
42 Mordecai Brown: 500.00 250.00
Chicago NL
Chicago down front of shirt
43 Mordecai Brown: 500.00 250.00
Chicago NL
Cubs Shirt
44 Al Burch: Brooklyn 60.00 30.00
Fielding
45 Al Burch: Brooklyn 125.00 60.00
Batting
46 Bill Burns 60.00 30.00
47 Donie Bush 75.00 38.00
48 Bobby Byrne 60.00 30.00
49 Howie Camnitz: 75.00 38.00
Pitt
Arms folded over chest
50 Howie Camnitz: 60.00 30.00
Pitt
Hands over head
51 Howie Camnitz: 60.00 30.00
Pitt.
Throwing
52 Billy Campbell 60.00 30.00
53 Bill Carrigan 60.00 30.00
54 Frank Chance: 400.00 200.00
Chicago NL
Cubs across chest
55 Frank Chance: 400.00 200.00
Chicago NL
Chicago down front of shirt
56 Frank Chance: 300.00 150.00
Chicago NL
Batting
57 Chappy Charles 60.00 30.00
58 Hal Chase 125.00 60.00
N.Y. AL
Port. blue bkgd.
59 Hal Chase 200.00 100.00
N.Y. AL
Port., pink bkgd.
60 Hal Chase 125.00 60.00
N.Y. AL
Holding cup
61 Hal Chase 125.00 60.00
N.Y. AL
Throwing, dark cap
62 Hal Chase 150.00 75.00
N.Y. AL
Throwing, white cap
63 Jack Chesbro 250.00 125.00
64 Eddie Cicotte 200.00 100.00
65 Fred Clarke: Pitt. 200.00 100.00
Portrait
66 Fred Clarke: Pitt. 200.00 100.00
67 Nig Clarke 75.00 38.00
68 Ty Cobb: Detroit 2500.00 1250.00
Port., red bkgd.
69 Ty Cobb: Detroit 3500.00 1800.00
Port., green background
70 Ty Cobb: Detroit 2500.00 1250.00
Bat on shoulder
71 Ty Cobb: Detroit 2500.00 1250.00
Bat away from shoulder
72 Eddie Collins: 300.00 150.00
Phila. AL
73 Wid Conroy: 75.00 38.00
Washington
Fielding
74 Wid Conroy 60.00 30.00
Washington
Bat on shoulder
75 Harry Covaleski: 75.00 38.00
Phila. NL
76 Doc Crandall 60.00 30.00
N.Y. NL,
without cap
77 Doc Crandall 60.00 30.00
N.Y. NL
sweater and cap
78 Sam Crawford: 400.00 200.00
Detroit, Batting
79 Sam Crawford: 400.00 200.00
Detroit, Throwing
80 Birdie Cree 60.00 30.00
81 Lou Criger 75.00 38.00
82 Dode Criss 75.00 38.00
83 Bill Dahlen: 125.00 60.00
Boston NL
84 Bill Dahlen: 200.00 100.00
Brooklyn
85 George Davis 200.00 100.00
86 Harry Davis 60.00 30.00
Phila. AL
Davis on card
87 Harry Davis 75.00 38.00
Phila. AL
H.Davis on card
88 Jim Delehanty 75.00 38.00
Sic, Delahanty
89 Ray Demmitt 4500.00 2200.00
St.L. AL
90 Ray Demmitt 75.00 38.00
N.Y. AL
91 Art Devlin 75.00 38.00
92 Josh Devore 60.00 30.00
93 Bill Dineen 60.00 30.00
94 Mike Donlin 125.00 60.00
N.Y. NL
Fielding
95 Mike Donlin 125.00 60.00
N.Y. NL
Sitting
96 Mike Donlin 75.00 38.00
N.Y. NL
Batting
97 Jiggs Donohue 75.00 38.00
98 Bill Donovan: 75.00 38.00
Detroit
Portrait
99 Bill Donovan: 60.00 30.00
Detroit
Throwing
100 Red Dooin 75.00 38.00
101 Mickey Doolan: 60.00 30.00
Phila. NL
Fielding
102 Mickey Doolan: 60.00 30.00
Phila. NL
Batting
103 Mickey Doolin (Sic, 75.00 38.00
Doolan): Phila. NL
104 Patsy Dougherty: 75.00 38.00
Chicago AL
Portrait
105 Patsy Dougherty: 60.00 30.00
Chicago AL
Fielding
106 Tom Downey: Cinc. 60.00 30.00
Batting
107 Tom Downey: Cinc. 60.00 30.00
Fielding
108A Joe Doyle: N.Y. 125.00 60.00
Hands over head
108B Joe Doyle: N.Y. 60000.00 30000.00
NAT'L
hands
over head)
109 Larry Doyle: N.Y. 75.00 38.00
NL
Sweater
110 Larry Doyle: N.Y. 125.00 60.00
NL
Throwing
111 Larry Doyle: N.Y. 75.00 38.00
NL
Bat on shoulder
112 Jean Dubuc 60.00 30.00
113 Hugh Duffy 300.00 150.00
114 Joe Dunn 60.00 30.00
115 Bull Durham 75.00 38.00
116 Jimmy Dygert 60.00 30.00
117 Ted Easterly 60.00 30.00
118 Dick Egan 60.00 30.00
119 Kid Elberfeld 60.00 30.00
Wash.
Fielding
120 Kid Elberfeld 1000.00 500.00
Wash.
Portrait
121 Kid Elberfeld 75.00 38.00
N.Y. AL
Portrait
122 Clyde Engle 60.00 30.00
123 Steve Evans 60.00 30.00
124 Johnny Evers: 500.00 250.00
Chicago NL
Portrait
125 Johnny Evers: 300.00 150.00
Chicago NL
Cubs across chest
126 Johnny Evers: 300.00 150.00
Chicago NL
Chicago down front of shirt
127 Bob Ewing 75.00 38.00
128 George Ferguson 60.00 30.00
129 Hobe Ferris 75.00 38.00
130 Lou Fiene 60.00 30.00
Chicago AL
Portrait
131 Lou Fiene 60.00 30.00
Chicago AL
Throwing
132 Art Fletcher 60.00 30.00
133 Elmer Flick 300.00 150.00
134 Russ Ford 60.00 30.00
135 John Frill 60.00 30.00
136 Art Fromme 60.00 30.00
137 Chick Gandil 250.00 125.00
138 Bob Ganley 75.00 38.00
139 Harry Gasper 60.00 30.00
140 Rube Geyer 60.00 30.00
141 George Gibson 75.00 38.00
142 Billy Gilbert 75.00 38.00
143 Wilbur Goode 75.00 38.00
Sic, Good
144 Bill Graham 60.00 30.00
145 Peaches Graham 60.00 30.00
146 Dolly Gray 75.00 38.00
147 Clark Griffith: 250.00 125.00
Cinc.
Portrait
148 Clark Griffith: 250.00 125.00
Cinc.
Batting
149 Bob Groom 60.00 30.00
150 Ed Hahn 75.00 38.00
151 Topsy Hartsel 60.00 30.00
152 Charlie Hemphill 75.00 38.00
153 Buck Herzog 75.00 38.00
N.Y. NL
154 Buck Herzog 60.00 30.00
Boston NL
155 Bill Hinchman 75.00 38.00
156 Doc Hoblitzell 60.00 30.00
157 Danny Hoffman 60.00 30.00
158 Solly Hofman 60.00 30.00
159 Del Howard 60.00 30.00
160 Harry Howell 60.00 30.00
St.L. AL
Portrait
161 Harry Howell 60.00 30.00
St.L. AL
Left hand on hip
162 Miller Huggins: 400.00 200.00
Cinc.
Portrait
163 Miller Huggins: 400.00 200.00
Cinc.
Hands to Mouth
164 Rudy Hulswitt 60.00 30.00
165 John Hummel 60.00 30.00
166 George Hunter 60.00 30.00
167 Frank Isbell 75.00 38.00
168 Fred Jacklitsch 75.00 38.00
169 Hughie Jennings MG: 400.00 200.00
Detroit
Portrait
170 Hughie Jennings MG: 400.00 200.00
Detroit
One
171 Hughie Jennings MG: 400.00 200.00
Detroit
Dancing
for joy
172 Walter Johnson: 1500.00 750.00
Washington
Portrait
173 Walter Johnson: 1200.00 600.00
Washington
Hands at Chest
174 Davy Jones 60.00 30.00
175 Fielder Jones 75.00 38.00
Chic. AL
Portrait
176 Fielder Jones 75.00 38.00
Chic AL
Hands on hips
177 Tom Jones 75.00 38.00
178 Tim Jordan: 75.00 38.00
Brooklyn
Portrait
179 Tim Jordan: 60.00 30.00
Brooklyn
Batting
180 Addie Joss: 500.00 250.00
Cleveland
Portrait
181 Addie Joss: 400.00 200.00
Cleveland
Ready to pitch
182 Ed Karger 75.00 38.00
183 Willie Keeler 500.00 250.00
N.Y. AL
Portrait
184 Willie Keeler 400.00 200.00
N.Y. AL
Batting
185 Ed Killian: Detroit 75.00 38.00
Portrait
186 Ed Killian: Detroit 60.00 30.00
Pitching
187 Red Kleinow 75.00 38.00
N.Y. AL
Batting
188 Red Kleinow 60.00 30.00
N.Y. AL
Catching
189 Red Kleinow 800.00 400.00
Boston AL
Catching
190 Johnny Kling: 75.00 38.00
Chicago NL
191 Otto Knabe 60.00 30.00
192 John Knight 60.00 30.00
N.Y. AL
Portrait

193 John Knight 60.00 30.00
N.Y. AL
Batting
194 Ed Konetchy 60.00 30.00
St.L. NL
Awaiting low ball
195 Ed Konetchy 75.00 38.00
St.L. NL
Glove above head
196 Harry Krause 60.00 30.00
Phila. AL
Portrait
197 Harry Krause 60.00 30.00
Phila. AL
Pitching
198 Rube Kroh 60.00 30.00
199 Nap Lajoie: 800.00 400.00
Cleveland
Portrait
200 Nap Lajoie: 600.00 300.00
Cleveland
Batting
201 Nap Lajoie: 600.00 300.00
Cleveland
Throwing
202 Joe Lake 75.00 38.00
N.Y. AL
203 Joe Lake 60.00 30.00
St.L. AL
Hands over head
204 Joe Lake 60.00 30.00
St.L. AL
Throwing
205 Frank LaPorte 60.00 30.00
206 Arlie Latham 75.00 38.00
207 Tommy Leach: Pitt. 75.00 38.00
Portrait
208 Tommy Leach: Pitt. 60.00 30.00
In fielding position
209 Lefty Leifield: 60.00 30.00
Pitt.
Batting
210 Lefty Leifield: 75.00 38.00
Pitt.
Hands behind head
211 Ed Lennox 60.00 30.00
212 Glenn Liebhardt 75.00 38.00
213 Vive Lindaman 125.00 60.00
214 Paddy Livingstone 60.00 30.00
215 Hans Lobert 75.00 38.00
216 Harry Lord 60.00 30.00
217 Harry Lumley 75.00 38.00
218 Carl Lundgren 300.00 150.00
219 Nick Maddox. 60.00 30.00
220 Sherry Magee 125.00 60.00
Phila. NL
Portrait
221 Sherry Magee 60.00 30.00
Phila. NL
Batting
222 Sherry Magie 15000.00 7500.00
Phila. NL
Sic, Magee
Portrait,
name misspelled
223 Rube Manning 75.00 38.00
N.Y. AL
Batting
224 Rube Manning 60.00 30.00
N.Y. AL
Hands over head
225 Rube Marquard 400.00 200.00
N.Y. NL
Portrait
226 Rube Marquard 300.00 150.00
N.Y. NL
Pitching
227 Rube Marquard 300.00 150.00
N.Y. NL
Standing
228 Doc Marshall 60.00 30.00
229 Christy Mathewson: 1500.00 750.00
N.Y. NL
Portrait
230 Christy Mathewson: 1200.00 600.00
N.Y. NL
Pitching, white cap
231 Christy Mathewson: 1200.00 600.00
N.Y. NL
Pitching, dark cap
232 Al Mattern 60.00 30.00
233 Jack McAleese 60.00 30.00
234 George McBride 60.00 30.00
235 Moose McCormick 60.00 30.00
236 Pryor McElveen 60.00 30.00
237 John McGraw 400.00 200.00
N.Y. NL
Portrait, no cap
238 John McGraw 400.00 200.00
N.Y. NL
Wearing sweater
239 John McGraw 400.00 200.00
N.Y. NL
pointing
240 John McGraw 400.00 200.00
N.Y. NL
Glove on hip
241 Matty McIntyre: 75.00 38.00
Brooklyn
242 Matty McIntyre: 60.00 30.00
Brooklyn and
Chicago NL
243 Mike McIntyre: 60.00 30.00
Detroit
244 Larry McLean 60.00 30.00
245 George McQuillan: 75.00 38.00
Phila. NL
Throwing
246 George McQuillan: 60.00 30.00
Phila. NL
Batting
247 Fred Merkle 125.00 60.00
N.Y. NL
Portrait
248 Fred Merkle 125.00 60.00
N.Y. NL
Throwing
249 Chief Meyers 60.00 30.00
250 Chief Meyers 60.00 30.00
Sic, Myers)
N.Y. NL
Fielding
251 Chief Meyers 75.00 38.00
Sic, Myers)
N.Y. NL
Batting
252 Clyde Milan 60.00 30.00
253 Dots Miller 60.00 30.00
254 Mike Mitchell 60.00 30.00
255 Pat Moran 60.00 30.00
256 George Moriarty 60.00 30.00
257 Mike Mowrey 60.00 30.00
258 George Mullin: 60.00 30.00
Detroit
Sic, Mullen
259 George Mullin: 75.00 38.00
Detroit
Throwing
260 George Mullin: 60.00 30.00
Detroit
Batting
261 Danny Murphy 75.00 38.00
Phila. AL
Throwing
262 Danny Murphy 60.00 30.00
Phila. AL
Bat on shoulder
263 Red Murray 60.00 30.00
N.Y. NL
Sweater
264 Red Murray 60.00 30.00
N.Y. NL
Bat on shoulder
265 Tom Needham 60.00 30.00
266 Simon Nicholls 75.00 38.00
Phila AL
267 Simon Nicholls 60.00 30.00
Sic, Nichols:
Phila. AL
268 Harry Niles 75.00 38.00
269 Rebel Oakes 60.00 30.00
270 Bill O'Hara: N.Y. NL 60.00 30.00
271 Bill O'Hara: 5000.00 2500.00
St. Louis NL
272 Rube Oldring 75.00 38.00
Phila. AL
Fielding
273 Rube Oldring 75.00 38.00
Phila. AL
Bat on shoulder
274 Charley O'Leary: 75.00 38.00
Detroit
Portrait
275 Charley O'Leary: 60.00 30.00
Detroit
Hands on knees
276 Orval Overall: 75.00 38.00
Chicago NL
Portrait
277 Orval Overall: 60.00 30.00
Chicago NL
Pitching follow thru
278 Orval Overall: 60.00 30.00
Chicago NL,
Pitching hiding
ball in glove
279 Frank Owen 75.00 38.00
Chicago AL
Sic, Owens)
280 Freddy Parent 75.00 38.00
281 Dode Paskert 60.00 30.00
282 Jim Pastorius 75.00 38.00
283 Harry Pattee 150.00 75.00
284 Fred Payne 60.00 30.00
285 Barney Pelty 125.00 60.00
St.L. AL
HOR
286 Barney Pelty 60.00 30.00
St.L. AL
VERT
287 George Perring 60.00 30.00
288 Jeff Pfeffer 60.00 30.00
289 Jack Pfeister 60.00 30.00
Chic. NL
Sitting
290 Jack Pfeister 60.00 30.00
Chic. NL
Pitching
291 Ed Phelps 60.00 30.00
292 Deacon Phillippe. 125.00 60.00
293 Eddie Plank 30000.00 15000.00
294 Jack Powell 75.00 38.00
295 Mike Powers 125.00 60.00
296 Billy Purtell 60.00 30.00
297 Jack Quinn 60.00 30.00
298 Bugs Raymond 75.00 38.00
299 Ed Reulbach 125.00 60.00
Chicago NL
Pitching
300 Ed Reulbach 125.00 60.00
Chicago NL
Hands at side
301 Bob Rhoades 60.00 30.00
sic,Rhoads
Cleveland
Hand in air
302 Bob Rhoades 60.00 30.00
sic, Rhoads
Cleveland
Ready to pitch
303 Charlie Rhodes 60.00 30.00
304 Claude Ritchey 75.00 38.00
305 Claude Rossman 60.00 30.00
306 Nap Rucker: 125.00 60.00
Brooklyn
Portrait
307 Nap Rucker: 75.00 38.00
Brooklyn
Pitching
308 Germany Schaefer: 75.00 38.00
Washington
309 Germany Schaefer: 75.00 38.00
Detroit
310 Admiral Schlei 60.00 30.00
N.Y. NL
Sweater
311 Admiral Schlei 60.00 30.00
N.Y. NL
Batting
312 Admiral Schlei 75.00 38.00
N.Y. NL
Fielding
313 Boss Schmidt: 60.00 30.00
Detroit
Portrait
314 Boss Schmidt: 75.00 38.00
Detroit
Throwing
315 Frank Schulte: 60.00 30.00
Chicago NL
Batting, back turned
316 Frank Schulte: 75.00 38.00
Chicago NL
Batting, front pose
317 Jim Scott 60.00 30.00
318 Cy Seymour 60.00 30.00
N.Y. NL
Portrait
319 Cy Seymour 60.00 30.00
N.Y. NL
Throwing
320 Cy Seymour 75.00 38.00
N.Y. NL
Batting
321 Al Shaw 75.00 38.00
322 Jimmy Sheckard: 60.00 30.00
Chicago NL
Throwing
323 Jimmy Sheckard: 75.00 38.00
Chicago NL
Side view
324 Bill Shipke 75.00 38.00
325 Frank Smith 60.00 30.00
Chicago AL
Listed as Smith
326 Frank Smith 400.00 200.00
Chicago and Boston AL
327 Frank Smith 75.00 38.00
Chicago AL
Listed as F.Smith
328 Happy Smith 60.00 30.00
329 Fred Snodgrass 75.00 38.00
N.Y. NL
Batting
329A Fred Snodgrass 3000.00 1500.00
N.Y., Battting
Card spelled Nodgrass
Due to a printing glitch
330 Fred Snodgrass 75.00 38.00
N.Y. NL
Catching
331 Bob Spade 75.00 38.00
332 Tris Speaker 800.00 400.00
333 Tubby Spencer 75.00 38.00
334 Jake Stahl: 75.00 38.00
Boston AL
Catching fly ball
335 Jake Stahl: 75.00 38.00
Boston AL
Standing, arms down
336 Oscar Stanage 60.00 30.00
337 Charlie Starr 60.00 30.00
338 Harry Steinfeldt: 125.00 60.00
Chicago NL
Portrait
339 Harry Steinfeldt: 75.00 38.00
Chicago NL
Batting
340 Jim Stephens 60.00 30.00
341 George Stone 75.00 38.00
342 George Stovall: 75.00 38.00
Cleveland
Portrait
343 George Stovall: 60.00 30.00
Cleveland
Batting
344 Gabby Street: 75.00 38.00
Washington
Portrait
345 Gabby Street: 60.00 30.00
Washington
Catching
346 Billy Sullivan 75.00 38.00
347 Ed Summers 60.00 30.00
348 Jeff Sweeney 60.00 30.00
349 Bill Sweeney 60.00 30.00
350 Jesse Tannehill 60.00 30.00
351 Lee Tannehill: 75.00 38.00
Chicago AL
Listed as L.Tannehill
352 Lee Tannehill: 60.00 30.00
Chicago AL
Listed as Tannehill
353 Fred Tenney 75.00 38.00
354 Ira Thomas 60.00 30.00
355 Joe Tinker 600.00 300.00
Chicago NL
Bat Off Shoulder
356 Joe Tinker 600.00 300.00
Chicago NL
Bat on Shoulder
357 Joe Tinker 600.00 300.00
Chicago NL
Portrait
358 Joe Tinker 600.00 300.00
Chicago NL
Hands on knees
359 John Titus 60.00 30.00
360 Terry Turner 75.00 38.00
361 Bob Unglaub 60.00 30.00
362 Rube Waddell 500.00 250.00
St.L. AL
Portrait
363 Rube Waddell 400.00 200.00
St.L. AL
Pitching
364 Heinie Wagner: 125.00 60.00
Boston AL
Bat on left shoulder
365 Heinie Wagner: 75.00 38.00
Boston AL
Bat on right shoulder
366 Honus Wagner 400000.00 200000.00
367 Bobby Wallace 300.00 150.00
368 Ed Walsh 500.00 250.00
369 Jack Warhop: N.Y. AL 60.00 30.00
370 Jake Weimer: N.Y. NL 75.00 38.00
371 Zach Wheat 300.00 150.00
372 Doc White 75.00 38.00
Chicago AL
Portrait
373 Doc White 60.00 30.00
Chicago AL
Pitching
374 Kaiser Wilhelm: 60.00 30.00
Brooklyn
Batting
375 Kaiser Wilhelm: 75.00 38.00
Brooklyn
Hands to chest
376 Ed Willett: Detroit 60.00 30.00
Batting
377 Ed Willett 60.00 30.00
Sic, Willetts
Detroit
Pitching
378 Jimmy Williams 75.00 38.00
379 Vic Willis: Pitt. 250.00 125.00
380 Vic Willis 200.00 100.00
St.L. NL
Pitching
381 Vic Willis 200.00 100.00
St.L. NL
Batting
382 Chief Wilson 60.00 30.00
383 Hooks Wiltse 75.00 38.00
N.Y. NL
Portrait
384 Hooks Wiltse 60.00 30.00
N.Y.NL
Sweater
385 Hooks Wiltse 60.00 30.00
N.Y. NL
Pitching
386 Cy Young 1200.00 600.00
Cleveland
Portrait
387 Cy Young 1000.00 500.00
Cleveland
Pitch, front view
388 Cy Young 1000.00 500.00
Cleveland
Pitch, side view
389 Heinie Zimmerman: 60.00 30.00
390 Fred Abbott 50.00 25.00
391 Merle(Doc) Adkins 50.00 25.00
392 John Anderson 50.00 25.00
393 Herman Armbruster 50.00 25.00
394 Harry Arndt 50.00 25.00
395 Cy Barger 60.00 30.00
396 John Barry 50.00 25.00
397 Emil H. Batch 50.00 25.00
398 Jake Beckley 250.00 125.00
399 Lena Blackburne 75.00 38.00
400 David Brain 50.00 25.00
401 Roy Brashear 50.00 25.00
402 Fred Burchell 50.00 25.00
403 Jimmy Burke 50.00 25.00
404 John Butler 50.00 25.00
405 Charles Carr 50.00 25.00
406 Doc Casey 50.00 25.00
407 Peter Cassidy 50.00 25.00
408 Wm. Chappelle 60.00 30.00
409 Wm. Clancy 50.00 25.00
410 Joshua Clarke 50.00 25.00
Sic, Clark
411 William Clymer 50.00 25.00
412 Jimmy Collins 400.00 200.00
413 Bunk Congalton 50.00 25.00
414 Gavvy Cravath 125.00 60.00
415 Monte Cross 60.00 30.00
416 Paul Davidson 50.00 25.00
417 Frank Delehanty 75.00 38.00
Sic, Delahanty
418 Rube Dessau 50.00 25.00
419 Gus Dorner 50.00 25.00
420 Jerome Downs 50.00 25.00
421 Jack Dunn 75.00 38.00
422 James Flanagan 50.00 25.00
423 James Freeman 50.00 25.00
424 John Ganzel 50.00 25.00
425 Myron Grimshaw 50.00 25.00
426 Robert Hall 50.00 25.00
427 William Hallman 60.00 30.00
428 John Hannifan 50.00 25.00
429 Jack Hayden 50.00 25.00
430 Harry Hinchman 50.00 25.00
431 Harry C. Hoffman 50.00 25.00
432 James B. Jackson 60.00 30.00
433 Joe Kelley 250.00 125.00
434 Rube Kissinger 60.00 30.00
Sic, Kisinger
435 Otto Krueger 50.00 25.00
Sic, Kruger
436 Wm. Lattimore 50.00 25.00
437 James Lavender 50.00 25.00
438 Carl Lundgren 50.00 25.00
439 Wm. Malarkey 60.00 30.00
440 Wm. Maloney 50.00 25.00
441 Dennis McGann 50.00 25.00
442 James McGinley 50.00 25.00
443 Joe McGinnity 250.00 125.00
444 Ulysses McGlynn 50.00 25.00
445 George Merritt 50.00 25.00
446 Wm. Milligan 50.00 25.00
447 Fred Mitchell. 50.00 25.00
448 Dan Moeller 50.00 25.00
449 Joseph H. Moran 50.00 25.00
450 Wm. Nattress 50.00 25.00
451 Frank Oberlin 50.00 25.00
452 Peter O'Brien 50.00 25.00
453 Wm. O'Neil 50.00 25.00
454 James Phelan 50.00 25.00
455 Oliver Pickering 50.00 25.00
456 Philip Poland 50.00 25.00
457 Ambrose Puttman 50.00 25.00
458 Lee Quillen 50.00 25.00
459 Newton Randall 50.00 25.00
460 Louis Ritter 50.00 25.00
461 Dick Rudolph 50.00 25.00
462 George Schirm 50.00 25.00
463 Larry Schlafly 50.00 25.00
464 Ossie Schreckengost 60.00 30.00
Sic Schreck
465 William Shannon 50.00 25.00
466 Bayard Sharpe 50.00 25.00
466A Bayard Sharpe 500.00 250.00
Name is spelled Shappe on front
467 Royal Shaw 50.00 25.00
468 James Slagle 50.00 25.00
469 George Henry Smith 50.00 25.00
470 Samuel Strang 50.00 25.00
471 Dummy Taylor 125.00 60.00
472 John Thielman 50.00 25.00
473 John F. White 50.00 25.00
474 William Wright 50.00 25.00
475 Irving M. Young 60.00 30.00
476 Jack Bastian 125.00 60.00
477 Harry Bay 125.00 60.00
478 Wm. Bernhard 125.00 60.00
479 Ted Breitenstein 125.00 60.00
480 Scoops Carey 125.00 60.00
481 Cad Coles 125.00 60.00
482 Wm. Cranston 125.00 60.00
483 Roy Ellam 125.00 60.00
484 Edward Foster 125.00 60.00
485 Charles Fritz 125.00 60.00
486 Ed Greminger 125.00 60.00
487 Guiheen 125.00 60.00
488 William F. Hart 125.00 60.00
489 James Henry Hart 125.00 60.00
490 J.R. Helm 125.00 60.00
491 Gordon Hickman 125.00 60.00
492 Buck Hooker 125.00 60.00
493 Ernie Howard 125.00 60.00
494 A.O. Jordan 125.00 60.00
495 J.F. Kiernan 125.00 60.00
496 Frank King 125.00 60.00
497 James LaFitte 125.00 60.00
498 Harry Sentz 125.00 60.00
Sic, Lentz
499 Perry Lipe 125.00 60.00
500 George Manion 125.00 60.00
501 McCauley 125.00 60.00
502 Charles B. Miller 125.00 60.00
503 Carlton Molesworth 125.00 60.00
504 Dominic Mullaney 125.00 60.00
505 Albert Orth 125.00 60.00
506 William Otey 125.00 60.00
507 George Paige 125.00 60.00
508 Hub Perdue. 150.00 75.00
509 Archie Persons 125.00 60.00
510 Edward Reagan 125.00 60.00
511 R.H. Revelle 125.00 60.00
512 Isaac Rockenfeld 125.00 60.00
513 Ray Ryan 125.00 60.00
514 Charles Seitz 125.00 60.00
515 Frank "Shag" Shaughnessy 150.00 75.00
516 Carlos Smith 125.00 60.00
517 Sid Smith 125.00 60.00
518 Dolly Stark 150.00 75.00
519 Tony Thebo 125.00 60.00
520 Woodie Thornton 125.00 60.00
521 Juan Viola 125.00 60.00
Sic, Violat
522 James Westlake 125.00 60.00
523 Foley White 125.00 60.00

1912 T207 Brown Background

The cards in this 207-card set measure approximately 1 1/2" by 2 5/8". The T207 set, also known as the "Brown Background" set was issued beginning in May with Broadleaf, Cycle, Napoleon, Recruit and anonymous (Factories no. 2, 3 or 25) backs in 1912. Broadleaf, Cycle and anonymous backs are difficult to obtain. Although many scarcities and cards with varying degrees of difficulty to obtain exist (see prices below), the Loudermilk, Lewis (Boston NL) and Miller (Chicago NL) cards are the rarest, followed by Saier and Tyler. The cards are numbered below for reference in alphabetical order by player's name. The complete set price below does include the Lewis variation missing the Braves patch on the sleeve.

Ex-Mt VG
COMPLETE SET (208) 30000.00 15000.00
1 Bert Adams 100.00 50.00
2 Eddie Ainsmith 60.00 30.00
3 Rafael Almeida 100.00 50.00
4 Jimmy Austin 60.00 30.00
StL AL
with StL on shirt
5 Jimmy Austin 120.00 60.00
StL AL
without StL on shirt
6 Neal Ball 60.00 30.00
7 Cy Barger 60.00 30.00
8 Jack Barry 60.00 30.00
9 Paddy Bauman 120.00 60.00
10 Beals Becker 60.00 30.00
11 Chief Bender 200.00 100.00
12 Joe Benz 100.00 50.00
13 Bob Bescher 60.00 30.00
14 Joe Birmingham 100.00 50.00
15 Lena Blackburne 100.00 50.00
16 Fred Blanding 100.00 50.00
17 Bruno Block 60.00 30.00
18 Ping Bodie 60.00 30.00
19 Hugh Bradley 60.00 30.00
20 Roger Bresnahan 200.00 100.00
21 Jack Bushelman 100.00 50.00
22 Hank Butcher 100.00 50.00
23 Bobby Byrne 60.00 30.00
24 Nixey Callahan 60.00 30.00
25 Howie Camnitz 60.00 30.00
26 Max Carey 120.00 60.00
27 Bill Carrigan: Bos AL 60.00 30.00
correct back
28 Bill Carrigan: Bos AL 120.00 60.00
Wagner back
29 George Chalmers 60.00 30.00
30 Frank Chance 250.00 125.00
31 Eddie Cicotte 200.00 100.00
32 Tommy Clarke 60.00 30.00
33 King Cole 60.00 30.00
34 Shano Collins 60.00 30.00

35 Bob Coulson 60.00 30.00
36 Tex Covington 60.00 30.00
37 Doc Crandall 60.00 30.00
38 Bill Cunningham 100.00 50.00
39 Dave Danforth 60.00 30.00
40 Bert Daniels 60.00 30.00
41 Jake Daubert 100.00 50.00
42 Harry Davis 60.00 30.00
43 Jim Delahanty 80.00 40.00
44 Claud Derrick 60.00 30.00
45 Art Devlin 60.00 30.00
46 Josh Devore 60.00 30.00
47 Mike Donlin 100.00 50.00
48 Ed Donnelly 100.00 50.00
49 Red Dooin 60.00 30.00
50 Tom Downey 100.00 50.00
51 Larry Doyle 80.00 40.00
52 Dellos Drake 60.00 30.00
53 Ted Easterly 60.00 30.00
54 Rube Ellis 60.00 30.00
55 Clyde Engle 60.00 30.00
56 Tex Erwin 60.00 30.00
57 Steve Evans 60.00 30.00
58 Jack Ferry 60.00 30.00
59 Ray Fisher: NY AL 120.00 60.00
white cap
60 Ray Fisher: NY AL 100.00 50.00
blue cap
61 Art Fletcher 60.00 30.00
62 Jack Fournier 100.00 50.00
63 Art Fromme 60.00 30.00
64 Del Gainor 60.00 30.00
65 Larry Gardner 60.00 30.00
66 Lefty George 60.00 30.00
67 Roy Golden 60.00 30.00
68 Hank Gowdy 80.00 40.00
69 Peaches Graham 100.00 50.00
70 Jack Graney 80.00 40.00
71 Vean Gregg 100.00 50.00
72 Casey Hageman 60.00 30.00
73 Sea Lion Hall 60.00 30.00
74 Ed Hallinan 60.00 30.00
75 Earl Hamilton 60.00 30.00
76 Bob Harmon 60.00 30.00
77 Grover Hartley 100.00 50.00
78 Olaf Henriksen 60.00 30.00
79 John Henry 100.00 50.00
80 Buck Herzog 100.00 50.00
81 Bob Higgins 60.00 30.00
82 Red Hoff 100.00 50.00
83 Willie Hogan 60.00 30.00
84 Harry Hooper 400.00 200.00
85 Ben Houser 100.00 50.00
86 Ham Hyatt 100.00 50.00
87 Walter Johnson 1000.00 500.00
88 George Kahler 60.00 30.00
89 Billy Kelly 100.00 50.00
90 Jay Kirke 100.00 50.00
91 Johnny Kling 60.00 30.00
92 Otto Knabe 60.00 30.00
93 Elmer Knetzer 60.00 30.00
94 Ed Konetchy 60.00 30.00
95 Harry Krause 60.00 30.00
96 Walt Kuhn 100.00 50.00
97 Joe Kutina 100.00 50.00
98 Frank Lange 100.00 50.00
99 Jack Lapp 60.00 30.00
100 Arlie Latham 60.00 30.00
101 Tommy Leach 60.00 30.00
102 Lefty Leifield 60.00 30.00
103 Ed Lennox 60.00 30.00
104 Duffy Lewis 60.00 30.00
105A Irving Lewis: Bos NL 2000.00 1000.00
Braves patch on sleeve
105B Irving Lewis: Bos NL 2500.00 1250.00
Nothing on sleeve
106 Jack Lively 60.00 30.00
107 Paddy Livingston: 250.00 125.00
Cleve "A" shirt
108 Paddy Livingston: 250.00 125.00
Cleve "C" shirt
109 Paddy Livingston: 100.00 50.00
Cleve "c" shirt
110 Bris Lord 60.00 30.00
111 Harry Lord 60.00 30.00
112 Louis Lowdermilk 2500.00 1250.00
113 Rube Marquard 200.00 100.00
114 Armando Marsans 100.00 50.00
115 George McBride 60.00 30.00
116 Alex McCarthy 120.00 60.00
117 Ed McDonald 60.00 30.00
118 John McGraw 250.00 125.00
119 Harry McIntire 60.00 30.00
120 Matty McIntyre 60.00 30.00
121 Bill McKechnie 400.00 200.00
122 Larry McLean 60.00 30.00
123 Clyde Milan 80.00 40.00
124 Dots Miller 60.00 30.00
125 Ward Miller 1500.00 750.00
126 Otto Miller 100.00 50.00
127 Doc Miller 100.00 50.00
128 Mike Mitchell 60.00 30.00
129 Willie Mitchell 100.00 50.00
130 George Mogridge 100.00 50.00
131 Earl Moore 100.00 50.00
132 Pat Moran 60.00 30.00
133 Cy Morgan 60.00 30.00
134 Ray Morgan 60.00 30.00
135 George Moriarity 100.00 50.00
136 George Mullin: Det 100.00 50.00
With "D" on cap
137 George Mullin: Det 200.00 100.00
Without "D" on cap
138 Tom Needham 60.00 30.00
139 Red Nelson 100.00 50.00
140 Hub Northen 60.00 30.00
141 Les Nunamaker 60.00 30.00
142 Rebel Oakes 60.00 30.00
143 Buck O'Brien 60.00 30.00
144 Rube Oldring 80.00 40.00
145 Ivy Olson 60.00 30.00
146 Marty O'Toole 60.00 30.00
147 Dode Paskert 60.00 30.00
148 Barney Pelty 100.00 50.00
149 Hub Perdue 80.00 40.00
150 Rube Peters 100.00 50.00
151 Art Phelan 100.00 50.00
152 Jack Quinn 80.00 40.00
153 Pat Ragan 400.00 200.00
154 Rasmussen: Phil NL 400.00 200.00
155 Morrie Rath 100.00 50.00
156 Ed Reulbach 80.00 40.00
157 Nap Rucker 80.00 40.00
158 Bud Ryan 100.00 50.00
159 Vic Saier 1000.00 500.00
160 Scanlon 60.00 30.00
161 Germany Schaefer 80.00 40.00
162 Bill Schardt 60.00 30.00
163 Frank Schulte 80.00 40.00
164 Jim Scott 60.00 30.00
165 Hank Severeid 60.00 30.00
166 Mike Simon 60.00 30.00
167 Wally Smith 60.00 30.00
168 Frank Smith 60.00 30.00
169 Fred Snodgrass 100.00 50.00
170 Tris Speaker 1200.00 600.00
171 Harry Spratt 60.00 30.00
172 Eddie Stack 60.00 30.00
173 Oscar Stanage 60.00 30.00
174 Bill Steele 60.00 30.00
175 Harry Steinfeldt 80.00 40.00
176 George Stovall 60.00 30.00
177 Gabby Street 80.00 40.00
178 Amos Strunk 60.00 30.00
179 Billy Sullivan 80.00 40.00
180 Bill Sweeney 120.00 60.00
181 Lee Tannehill 60.00 30.00
182 Claude Thomas 60.00 30.00
183 Joe Tinker 250.00 125.00
184 Bert Tooley 60.00 30.00
185 Terry Turner 60.00 30.00
186 Lefty Tyler 600.00 300.00
187 Hippo Vaughn 60.00 30.00
188 Heine Wagner 100.00 50.00
Bos AL, correct back
189 Heine Wagner 200.00 100.00
Bos AL, Carrigan back
190 Dixie Walker 60.00 30.00
191 Bobby Wallace 200.00 100.00
192 Jack Warhop 60.00 30.00
193 Buck Weaver 600.00 300.00
194 Zack Wheat 200.00 100.00
195 Doc White 100.00 50.00
196 Dewey Wilie 100.00 50.00
197 Bob Williams 60.00 30.00
198 Art Wilson 60.00 30.00
199 Chief Wilson 100.00 50.00
200 Hooks Wiltse 60.00 30.00
201 Ivey Wingo 60.00 30.00
202 Harry Wolverton 60.00 30.00
203 Joe Wood 200.00 100.00
204 Gene Woodburn 120.00 60.00
205 Ralph Works 300.00 150.00
206 Steve Yerkes 60.00 30.00
207 Rollie Zeider 120.00 60.00

1912 T227 Series of Champions

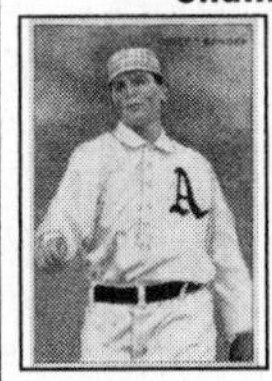

The cards in this four-card set measure approximately 2 5/16" by 3 3/8". Actually these four baseball players are but a small part of a larger set featuring a total of 21 other "Champions." The set was produced in 1912. These cards are unnumbered; the players have been alphabetized and numbered for reference in the checklist below. Card backs can be found with either Miners Extra or Honest Long Cut. The complete set price refers only to the 4 subjects listed immediately below and does not include any non-baseball subjects that may be in the set.

Ex-Mt VG
COMPLETE SET (4) 6000.00 3000.00
1 Frank Baker 800.00 400.00
2 Chief Bender 600.00 300.00
3 Ty Cobb 4000.00 2000.00
4 Rube Marquard 600.00 300.00

1916 Tango Brand Eggs

This 20-card set of 1916 Tango Brand Eggs Baseball cards was issued by the L. Frank Company in New Orleans as a promotion to increase egg sales. Less than 500 examples are known to exist, with some of the cards having quantities of less than 10 copies found. The cards have a glazed finish, a process used in several other sets of this vintage (E106, D303, T213 and T216). The fronts display a player color photo in a mix of poses (portrait, throwing, fielding, and batting). The player's name, position, and team are printed below the photo. Some of the cards are off center and poorly cut. The backs carry promotional information for the Tango Brand Eggs. The cards do not carry the Federal League designation since the league dissolved in 1915 and players moved back to the National and American League teams. One irregularity is the fact that Demmitt, Dooin, Jacklitsch, and Tinker of the E106 set appear as cards of Meyer, Morgan, Meyer, and Weaver in the Tango Brand Egg set. The set can be dated 1916, as "Germany" Schaefer appears in the set as a Brooklyn player, and prior to that year he played for Neward of the Federal League. During the 1916 season he was sold to the New York Americans, making that the only year he played for Brooklyn. The cards are unnumbered and checklisted below alphabetically.

Ex-Mt VG
COMPLETE SET (20) 10000.00 5000.00
1 Bob Bescher 150.00 75.00
2 Roger Bresnahan 250.00 125.00
3 Al Bridwell 150.00 75.00
4 Hal Chase 250.00 125.00
5 Ty Cobb 6000.00 3000.00
6 Eddie Collins 1500.00 750.00
7 Sam Crawford 1500.00 750.00
8 Red Dooin 150.00 75.00
9 Johnny Evers 300.00 150.00
10 Hap Felsch 300.00 150.00
Photo of Ray Demmitt
11 Hugh Jennings 250.00 125.00
12 George McQuillen 150.00 75.00
13 Billy Meyer 200.00 100.00
Photo of Fred Jacklitsch
14 Ray Morgan 200.00 100.00
Photo of Red Dooin
15 Eddie Murphy 150.00 75.00
16 Germany Schaefer 200.00 100.00
17 Joe Tinker 300.00 150.00
18 Honus Wagner 500.00 250.00
19 Buck Weaver 1000.00 500.00
Photo of Joe Tinker
20 Heinie Zimmerman 150.00 75.00

1934 Tarzan Thoro Bread D382

These cards measuring approximately 2 1/2"" by 3 1/8"and featuring attractive black and white photos were issued with Tarzan Thoro Bread. The players name is in the upper right hand corner. Since the cards are unnumbered, we have sequenced them in alphabetical order.

Ex-Mt VG
COMPLETE SET 7500.00 3800.00
1 Sparky Adams 300.00 150.00
2 Walter Betts 300.00 150.00
3 Edward Brandt 300.00 150.00
4 Tommy Bridges 400.00 200.00
5 Irving 'Jack' Burns 300.00 150.00
6 Bruce Campbell 300.00 150.00
7 Tex Carleton 300.00 150.00
8 Dick Coffman 300.00 150.00
9 George Connally 300.00 150.00
10 Tony Cuccinello 300.00 150.00
11 Debs Garms 300.00 150.00
12 Alex Gaston 300.00 150.00
13 Bill Hallahan 300.00 150.00
14 Myril Hoag 300.00 150.00
15 Chief Hogsett 300.00 150.00
16 Arndt Jorgens 300.00 150.00
17 Tom Zachary 300.00 150.00
17 Willie Kamm 400.00 200.00
18 Dutch Leonard 300.00 150.00
19 Clyde Manion 300.00 150.00
20 Eric McNair 300.00 150.00
21 Oscar Mellilo 300.00 150.00
22 Bob O'Farrell 300.00 150.00
23 Gus Suhr 300.00 150.00
24 Evar Swanson 300.00 150.00
25 Billy Urbanski 300.00 150.00
26 Johnny Vergez 300.00 150.00
27 Red Worthington 300.00 150.00

1969 Tasco Associates

These oversized crude caricatures were issued by Tasco Associates and featured some of the leading players in baseball. It is presumed that the set was skewed towards the more popular teams since certain teams have many more players known to exist than other less popular teams. This checklist may be incomplete so any additions are appreciated. We have sequenced this set in alphabetical order.

NM Ex
COMPLETE SET 250.00 100.00
1 Hank Aaron 15.00 6.00
2 Richie Allen 8.00 3.20
3 Mike Andrews 5.00 2.00
4 Luis Aparicio 10.00 4.00
5 Ernie Banks 10.00 4.00
6 Glenn Beckert 5.00 2.00
7 Johnny Bench 15.00 6.00
8 Norm Cash 8.00 3.20
9 Danny Cater 5.00 2.00
10 Tony Conigliaro 8.00 3.20
11 Ray Culp 5.00 2.00
12 Don Drysdale 10.00 4.00
13 Bill Freehan 6.00 2.40
14 Jim Fregosi 5.00 2.00
15 Bob Gibson 10.00 4.00
16 Bill Hands 5.00 2.00
17 Ken Holtzman 5.00 2.00
18 Frank Howard 6.00 2.40
19 Randy Hundley 5.00 2.00
20 Ferguson Jenkins 10.00 4.00
21 Jerry Koosman
22 Juan Marichal 10.00 4.00
23 Willie Mays 15.00 6.00
24 Bill Mazeroski 10.00 4.00
25 Dick McAuliffe 5.00 2.00
26 Dave McNally 5.00 2.00
27 Jim Northrup 5.00 2.00
28 Tony Oliva 8.00 3.20
29 Rico Petrocelli 5.00 2.00
30 Adolpho Phillips 5.00 2.00
31 Brooks Robinson 10.00 4.00
32 Pete Rose 15.00 6.00
33 Ron Santo 8.00 3.20
34 George Scott 5.00 2.00
35 Reggie Smith 6.00 2.40
36 Mel Stottlemyre 5.00 2.00
37 Luis Tiant 6.00 2.40
38 Billy Williams 10.00 4.00
39 Carl Yastrzemski 12.00 4.80

1978 Tastee-Freez Discs

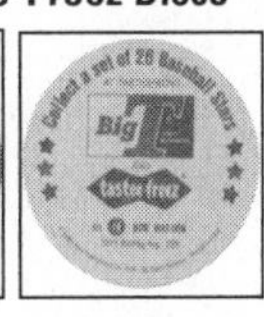

This set of 26 discs were given out at participating Big T and Tastee-Freez restaurants. The discs measure 3 3/8" in diameter and were produced by MSA. The front design features a black and white headshot inside a white baseball diamond pattern. Four red stars adorn the top of the discs, and the white diamond is bordered by various colors on different discs. The backs are printed in red and blue on white and provide the disc number, player's name, his batting average or won/loss record, and sponsors' advertisements.

NM Ex
COMPLETE SET (26) 35.00 14.00
1 Buddy Bell 1.00 .40
2 Jim Palmer 4.00 1.60
3 Steve Garvey 1.50 .60
4 Jeff Burroughs .50 .20
5 Greg Luzinski 1.00 .40
6 Lou Brock 3.00 1.20
7 Thurman Munson 2.00 .80
8 Rod Carew 3.00 1.20
9 George Brett 10.00 4.00
10 Tom Seaver 4.00 1.60
11 Willie Stargell 3.00 1.20
12 Jerry Koosman .50 .20
13 Bill North .50 .20
14 Richie Zisk .50 .20
15 Bill Madlock 1.00 .40
16 Carl Yastrzemski 3.00 1.20
17 Dave Cash .50 .20
18 Bob Watson 1.00 .40
19 Dave Kingman 2.00 .80
20 Gene Tenace .50 .20
21 Ralph Garr .50 .20
22 Mark Fidrych 3.00 1.20
23 Frank Tanana 1.00 .40
24 Larry Hisle .50 .20
25 Bruce Bochte .50 .20
26 Bob Bailor .50 .20

1933 Tatoo Orbit R305

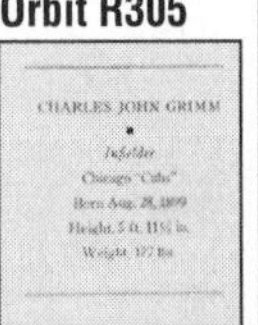

The cards in this 60-card set measure 2" by 2 1/4". The 1933 Tatoo Orbit set contains unnumbered, color cards. Blaeholder and Hadley, and to a lesser degree Andrews and Hornsby are considered more difficult to obtain than the other cards in this set. The cards are ordered and numbered below alphabetically by the player's name.

Ex-Mt VG
COMPLETE SET (60) 3500.00 1800.00
1 Dale Alexander 40.00 20.00
2 Ivy Andrews 120.00 60.00
3 Earl Averill 80.00 40.00
4 Dick Bartell 40.00 20.00
5 Wally Berger 40.00 20.00
6 George Blaeholder 200.00 100.00
7 Irving Burns 40.00 20.00
8 Guy Bush 40.00 20.00
9 Bruce Campbell 40.00 20.00
10 Chalmers Cissell 40.00 20.00
11 Watson Clark 40.00 20.00
12 Mickey Cochrane 120.00 60.00
13 Phil Collins 40.00 20.00
14 Kiki Cuyler 80.00 40.00
15 Dizzy Dean 200.00 100.00
16 Jimmy Dykes 50.00 25.00
17 George Earnshaw 40.00 20.00
18 Woody English 40.00 20.00
19 Lou Fonseca 40.00 20.00
20 Jimmy Foxx 150.00 75.00
21 Burleigh Grimes 80.00 40.00
22 Charlie Grimm 60.00 30.00
23 Lefty Grove 120.00 60.00
24 Frank Grube 40.00 20.00
25 George Haas 40.00 20.00
26 Bump Hadley 200.00 100.00
27 Chick Hafey 80.00 40.00
28 Jess Haines 80.00 40.00
29 Bill Hallahan 40.00 20.00
30 Mel Harder 50.00 25.00
31 Gabby Hartnett 80.00 40.00
32 Babe Herman 60.00 36.00
33 Billy Herman 80.00 40.00
34 Rogers Hornsby 250.00 125.00
35 Roy Johnson 40.00 20.00
36 Smead Jolley 40.00 20.00
37 Billy Jurges 40.00 20.00
38 Willie Kamm 40.00 20.00
39 Mark Koenig 40.00 20.00
40 Jim Levey 40.00 20.00
41 Ernie Lombardi 80.00 40.00
42 Red Lucas 40.00 20.00
43 Ted Lyons 80.00 40.00
44 Connie Mack MG 100.00 50.00
45 Pat Malone 40.00 20.00
46 Pepper Martin 60.00 30.00
47 Marty McManus 40.00 20.00
48 Lefty O'Doul 60.00 30.00
49 Dick Porter 40.00 20.00
50 Carl N. Reynolds 40.00 20.00
51 Charlie Root 50.00 25.00
52 Bob Seeds 40.00 20.00
53 Al Simmons 80.00 40.00
54 Riggs Stephenson 50.00 25.00
55 Lyle Tinning 40.00 20.00
56 Joe Vosmik 40.00 20.00
57 Rube Walberg 40.00 20.00
58 Paul Waner 80.00 40.00
59 Lon Warneke 40.00 20.00
60 Arthur Whitney 40.00 20.00

1933 Tatoo Orbit Self Develop R308

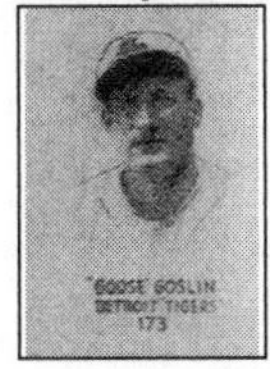

These very small (1 1/4" by 1 7/8") and unattractive cards are very scarce. They were produced by Tatoo Orbit around 1933. The set is presumed to include the numbers between 151 and 210; a few of the numbers are still unknown at this time. Badly over exposed cards are very difficult to identify and are considered (graded) fair at best. Two types of these cards are known: A larger card (of which only very few are known) and are very rare, and a smaller type -- which is considered the normal card. We are pricing the smaller cards.

Ex-Mt VG
COMPLETE SET 4000.00 2000.00
151 Vernon Gomez 120.00 60.00
152 Kiki Cuyler 100.00 50.00
153 Jimmy Foxx 300.00 150.00
154 Al Simmons 120.00 60.00
155 Gordon Cochrane 120.00 60.00
156 Woody English 60.00 30.00
157 Chuck Klein 100.00 50.00
158 Dick Bartell 60.00 30.00
159 Pepper Martin 80.00 40.00
160 Earl Averill 100.00 50.00
161 William Dickey 120.00 60.00
162 Wesley Ferrell 80.00 40.00
163 Oral Hildebrand 60.00 30.00
164 Willie Kamm 60.00 30.00
165 Earl Whitehill 60.00 30.00
166 Charles Fullis 60.00 30.00
167 Jimmy Dykes 60.00 30.00
168 Ben Cantwell 60.00 30.00
169 George Earnshaw 60.00 30.00
170 Jackson Stephenson 80.00 40.00
171 Randy Moore 60.00 30.00
172 Ted Lyons 100.00 50.00
173 Goose Goslin 100.00 50.00
174 Evar Swanson 60.00 30.00
175 Leroy Mahaffey 60.00 30.00
176 Joe Cronin 120.00 60.00
177 Tom Bridges 60.00 30.00
178 Henry Manush 100.00 50.00
179 Walter Stewart 60.00 30.00
180 Frank Pytlak 60.00 30.00
181 Dale Alexander 60.00 30.00
182 Robert Grove 150.00 75.00
183 Charles Gehringer 120.00 60.00
184 Lewis Fonseca 60.00 30.00
185 Alvin Crowder 60.00 30.00
186 Mickey Cochrane 120.00 60.00
187 Max Bishop 60.00 30.00
188 Connie Mack MG 120.00 60.00
189 Guy Bush 60.00 30.00
190 Charlie Root 60.00 30.00
191 Burleigh Grimes 100.00 50.00
Gabby Hartnett
192 Pat Malone 60.00 30.00
193 Woody English 60.00 30.00
194 Lonnie Warneke 60.00 30.00
195 Babe Herman 80.00 40.00
200 Gabby Hartnett 100.00 50.00
201 Paul Waner 120.00 60.00
202 Dizzy Dean 300.00 150.00
205 Jim Bottomley 100.00 50.00
207 Charles Hafey 100.00 50.00

1976 Taylor/Schmierer Bowman 47

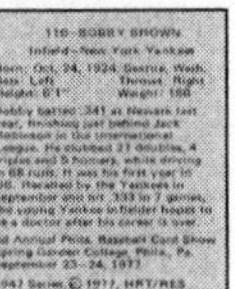

This set which measures 2 1/16" by 2 1/2" was issued by show promoters Bob Schmierer and Ted Taylor to promote what would become their long running EPSCC shows in the Philadelphia area. The set is designed in the style of the 1948 Bowman set and according to stories even some of the same paper stock was used for these sets as was used in 1948. The first series (1-49) cards sell for considerably more than the later two series. A reprint card of the T-206 Wagner along with a card of show promoter and long time hobbyist Ted Taylor were also produced. They are not considered part of the complete set.

NM Ex
COMPLETE SET (113) 200.00 80.00
COMMON CARD (1-49) 1.00 .40
COMMON CARD (50-113) .25 .10

1 Bobby Doerr 4.00 1.60
2 Stan Musial 10.00 4.00
3 Babe Ruth 20.00 8.00
4 Joe DiMaggio 15.00 6.00
5 Andy Pafko 1.00 .40
6 Johnny Pesky 1.00 .40
7 Gil Hodges 8.00 3.20
8 Tommy Holmes 1.00 .40
9 Ralph Kiner 8.00 3.20
10 Yogi Berra 10.00 4.00
11 Bob Feller 4.00 1.60
12 Sid Gordon 1.00 .40
13 Eddie Joost 1.00 .40
14 Del Ennis 1.00 .40
15 Johnny Mize 8.00 3.20
16 Pee Wee Reese 10.00 4.00
17 Jackie Robinson 15.00 6.00
18 Enos Slaughter 4.00 1.60
19 Vern Stephens 1.00 .40
20 Bobby Thomson 2.00 .80
21 Ted Williams 15.00 6.00
22 Bob Elliott 1.00 .40
23 Mickey Vernon 1.00 .40
24 Ewell Blackwell 1.00 .40
25 Lou Boudreau 4.00 1.60
26 Ralph Branca 1.00 .40
27 Harry Breechen 1.00 .40
28 Dom DiMaggio 3.00 1.20
29 Bruce Edwards 1.00 .40
30 Sam Chapman 1.00 .40
31 George Kell 4.00 1.60
32 Jack Kramer 1.00 .40
33 Hal Newhouser 4.00 1.60
34 Charlie Keller 1.00 .40
35 Ken Keltner 1.00 .40
36 Hank Greenberg 8.00 3.20
37 Howie Pollet 1.00 .40
38 Luke Appling 4.00 1.60
39 Pete Suder 1.00 .40
40 Johnny Sain 3.00 1.20
41 Phil Cavaretta 2.00 .80
42 Johnny Vander Meer 2.00 .80
43 Mel Ott 8.00 3.20
44 Walker Cooper 1.00 .40
45 Birdie Tebbetts 1.00 .40
46 Snuffy Stirnweiss 1.00 .40
47 Connie Mack MG 4.00 1.60
48 Jimmie Foxx 8.00 3.20
49 Joe DiMaggio 15.00 6.00
Babe Ruth
Checklist Back
50 Schoolboy Rowe .25 .10
51 Andy Seminick .25 .10
52 Dixie Walker .25 .10
53 Virgil Trucks .25 .10
54 Dizzy Trout .25 .10
55 Hoot Evers .25 .10
56 Thurman Tucker .25 .10
57 Fritz Ostermuller .25 .10
58 Augie Galan .25 .10
59 Babe Young .25 .10
60 Skeeter Newsome .25 .10
61 Jack Lohrke .25 .10
62 Rudy York .50 .20
63 Tex Hughson .25 .10
64 Sam Mele .25 .10
65 Fred Hutchinson .50 .20
66 Don Black .25 .10
67 Les Fleming .25 .10
68 George McQuinn .25 .10
69 Mike McCormick .25 .10
70 Mickey Witek .25 .10
71 Blix Donnelly .25 .10
72 Elbie Fletcher .25 .10
73 Hal Gregg .25 .10
74 Dick Whitman .25 .10
75 Johnny Neun MG .25 .10
76 Doyle Lade .25 .10
77 Ron Northey .25 .10
78 Mort Cooper .25 .10
79 Warren Spahn 3.00 1.20
80 Happy Chandler COMM 1.00 .40
81 Connie Mack 1.00 .40
Roy Mack
Connie Mack III
Checklist Back
82 Earle Mack Asst MG .25 .10
83 Buddy Rosar .25 .10
84 Walt Judnich .25 .10
85 Bob Kennedy .25 .10
86 Mike Tresh .25 .10
87 Sid Hudson .25 .10
88 Gene Thompson .25 .10
89 Bill Nicholson .25 .10
90 Stan Hack .25 .10
91 Terry Moore .50 .20
92 Ted Lyons MG 1.00 .40
93 Barney McCoskey .25 .10
94 Stan Spence .25 .10
95 Larry Jansen .25 .10
96 Whitey Kurowski .25 .10
97 Honus Wagner CO 4.00 1.60
98 Billy Herman MG 1.00 .40
99 Jim Tabor .25 .10
100 Phil Marchidon .25 .10
101 Dave Ferriss .25 .10
102 Al Zarilla .25 .10
103 Bob Dillinger .50 .20
104 Bob Lemon 2.00 .80
105 Jim Hegan .25 .10
106 Johnny Lindell .25 .10
107 Williard Marshall .25 .10
108 Walt Masterson .25 .10
109 Carl Scheib .25 .10
110 Bobby Brown .75 .30
111 Cy Block .25 .10
112 Sid Gordon .50 .20
113 Ty Cobb 8.00 3.20
Babe Ruth
Tris Speaker
Checklist Back
NNO Honus Wagner 5.00 2.00
NNO Ted Taylor .25 .10

1972 TCMA the 1930's Panels

This set consists of two 9" by 12" panels of 12 uncut cards each which feature black-and-white photos of players who played during the 1930's. The photos measure approximately 2 1/16" by 2 7/8" each. One panel contains cards #169-180, while the other panel consists of cards #193-204.

NM Ex
COMPLETE SET 30.00 12.00
169 Alvin Crowder 1.00 .40
170 August Suhr 1.00 .40
171 Monty Stratton 2.00 .80
172 Louis Berger 1.00 .40
173 John Whitehead 1.00 .40
174 Joe Heving 1.00 .40
175 Mervyn Shea 1.00 .40
176 Ed Durham 1.00 .40
177 Buddy Myer 2.00 .80
178 Carl Whitehill 1.00 .40
179 Joe Cronin 4.00 1.60
180 Zeke Bonura 2.00 .80
193 George Myatt 1.00 .40
194 Bill Werber 2.00 .80
195 Red Lucas 1.00 .40
196 Hal Luby 1.00 .40
197 Vic Sorrell 1.00 .40
198 Mickey Cochrane 4.00 1.60
199 Rudy York 2.00 .80
200 Ray Mack 1.00 .40
201 Vince DiMaggio 2.00 .80
202 Mel Ott 4.00 1.60
203 John Lucadello 1.00 .40
204 Debs Garms 1.00 .40

1972 TCMA's the 30's

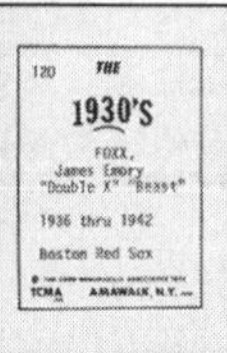

This 120-card set features borderless black-and-white photos of players who played during the 1930's and measures approximately 2" by 2 7/8". The backs carry the player's name, team and years during the 1930's in which he played. Cards numbered 1-72 are unnumbered and checklisted below alphabetically. Cards numbered 73-120 are listed according to the number on their backs.

NM Ex
COMPLETE SET (120) 75.00 30.00
1 Beau Bell .50 .20
2 Max Bishop .50 .20
3 Robert Boken .50 .20
4 Cliff Bolton .50 .20
5 John Broaca .50 .20
6 Bill Brubaker .50 .20
7 Slick Castleman .50 .20
8 Dick Coffman .50 .20
9 Philip Collins .50 .20
10 Earle Combs 2.00 .80
11 Doc Cramer 1.00 .40
12 Joseph Cronin 2.00 .80
13 Jack Crouch .50 .20
14 Anthony Cuccinello .50 .20
15 Babe Dahlgren 1.00 .40
16 Spud Davis .50 .20
17 Daffy Dean 1.00 .40
18 Dizzy Dean 3.00 1.20
19 Bill Dickey 2.00 .80
20 Joe DiMaggio 8.00 3.20
21 George Earnshaw .50 .20
22 Woody English .50 .20
(Portrait)
23 Woody English .50 .20
(Batting)
24 Harold Finney .50 .20
25 Freddie Fitzsimmons 1.00 .40
Hadley Fitzsimmons
26 Tony Freitas .50 .20
27 Frank Frisch 2.00 .80
28 Milt Gaston .50 .20
29 Sidney Gautreaux .50 .20
30 Charles Gehringer 2.00 .80
31 Charles Gelbert .50 .20
32 Lefty Gomez 2.00 .80
33 Lefty Grove 2.00 .80
34 Charles Hafey 1.50 .60
35 Jesse Haines 1.50 .60
36 William Hallahan 1.00 .40
37 Stanley Harris 2.00 .80
38 Edward Heusser .50 .20
39 Carl Hubbell 2.00 .80
(Portrait)
40 Carl Hubbell 2.00 .80
(Throwing)
41 James Jordan .50 .20
42 Joseph Judge 1.00 .40
43 Leonard Koenecke .50 .20
44 Mark Koenig 1.00 .40
45 Cookie Lavagetto 1.00 .40
46 Alfred Lawson .50 .20
47 Tony Lazzeri 2.00 .80
48 Gus Mancuso .50 .20
49 John McCarthy .50 .20
50 Joe Medwick 2.00 .80
51 Clifford Melton .50 .20
52 Terry Moore 1.50 .60
53 John Murphy 1.00 .40
54 Ken O'Dea .50 .20
55 Robert O'Farrell .50 .20
56 Manuel Onis .50 .20
57 Monte Pearson .50 .20
58 Paul Richards 1.00 .40
59 Max Rosenfeld .50 .20
60 Red Ruffing 2.00 .80
(Side view throwing)
61 Red Ruffing 2.00 .80
(Front view throwing)
62 Harold Schumacher 1.00 .40
63 George Selkirk .50 .20
64 Joseph Shaute .50 .20
65 Gordon Slade .50 .20
66 Lindo Storti .50 .20
67 Stephen Sundra .50 .20
68 Bill Terry 2.00 .80
69 John Tising .50 .20
70 Joseph Vance .50 .20
71 Rube Walberg 1.00 .40
72 Samuel West 1.00 .40
73 Vic Tamulis .50 .20
74 Kemp Wicker .50 .20
75 Robert Seeds .50 .20
76 Jack Saltzgaver .50 .20
77 Walter Brown .50 .20
78 Spud Chandler 1.00 .40
79 Myril Hoag .50 .20
80 Joseph Glenn .50 .20
81 Lefty Gomez 2.00 .80
82 Art Jorgens .50 .20
83 Jesse Hill .50 .20
84 Red Rolfe 1.50 .60
85 Wesley Ferrell 1.50 .60
86 Joseph Morrissey .50 .20
87 Anthony Piet .50 .20
88 Fred Walker 1.50 .60
89 William Dietrich .50 .20
90 Lynford Lary .50 .20
(Portrait)
91 Lynford Lary .50 .20
(Batting)
92 Lynford Lary .50 .20
(Batting in striped uniform)
93 Lynford Lary .50 .20
(Batting facing forward)
94 Ralph Boyle .50 .20
95 Tony Malinosky .50 .20
96 Al Lopez 2.00 .80
97 Lonny Frey .50 .20
98 Anthony Malinosky .50 .20
99 Owen Carroll .50 .20
100 John Hassett .50 .20
101 Gib Brack .50 .20
102 Samuel Leslie .50 .20
103 Fred Heimach .50 .20
104 Burleigh Grimes 2.00 .80
105 Ray Benge .50 .20
106 Joseph Stripp .50 .20
107 Joseph Becker .50 .20
108 Oscar Melillo .50 .20
109 Charles O'Leary CO 2.00 .80
Roger Hornsby MG
110 Luke Appling 2.00 .80
111 Stanley Hack 1.00 .40
112 Raymond Hayworth .50 .20
113 Charles Wilson .50 .20
114 Hal Trosky 1.50 .60
115 Wes Ferrell 1.50 .60
116 Lyn Lary .50 .20
(Throwing)
117 Nathaniel Gaston .50 .20
118 Eldon Auker 1.00 .40
119 Heinie Manush 2.00 .80
120 James Foxx 5.00 2.00

1973-79 TCMA All-Time Greats

This set eatures black-and-white photos of some of the greatest baseball players of all time. These cards measure approximately 3 1/2" by 5 1/2". The cards are unnumbered and checklisted below in alphabetical order in order of the series they were released in. The Cy Young card in 1st series of 1973 did not have the 1973 information on the back.

NM Ex
COMPLETE SET 250.00 100.00
1 Luke Appling 1.00 .40
2 Mickey Cochrane 2.00 .80
3 Eddie Collins 2.50 1.00
4 Kiki Cuyler 1.00 .40
5 Bill Dickey 1.50 .60
6 Joe DiMaggio 10.00 4.00
7 Bob Feller 4.00 1.60
8 Frankie Frisch 1.50 .60
9 Lou Gehrig 6.00 2.40
10 Goose Goslin 1.00 .40
11 Chick Hafey 1.00 .40
12 Gabby Hartnett 1.50 .60
13 Rogers Hornsby 2.50 1.00
14 Ted Lyons 1.00 .40
15 Connie Mack 1.50 .60
16 Heinie Manush 1.00 .40
17 Rabbit Maranville 1.00 .40
18 Joe Medwick 1.00 .40
19 Al Simmons 1.50 .60
20 Bill Terry 1.50 .60
21 Pie Traynor 1.50 .60
22 Dazzy Vance 1.00 .40
23 Cy Young 4.00 1.60
24 Gabby Hartnett 5.00 2.00
Babe Ruth
25 Roger Bresnahan 1.00 .40
26 Dizzy Dean 2.00 .80
27 Buck Ewing 1.00 .40
Mascot
28 Jimmy Foxx 2.50 1.00
29 Hank Greenberg 2.50 1.00
30 Burleigh Grimes 1.00 .40
31 Harry Heilmann 1.00 .40
32 Waite Hoyt 1.00 .40
33 Walter Johnson 2.50 1.00
34 George Kelly 1.00 .40
35 Stan Musial 5.00 2.00
36 Christy Mathewson 2.50 1.00
37 John McGraw 1.50 .60
38 Mel Ott 2.50 1.00
39 Satchel Paige 2.50 1.00
40 Sam Rice 1.00 .40
41 Edd Roush 1.00 .40
42 Red Ruffing 1.00 .40
43 Casey Stengel 2.00 .80
44 Harry Wright 1.00 .40
45 Paul Waner 1.50 .60
46 Honus Wagner 2.50 1.00
47 Lloyd Waner 1.00 .40
48 Ross Youngs 1.00 .40
49 Frank Baker 1.50 .60
50 Chief Bender 1.50 .60
51 Jim Bottomley 1.00 .40
52 Lou Boudreau 1.50 .60
53 Mordecai Brown 2.00 .80
54 Roy Campanella 2.50 1.00
55 Max Carey 1.00 .40
56 Ty Cobb 5.00 2.00
57 Earle Combs 1.50 .60
58 Jocko Conlan 1.00 .40
59 Hugh Duffy 1.00 .40
60 Red Faber 1.00 .40
61 Lefty Grove 2.50 1.00
62 Kennesaw M. Landis 1.00 .40
63 Eddie Plank 1.50 .60
64 Hoss Radbourne 1.00 .40
Sic, spelled without an E
65 Eppa Rixey 1.00 .40
66 Jackie Robinson 6.00 2.40
67 Babe Ruth 10.00 4.00
68 George Sisler 1.50 .60
69 Zack Wheat 1.50 .60
70 Ted Williams 8.00 3.20
71 Mel Ott 6.00 2.40
Babe Ruth
72 Tris Speaker 2.50 1.00
Wilbert Robinson
109 Dave Bancroft 1.00 .40
110 Ernie Banks 3.00 1.20
111 Frank Chance 2.50 1.00
112 Stan Covaleskie 1.00 .40
113 Billy Evans 1.00 .40
114 Clark Griffith 1.50 .60
115 Jesse Haines 1.00 .40
116 Will Harridge 1.00 .40
117 Harry Hooper 1.00 .40
118 Cal Hubbard 1.00 .40
119 Hugh Jennings 1.50 .60
120 Willie Keeler 2.50 1.00
121 Fred Lindstrom 1.00 .40
122 John Henry Lloyd 2.00 .80
123 Al Lopez 1.00 .40
124 Robin Roberts 2.50 1.00
125 Amos Rusie 1.00 .40
126 Ray Schalk 1.00 .40
127 Joe Sewell 1.00 .40
128 Rube Waddell 1.50 .60
129 George Weiss 1.00 .40
130 Dizzy Dean 1.50 .60
Gabby Hartnett
131 Joe DiMaggio 10.00 4.00
Mickey Mantle
132 Ted Williams 10.00 4.00
Joe DiMaggio
133 Jack Chesbro 1.00 .40
134 Tom Connolly 1.00 .40
135 Sam Crawford 1.50 .60
136 Elmer Flick 1.00 .40
137 Charlie Gehringer 1.50 .60
138 Warren Giles 1.00 .40
139 Ban Johnson 1.00 .40
140 Addie Joss 1.00 .40
141 Al Kaline 3.00 1.20
142 Willie Mays 5.00 2.00
143 Joe McGinnity 1.00 .40
144 Larry MacPhail 1.00 .40
145 Branch Rickey 1.00 .40
146 Wilbert Robinson 1.00 .40
147 Duke Snider 4.00 1.60
148 Tris Speaker 2.50 1.00
149 Bobby Wallace 1.00 .40
150 Hack Wilson 1.00 .40
151 Yogi Berra 5.00 2.00
Casey Stengel
152 Warren Giles PRES 5.00 2.00
Roberto Clemente
153 Mickey Mantle 10.00 4.00
Willie Mays
154 John McGraw 6.00 2.40
Babe Ruth
155 Satchel Paige 6.00 2.40
Bob Feller
156 Paul Waner 5.00 2.00
Lloyd Waner

1974 TCMA Nicknames

This 27-card set features black-and-white player photos with red printing and measures approximately 2 1/4" by 3 1/2". The backs carry player information.

NM Ex
COMPLETE SET (27) 40.00 16.00
1 Bob Feller 2.50 1.00
2 Babe Ruth 10.00 4.00
3 Spud Chandler 1.50 .60
4 Ducky Medwick 2.50 1.00
5 Cal Benge 1.00 .40
6 Goose Goslin 2.50 1.00
7 Mule Haas 1.00 .40
8 Dizzy Dean 2.50 1.00
9 Ray Harrell 1.00 .40
10 Ralph Boyle 1.00 .40
11 Curtis Davis 1.00 .40
12 Moose Solters 1.00 .40
13 Sam Jones 1.00 .40
14 Bad News Hale 1.00 .40
15 Bucky Harris 2.50 1.00
16 Jim Jordan 1.00 .40
17 Zeke Bonura 1.50 .60
19 Virgil Davis 1.00 .40
20 Bing Miller 1.00 .40
21 Preacher Roe 1.50 .60
22 Bill Hallahan 1.00 .40
23 Bob Johnson 1.00 .40
24 Joe Gordon 1.50 .60
25 Tot Presnell 1.00 .40
26 Luke Hamlin 1.00 .40
27 Tommy Henrich 2.00 .80
28 Tom Hafey 1.00 .40

1975 TCMA All-Time Greats

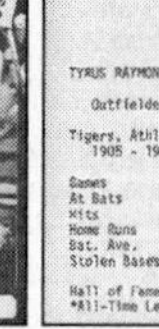

This 36-card set measures approximately 2 3/8" by 3 3/4" and features blue-and white player photos. The pictures are framed in blue with a bat and ball in each top corner. The card name and player's name are in the top and bottom margins respectively. The backs carry the player's name, position, team name and career stats. The cards are unnumbered and checklisted below in alphabetical order.

NM Ex
COMPLETE SET (36) 50.00 20.00
1 Earl Averill 1.00 .40
2 Jim Bottomley 1.00 .40
3 Lou Boudreau 1.00 .40
4 Fred Clarke 1.00 .40
5 Roberto Clemente 5.00 2.00
6 Ty Cobb 5.00 2.00
7 Jocko Conlon 1.00 .40
8 Hugh Duffy 1.00 .40
9 Red Faber 1.00 .40
10 Whitey Ford 2.50 1.00
11 Jimmy Foxx 2.50 1.00
12 Burleigh Grimes 1.00 .40
13 Lefty Grove 2.00 .80
14 Bucky Harris 1.00 .40
15 Billy Herman 1.00 .40
16 Miller Huggins 1.00 .40
17 Monte Irvin 1.00 .40
18 Ralph Kiner 2.00 .80
19 Sandy Koufax 2.50 1.00
20 Judge Landis 1.00 .40
21 Mickey Mantle 5.00 2.00
22 Joe McCarthy 1.00 .40
23 John McGraw 1.00 .40
24 Bill McKechnie 1.00 .40
25 Ducky Medwick 1.00 .40
26 Hoss Radborn 1.00 .40
27 Sam Rice 1.00 .40
28 Jackie Robinson 5.00 2.00
29 Wilbert Robinson 1.00 .40
30 Babe Ruth 8.00 3.20
31 Babe Ruth 8.00 3.20
(Closer head photo)
32 George Sisler 1.00 .40
33 Tris Speaker 1.00 .40
34 Zack Wheat 1.00 .40
35 Ted Williams 5.00 2.00
36 Ross Youngs 1.00 .40

1975 TCMA Guam

This 18-card set measures approximately 3 1/2" by 5 1/2" and features black and white photos of baseball players who served in the Navy in Guam during World War II. The backs display an on-going story about the team by Harrington Crissey.

NM Ex
COMPLETE SET (18) 20.00 8.00
1 Phil Rizzuto 2.50 1.00
Terry Moore
2 Gab Gab Guam 1945 1.00 .40
3 Team Photo 1.00 .40
4 Merrill May 1.00 .40
Pee Wee Reese
Johnny Vander Meer
5 Team Photo 1.00 .40
6 Team Photo 1.00 .40
7 Del Ennis 1.50 .60
8 Mace Brown 1.50 .60
9 Pee Wee Reese 2.50 1.00
Joe Gordon
Bill Dickey
10 Glenn McQuillen 1.00 .40
11 Mike Budnick 1.00 .40
12 Team Photo 1.00 .40
13 George "Skeets" Dickey 1.00 .40
14 Connie Ryan 1.00 .40
15 Hal White 1.00 .40
16 Mickey Cochrane 2.50 1.00
17 Barney McCosky 1.00 .40
18 Ben Huffman 1.00 .40

1975 TCMA House of Jazz

This 35-card set features black-and-white player photos printed on thin card stock and measuring approximately 2 3/8" by 3 1/2". The cards are unnumbered and checklisted below in alphabetical order.

NM Ex
COMPLETE SET (35) 60.00 24.00
1 John Antonelli .50 .20
2 Richie Ashburn 2.00 .80
3 Ernie Banks 3.00 1.20
4 Hank Bauer 1.00 .40
5 Joe DiMaggio 5.00 2.00
6 Bobby Doerr .50 .20
7 Herman Franks .50 .20
8 Lou Gehrig 5.00 2.00
9 Granny Hamner .50 .20
10 Al Kaline 2.00 .80
11 Harmon Killebrew 2.00 .80
12 Jim Konstanty .50 .20
13 Bob Lemon 1.50 .60
14 Ed Lopat .50 .20
15 Stan Lopata .50 .20
16 Peanuts Lowrey .50 .20
17 Mickey Mantle 8.00 3.20
18 Phil Marchildon .50 .20
19 Walt Masterson .50 .20

20 Ed Mathews 2.00 .80
21 Willie Mays 5.00 2.00
22 Don Newcombe 1.00 .40
23 Joe Nuxhall .50 .20
24 Satchel Paige 4.00 1.60
25 Roy Partee .50 .20
26 Jackie Robinson 5.00 2.00
27 Babe Ruth 8.00 3.20
28 Carl Scheib .50 .20
29 Bobby Shantz .50 .20
30 Burt Shotten .50 .20
31 Duke Snider 2.00 .80
32 Warren Spahn 2.00 .80
33 Johnny Temple .50 .20
34 Ted Williams 5.00 2.00
35 Early Wynn 2.00 .80

1975 TCMA Larry French Postcards

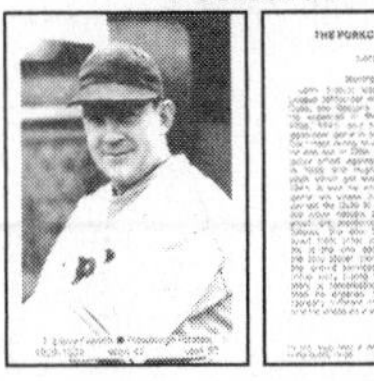
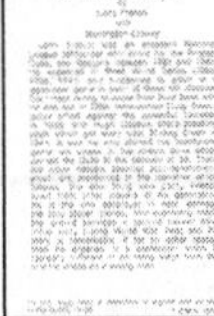

This six-card set features black-and-white pictures of Larry French printed in a postcard format. The backs when put together become a life story of French. It is written by French as told to Harrington Crissey.

NM Ex
COMPLETE SET (6) 20.00 8.00
COMMON CARD (1-6) 4.00 1.60
3 Bill Lee 4.00 1.60
Charlie Root
Larry French
Tuck Stainback
4 Larry French 4.00 1.60
Charlie Grimm
Fred Lindstrom
6 Larry French 4.00 1.60
Mickey Owen

1976 TCMA Umpires

This three-card set was produced by TCMA for the three umpires pictured on the cards and was distributed through the umpires themselves. The cards are unnumbered and checklisted below in alphabetical order.

NM Ex
COMPLETE SET (3) 5.00 2.00
1 Larry Barnett 2.00 .80
2 Don Denkinger 2.00 .80
3 Marty Springstead 2.00 .80

1977 TCMA The War Years

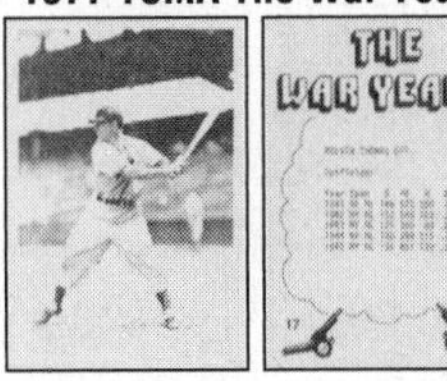

This standard-size set features players who stayed at home and played major league baseball during the Second World War.

NM Ex
COMPLETE SET 30.00 12.00
1 Sam Narron .25 .10
2 Ray Mack .25 .10
3 Mickey Owen .25 .10
4 John Gaston Peacock .25 .10
5 Dizzy Trout .25 .10
6 Birdie Tebbetts .25 .10
7 Alfred Todd .25 .10
8 Harland Clift .25 .10
9 Don Gilberto Nunez .25 .10
Gil Torres
10 Al Lopez 1.00 .40
11 Tony Lupien .25 .10
12 Luke Appling 1.00 .40
13 Pat Seerey .25 .10
14 Phil Masi .25 .10
15 Thomas Turner .25 .10
16 Nicholas Picciuto .25 .10
17 Mel Ott 2.00 .80
18 Red Treadway .25 .10
19 Samuel Naham .25 .10
20 Rip Sewell .25 .10
21 Roy Partee .25 .10
22 Richard Siebert .25 .10
23 Red Barrett .25 .10
24 Lefty O'Dea .25 .10
25 Louis Parisse .25 .10
26 Martin Marion .75 .30
27 Eugene Moore Jr. .25 .10
28 Walter "Boom Boom" Beck .25 .10
29 Donald Manno .25 .10
30 Hal Newhouser 1.00 .40
31 Gus Mancuso .25 .10
32 Pinky May .25 .10
33 Gerald Priddy .25 .10
34 Herman Besse .25 .10
35 Luis Olmo .25 .10
36 Robert O'Neill .25 .10
37 John Barrett .25 .10
38 Gordon Maltzberger .25 .10
39 William Nicholson .50 .20
40 Ron Northey .25 .10
41 Howard Pollet .25 .10
42 Aloysius Piechota .25 .10
43 Robert Shepard .25 .10
44 Alfred Anderson .25 .10
45 Damon Phillips .25 .10
46 Herman Franks .25 .10
47 Aldon Wilkie .25 .10
48 Max Macon .25 .10
49 Lester Webber .25 .10
50 Robert Swift .25 .10
51 Philip Weintraub .25 .10
52 Nicholas Strincevich .25 .10
53 Michael Tresh .25 .10
54 William Trotter .25 .10
55 Frankie Crosetti .75 .30
Bud Metheny
Billy Johnson
Charley Keller
Bill Dickey
Nick Etten
Joe Gordon
Johnny Lindell
Spud Chandler
John Sturm
57 Silas Johnson .25 .10
58 Don Kolloway .25 .10
59 Cecil Porter Vaughan .25 .10
60 George McQuinn .25 .10
Chet Laabs
Harlond Clift
Walt Judnich
61 Harold Wagner .25 .10
62 Alva Javery .25 .10
63 George Barnicle .50 .20
Bob Williams
Frank LaManna
Art Johnson
Ed Carnett
Casey Stengel MG
64 Dolf Camilli .75 .30
65 Mike McCormick .25 .10
66 Dick Wakefield .25 .10
67 Mickey Vernon .75 .30
68 John Vander Meer .75 .30
69 Mack McDonnell .25 .10
70 Thomas Jordan .25 .10
71 Maurice Van Robays .25 .10
72 Charles Stanceu .25 .10
73 Samuel Zoldak .25 .10
74 Ray Starr .25 .10
75 Roger Wolff .25 .10
76 Cecil Travis .50 .20
77 Arthur Johnson .25 .10
78 Louis Riggs .25 .10
79 Peter Suder .25 .10
80 Thomas Warren .25 .10
81 John Welaj .25 .10
82 Gee Walker .25 .10
83 Dee Williams .25 .10
84 Leonard Merullo .25 .10
85 Swede Johnson .25 .10
86 Junior Thompson .25 .10
87 William Zuber .25 .10
88 Earl Johnson .25 .10
89 Babe Young .25 .10
90 Jim Wallace .25 .10

1978 TCMA 60'S I

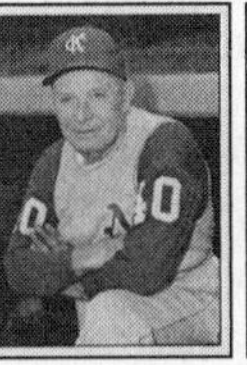

The 1960's
JAMES JOSEPH (JIMMIE) DYKES
Kansas City A's
Coach
Bats-R Throws-R
Ht 5-9 Wt 192
Bn 11-10-1896 D 6-15-76

The TCMA Stars of the 60's consists of 293 standard-size cards. This set was issued through hobby dealers at the time and was TCMA's second set of retired players. The set uses many photos from Mike Aronstein's library of photos. Many of the great and not so great players of the 60's are featured. No card numbers 43 or 98 were printed.

NM Ex
COMPLETE SET (293) 75.00 30.00
1 Smoky Burgess .20 .08
2 Juan Marichal 3.00 1.20
3 Don Drysdale 3.00 1.20
4 Jim Gentile .10 .04
5 Roy Face .20 .08
6 Joe Pepitone .20 .08
7 Joe Christopher .10 .04
8 Wayne Causey .10 .04
9 Frank Bolling .10 .04
10 Jim Maloney .20 .08
11 Roger Maris 4.00 1.60
12 Bill White .50 .20
13 Roberto Clemente 10.00 4.00
14 Bob Saverine .10 .04
15 Barney Schultz .10 .04
16 Albie Pearson .10 .04
17 Denny LeMaster .10 .04
18 Ernie Broglio .10 .04
19 Bobby Klaus .10 .04
20 Tony Cloninger .10 .04
21 Whitey Ford 3.00 1.20
22 Ron Santo 1.00 .40
23 Jim Duckworth .10 .04
24 Willie Davis .20 .08
25 Ed Charles .10 .04
26 Bob Allison .20 .08
27A Fritz Ackley 1.00 .40
27B Gary Kroll 1.00 .40
28 Ruben Amaro .10 .04
29 Johnny Callison .20 .08
30 Greg Bollo .10 .04
31 Felix Millan .10 .04
32 Camilo Pascual .20 .08
33 Jackie Brandt .10 .04
34 Don Lock .10 .04
35 Chico Ruiz .10 .04
36 Joe Azcue .10 .04
37 Ed Bailey .10 .04
38 Pete Ramos .10 .04
39 Eddie Bressoud .10 .04
40 Al Kaline 4.00 1.60
41 Ron Brand .10 .04
42 Bob Lillis .10 .04
44 Buster Narum .10 .04
45 Junior Gilliam .50 .20
46 Claude Raymond .10 .04
47 Billy Bryan .10 .04
48 Marshall Bridges .10 .04
49 Norm Cash .50 .20
50 Orlando Cepeda 1.50 .60
51 Lee Maye .10 .04
52 Andy Rodgers .10 .04
53 Ken Berry .10 .04
54 Don Mincher .10 .04
55 Jerry Lumpe .10 .04
56 Milt Pappas .10 .04
57 Steve Barber .10 .04
58 Dennis Menke .10 .04
59 Larry Maxie .10 .04
60 Bob Gibson 3.00 1.20
61 Larry Bearnarth .10 .04
62 Bill Mazeroski 1.50 .60
63 Bob Rodgers .10 .04
64 Jerry Arrigo .10 .04
65 Joe Nuxhall .20 .08
66 Dean Chance .20 .08
67 Ken Boyer 1.00 .40
68 John Odom .10 .04
69 Chico Cardenas .10 .04
70 Maury Wills 1.00 .40
71 Tony Oliva 1.00 .40
72 Don Nottebart .10 .04
73 Joe Adcock .20 .08
74 Felipe Alou .50 .20
75 Matty Alou .20 .08
76 Dick Radatz .10 .04
77 Jim Bouton .50 .20
78 John Blanchard .10 .04
79 Juan Pizarro .10 .04
80 Boog Powell 1.00 .40
81 Earl Robinson .10 .04
82 Bob Chance .10 .04
83 Max Alvis .10 .04
84 Don Blasingame .10 .04
85 Tom Cheney .10 .04
86 Jerry Arrigo .10 .04
87 Tommy Davis .20 .08
88 Steve Boros .10 .04
89 Don Cardwell .10 .04
90 Harmon Killebrew 2.00 .80
91 Jim Pagliaroni .10 .04
92 Jim O'Toole .10 .04
93 Dennis Bennett .10 .04
94 Dick McAuliffe .20 .08
95 Dick Brown .10 .04
96 Joe Amalfitano .10 .04
97 Phil Linz .10 .04
99 Dave Nicholson .10 .04
100 Hoyt Wilhelm 1.50 .60
101 Don Leppert .10 .04
102 Jose Pagan .10 .04
103 Sam McDowell .20 .08
104 Jack Baldschun .10 .04
105 Jim Perry .20 .08
106 Hal Reniff .10 .04
107 Lee Maye .10 .04
108 Joe Adcock .20 .08
109 Bob Bolin .10 .04
110 Don Leppert .10 .04
111 Bill Monbouquette .10 .04
112 Bobby Richardson .50 .20
113 Earl Battey .10 .04
114 Bob Veale .10 .04
115 Lou Jackson .10 .04
116 Frank Kreutzer .10 .04
117 Jerry Zimmerman .10 .04
118 Don Schwall .10 .04
119 Rich Rollins .10 .04
120 Pete Ward .10 .04
121 Moe Drabowsky .10 .04
122 Jesse Gonder .10 .04
123 Hal Woodeschick .10 .04
124 John Herrnstein .10 .04
125A Leon Wagner 1.00 .40
125B Gary Peters 1.00 .40
126 Dwight Siebler .10 .04
127 Gary Kroll .10 .04
128 Tony Horton .10 .04
129 John DeMerit .10 .04
130 Sandy Koufax 6.00 2.40
131 Jim Davenport .10 .04
132 Wes Covington .10 .04
133 Tony Taylor .20 .08
134 Jack Kralick .10 .04
135 Bill Pleis .10 .04
136 Russ Snyder .10 .04
137 Joe Torre 1.00 .40
138 Ted Wills .10 .04
139 Wes Stock .10 .04
140 Frank Robinson 3.00 1.20
141 Dave Stenhouse .10 .04
142 Ron Hansen .10 .04
143 Don Elston .10 .04
144 Del Crandall .10 .04
145 Bennie Daniels .10 .04
146 Vada Pinson .20 .08
147 Bill Spanswick .10 .04
148 Earl Wilson .10 .04
149 Ty Cline .10 .04
150 Dick Groat .20 .08
151 Jim Duckworth .10 .04
152 Jim Schaffer .10 .04
153 George Thomas .10 .04
154 Wes Stock .10 .04
155 Mike White .10 .04
156 John Podres .20 .08
157 Willie Crawford .10 .04
158 Fred Gladding .10 .04
159 John Wyatt .10 .04
160 Bob Friend .10 .04
161 Ted Uhlaender .10 .04
162 Dick Stigman .10 .04
163 Don Wert .10 .04
164 Eddie Bressoud .10 .04
165A Ed Roebuck 1.00 .40
165B Leon Wagner 1.00 .40
166 Al Spangler .10 .04
167 Bob Sadowski .10 .04
168 Ralph Terry .10 .04
169 Jim Schaffer .10 .04
170 Jim Fregosi .20 .08
170 Dick Hall .10 .04
171 Al Spangler .10 .04
172 Bob Tillman .10 .04
173 Ed Bailey .10 .04
174 Cesar Tovar .10 .04
175 Morrie Stevens .10 .04
176 Floyd Weaver .10 .04
177 Frank Malzone .10 .04
178 Norm Siebern .10 .04
179 Dick Phillips .10 .04
181 Bobby Wine .10 .04
182 Masanori Murakami 4.00 1.60
183 Chuck Schilling .10 .04
184 Jim Schaffer .10 .04
185 John Roseboro .20 .08
186 Jake Wood .10 .04
187 Dallas Green .20 .08
188 Tom Haller .10 .04
189 Chuck Cottier .10 .04
190 Brooks Robinson 3.00 1.20
191 Ty Cline .10 .04
192 Bubba Phillips .10 .04
193 Al Jackson .10 .04
194 Herm Starrette .10 .04
195 Dave Wickersham .10 .04
196 Vic Power .10 .04
197 Ray Culp .10 .04
198 Don Demeter .10 .04
199 Dick Schofield .10 .04
200 Mudcat Grant .10 .04
201 Roger Craig .20 .08
202 Dick Farrell .10 .04
203 Clay Dalrymple .10 .04
204 Jim Duffalo .10 .04
205 Tito Francona .10 .04
206 Tony Conigliaro 1.00 .40
207 Jim King .10 .04
208 Joel Gibson .10 .04
209 Arnold Earley .10 .04
210 Denny McLain .50 .20
211 Don Larsen .20 .08
212 Ron Hunt .10 .04
213 Deron Johnson .10 .04
214 Harry Bright .10 .04
215 Ernie Fazio .10 .04
216 Joey Jay .10 .04
217 Jim Coates .10 .04
218 Jerry Kindall .10 .04
219 Joe Gibbon .10 .04
220 Frank Howard .50 .20
221 Howie Koplitz .10 .04
222 Larry Jackson .10 .04
223 Dale Long .10 .04
224 Jimmy Dykes MG .20 .08
225 Hank Aguirre .10 .04
226 Earl Francis .10 .04
227 Vic Wertz .10 .04
228 Larry Haney .10 .04
229 Tony LaRussa 1.00 .40
230 Moose Skowron .20 .08
231 Lee Thomas .10 .04
231 Tito Francona .10 .04
232 Ken Johnson .10 .04
233 Dick Howser .10 .04
234 Bobby Knoop .10 .04
236 Elston Howard .50 .20
237 Donn Clendenon .10 .04
238 Jesse Gonder .10 .04
239 Vern Law .20 .08
240 Curt Flood .50 .20
241 Dal Maxvill .10 .04
242 Roy Sievers .20 .08
243 Jim Brewer .10 .04
244 Harry Craft MG .10 .04
245 Dave Eilers .10 .04
246 Dave DeBusschere .50 .20
247 Ken Harrelson .20 .08
248 Jim Duffalo UER .10 .04
Card numbered 249
249 Ed Kasko .10 .04
250 Luis Aparicio 1.50 .60
251 Ron Kline .10 .04
252 Chuck Hinton .10 .04
253 Frank Lary .10 .04
254 Stu Miller .10 .04
255 Ernie Banks 4.00 1.60
256 Dick Farrell .10 .04
257 Bud Daley .10 .04
258 Luis Arroyo .10 .04
259 Bob Del Greco .10 .04
260 Ted Williams 10.00 4.00
261 Mike Epstein .10 .04
262 Mickey Mantle 15.00 6.00
263 Jim LeFebvre .10 .04
264 Pat Jarvis .10 .04
265 Chuck Hinton .10 .04
266 Don Larsen .50 .20
267 Jim Coates .10 .04
268 Gary Kolb .10 .04
269 Jim Hart .10 .04
270 Dave McNally .20 .08
271 Jerry Kindall .10 .04
272 Hector Lopez .10 .04
273 Claude Osteen .10 .04
274 Jack Aker .10 .04
275 Mike Shannon .20 .08
276 Lew Burdette .20 .08
277 Mack Jones .10 .04
278 Art Shamsky .10 .04
279 Bob Johnson .10 .04
280 Willie Mays 8.00 3.20
281 Rich Nye .10 .04
282 Bill Cowan .10 .04
283 Gary Kolb .10 .04
284 Woody Held .10 .04
285 Bill Freehan .20 .08
286 Larry Jackson .10 .04
287 Mike Hershberger .10 .04
288 Julian Javier .10 .04
289 Charley Smith .10 .04
290 Hank Aaron 8.00 3.20
291 John Boccabella .10 .04
292 Charley James .10 .04
293 Sammy Ellis .10 .04

1979 TCMA 50'S

The TCMA Stars of the 50's set contains 291 standard-size cards featuring the players of the 50's. The set features a good mix of superstars and not so important players of the era. This set was TCMA's attempt at issuing cards after Topps successfully enjoined them from issuing current players. Using the style which was typical of most of the TCMA issues, the fronts

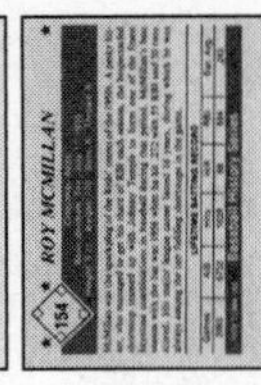

are clear with an informative biography on the back. The Hutchinson and Wertz cards were also issued with the word "SAMPLE" stamped on the back.

NM Ex
COMPLETE SET (291) 75.00 30.00
1 Joe DiMaggio 10.00 4.00
2 Yogi Berra 4.00 1.60
3 Warren Spahn 3.00 1.20
4 Robin Roberts 1.50 .60
5 Ernie Banks 4.00 1.60
6 Willie Mays 8.00 3.20
7 Mickey Mantle 15.00 6.00
8 Roy Campanella 4.00 1.60
9 Stan Musial 5.00 2.00
10 Ted Williams 10.00 4.00
11 Ed Bailey .10 .04
12 Ted Kluszewski 1.00 .40
13 Ralph Kiner 1.50 .60
14 Dick Littlefield .10 .04
15 Nellie Fox 1.50 .60
16 Billy Pierce .20 .08
17 Richie Ashburn 1.50 .60
18 Del Ennis .20 .08
19 Bob Lemon 1.50 .60
20 Early Wynn 1.50 .60
21 Joe Collins .10 .04
22 Hank Bauer .20 .08
23 Roberto Clemente 10.00 4.00
24 Frank Thomas .20 .08
25 Alvin Dark .20 .08
26 Whitey Lockman .10 .04
27 Larry Doby 1.50 .60
28 Bob Feller 4.00 1.60
29 Willie Jones .10 .04
30 Granny Hamner .10 .04
31 Clem Labine .20 .08
32 Ralph Branca .20 .08
33 Jack Harshman .10 .04
34 Dick Donovan .10 .04
35 Tommy Henrich .50 .20
36 Jerry Coleman .20 .08
37 Billy Hoeft .10 .04
38 Johnny Groth .10 .04
39 Harvey Haddix .20 .08
40 Gerry Staley .10 .04
41 Dale Long .10 .04
42 Vernon Law .20 .08
43 Duke Snider 2.00 .80
Gil Hodges
Roy Campanella
Carl Furillo
44 Sam Jethroe .20 .08
45 Vic Wertz .20 .08
45A Vic Wertz .20 .08
Sample Back
46 Wes Westrum .10 .04
47 Dee Fondy .10 .04
48 Gene Baker .10 .04
49 Sandy Koufax 5.00 2.00
50 Billy Loes .10 .04
51 Chuck Diering .10 .04
52 Joe Ginsberg .10 .04
53 Jim Konstanty .20 .08
54 Curt Simmons .20 .08
55 Alex Kellner .10 .04
56 Charlie Dressen MG .20 .08
57 Frank Sullivan .10 .04
58 Mel Parnell .10 .04
59 Bobby Hofman .10 .04
60 Bill Connelly .10 .04
61 Corky Valentine .10 .04
62 Johnny Klippstein .10 .04
63 Chuck Tanner .20 .08
64 Dick Drott .10 .04
65 Dean Stone .10 .04
66 Jim Busby .10 .04
67 Sid Gordon .10 .04
68 Del Crandall .20 .08
69 Walker Cooper .10 .04
70 Hank Sauer .20 .08
71 Gil Hodges 1.00 .40
72 Duke Snider 4.00 1.60
73 Sherman Lollar .10 .04
74 Chico Carrasquel .10 .04
75 Gus Triandos .20 .08
76 Bob Harrison .10 .04
77 Eddie Waitkus .10 .04
78 Ken Heintzelman .10 .04
79 Harry Simpson .10 .04
80 Luke Easter .20 .08
81 Ed Dick .10 .04
82 Jim DePalo .10 .04
83 Billy Cox .20 .08
84 Pee Wee Reese 3.00 1.20
85 Virgil Trucks .10 .04
86 George Kell 1.00 .40
87 Mickey Vernon .20 .08
88 Eddie Yost .10 .04
89 Gus Bell .10 .04
90 Dick Wakefield .10 .04
93 Solly Hemus .10 .04
94 Red Schoendienst 1.50 .60
95 Sammy White .10 .04
96 Billy Goodman .10 .04
97 Jim Hearn .10 .04
98 Ruben Gomez .10 .04
99 Marty Marion .20 .08
100 Bill Virdon .20 .08
101 Chuck Stobbs .10 .04
102 Ron Samford .10 .04
103 Bill Tuttle .10 .04
104 Harvey Kuenn .20 .08
105 Joe Cunningham .20 .08
106 Bill Sarni .10 .04
107 Jack Kramer .10 .04
108 Eddie Stanky .20 .08

109 Carmen Mauro .10 .04
110 Wayne Belardi .10 .04
111 Preston Ward .10 .04
112 Jack Shepard .10 .04
113 Buddy Kerr .10 .04
114 Vern Bickford .10 .04
115 Ellis Kinder .10 .04
116 Walt Dropo .10 .04
117 Duke Maas .10 .04
118 Billy Hunter .10 .04
119 Ewell Blackwell .20 .08
120 Hershell Freeman .10 .04
121 Freddie Martin .10 .04
122 Erv Dusak .10 .04
123 Roy Hartsfield .10 .04
124 Willard Marshall .10 .04
125 Jack Sanford .10 .04
126 Herman Wehmeier .10 .04
127 Hal Smith .10 .04
128 Jim Finigan .10 .04
129 Bob Hale .10 .04
130 Jim Wilson .10 .04
131 Bill Wight .10 .04
132 Mike Fornieles .10 .04
133 Steve Gromek .10 .04
134 Herb Score .20 .08
135 Ryne Duren .20 .08
136 Bob Turley .20 .08
137 Wally Moon .20 .08
138 Fred Hutchinson .20 .08
138A Fred Hutchinson .20 .08
Sample Back
139 Jim Hegan .10 .04
140 Dale Mitchell .10 .04
141 Walt Moryn .10 .04
142 Cal Neeman .10 .04
143 Billy Martin 1.00 .40
144 Phil Rizzuto 3.00 1.20
145 Preacher Roe .50 .20
146 Carl Erskine .50 .20
147 Vic Power .10 .04
148 Elmer Valo .10 .04
149 Don Mueller .20 .08
150 Hank Thompson .10 .04
151 Stan Lopata .10 .04
152 Dick Sisler .10 .04
153 Willard Schmidt .10 .04
154 Roy McMillan .10 .04
155 Gil McDougald .20 .08
156 Gene Woodling .20 .08
157 Eddie Mathews 2.00 .80
158 Johnny Logan .20 .08
159 Dan Bankhead .10 .04
160 Joe Black .20 .08
161 Roger Maris 5.00 2.00
162 Bob Cerv .10 .04
163 Paul Minner .10 .04
164 Bob Rush .10 .04
165 Gene Hermanski .10 .04
166 Harry Brecheen .10 .04
167 Davey Williams .10 .04
168 Monte Irvin 1.50 .60
169 Clint Courtney .10 .04
170 Sandy Consuegra .10 .04
171 Bobby Shantz .20 .08
172 Harry Byrd .10 .04
173 Marv Throneberry .20 .08
174 Woody Held .10 .04
175 Al Rosen .50 .20
176 Rance Pless .10 .04
177 Steve Bilko .10 .04
178 Joe Presko .10 .04
179 Ray Boone .10 .04
180 Jim Lemon .10 .04
181 Andy Pafko .20 .08
182 Don Newcombe .50 .20
183 Frank Lary .10 .04
184 Al Kaline 4.00 1.60
185 Allie Reynolds .50 .20
186 Vic Raschi .20 .08
187 Jake Pitler CO .50 .20
Walt Alston MG
Joe Becker CO
Billy Herman CO
188 Jimmy Piersall .20 .08
189 George Wilson .10 .04
190 Dusty Rhodes .10 .04
191 Duane Pillette .10 .04
192 Dave Philley .10 .04
193 Bobby Morgan .10 .04
194 Russ Meyer .10 .04
195 Hector Lopez .10 .04
196 Arnie Portocarrero .10 .04
197 Joe Page .20 .08
198 Tommy Byrne .10 .04
199 Ray Monzant .10 .04
200 John McCall .10 .04
201 Leo Durocher MG 1.00 .40
202 Bobby Thomson .50 .20
203 Jack Banta .10 .04
204 Joe Pignatano .10 .04
205 Carlos Paula .10 .04
206 Roy Sievers .20 .08
207 Mickey McDermott .10 .04
208 Ray Scarborough .10 .04
209 Bill Miller .10 .04
210 Bill Skowron .50 .20
211 Bob Nieman .10 .04
212 Al Pilarcik .10 .04
213 Jerry Priddy .10 .04
214 Frank House .10 .04
215 Don Mossi .20 .08
216 Rocky Colavito 1.00 .40
217 Brooks Lawrence .10 .04
218 Ted Wilks .10 .04
219 Zack Monroe .10 .04
220 Art Ditmar .10 .04
221 Cal McLish .10 .04
222 Gene Bearden .10 .04
223 Norm Siebern .10 .04
224 Bob Wiesler .10 .04
225 Foster Castleman .10 .04
226 Daryl Spencer .10 .04
227 Dick Williams .20 .08
228 Don Zimmer .20 .08
229 Jackie Jensen .20 .08
230 Billy Johnson .10 .04
231 Dave Koslo .10 .04
232 Al Corwin .10 .04
233 Erv Palica .10 .04
234 Bob Milliken .10 .04
235 Ray Kaat .10 .04
236 Sammy Calderone .10 .04
237 Don Demeter .10 .04
238 Karl Spooner .10 .04
239 Preacher Roe .20 .08
Johnny Podres
240 Enos Slaughter 1.00 .40
241 Dick Kryhoski .10 .04
242 Art Houtteman .10 .04
243 Andy Carey .10 .04
244 Tony Kubek .50 .20
245 Mike McCormick .10 .04
246 Bob Schmidt .10 .04
247 Nelson King .10 .04
248 Bob Skinner .10 .04
249 Dick Bokelmann .10 .04
250 Eddie Kazak .10 .04
251 Billy Klaus .10 .04
252 Norm Zauchin .10 .04
253 Art Schult .10 .04
254 Bob Martyn .10 .04
255 Larry Jansen .10 .04
256 Sal Maglie .20 .08
257 Bob Darnell .10 .04
258 Ken Lehman .10 .04
259 Jim Blackburn .10 .04
260 Bob Purkey .10 .04
261 Harry Walker .10 .04
262 Joe Garagiola 1.00 .40
263 Gus Zernial .10 .04
264 Walter Evers .10 .04
265 Mark Freeman .10 .04
266 Charlie Silvera .10 .04
267 Johnny Podres .50 .20
268 Jim Hughes .10 .04
269 Al Worthington .10 .04
270 Hoyt Wilhelm 1.00 .40
271 Elston Howard 1.00 .40
272 Don Larsen .50 .20
273 Don Hoak .10 .04
274 Chico Fernandez .10 .04
275 Gail Harris .10 .04
276 Valmy Thomas .10 .04
277 George Shuba .10 .04
278 Al Walker .10 .04
279 Willard Ramsdell .10 .04
280 Lindy McDaniel .10 .04
281 Bob Wilson .10 .04
282 Chuck Templeton .10 .04
283 Eddie Robinson .10 .04
284 Bob Porterfield .10 .04
285 Larry Miggins .10 .04
286 Minnie Minoso 1.00 .40
287 Lou Boudreau 1.00 .40
288 Jim Davenport .10 .04
289 Bob Miller .10 .04
290 Jim Gilliam .50 .20
291 Jackie Robinson 10.00 4.00

1981 TCMA 60's II

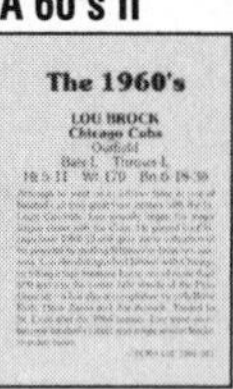

The cards in this 189-card set measure approximately 2 1/2" by 3 1/2". This set was actually a continuation of the prior TCMA Stars of the 1960's set and includes 189 additional cards for which the numbering sequence begins at number 294. They are similar in format to the first series, however, many new and different players are featured. The set was produced in 1981 and was only issued in complete set form. No card number 319 was made and there are two cards numbered at 399.

Nm-Mt Ex-Mt
COMPLETE SET (189) 75.00 30.00
294 Fritz Brickell .25 .10
295 Craig Anderson .25 .10
296 Cliff Cook .25 .10
297 Pumpsie Green .25 .10
298 ChooChoo Coleman .25 .10
299 Don Buford .25 .10
300 Sparky Anderson 1.00 .40
301 John Anderson .25 .10
302 Ted Beard .25 .10
303 Mickey Mantle 10.00 4.00
Roger Maris
304 Gene Freese .25 .10
305 Don Wilkinson .25 .10
306 Walter Alston MG 1.00 .40
307 George Bamberger .25 .10
308 Nelson Briles .25 .10
309 Dave Baldwin .25 .10
310 Bob Bailey .25 .10
311 Paul Blair .25 .10
312 Ken Boswell .25 .10
313 Sam Bowens .25 .10
314 Ray Barker .25 .10
315 Gil Hodges MG .75 .30
Tommie Agee
316 Elmer Valo .25 .10
317 Ken Walters .25 .10
318 Joel Horlen .25 .10
320 Charlie Maxwell .25 .10
321 Joe Foy .25 .10
322 Cleon Jones .25 .10
Tommie Agee
Ron Swoboda
323 Paul Foytack .25 .10
324 Ron Fairly .50 .20
325 Wilbur Wood .50 .20
326 Don Wilson .25 .10
327 Felix Mantilla .25 .10
328 Ed Bouchee .25 .10
329 Sandy Valdespino .25 .10
330 Al Ferrara .25 .10
331 Jose Tartabull .25 .10
332 Dick Kenworthy .25 .10
333 Don Pavletich .25 .10
334 Jim Fairey .25 .10
335 Rico Petrocelli .50 .20
336 Garry Roggenburk .25 .10
337 Rick Reichardt .25 .10
338 Ken McMullen .25 .10
339 Dooley Womack .25 .10
340 Joe Moock .25 .10
341 Lou Brock 4.00 1.60
342 Hector Torres .25 .10
343 Ted Savage .25 .10
344 Hobie Landrith .25 .10
345 Ed Lopat MG .50 .20
346 Mel Nelson .25 .10
347 Mickey Lolich .75 .30
348 Al Lopez MG 1.00 .40
349 ChiChi Olivo .25 .10
350 Bob Moose .25 .10
351 Bill McCool .25 .10
352 Ernie Bowman .25 .10
353 Tommy McCraw .25 .10
354 Sam Mele MG .25 .10
355 Len Boehmer .25 .10
356 Hank Aaron 10.00 4.00
357 Ron Hunt .25 .10
358 Luis Aparicio 1.50 .60
359 Gene Mauch MG .50 .20
360 Barry Moore .25 .10
361 John Buzhardt .25 .10
362 Solly Hemus MG .50 .20
Gussie Busch OWN
Bill Lewis CO
Johnny Grodzicki CO
363 Duke Snider 4.00 1.60
364 Billy Martin .75 .30
365 Wes Parker .50 .20
366 Dick Stuart .50 .20
367 Glenn Beckert .25 .10
368 Ollie Brown .25 .10
369 Stan Bahnsen .25 .10
370 Wesley(Lee) Bales .25 .10
371 Johnny Keane MG .25 .10
372 Wally Moon .50 .20
373 Larry Miller .25 .10
374 Fred Newman .25 .10
375 John Orsino .25 .10
376 Joe Pactwa .25 .10
377 John O'Donoghue .25 .10
378 Jim Ollom .25 .10
379 Ray Oyler .25 .10
380 Ron Nischwitz .25 .10
381 Ron Paul .25 .10
382 Roger Maris 2.50 1.00
homers on May 24, 1961
and is greeted by
Yogi Berra
Johnny Blanchard
383 Jim McKnight .25 .10
384 Gene Michael .50 .20
385 Dave May .25 .10
386 Tim McCarver 1.00 .40
387 Larry Mason .25 .10
388 Don Hoak .25 .10
389 Nate Oliver .25 .10
390 Phil Ortega .25 .10
391 Billy Madden .25 .10
392 John Miller .25 .10
393 Danny Murtaugh MG .50 .20
394 Nelson Mathews .25 .10
395 Red Schoendienst 1.00 .40
396 Roger Nelson .25 .10
397 Tom Matchick .25 .10
398 Dennis Musgraves .25 .10
399 Tommy Harper .50 .20
399 Chet Trail .25 .10
400 Francis Peters .25 .10
401 Tony Pierce .25 .10
402 Billy Williams 1.50 .60
403 Dave Boswell .25 .10
404 Ray Washburn .25 .10
405 Al Worthington .25 .10
406 Jesus Alou .25 .10
407 Gil Hodges MG 1.00 .40
Yogi Berra CO
Eddie Yost CO
Rube Walker CO
Joe Pignatano CO
408 Wally Bunker .25 .10
409 Jim Brenneman .25 .10
410 Bobby Bragan MG .25 .10
411 Cal McLish .25 .10
412 Curt Blefary .25 .10
413 Jim Bethke .25 .10
414 Bill White .50 .20
Julian Javier
Dick Groat
Ken Boyer
415 Richie Allen .75 .30
416 Larry Brown .25 .10
417 Mike Andrews .25 .10
418 Don Mossi .50 .20
419 J.C. Martin .25 .10
420 Dick Rustek .25 .10
421 Elly Rodriguez .25 .10
422 Casey Stengel MG 2.50 1.00
423 Gil Hodges MG .75 .30
Ed Vargo UMP
Argue Over Call
424 Johnny Briggs .25 .10
425 Bud Harrelson .25 .10
Al Weis
of Mets Turn a Double Play
426 Doc Edwards .25 .10
427 Joe Hague .25 .10
428 Lee Elia .25 .10
429 Billy Moran .25 .10
430 Al Moran .25 .10
431 Pete Mikkelsen .25 .10
432 Aurelio Monteagudo .25 .10
433 Ken Mackenzie .25 .10
434 Dick Egan .25 .10
435 Al McBean .25 .10
436 Mike Ferraro .25 .10
437 Gary Wagner .25 .10
438 Jerry Grote .25 .10
J.C. Martin
439 Ted Kluszewski 1.00 .40
440 Jerry Johnson .25 .10
441 Ross Moschitto .25 .10
442 Zoilo Versalles .25 .10
443 Dennis Ribant .25 .10
444 Ted Williams 8.00 3.20
445 Steve Whitaker .25 .10
446 Frank Bertaina .25 .10
447 Bo Belinsky .75 .30
448 Joe Moeller .25 .10
449 Ron Taylor .25 .10
Don Shaw
450 Al Downing .75 .30
Mel Stottlemyre
Fritz Peterson
Whitey Ford CO
451 Jack Tracy .25 .10
452 Tony Curry .25 .10
453 Roy White .50 .20
454 Jim Bunning 1.50 .60
455 Ralph Houk MG .50 .20
456 Bobby Shantz .50 .20
457 Bill Rigney MG .25 .10
458 Roger Repoz .25 .10
459 Bob Turley .50 .20
Robin Roberts
460 Gordon Richardson .25 .10
461 Dick Tracewski .25 .10
462 Thad Tillotson .25 .10
463 Bobo Osborne .25 .10
464 Larry Burright .25 .10
465 Alan Foster .25 .10
466 Ron Taylor .25 .10
467 Fred Talbot .25 .10
468 Bob Miller .25 .10
469 Frank Tepedino .50 .20
470 Danny Frisella .25 .10
471 Cecil Perkins .25 .10
472 Danny Napoleon .25 .10
473 John Upham .25 .10
474 Roger Maris 4.00 1.60
Yogi Berra
Mickey Mantle
Elston Howard
Moose Skowron
Johnny Blanchard
475 Al Weis .25 .10
476 Rich Beck .25 .10
477 Clete Boyer 1.00 .40
Tony Kubek
Bobby Richardson
Joe Pepitone
478 Jack Fisher .25 .10
479 Archie Moore .25 .10
480 Ralph Terry .25 .10
481 Jim Hegan CO .50 .20
Wally Moses CO
Ralph Houk MG
Frank Crosetti CO
Johnny Sain CO
482 Gil Hodges 2.00 .80
Clem Labine
Cookie Lavagetto CO
Roger Craig
Don Zimmer
Charlie Neal
Casey Stengel MG

1982 TCMA Greatest Pitchers

This-45 card set honors Baseball's greatest pitchers and features both color and black-and-white player photos with either thin red or green borders printed on white. The backs carry player information and career statistics.

Nm-Mt Ex-Mt
COMPLETE SET (45) 20.00 8.00
1 Bob Feller 1.50 .60
2 Bob Lemon 1.00 .40
3 Whitey Ford 1.50 .60
4 Joe Page .25 .10
5 Wilbur Wood .25 .10
6 Robin Roberts 1.00 .40
7 Warren Spahn 1.50 .60
8 Sandy Koufax 2.00 .80
9 Juan Marichal 1.00 .40
10 Don Newcombe .50 .20
11 Hoyt Wilhelm .75 .30
12 Roy Face .25 .10
13 Allie Reynolds .50 .20
14 Don Drysdale 1.00 .40
15 Bob Gibson 1.00 .40
16 Cy Young 2.00 .80
17 Walter Johnson 2.00 .80
18 Grover Alexander 1.50 .60
19 Jack Chesbro .25 .10
20 Lefty Gomez 1.00 .40
21 Wes Ferrell .25 .10
22 Hal Newhouser .50 .20
23 Early Wynn 1.00 .40
24 Denny McLain .50 .20
25 Catfish Hunter 1.00 .40
26 Jim Lonborg .25 .10
27 Frank Lary .25 .10
28 Red Ruffing 1.00 .40
29 Lefty Grove 1.50 .60
30 Herb Pennock .25 .10
31 Satchel Paige .25 .10
32 Joe McGinnity 1.00 .40
33 Christy Mathewson 1.50 .60
34 Mordecai"Three Finger" Brown 1.00 .40
35 Eppa Rixey .75 .30
36 Dizzy Dean 1.00 .40
37 Carl Hubbell 1.25 .50
38 Dazzy Vance 1.00 .40
39 Jim Bunning 1.00 .40
40 Joe Wood .75 .30
41 Freddie Fitzsimmons .50 .20
42 Rube Waddell 1.00 .40
43 Addie Joss 1.00 .40
44 Burleigh Grimes 1.00 .40
45 Chief Bender 1.00 .40

1982 TCMA Greatest Hitters

This-45 card set honors some of Baseball's greatest hitters and features both color and black-and-white player photos with either thin red or green borders printed on white. The backs carry player information and career statistics. All the "greatest" sets were available from TCMA for $4 each.

Nm-Mt Ex-Mt
COMPLETE SET (45) 25.00 10.00
1 Ted Williams 3.00 1.20
2 Stan Musial 2.50 1.00
3 Joe DiMaggio 3.00 1.20
4 Roberto Clemente 3.00 1.20
5 Jackie Robinson 3.00 1.20
6 Willie Mays 3.00 1.20
7 Lou Brock 1.00 .40
8 Al Kaline 1.00 .40
9 Richie Ashburn 1.00 .40
10 Tony Oliva .50 .20
11 Harvey Kuenn .25 .10
12 Mickey Vernon .25 .10
13 Tommy Davis .25 .10
14 Ty Cobb 3.00 1.20
15 Rogers Hornsby 1.00 .40
16 Joe Jackson 2.00 .80
17 Willie Keeler .25 .10
18 Tris Speaker .50 .20
19 Babe Ruth 5.00 2.00
20 Harry Heilmann .25 .10
21 Bill Terry .50 .20
22 George Sisler .50 .20
23 Lou Gehrig 3.00 1.20
24 Nap Lajoie 1.00 .40
25 Riggs Stephenson .25 .10
26 Al Simmons 1.00 .40
27 Cap Anson 1.00 .40
28 Paul Waner 1.00 .40
29 Eddie Collins 1.00 .40
30 Heinie Manush 1.00 .40
31 Honus Wagner 1.00 .40
32 Earle Combs .25 .10
33 Sam Rice .25 .10
34 Charlie Gehringer 1.00 .40
35 Chick Hafey .50 .20
36 Zack Wheat 1.00 .40
37 Frankie Frisch 1.00 .40
38 Bill Dickey 1.00 .40
39 Ernie Lombardi 1.00 .40
40 Joe Cronin 1.00 .40
41 Lefty O'Doul .50 .20
42 Luke Appling 1.00 .40
43 Ferris Fain .25 .10
44 Arky Vaughan .75 .30
45 Joe Medwick 1.00 .40

1982 TCMA Greatest Sluggers

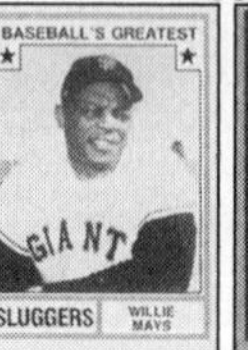

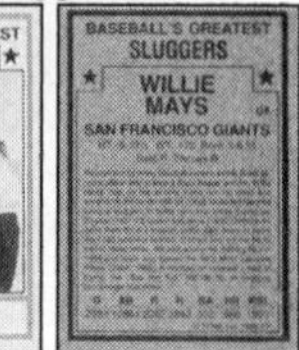

This-45 card set honors some of Baseball's greatest sluggers and features both color and black-and-white player photos with either thin red or green borders printed on white. The backs carry player information and career statistics.

Nm-Mt Ex-Mt
COMPLETE SET (45) 25.00 10.00
1 Harmon Killebrew 1.00 .40
2 Roger Maris 1.00 .40
3 Mickey Mantle 5.00 2.00
4 Hank Aaron 3.00 1.20
5 Ralph Kiner 1.00 .40
6 Willie McCovey 1.00 .40
7 Eddie Mathews 1.00 .40
8 Ernie Banks 1.00 .40
9 Duke Snider 1.00 .40
10 Frank Howard .50 .20
11 Ted Kluszewski .75 .30
12 Frank Robinson 1.00 .40
13 Billy Williams 1.00 .40
14 Gil Hodges .75 .30
15 Yogi Berra 1.00 .40
16 Richie Allen .75 .30
17 Joe Adcock .25 .10
18 Babe Ruth 5.00 2.00
19 Lou Gehrig 3.00 1.20
20 Jimmie Foxx 1.00 .40
21 Rogers Hornsby 1.00 .40
22 Ted Williams UER 3.00 1.20
Willie McCovey's name is misspelled
23 Hack Wilson 1.00 .40
24 Al Simmons 1.00 .40
25 John Mize 1.00 .40
26 Chuck Klein .75 .30
27 Hank Greenberg 1.00 .40
28 Babe Herman .50 .20
29 Norm Cash .25 .10
30 Rudy York .25 .10
31 Gavvy Cravath .25 .10
32 Mel Ott 1.00 .40
33 Orlando Cepeda .50 .20
34 Dolph Camilli .25 .10
35 Frank Baker .75 .30
36 Larry Doby 1.00 .40

37 Jim Gentile .25 .10
38 Harry Davis .25 .10
39 Rocky Colavito 1.00 .40
40 Cy Williams .50 .20
41 Roy Sievers .25 .10
42 Boog Powell .50 .20
43 Willie Mays 3.00 1.20
44 Joe DiMaggio 3.00 1.20
45 Earl Averill 1.00 .40

1982 TCMA Stars of the 50's

This 20-card set features color photos of great Baseball stars of the 1950s printed in a postcard format and measuring approximately 3 3/4" by 5 3/4".

Nm-Mt Ex-Mt
COMPLETE SET (20) 25.00 10.00
1 Roberto Clemente 5.00 2.00
2 Sandy Koufax 2.50 1.00
3 Phil Rizzuto 1.50 .60
4 Bob Feller 1.50 .60
5 Duke Snider 2.50 1.00
6 Hank Aaron 4.00 1.60
7 Eddie Mathews 1.50 .60
8 Roy Campanella 2.50 1.00
9 Willie Mays 4.00 1.60
10 Robin Roberts 1.00 .40
11 Nellie Fox 1.00 .40
12 Early Wynn 1.00 .40
13 Ted Williams 4.00 1.60
14 Warren Spahn 1.00 .40
15 Jackie Robinson 5.00 2.00
16 Joe DiMaggio 5.00 2.00
17 Frank Robinson 1.00 .40
18 Yogi Berra 2.00 .80
19 Mickey Mantle 6.00 2.40
20 Stan Musial 4.00 1.60

1983 TCMA Playball 1942

This 45-card standard-size set was printed in 1983 by TCMA and features sepia-tone posed and action player photos with white borders. A black-outline banner at the bottom contains the player's name and is accented with a baseball glove, bat, ball, and catchers mask icons. The backs are cardboard with navy blue print and display biography, player profile, and a Playball advertisement. All the TCMA Playball sets were available directly from TCMA for $4 each.

Nm-Mt Ex-Mt
COMPLETE SET (45) 8.00 3.20
1 Joe Gordon .20 .08
2 Joe DiMaggio 3.00 1.20
3 Bill Dickey .40 .16
4 Joe McCarthy MG .40 .16
5 Tex Hughson .10 .04
6 Ted Williams 3.00 1.20
7 Walt Judnich .10 .04
8 Vern Stephens .20 .08
9 Denny Galehouse .10 .04
10 Lou Boudreau P/MG .40 .16
11 Ken Keltner .20 .08
12 Jim Bagby .10 .04
13 Rudy York .10 .04
14 Barney McCosky .10 .04
15 Schoolboy Rowe .10 .04
16 Luke Appling .40 .16
17 Taffy Wright .10 .04
18 Ted Lyons .40 .16
19 Mickey Vernon .20 .08
20 George Case .10 .04
21 Bobo Newsom .20 .08
22 Bob Johnson .10 .04
23 Buddy Blair .10 .04
24 Pete Suder .10 .04
25 Terry Moore .10 .04
26 Stan Musial 1.50 .60
27 Marty Marion .30 .12
28 Pee Wee Reese 1.00 .40
29 Arky Vaughan .40 .16
30 Larry French .10 .04
31 Johnny Mize .40 .16
32 Mel Ott P/MG .40 .16
33 Willard Marshall .10 .04
34 Carl Hubbell .40 .16
35 Frank McCormick .10 .04
36 Linus Frey .10 .04
37 Bob Elliott .20 .08
38 Vince DiMaggio .10 .04
39 Al Lopez .40 .16
40 Stan Hack .20 .08
41 Lou Novikoff .10 .04
42 Casey Stengel MG .40 .16
43 Tommy Holmes .20 .08
44 Ron Northey .10 .04
45 Rube Melton .10 .04

1983 TCMA Playball 1943

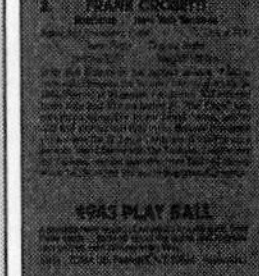

This 45-card standard-size set was printed in 1983 by TCMA and features sepia-tone posed and action player photos with white borders. A black-outline banner at the bottom contains the player's name and is accented with a baseball glove, bat, ball, and catchers mask icons. The backs are cardboard with navy blue print and display biography, player profile, and a Playball advertisement.

Nm-Mt Ex-Mt
COMPLETE SET (45) 5.00 2.00
1 Spud Chandler .20 .08
2 Frank Crosetti .20 .08
3 Johnny Lindell .10 .04
4 Dutch Leonard .10 .04
5 Stan Spence .10 .04
6 Ray Mack .10 .04
7 Hank Edwards .10 .04
8 Al Smith .10 .04
9 Mike Tresh .10 .04
10 Don Kolloway .10 .04
11 Orval Grove .10 .04
12 Doc Cramer .20 .08
13 Mike Higgins .10 .04
14 Dick Wakefield .10 .04
15 Harland Clift .10 .04
16 Chet Laabs .10 .04
17 George McQuinn .10 .04
18 Tony Lupien .10 .04
19 Oscar Judd .10 .04
20 Roy Partee .10 .04
21 Lum Harris .10 .04
22 Roger Wolf .10 .04
23 Dick Siebert .10 .04
24 Walker Cooper .20 .08
25 Mort Cooper .20 .08
26 Whitey Kurowski .10 .04
27 Eddie Miller .10 .04
28 Elmer Riddle .10 .04
29 Bucky Walters .20 .08
30 Whitlow Wyatt .20 .08
31 Dolph Camilli .20 .08
32 Elbie Fletcher .10 .04
33 Frank Gustine .10 .04
34 Rip Sewell .10 .04
35 Phil Cavarretta .20 .08
36 Bill(Swish) Nicholson .20 .08
37 Peanuts Lowery .10 .04
38 Phil Masi .10 .04
39 Al Javery .10 .04
40 Jim Tobin .10 .04
41 Glen Stewart .10 .04
42 Mickey Livingston .10 .04
43 Ace Adams .10 .04
44 Joe Medwick .40 .16
45 Sid Gordon .20 .08

1983 TCMA Playball 1944

This 45-card standard-size set was printed in 1983 by TCMA and features black and white posed and action player photos with white borders. A blue-outline banner at the bottom contains the player's name and is accented with a baseball glove, bat, ball and catchers mask icons. The backs are cardboard with black print and display biography, player profile, and a Playball advertisement.

Nm-Mt Ex-Mt
COMPLETE SET (45) 5.00 2.00
1 Don Gutteridge .10 .04
2 Mark Christman .10 .04
3 Mike Kreevich .10 .04
4 Jimmy Outlaw .10 .04
5 Paul Richards .20 .08
6 Hal Newhouser .40 .16
7 Bud Metheny .10 .04
8 Mike Garbark .10 .04
9 Hersh Martin .10 .04
10 Bob Johnson .10 .04
11 Mike Ryba .10 .04
12 Oris Hockett .10 .04
13 Ed Klieman .10 .04
14 Ford Garrison .10 .04
15 Irv Hall .10 .04
16 Ed Busch .10 .04
17 Ralph Hodgin .10 .04
18 Thurman Tucker .10 .04
19 Bill Dietrich .10 .04
20 Rick Ferrell .40 .16
21 John Sullivan .10 .04
22 Mickey Haefner .10 .04
23 Ray Sanders .10 .04
24 Johnny Hopp .10 .04
25 Ted Wilks .10 .04
26 John Barrett .10 .04
27 Jim Russell .10 .04
28 Nick Strincevich .10 .04
29 Eric Tipton .10 .04
30 Jim Konstanty .20 .08
31 Gee Walker .10 .04
32 Dom Dellessandro .10 .04
33 Bob Chipman .10 .04
34 Hank Wyse .10 .04
35 Phil Weintraub .10 .04
36 George Hausmann .10 .04
37 Bill Voiselle .10 .04
38 Whitey Wietelman .10 .04
39 Clyde Kluttz .10 .04
40 Connie Ryan .10 .04
41 Eddie Stanky .20 .08
42 Augie Galan .20 .08
43 Mickey Owen .10 .04
44 Charlie Schanz .10 .04
45 Bob Finley .10 .04

1983 TCMA Playball 1945

This 45-card standard-size set was printed in 1983 by TCMA and features black and white posed and action player photos with white borders. A blue-outline banner at the bottom contains the player's name and is accented with a baseball glove, bat, ball, and catchers mask icons. The backs are cardboard with black print and display biography, player profile, and a Playball advertisement.

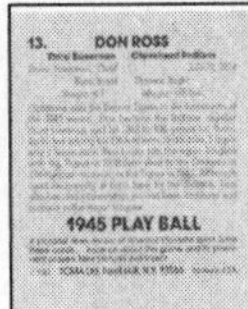

Nm-Mt Ex-Mt
COMPLETE SET (45) 5.00 2.00
1 Eddie Mayo .10 .04
2 Dizzy Trout .20 .08
3 Roy Cullenbine .10 .04
4 Joe Kuhel .10 .04
5 George Binks .10 .04
6 Roger Wolff .10 .04
7 Gene Moore .10 .04
8 Frank Mancuso .10 .04
9 Bob Muncrief .10 .04
10 Tuck Stainback .10 .04
11 Bill Bevens .10 .04
12 Snuffy Stirnweiss .20 .08
13 Don Ross .10 .04
14 Felix Mackiewicz .10 .04
15 Jeff Heath .20 .08
16 Johnny Dickshot .10 .04
17 Ed Lopat .30 .12
18 Skeeter Newsom .10 .04
19 Eddie Lake .10 .04
20 John Lazor .10 .04
21 Hal Peck .10 .04
22 Al Brancato .10 .04
23 Paul Derringer .20 .08
24 Stan Hack .10 .04
25 Lenny Merullo .10 .04
26 Emil Verban .10 .04
27 Ken O'Dea .10 .04
28 Red Barrett .10 .04
29 Eddie Basinski .10 .04
30 Dixie Walker .20 .08
31 Goody Rosen .10 .04
32 Preacher Roe .20 .08
33 Pete Coscarart .10 .04
34 Frankie Frisch MG .40 .16
35 Nap Reyes .10 .04
36 Danny Gardella .10 .04
37 Buddy Kerr .10 .04
38 Dick Culler .10 .04
39 Tommy Holmes .20 .08
40 Al Libke .10 .04
41 Howie Fox .10 .04
42 Johnny Riddle .10 .04
43 Andy Seminick .20 .08
44 Andy Karl .10 .04
45 Rene Monteguedo .10 .04

1983 TCMA Ruth

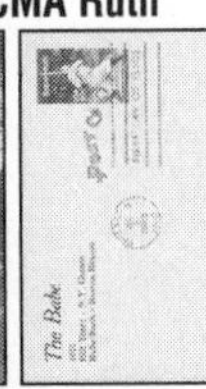

This six-card set features borderless black-and-white photos of Babe Ruth with other players and measures approximately 2 5/8" by 4". The backs display a postcard format and carry a cancelled Babe Ruth 20 cent postage stamp dated July 6, 1983, the first day of issue. The cards are unnumbered and checklisted below in alphabetical order.

Nm-Mt Ex-Mt
COMPLETE SET (6) 20.00 8.00
1 Earl Averill 4.00 1.60
Ben Chapman
Heinie Manush
Babe Ruth
Al Simmons
Sam West
2 Lou Gehrig 4.00 1.60
Joe McCarthy MG
Babe Ruth
3 Miller Huggins MG 4.00 1.60
Babe Ruth
4 Walter Johnson 4.00 1.60
Babe Ruth
5 Tony Lazzeri 4.00 1.60
Babe Ruth CO
6 Babe Ruth 4.00 1.60
Bill Terry

1984 TCMA All-Time All Stars

These standard-size cards were issued by TCMA and feature players who did exceptionally well in All-Star Games. The fronts have a player photo in a specially colored frame surrounded by white borders. The frames are red for National League players and blue for American League players. The player's name is in white against the blue frame. The back has information about the reason for this set as well as the player's All-Star game career record. Since these cards are unnumbered, we have sequenced them in alphabetical order.

Nm-Mt Ex-Mt
COMPLETE SET 10.00 4.00
1 Ernie Banks 1.00 .40
2 Roberto Clemente 2.00 .80
3 Jimmie Foxx 1.00 .40
4 Al Kaline 1.00 .40
5 Willie Mays 3.00 1.20
6 Stan Musial 2.00 .80
7 Ted Williams 4.00 1.60

1984 TCMA Bruce Stark Postcards

This five-card set features artwork of great players by Bruce Stark measuring approximately 3 3/4" by 5 3/4" and printed in a postcard format.

Nm-Mt Ex-Mt
COMPLETE SET (5) 15.00 6.00
BS1 Joe DiMaggio 5.00 2.00
BS2 Ted Williams 5.00 2.00
BS3 Ted Kluzewski UER 2.00 .80
misspelled Kluszewski
BS4 Mickey Vernon 1.00 .40
BS5 Stan Musial 4.00 1.60

1984 TCMA HOF Induction Postcards

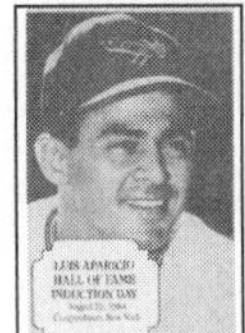

These two postcards feature some of the players who were inducted into Cooperstown in 1984. These cards are unnumbered so we have sequenced them in alphabetical order.

Nm-Mt Ex-Mt
COMPLETE SET (2) 3.00 1.20
1 Luis Aparicio 1.00 .40
2 Pee Wee Reese 2.00 .80

1984 TCMA Playball 1946

This 45-card standard-size set was printed in 1984 by TCMA and features black and white posed and action player photos with white borders. A green-outline banner at the bottom contains the player's name and is accented with a baseball glove, bat, ball, and catchers mask icons. The backs are cardboard with black print and display biography, player profile, and a Playball advertisement.

Nm-Mt Ex-Mt
COMPLETE SET (45) 6.00 2.40
1 Dom DiMaggio .30 .12
2 Boo Ferriss .10 .04
3 Johnny Pesky .20 .08
4 Hank Greenberg .75 .30
5 George Kell .40 .16
6 Virgil Trucks .10 .04
7 Phil Rizzuto .75 .30
8 Charlie Keller .20 .08
9 Tommy Henrich .30 .12
10 Cecil Travis .10 .04
11 Al Evans .10 .04
12 Buddy Lewis .10 .04
13 Edgar Smith .10 .04
14 Dario Lodigiani .10 .04
15 Earl Caldwell .10 .04
16 Jim Hegan .10 .04
17 Bob Feller .75 .30
18 John Berardino .20 .08
19 Jack Kramer .10 .04
20 John Lucadello .10 .04
21 Hank Majeski .10 .04
22 Elmer Valo .10 .04
23 Buddy Rosar .10 .04
24 Red Schoendienst .40 .16
25 Dick Sisler .10 .04
26 Johnny Beazley .10 .04
27 Vic Lombardi .10 .04
28 Dick Whitman .10 .04
29 Carl Furillo .30 .12
30 Billy Jurges .10 .04
31 Marv Rickert .10 .04
32 Clyde McCullough .10 .04
33 Johnny Hopp .10 .04
34 Mort Cooper .10 .04
35 Johnny Sain .20 .08
36 Del Ennis .20 .08
37 Roy Hughes .10 .04
38 Bert Haas .10 .04
39 Grady Hatton .10 .04
40 Ed Bahr .10 .04
41 Billy Cox .20 .08
42 Lee Handley .10 .04
43 Bill Rigney .10 .04
44 Babe Young .10 .04
45 Buddy Blattner .10 .04

1985 TCMA Home Run Champs

This 10-card set features color photos of players who hit home runs regularly in white borders with brown sun borders. The cards are unnumbered and checklisted below in alphabetical order.

Nm-Mt Ex-Mt
COMPLETE SET (10) 10.00 4.00
1 Hank Aaron 3.00 1.20
2 Orlando Cepeda 1.00 .40
3 Joe DiMaggio 3.00 1.20
4 Larry Doby 1.00 .40
5 Ralph Kiner 1.00 .40
6 Eddie Mathews 1.00 .40
7 Willie McCovey 1.00 .40
8 Al Rosen .25 .10
9 Duke Snider 1.00 .40
10 Ted Williams 3.00 1.20

1985 TCMA Photo Classics

This 40-card set features black-and-white photos of great Baseball players and measures approximately 3 1/2" by 5 1/2".

Nm-Mt Ex-Mt
COMPLETE SET (40) 50.00 20.00
1 Warren Spahn 1.50 .60
Johnny Sain
2 Jackie Robinson 5.00 2.00
3 Dwight D. Eisenhower PRES 2.00 .80
4 Babe Ruth 8.00 3.20
5 Joe McCarthy MG 2.50 1.00
Lou Gehrig
Joe DiMaggio
6 Bob Feller 2.50 1.00
7 Johnny Lindell 1.00 .40
Johnny Murphy
8 Babe Ruth 4.00 1.60
Claire Ruth
9 Babe Ruth 4.00 1.60
Joe Cook
10 Bobo Newsom 1.00 .40
11 Johnny Antonelli 1.00 .40
Robin Roberts
12 Joe Adcock 1.50 .60
Eddie Mathews
13 Al Lopez MG 1.00 .40
Mike Garcia
Bob Lemon
Early Wynn
14 Gil McDougald 2.00 .80
Roy Campanella
15 Ralph Branca 1.00 .40
Bobby Thomson
16 Lou Gehrig 1.00 .40
17 John Mize 2.00 .80
Bill Rigney
Mel Ott
18 Spider Jorgensen 2.50 1.00
Pee Wee Reese
Eddie Stanky
Jackie Robinson
19 Tommy Holmes 1.00 .40
Earl Torgeson
Jeff Heath
Connie Ryan
Billy Southworth MG
20 Ted Williams 2.50 1.00
Bobby Doerr
Dom DiMaggio
Vern Stephens
21 Chuck Schilling 1.50 .60
Carl Yasztremski
22 Roger Maris 4.00 1.60
Mickey Mantle
23 Rogers Hornsby 2.50 1.00
Gil McDougald
24 Jim Gentile 1.00 .40
Gus Triandos
25 Bobby Avila 2.50 1.00
Willie Mays
26 Joe Garagiola 2.00 .80
Ralph Kiner
27 Jim Gentile 2.50 1.00
Willie Mays
28 Red Schoendienst 1.50 .60
Marty Marion
29 Charlie Keller 1.00 .40
30 House of David team 1.00 .40
31 Harvey Kuenn 1.00 .40
Al Kaline
32 Hank Sauer 1.00 .40
33 Enos Slaughter 1.00 .40
34 Stan Musial 2.50 1.00
35 Willie Mays 5.00 2.00
36 William Bendix 4.00 1.60
Babe Ruth
37 Whitey Lockman 1.00 .40
Davey Williams
Hank Thompson
Alvin Dark
Don Mueller
Willie Mays
Monte Irvin
Wes Westrum
38 Pete Runnels 1.00 .40
Vic Wertz
39 Stan Musial 2.50 1.00
40 Dom DiMaggio 1.00 .40

1985 TCMA Playball 1947

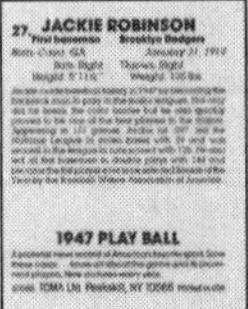

This 45-card standard-size set was printed in 1985 by TCMA and features black and white posed and action player photos with white borders. A blue-outline banner at the bottom contains the player's name and is accented with a baseball glove, bat, ball, and catchers mask icons. The backs are cardboard with black print and display biography, player profile, and a Playball advertisement.

Nm-Mt Ex-Mt
COMPLETE SET (45) 6.00 2.40
1 Hal Wagner .10 .04
2 Jake Jones .10 .04
3 Bobby Doerr .40 .16
4 Fred Hutchinson .20 .08
5 Bob Swift .10 .04
6 Pat Mullin .10 .04
7 Joe Page .20 .08
8 Allie Reynolds .20 .08
9 Billy Johnson .10 .04
10 Early Wynn .40 .16
11 Eddie Yost .10 .04
12 Floyd Baker .10 .04
13 Dave Philley .10 .04
14 George Dickey .10 .04
15 Dale Mitchell .20 .08

Card	Nm-Mt	Ex-Mt
16 Bob Lemon	.40	.16
17 Jerry Witte	.10	.04
18 Paul Lehner	.10	.04
19 Sam Zoldak	.10	.04
20 Sam Chapman	.10	.04
21 Eddie Joost	.20	.08
22 Ferris Fain	.20	.08
23 Erv Dusak	.10	.04
24 Joe Garagiola	.30	.12
25 Vernal "Nippy" Jones	.10	.04
26 Bobby Bragan	.10	.04
27 Jackie Robinson	3.00	1.20
28 Spider Jorgensen	.10	.04
29 Bob Scheffing	.10	.04
30 Johnny Schmitz	.10	.04
31 Doyle Lade	.10	.04
32 Earl Torgeson	.10	.04
33 Warren Spahn	.40	.16
34 Walt Lanfranconi	.10	.04
35 Johnny Wyrostek	.10	.04
36 Oscar Judd	.10	.04
37 Ewell Blackwell	.20	.08
38 Eddie Lukon	.10	.04
39 Benny Zientara	.10	.04
40 Gene Woodling	.20	.08
41 Ernie Bonham	.10	.04
42 Hank Greenberg	.40	.16
43 Bobby Thomson	.30	.12
44 Jack "Lucky" Lohrke	.10	.04
45 Dave Koslo	.10	.04

1985 TCMA Playball 1948

This 45-card set was printed in 1985 by TCMA and measures approximately 2 1/2" by 3 1/8". The fronts feature player photos with red trimming. The backs are cardboard with black print and display biography, player profile, and a Playball advertisement.

Card	Nm-Mt	Ex-Mt
COMPLETE SET (45)	6.00	2.40
1 Murry Dickson	.10	.04
2 Enos Slaughter	.40	.16
3 Don Lang	.10	.04
4 Joe Hatten	.10	.04
5 Gil Hodges	.30	.12
6 Gene Hermanski	.10	.04
7 Eddie Waitkus	.20	.08
8 Jesse Dobernic	.10	.04
9 Andy Pafko	.20	.08
10 Vern Bickford	.10	.04
11 Mike McCormick	.10	.04
12 Harry Walker	.20	.08
13 Putsy Caballero	.10	.04
14 Dutch Leonard	.10	.04
15 Frank Baumholtz	.10	.04
16 Ted Kluszewski	.30	.12
17 Virgil Stallcup	.10	.04
18 Bob Chesnes	.10	.04
19 Ted Beard	.10	.04
20 Wes Westrum	.10	.04
21 Clint Hartung	.10	.04
22 Whitey Lockman	.20	.08
23 Billy Goodman	.10	.04
24 Jack Kramer	.10	.04
25 Mel Parnell	.20	.08
26 George Vico	.10	.04
27 Walter Evers	.10	.04
28 Vic Wertz	.10	.04
29 Yogi Berra	.75	.30
30 Joe DiMaggio	3.00	1.20
31 Tommy Byrne	.10	.04
32 Al Kozar	.10	.04
33 Jake Early	.10	.04
34 Gil Coan	.10	.04
35 Pat Seerey	.10	.04
36 Ralph Hodgin	.10	.04
37 Allie Clark	.10	.04
38 Gene Bearden	.10	.04
39 Steve Gromek	.10	.04
40 Al Zarilla	.10	.04
41 Fred Sanford	.10	.04
42 Les Moss	.10	.04
43 Don White	.10	.04
44 Carl Scheib	.10	.04
45 Lou Brissie	.10	.04

1985 TCMA Playball 1949

This 45-card set was printed in 1985 by TCMA and measures approximately 2 1/2" by 3 1/8". The fronts feature player photos with red trimming. The backs are cardboard with black print and display biography, player profile, and a Playball advertisement.

Card	Nm-Mt	Ex-Mt
COMPLETE SET (45)	5.00	2.00
1 Al Brazle	.10	.04
2 Harry Brecheen	.10	.04
3 Howie Pollet	.10	.04
4 Cal Abrams	.10	.04
5 Ralph Branca	.20	.08
6 Duke Snider	1.50	.60
7 Charlie Grimm MG	.20	.08
8 Clarence Maddern	.10	.04
9 Hal Jeffcoat	.10	.04
10 John Antonelli	.20	.08
11 Alvin Dark	.30	.12
12 Nelson Potter	.10	.04
13 Granny Hamner	.20	.08
14 Willie Jones	.20	.08
15 Robin Roberts	.75	.30
16 Lloyd Merriman	.10	.04
17 Bobby Adams	.10	.04
18 Herm Wehmeier	.10	.04
19 Ralph Kiner	.75	.30
20 Dino Restelli	.10	.04
21 Larry Jansen	.20	.08
22 Sheldon Jones	.10	.04
23 Red Webb	.10	.04
24 Vern Stephens	.20	.08
25 Tex Hughson	.10	.04
26 Ellis Kinder	.10	.04
27 Neil Berry	.10	.04
28 Johnny Groth	.10	.04
29 Art Houteman	.10	.04
30 Hank Bauer	.20	.08
31 Vic Raschi	.20	.08
32 Bobby Brown	.20	.08
33 Joe Haynes	.10	.04
34 Eddie Robinson	.10	.04
35 Sam Dente	.10	.04
36 Herb Adams	.10	.04
37 Don Wheeler	.10	.04
38 Randy Gumpert	.10	.04
39 Ray Boone	.10	.04
40 Larry Doby	.40	.16
41 Jack Graham	.10	.04
42 Bob Dillinger	.20	.08
43 Dick Kokos	.10	.04
44 Wally Moses	.10	.04
45 Mike Guerra	.10	.04

1986 TCMA

The 1986 TCMA set is comprised of 20 cards measure 2 5/16" by 3 1/2". The cards were styled after the 1953 Bowman Black and White set. The fronts feature posed and action black-and-white photos within a white outer border and an inner fine black line. The player's name does not appear on the front. The horizontal white backs contain biography within a red stripe, player profile and lifetime statistics are printed below. The card number appears in the top left corner on a diamond icon. The cards are numbered on the back.

Card	Nm-Mt	Ex-Mt
COMPLETE SET (20)	15.00	6.00
1 Roberto Clemente	2.00	.80
2 Duke Snider	1.00	.40
3 Sandy Koufax	1.50	.60
4 Carl Hubbell	.50	.20
5 Ty Cobb	2.00	.80
6 Willie Mays	2.00	.80
7 Jackie Robinson	2.00	.80
8 Joe DiMaggio	2.00	.80
9 Stan Musial	1.00	.40
10 Pie Traynor	.50	.20
11 Yogi Berra	1.00	.40
12 Babe Ruth	2.00	.80
13 Brooks Robinson	.50	.20
14 Walter Johnson	1.00	.40
15 Ted Williams	1.50	.60
16 Bill Dickey	.50	.20
17 Lou Gehrig	2.00	.80
18 Hank Aaron	1.50	.60
19 Eddie Mathews	.50	.20
20 Mickey Mantle	2.00	.80

1986 TCMA Limited Autographs

This card was issued by TCMA as a premium for collectors who purchased other product from TCMA. The front features a glossy photo along with an autograph signed in blue sharpie. The back has a "message" from the player thanking them for their purchase along with the player's 1985 statistics. There may be other cards in this set so any additions are appreciated.

Card	Nm-Mt	Ex-Mt
1 Tony Gwynn	75.00	30.00

1986 TCMA Superstars Simon

These 50 cards mesaure 2 3/4" by 3 1/2". The cards feature drawings from sports artist Robert Stephen Simon on the front. The backs have vital statistics and biographical information.

Card	Nm-Mt	Ex-Mt
COMPLETE SET (50)	15.00	6.00
1 Carl Erskine	.25	.10
2 Babe Ruth	1.00	.40
Hank Aaron		
3 Ted Williams	2.00	.80
4 Mickey Mantle	2.50	1.00
5 Gil Hodges	.50	.20
6 Roberto Clemente	2.00	.80
7 Mickey Mantle	2.50	1.00
8 Walter Johnson	.75	.30
9 Joe DiMaggio	1.50	.60
Mickey Mantle		
Whitey Ford		
Phil Rizzuto		
Roger Maris		
Casey Stengel MG		
Babe Ruth		
Lou Gehrig		
Yogi Berra		
10 Carl Yatrzemski	.50	.20
Ted Williams		
11 Mickey Mantle	2.50	1.00
12 Harmon Killebrew	.75	.30
13 Warren Spahn	.75	.30
14 Ralph Kiner	1.00	.40
Babe Ruth		
15 Bob Gibson	.75	.30
16 Pee Wee Reese	.75	.30
17 Billy Martin	.50	.20
18 Joe DiMaggio	2.00	.80
Mickey Mantle		
19 Phil Rizzuto	.75	.30
20 Sandy Koufax	1.00	.40
21 Jackie Robinson	2.00	.80
22 Don Drysdale	.75	.30
23 Mickey Mantle	2.50	1.00
24 Mickey Mantle	2.50	1.00
25 Joe DiMaggio	2.00	.80
26 Robin Roberts	.75	.30
27 Lou Brock	.75	.30
28 Lou Gehrig	2.00	.80
29 Willie Mays	1.50	.60
30 Brooks Robinson	.75	.30
31 Thurman Munson	.50	.20
32 Roger Maris	1.00	.40
33 Jim Palmer	.75	.30
34 Stan Musial	1.00	.40
35 Roy Campanella	1.00	.40
36 Joe Pepitone	.25	.10
37 Ebbetts Field	.25	.10
38 Honus Wagner	.75	.30
39 Yogi Berra	1.00	.40
40 Eddie Mathews	.75	.30
41 Carl Yastrzemski	.75	.30
42 Babe Ruth	2.50	1.00
43 Babe Ruth	2.50	1.00
44 Pete Reiser	.25	.10
45 Don Larsen	.25	.10
46 Ernie Banks	.75	.30
47 Casey Stengel	1.00	.40
48 Jackie Robinson	2.00	.80
49 Duke Snider	1.00	.40
50 Duke Snider CL	.50	.20

1996 Team Out

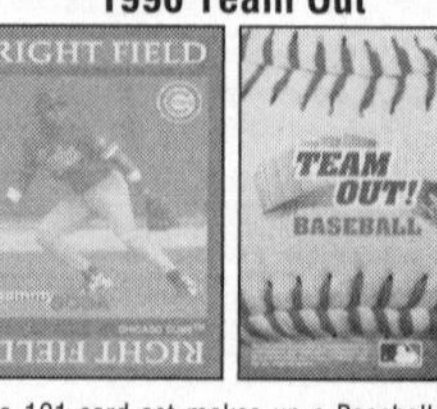

This 101-card set makes up a Baseball card game and is distributed in boxes of 60-card decks with a suggested retail of $12.95 a box. Each deck contains 34 player photo cards and 23 cartoon player cards. A total of 91 different player cards and 10 cartoon cards are available. The backs carry the name of the card game printed on a picture of a section of a baseball. The cards are unnumbered and checklisted below in alphabetical order with the last 10 cards being the cartoon cards and listed with a "C" prefix.

Card	Nm-Mt	Ex-Mt
COMPLETE SET (101)	50.00	15.00
COMMON CARD (1-91)	.10	.03
COMMON (C92-C101)	.10	.03
1 Roberto Alomar	.75	.23
2 Brady Anderson	.25	.07
3 Kevin Appier	.25	.07
4 Carlos Baerga	.25	.07
5 Jeff Bagwell	1.00	.30
6 Albert Belle	.25	.07
7 Dante Bichette	.25	.07
8 Craig Biggio	.50	.15
9 Wade Boggs	1.00	.30
10 Barry Bonds	2.00	.60
11 Kevin Brown	.50	.15
12 Jay Buhner	.25	.07
13 Ellis Burks	.25	.07
14 Ken Caminiti	.25	.07
15 Joe Carter	.25	.07
16 Vinny Castilla	.25	.07
17 Jeff Cirillo	.25	.07
18 Will Clark	.75	.23
19 Jeff Conine	.25	.07
20 Joey Cora	.10	.03
21 Marty Cordova	.10	.03
22 Eric Davis	.25	.07
23 Ray Durham	.25	.07
24 Jim Edmonds	.75	.23
25 Cecil Fielder	.25	.07
26 Travis Fryman	.25	.07
27 Jason Giambi	1.25	.35
28 Bernard Gilkey	.10	.03
29 Tom Glavine	1.00	.30
30 Juan Gonzalez	1.00	.30
31 Mark Grace	.50	.15
32 Ken Griffey Jr.	2.50	.75
33 Marquis Grissom	.25	.07
34 Mark Grudzielanek	.10	.03
35 Ozzie Guillen	.25	.07
36 Tony Gwynn	2.00	.60
37 Bobby Higginson	.25	.07
38 Todd Hundley	.25	.07
39 Derek Jeter	4.00	1.20
40 Lance Johnson	.10	.03
41 Randy Johnson	1.00	.30
42 Chipper Jones	2.00	.60
43 Brian Jordan	.25	.07
44 Wally Joyner	.25	.07
45 Jason Kendall	.25	.07
46 Chuck Knoblauch	.75	.23
47 Ray Lankford	.25	.07
48 Mike Lansing	.10	.03
49 Barry Larkin	.75	.23
50 Kenny Lofton	.50	.15
51 Javier Lopez	.50	.15
52 Mike Macfarlane	.10	.03
53 Greg Maddux	2.00	.60
54 Al Martin	.10	.03
55 Mark McGwire	3.00	.90
56 Brian McRae	.10	.03
57 Raul Mondesi	.25	.07
58 Denny Neagle	.10	.03
59 Hideo Nomo	.75	.23
60 John Olerud	.50	.15
61 Rey Ordonez	.10	.03
62 Troy Percival	.25	.07
63 Andy Pettitte	.50	.15
64 Mike Piazza	2.50	.75
65 Manny Ramirez	1.00	.30
66 Cal Ripken	4.00	1.20
67 Alex Rodriguez	2.50	.75
68 Ivan Rodriguez	1.00	.30
69 Tim Salmon	.75	.23
70 Ryne Sandberg	1.00	.30
71 Benito Santiago	.25	.07
72 Kevin Seitzer	.10	.03
73 Scott Servais	.10	.03
74 Gary Sheffield	1.00	.30
75 Ozzie Smith	2.00	.60
76 John Smoltz	.25	.07
77 Sammy Sosa	2.00	.60
78 Mike Stanley	.10	.03
79 Terry Steinbach	.10	.03
80 Frank Thomas	1.00	.30
81 Steve Trachsel	.10	.03
82 Jose Valentin	.10	.03
83 Mo Vaughn	.25	.07
84 Robin Ventura	.75	.23
85 Jose Vizcaino	.10	.03
86 Larry Walker	.25	.07
87 Walt Weiss	.10	.03
88 Bernie Williams	.75	.23
89 Matt Williams	.50	.15
90 Eric Young	.10	.03
91 Todd Zeile	.25	.07
C92 Roberto Alomar	.60	.18
C93 Albert Belle	.25	.07
Raul Mondesi		
C94 Barry Bonds	.60	.18
C95 Ken Griffey	2.00	.60
Sammy Sosa		
C96 Greg Maddux	.60	.18
C97 Mark McGwire	2.00	.60
Ozzie Smith		
Mo Vaughn		
C98 Mike Piazza	.40	.12
Matt Williams		
C99 Alex Rodriguez	1.25	.35
Cal Ripken		
C100 Frank Thomas	1.50	.45
C101 G.T. Roped	.10	.03

1993 Ted Williams Promos

These three standard-size promo cards were issued to preview the design of the forthcoming 1993 Ted Williams baseball set. Though the cards differ from the corresponding numbered cards in the regular series, the promos are not marked as such. Promo card 1 features a different action photo on its front as well as a different ghosted background picture. Also the lettering of Ted Williams' name differs slightly in color, lime green on the promo, orange on the regular issue card. The layout of the backs is identical, but close inspection reveals that the career summaries on each card are slightly different. The promo is easily distinguished by the fact that the career summary begins with a quote by Williams himself. Promo cards 115 and 160 are easily distinguished from their counterparts in the regular issue; in the promo set, player cards have replaced the checklist cards from the regular series. The cards are unnumbered and checklisted below in alphabetical order.

Card	Nm-Mt	Ex-Mt
COMPLETE SET (3)	30.00	9.00
1 Ted Williams	15.00	4.50
115 Satchell Paige	6.00	1.80
160 Juan Gonzalez	10.00	3.00
The Measure of a Hitter		

1993 Ted Williams

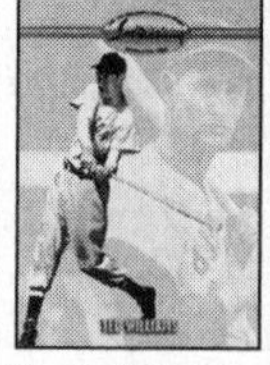

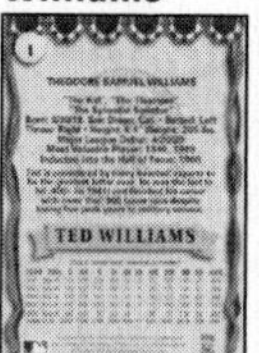

This set of 160 cards marks the inaugural effort of the Ted Williams Card Company. The standard-size cards are UV-coated, and bear the company's embossed logo. The card designs vary from subset to subset, and since the borderless cards feature players of the past (with only two exceptions), some of the photos on the fronts are black-and-white, some are color, and still others are sepia-toned. Generally, the backs carry Williams' comments on each player's abilities and career highlights. All the cards are grouped according to team. This set features these subsets: The Negro Leagues (97-115), All-American Girls' Professional Baseball League (116-120), Ted's Greatest Hitters (121-130), Barrier Breakers (131-140), Goin' North (141-150), and Dawning of a Legacy (151-160), which features cards of Juan Gonzalez and Jeff Bagwell, the only two current players in the set. Ted Williams personally signed 406 of his Locklear Collection insert card for this set and Juan Gonzalez signed 172 cards (43 each of his four different regular cards in this set) as well. Also, two POGs, or milk bottle caps, were inserted in each pack. These feature illustrations of former major and Negro league players, logos of their teams, and reproductions of selected signatures of former major league players.

Card	Nm-Mt	Ex-Mt
COMPLETE SET (160)	15.00	4.50
1 Ted Williams	2.00	.60
2 Rick Ferrell	.25	.07
3 Jim Lonborg	.05	.02
4 Mel Parnell	.05	.02
5 Jim Piersall	.10	.03
6 Luis Tiant	.10	.03
7 Carl Yastrzemski	.50	.15
8 Ralph Branca	.10	.03
9 Roy Campanella	.75	.23
10 Ron Cey	.10	.03
11 Tommy Davis	.10	.03
12 Don Drysdale	.40	.12
13 Carl Erskine	.10	.03
14 Steve Garvey	.15	.04
15 Don Newcombe	.15	.04
16 Duke Snider	.75	.23
17 Maury Wills	.15	.04
18 Jim Fregosi	.10	.03
19 Bobby Grich	.10	.03
20 Bill Buckner	.10	.03
21 Billy Herman UER	.25	.07
(Ted Williams stats on back)		
22 Ferguson Jenkins	.25	.07
23 Ron Santo	.15	.04
24 Billy Williams	.25	.07
25 Luis Aparicio	.25	.07
26 Luke Appling	.25	.07
27 Minnie Minoso	.15	.04
28 Johnny Bench	.50	.15
29 George Foster	.10	.03
30 Joe Morgan	.25	.07
31 Buddy Bell	.10	.03
32 Lou Boudreau	.25	.07
33 Rocky Colavito	.15	.04
34 Jim(Mudcat) Grant	.05	.02
35 Tris Speaker	.25	.07
36 Ray Boone	.05	.02
37 Darrell Evans	.10	.03
38 Al Kaline	.50	.15
39 George Kell	.25	.07
40 Mickey Lolich	.15	.04
41 Cesar Cedeno	.10	.03
42 Sal Bando	.05	.02
43 Vida Blue	.10	.03
44 Bert Campaneris	.05	.02
45 Ken Holtzman	.05	.02
46 Lew Burdette	.10	.03
47 Bob Horner	.05	.02
48 Warren Spahn	.25	.07
49 Cecil Cooper	.10	.03
50 Tony Oliva	.15	.04
51 Bobby Bonds	.15	.04
52 Alvin Dark	.10	.03
53 Dave Dravecky	.10	.03
54 Monte Irvin	.25	.07
55 Willie Mays	1.00	.30
56 Bud Harrelson	.10	.03
57 Dave Kingman UER	.10	.03
(Darrell Evans has 414 homers and is not in HOF)		
58 Yogi Berra	.50	.15
59 Don Baylor	.15	.04
60 Jim Bouton	.10	.03
61 Bobby Brown	.10	.03
62 Whitey Ford	.50	.15
63 Lou Gehrig	1.50	.45
64 Charlie Keller	.10	.03
65 Eddie Lopat	.10	.03
66 Johnny Mize	.25	.07
67 Bobby Murcer	.10	.03
68 Graig Nettles	.15	.04
69 Bobby Shantz	.05	.02
70 Richie Ashburn	.25	.07
71 Larry Bowa	.10	.03
72 Steve Carlton	.40	.12
73 Robin Roberts	.25	.07
74 Matty Alou	.05	.02
75 Harvey Haddix	.05	.02
76 Ralph Kiner	.25	.07
77 Bill Madlock	.10	.03
78 Bill Mazeroski	.15	.04
79 Al Oliver	.10	.03
80 Manny Sanguillen	.05	.02
81 Willie Stargell	.25	.07
82 Al Bumbry	.05	.02
83 Davey Johnson	.10	.03
84 Boog Powell	.15	.04
85 Earl Weaver MG	.15	.04
86 Lou Brock	.25	.07
87 Orlando Cepeda UER	.15	.04
(Born in Puerto Rico, not Dominican Republic)		
88 Curt Flood	.10	.03
89 Joe Garagiola	.15	.04
90 Bob Gibson	.25	.07
91 Rogers Hornsby UER	.25	.07
(Misspelled Rodgers on card front)		
92 Enos Slaughter	.25	.07
93 Joe Torre	.15	.04
94 Gaylord Perry	.25	.07
95 Checklist	.05	.02
96 Checklist	.05	.02
97 Cool Papa Bell	.25	.07
98 Garnett Blair	.10	.03
99 Gene Benson	.15	.04
100 Lyman Bostock Sr.	.10	.03
101 Marlin Carter	.10	.03
102 Oscar Charleston	.25	.07
103 Ray Dandridge	.25	.07
104 Mahlon Duckett	.10	.03
105 Josh Gibson	.75	.23
106 Cowan(Bubber) Hyde	.10	.03
107 William(Judy) Johnson	.25	.07
108 Buck Leonard	.25	.07
109 John Henry Lloyd	.25	.07
110 Lester Lockett	.10	.03
111 Max Manning	.10	.03
112 Satchel Paige	.75	.23
113 Armando Vazquez	.10	.03
114 Joe(Smokey) Williams	.25	.07
115 Checklist	.05	.02
116 Alice(Lefty) Hohlmeyer	.25	.07
117 Dotty Kamenshek	.25	.07
118 Lavonne(Pepper) Davis	.25	.07
119 Marge Wenzell	.25	.07
120 Checklist	.05	.02
121 Babe Ruth	2.50	.75
122 Lou Gehrig	1.50	.45
123 Jimmie Foxx	.50	.15
124 Rogers Hornsby	.50	.15
125 Ty Cobb	1.50	.45
126 Willie Mays	1.00	.30
127 Ralph Kiner	.40	.12
128 Tris Speaker	.40	.12
129 Johnny Mize	.25	.07
130 Checklist	.05	.02
131 Satchel Paige	.50	.15
132 Joe Black	.10	.03
133 Roy Campanella	.50	.15
134 Larry Doby UER	.15	.04
(Misspelled Dolby on card back)		
135 Jim Gilliam	.15	.04
136 Monte Irvin	.40	.12
137 Sam Jethroe	.10	.03
138 Willie Mays	1.00	.30
139 Don Newcombe	.10	.03
140 Checklist	.05	.02
141 Roy Campanella	.50	.15
142 Bob Gibson	.25	.07
143 Boog Powell	.15	.04
144 Willie Mays	1.00	.30
145 Johnny Mize	.25	.07
146 Monte Irvin	.25	.07
147 Earl Weaver MG	.15	.04
148 Ted Williams	1.50	.45
149 Jim Gilliam	.10	.03

150 Checklist .05 .02
151 Juan Gonzalez .50 .15
152 Juan Gonzalez .50 .15
153 Juan Gonzalez .50 .15
154 Juan Gonzalez .50 .15
155 Checklist 151-155 .05 .02
156 Jeff Bagwell .50 .15
157 Jeff Bagwell .50 .15
158 Jeff Bagwell .50 .15
159 Jeff Bagwell .50 .15
160 Checklist 156-160 .05 .02
AU151 Juan Gonzalez AU 250.00 75.00
(Certified autograph)
Footsteps to Greatness
AU152 Juan Gonzalez AU 250.00 75.00
(Certified autograph)
Sign 'em Up
AU153 Juan Gonzalez AU 250.00 75.00
(Certified autograph)
The Road to Success
AU154 Juan Gonzalez AU 250.00 75.00
(Certified autograph)
Looking Ahead

1993 Ted Williams Brooks Robinson

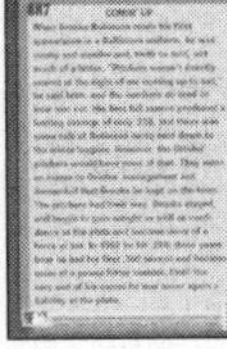

Randomly inserted in retail packs, this ten-card standard-size set features on its fronts borderless photos of Brooks Robinson. Certified Autographed cards of Robinson were randomly inserted into retail packs.

	Nm-Mt	Ex-Mt
COMPLETE SET (10)	15.00	4.50
COMMON CARD (1-10)	1.50	.45
AU Brooks Robinson AU	30.00	9.00

1993 Ted Williams Locklear Collection

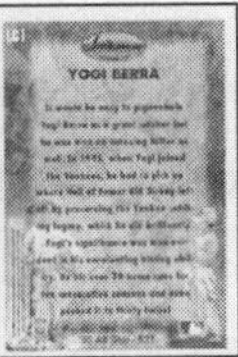

This ten-card standard-size set features the artwork of noted artist and former major league player Gene Locklear. The set includes famous players from the past. The cards are numbered on the back with an "LC" prefix with the order of players being alphabetical. The Ted Williams autograph cards can be differentiated by the serial numbering (to 406) on the back to go with the autograph on the front.

	Nm-Mt	Ex-Mt
COMPLETE SET (10)	35.00	10.50
1 Yogi Berra	6.00	1.80
2 Lou Brock	3.00	.90
3 Willie Mays	8.00	2.40
4 Johnny Mize	3.00	.90
5 Satchel Paige	6.00	1.80
6 Babe Ruth	8.00	2.40
7 Enos Slaughter	3.00	.90
8 Carl Yastrzemski	5.00	1.50
9 Ted Williams	8.00	2.40
10 Checklist	3.00	.90
AU9 Ted Williams AU/406 (Certified autograph)	500.00	150.00

1993 Ted Williams Memories

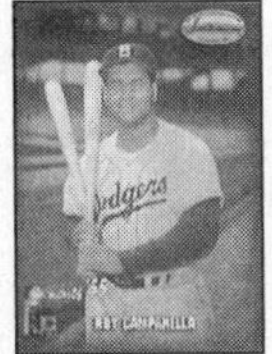

Individual cards from this special 20-card standard-size set were regionally but otherwise randomly inserted in foil hobby packs. For example, the 1973 Oakland A's cards were randomly inserted only in packs destined for shipment to the West Coast while the 1955 Brooklyn Dodgers cards were available only on the East Coast. The cards are numbered on the back with an "M" prefix.

	Nm-Mt	Ex-Mt
COMPLETE SET (20)	40.00	12.00
1 Roy Campanella	5.00	1.50
2 Jim Gilliam	2.00	.60
3 Gil Hodges	3.00	.90
4 Duke Snider	5.00	1.50
5 1955 Brooklyn Dodgers CL	1.50	.45
6 Don Drysdale	3.00	.90
7 Tommy Davis	1.50	.45
8 Johnny Podres	1.50	.45
9 Maury Wills	3.00	.90
10 1963 L.A. Dodgers CL	1.50	.45
11 Roberto Clemente	8.00	2.40
12 Al Oliver	2.00	.60
13 Manny Sanguillen	1.50	.45
14 Willie Stargell	3.00	.90
15 1971 Pitt. Pirates CL	1.50	.45
16 Johnny Bench	3.00	.90
17 George Foster	2.00	.60
18 Joe Morgan	3.00	.90
19 Tony Perez	3.00	.90
20 1975 Cinn. Reds CL	1.50	.45

1993 Ted Williams POG Cards

This set of 52 POGs was issued in pairs on 26 cards. The cards measure approximately 2 9/16" by 3 9/16" and are printed on a thick cardboard stock. Each POG measures 1 5/8" in diameter and is perforated for punch out. The fronts of the cards are black and the backs are white. The POGs consist of team logos, various special logos, and some players. The POGs are unnumbered and checklisted below alphabetically according to non-player cards (1-20) and cards which feature at least one player (21-26).

	Nm-Mt	Ex-Mt
COMPLETE SET (26)	6.00	1.80
1 Atlanta Black Crackers Baltimore Elite Giants	.25	.07
2 Atlanta Braves New York Mets	.25	.07
3 Baltimore Orioles 1993 All-Star Game 1993 World Series	.25	.07
4 Birmingham Black Barons New York Cuban Stars	.25	.07
5 Chicago Cubs Detroit Tigers	.25	.07
6 Cincinnati Reds Kansas City Royals 1969-1993	.25	.07
7 Classic Teams The Negro Leagues Negro League Baseball Players Assoc.	.25	.07
8 Cleveland Buckeyes Detroit Stars	.25	.07
9 Cleveland Indians Kansas City Athletics	.25	.07
10 Houston Colt .45s New York Yankees	.25	.07
11 Florida Marlins 1993 Inaugural Year Colorado Rockies 1993 Inaugural Year	.25	.07
12 Indianapolis ABCs New York Harlem Stars	.25	.07
13 Louisville Black Caps Philadelphia Stars	.25	.07
14 Minnesota Twins Boston Red Sox	.25	.07
15 Montreal Expos 1969-1993 San Diego Padres 1969-1993	.25	.07
16 New York Black Yankees Homestead Grays	.25	.07
17 New York Giants Milwaukee Braves	.25	.07
18 Oakland A's 21 (Clemente's number)	.25	.07
19 Pittsburgh Pirates St. Louis Cardinals	.25	.07
20 St. Louis Browns Brooklyn Dodgers	.25	.07
21 Yogi Berra Roy Campanella	1.00	.30
22 Brooklyn Dodgers Roy Campanella	.75	.23
23 Lou Gehrig Ted Williams	2.00	.60
24 Lou Gehrig New York Yankees	1.00	.30
25 Tommy Davis George Foster	.50	.15
26 Ted Williams 1941 - .406 Ted Williams	1.00	.30

1993 Ted Williams Roberto Clemente

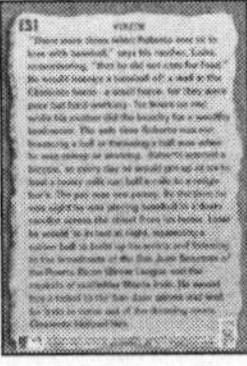

Randomly inserted in foil packs and subtitled "Etched in Stone," this ten-card standard-size set features on its fronts borderless photos of Roberto Clemente. The cards are numbered on the back with an "ES" prefix. The card numbering follows chronological order.

	Nm-Mt	Ex-Mt
COMPLETE SET (10)	20.00	6.00
COMMON CARD (1-10)	2.00	.60

1994 Ted Williams

The 1994 Ted Williams set comprises 162 standard-size cards distributed in 12-card packs. The series features former major league baseball players, players from the All-American Girls Professional Baseball League, 17 Negro

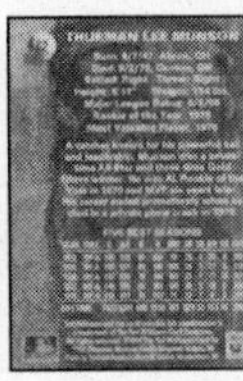

League stars, and 17 current top prospects. Topical subsets featured are Women in Baseball (93-99), The Negro League (100-117), The Campaign (118-135), Goin' North (136-144), Swinging for the Fences (145-153), and Dawning of a Legacy (154-162). A red foil version of the Ted Williams (LP1) and Larry Bird (LP2) insert cards were also produced. The values are the same as those listed below. Leon Day signed some cards for release in the packs. Packs of the football card product from the same year included a Ted Williams "Teddy Football" card and a numbered signed version of the same card seeded randomly. We've included pricing on those two cards below.

	Nm-Mt	Ex-Mt
COMPLETE SET (162)	10.00	3.00
1 Ted Williams	1.00	.30
2 Bernie Carbo	.05	.02
3 Bobby Doerr	.25	.07
4 Fred Lynn	.10	.03
5 John Pesky	.10	.03
6 Rico Petrocelli	.10	.03
7 Cy Young	.25	.07
8 Paul Blair	.05	.02
9 Andy Etchebarren	.05	.02
10 Brooks Robinson	.25	.07
11 Gil Hodges	.15	.04
12 Tommy John	.10	.03
13 Rick Monday	.05	.02
14 Dean Chance	.05	.02
15 Doug DeCinces	.05	.02
16 Gabby Hartnett	.25	.07
17 Don Kessinger	.05	.02
18 Bruce Sutter	.10	.03
19 Eddie Collins Sr.	.15	.04
20 Nellie Fox	.25	.07
21 Carlos May	.05	.02
22 Ted Kluszewski	.15	.04
23 Vada Pinson	.10	.03
24 Johnny Vander Meer	.10	.03
25 Bob Feller	.25	.07
26 Mike Garcia	.05	.02
27 Sam McDowell	.05	.02
28 Al Rosen	.10	.03
29 Norm Cash	.10	.03
30 Ty Cobb	.75	.23
31 Mark Fidrych	.10	.03
32 Hank Greenberg	.25	.07
33 Dennis McLain	.10	.03
34 Virgil Trucks	.05	.02
35 Enos Cabell	.05	.02
36 Mike Scott	.05	.02
37 Bob Watson	.10	.03
38 Amos Otis	.05	.02
39 Frank White	.10	.03
40 Joe Adcock	.10	.03
41 Rico Carty	.05	.02
42 Ralph Garr	.05	.02
43 Ed Mathews	.25	.07
44 Ben Oglivie	.05	.02
45 Gorman Thomas	.05	.02
46 Earl Battey	.05	.02
47 Rod Carew	.25	.07
48 Jim Kaat	.10	.03
49 Harmon Killebrew	.25	.07
50 Gary Carter	.15	.04
51 Steve Rogers	.05	.02
52 Rusty Staub	.10	.03
53 Sal Maglie	.10	.03
54 Juan Marichal	.25	.07
55 Mel Ott	.25	.07
56 Bobby Thomson	.15	.04
57 Tommie Agee	.05	.02
58 Tug McGraw	.10	.03
59 Elston Howard	.15	.04
60 Sparky Lyle	.10	.03
61 Billy Martin	.10	.03
62 Thurman Munson	.15	.04
63 Bobby Richardson	.10	.03
64 Bill Skowron	.10	.03
65 Mickey Cochrane	.25	.07
66 Rollie Fingers	.25	.07
67 Lefty Grove	.25	.07
68 James Hunter	.25	.07
69 Connie Mack MG	.25	.07
70 Al Simmons	.10	.03
71 Dick Allen	.15	.04
72 Bob Boone	.10	.03
73 Del Ennis	.05	.02
74 Chuck Klein	.25	.07
75 Mike Schmidt	.25	.07
76 Dock Ellis	.05	.02
77 Roy Face	.05	.02
78 Phil Garner	.05	.02
79 Bill Mazeroski	.15	.04
80 Pie Traynor	.25	.07
81 Honus Wagner	.25	.07
82 Dizzy Dean	.25	.07
83 Red Schoendienst	.25	.07
84 Randy Jones	.05	.02
85 Nate Colbert	.05	.02
86 Jeff Burroughs	.05	.02
87 Jim Sundberg	.05	.02
88 Frank Howard	.10	.03
89 Walter Johnson	.25	.07
90 Eddie Yost	.05	.02
91 Checklist 1	.05	.02
92 Checklist 2	.05	.02
93 Faye Dancer	.15	.04
94 Snookie Dayle	.10	.03
95 Maddy English	.10	.03
96 Nickie Fox	.10	.03
97 Sophie Kurys	.25	.07
98 Alma Ziegler	.10	.03
99 Checklist	.05	.02
100 Newton Allen	.10	.03
101 Willard Brown	.10	.03
102 Larry Brown	.10	.03
103 Leon Day	.25	.07
104 John Donaldson	.10	.03
105 Rube Foster	.15	.04
106 John Fowler	.10	.03
107 Elander Harris	.10	.03
108 Webster McDonald	.10	.03
109 Buck O'Neil	.25	.07
110 Ted "Double Duty" Radcliffe	.25	.07
111 Wilber Rogan	.10	.03
112 Marcenia Stone	.10	.03
113 James Taylor	.10	.03
114 Fleetwood Walker	.15	.04
115 George Wilson	.10	.03
116 Judson Wilson	.10	.03
117 Checklist	.05	.02
118 Howard Battle	.05	.02
119 John Burke	.05	.02
120 Brian Dubose	.05	.02
121 Alex Gonzalez	.15	.04
122 Jose Herrera	.05	.02
123 Jason Giambi	1.50	.45
124 Derek Jeter	4.00	1.20
125 Charles Johnson	.10	.03
126 Daron Kirkreit	.05	.02
127 Jason Moler	.05	.02
128 Vince Moore	.05	.02
129 Chad Mottola	.05	.02
130 Jose Silva	.05	.02
131 Mac Suzuki	.05	.02
132 Brien Taylor	.05	.02
133 Michael Tucker	.10	.03
134 Billy Wagner	.50	.15
135 Checklist	.05	.02
136 Gary Carter	.15	.04
137 Tony Conigliaro	.10	.03
138 Sparky Lyle	.10	.03
139 Roger Maris	.15	.04
140 Vada Pinson	.10	.03
141 Mike Schmidt	.25	.07
142 Frank White	.10	.03
143 Ted Williams	.75	.23
144 Checklist	.05	.02
145 Joe Adcock	.05	.02
146 Rocky Colavito	.15	.04
147 Lou Gehrig	1.00	.30
148 Gil Hodges	.10	.03
149 Bob Horner	.05	.02
150 Willie Mays	1.00	.30
151 Mike Schmidt	.25	.07
152 Pat Seerey	.05	.02
153 Checklist	.05	.02
154 Cliff Floyd	.30	.09
155 Cliff Floyd	.30	.09
156 Cliff Floyd	.30	.09
157 Cliff Floyd	.30	.09
158 Tim Salmon	.50	.15
159 Tim Salmon	.50	.15
160 Tim Salmon	.50	.15
161 Tim Salmon	.50	.15
162 Checklist	.05	.02
P1 Ted Williams Promo	2.00	.60
LP1 Larry Bird	5.00	1.50
LP2 Ted Williams	5.00	1.50
TW1 Ted Williams Teddy Football (issued in Football product packs)	2.00	.60
TW1AU Ted Williams AU/54 Teddy Football Autographed (issued in Football product packs)	500.00	150.00
NNO Leon Day AU	25.00	7.50

1994 Ted Williams 500 Club

Randomly inserted in foil packs, this nine-card standard-size set profiles members of baseball's elite 500 home run club. Cards numbers are prefixed with a "5C." A red foil version of this set was produced. The values are the same as those listed below.

	Nm-Mt	Ex-Mt
COMPLETE SET (9)	20.00	6.00
1 Hank Aaron	4.00	1.20
2 Reggie Jackson	3.00	.90
3 Harmon Killebrew	1.25	.35
4 Mickey Mantle	8.00	2.40
5 Jimmie Foxx	3.00	.90
6 Babe Ruth	6.00	1.80
7 Mike Schmidt	5.00	1.50
8 Ted Williams UER Card credits him with winning triple crown in 1940	6.00	1.80
9 Checklist	1.00	.30

1994 Ted Williams Dan Gardiner Collection

Randomly inserted in foil packs, this nine-card standard-size set presents top minor league prospects. Both sides display color paintings by noted artist Dan Gardiner. The backs also include a brief player profile.

	Nm-Mt	Ex-Mt
COMPLETE SET (9)	30.00	9.00
DG1 Michael Jordan	15.00	4.50
DG2 Michael Tucker	2.00	.60
DG3 Derek Jeter	15.00	4.50
DG4 Charles Johnson	1.00	.30
DG5 Howard Battle	.75	.23
DG6 Quilvio Veras	1.00	.30
DG7 Brian L. Hunter	.75	.23
DG8 Brien Taylor	.75	.23
DG9 Checklist	2.00	.60

1994 Ted Williams Locklear Collection

Randomly inserted in foil packs, this nine-card standard-size set again features the work of noted artist Gene Locklear. The numbering on the backs is in continuation of last year's Locklear Collection insert series.

	Nm-Mt	Ex-Mt
COMPLETE SET (9)	20.00	6.00
LC11 Ty Cobb	5.00	1.50
LC12 Bob Feller	2.50	.75
LC13 Lou Gehrig	8.00	2.40
LC14 Josh Gibson	3.00	.90
LC15 Walter Johnson	3.00	.90
LC16 Casey Stengel	3.00	.90
LC17 Honus Wagner	6.00	1.80
LC18 Cy Young	3.00	.90
LC19 Checklist	1.50	.45

1994 Ted Williams Memories

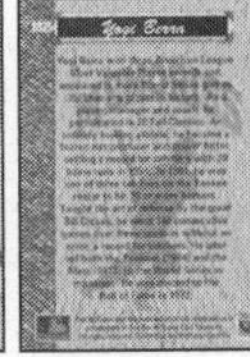

Randomly inserted only in hobby packs, this special regional insert set was sold on a regional basis, highlighting four great teams of the past. This year's set captures the 1954 New York Giants (M21-M24), the 1961 New York Yankees (M25-M28), the 1968 Detroit Tigers (M29-M32), and the 1975 Boston Red Sox (M33-M36). The numbering on the backs is in continuation of last year's Memories insert series.

	Nm-Mt	Ex-Mt
COMPLETE SET (17)	40.00	12.00
M21 Monte Irvin	2.50	.75
M22 Sal Maglie	2.50	.75
M23 Dusty Rhodes	1.50	.45
M24 Hank Thompson	1.50	.45
M25 Yogi Berra	5.00	1.50
M26 Elston Howard	4.00	1.20
M27 Roger Maris	6.00	1.80
M28 Bobby Richardson	2.50	.75
M29 Norm Cash	2.50	.75
M30 Al Kaline	6.00	1.80
M31 Mickey Lolich	2.00	.60
M32 Denny McLain	2.50	.75
M33 Bernie Carbo	1.50	.45
M34 Fred Lynn	2.00	.60
M35 Rico Petrocelli	2.00	.60
M36 Luis Tiant	2.00	.60
M37 Checklist	1.00	.30

1994 Ted Williams Mike Schmidt

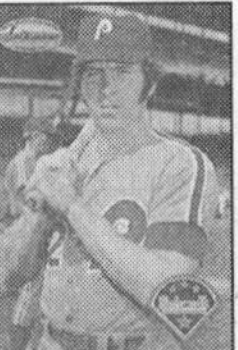
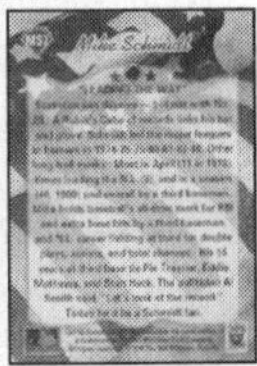

Randomly inserted one per jumbo pack, this nine-card standard-size set highlights the career of Mike Schmidt. These cards are all numbered with a "MS" prefix.

	Nm-Mt	Ex-Mt
COMPLETE SET (9)	6.00	1.80
COMMON CARD (MS1-MS8)	.75	.23

1994 Ted Williams Roger Maris

Randomly inserted in foil packs, this nine-card standard-size set highlights the career of Roger Maris. When placed in a nine-card plastic sheet, the background on the backs form a

composite "Etched in Stone" logo. A red foil version of this set was also produced. The values are the same as those listed below.

	Nm-Mt	Ex-Mt
COMPLETE SET (9)	12.00	3.60
COMMON CARD (ES1-ES8)	1.50	.45

1994 Ted Williams Trade for Babe

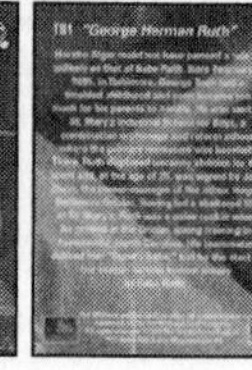

A special "Trade for Babe" chase card was randomly inserted throughout the packs. By mailing in the trade card plus 4.50 for shipping and handling, the collector received this nine-card standard-size set.

	Nm-Mt	Ex-Mt
COMPLETE SET (9)	40.00	12.00
COMMON CARD (T1-T8)	5.00	1.50
T9 Babe Ruth Checklist	4.00	1.20
NNO0 Trade Card	4.00	1.20

1988 Tetley Tea Discs

These discs, which are parallel to the 1988 MSA Iced Tea Discs, say Tetley Tea on the front. They are valued the same as the regular discs.

	Nm-Mt	Ex-Mt
COMPLETE SET (20)	10.00	4.00
1 Wade Boggs	1.00	.40
2 Ellis Burks	.75	.30
3 Don Mattingly	2.00	.80
4 Mark McGwire	3.00	1.20
5 Matt Nokes	.10	.04
6 Kirby Puckett	1.00	.40
7 Billy Ripken	.10	.04
8 Kevin Seitzer	.10	.04
9 Roger Clemens	2.00	.80
10 Will Clark	.75	.30
11 Vince Coleman	.10	.04
12 Eric Davis	.25	.10
13 Dave Magadan	.10	.04
14 Dale Murphy	.50	.20
15 Benito Santiago	.25	.10
16 Mike Schmidt	1.00	.40
17 Darryl Strawberry	.25	.10
18 Steve Bedrosian	.10	.04
19 Dwight Gooden	.25	.10
20 Fernando Valenzuela	.25	.10

1989 Tetley Tea Discs

For the second year, Tetlea tea was one of the companies distributing the MSA Iced Tea Discs. These Discs say Tetley on the front and are valued the same as the MSA Iced Tea Discs.

	Nm-Mt	Ex-Mt
COMPLETE SET (20)	50.00	20.00
1 Don Mattingly	6.00	2.40
2 Dave Cone	.50	.20
3 Mark McGwire	10.00	4.00
4 Will Clark	2.00	.80
5 Darryl Strawberry	1.00	.40
6 Dwight Gooden	1.00	.40
7 Wade Boggs	3.00	1.20
8 Roger Clemens	6.00	2.40
9 Benito Santiago	1.00	.40
10 Orel Hershiser	1.00	.40
11 Eric Davis	1.00	.40
12 Kirby Puckett	4.00	1.60
13 Dave Winfield	3.00	1.20
14 Andre Dawson	2.00	.80
15 Steve Bedrosian	.50	.20
16 Cal Ripken	12.00	4.80
17 Andy Van Slyke	.50	.20
18 Jose Canseco	2.50	1.00
19 Jose Oquendo	.50	.20
20 Dale Murphy	1.50	.60

1914 Texas Tommy E224

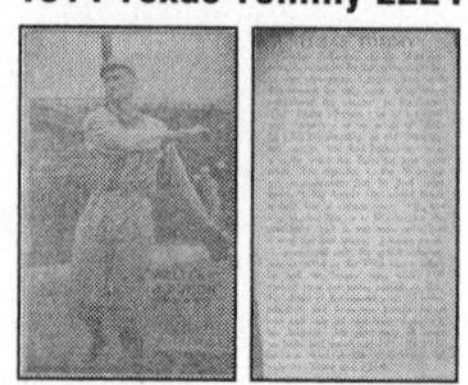

There are two types of these cards:Type I are 1-50 and Type II are 51-64. The type one cards measure 2 3/8" by 3 1/2" while the type two cards measure 1 7/8" by 3". The type one cards have stats on the back while the type 2 cards have blank backs. Harry Hooper and Rube Marquard only exist in type two fashion.

	Ex-Mt	VG
COMPLETE SET (64)	32000.00	16000.00
COMMON CARD (1-50)	250.00	125.00
COMMON CARD (51-64)	1000.00	500.00
1 Jimmy Archer	250.00	125.00
2 Jimmy Austin	250.00	125.00
3 Frank Baker	500.00	250.00
4 Chief Bender	500.00	250.00
5 Bob Bescher	250.00	125.00
6 Ping Bodie	300.00	150.00
7 Donie Bush	250.00	125.00
8 Bobby Byrne	250.00	125.00
9 Nixey Callahan	250.00	125.00
10 Howie Camnitz	250.00	125.00
11 Frank Chance	500.00	250.00
12 Hal Chase	500.00	250.00
13 Ty Cobb	3500.00	1800.00
14 Jack Coombs	300.00	150.00
15 Sam Crawford	500.00	250.00
16 Birdie Cree	250.00	125.00
17 Al Demaree	250.00	125.00
18 Red Dooin	300.00	150.00
19 Larry Doyle	500.00	250.00
20 Johnny Evers	500.00	250.00
21 Vean Gregg	250.00	125.00
22 Bob Harmon	250.00	125.00
23 Joe Jackson	4000.00	2000.00
24 Walter Johnson	800.00	400.00
25 Otto Knabe	250.00	125.00
26 Nap Lajoie	500.00	250.00
27 Bris Lord	250.00	125.00
28 Connie Mack MG	500.00	250.00
29 Armando Marsans	250.00	125.00
30 Christy Mathewson	800.00	400.00
31 George McBride	250.00	125.00
32 John McGraw MG	1000.00	500.00
33 Snuffy McInnis	300.00	150.00
34 Chief Meyers	300.00	150.00
35 Earl Moore	250.00	125.00
36 Mike Mowrey	250.00	125.00
37 Marty O'Toole	250.00	125.00
38 Eddie Plank	500.00	250.00
39 Jack Ryan	250.00	125.00
40 Tris Speaker	800.00	400.00
41 Jake Stahl	250.00	125.00
42 Oscar Stanage	250.00	125.00
43 Bill Sweeney	250.00	125.00
44 Honus Wagner	2000.00	1000.00
45 Ed Walsh	500.00	250.00
47 Harry Wolter	250.00	125.00
48 Joe Wood	500.00	250.00
49 Steve Yerkes	400.00	200.00
50 Heinie Zimmerman	300.00	150.00
51 Ping Bodie	1000.00	500.00
52 Larry Doyle	1500.00	750.00
53 Vean Gregg	1000.00	500.00
54 Harry Hooper	2000.00	1000.00
55 Walter Johnson	3000.00	1500.00
56 Connie Mack MG	2000.00	1000.00
57 Rube Marquard	2000.00	1000.00
58 Christy Mathewson	2000.00	1000.00
59 John McGraw MG	2000.00	1000.00
60 Chief Meyers	1200.00	600.00
61 Jake Stahl	1000.00	500.00
62 Honus Wagner	5000.00	2500.00
63 Steve Yerkes	1000.00	500.00
64 Joe Wood	2000.00	1000.00

1948 Thom McAn Feller

This one-card set was distributed by Thom McAn Shoe Stores and features a black-and-white picture of Bob Feller of the Cleveland Indians with a facsimile autograph. The back carrys a Baseball Quiz with the answers to the questions at the bottom.

	NM	Ex
1 Bob Feller	25.00	12.50

1985 Thom McAn Discs

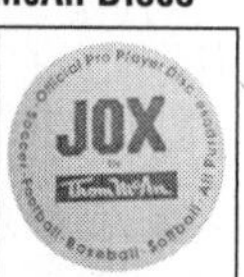

MSA (Michael Schechter Associates) produced this 46-disc set for Thom McAn to promote a specially developed line of boys' and young men's JOX all-turf cleat shoes. The give-away consisted of a set of 10 discs with every pair of shoes purchased. The production of the discs was discontinued when a decision was made to replace this line of shoes with a newer one. The discs measure 2 3/4" in diameter. The front design resembles a baseball, with a black and white headshot sandwiched between the two rows of stitching. Four stars appear above the player's picture, and the two ovals created by the stitching are colored yellow, green, red, or mustard. In addition, at least 8 players (Cedeno, Cooper, Cowens, Hargrove, Leonard, Valenzuela, Walker, and Zahn) had their photo and information printed in two different colors. The back of the discs are printed in black on white and have a Thom McAn advertisement. The discs are unnumbered and checklisted below alphabetically according to AL (1-24) and NL players (25-46).

	Nm-Mt	Ex-Mt
COMPLETE SET (46)	350.00	140.00
1 Benny Ayala	1.00	.40
2 Buddy Bell	2.00	.80
3 Juan Beniquez	1.00	.40
4 Tony Bernazard	1.00	.40
5 Mike Boddicker	1.00	.40
6 Bill Buckner	1.00	.40
7 Rod Carew	40.00	16.00
8 Onix Concepcion	1.00	.40
9 Cecil Cooper	2.00	.80
10 Al Cowens	1.00	.40
11 Ron Guidry	2.00	.80
12 Mike Hargrove	1.00	.40
13 Kent Hrbek	2.00	.80
14 Rick Langford	1.00	.40
15 Jack Morris	2.00	.80
16 Dan Quisenberry	1.00	.40
17 Cal Ripken	80.00	32.00
18 Ed Romero	1.00	.40
19 Tom Seaver	40.00	16.00
20 Alan Trammell	3.00	1.20
21 Greg Walker	1.00	.40
22 Willie Wilson	1.00	.40
23 Dave Winfield	40.00	16.00
24 Geoff Zahn	1.00	.40
25 Steve Carlton	40.00	16.00
26 Cesar Cedeno	1.00	.40
27 Jose Cruz	1.00	.40
28 Ivan DeJesus	1.00	.40
29 Luis DeLeon	1.00	.40
30 Rich Gossage	2.00	.80
31 Pedro Guerrero	1.00	.40
32 Tony Gwynn	60.00	24.00
33 Keith Hernandez	2.00	.80
34 Bob Horner	1.00	.40
35 Jeff Leonard	1.00	.40
36 Willie McGee	2.00	.80
37 Jesse Orosco	2.00	.80
38 Junior Ortiz	1.00	.40
39 Terry Puhl	1.00	.40
40 Johnny Ray	1.00	.40
41 Ryne Sandberg	50.00	20.00
42 Mike Schmidt	40.00	16.00
43 Rick Sutcliffe	1.00	.40
44 Bruce Sutter	2.00	.80
45 Fernando Valenzuela	2.00	.80
46 Ozzie Virgil	1.00	.40

1994 Frank Thomas Ameritech

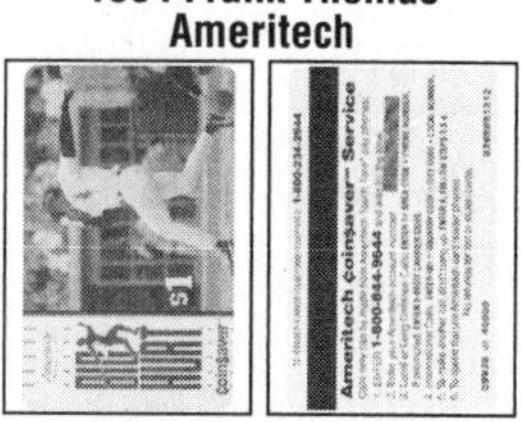

This phone card, with a $1 denomination, was issued in 1994. The front has a "Big Hurt" logo on the left with a full color photo next to it. The back has information on how to use the card. The cards are serial numbered to 40,000.

	Nm-Mt	Ex-Mt
1 Frank Thomas	5.00	1.50

1996 Thome Buick Postcard

Measuring approximately 4 1/2" by 6", this one card set featured star third baseman Jim Thome and was issued to promoted sales of Buicks in Northern Ohio. The front features a photo of Thome while the back has promotional information about various Buick automobiles.

	MINT	NRMT
1 Jim Thome	3.00	1.35

1907-09 Tigers A.C. Dietsche Postcards PC765

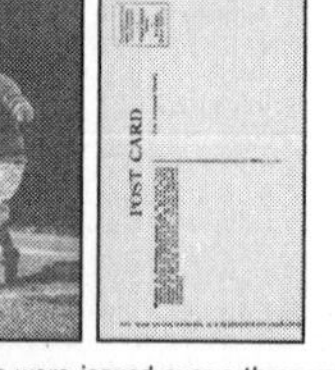

These postcards were issued over a three year period. The cards numbered from 1 through 15 are known as series one and issued in 1907 with a 1907 copyright. Cards numbered from 16 to 29 are known as series two and have 1908 or 1909 copyrights. An oversize team card has been rumored to exist but it has never been verified.

	Ex-Mt	VG
COMPLETE SET (29)	1500.00	750.00
1 Ty Cobb	250.00	125.00
2 William Coughlin	50.00	25.00
3 Sam Crawford	100.00	50.00
4 Bill Donovan	60.00	30.00
5 Jerome W. Downs	50.00	25.00
6 Hugh Jennings MG	100.00	50.00
7 Davy Jones	50.00	25.00
8 Ed Killian	50.00	25.00
9 George Mullin	50.00	25.00
10 Charles O'Leary	50.00	25.00
11 Fred T. Payne	50.00	25.00
12 Claude Rossman	50.00	25.00
13 Germany Schaefer	60.00	30.00
14 Boss Schmidt	50.00	25.00
15 Edward Siever	50.00	25.00
16 Henry Beckendorf 08	50.00	25.00
17 Owen Bush 08	50.00	25.00
18 Ty Cobb 08 (batting)	250.00	125.00
19 James Delehanty 09	50.00	25.00
20 Bill Donovan 08	60.00	30.00
21 Hugh Jennings MG 08	100.00	50.00
22 Tom Jones 09	50.00	25.00
23 Matthew McIntyre 08	50.00	25.00
24 George Moriarty 08	50.00	25.00
25 Oscar Stanage 08	50.00	25.00
26 Oren Edgar Summers 08	50.00	25.00
27 Edgar Willett 08	50.00	25.00
28 Ralph Works 09	50.00	25.00
29 Team Picture 09	80.00	40.00

1908 Tigers Fred G.Wright Postcard

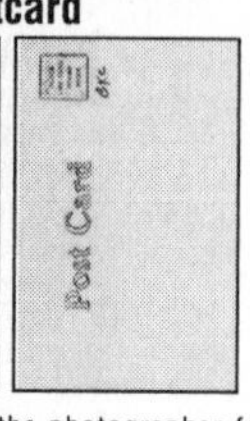

Fred G. Wright was the photographer for several cards including the Detroit Tigers set produced by H.M. Taylor, established his own company. The only card positively identified is one of "Wild Bill" Donovan, a star pitcher for the Tigers. All additions to this checklist are appreciated.

	Ex-Mt	VG
1 Bill Donovan	200.00	100.00

1909-11 Tigers H.M. Taylor PC773-2

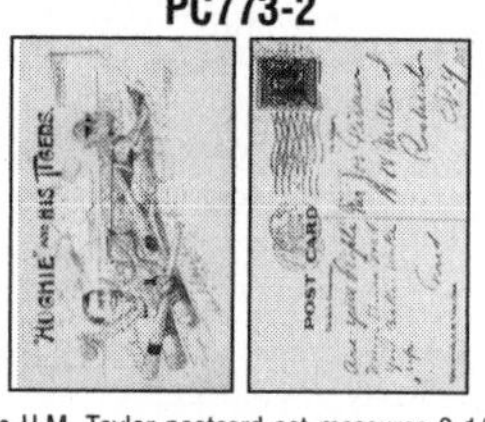

The H.M. Taylor postcard set measures 3 1/2" by 5 1/2" and was issued during the 1909-11 time period and features Detroit Tigers players only. The cards are black and white with a rather large border around the card. The H.M Taylor identification is presented on the back of the card.

	Ex-Mt	VG
COMPLETE SET (9)	2750.00	1400.00
1 Ty Cobb At Bat	1200.00	600.00
2 Bill Coughlin Batting	150.00	75.00
3 Sam Crawford Ready for the ball	250.00	125.00
4 Detroit Team Card	600.00	300.00
5 Wild Bill Donovan Floral Horseshoe presented at Philadelphia	150.00	75.00
6 Wild Bill Donovan Batting	150.00	75.00
7 Hugh Jennings Wee Ah; Yours Truly	300.00	150.00
8 Wild Bill Donovan Hugh Jennings Frank Chance In Dugout	150.00	75.00
9 Hugh Jennings MG and his Tigers Drawing	250.00	125.00

1909-10 Tigers Topping and Company PC773-1

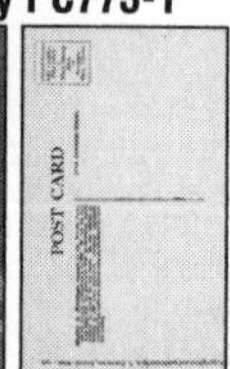

This set of Detroit Tiger stars is believed to have been issued in late 1909 and early 1910. This distinctive set features yellow bands at the top and bottom and a face shot of the player in a center of a six-pointed star, which also contains a yellow outline. The words "Tiger Stars" are printed in the upper yellow band whereas the player's name and position appears in the lower band. Topping and Publishers Company, Detroit, is identified on the reverse.

	Ex-Mt	VG
COMPLETE SET (20)	4500.00	2200.00
1 Henry Beckendorf	150.00	75.00
2 Donie Bush	150.00	75.00
3 Ty Cobb	2000.00	1000.00
4 Sam Crawford	300.00	150.00
5 Jim Delahanty	150.00	75.00
6 Bill Donovan	150.00	75.00
7 Hugh Jennings MG	300.00	150.00
8 Davy Jones	150.00	75.00
9 Tom Jones	150.00	75.00
10 Ed Killian	150.00	75.00
11 Matty McIntyre	150.00	75.00
12 George Moriarty	150.00	75.00
13 George Mullin	200.00	100.00
14 Charlie O'Leary	150.00	75.00
15 Charlie Schmidt	150.00	75.00
16 George Speer	150.00	75.00
17 Oscar Stanage	150.00	75.00
18 Eddie Summers	150.00	75.00
19 Edgar Willet	150.00	75.00
20 Ralph Works	150.00	75.00

1909 Tigers Wolverine News Postcards PC773-3

The Wolverine News Company features Detroit Tigers. Two poses each of Ty Cobb and Sam

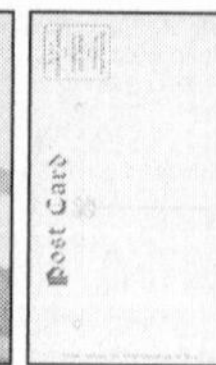

Crawford highlight this black and white set. The Wolverine News Company identification is printed on the back of the card.

	Ex-Mt	VG
COMPLETE SET	2000.00	1000.00
1 Ty Cobb at bat	600.00	300.00
2 Ty Cobb Portrait	600.00	300.00
3 Bill Coughlin Capt. and Third Baseman	60.00	30.00
4 Sam Crawford Bunting	120.00	60.00
5 Sam Crawford Center Field	120.00	60.00
6 Wild Bill Donovan Pitcher	80.00	40.00
7 Wild Bill Donovan At the Water Wagon	80.00	40.00
8 Jerry Downs Utility	60.00	30.00
9 Hugh Jennings MG On the Coaching Line HOR	120.00	60.00
10 Hugh (ey) Jennings Manager	120.00	60.00
11 Davy Jones Left Fielder	60.00	30.00
12 Ed Killian Pitcher	60.00	30.00
13 George Mullin Pitcher	60.00	30.00
14 Charlie O'Leary Short Stop	60.00	30.00
15 Fred Payne Catcher	60.00	30.00
16 Claude Rossman 1st Baseman	60.00	30.00
17 Herman Schaefer 2d. Baseman	60.00	30.00
18 Germany Schaefer Charlie O'Leary working double play HOR	80.00	40.00
19 Charlie Schmidt Catcher	60.00	30.00
20 Eddie Siever Pitcher	60.00	30.00

1934 Tigers Team Issue

These 23 photos features members of the 1934 Tigers. The set is identifiable by the Frank Doljack photo who only played for the Tigers in 1934. The player's name and position is located in the upper left corner. This set is also known as W-UNC.

	Ex-Mt	VG
COMPLETE SET (23)	250.00	125.00
1 Eldon Auker	10.00	5.00
2 Del Baker CO	10.00	5.00
3 Tommy Bridges	15.00	7.50
4 Mickey Cochrane	30.00	15.00
5 Alvin Crowder	10.00	5.00
6 Frank Doljack	10.00	5.00
7 Carl Fischer	10.00	5.00
8 Pete Fox	10.00	5.00
9 Charlie Gehringer	30.00	15.00
10 Goose Goslin	20.00	10.00
11 Hank Greenberg	40.00	20.00
12 Luke Hamlin	10.00	5.00
13 Ray Hayworth	10.00	5.00
14 Chief Hogsett	10.00	5.00
15 Firpo Marberry	10.00	5.00
16 Marv Owen	10.00	5.00
17 Cy Perkins CO	10.00	5.00
18 Bill Rogell	10.00	5.00
19 Schoolboy Rowe	10.00	5.00
20 Heinie Schuble	10.00	5.00
21 Vic Sorrell	10.00	5.00
22 Gee Walker	10.00	5.00
23 Jo Jo White	10.00	5.00

1939 Tigers Sportservice

These cards which measure 6 3/8" by 4 1/8" are sepia toned and feature members of the 1939 Detroit Tigers. The fronts feature a player photo as well as a short biography. There may be more cards so any additions are appreciated.

	Ex-Mt	VG
COMPLETE SET	120.00	60.00
1 Earl Averill	30.00	15.00
2 Beau Bell	15.00	7.50
3 Tommy Bridges	15.00	7.50
4 Pinky Higgins	15.00	7.50
5 Red Kress	15.00	7.50

6 Barney McCoskey	15.00	7.50
7 Bobo Newsom	15.00	7.50
8 Birdie Tebbetts	15.00	7.50

1953 Tigers Glendale

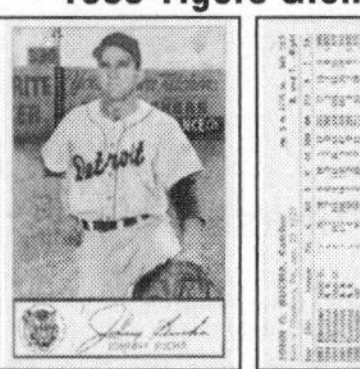

The cards in this 28-card set measure approximately 2 5/8" by 3 3/4". The 1953 Glendale Meats set of full-color, unnumbered cards features Detroit Tiger ballplayers exclusively and was distributed one per package of Glendale Meats in the Detroit area. The back contains the complete major and minor league record through the 1952 season. The scarcer cards of the set command higher prices, with the Houtteman card being the most difficult to find. There is an album associated with the set (which also is quite scarce now). The catalog designation for this scarce regional set is F151. Since the cards are unnumbered, they are ordered below alphabetically.

	NM	Ex
COMPLETE SET (28)	5000.00	2500.00
COMMON CARD (1-28)	150.00	75.00
COMMON SP	250.00	125.00
1 Matt Batts	150.00	75.00
2 Johnny Bucha	150.00	75.00
3 Frank Carswell	150.00	75.00
4 Jim Delsing	180.00	90.00
5 Walt Dropo	180.00	90.00
6 Hal Erickson	150.00	75.00
7 Paul Foytack	150.00	75.00
8 Owen Friend	150.00	75.00
9 Ned Garver	180.00	90.00
10 Joe Ginsberg SP	500.00	250.00
11 Ted Gray	150.00	75.00
12 Fred Hatfield	150.00	75.00
13 Ray Herbert	150.00	75.00
14 Billy Hitchcock	150.00	75.00
15 Billy Hoeft SP	250.00	125.00
16 Art Houtteman SP	2000.00	1000.00
17 Milt Jordan	150.00	75.00
18 Harvey Kuenn	500.00	250.00
19 Don Lund	150.00	75.00
20 Dave Madison	150.00	75.00
21 Dick Marlowe	150.00	75.00
22 Pat Mullin	150.00	75.00
23 Bob Nieman	150.00	75.00
24 Johnny Pesky	180.00	90.00
25 Jerry Priddy	150.00	75.00
26 Steve Souchock	150.00	75.00
27 Russ Sullivan	150.00	75.00
28 Bill Wight	150.00	75.00

1959 Tigers Graphic Arts Service PC749

The Graphic Art Service postcards were issued in the late 1950's and early 60's in Cincinnati, Ohio. Despite being issued in Cincinnati, the players featured are all Detroit Tigers. These black and white, unnumbered cards feature facsimile autographs on the front. Two poses of Reno Bertoia exist.

	NM	Ex
COMPLETE SET (16)	75.00	38.00
1 Al Aber	3.00	1.50
2 Hank Aguirre	5.00	2.50
3 Reno Bertoia (2)	3.00	1.50
4 Frank Bolling	3.00	1.50
5 Jim Bunning	15.00	7.50
6 Paul Foytack	3.00	1.50
7 Jim Hegan	3.00	1.50
8 Tom Henrich CO	10.00	5.00
9 Bill Hoeft	3.00	1.50
10 Frank House	3.00	1.50
11 Harvey Kuenn	5.00	2.50
12 Billy Martin	10.00	5.00
13 Tom Morgan	5.00	2.50
14 Bob Shaw	3.00	1.50
15 Lou Slater	3.00	1.50
16 Tim Thompson	3.00	1.50

1960 Tigers Jay Publishing

This 12-card set of the Detroit Tigers measures approximately 5" by 7" and features black-and-white player photos in a white border. These cards were packaged 12 to a packet. The backs are blank. The cards are unnumbered and checklisted below in alphabetical order.

	NM	Ex
COMPLETE SET (12)	45.00	18.00
1 Lou Berberet	2.50	1.00
2 Frank Bolling	2.50	1.00
3 Rocky Bridges	2.50	1.00
4 Jim Bunning	8.00	3.20
5 Rocky Colavito	5.00	2.00
6 Paul Foytack	2.50	1.00
7 Al Kaline	12.00	4.80
8 Frank Lary	2.50	1.00
9 Charlie Maxwell	2.50	1.00
10 Don Mossi	3.00	1.20
11 Ray Narleski	2.50	1.00
12 Eddie Yost	2.50	1.00

1961 Tigers Jay Publishing

This 12-card set of the Detroit Tigers measures approximately 5" by 7". The fronts feature black-and-white posed player photos with the player's and team name printed below in the white border. These cards were packaged 12 in a packet. The backs are blank. The cards are unnumbered and checklisted below in alphabetical order.

	NM	Ex
COMPLETE SET (12)	40.00	16.00
1 Steve Boros	2.50	1.00
2 Dick Brown	2.50	1.00
3 Bill Bruton	2.50	1.00
4 Jim Bunning	8.00	3.20
5 Norm Cash	4.00	1.60
6 Rocky Colavito	5.00	2.00
7 Chuck Cottier	2.50	1.00
8 Dick Gernert	2.50	1.00
9 Al Kaline	12.00	4.80
10 Frank Lary	2.50	1.00
11 Charlie Maxwell	2.50	1.00
12 Bob Sheffing MG	2.50	1.00

1962 Tigers Jay Publishing

This 12-card set of the Detroit Tigers measures approximately 5" by 7". The fronts feature black-and-white posed player photos with the player's and team name printed below in the white border. These cards were packaged 12 in a packet. The backs are blank. The cards are unnumbered and checklisted below in alphabetical order.

	NM	Ex
COMPLETE SET (12)	40.00	16.00
1 Steve Boros	2.50	1.00
2 Dick Brown	2.50	1.00
3 Jim Bunning	8.00	3.20
4 Norm Cash	5.00	2.00
5 Rocky Colavito	8.00	3.20
6 Chico Fernandez	2.50	1.00
7 Al Kaline	12.00	4.80
8 Frank Lary	2.50	1.00
9 Charley Maxwell	2.50	1.00
10 Don Mossi	3.00	1.20
11 Bob Scheffing MG	2.50	1.00
12 Jake Wood	2.50	1.00

1962 Tigers Post Cards Ford

These postcards feature members of the 1962 Detroit Tigers. They are unnumbered and we have sequenced them in alphabetical order. These cards are usually seen with real autographs.

	NM	Ex
COMPLETE SET	1000.00	400.00
1 Hank Aguirre	60.00	24.00
2 Steve Boros	50.00	20.00
3 Dick Brown	50.00	20.00
4 Jim Bunning	150.00	60.00
5 Phil Cavarretta CO	60.00	24.00
6 Rocky Colavito	120.00	47.50
7 Terry Fox	50.00	20.00
8 Purnal Goldy	50.00	20.00
9 Jack Hommel TR	50.00	20.00
10 Dave Jolley	50.00	20.00
11 Ron Kline	50.00	20.00
12 Don Mossi	60.00	24.00
13 George Myatt CO	60.00	24.00
14 Ron Nischwitz	50.00	20.00
15 Larry Osborne	50.00	20.00
16 Phil Regan	50.00	20.00
17 Mike Roarke	50.00	20.00

1963 Tigers Jay Publishing

This 12-card set of the Detroit Tigers measures approximately 5" by 7". The fronts feature black-and-white posed player photos with the player's and team name printed below in the white border. These cards were packaged 12 in a packet. The backs are blank. The cards are unnumbered and checklisted below in alphabetical order.

	NM	Ex
COMPLETE SET (12)	35.00	14.00
1 Hank Aguirre	2.00	.80
2 Bill Bruton	2.00	.80
3 Jim Bunning	8.00	3.20
4 Norm Cash	4.00	1.60
5 Rocky Colavito	6.00	2.40
6 Chico Fernandez	2.00	.80
7 Paul Foytack	2.00	.80
8 Al Kaline	12.00	4.80
9 Frank Lary	2.50	1.00
10 Bob Scheffing MG	2.00	.80
11 Gus Triandos	2.50	1.00
12 Jake Wood	2.00	.80

1964 Tigers Jay Publishing

This 12-card set of the Detroit Tigers measures approximately 5" by 7". The fronts feature black-and-white posed player photos with the player's and team name printed below in the white border. These cards were packaged 12 in a packet. The backs are blank. The cards are unnumbered and checklisted below in alphabetical order.

	NM	Ex
COMPLETE SET (12)	35.00	14.00
1 Hank Aguirre	2.00	.80
2 Bill Bruton	2.00	.80
3 Norm Cash	4.00	1.60
4 Chuck Dressen MG	2.50	1.00
5 Bill Freehan	4.00	1.60
6 Al Kaline	12.00	4.80
7 Frank Lary	2.50	1.00
8 Jerry Lumpe	2.00	.80
9 Ed Rakow	2.00	.80
10 Phil Regan	2.00	.80
11 Mike Roarke	2.00	.80
12 Jake Wood	2.00	.80

1964 Tigers Lids

This set of 14 lids was produced in 1964 and features members of the Detroit Tigers. The catalog designation for this set is F96-5. These lids are actually milk bottle caps. Each lid is blank backed and measures approximately 1 1/4" in diameter. Since the lids are unnumbered, they are ordered below in alphabetical order. The players are drawn on the lids in blue and the player's name is written in orange. The lids say "Visit Tiger Stadium" at the top and "See the Tigers More in '64" at the bottom of every lid.

	NM	Ex
COMPLETE SET	100.00	40.00
1 Hank Aguirre	5.00	2.00
2 Billy Bruton	5.00	2.00
3 Norm Cash	10.00	4.00
4 Don Demeter	5.00	2.00
5 Chuck Dressen MG	6.00	2.40
6 Bill Freehan	10.00	4.00
7 Al Kaline	50.00	20.00
8 Frank Lary	6.00	2.40
9 Jerry Lumpe	5.00	2.00
10 Dick McAuliffe	6.00	2.40
11 Bubba Phillips	5.00	2.00
12 Ed Rakow	5.00	2.00
13 Phil Regan	5.00	2.00
14 Dave Wickersham	5.00	2.00

1965 Tigers Jay Publishing

These blank-backed photos measure approximately 5" by 7" and feature white-bordered black-and-white posed player photos. The photos are printed on thin paper stock. The player's name and team appear below the photo within the bottom margin. The cards are unnumbered and checklisted below in alphabetical order. More than 12 photos are listed since the players were changed during the season

	NM	Ex
COMPLETE SET (19)	40.00	16.00
1 Hank Aguirre	2.00	.80
2 Gates Brown	2.00	.80
3 Norm Cash	4.00	1.60
4 Don Demeter	2.00	.80
5 Charlie Dressen MG	2.50	1.00
6 Bill Faul	2.00	.80
7 Bill Freehan	3.00	1.20
8 Al Kaline	12.00	4.80
9 Mickey Lolich	4.00	1.60
10 Jerry Lumpe	2.00	.80
11 Dick McAuliffe	2.50	1.00
12 Bubba Phillips	2.00	.80
13 Ed Rakow	2.00	.80
14 Phil Regan	2.00	.80
15 Larry Sherry	2.00	.80
16 George Thomas	2.00	.80
17 Don Wert	2.00	.80
18 Dave Wickersham	2.00	.80
19 Jake Wood	2.00	.80

1966 Tigers Team Issue

This 24 card issue measures 9 13/16" by 7 11/16" and features full color photos of members of the 1966 Detroit Tigers. Since the cards are unnumbered, we have sequenced them in alphabetical order.

	NM	Ex
COMPLETE SET (24)	60.00	24.00
1 Hank Aguirre	2.00	.80
2 Gates Brown	2.00	.80
3 Norm Cash	5.00	2.00
4 Don Demeter	2.00	.80
5 Chuck Dressen MG	2.00	.80
6 Bill Freehan	4.00	1.60
7 Fred Gladding	2.00	.80
8 Willie Horton	3.00	1.20
9 Al Kaline	10.00	4.00
10 Mickey Lolich	5.00	2.00
11 Jerry Lumpe	2.00	.80
12 Dick McAuliffe	3.00	1.20
13 Denny McLain	6.00	2.40
14 Bill Monbouquette	2.00	.80
15 Jim Northrup	3.00	1.20
16 Ray Oyler	2.00	.80
17 Orlando Pena	2.00	.80
18 Larry Sherry	2.00	.80
19 Joe Sparma	2.00	.80
20 Mickey Stanley	3.00	1.20
21 Dick Tracewski	2.00	.80
22 Don Wert	2.00	.80
23 Dave Wickersham	2.00	.80
24 Jake Wood	2.00	.80

1967 Tigers Dexter Press

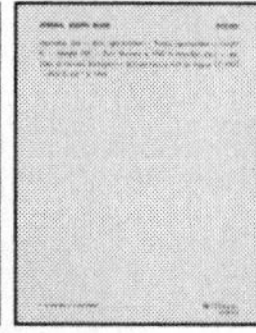

This set, which features 11 photo cards that measure approximately 5 1/2" by 7", has white-bordered posed color player photos on its fronts. The set was produced by Dexter Press located in West Nyack, New York and features Detroit Tigers' players. A facsimile autograph is printed across the top of the picture. The white backs carry a short biography printed in blue ink, with only one line providing statistics for the 1966 season. The cards are unnumbered and checklisted below in alphabetical order.

	NM	Ex
COMPLETE SET (11)	30.00	12.00
1 Norm Cash	5.00	2.00
2 Bill Freehan	4.00	1.60
3 Willie Horton	3.00	1.20
4 Al Kaline	8.00	3.20
5 Jerry Lumpe	2.50	1.00
6 Dick McAuliffe	3.00	1.20
7 Johnny Podres	3.00	1.20
8 Joe Sparma	2.50	1.00
9 Don Wert	2.50	1.00
10 Dave Wickersham	2.50	1.00
11 Earl Wilson	2.50	1.00

1968 Tigers Detroit Free Press Bubblegumless

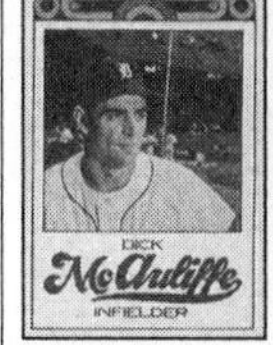

This set features members of the World Champion 1968 Detroit Tigers. The cards are unnumbered so we have sequenced them in alphabetical order.

	NM	Ex
COMPLETE SET	60.00	24.00
1 Gates Brown	1.50	.60
2 Norm Cash	5.00	2.00
3 Tony Cuccinello CO	1.50	.60
4 Pat Dobson	1.50	.60
5 Bill Freehan	5.00	2.00
6 John Hiller	1.50	.60
7 Willie Horton	2.50	1.00
8 Al Kaline	10.00	4.00
9 Fred Lasher	1.50	.60
10 Mickey Lolich	5.00	2.00
11 Dick McAuliffe	2.00	.80
12 Denny McLain	5.00	2.00
13 Don McMahon	1.50	.60
14 Tom Matchick	1.50	.60
15 Wally Moses CO	1.50	.60
16 Jim Northrup	2.00	.80
17 Ray Oyler	1.50	.60
18 Jim Price	1.50	.60
19 Daryl Patterson	1.50	.60
20 Johnny Sain CO	2.50	1.00
21 Mayo Smith MG	1.50	.60
22 Joe Sparma	1.50	.60
23 Mickey Stanley	2.00	.80
24 Dick Tracewski	1.50	.60
25 Jon Warden	1.50	.60
26 Don Wert	1.50	.60
27 Earl Wilson	1.50	.60
28 John Wyatt	1.50	.60

1968 Tigers News Super Posters

Issued to commemorate the Detroit Tigers would championship in 1968, these posters which measure approximately 13 1/2" by 23" feature all the players who participated in the World Series that year. Since these are unnumbered, we have sequenced them in alphabetical order.

	NM	Ex
COMPLETE SET (26)	150.00	60.00
1 Gates Brown	5.00	2.00
2 Norm Cash	8.00	3.20

3 Wayne Comer	5.00	2.00
4 Pat Dobson	5.00	2.00
5 Bill Freehan	6.00	2.40
6 John Hiller	5.00	2.00
7 Willie Horton	6.00	2.40
8 Al Kaline	15.00	6.00
9 Fred Lasher	5.00	2.00
10 Mickey Lolich	6.00	2.40
11 Tom Matchick	5.00	2.00
12 Eddie Mathews	12.00	4.80
13 Dick McAuliffe	6.00	2.40
14 Denny McLain	10.00	4.00
15 Don McMahon	5.00	2.00
16 Jim Northrup	6.00	2.40
17 Ray Oyler	5.00	2.00
18 Daryl Patterson	5.00	2.00
19 Jim Price	5.00	2.00
20 Mayo Smith MG	5.00	2.00
21 Joe Sparma	5.00	2.00
22 Mickey Stanley	6.00	2.40
23 Dick Tracewski	5.00	2.00
24 Jon Warden	5.00	2.00
25 Don Wert	5.00	2.00
26 Earl Wilson	5.00	2.00
27 John Wyatt	5.00	2.00
28 Detroit Tigers team	6.00	2.40

1968 Tigers Team Issue

These blank-backed cards, which measure approximately 5" by 7" feature members of the World Champion Detroit Tigers. Since these cards are unnumbered, we have sequenced them in alphabetical order. Since different players were substituted during the season -- there are more than 12 players in this set.

	NM	Ex
COMPLETE SET (12)	30.00	12.00
1 Norm Cash	4.00	1.60
2 Bill Freehan	2.50	1.00
3 Willie Horton	2.50	1.00
4 Al Kaline	8.00	3.20
5 Mike Kilkenny	2.00	.80
6 Eddie Mathews	5.00	2.00
7 Dick McAuliffe	2.50	1.00
8 Denny McLain	4.00	1.60
9 Jim Northrup	2.50	1.00
10 Mayo Smith MG	2.00	.80
11 Mickey Stanley	2.00	.80
12 Don Wert	2.00	.80
13 Earl Wilson	2.00	.80

1969 Tigers Farmer Jack

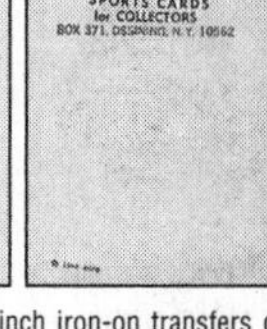

This set features six-inch iron-on transfers of player faces of the 1969 Detroit Tigers team and was distributed by Farmer Jack's Supermarket. An iron-on facsimile autograph is printed below the head. The transfers are unnumbered and checklisted below in alphabetical order. The checklist may be incomplete and additions are welcomed.

	NM	Ex
COMPLETE SET	50.00	20.00
1 Gates Brown	3.00	1.20
2 Norm Cash	6.00	2.40
3 Bill Freehan	5.00	2.00
4 Willie Horton	4.00	1.60
5 Al Kaline	15.00	6.00
6 Mickey Lolich	6.00	2.40
7 Dick McAuliffe	3.00	1.20
8 Denny McLain	6.00	2.40
9 Jim Northrup	4.00	1.60
10 Joe Sparma	3.00	1.20
11 Mickey Stanley	4.00	1.60
12 Earl Wilson	3.00	1.20

1969 Tigers Strip-Posters

Inserted into each Sunday issue of the Detroit Free Press were these "strip-posters" which featured various members of the Detroit Tigers. When properly cut out of the paper, these color drawings (by Dick Mayer) measure 4: by 15". Please note that this checklist is far from complete and any additions are greatly appreciated.

	MINT	NRMT
COMPLETE SET	25.00	11.00
1 Bill Freehan	8.00	3.60
2 Denny McLain	10.00	4.50
3 Jim Northrup	6.00	2.70
4 Mickey Stanley	5.00	2.20

1969 Tigers Team Issue

This 12-card set of the Detroit Tigers measures approximately 4 1/4" by 7". The fronts display black-and-white player portraits bordered in white. The player's name and team are printed in the top margin. The backs are blank. The cards are unnumbered and checklisted below in alphabetical order.

	NM	Ex
COMPLETE SET (12)	25.00	10.00
1 Norm Cash	3.00	1.20
2 Bill Freehan	3.00	1.20
3 Willie Horton	2.00	.80
4 Al Kaline	6.00	2.40
5 Mike Kilkenny	1.50	.60
6 Mickey Lolich	3.00	1.20
7 Dick McAuliffe	2.00	.80
8 Denny McLain	3.00	1.20
9 Jim Northrup	2.50	1.00
10 Mayo Smith MG	1.50	.60
11 Mickey Stanley	2.00	.80
12 Don Wert	1.50	.60

1969 Tigers Team Issue Color

This 20-card set of the Detroit Tigers measures approximately 7" by 8 3/4" with the fronts featuring white-bordered color player photos. The player's name and team is printed in black in the white margin below the picture. The backs are blank. The cards are unnumbered and checklisted below in alphabetical order.

	NM	Ex
COMPLETE SET (20)	50.00	20.00
1 Gates Brown	2.00	.80
2 Norm Cash	4.00	1.60
3 Pat Dobson	2.00	.80
4 Bill Freehan	4.00	1.60
5 John Hiller	2.00	.80
6 Willie Horton	2.50	1.00
7 Al Kaline	10.00	4.00
8 Fred Lasher	2.00	.80
9 Mickey Lolich	4.00	1.60
10 Tom Matchick	2.00	.80
11 Dick McAuliffe	2.50	1.00
12 Denny McLain	4.00	1.60
13 Jim Northrup	3.00	1.20
14 Jim Price	2.00	.80
15 Mayo Smith MG	2.00	.80
16 Joe Sparma	2.00	.80
17 Mickey Stanley	2.50	1.00
18 Dick Tracewski	2.00	.80
19 Don Wert	2.00	.80
20 Earl Wilson	2.00	.80

1972 Tigers Team Issue

This 12-card set of the Detroit Tigers measures approximately 4 1/4" by 7". The fronts display black-and-white player portraits bordered in white. The player's name and team are printed in the top margin. The backs are blank. The cards are unnumbered and checklisted below in alphabetical order.

	NM	Ex
COMPLETE SET (12)	20.00	8.00
1 Ed Brinkman	1.00	.40
2 Norm Cash	2.50	1.00
3 Joe Coleman	1.00	.40
4 Bill Freehan	2.00	.80
5 Willie Horton	1.50	.60
6 Al Kaline	5.00	2.00
7 Mickey Lolich	2.50	1.00
8 Billy Martin MG	3.00	1.20
9 Dick McAuliffe	1.50	.60
10 Jim Northrup	1.50	.60
11 Aurelio Rodriguez	1.00	.40
12 Mickey Stanley	1.00	.40

1973 Tigers Jewel

This 20-card set of the Detroit Tigers was produced by Jewel Food Stores and was issued in two series of ten cards each. Measuring approximately 7" by 8 3/4", the set features color posed player photos with white borders with blank backs. The cards are unnumbered and checklisted below in alphabetical order.

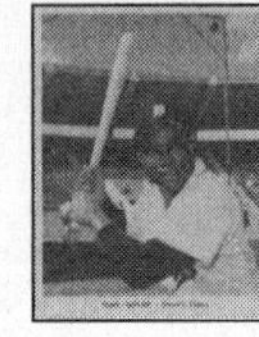

	NM	Ex
COMPLETE SET (20)	80.00	32.00
1 Ed Brinkman	4.00	1.60
2 Gates Brown	4.00	1.60
3 Ike Brown	4.00	1.60
4 Les Cain	4.00	1.60
5 Norman Cash	8.00	3.20
6 Joe Coleman	4.00	1.60
7 Bill Freehan	8.00	3.20
8 Tom Haller	4.00	1.60
9 Willie Horton	6.00	2.40
10 Al Kaline	15.00	6.00
11 Mickey Lolich	6.00	2.40
12 Billy Martin MG	8.00	3.20
13 Dick McAuliffe	5.00	2.00
14 Joe Niekro	5.00	2.00
15 Jim Northrup	5.00	2.00
16 Aurelio Rodriguez	4.00	1.60
17 Fred Scherman	4.00	1.60
18 Mickey Stanley	6.00	2.40
19 Tony Taylor	4.00	1.60
20 Tom Timmerman	4.00	1.60

1974 Tigers

This 12-piece set of photos are blank-backed, white-bordered and 7" X 8 3/4". The player's name and team in black are within lower margin. The photos are unnumbered and checklisted below in alphabetical order.

	NM	Ex
COMPLETE SET (12)	20.00	8.00
1 Gates Brown	2.00	.80
2 Ron Cash	1.50	.60
3 Joe Coleman	1.50	.60
4 Bill Freehan	3.00	1.20
5 John Hiller	1.50	.60
6 Al Kaline	5.00	2.00
7 John Knox	1.50	.60
8 Jim Northrup	2.00	.80
9 Ben Oglivie	2.00	.80
10 Jim Ray	1.50	.60
11 Chuck Seelbach	1.50	.60
12 Dick Sharon	1.50	.60

1974 Tigers TCMA 1934-35 AL Champions

This 36-card set of the 1934-35 American League Champion Detroit Tigers features black-and-white player photos measuring approximately 2 1/8" by 3 11/16". The backs carry 1934 and 1935 player statistics. The cards are unnumbered and checklisted below in alphabetical order with cards 35 and 36 being jumbo cards.

	NM	Ex
COMPLETE SET (36)	25.00	10.00
1 Elden Auker	.50	.20
2 Del Baker CO	.50	.20
3 Tommy Bridges	.50	.20
4 Flea Clifton	.50	.20
5 Mickey Cochrane	2.00	.80
6 Alvin Crowder	.50	.20
7 Frank Doljack	.50	.20
8 Carl Fisher	.50	.20
9 Pete Fox	.50	.20
10 Vic Frasier	.50	.20
11 Charles Gehringer	2.00	.80
12 Goose Goslin	2.00	.80
13 Hank Greenberg	3.00	1.20
14 Luke Hamlin	.50	.20
15 Clyde Hatter	.50	.20
16 Ray Hayworth	.50	.20
17 Chief Hogsett	.50	.20
18 Roxie Lawson	.50	.20
19 Fred Marberry	.50	.20
20 Chet Morgan	.50	.20
21 Marv Owen	.50	.20
22 Cy Perkins CO	.50	.20
23 Red Phillips	.50	.20
24 Frank Reiber	.50	.20
25 Bill Rogell	.50	.20
26 Schoolboy Rowe	1.50	.60
27 Henry Schuble	.50	.20
28 Hugh Shelly	.50	.20
29 Vic Sorrell	.50	.20
30 Joe Sullivan	.50	.20
31 Gee Walker	.50	.20
32 Harvey Walker	.50	.20
33 Jo Jo White	.50	.20
34 Rudy York	1.00	.40
35 Elden Auker Firpo Marberry Tommy Bridges Schoolboy Rowe	2.00	.80
36 Goose Goslin Jo Jo White Pete Fox	2.00	.80

1975 Tigers Postcards

This 36-card set of the Detroit Tigers features player photos on postcard-size cards. The cards are unnumbered and checklisted below in alphabetical order.

	NM	Ex
COMPLETE SET (36)	20.00	8.00
1 Fred Arroyo	.50	.20
2 Billy Baldwin	.50	.20
3 Ray Bare	.50	.20
4 Gates Brown	.75	.30
5 Nate Colbert	.50	.20
6 Joe Coleman	.50	.20
7 Bill Freehan	1.00	.40
8 Steve Hamilton CO	.50	.20
9 Jim Hegan CO	.50	.20
10 John Hiller	.75	.30
11 Ralph Houk MG	.75	.30
12 Willie Horton	1.50	.60
13 Terry Humphrey	.50	.20
14 Art James	.50	.20
15 John Knox	.50	.20
16 Lerrin LaGrow	.50	.20
17 Gene Lamont	.50	.20
18 Ron LeFlore	1.00	.40
19 Dave Lemanczyk	.50	.20
20 Mickey Lolich	1.50	.60
21 Dan Meyer	.50	.20
22 Gene Michael	.75	.30
23 Ben Oglivie	.75	.30
24 Gene Pentz	.50	.20
25 Jack Pierce	.50	.20
26 Bob Reynolds	.50	.20
27 Leon Roberts	.50	.20
28 Aurelio Rodriguez	.50	.20
29 Vern Ruhle	.50	.20
30 Joe Schultz CO	.50	.20
31 Mickey Stanley	.50	.20
32 Gary Sutherland	.50	.20
33 Dick Tracewski CO	.50	.20
34 Tom Veryzer	.50	.20
35 Tom Walker	.50	.20
36 John Wockenfuss	.50	.20

1976 Tigers Old-Timers Troy Show

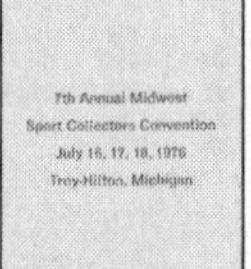

This 23-card set was available at the 7th Annual Midwest Sports Collectors Convention held July 16-18, 1976 in Troy-Hilton, Michigan. The cards measure 2 3/8" by 2 7/8" and feature portrait and action black-and-white illustrations of players. The player's name is near the top as is a small paragraph giving career history. A box at the bottom contains unusual personal facts. The backs carry information about the card show. The cards are unnumbered and checklisted below in alphabetical order.

	NM	Ex
COMPLETE SET (23)	12.50	5.00
1 Elden Auker	.25	.10
2 Tommy Bridges	.75	.30
3 Flea Clifton	.25	.10
4 Mickey Cochrane	1.00	.40
5 General Crowder	.25	.10
6 Frank Doljack	.25	.10
7 Carl Fischer	.25	.10
8 Pete Fox	.25	.10
9 Charles Gehringer	1.00	.40
10 Goose Goslin	1.00	.40
11 Hank Greenberg	1.00	.40
12 Luke Hamlin	.25	.10
13 Ray Hayworth	.25	.10
14 Chief Hogsett	.25	.10
15 Firpo Marberry	.25	.10
16 Marvin Owen	.75	.30
17 Cy Perkins	.25	.10
18 Bill Rogell	.25	.10
19 Schoolboy Rowe	1.00	.40
20 Heinie Schuble	.25	.10
21 Vic Sorrell	.25	.10
22 Gerald Walker	.25	.10
23 Jo Jo White	.25	.10

1976 Tigers Postcards

This 35-card set of the Detroit Tigers features player photos on postcard-size cards. The cards are unnumbered and checklisted below in alphabetical order.

	NM	Ex
COMPLETE SET (35)	20.00	8.00
1 Ray Bare	.50	.20
2 Joe Coleman	.50	.20
3 Jim Crawford	.50	.20
4 Mark Fidrych	4.00	1.60
5 Bill Freehan	1.00	.40
6 Pedro Garcia	.50	.20
7 Fred Gladding CO	.50	.20
8 Steve Grilli	.50	.20
9 Jim Hegan CO	.50	.20
10 John Hiller	.75	.30
11 Willie Horton	1.00	.40
12 Ralph Houk MG	.75	.30
13 Alex Johnson	.50	.20
14 Bruce Kimm	.50	.20
15 Bill Laxton	.50	.20
16 Ron LeFlore	.75	.30
17 Dave Lemanczyk	.50	.20
18 Frank MacCormack	.50	.20
19 Jerry Manuel	.75	.30
20 Milt May	.50	.20
21 Dan Meyer	.50	.20
22 Ben Oglivie	.75	.30
23 Dave Roberts	.50	.20
24 Aurelio Rodriguez	.50	.20
25 Vern Ruhle	.50	.20
26 Joe Schultz CO	.50	.20
27 Chuck Scrivener	.50	.20
28 Mickey Stanley	.50	.20
29 Rusty Staub	1.00	.40
30 Gary Sutherland	.50	.20
31 Jason Thompson	1.50	.60
32 Dick Tracewski CO	.50	.20
33 Tom Veryzer	.50	.20
34 John Wockenfuss	.50	.20
35 Tiger Stadium	.50	.20

1977 Tigers Burger King

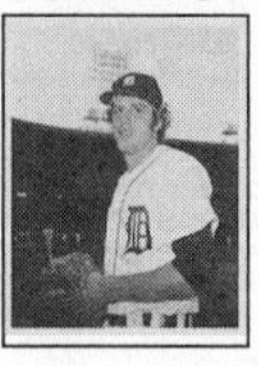

This four-card set was issued in 1977 by Burger King and features Detroit Tigers. The photo cards measure approximately 8" by 10" and carry posed player color portraits. The backs are blank and the set is checklisted below in alphabetical order.

	NM	Ex
COMPLETE SET (4)	10.00	4.00
1 Mark Fidyrich	4.00	1.60
2 Ron LeFlore	2.50	1.00
3 Dave Rozema	2.00	.80
4 Mickey Stanley	2.50	1.00

1978 Tigers Burger King

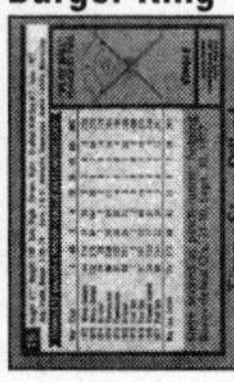

The cards in this 23-card set measure 2 1/2" by 3 1/2". Twenty-three color cards, 22 players and one numbered checklist, comprise the 1978 Burger King Tigers set issued in the Detroit area. The cards marked with an asterisk contain photos different from those appearing on the Topps regular issue cards of that year. For example, Jack Morris, Alan Trammell, and Lou Whitaker (in the 1978 Topps regular issue cards) each appear on rookie prospect cards with three other young players; whereas in this Burger King set, each has his own individual card.

	NM	Ex
COMPLETE SET (23)	40.00	16.00
1 Ralph Houk MG	.75	.30
2 Milt May	.25	.10
3 John Wockenfuss	.25	.10
4 Mark Fidrych	.75	.30
5 Dave Rozema	.25	.10
6 Jack Billingham *	.25	.10
7 Jim Slaton *	.25	.10
8 Jack Morris *	5.00	2.00
9 John Hiller	.50	.20
10 Steve Foucault	.25	.10
11 Milt Wilcox	.25	.10
12 Jason Thompson	.75	.30
13 Lou Whitaker *	10.00	4.00
14 Aurelio Rodriguez	.25	.10
15 Alan Trammell *	25.00	10.00
16 Steve Dillard *	.25	.10
17 Phil Mankowski	.25	.10
18 Steve Kemp	.50	.20
19 Ron LeFlore	.75	.30
20 Tim Corcoran	.25	.10
21 Mickey Stanley	.75	.30
22 Rusty Staub	1.00	.40
NNO Checklist Card TP	.15	.06

1978-80 Tigers Dearborn Card Show

These 2 5/8" by 3 5/8" cards were issued in conjunction with the annual Detroit area Dearborn card show. They feature Tiger greats from the past. For the 1978 set, 1,200 of each set were printed; 900 for promotional purposes and 300 for collector sales. For the 1980 set (issued in 1979), 1000 sets were produced; 600 for promotional purposes and 400 for collector sales. The first 18 cards were originally available for $2 per set.

	NM	Ex
COMPLETE SET	30.00	12.00
1 Rocky Colavito	2.00	.80
2 Ervin Fox	.75	.30
3 Schoolboy Rowe	.75	.30
4 Gerald Walker	.75	.30
5 Leon Goslin	1.50	.60
6 Harvey Kuenn	1.00	.40
7 Frank Howard	1.00	.40
8 Woodie Fryman	.75	.30
9 Don Wert	.75	.30
10 Jim Perry	1.00	.40
11 Mayo Smith MG	.75	.30
12 Al Kaline	3.00	1.20
13 Norm Cash	1.50	.60
14 Mickey Cochrane	1.00	.40
15 Fred Marberry	.75	.30
16 Bill Freehan	1.00	.40
17 Charley Gehringer	1.50	.60
18 Jim Northrup	.75	.30
19 Slick Coffman	.75	.30
20 Bruce Campbell	.75	.30
21 Jack Burns	.75	.30
22 Herman "Flea" Clifton	.75	.30
23 Vic Frasier	.75	.30
24 Pete Fox	.75	.30
25 Al Simmons	2.00	.80
26 Woodrow Davis	.75	.30
27 Dick Conger	.75	.30
28 John Corsica	.75	.30
29 Frank Croucher	.75	.30
30 Hank Greenberg	3.00	1.20
31 Tommy Bridges	.75	.30
32 William Hargrave	.75	.30
33 Chad Kimsey	.75	.30
34 Harry Eisenstat	.75	.30
35 Gene Desaultels	.75	.30
36 Dizzy Trout	1.00	.40

1978 Tigers Team Issue

These 3" by 5" photos feature the members of the 1978 Detroit Tigers. They are unnumbered so we have sequenced them in alphabetical order. Photos of Alan Trammell, Lou Whitaker, Jack Morris and Lance Parrish are included in their rookie season.

	NM	Ex
COMPLETE SET	40.00	16.00
1 Fernando Arroyo	.50	.20
2 Steve Baker	.50	.20
3 Jack Billingham	.50	.20
4 Gates Brown CO	.50	.20
5 Tim Corcoran	.50	.20
6 Jim Crawford	.50	.20
7 Steve Dillard	.50	.20
8 Mark Fidrych	1.50	.60
9 Steve Foucault	.50	.20
10 Fred Gladding CO	.50	.20
11 Fred Hatfield CO	.50	.20
12 Steve Hackett	.50	.20
13 Jim Hegan CO	.50	.20
14 John Hiller	.50	.20
15 Ralph Houk MG	.50	.20
16 Steve Kemp	.75	.30
17 Ron LeFlore	.75	.30
18 Phil Mankowski	.50	.20
19 Milt May	.50	.20
20 Jack Morris	8.00	3.20
21 Lance Parrish	4.00	1.60
22 Aurelio Rodriguez	.50	.20
23 Dave Rozema	.50	.20
24 Jim Slaton	.50	.20
25 Charlie Spikes	.50	.20
26 Mickey Stanley	.50	.20
27 Rusty Staub	1.00	.40
28 Bob Sykes	.50	.20
29 Bruce Taylor	.50	.20
30 Jason Thompson	.50	.20
31 Dick Tracewski CO	.50	.20
32 Alan Trammell	10.00	4.00
33 Mark Wayne	.50	.20
34 Lou Whitaker	8.00	3.20
35 Milt Wilcox	.50	.20
36 John Wockenfuss	.50	.20
37 Tiger Stadium	.50	.20

1979 Tigers Free Press

These 10" by 15" posters was published in the Detroit Free Press Newspaper and displays a black-and-white player photo with player information and statistics including a printed feature on the player with his career highlights. There may be even more posters and all additions to the checklist are welcomed.

	NM	Ex
COMPLETE SET	15.00	6.00
1 Jason Thompson	3.00	1.20
4 Ron LeFlore	3.00	1.20
5 Dave Rozema	3.00	1.20
6 Mickey Stanley	4.00	1.60
8 Milt May	3.00	1.20
9 Jim Slaton	3.00	1.20

1979 Tigers Team Issue

These cards, which originally sold from the Tigers directly for 20 cents each, feature members of the 1979 Detroit Tigers. This list consists solely of the new members of the 1979 Tigers that season and since they are unnumbered are sequenced in alphabetical order. Please note that there are 2 different manager cards as Sparky Anderson replaced Les Moss early in the 1979 season.

	NM	Ex
COMPLETE SET	10.00	4.00
1 Sparky Anderson MG	2.50	1.00
2 Steve Baker	.50	.20
3 Tom Brookens	.50	.20
4 Sheldon Burnside	.50	.20
5 Steve Baker	.50	.20
6 Mike Chris	.50	.20
7 Billy Consolo CO	.50	.20
8 Tim Corcoran	.50	.20
9 Danny Gonzalez	.50	.20
10 Al Greene	.50	.20
11 John Grodzicki CO	.50	.20
12 John Hiller	.75	.30
13 Lynn Jones	.50	.20
14 Aurelio Lopez	.50	.20
15 Dave Machemer	.50	.20
16 Milt May	.50	.20
17 Jerry Morales	.50	.20
18 Les Moss MG	.75	.30
19 Dan Petry	.75	.30
20 Ed Putnam	.50	.20
21 Bruce Robbins	.50	.20
22 Champ Summers	.50	.20
23 Dave Tobik	.50	.20
24 Pat Underwood	.50	.20
25 Kip Young	.50	.20

1980 Tigers Greats TCMA

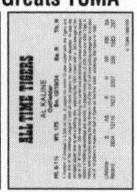

This 12-card standard-size set features some of the best Detroit Tigers of all time. The fronts have a black-and-white player photo while the horizontal backs have vital statistics, a biography and career statistics.

	NM	Ex
COMPLETE SET (12)	6.00	2.40
1 George Kell	.50	.20
2 Billy Rogell	.25	.10
3 Ty Cobb	1.00	.40
4 Hank Greenberg	1.00	.40
5 Al Kaline	1.00	.40
6 Charlie Gehringer	.75	.30
7 Harry Heilmann	.50	.20
8 Hal Newhouser	.50	.20
9 Steve O'Neill MG	.25	.10
10 Denny McLain	.50	.20
11 Mickey Cochrane	.75	.30
12 John Hiller	.25	.10

1981 Tigers Detroit News

This 135-card, standard-size set was issued in 1981 to celebrate the centennial of professional baseball in Detroit. This set features black and white photos surrounded by solid red borders, while the back provides information about either the player or event featured on the front of the card. This set was issued by the Detroit newspaper, the Detroit News and covered players from the nineteenth century right up to players and other personnel active at the time of issue.

	Nm-Mt	Ex-Mt
COMPLETE SET (135)	20.00	8.00
1 Detroit's Boys of Summer 100th Anniversary	.50	.20
2 Charles W. Bennett	.10	.04
3 Mickey Cochrane	.75	.30
4 Harry Heilmann	.50	.20
5 Walter O. Briggs OWN	.10	.04
6 Mark Fidrych	.50	.20
7 1887 Tigers	.10	.04
8 Tiger Stadium	.10	.04
9 Rudy York	.10	.04
10 George Kell	.50	.20
11 Steve O'Neill MG	.10	.04
12 John Hiller	.10	.04
13 1934 Tigers	.10	.04
14 Charlie Gehringer	.75	.30
15 Denny McLain	.50	.20
16 Billy Rogell	.10	.04
17 Ty Cobb	3.00	1.20
18 Sparky Anderson MG	.50	.20
19 Davy Jones	.10	.04
20 Kirk Gibson	.75	.30
21 Pat Mullin	.10	.04
22 1972 Tigers	.10	.04
23 What A Night	.10	.04
24 Doc Cramer	.10	.04
25 Mickey Stanley	.10	.04
26 John Lipon	.10	.04
27 Jo Jo White	.10	.04
28 Recreation Park	.10	.04
29 Wild Bill Donovan	.10	.04
30 Ray Oyler	.10	.04
31 Earl Whitehill	.10	.04
32 Billy Hoeft	.10	.04
33 Johnny Groth	.10	.04
34 Hughie Jennings P/MG	.50	.20
35 Mayo Smith MG	.10	.04
36 Bennett Park	.10	.04
37 Tigers Win	.10	.04
38 Donie Bush P/MG	.10	.04
39 Harry Coveleski	.10	.04
40 Paul Richards	.10	.04
41 Jonathon Stone	.10	.04
42 Bob Swift	.10	.04
43 Roy Cullenbine	.10	.04
44 Hoot Evers	.10	.04
45 Tigers Win Series	.10	.04
46 Art Houtteman	.10	.04
47 Aurelio Rodriguez	.10	.04
48 Fred Hutchinson P/MG	.10	.04
49 Don Mossi	.25	.10
50 Lou Gehrig Streak Ends in Detroit At 2130 Games	.75	.30
51 Earl Wilson	.10	.04
52 Jim Northrup	.10	.04
53 1907 Tigers	.10	.04
54 Hank Greenberg Hits 2 Homers to Draw Even With Ruth	.75	.30
55 Mickey Lolich	.50	.20
56 Tommy Bridges	.10	.04
57 Al Benton	.10	.04
58 Del Baker MG	.10	.04
59 Lou Whitaker	.75	.30
60 Navin Field	.10	.04
61 1945 Tigers	.10	.04
62 Ernie Harwell ANN	.50	.20
63 Tigers League Champs	.10	.04
64 Bobo Newsom	.25	.10
65 Don Wert	.10	.04
66 Ed Summers	.10	.04
67 Billy Martin MG	.75	.30
68 Alan Trammell	1.25	.50
69 Dale Alexander	.10	.04
70 Ed Brinkman	.10	.04
71 Right Man in Right Place in Right Park Wins Game	.10	.04
72 Bill Freehan	.25	.10
73A Norm Cash (Red border)	.50	.20
73B Norm Cash (Black border)	.50	.20
74 George Dauss	.10	.04
75 Aurelio Lopez	.10	.04
76 Charlie Maxwell	.10	.04
77 Ed Barrow MG	.25	.10
78 Willie Horton	.25	.10
79 Denny McLain Sets Record 31 Wins	.50	.20
80 Dan Brouthers	.75	.30
81 John E. Fetzer OWN	.10	.04
82A Heinie Manush (Red border)	.50	.20
82B Heinie Manush (Black border)	.50	.20
83 1935 Tigers	.10	.04
84 Ray Boone	.25	.10
85 Bob Fothergill	.10	.04
86 Steve Kemp	.10	.04
87 Ed Killian	.10	.04
88 Floyd Giebell Ineligible for Series, But ...	.10	.04
89 Pinky Higgins	.10	.04
90 Lance Parrish	.25	.10
91 Eldon Auker	.10	.04
92 Birdie Tebbetts	.10	.04
93 Schoolboy Rowe	.25	.10
94 Tiger Rally Gives Denny McLain 30	.50	.20
95 1909 Tigers	.10	.04
96 Harvey Kuenn	.50	.20
97 Jim Bunning	.50	.20
98 1940 Tigers	.10	.04
99 Rocky Colavito	.50	.20
100 Al Kaline Enters Hall Of Fame	1.25	.50
101 Billy Bruton	.10	.04
102 Germany Schaefer	.25	.10
103 Frank Bolling	.10	.04
104 Briggs Stadium	.10	.04
105 Bucky Harris P/MG	.25	.10
106 Gates Brown	.10	.04
107 Billy Martin Made the Difference	.50	.20
108 1908 Tigers	.10	.04
109 Gee Walker	.10	.04
110 Pete Fox	.10	.04
111 Virgil Trucks	.10	.04
112 1968 Tigers	.25	.10
113 Dizzy Trout	.10	.04
114 Barney McCosky	.10	.04
115 Lu Blue	.10	.04
116 Hal Newhouser	.75	.30
117 Tigers Are Home To Prepare For World's Championship Series	.10	.04
118 Bobby Veach	.10	.04
119 George Mullin	.10	.04
120 Reggie Jackson Super Homer Ignites A.L.	.75	.30
121 Sam Crawford	.50	.20
122 Hank Aguirre	.10	.04
123 Vic Wertz	.25	.10
124 Goose Goslin	.50	.20
125 Frank Lary	.25	.10
126 Joe Coleman	.10	.04
127 Ed Katalinas Scout	.10	.04
128 Jack Morris	.75	.30
129 Tigers Picked As Winners Of Pirate Battle	.10	.04
130 James A. Campbell GM	.25	.10
131 Ted Gray	.10	.04
132 Al Kaline	2.50	1.00
133 Hank Greenberg	.75	.30
134 Dick McAuliffe	.25	.10
135 Ozzie Virgil	.10	.04

1981 Tigers Pepsi Trammell

This one-card set produced by Pepsi-Cola features a small color photo of Detroit Tigers player, Alan Trammell, and was an invitation to kids to join the Pepsi-Tiger Fan Club. The back displays the official application form.

	Nm-Mt	Ex-Mt
1 Alan Trammell	5.00	2.00

1981 Tigers Second National Plymouth

This set was issued in conjuction with the Second National Sports Collectors Convention held in Plymouth, Michigan. The fronts have a photo, the player's name and his years as a Tiger. The backs are blank.

	Nm-Mt	Ex-Mt
COMPLETE SET (32)	20.00	8.00
1 Ty Cobb	3.00	1.20
2 Hughie Jennings MG	1.50	.60
3 Heinie Manush	1.50	.60
4 George Mullin	.75	.30
5 Donie Bush	.50	.20
6 Bobby Veach	.50	.20
7 Wild Bill Donovan	.50	.20
8 Harry Heilmann	1.00	.40
9 Sam Crawford	1.00	.40
10 Lu Blue	.50	.20
11 Bob Fothergill	.50	.20
12 Harry Coveleski	.50	.20
13 Dale Alexander	.50	.20
14 Charlie Gehringer	1.50	.60
15 Tommy Bridges	.75	.30
16 1935 Detroit Tigers	.50	.20
17 Hank Greenberg	1.50	.60
18 Goose Goslin	1.00	.40
19 Firpo Marberry	.50	.20
20 Hal Newhouser	1.00	.40
21 Schoolboy Rowe	.75	.30
22 Mickey Cochrane	1.00	.40
23 Gee Walker	.50	.20
24 Marv Owen	.50	.20
25 Barney McCosky	.50	.20
26 Rudy York	.75	.30
27 Pete Fox	.50	.20
28 Al Benton	.50	.20
29 Billy Rogell	.50	.20
30 JoJo White	.50	.20
31 Dizzy Trout	.50	.20
32 1945 Detroit Tigers	.50	.20

1983 Tigers Postcards

This set features members of the 1983 Detroit Tigers. Since these cards are unnumbered we have checklisted them below in alphabetical order.

	Nm-Mt	Ex-Mt
COMPLETE SET (32)	10.00	4.00
1 Sparky Anderson MG	.75	.30
2 Sal Butera	.25	.10
3 Howard Bailey	.25	.10
4 Juan Berenguer	.25	.10
5 Tom Brookens	.25	.10
6 Gates Brown CO	.25	.10
7 Enos Cabell	.25	.10
8 Bill Consolo CO	.25	.10
9 Roger Craig CO	.25	.10
10 Bill Fahey	.25	.10
11 Kirk Gibson	2.00	.80
12 Alex Grammas CO	.25	.10
13 John Grubb	.25	.10
14 Larry Herndon	.25	.10
15 Mike Ivie	.25	.10
16 Howard Johnson	1.00	.40
17 Lynn Jones	.25	.10
18 Rick Leach	.25	.10
19 Chet Lemon	.50	.20
20 Aurelio Lopez	.25	.10
21 Jack Morris	1.00	.40
22 Lance Parrish	.75	.30
23 Larry Pashnick	.25	.10
24 Dan Petry	.25	.10
25 Dave Rozema	.25	.10
26 Dave Rucker	.25	.10
27 Dick Tracewski CO	.25	.10
28 Alan Trammell	2.00	.80
29 Jerry Ujdur	.25	.10
30 Pat Underwood	.25	.10
31 Lou Whitaker	1.00	.40
32 Milt Wilcox	.25	.10
33 Glenn Wilson	.25	.10
34 John Wockenfuss	.25	.10
35 Tiger Stadium	.25	.10

1983 Tigers Al Kaline Story

This 72-card set was issued in 1983 to celebrate Al Kaline's thirtieth year of association with the Detroit Tigers. The set was issued in its own orange box and most of the cards in the series have orange borders. There are some cards which have black borders and those cards are the cards in the set which feature color photos. The set is basically in chronological order and covers events crucial to Kaline's career and the backs of the cards give further details about the picture on the front. The set was produced by Homeplate Sports Cards.

	Nm-Mt	Ex-Mt
COMPLETE SET (73)	20.00	8.00
COMMON CARD (1-72)	.25	.10
COMMON CARD COLOR	.40	.16
1A Autographed Title Card (Color)	10.00	4.00
1B Al Kaline I'd play for nothing (Color)	.60	.24
7 Al Kaline Louise Kaline	.40	.16
8 Al Kaline Pat Mullin	.25	.10
12 Al Kaline George Stark	.25	.10
13 Al Kaline Gordie Howe Howe taking batting practice	1.50	.60
14 Al Kaline Mickey Mantle	2.50	1.00
15 Jim Hegan Billy Martin Ray Boone Harvey Kuenn Jim Bunning Al Kaline	.60	.24
16 Billy Martin Al Kaline Harvey Kuenn Mickey Mantle Whitey Ford (color)	1.50	.60
18 Bill Skowron Al Kaline	.60	.24
19 Norm Cash Rocky Colavito Al Kaline	.75	.30
20 Al Kaline Nellie Fox Kaline Slides Under Fox	.75	.30
21 Al Kaline 1961 Gold Glove	.40	.16
22 Al Kaline Jim Campbell GM Norm Cash	.40	.16
24 Jim Bunning Al Kaline Norm Cash and others Japan Tour, 1962	.60	.24
26 Ernie Harwell ANN Al Kaline George Kell ANN	.75	.30
28 Al Kaline Michael Kaline Mark Kaline	.25	.10
29 Al Kaline Charlie Dressen MG	.25	.10
30 George Kell Al Kaline	.60	.24
31 Al Kaline Hal Newhouser	.60	.24
32 Michael Kaline Louise Kaline Al Kaline Mark Kaline	.25	.10
33 Al Kaline Charlie Gehringer Bill Freehan	.75	.30
34 Al Kaline Rapping a Hit, 1967 Color	.60	.24
35 Mickey Mantle Al Kaline	2.50	1.00
39 Hank Greenberg Hal Newhouser Billy Rogell Al Kaline John Fetzer OWN Dennis McLain George Kell Charlie Gehringer	.60	.24
41 Al Kaline Family Portrait, Color	.60	.24
43 Billy Martin Al Kaline	.60	.24
44 Al Kaline John Fetzer OWN Jim Campbell GM	.40	.16
45 Al Kaline On Deck, 1972; Color	.60	.24
48 Al Kaline Hit Number 3,000	.40	.16
51 Al Kaline Orlando Cepeda	.60	.24
52 Al Kaline John Hiller Jim Northrup	.40	.16
53 Al Kaline Day; Color	.60	.24
54 Al Kaline Lee McPhail PRES Jim Campbell GM Nicholas Kaline Naomi Kaline	.40	.16
57 Al Kaline George Kell Color	.75	.30
58 Al Kaline George Kell	.60	.24
59 Al Kaline Tiger Record Setter; Color	.60	.24
60 Al Kaline Last All-Star Team; Color	.60	.24
61 Pat Mullin Al Kaline	.25	.10
62 Al Kaline Mickey Lolich Color	.60	.24
64 Al Kaline Bowie Kuhn COMM Color	.60	.24
65 Al Kaline Nicholas Kaline Naomi Kaline) (color)	.40	.16
66 Al Kaline Kaline Family at Hall; color	.40	.16
67 Stan Musial Al Kaline	.75	.30
68 Ted Williams Al Kaline	1.50	.60
69 Al Kaline Brooks Robinson color	.75	.30
70 Al Kaline Pat Underwood	.25	.10
72 Al Kaline A Tiger Forever; Color	.75	.30

1984 Tigers Detroit News

These newspaper clippings, which measure approximately 13 1/2" by 8" feature the members of the 1984 World Champion Detroit Tigers. These newspaper clippings feature a large color photo of the featured player along with a box with biographical and personal information about the featured player. Since these are unnumbered, we have sequenced them in alphabetical order.

	MINT	NRMT
COMPLETE SET	50.00	22.00
1 Sparky Anderson MG	3.00	1.35
2 Doug Bair	2.00	.90
3 Doug Baker	2.00	.90
4 Dave Bergman	2.00	.90
5 Tom Brookens	2.00	.90
6 Marty Castillo	2.00	.90
7 Darrell Evans	2.50	1.10
8 Barbero Garbey	2.00	.90
9 Kirk Gibson	4.00	1.80
10 John Grubb	2.00	.90
11 Willie Hernandez	2.50	1.10
12 Larry Herndon	2.00	.90
13 Howard Johnson	2.50	1.10
14 Ruppert Jones	2.00	.90
15 Rusty Kuntz	2.00	.90
16 Chet Lemon	2.00	.90
17 Sid Monge	2.00	.90
18 Jack Morris	4.00	1.80
19 Lance Parrish	3.00	1.35
20 Dan Petry	2.00	.90
21 Dave Rozema	2.00	.90
22 Bill Scherrer	2.00	.90
23 Alan Trammell	4.00	1.80
24 Lou Whitaker	3.00	1.35

1984 Tigers Farmer Jack

These 16 photo cards were sponsored by the Farmer Jack grocery store chain in the upper Midwest in 1984, to honor the 1984 World Champion Detroit Tigers. The photos were a promotional item given away singly with a purchase. The cards measure approximately 6" by 9" and are printed on photographic paper stock. The white bordered fronts feature color player portraits with an autograph facsimile superimposed on the photo. The backs are blank. The cards are unnumbered and are checklisted alphabetically below.

	Nm-Mt	Ex-Mt
COMPLETE SET (16)	12.00	4.80
1 Dave Bergman	.50	.20
2 Darrell Evans	1.00	.40
3 Barbaro Garbey	.50	.20
4 Kirk Gibson	1.50	.60
5 John Grubb	.50	.20
6 Willie Hernandez	.75	.30
7 Larry Herndon	.50	.20
8 Howard Johnson	1.00	.40
9 Chet Lemon	.50	.20
10 Jack Morris	1.50	.60
11 Lance Parrish	1.00	.40
12 Dan Petry	.75	.30
13 Dave Rozema	.50	.20
14 Alan Trammell	3.00	1.20
15 Lou Whitaker	2.50	1.00
16 Milt Wilcox	.50	.20

1984 Tigers Team Issue

These photos were issued by the Detroit Tigers during the 1984 season and featured the players who would go to become the World Champions. The photos are unnumbered so we have sequenced them in alphabetical order

	Nm-Mt	Ex-Mt
COMPLETE SET	12.00	4.80
1 Tiger Stadium	.50	.20
2 Detroit Tigers	.50	.20
3 Glenn Abbott	.50	.20
4 Rod Allen	.50	.20
5 Doug Bair	.50	.20
6 Juan Berenguer	.50	.20
7 Dave Bergman	.50	.20
8 Tom Brookens	.50	.20
9 Gates Brown CO	.50	.20
10 Marty Castillo	.50	.20
11 Billy Consolo CO	.50	.20
12 Roger Craig MG	.50	.20
13 Darrell Evans	.75	.30
14 Barbaro Garbey	.50	.20
15 Kirk Gibson	1.50	.60
16 Alex Grammas CO	.50	.20
17 John Grubb	.50	.20
18 Larry Herndon	.50	.20
19 Willie Hernandez	.75	.30
20 Howard Johnson	.75	.30
21 Rusty Kuntz	.50	.20
22 Chet Lemon	.50	.20
23 Aurelio Lopez	.50	.20

	Nm-Mt	Ex-Mt
24 Dwight Lowry	.50	.20
25 Jack Morris	1.50	.60
26 Lance Parrish	1.00	.40
27 Dan Petry	.50	.20
28 Dave Rozema	.50	.20
29 Dick Tracewski CO	.50	.20
30 Alan Trammell	1.50	.60
31 Lou Whitaker	1.00	.40
32 Milt Wilcox	.50	.20

1984 Tigers Wave Postcards

During the 1984 Tigers World Championship season, these post cards were issued by Batter-Up, Inc. The fronts have two drawings; one of which is a head shot while the other one is an action pose. These cards are unnumbered and we have sequenced them in alphabetical order.

	Nm-Mt	Ex-Mt
COMPLETE SET (35)	15.00	6.00
1 Sparky Anderson MG	1.00	.40
2 Glenn Abbott	.50	.20
3 Doug Bair	.50	.20
4 Doug Baker	.50	.20
5 Bill Behm	.50	.20
6 Juan Berenguer	.50	.20
7 Dave Bergman	.50	.20
8 Tom Brookens	.50	.20
9 Gates Brown CO	.50	.20
10 Marty Castillo	.50	.20
11 Billy Consolo CO	.50	.20
12 Roger Craig CO	.75	.30
13 Pio DiSalvo	.50	.20
14 Darrell Evans	.75	.30
15 Barbaro Garbey	.50	.20
16 Kirk Gibson	1.50	.60
17 Alex Grammas CO	.50	.20
18 John Grubb	.50	.20
19 Willie Hernandez	.75	.30
20 Larry Herndon	.50	.20
21 Howard Johnson	1.00	.40
22 Ruppert Jones	.50	.20
23 Chet Lemon	.50	.20
24 Rusty Kuntz	.50	.20
25 Aurelio Lopez	.50	.20
26 Sid Monge	.50	.20
27 Jack Morris	1.50	.60
28 Lance Parrish	.75	.30
29 Dan Petry	.50	.20
30 Dave Rozema	.50	.20
31 Jim Schmakel	.50	.20
32 Dick Tracewski CO	.50	.20
33 Alan Trammell	3.00	1.20
34 Lou Whitaker	1.50	.60
35 Milt Wilcox	.50	.20

1985 Tigers Cain's Discs

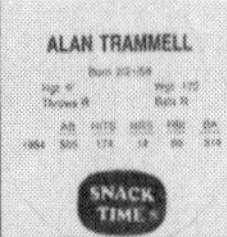

This set of discs was distributed by Cain's Potato Chips in 1985 to commemorate the Tigers' World Championship in 1984. Each disc measures 2 3/4" in diameter. Each disc has a distinctive yellow border on the front. Inside this yellow border is a full color photo of the player with his hat on. The statistics on back of the disc give the player's his 1984 pitching or hitting record as well as his vital statistics. The discs are not numbered; hence they are listed below in alphabetical order.

	Nm-Mt	Ex-Mt
COMPLETE SET (20)	35.00	14.00
1 Doug Bair	1.00	.40
2 Juan Berenguer	1.00	.40
3 Dave Bergman	1.00	.40
4 Tom Brookens	1.00	.40
5 Marty Castillo	1.00	.40
6 Darrell Evans	2.50	1.00
7 Barbaro Garbey	1.00	.40
8 Kirk Gibson	5.00	2.00
9 John Grubb	1.00	.40
10 Willie Hernandez	1.50	.60
11 Larry Herndon	1.00	.40
12 Chet Lemon	1.50	.60
13 Aurelio Lopez	1.00	.40
14 Jack Morris	4.00	1.60
15 Lance Parrish	2.50	1.00
16 Dan Petry	1.00	.40
17 Bill Scherrer	1.00	.40
18 Alan Trammell	6.00	2.40
19 Lou Whitaker	5.00	2.00
20 Milt Wilcox	1.00	.40

1985 Tigers Wendy's/Coke

This 22-card standard-size set features Detroit Tigers. The set was co-sponsored by Wendy's and Coca-Cola and was distributed in the Detroit metropolitan area. Coca-Cola purchasers were given a pack which contained three Tiger cards plus a header card. The orange-bordered player photos are different from those used by Topps in their regular set. The cards were produced by Topps as evidenced by the similarity of the card backs with the Topps regular set backs. The set is numbered on the back; the order corresponds to the alphabetical order of the player's names.

	Nm-Mt	Ex-Mt
COMPLETE SET (22)	6.00	2.40
1 Sparky Anderson MG CL	.50	.20
2 Doug Bair	.10	.04
3 Juan Berenguer	.10	.04
4 Dave Bergman	.10	.04
5 Tom Brookens	.10	.04
6 Marty Castillo	.10	.04
7 Darrell Evans	.30	.12
8 Barbaro Garbey	.10	.04
9 Kirk Gibson	1.25	.50
10 Johnny Grubb	.10	.04
11 Willie Hernandez	.20	.08
12 Larry Herndon	.10	.04
13 Rusty Kuntz	.10	.04
14 Chet Lemon	.20	.08
15 Aurelio Lopez	.10	.04
16 Jack Morris	1.25	.50
17 Lance Parrish	.50	.20
18 Dan Petry	.20	.08
19 Bill Scherrer	.10	.04
20 Alan Trammell	2.50	1.00
21 Lou Whitaker	1.50	.60
22 Milt Wilcox	.10	.04

1986 Tigers Cain's Discs

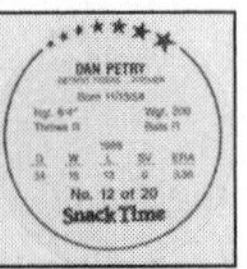

This set of 20 discs was distributed by Cain's Potato Chips in 1986 and consists solely of Detroit Tigers. Each disc measures 2 3/4" in diameter. The statistics on back of the disc give the player's his 1985 pitching or hitting record as well as his vital statistics. The discs are not numbered; hence they are listed below in alphabetical order.

	Nm-Mt	Ex-Mt
COMPLETE SET (20)	35.00	14.00
1 Dave Bergman	1.00	.40
2 Tom Brookens	1.00	.40
3 Dave Collins	1.00	.40
4 Darrell Evans	2.50	1.00
5 Doug Flynn	1.00	.40
6 Kirk Gibson	5.00	2.00
7 John Grubb	1.00	.40
8 Willie Hernandez	1.50	.60
9 Larry Herndon	1.00	.40
10 Dave LaPoint	1.00	.40
11 Chet Lemon	1.00	.40
12 Jack Morris	4.00	1.60
13 Randy O'Neal	1.00	.40
14 Lance Parrish	2.50	1.00
15 Dan Petry	1.00	.40
16 Nelson Simmons	1.00	.40
17 Frank Tanana	1.50	.60
18 Walt Terrell	1.00	.40
19 Alan Trammell	6.00	2.40
20 Lou Whitaker	5.00	2.00

1986 Tigers Sports Design

This 22-card standard-size set displays an unknown artist's portrait of "All-Time Great Tigers." The fronts are bordered in white with an inner black border. The player's name is printed across the bottom with a blue line above and below. The horizontal backs are printed in blue over a light gray background with a ghosted design that includes several bats and balls. Player statistics, biography and career summary are included.

	Nm-Mt	Ex-Mt
COMPLETE SET (22)	8.00	3.20
1 Ty Cobb	1.50	.60
2 Hughie Jennings	.75	.30
3 Harry Heilmann	.75	.30
4 Charlie Gehringer	.75	.30
5 Mickey Cochrane	.75	.30
6 Hank Greenberg	1.00	.40
7 Billy Rogell	.25	.10
8 Schoolboy Rowe	.25	.10
9 Hal Newhouser	.75	.30
10 George Kell	.75	.30
11 Harvey Kuenn	.50	.20
12 Al Kaline	1.00	.40
13 Jim Bunning	.75	.30
14 Norm Cash	.50	.20
15 Mickey Stanley	.25	.10
16 Jim Northrup	.25	.10
17 Bill Freehan	.50	.20
18 Gates Brown	.50	.20
19 Willie Horton	.50	.20
20 Mickey Lolich	.50	.20
21 Denny McLain	.50	.20
22 John Hiller	.25	.10

1987 Tigers Cain's Discs

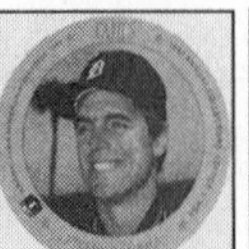

This set of 20 discs was distributed by Cain's Potato Chips in 1987 and consists solely of Detroit Tigers. Each disc measures 2 3/4" in diameter. The statistics on back of the disc give the player's 1986 pitching or hitting record as well as his vital statistics. The discs are numbered on the back and have a distinctive orange border on the front of the disc.

	Nm-Mt	Ex-Mt
COMPLETE SET (20)	25.00	10.00
1 Tom Brookens	1.00	.40
2 Darnell Coles	1.00	.40
3 Mike Heath	1.00	.40
4 Dave Bergman	1.00	.40
5 Dwight Lowry	1.00	.40
6 Darrell Evans	1.50	.60
7 Alan Trammell	5.00	2.00
8 Lou Whitaker	4.00	1.60
9 Kirk Gibson	4.00	1.60
10 Chet Lemon	1.00	.40
11 Larry Herndon	1.00	.40
12 John Grubb	1.00	.40
13 Willie Hernandez	1.50	.60
14 Jack Morris	2.50	1.00
15 Dan Petry	1.00	.40
16 Walt Terrell	1.00	.40
17 Mark Thurmond	1.00	.40
18 Pat Sheridan	1.00	.40
19 Eric King	1.00	.40
20 Frank Tanana	1.50	.60

1987 Tigers Coke

Coca-Cola, in collaboration with S. Abraham and Sons, issued a set of 18 cards featuring the Detroit Tigers. The cards are numbered on the back. The cards are distinguished by the bright yellow border framing the full-color picture of the player on the front. The cards were issued in panels of four: three player cards and a team logo card. The cards measure the standard size and were produced by MSA, Mike Schechter Associates.

	Nm-Mt	Ex-Mt
COMPLETE SET (18)	6.00	2.40
1 Kirk Gibson	1.25	.50
2 Larry Herndon	.10	.04
3 Walt Terrell	.10	.04
4 Alan Trammell	2.00	.80
5 Frank Tanana	.25	.10
6 Pat Sheridan	.10	.04
7 Jack Morris	1.25	.50
8 Mike Heath	.10	.04
9 Dave Bergman	.10	.04
10 Chet Lemon	.25	.10
11 Dwight Lowry	.10	.04
12 Dan Petry	.10	.04
13 Darrell Evans	.50	.20
14 Darnell Coles	.10	.04
15 Willie Hernandez	.25	.10
16 Lou Whitaker	1.50	.60
17 Tom Brookens	.10	.04
18 John Grubb	.10	.04

1988 Tigers Domino's

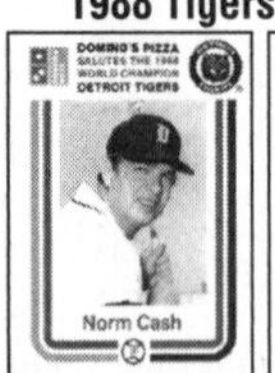

This rather unattractive set commemorates the 20th anniversary of the Detroit Tigers' World Championship season in 1968. The card stock used is rather thin. The cards measure approximately 2 1/2" by 3 1/2". There are a number of errors in the set including biographical errors, misspellings, and photo misidentifications. Players are pictured in black and white inside a red and blue horseshoe. The numerous factual errors in the set detract from the set's collectibility in the eyes of many collectors. The set numbering is in alphabetical order by player's name.

	Nm-Mt	Ex-Mt
COMPLETE SET (28)	4.00	1.60
1 Gates Brown	.25	.10
2 Norm Cash	.50	.20
3 Wayne Comer	.10	.04
4 Pat Dobson	.25	.10
5 Bill Freehan	.50	.20
6 Ernie Harwell ANN	.50	.20
7 John Hiller	.25	.10
8 Willie Horton	.25	.10
9 Al Kaline	1.25	.50
10 Fred Lasher	.10	.04
11 Mickey Lolich	.50	.20
12 Tom Matchick	.10	.04
13 Ed Mathews	.75	.30
14 Dick McAuliffe	.25	.10
15 Denny McLain	.50	.20
16 Don McMahon	.10	.04
17 Jim Northrup	.25	.10
18 Ray Oyler	.10	.04
19 Daryl Patterson	.10	.04
20 Jim Price	.10	.04
21 Joe Sparma	.10	.04
22 Mickey Stanley	.25	.10
23 Dick Tracewski	.10	.04
24 Jon Warden	.10	.04
25 Don Wert	.10	.04
26 Earl Wilson	.10	.04
27 Pizza Buck Coupon	.10	.04
28 Title Card	.10	.04
Old Timers Game 1988		

1988 Tigers Pepsi/Kroger

This set of 25 cards features members of the Detroit Tigers and was sponsored by Pepsi Cola and Kroger. The cards are in full color on the fronts and measure approximately 2 7/8" by 4 1/4". The card backs contain complete Major and Minor League season-by-season statistics. The cards are unnumbered so they are listed below by uniform number, which is given on the card.

	Nm-Mt	Ex-Mt
COMPLETE SET (25)	12.00	4.80
1 Lou Whitaker	2.00	.80
2 Alan Trammell	3.00	1.20
8 Mike Heath	.25	.10
11 Sparky Anderson MG	1.00	.40
12 Luis Salazar	.25	.10
14 Dave Bergman	.25	.10
15 Pat Sheridan	.25	.10
16 Tom Brookens	.25	.10
19 Doyle Alexander	.50	.20
21 Willie Hernandez	.50	.20
22 Ray Knight	.25	.10
24 Gary Pettis	.25	.10
25 Eric King	.25	.10
26 Frank Tanana	.50	.20
31 Larry Herndon	.25	.10
32 Jim Walewander	.25	.10
33 Matt Nokes	.75	.30
34 Chet Lemon	.50	.20
35 Walt Terrell	.25	.10
39 Mike Henneman	1.00	.40
41 Darrell Evans	.50	.20
44 Jeff M. Robinson	.25	.10
47 Jack Morris	1.00	.40
48 Paul Gibson	.25	.10
NNO Billy Consolo CO	.25	.10
Alex Grammas CO		
Billy Muffett CO		
Vada Pinson CO		
Dick Tracewski CO		

1988 Tigers Police

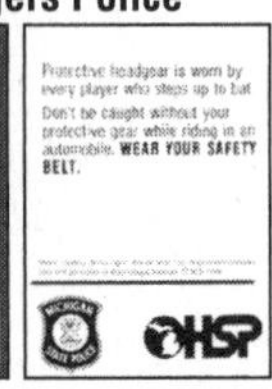

This set was sponsored by the Michigan State Police and the Detroit Tigers organization. There are 14 blue-bordered cards in the set; each card measures approximately 2 1/2" by 3 1/2". The cards are completely unnumbered as there is not even any reference to uniform numbers on the cards; the cards are listed below in alphabetical order.

	Nm-Mt	Ex-Mt
COMPLETE SET (14)	30.00	12.00
1 Doyle Alexander	1.50	.60
2 Sparky Anderson MG	3.00	1.20
3 Dave Bergman	1.50	.60
4 Tom Brookens	1.50	.60
5 Darrell Evans	2.50	1.00
6 Larry Herndon	1.50	.60
7 Chet Lemon	1.50	.60
8 Jack Morris	8.00	3.20
9 Matt Nokes	2.50	1.00
10 Jeff M. Robinson	1.50	.60
11 Frank Tanana	2.00	.80
12 Walt Terrell	1.50	.60
13 Alan Trammell	12.00	4.80
14 Lou Whitaker	8.00	3.20

1989 Tigers Marathon

The 1989 Marathon Tigers set features 28 cards measuring approximately 2 3/4" by 4 1/2". The set features color photos surrounded by blue borders and a white background. The Tigers logo is featured prominently under the photo and then the players uniform number name and position is underneath the Tiger logo. The horizontally oriented backs show career stats. The set was given away at the July 15, 1989 Tigers home game against the Seattle Mariners. The cards are numbered by the players' uniform numbers.

	Nm-Mt	Ex-Mt
COMPLETE SET (28)	10.00	4.00
1 Lou Whitaker	2.00	.80
3 Alan Trammell	2.50	1.00
8 Mike Heath	.25	.10
9 Fred Lynn	.50	.20
10 Keith Moreland	.25	.10
11 Sparky Anderson MG	.75	.30
12 Mike Brumley	.25	.10
14 Dave Bergman	.25	.10
15 Pat Sheridan	.25	.10
17 Al Pedrique	.25	.10
18 Ramon Pena	.25	.10
19 Doyle Alexander	.25	.10
21 Willie Hernandez	.50	.20
23 Torey Lovullo	.25	.10
24 Gary Pettis	.25	.10
25 Ken Williams	.50	.20
26 Frank Tanana	.75	.30
27 Charles Hudson	.25	.10
32 Gary Ward	.25	.10
33 Matt Nokes	.75	.30
34 Chet Lemon	.50	.20
35 Rick Schu	.25	.10
36 Frank Williams	.25	.10
39 Mike Henneman	.75	.30
44 Jeff M. Robinson	.25	.10
47 Jack Morris	1.00	.40
48 Paul Gibson	.25	.10
NNO Billy Consolo CO	.25	.10
Alex Grammas CO		
Billy Muffett CO		
Vada Pinson CO		
Dick Tracewski CO		

1989 Tigers Police

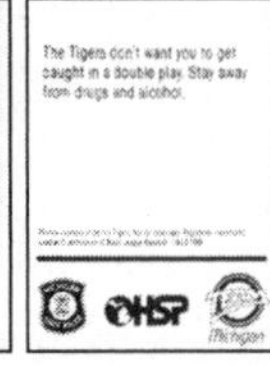

The 1989 Police Detroit Tigers set contains 14 standard-size cards. The fronts have color photos with blue and orange borders; the backs feature safety tips. These unnumbered cards were given away by the Michigan state police. The cards are numbered below according to uniform number.

	Nm-Mt	Ex-Mt
COMPLETE SET (14)	12.00	4.80
1 Lou Whitaker	3.00	1.20
3 Alan Trammell	4.00	1.60
9 Fred Lynn	1.00	.40
14 Dave Bergman	.50	.20
15 Pat Sheridan	.50	.20
19 Doyle Alexander	.50	.20
21 Willie Hernandez	.75	.30
26 Frank Tanana	1.00	.40
33 Matt Nokes	.75	.30
34 Chet Lemon	.75	.30
39 Mike Henneman	1.00	.40
44 Jeff M. Robinson	.50	.20
47 Jack Morris	1.50	.60
NNO Sparky Anderson MG	1.50	.60

1990 Tigers Coke/Kroger

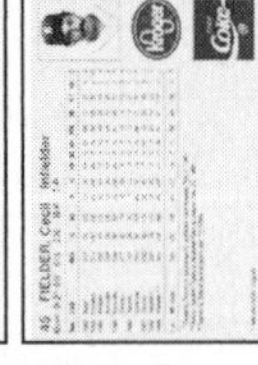

The 1990 Coke/Kroger Detroit Tigers set contains 28 cards, measuring approximately 2 7/8" by 4 1/4", which was used as a giveaway at the July 14th Detroit Tigers home game. The player photo is surrounded by green borders with complete career statistical information printed on the back of each card. This set is checklisted alphabetically in the listings below.

	Nm-Mt	Ex-Mt
COMPLETE SET (28)	8.00	2.40
1 Sparky Anderson MG	.75	.23
2 Dave Bergman	.25	.07
3 Brian DuBois	.25	.07
4 Cecil Fielder	.50	.15
5 Paul Gibson	.25	.07
6 Jerry Don Gleaton	.25	.07
7 Mike Heath	.25	.07
8 Mike Henneman	.50	.15
9 Tracy Jones	.25	.07
10 Chet Lemon	.50	.15
11 Urbano Lugo	.25	.07
12 Jack Morris	1.00	.30
13 Lloyd Moseby	.25	.07
14 Matt Nokes	.50	.15
15 Edwin Nunez	.25	.07
16 Dan Petry	.25	.07
17 Tony Phillips	.25	.07
18 Kevin Ritz	.25	.07
19 Jeff M. Robinson	.25	.07
20 Ed Romero	.25	.07
21 Mark Salas	.25	.07
22 Larry Sheets	.25	.07
23 Frank Tanana	.75	.23
24 Alan Trammell	2.00	.60
25 Gary Ward	.25	.07
26 Lou Whitaker	1.50	.45
27 Ken Williams	.50	.15
28 Billy Consolo CO	.50	.15
Alex Grammas CO		
Billy Muffett CO UER		
Sic, Muffet		

Card	Nm-Mt	Ex-Mt
Vada Pinson CO		
Dick Tracewski CO		

1990 Tigers Milk Henneman

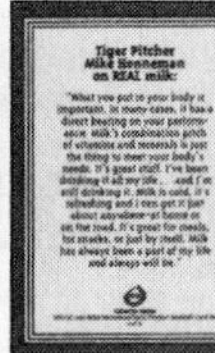

This eight-card standard-size set was a collector series issued by Real Milk Co. The set includes a title card and a membership card that enabled the consumer to mail in the card and become a Tiger Clubhouse Member. All the cards picture Mike Henneman and a carton of Real milk. The cards are numbered on the back and front.

	Nm-Mt	Ex-Mt
COMPLETE SET (8)	8.00	2.40
COMMON CARD (1-6)	.75	.23
COMMON HENNEMAN	2.00	.60
NNO Title card	.75	.23
NNO Membership card	.75	.23

1991 Tigers Coke/Kroger

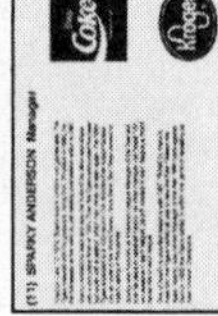

The 1991 Coke/Kroger Tigers set contains 27 cards measuring approximately 2 7/8" by 4 1/4". The set is skip-numbered by uniform number and checklisted accordingly. The Mike Dalton card (number 42) exists. However, most were produced with a stain on his face and were pulled from circulation. We are calling this card a SP and are not including it in the complete set price.

	Nm-Mt	Ex-Mt
COMPLETE SET (27)	10.00	3.00
COMMON SP	5.00	1.50
1 Lou Whitaker	1.00	.30
3 Alan Trammell	2.00	.60
4 Tony Phillips	.25	.07
10 Andy Allanson	.25	.07
11 Sparky Anderson MG	.75	.23
14 Dave Bergman	.25	.07
15 Lloyd Moseby	.25	.07
19 Jerry Don Gleaton	.25	.07
20 Mickey Tettleton	1.00	.30
22 Milt Cuyler	.25	.07
23 Mark Leiter	.25	.07
24 Travis Fryman	1.00	.30
25 John Shelby	.25	.07
26 Frank Tanana	.75	.23
27 Mark Salas	.25	.07
29 Pete Incaviglia	.50	.15
31 Kevin Ritz	.25	.07
35 Walt Terrell	.25	.07
36 Bill Gullickson	.25	.07
39 Mike Henneman	.50	.15
42 Mike Dalton SP	5.00	1.50
44 Rob Deer	.25	.07
45 Cecil Fielder	1.00	.30
46 Dan Petry	.25	.07
48 Paul Gibson	.25	.07
49 Steve Searcy	.25	.07
55 John Cerutti	.25	.07
NNO Billy Consolo CO	.25	.07
Jim Davenport CO		
Alex Grammas CO		
Billy Muffett CO		
Vada Pinson CO		
Dick Tracewski CO		

1991 Tigers Police

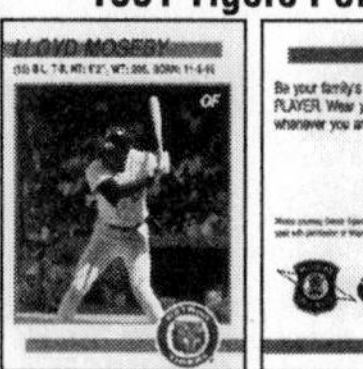

This 14-card standard-sized set was sponsored by the Michigan State Police, HSP, and Team Michigan, and their sponsor logos appear on the backs. The cards feature a mix of posed and action color player photos. The player's name appears in blue lettering in an orange stripe above the picture, while a second orange stripe below the picture intersects the team logo at the lower right corner. The backs contain safety tips. The cards are unnumbered and checklisted below in alphabetical order.

	Nm-Mt	Ex-Mt
COMPLETE SET (14)	25.00	7.50
1 Sparky Anderson MG	2.50	.75
2 Dave Bergman	1.00	.30
3 Cecil Fielder	2.50	.75
4 Travis Fryman	8.00	2.40
5 Paul Gibson	1.00	.30
6 Jerry Don Gleaton	1.00	.30
7 Lloyd Moseby	1.00	.30
8 Dan Petry	1.00	.30
9 Tony Phillips	1.00	.30
10 Mark Salas	1.00	.30
11 John Shelby	1.00	.30
12 Frank Tanana	1.50	.45
13 Alan Trammell	8.00	2.40
14 Lou Whitaker	4.00	1.20

1992 Tigers Kroger

This 28-card set measures approximately 2 7/8" by 4 1/4" and features color action photos of the 1992 Detroit Tigers with white borders. The backs display player information and career statistics. The cards are unnumbered and checklisted below in alphabetical order.

	Nm-Mt	Ex-Mt
COMPLETE SET (28)	10.00	3.00
1 Sparky Anderson MG	1.00	.30
2 Skeeter Barnes	.25	.07
3 Dave Bergman	.25	.07
4 Mark Carreon	.25	.07
5 Milt Cuyler	.25	.07
6 Rob Deer	.25	.07
7 John Doherty	.25	.07
8 Cecil Fielder	1.50	.45
9 Travis Fryman	1.00	.30
10 Dan Gladden	.25	.07
11 Bill Gullickson	.25	.07
12 Mike Henneman	.50	.15
13 John Kiely	.25	.07
14 Kurt Knudsen	.25	.07
15 Chad Kreuter	.25	.07
16 Mark Leiter	.25	.07
17 Les Lancaster	.25	.07
18 Scott Livingstone	.25	.07
19 Mike Munoz	.25	.07
20 Gary Pettis	.25	.07
21 Tony Phillips	.25	.07
22 Kevin Ritz	.25	.07
23 Frank Tanana	.50	.15
24 Walt Terrell	.25	.07
25 Mickey Tettleton	.75	.23
26 Alan Trammell	2.00	.60
27 Lou Whitaker	1.00	.30
28 Billy Consolo CO	.25	.07
Larry Herndon CO		
Billy Muffett CO		
Gene Roof CO		
Dick Tracewski CO		
Dan Whitmer		

1993 Tigers Gatorade

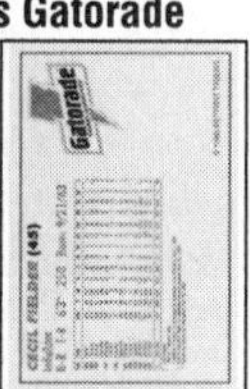

Sponsored by Gatorade, this 28-card set measures approximately 2 7/8" by 4 1/4". The cards are unnumbered and checklisted below in alphabetical order.

	Nm-Mt	Ex-Mt
COMPLETE SET (28)	8.00	2.40
1 Sparky Anderson MG	1.00	.30
2 Skeeter Barnes	.25	.07
3 Tom Bolton	.25	.07
4 Milt Cuyler	.25	.07
5 Rob Deer	.25	.07
6 John Doherty	.25	.07
7 Cecil Fielder	1.00	.30
8 Travis Fryman	1.00	.30
9 Kirk Gibson	.75	.23
10 Dan Gladden	.25	.07
11 Buddy Groom	.25	.07
12 Bill Gullickson	.25	.07
13 David Haas	.25	.07
14 Mike Henneman	.50	.15
15 Kurt Knudsen	.25	.07
16 Chad Kreuter	.25	.07
17 Bill Krueger	.25	.07
18 Mark Leiter	.25	.07
19 Scott Livingstone	.25	.07
20 Bob MacDonald	.25	.07
21 Mike Moore	.25	.07
22 Tony Phillips	.25	.07
23 Mickey Tettleton	.75	.23
24 Gary Thurman	.25	.07
25 Alan Trammell	1.50	.45
26 David Wells	.75	.23
27 Lou Whitaker	1.00	.30
28 Dick Tracewski CO	.25	.07
Billy Muffett CO		
Larry Herndon CO		
Gene Roof CO		
Dan Whitmer CO		

1993 Tigers Little Caesars

Issued as a seven-card/pin set, the '93 Tigers Little Caesars set spotlights the Tigers' World Series victories. The cards measure 2 1/2" by 5 1/4", are printed on thin white card stock, and have black-and-white or color photos on their fronts. The backs carry information regarding the particular Tigers team that won that World Series. The brass pins are affixed to the cards near the bottom. Cards 1-4 are unnumbered as such on their backs; cards 5-7 are unnumbered and so are checklisted below in chronological order.

	Nm-Mt	Ex-Mt
COMPLETE SET (7)	10.00	3.00
1 1935 World Champions	1.50	.45
2 1945 World Champions	1.50	.45
3 1968 World Champions	1.50	.45
4 1984 World Champions	1.50	.45
5 Denny McLain 31 Win Season	3.00	.90
6 1968 Tigers Celebration	1.50	.45
7 Mickey Lolich World Series MVP	3.00	.90

1996 Tigers Hebrew National

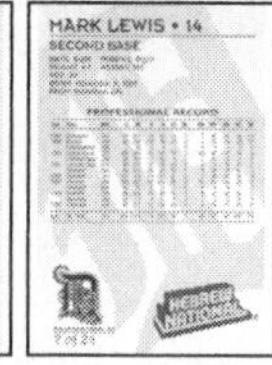

This 25-card set measures approximately 2 7/8" by 4 1/4" and features color photos of the Detroit Tigers in white borders. The backs carry biographical information and career statistics. Cards numbers 4 and 6 were supposed to be Chad Curtis and Cecil Fielder, but they do not exist. There is no card number 5. Card 3, Tony Clark, and card 28, the Coaches card, were not issued at the same time as the rest of the set.

	Nm-Mt	Ex-Mt
COMPLETE SET (25)	8.00	2.40
1 Kimera Bartee	.25	.07
2 Jose Lima	.25	.07
3 Tony Clark	1.00	.30
7 Bobby Higginson	.75	.23
8 Greg Keagle	.25	.07
9 Mark Lewis	.25	.07
10 Richie Lewis	.25	.07
11 Felipe Lira	.25	.07
12 Mike Myers	.25	.07
13 Melvin Nieves	.25	.07
14 Alan Trammell	1.50	.45
15 Tom Urbani	.25	.07
16 Brian Williams	.25	.07
17 Eddie Williams	.25	.07
18 Curtis Pride	.25	.07
19 Mark Parent	.25	.07
20 Raul Casanova	.25	.07
21 Omar Olivares	.25	.07
22 Gregg Olson	.50	.15
23 Justin Thompson	.25	.07
24 Brad Ausmus	.25	.07
25 Andujar Cedeno	.25	.07
26 Buddy Bell MG	.50	.15
27 Paws(Mascot)	.25	.07
28 Glenn Ezell CO	.25	.07
Terry Francona CO		
Larry Herndon CO		
Fred Kendall CO		
John Matlack CO		
Ron Oester CO		

1996 Tigers Postcards

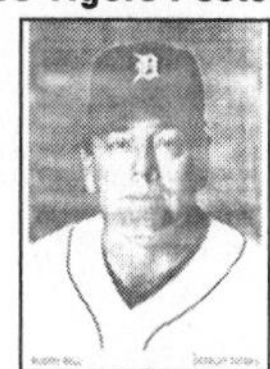

These 38 cards, which measure approximately 3 34/" by 5 1/4" and are blank backed feature members of the 1996 Detroit Tigers. Some of these cards also appear with a "coke" emblem. Since these cards are unnumbered, we have sequenced them in alphabetical order.

	Nm-Mt	Ex-Mt
COMPLETE SET	20.00	6.00
1 Rick Adair CO	.50	.15
2 Scott Aldred	.50	.15
3 Brad Ausmus	.50	.15
4 Kimera Bartee	.50	.15
5 Danny Bautista	.50	.15
6 Buddy Bell MG Has the Coke emblem	.75	.23
7 Doug Brocail	.50	.15
8 Raul Casanova	.50	.15
9 Mike Christopher	.50	.15
10 Chad Curtis	.50	.15
11 Glenn Ezell CO	.50	.15
12 Cecil Fielder	1.50	.45
13 John Flaherty	.50	.15
14 Terry Francona CO	.50	.15
15 Travis Fryman	1.00	.30
16 Greg Gohr	.50	.15
17 Chris Gomez	.50	.15
18 Larry Herndon CO	.50	.15
19 Bobby Higginson	1.50	.45
20 Greg Keagle	.50	.15
21 Fred Kendall CO	.50	.15
22 Mark Lewis	.50	.15
23 Richie Lewis	.50	.15
24 Jose Lima	.50	.15
25 Felipe Lira	.50	.15
26 Jon Matlack CO	.50	.15
27 Mike Myers	.50	.15
28 Melvin Nieves	.50	.15
29 C.J. Nitkowski	.50	.15
30 Ron Oester CO	.50	.15
31 Omar Olivares	.50	.15
32 Mark Parent	.50	.15
33 Curtis Pride Has the Coke Emblem	.50	.15
34 Justin Thompson Has the Coke Emblem	.50	.15
35 Alan Trammell CO	1.00	.30
36 Randy Veres	.50	.15
37 Brian Williams	.50	.15
38 Eddie Williams	.50	.15

1997 Tigers Hebrew National

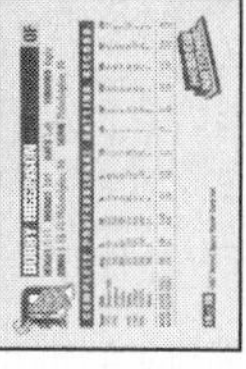

This 28 standard-size card set features members of the 1997 Detroit Tigers. The full-bleed borders have the player photo in the middle with the Detroit Tigers name on the top and the players name, small inset photo and position on the bottom. The horizontal backs have the players vital stats as well as their career records.

	Nm-Mt	Ex-Mt
COMPLETE SET (28)	15.00	4.50
1 Jose Bautista	.50	.15
2 Willie Blair	.50	.15
3 Doug Brocail	.50	.15
4 Raul Casanova	.50	.15
5 Tony Clark	1.50	.45
6 Deivi Cruz	.50	.15
7 John Cummings	.50	.15
8 Damion Easley	.50	.15
9 Travis Fryman	1.00	.30
10 Bobby Higginson	1.50	.45
11 Brian L. Hunter	.50	.15
12 Brian Johnson	.50	.15
13 Todd Jones	.50	.15
14 Felipe Lira	.50	.15
15 Dan Miceli	.50	.15
16 Brian Moehler	.50	.15
17 Mike Myers	.50	.15
18 Phil Nevin	1.50	.45
19 Melvin Nieves	.50	.15
20 Omar Oliveres	.50	.15
21 Curtis Pride	.50	.15
22 A.J. Sager	.50	.15
23 Justin Thompson	.50	.15
24 Matt Walbeck	.50	.15
25 Jody Reed	.50	.15
26 Bob Hamelin	.50	.15
27 Buddy Bell MG	.75	.23
28 Rick Adair CO	.50	.15
Larry Herndon CO		
Perry Hill CO		
Fred Kendall CO		
Larry Parrish CO		
Jerry White CO		

1997 Tigers Postcards

These 33 blank-backed postcards, which measure approximately 3 3/4" by 5 1/4", feature members of the 1997 Detroit Tigers. Since these cards are not numbered, we have sequenced them in alphabetical order.

	Nm-Mt	Ex-Mt
COMPLETE SET	15.00	4.50
1 Rick Adair CO	.50	.15
2 Buddy Bell MG	.75	.23
3 Willie Blair	.50	.15
4 Doug Brocail	.50	.15
5 Tony Clark	1.50	.45
6 Deivi Cruz	.50	.15
7 John Cummings	.50	.15
8 Damion Easley	.50	.15
9 Travis Fryman	.50	.15
10 Bob Hamelin	.50	.15
11 Larry Herndon CO	.50	.15
12 Bobby Higginson	1.50	.45
13 Perry Hill CO	.50	.15
14 Brian Hunter	.50	.15
15 Brian Johnson	.50	.15
16 Todd Jones	.50	.15
17 Fred Kendall CO	.50	.15
18 Felipe Lira	.50	.15
19 Dan Miceli	.50	.15
20 Orlando Miller	.50	.15
21 Brian Moehler	.50	.15
22 Mike Myers	.50	.15
23 Phil Nevin	1.50	.45
24 Melvin Nieves	.50	.15
25 Omar Olivares	.50	.15
26 Larry Parrish CO	.50	.15
27 Curtis Pride	.50	.15
28 Jody Reed	.50	.15
29 A.J. Sager	.50	.15
30 Justin Thompson	.50	.15
31 Bubba Trammell	.75	.23
32 Matt Walbeck	.50	.15
33 Jerry White CO	.50	.15

1998 Tigers Ball Park

This 26 card standard-size set features members of the 1998 Detroit Tigers. The fronts have the players name and position on the left side and the rest of the white bordered card has an action photo of the player. The horizontal backs have complete statistics along with biographical information and a brief blurb with a highlight from the players 1997 season. In additon, the Ball Park Franks logo is in the lower right on the back.

	Nm-Mt	Ex-Mt
COMPLETE SET (26)	6.00	1.80
1 Gabe Alvarez	.25	.07
2 Matt Anderson	.50	.15
3 Paul Bako	.25	.07
4 Trey Beamon	.25	.07
5 Buddy Bell MG	.50	.15
6 Geronimo Berroa	.25	.07
7 Doug Bochtler	.25	.07
8 Doug Brocail	.25	.07
9 Raul Casanova	.25	.07
10 Frank Castillo	.25	.07
11 Frank Catalanotto	1.50	.45
12 Tony Clark	.75	.23
13 Dean Crow	.25	.07
14 Deivi Cruz	.25	.07
15 Damion Easley	.25	.07
16 Bryce Florie	.25	.07
17 Luis Gonzalez	1.00	.30
18 Seth Greisinger	.25	.07
19 Bobby Higginson	.50	.15
20 Brian Hunter	.25	.07
21 Todd Jones	.25	.07
22 Brian Moehler	.25	.07
23 Brian Powell	.25	.07
24 Joe Randa	.25	.07
25 Sean Runyan	.25	.07
26 Justin Thompson	.25	.07

1998 Tigers Postcards

These blank-backed 3 3/4" by 5 1/4" postcards featuring members of the 1998 Detroit Tigers and were issued with black and white photos. We have split this checklist into three sections; of which all are in alphabetical order by group: The first 20 postcards have new poses for 1998; the next nine have the same pose as 1997 and the final 11 were late season additions

	Nm-Mt	Ex-Mt
COMPLETE SET (39)	20.00	6.00
1 Willie Blair	.50	.15
2 Raul Casanova	.50	.15
3 Frank Castillo	.50	.15
4 Frank Catalanotto	2.00	.60
5 Tony Clark	1.00	.30
6 Deivi Cruz	.50	.15
7 Damion Easley	.50	.15
8 Bryce Florie	.50	.15
9 Luis Gonzalez	1.50	.45
10 Bobby Higginson	.75	.23
11 Perry Hill CO	.50	.15
12 Brian L. Hunter	.50	.15
13 Todd Jones	.50	.15
14 Greg Keagle	.50	.15
15 Joe Oliver	.50	.15
16 Joe Randa	.50	.15
17 Bill Ripken	.50	.15
18 Bip Roberts	.50	.15
19 Sean Runyan	.50	.15
20 Justin Thompson	.50	.15
21 Tim Worrell	.50	.15
22 Rick Adair CO	.50	.15
23 Buddy Bell MG	.75	.23
24 Doug Brocail	.50	.15
25 Larry Herndon CO	.50	.15
26 Fred Kendall CO	.50	.15
27 Brian Moehler	.50	.15
28 Larry Parrish CO	.50	.15
29 A.J. Sager	.50	.15
30 Jerry White CO	.50	.15
31 Gabe Alvarez	.50	.15
32 Matt Anderson	.75	.23
33 Paul Bako	.50	.15
34 Trey Beamon	.50	.15
35 Kimera Bartee	.50	.15
36 Geronimo Berroa	.50	.15
37 Dean Crow	.50	.15
38 Seth Greisinger	.50	.15
39 Brian Powell	.50	.15
40 Roberto Duran	.50	.15

1999 Tigers Pop Secret

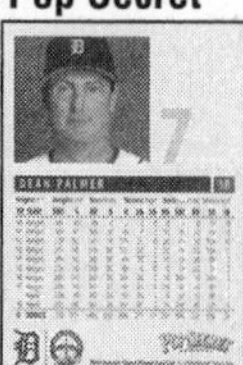

This 26 card standard-size set features members of the 1999 Detroit Tigers. The cards have a black and blue stripes going down the side with the player name and position printed in the black stripe. The rest of the borderless card features an action player photo. The back has a player portrait, biographical information and complete career stats. The cards are unnumbered except for the uniform number so we have sequenced them in alphabetical order.

	Nm-Mt	Ex-Mt
COMPLETE SET (26)	8.00	2.40
1 Matt Anderson	.25	.07

2 Brad Ausmus .25 .07
3 Willie Blair .25 .07
4 Doug Brocail .25 .07
5 Frank Catalanotto .75 .23
6 Tony Clark .75 .23
7 Deivi Cruz .25 .07
8 Damion Easley .25 .07
9 Juan Encarnacion 1.00 .30
10 Karim Garcia 1.00 .30
11 Seth Greisinger .25 .07
12 Bill Haselman .25 .07
13 Bobby Higginson .50 .15
14 Gregg Jefferies .25 .07
15 Todd Jones .25 .07
16 Gabe Kapler .50 .15
17 Masao Kida .25 .07
18 Dave Mlicki .25 .07
19 Brian Moehler .25 .07
20 C.J. Nitkowski .25 .07
21 Dean Palmer .50 .15
22 Larry Parrish MG .25 .07
23 Luis Polonia .25 .07
24 Justin Thompson .25 .07
25 Jeff Weaver 1.50 .45
26 The Corner .25 .07
Tiger Stadium

1999 Tigers Postcards

These blank backed postcards measure 3 3/4" by 5 1/4" and feature members of the 1999 Detroit Tigers. The cards are unnumbered so we have sequenced them in alphabetical order.

	Nm-Mt	Ex-Mt
COMPLETE SET	10.00	3.00
1 Rick Adair CO	.25	.07
2 Gabe Alvarez	.25	.07
3 Matt Anderson	.25	.07
4 Brad Ausmus	.25	.07
5 Willie Blair	.25	.07
6 Doug Brocail	.25	.07
7 Will Brunson	.25	.07
8 Frank Catalanotto	.75	.23
9 Tony Clark	.75	.23
10 Deivi Cruz	.25	.07
11 Nelson Cruz	.25	.07
12 Damion Easley	.25	.07
13 Juan Encarnacion	1.00	.30
14 Bryce Florie	.25	.07
15 Karim Garcia	1.00	.30
16 Seth Greisinger	.25	.07
17 Bill Haselman	.25	.07
18 Bobby Higginson	.50	.15
19 Perry Hill CO	.25	.07
20 Gregg Jefferies	.25	.07
21 Jeff Jones CO	.25	.07
22 Todd Jones	.25	.07
23 Gabe Kapler	.50	.15
24 Masao Kida	.25	.07
25 Dave Mlicki	.25	.07
26 Brian Moehler	.25	.07
27 C.J. Nitkowski	.25	.07
28 Dean Palmer	.50	.15
29 Lance Parrish CO	.25	.07
30 Larry Parrish MG	.25	.07
31 Dean Palmer	.75	.23
32 Luis Polonia	.25	.07
33 Sean Runyan	.25	.07
34 Justin Thompson	.25	.07
35 Alan Trammell CO	.75	.23
36 Jeff Weaver	1.50	.45
37 Jason Wood	.25	.07

2000 Tigers Postcards

These 39 cards, which measure approximately 3 3/4" by 5 1/4" and are blank backed feature members of the 2000 Detroit Tigers. Since these cards are not numbered, we have sequenced them in alphabetical order.

	Nm-Mt	Ex-Mt
COMPLETE SET	12.00	3.60
1 Matt Anderson	.25	.07
2 Brad Ausmus	.25	.07
3 Rich Becker	.25	.07
4 Willie Blair	.25	.07
5 Dave Borkowski	.25	.07
6 Doug Brocail	.25	.07
7 Javier Cardona	.25	.07
8 Tony Clark	.50	.15
9 Deivi Cruz	.25	.07
10 Nelson Cruz	.25	.07
11 Damion Easley	.25	.07
12 Juan Encarnacion	.75	.23
14 Phil Garner MG	.25	.07
14 Robert Fick	.50	.15
15 Juan Gonzalez	1.25	.35
16 Seth Greisinger	.25	.07
17 Shane Halter	.25	.07
18 Bobby Higginson	.50	.15
19 Chris Holt	.25	.07
20 Gregg Jefferies	.25	.07
21 Mark Johnson	.25	.07
22 Todd Jones	.25	.07
23 Jose Macias	.25	.07
24 Bill Madlock CO	.50	.15
25 Doug Mansolino CO	.25	.07
26 Allen McDill	.25	.07
27 Wendell Magee	.25	.07
28 Dave Mlicki	.25	.07
29 Brian Moehler	.25	.07
30 Eric Munson	.75	.23
31 C.J. Nitkowski	.25	.07
32 Hideo Nomo	2.00	.60
33 Dean Palmer	.50	.15
34 Danny Patterson	.25	.07
35 Lance Parrish CO	.50	.15
36 Luis Polonia	.25	.07
37 Juan Samuel CO	.25	.07
38 Dan Warthen CO	.25	.07
39 Jeff Weaver	.75	.23

2000 Tigers Upper Deck Pepsi

Issued as a premium in the Detroit area, these 15 cards feature members of the 2000 Detroit Tigers. The horizontal fronts feature two posed player photos while the backs have a blurb along with season and career stats.

	Nm-Mt	Ex-Mt
COMPLETE SET	6.00	1.80
1 Damion Easley	.25	.07
2 Dave Mlicki	.25	.07
3 Jeff Weaver	.75	.23
4 Deivi Cruz	.25	.07
5 Juan Encarnacion	.75	.23
6 Brian Moehler	.25	.07
7 Robert Fick	.50	.15
8 Phil Garner MG	.25	.07
9 Juan Gonzalez	1.50	.45
10 Brad Ausmus	.25	.07
11 Todd Jones	.25	.07
12 Bobby Higginson	.50	.15
13 Tony Clark	.50	.15
14 Dean Palmer	.50	.15
15 Doug Brocail	.25	.07

2001 Tigers Postcards

These 39 blank-back cards, which measure 3 3./4" by 5 1/4" were issued by the Detroit Tigers and features a mix of new poses and poses utilized in previous years. Since these postcards are unnumbered, we have sequenced them in alphabetical order.

	Nm-Mt	Ex-Mt
COMPLETE SET	12.00	3.60
1 Matt Anderson	.25	.07
2 Frank Beckerman ANN	.25	.07
3 Adam Bernero	.25	.07
4 Javier Cardona	.25	.07
5 Roger Cedeno	.50	.15
6 Tony Clark	.50	.15
7 Deivi Cruz	.25	.07
8 Damion Easley	.25	.07
9 Juan Encarnacion	.50	.15
10 Robert Fick	.50	.15
11 Phil Garner MG	.25	.07
12 Shane Halter	.25	.07
13 Ernie Harwell ANN	1.00	.30
14 Bobby Higginson	.50	.15
15 Brandon Inge	.25	.07
16 Ryan Jackson	.25	.07
17 Al Kaline ANN	2.00	.60
18 Bill Madlock CO	.50	.15
19 Doug Mansolino	.25	.07
20 Wendell Magee	.25	.07
21 Billy McMillon	.25	.07
22 Mitch Meluskey	.25	.07
23 Brian Moehler	.25	.07
24 Heath Murray	.25	.07
25 C.J. Nitkowski	.25	.07
26 Ed Ott CO	.25	.07
27 Dean Palmer	.50	.15
28 Lance Parrish CO	.50	.15
29 Danny Patterson	.25	.07
30 Adam Pettyjohn	.25	.07
31 Jim Price ANN	.25	.07
32 Juan Samuel CO	.25	.07
33 Victor Santos	.25	.07
34 Randall Simon	.50	.15
35 Randy Smith GM	.25	.07
36 Steve Sparks	.25	.07
37 Dan Warthen CO	.25	.07
38 Jeff Weaver	.75	.23
39 Matt Wheatland	.25	.07

2002 Tigers Team Issue

This blank-backed set, which measure approximately 4" by 5" feature the player's photo set against white borders. It is believed that some of the photos used were used during the 2001 season as well. Since this set is unnumbered, we have sequenced these cards in alphabetical order in our checklist.

	Nm-Mt	Ex-Mt
COMPLETE SET	15.00	4.50
1 Juan Acevedo	.50	.15
2 Felipe Alou CO	.75	.23
3 Matt Anderson	.50	.15
4 Dave Borkowski	.50	.15
5 Nate Cornejo	.50	.15
6 Jacob Cruz	.50	.15
7 David Dombrowski GM	.50	.15
8 Damion Easley	.50	.15
9 Jeff Farnsworth	.50	.15
10 Robert Fick	.75	.23
11 Seth Greisinger	.50	.15
12 Shane Halter	.50	.15
13 Bobby Higginson	.75	.23
14 Damian Jackson	.50	.15
15 Ryan Jackson	.50	.15
16 Jeff Jones	.50	.15
17 Al Kaline	3.00	.90
18 Rafael Landestoy	.50	.15
19 Jose Lima	.50	.15
20 Wendell Magee	.50	.15
21 Mitch Meluskey	.50	.15
22 Steve McCatty CO	.50	.15
23 Eric Munson	.75	.23
24 Dean Palmer	.75	.23
25 Jose Paniagua	.50	.15
26 Lance Parrish CO	.50	.15
27 Adam Pettyjohn	.50	.15
28 Craig Paquette	.50	.15
29 Luis Pujols MG	.50	.15
30 Mark Redman	.50	.15
31 Merv Rettenmund CO	.50	.15
32 Michael Rivera	.50	.15
33 Juan Samuel CO	.50	.15
34 Randall Simon	.75	.23
35 Steve Sparks	.50	.15
36 Dmitri Young	.75	.23

2003 Tigers Team Issue

These cards which measure approximately 4" by 5" feature members of the 2003 Detroit Tigers, who came real close to establishing modern records for most losses in a season. These cards are black and white with the player's name and Detroit Tigers in the white border on the bottom. Since these cards are unnumberedm, we have sequenced them in alphabetical order. This list is incomplete and any additions are appreciated.

	MINT	NRMT
COMPLETE SET	10.00	4.50
1 Nate Cornejo	.50	.23
2 Kirk Gibson CO	1.50	.70
3 Shane Halter	.50	.23
4 Bobby Higginson	.75	.35
5 Brandon Inge	.50	.23
6 Mick Kelleher CO	.50	.23
7 Mike Maroth	.50	.23
8 Craig Monroe	.75	.35
9 Eric Munson	.75	.35
10 Lance Parrish CO	.75	.35
11 Carlos Pena	.75	.35
12 Matt Roney	.50	.23
13 Juan Samuel CO	.50	.23
14 Ramon Santiago	.50	.23
15 Andres Torres	.50	.23
16 Alan Trammell MG	1.50	.70
17 Matt Walbeck	.50	.23
18 Jamie Walker	.50	.23

2003 Timeless Treasures

This 100 card standard-size set was released in July, 2003. These cards were issued in four card tins with an $100 SRP which came one group of cards to a tin and 15 tins to a case. Please note that these cards are sequenced in alphabetical order by the player's first name.

	Nm-Mt	Ex-Mt
STATED PRINT RUN 900 SERIAL #'d SETS		
PRODUCED BY DONRUSS/PLAYOFF		
1 Adam Dunn	4.00	1.20
2 Al Kaline	6.00	1.80
3 Alan Trammell	4.00	1.20
4 Albert Pujols	12.00	3.60
5 Alex Rodriguez	10.00	3.00
6 Alfonso Soriano	4.00	1.20
7 Andre Dawson	4.00	1.20
8 Andruw Jones	4.00	1.20
9 Austin Kearns	4.00	1.20
10 Babe Ruth	15.00	4.50
11 Barry Bonds	15.00	4.50
12 Barry Larkin	6.00	1.80
13 Barry Zito	4.00	1.20
14 Bernie Williams	4.00	1.20
15 Bo Jackson	6.00	1.80
16 Brooks Robinson	6.00	1.80
17 Cal Ripken	20.00	6.00
18 Carlton Fisk	4.00	1.20
19 Chipper Jones	6.00	1.80
20 Curt Schilling	4.00	1.20
21 Dale Murphy	6.00	1.80
22 Derek Jeter	15.00	4.50
23 Don Mattingly	15.00	4.50
24 Duke Snider	4.00	1.20
25 Eddie Mathews	6.00	1.80
26 Frank Robinson	4.00	1.20
27 Frank Thomas	6.00	1.80
28 Garret Anderson	4.00	1.20
29 Gary Carter	4.00	1.20
30 George Brett	15.00	4.50
31 Greg Maddux	10.00	3.00
32 Harmon Killebrew	6.00	1.80
33 Hideki Matsui RC	20.00	6.00
34 Hideo Nomo	6.00	1.80
35 Ichiro Suzuki	10.00	3.00
36 Ivan Rodriguez	6.00	1.80
37 Jackie Robinson	8.00	2.40
38 Jason Giambi	6.00	1.80
39 Jeff Bagwell	4.00	1.20
40 Jim Edmonds	4.00	1.20
41 Jim Palmer	4.00	1.20
42 Jim Thome	6.00	1.80
43 Joe Morgan	4.00	1.20
44 Jorge Posada	4.00	1.20
45 Jose Contreras RC	10.00	3.00
46 Juan Gonzalez	6.00	1.80
47 Kazuhisa Ishii	4.00	1.20
48 Ken Griffey Jr.	10.00	3.00
49 Kerry Wood	6.00	1.80
50 Kirby Puckett	6.00	1.80
51 Lance Berkman	4.00	1.20
52 Larry Walker	4.00	1.20
53 Lou Brock	4.00	1.20
54 Lou Gehrig	10.00	3.00
55 Magglio Ordonez	4.00	1.20
56 Mark Prior	12.00	3.60
57 Miguel Tejada	4.00	1.20
58 Mike Mussina	6.00	1.80
59 Mike Piazza	10.00	3.00
60 Mike Schmidt	12.00	3.60
61 Nolan Ryan	15.00	4.50
62 Nomar Garciaparra	10.00	3.00
63 Ozzie Smith	10.00	3.00
64 Pat Burrell	4.00	1.20
65 Pedro Martinez	6.00	1.80
66 Pee Wee Reese	4.00	1.20
67 Phil Rizzuto	4.00	1.20
68 Rafael Palmeiro	4.00	1.20
69 Randy Johnson	6.00	1.80
70 Reggie Jackson	4.00	1.20
71 Richie Ashburn	4.00	1.20
72 Rickey Henderson	6.00	1.80
73 Roberto Alomar	6.00	1.80
74 Roberto Clemente	12.00	3.60
75 Robin Yount	10.00	3.00
76 Rod Carew	4.00	1.20
77 Roger Clemens	12.00	3.60
78 Rogers Hornsby	6.00	1.80
79 Roy Oswalt	4.00	1.20
80 Ryan Klesko	4.00	1.20
81 Ryne Sandberg	12.00	3.60
82 Sammy Sosa	10.00	3.00
83 Scott Rolen	4.00	1.20
84 Shawn Green	4.00	1.20
85 Stan Musial	10.00	3.00
86 Steve Carlton	4.00	1.20
87 Thurman Munson	8.00	2.40
88 Todd Helton	4.00	1.20
89 Tom Glavine	4.00	1.20
90 Tom Seaver	4.00	1.20
91 Tony Gwynn	8.00	2.40
92 Tony Perez	4.00	1.20
93 Torii Hunter	4.00	1.20
94 Troy Glaus	4.00	1.20
95 Ty Cobb	10.00	3.00
96 Vernon Wells	4.00	1.20
97 Vladimir Guerrero	6.00	1.80
98 Warren Spahn	4.00	1.20
99 Willie McCovey	4.00	1.20
100 Yogi Berra	6.00	1.80

2003 Timeless Treasures Gold

Nm-Mt Ex-Mt
RANDOM INSERTS IN PACKS
STATED PRINT RUN 10 SERIAL #'d SETS
NO PRICING DUE TO SCARCITY

2003 Timeless Treasures Platinum

Nm-Mt Ex-Mt
RANDOM INSERTS IN PACKS
STATED PRINT RUN 1 SERIAL #'d SETS
NO PRICING DUE TO SCARCITY

2003 Timeless Treasures Silver

	Nm-Mt	Ex-Mt
*ACTIVE STARS: 1.5X TO 4X BASIC		
*RETIRED POST-WAR STARS: 2X TO 5X		
*RETIRED PRE-WAR STARS: 1.25X TO 3X		
*ROOKIES: 1.25X TO 3X BASIC		
RANDOM INSERTS IN PACKS		
STATED PRINT RUN 50 SERIAL #'d SETS		
33 Hideki Matsui	60.00	18.00

2003 Timeless Treasures Award

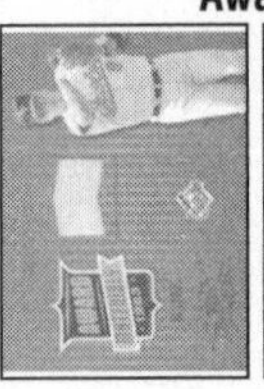

	Nm-Mt	Ex-Mt
RANDOM INSERTS IN PACKS		
PRINT RUNS B/WN 50-100 COPIES PER CARD		
1 Ivan Rodriguez Bat/100	20.00	6.00
2 Mike Schmidt Bat-Jsy/50	150.00	45.00
3 Roberto Clemente Bat/50	120.00	36.00
4 Roger Clemens Jsy/50	60.00	18.00
5 Randy Johnson Jsy/100	20.00	6.00
6 Pedro Martinez Jsy/100	20.00	6.00
7 Ivan Rodriguez Chest/100	20.00	6.00
8 Jeff Bagwell Pants/100	20.00	6.00
9 Frank Thomas Jsy/100	20.00	6.00
10 Cal Ripken Bat/75	100.00	30.00
11 Tom Seaver Jsy/50	40.00	12.00

2003 Timeless Treasures Award Autographs

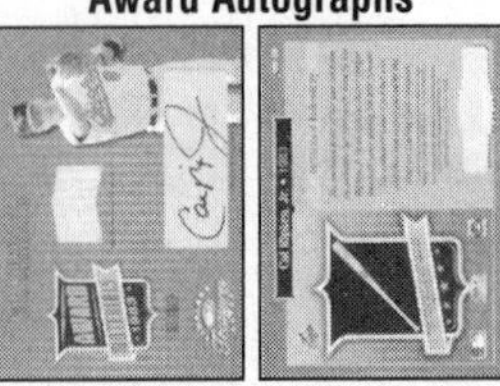

Nm-Mt Ex-Mt
RANDOM INSERTS IN PACKS
PRINT RUNS B/WN 5-15 COPIES PER CARD
NO PRICING DUE TO SCARCITY
2 Mike Schmidt Bat-Jsy/15
4 Roger Clemens Jsy/5
5 Randy Johnson Jsy/5
6 Pedro Martinez Jsy/5
8 Jeff Bagwell Pants/5
9 Frank Thomas Jsy/5
10 Cal Ripken Bat/15
11 Tom Seaver Jsy/10

2003 Timeless Treasures Award MLB Logos

Nm-Mt Ex-Mt
RANDOM INSERTS IN PACKS
STATED PRINT RUN 1 SERIAL #'d SET
NO PRICING DUE TO SCARCITY
5 Randy Johnson
6 Pedro Martinez

2003 Timeless Treasures Award Prime

	Nm-Mt	Ex-Mt
RANDOM INSERTS IN PACKS		
PRINT RUNS B/WN 15-50 COPIES PER CARD		
NO PRICING ON QTY OF 30 OR LESS.		
2 Mike Schmidt Bat-Jsy/25		
4 Roger Clemens Jsy/30		
5 Randy Johnson Jsy/30		
6 Pedro Martinez Jsy/50	60.00	18.00
9 Frank Thomas Jsy/50	60.00	18.00
11 Tom Seaver Jsy/15		

2003 Timeless Treasures Award Prime Autographs

Nm-Mt Ex-Mt
RANDOM INSERTS IN PACKS
STATED PRINT RUN 1 SERIAL #'d SET
NO PRICING DUE TO SCARCITY
2 Mike Schmidt Bat-Jsy
4 Roger Clemens Jsy
5 Randy Johnson Jsy
6 Pedro Martinez Jsy
9 Frank Thomas Jsy
11 Tom Seaver Jsy

2003 Timeless Treasures Classic Combos

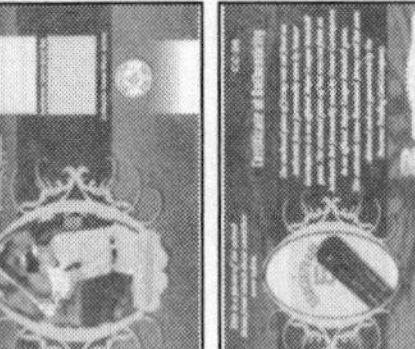

	Nm-Mt	Ex-Mt
RANDOM INSERTS IN PACKS		
STATED PRINT RUN 100 SERIAL #'d SETS		
1 Jason Giambi Hat-Jsy	25.00	7.50
2 Adrian Beltre Hat-Shoes	20.00	6.00
3 Alex Rodriguez Bat-Jsy	40.00	12.00
4 Alfonso Soriano Bat-Jsy	25.00	7.50
5 Andruw Jones Fld Glv-Jsy	20.00	6.00
6 Andre Dawson ST Bat-Jsy	20.00	6.00
7 Barry Larkin Bat-Jsy	25.00	7.50
8 Barry Zito Fld Glv-Jsy	25.00	7.50
9 Cal Ripken Bat-Jsy	100.00	30.00
10 Chipper Jones Bat-Jsy	25.00	7.50
11 Don Mattingly Bat-Jsy	80.00	24.00
12 Eric Chavez Bat-Jsy	20.00	6.00
13 Frank Thomas Bat-Jsy	25.00	7.50
14 Greg Maddux Bat-Jsy	40.00	12.00
15 Ivan Rodriguez Fld Glv-Jsy	25.00	7.50
16 Jeff Bagwell Bat-Jsy	25.00	7.50
17 Jim Thome Bat-Jsy	25.00	7.50
18 Juan Gonzalez Bat-Jsy	25.00	7.50
19 Kazuhisa Ishii Bat-Jsy	20.00	6.00
20 Kerry Wood Jsy-Shoes	25.00	7.50
21 Lance Berkman Fld Glv-Jsy	20.00	6.00
22 Magglio Ordonez Bat-Jsy	20.00	6.00
23 Manny Ramirez Bat-Jsy	20.00	6.00
24 Miguel Tejada Hat-Jsy	20.00	6.00
25 Mike Piazza Bat-Jsy	40.00	12.00
26 Nomar Garciaparra Bat-Jsy	50.00	15.00
27 Pedro Martinez Bat-Jsy	25.00	7.50
28 Randy Johnson Bat-Jsy	25.00	7.50
29 Rickey Henderson Bat-Jsy	25.00	7.50
30 Ryne Sandberg Bat-Jsy	80.00	24.00
31 Sammy Sosa Bat-Jsy		
32 Shawn Green Bat-Jsy	20.00	6.00
33 Todd Helton Bat-Jsy	25.00	7.50
34 Tony Gwynn Bat-Jsy	50.00	15.00
35 Vladimir Guerrero Bat-Jsy	25.00	7.50

2003 Timeless Treasures Classic Combos Autographs

Nm-Mt Ex-Mt
RANDOM INSERTS IN PACKS

PRINT RUNS B/WN 5-50 COPIES PER CARD
NO PRICING ON QTY OF 25 OR LESS.
3 Alex Rodriguez Bat-Jsy/15
4 Alfonso Soriano Bat-Jsy/5
5 Andruw Jones Fld Glv-Jsy/10
6 Andre Dawson Bat-ST Jsy/50. 60.00 18.00
7 Barry Larkin Bat-Jsy/25
8 Barry Zito Fld Glv-Jsy/25
9 Cal Ripken Bat-Jsy/25
10 Chipper Jones Bat-Jsy/5
11 Don Mattingly Bat-Jsy/25
12 Eric Chavez Bat-Jsy/15
13 Frank Thomas Bat-Jsy/5
14 Greg Maddux Bat-Jsy/25
17 Jim Thome Bat-Jsy/10
19 Kazuhisa Ishii Bat-Jsy/25
20 Kerry Wood Jsy-Shoes/15
21 Lance Berkman Fld Glv-Jsy/15
22 Magglio Ordonez Bat-Jsy/25
24 Miguel Tejada Hat-Jsy/15
27 Pedro Martinez Bat-Jsy/10
28 Randy Johnson Bat-Jsy/10
29 Rickey Henderson Bat-Jsy/10
30 Ryne Sandberg Bat-Jsy/50. 200.00 60.00
32 Shawn Green Bat-Jsy/25
33 Todd Helton Bat-Jsy/15
34 Tony Gwynn Bat-Jsy/25
35 Vladimir Guerrero Bat-Jsy/50 100.00 30.00

2003 Timeless Treasures Classic Prime Combos

Nm-Mt Ex-Mt
RANDOM INSERTS IN PACKS
STATED PRINT RUN 25 SERIAL #'d SETS
NO PRICING DUE TO SCARCITY

2003 Timeless Treasures Classic Prime Combos Autographs

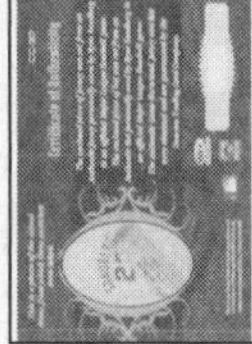

Nm-Mt Ex-Mt
RANDOM INSERTS IN PACKS
STATED PRINT RUN 1 SERIAL #'d SET
NO PRICING DUE TO SCARCITY
3 Alex Rodriguez Bat-Jsy
4 Alfonso Soriano Bat-Jsy
5 Andruw Jones Fld Glv-Jsy
6 Andre Dawson Bat-ST Jsy
7 Barry Larkin Bat-Jsy
8 Barry Zito Hat-Jsy
9 Cal Ripken Bat-Jsy
10 Chipper Jones Bat-Jsy
11 Don Mattingly Bat-Jsy
12 Eric Chavez Bat-Jsy
13 Frank Thomas Bat-Jsy
14 Greg Maddux Bat-Jsy
17 Jim Thome Bat-Jsy
19 Kazuhisa Ishii Bat-Jsy
20 Kerry Wood Jsy-Shoes
21 Lance Berkman Fld Glv-Jsy
22 Magglio Ordonez Bat-Jsy
24 Miguel Tejada Hat-Jsy
27 Pedro Martinez Bat-Jsy
28 Randy Johnson Bat-Jsy
29 Rickey Henderson Bat-Jsy
30 Ryne Sandberg Bat-Jsy
32 Shawn Green Bat-Jsy
33 Todd Helton Bat-Jsy
34 Tony Gwynn Bat-Jsy
35 Vladimir Guerrero Bat-Jsy

2003 Timeless Treasures Game Day

Nm-Mt Ex-Mt
RANDOM INSERTS IN PACKS
BAT-HAT-JSY PRINT RUN 100 #'d SETS
BALL PRINT RUN 20 SERIAL #'d SETS
NO BALL PRICING DUE TO SCARCITY
1 Tony Gwynn Bat 40.00 12.00
2 Magglio Ordonez Hat 15.00 4.50
3 George Brett Bat 60.00 18.00
4 Rickey Henderson Jsy 20.00 6.00
5 Billy Williams Bat 15.00 4.50
6 Frank Thomas Bat 20.00 6.00
7 Tony Gwynn Jsy 40.00 12.00
8 Billy Williams Ball/20
9 Frank Robinson Ball/20
10 Ryne Sandberg Bat 60.00 18.00
11 Miguel Tejada Jsy 15.00 4.50

2003 Timeless Treasures Game Day Autographs

Nm-Mt Ex-Mt
RANDOM INSERTS IN PACKS
PRINT RUNS B/WN 1-25 COPIES PER CARD
NO PRICING DUE TO SCARCITY
1 Tony Gwynn Bat/10
2 Magglio Ordonez Hat/10
3 George Brett Bat/15
4 Rickey Henderson Jsy/5
5 Billy Williams Bat/25

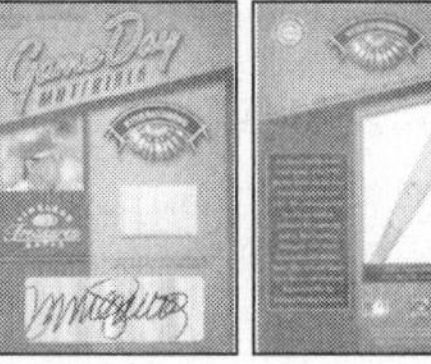

6 Frank Thomas Bat/1
7 Tony Gwynn Jsy/10
8 Billy Williams Ball/5
9 Frank Robinson Ball/5
10 Ryne Sandberg Bat/25
11 Miguel Tejada Jsy/25

2003 Timeless Treasures Game Day Prime

Nm-Mt Ex-Mt
RANDOM INSERTS IN PACKS
PRINT RUNS B/WN 5-75 COPIES PER CARD
NO PRICING ON QTY OF 25 OR LESS.
2 Magglio Ordonez Hat/5
4 Rickey Henderson Jsy/75 50.00 15.00
7 Tony Gwynn Jsy/75 80.00 24.00
11 Miguel Tejada Jsy/75 30.00 9.00

2003 Timeless Treasures Game Day Prime Autographs

Nm-Mt Ex-Mt
RANDOM INSERTS IN PACKS
STATED PRINT RUN 1 SERIAL #'d SET
NO PRICING DUE TO SCARCITY
2 Magglio Ordonez Hat
4 Rickey Henderson Jsy
7 Tony Gwynn Jsy
11 Miguel Tejada Jsy

2003 Timeless Treasures HOF Combos

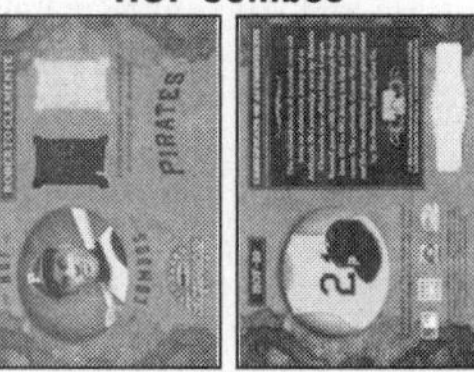

Nm-Mt Ex-Mt
RANDOM INSERTS IN PACKS
PRINT RUNS B/WN 25-100 COPIES PER CARD
NO PRICING ON QTY 25 OR LESS
1 Al Kaline Bat-Jsy/50 80.00 24.00
2 Babe Ruth Bat-Jsy/25
3 Eddie Mathews Bat-Jsy/50 60.00 18.00
4 Kirby Puckett Bat-Hat/75 50.00 15.00
5 Lou Gehrig Bat-Jsy/25
6 Mike Schmidt Bat-Jsy/100 80.00 24.00
7 Nolan Ryan Fld Glv-Jsy/50 150.00 45.00
8 Phil Rizzuto Bat-Jsy/50 60.00 18.00
9 Reggie Jackson Hat-Jsy/25
10 Roberto Clemente Hat-Jsy/25
11 Rod Carew Bat-Jsy/100 50.00 15.00
12 Stan Musial Bat-Jsy/25
13 Ty Cobb Bat-Pants/25
14 George Brett Bat-Hat/50 150.00 45.00
15 Carlton Fisk Bat-Jsy/100 50.00 15.00

2003 Timeless Treasures HOF Combos Autographs

Nm-Mt Ex-Mt
RANDOM INSERTS IN PACKS
PRINT RUNS B/WN 1-25 COPIES PER CARD
NO PRICING DUE TO SCARCITY
1 Al Kaline Bat-Jsy/25
4 Kirby Puckett Bat-Hat/25
6 Mike Schmidt Bat-Jsy/15
7 Nolan Ryan Fld Glv-Jsy/25
8 Phil Rizzuto Bat-Jsy/25
9 Reggie Jackson Hat-Jsy/1
11 Rod Carew Bat-Jsy/10
12 Stan Musial Bat-Jsy/25
14 George Brett Bat-Hat/15
15 Carlton Fisk Bat-Jsy/25

2003 Timeless Treasures HOF Cuts

Nm-Mt Ex-Mt
RANDOM INSERTS IN PACKS
STATED PRINT RUN 1 SERIAL #'d SET
NO PRICING DUE TO SCARCITY
1 Ty Cobb
2 Babe Ruth
3 Jackie Robinson
4 Pee Wee Reese

2003 Timeless Treasures HOF Induction Year Combos

Nm-Mt Ex-Mt
RANDOM INSERTS IN PACKS
STATED PRINT RUN 25 SERIAL #'d SETS
NO PRICING DUE TO SCARCITY

1 Ty Cobb Bat
Babe Ruth Bat
2 Mel Ott Bat
Jimmie Foxx Bat
3 Yogi Berra Jsy
Early Wynn Jsy
4 Roberto Clemente Jsy
Warren Spahn Jsy
5 Al Kaline Jsy
Duke Snider Jsy
6 Lou Brock Jsy
Enos Slaughter Jsy
7 Jim Palmer Jsy
Joe Morgan Jsy
8 Steve Carlton Jsy
Phil Rizzuto Jsy
9 Mike Schmidt Bat
Richie Ashburn Bat
10 George Brett Jsy
Robin Yount Jsy

2003 Timeless Treasures HOF Induction Year Combos Autographs

Nm-Mt Ex-Mt
RANDOM INSERTS IN PACKS
STATED PRINT RUN 5 SERIAL #'d SETS
NO PRICING DUE TO SCARCITY
5 Al Kaline Jsy
Duke Snider Jsy
7 Jim Palmer Jsy
Joe Morgan Jsy
8 Steve Carlton Jsy
Phil Rizzuto Jsy
10 George Brett Jsy
Robin Yount Jsy

2003 Timeless Treasures HOF Letters

Nm-Mt Ex-Mt
RANDOM INSERTS IN PACKS
PRINT RUNS B/WN 5-25 COPIES PER CARD
NO PRICING DUE TO SCARCITY
28 Brooks Robinson/5
32 Joe Morgan/5
33 Lou Brock/10
35 Mike Schmidt/25
36 Nolan Ryan Angels/15
37 Nolan Ryan Astros/15
38 Nolan Ryan Rangers/15
41 Reggie Jackson/15
44 Rod Carew/20
46 Tom Seaver/25
47 Steve Carlton/15

2003 Timeless Treasures HOF Letters Autographs

Nm-Mt Ex-Mt
RANDOM INSERTS IN PACKS
STATED PRINT RUN 1 SERIAL #'d SET
NO PRICING DUE TO SCARCITY
28 Brooks Robinson
32 Joe Morgan
33 Lou Brock
35 Mike Schmidt
36 Nolan Ryan Angels
37 Nolan Ryan Astros
38 Nolan Ryan Rangers
41 Reggie Jackson
44 Rod Carew
46 Tom Seaver
47 Steve Carlton

2003 Timeless Treasures HOF Logos

Nm-Mt Ex-Mt
RANDOM INSERTS IN PACKS
PRINT RUNS B/WN 1-35 COPIES PER CARD
NO PRICING ON QTY OF 25 OR LESS.
25 Al Kaline/15
27 Bobby Doerr/15
28 Brooks Robinson/10
29 Eddie Mathews/35 80.00 24.00
32 Joe Morgan/5
33 Lou Brock/10
35 Mike Schmidt/25
36 Nolan Ryan Angels/35 150.00 45.00
37 Nolan Ryan Astros/35 150.00 45.00
38 Nolan Ryan Rangers/25
39 Phil Rizzuto/5
41 Reggie Jackson/15
42 Roberto Clemente/15
43 Robin Yount/35 100.00 30.00
44 Rod Carew/35 60.00 18.00
45 Stan Musial/1
49 Pee Wee Reese/15
50 Jackie Robinson/5

2003 Timeless Treasures HOF Logos Autographs

Nm-Mt Ex-Mt
RANDOM INSERTS IN PACKS
STATED PRINT RUN 1 SERIAL #'d SET
NO PRICING DUE TO SCARCITY
25 Al Kaline
27 Bobby Doerr
28 Brooks Robinson
32 Joe Morgan
33 Lou Brock
35 Mike Schmidt
36 Nolan Ryan Angels
37 Nolan Ryan Astros
38 Nolan Ryan Rangers
39 Phil Rizzuto
40 Reggie Jackson Yanks
41 Reggie Jackson A's
43 Robin Yount
44 Rod Carew
45 Stan Musial

2003 Timeless Treasures HOF Materials

Nm-Mt Ex-Mt
RANDOM INSERTS IN PACKS
PRINT RUNS B/WN 25-100 COPIES PER CARD
NO PRICING ON QTY OF 25 OR LESS.
1 Al Kaline Bat/100 40.00 12.00
2 Babe Ruth Bat/75 250.00 75.00
3 Carlton Fisk Bat/100 25.00 7.50
4 Eddie Mathews Bat/100 40.00 12.00
5 Gary Carter Bat/100 25.00 7.50
6 George Brett Bat/100 60.00 18.00
7 Harmon Killebrew Bat/100 40.00 12.00
8 Joe Morgan Bat/100 20.00 6.00
9 Kirby Puckett Bat/100 25.00 7.50
10 Lou Gehrig Bat/100 150.00 45.00
11 Luis Aparicio Bat/100 20.00 6.00
12 Mike Schmidt Bat/100 50.00 15.00
13 Ozzie Smith Bat/100 40.00 12.00
14 Phil Rizzuto Bat/100 25.00 7.50
15 Reggie Jackson Bat/100 25.00 7.50
16 Richie Ashburn Bat/100 25.00 7.50
17 Roberto Clemente Bat/100 . 100.00 30.00
18 Robin Yount Bat/100 40.00 12.00
19 Rod Carew Bat/100 25.00 7.50
20 Rogers Hornsby Bat/100 60.00 18.00
21 Stan Musial Bat/100 50.00 15.00
22 Ty Cobb Bat/100 150.00 45.00
23 Willie McCovey Bat/100 25.00 7.50
24 Yogi Berra Bat/100 25.00 7.50
25 Al Kaline Jsy/100 40.00 12.00
26 Babe Ruth Jsy/50 450.00 135.00
27 Bobby Doerr Jsy/100 20.00 6.00
28 Brooks Robinson Jsy/100 25.00 7.50
29 Eddie Mathews Jsy/100 40.00 12.00
30 Harmon Killebrew Jsy/100 40.00 12.00
31 Ty Cobb Pants/50 150.00 45.00
32 Joe Morgan Jsy/100 20.00 6.00
33 Lou Brock Jsy/100 25.00 7.50
34 Lou Gehrig Jsy/50 300.00 90.00
35 Mike Schmidt Jsy/100 50.00 15.00
36 Nolan Ryan Angels Jsy/100 80.00 24.00
37 Nolan Ryan Astros Jsy/100 60.00 18.00
38 Nolan Ryan Rangers Jsy/100 80.00 24.00
39 Phil Rizzuto Jsy/100 25.00 7.50
40 Reggie Jackson Yanks Jsy/25
41 Reggie Jackson A's Jsy/100. 25.00 7.50
42 Roberto Clemente Jsy/50 150.00 45.00
43 Robin Yount Jsy/100 40.00 12.00
44 Rod Carew Jsy/100 25.00 7.50
45 Stan Musial Jsy/100 60.00 18.00
46 Tom Seaver Jsy/100 25.00 7.50
47 Steve Carlton Jsy/100 20.00 6.00
48 Carlton Fisk Jsy/100 25.00 7.50
49 Pee Wee Reese Jsy/100 25.00 7.50
50 Jackie Robinson Jsy/50 100.00 30.00

2003 Timeless Treasures HOF Materials Autographs

Nm-Mt Ex-Mt
RANDOM INSERTS IN PACKS
PRINT RUNS B/WN 5-50 COPIES PER CARD
NO PRICING ON QTY OF 25 OR LESS.
1 Al Kaline Bat/15
3 Carlton Fisk Bat/15
5 Gary Carter Bat/25
6 George Brett Bat/25
7 Harmon Killebrew Bat/25
8 Joe Morgan Bat/15
9 Kirby Puckett Bat/25
11 Luis Aparicio Bat/25
12 Mike Schmidt Bat/15
13 Ozzie Smith Bat/10
14 Phil Rizzuto Bat/15
15 Reggie Jackson Bat/10
18 Robin Yount Bat/15
19 Rod Carew Bat/10
21 Stan Musial Bat/25
23 Willie McCovey Bat/25
24 Yogi Berra Bat/15
25 Al Kaline Jsy/25
27 Bobby Doerr Jsy/25
28 Brooks Robinson Jsy/25
30 Harmon Killebrew Jsy/50 100.00 30.00
32 Joe Morgan Jsy/25
33 Lou Brock Jsy/50 80.00 24.00
35 Mike Schmidt Jsy/25
36 Nolan Ryan Angels Jsy/25
37 Nolan Ryan Astros Jsy/25
38 Nolan Ryan Rangers Jsy/25
39 Phil Rizzuto Jsy/25
40 Reggie Jackson Yanks Jsy/5
41 Reggie Jackson A's Jsy/15
43 Robin Yount Jsy/25
44 Rod Carew Jsy/15
45 Stan Musial Jsy/50 150.00 45.00
46 Tom Seaver Jsy/25
47 Steve Carlton Jsy/25
48 Carlton Fisk Jsy/25

2003 Timeless Treasures HOF Numbers

Nm-Mt Ex-Mt
RANDOM INSERTS IN PACKS
PRINT RUNS B/WN 5-50 COPIES PER CARD
NO PRICING ON QTY OF 30 OR LESS.
26 Babe Ruth/5
28 Brooks Robinson/5
29 Eddie Mathews/35 80.00 24.00
33 Lou Brock/25
34 Lou Gehrig/5
35 Mike Schmidt/50 100.00 30.00
36 Nolan Ryan Angels/35 200.00 60.00
37 Nolan Ryan Rangers/25
38 Nolan Ryan Rangers/5
39 Phil Rizzuto/10
41 Reggie Jackson/25
42 Roberto Clemente/15
43 Robin Yount/35 100.00 30.00
44 Rod Carew/25
45 Stan Musial/10
46 Tom Seaver/35 60.00 18.00
47 Steve Carlton/40 50.00 15.00
48 Carlton Fisk/35 60.00 18.00
49 Pee Wee Reese/10
50 Jackie Robinson/5

2003 Timeless Treasures HOF Numbers Autographs

Nm-Mt Ex-Mt
RANDOM INSERTS IN PACKS
STATED PRINT RUN 1 SERIAL #'d SET
NO PRICING DUE TO SCARCITY
25 Al Kaline
28 Brooks Robinson
32 Joe Morgan
33 Lou Brock
35 Mike Schmidt
36 Nolan Ryan Angels
37 Nolan Ryan Astros
38 Nolan Ryan Rangers
39 Phil Rizzuto
41 Reggie Jackson
43 Robin Yount
44 Rod Carew

45 Stan Musial
46 Tom Seaver
47 Steve Carlton
48 Carlton Fisk

2003 Timeless Treasures HOF Prime Combos

Nm-Mt Ex-Mt
RANDOM INSERTS IN PACKS
PRINT RUNS B/WN 5-25 COPIES PER CARD
NO PRICING DUE TO SCARCITY
1 Al Kaline Bat-Jsy/5
2 Babe Ruth Bat-Jsy/5
3 Eddie Mathews Bat-Jsy/25
4 Kirby Puckett Bat-Hat/15
6 Mike Schmidt Bat-Jsy/25
7 Nolan Ryan Fld Glv-Jsy/15
8 Phil Rizzuto Bat-Jsy/5
10 Roberto Clemente Hat-Jsy/5
11 Rod Carew Bat-Jsy/5
14 George Brett Bat-Hat/10
15 Carlton Fisk Bat-Jsy/5

2003 Timeless Treasures HOF Prime Combos Autographs

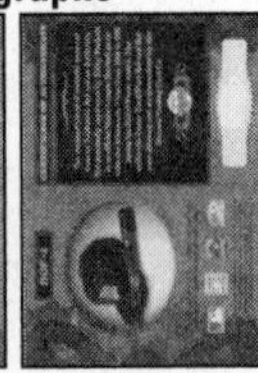

Nm-Mt Ex-Mt
RANDOM INSERTS IN PACKS
STATED PRINT RUN 1 SERIAL #'d SET
NO PRICING DUE TO SCARCITY
1 Al Kaline Bat-Jsy
4 Kirby Puckett Bat-Hat
6 Mike Schmidt Bat-Jsy
7 Nolan Ryan Fld Glv-Jsy
8 Phil Rizzuto Bat-Jsy
9 Reggie Jackson Hat-Jsy
11 Rod Carew Bat-Jsy
14 George Brett Bat-Hat
15 Carlton Fisk Bat-Jsy

2003 Timeless Treasures Home Run

Nm-Mt Ex-Mt
RANDOM INSERTS IN PACKS
BAT-JSY PRINT RUN 100 SERIAL #'d SETS
BALL PRINT RUN 20 SERIAL #'d SETS
NO BALL PRICING DUE TO SCARCITY
1 Harmon Killebrew HR 570 Bat 40.00 12.00
2 Harmon Killebrew HR 565 Bat 40.00 12.00
3 Jose Canseco HR 311 Bat 40.00 12.00
4 Magglio Ordonez 00 HR 17 Bat 15.00 4.50
5 Rafael Palmeiro HR 425 Bat 20.00 6.00
6 Rafael Palmeiro HR 440 Bat 20.00 6.00
7 Rafael Palmeiro HR 448 Jsy 20.00 6.00
8 Alex Rodriguez 00 HR 36 Bat 25.00 7.50
9 Alex Rodriguez 00 HR 37 Bat 25.00 7.50
10 Alex Rodriguez 00 HR 33 Bat 25.00 7.50
11 Alex Rodriguez 98 HR 23 Ball/20
12 Adam Dunn 00 HR 9 Jsy 15.00 4.50

2003 Timeless Treasures Home Run Autographs

Nm-Mt Ex-Mt
RANDOM INSERTS IN PACKS
PRINT RUNS B/WN 1-25 COPIES PER CARD
NO PRICING DUE TO SCARCITY
1 Harmon Killebrew HR 570 Bat/25
2 Harmon Killebrew HR 565 Bat/25
3 Jose Canseco HR 311 Bat/25
4 Magglio Ordonez 00 HR 17 Bat/15
5 Rafael Palmeiro HR 425 Bat/1
6 Rafael Palmeiro HR 440 Bat/1
7 Rafael Palmeiro HR 448 Jsy/1
8 Alex Rodriguez 00 HR 36 Bat/15
9 Alex Rodriguez 00 HR 37 Bat/15
10 Alex Rodriguez 00 HR 33 Bat/15
11 Alex Rodriguez 98 HR 23 Ball/5
12 Adam Dunn 00 HR 9 Jsy/25

2003 Timeless Treasures Home Run MLB Logos

Nm-Mt Ex-Mt
RANDOM INSERTS IN PACKS
STATED PRINT RUN 1 SERIAL #'d SET
NO PRICING DUE TO SCARCITY
7 Rafael Palmeiro HR 448
12 Adam Dunn 00 HR 9

2003 Timeless Treasures Material Ink

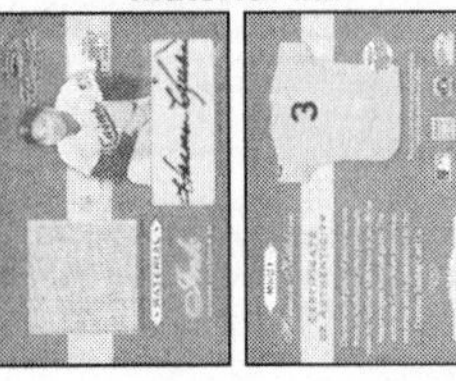

Nm-Mt Ex-Mt
COMMON CARD p/r 75-100 40.00 12.00
COMMON CARD p/r 50 60.00 18.00
RANDOM INSERTS IN PACKS
PRINT RUNS B/WN 25-100 COPIES PER CARD
NO PRICING ON QTY OF 25 OR LESS.
1 Adam Dunn/50 80.00 24.00
2 Alan Trammell/100 60.00 18.00
3 Alex Rodriguez White Jsy/25
4 Alex Rodriguez Blue Jsy/25
5 Andre Dawson/100 40.00 12.00
6 Barry Zito/50 80.00 24.00
7 Bo Jackson/100 100.00 30.00
8 Bob Feller/25
9 Bobby Doerr/50 60.00 18.00
10 Brooks Robinson/50
11 Cal Ripken No Sleeve/50 300.00 90.00
12 Cal Ripken Black Sleeve/50 300.00 90.00
13 Cal Ripken Throwing/25
14 Dale Murphy/50 80.00 24.00
15 Dave Parker/75 40.00 12.00
16 David Cone/100 40.00 12.00
17 Don Mattingly/100 150.00 45.00
18 Duke Snider/25
19 Edgar Martinez/50 80.00 24.00
20 Gary Carter/100 40.00 12.00
21 Harmon Killebrew/75 100.00 30.00
22 Jim Edmonds/25
23 Jim Thome/50 80.00 24.00
24 Joe Carter/100 40.00 12.00
25 Jose Canseco/50 80.00 24.00
26 Jose Vidro/100 40.00 12.00
27 Kazuhisa Ishii/100 40.00 12.00
28 Kerry Wood/50 80.00 24.00
29 Lance Berkman/50 60.00 18.00
30 Mark Mulder/25
31 Mark Prior/50
32 Mike Schmidt/50 150.00 45.00
33 Nick Johnson/100 40.00 12.00
34 Nolan Ryan Astros/25
35 Nolan Ryan Rangers/25
36 Nolan Ryan Angels/25
37 Paul LoDuca/100 40.00 12.00
38 Paul Molitor/50 80.00 24.00
39 Randy Johnson/25
40 Reggie Jackson/25
41 Roberto Alomar Mets/50 80.00 24.00
42 Roberto Alomar Indians/100 60.00 18.00
43 Robin Yount/50 150.00 45.00
44 Rod Carew/25
45 Roger Clemens Yanks/25
46 Roger Clemens Sox/25
47 Ryan Klesko/75 40.00 12.00
48 Ryne Sandberg/25
50 Shawn Green/25
51 Stan Musial/25
52 Steve Carlton Giants/100 60.00 18.00
53 Steve Carlton Sox/100 60.00 18.00
54 Todd Helton/50 80.00 24.00
55 Tom Seaver/50 80.00 24.00
56 Tony Gwynn/25
57 Torii Hunter/100 40.00 12.00
58 Vladimir Guerrero/100 60.00 18.00
59 Will Clark/50 120.00 36.00

2003 Timeless Treasures Milestone

Nm-Mt Ex-Mt
RANDOM INSERTS IN PACKS
JSY PRINT RUN 100 SERIAL #'d SETS
BALL PRINT RUN 24 SERIAL #'d SETS
NO BALL PRICING DUE TO SCARCITY
1 Cal Ripken Ball/24
2 Willie McCovey Ball/24
3 R.Henderson Padres Jsy/100 25.00 7.50
4 Gaylord Perry Jsy/100 20.00 6.00
5 R.Henderson A's Jsy/100 25.00 7.50

2003 Timeless Treasures Milestone Autographs

Nm-Mt Ex-Mt
RANDOM INSERTS IN PACKS
STATED PRINT RUN 1 SERIAL #'d SET
NO PRICING DUE TO SCARCITY
1 Cal Ripken Ball

2 Willie McCovey Ball
3 Rickey Henderson Padres Jsy
5 Rickey Henderson A's Jsy

2003 Timeless Treasures MLB Logo Ink

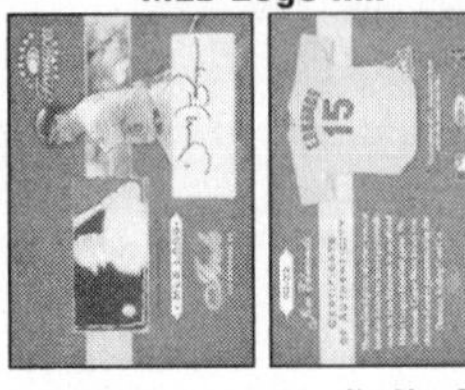

Nm-Mt Ex-Mt
RANDOM INSERTS IN PACKS
STATED PRINT RUN 1 SERIAL #'d SET
NO PRICING DUE TO SCARCITY
3 Alex Rodriguez White Jsy
4 Alex Rodriguez Blue Jsy
6 Barry Zito
13 Cal Ripken Throwing
19 Edgar Martinez
22 Jim Edmonds
23 Jim Thome
26 Jose Vidro
27 Kazuhisa Ishii
28 Kerry Wood
29 Lance Berkman
30 Mark Mulder
31 Mark Prior
33 Nick Johnson
37 Paul LoDuca
39 Randy Johnson
42 Roberto Alomar Indians
45 Roger Clemens Yanks
47 Ryan Klesko
50 Shawn Green
54 Todd Helton
57 Torii Hunter

2003 Timeless Treasures Past and Present

Nm-Mt Ex-Mt
RANDOM INSERTS IN PACKS
STATED PRINT RUN 100 SERIAL #'d SETS
1 Alex Rodriguez 40.00 12.00
2 Hideo Nomo 25.00 7.50
3 Jason Giambi 25.00 7.50
4 Juan Gonzalez 25.00 7.50
5 Mike Piazza 40.00 12.00
6 Pedro Martinez 25.00 7.50
7 Randy Johnson 25.00 7.50
8 Rickey Henderson 25.00 7.50
9 Roberto Alomar 25.00 7.50
10 Roger Clemens 40.00 12.00
11 Sammy Sosa 40.00 12.00

2003 Timeless Treasures Past and Present Autographs

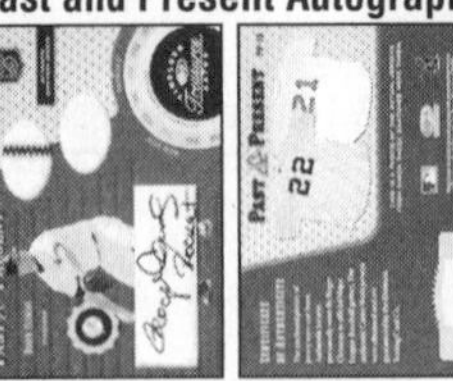

Nm-Mt Ex-Mt
RANDOM INSERTS IN PACKS
PRINT RUNS B/WN 5-25 COPIES PER CARD
NO PRICING DUE TO SCARCITY
1 Alex Rodriguez/25
6 Pedro Martinez/5
7 Randy Johnson/5
8 Rickey Henderson/10
9 Roberto Alomar/25
10 Roger Clemens/15

2003 Timeless Treasures Past and Present Letters

Nm-Mt Ex-Mt
RANDOM INSERTS IN PACKS
PRINT RUNS B/WN 25-75 COPIES PER CARD
NO PRICING ON QTY OF 25 OR LESS.
1 Alex Rodriguez/75 80.00 24.00
2 Hideo Nomo/25
4 Juan Gonzalez/50 60.00 18.00
6 Pedro Martinez/75 50.00 15.00
7 Randy Johnson/75 50.00 15.00
9 Roberto Alomar/25

2003 Timeless Treasures Past and Present Letters Autographs

Nm-Mt Ex-Mt
RANDOM INSERTS IN PACKS
STATED PRINT RUN 1 SERIAL #'d SET
NO PRICING DUE TO SCARCITY
1 Alex Rodriguez
7 Randy Johnson
9 Roberto Alomar

2003 Timeless Treasures Past and Present Logos

Nm-Mt Ex-Mt
RANDOM INSERTS IN PACKS
PRINT RUNS B/WN 5-75 COPIES PER CARD
NO PRICING ON QTY OF 25 OR LESS.
1 Alex Rodriguez/60 80.00 24.00
2 Hideo Nomo/25
3 Jason Giambi/75 50.00 15.00
4 Juan Gonzalez/25
5 Mike Piazza/50 80.00 24.00
7 Randy Johnson/5
8 Rickey Henderson/25
10 Roger Clemens/35 100.00 30.00
11 Sammy Sosa/25

2003 Timeless Treasures Past and Present Logos Autographs

Nm-Mt Ex-Mt
RANDOM INSERTS IN PACKS
STATED PRINT RUN 1 SERIAL #'d SET
NO PRICING DUE TO SCARCITY
1 Alex Rodriguez
7 Randy Johnson
8 Rickey Henderson
10 Roger Clemens

2003 Timeless Treasures Past and Present Numbers

Nm-Mt Ex-Mt
RANDOM INSERTS IN PACKS
PRINT RUNS B/WN 5-75 COPIES PER CARD
NO PRICING ON QTY OF 25 OR LESS.
1 Alex Rodriguez/35 100.00 30.00
2 Hideo Nomo/25
3 Jason Giambi/75 50.00 15.00
4 Juan Gonzalez/25
5 Mike Piazza/5
6 Pedro Martinez/50 60.00 18.00
7 Randy Johnson/50 60.00 18.00
8 Rickey Henderson /25
11 Sammy Sosa/25

2003 Timeless Treasures Past and Present Numbers Autographs

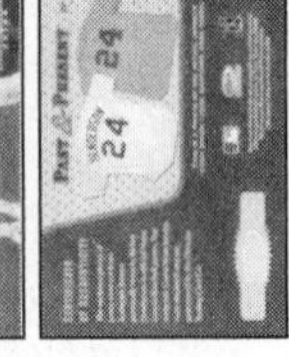

Nm-Mt Ex-Mt
RANDOM INSERTS IN PACKS
STATED PRINT RUN 1 SERIAL #'d SET
NO PRICING DUE TO SCARCITY
1 Alex Rodriguez
6 Pedro Martinez
7 Randy Johnson
8 Rickey Henderson

2003 Timeless Treasures Past and Present Patches

Nm-Mt Ex-Mt
RANDOM INSERTS IN PACKS
PRINT RUNS B/WN 5-20 COPIES PER CARD
NO PRICING DUE TO SCARCITY
1 Alex Rodriguez/10
5 Mike Piazza/15
6 Pedro Martinez/5
8 Rickey Henderson/5
9 Roberto Alomar/20

2003 Timeless Treasures Past and Present Patches Autographs

Nm-Mt Ex-Mt
RANDOM INSERTS IN PACKS
STATED PRINT RUN 1 SERIAL #'d SET
NO PRICING DUE TO SCARCITY
1 Alex Rodriguez
6 Pedro Martinez
8 Rickey Henderson
9 Roberto Alomar

2003 Timeless Treasures Post Season

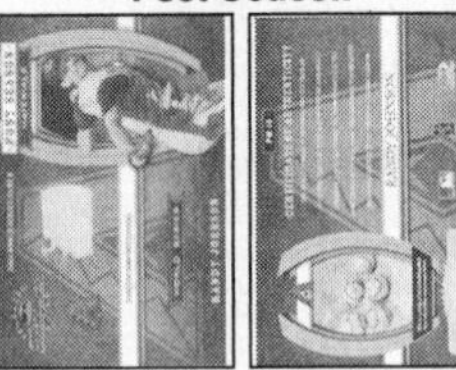

Nm-Mt Ex-Mt
RANDOM INSERTS IN PACKS
PRINT RUNS B/WN 25-100 COPIES PER CARD
NO PRICING ON QTY OF 25 OR LESS.
1 Ozzie Smith Jsy/100 40.00 12.00
2 Tom Glavine Jsy/50 40.00 12.00
3 Bernie Williams Bat/100 20.00 6.00
4 Roger Clemens Jsy/100 40.00 12.00
5 Babe Ruth Ball/25
6 Christy Mathewson Seat/100 50.00 15.00
7 Derek Jeter Ball/25
8 Alfonso Soriano Ball/25
9 Randy Johnson NLCS Ball/25
10 Ichiro Suzuki Ball/25
11 Curt Schilling Ball/25
12 Randy Johnson WS Ball/25

2003 Timeless Treasures Post Season Autographs

Nm-Mt Ex-Mt
RANDOM INSERTS IN PACKS
PRINT RUNS B/WN 5-15 COPIES PER CARD
NO PRICING DUE TO SCARCITY
1 Ozzie Smith Jsy/15
3 Bernie Williams Bat/5
4 Roger Clemens Jsy/10
8 Alfonso Soriano Ball/5
9 Randy Johnson NLCS Ball/5
12 Randy Johnson WS Ball/5

2003 Timeless Treasures Post Season Prime

Nm-Mt Ex-Mt
RANDOM INSERTS IN PACKS
PRINT RUNS B/WN 5-75 COPIES PER CARD
NO PRICING ON QTY OF 25 OR LESS.
1 Ozzie Smith Jsy/75 60.00 18.00
2 Tom Glavine Jsy/25
4 Roger Clemens Jsy/15
7 Derek Jeter Ball/5
8 Alfonso Soriano Ball/5
9 Randy Johnson NLCS Ball/5
10 Ichiro Suzuki Ball/5
11 Curt Schilling Ball/5
12 Randy Johnson WS Ball/5

2003 Timeless Treasures Post Season Prime Autographs

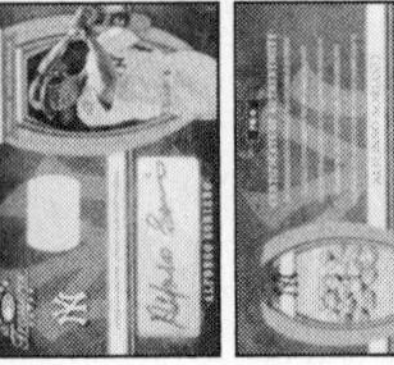

Nm-Mt Ex-Mt
RANDOM INSERTS IN PACKS
STATED PRINT RUN 1 SERIAL #'d SET
NO PRICING DUE TO SCARCITY
1 Ozzie Smith Jsy
2 Tom Glavine Jsy
4 Roger Clemens Jsy
8 Alfonso Soriano Ball
9 Randy Johnson NLCS Ball
12 Randy Johnson WS Ball

2003 Timeless Treasures Prime Ink

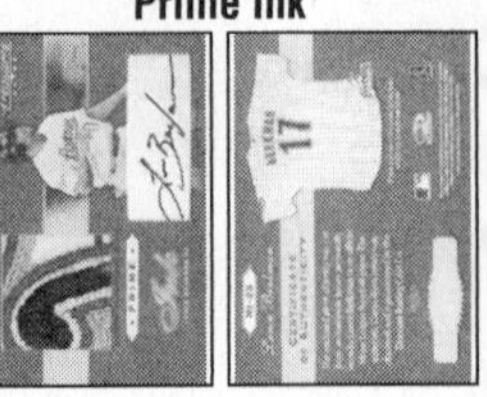

Nm-Mt Ex-Mt
RANDOM INSERTS IN PACKS
PRINT RUNS B/WN 5-50 COPIES PER CARD
NO PRICING ON QTY OF 25 OR LESS.
1 Adam Dunn/10
2 Alan Trammell/50 100.00 30.00
3 Alex Rodriguez White Jsy/10
4 Alex Rodriguez Blue Jsy/5
5 Andre Dawson/25
6 Barry Zito/10
7 Bo Jackson/50 200.00 60.00
8 Bob Feller/5
10 Brooks Robinson/10
11 Cal Ripken No Sleeve/25
12 Cal Ripken Black Sleeve/25
13 Cal Ripken Throwing/5
14 Dale Murphy/15
15 Dave Parker/15
16 David Cone/25
19 Edgar Martinez/10
20 Gary Carter/50 80.00 24.00
21 Harmon Killebrew/15

22 Jim Edmonds/5
23 Jim Thome/10
24 Joe Carter/50 80.00 24.00
25 Jose Canseco/15
26 Jose Vidro/25
27 Kazuhisa Ishii/50 80.00 24.00
28 Kerry Wood/10
29 Lance Berkman/10
30 Mark Mulder/5
31 Mark Prior/10
32 Mike Schmidt/10
33 Nick Johnson/50 80.00 24.00
34 Nolan Ryan Astros/5
37 Paul LoDuca/25
38 Paul Molitor/10
39 Randy Johnson/5
40 Reggie Jackson/5
41 Roberto Alomar Mets/10
42 Roberto Alomar Indians/25
43 Robin Yount/10
44 Rod Carew/5
45 Roger Clemens Yanks/5
46 Roger Clemens Sox/5
47 Ryan Klesko/25
48 Ryne Sandberg/5
50 Shawn Green/5
52 Steve Carlton Giants/50 100.00 30.00
53 Steve Carlton Sox/50 100.00 30.00
54 Todd Helton/10
56 Tony Gwynn/10
57 Torii Hunter/50 80.00 24.00
58 Vladimir Guerrero/50 120.00 36.00
59 Will Clark/25

2003 Timeless Treasures Rookie Year

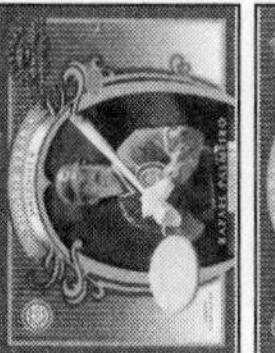

MINT NRMT
COMMON ACTIVE p/r 100 15.00 6.75
COMMON RETIRED p/r 100 15.00 6.75
PRINT RUNS B/WN 50-100 COPIES PER CARD

*PARALLEL p/r 75-100: .4X TO 1X BASIC RY
*PARALLEL p/r 61-68: .5X TO 1.2X BASIC RY
*PARALLEL p/r 42-47: .6X TO 1.5X BASIC RY
PARALLEL PRINT B/WN 42-100 COPIES PER
RANDOM INSERTS IN PACKS
1 Cal Ripken Bat/100 80.00 36.00
2 Mike Schmidt Bat/50 60.00 27.00
3 Rafael Palmeiro Bat/100 20.00 9.00
4 Nomar Garciaparra Jsy/100 40.00 18.00
5 Sean Casey Jsy/100 15.00 6.75
6 Stan Musial Jsy/100 50.00 22.00
7 Yogi Berra Jsy/100 40.00 18.00
8 Bernie Williams Bat/100 20.00 9.00
9 Ivan Rodriguez Jsy/100 20.00 9.00
10 J.D. Drew Jsy/100 15.00 6.75
11 Scott Rolen Jsy/100 20.00 9.00
12 Vladimir Guerrero Jsy/100 20.00 9.00
13 Johnny Bench Bat/100 25.00 11.00
14 Ivan Rodriguez Bat/100 20.00 9.00
15 Andruw Jones Jsy/100 15.00 6.75
16 Andruw Jones Bat/100 15.00 6.75
17 Fred Lynn Jsy/100 15.00 6.75
18 Jeff Kent Jsy/100 15.00 6.75
19 Gary Sheffield Jsy/100 15.00 6.75
20 Ron Santo Bat/100 25.00 11.00
21 Juan Gonzalez Jsy/100 20.00 9.00
22 Alfonso Soriano Jsy/100 20.00 9.00
23 Ryan Klesko Jsy/100 15.00 6.75
24 Adam Dunn Btg Glv/100 15.00 6.75
25 Hideo Nomo Jsy/100 20.00 9.00
26 Mark Prior Jsy/100 40.00 18.00
27 Pat Burrell Bat/50 25.00 11.00
28 Magglio Ordonez Bat/100 15.00 6.75
29 Kirby Puckett Bat/100 40.00 18.00
30 Albert Pujols Jsy/100 40.00 18.00
31 Albert Pujols Bat/100 40.00 18.00

2003 Timeless Treasures Rookie Year Autographs

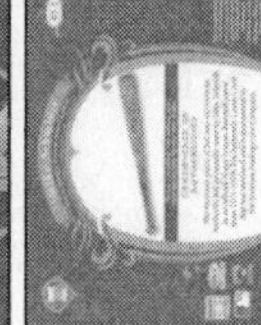

MINT NRMT
RANDOM INSERTS IN PACKS
PRINT RUNS B/WN 10-25 COPIES PER CARD
NO PRICING DUE TO SCARCITY
1 Cal Ripken Bat/25
2 Mike Schmidt Bat/25
6 Stan Musial Jsy/25
7 Yogi Berra Jsy/15
8 Bernie Williams Bat/25
12 Vladimir Guerrero Jsy/25
13 Johnny Bench Bat/25
15 Andruw Jones Jsy/10
16 Andruw Jones Bat/10
17 Fred Lynn Jsy/25
19 Gary Sheffield Jsy/10
20 Ron Santo Bat/25
22 Alfonso Soriano Jsy/10
23 Ryan Klesko Jsy/25
24 Adam Dunn Btg Glv/10
26 Mark Prior Jsy/25
27 Pat Burrell Bat/10
28 Magglio Ordonez Bat/25
29 Kirby Puckett Bat/15

2003 Timeless Treasures Rookie Year Combos

Nm-Mt Ex-Mt
RANDOM INSERTS IN PACKS
PRINT RUNS B/WN 25-50 COPIES PER CARD
NO PRICJNG ON QTY OF 25 OR LESS
1 Alfonso Soriano Btg Glv-Hat/25
2 Adam Dunn Hat-Shoes/25
3 Andruw Jones Bat-Jsy/50 30.00 9.00
4 Ivan Rodriguez Bat-Jsy/50 50.00 15.00
5 Hank Blalock Bat-ST Jsy/25
6 Mark Prior Hat-Jsy/50 100.00 30.00
7 Albert Pujols Bat-Jsy/50 100.00 30.00

2003 Timeless Treasures Rookie Year Combos Autographs

Nm-Mt Ex-Mt
RANDOM INSERTS IN PACKS
STATED PRINT RUN 1 SERIAL #'d SET
NO PRICING DUE TO SCARCITY
1 Alfonso Soriano Btg Glv-Hat
2 Adam Dunn Hat-Shoes
3 Andruw Jones Bat-Jsy
5 Hank Blalock Bat-ST Jsy
6 Mark Prior Hat-Jsy

2003 Timeless Treasures Rookie Year Letters

Nm-Mt Ex-Mt
RANDOM INSERTS IN PACKS
PRINT RUNS B/WN 15-35 COPIES PER CARD
NO PRICJNG ON QTY OF 25 OR LESS.
4 Nomar Garciaparra/35 60.00 18.00
5 Sean Casey/25
9 Ivan Rodriguez/35 50.00 15.00
10 J.D. Drew/15
11 Scott Rolen/15
12 Vladimir Guerrero/35 50.00 15.00
15 Andruw Jones/25
18 Jeff Kent/15
23 Ryan Klesko/15
25 Hideo Nomo/25
30 Albert Pujols/25

2003 Timeless Treasures Rookie Year Letters Autographs

Nm-Mt Ex-Mt
RANDOM INSERTS IN PACKS
STATED PRINT RUN 1 SERIAL #'d SET
NO PRICING DUE TO SCARCITY
11 Scott Rolen
12 Vladimir Guerrero
15 Andruw Jones
19 Gary Sheffield
23 Ryan Klesko
26 Mark Prior

2003 Timeless Treasures Rookie Year Logos

Nm-Mt Ex-Mt
RANDOM INSERTS IN PACKS
PRINT RUNS B/WN 10-50 COPIES PER CARD
NO PRICING ON QTY OF 25 OR LESS
4 Nomar Garciaparra/15
5 Sean Casey/50 40.00 12.00
6 Stan Musial/15
7 Yogi Berra/10
9 Ivan Rodriguez/10
10 J.D. Drew/50 40.00 12.00
11 Scott Rolen/50 50.00 15.00
12 Vladimir Guerrero/50 50.00 15.00
15 Andruw Jones/50 40.00 12.00
17 Fred Lynn/25
18 Jeff Kent/50 40.00 12.00
19 Gary Sheffield/50 40.00 12.00
21 Juan Gonzalez/25
22 Alfonso Soriano/20
23 Ryan Klesko/50 40.00 12.00
25 Hideo Nomo/25
26 Mark Prior/25
30 Albert Pujols/50 100.00 30.00

2003 Timeless Treasures Rookie Year Logos Autographs

Nm-Mt Ex-Mt
RANDOM INSERTS IN PACKS
STATED PRINT RUN 1 SERIAL #'d SET
NO PRICING DUE TO SCARCITY
6 Stan Musial
7 Yogi Berra
11 Scott Rolen
12 Vladimir Guerrero
15 Andruw Jones
17 Fred Lynn
19 Gary Sheffield
22 Alfonso Soriano
23 Ryan Klesko
26 Mark Prior

2003 Timeless Treasures Rookie Year Numbers

MINT NRMT
RANDOM INSERTS IN PACKS
PRINT RUNS B/WN 15-50 COPIES PER CARD
NO PRICING ON QTY OF 30 OR LESS.
5 Sean Casey/30
6 Stan Musial/15
7 Yogi Berra/15
9 Ivan Rodriguez/15
10 J.D. Drew/25
11 Scott Rolen/30
12 Vladimir Guerrero/50 50.00 22.00
15 Andruw Jones/50 40.00 18.00
17 Fred Lynn/30
18 Jeff Kent/25
19 Gary Sheffield/25
21 Juan Gonzalez/30
22 Alfonso Soriano/35 50.00 22.00
23 Ryan Klesko/35 40.00 18.00
25 Hideo Nomo/25
26 Mark Prior/35 80.00 36.00
30 Albert Pujols/25

2003 Timeless Treasures Rookie Year Numbers Autographs

MINT NRMT
RANDOM INSERTS IN PACKS
STATED PRINT RUN 1 SERIAL #'d SET
NO PRICING DUE TO SCARCITY
6 Stan Musial
7 Yogi Berra
12 Vladimir Guerrero
15 Andruw Jones
17 Fred Lynn
19 Gary Sheffield
22 Alfonso Soriano
23 Ryan Klesko
26 Mark Prior

2003 Timeless Treasures Rookie Year Parallel

MINT NRMT
*PARALLEL p/r 75-99: .4X TO 1X BASIC RYM
*PARALLEL p/r 61-68: .5X TO 1.2X BASIC RYM
*PARALLEL p/r 42-47: .4X TO 1X BASIC RYM
RANDOM INSERTS IN PACKS
PRINT RUNS B/WN 42-99 COPIES PER CARD
1 Cal Ripken Bat/82 80.00 36.00
3 Rafael Palmeiro Bat/86 20.00 9.00
5 Sean Casey Jsy/97 15.00 6.75
6 Stan Musial Jsy/42 80.00 36.00
7 Yogi Berra Jsy/47 60.00 27.00
8 Bernie Williams Bat/91 20.00 9.00
9 Ivan Rodriguez Jsy/91 20.00 9.00
10 J.D. Drew Jsy/99 15.00 6.75
11 Scott Rolen Jsy/96 20.00 9.00
12 Vladimir Guerrero Jsy/97 25.00 11.00
13 Johnny Bench Bat/68 25.00 11.00
14 Ivan Rodriguez Bat/91 20.00 9.00
15 Andruw Jones Jsy/96 15.00 6.75
16 Andruw Jones Bat/96 15.00 6.75
17 Fred Lynn Jsy/75 15.00 6.75
18 Jeff Kent Jsy/92 15.00 6.75
19 Gary Sheffield Jsy/89 15.00 6.75
20 Ron Santo Bat/61 30.00 13.50
21 Juan Gonzalez Jsy/89 20.00 9.00
23 Ryan Klesko Jsy/92 15.00 6.75
25 Hideo Nomo Jsy/95 20.00 9.00
27 Pat Burrell Bat/99 25.00 11.00
28 Magglio Ordonez Bat/98 15.00 6.75
29 Kirby Puckett Bat/84 40.00 18.00

2003 Timeless Treasures Rookie Year Patches

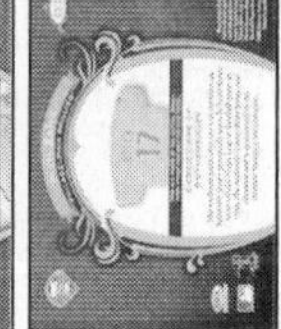

MINT NRMT
RANDOM INSERTS IN PACKS
PRINT RUNS B/WN 10-15 COPIES PER CARD
NO PRICING DUE TO SCARCITY
5 Sean Casey/15
11 Scott Rolen/10
12 Vladimir Guerrero/15
22 Alfonso Soriano/10
26 Mark Prior/10

2003 Timeless Treasures Rookie Year Patches Autographs

MINT NRMT
RANDOM INSERTS IN PACKS
STATED PRINT RUN 1 SERIAL #'d SET
NO PRICING DUE TO SCARCITY
12 Vladimir Guerrero
22 Alfonso Soriano
23 Ryan Klesko
26 Mark Prior

1947 Tip Top

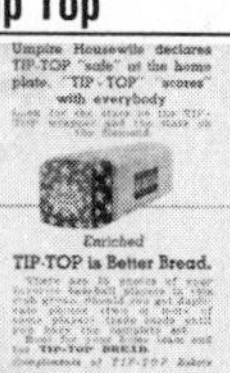

The cards in this 163-card set measure approximately 2 1/4" by 3". The 1947 Tip Top Bread issue contains unnumbered cards with black and white player photos. The set is of interest to baseball historians in that it contains cards of many players not appearing in any other card sets. The cards were issued locally for the eleven following teams: Red Sox (1-15), White Sox (16-30), Tigers (31-45), Yankees (46-60), Browns (61-75), Braves (76-90), Dodgers (91-104), Cubs (105-119), Giants (120-134), Pirates (135-148), and Cardinals (149-163). Players of the Red Sox, Tigers, White Sox, Braves, and the Cubs are scarcer than those of the other teams; players from these tougher teams are marked by SP below to indicate their scarcity. The catalog designation is D323. These unnumbered cards are listed in alphabetical order within teams (with teams also alphabetized within league) for convenience. It was thought that a card for the Giants Eugene Thompson was to be issued but it does not exist.

Ex-Mt VG
COMPLETE SET (163) 9000.00 4500.00
COMMON CARD (1-163) 25.00 12.50
COMMON SP PLAYER 80.00 40.00
1 Leon Culberson SP 80.00 40.00
2 Dom DiMaggio SP 150.00 75.00
3 Joe Dobson SP 80.00 40.00
4 Bob Doerr SP 300.00 150.00
5 Dave(Boo) Ferris SP 80.00 40.00
6 Mickey Harris SP 80.00 40.00
7 Frank Hayes SP 80.00 40.00
8 Cecil Hughson SP 80.00 40.00
9 Earl Johnson SP 80.00 40.00
10 Roy Partee SP 80.00 40.00
11 Johnny Pesky SP 100.00 50.00
12 Rip Russell SP 80.00 40.00
13 Hal Wagner SP 80.00 40.00
14 Rudy York SP 100.00 50.00
15 Bill Zuber SP 80.00 40.00
16 Floyd Baker SP 80.00 40.00
17 Earl Caldwell SP 80.00 40.00
18 Loyd Christopher SP 80.00 40.00
19 George Dickey SP 80.00 40.00
20 Ralph Hodgin SP 80.00 40.00
21 Bob Kennedy SP 80.00 40.00
22 Joe Kuhel SP 80.00 40.00
23 Thornton Lee SP 80.00 40.00
24 Ed Lopat SP 150.00 75.00
25 Cass Michaels SP 80.00 40.00
26 John Rigney SP 80.00 40.00
27 Mike Tresh SP 80.00 40.00
28 Thurman Tucker SP 80.00 40.00
29 Jack Wallasca SP 80.00 40.00
30 Taft Wright SP 80.00 40.00
31 Walter(Hoot)Evers SP 80.00 40.00
32 John Gorsica SP 80.00 40.00
33 Fred Hutchinson SP 100.00 50.00
34 George Kell SP 400.00 200.00
35 Eddie Lake SP 80.00 40.00
36 Ed Mayo SP 80.00 40.00
37 Arthur Mills SP 80.00 40.00
38 Pat Mullin SP 80.00 40.00
39 James Outlaw SP 80.00 40.00
40 Frank Overmire SP 80.00 40.00
41 Bob Swift SP 80.00 40.00
42 Birdie Tebbetts SP 80.00 40.00
43 Dizzy Trout SP 100.00 50.00
44 Virgil Trucks SP 100.00 50.00
45 Dick Wakefield SP 80.00 40.00
46 Yogi Berra 400.00 200.00
(Listed as Larry on card)
47 Floyd(Bill) Bevans 25.00 12.50
48 Bobby Brown 30.00 15.00
49 Thomas Byrne 25.00 12.50
50 Frank Crosetti 40.00 20.00
51 Tommy Henrich 40.00 20.00
52 Charlie Keller 40.00 20.00
53 Johnny Lindell 25.00 12.50
54 Joe Page 30.00 15.00
55 Mel Queen 25.00 12.50
56 Allie Reynolds 40.00 20.00
57 Phil Rizzuto 150.00 75.00
58 Aaron Robinson 25.00 12.50
59 George Stirnweiss 25.00 12.50
60 Charles Wensloff 25.00 12.50
61 John Berardino 40.00 20.00
62 Clifford Fannin 25.00 12.50
63 Dennis Galehouse 25.00 12.50
64 Jeff Heath 25.00 12.50
65 Walter Judnich 25.00 12.50
66 Jack Kramer 25.00 12.50
67 Paul Lehner 25.00 12.50
68 Les Moss 25.00 12.50
69 Bob Muncrief 25.00 12.50
70 Nelson Potter 25.00 12.50
71 Fred Sanford 25.00 12.50
72 Joe Schultz 25.00 12.50
73 Vern Stephens 30.00 15.00
74 Jerry Witte 25.00 12.50
75 Al Zarilla 25.00 12.50
76 Charles Barrett SP 80.00 40.00
77 Hank Camelli SP 80.00 40.00
78 Dick Culler SP 80.00 40.00
79 Nanny Fernandez SP 80.00 40.00
80 Si Johnson SP 80.00 40.00
81 Danny Litwhiler SP 80.00 40.00
82 Phil Masi SP 80.00 40.00
83 Carvel Rowell SP 80.00 40.00
84 Connie Ryan SP 80.00 40.00
85 John Sain SP 120.00 60.00
86 Ray Sanders SP 80.00 40.00
87 Sibby Sisti SP 80.00 40.00
88 B.Southworth SP MG 100.00 50.00
89 Warren Spahn SP 500.00 250.00
90 Ed Wright SP 80.00 40.00
91 Bob Bragan 30.00 15.00
92 Ralph Branca 30.00 15.00
93 Hugh Casey 25.00 12.50
94 Bruce Edwards 25.00 12.50
95 Hal Gregg 25.00 12.50
96 Joe Hatten 25.00 12.50
97 Gene Hermanski 25.00 12.50
98 John Jorgensen 25.00 12.50
99 Harry Lavagetto 30.00 15.00
100 Vic Lombardi 25.00 12.50
101 Frank Melton 25.00 12.50
102 Ed Miksis 25.00 12.50
103 Marv Rackley 25.00 12.50
104 Ed Stevens 25.00 12.50
105 Phil Cavarretta SP 120.00 60.00
106 Bob Chipman SP 80.00 40.00
107 Stan Hack SP 100.00 50.00
108 Don Johnson SP 80.00 40.00
109 Emil Kush SP 80.00 40.00
110 Bill Lee SP 100.00 50.00
111 Mickey Livingston SP 80.00 40.00
112 Harry Lowrey SP 80.00 40.00
113 Clyde McCullough SP 80.00 40.00
114 Andy Pafko SP 100.00 50.00
115 Marv Rickert SP 80.00 40.00
116 John Schmitz SP 80.00 40.00
117 Bobby Sturgeon SP 80.00 40.00
118 Ed Waitkus SP 100.00 50.00
119 Henry Wyse SP 80.00 40.00
120 Bill Ayers 25.00 12.50
121 Buddy Blattner 25.00 12.50
122 Mike Budnick 25.00 12.50
123 Sid Gordon 25.00 12.50
124 Clint Hartung 25.00 12.50
125 Monte Kennedy 25.00 12.50
126 Dave Koslo 25.00 12.50
127 Whitey Lockman 30.00 15.00
128 Jack Lohrke 25.00 12.50
129 Ernie Lombardi 80.00 40.00
130 Willard Marshall 25.00 12.50
131 John Mize 120.00 60.00
132 Ken Trinkle 25.00 12.50
133 Bill Voiselle 25.00 12.50
134 Mickey Witek 25.00 12.50
135 Eddie Basinski 25.00 12.50
136 Ernie Bonham 25.00 12.50
137 Billy Cox 30.00 15.00
138 Elbie Fletcher 25.00 12.50
139 Frank Gustine 25.00 12.50
140 Kirby Higbe 25.00 12.50
141 Leroy Jarvis 25.00 12.50
142 Ralph Kiner 120.00 60.00
143 Fred Ostermueller 25.00 12.50
144 Preacher Roe 40.00 20.00
145 Jim Russell 25.00 12.50
146 Rip Sewell 25.00 12.50
147 Nick Strincevich 25.00 12.50
148 Honus Wagner CO 120.00 60.00
149 Alpha Brazle 25.00 12.50
150 Ken Burkhart 25.00 12.50
151 Bernard Creger 25.00 12.50
152 Joffre Cross 25.00 12.50
153 Chuck Diering 25.00 12.50
154 Ervin Dusak 25.00 12.50
155 Joe Garagiola 80.00 40.00
156 Tony Kaufmann 25.00 12.50
157 Whitey Kurowski 25.00 12.50
158 Marty Marion 40.00 20.00
159 George Munger 25.00 12.50
160 Del Rice 25.00 12.50
161 Dick Sisler 30.00 15.00
162 Enos Slaughter 120.00 60.00
163 Ted Wilks 25.00 12.50

1952 Tip Top

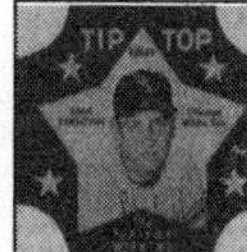

This set of 48 bread end-labels was issued by Tip Top in 1952. The labels measure 2 3/4" by 2 1/2". An album distributed with the labels names 47 ball players and has one blank slot with advertising. A second pose of Rizzuto -- which appears "cropped" from the first photo -- suggests either a last minute substitution for another player, or simply his popularity in the market area. These labels are unnumbered so we have sequenced them in alphabetical order. The catalog designation is D290-1.

NM Ex
COMPLETE SET (48) 6000.00 3000.00
1 Hank Bauer 100.00 50.00
2 Yogi Berra 250.00 125.00
3 Ralph Branca 100.00 50.00
4 Lou Brissie 60.00 30.00
5 Roy Campanella 250.00 125.00
6 Phil Cavarretta 100.00 50.00
7 Murry Dickson 60.00 30.00
8 Ferris Fain 60.00 30.00
9 Carl Furillo 120.00 60.00
10 Ned Garver 60.00 30.00
11 Sid Gordon 100.00 50.00
12 Johnny Groth 60.00 30.00
13 Granny Hamner 60.00 30.00
14 Jim Hearn 60.00 30.00
15 Gene Hermanski 60.00 30.00
16 Gil Hodges 200.00 100.00
17 Larry Jansen 80.00 40.00
18 Eddie Joost 60.00 30.00
19 George Kell 150.00 75.00
20 Dutch Leonard 60.00 30.00
21 Whitey Lockman 60.00 30.00
22 Eddie Lopat 100.00 50.00

23 Sal Maglie	100.00	50.00
24 Mickey Mantle	2000.00	1000.00
25 Gil McDougald	100.00	50.00
26 Dale Mitchell	80.00	40.00
27 Don Mueller	60.00	30.00
28 Andy Pafko	60.00	30.00
29 Bob Porterfield	60.00	30.00
30 Ken Raffensberger	60.00	30.00
31 Allie Reynolds	100.00	50.00
32 Phil Rizzuto (large)	120.00	60.00
33 Phil Rizzuto (small)	120.00	60.00
34 Robin Roberts	200.00	100.00
35 Saul Rogovin	60.00	30.00
36 Ray Scarborough	60.00	30.00
37 Red Schoendienst	120.00	60.00
38 Dick Sisler	60.00	30.00
39 Enos Slaughter	150.00	75.00
40 Duke Snider	250.00	125.00
41 Warren Spahn	200.00	100.00
42 Vern Stephens	60.00	30.00
43 Earl Torgeson	60.00	30.00
44 Mickey Vernon	80.00	40.00
45 Eddie Waitkus	60.00	30.00
46 Wes Westrum	60.00	30.00
47 Eddie Yost	60.00	30.00
48 Al Zarilla	60.00	30.00

1887 Tobin Lithographs

This 11 card set measures 3" by 4 1/2" and were issued in either black and white or color. The color cards have "56" listed in the lower left hand corner with and advertisement in the upper right corner. The card features a player drawing along with an humourus statement. The player's team identification is in the upper left corner. The backs come with or without advertising. We have listed these cards in alphabetical order with the description afterwards.

	Ex-Mt	VG
COMPLETE SET	2000.00	1000.00
1 Ed Andrews	150.00	75.00
Go it Old Boy		
2 Cap Anson	300.00	150.00
Oh, Come Off		
3 Dan Brouthers	250.00	125.00
Watch me soak it		
4 Charlie Ferguson	150.00	75.00
Not onto it		
5 Jack Glasscock	150.00	75.00
Struck by a cyclone		
6 Paul Hines	150.00	75.00
An Anxious Moment		
7 Tim Keefe	250.00	125.00
Where'l you have it		
8 Mike "King" Kelly	300.00	150.00
The Flower of our Flock		
Identified as our own Kelly		
9 Mike "King" Kelly	300.00	150.00
15,000 in his pocket		
Black and White		
Measures approximately 2 1/2" by 4"		
Does not have "56" in corner		
10 Jim McCormick	150.00	75.00
A slide for Hoome		
11 Mickey Welch	250.00	125.00
Aint it a daisy		

1913 Tom Barker WG6

These cards were distributed as part of a baseball game produced in 1913 as indicated by the patent date on the backs of the cards. The cards each measure approximately 2 7/16" by 3 7/16" and have rounded corners. The card fronts show a sepia photo of the player, his name, his team, and the game outcome associated with that particular card. The card backs are all the same, each showing an ornate red and white design with "Tom Barker Baseball Card Game" at the bottom under a drawing of a lefthanded batter all surrounded by a thick white outer border. Since the cards are unnumbered, they are listed below in alphabetical order. Some of the card photos are oriented horizontally (HOR). There are a number of cards without player identification. These action scenes are not explicitly listed in the checklist below and are valued as a "common" card unless a positive identification can be made of a major Hall of Famer in the action scene on the card.

	Ex-Mt	VG
COMPLETE SET	3000.00	1500.00
COMMON ACTION CARD	15.00	7.50
1 Grover Alexander	100.00	50.00
2 Chief Bender	60.00	30.00
3 Bob Bescher	30.00	15.00
4 Joe Birmingham	30.00	15.00
5 Roger Bresnahan	60.00	30.00
6 Nixey Callahan	30.00	15.00
7 Bill Carrigan	30.00	15.00
8 Frank Chance	60.00	30.00
9 Hal Chase	50.00	25.00
10 Fred Clarke	60.00	30.00
11 Ty Cobb	300.00	150.00
12 Sam Crawford	60.00	30.00
13 Jake Daubert	40.00	20.00
14 Red Dooin	30.00	15.00
15 Johnny Evers	60.00	30.00
16 Vean Gregg	30.00	15.00
17 Clark Griffith MG	60.00	30.00
18 Dick Hoblitzel	30.00	15.00
19 Miller Huggins	60.00	30.00
20 Joe Jackson	500.00	250.00
21 Hugh Jennings MG	60.00	30.00
22 Walter Johnson	150.00	75.00
23 Ed Konetchy	30.00	15.00
24 Nap Lajoie	120.00	60.00
25 Connie Mack MG	120.00	60.00
26 Rube Marquard	60.00	30.00
27 Christy Mathewson	150.00	75.00
28 John McGraw MG	120.00	60.00
29 Chief Meyers	40.00	20.00
30 Clyde Milan	40.00	20.00
31 Marty O'Toole	30.00	15.00
32 Nap Rucker	30.00	15.00
33 Tris Speaker	120.00	60.00
34 George Stallings MG	30.00	15.00
35 Bill Sweeney	30.00	15.00
36 Joe Tinker	60.00	30.00
37 Honus Wagner	150.00	75.00
38 Ed Walsh	60.00	30.00
39 Zack Wheat	60.00	30.00
40 Ivy Wingo	30.00	15.00
41 Joe Wood	50.00	25.00
42 Cy Young	120.00	60.00

1994 Tombstone Pizza

Produced by Michael Schlechter Associates for Pinnacle and sponsored by Tombstone Pizza, this 30-card standard-size set showcases 15 of the hottest players from the National (1-15) and American (16-30) Leagues. The promotion ran from May 15 to July 4, 1994, or while supplies lasted. One card was packaged in each Tombstone pizza. Collectors could obtain the complete set by sending in five proofs-of-purchase and 1.00 for shipping and handling. Like most MSA sets, the team logos have been airbrushed away. The cards are arranged alphabetically within each league.

	Nm-Mt	Ex-Mt
COMPLETE SET (30)	15.00	4.50
1 Jeff Bagwell	.75	.23
2 Jay Bell	.10	.03
3 Barry Bonds	1.50	.45
4 Bobby Bonilla	.20	.06
5 Andres Galarraga	.40	.12
6 Mark Grace	.30	.09
7 Marquis Grissom	.10	.03
8 Tony Gwynn	1.50	.45
9 Bryan Harvey	.10	.03
10 Gregg Jefferies	.10	.03
11 David Justice	.40	.12
12 John Kruk	.20	.06
13 Barry Larkin	.40	.12
14 Greg Maddux	2.00	.60
15 Mike Piazza	2.00	.60
16 Jim Abbott	.20	.06
17 Albert Belle	.20	.06
18 Cecil Fielder	.20	.06
19 Juan Gonzalez	.75	.23
20 Mike Greenwell	.10	.03
21 Ken Griffey Jr.	2.00	.60
22 Jack McDowell	.10	.03
23 Jeff Montgomery	.10	.03
24 John Olerud	.20	.06
25 Kirby Puckett	.75	.23
26 Cal Ripken	3.00	.90
27 Tim Salmon	.40	.12
28 Ruben Sierra	.20	.06
29 Frank Thomas	.75	.23
30 Robin Yount	.75	.23

1995 Tombstone Pizza

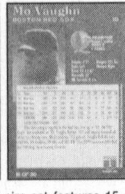

This 30-card standard-size set features 15 of the hottest players each from the National and the American Leagues. One card was packaged in each Tombstone Pizza. Six thousand classic player cards, autographed by Johnny Bench, George Brett or Bob Gibson, were randomly packed. Collectors who pulled one of these autograph cards could receive an 8 1/2" by 11" certificate of authenticity through a mail-in offer. Also collectors could obtain the complete set by sending in five proofs-of-purchase. The limit was two sets per family, and the offer expired December 31, 1995, or while supplies lasted. The cards are numbered on the back "X of 30."

	Nm-Mt	Ex-Mt
COMPLETE SET (30)	15.00	4.50
1 Frank Thomas	.75	.23
2 David Cone	.30	.09
3 Bob Hamelin	.10	.03
4 Jeff Bagwell	.75	.23
5 Greg Maddux	2.00	.60
6 Raul Mondesi	.30	.09
7 Chili Davis	.20	.06
8 Cecil Fielder	.20	.06
9 Ken Griffey Jr.	2.00	.60
10 Jimmy Key	.20	.06
11 Kenny Lofton	.30	.09
12 Paul Molitor	.75	.23
13 Kirby Puckett	.75	.23
14 Cal Ripken	3.00	.90
15 Ivan Rodriguez	.75	.23
16 Kevin Seitzer	.10	.03
17 Ruben Sierra	.20	.06
18 Mo Vaughn	.20	.06
19 Moises Alou	.20	.06
20 Barry Bonds	1.50	.45
21 Jeff Conine	.10	.03
22 Lenny Dykstra	.10	.03
23 Andres Galarraga	.50	.15
24 Tony Gwynn	1.50	.45
25 Barry Larkin	.50	.15
26 Fred McGriff	.30	.09
27 Orlando Merced	.10	.03
28 Bret Saberhagen	.20	.06
29 Ozzie Smith	.75	.23
30 Sammy Sosa	1.50	.45
AU1 Johnny Bench AU	30.00	9.00
AU2 George Brett AU	75.00	22.00
AU3 Bob Gibson AU	20.00	6.00

1951 Topps Blue Backs

The cards in this 52-card set measure approximately 2" by 2 5/8". The 1951 Topps series of blue-backed baseball cards could be used to play a baseball game by shuffling the cards and drawing them from a pile. These cards (packaged two adjoined in a penny pack) were marketed with a piece of caramel candy, which often melted or was squashed in such a way as to damage the card and wrapper (despite the fact that a paper shield was inserted between candy and card). Blue Backs are more difficult to obtain than the similarly styled Red Backs. The set is denoted on the cards as "Set B" and the Red Back set is correspondingly Set A. The only notable Rookie Card in the set is Billy Pierce.

	NM	Ex
COMPLETE SET (52)	1700.00	850.00
WRAPPER (1-CENT)	200.00	100.00
1 Eddie Yost	60.00	18.00
2 Hank Majeski	30.00	15.00
3 Richie Ashburn	200.00	100.00
4 Del Ennis	30.00	15.00
5 Johnny Pesky	30.00	15.00
6 Red Schoendienst	100.00	50.00
7 Gerry Staley	30.00	15.00
8 Dick Sisler	30.00	15.00
9 Johnny Sain	50.00	25.00
10 Joe Page	50.00	25.00
11 Johnny Groth	30.00	15.00
12 Sam Jethroe	40.00	20.00
13 Mickey Vernon	30.00	15.00
14 George Munger	30.00	15.00
15 Eddie Joost	30.00	15.00
16 Murry Dickson	30.00	15.00
17 Roy Smalley	30.00	15.00
18 Ned Garver	30.00	15.00
19 Phil Masi	30.00	15.00
20 Ralph Branca	50.00	25.00
21 Billy Johnson	30.00	15.00
22 Bob Kuzava	30.00	15.00
23 Dizzy Trout	40.00	20.00
24 Sherman Lollar	30.00	15.00
25 Sam Mele	30.00	15.00
26 Chico Carrasquel RC	40.00	20.00
27 Andy Pafko	30.00	15.00
28 Harry Brecheen	30.00	15.00
29 Granville Hamner	30.00	15.00
30 Enos Slaughter	100.00	50.00
31 Lou Brissie	30.00	15.00
32 Bob Elliott	40.00	20.00
33 Don Lenhardt	30.00	15.00
34 Earl Torgeson	30.00	15.00
35 Tommy Byrne	30.00	15.00
36 Cliff Fannin	30.00	15.00
37 Bobby Doerr	100.00	50.00
38 Irv Noren	30.00	15.00
39 Ed Lopat	50.00	25.00
40 Vic Wertz	30.00	15.00
41 Johnny Schmitz	30.00	15.00
42 Bruce Edwards	30.00	15.00
43 Willie Jones	30.00	15.00
44 Johnny Wyrostek	30.00	15.00
45 Billy Pierce RC	50.00	25.00
46 Gerry Priddy	30.00	15.00
47 Herman Wehmeier	30.00	15.00
48 Billy Cox	40.00	20.00
49 Hank Sauer	40.00	20.00
50 Johnny Mize	100.00	50.00
51 Eddie Waitkus	40.00	20.00
52 Sam Chapman	50.00	17.00

1951 Topps Red Backs

The cards in this 52-card set measure approximately 2" by 2 5/8". The 1951 Topps Red Back set is identical in style to the Blue Back set of the same year. The cards have rounded corners and were designed to be used as a baseball game. Zernial, number 36, is listed with either the White Sox or Athletics, and Holmes, number 52, with either the Braves or Hartford. The set is denoted on the cards as "Set A" and the Blue Back set is correspondingly Set B. The cards were packaged as two connected cards along with a piece of caramel in a penny pack. The most notable Rookie Card in the set is Monte Irvin.

	NM	Ex
COMPLETE SET (54)	850.00	425.00
WRAPPER (1-CENT)	5.00	2.50
1 Yogi Berra	125.00	45.00
2 Sid Gordon	10.00	5.00
3 Ferris Fain	12.00	6.00
4 Vern Stephens	12.00	6.00
5 Phil Rizzuto	60.00	30.00
6 Allie Reynolds	20.00	10.00
7 Howie Pollet	10.00	5.00
8 Early Wynn	25.00	12.50
9 Roy Sievers	15.00	7.50
10 Mel Parnell	12.00	6.00
11 Gene Hermanski	12.00	6.00
12 Jim Hegan	12.00	6.00
13 Dale Mitchell	12.00	6.00
14 Wayne Terwilliger	10.00	5.00
15 Ralph Kiner	25.00	12.50
16 Preacher Roe	15.00	7.50
17 Gus Bell RC	15.00	7.50
18 Jerry Coleman	15.00	7.50
19 Dick Kokos	10.00	5.00
20 Dom DiMaggio	20.00	10.00
21 Larry Jansen	12.00	6.00
22 Bob Feller	60.00	30.00
23 Ray Boone RC	15.00	7.50
24 Hank Bauer	20.00	10.00
25 Cliff Chambers	10.00	5.00
26 Luke Easter RC	15.00	7.50
27 Wally Westlake	12.00	6.00
28 Elmer Valo	10.00	5.00
29 Bob Kennedy	12.00	6.00
30 Warren Spahn	60.00	30.00
31 Gil Hodges	50.00	25.00
32 Henry Thompson	12.00	6.00
33 William Werle	10.00	5.00
34 Grady Hatton	10.00	5.00
35 Al Rosen	15.00	7.50
36A Gus Zernial	40.00	20.00
(Chicago)		
36B Gus Zernial	20.00	10.00
(Philadelphia)		
37 Wes Westrum	12.00	6.00
38 Duke Snider	60.00	30.00
39 Ted Kluszewski	25.00	12.50
40 Mike Garcia	15.00	7.50
41 Whitey Lockman	12.00	6.00
42 Ray Scarborough	10.00	5.00
43 Maurice McDermott	10.00	5.00
44 Sid Hudson	10.00	5.00
45 Andy Seminick	12.00	6.00
46 Billy Goodman	12.00	6.00
47 Tommy Glaviano	10.00	5.00
48 Eddie Stanky	12.00	6.00
49 Al Zarilla	10.00	5.00
50 Monte Irvin RC	40.00	20.00
51 Eddie Robinson	10.00	5.00
52A Tommy Holmes	40.00	10.00
(Boston)		
52B Tommy Holmes	25.00	6.25
(Hartford)		

1951 Topps Connie Mack All-Stars

The cards in this 11-card set measure approximately 2 1/16" by 5 1/4". The series of die-cut cards which comprise the set entitled Connie Mack All-Stars was one of Topps' most distinctive and fragile card designs. Printed on thin cardboard, these elegant cards were protected in the wrapper by panels of accompanying Red Backs, but once removed were easily damaged (after all, they were intended to be folded and used as toy figures). Cards without tops have a value less than one-half of that listed below. The cards are unnumbered and are listed below in alphabetical order.

	NM	Ex
COMPLETE SET (11)	7000.00	3500.00
WRAPPER (1-CENT)	350.00	180.00
1 Grover C. Alexander	400.00	200.00
2 Mickey Cochrane	300.00	150.00
3 Eddie Collins	150.00	75.00
4 Jimmy Collins	150.00	75.00
5 Lou Gehrig	2000.00	1000.00
6 Walter Johnson	700.00	350.00
7 Connie Mack	300.00	150.00
8 Christy Mathewson	500.00	250.00
9 Babe Ruth	2500.00	1250.00
10 Tris Speaker	250.00	125.00
11 Honus Wagner	400.00	200.00

1951 Topps Current All-Stars

The cards in this 11-card set measure approximately 2 1/16" by 5 1/4". The 1951 Topps Current All-Star series is probably the rarest of all legitimate, nationally issued, post war baseball issues. The set price listed below does not include the prices for the cards of Konstanty, Roberts and Stanky, which likely never were released to the public in gum packs. These three cards (SP in the checklist below) were probably obtained directly from the

company and exist in extremely limited numbers. As with the Connie Mack set, cards without the die-cut background are worth half of the value listed below. The cards are unnumbered and are listed below in alphabetical order. These cards were issued in two card packs (one being a Current AS the other being a Topps Team card).

	NM	Ex
COMPLETE SET (8)	4500.00	2200.00
WRAPPER (1-CENT)	500.00	250.00
1 Yogi Berra	1500.00	750.00
2 Larry Doby	400.00	200.00
3 Walt Dropo	250.00	125.00
4 Hoot Evers	250.00	125.00
5 George Kell	600.00	300.00
6 Ralph Kiner	750.00	375.00
7 Jim Konstanty SP	12500.00	6200.00
8 Bob Lemon	600.00	300.00
9 Phil Rizzuto	800.00	400.00
10 Robin Roberts SP	15000.00	7500.00
11 Eddie Stanky SP	12500.00	6200.00

1951 Topps Teams

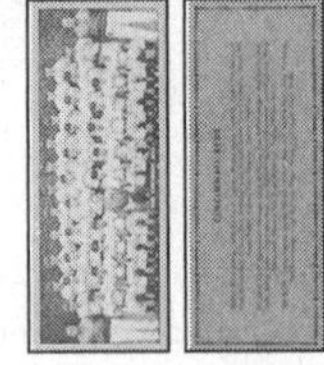

The cards in this nine-card set measure approximately 2 1/16" by 5 1/4". These unnumbered team cards issued by Topps in 1951 carry black and white photographs framed by a yellow border. These cards were issued in the same five-cent wrapper as the Connie Mack and Current All Stars. They have been assigned reference numbers in the checklist alphabetically by team city and name. They are found with or without "1950" printed in the name panel before the team name. Although the dated variations are slightly more difficult to find, there is usually no difference in value.

	NM	Ex
COMPLETE SET (9)	2250.00	1100.00
1 Boston Red Sox	350.00	180.00
2 Brooklyn Dodgers	350.00	180.00
3 Chicago White Sox	200.00	100.00
4 Cincinnati Reds	200.00	100.00
5 New York Giants	250.00	125.00
6 Philadelphia Athletics	200.00	100.00
7 Philadelphia Phillies	200.00	100.00
8 St. Louis Cardinals	350.00	180.00
9 Washington Senators	200.00	100.00

1952 Topps

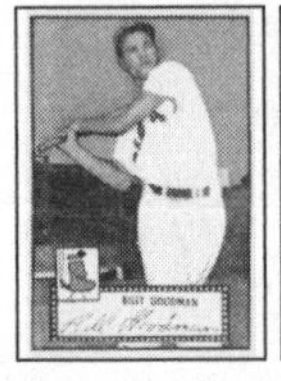

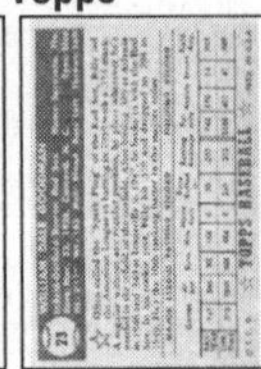

The cards in this 407-card set measure approximately 2 5/8" by 3 3/4". The 1952 Topps set is Topps' first truly major set. Card numbers 1 to 80 were issued with red or black backs, both of which are less plentiful than card numbers 81 to 250. In fact, the first series is considered the most difficult with respect to finding perfect condition cards. Card number 48 (Joe Page) and number 49 (Johnny Sain) can be found with each other's write-up on their back. However, many dealers today believe that all cards numbered 1-250 are valued the same. Card numbers 251 to 310 are somewhat scarce and numbers 311 to 407 are quite scarce. Cards 281-300 were single printed compared to the other cards in the next to last series. Cards 311-313 were double printed on the last high number printing sheet. The key card in the set is obviously Mickey Mantle, number 311, Mickey's first of many Topps cards. A really obscure variation on cards from 311 through 313 is that they exist with the stitching on the number circle in the back either clockwise or counter clockwise. There is no price differential for either variation. Card number 307, Frank Campos has been discovered to have a black star next to the words "Topps Baseball" on the back. This card is very scarce but since it is rarely traded in the secondary market -- no value can be established at this time. Many collectors are not aware of this variation. In the early 1980's, Topps issued a standard-size reprint set of the 52 Topps set. These cards were issued only as a factory set and have a current market value of between two and three hundred dollars. Five people portrayed in the regular set: Billy Loes (number 20), Dom DiMaggio (number 22), Saul Rogovin (number 159), Solly Hemus (number 196) and Tommy Holmes (number

289) are not in the reprint set. Although rarely seen, there exist salesman sample panels of three cards containing the fronts of regular cards with ad information on the back. Panels which have been seen are Bob Mahoney/Robin Roberts/Sid Hudson, Bob Wellman/Lou Kretlow/Ray Scarborough, Wally Westlake/Dizzy Trout/Irv Noren and Eddie Joost/Willie Jones/Gordon Goldsberry. The cards were issued in one-card penny packs and six-card nickle packs. The five cent packs were issued 24 packs to a box. The key Rookie Cards in this set are Billy Martin, Eddie Mathews (the last card in the set), and Hoyt Wilhelm. Some cards issued in Canada, (131-190) have also been reported, these cards have a "muted" tone on the front and use a grey stock reverse.

	NM	Ex
COMP.MASTER SET (487)	80000.00	40000.00
COMPLETE SET (407)	65000.00	32500.00
COMMON CARD (1-80)	60.00	30.00
COMMON CARD (81-250)	40.00	20.00
COMMON (251-310)	50.00	25.00
COMMON (311-407)	250.00	125.00
WRAPPER (1-cent)	250.00	125.00
WRAPPER (5-cent)	100.00	50.00
1 Andy Pafko	5000.00	500.00
1A Andy Pafko Black	3000.00	300.00
2 Pete Runnels RC	250.00	125.00
2A Pete Runnels RC Black	250.00	125.00
3 Hank Thompson	70.00	35.00
3A Hank Thompson Black	70.00	35.00
4 Don Lenhardt	60.00	30.00
4A Don Lenhardt Black	60.00	30.00
5 Larry Jansen	70.00	35.00
5A Larry Jansen Black	70.00	35.00
6 Grady Hatton	60.00	30.00
6A Grady Hatton Black	60.00	30.00
7 Wayne Terwilliger	60.00	30.00
7A W. Terwilliger Black	60.00	30.00
8 Fred Marsh	60.00	30.00
8A Fred Marsh Black	60.00	30.00
9 Robert Hogue	60.00	30.00
9A Robert Hogue Black	60.00	30.00
10 Al Rosen	70.00	35.00
10A Al Rosen Black	70.00	35.00
11 Phil Rizzuto	400.00	200.00
11A Phil Rizzuto Black	350.00	180.00
12 Monty Basgall	60.00	30.00
12A Monty Basgall Black	60.00	30.00
13 Johnny Wyrostek	60.00	30.00
13A J. Wyrostek Black	60.00	30.00
14 Bob Elliott	70.00	35.00
14A Bob Elliott Black	70.00	35.00
15 Johnny Pesky	70.00	35.00
15A Johnny Pesky Black	70.00	35.00
16 Gene Hermanski	60.00	30.00
16A G. Hermanski Black	60.00	30.00
17 Jim Hegan	70.00	35.00
17A Jim Hegan Black	70.00	35.00
18 Merrill Combs	60.00	30.00
18A Merrill Combs Black	60.00	30.00
19 Johnny Bucha	60.00	30.00
19A Johnny Bucha Black	60.00	30.00
20 Billy Loes RC	125.00	60.00
20A Billy Loes RC Black	125.00	60.00
21 Ferris Fain	70.00	35.00
21A Ferris Fain Black	70.00	35.00
22 Dom DiMaggio	100.00	50.00
22A Dom DiMaggio Black	100.00	50.00
23 Billy Goodman	70.00	35.00
23A Billy Goodman Black	70.00	35.00
24 Luke Easter	80.00	40.00
24A Luke Easter Black	80.00	40.00
25 Johnny Groth	60.00	30.00
25A Johnny Groth Black	60.00	30.00
26 Monte Irvin	150.00	75.00
26A Monte Irvin Black	125.00	60.00
27 Sam Jethroe	70.00	35.00
27A Sam Jethroe Black	70.00	35.00
28 Jerry Priddy	60.00	30.00
28A Jerry Priddy Black	60.00	30.00
29 Ted Kluszewski	125.00	60.00
29A Ted Kluszewski Black	125.00	60.00
30 Mel Parnell	70.00	35.00
30A Mel Parnell Black	70.00	35.00
31 Gus Zernial	80.00	40.00
Posed with seven baseballs		
31A Gus Zernial Black	80.00	40.00
Posed with seven baseballs		
32 Eddie Robinson	60.00	30.00
32A Eddie Robinson Black	60.00	30.00
33 Warren Spahn	300.00	150.00
33A Warren Spahn Black	250.00	125.00
34 Elmer Valo	60.00	30.00
34A Elmer Valo Black	60.00	30.00
35 Hank Sauer	70.00	35.00
35A Hank Sauer Black	70.00	35.00
36 Gil Hodges	300.00	150.00
36A Gil Hodges Black	250.00	125.00
37 Duke Snider	500.00	250.00
37A Duke Snider Black	400.00	200.00
38 Wally Westlake	60.00	30.00
38A Wally Westlake Black	60.00	30.00
39 Dizzy Trout	70.00	35.00
39A Dizzy Trout Black	70.00	35.00
40 Irv Noren	70.00	35.00
40A Irv Noren Black	70.00	35.00
41 Bob Wellman	60.00	30.00
41A Bob Wellman Black	60.00	30.00
42 Lou Kretlow	60.00	30.00
42A Lou Kretlow Black	60.00	30.00
43 Ray Scarborough	60.00	30.00
43A R. Scarbourough Black	60.00	30.00
44 Con Dempsey	60.00	30.00
44A Con Dempsey Black	60.00	30.00
45 Eddie Joost	60.00	30.00
45A Eddie Joost Black	60.00	30.00
46 Gordon Goldsberry	60.00	30.00
46A G. Goldsberry Black	60.00	30.00
47 Willie Jones	70.00	35.00
47A Willie Jones Black	70.00	35.00
48A Joe Page ERR	400.00	200.00
Bio for Sain		
Black Back		
48B Joe Page COR	125.00	60.00
Black Back		
48C Joe Page COR	125.00	60.00
Red Back		
49A John Sain ERR	400.00	200.00
Bio for Page		
Black Back		
49B John Sain COR	125.00	60.00
Black Back		
49C John Sain COR	125.00	60.00
Red Back		
50 Marv Rickert	60.00	30.00
50A Marv Richert Black	60.00	30.00
51 Jim Russell	60.00	30.00
51A Jim Russell Black	60.00	30.00
52 Don Mueller	70.00	35.00
52A Don Mueller Black	70.00	35.00
53 Chris Van Cuyk	60.00	30.00
53A Chris Van Cuyk Black	60.00	30.00
54 Leo Kiely	60.00	30.00
54A Leo Kiely Black	60.00	30.00
55 Ray Boone	80.00	40.00
55A Ray Boone Black	80.00	40.00
56 Tommy Glaviano	60.00	30.00
56A T. Glaviano Black	60.00	30.00
57 Ed Lopat	100.00	50.00
57A Ed Lopat Black	100.00	50.00
58 Bob Mahoney	60.00	30.00
58A Bob Mahoney Black	60.00	30.00
59 Robin Roberts	175.00	90.00
59A Robin Roberts Black	175.00	90.00
60 Sid Hudson	60.00	30.00
60A Sid Hudson Black	60.00	30.00
61 Tookie Gilbert	60.00	30.00
61A Tookie Gilbert Black	60.00	30.00
62 Chuck Stobbs	60.00	30.00
62A Chuck Stobbs Black	60.00	30.00
63 Howie Pollet	60.00	30.00
63A Howie Pollet Black	60.00	30.00
64 Roy Sievers	70.00	35.00
64A Roy Sievers Black	70.00	35.00
65 Enos Slaughter	175.00	90.00
65A Enos Slaughter Black	175.00	90.00
66 Preacher Roe	100.00	50.00
66A Preacher Roe Black	100.00	50.00
67 Allie Reynolds	125.00	60.00
67A Allie Reynolds Black	100.00	50.00
68 Cliff Chambers	60.00	30.00
68A Cliff Chambers Black	60.00	30.00
69 Virgil Stallcup	60.00	30.00
69A Virgil Stallcup Black	60.00	30.00
70 Al Zarilla	60.00	30.00
70A Al Zarilla Black	60.00	30.00
71 Tom Upton	60.00	30.00
71A Tom Upton Black	60.00	30.00
72 Karl Olson	60.00	30.00
72A Karl Olson Black	60.00	30.00
73 Bill Werle	60.00	30.00
73A Bill Werle Black	60.00	30.00
74 Andy Hansen	60.00	30.00
74A Andy Hansen Black	60.00	30.00
75 Wes Westrum	70.00	35.00
75A Wes Westrum Black	70.00	35.00
76 Eddie Stanky	70.00	35.00
76A Eddie Stanky Black	70.00	35.00
77 Bob Kennedy	70.00	35.00
77A Bob Kennedy Black	70.00	35.00
78 Ellis Kinder	60.00	30.00
78A Ellis Kinder Black	60.00	30.00
79 Gerry Staley	60.00	30.00
79A Gerry Staley Black	60.00	30.00
80 Herman Wehmeier	80.00	40.00
80A H. Wehmeier Black	80.00	40.00
81 Vernon Law	80.00	40.00
82 Duane Pillette	40.00	20.00
83 Billy Johnson	40.00	20.00
84 Vern Stephens	50.00	25.00
85 Bob Kuzava	50.00	25.00
86 Ted Gray	40.00	20.00
87 Dale Coogan	40.00	20.00
88 Bob Feller	250.00	125.00
89 Johnny Lipon	40.00	20.00
90 Mickey Grasso	40.00	20.00
91 Red Schoendienst	100.00	50.00
92 Dale Mitchell	50.00	25.00
93 Al Sima	40.00	20.00
94 Sam Mele	40.00	20.00
95 Ken Holcombe	40.00	20.00
96 Willard Marshall	40.00	20.00
97 Earl Torgeson	40.00	20.00
98 Billy Pierce	50.00	25.00
99 Gene Woodling	60.00	30.00
100 Del Rice	40.00	20.00
101 Max Lanier	40.00	20.00
102 Bill Kennedy	40.00	20.00
103 Cliff Mapes	40.00	20.00
104 Don Kolloway	40.00	20.00
105 Johnny Pramesa	40.00	20.00
106 Mickey Vernon	60.00	30.00
107 Connie Ryan	40.00	20.00
108 Jim Konstanty	60.00	30.00
109 Ted Wilks	40.00	20.00
110 Dutch Leonard	40.00	20.00
111 Peanuts Lowrey	40.00	20.00
112 Hank Majeski	40.00	20.00
113 Dick Sisler	50.00	25.00
114 Willard Ramsdell	40.00	20.00
115 George Munger	40.00	20.00
116 Carl Scheib	40.00	20.00
117 Sherm Lollar	50.00	25.00
118 Ken Raffensberger	40.00	20.00
119 Mickey McDermott	40.00	20.00
120 Bob Chakales	40.00	20.00
121 Gus Niarhos	40.00	20.00
122 Jackie Jensen	80.00	40.00
123 Eddie Yost	50.00	25.00
124 Monte Kennedy	40.00	20.00
125 Bill Rigney	50.00	25.00
126 Fred Hutchinson	50.00	25.00
127 Paul Minner	40.00	20.00
128 Don Bollweg	40.00	20.00
129 Johnny Mize	150.00	75.00
130 Sheldon Jones	40.00	20.00
131 Morrie Martin	40.00	20.00
132 Clyde Kluttz	40.00	20.00
133 Al Widmar	40.00	20.00
134 Joe Tipton	40.00	20.00
135 Dixie Howell	40.00	20.00
136 Johnny Schmitz	40.00	20.00
137 Roy McMillan RC	50.00	25.00
138 Bill MacDonald	40.00	20.00
139 Ken Wood	40.00	20.00
140 Johnny Antonelli	60.00	30.00
141 Clint Hartung	40.00	20.00
142 Harry Perkowski	40.00	20.00
143 Les Moss	40.00	20.00
144 Ed Blake	40.00	20.00
145 Joe Haynes	40.00	20.00
146 Frank House	40.00	20.00
147 Bob Young	40.00	20.00
148 Johnny Klippstein	40.00	20.00
149 Dick Kryhoski	40.00	20.00
150 Ted Beard	40.00	20.00
151 Wally Post RC	50.00	25.00
152 Al Evans	40.00	20.00
153 Bob Rush	40.00	20.00
154 Joe Muir	40.00	20.00
155 Frank Overmire	40.00	20.00
156 Frank Hiller	40.00	20.00
157 Bob Usher	40.00	20.00
158 Eddie Waitkus	40.00	20.00
159 Saul Rogovin	40.00	20.00
160 Owen Friend	40.00	20.00
161 Bud Byerly	40.00	20.00
162 Del Crandall	50.00	25.00
163 Stan Rojek	40.00	20.00
164 Walt Dubiel	40.00	20.00
165 Eddie Kazak	40.00	20.00
166 Paul LaPalme	40.00	20.00
167 Bill Howerton	40.00	20.00
168 Charlie Silvera RC	60.00	30.00
169 Howie Judson	40.00	20.00
170 Gus Bell	50.00	25.00
171 Ed Erautt	40.00	20.00
172 Eddie Miksis	40.00	20.00
173 Roy Smalley	40.00	20.00
174 Clarence Marshall	60.00	30.00
175 Billy Martin RC	500.00	250.00
176 Hank Edwards	40.00	20.00
177 Bill Wight	40.00	20.00
178 Cass Michaels	40.00	20.00
179 Frank Smith	40.00	20.00
180 Charlie Maxwell RC	50.00	25.00
181 Bob Swift	40.00	20.00
182 Billy Hitchcock	40.00	20.00
183 Erv Dusak	40.00	20.00
184 Bob Ramazzotti	40.00	20.00
185 Bill Nicholson	50.00	25.00
186 Walt Masterson	40.00	20.00
187 Bob Miller	40.00	20.00
188 Clarence Podbielan	40.00	20.00
189 Pete Reiser	60.00	30.00
190 Don Johnson	40.00	20.00
191 Yogi Berra	800.00	400.00
192 Myron Ginsberg	40.00	20.00
193 Harry Simpson	50.00	25.00
194 Joe Hatton	40.00	20.00
195 Minnie Minoso RC	150.00	75.00
196 Solly Hemus RC	60.00	30.00
197 George Strickland	40.00	20.00
198 Phil Haugstad	40.00	20.00
199 George Zuverink	40.00	20.00
200 Ralph Houk RC	80.00	40.00
201 Alex Kellner	40.00	20.00
202 Joe Collins RC	60.00	30.00
203 Curt Simmons	60.00	30.00
204 Ron Northey	40.00	20.00
205 Clyde King	60.00	30.00
206 Joe Ostrowski	40.00	20.00
207 Mickey Harris	40.00	20.00
208 Marlin Stuart	40.00	20.00
209 Howie Fox	40.00	20.00
210 Dick Fowler	40.00	20.00
211 Ray Coleman	40.00	20.00
212 Ned Garver	40.00	20.00
213 Nippy Jones	40.00	20.00
214 Johnny Hopp	50.00	25.00
215 Hank Bauer	100.00	50.00
216 Richie Ashburn	250.00	125.00
217 Snuffy Stirnweiss	50.00	25.00
218 Clyde McCullough	40.00	20.00
219 Bobby Shantz	60.00	30.00
220 Joe Presko	40.00	20.00
221 Granny Hamner	40.00	20.00
222 Hoot Evers	40.00	20.00
223 Del Ennis	50.00	25.00
224 Bruce Edwards	40.00	20.00
225 Frank Baumholtz	40.00	20.00
226 Dave Philley	40.00	20.00
227 Joe Garagiola	80.00	40.00
228 Al Brazle	40.00	20.00
229 Gene Beardon UER	40.00	20.00
(Misspelled Beardon)		
230 Matt Batts	40.00	20.00
231 Sam Zoldak	40.00	20.00
232 Billy Cox	50.00	25.00
233 Bob Friend RC	80.00	40.00
234 Steve Souchock	40.00	20.00
235 Walt Dropo	40.00	20.00
236 Ed Fitzgerald	40.00	20.00
237 Jerry Coleman	60.00	30.00
238 Art Houtteman	40.00	20.00
239 Rocky Bridges	50.00	25.00
240 Jack Phillips	40.00	20.00
241 Tommy Byrne	40.00	20.00
242 Tom Poholsky	40.00	20.00
243 Larry Doby	80.00	40.00
244 Vic Wertz	40.00	20.00
245 Sherry Robertson	40.00	20.00
246 George Kell	80.00	40.00
247 Randy Gumpert	40.00	20.00
248 Frank Shea	40.00	20.00
249 Bobby Adams	40.00	20.00
250 Carl Erskine	100.00	50.00
251 Chico Carrasquel	50.00	25.00
252 Vern Bickford	50.00	25.00
253 Johnny Berardino	100.00	50.00
254 Joe Dobson	50.00	25.00
255 Clyde Vollmer	50.00	25.00
256 Pete Suder	50.00	25.00
257 Bobby Avila	60.00	30.00
258 Steve Gromek	60.00	30.00
259 Bob Addis	50.00	25.00
260 Pete Castiglione	50.00	25.00
261 Willie Mays	3000.00	1500.00
262 Virgil Trucks	60.00	30.00
263 Harry Brecheen	60.00	30.00
264 Roy Hartsfield	50.00	25.00
265 Chuck Diering	50.00	25.00
266 Murry Dickson	50.00	25.00
267 Sid Gordon	50.00	25.00
268 Bob Lemon	150.00	75.00
269 Willard Nixon	50.00	25.00
270 Lou Brissie	50.00	25.00
271 Jim Delsing	60.00	30.00
272 Mike Garcia	80.00	40.00
273 Erv Palica	50.00	25.00
274 Ralph Branca	125.00	60.00
275 Pat Mullin	50.00	25.00
276 Jim Wilson RC	50.00	25.00
277 Early Wynn	175.00	90.00
278 Allie Clark	50.00	25.00
279 Eddie Stewart	50.00	25.00
280 Cloyd Boyer	80.00	40.00
281 Tommy Brown SP	80.00	40.00
282 Birdie Tebbetts SP	80.00	40.00
283 Phil Masi SP	60.00	30.00
284 Hank Arft SP	60.00	30.00
285 Cliff Fannin SP	60.00	30.00
286 Joe DeMaestri SP	60.00	30.00
287 Steve Bilko SP	60.00	30.00
288 Chet Nichols SP	80.00	40.00
289 Tommy Holmes SP	100.00	50.00
290 Joe Astroth SP	60.00	30.00
291 Gil Coan SP	60.00	30.00
292 Floyd Baker SP	60.00	30.00
293 Sibby Sisti SP	60.00	30.00
294 Walker Cooper SP	60.00	30.00
295 Phil Cavarretta SP	80.00	40.00
296 Red Rolfe MG SP	60.00	30.00
297 Andy Seminick SP	60.00	30.00
298 Bob Ross SP	60.00	30.00
299 Ray Murray SP	80.00	40.00
300 Barney McCosky SP	80.00	40.00
301 Bob Porterfield	50.00	25.00
302 Max Surkont	50.00	25.00
303 Harry Dorish	50.00	25.00
304 Sam Dente	50.00	25.00
305 Paul Richards MG	60.00	30.00
306 Lou Sleater	50.00	25.00
307 Frank Campos	50.00	25.00
307A Frank Campos		
Black Star on Back		
308 Luis Aloma	50.00	25.00
309 Jim Busby	60.00	30.00
310 George Metkovich	100.00	50.00
311 Mickey Mantle DP	18000.00	9000.00
312 Jackie Robinson DP	2000.00	1000.00
313 Bobby Thomson DP	350.00	180.00
314 Roy Campanella	2500.00	1250.00
315 Leo Durocher MG	600.00	300.00
316 Dave Williams RC	300.00	150.00
317 Conrado Marrero	300.00	150.00
318 Harold Gregg	300.00	150.00
319 Rube Walker	250.00	125.00
320 John Rutherford RC	300.00	150.00
321 Joe Black RC	350.00	180.00
322 Randy Jackson	300.00	150.00
323 Bubba Church	250.00	125.00
324 Warren Hacker	250.00	125.00
325 Bill Serena	300.00	150.00
326 George Shuba RC	400.00	200.00
327 Al Wilson	250.00	125.00
328 Bob Borkowski	300.00	150.00
329 Ike Delock	300.00	150.00
330 Turk Lown	300.00	150.00
331 Tom Morgan	300.00	150.00
332 Anthony Bartirome	300.00	150.00
333 Pee Wee Reese	1800.00	900.00
334 Wilmer Mizell RC	300.00	150.00
335 Ted Lepcio	250.00	125.00
336 Dave Koslo	250.00	125.00
337 Jim Hearn	300.00	150.00
338 Sal Yvars	300.00	150.00
339 Russ Meyer	300.00	150.00
340 Bob Hooper	300.00	150.00
341 Hal Jeffcoat	300.00	150.00
342 Clem Labine RC	400.00	200.00
343 Dick Gernert	250.00	125.00
344 Ewell Blackwell	300.00	150.00
345 Sammy White	300.00	150.00
346 George Spencer	250.00	125.00
347 Joe Adcock	400.00	200.00
348 Robert Kelly	300.00	150.00
349 Bob Cain	300.00	150.00
350 Cal Abrams	300.00	150.00
351 Alvin Dark	300.00	150.00
352 Karl Drews	300.00	150.00
353 Bobby Del Greco	300.00	150.00
354 Fred Hatfield	300.00	150.00
355 Bobby Morgan	300.00	150.00
356 Toby Atwell	300.00	150.00
357 Smoky Burgess	300.00	150.00
358 John Kucab	300.00	150.00
359 Dee Fondy	250.00	125.00
360 George Crowe RC	250.00	125.00
361 William Posedel CO	250.00	125.00
362 Ken Heintzelman	300.00	150.00
363 Dick Rozek	300.00	150.00
364 Clyde Sukeforth CO	300.00	150.00
365 Cookie Lavagetto CO	400.00	200.00
366 Dave Madison	250.00	125.00
367 Ben Thorpe	250.00	125.00
368 Ed Wright	300.00	150.00
369 Dick Groat RC	400.00	200.00
370 Billy Hoeft RC	300.00	150.00
371 Bobby Hofman	250.00	125.00
372 Gil McDougald RC	500.00	250.00
373 Jim Turner RC CO	400.00	200.00
374 John Benton	250.00	125.00
375 John Merson	250.00	125.00
376 Faye Throneberry	250.00	125.00
377 Chuck Dressen MG	400.00	200.00
378 Leroy Fusselman	300.00	150.00
379 Joe Rossi	250.00	125.00
380 Clem Koshorek	250.00	125.00
381 Milton Stock CO	300.00	150.00
382 Sam Jones RC	350.00	180.00
383 Del Wilber	250.00	125.00
384 Frank Crosetti CO	500.00	250.00
385 H.Franks CO RC	250.00	125.00
386 John Yuhas	250.00	125.00
387 Billy Meyer MG	250.00	125.00
388 Bob Chipman	250.00	125.00
389 Ben Wade	300.00	150.00
390 Glenn Nelson	300.00	150.00
391 B.Chapman UER CO	250.00	125.00
Photo actually		
Sam Chapman		
392 Hoyt Wilhelm RC	800.00	400.00
393 Ebba St.Claire	300.00	150.00
394 Billy Herman CO	600.00	300.00
395 Jake Pitler CO	300.00	150.00
396 Dick Williams RC	400.00	200.00
397 Forrest Main	250.00	125.00
398 Hal Rice	250.00	125.00
399 Jim Fridley	250.00	125.00
400 Bill Dickey CO	1000.00	500.00
401 Bob Schultz	300.00	150.00
402 Earl Harrist	300.00	150.00
403 Bill Miller	300.00	150.00
404 Dick Brodowski	300.00	150.00
405 Eddie Pellagrini	300.00	150.00
406 Joe Nuxhall RC	400.00	200.00
407 E.Mathews RC	10000.00	2500.00

1953 Topps

The cards in this 274-card set measure 2 5/8" by 3 3/4". Card number 69, Dick Brodowksi, features the first known drawing of a player during a night game. Although the last card is numbered 280, there are only 274 cards in the set since numbers 253, 261, 267, 268, 271, and 275 were never issued. The 1953 Topps series contains line drawings of players in full color. The name and team panel at the card base is easily damaged, making it very difficult to complete a mint set. The high number series, 221 to 280, was produced in shorter supply late in the year and hence is more difficult to complete than the lower numbers. The key cards in the set are Mickey Mantle (82) and Willie Mays (244). The key Rookie Cards in this set are Roy Face, Jim Gilliam, and Johnny Podres, all from the last series. There are a number of double-printed cards (actually not double but 50 percent more of each of these numbers were printed compared to the other cards in the series) indicated by DP in the checklist below. There were five players (10 Smoky Burgess, 44 Ellis Kinder, 61 Early Wynn, 72 Fred Hutchinson, and 81 Joe Black) held out of the first run of 1-85 (but printed in with numbers 86-165), who are each marked by SP in the checklist below. In addition, there are five numbers which were printed with the more plentiful series 166-220; these cards (94, 107, 131, 145, and 156) are also indicated by DP in the checklist below. All these aforementioned cards from 86 through 165 and the five short prints come with the biographical information on the back in either white or black lettering. These seem to be printed in equal quantities and no price differential is given for either variety. The cards were issued in one-card penny packs or six-card nickel packs. The nickel packs were issued 24 to a box. There were some three-card advertising panels produced by Topps; the players include Johnny Mize/Clem Koshorek/Toby Atwell; Jim Hearn/Johnny Groth/Sherman Lollar and Mickey Mantle/Johnny Wyrostek/Sal Yvars. When cut apart, these advertising cards are distinguished by the non-standard card back, i.e., part of an advertisement for the 1953 Topps set instead of the typical statistics and biographical information about the player pictured.

	NM	Ex
COMPLETE SET (274)	15000.00	7500.00
COMMON CARD (1-165)	30.00	15.00
COMMON (166-220)	25.00	12.50
COMMON DP (1-220)	15.00	7.50
COMMON (221-280)	100.00	50.00
NOT ISSUED (253/261/267)		
NOT ISSUED (268/271/275)		
WRAP.(1-CENT, DATED)	200.00	100.00
WRAP.(1-CENT, UNDATED)	300.00	150.00
WRAP.(5-CENT, DATED)	400.00	200.00
WRAP.(5-CENT, UNDATED)	350.00	180.00
1 Jackie Robinson DP	800.00	220.00
2 Luke Easter DP	20.00	10.00
3 George Crowe	40.00	20.00
4 Ben Wade	30.00	15.00
5 Joe Dobson	30.00	15.00
6 Sam Jones	40.00	20.00
7 Bob Borkowski DP	15.00	7.50
8 Clem Koshorek DP	15.00	7.50
9 Joe Collins	60.00	30.00
10 Smoky Burgess SP	80.00	40.00
11 Sal Yvars	30.00	15.00
12 Howie Judson DP	15.00	7.50
13 Conrado Marrero DP	15.00	7.50
14 Clem Labine DP	20.00	10.00
15 Bobo Newsom DP	20.00	10.00
16 Peanuts Lowrey DP	15.00	7.50
17 Billy Hitchcock	30.00	15.00
18 Ted Lepcio DP	15.00	7.50
19 Mel Parnell DP	20.00	10.00
20 Hank Thompson	40.00	20.00
21 Billy Johnson	30.00	15.00
22 Howie Fox	30.00	15.00
23 Toby Atwell DP	15.00	7.50
24 Ferris Fain	40.00	20.00
25 Ray Boone	40.00	20.00
26 Dale Mitchell DP	20.00	10.00
27 Roy Campanella DP	300.00	150.00
28 Eddie Pellagrini	30.00	15.00
29 Hal Jeffcoat	30.00	15.00
30 Willard Nixon	30.00	15.00
31 Ewell Blackwell	60.00	30.00
32 Clyde Vollmer	30.00	15.00
33 Bob Kennedy DP	15.00	7.50
34 George Shuba	40.00	20.00
35 Irv Noren DP	15.00	7.50
36 Johnny Groth DP	15.00	7.50
37 Eddie Mathews DP	250.00	125.00
38 Jim Hearn DP	15.00	7.50
39 Eddie Miksis	30.00	15.00
40 John Lipon	30.00	15.00

41 Enos Slaughter 80.00 40.00
42 Gus Zernial DP 20.00 10.00
43 Gil McDougald 60.00 30.00
44 Ellis Kinder SP 50.00 25.00
45 Grady Hatton DP 15.00 7.50
46 Johnny Klippstein DP 15.00 7.50
47 Bubba Church DP 15.00 7.50
48 Bob Del Greco DP 15.00 7.50
49 Faye Throneberry DP 15.00 7.50
50 Chuck Dressen MG DP 20.00 10.00
51 Frank Campos DP 15.00 7.50
52 Ted Gray DP 15.00 7.50
53 Sherm Lollar DP 20.00 10.00
54 Bob Feller DP 150.00 75.00
55 Maurice McDermott DP 15.00 7.50
56 Gerry Staley DP 15.00 7.50
57 Carl Scheib 30.00 15.00
58 George Metkovich 30.00 15.00
59 Karl Drews DP 15.00 7.50
60 Cloyd Boyer DP 15.00 7.50
61 Early Wynn SP 125.00 60.00
62 Monte Irvin DP 50.00 25.00
63 Gus Niarhos DP 15.00 7.50
64 Dave Philley 30.00 15.00
65 Earl Harrist 30.00 15.00
66 Minnie Minoso 60.00 30.00
67 Roy Sievers DP 20.00 10.00
68 Del Rice 30.00 15.00
69 Dick Brodowski 30.00 15.00
70 Ed Yuhas 30.00 15.00
71 Tony Bartirome 30.00 15.00
72 F.Hutchinson MG SP 50.00 25.00
73 Eddie Robinson 30.00 15.00
74 Joe Rossi 30.00 15.00
75 Mike Garcia 40.00 20.00
76 Pee Wee Reese 175.00 90.00
77 Johnny Mize DP 80.00 40.00
78 Red Schoendienst 80.00 40.00
79 Johnny Wyrostek 30.00 15.00
80 Jim Hegan 40.00 20.00
81 Joe Black SP 80.00 40.00
82 Mickey Mantle 3500.00 1800.00
83 Howie Pollet 30.00 15.00
84 Bob Hooper DP 15.00 7.50
85 Bobby Morgan DP 15.00 7.50
86 Billy Martin 125.00 60.00
87 Ed Lopat 60.00 30.00
88 Willie Jones DP 15.00 7.50
89 Chuck Stobbs DP 15.00 7.50
90 Hank Edwards DP 15.00 7.50
91 Ebba St.Claire DP 15.00 7.50
92 Paul Minner DP 15.00 7.50
93 Hal Rice DP 15.00 7.50
94 Bill Kennedy DP 15.00 7.50
95 Willard Marshall DP 15.00 7.50
96 Virgil Trucks 40.00 20.00
97 Don Kolloway DP 15.00 7.50
98 Cal Abrams DP 15.00 7.50
99 Dave Madison 30.00 15.00
100 Bill Miller 30.00 15.00
101 Ted Wilks 30.00 15.00
102 Connie Ryan DP 15.00 7.50
103 Joe Astroth DP 15.00 7.50
104 Yogi Berra 300.00 150.00
105 Joe Nuxhall DP 20.00 10.00
106 Johnny Antonelli 40.00 20.00
107 Danny O'Connell DP 15.00 7.50
108 Bob Porterfield DP 15.00 7.50
109 Alvin Dark 60.00 30.00
110 Herman Wehmeier DP 15.00 7.50
111 Hank Sauer DP 15.00 7.50
112 Ned Garver DP 15.00 7.50
113 Jerry Priddy 30.00 15.00
114 Phil Rizzuto 250.00 125.00
115 George Spencer 30.00 15.00
116 Frank Smith DP 15.00 7.50
117 Sid Gordon DP 15.00 7.50
118 Gus Bell DP 20.00 10.00
119 Johnny Sain SP 60.00 30.00
120 Davey Williams 40.00 20.00
121 Walt Dropo 40.00 20.00
122 Elmer Valo 30.00 15.00
123 Tommy Byrne DP 15.00 7.50
124 Sibby Sisti DP 15.00 7.50
125 Dick Williams DP 20.00 10.00
126 Bill Connelly DP 15.00 7.50
127 Clint Courtney DP 15.00 7.50
128 Wilmer Mizell DP 20.00 10.00
(Inconsistent design, logo on front with black birds)
129 Keith Thomas 30.00 15.00
130 Turk Lown DP 15.00 7.50
131 Harry Byrd DP 15.00 7.50
132 Tom Morgan 30.00 15.00
133 Gil Coan 30.00 15.00
134 Rube Walker 40.00 20.00
135 Al Rosen DP 20.00 10.00
136 Ken Heintzelman DP 15.00 7.50
137 John Rutherford DP 15.00 7.50
138 George Kell 80.00 40.00
139 Sammy White 30.00 15.00
140 Tommy Glaviano 30.00 15.00
141 Allie Reynolds DP 50.00 25.00
142 Vic Wertz 40.00 20.00
143 Billy Pierce 60.00 30.00
144 Bob Schultz DP 15.00 7.50
145 Harry Dorish DP 15.00 7.50
146 Granny Hamner 30.00 15.00
147 Warren Spahn 175.00 90.00
148 Mickey Grasso 30.00 15.00
149 Dom DiMaggio DP 50.00 25.00
150 Harry Simpson DP 15.00 7.50
151 Hoyt Wilhelm 100.00 50.00
152 Bob Adams DP 15.00 7.50
153 Andy Seminick DP 15.00 7.50
154 Dick Groat 40.00 20.00
155 Dutch Leonard 30.00 15.00
156 Jim Rivera DP 20.00 10.00
157 Bob Addis DP 15.00 7.50
158 Johnny Logan RC 40.00 20.00
159 Wayne Terwilliger DP 15.00 7.50
160 Bob Young 30.00 15.00
161 Vern Bickford DP 15.00 7.50
162 Ted Kluszewski 60.00 30.00
163 Fred Hatfield DP 15.00 7.50
164 Frank Shea DP 15.00 7.50
165 Billy Hoeft 30.00 15.00
166 Billy Hunter 25.00 12.50
167 Art Schult 25.00 12.50
168 Willard Schmidt 25.00 12.50
169 Dizzy Trout 30.00 15.00
170 Bill Werle 25.00 12.50
171 Bill Glynn 25.00 12.50
172 Rip Repulski 25.00 12.50
173 Preston Ward 25.00 12.50
174 Billy Loes 30.00 15.00
175 Ron Kline 25.00 12.50
176 Don Hoak RC 40.00 20.00
177 Jim Dyck 25.00 12.50
178 Jim Waugh 25.00 12.50
179 Gene Hermanski 25.00 12.50
180 Virgil Stallcup 25.00 12.50
181 Al Zarilla 25.00 12.50
182 Bobby Hofman 25.00 12.50
183 Stu Miller RC 40.00 20.00
184 Hal Brown 25.00 12.50
185 Jim Pendleton 25.00 12.50
186 Charlie Bishop 25.00 12.50
187 Jim Fridley 25.00 12.50
188 Andy Carey RC 40.00 20.00
189 Ray Jablonski 25.00 12.50
190 Dixie Walker CO 30.00 15.00
191 Ralph Kiner 80.00 40.00
192 Wally Westlake 25.00 12.50
193 Mike Clark 25.00 12.50
194 Eddie Kazak 25.00 12.50
195 Ed McGhee 25.00 12.50
196 Bob Keegan 25.00 12.50
197 Del Crandall 40.00 20.00
198 Forrest Main 25.00 12.50
199 Marion Fricano 25.00 12.50
200 Gordon Goldsberry 25.00 12.50
201 Paul LaPalme 25.00 12.50
202 Carl Sawatski 25.00 12.50
203 Cliff Fannin 25.00 12.50
204 Dick Bokelman 25.00 12.50
205 Vern Benson 25.00 12.50
206 Ed Bailey RC 30.00 15.00
207 Whitey Ford 200.00 100.00
208 Jim Wilson 25.00 12.50
209 Jim Greengrass 25.00 12.50
210 Bob Cerv RC 40.00 20.00
211 J.W. Porter 25.00 12.50
212 Jack Dittmer 25.00 12.50
213 Ray Scarborough 25.00 12.50
214 Bill Bruton RC 40.00 20.00
215 Gene Conley RC 30.00 15.00
216 Jim Hughes 25.00 12.50
217 Murray Wall 25.00 12.50
218 Les Fusselman 25.00 12.50
219 Pete Runnels UER 30.00 15.00
(Photo actually Don Johnson)
220 Satchel Paige UER 600.00 300.00
(Misspelled Satchell on card front)
221 Bob Milliken 100.00 50.00
222 Vic Janowicz DP RC 60.00 30.00
223 Johnny O'Brien DP 50.00 25.00
224 Lou Sleater DP 50.00 25.00
225 Bobby Shantz 125.00 60.00
226 Ed Erautt 100.00 50.00
227 Morrie Martin 100.00 50.00
228 Hal Newhouser 150.00 75.00
229 Rocky Krsnich 100.00 50.00
230 Johnny Lindell DP 50.00 25.00
231 Solly Hemus DP 50.00 25.00
232 Dick Kokos 100.00 50.00
233 Al Aber 100.00 50.00
234 Ray Murray DP 50.00 25.00
235 John Hetki DP 50.00 25.00
236 Harry Perkowski DP 50.00 25.00
237 Bud Podbielan DP 50.00 25.00
238 Cal Hogue DP 50.00 25.00
239 Jim Delsing 100.00 50.00
240 Fred Marsh 100.00 50.00
241 Al Sima DP 50.00 25.00
242 Charlie Silvera 125.00 60.00
243 Carlos Bernier DP 50.00 25.00
244 Willie Mays 2500.00 1250.00
245 Bill Norman CO 100.00 50.00
246 Roy Face DP RC 80.00 40.00
247 Mike Sandlock DP 50.00 25.00
248 Gene Stephens DP 50.00 25.00
249 Eddie O'Brien 100.00 50.00
250 Bob Wilson 100.00 50.00
251 Sid Hudson 100.00 50.00
252 Hank Foiles 100.00 50.00
253 Does not exist
254 Preacher Roe DP 80.00 40.00
255 Dixie Howell 100.00 50.00
256 Les Peden 100.00 50.00
257 Bob Boyd 100.00 50.00
258 Jim Gilliam RC 400.00 200.00
259 Roy McMillan DP 50.00 25.00
260 Sam Calderone 100.00 50.00
261 Does not exist
262 Bob Oldis 100.00 50.00
263 Johnny Podres RC 300.00 150.00
264 Gene Woodling DP 60.00 30.00
265 Jackie Jensen 125.00 60.00
266 Bob Cain 100.00 50.00
267 Does not exist
268 Does not exist
269 Duane Pillette 100.00 50.00
270 Vern Stephens 125.00 60.00
271 Does not exist
272 Bill Antonello 100.00 50.00
273 Harvey Haddix RC 150.00 75.00
274 John Riddle CO 100.00 50.00
275 Does not exist
276 Ken Raffensberger 100.00 50.00
277 Don Lund 100.00 50.00
278 Willie Miranda 100.00 50.00
279 Joe Coleman DP 50.00 25.00
280 Milt Bolling RC 350.00 57.50

1954 Topps

The cards in this 250-card set measure approximately 2 5/8" by 3 3/4". Each of the cards in the 1954 Topps set contains a large "head" shot of the player in color plus a smaller full-length photo in black and white set against a color background. The cards were issued in one-card penny packs or five-card nickel packs. Fifteen-card cello packs have also been seen. The penny packs came 120 to a box. This set contains the Rookie Cards of Hank Aaron, Ernie Banks, and Al Kaline and two separate cards of Ted Williams (number 1 and number 250). Conspicuous by his absence is Mickey Mantle who apparently was the exclusive property of Bowman during 1954 (and 1955). The first two issues of Sports Illustrated magazine contained "card" inserts on regular paper stock. The first issue showed actual cards in the set in color, while the second issue showed some created cards of New York Yankees players in black and white, including Mickey Mantle. There was also a Canadian printing of the first 50 cards. These cards can be easily discerned as they have "grey" backs rather than the white backs of the American printed cards.

NM Ex
COMPLETE SET (250) 8000.00 4000.00
COMMON (1-50/76-250) 15.00 7.50
COMMON CARD (51-75) 25.00 12.50
WRAP.(1-CENT, DATED) 200.00 100.00
WRAP.(1-CENT, UNDATED) 150.00 75.00
WRAP.(5-CENT, DATED) 300.00 150.00
WRAP.(5-CENT, UNDATED) 250.00 125.00
1 Ted Williams 800.00 275.00
2 Gus Zernial 25.00 12.50
3 Monte Irvin 50.00 25.00
4 Hank Sauer 25.00 12.50
5 Ed Lopat 25.00 12.50
6 Pete Runnels 25.00 12.50
7 Ted Kluszewski 50.00 25.00
8 Bob Young 15.00 7.50
9 Harvey Haddix 25.00 12.50
10 Jackie Robinson 400.00 200.00
11 Paul Leslie Smith 15.00 7.50
12 Del Crandall 25.00 12.50
13 Billy Martin 100.00 50.00
14 Preacher Roe 25.00 12.50
15 Al Rosen 25.00 12.50
16 Vic Janowicz 25.00 12.50
17 Phil Rizzuto 125.00 60.00
18 Walt Dropo 25.00 12.50
19 Johnny Lipon 15.00 7.50
Orioles Team Name on Front
White Sox team on Back
Wearing a Red Sox cap
20 Warren Spahn 125.00 60.00
21 Bobby Shantz 25.00 12.50
22 Jim Greengrass 15.00 7.50
23 Luke Easter 25.00 12.50
24 Granny Hamner 15.00 7.50
25 Harvey Kuenn RC 40.00 20.00
26 Ray Jablonski 15.00 7.50
27 Ferris Fain 25.00 12.50
28 Paul Minner 15.00 7.50
29 Jim Hegan 25.00 12.50
30 Eddie Mathews 100.00 50.00
31 Johnny Klippstein 15.00 7.50
32 Duke Snider 200.00 100.00
33 Johnny Schmitz 15.00 7.50
34 Jim Rivera 15.00 7.50
35 Jim Gilliam 50.00 25.00
36 Hoyt Wilhelm 50.00 25.00
37 Whitey Ford 200.00 100.00
38 Eddie Stanky MG 25.00 12.50
39 Sherm Lollar 25.00 12.50
40 Mel Parnell 25.00 12.50
41 Willie Jones 15.00 7.50
42 Don Mueller 25.00 12.50
43 Dick Groat 25.00 12.50
44 Ned Garver 15.00 7.50
45 Richie Ashburn 80.00 40.00
46 Ken Raffensberger 15.00 7.50
47 Ellis Kinder 15.00 7.50
48 Billy Hunter 15.00 7.50
49 Ray Murray 15.00 7.50
50 Yogi Berra 250.00 125.00
51 Johnny Lindell 25.00 12.50
52 Vic Power RC 30.00 15.00
53 Jack Dittmer 25.00 12.50
54 Vern Stephens 30.00 15.00
55 Phil Cavarretta MG 30.00 15.00
56 Willie Miranda 25.00 12.50
57 Luis Aloma 25.00 12.50
58 Bob Wilson 25.00 12.50
59 Gene Conley 30.00 15.00
60 Frank Baumholtz 25.00 12.50
61 Bob Cain 25.00 12.50
62 Eddie Robinson 25.00 12.50
63 Johnny Pesky 30.00 15.00
64 Hank Thompson 25.00 12.50
65 Bob Swift CO 25.00 12.50
66 Ted Lepcio 25.00 12.50
67 Jim Willis 25.00 12.50
68 Sam Calderone 25.00 12.50
69 Bud Podbielan 25.00 12.50
70 Larry Doby 60.00 30.00
71 Frank Smith 25.00 12.50
72 Preston Ward 25.00 12.50
73 Wayne Terwilliger 25.00 12.50
74 Bill Taylor 25.00 12.50
75 Fred Haney MG 25.00 12.50
76 Bob Scheffing CO 15.00 7.50
77 Ray Boone 25.00 12.50
78 Ted Kazanski 15.00 7.50
79 Andy Pafko 25.00 12.50
80 Jackie Jensen 25.00 12.50
81 Dave Hoskins 15.00 7.50
82 Milt Bolling 15.00 7.50
83 Joe Collins 25.00 12.50
84 Dick Cole 15.00 7.50
85 Bob Turley RC 40.00 20.00
86 Billy Herman CO 25.00 12.50
87 Roy Face 25.00 12.50
88 Matt Batts 15.00 7.50
89 Howie Pollet 15.00 7.50
90 Willie Mays 800.00 400.00
91 Bob Oldis 15.00 7.50
92 Wally Westlake 15.00 7.50
93 Sid Hudson 15.00 7.50
94 Ernie Banks RC 1000.00 500.00
95 Hal Rice 15.00 7.50
96 Charlie Silvera 25.00 12.50
97 Jerald Hal Lane 15.00 7.50
98 Joe Black 40.00 20.00
99 Bobby Hofman 15.00 7.50
100 Bob Keegan 15.00 7.50
101 Gene Woodling 25.00 12.50
102 Gil Hodges 80.00 40.00
103 Jim Lemon RC 15.00 7.50
104 Mike Sandlock 15.00 7.50
105 Andy Carey 25.00 12.50
106 Dick Kokos 15.00 7.50
107 Duane Pillette 15.00 7.50
108 Thornton Kipper 15.00 7.50
109 Bill Bruton 25.00 12.50
110 Harry Dorish 15.00 7.50
111 Jim Delsing 15.00 7.50
112 Bill Renna 15.00 7.50
113 Bob Boyd 15.00 7.50
114 Dean Stone 15.00 7.50
115 Rip Repulski 15.00 7.50
116 Steve Bilko 15.00 7.50
117 Solly Hemus 15.00 7.50
118 Carl Scheib 15.00 7.50
119 Johnny Antonelli 25.00 12.50
120 Roy McMillan 25.00 12.50
121 Clem Labine 25.00 12.50
122 Johnny Logan 25.00 12.50
123 Bobby Adams 15.00 7.50
124 Marion Fricano 15.00 7.50
125 Harry Perkowski 15.00 7.50
126 Ben Wade 15.00 7.50
127 Steve O'Neill MG 15.00 7.50
128 Hank Aaron RC 1500.00 750.00
129 Forrest Jacobs 15.00 7.50
130 Hank Bauer 25.00 12.50
131 Reno Bertoia 25.00 12.50
132 Tommy Lasorda RC 250.00 125.00
133 Del Baker CO 15.00 7.50
134 Cal Hogue 15.00 7.50
135 Joe Presko 15.00 7.50
136 Connie Ryan 15.00 7.50
137 Wally Moon RC 40.00 20.00
138 Bob Borkowski 15.00 7.50
139 The O'Briens 50.00 25.00
Johnny O'Brien
Eddie O'Brien
140 Tom Wright 15.00 7.50
141 Joey Jay RC 25.00 12.50
142 Tom Poholsky 15.00 7.50
143 Rollie Hemsley CO 15.00 7.50
144 Bill Werle 15.00 7.50
145 Elmer Valo 15.00 7.50
146 Don Johnson 15.00 7.50
147 Johnny Riddle CO 15.00 7.50
148 Bob Trice 15.00 7.50
149 Al Robertson 15.00 7.50
150 Dick Kryhoski 15.00 7.50
151 Alex Grammas 15.00 7.50
152 Michael Blyzka 15.00 7.50
153 Al Walker 25.00 12.50
154 Mike Fornieles 25.00 12.50
155 Bob Kennedy 25.00 12.50
156 Joe Coleman 25.00 12.50
157 Don Lenhardt 25.00 12.50
158 Peanuts Lowrey 15.00 7.50
159 Dave Philley 15.00 7.50
160 Ralph Kress CO 15.00 7.50
161 John Hetki 15.00 7.50
162 Herman Wehmeier 15.00 7.50
163 Frank House 15.00 7.50
164 Stu Miller 25.00 12.50
165 Jim Pendleton 15.00 7.50
166 Johnny Podres 40.00 20.00
167 Don Lund 15.00 7.50
168 Morrie Martin 25.00 12.50
169 Jim Hughes 40.00 20.00
170 Dusty Rhodes RC 25.00 12.50
171 Leo Kiely 15.00 7.50
172 Harold Brown 15.00 7.50
173 Jack Harshman 15.00 7.50
174 Tom Qualters 15.00 7.50
175 Frank Leja RC 25.00 12.50
176 Robert Keely CO 15.00 7.50
177 Bob Milliken 15.00 7.50
178 Bill Glynn UER 15.00 7.50
Spelled Gylnn on the front
179 Gair Allie 15.00 7.50
180 Wes Westrum 25.00 12.50
181 Mel Roach 15.00 7.50
182 Chuck Harmon 15.00 7.50
183 Earle Combs CO 25.00 12.50
184 Ed Bailey 15.00 7.50
185 Chuck Stobbs 15.00 7.50
186 Karl Olson 15.00 7.50
187 Heinie Manush CO 25.00 12.50
188 Dave Jolly 15.00 7.50
189 Bob Ross 15.00 7.50
190 Ray Herbert 15.00 7.50
191 John(Dick) Schofield RC 25.00 12.50
192 Ellis Deal CO 15.00 7.50
193 Johnny Hopp CO 25.00 12.50
194 Bill Sarni 15.00 7.50
195 Billy Consolo RC 15.00 7.50
196 Stan Jok 15.00 7.50
197 Lynwood Rowe CO 25.00 12.50
("Schoolboy")
198 Carl Sawatski 15.00 7.50
199 Glenn(Rocky) Nelson 15.00 7.50
200 Larry Jansen 25.00 12.50
201 Al Kaline RC 700.00 350.00
202 Bob Purkey RC 25.00 12.50
203 Harry Brecheen CO 25.00 12.50
204 Angel Scull 15.00 7.50
205 Johnny Sain 40.00 20.00
206 Ray Crone 15.00 7.50
207 Tom Oliver CO 15.00 7.50
208 Grady Hatton 15.00 7.50
209 Chuck Thompson 15.00 7.50
210 Bob Buhl RC 25.00 12.50
211 Don Hoak 15.00 7.50
212 Bob Micelotta 15.00 7.50
213 Johnny Fitzpatrick CO 15.00 7.50
214 Arnie Portocarrero 15.00 7.50
215 Ed McGhee 25.00 12.50
216 Al Sima 15.00 7.50
217 Paul Schreiber CO 15.00 7.50
218 Fred Marsh 15.00 7.50
219 Chuck Kress 15.00 7.50
220 Ruben Gomez 25.00 12.50
221 Dick Brodowski 15.00 7.50
222 Bill Wilson 15.00 7.50
223 Joe Haynes CO 15.00 7.50
224 Dick Weik 15.00 7.50
225 Don Liddle 15.00 7.50
226 Jehosie Heard 25.00 12.50
227 Buster Mills CO 15.00 7.50
228 Gene Hermanski 15.00 7.50
229 Bob Talbot 15.00 7.50
230 Bob Kuzava 25.00 12.50
231 Roy Smalley 15.00 7.50
232 Lou Limmer 15.00 7.50
233 Augie Galan CO 15.00 7.50
234 Jerry Lynch RC 15.00 7.50
235 Vern Law 25.00 12.50
236 Paul Penson 15.00 7.50
237 Mike Ryba CO 15.00 7.50
238 Al Aber 15.00 7.50
239 Bill Skowron RC 100.00 50.00
240 Sam Mele 25.00 12.50
241 Robert Miller 15.00 7.50
242 Curt Roberts 15.00 7.50
243 Ray Blades CO 15.00 7.50
244 Leroy Wheat 15.00 7.50
245 Roy Sievers 25.00 12.50
246 Howie Fox 15.00 7.50
247 Ed Mayo CO 15.00 7.50
248 Al Smith RC 25.00 12.50
249 Wilmer Mizell 25.00 12.50
250 Ted Williams 800.00 325.00

1955 Topps

The cards in this 206-card set measure approximately 2 5/8" by 3 3/4". Both the large "head" shot and the smaller full-length photos used on each card of the 1955 Topps set are in color. The card fronts were designed horizontally for the first time in Topps' history. The first card features Dusty Rhodes, hitting star and MVP in the New York Giants' 1954 World Series sweep over the Cleveland Indians. A "high" series, 161 to 210, is more difficult to find than cards 1 to 160. Numbers 175, 186, 203, and 209 were never issued. To fill in for the four cards not issued in the high number series, Topps double printed four players, those appearing on cards 170, 172, 184, and 188. Cards were issued in one-card penny packs or six-card nickel packs and 15-card cello packs (rarely seen). Although rarely seen, there exist salesman sample panels of three cards containing the fronts of regular cards with ad information for the 1955 Topps regular and the 1955 Topps Doubleheaders on the back. One panel depicts (from top to bottom) Danny Schell, Jake Thies, and Howie Pollet. Another Panel consists of Jackie Robinson, Bill Taylor and Curt Roberts. The key Rookie Cards in this set are Ken Boyer, Roberto Clemente, Harmon Killebrew, and Sandy Koufax.

NM Ex
COMPLETE SET (206) 8000.00 4000.00
COMMON CARD (1-150) 12.00 6.00
COMMON (151-160) 20.00 10.00
COMMON (161-210) 30.00 15.00
NOT ISSUED (175/186/203/209)
WRAP.(1-CENT, DATED) 150.00 75.00
WRAP.(1-CENT, UNDATED) 50.00 25.00
WRAP.(5-CENT, DATED) 150.00 75.00
WRAP.(5-CENT, UNDATED) 100.00 50.00
1 Dusty Rhodes 125.00 25.00
2 Ted Williams 600.00 300.00
3 Art Fowler 15.00 7.50
4 Al Kaline 150.00 75.00
5 Jim Gilliam 40.00 20.00
6 Stan Hack MG 25.00 12.50
7 Jim Hegan 15.00 7.50
8 Harold Smith 12.00 6.00
9 Robert Miller 12.00 6.00
10 Bob Keegan 12.00 6.00
11 Ferris Fain 15.00 7.50
12 Vernon(Jake) Thies 12.00 6.00
13 Fred Marsh 12.00 6.00
14 Jim Finigan 12.00 6.00
15 Jim Pendleton 12.00 6.00
16 Roy Sievers 15.00 7.50
17 Bobby Hofman 12.00 6.00
18 Russ Kemmerer 12.00 6.00
19 Billy Herman CO 15.00 7.50
20 Andy Carey 15.00 7.50
21 Alex Grammas 12.00 6.00
22 Bill Skowron 40.00 20.00
23 Jack Parks 12.00 6.00
24 Hal Newhouser 40.00 20.00
25 Johnny Podres 25.00 12.50
26 Dick Groat 15.00 7.50
27 Billy Gardner RC 15.00 7.50
28 Ernie Banks 200.00 100.00
29 Herman Wehmeier 12.00 6.00
30 Vic Power 15.00 7.50
31 Warren Spahn 100.00 50.00
32 Warren McGhee 12.00 6.00
33 Tom Qualters 12.00 6.00
34 Wayne Terwilliger 12.00 6.00
35 Dave Jolly 12.00 6.00
36 Leo Kiely 12.00 6.00
37 Joe Cunningham RC 15.00 7.50
38 Bob Turley 15.00 7.50
39 Bill Glynn 12.00 6.00
40 Don Hoak 15.00 7.50
41 Chuck Stobbs 12.00 6.00
42 John(Windy) McCall 12.00 6.00
43 Harvey Haddix 15.00 7.50
44 Harold Valentine 12.00 6.00
45 Hank Sauer 15.00 7.50
46 Ted Kazanski 12.00 6.00
47 Hank Aaron UER 400.00 200.00
(Birth incorrectly

listed as 2/10)
48 Bob Kennedy 15.00 7.50
49 J.W. Porter 12.00 6.00
50 Jackie Robinson 500.00 250.00
51 Jim Hughes 15.00 7.50
52 Bill Tremel 12.00 6.00
53 Bill Taylor 12.00 6.00
54 Lou Limmer 12.00 6.00
55 Rip Repulski 12.00 6.00
56 Ray Jablonski 12.00 6.00
57 Billy O'Dell 12.00 6.00
58 Jim Rivera 12.00 6.00
59 Gair Allie 12.00 6.00
60 Dean Stone 12.00 6.00
61 Forrest Jacobs 12.00 6.00
62 Thornton Kipper 12.00 6.00
63 Joe Collins 15.00 7.50
64 Gus Triandos RC 15.00 7.50
65 Ray Boone 15.00 7.50
66 Ron Jackson RC 12.00 6.00
67 Wally Moon 15.00 7.50
68 Jim Davis 12.00 6.00
69 Ed Bailey 15.00 7.50
70 Al Rosen 15.00 7.50
71 Ruben Gomez 12.00 6.00
72 Karl Olson 12.00 6.00
73 Jack Shepard 12.00 6.00
74 Bob Borkowski 12.00 6.00
75 Sandy Amoros RC 40.00 20.00
76 Howie Pollet 12.00 6.00
77 Arnie Portocarrero 12.00 6.00
78 Gordon Jones 12.00 6.00
79 Clyde(Danny) Schell 12.00 6.00
80 Bob Grim RC 15.00 7.50
81 Gene Conley 15.00 7.50
82 Chuck Harmon 12.00 6.00
83 Tom Brewer 12.00 6.00
84 Camilo Pascual RC 15.00 7.50
85 Don Mossi RC 25.00 12.50
86 Bill Wilson 12.00 6.00
87 Frank House 12.00 6.00
88 Bob Skinner RC 15.00 7.50
89 Joe Frazier 15.00 7.50
90 Karl Spooner RC 15.00 7.50
91 Milt Bolling 12.00 6.00
92 Don Zimmer RC 25.00 12.50
93 Steve Bilko 12.00 6.00
94 Reno Bertoia 12.00 6.00
95 Preston Ward 12.00 6.00
96 Chuck Bishop 12.00 6.00
97 Carlos Paula 12.00 6.00
98 John Riddle CO 12.00 6.00
99 Frank Leja 12.00 6.00
100 Monte Irvin 40.00 20.00
101 Johnny Gray 12.00 6.00
102 Wally Westlake 12.00 6.00
103 Chuck White 12.00 6.00
104 Jack Harshman 12.00 6.00
105 Chuck Diering 12.00 6.00
106 Frank Sullivan 12.00 6.00
107 Curt Roberts 12.00 6.00
108 Rube Walker 15.00 7.50
109 Ed Lopat 15.00 7.50
110 Gus Zernial 15.00 7.50
111 Bob Milliken 15.00 7.50
112 Nelson King 12.00 6.00
113 Harry Brecheen CO 15.00 7.50
114 Louis Ortiz 12.00 6.00
115 Ellis Kinder 12.00 6.00
116 Tom Hurd 12.00 6.00
117 Mel Roach 12.00 6.00
118 Bob Purkey 12.00 6.00
119 Bob Lennon 12.00 6.00
120 Ted Kluszewski 80.00 40.00
121 Bill Renna 12.00 6.00
122 Carl Sawatski 12.00 6.00
123 Sandy Koufax RC 800.00 400.00
124 Harmon Killebrew RC 250.00 125.00
125 Ken Boyer RC 80.00 40.00
126 Dick Hall 12.00 6.00
127 Dale Long RC 15.00 7.50
128 Ted Lepcio 12.00 6.00
129 Elvin Tappe 15.00 7.50
130 Mayo Smith MG 12.00 6.00
131 Grady Hatton 12.00 6.00
132 Bob Trice 12.00 6.00
133 Dave Hoskins 12.00 6.00
134 Joey Jay 15.00 7.50
135 Johnny O'Brien 15.00 7.50
136 Veston(Bunky)Stewart 12.00 6.00
137 Harry Elliott 12.00 6.00
138 Ray Herbert 12.00 6.00
139 Steve Kraly 12.00 6.00
140 Mel Parnell 15.00 7.50
141 Tom Wright 12.00 6.00
142 Jerry Lynch 15.00 7.50
143 John(Dick) Schofield 15.00 7.50
144 John(Joe) Amalfitano RC 12.00 6.00
145 Elmer Valo 12.00 6.00
146 Dick Donovan RC 12.00 6.00
147 Hugh Pepper 12.00 6.00
148 Hector Brown 12.00 6.00
149 Ray Crone 12.00 6.00
150 Mike Higgins MG 12.00 6.00
151 Ralph Kress CO 20.00 10.00
152 Harry Agganis RC 100.00 50.00
153 Bud Podbielan 25.00 12.50
154 Willie Miranda 20.00 10.00
155 Eddie Mathews 125.00 60.00
156 Joe Black 50.00 25.00
157 Robert Miller 20.00 10.00
158 Tommy Carroll 25.00 12.50
159 Johnny Schmitz 20.00 10.00
160 Ray Narleski RC 20.00 10.00
161 Chuck Tanner RC 40.00 20.00
162 Joe Coleman 30.00 15.00
163 Faye Throneberry 30.00 15.00
164 Roberto Clemente RC 2000.00 1000.00
165 Don Johnson 30.00 15.00
166 Hank Bauer 80.00 40.00
167 Tom Casagrande 30.00 15.00
168 Duane Pillette 30.00 15.00
169 Bob Oldis 40.00 20.00
170 Jim Pearce DP 15.00 7.50
171 Dick Brodowski 30.00 15.00
172 Frank Baumholtz DP 15.00 7.50
173 Bob Kline 30.00 15.00
174 Rudy Minarcin 30.00 15.00
175 Does not exist
176 Norm Zauchin 30.00 15.00
177 Al Robertson 30.00 15.00
178 Bobby Adams 30.00 15.00
179 Jim Bolger 30.00 15.00
180 Clem Labine 60.00 30.00
181 Roy McMillan 40.00 20.00
182 Humberto Robinson 30.00 15.00
183 Anthony Jacobs 30.00 15.00
184 Harry Perkowski DP 15.00 7.50
185 Don Ferrarese 30.00 15.00
186 Does not exist
187 Gil Hodges 175.00 90.00
188 Charlie Silvera DP 15.00 7.50
189 Phil Rizzuto 175.00 90.00
190 Gene Woodling 40.00 20.00
191 Eddie Stanky MG 40.00 20.00
192 Jim Delsing 40.00 20.00
193 Johnny Sain 60.00 30.00
194 Willie Mays 600.00 300.00
195 Ed Roebuck RC 60.00 30.00
196 Gale Wade 30.00 15.00
197 Al Smith 60.00 30.00
198 Yogi Berra 300.00 150.00
199 Bert Hamric 40.00 20.00
200 Jackie Jensen 60.00 30.00
201 Sherman Lollar 40.00 20.00
202 Jim Owens 30.00 15.00
203 Does not exist
204 Frank Smith 30.00 15.00
205 Gene Freese RC 40.00 20.00
206 Pete Daley 30.00 15.00
207 Billy Consolo 30.00 15.00
208 Ray Moore 40.00 20.00
209 Does not exist
210 Duke Snider 600.00 180.00

1955 Topps Double Header

The cards in this 66-card set measure approximately 2 1/16" by 4 7/8". Borrowing a design from the T201 Mecca series, Topps issued a 132-player "Double Header" set in a separate wrapper in 1955. Each player is numbered in the biographical section on the reverse. When open, with perforated flap up, one player is revealed; when the flap is lowered, or closed, the player design on top incorporates a portion of the inside player artwork. When the cards are placed side by side, a continuous ballpark background is formed. Some cards have been found without perforations, and all players pictured appear in the low series of the 1955 regular issue. The cards were issued in one-card penny packs with a piece of bubble gum.

NM Ex
COMPLETE SET (66) 4000.00 2000.00
WRAPPER (1-CENT) 200.00 100.00
1 Al Rosen and 50.00 25.00
2 Chuck Diering
3 Monte Irvin and 75.00 38.00
4 Russ Kemmerer
5 Ted Kazanski and 40.00 20.00
6 Gordon Jones
7 Bill Taylor and 40.00 20.00
8 Billy O'Dell
9 J.W. Porter and 40.00 20.00
10 Thornton Kipper
11 Curt Roberts and 40.00 20.00
12 Arnie Portocarrero
13 Wally Westlake and 50.00 25.00
14 Frank House
15 Rube Walker and 50.00 25.00
16 Lou Limmer
17 Dean Stone and 40.00 20.00
18 Charlie White
19 Karl Spooner and 50.00 25.00
20 Jim Hughes
21 Bill Skowron and 60.00 30.00
22 Frank Sullivan
23 Jack Shepard and 40.00 20.00
24 Stan Hack MG
25 Jackie Robinson and 300.00 150.00
26 Don Hoak
27 Dusty Rhodes and 50.00 25.00
28 Jim Davis
29 Vic Power and 40.00 20.00
30 Ed Bailey
31 Howie Pollet and 225.00 110.00
32 Ernie Banks
33 Jim Pendleton and 40.00 20.00
34 Gene Conley
35 Karl Olson and 40.00 20.00
36 Andy Carey
37 Wally Moon and 50.00 25.00
38 Joe Cunningham
39 Freddie Marsh and 40.00 20.00
40 Vernon Thies
41 Eddie Lopat and 60.00 30.00
42 Harvey Haddix
43 Leo Kiely and 40.00 20.00
44 Chuck Stobbs
45 Al Kaline and 225.00 110.00
46 Harold Valentine
47 Forrest Jacobs and 40.00 20.00
48 Johnny Gray
49 Ron Jackson and 40.00 20.00
50 Jim Finigan
51 Ray Jablonski and 40.00 20.00
52 Bob Keegan
53 Billy Herman CO and 75.00 38.00
54 Sandy Amoros
55 Chuck Harmon and 40.00 20.00
56 Bob Skinner
57 Dick Hall and 40.00 20.00
58 Bob Grim
59 Billy Glynn and 50.00 25.00
60 Bob Miller
61 Billy Gardner and 40.00 20.00
62 John Hetki
63 Bob Borkowski and 40.00 20.00
64 Bob Turley
65 Joe Collins and 40.00 20.00
66 Jack Harshman
67 Jim Hegan and 40.00 20.00
68 Jack Parks
69 Ted Williams and 400.00 200.00
70 Mayo Smith MG
71 Gair Allie and 40.00 20.00
72 Grady Hatton
73 Jerry Lynch and 40.00 20.00
74 Harry Brecheen CO
75 Tom Wright and 40.00 20.00
76 Vernon Stewart
77 Dave Hoskins and 40.00 20.00
78 Warren McGhee
79 Roy Sievers and 50.00 25.00
80 Art Fowler
81 Danny Schell and 40.00 20.00
82 Gus Triandos
83 Joe Frazier and 40.00 20.00
84 Don Mossi
85 Elmer Valo and 40.00 20.00
86 Hector Brown
87 Bob Kennedy and 50.00 25.00
88 Windy McCall
89 Ruben Gomez and 40.00 20.00
90 Jim Rivera
91 Louis Ortiz and 40.00 20.00
92 Milt Bolling
93 Carl Sawatski and 40.00 20.00
94 El Tappe
95 Dave Jolly and 40.00 20.00
96 Bobby Hofman
97 Preston Ward and 60.00 30.00
98 Don Zimmer
99 Bill Renna and 50.00 25.00
100 Dick Groat
101 Bill Wilson and 40.00 20.00
102 Bill Tremel
103 Hank Sauer and 50.00 25.00
104 Camilo Pascual
105 Hank Aaron and 500.00 250.00
106 Ray Herbert
107 Alex Grammas and 40.00 20.00
108 Tom Qualters
109 Hal Newhouser and 75.00 38.00
110 Chuck Bishop
111 Harmon Killebrew and 200.00 100.00
112 John Podres
113 Ray Boone and 40.00 20.00
114 Bob Purkey
115 Dale Long and 50.00 25.00
116 Ferris Fain
117 Steve Bilko and 40.00 20.00
118 Bob Milliken
119 Mel Parnell and 50.00 25.00
120 Tom Hurd
121 Ted Kluszewski and 75.00 38.00
122 Jim Owens
123 Gus Zernial and 40.00 20.00
124 Bob Trice
125 Rip Repulski and 40.00 20.00
126 Ted Lepcio
127 Warren Spahn and 200.00 100.00
128 Tom Brewer
129 Jim Gilliam and 75.00 38.00
130 Ellis Kinder
131 Herm Wehmeier and 40.00 20.00
132 Wayne Terwilliger

1955 Topps Test Stamps

These test issues stamps "are full-size versions of regular first series cards, but with blank, gummed backs and perforated edges." These stamps are listed in alphabetical order with their corresponding card number listed immediately after their name. Since these "stamps" show up very infrequently in the hobby -- any additions to this checklist are appreciated.

NM Ex
COMPLETE SET 6000.00 3000.00
1 Ray Boone 300.00 150.00
Card number 65
2 Joe Cunningham 300.00 150.00
Card number 37
3 Jim Davis 300.00 150.00
Card number 68
4 Ruben Gomez 300.00 150.00
Card number 71
5 Alex Grammas 300.00 150.00
Card number 21
6 Stan Hack MG 400.00 200.00
Card number 6
7 Harvey Haddix 300.00 150.00
Card number 43
8 Bobby Hofman 300.00 150.00
Card number 17
9 Ray Jablonski 300.00 150.00
Card number 56
10 Dave Jolly 300.00 150.00
Card number 35
11 Don Mossi 500.00 250.00
Card number 85
12 Jim Pendleton 300.00 150.00
Card number 15
13 Howie Pollet 300.00 150.00
Card number 76
14 Jack Shepard 300.00 150.00
Card number 73
15 Bob Skinner 400.00 200.00
Card number 88
16 Bill Skowron 600.00 300.00
Card number 22
17 Karl Spooner 400.00 200.00
Card number 90
18 Rube Walker 400.00 200.00
Card number 108
19 Charlie White 300.00 150.00
Card number 103

1956 Topps

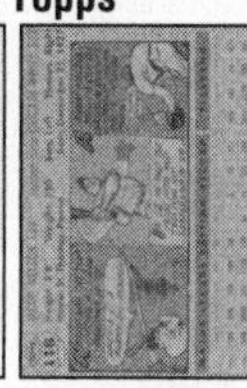

The cards in this 340-card set measure approximately 2 5/8" by 3 3/4". Following up with another horizontally oriented card in 1956, Topps improved the format by layering the color "head" shot onto an actual action sequence involving the player. Cards 1 to 180 come with either white or gray backs: in the 1 to 100 sequence, gray backs are less common (worth about 10 percent more) and in the 101 to 180 sequence, white backs are less common (worth 30 percent more). The team cards, used for the first time in a regular set by Topps, are found dated 1955, or undated, with the team name appearing on either side. The dated team cards in the first series were not printed on the gray stock. The two unnumbered checklist cards are highly prized (must be unmarked to qualify as excellent or mint). The complete set price below does not include the unnumbered checklist cards or any of the variations. The set was issued in one-card penny packs or six-card nickel packs. The six card nickel packs came 24 to a box with 24 boxes in a case. Both types of packs included a piece of bubble gum. Promotional three card strips were issued for this set. Among those strips were one featuring Johnny O'Brien/Harvey Haddix and Frank House. The key Rookie Cards in this set are Walt Alston, Luis Aparicio, and Roger Craig. There are ten double-printed cards in the first series as evidenced by the discovery of an uncut sheet of 110 cards (10 by 11); these DP's are listed below.

NM Ex
COMPLETE SET (340) 8000.00 4000.00
COMMON CARD (1-100) 10.00 5.00
COMMON (101-180) 12.00 6.00
COMMON (261-340) 12.00 6.00
COMMON (181-260) 15.00 7.50
WRAPPER (1-CENT) 250.00 125.00
WRAP.(1-CENT, REPEAT) 100.00 50.00
WRAPPER (5-CENT) 200.00 100.00
1 W.Harridge PRES RC 125.00 35.00
2 W. Giles PRES RC DP 50.00 25.00
3 Elmer Valo 15.00 7.50
4 Carlos Paula 15.00 7.50
5 Ted Williams 500.00 250.00
6 Ray Boone 25.00 12.50
7 Ron Negray 10.00 5.00
8 Walter Alston MG RC 40.00 20.00
9 Ruben Gomez DP 10.00 5.00
10 Warren Spahn 100.00 50.00
11A Chicago Cubs 30.00 15.00
(Centered)
11B Cubs Team 80.00 40.00
(Dated 1955)
11C Cubs Team 30.00 15.00
(Name at far left)
12 Andy Carey 15.00 7.50
13 Roy Face 15.00 7.50
14 Ken Boyer DP 15.00 7.50
15 Ernie Banks DP 100.00 50.00
16 Hector Lopez RC 15.00 7.50
17 Gene Conley 15.00 7.50
18 Dick Donovan 10.00 5.00
19 Chuck Diering DP 10.00 5.00
20 Al Kaline 125.00 60.00
21 Joe Collins DP 15.00 7.50
22 Jim Finigan 10.00 5.00
23 Fred Marsh 10.00 5.00
24 Dick Groat 15.00 7.50
25 Ted Kluszewski 80.00 40.00
26 Grady Hatton 10.00 5.00
27 Nelson Burbrink DP 10.00 5.00
28 Bobby Hofman 10.00 5.00
29 Jack Harshman 10.00 5.00
30 Jackie Robinson DP 250.00 125.00
31 Hank Aaron UER DP 350.00 180.00
(Small photo
actually Willie Mays)
32 Frank House 10.00 5.00
33 Roberto Clemente 400.00 200.00
34 Tom Brewer DP 10.00 5.00
35 Al Rosen 15.00 7.50
36 Rudy Minarcin 15.00 7.50
37 Alex Grammas 10.00 5.00
38 Bob Kennedy 15.00 7.50
39 Don Mossi 15.00 7.50
40 Bob Turley 15.00 7.50
41 Hank Sauer 15.00 7.50
42 Sandy Amoros 25.00 12.50
43 Ray Moore 10.00 5.00
44 Windy McCall 15.00 7.50
45 Gus Zernial 15.00 7.50
46 Gene Freese DP 10.00 5.00
47 Art Fowler 10.00 5.00
48 Jim Hegan 15.00 7.50
49 Pedro Ramos 10.00 5.00
50 Dusty Rhodes DP 15.00 7.50
51 Ernie Oravetz 10.00 5.00
52 Bob Grim DP 15.00 7.50
53 Arnie Portocarrero 10.00 5.00
54 Bob Keegan 10.00 5.00
55 Wally Moon 15.00 7.50
56 Dale Long 15.00 7.50
57 Duke Maas 10.00 5.00
58 Ed Roebuck 25.00 12.50
59 Jose Santiago 10.00 5.00
60 Mayo Smith MG DP 10.00 5.00
61 Bill Skowron 25.00 12.50
62 Hal Smith 15.00 7.50
63 Roger Craig RC 40.00 20.00
64 Luis Arroyo RC 10.00 5.00
65 Johnny O'Brien 15.00 7.50
66 Bob Speake DP 10.00 5.00
67 Vic Power 15.00 7.50
68 Chuck Stobbs 10.00 5.00
69 Chuck Tanner 15.00 7.50
70 Jim Rivera 10.00 5.00
71 Frank Sullivan 10.00 5.00
72A Phillies Team 30.00 15.00
(Centered)
72B Phillies Team 80.00 40.00
(Dated 1955)
72C Phillies Team DP 30.00 15.00
(Name at far left)
73 Wayne Terwilliger 10.00 5.00
74 Jim King 10.00 5.00
75 Roy Sievers DP 15.00 7.50
76 Ray Crone 10.00 5.00
77 Harvey Haddix 15.00 7.50
78 Herman Wehmeier 10.00 5.00
79 Sandy Koufax 350.00 180.00
80 Gus Triandos DP 10.00 5.00
81 Wally Westlake 10.00 5.00
82 Bill Renna DP 10.00 5.00
83 Karl Spooner 15.00 7.50
84 Babe Birrer 10.00 5.00
85A Cleveland Indians 30.00 15.00
(Centered)
85B Indians Team 80.00 40.00
(Dated 1955)
85C Indians Team 30.00 15.00
(Name at far left)
86 Ray Jablonski DP 10.00 5.00
87 Dean Stone 10.00 5.00
88 Johnny Kucks RC 15.00 7.50
89 Norm Zauchin 10.00 5.00
90A Cincinnati Redlegs 30.00 15.00
Team (Centered)
90B Reds Team 80.00 40.00
(Dated 1955)
90C Reds Team 30.00 15.00
(Name at far left)
91 Gail Harris 10.00 5.00
92 Bob(Red) Wilson 10.00 5.00
93 George Susce 10.00 5.00
94 Ron Kline 10.00 5.00
95A Milwaukee Braves 40.00 20.00
Team (Centered)
95B Braves Team 80.00 40.00
(Dated 1955)
95C Braves Team 40.00 20.00
(Name at far left)
96 Bill Tremel 10.00 5.00
97 Jerry Lynch 15.00 7.50
98 Camilo Pascual 15.00 7.50
99 Don Zimmer 25.00 12.50
100A Baltimore Orioles 40.00 20.00
Team (centered)
100B Orioles Team 80.00 40.00
(Dated 1955)
100C Orioles Team 40.00 20.00
(Name at far left)
101 Roy Campanella 150.00 75.00
102 Jim Davis 12.00 6.00
103 Willie Miranda 12.00 6.00
104 Bob Lennon 12.00 6.00
105 Al Smith 12.00 6.00
106 Joe Astroth 12.00 6.00
107 Eddie Mathews 100.00 50.00
108 Laurin Pepper 12.00 6.00
109 Enos Slaughter 40.00 20.00
110 Yogi Berra 175.00 90.00
111 Boston Red Sox 40.00 20.00
Team Card
112 Dee Fondy 12.00 6.00
113 Phil Rizzuto 150.00 75.00
114 Jim Owens 15.00 7.50
115 Jackie Jensen 15.00 7.50
116 Eddie O'Brien 12.00 6.00
117 Virgil Trucks 15.00 7.50
118 Nellie Fox 80.00 40.00
119 Larry Jackson RC 15.00 7.50
120 Richie Ashburn 60.00 30.00
121 Pittsburgh Pirates 40.00 20.00
Team Card
122 Willard Nixon 12.00 6.00
123 Roy McMillan 15.00 7.50
124 Don Kaiser 12.00 6.00
125 Minnie Minoso 40.00 20.00
126 Jim Brady 12.00 6.00
127 Willie Jones 15.00 7.50
128 Eddie Yost 15.00 7.50
129 Jake Martin 12.00 6.00
130 Willie Mays 300.00 150.00
131 Bob Roselli 12.00 6.00
132 Bobby Avila 12.00 6.00
133 Ray Narleski 12.00 6.00
134 St. Louis Cardinals 40.00 20.00
Team Card
135 Mickey Mantle 1500.00 750.00
136 Johnny Logan 15.00 7.50
137 Al Silvera 12.00 6.00
138 Johnny Antonelli 15.00 7.50
139 Tommy Carroll 15.00 7.50
140 Herb Score RC 60.00 30.00
141 Joe Frazier 12.00 6.00
142 Gene Baker 12.00 6.00
143 Jim Piersall 15.00 7.50
144 Leroy Powell 12.00 6.00
145 Gil Hodges 60.00 30.00
146 Washington Nationals 40.00 20.00
Team Card
147 Earl Torgeson 12.00 6.00
148 Alvin Dark 15.00 7.50
149 Dixie Howell 12.00 6.00
150 Duke Snider 125.00 60.00
151 Spook Jacobs 15.00 7.50
152 Billy Hoeft 15.00 7.50
153 Frank Thomas 15.00 7.50
154 Dave Pope 12.00 6.00
155 Harvey Kuenn 15.00 7.50
156 Wes Westrum 15.00 7.50
157 Dick Brodowski 12.00 6.00
158 Wally Post 15.00 7.50
159 Clint Courtney 12.00 6.00
160 Billy Pierce 15.00 7.50
161 Joe DeMaestri 12.00 6.00
162 Dave(Gus) Bell 15.00 7.50

163 Gene Woodling 15.00 7.50
164 Harmon Killebrew 100.00 50.00
165 Red Schoendienst 40.00 20.00
166 Brooklyn Dodgers 200.00 100.00
Team Card
167 Harry Dorish 12.00 6.00
168 Sammy White 12.00 6.00
169 Bob Nelson 12.00 6.00
170 Bill Virdon 15.00 7.50
171 Jim Wilson 12.00 6.00
172 Frank Torre RC 15.00 7.50
173 Johnny Podres 25.00 12.50
174 Glen Gorbous 12.00 6.00
175 Del Crandall 15.00 7.50
176 Alex Kellner 12.00 6.00
177 Hank Bauer 25.00 12.50
178 Joe Black 15.00 7.50
179 Harry Chiti 12.00 6.00
180 Robin Roberts 50.00 25.00
181 Billy Martin 100.00 50.00
182 Paul Minner 15.00 7.50
183 Stan Lopata 20.00 10.00
184 Don Bessent 20.00 10.00
185 Bill Bruton 20.00 10.00
186 Ron Jackson 15.00 7.50
187 Early Wynn 50.00 25.00
188 Chicago White Sox 50.00 25.00
Team Card
189 Ned Garver 15.00 7.50
190 Carl Furillo 30.00 15.00
191 Frank Lary 20.00 10.00
192 Smoky Burgess 20.00 10.00
193 Wilmer Mizell 20.00 10.00
194 Monte Irvin 30.00 15.00
195 George Kell 30.00 15.00
196 Tom Poholsky 15.00 7.50
197 Granny Hamner 15.00 7.50
198 Ed Fitzgerald 15.00 7.50
199 Hank Thompson 20.00 10.00
200 Bob Feller 125.00 60.00
201 Rip Repulski 15.00 7.50
202 Jim Hearn 15.00 7.50
203 Bill Tuttle 15.00 7.50
204 Art Swanson 15.00 7.50
205 Whitey Lockman 20.00 10.00
206 Erv Palica 15.00 7.50
207 Jim Small 15.00 7.50
208 Elston Howard 60.00 30.00
209 Max Surkont 15.00 7.50
210 Mike Garcia 20.00 10.00
211 Murry Dickson 15.00 7.50
212 Johnny Temple 15.00 7.50
213 Detroit Tigers 60.00 30.00
Team Card
214 Bob Rush 15.00 7.50
215 Tommy Byrne 20.00 10.00
216 Jerry Schoonmaker 15.00 7.50
217 Billy Klaus 15.00 7.50
218 Joe Nuxhall UER 20.00 10.00
(Misspelled Nuxall)
219 Lew Burdette 20.00 10.00
220 Del Ennis 20.00 10.00
221 Bob Friend 20.00 10.00
222 Dave Philley 15.00 7.50
223 Randy Jackson 15.00 7.50
224 Bud Podbielan 15.00 7.50
225 Gil McDougald 50.00 25.00
226 New York Giants 80.00 40.00
Team Card
227 Russ Meyer 15.00 7.50
228 Mickey Vernon 20.00 10.00
229 Harry Brecheen CO 20.00 10.00
230 Chico Carrasquel 15.00 7.50
231 Bob Hale 15.00 7.50
232 Toby Atwell 15.00 7.50
233 Carl Erskine 30.00 15.00
234 Pete Runnels 15.00 7.50
235 Don Newcombe 50.00 25.00
236 Kansas City Athletics 40.00 20.00
Team Card
237 Jose Valdivielso 15.00 7.50
238 Walt Dropo 20.00 10.00
239 Harry Simpson 15.00 7.50
240 Whitey Ford 125.00 60.00
241 Don Mueller UER 20.00 10.00
6" tall
242 Hershell Freeman 15.00 7.50
243 Sherm Lollar 20.00 10.00
244 Bob Buhl 30.00 15.00
245 Billy Goodman 20.00 10.00
246 Tom Gorman 15.00 7.50
247 Bill Sarni 15.00 7.50
248 Bob Porterfield 15.00 7.50
249 Johnny Klippstein 15.00 7.50
250 Larry Doby 30.00 15.00
251 New York Yankees 250.00 125.00
Team Card UER
(Don Larsen misspelled
as Larson on front)
252 Vern Law 20.00 10.00
253 Irv Noren 30.00 15.00
254 George Crowe 15.00 7.50
255 Bob Lemon 50.00 25.00
256 Tom Hurd 15.00 7.50
257 Bobby Thomson 30.00 15.00
258 Art Ditmar 15.00 7.50
259 Sam Jones 20.00 10.00
260 Pee Wee Reese 150.00 75.00
261 Bobby Shantz 15.00 7.50
262 Howie Pollet 12.00 6.00
263 Bob Miller 12.00 6.00
264 Ray Monzant 12.00 6.00
265 Sandy Consuegra 12.00 6.00
266 Don Ferrarese 12.00 6.00
267 Bob Nieman 12.00 6.00
268 Dale Mitchell 15.00 7.50
269 Jack Meyer 12.00 6.00
270 Billy Loes 15.00 7.50
271 Foster Castleman 12.00 6.00
272 Danny O'Connell 12.00 6.00
273 Walker Cooper 12.00 6.00
274 Frank Baumholtz 12.00 6.00
275 Jim Greengrass 12.00 6.00
276 George Zuverink 12.00 6.00
277 Daryl Spencer 12.00 6.00
278 Chet Nichols 12.00 6.00
279 Johnny Groth 12.00 6.00
280 Jim Gilliam 40.00 20.00
281 Art Houtteman 12.00 6.00
282 Warren Hacker 12.00 6.00
283 Hal Smith RC 15.00 7.50
284 Ike Delock 12.00 6.00
285 Eddie Miksis 12.00 6.00
286 Bill Wight 12.00 6.00
287 Bobby Adams 12.00 6.00
288 Bob Cerv 40.00 20.00
289 Hal Jeffcoat 12.00 6.00
290 Curt Simmons 15.00 7.50
291 Frank Kellert 12.00 6.00
292 Luis Aparicio RC 150.00 75.00
293 Stu Miller 25.00 12.50
294 Ernie Johnson 15.00 7.50
295 Clem Labine 15.00 7.50
296 Andy Seminick 12.00 6.00
297 Bob Skinner 15.00 7.50
298 Johnny Schmitz 12.00 6.00
299 Charlie Neal 40.00 20.00
300 Vic Wertz 15.00 7.50
301 Marv Grissom 12.00 6.00
302 Eddie Robinson 12.00 6.00
303 Jim Dyck 12.00 6.00
304 Frank Malzone 15.00 7.50
305 Brooks Lawrence 12.00 6.00
306 Curt Roberts 12.00 6.00
307 Hoyt Wilhelm 40.00 20.00
308 Chuck Harmon 12.00 6.00
309 Don Blasingame RC 15.00 7.50
310 Steve Gromek 12.00 6.00
311 Hal Naragon 12.00 6.00
312 Andy Pafko 15.00 7.50
313 Gene Stephens 12.00 6.00
314 Hobie Landrith 12.00 6.00
315 Milt Bolling 12.00 6.00
316 Jerry Coleman 15.00 7.50
317 Al Aber 12.00 6.00
318 Fred Hatfield 12.00 6.00
319 Jack Crimian 12.00 6.00
320 Joe Adcock 15.00 7.50
321 Jim Konstanty 15.00 7.50
322 Karl Olson 12.00 6.00
323 Willard Schmidt 12.00 6.00
324 Rocky Bridges 15.00 7.50
325 Don Liddle 12.00 6.00
326 Connie Johnson 12.00 6.00
327 Bob Wiesler 12.00 6.00
328 Preston Ward 12.00 6.00
329 Lou Berberet 12.00 6.00
330 Jim Busby 15.00 7.50
331 Dick Hall 12.00 6.00
332 Don Larsen 60.00 30.00
333 Rube Walker 12.00 6.00
334 Bob Miller 15.00 7.50
335 Don Hoak 15.00 7.50
336 Ellis Kinder 12.00 6.00
337 Bobby Morgan 12.00 6.00
338 Jim Delsing 12.00 6.00
339 Rance Pless 12.00 6.00
340 Mickey McDermott 60.00 12.00
NNO Checklist 1/3 300.00 95.00
NNO Checklist 2/4 300.00 95.00

1956 Topps Hocus Focus

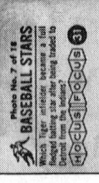

This 1956 Topps issue is often confused with the Magic Photos issue of 1950. The R714-26 (catalog designation) set comes in two types, which we have arbitrarily labeled A and B. Style A, the larger size (1" by 1 5/8"), contains 18 baseball subjects with the ones known checklisted below. Type B, the smaller size (7/8" by 1 3/8"), is reported to contain baseball subjects, those known are checklisted below. Like the Magic Photo set, these cards were "developed" by sunlight. The baseball players in these sets are but a portion of the total cards in the set. Dogs, personalities and other subjects were also featured.

NM Ex
COMP.BASEBALL PLAYERS . 2000.00 1000.00
COMMON A CARD 30.00 15.00
COMMON B CARD 40.00 20.00
A9 Mayo Smith MG 51 30.00 15.00
A1 Dick Groat 43 40.00 20.00
A2 Ed Lopat 44 50.00 25.00
A3 Hank Sauer 30 40.00 20.00
A4 Dusty Rhodes 86 30.00 15.00
A5 Ted Williams 5 200.00 100.00
A6 Harvey Haddix 26 30.00 15.00
A7 Ray Boone 31 30.00 15.00
A8 Al Rosen 69 50.00 25.00
A10 Warren Spahn 87 100.00 50.00
A11 Jim Rivera 67 30.00 15.00
A12 Ted Kluszewski 79 60.00 30.00
A13 Gus Zernial 49 30.00 15.00
A14 Jackie Robinson 13 200.00 100.00
A15 Hal Smith 42 30.00 15.00
A16 Johnny Schmitz 84 30.00 15.00
A17 Spook Jacobs 60 30.00 15.00
A18 Mel Parnell 18 40.00 20.00
B1 Babe Ruth 117 400.00 200.00
B3 Dick Groat 43 50.00 25.00
B6 Dusty Rhodes 86 50.00 25.00
B7 Ted Williams 5 250.00 125.00
B8 Harvey Haddix 26 40.00 20.00
B9 Ray Boone 31 40.00 20.00
B12 Warren Spahn 87 120.00 60.00
B13 Jim Rivera 67 40.00 20.00
B14 Ted Kluszewski 79 80.00 40.00
B15 Gus Zernial 49 40.00 20.00
B18 Johnny Schmitz 84 40.00 20.00
B20 Karl Spooner 122 40.00 20.00
B21 Ed Mathews 109 120.00 60.00

1956 Topps Pins

This set of 60 full-color pins was Topps first and only baseball player pin set. Each pin measures 1 3/16" in diameter. Although the set was advertised to contain 90 pins, only 60 were issued. The checklist below lists the players in alphabetical order within team, e.g., Baltimore Orioles (1-4), Chicago Cubs (5-7), Cleveland Indians (8-11), Kansas City A's (12-15), Milwaukee Braves (16-19), Philadelphia Phillies (20-22), Boston Red Sox (23-26), New York Yankees (27-31), Chicago White Sox (32-35), Detroit Tigers (36-38), New York Giants (39-41), Pittsburgh Pirates (42-44), St. Louis Cardinals (45-48), Brooklyn Dodgers (49-53), Cincinnati Redlegs (54-57) and Washington Senators (58-60). Chuck Diering, Hector Lopez and Chuck Stobbs (noted below with SP) are more difficult to obtain than other pins in the set. The pins were issued one per box along with a piece of bubble gum. The box featured a photo of Ted Williams on the front.

NM Ex
COMPLETE SET (60) 2250.00 1100.00
PIN BOX (5-CENT) 200.00 100.00
1 Chuck Diering SP 250.00 125.00
2 Willie Miranda 15.00 7.50
3 Hal Smith 15.00 7.50
4 Gus Triandos 20.00 10.00
5 Ernie Banks 75.00 38.00
6 Hank Sauer 20.00 10.00
7 Bill Tremel 15.00 7.50
8 Jim Hegan 15.00 7.50
9 Don Mossi 20.00 10.00
10 Al Rosen 30.00 15.00
11 Al Smith 15.00 7.50
12 Jim Finigan 15.00 7.50
13 Hector Lopez SP 200.00 100.00
14 Vic Power 15.00 7.50
15 Gus Zernial 20.00 10.00
16 Hank Aaron 125.00 60.00
17 Gene Conley 15.00 7.50
18 Eddie Mathews 75.00 38.00
19 Warren Spahn 75.00 38.00
20 Ron Negray 15.00 7.50
21 Mayo Smith MG 15.00 7.50
22 Herman Wehmeier 15.00 7.50
23 Grady Hatton 15.00 7.50
24 Jackie Jensen 30.00 15.00
25 Frank Sullivan 15.00 7.50
26 Ted Williams 150.00 75.00
27 Yogi Berra 100.00 50.00
28 Joe Collins 20.00 10.00
29 Phil Rizzuto 50.00 25.00
30 Bill Skowron 30.00 15.00
31 Bob Turley 30.00 15.00
32 Dick Donovan 15.00 7.50
33 Jack Harshman 15.00 7.50
34 Bob Kennedy 15.00 7.50
35 Jim Rivera 15.00 7.50
36 Ray Boone 20.00 10.00
37 Frank House 15.00 7.50
38 Al Kaline 75.00 38.00
39 Ruben Gomez 15.00 7.50
40 Bobby Hofman 15.00 7.50
41 Willie Mays 125.00 60.00
42 Dick Groat 30.00 15.00
43 Dale Long 20.00 10.00
44 Johnny O'Brien 15.00 7.50
45 Luis Arroyo 15.00 7.50
46 Ken Boyer 30.00 15.00
47 Harvey Haddix 20.00 10.00
48 Wally Moon 20.00 10.00
49 Sandy Amoros 20.00 10.00
50 Gil Hodges 50.00 25.00
51 Jackie Robinson 125.00 60.00
52 Duke Snider 100.00 50.00
53 Karl Spooner 20.00 10.00
54 Joe Black 25.00 12.50
55 Art Fowler 15.00 7.50
56 Ted Kluszewski 30.00 15.00
57 Roy McMillan 15.00 7.50
58 Carlos Paula 15.00 7.50
59 Roy Sievers 15.00 7.50
60 Chuck Stobbs SP 200.00 100.00

1957 Topps

The cards in this 407-card set measure 2 1/2" by 3 1/2". In 1957, Topps returned to the vertical obverse, adopted what we now call the standard card size, and used a large, uncluttered color photo for the first time since 1952. Cards in the series 265 to 352 and the unnumbered checklist cards are scarcer than other cards in the set. However within this scarce series (265-352) there are 22 cards which were printed in double the quantity of the other cards in the series; these 22 double prints are indicated by DP in the checklist below. The first star combination cards, cards 400 and 407, are quite popular with collectors. They feature the big stars of the previous season's World Series teams, the Dodgers (Furillo, Hodges, Campanella, and Snider) and Yankees (Berra and Mantle). The complete set price below does not include the unnumbered checklist cards. Confirmed packaging includes one-cent penny packs and six-card nickel packs. Cello packs are definately known to exist and some collectors remember buying rack packs of 57's as well. The key Rookie Cards in this set are Jim Bunning, Rocky Colavito, Don Drysdale, Whitey Herzog, Tony Kubek, Bill Mazeroski, Bobby Richardson, Brooks Robinson, and Frank Robinson.

NM Ex
COMPLETE SET (407) 10000.00 5000.00
COMMON CARD (1-88) 10.00 5.00
COMMON CARD (89-176) 8.00 4.00
COMMON (177-264) 8.00 4.00
COMMON (265-352) 20.00 10.00
COMMON (353-407) 8.00 4.00
COMMON DP (265-352) 12.00 6.00
WRAPPER (1-CENT) 300.00 150.00
WRAPPER (5-CENT) 200.00 100.00
1 Ted Williams 500.00 150.00
2 Yogi Berra 200.00 100.00
3 Dale Long 20.00 10.00
4 Johnny Logan 20.00 10.00
5 Sal Maglie 20.00 10.00
6 Hector Lopez 15.00 7.50
7 Luis Aparicio 30.00 15.00
8 Don Mossi 15.00 7.50
9 Johnny Temple 15.00 7.50
10 Willie Mays 250.00 125.00
11 George Zuverink 10.00 5.00
12 Dick Groat 20.00 10.00
13 Wally Burnette 10.00 5.00
14 Bob Nieman 10.00 5.00
15 Robin Roberts 30.00 15.00
16 Walt Moryn 10.00 5.00
17 Billy Gardner 10.00 5.00
18 Don Drysdale RC 250.00 125.00
19 Bob Wilson 10.00 5.00
20 Hank Aaron UER 300.00 150.00
(Reverse negative
photo on front)
21 Frank Sullivan 10.00 5.00
22 Jerry Snyder UER 10.00 5.00
Photo actually Ed Fitzgerald
23 Sherm Lollar 15.00 7.50
24 Bill Mazeroski RC 80.00 40.00
25 Whitey Ford 150.00 75.00
26 Bob Boyd 10.00 5.00
27 Ted Kazanski 10.00 5.00
28 Gene Conley 15.00 7.50
29 Whitey Herzog RC 30.00 15.00
30 Pee Wee Reese 80.00 40.00
31 Ron Northey 10.00 5.00
32 Hershell Freeman 10.00 5.00
33 Jim Small 10.00 5.00
34 Tom Sturdivant 15.00 7.50
35 Frank Robinson RC 250.00 125.00
36 Bob Grim 10.00 5.00
37 Frank Torre 15.00 7.50
38 Nellie Fox 50.00 25.00
39 Al Worthington 10.00 5.00
40 Early Wynn 30.00 15.00
41 Hal W. Smith 10.00 5.00
42 Dee Fondy 10.00 5.00
43 Connie Johnson 10.00 5.00
44 Joe DeMaestri 10.00 5.00
45 Carl Furillo 30.00 15.00
46 Robert J. Miller 10.00 5.00
47 Don Blasingame 10.00 5.00
48 Bill Bruton 10.00 5.00
49 Daryl Spencer 10.00 5.00
50 Herb Score 30.00 15.00
51 Clint Courtney 10.00 5.00
52 Lee Walls 10.00 5.00
53 Clem Labine 20.00 10.00
54 Elmer Valo 10.00 5.00
55 Ernie Banks 125.00 60.00
56 Dave Sisler 10.00 5.00
57 Jim Lemon 15.00 7.50
58 Ruben Gomez 10.00 5.00
59 Dick Williams 15.00 7.50
60 Billy Hoeft 15.00 7.50
61 Dusty Rhodes 15.00 7.50
62 Billy Martin 60.00 30.00
63 Ike Delock 10.00 5.00
64 Pete Runnels 15.00 7.50
65 Wally Moon 15.00 7.50
66 Brooks Lawrence 10.00 5.00
67 Chico Carrasquel 10.00 5.00
68 Ray Crone 10.00 5.00
69 Roy McMillan 15.00 7.50
70 Richie Ashburn 50.00 25.00
71 Murry Dickson 10.00 5.00
72 Bill Tuttle 10.00 5.00
73 George Crowe 10.00 5.00
74 Vito Valentinetti 10.00 5.00
75 Jimmy Piersall 15.00 7.50
76 Roberto Clemente 300.00 150.00
77 Paul Foytack 10.00 5.00
78 Vic Wertz 15.00 7.50
79 Lindy McDaniel RC 15.00 7.50
80 Gil Hodges 50.00 25.00
81 Herman Wehmeier 10.00 5.00
82 Elston Howard 30.00 15.00
83 Lou Skizas 10.00 5.00
84 Moe Drabowsky 15.00 7.50
85 Larry Doby 30.00 15.00
86 Bill Sarni 10.00 5.00
87 Tom Gorman 10.00 5.00
88 Harvey Kuenn 15.00 7.50
89 Roy Sievers 15.00 7.50
90 Warren Spahn 80.00 40.00
91 Mack Burk 8.00 4.00
92 Mickey Vernon 15.00 7.50
93 Hal Jeffcoat 8.00 4.00
94 Bobby Del Greco 8.00 4.00
95 Mickey Mantle 1200.00 600.00
96 Hank Aguirre 8.00 4.00
97 New York Yankees 100.00 50.00
Team Card
98 Alvin Dark 15.00 7.50
99 Bob Keegan 8.00 4.00
100 Warren Giles PRES 15.00 7.50
Will Harridge PRES
101 Chuck Stobbs 8.00 4.00
102 Ray Boone 15.00 7.50
103 Joe Nuxhall 15.00 7.50
104 Hank Foiles 8.00 4.00
105 Johnny Antonelli 15.00 7.50
106 Ray Moore 8.00 4.00
107 Jim Rivera 8.00 4.00
108 Tommy Byrne 15.00 7.50
109 Hank Thompson 8.00 4.00
110 Bill Virdon 15.00 7.50
111 Hal R. Smith 8.00 4.00
112 Tom Brewer 8.00 4.00
113 Wilmer Mizell 15.00 7.50
114 Milwaukee Braves 20.00 10.00
Team Card
115 Jim Gilliam 15.00 7.50
116 Mike Fornieles 8.00 4.00
117 Joe Adcock 20.00 10.00
118 Bob Porterfield 8.00 4.00
119 Stan Lopata 8.00 4.00
120 Bob Lemon 30.00 15.00
121 Clete Boyer RC 30.00 15.00
122 Ken Boyer 20.00 10.00
123 Steve Ridzik 8.00 4.00
124 Dave Philley 8.00 4.00
125 Al Kaline 100.00 50.00
126 Bob Wiesler 8.00 4.00
127 Bob Buhl 15.00 7.50
128 Ed Bailey 15.00 7.50
129 Saul Rogovin 8.00 4.00
130 Don Newcombe 20.00 10.00
131 Milt Bolling 8.00 4.00
132 Art Ditmar 15.00 7.50
133 Del Crandall 15.00 7.50
134 Don Kaiser 8.00 4.00
135 Bill Skowron 20.00 10.00
136 Jim Hegan 15.00 7.50
137 Bob Rush 8.00 4.00
138 Minnie Minoso 20.00 10.00
139 Lou Kretlow 8.00 4.00
140 Frank Thomas 15.00 7.50
141 Al Aber 8.00 4.00
142 Charley Thompson 8.00 4.00
143 Andy Pafko 15.00 7.50
144 Ray Narleski 8.00 4.00
145 Al Smith 8.00 4.00
146 Don Ferrarese 8.00 4.00
147 Al Walker 8.00 4.00
148 Don Mueller 15.00 7.50
149 Bob Kennedy 15.00 7.50
150 Bob Friend 15.00 7.50
151 Willie Miranda 8.00 4.00
152 Jack Harshman 8.00 4.00
153 Karl Olson 8.00 4.00
154 Red Schoendienst 30.00 15.00
155 Jim Brosnan 15.00 7.50
156 Gus Triandos 15.00 7.50
157 Wally Post 15.00 7.50
158 Curt Simmons 15.00 7.50
159 Solly Drake 8.00 4.00
160 Billy Pierce 15.00 7.50
161 Pittsburgh Pirates 15.00 7.50
Team Card
162 Jack Meyer 8.00 4.00
163 Sammy White 8.00 4.00
164 Tommy Carroll 8.00 4.00
165 Ted Kluszewski 100.00 50.00
166 Roy Face 15.00 7.50
167 Vic Power 15.00 7.50
168 Frank Lary 15.00 7.50
169 Herb Plews 8.00 4.00
170 Duke Snider 125.00 60.00
171 Boston Red Sox 15.00 7.50
Team Card
172 Gene Woodling 15.00 7.50
173 Roger Craig 15.00 7.50
174 Willie Jones 8.00 4.00
175 Don Larsen 30.00 15.00
176A Gene Baker ERR 350.00 180.00
(Misspelled Bakep
on card back)
176B Gene Baker COR 15.00 7.50
177 Eddie Yost 15.00 7.50
178 Don Bessent 8.00 4.00
179 Ernie Oravetz 8.00 4.00
180 Gus Bell 15.00 7.50
181 Dick Donovan 8.00 4.00
182 Hobie Landrith 8.00 4.00
183 Chicago Cubs 15.00 7.50
Team Card
184 Tito Francona RC 8.00 4.00
185 Johnny Kucks 15.00 7.50
186 Jim King 15.00 7.50
187 Virgil Trucks 15.00 7.50
188 Felix Mantilla RC 15.00 7.50
189 Willard Nixon 8.00 4.00
190 Randy Jackson 8.00 4.00
191 Joe Margoneri 8.00 4.00
192 Jerry Coleman 15.00 7.50
193 Del Rice 8.00 4.00
194 Hal Brown 8.00 4.00
195 Bobby Avila 8.00 4.00
196 Larry Jackson 15.00 7.50
197 Hank Sauer 15.00 7.50
198 Detroit Tigers 15.00 7.50
Team Card
199 Vern Law 15.00 7.50
200 Gil McDougald 15.00 7.50
201 Sandy Amoros 15.00 7.50
202 Dick Gernert 8.00 4.00
203 Hoyt Wilhelm 30.00 15.00
204 Kansas City Athletics 15.00 7.50
Team Card
205 Charlie Maxwell 15.00 7.50
206 Willard Schmidt 8.00 4.00
207 Gordon(Billy) Hunter 8.00 4.00
208 Lou Burdette 15.00 7.50
209 Bob Skinner 15.00 7.50
210 Roy Campanella 150.00 75.00
211 Camilo Pascual 15.00 7.50
212 Rocky Colavito RC 125.00 60.00
213 Les Moss 8.00 4.00
214 Philadelphia Phillies 15.00 7.50
Team Card
215 Enos Slaughter 30.00 15.00
216 Marv Grissom 8.00 4.00
217 Gene Stephens 8.00 4.00
218 Ray Jablonski 8.00 4.00
219 Tom Acker 8.00 4.00
220 Jackie Jensen 20.00 10.00
221 Dixie Howell 8.00 4.00
222 Alex Grammas 8.00 4.00
223 Frank House 8.00 4.00
224 Marv Blaylock 8.00 4.00
225 Harry Simpson 8.00 4.00
226 Preston Ward 8.00 4.00
227 Gerry Staley 8.00 4.00
228 Smoky Burgess UER 15.00 7.50
(Misspelled Smokey
on card back)
229 George Susce 8.00 4.00
230 George Kell 30.00 15.00
231 Solly Hemus 8.00 4.00
232 Whitey Lockman 15.00 7.50
233 Art Fowler 8.00 4.00

234 Dick Cole 8.00 4.00
235 Tom Poholsky 8.00 4.00
236 Joe Ginsberg 8.00 4.00
237 Foster Castleman 8.00 4.00
238 Eddie Robinson 8.00 4.00
239 Tom Morgan 8.00 4.00
240 Hank Bauer 15.00 7.50
241 Joe Lonnett 8.00 4.00
242 Charlie Neal 15.00 7.50
243 St. Louis Cardinals 15.00 7.50
Team Card
244 Billy Loes 15.00 7.50
245 Rip Repulski 8.00 4.00
246 Jose Valdivielso 8.00 4.00
247 Turk Lown 8.00 4.00
248 Jim Finigan 8.00 4.00
249 Dave Pope 8.00 4.00
250 Eddie Mathews 50.00 25.00
251 Baltimore Orioles 15.00 7.50
Team Card
252 Carl Erskine 15.00 7.50
253 Gus Zernial 15.00 7.50
254 Ron Negray 8.00 4.00
255 Charlie Silvera 15.00 7.50
256 Ron Kline 8.00 4.00
257 Walt Dropo 8.00 4.00
258 Steve Gromek 8.00 4.00
259 Eddie O'Brien 8.00 4.00
260 Del Ennis 15.00 7.50
261 Bob Chakales 8.00 4.00
262 Bobby Thomson 15.00 7.50
263 George Strickland 8.00 4.00
264 Bob Turley 15.00 7.50
265 Harvey Haddix DP 12.00 6.00
266 Ken Kuhn DP 12.00 6.00
267 Danny Kravitz 20.00 10.00
268 Jack Collum 20.00 10.00
269 Bob Cerv 30.00 15.00
270 Washington Senators 60.00 30.00
Team Card
271 Danny O'Connell DP 12.00 6.00
272 Bobby Shantz 30.00 15.00
273 Jim Davis 20.00 10.00
274 Don Hoak 15.00 7.50
275 Cleveland Indians 60.00 30.00
Team Card UER
(Text on back credits Tribe
with winning AL title in '28.
The Yankees won that year.)
276 Jim Pyburn 20.00 10.00
277 Johnny Podres DP 40.00 20.00
278 Fred Hatfield DP 12.00 6.00
279 Bob Thurman 20.00 10.00
280 Alex Kellner 20.00 10.00
281 Gail Harris 20.00 10.00
282 Jack Dittmer DP 12.00 6.00
283 Wes Covington DP 12.00 6.00
284 Don Zimmer 40.00 20.00
285 Ned Garver 20.00 10.00
286 Bobby Richardson RC 125.00 60.00
287 Sam Jones 20.00 10.00
288 Ted Lepcio 20.00 10.00
289 Jim Bolger DP 12.00 6.00
290 Andy Carey DP 40.00 20.00
291 Windy McCall 20.00 10.00
292 Billy Klaus 20.00 10.00
293 Ted Abernathy 20.00 10.00
294 Rocky Bridges DP 12.00 6.00
295 Joe Collins DP 40.00 20.00
296 Johnny Klippstein 20.00 10.00
297 Jack Crimian 20.00 10.00
298 Irv Noren DP 12.00 6.00
299 Chuck Harmon 20.00 10.00
300 Mike Garcia 30.00 15.00
301 Sammy Esposito DP 20.00 10.00
302 Sandy Koufax DP 300.00 150.00
303 Billy Goodman 30.00 15.00
304 Joe Cunningham 30.00 15.00
305 Chico Fernandez 20.00 10.00
306 Darrell Johnson DP 12.00 6.00
307 Jack D. Phillips DP 12.00 6.00
308 Dick Hall 20.00 10.00
309 Jim Busby DP 12.00 6.00
310 Max Surkont DP 12.00 6.00
311 Al Pilarcik DP 12.00 6.00
312 Tony Kubek DP RC 100.00 50.00
313 Mel Parnell 15.00 7.50
314 Ed Bouchee DP 12.00 6.00
315 Lou Berberet DP 12.00 6.00
316 Billy O'Dell 20.00 10.00
317 New York Giants 80.00 40.00
Team Card
318 Mickey McDermott 20.00 10.00
319 Gino Cimoli RC 20.00 10.00
320 Neil Chrisley 20.00 10.00
321 John(Red) Murff 20.00 10.00
322 Cincinnati Reds 80.00 40.00
Team Card
323 Wes Westrum 30.00 15.00
324 Brooklyn Dodgers 150.00 75.00
Team Card
325 Frank Bolling 20.00 10.00
326 Pedro Ramos 20.00 10.00
327 Jim Pendleton 20.00 10.00
328 Brooks Robinson RC 400.00 200.00
329 Chicago White Sox 60.00 30.00
Team Card
330 Jim Wilson 20.00 10.00
331 Ray Katt 20.00 10.00
332 Bob Bowman 20.00 10.00
333 Ernie Johnson 20.00 10.00
334 Jerry Schoonmaker 20.00 10.00
335 Granny Hamner 20.00 10.00
336 Haywood Sullivan RC 40.00 20.00
337 Rene Valdes 20.00 10.00
338 Jim Bunning RC 150.00 75.00
339 Bob Speake 20.00 10.00
340 Bill Wight 20.00 10.00
341 Don Gross 20.00 10.00
342 Gene Mauch 30.00 15.00
343 Taylor Phillips 15.00 7.50
344 Paul LaPalme 20.00 10.00
345 Paul Smith 20.00 10.00
346 Dick Littlefield 20.00 10.00
347 Hal Naragon 20.00 10.00
348 Jim Hearn 20.00 10.00
349 Nellie King 20.00 10.00
350 Eddie Miksis 20.00 10.00
351 Dave Hillman 20.00 10.00
352 Ellis Kinder 20.00 10.00
353 Cal Neeman 8.00 4.00
354 Rip Coleman 8.00 4.00
355 Frank Malzone 15.00 7.50
356 Faye Throneberry 8.00 4.00
357 Earl Torgeson 8.00 4.00
358 Jerry Lynch 15.00 7.50
359 Tom Cheney 8.00 4.00
360 Johnny Groth 8.00 4.00
361 Curt Barclay 8.00 4.00
362 Roman Mejias 15.00 7.50
363 Eddie Kasko 8.00 4.00
364 Cal McLish 15.00 7.50
365 Ozzie Virgil 8.00 4.00
366 Ken Lehman 8.00 4.00
367 Ed Fitzgerald 8.00 4.00
368 Bob Purkey 8.00 4.00
369 Milt Graff 8.00 4.00
370 Warren Hacker 8.00 4.00
371 Bob Lennon 8.00 4.00
372 Norm Zauchin 8.00 4.00
373 Pete Whisenant 8.00 4.00
374 Don Cardwell 8.00 4.00
375 Jim Landis 15.00 7.50
376 Don Elston 8.00 4.00
377 Andre Rodgers 8.00 4.00
378 Elmer Singleton 8.00 4.00
379 Don Lee 8.00 4.00
380 Walker Cooper 8.00 4.00
381 Dean Stone 8.00 4.00
382 Jim Brideweser 8.00 4.00
383 Juan Pizarro 8.00 4.00
384 Bobby G. Smith 8.00 4.00
385 Art Houtteman 8.00 4.00
386 Lyle Luttrell 8.00 4.00
387 Jack Sanford RC 15.00 7.50
388 Pete Daley 8.00 4.00
389 Dave Jolly 8.00 4.00
390 Reno Bertoia 8.00 4.00
391 Ralph Terry RC 15.00 7.50
392 Chuck Tanner 15.00 7.50
393 Raul Sanchez 8.00 4.00
394 Luis Arroyo 15.00 7.50
395 Bubba Phillips 8.00 4.00
396 Casey Wise 8.00 4.00
397 Roy Smalley 8.00 4.00
398 Al Cicotte 15.00 7.50
399 Billy Consolo 8.00 4.00
400 Carl Furillo 250.00 125.00
Gil Hodges
Roy Campanella
Duke Snider
401 Earl Battey RC 15.00 7.50
402 Jim Pisoni 8.00 4.00
403 Dick Hyde 8.00 4.00
404 Harry Anderson 8.00 4.00
405 Duke Maas 8.00 4.00
406 Bob Hale 8.00 4.00
407 Mickey Mantle 500.00 150.00
Yogi Berra
CC1 Contest Card 100.00 25.00
Saturday, May 4th
Boston Red Sox
vs. Cleveland Indians
Cincinnati Redlegs
vs. New York Giants
CC2 Contest Card 100.00 25.00
Saturday, May 25th
Detroit Tigers
vs. Kansas City Athletics
Pittsburgh Pirates
vs. Philadelphia Phillies
CC3 Contest Card 125.00 31.00
Saturday, June 22nd
Brooklyn Dodgers
vs. St. Louis Cardinals
Chicago White Sox
vs. New York Yankees
CC4 Contest Card 125.00 31.00
Saturday, July 19th
Milwaukee Braves
vs. New York Giants
Baltimore Orioles
vs. Kansas City Athletics
NNO Checklist 1/2 250.00 75.00
Bazooka Back
NNO Checklist 1/2 250.00 125.00
Blony Back
NNO Checklist 2/3 400.00 100.00
Bazooka Back
NNO Checklist 2/3 400.00 200.00
Blony Back
NNO Checklist 3/4 800.00 190.00
Bazooka Back
NNO Checklist 3/4 600.00 300.00
Blony Back
NNO Checklist 4/5 1000.00 220.00
Bazooka Back
NNO Checklist 4/5 800.00 400.00
Blony Back
NNO Lucky Penny Charm 100.00 50.00
and Key Chain
offer card

1958 Topps

This is a 494-card standard-size set. Card number 145, which was supposedly to be Ed Bouchee, was not issued. The 1958 Topps set contains the first Sport Magazine All-Star Selection series (475-495) and expanded use of combination cards. For the first time team cards carried series checklists on back (Milwaukee, Detroit, Baltimore, and Cincinnati are also found with players listed alphabetically). In the first series some cards were issued with yellow name (YL) or team (YT) lettering, as opposed to the common white lettering. They are explicity noted below. Cards were issued in one-card penny packs or six-card nickel packs. In the last series, All-Star cards of Stan Musial and Mickey Mantle were triple printed; the cards they replaced (443, 446, 450, and 462) on the printing sheet were hence printed in shorter supply than other cards in the last series and are marked with an SP in the list below. The All-Star card of Musial marked his first appearence on a Topps card. Technically the New York Giants team card (19) is an error as the Giants had already moved to San Francisco. The key Rookie Cards in this set are Orlando Cepeda, Curt Flood, Roger Maris, and Vada Pinson. These cards were issued in varying formats, including one cent packs which were issued 120 to a box.

	NM	Ex
COMP. MASTER (534)	12000.00	6000.00
COMPLETE SET (494)	6000.00	3000.00
COMMON CARD (1-110)	12.00	6.00
COMMON (111-495)	8.00	4.00
WRAPPER (1-CENT)	100.00	50.00
WRAPPER (5-CENT)	125.00	60.00

1 Ted Williams 600.00 210.00
2A Bob Lemon 30.00 15.00
2B Bob Lemon YT 60.00 30.00
3 Alex Kellner 12.00 6.00
4 Hank Foiles 12.00 6.00
5 Willie Mays 300.00 150.00
6 George Zuverink 12.00 6.00
7 Dale Long 15.00 7.50
8A Eddie Kasko 12.00 6.00
8B Eddie Kasko YN 40.00 20.00
9 Hank Bauer 20.00 10.00
10 Lou Burdette 20.00 10.00
11A Jim Rivera 12.00 6.00
11B Jim Rivera YT 40.00 20.00
12 George Crowe 12.00 6.00
13A Billy Hoeft 12.00 6.00
13B Billy Hoeft YN 40.00 20.00
14 Rip Repulski 12.00 6.00
15 Jim Lemon 15.00 7.50
16 Charlie Neal 15.00 7.50
17 Felix Mantilla 12.00 6.00
18 Frank Sullivan 12.00 6.00
19 Giants Team Card CL 40.00 8.00
20A Gil McDougald 20.00 10.00
20B Gil McDougald YN 60.00 30.00
21 Curt Barclay 12.00 6.00
22 Hal Naragon 12.00 6.00
23A Bill Tuttle 12.00 6.00
23B Bill Tuttle YN 40.00 20.00
24A Hobie Landrith 12.00 6.00
24B Hobie Landrith YN 40.00 20.00
25 Don Drysdale 100.00 50.00
26 Ron Jackson 12.00 6.00
27 Bud Freeman 12.00 6.00
28 Jim Busby 12.00 6.00
29 Ted Lepcio 12.00 6.00
30A Hank Aaron 200.00 100.00
30B Hank Aaron YN 500.00 250.00
31 Tex Clevenger 12.00 6.00
32A J.W. Porter 12.00 6.00
32B J.W. Porter YN 40.00 20.00
33A Cal Neeman 12.00 6.00
33B Cal Neeman YT 40.00 20.00
34 Bob Thurman 12.00 6.00
35A Don Mossi 15.00 7.50
35B Don Mossi YT 40.00 20.00
36 Ted Kazanski 12.00 6.00
37 Mike McCormick RC 15.00 7.50
UER Photo actually
Ray Monzant
38 Dick Gernert 12.00 6.00
39 Bob Martyn 12.00 6.00
40 George Kell 30.00 15.00
41 Dave Hillman 12.00 6.00
42 John Roseboro RC 30.00 15.00
43 Sal Maglie 15.00 7.50
44 Washington Senators 20.00 4.00
Team Card CL
45 Dick Groat 15.00 7.50
46A Lou Sleater 12.00 6.00
46B Lou Sleater YN 40.00 20.00
47 Roger Maris RC 500.00 250.00
48 Chuck Harmon 12.00 6.00
49 Smoky Burgess 15.00 7.50
50A Billy Pierce 15.00 7.50
50B Billy Pierce YT 40.00 20.00
51 Del Rice 12.00 6.00
52A Roberto Clemente 300.00 150.00
52B Roberto Clemente YT 500.00 250.00
53A Morrie Martin 12.00 6.00
53B Morrie Martin YN 40.00 20.00
54 Norm Siebern RC 20.00 10.00
55 Chico Carrasquel 12.00 6.00
56 Bill Fischer 12.00 6.00
57A Tim Thompson 12.00 6.00
57B Tim Thompson YN 40.00 20.00
58A Art Schult 12.00 6.00
58B Art Schult YT 40.00 20.00
59 Dave Sisler 12.00 6.00
60A Del Ennis 15.00 7.50
60B Del Ennis YN 40.00 20.00
61A Darrell Johnson 12.00 6.00
61B Darrell Johnson YN 40.00 20.00
62 Joe DeMaestri 12.00 6.00
63 Joe Nuxhall 15.00 7.50
64 Joe Lonnett 12.00 6.00
65A Von McDaniel RC 12.00 6.00
65B Von McDaniel YL RC 40.00 20.00
66 Lee Walls 12.00 6.00
67 Joe Ginsberg 12.00 6.00
68 Daryl Spencer 12.00 6.00
69 Wally Burnette 12.00 6.00
70A Al Kaline 100.00 50.00
70B Al Kaline YN 250.00 125.00
71 Dodgers Team CL 60.00 12.00
72 Bud Byerly 12.00 6.00
73 Pete Daley 12.00 6.00
74 Roy Face 15.00 7.50
75 Gus Bell 15.00 7.50
76A Dick Farrell 12.00 6.00
76B Dick Farrell YT 40.00 20.00
77A Don Zimmer 15.00 7.50
77B Don Zimmer YT 40.00 20.00
78A Ernie Johnson 15.00 7.50
78B Ernie Johnson YN 40.00 20.00
79A Dick Williams 15.00 7.50
79B Dick Williams YT 40.00 20.00
80 Dick Drott 12.00 6.00
81A Steve Boros RC 12.00 6.00
81B Steve Boros YT RC 40.00 20.00
82 Ron Kline 12.00 6.00
83 Bob Hazle RC 12.00 6.00
84 Billy O'Dell 12.00 6.00
85A Luis Aparicio 30.00 15.00
85B Luis Aparicio YT 80.00 40.00
86 Valmy Thomas 12.00 6.00
87 Johnny Kucks 12.00 6.00
88 Duke Snider 80.00 40.00
89 Billy Klaus 12.00 6.00
90 Robin Roberts 30.00 15.00
91 Chuck Tanner 15.00 7.50
92A Clint Courtney 12.00 6.00
92B Clint Courtney YN 40.00 20.00
93 Sandy Amoros 15.00 7.50
94 Bob Skinner 15.00 7.50
95 Frank Bolling 12.00 6.00
96 Joe Durham 12.00 6.00
97A Larry Jackson 12.00 6.00
97B Larry Jackson YN 40.00 20.00
98A Billy Hunter 12.00 6.00
98B Billy Hunter YN 40.00 20.00
99 Bobby Adams 12.00 6.00
100A Early Wynn 30.00 15.00
100B Early Wynn YT 80.00 40.00
101A Bobby Richardson 30.00 15.00
101B B.Richardson YN 60.00 30.00
102 George Strickland 12.00 6.00
103 Jerry Lynch 15.00 7.50
104 Jim Pendleton 12.00 6.00
105 Billy Gardner 12.00 6.00
106 Dick Schofield 15.00 7.50
107 Ossie Virgil 12.00 6.00
108A Jim Landis 12.00 6.00
108B Jim Landis YT 40.00 20.00
109 Herb Plews 12.00 6.00
110 Johnny Logan 15.00 7.50
111 Stu Miller 10.00 5.00
112 Gus Zernial 10.00 5.00
113 Jerry Walker RC 8.00 4.00
114 Irv Noren 10.00 5.00
115 Jim Bunning 30.00 15.00
116 Dave Philley 8.00 4.00
117 Frank Torre 10.00 5.00
118 Harvey Haddix 10.00 5.00
119 Harry Chiti 8.00 4.00
120 Johnny Podres 10.00 5.00
121 Eddie Miksis 8.00 4.00
122 Walt Moryn 8.00 4.00
123 Dick Tomanek 8.00 4.00
124 Bobby Usher 8.00 4.00
125 Alvin Dark 10.00 5.00
126 Stan Palys 8.00 4.00
127 Tom Sturdivant 10.00 5.00
128 Willie Kirkland 8.00 4.00
129 Jim Derrington 8.00 4.00
130 Jackie Jensen 10.00 5.00
131 Bob Henrich 8.00 4.00
132 Vern Law 10.00 5.00
133 Russ Nixon RC 8.00 4.00
134 Philadelphia Phillies 15.00 3.00
Team Card CL
135 Mike(Moe)Drabowsky 10.00 5.00
136 Jim Finigan 8.00 4.00
137 Russ Kemmerer 8.00 4.00
138 Earl Torgeson 8.00 4.00
139 George Brunet 8.00 4.00
140 Wes Covington 10.00 5.00
141 Ken Lehman 8.00 4.00
142 Enos Slaughter 25.00 12.50
143 Billy Muffett RC 8.00 4.00
144 Bobby Morgan 8.00 4.00
145 Never issued
146 Dick Gray 8.00 4.00
147 Don McMahon RC 8.00 4.00
148 Billy Consolo 8.00 4.00
149 Tom Acker 8.00 4.00
150 Mickey Mantle 800.00 400.00
151 Buddy Pritchard 8.00 4.00
152 Johnny Antonelli 10.00 5.00
153 Les Moss 8.00 4.00
154 Harry Byrd 8.00 4.00
155 Hector Lopez 10.00 5.00
156 Dick Hyde 8.00 4.00
157 Dee Fondy 8.00 4.00
158 Cleveland Indians 15.00 3.00
Team Card CL
159 Taylor Phillips 8.00 4.00
160 Don Hoak 10.00 5.00
161 Don Larsen 15.00 7.50
162 Gil Hodges 40.00 20.00
163 Jim Wilson 8.00 4.00
164 Bob Taylor 8.00 4.00
165 Bob Nieman 8.00 4.00
166 Danny O'Connell 8.00 4.00
167 Frank Baumann 8.00 4.00
168 Joe Cunningham 8.00 4.00
169 Ralph Terry 10.00 5.00
170 Vic Wertz 10.00 5.00
171 Harry Anderson 8.00 4.00
172 Don Gross 8.00 4.00
173 Eddie Yost 8.00 4.00
174 K.C. Athletics Team CL 15.00 3.00
175 Marv Throneberry RC 15.00 7.50
176 Bob Buhl 10.00 5.00
177 Al Smith 8.00 4.00
178 Ted Kluszewski 25.00 12.50
179 Willie Miranda 8.00 4.00
180 Lindy McDaniel 10.00 5.00
181 Willie Jones 8.00 4.00
182 Joe Caffie 8.00 4.00
183 Dave Jolly 8.00 4.00
184 Elvin Tappe 8.00 4.00
185 Ray Boone 8.00 4.00
186 Jack Meyer 8.00 4.00
187 Sandy Koufax 200.00 100.00
188 Milt Bolling UER 8.00 4.00
(Photo actually
Lou Berberet)
189 George Susce 8.00 4.00
190 Red Schoendienst 25.00 12.50
191 Art Ceccarelli 8.00 4.00
192 Milt Graff 8.00 4.00
193 Jerry Lumpe RC 8.00 4.00
194 Roger Craig 10.00 5.00
195 Whitey Lockman 10.00 5.00
196 Mike Garcia 10.00 5.00
197 Haywood Sullivan 10.00 5.00
198 Bill Virdon 10.00 5.00
199 Don Blasingame 8.00 4.00
200 Bob Keegan 8.00 4.00
201 Jim Bolger 8.00 4.00
202 Woody Held RC 8.00 4.00
203 Al Walker 8.00 4.00
204 Leo Kiely 8.00 4.00
205 Johnny Temple 10.00 5.00
206 Bob Shaw RC 8.00 4.00
207 Solly Hemus 8.00 4.00
208 Cal McLish 8.00 4.00
209 Bob Anderson 8.00 4.00
210 Wally Moon 10.00 5.00
211 Pete Burnside 8.00 4.00
212 Bubba Phillips 8.00 4.00
213 Red Wilson 8.00 4.00
214 Willard Schmidt 8.00 4.00
215 Jim Gilliam 15.00 7.50
216 St. Louis Cardinals 15.00 3.00
Team Card CL
217 Jack Harshman 8.00 4.00
218 Dick Rand 8.00 4.00
219 Camilo Pascual 10.00 5.00
220 Tom Brewer 8.00 4.00
221 Jerry Kindall RC 8.00 4.00
222 Bud Daley 8.00 4.00
223 Andy Pafko 10.00 5.00
224 Bob Grim 10.00 5.00
225 Billy Goodman 10.00 5.00
226 Bob Smith 8.00 4.00
227 Gene Stephens 8.00 4.00
228 Duke Maas 8.00 4.00
229 Frank Zupo 8.00 4.00
230 Richie Ashburn 40.00 20.00
231 Lloyd Merritt 8.00 4.00
232 Reno Bertoia 8.00 4.00
233 Mickey Vernon 10.00 5.00
234 Carl Sawatski 8.00 4.00
235 Tom Gorman 8.00 4.00
236 Ed Fitzgerald 8.00 4.00
237 Bill Wight 8.00 4.00
238 Bill Mazeroski 30.00 15.00
239 Chuck Stobbs 8.00 4.00
240 Bill Skowron 25.00 12.50
241 Dick Littlefield 8.00 4.00
242 Johnny Klippstein 8.00 4.00
243 Larry Raines 8.00 4.00
244 Don Demeter 8.00 4.00
245 Frank Lary 10.00 5.00
246 New York Yankees 100.00 20.00
Team Card CL
247 Casey Wise 8.00 4.00
248 Herman Wehmeier 8.00 4.00
249 Ray Moore 8.00 4.00
250 Roy Sievers 10.00 5.00
251 Warren Hacker 8.00 4.00
252 Bob Trowbridge 8.00 4.00
253 Don Mueller 10.00 5.00
254 Alex Grammas 8.00 4.00
255 Bob Turley 10.00 5.00
256 Chicago White Sox 15.00 3.00
Team Card CL
257 Hal Smith 8.00 4.00
258 Carl Erskine 15.00 7.50
259 Al Pilarcik 8.00 4.00
260 Frank Malzone 10.00 5.00
261 Turk Lown 8.00 4.00
262 Johnny Groth 8.00 4.00
263 Eddie Bressoud 10.00 5.00
264 Jack Sanford 10.00 5.00
265 Pete Runnels 10.00 5.00
266 Connie Johnson 8.00 4.00
267 Sherm Lollar 10.00 5.00
268 Granny Hamner 8.00 4.00
269 Paul Smith 8.00 4.00
270 Warren Spahn 60.00 30.00
271 Billy Martin 40.00 20.00
272 Ray Crone 8.00 4.00
273 Hal Smith 8.00 4.00
274 Rocky Bridges 8.00 4.00
275 Elston Howard 15.00 7.50
276 Bobby Avila 8.00 4.00
277 Virgil Trucks 10.00 5.00
278 Mack Burk 8.00 4.00
279 Bob Boyd 8.00 4.00
280 Jim Piersall 10.00 5.00
281 Sammy Taylor 8.00 4.00
282 Paul Foytack 8.00 4.00
283 Ray Shearer 8.00 4.00
284 Ray Katt 8.00 4.00
285 Frank Robinson 100.00 50.00
286 Gino Cimoli 8.00 4.00
287 Sam Jones 10.00 5.00
288 Harmon Killebrew 100.00 50.00
289 Lou Burdette 10.00 5.00
Bobby Shantz
290 Dick Donovan 8.00 4.00
291 Don Landrum 8.00 4.00
292 Ned Garver 8.00 4.00
293 Gene Freese 8.00 4.00
294 Hal Jeffcoat 8.00 4.00
295 Minnie Minoso 25.00 12.50
296 Ryne Duren RC 15.00 7.50
297 Don Buddin 8.00 4.00
298 Jim Hearn 8.00 4.00
299 Harry Simpson 8.00 4.00
300 Will Harridge PRES 15.00 7.50
Warren Giles
301 Randy Jackson 8.00 4.00
302 Mike Baxes 8.00 4.00
303 Neil Chrisley 8.00 4.00
304 Harvey Kuenn 25.00 12.50
Al Kaline
305 Clem Labine 10.00 5.00
306 Whammy Douglas 8.00 4.00
307 Brooks Robinson 100.00 50.00
308 Paul Giel 10.00 5.00
309 Gail Harris 8.00 4.00
310 Ernie Banks 100.00 50.00
311 Bob Purkey 8.00 4.00
312 Boston Red Sox 15.00 3.00
Team Card CL
313 Bob Rush 8.00 4.00
314 Duke Snider 50.00 25.00
Walt Alston MG
315 Bob Friend 10.00 5.00
316 Tito Francona 10.00 5.00
317 Albie Pearson 10.00 5.00
318 Frank House 8.00 4.00
319 Lou Skizas 8.00 4.00

320 Whitey Ford 60.00 30.00
321 Ted Kluszewski 100.00 50.00
Ted Williams
322 Harding Peterson 10.00 5.00
323 Elmer Valo 8.00 4.00
324 Hoyt Wilhelm 25.00 12.50
325 Joe Adcock 10.00 5.00
326 Bob Miller 8.00 4.00
327 Chicago Cubs 15.00 3.00
Team Card CL
328 Ike Delock 8.00 4.00
329 Bob Cerv 10.00 5.00
330 Ed Bailey 10.00 5.00
331 Pedro Ramos 8.00 4.00
332 Jim King 8.00 4.00
333 Andy Carey 10.00 5.00
334 Bob Friend 10.00 5.00
Billy Pierce
335 Ruben Gomez 8.00 4.00
336 Bert Hamric 8.00 4.00
337 Hank Aguirre 8.00 4.00
338 Walt Dropo 10.00 5.00
339 Fred Hatfield 8.00 4.00
340 Don Newcombe 15.00 7.50
341 Pittsburgh Pirates 15.00 3.00
Team Card CL
342 Jim Brosnan 10.00 5.00
343 Orlando Cepeda RC 100.00 50.00
344 Bob Porterfield 8.00 4.00
345 Jim Hegan 10.00 5.00
346 Steve Bilko 8.00 4.00
347 Don Rudolph 8.00 4.00
348 Chico Fernandez 8.00 4.00
349 Murry Dickson 8.00 4.00
350 Ken Boyer 25.00 12.50
351 Del Crandall 40.00 20.00
Eddie Mathews
Hank Aaron
Joe Adcock
352 Herb Score 15.00 7.50
353 Stan Lopata 8.00 4.00
354 Art Ditmar 10.00 5.00
355 Bill Bruton 10.00 5.00
356 Bob Malkmus 8.00 4.00
357 Danny McDevitt 8.00 4.00
358 Gene Baker 8.00 4.00
359 Billy Loes 10.00 5.00
360 Roy McMillan 10.00 5.00
361 Mike Fornieles 8.00 4.00
362 Ray Jablonski 8.00 4.00
363 Don Elston 8.00 4.00
364 Earl Battey 8.00 4.00
365 Tom Morgan 8.00 4.00
366 Gene Green 8.00 4.00
367 Jack Urban 8.00 4.00
368 Rocky Colavito 50.00 25.00
369 Ralph Lumenti 8.00 4.00
370 Yogi Berra 100.00 50.00
371 Marty Keough 8.00 4.00
372 Don Cardwell 8.00 4.00
373 Joe Pignatano 8.00 4.00
374 Brooks Lawrence 8.00 4.00
375 Pee Wee Reese 80.00 40.00
376 Charley Rabe 8.00 4.00
377A Milwaukee Braves 15.00 7.50
Team Card
(Alphabetical)
377B Milwaukee Team 100.00 20.00
numerical checklist
378 Hank Sauer 10.00 5.00
379 Ray Herbert 8.00 4.00
380 Charlie Maxwell 10.00 5.00
381 Hal Brown 8.00 4.00
382 Al Cicotte 8.00 4.00
383 Lou Berberet 8.00 4.00
384 John Goryl 8.00 4.00
385 Wilmer Mizell 10.00 5.00
386 Ed Bailey 15.00 7.50
Birdie Tebbetts MG
Frank Robinson
387 Wally Post 10.00 5.00
388 Billy Moran 8.00 4.00
389 Bill Taylor 8.00 4.00
390 Del Crandall 10.00 5.00
391 Dave Melton 8.00 4.00
392 Bennie Daniels 8.00 4.00
393 Tony Kubek 30.00 15.00
394 Jim Grant RC 8.00 4.00
395 Willard Nixon 8.00 4.00
396 Dutch Dotterer 8.00 4.00
397A Detroit Tigers 15.00 7.50
Team Card
(Alphabetical)
397B Detroit Team 100.00 20.00
numerical checklist
398 Gene Woodling 10.00 5.00
399 Marv Grissom 8.00 4.00
400 Nellie Fox 40.00 20.00
401 Don Bessent 8.00 4.00
402 Bobby Gene Smith 8.00 4.00
403 Steve Korcheck 8.00 4.00
404 Curt Simmons 10.00 5.00
405 Ken Aspromonte 8.00 4.00
406 Vic Power 10.00 5.00
407 Carlton Willey 10.00 5.00
408A Baltimore Orioles 15.00 7.50
Team Card
(Alphabetical)
408B Baltimore Team 100.00 20.00
numerical checklist
409 Frank Thomas 10.00 5.00
410 Murray Wall 8.00 4.00
411 Tony Taylor RC 10.00 5.00
412 Gerry Staley 8.00 4.00
413 Jim Davenport RC 8.00 4.00
414 Sammy White 8.00 4.00
415 Bob Bowman 8.00 4.00
416 Foster Castleman 8.00 4.00
417 Carl Furillo 15.00 7.50
418 Mickey Mantle 400.00 200.00
Hank Aaron
419 Bobby Shantz 10.00 5.00
420 Vada Pinson RC 40.00 20.00
421 Dixie Howell 8.00 4.00
422 Norm Zauchin 8.00 4.00
423 Phil Clark 8.00 4.00
424 Larry Doby 25.00 12.50
425 Sammy Esposito 8.00 4.00
426 Johnny O'Brien 10.00 5.00
427 Al Worthington 8.00 4.00
428A Cincinnati Reds 15.00 7.50
Team Card
(Alphabetical)
428B Cincinnati Team 100.00 20.00
numerical checklist
429 Gus Triandos 10.00 5.00
430 Bobby Thomson 10.00 5.00
431 Gene Conley 10.00 5.00
432 John Powers 8.00 4.00
433A Pancho Herrer ERR 600.00 300.00
433B Pancho Herrera COR 10.00 5.00
434 Harvey Kuenn 10.00 5.00
435 Ed Roebuck 10.00 5.00
436 Willie Mays 100.00 50.00
Duke Snider
437 Bob Speake 8.00 4.00
438 Whitey Herzog 10.00 5.00
439 Ray Narleski 8.00 4.00
440 Eddie Mathews 80.00 40.00
441 Jim Marshall 10.00 5.00
442 Phil Paine 8.00 4.00
443 Billy Harrell SP 20.00 10.00
444 Danny Kravitz 8.00 4.00
445 Bob Smith 8.00 4.00
446 Carroll Hardy SP 20.00 10.00
447 Ray Monzant 8.00 4.00
448 Charlie Lau RC 10.00 5.00
449 Gene Fodge 8.00 4.00
450 Preston Ward SP 20.00 10.00
451 Joe Taylor 8.00 4.00
452 Roman Mejias 8.00 4.00
453 Tom Qualters 8.00 4.00
454 Harry Hanebrink 8.00 4.00
455 Hal Griggs 8.00 4.00
456 Dick Brown 8.00 4.00
457 Milt Pappas RC 10.00 5.00
458 Julio Becquer 8.00 4.00
459 Ron Blackburn 8.00 4.00
460 Chuck Essegian 8.00 4.00
461 Ed Mayer 8.00 4.00
462 Gary Geiger SP 20.00 10.00
463 Vito Valentinetti 8.00 4.00
464 Curt Flood RC 30.00 15.00
465 Arnie Portocarrero 8.00 4.00
466 Pete Whisenant 8.00 4.00
467 Glen Hobbie 8.00 4.00
468 Bob Schmidt 8.00 4.00
469 Don Ferrarese 8.00 4.00
470 R.C. Stevens 8.00 4.00
471 Lenny Green 8.00 4.00
472 Joey Jay 10.00 5.00
473 Bill Renna 8.00 4.00
474 Roman Semproch 8.00 4.00
475 Fred Haney AS MG 25.00 7.50
Casey Stengel AS MG CL
476 Stan Musial AS TP 50.00 25.00
477 Bill Skowron AS 10.00 5.00
478 J.Temple AS UER 8.00 4.00
Card says record vs American League
Temple was NL AS
479 Nellie Fox AS 15.00 7.50
480 Eddie Mathews AS 30.00 15.00
481 Frank Malzone AS 8.00 4.00
482 Ernie Banks AS 40.00 20.00
483 Luis Aparicio AS 15.00 7.50
484 Frank Robinson AS 40.00 20.00
485 Ted Williams AS 150.00 75.00
486 Willie Mays AS 60.00 30.00
487 Mickey Mantle AS TP 175.00 90.00
488 Hank Aaron AS 60.00 30.00
489 Jackie Jensen AS 10.00 5.00
490 Ed Bailey AS 8.00 4.00
491 Sherm Lollar AS 8.00 4.00
492 Bob Friend AS 8.00 4.00
493 Bob Turley AS 10.00 5.00
494 Warren Spahn AS 25.00 12.50
495 Herb Score AS 15.00 3.00
NNO Contest Cards 40.00 20.00

1959 Topps

The cards in this 572-card set measure 2 1/2" by 3 1/2". The 1959 Topps set contains bust pictures of the players in a colored circle. Card numbers 551 to 572 are Sporting News All-Star Selections. High numbers 507 to 572 have the card number in a black background on the reverse rather than a green background as in the lower numbers. The high numbers are more difficult to obtain. Several cards in the 300s exist with or without an extra traded or option line on the back of the card. Cards 199 to 286 exist with either white or gray backs. There is no price differential for either colored back. Cards 461 to 470 contain "Highlights" while cards 116 to 146 give an alphabetically ordered listing of "Rookie Prospects." These Rookie Prospects (RP) were Topps' first organized inclusion of untested "Rookie" cards. Card 440 features Lew Burdette erroneously posing as a left-handed pitcher. Cards were issued in one-card penny packs or six-card nickel packs. There were some three-card advertising panels produced by Topps; the players included are from the first series. Panels which had Ted Kluszewski's card back on the back included Don McMahon/Red Wilson/Bob Boyd; Joe Pignatano/Sam Jones/Jack Urban also with Kluszewski's card back on back, Strips with Nellie Fox on the back included Billy Hunter/Chuck Stobbs/Carl Sawatski; Vito Valentinetti/Ken Lehman/Ed Bouchee; Mel Roach/Brooks Lawrence/Warren Spahn. Other panels include Harvey Kuenn/Alex Grammas/ Bob Cerv; and Bob Cerv/Jim Bolger/Mickey Mantle. When separated, these advertising cards are distinguished by the non-standard card back, i.e., part of an advertisement for the 1959 Topps set instead of the typical statistics and biographical information about the player pictured. The key Rookie Cards in this set are Felipe Alou, Sparky Anderson (called George on the card), Norm Cash, Bob Gibson, and Bill White.

	NM	Ex
COMPLETE SET (572)	5000.00	2500.00
COMMON CARD (1-110)	6.00	3.00
COMMON (111-506)	4.00	2.00
COMMON (507-572)	15.00	7.50
WRAPPER (1-CENT)	125.00	60.00
WRAPPER (5-CENT)	100.00	50.00

1 Ford Frick COMM RC 60.00 16.50
2 Eddie Yost 8.00 4.00
3 Don McMahon 8.00 4.00
4 Albie Pearson 8.00 4.00
5 Dick Donovan 8.00 4.00
6 Alex Grammas 6.00 3.00
7 Al Pilarcik 6.00 3.00
8 Phillies Team CL 80.00 16.00
9 Paul Giel 8.00 4.00
10 Mickey Mantle 700.00 350.00
11 Billy Hunter 8.00 4.00
12 Vern Law 8.00 4.00
13 Dick Gernert 6.00 3.00
14 Pete Whisenant 6.00 3.00
15 Dick Drott 6.00 3.00
16 Joe Pignatano 6.00 3.00
17 Frank Thomas 8.00 4.00
Danny Murtaugh MG
Ted Kluszewski
18 Jack Urban 6.00 3.00
19 Eddie Bressoud 6.00 3.00
20 Duke Snider 60.00 30.00
21 Connie Johnson 6.00 3.00
22 Al Smith 8.00 4.00
23 Murry Dickson 8.00 4.00
24 Red Wilson 6.00 3.00
25 Don Hoak 8.00 4.00
26 Chuck Stobbs 6.00 3.00
27 Andy Pafko 8.00 4.00
28 Al Worthington 6.00 3.00
29 Jim Bolger 6.00 3.00
30 Nellie Fox 30.00 15.00
31 Ken Lehman 6.00 3.00
32 Don Buddin 6.00 3.00
33 Ed Fitzgerald 6.00 3.00
34 Al Kaline 20.00 10.00
Charley Maxwell
35 Ted Kluszewski 12.00 6.00
36 Hank Aguirre 6.00 3.00
37 Gene Green 6.00 3.00
38 Morrie Martin 6.00 3.00
39 Ed Bouchee 6.00 3.00
40A Warren Spahn ERR 80.00 40.00
(Born 1931)
40B Warren Spahn ERR 100.00 50.00
(Born 1931, but three
is partially obscured)
40C Warren Spahn COR 60.00 30.00
(Born 1921)
41 Bob Martyn 6.00 3.00
42 Murray Wall 6.00 3.00
43 Steve Bilko 6.00 3.00
44 Vito Valentinetti 6.00 3.00
45 Andy Carey 8.00 4.00
46 Bill R. Henry 6.00 3.00
47 Jim Finigan 6.00 3.00
48 Orioles Team CL 25.00 5.00
49 Bill Hall 6.00 3.00
50 Willie Mays 150.00 75.00
51 Rip Coleman 6.00 3.00
52 Coot Veal 6.00 3.00
53 Stan Williams RC 8.00 4.00
54 Mel Roach 6.00 3.00
55 Tom Brewer 6.00 3.00
56 Carl Sawatski 6.00 3.00
57 Al Cicotte 6.00 3.00
58 Eddie Miksis 6.00 3.00
59 Irv Noren 8.00 4.00
60 Bob Turley 8.00 4.00
61 Dick Brown 6.00 3.00
62 Tony Taylor 8.00 4.00
63 Jim Hearn 6.00 3.00
64 Joe DeMaestri 6.00 3.00
65 Frank Torre 8.00 4.00
66 Joe Ginsberg 6.00 3.00
67 Brooks Lawrence 6.00 3.00
68 Dick Schofield 8.00 4.00
69 Giants Team CL 25.00 5.00
70 Harvey Kuenn 8.00 4.00
71 Don Bessent 6.00 3.00
72 Bill Renna 6.00 3.00
73 Ron Jackson 8.00 4.00
74 Jim Lemon 8.00 4.00
Cookie Lavagetto MG
Roy Sievers
75 Sam Jones 8.00 4.00
76 Bobby Richardson 20.00 10.00
77 John Goryl 6.00 3.00
78 Pedro Ramos 6.00 3.00
79 Harry Chiti 6.00 3.00
80 Minnie Minoso 12.00 6.00
81 Hal Jeffcoat 6.00 3.00
82 Bob Boyd 6.00 3.00
83 Bob Smith 6.00 3.00
84 Reno Bertoia 6.00 3.00
85 Harry Anderson 6.00 3.00
86 Bob Keegan 8.00 4.00
87 Danny O'Connell 6.00 3.00
88 Herb Score 12.00 6.00
89 Billy Gardner 6.00 3.00
90 Bill Skowron 12.00 6.00
91 Herb Moford 6.00 3.00
92 Dave Philley 6.00 3.00
93 Julio Becquer 6.00 3.00
94 White Sox Team CL 40.00 8.00
95 Carl Willey 6.00 3.00
96 Lou Berberet 6.00 3.00
97 Jerry Lynch 8.00 4.00
98 Arnie Portocarrero 6.00 3.00
99 Ted Kazanski 6.00 3.00
100 Bob Cerv 8.00 4.00
101 Alex Kellner 6.00 3.00
102 Felipe Alou RC 30.00 15.00
103 Billy Goodman 8.00 4.00
104 Del Rice 8.00 4.00
105 Lee Walls 6.00 3.00
106 Hal Woodeshick 6.00 3.00
107 Norm Larker 8.00 4.00
108 Zack Monroe 8.00 4.00
109 Bob Schmidt 6.00 3.00
110 George Witt 8.00 4.00
111 Redlegs Team CL 15.00 3.00
112 Billy Consolo 4.00 2.00
113 Taylor Phillips 4.00 2.00
114 Earl Battey 8.00 4.00
115 Mickey Vernon 8.00 4.00
116 Bob Allison RP RC 12.00 6.00
117 J.Blanchard RP RC 12.00 6.00
118 John Buzhardt RP 5.00 2.50
119 John Callison RP RC 12.00 6.00
120 Chuck Coles RP 5.00 2.50
121 Bob Conley RP 5.00 2.50
122 Bennie Daniels RP 5.00 2.50
123 Don Dillard RP 5.00 2.50
124 Dan Dobbek RP 5.00 2.50
125 Ron Fairly RP RC 12.00 6.00
126 Eddie Haas RP 5.00 2.50
127 Kent Hadley RP 5.00 2.50
128 Bob Hartman RP 5.00 2.50
129 Frank Herrera RP 5.00 2.50
130 Lou Jackson RP 5.00 2.50
131 Deron Johnson RP RC 12.00 6.00
132 Don Lee RP 5.00 2.50
133 Bob Lillis RP RC 5.00 2.50
134 Jim McDaniel RP 5.00 2.50
135 Gene Oliver RP 5.00 2.50
136 Jim O'Toole RP RC 5.00 2.50
137 Dick Ricketts RP 5.00 2.50
138 John Romano RP RC 5.00 2.50
139 Ed Sadowski RP 5.00 2.50
140 Charlie Secrest RP 5.00 2.50
141 Joe Shipley RP 5.00 2.50
142 Dick Stigman RP 5.00 2.50
143 Willie Tasby RP RC 5.00 2.50
144 Jerry Walker RP 5.00 2.50
145 Dom Zanni RP 5.00 2.50
146 Jerry Zimmerman RP 5.00 2.50
147 Dale Long 30.00 15.00
Ernie Banks
Walt Moryn
148 Mike McCormick 8.00 4.00
149 Jim Bunning 20.00 10.00
150 Stan Musial 125.00 60.00
151 Bob Malkmus 4.00 2.00
152 Johnny Klippstein 4.00 2.00
153 Jim Marshall 4.00 2.00
154 Ray Herbert 4.00 2.00
155 Enos Slaughter 20.00 10.00
156 Billy Pierce 12.00 6.00
Robin Roberts
157 Felix Mantilla 4.00 2.00
158 Walt Dropo 4.00 2.00
159 Bob Shaw 8.00 4.00
160 Dick Groat 8.00 4.00
161 Frank Baumann 4.00 2.00
162 Bobby G. Smith 4.00 2.00
163 Sandy Koufax 150.00 75.00
164 Johnny Groth 4.00 2.00
165 Bill Bruton 4.00 2.00
166 Minnie Minoso 30.00 15.00
Rocky Colavito
(Misspelled Colovito
on card back)
Larry Doby
167 Duke Maas 4.00 2.00
168 Carroll Hardy 4.00 2.00
169 Ted Abernathy 4.00 2.00
170 Gene Woodling 8.00 4.00
171 Willard Schmidt 4.00 2.00
172 Athletics Team CL 15.00 3.00
173 Bill Monbouquette 8.00 4.00
174 Jim Pendleton 4.00 2.00
175 Dick Farrell 8.00 4.00
176 Preston Ward 4.00 2.00
177 John Briggs 4.00 2.00
178 Ruben Amaro RC 12.00 6.00
179 Don Rudolph 4.00 2.00
180 Yogi Berra 80.00 40.00
181 Bob Porterfield 4.00 2.00
182 Milt Graff 4.00 2.00
183 Stu Miller 8.00 4.00
184 Harvey Haddix 8.00 4.00
185 Jim Busby 8.00 4.00
186 Mudcat Grant 8.00 4.00
187 Bubba Phillips 8.00 4.00
188 Juan Pizarro 4.00 2.00
189 Neil Chrisley 4.00 2.00
190 Bill Virdon 8.00 4.00
191 Russ Kemmerer 4.00 2.00
192 Charlie Beamon 4.00 2.00
193 Sammy Taylor 4.00 2.00
194 Jim Brosnan 8.00 4.00
195 Rip Repulski 4.00 2.00
196 Billy Moran 4.00 2.00
197 Ray Semproch 4.00 2.00
198 Jim Davenport 8.00 4.00
199 Leo Kiely 4.00 2.00
200 W.Giles NL PRES 8.00 4.00
201 Tom Acker 4.00 2.00
202 Roger Maris 125.00 60.00
203 Ossie Virgil 4.00 2.00
204 Casey Wise 4.00 2.00
205 Don Larsen 8.00 4.00
206 Carl Furillo 12.00 6.00
207 George Strickland 4.00 2.00
208 Willie Jones 4.00 2.00
209 Lenny Green 4.00 2.00
210 Ed Bailey 4.00 2.00
211 Bob Blaylock 4.00 2.00
212 Hank Aaron 80.00 40.00
Eddie Mathews
213 Jim Rivera 8.00 4.00
214 Marcelino Solis 4.00 2.00
215 Jim Lemon 8.00 4.00
216 Andre Rodgers 4.00 2.00
217 Carl Erskine 12.00 6.00
218 Roman Mejias 4.00 2.00
219 George Zuverink 4.00 2.00
220 Frank Malzone 8.00 4.00
221 Bob Bowman 4.00 2.00
222 Bobby Shantz 8.00 4.00
223 Cardinals Team CL 15.00 3.00
224 Claude Osteen RC 8.00 4.00
225 Johnny Logan 8.00 4.00
226 Art Ceccarelli 4.00 2.00
227 Hal W. Smith 4.00 2.00
228 Don Gross 4.00 2.00
229 Vic Power 8.00 4.00
230 Bill Fischer 4.00 2.00
231 Ellis Burton 4.00 2.00
232 Eddie Kasko 4.00 2.00
233 Paul Foytack 4.00 2.00
234 Chuck Tanner 8.00 4.00
235 Valmy Thomas 4.00 2.00
236 Ted Bowsfield 4.00 2.00
237 Gil McDougald 12.00 6.00
Bob Turley
Bobby Richardson
238 Gene Baker 4.00 2.00
239 Bob Trowbridge 4.00 2.00
240 Hank Bauer 12.00 6.00
241 Billy Muffett 4.00 2.00
242 Ron Samford 4.00 2.00
243 Marv Grissom 4.00 2.00
244 Ted Gray 4.00 2.00
245 Ned Garver 4.00 2.00
246 J.W. Porter 4.00 2.00
247 Don Ferrarese 4.00 2.00
248 Red Sox Team CL 15.00 3.00
249 Bobby Adams 4.00 2.00
250 Billy O'Dell 4.00 2.00
251 Clete Boyer 12.00 6.00
252 Ray Boone 8.00 4.00
253 Seth Morehead 4.00 2.00
254 Zeke Bella 4.00 2.00
255 Del Ennis 8.00 4.00
256 Jerry Davie 4.00 2.00
257 Leon Wagner RC 8.00 4.00
258 Fred Kipp 4.00 2.00
259 Jim Pisoni 4.00 2.00
260 Early Wynn UER 20.00 10.00
1957 Cleveland
261 Gene Stephens 4.00 2.00
262 Johnny Podres 12.00 6.00
Clem Labine
Don Drysdale
263 Bud Daley 4.00 2.00
264 Chico Carrasquel 4.00 2.00
265 Ron Kline 4.00 2.00
266 Woody Held 4.00 2.00
267 John Romonosky 4.00 2.00
268 Tito Francona 8.00 4.00
269 Jack Meyer 4.00 2.00
270 Gil Hodges 30.00 15.00
271 Orlando Pena 4.00 2.00
272 Jerry Lumpe 4.00 2.00
273 Joey Jay 8.00 4.00
274 Jerry Kindall 8.00 4.00
275 Jack Sanford 8.00 4.00
276 Pete Daley 4.00 2.00
277 Turk Lown 8.00 4.00
278 Chuck Essegian 4.00 2.00
279 Ernie Johnson 4.00 2.00
280 Frank Bolling 4.00 2.00
281 Walt Craddock 4.00 2.00
282 R.C. Stevens 4.00 2.00
283 Russ Heman 4.00 2.00
284 Steve Korcheck 4.00 2.00
285 Joe Cunningham 4.00 2.00
286 Dean Stone 4.00 2.00
287 Don Zimmer 12.00 6.00
288 Dutch Dotterer 4.00 2.00
289 Johnny Kucks 8.00 4.00
290 Wes Covington 4.00 2.00
291 Pedro Ramos 4.00 2.00
Camilo Pascual
292 Dick Williams 8.00 4.00
293 Ray Moore 4.00 2.00
294 Hank Foiles 4.00 2.00
295 Billy Martin 30.00 15.00
296 Ernie Broglio RC 4.00 2.00
297 Jackie Brandt 4.00 2.00
298 Tex Clevenger 4.00 2.00
299 Billy Klaus 4.00 2.00
300 Richie Ashburn 30.00 15.00
301 Earl Averill 4.00 2.00
302 Don Mossi 8.00 4.00
303 Marty Keough 4.00 2.00
304 Cubs Team CL 15.00 3.00
305 Curt Raydon 4.00 2.00
306 Jim Gilliam 8.00 4.00
307 Curt Barclay 4.00 2.00
308 Norm Siebern 4.00 2.00
309 Sal Maglie 8.00 4.00
310 Luis Aparicio 20.00 10.00
311 Norm Zauchin 4.00 2.00
312 Don Newcombe 8.00 4.00
313 Frank House 4.00 2.00
314 Don Cardwell 4.00 2.00
315 Joe Adcock 8.00 4.00
316A Ralph Lumenti UER 4.00 2.00
(Option)
(Photo actually
Camilo Pascual)
316B Ralph Lumenti UER 80.00 40.00
(No option)
(Photo actually
Camilo Pascual)
317 Willie Mays 80.00 40.00
Richie Ashburn
318 Rocky Bridges 4.00 2.00
319 Dave Hillman 4.00 2.00
320 Bob Skinner 8.00 4.00
321A Bob Giallombardo 8.00 4.00
(Option)
321B Bob Giallombardo 80.00 40.00
(No option)
322A Harry Hanebrink 8.00 4.00
(Traded)
322B Harry Hanebrink 80.00 40.00
(No trade)
323 Frank Sullivan 4.00 2.00
324 Don Demeter 4.00 2.00
325 Ken Boyer 12.00 6.00
326 Marv Throneberry 8.00 4.00
327 Gary Bell 4.00 2.00
328 Lou Skizas 4.00 2.00
329 Tigers Team CL 15.00 3.00
330 Gus Triandos 8.00 4.00
331 Steve Boros 4.00 2.00
332 Ray Monzant 4.00 2.00
333 Harry Simpson 4.00 2.00
334 Glen Hobbie 4.00 2.00
335 Johnny Temple 8.00 4.00
336A Billy Loes 8.00 4.00
(With traded line)
336B Billy Loes 80.00 40.00
(No trade)
337 George Crowe 4.00 2.00
338 Sparky Anderson RC 60.00 30.00
339 Roy Face 8.00 4.00

340 Roy Sievers 8.00 4.00
341 Tom Qualters 4.00 2.00
342 Ray Jablonski 4.00 2.00
343 Billy Hoeft 4.00 2.00
344 Russ Nixon 4.00 2.00
345 Gil McDougald 12.00 6.00
346 Dave Sisler 4.00 2.00
Tom Brewer
347 Bob Buhl 4.00 2.00
348 Ted Lepcio 4.00 2.00
349 Hoyt Wilhelm 20.00 10.00
350 Ernie Banks 80.00 40.00
351 Earl Torgeson 4.00 2.00
352 Robin Roberts 20.00 10.00
353 Curt Flood 8.00 4.00
354 Pete Burnside 4.00 2.00
355 Jimmy Piersall 8.00 4.00
356 Bob Mabe 4.00 2.00
357 Dick Stuart RC 8.00 4.00
358 Ralph Terry 8.00 4.00
359 Bill White RC 20.00 10.00
360 Al Kaline 60.00 30.00
361 Willard Nixon 4.00 2.00
362A Dolan Nichols 4.00 2.00
(With option line)
362B Dolan Nichols 80.00 40.00
(No option)
363 Bobby Avila 4.00 2.00
364 Danny McDevitt 4.00 2.00
365 Gus Bell 8.00 4.00
366 Humberto Robinson 4.00 2.00
367 Cal Neeman 4.00 2.00
368 Don Mueller 8.00 4.00
369 Dick Tomanek 4.00 2.00
370 Pete Runnels 8.00 4.00
371 Dick Brodowski 4.00 2.00
372 Jim Hegan 8.00 4.00
373 Herb Plews 4.00 2.00
374 Art Ditmar 8.00 4.00
375 Bob Nieman 4.00 2.00
376 Hal Naragon 4.00 2.00
377 John Antonelli 8.00 4.00
378 Gail Harris 4.00 2.00
379 Bob Miller 4.00 2.00
380 Hank Aaron 125.00 60.00
381 Mike Baxes 4.00 2.00
382 Curt Simmons 8.00 4.00
383 Don Larsen 12.00 6.00
Casey Stengel MG
384 Dave Sisler 4.00 2.00
385 Sherm Lollar 8.00 4.00
386 Jim Delsing 4.00 2.00
387 Don Drysdale 50.00 25.00
388 Bob Will 4.00 2.00
389 Joe Nuxhall 8.00 4.00
390 Orlando Cepeda 20.00 10.00
391 Milt Pappas 8.00 4.00
392 Whitey Herzog 8.00 4.00
393 Frank Lary 8.00 4.00
394 Randy Jackson 4.00 2.00
395 Elston Howard 12.00 6.00
396 Bob Rush 4.00 2.00
397 Senators Team CL 15.00 3.00
398 Wally Post 8.00 4.00
399 Larry Jackson 4.00 2.00
400 Jackie Jensen 8.00 4.00
401 Ron Blackburn 4.00 2.00
402 Hector Lopez 8.00 4.00
403 Clem Labine 8.00 4.00
404 Hank Sauer 8.00 4.00
405 Roy McMillan 8.00 4.00
406 Solly Drake 4.00 2.00
407 Moe Drabowsky 8.00 4.00
408 Nellie Fox 40.00 20.00
Luis Aparicio
409 Gus Zernial 8.00 4.00
410 Billy Pierce 8.00 4.00
411 Whitey Lockman 8.00 4.00
412 Stan Lopata 4.00 2.00
413 Camilo Pascual UER 8.00 4.00
(Listed as Camillo
on front and Pasqual
on back)
414 Dale Long 8.00 4.00
415 Bill Mazeroski 12.00 6.00
416 Haywood Sullivan 8.00 4.00
417 Virgil Trucks 8.00 4.00
418 Gino Cimoli 4.00 2.00
419 Braves Team CL 15.00 3.00
420 Rocky Colavito 30.00 15.00
421 Herman Wehmeier 4.00 2.00
422 Hobie Landrith 4.00 2.00
423 Bob Grim 8.00 4.00
424 Ken Aspromonte 4.00 2.00
425 Del Crandall 8.00 4.00
426 Gerry Staley 8.00 4.00
427 Charlie Neal 8.00 4.00
428 Ron Kline 4.00 2.00
Bob Friend
Vernon Law
Roy Face
429 Bobby Thomson 8.00 4.00
430 Whitey Ford 60.00 30.00
431 Whammy Douglas 4.00 2.00
432 Smoky Burgess 8.00 4.00
433 Billy Harrell 4.00 2.00
434 Hal Griggs 4.00 2.00
435 Frank Robinson 50.00 25.00
436 Granny Hamner 4.00 2.00
437 Ike Delock 4.00 2.00
438 Sammy Esposito 4.00 2.00
439 Brooks Robinson 50.00 25.00
440 Lou Burdette 8.00 4.00
(Posing as if
lefthanded)
441 John Roseboro 8.00 4.00
442 Ray Narleski 4.00 2.00
443 Daryl Spencer 4.00 2.00
444 Ron Hansen RC 8.00 4.00
445 Cal McLish 4.00 2.00
446 Rocky Nelson 4.00 2.00
447 Bob Anderson 4.00 2.00
448 Vada Pinson UER 12.00 6.00
(Born: 8/8/38
should be 8/11/38)
449 Tom Gorman 4.00 2.00
450 Eddie Mathews 40.00 20.00
451 Jimmy Constable 4.00 2.00
452 Chico Fernandez 4.00 2.00
453 Les Moss 4.00 2.00
454 Phil Clark 4.00 2.00
455 Larry Doby 12.00 6.00
456 Jerry Casale 4.00 2.00
457 Dodgers Team CL 30.00 6.00
458 Gordon Jones 4.00 2.00
459 Bill Tuttle 4.00 2.00
460 Bob Friend 8.00 4.00
461 Mickey Mantle HL 125.00 60.00
462 Rocky Colavito HL 12.00 6.00
463 Al Kaline HL 30.00 15.00
464 Willie Mays HL 40.00 20.00
54 World Series Catch
465 Roy Sievers HL 8.00 4.00
466 Billy Pierce HL 8.00 4.00
467 Hank Aaron HL 40.00 20.00
468 Duke Snider HL 20.00 10.00
469 Ernie Banks HL 20.00 10.00
470 Stan Musial HL 30.00 15.00
3,000 Hits
471 Tom Sturdivant 4.00 2.00
472 Gene Freese 4.00 2.00
473 Mike Fornieles 4.00 2.00
474 Moe Thacker 4.00 2.00
475 Jack Harshman 4.00 2.00
476 Indians Team CL 15.00 3.00
477 Barry Latman 4.00 2.00
478 Roberto Clemente 175.00 90.00
479 Lindy McDaniel 8.00 4.00
480 Red Schoendienst 12.00 6.00
481 Charlie Maxwell 8.00 4.00
482 Russ Meyer 4.00 2.00
483 Clint Courtney 4.00 2.00
484 Willie Kirkland 4.00 2.00
485 Ryne Duren 8.00 4.00
486 Sammy White 4.00 2.00
487 Hal Brown 4.00 2.00
488 Walt Moryn 4.00 2.00
489 John Powers 4.00 2.00
490 Frank Thomas 8.00 4.00
491 Don Blasingame 4.00 2.00
492 Gene Conley 8.00 4.00
493 Jim Landis 8.00 4.00
494 Don Pavletich 4.00 2.00
495 Johnny Podres 12.00 6.00
496 W.Terwilliger UER 4.00 2.00
Athlftics on front
497 Hal R. Smith 4.00 2.00
498 Dick Hyde 4.00 2.00
499 Johnny O'Brien 8.00 4.00
500 Vic Wertz 8.00 4.00
501 Bob Tiefenauer 4.00 2.00
502 Alvin Dark 8.00 4.00
503 Jim Owens 4.00 2.00
504 Ossie Alvarez 4.00 2.00
505 Tony Kubek 12.00 6.00
506 Bob Purkey 4.00 2.00
507 Bob Hale 15.00 7.50
508 Art Fowler 15.00 7.50
509 Norm Cash RC 80.00 40.00
510 Yankees Team CL 125.00 25.00
511 George Susce 15.00 7.50
512 George Altman 15.00 7.50
513 Tommy Carroll 15.00 7.50
514 Bob Gibson RC 250.00 125.00
515 Harmon Killebrew 125.00 60.00
516 Mike Garcia 20.00 10.00
517 Joe Koppe 15.00 7.50
518 Mike Cueller UER RC 30.00 15.00
Sic, Cuellar
519 Pete Runnels 20.00 10.00
Dick Gernert
Frank Malzone
520 Don Elston 15.00 7.50
521 Gary Geiger 15.00 7.50
522 Gene Snyder 15.00 7.50
523 Harry Bright 15.00 7.50
524 Larry Osborne 15.00 7.50
525 Jim Coates 20.00 10.00
526 Bob Speake 15.00 7.50
527 Solly Hemus 15.00 7.50
528 Pirates Team CL 80.00 16.00
529 G.Bamberger RC 20.00 10.00
530 Wally Moon 20.00 10.00
531 Ray Webster 15.00 7.50
532 Mark Freeman 15.00 7.50
533 Darrell Johnson 20.00 10.00
534 Faye Throneberry 15.00 7.50
535 Ruben Gomez 15.00 7.50
536 Danny Kravitz 15.00 7.50
537 Rudolph Arias 15.00 7.50
538 Chick King 15.00 7.50
539 Gary Blaylock 15.00 7.50
540 Willie Miranda 15.00 7.50
541 Bob Thurman 15.00 7.50
542 Jim Perry RC 30.00 15.00
543 Bob Skinner 125.00 60.00
Bill Virdon
Roberto Clemente
544 Lee Tate 15.00 7.50
545 Tom Morgan 15.00 7.50
546 Al Schroll 15.00 7.50
547 Jim Baxes 15.00 7.50
548 Elmer Singleton 15.00 7.50
549 Howie Nunn 15.00 7.50
550 Roy Campanella 150.00 75.00
(Symbol of Courage)
551 Fred Haney AS MG 15.00 7.50
552 Casey Stengel AS MG 30.00 15.00
553 Orlando Cepeda AS 30.00 15.00
554 Bill Skowron AS 20.00 10.00
555 Bill Mazeroski AS 30.00 15.00
556 Nellie Fox AS 40.00 20.00
557 Ken Boyer AS 30.00 15.00
558 Frank Malzone AS 15.00 7.50
559 Ernie Banks AS 60.00 30.00
560 Luis Aparicio AS 40.00 20.00
561 Hank Aaron AS 125.00 60.00
562 Al Kaline AS 60.00 30.00
563 Willie Mays AS 125.00 60.00
564 Mickey Mantle AS 300.00 150.00
565 Wes Covington AS 20.00 10.00
566 Roy Sievers AS 15.00 7.50
567 Del Crandall AS 15.00 7.50
568 Gus Triandos AS 15.00 7.50
569 Bob Friend AS 15.00 7.50
570 Bob Turley AS 15.00 7.50
571 Warren Spahn AS 50.00 25.00
572 Billy Pierce AS 40.00 13.00

1959 Topps Venezuelan

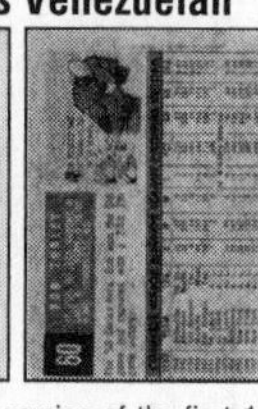

This set is a parallel version of the first 196 cards of the regular 1959 Topps set and is similar in design. The difference is found in the words "Impreso en Venezuela por Benco Co." printed on the bottom of the card back. The cards were issued for the Venezuelan market.

NM Ex
COMPLETE SET (196) 5000.00 2500.00
1 Ford Frick COMM 100.00 50.00
2 Eddie Yost 10.00 5.00
3 Don McMahon 10.00 5.00
4 Albie Pearson 10.00 5.00
5 Dick Donovan 10.00 5.00
6 Alex Grammas 10.00 5.00
7 Al Pilarcik 10.00 5.00
8 Phillies Team CL 120.00 60.00
9 Paul Giel 10.00 5.00
10 Mickey Mantle 1500.00 750.00
11 Billy Hunter 10.00 5.00
12 Vern Law 10.00 5.00
13 Dick Gernert 10.00 5.00
14 Pete Whisenant 10.00 5.00
15 Dick Drott 10.00 5.00
16 Joe Pignatano 10.00 5.00
17 Frank Thomas 15.00 7.50
Danny Murtaugh MG
Ted Kluszewski
18 Jack Urban 10.00 5.00
19 Eddie Bressoud 10.00 5.00
20 Duke Snider 150.00 75.00
21 Connie Johnson 10.00 5.00
22 Al Smith 10.00 5.00
23 Murry Dickson 10.00 5.00
24 Red Wilson 10.00 5.00
25 Don Hoak 10.00 5.00
26 Chuck Stobbs 10.00 5.00
27 Andy Pafko 10.00 5.00
28 Al Worthington 10.00 5.00
29 Jim Bolger 10.00 5.00
30 Nellie Fox 50.00 25.00
31 Ken Lehman 10.00 5.00
32 Don Buddin 10.00 5.00
33 Ed Fitzgerald 10.00 5.00
34 Al Kaline 40.00 20.00
Charley Maxwell
35 Ted Kluszewski 50.00 25.00
36 Hank Aguirre 10.00 5.00
37 Gene Green 10.00 5.00
38 Morrie Martin 10.00 5.00
39 Ed Bouchee 10.00 5.00
40 Warren Spahn 120.00 60.00
41 Bob Martyn 10.00 5.00
42 Murray Wall 10.00 5.00
43 Steve Bilko 10.00 5.00
44 Vito Valentinetti 10.00 5.00
45 Andy Carey 10.00 5.00
46 Bill R. Henry 10.00 5.00
47 Jim Finigan 10.00 5.00
48 Orioles Team CL 50.00 25.00
49 Bill Hall 10.00 5.00
50 Willie Mays 300.00 150.00
51 Rip Coleman 10.00 5.00
52 Coot Veal 10.00 5.00
53 Stan Williams 10.00 5.00
54 Mel Roach 10.00 5.00
55 Tom Brewer 10.00 5.00
56 Carl Sawatski 10.00 5.00
57 Al Cicotte 10.00 5.00
58 Eddie Miksis 10.00 5.00
59 Irv Noren 10.00 5.00
60 Bob Turley 15.00 7.50
61 Dick Brown 10.00 5.00
62 Tony Taylor 10.00 5.00
63 Jim Hearn 10.00 5.00
64 Joe DeMaestri 10.00 5.00
65 Frank Torre 10.00 5.00
66 Joe Ginsberg 10.00 5.00
67 Brooks Lawrence 10.00 5.00
68 Dick Schofield 10.00 5.00
69 Giants Team CL 50.00 25.00
70 Harvey Kuenn 15.00 7.50
71 Don Bessent 10.00 5.00
72 Bill Renna 10.00 5.00
73 Ron Jackson 10.00 5.00
74 Jim Lemon 10.00 5.00
Cookie Lavagetto MG
Roy Sievers
75 Sam Jones 10.00 5.00
76 Bobby Richardson 60.00 30.00
77 John Goryl 10.00 5.00
78 Pedro Ramos 10.00 5.00
79 Harry Chiti 10.00 5.00
80 Minnie Minoso 25.00 12.50
81 Hal Jeffcoat 10.00 5.00
82 Bob Boyd 10.00 5.00
83 Bob Smith 10.00 5.00
84 Reno Bertoia 10.00 5.00
85 Harry Anderson 10.00 5.00
86 Bob Keegan 10.00 5.00
87 Danny O'Connell 10.00 5.00
88 Herb Score 25.00 12.50
89 Billy Gardner 10.00 5.00
90 Bill Skowron 40.00 20.00
91 Herb Moford 10.00 5.00
92 Dave Philley 10.00 5.00
93 Julio Becquer 10.00 5.00
94 White Sox Team CL 80.00 40.00
95 Carl Willey 10.00 5.00
96 Lou Berberet 10.00 5.00
97 Jerry Lynch 10.00 5.00
98 Arnie Portocarrero 10.00 5.00
99 Ted Kazanski 10.00 5.00
100 Bob Cerv 10.00 5.00
101 Alex Kellner 10.00 5.00
102 Felipe Alou 80.00 40.00
103 Billy Goodman 10.00 5.00
104 Del Rice 10.00 5.00
105 Lee Walls 10.00 5.00
106 Hal Woodeshick 10.00 5.00
107 Norm Larker 10.00 5.00
108 Zack Monroe 10.00 5.00
109 Bob Schmidt 10.00 5.00
110 George Witt 10.00 5.00
111 Redlegs Team CL 25.00 12.50
112 Billy Consolo 10.00 5.00
113 Taylor Phillips 10.00 5.00
114 Earl Battey 10.00 5.00
115 Mickey Vernon 15.00 7.50
116 Bob Allison RP 20.00 10.00
117 John Blanchard RP 10.00 5.00
118 John Buzhardt RP 10.00 5.00
119 John Callison RP 25.00 12.50
120 Chuck Coles RP 10.00 5.00
121 Bob Conley RP 10.00 5.00
122 Bennie Daniels RP 10.00 5.00
123 Don Dillard RP 10.00 5.00
124 Dan Dobbek RP 10.00 5.00
125 Ron Fairly RP 20.00 10.00
126 Eddie Haas RP 10.00 5.00
127 Kent Hadley RP 10.00 5.00
128 Bob Hartman RP 10.00 5.00
129 Frank Herrera RP 10.00 5.00
130 Lou Jackson RP 10.00 5.00
131 Deron Johnson RP 10.00 5.00
132 Don Lee RP 10.00 5.00
133 Bob Lillis RP 10.00 5.00
134 Jim McDaniel RP 10.00 5.00
135 Gene Oliver RP 10.00 5.00
136 Jim O'Toole RP 10.00 5.00
137 Dick Ricketts RP 10.00 5.00
138 John Romano RP 10.00 5.00
139 Ed Sadowski RP 10.00 5.00
140 Charlie Secrest RP 10.00 5.00
141 Joe Shipley RP 10.00 5.00
142 Dick Stigman RP 10.00 5.00
143 Willie Tasby RP 10.00 5.00
144 Jerry Walker RP 10.00 5.00
145 Dom Zanni RP 10.00 5.00
146 Jerry Zimmerman RP 10.00 5.00
147 Dale Long 60.00 30.00
Ernie Banks
Walt Moryn
148 Mike McCormick 15.00 7.50
149 Jim Bunning 50.00 25.00
150 Stan Musial 300.00 150.00
151 Bob Malkmus 10.00 5.00
152 Johnny Klippstein 10.00 5.00
153 Jim Marshall 10.00 5.00
154 Ray Herbert 10.00 5.00
155 Enos Slaughter 50.00 25.00
156 Billy Pierce 25.00 12.50
Robin Roberts
157 Felix Mantilla 10.00 5.00
158 Walt Dropo 10.00 5.00
159 Bob Shaw 10.00 5.00
160 Dick Groat 15.00 7.50
161 Frank Baumann 10.00 5.00
162 Bobby G. Smith 10.00 5.00
163 Sandy Koufax 400.00 200.00
164 Johnny Groth 10.00 5.00
165 Bill Bruton 10.00 5.00
166 Minnie Minoso 50.00 25.00
Rocky Colavito
Misspelled Colovito on card back
Larry Doby
167 Duke Maas 10.00 5.00
168 Carroll Hardy 10.00 5.00
169 Ted Abernathy 10.00 5.00
170 Gene Woodling 10.00 5.00
171 Willard Schmidt 10.00 5.00
172 Athletics Team CL 25.00 12.50
173 Bill Monbouquette 10.00 5.00
174 Jim Pendleton 10.00 5.00
175 Dick Farrell 10.00 5.00
176 Preston Ward 10.00 5.00
177 John Briggs 10.00 5.00
178 Ruben Amaro 10.00 5.00
179 Don Rudolph 10.00 5.00
180 Yogi Berra 200.00 100.00
181 Bob Porterfield 10.00 5.00
182 Milt Graff 10.00 5.00
183 Stu Miller 10.00 5.00
184 Harvey Haddix 10.00 5.00
185 Jim Busby 10.00 5.00
186 Mudcat Grant 10.00 5.00
187 Bubba Phillips 10.00 5.00
188 Juan Pizarro 10.00 5.00
189 Neil Chrisley 10.00 5.00
190 Bill Virdon 10.00 5.00
191 Russ Kemmerer 10.00 5.00
192 Charlie Beamon 10.00 5.00
193 Sammy Taylor 10.00 5.00
194 Jim Brosnan 10.00 5.00
195 Rip Reuplski 10.00 5.00
196 Billy Moran 10.00 5.00

1960 Topps

The cards in this 572-card set measure 2 1/2" by 3 1/2". The 1960 Topps set is the only Topps standard size issue to use a horizontally oriented front. World Series cards appeared for the first time (385 to 391), and there is a Rookie Prospect (RP) series (117-148), the most famous of which is Carl Yastrzemski, and a Sport Magazine All-Star Selection (AS) series (553-572). There are 16 manager cards listed alphabetically from 212 through 227. The 1959 Topps All-Rookie team is featured on cards 316-325. The coaching staff of each team was also afforded their own card in a 16-card subset (455-470). There is no price differential for either color back. The high series (507-572) were printed on a more limited basis than the rest of the set. The team cards have series checklists on the reverse. Cards were issued in one-card penny packs and six-card nickel packs. Three card ad-sheets have been seen. One such sheet features Wayne Terwilliger, Kent Hadley and Faye Throneberry on the front with Gene Woodling and an Ad on the back. Another sheet featured Hank Foiles/Hobie Landrith and Hal Smith on the front. The key Rookie Cards in this set are Jim Kaat, Willie McCovey and Carl Yastrzemski. Recently, a Kent Hadley was discovered with a Kansas City A's logo on the front, while this card was rumoured to exist for years, this is the first known spotting of the card. Each series of this set had different card backs. Cards numbered 1-110 had cream colored white back, cards numbered 111-198 had grey backs, cards numbered 119-286 had cream colored white backs, cards numbered 287-374 had grey backs. Cards 375 to 440 come with either gray, white or cream-colored white backs. It is believed that the pure white backs are the most difficult of the three colors in this card range. Cards numbered 441-572 conclude this set and they all have grey backs.

NM Ex
COMPLETE SET (572) 5000.00 2000.00
COMMON CARD (1-440) 4.00 1.60
COMMON (441-506) 8.00 3.20
COMMON (507-572) 15.00 6.00
WRAPPER (1-CENT) 900.00 350.00
WRAP. (1-CENT REPEAT) 500.00 200.00
WRAPPER (5-CENT) 40.00 16.00
1 Early Wynn 40.00 10.00
2 Roman Mejias 4.00 1.60
3 Joe Adcock 6.00 2.40
4 Bob Purkey 4.00 1.60
5 Wally Moon 6.00 2.40
6 Lou Berberet 4.00 1.60
7 Willie Mays 25.00 10.00
Bill Rigney MG
8 Bud Daley 4.00 1.60
9 Faye Throneberry 4.00 1.60
10 Ernie Banks 50.00 20.00
11 Norm Siebern 4.00 1.60
12 Milt Pappas 6.00 2.40
13 Wally Post 6.00 2.40
14 Jim Grant 6.00 2.40
15 Pete Runnels 6.00 2.40
16 Ernie Broglio 6.00 2.40
17 Johnny Callison 6.00 2.40
18 Dodgers Team CL 50.00 10.00
19 Felix Mantilla 4.00 1.60
20 Roy Face 6.00 2.40
21 Dutch Dotterer 4.00 1.60
22 Rocky Bridges 4.00 1.60
23 Eddie Fisher 4.00 1.60
24 Dick Gray 4.00 1.60
25 Roy Sievers 6.00 2.40
26 Wayne Terwilliger 4.00 1.60
27 Dick Drott 4.00 1.60
28 Brooks Robinson 50.00 20.00
29 Clem Labine 6.00 2.40
30 Tito Francona 4.00 1.60
31 Sammy Esposito 4.00 1.60
32 Jim O'Toole 4.00 1.60
Vada Pinson
33 Tom Morgan 4.00 1.60
34 Sparky Anderson 15.00 6.00
35 Whitey Ford 50.00 20.00
36 Russ Nixon 4.00 1.60
37 Bill Bruton 4.00 1.60
38 Jerry Casale 4.00 1.60
39 Earl Averill 4.00 1.60
40 Joe Cunningham 4.00 1.60
41 Barry Latman 4.00 1.60
42 Hobie Landrith 4.00 1.60
43 Senators Team CL 10.00 2.00
44 Bobby Locke 4.00 1.60
45 Roy McMillan 6.00 2.40
46 Jerry Fisher 4.00 1.60
47 Don Zimmer 6.00 2.40
48 Hal W. Smith 4.00 1.60
49 Curt Raydon 4.00 1.60
50 Al Kaline 50.00 20.00
51 Jim Coates 6.00 2.40
52 Dave Philley 4.00 1.60
53 Jackie Brandt 4.00 1.60
54 Mike Fornieles 4.00 1.60
55 Bill Mazeroski 15.00 6.00
56 Steve Korcheck 4.00 1.60
57 Turk Lown 4.00 1.60
Gerry Staley
58 Gino Cimoli 4.00 1.60
58A Gino Cimoli
Cardinals Team Logo
59 Juan Pizarro 4.00 1.60
60 Gus Triandos 6.00 2.40
61 Eddie Kasko 4.00 1.60
62 Roger Craig 6.00 2.40
63 George Strickland 4.00 1.60
64 Jack Meyer 4.00 1.60
65 Elston Howard 6.00 2.40
66 Bob Trowbridge 4.00 1.60
67 Jose Pagan 4.00 1.60
68 Dave Hillman 4.00 1.60
69 Billy Goodman 6.00 2.40
70 Lew Burdette 6.00 2.40
Card spelled as Lou on front and back
71 Marty Keough 4.00 1.60
72 Tigers Team CL 25.00 5.00
73 Bob Gibson 50.00 20.00
74 Walt Moryn 4.00 1.60
75 Vic Power 6.00 2.40
76 Bill Fischer 4.00 1.60
77 Hank Foiles 4.00 1.60
78 Bob Grim 4.00 1.60
79 Walt Dropo 4.00 1.60
80 Johnny Antonelli 6.00 2.40
81 Russ Snyder 4.00 1.60
82 Ruben Gomez 4.00 1.60
83 Tony Kubek 15.00 6.00
84 Hal R. Smith 4.00 1.60
85 Frank Lary 6.00 2.40
86 Dick Gernert 4.00 1.60
87 John Romonosky 4.00 1.60
88 John Roseboro 6.00 2.40
89 Hal Brown 4.00 1.60
90 Bobby Avila 4.00 1.60

91 Bennie Daniels........ 4.00 1.60
92 Whitey Herzog........ 6.00 2.40
93 Art Schult........ 4.00 1.60
94 Leo Kiely........ 4.00 1.60
95 Frank Thomas........ 6.00 2.40
96 Ralph Terry........ 6.00 2.40
97 Ted Lepcio........ 4.00 1.60
98 Gordon Jones........ 4.00 1.60
99 Lenny Green........ 4.00 1.60
100 Nellie Fox........ 20.00 8.00
101 Bob Miller........ 4.00 1.60
102 Kent Hadley........ 4.00 1.60
102A Kent Hadley........
Athletics Team Logo
103 Dick Farrell........ 6.00 2.40
104 Dick Schofield........ 6.00 2.40
105 Larry Sherry RC........ 6.00 2.40
106 Billy Gardner........ 4.00 1.60
107 Carlton Willey........ 4.00 1.60
108 Pete Daley........ 4.00 1.60
109 Clete Boyer........ 15.00 6.00
110 Cal McLish........ 4.00 1.60
111 Vic Wertz........ 6.00 2.40
112 Jack Harshman........ 4.00 1.60
113 Bob Skinner........ 4.00 1.60
114 Ken Aspromonte........ 4.00 1.60
115 Roy Face........ 6.00 2.40
Hoyt Wilhelm
116 Jim Rivera........ 4.00 1.60
117 Tom Borland RP........ 4.00 1.60
118 Bob Bruce RP........ 4.00 1.60
119 Chico Cardenas RP........ 6.00 2.40
120 Duke Carmel RP........ 4.00 1.60
121 Camilo Carreon RP........ 4.00 1.60
122 Don Dillard RP........ 4.00 1.60
123 Dan Dobbek RP........ 4.00 1.60
124 Jim Donohue RP........ 4.00 1.60
125 Dick Ellsworth RP RC........ 6.00 2.40
126 Chuck Estrada RP RC........ 4.00 1.60
127 Ron Hansen RP........ 6.00 2.40
128 Bill Harris RP........ 4.00 1.60
129 Bob Hartman RP........ 4.00 1.60
130 Frank Herrera RP........ 4.00 1.60
131 Ed Hobaugh RP........ 4.00 1.60
132 Frank Howard RP RC........ 25.00 10.00
133 Manuel Javier RC RP........ 6.00 2.40
(Sic, Julian)
134 Deron Johnson RP........ 6.00 2.40
135 Ken Johnson RP........ 4.00 1.60
136 Jim Kaat RP RC........ 40.00 16.00
137 Lou Klimchock RP........ 4.00 1.60
138 Art Mahaffey RP RC........ 6.00 2.40
139 Carl Mathias RP........ 4.00 1.60
140 Julio Navarro RP RC........ 4.00 1.60
141 Jim Proctor RP........ 4.00 1.60
142 Bill Short RP........ 4.00 1.60
143 Al Spangler RP........ 4.00 1.60
144 Al Stieglitz RP........ 4.00 1.60
145 Jim Umbricht RP........ 4.00 1.60
146 Ted Wieand RP........ 4.00 1.60
147 Bob Will RP........ 4.00 1.60
148 C.Yastrzemski RP RC........ 175.00 70.00
149 Bob Nieman........ 4.00 1.60
150 Billy Pierce........ 6.00 2.40
151 Giants Team CL........ 10.00 2.00
152 Gail Harris........ 4.00 1.60
153 Bobby Thomson........ 6.00 2.40
154 Jim Davenport........ 6.00 2.40
155 Charlie Neal........ 6.00 2.40
156 Art Ceccarelli........ 4.00 1.60
157 Rocky Nelson........ 6.00 2.40
158 Wes Covington........ 6.00 2.40
159 Jim Piersall........ 6.00 2.40
160 Mickey Mantle........ 125.00 50.00
Ken Boyer
161 Ray Narleski........ 4.00 1.60
162 Sammy Taylor........ 4.00 1.60
163 Hector Lopez........ 6.00 2.40
164 Reds Team CL........ 10.00 2.00
165 Jack Sanford........ 6.00 2.40
166 Chuck Essegian........ 4.00 1.60
167 Valmy Thomas........ 4.00 1.60
168 Alex Grammas........ 4.00 1.60
169 Jake Striker........ 4.00 1.60
170 Del Crandall........ 6.00 2.40
171 Johnny Groth........ 4.00 1.60
172 Willie Kirkland........ 4.00 1.60
173 Billy Martin........ 20.00 8.00
174 Indians Team CL........ 10.00 2.00
175 Pedro Ramos........ 4.00 1.60
176 Vada Pinson........ 6.00 2.40
177 Johnny Kucks........ 4.00 1.60
178 Woody Held........ 4.00 1.60
179 Rip Coleman........ 4.00 1.60
180 Harry Simpson........ 4.00 1.60
181 Billy Loes........ 6.00 2.40
182 Glen Hobbie........ 4.00 1.60
183 Eli Grba........ 4.00 1.60
184 Gary Geiger........ 4.00 1.60
185 Jim Owens........ 4.00 1.60
186 Dave Sisler........ 4.00 1.60
187 Jay Hook........ 4.00 1.60
188 Dick Williams........ 6.00 2.40
189 Don McMahon........ 4.00 1.60
190 Gene Woodling........ 6.00 2.40
191 Johnny Klippstein........ 4.00 1.60
192 Danny O'Connell........ 4.00 1.60
193 Dick Hyde........ 4.00 1.60
194 Bobby Gene Smith........ 4.00 1.60
195 Lindy McDaniel........ 6.00 2.40
196 Andy Carey........ 6.00 2.40
197 Ron Kline........ 4.00 1.60
198 Jerry Lynch........ 6.00 2.40
199 Dick Donovan........ 6.00 2.40
200 Willie Mays........ 125.00 50.00
201 Larry Osborne........ 4.00 1.60
202 Fred Kipp........ 4.00 1.60
203 Sammy White........ 4.00 1.60
204 Ryne Duren........ 6.00 2.40
205 Johnny Logan........ 6.00 2.40
206 Claude Osteen........ 6.00 2.40
207 Bob Boyd........ 4.00 1.60
208 White Sox Team CL........ 10.00 2.00
209 Ron Blackburn........ 4.00 1.60
210 Harmon Killebrew........ 40.00 16.00
211 Taylor Phillips........ 4.00 1.60
212 Walter Alston MG........ 10.00 4.00
213 Chuck Dressen MG........ 6.00 2.40
214 Jimmy Dykes MG........ 6.00 2.40
215 Bob Elliott MG........ 6.00 2.40
216 Joe Gordon MG........ 6.00 2.40
217 Charlie Grimm MG........ 6.00 2.40
218 Solly Hemus MG........ 4.00 1.60
219 Fred Hutchinson MG........ 6.00 2.40
220 Billy Jurges MG........ 4.00 1.60
221 Cookie Lavagetto MG........ 4.00 1.60
222 Al Lopez MG........ 10.00 4.00
223 Danny Murtaugh MG........ 6.00 2.40
224 Paul Richards MG........ 6.00 2.40
225 Bill Rigney MG........ 4.00 1.60
226 Eddie Sawyer MG........ 4.00 1.60
227 Casey Stengel MG........ 15.00 6.00
228 Ernie Johnson........ 6.00 2.40
229 Joe M. Morgan........ 4.00 1.60
230 Lou Burdette........ 10.00 4.00
Warren Spahn
Bob Buhl
231 Hal Naragon........ 4.00 1.60
232 Jim Busby........ 4.00 1.60
233 Don Elston........ 4.00 1.60
234 Don Demeter........ 4.00 1.60
235 Gus Bell........ 6.00 2.40
236 Dick Ricketts........ 4.00 1.60
237 Elmer Valo........ 4.00 1.60
238 Danny Kravitz........ 4.00 1.60
239 Joe Shipley........ 4.00 1.60
240 Luis Aparicio........ 15.00 6.00
241 Albie Pearson........ 6.00 2.40
242 Cardinals Team CL........ 10.00 2.00
243 Bubba Phillips........ 4.00 1.60
244 Hal Griggs........ 4.00 1.60
245 Eddie Yost........ 6.00 2.40
246 Lee Maye........ 6.00 2.40
247 Gil McDougald........ 10.00 4.00
248 Del Rice........ 4.00 1.60
249 Earl Wilson RC........ 6.00 2.40
250 Stan Musial........ 100.00 40.00
251 Bob Malkmus........ 4.00 1.60
252 Ray Herbert........ 4.00 1.60
253 Eddie Bressoud........ 4.00 1.60
254 Arnie Portocarrero........ 4.00 1.60
255 Jim Gilliam........ 6.00 2.40
256 Dick Brown........ 4.00 1.60
257 Gordy Coleman RC........ 4.00 1.60
258 Dick Groat........ 6.00 2.40
259 George Altman........ 4.00 1.60
260 Rocky Colavito........ 15.00 6.00
Tito Francona
261 Pete Burnside........ 4.00 1.60
262 Hank Bauer........ 6.00 2.40
263 Darrell Johnson........ 4.00 1.60
264 Robin Roberts........ 15.00 6.00
265 Rip Repulski........ 4.00 1.60
266 Joey Jay........ 6.00 2.40
267 Jim Marshall........ 4.00 1.60
268 Al Worthington........ 4.00 1.60
269 Gene Green........ 4.00 1.60
270 Bob Turley........ 6.00 2.40
271 Julio Becquer........ 4.00 1.60
272 Fred Green........ 6.00 2.40
273 Neil Chrisley........ 4.00 1.60
274 Tom Acker........ 4.00 1.60
275 Curt Flood........ 6.00 2.40
276 Ken McBride........ 4.00 1.60
277 Harry Bright........ 4.00 1.60
278 Stan Williams........ 6.00 2.40
279 Chuck Tanner........ 6.00 2.40
280 Frank Sullivan........ 4.00 1.60
281 Ray Boone........ 6.00 2.40
282 Joe Nuxhall........ 6.00 2.40
283 John Blanchard........ 6.00 2.40
284 Don Gross........ 4.00 1.60
285 Harry Anderson........ 4.00 1.60
286 Ray Semproch........ 4.00 1.60
287 Felipe Alou........ 6.00 2.40
288 Bob Mabe........ 4.00 1.60
289 Willie Jones........ 4.00 1.60
290 Jerry Lumpe........ 4.00 1.60
291 Bob Keegan........ 4.00 1.60
292 Joe Pignatano........ 6.00 2.40
John Roseboro
293 Gene Conley........ 6.00 2.40
294 Tony Taylor........ 6.00 2.40
295 Gil Hodges........ 25.00 10.00
296 Nelson Chittum........ 4.00 1.60
297 Reno Bertoia........ 4.00 1.60
298 George Witt........ 4.00 1.60
299 Earl Torgeson........ 4.00 1.60
300 Hank Aaron........ 125.00 50.00
301 Jerry Davie........ 4.00 1.60
302 Phillies Team CL........ 10.00 2.00
303 Billy O'Dell........ 4.00 1.60
304 Joe Ginsberg........ 4.00 1.60
305 Richie Ashburn........ 20.00 8.00
306 Frank Baumann........ 4.00 1.60
307 Gene Oliver........ 4.00 1.60
308 Dick Hall........ 4.00 1.60
309 Bob Hale........ 4.00 1.60
310 Frank Malzone........ 6.00 2.40
311 Raul Sanchez........ 4.00 1.60
312 Charley Lau........ 6.00 2.40
313 Turk Lown........ 4.00 1.60
314 Chico Fernandez........ 4.00 1.60
315 Bobby Shantz........ 10.00 4.00
316 Willie McCovey RC........ 125.00 50.00
317 Pumpsie Green........ 6.00 2.40
318 Jim Baxes........ 6.00 2.40
319 Joe Koppe........ 6.00 2.40
320 Bob Allison........ 6.00 2.40
321 Ron Fairly........ 6.00 2.40
322 Willie Tasby........ 6.00 2.40
323 John Romano........ 6.00 2.40
324 Jim Perry........ 6.00 2.40
325 Jim O'Toole........ 6.00 2.40
326 Roberto Clemente........ 175.00 70.00
327 Ray Sadecki RC........ 4.00 1.60
328 Earl Battey........ 4.00 1.60
329 Zack Monroe........ 4.00 1.60
330 Harvey Kuenn........ 6.00 2.40
331 Henry Mason........ 4.00 1.60
332 Yankees Team CL........ 80.00 16.00
333 Danny McDevitt........ 4.00 1.60
334 Ted Abernathy........ 4.00 1.60
335 Red Schoendienst........ 15.00 6.00
336 Ike Delock........ 4.00 1.60
337 Cal Neeman........ 4.00 1.60
338 Ray Monzant........ 4.00 1.60
339 Harry Chiti........ 4.00 1.60
340 Harvey Haddix........ 6.00 2.40
341 Carroll Hardy........ 4.00 1.60
342 Casey Wise........ 4.00 1.60
343 Sandy Koufax........ 125.00 50.00
344 Clint Courtney........ 4.00 1.60
345 Don Newcombe........ 6.00 2.40
346 J.C. Martin UER........ 6.00 2.40
(Face actually
Gary Peters)
347 Ed Bouchee........ 4.00 1.60
348 Barry Shetrone........ 4.00 1.60
349 Moe Drabowsky........ 6.00 2.40
350 Mickey Mantle........ 500.00 200.00
351 Don Nottebart........ 4.00 1.60
352 Gus Bell........ 10.00 4.00
Frank Robinson
Jerry Lynch
353 Don Larsen........ 6.00 2.40
354 Bob Lillis........ 4.00 1.60
355 Bill White........ 6.00 2.40
356 Joe Amalfitano........ 4.00 1.60
357 Al Schroll........ 4.00 1.60
358 Joe DeMaestri........ 4.00 1.60
359 Buddy Gilbert........ 4.00 1.60
360 Herb Score........ 6.00 2.40
361 Bob Oldis........ 6.00 2.40
362 Russ Kemmerer........ 4.00 1.60
363 Gene Stephens........ 4.00 1.60
364 Paul Foytack........ 4.00 1.60
365 Minnie Minoso........ 10.00 4.00
366 Dallas Green RC........ 10.00 4.00
367 Bill Tuttle........ 4.00 1.60
368 Daryl Spencer........ 4.00 1.60
369 Billy Hoeft........ 4.00 1.60
370 Bill Skowron........ 10.00 4.00
371 Bud Byerly........ 4.00 1.60
372 Frank House........ 4.00 1.60
373 Don Hoak........ 6.00 2.40
374 Bob Buhl........ 6.00 2.40
375 Dale Long........ 10.00 4.00
376 John Briggs........ 4.00 1.60
377 Roger Maris........ 100.00 40.00
378 Stu Miller........ 6.00 2.40
379 Red Wilson........ 4.00 1.60
380 Bob Shaw........ 4.00 1.60
381 Braves Team CL........ 10.00 2.00
382 Ted Bowsfield........ 4.00 1.60
383 Leon Wagner........ 4.00 1.60
384 Don Cardwell........ 4.00 1.60
385 Charlie Neal WS........ 8.00 3.20
386 Charlie Neal WS........ 8.00 3.20
387 Carl Furillo WS........ 8.00 3.20
388 Gil Hodges WS........ 10.00 4.00
389 Luis Aparicio WS........ 12.00 4.80
Maury Wills
390 World Series Game 6........ 8.00 3.20
391 WS Summary........ 8.00 3.20
The Champs Celebrate
392 Tex Clevenger........ 4.00 1.60
393 Smoky Burgess........ 6.00 2.40
394 Norm Larker........ 6.00 2.40
395 Hoyt Wilhelm........ 15.00 6.00
396 Steve Bilko........ 4.00 1.60
397 Don Blasingame........ 4.00 1.60
398 Mike Cuellar........ 6.00 2.40
399 Milt Pappas........ 6.00 2.40
Jack Fisher
Jerry Walker
400 Rocky Colavito........ 20.00 8.00
401 Bob Duliba........ 4.00 1.60
402 Dick Stuart........ 15.00 6.00
403 Ed Sadowski........ 4.00 1.60
404 Bob Rush........ 4.00 1.60
405 Bobby Richardson........ 15.00 6.00
406 Billy Klaus........ 4.00 1.60
407 Gary Peters RC UER........ 6.00 2.40
(Face actually
J.C. Martin)
408 Carl Furillo........ 10.00 4.00
409 Ron Samford........ 4.00 1.60
410 Sam Jones........ 6.00 2.40
411 Ed Bailey........ 4.00 1.60
412 Bob Anderson........ 4.00 1.60
413 Athletics Team CL........ 10.00 2.00
414 Don Williams........ 4.00 1.60
415 Bob Cerv........ 4.00 1.60
416 Humberto Robinson........ 4.00 1.60
417 Chuck Cottier RC........ 4.00 1.60
418 Don Mossi........ 6.00 2.40
419 George Crowe........ 4.00 1.60
420 Eddie Mathews........ 40.00 16.00
421 Duke Maas........ 4.00 1.60
422 John Powers........ 4.00 1.60
423 Ed Fitzgerald........ 4.00 1.60
424 Pete Whisenant........ 4.00 1.60
425 Johnny Podres........ 6.00 2.40
426 Ron Jackson........ 4.00 1.60
427 Al Grunwald........ 4.00 1.60
428 Al Smith........ 4.00 1.60
429 Nellie Fox........ 10.00 4.00
Harvey Kuenn
430 Art Ditmar........ 4.00 1.60
431 Andre Rodgers........ 4.00 1.60
432 Chuck Stobbs........ 4.00 1.60
433 Irv Noren........ 4.00 1.60
434 Brooks Lawrence........ 6.00 2.40
435 Gene Freese........ 4.00 1.60
436 Marv Throneberry........ 6.00 2.40
437 Bob Friend........ 6.00 2.40
438 Jim Coker........ 4.00 1.60
439 Tom Brewer........ 4.00 1.60
440 Jim Lemon........ 6.00 2.40
441 Gary Bell........ 10.00 4.00
442 Joe Pignatano........ 8.00 3.20
443 Charlie Maxwell........ 8.00 3.20
444 Jerry Kindall........ 8.00 3.20
445 Warren Spahn........ 50.00 20.00
446 Ellis Burton........ 8.00 3.20
447 Ray Moore........ 8.00 3.20
448 Jim Gentile RC........ 15.00 6.00
449 Jim Brosnan........ 8.00 3.20
450 Orlando Cepeda........ 25.00 10.00
451 Curt Simmons........ 8.00 3.20
452 Ray Webster........ 8.00 3.20
453 Vern Law........ 25.00 10.00
454 Hal Woodeshick........ 8.00 3.20
455 Eddie Robinson CO........ 8.00 3.20
Harry Brecheen CO
Luman Harris CO
456 Rudy York CO........ 10.00 4.00
Billy Herman CO
Sal Maglie CO
Del Baker CO
457 Charlie Root CO........ 8.00 3.20
Lou Klein CO
Elvin Tappe CO
458 Johnny Cooney CO........ 8.00 3.20
Don Gutteridge CO
Tony Cuccinello CO
Ray Berres CO
459 Reggie Otero CO........ 8.00 3.20
Cot Deal CO
Wally Moses CO
460 Mel Harder CO........ 15.00 6.00
Jo-Jo White CO
Bob Lemon CO
Ralph(Red) Kress CO
461 Tom Ferrick CO........ 10.00 4.00
Luke Appling CO
Billy Hitchcock CO
462 Fred Fitzsimmons CO........ 8.00 3.20
Don Heffner CO
Walker Cooper CO
463 Bobby Bragan CO........ 8.00 3.20
Pete Reiser CO
Joe Becker CO
Greg Mulleavy CO
464 Bob Scheffing CO........ 8.00 3.20
Whitlow Wyatt CO
Andy Pafko CO
George Myatt CO
465 Bill Dickey CO........ 25.00 10.00
Ralph Houk CO
Frank Crosetti CO
Ed Lopat CO
466 Ken Silvestri CO........ 8.00 3.20
Dick Carter CO
Andy Cohen CO
467 Mickey Vernon CO........ 8.00 3.20
Frank Oceak CO
Sam Narron CO
Bill Burwell CO
468 Johnny Keane CO........ 8.00 3.20
Howie Pollet CO
Ray Katt CO
Harry Walker CO
469 Wes Westrum CO........ 8.00 3.20
Salty Parker CO
Bill Posedel CO
470 Bob Swift CO........ 8.00 3.20
Ellis Clary CO
Sam Mele CO
471 Ned Garver........ 8.00 3.20
472 Alvin Dark........ 8.00 3.20
473 Al Cicotte........ 8.00 3.20
474 Haywood Sullivan........ 8.00 3.20
475 Don Drysdale........ 40.00 16.00
476 Lou Johnson........ 8.00 3.20
477 Don Ferrarese........ 8.00 3.20
478 Frank Torre........ 8.00 3.20
479 Georges Maranda........ 8.00 3.20
480 Yogi Berra........ 80.00 32.00
481 Wes Stock........ 8.00 3.20
482 Frank Bolling........ 8.00 3.20
483 Camilo Pascual........ 8.00 3.20
484 Pirates Team CL........ 40.00 8.00
485 Ken Boyer........ 15.00 6.00
486 Bobby Del Greco........ 8.00 3.20
487 Tom Sturdivant........ 8.00 3.20
488 Norm Cash........ 25.00 10.00
Shown with Indians Cap but listed as a Tiger
489 Steve Ridzik........ 8.00 3.20
490 Frank Robinson........ 50.00 20.00
491 Mel Roach........ 8.00 3.20
492 Larry Jackson........ 8.00 3.20
493 Duke Snider........ 50.00 20.00
494 Orioles Team CL........ 25.00 5.00
495 Sherm Lollar........ 8.00 3.20
496 Bill Virdon........ 10.00 4.00
497 John Tsitouris........ 8.00 3.20
498 Al Pilarcik........ 8.00 3.20
499 Johnny James........ 10.00 4.00
500 Johnny Temple........ 8.00 3.20
501 Bob Schmidt........ 8.00 3.20
502 Jim Bunning........ 25.00 10.00
503 Don Lee........ 8.00 3.20
504 Seth Morehead........ 8.00 3.20
505 Ted Kluszewski........ 25.00 10.00
506 Lee Walls........ 8.00 3.20
507 Dick Stigman........ 15.00 6.00
508 Billy Consolo........ 15.00 6.00
509 Tommy Davis RC........ 25.00 10.00
510 Gerry Staley........ 15.00 6.00
511 Ken Walters........ 15.00 6.00
512 Joe Gibbon........ 15.00 6.00
513 Chicago Cubs........ 30.00 6.00
Team Card CL
514 Steve Barber RC........ 15.00 6.00
515 Stan Lopata........ 15.00 6.00
516 Marty Kutyna........ 15.00 6.00
517 Charlie James........ 25.00 10.00
518 Tony Gonzalez........ 15.00 6.00
519 Ed Roebuck........ 15.00 6.00
520 Don Buddin........ 15.00 6.00
521 Mike Lee........ 15.00 6.00
522 Ken Hunt........ 30.00 12.00
523 Clay Dalrymple........ 15.00 6.00
524 Bill Henry........ 15.00 6.00
525 Marv Breeding........ 15.00 6.00
526 Paul Giel........ 25.00 10.00
527 Jose Valdivielso........ 25.00 10.00
528 Ben Johnson........ 15.00 6.00
529 Norm Sherry RC........ 20.00 8.00
530 Mike McCormick........ 15.00 6.00
531 Sandy Amoros........ 20.00 8.00
532 Mike Garcia........ 20.00 8.00
533 Lu Clinton........ 15.00 6.00
534 Ken MacKenzie........ 15.00 6.00
535 Whitey Lockman........ 15.00 6.00
536 Wynn Hawkins........ 15.00 6.00
537 Boston Red Sox........ 30.00 6.00
Team Card CL
538 Frank Barnes........ 15.00 6.00
539 Gene Baker........ 15.00 6.00
540 Jerry Walker........ 15.00 6.00
541 Tony Curry........ 15.00 6.00
542 Ken Hamlin........ 15.00 6.00
543 Elio Chacon........ 15.00 6.00
544 Bill Monbouquette........ 20.00 8.00
545 Carl Sawatski........ 15.00 6.00
546 Hank Aguirre........ 15.00 6.00
547 Bob Aspromonte........ 20.00 8.00
548 Don Mincher........ 20.00 8.00
549 John Buzhardt........ 15.00 6.00
550 Jim Landis........ 15.00 6.00
551 Ed Rakow........ 15.00 6.00
552 Walt Bond........ 15.00 6.00
553 Bill Skowron AS........ 20.00 8.00
554 Willie McCovey AS........ 40.00 16.00
555 Nellie Fox AS........ 30.00 12.00
556 Charlie Neal AS........ 15.00 6.00
557 Frank Malzone AS........ 15.00 6.00
558 Eddie Mathews AS........ 40.00 16.00
559 Luis Aparicio AS........ 30.00 12.00
560 Ernie Banks AS........ 60.00 24.00
561 Al Kaline AS........ 60.00 24.00
562 Joe Cunningham AS........ 15.00 6.00
563 Mickey Mantle AS........ 250.00 100.00
564 Willie Mays AS........ 100.00 40.00
565 Roger Maris AS........ 100.00 40.00
566 Hank Aaron AS........ 100.00 40.00
567 Sherm Lollar AS........ 15.00 6.00
568 Del Crandall AS........ 15.00 6.00
569 Camilo Pascual AS........ 15.00 6.00
570 Don Drysdale AS........ 40.00 16.00
571 Billy Pierce AS........ 15.00 6.00
572 Johnny Antonelli AS........ 20.00 9.00
NNO Iron-on team transfer........ 5.00 2.00

1960 Topps Tattoos

In 1960 this tattoo set was issued separately by both Topps and O-Pee-Chee. They are actually the reverses (inside surfaces) of the wrappers in which the (one cent) product "Tattoo Bubble Gum" was packaged. The dimensions given (1 9/16" by 3 1/2") are for the entire wrapper. The wrapper lists instructions on how to apply the tattoo. The "tattoos" were to be applied by moistening the skin and then pressing the tattoo to the moistened spot. The tattoos are unnumbered and are colored. There are 96 tattoos in the set: 55 players, 16 team logos, 15 action shots and ten autographed balls. In the checklist below the player tattoos are numbered 1-55 in alphabetical order, the team tattoos (56-71) are numbered in alphabetical team order (within league), the action photos (72-86) are numbered in alphabetical order by title and the facsimile autographed ball tattoos (87-96) are numbered in alphabetical order according to the autographing player.

NM Ex
COMPLETE SET (96)........ 1800.00 700.00
COMMON TATTOO (1-55)........ 6.00 2.40
COMMON TEAM (56-71)........ 5.00 2.00
COMM.ACTION (72-86)........ 2.50 1.00
COMMON BALL (87-96)........ 2.50 1.00
WRAPPER........ 10.00 4.00
1 Hank Aaron........ 120.00 47.50
2 Bob Allison........ 8.00 3.20
3 Johnny Antonelli........ 8.00 3.20
4 Richie Ashburn........ 30.00 12.00
5 Ernie Banks........ 50.00 20.00
6 Yogi Berra........ 100.00 40.00
7 Lew Burdette........ 8.00 3.20
8 Orlando Cepeda........ 25.00 10.00
9 Rocky Colavito........ 25.00 10.00
10 Joe Cunningham........ 8.00 3.20
11 Bud Daley........ 6.00 2.40
12 Don Drysdale........ 40.00 16.00
13 Ryne Duren........ 10.00 4.00
14 Roy Face........ 10.00 4.00
15 Whitey Ford........ 40.00 16.00
16 Nellie Fox........ 30.00 12.00
17 Tito Francona........ 6.00 2.40
18 Gene Freese........ 6.00 2.40
19 Jim Gilliam........ 15.00 6.00
20 Dick Groat........ 10.00 4.00
21 Ray Herbert........ 6.00 2.40
22 Glen Hobbie........ 6.00 2.40
23 Jackie Jensen........ 15.00 6.00
24 Sam Jones........ 6.00 2.40
25 Al Kaline........ 50.00 20.00
26 Harmon Killebrew........ 40.00 16.00
27 Harvey Kuenn........ 15.00 6.00
28 Frank Lary........ 8.00 3.20
29 Vern Law........ 10.00 4.00
30 Frank Malzone........ 8.00 3.20
31 Mickey Mantle........ 400.00 160.00
32 Roger Maris........ 50.00 20.00
33 Eddie Mathews........ 40.00 16.00
34 Willie Mays........ 150.00 60.00
35 Cal McLish........ 6.00 2.40
36 Wally Moon........ 8.00 3.20
37 Walt Moryn........ 6.00 2.40
38 Don Mossi........ 8.00 3.20
39 Stan Musial........ 80.00 32.00
40 Charlie Neal........ 8.00 3.20
41 Don Newcombe........ 10.00 4.00
42 Milt Pappas........ 8.00 3.20
43 Camilo Pascual........ 8.00 3.20
44 Billy Pierce........ 8.00 3.20
45 Robin Roberts........ 30.00 12.00
46 Frank Robinson........ 40.00 16.00
47 Pete Runnels........ 8.00 3.20
48 Herb Score........ 10.00 4.00
49 Warren Spahn........ 40.00 16.00
50 Johnny Temple........ 8.00 3.20
51 Gus Triandos........ 8.00 3.20
52 Jerry Walker........ 6.00 2.40
53 Bill White........ 15.00 6.00
54 Gene Woodling........ 8.00 3.20
55 Early Wynn........ 30.00 12.00
56 Chicago Cubs........ 5.00 2.00
57 Cincinnati Reds........ 5.00 2.00
58 Los Angeles Dodgers........ 8.00 3.20
59 Milwaukee Braves........ 5.00 2.00
60 Philadelphia Phillies........ 5.00 2.00
61 Pittsburgh Pirates........ 5.00 2.00
62 St. Louis Cardinals........ 5.00 2.00
63 San Francisco Giants........ 5.00 2.00
64 Baltimore Orioles........ 5.00 2.00

65 Boston Red Sox 8.00 3.20
66 Chicago White Sox 5.00 2.00
67 Cleveland Indians 5.00 2.00
68 Detroit Tigers 5.00 2.00
69 Kansas City Athletics 5.00 2.00
70 New York Yankees 10.00 4.00
71 Washington Senators 5.00 2.00
72 Circus Catch 2.50 1.00
73 Double Play 2.50 1.00
74 Grand Slam Homer 2.50 1.00
75 Great Catch 2.50 1.00
76 Left Hand Batter 2.50 1.00
77 Left Hand Pitcher 2.50 1.00
78 Out at First 2.50 1.00
79 Out at Home 2.50 1.00
80 Right Hand Batter 2.50 1.00
81 Right Hand Pitcher 2.50 1.00
82 Right Hand Pitcher 2.50 1.00
(Different pose)
83 Run Down 2.50 1.00
84 Stolen Base 2.50 1.00
85 The Final Word 2.50 1.00
86 Twisting Foul 2.50 1.00
87 Richie Ashburn 8.00 3.20
(Autographed ball)
88 Rocky Colavito 8.00 3.20
(Autographed ball)
89 Roy Face 2.50 1.00
(Autographed ball)
90 Jackie Jensen 4.00 1.60
(Autographed ball)
91 Harmon Killebrew 10.00 4.00
(Autographed ball)
92 Mickey Mantle 200.00 80.00
(Autographed ball)
93 Willie Mays 40.00 16.00
(Autographed ball)
94 Stan Musial 25.00 10.00
(Autographed ball)
95 Billy Pierce 3.00 1.20
(Autographed ball)
96 Jerry Walker 2.50 1.00
(Autographed ball)

1960 Topps Venezuelan

This set is a parallel version of the first 196 cards of the regular 1960 Topps set and are similar in design. The cards were issued for the Venezuelan market. Although the cards were printed in the United States, they are faded compared to the American issued cards.

NM Ex
COMPLETE SET (196) 3500.00 1400.00
1 Early Wynn 80.00 32.00
2 Roman Mejias 10.00 4.00
3 Joe Adcock 15.00 6.00
4 Bob Purkey 10.00 4.00
5 Wally Moon 10.00 4.00
6 Lou Berberet 10.00 4.00
7 Willie Mays 60.00 24.00
Bill Rigney MG
8 Bud Daley 10.00 4.00
9 Faye Throneberry 10.00 4.00
10 Ernie Banks 120.00 47.50
11 Norm Siebern 10.00 4.00
12 Milt Pappas 15.00 6.00
13 Wally Post 10.00 4.00
14 Jim Grant 10.00 4.00
15 Pete Runnels 10.00 4.00
16 Ernie Broglio 10.00 4.00
17 Johnny Callison 10.00 4.00
18 Dodgers Team CL 100.00 40.00
19 Felix Mantilla 10.00 4.00
20 Roy Face 15.00 6.00
21 Dutch Dotterer 10.00 4.00
22 Rocky Bridges 10.00 4.00
23 Eddie Fisher 10.00 4.00
24 Dick Gray 10.00 4.00
25 Roy Sievers 15.00 6.00
26 Wayne Terwilliger 10.00 4.00
27 Dick Drott 10.00 4.00
28 Brooks Robinson 120.00 47.50
29 Clem Labine 10.00 4.00
30 Tito Francona 10.00 4.00
31 Sammy Esposito 10.00 4.00
32 Jim O'Toole 10.00 4.00
Vada Pinson
33 Tom Morgan 10.00 4.00
34 Sparky Anderson 40.00 16.00
35 Whitey Ford 120.00 47.50
36 Russ Nixon 10.00 4.00
37 Bill Bruton 10.00 4.00
38 Jerry Casale 10.00 4.00
39 Earl Averill 10.00 4.00
40 Joe Cunningham 15.00 6.00
41 Barry Latman 10.00 4.00
42 Hobie Landrith 10.00 4.00
43 Senators Team CL 20.00 8.00
44 Bobby Locke 10.00 4.00
45 Roy McMillan 10.00 4.00
46 Jerry Fisher 10.00 4.00
47 Don Zimmer 10.00 4.00
48 Hal W. Smith 10.00 4.00
49 Curt Raydon 10.00 4.00
50 Al Kaline 120.00 47.50
51 Jim Coates 10.00 4.00
52 Dave Philley 10.00 4.00
53 Jackie Brandt 10.00 4.00
54 Mike Fornieles 10.00 4.00
55 Bill Mazeroski 40.00 16.00
56 Steve Korcheck 10.00 4.00
57 Turk Lown 10.00 4.00
Gerry Staley
58 Gino Cimoli 10.00 4.00
59 Juan Pizarro 10.00 4.00
60 Gus Triandos 10.00 4.00
61 Eddie Kasko 10.00 4.00
62 Roger Craig 10.00 4.00
63 George Strickland 10.00 4.00
64 Jack Meyer 10.00 4.00
65 Elston Howard 15.00 6.00
66 Bob Trowbridge 10.00 4.00
67 Jose Pagan 10.00 4.00
68 Dave Hillman 10.00 4.00
69 Billy Goodman 10.00 4.00
70 Lew Burdette 15.00 6.00
71 Marty Keough 10.00 4.00
72 Tigers Team CL 40.00 16.00
73 Bob Gibson 120.00 47.50
74 Walt Moryn 10.00 4.00
75 Vic Power 10.00 4.00
76 Bill Fischer 10.00 4.00
77 Hank Foiles 10.00 4.00
78 Bob Grim 10.00 4.00
79 Walt Dropo 10.00 4.00
80 Johnny Antonelli 10.00 4.00
81 Russ Snyder 10.00 4.00
82 Ruben Gomez 10.00 4.00
83 Tony Kubek 15.00 6.00
84 Hal R. Smith 10.00 4.00
85 Frank Lary 10.00 4.00
86 Dick Gernert 10.00 4.00
87 John Romonosky 10.00 4.00
88 John Roseboro 10.00 4.00
89 Hal Brown 10.00 4.00
90 Bobby Avila 10.00 4.00
91 Bennie Daniels 10.00 4.00
92 Whitey Herzog 10.00 4.00
93 Art Schult 10.00 4.00
94 Leo Kiely 10.00 4.00
95 Frank Thomas 10.00 4.00
96 Ralph Terry 10.00 4.00
97 Ted Lepcio 10.00 4.00
98 Gordon Jones 10.00 4.00
99 Lenny Green 10.00 4.00
100 Nellie Fox 40.00 16.00
101 Bob Miller 10.00 4.00
102 Kent Hadley 10.00 4.00
103 Dick Farrell 10.00 4.00
104 Dick Schofield 10.00 4.00
105 Larry Sherry 10.00 4.00
106 Billy Gardner 10.00 4.00
107 Carlton Willey 10.00 4.00
108 Pete Daley 10.00 4.00
109 Clete Boyer 10.00 4.00
110 Cal McLish 10.00 4.00
111 Vic Wertz 10.00 4.00
112 Jack Harshman 10.00 4.00
113 Bob Skinner 10.00 4.00
114 Ken Aspromonte 10.00 4.00
115 Roy Face 15.00 6.00
Hoyt Wilhelm
116 Jim Rivera 10.00 4.00
117 Tom Borland RP 10.00 4.00
118 Bob Bruce RP 10.00 4.00
119 Chico Cardenas RP 10.00 4.00
120 Duke Carmel RP 10.00 4.00
121 Camilo Carreon RP 10.00 4.00
122 Don Dillard RP 10.00 4.00
123 Dan Dobbek RP 10.00 4.00
124 Jim Donohue RP 10.00 4.00
125 Dick Ellsworth RP 10.00 4.00
126 Chuck Estrada RP 10.00 4.00
127 Ron Hansen RP 10.00 4.00
128 Bill Harris RP 10.00 4.00
129 Bob Hartman RP 10.00 4.00
130 Frank Herrera RP 10.00 4.00
131 Ed Hobaugh RP 10.00 4.00
132 Frank Howard RP 50.00 20.00
133 Manuel Javier RP 10.00 4.00
(Sic, Julian)
134 Deron Johnson RP 10.00 4.00
135 Ken Johnson RP 10.00 4.00
136 Jim Kaat RP 100.00 40.00
137 Lou Klimchock RP 10.00 4.00
138 Art Mahaffey RP 10.00 4.00
139 Carl Mathias RP 10.00 4.00
140 Julio Navarro RP 10.00 4.00
141 Jim Proctor RP 10.00 4.00
142 Bill Short RP 10.00 4.00
143 Al Spangler RP 10.00 4.00
144 Al Stieglitz RP 10.00 4.00
145 Jim Umbricht RP 10.00 4.00
146 Ted Wieand RP 10.00 4.00
147 Bob Will RP 10.00 4.00
148 Carl Yastrzemski RP 300.00 120.00
149 Bob Nieman 10.00 4.00
150 Billy Pierce 15.00 6.00
151 Giants Team CL 20.00 8.00
152 Gail Harris 10.00 4.00
153 Bobby Thomson 15.00 6.00
154 Jim Davenport 10.00 4.00
155 Charlie Neal 10.00 4.00
156 Art Ceccarelli 10.00 4.00
157 Rocky Nelson 10.00 4.00
158 Wes Covington 10.00 4.00
159 Jim Piersall 15.00 6.00
160 Mickey Mantle 400.00 160.00
Ken Boyer
161 Ray Narleski 10.00 4.00
162 Sammy Taylor 10.00 4.00
163 Hector Lopez 10.00 4.00
164 Reds Team CL 20.00 8.00
165 Jack Sanford 10.00 4.00
166 Chuck Essegian 10.00 4.00
167 Valmy Thomas 10.00 4.00
168 Alex Grammas 10.00 4.00
169 Jake Striker 10.00 4.00
170 Del Crandall 10.00 4.00
171 Johnny Groth 10.00 4.00
172 Willie Kirkland 10.00 4.00
173 Billy Martin 40.00 16.00
174 Indians Team CL 20.00 8.00
175 Pedro Ramos 10.00 4.00
176 Vada Pinson 15.00 6.00
177 Johnny Kucks 10.00 4.00
178 Woody Held 10.00 4.00
179 Rip Coleman 10.00 4.00
180 Harry Simpson 10.00 4.00
181 Billy Loes 10.00 4.00
182 Glen Hobbie 10.00 4.00
183 Eli Grba 10.00 4.00
184 Gary Geiger 10.00 4.00
185 Jim Owens 10.00 4.00
186 Dave Sisler 10.00 4.00
187 Jay Hook 10.00 4.00
188 Dick Williams 10.00 4.00
189 Don McMahon 10.00 4.00
190 Gene Woodling 10.00 4.00
191 Johnny Klippstein 10.00 4.00
192 Danny O'Connell 10.00 4.00
193 Dick Hyde 10.00 4.00
194 Bobby Gene Smith 10.00 4.00
195 Lindy McDaniel 10.00 4.00
196 Andy Carey 10.00 4.00

1961 Topps

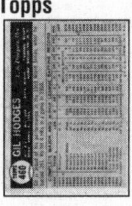

The cards in this 587-card set measure 2 1/2" by 3 1/2". In 1961, Topps returned to the vertical obverse format. Introduced for the first time were "League Leaders" (41-50) and separate, numbered checklist cards. Two number 463s exist: the Braves team card carrying that number was meant to be number 426. There are three versions of the second series checklist card number 98; the variations are distinguished by the color of the "CHECKLIST" headline on the front of the card, the color of the printing of the card number on the bottom of the reverse, and the presence of the copyright notice running vertically on the card back. There are two groups of managers (131-139/219-226) as well as separate subsets of World Series cards (306-313), Baseball Thrills (401-410), MVP's of the 1950's (AL 471-478/NL 479-486) and Sporting News All-Stars (566-589). The usual last series scarcity (523-589) exists. Some collectors believe that 61 high numbers are the toughest of all the Topps hi numbers. The set actually totals 587 cards since numbers 587 and 588 were never issued. These card advertising promos have been seen: Dan Dobbek/Russ Nixon/60 NL Pitching Leaders on the front along with an ad and Roger Maris on the back.Other strips feature Jack Kralick/Dick Stigman/Joe Christopher; Ed Roebuck/Bob Schmidt/Zoilo Versalles; Lindy (McDaniel) Shows Larry (Jackson)/John Blanchard/Johnny Kucks. Cards were issued in one-card penny packs as well as five-card nickel packs. The one card packs came 120 to a box. The key Rookie Cards in this set are Juan Marichal, Ron Santo and Billy Williams.

NM Ex
COMPLETE SET (587) 7000.00 2800.00
COMMON CARD (1-370) 3.00 1.20
COMMON (371-446) 4.00 1.60
COMMON (447-522) 8.00 3.20
COMMON (523-589) 30.00 12.00
NOT ISSUED (587/588)
WRAPPER (1-CENT) 200.00 80.00
WRAP.(1-CENT, REPEAT) 100.00 40.00
WRAPPER (5-CENT) 40.00 16.00
1 Dick Groat 30.00 6.00
2 Roger Maris 200.00 80.00
3 John Buzhardt 3.00 1.20
4 Lenny Green 3.00 1.20
5 John Romano 3.00 1.20
6 Ed Roebuck 3.00 1.20
7 White Sox Team 8.00 3.20
8 Dick Williams 6.00 2.40
9 Bob Purkey 3.00 1.20
10 Brooks Robinson 50.00 20.00
11 Curt Simmons 6.00 2.40
12 Moe Thacker 3.00 1.20
13 Chuck Cottier 3.00 1.20
14 Don Mossi 6.00 2.40
15 Willie Kirkland 3.00 1.20
16 Billy Muffett 3.00 1.20
17 Checklist 1 10.00 2.00
18 Jim Grant 6.00 2.40
19 Clete Boyer 8.00 3.20
20 Robin Roberts 15.00 6.00
21 Zorro Versalles 8.00 3.20
UER RC
First name should
be Zoilo
22 Clem Labine 6.00 2.40
23 Don Demeter 3.00 1.20
24 Ken Johnson 6.00 2.40
25 Vada Pinson 8.00 3.20
Gus Bell
Frank Robinson
26 Wes Stock 3.00 1.20
27 Jerry Kindall 3.00 1.20
28 Hector Lopez 6.00 2.40
29 Don Nottebart 3.00 1.20
30 Nellie Fox 15.00 6.00
31 Bob Schmidt 3.00 1.20
32 Ray Sadecki 3.00 1.20
33 Gary Geiger 3.00 1.20
34 Wynn Hawkins 3.00 1.20
35 Ron Santo RC 40.00 16.00
36 Jack Kralick 3.00 1.20
37 Charley Maxwell 6.00 2.40
38 Bob Lillis 3.00 1.20
39 Leo Posada 3.00 1.20
40 Bob Turley 6.00 2.40
41 Dick Groat 40.00 16.00
Norm Larker
Willie Mays
Roberto Clemente LL
42 Pete Runnels 8.00 3.20
Al Smith
Minnie Minoso
Bill Skowron LL
43 Ernie Banks 30.00 12.00
Hank Aaron
Ed Mathews
Ken Boyer LL
44 Mickey Mantle 80.00 32.00
Roger Maris
Jim Lemon
Rocky Colavito LL
45 Mike McCormick 8.00 3.20
Ernie Broglio
Don Drysdale
Bob Friend
Stan Williams LL
46 Frank Baumann 8.00 3.20
Jim Bunning
Art Ditmar
Hal Brown LL
47 Ernie Broglio 8.00 3.20
Warren Spahn
Vern Law
Lou Burdette LL
48 Chuck Estrada 8.00 3.20
Jim Perry UER
(Listed as an Oriole)
Bud Daley
Art Ditmar
Frank Lary
Milt Pappas LL
49 Don Drysdale 20.00 8.00
Sandy Koufax
Sam Jones
Ernie Broglio LL
50 Jim Bunning 8.00 3.20
Pedro Ramos
Early Wynn
Frank Lary LL
51 Detroit Tigers 8.00 3.20
Team Card
52 George Crowe 3.00 1.20
53 Russ Nixon 3.00 1.20
54 Earl Francis 3.00 1.20
55 Jim Davenport 6.00 2.40
56 Russ Kemmerer 3.00 1.20
57 Marv Throneberry 6.00 2.40
58 Joe Schaffernoth 3.00 1.20
59 Jim Woods 3.00 1.20
60 Woody Held 3.00 1.20
61 Ron Piche 3.00 1.20
62 Al Pilarcik 3.00 1.20
63 Jim Kaat 8.00 3.20
64 Alex Grammas 3.00 1.20
65 Ted Kluszewski 8.00 3.20
66 Bill Henry 3.00 1.20
67 Ossie Virgil 3.00 1.20
68 Deron Johnson 6.00 2.40
69 Earl Wilson 6.00 2.40
70 Bill Virdon 6.00 2.40
71 Jerry Adair 3.00 1.20
72 Stu Miller 6.00 2.40
73 Al Spangler 3.00 1.20
74 Joe Pignatano 3.00 1.20
75 Lindy McDaniel 6.00 2.40
Larry Jackson
76 Harry Anderson 3.00 1.20
77 Dick Stigman 3.00 1.20
78 Lee Walls 6.00 2.40
79 Joe Ginsberg 3.00 1.20
80 Harmon Killebrew 20.00 8.00
81 Tracy Stallard 3.00 1.20
82 Joe Christopher 3.00 1.20
83 Bob Bruce 3.00 1.20
84 Lee Maye 3.00 1.20
85 Jerry Walker 3.00 1.20
86 Los Angeles Dodgers 8.00 3.20
Team Card
87 Joe Amalfitano 3.00 1.20
88 Richie Ashburn 15.00 6.00
89 Billy Martin 15.00 6.00
90 Gerry Staley 3.00 1.20
91 Walt Moryn 3.00 1.20
92 Hal Naragon 3.00 1.20
93 Tony Gonzalez 3.00 1.20
94 Johnny Kucks 3.00 1.20
95 Norm Cash 8.00 3.20
96 Billy O'Dell 3.00 1.20
97 Jerry Lynch 6.00 2.40
98A Checklist 2 10.00 2.00
(Red "Checklist"
98 black on white)
98B Checklist 2 10.00 2.00
(Yellow "Checklist"
98 black on white)
98C Checklist 2 10.00 2.00
(Yellow "Checklist"
98 white on black
no copyright)
99 Don Buddin UER 3.00 1.20
(66 HR's)
100 Harvey Haddix 6.00 2.40
101 Bubba Phillips 3.00 1.20
102 Gene Stephens 3.00 1.20
103 Ruben Amaro 3.00 1.20
104 John Blanchard 8.00 3.20
105 Carl Willey 3.00 1.20
106 Whitey Herzog 3.00 1.20
107 Seth Morehead 3.00 1.20
108 Dan Dobbek 3.00 1.20
109 Johnny Podres 8.00 3.20
110 Vada Pinson 8.00 3.20
111 Jack Meyer 3.00 1.20
112 Chico Fernandez 3.00 1.20
113 Mike Fornieles 3.00 1.20
114 Hobie Landrith 3.00 1.20
115 Johnny Antonelli 6.00 2.40
116 Joe DeMaestri 3.00 1.20
117 Dale Long 6.00 2.40
118 Chris Cannizzaro 3.00 1.20
119 Norm Siebern 6.00 2.40
Hank Bauer
Jerry Lumpe
120 Eddie Mathews 30.00 12.00
121 Eli Grba 6.00 2.40
122 Chicago Cubs 8.00 3.20
Team Card
123 Billy Gardner 3.00 1.20
124 J.C. Martin 3.00 1.20
125 Steve Barber 3.00 1.20
126 Dick Stuart 6.00 2.40
127 Ron Kline 3.00 1.20
128 Rip Repulski 3.00 1.20
129 Ed Hobaugh 3.00 1.20
130 Norm Larker 3.00 1.20
131 Paul Richards MG 6.00 2.40
132 Al Lopez MG 8.00 3.20
133 Ralph Houk MG 6.00 2.40
134 Mickey Vernon MG 6.00 2.40
135 Fred Hutchinson MG 6.00 2.40
136 Walter Alston MG 8.00 3.20
137 Chuck Dressen MG 6.00 2.40
138 Danny Murtaugh MG 6.00 2.40
139 Solly Hemus MG 6.00 2.40
140 Gus Triandos 6.00 2.40
141 Billy Williams RC 60.00 24.00
142 Luis Arroyo 6.00 2.40
143 Russ Snyder 3.00 1.20
144 Jim Coker 3.00 1.20
145 Bob Buhl 6.00 2.40
146 Marty Keough 3.00 1.20
147 Ed Rakow 3.00 1.20
148 Julian Javier 6.00 2.40
149 Bob Oldis 3.00 1.20
150 Willie Mays 100.00 40.00
151 Jim Donohue 3.00 1.20
152 Earl Torgeson 3.00 1.20
153 Don Lee 3.00 1.20
154 Bobby Del Greco 3.00 1.20
155 Johnny Temple 6.00 2.40
156 Ken Hunt 6.00 2.40
157 Cal McLish 3.00 1.20
158 Pete Daley 3.00 1.20
159 Orioles Team 8.00 3.20
160 Whitey Ford UER 50.00 20.00
Incorrectly listed
as 5'0" tall
161 Sherman Jones UER 3.00 1.20
(Photo actually
Eddie Fisher)
162 Jay Hook 3.00 1.20
163 Ed Sadowski 3.00 1.20
164 Felix Mantilla 3.00 1.20
165 Gino Cimoli 3.00 1.20
166 Danny Kravitz 3.00 1.20
167 San Francisco Giants 8.00 3.20
Team Card
168 Tommy Davis 8.00 3.20
169 Don Elston 3.00 1.20
170 Al Smith 3.00 1.20
171 Paul Foytack 3.00 1.20
172 Don Dillard 3.00 1.20
173 Frank Malzone 6.00 2.40
Vic Wertz
Jackie Jensen
174 Ray Semproch 3.00 1.20
175 Gene Freese 3.00 1.20
176 Ken Aspromonte 3.00 1.20
177 Don Larsen 6.00 2.40
178 Bob Nieman 3.00 1.20
179 Joe Koppe 3.00 1.20
180 Bobby Richardson 12.00 4.80
181 Fred Green 3.00 1.20
182 Dave Nicholson 3.00 1.20
183 Andre Rodgers 3.00 1.20
184 Steve Bilko 6.00 2.40
185 Herb Score 6.00 2.40
186 Elmer Valo 6.00 2.40
187 Billy Klaus 3.00 1.20
188 Jim Marshall 3.00 1.20
189A Checklist 3 10.00 2.00
(Copyright symbol
almost adjacent to
263 Ken Hamlin)
189B Checklist 3 10.00 2.00
(Copyright symbol
adjacent to
264 Glen Hobbie)
190 Stan Williams 6.00 2.40
191 Mike de la Hoz 3.00 1.20
192 Dick Brown 3.00 1.20
193 Gene Conley 6.00 2.40
194 Gordy Coleman 6.00 2.40
195 Jerry Casale 3.00 1.20
196 Ed Bouchee 3.00 1.20
197 Dick Hall 3.00 1.20
198 Carl Sawatski 3.00 1.20
199 Bob Boyd 3.00 1.20
200 Warren Spahn 40.00 16.00
201 Pete Whisenant 3.00 1.20
202 Al Neiger 3.00 1.20
203 Eddie Bressoud 3.00 1.20
204 Bob Skinner 6.00 2.40
205 Billy Pierce 6.00 2.40
206 Gene Green 3.00 1.20
207 Sandy Koufax 30.00 12.00
Johnny Podres
208 Larry Osborne 3.00 1.20
209 Ken McBride 3.00 1.20
210 Pete Runnels 6.00 2.40
211 Bob Gibson 40.00 16.00
212 Haywood Sullivan 6.00 2.40
213 Bill Stafford 3.00 1.20
214 Danny Murphy 6.00 2.40
215 Gus Bell 6.00 2.40
216 Ted Bowsfield 3.00 1.20
217 Mel Roach 3.00 1.20
218 Hal Brown 3.00 1.20
219 Gene Mauch MG 6.00 2.40
220 Alvin Dark MG 6.00 2.40
221 Mike Higgins MG 3.00 1.20
222 Jimmy Dykes MG 6.00 2.40
223 Bob Scheffing MG 3.00 1.20
224 Joe Gordon MG 6.00 2.40
225 Bill Rigney MG 6.00 2.40
226 Cookie Lavagetto MG 6.00 2.40
227 Juan Pizarro 3.00 1.20
228 New York Yankees 60.00 24.00
Team Card
229 Rudy Hernandez 3.00 1.20
230 Don Hoak 3.00 1.20
231 Dick Drott 3.00 1.20
232 Bill White 6.00 2.40
233 Joey Jay 6.00 2.40
234 Ted Lepcio 3.00 1.20
235 Camilo Pascual 6.00 2.40
236 Don Gile 3.00 1.20
237 Billy Loes 6.00 2.40
238 Jim Gilliam 6.00 2.40
239 Dave Sisler 3.00 1.20
240 Ron Hansen 3.00 1.20
241 Al Cicotte 3.00 1.20
242 Hal Smith 3.00 1.20
243 Frank Lary 6.00 2.40
244 Chico Cardenas 6.00 2.40
245 Joe Adcock 6.00 2.40
246 Bob Davis 3.00 1.20
247 Billy Goodman 6.00 2.40
248 Ed Keegan 3.00 1.20
249 Cincinnati Reds 8.00 3.20

Card	NM	Ex
Team Card		
250 Vern Law	6.00	2.40
Roy Face		
251 Bill Bruton	3.00	1.20
252 Bill Short	3.00	1.20
253 Sammy Taylor	3.00	1.20
254 Ted Sadowski	6.00	2.40
255 Vic Power	6.00	2.40
256 Billy Hoeft	3.00	1.20
257 Carroll Hardy	3.00	1.20
258 Jack Sanford	6.00	2.40
259 John Schaive	3.00	1.20
260 Don Drysdale	30.00	12.00
261 Charlie Lau	6.00	2.40
262 Tony Curry	3.00	1.20
263 Ken Hamlin	3.00	1.20
264 Glen Hobbie	3.00	1.20
265 Tony Kubek	12.00	4.80
266 Lindy McDaniel	6.00	2.40
267 Norm Siebern	3.00	1.20
268 Ike Delock	3.00	1.20
269 Harry Chiti	3.00	1.20
270 Bob Friend	6.00	2.40
271 Jim Landis	3.00	1.20
272 Tom Morgan	3.00	1.20
273A Checklist 4	15.00	3.00
(Copyright symbol adjacent to 336 Don Mincher)		
273B Checklist 4	10.00	2.00
(Copyright symbol adjacent to 339 Gene Baker)		
274 Gary Bell	3.00	1.20
275 Gene Woodling	6.00	2.40
276 Ray Rippelmeyer	3.00	1.20
277 Hank Foiles	3.00	1.20
278 Don McMahon	3.00	1.20
279 Jose Pagan	3.00	1.20
280 Frank Howard	8.00	3.20
281 Frank Sullivan	3.00	1.20
282 Faye Throneberry	3.00	1.20
283 Bob Anderson	3.00	1.20
284 Dick Gernert	3.00	1.20
285 Sherm Lollar	6.00	2.40
286 George Witt	3.00	1.20
287 Carl Yastrzemski	50.00	20.00
288 Albie Pearson	6.00	2.40
289 Ray Moore	3.00	1.20
290 Stan Musial	100.00	40.00
291 Tex Clevenger	3.00	1.20
292 Jim Baumer	3.00	1.20
293 Tom Sturdivant	3.00	1.20
294 Don Blasingame	3.00	1.20
295 Milt Pappas	6.00	2.40
296 Wes Covington	6.00	2.40
297 Athletics Team	8.00	3.20
298 Jim Golden	3.00	1.20
299 Clay Dalrymple	3.00	1.20
300 Mickey Mantle	400.00	160.00
301 Chet Nichols	3.00	1.20
302 Al Heist	3.00	1.20
303 Gary Peters	6.00	2.40
304 Rocky Nelson	3.00	1.20
305 Mike McCormick	6.00	2.40
306 Bill Virdon WS	10.00	4.00
307 Mickey Mantle WS	80.00	32.00
308 B.Richardson WS	12.00	4.80
309 Gino Cimoli WS	10.00	4.00
310 Roy Face WS	10.00	4.00
311 Whitey Ford WS	15.00	6.00
312 Bill Mazeroski WS	20.00	8.00
Mazeroski Homer Wins it		
313 WS Summary	15.00	6.00
Pirates Celebrate		
314 Bob Miller	3.00	1.20
315 Earl Battey	6.00	2.40
316 Bobby Gene Smith	3.00	1.20
317 Jim Brewer	3.00	1.20
318 Danny O'Connell	3.00	1.20
319 Valmy Thomas	3.00	1.20
320 Lou Burdette	6.00	2.40
321 Marv Breeding	3.00	1.20
322 Bill Kunkel	6.00	2.40
323 Sammy Esposito	3.00	1.20
324 Hank Aguirre	3.00	1.20
325 Wally Moon	6.00	2.40
326 Dave Hillman	3.00	1.20
327 Matty Alou RC	12.00	4.80
328 Jim O'Toole	6.00	2.40
329 Julio Becquer	3.00	1.20
330 Rocky Colavito	20.00	8.00
331 Ned Garver	3.00	1.20
332 Dutch Dotterer UER	3.00	1.20
(Photo actually Tommy Dotterer Dutch's brother)		
333 Fritz Brickell	3.00	1.20
334 Walt Bond	3.00	1.20
335 Frank Bolling	3.00	1.20
336 Don Mincher	6.00	2.40
337 Early Wynn	8.00	3.20
Al Lopez		
Herb Score		
338 Don Landrum	3.00	1.20
339 Gene Baker	3.00	1.20
340 Vic Wertz	6.00	2.40
341 Jim Owens	3.00	1.20
342 Clint Courtney	3.00	1.20
343 Earl Robinson	3.00	1.20
344 Sandy Koufax	100.00	40.00
345 Jimmy Piersall	8.00	3.20
346 Howie Nunn	3.00	1.20
347 St. Louis Cardinals	8.00	3.20
Team Card		
348 Steve Boros	3.00	1.20
349 Danny McDevitt	3.00	1.20
350 Ernie Banks	40.00	16.00
351 Jim King	3.00	1.20
352 Bob Shaw	3.00	1.20
353 Howie Bedell	3.00	1.20
354 Billy Harrell	6.00	2.40
355 Bob Allison	8.00	3.20
356 Ryne Duren	3.00	1.20
357 Daryl Spencer	3.00	1.20
358 Earl Averill	6.00	2.40
359 Dallas Green	3.00	1.20
360 Frank Robinson	40.00	16.00
361A Checklist 5	15.00	3.00
(No ad on back)		
361B Checklist 5	15.00	3.00
(Special Feature ad on back)		
362 Frank Funk	3.00	1.20
363 John Roseboro	6.00	2.40
364 Moe Drabowsky	6.00	2.40
365 Jerry Lumpe	3.00	1.20
366 Eddie Fisher	3.00	1.20
367 Jim Rivera	3.00	1.20
368 Bennie Daniels	3.00	1.20
369 Dave Philley	3.00	1.20
370 Roy Face	6.00	2.40
371 Bill Skowron SP	50.00	20.00
372 Bob Hendley	4.00	1.60
373 Boston Red Sox	8.00	3.20
Team Card		
374 Paul Giel	4.00	1.60
375 Ken Boyer	12.00	4.80
376 Mike Roarke RC	6.00	2.40
377 Ruben Gomez	4.00	1.60
378 Wally Post	6.00	2.40
379 Bobby Shantz	4.00	1.60
380 Minnie Minoso	8.00	3.20
381 Dave Wickersham	4.00	1.60
382 Frank Thomas	6.00	2.40
383 Mike McCormick	6.00	2.40
Jack Sanford		
Billy O'Dell		
384 Chuck Essegian	4.00	1.60
385 Jim Perry	6.00	2.40
386 Joe Hicks	4.00	1.60
387 Duke Maas	4.00	1.60
388 Roberto Clemente	125.00	50.00
389 Ralph Terry	6.00	2.40
390 Del Crandall	8.00	3.20
391 Winston Brown	4.00	1.60
392 Reno Bertoia	4.00	1.60
393 Don Cardwell	4.00	1.60
Glen Hobbie		
394 Ken Walters	4.00	1.60
395 Chuck Estrada	6.00	2.40
396 Bob Aspromonte	4.00	1.60
397 Hal Woodeshick	4.00	1.60
398 Hank Bauer	6.00	2.40
399 Cliff Cook	4.00	1.60
400 Vern Law	6.00	2.40
401 Babe Ruth HL	60.00	24.00
60th HR		
402 Don Larsen HL SP	25.00	10.00
WS Perfect Game		
403 Joe Oeschger HL	8.00	3.20
Leon Cadore		
26 Inning Tie		
404 Rogers Hornsby HL	12.00	4.80
.424 Season BA		
405 Lou Gehrig HL	80.00	32.00
Consecutive Game Streak		
406 Mickey Mantle HL	100.00	40.00
565 foot HR		
407 Jack Chesbro HL	8.00	3.20
41 victories		
408 C. Mathewson HL SP	20.00	8.00
267 Strikeouts		
409 Walter Johnson SL	12.00	4.80
3 Shutouts in 4 days		
410 Harvey Haddix HL	8.00	3.20
12 Perfect Innings		
411 Tony Taylor	6.00	2.40
412 Larry Sherry	6.00	2.40
413 Eddie Yost	6.00	2.40
414 Dick Donovan	6.00	2.40
415 Hank Aaron	125.00	50.00
416 Dick Howser RC	8.00	3.20
417 Juan Marichal SP RC	100.00	40.00
418 Ed Bailey	6.00	2.40
419 Tom Borland	4.00	1.60
420 Ernie Broglio	6.00	2.40
421 Ty Cline SP	20.00	8.00
422 Bud Daley	4.00	1.60
423 Charlie Neal SP	20.00	8.00
424 Turk Lown	4.00	1.60
425 Yogi Berra	80.00	32.00
426 Milwaukee Braves	12.00	4.80
Team Card		
(Back numbered 463)		
427 Dick Ellsworth	6.00	2.40
428 Ray Barker SP	20.00	8.00
429 Al Kaline	50.00	20.00
430 Bill Mazeroski SP	50.00	20.00
431 Chuck Stobbs	4.00	1.60
432 Coot Veal	6.00	2.40
433 Art Mahaffey	4.00	1.60
434 Tom Brewer	4.00	1.60
435 Orlando Cepeda UER	12.00	4.80
(San Francis on card front)		
436 Jim Maloney SP RC	20.00	8.00
437A Checklist 6	15.00	3.00
440 Louis Aparicio		
437B Checklist 6	15.00	3.00
440 Luis Aparicio		
438 Curt Flood	8.00	3.20
439 Phil Regan RC	6.00	2.40
440 Luis Aparicio	12.00	4.80
441 Dick Bertell	4.00	1.60
442 Gordon Jones	4.00	1.60
443 Duke Snider	50.00	20.00
444 Joe Nuxhall	6.00	2.40
445 Frank Malzone	6.00	2.40
446 Bob Taylor	4.00	1.60
447 Harry Bright	8.00	3.20
448 Del Rice	15.00	6.00
449 Bob Bolin	8.00	3.20
450 Jim Lemon	8.00	3.20
451 Daryl Spencer	8.00	3.20
Bill White		
Ernie Broglio		
452 Bob Allen	8.00	3.20
453 Dick Schofield	8.00	3.20
454 Pumpsie Green	8.00	3.20
455 Early Wynn	15.00	6.00
456 Hal Bevan	8.00	3.20
457 Johnny James	8.00	3.20
(Listed as Angel, but wearing Yankee uniform and cap)		
458 Willie Tasby	8.00	3.20
459 Terry Fox RC	10.00	4.00
460 Gil Hodges	25.00	10.00
461 Smoky Burgess	15.00	6.00
462 Lou Klimchock	8.00	3.20
463 Jack Fisher	8.00	3.20
(See also 426)		
464 Lee Thomas RC	10.00	4.00
(Pictured with Yankee cap but listed as Los Angeles Angel)		
465 Roy McMillan	15.00	6.00
466 Ron Moeller	8.00	3.20
467 Cleveland Indians	12.00	4.80
Team Card		
468 John Callison	10.00	4.00
469 Ralph Lumenti	8.00	3.20
470 Roy Sievers	10.00	4.00
471 Phil Rizzuto MVP	25.00	10.00
472 Yogi Berra MVP	50.00	20.00
473 Bob Shantz MVP	8.00	3.20
474 Al Rosen MVP	10.00	4.00
475 Mickey Mantle MVP	200.00	80.00
476 Jackie Jensen MVP	10.00	4.00
477 Nellie Fox MVP	15.00	6.00
478 Roger Maris MVP	60.00	24.00
479 Jim Konstanty MVP	8.00	3.20
480 Roy Campanella MVP	40.00	16.00
481 Hank Sauer MVP	8.00	3.20
482 Willie Mays MVP	50.00	20.00
483 Don Newcombe MVP	10.00	4.00
484 Hank Aaron MVP	50.00	20.00
485 Ernie Banks MVP	40.00	16.00
486 Dick Groat MVP	10.00	4.00
487 Gene Oliver	8.00	3.20
488 Joe McClain	10.00	4.00
489 Walt Dropo	8.00	3.20
490 Jim Bunning	25.00	10.00
491 Philadelphia Phillies	12.00	4.80
Team Card		
492 Ron Fairly	10.00	4.00
493 Don Zimmer UER	10.00	4.00
(Brooklyn A.L.)		
494 Tom Cheney	15.00	6.00
495 Elston Howard	10.00	4.00
496 Ken MacKenzie	8.00	3.20
497 Willie Jones	8.00	3.20
498 Ray Herbert	8.00	3.20
499 Chuck Schilling RC	8.00	3.20
500 Harvey Kuenn	10.00	4.00
501 John DeMerit	8.00	3.20
502 Clarence Coleman RC	10.00	4.00
503 Tito Francona	8.00	3.20
504 Billy Consolo	8.00	3.20
505 Red Schoendienst	15.00	6.00
506 Willie Davis RC	15.00	6.00
507 Pete Burnside	8.00	3.20
508 Rocky Bridges	8.00	3.20
509 Camilo Carreon	8.00	3.20
510 Art Ditmar	8.00	3.20
511 Joe M. Morgan	8.00	3.20
512 Bob Will	8.00	3.20
513 Jim Brosnan	8.00	3.20
514 Jake Wood	8.00	3.20
515 Jackie Brandt	8.00	3.20
516 Checklist 7	15.00	3.00
517 Willie McCovey	40.00	16.00
518 Andy Carey	8.00	3.20
519 Jim Pagliaroni	8.00	3.20
520 Joe Cunningham	8.00	3.20
521 Norm Sherry	8.00	3.20
Larry Sherry		
522 Dick Farrell UER	15.00	6.00
(Phillies cap but listed on Dodgers)		
523 Joe Gibbon	30.00	12.00
524 Johnny Logan	30.00	12.00
525 Ron Perranoski RC	60.00	24.00
526 R.C. Stevens	30.00	12.00
527 Gene Leek	30.00	12.00
528 Pedro Ramos	30.00	12.00
529 Bob Roselli	30.00	12.00
530 Bob Malkmus	30.00	12.00
531 Jim Coates	50.00	20.00
532 Bob Hale	30.00	12.00
533 Jack Curtis	30.00	12.00
534 Eddie Kasko	40.00	16.00
535 Larry Jackson	30.00	12.00
536 Bill Tuttle	30.00	12.00
537 Bobby Locke	30.00	12.00
538 Chuck Hiller	30.00	12.00
539 Johnny Klippstein	30.00	12.00
540 Jackie Jensen	40.00	16.00
541 Roland Sheldon RC	50.00	20.00
542 Minnesota Twins	60.00	24.00
Team Card		
543 Roger Craig	40.00	16.00
544 George Thomas	50.00	20.00
545 Hoyt Wilhelm	60.00	24.00
546 Marty Kutyna	30.00	12.00
547 Leon Wagner	30.00	12.00
548 Ted Wills	30.00	12.00
549 Hal R. Smith	30.00	12.00
550 Frank Baumann	30.00	12.00
551 George Altman	40.00	16.00
552 Jim Archer	30.00	12.00
553 Bill Fischer	30.00	12.00
554 Pittsburgh Pirates	80.00	32.00
Team Card		
555 Sam Jones	30.00	12.00
556 Ken R. Hunt	30.00	12.00
557 Jose Valdivielso	30.00	12.00
558 Don Ferrarese	30.00	12.00
559 Jim Gentile	60.00	24.00
560 Barry Latman	40.00	16.00
561 Charley James	30.00	12.00
562 Bill Monbouquette	30.00	12.00
563 Bob Cerv	60.00	24.00
564 Don Cardwell	30.00	12.00
565 Felipe Alou	50.00	20.00
566 Paul Richards AS MG	30.00	12.00
567 D.Murtaugh AS MG	30.00	12.00
568 Bill Skowron AS	50.00	20.00
569 Frank Herrera AS	40.00	16.00
570 Nellie Fox AS	60.00	24.00
571 Bill Mazeroski AS	60.00	24.00
572 Brooks Robinson AS	80.00	32.00
573 Ken Boyer AS	50.00	20.00
574 Luis Aparicio AS	60.00	24.00
575 Ernie Banks AS	80.00	32.00
576 Roger Maris AS	175.00	70.00
577 Hank Aaron AS	150.00	60.00
578 Mickey Mantle AS	400.00	160.00
579 Willie Mays AS	150.00	60.00
580 Al Kaline AS	80.00	32.00
581 Frank Robinson AS	80.00	32.00
582 Earl Battey AS	30.00	12.00
583 Del Crandall AS	30.00	12.00
584 Jim Perry AS	30.00	12.00
585 Bob Friend AS	30.00	12.00
586 Whitey Ford AS	100.00	40.00
589 Warren Spahn AS	100.00	30.00

1961 Topps Magic Rub-Offs

There are 36 "Magic Rub-Offs" in this set of inserts also marketed in packages of 1961 Topps baseball cards. Each rub off measures 2 1/16" by 3 1/16". Of this number, 18 are team designs (numbered 1-18 below), while the remaining 18 depict players (numbered 19-36 below). The latter, one from each team, were apparently selected for their unusual nicknames. Note: The Duke Maas insert is misspelled "Mass".

	NM	Ex
COMPLETE SET (36)	140.00	55.00
COMMON RUB-OFF (1-18)	2.00	.80
COMMON CARD (19-36)	5.00	2.00
1 Detroit Tigers	3.00	1.20
2 New York Yankees	4.00	1.60
3 Minnesota Twins	2.00	.80
4 Washington Senators	2.00	.80
5 Boston Red Sox	3.00	1.20
6 Los Angeles Angels	2.00	.80
7 Kansas City A's	2.00	.80
8 Baltimore Orioles	2.00	.80
9 Chicago White Sox	2.00	.80
10 Cleveland Indians	2.00	.80
11 Pittsburgh Pirates	2.00	.80
12 San Francisco Giants	2.00	.80
13 Los Angeles Dodgers	4.00	1.60
14 Philadelphia Phillies	2.00	.80
15 Cincinnati Redlegs	2.00	.80
16 St. Louis Cardinals	2.00	.80
17 Chicago Cubs	2.00	.80
18 Milwaukee Braves	2.00	.80
19 John Romano	5.00	2.00
20 Ray Moore	5.00	2.00
21 Ernie Banks	25.00	10.00
22 Charlie Maxwell	5.00	2.00
23 Yogi Berra	25.00	10.00
24 Henry "Dutch" Dotterer	5.00	2.00
25 Jim Brosnan	5.00	2.00
26 Billy Martin	10.00	4.00
27 Jackie Brandt	5.00	2.00
28 Duke Maas	6.00	2.40
sic, Mass		
29 Pete Runnels	6.00	2.40
30 Joe Gordon MG	6.00	2.40
31 Sam Jones	5.00	2.00
32 Walt Moryn	5.00	2.00
33 Harvey Haddix	6.00	2.40
34 Frank Howard	8.00	3.20
35 Turk Lown	5.00	2.00
36 Frank Herrera	5.00	2.00

1961 Topps Stamps Inserts

There are 207 different baseball players depicted in this stamp series, which was issued as an insert in packages of the regular Topps cards of 1961. The set is actually comprised of 208 stamps: 104 players are pictured on brown stamps and 104 players appear on green stamps, with Kaline found in both colors. The stamps were issued in attached pairs and an album was sold separately (10 cents) at retail outlets. Each stamp measures 1 3/8" by 1 3/16". Stamps are unnumbered but are presented here in alphabetical order by team, Chicago Cubs (1-12), Cincinnati Reds (13-24), Los Angeles Dodgers (25-36), Milwaukee Braves (37-48), Philadelphia Phillies (49-60), Pittsburgh Pirates (61-72), San Francisco Giants (73-84), St. Louis Cardinals (85-96), Baltimore Orioles AL (97-107), Boston Red Sox (108-119), Chicago White Sox (120-131), Cleveland Indians (132-143), Detroit Tigers (144-155), Kansas City A's (156-168), Los Angeles Angels (169-175), Minnesota Twins (176-187), New York Yankees (188-200) and Washington Senators (201-207).

	NM	Ex
COMPLETE SET (207)	350.00	140.00
1 George Altman	.75	.30
2 Bob Anderson	.75	.30
brown		
3 Richie Ashburn	5.00	2.00
4 Ernie Banks	8.00	3.20
5 Ed Bouchee	.75	.30
6 Jim Brewer	.75	.30
7 Dick Ellsworth	.75	.30
8 Don Elston	.75	.30
9 Ron Santo	5.00	2.00
10 Sammy Taylor	.75	.30
11 Bob Will	.75	.30
12 Billy Williams	5.00	2.00
13 Ed Bailey	.75	.30
14 Gus Bell	1.00	.40
15 Jim Brosnan	.75	.30
brown		
16 Chico Cardenas	.75	.30
17 Gene Freese	.75	.30
18 Eddie Kasko	.75	.30
19 Jerry Lynch	.75	.30
20 Billy Martin	3.00	1.20
21 Jim O'Toole	.75	.30
22 Vada Pinson	1.50	.60
23 Wally Post	.75	.30
brown		
24 Frank Robinson	8.00	3.20
25 Tommy Davis	1.50	.60
26 Don Drysdale	6.00	2.40
27 Frank Howard	1.50	.60
brown		
28 Norm Larker	1.00	.40
29 Wally Moon	1.25	.50
brown		
30 Charlie Neal	1.00	.40
31 Johnny Podres	1.50	.60
32 Ed Roebuck	1.00	.40
33 Johnny Roseboro	1.00	.40
34 Larry Sherry	1.00	.40
35 Duke Snider	6.00	2.40
36 Stan Williams	1.00	.40
37 Hank Aaron	20.00	8.00
38 Joe Adcock	1.00	.40
39 Bill Bruton	.75	.30
40 Bob Buhl	.75	.30
41 Wes Covington	.75	.30
brown		
42 Del Crandall	1.00	.40
43 Joey Jay	.75	.30
44 Felix Mantilla	.75	.30
45 Eddie Mathews	6.00	2.40
46 Roy McMillan	.75	.30
47 Warren Spahn	8.00	3.20
48 Carlton Willey	.75	.30
brown		
49 John Buzhardt	.75	.30
50 Johnny Callison	1.00	.40
51 Tony Curry	.75	.30
52 Clay Dalrymple	.75	.30
brown		
53 Bobby Del Greco	.75	.30
brown		
54 Dick Farrell	.75	.30
brown		
55 Tony Gonzalez	.75	.30
56 Pancho Herrera	.75	.30
57 Art Mahaffey	.75	.30
58 Robin Roberts	5.00	2.00
brown		
59 Tony Taylor	1.00	.40
60 Lee Walls	.75	.30
61 Smoky Burgess	1.00	.40
62 Roy Face (brown)	1.25	.50
63 Bob Friend	1.00	.40
64 Dick Groat	1.50	.60
65 Don Hoak	.75	.30
66 Vern Law	1.25	.50
67 Bill Mazeroski	5.00	2.00
68 Rocky Nelson	.75	.30
69 Bob Skinner	.75	.30
70 Hal Smith	.75	.30
71 Dick Stuart	1.25	.50
72 Bill Virdon	1.25	.50
73 Don Blasingame	.75	.30
74 Eddie Bressoud	.75	.30
brown		
75 Orlando Cepeda	5.00	2.00
76 Jim Davenport	.75	.30
77 Harvey Kuenn	1.50	.60
brown		
78 Hobie Landrith	.75	.30
79 Juan Marichal	6.00	2.40
80 Willie Mays	20.00	8.00
81 Mike McCormick	1.00	.40
82 Willie McCovey	8.00	3.20
83 Billy O'Dell	.75	.30
84 Jack Sanford	.75	.30
85 Ken Boyer	1.50	.60
86 Curt Flood	1.25	.50
87 Alex Grammas	.75	.30
brown		
88 Larry Jackson	.75	.30
89 Julian Javier	.75	.30
90 Ron Kline	.75	.30
brown		
91 Lindy McDaniel	.75	.30
92 Stan Musial	15.00	6.00
93 Curt Simmons	.75	.30
brown		
94 Hal Smith	.75	.30
95 Daryl Spencer	.75	.30
96 Bill White	1.25	.50
brown		
97 Steve Barber	.75	.30
98 Jackie Brandt	.75	.30
brown		
99 Marv Breeding	.75	.30
100 Chuck Estrada	.75	.30
101 Jim Gentile	1.00	.40
102 Ron Hansen	.75	.30
103 Milt Pappas	1.00	.40
104 Brooks Robinson	8.00	3.20
105 Gene Stephens	.75	.30
106 Gus Triandos	1.00	.40
107 Hoyt Wilhelm	5.00	2.00
108 Tom Brewer	.75	.30
109 Gene Conley	.75	.30
brown		
110 Ike Delock	.75	.30
brown		
111 Gary Geiger	.75	.30
112 Jackie Jensen	1.50	.60
113 Frank Malzone	1.00	.40
114 Bill Monbouquette	.75	.30
115 Russ Nixon	.75	.30
116 Pete Runnels	1.00	.40
117 Willie Tasby	.75	.30
118 Vic Wertz	1.00	.40
brown		
119 Carl Yastrzemski	15.00	6.00
120 Luis Aparicio	5.00	2.00
121 Russ Kemmerer	.75	.30
brown		
122 Jim Landis	.75	.30
123 Sherman Lollar	.75	.30
124 J.C. Martin	.75	.30
125 Minnie Minoso	1.50	.60
126 Billy Pierce	1.25	.50
127 Bob Shaw	.75	.30

128 Roy Sievers 1.25 .50
129 Al Smith .75 .30
130 Gerry Staley .75 .30
brown
131 Early Wynn 5.00 2.00
132 Johnny Antonelli 1.00 .40
brown
133 Ken Aspromonte .75 .30
134 Tito Francona .75 .30
135 Jim Grant .75 .30
136 Woody Held .75 .30
137 Barry Latman .75 .30
138 Jim Perry 1.00 .40
139 Jimmy Piersall 1.50 .60
140 Bubba Phillips .75 .30
141 Vic Power .75 .30
142 John Romano .75 .30
143 Johnny Temple .75 .30
144 Hank Aguirre .75 .30
brown
145 Frank Bolling .75 .30
146 Steve Boros .75 .30
brown
147 Jim Bunning 5.00 2.00
brown
148 Norm Cash 1.50 .60
149 Harry Chiti .75 .30
150 Chico Fernandez .75 .30
151 Dick Gernert .75 .30
152A Al Kaline (green) 8.00 3.20
152B Al Kaline (brown) 8.00 3.20
153 Frank Lary 1.00 .40
154 Charlie Maxwell .75 .30
155 Dave Sisler .75 .30
156 Hank Bauer 1.00 .40
157 Bob Boyd (brown) .75 .30
158 Andy Carey .75 .30
159 Bud Daley .75 .30
160 Dick Hall .75 .30
161 J.C. Hartman .75 .30
162 Ray Herbert .75 .30
163 Whitey Herzog 1.50 .60
164 Jerry Lumpe .75 .30
brown
165 Norm Siebern .75 .30
166 Marv Throneberry 1.50 .60
167 Bill Tuttle .75 .30
168 Dick Williams 1.00 .40
169 Jerry Casale .75 .30
brown
170 Bob Cerv 1.00 .40
171 Ned Garver .75 .30
172 Ron Hunt .75 .30
173 Ted Kluszewski 3.00 1.20
174 Ed Sadowski .75 .30
brown
175 Eddie Yost .75 .30
176 Bob Allison 1.00 .40
177 Earl Battey .75 .30
brown
178 Reno Bertoia .75 .30
179 Billy Gardner 1.00 .40
180 Jim Kaat 3.00 1.20
181 Harmon Killebrew 6.00 2.40
182 Jim Lemon 1.00 .40
183 Camilo Pascual 1.00 .40
184 Pedro Ramos .75 .30
185 Chuck Stobbs .75 .30
186 Zoilo Versalles .75 .30
187 Pete Whisenant .75 .30
188 Luis Arroyo 1.00 .40
brown
189 Yogi Berra 12.50 5.00
190 John Blanchard 1.00 .40
191 Clete Boyer 1.50 .60
192 Art Ditmar 1.00 .40
193 Whitey Ford 12.50 5.00
194 Elston Howard 3.00 1.20
195 Tony Kubek 3.00 1.20
196 Mickey Mantle 60.00 24.00
197 Roger Maris 25.00 10.00
198 Bobby Shantz 1.25 .50
199 Bill Stafford 1.00 .40
200 Bob Turley 1.25 .50
201 Bud Daley 1.00 .40
brown
202 Dick Donovan .75 .30
203 Bobby Klaus .75 .30
204 Johnny Klippstein .75 .30
205 Dale Long 1.00 .40
206 Ray Semproch .75 .30
207 Gene Woodling 1.00 .40
XX Stamp Album 20.00 8.00

1961 Topps Dice Game

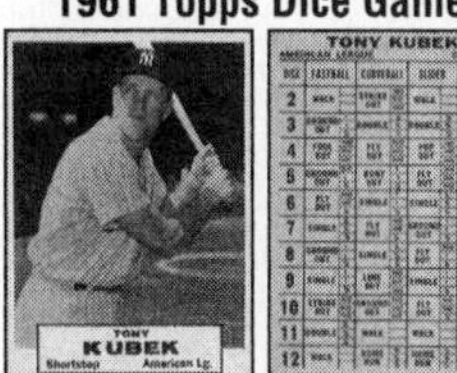

This 18-card standard-size set may never have been issued by Topps; it is considered a very obscure "test" issue and is quite scarce. The cards are printed completely in black and white on white card stock. There is no reference to Topps anywhere on the front or back of the card. The card back lays out the batter's outcome depending on the type of pitch thrown and the sum of two dice rolled. The cards are unnumbered and hence they are ordered below and assigned numbers alphabetically.

NM Ex
COMPLETE SET (18) 7000.00 2800.00
1 Earl Battey 100.00 40.00
2 Del Crandall 100.00 40.00
3 Jim Davenport 100.00 40.00
4 Don Drysdale 300.00 120.00
5 Dick Groat 120.00 47.50
6 Al Kaline 500.00 200.00
7 Tony Kubek 150.00 60.00
8 Mickey Mantle 3000.00 1200.00
9 Willie Mays 1000.00 400.00
10 Bill Mazeroski 200.00 80.00
11 Stan Musial 800.00 325.00
12 Camilo Pascual 100.00 40.00
13 Bobby Richardson 150.00 60.00
14 Brooks Robinson 500.00 200.00
15 Frank Robinson 400.00 160.00
16 Norm Siebern 100.00 40.00
17 Leon Wagner 100.00 40.00
18 Bill White 120.00 47.50

1962 Topps

The cards in this 598-card set measure 2 1/2" by 3 1/2". The 1962 Topps set contains a mini-series spotlighting Babe Ruth (135-144). Other subsets in the set include League Leaders (51-60), World Series cards (232-237), In Action cards (311-319), NL All Stars (390-399), AL All Stars (466-475), and Rookie Prospects (591-598). The All-Star selections were again provided by Sport Magazine, as in 1958 and 1960. The second series had two distinct printings which are distinguishable by numerous color and pose variations. Those cards with a distinctive "green tint" are valued at a slight premuim as they are basically the result of a flawed printing process occurring early in the second series run. Card number 139 exists as A: Babe Ruth Special card, B: Hal Reniff with arms over head, or C: Hal Reniff in the same pose as card number 159. In addition, two poses exist for these cards: 129, 132, 134, 147, 174, 176, and 190. The high number series, 523 to 598, is somewhat more difficult to obtain than other cards in the set. Within the last series (523-598) there are 43 cards which were printed in lesser quantities; these are marked SP in the checklist below. In particular, the Rookie Parade subset (591-598) of this last series is even more difficult. This was the first year Topps produced multi-player Rookie Cards. The set price listed does not include the pose variations (see checklist below for individual values). A three card ad sheet has been seen. The players on the front include AL HR leaders, Barney Schultz and Carl Sawatski, while the back features an ad and a Roger Maris card. Cards were issued in one-card penny packs as well as five-card nickel packs. The five card packs came 24 to a box. The key Rookie Cards in this set are Lou Brock, Tim McCarver, Gaylord Perry, and Bob Uecker.

NM Ex
COMP. MASTER (688) 7000.00 2800.00
COMPLETE SET (598) 6000.00 2400.00
COMMON CARD (1-370) 5.00 2.00
COMMON (371-446) 6.00 2.40
COMMON (447-522) 12.00 4.80
COMMON (523-598) 20.00 8.00
WRAPPER (1-CENT) 100.00 40.00
WRAPPER (5-CENT) 30.00 12.00
1 Roger Maris 300.00 75.00
2 Jim Brosnan 5.00 2.00
3 Pete Runnels 5.00 2.00
4 John DeMerit 8.00 3.20
5 Sandy Koufax UER 150.00 60.00
Struck ou 18
6 Marv Breeding 5.00 2.00
7 Frank Thomas 10.00 4.00
8 Ray Herbert 5.00 2.00
9 Jim Davenport 8.00 3.20
10 Roberto Clemente 175.00 70.00
11 Tom Morgan 5.00 2.00
12 Harry Craft MG 8.00 3.20
13 Dick Howser 8.00 3.20
14 Bill White 8.00 3.20
15 Dick Donovan 5.00 2.00
16 Darrell Johnson 5.00 2.00
17 Johnny Callison 8.00 3.20
18 Mickey Mantle 175.00 70.00
Willie Mays
19 Ray Washburn 5.00 2.00
20 Rocky Colavito 15.00 6.00
21 Jim Kaat 8.00 3.20
22A Checklist 1 ERR 12.00 2.40
(121-176 on back)
22B Checklist 1 COR 12.00 2.40
23 Norm Larker 5.00 2.00
24 Tigers Team 10.00 4.00
25 Ernie Banks 50.00 20.00
26 Chris Cannizzaro 8.00 3.20
27 Chuck Cottier 5.00 2.00
28 Minnie Minoso 10.00 4.00
29 Casey Stengel MG 20.00 8.00
30 Eddie Mathews 40.00 16.00
31 Tom Tresh RC 15.00 6.00
32 John Roseboro 8.00 3.20
33 Don Larsen 8.00 3.20
34 Johnny Temple 8.00 3.20
35 Don Schwall 10.00 4.00
36 Don Leppert 5.00 2.00
37 Barry Latman 5.00 2.00
Dick Stigman
Jim Perry
38 Gene Stephens 5.00 2.00
39 Joe Koppe 5.00 2.00
40 Orlando Cepeda 15.00 6.00
41 Cliff Cook 5.00 2.00
42 Jim King 5.00 2.00
43 Los Angeles Dodgers 10.00 4.00
Team Card
44 Don Taussig 5.00 2.00
45 Brooks Robinson 50.00 20.00
46 Jack Baldschun 5.00 2.00
47 Bob Will 5.00 2.00
48 Ralph Terry 8.00 3.20
49 Hal Jones 5.00 2.00
50 Stan Musial 100.00 40.00
51 Norm Cash 8.00 3.20
Jim Piersall
Al Kaline
Elston Howard LL
52 Roberto Clemente 20.00 8.00
Vada Pinson
Ken Boyer
Wally Moon LL
53 Roger Maris 100.00 40.00
Mickey Mantle
Jim Gentile
Harmon Killebrew LL
54 Orlando Cepeda 20.00 8.00
Willie Mays
Frank Robinson LL
55 Dick Donovan 8.00 3.20
Bill Stafford
Don Mossi
Milt Pappas LL
56 Warren Spahn 8.00 3.20
Jim O'Toole
Curt Simmons
Mike McCormick LL
57 Whitey Ford 8.00 3.20
Frank Lary
Steve Barber
Jim Bunning LL
58 Warren Spahn 8.00 3.20
Joe Jay
Jim O'Toole LL
59 Camilo Pascual 8.00 3.20
Whitey Ford
Jim Bunning
Juan Pizzaro LL
60 Sandy Koufax 20.00 8.00
Stan Williams
Don Drysdale
Jim O'Toole LL
61 Cardinals Team 10.00 4.00
62 Steve Boros 5.00 2.00
63 Tony Cloninger RC 8.00 3.20
64 Russ Snyder 5.00 2.00
65 Bobby Richardson 10.00 4.00
66 Cuno Barragan 5.00 2.00
67 Harvey Haddix 8.00 3.20
68 Ken Hunt 5.00 2.00
69 Phil Ortega 5.00 2.00
70 Harmon Killebrew 25.00 10.00
71 Dick LeMay 5.00 2.00
72 Steve Boros 5.00 2.00
Bob Scheffing MG
Jake Wood
73 Nellie Fox 20.00 8.00
74 Bob Lillis 8.00 3.20
75 Milt Pappas 8.00 3.20
76 Howie Bedell 5.00 2.00
77 Tony Taylor 8.00 3.20
78 Gene Green 5.00 2.00
79 Ed Hobaugh 5.00 2.00
80 Vada Pinson 8.00 3.20
81 Jim Pagliaroni 5.00 2.00
82 Deron Johnson 8.00 3.20
83 Larry Jackson 5.00 2.00
84 Lenny Green 5.00 2.00
85 Gil Hodges 20.00 8.00
86 Donn Clendenon RC 8.00 3.20
87 Mike Roarke 5.00 2.00
88 Ralph Houk MG 8.00 3.20
(Berra in background)
89 Barney Schultz 5.00 2.00
90 Jimmy Piersall 8.00 3.20
91 J.C. Martin 5.00 2.00
92 Sam Jones 5.00 2.00
93 John Blanchard 8.00 3.20
94 Jay Hook 8.00 3.20
95 Don Hoak 8.00 3.20
96 Eli Grba 5.00 2.00
97 Tito Francona 5.00 2.00
98 Checklist 2 12.00 2.40
99 John (Boog) Powell RC 30.00 12.00
100 Warren Spahn 40.00 16.00
101 Carroll Hardy 5.00 2.00
102 Al Schroll 5.00 2.00
103 Don Blasingame 5.00 2.00
104 Ted Savage 5.00 2.00
105 Don Mossi 8.00 3.20
106 Carl Sawatski 5.00 2.00
107 Mike McCormick 8.00 3.20
108 Willie Davis 8.00 3.20
109 Bob Shaw 5.00 2.00
110 Bill Skowron 8.00 3.20
110A Bill Skowron 8.00 3.20
Green Tint
111 Dallas Green 8.00 3.20
111A Dallas Green 8.00 3.20
Green Tint
112 Hank Foiles 5.00 2.00
112A Hank Foiles 5.00 2.00
Green Tint
113 Chicago White Sox 10.00 4.00
Team Card
113A Chicago White Sox 10.00 4.00
Team Card
Green Tint
114 Howie Koplitz 5.00 2.00
114A Howie Koplitz 5.00 2.00
Green Tint
115 Bob Skinner 8.00 3.20
115A Bob Skinner 8.00 3.20
Green Tint
116 Herb Score 8.00 3.20
116A Herb Score 8.00 3.20
Green Tint
117 Gary Geiger 8.00 3.20
117A Gary Geiger 8.00 3.20
Green Tint
118 Julian Javier 8.00 3.20
118A Julian Javier 8.00 3.20
Green Tint
119 Danny Murphy 5.00 2.00
119A Danny Murphy 5.00 2.00
Green Tint
120 Bob Purkey 5.00 2.00
120A Bob Purkey 5.00 2.00
Green Tint
121 Billy Hitchcock MG 5.00 2.00
121A Billy Hitchcock 5.00 2.00
Green Tint
122 Norm Bass 5.00 2.00
122A Norm Bass 5.00 2.00
Green Tint
123 Mike de la Hoz 5.00 2.00
123A Mike de la Hoz 5.00 2.00
Green Tint
124 Bill Pleis 5.00 2.00
124A Bill Pleis 5.00 2.00
Green Tint
125 Gene Woodling 8.00 3.20
125A Gene Woodling 8.00 3.20
Green Tint
126 Al Cicotte 5.00 2.00
126A Al Cicotte 5.00 2.00
Green Tint
127 Norm Siebern 5.00 2.00
Hank Bauer MG
Jerry Lumpe
127A Norm Siebern 5.00 2.00
Hank Bauer MG
Jerry Lumpe
Green Tint
128 Art Fowler 5.00 2.00
128A Art Fowler 5.00 2.00
Green Tint
129A Lee Walls 5.00 2.00
(Facing right)
129B Lee Walls 30.00 12.00
(Facing left)
130 Frank Bolling 5.00 2.00
130A Frank Bolling 5.00 2.00
Green Tint
131 Pete Richert 5.00 2.00
131A Pete Richert 5.00 2.00
Green Tint
132A Angels Team 10.00 4.00
(Without photo)
132B Angels Team 30.00 12.00
(With photo)
133 Felipe Alou 8.00 3.20
133A Felipe Alou 8.00 3.20
Green Tint
134A Billy Hoeft 5.00 2.00
134B Billy Hoeft 30.00 12.00
Green Tint
135 Babe Ruth Special 1 20.00 8.00
Babe as a Boy
135A Babe Ruth Special 20.00 8.00
Base as a Boy
136 Babe Ruth Special 2 20.00 8.00
Jacob Ruppert OWN
Babe Joins Yanks
136A Babe Ruth Special 20.00 8.00
Jacob Ruppert OWN
Babe Joins Yanks
Green Tint
137 Babe Ruth Special 3 20.00 8.00
With Miller Huggins
137A Babe Ruth Special 20.00 8.00
With Miller Huggins
Green Tint
138 Babe Ruth Special 4 20.00 8.00
Famous Slugger
138A Babe Ruth Special 20.00 8.00
Famous Slugger
Green Tint
139A Babe Ruth Special 5 30.00 12.00
Babe Hits 60
139B Hal Reniff PORT RC 15.00 6.00
139C Hal Reniff RC 60.00 24.00
Pitching
140 Babe Ruth Special 6 60.00 24.00
With Lou Gehrig
140A Babe Ruth Special 60.00 24.00
Lou Gehrig
Green Tint
141 Babe Ruth Special 7 20.00 8.00
Twilight Years
141A Babe Ruth Special 20.00 8.00
Twilight Years
Green Tint
142 Babe Ruth Special 8 20.00 8.00
Coaching Dodgers
142A Babe Ruth Special 20.00 8.00
Coaching Dodgers
Green Tint
143 Babe Ruth Special 9 20.00 8.00
Greatest Sports Hero
143A Babe Ruth Special 20.00 8.00
Greatest Sports Hero
Green Tint
144 Babe Ruth Special 10 20.00 8.00
Farewell Speech
144A Babe Ruth Special 20.00 8.00
Babe Ruth Special
Farewell Speech
145 Barry Latman 5.00 2.00
145A Barry Latman 5.00 2.00
Green Tint
146 Don Demeter 5.00 2.00
146A Don Demeter 5.00 2.00
Green Tint
147A Bill Kunkel PORT 5.00 2.00
147B Bill Kunkel 30.00 12.00
(Pitching pose)
148 Wally Post 5.00 2.00
148A Wally Post 5.00 2.00
Green Tint
149 Bob Duliba 5.00 2.00
149A Bob Duliba 5.00 2.00
Green Tint
150 Al Kaline 50.00 20.00
150A Al Kaline 50.00 20.00
Green Tint
151 Johnny Klippstein 5.00 2.00
151A Johnny Klippstein 5.00 2.00
Green Tint
152 Mickey Vernon MG 8.00 3.20
152A Mickey Vernon MG 8.00 3.20
Green Tint
153 Pumpsie Green 6.00 2.40
153A Pumpsie Green 6.00 2.40
Green Tint
154 Lee Thomas 6.00 2.40
154A Lee Thomas 6.00 2.40
Green Tint
155 Stu Miller 6.00 2.40
155A Stu Miller 6.00 2.40
Green Tint
156 Merritt Ranew 5.00 2.00
156A Merritt Ranew 5.00 2.00
Green Tint
157 Wes Covington 8.00 3.20
157A Wes Covington 8.00 3.20
Green Tint
158 Braves Team 10.00 4.00
158A Braves Team 15.00 6.00
Green Tint
159 Hal Reniff RC 8.00 3.20
160 Dick Stuart 8.00 3.20
160A Dick Stuart 8.00 3.20
Green Tint
161 Frank Baumann 5.00 2.00
161A Frank Baumann 5.00 2.00
Green Tint
162 Sammy Drake 5.00 2.00
162A Sammy Drake 5.00 2.00
Green Tint
163 Billy Gardner 8.00 3.20
Cletis Boyer
163A Billy Gardner 8.00 3.20
Clete Boyer
Green Tint
164 Hal Naragon 5.00 2.00
164A Hal Naragon 5.00 2.00
Green Tint
165 Jackie Brandt 5.00 2.00
165A Jackie Brandt 5.00 2.00
Green Tint
166 Don Lee 5.00 2.00
166A Don Lee 5.00 2.00
Green Tint
167 Tim McCarver RC 30.00 12.00
167A Tim McCarver RC 30.00 12.00
Green Tint
168 Leo Posada 5.00 2.00
168A Leo Posada 5.00 2.00
Green Tint
169 Bob Cerv 10.00 4.00
169A Bob Cerv 10.00 4.00
Green Tint
170 Ron Santo 15.00 6.00
170A Ron Santo 15.00 6.00
Green Tint
171 Dave Sisler 5.00 2.00
171A Dave Sisler 5.00 2.00
Green Tint
172 Fred Hutchinson MG 8.00 3.20
172A Fred Hutchinson MG 8.00 3.20
Green Tint
173 Chico Fernandez 5.00 2.00
173A Chico Fernandez 5.00 2.00
Green Tint
174A Carl Willey 5.00 2.00
(Capless)
174B Carl Willey 30.00 12.00
(With cap)
175 Frank Howard 10.00 4.00
175A Frank Howard 10.00 4.00
Green Tint
176A Eddie Yost PORT 5.00 2.00
176B Eddie Yost BATTING 30.00 12.00
177 Bobby Shantz 8.00 3.20
177A Bobby Shantz 8.00 3.20
Green Tint
178 Camilo Carreon 5.00 2.00
178A Camilo Carreon 5.00 2.00
Green Tint
179 Tom Sturdivant 5.00 2.00
179A Tom Sturdivant 5.00 2.00
Green Tint
180 Bob Allison 10.00 4.00
180A Bob Allison 10.00 4.00
Green Tint
181 Paul Brown 5.00 2.00
181A Paul Brown 5.00 2.00
Green Tint
182 Bob Nieman 5.00 2.00
182A Bob Nieman 5.00 2.00
Green Tint
183 Roger Craig 8.00 3.20
183A Roger Craig 8.00 3.20
Green Tint
184 Haywood Sullivan 8.00 3.20
184A Haywood Sullivan 8.00 3.20
Green Tint
185 Roland Sheldon 10.00 4.00
185A Roland Sheldon 10.00 4.00
Green Tint
186 Mack Jones 5.00 2.00
186A Mack Jones 5.00 2.00
Green Tint
187 Gene Conley 5.00 2.00
187A Gene Conley 5.00 2.00
Green Tint
188 Chuck Hiller 5.00 2.00
188A Chuck Hiller 5.00 2.00
Green Tint
189 Dick Hall 5.00 2.00
189A Dick Hall 5.00 2.00
Green Tint
190A Wally Moon PORT 8.00 3.20
190B W.Moon BATTING 30.00 12.00
191 Jim Brewer 5.00 2.00
191A Jim Brewer 5.00 2.00
Green Tint
192A Checklist 3 12.00 2.40
(Without comma)
192B Checklist 3 15.00 3.00
(Comma after
Checklist)
193 Eddie Kasko 5.00 2.00
193A Eddie Kasko 5.00 2.00
Green Tint
194 Dean Chance RC 8.00 3.20
194A Dean Chance RC 8.00 3.20
Green Tint
195 Joe Cunningham 5.00 2.00
195A Joe Cunningham 5.00 2.00
Green Tint
196 Terry Fox 5.00 2.00
196A Terry Fox 5.00 2.00
Green Tint
197 Daryl Spencer 5.00 2.00
198 Johnny Keane MG 5.00 2.00
199 Gaylord Perry RC 80.00 32.00
200 Mickey Mantle 500.00 200.00
201 Ike Delock 5.00 2.00
202 Carl Warwick 5.00 2.00
203 Jack Fisher 5.00 2.00
204 Johnny Weekly 5.00 2.00
205 Gene Freese 5.00 2.00

206 Senators Team 10.00 4.00
207 Pete Burnside 5.00 2.00
208 Billy Martin 20.00 8.00
209 Jim Fregosi RC 15.00 6.00
210 Roy Face 8.00 3.20
211 Frank Bolling 5.00 2.00
Roy McMillan
212 Jim Owens 5.00 2.00
213 Richie Ashburn 20.00 8.00
214 Dom Zanni 5.00 2.00
215 Woody Held 5.00 2.00
216 Ron Kline 5.00 2.00
217 Walter Alston MG 10.00 4.00
218 Joe Torre RC 40.00 16.00
219 Al Downing RC 8.00 3.20
220 Roy Sievers 8.00 3.20
221 Bill Short 5.00 2.00
222 Jerry Zimmerman 5.00 2.00
223 Alex Grammas 5.00 2.00
224 Don Rudolph 5.00 2.00
225 Frank Malzone 8.00 3.20
226 San Francisco Giants 10.00 4.00
Team Card
227 Bob Tiefenauer 5.00 2.00
228 Dale Long 10.00 4.00
229 Jesus McFarlane 5.00 2.00
230 Camilo Pascual 8.00 3.20
231 Ernie Bowman 5.00 2.00
232 World Series Game 1 10.00 4.00
Yanks win opener
233 Joey Jay WS 10.00 4.00
234 Roger Maris WS 25.00 10.00
235 Whitey Ford WS 15.00 6.00
sets new mark
236 World Series Game 5 10.00 4.00
Yanks crush Reds
237 WS Summary 10.00 4.00
Yanks celebrate
238 Norm Sherry 5.00 2.00
239 Cecil Butler 5.00 2.00
240 George Altman 5.00 2.00
241 Johnny Kucks 5.00 2.00
242 Mel McGaha MG 5.00 2.00
243 Robin Roberts 15.00 6.00
244 Don Gile 5.00 2.00
245 Ron Hansen 5.00 2.00
246 Art Ditmar 5.00 2.00
247 Joe Pignatano 5.00 2.00
248 Bob Aspromonte 8.00 3.20
249 Ed Keegan 5.00 2.00
250 Norm Cash 10.00 4.00
251 New York Yankees 50.00 20.00
Team Card
252 Earl Francis 5.00 2.00
253 Harry Chiti CO 5.00 2.00
254 Gordon Windhorn 5.00 2.00
255 Juan Pizarro 5.00 2.00
256 Elio Chacon 8.00 3.20
257 Jack Spring 5.00 2.00
258 Marty Keough 5.00 2.00
259 Lou Klimchock 5.00 2.00
260 Billy Pierce 8.00 3.20
261 George Alusik 5.00 2.00
262 Bob Schmidt 5.00 2.00
263 Bob Purkey 5.00 2.00
Jim Turner CO
Joe Jay
264 Dick Ellsworth 8.00 3.20
265 Joe Adcock 8.00 3.20
266 John Anderson 5.00 2.00
267 Dan Dobbek 5.00 2.00
268 Ken McBride 5.00 2.00
269 Bob Oldis 5.00 2.00
270 Dick Groat 8.00 3.20
271 Ray Rippelmeyer 5.00 2.00
272 Earl Robinson 5.00 2.00
273 Gary Bell 5.00 2.00
274 Sammy Taylor 5.00 2.00
275 Norm Siebern 5.00 2.00
276 Hal Kolstad 5.00 2.00
277 Checklist 4 15.00 3.00
278 Ken Johnson 8.00 3.20
279 Hobie Landrith UER 8.00 3.20
(Wrong birthdate)
280 Johnny Podres 8.00 3.20
281 Jake Gibbs 10.00 4.00
282 Dave Hillman 5.00 2.00
283 Charlie Smith 5.00 2.00
284 Ruben Amaro 5.00 2.00
285 Curt Simmons 8.00 3.20
286 Al Lopez MG 10.00 4.00
287 George Witt 5.00 2.00
288 Billy Williams 30.00 12.00
289 Mike Krsnich 5.00 2.00
290 Jim Gentile 8.00 3.20
291 Hal Stowe 5.00 2.00
292 Jerry Kindall 5.00 2.00
293 Bob Miller 8.00 3.20
294 Phillies Team 10.00 4.00
295 Vern Law 8.00 3.20
296 Ken Hamlin 5.00 2.00
297 Ron Perranoski 8.00 3.20
298 Bill Tuttle 5.00 2.00
299 Don Wert 5.00 2.00
300 Willie Mays 200.00 80.00
301 Galen Cisco RC 5.00 2.00
302 Johnny Edwards 5.00 2.00
303 Frank Torre 8.00 3.20
304 Dick Farrell 8.00 3.20
305 Jerry Lumpe 5.00 2.00
306 Lindy McDaniel 5.00 2.00
Larry Jackson
307 Jim Grant 8.00 3.20
308 Neil Chrisley 8.00 3.20
309 Moe Morhardt 5.00 2.00
310 Whitey Ford 50.00 20.00
311 Tony Kubek IA 8.00 3.20
312 Warren Spahn IA 15.00 6.00
313 Roger Maris IA 80.00 32.00
Blasts 61th
314 Rocky Colavito IA 8.00 3.20
315 Whitey Ford IA 15.00 6.00
316 Harmon Killebrew IA 15.00 6.00
317 Stan Musial IA 20.00 8.00
318 Mickey Mantle IA 150.00 60.00
319 Mike McCormick IA 5.00 2.00
320 Hank Aaron 150.00 60.00
321 Lee Stange 5.00 2.00
322 Alvin Dark MG 8.00 3.20
323 Don Landrum 5.00 2.00
324 Joe McClain 5.00 2.00
325 Luis Aparicio 15.00 6.00
326 Tom Parsons 5.00 2.00
327 Ozzie Virgil 5.00 2.00
328 Ken Walters 5.00 2.00
329 Bob Bolin 5.00 2.00
330 John Romano 5.00 2.00
331 Moe Drabowsky 8.00 3.20
332 Don Buddin 5.00 2.00
333 Frank Cipriani 5.00 2.00
334 Boston Red Sox 10.00 4.00
Team Card
335 Bill Bruton 5.00 2.00
336 Billy Muffett 5.00 2.00
337 Jim Marshall 8.00 3.20
338 Billy Gardner 5.00 2.00
339 Jose Valdivielso 5.00 2.00
340 Don Drysdale 50.00 20.00
341 Mike Hershberger 5.00 2.00
342 Ed Rakow 5.00 2.00
343 Albie Pearson 8.00 3.20
344 Ed Bauta 5.00 2.00
345 Chuck Schilling 5.00 2.00
346 Jack Kralick 5.00 2.00
347 Chuck Hinton 5.00 2.00
348 Larry Burright 8.00 3.20
349 Paul Foytack 5.00 2.00
350 Frank Robinson 50.00 20.00
351 Joe Torre 8.00 3.20
Del Crandall
352 Frank Sullivan 5.00 2.00
353 Bill Mazeroski 15.00 6.00
354 Roman Mejias 8.00 3.20
355 Steve Barber 5.00 2.00
356 Tom Haller RC 5.00 2.00
357 Jerry Walker 5.00 2.00
358 Tommy Davis 8.00 3.20
359 Bobby Locke 5.00 2.00
360 Yogi Berra 80.00 32.00
361 Bob Hendley 5.00 2.00
362 Ty Cline 5.00 2.00
363 Bob Roselli 5.00 2.00
364 Ken Hunt 5.00 2.00
365 Charlie Neal 8.00 3.20
366 Phil Regan 8.00 3.20
367 Checklist 5 15.00 3.00
368 Bob Tillman 5.00 2.00
369 Ted Bowsfield 5.00 2.00
370 Ken Boyer 10.00 4.00
371 Earl Battey 6.00 2.40
372 Jack Curtis 6.00 2.40
373 Al Heist 6.00 2.40
374 Gene Mauch MG 10.00 4.00
375 Ron Fairly 10.00 4.00
376 Bud Daley 8.00 3.20
377 John Orsino 6.00 2.40
378 Bennie Daniels 6.00 2.40
379 Chuck Essegian 6.00 2.40
380 Lou Burdette 10.00 4.00
381 Chico Cardenas 10.00 4.00
382 Dick Williams 8.00 3.20
383 Ray Sadecki 6.00 2.40
384 K.C. Athletics 10.00 4.00
Team Card
385 Early Wynn 15.00 6.00
386 Don Mincher 8.00 3.20
387 Lou Brock RC 125.00 50.00
388 Ryne Duren 8.00 3.20
389 Smoky Burgess 10.00 4.00
390 Orlando Cepeda AS 10.00 4.00
391 Bill Mazeroski AS 10.00 4.00
392 Ken Boyer AS UER 8.00 3.20
Batting Average mistakenly listed as .392
393 Roy McMillan AS 6.00 2.40
394 Hank Aaron AS 50.00 20.00
395 Willie Mays AS 50.00 20.00
396 Frank Robinson AS 15.00 6.00
397 John Roseboro AS 6.00 2.40
398 Don Drysdale AS 15.00 6.00
399 Warren Spahn AS 15.00 6.00
400 Elston Howard 10.00 4.00
401 Roger Maris 60.00 24.00
Orlando Cepeda
402 Gino Cimoli 6.00 2.40
403 Chet Nichols 6.00 2.40
404 Tim Harkness 8.00 3.20
405 Jim Perry 8.00 3.20
406 Bob Taylor 6.00 2.40
407 Hank Aguirre 6.00 2.40
408 Gus Bell 8.00 3.20
409 Pittsburgh Pirates 10.00 4.00
Team Card
410 Al Smith 6.00 2.40
411 Danny O'Connell 6.00 2.40
412 Charlie James 6.00 2.40
413 Matty Alou 10.00 4.00
414 Joe Gaines 6.00 2.40
415 Bill Virdon 10.00 4.00
416 Bob Scheffing MG 6.00 2.40
417 Joe Azcue 6.00 2.40
418 Andy Carey 6.00 2.40
419 Bob Bruce 8.00 3.20
420 Gus Triandos 8.00 3.20
421 Ken MacKenzie 8.00 3.20
422 Steve Bilko 6.00 2.40
423 Roy Face 10.00 4.00
Hoyt Wilhelm
424 Al McBean RC 6.00 2.40
425 Carl Yastrzemski 125.00 50.00
426 Bob Farley 6.00 2.40
427 Jake Wood 6.00 2.40
428 Joe Hicks 6.00 2.40
429 Billy O'Dell 6.00 2.40
430 Tony Kubek 15.00 6.00
431 Bob Rodgers RC 8.00 3.20
432 Jim Pendleton 6.00 2.40
433 Jim Archer 6.00 2.40
434 Clay Dalrymple 6.00 2.40
435 Larry Sherry 8.00 3.20
436 Felix Mantilla 8.00 3.20
437 Ray Moore 6.00 2.40
438 Dick Brown 6.00 2.40
439 Jerry Buchek 6.00 2.40
440 Joey Jay 6.00 2.40
441 Checklist 6 15.00 6.00
442 Wes Stock 6.00 2.40
443 Del Crandall 8.00 3.20
444 Ted Wills 6.00 2.40
445 Vic Power 8.00 3.20
446 Don Elston 6.00 2.40
447 Willie Kirkland 12.00 4.80
448 Joe Gibbon 12.00 4.80
449 Jerry Adair 12.00 4.80
450 Jim O'Toole 15.00 6.00
451 Jose Tartabull RC 15.00 6.00
452 Earl Averill Jr. 12.00 4.80
453 Cal McLish 12.00 4.80
454 Floyd Robinson 12.00 4.80
455 Luis Arroyo 15.00 6.00
456 Joe Amalfitano 15.00 6.00
457 Lou Clinton 12.00 4.80
458A Bob Buhl 15.00 6.00
(Braves emblem on cap)
458B Bob Buhl 50.00 20.00
(No emblem on cap)
459 Ed Bailey 12.00 4.80
460 Jim Bunning 20.00 8.00
461 Ken Hubbs RC 30.00 12.00
462A Willie Tasby 12.00 4.80
(Senators emblem on cap)
462B Willie Tasby 50.00 20.00
(No emblem on cap)
463 Hank Bauer MG 15.00 6.00
464 Al Jackson RC 12.00 4.80
465 Reds Team 20.00 8.00
466 Norm Cash AS 15.00 6.00
467 Chuck Schilling AS 12.00 4.80
468 Brooks Robinson AS 25.00 10.00
469 Luis Aparicio AS 15.00 6.00
470 Al Kaline AS 25.00 10.00
471 Mickey Mantle AS 200.00 80.00
472 Rocky Colavito AS 15.00 6.00
473 Elston Howard AS 15.00 6.00
474 Frank Lary AS 12.00 4.80
475 Whitey Ford AS 20.00 8.00
476 Orioles Team 20.00 8.00
477 Andre Rodgers 12.00 4.80
478 Don Zimmer 20.00 8.00
Shown with Mets cap, but listed with Cincinnati
479 Joel Horlen RC 12.00 4.80
480 Harvey Kuenn 15.00 6.00
481 Vic Wertz 15.00 6.00
482 Sam Mele MG 12.00 4.80
483 Don McMahon 12.00 4.80
484 Dick Schofield 12.00 4.80
485 Pedro Ramos 12.00 4.80
486 Jim Gilliam 15.00 6.00
487 Jerry Lynch 12.00 4.80
488 Hal Brown 12.00 4.80
489 Julio Gotay 12.00 4.80
490 Clete Boyer UER 15.00 6.00
Reversed Negative
491 Leon Wagner 12.00 4.80
492 Hal W. Smith 15.00 6.00
493 Danny McDevitt 12.00 4.80
494 Sammy White 12.00 4.80
495 Don Cardwell 12.00 4.80
496 Wayne Causey 12.00 4.80
497 Ed Bouchee 15.00 6.00
498 Jim Donohue 12.00 4.80
499 Zoilo Versalles 15.00 6.00
500 Duke Snider 60.00 24.00
501 Claude Osteen 15.00 6.00
502 Hector Lopez 15.00 6.00
503 Danny Murtaugh MG 15.00 6.00
504 Eddie Bressoud 12.00 4.80
505 Juan Marichal 40.00 16.00
506 Charlie Maxwell 15.00 6.00
507 Ernie Broglio 15.00 6.00
508 Gordy Coleman 15.00 6.00
509 Dave Giusti RC 15.00 6.00
510 Jim Lemon 12.00 4.80
511 Bubba Phillips 12.00 4.80
512 Mike Fornieles 12.00 4.80
513 Whitey Herzog 15.00 6.00
514 Sherm Lollar 15.00 6.00
515 Stan Williams 15.00 6.00
516A Checklist 7 15.00 3.00
White Boxes
516B Checklist 7 15.00 6.00
Yellow Boxes
517 Dave Wickersham 12.00 4.80
518 Lee Maye 12.00 4.80
519 Bob Johnson 12.00 4.80
520 Bob Friend 15.00 6.00
521 Jacke Davis UER 12.00 4.80
(Listed as OF on front and P on back)
522 Lindy McDaniel 15.00 6.00
523 Russ Nixon SP 30.00 12.00
524 Howie Nunn SP 30.00 12.00
525 George Thomas 20.00 8.00
526 Hal Woodeshick SP 30.00 12.00
527 Dick McAuliffe RC 30.00 12.00
528 Turk Lown 20.00 8.00
529 John Schaive SP 30.00 12.00
530 Bob Gibson SP 125.00 50.00
531 Bobby G. Smith 20.00 8.00
532 Dick Stigman 20.00 8.00
533 Charley Lau SP 30.00 12.00
534 Tony Gonzalez SP 30.00 12.00
535 Ed Roebuck 20.00 8.00
536 Dick Gernert 20.00 8.00
537 Cleveland Indians 50.00 20.00
Team Card
538 Jack Sanford 20.00 8.00
539 Billy Moran 20.00 8.00
540 Jim Landis SP 30.00 12.00
541 Don Nottebart SP 30.00 12.00
542 Dave Philley 20.00 8.00
543 Bob Allen SP 30.00 12.00
544 Willie McCovey SP 125.00 50.00
545 Hoyt Wilhelm SP 50.00 20.00
546 Moe Thacker SP 30.00 12.00
547 Don Ferrarese 20.00 8.00
548 Bobby Del Greco 20.00 8.00
549 Bill Rigney MG SP 30.00 12.00
550 Art Mahaffey SP 30.00 12.00
551 Harry Bright 20.00 8.00
552 Chicago Cubs SP 50.00 20.00
Team Card
553 Jim Coates 30.00 12.00
554 Bubba Morton SP 30.00 12.00
555 John Buzhardt SP 30.00 12.00
556 Al Spangler 20.00 8.00
557 Bob Anderson SP 30.00 12.00
558 John Goryl 20.00 8.00
559 Mike Higgins MG 20.00 8.00
560 Chuck Estrada SP 30.00 12.00
561 Gene Oliver SP 30.00 12.00
562 Bill Henry 20.00 8.00
563 Ken Aspromonte 20.00 8.00
564 Bob Grim 20.00 8.00
565 Jose Pagan 20.00 8.00
566 Marty Kutyna SP 30.00 12.00
567 Tracy Stallard SP 30.00 12.00
568 Jim Golden 20.00 8.00
569 Ed Sadowski SP 30.00 12.00
570 Bill Stafford SP 30.00 12.00
571 Billy Klaus SP 30.00 12.00
572 Bob G. Miller SP 30.00 12.00
573 Johnny Logan 20.00 8.00
574 Dean Stone 20.00 8.00
575 Red Schoendienst SP 50.00 20.00
576 Russ Kemmerer SP 30.00 12.00
577 Dave Nicholson SP 30.00 12.00
578 Jim Duffalo 20.00 8.00
579 Jim Schaffer SP 30.00 12.00
580 Bill Monbouquette 20.00 8.00
581 Mel Roach 20.00 8.00
582 Ron Piche 20.00 8.00
583 Larry Osborne 20.00 8.00
584 Minnesota Twins SP 60.00 24.00
Team Card
585 Glen Hobbie SP 30.00 12.00
586 Sammy Esposito SP 30.00 12.00
587 Frank Funk SP 30.00 12.00
588 Birdie Tebbetts MG 20.00 8.00
589 Bob Turley 30.00 12.00
590 Curt Flood 30.00 12.00
591 Sam McDowell RC 80.00 32.00
Ron Taylor
Ron Nischwitz
Art Quirk
Dick Radatz SP
592 Dan Pfister 80.00 32.00
Bo Belinsky
Dave Stenhouse
Jim Bouton RC
Joe Bonikowski SP
593 Jack Lamabe 50.00 20.00
Craig Anderson
Jack Hamilton
Bob Moorhead
Bob Veale SP
594 Doc Edwards 80.00 32.00
Ken Retzer
Bob Uecker RC
Doug Camilli
Don Pavletich SP
595 Bob Sadowski 50.00 20.00
Felix Torres
Marlan Coughtry
Ed Charles SP
596 Bernie Allen 80.00 32.00
Joe Pepitone RC
Phil Linz
Rich Rollins SP
597 Jim McKnight 50.00 20.00
Rod Kanehl
Amado Samuel
Denis Menke RC SP
598 Al Luplow 80.00 23.00
Manny Jimenez
Howie Goss
Jim Hickman
Ed Olivares SP

1962 Topps Bucks

There are 96 "Baseball Bucks" in this unusual set released in its own one-cent package in 1962. Each "buck" measures 1 3/4" by 4 1/8". Each depicts a player with accompanying biography and facsimile autograph to the left. To the right is found a drawing of the player's home stadium. His team and position are listed under the ribbon design containing his name. The team affiliation and league are also indicated within circles on the reverse.

	NM	Ex
COMPLETE SET (96)	1250.00	500.00
WRAPPER (1-CENT)	50.00	20.00
1 Hank Aaron	60.00	24.00
2 Joe Adcock	6.00	2.40
3 George Altman	5.00	2.00
4 Jim Archer	5.00	2.00
5 Richie Ashburn	25.00	10.00
6 Ernie Banks	35.00	14.00
7 Earl Battey	5.00	2.00
8 Gus Bell	5.00	2.00
9 Yogi Berra	40.00	16.00
10 Ken Boyer	8.00	3.20
11 Jackie Brandt	5.00	2.00
12 Jim Bunning	25.00	10.00
13 Lew Burdette	6.00	2.40
14 Don Cardwell	5.00	2.00
15 Norm Cash	8.00	3.20
16 Orlando Cepeda	20.00	8.00
17 Roberto Clemente	100.00	40.00
18 Rocky Colavito	15.00	6.00
19 Chuck Cottier	5.00	2.00
20 Roger Craig	6.00	2.40
21 Bennie Daniels	5.00	2.00
22 Don Demeter	5.00	2.00
23 Don Drysdale	30.00	12.00
24 Chuck Estrada	5.00	2.00
25 Dick Farrell	5.00	2.00
26 Whitey Ford	40.00	16.00
27 Nellie Fox	25.00	10.00
28 Tito Francona	5.00	2.00
29 Bob Friend	5.00	2.00
30 Jim Gentile	6.00	2.40
31 Dick Gernert	5.00	2.00
32 Lenny Green	5.00	2.00
33 Dick Groat	6.00	2.40
34 Woodie Held	5.00	2.00
35 Don Hoak	5.00	2.00
36 Gil Hodges	25.00	10.00
37 Elston Howard	15.00	6.00
38 Frank Howard	8.00	3.20
39 Dick Howser	6.00	2.40
40 Ken Hunt	5.00	2.00
41 Larry Jackson	5.00	2.00
42 Joey Jay	5.00	2.00
43 Al Kaline	35.00	14.00
44 Harmon Killebrew	25.00	10.00
45 Sandy Koufax	60.00	24.00
46 Harvey Kuenn	6.00	2.40
47 Jim Landis	5.00	2.00
48 Norm Larker	5.00	2.00
49 Frank Lary	5.00	2.00
50 Jerry Lumpe	5.00	2.00
51 Art Mahaffey	5.00	2.00
52 Frank Malzone	5.00	2.00
53 Felix Mantilla	5.00	2.00
54 Mickey Mantle	200.00	80.00
55 Roger Maris	50.00	20.00
56 Eddie Mathews	25.00	10.00
57 Willie Mays	65.00	26.00
58 Ken McBride	5.00	2.00
59 Mike McCormick	5.00	2.00
60 Stu Miller	5.00	2.00
61 Minnie Minoso	8.00	3.20
62 Wally Moon	6.00	2.40
63 Stan Musial	60.00	24.00
64 Danny O'Connell	5.00	2.00
65 Jim O'Toole	5.00	2.00
66 Camilo Pascual	5.00	2.00
67 Jim Perry	6.00	2.40
68 Jimmy Piersall	6.00	2.40
69 Vada Pinson	8.00	3.20
70 Juan Pizarro	5.00	2.00
71 Johnny Podres	6.00	2.40
72 Vic Power	5.00	2.00
73 Bob Purkey	5.00	2.00
74 Pedro Ramos	5.00	2.00
75 Brooks Robinson	35.00	14.00
76 Floyd Robinson	5.00	2.00
77 Frank Robinson	35.00	14.00
78 John Romano	5.00	2.00
79 Pete Runnels	5.00	2.00
80 Don Schwall	5.00	2.00
81 Bobby Shantz	5.00	2.00
82 Norm Siebern	5.00	2.00
83 Roy Sievers	5.00	2.00
84 Hal Smith	5.00	2.00
85 Warren Spahn	25.00	10.00
86 Dick Stuart	6.00	2.40
87 Tony Taylor	5.00	2.00
88 Lee Thomas	6.00	2.40
89 Gus Triandos	5.00	2.00
90 Leon Wagner	5.00	2.00
91 Jerry Walker	5.00	2.00
92 Bill White	8.00	3.20
93 Billy Williams	25.00	10.00
94 Gene Woodling	6.00	2.40
95 Early Wynn	25.00	10.00
96 Carl Yastrzemski	35.00	14.00

1962 Topps Stamps Inserts

The 201 baseball player stamps inserted into the Topps regular issue of 1962 are color photos set upon red or yellow backgrounds (100 players for each color). They came in two-stamp panels with a small additional strip which contained advertising for an album. Roy Sievers appears with Kansas City or Philadelphia; the set price includes both versions. Each stamp measures 1 3/8" by 1 7/8". Stamps are unnumbered but are presented here in alphabetical order by team, Baltimore Orioles AL (1-10), Boston Red Sox (11-20), Chicago White Sox (21-30), Cleveland Indians (31-40), Detroit Tigers (41-50), Kansas City A's (51-61), Los Angeles Angels (62-71), Minnesota Twins (72-81), New York Yankees (82-91), Washington Senators (92-101), Chicago Cubs NL (102-111), Cincinnati Reds (112-121), Houston Colt .45's (122-131), Los Angeles Dodgers (132-141), Milwaukee Braves (142-151), New York Mets (152-161), Philadelphia Phillies (162-171), Pittsburgh Pirates (172-181), St. Louis Cardinals (182-191) and San Francisco Giants (192-201).

	NM	Ex
COMPLETE SET (201)	400.00	160.00
1 Baltimore Emblem	.75	.30
2 Jerry Adair	.75	.30
3 Jackie Brandt	.75	.30
4 Chuck Estrada	.75	.30
5 Jim Gentile	1.00	.40
6 Ron Hansen	.75	.30
7 Milt Pappas	1.00	.40
8 Brooks Robinson	8.00	3.20
9 Gus Triandos	1.00	.40
10 Hoyt Wilhelm	5.00	2.00
11 Boston Emblem	.75	.30
12 Mike Fornieles	.75	.30
13 Gary Geiger	.75	.30
14 Frank Malzone	1.00	.40
15 Bill Monbouquette	.75	.30
16 Russ Nixon	.75	.30
17 Pete Runnels	1.00	.40
18 Chuck Schilling	.75	.30
19 Don Schwall	.75	.30
20 Carl Yastrzemski	12.50	5.00
21 Chicago Emblem	.75	.30
22 Luis Aparicio	5.00	2.00
23 Camilo Carreon	.75	.30
24 Nellie Fox	5.00	2.00
25 Ray Herbert	.75	.30
26 Jim Landis	.75	.30
27 J.C. Martin	.75	.30

28 Juan Pizzaro .75 .30
29 Floyd Robinson .75 .30
30 Early Wynn 5.00 2.00
31 Cleveland Emblem .75 .30
32 Ty Cline .75 .30
33 Dick Donovan .75 .30
34 Tito Francona .75 .30
35 Woody Held .75 .30
36 Barry Latman .75 .30
37 Jim Perry 1.00 .40
38 Bubba Phillips .75 .30
39 Vic Power .75 .30
40 Johnny Romano .75 .30
41 Detroit Emblem .75 .30
42 Steve Boros .75 .30
43 Bill Bruton .75 .30
44 Jim Bunning 5.00 2.00
45 Norm Cash 1.50 .60
46 Rocky Colavito 5.00 2.00
47 Al Kaline 8.00 3.20
48 Frank Lary 1.00 .40
49 Don Mossi 1.00 .40
50 Jake Wood .75 .30
51 Kansas City Emblem .75 .30
52 Jim Archer .75 .30
53 Dick Howser 1.50 .60
54 Jerry Lumpe .75 .30
55 Leo Posada .75 .30
56 Bob Shaw .75 .30
57 Norm Siebern .75 .30
58 Roy Sievers 1.50 .60
(A's, see also 169
59 Gene Stephens .75 .30
60 Haywood Sullivan .75 .30
61 Jerry Walker .75 .30
62 Los Angeles Emblem .75 .30
63 Steve Bilko .75 .30
64 Ted Bowsfield .75 .30
65 Ken Hunt .75 .30
66 Ken McBride .75 .30
67 Albie Pearson .75 .30
68 Bob Rodgers 1.00 .40
69 George Thomas .75 .30
70 Lee Thomas 1.00 .40
71 Leon Wagner .75 .30
72 Minnesota Emblem .75 .30
73 Bob Allison 1.00 .40
74 Earl Battey .75 .30
75 Lenny Green .75 .30
76 Harmon Killebrew 6.00 2.40
77 Jack Kralick .75 .30
78 Camilo Pascual 1.00 .40
79 Pedro Ramos .75 .30
80 Bill Tuttle .75 .30
81 Zoilo Versailles .75 .30
82 New York Emblem 1.00 .40
83 Yogi Berra 12.50 5.00
84 Clete Boyer 1.25 .50
85 Whitey Ford 10.00 4.00
86 Elston Howard 3.00 1.20
87 Tony Kubek 3.00 1.20
88 Mickey Mantle 60.00 24.00
89 Roger Maris 20.00 8.00
90 Bobby Richardson 3.00 1.20
91 Bill Skowron 1.50 .60
92 Washington Emblem .75 .30
93 Chuck Cottier .75 .30
94 Pete Daley .75 .30
95 Bennie Daniels .75 .30
96 Chuck Hinton .75 .30
97 Bob Johnson .75 .30
98 Joe McClain .75 .30
99 Danny O'Connell .75 .30
100 Jimmy Piersall 1.50 .60
101 Gene Woodling 1.00 .40
102 Chicago Emblem .75 .30
103 George Altman .75 .30
104 Ernie Banks 8.00 3.20
105 Dick Bertell .75 .30
106 Don Cardwell .75 .30
107 Dick Ellsworth .75 .30
108 Glen Hobbie .75 .30
109 Ron Santo 1.50 .60
110 Barney Schultz .75 .30
111 Billy Williams 5.00 2.00
112 Cincinnati Emblem .75 .30
113 Gordon Coleman .75 .30
114 Johnny Edwards .75 .30
115 Gene Freese .75 .30
116 Joey Jay .75 .30
117 Eddie Kasko .75 .30
118 Jim O'Toole .75 .30
119 Vada Pinson 1.50 .60
120 Bob Purkey .75 .30
121 Frank Robinson 8.00 3.20
122 Houston Emblem .75 .30
123 Joe Amalfitano .75 .30
124 Bob Aspromonte .75 .30
125 Dick Farrell .75 .30
126 Al Heist .75 .30
127 Sam Jones .75 .30
128 Bobby Shantz 1.00 .40
129 Hal W. Smith .75 .30
130 Al Spangler .75 .30
131 Bob Tiefenauer .75 .30
132 Los Angeles Emblem .75 .30
133 Don Drysdale 6.00 2.40
134 Ron Fairly 1.00 .40
135 Frank Howard 1.50 .60
136 Sandy Koufax 15.00 6.00
137 Wally Moon 1.00 .40
138 Johnny Podres 1.50 .60
139 John Roseboro .75 .30
140 Duke Snider 10.00 4.00
141 Daryl Spencer .75 .30
142 Milwaukee Emblem .75 .30
143 Hank Aaron 15.00 6.00
144 Joe Adcock 1.00 .40
145 Frank Bolling .75 .30
146 Lou Burdette 1.50 .60
147 Del Crandall .75 .30
148 Eddie Mathews 6.00 2.40
149 Roy McMillan .75 .30
150 Warren Spahn 8.00 3.20
151 Joe Torre 3.00 1.20
152 New York Emblem 1.00 .40
153 Gus Bell 1.00 .40
154 Roger Craig 1.50 .60
155 Gil Hodges 6.00 2.40
156 Jay Hook 1.00 .40
157 Hobie Landrith 1.00 .40
158 Felix Mantilla 1.00 .40
159 Bob L. Miller 1.00 .40
160 Lee Walls 1.00 .40
161 Don Zimmer 1.50 .60
162 Philadelphia Emblem .75 .30
163 Ruben Amaro .75 .30
164 Jack Baldschun .75 .30
165 Johnny Callison UER 1.00 .40
Name spelled Callizon
166 Clay Dalrymple .75 .30
167 Don Demeter .75 .30
168 Tony Gonzalez .75 .30
169 Roy Sievers 1.50 .60
Phils, see also 58
170 Tony Taylor 1.00 .40
171 Art Mahaffey .75 .30
172 Pittsburgh Emblem .75 .30
173 Smoky Burgess 1.00 .40
174 Roberto Clemente 40.00 16.00
175 Roy Face 1.50 .60
176 Bob Friend 1.00 .40
177 Dick Groat 1.50 .60
178 Don Hoak .75 .30
179 Bill Mazeroski 5.00 2.00
180 Dick Stuart 1.25 .50
181 Bill Virdon 1.50 .60
182 St. Louis Emblem .75 .30
183 Ken Boyer 1.50 .60
184 Larry Jackson .75 .30
185 Julian Javier .75 .30
186 Tim McCarver 3.00 1.20
187 Lindy McDaniel .75 .30
188 Minnie Minoso 1.50 .60
189 Stan Musial 15.00 6.00
190 Ray Sadecki .75 .30
191 Bill White 1.50 .60
192 S.F. Emblem .75 .30
193 Felipe Alou 1.25 .50
194 Ed Bailey .75 .30
195 Orlando Cepeda 5.00 2.00
196 Jim Davenport .75 .30
197 Harvey Kuenn 1.50 .60
198 Juan Marichal 5.00 2.00
199 Willie Mays 18.00 7.25
200 Mike McCormick 1.00 .40
201 Stu Miller .75 .30
NNO Stamp Album 20.00 8.00

1962 Topps Venezuelan

These 198 cards are parallel to the first 198 cards of the regular 1962 Topps set. They were issued for the Venezuelan market and are printed in Spanish. Also note this is not quite an exact parallel as cards numbered 197 and 198 were not printed but were replaced by Elio Chacon and Luis Aparicio as cards numbered 199 and 200. Both Chacon and Aparicio were natives of Venezuela.

NM Ex
COMPLETE SET (198) 5500.00 2200.00
1 Roger Maris 500.00 125.00
2 Jim Brosnan 10.00 4.00
3 Pete Runnels 10.00 4.00
4 John DeMerit 10.00 4.00
5 Sandy Koufax UER 500.00 200.00
(Struck ou 18)
6 Marv Breeding 10.00 4.00
7 Frank Thomas 10.00 4.00
8 Ray Herbert 10.00 4.00
9 Jim Davenport 10.00 4.00
10 Roberto Clemente 600.00 240.00
11 Tom Morgan 10.00 4.00
12 Harry Craft MG 10.00 4.00
13 Dick Howser 10.00 4.00
14 Bill White 15.00 6.00
15 Dick Donovan 10.00 4.00
16 Darrell Johnson 10.00 4.00
17 John Callison 10.00 4.00
18 Mickey Mantle 500.00 200.00
Willie Mays
19 Ray Washburn 10.00 4.00
20 Rocky Colavito 50.00 20.00
21 Jim Kaat 30.00 12.00
22 Checklist 1 25.00 5.00
23 Norm Larker 10.00 4.00
24 Tigers Team 20.00 8.00
25 Ernie Banks 120.00 47.50
26 Chris Cannizzaro 10.00 4.00
27 Chuck Cottier 10.00 4.00
28 Minnie Minoso 20.00 8.00
29 Casey Stengel MG 50.00 20.00
30 Eddie Mathews 60.00 24.00
31 Tom Tresh RC 40.00 16.00
32 John Roseboro 10.00 4.00
33 Don Larsen 15.00 6.00
34 Johnny Temple 10.00 4.00
35 Don Schwall 10.00 4.00
36 Don Leppert 10.00 4.00
37 Barry Latman 10.00 4.00
Dick Stigman
Jim Perry
38 Gene Stephens 10.00 4.00
39 Joe Koppe 10.00 4.00
40 Orlando Cepeda 40.00 16.00
41 Cliff Cook 10.00 4.00
42 Jim King 10.00 4.00
43 Los Angeles Dodgers 20.00 8.00
Team Card
44 Don Taussig 10.00 4.00
45 Brooks Robinson 120.00 47.50
46 Jack Baldschun 10.00 4.00
47 Bob Will 10.00 4.00
48 Ralph Terry 10.00 4.00
49 Hal Jones 10.00 4.00
50 Stan Musial 250.00 100.00
51 Norm Cash 15.00 6.00
Jim Piersall
Al Kaline
Elston Howard LL
52 Bob Clemente 30.00 12.00
Vada Pinson
Ken Boyer
Wally Moon LL
53 Roger Maris 250.00 100.00
Mickey Mantle
Jim Gentile
Harmon Killebrew LL
54 Orlando Cepeda 40.00 16.00
Willie Mays
Frank Robinson LL
55 Dick Donovan 15.00 6.00
Bill Stafford
Don Mossi
Milt Pappas LL
56 Warren Spahn 15.00 6.00
Jim O'Toole
Curt Simmons
Mike McCormick LL
57 Whitey Ford 15.00 6.00
Frank Lary
Steve Barber
Jim Bunning LL
58 Warren Spahn 15.00 6.00
Joe Jay
Jim O'Toole LL
59 Camilo Pascual 15.00 6.00
Whitey Ford
Jim Bunning
Juan Pizzaro LL
60 Sandy Koufax 25.00 10.00
Stan Williams
Don Drysdale
Jim O'Toole LL
61 Cardinals Team 20.00 8.00
62 Steve Boros 10.00 4.00
63 Tony Cloninger RC 10.00 4.00
64 Russ Snyder 10.00 4.00
65 Bobby Richardson 25.00 10.00
66 Cuno Barragan 10.00 4.00
67 Harvey Haddix 10.00 4.00
68 Ken Hunt 10.00 4.00
69 Phil Ortega 10.00 4.00
70 Harmon Killebrew 60.00 24.00
71 Dick LeMay 10.00 4.00
72 Steve Boros 10.00 4.00
Bob Scheffing MG
Jake Wood
73 Nellie Fox 25.00 10.00
74 Bob Lillis 10.00 4.00
75 Milt Pappas 15.00 6.00
76 Howie Bedell 10.00 4.00
77 Tony Taylor 10.00 4.00
78 Gene Green 10.00 4.00
79 Ed Hobaugh 10.00 4.00
80 Vada Pinson 15.00 6.00
81 Jim Pagliaroni 10.00 4.00
82 Deron Johnson 10.00 4.00
83 Larry Jackson 10.00 4.00
84 Lenny Green 10.00 4.00
85 Gil Hodges 40.00 16.00
86 Donn Clendenon RC 10.00 4.00
87 Mike Roarke 10.00 4.00
88 Ralph Houk MG 10.00 4.00
(Berra in background)
89 Barney Schultz 10.00 4.00
90 Jim Piersall 15.00 6.00
91 J.C. Martin 10.00 4.00
92 Sam Jones 10.00 4.00
93 John Blanchard 15.00 6.00
94 Jay Hook 10.00 4.00
95 Don Hoak 10.00 4.00
96 Eli Grba 10.00 4.00
97 Tito Francona 10.00 4.00
98 Checklist 2 25.00 5.00
99 John (Boog) Powell RC 80.00 32.00
100 Warren Spahn 80.00 32.00
101 Carroll Hardy 10.00 4.00
102 Al Schroll 10.00 4.00
103 Don Blasingame 10.00 4.00
104 Ted Savage 10.00 4.00
105 Don Mossi 10.00 4.00
106 Carl Sawatski 10.00 4.00
107 Mike McCormick 10.00 4.00
108 Willie Davis 10.00 4.00
109 Bob Shaw 10.00 4.00
110 Bill Skowron 15.00 6.00
111 Dallas Green 10.00 4.00
112 Hank Foiles 10.00 4.00
113 Chicago White Sox 20.00 8.00
Team Card
114 Howie Koplitz 10.00 4.00
115 Bob Skinner 10.00 4.00
116 Herb Score 15.00 6.00
117 Gary Geiger 10.00 4.00
118 Julian Javier 10.00 4.00
119 Danny Murphy 10.00 4.00
120 Bob Purkey 10.00 4.00
121 Billy Hitchcock MG 10.00 4.00
122 Norm Bass 10.00 4.00
123 Mike de la Hoz 10.00 4.00
124 Bill Pleis 10.00 4.00
125 Gene Woodling 10.00 4.00
126 Al Cicotte 10.00 4.00
127 Norm Siebern 10.00 4.00
Hank Bauer MG
Jerry Lumpe
128 Art Fowler 10.00 4.00
129 Lee Walls 10.00 4.00
130 Frank Bolling 10.00 4.00
131 Pete Richert 10.00 4.00
132 Angels Team 20.00 8.00
133 Felipe Alou 15.00 6.00
134 Billy Hoeft 10.00 4.00
135 Babe Ruth Special 1 50.00 20.00
Babe as a Boy
136 Babe Ruth Special 2 50.00 20.00
Jacob Ruppert OWN
Babe Joins Yanks
137 Babe Ruth Special 3 50.00 20.00
With Miller Huggins
138 Babe Ruth Special 4 50.00 20.00
Famous Slugger
139 Babe Ruth Special 5 60.00 24.00
Babe Hits 60
140 Babe Ruth Special 6 50.00 20.00
With Lou Gehrig
141 Babe Ruth Special 7 50.00 20.00
Twilight Years
142 Babe Ruth Special 8 50.00 20.00
Coaching Dodgers
143 Babe Ruth Special 9 50.00 20.00
Greatest Sports Hero
144 Babe Ruth Special 10 50.00 20.00
Farewell Speech
145 Barry Latman 10.00 4.00
146 Don Demeter 10.00 4.00
147 Bill Kunkel 10.00 4.00
148 Wally Post 10.00 4.00
149 Bob Duliba 10.00 4.00
150 Al Kaline 120.00 47.50
151 Johnny Klippstein 10.00 4.00
152 Mickey Vernon MG 10.00 4.00
153 Pumpsie Green 10.00 4.00
154 Lee Thomas 10.00 4.00
155 Stu Miller 10.00 4.00
156 Merritt Ranew 10.00 4.00
157 Wes Covington 15.00 6.00
158 Braves Team 20.00 8.00
159 Hal Reniff RC 10.00 4.00
160 Dick Stuart 10.00 4.00
161 Frank Baumann 10.00 4.00
162 Sammy Drake 10.00 4.00
163 Billy Gardner 10.00 4.00
Cletis Boyer
164 Hal Naragon 10.00 4.00
165 Jackie Brandt 10.00 4.00
166 Don Lee 10.00 4.00
167 Tim McCarver RC 80.00 32.00
168 Leo Posada 10.00 4.00
169 Bob Cerv 10.00 4.00
170 Ron Santo 40.00 16.00
171 Dave Sisler 10.00 4.00
172 Fred Hutchinson MG 10.00 4.00
173 Chico Fernandez 10.00 4.00
174 Carl Willey 10.00 4.00
175 Frank Howard 15.00 6.00
176 Eddie Yost 10.00 4.00
177 Bobby Shantz 10.00 4.00
178 Camilo Carreon 10.00 4.00
179 Tom Sturdivant 10.00 4.00
180 Bob Allison 10.00 4.00
181 Paul Brown 10.00 4.00
182 Bob Nieman 10.00 4.00
183 Roger Craig 10.00 4.00
184 Haywood Sullivan 10.00 4.00
185 Roland Sheldon 10.00 4.00
186 Mack Jones 10.00 4.00
187 Gene Conley 10.00 4.00
188 Chuck Hiller 10.00 4.00
189 Dick Hall 10.00 4.00
190 Wally Moon 10.00 4.00
191 Jim Brewer 10.00 4.00
192 Checklist 3 25.00 5.00
193 Eddie Kasko 10.00 4.00
194 Dean Chance RC 10.00 4.00
195 Joe Cunningham 10.00 4.00
196 Terry Fox 10.00 4.00
199 Elio Chacon 25.00 10.00
200 Luis Aparicio 50.00 20.00

1963 Topps

The cards in this 576-card set measure 2 1/2" by 3 1/2". The sharp color photographs of the 1963 set are a vivid contrast to the drab pictures of 1962. In addition to the "League Leaders" series (1-10) and World Series cards (142-148), the seventh and last series of cards (523-576) contains seven rookie cards (each depicting four players). Cards were issued, among other ways, in one-card penny packs and five-card nickel packs. There were some three-card advertising panels produced by Topps; the players included are from the first series; one panel shows Hoyt Wilhelm, Don Lock, and Bob Duliba on the front with a Stan Musial ad/endorsement on one of the backs. Key Rookie Cards in this set are Bill Freehan, Tony Oliva, Pete Rose, Willie Stargell and Rusty Staub.

NM Ex
COMPLETE SET (576) 5000.00 2000.00
COMMON CARD (1-196) 4.00 1.60
COMMON (197-283) 5.00 2.00
COMMON (284-370) 5.00 2.00
COMMON (371-446) 5.00 2.00
COMMON (447-522) 25.00 10.00
COMMON (523-576) 15.00 6.00
WRAPPER (1-CENT) 40.00 16.00
WRAPPER (5-CENT) 30.00 12.00
1 Tommy Davis 40.00 8.00
Frank Robinson
Stan Musial
Hank Aaron
Bill White LL
2 Pete Runnels 50.00 20.00
Mickey Mantle
Floyd Robinson
Norm Siebern
Chuck Hinton LL
3 Willie Mays 40.00 16.00
Hank Aaron
Frank Robinson
Orlando Cepeda
Ernie Banks LL
4 Harmon Killebrew 20.00 8.00
Norm Cash
Rocky Colavito
Roger Maris
Jim Gentile
Leon Wagner LL
5 Sandy Koufax 25.00 10.00
Bob Shaw
Bob Purkey
Bob Gibson
Don Drysdale LL
6 Hank Aguirre 10.00 4.00
Robin Roberts
Whitey Ford
Eddie Fisher
Dean Chance LL
7 Don Drysdale 10.00 4.00
Jack Sanford
Bob Purkey
Billy O'Dell
Art Mahaffey
Joe Jay LL
8 Ralph Terry 8.00 3.20
Dick Donovan
Ray Herbert
Jim Bunning
Camilo Pascual LL
9 Don Drysdale 30.00 12.00
Sandy Koufax
Bob Gibson
Billy O'Dell
Dick Farrell LL
10 Camilo Pascual 8.00 3.20
Jim Bunning
Ralph Terry
Juan Pizarro
Jim Kaat LL
11 Lee Walls 4.00 1.60
12 Steve Barber 4.00 1.60
13 Philadelphia Phillies 8.00 3.20
Team Card
14 Pedro Ramos 4.00 1.60
15 Ken Hubbs UER 10.00 4.00
(No position listed
on front of card)
16 Al Smith 4.00 1.60
17 Ryne Duren 8.00 3.20
18 Smoky Burgess 80.00 32.00
Dick Stuart
Bob Clemente
Bob Skinner
19 Pete Burnside 4.00 1.60
20 Tony Kubek 10.00 4.00
21 Marty Keough 4.00 1.60
22 Curt Simmons 8.00 3.20
23 Ed Lopat MG 8.00 3.20
24 Bob Bruce 4.00 1.60
25 Al Kaline 50.00 20.00
26 Ray Moore 4.00 1.60
27 Choo Choo Coleman 8.00 3.20
28 Mike Fornieles 4.00 1.60
29A 1962 Rookie Stars 10.00 4.00
Sammy Ellis
Ray Culp
John Boozer
Jesse Gonder
29B 1963 Rookie Stars 4.00 1.60
Sammy Ellis
Ray Culp
John Boozer
Jesse Gonder
30 Harvey Kuenn 8.00 3.20
31 Cal Koonce 4.00 1.60
32 Tony Gonzalez 4.00 1.60
33 Bo Belinsky 8.00 3.20
34 Dick Schofield 4.00 1.60
35 John Buzhardt 4.00 1.60
36 Jerry Kindall 4.00 1.60
37 Jerry Lynch 4.00 1.60
38 Bud Daley 8.00 3.20
39 Angels Team 8.00 3.20
40 Vic Power 8.00 3.20
41 Charley Lau 8.00 3.20
42 Stan Williams 8.00 3.20
(Listed as Yankee on
card but LA cap)
43 Casey Stengel MG 8.00 3.20
Gene Woodling
44 Terry Fox 4.00 1.60
45 Bob Aspromonte 4.00 1.60
46 Tommie Aaron RC 8.00 3.20
47 Don Lock 4.00 1.60
48 Birdie Tebbetts MG 8.00 3.20
49 Dal Maxvill RC 8.00 3.20
50 Billy Pierce 8.00 3.20
51 George Alusik 4.00 1.60
52 Chuck Schilling 4.00 1.60
53 Joe Moeller 8.00 3.20
54A 1962 Rookie Stars 15.00 6.00
Nelson Mathews
Harry Fanok
Jack Cullen
Dave DeBusschere RC
54B 1963 Rookie Stars 8.00 3.20
Nelson Mathews
Harry Fanok
Jack Cullen
Dave DeBusschere RC
55 Bill Virdon 8.00 3.20
56 Dennis Bennett 4.00 1.60
57 Billy Moran 4.00 1.60
58 Bob Will 4.00 1.60
59 Craig Anderson 4.00 1.60
60 Elston Howard 8.00 3.20
61 Ernie Bowman 4.00 1.60
62 Bob Hendley 4.00 1.60
63 Reds Team 8.00 3.20
64 Dick McAuliffe 8.00 3.20
65 Jackie Brandt 4.00 1.60
66 Mike Joyce 4.00 1.60
67 Ed Charles 4.00 1.60
68 Duke Snider 25.00 10.00
Gil Hodges
69 Bud Zipfel 4.00 1.60
70 Jim O'Toole 8.00 3.20
71 Bobby Wine 8.00 3.20
72 Johnny Romano 8.00 3.20
73 Bobby Bragan MG RC 8.00 3.20
74 Denny Lemaster 4.00 1.60
75 Bob Allison 8.00 3.20
76 Earl Wilson 8.00 3.20
77 Al Spangler 4.00 1.60
78 Marv Throneberry 8.00 3.20
79 Checklist 1 12.00 2.40
80 Jim Gilliam 8.00 3.20
81 Jim Schaffer 4.00 1.60
82 Ed Rakow 4.00 1.60
83 Charley James 4.00 1.60
84 Ron Kline 4.00 1.60

85 Tom Haller 8.00 3.20
86 Charley Maxwell 8.00 3.20
87 Bob Veale 8.00 3.20
88 Ron Hansen 4.00 1.60
89 Dick Stigman 4.00 1.60
90 Gordy Coleman 8.00 3.20
91 Dallas Green 8.00 3.20
92 Hector Lopez 8.00 3.20
93 Galen Cisco 4.00 1.60
94 Bob Schmidt 4.00 1.60
95 Larry Jackson 4.00 1.60
96 Lou Clinton 4.00 1.60
97 Bob Duliba 4.00 1.60
98 George Thomas 4.00 1.60
99 Jim Umbricht 4.00 1.60
100 Joe Cunningham 4.00 1.60
101 Joe Gibbon 4.00 1.60
102A Checklist 2 12.00 2.40
(Red on yellow)
102B Checklist 2 12.00 2.40
(White on red)
103 Chuck Essegian 4.00 1.60
104 Lew Krausse 4.00 1.60
105 Ron Fairly 8.00 3.20
106 Bobby Bolin 4.00 1.60
107 Jim Hickman 8.00 3.20
108 Hoyt Wilhelm 10.00 4.00
109 Lee Maye 4.00 1.60
110 Rich Rollins 8.00 3.20
111 Al Jackson 4.00 1.60
112 Dick Brown 4.00 1.60
113 Don Landrum UER 4.00 1.60
(Photo actually
Ron Santo)
114 Dan Osinski 4.00 1.60
115 Carl Yastrzemski 40.00 16.00
116 Jim Brosnan 8.00 3.20
117 Jacke Davis 4.00 1.60
118 Sherm Lollar 4.00 1.60
119 Bob Lillis 4.00 1.60
120 Roger Maris 80.00 32.00
121 Jim Hannan 4.00 1.60
122 Julio Gotay 4.00 1.60
123 Frank Howard 8.00 3.20
124 Dick Howser 8.00 3.20
125 Robin Roberts 15.00 6.00
126 Bob Uecker 15.00 6.00
127 Bill Tuttle 4.00 1.60
128 Matty Alou 8.00 3.20
129 Gary Bell 4.00 1.60
130 Dick Groat 8.00 3.20
131 Washington Senators 8.00 3.20
Team Card
132 Jack Hamilton 4.00 1.60
133 Gene Freese 4.00 1.60
134 Bob Scheffing MG 4.00 1.60
135 Richie Ashburn 20.00 8.00
136 Ike Delock 4.00 1.60
137 Mack Jones 4.00 1.60
138 Willie Mays 80.00 32.00
Stan Musial
139 Earl Averill 4.00 1.60
140 Frank Lary 8.00 3.20
141 Manny Mota RC 8.00 3.20
142 Whitey Ford WS 10.00 4.00
143 Jack Sanford WS 8.00 3.20
144 Roger Maris WS 15.00 6.00
145 Chuck Hiller WS 8.00 3.20
146 Tom Tresh WS 8.00 3.20
147 Billy Pierce WS 8.00 3.20
148 Ralph Terry WS 8.00 3.20
149 Marv Breeding 4.00 1.60
150 Johnny Podres 8.00 3.20
151 Pirates Team 8.00 3.20
152 Ron Nischwitz 4.00 1.60
153 Hal Smith 4.00 1.60
154 Walter Alston MG 8.00 3.20
155 Bill Stafford 4.00 1.60
156 Roy McMillan 8.00 3.20
157 Diego Segui RC 8.00 3.20
158 Rogelio Alvares 8.00 3.20
Dave Roberts
Tommy Harper RC
Bob Saverine
159 Jim Pagliaroni 4.00 1.60
160 Juan Pizarro 4.00 1.60
161 Frank Torre 8.00 3.20
162 Twins Team 8.00 3.20
163 Don Larsen 8.00 3.20
164 Bubba Morton 4.00 1.60
165 Jim Kaat 8.00 3.20
166 Johnny Keane MG 4.00 1.60
167 Jim Fregosi 8.00 3.20
168 Russ Nixon 4.00 1.60
169 Dick Egan 25.00 10.00
Julio Navarro
Tommie Sisk
Gaylord Perry
170 Joe Adcock 8.00 3.20
171 Steve Hamilton 4.00 1.60
172 Gene Oliver 4.00 1.60
173 Tom Tresh 150.00 60.00
Mickey Mantle
Bobby Richardson
174 Larry Burright 4.00 1.60
175 Bob Buhl 8.00 3.20
176 Jim King 4.00 1.60
177 Bubba Phillips 4.00 1.60
178 Johnny Edwards 4.00 1.60
179 Ron Piche 4.00 1.60
180 Bill Skowron 8.00 3.20
181 Sammy Esposito 4.00 1.60
182 Albie Pearson 8.00 3.20
183 Joe Pepitone 8.00 3.20
184 Vern Law 8.00 3.20
185 Chuck Hiller 4.00 1.60
186 Jerry Zimmerman 4.00 1.60
187 Willie Kirkland 4.00 1.60
188 Eddie Bressoud 4.00 1.60
189 Dave Giusti 8.00 3.20
190 Minnie Minoso 8.00 3.20
191 Checklist 3 12.00 2.40
192 Clay Dalrymple 4.00 1.60
193 Andre Rodgers 4.00 1.60
194 Joe Nuxhall 8.00 3.20
195 Manny Jimenez 4.00 1.60
196 Doug Camilli 4.00 1.60
197 Roger Craig 8.00 3.20
198 Lenny Green 5.00 2.00
199 Joe Amalfitano 5.00 2.00
200 Mickey Mantle 500.00 200.00
201 Cecil Butler 5.00 2.00
202 Boston Red Sox 8.00 3.20
Team Card
203 Chico Cardenas 8.00 3.20
204 Don Nottebart 5.00 2.00
205 Luis Aparicio 15.00 6.00
206 Ray Washburn 5.00 2.00
207 Ken Hunt 5.00 2.00
208 Ron Herbel 5.00 2.00
John Miller
Wally Wolf
Ron Taylor
209 Hobie Landrith 5.00 2.00
210 Sandy Koufax 150.00 60.00
211 Fred Whitfield 5.00 2.00
212 Glen Hobbie 5.00 2.00
213 Billy Hitchcock MG 5.00 2.00
214 Orlando Pena 5.00 2.00
215 Bob Skinner 8.00 3.20
216 Gene Conley 8.00 3.20
217 Joe Christopher 5.00 2.00
218 Frank Lary 8.00 3.20
Don Mossi
Jim Bunning
219 Chuck Cottier 5.00 2.00
220 Camilo Pascual 8.00 3.20
221 Cookie Rojas RC 8.00 3.20
222 Cubs Team 8.00 3.20
223 Eddie Fisher 5.00 2.00
224 Mike Roarke 5.00 2.00
225 Joey Jay 5.00 2.00
226 Julian Javier 8.00 3.20
227 Jim Grant 8.00 3.20
228 Max Alvis 50.00 20.00
Bob Bailey
Tony Oliva
(Listed as Pedro)
Ed Kranepool RC
229 Willie Davis 8.00 3.20
230 Pete Runnels 8.00 3.20
231 Eli Grba UER 5.00 2.00
(Large photo is
Ryne Duren)
232 Frank Malzone 8.00 3.20
233 Casey Stengel MG 20.00 8.00
234 Dave Nicholson 5.00 2.00
235 Billy O'Dell 5.00 2.00
236 Bill Bryan 5.00 2.00
237 Jim Coates 8.00 3.20
238 Lou Johnson 5.00 2.00
239 Harvey Haddix 8.00 3.20
240 Rocky Colavito 15.00 6.00
241 Bob Smith 5.00 2.00
242 Ernie Banks 60.00 24.00
Hank Aaron
243 Don Leppert 5.00 2.00
244 John Tsitouris 5.00 2.00
245 Gil Hodges 20.00 8.00
246 Lee Stange 5.00 2.00
247 Yankees Team 50.00 20.00
248 Tito Francona 5.00 2.00
249 Leo Burke 5.00 2.00
250 Stan Musial 100.00 40.00
251 Jack Lamabe 5.00 2.00
252 Ron Santo 10.00 4.00
253 Len Gabrielson 5.00 2.00
Pete Jernigan
John Wojcik
Deacon Jones
254 Mike Hershberger 5.00 2.00
255 Bob Shaw 5.00 2.00
256 Jerry Lumpe 5.00 2.00
257 Hank Aguirre 5.00 2.00
258 Alvin Dark MG 8.00 3.20
259 Johnny Logan 8.00 3.20
260 Jim Gentile 8.00 3.20
261 Bob Miller 5.00 2.00
262 Ellis Burton 5.00 2.00
263 Dave Stenhouse 5.00 2.00
264 Phil Linz 5.00 2.00
265 Vada Pinson 8.00 3.20
266 Bob Allen 5.00 2.00
267 Carl Sawatski 5.00 2.00
268 Don Demeter 5.00 2.00
269 Don Mincher 5.00 2.00
270 Felipe Alou 8.00 3.20
271 Dean Stone 5.00 2.00
272 Danny Murphy 5.00 2.00
273 Sammy Taylor 5.00 2.00
274 Checklist 4 12.00 2.40
275 Eddie Mathews 30.00 12.00
276 Barry Shetrone 5.00 2.00
277 Dick Farrell 5.00 2.00
278 Chico Fernandez 5.00 2.00
279 Wally Moon 8.00 3.20
280 Bob Rodgers 5.00 2.00
281 Tom Sturdivant 5.00 2.00
282 Bobby Del Greco 5.00 2.00
283 Roy Sievers 8.00 3.20
284 Dave Sisler 5.00 2.00
285 Dick Stuart 8.00 3.20
286 Stu Miller 8.00 3.20
287 Dick Bertell 5.00 2.00
288 Chicago White Sox 10.00 4.00
Team Card
289 Hal Brown 5.00 2.00
290 Bill White 8.00 3.20
291 Don Rudolph 5.00 2.00
292 Pumpsie Green 8.00 3.20
293 Bill Pleis 5.00 2.00
294 Bill Rigney MG 5.00 2.00
295 Ed Roebuck 5.00 2.00
296 Doc Edwards 5.00 2.00
297 Jim Golden 5.00 2.00
298 Don Dillard 5.00 2.00
299 Dave Morehead 8.00 3.20
Bob Dustal
Tom Butters
Dan Schneider
300 Willie Mays 150.00 60.00
301 Bill Fischer 5.00 2.00
302 Whitey Herzog 8.00 3.20
303 Earl Francis 5.00 2.00
304 Harry Bright 5.00 2.00
305 Don Hoak 5.00 2.00
306 Earl Battey 10.00 4.00
Elston Howard
307 Chet Nichols 5.00 2.00
308 Camilo Carreon 5.00 2.00
309 Jim Brewer 5.00 2.00
310 Tommy Davis 8.00 3.20
311 Joe McClain 5.00 2.00
312 Houston Colts 25.00 10.00
Team Card
313 Ernie Broglio 5.00 2.00
314 John Goryl 5.00 2.00
315 Ralph Terry 8.00 3.20
316 Norm Sherry 8.00 3.20
317 Sam McDowell 8.00 3.20
318 Gene Mauch MG 8.00 3.20
319 Joe Gaines 5.00 2.00
320 Warren Spahn 60.00 24.00
321 Gino Cimoli 5.00 2.00
322 Bob Turley 8.00 3.20
323 Bill Mazeroski 15.00 6.00
324 George Williams 8.00 3.20
Pete Ward
Phil Roof
Vic Davalillo
325 Jack Sanford 5.00 2.00
326 Hank Foiles 5.00 2.00
327 Paul Foytack 5.00 2.00
328 Dick Williams 8.00 3.20
329 Lindy McDaniel 8.00 3.20
330 Chuck Hinton 5.00 2.00
331 Bill Stafford 8.00 3.20
Bill Pierce
332 Joel Horlen 8.00 3.20
333 Carl Warwick 5.00 2.00
334 Wynn Hawkins 5.00 2.00
335 Leon Wagner 5.00 2.00
336 Ed Bauta 5.00 2.00
337 Dodgers Team 25.00 10.00
338 Russ Kemmerer 5.00 2.00
339 Ted Bowsfield 5.00 2.00
340 Yogi Berra P/CO 100.00 40.00
341 Jack Baldschun 5.00 2.00
342 Gene Woodling 8.00 3.20
343 Johnny Pesky MG 8.00 3.20
344 Don Schwall 5.00 2.00
345 Brooks Robinson 60.00 24.00
346 Billy Hoeft 5.00 2.00
347 Joe Torre 15.00 6.00
348 Vic Wertz 8.00 3.20
349 Zoilo Versalles 8.00 3.20
350 Bob Purkey 5.00 2.00
351 Al Luplow 5.00 2.00
352 Ken Johnson 5.00 2.00
353 Billy Williams 30.00 12.00
354 Dom Zanni 5.00 2.00
355 Dean Chance 8.00 3.20
356 John Schaive 5.00 2.00
357 George Altman 5.00 2.00
358 Milt Pappas 8.00 3.20
359 Haywood Sullivan 8.00 3.20
360 Don Drysdale 60.00 24.00
361 Clete Boyer 10.00 4.00
362 Checklist 5 12.00 2.40
363 Dick Radatz 8.00 3.20
364 Howie Goss 5.00 2.00
365 Jim Bunning 20.00 8.00
366 Tony Taylor 8.00 3.20
367 Tony Cloninger 5.00 2.00
368 Ed Bailey 5.00 2.00
369 Jim Lemon 5.00 2.00
370 Dick Donovan 5.00 2.00
371 Rod Kanehl 8.00 3.20
372 Don Lee 5.00 2.00
373 Jim Campbell 5.00 2.00
374 Claude Osteen 8.00 3.20
375 Ken Boyer 15.00 6.00
376 John Wyatt 5.00 2.00
377 Baltimore Orioles 10.00 4.00
Team Card
378 Bill Henry 5.00 2.00
379 Bob Anderson 5.00 2.00
380 Ernie Banks UER 100.00 40.00
(Back has career Major
and Minor, but he
never played in Minors)
381 Frank Baumann 5.00 2.00
382 Ralph Houk MG 10.00 4.00
383 Pete Richert 5.00 2.00
384 Bob Tillman 5.00 2.00
385 Art Mahaffey 5.00 2.00
386 Ed Kirkpatrick 5.00 2.00
John Bateman RC
Larry Bearnarth
Garry Roggenburk
387 Al McBean 5.00 2.00
388 Jim Davenport 8.00 3.20
389 Frank Sullivan 5.00 2.00
390 Hank Aaron 150.00 60.00
391 Bill Dailey 5.00 2.00
392 Johnny Romano 5.00 2.00
Tito Francona
393 Ken MacKenzie 8.00 3.20
394 Tim McCarver 15.00 6.00
395 Don McMahon 5.00 2.00
396 Joe Koppe 5.00 2.00
397 Kansas City Athletics 10.00 4.00
Team Card
398 Boog Powell 25.00 10.00
399 Dick Ellsworth 5.00 2.00
400 Frank Robinson 60.00 24.00
401 Jim Bouton 15.00 6.00
402 Mickey Vernon MG 8.00 3.20
403 Ron Perranoski 8.00 3.20
404 Bob Oldis 5.00 2.00
405 Floyd Robinson 5.00 2.00
406 Howie Koplitz 5.00 2.00
407 Frank Kostro 8.00 3.20
Chico Ruiz
Larry Elliot
Dick Simpson
408 Billy Gardner 5.00 2.00
409 Roy Face 8.00 3.20
410 Earl Battey 5.00 2.00
411 Jim Constable 5.00 2.00
412 Johnny Podres 50.00 20.00
Don Drysdale
Sandy Koufax
413 Jerry Walker 5.00 2.00
414 Ty Cline 5.00 2.00
415 Bob Gibson 60.00 24.00
416 Alex Grammas 5.00 2.00
417 Giants Team 10.00 4.00
418 John Orsino 5.00 2.00
419 Tracy Stallard 5.00 2.00
420 Bobby Richardson 15.00 6.00
421 Tom Morgan 5.00 2.00
422 Fred Hutchinson MG 8.00 3.20
423 Ed Hobaugh 5.00 2.00
424 Charlie Smith 5.00 2.00
425 Smoky Burgess 8.00 3.20
426 Barry Latman 5.00 2.00
427 Bernie Allen 5.00 2.00
428 Carl Boles 5.00 2.00
429 Lou Burdette 8.00 3.20
430 Norm Siebern 5.00 2.00
431A Checklist 6 12.00 2.40
(White on red)
431B Checklist 6 30.00 6.00
(Black on orange)
432 Roman Mejias 5.00 2.00
433 Denis Menke 5.00 2.00
434 John Callison 8.00 3.20
435 Woody Held 5.00 2.00
436 Tim Harkness 8.00 3.20
437 Bill Bruton 5.00 2.00
438 Wes Stock 5.00 2.00
439 Don Zimmer 8.00 3.20
440 Juan Marichal 30.00 12.00
441 Lee Thomas 8.00 3.20
442 J.C. Hartman 5.00 2.00
443 Jimmy Piersall 8.00 3.20
444 Jim Maloney 8.00 3.20
445 Norm Cash 10.00 4.00
446 Whitey Ford 60.00 24.00
447 Felix Mantilla 25.00 10.00
448 Jack Kralick 25.00 10.00
449 Jose Tartabull 25.00 10.00
450 Bob Friend 30.00 12.00
451 Indians Team 40.00 16.00
452 Barney Schultz 25.00 10.00
453 Jake Wood 25.00 10.00
454A Art Fowler 25.00 10.00
(Card number on
white background)
454B Art Fowler 30.00 12.00
(Card number on
orange background)
455 Ruben Amaro 25.00 10.00
456 Jim Coker 25.00 10.00
457 Tex Clevenger 25.00 10.00
458 Al Lopez MG 30.00 12.00
459 Dick LeMay 25.00 10.00
460 Del Crandall 30.00 12.00
461 Norm Bass 25.00 10.00
462 Wally Post 25.00 10.00
463 Joe Schaffernoth 25.00 10.00
464 Ken Aspromonte 25.00 10.00
465 Chuck Estrada 25.00 10.00
466 Nate Oliver 60.00 24.00
Tony Martinez
Bill Freehan RC
Jerry Robinson SP
467 Phil Ortega 25.00 10.00
468 Carroll Hardy 30.00 12.00
469 Jay Hook 30.00 12.00
470 Tom Tresh SP 60.00 24.00
471 Ken Retzer 25.00 10.00
472 Lou Brock 80.00 32.00
473 New York Mets 100.00 40.00
Team Card
474 Jack Fisher 25.00 10.00
475 Gus Triandos 30.00 12.00
476 Frank Funk 25.00 10.00
477 Donn Clendenon 30.00 12.00
478 Paul Brown 25.00 10.00
479 Ed Brinkman 25.00 10.00
480 Bill Monbouquette 25.00 10.00
481 Bob Taylor 25.00 10.00
482 Felix Torres 25.00 10.00
483 Jim Owens UER 25.00 10.00
(Stat column for Wins
has an R instead)
484 Dale Long SP 30.00 12.00
485 Jim Landis 25.00 10.00
486 Ray Sadecki 25.00 10.00
487 John Roseboro 30.00 12.00
488 Jerry Adair 25.00 10.00
489 Paul Toth 25.00 10.00
490 Willie McCovey 100.00 40.00
491 Harry Craft MG 25.00 10.00
492 Dave Wickersham 25.00 10.00
493 Walt Bond 25.00 10.00
494 Phil Regan 25.00 10.00
495 Frank Thomas SP 30.00 12.00
496 Steve Dalkowski RC 30.00 12.00
Fred Newman
Jack Smith
Carl Bouldin
497 Bennie Daniels 25.00 10.00
498 Eddie Kasko 25.00 10.00
499 J.C. Martin 25.00 10.00
500 Harmon Killebrew SP 150.00 60.00
501 Joe Azcue 25.00 10.00
502 Daryl Spencer 25.00 10.00
503 Braves Team 40.00 16.00
504 Bob Johnson 25.00 10.00
505 Curt Flood 40.00 16.00
506 Gene Green 25.00 10.00
507 Roland Sheldon 30.00 12.00
508 Ted Savage 25.00 10.00
509A Checklist 7 30.00 6.00
(Copyright centered)
509B Checklist 7 30.00 6.00
(Copyright to right)
510 Ken McBride 25.00 10.00
511 Charlie Neal 30.00 12.00
512 Cal McLish 25.00 10.00
513 Gary Geiger 25.00 10.00
514 Larry Osborne 25.00 10.00
515 Don Elston 25.00 10.00
516 Purnell Goldy 25.00 10.00
517 Hal Woodeshick 25.00 10.00
518 Don Blasingame 25.00 10.00
519 Claude Raymond RC 25.00 10.00
520 Orlando Cepeda 40.00 16.00
521 Dan Pfister 25.00 10.00
522 Mel Nelson 30.00 12.00
Gary Peters
Jim Roland
Art Quirk
523 Bill Kunkel 15.00 6.00
524 Cardinals Team 30.00 12.00
525 Nellie Fox 50.00 20.00
526 Dick Hall 15.00 6.00
527 Ed Sadowski 15.00 6.00
528 Carl Willey 15.00 6.00
529 Wes Covington 15.00 6.00
530 Don Mossi 20.00 8.00
531 Sam Mele MG 15.00 6.00
532 Steve Boros 15.00 6.00
533 Bobby Shantz 20.00 8.00
534 Ken Walters 15.00 6.00
535 Jim Perry 20.00 8.00
536 Norm Larker 15.00 6.00
537 Pedro Gonzalez 800.00 325.00
Ken McMullen
Al Weis
Pete Rose RC
538 George Brunet 15.00 6.00
539 Wayne Causey 15.00 6.00
540 Roberto Clemente 250.00 100.00
541 Ron Moeller 15.00 6.00
542 Lou Klimchock 15.00 6.00
543 Russ Snyder 15.00 6.00
544 Duke Carmel 50.00 20.00
Bill Haas
Rusty Staub RC
Dick Phillips
545 Jose Pagan 15.00 6.00
546 Hal Reniff 20.00 8.00
547 Gus Bell 15.00 6.00
548 Tom Satriano 15.00 6.00
549 Marcelino Lopez 15.00 6.00
Pete Lovrich
Paul Ratliff
Elmo Plaskett
550 Duke Snider 80.00 32.00
551 Billy Klaus 15.00 6.00
552 Detroit Tigers 50.00 20.00
Team Card
553 Brock Davis 125.00 50.00
Jim Gosger
Willie Stargell RC
John Herrnstein
554 Hank Fischer 15.00 6.00
555 John Blanchard 20.00 8.00
556 Al Worthington 15.00 6.00
557 Cuno Barragan 15.00 6.00
558 Bill Faul 20.00 8.00
Ron Hunt RC
Al Moran
Bob Lipski
559 Danny Murtaugh MG 15.00 6.00
560 Ray Herbert 15.00 6.00
561 Mike De La Hoz 15.00 6.00
562 Randy Cardinal 30.00 12.00
Dave McNally RC
Ken Rowe
Don Rowe
563 Mike McCormick 15.00 6.00
564 George Banks 15.00 6.00
565 Larry Sherry 15.00 6.00
566 Cliff Cook 15.00 6.00
567 Jim Duffalo 15.00 6.00
568 Bob Sadowski 15.00 6.00
569 Luis Arroyo 20.00 8.00
570 Frank Bolling 15.00 6.00
571 Johnny Klippstein 15.00 6.00
572 Jack Spring 15.00 6.00
573 Coot Veal 15.00 6.00
574 Hal Kolstad 15.00 6.00
575 Don Cardwell 15.00 6.00
576 Johnny Temple 30.00 11.00

1963 Topps Stick-Ons Inserts

Stick-on inserts were found in several series of the 1963 Topps cards. Each sticker measures 1 1/4" by 2 3/4". They are found either with blank backs or with instructions on the reverse. Stick-ons with the instruction backs are a little tougher to find. The player photo is in color inside an oval with name, team and postion below. Since these inserts were unnumbered, they are ordered below alphabetically.

NM Ex
COMPLETE SET (46) 300.00 120.00
1 Hank Aaron 30.00 12.00
2 Luis Aparicio 10.00 4.00
3 Richie Ashburn 12.00 4.80
4 Bob Aspromonte 3.00 1.20
5 Ernie Banks 15.00 6.00
6 Ken Boyer 6.00 2.40
7 Jim Bunning 10.00 4.00
8 Johnny Callison 3.00 1.20
9 Roberto Clemente 50.00 20.00
10 Orlando Cepeda 10.00 4.00
11 Rocky Colavito 8.00 3.20
12 Tommy Davis 4.00 1.60
13 Dick Donovan 3.00 1.20
14 Don Drysdale 12.00 4.80
15 Dick Farrell 3.00 1.20
16 Jim Gentile 4.00 1.60
17 Ray Herbert 3.00 1.20
18 Chuck Hinton 3.00 1.20
19 Ken Hubbs 6.00 2.40
20 Al Jackson 3.00 1.20
21 Al Kaline 15.00 6.00
22 Harmon Killebrew 10.00 4.00
23 Sandy Koufax 25.00 10.00
24 Jerry Lumpe 3.00 1.20
25 Art Mahaffey 3.00 1.20
26 Mickey Mantle 80.00 32.00
27 Willie Mays 35.00 14.00
28 Bill Mazeroski 8.00 3.20
29 Bill Monbouquette 3.00 1.20
30 Stan Musial 25.00 10.00
31 Camilo Pascual 3.00 1.20
32 Bob Purkey 3.00 1.20
33 Bobby Richardson 6.00 2.40
34 Brooks Robinson 15.00 6.00
35 Floyd Robinson 3.00 1.20
36 Frank Robinson 15.00 6.00
37 Bob Rodgers 3.00 1.20
38 Johnny Romano 3.00 1.20
39 Jack Sanford 3.00 1.20

40 Norm Siebern 3.00 1.20
41 Warren Spahn 10.00 4.00
42 Dave Stenhouse 3.00 1.20
43 Ralph Terry 3.00 1.20
44 Lee Thomas 4.00 1.60
45 Bill White 4.00 1.60
46 Carl Yastrzemski 20.00 8.00

1964 Topps

The cards in this 587-card set measure 2 1/2" by 3 1/2". Players in the 1964 Topps baseball series were easy to sort by team due to the giant block lettering found at the top of each card. The name and position of the player are found underneath the picture, and the card is numbered in a ball design on the orange-colored back. The usual last series scarcity holds for this set (523 to 587). Subsets within this set include League Leaders (1-12) and World Series cards (136-140). Among other vehicles, cards were issued in one-card penny packs as well as five-card nickel packs. There were some three-card advertising panels produced by Topps; the players included are from the first series; Panels with Mickey Mantle card backs include Walt Alston/Bill Henry/Vada Pinson; Carl Willey/White Sox Rookies/Bob Friend; and Jimmie Hall/Ernie Broglio/A.L. ERA Leaders on the front with a Mickey Mantle card back on one of the backs. The key Rookie Cards in this set are Richie Allen, Tony Conigliaro, Tommy John, Tony LaRussa, Phil Niekro and Lou Piniella.

	NM	Ex
COMPLETE SET (587)	4500.00	1800.00
COMMON CARD (1-196)	3.00	1.20
COMMON (197-370)	4.00	1.60
COMMON (371-522)	8.00	3.20
COMMON (523-587)	15.00	6.00
WRAPPER (1-CENT)	100.00	40.00
WRAP. (1-CENT, REPEAT)	125.00	50.00
WRAPPER (5-CENT)	30.00	12.00
WRAP.(5-CENT, COIN)	40.00	16.00

1 Sandy Koufax 30.00 9.00
Dick Ellsworth
Bob Friend LL
2 Gary Peters 8.00 3.20
Juan Pizarro
Camilo Pascual LL
3 Sandy Koufax 20.00 8.00
Juan Marichal
Warren Spahn
Jim Maloney LL
4 Whitey Ford 8.00 3.20
Camilo Pascual
Jim Bouton LL
5 Sandy Koufax 15.00 6.00
Jim Maloney
Don Drysdale LL
6 Camilo Pascual 8.00 3.20
Jim Bunning
Dick Stigman LL
7 Tommy Davis 20.00 8.00
Roberto Clemente
Dick Groat
Hank Aaron LL
8 Carl Yastrzemski 15.00 6.00
Al Kaline
Rich Rollins LL
9 Hank Aaron 30.00 12.00
Willie McCovey
Willie Mays
Orlando Cepeda LL
10 Harmon Killebrew 8.00 3.20
Dick Stuart
Bob Allison LL
11 Hank Aaron 15.00 6.00
Ken Boyer
Bill White LL
12 Dick Stuart 8.00 3.20
Al Kaline
Harmon Killebrew LL
13 Hoyt Wilhelm 12.00 4.80
14 Dick Nen RC 3.00 1.20
Nick Willhite
15 Zoilo Versalles 6.00 2.40
16 John Boozer 3.00 1.20
17 Willie Kirkland 3.00 1.20
18 Billy O'Dell 3.00 1.20
19 Don Wert 3.00 1.20
20 Bob Friend 6.00 2.40
21 Yogi Berra MG 40.00 16.00
22 Jerry Adair 3.00 1.20
23 Chris Zachary 3.00 1.20
24 Carl Sawatski 3.00 1.20
25 Bill Monbouquette 3.00 1.20
26 Gino Cimoli 3.00 1.20
27 New York Mets 8.00 3.20
Team Card
28 Claude Osteen 6.00 2.40
29 Lou Brock 40.00 16.00
30 Ron Perranoski 6.00 2.40
31 Dave Nicholson 3.00 1.20
32 Dean Chance 6.00 2.40
33 Sammy Ellis 6.00 2.40
Mel Queen
34 Jim Perry 6.00 2.40
35 Eddie Mathews 20.00 8.00
36 Hal Reniff 3.00 1.20
37 Smoky Burgess 6.00 2.40
38 Jim Wynn RC 8.00 3.20
39 Hank Aguirre 3.00 1.20
40 Dick Groat 6.00 2.40
41 Willie McCovey 8.00 3.20
Leon Wagner
42 Moe Drabowsky 6.00 2.40
43 Roy Sievers 6.00 2.40
44 Duke Carmel 3.00 1.20
45 Milt Pappas 6.00 2.40
46 Ed Brinkman 3.00 1.20
47 Jesus Alou RC 6.00 2.40
Ron Herbel
48 Bob Perry 3.00 1.20
49 Bill Henry 3.00 1.20
50 Mickey Mantle 300.00 120.00
51 Pete Richert 3.00 1.20
52 Chuck Hinton 3.00 1.20
53 Denis Menke 3.00 1.20
54 Sam Mele MG 3.00 1.20
55 Ernie Banks 40.00 16.00
56 Hal Brown 3.00 1.20
57 Tim Harkness 6.00 2.40
58 Don Demeter 6.00 2.40
59 Ernie Broglio 3.00 1.20
60 Frank Malzone 6.00 2.40
61 Bob Rodgers 6.00 2.40
Ed Sadowski
62 Ted Savage 3.00 1.20
63 John Orsino 3.00 1.20
64 Ted Abernathy 3.00 1.20
65 Felipe Alou 6.00 2.40
66 Eddie Fisher 3.00 1.20
67 Tigers Team 6.00 2.40
68 Willie Davis 6.00 2.40
69 Clete Boyer 6.00 2.40
70 Joe Torre 8.00 3.20
71 Jack Spring 3.00 1.20
72 Chico Cardenas 6.00 2.40
73 Jimmie Hall 8.00 3.20
74 Bob Priddy 3.00 1.20
Tom Butters
75 Wayne Causey 3.00 1.20
76 Checklist 1 10.00 2.00
77 Jerry Walker 3.00 1.20
78 Merritt Ranew 3.00 1.20
79 Bob Heffner 3.00 1.20
80 Vada Pinson 8.00 3.20
81 Nellie Fox 12.00 4.80
Harmon Killebrew
82 Jim Davenport 6.00 2.40
83 Gus Triandos 6.00 2.40
84 Carl Willey 3.00 1.20
85 Pete Ward 3.00 1.20
86 Al Downing 6.00 2.40
87 St. Louis Cardinals 6.00 2.40
Team Card
88 John Roseboro 6.00 2.40
89 Boog Powell 6.00 2.40
90 Earl Battey 3.00 1.20
91 Bob Bailey 6.00 2.40
92 Steve Ridzik 3.00 1.20
93 Gary Geiger 3.00 1.20
94 Jim Britton 3.00 1.20
Larry Maxie
95 George Altman 3.00 1.20
96 Bob Buhl 6.00 2.40
97 Jim Fregosi 6.00 2.40
98 Bill Bruton 3.00 1.20
99 Al Stanek 3.00 1.20
100 Elston Howard 6.00 2.40
101 Walt Alston MG 8.00 3.20
102 Checklist 2 10.00 2.00
103 Curt Flood 6.00 2.40
104 Art Mahaffey 6.00 2.40
105 Woody Held 3.00 1.20
106 Joe Nuxhall 6.00 2.40
107 Bruce Howard 3.00 1.20
Frank Kreutzer
108 John Wyatt 3.00 1.20
109 Rusty Staub 6.00 2.40
110 Albie Pearson 6.00 2.40
111 Don Elston 3.00 1.20
112 Bob Tillman 3.00 1.20
113 Grover Powell 6.00 2.40
114 Don Lock 3.00 1.20
115 Frank Bolling 3.00 1.20
116 Jay Ward 12.00 4.80
Tony Oliva
117 Earl Francis 3.00 1.20
118 John Blanchard 6.00 2.40
119 Gary Kolb 3.00 1.20
120 Don Drysdale 20.00 8.00
121 Pete Runnels 6.00 2.40
122 Don McMahon 3.00 1.20
123 Jose Pagan 3.00 1.20
124 Orlando Pena 3.00 1.20
125 Pete Rose 250.00 100.00
126 Russ Snyder 3.00 1.20
127 Aubrey Gatewood 3.00 1.20
Dick Simpson
128 Mickey Lolich RC 20.00 8.00
129 Amado Samuel 3.00 1.20
130 Gary Peters 6.00 2.40
131 Steve Boros 3.00 1.20
132 Braves Team 6.00 2.40
133 Jim Grant 6.00 2.40
134 Don Zimmer 6.00 2.40
135 Johnny Callison 6.00 2.40
136 Sandy Koufax WS 20.00 8.00
strikes out 15
137 Willie Davis WS 8.00 3.20
138 Ron Fairly WS 8.00 3.20
139 Frank Howard WS 8.00 3.20
140 WS Summary 8.00 3.20
Dodgers celebrate
141 Danny Murtaugh MG 6.00 2.40
142 John Bateman 3.00 1.20
143 Bubba Phillips 3.00 1.20
144 Al Worthington 3.00 1.20
145 Norm Siebern 3.00 1.20
146 Tommy John RC 30.00 12.00
Bob Chance
147 Ray Sadecki 3.00 1.20
148 J.C. Martin 3.00 1.20
149 Paul Foytack 3.00 1.20
150 Willie Mays 125.00 50.00
151 Athletics Team 6.00 2.40
152 Denny Lemaster 3.00 1.20
153 Dick Williams 6.00 2.40
154 Dick Tracewski RC 6.00 2.40
155 Duke Snider 30.00 12.00
156 Bill Dailey 3.00 1.20
157 Gene Mauch MG 6.00 2.40
158 Ken Johnson 3.00 1.20
159 Charlie Dees 3.00 1.20
160 Ken Boyer 6.00 2.40
161 Dave McNally 6.00 2.40
162 Dick Sisler CO 6.00 2.40
Vada Pinson
163 Donn Clendenon 6.00 2.40
164 Bud Daley 3.00 1.20
165 Jerry Lumpe 3.00 1.20
166 Marty Keough 3.00 1.20
167 Mike Brumley 30.00 12.00
Lou Piniella RC
168 Al Weis 3.00 1.20
169 Del Crandall 6.00 2.40
170 Dick Radatz 6.00 2.40
171 Ty Cline 3.00 1.20
172 Indians Team 6.00 2.40
173 Ryne Duren 6.00 2.40
174 Doc Edwards 3.00 1.20
175 Billy Williams 12.00 4.80
176 Tracy Stallard 3.00 1.20
177 Harmon Killebrew 20.00 8.00
178 Hank Bauer MG 6.00 2.40
179 Carl Warwick 3.00 1.20
180 Tommy Davis 6.00 2.40
181 Dave Wickersham 3.00 1.20
182 Carl Yastrzemski 15.00 6.00
Chuck Schilling
183 Ron Taylor 3.00 1.20
184 Al Luplow 3.00 1.20
185 Jim O'Toole 6.00 2.40
186 Roman Mejias 3.00 1.20
187 Ed Roebuck 3.00 1.20
188 Checklist 3 10.00 2.00
189 Bob Hendley 3.00 1.20
190 Bobby Richardson 8.00 3.20
191 Clay Dalrymple 6.00 2.40
192 John Boccabella 3.00 1.20
Billy Cowan
193 Jerry Lynch 3.00 1.20
194 John Goryl 3.00 1.20
195 Floyd Robinson 3.00 1.20
196 Jim Gentile 3.00 1.20
197 Frank Lary 6.00 2.40
198 Len Gabrielson 4.00 1.60
199 Joe Azcue 4.00 1.60
200 Sandy Koufax 100.00 40.00
201 Sam Bowens 6.00 2.40
Wally Bunker
202 Galen Cisco 6.00 2.40
203 John Kennedy 6.00 2.40
204 Matty Alou 6.00 2.40
205 Nellie Fox 12.00 4.80
206 Steve Hamilton 6.00 2.40
207 Fred Hutchinson MG 6.00 2.40
208 Wes Covington 6.00 2.40
209 Bob Allen 4.00 1.60
210 Carl Yastrzemski 40.00 16.00
211 Jim Coker 4.00 1.60
212 Pete Lovrich 4.00 1.60
213 Angels Team 6.00 2.40
214 Ken McMullen 6.00 2.40
215 Ray Herbert 4.00 1.60
216 Mike de la Hoz 4.00 1.60
217 Jim King 4.00 1.60
218 Hank Fischer 4.00 1.60
219 Al Downing 6.00 2.40
Jim Bouton
220 Dick Ellsworth 6.00 2.40
221 Bob Saverine 4.00 1.60
222 Billy Pierce 6.00 2.40
223 George Banks 4.00 1.60
224 Tommie Sisk 4.00 1.60
225 Roger Maris 60.00 24.00
226 Jerry Grote RC 6.00 2.40
Larry Yellen
227 Barry Latman 4.00 1.60
228 Felix Mantilla 4.00 1.60
229 Charley Lau 6.00 2.40
230 Brooks Robinson 40.00 16.00
231 Dick Calmus 4.00 1.60
232 Al Lopez MG 8.00 3.20
233 Hal Smith 4.00 1.60
234 Gary Bell 4.00 1.60
235 Ron Hunt 4.00 1.60
236 Bill Faul 4.00 1.60
237 Cubs Team 6.00 2.40
238 Roy McMillan 6.00 2.40
239 Herm Starrette 4.00 1.60
240 Bill White 6.00 2.40
241 Jim Owens 4.00 1.60
242 Harvey Kuenn 6.00 2.40
243 Richie Allen RC 30.00 12.00
John Herrnstein
244 Tony LaRussa RC 30.00 12.00
245 Dick Stigman 4.00 1.60
246 Manny Mota 6.00 2.40
247 Dave DeBusschere 6.00 2.40
248 Johnny Pesky MG 6.00 2.40
249 Doug Camilli 4.00 1.60
250 Al Kaline 40.00 16.00
251 Choo Choo Coleman 6.00 2.40
252 Ken Aspromonte 4.00 1.60
253 Wally Post 6.00 2.40
254 Don Hoak 6.00 2.40
255 Lee Thomas 6.00 2.40
256 Johnny Weekly 4.00 1.60
257 San Francisco Giants 6.00 2.40
Team Card
258 Garry Roggenburk 4.00 1.60
259 Harry Bright 4.00 1.60
260 Frank Robinson 40.00 16.00
261 Jim Hannan 4.00 1.60
262 Mike Shannon RC 8.00 3.20
Harry Fanok
263 Chuck Estrada 4.00 1.60
264 Jim Landis 4.00 1.60
265 Jim Bunning 12.00 4.80
266 Gene Freese 4.00 1.60
267 Wilbur Wood RC 6.00 2.40
268 Danny Murtaugh MG 6.00 2.40
Bill Virdon
269 Ellis Burton 4.00 1.60
270 Rich Rollins 6.00 2.40
271 Bob Sadowski 4.00 1.60
272 Jake Wood 4.00 1.60
273 Mel Nelson 4.00 1.60
274 Checklist 4 10.00 2.00
275 John Tsitouris 4.00 1.60
276 Jose Tartabull 6.00 2.40
277 Ken Retzer 4.00 1.60
278 Bobby Shantz 6.00 2.40
279 Joe Koppe UER 4.00 1.60
(Glove on wrong hand)
280 Juan Marichal 15.00 6.00
281 Jake Gibbs 6.00 2.40
Tom Metcalf
282 Bob Bruce 4.00 1.60
283 Tom McCraw RC 4.00 1.60
284 Dick Schofield 4.00 1.60
285 Robin Roberts 15.00 6.00
286 Don Landrum 4.00 1.60
287 Tony Conigliaro RC 50.00 20.00
Bill Spanswick
288 Al Moran 4.00 1.60
289 Frank Funk 4.00 1.60
290 Bob Allison 6.00 2.40
291 Phil Ortega 4.00 1.60
292 Mike Roarke 4.00 1.60
293 Phillies Team 6.00 2.40
294 Ken L. Hunt 4.00 1.60
295 Roger Craig 6.00 2.40
296 Ed Kirkpatrick 4.00 1.60
297 Ken MacKenzie 4.00 1.60
298 Harry Craft MG 4.00 1.60
299 Bill Stafford 4.00 1.60
300 Hank Aaron 100.00 40.00
301 Larry Brown 4.00 1.60
302 Dan Pfister 4.00 1.60
303 Jim Campbell 4.00 1.60
304 Bob Johnson 4.00 1.60
305 Jack Lamabe 4.00 1.60
306 Willie Mays 40.00 16.00
Orlando Cepeda
307 Joe Gibbon 4.00 1.60
308 Gene Stephens 4.00 1.60
309 Paul Toth 4.00 1.60
310 Jim Gilliam 6.00 2.40
311 Tom Brown RC 6.00 2.40
312 Fritz Fisher 4.00 1.60
Fred Gladding
313 Chuck Hiller 4.00 1.60
314 Jerry Buchek 4.00 1.60
315 Bo Belinsky 6.00 2.40
316 Gene Oliver 4.00 1.60
317 Al Smith 4.00 1.60
318 Minnesota Twins 6.00 2.40
Team Card
319 Paul Brown 4.00 1.60
320 Rocky Colavito 12.00 4.80
321 Bob Lillis 4.00 1.60
322 George Brunet 4.00 1.60
323 John Buzhardt 4.00 1.60
324 Casey Stengel MG 15.00 6.00
325 Hector Lopez 6.00 2.40
326 Ron Brand 4.00 1.60
327 Don Blasingame 4.00 1.60
328 Bob Shaw 4.00 1.60
329 Russ Nixon 4.00 1.60
330 Tommy Harper 6.00 2.40
331 Roger Maris 150.00 60.00
Norm Cash
Mickey Mantle
Al Kaline
332 Ray Washburn 4.00 1.60
333 Billy Moran 4.00 1.60
334 Lew Krausse 4.00 1.60
335 Don Mossi 6.00 2.40
336 Andre Rodgers 4.00 1.60
337 Al Ferrara 6.00 2.40
Jeff Torborg RC
338 Jack Kralick 4.00 1.60
339 Walt Bond 4.00 1.60
340 Joe Cunningham 4.00 1.60
341 Jim Roland 4.00 1.60
342 Willie Stargell 30.00 12.00
343 Senators Team 6.00 2.40
344 Phil Linz 6.00 2.40
345 Frank Thomas 8.00 3.20
346 Joey Jay 4.00 1.60
347 Bobby Wine 6.00 2.40
348 Ed Lopat MG 6.00 2.40
349 Art Fowler 4.00 1.60
350 Willie McCovey 25.00 10.00
351 Dan Schneider 4.00 1.60
352 Eddie Bressoud 4.00 1.60
353 Wally Moon 6.00 2.40
354 Dave Giusti 4.00 1.60
355 Vic Power 6.00 2.40
356 Bill McCool 6.00 2.40
Chico Ruiz
357 Charley James 4.00 1.60
358 Ron Kline 4.00 1.60
359 Jim Schaffer 4.00 1.60
360 Joe Pepitone 12.00 4.80
361 Jay Hook 4.00 1.60
362 Checklist 5 10.00 2.00
363 Dick McAuliffe 6.00 2.40
364 Joe Gaines 4.00 1.60
365 Cal McLish 6.00 2.40
366 Nelson Mathews 4.00 1.60
367 Fred Whitfield 4.00 1.60
368 Fritz Ackley 6.00 2.40
Don Buford RC
369 Jerry Zimmerman 4.00 1.60
370 Hal Woodeshick 4.00 1.60
371 Frank Howard 8.00 3.20
372 Howie Koplitz 8.00 3.20
373 Pirates Team 12.00 4.80
374 Bobby Bolin 8.00 3.20
375 Ron Santo 10.00 4.00
376 Dave Morehead 8.00 3.20
377 Bob Skinner 8.00 3.20
378 Woody Woodward RC 10.00 4.00
Jack Smith
379 Tony Gonzalez 8.00 3.20
380 Whitey Ford 40.00 16.00
381 Bob Taylor 8.00 3.20
382 Wes Stock 8.00 3.20
383 Bill Rigney MG 8.00 3.20
384 Ron Hansen 8.00 3.20
385 Curt Simmons 10.00 4.00
386 Lenny Green 8.00 3.20
387 Terry Fox 8.00 3.20
388 John O'Donoghue RC 10.00 4.00
George Williams
389 Jim Umbricht 10.00 4.00
(Card back mentions
his death)
390 Orlando Cepeda 25.00 10.00
391 Sam McDowell 10.00 4.00
392 Jim Pagliaroni 8.00 3.20
393 Casey Stengel MG 15.00 6.00
Ed Kranepool
394 Bob Miller 8.00 3.20
395 Tom Tresh 10.00 4.00
396 Dennis Bennett 8.00 3.20
397 Chuck Cottier 8.00 3.20
398 Bill Haas 10.00 4.00
Dick Smith
399 Jackie Brandt 8.00 3.20
400 Warren Spahn 40.00 16.00
401 Charlie Maxwell 8.00 3.20
402 Tom Sturdivant 8.00 3.20
403 Reds Team 12.00 4.80
404 Tony Martinez 8.00 3.20
405 Ken McBride 8.00 3.20
406 Al Spangler 8.00 3.20
407 Bill Freehan 10.00 4.00
408 Jim Stewart 8.00 3.20
Fred Burdette
409 Bill Fischer 8.00 3.20
410 Dick Stuart 10.00 4.00
411 Lee Walls 8.00 3.20
412 Ray Culp 10.00 4.00
413 Johnny Keane MG 8.00 3.20
414 Jack Sanford 8.00 3.20
415 Tony Kubek 15.00 6.00
416 Lee Maye 8.00 3.20
417 Don Cardwell 8.00 3.20
418 Darold Knowles 10.00 4.00
Buster Narum
419 Ken Harrelson RC 15.00 6.00
420 Jim Maloney 10.00 4.00
421 Camilo Carreon 8.00 3.20
422 Jack Fisher 8.00 3.20
423 Hank Aaron 125.00 50.00
Willie Mays
424 Dick Bertell 8.00 3.20
425 Norm Cash 10.00 4.00
426 Bob Rodgers 8.00 3.20
427 Don Rudolph 8.00 3.20
428 Archie Skeen 8.00 3.20
Pete Smith
(Back states Archie
has retired)
429 Tim McCarver 10.00 4.00
430 Juan Pizarro 8.00 3.20
431 George Alusik 8.00 3.20
432 Ruben Amaro 10.00 4.00
433 Yankees Team 40.00 16.00
434 Don Nottebart 8.00 3.20
435 Vic Davalillo 8.00 3.20
436 Charlie Neal 10.00 4.00
437 Ed Bailey 8.00 3.20
438 Checklist 6 15.00 3.00
439 Harvey Haddix 10.00 4.00
440 R.Clemente UER 250.00 100.00
1960 Pittsburfh
441 Bob Duliba 8.00 3.20
442 Pumpsie Green 10.00 4.00
443 Chuck Dressen MG 10.00 4.00
444 Larry Jackson 8.00 3.20
445 Bill Skowron 10.00 4.00
446 Julian Javier 15.00 6.00
447 Ted Bowsfield 8.00 3.20
448 Cookie Rojas 10.00 4.00
449 Deron Johnson 10.00 4.00
450 Steve Barber 8.00 3.20
451 Joe Amalfitano 8.00 3.20
452 Gil Garrido 10.00 4.00
Jim Ray Hart RC
453 Frank Baumann 8.00 3.20
454 Tommie Aaron 10.00 4.00
455 Bernie Allen 8.00 3.20
456 Wes Parker RC 10.00 4.00
John Werhas
457 Jesse Gonder 8.00 3.20
458 Ralph Terry 10.00 4.00
459 Pete Charton 8.00 3.20
Dalton Jones
460 Bob Gibson 40.00 16.00
461 George Thomas 8.00 3.20
462 Birdie Tebbetts MG 8.00 3.20
463 Don Leppert 8.00 3.20
464 Dallas Green 15.00 6.00
465 Mike Hershberger 8.00 3.20
466 Dick Green 10.00 4.00
Aurelio Monteagudo
467 Bob Aspromonte 8.00 3.20
468 Gaylord Perry 40.00 16.00
469 Fred Norman 10.00 4.00
Sterling Slaughter
470 Jim Bouton 10.00 4.00
471 Gates Brown RC 10.00 4.00
472 Vern Law 10.00 4.00
473 Baltimore Orioles 12.00 4.80
Team Card
474 Larry Sherry 10.00 4.00
475 Ed Charles 8.00 3.20
476 Rico Carty RC 15.00 6.00
Dick Kelley
477 Mike Joyce 8.00 3.20
478 Dick Howser 10.00 4.00
479 Dave Bakenhaster 8.00 3.20
Johnny Lewis
480 Bob Purkey 8.00 3.20
481 Chuck Schilling 8.00 3.20
482 John Briggs 10.00 4.00
Danny Cater
483 Fred Valentine 8.00 3.20
484 Bill Pleis 8.00 3.20
485 Tom Haller 8.00 3.20
486 Bob Kennedy MG 8.00 3.20
487 Mike McCormick 10.00 4.00
488 Pete Mikkelsen 15.00 6.00
Bob Meyer
489 Julio Navarro 8.00 3.20
490 Ron Fairly 10.00 4.00
491 Ed Rakow 8.00 3.20
492 Jim Beauchamp RC 8.00 3.20
Mike White
493 Don Lee 8.00 3.20
494 Al Jackson 8.00 3.20
495 Bill Virdon 10.00 4.00
496 White Sox Team 12.00 4.80
497 Jeoff Long 8.00 3.20
498 Dave Stenhouse 8.00 3.20
499 Chico Salmon 8.00 3.20
Gordon Seyfried
500 Camilo Pascual 10.00 4.00
501 Bob Veale 10.00 4.00
502 Bobby Knoop RC 8.00 3.20
Bob Lee

503 Earl Wilson 8.00 3.20
504 Claude Raymond 8.00 3.20
505 Stan Williams 8.00 3.20
506 Bobby Bragan MG 8.00 3.20
507 Johnny Edwards 8.00 3.20
508 Diego Segui 8.00 3.20
509 Gene Alley RC 10.00 4.00
Orlando McFarlane
510 Lindy McDaniel 10.00 4.00
511 Lou Jackson 10.00 4.00
512 Willie Horton RC 15.00 6.00
Joe Sparma
513 Don Larsen 10.00 4.00
514 Jim Hickman 10.00 4.00
515 Johnny Romano 8.00 3.20
516 Jerry Arrigo 8.00 3.20
Dwight Siebler
517A Checklist 7 ERR 25.00 5.00
(Incorrect numbering sequence on back)
517B Checklist 7 COR 15.00 3.00
(Correct numbering on back)
518 Carl Bouldin 8.00 3.20
519 Charlie Smith 8.00 3.20
520 Jack Baldschun 10.00 4.00
521 Tom Satriano 8.00 3.20
522 Bob Tiefenauer 8.00 3.20
523 Lou Burdette UER 20.00 8.00
(Pitching lefty)
524 Jim Dickson 15.00 6.00
Bobby Klaus
525 Al McBean 15.00 6.00
526 Lou Clinton 15.00 6.00
527 Larry Bearnarth 15.00 6.00
528 Dave Duncan RC 20.00 8.00
Tommie Reynolds
529 Alvin Dark MG 20.00 8.00
530 Leon Wagner 15.00 6.00
531 Los Angeles Dodgers 25.00 10.00
Team Card
532 Bud Bloomfield 15.00 6.00
(Bloomfield photo actually Jay Ward)
Joe Nossek RC
533 Johnny Klippstein 15.00 6.00
534 Gus Bell 15.00 6.00
535 Phil Regan 15.00 6.00
536 Larry Elliot 15.00 6.00
John Stephenson
537 Dan Osinski 15.00 6.00
538 Minnie Minoso 20.00 8.00
539 Roy Face 20.00 8.00
540 Luis Aparicio 40.00 16.00
541 Phil Roof 80.00 32.00
Phil Niekro RC
542 Don Mincher 15.00 6.00
543 Bob Uecker 40.00 16.00
544 Steve Hertz 15.00 6.00
Joe Hoerner
545 Max Alvis 15.00 6.00
546 Joe Christopher 15.00 6.00
547 Gil Hodges MG 30.00 12.00
548 Wayne Schurr 20.00 8.00
Paul Speckenbach
549 Joe Moeller 15.00 6.00
550 Ken Hubbs MEM 40.00 16.00
551 Billy Hoeft 15.00 6.00
552 Tom Kelley 15.00 6.00
Sonny Siebert
553 Jim Brewer 15.00 6.00
554 Hank Foiles 15.00 6.00
555 Lee Stange 15.00 6.00
556 Steve Dillon 15.00 6.00
Ron Locke
557 Leo Burke 15.00 6.00
558 Don Schwall 15.00 6.00
559 Dick Phillips 15.00 6.00
560 Dick Farrell 15.00 6.00
561 Dave Bennett UER 20.00 8.00
(19 ... is 18)
Rick Wise RC
562 Pedro Ramos 15.00 6.00
563 Dal Maxvill 20.00 8.00
564 Joe McCabe 20.00 8.00
Jerry McNertney
565 Stu Miller 15.00 6.00
566 Ed Kranepool 20.00 8.00
567 Jim Kaat 20.00 8.00
568 Phil Gagliano 15.00 6.00
Cap Peterson
569 Fred Newman 15.00 6.00
570 Bill Mazeroski 40.00 16.00
571 Gene Conley 15.00 6.00
572 Dave Gray 15.00 6.00
Dick Egan
573 Jim Duffalo 15.00 6.00
574 Manny Jimenez 15.00 6.00
575 Tony Cloninger 15.00 6.00
576 Jerry Hinsley 15.00 6.00
Bill Wakefield
577 Gordy Coleman 15.00 6.00
578 Glen Hobbie 15.00 6.00
579 Red Sox Team 25.00 10.00
580 Johnny Podres 20.00 8.00
581 Pedro Gonzalez 20.00 8.00
Archie Moore
582 Rod Kanehl 20.00 8.00
583 Tito Francona 15.00 6.00
584 Joel Horlen 15.00 6.00
585 Tony Taylor 20.00 8.00
586 Jimmy Piersall 20.00 8.00
587 Bennie Daniels 20.00 8.00

1964 Topps Coins Inserts

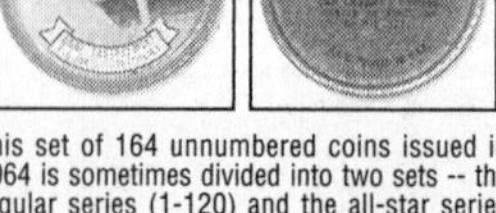

This set of 164 unnumbered coins issued in 1964 is sometimes divided into two sets -- the regular series (1-120) and the all-star series (121-164). Each metal coin is approximately 1 1/2" in diameter. The regular series features gold and silver coins with a full color photo of the player, including the background of the photo. The player's name, team and position are delineated on the coin front. The back includes the line "Collect the entire set of 120 all-stars". The all-star series (denoted AS in the checklist below) contains a full color cutout photo of the player on a solid background. The fronts feature the line "1964 All-stars" along with the name only of the player. The backs contain the line "Collect all 44 special stars". Mantle, Causey and Hinton appear in two variations each. The complete set price below includes all variations. Some dealers believe the following coins are short printed: Callison, Tresh, Rollins, Santo, Pappas, Freehan, Hendley, Staub, Bateman and O'Dell.

NM Ex
COMPLETE SET (167) 600.00 240.00
1 Don Zimmer 1.50 .60
2 Jim Wynn 2.00 .80
3 Johnny Orsino 1.00 .40
4 Jim Bouton 2.00 .80
5 Dick Groat 1.50 .60
6 Leon Wagner 1.00 .40
7 Frank Malzone 1.00 .40
8 Steve Barber 1.00 .40
9 Johnny Romano 1.00 .40
10 Tom Tresh 3.00 1.20
11 Felipe Alou 1.50 .60
12 Dick Stuart 3.00 1.20
13 Claude Osteen 1.00 .40
14 Juan Pizarro 1.00 .40
15 Donn Clendenon 1.00 .40
16 Jimmie Hall 1.00 .40
17 Al Jackson 1.00 .40
18 Brooks Robinson 15.00 6.00
19 Bob Allison 1.50 .60
20 Ed Roebuck 1.00 .40
21 Pete Ward 1.00 .40
22 Willie McCovey 10.00 4.00
23 Elston Howard 3.00 1.20
24 Diego Segui 1.00 .40
25 Ken Boyer 3.00 1.20
26 Carl Yastrzemski 20.00 8.00
27 Bill Mazeroski 8.00 3.20
28 Jerry Lumpe 1.00 .40
29 Woody Held 1.00 .40
30 Dick Radatz 1.00 .40
31 Luis Aparicio 8.00 3.20
32 Dave Nicholson 1.00 .40
33 Eddie Mathews 15.00 6.00
34 Don Drysdale 10.00 4.00
35 Ray Culp 1.00 .40
36 Juan Marichal 10.00 4.00
37 Frank Robinson 20.00 8.00
38 Chuck Hinton 1.00 .40
39 Floyd Robinson 1.50 .60
40 Tommy Harper 1.50 .60
41 Ron Hansen 1.00 .40
42 Ernie Banks 15.00 6.00
43 Jesse Gonder 1.00 .40
44 Billy Williams 10.00 4.00
45 Vada Pinson 2.00 .80
46 Rocky Colavito 5.00 2.00
47 Bill Monbouquette 1.00 .40
48 Max Alvis 1.00 .40
49 Norm Siebern 1.00 .40
50 Johnny Callison 2.00 .80
51 Rich Rollins 1.50 .60
52 Ken McBride 1.00 .40
53 Don Lock 1.00 .40
54 Ron Fairly 1.50 .60
55 Roberto Clemente 40.00 16.00
56 Dick Ellsworth 1.00 .40
57 Tommy Davis 1.50 .60
58 Tony Gonzalez 1.50 .60
59 Bob Gibson 10.00 4.00
60 Jim Maloney 1.50 .60
61 Frank Howard 3.00 1.20
62 Jim Pagliaroni 1.00 .40
63 Orlando Cepeda 8.00 3.20
64 Ron Perranoski 1.00 .40
65 Curt Flood 2.00 .80
66 Alvin McBean 1.00 .40
67 Dean Chance 1.00 .40
68 Ron Santo 3.00 1.20
69 Jack Baldschun 1.00 .40
70 Milt Pappas 1.50 .60
71 Gary Peters 1.00 .40
72 Bobby Richardson 3.00 1.20
73 Frank Thomas 1.00 .40
74 Hank Aguirre 1.00 .40
75 Carlton Willey 1.00 .40
76 Camilo Pascual 1.50 .60
77 Bob Friend 1.50 .60
78 Bill White 1.50 .60
79 Norm Cash 2.00 .80
80 Willie Mays 40.00 16.00
81 Leon Carmel 1.00 .40
82 Pete Rose 40.00 16.00
83 Hank Aaron 30.00 12.00
84 Bob Aspromonte 1.00 .40
85 Jim O'Toole 1.00 .40
86 Vic Davalillo 1.50 .60
87 Bill Freehan 2.00 .80
88 Warren Spahn 10.00 4.00
89 Ken Hunt 1.00 .40
90 Denis Menke 1.00 .40
91 Dick Farrell 1.00 .40
92 Jim Hickman 1.50 .60
93 Jim Bunning 8.00 3.20
94 Bob Hendley 2.00 .80
95 Ernie Broglio 1.00 .40
96 Rusty Staub 3.00 1.20
97 Lou Brock 10.00 4.00
98 Jim Fregosi 2.00 .80
99 Jim Grant 1.00 .40
100 Al Kaline 10.00 4.00
101 Earl Battey 2.00 .80
102 Wayne Causey 1.00 .40
103 Chuck Schilling 1.00 .40
104 Boog Powell 2.00 .80
105 Dave Wickersham 1.00 .40
106 Sandy Koufax 20.00 8.00
107 John Bateman 1.50 .60
108 Ed Brinkman 1.00 .40
109 Al Downing 1.00 .40
110 Joe Azcue 1.00 .40
111 Albie Pearson 1.00 .40
112 Harmon Killebrew 10.00 4.00
113 Tony Taylor 2.00 .80
114 Larry Jackson 1.00 .40
115 Billy O'Dell 2.00 .80
116 Don Demeter 1.50 .60
117 Ed Charles 1.00 .40
118 Joe Torre 3.00 1.20
119 Don Nottebart 1.00 .40
120 Mickey Mantle 60.00 24.00
121 Joe Pepitone AS 2.00 .80
122 Dick Stuart AS 1.50 .60
123 Bobby Richardson AS 3.00 1.20
124 Jerry Lumpe AS 1.00 .40
125 Brooks Robinson AS 10.00 4.00
126 Frank Malzone AS 1.00 .40
127 Luis Aparicio AS 6.00 2.40
128 Jim Fregosi AS 1.50 .60
129 Al Kaline AS 8.00 3.20
130 Leon Wagner AS 1.00 .40
131A Mickey Mantle AS 50.00 20.00
(right handed)
131B Mickey Mantle AS 50.00 20.00
(left handed)
132 Albie Pearson AS 1.00 .40
133 Harmon Killebrew AS 8.00 3.20
134 Carl Yastrzemski AS 15.00 6.00
135 Elston Howard AS 3.00 1.20
136 Earl Battey AS 1.00 .40
137 Camilo Pascual AS 1.00 .40
138 Jim Bouton AS 2.00 .80
139 Whitey Ford AS 10.00 4.00
140 Gary Peters AS 1.00 .40
141 Bill White AS 1.50 .60
142 Orlando Cepeda AS 6.00 2.40
143 Bill Mazeroski AS 6.00 2.40
144 Tony Taylor AS 1.00 .40
145 Ken Boyer AS 2.00 .80
146 Ron Santo AS 2.00 .80
147 Dick Groat AS 1.50 .60
148 Roy McMillan AS 1.00 .40
149 Hank Aaron AS 25.00 10.00
150 Roberto Clemente AS 30.00 12.00
151 Willie Mays AS 30.00 12.00
152 Vada Pinson AS 1.50 .60
153 Tommy Davis AS 1.50 .60
154 Frank Robinson AS 10.00 4.00
155 Joe Torre AS 3.00 1.20
156 Tim McCarver AS 3.00 1.20
157 Juan Marichal AS 8.00 3.20
158 Jim Maloney AS 1.50 .60
159 Sandy Koufax AS 15.00 6.00
160 Warren Spahn AS 8.00 3.20
161A Wayne Causey AS 8.00 3.20
National League
161B Wayne Causey AS 1.50 .60
American League
162A Chuck Hinton AS 10.00 4.00
National League
162B Chuck Hinton AS 1.50 .60
American League
163 Bob Aspromonte AS 1.00 .40
164 Ron Hunt AS 1.00 .40

1964 Topps Giants

The cards in this 60-card set measure approximately 3 1/8" by 5 1/4". The 1964 Topps Giants are postcard size cards containing color player photographs. They are numbered on the backs, which also contain biographical information presented in a newspaper format. These "giant size" cards were distributed in both cellophane and waxed gum packs apart from the Topps regular issue of 1964. The gum packs contain three cards. The Cards 3, 28, 42, 45, 47, 51 and 60 are more difficult to find and are indicated by SP in the checklist below.

NM Ex
COMPLETE SET (60) 250.00 100.00
COMMON CARD (1-60) .50 .20
COMMON SP'S 10.00 4.00
WRAPPER (5-CENT) 35.00 14.00
1 Gary Peters 1.00 .40
2 Ken Johnson .50 .20
3 Sandy Koufax SP 40.00 16.00
4 Bob Bailey .50 .20
5 Milt Pappas 1.00 .40
6 Ron Hunt .50 .20
7 Whitey Ford 4.00 1.60
8 Roy McMillan .50 .20
9 Rocky Colavito 2.00 .80
10 Jim Bunning 3.00 1.20
11 Roberto Clemente 30.00 12.00
12 Al Kaline 5.00 2.00
13 Nellie Fox 3.00 1.20
14 Tony Gonzalez .50 .20
15 Jim Gentile 1.00 .40
16 Dean Chance 1.00 .40
17 Dick Ellsworth 1.00 .40
18 Jim Fregosi 1.00 .40
19 Dick Groat 1.50 .60
20 Chuck Hinton .50 .20
21 Elston Howard 1.50 .60
22 Dick Farrell .50 .20
23 Albie Pearson .50 .20
24 Frank Howard 1.50 .60
25 Mickey Mantle 50.00 20.00
26 Joe Torre 2.00 .80
27 Eddie Brinkman .50 .20
28 Bob Friend SP 10.00 4.00
29 Frank Robinson 5.00 2.00
30 Bill Freehan 1.00 .40
31 Warren Spahn 4.00 1.60
32 Camilo Pascual 1.00 .40
33 Pete Ward .50 .20
34 Jim Maloney 1.00 .40
35 Dave Wickersham .50 .20
36 Johnny Callison 1.00 .40
37 Juan Marichal 4.00 1.60
38 Harmon Killebrew 4.00 1.60
39 Luis Aparicio 3.00 1.20
40 Dick Radatz .50 .20
41 Bob Gibson 4.00 1.60
42 Dick Stuart SP 10.00 4.00
43 Tommy Davis 1.00 .40
44 Tony Oliva 2.00 .80
45 Wayne Causey SP 10.00 4.00
46 Max Alvis .50 .20
47 Galen Cisco SP 10.00 4.00
48 Carl Yastrzemski 5.00 2.00
49 Hank Aaron 10.00 4.00
50 Brooks Robinson 5.00 2.00
51 Willie Mays SP 50.00 20.00
52 Billy Williams 3.00 1.20
53 Juan Pizarro .50 .20
54 Leon Wagner .50 .20
55 Orlando Cepeda 3.00 1.20
56 Vada Pinson 1.50 .60
57 Ken Boyer 1.50 .60
58 Ron Santo 1.50 .60
59 John Romano .50 .20
60 Bill Skowron SP 15.00 6.00

1964 Topps Rookie All-Star Banquet

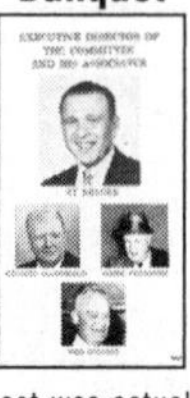

This 35-card set was actually the dinner program for the 1964 annual Topps Rookie All-Star Banquet and was housed in its own special presentation box. The first seven cards featured black and white photos of sport and media people and measured approximately 3" by 5 1/4". Cards 8-13 depicted the previous years' Rookie All-Star Teams each with black-and-white head shots of 10 players of that year on a light blue background. Cards 14-34A each displayed 3" by 3 1/4" black-and-white photos of one of the 1964 rookies being honored at the banquet or a photo of the PR Director for the team with a write-up of that team's rookie player.

NM Ex
COMPLETE SET (35) 1200.00 475.00
1 Title Card 20.00 8.00
2 Tommy Davis 40.00 16.00
Jeff Torborg
Ron Santo
Billy Williams
3 Luis Aparicio 40.00 16.00
Sam Bowens
Tom Tresh
Pedro Gonzalez
Bob Bruce
Walt Bond
Mike White
Bob Rodgers
Dean Chance
Lee Thomas
Ray Culp
Dalton Jones
Tony Conigliaro
Dave Gray
4 Hank Greenberg HOF 40.00 16.00
Frank Frisch HOF
Tim Cohane
D. Grote NL DIR
Carl Lindemann NBC
Bill MacPhail CBS
5 Jackie Robinson HOF 100.00 40.00
J. McDermott
J. McKenney AL DIR
Frank Shaughnessy PR INT'L
Joel Shorin
Al Silverman
Charles Spink
6 Sy Berger 25.00 10.00
G. MacDonald
H. Feimister
T. Wright
7 Joe Garagiola TRIB 40.00 16.00
8 Willie McCovey 80.00 32.00
Pumpsie Green
Joe Koppe
Jim Baxes
Bob Allison
Ron Fairly
Willie Tasby
John Romano
Jim Perry
Jim O'Toole
9 Jim Gentile 40.00 16.00
Stan Javier
Ron Hansen
Ron Santo
Tommy Davis
Frank Howard
Tony Curry
Jimmy Coker
Chuck Estrada
Dick Stigman
10 J.C. Martin 80.00 32.00
Jake Wood
Dick Howser
Charlie Smith
Billy Williams
Lee Thomas
Floyd Robinson
Joe Torre
Don Schwall
Jack Curtis
11 Fred Whitfield 40.00 16.00
Bernie Allen
Tom Tresh
Ed Charles
Manny Jimenez
Al Luplow
Boog Powell
Bob Rodgers
Dean Chance
Al Jackson
12 Pete Rose 200.00 80.00
Rusty Staub
Al Weis
Pete Ward
Jimmie Hall
Vic Davalillo
Tommy Harper
Jesse Gonder
Ray Culp
Gary Peters
13 64 Rookie AS Title Card 20.00 8.00
14 Ed Uhas DIR 20.00 8.00
15 Bob Chance 25.00 10.00
16 Garry Schumacher DIR 20.00 8.00
17 Hal Lanier 25.00 10.00
18 Larry Shenk DIR 20.00 8.00
19 Richie Allen 80.00 32.00
20 Jim Schaaf DIR 20.00 8.00
21 Bert Campaneris 30.00 12.00
22 Ernie Johnson DIR 20.00 8.00
23 Rico Carty 30.00 12.00
24 Bill Crowley DIR 20.00 8.00
25 Tony Conigliaro 40.00 16.00
26 Tom Mee DIR 20.00 8.00
27 Tony Oliva 60.00 24.00
28 Burt Hawkins DIR 20.00 8.00
29 Mike Brumley 25.00 10.00
30 Hank Zureick DIR 20.00 8.00
31 Billy McCool 25.00 10.00
32 Rob Brown DIR 20.00 8.00
33 Wally Bunker 25.00 10.00
34 Minor League POY Title Card 20.00 8.00
34A Luis Tiant 30.00 12.00

1964 Topps Stand Ups

In 1964 Topps produced a die-cut "Stand-Up" card design for the first time since their Connie Mack and Current All Stars of 1951. These cards were issued in both one cent and five cent packs. The cards have full-length, color player photos set against a green and yellow background. Of the 77 cards in the set, 22 were single printed and these are marked in the checklist below with an SP. These unnumbered cards are standard-size (2 1/2" by 3 1/2"), blank backed, and have been numbered here for reference in alphabetical order of players. Interestingly there were four different wrapper designs used for this set. All the design variations are valued at the same price.

NM Ex
COMPLETE SET (77) 3500.00 1400.00
COMMON CARD (1-77) 10.00 4.00
COMMON CARD SP 40.00 16.00
WRAPPER (1-CENT) 150.00 60.00
WRAPPER (5-CENT) 325.00 130.00
1 Hank Aaron 150.00 60.00
2 Hank Aguirre 10.00 4.00
3 George Altman 15.00 6.00
4 Max Alvis 10.00 4.00
5 Bob Aspromonte 10.00 4.00
6 Jack Baldschun SP 40.00 16.00
7 Ernie Banks 80.00 32.00
8 Steve Barber 10.00 4.00
9 Earl Battey 10.00 4.00
10 Ken Boyer 20.00 8.00
11 Ernie Broglio 10.00 4.00
12 John Callison 15.00 6.00
13 Norm Cash SP 60.00 24.00
14 Wayne Causey 10.00 4.00
15 Orlando Cepeda 50.00 20.00
16 Ed Charles 15.00 6.00
17 Roberto Clemente 225.00 90.00
18 Donn Clendenon SP 40.00 16.00
19 Rocky Colavito 40.00 16.00
20 Ray Culp SP 50.00 20.00
21 Tommy Davis 15.00 6.00
22 Don Drysdale SP 125.00 50.00
23 Dick Ellsworth 10.00 4.00
24 Dick Farrell 10.00 4.00
25 Jim Fregosi 15.00 6.00
26 Bob Friend 10.00 4.00
27 Jim Gentile 15.00 6.00
28 Jesse Gonder SP 40.00 16.00
29 Tony Gonzalez SP 40.00 16.00
30 Dick Groat 20.00 8.00
31 Woody Held 10.00 4.00
32 Chuck Hinton 10.00 4.00
33 Elston Howard 20.00 8.00
34 Frank Howard SP 60.00 24.00
35 Ron Hunt 15.00 6.00
36 Al Jackson 10.00 4.00
37 Ken Johnson 10.00 4.00
38 Al Kaline 80.00 32.00
39 Harmon Killebrew 70.00 28.00
40 Sandy Koufax 150.00 60.00
41 Don Lock SP 40.00 16.00
42 Jerry Lumpe SP 40.00 16.00
43 Jim Maloney 15.00 6.00
44 Frank Malzone 10.00 4.00
45 Mickey Mantle 500.00 200.00
46 Juan Marichal SP 100.00 40.00
47 Eddie Mathews SP 125.00 50.00
48 Willie Mays 250.00 100.00
49 Bill Mazeroski 30.00 12.00
50 Ken McBride 10.00 4.00
51 Willie McCovey SP 100.00 40.00
52 Claude Osteen 15.00 6.00
53 Jim O'Toole 10.00 4.00
54 Camilo Pascual 15.00 6.00
55 Albie Pearson SP 50.00 20.00
56 Gary Peters 10.00 4.00
57 Vada Pinson 20.00 8.00
58 Juan Pizarro 10.00 4.00

59 Boog Powell 20.00 8.00
60 Bobby Richardson 30.00 12.00
61 Brooks Robinson 80.00 32.00
62 Floyd Robinson 10.00 4.00
63 Frank Robinson 80.00 32.00
64 Ed Roebuck SP 40.00 16.00
65 Rich Rollins 10.00 4.00
66 John Romano 10.00 4.00
67 Ron Santo SP 60.00 24.00
68 Norm Siebern 10.00 4.00
69 Warren Spahn SP 125.00 50.00
70 Dick Stuart SP 50.00 20.00
71 Lee Thomas 10.00 4.00
72 Joe Torre 20.00 8.00
73 Pete Ward 10.00 4.00
74 Bill White SP 50.00 20.00
75 Billy Williams SP 100.00 40.00
76 Hal Woodeshick SP 40.00 16.00
77 Carl Yastrzemski SP 400.00 160.00

1964 Topps Tattoos Inserts

These tattoos measure 1 9/16" by 3 1/2" and are printed in color on very thin paper. One side gives instructions for applying the tattoo. The picture side gives either the team logo and name (on tattoos numbered 1-20 below) or the player's face, name and team (21-75 below). The tattoos are unnumbered and are presented below in alphabetical order within type for convenience. This set was issued in one cent packs which came 120 to a box. The boxes had photos of Whitey Ford on them.

NM Ex
COMPLETE SET (75) 1350.00 550.00
COMMON TATTOO (1-20) 4.00 1.60
COMMON TATTOO (21-75) 8.00 3.20
8 Detroit Tigers 5.00 2.00
11 Los Angeles Dodgers 12.00 4.80
14 New York Mets 5.00 2.00
15 New York Yankees 12.00 4.80
21 Hank Aaron 110.00 45.00
22 Max Alvis 8.00 3.20
23 Hank Aguirre 8.00 3.20
24 Ernie Banks 60.00 24.00
25 Steve Barber 8.00 3.20
26 Ken Boyer 12.00 4.80
27 John Callison 8.00 3.20
28 Norm Cash 10.00 4.00
29 Wayne Causey 8.00 3.20
30 Orlando Cepeda 20.00 8.00
31 Rocky Colavito 20.00 8.00
32 Ray Culp 8.00 3.20
33 Vic Davalillo 8.00 3.20
34 Moe Drabowsky 8.00 3.20
35 Dick Ellsworth 8.00 3.20
36 Curt Flood 12.00 4.80
37 Bill Freehan 10.00 4.00
38 Jim Fregosi 10.00 4.00
39 Bob Friend 8.00 3.20
40 Dick Groat 12.00 4.80
41 Woody Held 8.00 3.20
42 Frank Howard 12.00 4.80
43 Al Jackson 8.00 3.20
44 Larry Jackson 8.00 3.20
45 Ken Johnson 8.00 3.20
46 Al Kaline 60.00 24.00
47 Harmon Killebrew 40.00 16.00
48 Sandy Koufax 110.00 45.00
49 Don Lock 8.00 3.20
50 Frank Malzone 10.00 4.00
51 Mickey Mantle 300.00 120.00
52 Eddie Mathews 50.00 20.00
53 Willie Mays 125.00 50.00
54 Bill Mazeroski 15.00 6.00
55 Ken McBride 8.00 3.20
56 Bill Monbouquette 8.00 3.20
57 Dave Nicholson 8.00 3.20
58 Claude Osteen 8.00 3.20
59 Milt Pappas 10.00 4.00
60 Camilo Pascual 8.00 3.20
61 Albie Pearson 8.00 3.20
62 Ron Perranoski 8.00 3.20
63 Gary Peters 8.00 3.20
64 Boog Powell 12.00 4.80
65 Frank Robinson 50.00 20.00
66 Johnny Romano 8.00 3.20
67 Norm Siebern 8.00 3.20
68 Warren Spahn 50.00 20.00
69 Dick Stuart 10.00 4.00
70 Lee Thomas 8.00 3.20
71 Joe Torre 15.00 6.00
72 Pete Ward 8.00 3.20
73 Carlton Willey 8.00 3.20
74 Billy Williams 40.00 16.00
75 Carl Yastrzemski 60.00 24.00

1964 Topps Venezuelan

This set is a parallel version of the first 370 cards in the regular 1964 Topps set and is similar in design. The major difference is the black margin featured on the card back. The cards were issued for the Venezuelan market.

NM Ex
COMPLETE SET (370) 7000.00 2800.00
1 Sandy Koufax 60.00 24.00
Dick Ellsworth
Bob Friend LL
2 Gary Peters 10.00 4.00
Juan Pizarro
Camilo Pascual LL
3 Sandy Koufax 50.00 20.00
Juan Marichal
Warren Spahn
Jim Maloney LL
4 Whitey Ford 25.00 10.00
Camilo Pascual
Jim Bouton LL
5 Sandy Koufax 40.00 16.00
Jim Maloney
Don Drysdale LL
6 Camilo Pascual 10.00 4.00
Jim Bunning
Dick Stigman LL
7 Tommy Davis 50.00 20.00
Bob Clemente
Dick Groat
Hank Aaron LL
8 Carl Yastrzemski 30.00 12.00
Al Kaline
Rich Rollins LL
9 Hank Aaron 80.00 32.00
Willie McCovey
Willie Mays
Orlando Cepeda LL
10 Harmon Killebrew 25.00 10.00
Dick Stuart
Bob Allison LL
11 Hank Aaron 30.00 12.00
Ken Boyer
Bill White LL
12 Dick Stuart 25.00 10.00
Al Kaline
Harmon Killebrew LL
13 Hoyt Wilhelm 25.00 10.00
14 Dick Nen 8.00 3.20
Nick Willhite
15 Zoilo Versalles 8.00 3.20
16 John Boozer 8.00 3.20
17 Willie Kirkland 8.00 3.20
18 Billy O'Dell 8.00 3.20
19 Don Wert 8.00 3.20
20 Bob Friend 8.00 3.20
21 Yogi Berra MG 80.00 32.00
22 Jerry Adair 8.00 3.20
23 Chris Zachary 8.00 3.20
24 Carl Sawatski 8.00 3.20
25 Bill Monbouquette 8.00 3.20
26 Gino Cimoli 8.00 3.20
27 New York Mets 15.00 6.00
Team Card
28 Claude Osteen 8.00 3.20
29 Lou Brock 80.00 32.00
30 Ron Perranoski 8.00 3.20
31 Dave Nicholson 8.00 3.20
32 Dean Chance 8.00 3.20
33 Sammy Ellis 8.00 3.20
Mel Queen
34 Jim Perry 8.00 3.20
35 Eddie Mathews 40.00 16.00
36 Hal Reniff 8.00 3.20
37 Smoky Burgess 8.00 3.20
38 Jim Wynn 15.00 6.00
39 Hank Aguirre 8.00 3.20
40 Dick Groat 8.00 3.20
41 Willie McCovey 15.00 6.00
Leon Wagner
42 Moe Drabowsky 8.00 3.20
43 Roy Sievers 8.00 3.20
44 Duke Carmel 8.00 3.20
45 Milt Pappas 8.00 3.20
46 Ed Brinkman 8.00 3.20
47 Jesus Alou 8.00 3.20
Ron Herbel
48 Bob Perry 8.00 3.20
49 Bill Henry 8.00 3.20
50 Mickey Mantle 800.00 325.00
51 Pete Richert 8.00 3.20
52 Chuck Hinton 8.00 3.20
53 Denis Menke 8.00 3.20
54 Sam Mele MG 8.00 3.20
55 Ernie Banks 80.00 32.00
56 Hal Brown 8.00 3.20
57 Tim Harkness 8.00 3.20
58 Don Demeter 8.00 3.20
59 Ernie Broglio 8.00 3.20
60 Frank Malzone 8.00 3.20
61 Bob Rodgers 8.00 3.20
Ed Sadowski
62 Ted Savage 8.00 3.20
63 John Orsino 8.00 3.20
64 Ted Abernathy 8.00 3.20
65 Felipe Alou 15.00 6.00
66 Eddie Fisher 8.00 3.20
67 Tigers Team 15.00 6.00
68 Willie Davis 8.00 3.20
69 Clete Boyer 10.00 4.00
70 Joe Torre 20.00 8.00
71 Jack Spring 8.00 3.20
72 Chico Cardenas 8.00 3.20
73 Jimmie Hall 8.00 3.20
74 Bob Priddy 8.00 3.20
Tom Butters
75 Wayne Causey 8.00 3.20
76 Checklist 1 20.00 8.00
77 Jerry Walker 8.00 3.20
78 Merritt Ranew 8.00 3.20
79 Bob Heffner 8.00 3.20
80 Vada Pinson 10.00 4.00
81 Nellie Fox 20.00 8.00
Harmon Killebrew
82 Jim Davenport 8.00 3.20
83 Gus Triandos 8.00 3.20
84 Carl Willey 8.00 3.20
85 Pete Ward 8.00 3.20
86 Al Downing 8.00 3.20
87 St. Louis Cardinals 15.00 6.00
Team Card
88 John Roseboro 8.00 3.20
89 Boog Powell 15.00 6.00
90 Earl Battey 8.00 3.20
91 Bob Bailey 8.00 3.20
92 Steve Ridzik 8.00 3.20
93 Gary Geiger 8.00 3.20
94 Jim Britton 8.00 3.20
Larry Maxie
95 George Altman 8.00 3.20
96 Bob Buhl 8.00 3.20
97 Jim Fregosi 8.00 3.20
98 Bill Bruton 8.00 3.20
99 Al Stanek 8.00 3.20
100 Elston Howard 10.00 4.00
101 Walt Alston MG 15.00 6.00
102 Checklist 2 20.00 8.00
103 Curt Flood 10.00 4.00
104 Art Mahaffey 8.00 3.20
105 Woody Held 8.00 3.20
106 Joe Nuxhall 8.00 3.20
107 Bruce Howard 8.00 3.20
Frank Kreutzer
108 John Wyatt 8.00 3.20
109 Rusty Staub 15.00 6.00
110 Albie Pearson 8.00 3.20
111 Don Elston 8.00 3.20
112 Bob Tillman 8.00 3.20
113 Grover Powell 8.00 3.20
114 Don Lock 8.00 3.20
115 Frank Bolling 8.00 3.20
116 Jay Ward 30.00 12.00
Tony Oliva
117 Earl Francis 8.00 3.20
118 John Blanchard 8.00 3.20
119 Gary Kolb 8.00 3.20
120 Don Drysdale 50.00 20.00
121 Pete Runnels 8.00 3.20
122 Don McMahon 8.00 3.20
123 Jose Pagan 8.00 3.20
124 Orlando Pena 8.00 3.20
125 Pete Rose 400.00 160.00
126 Russ Snyder 8.00 3.20
127 Aubrey Gatewood 8.00 3.20
Dick Simpson
128 Mickey Lolich 50.00 20.00
129 Amado Samuel 8.00 3.20
130 Gary Peters 8.00 3.20
131 Steve Boros 8.00 3.20
132 Braves Team 15.00 6.00
133 Jim Grant 8.00 3.20
134 Don Zimmer 8.00 3.20
135 Johnny Callison 8.00 3.20
136 Sandy Koufax WS 40.00 16.00
Strikes out 15
137 Tommy Davis WS 10.00 4.00
138 Ron Fairly WS 10.00 4.00
139 Frank Howard WS 10.00 4.00
140 World Series Summary 10.00 4.00
Dodgers celebrate
141 Danny Murtaugh MG 8.00 3.20
142 John Bateman 8.00 3.20
143 Bubba Phillips 8.00 3.20
144 Al Worthington 8.00 3.20
145 Norm Siebern 8.00 3.20
146 Tommy John 80.00 32.00
Bob Chance
147 Ray Sadecki 8.00 3.20
148 J.C. Martin 8.00 3.20
149 Paul Foytack 8.00 3.20
150 Willie Mays 250.00 100.00
151 Athletics Team 15.00 6.00
152 Denny Lemaster 8.00 3.20
153 Dick Williams 10.00 4.00
154 Dick Tracewski 8.00 3.20
155 Duke Snider 80.00 32.00
156 Bill Dailey 8.00 3.20
157 Gene Mauch MG 8.00 3.20
158 Ken Johnson 8.00 3.20
159 Charlie Dees 8.00 3.20
160 Ken Boyer 15.00 6.00
161 Dave McNally 8.00 3.20
162 Dick Sisler CO 8.00 3.20
Vada Pinson
163 Donn Clendenon 8.00 3.20
164 Bud Daley 8.00 3.20
165 Jerry Lumpe 8.00 3.20
166 Marty Keough 8.00 3.20
167 Mike Brumley 80.00 32.00
Lou Piniella
168 Al Weis 8.00 3.20
169 Del Crandall 8.00 3.20
170 Dick Radatz 8.00 3.20
171 Ty Cline 8.00 3.20
172 Indians Team 15.00 6.00
173 Ryne Duren 8.00 3.20
174 Doc Edwards 8.00 3.20
175 Billy Williams 40.00 16.00
176 Tracy Stallard 8.00 3.20
177 Harmon Killebrew 50.00 20.00
178 Hank Bauer MG 8.00 3.20
179 Carl Warwick 8.00 3.20
180 Tommy Davis 8.00 3.20
181 Dave Wickersham 8.00 3.20
182 Carl Yastrzemski 40.00 16.00
Chuck Schilling
183 Ron Taylor 8.00 3.20
184 Al Luplow 8.00 3.20
185 Jim O'Toole 8.00 3.20
186 Roman Mejias 8.00 3.20
187 Ed Roebuck 8.00 3.20
188 Checklist 3 20.00 8.00
189 Bob Hendley 8.00 3.20
190 Bobby Richardson 20.00 8.00
191 Clay Dalrymple 8.00 3.20
192 John Boccabella 8.00 3.20
Billy Cowan
193 Jerry Lynch 8.00 3.20
194 John Goryl 8.00 3.20
195 Floyd Robinson 8.00 3.20
196 Jim Gentile 8.00 3.20
197 Frank Lary 8.00 3.20
198 Len Gabrielson 8.00 3.20
199 Joe Azcue 8.00 3.20
200 Sandy Koufax 250.00 100.00
201 Sam Bowens 8.00 3.20
Wally Bunker
202 Galen Cisco 8.00 3.20
203 John Kennedy 8.00 3.20
204 Matty Alou 10.00 4.00
205 Nellie Fox 25.00 10.00
206 Steve Hamilton 8.00 3.20
207 Fred Hutchinson MG 8.00 3.20
208 Wes Covington 8.00 3.20
209 Bob Allen 8.00 3.20
210 Carl Yastrzemski 80.00 32.00
211 Jim Coker 8.00 3.20
212 Pete Lovrich 8.00 3.20
213 Angels Team 15.00 6.00
214 Ken McMullen 8.00 3.20
215 Ray Herbert 8.00 3.20
216 Mike de la Hoz 8.00 3.20
217 Jim King 8.00 3.20
218 Hank Fischer 8.00 3.20
219 Al Downing 8.00 3.20
Jim Bouton
220 Dick Ellsworth 8.00 3.20
221 Bob Saverine 8.00 3.20
222 Billy Pierce 10.00 4.00
223 George Banks 8.00 3.20
224 Tommie Sisk 8.00 3.20
225 Roger Maris 120.00 47.50
226 Jerry Grote 10.00 4.00
Larry Yellen
227 Barry Latman 8.00 3.20
228 Felix Mantilla 8.00 3.20
229 Charley Lau 8.00 3.20
230 Brooks Robinson 80.00 32.00
231 Dick Calmus 8.00 3.20
232 Al Lopez MG 15.00 6.00
233 Hal Smith 8.00 3.20
234 Gary Bell 8.00 3.20
235 Ron Hunt 8.00 3.20
236 Bill Faul 8.00 3.20
237 Cubs Team 15.00 6.00
238 Roy McMillan 8.00 3.20
239 Herm Starrette 8.00 3.20
240 Bill White 10.00 4.00
241 Jim Owens 8.00 3.20
242 Harvey Kuenn 8.00 3.20
243 Richie Allen 80.00 32.00
John Herrnstein
244 Tony LaRussa 80.00 32.00
245 Dick Stigman 8.00 3.20
246 Manny Mota 10.00 4.00
247 Dave DeBusschere 15.00 6.00
248 Johnny Pesky MG 8.00 3.20
249 Doug Camilli 8.00 3.20
250 Al Kaline 100.00 40.00
251 Choo Choo Coleman 8.00 3.20
252 Ken Aspromonte 8.00 3.20
253 Wally Post 8.00 3.20
254 Don Hoak 8.00 3.20
255 Lee Thomas 8.00 3.20
256 Johnny Weekly 8.00 3.20
257 San Francisco Giants 15.00 6.00
Team Card
258 Garry Roggenburk 8.00 3.20
259 Harry Bright 8.00 3.20
260 Frank Robinson 80.00 32.00
261 Jim Hannan 8.00 3.20
262 Mike Shannon 20.00 8.00
Harry Fanok
263 Chuck Estrada 8.00 3.20
264 Jim Landis 8.00 3.20
265 Jim Bunning 40.00 16.00
266 Gene Freese 8.00 3.20
267 Wilbur Wood 10.00 4.00
268 Danny Murtaugh 8.00 3.20
Bill Virdon MG
269 Ellis Burton 8.00 3.20
270 Rich Rollins 8.00 3.20
271 Bob Sadowski 8.00 3.20
272 Jake Wood 8.00 3.20
273 Mel Nelson 8.00 3.20
274 Checklist 4 20.00 8.00
275 John Tsitouris 8.00 3.20
276 Jose Tartabull 8.00 3.20
277 Ken Retzer 8.00 3.20
278 Bobby Shantz 8.00 3.20
279 Joe Koppe UER 8.00 3.20
(Glove on wrong hand)
280 Juan Marichal 40.00 16.00
281 Jake Gibbs 8.00 3.20
Tom Metcalf
282 Bob Bruce 8.00 3.20
283 Tom McCraw 8.00 3.20
284 Dick Schofield 8.00 3.20
285 Robin Roberts 40.00 16.00
286 Don Landrum 8.00 3.20
287 Tony Conigliaro 120.00 47.50
Bill Spanswick
288 Al Moran 8.00 3.20
289 Frank Funk 8.00 3.20
290 Bob Allison 8.00 3.20
291 Phil Ortega 8.00 3.20
292 Mike Roarke 8.00 3.20
293 Phillies Team 15.00 6.00
294 Ken L. Hunt 8.00 3.20
295 Roger Craig 8.00 3.20
296 Ed Kirkpatrick 8.00 3.20
297 Ken MacKenzie 8.00 3.20
298 Harry Craft MG 8.00 3.20
299 Bill Stafford 8.00 3.20
300 Hank Aaron 200.00 80.00
301 Larry Brown 8.00 3.20
302 Dan Pfister 8.00 3.20
303 Jim Campbell 8.00 3.20
304 Bob Johnson 8.00 3.20
305 Jack Lamabe 8.00 3.20
306 Willie Mays 80.00 32.00
Orlando Cepeda
307 Joe Gibbon 8.00 3.20
308 Gene Stephens 8.00 3.20
309 Paul Toth 8.00 3.20
310 Jim Gilliam 10.00 4.00
311 Tom Brown 8.00 3.20
312 Fritz Fisher 8.00 3.20
Fred Gladding
313 Chuck Hiller 8.00 3.20
314 Jerry Buchek 8.00 3.20
315 Bo Belinsky 10.00 4.00
316 Gene Oliver 8.00 3.20
317 Al Smith 8.00 3.20
318 Minnesota Twins 15.00 6.00
Team Card
319 Paul Brown 8.00 3.20
320 Rocky Colavito 40.00 16.00
321 Bob Lillis 8.00 3.20
322 George Brunet 8.00 3.20
323 John Buzhardt 8.00 3.20
324 Casey Stengel MG 40.00 16.00
325 Hector Lopez 8.00 3.20
326 Ron Brand 8.00 3.20
327 Don Blasingame 8.00 3.20
328 Bob Shaw 8.00 3.20
329 Russ Nixon 8.00 3.20
330 Tommy Harper 8.00 3.20
331 Roger Maris 500.00 200.00
Norm Cash
Mickey Mantle
Al Kaline
332 Ray Washburn 8.00 3.20
333 Billy Moran 8.00 3.20
334 Lew Krausse 8.00 3.20
335 Don Mossi 8.00 3.20
336 Andre Rodgers 8.00 3.20
337 Al Ferrara 8.00 3.20
Jeff Torborg
338 Jack Kralick 8.00 3.20
339 Walt Bond 8.00 3.20
340 Joe Cunningham 8.00 3.20
341 Jim Roland 8.00 3.20
342 Willie Stargell 80.00 32.00
343 Senators Team 15.00 6.00
344 Phil Linz 8.00 3.20
345 Frank Thomas 8.00 3.20
346 Joey Jay 8.00 3.20
347 Bobby Wine 8.00 3.20
348 Ed Lopat MG 8.00 3.20
349 Art Fowler 8.00 3.20
350 Willie McCovey 50.00 20.00
351 Dan Schneider 8.00 3.20
352 Eddie Bressoud 8.00 3.20
353 Wally Moon 8.00 3.20
354 Dave Giusti 8.00 3.20
355 Vic Power 8.00 3.20
356 Bill McCool 8.00 3.20
Chico Ruiz
357 Charley James 8.00 3.20
358 Ron Kline 8.00 3.20
359 Jim Schaffer 8.00 3.20
360 Joe Pepitone 8.00 3.20
361 Jay Hook 8.00 3.20
362 Checklist 5 20.00 8.00
363 Dick McAuliffe 8.00 3.20
364 Joe Gaines 8.00 3.20
365 Cal McLish 8.00 3.20
366 Nelson Mathews 8.00 3.20
367 Fred Whitfield 8.00 3.20
368 Fritz Ackley 8.00 3.20
Don Buford
369 Jerry Zimmerman 8.00 3.20
370 Hal Woodeshick 8.00 3.20

1965 Topps

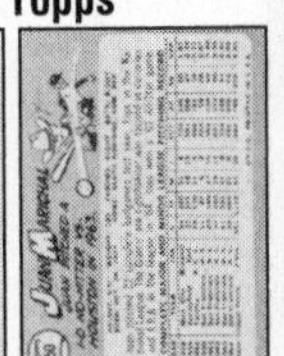

The cards in this 598-card set measure 2 1/2" by 3 1/2". The cards comprising the 1965 Topps set have team names located within a distinctive pennant design below the picture. The cards have blue borders on the reverse and were issued by series. Within this last series (523-598) there are 44 cards that were printed in lesser quantities than the other cards in that series; these shorter-printed cards are marked by SP in the checklist below. Featured subsets within this set include League Leaders (1-12) and World Series cards (132-139). This was the last year Topps issued one-card penny packs. Card were also issued in five-card nickel packs. The key Rookie Cards in this set are Steve Carlton, Jim "Catfish" Hunter, Joe Morgan, Mansori Murakami and Tony Perez.

NM Ex
COMPLETE SET (598) 4500.00 1800.00
COMMON CARD (1-196) 2.00 .80
COMMON (197-283) 2.50 1.00
COMMON (284-370) 4.00 1.60
COMMON (371-598) 8.00 3.20
WRAPPER (1-CENT) 125.00 50.00
WRAPPER (5-CENT) 100.00 40.00
1 Tony Oliva 20.00 6.00
Elston Howard
Brooks Robinson LL
2 Roberto Clemente 25.00 10.00
Hank Aaron
Rico Carty LL
3 Harmon Killebrew 50.00 20.00
Mickey Mantle
Boog Powell LL
4 Willie Mays 15.00 6.00
Billy Williams
Jim Ray Hart
Orlando Cepeda
Johnny Callison LL
5 Brooks Robinson 40.00 16.00
Harmon Killebrew
Mickey Mantle
Dick Stuart LL
6 Ken Boyer 12.00 4.80
Willie Mays
Ron Santo LL
7 Dean Chance 5.00 2.00
Joel Horlen LL
8 Sandy Koufax 20.00 8.00
Don Drysdale LL
9 Dean Chance 5.00 2.00
Gary Peters
Dave Wickersham
Juan Pizarro
Wally Bunker LL
10 Larry Jackson 5.00 2.00
Ray Sadecki
Juan Marichal LL
11 Al Downing 5.00 2.00
Dean Chance
Camilo Pascual LL
12 Bob Veale 10.00 4.00
Don Drysdale
Bob Gibson LL
13 Pedro Ramos 4.00 1.60
14 Len Gabrielson 2.00 .80
15 Robin Roberts 10.00 4.00
16 Joe Morgan RC 60.00 24.00
Sonny Jackson DP

17 Johnny Romano 2.00 .80
18 Bill McCool 2.00 .80
19 Gates Brown 4.00 1.60
20 Jim Bunning 10.00 4.00
21 Don Blasingame 2.00 .80
22 Charlie Smith 2.00 .80
23 Bob Tiefenauer 2.00 .80
24 Minnesota Twins 6.00 2.40
Team Card
25 Al McBean 2.00 .80
26 Bobby Knoop 2.00 .80
27 Dick Bertell 2.00 .80
28 Barney Schultz 2.00 .80
29 Felix Mantilla 2.00 .80
30 Jim Bouton 6.00 2.40
31 Mike White 2.00 .80
32 Herman Franks MG 2.00 .80
33 Jackie Brandt 2.00 .80
34 Cal Koonce 2.00 .80
35 Ed Charles 2.00 .80
36 Bobby Wine 2.00 .80
37 Fred Gladding 2.00 .80
38 Jim King 2.00 .80
39 Gerry Arrigo 2.00 .80
40 Frank Howard 6.00 2.40
41 Bruce Howard 2.00 .80
Marv Staehle
42 Earl Wilson 4.00 1.60
43 Mike Shannon 4.00 1.60
(Name in red, other
Cardinals in yellow)
44 Wade Blasingame 2.00 .80
45 Roy McMillan 4.00 1.60
46 Bob Lee 2.00 .80
47 Tommy Harper 4.00 1.60
48 Claude Raymond 4.00 1.60
49 Curt Blefary RC 4.00 1.60
John Miller
50 Juan Marichal 10.00 4.00
51 Bill Bryan 2.00 .80
52 Ed Roebuck 2.00 .80
53 Dick McAuliffe 4.00 1.60
54 Joe Gibbon 2.00 .80
55 Tony Conigliaro 15.00 6.00
56 Ron Kline 2.00 .80
57 Cardinals Team 6.00 2.40
58 Fred Talbot 2.00 .80
59 Nate Oliver 2.00 .80
60 Jim O'Toole 4.00 1.60
61 Chris Cannizzaro 2.00 .80
62 Jim Kaat UER DP 6.00 2.40
(Misspelled Katt)
63 Ty Cline 2.00 .80
64 Lou Burdette 4.00 1.60
65 Tony Kubek 10.00 4.00
66 Bill Rigney MG 2.00 .80
67 Harvey Haddix 4.00 1.60
68 Del Crandall 4.00 1.60
69 Bill Virdon 4.00 1.60
70 Bill Skowron 6.00 2.40
71 John O'Donoghue 2.00 .80
72 Tony Gonzalez 2.00 .80
73 Dennis Ribant 2.00 .80
74 Rico Petrocelli RC 10.00 4.00
Jerry Stephenson
75 Deron Johnson 4.00 1.60
76 Sam McDowell 6.00 2.40
77 Doug Camilli 2.00 .80
78 Dal Maxvill 2.00 .80
79A Checklist 1 10.00 2.00
(61 Cannizzaro)
79B Checklist 1 10.00 2.00
(61 C.Cannizzaro)
80 Turk Farrell 2.00 .80
81 Don Buford 4.00 1.60
82 Santos Alomar RC 6.00 2.40
John Braun
83 George Thomas 2.00 .80
84 Ron Herbel 2.00 .80
85 Willie Smith 2.00 .80
86 Buster Narum 2.00 .80
87 Nelson Mathews 2.00 .80
88 Jack Lamabe 2.00 .80
89 Mike Hershberger 2.00 .80
90 Rich Rollins 4.00 1.60
91 Cubs Team 6.00 2.40
92 Dick Howser 4.00 1.60
93 Jack Fisher 2.00 .80
94 Charlie Lau 4.00 1.60
95 Bill Mazeroski DP 6.00 2.40
96 Sonny Siebert 4.00 1.60
97 Pedro Gonzalez 2.00 .80
98 Bob Miller 2.00 .80
99 Gil Hodges MG 6.00 2.40
100 Ken Boyer 10.00 4.00
101 Fred Newman 2.00 .80
102 Steve Boros 2.00 .80
103 Harvey Kuenn 4.00 1.60
104 Checklist 2 10.00 2.00
105 Chico Salmon 2.00 .80
106 Gene Oliver 2.00 .80
107 Pat Corrales RC 4.00 1.60
Costen Shockley
108 Don Mincher 2.00 .80
109 Walt Bond 2.00 .80
110 Ron Santo 6.00 2.40
111 Lee Thomas 4.00 1.60
112 Derrell Griffith 2.00 .80
113 Steve Barber 2.00 .80
114 Jim Hickman 4.00 1.60
115 Bobby Richardson 10.00 4.00
116 Dave Dowling 4.00 1.60
Bob Tolan RC
117 Wes Stock 2.00 .80
118 Hal Lanier 4.00 1.60
119 John Kennedy 2.00 .80
120 Frank Robinson 40.00 16.00
121 Gene Alley 4.00 1.60
122 Bill Pleis 2.00 .80
123 Frank Thomas 4.00 1.60
124 Tom Satriano 2.00 .80
125 Juan Pizarro 2.00 .80
126 Dodgers Team 6.00 2.40
127 Frank Lary 2.00 .80
128 Vic Davalillo 2.00 .80
129 Bennie Daniels 2.00 .80
130 Al Kaline 40.00 16.00
131 Johnny Keane MG 2.00 .80
132 Mike Shannon WS 10.00 4.00
133 Mel Stottlemyre WS 6.00 2.40
134 Mickey Mantle WS 80.00 32.00
Mantle's Clutch HR UER
Mantle is shown wearing a road uniform
That game was played in New York
135 Ken Boyer WS 10.00 4.00
136 Tim McCarver WS 6.00 2.40
137 Jim Bouton WS 6.00 2.40
138 Bob Gibson WS 12.00 4.80
139 WS Summary 6.00 2.40
Cards celebrate
140 Dean Chance 4.00 1.60
141 Charlie James 2.00 .80
142 Bill Monbouquette 2.00 .80
143 John Gelnar 2.00 .80
Jerry May
144 Ed Kranepool 4.00 1.60
145 Luis Tiant RC 10.00 4.00
146 Ron Hansen 2.00 .80
147 Dennis Bennett 2.00 .80
148 Willie Kirkland 2.00 .80
149 Wayne Schurr 2.00 .80
150 Brooks Robinson 40.00 16.00
151 Athletics Team 6.00 2.40
152 Phil Ortega 2.00 .80
153 Norm Cash 6.00 2.40
154 Bob Humphreys 2.00 .80
155 Roger Maris 60.00 24.00
156 Bob Sadowski 2.00 .80
157 Zoilo Versalles 4.00 1.60
158 Dick Sisler 2.00 .80
159 Jim Duffalo 2.00 .80
160 R.Clemente UER 175.00 70.00
1960 Pittsburfh
161 Frank Baumann 2.00 .80
162 Russ Nixon 2.00 .80
163 Johnny Briggs 2.00 .80
164 Al Spangler 2.00 .80
165 Dick Ellsworth 2.00 .80
166 George Culver 4.00 1.60
Tommie Agee RC
167 Bill Wakefield 2.00 .80
168 Dick Green 2.00 .80
169 Dave Vineyard 2.00 .80
170 Hank Aaron 125.00 50.00
171 Jim Roland 2.00 .80
172 Jimmy Piersall 6.00 2.40
173 Detroit Tigers 6.00 2.40
Team Card
174 Joey Jay 2.00 .80
175 Bob Aspromonte 2.00 .80
176 Willie McCovey 20.00 8.00
177 Pete Mikkelsen 2.00 .80
178 Dalton Jones 2.00 .80
179 Hal Woodeshick 2.00 .80
180 Bob Allison 4.00 1.60
181 Don Loun 2.00 .80
Joe McCabe
182 Mike de la Hoz 2.00 .80
183 Dave Nicholson 2.00 .80
184 John Boozer 2.00 .80
185 Max Alvis 2.00 .80
186 Billy Cowan 2.00 .80
187 Casey Stengel MG 15.00 6.00
188 Sam Bowens 2.00 .80
189 Checklist 3 10.00 2.00
190 Bill White 6.00 2.40
191 Phil Regan 4.00 1.60
192 Jim Coker 2.00 .80
193 Gaylord Perry 15.00 6.00
194 Bill Kelso 2.00 .80
Rick Reichardt
195 Bob Veale 4.00 1.60
196 Ron Fairly 4.00 1.60
197 Diego Segui 2.50 1.00
198 Smoky Burgess 4.00 1.60
199 Bob Heffner 2.50 1.00
200 Joe Torre 6.00 2.40
201 Sandy Valdespino 4.00 1.60
Cesar Tovar RC
202 Leo Burke 2.50 1.00
203 Dallas Green 4.00 1.60
204 Russ Snyder 2.50 1.00
205 Warren Spahn 30.00 12.00
206 Willie Horton 4.00 1.60
207 Pete Rose 175.00 70.00
208 Tommy John 6.00 2.40
209 Pirates Team 6.00 2.40
210 Jim Fregosi 4.00 1.60
211 Steve Ridzik 2.50 1.00
212 Ron Brand 2.50 1.00
213 Jim Davenport 2.50 1.00
214 Bob Purkey 2.50 1.00
215 Pete Ward 2.50 1.00
216 Al Worthington 2.50 1.00
217 Walter Alston MG 6.00 2.40
218 Dick Schofield 2.50 1.00
219 Bob Meyer 2.50 1.00
220 Billy Williams 10.00 4.00
221 John Tsitouris 2.50 1.00
222 Bob Tillman 2.50 1.00
223 Dan Osinski 2.50 1.00
224 Bob Chance 2.50 1.00
225 Bo Belinsky 4.00 1.60
226 Elvio Jimenez 6.00 2.40
Jake Gibbs
227 Bobby Klaus 2.50 1.00
228 Jack Sanford 2.50 1.00
229 Lou Clinton 2.50 1.00
230 Ray Sadecki 2.50 1.00
231 Jerry Adair 2.50 1.00
232 Steve Blass RC 4.00 1.60
233 Don Zimmer 4.00 1.60
234 White Sox Team 6.00 2.40
235 Chuck Hinton 2.50 1.00
236 Denny McLain RC 25.00 10.00
237 Bernie Allen 2.50 1.00
238 Joe Moeller 2.50 1.00
239 Doc Edwards 2.50 1.00
240 Bob Bruce 2.50 1.00
241 Mack Jones 2.50 1.00
242 George Brunet 2.50 1.00
243 Ted Davidson 4.00 1.60
Tommy Helms RC
244 Lindy McDaniel 4.00 1.60
245 Joe Pepitone 6.00 2.40
246 Tom Butters 4.00 1.60
247 Wally Moon 4.00 1.60
248 Gus Triandos 4.00 1.60
249 Dave McNally 4.00 1.60
250 Willie Mays 150.00 60.00
251 Billy Herman MG 4.00 1.60
252 Pete Richert 2.50 1.00
253 Danny Cater 2.50 1.00
254 Roland Sheldon 2.50 1.00
255 Camilo Pascual 4.00 1.60
256 Tito Francona 2.50 1.00
257 Jim Wynn 4.00 1.60
258 Larry Bearnarth 2.50 1.00
259 Jim Northrup RC 6.00 2.40
Ray Oyler
260 Don Drysdale 20.00 8.00
261 Duke Carmel 2.50 1.00
262 Bud Daley 2.50 1.00
263 Marty Keough 2.50 1.00
264 Bob Buhl 4.00 1.60
265 Jim Pagliaroni 2.50 1.00
266 Bert Campaneris RC 10.00 4.00
267 Senators Team 6.00 2.40
268 Ken McBride 2.50 1.00
269 Frank Bolling 2.50 1.00
270 Milt Pappas 4.00 1.60
271 Don Wert 4.00 1.60
272 Chuck Schilling 2.50 1.00
273 Checklist 4 10.00 2.00
274 Lum Harris MG 2.50 1.00
275 Dick Groat 6.00 2.40
276 Hoyt Wilhelm 10.00 4.00
277 Johnny Lewis 2.50 1.00
278 Ken Retzer 2.50 1.00
279 Dick Tracewski 2.50 1.00
280 Dick Stuart 4.00 1.60
281 Bill Stafford 2.50 1.00
282 Dick Estelle 40.00 16.00
Masanori Murakami RC
283 Fred Whitfield 2.50 1.00
284 Nick Willhite 4.00 1.60
285 Ron Hunt 4.00 1.60
286 Jim Dickson 4.00 1.60
Aurelio Monteagudo
287 Gary Kolb 4.00 1.60
288 Jack Hamilton 4.00 1.60
289 Gordy Coleman 6.00 2.40
290 Wally Bunker 6.00 2.40
291 Jerry Lynch 4.00 1.60
292 Larry Yellen 4.00 1.60
293 Angels Team 6.00 2.40
294 Tim McCarver 10.00 4.00
295 Dick Radatz 6.00 2.40
296 Tony Taylor 6.00 2.40
297 Dave DeBusschere 10.00 4.00
298 Jim Stewart 4.00 1.60
299 Jerry Zimmerman 4.00 1.60
300 Sandy Koufax 100.00 40.00
301 Birdie Tebbetts MG 6.00 2.40
302 Al Stanek 4.00 1.60
303 John Orsino 4.00 1.60
304 Dave Stenhouse 4.00 1.60
305 Rico Carty 6.00 2.40
306 Bubba Phillips 4.00 1.60
307 Barry Latman 4.00 1.60
308 Cleon Jones RC 6.00 2.40
Tom Parsons
309 Steve Hamilton 6.00 2.40
310 Johnny Callison 6.00 2.40
311 Orlando Pena 4.00 1.60
312 Joe Nuxhall 4.00 1.60
313 Jim Schaffer 4.00 1.60
314 Sterling Slaughter 4.00 1.60
315 Frank Malzone 6.00 2.40
316 Reds Team 6.00 2.40
317 Don McMahon 4.00 1.60
318 Matty Alou 6.00 2.40
319 Ken McMullen 4.00 1.60
320 Bob Gibson 50.00 20.00
321 Rusty Staub 10.00 4.00
322 Rick Wise 6.00 2.40
323 Hank Bauer MG 6.00 2.40
324 Bobby Locke 4.00 1.60
325 Donn Clendenon 6.00 2.40
326 Dwight Siebler 4.00 1.60
327 Denis Menke 4.00 1.60
328 Eddie Fisher 4.00 1.60
329 Hawk Taylor 4.00 1.60
330 Whitey Ford 40.00 16.00
331 Al Ferrara 6.00 2.40
John Purdin
332 Ted Abernathy 4.00 1.60
333 Tom Reynolds 4.00 1.60
334 Vic Roznovsky 4.00 1.60
335 Mickey Lolich 6.00 2.40
336 Woody Held 4.00 1.60
337 Mike Cuellar 6.00 2.40
338 Philadelphia Phillies 6.00 2.40
Team Card
339 Ryne Duren 6.00 2.40
340 Tony Oliva 20.00 8.00
341 Bob Bolin 4.00 1.60
342 Bob Rodgers 6.00 2.40
343 Mike McCormick 6.00 2.40
344 Wes Parker 6.00 2.40
345 Floyd Robinson 4.00 1.60
346 Bobby Bragan MG 4.00 1.60
347 Roy Face 6.00 2.40
348 George Banks 4.00 1.60
349 Larry Miller 4.00 1.60
350 Mickey Mantle 500.00 200.00
351 Jim Perry 6.00 2.40
352 Alex Johnson RC 6.00 2.40
353 Jerry Lumpe 4.00 1.60
354 Billy Ott 4.00 1.60
Jack Warner
355 Vada Pinson 10.00 4.00
356 Bill Spanswick 4.00 1.60
357 Carl Warwick 4.00 1.60
358 Albie Pearson 6.00 2.40
359 Ken Johnson 4.00 1.60
360 Orlando Cepeda 15.00 6.00
361 Checklist 5 12.00 2.40
362 Don Schwall 4.00 1.60
363 Bob Johnson 4.00 1.60
364 Galen Cisco 4.00 1.60
365 Jim Gentile 6.00 2.40
366 Dan Schneider 4.00 1.60
367 Leon Wagner 4.00 1.60
368 Ken Berry 6.00 2.40
Joel Gibson
369 Phil Linz 6.00 2.40
370 Tommy Davis 6.00 2.40
371 Frank Kreutzer 8.00 3.20
372 Clay Dalrymple 8.00 3.20
373 Curt Simmons 8.00 3.20
374 Jose Cardenal RC 8.00 3.20
Dick Simpson
375 Dave Wickersham 8.00 3.20
376 Jim Landis 8.00 3.20
377 Willie Stargell 25.00 10.00
378 Chuck Estrada 8.00 3.20
379 Giants Team 8.00 3.20
380 Rocky Colavito 25.00 10.00
381 Al Jackson 8.00 3.20
382 J.C. Martin 8.00 3.20
383 Felipe Alou 15.00 6.00
384 Johnny Klippstein 8.00 3.20
385 Carl Yastrzemski 60.00 24.00
386 Paul Jaeckel 8.00 3.20
Fred Norman
387 Johnny Podres 15.00 6.00
388 John Blanchard 15.00 6.00
389 Don Larsen 15.00 6.00
390 Bill Freehan 15.00 6.00
391 Mel McGaha MG 8.00 3.20
392 Bob Friend 15.00 6.00
393 Ed Kirkpatrick 8.00 3.20
394 Jim Hannan 8.00 3.20
395 Jim Ray Hart 8.00 3.20
396 Frank Bertaina 8.00 3.20
397 Jerry Buchek 8.00 3.20
398 Dan Neville 15.00 6.00
Art Shamsky
399 Ray Herbert 8.00 3.20
400 Harmon Killebrew 50.00 20.00
401 Carl Willey 8.00 3.20
402 Joe Amalfitano 8.00 3.20
403 Boston Red Sox 8.00 3.20
Team Card
404 Stan Williams 8.00 3.20
(Listed as Indian
but Yankee cap)
405 John Roseboro 20.00 8.00
406 Ralph Terry 15.00 6.00
407 Lee Maye 8.00 3.20
408 Larry Sherry 8.00 3.20
409 Jim Beauchamp 15.00 6.00
Larry Dierker RC
410 Luis Aparicio 25.00 10.00
411 Roger Craig 15.00 6.00
412 Bob Bailey 8.00 3.20
413 Hal Reniff 8.00 3.20
414 Al Lopez MG 15.00 6.00
415 Curt Flood 15.00 6.00
416 Jim Brewer 8.00 3.20
417 Ed Brinkman 8.00 3.20
418 Johnny Edwards 8.00 3.20
419 Ruben Amaro 8.00 3.20
420 Larry Jackson 8.00 3.20
421 Gary Dotter 8.00 3.20
Jay Ward
422 Aubrey Gatewood 8.00 3.20
423 Jesse Gonder 8.00 3.20
424 Gary Bell 8.00 3.20
425 Wayne Causey 8.00 3.20
426 Braves Team 8.00 3.20
427 Bob Saverine 8.00 3.20
428 Bob Shaw 8.00 3.20
429 Don Demeter 8.00 3.20
430 Gary Peters 8.00 3.20
431 Nelson Briles RC 15.00 6.00
Wayne Spiezio
432 Jim Grant 15.00 6.00
433 John Bateman 8.00 3.20
434 Dave Morehead 8.00 3.20
435 Willie Davis 15.00 6.00
436 Don Elston 8.00 3.20
437 Chico Cardenas 15.00 6.00
438 Harry Walker MG 8.00 3.20
439 Moe Drabowsky 15.00 6.00
440 Tom Tresh 15.00 6.00
441 Denny Lemaster 8.00 3.20
442 Vic Power 8.00 3.20
443 Checklist 6 12.00 2.40
444 Bob Hendley 8.00 3.20
445 Don Lock 8.00 3.20
446 Art Mahaffey 8.00 3.20
447 Julian Javier 15.00 6.00
448 Lee Stange 8.00 3.20
449 Jerry Hinsley 15.00 6.00
Gary Kroll
450 Elston Howard 15.00 6.00
451 Jim Owens 8.00 3.20
452 Gary Geiger 8.00 3.20
453 Willie Crawford 15.00 6.00
John Werhas
454 Ed Rakow 8.00 3.20
455 Norm Siebern 8.00 3.20
456 Bill Henry 8.00 3.20
457 Bob Kennedy MG 15.00 6.00
458 John Buzhardt 8.00 3.20
459 Frank Kostro 8.00 3.20
460 Richie Allen 40.00 16.00
461 Clay Carroll RC 50.00 20.00
Phil Niekro
462 Lew Krausse UER 8.00 3.20
(Photo actually
Pete Lovrich)
463 Manny Mota 15.00 6.00
464 Ron Piche 8.00 3.20
465 Tom Haller 15.00 6.00
466 Pete Craig 8.00 3.20
Dick Nen
467 Ray Washburn 8.00 3.20
468 Larry Brown 8.00 3.20
469 Don Nottebart 8.00 3.20
470 Yogi Berra P/CO 50.00 20.00
471 Billy Hoeft 8.00 3.20
472 Don Pavletich UER 8.00 3.20
Listed as a pitcher
473 Paul Blair 15.00 6.00
Davey Johnson RC
474 Cookie Rojas 15.00 6.00
475 Clete Boyer 15.00 6.00
476 Billy O'Dell 8.00 3.20
477 Fritz Ackley 150.00 60.00
Steve Carlton RC
478 Wilbur Wood 15.00 6.00
479 Ken Harrelson 15.00 6.00
480 Joel Horlen 8.00 3.20
481 Cleveland Indians 10.00 4.00
Team Card
482 Bob Priddy 8.00 3.20
483 George Smith 8.00 3.20
484 Ron Perranoski 20.00 8.00
485 Nellie Fox P/CO 25.00 10.00
486 Tom Egan 8.00 3.20
Pat Rogan
487 Woody Woodward 15.00 6.00
488 Ted Wills 8.00 3.20
489 Gene Mauch MG 15.00 6.00
490 Earl Battey 8.00 3.20
491 Tracy Stallard 8.00 3.20
492 Gene Freese 8.00 3.20
493 Bill Roman 8.00 3.20
Bruce Brubaker
494 Jay Ritchie 8.00 3.20
495 Joe Christopher 8.00 3.20
496 Joe Cunningham 8.00 3.20
497 Ken Henderson 15.00 6.00
Jack Hiatt
498 Gene Stephens 8.00 3.20
499 Stu Miller 15.00 6.00
500 Eddie Mathews 40.00 16.00
501 Ralph Gagliano 8.00 3.20
Jim Rittwage
502 Don Cardwell 8.00 3.20
503 Phil Gagliano 8.00 3.20
504 Jerry Grote 15.00 6.00
505 Ray Culp 8.00 3.20
506 Sam Mele MG 8.00 3.20
507 Sammy Ellis 8.00 3.20
508 Checklist 7 12.00 2.40
509 Bob Guindon 8.00 3.20
Gerry Vezendy
510 Ernie Banks 80.00 32.00
511 Ron Locke 8.00 3.20
512 Cap Peterson 8.00 3.20
513 New York Yankees 40.00 16.00
Team Card
514 Joe Azcue 8.00 3.20
515 Vern Law 15.00 6.00
516 Al Weis 8.00 3.20
517 Paul Schaal 15.00 6.00
Jack Warner
518 Ken Rowe 8.00 3.20
519 Bob Uecker UER 30.00 12.00
(Posing as a left-
handed batter)
520 Tony Cloninger 8.00 3.20
521 Dave Bennett 8.00 3.20
Morrie Stevens
522 Hank Aguirre 8.00 3.20
523 Mike Brumley SP 12.00 4.80
524 Dave Giusti SP 12.00 4.80
525 Eddie Bressoud 8.00 3.20
526 Rene Lachemann 80.00 32.00
Johnny Odom
Jim Hunter RC UER
(Tim on back)
Skip Lockwood SP
527 Jeff Torborg SP 12.00 4.80
528 George Altman 8.00 3.20
529 Jerry Fosnow SP 12.00 4.80
530 Jim Maloney 15.00 6.00
531 Chuck Hiller 8.00 3.20
532 Hector Lopez 15.00 6.00
533 Dan Napoleon 25.00 10.00
Ron Swoboda RC
Tug McGraw RC
Jim Bethke SP
534 John Herrnstein 8.00 3.20
535 Jack Kralick SP 12.00 4.80
536 Andre Rodgers SP 12.00 4.80
537 Marcelino Lopez 8.00 3.20
Phil Roof
Rudy May RC
538 C.Dressen SP MG 12.00 4.80
539 Herm Starrette 8.00 3.20
540 Lou Brock SP 50.00 20.00
541 Greg Bollo 8.00 3.20
Bob Locker
542 Lou Klimchock 8.00 3.20
543 Ed Connolly SP 12.00 4.80
544 Howie Reed 8.00 3.20
545 Jesus Alou SP 15.00 6.00
546 Bill Davis 8.00 3.20
Mike Hedlund
Ray Barker
Floyd Weaver
547 Jake Wood SP 12.00 4.80
548 Dick Stigman 8.00 3.20
549 Roberto Pena 20.00 8.00
Glenn Beckert RC
550 M.Stottlemyre RC SP 30.00 12.00
551 New York Mets SP 30.00 12.00
Team Card
552 Julio Gotay 8.00 3.20
553 Dan Coombs 8.00 3.20
Gene Ratliff
Jack McClure
554 Chico Ruiz SP 12.00 4.80
555 Jack Baldschun SP 12.00 4.80
556 Red Schoendienst 25.00 10.00
SP MG
557 Jose Santiago 8.00 3.20
558 Tommie Sisk 8.00 3.20
559 Ed Bailey SP 12.00 4.80
560 Boog Powell SP 25.00 10.00
561 Dennis Daboll 15.00 6.00
Mike Kekich
Hector Valle
Jim Lefebvre RC
562 Billy Moran 8.00 3.20
563 Julio Navarro 8.00 3.20
564 Mel Nelson 8.00 3.20
565 Ernie Broglio SP 12.00 4.80
566 Gil Blanco 12.00 4.80
Ross Moschitto
Art Lopez SP
567 Tommie Aaron 8.00 3.20
568 Ron Taylor SP 12.00 4.80
569 Gino Cimoli SP 12.00 4.80
570 Claude Osteen SP 15.00 6.00
571 Ossie Virgil SP 12.00 4.80
572 Baltimore Orioles SP 25.00 10.00
Team Card
573 Jim Lonborg RC 25.00 10.00
Gerry Moses
Bill Schlesinger
Mike Ryan SP
574 Roy Sievers 15.00 6.00
575 Jose Pagan 8.00 3.20
576 Terry Fox SP 12.00 4.80
577 Darold Knowles 12.00 4.80
Don Buschhorn
Richie Scheinblum SP
578 Camilo Carreon SP 12.00 4.80
579 Dick Smith SP 12.00 4.80

580 Jimmie Hall SP 12.00 4.80
581 Tony Perez RC 80.00 32.00
Dave Ricketts
Kevin Collins SP
582 Bob Schmidt SP 12.00 4.80
583 Wes Covington SP 12.00 4.80
584 Harry Bright 15.00 6.00
585 Hank Fischer 8.00 3.20
586 Tom McCraw SP 12.00 4.80
587 Joe Sparma 8.00 3.20
588 Lenny Green 8.00 3.20
589 Frank Linzy 12.00 4.80
Bob Schroder SP
590 John Wyatt 8.00 3.20
591 Bob Skinner SP 12.00 4.80
592 Frank Bork SP 12.00 4.80
593 Jackie Moore RC 12.00 4.80
John Sullivan SP
594 Joe Gaines 8.00 3.20
595 Don Lee 8.00 3.20
596 Don Landrum SP 12.00 4.80
597 Joe Nossek 8.00 3.20
John Sevcik
Dick Reese
598 Al Downing SP 25.00 7.50

1965 Topps Embossed Inserts

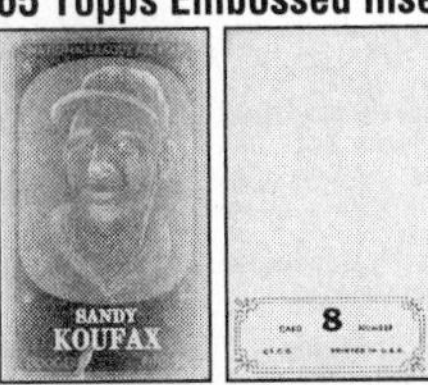

The cards in this 72-card set measure approximately 2 1/8" by 3 1/2". The 1965 Topps Embossed set contains gold foil cameo player portraits. Each league had 36 representatives set on blue backgrounds for the AL and red backgrounds for the NL. The Topps embossed set was distributed as inserts in packages of the regular 1965 baseball series.

	NM	Ex
COMPLETE SET (72)	200.00	80.00
1 Carl Yastrzemski	7.00	2.80
2 Ron Fairly	1.25	.50
3 Max Alvis	1.25	.50
4 Jim Ray Hart	1.25	.50
5 Bill Skowron	2.00	.80
6 Ed Kranepool	1.25	.50
7 Tim McCarver	2.00	.80
8 Sandy Koufax	15.00	6.00
9 Donn Clendenon	1.25	.50
10 John Romano	1.25	.50
11 Mickey Mantle	75.00	30.00
12 Joe Torre	2.50	1.00
13 Al Kaline	7.00	2.80
14 Al McBean	1.25	.50
15 Don Drysdale	5.00	2.00
16 Brooks Robinson	7.00	2.80
17 Jim Bunning	4.00	1.60
18 Gary Peters	1.25	.50
19 Roberto Clemente	35.00	14.00
20 Milt Pappas	1.25	.50
21 Wayne Causey	1.25	.50
22 Frank Robinson	7.00	2.80
23 Bill Mazeroski	3.00	1.20
24 Diego Segui	1.25	.50
25 Jim Bouton	2.00	.80
26 Eddie Mathews	4.00	1.60
27 Willie Mays	20.00	8.00
28 Ron Santo	2.00	.80
29 Boog Powell	2.00	.80
30 Ken McBride	1.25	.50
31 Leon Wagner	1.25	.50
32 Johnny Callison	1.25	.50
33 Zoilo Versalles	1.25	.50
34 Jack Baldschun	1.25	.50
35 Ron Hunt	1.25	.50
36 Richie Allen	2.50	1.00
37 Frank Malzone	1:25	.50
38 Bob Allison	1.25	.50
39 Jim Fregosi	2.00	.80
40 Billy Williams	4.00	1.60
41 Bill Freehan	2.00	.80
42 Vada Pinson	2.00	.80
43 Bill White	2.00	.80
44 Roy McMillan	1.25	.50
45 Orlando Cepeda	4.00	1.60
46 Rocky Colavito	3.00	1.20
47 Ken Boyer	2.00	.80
48 Dick Radatz	1.25	.50
49 Tommy Davis	2.00	.80
50 Walt Bond	1.25	.50
51 John Orsino	1.25	.50
52 Joe Christopher	1.25	.50
53 Al Spangler	1.25	.50
54 Jim King	1.25	.50
55 Mickey Lolich	2.00	.80
56 Harmon Killebrew	4.00	1.60
57 Bob Shaw	1.25	.50
58 Ernie Banks	7.00	2.80
59 Hank Aaron	20.00	8.00
60 Chuck Hinton	1.25	.50
61 Bob Aspromonte	1.25	.50
62 Lee Maye	1.25	.50
63 Joe Cunningham	1.25	.50
64 Pete Ward	1.25	.50
65 Bobby Richardson	2.00	.80
66 Dean Chance	1.25	.50
67 Dick Ellsworth	1.25	.50
68 Jim Maloney	1.25	.50
69 Bob Gibson	4.00	1.60
70 Earl Battey	1.25	.50
71 Tony Kubek	2.00	.80
72 Jack Kralick	1.25	.50

1965 Topps Transfers Inserts

The 1965 Topps transfers (2" by 3") were issued in series of 24 each as inserts in three of the regular 1965 Topps cards series. Thirty-six of the transfers feature blue bands at the top and bottom while 36 feature red bands at the top and bottom. The team name and position are listed in the top band while the player's name is listed in the bottom band. Transfers 1-36 have blue panels whereas 37-72 have red panels. These unnumbered transfers are ordered below alphabetically by player's name within each color group. Transfers of Bob Veale and Carl Yastrzemski are supposedly tougher to find than the others in the set; they are marked below by SP.

	NM	Ex
COMPLETE SET (72)	400.00	160.00
1 Bob Allison	1.50	.60
2 Max Alvis	1.50	.60
3 Luis Aparicio	6.00	2.40
4 Walt Bond	1.50	.60
5 Jim Bouton	2.00	.80
6 Jim Bunning	4.00	1.60
7 Rico Carty	2.00	.80
8 Wayne Causey	1.50	.60
9 Orlando Cepeda	4.00	1.60
10 Dean Chance	1.50	.60
11 Tony Conigliaro	2.00	.80
12 Bill Freehan	2.00	.80
13 Jim Fregosi	2.00	.80
14 Bob Gibson	10.00	4.00
15 Dick Groat	2.00	.80
16 Tom Haller	1.50	.60
17 Al Jackson	1.50	.60
18 Bobby Knoop	1.50	.60
19 Jim Maloney	2.00	.80
20 Juan Marichal	6.00	2.40
21 Lee Maye	1.50	.60
22 Jim O'Toole	1.50	.60
23 Camilo Pascual	1.50	.60
24 Vada Pinson	2.00	.80
25 Juan Pizarro	1.50	.60
26 Bobby Richardson	3.00	1.20
27 Bob Rodgers	1.50	.60
28 John Roseboro	1.50	.60
29 Dick Stuart	2.00	.80
30 Luis Tiant	3.00	1.20
31 Joe Torre	3.00	1.20
32 Bob Veale SP	10.00	4.00
33 Leon Wagner	1.50	.60
34 Dave Wickersham	1.50	.60
35 Billy Williams	5.00	2.00
36 Carl Yastrzemski SP	40.00	16.00
37 Hank Aaron	30.00	12.00
38 Richie Allen	4.00	1.60
39 Ken Aspromonte	1.50	.60
40 Ken Boyer	3.00	1.20
41 Johnny Callison	2.00	.80
42 Dean Chance	1.50	.60
43 Joe Christopher	1.50	.60
44 Roberto Clemente	50.00	20.00
45 Rocky Colavito	4.00	1.60
46 Tommy Davis	2.00	.80
47 Don Drysdale	12.00	4.80
48 Chuck Hinton	1.50	.60
49 Frank Howard	3.00	1.20
50 Ron Hunt	1.50	.60
51 Al Kaline	15.00	6.00
52 Harmon Killebrew	10.00	4.00
53 Jim King	1.50	.60
54 Ron Kline	1.50	.60
55 Sandy Koufax	30.00	12.00
56 Ed Kranepool	1.50	.60
57 Mickey Mantle	100.00	40.00
58 Willie Mays	35.00	14.00
59 Bill Mazeroski	4.00	1.60
60 Tony Oliva	4.00	1.60
61 Milt Pappas	1.50	.60
62 Gary Peters	1.50	.60
63 Boog Powell	3.00	1.20
64 Dick Radatz	1.50	.60
65 Brooks Robinson	15.00	6.00
66 Frank Robinson	15.00	6.00
67 Ron Santo	3.00	1.20
68 Diego Segui	1.50	.60
69 Bill Skowron	2.00	.80
70 Al Spangler	1.50	.60
71 Pete Ward	1.50	.60
72 Bill White	2.00	.80

1966 Topps

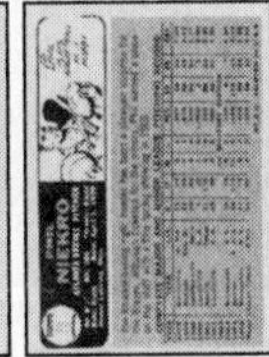

The cards in this 598-card set measure 2 1/2" by 3 1/2". There are the same number of cards as in the 1965 set. Once again, the seventh series cards (523 to 598) are considered more difficult to obtain than the cards of any other series in the set. Within this last series there are 43 cards that were printed in lesser quantities than the other cards in that series; these shorter-printed cards are marked by SP in the checklist below. Among other ways, cards were issued in five-card nickel wax packs and in 12-card dime cello packs which came 36 packs to a box. The only featured subset within this set is League Leaders (215-226). Noteworthy Rookie Cards in the set include Jim Palmer (126), Ferguson Jenkins (254), and Don Sutton (288). Jim Palmer is described in the bio (on his card back) as a left-hander.

	NM	Ex
COMPLETE SET (598)	4000.00	1600.00
COMMON CARD (1-109)	1.50	.60
COMMON (110-283)	2.00	.80
COMMON (284-370)	3.00	1.20
COMMON (371-446)	5.00	2.00
COMMON (447-522)	10.00	4.00
COMMON (523-598)	15.00	6.00
COMMON SP (523-598)	30.00	12.00
WRAPPER (5-CENT)	25.00	10.00
1 Willie Mays	300.00	95.00
2 Ted Abernathy	1.50	.60
3 Sam Mele MG	1.50	.60
4 Ray Culp	1.50	.60
5 Jim Fregosi	2.00	.80
6 Chuck Schilling	1.50	.60
7 Tracy Stallard	1.50	.60
8 Floyd Robinson	1.50	.60
9 Clete Boyer	2.00	.80
10 Tony Cloninger	1.50	.60
11 Brant Alyea Pete Craig	1.50	.60
12 John Tsitouris	1.50	.60
13 Lou Johnson	2.00	.80
14 Norm Siebern	1.50	.60
15 Vern Law	2.00	.80
16 Larry Brown	1.50	.60
17 John Stephenson	1.50	.60
18 Roland Sheldon	1.50	.60
19 San Francisco Giants Team Card	5.00	2.00
20 Willie Horton	2.00	.80
21 Don Nottebart	1.50	.60
22 Joe Nossek	1.50	.60
23 Jack Sanford	1.50	.60
24 Don Kessinger RC	4.00	1.60
25 Pete Ward	1.50	.60
26 Ray Sadecki	1.50	.60
27 Darold Knowles Andy Etchebarren	1.50	.60
28 Phil Niekro	20.00	8.00
29 Mike Brumley	1.50	.60
30 Pete Rose DP	100.00	40.00
31 Jack Cullen	2.00	.80
32 Adolfo Phillips	1.50	.60
33 Jim Pagliaroni	1.50	.60
34 Checklist 1	8.00	1.60
35 Ron Swoboda	4.00	1.60
36 Jim Hunter UER Stats say 1963 and 1964 should be 1964 and 1965	20.00	8.00
37 Billy Herman MG	2.00	.80
38 Ron Nischwitz	1.50	.60
39 Ken Henderson	1.50	.60
40 Jim Grant	1.50	.60
41 Don LeJohn	1.50	.60
42 Aubrey Gatewood	1.50	.60
43A Don Landrum (Dark button on pants showing)	2.00	.80
43B Don Landrum (Button on pants partially airbrushed)	20.00	8.00
43C Don Landrum (Button on pants not showing)	2.00	.80
44 Bill Davis Tom Kelley	1.50	.60
45 Jim Gentile	2.00	.80
46 Howie Koplitz	1.50	.60
47 J.C. Martin	1.50	.60
48 Paul Blair	2.00	.80
49 Woody Woodward	2.00	.80
50 Mickey Mantle DP	250.00	100.00
51 Gordon Richardson	1.50	.60
52 Wes Covington Johnny Callison	4.00	1.60
53 Bob Duliba	1.50	.60
54 Jose Pagan	1.50	.60
55 Ken Harrelson	2.00	.80
56 Sandy Valdespino	1.50	.60
57 Jim Lefebvre	2.00	.80
58 Dave Wickersham	1.50	.60
59 Reds Team	5.00	2.00
60 Curt Flood	4.00	1.60
61 Bob Bolin	1.50	.60
62A Merritt Ranew (With sold line)	2.00	.80
62B Merritt Ranew (Without sold line)	30.00	12.00
63 Jim Stewart	1.50	.60
64 Bob Bruce	1.50	.60
65 Leon Wagner	1.50	.60
66 Al Weis	1.50	.60
67 Cleon Jones Dick Selma	4.00	1.60
68 Hal Reniff	1.50	.60
69 Ken Hamlin	1.50	.60
70 Carl Yastrzemski	30.00	12.00
71 Frank Carpin	1.50	.60
72 Tony Perez	25.00	10.00
73 Jerry Zimmerman	1.50	.60
74 Don Mossi	2.00	.80
75 Tommy Davis	2.00	.80
76 Red Schoendienst MG	4.00	1.60
77 John Orsino	1.50	.60
78 Frank Linzy	1.50	.60
79 Joe Pepitone	4.00	1.60
80 Richie Allen	6.00	2.40
81 Ray Oyler	1.50	.60
82 Bob Hendley	1.50	.60
83 Albie Pearson	2.00	.80
84 Jim Beauchamp Dick Kelley	1.50	.60
85 Eddie Fisher	1.50	.60
86 John Bateman	1.50	.60
87 Dan Napoleon	1.50	.60
88 Fred Whitfield	1.50	.60
89 Ted Davidson	1.50	.60
90 Luis Aparicio	8.00	3.20
91A Bob Uecker TR	10.00	4.00
91B Bob Uecker NTR	40.00	16.00
92 Yankees Team	15.00	6.00
93 Jim Lonborg	2.00	.80
94 Matty Alou	2.00	.80
95 Pete Richert	1.50	.60
96 Felipe Alou	4.00	1.60
97 Jim Merritt	1.50	.60
98 Don Demeter	1.50	.60
99 Willie Stargell Donn Clendenon	6.00	2.40
100 Sandy Koufax	80.00	32.00
101A Checklist 2 (115 W. Spahn) ERR	15.00	3.00
101B Checklist 2 (115 Bill Henry) COR	10.00	2.00
102 Ed Kirkpatrick	1.50	.60
103A Dick Groat TR	2.00	.80
103B Dick Groat NTR	40.00	16.00
104A Alex Johnson TR	2.00	.80
104B Alex Johnson NTR	30.00	12.00
105 Milt Pappas	2.00	.80
106 Rusty Staub	4.00	1.60
107 Larry Stahl Ron Tompkins	1.50	.60
108 Bobby Klaus	1.50	.60
109 Ralph Terry	2.00	.80
110 Ernie Banks	30.00	12.00
111 Gary Peters	2.00	.80
112 Manny Mota	4.00	1.60
113 Hank Aguirre	2.00	.80
114 Jim Gosger	2.00	.80
115 Bill Henry	2.00	.80
116 Walter Alston MG	6.00	2.40
117 Jake Gibbs	2.00	.80
118 Mike McCormick	2.00	.80
119 Art Shamsky	2.00	.80
120 Harmon Killebrew	15.00	6.00
121 Ray Herbert	2.00	.80
122 Joe Gaines	2.00	.80
123 Frank Bork Jerry May	2.00	.80
124 Tug McGraw	4.00	1.60
125 Lou Brock	20.00	8.00
126 Jim Palmer RC UER Described as a lefthander on card back	100.00	40.00
127 Ken Berry	2.00	.80
128 Jim Landis	2.00	.80
129 Jack Kralick	2.00	.80
130 Joe Torre	6.00	2.40
131 Angels Team	5.00	2.00
132 Orlando Cepeda	8.00	3.20
133 Don McMahon	2.00	.80
134 Wes Parker	4.00	1.60
135 Dave Morehead	2.00	.80
136 Woody Held	2.00	.80
137 Pat Corrales	2.00	.80
138 Roger Repoz	2.00	.80
139 Byron Browne Don Young	2.00	.80
140 Jim Maloney	4.00	1.60
141 Tom McCraw	2.00	.80
142 Don Dennis	2.00	.80
143 Jose Tartabull	4.00	1.60
144 Don Schwall	2.00	.80
145 Bill Freehan	4.00	1.60
146 George Altman	2.00	.80
147 Lum Harris MG	2.00	.80
148 Bob Johnson	2.00	.80
149 Dick Nen	2.00	.80
150 Rocky Colavito	8.00	3.20
151 Gary Wagner	2.00	.80
152 Frank Malzone	4.00	1.60
153 Rico Carty	4.00	1.60
154 Chuck Hiller	2.00	.80
155 Marcelino Lopez	2.00	.80
156 Dick Schofield Hal Lanier	2.00	.80
157 Rene Lachemann	2.00	.80
158 Jim Brewer	2.00	.80
159 Chico Ruiz	2.00	.80
160 Whitey Ford	30.00	12.00
161 Jerry Lumpe	2.00	.80
162 Lee Maye	2.00	.80
163 Tito Francona	2.00	.80
164 Tommie Agee Marv Staehle	4.00	1.60
165 Don Lock	2.00	.80
166 Chris Krug	2.00	.80
167 Boog Powell	6.00	2.40
168 Dan Osinski	2.00	.80
169 Duke Sims	2.00	.80
170 Cookie Rojas	4.00	1.60
171 Nick Willhite	2.00	.80
172 Mets Team	5.00	2.00
173 Al Spangler	2.00	.80
174 Ron Taylor	2.00	.80
175 Bert Campaneris	4.00	1.60
176 Jim Davenport	2.00	.80
177 Hector Lopez	2.00	.80
178 Bob Tillman	2.00	.80
179 Dennis Aust Bob Tolan	4.00	1.60
180 Vada Pinson	4.00	1.60
181 Al Worthington	2.00	.80
182 Jerry Lynch	2.00	.80
183A Checklist 3 (Large print on front)	8.00	1.60
183B Checklist 3 (Small print on front)	8.00	1.60
184 Denis Menke	2.00	.80
185 Bob Buhl	4.00	1.60
186 Ruben Amaro	2.00	.80
187 Chuck Dressen MG	4.00	1.60
188 Al Luplow	2.00	.80
189 John Roseboro	4.00	1.60
190 Jimmie Hall	2.00	.80
191 Darrell Sutherland	2.00	.80
192 Vic Power	4.00	1.60
193 Dave McNally	4.00	1.60
194 Senators Team	5.00	2.00
195 Joe Morgan	15.00	6.00
196 Don Pavletich	2.00	.80
197 Sonny Siebert	2.00	.80
198 Mickey Stanley RC	6.00	2.40
199 Bill Skowron Johnny Romano Floyd Robinson	4.00	1.60
200 Eddie Mathews	15.00	6.00
201 Jim Dickson	2.00	.80
202 Clay Dalrymple	2.00	.80
203 Jose Santiago	2.00	.80
204 Cubs Team	5.00	2.00
205 Tom Tresh	4.00	1.60
206 Al Jackson	2.00	.80
207 Frank Quilici	2.00	.80
208 Bob Miller	2.00	.80
209 Fritz Fisher John Hiller RC	4.00	1.60
210 Bill Mazeroski	8.00	3.20
211 Frank Kreutzer	2.00	.80
212 Ed Kranepool	4.00	1.60
213 Fred Newman	2.00	.80
214 Tommy Harper	4.00	1.60
215 Bob Clemente Hank Aaron Willie Mays LL	50.00	20.00
216 Tony Oliva Carl Yastrzemski Vic Davalillo LL	5.00	2.00
217 Willie Mays Willie McCovey Billy Williams LL	20.00	8.00
218 Tony Conigliaro Norm Cash Willie Horton LL	5.00	2.00
219 Deron Johnson Frank Robinson Willie Mays LL	12.00	4.80
220 Rocky Colavito Willie Horton Tony Oliva LL	5.00	2.00
221 Sandy Koufax Juan Marichal Vern Law LL	12.00	4.80
222 Sam McDowell Eddie Fisher Sonny Siebert LL	5.00	2.00
223 Sandy Koufax Tony Cloninger Don Drysdale LL	12.00	4.80
224 Jim Grant Mel Stottlemyre Jim Kaat LL	5.00	2.00
225 Sandy Koufax Bob Veale Bob Gibson LL	12.00	4.80
226 Sam McDowell Mickey Lolich Dennis McLain Sonny Siebert LL	5.00	2.00
227 Russ Nixon	2.00	.80
228 Larry Dierker	4.00	1.60
229 Hank Bauer MG	4.00	1.60
230 Johnny Callison	4.00	1.60
231 Floyd Weaver	2.00	.80
232 Glenn Beckert	4.00	1.60
233 Dom Zanni	2.00	.80
234 Rich Beck Roy White RC	8.00	3.20
235 Don Cardwell	2.00	.80
236 Mike Hershberger	2.00	.80
237 Billy O'Dell	2.00	.80
238 Dodgers Team	5.00	2.00
239 Orlando Pena	2.00	.80
240 Earl Battey	2.00	.80
241 Dennis Ribant	2.00	.80
242 Jesus Alou	2.00	.80
243 Nelson Briles	4.00	1.60
244 Chuck Harrison Sonny Jackson	2.00	.80
245 John Buzhardt	2.00	.80
246 Ed Bailey	2.00	.80
247 Carl Warwick	2.00	.80
248 Pete Mikkelsen	2.00	.80
249 Bill Rigney MG	2.00	.80
250 Sammy Ellis	2.00	.80
251 Ed Brinkman	2.00	.80
252 Denny Lemaster	2.00	.80
253 Don Wert	2.00	.80
254 Fergie Jenkins RC Bill Sorrell	60.00	24.00
255 Willie Stargell	20.00	8.00
256 Lew Krausse	2.00	.80
257 Jeff Torborg	4.00	1.60
258 Dave Giusti	2.00	.80
259 Boston Red Sox Team Card	5.00	2.00
260 Bob Shaw	2.00	.80
261 Ron Hansen	2.00	.80
262 Jack Hamilton	2.00	.80
263 Tom Egan	2.00	.80
264 Andy Kosco Ted Uhlaender	2.00	.80
265 Stu Miller	4.00	1.60
266 Pedro Gonzalez UER (Misspelled Gonzales on card back)	2.00	.80
267 Joe Sparma	2.00	.80
268 John Blanchard	2.00	.80
269 Don Heffner MG	2.00	.80
270 Claude Osteen	4.00	1.60
271 Hal Lanier	2.00	.80
272 Jack Baldschun	2.00	.80
273 Bob Aspromonte Rusty Staub	4.00	1.60
274 Buster Narum	2.00	.80
275 Tim McCarver	4.00	1.60
276 Jim Bouton	4.00	1.60
277 George Thomas	2.00	.80
278 Cal Koonce	2.00	.80
279A Checklist 4 (Player's cap black)	8.00	1.60
279B Checklist 4 (Player's cap red)	8.00	1.60
280 Bobby Knoop	2.00	.80
281 Bruce Howard	2.00	.80
282 Johnny Lewis	2.00	.80
283 Jim Perry	4.00	1.60
284 Bobby Wine	3.00	1.20
285 Luis Tiant	5.00	2.00
286 Gary Geiger	3.00	1.20
287 Jack Aker	3.00	1.20
288 Bill Singer Don Sutton RC	50.00	20.00
289 Larry Sherry	3.00	1.20
290 Ron Santo	5.00	2.00
291 Moe Drabowsky	5.00	2.00
292 Jim Coker	3.00	1.20
293 Mike Shannon	5.00	2.00
294 Steve Ridzik	3.00	1.20
295 Jim Ray Hart	5.00	2.00
296 Johnny Keane MG	5.00	2.00
297 Jim Owens	3.00	1.20
298 Rico Petrocelli	5.00	2.00
299 Lou Burdette	5.00	2.00

300 Bob Clemente 150.00 60.00
301 Greg Bollo 3.00 1.20
302 Ernie Bowman 3.00 1.20
303 Cleveland Indians 5.00 2.00
Team Card
304 John Herrnstein 3.00 1.20
305 Camilo Pascual 5.00 2.00
306 Ty Cline 3.00 1.20
307 Clay Carroll 5.00 2.00
308 Tom Haller 5.00 2.00
309 Diego Segui 3.00 1.20
310 Frank Robinson 40.00 16.00
311 Tommy Helms 5.00 2.00
Dick Simpson
312 Bob Saverine 3.00 1.20
313 Chris Zachary 3.00 1.20
314 Hector Valle 3.00 1.20
315 Norm Cash 5.00 2.00
316 Jack Fisher 3.00 1.20
317 Dalton Jones 3.00 1.20
318 Harry Walker MG 3.00 1.20
319 Gene Freese 3.00 1.20
320 Bob Gibson 25.00 10.00
321 Rick Reichardt 3.00 1.20
322 Bill Faul 3.00 1.20
323 Ray Barker 3.00 1.20
324 John Boozer 3.00 1.20
325 Vic Davalillo 3.00 1.20
326 Braves Team 5.00 2.00
327 Bernie Allen 3.00 1.20
328 Jerry Grote 5.00 2.00
329 Pete Charton 3.00 1.20
330 Ron Fairly 5.00 2.00
331 Ron Herbel 3.00 1.20
332 Bill Bryan 3.00 1.20
333 Joe Coleman RC 3.00 1.20
Jim French
334 Marty Keough 3.00 1.20
335 Juan Pizarro 3.00 1.20
336 Gene Alley 5.00 2.00
337 Fred Gladding 3.00 1.20
338 Dal Maxvill 3.00 1.20
339 Del Crandall 5.00 2.00
340 Dean Chance 5.00 2.00
341 Wes Westrum MG 5.00 2.00
342 Bob Humphreys 3.00 1.20
343 Joe Christopher 3.00 1.20
344 Steve Blass 5.00 2.00
345 Bob Allison 5.00 2.00
346 Mike de la Hoz 3.00 1.20
347 Phil Regan 5.00 2.00
348 Orioles Team 8.00 3.20
349 Cap Peterson 3.00 1.20
350 Mel Stottlemyre 8.00 3.20
351 Fred Valentine 3.00 1.20
352 Bob Aspromonte 3.00 1.20
353 Al McBean 3.00 1.20
354 Smoky Burgess 5.00 2.00
355 Wade Blasingame 3.00 1.20
356 Owen Johnson 3.00 1.20
Ken Sanders
357 Gerry Arrigo 3.00 1.20
358 Charlie Smith 3.00 1.20
359 Johnny Briggs 3.00 1.20
360 Ron Hunt 3.00 1.20
361 Tom Satriano 3.00 1.20
362 Gates Brown 5.00 2.00
363 Checklist 5 10.00 2.00
364 Nate Oliver 3.00 1.20
365 Roger Maris UER 50.00 20.00
Wrong birth year listed on card
366 Wayne Causey 3.00 1.20
367 Mel Nelson 3.00 1.20
368 Charlie Lau 5.00 2.00
369 Jim King 3.00 1.20
370 Chico Cardenas 3.00 1.20
371 Lee Stange 5.00 2.00
372 Harvey Kuenn 8.00 3.20
373 Jack Hiatt 8.00 3.20
Dick Estelle
374 Bob Locker 5.00 2.00
375 Donn Clendenon 8.00 3.20
376 Paul Schaal 5.00 2.00
377 Turk Farrell 5.00 2.00
378 Dick Tracewski 5.00 2.00
379 Cardinal Team 10.00 4.00
380 Tony Conigliaro 10.00 4.00
381 Hank Fischer 5.00 2.00
382 Phil Roof 5.00 2.00
383 Jackie Brandt 5.00 2.00
384 Al Downing 8.00 3.20
385 Ken Boyer 10.00 4.00
386 Gil Hodges MG 8.00 3.20
387 Howie Reed 5.00 2.00
388 Don Mincher 5.00 2.00
389 Jim O'Toole 8.00 3.20
390 Brooks Robinson 50.00 20.00
391 Chuck Hinton 5.00 2.00
392 Bill Hands 8.00 3.20
Randy Hundley RC
393 George Brunet 5.00 2.00
394 Ron Brand 5.00 2.00
395 Len Gabrielson 5.00 2.00
396 Jerry Stephenson 5.00 2.00
397 Bill White 8.00 3.20
398 Danny Cater 5.00 2.00
399 Ray Washburn 5.00 2.00
400 Zoilo Versalles 8.00 3.20
401 Ken McMullen 5.00 2.00
402 Jim Hickman 5.00 2.00
403 Fred Talbot 5.00 2.00
404 Pittsburgh Pirates 10.00 4.00
Team Card
405 Elston Howard 8.00 3.20
406 Joey Jay 5.00 2.00
407 John Kennedy 5.00 2.00
408 Lee Thomas 8.00 3.20
409 Billy Hoeft 5.00 2.00
410 Al Kaline 40.00 16.00
411 Gene Mauch MG 5.00 2.00
412 Sam Bowens 5.00 2.00
413 Johnny Romano 5.00 2.00
414 Dan Coombs 5.00 2.00
415 Max Alvis 5.00 2.00
416 Phil Ortega 5.00 2.00
417 Jim McGlothlin 5.00 2.00
Ed Sukla
418 Phil Gagliano 5.00 2.00
419 Mike Ryan 5.00 2.00
420 Juan Marichal 15.00 6.00
421 Roy McMillan 8.00 3.20
422 Ed Charles 5.00 2.00
423 Ernie Broglio 5.00 2.00
424 Lee May RC 10.00 4.00
Darrell Osteen
425 Bob Veale 8.00 3.20
426 White Sox Team 10.00 4.00
427 John Miller 5.00 2.00
428 Sandy Alomar 5.00 2.00
429 Bill Monbouquette 5.00 2.00
430 Don Drysdale 20.00 8.00
431 Walt Bond 5.00 2.00
432 Bob Heffner 5.00 2.00
433 Alvin Dark MG 8.00 3.20
434 Willie Kirkland 5.00 2.00
435 Jim Bunning 15.00 6.00
436 Julian Javier 8.00 3.20
437 Al Stanek 5.00 2.00
438 Willie Smith 5.00 2.00
439 Pedro Ramos 5.00 2.00
440 Deron Johnson 8.00 3.20
441 Tommie Sisk 5.00 2.00
442 Ed Barnowski 5.00 2.00
Eddie Watt
443 Bill Wakefield 3.00 1.20
444 Checklist 6 10.00 2.00
445 Jim Kaat 10.00 4.00
446 Mack Jones 5.00 2.00
447 Dick Ellsworth UER 15.00 6.00
(Photo actually
Ken Hubbs)
448 Eddie Stanky MG 10.00 4.00
449 Joe Moeller 10.00 4.00
450 Tony Oliva 15.00 6.00
451 Barry Latman 10.00 4.00
452 Joe Azcue 10.00 4.00
453 Ron Kline 10.00 4.00
454 Jerry Buchek 10.00 4.00
455 Mickey Lolich 15.00 6.00
456 Darrell Brandon 10.00 4.00
Joe Foy
457 Joe Gibbon 10.00 4.00
458 Manny Jiminez 10.00 4.00
459 Bill McCool 10.00 4.00
460 Curt Blefary 10.00 4.00
461 Roy Face 15.00 6.00
462 Bob Rodgers 10.00 4.00
463 Philadelphia Phillies 15.00 6.00
Team Card
464 Larry Bearnarth 10.00 4.00
465 Don Buford 10.00 4.00
466 Ken Johnson 10.00 4.00
467 Vic Roznovsky 10.00 4.00
468 Johnny Podres 15.00 6.00
469 Bobby Murcer RC 30.00 12.00
Dooley Womack
470 Sam McDowell 15.00 6.00
471 Bob Skinner 10.00 4.00
472 Terry Fox 10.00 4.00
473 Rich Rollins 10.00 4.00
474 Dick Schofield 10.00 4.00
475 Dick Radatz 10.00 4.00
476 Bobby Bragan MG 10.00 4.00
477 Steve Barber 10.00 4.00
478 Tony Gonzalez 10.00 4.00
479 Jim Hannan 10.00 4.00
480 Dick Stuart 10.00 4.00
481 Bob Lee 10.00 4.00
482 John Boccabella 10.00 4.00
Dave Dowling
483 Joe Nuxhall 10.00 4.00
484 Wes Covington 10.00 4.00
485 Bob Bailey 10.00 4.00
486 Tommy John 15.00 6.00
487 Al Ferrara 10.00 4.00
488 George Banks 10.00 4.00
489 Curt Simmons 10.00 4.00
490 Bobby Richardson 25.00 10.00
491 Dennis Bennett 10.00 4.00
492 Athletics Team 15.00 6.00
493 Johnny Klippstein 10.00 4.00
494 Gordy Coleman 10.00 4.00
495 Dick McAuliffe 15.00 6.00
496 Lindy McDaniel 10.00 4.00
497 Chris Cannizzaro 10.00 4.00
498 Luke Walker 10.00 4.00
Woody Fryman
499 Wally Bunker 10.00 4.00
500 Hank Aaron 125.00 50.00
501 John O'Donoghue 10.00 4.00
502 Lenny Green UER 10.00 4.00
Born: aJn. 6, 1933
503 Steve Hamilton 15.00 6.00
504 Grady Hatton MG 10.00 4.00
505 Jose Cardenal 10.00 4.00
506 Bo Belinsky 15.00 6.00
507 Johnny Edwards 10.00 4.00
508 Steve Hargan RC 15.00 6.00
509 Jake Wood 10.00 4.00
510 Hoyt Wilhelm 25.00 10.00
511 Bob Barton 10.00 4.00
Tito Fuentes RC
512 Dick Stigman 10.00 4.00
513 Camilo Carreon 10.00 4.00
514 Hal Woodeshick 10.00 4.00
515 Frank Howard 15.00 6.00
516 Eddie Bressoud 10.00 4.00
517A Checklist 7 15.00 3.00
529 White Sox Rookies
544 Cardinals Rookies
517B Checklist 7 15.00 3.00
529 W. Sox Rookies
544 Cards Rookies
518 Herb Hippauf 10.00 4.00
Arnie Umbach
519 Bob Friend 15.00 6.00
520 Jim Wynn 15.00 6.00
521 John Wyatt 10.00 4.00
522 Phil Linz 10.00 4.00
523 Bob Sadowski 10.00 4.00
524 Ollie Brown 30.00 12.00
Don Mason SP
525 Gary Bell SP 30.00 12.00
526 Twins Team SP 100.00 40.00
527 Julio Navarro 15.00 6.00
528 Jesse Gonder SP 30.00 12.00
529 Lee Elia 15.00 6.00
Dennis Higgins
Bill Voss
530 Robin Roberts 50.00 20.00
531 Joe Cunningham 15.00 6.00
532 A.Monteagudo SP 30.00 12.00
533 Jerry Adair SP 30.00 12.00
534 Dave Eilers 15.00 6.00
Rob Gardner
535 Willie Davis SP 40.00 16.00
536 Dick Egan 15.00 6.00
537 Herman Franks MG 15.00 6.00
538 Bob Allen SP 30.00 12.00
539 Bill Heath 25.00 10.00
Carroll Sembera
540 Denny McLain SP 60.00 24.00
541 Gene Oliver SP 30.00 12.00
542 George Smith 15.00 6.00
543 Roger Craig SP 30.00 12.00
544 Joe Hoerner 30.00 12.00
George Kernek
Jimy Williams RC UER SP
(Misspelled Jimmy
on card)
545 Dick Green SP 30.00 12.00
546 Dwight Siebler 25.00 10.00
547 Horace Clarke RC SP 40.00 16.00
548 Gary Kroll SP 30.00 12.00
549 Al Closter 15.00 6.00
Casey Cox
550 Willie McCovey SP 100.00 40.00
551 Bob Purkey SP 30.00 12.00
552 Birdie Tebbetts 30.00 12.00
MG SP
553 Pat Garrett 15.00 6.00
Jackie Warner
554 Jim Northrup SP 30.00 12.00
555 Ron Perranoski SP 30.00 12.00
556 Mel Queen SP 30.00 12.00
557 Felix Mantilla SP 30.00 12.00
558 Guido Grilli 20.00 8.00
Pete Magrini
George Scott RC
559 Roberto Pena SP 30.00 12.00
560 Joel Horlen 15.00 6.00
561 Choo Choo Coleman SP 30.00 12.00
562 Russ Snyder 25.00 10.00
563 Pete Cimino 15.00 6.00
Cesar Tovar
564 Bob Chance SP 30.00 12.00
565 Jimmy Piersall SP 40.00 16.00
566 Mike Cuellar SP 30.00 12.00
567 Dick Howser SP 40.00 16.00
568 Paul Lindblad 15.00 6.00
Ron Stone
569 Orlando McFarlane SP 30.00 12.00
570 Art Mahaffey SP 30.00 12.00
571 Dave Roberts SP 30.00 12.00
572 Bob Priddy 15.00 6.00
573 Derrell Griffith 15.00 6.00
574 Bill Hepler 15.00 6.00
Bill Murphy
575 Earl Wilson 15.00 6.00
576 Dave Nicholson SP 30.00 12.00
577 Jack Lamabe SP 30.00 12.00
578 Chi Chi Olivo SP 30.00 12.00
579 Frank Bertaina 20.00 8.00
Gene Brabender
Dave Johnson
580 Billy Williams SP 60.00 24.00
581 Tony Martinez 15.00 6.00
582 Garry Roggenburk 15.00 6.00
583 Tigers Team SP UER 125.00 50.00
Text on back states Tigers
finished third in 1965 instead
of fourth
584 Frank Fernandez 15.00 6.00
Fritz Peterson
585 Tony Taylor 25.00 10.00
586 Claude Raymond SP 30.00 12.00
587 Dick Bertell 15.00 6.00
588 Chuck Dobson 15.00 6.00
Ken Suarez
589 Lou Klimchock SP 30.00 12.00
590 Bill Skowron SP 40.00 16.00
591 Bart Shirley 40.00 16.00
Grant Jackson RC SP
592 Andre Rodgers 15.00 6.00
593 Doug Camilli SP 30.00 12.00
594 Chico Salmon 15.00 6.00
595 Larry Jackson 15.00 6.00
596 Nate Colbert RC 30.00 12.00
Greg Sims SP
597 John Sullivan 15.00 6.00
598 Gaylord Perry SP 175.00 50.00

1966 Topps Rub-Offs Inserts

There are 120 "rub-offs" in the Topps insert set of 1966, of which 100 depict players and the remaining 20 show team pennants. Each rub off measures 2 1/16" by 3". The color player photos are vertical while the team pennants are horizontal; both types of transfer have a large black printer's mark. These rub-offs were originally printed in rolls of 20 and are frequently still found this way. Since these rub-offs are unnumbered, they are ordered below alphabetically within type, players (1-100) and team pennants (101-120).

NM Ex
COMPLETE SET (120) 375.00 150.00
COMMON (1-100) 1.00 .40
COMMON (101-120) .75 .30
1 Hank Aaron 30.00 12.00
2 Jerry Adair 1.00 .40
3 Richie Allen 2.00 .80
4 Jesus Alou 1.50 .60
5 Max Alvis 1.00 .40
6 Bob Aspromonte 1.00 .40
7 Ernie Banks 10.00 4.00
8 Earl Battey 1.00 .40
9 Curt Blefary 1.00 .40
10 Ken Boyer 2.00 .80
11 Bob Bruce 1.00 .40
12 Jim Bunning 6.00 2.40
13 Johnny Callison 1.50 .60
14 Bert Campaneris 1.50 .60
15 Jose Cardenal 1.00 .40
16 Dean Chance 1.50 .60
17 Ed Charles 1.00 .40
18 Roberto Clemente 50.00 20.00
19 Tony Cloninger 1.00 .40
20 Rocky Colavito 3.00 1.20
21 Tony Conigliaro 2.00 .80
22 Vic Davalillo 1.00 .40
23 Willie Davis 1.50 .60
24 Don Drysdale 8.00 3.20
25 Sammy Ellis 1.00 .40
26 Dick Ellsworth 1.00 .40
27 Ron Fairly 1.50 .60
28 Dick Farrell 1.00 .40
29 Eddie Fisher 1.00 .40
30 Jack Fisher 1.00 .40
31 Curt Flood 2.00 .80
32 Whitey Ford 8.00 3.20
33 Bill Freehan 1.50 .60
34 Jim Fregosi 1.50 .60
35 Bob Gibson 8.00 3.20
36 Jim Grant 1.00 .40
37 Jimmie Hall 1.00 .40
38 Ken Harrelson 1.50 .60
39 Jim Ray Hart 1.00 .40
40 Joel Horlen 1.00 .40
41 Willie Horton 1.50 .60
42 Frank Howard 2.00 .80
43 Deron Johnson 1.00 .40
44 Al Kaline 10.00 4.00
45 Harmon Killebrew 8.00 3.20
46 Bobby Knoop 1.00 .40
47 Sandy Koufax 15.00 6.00
48 Ed Kranepool 1.00 .40
49 Gary Kroll 1.00 .40
50 Don Landrum 1.00 .40
51 Vern Law 1.50 .60
52 Johnny Lewis 1.00 .40
53 Don Lock 1.00 .40
54 Mickey Lolich 2.00 .80
55 Jim Maloney 1.50 .60
56 Felix Mantilla 1.00 .40
57 Mickey Mantle 100.00 40.00
58 Juan Marichal 6.00 2.40
59 Eddie Mathews 6.00 2.40
60 Willie Mays 30.00 12.00
61 Bill Mazeroski 4.00 1.60
62 Dick McAuliffe 1.50 .60
63 Tim McCarver 2.00 .80
64 Willie McCovey 6.00 2.40
65 Sam McDowell 1.50 .60
66 Ken McMullen 1.00 .40
67 Denis Menke 1.00 .40
68 Bill Monbouquette 1.00 .40
69 Joe Morgan 8.00 3.20
70 Fred Newman 1.00 .40
71 John O'Donoghue 1.00 .40
72 Tony Oliva 3.00 1.20
73 Johnny Orsino 1.00 .40
74 Phil Ortega 1.00 .40
75 Milt Pappas 1.50 .60
76 Dick Radatz 1.50 .60
77 Bobby Richardson 3.00 1.20
78 Pete Richert 1.00 .40
79 Brooks Robinson 10.00 4.00
80 Floyd Robinson 1.00 .40
81 Frank Robinson 10.00 4.00
82 Cookie Rojas 1.00 .40
83 Pete Rose 30.00 12.00
84 John Roseboro 1.50 .60
85 Ron Santo 2.00 .80
86 Bill Skowron 1.50 .60
87 Willie Stargell 6.00 2.40
88 Mel Stottlemyre 2.00 .80
89 Dick Stuart 2.00 .80
90 Ron Swoboda 1.50 .60
91 Fred Talbot 1.00 .40
92 Ralph Terry 1.50 .60
93 Joe Torre 3.00 1.20
94 Tom Tresh 2.00 .80
95 Bob Veale 1.00 .40
96 Pete Ward 1.00 .40
97 Bill White 1.50 .60
98 Billy Williams 6.00 2.40
99 Jim Wynn 1.50 .60
100 Carl Yastrzemski 10.00 4.00
101 Baltimore Orioles 1.50 .60
102 Boston Red Sox 1.50 .60
111 Los Angeles Dodgers 1.50 .60
114 New York Mets 1.50 .60
115 New York Yankees 2.00 .80
120 Washington Senators 1.50 .60

1966 Topps Venezuelan

This set is a parallel version of the first 370 cards of the regular 1966 Topps set and is similar in design. The cards were issued for the Venezuelan market. The backs of these cards are noticably darker than their American counterparts.

NM Ex
COMPLETE SET (370) 8000.00 3200.00
1 Willie Mays 600.00 240.00
2 Ted Abernathy 10.00 4.00
3 Sam Mele MG 10.00 4.00
4 Ray Culp 10.00 4.00
5 Jim Fregosi 10.00 4.00
6 Chuck Schilling 10.00 4.00
7 Tracy Stallard 10.00 4.00
8 Floyd Robinson 10.00 4.00
9 Clete Boyer 15.00 6.00
10 Tony Cloninger 10.00 4.00
11 Brant Alyea 10.00 4.00
Pete Craig
12 John Tsitouris 10.00 4.00
13 Lou Johnson 10.00 4.00
14 Norm Siebern 10.00 4.00
15 Vern Law 10.00 4.00
16 Larry Brown 10.00 4.00
17 John Stephenson 10.00 4.00
18 Roland Sheldon 10.00 4.00
19 San Francisco Giants 20.00 8.00
Team Card
20 Willie Horton 15.00 6.00
21 Don Nottebart 10.00 4.00
22 Joe Nossek 10.00 4.00
23 Jack Sanford 10.00 4.00
24 Don Kessinger 15.00 6.00
25 Pete Ward 10.00 4.00
26 Ray Sadecki 10.00 4.00
27 Darold Knowles 10.00 4.00
Andy Etchebarren
28 Phil Niekro 80.00 32.00
29 Mike Brumley 10.00 4.00
30 Pete Rose 120.00 47.50
31 Jack Cullen 10.00 4.00
32 Adolfo Phillips 10.00 4.00
33 Jim Pagliaroni 10.00 4.00
34 Checklist 1 30.00 12.00
35 Ron Swoboda 10.00 4.00
36 Jim Hunter UER 80.00 32.00
(Stats say 1963 and 1964, should be
1964 and 1965)
37 Billy Herman MG 15.00 6.00
38 Ron Nischwitz 10.00 4.00
39 Ken Henderson 10.00 4.00
40 Jim Grant 10.00 4.00
41 Don LeJohn 10.00 4.00
42 Aubrey Gatewood 10.00 4.00
43 Don Landrum 10.00 4.00
44 Bill Davis 10.00 4.00
Tom Kelley
45 Jim Gentile 10.00 4.00
46 Howie Koplitz 10.00 4.00
47 J.C. Martin 10.00 4.00
48 Paul Blair 10.00 4.00
49 Woody Woodward 10.00 4.00
50 Mickey Mantle DP 800.00 325.00
51 Gordon Richardson 10.00 4.00
52 Wes Covington 10.00 4.00
Johnny Callison
53 Bob Duliba 10.00 4.00
54 Jose Pagan 10.00 4.00
55 Ken Harrelson 15.00 6.00
56 Sandy Valdespino 10.00 4.00
57 Jim Lefebvre 10.00 4.00
58 Dave Wickersham 10.00 4.00
59 Reds Team 20.00 8.00
60 Curt Flood 15.00 6.00
61 Bob Bolin 10.00 4.00
62 Merritt Ranew 10.00 4.00
63 Jim Stewart 10.00 4.00
64 Bob Bruce 10.00 4.00
65 Leon Wagner 10.00 4.00
66 Al Weis 10.00 4.00
67 Cleon Jones 10.00 4.00
Dick Selma
68 Hal Reniff 10.00 4.00
69 Ken Hamlin 10.00 4.00
70 Carl Yastrzemski 100.00 40.00
71 Frank Carpin 10.00 4.00
72 Tony Perez 100.00 40.00
73 Jerry Zimmerman 10.00 4.00
74 Don Mossi 10.00 4.00
75 Tommy Davis 15.00 6.00
76 Red Schoendienst MG 15.00 6.00
77 John Orsino 10.00 4.00
78 Frank Linzy 10.00 4.00
79 Joe Pepitone 10.00 4.00
80 Richie Allen 30.00 12.00
81 Ray Oyler 10.00 4.00
82 Bob Hendley 10.00 4.00
83 Albie Pearson 10.00 4.00
84 Jim Beauchamp 10.00 4.00
Dick Kelley
85 Eddie Fisher 10.00 4.00
86 John Bateman 10.00 4.00
87 Dan Napoleon 10.00 4.00
88 Fred Whitfield 10.00 4.00
89 Ted Davidson 10.00 4.00
90 Luis Aparicio 30.00 12.00
91 Bob Uecker 40.00 16.00
92 Yankes Team 50.00 20.00
93 Jim Lonborg 10.00 4.00
94 Matty Alou 15.00 6.00
95 Pete Richert 10.00 4.00
96 Felipe Alou 15.00 6.00
97 Jim Merritt 10.00 4.00
98 Don Demeter 10.00 4.00
99 Willie Stargell 30.00 12.00
Donn Clendenon
100 Sandy Koufax 300.00 120.00
101 Checklist 2 30.00 12.00
102 Ed Kirkpatrick 10.00 4.00
103 Dick Groat 10.00 4.00
104 Alex Johnson 10.00 4.00
105 Milt Pappas 15.00 6.00
106 Rusty Staub 15.00 6.00
107 Larry Stahl 10.00 4.00
Ron Tompkins
108 Bobby Klaus 10.00 4.00
109 Ralph Terry 10.00 4.00
110 Ernie Banks 120.00 47.50
111 Gary Peters 10.00 4.00
112 Manny Mota 15.00 6.00
113 Hank Aguirre 10.00 4.00
114 Jim Gosger 10.00 4.00
115 Bill Henry 10.00 4.00
116 Walt Alston MG 15.00 6.00
117 Jake Gibbs 10.00 4.00
118 Mike McCormick 10.00 4.00
119 Art Shamsky 10.00 4.00
120 Harmon Killebrew 60.00 24.00
121 Ray Herbert 10.00 4.00
122 Joe Gaines 10.00 4.00
123 Frank Bork 10.00 4.00
Jerry May
124 Tug McGraw 15.00 6.00
125 Lou Brock 80.00 32.00
126 Jim Palmer UER 400.00 160.00
(Described as a lefthander on card back)
127 Ken Berry 10.00 4.00
128 Jim Landis 10.00 4.00
129 Jack Kralick 10.00 4.00

130 Joe Torre 30.00 12.00
131 Angels Team 20.00 8.00
132 Orlando Cepeda 40.00 16.00
133 Don McMahon 10.00 4.00
134 Wes Parker 10.00 4.00
135 Dave Morehead 10.00 4.00
136 Woody Held 10.00 4.00
137 Pat Corrales 10.00 4.00
138 Roger Repoz 10.00 4.00
139 Byron Browne 10.00 4.00
Don Young
140 Jim Maloney 10.00 4.00
141 Tom McCraw 10.00 4.00
142 Don Dennis 10.00 4.00
143 Jose Tartabull 10.00 4.00
144 Don Schwall 10.00 4.00
145 Bill Freehan 15.00 6.00
146 George Altman 10.00 4.00
147 Lum Harris MG 10.00 4.00
148 Bob Johnson 10.00 4.00
149 Dick Nen 10.00 4.00
150 Rocky Colavito 30.00 12.00
151 Gary Wagner 10.00 4.00
152 Frank Malzone 10.00 4.00
153 Rico Carty 15.00 6.00
154 Chuck Hiller 10.00 4.00
155 Marcelino Lopez 10.00 4.00
156 Dick Schofield 10.00 4.00
Hal Lanier
157 Rene Lachemann 10.00 4.00
158 Jim Brewer 10.00 4.00
159 Chico Ruiz 10.00 4.00
160 Whitey Ford 100.00 40.00
161 Jerry Lumpe 10.00 4.00
162 Lee Maye 10.00 4.00
163 Tito Francona 10.00 4.00
164 Tommie Agee 10.00 4.00
Marv Staehle
165 Don Lock 10.00 4.00
166 Chris Krug 10.00 4.00
167 Boog Powell 30.00 12.00
168 Dan Osinski 10.00 4.00
169 Duke Sims 10.00 4.00
170 Cookie Rojas 10.00 4.00
171 Nick Willhite 10.00 4.00
172 Mets Team 20.00 8.00
173 Al Spangler 10.00 4.00
174 Ron Taylor 10.00 4.00
175 Bert Campaneris 15.00 6.00
176 Jim Davenport 10.00 4.00
177 Hector Lopez 10.00 4.00
178 Bob Tillman 10.00 4.00
179 Dennis Aust 10.00 4.00
Bob Tolan
180 Vada Pinson 15.00 6.00
181 Al Worthington 10.00 4.00
182 Jerry Lynch 10.00 4.00
183 Checklist 3 30.00 9.00
184 Denis Menke 10.00 4.00
185 Bob Buhl 10.00 4.00
186 Ruben Amaro 10.00 4.00
187 Chuck Dressen MG 10.00 4.00
188 Al Luplow 10.00 4.00
189 John Roseboro 10.00 4.00
190 Jimmie Hall 10.00 4.00
191 Darrell Sutherland 10.00 4.00
192 Vic Power 10.00 4.00
193 Dave McNally 10.00 4.00
194 Senators Team 10.00 4.00
195 Joe Morgan 60.00 24.00
196 Don Pavletich 10.00 4.00
197 Sonny Siebert 10.00 4.00
198 Mickey Stanley 10.00 4.00
199 Bill Skowron 10.00 4.00
Johnny Romano
Floyd Robinson
200 Eddie Mathews 60.00 24.00
201 Jim Dickson 10.00 4.00
202 Clay Dalrymple 10.00 4.00
203 Jose Santiago 10.00 4.00
204 Cubs Team 20.00 8.00
205 Tom Tresh 15.00 6.00
206 Al Jackson 10.00 4.00
207 Frank Quilici 10.00 4.00
208 Bob Miller 10.00 4.00
209 Fritz Fisher 10.00 4.00
John Hiller
210 Bill Mazeroski 50.00 20.00
211 Frank Kreutzer 10.00 4.00
212 Ed Kranepool 10.00 4.00
213 Fred Newman 10.00 4.00
214 Tommy Harper 10.00 4.00
215 Bob Clemente 200.00 80.00
Hank Aaron
Willie Mays LL
216 Tony Oliva 30.00 12.00
Carl Yastrzemski
Vic Davalillo LL
217 Willie Mays 80.00 32.00
Willie McCovey
Billy Williams LL
218 Tony Conigliaro 20.00 8.00
Norm Cash
Willie Horton LL
219 Deron Johnson 40.00 16.00
Frank Robinson
Willie Mays LL
220 Rocky Colavito 20.00 8.00
Willie Horton
Tony Oliva LL
221 Sandy Koufax 40.00 16.00
Juan Marichal
Vern Law LL
222 Sam McDowell 20.00 8.00
Eddie Fisher
Sonny Siebert LL
223 Sandy Koufax 40.00 16.00
Tony Cloninger
Don Drysdale LL
224 Jim Grant 20.00 8.00
Mel Stottlemyre
Jim Kaat LL
225 Sandy Koufax 40.00 16.00
Bob Veale
Bob Gibson LL
226 Sam McDowell 20.00 8.00
Mickey Lolich
Dennis McLain
Sonny Siebert LL
227 Russ Nixon 10.00 4.00
228 Larry Dierker 10.00 4.00
229 Hank Bauer MG 10.00 4.00
230 Johnny Callison 10.00 4.00
231 Floyd Weaver 10.00 4.00
232 Glenn Beckert 10.00 4.00
233 Dom Zanni 10.00 4.00
234 Rich Beck 15.00 6.00
Roy White
235 Don Cardwell 10.00 4.00
236 Mike Hershberger 10.00 4.00
237 Billy O'Dell 10.00 4.00
238 Dodgers Team 20.00 8.00
239 Orlando Pena 10.00 4.00
240 Earl Battey 10.00 4.00
241 Dennis Ribant 10.00 4.00
242 Jesus Alou 10.00 4.00
243 Nelson Briles 10.00 4.00
244 Chuck Harrison 10.00 4.00
Sonny Jackson
245 John Buzhardt 10.00 4.00
246 Ed Bailey 10.00 4.00
247 Carl Warwick 10.00 4.00
248 Pete Mikkelsen 10.00 4.00
249 Bill Rigney MG 10.00 4.00
250 Sammy Ellis 10.00 4.00
251 Ed Brinkman 10.00 4.00
252 Denny Lemaster 10.00 4.00
253 Don Wert 10.00 4.00
254 Fergie Jenkins 300.00 120.00
Bill Sorrell
255 Willie Stargell 80.00 32.00
256 Lew Krausse 10.00 4.00
257 Jeff Torborg 10.00 4.00
258 Dave Giusti 10.00 4.00
259 Boston Red Sox 20.00 8.00
Team Card
260 Bob Shaw 10.00 4.00
261 Ron Hansen 10.00 4.00
262 Jack Hamilton 10.00 4.00
263 Tom Egan 10.00 4.00
264 Andy Kosco 10.00 4.00
Ted Uhlaender
265 Stu Miller 10.00 4.00
266 Pedro Gonzalez UER 10.00 4.00
Misspelled Gonzales on card back
267 Joe Sparma 10.00 4.00
268 John Blanchard 10.00 4.00
269 Don Heffner MG 10.00 4.00
270 Claude Osteen 10.00 4.00
271 Hal Lanier 10.00 4.00
272 Jack Bladschun 10.00 4.00
273 Bob Aspromonte 10.00 4.00
Rusty Staub
274 Buster Narum 10.00 4.00
275 Tim McCarver 20.00 8.00
276 Jim Bouton 15.00 6.00
277 George Thomas 10.00 4.00
278 Cal Koonce 10.00 4.00
279 Checklist 4 20.00 6.00
280 Bobby Knoop 10.00 4.00
281 Bruce Howard 10.00 4.00
282 Johnny Lewis 10.00 4.00
283 Jim Perry 15.00 6.00
284 Bobby Wine 10.00 4.00
285 Luis Tiant 20.00 8.00
286 Gary Geiger 10.00 4.00
287 Jack Aker 10.00 4.00
288 Bill Singer 150.00 60.00
Don Sutton
289 Larry Sherry 10.00 4.00
290 Ron Santo 30.00 12.00
291 Moe Drabowsky 10.00 4.00
292 Jim Coker 10.00 4.00
293 Mike Shannon 10.00 4.00
294 Steve Ridzik 10.00 4.00
295 Jim Ray Hart 10.00 4.00
296 Johnny Keane MG 10.00 4.00
297 Jim Owens 10.00 4.00
298 Rico Petrocelli 10.00 4.00
299 Lou Burdette 15.00 6.00
300 Roberto Clemente 600.00 240.00
301 Greg Bollo 10.00 4.00
302 Ernie Bowman 10.00 4.00
303 Cleveland Indians 20.00 8.00
Team Card
304 John Herrnstein 10.00 4.00
305 Camilo Pascual 10.00 4.00
306 Ty Cline 10.00 4.00
307 Clay Carroll 10.00 4.00
308 Tom Haller 10.00 4.00
309 Diego Segui 10.00 4.00
310 Frank Robinson 120.00 47.50
311 Tommy Helms 10.00 4.00
Dick Simpson
312 Bob Saverine 10.00 4.00
313 Chris Zachary 10.00 4.00
314 Hector Valle 10.00 4.00
315 Norm Cash 20.00 8.00
316 Jack Fisher 10.00 4.00
317 Dalton Jones 10.00 4.00
318 Harry Walker MG 10.00 4.00
319 Gene Freese 10.00 4.00
320 Bob Gibson 100.00 40.00
321 Rick Reichardt 10.00 4.00
322 Bill Faul 10.00 4.00
323 Ray Barker 10.00 4.00
324 John Boozer 10.00 4.00
325 Vic Davlillo 10.00 4.00
326 Braves Team 20.00 8.00
327 Bernie Allen 10.00 4.00
328 Jerry Grote 10.00 4.00
329 Pete Charton 10.00 4.00
330 Ron Fairly 15.00 6.00
331 Ron Herbel 10.00 4.00
332 Bill Bryan 10.00 4.00
333 Joe Coleman 10.00 4.00
Jim French
334 Marty Keough 10.00 4.00
335 Juan Pizarro 10.00 4.00
336 Gene Alley 10.00 4.00
337 Fred Gladding 10.00 4.00
338 Dal Maxvill 10.00 4.00
339 Del Crandall 10.00 4.00
340 Dean Chance 10.00 4.00
341 Wes Westrum MG 10.00 4.00
342 Bob Humphreys 10.00 4.00
343 Joe Christopher 10.00 4.00
344 Steve Blass 10.00 4.00
345 Bob Allison 10.00 4.00
346 Mike de la Hoz 10.00 4.00
347 Phil Regan 10.00 4.00
348 Orioles Team 30.00 12.00
349 Cap Peterson 10.00 4.00
350 Mel Stottlemyre 15.00 6.00
351 Fred Valentine 10.00 4.00
352 Bob Aspromonte 10.00 4.00
353 Al McBean 10.00 4.00
354 Smoky Burgess 10.00 4.00
355 Wade Blasingame 10.00 4.00
356 Owen Johnson 10.00 4.00
Ken Sanders
357 Gerry Arrigo 10.00 4.00
358 Charlie Smith 10.00 4.00
359 Johnny Briggs 10.00 4.00
360 Ron Hunt 10.00 4.00
361 Tom Satriano 10.00 4.00
362 Gates Brown 10.00 4.00
363 Checklist 5 30.00 9.00
364 Nate Oliver 10.00 4.00
365 Roger Maris 120.00 47.50
366 Wayne Causey 10.00 4.00
367 Mel Nelson 10.00 4.00
368 Charlie Lau 10.00 4.00
369 Jim King 10.00 4.00
370 Chico Cardenas 10.00 4.00

1967 Topps

The cards in this 609-card set measure 2 1/2" by 3 1/2". The 1967 Topps series is considered by some collectors to be one of the company's finest accomplishments in baseball card production. Excellent color photographs are combined with easy-to-read backs. Cards 458 to 533 are slightly harder to find than numbers 1 to 457, and the inevitable high series (534 to 609) exists. Each checklist card features a small circular picture of a popular player included in that series. Printing discrepancies resulted in some high series cards being in shorter supply. The checklist below identifies (by DP) 22 double-printed high numbers; of the 76 cards in the last series, 54 cards were short printed and the other 22 cards are much more plentiful. Featured subsets within this set include World Series cards (151-155) and League Leaders (233-244). A limited number of "proof" Roger Maris cards were produced. These cards are blank backed and Maris is listed as a New York Yankee on it. Some Bob Bolin cards: (number 252) have a white smear in between his names. Another tough variation that has been recently discovered involves card number 58 Paul Schaal. The tough version has a green bat above his name. The key Rookie Cards in the set are high number cards of Rod Carew and Tom Seaver. Confirmed methods of selling these cards include five-card nickel wax packs. Although rarely seen, there exists a salesman's sample panel of three cards that pictures Earl Battey, Manny Mota, and Gene Brabender with ad information on the back about the "new" Topps cards.

	NM	Ex
COMPLETE SET (609)	5000.00	2000.00
COMMON CARD (1-109)	1.50	.60
COMMON (110-283)	2.00	.80
COMMON (284-370)	2.50	1.00
COMMON (371-457)	4.00	1.60
COMMON (458-533)	6.00	2.40
COMMON (534-609)	15.00	6.00
COMMON DP (534-609)	8.00	3.20
WRAPPER (5-CENT)	25.00	10.00

1 Frank Robinson 25.00 7.50
Hank Bauer MG
Brooks Robinson DP
2 Jack Hamilton 1.50 .60
3 Duke Sims 1.50 .60
4 Hal Lanier 1.50 .60
5 Whitey Ford UER 20.00 8.00
(1953 listed as
1933 in stats on back)
6 Dick Simpson 1.50 .60
7 Don McMahon 1.50 .60
8 Chuck Harrison 1.50 .60
9 Ron Hansen 1.50 .60
10 Matty Alou 4.00 1.60
11 Barry Moore 1.50 .60
12 Jim Campanis 1.50 .60
Bill Singer
13 Joe Sparma 1.50 .60
14 Phil Linz 4.00 1.60
15 Earl Battey 1.50 .60
16 Bill Hands 1.50 .60
17 Jim Gosger 1.50 .60
18 Gene Oliver 1.50 .60
19 Jim McGlothlin 1.50 .60
20 Orlando Cepeda 8.00 3.20
21 Dave Bristol MG 1.50 .60
22 Gene Brabender 1.50 .60
23 Larry Elliot 1.50 .60
24 Bob Allen 1.50 .60
25 Elston Howard 4.00 1.60
26A Bob Priddy NTR 30.00 12.00
26B Bob Priddy TR 4.00 1.60
27 Bob Saverine 1.50 .60
28 Barry Latman 1.50 .60
29 Tom McCraw 1.50 .60
30 Al Kaline DP 20.00 8.00
31 Jim Brewer 1.50 .60
32 Bob Bailey 4.00 1.60
33 Sal Bando RC 6.00 2.40
Randy Schwartz
34 Pete Cimino 1.50 .60
35 Rico Carty 4.00 1.60
36 Bob Tillman 1.50 .60
37 Rick Wise 4.00 1.60
38 Bob Johnson 1.50 .60
39 Curt Simmons 4.00 1.60
40 Rick Reichardt 1.50 .60
41 Joe Hoerner 1.50 .60
42 Mets Team 10.00 4.00
43 Chico Salmon 1.50 .60
44 Joe Nuxhall 4.00 1.60
45 Roger Maris 50.00 20.00
45A Roger Maris 1000.00 400.00
Yankees listed as team
Blank Back
46 Lindy McDaniel 4.00 1.60
47 Ken McMullen 1.50 .60
48 Bill Freehan 4.00 1.60
49 Roy Face 4.00 1.60
50 Tony Oliva 6.00 2.40
51 Dave Adlesh 1.50 .60
Wes Bales
52 Dennis Higgins 1.50 .60
53 Clay Dalrymple 1.50 .60
54 Dick Green 1.50 .60
55 Don Drysdale 15.00 6.00
56 Jose Tartabull 4.00 1.60
57 Pat Jarvis RC 4.00 1.60
58A Paul Schaal 20.00 8.00
Green Bat
58B Paul Schaal 1.50 .60
Normal Colored Bat
59 Ralph Terry 4.00 1.60
60 Luis Aparicio 8.00 3.20
61 Gordy Coleman 1.50 .60
62 Frank Robinson CL 8.00 1.60
63 Lou Brock 8.00 3.20
Curt Flood
64 Fred Valentine 1.50 .60
65 Tom Haller 4.00 1.60
66 Manny Mota 4.00 1.60
67 Ken Berry 1.50 .60
68 Bob Buhl 4.00 1.60
69 Vic Davalillo 1.50 .60
70 Ron Santo 6.00 2.40
71 Camilo Pascual 4.00 1.60
72 George Korince 1.50 .60
(Photo actually
James Murray Brown)
John (Tom) Matchick
73 Rusty Staub 6.00 2.40
74 Wes Stock 1.50 .60
75 George Scott 4.00 1.60
76 Jim Barbieri 1.50 .60
77 Dooley Womack 4.00 1.60
78 Pat Corrales 1.50 .60
79 Bubba Morton 1.50 .60
80 Jim Maloney 4.00 1.60
81 Eddie Stanky MG 4.00 1.60
82 Steve Barber 1.50 .60
83 Ollie Brown 1.50 .60
84 Tommie Sisk 1.50 .60
85 Johnny Callison 4.00 1.60
86A Mike McCormick NTR 30.00 12.00
(Senators on front
and Senators on back)
86B Mike McCormick TR 4.00 1.60
(Traded line
at end of bio;
Senators on front,
but Giants on back)
87 George Altman 1.50 .60
88 Mickey Lolich 4.00 1.60
89 Felix Millan 4.00 1.60
90 Jim Nash 1.50 .60
91 Johnny Lewis 1.50 .60
92 Ray Washburn 1.50 .60
93 Stan Bahnsen RC 4.00 1.60
Bobby Murcer
94 Ron Fairly 4.00 1.60
95 Sonny Siebert 1.50 .60
96 Art Shamsky 1.50 .60
97 Mike Cuellar 4.00 1.60
98 Rich Rollins 1.50 .60
99 Lee Stange 1.50 .60
100 Frank Robinson DP 15.00 6.00
101 Ken Johnson 1.50 .60
102 Philadelphia Phillies 4.00 1.60
Team Card
103 Mickey Mantle CL 20.00 4.00
104 Minnie Rojas 1.50 .60
105 Ken Boyer 6.00 2.40
106 Randy Hundley 4.00 1.60
107 Joel Horlen 1.50 .60
108 Alex Johnson 4.00 1.60
109 Rocky Colavito 6.00 2.40
Leon Wagner
110 Jack Aker 4.00 1.60
111 John Kennedy 2.00 .80
112 Dave Wickersham 2.00 .80
113 Dave Nicholson 2.00 .80
114 Jack Baldschun 2.00 .80
115 Paul Casanova 2.00 .80
116 Herman Franks MG 2.00 .80
117 Darrell Brandon 2.00 .80
118 Bernie Allen 2.00 .80
119 Wade Blasingame 2.00 .80
120 Floyd Robinson 2.00 .80
121 Eddie Bressoud 2.00 .80
122 George Brunet 2.00 .80
123 Jim Price 4.00 1.60
Luke Walker
124 Jim Stewart 2.00 .80
125 Moe Drabowsky 4.00 1.60
126 Tony Taylor 2.00 .80
127 John O'Donoghue 2.00 .80
128 Ed Spiezio 2.00 .80
129 Phil Roof 2.00 .80
130 Phil Regan 4.00 1.60
131 Yankees Team 10.00 4.00
132 Ozzie Virgil 2.00 .80
133 Ron Kline 2.00 .80
134 Gates Brown 6.00 2.40
135 Deron Johnson 4.00 1.60
136 Carroll Sembera 2.00 .80
137 Ron Clark 2.00 .80
Jim Ollum
138 Dick Kelley 2.00 .80
139 Dalton Jones 4.00 1.60
140 Willie Stargell 20.00 8.00
141 John Miller 2.00 .80
142 Jackie Brandt 2.00 .80
143 Pete Ward 2.00 .80
Don Buford
144 Bill Hepler 2.00 .80
145 Larry Brown 2.00 .80
146 Steve Carlton 50.00 20.00
147 Tom Egan 2.00 .80
148 Adolfo Phillips 2.00 .80
149 Joe Moeller 2.00 .80
150 Mickey Mantle 250.00 100.00
151 Moe Drabowsky WS 5.00 2.00
152 Jim Palmer WS 8.00 3.20
153 Paul Blair WS 5.00 2.00
154 Brooks Robinson WS 5.00 2.00
Dave McNally
155 WS Summary 5.00 2.00
Winners celebrate
156 Ron Herbel 2.00 .80
157 Danny Cater 2.00 .80
158 Jimmie Coker 2.00 .80
159 Bruce Howard 2.00 .80
160 Willie Davis 4.00 1.60
161 Dick Williams MG 4.00 1.60
162 Billy O'Dell 2.00 .80
163 Vic Roznovsky 2.00 .80
164 Dwight Siebler UER 2.00 .80
(Last line of stats
shows 1960 Minnesota)
165 Cleon Jones 4.00 1.60
166 Eddie Mathews 15.00 6.00
167 Joe Coleman 2.00 .80
Tim Cullen
168 Ray Culp 2.00 .80
169 Horace Clarke 4.00 1.60
170 Dick McAuliffe 4.00 1.60
171 Cal Koonce 2.00 .80
172 Bill Heath 2.00 .80
173 St. Louis Cardinals 4.00 1.60
Team Card
174 Dick Radatz 4.00 1.60
175 Bobby Knoop 2.00 .80
176 Sammy Ellis 2.00 .80
177 Tito Fuentes 1.50 .60
178 John Buzhardt 2.00 .80
179 Charles Vaughan 4.00 1.60
Cecil Upshaw
180 Curt Blefary 2.00 .80
181 Terry Fox 2.00 .80
182 Ed Charles 2.00 .80
183 Jim Pagliaroni 2.00 .80
184 George Thomas 2.00 .80
185 Ken Holtzman RC 4.00 1.60
186 Ed Kranepool 4.00 1.60
Ron Swoboda
187 Pedro Ramos 2.00 .80
188 Ken Harrelson 4.00 1.60
189 Chuck Hinton 2.00 .80
190 Turk Farrell 2.00 .80
191A Willie Mays CL 10.00 2.00
214 Tom Kelley
191B Willie Mays CL 12.00 2.40
214 Dick Kelley
192 Fred Gladding 2.00 .80
193 Jose Cardenal 4.00 1.60
194 Bob Allison 4.00 1.60
195 Al Jackson 2.00 .80
196 Johnny Romano 2.00 .80
197 Ron Perranoski 4.00 1.60
198 Chuck Hiller 2.00 .80
199 Billy Hitchcock MG 2.00 .80
200 Willie Mays UER 100.00 40.00
('63 Sna Francisco
on card back stats)
201 Hal Reniff 4.00 1.60
202 Johnny Edwards 2.00 .80
203 Al McBean 2.00 .80
204 Mike Epstein 6.00 2.40
Tom Phoebus
205 Dick Groat 4.00 1.60
206 Dennis Bennett 2.00 .80
207 John Orsino 2.00 .80
208 Jack Lamabe 2.00 .80
209 Joe Nossek 2.00 .80
210 Bob Gibson 20.00 8.00
211 Twins Team 4.00 1.60
212 Chris Zachary 2.00 .80
213 Jay Johnstone RC 4.00 1.60
214 Dick Kelley 2.00 .80
215 Ernie Banks 20.00 8.00
216 Norm Cash 8.00 3.20
Al Kaline
217 Rob Gardner 2.00 .80
218 Wes Parker 4.00 1.60
219 Clay Carroll 4.00 1.60
220 Jim Ray Hart 4.00 1.60
221 Woody Fryman 4.00 1.60
222 Darrell Osteen 4.00 1.60
Lee May
223 Mike Ryan 4.00 1.60
224 Walt Bond 2.00 .80
225 Mel Stottlemyre 6.00 2.40
226 Julian Javier 4.00 1.60
227 Paul Lindblad 2.00 .80
228 Gil Hodges MG 6.00 2.40
229 Larry Jackson 2.00 .80
230 Boog Powell 6.00 2.40
231 John Bateman 2.00 .80
232 Don Buford 2.00 .80
233 Gary Peters 4.00 1.60
Joel Horlen
Steve Hargan LL
234 Sandy Koufax 15.00 6.00
Mike Cuellar
Juan Marichal LL
235 Jim Kaat 6.00 2.40
Denny McLain
Earl Wilson LL
236 Sandy Koufax 25.00 10.00
Juan Marichal
Bob Gibson
Gaylord Perry LL
237 Sam McDowell 6.00 2.40
Jim Kaat
Earl Wilson LL
238 Sandy Koufax 12.00 4.80
Jim Bunning
Bob Veale LL
239 Frank Robinson 10.00 4.00
Tony Oliva
Al Kaline LL
240 Matty Alou 6.00 2.40
Felipe Alou
Rico Carty LL
241 Frank Robinson 10.00 4.00

Harmon Killebrew		
Boog Powell LL		
242 Hank Aaron	25.00	10.00
Bob Clemente		
Richie Allen LL		
243 Frank Robinson	10.00	4.00
Harmon Killebrew		
Boog Powell LL		
244 Hank Aaron	20.00	8.00
Richie Allen		
Willie Mays LL		
245 Curt Flood	6.00	2.40
246 Jim Perry	4.00	1.60
247 Jerry Lumpe	2.00	.80
248 Gene Mauch MG	4.00	1.60
249 Nick Willhite	2.00	.80
250 Hank Aaron UER	80.00	32.00
(Second 1961 in stats should be 1962)		
251 Woody Held	2.00	.80
252 Bob Bolin	2.00	.80
253 Bill Davis	2.00	.80
Gus Gil		
254 Milt Pappas	4.00	1.60
(No facsimile autograph on card front)		
255 Frank Howard	4.00	1.60
256 Bob Hendley	2.00	.80
257 Charlie Smith	2.00	.80
258 Lee Maye	2.00	.80
259 Don Dennis	2.00	.80
260 Jim Lefebvre	4.00	1.60
261 John Wyatt	2.00	.80
262 Athletics Team	4.00	1.60
263 Hank Aguirre	2.00	.80
264 Ron Swoboda	4.00	1.60
265 Lou Burdette	4.00	1.60
266 Willie Stargell	4.00	1.60
Donn Clendenon		
267 Don Schwall	2.00	.80
268 Johnny Briggs	2.00	.80
269 Don Nottebart	2.00	.80
270 Zoilo Versalles	2.00	.80
271 Eddie Watt	2.00	.80
272 Bill Connors RC	4.00	1.60
Dave Dowling		
273 Dick Lines	2.00	.80
274 Bob Aspromonte	2.00	.80
275 Fred Whitfield	2.00	.80
276 Bruce Brubaker	2.00	.80
277 Steve Whitaker	6.00	2.40
278 Jim Kaat CL	8.00	1.60
279 Frank Linzy	2.00	.80
280 Tony Conigliaro	8.00	3.20
281 Bob Rodgers	2.00	.80
282 John Odom	2.00	.80
283 Gene Alley	4.00	1.60
284 Johnny Podres	4.00	1.60
285 Lou Brock	20.00	8.00
286 Wayne Causey	2.50	1.00
287 Greg Goossen	2.50	1.00
Bart Shirley		
288 Denny Lemaster	2.50	1.00
289 Tom Tresh	5.00	2.00
290 Bill White	5.00	2.00
291 Jim Hannan	2.50	1.00
292 Don Pavletich	2.50	1.00
293 Ed Kirkpatrick	2.50	1.00
294 Walter Alston MG	8.00	3.20
295 Sam McDowell	5.00	2.00
296 Glenn Beckert	5.00	2.00
297 Dave Morehead	5.00	2.00
298 Ron Davis	2.50	1.00
299 Norm Siebern	2.50	1.00
300 Jim Kaat	5.00	2.00
301 Jesse Gonder	2.50	1.00
302 Orioles Team	8.00	3.20
303 Gil Blanco	2.50	1.00
304 Phil Gagliano	2.50	1.00
305 Earl Wilson	5.00	2.00
306 Bud Harrelson RC	5.00	2.00
307 Jim Beauchamp	2.50	1.00
308 Al Downing	5.00	2.00
309 Johnny Callison	5.00	2.00
Richie Allen		
310 Gary Peters	2.50	1.00
311 Ed Brinkman	2.50	1.00
312 Don Mincher	2.50	1.00
313 Bob Lee	2.50	1.00
314 Mike Andrews	8.00	3.20
Reggie Smith RC		
315 Billy Williams	15.00	6.00
316 Jack Kralick	2.50	1.00
317 Cesar Tovar	2.50	1.00
318 Dave Giusti	2.50	1.00
319 Paul Blair	5.00	2.00
320 Gaylord Perry	15.00	6.00
321 Mayo Smith MG	2.50	1.00
322 Jose Pagan	2.50	1.00
323 Mike Hershberger	2.50	1.00
324 Hal Woodeshick	2.50	1.00
325 Chico Cardenas	5.00	2.00
326 Bob Uecker	10.00	4.00
327 California Angels	8.00	3.20
Team Card		
328 Clete Boyer UER	5.00	2.00
(Stats only go up through 1965)		
329 Charlie Lau	5.00	2.00
330 Claude Osteen	5.00	2.00
331 Joe Foy	5.00	2.00
332 Jesus Alou	2.50	1.00
333 Fergie Jenkins	20.00	8.00
334 Bob Allison	10.00	4.00
Harmon Killebrew		
335 Bob Veale	5.00	2.00
336 Joe Azcue	2.50	1.00
337 Joe Morgan	15.00	6.00
338 Bob Locker	2.50	1.00
339 Chico Ruiz	2.50	1.00
340 Joe Pepitone	8.00	3.20
341 Dick Dietz	2.50	1.00
Bill Sorrell		
342 Hank Fischer	2.50	1.00
343 Tom Satriano	2.50	1.00
344 Ossie Chavarria	2.50	1.00
345 Stu Miller	5.00	2.00
346 Jim Hickman	2.50	1.00
347 Grady Hatton MG	2.50	1.00
348 Tug McGraw	5.00	2.00
349 Bob Chance	2.50	1.00
350 Joe Torre	8.00	3.20
351 Vern Law	5.00	2.00
352 Ray Oyler	2.50	1.00
353 Bill McCool	2.50	1.00
354 Cubs Team	8.00	3.20
355 Carl Yastrzemski	60.00	24.00
356 Larry Jaster	2.50	1.00
357 Bill Skowron	5.00	2.00
358 Ruben Amaro	2.50	1.00
359 Dick Ellsworth	2.50	1.00
360 Leon Wagner	2.50	1.00
361 Roberto Clemente CL	15.00	3.00
362 Darold Knowles	2.50	1.00
363 Davey Johnson	5.00	2.00
364 Claude Raymond	2.50	1.00
365 John Roseboro	5.00	2.00
366 Andy Kosco	2.50	1.00
367 Bill Kelso	2.50	1.00
Don Wallace		
368 Jack Hiatt	2.50	1.00
369 Jim Hunter	15.00	6.00
370 Tommy Davis	5.00	2.00
371 Jim Lonborg	8.00	3.20
372 Mike de la Hoz	4.00	1.60
373 Duane Josephson	4.00	1.60
Fred Klages DP		
374A Mel Queen ERR DP	20.00	8.00
(Incomplete stat line on back)		
374B Mel Queen COR DP	4.00	1.60
(Complete stat line on back)		
375 Jake Gibbs	8.00	3.20
376 Don Lock DP	4.00	1.60
377 Luis Tiant	8.00	3.20
378 Detroit Tigers	8.00	3.20
Team Card UER		
(Willie Horton with 262 RBI's in 1966)		
379 Jerry May DP	4.00	1.60
380 Dean Chance DP	4.00	1.60
381 Dick Schofield DP	4.00	1.60
382 Dave McNally	8.00	3.20
383 Ken Henderson DP	4.00	1.60
384 Jim Cosman	4.00	1.60
Dick Hughes		
385 Jim Fregosi	8.00	3.20
(Batting wrong)		
386 Dick Selma DP	4.00	1.60
387 Cap Peterson DP	4.00	1.60
388 Arnold Earley DP	4.00	1.60
389 Alvin Dark MG DP	8.00	3.20
390 Jim Wynn DP	8.00	3.20
391 Wilbur Wood DP	8.00	3.20
392 Tommy Harper DP	8.00	3.20
393 Jim Bouton DP	8.00	3.20
394 Jake Wood DP	4.00	1.60
395 Chris Short	8.00	3.20
396 Denis Menke	4.00	1.60
Tony Cloninger		
397 Willie Smith DP	4.00	1.60
398 Jeff Torborg	8.00	3.20
399 Al Worthington DP	4.00	1.60
400 Bob Clemente DP	100.00	40.00
401 Jim Coates	4.00	1.60
402A Phillies Rookies DP	20.00	8.00
Grant Jackson		
Billy Wilson		
Incomplete stat line		
402B Phillies Rookies DP	8.00	3.20
Grant Jackson		
Billy Wilson		
403 Dick Nen	4.00	1.60
404 Nelson Briles	8.00	3.20
405 Russ Snyder	4.00	1.60
406 Lee Elia DP	4.00	1.60
407 Reds Team	8.00	3.20
408 Jim Northrup DP	8.00	3.20
409 Ray Sadecki	4.00	1.60
410 Lou Johnson DP	4.00	1.60
411 Dick Howser DP	4.00	1.60
412 Norm Miller	8.00	3.20
Doug Rader RC		
413 Jerry Grote	4.00	1.60
414 Casey Cox	4.00	1.60
415 Sonny Jackson	4.00	1.60
416 Roger Repoz	4.00	1.60
417A Bob Bruce ERR DP	30.00	12.00
(RBAVES on back)		
417B Bob Bruce COR DP	4.00	1.60
418 Sam Mele MG	4.00	1.60
419 Don Kessinger DP	8.00	3.20
420 Denny McLain	12.00	4.80
421 Dal Maxvill DP	4.00	1.60
422 Hoyt Wilhelm	15.00	6.00
423 Willie Mays	25.00	10.00
Willie McCovey DP		
424 Pedro Gonzalez	4.00	1.60
425 Pete Mikkelsen	4.00	1.60
426 Lou Clinton	4.00	1.60
427A R.Gomez ERR DP	20.00	8.00
Incomplete stat line on back		
427B R.Gomez COR DP	4.00	1.60
Complete stat line on back		
428 Tom Hutton RC	8.00	3.20
Gene Michael DP		
429 Garry Roggenburk DP	4.00	1.60
430 Pete Rose	100.00	40.00
431 Ted Uhlaender	4.00	1.60
432 Jimmie Hall DP	4.00	1.60
433 Al Luplow DP	4.00	1.60
434 Eddie Fisher DP	4.00	1.60
435 Mack Jones DP	4.00	1.60
436 Pete Ward	4.00	1.60
437 Senators Team	8.00	3.20
438 Chuck Dobson	4.00	1.60
439 Byron Browne	4.00	1.60
440 Steve Hargan	4.00	1.60
441 Jim Davenport	4.00	1.60
442 Bill Robinson RC	8.00	3.20
Joe Verbanic DP		
443 Tito Francona DP	4.00	1.60
444 George Smith	4.00	1.60
445 Don Sutton	25.00	10.00
446 Russ Nixon DP	4.00	1.60
447A Bo Belinsky ERR DP	5.00	2.00
(Incomplete stat line on back)		
447B Bo Belinsky COR DP	8.00	3.20
(Complete stat line on back)		
448 Harry Walker DP MG	4.00	1.60
449 Orlando Pena	4.00	1.60
450 Richie Allen	8.00	3.20
451 Fred Newman DP	4.00	1.60
452 Ed Kranepool	8.00	3.20
453 A.Monteagudo DP	4.00	1.60
454A Juan Marichal CL	12.00	2.40
Missing left ear		
454B Juan Marichal CL	12.00	2.40
left ear showing		
455 Tommie Agee	8.00	3.20
456 Phil Niekro	15.00	6.00
457 Andy Etchebarren DP	8.00	3.20
458 Lee Thomas	6.00	2.40
459 Dick Bosman RC	6.00	2.40
Pete Craig		
460 Harmon Killebrew	60.00	24.00
461 Bob Miller	12.00	4.80
462 Bob Barton	6.00	2.40
463 Sam McDowell	12.00	4.80
Sonny Siebert		
464 Dan Coombs	6.00	2.40
465 Willie Horton	12.00	4.80
466 Bobby Wine	6.00	2.40
467 Jim O'Toole	6.00	2.40
468 Ralph Houk MG	6.00	2.40
469 Len Gabrielson	6.00	2.40
470 Bob Shaw	6.00	2.40
471 Rene Lachemann	6.00	2.40
472 John Gelnar	6.00	2.40
George Spriggs		
473 Jose Santiago	6.00	2.40
474 Bob Tolan	6.00	2.40
475 Jim Palmer	80.00	32.00
476 Tony Perez SP	60.00	24.00
477 Braves Team	15.00	6.00
478 Bob Humphreys	6.00	2.40
479 Gary Bell	6.00	2.40
480 Willie McCovey	40.00	16.00
481 Leo Durocher MG	20.00	8.00
482 Bill Monbouquette	6.00	2.40
483 Jim Landis	6.00	2.40
484 Jerry Adair	6.00	2.40
485 Tim McCarver	25.00	10.00
486 Rich Reese	6.00	2.40
Bill Whitby		
487 Tommie Reynolds	6.00	2.40
488 Gerry Arrigo	6.00	2.40
489 Doug Clemens	6.00	2.40
490 Tony Cloninger	6.00	2.40
491 Sam Bowens	6.00	2.40
492 Pittsburgh Pirates	15.00	6.00
Team Card		
493 Phil Ortega	6.00	2.40
494 Bill Rigney MG	6.00	2.40
495 Fritz Peterson	6.00	2.40
496 Orlando McFarlane	6.00	2.40
497 Ron Campbell	6.00	2.40
498 Larry Dierker	12.00	4.80
499 George Culver	6.00	2.40
Jose Vidal		
500 Juan Marichal	25.00	10.00
501 Jerry Zimmerman	6.00	2.40
502 Derrell Griffith	6.00	2.40
503 Los Angeles Dodgers	20.00	8.00
Team Card		
504 Orlando Martinez	6.00	2.40
505 Tommy Helms	12.00	4.80
506 Smoky Burgess	6.00	2.40
507 Ed Barnowski	6.00	2.40
Larry Haney RC		
508 Dick Hall	6.00	2.40
509 Jim King	6.00	2.40
510 Bill Mazeroski	25.00	10.00
511 Don Wert	6.00	2.40
512 Red Schoendienst MG	25.00	10.00
513 Marcelino Lopez	6.00	2.40
514 John Werhas	6.00	2.40
515 Bert Campaneris	12.00	4.80
516 Giants Team	15.00	6.00
517 Fred Talbot	12.00	4.80
518 Denis Menke	6.00	2.40
519 Ted Davidson	6.00	2.40
520 Max Alvis	6.00	2.40
521 Boog Powell	12.00	4.80
Curt Blefary		
522 John Stephenson	6.00	2.40
523 Jim Merritt	6.00	2.40
524 Felix Mantilla	6.00	2.40
525 Ron Hunt	6.00	2.40
526 Pat Dobson RC	6.00	2.40
George Korince		
(See 67T-72)		
527 Dennis Ribant	6.00	2.40
528 Rico Petrocelli	20.00	8.00
529 Gary Wagner	6.00	2.40
530 Felipe Alou	12.00	4.80
531 Brooks Robinson CL	15.00	3.00
532 Jim Hicks	6.00	2.40
533 Jack Fisher	6.00	2.40
534 Hank Bauer MG DP	8.00	3.20
535 Donn Clendenon	25.00	10.00
536 Joe Niekro RC	50.00	20.00
Paul Popovich		
537 Chuck Estrada DP	8.00	3.20
538 J.C. Martin	15.00	6.00
539 Dick Egan DP	8.00	3.20
540 Norm Cash	50.00	20.00
541 Joe Gibbon	15.00	6.00
542 Rick Monday RC	15.00	6.00
Tony Pierce DP		
543 Dan Schneider	15.00	6.00
544 Cleveland Indians	30.00	12.00
Team Card		
545 Jim Grant	25.00	10.00
546 Woody Woodward	25.00	10.00
547 Russ Gibson	8.00	3.20
Bill Rohr DP		
548 Tony Gonzalez DP	8.00	3.20
549 Jack Sanford	15.00	6.00
550 Vada Pinson DP	10.00	4.00
551 Doug Camilli DP	8.00	3.20
552 Ted Savage	25.00	10.00
553 Mike Hegan RC	40.00	16.00
Thad Tillotson		
554 Andre Rodgers DP	8.00	3.20
555 Don Cardwell	25.00	10.00
556 Al Weis DP	8.00	3.20
557 Al Ferrara	25.00	10.00
558 Mark Belanger RC	50.00	20.00
Bill Dillman		
559 Dick Tracewski DP	8.00	3.20
560 Jim Bunning	60.00	24.00
561 Sandy Alomar	40.00	16.00
562 Steve Blass DP	8.00	3.20
563 Joe Adcock	40.00	16.00
564 Alonzo Harris	8.00	3.20
Aaron Pointer		
565 Lew Krausse	25.00	10.00
566 Gary Geiger DP	8.00	3.20
567 Steve Hamilton	40.00	16.00
568 John Sullivan	40.00	16.00
569 Rod Carew RC	200.00	80.00
Hank Allen DP		
570 Maury Wills	80.00	32.00
571 Larry Sherry	25.00	10.00
572 Don Demeter	25.00	10.00
573 Chicago White Sox	30.00	12.00
Team Card UER		
(Indians team stats on back)		
574 Jerry Buchek	25.00	10.00
575 Dave Boswell	15.00	6.00
576 Ramon Hernandez	40.00	16.00
Norm Gigon RC		
577 Bill Short	15.00	6.00
578 John Boccabella	15.00	6.00
579 Bill Henry	15.00	6.00
580 Rocky Colavito	125.00	50.00
581 Bill Denehy	500.00	200.00
Tom Seaver RC		
582 Jim Owens DP	8.00	3.20
583 Ray Barker	40.00	16.00
584 Jimmy Piersall	40.00	16.00
585 Wally Bunker	25.00	10.00
586 Manny Jimenez	15.00	6.00
587 Don Shaw	40.00	16.00
Gary Sutherland RC		
588 Johnny Klippstein DP	8.00	3.20
589 Dave Ricketts DP	8.00	3.20
590 Pete Richert	15.00	6.00
591 Ty Cline	25.00	10.00
592 Jim Shellenback	25.00	10.00
Ron Willis RC		
593 Wes Westrum MG	50.00	20.00
594 Dan Osinski	40.00	16.00
595 Cookie Rojas	25.00	10.00
596 Galen Cisco DP	8.00	3.20
597 Ted Abernathy	15.00	6.00
598 Walt Williams	25.00	10.00
Ed Stroud		
599 Bob Duliba DP	8.00	3.20
600 Brooks Robinson	250.00	100.00
601 Bill Bryan DP	8.00	3.20
602 Juan Pizarro	40.00	16.00
603 Tim Talton	25.00	10.00
Ramon Webster		
604 Red Sox Team	125.00	50.00
605 Mike Shannon	50.00	20.00
606 Ron Taylor	25.00	10.00
607 Mickey Stanley	50.00	20.00
608 Rich Nye	8.00	3.20
John Upham DP		
609 Tommy John	80.00	27.00

1967 Topps Posters Inserts

The wrappers of the 1967 Topps cards have this 32-card set advertised as follows: 'Extra -- All Star Pin-Up Inside.' Printed on (5" by 7") paper in full color, these "All-Star" inserts have fold lines which are generally not very noticeable when stored carefully. They are numbered, blank-backed, and carry a facsimile autograph.

	NM	Ex
COMPLETE SET (32)	60.00	24.00
1 Boog Powell	1.50	.60
2 Bert Campaneris	1.00	.40
3 Brooks Robinson	4.00	1.60
4 Tommie Agee	.75	.30
5 Carl Yastrzemski	4.00	1.60
6 Mickey Mantle	20.00	8.00
7 Frank Howard	1.00	.40
8 Sam McDowell	1.00	.40
9 Orlando Cepeda	2.00	.80
10 Chico Cardenas	.75	.30
11 Roberto Clemente	10.00	4.00
12 Willie Mays	8.00	3.20
13 Cleon Jones	.75	.30
14 Johnny Callison	1.00	.40
15 Hank Aaron	6.00	2.40
16 Don Drysdale	3.00	1.20
17 Bobby Knoop	.75	.30
18 Tony Oliva	1.50	.60
19 Frank Robinson	4.00	1.60
20 Denny McLain	1.50	.60
21 Al Kaline	4.00	1.60
22 Joe Pepitone	1.50	.60
23 Harmon Killebrew	3.00	1.20
24 Leon Wagner	.75	.30
25 Joe Morgan	3.00	1.20
26 Ron Santo	1.50	.60
27 Joe Torre	1.50	.60
28 Juan Marichal	3.00	1.20
29 Matty Alou	.75	.30
30 Felipe Alou	1.00	.40
31 Ron Hunt	.75	.30
32 Willie McCovey	3.00	1.20

1967 Topps Test Foil

This 24-card set of all-stars is know only in proof form and was intended to be pressed onto a pin-back button issue which never materialized. The set measures approximately 2 3/8" square and features a color player head photo in a 2 1/4" white circle on a silver foil

background with the player's name and position printed in black across the neck. The word "Japan" is printed in tiny black letters at the top-left apparently intended to be folded under the rim of the button. The backs are blank. The cards are unnumbered and checklisted below in alphabetical order.

	NM	Ex
COMPLETE SET (23)	3000.00	1200.00
1 Hank Aaron	250.00	100.00
2 Johnny Callison	50.00	20.00
3 Bert Campaneris	80.00	32.00
4 Leo Cardenas	50.00	20.00
5 Orlando Cepeda	150.00	60.00
6 Roberto Clemente	300.00	120.00
7 Frank Howard	80.00	32.00
8 Cleon Jones	50.00	20.00
9 Bobby Knoop	50.00	20.00
10 Sandy Koufax	250.00	100.00
11 Mickey Mantle	400.00	160.00
12 Juan Marichal	150.00	60.00
13 Willie Mays	250.00	100.00
14 Sam McDowell	50.00	20.00
15 Denny McLain	80.00	32.00
16 Joe Morgan	150.00	60.00
17 Tony Oliva	80.00	32.00
18 Boog Powell	80.00	32.00
19 Brooks Robinson	150.00	60.00
20 Frank Robinson	150.00	60.00
21 Ron Santo	100.00	40.00
22 Joe Torre	100.00	40.00
23 Carl Yastrzemski	150.00	60.00

1967 Topps Venezuelan

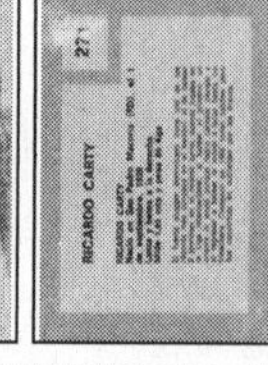

This set features color player photos in a white border on the fronts. The horizontal backs carry player information. The cards are printed in Spanish and were issued for the Venezuelan market. Cards from 139 through 188 feature retired players while the rest of the set features active players. The cards which feature the same photos as the 67 Topps cards seemed trimmed. However, by checking the back -- any collector should have confidence in what they are buying. The first 138 cards in this set feature players who were then playing in the Venezuelan Winter league. Those first 138 cards have red backs. Cards numbered 139 through 188 have green backs. The rest of the set (189-338) have a light blue back. Both Bobby Cox and Dave Concepcion have cards in this set which significantly predate their Topps Rookie Cards.

	NM	Ex
COMPLETE SET	15000.00	6000.00
COMMON CARD (1-138)	30.00	12.00
COMMON CARD (139-188)	40.00	16.00
COMMON CARD (189-338)	5.00	2.00
1 Regino Otero	30.00	12.00
2 Alejandro Carrasquel	30.00	12.00
3 Pompeyo Davalillo	30.00	12.00
4 Gonzalo Marquez	30.00	12.00
5 Cookie Rojas	35.00	14.00
6 Teodoro Obregon	30.00	12.00
7 Paul Schall	35.00	14.00
8 Juan Francia	30.00	12.00
9 Luis Tiant	50.00	20.00
10 Jose Tartabull	30.00	12.00
10A Jose Tartabull	30.00	12.00
Blue Back		
11 Vic Davalillo	30.00	12.00
12 Cesar Tovar	30.00	12.00
13 Ron Klimkowski	30.00	12.00
14 Diego Segui	30.00	12.00
15 Luis Penalver	30.00	12.00
16 Urbano Lugo	30.00	12.00
17 Aurelio Monteagudo	30.00	12.00
18 Richard Underwood	30.00	12.00
19 Nelson Castellanos	30.00	12.00
20 Manuel Mendible	30.00	12.00
21 Fidel Garcia	30.00	12.00
22 Luis Cordoba	30.00	12.00
23 Jesus Padron	30.00	12.00
24 Lorenzo Fernandez	30.00	12.00
25 Leopoldo Tovar	30.00	12.00
26 Carlos Loreto	30.00	12.00
27 Ossie Blanco	30.00	12.00
28 Syd O'Brien	30.00	12.00
29 Cesar Gutierrerz	30.00	12.00
30 Luis Garcia	30.00	12.00
31 Fred Klages	30.00	12.00
32 Isasis Chavez	30.00	12.00
33 Walt Williams	30.00	12.00
34 Jim Hicks	30.00	12.00
35 Gustavo Sposito	30.00	12.00
36 Cisco Carlos	30.00	12.00
37 Jim Mooring	30.00	12.00
38 Alonso Olivares	30.00	12.00
39 Gracilliano Parra	30.00	12.00
40 Merritt Ranew	30.00	12.00
41 Everest Contramaestre	30.00	12.00
42 Orlando Reyes	30.00	12.00
43 Edicto Arteaga	30.00	12.00
44 Francisco Diaz	30.00	12.00
45 Victor Diaz	30.00	12.00
46 Ramon Diaz	30.00	12.00
46A Francisco Diaz	30.00	12.00

Blue Back
47 Luis Aparicio 80.00 32.00
48 Reynaldo Cordeiro CO 30.00 12.00
49 Luis Aparicio 80.00 32.00
50 Ramon Webster 30.00 12.00
51 Remigio Hermoso 30.00 12.00
52 Mike de la Hoz 30.00 12.00
53 Enzo Hernandez 30.00 12.00
54 Ed Watt 30.00 12.00
55 Angel Bravo 30.00 12.00
56 Merv Rettenmund 30.00 12.00
57 Jose Herrera 30.00 12.00
58 Tom Fisher 30.00 12.00
59 Jim Weaver 30.00 12.00
60 Juan Quintana 30.00 12.00
60A Frank Fernandez 30.00 12.00
Blue Back
61 Hector Urbano 30.00 12.00
62A Hector Brito 30.00 12.00
Blue Back
63 Jesus Romero 30.00 12.00
64 Carlos Moreno 30.00 12.00
65 Nestor Mendible 30.00 12.00
66 Armando Ortiz 30.00 12.00
67 Graciano Ravelo 30.00 12.00
68 Paul Knechtges 30.00 12.00
69 Marcelino Lopez 30.00 12.00
70 Wilfredo Calvino 30.00 12.00
71 Jesus Avila 30.00 12.00
72 Carlos Pascual 30.00 12.00
73 Bob Burda 30.00 12.00
73 Bob Burda 30.00 12.00
Blue Back
74 Elio Chacon 30.00 12.00
75 Jacinto Hernandez 30.00 12.00
76 Jose Tovar 30.00 12.00
77 Bill Whitby 30.00 12.00
78 Enrique Izquierdo 30.00 12.00
79 Sandy Valdespino 30.00 12.00
80 John Lewis 30.00 12.00
81 Hector Martinez 30.00 12.00
82 Rene Paredes 30.00 12.00
83 Danny Morris 30.00 12.00
84 Pedro Ramos 30.00 12.00
85 Jose Ramon Lopez 30.00 12.00
86 Jesus Rizales 30.00 12.00
87 Winston Acosta 30.00 12.00
88 Pablo Bello 30.00 12.00
89 Dave Concepcion 100.00 40.00
90 Manuel Garcia 30.00 12.00
91 Anibal Longa 30.00 12.00
92 Franscico Moscoso 30.00 12.00
93 Mel McGaha MG 30.00 12.00
94 Aquiles Gomez 30.00 12.00
95 Alfonso Carrasquel UER 30.00 12.00
Card numbered 115
95A Alfonso Carrasquel 30.00 12.00
Blue Back
96 Tom Murray 30.00 12.00
97 Gus Gil 30.00 12.00
98 Damaso Blanco 30.00 12.00
99 Alberto Cambero 30.00 12.00
100 Don Bryant 30.00 12.00
101 George Culver 30.00 12.00
102 Teolindo Acosta 30.00 12.00
103 Aaron Pointer 30.00 12.00
104 Ed Kirkpatrick 30.00 12.00
106 Mike Daniel 30.00 12.00
108 Juan Quiroz 30.00 12.00
109 Juan Campos 30.00 12.00
110 Freddy Rivero 30.00 12.00
111 Dick Lemay 30.00 12.00
112 Raul Ortega 30.00 12.00
113 Bruno Estaba 30.00 12.00
114 Evangelista Nunez 30.00 12.00
115 Roberto Munoz 30.00 12.00
116 Tony Castanos 30.00 12.00
117 Domingo Barboza 30.00 12.00
118 Lucio Celis 30.00 12.00
119 Carlos Santeliz 30.00 12.00
120 Bart Shirley 30.00 12.00
121 Nuedo Morales 30.00 12.00
122 Bobby Cox 100.00 40.00
123 Cruz Amaya 30.00 12.00
Blue Back
124 Jim Campanis 30.00 12.00
125 Dave Roberts 30.00 12.00
126 Jerrry Crider 30.00 12.00
127 Domingo Carrasquel 30.00 12.00
128 Leo Marentette 30.00 12.00
129 Frank Kreutzer 30.00 12.00
130 Jim Dickson 30.00 12.00
131 Bob Oliver 30.00 12.00
132 Pablo Torrealba 30.00 12.00
133 Pablo Torrealba 30.00 12.00
134 Iran Paz 30.00 12.00
135 Eliecer Bueno 30.00 12.00
136 Claudio Urdaneta 30.00 12.00
137 Faustino Zabala 30.00 12.00
138 Dario Chirinos 30.00 12.00
139 Walter Johnson 200.00 80.00
140 Bill Dickey 100.00 40.00
141 Lou Gehrig 400.00 160.00
142 Rogers Hornsby 200.00 80.00
143 Honus Wagner 250.00 100.00
144 Pie Traynor 100.00 40.00
145 Joe DiMaggio 400.00 160.00
146 Ty Cobb 400.00 160.00
147 Babe Ruth 500.00 200.00
148 Ted Williams 400.00 160.00
149 Mel Ott 100.00 40.00
150 Cy Young 200.00 80.00
151 Christy Matthewson 200.00 80.00
152 Warren Spahn 100.00 40.00
153 Mickey Cochrane 100.00 40.00
154 George Sisler 80.00 32.00
155 Jimmy Collins 60.00 24.00
156 Tris Speaker 150.00 60.00
157 Stan Musial 200.00 80.00
158 Luke Appling 80.00 32.00
159 Nap Lajoie 150.00 60.00
160 Bob Feller 200.00 80.00
161 Bill Terry 60.00 24.00
162 Sandy Koufax 250.00 100.00
163 Jimmy Foxx 200.00 80.00
164 Joe Cronin 80.00 32.00
165 Frank Frisch 80.00 32.00
166 Paul Waner 100.00 40.00
167 Lloyd Waner 80.00 32.00
168 Lefty Grove 150.00 60.00
169 Bobby Doerr 60.00 24.00
170 Al Simmons 80.00 32.00
171 Grover Alexander 200.00 80.00
172 Carl Hubbell 200.00 80.00
173 Mordecai Brown 150.00 60.00
174 Ted Lyons 80.00 32.00
175 Johnny Vander Meer 60.00 24.00
176 Alex Carrasquel 40.00 16.00
177 Satchel Paige 300.00 120.00
178 Whitey Ford 150.00 60.00
179 Yogi Berra 150.00 60.00
180 Roy Campanella 150.00 60.00
181 Chico Carrasquel 40.00 16.00
182 Johnny Mize 80.00 32.00
183 Ted Kluszewski 40.00 16.00
Ray Herbert
184 Jackie Robinson 400.00 160.00
185 Beto Avila 40.00 16.00
186 Phil Rizzuto 150.00 60.00
187 Minnie Minoso 60.00 24.00
188 Conrado Marrero 40.00 16.00
189 Luis Aparicio 15.00 6.00
190 Vic Davalillo 5.00 2.00
191 Cesar Tovar 5.00 2.00
192 Mickey Mantle 800.00 325.00
193 Carl Yastrzemski 120.00 47.50
194 Frank Robinson 40.00 16.00
195 Willie Horton 6.00 2.40
196 Gary Peters 5.00 2.00
197 Bert Campaneris 5.00 2.00
198 Norm Cash 8.00 3.20
199 Boog Powell 15.00 6.00
200 George Scott 5.00 2.00
201 Frank Howard 6.00 2.40
202 Rick Reichardt 5.00 2.00
203 Jose Cardenal 5.00 2.00
204 Rico Petrocelli 5.00 2.00
205 Lew Krausse 5.00 2.00
206 Harmon Killebrew 40.00 16.00
207 Leon Wagner 5.00 2.00
208 Joe Foy 5.00 2.00
209 Joe Pepitone 6.00 2.40
210 Al Kaline 40.00 16.00
211 Brooks Robinson 50.00 20.00
212 Bill Freehan 5.00 2.00
213 Jim Lonborg 5.00 2.00
214 Ed Mathews 40.00 16.00
215 Dick Green 5.00 2.00
216 Tom Tresh 5.00 2.00
217 Dean Chance 5.00 2.00
218 Paul Blair 5.00 2.00
219 Larry Brown 5.00 2.00
220 Fred Valentine 5.00 2.00
221 Al Downing 5.00 2.00
222 Earl Battey 5.00 2.00
223 Don Mincher 5.00 2.00
224 Tommie Agee 5.00 2.00
225 Jim McGlothlin 5.00 2.00
226 Zolio Versalles 5.00 2.00
227 Curt Blefary 5.00 2.00
228 Joel Horlen 5.00 2.00
229 Stu Miller 5.00 2.00
230 Tony Oliva 8.00 3.20
231 Paul Casanova 5.00 2.00
232 Orlando Pena 5.00 2.00
233 Ron Hansen 5.00 2.00
234 Earl Wilson 5.00 2.00
235 Ken Boyer 6.00 2.40
236 Jim Kaat 8.00 3.20
237 Dalton Jones 5.00 2.00
238 Pete Ward 5.00 2.00
239 Mickey Lolich 6.00 2.40
240 Jose Santiago 5.00 2.00
241 Dick McAuliffe 5.00 2.00
242 Mel Stottlemyre 6.00 2.40
243 Camilo Pascual 5.00 2.00
244 Jim Fregosi 6.00 2.40
245 Tony Conigliaro 25.00 10.00
246 Sonny Siebert 5.00 2.00
247 Jim Perry 5.00 2.00
248 Dave McNally 5.00 2.00
249 Fred Whitfield 5.00 2.00
250 Ken Berry 5.00 2.00
251 Jim Grant 5.00 2.00
252 Hank Aguirre 5.00 2.00
253 Don Wert 5.00 2.00
254 Wally Bunker 5.00 2.00
255 Elston Howard 8.00 3.20
256 Dave Johnson 5.00 2.00
257 Hoyt Wilhelm 25.00 10.00
258 Dick Buford 5.00 2.00
259 Sam McDowell 5.00 2.00
260 Bobby Knoop 5.00 2.00
261 Denny McLain 15.00 6.00
262 Steve Hargan 5.00 2.00
263 Jim Nash 5.00 2.00
264 Jerry Adair 5.00 2.00
265 Tony Gonzalez 5.00 2.00
266 Mike Shannon 5.00 2.00
267 Bob Gibson 50.00 20.00
268 John Roseboro 5.00 2.00
269 Bob Aspromonte 5.00 2.00
270 Pete Rose 200.00 80.00
271 Rico Carty 5.00 2.00
272 Juan Pizarro 5.00 2.00
273 Willie Mays 200.00 80.00
274 Jim Bunning 80.00 32.00
275 Ernie Banks 50.00 20.00
276 Curt Flood 6.00 2.40
277 Mack Jones 5.00 2.00
278 Roberto Clemente 250.00 100.00
279 Sammy Ellis 5.00 2.00
280 Willie Stargell 50.00 20.00
281 Felipe Alou 6.00 2.40
282 Ed Kranepool 5.00 2.00
283 Nelson Briles 5.00 2.00
284 Hank Aaron 200.00 80.00
285 Vada Pinson 6.00 2.40
286 Jim LeFebvre 5.00 2.00
287 Hal Lanier 5.00 2.00
288 Ron Swoboda 5.00 2.00
289 Mike McCormick 5.00 2.00
290 Lou Johnson 5.00 2.00
291 Orlando Cepeda 15.00 6.00
292 Rusty Staub 8.00 3.20
293 Manny Mota 6.00 2.40
294 Tommy Harper 5.00 2.00
295 Don Drysdale 40.00 16.00
296 Mel Queen 5.00 2.00
297 Red Schoendienst MG 20.00 8.00
298 Matty Alou 6.00 2.40
299 Johnny Callison 5.00 2.00
300 Juan Marichal 40.00 16.00
301 Al McBean 5.00 2.00
302 Claude Osteen 5.00 2.00
303 Willie McCovey 50.00 20.00
304 Jim Owens 5.00 2.00
305 Chico Ruiz 5.00 2.00
306 Fergie Jenkins 40.00 16.00
307 Lou Brock 50.00 20.00
308 Joe Morgan 40.00 16.00
309 Ron Santo 8.00 3.20
310 Chico Cardenas 5.00 2.00
311 Richie Allen 6.00 2.40
312 Gaylord Perry 40.00 16.00
313 Bill Mazeroski 20.00 8.00
314 Tony Taylor 5.00 2.00
315 Tommy Helms 5.00 2.00
316 Jim Wynn 6.00 2.40
317 Don Sutton 40.00 16.00
318 Mike Cuellar 6.00 2.40
319 Willie Davis 5.00 2.00
320 Julian Javier 5.00 2.00
321 Maury Willis 6.00 2.40
322 Gene Alley 5.00 2.00
323 Ray Sadecki 5.00 2.00
324 Joe Torre 8.00 3.20
325 Jim Maloney 5.00 2.00
326 Jim Davenport 5.00 2.00
327 Tony Perez 30.00 12.00
328 Roger Maris 80.00 32.00
329 Chris Short 5.00 2.00
330 Jesus Alou 5.00 2.00
331 Deron Johnson 5.00 2.00
332 Tommy Davis 6.00 2.40
333 Bob Veale 5.00 2.00
334 Bill McCool 5.00 2.00
335 Jim Hart 5.00 2.00
336 Roy Face 6.00 2.40
337 Billy Williams 25.00 10.00
338 Dick Groat 6.00 2.40

1967 Topps Who am I

These are just the "baseball" players issued by Topps in this set which features famous people. The front features a drawing of the person along with their name and claim to fame on the top. The back asks some questions about the person. We are just cataloguing the baseball players here.

	NM	Ex
COMPLETE SET	250.00	100.00
12 Babe Ruth	100.00	40.00
22 Mickey Mantle	80.00	32.00
33 Willie Mays	50.00	20.00
41 Sandy Koufax	50.00	20.00

1968 Topps

The cards in this 598-card set measure 2 1/2" by 3 1/2". The 1968 Topps set includes Sporting News All-Star Selections as card numbers 361 to 380. Other subsets in the set include League Leaders (1-12) and World Series cards (151-158). The front of each checklist card features a picture of a popular player inside a circle. Higher numbers 458 to 598 are slightly more difficult to obtain. The first series looks different from the other series, as it has a lighter, wider mesh background on the card front. The later series all had a much darker, finer mesh pattern. Among other fashions, cards were issued in five-card nickel packs. The five cent packs were issued 24 packs to a box. The key Rookie Cards in the set are Johnny Bench and Nolan Ryan. Lastly, some cards were also issued along with the "Win-A-Card" board game from Milton Bradley that included cards from the 1965 Topps Hot Rods and 1967 Topps football card sets. This version of these cards is somewhat difficult to distinguish, but are often found with a slight touch of the 1967 football set white border on the front top or bottom edge as well as a brighter yellow card back instead of the darker yellow or gold color. The known cards from this product include card numbers 16, 20, 34, 45, 108, and 149.

	NM	Ex
COMPLETE SET (598)	3000.00	1200.00
COMMON CARD (1-457)	2.00	.80
COMMON (458-598)	4.00	1.60
WRAPPER (5-CENT)	25.00	10.00

1 Roberto Clemente 30.00 12.00
Tony Gonzalez
Matty Alou LL
2 Carl Yastrzemski 15.00 6.00
Frank Robinson
Al Kaline LL
3 Orlando Cepeda 20.00 8.00
Roberto Clemente
Hank Aaron LL
4 Carl Yastrzemski 15.00 6.00
Harmon Killebrew
Frank Robinson LL
5 Hank Aaron 8.00 3.20
Jim Wynn
Ron Santo
Willie McCovey LL
6 Carl Yastrzemski 8.00 3.20
Harmon Killebrew
Frank Howard LL
7 Phil Niekro 4.00 1.60
Jim Bunning
Chris Short LL
8 Joel Horlen 4.00 1.60
Gary Peters
Sonny Siebert LL
9 Mike McCormick 4.00 1.60
Ferguson Jenkins
Jim Bunning
Claude Osteen LL
10A Jim Lonborg ERR 4.00 1.60
(Misspelled Lonberg on card back)
Earl Wilson
Dean Chance LL
10B Jim Lonborg COR 4.00 1.60
Earl Wilson
Dean Chance LL
11 Jim Bunning 6.00 2.40
Ferguson Jenkins
Gaylord Perry LL
12 Jim Lonborg UER 4.00 1.60
(Misspelled Longberg on card back)
Sam McDowell
Dean Chance LL
13 Chuck Hartenstein 2.00 .80
14 Jerry McNertney 2.00 .80
15 Ron Hunt 2.00 .80
16 Lou Piniella 6.00 2.40
Richie Scheinblum
17 Dick Hall 2.00 .80
18 Mike Hershberger 2.00 .80
19 Juan Pizarro 2.00 .80
20 Brooks Robinson 25.00 10.00
21 Ron Davis 2.00 .80
22 Pat Dobson 4.00 1.60
23 Chico Cardenas 4.00 1.60
24 Bobby Locke 2.00 .80
25 Julian Javier 4.00 1.60
26 Darrell Brandon 2.00 .80
27 Gil Hodges MG 8.00 3.20
28 Ted Uhlaender 2.00 .80
29 Joe Verbanic 2.00 .80
30 Joe Torre 6.00 2.40
31 Ed Stroud 2.00 .80
32 Joe Gibbon 2.00 .80
33 Pete Ward 2.00 .80
34 Al Ferrara 2.00 .80
35 Steve Hargan 2.00 .80
36 Bob Moose 4.00 1.60
Bob Robertson
37 Billy Williams 8.00 3.20
38 Tony Pierce 2.00 .80
39 Cookie Rojas 2.00 .80
40 Denny McLain 8.00 3.20
41 Julio Gotay 2.00 .80
42 Larry Haney 2.00 .80
43 Gary Bell 2.00 .80
44 Frank Kostro 2.00 .80
45 Tom Seaver 50.00 20.00
46 Dave Ricketts 2.00 .80
47 Ralph Houk MG 4.00 1.60
48 Ted Davidson 2.00 .80
49A Eddie Brinkman 2.00 .80
(White team name)
49B Eddie Brinkman 50.00 20.00
(Yellow team name)
50 Willie Mays 60.00 24.00
51 Bob Locker 2.00 .80
52 Hawk Taylor 2.00 .80
53 Gene Alley 4.00 1.60
54 Stan Williams 2.00 .80
55 Felipe Alou 4.00 1.60
56 Dave Leonhard 2.00 .80
Dave May RC
57 Dan Schneider 2.00 .80
58 Eddie Mathews 15.00 6.00
59 Don Lock 2.00 .80
60 Ken Holtzman 4.00 1.60
61 Reggie Smith 4.00 1.60
62 Chuck Dobson 2.00 .80
63 Dick Kenworthy 2.00 .80
64 Jim Merritt 2.00 .80
65 John Roseboro 4.00 1.60
66A Casey Cox 2.00 .80
(White team name)
66B Casey Cox 100.00 40.00
(Yellow team name)
67 Jim Kaat CL 6.00 1.20
68 Ron Willis 2.00 .80
69 Tom Tresh 4.00 1.60
70 Bob Veale 4.00 1.60
71 Vern Fuller 2.00 .80
72 Tommy John 6.00 2.40
73 Jim Ray Hart 4.00 1.60
74 Milt Pappas 4.00 1.60
75 Don Mincher 2.00 .80
76 Jim Britton 4.00 1.60
Ron Reed
77 Don Wilson 4.00 1.60
78 Jim Northrup 6.00 2.40
79 Ted Kubiak 2.00 .80
80 Rod Carew 50.00 20.00
81 Larry Jackson 2.00 .80
82 Sam Bowens 2.00 .80
83 John Stephenson 2.00 .80
84 Bob Tolan 2.00 .80
85 Gaylord Perry 8.00 3.20
86 Willie Stargell 8.00 3.20
87 Dick Williams MG 4.00 1.60
88 Phil Regan 4.00 1.60
89 Jake Gibbs 4.00 1.60
90 Vada Pinson 4.00 1.60
91 Jim Ollom 2.00 .80
92 Ed Kranepool 4.00 1.60
93 Tony Cloninger 2.00 .80
94 Lee Maye 2.00 .80
95 Bob Aspromonte 2.00 .80
96 Frank Coggins 2.00 .80
Dick Nold
97 Tom Phoebus 2.00 .80
98 Gary Sutherland 2.00 .80
99 Rocky Colavito 8.00 3.20
100 Bob Gibson 25.00 10.00
101 Glenn Beckert 4.00 1.60
102 Jose Cardenal 4.00 1.60
103 Don Sutton 8.00 3.20
104 Dick Dietz 2.00 .80
105 Al Downing 4.00 1.60
106 Dalton Jones 2.00 .80
107A Juan Marichal CL 6.00 1.20
Tan wide mesh
107B Juan Marichal CL 6.00 1.20
Brown fine mesh
108 Don Pavletich 2.00 .80
109 Bert Campaneris 4.00 1.60
110 Hank Aaron 60.00 24.00
111 Rich Reese 2.00 .80
112 Woody Fryman 2.00 .80
113 Tom Matchick 4.00 1.60
Daryl Patterson
114 Ron Swoboda 4.00 1.60
115 Sam McDowell 4.00 1.60
116 Ken McMullen 2.00 .80
117 Larry Jaster 2.00 .80
118 Mark Belanger 4.00 1.60
119 Ted Savage 2.00 .80
120 Mel Stottlemyre 4.00 1.60
121 Jimmie Hall 2.00 .80
122 Gene Mauch MG 4.00 1.60
123 Jose Santiago 2.00 .80
124 Nate Oliver 2.00 .80
125 Joel Horlen 2.00 .80
126 Bobby Etheridge 2.00 .80
127 Paul Lindblad 2.00 .80
128 Tom Dukes 2.00 .80
Alonzo Harris
129 Mickey Stanley 6.00 2.40
130 Tony Perez 8.00 3.20
131 Frank Bertaina 2.00 .80
132 Bud Harrelson 4.00 1.60
133 Fred Whitfield 2.00 .80
134 Pat Jarvis 2.00 .80
135 Paul Blair 4.00 1.60
136 Randy Hundley 4.00 1.60
137 Twins Team 4.00 1.60
138 Ruben Amaro 2.00 .80
139 Chris Short 2.00 .80
140 Tony Conigliaro 8.00 3.20
141 Dal Maxvill 2.00 .80
142 Buddy Bradford 2.00 .80
Bill Voss
143 Pete Cimino 2.00 .80
144 Joe Morgan 12.00 4.80
145 Don Drysdale 12.00 4.80
146 Sal Bando 4.00 1.60
147 Frank Linzy 2.00 .80
148 Dave Bristol MG 2.00 .80
149 Bob Saverine 2.00 .80
150 Roberto Clemente 80.00 32.00
151 Lou Brock WS 10.00 4.00
152 Carl Yastrzemski WS 10.00 4.00
153 Nellie Briles WS 5.00 2.00
154 Bob Gibson WS 10.00 4.00
155 Jim Lonborg WS 5.00 2.00
156 Rico Petrocelli WS 5.00 2.00
157 World Series Game 7 5.00 2.00
St. Louis wins it
158 WS Summary 5.00 2.00
Cardinals celebrate
159 Don Kessinger 4.00 1.60
160 Earl Wilson 4.00 1.60
161 Norm Miller 2.00 .80
162 Hal Gilson 4.00 1.60
Mike Torrez
163 Gene Brabender 2.00 .80
164 Ramon Webster 2.00 .80
165 Tony Oliva 6.00 2.40
166 Claude Raymond 2.00 .80
167 Elston Howard 6.00 2.40
168 Dodgers Team 4.00 1.60
169 Bob Bolin 2.00 .80
170 Jim Fregosi 4.00 1.60
171 Don Nottebart 2.00 .80
172 Walt Williams 2.00 .80
173 John Boozer 2.00 .80
174 Bob Tillman 2.00 .80
175 Maury Wills 6.00 2.40
176 Bob Allen 2.00 .80
177 Jerry Koosman RC 500.00 200.00
Nolan Ryan RC
178 Don Wert 4.00 1.60
179 Bill Stoneman 2.00 .80
180 Curt Flood 6.00 2.40
181 Jerry Zimmerman 2.00 .80
182 Dave Giusti 2.00 .80
183 Bob Kennedy MG 4.00 1.60
184 Lou Johnson 2.00 .80
185 Tom Haller 2.00 .80
186 Eddie Watt 2.00 .80
187 Sonny Jackson 2.00 .80
188 Cap Peterson 2.00 .80
189 Bill Landis 2.00 .80
190 Bill White 4.00 1.60
191 Dan Frisella 2.00 .80
192A Carl Yastrzemski CL 8.00 1.60
Special Baseball Playing Card
192B Carl Yastrzemski CL 8.00 1.60
Special Baseball
Playing Card Game
193 Jack Hamilton 2.00 .80
194 Don Buford 2.00 .80
195 Joe Pepitone 4.00 1.60
196 Gary Nolan 4.00 1.60
197 Larry Brown 2.00 .80
198 Roy Face 4.00 1.60
199 Roberto Rodriquez 2.00 .80
Darrell Osteen
200 Orlando Cepeda 8.00 3.20
201 Mike Marshall RC 4.00 1.60
202 Adolfo Phillips 2.00 .80
203 Dick Kelley 2.00 .80
204 Andy Etchebarren 2.00 .80
205 Juan Marichal 8.00 3.20
206 Cal Ermer MG 2.00 .80
207 Carroll Sembera 2.00 .80
208 Willie Davis 4.00 1.60
209 Tim Cullen 2.00 .80
210 Gary Peters 2.00 .80
211 J.C. Martin 2.00 .80
212 Dave Morehead 2.00 .80
213 Chico Ruiz 2.00 .80

214 Stan Bahnsen 4.00 1.60
Frank Fernandez
215 Jim Bunning 8.00 3.20
216 Bubba Morton 2.00 .80
217 Dick Farrell 2.00 .80
218 Ken Suarez 2.00 .80
219 Rob Gardner 2.00 .80
220 Harmon Killebrew 15.00 6.00
221 Braves Team 4.00 1.60
222 Jim Hardin 2.00 .80
223 Ollie Brown 2.00 .80
224 Jack Aker 2.00 .80
225 Richie Allen 6.00 2.40
226 Jimmie Price 2.00 .80
227 Joe Hoerner 2.00 .80
228 Jack Billingham 4.00 1.60
Jim Fairey
229 Fred Klages 2.00 .80
230 Pete Rose 60.00 24.00
231 Dave Baldwin 2.00 .80
232 Denis Menke 2.00 .80
233 George Scott 4.00 1.60
234 Bill Monbouquette 2.00 .80
235 Ron Santo 8.00 3.20
236 Tug McGraw 6.00 2.40
237 Alvin Dark MG 4.00 1.60
238 Tom Satriano 2.00 .80
239 Bill Henry 2.00 .80
240 Al Kaline 40.00 16.00
241 Felix Millan 2.00 .80
242 Moe Drabowsky 4.00 1.60
243 Rich Rollins 2.00 .80
244 John Donaldson 2.00 .80
245 Tony Gonzalez 2.00 .80
246 Fritz Peterson 4.00 1.60
247 Johnny Bench RC 125.00 50.00
Ron Tompkins
248 Fred Valentine 2.00 .80
249 Bill Singer 2.00 .80
250 Carl Yastrzemski 30.00 12.00
251 Manny Sanguillen RC 6.00 2.40
252 Angels Team 4.00 1.60
253 Dick Hughes 2.00 .80
254 Cleon Jones 4.00 1.60
255 Dean Chance 4.00 1.60
256 Norm Cash 6.00 2.40
257 Phil Niekro 8.00 3.20
258 Jose Arcia 2.00 .80
Bill Schlesinger
259 Ken Boyer 6.00 2.40
260 Jim Wynn 4.00 1.60
261 Dave Duncan 4.00 1.60
262 Rick Wise 4.00 1.60
263 Horace Clarke 4.00 1.60
264 Ted Abernathy 2.00 .80
265 Tommy Davis 4.00 1.60
266 Paul Popovich 2.00 .80
267 Herman Franks MG 2.00 .80
268 Bob Humphreys 2.00 .80
269 Bob Tiefenauer 2.00 .80
270 Matty Alou 4.00 1.60
271 Bobby Knoop 2.00 .80
272 Ray Culp 2.00 .80
273 Dave Johnson 4.00 1.60
274 Mike Cuellar 4.00 1.60
275 Tim McCarver 6.00 2.40
276 Jim Roland 2.00 .80
277 Jerry Buchek 2.00 .80
278 Orlando Cepeda CL 6.00 1.20
279 Bill Hands 2.00 .80
280 Mickey Mantle 250.00 100.00
281 Jim Campanis 2.00 .80
282 Rick Monday 4.00 1.60
283 Mel Queen 2.00 .80
284 Johnny Briggs 2.00 .80
285 Dick McAuliffe 6.00 2.40
286 Cecil Upshaw 2.00 .80
287 Mickey Abarbanel 2.00 .80
Cisco Carlos
288 Dave Wickersham 2.00 .80
289 Woody Held 2.00 .80
290 Willie McCovey 12.00 4.80
291 Dick Lines 2.00 .80
292 Art Shamsky 2.00 .80
293 Bruce Howard 2.00 .80
294 Red Schoendienst MG 6.00 2.40
295 Sonny Siebert 2.00 .80
296 Byron Browne 2.00 .80
297 Russ Gibson 2.00 .80
298 Jim Brewer 2.00 .80
299 Gene Michael 4.00 1.60
300 Rusty Staub 4.00 1.60
301 George Mitterwald 2.00 .80
Rick Renick
302 Gerry Arrigo 2.00 .80
303 Dick Green 4.00 1.60
304 Sandy Valdespino 2.00 .80
305 Minnie Rojas 2.00 .80
306 Mike Ryan 2.00 .80
307 John Hiller 4.00 1.60
308 Pirates Team 4.00 1.60
309 Ken Henderson 2.00 .80
310 Luis Aparicio 8.00 3.20
311 Jack Lamabe 2.00 .80
312 Curt Blefary 2.00 .80
313 Al Weis 2.00 .80
314 Bill Rohr 2.00 .80
George Spriggs
315 Zoilo Versalles 2.00 .80
316 Steve Barber 2.00 .80
317 Ron Brand 2.00 .80
318 Chico Salmon 2.00 .80
319 George Culver 2.00 .80
320 Frank Howard 4.00 1.60
321 Leo Durocher MG 6.00 2.40
322 Dave Boswell 2.00 .80
323 Deron Johnson 4.00 1.60
324 Jim Nash 2.00 .80
325 Manny Mota 4.00 1.60
326 Dennis Ribant 2.00 .80
327 Tony Taylor 4.00 1.60
328 Chuck Vinson 2.00 .80
Jim Weaver
329 Duane Josephson 2.00 .80
330 Roger Maris 50.00 20.00
331 Dan Osinski 2.00 .80
332 Doug Rader 4.00 1.60
333 Ron Herbel 2.00 .80
334 Orioles Team 4.00 1.60
335 Bob Allison 4.00 1.60
336 John Purdin 2.00 .80
337 Bill Robinson 4.00 1.60
338 Bob Johnson 2.00 .80
339 Rich Nye 2.00 .80
340 Max Alvis 2.00 .80
341 Jim Lemon MG 2.00 .80
342 Ken Johnson 2.00 .80
343 Jim Gosger 2.00 .80
344 Donn Clendenon 4.00 1.60
345 Bob Hendley 2.00 .80
346 Jerry Adair 2.00 .80
347 George Brunet 2.00 .80
348 Larry Colton 2.00 .80
Dick Thoenen
349 Ed Spiezio 4.00 1.60
350 Hoyt Wilhelm 8.00 3.20
351 Bob Barton 2.00 .80
352 Jackie Hernandez 2.00 .80
353 Mack Jones 2.00 .80
354 Pete Richert 2.00 .80
355 Ernie Banks 25.00 10.00
356A Ken Holtzman CL 6.00 1.20
Head centered within circle
356B Ken Holtzman 6.00 1.20
Head shifted right
within circle
357 Len Gabrielson 2.00 .80
358 Mike Epstein 2.00 .80
359 Joe Moeller 2.00 .80
360 Willie Horton 6.00 2.40
361 Harmon Killebrew AS 8.00 3.20
362 Orlando Cepeda AS 6.00 2.40
363 Rod Carew AS 8.00 3.20
364 Joe Morgan AS 8.00 3.20
365 Brooks Robinson AS 8.00 3.20
366 Ron Santo AS 6.00 2.40
367 Jim Fregosi AS 4.00 1.60
368 Gene Alley AS 4.00 1.60
369 Carl Yastrzemski AS 10.00 4.00
370 Hank Aaron AS 20.00 8.00
371 Tony Oliva AS 6.00 2.40
372 Lou Brock AS 8.00 3.20
373 Frank Robinson AS 8.00 3.20
374 Bob Clemente AS 30.00 12.00
375 Bill Freehan AS 4.00 1.60
376 Tim McCarver AS 4.00 1.60
377 Joel Horlen AS 4.00 1.60
378 Bob Gibson AS 8.00 3.20
379 Gary Peters AS 4.00 1.60
380 Ken Holtzman AS 4.00 1.60
381 Boog Powell 4.00 1.60
382 Ramon Hernandez 2.00 .80
383 Steve Whitaker 2.00 .80
384 Bill Henry 6.00 2.40
Hal McRae RC
385 Jim Hunter 10.00 4.00
386 Greg Goossen 2.00 .80
387 Joe Foy 2.00 .80
388 Ray Washburn 2.00 .80
389 Jay Johnstone 4.00 1.60
390 Bill Mazeroski 8.00 3.20
391 Bob Priddy 2.00 .80
392 Grady Hatton MG 2.00 .80
393 Jim Perry 4.00 1.60
394 Tommie Aaron 6.00 2.40
395 Camilo Pascual 4.00 1.60
396 Bobby Wine 2.00 .80
397 Vic Davalillo 2.00 .80
398 Jim Grant 2.00 .80
399 Ray Oyler 4.00 1.60
400A Mike McCormick 4.00 1.60
(Yellow letters)
400B Mike McCormick 150.00 60.00
(Team name in
white letters)
401 Mets Team 4.00 1.60
402 Mike Hegan 4.00 1.60
403 John Buzhardt 2.00 .80
404 Floyd Robinson 2.00 .80
405 Tommy Helms 4.00 1.60
406 Dick Ellsworth 2.00 .80
407 Gary Kolb 2.00 .80
408 Steve Carlton 30.00 12.00
409 Frank Peters 2.00 .80
Ron Stone
410 Ferguson Jenkins 10.00 4.00
411 Ron Hansen 2.00 .80
412 Clay Carroll 4.00 1.60
413 Tom McCraw 2.00 .80
414 Mickey Lolich 8.00 3.20
415 Johnny Callison 4.00 1.60
416 Bill Rigney MG 2.00 .80
417 Willie Crawford 2.00 .80
418 Eddie Fisher 2.00 .80
419 Jack Hiatt 2.00 .80
420 Cesar Tovar 2.00 .80
421 Ron Taylor 2.00 .80
422 Rene Lachemann 2.00 .80
423 Fred Gladding 2.00 .80
424 Chicago White Sox 4.00 1.60
Team Card
425 Jim Maloney 4.00 1.60
426 Hank Allen 2.00 .80
427 Dick Calmus 2.00 .80
428 Vic Roznovsky 2.00 .80
429 Tommie Sisk 2.00 .80
430 Rico Petrocelli 4.00 1.60
431 Dooley Womack 2.00 .80
432 Bill Davis 2.00 .80
Jose Vidal
433 Bob Rodgers 2.00 .80
434 Ricardo Joseph 2.00 .80
435 Ron Perranoski 4.00 1.60
436 Hal Lanier 2.00 .80
437 Don Cardwell 2.00 .80
438 Lee Thomas 4.00 1.60
439 Lum Harris MG 2.00 .80
440 Claude Osteen 4.00 1.60
441 Alex Johnson 4.00 1.60
442 Dick Bosman 2.00 .80
443 Joe Azcue 2.00 .80
444 Jack Fisher 2.00 .80
445 Mike Shannon 4.00 1.60
446 Ron Kline 2.00 .80
447 George Korince 4.00 1.60
Fred Lasher
448 Gary Wagner 2.00 .80
449 Gene Oliver 2.00 .80
450 Jim Kaat 6.00 2.40
451 Al Spangler 2.00 .80
452 Jesus Alou 2.00 .80
453 Sammy Ellis 2.00 .80
454A Frank Robinson CL 8.00 1.60
Cap complete within circle
454B Frank Robinson CL 8.00 1.60
Cap partially within circle
455 Rico Carty 4.00 1.60
456 John O'Donoghue 2.00 .80
457 Jim Lefebvre 4.00 1.60
458 Lew Krausse 6.00 2.40
459 Dick Simpson 4.00 1.60
460 Jim Lonborg 6.00 2.40
461 Chuck Hiller 4.00 1.60
462 Barry Moore 4.00 1.60
463 Jim Schaffer 4.00 1.60
464 Don McMahon 4.00 1.60
465 Tommie Agee 10.00 4.00
466 Bill Dillman 4.00 1.60
467 Dick Howser 10.00 4.00
468 Larry Sherry 4.00 1.60
469 Ty Cline 4.00 1.60
470 Bill Freehan 10.00 4.00
471 Orlando Pena 4.00 1.60
472 Walter Alston MG 6.00 2.40
473 Al Worthington 4.00 1.60
474 Paul Schaal 4.00 1.60
475 Joe Niekro 6.00 2.40
476 Woody Woodward 4.00 1.60
477 Philadelphia Phillies 8.00 3.20
Team Card
478 Dave McNally 6.00 2.40
479 Phil Gagliano 6.00 2.40
480 Tony Oliva 80.00 32.00
Chico Cardenas
Bob Clemente
481 John Wyatt 4.00 1.60
482 Jose Pagan 4.00 1.60
483 Darold Knowles 4.00 1.60
484 Phil Roof 4.00 1.60
485 Ken Berry 6.00 2.40
486 Cal Koonce 4.00 1.60
487 Lee May 10.00 4.00
488 Dick Tracewski 6.00 2.40
489 Wally Bunker 4.00 1.60
490 Harmon Killebrew 150.00 60.00
Willie Mays
Mickey Mantle
491 Denny Lemaster 4.00 1.60
492 Jeff Torborg 6.00 2.40
493 Jim McGlothlin 4.00 1.60
494 Ray Sadecki 4.00 1.60
495 Leon Wagner 4.00 1.60
496 Steve Hamilton 6.00 2.40
497 Cardinals Team 8.00 3.20
498 Bill Bryan 6.00 2.40
499 Steve Blass 6.00 2.40
500 Frank Robinson 30.00 12.00
501 John Odom 6.00 2.40
502 Mike Andrews 4.00 1.60
503 Al Jackson 6.00 2.40
504 Russ Snyder 4.00 1.60
505 Joe Sparma 10.00 4.00
506 Clarence Jones RC 4.00 1.60
507 Wade Blasingame 4.00 1.60
508 Duke Sims 4.00 1.60
509 Dennis Higgins 4.00 1.60
510 Ron Fairly 10.00 4.00
511 Bill Kelso 4.00 1.60
512 Grant Jackson 4.00 1.60
513 Hank Bauer MG 6.00 2.40
514 Al McBean 4.00 1.60
515 Russ Nixon 4.00 1.60
516 Pete Mikkelsen 4.00 1.60
517 Diego Segui 6.00 2.40
518A Clete Boyer CL ERR 12.00 2.40
539 AL Rookies
518B Clete Boyer CL COR 12.00 2.40
539 ML Rookies
519 Jerry Stephenson 4.00 1.60
520 Lou Brock 25.00 10.00
521 Don Shaw 4.00 1.60
522 Wayne Causey 4.00 1.60
523 John Tsitouris 4.00 1.60
524 Andy Kosco 6.00 2.40
525 Jim Davenport 4.00 1.60
526 Bill Denehy 4.00 1.60
527 Tito Francona 4.00 1.60
528 Tigers Team 60.00 24.00
529 Bruce Von Hoff 4.00 1.60
530 Brooks Robinson 40.00 16.00
Frank Robinson
531 Chuck Hinton 4.00 1.60
532 Luis Tiant 6.00 2.40
533 Wes Parker 6.00 2.40
534 Bob Miller 6.00 2.40
535 Danny Cater 6.00 2.40
536 Bill Short 4.00 1.60
537 Norm Siebern 6.00 2.40
538 Manny Jimenez 6.00 2.40
539 Jim Ray 4.00 1.60
Mike Ferraro
540 Nelson Briles 6.00 2.40
541 Sandy Alomar 6.00 2.40
542 John Boccabella 4.00 1.60
543 Bob Lee 4.00 1.60
544 Mayo Smith MG 12.00 4.80
545 Lindy McDaniel 6.00 2.40
546 Roy White 6.00 2.40
547 Dan Coombs 4.00 1.60
548 Bernie Allen 4.00 1.60
549 Curt Motton 4.00 1.60
Roger Nelson
550 Clete Boyer 6.00 2.40
551 Darrell Sutherland 4.00 1.60
552 Ed Kirkpatrick 4.00 1.60
553 Hank Aguirre 4.00 1.60
554 A's Team 10.00 4.00
555 Jose Tartabull 6.00 2.40
556 Dick Selma 4.00 1.60
557 Frank Quilici 6.00 2.40
558 Johnny Edwards 4.00 1.60
559 Carl Taylor 4.00 1.60
Luke Walker
560 Paul Casanova 4.00 1.60
561 Lee Elia 6.00 2.40
562 Jim Bouton 6.00 2.40
563 Ed Charles 6.00 2.40
564 Eddie Stanky MG 6.00 2.40
565 Larry Dierker 6.00 2.40
566 Ken Harrelson 6.00 2.40
567 Clay Dalrymple 4.00 1.60
568 Willie Smith 4.00 1.60
569 Ivan Murrell 4.00 1.60
Les Rohr
570 Rick Reichardt 4.00 1.60
571 Tony LaRussa 12.00 4.80
572 Don Bosch 4.00 1.60
573 Joe Coleman 4.00 1.60
574 Cincinnati Reds 10.00 4.00
Team Card
575 Jim Palmer 40.00 16.00
576 Dave Adlesh 4.00 1.60
577 Fred Talbot 4.00 1.60
578 Orlando Martinez 4.00 1.60
579 Larry Hisle RC 10.00 4.00
Mike Lum
580 Bob Bailey 4.00 1.60
581 Garry Roggenburk 4.00 1.60
582 Jerry Grote 10.00 4.00
583 Gates Brown 10.00 4.00
584 Larry Shepard MG 4.00 1.60
585 Wilbur Wood 6.00 2.40
586 Jim Pagliaroni 6.00 2.40
587 Roger Repoz 4.00 1.60
588 Dick Schofield 4.00 1.60
589 Ron Clark 4.00 1.60
Moe Ogier
590 Tommy Harper 6.00 2.40
591 Dick Nen 4.00 1.60
592 John Bateman 4.00 1.60
593 Lee Stange 4.00 1.60
594 Phil Linz 6.00 2.40
595 Phil Ortega 4.00 1.60
596 Charlie Smith 4.00 1.60
597 Bill McCool 4.00 1.60
598 Jerry May 6.00 1.85

1968 Topps Game Card Inserts

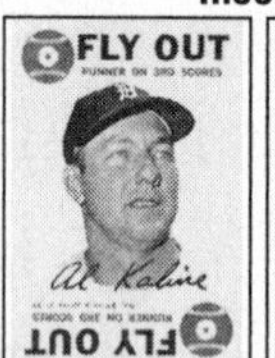

The cards in this 33-card set measure approximately 2 1/4" by 3 1/4". This "Game" card set of players, issued as inserts with the regular third series 1968 Topps baseball cards, was patterned directly after the Red Back and Blue Back sets of 1951. Each card has a color player photo set upon a pure white background, with a facsimile autograph underneath the picture. The cards have blue backs, and were also sold in boxed sets on a limited basis.

	NM	Ex
COMPLETE SET (33)	125.00	50.00
COMP.FACT SET (33)	125.00	50.00
1 Matty Alou	1.00	.40
2 Mickey Mantle	40.00	16.00
3 Carl Yastrzemski	5.00	2.00
4 Hank Aaron	15.00	6.00
5 Harmon Killebrew	3.00	1.20
6 Roberto Clemente	25.00	10.00
7 Frank Robinson	5.00	2.00
8 Willie Mays	20.00	8.00
9 Brooks Robinson	5.00	2.00
10 Tommy Davis	.75	.30
11 Bill Freehan	1.00	.40
12 Claude Osteen	.75	.30
13 Gary Peters	.75	.30
14 Jim Lonborg	.75	.30
15 Steve Hargan	.75	.30
16 Dean Chance	.75	.30
17 Mike McCormick	.75	.30
18 Tim McCarver	1.00	.40
19 Ron Santo	1.25	.50
20 Tony Gonzalez	.75	.30
21 Frank Howard	1.25	.50
22 George Scott	.75	.30
23 Richie Allen	1.25	.50
24 Jim Wynn	1.00	.40
25 Gene Alley	.75	.30
26 Rick Monday	.75	.30
27 Al Kaline	5.00	2.00
28 Rusty Staub	1.00	.40
29 Rod Carew	5.00	2.00
30 Pete Rose	10.00	4.00
31 Joe Torre	1.50	.60
32 Orlando Cepeda	1.50	.60
33 Jim Fregosi	1.00	.40

1968 Topps 3-D

The cards in this 12-card set measure 2 1/4" by 3 1/2". Topps' experiment with "3-D" cards came two years before Kellogg's inaugural set. These cards are considered to be quite rare. This was a "test set" sold in a plain white wrapper with a sticker attached as a design, a device used by Topps for limited marketing. The cards employ a sharp foreground picture set against an indistinct background, covered by a layer of plastic to produce the "3-D" effect. The checklist below is ordered alphabetically. A test 3D card of Brooks Robinson was issued before this 12 card set was released. The Robinson card measures 2 1/4" by 3 1/4" and has the team name on the top but with no player identification.

	NM	Ex
COMPLETE SET (12)	12000.00	4800.00
WRAPPER (10-CENTS)	1000.00	400.00
1 Roberto Clemente	5000.00	2000.00
2 Willie Davis	1000.00	400.00
3 Ron Fairly	600.00	240.00
4 Curt Flood	1000.00	400.00
5 Jim Lonborg	1000.00	400.00
6 Jim Maloney	1000.00	400.00
7 Tony Perez	1500.00	600.00
8 Boog Powell	1200.00	475.00
9 Bill Robinson	600.00	240.00
10 Rusty Staub	1000.00	400.00
11 Mel Stottlemyre	1000.00	400.00
12 Ron Swoboda	600.00	240.00

1968 Topps Action Stickers

This test issue is a set of 16 long stickers which is perforated and can be divided into three stickers. The middle sticker features a large sticker depicting only one player, whereas the top and bottom stickers feature three smaller stickers. These stickers are attractive and colorful. These cane packed 12 packs to a box with 24 boxes in a case.

	NM	Ex
COMPLETE SET (48)	1800.00	700.00
COMMON INDIV. PANEL	8.00	3.20
COMMON TRIPLE PANEL	15.00	6.00
WRAPPER (10-CENT)	400.00	160.00
1A Joel Horlen Orlando Cepeda Bill Mazeroski	8.00	3.20
1B Carl Yastrzemski	120.00	47.50
1C Mel Stottlemyre Al Kaline Claude Osteen	20.00	8.00
2A Pete Ward Mike McCormick Ron Swoboda	8.00	3.20
2B Harmon Killebrew	60.00	24.00
2C George Scott Tom Phoebus Don Drysdale	15.00	6.00
3A Jim Maloney Joe Pepitone Henry Aaron	20.00	8.00
3B Frank Robinson	80.00	32.00
3C Paul Casanova Rick Reichardt Tom Seaver	20.00	8.00
4A Frank Robinson Jim Lefebvre Dean Chance	15.00	6.00
4B Ron Santo	20.00	8.00
4C Johnny Callison Jim Lonborg Bob Aspromonte	8.00	3.20
5A Bert Campaneris Ron Santo Al Downing	8.00	3.20
5B Willie Mays	150.00	60.00
5C Pete Rose Ed Kranepool Willie Horton	80.00	32.00
6A Carl Yastrzemski Max Alvis Walt Williams	40.00	16.00
6B Al Kaline	100.00	40.00
6C Ernie Banks Tim McCarver Rusty Staub	40.00	16.00
7A Willie McCovey Rick Monday Steve Hargan	20.00	8.00
7B Mickey Mantle	400.00	160.00
7C Rod Carew Tony Gonzalez Billy Williams	25.00	10.00
8A Ken Boyer Don Mincher Jim Bunning	15.00	6.00
8B Joel Horlen	20.00	8.00
8C Tony Conigliaro Ken McMullen Mike Cuellar	8.00	3.20
9A Harmon Killebrew Jim Fregosi Earl Wilson	15.00	6.00
9B Orlando Cepeda	40.00	16.00
9C Roberto Clemente Willie Mays Chris Short	120.00	47.50
10A Mickey Mantle Jim Hunter Vada Pinson	100.00	40.00
10B Hank Aaron	150.00	60.00
10C Gary Peters Bob Gibson Ken Harrelson	15.00	6.00
11A Tony Oliva Bob Veale Bill Freehan	8.00	3.20
11B Don Drysdale	60.00	24.00
11C Frank Howard Fergie Jenkins Jim Wynn	8.00	3.20
12A Joe Torre Dick Allen Jim McGlothlin	8.00	3.20
12B Roberto Clemente	200.00	80.00
12C Brooks Robinson Tony Perez Sam McDowell	25.00	10.00
13A Frank Robinson Jim Lefebvre Dean Chance	20.00	8.00
13B Carl Yastrzemski	120.00	47.50
13C Tom Phoebus George Scott	15.00	6.00

Don Drysdale
14A Joel Horlen 8.00 3.20
Orlando Cepeda
Bill Mazeroski
14B Harmon Killebrew 60.00 24.00
14C Paul Casanova 20.00 8.00
Rick Reichardt
Tom Seaver
15A Pete Ward 8.00 3.20
Mike McCormick
Ron Swoboda
15B Frank Robinson 100.00 40.00
15C Johnny Callison 8.00 3.20
Jim Lonborg
Bob Aspromonte
16A Jim Maloney 20.00 8.00
Joe Pepitone
Henry Aaron
16B Ron Santo 20.00 8.00
16C Mel Stottlemyre 20.00 8.00
Al Kaline
Claude Osteen

1968 Topps Giant Stand Ups

This test issue is quite scarce. The set features a color portrait photo of the player on a distinctive black background on heavy card stock. Each card measures 3 1/16" by 5 1/4" and is blank backed. The cards are numbered on the front in the lower left corner. Cards are found both with and without the stand up die cut.

NM Ex
COMPLETE SET (24) 20000.00 8000.00
1 Pete Rose 2500.00 1000.00
2 Gary Peters 200.00 80.00
3 Frank Robinson 500.00 200.00
4 Jim Lonborg 200.00 80.00
5 Ron Swoboda 200.00 80.00
6 Harmon Killebrew 500.00 200.00
7 Roberto Clemente 3000.00 1200.00
8 Mickey Mantle 5000.00 2000.00
9 Jim Fregosi 200.00 80.00
10 Al Kaline 500.00 200.00
11 Don Drysdale 500.00 200.00
12 Dean Chance 200.00 80.00
13 Orlando Cepeda 250.00 100.00
14 Tim McCarver 250.00 100.00
15 Frank Howard 250.00 100.00
16 Max Alvis 200.00 80.00
17 Rusty Staub 250.00 100.00
18 Richie Allen 250.00 100.00
19 Willie Mays 2500.00 1000.00
20 Hank Aaron 2500.00 1000.00
21 Carl Yastrzemski 2000.00 800.00
22 Ron Santo 250.00 100.00
23 Jim Hunter 500.00 200.00
24 Jim Wynn 200.00 80.00

1968 Topps Plaks

These brown plastic "busts," measue roughly 1" by 2". One Checklist per pack was included with these plaks, which were issued three to a 10 cent pack, which measured 2 1/8" by 4". The set is sequenced and therefore checklisted in alphabetical order within each league.

NM Ex
COMPLETE SET (26) 6500.00 2600.00
*WRAPPER (10-CENT)
1 Max Alvis 80.00 32.00
2 Dean Chance 100.00 40.00
3 Jim Fregosi 100.00 40.00
4 Frank Howard 150.00 60.00
5 Jim Hunter 200.00 80.00
6 Al Kaline 400.00 160.00
7 Harmon Killebrew 250.00 100.00
8 Jim Lonborg 100.00 40.00
9 Mickey Mantle 1500.00 600.00
10 Gary Peters 80.00 32.00
11 Frank Robinson 250.00 100.00
12 Carl Yastrzemski 300.00 120.00
13 Hank Aaron 800.00 325.00
14 Richie Allen 150.00 60.00
15 Orlando Cepeda 200.00 80.00
16 Roberto Clemente 1000.00 400.00
17 Tommy Davis 100.00 40.00
18 Don Drysdale 250.00 100.00
19 Willie Mays 800.00 325.00
20 Tim McCarver 150.00 60.00
21 Pete Rose 800.00 325.00
22 Ron Santo 150.00 60.00
23 Rusty Staub 100.00 40.00
24 Jim Wynn 100.00 40.00
NNO Checklist Card 1-12 80.00 32.00
NNO Checklist Card 13-24 80.00 32.00

1968 Topps Plaks Checklists

These two cards, which measure 2 /18" by 4", were inserted one per 1968 Topps Plak pack. Each checklist card featured all the players each league that were available in the packs.

NM Ex
COMPLETE SET 1500.00 600.00
1 Max Alvis 800.00 325.00
Dean Chance
Jim Fregosi
Frank Howard
Jim Hunter
Al Kaline
Harmon Killebrew
Jim Lonborg
Mickey Mantle
Gary Peters
Frank Robinson
Carl Yastrzemski
2 Hank Aaron 800.00 325.00
Richie Allen
Orlando Cepeda
Roberto Clemente
Tommy Davis
Don Drysdale
Willie Mays
Tim McCarver
Ron Santo
Rusty Staub
Pete Rose
Jim Wynn

1968 Topps Posters

This 1968 color poster set is not an "insert" but was issued separately with a piece of gum and in its own wrapper. The posters are numbered at the lower left and the player's name and team appear in a large star. The poster was folded six times to fit into the package, so fold lines are a factor in grading. Each poster measures 9 3/4" by 18 1/8".

NM Ex
COMPLETE SET (24) 300.00 120.00
WRAPPER (5-CENT) 30.00 12.00
1 Dean Chance 2.50 1.00
2 Max Alvis 2.50 1.00
3 Frank Howard 4.00 1.60
4 Jim Fregosi 2.50 1.00
5 Jim Hunter 10.00 4.00
6 Roberto Clemente 60.00 24.00
7 Don Drysdale 10.00 4.00
8 Jim Wynn 2.50 1.00
9 Al Kaline 15.00 6.00
10 Harmon Killebrew 12.00 4.80
11 Jim Lonborg 2.50 1.00
12 Orlando Cepeda 6.00 2.40
13 Gary Peters 2.50 1.00
14 Hank Aaron 20.00 8.00
15 Richie Allen 4.00 1.60
16 Carl Yastrzemski 15.00 6.00
17 Ron Swoboda 2.50 1.00
18 Mickey Mantle 80.00 32.00
19 Tim McCarver 4.00 1.60
20 Willie Mays 20.00 8.00
21 Ron Santo 4.00 1.60
22 Rusty Staub 4.00 1.60
23 Pete Rose 40.00 16.00
24 Frank Robinson 15.00 6.00

1968 Topps Test Discs

These six discs, which measure 2 1/4" were designed to be into a pin set but were not ever produced. These discs feature a player photo surrounded by the team name on the sides and the player's name on the bottom. Since these were never numbered, we have sequenced them in alphabetical order. This might be an incomplete checklist so all additions are appreciated.

NM Ex
1 Dean Chance 50.00 20.00
2 Bill Freehan 60.00 24.00
3 Jim Fregosi 50.00 20.00
4 Steve Hargan 50.00 20.00
5 Sam McDowell 60.00 24.00
5 Joe Torre 100.00 40.00

1968 Topps Venezuelan

This set is a parallel version of the first 370 cards of the regular 1968 Topps set and is similar in design. A major difference is that the Venezuelan cards are printed on a gray stock and have an orange background compared to the American Topps. There is also the "Hecho en Venezulela - C. A. Litoven" printed in faint white type at the bottom on the back of the card. However, not all of the cards have that expression printed on the bottom. Among the notable cards which do not is the Tom Seaver (number 45) card.

NM Ex
COMPLETE SET (370) 7000.00 2800.00
1 Roberto Clemente 60.00 24.00
Tony Gonzalez
Matty Alou LL
2 Carl Yastrzemski 30.00 12.00
Frank Robinson
Al Kaline LL
3 Orlando Cepeda 40.00 16.00
Roberto Clemente
Hank Aaron LL
4 Carl Yastrzemski 25.00 10.00
Harmon Killebrew
Frank Robinson LL
5 Hank Aaron 15.00 6.00
John Wynn
Ron Santo
Willie McCovey LL
6 Carl Yastrzemski 15.00 6.00
Harmon Killebrew
Frank Howard LL
7 Phil Neikro 8.00 3.20
Jim Bunning
Chris Short LL
8 Joel Horlen 8.00 3.20
Gary Peters
Sonny Siebert LL
9 Mike McCormick 8.00 3.20
Ferguson Jenkins
Jim Bunning
Claude Osteen LL
10 Jim Lonborg 8.00 3.20
Earl Wilson
Dean Chance LL
11 Jim Bunning 10.00 4.00
Ferguson Jenkins
Gaylor Perry LL
12 Jim Lonborg UER 10.00 4.00
(Misspelled Longberg on card back)
Sam McDowell
Dean Chance LL
13 Chuck Hartenstein 4.00 1.60
14 Jerry McNertney 4.00 1.60
15 Ron Hunt 4.00 1.60
16 Lou Piniella 8.00 3.20
Richie Scheinblum
17 Dick Hall 4.00 1.60
18 Mike Hershberger 4.00 1.60
19 Juan Pizarro 4.00 1.60
20 Brooks Robinson 60.00 24.00
21 Ron Davis 4.00 1.60
22 Pat Dobson 4.00 1.60
23 Chico Cardenas 4.00 1.60
24 Bobby Locke 4.00 1.60
25 Julian Javier 4.00 1.60
26 Darrell Brandon 4.00 1.60
27 Gil Hodges MG 20.00 8.00
28 Ted Uhlaender 4.00 1.60
29 Joe Verbanic 4.00 1.60
30 Joe Torre 10.00 4.00
31 Ed Stroud 4.00 1.60
32 Joe Gibbon 4.00 1.60
33 Pete Ward 4.00 1.60
34 Al Ferrara 4.00 1.60
35 Steve Hargan 4.00 1.60
36 Bob Moose 4.00 1.60
Bob Robertson
37 Billy Williams 25.00 10.00
38 Tony Pierce 4.00 1.60
39 Cookie Rojas 4.00 1.60
40 Denny McLain 25.00 10.00
41 Julio Gotay 4.00 1.60
42 Larry Haney 4.00 1.60
43 Gary Bell 4.00 1.60
44 Frank Kostro 4.00 1.60
45 Tom Seaver 120.00 47.50
46 Dave Ricketts 4.00 1.60
47 Ralph Houk MG 4.00 1.60
48 Ted Davidson 4.00 1.60
49 Eddie Brinkman 4.00 1.60
50 Willie Mays 150.00 60.00
51 Bob Locker 4.00 1.60
52 Hawk Taylor 4.00 1.60
53 Gene Alley 4.00 1.60
54 Stan Williams 4.00 1.60
55 Felipe Alou 8.00 3.20
56 Dave Leonhard 4.00 1.60
Dave May
57 Dan Schneider 4.00 1.60
58 Eddie Mathews 40.00 16.00
59 Don Lock 4.00 1.60
60 Ken Holtzman 4.00 1.60
61 Reggie Smith 6.00 2.40
62 Chuck Dobson 4.00 1.60
63 Dick Kenworthy 4.00 1.60
64 Jim Merritt 4.00 1.60
65 John Roseboro 4.00 1.60
66 Casey Cox 4.00 1.60
67 Jim Kaat CL 10.00 3.00
68 Ron Willis 4.00 1.60
69 Tom Tresh 6.00 2.40
70 Bob Veale 4.00 1.60
71 Vern Fuller 4.00 1.60
72 Tommy John 10.00 4.00
73 Jim Ray Hart 4.00 1.60
74 Milt Pappas 4.00 1.60
75 Don Mincher 4.00 1.60
76 Jim Britton 4.00 1.60
Ron Reed
77 Don Wilson 4.00 1.60
78 Jim Northrup 4.00 1.60
79 Ted Kubiak 4.00 1.60
80 Rod Carew 120.00 47.50
81 Larry Jackson 4.00 1.60
83 John Stephenson 4.00 1.60
83 Sam Bowens 4.00 1.60
84 Bob Tolan 4.00 1.60
85 Gaylord Perry 20.00 8.00
86 Willie Stargell 20.00 8.00
87 Dick Williams MG 6.00 2.40
88 Phil Regan 4.00 1.60
89 Jake Gibbs 4.00 1.60
90 Vada Pinson 10.00 4.00
91 Jim Ollom 4.00 1.60
92 Ed Kranepool 6.00 2.40
93 Tony Cloninger 4.00 1.60
94 Lee Maye 4.00 1.60
95 Bob Aspromonte 4.00 1.60
96 Frank Coggins 4.00 1.60
Dick Nold
97 Tom Phoebus 4.00 1.60
98 Gary Sutherland 4.00 1.60
99 Rocky Colavito 20.00 8.00
100 Bob Gibson 60.00 24.00
101 Glenn Beckert 4.00 1.60
102 Jose Cardenal 4.00 1.60
103 Don Sutton 15.00 6.00
104 Dick Dietz 4.00 1.60
105 Al Downing 4.00 1.60
106 Dalton Jones 4.00 1.60
107 Juan Marichal CL 10.00 3.00
108 Don Pavletich 4.00 1.60
109 Bert Campaneris 6.00 2.40
110 Hank Aaron 150.00 60.00
111 Rich Reese 4.00 1.60
112 Woody Fryman 4.00 1.60
113 Tom Matchick 4.00 1.60
Daryl Patterson
114 Ron Swoboda 6.00 2.40
115 Sam McDowell 4.00 1.60
116 Ken McMullen 4.00 1.60
117 Larry Jaster 4.00 1.60
118 Mark Belanger 4.00 1.60
119 Ted Savage 4.00 1.60
120 Mel Stottlemyre 6.00 2.40
121 Jimmie Hall 4.00 1.60
122 Gene Mauch MG 4.00 1.60
123 Jose Santiago 4.00 1.60
124 Nate Oliver 4.00 1.60
125 Joel Horlen 4.00 1.60
126 Bobby Etheridge 4.00 1.60
127 Paul Lindblad 4.00 1.60
128 Tom Dukes 4.00 1.60
Alonzo Harris
129 Mickey Stanley 4.00 1.60
130 Tony Perez 20.00 8.00
131 Frank Bertaina 4.00 1.60
132 Bud Harrelson 4.00 1.60
133 Fred Whitfield 4.00 1.60
134 Pat Jarvis 4.00 1.60
135 Paul Blair 4.00 1.60
136 Randy Hundley 4.00 1.60
137 Twins Team 8.00 3.20
138 Ruben Amaro 4.00 1.60
139 Chris Short 4.00 1.60
140 Tony Conigliaro 20.00 8.00
141 Dal Maxvill 4.00 1.60
142 Buddy Bradford 4.00 1.60
Bill Voss
143 Pete Cimino 4.00 1.60
144 Joe Morgan 30.00 12.00
145 Don Drysdale 30.00 12.00
146 Sal Bando 4.00 1.60
147 Frank Linzy 4.00 1.60
148 Dave Bristol MG 4.00 1.60
149 Bob Saverine 4.00 1.60
150 Roberto Clemente 200.00 80.00
151 Lou Brock WS 25.00 10.00
152 Carl Yastrzemski WS 25.00 10.00
153 Nellie Briles WS 10.00 4.00
154 Bob Gibson WS 20.00 8.00
155 Jim Lonborg WS 10.00 4.00
156 Rico Petrocelli WS 10.00 4.00
157 World Series Game 7 10.00 4.00
St. Louis wins it
158 World Series Summary 10.00 4.00
Cardinals celebrate
159 Don Kessinger 4.00 1.60
160 Earl Wilson 4.00 1.60
161 Norm Miller 4.00 1.60
162 Hal Gibson 4.00 1.60
Mike Torrez
163 Gene Brabender 4.00 1.60
164 Ramon Webster 4.00 1.60
165 Tony Oliva 10.00 4.00
166 Claude Raymond 4.00 1.60
167 Elston Howard 10.00 4.00
168 Dodgers Team 10.00 4.00
169 Bob Bolin 4.00 1.60
170 Jim Fregosi 6.00 2.40
171 Don Nottebart 4.00 1.60
172 Walt Williams 4.00 1.60
173 John Boozer 4.00 1.60
174 Bob Tillman 4.00 1.60
175 Maury Wills 10.00 4.00
176 Bob Allen 4.00 1.60
177 Jerry Koosman 3000.00 1200.00
Nolan Ryan
178 Don Wert 4.00 1.60
179 Bill Stoneman 4.00 1.60
180 Curt Flood 8.00 3.20
181 Jerry Zimmerman 4.00 1.60
182 Dave Giusti 4.00 1.60
183 Bob Kennedy MG 4.00 1.60
184 Lou Johnson 4.00 1.60
185 Tom Haller 4.00 1.60
186 Eddie Watt 4.00 1.60
187 Sonny Jackson 4.00 1.60
188 Cap Peterson 4.00 1.60
189 Bill Landis 4.00 1.60
190 Bill White 10.00 4.00
191 Dan Frisella 4.00 1.60
192 Carl Yastrzemski CL 20.00 6.00
193 Jack Hamilton 4.00 1.60
194 Don Buford 4.00 1.60
195 Joe Pepitone 4.00 1.60
196 Gary Nolan 4.00 1.60
197 Larry Brown 4.00 1.60
198 Roy Face 6.00 2.40
199 Roberto Rodriguez 4.00 1.60
Darrell fOsteen
200 Orlando Cepeda 15.00 6.00
201 Mike Marshall 6.00 2.40
202 Adolfo Phillips 4.00 1.60
203 Dick Kelley 4.00 1.60
204 Andy Etchebarren 4.00 1.60
205 Juan Marichal 20.00 8.00
206 Cal Ermer MG 4.00 1.60
207 Carroll Sembera 4.00 1.60
208 Willie Davis 4.00 1.60
209 Tim Cullen 4.00 1.60
210 Gary Peters 4.00 1.60
211 J.C. Martin 4.00 1.60
212 Dave Morehead 4.00 1.60
213 Chico Ruiz 4.00 1.60
214 Stan Bahnsen 4.00 1.60
Frank Fernandez
215 Jim Bunning 20.00 8.00
216 Bubba Morton 4.00 1.60
217 Dick Farrell 4.00 1.60
218 Ken Suarez 4.00 1.60
219 Rob Gardner 4.00 1.60
220 Harmon Killebrew 40.00 16.00
221 Braves Team 8.00 3.20
222 Jim Hardin 4.00 1.60
223 Ollie Brown 4.00 1.60
224 Jack Aker 4.00 1.60
225 Richie Allen 15.00 6.00
226 Jimmie Price 4.00 1.60
227 Joe Hoerner 4.00 1.60
228 Jack Billingham 4.00 1.60
Jim Fairey
229 Fred Klages 4.00 1.60
230 Pete Rose 100.00 40.00
231 Dave Baldwin 4.00 1.60
232 Denis Manke 4.00 1.60
233 George Scott 4.00 1.60
234 Bill Monbouquette 4.00 1.60
235 Ron Santo 10.00 4.00
236 Tug McGraw 8.00 3.20
237 Alvin Dark MG 6.00 2.40
238 Tom Satriano 4.00 1.60
239 Bill Henry 4.00 1.60
240 Al Kaline 60.00 24.00
241 Felix Millan 4.00 1.60
242 Moe Drabowsky 4.00 1.60
243 Rich Rollins 4.00 1.60
244 John Donaldson 4.00 1.60
245 Tony Gonzalez 4.00 1.60
246 Fritz Peterson 4.00 1.60
247 Johnny Bench 300.00 120.00
Ron Tompkins
248 Fred Valentine 4.00 1.60
249 Bill Singer 4.00 1.60
250 Carl Yastrzemski 60.00 24.00
251 Manny Sanguillen 10.00 4.00
252 Angels Team 8.00 3.20
253 Dick Hughes 4.00 1.60
254 Cleon Jones 4.00 1.60
255 Dean Chance 4.00 1.60
256 Norm Cash 15.00 6.00
257 Phil Niekro 20.00 8.00
258 Jose Arcia 4.00 1.60
Bill Schlesinger
259 Ken Boyer 8.00 3.20
260 Jim Wynn 4.00 1.60
261 Dave Duncan 4.00 1.60
262 Rick Wise 4.00 1.60
263 Horace Clarke 4.00 1.60
264 Ted Abernathy 4.00 1.60
265 Tommy Davis 4.00 1.60
266 Paul Popovich 4.00 1.60
267 Herman Franks MG 4.00 1.60
268 Bob Humphreys 4.00 1.60
269 Bob Tiefenauer 4.00 1.60
270 Matty Alou 6.00 2.40
271 Bobby Knoop 4.00 1.60
272 Ray Culp 4.00 1.60
273 Dave Johnson 8.00 3.20
274 Mike Cuellar 6.00 2.40
275 Tim McCarver 10.00 4.00
276 Jim Roland 4.00 1.60
277 Jerry Buchek 4.00 1.60
278 Orlando Cepeda CL 10.00 3.00
279 Bill Hands 4.00 1.60
280 Mickey Mantle 600.00 240.00
281 Jim Campanis 4.00 1.60
282 Rick Monday 4.00 1.60
283 Mel Queen 4.00 1.60
284 Johnny Briggs 4.00 1.60
285 Dick McAuliffe 4.00 1.60
286 Cecil Upshaw 4.00 1.60
287 Mickey Abarbanel 4.00 1.60
Cisco Carlos
288 Dave Wickersham 4.00 1.60
289 Woody Held 4.00 1.60
290 Willie McCovey 30.00 12.00
291 Dick Lines 4.00 1.60
292 Art Shamsky 4.00 1.60
293 Bruce Howard 4.00 1.60
294 Red Schoendienst MG 10.00 4.00
295 Sonny Siebert 4.00 1.60
296 Byron Browne 4.00 1.60
297 Russ Gibson 4.00 1.60
298 Jim Brewer 4.00 1.60
299 Gene Michael 4.00 1.60
300 Rusty Staub 8.00 3.20
301 George Mitterwald 4.00 1.60
Rick Renick
302 Gerry Arrigo 4.00 1.60
303 Dick Green 4.00 1.60
304 Sandy Valdespino 4.00 1.60
305 Minnie Rojas 4.00 1.60
306 Mike Ryan 4.00 1.60
307 John Hiller 4.00 1.60
308 Pirates Team 8.00 3.20
309 Ken Henderson 4.00 1.60
310 Luis Aparicio 20.00 8.00
311 Jack Lamabe 4.00 1.60
312 Curt Blefary 4.00 1.60
313 Al Weis 4.00 1.60
314 Bill Rohr 4.00 1.60
George Spriggs
315 Zoilo Versalles 4.00 1.60
316 Steve Barber 4.00 1.60
317 Ron Brand 4.00 1.60
318 Chico Salmon 4.00 1.60
319 George Culver 4.00 1.60
320 Frank Howard 6.00 2.40
321 Leo Durocher MG 10.00 4.00
322 Dave Boswell 4.00 1.60
323 Deron Johnson 4.00 1.60
324 Jim Nash 4.00 1.60
325 Manny Mota 6.00 2.40
326 Dennis Ribant 4.00 1.60
327 Tony Taylor 4.00 1.60
328 Chuck Vinson 4.00 1.60
Jim Weaver
329 Duane Josephson 4.00 1.60
330 Roger Maris 80.00 32.00
331 Dan Osinski 4.00 1.60
332 Doug Rader 4.00 1.60
333 Ron Herbel 4.00 1.60
334 Orioles Team 8.00 3.20
335 Bob Allison 4.00 1.60
336 John Purdin 4.00 1.60
337 Bill Robinson 4.00 1.60
338 Bob Johnson 4.00 1.60
339 Rich Nye 4.00 1.60
340 Max Alvis 4.00 1.60
341 Jim Lemon MG 4.00 1.60
342 Ken Johnson 4.00 1.60
343 Jim Gosger 4.00 1.60
344 Donn Clendenon 4.00 1.60
345 Bob Hendley 4.00 1.60
346 Jerry Adair 4.00 1.60
347 George Brunet 4.00 1.60
348 Larry Colton 4.00 1.60
Dick Thoenen
349 Ed Spiezio 4.00 1.60

350 Hoyt Wilhelm 15.00 6.00
351 Bob Barton 4.00 1.60
352 Jackie Hernandez 4.00 1.60
353 Mack Jones 4.00 1.60
354 Pete Richert 4.00 1.60
355 Ernie Banks 60.00 24.00
356 Ken Holtzman CL 10.00 4.00
357 Len Gabrielson 4.00 1.60
358 Mike Epstein 4.00 1.60
359 Joe Moeller 4.00 1.60
360 Willie Horton 8.00 3.20
361 Harmon Killebrew AS 15.00 6.00
362 Orlando Cepeda AS 10.00 4.00
363 Rod Carew AS 15.00 6.00
364 Joe Morgan AS 15.00 6.00
365 Brooks Robinson AS 15.00 6.00
366 Ron Santo AS 8.00 3.20
367 Jim Fregosi AS 4.00 1.60
368 Gene Alley AS 4.00 1.60
369 Carl Yastrzemski AS 25.00 10.00
370 Hank Aaron AS 50.00 20.00

1969 Topps

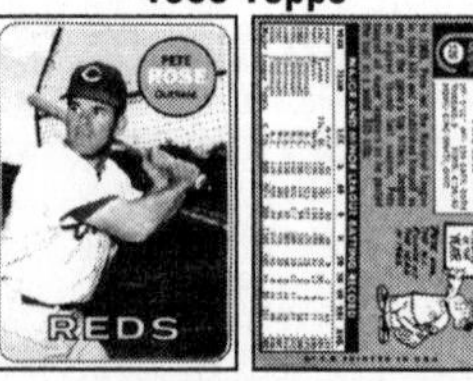

The cards in this 664-card set measure 2 1/2" by 3 1/2". The 1969 Topps set includes Sporting News All-Star Selections as card numbers 416 to 435. Other popular subsets within this set include League Leaders (1-12) and World Series cards (162-169). The fifth series contains several variations; the more difficult variety consists of cards with the player's first name, last name, and/or position in white letters instead of lettering in some other color. These are designated in the checklist below by WL (white letters). Each checklist card features a different popular player's picture inside a circle on the front of the checklist card. Two different team identifications of Clay Dalrymple and Donn Clendenon exist, as indicated in the checklist. The key Rookie Cards in this set are Rollie Fingers, Reggie Jackson, and Graig Nettles. This was the last year that Topps issued multi-player special star cards, ending a 13-year tradition, which they had begun in 1957. There were cropping differences in checklist cards 57, 214, and 412, due to their each being printed with two different series. The differences are difficult to explain and have not been greatly sought by collectors; hence they are not listed explicitly in the list below. The All-Star cards 426-435, when turned over and placed together, form a puzzle back of Pete Rose. This would turn out to be the final year that Topps issued cards in five-card nickel wax packs.

NM Ex
COMP. MASTER (695) 5000.00 2000.00
COMPLETE SET (664) 2800.00 1100.00
COMMON (1-218/328-512) 1.50 .60
COMMON (219-327) 2.50 1.00
COMMON (513-588) 2.00 .80
COMMON (589-664) 3.00 1.20
WRAPPER (5-CENT) 20.00 8.00
1 Carl Yastrzemski 15.00 5.25
Danny Cater
Tony Oliva LL
2 Pete Rose 8.00 3.20
Matty Alou
Felipe Alou LL
3 Ken Harrelson 4.00 1.60
Frank Howard
Jim Northrup LL
4 Willie McCovey 6.00 2.40
Ron Santo
Billy Williams LL
5 Frank Howard 4.00 1.60
Willie Horton
Ken Harrelson LL
6 Willie McCovey 6.00 2.40
Richie Allen
Ernie Banks LL
7 Luis Tiant 4.00 1.60
Sam McDowell
Dave McNally LL
8 Bob Gibson 6.00 2.40
Bobby Bolin
Bob Veale LL
9 Denny McLain 4.00 1.60
Dave McNally
Luis Tiant
Mel Stottlemyre LL
10 Juan Marichal 8.00 3.20
Bob Gibson
Fergie Jenkins LL
11 Sam McDowell 4.00 1.60
Denny McLain
Luis Tiant LL
12 Bob Gibson 4.00 1.60
Fergie Jenkins
Bill Singer LL
13 Mickey Stanley 2.50 1.00
14 Al McBean 1.50 .60
15 Boog Powell 4.00 1.60
16 Cesar Gutierrez 1.50 .60
Rich Robertson
17 Mike Marshall 2.50 1.00
18 Dick Schofield 1.50 .60
19 Ken Suarez 1.50 .60
20 Ernie Banks 20.00 8.00
21 Jose Santiago 1.50 .60
22 Jesus Alou 2.50 1.00
23 Lew Krausse 1.50 .60
24 Walt Alston MG 4.00 1.60
25 Roy White 2.50 1.00
26 Clay Carroll 2.50 1.00
27 Bernie Allen 1.50 .60
28 Mike Ryan 1.50 .60
29 Dave Morehead 1.50 .60
30 Bob Allison 2.50 1.00
31 Gary Gentry RC 2.50 1.00
Amos Otis RC
32 Sammy Ellis 1.50 .60
33 Wayne Causey 1.50 .60
34 Gary Peters 1.50 .60
35 Joe Morgan 10.00 4.00
36 Luke Walker 1.50 .60
37 Curt Motton 1.50 .60
38 Zoilo Versalles 2.50 1.00
39 Dick Hughes 1.50 .60
40 Mayo Smith MG 1.50 .60
41 Bob Barton 1.50 .60
42 Tommy Harper 2.50 1.00
43 Joe Niekro 2.50 1.00
44 Danny Cater 1.50 .60
45 Maury Wills 2.50 1.00
46 Fritz Peterson 2.50 1.00
47A Paul Popovich 2.50 1.00
No helmet emblem, thick airbrushing
47B Paul Popovich 2.50 1.00
No helmet emblem, light airbrushing
47C Paul Popovich 25.00 10.00
(C emblem on helmet)
48 Brant Alyea 1.50 .60
49A Royals Rookies ERR 25.00 10.00
Steve Jones
E. Rodriguez
49B Royals Rookies COR 1.50 .60
Steve Jones
E. Rodriguez
50 Roberto Clemente UER 60.00 24.00
Bats Right listed twice
51 Woody Fryman 2.50 1.00
52 Mike Andrews 1.50 .60
53 Sonny Jackson 1.50 .60
54 Cisco Carlos 1.50 .60
55 Jerry Grote 2.50 1.00
56 Rich Reese 1.50 .60
57 Denny McLain CL 6.00 1.20
58 Fred Gladding 1.50 .60
59 Jay Johnstone 2.50 1.00
60 Nelson Briles 2.50 1.00
61 Jimmie Hall 1.50 .60
62 Chico Salmon 1.50 .60
63 Jim Hickman 2.50 1.00
64 Bill Monbouquette 1.50 .60
65 Willie Davis 2.50 1.00
66 Mike Adamson 1.50 .60
Merv Rettenmund
67 Bill Stoneman 2.50 1.00
68 Dave Duncan 2.50 1.00
69 Steve Hamilton 2.50 1.00
70 Tommy Helms 2.50 1.00
71 Steve Whitaker 2.50 1.00
72 Ron Taylor 1.50 .60
73 Johnny Briggs 1.50 .60
74 Preston Gomez MG 2.50 1.00
75 Luis Aparicio 6.00 2.40
76 Norm Miller 1.50 .60
77A Ron Perranoski 2.50 1.00
(No emblem on cap)
77B Ron Perranoski 25.00 10.00
(LA on cap)
78 Tom Satriano 1.50 .60
79 Milt Pappas 2.50 1.00
80 Norm Cash 2.50 1.00
81 Mel Queen 1.50 .60
82 Rich Hebner RC 8.00 3.20
Al Oliver RC
83 Mike Ferraro 2.50 1.00
84 Bob Humphreys 1.50 .60
85 Lou Brock 20.00 8.00
86 Pete Richert 1.50 .60
87 Horace Clarke 2.50 1.00
88 Rich Nye 1.50 .60
89 Russ Gibson 1.50 .60
90 Jerry Koosman 2.50 1.00
91 Alvin Dark MG 2.50 1.00
92 Jack Billingham 2.50 1.00
93 Joe Foy 2.50 1.00
94 Hank Aguirre 1.50 .60
95 Johnny Bench 50.00 20.00
96 Denny Lemaster 1.50 .60
97 Buddy Bradford 1.50 .60
98 Dave Giusti 1.50 .60
99A Twins Rookies 15.00 6.00
Danny Morris
Graig Nettles RC
(No loop)
99B Twins Rookies 15.00 6.00
Danny Morris
Graig Nettles RC
(Errant loop in
upper left corner
of obverse)
100 Hank Aaron 50.00 20.00
101 Daryl Patterson 1.50 .60
102 Jim Davenport 1.50 .60
103 Roger Repoz 1.50 .60
104 Steve Blass 1.50 .60
105 Rick Monday 2.50 1.00
106 Jim Hannan 1.50 .60
107A Bob Gibson CL ERR 6.00 1.20
161 Jim Purdin
107B Bob Gibson CL COR 8.00 1.60
161 John Purdin
108 Tony Taylor 2.50 1.00
109 Jim Lonborg 2.50 1.00
110 Mike Shannon 2.50 1.00
111 John Morris RC 1.50 .60
112 J.C. Martin 2.50 1.00
113 Dave May 1.50 .60
114 Alan Closter 2.50 1.00
John Cumberland
115 Bill Hands 1.50 .60
116 Chuck Harrison 1.50 .60
117 Jim Fairey 2.50 1.00
118 Stan Williams 1.50 .60
119 Doug Rader 2.50 1.00
120 Pete Rose 50.00 20.00
121 Joe Grzenda 1.50 .60
122 Ron Fairly 2.50 1.00
123 Wilbur Wood 2.50 1.00
124 Hank Bauer MG 2.50 1.00
125 Ray Sadecki 1.50 .60
126 Dick Tracewski 1.50 .60
127 Kevin Collins 2.50 1.00
128 Tommie Aaron 2.50 1.00
129 Bill McCool 1.50 .60
130 Carl Yastrzemski 20.00 8.00
131 Chris Cannizzaro 1.50 .60
132 Dave Baldwin 1.50 .60
133 Johnny Callison 2.50 1.00
134 Jim Weaver 1.50 .60
135 Tommy Davis 2.50 1.00
136 Steve Huntz 1.50 .60
Mike Torrez
137 Wally Bunker 1.50 .60
138 John Bateman 1.50 .60
139 Andy Kosco 1.50 .60
140 Jim Lefebvre 2.50 1.00
141 Bill Dillman 1.50 .60
142 Woody Woodward 1.50 .60
143 Joe Nossek 1.50 .60
144 Bob Hendley 2.50 1.00
145 Max Alvis 1.50 .60
146 Jim Perry 2.50 1.00
147 Leo Durocher MG 4.00 1.60
148 Lee Stange 1.50 .60
149 Ollie Brown 2.50 1.00
150 Denny McLain 4.00 1.60
151A Clay Dalrymple 1.50 .60
Portrait, Orioles
151B Clay Dalrymple 15.00 6.00
Catching, Phillies
152 Tommie Sisk 1.50 .60
153 Ed Brinkman 1.50 .60
154 Jim Britton 1.50 .60
155 Pete Ward 1.50 .60
156 Hal Gilson 1.50 .60
Leon McFadden
157 Bob Rodgers 2.50 1.00
158 Joe Gibbon 1.50 .60
159 Jerry Adair 1.50 .60
160 Vada Pinson 2.50 1.00
161 John Purdin 1.50 .60
162 Bob Gibson WS 8.00 3.20
Fans 17
163 Willie Horton WS 6.00 2.40
164 Tim McCarver WS 12.00 4.80
Roger Maris
165 Lou Brock WS 8.00 3.20
166 Al Kaline WS 8.00 3.20
167 Jim Northrup WS 6.00 2.40
168 Mickey Lolich WS 8.00 3.20
Bob Gibson
169 Dick McAuliffe WS 6.00 2.40
Denny McLain
Willie Horton
170 Frank Howard 2.50 1.00
171 Glenn Beckert 2.50 1.00
172 Jerry Stephenson 1.50 .60
173 Bob Christian 1.50 .60
Gerry Nyman
174 Grant Jackson 1.50 .60
175 Jim Bunning 6.00 2.40
176 Joe Azcue 1.50 .60
177 Ron Reed 1.50 .60
178 Ray Oyler 2.50 1.00
179 Don Pavletich 1.50 .60
180 Willie Horton 2.50 1.00
181 Mel Nelson 1.50 .60
182 Bill Rigney MG 1.50 .60
183 Don Shaw 2.50 1.00
184 Roberto Pena 1.50 .60
185 Tom Phoebus 1.50 .60
186 Johnny Edwards 1.50 .60
187 Leon Wagner 1.50 .60
188 Rick Wise 2.50 1.00
189 Joe Lahoud 1.50 .60
John Thibodeau
190 Willie Mays 80.00 32.00
191 Lindy McDaniel 2.50 1.00
192 Jose Pagan 1.50 .60
193 Don Cardwell 2.50 1.00
194 Ted Uhlaender 1.50 .60
195 John Odom 1.50 .60
196 Lum Harris MG 1.50 .60
197 Dick Selma 1.50 .60
198 Willie Smith 1.50 .60
199 Jim French 1.50 .60
200 Bob Gibson 12.00 4.80
201 Russ Snyder 1.50 .60
202 Don Wilson 2.50 1.00
203 Dave Johnson 2.50 1.00
204 Jack Hiatt 1.50 .60
205 Rick Reichardt 1.50 .60
206 Larry Hisle 2.50 1.00
Barry Lersch
207 Roy Face 2.50 1.00
208A Donn Clendenon 2.50 1.00
Houston
208B Donn Clendenon 15.00 6.00
Expos
209 Larry Haney UER 1.50 .60
(Reverse negative)
210 Felix Millan 1.50 .60
211 Galen Cisco 1.50 .60
212 Tom Tresh 2.50 1.00
213 Gerry Arrigo 1.50 .60
214 Checklist 3 6.00 1.20
With 69T deckle CL
on back (no player)
215 Rico Petrocelli 2.50 1.00
216 Don Sutton 6.00 2.40
217 John Donaldson 1.50 .60
218 John Roseboro 2.50 1.00
219 Freddie Patek RC 4.00 1.60
220 Sam McDowell 4.00 1.60
221 Art Shamsky 4.00 1.60
222 Duane Josephson 2.50 1.00
223 Tom Dukes 4.00 1.60
224 Bill Harrelson 2.50 1.00
Steve Kealey
225 Don Kessinger 4.00 1.60
226 Bruce Howard 2.50 1.00
227 Frank Johnson 2.50 1.00
228 Dave Leonhard 2.50 1.00
229 Don Lock 2.50 1.00
230 Rusty Staub UER 4.00 1.60
For 1966 stats, Houston spelled
Huoston
231 Pat Dobson 4.00 1.60
232 Dave Ricketts 2.50 1.00
233 Steve Barber 4.00 1.60
234 Dave Bristol MG 2.50 1.00
235 Jim Hunter 10.00 4.00
236 Manny Mota 4.00 1.60
237 Bobby Cox RC 10.00 4.00
238 Ken Johnson 2.50 1.00
239 Bob Taylor 4.00 1.60
240 Ken Harrelson 4.00 1.60
241 Jim Brewer 2.50 1.00
242 Frank Kostro 2.50 1.00
243 Ron Kline 2.50 1.00
244 Ray Fosse RC 4.00 1.60
George Woodson
245 Ed Charles 4.00 1.60
246 Joe Coleman 2.50 1.00
247 Gene Oliver 2.50 1.00
248 Bob Priddy 2.50 1.00
249 Ed Spiezio 4.00 1.60
250 Frank Robinson 20.00 8.00
251 Ron Herbel 2.50 1.00
252 Chuck Cottier 2.50 1.00
253 Jerry Johnson 2.50 1.00
254 Joe Schultz MG 4.00 1.60
255 Steve Carlton 30.00 12.00
256 Gates Brown 4.00 1.60
257 Jim Ray 2.50 1.00
258 Jackie Hernandez 4.00 1.60
259 Bill Short 2.50 1.00
260 Reggie Jackson RC 200.00 80.00
261 Bob Johnson 2.50 1.00
262 Mike Kekich 4.00 1.60
263 Jerry May 2.50 1.00
264 Bill Landis 2.50 1.00
265 Chico Cardenas 4.00 1.60
266 Tom Hutton 4.00 1.60
Alan Foster
267 Vicente Romo 2.50 1.00
268 Al Spangler 2.50 1.00
269 Al Weis 4.00 1.60
270 Mickey Lolich 4.00 1.60
271 Larry Stahl 4.00 1.60
272 Ed Stroud 2.50 1.00
273 Ron Willis 2.50 1.00
274 Clyde King MG 2.50 1.00
275 Vic Davalillo 2.50 1.00
276 Gary Wagner 2.50 1.00
277 Elrod Hendricks RC 2.50 1.00
278 Gary Geiger UER 2.50 1.00
(Batting wrong)
279 Roger Nelson 4.00 1.60
280 Alex Johnson 4.00 1.60
281 Ted Kubiak 2.50 1.00
282 Pat Jarvis 2.50 1.00
283 Sandy Alomar 4.00 1.60
284 Jerry Robertson 4.00 1.60
Mike Wegener
285 Don Mincher 4.00 1.60
286 Dock Ellis RC 4.00 1.60
287 Jose Tartabull 4.00 1.60
288 Ken Holtzman 4.00 1.60
289 Bart Shirley 2.50 1.00
290 Jim Kaat 4.00 1.60
291 Vern Fuller 2.50 1.00
292 Al Downing 4.00 1.60
293 Dick Dietz 2.50 1.00
294 Jim Lemon MG 2.50 1.00
295 Tony Perez 12.00 4.80
296 Andy Messersmith RC 4.00 1.60
297 Deron Johnson 2.50 1.00
298 Dave Nicholson 4.00 1.60
299 Mark Belanger 4.00 1.60
300 Felipe Alou 4.00 1.60
301 Darrell Brandon 4.00 1.60
302 Jim Pagliaroni 2.50 1.00
303 Cal Koonce 4.00 1.60
304 Bill Davis 6.00 2.40
Clarence Gaston RC
305 Dick McAuliffe 4.00 1.60
306 Jim Grant 4.00 1.60
307 Gary Kolb 2.50 1.00
308 Wade Blasingame 2.50 1.00
309 Walt Williams 2.50 1.00
310 Tom Haller 2.50 1.00
311 Sparky Lyle RC 10.00 4.00
312 Lee Elia 2.50 1.00
313 Bill Robinson 4.00 1.60
314 Don Drysdale CL 6.00 1.20
315 Eddie Fisher 2.50 1.00
316 Hal Lanier 2.50 1.00
317 Bruce Look 2.50 1.00
318 Jack Fisher 2.50 1.00
319 Ken McMullen UER 2.50 1.00
(Headings on back
are for a pitcher)
320 Dal Maxvill 2.50 1.00
321 Jim McAndrew 4.00 1.60
322 Jose Vidal 4.00 1.60
323 Larry Miller 2.50 1.00
324 Les Cain 4.00 1.60
Dave Campbell RC
325 Jose Cardenal 4.00 1.60
326 Gary Sutherland 4.00 1.60
327 Willie Crawford 2.50 1.00
328 Joel Horlen 1.50 .60
329 Rick Joseph 1.50 .60
330 Tony Conigliaro 4.00 1.60
331 Gil Garrido 2.50 1.00
Tom House RC
332 Fred Talbot 1.50 .60
333 Ivan Murrell 1.50 .60
334 Phil Roof 1.50 .60
335 Bill Mazeroski 6.00 2.40
336 Jim Roland 1.50 .60
337 Marty Martinez 1.50 .60
338 Del Unser 1.50 .60
339 Steve Mingori 1.50 .60
Jose Pena
340 Dave McNally 2.50 1.00
341 Dave Adlesh 1.50 .60
342 Bubba Morton 1.50 .60
343 Dan Frisella 1.50 .60
344 Tom Matchick 1.50 .60
345 Frank Linzy 1.50 .60
346 Wayne Comer 1.50 .60
347 Randy Hundley 2.50 1.00
348 Steve Hargan 1.50 .60
349 Dick Williams MG 2.50 1.00
350 Richie Allen 4.00 1.60
351 Carroll Sembera 1.50 .60
352 Paul Schaal 2.50 1.00
353 Jeff Torborg 2.50 1.00
354 Nate Oliver 1.50 .60
355 Phil Niekro 6.00 2.40
356 Frank Quilici 1.50 .60
357 Carl Taylor 1.50 .60
358 George Lauzerique 1.50 .60
Roberto Rodriguez
359 Dick Kelley 1.50 .60
360 Jim Wynn 2.50 1.00
361 Gary Holman 1.50 .60
362 Jim Maloney 2.50 1.00
363 Russ Nixon 1.50 .60
364 Tommie Agee 4.00 1.60
365 Jim Fregosi 2.50 1.00
366 Bo Belinsky 2.50 1.00
367 Lou Johnson 2.50 1.00
368 Vic Roznovsky 1.50 .60
369 Bob Skinner MG 2.50 1.00
370 Juan Marichal 8.00 3.20
371 Sal Bando 2.50 1.00
372 Adolfo Phillips 1.50 .60
373 Fred Lasher 1.50 .60
374 Bob Tillman 1.50 .60
375 Harmon Killebrew 15.00 6.00
376 Mike Fiore 1.50 .60
Jim Rooker RC
377 Gary Bell 2.50 1.00
378 Jose Herrera 1.50 .60
379 Ken Boyer 2.50 1.00
380 Stan Bahnsen 2.50 1.00
381 Ed Kranepool 2.50 1.00
382 Pat Corrales 2.50 1.00
383 Casey Cox 1.50 .60
384 Larry Shepard MG 1.50 .60
385 Orlando Cepeda 6.00 2.40
386 Jim McGlothlin 1.50 .60
387 Bobby Klaus 1.50 .60
388 Tom McCraw 1.50 .60
389 Dan Coombs 1.50 .60
390 Bill Freehan 2.50 1.00
391 Ray Culp 1.50 .60
392 Bob Burda 1.50 .60
393 Gene Brabender 2.50 1.00
394 Lou Piniella 6.00 2.40
Marv Staehle
395 Chris Short 1.50 .60
396 Jim Campanis 1.50 .60
397 Chuck Dobson 1.50 .60
398 Tito Francona 1.50 .60
399 Bob Bailey 2.50 1.00
400 Don Drysdale 15.00 6.00
401 Jake Gibbs 2.50 1.00
402 Ken Boswell 2.50 1.00
403 Bob Miller 1.50 .60
404 Vic LaRose 2.50 1.00
Gary Ross
405 Lee May 2.50 1.00
406 Phil Ortega 1.50 .60
407 Tom Egan 1.50 .60
408 Nate Colbert 1.50 .60
409 Bob Moose 1.50 .60
410 Al Kaline 25.00 10.00
411 Larry Dierker 2.50 1.00
412 Mickey Mantle CL DP 15.00 3.00
413 Roland Sheldon 2.50 1.00
414 Duke Sims 1.50 .60
415 Ray Washburn 1.50 .60
416 Willie McCovey AS 8.00 3.20
417 Ken Harrelson AS 3.00 1.20
418 Tommy Helms AS 3.00 1.20
419 Rod Carew AS 10.00 4.00
420 Ron Santo AS 4.00 1.60
421 Brooks Robinson AS 8.00 3.20
422 Don Kessinger AS 3.00 1.20
423 Bert Campaneris AS 4.00 1.60
424 Pete Rose AS 15.00 6.00
425 Carl Yastrzemski AS 10.00 4.00
426 Curt Flood AS 4.00 1.60
427 Tony Oliva AS 4.00 1.60
428 Lou Brock AS 6.00 2.40
429 Willie Horton AS 3.00 1.20
430 Johnny Bench AS 10.00 4.00
431 Bill Freehan AS 4.00 1.60
432 Bob Gibson AS 6.00 2.40
433 Denny McLain AS 3.00 1.20
434 Jerry Koosman AS 3.00 1.20
435 Sam McDowell AS 2.50 1.00
436 Gene Alley 2.50 1.00
437 Luis Alcaraz 1.50 .60
438 Gary Waslewski 1.50 .60
439 Ed Herrmann 1.50 .60
Dan Lazar
440A Willie McCovey 15.00 6.00
440B Willie McCovey WL 100.00 40.00
(McCovey white)
441A Dennis Higgins 1.50 .60
441B Dennis Higgins WL 25.00 10.00
(Higgins white)
442 Ty Cline 1.50 .60
443 Don Wert 1.50 .60
444A Joe Moeller 1.50 .60
444B Joe Moeller WL 25.00 10.00
(Moeller white)
445 Bobby Knoop 1.50 .60
446 Claude Raymond 1.50 .60
447A Ralph Houk MG 2.50 1.00
447B Ralph Houk WL 25.00 10.00
MG (Houk white)
448 Bob Tolan 2.50 1.00
449 Paul Lindblad 1.50 .60
450 Billy Williams 8.00 3.20
451A Rich Rollins 2.50 1.00
451B Rich Rollins WL 25.00 10.00
(Rich and 3B white)
452A Al Ferrara 1.50 .60
452B Al Ferrara WL 25.00 10.00
(Al and OF white)
453 Mike Cuellar 2.50 1.00
454A Phillies Rookies 2.50 1.00
Larry Colton
Don Money
454B Phillies Rookies WL 25.00 10.00
Larry Colton
Don Money
(Names in white)
455 Sonny Siebert 1.50 .60
456 Bud Harrelson 2.50 1.00
457 Dalton Jones 1.50 .60
458 Curt Blefary 1.50 .60
459 Dave Boswell 1.50 .60
460 Joe Torre 4.00 1.60
461A Mike Epstein 1.50 .60

461B Mike Epstein WL 25.00 10.00
(Epstein white)
462 Red Schoendienst 2.50 1.00
MG
463 Dennis Ribant 1.50 .60
464A Dave Marshall 1.50 .60
464B Dave Marshall WL 25.00 10.00
(Marshall white)
465 Tommy John 4.00 1.60
466 John Boccabella 2.50 1.00
467 Tommie Reynolds 1.50 .60
468A Pirates Rookies 1.50 .60
Bruce Dal Canton
Bob Robertson
468B Pirates Rookies WL 25.00 10.00
Bruce Dal Canton
Bob Robertson
(Names in white)
469 Chico Ruiz 1.50 .60
470A Mel Stottlemyre 2.50 1.00
470B Mel Stottlemyre WL 30.00 12.00
(Stottlemyre white)
471A Ted Savage 1.50 .60
471B Ted Savage WL 25.00 10.00
(Savage white)
472 Jim Price 1.50 .60
473A Jose Arcia 1.50 .60
473B Jose Arcia WL 25.00 10.00
(Jose and 2B white)
474 Tom Murphy 1.50 .60
475 Tim McCarver 4.00 1.60
476A Boston Rookies 3.00 1.20
Ken Brett RC
Gerry Moses
476B Boston Rookies WL 30.00 12.00
Ken Brett RC
Gerry Moses
(Names in white)
477 Jeff James 1.50 .60
478 Don Buford 1.50 .60
479 Richie Scheinblum 1.50 .60
480 Tom Seaver 80.00 32.00
481 Bill Melton 2.50 1.00
482A Jim Gosger 1.50 .60
482B Jim Gosger WL 25.00 10.00
(Jim and OF white)
483 Ted Abernathy 1.50 .60
484 Joe Gordon MG 2.50 1.00
485A Gaylord Perry 10.00 4.00
485B Gaylord Perry WL 80.00 32.00
(Perry white)
486A Paul Casanova 1.50 .60
486B Paul Casanova WL 25.00 10.00
(Casanova white)
487 Denis Menke 1.50 .60
488 Joe Sparma 1.50 .60
489 Clete Boyer 2.50 1.00
490 Matty Alou 2.50 1.00
491A Twins Rookies 1.50 .60
Jerry Crider
George Mitterwald
491B Twins Rookies WL 25.00 10.00
Jerry Crider
George Mitterwald
(Names in white)
492 Tony Cloninger 1.50 .60
493A Wes Parker 2.50 1.00
493B Wes Parker WL 25.00 10.00
(Parker white)
494 Ken Berry 1.50 .60
495 Bert Campaneris 2.50 1.00
496 Larry Jaster 1.50 .60
497 Julian Javier 2.50 1.00
498 Juan Pizarro 2.50 1.00
499 Don Bryant 1.50 .60
Steve Shea
500A Mickey Mantle UER 300.00 120.00
(No Topps copy-
right on card back)
500B Mickey Mantle WL 2000.00 800.00
(Mantle in white;
no Topps copyright
on card back) UER
501A Tony Gonzalez 2.50 1.00
501B Tony Gonzalez WL 25.00 10.00
(Tony and OF white)
502 Minnie Rojas 1.50 .60
503 Larry Brown 1.50 .60
504 Brooks Robinson CL 8.00 1.60
505A Bobby Bolin 1.50 .60
505B Bobby Bolin WL 25.00 10.00
(Bolin white)
506 Paul Blair 2.50 1.00
507 Cookie Rojas 2.50 1.00
508 Moe Drabowsky 2.50 1.00
509 Manny Sanguillen 2.50 1.00
510 Rod Carew 40.00 16.00
511A Diego Segui 2.50 1.00
511B Diego Segui WL 25.00 10.00
(Diego and P white)
512 Cleon Jones 2.50 1.00
513 Camilo Pascual 3.00 1.20
514 Mike Lum 2.00 .80
515 Dick Green 2.00 .80
516 Earl Weaver RC MG 20.00 8.00
517 Mike McCormick 3.00 1.20
518 Fred Whitfield 2.00 .80
519 Jerry Kenney 2.00 .80
Len Boehmer
520 Bob Veale 3.00 1.20
521 George Thomas 2.00 .80
522 Joe Hoerner 2.00 .80
523 Bob Chance 2.00 .80
524 Jose Laboy 3.00 1.20
Floyd Wicker
525 Earl Wilson 3.00 1.20
526 Hector Torres 2.00 .80
527 Al Lopez MG 5.00 2.00
528 Claude Osteen 3.00 1.20
529 Ed Kirkpatrick 3.00 1.20
530 Cesar Tovar 2.00 .80
531 Dick Farrell 2.00 .80
532 Tom Phoebus 3.00 1.20
Jim Hardin
Dave McNally
Mike Cuellar
533 Nolan Ryan 250.00 100.00
534 Jerry McNertney 3.00 1.20
535 Phil Regan 3.00 1.20
536 Danny Breeden 2.00 .80
Dave Roberts
537 Mike Paul 2.00 .80
538 Charlie Smith 2.00 .80
539 Mike Epstein 12.00 4.80
Ted Williams MG
540 Curt Flood 3.00 1.20
541 Joe Verbanic 2.00 .80
542 Bob Aspromonte 2.00 .80
543 Fred Newman 2.00 .80
544 Mike Kilkenny 2.00 .80
Ron Woods
545 Willie Stargell 12.00 4.80
546 Jim Nash 2.00 .80
547 Billy Martin MG 5.00 2.00
548 Bob Locker 2.00 .80
549 Ron Brand 2.00 .80
550 Brooks Robinson 30.00 12.00
551 Wayne Granger 2.00 .80
552 Ted Sizemore RC 3.00 1.20
Bill Sudakis
553 Ron Davis 2.00 .80
554 Frank Bertaina 2.00 .80
555 Jim Ray Hart 3.00 1.20
556 Sal Bando 3.00 1.20
Bert Campaneris
Danny Cater
557 Frank Fernandez 2.00 .80
558 Tom Burgmeier 3.00 1.20
559 Joe Hague 2.00 .80
Jim Hicks
560 Luis Tiant 3.00 1.20
561 Ron Clark 2.00 .80
562 Bob Watson RC 8.00 3.20
563 Marty Pattin 3.00 1.20
564 Gil Hodges MG 10.00 4.00
565 Hoyt Wilhelm 8.00 3.20
566 Ron Hansen 2.00 .80
567 Elvio Jimenez 2.00 .80
Jim Shellenback
568 Cecil Upshaw 2.00 .80
569 Billy Harris 1.50 .60
570 Ron Santo 8.00 3.20
571 Cap Peterson 2.00 .80
572 Willie McCovey 15.00 6.00
Juan Marichal
573 Jim Palmer 30.00 12.00
574 George Scott 3.00 1.20
575 Bill Singer 3.00 1.20
576 Ron Stone 2.00 .80
Bill Wilson
577 Mike Hegan 3.00 1.20
578 Don Bosch 2.00 .80
579 Dave Nelson 2.00 .80
580 Jim Northrup 3.00 1.20
581 Gary Nolan 3.00 1.20
582A Tony Oliva CL 6.00 1.20
White circle on back
582B Tony Oliva CL 8.00 1.60
Red circle on back
583 Clyde Wright 2.00 .80
584 Don Mason 2.00 .80
585 Ron Swoboda 3.00 1.20
586 Tim Cullen 2.00 .80
587 Joe Rudi RC 8.00 3.20
588 Bill White 3.00 1.20
589 Joe Pepitone 5.00 2.00
590 Rico Carty 5.00 2.00
591 Mike Hedlund 3.00 1.20
592 Rafael Robles 5.00 2.00
Al Santorini
593 Don Nottebart 3.00 1.20
594 Dooley Womack 3.00 1.20
595 Lee Maye 3.00 1.20
596 Chuck Hartenstein 3.00 1.20
597 Bob Floyd 40.00 16.00
Larry Burchart
Rollie Fingers RC
598 Ruben Amaro 3.00 1.20
599 John Boozer 3.00 1.20
600 Tony Oliva 8.00 3.20
601 Tug McGraw 8.00 3.20
602 Alec Distaso 5.00 2.00
Don Young
Jim Qualls
603 Joe Keough 3.00 1.20
604 Bobby Etheridge 3.00 1.20
605 Dick Ellsworth 3.00 1.20
606 Gene Mauch MG 5.00 2.00
607 Dick Bosman 3.00 1.20
608 Dick Simpson 3.00 1.20
609 Phil Gagliano 3.00 1.20
610 Jim Hardin 3.00 1.20
611 Bob Didier 5.00 2.00
Walt Hriniak RC
Gary Neibauer
612 Jack Aker 5.00 2.00
613 Jim Beauchamp 3.00 1.20
614 Tom Griffin 3.00 1.20
Skip Guinn
615 Len Gabrielson 3.00 1.20
616 Don McMahon 3.00 1.20
617 Jesse Gonder 3.00 1.20
618 Ramon Webster 3.00 1.20
619 Bill Butler 5.00 2.00
Pat Kelly
Juan Rios
620 Dean Chance 5.00 2.00
621 Bill Voss 3.00 1.20
622 Dan Osinski 3.00 1.20
623 Hank Allen 3.00 1.20
624 Darrel Chaney 5.00 2.00
Duffy Dyer RC
Terry Harmon
625 Mack Jones UER 5.00 2.00
(Batting wrong)
626 Gene Michael 5.00 2.00
627 George Stone 3.00 1.20
628 Bill Conigliaro RC 5.00 2.00
Syd O'Brien
Fred Wenz
629 Jack Hamilton 3.00 1.20
630 Bobby Bonds RC 30.00 12.00
631 John Kennedy 5.00 2.00
632 Jon Warden 3.00 1.20
633 Harry Walker MG 3.00 1.20
634 Andy Etchebarren 3.00 1.20
635 George Culver 3.00 1.20
636 Woody Held 3.00 1.20
637 Jerry DaVanon 5.00 2.00
Frank Reberger
Clay Kirby
638 Ed Sprague RC 3.00 1.20
639 Barry Moore 3.00 1.20
640 Ferguson Jenkins 20.00 8.00
641 Bobby Darwin 5.00 2.00
John Miller
Tommy Dean
642 John Hiller 3.00 1.20
643 Billy Cowan 3.00 1.20
644 Chuck Hinton 3.00 1.20
645 George Brunet 3.00 1.20
646 Dan McGinn 5.00 2.00
Carl Morton
647 Dave Wickersham 3.00 1.20
648 Bobby Wine 5.00 2.00
649 Al Jackson 3.00 1.20
650 Ted Williams MG 20.00 8.00
651 Gus Gil 5.00 2.00
652 Eddie Watt 3.00 1.20
653 A.Rodriguez RC UER 5.00 2.00
Photo actually
Angels' batboy
654 Carlos May RC 5.00 2.00
Don Secrist
Rich Morales
655 Mike Hershberger 3.00 1.20
656 Dan Schneider 3.00 1.20
657 Bobby Murcer 8.00 3.20
658 Tom Hall 3.00 1.20
Bill Burbach
Jim Miles
659 Johnny Podres 5.00 2.00
660 Reggie Smith 5.00 2.00
661 Jim Merritt 3.00 1.20
662 Dick Drago 5.00 2.00
George Spriggs
Bob Oliver
663 Dick Radatz 5.00 2.00
664 Ron Hunt 5.00 1.35

1969 Topps Decals Inserts

The 1969 Topps Decal Inserts are a set of 48 unnumbered decals issued as inserts in packages of 1969 Topps regular issue cards. Each decal is approximately 1" by 1 1/2" although including the plain backing the measurement is 1 3/4" by 2 1/8". The decals appear to be miniature versions of the Topps regular issue of that year. The copyright notice on the side indicates that these decals were produced in the United Kingdom. Most of the players on the decals are stars.

NM Ex
COMPLETE SET (48) 500.00 200.00
1 Hank Aaron 50.00 20.00
2 Richie Allen 5.00 2.00
3 Felipe Alou 3.00 1.20
4 Matty Alou 3.00 1.20
5 Luis Aparicio 8.00 3.20
6 Roberto Clemente 60.00 24.00
7 Donn Clendenon 2.50 1.00
8 Tommy Davis 3.00 1.20
9 Don Drysdale 12.00 4.80
10 Joe Foy 2.50 1.00
11 Jim Fregosi 3.00 1.20
12 Bob Gibson 12.00 4.80
13 Tony Gonzalez 2.50 1.00
14 Tom Haller 2.50 1.00
15 Ken Harrelson 3.00 1.20
16 Tommy Helms 2.50 1.00
17 Willie Horton 3.00 1.20
18 Frank Howard 3.00 1.20
19 Reggie Jackson 50.00 20.00
20 Ferguson Jenkins 8.00 3.20
21 Harmon Killebrew 8.00 3.20
22 Jerry Koosman 3.00 1.20
23 Mickey Mantle 120.00 47.50
24 Willie Mays 50.00 20.00
25 Tim McCarver 5.00 2.00
26 Willie McCovey 12.00 4.80
27 Sam McDowell 3.00 1.20
28 Denny McLain 3.00 1.20
29 Dave McNally 3.00 1.20
30 Don Mincher 2.50 1.00
31 Rick Monday 2.50 1.00
32 Tony Oliva 4.00 1.60
33 Camilo Pascual 2.50 1.00
34 Rick Reichardt 2.50 1.00
35 Frank Robinson 15.00 6.00
36 Pete Rose 30.00 12.00
37 Ron Santo 5.00 2.00
38 Tom Seaver 30.00 12.00
39 Dick Selma 2.50 1.00
40 Chris Short 2.50 1.00
41 Rusty Staub 4.00 1.60
42 Mel Stottlemyre 3.00 1.20
43 Luis Tiant 3.00 1.20
44 Pete Ward 2.50 1.00
45 Hoyt Wilhelm 8.00 3.20
46 Maury Wills 5.00 2.00
47 Jim Wynn 3.00 1.20
48 Carl Yastrzemski 20.00 8.00

1969 Topps Deckle Inserts

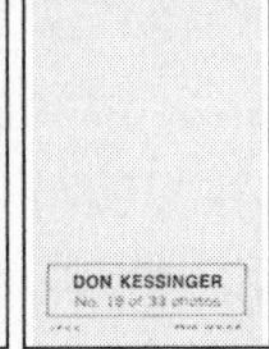

The cards in this 33-card set measure approximately 2 1/4" by 3 1/4". This unusual black and white insert set derives its name from the serrated border, or edge, of the cards. The cards were included as inserts in the regularly issued Topps baseball third series of 1969. Card number 11 is found with either Hoyt Wilhelm or Jim Wynn, and number 22 with either Rusty Staub or Joe Foy. The set price below does include all variations. The set numbering is arranged in team order by league except for cards 11 and 22.

NM Ex
COMPLETE SET (35) 100.00 40.00
1 Brooks Robinson 8.00 3.20
2 Boog Powell 2.00 .80
3 Ken Harrelson .75 .30
4 Carl Yastrzemski 6.00 2.40
5 Jim Fregosi 1.00 .40
6 Luis Aparicio 3.00 1.20
7 Luis Tiant 1.00 .40
8 Denny McLain 1.50 .60
9 Willie Horton 1.00 .40
10 Bill Freehan 1.00 .40
11A Hoyt Wilhelm 8.00 3.20
11B Jim Wynn 15.00 6.00
12 Rod Carew 5.00 2.00
13 Mel Stottlemyre 1.00 .40
14 Rick Monday .75 .30
15 Tommy Davis 1.00 .40
16 Frank Howard 1.00 .40
17 Felipe Alou 1.00 .40
18 Don Kessinger .75 .30
19 Ron Santo 2.00 .80
20 Tommy Helms .75 .30
21 Pete Rose 10.00 4.00
22A Rusty Staub 3.00 1.20
22B Joe Foy 12.00 4.80
23 Tom Haller .75 .30
24 Maury Wills 1.50 .60
25 Jerry Koosman 1.00 .40
26 Richie Allen 2.00 .80
27 Roberto Clemente 20.00 8.00
28 Curt Flood 1.50 .60
29 Bob Gibson 5.00 2.00
30 Al Ferrara .75 .30
31 Willie McCovey 4.00 1.60
32 Juan Marichal 4.00 1.60
33 Willie Mays 12.00 4.80

1969 Topps Four-in-One

This was a test issue consisting of 25 sticker cards (blank back). Each card measures 2 1/2" by 3 1/2" and features four mini-stickers. These unnumbered stickers are ordered in the checklist below alphabetically by the upper left player's name on each card. Each mini-card featured is from the 1969 Topps second series. Five of the cards were double printed (technically 50 percent more were printed) compared to the others in the set; these are marked below by DP.

NM Ex
COMPLETE SET (25) 800.00 325.00
1 Jerry Adair 100.00 40.00
Don Wilson
Willie Mays
John Morris
2 Hal Gilson 12.00 4.80
Leon McFadden
Wally Bunker
Joe Gibbon
Don Cardwell
3 Donn Clendenon 12.00 4.80
Woody Woodward
Tommie Aaron
Jim Britton
4 Tommy Davis 20.00 8.00
Don Pavletich
Lou Brock WS
Vada Pinson
5 Ron Fairly 12.00 4.80
Rick Wise
Max Alvis
Glenn Beckert
6 Jim French 12.00 4.80
Dick Selma
Johnny Callison
Lum Harris MG
7 Bob Gibson DP 40.00 16.00
Tim McCarver WS
Rick Reichardt
Larry Haney
8 Andy Kosco 15.00 6.00
Ron Reed
Jim Bunning
Ollie Brown
9 Jim Lefebvre 12.00 4.80
John Purdin
Bill Dillman
John Roseboro
10 Felix Millan DP 12.00 4.80
Bill Hands
Lindy McDaniel
Chuck Harrison
11 Mel Nelson 15.00 6.00
Dave Johnson
Jack Hiatt
Tommie Sisk
12 John Odom 15.00 6.00
Leo Durocher MG
Wilbur Wood
Clay Dalrymple
13 Ray Oyler DP 12.00 4.80
Hank Bauer MG
Kevin Collins
Russ Snyder
14 Jim Perry 15.00 6.00
Mickey Lolich WS
Bob Gibson WS
Gerry Arrigo
Joe Lahoud
John Thibodeau
15 Doug Rader 12.00 4.80
Bill McCool
Roberto Pena
Willie Horton WS
16 Bob Rodgers 15.00 6.00
Willie Horton
Roy Face
Ed Brinkman
17 Ray Sadecki 12.00 4.80
Dave Baldwin
J.C. Martin
Dave May
18 Mike Shannon DP 15.00 6.00
Bob Gibson WS
Jose Pagan
Tom Phoebus
19 Lee Stange 300.00 120.00
Don Sutton
Ted Uhlaender
Pete Rose
20 Jim Weaver 12.00 4.80
Dick Tracewski
Joe Grzenda
Frank Howard
21 Bob Christian 15.00 6.00
Gerry Nyman
Denny McLain
Grant Jackson
Joe Azcue
22 Stan Williams 12.00 4.80
John Edwards
Jim Fairey
Phillies Rookies
(Hisle/Lersch)
23 W.S. Celebration 12.00 4.80
(Tigers celebrate)
Leon Wagner
John Bateman
Willie Smith
24 Yankees Rookies 12.00 4.80
(Closter/Cumberland)
Chris Cannizzaro
W.S. Game 5
(Kaline's hit)
Bob Hendley
25 Carl Yastrzemski DP 200.00 80.00
Rico Petrocelli
Joe Nossek
Cards Rookies
(Huntz/Torrez)

1969 Topps Bowie Kuhn

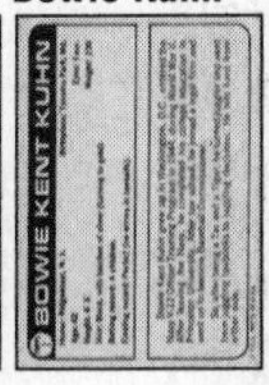

This one-card standard-size set was issued soon after Bowie Kuhn's elevation to Baseball Commissioner. The front features a superimposed photo of Kuhn in regal wear sitting on a base. The horizontal back features vital statistics as well as a brief biography.

NM Ex
1 Bowie Kuhn 40.00 16.00

1969 Topps Super

The cards in this 66-card set measure approximately 2 1/4" by 3 1/4". This beautiful Topps set was released independently of the regular baseball series of 1969. It is referred to as "Super Baseball" on the back of the card, a title which was also used for the postcard-size cards issued in 1970 and 1971. Complete sheets, and cards with square corners cut from these sheets, are sometimes encountered. The set numbering is in alphabetical order by teams within league. Cards from the far right of each row are usually found with a white line on the right edge. Although rarely seen, this set was issued in three-card cello packs. The set features Reggie Jackson in his Rookie Card year.

NM Ex
COMPLETE SET (66) 6000.00 2400.00
1 Dave McNally 15.00 6.00
2 Frank Robinson 200.00 80.00
3 Brooks Robinson 200.00 80.00
4 Ken Harrelson 20.00 8.00
5 Carl Yastrzemski 250.00 100.00
6 Ray Culp 15.00 6.00
7 Jim Fregosi 20.00 8.00
8 Rick Reichardt 15.00 6.00
9 Vic Davalillo 15.00 6.00
10 Luis Aparicio 80.00 32.00
11 Pete Ward 15.00 6.00
12 Joel Horlen 15.00 6.00
13 Luis Tiant 20.00 8.00
14 Sam McDowell 15.00 6.00
15 Jose Cardenal 15.00 6.00
16 Willie Horton 20.00 8.00
17 Denny McLain 25.00 10.00
18 Bill Freehan 20.00 8.00

19 Harmon Killebrew 150.00 60.00
20 Tony Oliva 30.00 12.00
21 Dean Chance 15.00 6.00
22 Joe Foy 15.00 6.00
23 Roger Nelson 15.00 6.00
24 Mickey Mantle 1000.00 400.00
25 Mel Stottlemyre 20.00 8.00
26 Roy White 20.00 8.00
27 Rick Monday 15.00 6.00
28 Reggie Jackson 500.00 200.00
29 Bert Campaneris 20.00 8.00
30 Frank Howard 25.00 10.00
31 Camilo Pascual 15.00 6.00
32 Tommy Davis 20.00 8.00
33 Don Mincher 15.00 6.00
34 Hank Aaron 500.00 200.00
35 Felipe Alou 25.00 10.00
36 Joe Torre 40.00 16.00
37 Ferguson Jenkins 80.00 32.00
38 Ron Santo 30.00 12.00
39 Billy Williams 80.00 32.00
40 Tommy Helms 15.00 6.00
41 Pete Rose 400.00 160.00
42 Joe Morgan 120.00 47.50
43 Jim Wynn 15.00 6.00
44 Curt Blefary 15.00 6.00
45 Willie Davis 15.00 6.00
46 Don Drysdale 100.00 40.00
47 Tom Haller 15.00 6.00
48 Rusty Staub 25.00 10.00
49 Maury Wills 30.00 12.00
50 Cleon Jones 15.00 6.00
51 Jerry Koosman 25.00 10.00
52 Tom Seaver 400.00 160.00
53 Richie Allen 25.00 10.00
54 Chris Short 15.00 6.00
55 Cookie Rojas 15.00 6.00
56 Matty Alou 15.00 6.00
57 Steve Blass 15.00 6.00
58 Roberto Clemente 600.00 240.00
59 Curt Flood 25.00 10.00
60 Bob Gibson 150.00 60.00
61 Tim McCarver 30.00 12.00
62 Dick Selma 15.00 6.00
63 Ollie Brown 15.00 6.00
64 Juan Marichal 100.00 40.00
65 Willie Mays 500.00 200.00
66 Willie McCovey 100.00 40.00

1969 Topps Stamps

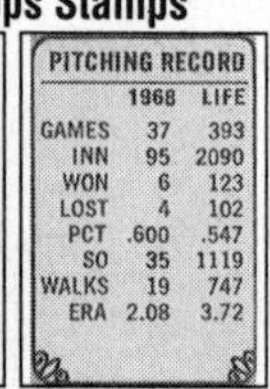

PITCHING RECORD	1968	LIFE
GAMES	37	393
INN	95	2090
WON	6	123
LOST	4	102
PCT	.600	.547
SO	35	1119
WALKS	19	747
ERA	2.08	3.72

The 1969 Topps set of baseball player stamps contains 240 individual stamps and 24 separate albums, 10 stamps and one album per major league team. The stamps were issued in strips of 12 and have gummed backs. Each stamp measures 1" by 1 7/16". The eight-page albums are bright orange and have an autograph feature on the back cover. The stamps are numbered here alphabetically within each team and the teams are listed in alphabetical order within league, e.g., Atlanta Braves NL (1-10), Chicago Cubs (11-20), Cincinnati Reds (21-30), Houston Astros (31-40), Los Angeles Dodgers (41-50), Montreal Expos (51-60), New York Mets (61-70), Philadelphia Phillies (71-80), Pittsburgh Pirates (81-90), San Diego Padres (91-100), San Francisco Giants (101-110), St. Louis Cardinals (111-120), Baltimore Orioles AL (121-130), Boston Red Sox (131-140), California Angels (141-150), Chicago White Sox (151-160), Cleveland Indians (161-170), Detroit Tigers (171-180), Kansas City Royals (181-190), Minnesota Twins (191-200), New York Yankees (201-210), Oakland A's (211-220), Seattle Pilots (221-230) and Washington Senators (231-240). Stamps still in the original uncut sheets are valued at twice the listed prices below.

NM Ex
COMPLETE SET (240) 200.00 80.00
WRAPPER (5-CENT)
1 Hank Aaron 12.00 4.80
2 Felipe Alou .75 .30
3 Clete Boyer .50 .20
4 Tito Francona .25 .10
5 Sonny Jackson .25 .10
6 Pat Jarvis .25 .10
7 Felix Millan .25 .10
8 Milt Pappas .50 .20
9 Ron Reed .25 .10
10 Joe Torre 1.50 .60
11 Ernie Banks 4.00 1.60
12 Glenn Beckert .25 .10
13 Bill Hands .25 .10
14 Randy Hundley .25 .10
15 Ferguson Jenkins 2.50 1.00
16 Don Kessinger .50 .20
17 Adolpho Phillips .25 .10
18 Phil Regan .25 .10
19 Ron Santo 1.50 .60
20 Billy Williams 2.50 1.00
21 Ted Abernathy .25 .10
22 Gerry Arrigo .25 .10
23 Johnny Bench 5.00 2.00
24 Tommy Helms .25 .10
25 Alex Johnson .25 .10
26 Jim Maloney .50 .20
27 Lee May .50 .20
28 Tony Perez 2.50 1.00
29 Pete Rose 15.00 6.00
30 Bobby Tolan .25 .10
31 Bob Aspromonte .25 .10
32 Larry Dierker .25 .10
33 Johnny Edwards .25 .10
34 Denny Lemaster .25 .10
35 Denis Menke .25 .10
36 Joe Morgan 3.00 1.20
37 Doug Rader .25 .10
38 Rusty Staub 1.00 .40
39 Don Wilson .25 .10
40 Jim Wynn .50 .20
41 Willie Davis .50 .20
42 Don Drysdale 2.50 1.00
43 Ron Fairly .25 .10
44 Len Gabrielson .25 .10
45 Tom Haller .25 .10
46 Jim LeFebvre .25 .10
47 Claude Osteen .50 .20
48 Paul Popovich .25 .10
49 Bill Singer .25 .10
50 Don Sutton 2.50 1.00
51 Jesus Alou .25 .10
52 Bob Bailey .25 .10
53 John Bateman .25 .10
54 Donn Clendenon .25 .10
55 Jim Grant .25 .10
56 Larry Jaster .25 .10
57 Mack Jones .25 .10
58 Manny Mota .50 .20
59 Gary Sutherland .25 .10
60 Maury Wills 1.00 .40
61 Tommie Agee .50 .20
62 Ed Charles .25 .10
63 Jerry Grote .25 .10
64 Bud Harrelson .25 .10
65 Cleon Jones .25 .10
66 Jerry Koosman .50 .20
67 Ed Kranepool .25 .10
68 Tom Seaver 8.00 3.20
69 Art Shamsky .25 .10
70 Ron Swoboda .25 .10
71 Richie Allen 1.00 .40
72 John Briggs .25 .10
73 Johnny Callison .50 .20
74 Clay Dalrymple .25 .10
75 Woodie Fryman .25 .10
76 Don Lock .25 .10
77 Cookie Rojas .50 .20
78 Chris Short .25 .10
79 Ron Taylor .25 .10
80 Rick Wise .25 .10
81 Gene Alley .25 .10
82 Matty Alou .50 .20
83 Steve Blass .25 .10
84 Jim Bunning 2.50 1.00
85 Roberto Clemente 20.00 8.00
86 Ron Kline .25 .10
87 Jerry May .25 .10
88 Bill Mazeroski 2.50 1.00
89 Willie Stargell 3.00 1.20
90 Bob Veale .25 .10
91 Jose Arcia .25 .10
92 Ollie Brown .25 .10
93 Al Ferrara .25 .10
94 Tony Gonzalez .25 .10
95 Dave Giusti .25 .10
96 Alvin McBean .25 .10
97 Roberto Pena .25 .10
98 Dick Selma .25 .10
99 Larry Stahl .25 .10
100 Zoilo Versalles .25 .10
101 Bobby Bolin .25 .10
102 Jim Davenport .25 .10
103 Dick Dietz .25 .10
104 Jim Ray Hart .25 .10
105 Ron Hunt .25 .10
106 Hal Lanier .25 .10
107 Juan Marichal 3.00 1.20
108 Willie Mays 10.00 4.00
109 Willie McCovey 3.00 1.20
110 Gaylord Perry 2.50 1.00
111 Nelson Briles .25 .10
112 Lou Brock 4.00 1.60
113 Orlando Cepeda 2.50 1.00
114 Curt Flood 1.00 .40
115 Bob Gibson 3.00 1.20
116 Julian Javier .25 .10
117 Dal Maxvill .25 .10
118 Tim McCarver 1.00 .40
119 Vada Pinson .75 .30
120 Mike Shannon .50 .20
121 Mark Belanger .50 .20
122 Curt Blefary .25 .10
123 Don Buford .25 .10
124 Jim Hardin .25 .10
125 Dave Johnson .75 .30
126 Dave McNally .50 .20
127 Tom Phoebus .25 .10
128 Boog Powell 1.00 .40
129 Brooks Robinson 4.00 1.60
130 Frank Robinson 4.00 1.60
131 Mike Andrews .25 .10
132 Ray Culp .25 .10
133 Russ Gibson .25 .10
134 Ken Harrelson .75 .01
135 Jim Lonborg .50 .20
136 Rico Petrocelli .50 .20
137 Jose Santiago .25 .10
138 George Scott .50 .20
139 Reggie Smith .75 .30
140 Carl Yastrzemski 5.00 2.00
141 George Brunet .25 .10
142 Vic Davalillo .25 .10
143 Eddie Fisher .25 .10
144 Jim Fregosi .50 .20
145 Bobby Knoop .25 .10
146 Jim McGlothlin .25 .10
147 Rick Reichardt .25 .10
148 Roger Repoz .25 .10
149 Bob Rodgers .25 .10
150 Tom Satriano .25 .10
151 Sandy Alomar .25 .10
152 Luis Aparicio 2.50 1.00
153 Ken Berry .25 .10
154 Joel Horlen .25 .10
155 Tommy John 1.50 .60
156 Duane Josephson .25 .10
157 Gary Peters .25 .10
158 Gary Wagner .25 .10
159 Pete Ward .25 .10
160 Wilbur Wood .25 .10
161 Max Alvis .25 .10
162 Joe Azcue .25 .10
163 Larry Brown .25 .10
164 Jose Cardenal .25 .10
165 Lee Maye .25 .10
166 Sam McDowell .50 .20
167 Sonny Siebert .25 .10
168 Duke Sims .25 .10
169 Luis Tiant 1.00 .40
170 Stan Williams .25 .10
171 Norm Cash 1.00 .40
172 Bill Freehan .50 .20
173 Willie Horton .50 .20
174 Al Kaline 4.00 1.60
175 Mickey Lolich .75 .30
176 Dick McAuliffe .25 .10
177 Denny McLain 1.00 .40
178 Jim Northrup .50 .20
179 Mickey Stanley .50 .20
180 Don Wert .25 .10
181 Jerry Adair .25 .10
182 Wally Bunker .25 .10
183 Moe Drabowsky .25 .10
184 Joe Foy .25 .10
185 Jackie Hernandez .25 .10
186 Roger Nelson .25 .10
187 Bob Oliver .25 .10
188 Paul Schaal .25 .10
189 Steve Whitaker .25 .10
190 Hoyt Wilhelm 2.50 1.00
191 Bob Allison .50 .20
192 Rod Carew 4.00 1.60
193 Dean Chance .50 .20
194 Jim Kaat 1.00 .40
195 Harmon Killebrew 3.00 1.20
196 Tony Oliva 1.50 .60
197 Ron Perranoski .25 .10
198 Johnny Roseboro .25 .10
199 Cesar Tovar .25 .10
200 Ted Uhlaender .25 .10
201 Stan Bahnsen .25 .10
202 Horace Clarke .25 .10
203 Jake Gibbs .25 .10
204 Andy Kosco .25 .10
205 Mickey Mantle 40.00 16.00
206 Joe Pepitone .50 .20
207 Bill Robinson .25 .10
208 Mel Stottlemyre .50 .20
209 Tom Tresh .50 .20
210 Roy White .50 .20
211 Sal Bando .50 .20
212 Bert Campaneris .50 .20
213 Danny Cater .25 .10
214 Dave Duncan .25 .10
215 Dick Green .25 .10
216 Jim Hunter 2.50 1.00
217 Lew Krausse .25 .10
218 Rick Monday .50 .20
219 Jim Nash .25 .10
220 John Odom .25 .10
221 Jack Aker .25 .10
222 Steve Barber .25 .10
223 Gary Bell .25 .10
224 Tommy Davis .50 .20
225 Tommy Harper .25 .10
226 Jerry McNertney .25 .10
227 Don Mincher .25 .10
228 Ray Oyler .25 .10
229 Rich Rollins .25 .10
230 Chico Salmon .25 .10
231 Bernie Allen .25 .10
232 Ed Brinkman .25 .10
233 Paul Casanova .25 .10
234 Joe Coleman .25 .10
235 Mike Epstein .25 .10
236 Jim Hannan .25 .10
237 Dennis Higgins .25 .10
238 Frank Howard 1.00 .40
239 Ken McMullen .25 .10
240 Camilo Pascual .25 .10

1969 Topps Stamp Albums

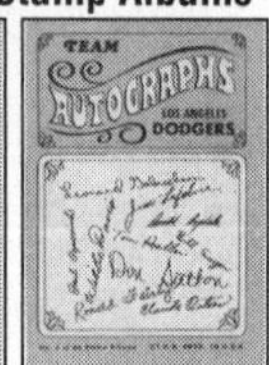

The 1969 Topps stamp set of baseball player stamps was intended to be mounted in 24 separate team albums, 10 stamps for that team's players going into that team's album. The eight-page albums are bright orange and have an autograph feature on the back cover. The albums measure approximately 2 1/2" by 3 1/2".

NM Ex
COMPLETE SET (24) 30.00 12.00
23 Seattle Pilots 2.50 1.00

1969 Topps Team Posters

This set was issued as a separate set by Topps, but was apparently not widely distributed. It was folded many times to fit the packaging and hence is typically found with relatively heavy fold creases. Each team poster measures approximately 12" by 20". These posters are in full color with a blank back. Each team features nine or ten individual players; a complete list is listed in the checklist below. Each player photo is accompanied by a facsimile autograph. The posters are numbered in the bottom left corner.

NM Ex
COMPLETE SET (24) 1200.00 475.00
WRAPPER (10-CENT)
1 Norm Cash 40.00 16.00
Al Kaline
Mickey Lolich
Denny McLain
Bill Freehan
Willie Horton
Dick McAuliffe
Jim Northrup
Mickey Stanley
Don Wert
Earl Wilson
2 Hank Aaron 60.00 24.00
Phil Niekro
Joe Torre
Felipe Alou
Clete Boyer
Rico Carty
Tito Francona
Sonny Jackson
Pat Jarvis
Felix Millan
Milt Pappas
3 Carl Yastrzemski 60.00 24.00
Mike Andrews
Tony Conigliaro
Ray Culp
Russ Gibson
Ken Harrelson
Jim Lonborg
Rico Petrocelli
Jose Santiago
George Scott
Reggie Smith
4 Ernie Banks 50.00 20.00
Billy Williams
Glenn Beckert
Bill Hands
Jim Hickman
Ken Holtzman
Randy Hundley
Fergie Jenkins
Don Kessinger
Adolpho Phillips
Ron Santo
5 Boog Powell 60.00 24.00
Brooks Robinson
Frank Robinson
Mark Belanger
Paul Blair
Don Buford
Andy Etchebarren
Jim Hardin
Dave Johnson
Dave McNally
Tom Phoebus
6 Joe Morgan 30.00 12.00
Curt Blefary
Donn Clendenon
Larry Dierker
John Edwards
Denny Lemaster
Denis Menke
Norm Miller
Doug Rader
Don Wilson
Jim Wynn
7 Wally Bunker 20.00 8.00
Jerry Adair
Mike Fiore
Joe Foy
Jackie Hernandez
Pat Kelly
Dave Morehead
Roger Nelson
Dave Nicholson
Ellie Rodriguez
Steve Whitaker
8 Richie Allen 20.00 8.00
John Callison
Woodie Fryman
Larry Hisle
Don Money
Cookie Rojas
Mike Ryan
Chris Short
Tony Taylor
Bill White
Rick Wise
9 Tommy Davis 40.00 16.00
Jack Aker
Steve Barber
Gary Bell
Jim Gosger
Tommy Harper
Jerry McNertney
Don Mincher
Ray Oyler
Rich Rollins
Chico Salmon
10 Rusty Staub 20.00 8.00
Maury Wills
Bob Bailey
John Bateman
Jack Billingham
Jim Grant
Larry Jaster
Mack Jones
Manny Mota
Gary Sutherland
Jimy Williams
11 Luis Aparicio 20.00 8.00
Tommy John
Sandy Alomar
Ken Berry
Buddy Bradford
Joel Horlen
Duane Josephson
Tom McCraw
Bill Melton
Pete Ward
Wilbur Wood
12 Ollie Brown 20.00 8.00
Jose Arcia
Danny Breeden
Bill Davis
Ron Davis
Tony Gonzalez
Dick Kelley
Al McBean
Roberto Pena
Dick Selma
Ed Spiezio
13 Luis Tiant 20.00 8.00
Max Alvis
Joe Azcue
Jose Cardenal
Vern Fuller
Lou Johnson
Sam McDowell
Sonny Siebert
Duke Sims
Russ Snyder
Zoilo Versalles
14 Juan Marichal 50.00 20.00
Willie Mays
Willie McCovey
Gaylord Perry
Bobby Bolin
Jim Davenport
Dick Dietz
Jim Ray Hart
Ron Hunt
Hal Lanier
Charley Smith
15 Rod Carew 30.00 12.00
Harmon Killebrew
Bob Allison
Chico Cardenas
Dean Chance
Jim Kaat
Tony Oliva
Jim Perry
John Roseboro
Cesar Tovar
Ted Uhlaender
16 Roberto Clemente 120.00 47.50
Willie Stargell
Gene Alley
Matty Alou
Steve Blass
Jim Bunning
Richie Hebner
Jerry May
Bill Mazeroski
Bob Robertson
Bob Veale
17 Hoyt Wilhelm 20.00 8.00
Ruben Amaro
George Brunet
Bob Chance
Vic Davalillo
Jim Fregosi
Bobby Knoop
Jim McGlothlin
Rick Reichardt
Roger Repoz
Bob Rodgers
18 Lou Brock 40.00 16.00
Orlando Cepeda
Curt Flood
Bob Gibson
Nellie Briles
Julian Javier
Dal Maxvill
Tim McCarver
Vada Pinson
Mike Shannon
Ray Washburn
19 Mickey Mantle 200.00 80.00
Mel Stottlemyre
Tom Tresh
Stan Bahnsen
Horace Clarke
Bobby Cox
Jake Gibbs
Joe Pepitone
Fritz Peterson
Bill Robinson
Roy White
20 Johnny Bench 100.00 40.00
Tony Perez
Pete Rose
Gerry Arrigo
Tommy Helms
Alex Johnson
Jim Maloney
Lee May
Gary Nolan
Bob Tolan
Woody Woodward
21 Jim Hunter 100.00 40.00
Reggie Jackson
Sal Bando
Bert Campaneris
Danny Cater
Dick Green
Mike Hershberger
Rick Monday
Jim Nash
John Odom
Jim Pagliaroni
22 Don Drysdale 30.00 12.00
Willie Crawford
Willie Davis
Ron Fairly
Tom Haller
Andy Kosco
Jim Lefevre
Claude Osteen
Paul Popovich
Bill Singer
Bill Sudakis
23 Frank Howard 20.00 8.00
Bernie Allen
Brant Alyea
Ed Brinkman
Paul Casanova
Joe Coleman
Mike Epstein
Jim Hannan
Ken McMullen
Camilo Pascual
Del Unser
24 Tom Seaver 100.00 40.00
Tommie Agee
Ken Boswell
Ed Charles
Jerry Grote
Bud Harrelson
Cleon Jones
Jerry Koosman
Ed Kranepool
Jim McAndrew
Ron Swoboda

1970 Topps

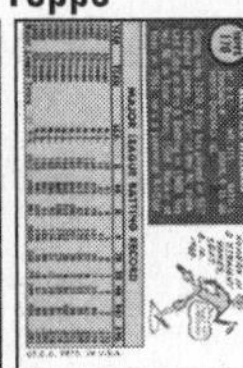

The cards in this 720-card set measure 2 1/2" by 3 1/2". The Topps set for 1970 has color photos surrounded by white frame lines and gray borders. The backs have a blue biographical section and a yellow record section. All-Star selections are featured on cards 450 to 469. Other topical subsets within this set include League Leaders (61-72), Playoffs cards (195-202), and World Series cards (305-310). There are graduations of scarcity, terminating in the high series (634-720), which are outlined in the value summary. Cards were issued in ten-card dime packs as well as thirty-three card cello packs quarter back encased in a small Topps box. The key Rookie Card in this set is Thurman Munson.

NM Ex
COMPLETE SET (720) 2500.00 1000.00
COMMON CARD (1-132) .75 .30
COMMON (373-459) 1.00 .40
COMMON CARD (373-459) 1.50 .60
COMMON (460-546) 2.00 .80
COMMON (547-633) 4.00 1.60
COMMON (634-720) 10.00 4.00
WRAPPER (10-CENT) 20.00 8.00
1 New York Mets 30.00 9.50
Team Card
2 Diego Segui 1.00 .40
3 Darrel Chaney .75 .30
4 Tom Egan .75 .30
5 Wes Parker 1.00 .40
6 Grant Jackson .75 .30
7 Gary Boyd .75 .30
Russ Nagelson
8 Jose Martinez .75 .30
9 Checklist 1 12.00 2.40
10 Carl Yastrzemski 20.00 8.00
11 Nate Colbert .75 .30
12 John Hiller .75 .30
13 Jack Hiatt .75 .30
14 Hank Allen .75 .30
15 Larry Dierker .75 .30
16 Charlie Metro MG .75 .30
17 Hoyt Wilhelm 4.00 1.60
18 Carlos May 1.00 .40
19 John Boccabella .75 .30
20 Dave McNally 1.00 .40
21 Vida Blue RC 4.00 1.60
Gene Tenace RC
22 Ray Washburn .75 .30
23 Bill Robinson 1.00 .40
24 Dick Selma .75 .30
25 Cesar Tovar .75 .30
26 Tug McGraw 2.00 .80
27 Chuck Hinton .75 .30
28 Billy Wilson .75 .30
29 Sandy Alomar 1.00 .40
30 Matty Alou 1.00 .40
31 Marty Pattin 1.00 .40
32 Harry Walker MG .75 .30
33 Don Wert .75 .30
34 Willie Crawford .75 .30
35 Joel Horlen .75 .30
36 Danny Breeden 1.00 .40
Bernie Carbo
37 Dick Drago .75 .30
38 Mack Jones .75 .30
39 Mike Nagy .75 .30
40 Rich Allen 2.00 .80
41 George Lauzerique .75 .30
42 Tito Fuentes .75 .30
43 Jack Aker .75 .30
44 Roberto Pena .75 .30
45 Dave Johnson 1.00 .40
46 Ken Rudolph .75 .30
47 Bob Miller .75 .30
48 Gil Garrido .75 .30
49 Tim Cullen .75 .30
50 Tommie Agee 1.00 .40
51 Bob Christian .75 .30
52 Bruce Dal Canton .75 .30
53 John Kennedy .75 .30
54 Jeff Torborg 1.00 .40
55 John Odom .75 .30
56 Joe Lis .75 .30
Scott Reid
57 Pat Kelly .75 .30
58 Dave Marshall .75 .30
59 Dick Ellsworth .75 .30
60 Jim Wynn 1.00 .40
61 Pete Rose 12.00 4.80
Bob Clemente
Cleon Jones LL
62 Rod Carew 2.00 .80
Reggie Smith
Tony Oliva LL
63 Willie McCovey 2.00 .80
Ron Santo
Tony Perez LL
64 Harmon Killebrew 4.00 1.60
Boog Powell
Reggie Jackson LL
65 Willie McCovey 4.00 1.60
Hank Aaron
Lee May LL
66 Harmon Killebrew 4.00 1.60
Frank Howard
Reggie Jackson LL
67 Juan Marichal 4.00 1.60
Steve Carlton
Bob Gibson LL
68 Dick Bosman 1.00 .40
Jim Palmer
Mike Cuellar LL
69 Tom Seaver 4.00 1.60
Phil Niekro
Fergie Jenkins
Juan Marichal LL
70 Dennis McLain 1.00 .40
Mike Cuellar
Dave Boswell
Dave McNally
Jim Perry
Mel Stottlemyre LL
71 Fergie Jenkins 2.00 .80
Bob Gibson
Bill Singer LL
72 Sam McDowell 1.00 .40
Mickey Lolich
Andy Messersmith LL
73 Wayne Granger .75 .30
74 Greg Washburn .75 .30
Wally Wolf
75 Jim Kaat 1.00 .40
76 Carl Taylor .75 .30
77 Frank Linzy .75 .30
78 Joe Lahoud .75 .30
79 Clay Kirby .75 .30
80 Don Kessinger 1.00 .40
81 Dave May .75 .30
82 Frank Fernandez .75 .30
83 Don Cardwell .75 .30
84 Paul Casanova .75 .30
85 Max Alvis .75 .30
86 Lum Harris MG .75 .30
87 Steve Renko RC .75 .30
88 Miguel Fuentes 1.00 .40
Dick Baney
89 Juan Rios .75 .30
90 Tim McCarver 1.00 .40
91 Rich Morales .75 .30
92 George Culver .75 .30
93 Rick Renick .75 .30
94 Freddie Patek 1.00 .40
95 Earl Wilson 1.00 .40
96 Leron Lee 1.00 .40
Jerry Reuss RC
97 Joe Moeller .75 .30
98 Gates Brown 1.00 .40
99 Bobby Pfeil .75 .30
100 Mel Stottlemyre 1.00 .40
101 Bobby Floyd .75 .30
102 Joe Rudi 1.00 .40
103 Frank Reberger .75 .30
104 Gerry Moses .75 .30
105 Tony Gonzalez .75 .30
106 Darold Knowles .75 .30
107 Bobby Etheridge .75 .30
108 Tom Burgmeier .75 .30
109 Garry Jestadt .75 .30
Carl Morton
110 Bob Moose .75 .30
111 Mike Hegan 1.00 .40
112 Dave Nelson .75 .30
113 Jim Ray .75 .30
114 Gene Michael 1.00 .40
115 Alex Johnson 1.00 .40
116 Sparky Lyle 1.00 .40
117 Don Young .75 .30
118 George Mitterwald .75 .30
119 Chuck Taylor .75 .30
120 Sal Bando 1.00 .40
121 Fred Beene .75 .30
Terry Crowley
122 George Stone .75 .30
123 Don Gutteridge MG .75 .30
124 Larry Jaster .75 .30
125 Deron Johnson .75 .30
126 Marty Martinez .75 .30
127 Joe Coleman .75 .30
128A Checklist 2 ERR 6.00 1.20
(226 R Perranoski)
128B Checklist 2 COR 6.00 1.20
(226 R. Perranoski)
129 Jimmie Price .75 .30
130 Ollie Brown .75 .30
131 Ray Lamb .75 .30
Bob Stinson
132 Jim McGlothlin .75 .30
133 Clay Carroll 1.00 .40
134 Danny Walton 1.00 .40
135 Dick Dietz 1.00 .40
136 Steve Hargan 1.00 .40
137 Art Shamsky 1.00 .40
138 Joe Foy 1.00 .40
139 Rich Nye 1.00 .40
140 Reggie Jackson 50.00 20.00
141 Dave Cash RC 1.50 .60
Johnny Jeter
142 Fritz Peterson 1.00 .40
143 Phil Gagliano 1.00 .40
144 Ray Culp 1.00 .40
145 Rico Carty 1.50 .60
146 Danny Murphy 1.00 .40
147 Angel Hermoso 1.00 .40
148 Earl Weaver MG 3.00 1.20
149 Billy Champion 1.00 .40
150 Harmon Killebrew 8.00 3.20
151 Dave Roberts 1.00 .40
152 Ike Brown 1.00 .40
153 Gary Gentry 1.00 .40
154 Jim Miles 1.00 .40
Jan Dukes
155 Denis Menke 1.00 .40
156 Eddie Fisher 1.00 .40
157 Manny Mota 1.50 .60
158 Jerry McNertney 1.50 .60
159 Tommy Helms 1.50 .60
160 Phil Niekro 5.00 2.00
161 Richie Scheinblum 1.00 .40
162 Jerry Johnson 1.00 .40
163 Syd O'Brien 1.00 .40
164 Ty Cline 1.00 .40
165 Ed Kirkpatrick 1.00 .40
166 Al Oliver 3.00 1.20
167 Bill Burbach 1.00 .40
168 Dave Watkins 1.00 .40
169 Tom Hall 1.00 .40
170 Billy Williams 5.00 2.00
171 Jim Nash 1.00 .40
172 Garry Hill 1.50 .60
Ralph Garr RC
173 Jim Hicks 1.00 .40
174 Ted Sizemore 1.50 .60
175 Dick Bosman 1.00 .40
176 Jim Ray Hart 1.50 .60
177 Jim Northrup 1.50 .60
178 Denny Lemaster 1.00 .40
179 Ivan Murrell 1.00 .40
180 Tommy John 1.50 .60
181 Sparky Anderson MG 5.00 2.00
182 Dick Hall 1.00 .40
183 Jerry Grote 1.50 .60
184 Ray Fosse 1.00 .40
185 Don Mincher 1.50 .60
186 Rick Joseph 1.00 .40
187 Mike Hedlund 1.00 .40
188 Manny Sanguillen 1.50 .60
189 Thurman Munson RC 80.00 32.00
Dave McDonald
190 Joe Torre 3.00 1.20
191 Vicente Romo 1.00 .40
192 Jim Qualls 1.00 .40
193 Mike Wegener 1.00 .40
194 Chuck Manuel 1.00 .40
195 Tom Seaver NLCS 15.00 6.00
196 Ken Boswell NLCS 2.00 .80
197 Nolan Ryan NLCS 30.00 12.00
198 NL Playoff Summary 15.00 6.00
Mets celebrate
(Nolan Ryan)
199 Mike Cuellar ALCS 2.00 .80
200 Boog Powell ALCS 3.00 1.20
201 Boog Powell ALCS 2.00 .80
Andy Etchebarren)
202 AL Playoff Summary 2.00 .80
Orioles celebrate
203 Rudy May 1.00 .40
204 Len Gabrielson 1.00 .40
205 Bert Campaneris 1.50 .60
206 Clete Boyer 1.50 .60
207 Norman McRae 1.00 .40
Bob Reed
208 Fred Gladding 1.00 .40
209 Ken Suarez 1.00 .40
210 Juan Marichal 5.00 2.00
211 Ted Williams MG UER 15.00 6.00
Throwing information on back incorrect
212 Al Santorini 1.00 .40
213 Andy Etchebarren 1.00 .40
214 Ken Boswell 1.00 .40
215 Reggie Smith 1.50 .60
216 Chuck Hartenstein 1.00 .40
217 Ron Hansen 1.00 .40
218 Ron Stone 1.00 .40
219 Jerry Kenney 1.00 .40
220 Steve Carlton 15.00 6.00
221 Ron Brand 1.00 .40
222 Jim Rooker 1.00 .40
223 Nate Oliver 1.00 .40
224 Steve Barber 1.50 .60
225 Lee May 1.50 .60
226 Ron Perranoski 1.00 .40
227 John Mayberry RC 1.50 .60
Bob Watkins
228 Aurelio Rodriguez 1.00 .40
229 Rich Robertson 1.00 .40
230 Brooks Robinson 15.00 6.00
231 Luis Tiant 1.50 .60
232 Bob Didier 1.00 .40
233 Lew Krausse 1.00 .40
234 Tommy Dean 1.00 .40
235 Mike Epstein 1.00 .40
236 Bob Veale 1.00 .40
237 Russ Gibson 1.00 .40
238 Jose Laboy 1.00 .40
239 Ken Berry 1.00 .40
240 Ferguson Jenkins 5.00 2.00
241 Al Fitzmorris 1.00 .40
Scott Northey
242 Walter Alston MG 3.00 1.20
243 Joe Sparma 1.00 .40
244A Checklist 3 6.00 1.20
(Red bat on front)
244B Checklist 3 6.00 1.20
(Brown bat on front)
245 Leo Cardenas 1.00 .40
246 Jim McAndrew 1.00 .40
247 Lou Klimchock 1.00 .40
248 Jesus Alou 1.00 .40
249 Bob Locker 1.00 .40
250 Willie McCovey UER 10.00 4.00
(1963 San Francisci)
251 Dick Schofield 1.00 .40
252 Lowell Palmer 1.00 .40
253 Ron Woods 1.00 .40
254 Camilo Pascual 1.00 .40
255 Jim Spencer 1.00 .40
256 Vic Davalillo 1.00 .40
257 Dennis Higgins 1.00 .40
258 Paul Popovich 1.00 .40
259 Tommie Reynolds 1.00 .40
260 Claude Osteen 1.00 .40
261 Curt Motton 1.00 .40
262 Jerry Morales 1.00 .40
Jim Williams
263 Duane Josephson 1.00 .40
264 Rich Hebner 1.00 .40
265 Randy Hundley 1.00 .40
266 Wally Bunker 1.00 .40
267 Herman Hill 1.00 .40
Paul Ratliff
268 Claude Raymond 1.00 .40
269 Cesar Gutierrez 1.00 .40
270 Chris Short 1.00 .40
271 Greg Goossen 1.50 .60
272 Hector Torres 1.00 .40
273 Ralph Houk MG 1.50 .60
274 Gerry Arrigo 1.00 .40
275 Duke Sims 1.00 .40
276 Ron Hunt 1.00 .40
277 Paul Doyle 1.00 .40
278 Tommie Aaron 1.00 .40
279 Bill Lee RC 1.50 .60
280 Donn Clendenon 1.50 .60
281 Casey Cox 1.00 .40
282 Steve Huntz 1.00 .40
283 Angel Bravo 1.00 .40
284 Jack Baldschun 1.00 .40
285 Paul Blair 1.50 .60
286 Jack Jenkins 5.00 2.00
Bill Buckner RC
287 Fred Talbot 1.00 .40
288 Larry Hisle 1.50 .60
289 Gene Brabender 1.00 .40
290 Rod Carew 15.00 6.00
291 Leo Durocher MG 3.00 1.20
292 Eddie Leon 1.00 .40
293 Bob Bailey 1.50 .60
294 Jose Azcue 1.00 .40
295 Cecil Upshaw 1.00 .40
296 Woody Woodward 1.00 .40
297 Curt Blefary 1.00 .40
298 Ken Henderson 1.00 .40
299 Buddy Bradford 1.00 .40
300 Tom Seaver 30.00 12.00
301 Chico Salmon 1.00 .40
302 Jeff James 1.00 .40
303 Brant Alyea 1.00 .40
304 Bill Russell RC 5.00 2.00
305 Don Buford WS 4.00 1.60
306 Donn Clendenon WS 4.00 1.60
307 Tommie Agee WS 4.00 1.60
308 J.C. Martin WS 4.00 1.60
309 Jerry Koosman WS 4.00 1.60
310 WS Summary 5.00 2.00
Mets whoop it up
311 Dick Green 1.00 .40
312 Mike Torrez 1.00 .40
313 Mayo Smith MG 1.00 .40
314 Bill McCool 1.00 .40
315 Luis Aparicio 5.00 2.00
316 Skip Guinn 1.00 .40
317 Billy Conigliaro 1.50 .60
Luis Alvarado
318 Willie Smith 1.00 .40
319 Clay Dalrymple 1.00 .40
320 Jim Maloney 1.50 .60
321 Lou Piniella 1.50 .60
322 Luke Walker 1.00 .40
323 Wayne Comer 1.00 .40
324 Tony Taylor 1.50 .60
325 Dave Boswell 1.00 .40
326 Bill Voss 1.00 .40
327 Hal King 1.00 .40
328 George Brunet 1.00 .40
329 Chris Cannizzaro 1.00 .40
330 Lou Brock 10.00 4.00
331 Chuck Dobson 1.00 .40
332 Bobby Wine 1.00 .40
333 Bobby Murcer 1.50 .60
334 Phil Regan 1.00 .40
335 Bill Freehan 1.50 .60
336 Del Unser 1.00 .40
337 Mike McCormick 1.50 .60
338 Paul Schaal 1.00 .40
339 Johnny Edwards 1.00 .40
340 Tony Conigliaro 3.00 1.20
341 Bill Sudakis 1.00 .40
342 Wilbur Wood 1.50 .60
343A Checklist 4 6.00 1.20
(Red bat on front)
343B Checklist 4 6.00 1.20
(Brown bat on front)
344 Marcelino Lopez 1.00 .40
345 Al Ferrara 1.00 .40
346 Red Schoendienst MG 1.50 .60
347 Russ Snyder 1.00 .40
348 Mike Jorgensen 1.50 .60
Jesse Hudson
349 Steve Hamilton 1.00 .40
350 Roberto Clemente 60.00 24.00
351 Tom Murphy 1.00 .40
352 Bob Barton 1.00 .40
353 Stan Williams 1.00 .40
354 Amos Otis 1.50 .60
355 Doug Rader 1.00 .40
356 Fred Lasher 1.00 .40
357 Bob Burda 1.00 .40
358 Pedro Borbon RC 1.50 .60
359 Phil Roof 1.50 .60
360 Curt Flood 1.50 .60
361 Ray Jarvis 1.00 .40
362 Joe Hague 1.00 .40
363 Tom Shopay 1.00 .40
364 Dan McGinn 1.00 .40
365 Zoilo Versalles 1.00 .40
366 Barry Moore 1.00 .40
367 Mike Lum 1.00 .40
368 Ed Herrmann 1.00 .40
369 Alan Foster 1.00 .40
370 Tommy Harper 1.50 .60
371 Rod Gaspar 1.00 .40
372 Dave Giusti 1.00 .40
373 Roy White 2.00 .80
374 Tommie Sisk 1.50 .60
375 Johnny Callison 2.00 .80
376 Lefty Phillips MG 1.50 .60
377 Bill Butler 1.50 .60
378 Jim Davenport 1.50 .60
379 Tom Tischinski 1.50 .60
380 Tony Perez 6.00 2.40
381 Bobby Brooks 1.50 .60
Mike Olivo
382 Jack DiLauro 1.50 .60
383 Mickey Stanley 2.00 .80
384 Gary Neibauer 1.50 .60
385 George Scott 2.00 .80
386 Bill Dillman 1.50 .60
387 Baltimore Orioles 3.00 1.20
Team Card
388 Byron Browne 1.50 .60
389 Jim Shellenback 1.50 .60
390 Willie Davis 2.00 .80
391 Larry Brown 1.50 .60
392 Walt Hriniak 2.00 .80
393 John Gelnar 1.50 .60
394 Gil Hodges MG 4.00 1.60
395 Walt Williams 1.50 .60
396 Steve Blass 2.00 .80
397 Roger Repoz 1.50 .60
398 Bill Stoneman 1.50 .60
399 New York Yankees 3.00 1.20
Team Card
400 Denny McLain 4.00 1.60
401 John Harrell 1.50 .60
Bernie Williams
402 Ellie Rodriguez 1.50 .60
403 Jim Bunning 6.00 2.40
404 Rich Reese 1.50 .60
405 Bill Hands 1.50 .60
406 Mike Andrews 1.50 .60
407 Bob Watson 2.00 .80
408 Paul Lindblad 1.50 .60
409 Bob Tolan 1.50 .60
410 Boog Powell 4.00 1.60
411 Los Angeles Dodgers 3.00 1.20
Team Card
412 Larry Burchart 1.50 .60
413 Sonny Jackson 1.50 .60
414 Paul Edmondson 1.50 .60
415 Julian Javier 2.00 .80
416 Joe Verbanic 1.50 .60
417 John Bateman 1.50 .60
418 John Donaldson 1.50 .60
419 Ron Taylor 1.50 .60
420 Ken McMullen 2.00 .80
421 Pat Dobson 2.00 .80
422 Royals Team 3.00 1.20
423 Jerry May 1.50 .60
424 Mike Kilkenny 1.50 .60
(Inconsistent design
card number in
white circle)
425 Bobby Bonds 6.00 2.40
426 Bill Rigney MG 1.50 .60
427 Fred Norman 1.50 .60
428 Don Buford 1.50 .60
429 Randy Bobb 1.50 .60
Jim Cosman
430 Andy Messersmith 2.00 .80
431 Ron Swoboda 2.00 .80
432A Checklist 5 6.00 1.20
(Baseball in
yellow letters)
432B Checklist 5 6.00 1.20
(Baseball in
white letters)
433 Ron Bryant 1.50 .60
434 Felipe Alou 2.00 .80
435 Nelson Briles 2.00 .80
436 Philadelphia Phillies 3.00 1.20
Team Card
437 Danny Cater 1.50 .60
438 Pat Jarvis 1.50 .60
439 Lee Maye 1.50 .60
440 Bill Mazeroski 6.00 2.40
441 John O'Donoghue 1.50 .60
442 Gene Mauch MG 2.00 .80
443 Al Jackson 1.50 .60
444 Billy Farmer 1.50 .60
John Matias
445 Vada Pinson 2.00 .80
446 Billy Grabarkewitz 1.50 .60
447 Lee Stange 1.50 .60
448 Houston Astros 3.00 1.20
Team Card
449 Jim Palmer 12.00 4.80
450 Willie McCovey AS 6.00 2.40
451 Boog Powell AS 4.00 1.60
452 Felix Millan AS 2.00 .80
453 Rod Carew AS 6.00 2.40
454 Ron Santo AS 4.00 1.60
455 Brooks Robinson AS 6.00 2.40
456 Don Kessinger AS 2.00 .80
457 Rico Petrocelli AS 4.00 1.60
458 Pete Rose AS 15.00 6.00
459 Reggie Jackson AS 12.00 4.80
460 Matty Alou AS 3.00 1.20
461 Carl Yastrzemski AS 10.00 4.00
462 Hank Aaron AS 15.00 6.00
463 Frank Robinson AS 8.00 3.20
464 Johnny Bench AS 15.00 6.00
465 Bill Freehan AS 3.00 1.20
466 Juan Marichal AS 5.00 2.00
467 Denny McLain AS 3.00 1.20
468 Jerry Koosman AS 3.00 1.20
469 Sam McDowell AS 3.00 1.20
470 Willie Stargell 10.00 4.00
471 Chris Zachary 2.00 .80
472 Braves Team 4.00 1.60
473 Don Bryant 2.00 .80
474 Dick Kelley 2.00 .80
475 Dick McAuliffe 3.00 1.20
476 Don Shaw 2.00 .80
477 Al Severinsen 2.00 .80
Roger Freed
478 Bobby Heise 2.00 .80
479 Dick Woodson 2.00 .80
480 Glenn Beckert 3.00 1.20
481 Jose Tartabull 2.00 .80
482 Tom Hilgendorf 2.00 .80
483 Gail Hopkins 2.00 .80
484 Gary Nolan 3.00 1.20
485 Jay Johnstone 3.00 1.20
486 Terry Harmon 2.00 .80
487 Cisco Carlos 2.00 .80
488 J.C. Martin 2.00 .80
489 Eddie Kasko MG 2.00 .80
490 Bill Singer 3.00 1.20
491 Graig Nettles 5.00 2.00
492 Keith Lampard 2.00 .80
Scipio Spinks
493 Lindy McDaniel 3.00 1.20
494 Larry Stahl 2.00 .80
495 Dave Morehead 2.00 .80
496 Steve Whitaker 2.00 .80
497 Eddie Watt 2.00 .80
498 Al Weis 2.00 .80
499 Skip Lockwood 3.00 1.20
500 Hank Aaron 50.00 20.00
501 Chicago White Sox 4.00 1.60
Team Card
502 Rollie Fingers 10.00 4.00
503 Dal Maxvill 2.00 .80
504 Don Pavletich 2.00 .80
505 Ken Holtzman 3.00 1.20
506 Ed Stroud 2.00 .80
507 Pat Corrales 2.00 .80
508 Joe Niekro 3.00 1.20
509 Montreal Expos 4.00 1.60
Team Card
510 Tony Oliva 5.00 2.00
511 Joe Hoerner 2.00 .80
512 Billy Harris 2.00 .80
513 Preston Gomez MG 2.00 .80
514 Steve Hovley 2.00 .80
515 Don Wilson 3.00 1.20
516 John Ellis 2.00 .80
Jim Lyttle
517 Joe Gibbon 2.00 .80
518 Bill Melton 2.00 .80
519 Don McMahon 2.00 .80
520 Willie Horton 3.00 1.20
521 Cal Koonce 2.00 .80
522 Angels Team 4.00 1.60

Card	NM	Ex
523 Jose Pena	2.00	.80
524 Alvin Dark MG	3.00	1.20
525 Jerry Adair	2.00	.80
526 Ron Herbel	2.00	.80
527 Don Bosch	2.00	.80
528 Elrod Hendricks	2.00	.80
529 Bob Aspromonte	2.00	.80
530 Bob Gibson	15.00	6.00
531 Ron Clark	2.00	.80
532 Danny Murtaugh MG	3.00	1.20
533 Buzz Stephen	2.00	.80
534 Minnesota Twins	4.00	1.60
Team Card		
535 Andy Kosco	2.00	.80
536 Mike Kekich	2.00	.80
537 Joe Morgan	10.00	4.00
538 Bob Humphreys	2.00	.80
539 Denny Doyle	8.00	3.20
Larry Bowa RC		
540 Gary Peters	2.00	.80
541 Bill Heath	2.00	.80
542 Checklist 6	6.00	1.20
543 Clyde Wright	2.00	.80
544 Cincinnati Reds	4.00	1.60
Team Card		
545 Ken Harrelson	3.00	1.20
546 Ron Reed	2.00	.80
547 Rick Monday	6.00	2.40
548 Howie Reed	4.00	1.60
549 St. Louis Cardinals	6.00	2.40
Team Card		
550 Frank Howard	6.00	2.40
551 Dock Ellis	6.00	2.40
552 Don O'Riley	4.00	1.60
Dennis Paepke		
Fred Rico		
553 Jim Lefebvre	6.00	2.40
554 Tom Timmermann	4.00	1.60
555 Orlando Cepeda	12.00	4.80
556 Dave Bristol MG	6.00	2.40
557 Ed Kranepool	6.00	2.40
558 Vern Fuller	4.00	1.60
559 Tommy Davis	6.00	2.40
560 Gaylord Perry	12.00	4.80
561 Tom McCraw	4.00	1.60
562 Ted Abernathy	4.00	1.60
563 Boston Red Sox	6.00	2.40
Team Card		
564 Johnny Briggs	4.00	1.60
565 Jim Hunter	12.00	4.80
566 Gene Alley	6.00	2.40
567 Bob Oliver	4.00	1.60
568 Stan Bahnsen	6.00	2.40
569 Cookie Rojas	6.00	2.40
570 Jim Fregosi	6.00	2.40
White Chevy Pick-Up in Background		
571 Jim Brewer	4.00	1.60
572 Frank Quilici	4.00	1.60
573 Mike Corkins	4.00	1.60
Rafael Robles		
Ron Slocum		
574 Bobby Bolin	6.00	2.40
575 Cleon Jones	6.00	2.40
576 Milt Pappas	6.00	2.40
577 Bernie Allen	4.00	1.60
578 Tom Griffin	4.00	1.60
579 Detroit Tigers	6.00	2.40
Team Card		
580 Pete Rose	60.00	24.00
581 Tom Satriano	4.00	1.60
582 Mike Paul	4.00	1.60
583 Hal Lanier	4.00	1.60
584 Al Downing	6.00	2.40
585 Rusty Staub	8.00	3.20
586 Rickey Clark	4.00	1.60
587 Jose Arcia	4.00	1.60
588A Checklist 7 ERR	8.00	1.60
(666 Adolfo)		
588B Checklist 7 COR	6.00	1.20
(666 Adolpho)		
589 Joe Keough	4.00	1.60
590 Mike Cuellar	6.00	2.40
591 Mike Ryan UER	4.00	1.60
(Pitching Record		
header on card back)		
592 Daryl Patterson	4.00	1.60
593 Chicago Cubs	8.00	3.20
Team Card		
594 Jake Gibbs	4.00	1.60
595 Maury Wills	8.00	3.20
596 Mike Hershberger	6.00	2.40
597 Sonny Siebert	4.00	1.60
598 Joe Pepitone	6.00	2.40
599 Dick Stelmaszek	4.00	1.60
Gene Martin		
Dick Such		
600 Willie Mays	80.00	32.00
601 Pete Richert	4.00	1.60
602 Ted Savage	4.00	1.60
603 Ray Oyler	4.00	1.60
604 Clarence Gaston	6.00	2.40
605 Rick Wise	6.00	2.40
606 Chico Ruiz	4.00	1.60
607 Gary Waslewski	4.00	1.60
608 Pittsburgh Pirates	6.00	2.40
Team Card		
609 Buck Martinez RC	6.00	2.40
(Inconsistent design		
card number in		
white circle)		
610 Jerry Koosman	8.00	3.20
611 Norm Cash	6.00	2.40
612 Jim Hickman	6.00	2.40
613 Dave Baldwin	6.00	2.40
614 Mike Shannon	6.00	2.40
615 Mark Belanger	6.00	2.40
616 Jim Merritt	4.00	1.60
617 Jim French	4.00	1.60
618 Billy Wynne	4.00	1.60
619 Norm Miller	4.00	1.60
620 Jim Perry	6.00	2.40
621 Mike McQueen	12.00	4.80
Darrell Evans RC		
Rick Kester		
622 Don Sutton	12.00	4.80
623 Horace Clarke	6.00	2.40
624 Clyde King MG	4.00	1.60
625 Dean Chance	4.00	1.60
626 Dave Ricketts	4.00	1.60
627 Gary Wagner	4.00	1.60
628 Wayne Garrett	4.00	1.60
629 Merv Rettenmund	4.00	1.60
630 Ernie Banks	50.00	20.00
631 Oakland Athletics	6.00	2.40
Team Card		
632 Gary Sutherland	4.00	1.60
633 Roger Nelson	4.00	1.60
634 Bud Harrelson	15.00	6.00
635 Bob Allison	15.00	6.00
636 Jim Stewart	10.00	4.00
637 Cleveland Indians	12.00	4.80
Team Card		
638 Frank Bertaina	10.00	4.00
639 Dave Campbell	15.00	6.00
640 Al Kaline	50.00	20.00
641 Al McBean	10.00	4.00
642 Greg Garrett	10.00	4.00
Gordon Lund		
Jarvis Tatum		
643 Jose Pagan	10.00	4.00
644 Gerry Nyman	10.00	4.00
645 Don Money	15.00	6.00
646 Jim Britton	10.00	4.00
647 Tom Matchick	10.00	4.00
648 Larry Haney	10.00	4.00
649 Jimmie Hall	10.00	4.00
650 Sam McDowell	15.00	6.00
651 Jim Gosger	10.00	4.00
652 Rich Rollins	15.00	6.00
653 Moe Drabowsky	10.00	4.00
654 Oscar Gamble RC	15.00	6.00
Boots Day		
Angel Mangual		
655 John Roseboro	15.00	6.00
656 Jim Hardin	10.00	4.00
657 San Diego Padres	12.00	4.80
Team Card		
658 Ken Tatum	10.00	4.00
659 Pete Ward	10.00	4.00
660 Johnny Bench	80.00	32.00
661 Jerry Robertson	10.00	4.00
662 Frank Lucchesi MG	10.00	4.00
663 Tito Francona	10.00	4.00
664 Bob Robertson	10.00	4.00
665 Jim Lonborg	15.00	6.00
666 Adolpho Phillips	10.00	4.00
667 Bob Meyer	15.00	6.00
668 Bob Tillman	10.00	4.00
669 Bart Johnson	10.00	4.00
Dan Lazar		
Mickey Scott		
670 Ron Santo	15.00	6.00
671 Jim Campanis	10.00	4.00
672 Leon McFadden	10.00	4.00
673 Ted Uhlaender	10.00	4.00
674 Dave Leonhard	10.00	4.00
675 Jose Cardenal	15.00	6.00
676 Washington Senators	12.00	4.80
Team Card		
677 Woodie Fryman	10.00	4.00
678 Dave Duncan	15.00	6.00
679 Ray Sadecki	10.00	4.00
680 Rico Petrocelli	15.00	6.00
681 Bob Garibaldi	10.00	4.00
682 Dalton Jones	10.00	4.00
683 Vern Geishert	15.00	6.00
Hal McRae		
Wayne Simpson		
684 Jack Fisher	10.00	4.00
685 Tom Haller	10.00	4.00
686 Jackie Hernandez	10.00	4.00
687 Bob Priddy	10.00	4.00
688 Ted Kubiak	15.00	6.00
689 Frank Tepedino	15.00	6.00
690 Ron Fairly	15.00	6.00
691 Joe Grzenda	10.00	4.00
692 Duffy Dyer	10.00	4.00
693 Bob Johnson	10.00	4.00
694 Gary Ross	10.00	4.00
695 Bobby Knoop	10.00	4.00
696 San Francisco Giants	12.00	4.80
Team Card		
697 Jim Hannan	10.00	4.00
698 Tom Tresh	15.00	6.00
699 Hank Aguirre	10.00	4.00
700 Frank Robinson	50.00	20.00
701 Jack Billingham	10.00	4.00
702 Bob Johnson	10.00	4.00
Ron Klimkowski		
Bill Zepp		
703 Lou Marone	10.00	4.00
704 Frank Baker	10.00	4.00
705 Tony Cloninger UER	10.00	4.00
(Batter headings		
on card back)		
706 John McNamara MG	10.00	4.00
707 Kevin Collins	10.00	4.00
708 Jose Santiago	10.00	4.00
709 Mike Fiore	10.00	4.00
710 Felix Millan	10.00	4.00
711 Ed Brinkman	10.00	4.00
712 Nolan Ryan	200.00	80.00
713 Seattle Pilots	25.00	10.00
Team Card		
714 Al Spangler	10.00	4.00
715 Mickey Lolich	15.00	6.00
716 Sal Campisi	15.00	6.00
Reggie Cleveland		
Santiago Guzman		
717 Tom Phoebus	10.00	4.00
718 Ed Spiezio	10.00	4.00
719 Jim Roland	10.00	4.00
720 Rick Reichardt	15.00	5.00

1970 Topps Booklets

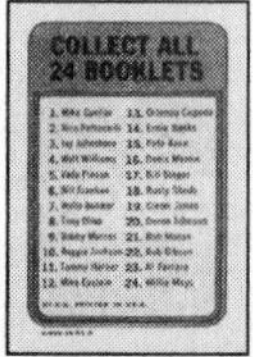

Inserted into packages of the 1970 Topps (and O-Pee-Chee) regular issue of cards, there are 24 miniature biographies of ballplayers in the set. Each numbered paper booklet contains six pages of comic book style story and a checklist of the booklet is available on the back page. These little booklets measure approximately 2 1/2" by 3 7/16".

	NM	Ex
COMPLETE SET (24)	40.00	16.00
COMMON CARD (1-16)	.75	.30
COMMON CARD (17-24)	1.00	.01
1 Mike Cuellar	.75	.30
2 Rico Petrocelli	1.00	.40
3 Jay Johnstone	1.00	.40
4 Walt Williams	.75	.30
5 Vada Pinson	1.25	.50
6 Bill Freehan	1.25	.50
7 Wally Bunker	.75	.30
8 Tony Oliva	1.50	.60
9 Bobby Murcer	1.25	.50
10 Reggie Jackson	6.00	2.40
11 Tommy Harper	.75	.30
12 Mike Epstein	.75	.30
13 Orlando Cepeda	3.00	1.20
14 Ernie Banks	5.00	2.00
15 Pete Rose	6.00	2.40
16 Denis Menke	.75	.30
17 Bill Singer	1.00	.40
18 Rusty Staub	1.25	.50
19 Cleon Jones	1.00	.40
20 Deron Johnson	1.00	.40
21 Bob Moose	1.00	.40
22 Bob Gibson	5.00	2.00
23 Al Ferrara	1.00	.40
24 Willie Mays	8.00	3.20

1970 Topps Candy Lid

This 24-card set features color player portraits printed on the bottom of candy lids and measures approximately 1 7/8" in diameter. The lids are unnumbered and checklisted below in alphabetical order.

	NM	Ex
COMPLETE SET (24)	2000.00	800.00
1 Hank Aaron	250.00	100.00
2 Rich Allen	80.00	32.00
3 Luis Aparicio	100.00	40.00
4 Johnny Bench	200.00	80.00
5 Ollie Brown	50.00	20.00
6 Willie Davis	50.00	20.00
7 Jim Fregosi	50.00	20.00
8 Mike Hegan	50.00	20.00
9 Frank Howard	60.00	24.00
10 Reggie Jackson	250.00	100.00
11 Fergie Jenkins	120.00	47.50
12 Harmon Killebrew	120.00	47.50
13 Bill Mazeroski	100.00	40.00
14 Juan Marichal	120.00	47.50
15 Tim McCarver	60.00	24.00
16 Sam McDowell	50.00	20.00
17 Denny McLain	50.00	20.00
18 Lou Piniella	50.00	20.00
19 Frank Robinson	150.00	60.00
20 Tom Seaver	150.00	60.00
21 Rusty Staub	50.00	20.00
22 Mel Stottlemyre	50.00	20.00
23 Jim Wynn	50.00	20.00
24 Carl Yastrzemski	150.00	60.00

1970 Topps Cloth Stickers

These stickers measure the standard size, and so far all found seem to be all from the 2nd series in 1970. These cards were intended to be pasted on jackets. Obviously this checklist is far from complete so any further information is greatly appreciated.

	NM	Ex
216 Chuck Hartenstein	500.00	200.00
226 Ron Perranoski	500.00	200.00
238 Coco Laboy	500.00	200.00
257 Dennis Higgins	500.00	200.00

1970 Topps Posters Inserts

In 1970 Topps raised its price per package of cards to ten cents, and a series of 24 color posters was included as a bonus to the collector. Each thin-paper poster is numbered and features a large portrait and a smaller black and white action pose. It was folded five times to fit in the packaging. Each poster measures 8 11/16" by 9 5/8".

	NM	Ex
COMPLETE SET (24)	60.00	24.00
1 Joe Horlen	1.00	.40
2 Phil Niekro	4.00	1.60
3 Willie Davis	1.50	.60
4 Lou Brock	5.00	2.00
5 Ron Santo	3.00	1.20
6 Ken Harrelson	1.50	.60
7 Willie McCovey	5.00	2.00
8 Rick Wise	1.00	.40
9 Andy Messersmith	1.00	.40
10 Ron Fairly	1.00	.40
11 Johnny Bench	10.00	4.00
12 Frank Robinson	8.00	3.20
13 Tommie Agee	1.50	.60
14 Roy White	1.50	.60
15 Larry Dierker	1.00	.40
16 Rod Carew	6.00	2.40
17 Don Mincher	1.00	.40
18 Ollie Brown	1.00	.40
19 Ed Kirkpatrick	1.00	.40
20 Reggie Smith	1.50	.60
21 Roberto Clemente	20.00	8.00
22 Frank Howard	2.00	.80
23 Bert Campaneris	1.00	.40
24 Denny McLain	2.00	.80

1970 Topps Scratchoffs

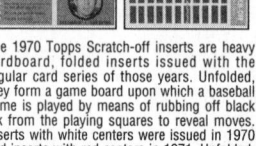

The 1970 Topps Scratch-off inserts are heavy cardboard, folded inserts issued with the regular card series of those years. Unfolded, they form a game board upon which a baseball game is played by means of rubbing off black ink from the playing squares to reveal moves. Inserts with white centers were issued in 1970 and inserts with red centers in 1971. Unfolded, these inserts measure 3 3/8" by 5". Obviously, a card which has been scratched off can be considered to be in no better than vg condition.

	NM	Ex
COMPLETE SET (24)	50.00	20.00
1 Hank Aaron	8.00	3.20
2 Rich Allen	1.50	.60
3 Luis Aparicio	4.00	1.60
4 Sal Bando	.75	.30
5 Glenn Beckert	.75	.30
6 Dick Bosman	.75	.30
7 Nate Colbert	.75	.30
8 Mike Hegan	.75	.30
9 Mack Jones	.75	.30
10 Al Kaline	4.00	1.60
11 Harmon Killebrew	4.00	1.60
12 Juan Marichal	4.00	1.60
13 Tim McCarver	2.00	.80
14 Sam McDowell	1.00	.40
15 Claude Osteen	.75	.30
16 Tony Perez	4.00	1.60
17 Lou Piniella	1.50	.60
18 Boog Powell	1.50	.60
19 Tom Seaver	6.00	2.40
20 Jim Spencer	.75	.30
21 Willie Stargell	4.00	1.60
22 Mel Stottlemyre	1.00	.40
23 Jim Wynn	1.00	.40
24 Carl Yastrzemski	4.00	1.60

1970 Topps Super

The cards in this 42-card set measure approximately 3 1/8" by 5 1/4". The 1970 Topps Super set was a separate Topps issue printed on heavy stock and marketed in its own wrapper with gum. The blue and yellow backs are identical to the respective player's backs in the 1970 Topps regular issue. Cards 38, Boog Powell, is the key card of the set; other short print run cards are listed in the checklist with SP. The obverse pictures are borderless and contain a facsimile autograph. The set was issued in three-card wax packs which came 24 packs to a box and 24 boxes to a case.

	NM	Ex
COMPLETE SET (42)	250.00	100.00
COMMON CARD (1-42)	2.00	.80
WRAPPER (10-CENT)		
COMMON SP	4.00	1.60
1 Claude Osteen SP	4.00	1.60
2 Sal Bando SP	4.00	1.60
3 Luis Aparicio SP	5.00	2.00
4 Harmon Killebrew	5.00	2.00
5 Tom Seaver SP	25.00	10.00
6 Larry Dierker	2.50	1.00
7 Bill Freehan	2.50	1.00
8 Johnny Bench	15.00	6.00
9 Tommy Harper	2.00	.80
10 Sam McDowell	2.00	.80
11 Lou Brock	5.00	2.00
12 Roberto Clemente	30.00	12.00
13 Willie McCovey	5.00	2.00
14 Rico Petrocelli	2.00	.80
15 Phil Niekro	4.00	1.60
16 Frank Howard	2.50	1.00
17 Denny McLain	2.50	1.00
18 Willie Mays	20.00	8.00
19 Willie Stargell	5.00	2.00
20 Joel Horlen	2.00	.80
21 Ron Santo	3.00	1.20
22 Dick Bosman	2.00	.80
23 Tim McCarver	3.00	1.20
24 Hank Aaron	20.00	8.00
25 Andy Messersmith	2.00	.80
26 Tony Oliva	3.00	1.20
27 Mel Stottlemyre	2.50	1.00
28 Reggie Jackson	15.00	6.00
29 Carl Yastrzemski	15.00	6.00
30 Jim Fregosi	2.50	1.00
31 Vada Pinson	2.50	1.00
32 Lou Piniella	3.00	1.20
33 Bob Gibson	5.00	2.00
34 Pete Rose	20.00	8.00
35 Jim Wynn	2.50	1.00
36 Ollie Brown SP	6.00	2.40
37 Frank Robinson SP	20.00	8.00
38 Boog Powell SP	50.00	20.00
39 Willie Davis SP	4.00	1.60
40 Billy Williams SP	10.00	4.00
41 Rusty Staub	3.00	1.20
42 Tommie Agee	2.50	1.00

1971 Topps

The cards in this 752-card set measure 2 1/2" by 3 1/2". The 1971 Topps set is a challenge to complete in strict mint condition because the black obverse border is easily scratched and damaged. An unusual feature of this set is that the player is also pictured in black and white on the back of the card. Featured subsets within this set include League Leaders (61-72), Playoffs cards (195-202), and World Series cards (327-332). Cards 524-643 and the last series (644-752) are somewhat scarce. The last series was printed in two sheets of 132. On the printing sheets 44 cards were printed in 50 percent greater quantity than the other 66 cards. These 66 (slightly) shorter-printed numbers are identified in the checklist below by SP. The key Rookie Cards in this set are the multi-player Rookie Card of Dusty Baker and Don Baylor and the individual cards of Bert Blyleven, Dave Concepcion, Steve Garvey, and Ted Simmons. The Jim Northrup and Jim Nash cards have been seen with our without printing "blotches" on the card. There is still debate on whether those two cards are just printing issues or legitimate variations.

	NM	Ex
COMPLETE SET (752)	2500.00	1000.00
COMMON CARD (1-393)	1.50	.60
COMMON (394-523)	2.50	1.00
COMMON (524-643)	4.00	1.60
COMMON (644-752)	8.00	3.20
COMMON SP (644-752)	12.00	4.80
WRAPPER (10-CENT)	15.00	6.00
1 Baltimore Orioles	20.00	6.75
Team Card		
2 Dock Ellis	1.50	.60
3 Dick McAuliffe	2.00	.80
4 Vic Davalillo	1.50	.60
5 Thurman Munson	60.00	24.00
6 Ed Spiezio	1.50	.60
7 Jim Holt	1.50	.60
8 Mike McQueen	1.50	.60
9 George Scott	2.00	.80
10 Claude Osteen	2.00	.80
11 Elliott Maddox	1.50	.60
12 Johnny Callison	2.00	.80
13 Charlie Brinkman	1.50	.60
Dick Moloney		
14 Dave Concepcion RC	15.00	6.00
15 Andy Messersmith	2.00	.80
16 Ken Singleton RC	4.00	1.60
17 Billy Sorrell	1.50	.60
18 Norm Miller	1.50	.60
19 Skip Pitlock	1.50	.60
20 Reggie Jackson	50.00	20.00
21 Dan McGinn	1.50	.60
22 Phil Roof	1.50	.60
23 Oscar Gamble	1.50	.60
24 Rich Hand	1.50	.60
25 Clarence Gaston	2.00	.80
26 Bert Blyleven RC	20.00	8.00
27 Fred Cambria	1.50	.60
Gene Clines		
28 Ron Klimkowski	1.50	.60
29 Don Buford	1.50	.60
30 Phil Niekro	6.00	2.40
31 Eddie Kasko MG	1.50	.60
32 Jerry DaVanon	1.50	.60
33 Del Unser	1.50	.60
34 Sandy Vance	1.50	.60
35 Lou Piniella	2.00	.80
36 Dean Chance	2.00	.80
37 Rich McKinney	1.50	.60
38 Jim Colborn	1.50	.60
39 Lerrin LaGrow	2.00	.80
Gene Lamont RC		
40 Lee May	2.00	.80
41 Rick Austin	1.50	.60
42 Boots Day	1.50	.60
43 Steve Kealey	1.50	.60
44 Johnny Edwards	1.50	.60
45 Jim Hunter	6.00	2.40
46 Dave Campbell	2.00	.80
47 Johnny Jeter	1.50	.60
48 Dave Baldwin	1.50	.60
49 Don Money	1.50	.60
50 Willie McCovey	10.00	4.00
51 Steve Kline	1.50	.60
52 Oscar Brown	1.50	.60
Earl Williams RC		
53 Paul Blair	2.00	.80
54 Checklist 1	10.00	2.00
55 Steve Carlton	20.00	8.00
56 Duane Josephson	1.50	.60
57 Von Joshua	1.50	.60
58 Bill Lee	2.00	.80
59 Gene Mauch MG	2.00	.80
60 Dick Bosman	1.50	.60
61 Alex Johnson	4.00	1.60
Carl Yastrzemski		
Tony Oliva LL		
62 Rico Carty	2.00	.80

Joe Torre
Manny Sanguillen LL
63 Frank Howard 4.00 1.60
Tony Conigliaro
Boog Powell LL
64 Johnny Bench 6.00 2.40
Tony Perez
Billy Williams LL
65 Frank Howard 4.00 1.60
Harmon Killebrew
Carl Yastrzemski LL
66 Johnny Bench 6.00 2.40
Billy Williams
Tony Perez LL
67 Diego Segui 4.00 1.60
Jim Palmer
Clyde Wright LL
68 Tom Seaver 4.00 1.60
Wayne Simpson
Luke Walker LL
69 Mike Cuellar 2.00 .80
Dave McNally
Jim Perry LL
70 Bob Gibson 6.00 2.40
Gaylord Perry
Fergie Jenkins LL
71 Sam McDowell 2.00 .80
Mickey Lolich
Bob Johnson LL
72 Tom Seaver 6.00 2.40
Bob Gibson
Fergie Jenkins LL
73 George Brunet 1.50 .60
74 Pete Hamm 1.50 .60
Jim Nettles
75 Gary Nolan 2.00 .80
76 Ted Savage 1.50 .60
77 Mike Compton 1.50 .60
78 Jim Spencer 1.50 .60
79 Wade Blasingame 1.50 .60
80 Bill Melton 1.50 .60
81 Felix Millan 1.50 .60
82 Casey Cox 1.50 .60
83 Tim Foli RC 2.00 .80
Randy Bobb
84 Marcel Lachemann RC 1.50 .60
85 Billy Grabarkewitz 1.50 .60
86 Mike Kilkenny 1.50 .60
87 Jack Heidemann 1.50 .60
88 Hal King 1.50 .60
89 Ken Brett 1.50 .60
90 Joe Pepitone 2.00 .80
91 Bob Lemon MG 2.00 .80
92 Fred Wenz 1.50 .60
93 Norm McRae 1.50 .60
Denny Riddleberger
94 Don Hahn 1.50 .60
95 Luis Tiant 2.00 .80
96 Joe Hague 1.50 .60
97 Floyd Wicker 1.50 .60
98 Joe Decker 1.50 .60
99 Mark Belanger 2.00 .80
100 Pete Rose 80.00 32.00
101 Les Cain 1.50 .60
102 Ken Forsch 2.00 .80
Larry Howard
103 Rich Severson 1.50 .60
104 Dan Frisella 1.50 .60
105 Tony Conigliaro 2.00 .80
106 Tom Dukes 1.50 .60
107 Roy Foster 1.50 .60
108 John Cumberland 1.50 .60
109 Steve Hovley 1.50 .60
110 Bill Mazeroski 6.00 2.40
111 Loyd Colson 1.50 .60
Bobby Mitchell
112 Manny Mota 2.00 .80
113 Jerry Crider 1.50 .60
114 Billy Conigliaro 2.00 .80
115 Donn Clendenon 2.00 .80
116 Ken Sanders 1.50 .60
117 Ted Simmons RC 8.00 3.20
118 Cookie Rojas 2.00 .80
119 Frank Lucchesi MG 1.50 .60
120 Willie Horton 2.00 .80
121 Jim Dunegan 1.50 .60
Roe Skidmore
122 Eddie Watt 1.50 .60
123A Checklist 2 10.00 2.00
(Card number
at bottom right)
123B Checklist 2 10.00 2.00
(Card number
centered)
124 Don Gullett RC 2.00 .80
125 Ray Fosse 1.50 .60
126 Danny Coombs 1.50 .60
127 Danny Thompson 2.00 .80
128 Frank Johnson 1.50 .60
129 Aurelio Monteagudo 1.50 .60
130 Denis Menke 1.50 .60
131 Curt Blefary 1.50 .60
132 Jose Laboy 1.50 .60
133 Mickey Lolich 2.00 .80
134 Jose Arcia 1.50 .60
135 Rick Monday 2.00 .80
136 Duffy Dyer 1.50 .60
137 Marcelino Lopez 1.50 .60
138 Joe Lis 2.00 .80
Willie Montanez
139 Paul Casanova 1.50 .60
140 Gaylord Perry 6.00 2.40
141 Frank Quilici 1.50 .60
142 Mack Jones 1.50 .60
143 Steve Blass 2.00 .80
144 Jackie Hernandez 1.50 .60
145 Bill Singer 2.00 .80
146 Ralph Houk MG 2.00 .80
147 Bob Priddy 1.50 .60
148 John Mayberry 2.00 .80
149 Mike Hershberger 1.50 .60
150 Sam McDowell 2.00 .80
151 Tommy Davis 2.00 .80
152 Lloyd Allen 1.50 .60
Winston Llenas
153 Gary Ross 1.50 .60
154 Cesar Gutierrez 1.50 .60
155 Ken Henderson 1.50 .60
156 Bart Johnson 1.50 .60
157 Bob Bailey 2.00 .80
158 Jerry Reuss 2.00 .80
159 Jarvis Tatum 1.50 .60
160 Tom Seaver 30.00 12.00
161 Coin Checklist 10.00 2.00
162 Jack Billingham 1.50 .60
163 Buck Martinez 2.00 .80
164 Frank Duffy 2.00 .80
Milt Wilcox
165 Cesar Tovar 1.50 .60
166 Joe Hoerner 1.50 .60
167 Tom Grieve RC 2.00 .80
168 Bruce Dal Canton 1.50 .60
169 Ed Herrmann 1.50 .60
170 Mike Cuellar 2.00 .80
171 Bobby Wine 1.50 .60
172 Duke Sims 1.50 .60
173 Gil Garrido 1.50 .60
174 Dave LaRoche 1.50 .60
175 Jim Hickman 1.50 .60
176 Bob Montgomery RC 2.00 .80
Doug Griffin
177 Hal McRae 2.00 .80
178 Dave Duncan 2.00 .80
179 Mike Corkins 1.50 .60
180 Al Kaline UER 20.00 8.00
(Home instead
of Birth)
181 Hal Lanier 1.50 .60
182 Al Downing 2.00 .80
183 Gil Hodges MG 4.00 1.60
184 Stan Bahnsen 1.50 .60
185 Julian Javier 1.50 .60
186 Bob Spence 1.50 .60
187 Ted Abernathy 1.50 .60
188 Bob Valentine RC 6.00 2.40
Mike Strahler
189 George Mitterwald 1.50 .60
190 Bob Tolan 1.50 .60
191 Mike Andrews 1.50 .60
192 Billy Wilson 1.50 .60
193 Bob Grich RC 4.00 1.60
194 Mike Lum 1.50 .60
195 Boog Powell ALCS 2.00 .80
196 Dave McNally ALCS 2.00 .80
197 Jim Palmer ALCS 4.00 1.60
198 AL Playoff Summary 2.00 .80
Orioles celebrate
199 Ty Cline NLCS 2.00 .80
200 Bobby Tolan NLCS 2.00 .80
201 Ty Cline NLCS 2.00 .80
202 NL Playoff Summary 2.00 .80
Reds celebrate
203 Larry Gura 2.00 .80
204 Bernie Smith 1.50 .60
George Kopacz
205 Gerry Moses 1.50 .60
206 Checklist 3 10.00 2.00
207 Alan Foster 1.50 .60
208 Billy Martin MG 4.00 1.60
209 Steve Renko 1.50 .60
210 Rod Carew 15.00 6.00
211 Phil Hennigan 1.50 .60
212 Rich Hebner 2.00 .80
213 Frank Baker 1.50 .60
214 Al Ferrara 1.50 .60
215 Diego Segui 1.50 .60
216 Reggie Cleveland 1.50 .60
Luis Melendez
217 Ed Stroud 1.50 .60
218 Tony Cloninger 1.50 .60
219 Elrod Hendricks 1.50 .60
220 Ron Santo 4.00 1.60
221 Dave Morehead 1.50 .60
222 Bob Watson 2.00 .80
223 Cecil Upshaw 1.50 .60
224 Alan Gallagher 1.50 .60
225 Gary Peters 1.50 .60
226 Bill Russell 2.00 .80
227 Floyd Weaver 1.50 .60
228 Wayne Garrett 1.50 .60
229 Jim Hannan 1.50 .60
230 Willie Stargell 15.00 6.00
231 Vince Colbert 2.00 .80
John Lowenstein RC
232 John Strohmayer 1.50 .60
233 Larry Bowa 2.00 .80
234 Jim Lyttle 1.50 .60
235 Nate Colbert 1.50 .60
236 Bob Humphreys 1.50 .60
237 Cesar Cedeno RC 2.00 .80
238 Chuck Dobson 1.50 .60
239 Red Schoendienst MG 2.00 .80
240 Clyde Wright 1.50 .60
241 Dave Nelson 1.50 .60
242 Jim Ray 1.50 .60
243 Carlos May 1.50 .60
244 Bob Tillman 1.50 .60
245 Jim Kaat 2.00 .80
246 Tony Taylor 1.50 .60
247 Jerry Cram 2.00 .80
Paul Splittorff
248 Hoyt Wilhelm 6.00 2.40
249 Chico Salmon 1.50 .60
250 Johnny Bench 50.00 20.00
251 Frank Reberger 1.50 .60
252 Eddie Leon 1.50 .60
253 Bill Sudakis 1.50 .60
254 Cal Koonce 1.50 .60
255 Bob Robertson 2.00 .80
256 Tony Gonzalez 1.50 .60
257 Nelson Briles 2.00 .80
258 Dick Green 1.50 .60
259 Dave Marshall 1.50 .60
260 Tommy Harper 2.00 .80
261 Darold Knowles 1.50 .60
262 Jim Williams 1.50 .60
Dave Robinson
263 John Ellis 1.50 .60
264 Joe Morgan 8.00 3.20
265 Jim Northrup 2.00 .80
266 Bill Stoneman 1.50 .60
267 Rich Morales 1.50 .60
268 Philadelphia Phillies 4.00 1.60
Team Card
269 Gail Hopkins 1.50 .60
270 Rico Carty 2.00 .80
271 Bill Zepp 1.50 .60
272 Tommy Helms 2.00 .80
273 Pete Richert 1.50 .60
274 Ron Slocum 1.50 .60
275 Vada Pinson 2.00 .80
276 Mike Davison 8.00 3.20
George Foster RC
277 Gary Waslewski 1.50 .60
278 Jerry Grote 2.00 .80
279 Lefty Phillips MG 1.50 .60
280 Ferguson Jenkins 6.00 2.40
281 Danny Walton 1.50 .60
282 Jose Pagan 1.50 .60
283 Dick Such 1.50 .60
284 Jim Gosger 1.50 .60
285 Sal Bando 2.00 .80
286 Jerry McNertney 1.50 .60
287 Mike Fiore 1.50 .60
288 Joe Moeller 1.50 .60
289 Chicago White Sox 4.00 1.60
Team Card
290 Tony Oliva 4.00 1.60
291 George Culver 1.50 .60
292 Jay Johnstone 2.00 .80
293 Pat Corrales 2.00 .80
294 Steve Dunning 1.50 .60
295 Bobby Bonds 4.00 1.60
296 Tom Timmermann 1.50 .60
297 Johnny Briggs 1.50 .60
298 Jim Nelson 1.50 .60
299 Ed Kirkpatrick 1.50 .60
300 Brooks Robinson 20.00 8.00
301 Earl Wilson 1.50 .60
302 Phil Gagliano 1.50 .60
303 Lindy McDaniel 2.00 .80
304 Ron Brand 1.50 .60
305 Reggie Smith 2.00 .80
306 Jim Nash 1.50 .60
307 Don Wert 1.50 .60
308 St. Louis Cardinals 4.00 1.60
Team Card
309 Dick Ellsworth 1.50 .60
310 Tommie Agee 2.00 .80
311 Lee Stange 1.50 .60
312 Harry Walker MG 1.50 .60
313 Tom Hall 1.50 .60
314 Jeff Torborg 2.00 .80
315 Ron Fairly 2.00 .80
316 Fred Scherman 1.50 .60
317 Jim Driscoll 1.50 .60
Angel Mangual
318 Rudy May 1.50 .60
319 Ty Cline 1.50 .60
320 Dave McNally 2.00 .80
321 Tom Matchick 1.50 .60
322 Jim Beauchamp 1.50 .60
323 Billy Champion 1.50 .60
324 Graig Nettles 2.00 .80
325 Juan Marichal 8.00 3.20
326 Richie Scheinblum 1.50 .60
327 Boog Powell WS 2.00 .80
328 Don Buford WS 2.00 .80
329 Frank Robinson WS 4.00 1.60
330 World Series Game 4 2.00 .80
Reds stay alive
331 Brooks Robinson WS 6.00 2.40
commits robbery
332 WS Summary 2.00 .80
Orioles celebrate
333 Clay Kirby 1.50 .60
334 Roberto Pena 1.50 .60
335 Jerry Koosman 2.00 .80
336 Detroit Tigers 4.00 1.60
Team Card
337 Jesus Alou 1.50 .60
338 Gene Tenace 2.00 .80
339 Wayne Simpson 1.50 .60
340 Rico Petrocelli 2.00 .80
341 Steve Garvey RC 40.00 16.00
342 Frank Tepedino 2.00 .80
343 Ed Acosta 2.00 .80
Milt May RC
344 Ellie Rodriguez 1.50 .60
345 Joel Horlen 1.50 .60
346 Lum Harris MG 1.50 .60
347 Ted Uhlaender 1.50 .60
348 Fred Norman 1.50 .60
349 Rich Reese 1.50 .60
350 Billy Williams 6.00 2.40
351 Jim Shellenback 1.50 .60
352 Denny Doyle 1.50 .60
353 Carl Taylor 1.50 .60
354 Don McMahon 1.50 .60
355 Bud Harrelson 4.00 1.60
(Nolan Ryan in photo)
356 Bob Locker 1.50 .60
357 Cincinnati Reds 4.00 1.60
Team Card
358 Danny Cater 1.50 .60
359 Ron Reed 1.50 .60
360 Jim Fregosi 2.00 .80
361 Don Sutton 6.00 2.40
362 Mike Adamson 1.50 .60
Roger Freed
363 Mike Nagy 1.50 .60
364 Tommy Dean 1.50 .60
365 Bob Johnson 1.50 .60
366 Ron Stone 1.50 .60
367 Dalton Jones 1.50 .60
368 Bob Veale 2.00 .80
369 Checklist 4 10.00 2.00
370 Joe Torre 4.00 1.60
371 Jack Hiatt 1.50 .60
372 Lew Krausse 1.50 .60
373 Tom McCraw 1.50 .60
374 Clete Boyer 2.00 .80
375 Steve Hargan 1.50 .60
376 Clyde Mashore 1.50 .60
Ernie McAnally
377 Greg Garrett 1.50 .60
378 Tito Fuentes 1.50 .60
379 Wayne Granger 1.50 .60
380 Ted Williams MG 12.00 4.80
381 Fred Gladding 1.50 .60
382 Jake Gibbs 1.50 .60
383 Rod Gaspar 1.50 .60
384 Rollie Fingers 6.00 2.40
385 Maury Wills 4.00 1.60
386 Boston Red Sox 2.00 .80
Team Card
387 Ron Herbel 1.50 .60
388 Al Oliver 4.00 1.60
389 Ed Brinkman 1.50 .60
390 Glenn Beckert 2.00 .80
391 Steve Brye 2.00 .80
Cotton Nash
392 Grant Jackson 1.50 .60
393 Merv Rettenmund 2.00 .80
394 Clay Carroll 2.50 1.00
395 Roy White 4.00 1.60
396 Dick Schofield 2.50 1.00
397 Alvin Dark MG 4.00 1.60
398 Howie Reed 2.50 1.00
399 Jim French 2.50 1.00
400 Hank Aaron 60.00 24.00
401 Tom Murphy 2.50 1.00
402 Los Angeles Dodgers 6.00 2.40
Team Card
403 Joe Coleman 2.50 1.00
404 Buddy Harris 2.50 1.00
Roger Metzger
405 Leo Cardenas 2.50 1.00
406 Ray Sadecki 2.50 1.00
407 Joe Rudi 4.00 1.60
408 Rafael Robles 2.50 1.00
409 Don Pavletich 2.50 1.00
410 Ken Holtzman 4.00 1.60
411 George Spriggs 2.50 1.00
412 Jerry Johnson 2.50 1.00
413 Pat Kelly 2.50 1.00
414 Woodie Fryman 2.50 1.00
415 Mike Hegan 2.50 1.00
416 Gene Alley 2.50 1.00
417 Dick Hall 2.50 1.00
418 Adolfo Phillips 2.50 1.00
419 Ron Hansen 2.50 1.00
420 Jim Merritt 2.50 1.00
421 John Stephenson 2.50 1.00
422 Frank Bertaina 2.50 1.00
423 Dennis Saunders 2.50 1.00
Tim Marting
424 Roberto Rodriquez 2.50 1.00
425 Doug Rader 4.00 1.60
426 Chris Cannizzaro 2.50 1.00
427 Bernie Allen 2.50 1.00
428 Jim McAndrew 2.50 1.00
429 Chuck Hinton 2.50 1.00
430 Wes Parker 4.00 1.60
431 Tom Burgmeier 2.50 1.00
432 Bob Didier 2.50 1.00
433 Skip Lockwood 2.50 1.00
434 Gary Sutherland 2.50 1.00
435 Jose Cardenal 4.00 1.60
436 Wilbur Wood 4.00 1.60
437 Danny Murtaugh MG 4.00 1.60
438 Mike McCormick 4.00 1.60
439 Greg Luzinski RC 6.00 2.40
Scott Reid
440 Bert Campaneris 4.00 1.60
441 Milt Pappas 4.00 1.60
442 California Angels 4.00 1.60
Team Card
443 Rich Robertson 2.50 1.00
444 Jimmie Price 2.50 1.00
445 Art Shamsky 2.50 1.00
446 Bobby Bolin 2.50 1.00
447 Cesar Geronimo 4.00 1.60
448 Dave Roberts 2.50 1.00
449 Brant Alyea 2.50 1.00
450 Bob Gibson 15.00 6.00
451 Joe Keough 2.50 1.00
452 John Boccabella 2.50 1.00
453 Terry Crowley 2.50 1.00
454 Mike Paul 2.50 1.00
455 Don Kessinger 4.00 1.60
456 Bob Meyer 2.50 1.00
457 Willie Smith 2.50 1.00
458 Ron Lolich 2.50 1.00
Dave Lemonds
459 Jim Lefebvre 2.50 1.00
460 Fritz Peterson 2.50 1.00
461 Jim Ray Hart 2.50 1.00
462 Washington Senators 6.00 2.40
Team Card
463 Tom Kelley 2.50 1.00
464 Aurelio Rodriguez 2.50 1.00
465 Tim McCarver 6.00 2.40
466 Ken Berry 2.50 1.00
467 Al Santorini 2.50 1.00
468 Frank Fernandez 2.50 1.00
469 Bob Aspromonte 2.50 1.00
470 Bob Oliver 2.50 1.00
471 Tom Griffin 2.50 1.00
472 Ken Rudolph 2.50 1.00
473 Gary Wagner 2.50 1.00
474 Jim Fairey 2.50 1.00
475 Ron Perranoski 2.50 1.00
476 Dal Maxvill 2.50 1.00
477 Earl Weaver MG 6.00 2.40
478 Bernie Carbo 2.50 1.00
479 Dennis Higgins 2.50 1.00
480 Manny Sanguillen 4.00 1.60
481 Daryl Patterson 2.50 1.00
482 San Diego Padres 6.00 2.40
Team Card
483 Gene Michael 2.50 1.00
484 Don Wilson 2.50 1.00
485 Ken McMullen 2.50 1.00
486 Steve Huntz 2.50 1.00
487 Paul Schaal 2.50 1.00
488 Jerry Stephenson 2.50 1.00
489 Luis Alvarado 2.50 1.00
490 Deron Johnson 2.50 1.00
491 Jim Hardin 2.50 1.00
492 Ken Boswell 2.50 1.00
493 Dave May 2.50 1.00
494 Ralph Garr 4.00 1.60
Rick Kester
495 Felipe Alou 4.00 1.60
496 Woody Woodward 2.50 1.00
497 Horacio Pina 2.50 1.00
498 John Kennedy 2.50 1.00
499 Checklist 5 10.00 2.00
500 Jim Perry 4.00 1.60
501 Andy Etchebarren 2.50 1.00
502 Chicago Cubs 6.00 2.40
Team Card
503 Gates Brown 4.00 1.60
504 Ken Wright 2.50 1.00
505 Ollie Brown 2.50 1.00
506 Bobby Knoop 2.50 1.00
507 George Stone 2.50 1.00
508 Roger Repoz 2.50 1.00
509 Jim Grant 2.50 1.00
510 Ken Harrelson 4.00 1.60
511 Chris Short 4.00 1.60
(Pete Rose leading off second)
512 Dick Mills 2.50 1.00
Mike Garman
513 Nolan Ryan 150.00 60.00
514 Ron Woods 2.50 1.00
515 Carl Morton 2.50 1.00
516 Ted Kubiak 2.50 1.00
517 Charlie Fox MG 2.50 1.00
518 Joe Grzenda 2.50 1.00
519 Willie Crawford 2.50 1.00
520 Tommy John 6.00 2.40
521 Leron Lee 2.50 1.00
522 Minnesota Twins 6.00 2.40
Team Card
523 John Odom 2.50 1.00
524 Mickey Stanley 6.00 2.40
525 Ernie Banks 50.00 20.00
526 Ray Jarvis 4.00 1.60
527 Cleon Jones 6.00 2.40
528 Wally Bunker 4.00 1.60
529 Enzo Hernandez 6.00 2.40
Bill Buckner
Marty Perez
530 Carl Yastrzemski 30.00 12.00
531 Mike Torrez 4.00 1.60
532 Bill Rigney MG 4.00 1.60
533 Mike Ryan 4.00 1.60
534 Luke Walker 4.00 1.60
535 Curt Flood 6.00 2.40
536 Claude Raymond 4.00 1.60
537 Tom Egan 4.00 1.60
538 Angel Bravo 4.00 1.60
539 Larry Brown 4.00 1.60
540 Larry Dierker 6.00 2.40
541 Bob Burda 4.00 1.60
542 Bob Miller 4.00 1.60
543 New York Yankees 10.00 4.00
Team Card
544 Vida Blue 6.00 2.40
545 Dick Dietz 4.00 1.60
546 John Matias 4.00 1.60
547 Pat Dobson 6.00 2.40
548 Don Mason 4.00 1.60
549 Jim Brewer 6.00 2.40
550 Harmon Killebrew 25.00 10.00
551 Frank Linzy 4.00 1.60
552 Buddy Bradford 4.00 1.60
553 Kevin Collins 4.00 1.60
554 Lowell Palmer 4.00 1.60
555 Walt Williams 4.00 1.60
556 Jim McGlothlin 4.00 1.60
557 Tom Satriano 4.00 1.60
558 Hector Torres 4.00 1.60
559 Terry Cox 4.00 1.60
Bill Gogolewski
Gary Jones
560 Rusty Staub 6.00 2.40
561 Syd O'Brien 4.00 1.60
562 Dave Giusti 4.00 1.60
563 San Francisco Giants 8.00 3.20
Team Card
564 Al Fitzmorris 4.00 1.60
565 Jim Wynn 6.00 2.40
566 Tim Cullen 4.00 1.60
567 Walt Alston MG 8.00 3.20
568 Sal Campisi 4.00 1.60
569 Ivan Murrell 4.00 1.60
570 Jim Palmer 30.00 12.00
571 Ted Sizemore 4.00 1.60
572 Jerry Kenney 4.00 1.60
573 Ed Kranepool 6.00 2.40
574 Jim Bunning 8.00 3.20
575 Bill Freehan 6.00 2.40
576 Adrian Garrett 4.00 1.60
Brock Davis
Garry Jestadt
577 Jim Lonborg 6.00 2.40
578 Ron Hunt 4.00 1.60
579 Marty Pattin 4.00 1.60
580 Tony Perez 20.00 8.00
581 Roger Nelson 4.00 1.60
582 Dave Cash 6.00 2.40
583 Ron Cook 4.00 1.60
584 Cleveland Indians 8.00 3.20
Team Card
585 Willie Davis 6.00 2.40
586 Dick Woodson 4.00 1.60
587 Sonny Jackson 4.00 1.60
588 Tom Bradley 4.00 1.60
589 Bob Barton 4.00 1.60
590 Alex Johnson 6.00 2.40
591 Jackie Brown 4.00 1.60
592 Randy Hundley 6.00 2.40
593 Jack Aker 4.00 1.60
594 Bob Chlupsa 6.00 2.40
Bob Stinson
Al Hrabosky RC
595 Dave Johnson 6.00 2.40
596 Mike Jorgensen 4.00 1.60
597 Ken Suarez 4.00 1.60
598 Rick Wise 6.00 2.40
599 Norm Cash 6.00 2.40
600 Willie Mays 100.00 40.00
601 Ken Tatum 4.00 1.60
602 Marty Martinez 4.00 1.60
603 Pittsburgh Pirates 8.00 3.20
Team Card
604 John Gelnar 4.00 1.60
605 Orlando Cepeda 8.00 3.20
606 Chuck Taylor 4.00 1.60
607 Paul Ratliff 4.00 1.60
608 Mike Wegener 4.00 1.60
609 Leo Durocher MG 8.00 3.20
610 Amos Otis 6.00 2.40
611 Tom Phoebus 4.00 1.60
612 Lou Camilli 4.00 1.60
Ted Ford
Steve Mingori
613 Pedro Borbon 4.00 1.60
614 Billy Cowan 4.00 1.60
615 Mel Stottlemyre 6.00 2.40
616 Larry Hisle 6.00 2.40
617 Clay Dalrymple 4.00 1.60
618 Tug McGraw 6.00 2.40
619A Checklist 6 ERR 10.00 2.00
(No copyright)
619B Checklist 6 COR 6.00 1.20
(Copyright on back)

Card	NM	Ex
620 Frank Howard	6.00	2.40
621 Ron Bryant	4.00	1.60
622 Joe Lahoud	4.00	1.60
623 Pat Jarvis	4.00	1.60
624 Oakland Athletics	8.00	3.20
Team Card		
625 Lou Brock	30.00	12.00
626 Freddie Patek	6.00	2.40
627 Steve Hamilton	4.00	1.60
628 John Bateman	4.00	1.60
629 John Hiller	6.00	2.40
630 Roberto Clemente	150.00	60.00
631 Eddie Fisher	4.00	1.60
632 Darrel Chaney	4.00	1.60
633 Bobby Brooks	4.00	1.60
Pete Koegel		
Scott Northey		
634 Phil Regan	4.00	1.60
635 Bobby Murcer	6.00	2.40
636 Denny Lemaster	4.00	1.60
637 Dave Bristol MG	4.00	1.60
638 Stan Williams	4.00	1.60
639 Tom Haller	4.00	1.60
640 Frank Robinson	40.00	16.00
641 New York Mets	15.00	6.00
Team Card		
642 Jim Roland	4.00	1.60
643 Rick Reichardt	4.00	1.60
644 Jim Stewart SP	12.00	4.80
645 Jim Maloney SP	15.00	6.00
646 Bobby Floyd SP	12.00	4.80
647 Juan Pizarro	8.00	3.20
648 Rich Folkers	25.00	10.00
Ted Martinez		
John Matlack RC SP		
649 Sparky Lyle SP	15.00	6.00
650 Rich Allen SP	30.00	12.00
651 Jerry Robertson SP	12.00	4.80
652 Atlanta Braves	12.00	4.80
Team Card		
653 Russ Snyder SP	12.00	4.80
654 Don Shaw SP	12.00	4.80
655 Mike Epstein SP	12.00	4.80
656 Gerry Nyman SP	12.00	4.80
657 Jose Azcue	8.00	3.20
658 Paul Lindblad SP	12.00	4.80
659 Byron Browne SP	12.00	4.80
660 Ray Culp	8.00	3.20
661 Chuck Tanner MG SP	15.00	6.00
662 Mike Hedlund SP	12.00	4.80
663 Marv Staehle	8.00	3.20
664 Archie Reynolds	12.00	4.80
Bob Reynolds		
Ken Reynolds SP		
665 Ron Swoboda SP	15.00	6.00
666 Gene Brabender SP	12.00	4.80
667 Pete Ward	8.00	3.20
668 Gary Neibauer	8.00	3.20
669 Ike Brown SP	12.00	4.80
670 Bill Hands	8.00	3.20
671 Bill Voss SP	12.00	4.80
672 Ed Crosby SP	12.00	4.80
673 Gerry Janeski SP	12.00	4.80
674 Montreal Expos	12.00	4.80
Team Card		
675 Dave Boswell	8.00	3.20
676 Tommie Reynolds	8.00	3.20
677 Jack DiLauro SP	12.00	4.80
678 George Thomas	8.00	3.20
679 Don O'Riley	8.00	3.20
680 Don Mincher SP	12.00	4.80
681 Bill Butler	8.00	3.20
682 Terry Harmon	8.00	3.20
683 Bill Burbach SP	12.00	4.80
684 Curt Motton	8.00	3.20
685 Moe Drabowsky	8.00	3.20
686 Chico Ruiz SP	12.00	4.80
687 Ron Taylor SP	12.00	4.80
688 S.Anderson MG SP	30.00	12.00
689 Frank Baker	8.00	3.20
690 Bob Moose	8.00	3.20
691 Bobby Heise	8.00	3.20
692 Hal Haydel	12.00	4.80
Rogelio Moret		
Wayne Twitchell SP		
693 Jose Pena SP	12.00	4.80
694 Rick Renick SP	12.00	4.80
695 Joe Niekro	12.00	4.80
696 Jerry Morales	8.00	3.20
697 Rickey Clark SP	12.00	4.80
698 M. Brewers SP	20.00	8.00
Team Card		
699 Jim Britton	8.00	3.20
700 Boog Powell SP	25.00	10.00
701 Bob Garibaldi	8.00	3.20
702 Milt Ramirez	8.00	3.20
703 Mike Kekich	8.00	3.20
704 J.C. Martin SP	12.00	4.80
705 Dick Selma SP	12.00	4.80
706 Joe Foy SP	12.00	4.80
707 Fred Lasher	8.00	3.20
708 Russ Nagelson SP	12.00	4.80
709 Dusty Baker RC	80.00	32.00
Don Baylor RC		
Tom Paciorek RC SP		
710 Sonny Siebert	8.00	3.20
711 Larry Stahl SP	12.00	4.80
712 Jose Martinez	8.00	3.20
713 Mike Marshall SP	15.00	6.00
714 Dick Williams MG SP	15.00	6.00
715 Horace Clarke SP	15.00	6.00
716 Dave Leonhard	8.00	3.20
717 Tommie Aaron SP	12.00	4.80
718 Billy Wynne	8.00	3.20
719 Jerry May SP	12.00	4.80
720 Matty Alou	12.00	4.80
721 John Morris	8.00	3.20
722 Houston Astros SP	20.00	8.00
Team Card		
723 Vicente Romo SP	12.00	4.80
724 Tom Tischinski SP	12.00	4.80
725 Gary Gentry SP	12.00	4.80
726 Paul Popovich	8.00	3.20
727 Ray Lamb SP	12.00	4.80
728 Wayne Redmond	8.00	3.20
Keith Lampard		
Bernie Williams		
729 Dick Billings	8.00	3.20
730 Jim Rooker	8.00	3.20
731 Jim Qualls SP	12.00	4.80
732 Bob Reed	8.00	3.20
733 Lee Maye SP	12.00	4.80
734 Rob Gardner SP	12.00	4.80
735 Mike Shannon SP	15.00	6.00
736 Mel Queen SP	12.00	4.80
737 P.Gomez SP MG	12.00	4.80
738 Russ Gibson SP	12.00	4.80
739 Barry Lersch SP	12.00	4.80
740 Luis Aparicio SP UER	30.00	12.00
(Led AL in steals from 1965 to 1964, should be 1956 to 1964)		
741 Skip Guinn	8.00	3.20
742 Kansas City Royals	12.00	4.80
Team Card		
743 John O'Donoghue SP	12.00	4.80
744 Chuck Manuel SP	12.00	4.80
745 Sandy Alomar SP	12.00	4.80
746 Andy Kosco	8.00	3.20
747 Al Severinsen	8.00	3.20
Scipio Spinks		
Balor Moore		
748 John Purdin SP	12.00	4.80
749 Ken Szotkiewicz	8.00	3.20
750 Denny McLain SP	25.00	10.00
751 Al Weis SP	15.00	6.00
752 Dick Drago	12.00	2.90

1971 Topps Coins Inserts

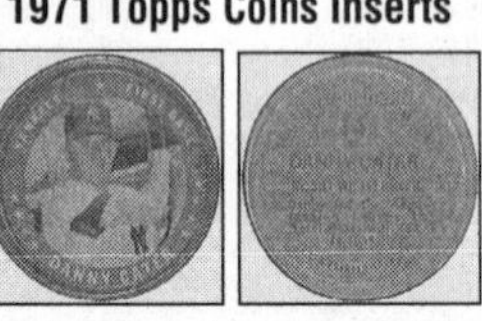

This full-color set of 153 coins, which were inserted into packs, contains the photo of the player surrounded by a colored band, which contains the player's name, his team, his position and several stars. The backs contain the coin number, short biographical data and the line "Collect the entire set of 153 coins." The set was evidently produced in three groups of 51 as coins 1-51 have brass backs, coins 52-102 have chrome backs and coins 103-153 have blue backs. In fact it has been verified that the coins were printed in three sheets of 51 coins comprised of three rows of 17 coins. Each coin measures approximately 1 1/2" in diameter.

	NM	Ex
COMPLETE SET (153)	350.00	140.00
1 Clarence Gaston	1.25	.50
2 Dave Johnson	1.25	.50
3 Jim Bunning	5.00	2.00
4 Jim Spencer	1.00	.40
5 Felix Millan	1.00	.40
6 Gerry Moses	1.00	.40
7 Ferguson Jenkins	5.00	2.00
8 Felipe Alou	1.25	.50
9 Jim McGlothlin	1.00	.40
10 Dick McAuliffe	1.00	.40
11 Joe Torre	4.00	1.60
12 Jim Perry	1.25	.50
13 Bobby Bonds	2.00	.80
14 Danny Cater	1.00	.40
15 Bill Mazeroski	3.00	1.20
16 Luis Aparicio	5.00	2.00
17 Doug Rader	1.00	.40
18 Vada Pinson	1.50	.60
19 John Bateman	1.00	.40
20 Lew Krausse	1.00	.40
21 Billy Grabarkewitz	1.00	.40
22 Frank Howard	1.50	.60
23 Jerry Koosman	1.50	.60
24 Rod Carew	8.00	3.20
25 Al Ferrara	1.00	.40
26 Dave McNally	1.25	.50
27 Jim Hickman	1.00	.40
28 Sandy Alomar	1.25	.50
29 Lee May	1.25	.50
30 Rico Petrocelli	1.25	.50
31 Don Money	1.00	.40
32 Jim Rooker	1.00	.40
33 Dick Dietz	1.00	.40
34 Roy White	1.25	.50
35 Carl Morton	1.00	.40
36 Walt Williams	1.00	.40
37 Phil Niekro	4.00	1.60
38 Bill Freehan	1.25	.50
39 Julian Javier	1.00	.40
40 Rick Monday	1.25	.50
41 Don Wilson	1.00	.40
42 Ray Fosse	1.25	.50
43 Art Shamsky	1.00	.40
44 Ted Savage	1.00	.40
45 Claude Osteen	1.25	.50
46 Ed Brinkman	1.00	.40
47 Matty Alou	1.25	.50
48 Bob Oliver	1.00	.40
49 Danny Coombs	1.00	.40
50 Frank Robinson	8.00	3.20
51 Randy Hundley	1.00	.40
52 Cesar Tovar	1.25	.50
53 Wayne Simpson	1.00	.40
54 Bobby Murcer	1.50	.60
55 Carl Taylor	1.00	.40
56 Tommy John	2.00	.80
57 Willie McCovey	8.00	3.20
58 Carl Yastrzemski	8.00	3.20
59 Bob Bailey	1.00	.40
60 Clyde Wright	1.00	.40
61 Orlando Cepeda	4.00	1.60
62 Al Kaline	8.00	3.20
63 Bob Gibson	8.00	3.20
64 Bert Campaneris	1.25	.50
65 Ted Sizemore	1.00	.40
66 Duke Sims	1.00	.40
67 Bud Harrelson	1.00	.40
68 Gerald McNertney	1.00	.40
69 Jim Wynn	1.25	.50
70 Dick Bosman	1.00	.40
71 Roberto Clemente	25.00	10.00
72 Rich Reese	1.00	.40
73 Gaylord Perry	5.00	2.00
74 Boog Powell	2.00	.80
75 Billy Williams	5.00	2.00
76 Bill Melton	1.00	.40
77 Nate Colbert	1.00	.40
78 Reggie Smith	1.25	.50
79 Deron Johnson	1.00	.40
80 Jim Hunter	5.00	2.00
81 Bobby Tolan	1.25	.50
82 Jim Northrup	1.00	.40
83 Ron Fairly	1.25	.50
84 Alex Johnson	1.00	.40
85 Pat Jarvis	1.00	.40
86 Sam McDowell	1.25	.50
87 Lou Brock	8.00	3.20
88 Danny Walton	1.00	.40
89 Denis Menke	1.00	.40
90 Jim Palmer	8.00	3.20
91 Tommy Agee	1.25	.50
92 Duane Josephson	1.00	.40
93 Willie Davis	1.25	.50
94 Mel Stottlemyre	1.25	.50
95 Ron Santo	1.50	.60
96 Amos Otis	1.25	.50
97 Ken Henderson	1.00	.40
98 George Scott	1.25	.50
99 Dock Ellis	1.25	.50
100 Harmon Killebrew	8.00	3.20
101 Pete Rose	12.00	4.80
102 Rick Reichardt	1.00	.40
103 Cleon Jones	1.00	.40
104 Ron Perranoski	1.00	.40
105 Tony Perez	4.00	1.60
106 Mickey Lolich	2.00	.80
107 Tim McCarver	1.50	.60
108 Reggie Jackson	12.00	4.80
109 Chris Cannizzaro	1.00	.40
110 Steve Hargan	1.00	.40
111 Rusty Staub	2.00	.80
112 Andy Messersmith	1.25	.50
113 Rico Carty	1.25	.50
114 Brooks Robinson	10.00	4.00
115 Steve Carlton	10.00	4.00
116 Mike Hegan	1.00	.40
117 Joe Morgan	8.00	3.20
118 Thurman Munson	8.00	3.20
119 Don Kessinger	1.00	.40
120 Joel Horlen	1.00	.40
121 Wes Parker	1.25	.50
122 Sonny Siebert	1.00	.40
123 Willie Stargell	8.00	3.20
124 Ellie Rodriguez	1.00	.40
125 Juan Marichal	8.00	3.20
126 Mike Epstein	1.00	.40
127 Tom Seaver	12.00	4.80
128 Tony Oliva	2.00	.80
129 Jim Merritt	1.00	.40
130 Willie Horton	1.25	.50
131 Rick Wise	1.00	.40
132 Sal Bando	1.25	.50
133 Ollie Brown	1.00	.40
134 Ken Harrelson	1.25	.50
135 Mack Jones	1.00	.40
136 Jim Fregosi	1.25	.50
137 Hank Aaron	15.00	6.00
138 Fritz Peterson	1.00	.40
139 Joe Hague	1.00	.40
140 Tommy Harper	1.00	.40
141 Larry Dierker	1.25	.50
142 Tony Conigliaro	1.50	.60
143 Glenn Beckert	1.00	.40
144 Carlos May	1.00	.40
145 Don Sutton	4.00	1.60
146 Paul Casanova	1.00	.40
147 Bob Moose	1.00	.40
148 Chico Cardenas	1.00	.40
149 Johnny Bench	12.00	4.80
150 Mike Cuellar	1.25	.50
151 Donn Clendenon	1.00	.40
152 Lou Piniella	2.00	.80
153 Willie Mays	20.00	8.00

1971 Topps Scratchoffs

These pack inserts featured the same players are the 1970 Topps Scratchoffs. However, the only difference is that the center of the game is red rather than black.

	NM	Ex
COMPLETE SET (24)	40.00	16.00
1 Hank Aaron	8.00	3.20
2 Rich Allen	1.50	.60
3 Luis Aparicio	4.00	1.60
4 Sal Bando	1.00	.40
5 Glenn Beckert	1.00	.40
6 Dick Bosman	1.00	.40
7 Nate Colbert	1.00	.40
8 Mike Hegan	1.00	.40
9 Mack Jones	1.00	.40
10 Al Kaline	5.00	2.00
11 Harmon Killebrew	5.00	2.00
12 Juan Marichal	4.00	1.60
13 Tim McCarver	2.00	.80
14 Sam McDowell	1.25	.50
15 Claude Osteen	1.00	.40
16 Tony Perez	3.00	1.20
17 Lou Piniella	1.50	.60
18 Boog Powell	1.50	.60
19 Tom Seaver	6.00	2.40
20 Jim Spencer	1.00	.40
21 Willie Stargell	5.00	2.00
22 Mel Stottlemyre	1.25	.50
23 Jim Wynn	1.25	.50
24 Carl Yastrzemski	5.00	2.00

1971 Topps Greatest Moments

The cards in this 55-card set measure 2 1/2" by 4 3/4". The 1971 Topps Greatest Moments set contains numbered cards depicting specific career highlights of current players. The obverses are black bordered and contain a small cameo picture of the left side; a deckle-bordered black and white action photo dominates the rest of the card. The backs are designed in newspaper style. Sometimes found in uncut sheets, this test set was retailed in gum packs on a very limited basis. Double prints (DP) are listed in the checklist below; there were 22 double prints and 33 single prints.

	NM	Ex
COMPLETE SET (55)	1500.00	600.00
COMMON CARD (1-55)	20.00	8.00
COMMON DP	6.00	2.40
1 Thurman Munson DP	30.00	12.00
2 Hoyt Wilhelm	40.00	16.00
3 Rico Carty	20.00	8.00
4 Carl Morton DP	6.00	2.40
5 Sal Bando DP	8.00	3.20
6 Bert Campaneris DP	8.00	3.20
7 Jim Kaat	30.00	12.00
8 Harmon Killebrew	75.00	30.00
9 Brooks Robinson	75.00	30.00
10 Jim Perry	20.00	8.00
11 Tony Oliva	35.00	14.00
12 Vada Pinson	25.00	10.00
13 Johnny Bench	125.00	50.00
14 Tony Perez	40.00	16.00
15 Pete Rose DP	75.00	30.00
16 Jim Fregosi DP	8.00	3.20
17 Alex Johnson DP	6.00	2.40
18 Clyde Wright DP	6.00	2.40
19 Al Kaline DP	30.00	12.00
20 Denny McLain	35.00	14.00
21 Jim Northrup	20.00	8.00
22 Bill Freehan	20.00	8.00
23 Mickey Lolich	25.00	10.00
24 Bob Gibson DP	30.00	12.00
25 Tim McCarver DP	6.00	2.40
26 Orlando Cepeda DP	20.00	8.00
27 Lou Brock DP	30.00	12.00
28 Nate Colbert DP	6.00	2.40
29 Maury Wills	35.00	14.00
30 Wes Parker	20.00	8.00
31 Jim Wynn	25.00	10.00
32 Larry Dierker	25.00	10.00
33 Bill Melton	20.00	8.00
34 Joe Morgan	40.00	16.00
35 Rusty Staub	30.00	12.00
36 Ernie Banks DP	35.00	14.00
37 Billy Williams	40.00	16.00
38 Lou Piniella	30.00	12.00
39 Rico Petrocelli DP	8.00	3.20
40 Carl Yastrzemski DP	50.00	20.00
41 Willie Mays DP	100.00	40.00
42 Tommy Harper	20.00	8.00
43 Jim Bunning DP	15.00	6.00
44 Fritz Peterson	25.00	10.00
45 Roy White	30.00	12.00
46 Bobby Murcer	35.00	14.00
47 Reggie Jackson	200.00	80.00
48 Frank Howard	30.00	12.00
49 Dick Bosman	20.00	8.00
50 Sam McDowell DP	8.00	3.20
51 Luis Aparicio DP	15.00	6.00
52 Willie McCovey DP	20.00	8.00
53 Joe Pepitone	30.00	12.00
54 Jerry Grote	25.00	10.00
55 Bud Harrelson	20.00	8.00

1971 Topps Super

The cards in this 63-card set measure 3 1/8" by 5 1/4". The obverse format of the Topps Super set of 1971 is identical to that of the 1970 set, that is, a borderless color photograph with a facsimile autograph printed on it. The backs are enlargements of the respective player's cards of the 1971 regular baseball issue. There are no reported scarcities in the set. Just as in 1970, this set was issued in three-card wax packs.

	NM	Ex
COMPLETE SET (63)	250.00	100.00
WRAPPER (10-CENT)		
1 Reggie Smith	2.00	.80
2 Gaylord Perry	4.00	1.60
3 Ted Savage	1.50	.60
4 Donn Clendenon	1.50	.60
5 Boog Powell	2.50	1.00
6 Tony Perez	4.00	1.60
7 Dick Bosman	1.50	.60
8 Alex Johnson	1.50	.60
9 Rusty Staub	2.50	1.00
10 Mel Stottlemyre	2.50	1.00
11 Tony Oliva	2.50	1.00
12 Bill Freehan	2.00	.80
13 Fritz Peterson	1.50	.60
14 Wes Parker	2.00	.80
15 Cesar Cedeno	2.00	.80
16 Sam McDowell	2.00	.80
17 Frank Howard	2.00	.80
18 Dave McNally	2.00	.80
19 Rico Petrocelli	2.00	.80
20 Pete Rose	25.00	10.00
21 Luke Walker	1.50	.60
22 Nate Colbert	1.50	.60
23 Luis Aparicio	4.00	1.60
24 Jim Perry	2.00	.80
25 Lou Brock	5.00	2.00
26 Roy White	2.00	.80
27 Claude Osteen	1.50	.60
28 Carl Morton	1.50	.60
29 Rico Carty	2.00	.80
30 Larry Dierker	1.50	.60
31 Bert Campaneris	2.00	.80
32 Johnny Bench	15.00	6.00
33 Felix Millan	1.50	.60
34 Tim McCarver	2.50	1.00
35 Ron Santo	2.50	1.00
36 Tommie Agee	2.00	.80
37 Roberto Clemente	30.00	12.00
38 Reggie Jackson	15.00	6.00
39 Clyde Wright	1.50	.60
40 Rich Allen	2.50	1.00
41 Curt Flood	2.00	.80
42 Ferguson Jenkins	4.00	1.60
43 Willie Stargell	4.00	1.60
44 Hank Aaron	15.00	6.00
45 Amos Otis	2.00	.80
46 Willie McCovey	5.00	2.00
47 Bill Melton	1.50	.60
48 Bob Gibson	5.00	2.00
49 Carl Yastrzemski	10.00	4.00
50 Glenn Beckert	1.50	.60
51 Ray Fosse	1.50	.60
52 Cito Gaston	2.00	.80
53 Tom Seaver	10.00	4.00
54 Al Kaline	8.00	3.20
55 Jim Northrup	2.00	.80
56 Willie Mays	18.00	7.25
57 Sal Bando	2.00	.80
58 Deron Johnson	1.50	.60
59 Brooks Robinson	8.00	3.20
60 Harmon Killebrew	5.00	2.00
61 Joe Torre	4.00	1.60
62 Lou Piniella	2.50	1.00
63 Tommy Harper	1.50	.60

1971 Topps Tattoos

There are 16 different sheets (3 1/2" X 14 1/4") of baseball tattoos issued by Topps in 1971. Each contains two distinct sizes (1 3/4" by 2 3/8" and 1 3/16" by 1 3/4") of tattoos; those of players feature flesh-tone faces on red or yellow backgrounds; those of baseball figures, facsimile autographs (these are denoted by FAC in the checklist) and team pennants are one-half the player tattoo size. The "Baseball Tattoos" logo panel at the top of each sheet contains the sheet number; the sheet number is given (with an S prefix) in the checklist below after the name. The small baseball figures are not priced in the checklist. The complete tattoo panel prices can be figured as the sum of the individual (player, team and autograph) tattoos.

	NM	Ex
COMPLETE SET (134)	175.00	70.00
1 Sal Bando S1	1.00	.40
2 Dick Bosman S1	.75	.30
3 Nate Colbert S1	.75	.30
4 Cleon Jones S1	.75	.30
5 Juan Marichal S1	4.00	1.60
6 Brooks Robinson S1	6.00	2.40
7 Brooks Robinson FAC S1	2.00	.80
8 Montreal Expos S1	.75	.30
9 San Fran. Giants S1	.75	.30
10 Glenn Beckert S2	.75	.30
11 Tommy Harper S2	.75	.30
12 Ken Henderson S2	.75	.30
13 Carl Yastrzemski S2	6.00	2.40
14 Carl Yastrzemski FAC S2	2.00	.80
15 Boston Red Sox S2	.75	.30
16 New York Mets S2	.75	.30
17 Orlando Cepeda S3	2.00	.80
18 Jim Fregosi S3	1.00	.40
19 Jim Fregosi FAC S3	.75	.30
20 Randy Hundley S3	.75	.30
21 Reggie Jackson S3	8.00	3.20
22 Jerry Koosman S3	1.50	.60
23 Jim Palmer S3	4.00	1.60
24 Phila. Phillies S3	.75	.30
25 New York Yankees S3	1.00	.40
26 Dick Dietz S4	.75	.30
27 Clarence Gaston S4	1.00	.40
28 Dave Johnson S4	1.50	.60
29 Sam McDowell S4	1.00	.40
30 Sam McDowell FAC S4	.75	.30
31 Gary Nolan S4	.75	.30
32 Amos Otis S4	1.00	.40
33 Kansas City Royals S4	.75	.30
34 Oakland A's S4	.75	.30
35 Billy Grabarkewitz S5	.75	.30
36 Al Kaline S5	6.00	2.40
37 Al Kaline FAC S5	1.50	.60
38 Lee May S5	1.00	.40
39 Tom Murphy S5	.75	.30
40 Vada Pinson S5	1.50	.60
41 Manny Sanguillen S5	.75	.30
42 Atlanta Braves S5	.75	.30
43 Los Angeles Dodgers S5	.75	.30
44 Luis Aparicio S6	4.00	1.60
45 Paul Blair S6	.75	.30
46 Chris Cannizzaro S6	.75	.30
47 Donn Clendenon S6	.75	.30
48 Larry Dierker S6	.75	.30
49 Harmon Killebrew S6	4.00	1.60
50 Harmon Killebrew FAC S6	1.50	.60
51 Chicago Cubs S6	.75	.30
52 Cincinnati Reds S6	.75	.30
53 Rich Allen S7	2.00	.80
54 Bert Campaneris S7	1.00	.40
55 Don Money S7	.75	.30
56 Boog Powell S7	2.00	.80
57 Boog Powell FAC S7	1.00	.40
58 Ted Savage S7	.75	.01
59 Rusty Staub S7	1.50	.60
60 Cleveland Indians S7	.75	.30
61 Milwaukee Brewers S7	.75	.30
62 Leo Cardenas S8	.75	.30
63 Bill Hands S8	.75	.30
64 Frank Howard S8	1.50	.60
65 Frank Howard FAC S8	1.00	.40
66 Wes Parker S8	.75	.30
67 Reggie Smith S8	1.00	.40

68 Willie Stargell S8 4.00 1.60
69 Chicago White Sox S8 .75 .30
70 San Diego Padres S8 .75 .30
71 Hank Aaron S9 10.00 4.00
72 Hank Aaron FAC S9 2.00 .80
73 Tommy Agee S9 .75 .30
74 Jim Hunter S9 4.00 1.60
75 Dick McAuliffe S9 .75 .30
76 Tony Perez S9 3.00 1.20
77 Lou Piniella S9 1.50 .60
78 Detroit Tigers S9 .75 .30
79 Roberto Clemente S10 15.00 6.00
80 Tony Conigliaro S10 1.00 .40
81 Fergie Jenkins S10 4.00 1.60
82 Fergie Jenkins FAC S10 1.50 .60
83 Thurman Munson S10 5.00 2.00
84 Gary Peters S10 .75 .30
85 Joe Torre S10 1.50 .60
86 Baltimore Orioles S10 .75 .30
87 Johnny Bench S11 6.00 2.40
88 Johnny Bench FAC S11 1.50 .60
89 Rico Carty S11 1.00 .40
90 Bill Mazeroski S11 3.00 1.20
91 Bob Oliver S11 .75 .30
92 Rico Petrocelli S11 1.00 .40
93 Frank Robinson S11 5.00 2.00
94 Washington Senators S11 .75 .30
95 Bill Freehan S12 1.00 .40
96 Dave McNally S12 .75 .30
97 Felix Millan S12 .75 .30
98 Mel Stottlemyre S12 1.00 .40
99 Bob Tolan S12 .75 .30
100 Billy Williams S12 4.00 1.60
101 Billy Williams FAC S12 1.50 .60
102 Houston Astros S12 .75 .30
103 Ray Culp S13 .75 .30
104 Bud Harrelson S13 .75 .30
105 Mickey Lolich S13 1.50 .60
106 Willie McCovey S13 4.00 1.60
107 Willie McCovey FAC S13 1.50 .60
108 Ron Santo S13 2.00 .80
109 Roy White S13 1.00 .40
110 Pittsburgh Pirates S13 .75 .30
111 Bill Melton S14 .75 .30
112 Jim Perry S14 1.00 .40
113 Pete Rose S14 10.00 4.00
114 Tom Seaver S14 8.00 3.20
115 Tom Seaver FAC S14 2.00 .80
116 Maury Wills S14 1.50 .60
117 Clyde Wright S14 .75 .30
118 Minnesota Twins S14 .75 .30
119 Rod Carew S15 6.00 2.40
120 Bob Gibson S15 6.00 2.40
121 Bob Gibson FAC S15 1.50 .60
122 Alex Johnson S15 .75 .30
123 Don Kessinger S15 .75 .30
124 Jim Merritt S15 .75 .30
125 Rick Monday S15 .75 .30
126 St. Louis Cardinals S15 .75 .30
127 Larry Bowa S16 1.00 .40
128 Mike Cuellar S16 1.00 .40
129 Ray Fosse S16 .75 .30
130 Willie Mays S16 12.00 4.80
131 Willie Mays FAC S16 2.00 .80
132 Carl Morton S16 .75 .30
133 Tony Oliva S16 2.50 1.00
134 California Angels S16 .75 .30

1972 Topps

The cards in this 787-card set measure 2 1/2" by 3 1/2". The 1972 Topps set contained the most cards ever for a Topps set to that point in time. Features appearing for the first time were "Boyhood Photos" (341-348/491-498), Awards and Trophy cards (621-626), "In Action" (distributed throughout the set), and "Traded Cards" (751-757). Other subsets included League Leaders (85-96), Playoffs cards (221-222), and World Series cards (223-230). The curved lines of the color picture are a departure from the rectangular designs of other years. There is a series of intermediate scarcity (526-656) and the usual high numbers (657-787). The backs of cards 692, 694, 696, 700, 706 and 710 form a picture back of Tom Seaver. The backs of cards 698, 702, 704, 708, 712, 714 form a picture back of Tony Oliva. As in previous years, cards were issued in a variety of ways including ten-card wax packs which cost a dime and 28 card cello packs which cost a quarter. The 10 cents wax packs were issued 24 packs to a box while the cello packs were also issued 24 packs to a box. Rookie Cards in this set include Ron Cey and Carlton Fisk.

NM Ex
COMPLETE SET (787) 1800.00 700.00
COMMON CARD (1-132) .60 .24
COMMON (133-263) 1.00 .40
COMMON (264-394) 1.25 .50
COMMON (395-525) 1.50 .60
COMMON (526-656) 4.00 1.60
COMMON (657-787) 12.00 4.80
WRAPPER (10-CENT) 15.00 6.00
1 Pittsburgh Pirates 8.00 2.90
Team Card
2 Ray Culp .60 .24
3 Bob Tolan .60 .24
4 Checklist 1-132 6.00 1.20
5 John Bateman .60 .24
6 Fred Scherman .60 .24
7 Enzo Hernandez .60 .24
8 Ron Swoboda 1.25 .50
9 Stan Williams .60 .24
10 Amos Otis 1.25 .50
11 Bobby Valentine 1.25 .50
12 Jose Cardenal .60 .24
13 Joe Grzenda .60 .24
14 Pete Koegel .60 .24
Mike Anderson
Wayne Twitchell
15 Walt Williams .60 .24
16 Mike Jorgensen .60 .24
17 Dave Duncan 1.25 .50
18A Juan Pizarro .60 .24
(Yellow underline
C and S of Cubs)
18B Juan Pizarro 5.00 2.00
(Green underline
C and S of Cubs)
19 Billy Cowan .60 .24
20 Don Wilson .60 .24
21 Atlanta Braves 1.50 .60
Team Card
22 Rob Gardner .60 .24
23 Ted Kubiak .60 .24
24 Ted Ford .60 .24
25 Bill Singer .60 .24
26 Andy Etchebarren .60 .24
27 Bob Johnson .60 .24
28 Bob Gebhard .60 .24
Steve Brye
Hal Haydel
29A Bill Bonham .60 .24
(Yellow underline
C and S of Cubs)
29B Bill Bonham 5.00 2.00
(Green underline
C and S of Cubs)
30 Rico Petrocelli 1.25 .50
31 Cleon Jones 1.25 .50
32 Cleon Jones IA .60 .24
33 Billy Martin MG 4.00 1.60
34 Billy Martin IA 2.50 1.00
35 Jerry Johnson .60 .24
36 Jerry Johnson IA .60 .24
37 Carl Yastrzemski 10.00 4.00
38 Carl Yastrzemski IA 6.00 2.40
39 Bob Barton .60 .24
40 Bob Barton IA .60 .24
41 Tommy Davis 1.25 .50
42 Tommy Davis IA 1.25 .50
43 Rick Wise 1.25 .50
44 Rick Wise IA .60 .24
45A Glenn Beckert 1.25 .50
(Yellow underline
C and S of Cubs)
45B Glenn Beckert 5.00 2.00
(Green underline
C and S of Cubs)
46 Glenn Beckert IA .60 .24
47 John Ellis .60 .24
48 John Ellis IA .60 .24
49 Willie Mays 40.00 16.00
50 Willie Mays IA 20.00 8.00
51 Harmon Killebrew 8.00 3.20
52 Harmon Killebrew IA 4.00 1.60
53 Bud Harrelson 1.25 .50
54 Bud Harrelson IA .60 .24
55 Clyde Wright .60 .24
56 Rich Chiles .60 .24
57 Bob Oliver .60 .24
58 Ernie McAnally .60 .24
59 Fred Stanley .60 .24
60 Manny Sanguillen 1.25 .50
61 Burt Hooton RC 1.25 .50
Gene Hiser
Earl Stephenson
62 Angel Mangual .60 .24
63 Duke Sims .60 .24
64 Pete Broberg .60 .24
65 Cesar Cedeno 1.25 .50
66 Ray Corbin .60 .24
67 Red Schoendienst MG 2.50 1.00
68 Jim York .60 .24
69 Roger Freed .60 .24
70 Mike Cuellar 1.25 .50
71 California Angels 1.50 .60
Team Card
72 Bruce Kison RC .60 .24
73 Steve Huntz .60 .24
74 Cecil Upshaw .60 .24
75 Bert Campaneris 1.25 .50
76 Don Carrithers .60 .24
77 Ron Theobald .60 .24
78 Steve Arlin .60 .24
79 Mike Garman 50.00 20.00
Cecil Cooper RC
Carlton Fisk RC
80 Tony Perez 4.00 1.60
81 Mike Hedlund .60 .24
82 Ron Woods .60 .24
83 Dalton Jones .60 .24
84 Vince Colbert .60 .24
85 Joe Torre 2.50 1.00
Ralph Garr
Glenn Beckert LL
86 Tony Oliva 2.50 1.00
Bobby Murcer
Merv Rettenmund LL
87 Joe Torre 4.00 1.60
Willie Stargell
Hank Aaron LL
88 Harmon Killebrew 4.00 1.60
Frank Robinson
Reggie Smith LL
89 Willie Stargell 2.50 1.00
Hank Aaron
Lee May LL
90 Bill Melton 2.50 1.00
Norm Cash
Reggie Jackson LL
91 Tom Seaver 2.50 1.00
Dave Roberts UER
(Photo actually
Danny Coombs)
Don Wilson LL
92 Vida Blue 2.50 1.00
Wilbur Wood
Jim Palmer LL
93 Fergie Jenkins 4.00 1.60
Steve Carlton
Al Downing
Tom Seaver LL
94 Mickey Lolich 2.50 1.00
Vida Blue
Wilbur Wood LL
95 Tom Seaver 4.00 1.60
Fergie Jenkins
Bill Stoneman LL
96 Mickey Lolich 2.50 1.00
Vida Blue
Joe Coleman LL
97 Tom Kelley .60 .24
98 Chuck Tanner MG 1.25 .50
99 Ross Grimsley .60 .24
100 Frank Robinson 8.00 3.20
101 Bill Greif 2.50 1.00
J.R. Richard RC
Ray Busse
102 Lloyd Allen .60 .24
103 Checklist 133-263 6.00 1.20
104 Toby Harrah RC 1.25 .50
105 Gary Gentry .60 .24
106 Milwaukee Brewers 1.50 .60
Team Card
107 Jose Cruz RC 1.25 .50
108 Gary Waslewski .60 .24
109 Jerry May .60 .24
110 Ron Hunt .60 .24
111 Jim Grant .60 .24
112 Greg Luzinski 1.25 .50
113 Rogelio Moret .60 .24
114 Bill Buckner 1.25 .50
115 Jim Fregosi 1.25 .50
116 Ed Farmer .60 .24
117A Cleo James .60 .24
(Yellow underline
C and S of Cubs)
117B Cleo James 5.00 2.00
(Green underline
C and S of Cubs)
118 Skip Lockwood .60 .24
119 Marty Perez .60 .24
120 Bill Freehan 1.25 .50
121 Ed Sprague .60 .24
122 Larry Biittner .60 .24
123 Ed Acosta .60 .24
124 Alan Closter .60 .24
Rusty Torres
Roger Hambright
125 Dave Cash 1.25 .50
126 Bart Johnson .60 .24
127 Duffy Dyer .60 .24
128 Eddie Watt .60 .24
129 Charlie Fox MG .60 .24
130 Bob Gibson 8.00 3.20
131 Jim Nettles .60 .24
132 Joe Morgan 6.00 2.40
133 Joe Keough 1.00 .40
134 Carl Morton 1.00 .40
135 Vada Pinson 2.00 .80
136 Darrel Chaney 1.00 .40
137 Dick Williams MG 2.00 .80
138 Mike Kekich 1.00 .40
139 Tim McCarver 2.00 .80
140 Pat Dobson 2.00 .80
141 Buzz Capra 2.00 .80
Lee Stanton
Jon Matlack
142 Chris Chambliss RC 4.00 1.60
143 Garry Jestadt 1.00 .40
144 Marty Pattin 1.00 .40
145 Don Kessinger 2.00 .80
146 Steve Kealey 1.00 .40
147 Dave Kingman RC 6.00 2.40
148 Dick Billings 1.00 .40
149 Gary Neibauer 1.00 .40
150 Norm Cash 2.00 .80
151 Jim Brewer 1.00 .40
152 Gene Clines 1.00 .40
153 Rick Auerbach 1.00 .40
154 Ted Simmons 4.00 1.60
155 Larry Dierker 1.00 .40
156 Minnesota Twins 2.00 .80
Team Card
157 Don Gullett 1.00 .40
158 Jerry Kenney 1.00 .40
159 John Boccabella 1.00 .40
160 Andy Messersmith 2.00 .80
161 Brock Davis 1.00 .40
162 Jerry Bell 2.00 .80
Darrell Porter RC
Bob Reynolds UER
(Porter and Bell
photos switched)
163 Tug McGraw 4.00 1.60
164 Tug McGraw IA 2.00 .80
165 Chris Speier RC 2.00 .80
166 Chris Speier IA 1.00 .40
167 Deron Johnson 1.00 .40
168 Deron Johnson IA 1.00 .40
169 Vida Blue 4.00 1.60
170 Vida Blue IA 2.00 .80
171 Darrell Evans 4.00 1.60
172 Darrell Evans IA 2.00 .80
173 Clay Kirby 1.00 .40
174 Clay Kirby IA 1.00 .40
175 Tom Haller 1.00 .40
176 Tom Haller IA 1.00 .40
177 Paul Schaal 1.00 .40
178 Paul Schaal IA 1.00 .40
179 Dock Ellis 1.00 .40
180 Dock Ellis IA 1.00 .40
181 Ed Kranepool 2.00 .80
182 Ed Kranepool IA 1.00 .40
183 Bill Melton 1.00 .40
184 Bill Melton IA 1.00 .40
185 Ron Bryant 1.00 .40
186 Ron Bryant IA 1.00 .40
187 Gates Brown 1.00 .40
188 Frank Lucchesi MG 1.00 .40
189 Gene Tenace 2.00 .80
190 Dave Giusti 1.00 .40
191 Jeff Burroughs RC 4.00 1.60
192 Chicago Cubs 2.00 .80
Team Card
193 Kurt Bevacqua 1.00 .40
194 Fred Norman 1.00 .40
195 Orlando Cepeda 6.00 2.40
196 Mel Queen 1.00 .40
197 Johnny Briggs 1.00 .40
198 Charlie Hough RC 6.00 2.40
Bob O'Brien
Mike Strahler
199 Mike Fiore 1.00 .40
200 Lou Brock 8.00 3.20
201 Phil Roof 1.00 .40
202 Scipio Spinks 1.00 .40
203 Ron Blomberg 1.00 .40
204 Tommy Helms 1.00 .40
205 Dick Drago 1.00 .40
206 Dal Maxvill 1.00 .40
207 Tom Egan 1.00 .40
208 Milt Pappas 2.00 .80
209 Joe Rudi 2.00 .80
210 Denny McLain 2.00 .80
211 Gary Sutherland 1.00 .40
212 Grant Jackson 1.00 .40
213 Billy Parker 1.00 .40
Art Kusnyer
Tom Silverio
214 Mike McQueen 1.00 .40
215 Alex Johnson 2.00 .80
216 Joe Niekro 2.00 .80
217 Roger Metzger 1.00 .40
218 Eddie Kasko MG 1.00 .40
219 Rennie Stennett 2.00 .80
220 Jim Perry 2.00 .80
221 NL Playoffs 2.00 .80
Bucs champs
222 Br. Robinson ALCS 4.00 1.60
223 Dave McNally WS 2.00 .80
224 Dave Johnson WS 2.00 .80
Mark Belanger
225 Manny Sanguillen WS 2.00 .80
226 Roberto Clemente WS 8.00 3.20
227 Nellie Briles WS 2.00 .80
228 Frank Robinson WS 2.00 .80
Manny Sanguillen
229 Steve Blass WS 2.00 .80
230 WS Summary 2.00 .80
Pirates celebrate
231 Casey Cox 1.00 .40
232 Chris Arnold 1.00 .40
Jim Barr
Dave Rader
233 Jay Johnstone 2.00 .80
234 Ron Taylor 1.00 .40
235 Merv Rettenmund 1.00 .40
236 Jim McGlothlin 1.00 .40
237 New York Yankees 2.00 .80
Team Card
238 Leron Lee 1.00 .40
239 Tom Timmermann 1.00 .40
240 Rich Allen 2.00 .80
241 Rollie Fingers 6.00 2.40
242 Don Mincher 1.00 .40
243 Frank Linzy 1.00 .40
244 Steve Braun 1.00 .40
245 Tommie Agee 2.00 .80
246 Tom Burgmeier 1.00 .40
247 Milt May 1.00 .40
248 Tom Bradley 1.00 .40
249 Harry Walker MG 1.00 .40
250 Boog Powell 2.00 .80
251 Checklist 264-394 6.00 1.20
252 Ken Reynolds 1.00 .40
253 Sandy Alomar 2.00 .80
254 Boots Day 1.00 .40
255 Jim Lonborg 2.00 .80
256 George Foster 2.00 .80
257 Jim Foor 1.00 .40
Tim Hosley
Paul Jata
258 Randy Hundley 1.00 .40
259 Sparky Lyle 2.00 .80
260 Ralph Garr 2.00 .80
261 Steve Mingori 1.00 .40
262 San Diego Padres 2.00 .80
Team Card
263 Felipe Alou 2.00 .80
264 Tommy John 2.00 .80
265 Wes Parker 2.00 .80
266 Bobby Bolin 1.25 .50
267 Dave Concepcion 4.00 1.60
268 Dwain Anderson 1.25 .50
Chris Floethe
269 Don Hahn 1.25 .50
270 Jim Palmer 8.00 3.20
271 Ken Rudolph 1.25 .50
272 Mickey Rivers RC 2.00 .80
273 Bobby Floyd 1.25 .50
274 Al Severinsen 1.25 .50
275 Cesar Tovar 1.25 .50
276 Gene Mauch MG 2.00 .80
277 Elliott Maddox 1.25 .50
278 Dennis Higgins 1.25 .50
279 Larry Brown 1.25 .50
280 Willie McCovey 6.00 2.40
281 Bill Parsons 1.25 .50
282 Houston Astros 2.00 .80
Team Card
283 Darrell Brandon 1.25 .50
284 Ike Brown 1.25 .50
285 Gaylord Perry 6.00 2.40
286 Gene Alley 1.25 .50
287 Jim Hardin 1.25 .50
288 Johnny Jeter 1.25 .50
289 Syd O'Brien 1.25 .50
290 Sonny Siebert 1.25 .50
291 Hal McRae 2.00 .80
292 Hal McRae IA 1.25 .50
293 Dan Frisella 1.25 .50
294 Dan Frisella IA 1.25 .50
295 Dick Dietz 1.25 .50
296 Dick Dietz IA 1.25 .50
297 Claude Osteen 2.00 .80
298 Claude Osteen IA 1.25 .50
299 Hank Aaron 40.00 16.00
300 Hank Aaron IA 20.00 8.00
301 George Mitterwald 1.25 .50
302 George Mitterwald IA 1.25 .50
303 Joe Pepitone 2.00 .80
304 Joe Pepitone IA 1.25 .50
305 Ken Boswell 1.25 .50
306 Ken Boswell IA 1.25 .50
307 Steve Renko 1.25 .50
308 Steve Renko IA 1.25 .50
309 Roberto Clemente 50.00 20.00
310 Roberto Clemente IA 25.00 10.00
311 Clay Carroll 1.25 .50
312 Clay Carroll IA 1.25 .50
313 Luis Aparicio 6.00 2.40
314 Luis Aparicio IA 2.00 .80
315 Paul Splittorff 1.25 .50
316 Jim Bibby 2.00 .80
Jorge Roque
Santiago Guzman
317 Rich Hand 1.25 .50
318 Sonny Jackson 1.25 .50
319 Aurelio Rodriguez 1.25 .50
320 Steve Blass 2.00 .80
321 Joe Lahoud 1.25 .50
322 Jose Pena 1.25 .50
323 Earl Weaver MG 4.00 1.60
324 Mike Ryan 1.25 .50
325 Mel Stottlemyre 2.00 .80
326 Pat Kelly 1.25 .50
327 Steve Stone RC 2.00 .80
328 Boston Red Sox 2.00 .80
Team Card
329 Roy Foster 1.25 .50
330 Jim Hunter 6.00 2.40
331 Stan Swanson 1.25 .50
332 Buck Martinez 1.25 .50
333 Steve Barber 1.25 .50
334 Bill Fahey 1.25 .50
Jim Mason
Tom Ragland
335 Bill Hands 1.25 .50
336 Marty Martinez 1.25 .50
337 Mike Kilkenny 1.25 .50
338 Bob Grich 2.00 .80
339 Ron Cook 1.25 .50
340 Roy White 2.00 .80
341 Joe Torre KP 1.25 .50
342 Wilbur Wood KP 1.25 .50
343 Willie Stargell KP 2.00 .80
344 Dave McNally KP 1.25 .50
345 Rick Wise KP 1.25 .50
346 Jim Fregosi KP 1.25 .50
347 Tom Seaver KP 4.00 1.60
348 Sal Bando KP 1.25 .50
349 Al Fitzmorris 1.25 .50
350 Frank Howard 2.00 .80
351 Tom House 2.00 .80
Rick Kester
Jimmy Britton
352 Dave LaRoche 1.25 .50
353 Art Shamsky 1.25 .50
354 Tom Murphy 1.25 .50
355 Bob Watson 2.00 .80
356 Gerry Moses 1.25 .50
357 Woody Fryman 1.25 .50
358 Sparky Anderson MG 4.00 1.60
359 Don Pavletich 1.25 .50
360 Dave Roberts 1.25 .50
361 Mike Andrews 1.25 .50
362 New York Mets 2.00 .80
Team Card
363 Ron Klimkowski 1.25 .50
364 Johnny Callison 2.00 .80
365 Dick Bosman 2.00 .80
366 Jimmy Rosario 1.25 .50
367 Ron Perranoski 2.00 .80
368 Danny Thompson 1.25 .50
369 Jim Lefebvre 2.00 .80
370 Don Buford 1.25 .50
371 Denny Lemaster 1.25 .50
372 Lance Clemons 1.25 .50
Monty Montgomery
373 John Mayberry 2.00 .80
374 Jack Heidemann 1.25 .50
375 Reggie Cleveland 1.25 .50
376 Andy Kosco 1.25 .50
377 Terry Harmon 1.25 .50
378 Checklist 395-525 6.00 1.20
379 Ken Berry 1.25 .50
380 Earl Williams 1.25 .50
381 Chicago White Sox 2.00 .80
Team Card
382 Joe Gibbon 1.25 .50
383 Brant Alyea 1.25 .50
384 Dave Campbell 2.00 .80
385 Mickey Stanley 2.00 .80
386 Jim Colborn 1.25 .50
387 Horace Clarke 2.00 .80
388 Charlie Williams 1.25 .50
389 Bill Rigney MG 1.25 .50
390 Willie Davis 2.00 .80
391 Ken Sanders 1.25 .50
392 Fred Cambria 2.00 .80
Richie Zisk RC
393 Curt Motton 1.25 .50
394 Ken Forsch 2.00 .80
395 Matty Alou 2.00 .80
396 Paul Lindblad 1.50 .60
397 Philadelphia Phillies 2.00 .80
Team Card
398 Larry Hisle 2.00 .80
399 Milt Wilcox 2.00 .80
400 Tony Oliva 4.00 1.60
401 Jim Nash 1.50 .60
402 Bobby Heise 1.50 .60
403 John Cumberland 1.50 .60
404 Jeff Torborg 2.00 .80
405 Ron Fairly 2.00 .80
406 George Hendrick RC 2.00 .80
407 Chuck Taylor 1.50 .60
408 Jim Northrup 2.00 .80
409 Frank Baker 1.50 .60
410 Ferguson Jenkins 6.00 2.40
411 Bob Montgomery 1.50 .60
412 Dick Kelley 1.50 .60
413 Don Eddy 1.50 .60
Dave Lemonds
414 Bob Miller 1.50 .60
415 Cookie Rojas 2.00 .80
416 Johnny Edwards 1.50 .60
417 Tom Hall 1.50 .60
418 Tom Shopay 1.50 .60
419 Jim Spencer 1.50 .60
420 Steve Carlton 20.00 8.00
421 Ellie Rodriguez 1.50 .60
422 Ray Lamb 1.50 .60
423 Oscar Gamble 2.00 .80
424 Bill Gogolewski 1.50 .60
425 Ken Singleton 2.00 .80
426 Ken Singleton IA 1.50 .60
427 Tito Fuentes 1.50 .60
428 Tito Fuentes IA 1.50 .60
429 Bob Robertson 1.50 .60
430 Bob Robertson IA 1.50 .60
431 Clarence Gaston 2.00 .80
432 Clarence Gaston IA 2.00 .80
433 Johnny Bench 25.00 10.00
434 Johnny Bench IA 15.00 6.00

435 Reggie Jackson 30.00 12.00
436 Reggie Jackson IA 12.00 4.80
437 Maury Wills 2.00 .80
438 Maury Wills IA 2.00 .80
439 Billy Williams 6.00 2.40
440 Billy Williams IA 4.00 1.60
441 Thurman Munson 15.00 6.00
442 Thurman Munson IA 8.00 3.20
443 Ken Henderson 1.50 .60
444 Ken Henderson IA 1.50 .60
445 Tom Seaver 30.00 12.00
446 Tom Seaver IA 15.00 6.00
447 Willie Stargell 8.00 3.20
448 Willie Stargell IA 4.00 1.60
449 Bob Lemon MG 2.00 .80
450 Mickey Lolich 2.00 .80
451 Tony LaRussa 4.00 1.60
452 Ed Herrmann 1.50 .60
453 Barry Lersch 1.50 .60
454 Oakland A's 2.00 .80
Team Card
455 Tommy Harper 2.00 .80
456 Mark Belanger 2.00 .80
457 Darcy Fast 1.50 .60
Derrel Thomas
Mike Ivie
458 Aurelio Monteagudo 1.50 .60
459 Rick Renick 1.50 .60
460 Al Downing 1.50 .60
461 Tim Cullen 1.50 .60
462 Rickey Clark 1.50 .60
463 Bernie Carbo 1.50 .60
464 Jim Roland 1.50 .60
465 Gil Hodges MG 4.00 1.60
466 Norm Miller 1.50 .60
467 Steve Kline 1.50 .60
468 Richie Scheinblum 1.50 .60
469 Ron Herbel 1.50 .60
470 Ray Fosse 1.50 .60
471 Luke Walker 1.50 .60
472 Phil Gagliano 1.50 .60
473 Dan McGinn 1.50 .60
474 Don Baylor 15.00 6.00
Roric Harrison
Johnny Oates RC
475 Gary Nolan 2.00 .80
476 Lee Richard 1.50 .60
477 Tom Phoebus 1.50 .60
478 Checklist 526-656 6.00 1.20
479 Don Shaw 1.50 .60
480 Lee May 2.00 .80
481 Billy Conigliaro 2.00 .80
482 Joe Hoerner 1.50 .60
483 Ken Suarez 1.50 .60
484 Lum Harris MG 1.50 .60
485 Phil Regan 2.00 .80
486 John Lowenstein 1.50 .60
487 Detroit Tigers 2.00 .80
Team Card
488 Mike Nagy 1.50 .60
489 Terry Humphrey 1.50 .60
Keith Lampard
490 Dave McNally 2.00 .80
491 Lou Piniella KP 2.00 .80
492 Mel Stottlemyre KP 2.00 .80
493 Bob Bailey KP 2.00 .80
494 Willie Horton KP 2.00 .80
495 Bill Melton KP 2.00 .80
496 Bud Harrelson KP 2.00 .80
497 Jim Perry KP 2.00 .80
498 Brooks Robinson KP 4.00 1.60
499 Vicente Romo 1.50 .60
500 Joe Torre 4.00 1.60
501 Pete Hamm 1.50 .60
502 Jackie Hernandez 1.50 .60
503 Gary Peters 1.50 .60
504 Ed Spiezio 1.50 .60
505 Mike Marshall 2.00 .80
506 Terry Ley 1.50 .60
Jim Moyer
Dick Tidrow RC
507 Fred Gladding 1.50 .60
508 Elrod Hendricks 1.50 .60
509 Don McMahon 1.50 .60
510 Ted Williams MG 12.00 4.80
511 Tony Taylor 2.00 .80
512 Paul Popovich 1.50 .60
513 Lindy McDaniel 2.00 .80
514 Ted Sizemore 1.50 .60
515 Bert Blyleven 4.00 1.60
516 Oscar Brown 1.50 .60
517 Ken Brett 1.50 .60
518 Wayne Garrett 1.50 .60
519 Ted Abernathy 1.50 .60
520 Larry Bowa 2.00 .80
521 Alan Foster 1.50 .60
522 Los Angeles Dodgers 2.00 .80
Team Card
523 Chuck Dobson 1.50 .60
524 Ed Armbrister 1.50 .60
Mel Behney
525 Carlos May 2.00 .80
526 Bob Bailey 6.00 2.40
527 Dave Leonhard 4.00 1.60
528 Ron Stone 4.00 1.60
529 Dave Nelson 6.00 2.40
530 Don Sutton 12.00 4.80
531 Freddie Patek 6.00 2.40
532 Fred Kendall 4.00 1.60
533 Ralph Houk MG 6.00 2.40
534 Jim Hickman 6.00 2.40
535 Ed Brinkman 4.00 1.60
536 Doug Rader 6.00 2.40
537 Bob Locker 4.00 1.60
538 Charlie Sands 4.00 1.60
539 Terry Forster RC 6.00 2.40
540 Felix Millan 4.00 1.60
541 Roger Repoz 4.00 1.60
542 Jack Billingham 4.00 1.60
543 Duane Josephson 4.00 1.60
544 Ted Martinez 4.00 1.60
545 Wayne Granger 4.00 1.60
546 Joe Hague 4.00 1.60
547 Cleveland Indians 8.00 3.20
Team Card
548 Frank Reberger 4.00 1.60
549 Dave May 4.00 1.60
550 Brooks Robinson 25.00 10.00
551 Ollie Brown 4.00 1.60
552 Ollie Brown IA 4.00 1.60
553 Wilbur Wood 6.00 2.40
554 Wilbur Wood IA 4.00 1.60
555 Ron Santo 8.00 3.20
556 Ron Santo IA 6.00 2.40
557 John Odom 4.00 1.60
558 John Odom IA 4.00 1.60
559 Pete Rose 50.00 20.00
560 Pete Rose IA 25.00 10.00
561 Leo Cardenas 4.00 1.60
562 Leo Cardenas IA 4.00 1.60
563 Ray Sadecki 4.00 1.60
564 Ray Sadecki IA 4.00 1.60
565 Reggie Smith 6.00 2.40
566 Reggie Smith IA 4.00 1.60
567 Juan Marichal 12.00 4.80
568 Juan Marichal IA 6.00 2.40
569 Ed Kirkpatrick 4.00 1.60
570 Ed Kirkpatrick IA 4.00 1.60
571 Nate Colbert 4.00 1.60
572 Nate Colbert IA 4.00 1.60
573 Fritz Peterson 4.00 1.60
574 Fritz Peterson IA 4.00 1.60
575 Al Oliver 8.00 3.20
576 Leo Durocher MG 6.00 2.40
577 Mike Paul 6.00 2.40
578 Billy Grabarkewitz 4.00 1.60
579 Doyle Alexander RC 6.00 2.40
580 Lou Piniella 6.00 2.40
581 Wade Blasingame 4.00 1.60
582 Montreal Expos 8.00 3.20
Team Card
583 Darold Knowles 4.00 1.60
584 Jerry McNertney 4.00 1.60
585 George Scott 6.00 2.40
586 Denis Menke 4.00 1.60
587 Billy Wilson 4.00 1.60
588 Jim Holt 4.00 1.60
589 Hal Lanier 4.00 1.60
590 Graig Nettles 8.00 3.20
591 Paul Casanova 4.00 1.60
592 Lew Krausse 4.00 1.60
593 Rich Morales 4.00 1.60
594 Jim Beauchamp 4.00 1.60
595 Nolan Ryan 100.00 40.00
596 Manny Mota 6.00 2.40
597 Jim Magnuson 4.00 1.60
598 Hal King 6.00 2.40
599 Billy Champion 4.00 1.60
600 Al Kaline 25.00 10.00
601 George Stone 4.00 1.60
602 Dave Bristol MG 4.00 1.60
603 Jim Ray 4.00 1.60
604A Checklist 657-787 12.00 2.40
(Copyright on back
bottom right)
604B Checklist 657-787 12.00 2.40
(Copyright on back
bottom left)
605 Nelson Briles 6.00 2.40
606 Luis Melendez 4.00 1.60
607 Frank Duffy 4.00 1.60
608 Mike Corkins 4.00 1.60
609 Tom Grieve 6.00 2.40
610 Bill Stoneman 6.00 2.40
611 Rich Reese 4.00 1.60
612 Joe Decker 4.00 1.60
613 Mike Ferraro 4.00 1.60
614 Ted Uhlaender 4.00 1.60
615 Steve Hargan 4.00 1.60
616 Joe Ferguson RC 6.00 2.40
617 Kansas City Royals 8.00 3.20
Team Card
618 Rich Robertson 4.00 1.60
619 Rich McKinney 4.00 1.60
620 Phil Niekro 12.00 4.80
621 Comm. Award 8.00 3.20
622 MVP Award 8.00 3.20
623 Cy Young Award 8.00 3.20
624 Minor League Player 8.00 3.20
of the Year
625 Rookie of the Year 8.00 3.20
626 Babe Ruth Award 8.00 3.20
627 Moe Drabowsky 4.00 1.60
628 Terry Crowley 4.00 1.60
629 Paul Doyle 4.00 1.60
630 Rich Hebner 6.00 2.40
631 John Strohmayer 4.00 1.60
632 Mike Hegan 4.00 1.60
633 Jack Hiatt 4.00 1.60
634 Dick Woodson 4.00 1.60
635 Don Money 6.00 2.40
636 Bill Lee 6.00 2.40
637 Preston Gomez MG 4.00 1.60
638 Ken Wright 4.00 1.60
639 J.C. Martin 4.00 1.60
640 Joe Coleman 4.00 1.60
641 Mike Lum 4.00 1.60
642 Dennis Riddleberger 4.00 1.60
643 Russ Gibson 4.00 1.60
644 Bernie Allen 4.00 1.60
645 Jim Maloney 6.00 2.40
646 Chico Salmon 4.00 1.60
647 Bob Moose 4.00 1.60
648 Jim Lyttle 4.00 1.60
649 Pete Richert 4.00 1.60
650 Sal Bando 6.00 2.40
651 Cincinnati Reds 8.00 3.20
Team Card
652 Marcelino Lopez 4.00 1.60
653 Jim Fairey 4.00 1.60
654 Horacio Pina 6.00 2.40
655 Jerry Grote 4.00 1.60
656 Rudy May 4.00 1.60
657 Bobby Wine 12.00 4.80
658 Steve Dunning 12.00 4.80
659 Bob Aspromonte 12.00 4.80
660 Paul Blair 15.00 6.00
661 Bill Virdon MG 12.00 4.80
662 Stan Bahnsen 12.00 4.80
663 Fran Healy 15.00 6.00
664 Bobby Knoop 12.00 4.80
665 Chris Short 12.00 4.80
666 Hector Torres 12.00 4.80
667 Ray Newman 12.00 4.80
668 Texas Rangers 30.00 12.00
Team Card
669 Willie Crawford 12.00 4.80
670 Ken Holtzman 15.00 6.00
671 Donn Clendenon 15.00 6.00
672 Archie Reynolds 12.00 4.80
673 Dave Marshall 12.00 4.80
674 John Kennedy 12.00 4.80
675 Pat Jarvis 12.00 4.80
676 Danny Cater 12.00 4.80
677 Ivan Murrell 12.00 4.80
678 Steve Luebber 12.00 4.80
679 Bob Fenwick 12.00 4.80
Bob Stinson
680 Dave Johnson 15.00 6.00
681 Bobby Pfeil 12.00 4.80
682 Mike McCormick 15.00 6.00
683 Steve Hovley 12.00 4.80
684 Hal Breeden 12.00 4.80
685 Joel Horlen 12.00 4.80
686 Steve Garvey 40.00 16.00
687 Del Unser 12.00 4.80
688 St. Louis Cardinals 20.00 8.00
Team Card
689 Eddie Fisher 12.00 4.80
690 Willie Montanez 15.00 6.00
691 Curt Blefary 12.00 4.80
692 Curt Blefary IA 12.00 4.80
693 Alan Gallagher 12.00 4.80
694 Alan Gallagher IA 12.00 4.80
695 Rod Carew 50.00 20.00
696 Rod Carew IA 30.00 12.00
697 Jerry Koosman 15.00 6.00
698 Jerry Koosman IA 15.00 6.00
699 Bobby Murcer 15.00 6.00
700 Bobby Murcer IA 15.00 6.00
701 Jose Pagan 12.00 4.80
702 Jose Pagan IA 12.00 4.80
703 Doug Griffin 12.00 4.80
704 Doug Griffin IA 12.00 4.80
705 Pat Corrales 15.00 6.00
706 Pat Corrales IA 12.00 4.80
707 Tim Foli 12.00 4.80
708 Tim Foli IA 12.00 4.80
709 Jim Kaat 15.00 6.00
710 Jim Kaat IA 15.00 6.00
711 Bobby Bonds 20.00 8.00
712 Bobby Bonds IA 15.00 6.00
713 Gene Michael 20.00 8.00
714 Gene Michael IA 15.00 6.00
715 Mike Epstein 12.00 4.80
716 Jesus Alou 12.00 4.80
717 Bruce Dal Canton 12.00 4.80
718 Del Rice MG 12.00 4.80
719 Cesar Geronimo 12.00 4.80
720 Sam McDowell 15.00 6.00
721 Eddie Leon 12.00 4.80
722 Bill Sudakis 12.00 4.80
723 Al Santorini 12.00 4.80
724 John Curtis 12.00 4.80
Rich Hinton
Mickey Scott RC
725 Dick McAuliffe 15.00 6.00
726 Dick Selma 12.00 4.80
727 Jose Laboy 12.00 4.80
728 Gail Hopkins 12.00 4.80
729 Bob Veale 15.00 6.00
730 Rick Monday 15.00 6.00
731 Baltimore Orioles 20.00 8.00
Team Card
732 George Culver 12.00 4.80
733 Jim Ray Hart 15.00 6.00
734 Bob Burda 12.00 4.80
735 Diego Segui 12.00 4.80
736 Bill Russell 15.00 6.00
737 Len Randle 15.00 6.00
738 Jim Merritt 12.00 4.80
739 Don Mason 12.00 4.80
740 Rico Carty 15.00 6.00
741 Tom Hutton 15.00 6.00
John Milner
Rick Miller RC
742 Jim Rooker 12.00 4.80
743 Cesar Gutierrez 12.00 4.80
744 Jim Slaton 12.00 4.80
745 Julian Javier 15.00 6.00
746 Lowell Palmer 12.00 4.80
747 Jim Stewart 12.00 4.80
748 Phil Hennigan 12.00 4.80
749 Walter Alston MG 20.00 8.00
750 Willie Horton 15.00 6.00
751 Steve Carlton TR 40.00 16.00
752 Joe Morgan TR 40.00 16.00
753 Denny McLain TR 20.00 8.00
754 Frank Robinson TR 40.00 16.00
755 Jim Fregosi TR 15.00 6.00
756 Rick Wise TR 15.00 6.00
757 Jose Cardenal TR 15.00 6.00
758 Gil Garrido 12.00 4.80
759 Chris Cannizzaro 12.00 4.80
760 Bill Mazeroski 25.00 10.00
761 Ben Oglivie RC 25.00 10.00
Ron Cey RC
Bernie Williams
762 Wayne Simpson 12.00 4.80
763 Ron Hansen 12.00 4.80
764 Dusty Baker 20.00 8.00
765 Ken McMullen 12.00 4.80
766 Steve Hamilton 12.00 4.80
767 Tom McCraw 15.00 6.00
768 Denny Doyle 12.00 4.80
769 Jack Aker 12.00 4.80
770 Jim Wynn 15.00 6.00
771 San Francisco Giants 20.00 8.00
Team Card
772 Ken Tatum 12.00 4.80
773 Ron Brand 12.00 4.80
774 Luis Alvarado 12.00 4.80
775 Jerry Reuss 15.00 6.00
776 Bill Voss 12.00 4.80
777 Hoyt Wilhelm 25.00 10.00
778 Vic Albury 20.00 8.00
Rick Dempsey RC
Jim Strickland
779 Tony Cloninger 12.00 4.80
780 Dick Green 12.00 4.80
781 Jim McAndrew 12.00 4.80
782 Larry Stahl 12.00 4.80
783 Les Cain 12.00 4.80
784 Ken Aspromonte 12.00 4.80
785 Vic Davalillo 12.00 4.80
786 Chuck Brinkman 12.00 4.80
787 Ron Reed 15.00 5.25

1972 Topps Candy Lids

A cross in design between the 1970 and the 1973 Topps Candy Lids. These lids do not have borders. Since the lids are unnumbered we have sequenced them alphabetically. Any further information on these lids are appreciated. These have been dated 1972 by Ray Fosse being listed as a member of the Cleveland Indians.

NM Ex
COMPLETE SET 1500.00 600.00
1 Dick Allen 200.00 80.00
2 Carlton Fisk 400.00 160.00
3 Ray Fosse 100.00 40.00
4 Bob Gibson 200.00 80.00
5 Greg Luzinski 150.00 60.00
6 Thurman Munson 250.00 100.00
7 Gaylord Perry 200.00 80.00
8 Ellie Rodriguez 100.00 40.00

1972 Topps Posters

This giant (9 7/16" by 18"), full-color series of 24 paper-thin posters was issued as a separate set in 1972. The posters are individually numbered and unlike other Topps posters described in this book, are borderless. They are printed on thin paper and were folded five times to facilitate packaging.

NM Ex
COMPLETE SET (24) 800.00 325.00
WRAPPER (10-CENT)
1 Dave McNally 8.00 3.20
2 Carl Yastrzemski 80.00 32.00
3 Bill Melton 8.00 3.20
4 Ray Fosse 8.00 3.20
5 Mickey Lolich 10.00 4.00
6 Amos Otis 10.00 4.00
7 Tony Oliva 12.00 4.80
8 Vida Blue 10.00 4.00
9 Hank Aaron 100.00 40.00
10 Fergie Jenkins 20.00 8.00
11 Pete Rose 100.00 40.00
12 Willie Davis 10.00 4.00
13 Tom Seaver 80.00 32.00
14 Rick Wise 8.00 3.20
15 Willie Stargell 40.00 16.00
16 Joe Torre 12.00 4.80
17 Willie Mays 100.00 40.00
18 Andy Messersmith 10.00 4.00
19 Wilbur Wood 10.00 4.00
20 Harmon Killebrew 40.00 16.00
21 Billy Williams 40.00 16.00
22 Bud Harrelson 8.00 3.20
23 Roberto Clemente 150.00 60.00
24 Willie McCovey 40.00 16.00

1972 Topps Cloth Test

These "test" issue cards look like 1972 Topps cards except that they are on a "cloth sticker". Each card measures 2 1/2" by 3 1/2". The "cards" in this set are all taken from the third series of the 1972 Topps regular issue. Cards are blank backed and unnumbered. They are listed below in alphabetical order.

NM Ex
COMPLETE SET (33) 600.00 240.00
1 Hank Aaron 100.00 40.00
2 Luis Aparicio IA 30.00 12.00
3 Ike Brown 15.00 6.00
4 Johnny Callison 20.00 8.00
5 Checklist 264-319 15.00 6.00
6 Roberto Clemente 150.00 60.00
7 Dave Concepcion 25.00 10.00
8 Ron Cook 15.00 6.00
9 Willie Davis 20.00 8.00
10 Al Fitzmorris 15.00 6.00
11 Bobby Floyd 15.00 6.00
12 Roy Foster 15.00 6.00
13 Jim Fregosi KP 15.00 6.00
14 Danny Frisella IA 15.00 6.00
15 Woody Fryman 15.00 6.00
16 Terry Harmon 15.00 6.00
17 Frank Howard 20.00 8.00
18 Ron Klimkowski 15.00 6.00
19 Joe Lahoud 15.00 6.00
20 Jim Lefebvre 15.00 6.00
21 Elliott Maddox 15.00 6.00
22 Marty Martinez 15.00 6.00
23 Willie McCovey 60.00 24.00
24 Hal McRae 20.00 8.00
25 Syd O'Brien 15.00 6.00
26 Red Sox Team 20.00 8.00
27 Aurelio Rodriguez 15.00 6.00
28 Al Severinsen 15.00 6.00
29 Art Shamsky 15.00 6.00
30 Steve Stone 20.00 8.00
31 Stan Swanson 15.00 6.00
32 Bob Watson 20.00 8.00
33 Roy White 20.00 8.00

1972 Topps Test 53

These "test" issue cards were made to look like 1953 Topps cards as the cards show drawings rather than photos. The card number of the corresponding art from the 1953 Topps set is given in parentheses after the name of the player. For three of the cards in this set the

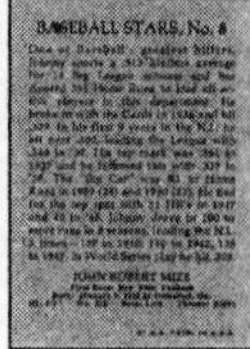

player pictured in the art is not the same player as listed on the card; in these cases the actual player pictured is also listed parenthetically in the checklist below. Each card measures 2 1/2" by 3 1/2". Printing on the back is in blue ink on gray card stock.

NM Ex
COMPLETE SET (8) 600.00 240.00
1 Satchel Paige UER 100.00 40.00
53 Topps 220, spelled Satchell
2 Jackie Robinson 100.00 40.00
53 Topps 1
3 Carl Furillo 60.00 24.00
53 Topps 272
picture actually
Bill Antonello
4 Al Rosen 60.00 24.00
53 Topps 187
picture actually
Jim Fridley
5 Hal Newhouser 80.00 32.00
53 Topps 228
6 Clyde McCullough 40.00 16.00
53 Topps 222
picture actually
Vic Janowicz
7 Peanuts Lowrey 40.00 16.00
53 Topps 16
8 Johnny Mize 100.00 40.00
53 Topps 77

1973 Topps

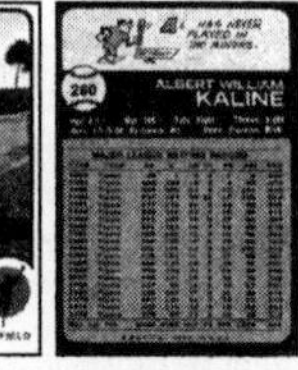

The cards in this 660-card set measure 2 1/2" by 3 1/2". The 1973 Topps set marked the last year in which Topps marketed baseball cards in consecutive series. The last series (529-660) is more difficult to obtain. In some parts of the country, however, all five series were distributed together. Beginning in 1974, all Topps cards were printed at the same time, thus eliminating the "high number" factor. The set features team leader cards with small individual pictures of the coaching staff members and a larger picture of the manager. The "background" variations below with respect to these leader cards are subtle and are best understood after a side-by-side comparison of the two varieties. An "All-Time Leaders" series (471-478) appeared for the first time in this set. Kid Pictures appeared again for the second year in a row (341-346). Other topical subsets within the set included League Leaders (61-68), Playoffs cards (201-202), World Series cards (203-210), and Rookie Prospects (601-616). For the fourth and final time, cards were issued in ten-card dime packs, cards were also released in 54-card rack packs. The key Rookie Cards in this set are all in the Rookie Prospect series: Bob Boone, Dwight Evans, and Mike Schmidt.

NM Ex
COMPLETE SET (660) 700.00 275.00
COMMON CARD (1-264) .50 .20
COMMON (265-396) .75 .30
COMMON (397-528) 1.25 .50
COMMON (529-660) 3.00 1.20
WRAP. (10-CENT, BAT) 15.00 6.00
WRAPPER (10-CENT) 15.00 6.00
1 Babe Ruth 714 40.00 11.50
Hank Aaron 673
Willie Mays 654 ATL
2 Rich Hebner 1.50 .60
3 Jim Lonborg 1.50 .60
4 John Milner .50 .20
5 Ed Brinkman .50 .20
6 Mac Scarce .50 .20
7 Texas Rangers 2.00 .80
Team Card
8 Tom Hall .50 .20
9 Johnny Oates 1.50 .60
10 Don Sutton 4.00 1.60
11 Chris Chambliss 1.50 .60
12A Don Zimmer MG 3.00 1.20
Dave Garcia CO
Johnny Podres CO
Bob Skinner CO
Whitey Wietelmann CO
(Podres no right ear)
12B Padres Leaders .75 .30
(Podres has right ear)
13 George Hendrick 1.50 .60
14 Sonny Siebert .50 .20
15 Ralph Garr 1.50 .60
16 Steve Braun .50 .20
17 Fred Gladding .50 .20
18 Leroy Stanton .50 .20
19 Tim Foli .50 .20
20 Stan Bahnsen .50 .20
21 Randy Hundley 1.50 .60
22 Ted Abernathy .50 .20
23 Dave Kingman 1.50 .60
24 Al Santorini .50 .20
25 Roy White 1.50 .60
26 Pittsburgh Pirates 2.00 .80

Team Card
27 Bill Gogolewski .50 .20
28 Hal McRae 1.50 .60
29 Tony Taylor 1.50 .60
30 Tug McGraw 1.50 .60
31 Buddy Bell RC 2.50 1.00
32 Fred Norman .50 .20
33 Jim Breazeale .50 .20
34 Pat Dobson .50 .20
35 Willie Davis 1.50 .60
36 Steve Barber .50 .20
37 Bill Robinson 1.50 .60
38 Mike Epstein .50 .20
39 Dave Roberts .50 .20
40 Reggie Smith 1.50 .60
41 Tom Walker .50 .20
42 Mike Andrews .50 .20
43 Randy Moffitt .50 .20
44 Rick Monday 1.50 .60
45 Ellie Rodriguez UER .50 .20
(Photo actually
John Felske)
46 Lindy McDaniel 1.50 .60
47 Luis Melendez .50 .20
48 Paul Splittorff .50 .20
49A Frank Quilici MG 3.00 1.20
Vern Morgan CO
Bob Rodgers CO
Ralph Rowe CO
Al Worthington CO
(Solid backgrounds)
49B Twins Leaders .75 .30
(Natural backgrounds)
50 Roberto Clemente 40.00 16.00
51 Chuck Seelbach .50 .20
52 Denis Menke .50 .20
53 Steve Dunning .50 .20
54 Checklist 1-132 3.00 .60
55 Jon Matlack 1.50 .60
56 Merv Rettenmund .50 .20
57 Derrel Thomas .50 .20
58 Mike Paul .50 .20
59 Steve Yeager RC 1.50 .60
60 Ken Holtzman 1.50 .60
61 Billy Williams 2.50 1.00
Rod Carew LL
62 Johnny Bench 2.50 1.00
Dick Allen LL
Home Run Leaders
63 Johnny Bench 2.50 1.00
Dick Allen
RBI Leaders
64 Lou Brock 1.50 .60
Bert Campaneris LL
65 Steve Carlton 1.50 .60
Luis Tiant LL
66 Steve Carlton 1.50 .60
Gaylord Perry
Wilbur Wood LL
67 Steve Carlton 25.00 10.00
Nolan Ryan LL
68 Clay Carroll 1.50 .60
Sparky Lyle LL
69 Phil Gagliano .50 .20
70 Milt Pappas 1.50 .60
71 Johnny Briggs .50 .20
72 Ron Reed .50 .20
73 Ed Herrmann .50 .20
74 Billy Champion .50 .20
75 Vada Pinson 1.50 .60
76 Doug Rader .50 .20
77 Mike Torrez 1.50 .60
78 Richie Scheinblum .50 .20
79 Jim Willoughby .50 .20
80 Tony Oliva UER 2.50 1.00
(Minnseota on front)
81A Whitey Lockman MG 1.50 .60
Hank Aguirre CO
Ernie Banks CO
Larry Jansen CO
Pete Reiser CO
(Solid backgrounds)
81B Cubs Leaders 1.50 .60
(Natural backgrounds)
82 Fritz Peterson .50 .20
83 Leron Lee .50 .20
84 Rollie Fingers 4.00 1.60
85 Ted Simmons 1.50 .60
86 Tom McCraw .50 .20
87 Ken Boswell .50 .20
88 Mickey Stanley 1.50 .60
89 Jack Billingham .50 .20
90 Brooks Robinson 8.00 3.20
91 Los Angeles Dodgers 2.00 .80
Team Card
92 Jerry Bell .50 .20
93 Jesus Alou .50 .20
94 Dick Billings .50 .20
95 Steve Blass 1.50 .60
96 Doug Griffin .50 .20
97 Willie Montanez 1.50 .60
98 Dick Woodson .50 .20
99 Carl Taylor .50 .20
100 Hank Aaron 40.00 16.00
101 Ken Henderson .50 .20
102 Rudy May .50 .20
103 Celerino Sanchez .50 .20
104 Reggie Cleveland .50 .20
105 Carlos May .50 .20
106 Terry Humphrey .50 .20
107 Phil Hennigan .50 .20
108 Bill Russell 1.50 .60
109 Doyle Alexander 1.50 .60
110 Bob Watson 1.50 .60
111 Dave Nelson .50 .20
112 Gary Ross .50 .20
113 Jerry Grote 1.50 .60
114 Lynn McGlothen .50 .20
115 Ron Santo 1.50 .60
116A Ralph Houk MG 3.00 1.20
Jim Hegan CO
Elston Howard CO
Dick Howser CO
Jim Turner CO
(Solid backgrounds)
116B Yankees Leaders .75 .30
(Natural backgrounds)
117 Ramon Hernandez .50 .20
118 John Mayberry 1.50 .60
119 Larry Bowa 1.50 .60
120 Joe Coleman .50 .20
121 Dave Rader .50 .20
122 Jim Strickland .50 .20
123 Sandy Alomar 1.50 .60
124 Jim Hardin .50 .20
125 Ron Fairly 1.50 .60
126 Jim Brewer .50 .20
127 Milwaukee Brewers 2.00 .80
Team Card
128 Ted Sizemore .50 .20
129 Terry Forster 1.50 .60
130 Pete Rose 30.00 12.00
131A Eddie Kasko MG 3.00 1.20
Doug Camilli CO
Don Lenhardt CO
Eddie Popowski CO
(No right ear)
Lee Stange CO
131B Red Sox Leaders 1.50 .60
(Popowski has right
ear showing)
132 Matty Alou 1.50 .60
133 Dave Roberts RC .50 .20
134 Milt Wilcox .50 .20
135 Lee May UER 1.50 .60
(Career average .000)
136A Earl Weaver MG 2.00 .80
George Bamberger CO
Jim Frey CO
Billy Hunter CO
George Staller CO
(Orange backgrounds)
136B Orioles Leaders 3.00 1.20
(Dark pale
backgrounds)
137 Jim Beauchamp .50 .20
138 Horacio Pina .50 .20
139 Carmen Fanzone .50 .20
140 Lou Piniella 2.50 1.00
141 Bruce Kison .50 .20
142 Thurman Munson 8.00 3.20
143 John Curtis .50 .20
144 Marty Perez .50 .20
145 Bobby Bonds 2.50 1.00
146 Woodie Fryman .50 .20
147 Mike Anderson .50 .20
148 Dave Goltz .50 .20
149 Ron Hunt .50 .20
150 Wilbur Wood 1.50 .60
151 Wes Parker 1.50 .60
152 Dave May .50 .20
153 Al Hrabosky 1.50 .60
154 Jeff Torborg 1.50 .60
155 Sal Bando 1.50 .60
156 Cesar Geronimo .50 .20
157 Denny Riddleberger .50 .20
158 Houston Astros 2.00 .80
Team Card
159 Clarence Gaston 1.50 .60
160 Jim Palmer 6.00 2.40
161 Ted Martinez .50 .20
162 Pete Broberg .50 .20
163 Vic Davalillo .50 .20
164 Monty Montgomery .50 .20
165 Luis Aparicio 4.00 1.60
166 Terry Harmon .50 .20
167 Steve Stone 1.50 .60
168 Jim Northrup 1.50 .60
169 Ron Schueler RC 1.50 .60
170 Harmon Killebrew 5.00 2.00
171 Bernie Carbo .50 .20
172 Steve Kline .50 .20
173 Hal Breeden .50 .20
174 Goose Gossage RC 6.00 2.40
175 Frank Robinson 6.00 2.40
176 Chuck Taylor .50 .20
177 Bill Plummer .50 .20
178 Don Rose .50 .20
179A Dick Williams MG 4.00 1.60
Jerry Adair CO
Vern Hoscheit CO
Irv Noren CO
Wes Stock CO
(Hoscheit left ear
showing)
179B A's Leaders 1.50 .60
(Hoscheit left ear
not showing)
180 Ferguson Jenkins 4.00 1.60
181 Jack Brohamer .50 .20
182 Mike Caldwell RC 1.50 .60
183 Don Buford .50 .20
184 Jerry Koosman 1.50 .60
185 Jim Wynn 1.50 .60
186 Bill Fahey .50 .20
187 Luke Walker .50 .20
188 Cookie Rojas 1.50 .60
189 Greg Luzinski 2.50 1.00
190 Bob Gibson 8.00 3.20
191 Detroit Tigers 2.50 1.00
Team Card
192 Pat Jarvis .50 .20
193 Carlton Fisk 10.00 4.00
194 Jorge Orta .50 .20
195 Clay Carroll .50 .20
196 Ken McMullen .50 .20
197 Ed Goodson .50 .20
198 Horace Clarke .50 .20
199 Bert Blyleven 2.50 1.00
200 Billy Williams 4.00 1.60
201 G. Hendrick ALCS 1.50 .60
202 George Foster NLCS 1.50 .60
203 Gene Tenace WS 1.50 .60
204 World Series Game 2 1.50 .60
A's two straight
205 Tony Perez WS 2.50 1.00
206 Gene Tenace WS 1.50 .60
207 Blue Moon Odom WS 1.50 .60
208 Johnny Bench WS6 5.00 2.00
209 Bert Campaneris WS 1.50 .60
210 W.S. Summary .50 .20
World champions:
A's Win
211 Balor Moore .50 .20
212 Joe Lahoud .50 .20
213 Steve Garvey 5.00 2.00
214 Dave Hamilton .50 .20
215 Dusty Baker 2.50 1.00
216 Toby Harrah 1.50 .60
217 Don Wilson .50 .20
218 Aurelio Rodriguez .50 .20
219 St. Louis Cardinals 2.50 1.00
Team Card
220 Nolan Ryan 60.00 24.00
221 Fred Kendall .50 .20
222 Rob Gardner .50 .20
223 Bud Harrelson 1.50 .60
224 Bill Lee 1.50 .60
225 Al Oliver 1.50 .60
226 Ray Fosse .50 .20
227 Wayne Twitchell .50 .20
228 Bobby Darwin .50 .20
229 Roric Harrison .50 .20
230 Joe Morgan 6.00 2.40
231 Bill Parsons .50 .20
232 Ken Singleton 1.50 .60
233 Ed Kirkpatrick .50 .20
234 Bill North .50 .20
235 Jim Hunter 4.00 1.60
236 Tito Fuentes .50 .20
237A Eddie Mathews MG 2.00 .80
Lew Burdette CO
Jim Busby CO
Roy Hartsfield CO
Ken Silvestri CO
(Burdette right ear
showing)
237B Braves Leaders 3.00 1.20
(Burdette right ear
not showing)
238 Tony Muser .50 .20
239 Pete Richert .50 .20
240 Bobby Murcer 1.50 .60
241 Dwain Anderson .50 .20
242 George Culver .50 .20
243 California Angels 2.50 1.00
Team Card
244 Ed Acosta .50 .20
245 Carl Yastrzemski 10.00 4.00
246 Ken Sanders .50 .20
247 Del Unser .50 .20
248 Jerry Johnson .50 .20
249 Larry Biittner .50 .20
250 Manny Sanguillen 1.50 .60
251 Roger Nelson .50 .20
252A Charlie Fox MG 4.00 1.60
Joe Amalfitano CO
Andy Gilbert CO
Don McMahon CO
John McNamara CO
(Orange backgrounds)
252B Giants Leaders 1.50 .60
(Dark pale
backgrounds)
253 Mark Belanger 1.50 .60
254 Bill Stoneman .50 .20
255 Reggie Jackson 15.00 6.00
256 Chris Zachary .50 .20
257A Yogi Berra MG 3.00 1.20
Roy McMillan CO
Joe Pignatano CO
Rube Walker CO
Eddie Yost CO
(Orange backgrounds)
257B Mets Leaders 5.00 2.00
(Dark pale
backgrounds)
258 Tommy John 1.50 .60
259 Jim Holt .50 .20
260 Gary Nolan 1.50 .60
261 Pat Kelly .50 .20
262 Jack Aker .50 .20
263 George Scott 1.50 .60
264 Checklist 133-264 3.00 .60
265 Gene Michael 1.50 .60
266 Mike Lum .75 .30
267 Lloyd Allen .75 .30
268 Jerry Morales .75 .30
269 Tim McCarver 1.50 .60
270 Luis Tiant 1.50 .60
271 Tom Hutton .75 .30
272 Ed Farmer .75 .30
273 Chris Speier .75 .30
274 Darold Knowles .75 .30
275 Tony Perez 4.00 1.60
276 Joe Lovitto .75 .30
277 Bob Miller .75 .30
278 Baltimore Orioles 1.50 .60
Team Card
279 Mike Strahler .75 .30
280 Al Kaline 8.00 3.20
281 Mike Jorgensen .75 .30
282 Steve Hovley .75 .30
283 Ray Sadecki .75 .30
284 Glenn Borgmann .75 .30
285 Don Kessinger 1.50 .60
286 Frank Linzy .75 .30
287 Eddie Leon .75 .30
288 Gary Gentry .75 .30
289 Bob Oliver .75 .30
290 Cesar Cedeno 1.50 .60
291 Rogelio Moret .75 .30
292 Jose Cruz 1.50 .60
293 Bernie Allen .75 .30
294 Steve Arlin .75 .30
295 Bert Campaneris 1.50 .60
296 Sparky Anderson MG 2.50 1.00
Alex Grammas CO
Ted Kluszewski CO
George Scherger CO
Larry Shepard CO
297 Walt Williams .75 .30
298 Ron Bryant .75 .30
299 Ted Ford .75 .30
300 Steve Carlton 10.00 4.00
301 Billy Grabarkewitz .75 .30
302 Terry Crowley .75 .30
303 Nelson Briles .75 .30
304 Duke Sims .75 .30
305 Willie Mays 40.00 16.00
306 Tom Burgmeier .75 .30
307 Boots Day .75 .30
308 Skip Lockwood .75 .30
309 Paul Popovich .75 .30
310 Dick Allen 1.50 .60
311 Joe Decker .75 .30
312 Oscar Brown .75 .30
313 Jim Ray .75 .30
314 Ron Swoboda 1.50 .60
315 John Odom .75 .30
316 San Diego Padres 1.50 .60
Team Card
317 Danny Cater .75 .30
318 Jim McGlothlin .75 .30
319 Jim Spencer .75 .30
320 Lou Brock 8.00 3.20
321 Rich Hinton .75 .30
322 Garry Maddox RC 1.50 .60
323 Billy Martin MG 1.50 .60
Art Fowler CO
Charlie Silvera CO
Dick Tracewski CO
Joe Schultz CO ERR
Schult's name not printed on card
324 Al Downing .75 .30
325 Boog Powell 1.50 .60
326 Darrell Brandon .75 .30
327 John Lowenstein .75 .30
328 Bill Bonham .75 .30
329 Ed Kranepool 1.50 .60
330 Rod Carew 8.00 3.20
331 Carl Morton .75 .30
332 John Felske .75 .30
333 Gene Clines .75 .30
334 Freddie Patek .75 .30
335 Bob Tolan .75 .30
336 Tom Bradley .75 .30
337 Dave Duncan 1.50 .60
338 Checklist 265-396 3.00 .60
339 Dick Tidrow .75 .30
340 Nate Colbert .75 .30
341 Jim Palmer KP 2.50 1.00
342 Sam McDowell KP .75 .30
343 Bobby Murcer KP .75 .30
344 Jim Hunter KP 2.50 1.00
345 Chris Speier KP .75 .30
346 Gaylord Perry KP 1.50 .60
347 Kansas City Royals 1.50 .60
Team Card
348 Rennie Stennett .75 .30
349 Dick McAuliffe .75 .30
350 Tom Seaver 12.00 4.80
351 Jimmy Stewart .75 .30
352 Don Stanhouse .75 .30
353 Steve Brye .75 .30
354 Billy Parker .75 .30
355 Mike Marshall 1.50 .60
356 Chuck Tanner MG 4.00 1.60
Joe Lonnett CO
Jim Mahoney CO
Al Monchak CO
Johnny Sain CO
357 Ross Grimsley .75 .30
358 Jim Nettles .75 .30
359 Cecil Upshaw .75 .30
360 Joe Rudi UER 1.50 .60
(Photo actually
Gene Tenace)
361 Fran Healy .75 .30
362 Eddie Watt .75 .30
363 Jackie Hernandez .75 .30
364 Rick Wise .75 .30
365 Rico Petrocelli 1.50 .60
366 Brock Davis .75 .30
367 Burt Hooton 1.50 .60
368 Bill Buckner 1.50 .60
369 Lerrin LaGrow .75 .30
370 Willie Stargell 5.00 2.00
371 Mike Kekich .75 .30
372 Oscar Gamble .75 .30
373 Clyde Wright .75 .30
374 Darrell Evans 1.50 .60
375 Larry Dierker 1.50 .60
376 Frank Duffy .75 .30
377 Gene Mauch MG 4.00 1.60
Dave Bristol CO
Larry Doby CO
Cal McLish CO
Jerry Zimmerman CO
378 Len Randle .75 .30
379 Cy Acosta .75 .30
380 Johnny Bench 12.00 4.80
381 Vicente Romo .75 .30
382 Mike Hegan .75 .30
383 Diego Segui .75 .30
384 Don Baylor 4.00 1.60
385 Jim Perry 1.50 .60
386 Don Money .75 .30
387 Jim Barr .75 .30
388 Ben Oglivie 1.50 .60
389 New York Mets 4.00 1.60
Team Card
390 Mickey Lolich 1.50 .60
391 Lee Lacy RC 1.50 .60
392 Dick Drago .75 .30
393 Jose Cardenal .75 .30
394 Sparky Lyle 1.50 .60
395 Roger Metzger .75 .30
396 Grant Jackson .75 .30
397 Dave Cash 1.25 .50
398 Rich Hand 1.25 .50
399 George Foster 2.00 .80
400 Gaylord Perry 5.00 2.00
401 Clyde Mashore 1.25 .50
402 Jack Hiatt 1.25 .50
403 Sonny Jackson 1.25 .50
404 Chuck Brinkman 1.25 .50
405 Cesar Tovar 1.25 .50
406 Paul Lindblad 1.25 .50
407 Felix Millan 1.25 .50
408 Jim Colborn 1.25 .50
409 Ivan Murrell 1.25 .50
410 Willie McCovey 6.00 2.40
(Bench behind plate)
411 Ray Corbin 1.25 .50
412 Manny Mota 2.00 .80
413 Tom Timmermann 1.25 .50
414 Ken Rudolph 1.25 .50
415 Marty Pattin 1.25 .50
416 Paul Schaal 1.25 .50
417 Scipio Spinks 1.25 .50
418 Bob Grich 2.00 .80
419 Casey Cox 1.25 .50
420 Tommie Agee 1.25 .50
421A Bobby Winkles MG 1.50 .60
Tom Morgan CO
Salty Parker CO
Jimmie Reese CO
John Roseboro CO
(Orange backgrounds)
421B Angels Leaders 3.00 1.20
(Dark pale
backgrounds)
422 Bob Robertson 1.25 .50
423 Johnny Jeter 1.25 .50
424 Denny Doyle 1.25 .50
425 Alex Johnson 1.25 .50
426 Dave LaRoche 1.25 .50
427 Rick Auerbach 1.25 .50
428 Wayne Simpson 1.25 .50
429 Jim Fairey 1.25 .50
430 Vida Blue 2.00 .80
431 Gerry Moses 1.25 .50
432 Dan Frisella 1.25 .50
433 Willie Horton 2.00 .80
434 San Francisco Giants 3.00 1.20
Team Card
435 Rico Carty 2.00 .80
436 Jim McAndrew 1.25 .50
437 John Kennedy 1.25 .50
438 Enzo Hernandez 1.25 .50
439 Eddie Fisher 1.25 .50
440 Glenn Beckert 1.25 .50
441 Gail Hopkins 1.25 .50
442 Dick Dietz 1.25 .50
443 Danny Thompson 1.25 .50
444 Ken Brett 1.25 .50
445 Ken Berry 1.25 .50
446 Jerry Reuss 2.00 .80
447 Joe Hague 1.25 .50
448 John Hiller 1.25 .50
449A Ken Aspromonte MG 4.00 1.60
Rocky Colavito CO
Joe Lutz CO
Warren Spahn CO
(Spahn's right
ear pointed)
449B Indians Leaders 4.00 1.60
(Spahn's right
ear round)
450 Joe Torre 3.00 1.20
451 John Vukovich 1.25 .50
452 Paul Casanova 1.25 .50
453 Checklist 397-528 3.00 .60
454 Tom Haller 1.25 .50
455 Bill Melton 1.25 .50
456 Dick Green 1.25 .50
457 John Strohmayer 1.25 .50
458 Jim Mason 1.25 .50
459 Jimmy Howarth 1.25 .50
460 Bill Freehan 2.00 .80
461 Mike Corkins 1.25 .50
462 Ron Blomberg 1.25 .50
463 Ken Tatum 1.25 .50
464 Chicago Cubs 3.00 1.20
Team Card
465 Dave Giusti 1.25 .50
466 Jose Arcia 1.25 .50
467 Mike Ryan 1.25 .50
468 Tom Griffin 1.25 .50
469 Dan Monzon 1.25 .50
470 Mike Cuellar 2.00 .80
471 Ty Cobb ATL 10.00 4.00
4191 Hits
472 Lou Gehrig ATL 15.00 6.00
23 Grand Slams
473 Hank Aaron ATL 10.00 4.00
6172 Total Bases
474 Babe Ruth ATL 20.00 8.00
2209 RBI
475 Ty Cobb ATL 8.00 3.20
.367 Batting Average
476 Walter Johnson ATL 3.00 1.20
113 Shutouts
477 Cy Young ATL 3.00 1.20
511 Victories
478 Walter Johnson ATL 3.00 1.20
3508 Strikeouts
479 Hal Lanier 1.25 .50
480 Juan Marichal 5.00 2.00
481 Chicago White Sox 3.00 1.20
Team Card
482 Rick Reuschel RC 3.00 1.20
483 Dal Maxvill 1.25 .50
484 Ernie McAnally 1.25 .50
485 Norm Cash 2.00 .80
486A Danny Ozark MG 1.50 .60
Carroll Beringer CO
Billy DeMars CO
Ray Rippelmeyer CO
Bobby Wine CO
(Orange backgrounds)
486B Phillies Leaders 3.00 1.20
(Dark pale
backgrounds)
487 Bruce Dal Canton 1.25 .50
488 Dave Campbell 2.00 .80
489 Jeff Burroughs 2.00 .80
490 Claude Osteen 2.00 .80
491 Bob Montgomery 1.25 .50
492 Pedro Borbon 1.25 .50
493 Duffy Dyer 1.25 .50
494 Rich Morales 1.25 .50
495 Tommy Helms 1.25 .50
496 Ray Lamb 1.25 .50
497A Red Schoendienst MG 2.00 .80
Vern Benson CO
George Kissell CO
Barney Schultz CO
(Orange backgrounds)
497B Cardinals Leaders 3.00 1.20
(Dark pale
backgrounds)
498 Graig Nettles 3.00 1.20
499 Bob Moose 1.25 .50
500 Oakland A's 3.00 1.20
Team Card
501 Larry Gura 1.25 .50
502 Bobby Valentine 3.00 1.20
503 Phil Niekro 5.00 2.00
504 Earl Williams 1.25 .50
505 Bob Bailey 1.25 .50
506 Bart Johnson 1.25 .50
507 Darrel Chaney 1.25 .50
508 Gates Brown 1.25 .50
509 Jim Nash 1.25 .50
510 Amos Otis 2.00 .80
511 Sam McDowell 2.00 .80
512 Dalton Jones 1.25 .50
513 Dave Marshall 1.25 .50

514 Jerry Kenney 1.25 .50
515 Andy Messersmith 2.00 .80
516 Danny Walton 1.25 .50
517A Bill Virdon MG 1.50 .60
Don Leppert CO
Bill Mazeroski CO
Dave Ricketts CO
Mel Wright CO
(Mazeroski has
no right ear)
517B Pirates Leaders 3.00 1.20
(Mazeroski has
right ear)
518 Bob Veale 1.25 .50
519 Johnny Edwards 1.25 .50
520 Mel Stottlemyre 2.00 .80
521 Atlanta Braves 3.00 1.20
Team Card
522 Leo Cardenas 1.25 .50
523 Wayne Granger 1.25 .50
524 Gene Tenace 2.00 .80
525 Jim Fregosi 2.00 .80
526 Ollie Brown 1.25 .50
527 Dan McGinn 1.25 .50
528 Paul Blair 1.25 .50
529 Milt May 3.00 1.20
530 Jim Kaat 5.00 2.00
531 Ron Woods 3.00 1.20
532 Steve Mingori 3.00 1.20
533 Larry Stahl 3.00 1.20
534 Dave Lemonds 3.00 1.20
535 Johnny Callison 5.00 2.00
536 Philadelphia Phillies 6.00 2.40
Team Card
537 Bill Slayback 3.00 1.20
538 Jim Ray Hart 5.00 2.00
539 Tom Murphy 3.00 1.20
540 Cleon Jones 5.00 2.00
541 Bob Bolin 3.00 1.20
542 Pat Corrales 5.00 2.00
543 Alan Foster 3.00 1.20
544 Von Joshua 3.00 1.20
545 Orlando Cepeda 8.00 3.20
546 Jim York 3.00 1.20
547 Bobby Heise 3.00 1.20
548 Don Durham 3.00 1.20
549 Whitey Herzog MG 5.00 2.00
Chuck Estrada CO
Chuck Hiller CO
Jackie Moore CO
550 Dave Johnson 5.00 2.00
551 Mike Kilkenny 3.00 1.20
552 J.C. Martin 3.00 1.20
553 Mickey Scott 3.00 1.20
554 Dave Concepcion 5.00 2.00
555 Bill Hands 3.00 1.20
556 New York Yankees 8.00 3.20
Team Card
557 Bernie Williams 3.00 1.20
558 Jerry May 3.00 1.20
559 Barry Lersch 3.00 1.20
560 Frank Howard 5.00 2.00
561 Jim Geddes 3.00 1.20
562 Wayne Garrett 3.00 1.20
563 Larry Haney 3.00 1.20
564 Mike Thompson 3.00 1.20
565 Jim Hickman 3.00 1.20
566 Lew Krausse 3.00 1.20
567 Bob Fenwick 3.00 1.20
568 Ray Newman 3.00 1.20
569 Walt Alston MG 8.00 3.20
Red Adams CO
Monty Basgall CO
Jim Gilliam CO
Tom Lasorda CO
570 Bill Singer 5.00 2.00
571 Rusty Torres 3.00 1.20
572 Gary Sutherland 3.00 1.20
573 Fred Beene 3.00 1.20
574 Bob Didier 3.00 1.20
575 Dock Ellis 3.00 1.20
576 Montreal Expos 6.00 2.40
Team Card
577 Eric Soderholm 3.00 1.20
578 Ken Wright 3.00 1.20
579 Tom Grieve 5.00 2.00
580 Joe Pepitone 5.00 2.00
581 Steve Kealey 3.00 1.20
582 Darrell Porter 5.00 2.00
583 Bill Grief 3.00 1.20
584 Chris Arnold 3.00 1.20
585 Joe Niekro 5.00 2.00
586 Bill Sudakis 3.00 1.20
587 Rich McKinney 3.00 1.20
588 Checklist 529-660 20.00 4.00
589 Ken Forsch 3.00 1.20
590 Deron Johnson 3.00 1.20
591 Mike Hedlund 3.00 1.20
592 John Boccabella 3.00 1.20
593 Jack McKeon MG 4.00 1.60
Galen Cisco CO
Harry Dunlop CO
Charlie Lau CO
594 Vic Harris 3.00 1.20
595 Don Gullett 5.00 2.00
596 Boston Red Sox 6.00 2.40
Team Card
597 Mickey Rivers 5.00 2.00
598 Phil Roof 3.00 1.20
599 Ed Crosby 3.00 1.20
600 Dave McNally 5.00 2.00
601 Sergio Robles 5.00 2.00
George Pena
Rick Stelmaszek
602 Mel Behney 5.00 2.00
Ralph Garcia
Doug Rau
603 Terry Hughes 5.00 2.00
Bill McNulty
Ken Reitz RC
604 Jesse Jefferson 5.00 2.00
Dennis O'Toole
Bob Strampe
605 Enos Cabell RC 5.00 2.00
Pat Bourque
Gonzalo Marquez
606 Gary Matthews RC 5.00 2.00
Tom Paciorek
Jorge Roque
607 Pepe Frias 5.00 2.00
Ray Busse
Mario Guerrero
608 Steve Busby RC 5.00 2.00
Dick Colpaert
George Medich RC
609 Larvell Blanks 5.00 2.00
Pedro Garcia
Dave Lopes RC
610 Jimmy Freeman 5.00 2.00
Charlie Hough
Hank Webb
611 Rich Coggins 5.00 2.00
Jim Wohlford
Richie Zisk
612 Steve Lawson 5.00 2.00
Bob Reynolds
Brent Strom
613 Bob Boone RC 15.00 6.00
Skip Jutze
Mike Ivie
614 Al Bumbry RC 20.00 8.00
Dwight Evans RC
Charlie Spikes
615 Ron Cey 150.00 60.00
John Hilton
Mike Schmidt RC
616 Norm Angelini 5.00 2.00
Steve Blateric
Mike Garman
617 Rich Chiles 3.00 1.20
618 Andy Etchebarren 3.00 1.20
619 Billy Wilson 3.00 1.20
620 Tommy Harper 5.00 2.00
621 Joe Ferguson 5.00 2.00
622 Larry Hisle 5.00 2.00
623 Steve Renko 3.00 1.20
624 Leo Durocher MG 5.00 2.00
Preston Gomez CO
Grady Hatton CO
Hub Kittle CO
Jim Owens CO
625 Angel Mangual 3.00 1.20
626 Bob Barton 3.00 1.20
627 Luis Alvarado 3.00 1.20
628 Jim Slaton 3.00 1.20
629 Cleveland Indians 6.00 2.40
Team Card
630 Denny McLain 8.00 3.20
631 Tom Matchick 3.00 1.20
632 Dick Selma 3.00 1.20
633 Ike Brown 3.00 1.20
634 Alan Closter 3.00 1.20
635 Gene Alley 5.00 2.00
636 Rickey Clark 3.00 1.20
637 Norm Miller 3.00 1.20
638 Ken Reynolds 3.00 1.20
639 Willie Crawford 3.00 1.20
640 Dick Bosman 3.00 1.20
641 Cincinnati Reds 6.00 2.40
Team Card
642 Jose Laboy 3.00 1.20
643 Al Fitzmorris 3.00 1.20
644 Jack Heidemann 3.00 1.20
645 Bob Locker 3.00 1.20
646 Del Crandall MG 4.00 1.60
Harvey Kuenn CO
Joe Nossek CO
Bob Shaw CO
Jim Walton CO
647 George Stone 3.00 1.20
648 Tom Egan 3.00 1.20
649 Rich Folkers 3.00 1.20
650 Felipe Alou 5.00 2.00
651 Don Carrithers 3.00 1.20
652 Ted Kubiak 3.00 1.20
653 Joe Hoerner 3.00 1.20
654 Minnesota Twins 6.00 2.40
Team Card
655 Clay Kirby 3.00 1.20
656 John Ellis 3.00 1.20
657 Bob Johnson 3.00 1.20
658 Elliott Maddox 3.00 1.20
659 Jose Pagan 3.00 1.20
660 Fred Scherman 5.00 1.95

1973 Topps Blue Team Checklists

This 24-card standard-size set is rather difficult to find. These blue-bordered team checklist cards are very similar in design to the mass produced red trim team checklist cards issued by Topps the next year. Reportedly these were inserts only found in the test packs that included all series. In addition, a collector could mail in 25 cents and receive a full uncut sheet of these cards. This offer was somewhat limited in terms of collectors mailing in for them.

	NM	Ex
COMPLETE SET (24)	175.00	52.50
COMMON TEAM (1-24)	8.00	2.40
16 New York Mets	10.00	3.00
17 New York Yankees	10.00	3.00

1973 Topps Pin-Ups

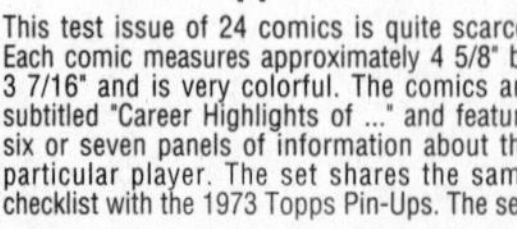

This test issue of 24 pin-ups is quite scarce. Each pin-up measures approximately 3 7/16" by 4 5/8" and is very colorful with a thick white border. The thin-paper pin-ups contain a facsimile autograph on the front of the card. The set shares the same checklist with the 1973 Topps Comics. The set is unnumbered and hence is ordered below alphabetically. The team insignia and logos on the cards have been airbrushed away, which is contra-indicative of a Topps issue.

	NM	Ex
COMPLETE SET (24)	5000.00	2000.00
1 Hank Aaron	400.00	160.00
2 Dick Allen	100.00	40.00
3 Johnny Bench	300.00	120.00
4 Steve Carlton	300.00	120.00
5 Nate Colbert	80.00	32.00
6 Willie Davis	80.00	32.00
7 Mike Epstein	80.00	32.00
8 Reggie Jackson	400.00	160.00
9 Harmon Killebrew	200.00	80.00
10 Mickey Lolich	100.00	40.00
11 Mike Marshall	80.00	32.00
12 Lee May	80.00	32.00
13 Willie McCovey	200.00	80.00
14 Bobby Murcer	100.00	40.00
15 Gaylord Perry	200.00	80.00
16 Lou Piniella	100.00	40.00
17 Brooks Robinson	300.00	120.00
18 Nolan Ryan	600.00	240.00
19 George Scott	80.00	32.00
20 Tom Seaver	400.00	160.00
21 Willie Stargell	200.00	80.00
22 Joe Torre	150.00	60.00
23 Billy Williams	200.00	80.00
24 Carl Yastrzemski	250.00	100.00

1973 Topps Candy Lids

One of Topps' most unusual test sets is this series of 55 color portraits of baseball players printed on the bottom of candy lids. These lids measure 1 7/8" in diameter. The product was called "Baseball Stars Bubble Gum" and consisted of a small tub of candy-coated gum kernels. Issued in 1973, the lids are unnumbered and each has a small tab. Underneath the picture is a small ribbon design which contains the player's name, team and position. It is believed that this set was mainly tested on the east coast with some light testing in the midwest.

	NM	Ex
COMPLETE SET (55)	600.00	240.00
1 Hank Aaron	40.00	16.00
2 Dick Allen	5.00	2.00
3 Dusty Baker	5.00	2.00
4 Sal Bando	3.00	1.20
5 Johnny Bench	25.00	10.00
6 Bobby Bonds	5.00	2.00
7 Dick Bosman	3.00	1.20
8 Lou Brock	15.00	6.00
9 Rod Carew	15.00	6.00
10 Steve Carlton	15.00	6.00
11 Nate Colbert	3.00	1.20
12 Willie Davis	3.00	1.20
13 Larry Dierker	3.00	1.20
14 Mike Epstein	3.00	1.20
15 Carlton Fisk	30.00	12.00
16 Tim Foli	3.00	1.20
17 Ray Fosse	3.00	1.20
18 Bill Freehan	5.00	2.00
19 Bob Gibson	15.00	6.00
20 Bud Harrelson	3.00	1.20
21 Jim Hunter	10.00	4.00
22 Reggie Jackson	25.00	10.00
23 Ferguson Jenkins	10.00	4.00
24 Al Kaline	15.00	6.00
25 Harmon Killebrew	15.00	6.00
26 Clay Kirby	3.00	1.20
27 Mickey Lolich	5.00	2.00
28 Greg Luzinski	5.00	2.00
29 Willie McCovey	15.00	6.00
30 Mike Marshall	3.00	1.20
31 Lee May	3.00	1.20
32 John Mayberry	3.00	1.20
33 Willie Mays	40.00	16.00
34 Thurman Munson	10.00	4.00
35 Bobby Murcer	5.00	2.00
36 Gary Nolan	3.00	1.20
37 Amos Otis	3.00	1.20
38 Jim Palmer	15.00	6.00
39 Gaylord Perry	10.00	4.00
40 Lou Piniella	5.00	2.00
41 Brooks Robinson	15.00	6.00
42 Frank Robinson	15.00	6.00
43 Ellie Rodriguez	3.00	1.20
44 Pete Rose	40.00	16.00
45 Nolan Ryan	100.00	40.00
46 Manny Sanguillen	3.00	1.20
47 George Scott	3.00	1.20
48 Tom Seaver	25.00	10.00
49 Chris Speier	3.00	1.20
50 Willie Stargell	15.00	6.00
51 Don Sutton	10.00	4.00
52 Joe Torre	8.00	3.20
53 Billy Williams	10.00	4.00
54 Wilbur Wood	3.00	1.20
55 Carl Yastrzemski	25.00	10.00

1973 Topps Comics

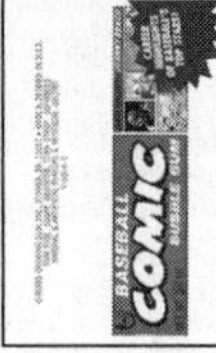

This test issue of 24 comics is quite scarce. Each comic measures approximately 4 5/8" by 3 7/16" and is very colorful. The comics are subtitled "Career Highlights of ..." and feature six or seven panels of information about the particular player. The set shares the same checklist with the 1973 Topps Pin-Ups. The set is unnumbered and hence is ordered below alphabetically. The team insignia and logos on the cards have been airbrushed away, which is contra-indicative of a Topps issue.

	NM	Ex
COMPLETE SET (24)	2500.00	1000.00
1 Hank Aaron	200.00	80.00
2 Dick Allen	80.00	32.00
3 Johnny Bench	150.00	60.00
4 Steve Carlton	150.00	60.00
5 Nate Colbert	40.00	16.00
6 Willie Davis	40.00	16.00
7 Mike Epstein	60.00	24.00
8 Reggie Jackson	200.00	80.00
9 Harmon Killebrew	100.00	40.00
10 Mickey Lolich	60.00	24.00
11 Mike Marshall	40.00	16.00
12 Lee May	60.00	24.00
13 Willie McCovey	120.00	47.50
14 Bobby Murcer	60.00	24.00
15 Gaylord Perry	120.00	47.50
16 Lou Piniella	60.00	24.00
17 Brooks Robinson	150.00	60.00
18 Nolan Ryan	600.00	240.00
19 George Scott	40.00	16.00
20 Tom Seaver	200.00	80.00
21 Willie Stargell	120.00	47.50
22 Joe Torre	80.00	32.00
23 Billy Williams	120.00	47.50
24 Carl Yastrzemski	200.00	80.00

1974 Topps

The cards in this 660-card set measure 2 1/2" by 3 1/2". This year marked the first time Topps issued all the cards of its baseball set at the same time rather than in series. Among other methods, cards were issued in eight-card dime wax packs and 42 card rack packs. The ten cent packs were issued 36 to a box. For the first time, factory sets were issued through the JC Penny's catalog. Sales were probably disappointing for it would be several years before factory sets were issued again. Some interesting variations were created by the rumored move of the San Diego Padres to Washington. Fifteen cards (13 players, the team card, and the rookie card (599) of the Padres were printed either as "San Diego" (SD) or "Washington." The latter are the scarcer variety and are denoted in the checklist below by WAS. Each team's manager and his coaches again have a combined card with small pictures of each coach below the larger photo of the team's manager. The first six cards in the set (1-6) feature Hank Aaron and his illustrious career. Other topical subsets included in the set are League Leaders (201-208), All-Star selections (331-339), Playoffs cards (470-471), World Series cards (472-479), and Rookie Prospects (596-608). The card backs for the All-Stars (331-339) have no statistics, but form a picture puzzle of Bobby Bonds, the 1973 All-Star Game MVP. The key Rookie Cards in this set are Ken Griffey Sr., Dave Parker and Dave Winfield.

	NM	Ex
COMPLETE SET (660)	400.00	160.00
COMP.FACT.SET (660)	600.00	240.00
WRAPPERS (10-CENTS)	10.00	4.00

1 Hank Aaron 715 40.00 12.00
2 Hank Aaron 54-57 8.00 3.20
3 Hank Aaron 58-61 8.00 3.20
4 Hank Aaron 62-65 8.00 3.20
5 Hank Aaron 66-69 8.00 3.20
6 Hank Aaron 70-73 8.00 3.20
7 Jim Hunter 4.00 1.60
8 George Theodore .50 .20
9 Mickey Lolich 1.00 .40
10 Johnny Bench 15.00 6.00
11 Jim Bibby .50 .20
12 Dave May .50 .20
13 Tom Hilgendorf .50 .20
14 Paul Popovich .50 .20
15 Joe Torre 2.00 .80
16 Baltimore Orioles 1.00 .40
Team Card
17 Doug Bird .50 .20
18 Gary Thomasson .50 .20
19 Gerry Moses .50 .20
20 Nolan Ryan 40.00 16.00
21 Bob Gallagher .50 .20
22 Cy Acosta .50 .20
23 Craig Robinson .50 .20
24 John Hiller 1.00 .40
25 Ken Singleton 1.00 .40
26 Bill Campbell .50 .20
27 George Scott 1.00 .40
28 Manny Sanguillen 1.00 .40
29 Phil Niekro 3.00 1.20
30 Bobby Bonds 2.00 .80
31 Preston Gomez MG 1.00 .40
Roger Craig CO
Hub Kittle CO
Grady Hatton CO
Bob Lillis CO
32A Johnny Grubb SD 1.00 .40
32B Johnny Grubb WASH 4.00 1.60
33 Don Newhauser .50 .20
34 Andy Kosco .50 .20
35 Gaylord Perry 3.00 1.20
36 St. Louis Cardinals 1.00 .40
Team Card
37 Dave Sells .50 .20
38 Don Kessinger 1.00 .40
39 Ken Suarez .50 .20
40 Jim Palmer 8.00 3.20
41 Bobby Floyd .50 .20
42 Claude Osteen 1.00 .40
43 Jim Wynn 1.00 .40
44 Mel Stottlemyre 1.00 .40
45 Dave Johnson 1.00 .40
46 Pat Kelly .50 .20
47 Dick Ruthven .50 .20
48 Dick Sharon .50 .20
49 Steve Renko .50 .20
50 Rod Carew 8.00 3.20
51 Bobby Heise .50 .20
52 Al Oliver 1.00 .40
53A Fred Kendall SD 1.00 .40
53B Fred Kendall WASH 4.00 1.60
54 Elias Sosa .50 .20
55 Frank Robinson 8.00 3.20
56 New York Mets 1.00 .40
Team Card
57 Darold Knowles .50 .20
58 Charlie Spikes .50 .20
59 Ross Grimsley .50 .20
60 Lou Brock 6.00 2.40
61 Luis Aparicio 3.00 1.20
62 Bob Locker .50 .20
63 Bill Sudakis .50 .20
64 Doug Rau .50 .20
65 Amos Otis 1.00 .40
66 Sparky Lyle 1.00 .40
67 Tommy Helms .50 .20
68 Grant Jackson .50 .20
69 Del Unser .50 .20
70 Dick Allen 2.00 .80
71 Dan Frisella .50 .20
72 Aurelio Rodriguez .50 .20
73 Mike Marshall 2.00 .80
74 Minnesota Twins 1.00 .40
Team Card
75 Jim Colborn .50 .20
76 Mickey Rivers 1.00 .40
77A Rich Troedson SD 1.00 .40
77B Rich Troedson WASH 4.00 1.60
78 Charlie Fox MG 1.00 .40
John McNamara CO
Joe Amalfitano CO
Andy Gilbert CO
Don McMahon CO
79 Gene Tenace 1.00 .40
80 Tom Seaver 12.00 4.80
81 Frank Duffy .50 .20
82 Dave Giusti .50 .20
83 Orlando Cepeda 3.00 1.20
84 Rick Wise .50 .20
85 Joe Morgan 8.00 3.20
86 Joe Ferguson 1.00 .40
87 Fergie Jenkins 3.00 1.20
88 Freddie Patek 1.00 .40
89 Jackie Brown .50 .20
90 Bobby Murcer 1.00 .40
91 Ken Forsch .50 .20
92 Paul Blair 1.00 .40
93 Rod Gilbreath .50 .20
94 Detroit Tigers 1.00 .40
Team Card
95 Steve Carlton 8.00 3.20
96 Jerry Hairston .50 .20
97 Bob Bailey .50 .20
98 Bert Blyleven 2.00 .80
99 Del Crandall MG 1.00 .40
Harvey Kuenn CO
Joe Nossek CO
Jim Walton CO
Al Widmar CO
100 Willie Stargell 6.00 2.40
101 Bobby Valentine 1.00 .40
102A Bill Greif SD 1.00 .40
102B Bill Greif WASH 4.00 1.60
103 Sal Bando 1.00 .40
104 Ron Bryant .50 .20
105 Carlton Fisk 12.00 4.80
106 Harry Parker .50 .20
107 Alex Johnson .50 .20
108 Al Hrabosky 1.00 .40
109 Bob Grich 1.00 .40
110 Billy Williams 3.00 1.20
111 Clay Carroll .50 .20
112 Dave Lopes 2.00 .80
113 Dick Drago .50 .20
114 Angels Team 1.00 .40
115 Willie Horton 1.00 .40
116 Jerry Reuss 1.00 .40
117 Ron Blomberg .50 .20
118 Bill Lee 1.00 .40
119 Danny Ozark MG 1.00 .40
Ray Ripplemeyer CO
Bobby Wine CO
Carroll Beringer CO
Billy DeMars CO
120 Wilbur Wood .50 .20
121 Larry Lintz .50 .20
122 Jim Holt .50 .20
123 Nelson Briles 1.00 .40
124 Bobby Coluccio .50 .20
125A Nate Colbert SD 1.00 .40
125B Nate Colbert WASH 4.00 1.60
126 Checklist 1-132 3.00 .60
127 Tom Paciorek 1.00 .40
128 John Ellis .50 .20
129 Chris Speier .50 .20
130 Reggie Jackson 15.00 6.00
131 Bob Boone 2.00 .80
132 Felix Millan .50 .20
133 David Clyde 1.00 .40
134 Denis Menke .50 .20
135 Roy White 1.00 .40
136 Rick Reuschel 1.00 .40
137 Al Bumbry 1.00 .40
138 Eddie Brinkman .50 .20
139 Aurelio Monteagudo .50 .20
140 Darrell Evans 2.00 .80

141 Pat Bourque .50 .20
142 Pedro Garcia .50 .20
143 Dick Woodson .50 .20
144 Walter Alston MG 3.00 1.20
Tom Lasorda CO
Jim Gilliam CO
Red Adams CO
Monty Basgall CO
145 Dock Ellis .50 .20
146 Ron Fairly 1.00 .40
147 Bart Johnson .50 .20
148A Dave Hilton SD 1.00 .40
148B Dave Hilton WASH 4.00 1.60
149 Mac Scarce .50 .20
150 John Mayberry 1.00 .40
151 Diego Segui .50 .20
152 Oscar Gamble 1.00 .40
153 Jon Matlack 1.00 .40
154 Houston Astros 1.00 .40
Team Card
155 Bert Campaneris 1.00 .40
156 Randy Moffitt .50 .20
157 Vic Harris .50 .20
158 Jack Billingham .50 .20
159 Jim Ray Hart .50 .20
160 Brooks Robinson 8.00 3.20
161 Ray Burris UER 1.00 .40
(Card number is
printed sideways)
162 Bill Freehan 1.00 .40
163 Ken Berry .50 .20
164 Tom House .50 .20
165 Willie Davis 1.00 .40
166 Jack McKeon MG 1.00 .40
Charlie Lau CO
Harry Dunlop CO
Galen Cisco CO
167 Luis Tiant 2.00 .80
168 Danny Thompson .50 .20
169 Steve Rogers RC 2.00 .80
170 Bill Melton .50 .20
171 Eduardo Rodriguez .50 .20
172 Gene Clines .50 .20
173A Randy Jones SD RC 2.00 .80
173B Randy Jones WASH 5.00 2.00
174 Bill Robinson 1.00 .40
175 Reggie Cleveland .50 .20
176 John Lowenstein .50 .20
177 Dave Roberts .50 .20
178 Garry Maddox 1.00 .40
179 Yogi Berra MG 5.00 2.00
Rube Walker CO
Eddie Yost CO
Roy McMillan CO
Joe Pignatano CO
180 Ken Holtzman 1.00 .40
181 Cesar Geronimo .50 .20
182 Lindy McDaniel 1.00 .40
183 Johnny Oates 1.00 .40
184 Texas Rangers 1.00 .40
Team Card
185 Jose Cardenal .50 .20
186 Fred Scherman .50 .20
187 Don Baylor 2.00 .80
188 Rudy Meoli .50 .20
189 Jim Brewer .50 .20
190 Tony Oliva 2.00 .80
191 Al Fitzmorris .50 .20
192 Mario Guerrero .50 .20
193 Tom Walker .50 .20
194 Darrell Porter 1.00 .40
195 Carlos May .50 .20
196 Jim Fregosi 1.00 .40
197A Vicente Romo SD 1.00 .40
197B V.Romo WASH 4.00 1.60
198 Dave Cash .50 .20
199 Mike Kekich .50 .20
200 Cesar Cedeno 1.00 .40
201 Rod Carew 6.00 2.40
Pete Rose LL
202 Reggie Jackson 5.00 2.00
Willie Stargell LL
203 Reggie Jackson 5.00 2.00
Willie Stargell LL
204 Tommy Harper 2.00 .80
Lou Brock LL
205 Wilbur Wood 1.00 .40
Ron Bryant LL
206 Jim Palmer 5.00 2.00
Tom Seaver LL
207 Nolan Ryan 12.00 4.80
Tom Seaver LL
208 John Hiller 1.00 .40
Mike Marshall LL
209 Ted Sizemore .50 .20
210 Bill Singer .50 .20
211 Chicago Cubs 1.00 .40
Team Card
212 Rollie Fingers 3.00 1.20
213 Dave Rader .50 .20
214 Billy Grabarkewitz .50 .20
215 Al Kaline UER 10.00 4.00
(No copyright on back)
216 Ray Sadecki .50 .20
217 Tim Foli .50 .20
218 Johnny Briggs .50 .20
219 Doug Griffin .50 .20
220 Don Sutton 3.00 1.20
221 Chuck Tanner MG 1.00 .40
Jim Mahoney CO
Alex Monchak CO
Johnny Sain CO
Joe Lonnett CO
222 Ramon Hernandez .50 .20
223 Jeff Burroughs 2.00 .80
224 Roger Metzger .50 .20
225 Paul Splittorff .50 .20
226A San Diego Padres 2.00 .80
Team Card San Diego Variation
226B San Diego Padres 8.00 3.20
Team Card Washington Variation
227 Mike Lum .50 .20
228 Ted Kubiak .50 .20
229 Fritz Peterson .50 .20
230 Tony Perez 4.00 1.60
231 Dick Tidrow .50 .20
232 Steve Brye .50 .20
233 Jim Barr .50 .20
234 John Milner .50 .20
235 Dave McNally 1.00 .40
236 Red Schoendienst MG 3.00 1.20
Barney Schultz CO
George Kissell CO
Johnny Lewis CO
Vern Benson CO
237 Ken Brett .50 .20
238 Fran Healy HOR .50 .20
(Munson sliding
in background)
239 Bill Russell 1.00 .40
240 Joe Coleman .50 .20
241A Glenn Beckert SD 1.00 .40
241B G.Beckert WASH 4.00 1.60
242 Bill Gogolewski .50 .20
243 Bob Oliver .50 .20
244 Carl Morton .50 .20
245 Cleon Jones .50 .20
246 Oakland Athletics 2.00 .80
Team Card
247 Rick Miller .50 .20
248 Tom Hall .50 .20
249 George Mitterwald .50 .20
250A Willie McCovey SD 8.00 3.20
250B W.McCovey WASH 25.00 10.00
251 Graig Nettles 2.00 .80
252 Dave Parker RC 10.00 4.00
253 John Boccabella .50 .20
254 Stan Bahnsen .50 .20
255 Larry Bowa 1.00 .40
256 Tom Griffin .50 .20
257 Buddy Bell 2.00 .80
258 Jerry Morales .50 .20
259 Bob Reynolds .50 .20
260 Ted Simmons 2.00 .80
261 Jerry Bell .50 .20
262 Ed Kirkpatrick .50 .20
263 Checklist 133-264 3.00 .60
264 Joe Rudi 1.00 .40
265 Tug McGraw 2.00 .80
266 Jim Northrup 1.00 .40
267 Andy Messersmith 1.00 .40
268 Tom Grieve 1.00 .40
269 Bob Johnson .50 .20
270 Ron Santo 2.00 .80
271 Bill Hands .50 .20
272 Paul Casanova .50 .20
273 Checklist 265-396 3.00 .60
274 Fred Beene .50 .20
275 Ron Hunt .50 .20
276 Bobby Winkles MG 1.00 .40
John Roseboro CO
Tom Morgan CO
Jimmie Reese CO
Salty Parker CO
277 Gary Nolan 1.00 .40
278 Cookie Rojas 1.00 .40
279 Jim Crawford .50 .20
280 Carl Yastrzemski 12.00 4.80
281 San Francisco Giants 1.00 .40
Team Card
282 Doyle Alexander 1.00 .40
283 Mike Schmidt 20.00 8.00
284 Dave Duncan 1.00 .40
285 Reggie Smith 1.00 .40
286 Tony Muser .50 .20
287 Clay Kirby .50 .20
288 Gorman Thomas RC 2.00 .80
289 Rick Auerbach .50 .20
290 Vida Blue 1.00 .40
291 Don Hahn .50 .20
292 Chuck Seelbach .50 .20
293 Milt May .50 .20
294 Steve Foucault .50 .20
295 Rick Monday 1.00 .40
296 Ray Corbin .50 .20
297 Hal Breeden .50 .20
298 Roric Harrison .50 .20
299 Gene Michael .50 .20
300 Pete Rose 25.00 10.00
301 Bob Montgomery .50 .20
302 Rudy May .50 .20
303 George Hendrick 1.00 .40
304 Don Wilson .50 .20
305 Tito Fuentes .50 .20
306 Earl Weaver MG 3.00 1.20
Jim Frey CO
George Bamberger CO
Billy Hunter CO
George Staller CO
307 Luis Melendez .50 .20
308 Bruce Dal Canton .50 .20
309A Dave Roberts SD 1.00 .40
309B Dave Roberts WASH 6.00 2.40
310 Terry Forster 1.00 .40
311 Jerry Grote 1.00 .40
312 Deron Johnson .50 .20
313 Barry Lersch .50 .20
314 Milwaukee Brewers 1.00 .40
Team Card
315 Ron Cey 2.00 .80
316 Jim Perry 1.00 .40
317 Richie Zisk 1.00 .40
318 Jim Merritt .50 .20
319 Randy Hundley .50 .20
320 Dusty Baker 2.00 .80
321 Steve Braun .50 .20
322 Ernie McAnally .50 .20
323 Richie Scheinblum .50 .20
324 Steve Kline .50 .20
325 Tommy Harper 1.00 .40
326 Sparky Anderson MG 3.00 1.20
Larry Shepard CO
George Scherger CO
Alex Grammas CO
Ted Kluszewski CO
327 Tom Timmermann .50 .20
328 Skip Jutze .50 .20
329 Mark Belanger 1.00 .40
330 Juan Marichal 5.00 2.00
331 Carlton Fisk 5.00 2.00
Johnny Bench AS
332 Dick Allen 8.00 3.20
Hank Aaron AS
333 Rod Carew 4.00 1.60
Joe Morgan AS
334 Brooks Robinson 3.00 1.20
Ron Santo AS
335 Bert Campaneris 1.00 .40
Chris Speier AS
336 Bobby Murcer 5.00 2.00
Pete Rose AS
337 Amos Otis 1.00 .40
Cesar Cedeno AS
338 Reggie Jackson 5.00 2.00
Billy Williams AS
339 Jim Hunter 3.00 1.20
Rick Wise AS
340 Thurman Munson 8.00 3.20
341 Dan Driessen RC 1.00 .40
342 Jim Lonborg 1.00 .40
343 Royals Team 1.00 .40
344 Mike Caldwell .50 .20
345 Bill North .50 .20
346 Ron Reed .50 .20
347 Sandy Alomar 1.00 .40
348 Pete Richert .50 .20
349 John Vukovich .50 .20
350 Bob Gibson 8.00 3.20
351 Dwight Evans 3.00 1.20
352 Bill Stoneman .50 .20
353 Rich Coggins .50 .20
354 Whitey Lockman MG 1.00 .40
J.C. Martin CO
Hank Aguirre CO
Al Spangler CO
Jim Marshall CO
355 Dave Nelson .50 .20
356 Jerry Koosman 1.00 .40
357 Buddy Bradford .50 .20
358 Dal Maxvill .50 .20
359 Brent Strom .50 .20
360 Greg Luzinski 2.00 .80
361 Don Carrithers .50 .20
362 Hal King .50 .20
363 New York Yankees 2.00 .80
Team Card
364A Cito Gaston SD 2.00 .80
364B Cito Gaston WASH 8.00 3.20
365 Steve Busby 1.00 .40
366 Larry Hisle 1.00 .40
367 Norm Cash 2.00 .80
368 Manny Mota 1.00 .40
369 Paul Lindblad .50 .20
370 Bob Watson 1.00 .40
371 Jim Slaton .50 .20
372 Ken Reitz .50 .20
373 John Curtis .50 .20
374 Marty Perez .50 .20
375 Earl Williams .50 .20
376 Jorge Orta .50 .20
377 Ron Woods .50 .20
378 Burt Hooton 1.00 .40
379 Billy Martin MG 2.00 .80
Frank Lucchesi CO
Art Fowler CO
Charlie Silvera CO
Jackie Moore CO
380 Bud Harrelson 1.00 .40
381 Charlie Sands .50 .20
382 Bob Moose .50 .20
383 Philadelphia Phillies 1.00 .40
Team Card
384 Chris Chambliss 1.00 .40
385 Don Gullett 1.00 .40
386 Gary Matthews 2.00 .80
387A Rich Morales SD 1.00 .40
387B Rich Morales WASH 6.00 2.40
388 Phil Roof .50 .20
389 Gates Brown .50 .20
390 Lou Piniella 2.00 .80
391 Billy Champion .50 .20
392 Dick Green .50 .20
393 Orlando Pena .50 .20
394 Ken Henderson .50 .20
395 Doug Rader .50 .20
396 Tommy Davis 1.00 .40
397 George Stone .50 .20
398 Duke Sims .50 .20
399 Mike Paul .50 .20
400 Harmon Killebrew 6.00 2.40
401 Elliott Maddox .50 .20
402 Jim Rooker .50 .20
403 Darrell Johnson MG 1.00 .40
Eddie Popowski CO
Lee Stange CO
Don Zimmer CO
Don Bryant CO
404 Jim Howarth .50 .20
405 Ellie Rodriguez .50 .20
406 Steve Arlin .50 .20
407 Jim Wohlford .50 .20
408 Charlie Hough 1.00 .40
409 Ike Brown .50 .20
410 Pedro Borbon .50 .20
411 Frank Baker .50 .20
412 Chuck Taylor .50 .20
413 Don Money 1.00 .40
414 Checklist 397-528 3.00 .60
415 Gary Gentry .50 .20
416 Chicago White Sox 1.00 .40
Team Card
417 Rich Folkers .50 .20
418 Walt Williams .50 .20
419 Wayne Twitchell .50 .20
420 Ray Fosse .50 .20
421 Dan Fife .50 .20
422 Gonzalo Marquez .50 .20
423 Fred Stanley .50 .20
424 Jim Beauchamp .50 .20
425 Pete Broberg .50 .20
426 Rennie Stennett .50 .20
427 Bobby Bolin .50 .20
428 Gary Sutherland .50 .20
429 Dick Lange .50 .20
430 Matty Alou 1.00 .40
431 Gene Garber RC 1.00 .40
432 Chris Arnold .50 .20
433 Lerrin LaGrow .50 .20
434 Ken McMullen .50 .20
435 Dave Concepcion 2.00 .80
436 Don Hood .50 .20
437 Jim Lyttle .50 .20
438 Ed Herrmann .50 .20
439 Norm Miller .50 .20
440 Jim Kaat 2.00 .80
441 Tom Ragland .50 .20
442 Alan Foster .50 .20
443 Tom Hutton .50 .20
444 Vic Davalillo .50 .20
445 George Medich .50 .20
446 Len Randle .50 .20
447 Frank Quilici MG 1.00 .40
Ralph Rowe CO
Bob Rodgers CO
Vern Morgan CO
448 Ron Hodges .50 .20
449 Tom McCraw .50 .20
450 Rich Hebner 1.00 .40
451 Tommy John 2.00 .80
452 Gene Hiser .50 .20
453 Balor Moore .50 .20
454 Kurt Bevacqua .50 .20
455 Tom Bradley .50 .20
456 Dave Winfield RC 40.00 16.00
457 Chuck Goggin .50 .20
458 Jim Ray .50 .20
459 Cincinnati Reds 2.00 .80
Team Card
460 Boog Powell 2.00 .80
461 John Odom .50 .20
462 Luis Alvarado .50 .20
463 Pat Dobson .50 .20
464 Jose Cruz 2.00 .80
465 Dick Bosman .50 .20
466 Dick Billings .50 .20
467 Winston Llenas .50 .20
468 Pepe Frias .50 .20
469 Joe Decker .50 .20
470 Reggie Jackson ALCS 5.00 2.00
471 Jon Matlack NLCS 1.00 .40
472 Darold Knowles WS1 1.00 .40
473 Willie Mays WS 8.00 3.20
474 Bert Campaneris WS3 1.00 .40
475 Rusty Staub WS4 1.00 .40
476 Cleon Jones WS5 1.00 .40
477 Reggie Jackson WS 5.00 2.00
478 Bert Campaneris WS7 1.00 .40
479 WS Summary 1.00 .40
A's celebrate; win
2nd consecutive
championship
480 Willie Crawford .50 .20
481 Jerry Terrell .50 .20
482 Bob Didier .50 .20
483 Atlanta Braves 1.00 .40
Team Card
484 Carmen Fanzone .50 .20
485 Felipe Alou 2.00 .80
486 Steve Stone 1.00 .40
487 Ted Martinez .50 .20
488 Andy Etchebarren .50 .20
489 Danny Murtaugh MG 1.00 .40
Don Osborn CO
Don Leppert CO
Bill Mazeroski CO
Bob Skinner CO
490 Vada Pinson 2.00 .80
491 Roger Nelson .50 .20
492 Mike Rogodzinski .50 .20
493 Joe Hoerner .50 .20
494 Ed Goodson .50 .20
495 Dick McAuliffe 1.00 .40
496 Tom Murphy .50 .20
497 Bobby Mitchell .50 .20
498 Pat Corrales .50 .20
499 Rusty Torres .50 .20
500 Lee May 1.00 .40
501 Eddie Leon .50 .20
502 Dave LaRoche .50 .20
503 Eric Soderholm .50 .20
504 Joe Niekro 1.00 .40
505 Bill Buckner 1.00 .40
506 Ed Farmer .50 .20
507 Larry Stahl .50 .20
508 Montreal Expos 1.00 .40
Team Card
509 Jesse Jefferson .50 .20
510 Wayne Garrett .50 .20
511 Toby Harrah 1.00 .40
512 Joe Lahoud .50 .20
513 Jim Campanis .50 .20
514 Paul Schaal .50 .20
515 Willie Montanez .50 .20
516 Horacio Pina .50 .20
517 Mike Hegan .50 .20
518 Derrel Thomas .50 .20
519 Bill Sharp .50 .20
520 Tim McCarver 2.00 .80
521 Ken Aspromonte MG 1.00 .40
Clay Bryant CO
Tony Pacheco CO
522 J.R. Richard 2.00 .80
523 Cecil Cooper 2.00 .80
524 Bill Plummer .50 .20
525 Clyde Wright .50 .20
526 Frank Tepedino 1.00 .40
527 Bobby Darwin .50 .20
528 Bill Bonham .50 .20
529 Horace Clarke 1.00 .40
530 Mickey Stanley 1.00 .40
531 Gene Mauch MG 1.00 .40
Dave Bristol CO
Cal McLish CO
Larry Doby CO
Jerry Zimmerman CO
532 Skip Lockwood .50 .20
533 Mike Phillips .50 .20
534 Eddie Watt .50 .20
535 Bob Tolan .50 .20
536 Duffy Dyer .50 .20
537 Steve Mingori .50 .20
538 Cesar Tovar .50 .20
539 Lloyd Allen .50 .20
540 Bob Robertson .50 .20
541 Cleveland Indians 1.00 .40
Team Card
542 Goose Gossage 2.00 .80
543 Danny Cater .50 .20
544 Ron Schueler .50 .20
545 Billy Conigliaro 1.00 .40
546 Mike Corkins .50 .20
547 Glenn Borgmann .50 .20
548 Sonny Siebert .50 .20
549 Mike Jorgensen .50 .20
550 Sam McDowell 1.00 .40
551 Von Joshua .50 .20
552 Denny Doyle .50 .20
553 Jim Willoughby .50 .20
554 Tim Johnson .50 .20
555 Woodie Fryman .50 .20
556 Dave Campbell 1.00 .40
557 Jim McGlothlin .50 .20
558 Bill Fahey .50 .20
559 Darrel Chaney .50 .20
560 Mike Cuellar 1.00 .40
561 Ed Kranepool 1.00 .40
562 Jack Aker .50 .20
563 Hal McRae 1.00 .40
564 Mike Ryan .50 .20
565 Milt Wilcox .50 .20
566 Jackie Hernandez .50 .20
567 Boston Red Sox 1.00 .40
Team Card
568 Mike Torrez 1.00 .40
569 Rick Dempsey 1.00 .40
570 Ralph Garr 1.00 .40
571 Rich Hand .50 .20
572 Enzo Hernandez .50 .20
573 Mike Adams .50 .20
574 Bill Parsons .50 .20
575 Steve Garvey 3.00 1.20
576 Scipio Spinks .50 .20
577 Mike Sadek .50 .20
578 Ralph Houk MG 1.00 .40
579 Cecil Upshaw .50 .20
580 Jim Spencer .50 .20
581 Fred Norman .50 .20
582 Bucky Dent RC 4.00 1.60
583 Marty Pattin .50 .20
584 Ken Rudolph .50 .20
585 Merv Rettenmund .50 .20
586 Jack Brohamer .50 .20
587 Larry Christenson .50 .20
588 Hal Lanier .50 .20
589 Boots Day .50 .20
590 Roger Moret .50 .20
591 Sonny Jackson .50 .20
592 Ed Bane .50 .20
593 Steve Yeager 1.00 .40
594 Leroy Stanton .50 .20
595 Steve Blass 1.00 .40
596 Wayne Garland .50 .20
Fred Holdsworth
Mark Littell
Dick Pole
597 Dave Chalk 1.00 .40
John Gamble
Pete MacKanin
Manny Trillo RC
598 Dave Augustine 12.00 4.80
Ken Griffey RC
Steve Ontiveros
Jim Tyrone
599A Rookie Pitchers WAS 2.00 .80
Ron Diorio
Dave Freisleben
Frank Riccelli
Greg Shanahan
599B Rookie Pitchers SD 3.00 1.20
(SD in large print)
599C Rookie Pitchers SD 6.00 2.40
(SD in small print)
600 Ron Cash 5.00 2.00
Jim Cox
Bill Madlock RC
Reggie Sanders
601 Ed Armbrister 3.00 1.20
Rich Bladt
Brian Downing RC
Bake McBride RC
602 Glen Abbott 1.00 .40
Rick Henninger
Craig Swan
Dan Vossler
603 Barry Foote 1.00 .40
Tom Lundstedt
Charlie Moore RC
Sergio Robles
604 Terry Hughes 5.00 2.00
John Knox
Andre Thornton RC
Frank White RC
605 Vic Albury 4.00 1.60
Ken Frailing
Kevin Kobel
Frank Tanana RC
606 Jim Fuller 1.00 .40
Wilbur Howard
Tommy Smith
Otto Velez
607 Leo Foster 1.00 .40
Tom Heintzelman
Dave Rosello
Frank Taveras RC
608A Rookie Pitchers ERR 2.00 .80
Bob Apodaco (sic)
Dick Baney
John D'Acquisto
Mike Wallace
608B Rookie Pitchers COR 1.00 .40
Bob Apodaca
Dick Baney
John D'Acquisto
Mike Wallace
609 Rico Petrocelli 1.00 .40
610 Dave Kingman 2.00 .80
611 Rich Stelmaszek .50 .20
612 Luke Walker .50 .20
613 Dan Monzon .50 .20
614 Adrian Devine .50 .20
615 Johnny Jeter UER .50 .20
(Misspelled Johnnie
on card back)
616 Larry Gura .50 .20
617 Ted Ford .50 .20
618 Jim Mason .50 .20
619 Mike Anderson .50 .20
620 Al Downing .50 .20
621 Bernie Carbo .50 .20
622 Phil Gagliano .50 .20
623 Celerino Sanchez .50 .20
624 Bob Miller .50 .20
625 Ollie Brown .50 .20
626 Pittsburgh Pirates 1.00 .40
Team Card
627 Carl Taylor .50 .20
628 Ivan Murrell .50 .20
629 Rusty Staub 2.00 .80
630 Tommie Agee 1.00 .40
631 Steve Barber .50 .20

	NM	Ex
632 George Culver	.50	.20
633 Dave Hamilton	.50	.20
634 Eddie Mathews MG Herm Starrette CO Connie Ryan CO Jim Busby CO Ken Silvestri CO	3.00	1.20
635 Johnny Edwards	.50	.20
636 Dave Goltz	.50	.20
637 Checklist 529-660	3.00	.60
638 Ken Sanders	.50	.20
639 Joe Lovitto	.50	.20
640 Milt Pappas	1.00	.40
641 Chuck Brinkman	.50	.20
642 Terry Harmon	.50	.20
643 Dodgers Team	1.00	.40
644 Wayne Granger	.50	.20
645 Ken Boswell	.50	.20
646 George Foster	2.00	.80
647 Juan Beniquez	.50	.20
648 Terry Crowley	.50	.20
649 Fernando Gonzalez RC	.50	.20
650 Mike Epstein	.50	.20
651 Leron Lee	.50	.20
652 Gail Hopkins	.50	.20
653 Bob Stinson	.50	.20
654A Jesus Alou ERR (No position)	4.00	1.60
654B Jesus Alou COR (Outfield)	1.00	.40
655 Mike Tyson	.50	.20
656 Adrian Garrett	.50	.20
657 Jim Shellenback	.50	.20
658 Lee Lacy	.50	.20
659 Joe Lis	.50	.20
660 Larry Dierker	2.00	.50

1974 Topps Traded

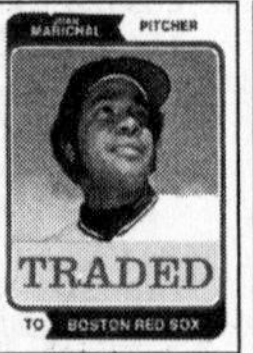

The cards in this 44-card set measure 2 1/2" by 3 1/2". The 1974 Topps Traded set contains 43 player cards and one unnumbered checklist card. The fronts have the word "traded" in block letters and the backs are designed in newspaper style. Card numbers are the same as in the regular set except they are followed by a "T." No known scarcities exist for this set. The cards were inserted in all packs toward the end of the production run. They were produced in large enough quantity that they are no scarcer than the regular Topps cards.

	NM	Ex
COMPLETE SET (44)	20.00	8.00
23T Craig Robinson	.50	.20
42T Claude Osteen	.75	.30
43T Jim Wynn	.75	.30
51T Bobby Heise	.50	.20
59T Ross Grimsley	.50	.20
62T Bob Locker	.50	.20
63T Bill Sudakis	.50	.20
73T Mike Marshall	.75	.30
123T Nelson Briles	.75	.30
139T Aurelio Monteagudo	.50	.20
151T Diego Segui	.50	.20
165T Willie Davis	.75	.30
175T Reggie Cleveland	.50	.20
182T Lindy McDaniel	.75	.30
186T Fred Scherman	.50	.20
249T George Mitterwald	.50	.20
262T Ed Kirkpatrick	.50	.20
269T Bob Johnson	.50	.20
270T Ron Santo	1.00	.40
313T Barry Lersch	.50	.20
319T Randy Hundley	.75	.30
330T Juan Marichal	2.00	.80
348T Pete Richert	.50	.20
373T John Curtis	.50	.20
390T Lou Piniella	1.00	.40
428T Gary Sutherland	.50	.20
454T Kurt Bevacqua	.50	.20
458T Jim Ray	.50	.20
485T Felipe Alou	1.00	.40
486T Steve Stone	.75	.30
496T Tom Murphy	.50	.20
516T Horacio Pina	.50	.20
534T Eddie Watt	.50	.20
538T Cesar Tovar	.50	.20
544T Ron Schueler	.50	.20
579T Cecil Upshaw	.50	.20
585T Merv Rettenmund	.50	.20
612T Luke Walker	.50	.20
616T Larry Gura	.75	.30
618T Jim Mason	.50	.20
630T Tommie Agee	.75	.30
648T Terry Crowley	.50	.20
649T Fernando Gonzalez	.50	.20
NNO Traded Checklist	1.50	.30

1974 Topps Team Checklists

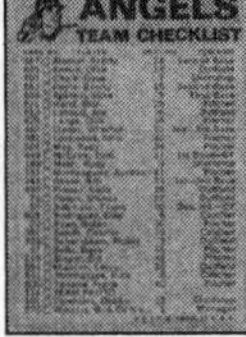

The cards in this 24-card set measure 2 1/2" by 3 1/2". The 1974 series of checklists was issued in packs with the regular cards for that year. The cards are unnumbered (arbitrarily numbered below alphabetically by team name) and have bright red borders. The year and team name appear in a green panel decorated by a crossed bats design, below which is a white area containing facsimile autographs of various players. The mustard-yellow and gray-colored backs list team members alphabetically, along with their card number, uniform number and position. Uncut sheets of these cards were also available through a wrapper mail-in offer. The uncut sheet value in NR/Mt or better condition is approximately $150.

	NM	Ex
COMPLETE SET (24)	20.00	6.00
COMMON TEAM (1-24)	1.00	.30

1974 Topps Deckle Edge

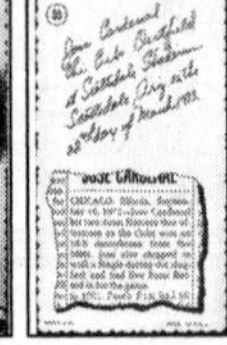

The cards in this 72-card set measure 2 7/8" by 5". Returning to a format first used in 1969, Topps produced a set of black and white photo cards in 1974 bearing an unusual serrated or "deckle" border. A facsimile autograph appears on the obverse while the backs contain the card number and a "newspaper-clipping" design detailing a milestone in the player's career. This was a test set and uncut sheets are sometimes found. Card backs are either white or gray; the white back cards are slightly tougher to obtain. The wrapper is also considered collectible. Wrappers featured Reggie Jackson and Tom Seaver and come with or without the phrase "With gum".

	NM	Ex
COMPLETE SET (72)	4500.00	1800.00
WRAPPER (With Gum)	20.00	8.00
WRAPPER (Without Gum)	20.00	8.00
1 Amos Otis	25.00	10.00
2 Darrell Evans	25.00	10.00
3 Bob Gibson	120.00	47.50
4 Dave Nelson	15.00	6.00
5 Steve Carlton	200.00	80.00
6 Jim Hunter	120.00	47.50
7 Thurman Munson	150.00	60.00
8 Bob Grich	25.00	10.00
9 Tom Seaver	250.00	100.00
10 Ted Simmons	25.00	10.00
11 Bobby Valentine	25.00	10.00
12 Don Sutton	80.00	32.00
13 Wilbur Wood	15.00	6.00
14 Doug Rader	15.00	6.00
15 Chris Chambliss	15.00	6.00
16 Pete Rose	250.00	100.00
17 John Hiller	15.00	6.00
18 Burt Hooton	15.00	6.00
19 Tim Foli	15.00	6.00
20 Lou Brock	120.00	47.50
21 Ron Bryant	15.00	6.00
22 Manny Sanguillen	15.00	6.00
23 Bob Tolan	15.00	6.00
24 Greg Luzinski	25.00	10.00
25 Brooks Robinson	200.00	80.00
26 Felix Millan	15.00	6.00
27 Luis Tiant	25.00	10.00
28 Willie McCovey	120.00	47.50
29 Chris Speier	15.00	6.00
30 George Scott	15.00	6.00
31 Willie Stargell	120.00	47.50
32 Rod Carew	150.00	60.00
33 Charlie Spikes	15.00	6.00
34 Nate Colbert	15.00	6.00
35 Rich Hebner	15.00	6.00
36 Bobby Bonds	25.00	10.00
37 Buddy Bell	25.00	10.00
38 Claude Osteen	15.00	6.00
39 Dick Allen	25.00	10.00
40 Bill Russell	15.00	6.00
41 Nolan Ryan	1500.00	600.00
42 Willie Davis	15.00	6.00
43 Carl Yastrzemski	150.00	60.00
44 Jon Matlack	15.00	6.00
45 Jim Palmer	150.00	60.00
46 Bert Campaneris	15.00	6.00
47 Bert Blyleven	25.00	10.00
48 Jeff Burroughs	15.00	6.00
49 Jim Colborn	15.00	6.00
50 Dave Johnson	25.00	10.00
51 John Mayberry	15.00	6.00
52 Don Kessinger	15.00	6.00
53 Joe Coleman	15.00	6.00
54 Tony Perez	80.00	32.00
55 Jose Cardenal	15.00	6.00
56 Paul Splittorff	15.00	6.00
57 Hank Aaron	250.00	100.00
58 Dave May	15.00	6.00
59 Fergie Jenkins	120.00	47.50
60 Ron Blomberg	15.00	6.00
61 Reggie Jackson	250.00	100.00
62 Tony Oliva	25.00	10.00
63 Bobby Murcer	25.00	10.00
64 Carlton Fisk	150.00	60.00
65 Steve Rogers	15.00	6.00
66 Frank Robinson	150.00	60.00
67 Joe Ferguson	15.00	6.00
68 Bill Melton	15.00	6.00
69 Bob Watson	15.00	6.00
70 Larry Bowa	25.00	10.00
71 Johnny Bench	200.00	80.00
72 Willie Horton	15.00	6.00

1974 Topps Puzzles

This set of 12 jigsaw puzzles was supposedly distributed by Topps in 1974 as a test issue. Each puzzle measures approximately 5" by 7 1/8" and shows a colorful picture of the player inside a white border. Puzzles contained 40 pieces. The wrapper for the puzzles is also collectible as it shows a picture of Tom Seaver. The wrapper comes two ways: either with a pre-printed price of 29 cents or 25 cents. The

puzzles are blank backed and unnumbered; they are listed below alphabetically.

	NM	Ex
COMPLETE SET (12)	1800.00	700.00
WRAPPER (25 cents)	20.00	8.00
WRAPPER (29 cents)	80.00	32.00
1 Hank Aaron	150.00	60.00
2 Dick Allen	40.00	16.00
3 Johnny Bench	100.00	40.00
4 Bobby Bonds	40.00	16.00
5 Bob Gibson	80.00	32.00
6 Reggie Jackson	200.00	80.00
7 Bobby Murcer	40.00	16.00
8 Jim Palmer	80.00	32.00
9 Nolan Ryan	1000.00	400.00
10 Tom Seaver	150.00	60.00
11 Willie Stargell	80.00	32.00
12 Carl Yastrzemski	100.00	40.00

1974 Topps Stamps

The 240 color portraits depicted on stamps in this 1974 Topps series have the player's name, team and position inside an oval below the picture area. Each stamp measures 1" by 1 1/2". The stamps were marketed in 12 stamp sheets, along with an album, in their own wrapper. The booklets have eight pages and measure 2 1/2" by 3 7/8". There are 24 albums, one for each team, designed to hold 10 stamps apiece. The stamps are numbered here alphabetically within each team and the teams are listed in alphabetical order within league, e.g., Atlanta Braves NL (1-10), Chicago Cubs (11-20), Cincinnati Reds (21-30), Houston Astros (31-40), Los Angeles Dodgers (41-50), Montreal Expos (51-60), New York Mets (61-70), Philadelphia Phillies (71-80), Pittsburgh Pirates (81-90), San Diego Padres (91-100), San Francisco Giants (101-110), St. Louis Cardinals (111-120), Baltimore Orioles AL (121-130), Boston Red Sox (131-140), California Angels (141-150), Chicago White Sox (151-160), Cleveland Indians (161-170), Detroit Tigers (171-180), Kansas City Royals (181-190), Milwaukee Brewers (191-200), Minnesota Twins (201-210), New York Yankees (211-220), Oakland A's (221-230) and Texas Rangers (231-240).

	NM	Ex
COMPLETE SET (240)	125.00	50.00
1 Hank Aaron	10.00	4.00
2 Dusty Baker	.50	.20
3 Darrell Evans	.50	.20
4 Ralph Garr	.30	.12
5 Roric Harrison	.15	.06
6 Dave Johnson	.75	.30
7 Mike Lum	.15	.06
8 Carl Morton	.15	.06
9 Phil Niekro	3.00	1.20
10 Johnny Oates	.15	.06
11 Glenn Beckert	.15	.06
12 Jose Cardenal	.15	.06
13 Vic Harris	.15	.06
14 Burt Hooton	.15	.06
15 Randy Hundley	.15	.06
16 Don Kessinger	.30	.12
17 Rick Monday	.30	.12
18 Rick Reuschel	.75	.30
19 Ron Santo	1.25	.50
20 Billy Williams	3.00	1.20
21 Johnny Bench	6.00	2.40
22 Jack Billingham	.15	.06
23 Pedro Borbon	.15	.06
24 Dave Concepcion	.75	.30
25 Dan Driessen	.30	.12
26 Cesar Geronimo	.15	.06
27 Don Gullett	.30	.12
28 Joe Morgan	4.00	1.60
29 Tony Perez	2.00	.80
30 Pete Rose	10.00	4.00
31 Cesar Cedeno	.30	.12
32 Tommy Helms	.15	.06
33 Lee May	.30	.12
34 Roger Metzger	.15	.06
35 Doug Rader	.15	.06
36 J.R. Richard	.30	.12
37 Dave Roberts	.15	.06
38 Jerry Reuss	.30	.12
39 Bob Watson	.30	.12
40 Jim Wynn	.30	.12
41 Bill Buckner	.50	.20
42 Ron Cey	.50	.20
43 Willie Crawford	.15	.06
44 Willie Davis	.30	.12
45 Joe Ferguson	.15	.06
46 Davey Lopes	.30	.12
47 Andy Messersmith	.30	.12
48 Claude Osteen	.30	.12
49 Bill Russell	.30	.12
50 Don Sutton	2.00	.80
51 Bob Bailey	.15	.06
52 John Boccabella	.15	.06
53 Ron Fairly	.30	.12
54 Tim Foli	.15	.06
55 Ron Hunt	.15	.06
56 Mike Jorgensen	.15	.06
57 Mike Marshall	.30	.12
58 Steve Renko	.15	.06
59 Steve Rogers	.30	.12
60 Ken Singleton	.50	.20
61 Wayne Garrett	.15	.06
62 Jerry Grote	.15	.06
63 Bud Harrelson	.30	.12
64 Cleon Jones	.15	.06
65 Jerry Koosman	.75	.30
66 Jon Matlack	.30	.12
67 Tug McGraw	.75	.30
68 Felix Millan	.15	.06
69 John Milner	.15	.06
70 Tom Seaver	6.00	2.40
71 Bob Boone	.75	.30
72 Larry Bowa	.30	.12
73 Steve Carlton	6.00	2.40
74 Bill Grabarkewitz	.15	.06
75 Jim Lonborg	.30	.12
76 Greg Luzinski	.50	.20
77 Willie Montanez	.15	.06
78 Bill Robinson	.30	.12
79 Wayne Twitchell	.15	.06
80 Del Unser	.15	.06
81 Nelson Briles	.30	.12
82 Dock Ellis	.15	.06
83 Dave Giusti	.15	.06
84 Richie Hebner	.15	.06
85 Al Oliver	.50	.20
86 Dave Parker	3.00	1.20
87 Manny Sanguillen	.30	.12
88 Willie Stargell	4.00	1.60
89 Rennie Stennett	.15	.06
90 Richie Zisk	.30	.12
91 Nate Colbert	.15	.06
92 Bill Grief	.15	.06
93 Johnny Grubb	.15	.06
94 Randy Jones	.30	.12
95 Fred Kendall	.15	.06
96 Clay Kirby	.15	.06
97 Willie McCovey	4.00	1.60
98 Jerry Morales	.15	.06
99 Dave Roberts	.15	.06
100 Dave Winfield	10.00	4.00
101 Bobby Bonds	.75	.30
102 Tom Bradley	.15	.06
103 Ron Bryant	.15	.06
104 Tito Fuentes	.15	.06
105 Ed Goodson	.15	.06
106 Dave Kingman	1.25	.50
107 Garry Maddox	.30	.12
108 Dave Rader	.15	.06
109 Elias Sosa	.15	.06
110 Chris Speier	.30	.12
111 Lou Brock	4.00	1.60
112 Reggie Cleveland	.15	.06
113 Jose Cruz	.50	.20
114 Bob Gibson	4.00	1.60
115 Tim McCarver	.50	.20
116 Ted Simmons	.50	.20
117 Ted Sizemore	.15	.06
118 Reggie Smith	.30	.12
119 Joe Torre	.75	.30
120 Mike Tyson	.15	.06
121 Don Baylor	.75	.30
122 Mark Belanger	.30	.12
123 Paul Blair	.15	.06
124 Tommy Davis	.30	.12
125 Bobby Grich	.30	.12
126 Grant Jackson	.15	.06
127 Dave McNally	.30	.12
128 Jim Palmer	3.00	1.20
129 Brooks Robinson	5.00	2.00
130 Earl Williams	.15	.06
131 Luis Aparicio	3.00	1.20
132 Orlando Cepeda	2.00	.80
133 Carlton Fisk	5.00	2.00
134 Tommy Harper	.15	.06
135 Bill Lee	.30	.12
136 Rick Miller	.15	.06
137 Roger Moret	.15	.06
138 Luis Tiant	.75	.30
139 Rick Wise	.15	.06
140 Carl Yastrzemski	6.00	2.40
141 Sandy Alomar	.15	.06
142 Mike Epstein	.15	.06
143 Bob Oliver	.15	.06
144 Vada Pinson	.50	.20
145 Frank Robinson	5.00	2.00
146 Ellie Rodriguez	.15	.06
147 Nolan Ryan	20.00	8.00
148 Richie Scheinblum	.15	.06
149 Bill Singer	.15	.06
150 Bobby Valentine	.30	.12
151 Dick Allen	.75	.30
152 Stan Bahnsen	.15	.06
153 Terry Forster	.30	.12
154 Ken Henderson	.15	.06
155 Ed Herrmann	.15	.06
156 Pat Kelly	.15	.06
157 Carlos May	.15	.06
158 Bill Melton	.15	.06
159 Jorge Orta	.15	.06
160 Wilbur Wood	.30	.12
161 Buddy Bell	.75	.30
162 Chris Chambliss	.50	.20
163 Frank Duffy	.15	.06
164 Dave Duncan	.15	.06
165 John Ellis	.15	.06
166 Oscar Gamble	.30	.12
167 George Hendrick	.30	.12
168 Gaylord Perry	3.00	1.20
169 Charlie Spikes	.15	.06
170 Dick Tidrow	.15	.06
171 Ed Brinkman	.15	.06
172 Norm Cash	.75	.30
173 Joe Coleman	.15	.06
174 Bill Freehan	.50	.20
175 John Hiller	.30	.12
176 Willie Horton	.30	.12
177 Al Kaline	6.00	2.40
178 Mickey Lolich	.75	.30
179 Aurelio Rodriguez	.15	.06
180 Mickey Stanley	.15	.06
181 Steve Busby	.30	.12
182 Fran Healy	.15	.06
183 Ed Kirkpatrick	.15	.06
184 John Mayberry	.30	.12
185 Amos Otis	.50	.20
186 Fred Patek	.15	.06
187 Marty Pattin	.15	.06
188 Lou Piniella	.75	.30
189 Cookie Rojas	.15	.06
190 Paul Splittorff	.15	.06
191 Jerry Bell	.15	.06
192 Johnny Briggs	.15	.06
193 Jim Colborn	.15	.06
194 Bob Collucio	.15	.06
195 Pedro Garcia	.15	.06
196 Dave May	.15	.06
197 Don Money	.15	.06
198 Darrell Porter	.30	.12
199 George Scott	.30	.12
200 Jim Slaton	.15	.06
201 Bert Blyleven	.75	.30
202 Steve Braun	.15	.06
203 Rod Carew	6.00	2.40
204 Ray Corbin	.15	.06
205 Bobby Darwin	.15	.06
206 Joe Decker	.15	.06
207 Jim Holt	.15	.06
208 Harmon Killebrew	4.00	1.60
209 George Mitterwald	.15	.06
210 Tony Oliva	.75	.30
211 Ron Blomberg	.15	.06
212 Sparky Lyle	.50	.20
213 George Medich	.15	.06
214 Gene Michael	.15	.06
215 Thurman Munson	5.00	2.00
216 Bobby Murcer	.50	.20
217 Graig Nettles	.75	.30
218 Mel Stottlemyre	.50	.20
219 Otto Velez	.15	.06
220 Roy White	.30	.12
221 Sal Bando	.30	.12
222 Vida Blue	.75	.30
223 Bert Campaneris	.30	.12
224 Ken Holtzman	.30	.12
225 Jim Hunter	3.00	1.20
226 Reggie Jackson	8.00	3.20
227 Deron Johnson	.15	.06
228 Bill North	.15	.06
229 Joe Rudi	.30	.12
230 Gene Tenace	.30	.12
231 Jim Bibby	.15	.06
232 Jeff Burroughs	.30	.12
233 David Clyde	.15	.06
234 Jim Fregosi	.50	.20
235 Toby Harrah	.30	.12
236 Ferguson Jenkins	3.00	1.20
237 Alex Johnson	.15	.06
238 Dave Nelson	.15	.06
239 Jim Spencer	.15	.06
240 Bill Sudakis	.15	.06

1974 Topps Stamp Albums

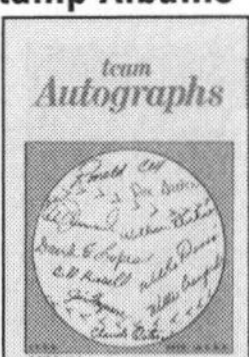

The 1974 Topps stamp set of baseball player stamps was intended to be mounted in 24 separate team albums, 10 stamps for that team's players going into that team's album. The albums measure approximately 2 1/2" by 3 1/2".

	NM	Ex
COMPLETE SET (24)	120.00	47.50
COMMON TEAM (1-24)	5.00	2.00
17 New York Yankees	6.00	2.40

1975 Topps

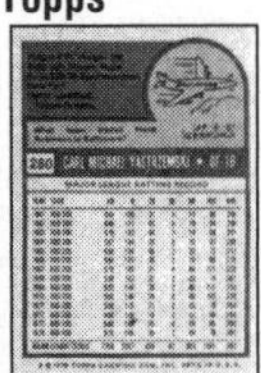

The 1975 Topps set consists of 660 standard size cards. The design was radically different in appearance from sets of the preceding years. The most prominent change was the use of a two-color frame surrounding the picture area rather than a single, subdued color. A facsimile autograph appears on the picture, and the backs are printed in red and green on gray. Cards were released in ten-card wax packs, 18-card cello packs as well as in 42-card rack packs. The cello packs were issued 24 to a box. Cards 189-212 depict the MVP's of both leagues from 1951 through 1974. The first seven cards (1-7) feature players (listed in alphabetical order) breaking records or achieving milestones during the previous season. Cards 306-313 picture league leaders in various statistical categories. Cards 459-466 depict the results of post-season action. Team cards feature a checklist back for players on that team and show a small inset photo of the manager on the front. The following players' regular issue cards are explicitly denoted as All-Stars, 1, 50, 80, 140, 170, 180, 260, 320, 350, 390, 400, 420, 440, 470, 530, 570, and 600. This set is quite popular with collectors, at least in part due to the fact that the Rookie Cards of George Brett, Gary Carter, Keith Hernandez, Fred Lynn, Jim Rice and Robin Yount are all in the set.

	NM	Ex
COMPLETE SET (660)	600.00	240.00
WRAPPER (15-CENT)	8.00	3.20
1 Hank Aaron HL	30.00	10.00
2 Lou Brock HL	3.00	1.20

3 Bob Gibson HL 3.00 1.20
4 Al Kaline HL 6.00 2.40
5 Nolan Ryan HL 15.00 6.00
6 Mike Marshall HL 1.00 .40
7 Steve Busby HL 8.00 3.20
Dick Bosman
Nolan Ryan
8 Rogelio Moret .50 .20
9 Frank Tepedino 1.00 .40
10 Willie Davis 1.00 .40
11 Bill Melton .50 .20
12 David Clyde .50 .20
13 Gene Locklear RC 1.00 .40
14 Milt Wilcox .50 .20
15 Jose Cardenal 1.00 .40
16 Frank Tanana 2.00 .80
17 Dave Concepcion 2.00 .80
18 Tigers Team CL 2.00 .40
Ralph Houk MG
19 Jerry Koosman 1.00 .40
20 Thurman Munson 8.00 3.20
21 Rollie Fingers 3.00 1.20
22 Dave Cash .50 .20
23 Bill Russell 1.00 .40
24 Al Fitzmorris .50 .20
25 Lee May 1.00 .40
26 Dave McNally 1.00 .40
27 Ken Reitz .50 .20
28 Tom Murphy .50 .20
29 Dave Parker 3.00 1.20
30 Bert Blyleven 2.00 .80
31 Dave Rader .50 .20
32 Reggie Cleveland .50 .20
33 Dusty Baker 2.00 .80
34 Steve Renko .50 .20
35 Ron Santo 1.00 .40
36 Joe Lovitto .50 .20
37 Dave Freisleben .50 .20
38 Buddy Bell 2.00 .80
39 Andre Thornton 1.00 .40
40 Bill Singer .50 .20
41 Cesar Geronimo 1.00 .40
42 Joe Coleman .50 .20
43 Cleon Jones 1.00 .40
44 Pat Dobson .50 .20
45 Joe Rudi 1.00 .40
46 Phillies Team CL 2.00 .40
Danny Ozark MG UER
Terry Harmon listed as 339
instead of 399
47 Tommy John 2.00 .80
48 Freddie Patek 1.00 .40
49 Larry Dierker 1.00 .40
50 Brooks Robinson 8.00 3.20
51 Bob Forsch RC 1.00 .40
52 Darrell Porter 1.00 .40
53 Dave Giusti .50 .20
54 Eric Soderholm .50 .20
55 Bobby Bonds 2.00 .80
56 Rick Wise 1.00 .40
57 Dave Johnson 1.00 .40
58 Chuck Taylor .50 .20
59 Ken Henderson .50 .20
60 Fergie Jenkins 3.00 1.20
61 Dave Winfield 15.00 6.00
62 Fritz Peterson .50 .20
63 Steve Swisher .50 .20
64 Dave Chalk .50 .20
65 Don Gullett 1.00 .40
66 Willie Horton 1.00 .40
67 Tug McGraw 1.00 .40
68 Ron Blomberg .50 .20
69 John Odom .50 .20
70 Mike Schmidt 20.00 8.00
71 Charlie Hough 1.00 .40
72 Royals Team CL 2.00 .40
Jack McKeon MG
73 J.R. Richard 1.00 .40
74 Mark Belanger 1.00 .40
75 Ted Simmons 2.00 .80
76 Ed Sprague .50 .20
77 Richie Zisk 1.00 .40
78 Ray Corbin .50 .20
79 Gary Matthews 1.00 .40
80 Carlton Fisk 8.00 3.20
81 Ron Reed .50 .20
82 Pat Kelly .50 .20
83 Jim Merritt .50 .20
84 Enzo Hernandez .50 .20
85 Bill Bonham .50 .20
86 Joe Lis .50 .20
87 George Foster 2.00 .80
88 Tom Egan .50 .20
89 Jim Ray .50 .20
90 Rusty Staub 2.00 .80
91 Dick Green .50 .20
92 Cecil Upshaw .50 .20
93 Dave Lopes 2.00 .80
94 Jim Lonborg 1.00 .40
95 John Mayberry 1.00 .40
96 Mike Cosgrove .50 .20
97 Earl Williams .50 .20
98 Rich Folkers .50 .20
99 Mike Hegan .50 .20
100 Willie Stargell 4.00 1.60
101 Expos Team CL 2.00 .40
Gene Mauch MG
102 Joe Decker .50 .20
103 Rick Miller .50 .20
104 Bill Madlock 2.00 .80
105 Buzz Capra .50 .20
106 M. Hargrove RC UER 3.00 1.20
Gastonia At-bats are wrong
107 Jim Barr .50 .20
108 Tom Hall .50 .20
109 George Hendrick 1.00 .40
110 Wilbur Wood .50 .20
111 Wayne Garrett .50 .20
112 Larry Hardy .50 .20
113 Elliott Maddox .50 .20
114 Dick Lange .50 .20
115 Joe Ferguson .50 .20
116 Lerrin LaGrow .50 .20
117 Orioles Team CL 3.00 .60
Earl Weaver MG
118 Mike Anderson .50 .20
119 Tommy Helms .50 .20
120 Steve Busby UER 1.00 .40
(Photo actually
Fran Healy)
121 Bill North .50 .20
122 Al Hrabosky 1.00 .40
123 Johnny Briggs .50 .20
124 Jerry Reuss 1.00 .40
125 Ken Singleton 1.00 .40
126 Checklist 1-132 3.00 .60
127 Glenn Borgmann .50 .20
128 Bill Lee 1.00 .40
129 Rick Monday 1.00 .40
130 Phil Niekro 3.00 1.20
131 Toby Harrah 1.00 .40
132 Randy Moffitt .50 .20
133 Dan Driessen 1.00 .40
134 Ron Hodges .50 .20
135 Charlie Spikes .50 .20
136 Jim Mason .50 .20
137 Terry Forster 1.00 .40
138 Del Unser .50 .20
139 Horacio Pina .50 .20
140 Steve Garvey 3.00 1.20
141 Mickey Stanley 1.00 .40
142 Bob Reynolds .50 .20
143 Cliff Johnson 1.00 .40
144 Jim Wohlford .50 .20
145 Ken Holtzman 1.00 .40
146 Padres Team CL 2.00 .40
John McNamara MG
147 Pedro Garcia .50 .20
148 Jim Rooker .50 .20
149 Tim Foli .50 .20
150 Bob Gibson 6.00 2.40
151 Steve Brye .50 .20
152 Mario Guerrero .50 .20
153 Rick Reuschel 1.00 .40
154 Mike Lum .50 .20
155 Jim Bibby .50 .20
156 Dave Kingman 2.00 .80
157 Pedro Borbon 1.00 .40
158 Jerry Grote .50 .20
159 Steve Arlin .50 .20
160 Graig Nettles 2.00 .80
161 Stan Bahnsen .50 .20
162 Willie Montanez .50 .20
163 Jim Brewer .50 .20
164 Mickey Rivers 1.00 .40
165 Doug Rader 1.00 .40
166 Woodie Fryman .50 .20
167 Rich Coggins .50 .20
168 Bill Greif .50 .20
169 Cookie Rojas .50 .20
170 Bert Campaneris 1.00 .40
171 Ed Kirkpatrick .50 .20
172 Red Sox Team CL 3.00 .60
Darrell Johnson MG
173 Steve Rogers 1.00 .40
174 Bake McBride 1.00 .40
175 Don Money 1.00 .40
176 Burt Hooton 1.00 .40
177 Vic Correll .50 .20
178 Cesar Tovar .50 .20
179 Tom Bradley .50 .20
180 Joe Morgan 6.00 2.40
181 Fred Beene .50 .20
182 Don Hahn .50 .20
183 Mel Stottlemyre 1.00 .40
184 Jorge Orta .50 .20
185 Steve Carlton 8.00 3.20
186 Willie Crawford .50 .20
187 Denny Doyle .50 .20
188 Tom Griffin .50 .20
189 Larry (Yogi) Berra 4.00 1.60
Roy Campanella MVP
Campanella card never issued
190 Bobby Shantz 2.00 .80
Hank Sauer MVP
191 Al Rosen 2.00 .80
Roy Campanella MVP
192 Yogi Berra 4.00 1.60
Willie Mays MVP
193 Yogi Berra 3.00 1.20
Roy Campanella MVP
Campanella card never issued
he is pictured with LA cap
194 Mickey Mantle 10.00 4.00
Don Newcombe MVP
195 Mickey Mantle 12.00 4.80
Hank Aaron MVP
196 Jackie Jensen 3.00 1.20
Ernie Banks MVP
197 Nellie Fox 2.00 .80
Ernie Banks MVP
198 Roger Maris 2.00 .80
Dick Groat MVP
199 Roger Maris 3.00 1.20
Frank Robinson MVP
200 Mickey Mantle 10.00 4.00
Maury Wills MVP
(Wills card never issued)
201 Elston Howard 2.00 .80
Sandy Koufax MVP
202 Brooks Robinson 2.00 .80
Ken Boyer MVP
203 Zoilo Versalles 2.00 .80
Willie Mays MVP
204 Frank Robinson 6.00 2.40
Bob Clemente MVP
205 Carl Yastrzemski 2.00 .80
Orlando Cepeda MVP
206 Denny McLain UER 2.00 .80
Bob Gibson MVP
On the back McLain is spelled McClain
207 Harmon Killebrew 2.00 .80
Willie McCovey MVP
208 Boog Powell 2.00 .80
Johnny Bench MVP
209 Vida Blue 2.00 .80
Joe Torre MVP
210 Rich Allen 2.00 .80
Johnny Bench MVP
211 Reggie Jackson 5.00 2.00
Pete Rose MVP
212 Jeff Burroughs 2.00 .80
Steve Garvey MVP
213 Oscar Gamble 1.00 .40
214 Harry Parker .50 .20
215 Bobby Valentine 1.00 .40
216 Giants Team CL 2.00 .40
Wes Westrum MG
217 Lou Piniella 2.00 .80
218 Jerry Johnson .50 .20
219 Ed Herrmann .50 .20
220 Don Sutton 3.00 1.20
221 Aurelio Rodriguez .50 .20
222 Dan Spillner .50 .20
223 Robin Yount RC 50.00 20.00
224 Ramon Hernandez .50 .20
225 Bob Grich 1.00 .40
226 Bill Campbell .50 .20
227 Bob Watson 1.00 .40
228 George Brett RC 80.00 32.00
229 Barry Foote .50 .20
230 Jim Hunter 4.00 1.60
231 Mike Tyson .50 .20
232 Diego Segui .50 .20
233 Billy Grabarkewitz .50 .20
234 Tom Grieve 1.00 .40
235 Jack Billingham 1.00 .40
236 Angels Team CL 2.00 .40
Dick Williams MG
237 Carl Morton 1.00 .40
238 Dave Duncan 1.00 .40
239 George Stone .50 .20
240 Garry Maddox 1.00 .40
241 Dick Tidrow .50 .20
242 Jay Johnstone 1.00 .40
243 Jim Kaat 2.00 .80
244 Bill Buckner 1.00 .40
245 Mickey Lolich 2.00 .80
246 Cardinals Team CL 2.00 .40
Red Schoendienst MG
247 Enos Cabell .50 .20
248 Randy Jones 2.00 .80
249 Danny Thompson .50 .20
250 Ken Brett .50 .20
251 Fran Healy .50 .20
252 Fred Scherman .50 .20
253 Jesus Alou .50 .20
254 Mike Torrez 1.00 .40
255 Dwight Evans 2.00 .80
256 Billy Champion .50 .20
257 Checklist: 133-264 3.00 .60
258 Dave LaRoche .50 .20
259 Len Randle .50 .20
260 Johnny Bench 15.00 6.00
261 Andy Hassler .50 .20
262 Rowland Office .50 .20
263 Jim Perry 1.00 .40
264 John Milner .50 .20
265 Ron Bryant .50 .20
266 Sandy Alomar 1.00 .40
267 Dick Ruthven .50 .20
268 Hal McRae 1.00 .40
269 Doug Rau .50 .20
270 Ron Fairly 1.00 .40
271 Gerry Moses .50 .20
272 Lynn McGlothen .50 .20
273 Steve Braun .50 .20
274 Vicente Romo .50 .20
275 Paul Blair 1.00 .40
276 White Sox Team CL 2.00 .40
Chuck Tanner MG
277 Frank Taveras .50 .20
278 Paul Lindblad .50 .20
279 Milt May .50 .20
280 Carl Yastrzemski 12.00 4.80
281 Jim Slaton .50 .20
282 Jerry Morales .50 .20
283 Steve Foucault .50 .20
284 Ken Griffey 4.00 1.60
285 Ellie Rodriguez .50 .20
286 Mike Jorgensen .50 .20
287 Roric Harrison .50 .20
288 Bruce Ellingsen .50 .20
289 Ken Rudolph .50 .20
290 Jon Matlack .50 .20
291 Bill Sudakis .50 .20
292 Ron Schueler .50 .20
293 Dick Sharon .50 .20
294 Geoff Zahn .50 .20
295 Vada Pinson 2.00 .80
296 Alan Foster .50 .20
297 Craig Kusick .50 .20
298 Johnny Grubb .50 .20
299 Bucky Dent 2.00 .80
300 Reggie Jackson 15.00 6.00
301 Dave Roberts .50 .20
302 Rick Burleson 1.00 .40
303 Grant Jackson .50 .20
304 Pirates Team CL 2.00 .40
Danny Murtaugh MG
305 Jim Colborn .50 .20
306 Rod Carew 2.00 .80
Ralph Garr LL
307 Dick Allen 4.00 1.60
Mike Schmidt LL
308 Jeff Burroughs 2.00 .80
Johnny Bench LL
309 Bill North 2.00 .80
Lou Brock LL
310 Jim Hunter 2.00 .80
Fergie Jenkins
Andy Messersmith
Phil Niekro LL
311 Jim Hunter 2.00 .80
Buzz Capra LL
312 Nolan Ryan 12.00 4.80
Steve Carlton LL
313 Terry Forster 1.00 .40
Mike Marshall LL
314 Buck Martinez .50 .20
315 Don Kessinger 1.00 .40
316 Jackie Brown .50 .20
317 Joe Lahoud .50 .20
318 Ernie McAnally .50 .20
319 Johnny Oates 1.00 .40
320 Pete Rose 30.00 12.00
321 Rudy May .50 .20
322 Ed Goodson .50 .20
323 Fred Holdsworth .50 .20
324 Ed Kranepool 1.00 .40
325 Tony Oliva 2.00 .80
326 Wayne Twitchell .50 .20
327 Jerry Hairston .50 .20
328 Sonny Siebert .50 .20
329 Ted Kubiak .50 .20
330 Mike Marshall 1.00 .40
331 Indians Team CL 2.00 .40
Frank Robinson MG
332 Fred Kendall .50 .20
333 Dick Drago .50 .20
334 Greg Gross .50 .20
335 Jim Palmer 6.00 2.40
336 Rennie Stennett .50 .20
337 Kevin Kobel .50 .20
338 Rich Stelmaszek .50 .20
339 Jim Fregosi 1.00 .40
340 Paul Splittorff .50 .20
341 Hal Breeden .50 .20
342 Leroy Stanton .50 .20
343 Danny Frisella .50 .20
344 Ben Oglivie 1.00 .40
345 Clay Carroll 1.00 .40
346 Bobby Darwin .50 .20
347 Mike Caldwell .50 .20
348 Tony Muser .50 .20
349 Ray Sadecki .50 .20
350 Bobby Murcer 1.00 .40
351 Bob Boone 2.00 .80
352 Darold Knowles .50 .20
353 Luis Melendez .50 .20
354 Dick Bosman .50 .20
355 Chris Cannizzaro .50 .20
356 Rico Petrocelli 1.00 .40
357 Ken Forsch UER .50 .20
Forsch is misspelled in blurb
358 Al Bumbry 1.00 .40
359 Paul Popovich .50 .20
360 George Scott 1.00 .40
361 Dodgers Team CL 2.00 .40
Walter Alston MG
362 Steve Hargan .50 .20
363 Carmen Fanzone .50 .20
364 Doug Bird .50 .20
365 Bob Bailey .50 .20
366 Ken Sanders .50 .20
367 Craig Robinson .50 .20
368 Vic Albury .50 .20
369 Merv Rettenmund .50 .20
370 Tom Seaver 12.00 4.80
371 Gates Brown .50 .20
372 John D'Acquisto .50 .20
373 Bill Sharp .50 .20
374 Eddie Watt .50 .20
375 Roy White 1.00 .40
376 Steve Yeager 1.00 .40
377 Tom Hilgendorf .50 .20
378 Derrel Thomas .50 .20
379 Bernie Carbo .50 .20
380 Sal Bando 1.00 .40
381 John Curtis .50 .20
382 Don Baylor 2.00 .80
383 Jim York .50 .20
384 Brewers Team 2.00 .40
Del Crandall MG
385 Dock Ellis .50 .20
386 Checklist: 265-396 UER 3.00 .60
Dick Sharon's name is misspelled
387 Jim Spencer .50 .20
388 Steve Stone 1.00 .40
389 Tony Solaita .50 .20
390 Ron Cey 2.00 .80
391 Don DeMola .50 .20
392 Bruce Bochte RC 1.00 .40
393 Gary Gentry .50 .20
394 Larvell Blanks .50 .20
395 Bud Harrelson 1.00 .40
396 Fred Norman 1.00 .40
397 Bill Freehan 1.00 .40
398 Elias Sosa .50 .20
399 Terry Harmon .50 .20
400 Dick Allen 2.00 .80
401 Mike Wallace .50 .20
402 Bob Tolan .50 .20
403 Tom Buskey .50 .20
404 Ted Sizemore .50 .20
405 John Montague .50 .20
406 Bob Gallagher .50 .20
407 Herb Washington RC 2.00 .80
408 Clyde Wright UER .50 .20
Listed with wrong 1974 team
409 Bob Robertson .50 .20
410 Mike Cueller UER 1.00 .40
Sic, Cuellar
411 George Mitterwald .50 .20
412 Bill Hands .50 .20
413 Marty Pattin .50 .20
414 Manny Mota 1.00 .40
415 John Hiller 1.00 .40
416 Larry Lintz .50 .20
417 Skip Lockwood .50 .20
418 Leo Foster .50 .20
419 Dave Goltz .50 .20
420 Larry Bowa 2.00 .80
421 Mets Team CL 3.00 .60
Yogi Berra MG
422 Brian Downing 1.00 .40
423 Clay Kirby .50 .20
424 John Lowenstein .50 .20
425 Tito Fuentes .50 .20
426 George Medich .50 .20
427 Clarence Gaston 1.00 .40
428 Dave Hamilton .50 .20
429 Jim Dwyer .50 .20
430 Luis Tiant 2.00 .80
431 Rod Gilbreath .50 .20
432 Ken Berry .50 .20
433 Larry Demery .50 .20
434 Bob Locker .50 .20
435 Dave Nelson .50 .20
436 Ken Frailing .50 .20
437 Al Cowens 1.00 .40
438 Don Carrithers .50 .20
439 Ed Brinkman .50 .20
440 Andy Messersmith 1.00 .40
441 Bobby Heise .50 .20
442 Maximino Leon .50 .20
443 Twins Team CL 2.00 .40
Frank Quilici MG
444 Gene Garber 1.00 .40
445 Felix Millan .50 .20
446 Bart Johnson .50 .20
447 Terry Crowley .50 .20
448 Frank Duffy .50 .20
449 Charlie Williams .50 .20
450 Willie McCovey 6.00 2.40
451 Rick Dempsey 1.00 .40
452 Angel Mangual .50 .20
453 Claude Osteen 1.00 .40
454 Doug Griffin .50 .20
455 Don Wilson .50 .20
456 Bob Coluccio .50 .20
457 Mario Mendoza .50 .20
458 Ross Grimsley .50 .20
459 1974 AL Champs 1.00 .40
A's over Orioles
(Second base action
pictured)
460 Steve Garvey NLCS 2.00 .80
Frank Taveras
461 Reggie Jackson WS 5.00 2.00
462 World Series Game 2 1.00 .40
(Dodger dugout)
463 Rollie Fingers WS 2.00 .80
464 World Series Game 4 1.00 .40
(A's batter)
465 Joe Rudi WS5 1.00 .40
466 WS Summary 2.00 .80
A's do it again;
win third straight
A's group picture
467 Ed Halicki .50 .20
468 Bobby Mitchell .50 .20
469 Tom Dettore .50 .20
470 Jeff Burroughs 1.00 .40
471 Bob Stinson .50 .20
472 Bruce Dal Canton .50 .20
473 Ken McMullen .50 .20
474 Luke Walker .50 .20
475 Darrell Evans 1.00 .40
476 Ed Figueroa .50 .20
477 Tom Hutton .50 .20
478 Tom Burgmeier .50 .20
479 Ken Boswell .50 .20
480 Carlos May .50 .20
481 Will McEnaney 1.00 .40
482 Tom McCraw .50 .20
483 Steve Ontiveros .50 .20
484 Glenn Beckert 1.00 .40
485 Sparky Lyle 1.00 .40
486 Ray Fosse .50 .20
487 Astros Team CL 2.00 .40
Preston Gomez MG
488 Bill Travers .50 .20
489 Cecil Cooper 2.00 .80
490 Reggie Smith 1.00 .40
491 Doyle Alexander 1.00 .40
492 Rich Hebner 1.00 .40
493 Don Stanhouse .50 .20
494 Pete LaCock .50 .20
495 Nelson Briles 1.00 .40
496 Pepe Frias .50 .20
497 Jim Nettles .50 .20
498 Al Downing .50 .20
499 Marty Perez .50 .20
500 Nolan Ryan 50.00 20.00
501 Bill Robinson 1.00 .40
502 Pat Bourque .50 .20
503 Fred Stanley .50 .20
504 Buddy Bradford .50 .20
505 Chris Speier .50 .20
506 Leron Lee .50 .20
507 Tom Carroll .50 .20
508 Bob Hansen .50 .20
509 Dave Hilton .50 .20
510 Vida Blue 1.00 .40
511 Rangers Team CL 2.00 .40
Billy Martin MG
512 Larry Milbourne .50 .20
513 Dick Pole .50 .20
514 Jose Cruz 2.00 .80
515 Manny Sanguillen 1.00 .40
516 Don Hood .50 .20
517 Checklist: 397-528 3.00 .60
518 Leo Cardenas .50 .20
519 Jim Todd .50 .20
520 Amos Otis 1.00 .40
521 Dennis Blair .50 .20
522 Gary Sutherland .50 .20
523 Tom Paciorek 1.00 .40
524 John Doherty .50 .20
525 Tom House .50 .20
526 Larry Hisle 1.00 .40
527 Mac Scarce .50 .20
528 Eddie Leon .50 .20
529 Gary Thomasson .50 .20
530 Gaylord Perry 3.00 1.20
531 Reds Team CL 5.00 1.00
Sparky Anderson MG
532 Gorman Thomas 1.00 .40
533 Rudy Meoli .50 .20
534 Alex Johnson .50 .20
535 Gene Tenace 1.00 .40
536 Bob Moose .50 .20
537 Tommy Harper 1.00 .40
538 Duffy Dyer .50 .20
539 Jesse Jefferson .50 .20
540 Lou Brock 6.00 2.40
541 Roger Metzger .50 .20
542 Pete Broberg .50 .20
543 Larry Biittner .50 .20
544 Steve Mingori .50 .20
545 Billy Williams 3.00 1.20
546 John Knox .50 .20
547 Von Joshua .50 .20
548 Charlie Sands .50 .20
549 Bill Butler .50 .20
550 Ralph Garr 1.00 .40
551 Larry Christenson .50 .20
552 Jack Brohamer .50 .20
553 John Boccabella .50 .20
554 Goose Gossage 2.00 .80
555 Al Oliver 2.00 .80
556 Tim Johnson .50 .20
557 Larry Gura .50 .20
558 Dave Roberts .50 .20
559 Bob Montgomery .50 .20
560 Tony Perez 4.00 1.60
561 A's Team CL 2.00 .40
Alvin Dark MG
562 Gary Nolan 1.00 .40
563 Wilbur Howard .50 .20
564 Tommy Davis 1.00 .40
565 Joe Torre 2.00 .80
566 Ray Burris .50 .20
567 Jim Sundberg RC 2.00 .80
568 Dale Murray .50 .20
569 Frank White 1.00 .40
570 Jim Wynn 1.00 .40
571 Dave Lemanczyk .50 .20
572 Roger Nelson .50 .20

573 Orlando Pena .50 .20
574 Tony Taylor .50 .20
575 Gene Clines .50 .20
576 Phil Roof .50 .20
577 John Morris .50 .20
578 Dave Tomlin .50 .20
579 Skip Pitlock .50 .20
580 Frank Robinson 6.00 2.40
581 Darrel Chaney .50 .20
582 Eduardo Rodriguez .50 .20
583 Andy Etchebarren .50 .20
584 Mike Garman .50 .20
585 Chris Chambliss 1.00 .40
586 Tim McCarver 2.00 .80
587 Chris Ward .50 .20
588 Rick Auerbach .50 .20
589 Braves Team CL 2.00 .40
Clyde King MG
590 Cesar Cedeno 1.00 .40
591 Glenn Abbott .50 .20
592 Balor Moore .50 .20
593 Gene Lamont .50 .20
594 Jim Fuller .50 .20
595 Joe Niekro 1.00 .40
596 Ollie Brown .50 .20
597 Winston Llenas .50 .20
598 Bruce Kison .50 .20
599 Nate Colbert .50 .20
600 Rod Carew 8.00 3.20
601 Juan Beniquez .50 .20
602 John Vukovich .50 .20
603 Lew Krausse .50 .20
604 Oscar Zamora .50 .20
605 John Ellis .50 .20
606 Bruce Miller .50 .20
607 Jim Holt .50 .20
608 Gene Michael .50 .20
609 Elrod Hendricks .50 .20
610 Ron Hunt .50 .20
611 Yankees Team CL 2.00 .40
Bill Virdon MG
612 Terry Hughes .50 .20
613 Bill Parsons .50 .20
614 Jack Kucek 1.00 .40
Dyar Miller
Vern Ruhle
Paul Siebert
615 Pat Darcy 2.00 .80
Dennis Leonard RC
Tom Underwood
Hank Webb
616 Dave Augustine 15.00 6.00
Pepe Mangual
Jim Rice RC
John Scott
617 Mike Cubbage 2.00 .80
Doug DeCinces RC
Reggie Sanders
Manny Trillo
618 Jamie Easterly 1.00 .40
Tom Johnson
Scott McGregor RC
Rick Rhoden
619 Benny Ayala 1.00 .40
Nyls Nyman
Tommy Smith
Jerry Turner
620 Gary Carter RC 15.00 6.00
Marc Hill
Danny Meyer
Leon Roberts
621 John Denny RC 2.00 .80
Rawly Eastwick
Jim Kern
Juan Veintidos
622 Ed Armbrister 8.00 3.20
Fred Lynn RC
Tom Poquette
Terry Whitfield UER
(Listed as Ney York)
623 Phil Garner 6.00 2.40
Keith Hernandez RC UER
(Sic, bats right)
Bob Sheldon
Tom Veryzer
624 Doug Konieczny 1.00 .40
Gary Lavelle
Jim Otten
Eddie Solomon
625 Boog Powell 2.00 .80
626 Larry Haney UER .50 .20
Photo actually
Dave Duncan
627 Tom Walker .50 .20
628 Ron LeFlore RC 1.00 .40
629 Joe Hoerner .50 .20
630 Greg Luzinski 2.00 .80
631 Lee Lacy .50 .20
632 Morris Nettles .50 .20
633 Paul Casanova .50 .20
634 Cy Acosta .50 .20
635 Chuck Dobson .50 .20
636 Charlie Moore .50 .20
637 Ted Martinez .50 .20
638 Cubs Team CL 2.00 .40
Jim Marshall MG
639 Steve Kline .50 .20
640 Harmon Killebrew 6.00 2.40
641 Jim Northrup 1.00 .40
642 Mike Phillips .50 .20
643 Brent Strom .50 .20
644 Bill Fahey .50 .20
645 Danny Cater .50 .20
646 Checklist: 529-660 3.00 .60
647 Cl. Washington RC 2.00 .80
648 Dave Pagan .50 .20
649 Jack Heidemann .50 .20
650 Dave May .50 .20
651 John Morlan .50 .20
652 Lindy McDaniel 1.00 .40
653 Lee Richard UER .50 .20
(Listed as Richards
on card front)
654 Jerry Terrell .50 .20
655 Rico Carty 1.00 .40
656 Bill Plummer .50 .20
657 Bob Oliver .50 .20
658 Vic Harris .50 .20
659 Bob Apodaca .50 .20
660 Hank Aaron 30.00 9.00

1975 Topps Mini

This set is a parallel to the regular 1975 Topps set. Each card measures 2 1/4" by 3 1/8" and the set was regionally issued. Michigan and California were among the two areas to receive this issue. These cards were also sporadically distributed in other areas as collectors have recalled getting them in their local areas other than those mentioned above. The cards are currently valued the same as the regular 75 Topps cards and have proven not to have remained as popular as the regular 1975 issue. These cards were issued in 10 card packs which cost 15 cents on issue and were packed 36 to a box.

NM Ex
COMPLETE SET (660) 800.00 325.00
*MINI STARS: .75X TO 1.5X BASIC CARDS
*MINI RC'S: .5X TO 1X BASIC ROOKIE CARDS

1975 Topps Team Checklist Sheet

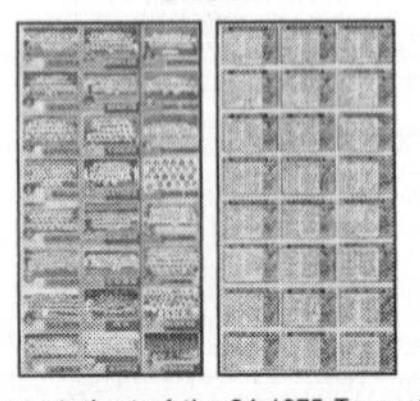

This uncut sheet of the 24 1975 Topps team checklists measures 10 1/2" by 20 1/8". The sheet was obtained by sending 40 cents plus one wrapper to Topps. When cut, each card measures the standard size.

NM Ex
1 Topps Team CL Sheet 50.00 20.00

1976 Topps

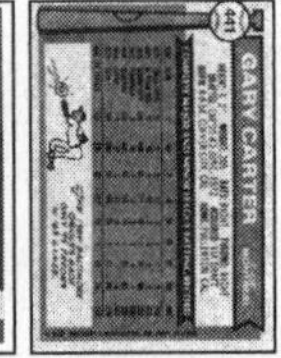

The 1976 Topps set of 660 standard-size cards is known for its sharp color photographs and interesting presentation of subjects. Cards were issued in ten-card wax packs, 42-card rack packs as well as cello packs and other options. Team cards feature a checklist back for players on that team and show a small inset photo of the manager on the front. A "Father and Son" series (66-70) spotlights five Major Leaguers whose fathers also made the "Big Show." Other subseries include "All Time All Stars" (341-350), "Record Breakers" from the previous season (1-6), League Leaders (191-205), Post-season cards (461-462), and Rookie Prospects (589-599). The following players' regular issue cards are explicitly denoted as All-Stars, 10, 48, 60, 140, 150, 165, 169, 240, 300, 370, 380, 395, 400, 420, 475, 500, 580, and 650. The key Rookie Cards in this set are Dennis Eckersley, Ron Guidry, and Willie Randolph. We've heard recent reports that this set was also issued in seven-card wax packs which cost a dime. Confirmation of that information would be appreciated.

NM Ex
COMPLETE SET (660) 250.00 100.00
1 Hank Aaron RB 15.00 4.70
2 Bobby Bonds RB 1.50 .60
3 Mickey Lolich RB .75 .30
4 Dave Lopes RB .75 .30
5 Tom Seaver RB 5.00 2.00
6 Rennie Stennett RB .75 .30
7 Jim Umbarger .40 .16
8 Tito Fuentes .40 .16
9 Paul Lindblad .40 .16
10 Lou Brock 5.00 2.00
11 Jim Hughes .40 .16
12 Richie Zisk .75 .30
13 John Wockenfuss .40 .16
14 Gene Garber .75 .30
15 George Scott .75 .30
16 Bob Apodaca .40 .16
17 New York Yankees 1.50 .30
Team Card CL
Billy Martin MG
18 Dale Murray .40 .16
19 George Brett 30.00 12.00
20 Bob Watson .75 .30
21 Dave LaRoche .40 .16
22 Bill Russell .75 .30
23 Brian Downing .40 .16
24 Cesar Geronimo .75 .30
25 Mike Torrez .75 .30
26 Andre Thornton .75 .30
27 Ed Figueroa .40 .16
28 Dusty Baker 1.50 .60
29 Rick Burleson .75 .30
30 John Montefusco .75 .30
31 Len Randle .40 .16
32 Danny Frisella .40 .16
33 Bill North .40 .16
34 Mike Garman .40 .16
35 Tony Oliva 1.50 .60
36 Frank Taveras .40 .16
37 John Hiller .75 .30
38 Garry Maddox .75 .30
39 Pete Broberg .40 .16
40 Dave Kingman 1.50 .60
41 Tippy Martinez .75 .30
42 Barry Foote .40 .16
43 Paul Splittorff .40 .16
44 Doug Rader .75 .30
45 Boog Powell 1.50 .60
46 Los Angeles Dodgers 1.50 .30
Team Card CL
Walter Alston MG
47 Jesse Jefferson .40 .16
48 Dave Concepcion 1.50 .60
49 Dave Duncan .75 .30
50 Fred Lynn 1.50 .60
51 Ray Burris .40 .16
52 Dave Chalk .40 .16
53 Mike Beard .40 .16
54 Dave Rader .40 .16
55 Gaylord Perry 2.50 1.00
56 Bob Tolan .40 .16
57 Phil Garner .75 .30
58 Ron Reed .40 .16
59 Larry Hisle .75 .30
60 Jerry Reuss .75 .30
61 Ron LeFlore .75 .30
62 Johnny Oates .75 .30
63 Bobby Darwin .40 .16
64 Jerry Koosman .75 .30
65 Chris Chambliss .75 .30
66 Gus Bell FS .75 .30
Buddy Bell
67 Ray Boone FS .75 .30
Bob Boone
68 Joe Coleman FS .40 .16
Joe Coleman Jr.
69 Jim Hegan FS .40 .16
Mike Hegan
70 Roy Smalley FS .75 .30
Roy Smalley Jr.
71 Steve Rogers .75 .30
72 Hal McRae .75 .30
73 Baltimore Orioles 1.50 .30
Team Card CL
Earl Weaver MG
74 Oscar Gamble .75 .30
75 Larry Dierker .75 .30
76 Willie Crawford .40 .16
77 Pedro Borbon .75 .30
78 Cecil Cooper .75 .30
79 Jerry Morales .40 .16
80 Jim Kaat 1.50 .60
81 Darrell Evans .75 .30
82 Von Joshua .40 .16
83 Jim Spencer .40 .16
84 Brent Strom .40 .16
85 Mickey Rivers .75 .30
86 Mike Tyson .40 .16
87 Tom Burgmeier .40 .16
88 Duffy Dyer .40 .16
89 Vern Ruhle .40 .16
90 Sal Bando .75 .30
91 Tom Hutton .40 .16
92 Eduardo Rodriguez .40 .16
93 Mike Phillips .40 .16
94 Jim Dwyer .40 .16
95 Brooks Robinson 6.00 2.40
96 Doug Bird .40 .16
97 Wilbur Howard .40 .16
98 Dennis Eckersley RC 25.00 10.00
99 Lee Lacy .40 .16
100 Jim Hunter 3.00 1.20
101 Pete LaCock .40 .16
102 Jim Willoughby .40 .16
103 Biff Pocoroba .40 .16
104 Cincinnati Reds 2.50 .50
Team Card CL
Sparky Anderson MG
105 Gary Lavelle .40 .16
106 Tom Grieve .75 .30
107 Dave Roberts .40 .16
108 Don Kirkwood .40 .16
109 Larry Lintz .40 .16
110 Carlos May .40 .16
111 Danny Thompson .40 .16
112 Kent Tekulve RC 1.50 .60
113 Gary Sutherland .40 .16
114 Jay Johnstone .75 .30
115 Ken Holtzman .75 .30
116 Charlie Moore .40 .16
117 Mike Jorgensen .40 .16
118 Boston Red Sox 1.50 .30
Team Card CL
Darrell Johnson MG
119 Checklist 1-132 1.50 .30
120 Rusty Staub .75 .30
121 Tony Solaita .40 .16
122 Mike Cosgrove .40 .16
123 Walt Williams .40 .16
124 Doug Rau .40 .16
125 Don Baylor 1.50 .60
126 Tom Dettore .40 .16
127 Larvell Blanks .40 .16
128 Ken Griffey Sr. 2.50 1.00
129 Andy Etchebarren .40 .16
130 Luis Tiant 1.50 .60
131 Bill Stein .40 .16
132 Don Hood .40 .16
133 Gary Matthews .75 .30
134 Mike Ivie .40 .16
135 Bake McBride .75 .30
136 Dave Goltz .40 .16
137 Bill Robinson .75 .30
138 Lerrin LaGrow .40 .16
139 Gorman Thomas .75 .30
140 Vida Blue .75 .30
141 Larry Parrish RC 1.50 .60
142 Dick Drago .40 .16
143 Jerry Grote .40 .16
144 Al Fitzmorris .40 .16
145 Larry Bowa .75 .30
146 George Medich .40 .16
147 Houston Astros 1.50 .30
Team Card CL
Bill Virdon MG
148 Stan Thomas .40 .16
149 Tommy Davis .75 .30
150 Steve Garvey 2.50 1.00
151 Bill Bonham .40 .16
152 Leroy Stanton .40 .16
153 Buzz Capra .40 .16
154 Bucky Dent .75 .30
155 Jack Billingham .75 .30
156 Rico Carty .75 .30
157 Mike Caldwell .40 .16
158 Ken Reitz .40 .16
159 Jerry Terrell .40 .16
160 Dave Winfield 10.00 4.00
161 Bruce Kison .40 .16
162 Jack Pierce .40 .16
163 Jim Slaton .40 .16
164 Pepe Mangual .40 .16
165 Gene Tenace .75 .30
166 Skip Lockwood .40 .16
167 Freddie Patek .75 .30
168 Tom Hilgendorf .40 .16
169 Graig Nettles 1.50 .60
170 Rick Wise .40 .16
171 Greg Gross .40 .16
172 Texas Rangers 1.50 .30
Team Card CL
Frank Lucchesi MG
173 Steve Swisher .40 .16
174 Charlie Hough .75 .30
175 Ken Singleton .75 .30
176 Dick Lange .40 .16
177 Marty Perez .40 .16
178 Tom Buskey .40 .16
179 George Foster 1.50 .60
180 Goose Gossage 1.50 .60
181 Willie Montanez .40 .16
182 Harry Rasmussen .40 .16
183 Steve Braun .40 .16
184 Bill Greif .40 .16
185 Dave Parker 1.50 .60
186 Tom Walker .40 .16
187 Pedro Garcia .40 .16
188 Fred Scherman .40 .16
189 Claudell Washington .75 .30
190 Jon Matlack .40 .16
191 Bill Madlock .75 .30
Ted Simmons
Manny Sanguillen LL
192 Rod Carew 2.50 1.00
Fred Lynn
Thurman Munson LL
193 Mike Schmidt 3.00 1.20
Dave Kingman
Greg Luzinski LL
194 Reggie Jackson 3.00 1.20
George Scott
John Mayberry LL
195 Greg Luzinski 1.50 .60
Johnny Bench
Tony Perez LL
196 George Scott .75 .30
John Mayberry
Fred Lynn LL
197 Dave Lopes 1.50 .60
Joe Morgan
Lou Brock LL
198 Mickey Rivers .75 .30
Claudell Washington
Amos Otis LL
199 Tom Seaver 2.50 1.00
Randy Jones
Andy Messersmith LL
200 Jim Hunter 1.50 .60
Jim Palmer
Vida Blue LL
201 Randy Jones 1.50 .60
Andy Messersmith
Tom Seaver LL
202 Jim Palmer 3.00 1.20
Jim Hunter
Dennis Eckersley LL
203 Tom Seaver 2.50 1.00
John Montefusco
Andy Messersmith LL
204 Frank Tanana .75 .30
Bert Blyleven
Gaylord Perry LL
205 Al Hrabosky .75 .30
Rich Gossage LL
206 Manny Trillo .40 .16
207 Andy Hassler .40 .16
208 Mike Lum .40 .16
209 Alan Ashby .75 .30
210 Lee May .75 .30
211 Clay Carroll .75 .30
212 Pat Kelly .40 .16
213 Dave Heaverlo .40 .16
214 Eric Soderholm .40 .16
215 Reggie Smith .75 .30
216 Montreal Expos 1.50 .30
Team Card CL
Karl Kuehl MG
217 Dave Freisleben .40 .16
218 John Knox .40 .16
219 Tom Murphy .40 .16
220 Manny Sanguillen .75 .30
221 Jim Todd .40 .16
222 Wayne Garrett .40 .16
223 Ollie Brown .40 .16
224 Jim York .40 .16
225 Roy White .75 .30
226 Jim Sundberg .75 .30
227 Oscar Zamora .40 .16
228 John Hale .40 .16
229 Jerry Remy .40 .16
230 Carl Yastrzemski 10.00 4.00
231 Tom House .40 .16
232 Frank Duffy .40 .16
233 Grant Jackson .40 .16
234 Mike Sadek .40 .16
235 Bert Blyleven 1.50 .60
236 Kansas City Royals 1.50 .30
Team Card CL
Whitey Herzog MG
237 Dave Hamilton .40 .16
238 Larry Biittner .40 .16
239 John Curtis .40 .16
240 Pete Rose 25.00 10.00
241 Hector Torres .40 .16
242 Dan Meyer .40 .16
243 Jim Rooker .40 .16
244 Bill Sharp .40 .16
245 Felix Millan .40 .16
246 Cesar Tovar .40 .16
247 Terry Harmon .40 .16
248 Dick Tidrow .40 .16
249 Cliff Johnson .75 .30
250 Fergie Jenkins 2.50 1.00
251 Rick Monday .75 .30
252 Tim Nordbrook .40 .16
253 Bill Buckner .75 .30
254 Rudy Meoli .40 .16
255 Fritz Peterson .40 .16
256 Rowland Office .40 .16
257 Ross Grimsley .40 .16
258 Nyls Nyman .40 .16
259 Darrel Chaney .40 .16
260 Steve Busby .40 .16
261 Gary Thomasson .40 .16
262 Checklist 133-264 1.50 .30
263 Lyman Bostock RC 1.50 .60
264 Steve Renko .40 .16
265 Willie Davis .75 .30
266 Alan Foster .40 .16
267 Aurelio Rodriguez .40 .16
268 Del Unser .40 .16
269 Rick Austin .40 .16
270 Willie Stargell 3.00 1.20
271 Jim Lonborg .75 .30
272 Rick Dempsey .75 .30
273 Joe Niekro .75 .30
274 Tommy Harper .75 .30
275 Rick Manning .40 .16
276 Mickey Scott .40 .16
277 Chicago Cubs 1.50 .30
Team Card CL
Jim Marshall MG
278 Bernie Carbo .40 .16
279 Roy Howell .40 .16
280 Burt Hooton .75 .30
281 Dave May .40 .16
282 Dan Osborn .40 .16
283 Merv Rettenmund .40 .16
284 Steve Ontiveros .40 .16
285 Mike Cuellar .75 .30
286 Jim Wohlford .40 .16
287 Pete Mackanin .40 .16
288 Bill Campbell .40 .16
289 Enzo Hernandez .40 .16
290 Ted Simmons .75 .30
291 Ken Sanders .40 .16
292 Leon Roberts .40 .16
293 Bill Castro .40 .16
294 Ed Kirkpatrick .40 .16
295 Dave Cash .40 .16
296 Pat Dobson .40 .16
297 Roger Metzger .40 .16
298 Dick Bosman .40 .16
299 Champ Summers .40 .16
300 Johnny Bench 12.00 4.80
301 Jackie Brown .40 .16
302 Rick Miller .40 .16
303 Steve Foucault .40 .16
304 California Angels 1.50 .30
Team Card CL
Dick Williams MG
305 Andy Messersmith .75 .30
306 Rod Gilbreath .40 .16
307 Al Bumbry .75 .30
308 Jim Barr .40 .16
309 Bill Melton .40 .16
310 Randy Jones .75 .30
311 Cookie Rojas .40 .16
312 Don Carrithers .40 .16
313 Dan Ford .40 .16
314 Ed Kranepool .40 .16
315 Al Hrabosky .75 .30
316 Robin Yount 15.00 6.00
317 John Candelaria RC 1.50 .60
318 Bob Boone 1.50 .60
319 Larry Gura .40 .16
320 Willie Horton .75 .30
321 Jose Cruz 1.50 .60
322 Glenn Abbott .40 .16
323 Rob Sperring .40 .16
324 Jim Bibby .40 .16
325 Tony Perez 3.00 1.20
326 Dick Pole .40 .16
327 Dave Moates .40 .16
328 Carl Morton .40 .16
329 Joe Ferguson .40 .16
330 Nolan Ryan 25.00 10.00
331 San Diego Padres 1.50 .30
Team Card CL
John McNamara MG
332 Charlie Williams .40 .16
333 Bob Coluccio .40 .16
334 Dennis Leonard .75 .30
335 Bob Grich .75 .30
336 Vic Albury .40 .16
337 Bud Harrelson .75 .30
338 Bob Bailey .40 .16
339 John Denny .75 .30
340 Jim Rice 4.00 1.60
341 Lou Gehrig ATG 12.00 4.80
342 Rogers Hornsby ATG 3.00 1.20
343 Pie Traynor ATG 1.50 .60
344 Honus Wagner ATG 5.00 2.00
345 Babe Ruth ATG 15.00 6.00
346 Ty Cobb ATG 12.00 4.80
347 Ted Williams ATG 12.00 4.80
348 Mickey Cochrane ATG 1.50 .60
349 Walter Johnson ATG 5.00 2.00
350 Lefty Grove ATG 1.50 .60
351 Randy Hundley .75 .30
352 Dave Giusti .40 .16
353 Sixto Lezcano .75 .30
354 Ron Blomberg .40 .16
355 Steve Carlton 6.00 2.40
356 Ted Martinez .40 .16
357 Ken Forsch .40 .16
358 Buddy Bell .75 .30
359 Rick Reuschel .75 .30
360 Jeff Burroughs .75 .30
361 Detroit Tigers 1.50 .30
Team Card CL
Ralph Houk MG
362 Will McEnaney .75 .30
363 Dave Collins RC .75 .30
364 Elias Sosa .40 .16
365 Carlton Fisk 6.00 2.40
366 Bobby Valentine .75 .30
367 Bruce Miller .40 .16
368 Wilbur Wood .40 .16
369 Frank White .75 .30
370 Ron Cey .75 .30
371 Elrod Hendricks .40 .16
372 Rick Baldwin .40 .16
373 Johnny Briggs .40 .16
374 Dan Warthen .40 .16
375 Ron Fairly .75 .30
376 Rich Hebner .75 .30
377 Mike Hegan .40 .16
378 Steve Stone .75 .30

379 Ken Boswell .40 .16
380 Bobby Bonds 1.50 .60
381 Denny Doyle .40 .16
382 Matt Alexander .40 .16
383 John Ellis .40 .16
384 Philadelphia Phillies 1.50 .30
Team Card CL
Danny Ozark MG
385 Mickey Lolich .75 .30
386 Ed Goodson .40 .16
387 Mike Miley .40 .16
388 Stan Perzanowski .40 .16
389 Glenn Adams .40 .16
390 Don Gullett .75 .30
391 Jerry Hairston .40 .16
392 Checklist 265-396 1.50 .30
393 Paul Mitchell .40 .16
394 Fran Healy .40 .16
395 Jim Wynn .75 .30
396 Bill Lee .40 .16
397 Tim Foli .40 .16
398 Dave Tomlin .40 .16
399 Luis Melendez .40 .16
400 Rod Carew 6.00 2.40
401 Ken Brett .40 .16
402 Don Money .75 .30
403 Geoff Zahn .40 .16
404 Enos Cabell .40 .16
405 Rollie Fingers 2.50 1.00
406 Ed Herrmann .40 .16
407 Tom Underwood .40 .16
408 Charlie Spikes .40 .16
409 Dave Lemanczyk .40 .16
410 Ralph Garr .75 .30
411 Bill Singer .40 .16
412 Toby Harrah .75 .30
413 Pete Varney .40 .16
414 Wayne Garland .40 .16
415 Vada Pinson 1.50 .60
416 Tommy John 1.50 .60
417 Gene Clines .40 .16
418 Jose Morales RC .40 .16
419 Reggie Cleveland .40 .16
420 Joe Morgan 5.00 2.00
421 Oakland A's 1.50 .30
Team Card CL
(No MG on front
422 Johnny Grubb .40 .16
423 Ed Halicki .40 .16
424 Phil Roof .40 .16
425 Rennie Stennett .40 .16
426 Bob Forsch .40 .16
427 Kurt Bevacqua .40 .16
428 Jim Crawford .40 .16
429 Fred Stanley .40 .16
430 Jose Cardenal .75 .30
431 Dick Ruthven .40 .16
432 Tom Veryzer .40 .16
433 Rick Waits .40 .16
434 Morris Nettles .40 .16
435 Phil Niekro 2.50 1.00
436 Bill Fahey .40 .16
437 Terry Forster .40 .16
438 Doug DeCinces .75 .30
439 Rick Rhoden .75 .30
440 John Mayberry .75 .30
441 Gary Carter 4.00 1.60
442 Hank Webb .40 .16
443 San Francisco Giants 1.50 .30
Team Card CL
(No MG on front
444 Gary Nolan .75 .30
445 Rico Petrocelli .75 .30
446 Larry Haney .40 .16
447 Gene Locklear .75 .30
448 Tom Johnson .40 .16
449 Bob Robertson .40 .16
450 Jim Palmer 5.00 2.00
451 Buddy Bradford .40 .16
452 Tom Hausman .40 .16
453 Lou Piniella 1.50 .60
454 Tom Griffin .40 .16
455 Dick Allen 1.50 .60
456 Joe Coleman .40 .16
457 Ed Crosby .40 .16
458 Earl Williams .40 .16
459 Jim Brewer .40 .16
460 Cesar Cedeno .75 .30
461 NL and AL Champs .75 .30
Reds sweep Bucs,
Bosox surprise A's
462 '75 World Series .75 .30
Reds Champs
463 Steve Hargan .40 .16
464 Ken Henderson .40 .16
465 Mike Marshall .75 .30
466 Bob Stinson .40 .16
467 Woodie Fryman .40 .16
468 Jesus Alou .40 .16
469 Rawly Eastwick .75 .30
470 Bobby Murcer .75 .30
471 Jim Burton .40 .16
472 Bob Davis .40 .16
473 Paul Blair .75 .30
474 Ray Corbin .40 .16
475 Joe Rudi .75 .30
476 Bob Moose .40 .16
477 Cleveland Indians 1.50 .30
Team Card CL
Frank Robinson MG
478 Lynn McGlothen .40 .16
479 Bobby Mitchell .40 .16
480 Mike Schmidt 15.00 6.00
481 Rudy May .40 .16
482 Tim Hosley .40 .16
483 Mickey Stanley .40 .16
484 Eric Raich .40 .16
485 Mike Hargrove .75 .30
486 Bruce Dal Canton .40 .16
487 Leron Lee .40 .16
488 Claude Osteen .75 .30
489 Skip Jutze .40 .16
490 Frank Tanana .75 .30
491 Terry Crowley .40 .16
492 Marty Pattin .40 .16
493 Derrel Thomas .40 .16
494 Craig Swan .75 .30
495 Nate Colbert .40 .16
496 Juan Beniquez .40 .16
497 Joe McIntosh .40 .16
498 Glenn Borgmann .40 .16
499 Mario Guerrero .40 .16
500 Reggie Jackson 12.00 4.80
501 Billy Champion .40 .16
502 Tim McCarver 1.50 .60
503 Elliott Maddox .40 .16
504 Pittsburgh Pirates 1.50 .30
Team Card CL
Danny Murtaugh MG
505 Mark Belanger .75 .30
506 George Mitterwald .40 .16
507 Ray Bare .40 .16
508 Duane Kuiper .40 .16
509 Bill Hands .40 .16
510 Amos Otis .75 .30
511 Jamie Easterley .40 .16
512 Ellie Rodriguez .40 .16
513 Bart Johnson .40 .16
514 Dan Driessen .75 .30
515 Steve Yeager .75 .30
516 Wayne Granger .40 .16
517 John Milner .40 .16
518 Doug Flynn .40 .16
519 Steve Brye .40 .16
520 Willie McCovey 5.00 2.00
521 Jim Colborn .40 .16
522 Ted Sizemore .40 .16
523 Bob Montgomery .40 .16
524 Pete Falcone .40 .16
525 Billy Williams 2.50 1.00
526 Checklist 397-528 1.50 .30
527 Mike Anderson .40 .16
528 Dock Ellis .40 .16
529 Deron Johnson .40 .16
530 Don Sutton 2.50 1.00
531 New York Mets 1.50 .30
Team Card CL
Joe Frazier MG
532 Milt May .40 .16
533 Lee Richard .40 .16
534 Stan Bahnsen .40 .16
535 Dave Nelson .40 .16
536 Mike Thompson .40 .16
537 Tony Muser .40 .16
538 Pat Darcy .40 .16
539 John Balaz .40 .16
540 Bill Freehan .75 .30
541 Steve Mingori .40 .16
542 Keith Hernandez 1.50 .60
543 Wayne Twitchell .40 .16
544 Pepe Frias .40 .16
545 Sparky Lyle .75 .30
546 Dave Rosello .40 .16
547 Roric Harrison .40 .16
548 Manny Mota .75 .30
549 Randy Tate .40 .16
550 Hank Aaron 25.00 10.00
551 Jerry DaVanon .40 .16
552 Terry Humphrey .40 .16
553 Randy Moffitt .40 .16
554 Ray Fosse .40 .16
555 Dyar Miller .40 .16
556 Minnesota Twins 1.50 .30
Team Card CL
Gene Mauch MG
557 Dan Spillner .40 .16
558 Clarence Gaston .75 .30
559 Clyde Wright .40 .16
560 Jorge Orta .40 .16
561 Tom Carroll .40 .16
562 Adrian Garrett .40 .16
563 Larry Demery .40 .16
564 Bubble Gum Champ 1.50 .60
Kurt Bevacqua
565 Tug McGraw .75 .30
566 Ken McMullen .40 .16
567 George Stone .40 .16
568 Rob Andrews .40 .16
569 Nelson Briles .75 .30
570 George Hendrick .75 .30
571 Don DeMola .40 .16
572 Rich Coggins .40 .16
573 Bill Travers .40 .16
574 Don Kessinger .75 .30
575 Dwight Evans 1.50 .60
576 Maximino Leon .40 .16
577 Marc Hill .40 .16
578 Ted Kubiak .40 .16
579 Clay Kirby .40 .16
580 Bert Campaneris .75 .30
581 St. Louis Cardinals 1.50 .30
Team Card CL
Red Schoendienst MG
582 Mike Kekich .40 .16
583 Tommy Helms .40 .16
584 Stan Wall .40 .16
585 Joe Torre 1.50 .60
586 Ron Schueler .40 .16
587 Leo Cardenas .40 .16
588 Kevin Kobel .40 .16
589 Santo Alcala 1.50 .60
Mike Flanagan RC
Joe Pactwa
Pablo Torrealba
590 Henry Cruz .75 .30
Chet Lemon RC
Ellis Valentine
Terry Whitfield
591 Steve Grilli .75 .30
Craig Mitchell
Jose Sosa
George Throop
592 Willie Randolph RC 6.00 2.40
Dave McKay
Jerry Royster
Roy Staiger
593 Larry Anderson .75 .30
Ken Crosby
Mark Littell
Butch Metzger
594 Andy Merchant .75 .30
Ed Ott
Royle Stillman
Jerry White
595 Art DeFillipis .75 .30
Randy Lerch
Sid Monge
Steve Barr
596 Craig Reynolds .75 .30
Lamar Johnson
Johnnie LeMaster
Jerry Manuel RC
597 Don Aase .75 .30
Jack Kucek
Frank LaCorte
Mike Pazik
598 Hector Cruz .75 .30
Jamie Quirk
Jerry Turner
Joe Wallis
599 Rob Dressler 6.00 2.40
Ron Guidry RC
Bob McClure
Pat Zachry
600 Tom Seaver 10.00 4.00
601 Ken Rudolph .40 .16
602 Doug Konieczny .40 .16
603 Jim Holt .40 .16
604 Joe Lovitto .40 .16
605 Al Downing .40 .16
606 Milwaukee Brewers 1.50 .30
Team Card CL
Alex Grammas MG
607 Rich Hinton .40 .16
608 Vic Correll .40 .16
609 Fred Norman .40 .16
610 Greg Luzinski 1.50 .60
611 Rich Folkers .40 .16
612 Joe Lahoud .40 .16
613 Tim Johnson .40 .16
614 Fernando Arroyo .40 .16
615 Mike Cubbage .40 .16
616 Buck Martinez .40 .16
617 Darold Knowles .40 .16
618 Jack Brohamer .40 .16
619 Bill Butler .40 .16
620 Al Oliver .75 .30
621 Tom Hall .40 .16
622 Rick Auerbach .40 .16
623 Bob Allietta .40 .16
624 Tony Taylor .40 .16
625 J.R. Richard .75 .30
626 Bob Sheldon .40 .16
627 Bill Plummer .40 .16
628 John D'Acquisto .40 .16
629 Sandy Alomar .75 .30
630 Chris Speier .40 .16
631 Atlanta Braves 1.50 .30
Team Card CL
Dave Bristol MG
632 Rogelio Moret .40 .16
633 John Stearns RC .75 .30
634 Larry Christenson .40 .16
635 Jim Fregosi .75 .30
636 Joe Decker .40 .16
637 Bruce Bochte .40 .16
638 Doyle Alexander .75 .30
639 Fred Kendall .40 .16
640 Bill Madlock 1.50 .60
641 Tom Paciorek .75 .30
642 Dennis Blair .40 .16
643 Checklist 529-660 1.50 .30
644 Tom Bradley .40 .16
645 Darrell Porter .75 .30
646 John Lowenstein .40 .16
647 Ramon Hernandez .40 .16
648 Al Cowens .40 .16
649 Dave Roberts .40 .16
650 Thurman Munson 6.00 2.40
651 John Odom .40 .16
652 Ed Armbrister .40 .16
653 Mike Norris RC .75 .30
654 Doug Griffin .40 .16
655 Mike Vail .40 .16
656 Chicago White Sox 1.50 .30
Team Card CL
Chuck Tanner MG
657 Roy Smalley RC .75 .30
658 Jerry Johnson .40 .16
659 Ben Oglivie .75 .30
660 Dave Lopes 1.50 .30

1976 Topps Traded

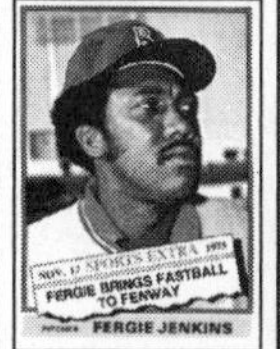

The cards in this 44-card set measure 2 1/2" by 3 1/2". The 1976 Topps Traded set contains 43 players and one unnumbered checklist card. The individuals pictured were traded after the Topps regular set was printed. A "Sports Extra" heading design is found on each picture and is also used to introduce the biographical section of the reverse. Each card is numbered according to the player's regular 1976 card with the addition of "T" to indicate his new status. As in 1974, the cards were inserted in all packs toward the end of the production run. According to published reports at the time, they were not released until April, 1976. Because they were produced in large quantities, they are no scarcer than the basic cards. Reports at the time indicated that a dealer could make approximately 35 sets from a vending case. The vending cases included both regular and traded cards.

NM Ex
COMPLETE SET (44) 30.00 12.00
27T Ed Figueroa .40 .16
28T Dusty Baker 1.50 .60
44T Doug Rader .75 .30
58T Ron Reed .40 .16
74T Oscar Gamble 1.50 .60
80T Jim Kaat 1.50 .60
83T Jim Spencer .40 .16
85T Mickey Rivers .75 .30
99T Lee Lacy .40 .16
120T Rusty Staub .75 .30
127T Larvell Blanks .40 .16
146T George Medich .40 .16
158T Ken Reitz .40 .16
208T Mike Lum .40 .16
211T Clay Carroll .40 .16
231T Tom House .40 .16
250T Fergie Jenkins 3.00 1.20
259T Darrel Chaney .40 .16
292T Leon Roberts .40 .16
296T Pat Dobson .40 .16
309T Bill Melton .40 .16
338T Bob Bailey .40 .16
380T Bobby Bonds 1.50 .60
383T John Ellis .40 .16
385T Mickey Lolich .75 .30
401T Ken Brett .40 .16
410T Ralph Garr .40 .16
411T Bill Singer .40 .16
428T Jim Crawford .40 .16
434T Morris Nettles .40 .16
464T Ken Henderson .40 .16
497T Joe McIntosh .40 .16
524T Pete Falcone .40 .16
527T Mike Anderson .40 .16
528T Dock Ellis .40 .16
532T Milt May .40 .16
554T Ray Fosse .40 .16
579T Clay Kirby .40 .16
583T Tommy Helms .40 .16
592T Willie Randolph 5.00 2.00
618T Jack Brohamer .40 .16
632T Rogelio Moret .40 .16
649T Dave Roberts .40 .16
NNO Traded Checklist 2.00 .40

1976 Topps Team Checklist Sheet

This uncut sheet of the 24 1976 Topps team checklists measures 10" by 21". The sheet was obtained by sending 50 cents plus one wrapper to Topps. When seperated, these cards measure the standard-size.

NM Ex
1 Topps Team CL Sheet 40.00 16.00

1976 Topps Cloth Sticker Test

Before releasing their 1977 Cloth Sticker set, Topps experimented and produced several type cards for a 1976 Cloth Sticker set. While these standard-size cards were never released to the public, a few have made their way into the secondary market. Any more information and additions to this checklist is appreciated.

NM Ex
1 Bob Apodaca 50.00 20.00
2 Duffy Dyer 50.00 20.00

1976 Topps Garagiola

This one-card set was produced by Topps in honor of catcher Joe Garagiola. The front features a color portrait of the player in a thin black fame with a white border. The back displays the player's name and business address in a black cut-out bubble with the player's information and statistics printed in the background.

NM Ex
1 Joe Garagiola 10.00 4.00

1977 Topps

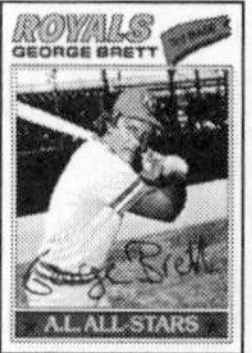

In 1977 for the fifth consecutive year, Topps produced a 660-card standard-size baseball set. Among other fashions, this set was released in 10-card wax packs as well as thirty-nine card rack packs. The player's name, team affiliation, and his position are compactly arranged over the picture area and a facsimile autograph appears on the photo. Team cards feature a checklist of that team's players in the set and a small picture of the manager on the front of the card. Appearing for the first time are the series "Brothers" (631-634) and "Turn Back the Clock" (433-437). Other subseries in the set are League Leaders (1-8), Record Breakers (231-234), Playoffs cards (276-277), World Series cards (411-413), and Rookie Prospects (472-479/487-494). The following players' regular issue cards are explicitly denoted as All-Stars, 30, 70, 100, 120, 170, 210, 240, 265, 301, 347, 400, 420, 450, 500, 521, 550, 560, and 580. The key Rookie Cards in the set are Jack Clark, Andre Dawson, Mark "The Bird" Fidrych, Dennis Martinez and Dale Murphy. Cards numbered 23 or lower, that feature Yankees and do not follow the numbering checklisted below, are not necessarily error cards. Those cards were issued in the NY area and distributed by Burger King. There was an aluminum version of the Dale Murphy rookie card number 476 produced (legally) in the early '80s; proceeds from the sales originally priced at 10.00) of this "card" went to the Huntington's Disease Foundation.

NM Ex
COMPLETE SET (660) 250.00 100.00
1 George Brett 8.00 2.30
Bill Madlock LL
2 Graig Nettles 2.50 1.00
Mike Schmidt LL
3 Lee May 1.50 .60
George Foster LL
4 Bill North .75 .30
Dave Lopes LL
5 Jim Palmer 1.50 .60
Randy Jones LL
6 Nolan Ryan 15.00 6.00
Tom Seaver LL
7 Mark Fidrych .75 .30
John Denny LL
8 Bill Campbell .75 .30
Rawly Eastwick LL
9 Doug Rader .30 .12
10 Reggie Jackson 10.00 4.00
11 Rob Dressler .30 .12
12 Larry Haney .30 .12
13 Luis Gomez .30 .12
14 Tommy Smith .30 .12
15 Don Gullett .75 .30
16 Bob Jones .30 .12
17 Steve Stone .75 .30
18 Indians Team CL 1.50 .30
Frank Robinson MG
19 John D'Acquisto .30 .12
20 Graig Nettles 1.50 .60
21 Ken Forsch .30 .12
22 Bill Freehan .75 .30
23 Dan Driessen .30 .12
24 Carl Morton .30 .12
25 Dwight Evans 1.50 .60
26 Ray Sadecki .30 .12
27 Bill Buckner .75 .30
28 Woodie Fryman .30 .12
29 Bucky Dent .75 .30
30 Greg Luzinski 1.50 .60
31 Jim Todd .30 .12
32 Checklist 1-132 1.50 .30
33 Wayne Garland .30 .12
34 Angels Team CL 1.50 .30
Norm Sherry MG
35 Rennie Stennett .30 .12
36 John Ellis .30 .12
37 Steve Hargan .30 .12
38 Craig Kusick .30 .12
39 Tom Griffin .30 .12
40 Bobby Murcer .75 .30
41 Jim Kern .30 .12
42 Jose Cruz .75 .30
43 Ray Bare .30 .12
44 Bud Harrelson .75 .30
45 Rawly Eastwick .30 .12
46 Buck Martinez .30 .12
47 Lynn McGlothen .30 .12
48 Tom Paciorek .75 .30
49 Grant Jackson .30 .12
50 Ron Cey .75 .30
51 Brewers Team CL 1.50 .30
Alex Grammas MG
52 Ellis Valentine .30 .12
53 Paul Mitchell .30 .12
54 Sandy Alomar .75 .30
55 Jeff Burroughs .75 .30
56 Rudy May .30 .12
57 Marc Hill .30 .12
58 Chet Lemon .75 .30
59 Larry Christenson .30 .12
60 Jim Rice 2.50 1.00
61 Manny Sanguillen .75 .30
62 Eric Raich .30 .12
63 Tito Fuentes .30 .12
64 Larry Biittner .30 .12
65 Skip Lockwood .30 .12
66 Roy Smalley .75 .30
67 Joaquin Andujar RC .75 .30
68 Bruce Bochte .30 .12
69 Jim Crawford .30 .12
70 Johnny Bench 10.00 4.00
71 Dock Ellis .30 .12
72 Mike Anderson .30 .12
73 Charlie Williams .30 .12
74 A's Team CL 1.50 .30
Jack McKeon MG
75 Dennis Leonard .75 .30
76 Tim Foli .30 .12
77 Dyar Miller .30 .12
78 Bob Davis .30 .12
79 Don Money .75 .30
80 Andy Messersmith .75 .30
81 Juan Beniquez .30 .12
82 Jim Rooker .30 .12
83 Kevin Bell .30 .12
84 Ollie Brown .30 .12
85 Duane Kuiper .30 .12
86 Pat Zachry .30 .12
87 Glenn Borgmann .30 .12
88 Stan Wall .30 .12
89 Butch Hobson RC .75 .30
90 Cesar Cedeno .75 .30
91 John Verhoeven .30 .12
92 Dave Rosello .30 .12
93 Tom Poquette .30 .12
94 Craig Swan .30 .12
95 Keith Hernandez .75 .30
96 Lou Piniella .75 .30
97 Dave Heaverlo .30 .12
98 Milt May .30 .12
99 Tom Hausman .30 .12
100 Joe Morgan 4.00 1.60
101 Dick Bosman .30 .12
102 Jose Morales .30 .12
103 Mike Bacsik .30 .12
104 Omar Moreno .75 .30

105 Steve Yeager .75 .30
106 Mike Flanagan .75 .30
107 Bill Melton .30 .12
108 Alan Foster .30 .12
109 Jorge Orta .30 .12
110 Steve Carlton 5.00 2.00
111 Rico Petrocelli .75 .30
112 Bill Greif .30 .12
113 Blue Jays Leaders 1.50 .30
Roy Hartsfield MG
Don Leppert CO
Bob Miller CO
Jackie Moore CO
Harry Warner CO
114 Bruce Dal Canton .30 .12
115 Rick Manning .30 .12
116 Joe Niekro .75 .30
117 Frank White .75 .30
118 Rick Jones .30 .12
119 John Stearns .30 .12
120 Rod Carew 5.00 2.00
121 Gary Nolan .30 .12
122 Ben Oglivie .75 .30
123 Fred Stanley .30 .12
124 George Mitterwald .30 .12
125 Bill Travers .30 .12
126 Rod Gilbreath .30 .12
127 Ron Fairly .75 .30
128 Tommy John 1.50 .60
129 Mike Sadek .30 .12
130 Al Oliver .75 .30
131 Orlando Ramirez .30 .12
132 Chip Lang .30 .12
133 Ralph Garr .75 .30
134 Padres Team CL 1.50 .30
John McNamara MG
135 Mark Belanger .75 .30
136 Jerry Mumphrey .75 .30
137 Jeff Terpko .30 .12
138 Bob Stinson .30 .12
139 Fred Norman .30 .12
140 Mike Schmidt 12.00 4.80
141 Mark Littell .30 .12
142 Steve Dillard .30 .12
143 Ed Herrmann .30 .12
144 Bruce Sutter RC 3.00 1.20
145 Tom Veryzer .30 .12
146 Dusty Baker 1.50 .60
147 Jackie Brown .30 .12
148 Fran Healy .30 .12
149 Mike Cubbage .30 .12
150 Tom Seaver 8.00 3.20
151 Johnny LeMaster .30 .12
152 Gaylord Perry 2.50 1.00
153 Ron Jackson RC .30 .12
154 Dave Giusti .30 .12
155 Joe Rudi .75 .30
156 Pete Mackanin .30 .12
157 Ken Brett .30 .12
158 Ted Kubiak .30 .12
159 Bernie Carbo .30 .12
160 Will McEnaney .30 .12
161 Garry Templeton RC 1.50 .60
162 Mike Cuellar .75 .30
163 Dave Hilton .30 .12
164 Tug McGraw .75 .30
165 Jim Wynn .75 .30
166 Bill Campbell .30 .12
167 Rich Hebner .75 .30
168 Charlie Spikes .30 .12
169 Darold Knowles .30 .12
170 Thurman Munson 5.00 2.00
171 Ken Sanders .30 .12
172 John Milner .30 .12
173 Chuck Scrivener .30 .12
174 Nelson Briles .75 .30
175 Butch Wynegar .75 .30
176 Bob Robertson .30 .12
177 Bart Johnson .30 .12
178 Bombo Rivera .30 .12
179 Paul Hartzell .30 .12
180 Dave Lopes .75 .30
181 Ken McMullen .30 .12
182 Dan Spillner .30 .12
183 Cardinals Team CL 1.50 .30
Vern Rapp MG
184 Bo McLaughlin .30 .12
185 Sixto Lezcano .30 .12
186 Doug Flynn .30 .12
187 Dick Pole .30 .12
188 Bob Tolan .30 .12
189 Rick Dempsey .75 .30
190 Ray Burris .30 .12
191 Doug Griffin .30 .12
192 Clarence Gaston .75 .30
193 Larry Gura .30 .12
194 Gary Matthews .75 .30
195 Ed Figueroa .30 .12
196 Len Randle .30 .12
197 Ed Ott .30 .12
198 Wilbur Wood .30 .12
199 Pepe Frias .30 .12
200 Frank Tanana .75 .30
201 Ed Kranepool .30 .12
202 Tom Johnson .30 .12
203 Ed Armbrister .30 .12
204 Jeff Newman .30 .12
205 Pete Falcone .30 .12
206 Boog Powell 1.50 .60
207 Glenn Abbott .30 .12
208 Checklist 133-264 1.50 .30
209 Rob Andrews .30 .12
210 Fred Lynn .75 .15
211 Giants Team CL 1.50 .60
Joe Altobelli MG
212 Jim Mason .30 .12
213 Maximino Leon .30 .12
214 Darrell Porter .75 .30
215 Butch Metzger .30 .12
216 Doug DeCinces .75 .30
217 Tom Underwood .30 .12
218 John Wathan RC .75 .30
219 Joe Coleman .30 .12
220 Chris Chambliss .75 .30
221 Bob Bailey .30 .12
222 Francisco Barrios .30 .12
223 Earl Williams .30 .12
224 Rusty Torres .30 .12
225 Bob Apodaca .30 .12
226 Leroy Stanton .75 .30
227 Joe Sambito .30 .12
228 Twins Team CL 1.50 .30
Gene Mauch MG
229 Don Kessinger .75 .30
230 Vida Blue .75 .30
231 George Brett RB 8.00 3.20
232 Minnie Minoso RB .75 .30
233 Jose Morales RB .30 .12
234 Nolan Ryan RB 15.00 6.00
235 Cecil Cooper .75 .30
236 Tom Buskey .30 .12
237 Gene Clines .30 .12
238 Tippy Martinez .30 .12
239 Bill Plummer .30 .12
240 Ron LeFlore .75 .30
241 Dave Tomlin .30 .12
242 Ken Henderson .30 .12
243 Ron Reed .30 .12
244 John Mayberry .75 .30
(Cartoon mentions
T206 Wagner)
245 Rick Rhoden .75 .30
246 Mike Vail .30 .12
247 Chris Knapp .30 .12
248 Wilbur Howard .30 .12
249 Pete Redfern .30 .12
250 Bill Madlock .75 .30
251 Tony Muser .30 .12
252 Dale Murray .30 .12
253 John Hale .30 .12
254 Doyle Alexander .30 .12
255 George Scott .75 .30
256 Joe Hoerner .30 .12
257 Mike Miley .30 .12
258 Luis Tiant .75 .30
259 Mets Team CL 1.50 .30
Joe Frazier MG
260 J.R. Richard .75 .30
261 Phil Garner .75 .30
262 Al Cowens .30 .12
263 Mike Marshall .75 .30
264 Tom Hutton .30 .12
265 Mark Fidrych RC 3.00 1.20
266 Derrel Thomas .30 .12
267 Ray Fosse .30 .12
268 Rick Sawyer .30 .12
269 Joe Lis .30 .12
270 Dave Parker 1.50 .60
271 Terry Forster .30 .12
272 Lee Lacy .30 .12
273 Eric Soderholm .30 .12
274 Don Stanhouse .30 .12
275 Mike Hargrove .75 .30
276 C.Chambliss ALCS 1.50 .60
homer decides it
277 Pete Rose NLCS 5.00 2.00
278 Danny Frisella .30 .12
279 Joe Wallis .30 .12
280 Jim Hunter 2.50 1.00
281 Roy Staiger .30 .12
282 Sid Monge .30 .12
283 Jerry DaVanon .30 .12
284 Mike Norris .30 .12
285 Brooks Robinson 5.00 2.00
286 Johnny Grubb .30 .06
287 Reds Team CL 1.50 .60
Sparky Anderson MG
288 Bob Montgomery .30 .12
289 Gene Garber .75 .30
290 Amos Otis .75 .30
291 Jason Thompson RC .75 .30
292 Rogelio Moret .30 .12
293 Jack Brohamer .30 .12
294 George Medich .30 .12
295 Gary Carter 2.50 1.00
296 Don Hood .30 .12
297 Ken Reitz .30 .12
298 Charlie Hough .75 .30
299 Otto Velez .30 .12
300 Jerry Koosman .75 .30
301 Toby Harrah .75 .30
302 Mike Garman .30 .12
303 Gene Tenace .75 .30
304 Jim Hughes .30 .12
305 Mickey Rivers .75 .30
306 Rick Waits .30 .12
307 Gary Sutherland .30 .12
308 Gene Pentz .30 .12
309 Red Sox Team CL 1.50 .30
Don Zimmer MG
310 Larry Bowa .75 .30
311 Vern Ruhle .30 .12
312 Rob Belloir .30 .12
313 Paul Blair .75 .30
314 Steve Mingori .30 .12
315 Dave Chalk .30 .12
316 Steve Rogers .30 .12
317 Kurt Bevacqua .30 .12
318 Duffy Dyer .30 .12
319 Goose Gossage 1.50 .60
320 Ken Griffey Sr. 1.50 .60
321 Dave Goltz .30 .12
322 Bill Russell .75 .30
323 Larry Lintz .30 .12
324 John Curtis .30 .12
325 Mike Ivie .30 .12
326 Jesse Jefferson .30 .12
327 Astros Team CL 1.50 .30
Bill Virdon MG
328 Tommy Boggs .30 .12
329 Ron Hodges .30 .12
330 George Hendrick .75 .30
331 Jim Colborn .30 .12
332 Elliott Maddox .30 .12
333 Paul Reuschel .30 .12
334 Bill Stein .30 .12
335 Bill Robinson .75 .30
336 Denny Doyle .30 .12
337 Ron Schueler .30 .12
338 Dave Duncan .75 .30
339 Adrian Devine .30 .12
340 Hal McRae .75 .30
341 Joe Kerrigan .30 .12
342 Jerry Remy .30 .12
343 Ed Halicki .30 .12
344 Brian Downing .75 .30
345 Reggie Smith .75 .30
346 Bill Singer .30 .12
347 George Foster 1.50 .60
348 Brent Strom .30 .12
349 Jim Holt .30 .12
350 Larry Dierker .75 .30
351 Jim Sundberg .75 .30
352 Mike Phillips .30 .12
353 Stan Thomas .30 .12
354 Pirates Team CL 1.50 .30
Chuck Tanner MG
355 Lou Brock 4.00 1.60
356 Checklist 265-396 1.50 .30
357 Tim McCarver 1.50 .60
358 Tom House .30 .12
359 Willie Randolph 1.50 .60
360 Rick Monday .75 .30
361 Eduardo Rodriguez .30 .12
362 Tommy Davis .75 .30
363 Dave Roberts .30 .12
364 Vic Correll .30 .12
365 Mike Torrez .75 .30
366 Ted Sizemore .30 .12
367 Dave Hamilton .30 .12
368 Mike Jorgensen .30 .12
369 Terry Humphrey .30 .12
370 John Montefusco .30 .12
371 Royals Team CL 1.50 .30
Whitey Herzog MG
372 Rich Folkers .30 .12
373 Bert Campaneris .75 .30
374 Kent Tekulve .75 .30
375 Larry Hisle .75 .30
376 Nino Espinosa .30 .12
377 Dave McKay .30 .12
378 Jim Umbarger .30 .12
379 Larry Cox .30 .12
380 Lee May .75 .30
381 Bob Forsch .30 .12
382 Charlie Moore .30 .12
383 Stan Bahnsen .30 .12
384 Darrel Chaney .30 .12
385 Dave LaRoche .30 .12
386 Manny Mota .75 .30
387 Yankees Team CL 2.50 .50
Billy Martin MG
388 Terry Harmon .30 .12
389 Ken Kravec .30 .12
390 Dave Winfield 6.00 2.40
391 Dan Warthen .30 .12
392 Phil Roof .30 .12
393 John Lowenstein .30 .12
394 Bill Laxton .30 .12
395 Manny Trillo .30 .12
396 Tom Murphy .30 .12
397 Larry Herndon RC .75 .30
398 Tom Burgmeier .30 .12
399 Bruce Boisclair .30 .12
400 Steve Garvey 2.50 1.00
401 Mickey Scott .30 .12
402 Tommy Helms .30 .12
403 Tom Grieve .75 .30
404 Eric Rasmussen .30 .12
405 Claudell Washington .75 .30
406 Tim Johnson .30 .12
407 Dave Freisleben .30 .12
408 Cesar Tovar .30 .12
409 Pete Broberg .30 .12
410 Willie Montanez .30 .12
411 Joe Morgan WS 2.50 1.00
Johnny Bench
412 Johnny Bench WS 2.50 1.00
413 WS Summary .75 .30
Cincy wins 2nd
straight series
414 Tommy Harper .75 .30
415 Jay Johnstone .75 .30
416 Chuck Hartenstein .30 .12
417 Wayne Garrett .30 .12
418 White Sox Team CL 1.50 .30
Bob Lemon MG
419 Steve Swisher .30 .12
420 Rusty Staub 1.50 .60
421 Doug Rau .30 .12
422 Freddie Patek .75 .30
423 Gary Lavelle .30 .12
424 Steve Brye .30 .12
425 Joe Torre 1.50 .60
426 Dick Drago .30 .12
427 Dave Rader .30 .12
428 Rangers Team CL 1.50 .30
Frank Lucchesi
429 Ken Boswell .30 .12
430 Fergie Jenkins 2.50 1.00
431 Dave Collins UER .75 .30
(Photo actually
Bobby Jones)
432 Buzz Capra .30 .12
433 Nate Colbert TBC .30 .12
(5 HR, 13 RBI)
434 Carl Yastrzemski TBC 1.50 .60
'67 Triple Crown
435 Maury Wills TBC .75 .30
104 steals
436 Bob Keegan TBC .30 .12
Majors' only no-hitter
437 Ralph Kiner TBC 1.50 .60
Leads NL in HR's
7th straight year
438 Marty Perez .30 .12
439 Gorman Thomas .75 .30
440 Jon Matlack .30 .12
441 Larvell Blanks .30 .12
442 Braves Team CL 1.50 .30
Dave Bristol MG
443 Lamar Johnson .30 .12
444 Wayne Twitchell .30 .12
445 Ken Singleton .75 .30
446 Bill Bonham .30 .12
447 Jerry Turner .30 .12
448 Ellie Rodriguez .30 .12
449 Al Fitzmorris .30 .12
450 Pete Rose 20.00 8.00
451 Checklist 397-528 1.50 .30
452 Mike Caldwell .30 .12
453 Pedro Garcia .30 .12
454 Andy Etchebarren .30 .12
455 Rick Wise .30 .12
456 Leon Roberts .30 .12
457 Steve Luebber .30 .12
458 Leo Foster .30 .12
459 Steve Foucault .30 .12
460 Willie Stargell 2.50 1.00
461 Dick Tidrow .30 .12
462 Don Baylor 1.50 .60
463 Jamie Quirk .30 .12
464 Randy Moffitt .30 .12
465 Rico Carty .75 .30
466 Fred Holdsworth .30 .12
467 Phillies Team CL 1.50 .30
Danny Ozark MG
468 Ramon Hernandez .30 .12
469 Pat Kelly .30 .12
470 Ted Simmons .75 .30
471 Del Unser .30 .12
472 Don Aase .30 .12
Bob McClure
Gil Patterson
Dave Wehrmeister
Sheldon Gill pictured instead of Gil
Patterson
473 Andre Dawson RC 20.00 8.00
Gene Richards
John Scott
Denny Walling
474 Bob Bailor .75 .30
Kiko Garcia
Craig Reynolds
Alex Taveras
475 Chris Batton .75 .30
Rick Camp
Scott McGregor
Manny Sarmiento
476 Gary Alexander 20.00 8.00
Rick Cerone
Dale Murphy RC
Kevin Pasley
477 Doug Ault .75 .30
Rich Dauer
Orlando Gonzalez
Phil Mankowski
478 Jim Gideon .75 .30
Leon Hooten
Dave Johnson
Mark Lemongello
479 Brian Asselstine .75 .30
Wayne Gross
Sam Mejias
Alvis Woods
480 Carl Yastrzemski 8.00 3.20
481 Roger Metzger .30 .12
482 Tony Solaita .30 .12
483 Richie Zisk .30 .12
484 Burt Hooton .75 .30
485 Roy White .75 .30
486 Ed Bane .30 .12
487 Larry Anderson .75 .30
Ed Glynn
Joe Henderson
Greg Terlecky
488 Jack Clark RC 3.00 1.20
Ruppert Jones RC
Lee Mazzilli RC
Dan Thomas
489 Len Barker RC .75 .30
Randy Lerch
Greg Minton
Mike Overy
490 Billy Almon .75 .30
Mickey Klutts
Tommy McMillan
Mark Wagner
491 Mike Dupree 5.00 2.00
Dennis Martinez RC
Craig Mitchell
Bob Sykes
492 Tony Armas RC .75 .30
Steve Kemp RC
Carlos Lopez
Gary Woods
493 Mike Krukow .75 .30
Jim Otten
Gary Wheelock
Mike Willis
494 Juan Bernhardt 1.50 .60
Mike Champion
Jim Gantner RC
Bump Wills
495 Al Hrabosky .30 .12
496 Gary Thomasson .30 .12
497 Clay Carroll .30 .12
498 Sal Bando .75 .30
499 Pablo Torrealba .30 .12
500 Dave Kingman 1.50 .60
501 Jim Bibby .30 .12
502 Randy Hundley .30 .12
503 Bill Lee .30 .12
504 Dodgers Team CL 1.50 .30
Tom Lasorda MG
505 Oscar Gamble .75 .30
506 Steve Grilli .30 .12
507 Mike Hegan .30 .12
508 Dave Pagan .30 .12
509 Cookie Rojas .75 .30
510 John Candelaria .30 .12
511 Bill Fahey .30 .12
512 Jack Billingham .30 .12
513 Jerry Terrell .30 .12
514 Cliff Johnson .30 .12
515 Chris Speier .30 .12
516 Bake McBride .75 .30
517 Pete Vuckovich RC .75 .30
518 Cubs Team CL 1.50 .30
Herman Franks MG
519 Don Kirkwood .30 .12
520 Garry Maddox .30 .12
521 Bob Grich .75 .30
Only card in set with no date of birth
522 Enzo Hernandez .30 .12
523 Rollie Fingers 2.50 1.00
524 Rowland Office .30 .12
525 Dennis Eckersley 5.00 2.00
526 Larry Parrish .75 .30
527 Dan Meyer .75 .30
528 Bill Castro .30 .12
529 Jim Essian .30 .12
530 Rick Reuschel .75 .30
531 Lyman Bostock .75 .30
532 Jim Willoughby .30 .12
533 Mickey Stanley .30 .12
534 Paul Splittorff .30 .12
535 Cesar Geronimo .30 .12
536 Vic Albury .30 .12
537 Dave Roberts .30 .12
538 Frank Taveras .30 .12
539 Mike Wallace .30 .12
540 Bob Watson .75 .30
541 John Denny .75 .30
542 Frank Duffy .30 .12
543 Ron Blomberg .30 .12
544 Gary Ross .30 .12
545 Bob Boone .75 .30
546 Oriole Team CL 1.50 .30
Earl Weaver MG
547 Willie McCovey 4.00 1.60
548 Joel Youngblood .30 .12
549 Jerry Royster .30 .12
550 Randy Jones .30 .12
551 Bill North .30 .12
552 Pepe Mangual .30 .12
553 Jack Heidemann .30 .12
554 Bruce Kimm .30 .12
555 Dan Ford .30 .12
556 Doug Bird .30 .12
557 Jerry White .30 .12
558 Elias Sosa .30 .12
559 Alan Bannister .30 .12
560 Dave Concepcion 1.50 .60
561 Pete LaCock .30 .12
562 Checklist 529-660 1.50 .30
563 Bruce Kison .30 .12
564 Alan Ashby .75 .30
565 Mickey Lolich .75 .30
566 Rick Miller .30 .12
567 Enos Cabell .30 .12
568 Carlos May .30 .12
569 Jim Lonborg .75 .30
570 Bobby Bonds 1.50 .60
571 Darrell Evans .75 .30
572 Ross Grimsley .30 .12
573 Joe Ferguson .30 .12
574 Aurelio Rodriguez .30 .12
575 Dick Ruthven .30 .12
576 Fred Kendall .30 .12
577 Jerry Augustine .30 .12
578 Bob Randall .30 .12
579 Don Carrithers .30 .12
580 George Brett 15.00 6.00
581 Pedro Borbon .30 .12
582 Ed Kirkpatrick .30 .12
583 Paul Lindblad .30 .12
584 Ed Goodson .30 .12
585 Rick Burleson .75 .30
586 Steve Renko .30 .12
587 Rick Baldwin .30 .12
588 Dave Moates .30 .12
589 Mike Cosgrove .30 .12
590 Buddy Bell .75 .30
591 Chris Arnold .30 .12
592 Dan Briggs .30 .12
593 Dennis Blair .30 .12
594 Biff Pocoroba .30 .12
595 John Hiller .30 .12
596 Jerry Martin .30 .12
597 Mariners Leaders CL 1.50 .30
Darrell Johnson MG
Don Bryant CO
Jim Busby CO
Vada Pinson CO
Wes Stock CO
598 Sparky Lyle .75 .30
599 Mike Tyson .30 .12
600 Jim Palmer 4.00 1.60
601 Mike Lum .30 .12
602 Andy Hassler .30 .12
603 Willie Davis .75 .30
604 Jim Slaton .30 .12
605 Felix Millan .30 .12
606 Steve Braun .30 .12
607 Larry Demery .30 .12
608 Roy Howell .30 .12
609 Jim Barr .30 .12
610 Jose Cardenal .75 .30
611 Dave Lemanczyk .30 .12
612 Barry Foote .30 .12
613 Reggie Cleveland .30 .12
614 Greg Gross .30 .12
615 Phil Niekro 2.50 1.00
616 Tommy Sandt .30 .12
617 Bobby Darwin .30 .12
618 Pat Dobson .30 .12
619 Johnny Oates .75 .30
620 Don Sutton 2.50 1.00
621 Tigers Team CL 1.50 .30
Ralph Houk MG
622 Jim Wohlford .30 .12
623 Jack Kucek .30 .12
624 Hector Cruz .30 .12
625 Ken Holtzman .75 .30
626 Al Bumbry .75 .30
627 Bob Myrick .30 .12
628 Mario Guerrero .30 .12
629 Bobby Valentine .75 .30
630 Bert Blyleven 1.50 .60
631 George Brett 6.00 2.40
Ken Brett
632 Bob Forsch .75 .30
Ken Forsch
633 Lee May .75 .30
Carlos May
634 Paul Reuschel .75 .30
Rick Reuschel UER
(Photos switched)
635 Robin Yount 8.00 3.20
636 Santo Alcala .30 .12
637 Alex Johnson .30 .12
638 Jim Kaat 1.50 .60
639 Jerry Morales .30 .12
640 Carlton Fisk 5.00 2.00
641 Dan Larson .30 .12
642 Willie Crawford .30 .12
643 Mike Pazik .30 .12
644 Matt Alexander .30 .12
645 Jerry Reuss .75 .30
646 Andres Mora .30 .12
647 Expos Team CL 1.50 .30
Dick Williams MG
648 Jim Spencer .30 .12
649 Dave Cash .30 .12
650 Nolan Ryan 30.00 12.00
651 Von Joshua .30 .12
652 Tom Walker .30 .12
653 Diego Segui .75 .30
654 Ron Pruitt .30 .12
655 Tony Perez 2.50 1.00
656 Ron Guidry 1.50 .60
657 Mick Kelleher .30 .12
658 Marty Pattin .30 .12

659 Merv Rettenmund .30 .12
660 Willie Horton 1.50 .30

1977 Topps Cloth Stickers

The "cards" in this 73-card set measure 2 1/2" by 3 1/2". The 1977 Cloth Stickers series was issued as a test set separately from the regular baseball series of that year. The packs of these cards contained two stickers as well as one "checklist puzzle" piece. The obverse pictures are identical to those appearing in the regular set, but the backs are completely different. There are 55 player cards and 18 unnumbered checklists, the latter bearing the title "Baseball Patches". The player cards are sequenced in alphabetical order. The checklists are puzzle pieces which, when properly arranged, form pictures of the A.L. and N.L. All-Star teams. Puzzle pieces are coded below by U (Upper), M (Middle), B (Bottom), L (left), C (Center), and R (Right). Cards marked with an SP in the checklist are in shorter supply than all others in the set. Even though we have assigned numbers 56 through 73 in our checklist for the puzzle cards, they are in fact all unnumbered.

NM Ex
COMPLETE SET (73) 125.00 50.00
COMMON CARD (1-55) .25 .10
COMMON SP (1-55) 1.00 .40
COM.PUZZLE (56-73) .10 .04
1 Alan Ashby .25 .10
2 Buddy Bell SP 1.25 .50
3 Johnny Bench 4.00 1.60
4 Vida Blue .75 .30
5 Bert Blyleven .75 .30
6 Steve Braun SP 1.00 .40
7 George Brett 10.00 4.00
8 Lou Brock 3.00 1.20
9 Jose Cardenal .25 .10
10 Rod Carew SP 6.00 2.40
11 Steve Carlton 4.00 1.60
12 Dave Cash .25 .10
13 Cesar Cedeno SP 1.25 .50
14 Ron Cey .75 .30
15 Mark Fidrych 5.00 2.00
16 Dan Ford .25 .10
17 Wayne Garland .25 .10
18 Ralph Garr .25 .10
19 Steve Garvey 3.00 1.20
20 Mike Hargrove .75 .30
21 Jim Hunter 2.00 .80
22 Reggie Jackson 4.00 1.60
23 Randy Jones .25 .10
24 Dave Kingman SP 1.25 .50
25 Bill Madlock .75 .30
26 Lee May SP 1.25 .50
27 John Mayberry .25 .10
28 John(Andy)Messersmith .25 .10
29 Willie Montanez .25 .10
30 John Montefusco SP 1.00 .40
31 Joe Morgan 2.00 .80
32 Thurman Munson 2.00 .80
33 Bobby Murcer .75 .30
34 Al Oliver SP 1.25 .50
35 Dave Pagan .25 .10
36 Jim Palmer SP 3.00 1.20
37 Tony Perez 2.00 .80
38 Pete Rose SP 12.00 4.80
39 Joe Rudi .50 .20
40 Nolan Ryan SP 60.00 24.00
41 Mike Schmidt 10.00 4.00
42 Tom Seaver 5.00 2.00
43 Ted Simmons .75 .30
44 Bill Singer .25 .10
45 Willie Stargell 3.00 1.20
46 Rusty Staub .75 .30
47 Don Sutton 2.00 .80
48 Luis Tiant .75 .30
49 Bill Travers .25 .10
50 Claudell Washington .75 .30
51 Bob Watson .75 .30
52 Dave Winfield 6.00 2.40
53 Carl Yastrzemski 4.00 1.60
54 Robin Yount 6.00 2.40
55 Richie Zisk .25 .10
56 AL Puzzle UL .10 .04
57 AL Puzzle UC .10 .04
58 AL Puzzle UR .10 .04
59 AL Puzzle ML .10 .04
60 AL Puzzle MC .10 .04
61 AL Puzzle MR .10 .04
62 AL Puzzle BL SP .20 .08
63 AL Puzzle BC SP .20 .08
64 AL Puzzle BR SP .20 .08
65 NL Puzzle UL .10 .04
66 NL Puzzle UC .10 .04
67 NL Puzzle UR .10 .04
68 NL Puzzle ML .10 .04
69 NL Puzzle MC .10 .04
70 NL Puzzle MR .10 .04
71 NL Puzzle BL .10 .04
72 NL Puzzle BC .10 .04
73 NL Puzzle BR .10 .04

1978 Topps

The cards in this 726-card set measure 2 1/2" by 3 1/2". As in previous years, this set was issued in many different ways: some of them include 14-card wax packs and 39-card rack packs. The 1978 Topps set experienced an increase in number of cards from the previous five regular issue sets of 660. Card numbers 1 through 7 feature Record Breakers (RB) of the 1977 season. Other subsets within this set include League Leaders (201-208), Post-season cards (411-413), and Rookie Prospects (701-711). The key Rookie Cards in this set are the multi-player Rookie Card of Paul Molitor and Alan Trammell, Jack Morris, Eddie Murray, Lance Parrish, and Lou Whitaker. Many of the Molitor/Trammell cards are found with black printing smudges. The manager cards in the set feature a "then and now" format on the card front showing the manager as he looked during his playing days. While no scarcities exist, 66 of the cards are more abundant in supply, as they were "double printed." These 66 double-printed cards are noted in the checklist by DP. Team cards again feature a checklist of that team's players in the set on the back. Cards numbered 23 or lower, that feature Astros, Rangers, Tigers, or Yankees and do not follow the numbering checklisted below, are not necessarily error cards. They are undoubtedly Burger King cards, separate sets with their own pricing and mass distribution. The Bump Wills card has been seen with either no black mark or a major black mark on the front of the card. We will continue to investigate this card and see whether or not it should be considered a variation.

NM Ex
COMPLETE SET (726) 200.00 80.00
COMMON CARD (1-726) .25 .10
COMMON CARD DP .15 .06
1 Lou Brock RB 3.00 .90
2 Sparky Lyle RB .60 .24
3 Willie McCovey RB 2.50 1.00
4 Brooks Robinson RB 2.50 1.00
5 Pete Rose RB 8.00 3.20
6 Nolan Ryan RB 15.00 6.00
7 Reggie Jackson RB 4.00 1.60
8 Mike Sadek .25 .10
9 Doug DeCinces .60 .24
10 Phil Niekro 2.50 1.00
11 Rick Manning .25 .10
12 Don Aase .25 .10
13 Art Howe RC .60 .24
14 Lerrin LaGrow .25 .10
15 Tony Perez DP 1.25 .50
16 Roy White .60 .24
17 Mike Krukow .25 .10
18 Bob Grich .60 .24
19 Darrell Porter .60 .24
20 Pete Rose DP 12.00 4.80
21 Steve Kemp .25 .10
22 Charlie Hough .60 .24
23 Bump Wills .25 .10
24 Don Money DP .15 .06
25 Jon Matlack .25 .10
26 Rich Hebner .60 .24
27 Geoff Zahn .25 .10
28 Ed Ott .25 .10
29 Bob Lacey .25 .10
30 George Hendrick .60 .24
31 Glenn Abbott .25 .10
32 Garry Templeton .60 .24
33 Dave Lemanczyk .25 .10
34 Willie McCovey 3.00 1.20
35 Sparky Lyle .60 .24
36 Eddie Murray RC 80.00 32.00
37 Rick Waits .25 .10
38 Willie Montanez .25 .10
39 Floyd Bannister RC .25 .10
40 Carl Yastrzemski 6.00 2.40
41 Burt Hooton .60 .24
42 Jorge Orta .25 .10
43 Bill Atkinson .25 .10
44 Toby Harrah .60 .24
45 Mark Fidrych 2.50 1.00
46 Al Cowens .25 .10
47 Jack Billingham .25 .10
48 Don Baylor 1.25 .50
49 Ed Kranepool .60 .24
50 Rick Reuschel .60 .24
51 Charlie Moore DP .15 .06
52 Jim Lonborg .60 .24
53 Phil Garner DP .25 .10
54 Tom Johnson .25 .10
55 Mitchell Page .25 .10
56 Randy Jones .25 .10
57 Dan Meyer .25 .10
58 Bob Forsch .25 .10
59 Otto Velez .25 .10
60 Thurman Munson 4.00 1.60
61 Larvell Blanks .25 .10
62 Jim Barr .25 .10
63 Don Zimmer MG .60 .24
64 Gene Pentz .25 .10
65 Ken Singleton .60 .24
66 Chicago White Sox 1.25 .25
Team Card CL
67 Claudell Washington .60 .24
68 Steve Foucault DP .15 .06
69 Mike Vail .25 .10
70 Goose Gossage 1.25 .50
71 Terry Humphrey .25 .10
72 Andre Dawson 4.00 1.60
73 Andy Hassler .25 .10
74 Checklist 1-121 1.25 .25
75 Dick Ruthven .25 .10
76 Steve Ontiveros .25 .10
77 Ed Kirkpatrick .25 .10
78 Pablo Torrealba .25 .10
79 Da.Johnson DP MG .15 .06
80 Ken Griffey Sr. 1.25 .50
81 Pete Redfern .25 .10
82 San Francisco Giants 1.25 .25
Team Card CL
83 Bob Montgomery .25 .10
84 Kent Tekulve .60 .24
85 Ron Fairly .60 .24
86 Dave Tomlin .25 .10
87 John Lowenstein .25 .10
88 Mike Phillips .25 .10
89 Ken Clay .25 .10
90 Larry Bowa 1.25 .50
91 Oscar Zamora .25 .10
92 Adrian Devine .25 .10
93 Bobby Cox DP .15 .06
94 Chuck Scrivener .25 .10
95 Jamie Quirk .25 .10
96 Baltimore Orioles 1.25 .25
Team Card CL
97 Stan Bahnsen .25 .10
98 Jim Essian .60 .24
99 Willie Hernandez RC 1.25 .50
100 George Brett 15.00 6.00
101 Sid Monge .25 .10
102 Matt Alexander .25 .10
103 Tom Murphy .25 .10
104 Lee Lacy .25 .10
105 Reggie Cleveland .25 .10
106 Bill Plummer .25 .10
107 Ed Halicki .25 .10
108 Von Joshua .25 .10
109 Joe Torre MG .60 .24
110 Richie Zisk .25 .10
111 Mike Tyson .25 .10
112 Houston Astros 1.25 .25
Team Card CL
113 Don Carrithers .25 .10
114 Paul Blair .60 .24
115 Gary Nolan .25 .10
116 Tucker Ashford .25 .10
117 John Montague .25 .10
118 Terry Harmon .25 .10
119 Dennis Martinez 2.50 1.00
120 Gary Carter 2.50 1.00
121 Alvis Woods .25 .10
122 Dennis Eckersley 3.00 1.20
123 Manny Trillo .25 .10
124 Dave Rozema RC .25 .10
125 George Scott .60 .24
126 Paul Moskau .25 .10
127 Chet Lemon .60 .24
128 Bill Russell .60 .24
129 Jim Colborn .25 .10
130 Jeff Burroughs .60 .24
131 Bert Blyleven 1.25 .50
132 Enos Cabell .25 .10
133 Jerry Augustine .25 .10
134 Steve Henderson .25 .10
135 Ron Guidry DP 1.25 .50
136 Ted Sizemore .25 .10
137 Craig Kusick .25 .10
138 Larry Demery .25 .10
139 Wayne Gross .25 .10
140 Rollie Fingers 2.50 1.00
141 Ruppert Jones .25 .10
142 John Montefusco .25 .10
143 Keith Hernandez .60 .24
144 Jesse Jefferson .25 .10
145 Rick Monday .60 .24
146 Doyle Alexander .60 .24
147 Lee Mazzilli .25 .10
148 Andre Thornton .60 .24
149 Dale Murray .25 .10
150 Bobby Bonds 1.25 .50
151 Milt Wilcox .25 .10
152 Ivan DeJesus .25 .10
153 Steve Stone .60 .24
154 Cecil Cooper DP .25 .10
155 Butch Hobson .25 .10
156 Andy Messersmith .60 .24
157 Pete LaCock DP .15 .06
158 Joaquin Andujar .60 .24
159 Lou Piniella .60 .24
160 Jim Palmer 3.00 1.20
161 Bob Boone 1.25 .50
162 Paul Thormodsgard .25 .10
163 Bill North .25 .10
164 Bob Owchinko .25 .10
165 Rennie Stennett .25 .10
166 Carlos Lopez .25 .10
167 Tim Foli .25 .10
168 Reggie Smith .60 .24
169 Jerry Johnson .25 .10
170 Lou Brock 3.00 1.20
171 Pat Zachry .25 .10
172 Mike Hargrove .60 .24
173 Robin Yount UER 5.00 2.00
(Played for Newark
in 1973, not 1971)
174 Wayne Garland .25 .10
175 Jerry Morales .25 .10
176 Milt May .25 .10
177 Gene Garber DP .25 .10
178 Dave Chalk .25 .10
179 Dick Tidrow .25 .10
180 Dave Concepcion 1.25 .50
181 Ken Forsch .25 .10
182 Jim Spencer .25 .10
183 Doug Bird .25 .10
184 Checklist 122-242 1.25 .25
185 Ellis Valentine .25 .10
186 Bob Stanley DP .15 .06
187 Jerry Royster DP .15 .06
188 Al Bumbry .60 .24
189 Tom Lasorda MG 2.50 1.00
190 John Candelaria .60 .24
191 Rodney Scott .60 .24
192 San Diego Padres 1.25 .25
Team Card CL
193 Rich Chiles .25 .10
194 Derrel Thomas .25 .10
195 Larry Dierker .60 .24
196 Bob Bailor .25 .10
197 Nino Espinosa .25 .10
198 Ron Pruitt .25 .10
199 Craig Reynolds .25 .10
200 Reggie Jackson 8.00 3.20
201 Dave Parker 1.25 .50
Rod Carew LL
202 George Foster .60 .24
Jim Rice LL DP
203 George Foster .60 .24
Larry Hisle LL
204 Frank Taveras .25 .10
Freddie Patek LL DP
205 Steve Carlton 2.50 1.00
Dave Goltz
Dennis Leonard
Jim Palmer LL
206 Phil Niekro 6.00 2.40
Nolan Ryan LL DP
207 John Candelaria .60 .24
Frank Tanana LL DP
208 Rollie Fingers 1.25 .50
Bill Campbell LL
209 Dock Ellis .25 .10
210 Jose Cardenal .25 .10
211 Earl Weaver MG DP 1.25 .50
212 Mike Caldwell .25 .10
213 Alan Bannister .25 .10
214 California Angels 1.25 .25
Team Card CL
215 Darrell Evans .60 .24
216 Mike Paxton .25 .10
217 Rod Gilbreath .25 .10
218 Marty Pattin .25 .10
219 Mike Cubbage .25 .10
220 Pedro Borbon .25 .10
221 Chris Speier .25 .10
222 Jerry Martin .25 .10
223 Bruce Kison .25 .10
224 Jerry Tabb .25 .10
225 Don Gullett DP .25 .10
226 Joe Ferguson .25 .10
227 Al Fitzmorris .25 .10
228 Manny Mota DP .25 .10
229 Leo Foster .25 .10
230 Al Hrabosky .25 .10
231 Wayne Nordhagen .25 .10
232 Mickey Stanley .25 .10
233 Dick Pole .25 .10
234 Herman Franks MG .25 .10
235 Tim McCarver .60 .24
236 Terry Whitfield .25 .10
237 Rich Dauer .25 .10
238 Juan Beniquez .25 .10
239 Dyar Miller .25 .10
240 Gene Tenace .60 .24
241 Pete Vuckovich .60 .24
242 Barry Bonnell DP .15 .06
243 Bob McClure .25 .10
244 Montreal Expos .60 .12
Team Card CL DP
245 Rick Burleson .60 .24
246 Dan Driessen .25 .10
247 Larry Christenson .25 .10
248 Frank White DP .60 .24
249 Dave Goltz DP .15 .06
250 Graig Nettles DP .60 .24
251 Don Kirkwood .25 .10
252 Steve Swisher DP .15 .06
253 Jim Kern .25 .10
254 Dave Collins .60 .24
255 Jerry Reuss .60 .24
256 Joe Altobelli MG .25 .10
257 Hector Cruz .25 .10
258 John Hiller .60 .24
259 Los Angeles Dodgers 1.25 .25
Team Card CL
260 Bert Campaneris .60 .24
261 Tim Hosley .25 .10
262 Rudy May .25 .10
263 Danny Walton .25 .10
264 Jamie Easterly .25 .10
265 Sal Bando DP .60 .24
266 Bob Shirley .25 .10
267 Doug Ault .25 .10
268 Gil Flores .25 .10
269 Wayne Twitchell .25 .10
270 Carlton Fisk 4.00 1.60
271 Randy Lerch DP .15 .06
272 Royle Stillman .25 .10
273 Fred Norman .25 .10
274 Freddie Patek .60 .24
275 Dan Ford .25 .10
276 Bill Bonham DP .15 .06
277 Bruce Boisclair .25 .10
278 Enrique Romo .25 .10
279 Bill Virdon MG .25 .10
280 Buddy Bell .60 .24
281 Eric Rasmussen DP .15 .06
282 New York Yankees 2.50 .50
Team Card CL
283 Omar Moreno .25 .10
284 Randy Moffitt .25 .10
285 Steve Yeager DP .60 .24
286 Ben Oglivie .60 .24
287 Kiko Garcia .25 .10
288 Dave Hamilton .25 .10
289 Checklist 243-363 1.25 .25
290 Willie Horton .60 .24
291 Gary Ross .25 .10
292 Gene Richards .25 .10
293 Mike Willis .25 .10
294 Larry Parrish .60 .24
295 Bill Lee .25 .10
296 Biff Pocoroba .25 .10
297 Warren Brusstar DP .15 .06
298 Tony Armas .60 .24
299 Whitey Herzog MG .60 .24
300 Joe Morgan 3.00 1.20
301 Buddy Schultz .25 .10
302 Chicago Cubs 1.25 .25
Team Card CL
303 Sam Hinds .25 .10
304 John Milner .25 .10
305 Rico Carty .60 .24
306 Joe Niekro .60 .24
307 Glenn Borgmann .25 .10
308 Jim Rooker .25 .10
309 Cliff Johnson .25 .10
310 Don Sutton 2.50 1.00
311 Jose Baez DP .15 .06
312 Greg Minton .25 .10
313 Andy Etchebarren .25 .10
314 Paul Lindblad .25 .10
315 Mark Belanger .60 .24
316 Henry Cruz DP .15 .06
317 Dave Johnson .25 .10
318 Tom Griffin .25 .10
319 Alan Ashby .25 .10
320 Fred Lynn .60 .24
321 Santo Alcala .25 .10
322 Tom Paciorek .60 .24
323 Jim Fregosi DP .25 .10
324 Vern Rapp MG .25 .10
325 Bruce Sutter 1.25 .50
326 Mike Lum DP .15 .06
327 Rick Langford DP .15 .06
328 Milwaukee Brewers 1.25 .25
Team Card CL
329 John Verhoeven .25 .10
330 Bob Watson .60 .24
331 Mark Littell .25 .10
332 Duane Kuiper .25 .10
333 Jim Todd .25 .10
334 John Stearns .25 .10
335 Bucky Dent .60 .24
336 Steve Busby .25 .10
337 Tom Grieve .60 .24
338 Dave Heaverlo .25 .10
339 Mario Guerrero .25 .10
340 Bake McBride .60 .24
341 Mike Flanagan .60 .24
342 Aurelio Rodriguez .25 .10
343 John Wathan DP .15 .06
344 Sam Ewing .25 .10
345 Luis Tiant .60 .24
346 Larry Biittner .25 .10
347 Terry Forster .25 .10
348 Del Unser .25 .10
349 Rick Camp DP .15 .06
350 Steve Garvey 2.50 1.00
351 Jeff Torborg .60 .24
352 Tony Scott .25 .10
353 Doug Bair .25 .10
354 Cesar Geronimo .25 .10
355 Bill Travers .25 .10
356 New York Mets 1.25 .25
Team Card CL
357 Tom Poquette .25 .10
358 Mark Lemongello .25 .10
359 Marc Hill .25 .10
360 Mike Schmidt 10.00 4.00
361 Chris Knapp .25 .10
362 Dave May .25 .10
363 Bob Randall .25 .10
364 Jerry Turner .25 .10
365 Ed Figueroa .25 .10
366 Larry Milbourne DP .15 .06
367 Rick Dempsey .60 .24
368 Balor Moore .25 .10
369 Tim Nordbrook .25 .10
370 Rusty Staub 1.25 .50
371 Ray Burris .25 .10
372 Brian Asselstine .25 .10
373 Jim Willoughby .25 .10
374 Jose Morales .25 .10
375 Tommy John 1.25 .50
376 Jim Wohlford .25 .10
377 Manny Sarmiento .25 .10
378 Bobby Winkles MG .25 .10
379 Skip Lockwood .25 .10
380 Ted Simmons .60 .24
381 Philadelphia Phillies 1.25 .25
Team Card CL
382 Joe Lahoud .25 .10
383 Mario Mendoza .25 .10
384 Jack Clark 1.25 .50
385 Tito Fuentes .25 .10
386 Bob Gorinski .25 .10
387 Ken Holtzman .60 .24
388 Bill Fahey DP .15 .06
389 Julio Gonzalez .25 .10
390 Oscar Gamble .60 .24
391 Larry Haney .25 .10
392 Billy Almon .25 .10
393 Tippy Martinez .60 .24
394 Roy Howell DP .15 .06
395 Jim Hughes .25 .10
396 Bob Stinson DP .15 .06
397 Greg Gross .25 .10
398 Don Hood .25 .10
399 Pete Mackanin .25 .10
400 Nolan Ryan 30.00 12.00
401 Sparky Anderson MG .60 .24
402 Dave Campbell .25 .10
403 Bud Harrelson .60 .24
404 Detroit Tigers 1.25 .25
Team Card CL
405 Rawly Eastwick .25 .10
406 Mike Jorgensen .25 .10
407 Odell Jones .25 .10
408 Joe Zdeb .25 .10
409 Ron Schueler .25 .10
410 Bill Madlock .60 .24
411 Mickey Rivers ALCS .60 .24
412 Davey Lopes NLCS .60 .24
413 Reggie Jackson WS 4.00 1.60
414 Darold Knowles DP .15 .06
415 Ray Fosse .25 .10
416 Jack Brohamer .25 .10
417 Mike Garman DP .15 .06
418 Tony Muser .25 .10
419 Jerry Garvin .25 .10
420 Greg Luzinski 1.25 .50
421 Junior Moore .25 .10
422 Steve Braun .25 .10
423 Dave Rosello .25 .10
424 Boston Red Sox 1.25 .25
Team Card CL
425 Steve Rogers DP .25 .10
426 Fred Kendall .25 .10
427 Mario Soto RC .60 .24
428 Joel Youngblood .25 .10
429 Mike Barlow .25 .10
430 Al Oliver .60 .24
431 Butch Metzger .25 .10
432 Terry Bulling .25 .10
433 Fernando Gonzalez .25 .10
434 Mike Norris .25 .10
435 Checklist 364-484 1.25 .25
436 Vic Harris DP .15 .06
437 Bo McLaughlin .25 .10
438 John Ellis .25 .10
439 Ken Kravec .25 .10
440 Dave Lopes .60 .24
441 Larry Gura .25 .10
442 Elliott Maddox .25 .10
443 Darrel Chaney .25 .10
444 Roy Hartsfield MG .25 .10
445 Mike Ivie .25 .10
446 Tug McGraw .60 .24
447 Leroy Stanton .25 .10
448 Bill Castro .25 .10
449 Tim Blackwell DP .15 .06
450 Tom Seaver 6.00 2.40
451 Minnesota Twins 1.25 .25

Team Card CL
452 Jerry Mumphrey .25 .10
453 Doug Flynn .25 .10
454 Dave LaRoche .25 .10
455 Bill Robinson .60 .24
456 Vern Ruhle .25 .10
457 Bob Bailey .25 .10
458 Jeff Newman .25 .10
459 Charlie Spikes .25 .10
460 Jim Hunter 2.50 1.00
461 Rob Andrews DP .15 .06
462 Rogelio Moret .25 .10
463 Kevin Bell .25 .10
464 Jerry Grote .25 .10
465 Hal McRae .60 .24
466 Dennis Blair .25 .10
467 Alvin Dark MG .60 .24
468 Warren Cromartie RC .60 .24
469 Rick Cerone .60 .24
470 J.R. Richard .60 .24
471 Roy Smalley .60 .24
472 Ron Reed .25 .10
473 Bill Buckner .60 .24
474 Jim Slaton .25 .10
475 Gary Matthews .60 .24
476 Bill Stein .25 .10
477 Doug Capilla .25 .10
478 Jerry Remy .25 .10
479 St. Louis Cardinals 1.25 .25
Team Card CL
480 Ron LeFlore .60 .24
481 Jackson Todd .25 .10
482 Rick Miller .25 .10
483 Ken Macha RC .25 .10
484 Jim Norris .25 .10
485 Chris Chambliss .60 .24
486 John Curtis .25 .10
487 Jim Tyrone .25 .10
488 Dan Spillner .25 .10
489 Rudy Meoli .25 .10
490 Amos Otis .60 .24
491 Scott McGregor .60 .24
492 Jim Sundberg .60 .24
493 Steve Renko .25 .10
494 Chuck Tanner MG .60 .24
495 Dave Cash .25 .10
496 Jim Clancy DP .15 .06
497 Glenn Adams .25 .10
498 Joe Sambito .25 .10
499 Seattle Mariners 1.25 .25
Team Card CL
500 George Foster 1.25 .50
501 Dave Roberts .25 .10
502 Pat Rockett .25 .10
503 Ike Hampton .25 .10
504 Roger Freed .25 .10
505 Felix Millan .25 .10
506 Ron Blomberg .25 .10
507 Willie Crawford .25 .10
508 Johnny Oates .60 .24
509 Brent Strom .25 .10
510 Willie Stargell 2.50 1.00
511 Frank Duffy .25 .10
512 Larry Herndon .25 .10
513 Barry Foote .25 .10
514 Rob Sperring .25 .10
515 Tim Corcoran .25 .10
516 Gary Beare .25 .10
517 Andres Mora .25 .10
518 Tommy Boggs DP .15 .06
519 Brian Downing .60 .24
520 Larry Hisle .25 .10
521 Steve Staggs .25 .10
522 Dick Williams MG .60 .24
523 Donnie Moore RC .25 .10
524 Bernie Carbo .25 .10
525 Jerry Terrell .25 .10
526 Cincinnati Reds 1.25 .25
Team Card CL
527 Vic Correll .25 .10
528 Rob Picciolo .25 .10
529 Paul Hartzell .25 .10
530 Dave Winfield 4.00 1.60
531 Tom Underwood .25 .10
532 Skip Jutze .25 .10
533 Sandy Alomar .60 .24
534 Wilbur Howard .25 .10
535 Checklist 485-605 1.25 .25
536 Roric Harrison .25 .10
537 Bruce Bochte .25 .10
538 Johnny LeMaster .25 .10
539 Vic Davalillo DP .15 .06
540 Steve Carlton 4.00 1.60
541 Larry Cox .25 .10
542 Tim Johnson .25 .10
543 Larry Harlow DP .15 .06
544 Len Randle DP .15 .06
545 Bill Campbell .25 .10
546 Ted Martinez .25 .10
547 John Scott .25 .10
548 Billy Hunter DP MG .15 .06
549 Joe Kerrigan .25 .10
550 John Mayberry .60 .24
551 Atlanta Braves 1.25 .25
Team Card CL
552 Francisco Barrios .25 .10
553 Terry Puhl .60 .24
554 Joe Coleman .25 .10
555 Butch Wynegar .25 .10
556 Ed Armbrister .25 .10
557 Tony Solaita .25 .10
558 Paul Mitchell .25 .10
559 Phil Mankowski .25 .10
560 Dave Parker 1.25 .50
561 Charlie Williams .25 .10
562 Glenn Burke .25 .10
563 Dave Rader .25 .10
564 Mick Kelleher .25 .10
565 Jerry Koosman .60 .24
566 Merv Rettenmund .25 .10
567 Dick Drago .25 .10
568 Tom Hutton .25 .10
569 Lary Sorensen .25 .10
570 Dave Kingman 1.25 .50
571 Buck Martinez .25 .10
572 Rick Wise .25 .10
573 Luis Gomez .25 .10
574 Bob Lemon MG 1.25 .50
575 Pat Dobson .25 .10
576 Sam Mejias .25 .10
577 Oakland A's 1.25 .25
Team Card CL
578 Buzz Capra .25 .10
579 Rance Mulliniks .25 .10
580 Rod Carew 4.00 1.60
581 Lynn McGlothen .25 .10
582 Fran Healy .25 .10
583 George Medich .25 .10
584 John Hale .25 .10
585 Woodie Fryman DP .15 .06
586 Ed Goodson .25 .10
587 John Urrea .25 .10
588 Jim Mason .25 .10
589 Bob Knepper .25 .10
590 Bobby Murcer .60 .24
591 George Zeber .25 .10
592 Bob Apodaca .25 .10
593 Dave Skaggs .25 .10
594 Dave Freisleben .25 .10
595 Sixto Lezcano .25 .10
596 Gary Wheelock .25 .10
597 Steve Dillard .25 .10
598 Eddie Solomon .25 .10
599 Gary Woods .25 .10
600 Frank Tanana .60 .24
601 Gene Mauch MG .60 .24
602 Eric Soderholm .25 .10
603 Will McEnaney .25 .10
604 Earl Williams .25 .10
605 Rick Rhoden .60 .24
606 Pittsburgh Pirates 1.25 .25
Team Card CL
607 Fernando Arroyo .25 .10
608 Johnny Grubb .25 .10
609 John Denny .25 .10
610 Garry Maddox .60 .24
611 Pat Scanlon .25 .10
612 Ken Henderson .25 .10
613 Marty Perez .25 .10
614 Joe Wallis .25 .10
615 Clay Carroll .25 .10
616 Pat Kelly .25 .10
617 Joe Nolan .25 .10
618 Tommy Helms .25 .10
619 Thad Bosley DP .15 .06
620 Willie Randolph 1.25 .50
621 Craig Swan DP .15 .06
622 Champ Summers .25 .10
623 Eduardo Rodriguez .25 .10
624 Gary Alexander DP .15 .06
625 Jose Cruz .60 .24
626 Toronto Blue Jays 1.25 .25
Team Card CL DP
627 David Johnson .25 .10
628 Ralph Garr .60 .24
629 Don Stanhouse .25 .10
630 Ron Cey 1.25 .50
631 Danny Ozark MG .25 .10
632 Rowland Office .25 .10
633 Tom Veryzer .25 .10
634 Len Barker .25 .10
635 Joe Rudi .60 .24
636 Jim Bibby .25 .10
637 Duffy Dyer .25 .10
638 Paul Splittorff .25 .10
639 Gene Clines .25 .10
640 Lee May DP .25 .10
641 Doug Rau .25 .10
642 Denny Doyle .25 .10
643 Tom House .25 .10
644 Jim Dwyer .25 .10
645 Mike Torrez .60 .24
646 Rick Auerbach DP .15 .06
647 Steve Dunning .25 .10
648 Gary Thomasson .25 .10
649 Moose Haas .25 .10
650 Cesar Cedeno .60 .24
651 Doug Rader .25 .10
652 Checklist 606-726 1.25 .25
653 Ron Hodges DP .15 .06
654 Pepe Frias .25 .10
655 Lyman Bostock .60 .24
656 Dave Garcia MG .25 .10
657 Bombo Rivera .25 .10
658 Manny Sanguillen .60 .24
659 Texas Rangers 1.25 .25
Team Card CL
660 Jason Thompson .60 .24
661 Grant Jackson .25 .10
662 Paul Dade .25 .10
663 Paul Reuschel .25 .10
664 Fred Stanley .25 .10
665 Dennis Leonard .60 .24
666 Billy Smith RC .25 .10
667 Jeff Byrd .25 .10
668 Dusty Baker 1.25 .50
669 Pete Falcone .25 .10
670 Jim Rice 1.25 .50
671 Gary Lavelle .25 .10
672 Don Kessinger .60 .24
673 Steve Brye .25 .10
674 Ray Knight RC 2.50 1.00
675 Jay Johnstone .60 .24
676 Bob Myrick .25 .10
677 Ed Herrmann .25 .10
678 Tom Burgmeier .25 .10
679 Wayne Garrett .25 .10
680 Vida Blue .60 .24
681 Rob Belloir .25 .10
682 Ken Brett .25 .10
683 Mike Champion .25 .10
684 Ralph Houk MG .60 .24
685 Frank Taveras .25 .10
686 Gaylord Perry 2.50 1.00
687 Julio Cruz RC .25 .10
688 George Mitterwald .25 .10
689 Cleveland Indians 1.25 .25
Team Card CL
690 Mickey Rivers .60 .24
691 Ross Grimsley .25 .10
692 Ken Reitz .25 .10
693 Lamar Johnson .25 .10
694 Elias Sosa .25 .10
695 Dwight Evans 1.25 .50
696 Steve Mingori .25 .10
697 Roger Metzger .25 .10
698 Juan Bernhardt .25 .10
699 Jackie Brown .25 .10
700 Johnny Bench 8.00 3.20
701 Tom Hume .60 .24
Larry Landreth
Steve McCatty
Bruce Taylor
702 Bill Nahorodny .60 .24
Kevin Pasley
Rick Sweet
Don Werner
703 Larry Andersen 5.00 2.00
Tim Jones
Mickey Mahler
Jack Morris RC DP
704 Garth Iorg 8.00 3.20
Dave Oliver
Sam Perlozzo
Lou Whitaker RC
705 Dave Bergman 1.25 .50
Miguel Dilone
Clint Hurdle
Willie Norwood
706 Wayne Cage .60 .24
Ted Cox
Pat Putnam
Dave Revering
707 Mickey Klutts 80.00 32.00
Paul Molitor RC
Alan Trammell RC
U.L. Washington
708 Bo Diaz 4.00 1.60
Dale Murphy
Lance Parrish RC
Ernie Whitt
709 Steve Burke .60 .24
Matt Keough
Lance Rautzhan
Dan Schatzeder
710 Dell Alston 1.25 .50
Rick Bosetti
Mike Easler RC
Keith Smith
711 Cardell Camper .25 .10
Dennis Lamp
Craig Mitchell
Roy Thomas DP
712 Bobby Valentine .60 .24
713 Bob Davis .25 .10
714 Mike Anderson .25 .10
715 Jim Kaat 1.25 .50
716 Clarence Gaston .60 .24
717 Nelson Briles .25 .10
718 Ron Jackson .25 .10
719 Randy Elliott .25 .10
720 Fergie Jenkins 2.50 1.00
721 Billy Martin MG 1.25 .50
722 Pete Broberg .25 .10
723 John Wockenfuss .25 .10
724 Kansas City Royals 1.25 .25
Team Card CL
725 Kurt Bevacqua .25 .10
726 Wilbur Wood 1.25 .30

1978 Topps Team Checklist Sheet

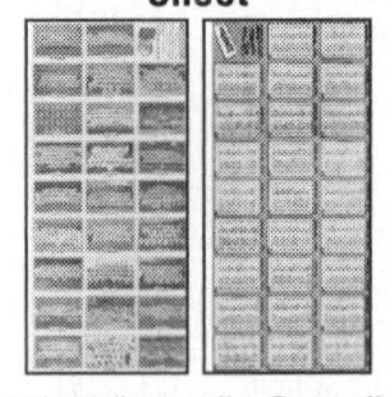

As part of a mail-away offer, Topps offered all 26 team checklist cards on an uncut sheet. These cards enabled the collector to have an easy reference for which card(s) he/she needed to finish their sets. When cut from the sheet, all cards measure the standard size.

NM Ex
1 Team Checklist Sheet 15.00 6.00

1978 Topps Zest

This set of five standard-size cards is very similar to the 1978 Topps regular issue. Although the cards were produced by Topps, they were used in a promotion for Zest Soap. The sponsor of the set, Zest Soap, is not mentioned anywhere on the cards. The card numbers are different and the backs are written in English and Spanish. By the choice of players in this small set, Zest appears to have been targeting the Hispanic community. Each player's card number in the regular 1978 Topps set is also given. A different photo was used for Montanez, showing his head and shoulders as a New York Met rather than as an Atlanta Brave in a batting stance as shown on Willie's Topps regular card.

NM Ex
COMPLETE SET (5) 6.00 2.40
1 Joaquin Andujar 1.50 .60
2 Bert Campaneris 2.00 .80
3 Ed Figueroa 1.00 .40
4 Willie Montanez 1.50 .60
different pose, New York Mets
5 Manny Mota 1.50 .60

1979 Topps

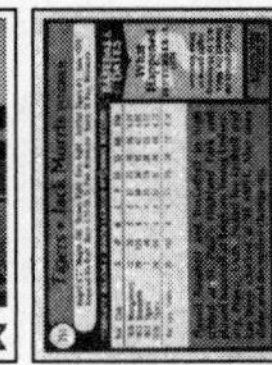

The cards in this 726-card set measure 2 1/2" by 3 1/2". Topps continued with the same number of cards as in 1978. As in previous years, this set was released in many different formats, among them are 12-card wax packs and 39-card rack packs. Various series spotlight League Leaders (1-8), "Season and Career Record Holders" (411-418), "Record Breakers" (201-206), and one "Prospects" card for each team (701-726). Team cards feature a checklist on back of that team's players in the set and a small picture of the manager on the front of the card. There are 66 cards that were double printed and these are noted in the checklist by the abbreviation DP. Bump Wills (369) was initially depicted in a Ranger uniform but with a Blue Jays affiliation; later printings correctly labeled him with Texas. The set price includes either Wills card. The key Rookie Cards in this set are Pedro Guerrero, Carney Lansford, Ozzie Smith, Bob Welch and Willie Wilson. Cards numbered 23 or lower, which feature Phillies or Yankees and do not follow the numbering checklisted below, are not necessarily error cards. They are undoubtedly Burger King cards, separate sets for each team with their own pricing and mass distribution.

NM Ex
COMPLETE SET (726) 175.00 70.00
COMMON CARD (1-726) .25 .10
COMMON CARD DP .15 .06
1 Rod Carew 2.50 .50
Dave Parker LL
2 Jim Rice 1.00 .40
George Foster LL
3 Jim Rice 1.00 .40
George Foster LL
4 Ron LeFlore .50 .20
Omar Moreno LL
5 Ron Guidry .50 .20
Gaylord Perry LL
6 Nolan Ryan 5.00 2.00
J.R. Richard LL
7 Ron Guidry .50 .20
Craig Swan LL
8 Rich Gossage 1.00 .40
Rollie Fingers LL
9 Dave Campbell .25 .10
10 Lee May .50 .20
11 Marc Hill .25 .10
12 Dick Drago .25 .10
13 Paul Dade .25 .10
14 Rafael Landestoy .25 .10
15 Ross Grimsley .25 .10
16 Fred Stanley .25 .10
17 Donnie Moore .25 .10
18 Tony Solaita .25 .10
19 Larry Gura DP .15 .06
20 Joe Morgan DP 2.00 .80
21 Kevin Kobel .25 .10
22 Mike Jorgensen .25 .10
23 Terry Forster .25 .10
24 Paul Molitor 12.00 4.80
25 Steve Carlton 3.00 1.20
26 Jamie Quirk .25 .10
27 Dave Goltz .25 .10
28 Steve Brye .25 .10
29 Rick Langford .25 .10
30 Dave Winfield 4.00 1.60
31 Tom House DP .15 .06
32 Jerry Mumphrey .25 .10
33 Dave Rozema .25 .10
34 Rob Andrews .25 .10
35 Ed Figueroa .25 .10
36 Alan Ashby .25 .10
37 Joe Kerrigan DP .15 .06
38 Bernie Carbo .25 .10
39 Dale Murphy 3.00 1.20
40 Dennis Eckersley 2.00 .80
41 Twins Team CL 1.00 .20
Gene Mauch MG
42 Ron Blomberg .25 .10
43 Wayne Twitchell .25 .10
44 Kurt Bevacqua .25 .10
45 Al Hrabosky .25 .10
46 Ron Hodges .25 .10
47 Fred Norman .25 .10
48 Merv Rettenmund .25 .10
49 Vern Ruhle .25 .10
50 Steve Garvey DP 1.00 .40
51 Ray Fosse DP .15 .06
52 Randy Lerch .25 .10
53 Mick Kelleher .25 .10
54 Dell Alston DP .15 .06
55 Willie Stargell 2.00 .80
56 John Hale .25 .10
57 Eric Rasmussen .25 .10
58 Bob Randall DP .15 .06
59 John Denny DP .25 .10
60 Mickey Rivers .50 .20
61 Bo Diaz .25 .10
62 Randy Moffitt .25 .10
63 Jack Brohamer .25 .10
64 Tom Underwood .25 .10
65 Mark Belanger .50 .20
66 Tigers Team CL 1.00 .20
Les Moss MG
67 Jim Mason DP .15 .06
68 Joe Niekro DP .25 .10
69 Elliott Maddox .25 .10
70 John Candelaria .50 .20
71 Brian Downing .50 .20
72 Steve Mingori .25 .10
73 Ken Henderson .25 .10
74 Shane Rawley .25 .10
75 Steve Yeager .50 .20
76 Warren Cromartie .50 .20
77 Dan Briggs DP .15 .06
78 Elias Sosa .25 .10
79 Ted Cox .25 .10
80 Jason Thompson .50 .20
81 Roger Erickson .25 .10
82 Mets Team CL 1.00 .20
Joe Torre MG
83 Fred Kendall .25 .10
84 Greg Minton .25 .10
85 Gary Matthews .50 .20
86 Rodney Scott .25 .10
87 Pete Falcone .25 .10
88 Bob Molinaro .25 .10
89 Dick Tidrow .25 .10
90 Bob Boone 1.00 .40
91 Terry Crowley .25 .10
92 Jim Bibby .25 .10
93 Phil Mankowski .25 .10
94 Len Barker .25 .10
95 Robin Yount 5.00 2.00
96 Indians Team CL 1.00 .20
Jeff Torborg
97 Sam Mejias .25 .10
98 Ray Burris .25 .10
99 John Wathan .50 .20
100 Tom Seaver DP 4.00 1.60
101 Roy Howell .25 .10
102 Mike Anderson .25 .10
103 Jim Todd .25 .10
104 Johnny Oates DP .25 .10
105 Rick Camp DP .15 .06
106 Frank Duffy .25 .10
107 Jesus Alou DP .15 .06
108 Eduardo Rodriguez .25 .10
109 Joel Youngblood .25 .10
110 Vida Blue .50 .20
111 Roger Freed .25 .10
112 Phillies Team 1.00 .20
Danny Ozark MG
113 Pete Redfern .25 .10
114 Cliff Johnson .25 .10
115 Nolan Ryan 20.00 8.00
116 Ozzie Smith RC 80.00 32.00
117 Grant Jackson .25 .10
118 Bud Harrelson .50 .20
119 Don Stanhouse .25 .10
120 Jim Sundberg .50 .20
121 Checklist 1-121 DP .50 .10
122 Mike Paxton .25 .10
123 Lou Whitaker 2.50 1.00
124 Dan Schatzeder .25 .10
125 Rick Burleson .25 .10
126 Doug Bair .25 .10
127 Thad Bosley .25 .10
128 Ted Martinez .25 .10
129 Marty Pattin DP .15 .06
130 Bob Watson DP .25 .10
131 Jim Clancy .25 .10
132 Rowland Office .25 .10
133 Bill Castro .25 .10
134 Alan Bannister .25 .10
135 Bobby Murcer .50 .20
136 Jim Kaat .50 .20
137 Larry Wolfe DP .15 .06
138 Mark Lee RC .25 .10
139 Luis Pujols .25 .10
140 Don Gullett .50 .20
141 Tom Paciorek .50 .20
142 Charlie Williams .25 .10
143 Tony Scott .25 .10
144 Sandy Alomar .25 .10
145 Rick Rhoden .25 .10
146 Duane Kuiper .25 .10
147 Dave Hamilton .25 .10
148 Bruce Boisclair .25 .10
149 Manny Sarmiento .25 .10
150 Wayne Cage .25 .10
151 John Hiller .25 .10
152 Rick Cerone .25 .10
153 Dennis Lamp .25 .10
154 Jim Gantner DP .25 .10
155 Dwight Evans 1.00 .40
156 Buddy Solomon .25 .10
157 U.L. Washington UER .25 .10
(Sic, bats left,
should be right)
158 Joe Sambito .25 .10
159 Roy White .50 .20
160 Mike Flanagan 1.00 .40
161 Barry Foote .25 .10
162 Tom Johnson .25 .10
163 Glenn Burke .25 .10
164 Mickey Lolich .50 .20
165 Frank Taveras .25 .10
166 Leon Roberts .25 .10
167 Roger Metzger DP .15 .06
168 Dave Freisleben .25 .10
169 Bill Nahorodny .25 .10
170 Don Sutton 2.00 .80
171 Gene Clines .25 .10
172 Mike Bruhert .25 .10
173 John Lowenstein .25 .10
174 Rick Auerbach .25 .10
175 George Hendrick 1.00 .40
176 Aurelio Rodriguez .25 .10
177 Ron Reed .25 .10
178 Alvis Woods .25 .10
179 Jim Beattie DP .15 .06
180 Larry Hisle .25 .10
181 Mike Garman .25 .10
182 Tim Johnson .25 .10
183 Paul Splittorff .25 .10
184 Darrel Chaney .25 .10
185 Mike Torrez .50 .20
186 Eric Soderholm .25 .10
187 Mark Lemongello .25 .10
188 Pat Kelly .25 .10
189 Eddie Whitson RC .25 .10
190 Ron Cey .50 .20
191 Mike Norris .25 .10
192 Cardinals Team CL 1.00 .20
Ken Boyer MG
193 Glenn Adams .25 .10
194 Randy Jones .25 .10
195 Bill Madlock .50 .20
196 Steve Kemp DP .25 .10
197 Bob Apodaca .25 .10
198 Johnny Grubb .25 .10
199 Larry Milbourne .25 .10
200 Johnny Bench DP 5.00 2.00
201 Mike Edwards RB .25 .10
202 Ron Guidry RB .50 .20
203 J.R. Richard RB .25 .10
204 Pete Rose RB 5.00 2.00
205 John Stearns RB .25 .10
206 Sammy Stewart RB .25 .10
207 Dave Lemanczyk .25 .10
208 Clarence Gaston .25 .10
209 Reggie Cleveland .25 .10

210 Larry Bowa .50 .20
211 Denny Martinez 2.00 .80
212 Carney Lansford RC 1.00 .40
213 Bill Travers .25 .10
214 Red Sox Team CL 1.00 .20
Don Zimmer MG
215 Willie McCovey 2.50 1.00
216 Wilbur Wood .25 .10
217 Steve Dillard .25 .10
218 Dennis Leonard .50 .20
219 Roy Smalley .50 .20
220 Cesar Geronimo .25 .10
221 Jesse Jefferson .25 .10
222 Bob Beall .25 .10
223 Kent Tekulve .50 .20
224 Dave Revering .25 .10
225 Goose Gossage 1.00 .40
226 Ron Pruitt .25 .10
227 Steve Stone .50 .20
228 Vic Davalillo .25 .10
229 Doug Flynn .25 .10
230 Bob Forsch .25 .10
231 John Wockenfuss .25 .10
232 Jimmy Sexton .25 .10
233 Paul Mitchell .25 .10
234 Toby Harrah .50 .20
235 Steve Rogers .25 .10
236 Jim Dwyer .25 .10
237 Billy Smith .25 .10
238 Balor Moore .25 .10
239 Willie Horton .50 .20
240 Rick Reuschel .50 .20
241 Checklist 122-242 DP .50 .10
242 Pablo Torrealba .25 .10
243 Buck Martinez DP .15 .06
244 Pirates Team CL 1.00 .20
Chuck Tanner MG
245 Jeff Burroughs .50 .20
246 Darrell Jackson .25 .10
247 Tucker Ashford DP .15 .06
248 Pete LaCock .25 .10
249 Paul Thormodsgard .25 .10
250 Willie Randolph .50 .20
251 Jack Morris 2.00 .80
252 Bob Stinson .25 .10
253 Rick Wise .25 .10
254 Luis Gomez .25 .10
255 Tommy John 1.00 .40
256 Mike Sadek .25 .10
257 Adrian Devine .25 .10
258 Mike Phillips .25 .10
259 Reds Team CL 1.00 .20
Sparky Anderson MG
260 Richie Zisk .25 .10
261 Mario Guerrero .25 .10
262 Nelson Briles .25 .10
263 Oscar Gamble .50 .20
264 Don Robinson RC .25 .10
265 Don Money .25 .10
266 Jim Willoughby .25 .10
267 Joe Rudi .50 .20
268 Julio Gonzalez .25 .10
269 Woodie Fryman .25 .10
270 Butch Hobson .50 .20
271 Rawly Eastwick .25 .10
272 Tim Corcoran .25 .10
273 Jerry Terrell .25 .10
274 Willie Norwood .25 .10
275 Junior Moore .25 .10
276 Jim Colborn .25 .10
277 Tom Grieve .50 .20
278 Andy Messersmith .50 .20
279 Jerry Grote DP .15 .06
280 Andre Thornton .50 .20
281 Vic Correll DP .15 .06
282 Blue Jays Team CL .50 .10
Roy Hartsfield MG
283 Ken Kravec .25 .10
284 Johnnie LeMaster .25 .10
285 Bobby Bonds 1.00 .40
286 Duffy Dyer .25 .10
287 Andres Mora .25 .10
288 Milt Wilcox .25 .10
289 Jose Cruz 1.00 .40
290 Dave Lopes .50 .20
291 Tom Griffin .25 .10
292 Don Reynolds .25 .10
293 Jerry Garvin .25 .10
294 Pepe Frias .25 .10
295 Mitchell Page .25 .10
296 Preston Hanna .25 .10
297 Ted Sizemore .25 .10
298 Rich Gale .25 .10
299 Steve Ontiveros .25 .10
300 Rod Carew 3.00 1.20
301 Tom Hume .25 .10
302 Braves Team CL 1.00 .20
Bobby Cox MG
303 Lary Sorensen DP .15 .06
304 Steve Swisher .25 .10
305 Willie Montanez .25 .10
306 Floyd Bannister .25 .10
307 Larvell Blanks .25 .10
308 Bert Blyleven 1.00 .40
309 Ralph Garr .50 .20
310 Thurman Munson 3.00 1.20
311 Gary Lavelle .25 .10
312 Bob Robertson .25 .10
313 Dyar Miller .25 .10
314 Larry Harlow .25 .10
315 Jon Matlack .25 .10
316 Milt May .25 .10
317 Jose Cardenal .50 .20
318 Bob Welch RC 2.00 .80
319 Wayne Garrett .25 .10
320 Carl Yastrzemski 5.00 2.00
321 Gaylord Perry 2.00 .80
322 Danny Goodwin .25 .10
323 Lynn McGlothen .25 .10
324 Mike Tyson .25 .10
325 Cecil Cooper .50 .20
326 Pedro Borbon .25 .10
327 Art Howe DP .25 .10
328 A's Team CL 1.00 .20
Jack McKeon MG
329 Joe Coleman .25 .10
330 George Brett 10.00 4.00
331 Mickey Mahler .25 .10
332 Gary Alexander .25 .10
333 Chet Lemon .50 .20
334 Craig Swan .25 .10
335 Chris Chambliss .50 .20
336 Bobby Thompson .25 .10
337 John Montague .25 .10
338 Vic Harris .25 .10
339 Ron Jackson .25 .10
340 Jim Palmer 2.50 1.00
341 Willie Upshaw .50 .20
342 Dave Roberts .25 .10
343 Ed Glynn .25 .10
344 Jerry Royster .25 .10
345 Tug McGraw .50 .20
346 Bill Buckner .50 .20
347 Doug Rau .25 .10
348 Andre Dawson 3.00 1.20
349 Jim Wright .25 .10
350 Garry Templeton .50 .20
351 Wayne Nordhagen DP .15 .06
352 Steve Renko .25 .10
353 Checklist 243-363 1.00 .20
354 Bill Bonham .25 .10
355 Lee Mazzilli .25 .10
356 Giants Team CL 1.00 .20
Joe Altobelli MG
357 Jerry Augustine .25 .10
358 Alan Trammell 3.00 1.20
359 Dan Spillner DP .15 .06
360 Amos Otis .50 .20
361 Tom Dixon .25 .10
362 Mike Cubbage .25 .10
363 Craig Skok .25 .10
364 Gene Richards .25 .10
365 Sparky Lyle .50 .20
366 Juan Bernhardt .25 .10
367 Dave Skaggs .25 .10
368 Don Aase .25 .10
369A Bump Wills ERR 3.00 1.20
(Blue Jays)
369B Bump Wills COR 3.00 1.20
(Rangers)
370 Dave Kingman 1.00 .40
371 Jeff Holly .25 .10
372 Lamar Johnson .25 .10
373 Lance Rautzhan .25 .10
374 Ed Herrmann .25 .10
375 Bill Campbell .25 .10
376 Gorman Thomas .50 .20
377 Paul Moskau .25 .10
378 Rob Picciolo DP .15 .06
379 Dale Murray .25 .10
380 John Mayberry .50 .20
381 Astros Team CL 1.00 .20
Bill Virdon MG
382 Jerry Martin .25 .10
383 Phil Garner .50 .20
384 Tommy Boggs .25 .10
385 Dan Ford .25 .10
386 Francisco Barrios .25 .10
387 Gary Thomasson .25 .10
388 Jack Billingham .25 .10
389 Joe Zdeb .25 .10
390 Rollie Fingers 2.00 .80
391 Al Oliver .50 .20
392 Doug Ault .25 .10
393 Scott McGregor .50 .20
394 Randy Stein .25 .10
395 Dave Cash .25 .10
396 Bill Plummer .25 .10
397 Sergio Ferrer .25 .10
398 Ivan DeJesus .25 .10
399 David Clyde .25 .10
400 Jim Rice 1.00 .40
401 Ray Knight .50 .20
402 Paul Hartzell .25 .10
403 Tim Foli .25 .10
404 White Sox Team CL 1.00 .20
Don Kessinger MG
405 Butch Wynegar DP .15 .06
406 Joe Wallis DP .15 .06
407 Pete Vuckovich .50 .20
408 Charlie Moore DP .15 .06
409 Willie Wilson RC 1.00 .40
410 Darrell Evans 1.00 .40
411 George Sisler ATL 2.50 1.00
Ty Cobb
412 Hack Wilson ATL 2.50 1.00
Hank Aaron
413 Roger Maris ATL 4.00 1.60
Hank Aaron
414 Rogers Hornsby ATL 2.50 1.00
Ty Cobb
415 Lou Brock ATL 1.00 .40
416 Jack Chesbro ATL .50 .20
Cy Young
417 Nolan Ryan ATL DP 5.00 2.00
Walter Johnson
418 D.Leonard ATL DP .25 .10
Walter Johnson
419 Dick Ruthven .25 .10
420 Ken Griffey Sr. .50 .20
421 Doug DeCinces .50 .20
422 Ruppert Jones .25 .10
423 Bob Montgomery .25 .10
424 Angels Team CL 1.00 .20
Jim Fregosi MG
425 Rick Manning .25 .10
426 Chris Speier .25 .10
427 Andy Replogle .25 .10
428 Bobby Valentine .50 .20
429 John Urrea DP .15 .06
430 Dave Parker .50 .20
431 Glenn Borgmann .25 .10
432 Dave Heaverlo .25 .10
433 Larry Biittner .25 .10
434 Ken Clay .25 .10
435 Gene Tenace .50 .20
436 Hector Cruz .25 .10
437 Rick Williams .25 .10
438 Horace Speed .25 .10
439 Frank White .50 .20
440 Rusty Staub 1.00 .40
441 Lee Lacy .25 .10
442 Doyle Alexander .25 .10
443 Bruce Bochte .25 .10
444 Aurelio Lopez .25 .10
445 Steve Henderson .25 .10
446 Jim Lonborg .50 .20
447 Manny Sanguillen .50 .20
448 Moose Haas .25 .10
449 Bombo Rivera .25 .10
450 Dave Concepcion 1.00 .40
451 Royals Team CL 1.00 .20
Whitey Herzog MG
452 Jerry Morales .25 .10
453 Chris Knapp .25 .10
454 Len Randle .25 .10
455 Bill Lee DP .15 .06
456 Chuck Baker .25 .10
457 Bruce Sutter .50 .20
458 Jim Essian .25 .10
459 Sid Monge .25 .10
460 Graig Nettles 1.00 .40
461 Jim Barr DP .15 .06
462 Otto Velez .25 .10
463 Steve Comer .25 .10
464 Joe Nolan .25 .10
465 Reggie Smith .50 .20
466 Mark Littell .25 .10
467 Don Kessinger DP .25 .10
468 Stan Bahnsen DP .15 .06
469 Lance Parrish 1.00 .40
470 Garry Maddox DP .25 .10
471 Joaquin Andujar .50 .20
472 Craig Kusick .25 .10
473 Dave Roberts .25 .10
474 Dick Davis .25 .10
475 Dan Driessen .25 .10
476 Tom Poquette .25 .10
477 Bob Grich .50 .20
478 Juan Beniquez .25 .10
479 Padres Team CL 1.00 .20
Roger Craig MG
480 Fred Lynn .50 .20
481 Skip Lockwood .25 .10
482 Craig Reynolds .25 .10
483 Checklist 364-484 DP .50 .10
484 Rick Waits .25 .10
485 Bucky Dent .50 .20
486 Bob Knepper .25 .10
487 Miguel Dilone .25 .10
488 Bob Owchinko .25 .10
489 Larry Cox UER .25 .10
(Photo actually
Dave Rader)
490 Al Cowens .25 .10
491 Tippy Martinez .25 .10
492 Bob Bailor .25 .10
493 Larry Christenson .25 .10
494 Jerry White .25 .10
495 Tony Perez 2.00 .80
496 Barry Bonnell DP .15 .06
497 Glenn Abbott .25 .10
498 Rich Chiles .25 .10
499 Rangers Team CL 1.00 .20
Pat Corrales MG
500 Ron Guidry .50 .20
501 Junior Kennedy .25 .10
502 Steve Braun .25 .10
503 Terry Humphrey .25 .10
504 Larry McWilliams .25 .10
505 Ed Kranepool .25 .10
506 John D'Acquisto .25 .10
507 Tony Armas .50 .20
508 Charlie Hough .50 .20
509 Mario Mendoza UER .25 .10
(Career BA .278,
should say .204)
510 Ted Simmons 1.00 .40
511 Paul Reuschel DP .15 .06
512 Jack Clark .50 .20
513 Dave Johnson .50 .20
514 Mike Proly .25 .10
515 Enos Cabell .25 .10
516 Champ Summers DP .15 .06
517 Al Bumbry .50 .20
518 Jim Umbarger .25 .10
519 Ben Oglivie .50 .20
520 Gary Carter 2.00 .80
521 Sam Ewing .25 .10
522 Ken Holtzman .50 .20
523 John Milner .25 .10
524 Tom Burgmeier .25 .10
525 Freddie Patek .25 .10
526 Dodgers Team CL 1.00 .20
Tom Lasorda MG
527 Lerrin LaGrow .25 .10
528 Wayne Gross DP .15 .06
529 Brian Asselstine .25 .10
530 Frank Tanana .50 .20
531 Fernando Gonzalez .25 .10
532 Buddy Schultz .25 .10
533 Leroy Stanton .25 .10
534 Ken Forsch .25 .10
535 Ellis Valentine .25 .10
536 Jerry Reuss .50 .20
537 Tom Veryzer .25 .10
538 Mike Ivie DP .15 .06
539 John Ellis .25 .10
540 Greg Luzinski .50 .20
541 Jim Slaton .25 .10
542 Rick Bosetti .25 .10
543 Kiko Garcia .25 .10
544 Fergie Jenkins 2.00 .80
545 John Stearns .25 .10
546 Bill Russell .50 .20
547 Clint Hurdle .25 .10
548 Enrique Romo .25 .10
549 Bob Bailey .25 .10
550 Sal Bando .50 .20
551 Cubs Team CL 1.00 .20
Herman Franks MG
552 Jose Morales .25 .10
553 Denny Walling .25 .10
554 Matt Keough .25 .10
555 Biff Pocoroba .25 .10
556 Mike Lum .25 .10
557 Ken Brett .25 .10
558 Jay Johnstone .50 .20
559 Greg Pryor .25 .10
560 John Montefusco .50 .20
561 Ed Ott .25 .10
562 Dusty Baker 1.00 .40
563 Roy Thomas .25 .10
564 Jerry Turner .25 .10
565 Rico Carty .50 .20
566 Nino Espinosa .25 .10
567 Richie Hebner .50 .20
568 Carlos Lopez .25 .10
569 Bob Sykes .25 .10
570 Cesar Cedeno .50 .20
571 Darrell Porter .50 .20
572 Rod Gilbreath .25 .10
573 Jim Kern .25 .10
574 Claudell Washington .50 .20
575 Luis Tiant .50 .20
576 Mike Parrott .25 .10
577 Brewers Team CL 1.00 .20
George Bamberger MG
578 Pete Broberg .25 .10
579 Greg Gross .25 .10
580 Ron Fairly .50 .20
581 Darold Knowles .25 .10
582 Paul Blair .50 .20
583 Julio Cruz .25 .10
584 Jim Rooker .25 .10
585 Hal McRae 1.00 .40
586 Bob Horner RC 1.00 .40
587 Ken Reitz .25 .10
588 Tom Murphy .25 .10
589 Terry Whitfield .25 .10
590 J.R. Richard .50 .20
591 Mike Hargrove .50 .20
592 Mike Krukow .25 .10
593 Rick Dempsey .50 .20
594 Bob Shirley .25 .10
595 Phil Niekro 2.00 .80
596 Jim Wohlford .25 .10
597 Bob Stanley .25 .10
598 Mark Wagner .25 .10
599 Jim Spencer .25 .10
600 George Foster .50 .20
601 Dave LaRoche .25 .10
602 Checklist 485-605 1.00 .20
603 Rudy May .25 .10
604 Jeff Newman .25 .10
605 Rick Monday DP .25 .10
606 Expos Team CL 1.00 .20
Dick Williams MG
607 Omar Moreno .25 .10
608 Dave McKay .25 .10
609 Silvio Martinez .25 .10
610 Mike Schmidt 8.00 3.20
611 Jim Norris .25 .10
612 Rick Honeycutt RC .50 .20
613 Mike Edwards .25 .10
614 Willie Hernandez .50 .20
615 Ken Singleton .50 .20
616 Billy Almon .25 .10
617 Terry Puhl .25 .10
618 Jerry Remy .25 .10
619 Ken Landreaux .50 .20
620 Bert Campaneris .50 .20
621 Pat Zachry .25 .10
622 Dave Collins .50 .20
623 Bob McClure .25 .10
624 Larry Herndon .25 .10
625 Mark Fidrych 2.00 .80
626 Yankees Team CL 1.00 .20
Bob Lemon MG
627 Gary Serum .25 .10
628 Del Unser .25 .10
629 Gene Garber .50 .20
630 Bake McBride .50 .20
631 Jorge Orta .25 .10
632 Don Kirkwood .25 .10
633 Rob Wilfong DP .15 .06
634 Paul Lindblad .25 .10
635 Don Baylor 1.00 .40
636 Wayne Garland .25 .10
637 Bill Robinson .50 .20
638 Al Fitzmorris .25 .10
639 Manny Trillo .25 .10
640 Eddie Murray 12.00 4.80
641 Bobby Castillo .25 .10
642 Wilbur Howard DP .15 .06
643 Tom Hausman .25 .10
644 Manny Mota .50 .20
645 George Scott DP .25 .10
646 Rick Sweet .25 .10
647 Bob Lacey .25 .10
648 Lou Piniella .50 .20
649 John Curtis .25 .10
650 Pete Rose 12.00 4.80
651 Mike Caldwell .25 .10
652 Stan Papi .25 .10
653 Warren Brusstar DP .15 .06
654 Rick Miller .25 .10
655 Jerry Koosman .50 .20
656 Hosken Powell .25 .10
657 George Medich .25 .10
658 Taylor Duncan .25 .10
659 Mariners Team CL 1.00 .20
Darrell Johnson MG
660 Ron LeFlore DP .25 .10
661 Bruce Kison .25 .10
662 Kevin Bell .25 .10
663 Mike Vail .25 .10
664 Doug Bird .25 .10
665 Lou Brock 2.50 1.00
666 Rich Dauer .25 .10
667 Don Hood .25 .10
668 Bill North .25 .10
669 Checklist 606-726 1.00 .20
670 Jim Hunter DP 1.00 .40
671 Joe Ferguson DP .15 .06
672 Ed Halicki .25 .10
673 Tom Hutton .25 .10
674 Dave Tomlin .25 .10
675 Tim McCarver 1.00 .40
676 Johnny Sutton .25 .10
677 Larry Parrish .50 .20
678 Geoff Zahn .25 .10
679 Derrel Thomas .25 .10
680 Carlton Fisk 3.00 1.20
681 John Henry Johnson .25 .10
682 Dave Chalk .25 .10
683 Dan Meyer DP .15 .06
684 Jamie Easterly DP .15 .06
685 Sixto Lezcano .25 .10
686 Ron Schueler DP .15 .06
687 Rennie Stennett .25 .10
688 Mike Willis .25 .10
689 Orioles Team CL 1.00 .20
Earl Weaver MG
690 Buddy Bell DP .25 .10
691 Dock Ellis DP .15 .06
692 Mickey Stanley .25 .10
693 Dave Rader .25 .10
694 Burt Hooton .50 .20
695 Keith Hernandez 1.00 .40
696 Andy Hassler .25 .10
697 Dave Bergman .25 .10
698 Bill Stein .25 .10
699 Hal Dues .25 .10
700 Reggie Jackson DP 5.00 2.00
701 Mark Corey .50 .20
John Flinn
Sammy Stewart
702 Joel Finch .50 .20
Garry Hancock
Allen Ripley
703 Jim Anderson .50 .20
Dave Frost
Bob Slater
704 Ross Baumgarten .50 .20
Mike Colbern
Mike Squires
705 Alfredo Griffin RC 1.00 .40
Tim Norrid
Dave Oliver
706 Dave Stegman .50 .20
Dave Tobik
Kip Young
707 Randy Bass RC 1.00 .40
Jim Gaudet
Randy McGilberry
708 Kevin Bass RC 1.00 .40
Eddie Romero
Ned Yost RC
709 Sam Perlozzo .50 .20
Rick Sofield
Kevin Stanfield
710 Brian Doyle .50 .20
Mike Heath
Dave Rajsich
711 Dwayne Murphy RC 1.00 .40
Bruce Robinson
Alan Wirth
712 Bud Anderson .50 .20
Greg Biercevicz
Byron McLaughlin
713 Danny Darwin RC 1.00 .40
Pat Putnam
Billy Sample
714 Victor Cruz .50 .20
Pat Kelly
Ernie Whitt
715 Bruce Benedict 1.00 .40
Glenn Hubbard RC
Larry Whisenton
716 Dave Geisel .50 .20
Karl Pagel
Scott Thompson
717 Mike LaCoss .50 .20
Ron Oester RC
Harry Spilman
718 Bruce Bochy .50 .20
Mike Fischlin
Don Pisker
719 Pedro Guerrero RC 1.00 .40
Rudy Law
Joe Simpson
720 Jerry Fry 1.00 .40
Jerry Pirtle
Scott Sanderson RC
721 Juan Berenguer .50 .20
Dwight Bernard
Dan Norman
722 Jim Morrison 1.00 .40
Lonnie Smith RC
Jim Wright
723 Dale Berra RC .50 .20
Eugenio Cotes
Ben Wiltbank
724 Tom Bruno 1.00 .40
George Frazier
Terry Kennedy RC
725 Jim Beswick .50 .20
Steve Mura
Broderick Perkins
726 Greg Johnston .50 .10
Joe Strain
John Tamargo

1979 Topps Comics

This 33 card (comic) set, which measures approximately 3" by 3 1/4", is rather plentiful in spite of the fact that it was originally touted as a limited edition "test" issue. This flimsy set has never been very popular with collectors. These waxy comics are numbered and are blank backed. Each comic also features an "Inside Baseball" tip in the lower right corner.

	NM	Ex
COMPLETE SET (33)	20.00	8.00
1 Eddie Murray	1.25	.50
2 Jim Rice	.30	.12
3 Carl Yastrzemski	1.00	.40
4 Nolan Ryan	4.00	1.60
5 Chet Lemon	.10	.04
6 Andre Thornton	.10	.04
7 Rusty Staub	.20	.08
8 Ron LeFlore	.10	.04
9 George Brett	3.00	1.20
10 Larry Hisle	.10	.04
11 Rod Carew	1.00	.40
12 Reggie Jackson	1.50	.60
13 Ron Guidry	.20	.08
14 Mitchell Page	.10	.04
15 Leon Roberts	.10	.04
16 Al Oliver	.20	.08
17 John Mayberry	.10	.04
18 Bob Horner	.20	.08
19 Phil Niekro	1.00	.40
20 Dave Kingman	.30	.12
21 Johnny Bench	1.25	.50
22 Tom Seaver	1.25	.50
23 J.R. Richard	.10	.04
24 Steve Garvey	.30	.12

25 Reggie Smith .10 .04
26 Ross Grimsley .10 .04
27 Craig Swan .10 .04
28 Pete Rose 1.50 .60
29 Dave Parker .20 .08
30 Ted Simmons .20 .08
31 Dave Winfield 1.00 .40
32 Jack Clark .20 .08
33 Vida Blue .10 .04

1979 Topps Team Checklist Sheet

As part of a mail-away offer, Topps offered all 26 1979 team cards checklist cards on an uncut sheet. These cards enabled the collector to have an easy reference for which card(s) he/she needed to finish their sets. When cut from the sheet, all cards measure the standard size.

NM Ex
1 Team Checklist Sheet 15.00 6.00

1980 Topps

The cards in this 726-card set measure the standard size. In 1980 Topps released another set of the same size and number of cards as the previous two years. Distribution for these cards included 15-card wax packs as well as 42-card rack packs. A special experiment in 1980 was the issuance of a 28-card cello pack with a three-pack of gum at the bottom so no cards would be damaged. As with those sets, Topps again produced 66 double-printed cards in the set; they are noted by DP in the checklist below. The player's name appears over the picture and his position and team are found in pennant design. Every card carries a facsimile autograph. Team cards feature a team checklist of players in the set on the back and the manager's name on the front. Cards 1-6 show Highlights (HL) of the 1979 season, cards 201-207 are League Leaders, and cards 661-686 feature American and National League rookie "Future Stars," one card for each team showing three young prospects. The key Rookie Card in this set is Rickey Henderson; other Rookie Cards included in this set are Dan Quisenberry, Dave Stieb and Rick Sutcliffe.

NM Ex
COMPLETE SET (726) 120.00 47.50
COMMON CARD (1-726) .25 .10
COMMON CARD DP .15 .06
1 Lou Brock HL 2.50 .50
Carl Yastrzemski
2 Willie McCovey HL .75 .30
3 Manny Mota HL .25 .10
4 Pete Rose HL 3.00 1.20
5 Garry Templeton HL .25 .10
6 Del Unser HL .25 .10
7 Mike Lum .25 .10
8 Craig Swan .25 .10
9 Steve Braun .25 .10
10 Dennis Martinez 1.25 .50
11 Jimmy Sexton .25 .10
12 John Curtis DP .15 .06
13 Ron Pruitt .25 .10
14 Dave Cash .25 .10
15 Bill Campbell .25 .10
16 Jerry Narron .25 .10
17 Bruce Sutter .75 .30
18 Ron Jackson .25 .10
19 Balor Moore .25 .10
20 Dan Ford .25 .10
21 Manny Sarmiento .25 .10
22 Pat Putnam .25 .10
23 Derrel Thomas .25 .10
24 Jim Slaton .25 .10
25 Lee Mazzilli .40 .16
26 Marty Pattin .25 .10
27 Del Unser .25 .10
28 Bruce Kison .25 .10
29 Mark Wagner .25 .10
30 Vida Blue .75 .30
31 Jay Johnstone .40 .16
32 Julio Cruz DP .15 .06
33 Tony Scott .25 .10
34 Jeff Newman DP .15 .06
35 Luis Tiant .40 .16
36 Rusty Torres .25 .10
37 Kiko Garcia .25 .10
38 Dan Spillner DP .15 .06
39 Rowland Office .25 .10
40 Carlton Fisk 2.00 .80
41 Rangers Team CL .75 .15
Pat Corrales MG
42 David Palmer .25 .10
43 Bombo Rivera .25 .10
44 Bill Fahey .25 .10
45 Frank White .75 .30
46 Rico Carty .40 .16
47 Bill Bonham DP .15 .06
48 Rick Miller .25 .10
49 Mario Guerrero .25 .10
50 J.R. Richard .40 .16
51 Joe Ferguson DP .15 .06
52 Warren Brusstar .25 .10
53 Ben Oglivie .40 .16
54 Dennis Lamp .25 .10
55 Bill Madlock .40 .16
56 Bobby Valentine .40 .16
57 Pete Vuckovich .25 .10
58 Doug Flynn .25 .10
59 Eddy Putman .25 .10
60 Bucky Dent .40 .16
61 Gary Serum .25 .10
62 Mike Ivie .25 .10
63 Bob Stanley .25 .10
64 Joe Nolan .25 .10
65 Al Bumbry .40 .16
66 Royals Team CL .75 .15
Jim Frey MG
67 Doyle Alexander .25 .10
68 Larry Harlow .25 .10
69 Rick Williams .25 .10
70 Gary Carter 1.25 .50
71 John Milner DP .15 .06
72 Fred Howard DP .15 .06
73 Dave Collins .25 .10
74 Sid Monge .25 .10
75 Bill Russell .40 .16
76 John Stearns .25 .10
77 Dave Stieb RC 1.25 .50
78 Ruppert Jones .25 .10
79 Bob Owchinko .25 .10
80 Ron LeFlore .40 .16
81 Ted Sizemore .25 .10
82 Astros Team CL .75 .15
Bill Virdon MG
83 Steve Trout .25 .10
84 Gary Lavelle .25 .10
85 Ted Simmons .40 .16
86 Dave Hamilton .25 .10
87 Pepe Frias .25 .10
88 Ken Landreaux .25 .10
89 Don Hood .25 .10
90 Manny Trillo .40 .16
91 Rick Dempsey .40 .16
92 Rick Rhoden .40 .16
93 Dave Roberts DP .15 .06
94 Neil Allen .40 .16
95 Cecil Cooper .40 .16
96 A's Team CL .75 .15
Jim Marshall MG
97 Bill Lee .40 .16
98 Jerry Terrell .25 .10
99 Victor Cruz .25 .10
100 Johnny Bench 4.00 1.60
101 Aurelio Lopez .25 .10
102 Rich Dauer .25 .10
103 Bill Caudill .25 .10
104 Manny Mota .40 .16
105 Frank Tanana .40 .16
106 Jeff Leonard RC .75 .30
107 Francisco Barrios .25 .10
108 Bob Horner .40 .16
109 Bill Travers .25 .10
110 Fred Lynn DP .40 .16
111 Bob Knepper .40 .16
112 White Sox Team CL .75 .15
Tony LaRussa MG
113 Geoff Zahn .25 .10
114 Juan Beniquez .25 .10
115 Sparky Lyle .40 .16
116 Larry Cox .25 .10
117 Dock Ellis .25 .10
118 Phil Garner .40 .16
119 Sammy Stewart .25 .10
120 Greg Luzinski .40 .16
121 Checklist 1-121 .75 .15
122 Dave Rosello DP .15 .06
123 Lynn Jones .25 .10
124 Dave Lemanczyk .25 .10
125 Tony Perez 1.25 .50
126 Dave Tomlin .25 .10
127 Gary Thomasson .25 .10
128 Tom Burgmeier .25 .10
129 Craig Reynolds .25 .10
130 Amos Otis .40 .16
131 Paul Mitchell .25 .10
132 Biff Pocoroba .25 .10
133 Jerry Turner .25 .10
134 Matt Keough .25 .10
135 Bill Buckner .40 .16
136 Dick Ruthven .25 .10
137 John Castino .25 .10
138 Ross Baumgarten .25 .10
139 Dane Iorg .25 .10
140 Rich Gossage .75 .30
141 Gary Alexander .25 .10
142 Phil Huffman .25 .10
143 Bruce Bochte DP .15 .06
144 Steve Comer .25 .10
145 Darrell Evans .40 .16
146 Bob Welch .40 .16
147 Terry Puhl .40 .16
148 Manny Sanguillen .40 .16
149 Tom Hume .25 .10
150 Jason Thompson .25 .10
151 Tom Hausman DP .15 .06
152 John Fulgham .25 .10
153 Tim Blackwell .25 .10
154 Lary Sorensen .25 .10
155 Jerry Remy .25 .10
156 Tony Brizzolara .25 .10
157 Willie Wilson DP .25 .10
158 Rob Picciolo DP .15 .06
159 Ken Clay .25 .10
160 Eddie Murray 5.00 2.00
161 Larry Christenson .25 .10
162 Bob Randall .25 .10
163 Steve Swisher .25 .10
164 Greg Pryor .25 .10
165 Omar Moreno .25 .10
166 Glenn Abbott .25 .10
167 Jack Clark .40 .16
168 Rick Waits .25 .10
169 Luis Gomez .25 .10
170 Burt Hooton .40 .16
171 Fernando Gonzalez .25 .10
172 Ron Hodges .25 .10
173 John Henry Johnson .25 .10
174 Ray Knight .40 .16
175 Rick Reuschel .40 .16
176 Champ Summers .25 .10
177 Dave Heaverlo .25 .10
178 Tim McCarver .75 .30
179 Ron Davis .25 .10
180 Warren Cromartie .25 .10
181 Moose Haas .25 .10
182 Ken Reitz .25 .10
183 Jim Anderson DP .15 .06
184 Steve Renko DP .15 .06
185 Hal McRae .40 .16
186 Junior Moore .25 .10
187 Alan Ashby .25 .10
188 Terry Crowley .25 .10
189 Kevin Kobel .25 .10
190 Buddy Bell .40 .16
191 Ted Martinez .25 .10
192 Braves Team CL .75 .15
Bobby Cox MG
193 Dave Goltz .25 .10
194 Mike Easler .25 .10
195 John Montefusco .25 .10
196 Lance Parrish .40 .16
197 Byron McLaughlin .25 .10
198 Dell Alston DP .15 .06
199 Mike LaCoss .25 .10
200 Jim Rice .40 .16
201 Keith Hernandez .75 .30
Fred Lynn LL
202 Dave Kingman .75 .30
Gorman Thomas LL
203 Dave Winfield 1.25 .50
Don Baylor LL
204 Omar Moreno .40 .16
Willie Wilson LL
205 Joe Niekro .75 .30
Phil Niekro
Mike Flanagan LL
206 J.R. Richard 5.00 2.00
Nolan Ryan LL
207 J.R. Richard .75 .30
Ron Guidry LL
208 Wayne Cage .25 .10
209 Von Joshua .25 .10
210 Steve Carlton 2.00 .80
211 Dave Skaggs DP .15 .06
212 Dave Roberts .25 .10
213 Mike Jorgensen DP .15 .06
214 Angels Team CL .75 .15
Jim Fregosi MG
215 Sixto Lezcano .25 .10
216 Phil Mankowski .25 .10
217 Ed Halicki .25 .10
218 Jose Morales .25 .10
219 Steve Mingori .25 .10
220 Dave Concepcion .75 .30
221 Joe Cannon .25 .10
222 Ron Hassey .25 .10
223 Bob Sykes .25 .10
224 Willie Montanez .25 .10
225 Lou Piniella .75 .30
226 Bill Stein .25 .10
227 Len Barker .25 .10
228 Johnny Oates .40 .16
229 Jim Bibby .25 .10
230 Dave Winfield 2.50 1.00
231 Steve McCatty .25 .10
232 Alan Trammell 1.25 .50
233 LaRue Washington .25 .10
234 Vern Ruhle .25 .10
235 Andre Dawson 1.50 .60
236 Marc Hill .25 .10
237 Scott McGregor .25 .10
238 Rob Wilfong .25 .10
239 Don Aase .25 .10
240 Dave Kingman .75 .30
241 Checklist 122-242 .75 .15
242 Lamar Johnson .25 .10
243 Jerry Augustine .25 .10
244 Cardinals Team CL .75 .15
Ken Boyer MG
245 Phil Niekro 1.25 .50
246 Tim Foli DP .15 .06
247 Frank Riccelli .25 .10
248 Jamie Quirk .25 .10
249 Jim Clancy .25 .10
250 Jim Kaat .75 .30
251 Kip Young .25 .10
252 Ted Cox .25 .10
253 John Montague .25 .10
254 Paul Dade DP .15 .06
255 Dusty Baker DP .40 .16
256 Roger Erickson .25 .10
257 Larry Herndon .25 .10
258 Paul Moskau .25 .10
259 Mets Team CL .75 .15
Joe Torre MG
260 Al Oliver .75 .30
261 Dave Chalk .25 .10
262 Benny Ayala .25 .10
263 Dave LaRoche DP .15 .06
264 Bill Robinson .25 .10
265 Robin Yount 3.00 1.20
266 Bernie Carbo .25 .10
267 Dan Schatzeder .25 .10
268 Rafael Landestoy .25 .10
269 Dave Tobik .25 .10
270 Mike Schmidt DP 3.00 1.20
271 Dick Drago DP .15 .06
272 Ralph Garr .40 .16
273 Eduardo Rodriguez .25 .10
274 Dale Murphy 1.25 .50
275 Jerry Koosman .40 .16
276 Tom Veryzer .25 .10
277 Rick Bosetti .25 .10
278 Jim Spencer .25 .10
279 Rob Andrews .25 .10
280 Gaylord Perry 1.25 .50
281 Paul Blair .40 .16
282 Mariners Team CL .75 .15
Darrell Johnson MG
283 John Ellis .25 .10
284 Larry Murray DP .15 .06
285 Don Baylor .75 .30
286 Darold Knowles DP .15 .06
287 John Lowenstein .25 .10
288 Dave Rozema .25 .10
289 Bruce Bochy .25 .10
290 Steve Garvey 1.25 .50
291 Randy Scarberry .25 .10
292 Dale Berra .25 .10
293 Elias Sosa .25 .10
294 Charlie Spikes .25 .10
295 Larry Gura .25 .10
296 Dave Rader .25 .10
297 Tim Johnson .25 .10
298 Ken Holtzman .40 .16
299 Steve Henderson .25 .10
300 Ron Guidry .40 .16
301 Mike Edwards .25 .10
302 Dodgers Team CL .75 .15
Tom Lasorda MG
303 Bill Castro .25 .10
304 Butch Wynegar .25 .10
305 Randy Jones .25 .10
306 Denny Walling .25 .10
307 Rick Honeycutt .25 .10
308 Mike Hargrove .40 .16
309 Larry McWilliams .25 .10
310 Dave Parker .75 .30
311 Roger Metzger .25 .10
312 Mike Barlow .25 .10
313 Johnny Grubb .25 .10
314 Tim Stoddard .25 .10
315 Steve Kemp .25 .10
316 Bob Lacey .25 .10
317 Mike Anderson DP .15 .06
318 Jerry Reuss .40 .16
319 Chris Speier .25 .10
320 Dennis Eckersley .75 .30
321 Keith Hernandez .40 .16
322 Claudell Washington .40 .16
323 Mick Kelleher .25 .10
324 Tom Underwood .25 .10
325 Dan Driessen .25 .10
326 Bo McLaughlin .25 .10
327 Ray Fosse DP .15 .06
328 Twins Team CL .75 .15
Gene Mauch MG
329 Bert Roberge .25 .10
330 Al Cowens .25 .10
331 Richie Hebner .40 .16
332 Enrique Romo .25 .10
333 Jim Norris DP .15 .06
334 Jim Beattie .25 .10
335 Willie McCovey 1.50 .60
336 George Medich .25 .10
337 Carney Lansford .40 .16
338 John Wockenfuss .25 .10
339 John D'Acquisto .25 .10
340 Ken Singleton .40 .16
341 Jim Essian .25 .10
342 Odell Jones .25 .10
343 Mike Vail .25 .10
344 Randy Lerch .25 .10
345 Larry Parrish .40 .16
346 Buddy Solomon .25 .10
347 Harry Chappas .25 .10
348 Checklist 243-363 .75 .15
349 Jack Brohamer .25 .10
350 George Hendrick .40 .16
351 Bob Davis .25 .10
352 Dan Briggs .25 .10
353 Andy Hassler .25 .10
354 Rick Auerbach .25 .10
355 Gary Matthews .40 .16
356 Padres Team CL .75 .15
Jerry Coleman MG
357 Bob McClure .25 .10
358 Lou Whitaker 1.25 .50
359 Randy Moffitt .25 .10
360 Darrell Porter DP .25 .10
361 Wayne Garland .25 .10
362 Danny Goodwin .25 .10
363 Wayne Gross .25 .10
364 Ray Burris .25 .10
365 Bobby Murcer .40 .16
366 Rob Dressler .25 .10
367 Billy Smith .25 .10
368 Willie Aikens .25 .10
369 Jim Kern .25 .10
370 Cesar Cedeno .40 .16
371 Jack Morris .75 .30
372 Joel Youngblood .25 .10
373 Dan Petry RC DP .25 .10
374 Jim Gantner .40 .16
375 Ross Grimsley .25 .10
376 Gary Allenson .25 .10
377 Junior Kennedy .25 .10
378 Jerry Mumphrey .25 .10
379 Kevin Bell .25 .10
380 Garry Maddox .40 .16
381 Cubs Team CL .75 .15
Preston Gomez MG
382 Dave Freisleben .25 .10
383 Ed Ott .25 .10
384 Joey McLaughlin .25 .10
385 Enos Cabell .25 .10
386 Darrell Jackson .25 .10
387A Fred Stanley YL 2.00 .80
387B Fred Stanley .25 .10
(Red name on front)
388 Mike Paxton .25 .10
389 Pete LaCock .25 .10
390 Fergie Jenkins 1.25 .50
391 Tony Armas DP .25 .10
392 Milt Wilcox .25 .10
393 Ozzie Smith 10.00 4.00
394 Reggie Cleveland .25 .10
395 Ellis Valentine .25 .10
396 Dan Meyer .25 .10
397 Roy Thomas DP .15 .06
398 Barry Foote .25 .10
399 Mike Proly DP .15 .06
400 George Foster .40 .16
401 Pete Falcone .25 .10
402 Merv Rettenmund .25 .10
403 Pete Redfern DP .15 .06
404 Orioles Team CL .75 .15
Earl Weaver MG
405 Dwight Evans .40 .16
406 Paul Molitor 5.00 2.00
407 Tony Solaita .25 .10
408 Bill North .25 .10
409 Paul Splittorff .25 .10
410 Bobby Bonds .75 .30
411 Frank LaCorte .25 .10
412 Thad Bosley .25 .10
413 Allen Ripley .25 .10
414 George Scott .40 .16
415 Bill Atkinson .25 .10
416 Tom Brookens .25 .10
417 Craig Chamberlain DP .15 .06
418 Roger Freed DP .15 .06
419 Vic Correll .25 .10
420 Butch Hobson .25 .10
421 Doug Bird .25 .10
422 Larry Milbourne .25 .10
423 Dave Frost .25 .10
424 Yankees Team CL .75 .15
Dick Howser MG
424A Yankees Team CL
Billy Martin MG
Card is believed to be a pre-production issue
425 Mark Belanger .40 .16
426 Grant Jackson .25 .10
427 Tom Hutton DP .15 .06
428 Pat Zachry .25 .10
429 Duane Kuiper .25 .10
430 Larry Hisle DP .15 .06
431 Mike Krukow .25 .10
432 Willie Norwood .25 .10
433 Rich Gale .25 .10
434 Johnnie LeMaster .25 .10
435 Don Gullett .40 .16
436 Billy Almon .25 .10
437 Joe Niekro .40 .16
438 Dave Revering .25 .10
439 Mike Phillips .25 .10
440 Don Sutton 1.25 .50
441 Eric Soderholm .25 .10
442 Jorge Orta .25 .10
443 Mike Parrott .25 .10
444 Alvis Woods .25 .10
445 Mark Fidrych 1.25 .50
446 Duffy Dyer .25 .10
447 Nino Espinosa .25 .10
448 Jim Wohlford .25 .10
449 Doug Bair .25 .10
450 George Brett 8.00 3.20
451 Indians Team CL .40 .08
Dave Garcia MG
452 Steve Dillard .25 .10
453 Mike Bacsik .25 .10
454 Tom Donohue .25 .10
455 Mike Torrez .25 .10
456 Frank Taveras .25 .10
457 Bert Blyleven .75 .30
458 Billy Sample .25 .10
459 Mickey Lolich DP .25 .10
460 Willie Randolph .40 .16
461 Dwayne Murphy .25 .10
462 Mike Sadek DP .15 .06
463 Jerry Royster .25 .10
464 John Denny .25 .10
465 Rick Monday .25 .10
466 Mike Squires .25 .10
467 Jesse Jefferson .25 .10
468 Aurelio Rodriguez .25 .10
469 Randy Niemann DP .15 .06
470 Bob Boone .75 .30
471 Hosken Powell DP .15 .06
472 Willie Hernandez .40 .16
473 Bump Wills .25 .10
474 Steve Busby .25 .10
475 Cesar Geronimo .25 .10
476 Bob Shirley .25 .10
477 Buck Martinez .25 .10
478 Gil Flores .25 .10
479 Expos Team CL .75 .15
Dick Williams MG
480 Bob Watson .40 .16
481 Tom Paciorek .40 .16
482 R.Henderson RC UER 70.00 28.00
7 steals at Modesto,
should be at Fresno
483 Bo Diaz .25 .10
484 Checklist 364-484 .75 .15
485 Mickey Rivers .40 .16
486 Mike Tyson DP .15 .06
487 Wayne Nordhagen .25 .10
488 Roy Howell .25 .10
489 Preston Hanna DP .15 .06
490 Lee May .40 .16
491 Steve Mura DP .15 .06
492 Todd Cruz .25 .10
493 Jerry Martin .25 .10
494 Craig Minetto .25 .10
495 Bake McBride .25 .10
496 Silvio Martinez .25 .10
497 Jim Mason .25 .10
498 Danny Darwin .25 .10
499 Giants Team CL .75 .15
Dave Bristol MG
500 Tom Seaver 3.00 1.20
501 Rennie Stennett .25 .10
502 Rich Wortham DP .15 .06
503 Mike Cubbage .25 .10
504 Gene Garber .40 .16
505 Bert Campaneris .40 .16
506 Tom Buskey .25 .10
507 Leon Roberts .25 .10
508 U.L. Washington .25 .10
509 Ed Glynn .25 .10
510 Ron Cey .75 .30
511 Eric Wilkins .25 .10
512 Jose Cardenal .25 .10
513 Tom Dixon DP .15 .06
514 Steve Ontiveros .25 .10
515 Mike Caldwell UER .25 .10
1979 loss total reads
96 instead of 6
516 Hector Cruz .25 .10
517 Don Stanhouse .25 .10
518 Nelson Norman .25 .10
519 Steve Nicosia .25 .10
520 Steve Rogers .25 .10
521 Ken Brett .25 .10
522 Jim Morrison .25 .10
523 Ken Henderson .25 .10
524 Jim Wright DP .15 .06
525 Clint Hurdle .25 .10
526 Phillies Team CL .75 .15
Dallas Green MG
527 Doug Rau DP .15 .06
528 Adrian Devine .25 .10
529 Jim Barr .25 .10
530 Jim Sundberg DP .25 .10
531 Eric Rasmussen .25 .10
532 Willie Horton .40 .16
533 Checklist 485-605 .75 .15
534 Andre Thornton .40 .16
535 Bob Forsch .25 .10
536 Lee Lacy .25 .10
537 Alex Trevino .25 .10

Card	NM	Ex
538 Joe Strain	.25	.10
539 Rudy May	.25	.10
540 Pete Rose	8.00	3.20
541 Miguel Dilone	.25	.10
542 Joe Coleman	.25	.10
543 Pat Kelly	.25	.10
544 Rick Sutcliffe RC	.75	.30
545 Jeff Burroughs	.40	.16
546 Rick Langford	.25	.10
547 John Wathan	.25	.10
548 Dave Rajsich	.25	.10
549 Larry Wolfe	.25	.10
550 Ken Griffey Sr.	.75	.30
551 Pirates Team CL	.75	.15
Chuck Tanner MG		
552 Bill Nahorodny	.25	.10
553 Dick Davis	.25	.10
554 Art Howe	.40	.16
555 Ed Figueroa	.25	.10
556 Joe Rudi	.40	.16
557 Mark Lee	.25	.10
558 Alfredo Griffin	.25	.10
559 Dale Murray	.25	.10
560 Dave Lopes	.40	.16
561 Eddie Whitson	.25	.10
562 Joe Wallis	.25	.10
563 Will McEnaney	.25	.10
564 Rick Manning	.25	.10
565 Dennis Leonard	.40	.16
566 Bud Harrelson	.40	.16
567 Skip Lockwood	.25	.10
568 Gary Roenicke	.40	.16
569 Terry Kennedy	.40	.16
570 Roy Smalley	.25	.10
571 Joe Sambito	.25	.10
572 Jerry Morales DP	.15	.06
573 Kent Tekulve	.40	.16
574 Scot Thompson	.25	.10
575 Ken Kravec	.25	.10
576 Jim Dwyer	.25	.10
577 Blue Jays Team CL	.75	.15
Bobby Mattick MG		
578 Scott Sanderson	.40	.16
579 Charlie Moore	.25	.10
580 Nolan Ryan	15.00	6.00
581 Bob Bailor	.25	.10
582 Brian Doyle	.25	.10
583 Bob Stinson	.25	.10
584 Kurt Bevacqua	.25	.10
585 Al Hrabosky	.25	.10
586 Mitchell Page	.25	.10
587 Garry Templeton	.25	.10
588 Greg Minton	.25	.10
589 Chet Lemon	.40	.16
590 Jim Palmer	1.50	.60
591 Rick Cerone	.25	.10
592 Jon Matlack	.25	.10
593 Jesus Alou	.25	.10
594 Dick Tidrow	.25	.10
595 Don Money	.25	.10
596 Rick Matula	.25	.10
597 Tom Poquette	.25	.10
598 Fred Kendall DP	.15	.06
599 Mike Norris	.25	.10
600 Reggie Jackson	4.00	1.60
601 Buddy Schultz	.25	.10
602 Brian Downing	.25	.10
603 Jack Billingham DP	.15	.06
604 Glenn Adams	.25	.10
605 Terry Forster	.25	.10
606 Reds Team CL	.75	.15
John McNamara MG		
607 Woodie Fryman	.25	.10
608 Alan Bannister	.25	.10
609 Ron Reed	.25	.10
610 Willie Stargell	1.25	.50
611 Jerry Garvin DP	.15	.06
612 Cliff Johnson	.25	.10
613 Randy Stein	.25	.10
614 John Hiller	.25	.10
615 Doug DeCinces	.40	.16
616 Gene Richards	.25	.10
617 Joaquin Andujar	.40	.16
618 Bob Montgomery DP	.40	.16
619 Sergio Ferrer	.25	.10
620 Richie Zisk	.25	.10
621 Bob Grich	.40	.16
622 Mario Soto	.40	.16
623 Gorman Thomas	.40	.16
624 Lerrin LaGrow	.25	.10
625 Chris Chambliss	.40	.16
626 Tigers Team CL	.75	.15
Sparky Anderson MG		
627 Pedro Borbon	.25	.10
628 Doug Capilla	.25	.10
629 Jim Todd	.25	.10
630 Larry Bowa	.40	.16
631 Mark Littell	.25	.10
632 Barry Bonnell	.25	.10
633 Bob Apodaca	.25	.10
634 Glenn Borgmann DP	.15	.06
635 John Candelaria	.40	.16
636 Toby Harrah	.40	.16
637 Joe Simpson	.25	.10
638 Mark Clear	.25	.10
639 Larry Biittner	.25	.10
640 Mike Flanagan	.40	.16
641 Ed Kranepool	.40	.16
642 Ken Forsch DP	.15	.06
643 John Mayberry	.40	.16
644 Charlie Hough	.40	.16
645 Rick Burleson	.25	.10
646 Checklist 606-726	.75	.15
647 Milt May	.25	.10
648 Roy White	.40	.16
649 Tom Griffin	.25	.10
650 Joe Morgan	1.50	.60
651 Rollie Fingers	1.25	.50
652 Mario Mendoza	.25	.10
653 Stan Bahnsen	.25	.10
654 Bruce Boisclair DP	.15	.06
655 Tug McGraw	.40	.16
656 Larvell Blanks	.25	.10
657 Dave Edwards	.25	.10
658 Chris Knapp	.25	.10
659 Brewers Team CL	.75	.15
George Bamberger MG		
660 Rusty Staub	.40	.16
661 Mark Corey	.40	.16
Dave Ford		
Wayne Krenchicki		
662 Joel Finch	.40	.16
Mike O'Berry		
Chuck Rainey		
663 Ralph Botting	.75	.30
Bob Clark		
Dickie Thon RC		
664 Mike Colbern	.40	.16
Guy Hoffman		
Dewey Robinson		
665 Larry Andersen	.75	.30
Bobby Cuellar		
Sandy Wihtol		
666 Mike Chris	.40	.16
Al Greene		
Bruce Robbins		
667 Renie Martin	.75	.30
Bill Paschall		
Dan Quisenberry RC		
668 Danny Boitano	.40	.16
Willie Mueller		
Lenn Sakata		
669 Dan Graham	.40	.16
Rick Sofield		
Gary Ward RC		
670 Bobby Brown	.40	.16
Brad Gulden		
Darryl Jones		
671 Derek Bryant	1.25	.50
Brian Kingman		
Mike Morgan RC		
672 Charlie Beamon	.40	.16
Rodney Craig		
Rafael Vasquez		
673 Brian Allard	.40	.16
Jerry Don Gleaton		
Greg Mahlberg		
674 Butch Edge	.40	.16
Pat Kelly		
Ted Wilborn		
675 Bruce Benedict	.40	.16
Larry Bradford		
Eddie Miller		
676 Dave Geisel	.40	.16
Steve Macko		
Karl Pagel		
677 Art DeFreites	.40	.16
Frank Pastore		
Harry Spilman		
678 Reggie Baldwin	.40	.16
Alan Knicely		
Pete Ladd		
679 Joe Beckwith	.75	.30
Mickey Hatcher RC		
Dave Patterson		
680 Tony Bernazard	.75	.30
Randy Miller		
John Tamargo		
681 Dan Norman	1.50	.60
Jesse Orosco RC		
Mike Scott RC		
682 Ramon Aviles	.40	.16
Dickie Noles		
Kevin Saucier		
683 Dorian Boyland	.40	.16
Alberto Lois		
Harry Saferight		
684 George Frazier	.75	.30
Tom Herr RC		
Dan O'Brien		
685 Tim Flannery	.40	.16
Brian Greer		
Jim Wilhelm		
686 Greg Johnston	.40	.16
Dennis Littlejohn		
Phil Nastu		
687 Mike Heath DP	.15	.06
688 Steve Stone	.40	.16
689 Red Sox Team CL	.75	.15
Don Zimmer MG		
690 Tommy John	.75	.30
691 Ivan DeJesus	.25	.10
692 Rawly Eastwick DP	.15	.06
693 Craig Kusick	.25	.10
694 Jim Rooker	.25	.10
695 Reggie Smith	.40	.16
696 Julio Gonzalez	.25	.10
697 David Clyde	.25	.10
698 Oscar Gamble	.40	.16
699 Floyd Bannister	.25	.10
700 Rod Carew DP	1.50	.60
701 Ken Oberkfell	.25	.10
702 Ed Farmer	.25	.10
703 Otto Velez	.25	.10
704 Gene Tenace	.40	.16
705 Freddie Patek	.25	.10
706 Tippy Martinez	.25	.10
707 Elliott Maddox	.25	.10
708 Bob Tolan	.25	.10
709 Pat Underwood	.25	.10
710 Graig Nettles	.75	.30
711 Bob Galasso	.25	.10
712 Rodney Scott	.25	.10
713 Terry Whitfield	.25	.10
714 Fred Norman	.25	.10
715 Sal Bando	.40	.16
716 Lynn McGlothen	.25	.10
717 Mickey Klutts DP	.15	.06
718 Greg Gross	.25	.10
719 Don Robinson	.40	.16
720 Carl Yastrzemski DP	2.00	.80
721 Paul Hartzell	.25	.10
722 Jose Cruz	.40	.16
723 Shane Rawley	.25	.10
724 Jerry White	.25	.10
725 Rick Wise	.25	.10
726 Steve Yeager	.75	.15

1980 Topps/O-Pee-Chee Retail Promotion Cards

This set features special promotional redemption cards from Mrs. Butterworth's Syrup and Kmart Stores that could be redeemed for an unopened pack of three standard Topps Baseball cards. A special "3000 or More Hits", "lifetime .300 hitters" or a "Major League Records" card came with the packs. Hunts bread did the same promotion up in

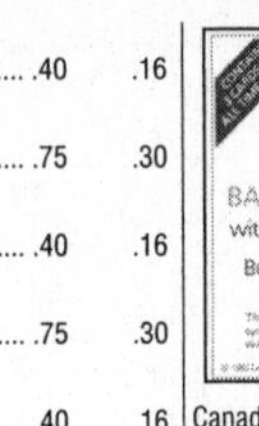

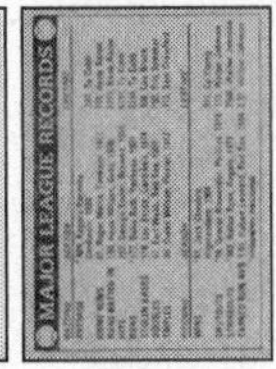

Canada. The promotion was limited to certain states and to certain stores.

	NM	Ex
COMPLETE SET	20.00	8.00
1 Mrs. Butterworth's	5.00	2.00
2 Kmart	5.00	2.00
3 Squirt	5.00	2.00
4 Hunts Bread	5.00	2.00

1980 Topps Super

This 60-card set, measuring 4 7/8" by 6 7/8", consists primarily of star players. A player photo comprises the entire front with a facsimile signature at the lower portion of the photo. The backs contain a large Topps logo and the player's name. The cards were issued with either white or gray backs. The white backs have thicker card stock than the gray. White back cards were issued in three-card cellophane packs and gray back cards were issued through various promotional means. The prices below reflect those of the gray back. There are a number of cards that were Triple Printed. They are indicated by below (TP).

	NM	Ex
COMPLETE SET (60)	15.00	6.00
COMMON CARD (1-60)	.10	.04
COMMON TP	.25	.10
*WHITE BACKS: 2X GRAY BACKS		
1 Willie Stargell	.75	.30
2 Mike Schmidt TP	1.00	.40
3 Johnny Bench	1.00	.40
4 Jim Palmer	.75	.30
5 Jim Rice	.25	.10
6 Reggie Jackson TP	1.00	.40
7 Ron Guidry	.25	.10
8 Lee Mazzilli	.25	.10
9 Don Baylor	.50	.20
10 Fred Lynn	.25	.10
11 Ken Singleton	.25	.10
12 Rod Carew TP	.75	.30
13 Steve Garvey TP	.50	.20
14 George Brett TP	1.50	.60
15 Tom Seaver	1.00	.40
16 Dave Kingman	.25	.10
17 Dave Parker TP	.25	.10
18 Dave Winfield	.75	.30
19 Pete Rose	.75	.30
20 Nolan Ryan	3.00	1.20
21 Graig Nettles	.25	.10
22 Carl Yastrzemski	.75	.30
23 Tommy John	.50	.20
24 George Foster	.25	.10
25 J.R. Richard	.10	.04
26 Keith Hernandez	.25	.10
27 Bob Horner	.10	.04
28 Eddie Murray	2.00	.80
29 Steve Kemp	.10	.04
30 Gorman Thomas	.10	.04
31 Sixto Lezcano	.10	.04
32 Bruce Sutter	.25	.10
33 Cecil Cooper	.25	.10
34 Larry Bowa	.25	.10
35 Al Oliver	.50	.20
36 Ted Simmons	.25	.10
37 Garry Templeton	.10	.04
38 Jerry Koosman	.25	.10
39 Darrell Porter	.10	.04
40 Roy Smalley	.10	.04
41 Craig Swan	.10	.04
42 Jason Thompson	.10	.04
43 Andre Thornton	.10	.04
44 Rick Manning	.10	.04
45 Kent Tekulve	.10	.04
46 Phil Niekro	.75	.30
47 Buddy Bell	.25	.10
48 Randy Jones	.10	.04
49 Brian Downing	.10	.04
50 Amos Otis	.10	.04
51 Rick Bosetti	.10	.04
52 Gary Carter	.75	.30
53 Larry Parrish	.25	.10
54 Jack Clark	.25	.10
55 Bruce Bochte	.10	.04
56 Cesar Cedeno	.10	.04
57 Chet Lemon	.10	.04
58 Dave Revering	.10	.04
59 Vida Blue	.25	.10
60 Dave Lopes	.25	.10

1980 Topps Team Checklist Sheet

As part of a mail-away offer, Topps offered all 26 1980 team checklist cards on an uncut sheet. These cards enabled the collector to have an easy reference for which card(s) he/she needed to finish their sets. When cut from the sheet, all cards measure the standard size.

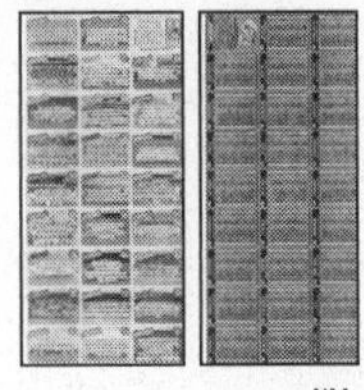

	NM	Ex
1 Team Checklist Sheet	15.00	6.00

1981 Topps

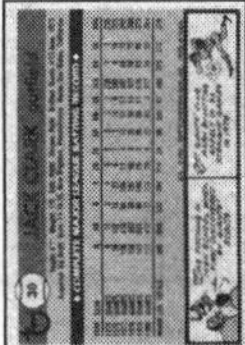

The cards in this 726-card set measure the standard size. This set was issued primarily in 15-card wax packs and 50-card rack packs. League Leaders (1-8), Record Breakers (201-208), and Post-season cards (401-404) are the topical subsets. The team cards are all grouped together (661-686) and feature team checklist backs and a very small photo of the team's manager in the upper right corner of the obverse. The obverses carry the player's position and team in a baseball cap design, and the company name is printed in a small baseball. The backs are red and gray. The 66 double-printed cards are noted in the checklist by DP. Notable Rookie Cards in the set include Harold Baines, Kirk Gibson, Tim Raines, Jeff Reardon, and Fernando Valenzuela. During 1981, a promotion existed where collectors could order complete set in sheet form from Topps for $24.

	Nm-Mt	Ex-Mt
COMPLETE SET (726)	60.00	24.00
COMMON CARD (1-726)	.15	.06
COMMON CARD DP	.07	.03
1 George Brett	3.00	1.20
Bill Buckner LL		
2 Reggie Jackson	1.50	.60
Ben Oglivie		
Mike Schmidt LL		
3 Cecil Cooper	1.50	.60
Mike Schmidt LL		
4 Rickey Henderson	3.00	1.20
Ron LeFlore LL		
5 Steve Stone	.40	.16
Steve Carlton LL		
6 Len Barker	.40	.16
Steve Carlton LL		
7 Rudy May	.75	.30
Don Sutton LL		
8 Dan Quisenberry	.40	.16
Rollie Fingers		
Tom Hume LL		
9 Pete LaCock DP	.07	.03
10 Mike Flanagan	.40	.16
11 Jim Wohlford DP	.07	.03
12 Mark Clear	.15	.06
13 Joe Charboneau RC	1.50	.60
14 John Tudor RC	.40	.16
15 Larry Parrish	.15	.06
16 Ron Davis	.15	.06
17 Cliff Johnson	.15	.06
18 Glenn Adams	.15	.06
19 Jim Clancy	.15	.06
20 Jeff Burroughs	.15	.06
21 Ron Oester	.15	.06
22 Danny Darwin	.15	.06
23 Alex Trevino	.15	.06
24 Don Stanhouse	.15	.06
25 Sixto Lezcano	.15	.06
26 U.L. Washington	.15	.06
27 Champ Summers DP	.07	.03
28 Enrique Romo	.15	.06
29 Gene Tenace	.40	.16
30 Jack Clark	.40	.16
31 Checklist 1-121 DP	.15	.06
32 Ken Oberkfell	.15	.06
33 Rick Honeycutt	.15	.06
34 Aurelio Rodriguez	.15	.06
35 Mitchell Page	.15	.06
36 Ed Farmer	.15	.06
37 Gary Roenicke	.15	.06
38 Win Remmerswaal	.15	.06
39 Tom Veryzer	.15	.06
40 Tug McGraw	.40	.16
41 Bob Babcock	.15	.06
John Butcher		
Jerry Don Gleaton		
42 Jerry White DP	.07	.03
43 Jose Morales	.15	.06
44 Larry McWilliams	.15	.06
45 Enos Cabell	.15	.06
46 Rick Bosetti	.15	.06
47 Ken Brett	.15	.06
48 Dave Skaggs	.15	.06
49 Bob Shirley	.15	.06
50 Dave Lopes	.40	.16
51 Bill Robinson DP	.15	.06
52 Hector Cruz	.15	.06
53 Kevin Saucier	.15	.06
54 Ivan DeJesus	.15	.06
55 Mike Norris	.15	.06
56 Buck Martinez	.15	.06
57 Dave Roberts	.15	.06
58 Joel Youngblood	.15	.06
59 Dan Petry	.15	.06
60 Willie Randolph	.40	.16
61 Butch Wynegar	.15	.06
62 Joe Pettini	.15	.06
63 Steve Renko DP	.07	.03
64 Brian Asselstine	.15	.06
65 Scott McGregor	.15	.06
66 Manny Castillo	.15	.06
Tim Ireland		
Mike Jones		
67 Ken Kravec	.15	.06
68 Matt Alexander DP	.07	.03
69 Ed Halicki	.15	.06
70 Al Oliver DP	.40	.16
71 Hal Dues	.15	.06
72 Barry Evans DP	.07	.03
73 Doug Bair	.15	.06
74 Mike Hargrove	.40	.16
75 Reggie Smith	.40	.16
76 Mario Mendoza	.15	.06
77 Mike Barlow	.15	.06
78 Steve Dillard	.15	.06
79 Bruce Robbins	.15	.06
80 Rusty Staub	.40	.16
81 Dave Stapleton	.15	.06
82 Danny Heep	.15	.06
Alan Knicely		
Bobby Sprowl		
83 Mike Proly	.15	.06
84 Johnnie LeMaster	.15	.06
85 Mike Caldwell	.15	.06
86 Wayne Gross	.15	.06
87 Rick Camp	.15	.06
88 Joe Lefebvre	.15	.06
89 Darrell Jackson	.15	.06
90 Bake McBride	.15	.06
91 Tim Stoddard DP	.07	.03
92 Mike Easler	.15	.06
93 Ed Glynn DP	.07	.03
94 Harry Spilman DP	.07	.03
95 Jim Sundberg	.40	.16
96 Dave Beard	.15	.06
Ernie Camacho		
Pat Dempsey		
97 Chris Speier	.15	.06
98 Clint Hurdle	.15	.06
99 Eric Wilkins	.15	.06
100 Rod Carew	.75	.30
101 Benny Ayala	.15	.06
102 Dave Tobik	.15	.06
103 Jerry Martin	.15	.06
104 Terry Forster	.15	.06
105 Jose Cruz	.40	.16
106 Don Money	.15	.06
107 Rich Wortham	.15	.06
108 Bruce Benedict	.15	.06
109 Mike Scott	.40	.16
110 Carl Yastrzemski	2.50	1.00
111 Greg Minton	.15	.06
112 Rusty Kuntz	.15	.06
Fran Mullins		
Leo Sutherland		
113 Mike Phillips	.15	.06
114 Tom Underwood	.15	.06
115 Roy Smalley	.15	.06
116 Joe Simpson	.15	.06
117 Pete Falcone	.15	.06
118 Kurt Bevacqua	.15	.06
119 Tippy Martinez	.15	.06
120 Larry Bowa	.40	.16
121 Larry Harlow	.15	.06
122 John Denny	.15	.06
123 Al Cowens	.15	.06
124 Jerry Garvin	.15	.06
125 Andre Dawson	.75	.30
126 Charlie Leibrandt RC	.75	.30
127 Rudy Law	.15	.06
128 Gary Allenson DP	.07	.03
129 Art Howe	.40	.16
130 Larry Gura	.15	.06
131 Keith Moreland	.40	.16
132 Tommy Boggs	.15	.06
133 Jeff Cox	.15	.06
134 Steve Mura	.15	.06
135 Gorman Thomas	.40	.16
136 Doug Capilla	.15	.06
137 Hosken Powell	.15	.06
138 Rich Dotson DP	.15	.06
139 Oscar Gamble	.15	.06
140 Bob Forsch	.15	.06
141 Miguel Dilone	.15	.06
142 Jackson Todd	.15	.06
143 Dan Meyer	.15	.06
144 Allen Ripley	.15	.06
145 Mickey Rivers	.40	.16
146 Bobby Castillo	.15	.06
147 Dale Berra	.15	.06
148 Randy Niemann	.15	.06
149 Joe Nolan	.15	.06
150 Mark Fidrych	1.50	.60
151 Claudell Washington	.15	.06
152 John Urrea	.15	.06
153 Tom Poquette	.15	.06
154 Rick Langford	.15	.06
155 Chris Chambliss	.40	.16
156 Bob McClure	.15	.06
157 John Wathan	.15	.06
158 Fergie Jenkins	.40	.16
159 Brian Doyle	.15	.06
160 Garry Maddox	.15	.06
161 Dan Graham	.15	.06
162 Doug Corbett	.15	.06
163 Bill Almon	.15	.06
164 LaMarr Hoyt RC	.40	.16
165 Tony Scott	.15	.06
166 Floyd Bannister	.15	.06
167 Terry Whitfield	.15	.06
168 Don Robinson DP	.07	.03
169 John Mayberry	.15	.06
170 Ross Grimsley	.15	.06
171 Gene Richards	.15	.06
172 Gary Woods	.15	.06
173 Bump Wills	.15	.06
174 Doug Rau	.15	.06
175 Dave Collins	.15	.06
176 Mike Krukow	.15	.06
177 Rick Peters	.15	.06
178 Jim Essian DP	.07	.03
179 Rudy May	.15	.06
180 Pete Rose	5.00	2.00
181 Elias Sosa	.15	.06
182 Bob Grich	.40	.16
183 Dick Davis DP	.07	.03
184 Jim Dwyer	.15	.06
185 Dennis Leonard	.15	.06
186 Wayne Nordhagen	.15	.06

187 Mike Parrott .15 .06
188 Doug DeCinces .40 .16
189 Craig Swan .15 .06
190 Cesar Cedeno .40 .16
191 Rick Sutcliffe .40 .16
192 Terry Harper .40 .16
Ed Miller
Rafael Ramirez
193 Pete Vuckovich .40 .16
194 Rod Scurry .15 .06
195 Rich Murray .15 .06
196 Duffy Dyer .15 .06
197 Jim Kern .15 .06
198 Jerry Dybzinski .15 .06
199 Chuck Rainey .15 .06
200 George Foster .40 .16
201 Johnny Bench RB .75 .30
202 Steve Carlton RB .15 .06
203 Bill Gullickson RB .75 .30
204 Ron LeFlore RB .40 .16
Rodney Scott
205 Pete Rose RB 1.50 .60
206 Mike Schmidt RB 1.50 .60
207 Ozzie Smith RB 2.00 .80
208 Willie Wilson RB .40 .16
209 Dickie Thon DP .40 .16
210 Jim Palmer .40 .16
211 Derrel Thomas .15 .06
212 Steve Nicosia .15 .06
213 Al Holland .15 .06
214 Ralph Botting .15 .06
Jim Dorsey
John Harris
215 Larry Hisle .15 .06
216 John Henry Johnson .15 .06
217 Rich Hebner .15 .06
218 Paul Splittorff .15 .06
219 Ken Landreaux .15 .06
220 Tom Seaver .75 .30
221 Bob Davis .15 .06
222 Jorge Orta .15 .06
223 Roy Lee Jackson .15 .06
224 Pat Zachry .15 .06
225 Ruppert Jones .15 .06
226 Manny Sanguillen DP .07 .03
227 Fred Martinez .15 .06
228 Tom Paciorek .40 .16
229 Rollie Fingers .40 .16
230 George Hendrick .40 .16
231 Joe Beckwith .15 .06
232 Mickey Klutts .15 .06
233 Skip Lockwood .15 .06
234 Lou Whitaker .75 .30
235 Scott Sanderson .15 .06
236 Mike Ivie .15 .06
237 Charlie Moore .15 .06
238 Willie Hernandez .40 .16
239 Rick Miller DP .07 .03
240 Nolan Ryan 8.00 3.20
241 Checklist 122-242 DP .15 .06
242 Chet Lemon .15 .06
243 Sal Butera .15 .06
244 Tito Landrum .15 .06
Al Olmsted
Andy Rincon
245 Ed Figueroa .15 .06
246 Ed Ott DP .07 .03
247 Glenn Hubbard DP .07 .03
248 Joey McLaughlin .15 .06
249 Larry Cox .15 .06
250 Ron Guidry .40 .16
251 Tom Brookens .15 .06
252 Victor Cruz .15 .06
253 Dave Bergman .15 .06
254 Ozzie Smith 5.00 2.00
255 Mark Littell .15 .06
256 Bombo Rivera .15 .06
257 Rennie Stennett .15 .06
258 Joe Price .15 .06
259 Juan Berenguer 1.50 .60
Hubie Brooks RC
Mookie Wilson
260 Ron Cey .40 .16
261 Rickey Henderson 10.00 4.00
262 Sammy Stewart .15 .06
263 Brian Downing .40 .16
264 Jim Norris .15 .06
265 John Candelaria .40 .16
266 Tom Herr .40 .16
267 Stan Bahnsen .15 .06
268 Jerry Royster .15 .06
269 Ken Forsch .15 .06
270 Greg Luzinski .40 .16
271 Bill Castro .15 .06
272 Bruce Kimm .15 .06
273 Stan Papi .15 .06
274 Craig Chamberlain .15 .06
275 Dwight Evans .75 .30
276 Dan Spillner .15 .06
277 Alfredo Griffin .15 .06
278 Rick Sofield .15 .06
279 Bob Knepper .15 .06
280 Ken Griffey .75 .30
281 Fred Stanley .15 .06
282 Rick Anderson .15 .06
Greg Biercevicz
Rodney Craig
283 Billy Sample .15 .06
284 Brian Kingman .15 .06
285 Jerry Turner .15 .06
286 Dave Frost .15 .06
287 Lenn Sakata .15 .06
288 Bob Clark .15 .06
289 Mickey Hatcher .40 .16
290 Bob Boone DP .40 .16
291 Aurelio Lopez .15 .06
292 Mike Squires .15 .06
293 Charlie Lea .15 .06
294 Mike Tyson DP .07 .03
295 Hal McRae .40 .16
296 Bill Nahorodny DP .07 .03
297 Bob Bailor .15 .06
298 Buddy Solomon .15 .06
299 Elliott Maddox .15 .06
300 Paul Molitor 1.50 .60
301 Matt Keough .15 .06
302 Jack Perconte 5.00 2.00
Mike Scioscia RC
Fernando Valenzuela RC
303 Johnny Oates .40 .16
304 John Castino .15 .06
305 Ken Clay .15 .06
306 Juan Beniquez DP .07 .03
307 Gene Garber .15 .06
308 Rick Manning .15 .06
309 Luis Salazar RC .15 .06
310 Vida Blue DP .15 .06
311 Freddie Patek .15 .06
312 Rick Rhoden .15 .06
313 Luis Pujols .15 .06
314 Rich Dauer .15 .06
315 Kirk Gibson RC 3.00 1.20
316 Craig Minetto .15 .06
317 Lonnie Smith .40 .16
318 Steve Yeager .15 .06
319 Rowland Office .15 .06
320 Tom Burgmeier .15 .06
321 Leon Durham .40 .16
322 Neil Allen .15 .06
323 Jim Morrison DP .07 .03
324 Mike Willis .15 .06
325 Ray Knight .40 .16
326 Biff Pocoroba .15 .06
327 Moose Haas .15 .06
328 Dave Engle .15 .06
Greg Johnston
Gary Ward
329 Joaquin Andujar .40 .16
330 Frank White .40 .16
331 Dennis Lamp .15 .06
332 Lee Lacy DP .07 .03
333 Sid Monge .15 .06
334 Dane Iorg .15 .06
335 Rick Cerone .15 .06
336 Eddie Whitson .15 .06
337 Lynn Jones .15 .06
338 Checklist 243-363 .75 .30
339 John Ellis .15 .06
340 Bruce Kison .15 .06
341 Dwayne Murphy .15 .06
342 Eric Rasmussen DP .07 .03
343 Frank Taveras .15 .06
344 Byron McLaughlin .15 .06
345 Warren Cromartie .15 .06
346 Larry Christenson DP .07 .03
347 Harold Baines RC 8.00 3.20
348 Bob Sykes .15 .06
349 Glenn Hoffman .15 .06
350 J.R. Richard .40 .16
351 Otto Velez .15 .06
352 Dick Tidrow DP .07 .03
353 Terry Kennedy .15 .06
354 Mario Soto .15 .06
355 Bob Horner .40 .16
356 George Stablein .15 .06
Craig Stimac
Tom Tellmann
357 Jim Slaton .15 .06
358 Mark Wagner .15 .06
359 Tom Hausman .15 .06
360 Willie Wilson .40 .16
361 Joe Strain .15 .06
362 Bo Diaz .15 .06
363 Geoff Zahn .15 .06
364 Mike Davis .15 .06
365 Graig Nettles DP .40 .16
366 Mike Ramsey RC .15 .06
367 Dennis Martinez .75 .30
368 Leon Roberts .15 .06
369 Frank Tanana .40 .16
370 Dave Winfield .75 .30
371 Charlie Hough .40 .16
372 Jay Johnstone .40 .16
373 Pat Underwood .15 .06
374 Tommy Hutton .15 .06
375 Dave Concepcion .40 .16
376 Ron Reed .15 .06
377 Jerry Morales .15 .06
378 Dave Rader .15 .06
379 Lary Sorensen .15 .06
380 Willie Stargell .75 .30
381 Carlos Lezcano .15 .06
Steve Macko
Randy Martz
382 Paul Mirabella .15 .06
383 Eric Soderholm DP .07 .03
384 Mike Sadek .15 .06
385 Joe Sambito .15 .06
386 Dave Edwards .15 .06
387 Phil Niekro .40 .16
388 Andre Thornton .40 .16
389 Marty Pattin .15 .06
390 Cesar Geronimo .15 .06
391 Dave Lemanczyk DP .07 .03
392 Lance Parrish .40 .16
393 Broderick Perkins .15 .06
394 Woodie Fryman .15 .06
395 Scot Thompson .15 .06
396 Bill Campbell .15 .06
397 Julio Cruz .15 .06
398 Ross Baumgarten .15 .06
399 Mike Boddicker RC 1.50 .60
Mark Corey
Floyd Rayford
400 Reggie Jackson .75 .30
401 George Brett ALCS 2.50 1.00
402 NL Champs .75 .30
Phillies squeak
past Astros
(Phillies celebrating)
403 Larry Bowa WS .75 .30
404 Tug McGraw WS .75 .30
405 Nino Espinosa .15 .06
406 Dickie Noles .15 .06
407 Ernie Whitt .15 .06
408 Fernando Arroyo .15 .06
409 Larry Herndon .15 .06
410 Bert Campaneris .40 .16
411 Terry Puhl .15 .06
412 Britt Burns .15 .06
413 Tony Bernazard .15 .06
414 John Pacella DP .07 .03
415 Ben Oglivie .40 .16
416 Gary Alexander .15 .06
417 Dan Schatzeder .15 .06
418 Bobby Brown .15 .06
419 Tom Hume .15 .06
420 Keith Hernandez .75 .30
421 Bob Stanley .15 .06
422 Dan Ford .15 .06
423 Shane Rawley .15 .06
424 Tim Lollar .15 .06
Bruce Robinson
Dennis Werth
425 Al Bumbry .40 .16
426 Warren Brusstar .15 .06
427 John D'Acquisto .15 .06
428 John Stearns .15 .06
429 Mick Kelleher .15 .06
430 Jim Bibby .15 .06
431 Dave Roberts .15 .06
432 Len Barker .15 .06
433 Rance Mulliniks .15 .06
434 Roger Erickson .15 .06
435 Jim Spencer .15 .06
436 Gary Lucas .15 .06
437 Mike Heath DP .07 .03
438 John Montefusco .15 .06
439 Denny Walling .15 .06
440 Jerry Reuss .40 .16
441 Ken Reitz .15 .06
442 Ron Pruitt .15 .06
443 Jim Beattie DP .07 .03
444 Garth Iorg .15 .06
445 Ellis Valentine .15 .06
446 Checklist 364-484 .75 .30
447 Junior Kennedy DP .07 .03
448 Tim Corcoran .15 .06
449 Paul Mitchell .15 .06
450 Dave Kingman DP .40 .16
451 Chris Bando .15 .06
Tom Brennan
Sandy Wihtol
452 Renie Martin .15 .06
453 Rob Wilfong DP .40 .16
454 Andy Hassler .15 .06
455 Rick Burleson .15 .06
456 Jeff Reardon RC 1.50 .60
457 Mike Lum .15 .06
458 Randy Jones .15 .06
459 Greg Gross .15 .06
460 Rich Gossage .75 .30
461 Dave McKay .15 .06
462 Jack Brohamer .15 .06
463 Milt May .15 .06
464 Adrian Devine .15 .06
465 Bill Russell .40 .16
466 Bob Molinaro .15 .06
467 Dave Stieb .40 .16
468 John Wockenfuss .15 .06
469 Jeff Leonard .40 .16
470 Manny Trillo .15 .06
471 Mike Vail .15 .06
472 Dyar Miller DP .07 .03
473 Jose Cardenal .15 .06
474 Mike LaCoss .15 .06
475 Buddy Bell .40 .16
476 Jerry Koosman .40 .16
477 Luis Gomez .15 .06
478 Juan Eichelberger .15 .06
479 Tim Raines RC 3.00 1.20
Roberto Ramos
Bobby Pate
480 Carlton Fisk .75 .30
481 Bob Lacey DP .07 .03
482 Jim Gantner .40 .16
483 Mike Griffin RC .15 .06
484 Max Venable DP .07 .03
485 Garry Templeton .15 .06
486 Marc Hill .15 .06
487 Dewey Robinson .15 .06
488 Damaso Garcia .15 .06
489 John Littlefield .15 .06
Photo on card believed to be Mark Riggins
490 Eddie Murray 2.50 1.00
491 Gordy Pladson .15 .06
492 Barry Foote .15 .06
493 Dan Quisenberry .40 .16
494 Bob Walk RC .40 .16
495 Dusty Baker .75 .30
496 Paul Dade .15 .06
497 Fred Norman .15 .06
498 Pat Putnam .15 .06
499 Frank Pastore .15 .06
500 Jim Rice .40 .16
501 Tim Foli DP .07 .03
502 Chris Bourjos .40 .16
Al Hargesheimer
Mike Rowland
503 Steve McCatty .15 .06
504 Dale Murphy 1.50 .60
505 Jason Thompson .15 .06
506 Phil Huffman .15 .06
507 Jamie Quirk .15 .06
508 Rob Dressler .15 .06
509 Pete Mackanin .15 .06
510 Lee Mazzilli .15 .06
511 Wayne Garland .15 .06
512 Gary Thomasson .15 .06
513 Frank LaCorte .15 .06
514 George Riley .15 .06
515 Robin Yount 2.50 1.00
516 Doug Bird .15 .06
517 Richie Zisk .15 .06
518 Grant Jackson .15 .06
519 John Tamargo DP .40 .16
520 Steve Stone .40 .16
521 Sam Mejias .15 .06
522 Mike Colbern .15 .06
523 John Fulgham .15 .06
524 Willie Aikens .15 .06
525 Mike Torrez .15 .06
526 Marty Bystrom .15 .06
Jay Loviglio
Jim Wright
527 Danny Goodwin .15 .06
528 Gary Matthews .40 .16
529 Dave LaRoche .15 .06
530 Steve Garvey .40 .16
531 John Curtis .15 .06
532 Bill Stein .15 .06
533 Jesus Figueroa .15 .06
534 Dave Smith RC .40 .16
535 Omar Moreno .15 .06
536 Bob Owchinko DP .07 .03
537 Ron Hodges .15 .06
538 Tom Griffin .15 .06
539 Rodney Scott .15 .06
540 Mike Schmidt DP 2.50 1.00
541 Steve Swisher .15 .06
542 Larry Bradford DP .07 .03
543 Terry Crowley .15 .06
544 Rich Gale .15 .06
545 Johnny Grubb .15 .06
546 Paul Moskau .15 .06
547 Mario Guerrero .15 .06
548 Dave Goltz .15 .06
549 Jerry Remy .15 .06
550 Tommy John .75 .30
551 Vance Law 1.50 .60
Tony Pena RC
Pascual Perez RC
552 Steve Trout .15 .06
553 Tim Blackwell .15 .06
554 Bert Blyleven UER .75 .30
(1 is missing from
1980 on card back)
555 Cecil Cooper .40 .16
556 Jerry Mumphrey .15 .06
557 Chris Knapp .15 .06
558 Barry Bonnell .15 .06
559 Willie Montanez .15 .06
560 Joe Morgan .75 .30
561 Dennis Littlejohn .15 .06
562 Checklist 485-605 .75 .30
563 Jim Kaat .40 .16
564 Ron Hassey DP .07 .03
565 Burt Hooton .15 .06
566 Del Unser .15 .06
567 Mark Bomback .15 .06
568 Dave Revering .15 .06
569 Al Williams DP .07 .03
570 Ken Singleton .40 .16
571 Todd Cruz .15 .06
572 Jack Morris .75 .30
573 Phil Garner .40 .16
574 Bill Caudill .15 .06
575 Tony Perez .75 .30
576 Reggie Cleveland .15 .06
577 Luis Leal .15 .06
Brian Milner
Ken Schrom
578 Bill Gullickson RC .75 .30
579 Tim Flannery .15 .06
580 Don Baylor .75 .30
581 Roy Howell .15 .06
582 Gaylord Perry .40 .16
583 Larry Milbourne .15 .06
584 Randy Lerch .15 .06
585 Amos Otis .40 .16
586 Silvio Martinez .15 .06
587 Jeff Newman .15 .06
588 Gary Lavelle .15 .06
589 Lamar Johnson .15 .06
590 Bruce Sutter .40 .16
591 John Lowenstein .15 .06
592 Steve Comer .15 .06
593 Steve Kemp .15 .06
594 Preston Hanna DP .07 .03
595 Butch Hobson .15 .06
596 Jerry Augustine .15 .06
597 Rafael Landestoy .15 .06
598 George Vukovich DP .07 .03
599 Dennis Kinney .15 .06
600 Johnny Bench 1.50 .60
601 Don Aase .15 .06
602 Bobby Murcer .40 .16
603 John Verhoeven .15 .06
604 Rob Picciolo .15 .06
605 Don Sutton 1.50 .60
606 Bruce Berenyi .15 .06
Geoff Combe
Paul Householder
607 David Palmer .15 .06
608 Greg Pryor .15 .06
609 Lynn McGlothen .15 .06
610 Darrell Porter .15 .06
611 Rick Matula DP .07 .03
612 Duane Kuiper .15 .06
613 Jim Anderson .15 .06
614 Dave Rozema .15 .06
615 Rick Dempsey .40 .16
616 Rick Wise .15 .06
617 Craig Reynolds .15 .06
618 John Milner .15 .06
619 Steve Henderson .15 .06
620 Dennis Eckersley .75 .30
621 Tom Donohue .15 .06
622 Randy Moffitt .15 .06
623 Sal Bando .40 .16
624 Bob Welch .40 .16
625 Bill Buckner .40 .16
626 Dave Steffen .15 .06
Jerry Ujdur
Roger Weaver
627 Luis Tiant .40 .16
628 Vic Correll .15 .06
629 Tony Armas .40 .16
630 Steve Carlton .40 .16
631 Ron Jackson .15 .06
632 Alan Bannister .15 .06
633 Bill Lee .40 .16
634 Doug Flynn .15 .06
635 Bobby Bonds .40 .16
636 Al Hrabosky .15 .06
637 Jerry Narron .15 .06
638 Checklist 606-726 .75 .30
639 Carney Lansford .40 .16
640 Dave Parker .40 .16
641 Mark Belanger .40 .16
642 Vern Ruhle .15 .06
643 Lloyd Moseby .40 .16
644 Ramon Aviles DP .07 .03
645 Rick Reuschel .40 .16
646 Marvis Foley .15 .06
647 Dick Drago .15 .06
648 Darrell Evans .40 .16
649 Manny Sarmiento .15 .06
650 Bucky Dent .40 .16
651 Pedro Guerrero .75 .30
652 John Montague .15 .06
653 Bill Fahey .15 .06
654 Ray Burris .15 .06
655 Dan Driessen .15 .06
656 Jon Matlack .15 .06
657 Mike Cubbage DP .07 .03
658 Milt Wilcox .15 .06
659 John Flinn .15 .06
Ed Romero
Ned Yost
660 Gary Carter .75 .30
661 Orioles Team CL .75 .30
Earl Weaver MG
662 Red Sox Team CL .75 .30
Ralph Houk MG
663 Angels Team CL .75 .30
Jim Fregosi MG
664 White Sox CL .75 .30
Tony LaRussa MG
665 Indians Team CL .75 .30
Dave Garcia MG
666 Tigers Team CL .75 .30
Sparky Anderson MG
667 Royals Team CL .75 .30
Jim Frey MG
668 Brewers Team CL .75 .30
Bob Rodgers MG
669 Twins Team CL .75 .30
John Goryl MG
670 Yankees Team CL .75 .30
Gene Michael MG
671 A's Team CL .75 .30
Billy Martin MG
672 Mariners Team CL .75 .30
Maury Wills MG
673 Rangers Team CL .75 .30
Don Zimmer MG
674 Blue Jays Team CL .75 .30
Bobby Mattick MG
675 Braves Team CL .75 .30
Bobby Cox MG
676 Cubs Team CL .75 .30
Joe Amalfitano MG
677 Reds Team CL .75 .30
John McNamara MG
678 Astros Team CL .75 .30
Bill Virdon MG
679 Dodgers Team CL .75 .30
Tom Lasorda MG
680 Expos Team CL .75 .30
Dick Williams MG
681 Mets Team CL .75 .30
Joe Torre MG
682 Phillies Team CL .75 .30
Dallas Green MG
683 Pirates Team CL .75 .30
Chuck Tanner MG
684 Cardinals Team CL .75 .30
Whitey Herzog MG
685 Padres Team CL .75 .30
Frank Howard MG
686 Giants Team CL .75 .30
Dave Bristol MG
687 Jeff Jones .15 .06
688 Kiko Garcia .15 .06
689 Bruce Hurst RC 1.50 .60
Keith MacWhorter
Reid Nichols
690 Bob Watson .40 .16
691 Dick Ruthven .15 .06
692 Lenny Randle .15 .06
693 Steve Howe .40 .16
694 Bud Harrelson DP .15 .06
695 Kent Tekulve .40 .16
696 Alan Ashby .15 .06
697 Rick Waits .15 .06
698 Mike Jorgensen .15 .06
699 Glenn Abbott .15 .06
700 George Brett 4.00 1.60
701 Joe Rudi .40 .16
702 George Medich .15 .06
703 Alvis Woods .15 .06
704 Bill Travers DP .07 .03
705 Ted Simmons .40 .16
706 Dave Ford .15 .06
707 Dave Cash .15 .06
708 Doyle Alexander .15 .06
709 Alan Trammell DP .75 .30
710 Ron LeFlore DP .15 .06
711 Joe Ferguson .15 .06
712 Bill Bonham .15 .06
713 Bill North .15 .06
714 Pete Redfern .15 .06
715 Bill Madlock .40 .16
716 Glenn Borgmann .15 .06
717 Jim Barr DP .07 .03
718 Larry Biittner .15 .06
719 Sparky Lyle .40 .16
720 Fred Lynn .40 .16
721 Toby Harrah .40 .16
722 Joe Niekro .40 .16
723 Bruce Bochte .15 .06
724 Lou Piniella .40 .16
725 Steve Rogers .15 .06
726 Rick Monday .40 .16

1981 Topps Traded

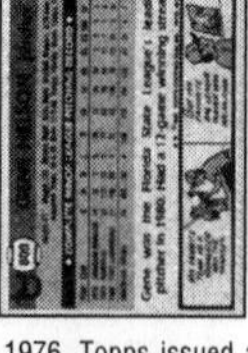

For the first time since 1976, Topps issued a 132-card factory boxed "traded" set in 1981, issued exclusively through hobby dealers. This set was sequentially numbered, alphabetically, from 727 to 858 and carries the same design as the regular issue 1981 Topps set. There are no key Rookie Cards in this set although Tim Raines, Jeff Reardon, and Fernando Valenzuela are depicted in their rookie year for cards. The key extended Rookie Card in the set is Danny Ainge.

Nm-Mt Ex-Mt
COMP.FACT.SET (132) 30.00 12.00
727 Danny Ainge XRC 5.00 2.00
728 Doyle Alexander .25 .10
729 Gary Alexander .25 .10
730 Bill Almon .25 .10
731 Joaquin Andujar 1.00 .40
732 Bob Bailor .25 .10
733 Juan Beniquez .25 .10
734 Dave Bergman .25 .10
735 Tony Bernazard .25 .10
736 Larry Biittner .25 .10

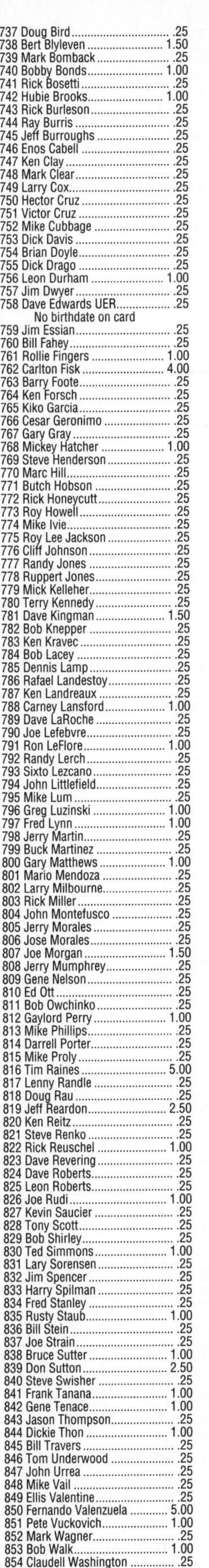
737 Doug Bird .25 .10
738 Bert Blyleven 1.50 .60
739 Mark Bomback .25 .10
740 Bobby Bonds 1.00 .40
741 Rick Bosetti .25 .10
742 Hubie Brooks 1.00 .40
743 Rick Burleson .25 .10
744 Ray Burris .25 .10
745 Jeff Burroughs .25 .10
746 Enos Cabell .25 .10
747 Ken Clay .25 .10
748 Mark Clear .25 .10
749 Larry Cox .25 .10
750 Hector Cruz .25 .10
751 Victor Cruz .25 .10
752 Mike Cubbage .25 .10
753 Dick Davis .25 .10
754 Brian Doyle .25 .10
755 Dick Drago .25 .10
756 Leon Durham 1.00 .40
757 Jim Dwyer .25 .10
758 Dave Edwards UER .25 .10
No birthdate on card
759 Jim Essian .25 .10
760 Bill Fahey .25 .10
761 Rollie Fingers 1.00 .40
762 Carlton Fisk 4.00 1.60
763 Barry Foote .25 .10
764 Ken Forsch .25 .10
765 Kiko Garcia .25 .10
766 Cesar Geronimo .25 .10
767 Gary Gray .25 .10
768 Mickey Hatcher 1.00 .40
769 Steve Henderson .25 .10
770 Marc Hill .25 .10
771 Butch Hobson .25 .10
772 Rick Honeycutt .25 .10
773 Roy Howell .25 .10
774 Mike Ivie .25 .10
775 Roy Lee Jackson .25 .10
776 Cliff Johnson .25 .10
777 Randy Jones .25 .10
778 Ruppert Jones .25 .10
779 Mick Kelleher .25 .10
780 Terry Kennedy .25 .10
781 Dave Kingman 1.50 .60
782 Bob Knepper .25 .10
783 Ken Kravec .25 .10
784 Bob Lacey .25 .10
785 Dennis Lamp .25 .10
786 Rafael Landestoy .25 .10
787 Ken Landreaux .25 .10
788 Carney Lansford 1.00 .40
789 Dave LaRoche .25 .10
790 Joe Lefebvre .25 .10
791 Ron LeFlore 1.00 .40
792 Randy Lerch .25 .10
793 Sixto Lezcano .25 .10
794 John Littlefield .25 .10
795 Mike Lum .25 .10
796 Greg Luzinski 1.00 .40
797 Fred Lynn 1.00 .40
798 Jerry Martin .25 .10
799 Buck Martinez .25 .10
800 Gary Matthews 1.00 .40
801 Mario Mendoza .25 .10
802 Larry Milbourne .25 .10
803 Rick Miller .25 .10
804 John Montefusco .25 .10
805 Jerry Morales .25 .10
806 Jose Morales .25 .10
807 Joe Morgan 1.50 .60
808 Jerry Mumphrey .25 .10
809 Gene Nelson .25 .10
810 Ed Ott .25 .10
811 Bob Owchinko .25 .10
812 Gaylord Perry 1.00 .40
813 Mike Phillips .25 .10
814 Darrell Porter .25 .10
815 Mike Proly .25 .10
816 Tim Raines 5.00 2.00
817 Lenny Randle .25 .10
818 Doug Rau .25 .10
819 Jeff Reardon 2.50 1.00
820 Ken Reitz .25 .10
821 Steve Renko .25 .10
822 Rick Reuschel 1.00 .40
823 Dave Revering .25 .10
824 Dave Roberts .25 .10
825 Leon Roberts .25 .10
826 Joe Rudi 1.00 .40
827 Kevin Saucier .25 .10
828 Tony Scott .25 .10
829 Bob Shirley .25 .10
830 Ted Simmons 1.00 .40
831 Lary Sorensen .25 .10
832 Jim Spencer .25 .10
833 Harry Spilman .25 .10
834 Fred Stanley .25 .10
835 Rusty Staub 1.00 .40
836 Bill Stein .25 .10
837 Joe Strain .25 .10
838 Bruce Sutter 1.00 .40
839 Don Sutton 2.50 1.00
840 Steve Swisher .25 .10
841 Frank Tanana 1.00 .40
842 Gene Tenace 1.00 .40
843 Jason Thompson .25 .10
844 Dickie Thon 1.00 .40
845 Bill Travers .25 .10
846 Tom Underwood .25 .10
847 John Urrea .25 .10
848 Mike Vail .25 .10
849 Ellis Valentine .25 .10
850 Fernando Valenzuela 5.00 2.00
851 Pete Vuckovich 1.00 .40
852 Mark Wagner .25 .10
853 Bob Walk 1.00 .40
854 Claudell Washington .25 .10
855 Dave Winfield 4.00 1.60
856 Geoff Zahn .25 .10
857 Richie Zisk .25 .10
858 Checklist 727-858 .25 .10

1981 Topps Scratchoffs

The cards in this 108-card set measure 1 13/16" by 3 1/4" in a three-card panel measuring 3 1/4" by 5 1/4". The 1981 Topps Scratch-Offs were issued in their own wrapper with bubble gum. The title "Scratch-Off" refers to the black dots of each card which, when rubbed or scraped with a hard edge, reveal a baseball game. While there are only 108 possible individual cards in the set, there are 144 possible panels combinations. The N.L. players appear with green backgrounds and A.L. players with red backgrounds. The numbering of the cards in the set is according to league with American Leaguers (1-54) and National Leaguers (55-108). Some cards are found without dots. An intact panel is worth 20 percent more than the sum of its individual cards.

Nm-Mt Ex-Mt
COMPLETE SET (108) 10.00 4.00
1 George Brett 1.00 .40
2 Cecil Cooper .15 .06
3 Reggie Jackson .60 .24
4 Al Oliver .15 .06
5 Fred Lynn .15 .06
6 Tony Armas .10 .04
7 Ben Oglivie .10 .04
8 Tony Perez .50 .20
9 Eddie Murray .60 .24
10 Robin Yount .50 .20
11 Steve Kemp .10 .04
12 Joe Charboneau .25 .10
13 Jim Rice .25 .10
14 Lance Parrish .15 .06
15 John Mayberry .10 .04
16 Richie Zisk .10 .04
17 Ken Singleton .10 .04
18 Rod Carew .50 .20
19 Rick Manning .10 .04
20 Willie Wilson .10 .04
21 Buddy Bell .15 .06
22 Dave Revering .10 .04
23 Tom Paciorek .10 .04
24 Champ Summers .10 .04
25 Carney Lansford .15 .06
26 Lamar Johnson .10 .04
27 Willie Aikens .10 .04
28 Rick Cerone .10 .04
29 Al Bumbry .10 .04
30 Bruce Bochte .10 .04
31 Mickey Rivers .15 .06
32 Mike Hargrove .15 .06
33 John Castino .10 .04
34 Chet Lemon .10 .04
35 Paul Molitor .50 .20
36 Willie Randolph .15 .06
37 Rick Burleson .10 .04
38 Alan Trammell .40 .16
39 Rickey Henderson 1.00 .40
40 Dan Meyer .10 .04
41 Ken Landreaux .10 .04
42 Damaso Garcia .10 .04
43 Roy Smalley .10 .04
44 Otto Velez .10 .04
45 Sixto Lezcano .10 .04
46 Toby Harrah .15 .06
47 Frank White .15 .06
48 Dave Stapleton .10 .04
49 Steve Stone .10 .04
50 Jim Palmer .50 .20
51 Larry Gura .10 .04
52 Tommy John .25 .10
53 Mike Norris .10 .04
54 Ed Farmer .10 .04
55 Bill Buckner .15 .06
56 Steve Garvey .25 .10
57 Reggie Smith .15 .06
58 Bake McBride .10 .04
59 Dave Parker .15 .06
60 Mike Schmidt .75 .30
61 Bob Horner .10 .04
62 Pete Rose .75 .30
63 Ted Simmons .15 .06
64 Johnny Bench .50 .20
65 George Foster .15 .06
66 Gary Carter .50 .20
67 Keith Hernandez .15 .06
68 Ozzie Smith .75 .30
69 Dave Kingman .15 .06
70 Jack Clark .15 .06
71 Dusty Baker .15 .06
72 Dale Murphy .40 .16
73 Ron Cey .15 .06
74 Greg Luzinski .15 .06
75 Lee Mazzilli .15 .06
76 Gary Matthews .15 .06
77 Cesar Cedeno .10 .04
78 Warren Cromartie .10 .04
79 Steve Henderson .10 .04
80 Ellis Valentine .10 .04
81 Mike Easler .10 .04
82 Garry Templeton .10 .04
83 Jose Cruz .15 .06
84 Dave Collins .10 .04
85 George Hendrick .10 .04
86 Gene Richards .10 .04
87 Terry Whitfield .10 .04
88 Terry Puhl .10 .04
89 Larry Parrish .10 .04
90 Andre Dawson .40 .16
91 Ken Griffey .15 .06
92 Dave Lopes .15 .06
93 Doug Flynn .10 .04
94 Ivan DeJesus .10 .04
95 Dave Concepcion .15 .06
96 John Stearns .10 .04
97 Jerry Mumphrey .10 .04
98 Jerry Martin .10 .04
99 Art Howe .15 .06
100 Omar Moreno .10 .04
101 Ken Reitz .10 .04
102 Phil Garner .10 .04
103 Jerry Reuss .15 .06
104 Steve Carlton .40 .16
105 Jim Bibby .10 .04
106 Steve Rogers .10 .04
107 Tom Seaver .50 .20
108 Vida Blue .15 .06

1981 Topps Stickers

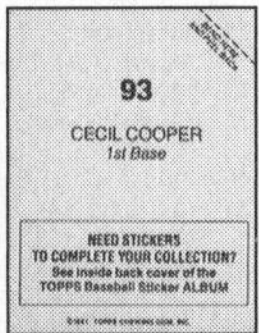

Made for Topps by Panini, an Italian company, these 262 stickers measure 1 15/16" by 2 9/16" and are numbered on both front and back. The set was the first of the Topps/O-Pee-Chee/Panini genre of sticker sets. The fronts feature white-bordered color player action shots. The backs carry the player's name and position. Team affiliations are not shown. An album onto which the stickers could be affixed was available at retail stores. The first 32 stickers depict 1980 major league pitching and batting leaders. Stickers 33-240 are arranged by teams as follows: Baltimore Orioles (33-40), Boston Red Sox (41-48), California Angels (49-56), Chicago White Sox (57-64), Cleveland Indians (65-72), Detroit Tigers (73-80), Kansas City Royals (81-88), Milwaukee Brewers (91-98), Minnesota Twins (99-106), New York Yankees (107-114), Oakland A's (115-122), Seattle Mariners (123-130), Texas Rangers (130-136), Toronto Blue Jays (137-143), Atlanta Braves (144-150), Chicago Cubs (151-158), Cincinnati Reds (159-166), Houston Astros (167-174), Los Angeles Dodgers (175-182), Montreal Expos (183-190), New York Mets (191-198), Philadelphia Phillies (199-208), Pittsburgh Pirates (209-216), St. Louis Cardinals (217-224), San Diego Padres (225-232) and San Francisco Giants (233-240). Stickers 241-262 have color photos of "All-Star" players printed on silver (AL) or gold (NL) foil.

Nm-Mt Ex-Mt
COMPLETE SET (262) 25.00 10.00
COMMON STICKER (1-240) .05 .02
COMMON FOIL (241-262) .10 .04
1 Steve Stone .05 .02
2 Tommy John .15 .06
Mike Norris
3 Rudy May .05 .02
4 Mike Norris .05 .02
5 Len Barker .05 .02
6 Mike Norris .05 .02
7 Dan Quisenberry .15 .06
8 Rich Gossage .25 .10
9 George Brett 2.50 1.00
10 Cecil Cooper .15 .06
11 Reggie Jackson .40 .16
Ben Oglivie
12 Gorman Thomas .05 .02
13 Cecil Cooper .15 .06
14 George Brett 1.25 .50
Ben Oglivie
15 Rickey Henderson 2.50 1.00
16 Willie Wilson .15 .06
17 Bill Buckner .15 .06
18 Keith Hernandez .15 .06
19 Mike Schmidt 1.50 .60
20 Bob Horner .05 .02
21 Mike Schmidt 1.50 .60
22 George Hendrick .05 .02
23 Ron LeFlore .15 .06
24 Omar Moreno .05 .02
25 Steve Carlton .60 .24
26 Joe Niekro .15 .06
27 Don Sutton .40 .16
28 Steve Carlton .60 .24
29 Steve Carlton .60 .24
30 Nolan Ryan 3.00 1.20
31 Rollie Fingers .15 .06
Tom Hume
32 Bruce Sutter .15 .06
33 Ken Singleton .05 .02
34 Eddie Murray 2.00 .80
35 Al Bumbry .05 .02
36 Rich Dauer .05 .02
37 Scott McGregor .05 .02
38 Rick Dempsey .05 .02
39 Jim Palmer .40 .16
40 Steve Stone .05 .02
41 Jim Rice .25 .10
42 Fred Lynn .15 .06
43 Carney Lansford .15 .06
44 Tony Perez .40 .16
45 Carl Yastrzemski .60 .24
46 Carlton Fisk .75 .30
47 Dave Stapleton .05 .02
48 Dennis Eckersley .40 .16
49 Rod Carew .60 .24
50 Brian Downing .05 .02
51 Don Baylor .25 .10
52 Rick Burleson .05 .02
53 Bobby Grich .15 .06
54 Butch Hobson .05 .02
55 Andy Hassler .05 .02
56 Frank Tanana .15 .06
57 Chet Lemon .05 .02
58 Lamar Johnson .05 .02
59 Wayne Nordhagen .05 .02
60 Jim Morrison .05 .02
61 Bob Molinaro .05 .02
62 Rich Dotson .05 .02
63 Britt Burns .05 .02
64 Ed Farmer .05 .02
65 Toby Harrah .15 .06
66 Joe Charboneau .40 .16
67 Miguel Dilone .05 .02
68 Mike Hargrove .15 .06
69 Rick Manning .05 .02
70 Andre Thornton .15 .06
71 Ron Hassey .05 .02
72 Len Barker .05 .02
73 Lance Parrish .15 .06
74 Steve Kemp .05 .02
75 Alan Trammell .75 .30
76 Champ Summers .05 .02
77 Rick Peters .05 .02
78 Kirk Gibson 1.25 .50
79 Johnny Wockenfuss .05 .02
80 Jack Morris .25 .10
81 Willie Wilson .15 .06
82 George Brett 2.50 1.00
83 Frank White .15 .06
84 Willie Aikens .05 .02
85 Clint Hurdle .05 .02
86 Hal McRae .15 .06
87 Dennis Leonard .05 .02
88 Larry Gura .05 .02
89 AL Pennant Winner .05 .02
90 AL Pennant Winner .05 .02
91 Paul Molitor 1.50 .60
92 Ben Oglivie .15 .06
93 Cecil Cooper .15 .06
94 Ted Simmons .15 .06
95 Robin Yount .75 .30
96 Gorman Thomas .05 .02
97 Mike Caldwell .05 .02
98 Moose Haas .05 .02
99 John Castino .05 .02
100 Roy Smalley .05 .02
101 Ken Landreaux .05 .02
102 Butch Wynegar .05 .02
103 Ron Jackson .05 .02
104 Jerry Koosman .15 .06
105 Roger Erickson .05 .02
106 Doug Corbett .05 .02
107 Reggie Jackson .75 .30
108 Willie Randolph .15 .06
109 Rick Cerone .05 .02
110 Bucky Dent .15 .06
111 Dave Winfield .75 .30
112 Ron Guidry .15 .06
113 Rich Gossage .25 .10
114 Tommy John .25 .10
115 Rickey Henderson 2.50 1.00
116 Tony Armas .05 .02
117 Dave Revering .05 .02
118 Wayne Gross .05 .02
119 Dwayne Murphy .05 .02
120 Jeff Newman .05 .02
121 Rick Langford .05 .02
122 Mike Norris .05 .02
123 Bruce Bochte .05 .02
124 Tom Paciorek .15 .06
125 Dan Meyer .05 .02
126 Julio Cruz .05 .02
127 Richie Zisk .05 .02
128 Floyd Bannister .05 .02
129 Shane Rawley .05 .02
130 Buddy Bell .15 .06
131 Al Oliver .15 .06
132 Mickey Rivers .15 .06
133 Jim Sundberg .15 .06
134 Bump Wills .05 .02
135 Jon Matlack .05 .02
136 Danny Darwin .15 .06
137 Damaso Garcia .05 .02
138 Otto Velez .05 .02
139 John Mayberry .05 .02
140 Alfredo Griffin .05 .02
141 Alvis Woods .05 .02
142 Dave Stieb .15 .06
143 Jim Clancy .05 .02
144 Gary Matthews .15 .06
145 Bob Horner .15 .06
146 Dale Murphy .40 .16
147 Chris Chambliss .15 .06
148 Phil Niekro .40 .16
149 Glenn Hubbard .05 .02
150 Rick Camp .05 .02
151 Dave Kingman .25 .10
152 Bill Caudill .05 .02
153 Bill Buckner .15 .06
154 Barry Foote .05 .02
155 Mike Tyson .05 .02
156 Ivan DeJesus .05 .02
157 Rick Reuschel .15 .06
158 Ken Reitz .05 .02
159 George Foster .15 .06
160 Johnny Bench .75 .30
161 Dave Concepcion .15 .06
162 Dave Collins .05 .02
163 Ken Griffey .15 .06
164 Dan Driessen .05 .02
165 Tom Seaver .75 .30
166 Tom Hume .05 .02
167 Cesar Cedeno .15 .06
168 Rafael Landestoy .05 .02
169 Jose Cruz .15 .06
170 Art Howe .05 .02
171 Terry Puhl .05 .02
172 Joe Sambito .05 .02
173 Nolan Ryan 3.00 1.20
174 Joe Niekro .15 .06
175 Dave Lopes .15 .06
176 Steve Garvey .40 .16
177 Ron Cey .15 .06
178 Reggie Smith .15 .06
179 Bill Russell .15 .06
180 Burt Hooton .05 .02
181 Jerry Reuss .15 .06
182 Dusty Baker .15 .06
183 Larry Parrish .05 .02
184 Gary Carter .40 .16
185 Rodney Scott .05 .02
186 Ellis Valentine .05 .02
187 Andre Dawson .75 .30
188 Warren Cromartie .05 .02
189 Chris Speier .05 .02
190 Steve Rogers .05 .02
191 Lee Mazzilli .05 .02
192 Doug Flynn .05 .02
193 Steve Henderson .05 .02
194 John Stearns .05 .02
195 Joel Youngblood .05 .02
196 Frank Taveras .05 .02
197 Pat Zachry .05 .02
198 Neil Allen .05 .02
199 Mike Schmidt 1.50 .60
200 Pete Rose 1.25 .50
201 Larry Bowa .15 .06
202 Bake McBride .05 .02
203 Bob Boone .15 .06
204 Garry Maddox .05 .02
205 Tug McGraw .15 .06
206 Steve Carlton .40 .16
207 NL Pennant Winner .05 .02
(World Champions)
208 NL Pennant Winner .05 .02
(World Champions)
209 Phil Garner .15 .06
210 Dave Parker .15 .06
211 Omar Moreno .05 .02
212 Mike Easler .05 .02
213 Bill Madlock .15 .06
214 Ed Ott .05 .02
215 Willie Stargell .40 .16
216 Jim Bibby .05 .02
217 Garry Templeton .05 .02
218 Sixto Lezcano .05 .02
219 Keith Hernandez .15 .06
220 George Hendrick .05 .02
221 Bruce Sutter .15 .06
222 Ken Oberkfell .05 .02
223 Tony Scott .05 .02
224 Darrell Porter .15 .06
225 Gene Richards .05 .02
226 Broderick Perkins .05 .02
227 Jerry Mumphrey .05 .02
228 Luis Salazar .05 .02
229 Jerry Turner .05 .02
230 Ozzie Smith 2.50 1.00
231 John Curtis .05 .02
232 Rick Wise .05 .02
233 Terry Whitfield .05 .02
234 Jack Clark .15 .06
235 Darrell Evans .15 .06
236 Larry Herndon .05 .02
237 Milt May .05 .02
238 Greg Minton .05 .02
239 Vida Blue .15 .06
240 Eddie Whitson .05 .02
241 Cecil Cooper FOIL .25 .10
242 Willie Randolph FOIL .15 .06
243 George Brett FOIL 3.00 1.20
244 Robin Yount FOIL 1.00 .40
245 Reggie Jackson FOIL 1.00 .40
246 Al Oliver FOIL .25 .10
247 Willie Wilson FOIL .25 .10
248 Rick Cerone FOIL .10 .04
249 Steve Stone FOIL .10 .04
250 Tommy John FOIL .25 .10
251 Rich Gossage FOIL .25 .10
252 Steve Garvey FOIL .25 .10
253 Phil Garner FOIL .15 .06
254 Mike Schmidt FOIL 2.00 .80
255 Garry Templeton FOIL .10 .04
256 George Hendrick FOIL .10 .04
257 Dave Parker FOIL .25 .10
258 Cesar Cedeno FOIL .25 .10
259 Gary Carter FOIL .40 .16
260 Jim Bibby FOIL .10 .04
261 Steve Carlton FOIL .75 .30
262 Tug McGraw FOIL .25 .10
NNO Album 1.00 .40

1981 Topps Super Home Team

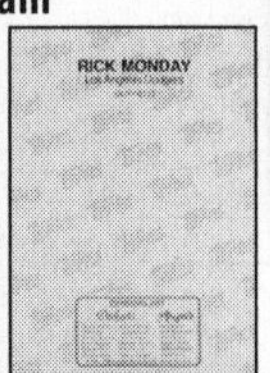

The cards in this 102-card set measure 4 7/8" by 6 7/8". In 1981 Topps issued an attractive series of photos of players from eleven AL and NL teams. The Phillies, Red Sox and Reds each were marketed in twelve-player subsets. Eighteen-player subsets were issued for the following areas: Chicago (nine White Sox and nine Cubs); New York (twelve Yankees and six Mets); Los Angeles (twelve Dodgers and six Angels); and Texas (six Rangers and six Astros). The cards of each subset contain a subset checklist on the reverse. Team sets could be obtained via a mail offer printed on the wrapper. These cards are often sold by the team or team pair. The checklist below is organized alphabetically by team(s); Boston (1-12), Chicago (13-30), Cincinnati (31-42), Los Angeles (43-60), New York (61-78), Philadelphia (79-90) and Texas (91-102).

Nm-Mt Ex-Mt
COMPLETE SET (102) 30.00 12.00
1 Tom Burgmeier .10 .04
2 Dennis Eckersley 1.00 .40
3 Dwight Evans .50 .20
4 Carlton Fisk 1.00 .40
5 Glenn Hoffman .10 .04
6 Carney Lansford .25 .10
7 Tony Perez 1.00 .40
8 Jim Rice .50 .20
9 Bob Stanley .10 .04
10 Dave Stapleton .10 .04
11 Frank Tanana .25 .10
12 Carl Yastrzemski 1.25 .50
13 Britt Burns .25 .10
14 Rich Dotson .25 .10
15 Ed Farmer .10 .04
16 Lamar Johnson .10 .04
17 Ron LeFlore .10 .04
18 Chet Lemon .10 .04
19 Bob Molinaro .10 .04
20 Jim Morrison .10 .04
21 Wayne Nordhagen .10 .04
22 Tim Blackwell .10 .04
23 Bill Buckner .25 .10
24 Ivan DeJesus .10 .04
25 Leon Durham .25 .10
26 Dave Kingman .50 .20

27 Mike Krukow .10 .04
28 Ken Reitz .10 .04
29 Rick Reuschel .25 .10
30 Mike Tyson .10 .04
31 Johnny Bench 1.50 .60
32 Dave Collins .10 .04
33 Dave Concepcion .25 .10
34 Dan Driessen .10 .04
35 George Foster .25 .10
36 Ken Griffey .25 .10
37 Tom Hume .10 .04
38 Ray Knight .10 .04
39 Joe Nolan .10 .04
40 Ron Oester .10 .04
41 Tom Seaver 1.50 .60
42 Mario Soto .10 .04
43 Dusty Baker .25 .10
44 Ron Cey .25 .10
45 Steve Garvey .50 .20
46 Burt Hooton .10 .04
47 Steve Howe .10 .04
48 Davey Lopes .25 .10
49 Rick Monday .25 .10
50 Jerry Reuss .25 .10
51 Bill Russell .25 .10
52 Reggie Smith .25 .10
53 Bob Welch .25 .10
54 Steve Yeager .10 .04
55 Don Baylor .50 .20
56 Rick Burleson .10 .04
57 Rod Carew 1.00 .40
58 Bobby Grich .25 .10
59 Butch Hobson .10 .04
60 Fred Lynn .25 .10
61 Rick Cerone .10 .04
62 Bucky Dent .25 .10
63 Rich Gossage .50 .20
64 Ron Guidry .25 .10
65 Reggie Jackson 1.25 .50
66 Tommy John .50 .20
67 Ruppert Jones .10 .04
68 Rudy May .10 .04
69 Graig Nettles .50 .20
70 Willie Randolph .25 .10
71 Bob Watson .50 .20
72 Dave Winfield 1.50 .60
73 Neil Allen .10 .04
74 Doug Flynn .10 .04
75 Lee Mazzilli .25 .10
76 Rusty Staub .25 .10
77 Frank Taveras .10 .04
78 Alex Trevino .10 .04
79 Bob Boone .25 .10
80 Larry Bowa .25 .10
81 Steve Carlton 1.00 .40
82 Greg Luzinski .25 .10
83 Garry Maddox .10 .04
84 Bake McBride .10 .04
85 Tug McGraw .25 .10
86 Pete Rose 1.25 .50
87 Dick Ruthven .10 .04
88 Mike Schmidt 1.25 .50
89 Manny Trillo .10 .04
90 Del Unser .10 .04
91 Buddy Bell .25 .10
92 Jon Matlack .10 .04
93 Al Oliver .25 .10
94 Mickey Rivers .25 .10
95 Jim Sundberg .25 .10
96 Bump Wills .10 .04
97 Cesar Cedeno .25 .10
98 Jose Cruz .25 .10
99 Art Howe .25 .10
100 Terry Puhl .10 .04
101 Nolan Ryan 3.00 1.20
102 Don Sutton 1.00 .40

1981 Topps Super National

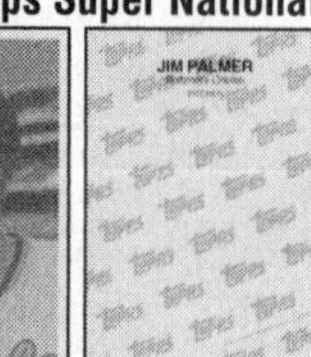

The cards in this 15-card set measure 4 7/8" by 6 7/8". In a format similar to the Home Team series of 1981 and the Super Star Photo set of 1980, these cards feature excellent photos of the top stars of 1981. The pictures of players appearing in both the regional Home Team and National sets are identical, but Brett, Cooper, Palmer, Parker and Simmons are unique to the latter and are indicated in the checklist below with an asterisk. The backs of the cards contain the player's name, team and position and a single copyright line.

Nm-Mt Ex-Mt
COMPLETE SET (15) 4.00 1.60
1 Buddy Bell .20 .08
2 Johnny Bench .50 .20
3 George Brett 1.00 .40
4 Rod Carew .50 .20
5 Cecil Cooper .10 .04
6 Steve Garvey .30 .12
7 Rich Gossage .20 .08
8 Reggie Jackson .50 .20
9 Jim Palmer .50 .20
10 Dave Parker .20 .08
11 Jim Rice .20 .08
12 Pete Rose .75 .30
13 Mike Schmidt .75 .30
14 Tom Seaver .50 .20
15 Ted Simmons .20 .08

1981 Topps Team Checklist Sheet

As part of a mail-away offer, Topps offered all 26 1981 team checklist cards on an uncut sheet. These cards enabled the collector to have an easy reference for which card(s) he/she needed to finish their sets. When cut

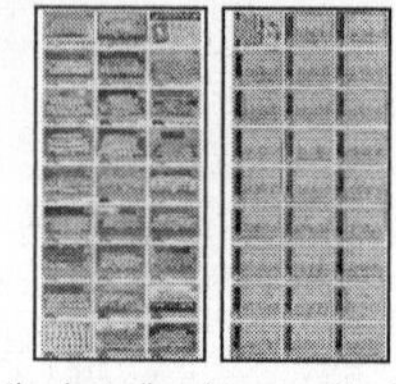

form the sheet, all cards measure the standard size.

Nm-Mt Ex-Mt
1 Team Checklist Sheet 15.00 6.00

1982 Topps

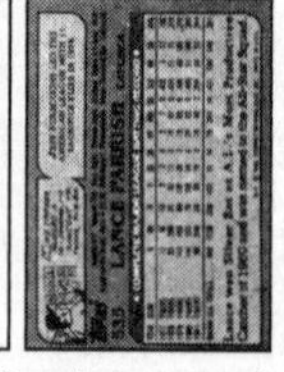

The cards in this 792-card set measure the standard size. Cards were primarily distributed in 15-card wax packs and 51-card rack packs. The 1982 baseball series was the first of the largest sets Topps issued at one printing. The 66-card increase from the previous year's total eliminated the "double print" practice, that had occurred in every regular issue since 1978. Cards 1-6 depict Highlights of the strike-shortened 1981 season, cards 161-168 picture League Leaders, and there are subsets of AL (547-557) and NL (337-347) All-Stars (AS). The abbreviation "SA" in the checklist is given for the 40 "Super Action" cards introduced in this set. The team cards are actually Team Leader (TL) cards picturing the batting average and ERA leader for that team with a checklist back. All 26 of these cards were available from Topps on a perforated sheet through an offer on wax pack wrappers. Notable Rookie Cards include Brett Butler, Chili Davis, Cal Ripken Jr., Lee Smith, and Dave Stewart. Be careful when purchasing blank-back Cal Ripken Jr. Rookie Cards. Those cards are extremely likely to be counterfeit.

Nm-Mt Ex-Mt
COMPLETE SET (792) 100.00 40.00
1 Steve Carlton HL .15 .06
2 Ron Davis HL .15 .06
3 Tim Raines HL .60 .24
4 Pete Rose HL .60 .24
5 Nolan Ryan HL 3.00 1.20
6 Fernando Valenzuela HL .60 .24
7 Scott Sanderson .15 .06
8 Rich Dauer .15 .06
9 Ron Guidry .30 .12
10 Ron Guidry SA .15 .06
11 Gary Alexander .15 .06
12 Moose Haas .15 .06
13 Lamar Johnson .15 .06
14 Steve Howe .15 .06
15 Ellis Valentine .15 .06
16 Steve Comer .15 .06
17 Darrell Evans .30 .12
18 Fernando Arroyo .15 .06
19 Ernie Whitt .15 .06
20 Garry Maddox .15 .06
21 Bob Bonner 50.00 20.00
Cal Ripken RC
Jeff Schneider
Birthdate for Jeff Scheider is wrong
22 Jim Beattie .15 .06
23 Willie Hernandez .30 .12
24 Dave Frost .15 .06
25 Jerry Remy .15 .06
26 Jorge Orta .15 .06
27 Tom Herr .30 .12
28 John Urrea .15 .06
29 Dwayne Murphy .15 .06
30 Tom Seaver .60 .24
31 Tom Seaver SA .30 .12
32 Gene Garber .15 .06
33 Jerry Morales .15 .06
34 Joe Sambito .15 .06
35 Willie Aikens .15 .06
36 Al Oliver .60 .24
Doc Medich TL
37 Dan Graham .15 .06
38 Charlie Lea .15 .06
39 Lou Whitaker .30 .12
40 Dave Parker .30 .12
41 Dave Parker SA .15 .06
42 Rick Sofield .15 .06
43 Mike Cubbage .15 .06
44 Britt Burns .15 .06
45 Rick Cerone .15 .06
46 Jerry Augustine .15 .06
47 Jeff Leonard .15 .06
48 Bobby Castillo .15 .06
49 Alvis Woods .15 .06
50 Buddy Bell .30 .12
51 Jay Howell RC .60 .24
Carlos Lezcano
Ty Waller
52 Larry Andersen .15 .06
53 Greg Gross .15 .06
54 Ron Hassey .15 .06
55 Rick Burleson .15 .06
56 Mark Littell .15 .06
57 Craig Reynolds .15 .06
58 John D'Acquisto .15 .06
59 Rich Gedman .30 .12
60 Tony Armas .15 .06
61 Tommy Boggs .15 .06
62 Mike Tyson .15 .06
63 Mario Soto .15 .06
64 Lynn Jones .15 .06
65 Terry Kennedy .15 .06
66 Art Howe 2.00 .80
Nolan Ryan TL
67 Rich Gale .15 .06
68 Roy Howell .15 .06
69 Al Williams .15 .06
70 Tim Raines 1.25 .50
71 Roy Lee Jackson .15 .06
72 Rick Auerbach .15 .06
73 Buddy Solomon .15 .06
74 Bob Clark .15 .06
75 Tommy John .60 .24
76 Greg Pryor .15 .06
77 Miguel Dilone .15 .06
78 George Medich .15 .06
79 Bob Bailor .15 .06
80 Jim Palmer .30 .12
81 Jim Palmer SA .15 .06
82 Bob Welch .30 .12
83 Steve Balboni RC .60 .24
Andy McGaffigan
Andre Robertson
84 Rennie Stennett .15 .06
85 Lynn McGlothen .15 .06
86 Dane Iorg .15 .06
87 Matt Keough .15 .06
88 Biff Pocoroba .15 .06
89 Steve Henderson .15 .06
90 Nolan Ryan 6.00 2.40
91 Carney Lansford .30 .12
92 Brad Havens .15 .06
93 Larry Hisle .15 .06
94 Andy Hassler .15 .06
95 Ozzie Smith 2.50 1.00
96 George Brett 1.25 .50
Larry Gura TL
97 Paul Moskau .15 .06
98 Terry Bulling .15 .06
99 Barry Bonnell .15 .06
100 Mike Schmidt 3.00 1.20
101 Mike Schmidt SA 1.25 .50
102 Dan Briggs .15 .06
103 Bob Lacey .15 .06
104 Rance Mulliniks .15 .06
105 Kirk Gibson 1.25 .50
106 Enrique Romo .15 .06
107 Wayne Krenchicki .15 .06
108 Bob Sykes .15 .06
109 Dave Revering .15 .06
110 Carlton Fisk .60 .24
111 Carlton Fisk SA .30 .12
112 Billy Sample .15 .06
113 Steve McCatty .15 .06
114 Ken Landreaux .15 .06
115 Gaylord Perry .30 .12
116 Jim Wohlford .15 .06
117 Rawly Eastwick .15 .06
118 Terry Francona RC .30 .12
Brad Mills
Bryn Smith RC
119 Joe Pittman .15 .06
120 Gary Lucas .15 .06
121 Ed Lynch .15 .06
122 Jamie Easterly UER .15 .06
(Photo actually
Reggie Cleveland)
123 Danny Goodwin .15 .06
124 Reid Nichols .15 .06
125 Danny Ainge 1.50 .60
126 Claudell Washington .60 .24
Rick Mahler TL
127 Lonnie Smith .30 .12
128 Frank Pastore .15 .06
129 Checklist 1-132 .60 .24
130 Julio Cruz .15 .06
131 Stan Bahnsen .15 .06
132 Lee May .30 .12
133 Pat Underwood .15 .06
134 Dan Ford .15 .06
135 Andy Rincon .15 .06
136 Lenn Sakata .15 .06
137 George Cappuzzello .15 .06
138 Tony Pena .30 .12
139 Jeff Jones .15 .06
140 Ron LeFlore .30 .12
141 Chris Bando .30 .12
Tom Brennan
Von Hayes RC
142 Dave LaRoche .15 .06
143 Mookie Wilson .30 .12
144 Fred Breining .15 .06
145 Bob Horner .30 .12
146 Mike Griffin .15 .06
147 Denny Walling .15 .06
148 Mickey Klutts .15 .06
149 Pat Putnam .15 .06
150 Ted Simmons .30 .12
151 Dave Edwards .15 .06
152 Ramon Aviles .15 .06
153 Roger Erickson .15 .06
154 Dennis Werth .15 .06
155 Otto Velez .15 .06
156 Rickey Henderson 1.25 .50
Steve McCatty TL
157 Steve Crawford .15 .06
158 Brian Downing .15 .06
159 Larry Biittner .15 .06
160 Luis Tiant .30 .12
161 Bill Madlock .30 .12
Carney Lansford LL
162 Mike Schmidt 1.25 .50
Tony Armas
Dwight Evans
Bobby Grich
Eddie Murray LL
163 Mike Schmidt 1.25 .50
Eddie Murray LL
164 Tim Raines 1.25 .50
Rickey Henderson LL
165 Tom Seaver .30 .12
Denny Martinez
Steve McCatty
Jack Morris
Pete Vuckovich LL
166 Fernando Valenzuela .30 .12
Len Barker LL
167 Nolan Ryan 2.00 .80
Steve McCatty LL
168 Bruce Sutter .30 .12
Rollie Fingers LL
169 Charlie Leibrandt .15 .06
170 Jim Bibby .15 .06
171 Bob Brenly RC 3.00 1.20
Chili Davis RC
Bob Tufts
172 Bill Gullickson .15 .06
173 Jamie Quirk .15 .06
174 Dave Ford .15 .06
175 Jerry Mumphrey .15 .06
176 Dewey Robinson .15 .06
177 John Ellis .15 .06
178 Dyar Miller .15 .06
179 Steve Garvey .30 .12
180 Steve Garvey SA .15 .06
181 Silvio Martinez .15 .06
182 Larry Herndon .15 .06
183 Mike Proly .15 .06
184 Mick Kelleher .15 .06
185 Phil Niekro .30 .12
186 Keith Hernandez .60 .24
Bob Forsch TL
187 Jeff Newman .15 .06
188 Randy Martz .15 .06
189 Glenn Hoffman .15 .06
190 J.R. Richard .30 .12
191 Tim Wallach RC .60 .24
192 Broderick Perkins .15 .06
193 Darrell Jackson .15 .06
194 Mike Vail .15 .06
195 Paul Molitor .60 .24
196 Willie Upshaw .15 .06
197 Shane Rawley .15 .06
198 Chris Speier .15 .06
199 Don Aase .15 .06
200 George Brett 3.00 1.20
201 George Brett SA 1.50 .60
202 Rick Manning .15 .06
203 Jesse Barfield RC .60 .24
Brian Milner
Boomer Wells
204 Gary Roenicke .15 .06
205 Neil Allen .15 .06
206 Tony Bernazard .15 .06
207 Rod Scurry .15 .06
208 Bobby Murcer .30 .12
209 Gary Lavelle .15 .06
210 Keith Hernandez .60 .24
211 Dan Petry .15 .06
212 Mario Mendoza .15 .06
213 Dave Stewart RC 1.50 .60
214 Brian Asselstine .15 .06
215 Mike Krukow .15 .06
216 Chet Lemon .60 .24
Dennis Lamp TL
217 Bo McLaughlin .15 .06
218 Dave Roberts .15 .06
219 John Curtis .15 .06
220 Manny Trillo .15 .06
221 Jim Slaton .15 .06
222 Butch Wynegar .15 .06
223 Lloyd Moseby .15 .06
224 Bruce Bochte .15 .06
225 Mike Torrez .15 .06
226 Checklist 133-264 .60 .24
227 Ray Burris .15 .06
228 Sam Mejias .15 .06
229 Geoff Zahn .15 .06
230 Willie Wilson .30 .12
231 Mark Davis RC .60 .24
Bob Dernier
Ozzie Virgil
232 Terry Crowley .15 .06
233 Duane Kuiper .15 .06
234 Ron Hodges .15 .06
235 Mike Easler .15 .06
236 John Martin RC .15 .06
237 Rusty Kuntz .15 .06
238 Kevin Saucier .15 .06
239 Jon Matlack .15 .06
240 Bucky Dent .30 .12
241 Bucky Dent SA .15 .06
242 Milt May .15 .06
243 Bob Owchinko .15 .06
244 Rufino Linares .15 .06
245 Ken Reitz .15 .06
246 Hubie Brooks .60 .24
Mike Scott TL
247 Pedro Guerrero .30 .12
248 Frank LaCorte .15 .06
249 Tim Flannery .15 .06
250 Tug McGraw .30 .12
251 Fred Lynn .30 .12
252 Fred Lynn SA .15 .06
253 Chuck Baker .15 .06
254 Jorge Bell RC 1.25 .50
255 Tony Perez .60 .24
256 Tony Perez SA .30 .12
257 Larry Harlow .15 .06
258 Bo Diaz .15 .06
259 Rodney Scott .15 .06
260 Bruce Sutter .30 .12
261 Howard Bailey .15 .06
Marty Castillo
Dave Rucker UER
(Rucker photo act-
ally Roger Weaver)
262 Doug Bair .15 .06
263 Victor Cruz .15 .06
264 Dan Quisenberry .30 .12
265 Al Bumbry .15 .06
266 Rick Leach .15 .06
267 Kurt Bevacqua .15 .06
268 Rickey Keeton .15 .06
269 Jim Essian .15 .06
270 Rusty Staub .30 .12
271 Larry Bradford .15 .06
272 Bump Wills .15 .06
273 Doug Bird .15 .06
274 Bob Ojeda RC .60 .24
275 Bob Watson .30 .12
276 Rod Carew .60 .24
Ken Forsch TL
277 Terry Puhl .15 .06
278 John Littlefield .15 .06
279 Bill Russell .30 .12
280 Ben Oglivie .30 .12
281 John Verhoeven .15 .06
282 Ken Macha .15 .06
283 Brian Allard .15 .06
284 Bobby Grich .30 .12
285 Sparky Lyle .30 .12
286 Bill Fahey .15 .06
287 Alan Bannister .15 .06
288 Garry Templeton .15 .06
289 Bob Stanley .15 .06
290 Ken Singleton .30 .12
291 Vance Law .30 .12
Bob Long
Johnny Ray RC
292 David Palmer .15 .06
293 Rob Picciolo .15 .06
294 Mike LaCoss .15 .06
295 Jason Thompson .15 .06
296 Bob Walk .15 .06
297 Clint Hurdle .15 .06
298 Danny Darwin .15 .06
299 Steve Trout .15 .06
300 Reggie Jackson .60 .24
301 Reggie Jackson SA .30 .12
302 Doug Flynn .15 .06
303 Bill Caudill .15 .06
304 Johnnie LeMaster .15 .06
305 Don Sutton 1.25 .50
306 Don Sutton SA .60 .24
307 Randy Bass RC .15 .06
308 Charlie Moore .15 .06
309 Pete Redfern .15 .06
310 Mike Hargrove .30 .12
311 Dusty Baker .60 .24
Burt Hooton TL
312 Lenny Randle .15 .06
313 John Harris .15 .06
314 Buck Martinez .15 .06
315 Burt Hooton .15 .06
316 Steve Braun .15 .06
317 Dick Ruthven .15 .06
318 Mike Heath .15 .06
319 Dave Rozema .15 .06
320 Chris Chambliss .30 .12
321 Chris Chambliss SA .15 .06
322 Garry Hancock .15 .06
323 Bill Lee .30 .12
324 Steve Dillard .15 .06
325 Jose Cruz .30 .12
326 Pete Falcone .15 .06
327 Joe Nolan .15 .06
328 Ed Farmer .15 .06
329 U.L. Washington .15 .06
330 Rick Wise .15 .06
331 Benny Ayala .15 .06
332 Don Robinson .15 .06
333 Frank DiPino .15 .06
Marshall Edwards
Chuck Porter
334 Aurelio Rodriguez .15 .06
335 Jim Sundberg .15 .06
336 Tom Paciorek .60 .24
Glenn Abbott TL
337 Pete Rose AS .60 .24
338 Dave Lopes AS .15 .06
339 Mike Schmidt AS 1.25 .50
340 Dave Concepcion AS .15 .06
341 Andre Dawson AS .15 .06
342A George Foster AS .30 .12
(With autograph)
342B George Foster AS 1.25 .50
(W/o autograph)
343 Dave Parker AS .15 .06
344 Gary Carter AS .30 .12
345 F. Valenzuela AS .60 .24
346 Tom Seaver AS ERR .30 .12
("t ed")
346B Tom Seaver AS COR .30 .12
("tied")
347 Bruce Sutter AS .15 .06
348 Derrel Thomas .15 .06
349 George Frazier .15 .06
350 Thad Bosley .15 .06
351 Scott Brown .15 .06
Geoff Combe
Paul Householder
352 Dick Davis .15 .06
353 Jack O'Connor .15 .06
354 Roberto Ramos .15 .06
355 Dwight Evans .60 .24
356 Denny Lewallyn .15 .06
357 Butch Hobson .15 .06
358 Mike Parrott .15 .06
359 Jim Dwyer .15 .06
360 Len Barker .15 .06
361 Rafael Landestoy .15 .06
362 Jim Wright UER .15 .06
(Wrong Jim Wright
pictured)
363 Bob Molinaro .15 .06
364 Doyle Alexander .15 .06
365 Bill Madlock .30 .12
366 Luis Salazar .60 .24
Juan Eichelberger TL
367 Jim Kaat .30 .12
368 Alex Trevino .15 .06
369 Champ Summers .15 .06
370 Mike Norris .15 .06
371 Jerry Don Gleaton .15 .06
372 Luis Gomez .15 .06
373 Gene Nelson .15 .06
374 Tim Blackwell .15 .06
375 Dusty Baker .60 .24
376 Chris Welsh .15 .06
377 Kiko Garcia .15 .06
378 Mike Caldwell .15 .06
379 Rob Wilfong .15 .06
380 Dave Stieb .30 .12
381 Bruce Hurst .30 .12
Dave Schmidt
Julio Valdez
382 Joe Simpson .15 .06
383A Pascual Perez ERR 40.00 16.00
(No position
on front)
383B Pascual Perez COR .30 .12
384 Keith Moreland .15 .06
385 Ken Forsch .15 .06
386 Jerry White .15 .06
387 Tom Veryzer .15 .06
388 Joe Rudi .15 .06
389 George Vukovich .15 .06
390 Eddie Murray 1.25 .50
391 Dave Tobik .15 .06
392 Rick Bosetti .15 .06
393 Al Hrabosky .15 .06
394 Checklist 265-396 .60 .24
395 Omar Moreno .15 .06
396 John Castino .60 .24

Fernando Arroyo TL
397 Ken Brett .15 .06
398 Mike Squires .15 .06
399 Pat Zachry .15 .06
400 Johnny Bench 1.25 .50
401 Johnny Bench SA .60 .24
402 Bill Stein .15 .06
403 Jim Tracy .15 .06
404 Dickie Thon .15 .06
405 Rick Reuschel .30 .12
406 Al Holland .15 .06
407 Danny Boone .15 .06
408 Ed Romero .15 .06
409 Don Cooper .15 .06
410 Ron Cey .30 .12
411 Ron Cey SA .15 .06
412 Luis Leal .15 .06
413 Dan Meyer .15 .06
414 Elias Sosa .15 .06
415 Don Baylor .60 .24
416 Marty Bystrom .15 .06
417 Pat Kelly .15 .06
418 John Butcher .15 .06
Bobby Johnson
Dave Schmidt
419 Steve Stone .30 .12
420 George Hendrick .15 .06
421 Mark Clear .15 .06
422 Cliff Johnson .15 .06
423 Stan Papi .15 .06
424 Bruce Benedict .15 .06
425 John Candelaria .15 .06
426 Eddie Murray .60 .24
Sammy Stewart
427 Ron Oester .15 .06
428 LaMarr Hoyt .15 .06
429 John Wathan .15 .06
430 Vida Blue .30 .12
431 Vida Blue SA .15 .06
432 Mike Scott .30 .12
433 Alan Ashby .15 .06
434 Joe Lefebvre .15 .06
435 Robin Yount 2.00 .80
436 Joe Strain .15 .06
437 Juan Berenguer .15 .06
438 Pete Mackanin .15 .06
439 Dave Righetti RC 1.25 .50
440 Jeff Burroughs .15 .06
441 Danny Heep .15 .06
Billy Smith
Bobby Sprowl
442 Bruce Kison .15 .06
443 Mark Wagner .15 .06
444 Terry Forster .15 .06
445 Larry Parrish .15 .06
446 Wayne Garland .15 .06
447 Darrell Porter .30 .12
448 Darrell Porter SA .15 .06
449 Luis Aguayo .15 .06
450 Jack Morris .30 .12
451 Ed Miller .15 .06
452 Lee Smith RC 3.00 1.20
453 Art Howe .30 .12
454 Rick Langford .15 .06
455 Tom Burgmeier .15 .06
456 Bill Buckner .60 .24
Randy Martz TL
457 Tim Stoddard .15 .06
458 Willie Montanez .15 .06
459 Bruce Berenyi .15 .06
460 Jack Clark .30 .12
461 Rich Dotson .15 .06
462 Dave Chalk .15 .06
463 Jim Kern .15 .06
464 Juan Bonilla RC .15 .06
465 Lee Mazzilli .15 .06
466 Randy Lerch .15 .06
467 Mickey Hatcher .15 .06
468 Floyd Bannister .15 .06
469 Ed Ott .15 .06
470 John Mayberry .15 .06
471 Atlee Hammaker .15 .06
Mike Jones
Darryl Motley
472 Oscar Gamble .15 .06
473 Mike Stanton .15 .06
474 Ken Oberkfell .15 .06
475 Alan Trammell .60 .24
476 Brian Kingman .15 .06
477 Steve Yeager .15 .06
478 Ray Searage .15 .06
479 Rowland Office .15 .06
480 Steve Carlton .30 .12
481 Steve Carlton SA .15 .06
482 Glenn Hubbard .15 .06
483 Gary Woods .15 .06
484 Ivan DeJesus .15 .06
485 Kent Tekulve .30 .12
486 Jerry Mumphrey .30 .12
Tommy John TL
487 Bob McClure .15 .06
488 Ron Jackson .15 .06
489 Rick Dempsey .30 .12
490 Dennis Eckersley .60 .24
491 Checklist 397-528 .60 .24
492 Joe Price .15 .06
493 Chet Lemon .15 .06
494 Hubie Brooks .30 .12
495 Dennis Leonard .15 .06
496 Johnny Grubb .15 .06
497 Jim Anderson .15 .06
498 Dave Bergman .15 .06
499 Paul Mirabella .15 .06
500 Rod Carew .60 .24
501 Rod Carew SA .60 .24
502 Steve Bedrosian RC UER 1.50 .60
Photo actually Larry Owen)
Brett Butler RC
Larry Owen
503 Julio Gonzalez .15 .06
504 Rick Peters .15 .06
505 Graig Nettles .30 .12
506 Graig Nettles SA .15 .06
507 Terry Harper .15 .06
508 Jody Davis .15 .06
509 Harry Spilman .15 .06
510 Fernando Valenzuela 1.25 .50
511 Ruppert Jones .15 .06
512 Jerry Dybzinski .15 .06
513 Rick Rhoden .15 .06
514 Joe Ferguson .15 .06
515 Larry Bowa .30 .12
516 Larry Bowa SA .15 .06
517 Mark Brouhard .15 .06
518 Garth Iorg .15 .06
519 Glenn Adams .15 .06
520 Mike Flanagan .30 .12
521 Bill Almon .15 .06
522 Chuck Rainey .15 .06
523 Gary Gray .15 .06
524 Tom Hausman .15 .06
525 Ray Knight .30 .12
526 Warren Cromartie .60 .24
Bill Gullickson TL
527 John Henry Johnson .15 .06
528 Matt Alexander .15 .06
529 Allen Ripley .15 .06
530 Dickie Noles .15 .06
531 Rich Bordi .15 .06
Mark Budaska
Kelvin Moore
532 Toby Harrah .30 .12
533 Joaquin Andujar .30 .12
534 Dave McKay .15 .06
535 Lance Parrish .60 .24
536 Rafael Ramirez .15 .06
537 Doug Capilla .15 .06
538 Lou Piniella .30 .12
539 Vern Ruhle .15 .06
540 Andre Dawson .30 .12
541 Barry Evans .15 .06
542 Ned Yost .15 .06
543 Bill Robinson .15 .06
544 Larry Christenson .15 .06
545 Reggie Smith .30 .12
546 Reggie Smith SA .15 .06
547 Rod Carew AS .30 .12
548 Willie Randolph AS .30 .12
549 George Brett AS 1.50 .60
550 Bucky Dent AS .15 .06
551 Reggie Jackson AS .30 .12
552 Ken Singleton AS .15 .06
553 Dave Winfield AS .15 .06
554 Carlton Fisk AS .60 .24
555 Scott McGregor AS .15 .06
556 Jack Morris AS .15 .06
557 Rich Gossage AS .30 .12
558 John Tudor .15 .06
559 Mike Hargrove .30 .12
Bert Blyleven TL
560 Doug Corbett .15 .06
561 Glenn Brummer .15 .06
Luis DeLeon
Gene Roof
562 Mike O'Berry .15 .06
563 Ross Baumgarten .15 .06
564 Doug DeCinces .30 .12
565 Jackson Todd .15 .06
566 Mike Jorgensen .15 .06
567 Bob Babcock .15 .06
568 Joe Pettini .15 .06
569 Willie Randolph .30 .12
570 Willie Randolph SA .30 .12
571 Glenn Abbott .15 .06
572 Juan Beniquez .15 .06
573 Rick Waits .15 .06
574 Mike Ramsey .15 .06
575 Al Cowens .15 .06
576 Milt May .60 .24
Vida Blue TL
577 Rick Monday .15 .06
578 Shooty Babitt .15 .06
579 Rick Mahler .15 .06
580 Bobby Bonds .30 .12
581 Ron Reed .15 .06
582 Luis Pujols .15 .06
583 Tippy Martinez .15 .06
584 Hosken Powell .15 .06
585 Rollie Fingers .30 .12
586 Rollie Fingers SA .30 .12
587 Tim Lollar .15 .06
588 Dale Berra .15 .06
589 Dave Stapleton .15 .06
590 Al Oliver .30 .12
591 Al Oliver SA .15 .06
592 Craig Swan .15 .06
593 Billy Smith .15 .06
594 Renie Martin .15 .06
595 Dave Collins .15 .06
596 Damaso Garcia .15 .06
597 Wayne Nordhagen .15 .06
598 Bob Galasso .15 .06
599 Jay Loviglio .15 .06
Reggie Patterson
Leo Sutherland
600 Dave Winfield .30 .12
601 Sid Monge .15 .06
602 Freddie Patek .15 .06
603 Rich Hebner .30 .12
604 Orlando Sanchez .15 .06
605 Steve Rogers .15 .06
606 John Mayberry .60 .24
Dave Stieb TL
607 Leon Durham .15 .06
608 Jerry Royster .15 .06
609 Rick Sutcliffe .30 .12
610 Rickey Henderson 4.00 1.60
611 Joe Niekro .30 .12
612 Gary Ward .15 .06
613 Jim Gantner .30 .12
614 Juan Eichelberger .15 .06
615 Bob Boone .30 .12
616 Bob Boone SA .15 .06
617 Scott McGregor .15 .06
618 Tim Foli .15 .06
619 Bill Campbell .15 .06
620 Ken Griffey .30 .12
621 Ken Griffey SA .15 .06
622 Dennis Lamp .15 .06
623 Ron Gardenhire RC .60 .24
Terry Leach
Tim Leary RC
624 Fergie Jenkins .30 .12
625 Hal McRae .30 .12
626 Randy Jones .15 .06
627 Enos Cabell .15 .06
628 Bill Travers .15 .06
629 John Wockenfuss .15 .06
630 Joe Charboneau .30 .12
631 Gene Tenace .30 .12
632 Bryan Clark RC .15 .06
633 Mitchell Page .15 .06
634 Checklist 529-660 .60 .24
635 Ron Davis .15 .06
636 Pete Rose 1.25 .50
Steve Carlton TL
637 Rick Camp .15 .06
638 John Milner .15 .06
639 Ken Kravec .15 .06
640 Cesar Cedeno .30 .12
641 Steve Mura .15 .06
642 Mike Scioscia .30 .12
643 Pete Vuckovich .15 .06
644 John Castino .15 .06
645 Frank White .30 .12
646 Frank White SA .15 .06
647 Warren Brusstar .15 .06
648 Jose Morales .15 .06
649 Ken Clay .15 .06
650 Carl Yastrzemski 2.00 .80
651 Carl Yastrzemski SA 1.25 .50
652 Steve Nicosia .15 .06
653 Tom Brunansky RC .60 .24
Luis Sanchez
Daryl Sconiers
654 Jim Morrison .15 .06
655 Joel Youngblood .15 .06
656 Eddie Whitson .15 .06
657 Tom Poquette .15 .06
658 Tito Landrum .15 .06
659 Fred Martinez .15 .06
660 Dave Concepcion .30 .12
661 Dave Concepcion SA .15 .06
662 Luis Salazar .15 .06
663 Hector Cruz .15 .06
664 Dan Spillner .15 .06
665 Jim Clancy .15 .06
666 Steve Kemp .60 .24
Dan Petry TL
667 Jeff Reardon .60 .24
668 Dale Murphy 1.25 .50
669 Larry Milbourne .15 .06
670 Steve Kemp .15 .06
671 Mike Davis .15 .06
672 Bob Knepper .15 .06
673 Keith Drumwright .15 .06
674 Dave Goltz .15 .06
675 Cecil Cooper .30 .12
676 Sal Butera .15 .06
677 Alfredo Griffin .15 .06
678 Tom Paciorek .30 .12
679 Sammy Stewart .15 .06
680 Gary Matthews .30 .12
681 Mike Marshall RC 1.25 .50
Ron Roenicke
Steve Sax RC
682 Jesse Jefferson .15 .06
683 Phil Garner .30 .12
684 Harold Baines 1.25 .50
685 Bert Blyleven .60 .24
686 Gary Allenson .15 .06
687 Greg Minton .15 .06
688 Leon Roberts .15 .06
689 Lary Sorensen .15 .06
690 Dave Kingman .30 .12
691 Dan Schatzeder .15 .06
692 Wayne Gross .15 .06
693 Cesar Geronimo .15 .06
694 Dave Wehrmeister .15 .06
695 Warren Cromartie .15 .06
696 Bill Madlock .60 .24
Eddie Solomon TL
697 John Montefusco .15 .06
698 Tony Scott .15 .06
699 Dick Tidrow .15 .06
700 George Foster .30 .12
701 George Foster SA .15 .06
702 Steve Renko .15 .06
703 Cecil Cooper .60 .24
Pete Vuckovich TL
704 Mickey Rivers .15 .06
705 Mickey Rivers SA .15 .06
706 Barry Foote .15 .06
707 Mark Bomback .15 .06
708 Gene Richards .15 .06
709 Don Money .15 .06
710 Jerry Reuss .30 .12
711 Dave Edler .60 .24
Dave Henderson RC
Reggie Walton
712 Dennis Martinez .60 .24
713 Del Unser .15 .06
714 Jerry Koosman .30 .12
715 Willie Stargell .60 .24
716 Willie Stargell SA .30 .12
717 Rick Miller .15 .06
718 Charlie Hough .30 .12
719 Jerry Narron .15 .06
720 Greg Luzinski .30 .12
721 Greg Luzinski SA .15 .06
722 Jerry Martin .15 .06
723 Junior Kennedy .15 .06
724 Dave Rosello .15 .06
725 Amos Otis .30 .12
726 Amos Otis SA .15 .06
727 Sixto Lezcano .15 .06
728 Aurelio Lopez .15 .06
729 Jim Spencer .15 .06
730 Gary Carter .60 .24
731 Mike Armstrong .15 .06
Doug Gwosdz
Fred Kuhaulua
732 Mike Lum .15 .06
733 Larry McWilliams .15 .06
734 Mike Ivie .15 .06
735 Rudy May .15 .06
736 Jerry Turner .15 .06
737 Reggie Cleveland .15 .06
738 Dave Engle .15 .06
739 Joey McLaughlin .15 .06
740 Dave Lopes .30 .12
741 Dave Lopes SA .15 .06
742 Dick Drago .15 .06
743 John Stearns .15 .06
744 Mike Witt .30 .12
745 Bake McBride .15 .06
746 Andre Thornton .15 .06
747 John Lowenstein .15 .06
748 Marc Hill .15 .06
749 Bob Shirley .15 .06
750 Jim Rice .30 .12
751 Rick Honeycutt .15 .06
752 Lee Lacy .15 .06
753 Tom Brookens .15 .06
754 Joe Morgan .60 .24
755 Joe Morgan SA .30 .12
756 Ken Griffey .30 .12
Tom Seaver TL
757 Tom Underwood .15 .06
758 Claudell Washington .15 .06
759 Paul Splittorff .15 .06
760 Bill Buckner .30 .12
761 Dave Smith .15 .06
762 Mike Phillips .15 .06
763 Tom Hume .15 .06
764 Steve Swisher .15 .06
765 Gorman Thomas .30 .12
766 Lenny Faedo 1.50 .60
Kent Hrbek RC
Tim Laudner
767 Roy Smalley .15 .06
768 Jerry Garvin .15 .06
769 Richie Zisk .15 .06
770 Rich Gossage .60 .24
771 Rich Gossage SA .30 .12
772 Bert Campaneris .30 .12
773 John Denny .15 .06
774 Jay Johnstone .30 .12
775 Bob Forsch .15 .06
776 Mark Belanger .15 .06
777 Tom Griffin .15 .06
778 Kevin Hickey RC .15 .06
779 Grant Jackson .15 .06
780 Pete Rose 4.00 1.60
781 Pete Rose SA 1.25 .50
782 Frank Taveras .15 .06
783 Greg Harris RC .15 .06
784 Milt Wilcox .15 .06
785 Dan Driessen .15 .06
786 Carney Lansford .60 .24
Mike Torrez TL
787 Fred Stanley .15 .06
788 Woodie Fryman .15 .06
789 Checklist 661-792 .60 .24
790 Larry Gura .15 .06
791 Bobby Brown .15 .06
792 Frank Tanana .30 .12

1982 Topps Sticker Variations

This 48-card (skip-numbered) set is actually a slightly different version of the 1982 Topps stickers. They are the same size (1 15/16" by 2 9/16") and are easily confused. They were produced for insertion into the regular packs of cards that year. They are distinguishable from the "other" sticker set by the fact that on their backs these say the Topps sticker album is "Coming Soon." There are no foils in this set. All of the stickers in this set depict a single player. Colored borders surround the posed color player photos on the fronts, blue for the NL and red for the AL. The player's name and position appear on the back. The stickers are numbered on the front and back. Choice of players for this small set appears to have been systematic, i.e., taking every fourth player between number 17 and number 109 and every fifth player between number 151 and number 251.

	Nm-Mt	Ex-Mt
COMPLETE SET (48)	4.00	1.60
17 Chris Chambliss	.10	.04
21 Bruce Benedict	.05	.02
25 Leon Durham	.05	.02
29 Bill Buckner	.10	.04
33 Dave Collins	.05	.02
37 Dave Concepcion	.10	.04
41 Nolan Ryan	2.00	.80
45 Bob Knepper	.05	.02
49 Ken Landreaux	.05	.02
53 Burt Hooton	.05	.02
57 Andre Dawson	.30	.12
61 Gary Carter	.40	.16
65 Joel Youngblood	.05	.02
69 Ellis Valentine	.05	.02
73 Garry Maddox	.05	.02
77 Bob Boone	.10	.04
81 Omar Moreno	.05	.02
85 Willie Stargell	.30	.12
89 Ken Oberkfell	.05	.02
93 Darrell Porter	.05	.02
97 Juan Eichelberger	.05	.02
101 Luis Salazar	.05	.02
105 Enos Cabell	.05	.02
109 Larry Herndon	.05	.02
143 Scott McGregor	.05	.02
148 Mike Flanagan	.10	.04
151 Mike Torrez	.05	.02
156 Carney Lansford	.10	.04
161 Fred Lynn	.10	.04
166 Rich Dotson	.05	.02
171 Tony Bernazard	.05	.02
176 Bo Diaz	.05	.02
181 Alan Trammell	.25	.10
186 Milt Wilcox	.05	.02
191 Dennis Leonard	.05	.02
196 Willie Aikens	.05	.02
201 Ted Simmons	.10	.04
206 Hosken Powell	.05	.02
211 Roger Erickson	.05	.02
215 Graig Nettles	.10	.04
216 Reggie Jackson	.50	.20
221 Rickey Henderson	1.00	.40
226 Cliff Johnson	.05	.02
231 Jeff Burroughs	.05	.02
236 Tom Paciorek	.05	.02
241 Pat Putnam	.05	.02
246 Lloyd Moseby	.05	.02
251 Barry Bonnell	.05	.02

1982 Topps Team Checklist Sheet

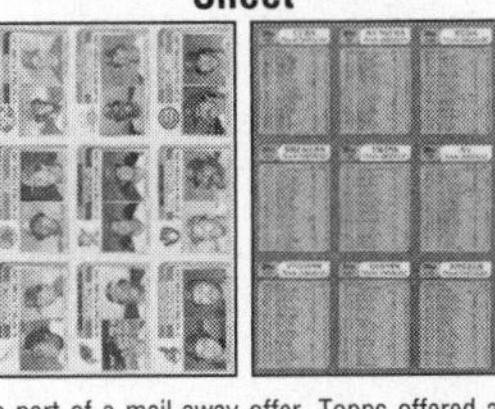

As part of a mail-away offer, Topps offered all 26 1982 team checklist cards on an uncut sheet. These cards enabled the collector to have an easy reference for which card(s) he/she needed to finish their sets. When cut from the sheet, all cards measure the standard-size.

	Nm-Mt	Ex-Mt
1 Team Checklist Sheet	10.00	4.00

1982 Topps Traded

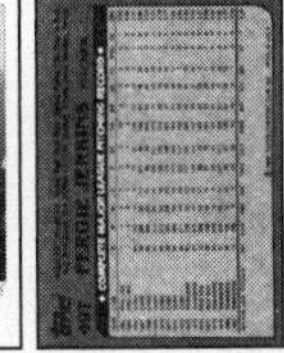

The cards in this 132-card set measure the standard size. The 1982 Topps Traded or extended series is distinguished by a "T" printed after the number (located on the reverse). This was the first time Topps began a tradition of newly numbering (and alphabetizing) their traded series from 1T to 132T. All 131 player photos used in the set are completely new. Of this total, 112 individuals are seen in the uniform of their new team, 11 youngsters have been elevated to single card status from multi-player "Future Stars" cards, and eight more are entirely new to the 1982 Topps lineup. The backs are almost completely red in color with black print. There are no key Rookie Cards in this set. Although the Cal Ripken card is this set's most valuable card, it is not his Rookie Card since he had already been included in the 1982 regular set, albeit on a multi-player card.

	Nm-Mt	Ex-Mt
COMP.FACT.SET (132)	150.00	60.00
1T Doyle Alexander	.50	.20
2T Jesse Barfield	1.00	.40
3T Ross Baumgarten	.50	.20
4T Steve Bedrosian	1.00	.40
5T Mark Belanger	1.00	.40
6T Kurt Bevacqua	.50	.20
7T Tim Blackwell	.50	.20
8T Vida Blue	1.00	.40
9T Bob Boone	1.00	.40
10T Larry Bowa	1.00	.40
11T Dan Briggs	.50	.20
12T Bobby Brown	.50	.20
13T Tom Brunansky	1.00	.40
14T Jeff Burroughs	.50	.20
15T Enos Cabell	.50	.20
16T Bill Campbell	.50	.20
17T Bobby Castillo	.50	.20
18T Bill Caudill	.50	.20
19T Cesar Cedeno	1.00	.40
20T Dave Collins	.50	.20
21T Doug Corbett	.50	.20
22T Al Cowens	.50	.20
23T Chili Davis	8.00	3.20
24T Dick Davis	.50	.20
25T Ron Davis	.50	.20
26T Doug DeCinces	1.00	.40
27T Ivan DeJesus	.50	.20
28T Bob Dernier	.50	.20
29T Bo Diaz	.50	.20
30T Roger Erickson	.50	.20
31T Jim Essian	.50	.20
32T Ed Farmer	.50	.20
33T Doug Flynn	.50	.20
34T Tim Foli	.50	.20
35T Dan Ford	.50	.20
36T George Foster	1.00	.40
37T Dave Frost	.50	.20
38T Rich Gale	.50	.20
39T Ron Gardenhire	.50	.20
40T Ken Griffey	1.00	.40
41T Greg Harris	.50	.20
42T Von Hayes	1.00	.40
43T Larry Herndon	.50	.20
44T Kent Hrbek	2.00	.80
45T Mike Ivie	.50	.20
46T Grant Jackson	.50	.20
47T Reggie Jackson	2.00	.80
48T Ron Jackson	.50	.20
49T Fergie Jenkins	1.00	.40
50T Lamar Johnson	.50	.20
51T Randy Johnson	.50	.20
52T Jay Johnstone	1.00	.40
53T Mick Kelleher	.50	.20
54T Steve Kemp	.50	.20
55T Junior Kennedy	.50	.20
56T Jim Kern	.50	.20
57T Ray Knight	1.00	.40
58T Wayne Krenchicki	.50	.20
59T Mike Krukow	.50	.20
60T Duane Kuiper	.50	.20
61T Mike LaCoss	.50	.20
62T Chet Lemon	.50	.20
63T Sixto Lezcano	.50	.20
64T Dave Lopes	1.00	.40

65T Jerry Martin .50 .20
66T Renie Martin .50 .20
67T John Mayberry .50 .20
68T Lee Mazzilli .50 .20
69T Bake McBride .50 .20
70T Dan Meyer .50 .20
71T Larry Milbourne .50 .20
72T Eddie Milner .50 .20
73T Sid Monge .50 .20
74T John Montefusco .50 .20
75T Jose Morales .50 .20
76T Keith Moreland .50 .20
77T Jim Morrison .50 .20
78T Rance Mulliniks .50 .20
79T Steve Mura .50 .20
80T Gene Nelson .50 .20
81T Joe Nolan .50 .20
82T Dickie Noles .50 .20
83T Al Oliver 1.00 .40
84T Jorge Orta .50 .20
85T Tom Paciorek 1.00 .40
86T Larry Parrish .50 .20
87T Jack Perconte .50 .20
88T Gaylord Perry 1.00 .40
89T Rob Picciolo .50 .20
90T Joe Pittman .50 .20
91T Hosken Powell .50 .20
92T Mike Proly .50 .20
93T Greg Pryor .50 .20
94T Charlie Puleo .50 .20
95T Shane Rawley .50 .20
96T Johnny Ray 1.00 .40
97T Dave Revering .50 .20
98T Cal Ripken 120.00 47.50
99T Allen Ripley .50 .20
100T Bill Robinson .50 .20
101T Aurelio Rodriguez .50 .20
102T Joe Rudi .50 .20
103T Steve Sax 4.00 1.60
104T Dan Schatzeder .50 .20
105T Bob Shirley .50 .20
106T Eric Show 1.00 .40
107T Roy Smalley .50 .20
108T Lonnie Smith 1.00 .40
109T Ozzie Smith 15.00 6.00
110T Reggie Smith 1.00 .40
111T Lary Sorensen .50 .20
112T Elias Sosa .50 .20
113T Mike Stanton .50 .20
114T Steve Stroughter .50 .20
115T Champ Summers .50 .20
116T Rick Sutcliffe 1.00 .40
117T Frank Tanana 1.00 .40
118T Frank Taveras .50 .20
119T Garry Templeton .50 .20
120T Alex Trevino .50 .20
121T Jerry Turner .50 .20
122T Ed VandeBerg .50 .20
123T Tom Veryzer .50 .20
124T Ron Washington .50 .20
125T Bob Watson 1.00 .40
126T Dennis Werth .50 .20
127T Eddie Whitson .50 .20
128T Rob Wilfong .50 .20
129T Bump Wills .50 .20
130T Gary Woods .50 .20
131T Butch Wynegar .50 .20
132T Checklist: 1-132 .50 .20

1982 Topps Stickers

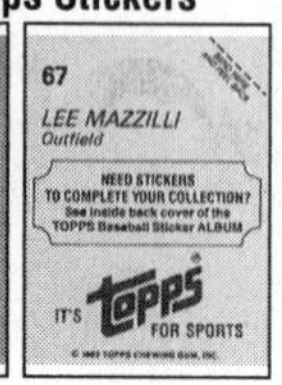

Made for Topps and O-Pee-Chee by Panini, an Italian company, these 260 stickers measure 1 15/16" by 2 9/16" and are numbered on both front and back. The fronts feature color player photos with color borders, blue for the NL and red for the AL. The backs carry the player's name and position and a bilingual ad for O-Pee-Chee. Team affiliations are not shown. The stickers were issued both as inserts in the regular 1982 issue and in individual gumless packs. An album onto which the stickers could be affixed was available at retail stores. The album and the sticker numbering are organized as follows: League Leaders (1-16), Atlanta Braves (17-24), Chicago Cubs (25-32), Cincinnati Reds (33-40), Houston Astros (41-48), Los Angeles Dodgers (49-56), Montreal Expos (57-65), New York Mets (66-72), Philadelphia Phillies (73-80), Pittsburgh Pirates (81-88), St. Louis Cardinals (89-96), San Diego Padres (97-104), San Francisco Giants (105-112), Highlights (113-120), NL Foil All-Stars (121-130), AL Foil All-Stars (131-140), Baltimore Orioles (141-148), Boston Red Sox (149-156), California Angels (157-164), Chicago White Sox (165-172) Cleveland Indians (173-180), Detroit Tigers (181-188), Kansas City Royals (189-196), Milwaukee Brewers (197-204), Minnesota Twins (205-212), New York Yankees (213-221), Oakland A's (222-228), Seattle Mariners (229-236), Texas Rangers (237-244), Toronto Blue Jays (245-252) and postseason games (253-260).

Nm-Mt Ex-Mt
COMPLETE SET (260) 15.00 6.00
COM. STICKER (1-120,141-260) .05 .02
COMMON FOIL (121-140) .10 .04
*TOPPS AND OPC: SAME VALUE
1 Bill Madlock LL .10 .04
2 Carney Lansford LL .10 .04
3 Mike Schmidt LL .60 .24
4 Tony Armas LL .25 .10
Bobby Grich
Dwight Evans
Eddie Murray
5 Mike Schmidt LL .60 .24
6 Eddie Murray LL .60 .24
7 Tim Raines LL .15 .06
8 Rickey Henderson LL .50 .24
9 Tom Seaver LL .40 .16
10 Steve McCatty LL .05 .02
Dennis Martinez
Pete Vuckovich
Jack Morris
11 Fernando Valenzuela LL .15 .06
12 Len Barker LL .05 .02
13 Nolan Ryan LL 1.50 .60
14 Steve McCatty LL .05 .02
15 Bruce Sutter LL .10 .04
16 Rollie Fingers LL .15 .06
17 Chris Chambliss .05 .02
18 Bob Horner .10 .04
19 Dale Murphy .40 .16
20 Phil Niekro .25 .10
21 Bruce Benedict .05 .02
22 Claudell Washington .05 .02
23 Glenn Hubbard .05 .02
24 Rick Camp .05 .02
25 Leon Durham .05 .02
26 Ken Reitz .05 .02
27 Dick Tidrow .05 .02
28 Tim Blackwell .05 .02
29 Bill Buckner .10 .04
30 Steve Henderson .05 .02
31 Mike Krukow .05 .02
32 Ivan DeJesus .05 .02
33 Dave Collins .05 .02
34 Ron Oester .05 .02
35 Johnny Bench .75 .30
36 Tom Seaver .75 .30
37 Dave Concepcion .10 .04
38 Tom Hume .05 .02
39 Ray Knight .05 .02
40 George Foster .10 .04
41 Nolan Ryan 3.00 1.20
42 Terry Puhl .05 .02
43 Art Howe .10 .04
44 Jose Cruz .10 .04
45 Bob Knepper .05 .02
46 Craig Reynolds .05 .02
47 Cesar Cedeno .10 .04
48 Alan Ashby .05 .02
49 Ken Landreaux .05 .02
50 Fernando Valenzuela .40 .16
51 Ron Cey .10 .04
52 Dusty Baker .10 .04
53 Burt Hooton .05 .02
54 Steve Garvey .15 .06
55 Pedro Guerrero .10 .04
56 Jerry Reuss .10 .04
57 Andre Dawson .60 .24
58 Chris Speier .05 .02
59 Steve Rogers .05 .02
60 Warren Cromartie .05 .02
61 Gary Carter .25 .10
62 Tim Raines .40 .16
63 Scott Sanderson .05 .02
64 Larry Parrish .05 .02
65 Joel Youngblood .05 .02
66 Neil Allen .05 .02
67 Lee Mazzilli .05 .02
68 Hubie Brooks .10 .04
69 Ellis Valentine .05 .02
70 Doug Flynn .05 .02
71 Pat Zachry .05 .02
72 Dave Kingman .10 .04
73 Garry Maddox .05 .02
74 Mike Schmidt 1.25 .50
75 Steve Carlton .60 .24
76 Manny Trillo .05 .02
77 Bob Boone .10 .04
78 Pete Rose 1.25 .50
79 Gary Matthews .10 .04
80 Larry Bowa .10 .04
81 Omar Moreno .05 .02
82 Rick Rhoden .05 .02
83 Bill Madlock .10 .04
84 Mike Easler .05 .02
85 Willie Stargell .40 .16
86 Jim Bibby .05 .02
87 Dave Parker .10 .04
88 Tim Foli .05 .02
89 Ken Oberkfell .05 .02
90 Bob Forsch .05 .02
91 George Hendrick .05 .02
92 Keith Hernandez .10 .04
93 Darrell Porter .05 .02
94 Bruce Sutter .10 .04
95 Sixto Lezcano .05 .02
96 Garry Templeton .05 .02
97 Juan Eichelberger .05 .02
98 Broderick Perkins .05 .02
99 Ruppert Jones .05 .02
100 Terry Kennedy .05 .02
101 Luis Salazar .05 .02
102 Gary Lucas .05 .02
103 Gene Richards .05 .02
104 Ozzie Smith 2.00 .80
105 Enos Cabell .05 .02
106 Jack Clark .10 .04
107 Greg Minton .05 .02
108 Johnnie LeMaster .05 .02
109 Larry Herndon .05 .02
110 Milt May .05 .02
111 Vida Blue .10 .04
112 Darrell Evans .10 .04
113 Len Barker HL .05 .02
114 Julio Cruz HL .05 .02
115 Billy Martin MG HL .10 .04
116 Tim Raines HL .15 .06
117 Pete Rose HL .60 .24
118 Bill Stein HL .05 .02
119 Fern.Valenzuela HL .15 .06
120 Carl Yastrzemski HL .25 .10
121 Pete Rose FOIL 1.50 .60
122 Manny Trillo FOIL .10 .04
123 Mike Schmidt FOIL 1.50 .60
124 Dave Concepcion FOIL .20 .08
125 Andre Dawson FOIL .75 .30
126 George Foster FOIL .20 .08
127 Dave Parker FOIL .30 .12
128 Gary Carter FOIL .40 .16
129 Steve Carlton FOIL .75 .30
130 Bruce Sutter FOIL .20 .08
131 Rod Carew FOIL .75 .30
132 Jerry Remy FOIL .10 .04
133 George Brett FOIL 2.50 1.00
134 Rick Burleson FOIL .10 .04
135 Dwight Evans FOIL .20 .08
136 Ken Singleton FOIL .10 .04
137 Dave Winfield FOIL .75 .30
138 Carlton Fisk FOIL .75 .30
139 Jack Morris FOIL .30 .12
140 Rich Gossage FOIL .30 .12
141 Al Bumbry .10 .04
142 Doug DeCinces .05 .02
143 Scott McGregor .05 .02
144 Ken Singleton .05 .02
145 Eddie Murray 1.50 .60
146 Jim Palmer .40 .16
147 Rich Dauer .05 .02
148 Mike Flanagan .10 .04
149 Jerry Remy .05 .02
150 Jim Rice .10 .04
151 Mike Torrez .05 .02
152 Tony Perez .25 .10
153 Dwight Evans .10 .04
154 Mark Clear .05 .02
155 Carl Yastrzemski .60 .24
156 Carney Lansford .10 .04
157 Rick Burleson .05 .02
158 Don Baylor .15 .06
159 Ken Forsch .05 .02
160 Rod Carew .60 .24
161 Fred Lynn .10 .04
162 Bob Grich .10 .04
163 Dan Ford .05 .02
164 Butch Hobson .05 .02
165 Greg Luzinski .10 .04
166 Rich Dotson .05 .02
167 Billy Almon .05 .02
168 Chet Lemon .05 .02
169 Steve Trout .05 .02
170 Carlton Fisk .60 .24
171 Tony Bernazard .05 .02
172 Ron LeFlore .10 .04
173 Bert Blyleven .15 .06
174 Andre Thornton .05 .02
175 Jorge Orta .05 .02
176 Bo Diaz .05 .02
177 Toby Harrah .10 .04
178 Len Barker .05 .02
179 Rick Manning .05 .02
180 Mike Hargrove .10 .04
181 Alan Trammell .40 .16
182 Al Cowens .05 .02
183 Jack Morris .10 .04
184 Kirk Gibson .25 .10
185 Steve Kemp .05 .02
186 Milt Wilcox .05 .02
187 Lou Whitaker .25 .10
188 Lance Parrish .15 .06
189 Willie Wilson .05 .02
190 George Brett 2.00 .80
191 Dennis Leonard .05 .02
192 John Wathan .05 .02
193 Frank White .10 .04
194 Amos Otis .10 .04
195 Larry Gura .05 .02
196 Willie Aikens .05 .02
197 Ben Oglivie .10 .04
198 Rollie Fingers .25 .10
199 Cecil Cooper .10 .04
200 Paul Molitor .75 .30
201 Ted Simmons .10 .04
202 Pete Vuckovich .05 .02
203 Robin Yount .60 .24
204 Gorman Thomas .10 .04
205 Rob Wilfong .05 .02
206 Hosken Powell .05 .02
207 Roy Smalley .05 .02
208 Butch Wynegar .05 .02
209 John Castino .05 .02
210 Doug Corbett .05 .02
211 Roger Erickson .05 .02
212 Mickey Hatcher .05 .02
213 Dave Winfield .60 .24
214 Tommy John .15 .06
215 Graig Nettles .10 .04
216 Reggie Jackson .75 .30
217 Rich Gossage .15 .06
218 Rick Cerone .05 .02
219 Willie Randolph .10 .04
220 Jerry Mumphrey .05 .02
221 Rickey Henderson 1.25 .50
222 Mike Norris .05 .02
223 Jim Spencer .05 .02
224 Tony Armas .05 .02
225 Matt Keough .05 .02
226 Cliff Johnson .05 .02
227 Dwayne Murphy .05 .02
228 Steve McCatty .05 .02
229 Richie Zisk .05 .02
230 Lenny Randle .05 .02
231 Jeff Burroughs .05 .02
232 Bruce Bochte .05 .02
233 Gary Gray .05 .02
234 Floyd Bannister .05 .02
235 Julio Cruz .05 .02
236 Tom Paciorek .10 .04
237 Danny Darwin .05 .02
238 Buddy Bell .15 .06
239 Al Oliver .15 .06
240 Jim Sundberg .10 .04
241 Pat Putnam .05 .02
242 Steve Comer .05 .02
243 Mickey Rivers .05 .02
244 Bump Wills .05 .02
245 Damaso Garcia .05 .02
246 Lloyd Moseby .10 .04
247 Ernie Whitt .05 .02
248 John Mayberry .05 .02
249 Otto Velez .05 .02
250 Dave Stieb .10 .04
251 Barry Bonnell .05 .02
252 Alfredo Griffin .05 .02
253 Gary Carter PLAY .10 .04
254 1981 AL Playoffs .05 .02
(Action at plate)
255 Dodgers Team .10 .04
World Champions
(Left half photo)
256 Dodgers Team .10 .04
World Champions
(Right half photo)
257 Fernando Valenzuela WS .15 .06
258 Steve Garvey WS .15 .06
259 Jerry Reuss WS .10 .04
Steve Yeager
260 Pedro Guerrero WS .10 .04
NNO Album 1.00 .40

1983 Topps

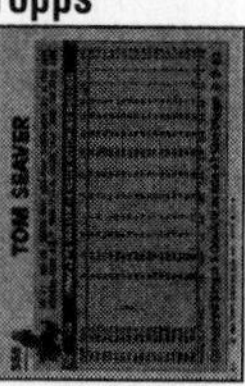

The cards in this 792-card set measure the standard size. Cards were primarily issued in 15-card wax packs and 51-card rack packs. Each player card front features a large action shot with a small cameo portrait at bottom right. There are special series for AL and NL All Stars (386-407), League Leaders (701-708), and Record Breakers (1-6). In addition, there are 34 "Super Veteran" (SV) cards and six numbered checklist cards. The Super Veteran cards are oriented horizontally and show two pictures of the featured player, a recent picture and a picture showing the player as a rookie. The team cards are actually Team Leader (TL) cards picturing the batting and pitching leader for that team with a checklist back. Notable Rookie Cards include Wade Boggs, Tony Gwynn and Ryne Sandberg. In each wax pack a game card was included which included prizes all the way up to a trip and tickets to the World Series. Card prizes possible from these cards included the 1983 Topps League Leaders sheet as well as with enough run accumulation, ordering of a part of the 1983 Topps Mail-Away glossy set. The factory sets were available in JC Penney's Christmas Catalog for $15.99.

Nm-Mt Ex-Mt
COMPLETE SET (792) 80.00 32.00
1 Tony Armas RB .30 .12
2 Rickey Henderson RB 1.25 .50
3 Greg Minton RB .15 .06
4 Lance Parrish RB .15 .06
5 Manny Trillo RB .15 .06
6 John Wathan RB .15 .06
7 Gene Richards .15 .06
8 Steve Balboni .15 .06
9 Joey McLaughlin .15 .06
10 Gorman Thomas .15 .06
11 Billy Gardner MG .15 .06
12 Paul Mirabella .15 .06
13 Larry Herndon .15 .06
14 Frank LaCorte .15 .06
15 Ron Cey .30 .12
16 George Vukovich .15 .06
17 Kent Tekulve .30 .12
18 Kent Tekulve SV .15 .06
19 Oscar Gamble .15 .06
20 Carlton Fisk .60 .24
21 Eddie Murray .60 .24
Jim Palmer TL
22 Randy Martz .15 .06
23 Mike Heath .15 .06
24 Steve Mura .15 .06
25 Hal McRae .30 .12
26 Jerry Royster .15 .06
27 Doug Corbett .15 .06
28 Bruce Bochte .15 .06
29 Randy Jones .15 .06
30 Jim Rice .30 .12
31 Bill Gullickson .15 .06
32 Dave Bergman .15 .06
33 Jack O'Connor .15 .06
34 Paul Householder .15 .06
35 Rollie Fingers .30 .12
36 Rollie Fingers SV .30 .12
37 Darrell Johnson MG .15 .06
38 Tim Flannery .15 .06
39 Terry Puhl .15 .06
40 Fernando Valenzuela .60 .24
41 Jerry Turner .15 .06
42 Dale Murray .15 .06
43 Bob Dernier .15 .06
44 Don Robinson .15 .06
45 John Mayberry .15 .06
46 Richard Dotson .15 .06
47 Dave McKay .15 .06
48 Lary Sorensen .15 .06
49 Willie McGee RC 3.00 1.20
50 Bob Horner UER .15 .06
('82 RBI total 7)
51 Leon Durham .15 .06
Fergie Jenkins TL
52 Onix Concepcion .15 .06
53 Mike Witt .15 .06
54 Jim Maler .15 .06
55 Mookie Wilson .30 .12
56 Chuck Rainey .15 .06
57 Tim Blackwell .15 .06
58 Al Holland .15 .06
59 Benny Ayala .15 .06
60 Johnny Bench 1.25 .50
61 Johnny Bench SV .60 .24
62 Bob McClure .15 .06
63 Rick Monday .15 .06
64 Bill Stein .15 .06
65 Jack Morris .30 .12
66 Bob Lillis MG .15 .06
67 Sal Butera .15 .06
68 Eric Show .15 .06
69 Lee Lacy .15 .06
70 Steve Carlton .30 .12
71 Steve Carlton SV .15 .06
72 Tom Paciorek .30 .12
73 Allen Ripley .15 .06
74 Julio Gonzalez .15 .06
75 Amos Otis .30 .12
76 Rick Mahler .15 .06
77 Hosken Powell .15 .06
78 Bill Caudill .15 .06
79 Mick Kelleher .15 .06
80 George Foster .30 .12
81 Jerry Mumphrey .30 .12
Dave Righetti TL
82 Bruce Hurst .15 .06
83 Ryne Sandberg RC 15.00 6.00
84 Milt May .15 .06
85 Ken Singleton .15 .06
86 Tom Hume .15 .06
87 Joe Rudi .15 .06
88 Jim Gantner .15 .06
89 Leon Roberts .15 .06
90 Jerry Reuss .30 .12
91 Larry Milbourne .15 .06
92 Mike LaCoss .15 .06
93 John Castino .15 .06
94 Dave Edwards .15 .06
95 Alan Trammell .60 .24
96 Dick Howser MG .15 .06
97 Ross Baumgarten .15 .06
98 Vance Law .15 .06
99 Dickie Noles .15 .06
100 Pete Rose 4.00 1.60
101 Pete Rose SV 1.25 .50
102 Dave Beard .15 .06
103 Darrell Porter .15 .06
104 Bob Walk .15 .06
105 Don Baylor .60 .24
106 Gene Nelson .15 .06
107 Mike Jorgensen .15 .06
108 Glenn Hoffman .15 .06
109 Luis Leal .15 .06
110 Ken Griffey .30 .12
111 Al Oliver .30 .12
Steve Rogers TL
112 Bob Shirley .15 .06
113 Ron Roenicke .15 .06
114 Jim Slaton .15 .06
115 Chili Davis 1.25 .50
116 Dave Schmidt .15 .06
117 Alan Knicely .15 .06
118 Chris Welsh .15 .06
119 Tom Brookens .15 .06
120 Len Barker .15 .06
121 Mickey Hatcher .15 .06
122 Jimmy Smith .15 .06
123 George Frazier .15 .06
124 Marc Hill .15 .06
125 Leon Durham .15 .06
126 Joe Torre MG .30 .12
127 Preston Hanna .15 .06
128 Mike Ramsey .15 .06
129 Checklist: 1-132 .30 .12
130 Dave Stieb .30 .12
131 Ed Ott .15 .06
132 Todd Cruz .15 .06
133 Jim Barr .15 .06
134 Hubie Brooks .30 .12
135 Dwight Evans .30 .12
136 Willie Aikens .15 .06
137 Woodie Fryman .15 .06
138 Rick Dempsey .30 .12
139 Bruce Berenyi .15 .06
140 Willie Randolph .30 .12
141 Toby Harrah .30 .12
Rick Sutcliffe TL
142 Mike Caldwell .15 .06
143 Joe Pettini .15 .06
144 Mark Wagner .15 .06
145 Don Sutton 1.25 .50
146 Don Sutton SV .60 .24
147 Rick Leach .15 .06
148 Dave Roberts .15 .06
149 Johnny Ray .15 .06
150 Bruce Sutter .30 .12
151 Bruce Sutter SV .15 .06
152 Jay Johnstone .30 .12
153 Jerry Koosman .30 .12
154 Johnnie LeMaster .15 .06
155 Dan Quisenberry .30 .12
156 Billy Martin MG .30 .12
157 Steve Bedrosian .30 .12
158 Rob Wilfong .15 .06
159 Mike Stanton .15 .06
160 Dave Kingman .60 .24
161 Dave Kingman SV .30 .12
162 Mark Clear .15 .06
163 Cal Ripken 10.00 4.00
164 David Palmer .15 .06
165 Dan Driessen .15 .06
166 John Pacella .15 .06
167 Mark Brouhard .15 .06
168 Juan Eichelberger .15 .06
169 Doug Flynn .15 .06
170 Steve Howe .15 .06
171 Joe Morgan .30 .12
Bill Laskey TL
172 Vern Ruhle .15 .06
173 Jim Morrison .15 .06
174 Jerry Ujdur .15 .06
175 Bo Diaz .15 .06
176 Dave Righetti .30 .12
177 Harold Baines 1.25 .50
178 Luis Tiant .30 .12
179 Luis Tiant SV .15 .06
180 Rickey Henderson 2.50 1.00
181 Terry Felton .15 .06
182 Mike Fischlin .15 .06
183 Ed VandeBerg .15 .06
184 Bob Clark .15 .06
185 Tim Lollar .15 .06
186 Whitey Herzog MG .30 .12
187 Terry Leach .15 .06
188 Rick Miller .15 .06
189 Dan Schatzeder .15 .06
190 Cecil Cooper .30 .12
191 Joe Price .15 .06
192 Floyd Rayford .15 .06
193 Harry Spilman .15 .06
194 Cesar Geronimo .15 .06
195 Bob Stoddard .15 .06
196 Bill Fahey .15 .06
197 Jim Eisenreich RC 1.25 .50
198 Kiko Garcia .15 .06
199 Marty Bystrom .15 .06
200 Rod Carew .60 .24
201 Rod Carew SV .30 .12
202 Damaso Garcia .30 .12
Dave Stieb TL
203 Mike Morgan .15 .06
204 Junior Kennedy .15 .06
205 Dave Parker .30 .12
206 Ken Oberkfell .15 .06
207 Rick Camp .15 .06
208 Dan Meyer .15 .06

209 Mike Moore RC .30 .12
210 Jack Clark .30 .12
211 John Denny .15 .06
212 John Stearns .15 .06
213 Tom Burgmeier .15 .06
214 Jerry White .15 .06
215 Mario Soto .15 .06
216 Tony LaRussa MG .30 .12
217 Tim Stoddard .15 .06
218 Roy Howell .15 .06
219 Mike Armstrong .15 .06
220 Dusty Baker .30 .12
221 Joe Niekro .30 .12
222 Damaso Garcia .15 .06
223 John Montefusco .15 .06
224 Mickey Rivers .15 .06
225 Enos Cabell .15 .06
226 Enrique Romo .15 .06
227 Chris Bando .15 .06
228 Joaquin Andujar .15 .06
229 Bo Diaz .15 .06
Steve Carlton TL
230 Fergie Jenkins .30 .12
231 Fergie Jenkins SV .15 .06
232 Tom Brunansky .30 .12
233 Wayne Gross .15 .06
234 Larry Andersen .15 .06
235 Claudell Washington .15 .06
236 Steve Renko .15 .06
237 Dan Norman .15 .06
238 Bud Black RC .30 .12
239 Dave Stapleton .15 .06
240 Rich Gossage .60 .24
241 Rich Gossage SV .30 .12
242 Joe Nolan .15 .06
243 Duane Walker .15 .06
244 Dwight Bernard .15 .06
245 Steve Sax .30 .12
246 G.Bamberger MG .15 .06
247 Dave Smith .15 .06
248 Bake McBride .15 .06
249 Checklist: 133-264 .30 .12
250 Bill Buckner .30 .12
251 Alan Wiggins .15 .06
252 Luis Aguayo .15 .06
253 Larry McWilliams .15 .06
254 Rick Cerone .15 .06
255 Gene Garber .15 .06
256 Gene Garber SV .15 .06
257 Jesse Barfield .30 .12
258 Manny Castillo .15 .06
259 Jeff Jones .15 .06
260 Steve Kemp .15 .06
261 Larry Herndon .30 .12
Dan Petry TL
262 Ron Jackson .15 .06
263 Renie Martin .15 .06
264 Jamie Quirk .15 .06
265 Joel Youngblood .15 .06
266 Paul Boris .15 .06
267 Terry Francona .15 .06
268 Storm Davis RC .15 .06
269 Ron Oester .15 .06
270 Dennis Eckersley .60 .24
271 Ed Romero .15 .06
272 Frank Tanana .30 .12
273 Mark Belanger .15 .06
274 Terry Kennedy .15 .06
275 Ray Knight .30 .12
276 Gene Mauch MG .15 .06
277 Rance Mulliniks .15 .06
278 Kevin Hickey .15 .06
279 Greg Gross .15 .06
280 Bert Blyleven .60 .24
281 Andre Robertson .15 .06
282 Reggie Smith 1.25 .50
(Ryne Sandberg
ducking back)
283 Reggie Smith SV .15 .06
284 Jeff Lahti .15 .06
285 Lance Parrish .30 .12
286 Rick Langford .15 .06
287 Bobby Brown .15 .06
288 Joe Cowley .15 .06
289 Jerry Dybzinski .15 .06
290 Jeff Reardon .30 .12
291 Bill Madlock .30 .12
John Candelaria TL
292 Craig Swan .15 .06
293 Glenn Gulliver .15 .06
294 Dave Engle .15 .06
295 Jerry Remy .15 .06
296 Greg Harris .15 .06
297 Ned Yost .15 .06
298 Floyd Chiffer .15 .06
299 George Wright RC .15 .06
300 Mike Schmidt 3.00 1.20
301 Mike Schmidt SV 1.25 .50
302 Ernie Whitt .15 .06
303 Miguel Dilone .15 .06
304 Dave Rucker .15 .06
305 Larry Bowa .30 .12
306 Tom Lasorda MG .60 .24
307 Lou Piniella .30 .12
308 Jesus Vega .15 .06
309 Jeff Leonard .15 .06
310 Greg Luzinski .30 .12
311 Glenn Brummer .15 .06
312 Brian Kingman .15 .06
313 Gary Gray .15 .06
314 Ken Dayley .15 .06
315 Rick Burleson .15 .06
316 Paul Splittorff .15 .06
317 Gary Rajsich .15 .06
318 John Tudor .15 .06
319 Lenn Sakata .15 .06
320 Steve Rogers .15 .06
321 Robin Yount 1.25 .50
Pete Vuckovich TL
322 Dave Van Gorder .15 .06
323 Luis DeLeon .15 .06
324 Mike Marshall .15 .06
325 Von Hayes .30 .12
326 Garth Iorg .15 .06
327 Bobby Castillo .15 .06
328 Craig Reynolds .15 .06
329 Randy Niemann .15 .06
330 Buddy Bell .30 .12
331 Mike Krukow .15 .06
332 Glenn Wilson .30 .12
333 Dave LaRoche .15 .06
334 Dave LaRoche SV .15 .06
335 Steve Henderson .15 .06
336 Rene Lachemann MG .15 .06
337 Tito Landrum .15 .06
338 Bob Owchinko .15 .06
339 Terry Harper .15 .06
340 Larry Gura .15 .06
341 Doug DeCinces .30 .12
342 Atlee Hammaker .15 .06
343 Bob Bailor .15 .06
344 Roger LaFrancois .15 .06
345 Jim Clancy .15 .06
346 Joe Pittman .15 .06
347 Sammy Stewart .15 .06
348 Alan Bannister .15 .06
349 Checklist: 265-396 .30 .12
350 Robin Yount 2.00 .80
351 Cesar Cedeno .30 .12
Mario Soto TL
352 Mike Scioscia .30 .12
353 Steve Comer .15 .06
354 Randy Johnson .15 .06
355 Jim Bibby .15 .06
356 Gary Woods .15 .06
357 Len Matuszek .15 .06
358 Jerry Garvin .15 .06
359 Dave Collins .15 .06
360 Nolan Ryan 6.00 2.40
361 Nolan Ryan SV 3.00 1.20
362 Bill Almon .15 .06
363 John Stuper .15 .06
364 Brett Butler 1.25 .50
365 Dave Lopes .30 .12
366 Dick Williams MG .15 .06
367 Bud Anderson .15 .06
368 Richie Zisk .15 .06
369 Jesse Orosco .15 .06
370 Gary Carter .60 .24
371 Mike Richardt .15 .06
372 Terry Crowley .15 .06
373 Kevin Saucier .15 .06
374 Wayne Krenchicki .15 .06
375 Pete Vuckovich .15 .06
376 Ken Landreaux .15 .06
377 Lee May .30 .12
378 Lee May SV .15 .06
379 Guy Sularz .15 .06
380 Ron Davis .15 .06
381 Jim Rice .30 .12
Bob Stanley TL
382 Bob Knepper .15 .06
383 Ozzie Virgil .15 .06
384 Dave Dravecky RC 1.25 .50
385 Mike Easler .15 .06
386 Rod Carew AS .30 .12
387 Bob Grich AS .15 .06
388 George Brett AS 1.50 .60
389 Robin Yount AS 1.25 .50
390 Reggie Jackson AS .30 .12
391 Rickey Henderson AS 1.25 .50
392 Fred Lynn AS .15 .06
393 Carlton Fisk AS .30 .12
394 Pete Vuckovich AS .15 .06
395 Larry Gura AS .15 .06
396 Dan Quisenberry AS .15 .06
397 Pete Rose AS .60 .24
398 Manny Trillo AS .15 .06
399 Mike Schmidt AS 1.25 .50
400 Dave Concepcion AS .15 .06
401 Dale Murphy AS .60 .24
402 Andre Dawson AS .15 .06
403 Tim Raines AS .30 .12
404 Gary Carter AS .30 .12
405 Steve Rogers AS .15 .06
406 Steve Carlton AS .15 .06
407 Bruce Sutter AS .15 .06
408 Rudy May .15 .06
409 Marvis Foley .15 .06
410 Phil Niekro .30 .12
411 Phil Niekro SV .30 .12
412 Buddy Bell .30 .12
Charlie Hough TL
413 Matt Keough .15 .06
414 Julio Cruz .15 .06
415 Bob Forsch .15 .06
416 Joe Ferguson .15 .06
417 Tom Hausman .15 .06
418 Greg Pryor .15 .06
419 Steve Crawford .15 .06
420 Al Oliver .30 .12
421 Al Oliver SV .15 .06
422 George Cappuzzello .15 .06
423 Tom Lawless .15 .06
424 Jerry Augustine .15 .06
425 Pedro Guerrero .30 .12
426 Earl Weaver MG .60 .24
427 Roy Lee Jackson .15 .06
428 Champ Summers .15 .06
429 Eddie Whitson .15 .06
430 Kirk Gibson 1.25 .50
431 Gary Gaetti RC 1.25 .50
432 Porfirio Altamirano .15 .06
433 Dale Berra .15 .06
434 Dennis Lamp .15 .06
435 Tony Armas .15 .06
436 Bill Campbell .15 .06
437 Rick Sweet .15 .06
438 Dave LaPoint .15 .06
439 Rafael Ramirez .15 .06
440 Ron Guidry .30 .12
441 Ray Knight .30 .12
Joe Niekro TL
442 Brian Downing .15 .06
443 Don Hood .15 .06
444 Wally Backman .15 .06
445 Mike Flanagan .30 .12
446 Reid Nichols .15 .06
447 Bryn Smith .15 .06
448 Darrell Evans .30 .12
449 Eddie Milner .15 .06
450 Ted Simmons .30 .12
451 Ted Simmons SV .15 .06
452 Lloyd Moseby .15 .06
453 Lamar Johnson .15 .06
454 Bob Welch .30 .12
455 Sixto Lezcano .15 .06
456 Lee Elia MG .15 .06
457 Milt Wilcox .15 .06
458 Ron Washington .15 .06
459 Ed Farmer .15 .06
460 Roy Smalley .15 .06
461 Steve Trout .15 .06
462 Steve Nicosia .15 .06
463 Gaylord Perry .30 .12
464 Gaylord Perry SV .15 .06
465 Lonnie Smith .15 .06
466 Tom Underwood .15 .06
467 Rufino Linares .15 .06
468 Dave Goltz .15 .06
469 Ron Gardenhire .15 .06
470 Greg Minton .15 .06
471 Willie Wilson .30 .12
Vida Blue TL
472 Gary Allenson .15 .06
473 John Lowenstein .15 .06
474 Ray Burris .15 .06
475 Cesar Cedeno .30 .12
476 Rob Picciolo .15 .06
477 Tom Niedenfuer .15 .06
478 Phil Garner .30 .12
479 Charlie Hough .30 .12
480 Toby Harrah .15 .06
481 Scot Thompson .15 .06
482 Tony Gwynn UER RC 25.00 10.00
No Topps logo under
card number on back
483 Lynn Jones .15 .06
484 Dick Ruthven .15 .06
485 Omar Moreno .15 .06
486 Clyde King MG .15 .06
487 Jerry Hairston .15 .06
488 Alfredo Griffin .15 .06
489 Tom Herr .30 .12
490 Jim Palmer .30 .12
491 Jim Palmer SV .15 .06
492 Paul Serna .15 .06
493 Steve McCatty .15 .06
494 Bob Brenly .15 .06
495 Warren Cromartie .15 .06
496 Tom Veryzer .15 .06
497 Rick Sutcliffe .30 .12
498 Wade Boggs RC 12.00 4.80
499 Jeff Little .15 .06
500 Reggie Jackson .60 .24
501 Reggie Jackson SV .30 .12
502 Dale Murphy .60 .24
Phil Niekro TL
503 Moose Haas .15 .06
504 Don Werner .15 .06
505 Garry Templeton .15 .06
506 Jim Gott RC .15 .06
507 Tony Scott .15 .06
508 Tom Filer .15 .06
509 Lou Whitaker .30 .12
510 Tug McGraw .30 .12
511 Tug McGraw SV .15 .06
512 Doyle Alexander .15 .06
513 Fred Stanley .15 .06
514 Rudy Law .15 .06
515 Gene Tenace .30 .12
516 Bill Virdon MG .15 .06
517 Gary Ward .15 .06
518 Bill Laskey .15 .06
519 Terry Bulling .15 .06
520 Fred Lynn .30 .12
521 Bruce Benedict .15 .06
522 Pat Zachry .15 .06
523 Carney Lansford .30 .12
524 Tom Brennan .15 .06
525 Frank White .30 .12
526 Checklist: 397-528 .30 .12
527 Larry Biittner .15 .06
528 Jamie Easterly .15 .06
529 Tim Laudner .15 .06
530 Eddie Murray 1.25 .50
531 Rickey Henderson 1.25 .50
Rick Langford TL
532 Dave Stewart .30 .12
533 Luis Salazar .15 .06
534 John Butcher .15 .06
535 Manny Trillo .15 .06
536 John Wockenfuss .15 .06
537 Rod Scurry .15 .06
538 Danny Heep .15 .06
539 Roger Erickson .15 .06
540 Ozzie Smith 2.00 .80
541 Britt Burns .15 .06
542 Jody Davis .15 .06
543 Alan Fowlkes .15 .06
544 Larry Whisenton .15 .06
545 Floyd Bannister .15 .06
546 Dave Garcia MG .15 .06
547 Geoff Zahn .15 .06
548 Brian Giles .15 .06
549 Charlie Puleo .15 .06
550 Carl Yastrzemski 2.00 .80
551 Carl Yastrzemski SV 1.25 .50
552 Tim Wallach .30 .12
553 Dennis Martinez .30 .12
554 Mike Vail .15 .06
555 Steve Yeager .15 .06
556 Willie Upshaw .15 .06
557 Rick Honeycutt .15 .06
558 Dickie Thon .15 .06
559 Pete Redfern .15 .06
560 Ron LeFlore .15 .06
561 Lonnie Smith .30 .12
Joaquin Andujar TL
562 Dave Rozema .15 .06
563 Juan Bonilla .15 .06
564 Sid Monge .15 .06
565 Bucky Dent .30 .12
566 Manny Sarmiento .15 .06
567 Joe Simpson .15 .06
568 Willie Hernandez .30 .12
569 Jack Perconte .15 .06
570 Vida Blue .30 .12
571 Mickey Klutts .15 .06
572 Bob Watson .30 .12
573 Andy Hassler .15 .06
574 Glenn Adams .15 .06
575 Neil Allen .15 .06
576 Frank Robinson MG .60 .24
577 Luis Aponte .15 .06
578 David Green RC .15 .06
579 Rich Dauer .15 .06
580 Tom Seaver .60 .24
581 Tom Seaver SV .30 .12
582 Marshall Edwards .15 .06
583 Terry Forster .15 .06
584 Dave Hostetler .15 .06
585 Jose Cruz .30 .12
586 Frank Viola RC 1.25 .50
587 Ivan DeJesus .15 .06
588 Pat Underwood .15 .06
589 Alvis Woods .15 .06
590 Tony Pena .15 .06
591 Greg Luzinski .30 .12
LaMarr Hoyt TL
592 Shane Rawley .15 .06
593 Broderick Perkins .15 .06
594 Eric Rasmussen .15 .06
595 Tim Raines 1.25 .50
596 Randy Johnson .15 .06
597 Mike Proly .15 .06
598 Dwayne Murphy .15 .06
599 Don Aase .15 .06
600 George Brett 3.00 1.20
601 Ed Lynch .15 .06
602 Rich Gedman .15 .06
603 Joe Morgan .60 .24
604 Joe Morgan SV .30 .12
605 Gary Roenicke .15 .06
606 Bobby Cox MG .30 .12
607 Charlie Leibrandt .15 .06
608 Don Money .15 .06
609 Danny Darwin .15 .06
610 Steve Garvey .30 .12
611 Bert Roberge .15 .06
612 Steve Swisher .15 .06
613 Mike Ivie .15 .06
614 Ed Glynn .15 .06
615 Garry Maddox .15 .06
616 Bill Nahorodny .15 .06
617 Butch Wynegar .15 .06
618 LaMarr Hoyt .30 .12
619 Keith Moreland .15 .06
620 Mike Norris .15 .06
621 Mookie Wilson .30 .12
Craig Swan TL
622 Dave Edler .15 .06
623 Luis Sanchez .15 .06
624 Glenn Hubbard .15 .06
625 Ken Forsch .15 .06
626 Jerry Martin .15 .06
627 Doug Bair .15 .06
628 Julio Valdez .15 .06
629 Charlie Lea .15 .06
630 Paul Molitor .60 .24
631 Tippy Martinez .15 .06
632 Alex Trevino .15 .06
633 Vicente Romo .15 .06
634 Max Venable .15 .06
635 Graig Nettles .30 .12
636 Graig Nettles SV .15 .06
637 Pat Corrales MG .15 .06
638 Dan Petry .15 .06
639 Art Howe .30 .12
640 Andre Thornton .15 .06
641 Billy Sample .15 .06
642 Checklist: 529-660 .30 .12
643 Bump Wills .15 .06
644 Joe Lefebvre .15 .06
645 Bill Madlock .30 .12
646 Jim Essian .15 .06
647 Bobby Mitchell .15 .06
648 Jeff Burroughs .15 .06
649 Tommy Boggs .15 .06
650 George Hendrick .15 .06
651 Rod Carew .30 .12
Mike Witt TL
652 Butch Hobson .15 .06
653 Ellis Valentine .15 .06
654 Bob Ojeda .15 .06
655 Al Bumbry .15 .06
656 Dave Frost .15 .06
657 Mike Gates .15 .06
658 Frank Pastore .15 .06
659 Charlie Moore .15 .06
660 Mike Hargrove .30 .12
661 Bill Russell .15 .06
662 Joe Sambito .15 .06
663 Tom O'Malley .15 .06
664 Bob Molinaro .15 .06
665 Jim Sundberg .30 .12
666 Sparky Anderson MG .30 .12
667 Dick Davis .15 .06
668 Larry Christenson .15 .06
669 Mike Squires .15 .06
670 Jerry Mumphrey .15 .06
671 Lenny Faedo .15 .06
672 Jim Kaat .30 .12
673 Jim Kaat SV .15 .06
674 Kurt Bevacqua .15 .06
675 Jim Slaton .15 .06
676 Biff Pocoroba .15 .06
677 Dave Revering .15 .06
678 Juan Beniquez .15 .06
679 Mike Scott .30 .12
680 Andre Dawson .30 .12
681 Pedro Guerrero .30 .12
Fernando Valenzuela TL
682 Bob Stanley .15 .06
683 Dan Ford .15 .06
684 Rafael Landestoy .15 .06
685 Lee Mazzilli .15 .06
686 Randy Lerch .15 .06
687 U.L. Washington .15 .06
688 Jim Wohlford .15 .06
689 Ron Hassey .15 .06
690 Kent Hrbek .30 .12
691 Dave Tobik .15 .06
692 Denny Walling .15 .06
693 Sparky Lyle .30 .12
694 Sparky Lyle SV .15 .06
695 Ruppert Jones .15 .06
696 Chuck Tanner MG .15 .06
697 Barry Foote .15 .06
698 Tony Bernazard .15 .06
699 Lee Smith 1.25 .50
700 Keith Hernandez .60 .24
701 Willie Wilson .30 .12
Al Oliver LL
702 Reggie Jackson .30 .12
Gorman Thomas
Dave Kingman LL
703 Hal McRae .60 .24
Dale Murphy
Al Oliver LL
704 Rickey Henderson 1.25 .50
Tim Raines LL
705 LaMarr Hoyt .30 .12
Steve Carlton LL
706 Floyd Bannister .30 .12
Steve Carlton LL
707 Rick Sutcliffe .30 .12
Steve Rogers LL
708 Dan Quisenberry .30 .12
Bruce Sutter LL
709 Jimmy Sexton .15 .06
710 Willie Wilson .30 .12
711 Bruce Bochte .30 .12
Jim Beattie TL
712 Bruce Kison .15 .06
713 Ron Hodges .15 .06
714 Wayne Nordhagen .15 .06
715 Tony Perez .60 .24
716 Tony Perez SV .30 .12
717 Scott Sanderson .15 .06
718 Jim Dwyer .15 .06
719 Rich Gale .15 .06
720 Dave Concepcion .30 .12
721 John Martin .15 .06
722 Jorge Orta .15 .06
723 Randy Moffitt .15 .06
724 Johnny Grubb .15 .06
725 Dan Spillner .15 .06
726 Harvey Kuenn MG .15 .06
727 Chet Lemon .15 .06
728 Ron Reed .15 .06
729 Jerry Morales .15 .06
730 Jason Thompson .15 .06
731 Al Williams .15 .06
732 Dave Henderson .15 .06
733 Buck Martinez .15 .06
734 Steve Braun .15 .06
735 Tommy John .60 .24
736 Tommy John SV .30 .12
737 Mitchell Page .15 .06
738 Tim Foli .15 .06
739 Rick Ownbey .15 .06
740 Rusty Staub .30 .12
741 Rusty Staub SV .15 .06
742 Terry Kennedy .30 .12
Tim Lollar
743 Mike Torrez .15 .06
744 Brad Mills .15 .06
745 Scott McGregor .15 .06
746 John Wathan .15 .06
747 Fred Breining .15 .06
748 Derrel Thomas .15 .06
749 Jon Matlack .15 .06
750 Ben Oglivie .15 .06
751 Brad Havens .15 .06
752 Luis Pujols .15 .06
753 Elias Sosa .15 .06
754 Bill Robinson .15 .06
755 John Candelaria .15 .06
756 Russ Nixon MG .15 .06
757 Rick Manning .15 .06
758 Aurelio Rodriguez .15 .06
759 Doug Bird .15 .06
760 Dale Murphy 1.25 .50
761 Gary Lucas .15 .06
762 Cliff Johnson .15 .06
763 Al Cowens .15 .06
764 Pete Falcone .15 .06
765 Bob Boone .30 .12
766 Barry Bonnell .15 .06
767 Duane Kuiper .15 .06
768 Chris Speier .15 .06
769 Checklist: 661-792 .30 .12
770 Dave Winfield .30 .12
771 Kent Hrbek .30 .12
Bobby Castillo TL
772 Jim Kern .15 .06
773 Larry Hisle .15 .06
774 Alan Ashby .15 .06
775 Burt Hooton .15 .06
776 Larry Parrish .15 .06
777 John Curtis .15 .06
778 Rich Hebner .30 .12
779 Rick Waits .15 .06
780 Gary Matthews .30 .12
781 Rick Rhoden .15 .06
782 Bobby Murcer .30 .12
783 Bobby Murcer SV .15 .06
784 Jeff Newman .15 .06
785 Dennis Leonard .15 .06
786 Ralph Houk MG .15 .06
787 Dick Tidrow .15 .06
788 Dane Iorg .15 .06
789 Bryan Clark .15 .06
790 Bob Grich .30 .12
791 Gary Lavelle .15 .06
792 Chris Chambliss .30 .12
XX Game Insert Card .10 .04

1983 Topps Glossy Send-Ins

The cards in this 40-card set measure the standard size. The 1983 Topps "Collector's Edition" or "All-Star Set" (popularly known as "Glossies") consists of color ballplayer picture cards with shiny, glazed surfaces. The player's name appears in small print outside the frame line at bottom left. The backs contain no biography or record and list only the set titles, the player's name, team, position, and the card number.

	Nm-Mt	Ex-Mt
COMPLETE SET (40)	15.00	6.00
1 Carl Yastrzemski	1.25	.50
2 Mookie Wilson	.20	.08
3 Andre Thornton	.10	.04
4 Keith Hernandez	.20	.08
5 Robin Yount	1.25	.50

6 Terry Kennedy .10 .04
7 Dave Winfield 1.25 .50
8 Mike Schmidt 1.50 .60
9 Buddy Bell .20 .08
10 Fernando Valenzuela .30 .12
11 Rich Gossage .20 .08
12 Bob Horner .10 .04
13 Toby Harrah .10 .04
14 Pete Rose 1.50 .60
15 Cecil Cooper .20 .08
16 Dale Murphy .50 .20
17 Carlton Fisk 1.25 .50
18 Ray Knight .10 .04
19 Jim Palmer 1.00 .40
20 Gary Carter 1.00 .40
21 Richie Zisk .10 .04
22 Dusty Baker .20 .08
23 Willie Wilson .10 .04
24 Bill Buckner .20 .08
25 Dave Stieb .10 .04
26 Bill Madlock .10 .04
27 Lance Parrish .20 .08
28 Nolan Ryan 5.00 2.00
29 Rod Carew 1.00 .40
30 Al Oliver .20 .08
31 George Brett 2.50 1.00
32 Jack Clark .10 .04
33 Rickey Henderson 2.00 .80
34 Dave Concepcion .20 .08
35 Kent Hrbek .20 .08
36 Steve Carlton 1.00 .40
37 Eddie Murray 1.25 .50
38 Ruppert Jones .10 .04
39 Reggie Jackson 1.25 .50
40 Bruce Sutter .20 .08

1983 Topps Traded

For the third year in a row, Topps issued a 132-card standard-size Traded (or extended) set featuring some of the year's top rookies and players who had changed teams during the year. The cards were available through hobby dealers only in factory set form and were printed in Ireland by the Topps affiliate in that country. The set is numbered alphabetically by player. The Darryl Strawberry card number 108 can be found with either one or two asterisks (in the lower left corner of the reverse). There is no difference in value for either version. The key (extended) Rookie Cards in this set include Julio Franco, Tony Phillips and Darryl Strawberry.

Nm-Mt Ex-Mt
COMP.FACT.SET (132) 40.00 16.00
1T Neil Allen .25 .10
2T Bill Almon .25 .10
3T Joe Altobelli MG .25 .10
4T Tony Armas .25 .10
5T Doug Bair .25 .10
6T Steve Baker .25 .10
7T Floyd Bannister .25 .10
8T Don Baylor 2.00 .80
9T Tony Bernazard .25 .10
10T Larry Biittner .25 .10
11T Dann Bilardello .25 .10
12T Doug Bird .25 .10
13T Steve Boros MG .25 .10
14T Greg Brock .50 .20
15T Mike C. Brown .25 .10
16T Tom Burgmeier .25 .10
17T Randy Bush .25 .10
18T Bert Campaneris 1.00 .40
19T Ron Cey 1.00 .40
20T Chris Codiroli .25 .10
21T Dave Collins .25 .10
22T Terry Crowley .25 .10
23T Julio Cruz .25 .10
24T Mike Davis .25 .10
25T Frank DiPino .25 .10
26T Bill Doran XRC 1.00 .40
27T Jerry Dybzinski .25 .10
28T Jamie Easterly .25 .10
29T Juan Eichelberger .25 .10
30T Jim Essian .25 .10
31T Pete Falcone .25 .10
32T Mike Ferraro MG .25 .10
33T Terry Forster .25 .10
34T Julio Franco XRC 4.00 1.60
35T Rich Gale .25 .10
36T Kiko Garcia .25 .10
37T Steve Garvey 1.00 .40
38T Johnny Grubb .25 .10
39T Mel Hall XRC* 1.00 .40
40T Von Hayes 1.00 .40
41T Danny Heep .25 .10
42T Steve Henderson .25 .10
43T Keith Hernandez 2.00 .80
44T Leo Hernandez .25 .10
45T Willie Hernandez 1.00 .40
46T Al Holland .25 .10
47T Frank Howard MG 1.00 .40
48T Bobby Johnson .25 .10
49T Cliff Johnson .25 .10
50T Odell Jones .25 .10
51T Mike Jorgensen .25 .10
52T Bob Kearney .25 .10
53T Steve Kemp .25 .10
54T Matt Keough .25 .10
55T Ron Kittle XRC* 2.00 .80
56T Mickey Klutts .25 .10
57T Alan Knicely .25 .10
58T Mike Krukow .25 .10
59T Rafael Landestoy .25 .10
60T Carney Lansford 1.00 .40
61T Joe Lefebvre .25 .10
62T Bryan Little .25 .10
63T Aurelio Lopez .25 .10
64T Mike Madden .25 .10
65T Rick Manning .25 .10
66T Billy Martin MG 1.00 .40
67T Lee Mazzilli .25 .10
68T Andy McGaffigan .25 .10
69T Craig McMurtry .25 .10
70T John McNamara MG .25 .10
71T Orlando Mercado .25 .10
72T Larry Milbourne .25 .10
73T Randy Moffitt .25 .10
74T Sid Monge .25 .10
75T Jose Morales .25 .10
76T Omar Moreno .25 .10
77T Joe Morgan 2.00 .80
78T Mike Morgan .25 .10
79T Dale Murray .25 .10
80T Jeff Newman .25 .10
81T Pete O'Brien XRC 1.00 .40
82T Jorge Orta .25 .10
83T Alejandro Pena XRC 1.00 .40
84T Pascual Perez .25 .10
85T Tony Perez 2.00 .80
86T Broderick Perkins .25 .10
87T Tony Phillips XRC 2.00 .80
88T Charlie Puleo .25 .10
89T Pat Putnam .25 .10
90T Jamie Quirk .25 .10
91T Doug Rader MG .25 .10
92T Chuck Rainey .25 .10
93T Bobby Ramos .25 .10
94T Gary Redus XRC 1.00 .40
95T Steve Renko .25 .10
96T Leon Roberts .25 .10
97T Aurelio Rodriguez .25 .10
98T Dick Ruthven .25 .10
99T Daryl Sconiers .25 .10
100T Mike Scott 1.00 .40
101T Tom Seaver 2.00 .80
102T John Shelby .25 .10
103T Bob Shirley .25 .10
104T Joe Simpson .25 .10
105T Doug Sisk .25 .10
106T Mike Smithson .25 .10
107T Elias Sosa .25 .10
108T D.Strawberry XRC 10.00 4.00
109T Tom Tellmann .25 .10
110T Gene Tenace 1.00 .40
111T Gorman Thomas .25 .10
112T Dick Tidrow .25 .10
113T Dave Tobik .25 .10
114T Wayne Tolleson .25 .10
115T Mike Torrez .25 .10
116T Manny Trillo .25 .10
117T Steve Trout .25 .10
118T Lee Tunnell .25 .10
119T Mike Vail .25 .10
120T Ellis Valentine .25 .10
121T Tom Veryzer .25 .10
122T George Vukovich .25 .10
123T Rick Waits .25 .10
124T Greg Walker 1.00 .40
125T Chris Welsh .25 .10
126T Len Whitehouse .25 .10
127T Eddie Whitson .25 .10
128T Jim Wohlford .25 .10
129T Matt Young XRC .25 .10
130T Joel Youngblood .25 .10
131T Pat Zachry .25 .10
132T Checklist 1T-132T .25 .10

1983 Topps Foldouts

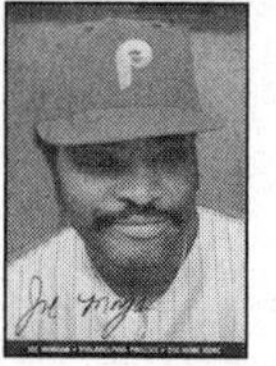

The cards in this 85-card (five folders with 17 photos in each folder) set measure 3 1/2" by 5 5/16". The 1983 Fold-Outs were an innovation by Topps featuring five sets of 17 postcard-size photos each. Each of the five sets had a theme of career leaders in a particular category. The five catagories -- batting leaders, home run leaders, stolen base leaders, pitching leaders and relief aces -- featured the 17 top active players in their respective categories. If a player were a leader in more than one category, he is pictured in more than one of the five sets. These foldout booklets are typically sold intact and are priced below at one price per complete panel. Each picture contains a facsimile autograph as well. The quality of the photos is very good. In the checklist below the leaders are listed in order of their career standing as shown on each foldout.

Nm-Mt Ex-Mt
COMPLETE SET (5) 5.00 2.00
1 Gaylord Perry 1.25 .02
Steve Carlton
Jim Kaat
Fergie Jenkins
Tom Seaver
Jim Palmer
Don Sutton
Phil Niekro
Tommy John
Nolan Ryan
Vida Blue
Jerry Koosman
Mike Torrez
Bert Blyleven
Joe Niekro
Jerry Reuss
Paul Splittorff
2 Reggie Jackson 1.50 .60
Carl Yastrzemski
Johnny Bench
Tony Perez
Mike Schmidt
Dave Kingman
Graig Nettles
Rusty Staub
Greg Luzinski
George Foster
John Mayberry
Bobby Murcer
Joe Morgan
Jim Rice
Rick Monday
Darrell Evans
Ron Cey
3 Rod Carew 1.50 .60
George Brett
Bill Madlock
Lonnie Smith
Willie Wilson
Pete Rose
Dave Parker
Cecil Cooper
Jim Rice
Al Oliver
Pedro Guerrero
Ken Griffey
Fred Lynn
Steve Garvey
Bake McBride
Keith Hernandez
Dane Iorg
4 Rollie Fingers 1.00 .40
Bruce Sutter
Rich Gossage
Tug McGraw
Gene Garber
Kent Tekulve
Bill Campbell
Terry Forster
Tom Burgmeier
Greg Lavelle
Dan Quisenberry
Jim Kern
Randy Moffitt
Ron Reed
EliasSosa
Ed Farmer
Greg Minton
5 Joe Morgan 1.00 .40
Cesar Cedeno
Ron LeFlore
Davey Lopes
Omar Moreno
Rod Carew
Amos Otis
Rickey Henderson
Larry Bowa
Willie Wilson
Don Baylor
Julio Cruz
Mickey Rivers
Dave Concepcion
Jose Cruz
Garry Maddox
Al Bumbry

1983 Topps Leader Sheet

The cards in this 8-player sheet measure 2 1/2" by 3 1/2". The full sheet is 7 1/2" by 10 1/2". The full sheet is typically kept intact as it has not been perforated. The sheet is blank backed and features the league statistical leaders from the previous season. The cards are unnumbered and are listed below in left to right order of appearance on the sheet.

Nm-Mt Ex-Mt
1 Willie Wilson 2.00 .80
Reggie Jackson
Gorman Thomas
Al Oliver
LaMarr Hoyt
Steve Carlton
Dan Quisenberry
Dave Kingman
Bruce Sutter

1983 Topps Stickers

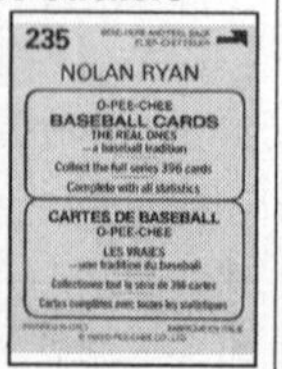

Made for Topps and O-Pee-Chee by Panini, an Italian company, these 330 stickers measure approximately 1 15/16" by 2 9/16" and are numbered on both front and back. The fronts feature white-bordered color player photos framed with a colored and a black line. The colored line is red for AL players and blue for NL players. The backs carry player names and a bilingual ad for the O-Pee-Chee sticker album. The album, onto which the stickers could be affixed, was available at retail stores. The album and the sticker numbering are organized as follows: Home Run Kings (1-14), AL Pitching and Batting Leaders (15-22), Baltimore Orioles (23-30), Boston Red Sox (31-38), California Angels (39-46), Chicago White Sox (47-54), Cleveland Indians (55-62), Detroit Tigers (63-70), Kansas City Royals (71-78), Milwaukee Brewers (79-86), Minnesota Twins (87-94), New York Yankees (95-102), Oakland A's (103-110), Seattle Mariners (111-118), Texas Rangers (119-126), Toronto Blue Jays (127-134), 1982 Record Breakers (135-146), 1982 Championship Series (147-158), AL and NL All-Stars (159-178), 1982 World Series (179-190), 1982 Record Breakers (191-202), NL Pitching and Batting Leaders (203-210), Atlanta Braves (211-218), Chicago Cubs (219-226), Cincinnati Reds (227-234), Houston Astros (235-242), Los Angeles Dodgers (243-250), Montreal Expos (251-258), New York Mets (259-266), Philadelphia Phillies (267-274), Pittsburgh Pirates (275-282), St. Louis Cardinals (283-290), San Diego Padres (291-298), San Francisco Giants (299-306), and Stars of the Future (307-330). Wade Boggs and Ryne Sandberg are featured during their Rookie Card year.

Nm-Mt Ex-Mt
COMPLETE SET (330) 15.00 6.00
COMMON STICKER (1-330) .05 .02
COMMON FOIL .10 .04
*OPC: 2X VALUES BELOW
1 Hank Aaron FOIL 1.25 .50
2 Babe Ruth FOIL 3.00 1.20
3 Willie Mays FOIL 1.50 .60
4 Frank Robinson FOIL .25 .10
5 Reggie Jackson .50 .20
6 Carl Yastrzemski .40 .16
7 Johnny Bench .50 .20
8 Tony Perez .15 .06
9 Lee May .10 .04
10 Mike Schmidt .60 .24
11 Dave Kingman .10 .04
12 Reggie Smith .10 .04
13 Graig Nettles .10 .04
14 Rusty Staub .10 .04
15 Willie Wilson .05 .02
16 LaMarr Hoyt .05 .02
17 Reggie Jackson and .15 .06
Gorman Thomas
18 Floyd Bannister .05 .02
19 Hal McRae .10 .04
20 Rick Sutcliffe .05 .02
21 Rickey Henderson .50 .20
22 Dan Quisenberry .05 .02
23 Jim Palmer FOIL .40 .16
24 John Lowenstein .05 .02
25 Mike Flanagan .10 .04
26 Cal Ripken 4.00 1.60
27 Rich Dauer .05 .02
28 Ken Singleton .10 .04
29 Eddie Murray .50 .20
30 Rick Dempsey .10 .04
31 Carl Yastrzemski FOIL .60 .24
32 Carney Lansford .10 .04
33 Jerry Remy .05 .02
34 Dennis Eckersley .15 .06
35 Dave Stapleton .05 .02
36 Mark Clear .05 .02
37 Jim Rice .10 .04
38 Dwight Evans .10 .04
39 Rod Carew .40 .16
40 Don Baylor .10 .04
41 Reggie Jackson FOIL .75 .30
42 Geoff Zahn .05 .02
43 Bobby Grich .10 .04
44 Fred Lynn .10 .04
45 Bob Boone .10 .04
46 Doug DeCinces .05 .02
47 Tom Paciorek .10 .04
48 Britt Burns .05 .02
49 Tony Bernazard .05 .02
50 Steve Kemp .05 .02
51 Greg Luzinski FOIL .15 .06
52 Harold Baines .15 .06
53 LaMarr Hoyt .05 .02
54 Carlton Fisk .25 .10
55 Andre Thornton FOIL .10 .04
56 Mike Hargrove .10 .04
57 Len Barker .05 .02
58 Toby Harrah .05 .02
59 Dan Spillner .05 .02
60 Rick Manning .05 .02
61 Rick Sutcliffe .05 .02
62 Ron Hassey .05 .02
63 Lance Parrish FOIL .15 .06
64 John Wockenfuss .05 .02
65 Lou Whitaker .15 .06
66 Alan Trammell .25 .10
67 Kirk Gibson .15 .06
68 Larry Herndon .05 .02
69 Jack Morris .10 .04
70 Dan Petry .05 .02
71 Frank White .10 .04
72 Amos Otis .10 .04
73 Willie Wilson FOIL .10 .04
74 Dan Quisenberry .05 .02
75 Hal McRae .10 .04
76 George Brett 1.50 .60
77 Larry Gura .05 .02
78 John Wathan .05 .02
79 Rollie Fingers .25 .10
80 Cecil Cooper .10 .04
81 Robin Yount FOIL .50 .20
82 Ben Oglivie .05 .02
83 Paul Molitor .40 .16
84 Gorman Thomas .05 .02
85 Ted Simmons .10 .04
86 Pete Vuckovich .05 .02
87 Gary Gaetti .25 .10
88 Kent Hrbek FOIL .25 .10
89 John Castino .05 .02
90 Tom Brunansky .05 .02
91 Bobby Mitchell .05 .02
92 Gary Ward .05 .02
93 Tim Laudner .05 .02
94 Ron Davis .05 .02
95 Willie Randolph .10 .04
96 Roy Smalley .05 .02
97 Jerry Mumphrey .05 .02
98 Ken Griffey .10 .04
99 Dave Winfield FOIL .50 .20
100 Rich Gossage .10 .04
101 Butch Wynegar .05 .02
102 Ron Guidry .10 .04
103 Rickey Henderson FOIL .75 .30
104 Mike Heath .05 .02
105 Dave Lopes .10 .04
106 Rick Langford .05 .02
107 Dwayne Murphy .05 .02
108 Tony Armas .05 .02
109 Matt Keough .05 .02
110 Danny Meyer .05 .02
111 Bruce Bochte .05 .02
112 Julio Cruz .05 .02
113 Floyd Bannister .05 .02
114 Gaylord Perry FOIL .25 .10
115 Al Cowens .05 .02
116 Richie Zisk .05 .02
117 Jim Essian .05 .02
118 Bill Caudill .05 .02
119 Buddy Bell FOIL .15 .06
120 Larry Parrish .05 .02
121 Danny Darwin .05 .02
122 Bucky Dent .10 .04
123 Johnny Grubb .05 .02
124 George Wright .05 .02
125 Charlie Hough .10 .04
126 Jim Sundberg .05 .02
127 Dave Stieb FOIL .10 .04
128 Willie Upshaw .05 .02
129 Alfredo Griffin .05 .02
130 Lloyd Moseby .05 .02
131 Ernie Whitt .05 .02
132 Jim Clancy .05 .02
133 Barry Bonnell .05 .02
134 Damaso Garcia .05 .02
135 Jim Kaat RB .10 .04
136 Jim Kaat RB .10 .04
137 Greg Minton RB .05 .02
138 Greg Minton RB .05 .02
139 Paul Molitor RB .15 .06
140 Paul Molitor RB .15 .06
141 Manny Trillo RB .05 .02
142 Manny Trillo RB .05 .02
143 Joel Youngblood RB .05 .02
144 Joel Youngblood RB .05 .02
145 Robin Yount RB .15 .06
146 Robin Yount RB .15 .06
147 Willie McGee LCS .10 .04
148 Darrell Porter LCS .05 .02
149 Darrell Porter LCS .05 .02
150 Robin Yount LCS .15 .06
151 Bruce Benedict LCS .05 .02
152 Bruce Benedict LCS .05 .02
153 George Hendrick LCS .05 .02
154 Bruce Benedict LCS .05 .02
155 Doug DeCinces LCS .05 .02
156 Paul Molitor LCS .15 .06
157 Charlie Moore LCS .05 .02
158 Fred Lynn LCS .10 .04
159 Rickey Henderson .50 .20
160 Dale Murphy .15 .06
161 Willie Wilson .05 .02
162 Jack Clark .10 .04
163 Reggie Jackson .50 .20
164 Andre Dawson .25 .10
165 Dan Quisenberry .05 .02
166 Bruce Sutter .10 .04
167 Robin Yount .25 .10
168 Ozzie Smith .75 .30
169 Frank White .10 .04
170 Phil Garner .10 .04
171 Doug DeCinces .05 .02
172 Mike Schmidt .60 .24
173 Cecil Cooper .10 .04
174 Al Oliver .10 .04
175 Jim Palmer .25 .10
176 Steve Carlton .40 .16
177 Carlton Fisk .25 .10
178 Gary Carter .10 .04
179 Joaquin Andujar WS .05 .02
180 Ozzie Smith WS .25 .10
181 Cecil Cooper WS .10 .04
182 Darrell Porter WS .05 .02
183 Darrell Porter WS .05 .02
184 Mike Caldwell WS .05 .02
185 Mike Caldwell WS .05 .02
186 Ozzie Smith WS .25 .10
187 Bruce Sutter WS .10 .04
188 Keith Hernandez WS .10 .04
189 Dane Iorg WS .05 .02
190 Dane Iorg WS .05 .02
191 Tony Armas RB .05 .02
192 Tony Armas RB .05 .02
193 Lance Parrish RB .10 .04
194 Lance Parrish RB .10 .04
195 John Wathan RB .05 .02
196 John Wathan RB .05 .02
197 Rickey Henderson RB .25 .10
198 Rickey Henderson RB .25 .10
199 Rickey Henderson RB .25 .10
200 Rickey Henderson RB .25 .10
201 Rickey Henderson RB .25 .10
202 Rickey Henderson RB .25 .10
203 Steve Carlton .40 .16
204 Steve Carlton .40 .16
205 Al Oliver .10 .04
206 Dale Murphy and .15 .06
Al Oliver
207 Dave Kingman .10 .04
208 Steve Rogers .05 .02
209 Bruce Sutter .10 .04
210 Tim Raines .15 .06
211 Dale Murphy FOIL .25 .10
212 Chris Chambliss .10 .04
213 Gene Garber .05 .02
214 Bob Horner .05 .02
215 Glenn Hubbard .05 .02
216 Claudell Washington .05 .02
217 Bruce Benedict .05 .02
218 Phil Niekro .25 .10
219 Leon Durham FOIL .10 .04
220 Jay Johnstone .10 .04
221 Larry Bowa .10 .04
222 Keith Moreland .05 .02
223 Bill Buckner .10 .04
224 Fergie Jenkins .25 .10
225 Dick Tidrow .05 .02
226 Jody Davis .05 .02
227 Dave Concepcion .10 .04
228 Dan Driessen .05 .02
229 Johnny Bench .50 .20
230 Ron Oester .05 .02
231 Cesar Cedeno .10 .04
232 Alex Trevino .05 .02
233 Tom Seaver .50 .20
234 Mario Soto .05 .02
235 Nolan Ryan FOIL 3.00 1.20
236 Art Howe .10 .04
237 Phil Garner .10 .04
238 Ray Knight .05 .02
239 Terry Puhl .05 .02

240 Joe Niekro .10 .04
241 Alan Ashby .05 .02
242 Jose Cruz .10 .04
243 Steve Garvey .15 .06
244 Ron Cey .10 .04
245 Dusty Baker .10 .04
246 Ken Landreaux .05 .02
247 Jerry Reuss .10 .04
248 Pedro Guerrero .10 .04
249 Bill Russell .10 .04
250 Fern.Valenzuela FOIL .20 .08
251 Al Oliver FOIL .20 .08
252 Andre Dawson .25 .10
253 Tim Raines .25 .10
254 Jeff Reardon .10 .04
255 Gary Carter .15 .06
256 Steve Rogers .05 .02
257 Tim Wallach .10 .04
258 Chris Speier .05 .02
259 Dave Kingman .15 .06
260 Bob Bailor .05 .02
261 Hubie Brooks .05 .02
262 Craig Swan .05 .02
263 George Foster .10 .04
264 John Stearns .05 .02
265 Neil Allen .05 .02
266 Mookie Wilson FOIL .15 .06
267 Steve Carlton FOIL .60 .24
268 Manny Trillo .05 .02
269 Gary Matthews .05 .02
270 Mike Schmidt .60 .24
271 Ivan DeJesus .05 .02
272 Pete Rose .75 .30
273 Bo Diaz .05 .02
274 Sid Monge .05 .02
275 Bill Madlock FOIL .20 .08
276 Jason Thompson .05 .02
277 Don Robinson .05 .02
278 Omar Moreno .05 .02
279 Dale Berra .05 .02
280 Dave Parker .10 .04
281 Tony Pena .10 .04
282 John Candelaria .05 .02
283 Lonnie Smith .05 .02
284 Bruce Sutter FOIL .15 .06
285 George Hendrick .05 .02
286 Tom Herr .10 .04
287 Ken Oberkfell .05 .02
288 Ozzie Smith .75 .30
289 Bob Forsch .05 .02
290 Keith Hernandez .10 .04
291 Garry Templeton .05 .02
292 Broderick Perkins .05 .02
293 Terry Kennedy FOIL .10 .04
294 Gene Richards .05 .02
295 Ruppert Jones .05 .02
296 Tim Lollar .05 .02
297 John Montefusco .05 .02
298 Sixto Lezcano .05 .02
299 Greg Minton .05 .02
300 Jack Clark FOIL .15 .06
301 Milt May .05 .02
302 Reggie Smith .10 .04
303 Joe Morgan .25 .10
304 John LeMaster .05 .02
305 Darrell Evans .10 .04
306 Al Holland .05 .02
307 Jesse Barfield .10 .04
308 Wade Boggs 3.00 1.20
309 Tom Brunansky .05 .02
310 Storm Davis .05 .02
311 Von Hayes .05 .02
312 Dave Hostetler .05 .02
313 Kent Hrbek .10 .04
314 Tim Laudner .05 .02
315 Cal Ripken 5.00 2.00
316 Andre Robertson .05 .02
317 Ed VandeBerg .05 .02
318 Glenn Wilson .05 .02
319 Chili Davis .25 .10
320 Bob Dernier .05 .02
321 Terry Francona .10 .04
322 Brian Giles .05 .02
323 David Green .05 .02
324 Atlee Hammaker .05 .02
325 Bill Laskey .05 .02
326 Willie McGee 1.00 .40
327 Johnny Ray .05 .02
328 Ryne Sandberg 6.00 2.40
329 Steve Sax .10 .04
330 Eric Show .05 .02
NNO Album 1.00 .40

1983 Topps Sticker Boxes

The cards in this eight (box) card set measure the standard size. The 1983 Topps baseball stickers were distributed in boxes which themselves contained a baseball card. In all there were eight different boxes each originally containing 30 stickers but no foils; hence, eight blank-backed cards comprise the box set. The box itself contained an offer for the sticker album and featured a Reggie Jackson photo. Stickers in the boxes came in six strips of five. The prices below reflect the value of the cards on the outside of the box only.

	Nm-Mt	Ex-Mt
COMPLETE SET (8)	10.00	4.00
1 Fernando Valenzuela	.75	.30
2 Gary Carter	1.50	.60
3 Mike Schmidt	2.00	.80
4 Reggie Jackson	2.00	.80
5 Jim Palmer	1.50	.60
6 Rollie Fingers	.75	.30
7 Pete Rose	2.00	.80
8 Rickey Henderson	2.00	.80

1983 Topps Gaylord Perry

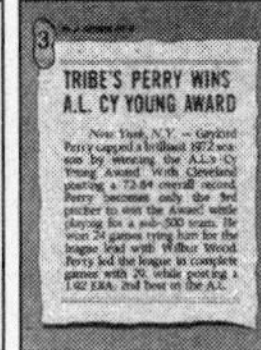

This six-card, standard-size, set depicts Gaylord Perry during various parts of his career. These cards have the looks of Topps cards and were produced by Topps but have no Topps logo on either the front or the back of the card.

	Nm-Mt	Ex-Mt
COMPLETE SET (6)	15.00	6.00
COMMON CARD (1-6)	3.00	1.20

1983 Topps Reprint 52

This 402 card standard-size set feature reprinted versions of the cards in the 52 Topps set. These sets were issued in complete form only available from Topps. Five players did not agree to be in this set, that is why the set only contains 402 cards. The five cards not in this set are Billy Loes (number 20), Dom DiMaggio (number 22), Saul Rogovin (number 159), Solly Hemus (number 196) and Tommy Holmes (number 289).

Nm-Mt Ex-Mt
COMP.FACT. SET (402) 200.00 80.00
1 Andy Pafko 2.50 1.00
2 Pete Runnels 1.00 .40
3 Hank Thompson 1.00 .40
4 Don Lenhardt .50 .20
5 Larry Jansen 1.00 .40
6 Grady Hatton .50 .20
7 Wayne Terwilliger 1.00 .40
8 Fred Marsh .50 .20
9 Robert Hogue .50 .20
10 Al Rosen 2.00 .80
11 Phil Rizzuto 10.00 4.00
12 Monty Basgall .50 .20
13 Johnny Wyrostek .50 .20
14 Bob Elliott 1.00 .40
15 Johnny Pesky 1.00 .40
16 Gene Hermanski .50 .20
17 Jim Hegan 1.00 .40
18 Merrill Combs .50 .20
19 Johnny Bucha .50 .20
21 Ferris Fain 1.00 .40
23 Billy Goodman 1.00 .40
24 Luke Easter 1.00 .40
25 Johnny Groth .50 .20
26 Monte Irvin 6.00 2.40
27 Sam Jethroe 1.00 .40
28 Jerry Priddy .50 .20
29 Ted Kluszewski 6.00 2.40
30 Mel Parnell 1.00 .40
31 Gus Zernial 2.50 1.00
32 Eddie Robinson .50 .20
33 Warren Spahn 10.00 4.00
34 Elmer Valo .50 .20
35 Hank Sauer 2.00 .80
36 Gil Hodges 10.00 4.00
37 Duke Snider 15.00 6.00
38 Wally Westlake .50 .20
39 Dizzy Trout 1.00 .40
40 Irv Noren 1.00 .40
41 Bob Wellman .50 .20
42 Lou Kretlow .50 .20
43 Ray Scarborough .50 .20
44 Con Dempsey .50 .20
45 Eddie Joost .50 .20
46 Gordon Goldsberry .50 .20
47 Willie Jones .50 .20
48 Joe Page 2.00 .80
49 Johnny Sain 2.00 .80
50 Marv Rickert .50 .20
51 Jim Russell .50 .20
52 Don Mueller 1.00 .40
53 Chris Van Cuyk .50 .20
54 Leo Kiely .50 .20
55 Ray Boone 1.00 .40
56 Tommy Glaviano .50 .20
57 Ed Lopat 2.50 1.00
58 Bob Mahoney .50 .20
59 Robin Roberts 10.00 4.00
60 Sid Hudson .50 .20
61 Tookie Gilbert .50 .20
62 Chuck Stobbs .50 .20
63 Howie Pollet .50 .20
64 Roy Sievers 1.00 .40
65 Enos Slaughter 10.00 4.00
66 Preacher Roe 2.50 1.00
67 Allie Reynolds 2.50 1.00
68 Cliff Chambers .50 .20
69 Virgil Stallcup .50 .20
70 Al Zarilla .50 .20
71 Tom Upton .50 .20
72 Karl Olson .50 .20
73 Bill Werle .50 .20
74 Andy Hansen .50 .20
75 Wes Westrum 1.00 .40
76 Eddie Stanky 1.00 .40
77 Bob Kennedy 1.00 .40
78 Ellis Kinder .50 .20
79 Gerry Staley .50 .20
80 Herman Wehmeier .50 .20
81 Vernon Law 1.00 .40
82 Duane Pillette .50 .20
83 Billy Johnson .50 .20
84 Vern Stephens 1.00 .40
85 Bob Kuzava 1.00 .40
86 Ted Gray .50 .20
87 Dale Coogan .50 .20
88 Bob Feller 15.00 6.00
89 Johnny Lipon .50 .20
90 Mickey Grasso .50 .20
91 Red Schoendienst 6.00 2.40
92 Dale Mitchell 1.00 .40
93 Al Sima .50 .20
94 Sam Mele .50 .20
95 Ken Holcombe .50 .20
96 Willard Marshall .50 .20
97 Earl Torgeson .50 .20
98 Billy Pierce 1.00 .40
99 Gene Woodling 2.00 .80
100 Del Rice .50 .20
101 Max Lanier .50 .20
102 Bill Kennedy .50 .20
103 Cliff Mapes .50 .20
104 Don Kolloway .50 .20
105 Johnny Pramesa .50 .20
106 Mickey Vernon 2.00 .80
107 Connie Ryan .50 .20
108 Jim Konstanty 2.00 .80
109 Ted Wilks .50 .20
110 Dutch Leonard .50 .20
111 Peanuts Lowrey .50 .20
112 Hank Majeski .50 .20
113 Dick Sisler 1.00 .40
114 Willard Ramsdell .50 .20
115 George Munger .50 .20
116 Carl Scheib .50 .20
117 Sherm Lollar 1.00 .40
118 Ken Raffensberger .50 .20
119 Mickey McDermott .50 .20
120 Bob Chakales .50 .20
121 Gus Niarhos .50 .20
122 Jackie Jensen 5.00 2.00
123 Eddie Yost 1.00 .40
124 Monte Kennedy .50 .20
125 Bill Rigney .50 .20
126 Fred Hutchinson 1.00 .40
127 Paul Minner .50 .20
128 Don Bollweg .50 .20
129 Johnny Mize 6.00 2.40
130 Sheldon Jones .50 .20
131 Morrie Martin .50 .20
132 Clyde Kluttz .50 .20
133 Al Widmar .50 .20
134 Joe Tipton .50 .20
135 Dixie Howell .50 .20
136 Johnny Schmitz .50 .20
137 Roy McMillan 1.00 .40
138 Bill MacDonald .50 .20
139 Ken Wood .50 .20
140 Johnny Antonelli 1.00 .40
141 Clint Hartung .50 .20
142 Harry Perkowski .50 .20
143 Les Moss .50 .20
144 Ed Blake .50 .20
145 Joe Haynes .50 .20
146 Frank House .50 .20
147 Bob Young .50 .20
148 Johnny Klippstein .50 .20
149 Dick Kryhoski .50 .20
150 Ted Beard .50 .20
151 Wally Post 1.00 .40
152 Al Evans .50 .20
153 Bob Rush .50 .20
154 Joe Muir .50 .20
155 Frank Overmire .50 .20
156 Frank Hiller .50 .20
157 Bob Usher .50 .20
158 Eddie Waitkus .50 .20
160 Owen Friend .50 .20
161 Bud Byerly .50 .20
162 Del Crandall 1.00 .40
163 Stan Rojek .50 .20
164 Walt Dubiel .50 .20
165 Eddie Kazak .50 .20
166 Paul LaPalme .50 .20
167 Bill Howerton .50 .20
168 Charlie Silvera 1.00 .40
169 Howie Judson .50 .20
170 Gus Bell 1.00 .40
171 Ed Erautt .50 .20
172 Eddie Miksis .50 .20
173 Roy Smalley .50 .20
174 Clarence Marshall .50 .20
175 Billy Martin 10.00 4.00
176 Hank Edwards .50 .20
177 Bill Wight .50 .20
178 Cass Michaels .50 .20
179 Frank Smith .50 .20
180 Charlie Maxwell 1.00 .40
181 Bob Swift .50 .20
182 Billy Hitchcock .50 .20
183 Erv Dusak .50 .20
184 Bob Ramazzotti .50 .20
185 Bill Nicholson 1.00 .40
186 Walt Masterson .50 .20
187 Bob Miller .50 .20
188 Clarence Podbielan .50 .20
189 Pete Reiser 2.00 .80
190 Don Johnson .50 .20
191 Yogi Berra 15.00 6.00
192 Myron Ginsberg .50 .20
193 Harry Simpson 1.00 .40
194 Joe Hatton .50 .20
195 Minnie Minoso 6.00 2.40
197 George Strickland .50 .20
198 Phil Haugstad .50 .20
199 George Zuverink .50 .20
200 Ralph Houk 2.50 1.00
201 Alex Kellner .50 .20
202 Joe Collins 2.00 .80
203 Curt Simmons 2.00 .80
204 Ron Northey .50 .20
205 Clyde King 1.00 .40
206 Joe Ostrowski .50 .20
207 Mickey Harris .50 .20
208 Marlin Stuart .50 .20
209 Howie Fox .50 .20
210 Dick Fowler .50 .20
211 Ray Coleman .50 .20
212 Ned Garver .50 .20
213 Nippy Jones .50 .20
214 Johnny Hopp 1.00 .40
215 Hank Bauer 2.50 1.00
216 Richie Ashburn 10.00 4.00
217 Snuffy Stirnweiss 1.00 .40
218 Clyde McCullough .50 .20
219 Bobby Shantz 2.00 .80
220 Joe Presko .50 .20
221 Granny Hamner .50 .20
222 Hoot Evers .50 .20
223 Del Ennis 1.00 .40
224 Bruce Edwards .50 .20
225 Frank Baumholtz .50 .20
226 Dave Philley .50 .20
227 Joe Garagiola 5.00 2.00
228 Al Brazle .50 .20
229 Gene Bearden UER .50 .20
(Misspelled Beardon)
230 Matt Batts .50 .20
231 Sam Zoldak .50 .20
232 Billy Cox .50 .20
233 Bob Friend 2.00 .80
234 Steve Souchock .50 .20
235 Walt Dropo .50 .20
236 Ed Fitzgerald .50 .20
237 Jerry Coleman 2.00 .80
238 Art Houtteman .50 .20
239 Rocky Bridges .50 .20
240 Jack Phillips .50 .20
241 Tommy Byrne .50 .20
242 Tom Poholsky .50 .20
243 Larry Doby 5.00 2.00
244 Vic Wertz 1.00 .40
245 Sherry Robertson .50 .20
246 George Kell 6.00 2.40
247 Randy Gumpert .50 .20
248 Frank Shea .50 .20
249 Bobby Adams .50 .20
250 Carl Erskine 2.50 1.00
251 Chico Carrasquel .50 .20
252 Vern Bickford .50 .20
253 Johnny Berardino 1.00 .40
254 Joe Dobson .50 .20
255 Clyde Vollmer .50 .20
256 Pete Suder .50 .20
257 Bobby Avila 1.00 .40
258 Steve Gromek .50 .20
259 Bob Addis .50 .20
260 Pete Castiglione .50 .20
261 Willie Mays 25.00 10.00
262 Virgil Trucks 1.00 .40
263 Harry Brecheen 1.00 .40
264 Roy Hartsfield .50 .20
265 Chuck Diering .50 .20
266 Murry Dickson .50 .20
267 Sid Gordon .50 .20
268 Bob Lemon 6.00 2.40
269 Willard Nixon .50 .20
270 Lou Brissie .50 .20
271 Jim Delsing .50 .20
272 Mike Garcia 1.00 .40
273 Erv Palica .50 .20
274 Ralph Branca 2.50 1.00
275 Pat Mullin .50 .20
276 Jim Wilson .50 .20
277 Early Wynn 6.00 2.40
278 Allie Clark .50 .20
279 Eddie Stewart .50 .20
280 Cloyd Boyer 1.00 .40
281 Tommy Brown .50 .20
282 Birdie Tebbetts 1.00 .40
283 Phil Masi .50 .20
284 Hank Arft .50 .20
285 Cliff Fannin .50 .20
286 Joe DeMaestri .50 .20
287 Steve Bilko .50 .20
288 Chet Nichols .50 .20
290 Joe Astroth .50 .20
291 Gil Coan .50 .20
292 Floyd Baker .50 .20
293 Sibby Sisti .50 .20
294 Walker Cooper .50 .20
295 Phil Cavarretta 1.00 .40
296 Red Rolfe MG 1.00 .40
297 Andy Seminick 1.00 .40
298 Bob Ross .50 .20
299 Ray Murray .50 .20
300 Barney McCosky .50 .20
301 Bob Porterfield .50 .20
302 Max Surkont .50 .20
303 Harry Dorish .50 .20
304 Sam Dente .50 .20
305 Paul Richards MG 1.00 .40
306 Lou Sleater .50 .20
307 Frank Campos .50 .20
308 Luis Aloma .50 .20
309 Jim Busby .50 .20
310 George Metkovich 1.00 .40
311 Mickey Mantle 50.00 20.00
312 Jackie Robinson 25.00 10.00
313 Bobby Thomson 5.00 2.00
314 Roy Campanella 10.00 4.00
315 Leo Durocher MG 6.00 2.40
316 Dave Williams 1.00 .40
317 Conrado Marrero 1.00 .40
318 Harold Gregg .50 .20
319 Al Walker .50 .20
320 John Rutherford 1.00 .40
321 Joe Black 5.00 2.00
322 Randy Jackson .50 .20
323 Bubba Church .50 .20
324 Warren Hacker .50 .20
325 Bill Serena .50 .20
326 George Shuba 2.00 .80
327 Al Wilson .50 .20
328 Bob Borkowski .50 .20
329 Ike Delock .50 .20
330 Turk Lown .50 .20
331 Tom Morgan .50 .20
332 Anthony Bartirome .50 .20
333 Pee Wee Reese 10.00 4.00
334 Wilmer Mizell 1.00 .40
335 Ted Lepcio .50 .20
336 Dave Koslo .50 .20
337 Jim Hearn .50 .20
338 Sal Yvars .50 .20
339 Russ Meyer .50 .20
340 Bob Hooper .50 .20
341 Hal Jeffcoat .50 .20
342 Clem Labine 5.00 2.00
343 Dick Gernert .50 .20
344 Ewell Blackwell 2.00 .80
345 Sammy White .50 .20
346 George Spencer .50 .20
347 Joe Adcock 2.00 .80
348 Robert Kelly .50 .20
349 Bob Cain .50 .20
350 Cal Abrams .50 .20
351 Alvin Dark 2.00 .80
352 Karl Drews .50 .20
353 Bobby Del Greco .50 .20
354 Fred Hatfield .50 .20
355 Bobby Morgan .50 .20
356 Toby Atwell .50 .20
357 Smoky Burgess 2.00 .80
358 John Kucab .50 .20
359 Dee Fondy .50 .20
360 George Crowe 1.00 .40
361 William Posedel CO .50 .20
362 Ken Heintzelman .50 .20
363 Dick Rozek .50 .20
364 Clyde Sukeforth CO .50 .20
365 Cookie Lavagetto CO 1.00 .40
366 Dave Madison .50 .20
367 Ben Thorpe .50 .20
368 Ed Wright .50 .20
369 Dick Groat 5.00 2.00
370 Billy Hoeft 1.00 .40
371 Bobby Hofman .50 .20
372 Gil McDougald 5.00 2.00
373 Jim Turner CO 2.00 .80
374 John Benton .50 .20
375 John Merson .50 .20
376 Faye Throneberry .50 .20
377 Chuck Dressen MG 1.00 .40
378 Leroy Fusselman .50 .20
379 Joe Rossi .50 .20
380 Clem Koshorek .50 .20
381 Milton Stock CO .50 .20
382 Sam Jones 2.00 .80
383 Del Wilber .50 .20
384 Frank Crosetti CO 5.00 2.00
385 Herman Franks CO .50 .20
386 John Yuhas .50 .20
387 Billy Meyer MG .50 .20
388 Bob Chipman .50 .20
389 Ben Wade .50 .20
390 Glenn Nelson .50 .20
391 B.Chapman UER CO .50 .20
Photo actually
Sam Chapman
392 Hoyt Wilhelm 6.00 2.40
393 Ebba St.Claire .50 .20
394 Billy Herman CO 5.00 2.00
395 Jake Pitler CO .50 .20
396 Dick Williams 5.00 2.00
397 Forrest Main .50 .20
398 Hal Rice .50 .20
399 Jim Fridley .50 .20
400 Bill Dickey CO 6.00 2.40
401 Bob Schultz .50 .20
402 Earl Harrist .50 .20
403 Bill Miller .50 .20
404 Dick Brodowski .50 .20
405 Eddie Pellagrini .50 .20
406 Joe Nuxhall 2.00 .80
407 Eddie Mathews 10.00 4.00

1983-91 Topps Traded Bronze Premiums

Dealers who ordered Topps Traded cases received these bronze replica cards as bonuses. These cards which measure approximately 1 1/4" by 1 3/4" started off by featuring current players but later switched to retired stars. We have sequenced this set by year of release.

	Nm-Mt	Ex-Mt
COMPLETE SET (9)	200.00	80.00
1 Steve Carlton	30.00	12.00
2 Darryl Strawberry	15.00	6.00
3 Pete Rose	15.00	6.00
4 Mickey Mantle	50.00	20.00
5 Willie Mays	25.00	10.00
6 Duke Snider	15.00	6.00
7 Hank Aaron	20.00	8.00
8 Jackie Robinson	20.00	8.00
9 Brooks Robinson	20.00	8.00

1984 Topps

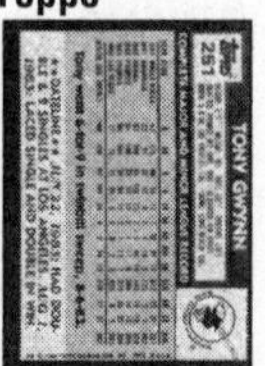

The cards in this 792-card set measure the standard size. Cards were primarily distributed in 15-card wax packs and 54-card rack packs. For the second year in a row, Topps utilized a dual picture on the front of the card. A portrait is shown in a square insert and an action shot is featured in the main photo. Card numbers 1-6 feature 1983 Highlights (HL), cards 131-138 depict League Leaders, card numbers 386-407 feature All-Stars, and card numbers 701-718 feature active Major League career leaders in various statistical categories. Each team leader (TL) card features the team's leading hitter and pitcher pictured on the front with a team checklist back. There are six numerical checklist cards in the set. The player cards feature team logos in the upper right corner of the reverse. The key Rookie Cards in this set are Don Mattingly and Darryl Strawberry. Topps tested a special send-in offer in Michigan and a few other states whereby collectors could obtain direct from Topps ten cards of their choice. Needless to say most people ordered the key (most valuable) players necessitating the printing of a special sheet to keep up with the demand. The special sheet had five cards of Darryl Strawberry, three cards of Don Mattingly, etc. The test was apparently a failure in Topps' eyes as they have never tried it again.

Nm-Mt Ex-Mt
COMPLETE SET (792) 50.00 20.00
1 Steve Carlton HL .15 .06
2 Rickey Henderson HL .60 .24
3 Dan Quisenberry HL .15 .06
4 Nolan Ryan HL 1.00 .40
Steve Carlton
Gaylord Perry
5 Dave Righetti HL .25 .10
Bob Forsch
Mike Warren
6 Johnny Bench HL .40 .16
Gaylord Perry
Carl Yastrzemski
7 Gary Lucas .15 .06
8 Don Mattingly RC 15.00 6.00
9 Jim Gott .15 .06
10 Robin Yount 1.00 .40
11 Kent Hrbek .25 .10
Ken Schrom TL
12 Billy Sample .15 .06
13 Scott Holman .15 .06
14 Tom Brookens .25 .10
15 Burt Hooton .15 .06
16 Omar Moreno .15 .06
17 John Denny .15 .06
18 Dale Berra .15 .06
19 Ray Fontenot .15 .06
20 Greg Luzinski .25 .10
21 Joe Altobelli MG .15 .06
22 Bryan Clark .15 .06
23 Keith Moreland .15 .06
24 John Martin .15 .06
25 Glenn Hubbard .15 .06
26 Bud Black .15 .06
27 Daryl Sconiers .15 .06
28 Frank Viola .40 .16
29 Danny Heep .15 .06
30 Wade Boggs 1.50 .60
31 Andy McGaffigan .15 .06
32 Bobby Ramos .15 .06
33 Tom Burgmeier .15 .06
34 Eddie Milner .15 .06
35 Don Sutton .60 .24
36 Denny Walling .15 .06
37 Buddy Bell .25 .10
Rick Honeycutt TL
38 Luis DeLeon .15 .06
39 Garth Iorg .15 .06
40 Dusty Baker .25 .10
41 Tony Bernazard .15 .06
42 Johnny Grubb .15 .06
43 Ron Reed .15 .06
44 Jim Morrison .15 .06
45 Jerry Mumphrey .15 .06
46 Ray Smith .15 .06
47 Rudy Law .15 .06
48 Julio Franco .40 .16
49 John Stuper .15 .06
50 Chris Chambliss .25 .10
51 Jim Frey MG .15 .06
52 Paul Splittorff .15 .06
53 Juan Beniquez .15 .06
54 Jesse Orosco .15 .06
55 Dave Concepcion .25 .10
56 Gary Allenson .15 .06
57 Dan Schatzeder .15 .06
58 Max Venable .15 .06
59 Sammy Stewart .15 .06
60 Paul Molitor UER .40 .16
('83 stats .272, 613, 167; should be .270, 608, 164)
61 Chris Codiroli .15 .06
62 Dave Hostetler .15 .06
63 Ed VandeBerg .15 .06
64 Mike Scioscia .15 .06
65 Kirk Gibson .60 .24
66 Jose Cruz 1.00 .40
Nolan Ryan TL
67 Gary Ward .15 .06
68 Luis Salazar .15 .06
69 Rod Scurry .15 .06
70 Gary Matthews .25 .10
71 Leo Hernandez .15 .06
72 Mike Squires .15 .06
73 Jody Davis .15 .06
74 Jerry Martin .15 .06
75 Bob Forsch .15 .06
76 Alfredo Griffin .15 .06
77 Brett Butler .40 .16
78 Mike Torrez .15 .06
79 Rob Wilfong .15 .06
80 Steve Rogers .15 .06
81 Billy Martin MG .25 .10
82 Doug Bird .15 .06
83 Richie Zisk .15 .06
84 Lenny Faedo .15 .06
85 Atlee Hammaker .15 .06
86 John Shelby .15 .06
87 Frank Pastore .15 .06
88 Rob Picciolo .15 .06
89 Mike Smithson .15 .06
90 Pedro Guerrero .25 .10
91 Dan Spillner .15 .06
92 Lloyd Moseby .15 .06
93 Bob Knepper .15 .06
94 Mario Ramirez .15 .06
95 Aurelio Lopez .25 .10
96 Hal McRae .25 .10
Larry Gura TL
97 LaMarr Hoyt .15 .06
98 Steve Nicosia .15 .06
99 Craig Lefferts RC .15 .06
100 Reggie Jackson .40 .16
101 Porfirio Altamirano .15 .06
102 Ken Oberkfell .15 .06
103 Dwayne Murphy .15 .06
104 Ken Dayley .15 .06
105 Tony Armas .15 .06
106 Tim Stoddard .15 .06
107 Ned Yost .15 .06
108 Randy Moffitt .15 .06
109 Brad Wellman .15 .06
110 Ron Guidry .25 .10
111 Bill Virdon MG .15 .06
112 Tom Niedenfuer .15 .06
113 Kelly Paris .15 .06
114 Checklist 1-132 .25 .10
115 Andre Thornton .15 .06
116 George Bjorkman .15 .06
117 Tom Veryzer .15 .06
118 Charlie Hough .25 .10
119 John Wockenfuss .15 .06
120 Keith Hernandez .40 .16
121 Pat Sheridan .15 .06
122 Cecilio Guante .15 .06
123 Butch Wynegar .15 .06
124 Damaso Garcia .15 .06
125 Britt Burns .15 .06
126 Dale Murphy .40 .16
Craig McMurtry TL
127 Mike Madden .15 .06
128 Rick Manning .15 .06
129 Bill Laskey .15 .06
130 Ozzie Smith 1.00 .40
131 Bill Madlock .60 .24
Wade Boggs LL
132 Mike Schmidt .60 .24
Jim Rice LL
133 Dale Murphy .40 .16
Cecil Cooper
Jim Rice LL
134 Tim Raines .60 .24
Rickey Henderson LL
135 John Denny .60 .24
LaMarr Hoyt LL
136 Steve Carlton .25 .10
Jack Morris LL
137 Atlee Hammaker .25 .10
Rick Honeycutt LL
138 Al Holland .25 .10
Dan Quisenberry LL
139 Bert Campaneris .25 .10
140 Storm Davis .15 .06
141 Pat Corrales MG .15 .06
142 Rich Gale .15 .06
143 Jose Morales .15 .06
144 Brian Harper RC .25 .10
145 Gary Lavelle .15 .06
146 Ed Romero .15 .06
147 Dan Petry .25 .10
148 Joe Lefebvre .15 .06
149 Jon Matlack .15 .06
150 Dale Murphy .60 .24
151 Steve Trout .15 .06
152 Glenn Brummer .15 .06
153 Dick Tidrow .15 .06
154 Dave Henderson .25 .10
155 Frank White .25 .10
156 Rickey Henderson .60 .24
Tim Conroy TL
157 Gary Gaetti .40 .16
158 John Curtis .15 .06
159 Darryl Cias .15 .06
160 Mario Soto .15 .06
161 Junior Ortiz .15 .06
162 Bob Ojeda .15 .06
163 Lorenzo Gray .15 .06
164 Scott Sanderson .15 .06
165 Ken Singleton .15 .06
166 Jamie Nelson .15 .06
167 Marshall Edwards .15 .06
168 Juan Bonilla .15 .06
169 Larry Parrish .15 .06
170 Jerry Reuss .15 .06
171 Frank Robinson MG .40 .16
172 Frank DiPino .15 .06
173 Marvell Wynne .15 .06
174 Juan Berenguer .15 .06
175 Graig Nettles .25 .10
176 Lee Smith .60 .24
177 Jerry Hairston .15 .06
178 Bill Krueger RC .15 .06
179 Buck Martinez .15 .06
180 Manny Trillo .15 .06
181 Roy Thomas .15 .06
182 Darryl Strawberry RC 1.00 .40
183 Al Williams .15 .06
184 Mike O'Berry .15 .06
185 Sixto Lezcano .15 .06
186 Lonnie Smith .25 .10
John Stuper TL
187 Luis Aponte .15 .06
188 Bryan Little .15 .06
189 Tim Conroy .15 .06
190 Ben Oglivie .15 .06
191 Mike Boddicker .15 .06
192 Nick Esasky .15 .06
193 Darrell Brown .15 .06
194 Domingo Ramos .15 .06
195 Jack Morris .25 .10
196 Don Slaught .25 .10
197 Garry Hancock .15 .06
198 Bill Doran RC* .25 .10
199 Willie Hernandez .25 .10
200 Andre Dawson .25 .10
201 Bruce Kison .15 .06
202 Bobby Cox MG .25 .10
203 Matt Keough .15 .06
204 Bobby Meacham .15 .06
205 Greg Minton .15 .06
206 Andy Van Slyke RC .60 .24
207 Donnie Moore .15 .06
208 Jose Oquendo RC .25 .10
209 Manny Sarmiento .15 .06
210 Joe Morgan .40 .16
211 Rick Sweet .15 .06
212 Broderick Perkins .15 .06
213 Bruce Hurst .15 .06
214 Paul Householder .15 .06
215 Tippy Martinez .15 .06
216 Carlton Fisk .25 .10
Richard Dotson TL
217 Alan Ashby .15 .06
218 Rick Waits .15 .06
219 Joe Simpson .15 .06
220 Fernando Valenzuela .25 .10
221 Cliff Johnson .15 .06
222 Rick Honeycutt .15 .06
223 Wayne Krenchicki .15 .06
224 Sid Monge .15 .06
225 Lee Mazzilli .15 .06
226 Juan Eichelberger .15 .06
227 Steve Braun .15 .06
228 John Rabb .15 .06
229 Paul Owens MG .15 .06
230 Rickey Henderson 1.00 .40
231 Gary Woods .15 .06
232 Tim Wallach .25 .10
233 Checklist 133-264 .25 .10
234 Rafael Ramirez .15 .06
235 Matt Young RC .15 .06
236 Ellis Valentine .15 .06
237 John Castino .15 .06
238 Reid Nichols .15 .06
239 Jay Howell .15 .06
240 Eddie Murray .60 .24
241 Bill Almon .15 .06
242 Alex Trevino .15 .06
243 Pete Ladd .15 .06
244 Candy Maldonado .15 .06
245 Rick Sutcliffe .25 .10
246 Mookie Wilson .25 .10
Tom Seaver TL
247 Onix Concepcion .15 .06
248 Bill Dawley .15 .06
249 Jay Johnstone .25 .10
250 Bill Madlock .25 .10
251 Tony Gwynn 2.50 1.00
252 Larry Christenson .15 .06
253 Jim Wohlford .15 .06
254 Shane Rawley .15 .06
255 Bruce Benedict .15 .06
256 Dave Geisel .15 .06
257 Julio Cruz .15 .06
258 Luis Sanchez .15 .06
259 Sparky Anderson MG .40 .16
260 Scott McGregor .15 .06
261 Bobby Brown .15 .06
262 Tom Candiotti RC .60 .24
263 Jack Fimple .15 .06
264 Doug Frobel .15 .06
265 Donnie Hill .15 .06
266 Steve Lubratich .15 .06
267 Carmelo Martinez .15 .06
268 Jack O'Connor .15 .06
269 Aurelio Rodriguez .15 .06
270 Jeff Russell RC .25 .10
271 Moose Haas .15 .06
272 Rick Dempsey .15 .06
273 Charlie Puleo .15 .06
274 Rick Monday .15 .06
275 Len Matuszek .15 .06
276 Rod Carew .25 .10
Geoff Zahn TL
277 Eddie Whitson .15 .06
278 Jorge Bell .40 .16
279 Ivan DeJesus .15 .06
280 Floyd Bannister .15 .06
281 Larry Milbourne .15 .06
282 Jim Barr .15 .06
283 Larry Biittner .15 .06
284 Howard Bailey .15 .06
285 Darrell Porter .15 .06
286 Lary Sorensen .15 .06
287 Warren Cromartie .15 .06
288 Jim Beattie .15 .06
289 Randy Johnson .15 .06
290 Dave Dravecky .25 .10
291 Chuck Tanner MG .15 .06
292 Tony Scott .15 .06
293 Ed Lynch .15 .06
294 U.L. Washington .15 .06
295 Mike Flanagan .15 .06
296 Jeff Newman .15 .06
297 Bruce Berenyi .15 .06
298 Jim Gantner .15 .06
299 John Butcher .15 .06
300 Pete Rose 2.00 .80
301 Frank LaCorte .15 .06
302 Barry Bonnell .15 .06
303 Marty Castillo .15 .06
304 Warren Brusstar .15 .06
305 Roy Smalley .15 .06
306 Pedro Guerrero .25 .10
Bob Welch TL
307 Bobby Mitchell .15 .06
308 Ron Hassey .15 .06
309 Tony Phillips RC .60 .24
310 Willie McGee .40 .16
311 Jerry Koosman .25 .10
312 Jorge Orta .15 .06
313 Mike Jorgensen .15 .06
314 Orlando Mercado .15 .06
315 Bobby Grich .25 .10
316 Mark Bradley .15 .06
317 Greg Pryor .15 .06
318 Bill Gullickson .15 .06
319 Al Bumbry .15 .06
320 Bob Stanley .15 .06
321 Harvey Kuenn MG .25 .10
322 Ken Schrom .15 .06
323 Alan Knicely .15 .06
324 Alejandro Pena RC* .25 .10
325 Darrell Evans .25 .10
326 Bob Kearney .15 .06
327 Ruppert Jones .15 .06
328 Vern Ruhle .15 .06
329 Pat Tabler .15 .06
330 John Candelaria .15 .06
331 Bucky Dent .25 .10
332 Kevin Gross RC .15 .06
333 Larry Herndon .25 .10
334 Chuck Rainey .15 .06
335 Don Baylor .40 .16
336 Pat Putnam .25 .10
Matt Young TL
337 Kevin Hagen .15 .06
338 Mike Warren .15 .06
339 Roy Lee Jackson .15 .06
340 Hal McRae .25 .10
341 Dave Tobik .15 .06
342 Tim Foli .15 .06
343 Mark Davis .15 .06
344 Rick Miller .15 .06
345 Kent Hrbek .25 .10
346 Kurt Bevacqua .15 .06
347 Allan Ramirez .15 .06
348 Toby Harrah .25 .10
349 Bob L. Gibson RC .15 .06
350 George Foster .25 .10
351 Russ Nixon MG .15 .06
352 Dave Stewart .25 .10
353 Jim Anderson .15 .06
354 Jeff Burroughs .15 .06
355 Jason Thompson .15 .06
356 Glenn Abbott .15 .06
357 Ron Cey .25 .10
358 Bob Dernier .15 .06
359 Jim Acker .15 .06
360 Willie Randolph .25 .10
361 Dave Smith .15 .06
362 David Green .15 .06
363 Tim Laudner .15 .06
364 Scott Fletcher .15 .06
365 Steve Bedrosian .15 .06
366 Terry Kennedy .25 .10
Dave Dravecky TL
367 Jamie Easterly .15 .06
368 Hubie Brooks .15 .06
369 Steve McCatty .15 .06
370 Tim Raines .40 .16
371 Dave Gumpert .15 .06
372 Gary Roenicke .15 .06
373 Bill Scherrer .15 .06
374 Don Money .15 .06
375 Dennis Leonard .15 .06
376 Dave Anderson RC .15 .06
377 Danny Darwin .15 .06
378 Bob Brenly .15 .06
379 Checklist 265-396 .25 .10
380 Steve Garvey .25 .10
381 Ralph Houk MG .25 .10
382 Chris Nyman .15 .06
383 Terry Puhl .15 .06
384 Lee Tunnell .15 .06
385 Tony Perez .40 .16
386 George Hendrick AS .15 .06
387 Johnny Ray AS .15 .06
388 Mike Schmidt AS .60 .24
389 Ozzie Smith AS .60 .24
390 Tim Raines AS .25 .10
391 Dale Murphy AS .40 .16
392 Andre Dawson AS .15 .06
393 Gary Carter AS .25 .10
394 Steve Rogers AS .15 .06
395 Steve Carlton AS .15 .06
396 Jesse Orosco AS .15 .06
397 Eddie Murray AS .40 .16
398 Lou Whitaker AS .15 .06
399 George Brett AS .60 .24
400 Cal Ripken AS 2.00 .80
401 Jim Rice AS .15 .06
402 Dave Winfield AS .15 .06
403 Lloyd Moseby AS .15 .06
404 Ted Simmons AS .15 .06
405 LaMarr Hoyt AS .15 .06
406 Ron Guidry AS .15 .06
407 Dan Quisenberry AS .15 .06
408 Lou Piniella .25 .10
409 Juan Agosto .15 .06
410 Claudell Washington .15 .06
411 Houston Jimenez .15 .06
412 Doug Rader MG .15 .06
413 Spike Owen RC .25 .10
414 Mitchell Page .15 .06
415 Tommy John .40 .16
416 Dane Iorg .15 .06
417 Mike Armstrong .15 .06
418 Ron Hodges .15 .06
419 John Henry Johnson .15 .06
420 Cecil Cooper .25 .10
421 Charlie Lea .15 .06
422 Jose Cruz .25 .10
423 Mike Morgan .15 .06
424 Dann Bilardello .15 .06
425 Steve Howe .15 .06
426 Cal Ripken 1.50 .60
Mike Boddicker TL
427 Rick Leach .15 .06
428 Fred Breining .15 .06
429 Randy Bush .15 .06
430 Rusty Staub .25 .10
431 Chris Bando .15 .06
432 Charles Hudson .15 .06
433 Rich Hebner .15 .06
434 Harold Baines .60 .24
435 Neil Allen .15 .06
436 Rick Peters .15 .06
437 Mike Proly .15 .06
438 Biff Pocoroba .15 .06
439 Bob Stoddard .15 .06
440 Steve Kemp .15 .06
441 Bob Lillis MG .15 .06
442 Byron McLaughlin .15 .06
443 Benny Ayala .15 .06
444 Steve Renko .15 .06
445 Jerry Remy .15 .06
446 Luis Pujols .15 .06
447 Tom Brunansky .25 .10
448 Ben Hayes .15 .06
449 Joe Pettini .15 .06
450 Gary Carter .40 .16
451 Bob Jones .15 .06
452 Chuck Porter .15 .06
453 Willie Upshaw .15 .06
454 Joe Beckwith .15 .06
455 Terry Kennedy .15 .06
456 Keith Moreland .15 .06
Fergie Jenkins TL
457 Dave Rozema .15 .06
458 Kiko Garcia .15 .06
459 Kevin Hickey .15 .06
460 Dave Winfield .25 .10
461 Jim Maler .15 .06
462 Lee Lacy .15 .06
463 Dave Engle .15 .06
464 Jeff A. Jones .15 .06
465 Mookie Wilson .25 .10
466 Gene Garber .15 .06
467 Mike Ramsey .15 .06
468 Geoff Zahn .15 .06
469 Tom O'Malley .15 .06
470 Nolan Ryan 3.00 1.20
471 Dick Howser MG .15 .06
472 Mike G. Brown RC .15 .06
473 Jim Dwyer .15 .06
474 Greg Bargar .15 .06
475 Gary Redus RC* .15 .06
476 Tom Tellmann .15 .06
477 Rafael Landestoy .15 .06
478 Alan Bannister .15 .06
479 Frank Tanana .25 .10
480 Ron Kittle .15 .06
481 Mark Thurmond .15 .06
482 Enos Cabell .15 .06
483 Fergie Jenkins .25 .10
484 Ozzie Virgil .15 .06
485 Rick Rhoden .15 .06
486 Don Baylor .25 .10
Ron Guidry TL
487 Ricky Adams .15 .06
488 Jesse Barfield .25 .10
489 Dave Von Ohlen .15 .06
490 Cal Ripken 4.00 1.60
491 Bobby Castillo .15 .06
492 Tucker Ashford .15 .06
493 Mike Norris .15 .06
494 Chili Davis .40 .16
495 Rollie Fingers .25 .10
496 Terry Francona .15 .06
497 Bud Anderson .15 .06
498 Rich Gedman .15 .06
499 Mike Witt .15 .06
500 George Brett 1.50 .60
501 Steve Henderson .15 .06
502 Joe Torre MG .25 .10
503 Elias Sosa .15 .06
504 Mickey Rivers .15 .06
505 Pete Vuckovich .15 .06
506 Ernie Whitt .15 .06
507 Mike LaCoss .15 .06
508 Mel Hall .25 .10
509 Brad Havens .15 .06
510 Alan Trammell .40 .16
511 Marty Bystrom .15 .06
512 Oscar Gamble .15 .06
513 Dave Beard .15 .06
514 Floyd Rayford .15 .06
515 Gorman Thomas .15 .06
516 Al Oliver .25 .10
Charlie Lea TL
517 John Moses .15 .06
518 Greg Walker .25 .10
519 Ron Davis .15 .06
520 Bob Boone .25 .10
521 Pete Falcone .15 .06
522 Dave Bergman .15 .06
523 Glenn Hoffman .15 .06
524 Carlos Diaz .15 .06
525 Willie Wilson .15 .06
526 Ron Oester .15 .06
527 Checklist 397-528 .25 .10
528 Mark Brouhard .15 .06
529 Keith Atherton .15 .06
530 Dan Ford .15 .06
531 Steve Boros MG .15 .06
532 Eric Show .15 .06
533 Ken Landreaux .15 .06
534 Pete O'Brien RC* .25 .10
535 Bo Diaz .15 .06
536 Doug Bair .15 .06
537 Johnny Ray .15 .06
538 Kevin Bass .15 .06
539 George Frazier .15 .06
540 George Hendrick .15 .06
541 Dennis Lamp .15 .06
542 Duane Kuiper .15 .06
543 Craig McMurtry .15 .06
544 Cesar Geronimo .15 .06
545 Bill Buckner .25 .10
546 Mike Hargrove .25 .10
Lary Sorensen TL
547 Mike Moore .15 .06
548 Ron Jackson .15 .06
549 Walt Terrell .15 .06
550 Jim Rice .25 .10
551 Scott Ullger .15 .06
552 Ray Burris .15 .06
553 Joe Nolan .15 .06
554 Ted Power .15 .06
555 Greg Brock .15 .06
556 Joey McLaughlin .15 .06
557 Wayne Tolleson .15 .06
558 Mike Davis .15 .06
559 Mike Scott .25 .10
560 Carlton Fisk .40 .16
561 Whitey Herzog MG .15 .06
562 Manny Castillo .15 .06
563 Glenn Wilson .25 .10
564 Al Holland .15 .06
565 Leon Durham .15 .06
566 Jim Bibby .15 .06
567 Mike Heath .15 .06
568 Pete Filson .15 .06
569 Bake McBride .15 .06
570 Dan Quisenberry .15 .06
571 Bruce Bochy .15 .06
572 Jerry Royster .15 .06
573 Dave Kingman .40 .16
574 Brian Downing .15 .06
575 Jim Clancy .15 .06
576 Jeff Leonard .25 .10
Atlee Hammaker TL
577 Mark Clear .15 .06
578 Lenn Sakata .15 .06
579 Bob James .15 .06
580 Lonnie Smith .15 .06
581 Jose DeLeon RC .15 .06
582 Bob McClure .15 .06
583 Derrel Thomas .15 .06
584 Dave Schmidt .15 .06
585 Dan Driessen .15 .06
586 Joe Niekro .25 .10
587 Von Hayes .15 .06
588 Milt Wilcox .15 .06
589 Mike Easler .15 .06
590 Dave Stieb .15 .06
591 Tony LaRussa MG .25 .10
592 Andre Robertson .15 .06
593 Jeff Lahti .15 .06
594 Gene Richards .15 .06
595 Jeff Reardon .25 .10
596 Ryne Sandberg 2.50 1.00
597 Rick Camp .15 .06
598 Rusty Kuntz .15 .06
599 Doug Sisk .15 .06
600 Rod Carew .40 .16
601 John Tudor .15 .06
602 John Wathan .15 .06
603 Renie Martin .15 .06
604 John Lowenstein .15 .06
605 Mike Caldwell .15 .06
606 Lloyd Moseby .25 .10
Dave Stieb TL
607 Tom Hume .15 .06
608 Bobby Johnson .15 .06
609 Dan Meyer .15 .06
610 Steve Sax .25 .10
611 Chet Lemon .15 .06
612 Harry Spilman .15 .06
613 Greg Gross .15 .06

614 Len Barker .15 .06
615 Garry Templeton .15 .06
616 Don Robinson .15 .06
617 Rick Cerone .15 .06
618 Dickie Noles .15 .06
619 Jerry Dybzinski .15 .06
620 Al Oliver .25 .10
621 Frank Howard MG .25 .10
622 Al Cowens .15 .06
623 Ron Washington .15 .06
624 Terry Harper .15 .06
625 Larry Gura .15 .06
626 Bob Clark .15 .06
627 Dave LaPoint .15 .06
628 Ed Jurak .15 .06
629 Rick Langford .15 .06
630 Ted Simmons .25 .10
631 Dennis Martinez .25 .10
632 Tom Foley .15 .06
633 Mike Krukow .15 .06
634 Mike Marshall .15 .06
635 Dave Righetti .25 .10
636 Pat Putnam .15 .06
637 Gary Matthews .25 .10
John Denny TL
638 George Vukovich .15 .06
639 Rick Lysander .15 .06
640 Lance Parrish .40 .16
641 Mike Richardt .15 .06
642 Tom Underwood .15 .06
643 Mike C. Brown .15 .06
644 Tim Lollar .15 .06
645 Tony Pena .15 .06
646 Checklist 529-660 .25 .10
647 Ron Roenicke .15 .06
648 Len Whitehouse .15 .06
649 Tom Herr .25 .10
650 Phil Niekro .25 .10
651 John McNamara MG .15 .06
652 Rudy May .15 .06
653 Dave Stapleton .15 .06
654 Bob Bailor .15 .06
655 Amos Otis .25 .10
656 Bryn Smith .15 .06
657 Thad Bosley .15 .06
658 Jerry Augustine .15 .06
659 Duane Walker .15 .06
660 Ray Knight .25 .10
661 Steve Yeager .15 .06
662 Tom Brennan .15 .06
663 Johnnie LeMaster .15 .06
664 Dave Stegman .15 .06
665 Buddy Bell .25 .10
666 Lou Whitaker .25 .10
Jack Morris TL
667 Vance Law .15 .06
668 Larry McWilliams .15 .06
669 Dave Lopes .25 .10
670 Rich Gossage .40 .16
671 Jamie Quirk .15 .06
672 Ricky Nelson .15 .06
673 Mike Walters .15 .06
674 Tim Flannery .15 .06
675 Pascual Perez .15 .06
676 Brian Giles .15 .06
677 Doyle Alexander .15 .06
678 Chris Speier .15 .06
679 Art Howe .15 .06
680 Fred Lynn .25 .10
681 Tom Lasorda MG .40 .16
682 Dan Morogiello .15 .06
683 Marty Barrett RC .25 .10
684 Bob Shirley .15 .06
685 Willie Aikens .15 .06
686 Joe Price .15 .06
687 Roy Howell .15 .06
688 George Wright .15 .06
689 Mike Fischlin .15 .06
690 Jack Clark .25 .10
691 Steve Lake .15 .06
692 Dickie Thon .15 .06
693 Alan Wiggins .15 .06
694 Mike Stanton .15 .06
695 Lou Whitaker .25 .10
696 Bill Madlock .25 .10
Rick Rhoden TL
697 Dale Murray .15 .06
698 Marc Hill .15 .06
699 Dave Rucker .15 .06
700 Mike Schmidt 1.50 .60
701 Bill Madlock .60 .24
Pete Rose
Dave Parker LL
702 Pete Rose .60 .24
Rusty Staub
Tony Perez LL
703 Mike Schmidt .60 .24
Tony Perez
Dave Kingman LL
704 Tony Perez .40 .16
Rusty Staub
Al Oliver LL
705 Joe Morgan .40 .16
Cesar Cedeno
Larry Bowa LL
706 Steve Carlton .25 .10
Fergie Jenkins
Tom Seaver LL
707 Steve Carlton 1.50 .60
Nolan Ryan
Tom Seaver LL
708 Tom Seaver .25 .10
Steve Carlton
Steve Rogers LL
709 Bruce Sutter .25 .10
Tug McGraw
Gene Garber LL
710 Rod Carew .40 .16
George Brett
Cecil Cooper LL
711 Rod Carew .25 .10
Bert Campaneris
Reggie Jackson LL
712 Reggie Jackson .25 .10
Graig Nettles
Greg Luzinski LL
713 Reggie Jackson .25 .10
Ted Simmons
Graig Nettles LL
714 Bert Campaneris .25 .10
Dave Lopes
Omar Moreno LL
715 Jim Palmer .25 .10
Don Sutton
Tommy John LL
716 Don Sutton .40 .16
Bert Blyleven
Jerry Koosman LL
717 Jim Palmer .25 .10
Rollie Fingers
Ron Guidry LL
718 Rollie Fingers .25 .10
Rich Gossage
Dan Quisenberry LL
719 Andy Hassler .15 .06
720 Dwight Evans .25 .10
721 Del Crandall MG .15 .06
722 Bob Welch .15 .06
723 Rich Dauer .15 .06
724 Eric Rasmussen .15 .06
725 Cesar Cedeno .25 .10
726 Ted Simmons .25 .10
Moose Haas TL
727 Joel Youngblood .15 .06
728 Tug McGraw .25 .10
729 Gene Tenace .25 .10
730 Bruce Sutter .25 .10
731 Lynn Jones .15 .06
732 Terry Crowley .15 .06
733 Dave Collins .15 .06
734 Odell Jones .15 .06
735 Rick Burleson .15 .06
736 Dick Ruthven .15 .06
737 Jim Essian .15 .06
738 Bill Schroeder .15 .06
739 Bob Watson .25 .10
740 Tom Seaver .40 .16
741 Wayne Gross .15 .06
742 Dick Williams MG .25 .10
743 Don Hood .15 .06
744 Jamie Allen .15 .06
745 Dennis Eckersley .40 .16
746 Mickey Hatcher .15 .06
747 Pat Zachry .15 .06
748 Jeff Leonard .15 .06
749 Doug Flynn .15 .06
750 Jim Palmer .25 .10
751 Charlie Moore .15 .06
752 Phil Garner .25 .10
753 Doug Gwosdz .15 .06
754 Kent Tekulve .25 .10
755 Garry Maddox .15 .06
756 Ron Oester .25 .10
Mario Soto TL
757 Larry Bowa .25 .10
758 Bill Stein .15 .06
759 Richard Dotson .15 .06
760 Bob Horner .15 .06
761 John Montefusco .15 .06
762 Rance Mulliniks .15 .06
763 Craig Swan .15 .06
764 Mike Hargrove .25 .10
765 Ken Forsch .15 .06
766 Mike Vail .15 .06
767 Carney Lansford .25 .10
768 Champ Summers .15 .06
769 Bill Caudill .15 .06
770 Ken Griffey .25 .10
771 Billy Gardner MG .15 .06
772 Jim Slaton .15 .06
773 Todd Cruz .15 .06
774 Tom Gorman .15 .06
775 Dave Parker .25 .10
776 Craig Reynolds .15 .06
777 Tom Paciorek .25 .10
778 Andy Hawkins .15 .06
779 Jim Sundberg .25 .10
780 Steve Carlton .25 .10
781 Checklist 661-792 .25 .10
782 Steve Balboni .15 .06
783 Luis Leal .15 .06
784 Leon Roberts .15 .06
785 Joaquin Andujar .15 .06
786 Wade Boggs .40 .16
Bob Ojeda TL
787 Bill Campbell .15 .06
788 Milt May .15 .06
789 Bert Blyleven .25 .10
790 Doug DeCinces .15 .06
791 Terry Forster .15 .06
792 Bill Russell .15 .06

1984 Topps Tiffany

This 792 card standard-size set was issued by Topps as a parallel to their regular issue. Printed in their Ireland facility, these cards are differentiated from the regular cards by the glossy fronts and pure white stock. These sets were available only through Topps' dealer network and sold only in factory set form. According to information from the time of issue, 10,000 of these sets were produced.

Nm-Mt Ex-Mt
COMP.FACT.SET (792) 200.00 80.00
*STARS: 3X TO 8X BASIC CARDS
*ROOKIES: 2.5X TO 6X BASIC CARDS

1984 Topps Glossy All-Stars

The cards in this 22-card set measure the standard size. Unlike the 1983 Topps Glossy set which was not distributed with its regular baseball cards, the 1984 Topps Glossy set was distributed as inserts in Topps Rak-Paks. The set features the nine American and National League All-Stars who started in the 1983 All Star game in Chicago. The managers and team captains (Yastrzemski and Bench) complete the set. The cards are numbered on the back and are ordered by position within league (AL: 1-11 and NL: 12-22).

Nm-Mt Ex-Mt
COMPLETE SET (22) 5.00 2.00
1 Harvey Kuenn MG .05 .02
2 Rod Carew .50 .20
3 Manny Trillo .05 .02
4 George Brett 1.00 .40
5 Robin Yount .50 .20
6 Jim Rice .10 .04
7 Fred Lynn .10 .04
8 Dave Winfield .50 .20
9 Ted Simmons .10 .04
10 Dave Stieb .05 .02
11 Carl Yastrzemski CAPT .50 .20
12 Whitey Herzog MG .05 .02
13 Al Oliver .10 .04
14 Steve Sax .10 .04
15 Mike Schmidt .75 .30
16 Ozzie Smith 1.00 .40
17 Tim Raines .15 .06
18 Andre Dawson .25 .10
19 Dale Murphy .25 .10
20 Gary Carter .40 .16
21 Mario Soto .05 .02
22 Johnny Bench CAPT .50 .20

1984 Topps Glossy Send-Ins

The cards in this 40-card set measure the standard size. Similar to last year's glossy set, this set was issued as a bonus prize to Topps All-Star Baseball Game cards found in wax packs. Twenty-five bonus runs from the game cards were necessary to obtain a five card subset of the series. There were eight different subsets of five cards. The cards are numbered and the set contains 20 stars from each league.

Nm-Mt Ex-Mt
COMPLETE SET (40) 12.00 4.80
1 Pete Rose 1.25 .50
2 Lance Parrish .20 .08
3 Steve Rogers .10 .04
4 Eddie Murray 1.00 .40
5 Johnny Ray .10 .04
6 Rickey Henderson 2.00 .80
7 Atlee Hammaker .10 .04
8 Wade Boggs 1.50 .60
9 Gary Carter 1.25 .50
10 Jack Morris .20 .08
11 Darrell Evans .20 .08
12 George Brett 2.50 1.00
13 Bob Horner .10 .04
14 Ron Guidry .20 .08
15 Nolan Ryan 5.00 2.00
16 Dave Winfield 1.00 .40
17 Ozzie Smith 2.00 .80
18 Ted Simmons .20 .08
19 Bill Madlock .10 .04
20 Tony Armas .10 .04
21 Al Oliver .20 .08
22 Jim Rice .20 .08
23 George Hendrick .10 .04
24 Dave Stieb .10 .04
25 Pedro Guerrero .10 .04
26 Rod Carew 1.00 .40
27 Steve Carlton .50 .20
28 Dave Righetti .20 .08
29 Darryl Strawberry .20 .08
30 Lou Whitaker .20 .08
31 Dale Murphy .30 .12
32 LaMarr Hoyt .10 .04
33 Jesse Orosco .20 .08
34 Cecil Cooper .20 .08
35 Andre Dawson .50 .20
36 Robin Yount 1.25 .50
37 Tim Raines .30 .12
38 Dan Quisenberry .10 .04
39 Mike Schmidt 2.00 .80
40 Carlton Fisk 1.50 .60

1984 Topps Traded

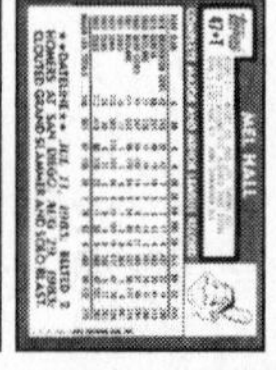

In now standard procedure, Topps issued its standard-size Traded (or extended) set for the fourth year in a row. Several of 1984's top rookies not contained in the regular set are pictured in the Traded set. Extended Rookie Cards in this set include Dwight Gooden, Jimmy Key, Mark Langston, Jose Rijo, and Bret Saberhagen. Again this year, the Topps affiliate in Ireland printed the cards, and the cards were available through hobby channels only in factory set form. The set numbering is in alphabetical order by player's name.

Nm-Mt Ex-Mt
COMP.FACT.SET (132) 30.00 12.00
1T Willie Aikens .40 .16
2T Luis Aponte .40 .16
3T Mike Armstrong .40 .16
4T Bob Bailor .40 .16
5T Dusty Baker .60 .24
6T Steve Balboni .40 .16
7T Alan Bannister .40 .16
8T Dave Beard .40 .16
9T Joe Beckwith .40 .16
10T Bruce Berenyi .40 .16
11T Dave Bergman .40 .16
12T Tony Bernazard .40 .16
13T Yogi Berra MG 1.50 .60
14T Barry Bonnell .40 .16
15T Phil Bradley .60 .24
16T Fred Breining .40 .16
17T Bill Buckner .60 .24
18T Ray Burris .40 .16
19T John Butcher .40 .16
20T Brett Butler 1.00 .40
21T Enos Cabell .40 .16
22T Bill Campbell .40 .16
23T Bill Caudill .40 .16
24T Bob Clark .40 .16
25T Bryan Clark .40 .16
26T Jaime Cocanower .40 .16
27T Ron Darling XRC* 1.00 .40
28T Alvin Davis XRC .60 .24
29T Ken Dayley .40 .16
30T Jeff Dedmon .40 .16
31T Bob Dernier .40 .16
32T Carlos Diaz .40 .16
33T Mike Easler .40 .16
34T Dennis Eckersley 1.00 .40
35T Jim Essian .40 .16
36T Darrell Evans .60 .24
37T Mike Fitzgerald .40 .16
38T Tim Foli .40 .16
39T George Frazier .40 .16
40T Rich Gale .40 .16
41T Barbaro Garbey .40 .16
42T Dwight Gooden XRC 5.00 2.00
43T Rich Gossage 1.00 .40
44T Wayne Gross .40 .16
45T Mark Gubicza XRC .60 .24
46T Jackie Gutierrez .40 .16
47T Mel Hall .60 .24
48T Toby Harrah .60 .24
49T Ron Hassey .40 .16
50T Rich Hebner .40 .16
51T Willie Hernandez .60 .24
52T Ricky Horton .40 .16
53T Art Howe .60 .24
54T Dane Iorg .40 .16
55T Brook Jacoby .60 .24
56T Mike Jeffcoat .40 .16
57T Dave Johnson MG .60 .24
58T Lynn Jones .40 .16
59T Ruppert Jones .40 .16
60T Mike Jorgensen .40 .16
61T Bob Kearney .40 .16
62T Jimmy Key XRC 1.00 .40
63T Dave Kingman 1.00 .40
64T Jerry Koosman .60 .24
65T Wayne Krenchicki .40 .16
66T Rusty Kuntz .40 .16
67T Rene Lachemann MG .40 .16
68T Frank LaCorte .40 .16
69T Dennis Lamp .40 .16
70T Mark Langston XRC 1.00 .40
71T Rick Leach .40 .16
72T Craig Lefferts .60 .24
73T Gary Lucas .40 .16
74T Jerry Martin .40 .16
75T Carmelo Martinez .40 .16
76T Mike Mason XRC .40 .16
77T Gary Matthews .60 .24
78T Andy McGaffigan .40 .16
79T Larry Milbourne .40 .16
80T Sid Monge .40 .16
81T Jackie Moore MG .40 .16
82T Joe Morgan 1.00 .40
83T Graig Nettles .60 .24
84T Phil Niekro .60 .24
85T Ken Oberkfell .40 .16
86T Mike O'Berry .40 .16
87T Al Oliver .60 .24
88T Jorge Orta .40 .16
89T Amos Otis .60 .24
90T Dave Parker .60 .24
91T Tony Perez 1.00 .40
92T Gerald Perry .60 .24
93T Gary Pettis .40 .16
94T Rob Picciolo .40 .16
95T Vern Rapp MG .40 .16
96T Floyd Rayford .40 .16
97T Randy Ready XRC .60 .24
98T Ron Reed .40 .16
99T Gene Richards .40 .16
100T Jose Rijo XRC 1.50 .60
101T Jeff D. Robinson .40 .16
102T Ron Romanick .40 .16
103T Pete Rose 5.00 2.00
104T B.Saberhagen XRC 3.00 1.20
105T Juan Samuel XRC* 1.00 .40
106T Scott Sanderson .40 .16
107T Dick Schofield XRC* .60 .24
108T Tom Seaver 1.00 .40
109T Jim Slaton .40 .16
110T Mike Smithson .40 .16
111T Lary Sorensen .40 .16
112T Tim Stoddard .40 .16
113T Champ Summers .40 .16
114T Jim Sundberg .60 .24
115T Rick Sutcliffe .60 .24
116T Craig Swan .40 .16
117T Tim Teufel XRC* .40 .16
118T Derrel Thomas .40 .16
119T Gorman Thomas .40 .16
120T Alex Trevino .40 .16
121T Manny Trillo .40 .16
122T John Tudor .40 .16
123T Tom Underwood .40 .16
124T Mike Vail .40 .16
125T Tom Waddell .40 .16
126T Gary Ward .40 .16
127T Curtis Wilkerson .40 .16
128T Frank Williams .40 .16
129T Glenn Wilson .40 .16
130T John Wockenfuss .40 .16
131T Ned Yost .40 .16
132T Checklist 1T-132T .40 .16

1984 Topps Traded Tiffany

This 132-card standard-size set was issued by Topps as a premium parallel to their regular issue. This set was printed in the Topps Ireland factory and are differentiated from the regular cards by their glossy sheen and clean backs. These sets were only available through the Topps hobby distribution system. Topps issued these sets only if a dealer ordered the regular Tiffany sets, therefore approximately 10,000 of these sets were produced as well.

Nm-Mt Ex-Mt
COMP.FACT.SET (132) 60.00 24.00
*STARS: .6X TO 1.5X BASIC CARDS ..
*ROOKIES: 1X TO 2.5X BASIC CARDS

1984 Topps Cereal

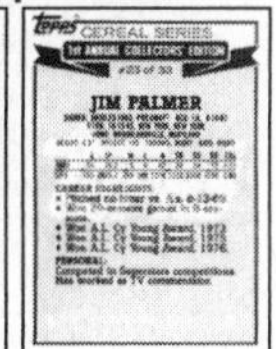

The cards in this 33-card set measure the standard size. The cards are numbered both on the front and the back. The 1984 Topps Cereal Series is exactly the same as the Ralston-Purina issue of this year except for a Topps logo and the words "Cereal Series" on the tops of the fronts of the cards in place of the Ralston checkerboard background. The checkerboard background is absent from the reverse, and a Topps logo is on the reverse of the cereal cards. These cards were distributed in unmarked boxes of Ralston-Purina cereal with a pack of four cards (three players and a checklist) being inside random cereal boxes. The back of the checklist details an offer to obtain any twelve cards direct from the issuer for only 1.50.

Nm-Mt Ex-Mt
COMPLETE SET (34) 12.00 4.80
1 Eddie Murray 1.50 .60
2 Ozzie Smith 2.00 .80
3 Ted Simmons .20 .08
4 Pete Rose 1.25 .50
5 Greg Luzinski .20 .08
6 Andre Dawson .50 .20
7 Dave Winfield 1.00 .40
8 Tom Seaver 1.00 .40
9 Jim Rice .20 .08
10 Fernando Valenzuela .20 .08
11 Wade Boggs 1.50 .60
12 Dale Murphy .40 .16
13 George Brett 2.00 .80
14 Nolan Ryan 4.00 1.60
15 Rickey Henderson 1.50 .60
16 Steve Carlton 1.00 .40
17 Rod Carew .75 .30
18 Steve Garvey .20 .08
19 Reggie Jackson 1.00 .40
20 Dave Concepcion .20 .08
21 Robin Yount 1.00 .40
22 Mike Schmidt 1.50 .60
23 Jim Palmer 1.00 .40
24 Bruce Sutter .20 .08
25 Dan Quisenberry .10 .04
26 Bill Madlock .10 .04
27 Cecil Cooper .20 .08
28 Gary Carter .75 .30
29 Fred Lynn .20 .08
30 Pedro Guerrero .20 .08
31 Ron Guidry .20 .08
32 Keith Hernandez .20 .08
33 Carlton Fisk 1.00 .40
NNO Checklist Card .10 .04

1984 Topps Gallery of Champions

These 12 "mini" cards were issued in set form only. These "Cards" measure approximately 1 1/4" by 1 3/4" and have the same design as the regular Topps cards from that year. In 1984 and 1985 no aluminum sets were issued. We have sequenced this set in alphabetical order. These cards were issued in bronze and silver versions. We have priced the bronze version. The silver versions are valued at approximately 2.5 times the values listed below.

Nm-Mt Ex-Mt
COMPLETE SET (12) 450.00 180.00
1 George Brett 60.00 24.00
2 Rod Carew 25.00 10.00
3 Steve Carlton 25.00 10.00
4 Rollie Fingers 10.00 4.00
5 Steve Garvey 25.00 10.00
6 Reggie Jackson 60.00 24.00
7 Joe Morgan 15.00 6.00
8 Jim Palmer 15.00 6.00
9 Pete Rose 40.00 16.00
10 Nolan Ryan 150.00 60.00
11 Mike Schmidt 50.00 20.00
12 Tom Seaver 40.00 16.00

1984 Topps Stickers

Made in Italy for Topps and O-Pee-Chee by Panini, these 386 stickers measure approximately 1 15/16" by 2 9/16" and are numbered on both front and back. The fronts feature white-bordered color player photos. The horizontal back carries the player's name and a bilingual ad for O-Pee-Chee in red lettering. The

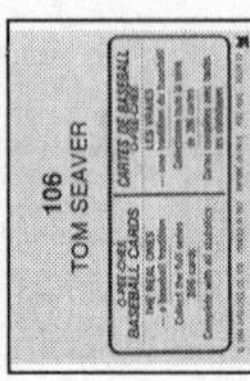

stickers were also issued boxes of seven strips of five stickers each. An album onto which the stickers could be affixed was available at retail stores. The album and the sticker numbering are organized as follows: 1983 Highlights (1-10), 1983 Championship Series (11-18), World Series (19-26), Atlanta Braves (27-38), Chicago Cubs (39-50), Cincinnati Reds (51-62), Houston Astros (63-74), Los Angeles Dodgers (75-86), Montreal Expos (87-98), 1983 Stat Leaders (99-102), New York Mets (103-114), Philadelphia Phillies (115-126), Pittsburgh Pirates (127-138), St. Louis Cardinals (139-150), San Diego Padres (151-162), San Francisco Giants (163-174), 1983 Stat Leaders (175-178), Foil All-Stars (179-198), 1983 Stat Leaders (199-202), Baltimore Orioles (203-214), Boston Red Sox (215-226), California Angels (227-238), Chicago White Sox (239-250), Cleveland Indians (251-262), Detroit Tigers (263-274), Kansas City Royals (275-286), 1983 Stat Leaders (287-290), Milwaukee Brewers (291-302), Minnesota Twins (303-314), New York Yankees (315-326), Oakland A's (327-338), Seattle Mariners (339-350), Texas Rangers (351-362), Toronto Blue Jays (363-374), and Stars of the Future (375-386). There were stickers issued which corresponded with Don Mattingly and Darryl Strawberry Rookie Year for cards.

Nm-Mt Ex-Mt
COMPLETE SET (386) 15.00 6.00
COMM. STICKER (1-178,199-386) .05 .02
COMMON FOIL (179-198) .10 .04
*TOPPS AND OPC: SAME VALUE
1 Steve Carlton .15 .06
(Top half)
2 Steve Carlton .15 .06
(Bottom half)
3 Rickey Henderson .15 .06
(Top half)
4 Rickey Henderson .15 .06
(Bottom half)
5 Fred Lynn .10 .04
(Top half)
6 Fred Lynn .10 .04
(Bottom half)
7 Greg Luzinski .10 .04
(Top half)
8 Greg Luzinski .10 .04
(Bottom half)
9 Dan Quisenberry .05 .02
(Top half)
10 Dan Quisenberry .05 .02
(Bottom half)
11 LaMarr Hoyt LCS .05 .02
12 Mike Flanagan LCS .05 .02
13 Mike Boddicker LCS .05 .02
14 Tito Landrum LCS .05 .02
15 Steve Carlton LCS .15 .06
16 Fern.Valenzuela LCS .10 .04
17 Charlie Hudson LCS .05 .02
18 Gary Matthews LCS .05 .02
19 John Denny WS .05 .02
20 John Lowenstein WS .05 .02
21 Jim Palmer WS .15 .06
22 Benny Ayala WS .05 .02
23 Rick Dempsey WS .05 .02
24 Cal Ripken WS 1.25 .50
25 Sammy Stewart WS .05 .02
26 Eddie Murray WS .15 .06
27 Dale Murphy .15 .06
28 Chris Chambliss .05 .02
29 Glenn Hubbard .05 .02
30 Bob Horner .05 .02
31 Phil Niekro .25 .10
32 Claudell Washington .05 .02
33 Rafael Ramirez (135) .05 .02
34 Bruce Benedict (82) .05 .02
35 Gene Garber (59) .05 .02
36 Pascual Perez (347) .05 .02
37 Jerry Royster (281) .05 .02
38 Steve Bedrosian(283) .05 .02
39 Keith Moreland .05 .02
40 Leon Durham .05 .02
41 Ron Cey .10 .04
42 Bill Buckner .10 .04
43 Jody Davis .05 .02
44 Lee Smith .25 .10
45 Ryne Sandberg (70) 1.25 .50
46 Larry Bowa (301) .10 .04
47 Chuck Rainey (247) .05 .02
48 Fergie Jenkins (170) .25 .10
49 Dick Ruthven (333) .05 .02
50 Jay Johnstone (298) .05 .02
51 Mario Soto .05 .02
52 Gary Redus .05 .02
53 Ron Oester .05 .02
54 Cesar Cedeno .10 .04
55 Dan Driessen .05 .02
56 Dave Concepcion .10 .04
57 Dann Bilardello(147) .05 .02
58 Joe Price (98) .05 .02
59 Tom Hume (35) .05 .02
60 Eddie Milner (84) .05 .02
61 Paul Householder .05 .02
(226)
62 Bill Scherrer (269) .05 .02
63 Phil Garner .10 .04
64 Dickie Thon .05 .02
65 Jose Cruz .10 .04
66 Nolan Ryan 2.00 .80
67 Terry Puhl .05 .02
68 Ray Knight .10 .04
69 Joe Niekro (312) .10 .04
70 Jerry Mumphrey (45) .05 .02
71 Bill Dawley (314) .05 .02
72 Alan Ashby (162) .05 .02
73 Denny Walling (81) .05 .02
74 Frank DiPino (360) .05 .02
75 Pedro Guerrero .10 .04
76 Ken Landreaux .05 .02
77 Bill Russell .10 .04
78 Steve Sax .10 .04
79 Fernando Valenzuela .10 .04
80 Dusty Baker .10 .04
81 Jerry Reuss (73) .05 .02
82 Alejandro Pena (34) .05 .02
83 Rick Monday .05 .02
84 Rick Honeycutt (60) .05 .02
85 Mike Marshall (245) .05 .02
86 Steve Yeager (284) .05 .02
87 Al Oliver .10 .04
88 Steve Rogers .05 .02
89 Jeff Reardon .10 .04
90 Gary Carter .25 .10
91 Tim Raines .25 .10
92 Andre Dawson .25 .10
93 Manny Trillo (137) .05 .02
94 Tim Wallach (348) .10 .04
95 Chris Speier (172) .05 .02
96 Bill Gullickson(134) .05 .02
97 Doug Flynn (271) .05 .02
98 Charlie Lea (58) .05 .02
99 Bill Madlock .10 .04
(102B/288B)
100 Wade Boggs .60 .24
(200B/287B)
101 Mike Schmidt (176) .60 .24
102A Jim Rice (287A/177) .10 .04
102B Reggie Jackson .50 .20
(99/288B)
103 Hubie Brooks .05 .02
104 Jesse Orosco .05 .02
105 George Foster .10 .04
106 Tom Seaver .50 .20
107 Keith Hernandez .10 .04
108 Mookie Wilson .10 .04
109 Bob Bailor (122) .05 .02
110 Walt Terrell (209) .05 .02
111 Brian Giles (126) .05 .02
112 Jose Oquendo (372) .05 .02
113 Mike Torrez (258) .05 .02
114 Junior Ortiz (371) .05 .02
115 Pete Rose .75 .30
116 Joe Morgan .25 .10
117 Mike Schmidt .60 .24
118 Gary Matthews .05 .02
119 Steve Carlton .40 .16
120 Bo Diaz .05 .02
121 Ivan DeJesus (210) .05 .02
122 John Denny (109) .05 .02
123 Garry Maddox (335) .05 .02
124 Von Hayes (224) .05 .02
125 Al Holland (158) .05 .02
126 Tony Perez (111) .25 .10
127 John Candelaria .05 .02
128 Jason Thompson .05 .02
129 Tony Pena .05 .02
130 Dave Parker .10 .04
131 Bill Madlock .05 .02
132 Kent Tekulve .10 .04
133 Larry McWilliams .05 .02
(146)
134 Johnny Ray (96) .05 .02
135 Marvell Wynne (33) .05 .02
136 Dale Berra (299) .05 .02
137 Mike Easler (93) .05 .02
138 Lee Lacy (233) .05 .02
139 George Hendrick .05 .02
140 Lonnie Smith .05 .02
141 Willie McGee .15 .06
142 Tom Herr .10 .04
143 Darrell Porter .05 .02
144 Ozzie Smith .40 .16
145 Bruce Sutter (221) .10 .04
146 Dave LaPoint (133) .05 .02
147 Neil Allen (57) .05 .02
148 Ken Oberkfell (238) .05 .02
149 David Green (324) .05 .02
150 Andy Van Slyke (235) .25 .10
151 Garry Templeton .05 .02
152 Juan Bonilla .05 .02
153 Alan Wiggins .05 .02
154 Terry Kennedy .05 .02
155 Dave Dravecky .10 .04
156 Steve Garvey .15 .06
157 Bobby Brown (361) .05 .02
158 Ruppert Jones (125) .05 .02
159 Luis Salazar (214) .05 .02
160 Tony Gwynn (212) 2.50 1.00
161 Gary Lucas (211) .05 .02
162 Eric Show (72) .05 .02
163 Darrell Evans .10 .04
164 Gary Lavelle .05 .02
165 Atlee Hammaker .05 .02
166 Jeff Leonard .05 .02
167 Jack Clark .10 .04
168 Johnny LeMaster .05 .02
169 Duane Kuiper (260) .05 .02
170 Tom O'Malley (48) .05 .02
171 Chili Davis (311) .10 .04
172 Bill Laskey (95) .05 .02
173 Joel Youngblood(300) .05 .02
174 Bob Brenly (225) .05 .02
175 Atlee Hammaker(202) .05 .02
176 Rick Honeycutt (101) .05 .02
177 John Denny .05 .02
(102A/287A)
178 LaMarr Hoyt .05 .02
(200A/288A)
179 Tim Raines FOIL .15 .06
180 Dale Murphy FOIL .40 .16
181 Andre Dawson FOIL .40 .16
182 Steve Rogers FOIL .10 .04
183 Gary Carter FOIL .25 .10
184 Steve Carlton FOIL .40 .16
185 George Hendrick FOIL .10 .04
186 Johnny Ray FOIL .10 .04
187 Ozzie Smith FOIL .40 .16
188 Mike Schmidt FOIL .75 .30
189 Jim Rice FOIL .10 .04
190 Dave Winfield FOIL .40 .16
191 Lloyd Moseby FOIL .10 .04
192 LaMarr Hoyt FOIL .10 .04
193 Ted Simmons FOIL .10 .04
194 Ron Guidry FOIL .15 .06
195 Eddie Murray FOIL .40 .16
196 Lou Whitaker FOIL .15 .06
197 Cal Ripken FOIL 3.00 1.20
198 George Brett FOIL 1.25 .50
199 Dale Murphy (290) .15 .06
200A Cecil Cooper .10 .04
(288A/178)
200B Jim Rice (287B/100) .10 .04
201 Tim Raines (289) .15 .06
202 Rickey Henderson .40 .16
(175)
203 Eddie Murray .40 .16
204 Cal Ripken 2.50 1.00
205 Gary Roenicke .05 .02
206 Ken Singleton .05 .02
207 Scott McGregor .05 .02
208 Tippy Martinez .05 .02
209 John Lowenstein(110) .05 .02
210 Mike Flanagan (121) .05 .02
211 Jim Palmer (161) .25 .10
212 Dan Ford (160) .05 .02
213 Rick Dempsey (234) .05 .02
214 Rich Dauer (159) .05 .02
215 Jerry Remy .05 .02
216 Wade Boggs .60 .24
217 Jim Rice .10 .04
218 Tony Armas .05 .02
219 Dwight Evans .10 .04
220 Bob Stanley (370) .05 .02
221 Dave Stapleton (145) .05 .02
222 Rich Gedman .05 .02
223 Glenn Hoffman (272) .05 .02
224 Dennis Eckersley .15 .06
(124)
225 John Tudor (174) .05 .02
226 Bruce Hurst (61) .05 .02
227 Rod Carew .40 .16
228 Bobby Grich .10 .04
229 Doug DeCinces .05 .02
230 Fred Lynn .10 .04
231 Reggie Jackson .50 .20
232 Tommy John .10 .04
233 Luis Sanchez (138) .05 .02
234 Bob Boone (213) .10 .04
235 Bruce Kison (150) .05 .02
236 Brian Downing (262) .05 .02
237 Ken Forsch (246) .05 .02
238 Rick Burleson (148) .05 .02
239 Dennis Lamp .05 .02
240 LaMarr Hoyt .05 .02
241 Richard Dotson .05 .02
242 Harold Baines .15 .06
243 Carlton Fisk .25 .10
244 Greg Luzinski .10 .04
245 Rudy Law (85) .05 .02
246 Tom Paciorek (237) .05 .02
247 Floyd Bannister(47) .05 .02
248 Julio Cruz (369) .05 .02
249 Vance Law (358) .05 .02
250 Scott Fletcher(270) .05 .02
251 Toby Harrah .10 .04
252 Pat Tabler .05 .02
253 Gorman Thomas .05 .02
254 Rick Sutcliffe .10 .04
255 Andre Thornton .05 .02
256 Bake McBride .05 .02
257 Alan Bannister(313) .05 .02
258 Jamie Easterly(113) .05 .02
259 Lary Sorensen (285) .05 .02
260 Mike Hargrove (169) .10 .04
261 Bert Blyleven (346) .10 .04
262 Ron Hassey (236) .05 .02
263 Jack Morris .10 .04
264 Larry Herndon .05 .02
265 Lance Parrish .10 .04
266 Alan Trammell .25 .10
267 Lou Whitaker .10 .04
268 Aurelio Lopez .05 .02
269 Dan Petry (62) .05 .02
270 Glenn Wilson (250) .05 .02
271 Chet Lemon (97) .05 .02
272 Kirk Gibson (223) .15 .06
273 Enos Cabell (338) .05 .02
274 John Wockenfuss(321) .05 .02
275 George Brett 1.00 .40
276 Willie Aikens .05 .02
277 Frank White .10 .04
278 Hal McRae .10 .04
279 Dan Quisenberry .05 .02
280 Willie Wilson .05 .02
281 Paul Splittorff(281) .05 .02
282 U.L. Washington(322) .05 .02
283 Bud Black (38) .05 .02
284 John Wathan (86) .05 .02
285 Larry Gura (259) .05 .02
286 Pat Sheridan (323) .05 .02
287A Rusty Staub .10 .04
(102A/177)
287B Dave Righetti .05 .02
(100/200B)
288A Bob Forsch .05 .02
(178/200A)
288B Mike Warren .05 .02
(99/102B)
289 Al Holland (201) .05 .02
290 Dan Quisenberry(199) .05 .02
291 Cecil Cooper .10 .04
292 Moose Haas .05 .02
293 Ted Simmons .10 .04
294 Paul Molitor .25 .10
295 Robin Yount .25 .10
296 Ben Oglivie .05 .02
297 Tom Tellman (325) .05 .02
298 Jim Gantner (50) .10 .04
299 Rick Manning (136) .05 .02
300 Don Sutton (173) .25 .10
301 Charlie Moore (46) .05 .02
302 Jim Slaton (337) .05 .02
303 Gary Ward .05 .02
304 Tom Brunansky .10 .04
305 Kent Hrbek .15 .06
306 Gary Gaetti .15 .06
307 John Castino .05 .02
308 Ken Schrom .05 .02
309 Ron Davis (334) .05 .02
310 Lenny Faedo (336) .05 .02
311 Darrell Brown (171) .05 .02
312 Frank Viola (69) .15 .06
313 Dave Engle (257) .05 .02
314 Randy Bush (71) .05 .02
315 Dave Righetti .10 .04
316 Rich Gossage .10 .04
317 Ken Griffey .10 .04
318 Ron Guidry .10 .04
319 Dave Winfield .25 .10
320 Don Baylor .10 .04
321 Butch Wynegar (274) .05 .02
322 Omar Moreno (282) .05 .02
323 Andre Robertson(286) .05 .02
324 Willie Randolph(149) .10 .04
325 Don Mattingly (297) 5.00 2.00
326 Graig Nettles .10 .04
327 Rickey Henderson .40 .16
328 Carney Lansford .10 .04
329 Jeff Burroughs .05 .02
330 Chris Codiroli .05 .02
331 Dave Lopes .10 .04
332 Dwayne Murphy .05 .02
333 Wayne Gross (49) .05 .02
334 Bill Almon (309) .05 .02
335 Tom Underwood (123) .05 .02
336 Dave Beard (310) .05 .02
337 Mike Heath (302) .05 .02
338 Mike Davis (273) .05 .02
339 Pat Putnam .05 .02
340 Tony Bernazard .05 .02
341 Steve Henderson .05 .02
342 Richie Zisk .05 .02
343 Dave Henderson .10 .04
344 Al Cowens .05 .02
345 Bill Caudill (359) .05 .02
346 Jim Beattie (261) .05 .02
347 Rick Nelson (36) .05 .02
348 Roy Thomas (94) .05 .02
349 Spike Owen (362) .10 .04
350 Jamie Allen (373) .05 .02
351 Buddy Bell .10 .04
352 Billy Sample .05 .02
353 George Wright .05 .02
354 Larry Parrish .05 .02
355 Jim Sundberg .10 .04
356 Charlie Hough .10 .04
357 Pete O'Brien .05 .02
358 Wayne Tolleson(249) .05 .02
359 Danny Darwin (345) .05 .02
360 Dave Stewart (74) .10 .04
361 Mickey Rivers (157) .05 .02
362 Bucky Dent (349) .10 .04
363 Willie Upshaw .05 .02
364 Damaso Garcia .05 .02
365 Lloyd Moseby .05 .02
366 Cliff Johnson .05 .02
367 Jim Clancy .05 .02
368 Dave Stieb .05 .02
369 Alfredo Griffin(248) .05 .02
370 Barry Bonnell (222) .05 .02
371 Luis Leal (114) .05 .02
372 Jesse Barfield(112) .05 .02
373 Ernie Whitt (350) .05 .02
374 Rance Mulliniks(326) .05 .02
375 Mike Boddicker .05 .02
376 Greg Brock .05 .02
377 Bill Doran .10 .04
378 Nick Esasky .05 .02
379 Julio Franco .25 .10
380 Mel Hall .05 .02
381 Bob Kearney .05 .02
382 Ron Kittle .05 .02
383 Carmelo Martinez .05 .02
384 Craig McMurtry .05 .02
385 Darryl Strawberry 1.25 .50
386 Matt Young .05 .02
NNO Album 1.00 .40

1984 Topps Sticker Boxes

The 24 cards in this set measure 2 1/2" by 3 1/2". For the second straight year, Topps issued blank-backed baseball cards on the boxes containing its stickers. Two cards per box were issued featuring "24 Leaders in Batting Average in 1983 -- Righties, Lefties and Switch Hitters." Officially called Super Bats Picture Cards, the player's name and 1983 batting average were featured within the dotted line cut-out around the card. The team name and batting side(s) of the player were on the outside of the dotted line. The price below includes only the cards on the box. Box 10 was not issued.

Nm-Mt Ex-Mt
COMPLETE SET (12) 10.00 4.00
1 Al Oliver .75 .30
Lou Whitaker
2 Ken Oberkfell .25 .10
Ted Simmons
3 Alan Wiggins .50 .20
Hal McRae
4 Tim Raines .75 .30
Lloyd Moseby
5 Lonnie Smith .25 .10
Willie Wilson
6 Keith Hernandez 1.25 .50
Robin Yount
7 Johnny Ray 2.00 .80
Wade Boggs
8 Willie McGee .75 .30
Ken Singleton
9 Ray Knight .75 .30
Alan Trammell
11 George Hendrick 1.25 .50
Rod Carew
12 Bill Madlock 1.25 .50
Eddie Murray
13 Jose Cruz 8.00 3.20
Cal Ripken

1984 Topps Rub Downs

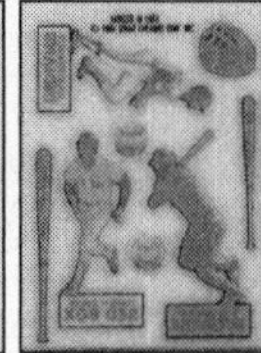

The cards in this 112-player (32 different sheets) set measure 2 3/8" by 3 5/16". The Topps Rub Downs set was actually similar to earlier Topps tatoo or decal-type offerings. The full color photo could be transfered from the rub down to another surface by rubbing a coin over the paper backing. Distributed in packages of two rub down sheets, some contained two or three player action poses, others head shots and various pieces of player equipment. Players from all teams were included in the set. Although the sheets are unnumbered, they are numbered here in alphabetical order based on each card first being placed in alphabetical order.

Nm-Mt Ex-Mt
COMPLETE SET (32) 8.00 3.20
1 Tony Armas .10 .04
Harold Baines
Lonnie Smith
2 Don Baylor .10 .04
George Hendrick
Ron Kittle
Johnnie LeMaster
3 Buddy Bell .20 .08
Ray Knight
Lloyd Moseby
4 Bruce Benedict .10 .04
Atlee Hammaker
Frank White
5 Wade Boggs .75 .30
Rick Dempsey
Keith Hernandez
6 George Brett 1.50 .60
Andre Dawson
Paul Molitor
Alan Wiggins
7 Tom Brunansky .75 .30
Pedro Guerrero
Darryl Strawberry
8 Bill Buckner .20 .08
Rich Gossage
Dave Stieb
Rick Sutcliffe
9 Rod Carew .75 .30
Carlton Fisk
Johnny Ray
Matt Young
10 Steve Carlton .40 .16
Bob Horner
Dan Quisenberry
11 Gary Carter .20 .08
Phil Garner
Ron Guidry
12 Ron Cey .20 .08
Steve Kemp
Greg Luzinski
Kent Tekulve
13 Chris Chambliss .40 .16
Dwight Evans
Julio Franco
14 Jack Clark .30 .12
Damaso Garcia
Hal McRae
Lance Parrish
15 Dave Concepcion .30 .12
Cecil Cooper
Fred Lynn
Jesse Orosco
16 Jose Cruz .30 .12
Gary Matthews
Jack Morris
Jim Rice
17 Ron Davis .60 .24
Kent Hrbek
Tom Seaver
18 John Denny .20 .08
Carney Lansford
Mario Soto
Lou Whitaker
19 Leon Durham .10 .04
Dave Lopes
Steve Sax
20 George Foster .30 .12
Gary Gaetti
Bobby Grich
Gary Redus
21 Steve Garvey .20 .08
Jerry Remy
Bill Russell
George Wright
22 Moose Haas .10 .04
Bruce Sutter
Dickie Thon
Andre Thornton
23 Toby Harrah .75 .30
Pat Putnam
Tim Raines
Mike Schmidt
24 Rickey Henderson 1.25 .50
Dave Righetti
Pete Rose
25 Steve Henderson .30 .12
Bill Madlock
Alan Trammell
26 LaMarr Hoyt 2.00 .80
Larry Parrish
Nolan Ryan
27 Reggie Jackson .40 .16
Eric Show
Jason Thompson
28 Tommy John 1.00 .40
Terry Kennedy
Eddie Murray
Ozzie Smith
29 Jeff Leonard .40 .16
Dale Murphy
Ken Singleton
Dave Winfield
30 Craig McMurtry 2.50 1.00
Cal Ripken
Steve Rogers

Willie Upshaw
31 Ben Oglivie .30 .12
Jim Palmer
Darrell Porter
32 Tony Pena .40 .16
Fernando Valenzuela
Robin Yount

1984 Topps Super

The cards in this 30-card set measure 4 7/8" by 6 7/8". The 1984 Topps Supers feature enlargements from the 1984 regular set. The cards differ from the corresponding cards of the regular set in size and number only. As one would expect, only those considered stars and superstars appear in this set.

Nm-Mt Ex-Mt
COMPLETE SET (30) 10.00 4.00
1 Cal Ripken 4.00 1.60
2 Dale Murphy .75 .30
3 LaMarr Hoyt .10 .04
4 John Denny .10 .04
5 Jim Rice .25 .10
6 Mike Schmidt 1.25 .50
7 Wade Boggs 1.50 .60
8 Bill Madlock .10 .04
9 Dan Quisenberry .10 .04
10 Al Holland .10 .04
11 Ron Kittle .10 .04
12 Darryl Strawberry 1.00 .40
13 George Brett 1.50 .60
14 Bill Buckner .25 .10
15 Carlton Fisk 1.00 .40
16 Steve Carlton 1.00 .40
17 Ron Guidry .25 .10
18 Gary Carter 1.00 .40
19 Rickey Henderson 1.50 .60
20 Andre Dawson .50 .20
21 Reggie Jackson 1.00 .40
22 Steve Garvey .25 .10
23 Fred Lynn .25 .10
24 Pedro Guerrero .25 .10
25 Eddie Murray 1.25 .50
26 Keith Hernandez .25 .10
27 Dave Winfield 1.00 .40
28 Nolan Ryan 3.00 1.20
29 Robin Yount 1.00 .40
30 Fernando Valenzuela .25 .10

1984-91 Topps Pewter Bonuses

During the eight year period that Topps issued their Gallery of Champions set, various other metal cards were issued as well. During that period, Topps issued Pewter cards as a premium. From 1984 to 1987 these Pewters were issued as a bonus for ordering "Tiffany" cases. From 1988-91, these Pewters were issued as bonuses for Gallery of Champion cases. The cards are sequenced in year order. A different Jose Canseco card was issued in 1987 and 1989.

Nm-Mt Ex-Mt
COMPLETE SET (8) 800.00 325.00
1 Tom Seaver '84 300.00 120.00
2 Dwight Gooden '85 50.00 20.00
3 Don Mattingly '86 80.00 32.00
4 Jose Canseco '87 50.00 20.00
5 Mark McGwire '88 80.00 32.00
6 Jose Canseco '89 30.00 12.00
7 Nolan Ryan '90 200.00 80.00
8 Rickey Henderson '91 50.00 20.00

1985 Topps

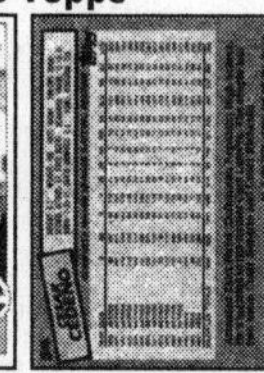

The 1985 Topps set contains 792 standard-size full-color cards. Cards were primarily distributed in 15-card wax packs, 51-card rack packs and factory (usually available through retail catalogs) sets. Manager cards feature the team checklist on the reverse. Full color card fronts feature both the Topps and team logos along with the team name, player's name, and his position. The first ten cards (1-10) are Record Breakers, cards 131-143 are Father and Sons, and cards 701 to 722 portray All-Star selections. Cards 271-282 represent "First Draft Picks" still active in professional baseball and cards 389-404 feature selected members of the 1984 U.S. Olympic Baseball Team. Rookie Cards include Roger Clemens, Eric Davis, Shawon Dunston, Dwight Gooden, Orel Hershiser, Jimmy Key, Mark Langston, Mark McGwire, Terry Pendleton, Kirby Puckett and Bret Saberhagen.

Nm-Mt Ex-Mt
COMPLETE SET (792) 100.00 40.00
COMP.FACT.SET (792) 200.00 80.00
1 Carlton Fisk RB .25 .10
2 Steve Garvey RB .15 .06
3 Dwight Gooden RB .60 .24
4 Cliff Johnson RB .15 .06
5 Joe Morgan RB .15 .06
6 Pete Rose RB .40 .16
7 Nolan Ryan RB 1.50 .60
8 Juan Samuel RB .15 .06
9 Bruce Sutter RB .15 .06
10 Don Sutton RB .25 .10
11 Ralph Houk MG .15 .06
12 Dave Lopes .25 .10
(Now with Cubs
on card front)
13 Tim Lollar .15 .06
14 Chris Bando .15 .06
15 Jerry Koosman .25 .10
16 Bobby Meacham .15 .06
17 Mike Scott .15 .06
18 Mickey Hatcher .15 .06
19 George Frazier .15 .06
20 Chet Lemon .15 .06
21 Lee Tunnell .15 .06
22 Duane Kuiper .15 .06
23 Bret Saberhagen RC .60 .24
24 Jesse Barfield .15 .06
25 Steve Bedrosian .15 .06
26 Roy Smalley .15 .06
27 Bruce Berenyi .15 .06
28 Dann Bilardello .15 .06
29 Odell Jones .15 .06
30 Cal Ripken 2.50 1.00
31 Terry Whitfield .15 .06
32 Chuck Porter .15 .06
33 Tito Landrum .15 .06
34 Ed Nunez .15 .06
35 Graig Nettles .25 .10
36 Fred Breining .15 .06
37 Reid Nichols .15 .06
38 Jackie Moore MG .15 .06
39 John Wockenfuss .15 .06
40 Phil Niekro .25 .10
41 Mike Fischlin .15 .06
42 Luis Sanchez .15 .06
43 Andre David .15 .06
44 Dickie Thon .15 .06
45 Greg Minton .15 .06
46 Gary Woods .15 .06
47 Dave Rozema .15 .06
48 Tony Fernandez .25 .10
49 Butch Davis .15 .06
50 John Candelaria .15 .06
51 Bob Watson .25 .10
52 Jerry Dybzinski .15 .06
53 Tom Gorman .15 .06
54 Cesar Cedeno .25 .10
55 Frank Tanana .15 .06
56 Jim Dwyer .15 .06
57 Pat Zachry .15 .06
58 Orlando Mercado .15 .06
59 Rick Waits .15 .06
60 George Hendrick .15 .06
61 Curt Kaufman .15 .06
62 Mike Ramsey .15 .06
63 Steve McCatty .15 .06
64 Mark Bailey .15 .06
65 Bill Buckner .25 .10
66 Dick Williams MG .25 .10
67 Rafael Santana .15 .06
68 Von Hayes .15 .06
69 Jim Winn .15 .06
70 Don Baylor .25 .10
71 Tim Laudner .15 .06
72 Rick Sutcliffe .25 .10
73 Rusty Kuntz .15 .06
74 Mike Krukow .15 .06
75 Willie Upshaw .15 .06
76 Alan Bannister .15 .06
77 Joe Beckwith .15 .06
78 Scott Fletcher .15 .06
79 Rick Mahler .15 .06
80 Keith Hernandez .40 .16
81 Lenn Sakata .15 .06
82 Joe Price .15 .06
83 Charlie Moore .15 .06
84 Spike Owen .15 .06
85 Mike Marshall .15 .06
86 Don Aase .15 .06
87 David Green .15 .06
88 Bryn Smith .15 .06
89 Jackie Gutierrez .15 .06
90 Rich Gossage .25 .10
91 Jeff Burroughs .15 .06
92 Paul Owens MG .15 .06
93 Don Schulze .15 .06
94 Toby Harrah .15 .06
95 Jose Cruz .25 .10
96 Johnny Ray .15 .06
97 Pete Filson .15 .06
98 Steve Lake .15 .06
99 Milt Wilcox .15 .06
100 George Brett 1.50 .60
101 Jim Acker .15 .06
102 Tommy Dunbar .15 .06
103 Randy Lerch .15 .06
104 Mike Fitzgerald .15 .06
105 Ron Kittle .15 .06
106 Pascual Perez .15 .06
107 Tom Foley .15 .06
108 Darnell Coles .15 .06
109 Gary Roenicke .15 .06
110 Alejandro Pena .15 .06
111 Doug DeCinces .15 .06
112 Tom Tellmann .15 .06
113 Tom Herr .15 .06
114 Bob James .15 .06
115 Rickey Henderson .75 .30
116 Dennis Boyd .15 .06
117 Greg Gross .15 .06
118 Eric Show .15 .06
119 Pat Corrales MG .15 .06
120 Steve Kemp .15 .06
121 Checklist: 1-132 .15 .06
122 Tom Brunansky .25 .10
123 Dave Smith .15 .06
124 Rich Hebner .15 .06
125 Kent Tekulve .15 .06
126 Ruppert Jones .15 .06
127 Mark Gubicza RC* .25 .10
128 Ernie Whitt .15 .06
129 Gene Garber .15 .06
130 Al Oliver .25 .10
131 Buddy Bell FS .25 .10
Gus Bell
132 Dale Berra FS .25 .10
Yogi Berra
133 Bob Boone FS .15 .06
Ray Boone
134 Terry Francona FS .15 .06
Tito Francona
135 Terry Kennedy FS .15 .06
Bob Kennedy
136 Jeff Kunkel FS .15 .06
Bill Kunkel
137 Vance Law FS .25 .10
Vern Law
138 Dick Schofield FS .15 .06
Dick Schofield
139 Joel Skinner FS .15 .06
Bob Skinner
140 Roy Smalley Jr. FS .15 .06
Roy Smalley
141 Mike Stenhouse FS .15 .06
Dave Stenhouse
142 Steve Trout FS .15 .06
Dizzy Trout
143 Ozzie Virgil FS .15 .06
Ossie Virgil
144 Ron Gardenhire .15 .06
145 Alvin Davis RC* .25 .10
146 Gary Redus .15 .06
147 Bill Swaggerty .15 .06
148 Steve Yeager .15 .06
149 Dickie Noles .15 .06
150 Jim Rice .25 .10
151 Moose Haas .15 .06
152 Steve Braun .15 .06
153 Frank LaCorte .15 .06
154 Angel Salazar .15 .06
155 Yogi Berra MG .40 .16
156 Craig Reynolds .15 .06
157 Tug McGraw .25 .10
158 Pat Tabler .15 .06
159 Carlos Diaz .15 .06
160 Lance Parrish .25 .10
161 Ken Schrom .15 .06
162 Benny Distefano .15 .06
163 Dennis Eckersley .40 .16
164 Jorge Orta .15 .06
165 Dusty Baker .25 .10
166 Keith Atherton .15 .06
167 Rufino Linares .15 .06
168 Garth Iorg .15 .06
169 Dan Spillner .15 .06
170 George Foster .25 .10
171 Bill Stein .15 .06
172 Jack Perconte .15 .06
173 Mike Young .15 .06
174 Rick Honeycutt .15 .06
175 Dave Parker .25 .10
176 Bill Schroeder .15 .06
177 Dave Von Ohlen .15 .06
178 Miguel Dilone .15 .06
179 Tommy John .40 .16
180 Dave Winfield .25 .10
181 Roger Clemens RC 25.00 10.00
182 Tim Flannery .15 .06
183 Larry McWilliams .15 .06
184 Carmen Castillo .15 .06
185 Al Holland .15 .06
186 Bob Lillis MG .15 .06
187 Mike Walters .15 .06
188 Greg Pryor .15 .06
189 Warren Brusstar .15 .06
190 Rusty Staub .25 .10
191 Steve Nicosia .15 .06
192 Howard Johnson .25 .10
193 Jimmy Key RC .60 .24
194 Dave Stegman .15 .06
195 Glenn Hubbard .15 .06
196 Pete O'Brien .15 .06
197 Mike Warren .15 .06
198 Eddie Milner .15 .06
199 Dennis Martinez .25 .10
200 Reggie Jackson .40 .16
201 Burt Hooton .15 .06
202 Gorman Thomas .15 .06
203 Bob McClure .15 .06
204 Art Howe .15 .06
205 Steve Rogers .15 .06
206 Phil Garner .25 .10
207 Mark Clear .15 .06
208 Champ Summers .15 .06
209 Bill Campbell .15 .06
210 Gary Matthews .15 .06
211 Clay Christiansen .15 .06
212 George Vukovich .15 .06
213 Billy Gardner MG .25 .10
214 John Tudor .15 .06
215 Bob Brenly .15 .06
216 Jerry Don Gleaton .15 .06
217 Leon Roberts .15 .06
218 Doyle Alexander .15 .06
219 Gerald Perry .15 .06
220 Fred Lynn .25 .10
221 Ron Reed .15 .06
222 Hubie Brooks .15 .06
223 Tom Hume .15 .06
224 Al Cowens .15 .06
225 Mike Boddicker .15 .06
226 Juan Beniquez .15 .06
227 Danny Darwin .15 .06
228 Dion James .15 .06
229 Dave LaPoint .15 .06
230 Gary Carter .40 .16
231 Dwayne Murphy .15 .06
232 Dave Beard .15 .06
233 Ed Jurak .15 .06
234 Jerry Narron .15 .06
235 Garry Maddox .15 .06
236 Mark Thurmond .15 .06
237 Julio Franco .40 .16
238 Jose Rijo RC .40 .16
239 Tim Teufel .15 .06
240 Dave Stieb .25 .10
241 Jim Frey MG .15 .06
242 Greg Harris .15 .06
243 Barbaro Garbey .15 .06
244 Mike Jones .15 .06
245 Chili Davis .25 .10
246 Mike Norris .15 .06
247 Wayne Tolleson .15 .06
248 Terry Forster .15 .06
249 Harold Baines .25 .10
250 Jesse Orosco .15 .06
251 Brad Gulden .15 .06
252 Dan Ford .15 .06
253 Sid Bream RC .25 .10
254 Pete Vuckovich .15 .06
255 Lonnie Smith .15 .06
256 Mike Stanton .15 .06
257 Bryan Little UER .15 .06
Name spelled Brian on front
258 Mike C. Brown .15 .06
259 Gary Allenson .15 .06
260 Dave Righetti .25 .10
261 Checklist: 133-264 .15 .06
262 Greg Booker .15 .06
263 Mel Hall .15 .06
264 Joe Sambito .15 .06
265 Juan Samuel .15 .06
266 Frank Viola .25 .10
267 Henry Cotto RC .15 .06
268 Chuck Tanner MG .25 .10
269 Doug Baker .15 .06
270 Dan Quisenberry .25 .10
271 Tim Foli FDP68 .15 .06
272 Jeff Burroughs FDP69 .15 .06
273 Bill Almon FDP74 .15 .06
274 F.Bannister FDP76 .15 .06
275 Harold Baines FDP77 .15 .06
276 Bob Horner FDP78 .15 .06
277 Al Chambers FDP79 .15 .06
278 Darryl Strawberry .40 .16
FDP80
279 Mike Moore FDP81 .15 .06
280 S.Dunston FDP82 RC .40 .16
281 T.Belcher RC FDP83 .60 .24
282 Shawn Abner FDP84 .15 .06
283 Fran Mullins .15 .06
284 Marty Bystrom .15 .06
285 Dan Driessen .15 .06
286 Rudy Law .15 .06
287 Walt Terrell .15 .06
288 Jeff Kunkel .15 .06
289 Tom Underwood .15 .06
290 Cecil Cooper .25 .10
291 Bob Welch .15 .06
292 Brad Komminsk .15 .06
293 Curt Young .15 .06
294 Tom Nieto .15 .06
295 Joe Niekro .15 .06
296 Ricky Nelson .15 .06
297 Gary Lucas .15 .06
298 Marty Barrett .15 .06
299 Andy Hawkins .15 .06
300 Rod Carew .40 .16
301 John Montefusco .15 .06
302 Tim Corcoran .15 .06
303 Mike Jeffcoat .15 .06
304 Gary Gaetti .25 .10
305 Dale Berra .15 .06
306 Rick Reuschel .15 .06
307 Sparky Anderson MG .25 .10
308 John Wathan .15 .06
309 Mike Witt .15 .06
310 Manny Trillo .15 .06
311 Jim Gott .15 .06
312 Marc Hill .15 .06
313 Dave Schmidt .15 .06
314 Ron Oester .15 .06
315 Doug Sisk .15 .06
316 John Lowenstein .15 .06
317 Jack Lazorko .15 .06
318 Ted Simmons .25 .10
319 Jeff Jones .15 .06
320 Dale Murphy .60 .24
321 Ricky Horton .15 .06
322 Dave Stapleton .15 .06
323 Andy McGaffigan .15 .06
324 Bruce Bochy .15 .06
325 John Denny .15 .06
326 Kevin Bass .15 .06
327 Brook Jacoby .15 .06
328 Bob Shirley .15 .06
329 Ron Washington .15 .06
330 Leon Durham .15 .06
331 Bill Laskey .15 .06
332 Brian Harper .15 .06
333 Willie Hernandez .15 .06
334 Dick Howser MG .25 .10
335 Bruce Benedict .15 .06
336 Rance Mulliniks .15 .06
337 Billy Sample .15 .06
338 Britt Burns .15 .06
339 Danny Heep .15 .06
340 Robin Yount 1.00 .40
341 Floyd Rayford .15 .06
342 Ted Power .15 .06
343 Bill Russell .15 .06
344 Dave Henderson .15 .06
345 Charlie Lea .15 .06
346 Terry Pendleton RC .60 .24
347 Rick Langford .15 .06
348 Bob Boone .25 .10
349 Domingo Ramos .15 .06
350 Wade Boggs .75 .30
351 Juan Agosto .15 .06
352 Joe Morgan .40 .16
353 Julio Solano .15 .06
354 Andre Robertson .15 .06
355 Bert Blyleven .25 .10
356 Dave Meier .15 .06
357 Rich Bordi .15 .06
358 Tony Pena .15 .06
359 Pat Sheridan .15 .06
360 Steve Carlton .25 .10
361 Alfredo Griffin .15 .06
362 Craig McMurtry .15 .06
363 Ron Hodges .15 .06
364 Richard Dotson .15 .06
365 Danny Ozark MG .15 .06
366 Todd Cruz .15 .06
367 Keefe Cato .15 .06
368 Dave Bergman .15 .06
369 R.J. Reynolds .15 .06
370 Bruce Sutter .25 .10
371 Mickey Rivers .15 .06
372 Roy Howell .15 .06
373 Mike Moore .15 .06
374 Brian Downing .15 .06
375 Jeff Reardon .25 .10
376 Jeff Newman .15 .06
377 Checklist: 265-396 .15 .06
378 Alan Wiggins .15 .06
379 Charles Hudson .15 .06
380 Ken Griffey .25 .10
381 Roy Smith .15 .06
382 Denny Walling .15 .06
383 Rick Lysander .15 .06
384 Jody Davis .15 .06
385 Jose DeLeon .15 .06
386 Dan Gladden RC .25 .10
387 Buddy Biancalana .15 .06
388 Bert Roberge .15 .06
389 Rod Dedeaux OLY CO .25 .10
390 Sid Akins OLY .15 .06
391 Flavio Alfaro OLY .15 .06
392 Don August OLY .15 .06
393 S.Bankhead RC OLY .15 .06
394 Bob Caffrey OLY .15 .06
395 Mike Dunne OLY .25 .10
396 Gary Green OLY .15 .06
397 John Hoover OLY .15 .06
398 Shane Mack RC OLY .60 .24
399 John Marzano OLY .25 .10
400 O.McDowell RC OLY .25 .10
401 M.McGwire OLY RC 50.00 20.00
402 Pat Pacillo OLY .25 .10
403 Cory Snyder RC OLY .40 .16
404 Billy Swift OLY RC .40 .16
405 Tom Veryzer .15 .06
406 Len Whitehouse .15 .06
407 Bobby Ramos .15 .06
408 Sid Monge .15 .06
409 Brad Wellman .15 .06
410 Bob Horner .15 .06
411 Bobby Cox MG .15 .06
412 Bud Black .15 .06
413 Vance Law .15 .06
414 Gary Ward .15 .06
415 Ron Darling UER .25 .10
(No trivia answer)
416 Wayne Gross .15 .06
417 John Franco RC .60 .24
418 Ken Landreaux .15 .06
419 Mike Caldwell .15 .06
420 Andre Dawson .25 .10
421 Dave Rucker .15 .06
422 Carney Lansford .25 .10
423 Barry Bonnell .15 .06
424 Al Nipper .15 .06
425 Mike Hargrove .25 .10
426 Vern Ruhle .15 .06
427 Mario Ramirez .15 .06
428 Larry Andersen .15 .06
429 Rick Cerone .15 .06
430 Ron Davis .15 .06
431 U.L. Washington .15 .06
432 Thad Bosley .15 .06
433 Jim Morrison .15 .06
434 Gene Richards .15 .06
435 Dan Petry .15 .06
436 Willie Aikens .15 .06
437 Al Jones .15 .06
438 Joe Torre MG .40 .16
439 Junior Ortiz .15 .06
440 Fernando Valenzuela .25 .10
441 Duane Walker .15 .06
442 Ken Forsch .15 .06
443 George Wright .15 .06
444 Tony Phillips .15 .06
445 Tippy Martinez .15 .06
446 Jim Sundberg .15 .06
447 Jeff Lahti .15 .06
448 Derrel Thomas .15 .06
449 Phil Bradley .25 .10
450 Steve Garvey .25 .10
451 Bruce Hurst .15 .06
452 John Castino .15 .06
453 Tom Waddell .15 .06
454 Glenn Wilson .15 .06
455 Bob Knepper .15 .06
456 Tim Foli .15 .06
457 Cecilio Guante .15 .06
458 Randy Johnson .15 .06
459 Charlie Leibrandt .15 .06
460 Ryne Sandberg 1.25 .50
461 Marty Castillo .15 .06
462 Gary Lavelle .15 .06
463 Dave Collins .15 .06
464 Mike Mason RC .15 .06
465 Bobby Grich .25 .10
466 Tony LaRussa MG .40 .16
467 Ed Lynch .15 .06
468 Wayne Krenchicki .15 .06
469 Sammy Stewart .15 .06
470 Steve Sax .15 .06
471 Pete Ladd .15 .06
472 Jim Essian .15 .06
473 Tim Wallach .25 .10
474 Kurt Kepshire .15 .06
475 Andre Thornton .15 .06
476 Jeff Stone .15 .06
477 Bob Ojeda .15 .06
478 Kurt Bevacqua .15 .06
479 Mike Madden .15 .06
480 Lou Whitaker .25 .10
481 Dale Murray .15 .06
482 Harry Spilman .15 .06
483 Mike Smithson .15 .06
484 Larry Bowa .25 .10
485 Matt Young .15 .06
486 Steve Balboni .15 .06
487 Frank Williams .15 .06
488 Joel Skinner .15 .06
489 Bryan Clark .15 .06
490 Jason Thompson .15 .06
491 Rick Camp .15 .06
492 Dave Johnson MG .25 .10
493 Orel Hershiser RC .75 .30
494 Rich Dauer .15 .06
495 Mario Soto .15 .06
496 Donnie Scott .15 .06
497 Gary Pettis UER .15 .06
(Photo actually
Gary's little
brother Lynn)
498 Ed Romero .15 .06
499 Danny Cox .15 .06
500 Mike Schmidt 1.50 .60
501 Dan Schatzeder .15 .06
502 Rick Miller .15 .06
503 Tim Conroy .15 .06
504 Jerry Willard .15 .06
505 Jim Beattie .15 .06
506 Franklin Stubbs .15 .06
507 Ray Fontenot .15 .06
508 John Shelby .15 .06
509 Milt May .15 .06
510 Kent Hrbek .25 .10
511 Lee Smith .40 .16
512 Tom Brookens .15 .06
513 Lynn Jones .15 .06
514 Jeff Cornell .15 .06
515 Dave Concepcion .25 .10
516 Roy Lee Jackson .15 .06
517 Jerry Martin .15 .06

518 Chris Chambliss .25 .10
519 Doug Rader MG .15 .06
520 LaMarr Hoyt .15 .06
521 Rick Dempsey .15 .06
522 Paul Molitor .40 .16
523 Candy Maldonado .15 .06
524 Rob Wilfong .15 .06
525 Darrell Porter .15 .06
526 David Palmer .15 .06
527 Checklist: 397-528 .15 .06
528 Bill Krueger .15 .06
529 Rich Gedman .15 .06
530 Dave Dravecky .25 .10
531 Joe Lefebvre .15 .06
532 Frank DiPino .15 .06
533 Tony Bernazard .15 .06
534 Brian Dayett .15 .06
535 Pat Putnam .15 .06
536 Kirby Puckett RC 6.00 2.40
537 Don Robinson .15 .06
538 Keith Moreland .15 .06
539 Aurelio Lopez .15 .06
540 Claudell Washington .15 .06
541 Mark Davis .15 .06
542 Don Slaught .15 .06
543 Mike Squires .15 .06
544 Bruce Kison .15 .06
545 Lloyd Moseby .15 .06
546 Brent Gaff .15 .06
547 Pete Rose MG .40 .16
548 Larry Parrish .15 .06
549 Mike Scioscia .15 .06
550 Scott McGregor .15 .06
551 Andy Van Slyke .25 .10
552 Chris Codiroli .15 .06
553 Bob Clark .15 .06
554 Doug Flynn .15 .06
555 Bob Stanley .15 .06
556 Sixto Lezcano .15 .06
557 Len Barker .15 .06
558 Carmelo Martinez .15 .06
559 Jay Howell .15 .06
560 Bill Madlock .25 .10
561 Darryl Motley .15 .06
562 Houston Jimenez .15 .06
563 Dick Ruthven .15 .06
564 Alan Ashby .15 .06
565 Kirk Gibson .25 .10
566 Ed VandeBerg .15 .06
567 Joel Youngblood .15 .06
568 Cliff Johnson .15 .06
569 Ken Oberkfell .15 .06
570 Darryl Strawberry .60 .24
571 Charlie Hough .25 .10
572 Tom Paciorek .25 .10
573 Jay Tibbs .15 .06
574 Joe Altobelli MG .15 .06
575 Pedro Guerrero .25 .10
576 Jaime Cocanower .15 .06
577 Chris Speier .15 .06
578 Terry Francona .15 .06
579 Ron Romanick .15 .06
580 Dwight Evans .25 .10
581 Mark Wagner .15 .06
582 Ken Phelps .15 .06
583 Bobby Brown .15 .06
584 Kevin Gross .15 .06
585 Butch Wynegar .15 .06
586 Bill Scherrer .15 .06
587 Doug Frobel .15 .06
588 Bobby Castillo .15 .06
589 Bob Dernier .15 .06
590 Ray Knight .15 .06
591 Larry Herndon .15 .06
592 Jeff D. Robinson .15 .06
593 Rick Leach .15 .06
594 Curt Wilkerson .15 .06
595 Larry Gura .15 .06
596 Jerry Hairston .15 .06
597 Brad Lesley .15 .06
598 Jose Oquendo .15 .06
599 Storm Davis .15 .06
600 Pete Rose 1.50 .60
601 Tom Lasorda MG .40 .16
602 Jeff Dedmon .15 .06
603 Rick Manning .15 .06
604 Daryl Sconiers .15 .06
605 Ozzie Smith 1.00 .40
606 Rich Gale .15 .06
607 Bill Almon .15 .06
608 Craig Lefferts .15 .06
609 Broderick Perkins .15 .06
610 Jack Morris .25 .10
611 Ozzie Virgil .15 .06
612 Mike Armstrong .15 .06
613 Terry Puhl .15 .06
614 Al Williams .15 .06
615 Marvell Wynne .15 .06
616 Scott Sanderson .15 .06
617 Willie Wilson .15 .06
618 Pete Falcone .15 .06
619 Jeff Leonard .15 .06
620 Dwight Gooden RC 1.00 .40
621 Marvis Foley .15 .06
622 Luis Leal .15 .06
623 Greg Walker .15 .06
624 Benny Ayala .15 .06
625 Mark Langston RC .40 .16
626 German Rivera .15 .06
627 Eric Davis RC 1.00 .40
628 Rene Lachemann MG .15 .06
629 Dick Schofield .15 .06
630 Tim Raines .25 .10
631 Bob Forsch .15 .06
632 Bruce Bochte .15 .06
633 Glenn Hoffman .15 .06
634 Bill Dawley .15 .06
635 Terry Kennedy .15 .06
636 Shane Rawley .15 .06
637 Brett Butler .25 .10
638 Mike Pagliarulo .15 .06
639 Ed Hodge .15 .06
640 Steve Henderson .15 .06
641 Rod Scurry .15 .06
642 Dave Owen .15 .06
643 Johnny Grubb .15 .06
644 Mark Huismann .15 .06
645 Damaso Garcia .15 .06
646 Scot Thompson .15 .06
647 Rafael Ramirez .15 .06
648 Bob Jones .15 .06
649 Sid Fernandez .25 .10
650 Greg Luzinski .25 .10
651 Jeff Russell .15 .06
652 Joe Nolan .15 .06
653 Mark Brouhard .15 .06
654 Dave Anderson .15 .06
655 Joaquin Andujar .15 .06
656 Chuck Cottier MG .15 .06
657 Jim Slaton .15 .06
658 Mike Stenhouse .15 .06
659 Checklist: 529-660 .15 .06
660 Tony Gwynn 1.25 .50
661 Steve Crawford .15 .06
662 Mike Heath .15 .06
663 Luis Aguayo .15 .06
664 Steve Farr RC .25 .10
665 Don Mattingly 2.50 1.00
666 Mike LaCoss .15 .06
667 Dave Engle .15 .06
668 Steve Trout .15 .06
669 Lee Lacy .15 .06
670 Tom Seaver .40 .16
671 Dane Iorg .15 .06
672 Juan Berenguer .15 .06
673 Buck Martinez .15 .06
674 Atlee Hammaker .15 .06
675 Tony Perez .40 .16
676 Albert Hall .15 .06
677 Wally Backman .15 .06
678 Joey McLaughlin .15 .06
679 Bob Kearney .15 .06
680 Jerry Reuss .15 .06
681 Ben Oglivie .15 .06
682 Doug Corbett .15 .06
683 Whitey Herzog MG .25 .10
684 Bill Doran .15 .06
685 Bill Caudill .15 .06
686 Mike Easler .15 .06
687 Bill Gullickson .15 .06
688 Len Matuszek .15 .06
689 Luis DeLeon .15 .06
690 Alan Trammell .40 .16
691 Dennis Rasmussen .15 .06
692 Randy Bush .15 .06
693 Tim Stoddard .15 .06
694 Joe Carter .60 .24
695 Rick Rhoden .15 .06
696 John Rabb .15 .06
697 Onix Concepcion .15 .06
698 Jorge Bell .25 .10
699 Donnie Moore .15 .06
700 Eddie Murray .60 .24
701 Eddie Murray AS .40 .16
702 Damaso Garcia AS .15 .06
703 George Brett AS .60 .24
704 Cal Ripken AS 1.50 .60
705 Dave Winfield AS .15 .06
706 Rickey Henderson AS .40 .16
707 Tony Armas AS .15 .06
708 Lance Parrish AS .15 .06
709 Mike Boddicker AS .15 .06
710 Frank Viola AS .15 .06
711 Dan Quisenberry AS .15 .06
712 Keith Hernandez AS .25 .10
713 Ryne Sandberg AS .60 .24
714 Mike Schmidt AS .60 .24
715 Ozzie Smith AS .60 .24
716 Dale Murphy AS .40 .16
717 Tony Gwynn AS 1.00 .40
718 Jeff Leonard AS .15 .06
719 Gary Carter AS .25 .10
720 Rick Sutcliffe AS .15 .06
721 Bob Knepper AS .15 .06
722 Bruce Sutter AS .15 .06
723 Dave Stewart .25 .10
724 Oscar Gamble .15 .06
725 Floyd Bannister .15 .06
726 Al Bumbry .15 .06
727 Frank Pastore .15 .06
728 Bob Bailor .15 .06
729 Don Sutton .60 .24
730 Dave Kingman .25 .10
731 Neil Allen .15 .06
732 John McNamara MG .15 .06
733 Tony Scott .15 .06
734 John Henry Johnson .15 .06
735 Garry Templeton .15 .06
736 Jerry Mumphrey .15 .06
737 Bo Diaz .15 .06
738 Omar Moreno .15 .06
739 Ernie Camacho .15 .06
740 Jack Clark .25 .10
741 John Butcher .15 .06
742 Ron Hassey .15 .06
743 Frank White .25 .10
744 Doug Bair .15 .06
745 Buddy Bell .25 .10
746 Jim Clancy .15 .06
747 Alex Trevino .15 .06
748 Lee Mazzilli .15 .06
749 Julio Cruz .15 .06
750 Rollie Fingers .25 .10
751 Kelvin Chapman .15 .06
752 Bob Owchinko .15 .06
753 Greg Brock .15 .06
754 Larry Milbourne .15 .06
755 Ken Singleton .15 .06
756 Rob Picciolo .15 .06
757 Willie McGee .25 .10
758 Ray Burris .15 .06
759 Jim Fanning MG .15 .06
760 Nolan Ryan 3.00 1.20
761 Jerry Remy .15 .06
762 Eddie Whitson .15 .06
763 Kiko Garcia .15 .06
764 Jamie Easterly .15 .06
765 Willie Randolph .25 .10
766 Paul Mirabella .15 .06
767 Darrell Brown .15 .06
768 Ron Cey .25 .10
769 Joe Cowley .15 .06
770 Carlton Fisk .40 .16
771 Geoff Zahn .15 .06
772 Johnnie LeMaster .15 .06
773 Hal McRae .25 .10
774 Dennis Lamp .15 .06
775 Mookie Wilson .25 .10
776 Jerry Royster .15 .06
777 Ned Yost .15 .06
778 Mike Davis .15 .06
779 Nick Esasky .15 .06
780 Mike Flanagan .15 .06
781 Jim Gantner .15 .06
782 Tom Niedenfuer .15 .06
783 Mike Jorgensen .15 .06
784 Checklist: 661-792 .15 .06
785 Tony Armas .15 .06
786 Enos Cabell .15 .06
787 Jim Wohlford .15 .06
788 Steve Comer .15 .06
789 Luis Salazar .15 .06
790 Ron Guidry .25 .10
791 Ivan DeJesus .15 .06
792 Darrell Evans .25 .10

1985 Topps Tiffany

For the second year, Topps issued a special glossy set through their hobby dealers. This set is a direct parallel to the regular Topps issue. These 792 cards are differentiated from the regular issue by their glossy fronts and very clear backs. These sets were only available through Topps' hobby dealers. According to original reports in 1985, only 5,000 of these sets were produced.

Nm-Mt Ex-Mt
COMP.FACT.SET (792) 600.00 240.00
*STARS: 3X TO 8X BASIC CARDS
*ROOKIES: 2.5X TO 6X BASIC CARDS

1985 Topps Glossy All-Stars

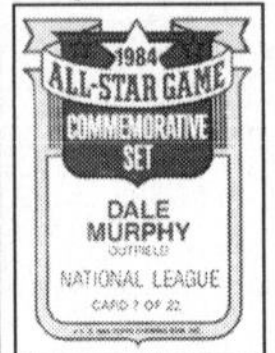

The cards in this 22-card set the standard size. Similar in design, both front and back, to last year's Glossy set, this edition features the managers, starting nine players and honorary captains of the National and American League teams in the 1984 All-Star game. The set is numbered on the reverse with players essentially ordered by position within league, NL: 1-11 and AL: 12-22.

Nm-Mt Ex-Mt
COMPLETE SET (22) 5.00 2.00
1 Paul Owens MG .05 .02
2 Steve Garvey .15 .06
3 Ryne Sandberg 1.00 .40
4 Mike Schmidt .75 .30
5 Ozzie Smith 1.00 .40
6 Tony Gwynn 1.25 .50
7 Dale Murphy .20 .08
8 Darryl Strawberry .10 .04
9 Gary Carter .50 .20
10 Charlie Lea .05 .02
11 Willie McCovey CAPT .10 .04
12 Joe Altobelli MG .05 .02
13 Rod Carew .50 .20
14 Lou Whitaker .10 .04
15 George Brett 1.00 .40
16 Cal Ripken 2.00 .80
17 Dave Winfield .50 .20
18 Chet Lemon .05 .02
19 Reggie Jackson .50 .20
20 Lance Parrish .05 .02
21 Dave Stieb .05 .02
22 Hank Greenberg CAPT .10 .04

1985 Topps Glossy Send-Ins

The cards in this 40-card set measure the standard size. Similar to last year's glossy set, this set was issued as a bonus prize to Topps All-Star Baseball Game cards found in wax packs. The set could be obtained by sending in the "Bonus Runs" from the "Winning Pitch" game insert cards. For 25 runs and 75 cents, a collector could send in for one of the eight different five card series plus automatically be entered in the Grand Prize Sweepstakes for a chance at a free trip to the All-Star game. The cards are numbered and contain 20 stars from each league.

Nm-Mt Ex-Mt
COMPLETE SET (40) 10.00 4.00
1 Dale Murphy .30 .12
2 Jesse Orosco .20 .08
3 Bob Brenly .20 .08
4 Mike Boddicker .10 .04
5 Dave Kingman .20 .08
6 Jim Rice .20 .08
7 Frank Viola .20 .08
8 Alvin Davis .10 .04
9 Rick Sutcliffe .10 .04
10 Pete Rose 1.25 .50
11 Leon Durham .10 .04
12 Joaquin Andujar .10 .04
13 Keith Hernandez .20 .08
14 Dave Winfield .75 .30
15 Reggie Jackson .75 .30
16 Alan Trammell .30 .12
17 Bert Blyleven .20 .08
18 Tony Armas .10 .04
19 Rich Gossage .20 .08
20 Jose Cruz .20 .08
21 Ryne Sandberg 2.00 .80
22 Bruce Sutter .20 .08
23 Mike Schmidt 1.25 .50
24 Cal Ripken 5.00 2.00
25 Dan Petry .10 .04
26 Jack Morris .20 .08
27 Don Mattingly 2.50 1.00
28 Eddie Murray 1.00 .40
29 Tony Gwynn 2.50 1.00
30 Charlie Lea .10 .04
31 Juan Samuel .10 .04
32 Phil Niekro .75 .30
33 Alejandro Pena .10 .04
34 Harold Baines .20 .08
35 Dan Quisenberry .10 .04
36 Gary Carter .75 .30
37 Mario Soto .10 .04
38 Dwight Gooden .50 .20
39 Tom Brunansky .10 .04
40 Dave Stieb .10 .04

1985 Topps Traded

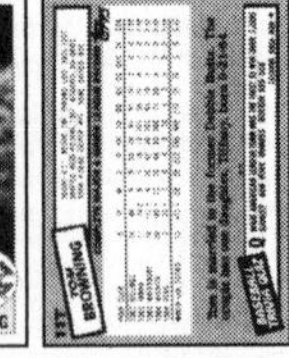

In its now standard procedure, Topps issued its standard-size Traded (or extended) set for the fifth year in a row. In addition to the typical factory set hobby distribution, Topps tested the limited issuance of these Traded cards in wax packs. Card design is identical to the regular-issue 1985 Topps set except for whiter card stock and T-suffixed numbering on back. The set numbering is in alphabetical order by player's name. The key extended Rookie Cards in this set include Vince Coleman, Ozzie Guillen, and Mickey Tettleton.

Nm-Mt Ex-Mt
COMP.FACT.SET (132) 6.00 2.40
1T Don Aase .15 .06
2T Bill Almon .15 .06
3T Benny Ayala .15 .06
4T Dusty Baker .40 .16
5T George Bamberger MG .15 .06
6T Dale Berra .15 .06
7T Rich Bordi .15 .06
8T Daryl Boston XRC* .15 .06
9T Hubie Brooks .15 .06
10T Chris Brown .15 .06
11T Tom Browning XRC* .40 .16
12T Al Bumbry .15 .06
13T Ray Burris .15 .06
14T Jeff Burroughs .15 .06
15T Bill Campbell .15 .06
16T Don Carman .15 .06
17T Gary Carter .75 .30
18T Bobby Castillo .15 .06
19T Bill Caudill .15 .06
20T Rick Cerone .15 .06
21T Bryan Clark .15 .06
22T Jack Clark .40 .16
23T Pat Clements .15 .06
24T Vince Coleman XRC 1.00 .40
25T Dave Collins .15 .06
26T Danny Darwin .15 .06
27T Jim Davenport MG .15 .06
28T Jerry Davis .15 .06
29T Brian Dayett .15 .06
30T Ivan DeJesus .15 .06
31T Ken Dixon .15 .06
32T Mariano Duncan XRC 1.00 .40
33T John Felske MG .15 .06
34T Mike Fitzgerald .15 .06
35T Ray Fontenot .15 .06
36T Greg Gagne XRC* .40 .16
37T Oscar Gamble .15 .06
38T Scott Garrelts .15 .06
39T Bob L. Gibson .15 .06
40T Jim Gott .15 .06
41T David Green .15 .06
42T Alfredo Griffin .15 .06
43T Ozzie Guillen XRC .75 .30
44T Eddie Haas MG .15 .06
45T Terry Harper .15 .06
46T Toby Harrah .15 .06
47T Greg Harris .15 .06
48T Ron Hassey .15 .06
49T Rickey Henderson 2.50 1.00
50T Steve Henderson .15 .06
51T George Hendrick .15 .06
52T Joe Hesketh .15 .06
53T Teddy Higuera XRC .40 .16
54T Donnie Hill .15 .06
55T Al Holland .15 .06
56T Burt Hooton .15 .06
57T Jay Howell .15 .06
58T Ken Howell .15 .06
59T LaMarr Hoyt .15 .06
60T Tim Hulett XRC* .15 .06
61T Bob James .15 .06
62T Steve Jeltz .15 .06
63T Cliff Johnson .15 .06
64T Howard Johnson .40 .16
65T Ruppert Jones .15 .06
66T Steve Kemp .15 .06
67T Bruce Kison .15 .06
68T Alan Knicely .15 .06
69T Mike LaCoss .15 .06
70T Lee Lacy .15 .06
71T Dave LaPoint .15 .06
72T Gary Lavelle .15 .06
73T Vance Law .15 .06
74T Johnnie LeMaster .15 .06
75T Sixto Lezcano .15 .06
76T Tim Lollar .15 .06
77T Fred Lynn .40 .16
78T Billy Martin MG .40 .16
79T Ron Mathis .15 .06
80T Len Matuszek .15 .06
81T Gene Mauch MG .40 .16
82T Oddibe McDowell .40 .16
83T Roger McDowell XRC .40 .16
84T John McNamara MG .15 .06
85T Donnie Moore .15
86T Gene Nelson .15
87T Steve Nicosia .15
88T Al Oliver .40
89T Joe Orsulak XRC .40
90T Rob Picciolo .15
91T Chris Pittaro .15
92T Jim Presley .40
93T Rick Reuschel .15
94T Bert Roberge .15
95T Bob Rodgers MG .15
96T Jerry Royster .15
97T Dave Rozema .15
98T Dave Rucker .15
99T Vern Ruhle .15
100T Paul Runge XRC .15
101T Mark Salas .15
102T Luis Salazar .15
103T Joe Sambito .15
104T Rick Schu .15
105T Donnie Scott .15
106T Larry Sheets .15
107T Don Slaught .15
108T Roy Smalley .15
109T Lonnie Smith .15
110T Nate Snell UER .15
(Headings on back for a batter)
111T Chris Speier .15
112T Mike Stenhouse .15
113T Tim Stoddard .15
114T Jim Sundberg .15
115T Bruce Sutter .40
116T Don Sutton 1.00
117T Kent Tekulve .15
118T Tom Tellmann .15
119T Walt Terrell .15
120T M.Tettleton XRC .75
121T Derrel Thomas .15
122T Rich Thompson .15
123T Alex Trevino .15
124T John Tudor .15
125T Jose Uribe .15
126T Bobby Valentine MG .15
127T Dave Von Ohlen .15
128T U.L. Washington .15
129T Earl Weaver MG .75
130T Eddie Whitson .15
131T Herm Winningham .15
132T Checklist 1-132 .15

1985 Topps Traded Tiffany

Just as in 1984, Topps issued an glossy upda set. The 132-card standard-size set is a paral to the Topps update issue. These sets we issued to the hobby through Topps deal network and were printed in Ireland. Again similar to the regular Tiffany issue -- it believed that 5,000 of these sets we produced.

Nm-Mt Ex-M
COMP.FACT.SET (132) 50.00 20.0
*STARS: 1.5X TO 4X BASIC CARDS
*ROOKIES: 1.5X TO 4X BASIC CARDS

1985 Topps 3-D

This innovative 30-card set was issued in pac of one. These large cards are very difficult store (due to the 3-D effect) as they are n really stackable and are crumpled if placed an album using plastic sheets. The cards a blank-backed except for two covered adhesi strips and measure approximately 4 1/4" by 7/8". Cards are numbered on the front a feature a prominent team logo on the front well.

Nm-Mt
COMPLETE SET (30) 12.00
1 Mike Schmidt 1.00
2 Eddie Murray 1.00
3 Dale Murphy .30
4 George Brett 2.00
5 Pete Rose 1.00
6 Jim Rice .20
7 Ryne Sandberg 1.50
8 Don Mattingly 2.00
9 Darryl Strawberry .20
10 Rickey Henderson .75
11 Keith Hernandez .20
12 Dave Kingman .10
13 Tony Gwynn 2.00
14 Reggie Jackson .75
15 Gary Carter .75
16 Cal Ripken 4.00 1.6
17 Tim Raines .20
18 Dave Winfield .75
19 Dwight Gooden .50
20 Dave Stieb .10
21 Fernando Valenzuela .20
22 Mark Langston .10
23 Bruce Sutter .20
24 Dan Quisenberry .10
25 Steve Carlton .75
26 Mike Boddicker .10
27 Rich Gossage .20
28 Jack Morris .20
29 Rick Sutcliffe .10
30 Tom Seaver 1.00

1985 Topps Gallery of Champions

This would be the second year that Top issued a 12-card set featuring baseball sta These "cards" were made of either silver bronze and measure approximately 1 1/4" by

3/4". Since the cards are replicas of the 1985 Topps cards and would be skip-numbered, we have sequenced these cards in alphabetical order. This would be the last year that no aluminum cards were produced. The silver cards are valued at 2.5X the bronze versions.

	Nm-Mt	Ex-Mt
COMPLETE SET (12)	350.00	140.00
1 Tony Armas	10.00	4.00
2 Alvin Davis	10.00	4.00
3 Dwight Gooden	30.00	12.00
4 Tony Gwynn	60.00	24.00
5 Willie Hernandez	10.00	4.00
6 Don Matttingly	60.00	24.00
7 Dale Murphy	40.00	16.00
8 Dan Quisenberry	10.00	4.00
9 Ryne Sandberg	60.00	24.00
10 Mike Schmidt	40.00	16.00
11 Rick Sutcliffe	10.00	4.00
12 Bruce Sutter	10.00	4.00

1985 Topps Stickers

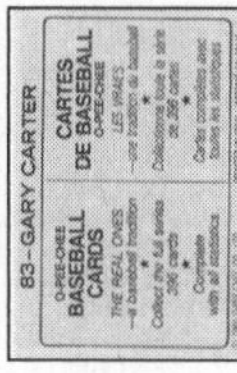

Made in Italy for Topps and O-Pee-Chee by Panini, these 376 stickers measure approximately 2 1/8" by 3" and are numbered on both front and back. Some stickers are player cutouts. The fronts feature white-bordered color player photos. The horizontal backs carry a bilingual ad for O-Pee-Chee in blue lettering. An album onto which the stickers could be affixed was available at retail stores. The album and the sticker numbering are organized as follows: 1984 Record Breakers (1-8), 1984 Championship Series (9-14), 1984 World Series (15-21), Atlanta Braves (22-33), Chicago Cubs (34-45), Cincinnati Reds (46-57), Houston Astros (58-69), Los Angeles Dodgers (70-81), Montreal Expos (82-93), 1984 Stat Leaders (94-97), New York Mets (98-109), Philadelphia Phillies (110-121), Pittsburgh Pirates (122-133), St. Louis Cardinals (134-145), San Diego Padres (146-157), San Francisco Giants (158-169), 1984 Stat Leaders (170-173), Foil All-Stars (174-191), 1984 Stat Leaders (192-195), Baltimore Orioles (196-207), Boston Red Sox (208-219), California Angels (220-231), Chicago White Sox (232-243), Cleveland Indians (244-255), Detroit Tigers (256-267), Kansas City Royals (268-279), 1984 Stat Leaders (280-283), Milwaukee Brewers (284-295), Minnesota Twins (296-307), New York Yankees (308-319), Oakland A's (320-331), Seattle Mariners (332-343), Texas Rangers (344-355), Toronto Blue Jays (356-367) and Future Stars (368-376). For those stickers featuring more than one player, the other numbers on that sticker are given below in parentheses. Kirby Puckett, Mark Langston and Dwight Gooden are featured in their Rookie Card year.

	Nm-Mt	Ex-Mt
COMPLETE SET (376)	15.00	6.00
COMMON STICKERS (1-376)	.05	.02
COMMON FOIL	.10	.04
*TOPPS AND OPC SAME VALUE		
1 Steve Garvey FOIL (Top half)	.15	.06
2 Steve Garvey FOIL (Bottom half)	.15	.06
3 Dwight Gooden (Top half)	.50	.20
4 Dwight Gooden (Bottom half)	.50	.20
5 Joe Morgan (Top half)	.10	.04
6 Joe Morgan (Bottom half)	.10	.04
7 Don Sutton (Top half)	.10	.04
8 Don Sutton (Bottom half)	.10	.04
9 AL Championships (Jack Morris)	.10	.04
10 AL Championships (Milt Wilcox)	.05	.02
11 AL Championships (Kirk Gibson)	.10	.04
12 NL Championships (Cubs at plate)	.05	.02
13 NL Championships (Steve Garvey swings)	.10	.04
14 NL Championships (Steve Garvey)	.10	.04
15 World Series (Jack Morris)	.10	.04
16 World Series (Kurt Bevacqua)	.05	.02
17 World Series (Milt Wilcox)	.05	.02
18 World Series (Alan Trammell ready to throw)	.10	.04
19 World Series (Kirk Gibson)	.10	.04
20 World Series (Alan Trammell)	.10	.04
21 World Series (Chet Lemon back)	.05	.02
22 Dale Murphy	.15	.06
23 Steve Bedrosian	.05	.02
24 Bob Horner	.05	.02
25 Claudell Washington	.05	.02
26 Rick Mahler (212)	.05	.02
27 Rafael Ramirez (213)	.05	.02
28 Craig McMurtry (214)	.05	.02
29 Chris Chambliss(215)	.10	.04
30 Alex Trevino (216)	.05	.02
31 Bruce Benedict (217)	.05	.02
32 Ken Oberkfell (218)	.05	.02
33 Glenn Hubbard (219)	.05	.02
34 Ryne Sandberg	1.25	.50
35 Rick Sutcliffe	.05	.02
36 Leon Durham	.05	.02
37 Jody Davis	.05	.02
38 Bob Dernier (224)	.05	.02
39 Keith Moreland(225)	.05	.02
40 Scott Sanderson(226)	.05	.02
41 Lee Smith (227)	.25	.10
42 Ron Cey (228)	.10	.04
43 Steve Trout (229)	.05	.02
44 Gary Matthews(230)	.05	.02
45 Larry Bowa (231)	.10	.04
46 Mario Soto	.05	.02
47 Dave Parker	.10	.04
48 Dave Concepcion	.10	.04
49 Gary Redus	.05	.02
50 Ted Power (236)	.05	.02
51 Nick Esasky (237)	.05	.02
52 Duane Walker (238)	.05	.02
53 Eddie Milner (239)	.05	.02
54 Ron Oester (240)	.05	.02
55 Cesar Cedeno (241)	.10	.04
56 Joe Price (242)	.05	.02
57 Pete Rose (243)	.75	.30
58 Nolan Ryan	2.50	1.00
59 Jose Cruz	.10	.04
60 Jerry Mumphrey	.05	.02
61 Enos Cabell	.05	.02
62 Bob Knepper (248)	.05	.02
63 Dickie Thon (249)	.05	.02
64 Phil Garner (250)	.10	.04
65 Craig Reynolds (251)	.05	.02
66 Frank DiPino (252)	.05	.02
67 Terry Puhl (253)	.05	.02
68 Bill Doran (254)	.05	.02
69 Joe Niekro (255)	.05	.02
70 Pedro Guerrero	.10	.04
71 Fernando Valenzuela	.10	.04
72 Mike Marshall	.05	.02
73 Alejandro Pena	.05	.02
74 Orel Hershiser(260)	.75	.30
75 Ken Landreaux (261)	.05	.02
76 Bill Russell (262)	.10	.04
77 Steve Sax (263)	.10	.04
78 Rick Honeycutt(264)	.05	.02
79 Mike Scioscia (265)	.10	.04
80 Tom Niedenfuer(266)	.05	.02
81 Candy Maldonado(267)	.05	.02
82 Tim Raines	.10	.04
83 Gary Carter	.15	.06
84 Charlie Lea	.05	.02
85 Jeff Reardon	.10	.04
86 Andre Dawson (272)	.15	.06
87 Tim Wallach (273)	.10	.04
88 Terry Francona (274)	.10	.04
89 Steve Rogers (275)	.05	.02
90 Bryn Smith (276)	.05	.02
91 Bill Gullickson(277)	.05	.02
92 Dan Driessen (278)	.05	.02
93 Doug Flynn (279)	.05	.02
94 Mike Schmidt (170/192/280)	.60	.24
95 Tony Armas (171/193/281)	.05	.02
96 Dale Murphy (172/194/282)	.15	.06
97 Rick Sutcliffe (173/195/283)	.05	.02
98 Keith Hernandez	.10	.04
99 George Foster	.10	.04
100 Darryl Strawberry	.05	.02
101 Jesse Orosco	.05	.02
102 Mookie Wilson (288)	.10	.04
103 Doug Sisk (289)	.05	.02
104 Hubie Brooks (290)	.05	.02
105 Ron Darling (291)	.10	.04
106 Wally Backman (292)	.05	.02
107 Dwight Gooden (293)	.75	.30
108 Mike Fitzgerald(294)	.05	.02
109 Walt Terrell (295)	.05	.02
110 Ozzie Virgil	.05	.02
111 Mike Schmidt	.60	.24
112 Steve Carlton	.40	.16
113 Al Holland	.05	.02
114 Juan Samuel (300)	.05	.02
115 Von Hayes (301)	.05	.02
116 Jeff Stone (302)	.05	.02
117 Jerry Koosman (303)	.10	.04
118 Al Oliver (304)	.10	.04
119 John Denny (305)	.05	.02
120 Charles Hudson (306)	.05	.02
121 Garry Maddox (307)	.05	.02
122 Bill Madlock	.10	.04
123 John Candelaria	.05	.02
124 Tony Pena	.05	.02
125 Jason Thompson	.05	.02
126 Lee Lacy (312)	.05	.02
127 Rick Rhoden (313)	.05	.02
128 Doug Frobel (314)	.05	.02
129 Kent Tekulve (315)	.05	.02
130 Johnny Ray (316)	.05	.02
131 Marvell Wynne (317)	.05	.02
132 Larry McWilliams (318)	.05	.02
133 Dale Berra (319)	.05	.02
134 George Hendrick	.05	.02
135 Bruce Sutter	.10	.04
136 Joaquin Andujar	.05	.02
137 Ozzie Smith	.40	.16
138 Andy Van Slyke (324)	.15	.06
139 Lonnie Smith (325)	.05	.02
140 Darrell Porter (326)	.05	.02
141 Willie McGee (327)	.10	.04
142 Tom Herr (328)	.10	.04
143 Dave LaPoint (329)	.05	.02
144 Neil Allen (330)	.05	.02
145 David Green (331)	.05	.02
146 Tony Gwynn	2.00	.80
147 Rich Gossage	.10	.04
148 Terry Kennedy	.05	.02
149 Steve Garvey	.15	.06
150 Alan Wiggins (336)	.05	.02
151 Garry Templeton(337)	.05	.02
152 Ed Whitson (338)	.05	.02
153 Tim Lollar (339)	.05	.02
154 Dave Dravecky (340)	.10	.04
155 Graig Nettles (341)	.10	.04
156 Eric Show (342)	.05	.02
157 Carmelo Martinez (343)	.05	.02
158 Bob Brenly	.05	.02
159 Gary Lavelle	.05	.02
160 Jack Clark	.10	.04
161 Jeff Leonard	.05	.02
162 Chili Davis (348)	.10	.04
163 Mike Krukow (349)	.05	.02
164 Johnnie LeMaster (350)	.05	.02
165 Atlee Hammaker (351)	.05	.02
166 Dan Gladden (352)	.05	.02
167 Greg Minton (353)	.05	.02
168 Joel Youngblood(354)	.05	.02
169 Frank Williams (355)	.05	.02
170 Tony Gwynn (94/192/280)	1.50	.60
171 Don Mattingly (95/193/281)	2.00	.80
172 Bruce Sutter (96/194/282)	.10	.04
173 Dan Quisenberry (97/195/283)	.05	.02
174 Tony Gwynn FOIL	2.50	1.00
175 Ryne Sandberg FOIL	1.50	.60
176 Steve Garvey FOIL	.25	.10
177 Dale Murphy FOIL	.25	.10
178 Mike Schmidt FOIL		
179 Darryl Strawberry FOIL	.50	.20
180 Gary Carter FOIL	.25	.10
181 Ozzie Smith FOIL	.60	.24
182 Charlie Lea FOIL	.10	.04
183 Lou Whitaker FOIL	.15	.06
184 Rod Carew FOIL	.60	.24
185 Cal Ripken FOIL	3.00	1.20
186 Dave Winfield FOIL	.50	.20
187 Reggie Jackson FOIL	.75	.30
188 George Brett FOIL	1.25	.50
189 Lance Parrish FOIL	.15	.06
190 Chet Lemon FOIL	.10	.04
191 Dave Stieb FOIL	.10	.04
192 Gary Carter (94/170/280)	.10	.04
193 Mike Schmidt (95/171/281)	.60	.24
194 Tony Armas (96/172/282)	.05	.02
195 Mike Witt (97/173/283)	.05	.02
196 Eddie Murray	.40	.16
197 Cal Ripken	2.50	1.00
198 Scott McGregor	.05	.02
199 Rick Dempsey	.05	.02
200 Tippy Martinez (360)	.05	.02
201 Ken Singleton (361)	.05	.02
202 Mike Boddicker (362)	.05	.02
203 Rich Dauer (363)	.05	.02
204 John Shelby (364)	.05	.02
205 Al Bumbry (365)	.05	.02
206 John Lowenstein(366)	.05	.02
207 Mike Flanagan (367)	.05	.02
208 Jim Rice	.10	.04
209 Tony Armas	.05	.02
210 Wade Boggs	.50	.20
211 Bruce Hurst	.05	.02
212 Dwight Evans (26)	.10	.04
213 Mike Easler (27)	.05	.02
214 Bill Buckner (28)	.10	.04
215 Bob Stanley (29)	.05	.02
216 Jackie Gutierrez(30)	.05	.02
217 Rich Gedman (31)	.05	.02
218 Jerry Remy (32)	.05	.02
219 Marty Barrett (33)	.05	.02
220 Reggie Jackson	.50	.20
221 Geoff Zahn	.05	.02
222 Doug DeCinces	.05	.02
223 Rod Carew	.40	.16
224 Brian Downing (38)	.10	.04
225 Fred Lynn (39)	.10	.04
226 Gary Pettis (40)	.05	.02
227 Mike Witt (41)	.05	.02
228 Bob Boone (42)	.10	.04
229 Tommy John (43)	.15	.06
230 Bobby Grich (44)	.10	.04
231 Ron Romanick (45)	.05	.02
232 Ron Kittle	.05	.02
233 Richard Dotson	.05	.02
234 Harold Baines	.10	.04
235 Tom Seaver	.50	.20
236 Greg Walker (50)	.05	.02
237 Roy Smalley (51)	.05	.02
238 Greg Luzinski (52)	.10	.04
239 Julio Cruz (53)	.05	.02
240 Scott Fletcher (54)	.05	.02
241 Rudy Law (55)	.05	.02
242 Vance Law (56)	.05	.02
243 Carlton Fisk (57)	.25	.10
244 Andre Thornton	.05	.02
245 Julio Franco	.10	.04
246 Brett Butler	.10	.04
247 Bert Blyleven	.10	.04
248 Mike Hargrove (62)	.10	.04
249 George Vukovich(63)	.05	.02
250 Pat Tabler (64)	.05	.02
251 Brook Jacoby (65)	.05	.02
252 Tony Bernazard (66)	.05	.02
253 Ernie Camacho (67)	.05	.02
254 Mel Hall (68)	.05	.02
255 Carmen Castillo (69)	.05	.02
256 Jack Morris	.10	.04
257 Willie Hernandez	.05	.02
258 Alan Trammell	.15	.06
259 Lance Parrish	.10	.04
260 Chet Lemon (74)	.05	.02
261 Lou Whitaker (75)	.15	.06
262 Howard Johnson (76)	.10	.04
263 Barbaro Garbey (77)	.05	.02
264 Dan Petry (78)	.05	.02
265 Aurelio Lopez (79)	.05	.02
266 Larry Herndon (80)	.05	.02
267 Kirk Gibson (81)	.10	.04
268 George Brett	.75	.30
269 Dan Quisenberry	.05	.02
270 Hal McRae	.10	.04
271 Steve Balboni	.05	.02
272 Pat Sheridan (86)	.05	.02
273 Jorge Orta (87)	.05	.02
274 Frank White (88)	.10	.04
275 Bud Black (89)	.05	.02
276 Darryl Motley (90)	.05	.02
277 Willie Wilson (91)	.10	.04
278 Larry Gura (92)	.05	.02
279 Don Slaught (93)	.05	.02
280 Dwight Gooden (94/170/192)	1.50	.60
281 Mark Langston (95/171/193)	.25	.10
282 Tim Raines (96/172/194)	.10	.04
283 Rickey Henderson (97/173/195/283)	.25	.10
284 Robin Yount	.25	.10
285 Rollie Fingers	.25	.10
286 Jim Sundberg	.05	.02
287 Cecil Cooper	.10	.04
288 Jamie Cocanower(102)	.05	.02
289 Mike Caldwell (103)	.05	.02
290 Don Sutton (104)	.25	.10
291 Rick Manning (105)	.05	.02
292 Ben Oglivie (106)	.05	.02
293 Moose Haas (107)	.05	.02
294 Ted Simmons (108)	.10	.04
295 Jim Gantner (109)	.05	.02
296 Kent Hrbek	.10	.04
297 Ron Davis	.05	.02
298 Dave Engle	.05	.02
299 Tom Brunansky	.10	.04
300 Frank Viola (114)	.10	.04
301 Mike Smithson (115)	.05	.02
302 Gary Gaetti (116)	.10	.04
303 Tim Teufel (117)	.05	.02
304 Mickey Hatcher(118)	.05	.02
305 John Butcher (119)	.05	.02
306 Darrell Brown (120)	.05	.02
307 Kirby Puckett (121)	5.00	2.00
308 Dave Winfield	.25	.10
309 Phil Niekro	.25	.10
310 Don Mattingly	2.00	.80
311 Don Baylor	.10	.04
312 Willie Randolph(126)	.10	.04
313 Ron Guidry (127)	.10	.04
314 Dave Righetti (128)	.10	.04
315 Bobby Meacham (129)	.05	.02
316 Butch Wynegar (130)	.05	.02
317 Mike Pagliarulo(131)	.05	.02
318 Joe Cowley (132)	.05	.02
319 John Montefusco(133)	.05	.02
320 Dave Kingman	.10	.04
321 Rickey Henderson	.50	.20
322 Bill Caudill	.05	.02
323 Dwayne Murphy	.05	.02
324 Steve McCatty (138)	.05	.02
325 Joe Morgan (139)	.25	.10
326 Mike Heath (140)	.05	.02
327 Chris Codiroli (141)	.05	.02
328 Ray Burris (142)	.05	.02
329 Tony Phillips (143)	.05	.02
330 Carney Lansford(144)	.10	.04
331 Bruce Bochte (145)	.05	.02
332 Alvin Davis	.10	.04
333 Al Cowens	.05	.02
334 Jim Beattie	.05	.02
335 Bob Kearney	.05	.02
336 Ed VandeBerg (150)	.05	.02
337 Mark Langston (151)	.25	.10
338 Dave Henderson (152)	.10	.04
339 Spike Owen (153)	.05	.02
340 Matt Young (154)	.05	.02
341 Jack Perconte (155)	.05	.02
342 Barry Bonnell (156)	.05	.02
343 Mike Stanton (157)	.05	.02
344 Pete O'Brien	.05	.02
345 Charlie Hough	.10	.04
346 Larry Parrish	.05	.02
347 Buddy Bell	.10	.04
348 Frank Tanana (162)	.05	.02
349 Curt Wilkerson (163)	.05	.02
350 Jeff Kunkel (164)	.05	.02
351 Billy Sample (165)	.05	.02
352 Danny Darwin (166)	.05	.02
353 Gary Ward (167)	.05	.02
354 Mike Mason (168)	.05	.02
355 Mickey Rivers (169)	.05	.02
356 Dave Stieb	.05	.02
357 Damaso Garcia	.05	.02
358 Willie Upshaw	.05	.02
359 Lloyd Moseby	.05	.02
360 George Bell (200)	.10	.04
361 Luis Leal (201)	.05	.02
362 Jesse Barfield (202)	.05	.02
363 Dave Collins (203)	.05	.02
364 Roy Lee Jackson(204)	.05	.02
365 Doyle Alexander(205)	.05	.02
366 Alfredo Griffin(206)	.05	.02
367 Cliff Johnson (207)	.05	.02
368 Alvin Davis	.10	.04
369 Juan Samuel	.05	.02
370 Brook Jacoby	.05	.02
371 Mark Langston and Dwight Gooden	.25	.10
372 Mike Fitzgerald	.05	.02
373 Jackie Gutierrez	.05	.02
374 Dan Gladden	.05	.02
375 Carmelo Martinez	.05	.02
376 Kirby Puckett	5.00	2.00
NNO Album	1.00	.40

1985 Topps/OPC Minis

This test issue looks exactly like the 1985 Topps standard-size counterparts, but measures a slightly smaller 2 3/8" by 3 9/32" and are printed on white OPC-like card stock. These cards were produced in extremely limited quantities and probably were supposed to be destroyed. Only one of the six 132-card sheets were produced in this fashion, thus none of the key Rookie Cards exist in mini form. It is estimated that 100 or less of each card exists. Approximately 2/3 of the cards were printed with the complete backs while the others are blank backed. Values for the blank back cards are from the same value to 1.5 times the prices listed below. Card numbering matches the 1985 Topps issues; therefore we have listed the cards in skip numbered fashion below.

	Nm-Mt	Ex-Mt
COMPLETE SET (132)	2000.00	800.00
12 Davey Lopes	20.00	8.00
15 Jerry Koosman	20.00	8.00
17 Mike Scott	20.00	8.00
25 Steve Bedrosian	10.00	4.00
44 Dickie Thon	10.00	4.00
65 Bill Buckner	20.00	8.00
68 Von Hayes	10.00	4.00
72 Rick Sutcliffe	20.00	8.00
75 Willie Upshaw	10.00	4.00
82 Joe Price	10.00	4.00
88 Bryn Smith	10.00	4.00
91 Jeff Burroughs	20.00	8.00
95 Jose Cruz	20.00	8.00
96 Johnny Ray	10.00	4.00
109 Gary Roenicke	10.00	4.00
113 Tom Herr	10.00	4.00
114 Bob James	10.00	4.00
117 Greg Gross	10.00	4.00
120 Steve Kemp	10.00	4.00
121 Checklist	10.00	4.00
128 Ernie Whitt	10.00	4.00
148 Steve Yeager	10.00	4.00
150 Jim Rice	40.00	16.00
151 Moose Haas	10.00	4.00
154 Angel Salazar	10.00	4.00
156 Craig Reynolds	10.00	4.00
160 Lance Parrish	20.00	8.00
165 Dusty Baker	40.00	16.00
170 George Foster	20.00	8.00
178 Miguel Dilone	10.00	4.00
185 Al Holland	10.00	4.00
190 Rusty Staub	20.00	8.00
198 Eddie Milner	10.00	4.00
201 Burt Hooton	10.00	4.00
205 Steve Rogers	10.00	4.00
209 Bill Campbell	10.00	4.00
210 Gary Matthews	10.00	4.00
218 Doyle Alexander	10.00	4.00
222 Hubie Brooks	10.00	4.00
223 Tom Hume	10.00	4.00
225 Mike Boddicker	10.00	4.00
229 Dave LaPoint	10.00	4.00
230 Gary Carter	80.00	32.00
235 Garry Maddox	10.00	4.00
236 Mark Thurmond	10.00	4.00
237 Julio Franco	20.00	8.00
239 Tim Teufel	10.00	4.00
248 Terry Forster	10.00	4.00
250 Jesse Orosco	20.00	8.00
251 Brad Gulden	10.00	4.00
255 Lonnie Smith	10.00	4.00
261 Checklist	10.00	4.00
263 Mel Hall	10.00	4.00
266 Frank Voila	20.00	8.00
287 Walt Terrell	10.00	4.00
306 Rick Reuschel	20.00	8.00
310 Manny Trillo	10.00	4.00
313 Dave Schmidt	10.00	4.00
325 John Denny	10.00	4.00
330 Leon Durham	10.00	4.00
333 Willie Hernandez	10.00	4.00
340 Robin Yount	80.00	32.00
343 Bill Russell	10.00	4.00
345 Charlie Lea	10.00	4.00
352 Joe Morgan	100.00	40.00
355 Bert Blyleven	40.00	16.00
358 Tony Pena	20.00	8.00
360 Steve Carlton	120.00	47.50
362 Craig McMurtry	10.00	4.00
375 Jeff Reardon	20.00	8.00
379 Charles Hudson	10.00	4.00
415 Ron Darling	10.00	4.00
445 Tippy Martinez	10.00	4.00
446 Jim Sundberg	10.00	4.00
450 Steve Garvey	40.00	16.00
452 John Castino	10.00	4.00
464 Mike Mason	10.00	4.00
470 Steve Sax	10.00	4.00
485 Matt Young	10.00	4.00
487 Frank Williams	10.00	4.00
489 Bryan Clark	10.00	4.00
491 Rick Camp	10.00	4.00
495 Mario Soto	10.00	4.00
500 Mike Schmidt	200.00	80.00
501 Dan Schatzeder	10.00	4.00
504 Jerry Willard	10.00	4.00
511 Lee Smith	40.00	16.00
515 Dave Concepcion	20.00	8.00
520 LaMarr Hoyt	10.00	4.00
526 Dave Palmer	10.00	4.00
530 Dave Dravecky	20.00	8.00
538 Keith Moreland	10.00	4.00
545 Lloyd Moseby	10.00	4.00
551 Andy Van Slyke	10.00	4.00
554 Doug Flynn	10.00	4.00
556 Sixto Lezcano	10.00	4.00
560 Bill Madlock	20.00	8.00
563 Dick Ruthven	10.00	4.00
566 Ed Vande Berg	10.00	4.00
568 Cliff Johnson	10.00	4.00
569 Ken Oberkfell	10.00	4.00
575 Pedro Guerrero	20.00	8.00
580 Dwight Evans	40.00	16.00
589 Bob Dernier	10.00	4.00
592 Jeff D. Robinson	10.00	4.00
603 Rick Manning	10.00	4.00
608 Craig Lefferts	10.00	4.00
610 Jack Morris	40.00	16.00
613 Terry Puhl	10.00	4.00
615 Marvell Wynne	10.00	4.00
619 Jeffrey Leonard	10.00	4.00
625 Mark Langston	40.00	16.00
630 Tim Raines	40.00	16.00
634 Bill Dawley	10.00	4.00
670 Tom Seaver	200.00	80.00
673 Buck Martinez	10.00	4.00
674 Atlee Hammaker	10.00	4.00

685 Bill Caudill 10.00 4.00
700 Eddie Murray.................... 250.00 100.00
725 Floyd Bannister 10.00 4.00
729 Don Sutton........................ 80.00 32.00
731 Neil Allen........................... 10.00 4.00
736 Jerry Mumphrey................. 10.00 4.00
748 Lee Mazzilli......................... 20.00 8.00
753 Greg Brock.......................... 10.00 4.00
755 Ken Singleton...................... 10.00 4.00
757 Willie McGee 40.00 16.00
760 Nolan Ryan....................... 400.00 160.00
762 Eddie Whitson..................... 10.00 4.00
775 Mookie Wilson 20.00 8.00
780 Mike Flanagan 10.00 4.00
782 Tom Neidenfuer................... 10.00 4.00

1985 Topps Rub Downs

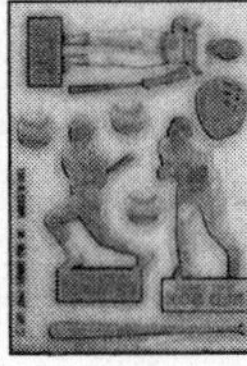

The cards in this 112 player (32 different sheets) set measure 2 3/8" by 3 5/16". The full color photo could be transfered from the rub down to another surface by rubbing a coin over the paper backing. Distributed in packages of two rub down sheets, some contained two or three player action poses, others head shots and various pieces of player equipment. Players from all teams were included in the set. Although the sheets are unnumbered, they are numbered here in alphabetical order based on each card first being placed in alphabetical order.

Nm-Mt Ex-Mt
COMPLETE SET (32)................ 15.00 6.00
1 Tony Armas............................... .10 .04
Harold Baines
Lonnie Smith
2 Don Baylor .... .10 .04
George Hendrick
Ron Kittle
Johnnie LeMaster
3 Buddy Bell .... 2.00 .80
Tony Gwynn
Lloyd Moseby
4 Bruce Benedict.......................... .10 .04
Atlee Hammaker
Frank White
5 Mike Boddicker .... 1.00 .40
Rod Carew
Carlton Fisk
Johnny Ray
6 Wade Boggs................................. .75 .30
Rick Dempsey
Keith Hernandez
7 George Brett............................ 1.50 .60
Andre Dawson
Paul Molitor
Alan Wiggins
8 Tom Brunansky............................ .30 .12
Pedro Guerrero
Darryl Strawberry
9 Bill Buckner............................. 2.00 .80
Tim Raines
Ryne Sandberg
Mike Schmidt
10 Steve Carlton.............................. .40 .16
Bob Horner
Dan Quisenberry
11 Gary Carter................................. .40 .16
Phil Garner
Ron Guidry
12 Jack Clark.................................. .20 .08
Damaso Garcia
Hal McRae
Lance Parrish
13 Dave Concepcion......................... .20 .08
Cecil Cooper
Fred Lynn
Jesse Orosco
14 Jose Cruz.................................... .30 .12
Jack Morris
Jim Rice
Rick Sutcliffe
15 Alvin Davis .... .20 .08
Steve Kemp
Greg Luzinski
Kent Tekulve
16 Ron Davis.................................... .10 .04
Kent Hrbek
Juan Samuel
17 John Denny .... .10 .04
Carney Lansford
Mario Soto
Lou Whitaker
18 Leon Durham .... .10 .04
Willie Hernandez
Steve Sax
19 Dwight Evans .... 1.00 .40
Julio Franco
Dwight Gooden
20 George Foster.............................. .20 .08
Gary Gaetti
Bobby Grich
Gary Redus
21 Steve Garvey .... .30 .12
Jerry Remy
Bill Russell
George Wright
22 Kirk Gibson 2.50 1.00
Rich Gossage
Don Mattingly
Dave Stieb
23 Moose Haas .... .10 .04
Bruce Sutter
Dickie Thon
Andre Thornton
24 Rickey Henderson .... 1.50 .60
Dave Righetti
Pete Rose
25 Steve Henderson .... .30 .12
Bill Madlock
Alan Trammell
26 LaMarr Hoyt 2.50 1.00
Larry Parrish
Nolan Ryan
27 Reggie Jackson .... .40 .16
Eric Show
Jason Thompson
28 Terry Kennedy .... 1.50 .60
Eddie Murray
Tom Seaver
Ozzie Smith
29 Mark Langston .... .40 .16
Ben Oglivie
Darrell Porter
30 Jeff Leonard .... .40 .16
Gary Matthews
Dale Murphy
Dave Winfield
31 Craig McMurtry .... 2.00 .80
Cal Ripken
Steve Rogers
Willie Upshaw
32 Tony Pena .... .40 .16
Fernando Valenzuela
Robin Yount

1985 Topps Super

This 60-card set was issued in packs of three. These large cards measure 4 7/8" by 6 7/8". The fronts of the cards are merely a blow-up of the Topps regular issue. In fact, the cards differ from the corresponding cards of the regular set in size and number only. As one would expect, only those considered stars and superstars appear in this set. Backs are green with maroon printing. A checklist for the set is contained on the back of the wrapper. The back of the wrapper also gives details of Topps' offer to send your "missing" cards.

Nm-Mt Ex-Mt
COMPLETE SET (60)................ 10.00 4.00
1 Ryne Sandberg.......................... 1.50 .60
2 Willie Hernandez .... .10 .04
3 Rick Sutcliffe.............................. .20 .08
4 Don Mattingly........................... 1.50 .60
5 Tony Gwynn .... 1.50 .60
6 Alvin Davis .... .10 .04
7 Dwight Gooden .... .40 .16
8 Dan Quisenberry .... .10 .04
9 Bruce Sutter .... .10 .04
10 Tony Armas............................... .10 .04
11 Dale Murphy.............................. .40 .16
12 Mike Schmidt............................ .75 .30
13 Gary Carter................................ .60 .24
14 Rickey Henderson .... 1.00 .40
15 Tim Raines .... .20 .08
16 Mike Boddicker .... .10 .04
17 Alejandro Pena .... .10 .04
18 Eddie Murray............................. .75 .30
19 Gary Matthews .... .10 .04
20 Mark Langston .... .10 .04
21 Mario Soto .... .10 .04
22 Dave Stieb................................. .10 .04
23 Nolan Ryan............................ 3.00 1.20
24 Steve Carlton............................. .75 .30
25 Alan Trammell........................... .40 .16
26 Steve Garvey .... .40 .16
27 Kirk Gibson .... .20 .08
28 Juan Samuel .... .10 .04
29 Reggie Jackson.......................... .75 .30
30 Darryl Strawberry .... .20 .08
31 Tom Seaver................................ .75 .30
32 Pete Rose.................................. .75 .30
33 Dwight Evans .... .20 .08
34 Jose Cruz .... .20 .08
35 Bert Blyleven .... .20 .08
36 Keith Hernandez .... .20 .08
37 Robin Yount .... .75 .30
38 Joaquin Andujar .... .10 .04
39 Lloyd Moseby............................ .10 .04
40 Chili Davis .... .20 .08
41 Kent Hrbek .... .20 .08
42 Dave Parker............................... .20 .08
43 Jack Morris .... .20 .08
44 Pedro Guerrero .... .10 .04
45 Mike Witt.................................. .10 .04
46 George Brett........................... 1.50 .60
47 Ozzie Smith .... 1.50 .60
48 Cal Ripken 3.00 1.20
49 Rich Gossage .... .20 .08
50 Jim Rice .... .20 .08
51 Harold Baines............................ .40 .16
52 Fernando Valenzuela .... .20 .08
53 Buddy Bell................................ .10 .04
54 Jesse Orosco.............................. .20 .08
55 Lance Parrish .... .10 .04
56 Jason Thompson........................ .10 .04
57 Tom Brunansky .... .10 .04
58 Dave Righetti............................. .10 .04
59 Dave Kingman .... .20 .08
60 Dave Winfield .... .75 .30

1986 Topps

This set consists of 792 standard-size cards. Cards were primarily distributed in 15-card wax packs, 48-card rack packs and factors sets. This was also the first year Topps offered a factory set to hobby dealers. Standard card fronts feature a black and white split border framing a color photo with team name on top and player name on bottom. Subsets include Pete Rose tribute (1-7), Record Breakers (201-207), Turn Back the Clock (401-405), All-Stars (701-722) and Team Leaders (seeded throughout the set). Manager cards feature the team checklist on the reverse. There are two uncorrected errors involving misnumbered cards; see card numbers 51, 57, 141, and 171 in the checklist below. The key Rookie Cards in this set are Darren Daulton, Len Dykstra, Cecil Fielder, and Mickey Tettleton.

Nm-Mt Ex-Mt
COMPLETE SET (792).............. 25.00 10.00
COMP.X-MAS.SET (792)......... 120.00 47.50
1 Pete Rose.............................. 2.00 .80
2 Pete Rose 63-66......................... .25 .10
3 Pete Rose 67-70......................... .25 .10
4 Pete Rose 71-74......................... .25 .10
5 Pete Rose 75-78......................... .25 .10
6 Pete Rose 79-82......................... .25 .10
7 Pete Rose 83-85......................... .25 .10
8 Dwayne Murphy .... .10 .04
9 Roy Smith .... .10 .04
10 Tony Gwynn .... .60 .24
11 Bob Ojeda.................................. .10 .04
12 Jose Uribe .... .10 .04
13 Bob Kearney.............................. .10 .04
14 Julio Cruz.................................. .10 .04
15 Eddie Whitson .... .10 .04
16 Rick Schu.................................. .10 .04
17 Mike Stenhouse......................... .10 .04
18 Brent Gaff.................................. .10 .04
19 Rich Hebner .... .10 .04
20 Lou Whitaker............................. .15 .06
21 George Bamberger MG............. .10 .04
22 Duane Walker............................ .10 .04
23 Manny Lee RC* .... .10 .04
24 Len Barker................................. .10 .04
25 Willie Wilson .... .10 .04
26 Frank DiPino.............................. .10 .04
27 Ray Knight................................. .15 .06
28 Eric Davis .... .25 .10
29 Tony Phillips .... .10 .04
30 Eddie Murray............................. .40 .16
31 Jamie Easterly .... .10 .04
32 Steve Yeager .... .10 .04
33 Jeff Lahti .... .10 .04
34 Ken Phelps................................. .10 .04
35 Jeff Reardon.............................. .10 .04
36 Lance Parrish TL .... .15 .06
37 Mark Thurmond .... .10 .04
38 Glenn Hoffman .... .10 .04
39 Dave Rucker.............................. .10 .04
40 Ken Griffey .... .15 .06
41 Brad Wellman............................ .10 .04
42 Geoff Zahn................................ .10 .04
43 Dave Engle .... .10 .04
44 Lance McCullers........................ .10 .04
45 Damaso Garcia.......................... .10 .04
46 Billy Hatcher.............................. .10 .04
47 Juan Berenguer .... .10 .04
48 Bill Almon.................................. .10 .04
49 Rick Manning .... .10 .04
50 Dan Quisenberry .... .10 .04
51 Bobby Wine MG ERR .... .10 .04
Number of card on
back is actually 57)
52 Chris Welsh............................... .10 .04
53 Len Dykstra RC .... .75 .30
54 John Franco .... .40 .16
55 Fred Lynn.................................. .15 .06
56 Tom Niedenfuer......................... .10 .04
57 Bill Doran .... .10 .04
(See also 51)
58 Bill Krueger .... .10 .04
59 Andre Thornton .... .10 .04
60 Dwight Evans .... .15 .06
61 Karl Best.................................... .10 .04
62 Bob Boone .... .15 .06
63 Ron Roenicke............................ .10 .04
64 Floyd Bannister .... .10 .04
65 Dan Driessen............................. .10 .04
66 Bob Forsch TL........................... .10 .04
67 Carmelo Martinez .... .10 .04
68 Ed Lynch .... .10 .04
69 Luis Aguayo .... .10 .04
70 Dave Winfield .... .15 .06
71 Ken Schrom .... .10 .04
72 Shawon Dunston........................ .15 .06
73 Randy O'Neal .... .10 .04
74 Rance Mulliniks......................... .10 .04
75 Jose DeLeon .... .10 .04
76 Dion James .... .10 .04
77 Charlie Leibrandt....................... .10 .04
78 Bruce Benedict .... .10 .04
79 Dave Schmidt............................ .10 .04
80 Darryl Strawberry .... .25 .10
81 Gene Mauch MG........................ .15 .06
82 Tippy Martinez........................... .10 .04
83 Phil Garner .... .15 .06
84 Curt Young................................. .10 .04
85 Tony Perez .... .25 .10
(Eric Davis also
shown on card)
86 Tom Waddell .... .10 .04
87 Candy Maldonado .... .10 .04
88 Tom Nieto .... .10 .04
89 Randy St.Claire.......................... .10 .04
90 Garry Templeton .... .10 .04
91 Steve Crawford.......................... .10 .04
92 Al Cowens .... .10 .04
93 Scot Thompson.......................... .10 .04
94 Rich Bordi .... .10 .04
95 Ozzie Virgil .... .10 .04
96 Jim Clancy TL............................ .10 .04
97 Gary Gaetti .... .15 .06
98 Dick Ruthven............................. .10 .04
99 Buddy Biancalana...................... .10 .04
100 Nolan Ryan........................... 2.00 .80
101 Dave Bergman......................... .10 .04
102 Joe Orsulak RC* .... .10 .04
103 Luis Salazar............................ .10 .04
104 Sid Fernandez......................... .15 .06
105 Gary Ward .... .10 .04
106 Ray Burris .... .10 .04
107 Rafael Ramirez .... .10 .04
108 Ted Power............................... .10 .04
109 Len Matuszek.......................... .10 .04
110 Scott McGregor....................... .10 .04
111 Roger Craig MG .... .15 .06
112 Bill Campbell .... .10 .04
113 U.L. Washington .... .10 .04
114 Mike C. Brown......................... .10 .04
115 Jay Howell............................... .10 .04
116 Brook Jacoby .... .10 .04
117 Bruce Kison............................. .10 .04
118 Jerry Royster........................... .10 .04
119 Barry Bonnell........................... .10 .04
120 Steve Carlton........................... .15 .06
121 Nelson Simmons...................... .10 .04
122 Pete Filson............................... .10 .04
123 Greg Walker .... .10 .04
124 Luis Sanchez........................... .10 .04
125 Dave Lopes .... .15 .06
126 Mookie Wilson TL .... .10 .04
127 Jack Howell............................. .10 .04
128 John Wathan........................... .10 .04
129 Jeff Dedmon............................ .10 .04
130 Alan Trammell......................... .25 .10
131 Checklist: 1-132 .... .15 .06
132 Razor Shines .... .10 .04
133 Andy McGaffigan..................... .10 .04
134 Carney Lansford...................... .15 .06
135 Joe Niekro .... .10 .04
136 Mike Hargrove......................... .15 .06
137 Charlie Moore.......................... .10 .04
138 Mark Davis .... .10 .04
139 Daryl Boston .... .10 .04
140 John Candelaria....................... .10 .04
141 Chuck Cottier MG .... .10 .04
See also 171
142 Bob Jones .... .10 .04
143 Dave Van Gorder .... .10 .04
144 Doug Sisk................................ .10 .04
145 Pedro Guerrero .... .15 .06
146 Jack Perconte.......................... .10 .04
147 Larry Sheets............................ .10 .04
148 Mike Heath .... .10 .04
149 Brett Butler .... .15 .06
150 Joaquin Andujar .... .10 .04
151 Dave Stapleton .... .10 .04
152 Mike Morgan........................... .10 .04
153 Ricky Adams .... .10 .04
154 Bert Roberge........................... .10 .04
155 Bobby Grich .... .15 .06
156 Richard Dotson TL .... .10 .04
157 Ron Hassey .... .10 .04
158 Derrel Thomas......................... .10 .04
159 Orel Hershiser UER .... .40 .16
(82 Alburquerque)
160 Chet Lemon............................. .10 .04
161 Lee Tunnell.............................. .10 .04
162 Greg Gagne .... .10 .04
163 Pete Ladd .... .10 .04
164 Steve Balboni .... .10 .04
165 Mike Davis............................... .10 .04
166 Dickie Thon .... .10 .04
167 Zane Smith.............................. .10 .04
168 Jeff Burroughs .... .10 .04
169 George Wright......................... .10 .04
170 Gary Carter.............................. .25 .10
171 Bob Rodgers MG ERR............ .10 .04
Number of card on
back actually 141)
172 Jerry Reed............................... .10 .04
173 Wayne Gross........................... .10 .04
174 Brian Snyder .... .10 .04
175 Steve Sax .... .10 .04
176 Jay Tibbs................................. .10 .04
177 Joel Youngblood .... .10 .04
178 Ivan DeJesus........................... .10 .04
179 Stu Cliburn.............................. .10 .04
180 Don Mattingly...................... 1.25 .50
181 Al Nipper .... .10 .04
182 Bobby Brown .... .10 .04
183 Larry Andersen........................ .10 .04
184 Tim Laudner............................ .10 .04
185 Rollie Fingers .... .15 .06
186 Jose Cruz TL .... .10 .04
187 Scott Fletcher .... .10 .04
188 Bob Dernier .... .10 .04
189 Mike Mason............................. .10 .04
190 George Hendrick .... .10 .04
191 Wally Backman........................ .10 .04
192 Milt Wilcox.............................. .10 .04
193 Daryl Sconiers......................... .10 .04
194 Craig McMurtry .... .10 .04
195 Dave Concepcion.................... .15 .06
196 Doyle Alexander .... .10 .04
197 Enos Cabell .... .10 .04
198 Ken Dixon................................ .10 .04
199 Dick Howser MG .... .15 .06
200 Mike Schmidt...................... 1.00 .40
201 Vince Coleman RB.................. .15 .06
202 Dwight Gooden RB................. .25 .10
203 Keith Hernandez RB .... .15 .06
204 Phil Niekro RB........................ .15 .06
205 Tony Perez RB........................ .15 .06
206 Pete Rose RB .... .40 .16
207 F. Valenzuela RB.................... .15 .06
208 Ramon Romero....................... .10 .04
209 Randy Ready .... .10 .04
210 Calvin Schiraldi .... .10 .04
211 Ed Wojna................................. .10 .04
212 Chris Speier............................ .10 .04
213 Bob Shirley............................. .10 .04
214 Randy Bush............................. .10 .04
215 Frank White............................ .15 .06
216 Dwayne Murphy TL .... .10 .04
217 Bill Scherrer .... .10 .04
218 Randy Hunt .... .10 .04
219 Dennis Lamp .... .10 .04
220 Bob Horner............................. .10 .04
221 Dave Henderson..................... .10 .04
222 Craig Gerber........................... .10 .04
223 Atlee Hammaker..................... .10 .04
224 Cesar Cedeno .... .15 .06
225 Ron Darling .... .10 .04
226 Lee Lacy.................................. .10 .04
227 Al Jones .... .10 .04
228 Tom Lawless .... .10 .04
229 Bill Gullickson .... .10 .04
230 Terry Kennedy........................ .10 .04
231 Jim Frey MG............................ .10 .04
232 Rick Rhoden............................ .10 .04
233 Steve Lyons............................. .10 .04
234 Doug Corbett........................... .10 .04
235 Butch Wynegar........................ .10 .04
236 Frank Eufemia .... .10 .04
237 Ted Simmons.......................... .15 .06
238 Larry Parrish .... .10 .04
239 Joel Skinner .... .10 .04
240 Tommy John........................... .40 .16
241 Tony Fernandez...................... .10 .04
242 Rich Thompson....................... .10 .04
243 Johnny Grubb .... .10 .04
244 Craig Lefferts.......................... .10 .04
245 Jim Sundberg.......................... .10 .04
246 Steve Carlton TL..................... .10 .04
247 Terry Harper........................... .10 .04
248 Spike Owen .... .10 .04
249 Rob Deer................................. .15 .06
250 Dwight Gooden .... .40 .16
251 Rich Dauer .... .10 .04
252 Bobby Castillo .... .10 .04
253 Dann Bilardello....................... .10 .04
254 Ozzie Guillen RC* .... .25 .10
255 Tony Armas............................. .10 .04
256 Kurt Kepshire .... .10 .04
257 Doug DeCinces........................ .10 .04
258 Tim Burke................................ .10 .04
259 Dan Pasqua .... .10 .04
260 Tony Pena .... .10 .04
261 Bobby Valentine MG............... .15 .06
262 Mario Ramirez......................... .10 .04
263 Checklist: 133-264 .... .15 .06
264 Darren Daulton RC .... .75 .30
265 Ron Davis................................ .10 .04
266 Keith Moreland....................... .10 .04
267 Paul Molitor............................ .25 .10
268 Mike Scott............................... .10 .04
269 Dane Iorg .... .10 .04
270 Jack Morris .... .15 .06
271 Dave Collins .... .10 .04
272 Tim Tolman............................. .10 .04
273 Jerry Willard............................ .10 .04
274 Ron Gardenhire....................... .10 .04
275 Charlie Hough .... .15 .06
276 Willie Randolph TL................. .15 .06
277 Jaime Cocanower.................... .10 .04
278 Sixto Lezcano.......................... .10 .04
279 Al Pardo .... .10 .04
280 Tim Raines .... .15 .06
281 Steve Mura.............................. .10 .04
282 Jerry Mumphrey...................... .10 .04
283 Mike Fischlin .... .10 .04
284 Brian Dayett............................ .10 .04
285 Buddy Bell .... .15 .06
286 Luis DeLeon .... .10 .04
287 John Christensen .... .10 .04
288 Don Aase................................. .10 .04
289 Johnnie LeMaster.................... .10 .04
290 Carlton Fisk .... .25 .10
291 Tom Lasorda MG .... .25 .10
292 Chuck Porter .... .10 .04
293 Chris Chambliss .... .15 .06
294 Danny Cox.............................. .10 .04
295 Kirk Gibson .... .15 .06
296 Geno Petralli........................... .10 .04
297 Tim Lollar................................ .10 .04
298 Craig Reynolds........................ .10 .04
299 Bryn Smith .... .10 .04
300 George Brett........................ 1.00 .40
301 Dennis Rasmussen .... .10 .04
302 Greg Gross.............................. .10 .04
303 Curt Wardle............................. .10 .04
304 Mike Gallego RC...................... .10 .04
305 Phil Bradley............................. .10 .04
306 Terry Kennedy TL.................... .10 .04
307 Dave Sax .... .10 .04
308 Ray Fontenot........................... .10 .04
309 John Shelby .... .10 .04
310 Greg Minton .... .10 .04
311 Dick Schofield .... .10 .04
312 Tom Filer................................. .10 .04
313 Joe DeSa................................. .10 .04
314 Frank Pastore .... .10 .04
315 Mookie Wilson .... .15 .06
316 Sammy Khalifa........................ .10 .04
317 Ed Romero.............................. .10 .04
318 Terry Whitfield........................ .10 .04
319 Rick Camp............................... .10 .04
320 Jim Rice .... .15 .06
321 Earl Weaver MG .... .40 .16
322 Bob Forsch.............................. .10 .04
323 Jerry Davis .... .10 .04
324 Dan Schatzeder .... .10 .04
325 Juan Beniquez......................... .10 .04
326 Kent Tekulve........................... .10 .04
327 Mike Pagliarulo .... .10 .04
328 Pete O'Brien .... .10 .04
329 Kirby Puckett.......................... .75 .30
330 Rick Sutcliffe .... .15 .06
331 Alan Ashby .... .10 .04
332 Darryl Motley.......................... .10 .04
333 Tom Henke.............................. .15 .06
334 Ken Oberkfell.......................... .10 .04
335 Don Sutton.............................. .40 .16
336 Andre Thornton TL .... .15 .06
337 Darnell Coles .... .10 .04
338 Jorge Bell .... .15 .06
339 Bruce Berenyi.......................... .10 .04
340 Cal Ripken .... 1.50 .60
341 Frank Williams........................ .10 .04
342 Gary Redus .... .10 .04
343 Carlos Diaz .... .10 .04
344 Jim Wohlford .... .10 .04
345 Donnie Moore .... .10 .04
346 Bryan Little............................. .10 .04
347 Teddy Higuera RC* .... .25 .10
348 Cliff Johnson.......................... .10 .04
349 Mark Clear.............................. .10 .04
350 Jack Clark............................... .15 .06
351 Chuck Tanner MG................... .10 .04
352 Harry Spilman .... .10 .04
353 Keith Atherton .... .10 .04
354 Tony Bernazard .... .10 .04
355 Lee Smith................................ .25 .10
356 Mickey Hatcher .... .10 .04
357 Ed VandeBerg......................... .10 .04
358 Rick Dempsey .... .10 .04
359 Mike LaCoss............................ .10 .04
360 Lloyd Moseby.......................... .10 .04
361 Shane Rawley.......................... .10 .04
362 Tom Paciorek........................... .15 .06
363 Terry Forster .... .10 .04
364 Reid Nichols............................ .10 .04
365 Mike Flanagan .... .10 .04
366 Dave Concepcion TL............... .15 .06
367 Aurelio Lopez .... .10 .04
368 Greg Brock.............................. .10 .04
369 Al Holland............................... .10 .04
370 Vince Coleman RC* .... .50 .20
371 Bill Stein.................................. .10 .04
372 Ben Oglivie .... .10 .04
373 Urbano Lugo .... .10 .04
374 Terry Francona........................ .10 .04
375 Rich Gedman........................... .10 .04

376 Bill Dawley .10 .04
377 Joe Carter .40 .16
378 Bruce Bochte .10 .04
379 Bobby Meacham .10 .04
380 LaMarr Hoyt .10 .04
381 Ray Miller MG .10 .04
382 Ivan Calderon RC* .25 .10
383 Chris Brown .10 .04
384 Steve Trout .10 .04
385 Cecil Cooper .15 .06
386 Cecil Fielder RC .75 .30
387 Steve Kemp .10 .04
388 Dickie Noles .10 .04
389 Glenn Davis .15 .06
390 Tom Seaver .25 .10
391 Julio Franco .15 .06
392 John Russell .10 .04
393 Chris Pittaro .10 .04
394 Checklist: 265-396 .15 .06
395 Scott Garrelts .10 .04
396 Dwight Evans TL .15 .06
397 Steve Buechele RC .25 .10
398 Earnie Riles .10 .04
399 Bill Swift .10 .04
400 Rod Carew .25 .10
401 Fernando Valenzuela TBC '81 .15 .06
402 Tom Seaver TBC '76 .15 .06
403 Willie Mays TBC '71 .25 .10
404 Frank Robinson TBC '66 .15 .06
405 Roger Maris TBC '61 .40 .16
406 Scott Sanderson .10 .04
407 Sal Butera .10 .04
408 Dave Smith .10 .04
409 Paul Runge RC .10 .04
410 Dave Kingman .15 .06
411 Sparky Anderson MG .25 .10
412 Jim Clancy .10 .04
413 Tim Flannery .10 .04
414 Tom Gorman .10 .04
415 Hal McRae .15 .06
416 Dennis Martinez .15 .06
417 R.J. Reynolds .10 .04
418 Alan Knicely .10 .04
419 Frank Wills .10 .04
420 Von Hayes .10 .04
421 David Palmer .10 .04
422 Mike Jorgensen .10 .04
423 Dan Spillner .10 .04
424 Rick Miller .10 .04
425 Larry McWilliams .10 .04
426 Charlie Moore TL .10 .04
427 Joe Cowley .10 .04
428 Max Venable .10 .04
429 Greg Booker .10 .04
430 Kent Hrbek .15 .06
431 George Frazier .10 .04
432 Mark Bailey .10 .04
433 Chris Codiroli .10 .04
434 Curt Wilkerson .10 .04
435 Bill Caudill .10 .04
436 Doug Flynn .10 .04
437 Rick Mahler .10 .04
438 Clint Hurdle .10 .04
439 Rick Honeycutt .10 .04
440 Alvin Davis .10 .04
441 Whitey Herzog MG .25 .10
442 Ron Robinson .10 .04
443 Bill Buckner .15 .06
444 Alex Trevino .10 .04
445 Bert Blyleven .15 .06
446 Lenn Sakata .10 .04
447 Jerry Don Gleaton .10 .04
448 Herm Winningham .10 .04
449 Rod Scurry .10 .04
450 Graig Nettles .15 .06
451 Mark Brown .10 .04
452 Bob Clark .10 .04
453 Steve Jeltz .10 .04
454 Burt Hooton .10 .04
455 Willie Randolph .15 .06
456 Dale Murphy TL .25 .10
457 Mickey Tettleton RC .25 .10
458 Kevin Bass .10 .04
459 Luis Leal .10 .04
460 Leon Durham .10 .04
461 Walt Terrell .10 .04
462 Domingo Ramos .10 .04
463 Jim Gott .10 .04
464 Ruppert Jones .10 .04
465 Jesse Orosco .10 .04
466 Tom Foley .10 .04
467 Bob James .10 .04
468 Mike Scioscia .10 .04
469 Storm Davis .10 .04
470 Bill Madlock .15 .06
471 Bobby Cox MG .15 .06
472 Joe Hesketh .10 .04
473 Mark Brouhard .10 .04
474 John Tudor .10 .04
475 Juan Samuel .10 .04
476 Ron Mathis .10 .04
477 Mike Easler .10 .04
478 Andy Hawkins .10 .04
479 Bob Melvin .10 .04
480 Oddibe McDowell .10 .04
481 Scott Bradley .10 .04
482 Rick Lysander .10 .04
483 George Vukovich .10 .04
484 Donnie Hill .10 .04
485 Gary Matthews .10 .04
486 Bobby Grich TL .10 .04
487 Bret Saberhagen .15 .06
488 Lou Thornton .10 .04
489 Jim Winn .10 .04
490 Jeff Leonard .10 .04
491 Pascual Perez .10 .04
492 Kelvin Chapman .10 .04
493 Gene Nelson .10 .04
494 Gary Roenicke .10 .04
495 Mark Langston .10 .04
496 Jay Johnstone .15 .06
497 John Stuper .10 .04
498 Tito Landrum .10 .04
499 Bob L. Gibson .10 .04
500 Rickey Henderson .40 .16
501 Dave Johnson MG .15 .06
502 Glen Cook .10 .04
503 Mike Fitzgerald .10 .04
504 Denny Walling .10 .04
505 Jerry Koosman .15 .06
506 Bill Russell .15 .06
507 Steve Ontiveros RC .10 .04
508 Alan Wiggins .10 .04
509 Ernie Camacho .10 .04
510 Wade Boggs .25 .10
511 Ed Nunez .10 .04
512 Thad Bosley .10 .04
513 Ron Washington .10 .04
514 Mike Jones .10 .04
515 Darrell Evans .15 .06
516 Greg Minton TL .10 .04
517 Milt Thompson RC .10 .04
518 Buck Martinez .10 .04
519 Danny Darwin .10 .04
520 Keith Hernandez .25 .10
521 Nate Snell .10 .04
522 Bob Bailor .10 .04
523 Joe Price .10 .04
524 Darrell Miller .10 .04
525 Marvell Wynne .10 .04
526 Charlie Lea .10 .04
527 Checklist: 397-528 .15 .06
528 Terry Pendleton .15 .06
529 Marc Sullivan .10 .04
530 Rich Gossage .15 .06
531 Tony LaRussa MG .15 .06
532 Don Carman .10 .04
533 Billy Sample .10 .04
534 Jeff Calhoun .10 .04
535 Toby Harrah .10 .04
536 Jose Rijo .10 .04
537 Mark Salas .10 .04
538 Dennis Eckersley .25 .10
539 Glenn Hubbard .10 .04
540 Dan Petry .10 .04
541 Jorge Orta .10 .04
542 Don Schulze .10 .04
543 Jerry Narron .10 .04
544 Eddie Milner .10 .04
545 Jimmy Key .40 .16
546 Dave Henderson TL .10 .04
547 Roger McDowell RC* .10 .04
548 Mike Young .10 .04
549 Bob Welch .10 .04
550 Tom Herr .10 .04
551 Dave LaPoint .10 .04
552 Marc Hill .10 .04
553 Jim Morrison .10 .04
554 Paul Householder .10 .04
555 Hubie Brooks .10 .04
556 John Denny .10 .04
557 Gerald Perry .10 .04
558 Tim Stoddard .10 .04
559 Tommy Dunbar .10 .04
560 Dave Righetti .10 .04
561 Bob Lillis MG .10 .04
562 Joe Beckwith .10 .04
563 Alejandro Sanchez .10 .04
564 Warren Brusstar .10 .04
565 Tom Brunansky .10 .04
566 Alfredo Griffin .10 .04
567 Jeff Barkley .10 .04
568 Donnie Scott .10 .04
569 Jim Acker .10 .04
570 Rusty Staub .15 .06
571 Mike Jeffcoat .10 .04
572 Paul Zuvella .10 .04
573 Tom Hume .10 .04
574 Ron Kittle .10 .04
575 Mike Boddicker .10 .04
576 Andre Dawson TL .10 .04
577 Jerry Reuss .10 .04
578 Lee Mazzilli .10 .04
579 Jim Slaton .10 .04
580 Willie McGee .15 .06
581 Bruce Hurst .10 .04
582 Jim Gantner .10 .04
583 Al Bumbry .10 .04
584 Brian Fisher RC .10 .04
585 Garry Maddox .10 .04
586 Greg Harris .10 .04
587 Rafael Santana .10 .04
588 Steve Lake .10 .04
589 Sid Bream .10 .04
590 Bob Knepper .10 .04
591 Jackie Moore MG .10 .04
592 Frank Tanana .10 .04
593 Jesse Barfield .10 .04
594 Chris Bando .10 .04
595 Dave Parker .15 .06
596 Onix Concepcion .10 .04
597 Sammy Stewart .10 .04
598 Jim Presley .10 .04
599 Rick Aguilera RC .25 .10
600 Dale Murphy .40 .16
601 Gary Lucas .10 .04
602 Mariano Duncan RC* .25 .10
603 Bill Laskey .10 .04
604 Gary Pettis .10 .04
605 Dennis Boyd .10 .04
606 Hal McRae TL .15 .06
607 Ken Dayley .10 .04
608 Bruce Bochy .10 .04
609 Barbaro Garbey .10 .04
610 Ron Guidry .15 .06
611 Gary Woods .10 .04
612 Richard Dotson .10 .04
613 Roy Smalley .10 .04
614 Rick Waits .10 .04
615 Johnny Ray .10 .04
616 Glenn Brummer .10 .04
617 Lonnie Smith .10 .04
618 Jim Pankovits .10 .04
619 Danny Heep .10 .04
620 Bruce Sutter .15 .06
621 John Felske MG .10 .04
622 Gary Lavelle .10 .04
623 Floyd Rayford .10 .04
624 Steve McCatty .10 .04
625 Bob Brenly .10 .04
626 Roy Thomas .10 .04
627 Ron Oester .10 .04
628 Kirk McCaskill RC .10 .04
629 Mitch Webster .10 .04
630 Fernando Valenzuela .15 .06
631 Steve Braun .10 .04
632 Dave Von Ohlen .10 .04
633 Jackie Gutierrez .10 .04
634 Roy Lee Jackson .10 .04
635 Jason Thompson .10 .04
636 Lee Smith TL .15 .06
637 Rudy Law .10 .04
638 John Butcher .10 .04
639 Bo Diaz .10 .04
640 Jose Cruz .15 .06
641 Wayne Tolleson .10 .04
642 Ray Searage .10 .04
643 Tom Brookens .10 .04
644 Mark Gubicza .10 .04
645 Dusty Baker .15 .06
646 Mike Moore .10 .04
647 Mel Hall .10 .04
648 Steve Bedrosian .10 .04
649 Ronn Reynolds .10 .04
650 Dave Stieb .10 .04
651 Billy Martin MG .15 .06
652 Tom Browning .10 .04
653 Jim Dwyer .10 .04
654 Ken Howell .10 .04
655 Manny Trillo .10 .04
656 Brian Harper .10 .04
657 Juan Agosto .10 .04
658 Rob Wilfong .10 .04
659 Checklist: 529-660 .15 .06
660 Steve Garvey .15 .06
661 Roger Clemens 1.50 .60
662 Bill Schroeder .10 .04
663 Neil Allen .10 .04
664 Tim Corcoran .10 .04
665 Alejandro Pena .10 .04
666 Charlie Hough TL .15 .06
667 Tim Teufel .10 .04
668 Cecilio Guante .10 .04
669 Ron Cey .15 .06
670 Willie Hernandez .10 .04
671 Lynn Jones .10 .04
672 Rob Picciolo .10 .04
673 Ernie Whitt .10 .04
674 Pat Tabler .10 .04
675 Claudell Washington .10 .04
676 Matt Young .10 .04
677 Nick Esasky .10 .04
678 Dan Gladden .10 .04
679 Britt Burns .10 .04
680 George Foster .15 .06
681 Dick Williams MG .15 .06
682 Junior Ortiz .10 .04
683 Andy Van Slyke .15 .06
684 Bob McClure .10 .04
685 Tim Wallach .10 .04
686 Jeff Stone .10 .04
687 Mike Trujillo .10 .04
688 Larry Herndon .10 .04
689 Dave Stewart .15 .06
690 Ryne Sandberg UER .75 .30
(No Topps logo on front)
691 Mike Madden .10 .04
692 Dale Berra .10 .04
693 Tom Tellmann .10 .04
694 Garth Iorg .10 .04
695 Mike Smithson .10 .04
696 Bill Russell TL .15 .06
697 Bud Black .10 .04
698 Brad Komminsk .10 .04
699 Pat Corrales MG .10 .04
700 Reggie Jackson .25 .10
701 Keith Hernandez AS .15 .06
702 Tom Herr AS .10 .04
703 Tim Wallach AS .10 .04
704 Ozzie Smith AS .40 .16
705 Dale Murphy AS .25 .10
706 Pedro Guerrero AS .10 .04
707 Willie McGee AS .10 .04
708 Gary Carter AS .15 .06
709 Dwight Gooden AS .25 .10
710 John Tudor AS .10 .04
711 Jeff Reardon AS .10 .04
712 Don Mattingly AS .60 .24
713 Damaso Garcia AS .10 .04
714 George Brett AS .40 .16
715 Cal Ripken AS .40 .16
716 Rickey Henderson AS .25 .10
717 Dave Winfield AS .10 .04
718 George Bell AS .10 .04
719 Carlton Fisk AS .15 .06
720 Bret Saberhagen AS .10 .04
721 Ron Guidry AS .15 .06
722 Dan Quisenberry AS .10 .04
723 Marty Bystrom .10 .04
724 Tim Hulett .10 .04
725 Mario Soto .10 .04
726 Rick Dempsey TL .15 .06
727 David Green .10 .04
728 Mike Marshall .10 .04
729 Jim Beattie .10 .04
730 Ozzie Smith .60 .24
731 Don Robinson .10 .04
732 Floyd Youmans .10 .04
733 Ron Romanick .10 .04
734 Marty Barrett .10 .04
735 Dave Dravecky .15 .06
736 Glenn Wilson .10 .04
737 Pete Vuckovich .10 .04
738 Andre Robertson .10 .04
739 Dave Rozema .10 .04
740 Lance Parrish .15 .06
741 Pete Rose MG .40 .16
742 Frank Viola .15 .06
743 Pat Sheridan .10 .04
744 Lary Sorensen .10 .04
745 Willie Upshaw .10 .04
746 Denny Gonzalez .10 .04
747 Rick Cerone .10 .04
748 Steve Henderson .10 .04
749 Ed Jurak .10 .04
750 Gorman Thomas .10 .04
751 Howard Johnson .15 .06
752 Mike Krukow .10 .04
753 Dan Ford .10 .04
754 Pat Clements .10 .04
755 Harold Baines .25 .10
756 Rick Rhoden TL .10 .04
757 Darrell Porter .15 .06
758 Dave Anderson .10 .04
759 Moose Haas .10 .04
760 Andre Dawson .15 .06
761 Don Slaught .10 .04
762 Eric Show .10 .04
763 Terry Puhl .10 .04
764 Kevin Gross .10 .04
765 Don Baylor .25 .10
766 Rick Langford .10 .04
767 Jody Davis .10 .04
768 Vern Ruhle .10 .04
769 Harold Reynolds RC .75 .30
770 Vida Blue .15 .06
771 John McNamara MG .10 .04
772 Brian Downing .10 .04
773 Greg Pryor .10 .04
774 Terry Leach .10 .04
775 Al Oliver .15 .06
776 Gene Garber .10 .04
777 Wayne Krenchicki .10 .04
778 Jerry Hairston .10 .04
779 Rick Reuschel .10 .04
780 Robin Yount .60 .24
781 Joe Nolan .10 .04
782 Ken Landreaux .10 .04
783 Ricky Horton .10 .04
784 Alan Bannister .10 .04
785 Bob Stanley .10 .04
786 Mickey Hatcher TL .10 .04
787 Vance Law .10 .04
788 Marty Castillo .10 .04
789 Kurt Bevacqua .10 .04
790 Phil Niekro .15 .06
791 Checklist: 661-792 .15 .06
792 Charles Hudson .10 .04

1986 Topps Tiffany

These 792 cards form a parallel to the regular Topps set. These cards, available only through the Topps dealer network were issued in factory sealed boxes. These cards have a "glossy" front and a very clear back. These cards were printed in the Topps Ireland plant. Reports within the hobby indicate that it is believed that 5,000 of these sets were produced.

	Nm-Mt	Ex-Mt
COMP.FACT.SET (792)	120.00	47.50
*STARS: 5X TO 12X BASIC CARDS		
*ROOKIES: 5X TO 12X BASIC CARDS		

1986 Topps Glossy All-Stars

This 22-card standard-size set was distributed as an insert, one card per rak pack. The players featured are the starting lineups of the 1985 All-Star Game played in Minnesota. The cards are very colorful and have a high gloss finish.

	Nm-Mt	Ex-Mt
COMPLETE SET (22)	5.00	2.00
1 Sparky Anderson MG	.05	.02
2 Eddie Murray	.50	.20
3 Lou Whitaker	.10	.04
4 George Brett	1.00	.40
5 Cal Ripken	2.00	.80
6 Jim Rice	.10	.04
7 Rickey Henderson	.50	.20
8 Dave Winfield	.50	.20
9 Carlton Fisk	.40	.16
10 Jack Morris	.10	.04
11 AL Team Photo	.05	.02
12 Dick Williams MG	.05	.02
13 Steve Garvey	.10	.04
14 Tom Herr	.05	.02
15 Graig Nettles	.10	.04
16 Ozzie Smith	1.00	.40
17 Tony Gwynn	1.00	.40
18 Dale Murphy	.20	.08
19 Darryl Strawberry	.10	.04
20 Terry Kennedy	.05	.02
21 LaMarr Hoyt	.05	.02
22 NL Team Photo	.05	.02

1986 Topps Glossy Send-Ins

This 60-card glossy standard-size set was produced by Topps and distributed ten cards at a time based on the offer found on the wax packs. Each series of ten cards was available by sending in 1.00 plus six "special offer" cards inserted one per wax pack. The card backs are printed in red and blue on white card stock. The card fronts feature a white border and a green frame surrounding a full-color photo of the player.

	Nm-Mt	Ex-Mt
COMPLETE SET (60)	12.00	4.80
1 Oddibe McDowell	.10	.04
2 Reggie Jackson	.75	.30
3 Fernando Valenzuela	.20	.08
4 Jack Clark	.10	.04
5 Rickey Henderson	1.25	.50
6 Steve Balboni	.10	.04
7 Keith Hernandez	.20	.08
8 Lance Parrish	.20	.08
9 Willie McGee	.20	.08
10 Chris Brown	.10	.04
11 Darryl Strawberry	.20	.08
12 Ron Guidry	.20	.08
13 Dave Parker	.20	.08
14 Cal Ripken	4.00	1.60
15 Tim Raines	.20	.08
16 Rod Carew	.75	.30
17 Mike Schmidt	1.00	.40
18 George Brett	2.00	.80
19 Joe Hesketh	.10	.04
20 Dan Pasqua	.10	.04
21 Vince Coleman	.20	.08
22 Tom Seaver	.75	.30
23 Gary Carter	.75	.30
24 Orel Hershiser	.20	.08
25 Pedro Guerrero	.10	.04
26 Wade Boggs	.75	.30
27 Bret Saberhagen	.20	.08
28 Carlton Fisk	.75	.30
29 Kirk Gibson	.20	.08
30 Brian Fisher	.10	.04
31 Don Mattingly	2.00	.80
32 Tom Herr	.10	.04
33 Eddie Murray	.75	.30
34 Ryne Sandberg	1.50	.60
35 Dan Quisenberry	.10	.04
36 Jim Rice	.20	.08
37 Dale Murphy	.30	.12
38 Steve Garvey	.20	.08
39 Roger McDowell	.10	.04
40 Earnie Riles	.10	.04
41 Dwight Gooden	.20	.08
42 Dave Winfield	.60	.24
43 Dave Stieb	.10	.04
44 Bob Horner	.10	.04
45 Nolan Ryan	4.00	1.60
46 Ozzie Smith	2.00	.80
47 George Bell	.10	.04
48 Gorman Thomas	.10	.04
49 Tom Browning	.10	.04
50 Larry Sheets	.10	.04
51 Pete Rose	1.00	.40
52 Brett Butler	.20	.08
53 John Tudor	.10	.04
54 Phil Bradley	.10	.04
55 Jeff Reardon	.20	.08
56 Rich Gossage	.20	.08
57 Tony Gwynn	2.00	.80
58 Ozzie Guillen	.30	.12
59 Glenn Davis	.10	.04
60 Darrell Evans	.10	.04

1986 Topps Wax Box Cards

Topps printed cards (each measuring the standard 2 1/2" by 3 1/2") on the bottoms of their wax pack boxes for their regular issue cards; there are four different boxes, each with four cards. These sixteen cards ("numbered" A through P) are listed below; they are not considered an integral part of the regular set but are considered a separate set. The order of the set is alphabetical by player's name. These wax box cards are styled almost exactly like the 1986 Topps regular issue cards. Complete boxes would be worth an additional 25 percent premium over the prices below. The card lettering is sequenced in alphabetical order.

	Nm-Mt	Ex-Mt
COMPLETE SET (16)	8.00	3.20
A George Bell	.20	.08
B Wade Boggs	1.00	.40
C George Brett	2.00	.80
D Vince Coleman	.40	.16
E Carlton Fisk	1.00	.40
F Dwight Gooden	.40	.16
G Pedro Guerrero	.40	.16
H Ron Guidry	.40	.16
I Reggie Jackson	1.00	.40
J Don Mattingly	2.00	.80
K Oddibe McDowell	.20	.08
L Willie McGee	.40	.16
M Dale Murphy	.60	.24
N Pete Rose	1.25	.50
O Bret Saberhagen	.40	.16
P Fernando Valenzuela	.40	.16

1986 Topps Traded

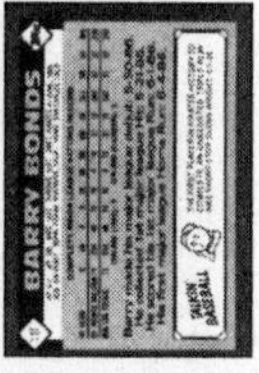

This 132-card standard-size Traded set was distributed in factory set form in a red and white box through hobby dealers. The cards are identical in style to regular-issue 1986 Topps cards except for whiter stock and t-suffixed numbering. The key extended Rookie Cards in this set are Barry Bonds, Bobby Bonilla, Jose Canseco, Will Clark, Andres Galarraga, Bo Jackson, Wally Joyner, John Kruk, and Kevin Mitchell.

	Nm-Mt	Ex-Mt
COMP.FACT.SET (132)	40.00	16.00
1T Andy Allanson	.10	.04
2T Neil Allen	.10	.04
3T Joaquin Andujar	.10	.04
4T Paul Assenmacher	.10	.04
5T Scott Bailes	.10	.04
6T Don Baylor	.25	.10
7T Steve Bedrosian	.10	.04
8T Juan Beniquez	.10	.04
9T Juan Berenguer	.10	.04
10T Mike Bielecki	.10	.04
11T Barry Bonds XRC	30.00	12.00
12T Bobby Bonilla XRC	.50	.20
13T Juan Bonilla	.10	.04
14T Rich Bordi	.10	.04
15T Steve Boros MG	.10	.04
16T Rick Burleson	.10	.04
17T Bill Campbell	.10	.04
18T Tom Candiotti	.10	.04
19T John Cangelosi	.10	.04
20T Jose Canseco XRC	1.50	.60

Card	Nm-Mt	Ex-Mt
21T Carmen Castillo	.10	.04
22T Rick Cerone	.10	.04
23T John Cerutti	.10	.04
24T Will Clark XRC	1.50	.60
25T Mark Clear	.10	.04
26T Darnell Coles	.10	.04
27T Dave Collins	.10	.04
28T Tim Conroy	.10	.04
29T Joe Cowley	.10	.04
30T Joel Davis	.10	.04
31T Rob Deer	.10	.04
32T John Denny	.10	.04
33T Mike Easler	.10	.04
34T Mark Eichhorn	.10	.04
35T Steve Farr	.10	.04
36T Scott Fletcher	.10	.04
37T Terry Forster	.10	.04
38T Terry Francona	.10	.04
39T Jim Fregosi MG	.10	.04
40T Andres Galarraga XRC	1.00	.40
41T Ken Griffey	.15	.06
42T Bill Gullickson	.10	.04
43T Jose Guzman XRC *	.10	.04
44T Moose Haas	.10	.04
45T Billy Hatcher	.10	.04
46T Mike Heath	.10	.04
47T Tom Hume	.10	.04
48T Pete Incaviglia XRC	.25	.10
49T Dane Iorg	.10	.04
50T Bo Jackson XRC	1.50	.60
51T Wally Joyner XRC	.50	.20
52T Charlie Kerfeld	.10	.04
53T Eric King	.10	.04
54T Bob Kipper	.10	.04
55T Wayne Krenchicki	.10	.04
56T John Kruk XRC	.75	.30
57T Mike LaCoss	.10	.04
58T Pete Ladd	.10	.04
59T Mike Laga	.10	.04
60T Hal Lanier MG	.10	.04
61T Dave LaPoint	.10	.04
62T Rudy Law	.10	.04
63T Rick Leach	.10	.04
64T Tim Leary	.10	.04
65T Dennis Leonard	.10	.04
66T Jim Leyland MG XRC	.25	.10
67T Steve Lyons	.10	.04
68T Mickey Mahler	.10	.04
69T Candy Maldonado	.10	.04
70T Roger Mason XRC *	.10	.04
71T Bob McClure	.10	.04
72T Andy McGaffigan	.10	.04
73T Gene Michael MG	.10	.04
74T Kevin Mitchell XRC	.50	.20
75T Omar Moreno	.10	.04
76T Jerry Mumphrey	.10	.04
77T Phil Niekro	.15	.06
78T Randy Niemann	.10	.04
79T Juan Nieves	.10	.04
80T Otis Nixon XRC*	.25	.10
81T Bob Ojeda	.10	.04
82T Jose Oquendo	.10	.04
83T Tom Paciorek	.15	.06
84T David Palmer	.10	.04
85T Frank Pastore	.10	.04
86T Lou Piniella MG	.15	.06
87T Dan Plesac	.10	.04
88T Darrell Porter	.15	.06
89T Rey Quinones	.10	.04
90T Gary Redus	.10	.04
91T Bip Roberts XRC	.25	.10
92T Billy Joe Robidoux	.10	.04
93T Jeff D. Robinson	.10	.04
94T Gary Roenicke	.10	.04
95T Ed Romero	.10	.04
96T Angel Salazar	.10	.04
97T Joe Sambito	.10	.04
98T Billy Sample	.10	.04
99T Dave Schmidt	.10	.04
100T Ken Schrom	.10	.04
101T Tom Seaver	.25	.10
102T Ted Simmons	.15	.06
103T Sammy Stewart	.10	.04
104T Kurt Stillwell	.10	.04
105T Franklin Stubbs	.10	.04
106T Dale Sveum	.10	.04
107T Chuck Tanner MG	.10	.04
108T Danny Tartabull	.15	.06
109T Tim Teufel	.10	.04
110T Bob Tewksbury XRC	.25	.10
111T Andres Thomas	.10	.04
112T Milt Thompson	.10	.04
113T R.Thompson XRC	.25	.10
114T Jay Tibbs	.10	.04
115T Wayne Tolleson	.10	.04
116T Alex Trevino	.10	.04
117T Manny Trillo	.10	.04
118T Ed VandeBerg	.10	.04
119T Ozzie Virgil	.10	.04
120T Bob Walk	.10	.04
121T Gene Walter	.10	.04
122T Claudell Washington	.10	.04
123T Bill Wegman XRC *	.10	.04
124T Dick Williams MG	.15	.06
125T Mitch Williams XRC	.25	.10
126T Bobby Witt XRC	.25	.10
127T Todd Worrell XRC *	.25	.10
128T George Wright	.10	.04
129T Ricky Wright	.10	.04
130T Steve Yeager	.10	.04
131T Paul Zuvella	.10	.04
132T Checklist 1T-132T	.10	.04

1986 Topps Traded Tiffany

For the third consecutive season, Topps issued a Tiffany Update issue to go with their regular issue. These 132 cards feature the same players as in the regular set but have a "glossy" front and very clear back. These cards, released through Topps hobby dealers, were sent out only if the dealer ordered the regular Tiffany set. These cards were printed in Topps' Ireland plant. Again, similar to the regular set, it is believed that 5,000 of these sets were produced.

	Nm-Mt	Ex-Mt
COMP.FACT.SET (132)	1000.00	400.00
*STARS: 5X TO 12X BASIC CARDS		
*ROOKIES: 5X TO 12X BASIC CARDS		

FACTORY SET PRICE IS FOR SEALED SETS
OPENED SETS SELL FOR 50-60% OF SEALED

1986 Topps 3-D

This set consists of 30 plastic-sculpted "cards" each measuring 4 3/8" by 6". Each card was individually wrapped in a red paper wrapper. The card back is blank except for two adhesive strips which could used for mounting the card. Cards are numbered on the front in the lower right corner above the name.

Card	Nm-Mt	Ex-Mt
COMPLETE SET (30)	25.00	10.00
1 Bert Blyleven	.25	.10
2 Gary Carter	1.25	.50
3 Wade Boggs	2.50	1.00
4 Dwight Gooden	.50	.20
5 George Brett	5.00	2.00
6 Rich Gossage	.50	.20
7 Darrell Evans	.25	.10
8 Pedro Guerrero	.25	.10
9 Ron Guidry	.50	.20
10 Keith Hernandez	.75	.30
11 Rickey Henderson	2.50	1.00
12 Orel Hershiser	.75	.30
13 Reggie Jackson	1.50	.60
14 Willie McGee	.75	.30
15 Don Mattingly	5.00	2.00
16 Dale Murphy	1.00	.40
17 Jack Morris	.50	.20
18 Dave Parker	.50	.20
19 Eddie Murray	1.50	.60
20 Jeff Reardon	.25	.10
21 Dan Quisenberry	.25	.10
22 Pete Rose	1.50	.60
23 Jim Rice	.75	.30
24 Mike Schmidt	1.50	.60
25 Bret Saberhagen	.50	.20
26 Darryl Strawberry	.50	.20
27 Dave Stieb	.25	.10
28 John Tudor	.25	.10
29 Dave Winfield	1.50	.60
30 Fernando Valenzuela	.50	.20

1986 Topps Gallery of Champions

This 12 card set features various 1985 league leaders or award winners. For the second straight year, these replica cards were issued in either aluminum, bronze or silver. The cards measure approximately 1 1/4" by 1 3/4" and we have sequenced the set in alphabetical order. The bronze cards are valued at 2X to 4X the aluminum cards while the silvers have a value between 5X and 10X of the aluminums.

Card	Nm-Mt	Ex-Mt
COMPLETE SET (12)	100.00	40.00
1 Wade Boggs	20.00	8.00
2 Vince Coleman	5.00	2.00
3 Darrell Evans	5.00	2.00
4 Dwight Gooden	10.00	4.00
5 Ozzie Guillen	5.00	2.00
6 Don Mattingly	25.00	10.00
7 Willie McGee	8.00	3.20
8 Dale Murphy	15.00	6.00
9 Dan Quisenberry	5.00	2.00
10 Jeff Reardon	5.00	2.00
11 Pete Rose	20.00	8.00
12 Bret Saberhagen	5.00	2.00

1986 Topps Mini Leaders

The 1986 Topps Mini set of Major League Leaders features 66 cards of leaders of the various statistical categories for the 1985 season. The cards are numbered on the back and measure approximately 2 1/8" by 2 15/16". They are very similar in design to the Team Leader "Dean" cards in the 1986 Topps regular issue. The order of the set numbering is alphabetical by player's name as well as alphabetical by team city name within league.

Card	Nm-Mt	Ex-Mt
COMPLETE SET (66)	4.00	1.60
1 Eddie Murray	.50	.20
2 Cal Ripken	2.00	.80
3 Wade Boggs	.50	.20
4 Dennis Boyd	.05	.02
5 Dwight Evans	.10	.04
6 Bruce Hurst	.05	.02
7 Gary Pettis	.05	.02
8 Harold Baines	.15	.06
9 Floyd Bannister	.05	.02
10 Britt Burns	.05	.02
11 Carlton Fisk	.50	.20
12 Brett Butler	.10	.04
13 Darrell Evans	.10	.04
14 Jack Morris	.10	.04
15 Lance Parrish	.05	.02
16 Walt Terrell	.05	.02
17 Steve Balboni	.05	.02
18 George Brett	1.00	.40
19 Charlie Leibrandt	.05	.02
20 Bret Saberhagen	.10	.04
21 Lonnie Smith	.05	.02
22 Willie Wilson	.05	.02
23 Bert Blyleven	.10	.04
24 Mike Smithson	.05	.02
25 Frank Viola	.10	.04
26 Ron Guidry	.10	.04
27 Rickey Henderson	.75	.30
28 Don Mattingly	1.00	.40
29 Dave Winfield	.40	.16
30 Mike Moore	.05	.02
31 Gorman Thomas	.05	.02
32 Toby Harrah	.05	.02
33 Charlie Hough	.05	.02
34 Doyle Alexander	.05	.02
35 Jimmy Key	.10	.04
36 Dave Stieb	.05	.02
37 Dale Murphy	.20	.08
38 Keith Moreland	.05	.02
39 Ryne Sandberg	.75	.30
40 Tom Browning	.05	.02
41 Dave Parker	.10	.04
42 Mario Soto	.05	.02
43 Nolan Ryan	2.00	.80
44 Pedro Guerrero	.05	.02
45 Orel Hershiser	.15	.06
46 Mike Scioscia	.10	.04
47 Fernando Valenzuela	.10	.04
48 Bob Welch	.05	.02
49 Tim Raines	.10	.04
50 Gary Carter	.50	.20
51 Sid Fernandez	.05	.02
52 Dwight Gooden	.10	.04
53 Keith Hernandez	.10	.04
54 Juan Samuel	.05	.02
55 Mike Schmidt	.50	.20
56 Glenn Wilson	.05	.02
57 Rick Reuschel	.05	.02
58 Joaquin Andujar	.05	.02
59 Jack Clark	.05	.02
60 Vince Coleman	.10	.04
61 Danny Cox	.05	.02
62 Tom Herr	.05	.02
63 Willie McGee	.10	.04
64 John Tudor	.05	.02
65 Tony Gwynn	1.00	.40
66 Checklist Card	.05	.02

1986 Topps Stickers

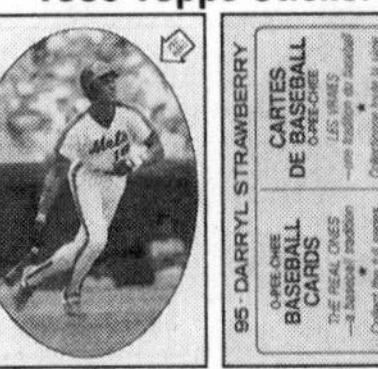

Made in Italy for O-Pee-Chee by Panini, these 315 stickers measure approximately 2 1/8" by 3" and are numbered on both front and back. The fronts feature white-bordered color player photos. The horizontal backs carry a bilingual ad for O-Pee-Chee. An album onto which the stickers could be affixed was available at retail stores. The album and the sticker numbering are organized as follows: 1985 Highlights (1-10), 1985 Championship Series (11-16), 1985 World Series (17-23), Houston Astros (24-33), Atlanta Braves (34-43), St. Louis Cardinals (44-53), Chicago Cubs (54-63), Los Angeles Dodgers (64-73), Montreal Expos (74-83), San Francisco Giants (84-93), New York Mets (94-103), San Diego Padres (104-113), Philadelphia Phillies (114-123), Pittsburgh Pirates (124-133), Cincinnati Reds (134-143), 1985 NL Stat Leaders (144, 145), Foil All-Stars (146-163), 1985 AL Stat Leaders (164, 165), Oakland A's (166-175), California Angels (176-185), Toronto Blue Jays (186-195), Milwaukee Brewers (196-205), Cleveland Indians (206-215), Seattle Mariners (216-225), Baltimore Orioles (226-235), Texas Rangers (236-245), Boston Red Sox (246-255), Kansas City Royals (256-265), Detroit Tigers (266-275), Minnesota Twins (276-285), Chicago White Sox (286-295), New York Yankees (296-305), and Future Stars (306-315). For those stickers featuring more than one player, the other numbers on that sticker are given below in parentheses. The Topps stickers contain offers on the back to obtain either a trip for four to Spring Training of the team of your choice or a complete set of Topps baseball cards directly from Topps.

Card	Nm-Mt	Ex-Mt
COMPLETE SET (315)	15.00	6.00
COMMON STICKER (1-315)	.05	.02
COMMON FOIL PLAYER	.10	.04
*TOPPS AND OPC: SAME VALUE		
1 Pete Rose FOIL (Top half)	.60	.24
2 Pete Rose FOIL (Bottom half)	.60	.24
3 George Brett (175)	.75	.30
4 Rod Carew (178)	.40	.16
5 Vince Coleman (179)	.15	.06
6 Dwight Gooden (180)	.25	.10
7 Phil Niekro (181)	.25	.10
8 Tony Perez (182)	.25	.10
9 Nolan Ryan (183)	2.00	.80
10 Tom Seaver (184)	.50	.20
11 NL Championship (Ozzie Smith batting)	.15	.06
12 NL Championship (Bill Madlock)	.10	.04
13 NL Championship (Cardinals celebrate)	.10	.04
14 AL Championship (Al Oliver swings)	.10	.04
15 AL Championship (Jim Sundberg)	.05	.02
16 AL Championship (George Brett swings)	.75	.30
17 World Series (Bret Saberhagen)	.10	.04
18 World Series (Dane Iorg swings)	.05	.02
19 World Series (Tito Landrum)	.05	.02
20 World Series (John Tudor)	.05	.02
21 World Series (Buddy Biancalana)	.05	.02
22 World Series (Darryl Motley)	.05	.02
23 World Series (George Brett and Frank White)	.25	.10
24 Nolan Ryan	2.00	.80
25 Bill Doran	.05	.02
26 Jose Cruz (185)	.10	.04
27 Mike Scott (188)	.05	.02
28 Kevin Bass (189)	.05	.02
29 Glenn Davis (190)	.10	.04
30 Mark Bailey (191)	.05	.02
31 Dave Smith (192)	.05	.02
32 Phil Garner (193)	.10	.04
33 Dickie Thon (194)	.05	.02
34 Bob Horner	.05	.02
35 Dale Murphy	.15	.06
36 Glenn Hubbard (195)	.05	.02
37 Bruce Sutter (198)	.10	.04
38 Ken Oberkfell (199)	.05	.02
39 Claudell Washington (200)	.05	.02
40 Steve Bedrosian (201)	.05	.02
41 Terry Harper (202)	.05	.02
42 Rafael Ramirez (203)	.05	.02
43 Rick Mahler (204)	.05	.02
44 Joaquin Andujar	.05	.02
45 Willie McGee	.15	.06
46 Ozzie Smith (205)	.40	.16
47 Vince Coleman (208)	.15	.06
48 Danny Cox (209)	.05	.02
49 Tom Herr (210)	.05	.02
50 Jack Clark (211)	.10	.04
51 Andy Van Slyke (212)	.10	.04
52 John Tudor (213)	.05	.02
53 Terry Pendleton(214)	.15	.06
54 Keith Moreland	.05	.02
55 Ryne Sandberg	.60	.24
56 Lee Smith (215)	.15	.06
57 Steve Trout (218)	.05	.02
58 Jody Davis (219)	.05	.02
59 Gary Matthews (220)	.05	.02
60 Leon Durham (221)	.05	.02
61 Rick Sutcliffe (222)	.05	.02
62 Dennis Eckersley (223)	.15	.06
63 Bob Dernier (224)	.05	.02
64 Fernando Valenzuela	.10	.04
65 Pedro Guerrero	.05	.02
66 Jerry Reuss (225)	.05	.02
67 Greg Brock (228)	.05	.02
68 Mike Scioscia (229)	.05	.02
69 Ken Howell (230)	.05	.02
70 Bill Madlock (231)	.10	.04
71 Mike Marshall (232)	.05	.02
72 Steve Sax (233)	.05	.02
73 Orel Hershiser (234)	.15	.06
74 Andre Dawson	.25	.10
75 Tim Raines	.10	.04
76 Jeff Reardon (235)	.10	.04
77 Hubie Brooks (238)	.05	.02
78 Bill Gullickson(239)	.05	.02
79 Bryn Smith (240)	.05	.02
80 Terry Francona (241)	.10	.04
81 Vance Law (242)	.05	.02
82 Tim Wallach (243)	.05	.02
83 He.Winningham (244)	.05	.02
84 Jeff Leonard	.05	.02
85 Chris Brown	.05	.02
86 Scott Garrelts (245)	.05	.02
87 Jose Uribe (248)	.05	.02
88 Manny Trillo (249)	.05	.02
89 Dan Driessen (250)	.05	.02
90 Dan Gladden (251)	.05	.02
91 Mark Davis (252)	.05	.02
92 Bob Brenly (253)	.05	.02
93 Mike Krukow (254)	.05	.02
94 Dwight Gooden	.25	.10
95 Darryl Strawberry	.15	.06
96 Gary Carter (255)	.10	.04
97 Wally Backman (258)	.05	.02
98 Ron Darling (259)	.05	.02
99 Keith Hernandez(260)	.10	.04
100 George Foster (261)	.10	.04
101 Howard Johnson (262)	.10	.04
102 Rafael Santana (263)	.05	.02
103 Roger McDowell (264)	.10	.04
104 Steve Garvey	.15	.06
105 Tony Gwynn	1.00	.40
106 Graig Nettles (265)	.10	.04
107 Rich Gossage (268)	.10	.04
108 Andy Hawkins (269)	.05	.02
109 Carmelo Martinez (270)	.05	.02
110 Garry Templeton(271)	.05	.02
111 Terry Kennedy (272)	.05	.02
112 Tim Flannery (273)	.05	.02
113 LaMarr Hoyt (274)	.05	.02
114 Mike Schmidt	.60	.24
115 Ozzie Virgil	.05	.02
116 Steve Carlton (275)	.40	.16
117 Garry Maddox (278)	.05	.02
118 Glenn Wilson (279)	.05	.02
119 Kevin Gross (280)	.05	.02
120 Von Hayes (281)	.05	.02
121 Juan Samuel (282)	.05	.02
122 Rick Schu (283)	.05	.02
123 Shane Rawley (284)	.05	.02
124 Johnny Ray	.05	.02
125 Tony Pena	.05	.02
126 Rick Reuschel (285)	.05	.02
127 Sammy Khalifa (288)	.05	.02
128 Marvell Wynne (289)	.05	.02
129 Jason Thompson (290)	.05	.02
130 Rick Rhoden (291)	.05	.02
131 Bill Almon (292)	.05	.02
132 Joe Orsulak (293)	.05	.02
133 Jim Morrison (294)	.05	.02
134 Pete Rose	.75	.30
135 Dave Parker	.10	.04
136 Mario Soto (295)	.05	.02
137 Dave Concepcion(298)	.10	.04
138 Ron Oester (299)	.05	.02
139 Buddy Bell (300)	.10	.04
140 Ted Power (301)	.05	.02
141 Tom Browning (302)	.05	.02
142 John Franco (303)	.15	.06
143 Tony Perez (304)	.15	.06
144 Willie McGee (305)	.10	.04
145 Dale Murphy (306)	.15	.06
146 Tony Gwynn FOIL	1.50	.60
147 Tom Herr FOIL	.10	.04
148 Steve Garvey FOIL	.25	.10
149 Dale Murphy FOIL	.20	.08
150 Darryl Strawberry FOIL	.25	.10
151 Graig Nettles FOIL	.20	.08
152 Terry Kennedy FOIL	.10	.04
153 Ozzie Smith FOIL	.60	.24
154 LaMarr Hoyt FOIL	.10	.04
155 Rickey Henderson FOIL	.40	.16
156 Lou Whitaker FOIL	.15	.06
157 George Brett FOIL	1.25	.50
158 Eddie Murray FOIL	.50	.20
159 Cal Ripken FOIL	3.00	1.20
160 Dave Winfield FOIL	.40	.16
161 Jim Rice FOIL	.15	.06
162 Carlton Fisk FOIL	.40	.16
163 Jack Morris FOIL	.15	.06
164 Wade Boggs (307)	.25	.10
165 Darrell Evans (308)	.10	.04
166 Mike Davis	.05	.02
167 Dave Kingman	.10	.04
168 Alfredo Griffin(309)	.05	.02
169 Carney Lansford(310)	.10	.04
170 Bruce Bochte (311)	.05	.02
171 Dwayne Murphy (312)	.05	.02
172 Dave Collins (313)	.05	.02
173 Chris Codiroli (314)	.05	.02
174 Mike Heath (315)	.05	.02
175 Jay Howell (3)	.05	.02
176 Rod Carew	.40	.16
177 Reggie Jackson	.50	.20
178 Doug DeCinces (4)	.05	.02
179 Bob Boone (5)	.10	.04
180 Ron Romanick (6)	.05	.02
181 Bob Grich (7)	.10	.04
182 Donnie Moore (8)	.05	.02
183 Brian Downing (9)	.05	.02
184 Ruppert Jones (10)	.05	.02
185 Juan Beniquez (26)	.05	.02
186 Dave Stieb	.05	.02
187 George Bell	.05	.02
188 Willie Upshaw (27)	.05	.02
189 Tom Henke (28)	.10	.04
190 Damaso Garcia (29)	.05	.02
191 Jimmy Key (30)	.15	.06
192 Jesse Barfield (31)	.05	.02
193 Dennis Lamp (32)	.05	.02
194 Tony Fernandez (33)	.05	.02
195 Lloyd Moseby (36)	.05	.02
196 Cecil Cooper	.10	.04
197 Robin Yount	.15	.06
198 Rollie Fingers (37)	.15	.06
199 Ted Simmons (38)	.10	.04
200 Ben Oglivie (39)	.05	.02
201 Moose Haas (40)	.05	.02
202 Jim Gantner (41)	.05	.02
203 Paul Molitor (42)	.15	.06
204 Charlie Moore (43)	.05	.02
205 Danny Darwin (46)	.05	.02
206 Brett Butler	.10	.04
207 Brook Jacoby	.05	.02
208 Andre Thornton (47)	.05	.02
209 Tom Waddell (48)	.05	.02
210 Tony Bernazard (49)	.05	.02
211 Julio Franco (50)	.10	.04
212 Pat Tabler (51)	.05	.02
213 Joe Carter (52)	.25	.10
214 George Vukovich (53)	.05	.02
215 Rich Thompson (56)	.05	.02
216 Gorman Thomas	.05	.02
217 Phil Bradley	.05	.02
218 Alvin Davis (57)	.05	.02
219 Jim Presley (58)	.05	.02
220 Matt Young (59)	.05	.02
221 Mike Moore (60)	.05	.02
222 Dave Henderson (61)	.05	.02
223 Ed Nunez (62)	.05	.02
224 Spike Owen (63)	.05	.02
225 Mark Langston (66)	.05	.02
226 Cal Ripken	2.00	.80
227 Eddie Murray	.25	.10
228 Fred Lynn (67)	.10	.04
229 Lee Lacy (68)	.05	.02
230 Scott McGregor (69)	.05	.02
231 Storm Davis (70)	.05	.02
232 Rick Dempsey (71)	.10	.04
233 Mike Boddicker (72)	.05	.02
234 Mike Young (73)	.05	.02
235 Sammy Stewart (76)	.05	.02
236 Pete O'Brien	.05	.02
237 Oddibe McDowell	.05	.02
238 Toby Harrah (77)	.05	.02
239 Gary Ward (78)	.05	.02
240 Larry Parrish (79)	.05	.02
241 Charlie Hough (80)	.10	.04
242 Burt Hooton (81)	.05	.02
243 Don Slaught (82)	.05	.02
244 Curt Wilkerson (83)	.05	.02
245 Greg Harris (86)	.05	.02
246 Jim Rice	.10	.04
247 Wade Boggs	.25	.10
248 Rich Gedman (87)	.05	.02
249 Dennis Boyd (88)	.05	.02
250 Marty Barrett (89)	.05	.02
251 Dwight Evans (90)	.10	.04
252 Bill Buckner (91)	.10	.04
253 Bob Stanley (92)	.05	.02
254 Tony Armas (93)	.05	.02
255 Mike Easler (96)	.05	.02
256 George Brett	.75	.30
257 Dan Quisenberry	.05	.02
258 Willie Wilson (97)	.05	.02
259 Jim Sundberg (98)	.05	.02
260 Bret Saberhagen (99)	.10	.04
261 Bud Black (100)	.05	.02
262 Charlie Leibrandt (101)	.05	.02
263 Frank White (102)	.10	.04
264 Lonnie Smith (103)	.05	.02
265 Steve Balboni (106)	.05	.02
266 Kirk Gibson	.10	.04
267 Alan Trammell	.15	.06
268 Jack Morris (107)	.10	.04
269 Darrell Evans (108)	.10	.04
270 Dan Petry (109)	.05	.02

271 Larry Herndon (110)	.05	.02
272 Lou Whitaker (111)	.10	.04
273 Lance Parrish (112)	.10	.04
274 Chet Lemon (113)	.05	.02
275 Willie Hernandez (116)	.05	.02
276 Tom Brunansky	.05	.02
277 Kent Hrbek	.10	.04
278 Mark Salas (117)	.05	.02
279 Bert Blyleven (118)	.10	.04
280 Tim Teufel (119)	.05	.02
281 Ron Davis (120)	.05	.02
282 Mike Smithson (121)	.05	.02
283 Gary Gaetti (122)	.10	.04
284 Frank Viola (123)	.10	.04
285 Kirby Puckett (126)	1.50	.60
286 Carlton Fisk	.25	.10
287 Tom Seaver	.50	.20
288 Harold Baines (127)	.10	.04
289 Ron Kittle (128)	.05	.02
290 Bob James (129)	.05	.02
291 Rudy Law (130)	.05	.02
292 Britt Burns (131)	.05	.02
293 Greg Walker (132)	.05	.02
294 Ozzie Guillen (133)	.15	.06
295 Tim Hulett (136)	.05	.02
296 Don Mattingly	1.50	.60
297 Rickey Henderson	.25	.10
298 Dave Winfield (137)	.25	.10
299 Butch Wynegar (138)	.05	.02
300 Don Baylor (139)	.10	.04
301 Eddie Whitson (140)	.05	.02
302 Ron Guidry (141)	.10	.04
303 Dave Righetti (142)	.05	.02
304 Bobby Meacham (143)	.05	.02
305 Willie Randolph(144)	.10	.04
306 Vince Coleman (145)	.15	.06
307 Oddibe McDowell(164)	.05	.02
308 Larry Sheets (165)	.05	.02
309 Ozzie Guillen (168)	.15	.06
310 Ernie Riles (169)	.05	.02
311 Chris Brown (170)	.05	.02
312 Brian Fisher and Roger McDowell (171)	.05	.02
313 Tom Browning (172)	.05	.02
314 Glenn Davis (173)	.05	.02
315 Mark Salas (174)	.05	.02
NNO Album	1.00	.40

1986 Topps Rose

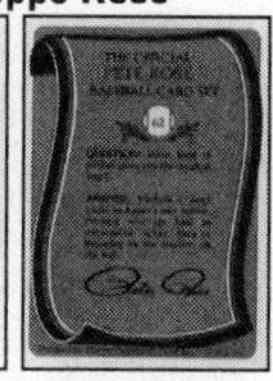

his set of 120 different standard-size cards is edicated to Pete Rose. The set was sold in a ed and white box and distributed by Renata alasso, Inc. The checklist below gives the istinguishing features of each of the cards. Many of the backs feature a question and nswer back. Since many of the pictures are imilar, the back question is frequently xcerpted below. The first three cards feature aditional statistical backs and the last 30 ards (91-120) feature backs that form a puzzle hich, when completely assembled, shows in olor all of Pete's Topps baseball cards up rough 1985. In the set there are several cards hich picture paintings of Pete at various tages of his career by artist Ron Lewis.

	Nm-Mt	Ex-Mt
OMP. FACT SET (120)	12.50	5.00
OMMON CARD (1-120)	.15	.06
Pete Rose	.40	.16
Statistics '60s; Lewis painting		
Pete Rose	.15	.06
Pete Rose Jr.		
hit number 3631		
6 Pete Rose	.15	.06
Tyler Rose		
with horse		
8 Pete Rose	.15	.06
Ray Fosse		
collision		
9 Pete Rose	.15	.06
Ray Fosse		
Pete got hurt in collision		
0 Pete Rose	.15	.06
Bud Harrelson		
fight; Lewis painting		
3 Pete Rose	.15	.06
Pete Rose Jr.		
Hugs		
7 Pete Rose	.15	.06
Babe Ruth		
8 Pete Rose	.15	.06
Talking to Reagan		
20 Pete Rose	.25	.10
Scoreboard		

1986 Topps Super

his 60-card set actually consists of giant-sized ersions of the Topps regular issue of some of e most popular players. The cards measure 4 "8" by 6 7/8". Cards are very similar to the opps regular issue; two exceptions are that on e back they are numbered differently and an dditional line of type is printed at the bottom the back noting an accomplishment of that ayer at the end of the 1985 season.

	Nm-Mt	Ex-Mt
OMPLETE SET (60)	20.00	8.00
Don Mattingly	2.00	.80
Willie McGee	.20	.08
Bret Saberhagen	.20	.08
Dwight Gooden	.20	.08
Dan Quisenberry	.10	.04
Jeff Reardon	.10	.04
Ozzie Guillen	.10	.04
Vince Coleman	.20	.08
9 Harold Baines	.30	.12
10 Jorge Bell	.10	.04
11 Bert Blyleven	.20	.08
12 Wade Boggs	1.00	.40
13 Phil Bradley	.10	.04
14 George Brett	2.00	.80
15 Hubie Brooks	.10	.04
16 Tom Browning	.10	.04
17 Bill Buckner	.10	.04
18 Brett Butler	.20	.08
19 Gary Carter	.75	.30
20 Cecil Cooper	.10	.04
21 Darrell Evans	.10	.04
22 Dwight Evans	.20	.08
23 Carlton Fisk	.50	.20
24 Steve Garvey	.30	.12
25 Kirk Gibson	.20	.08
26 Rich Gossage	.20	.08
27 Pedro Guerrero	.10	.04
28 Ron Guidry	.20	.08
29 Tony Gwynn	2.00	.80
30 Rickey Henderson	1.25	.50
31 Keith Hernandez	.20	.08
32 Tom Herr	.10	.04
33 Orel Hershiser	.30	.12
34 Jay Howell	.10	.04
35 Reggie Jackson	.75	.30
36 Bob James	.10	.04
37 Charlie Leibrandt	.10	.04
38 Jack Morris	.20	.08
39 Dale Murphy	.30	.12
40 Eddie Murray	.75	.30
41 Dave Parker	.20	.08
42 Tim Raines	.20	.08
43 Jim Rice	.20	.08
44 Dave Righetti	.10	.04
45 Cal Ripken	4.00	1.60
46 Pete Rose	1.00	.40
47 Nolan Ryan	4.00	1.60
48 Ryne Sandberg	2.00	.80
49 Mike Schmidt	.75	.30
50 Tom Seaver	.75	.30
51 Bryn Smith	.10	.04
52 Lee Smith	.30	.12
53 Ozzie Smith	2.00	.80
54 Dave Stieb	.10	.04
55 Darryl Strawberry	.20	.08
56 Gorman Thomas	.10	.04
57 John Tudor	.10	.04
58 Fernando Valenzuela	.20	.08
59 Willie Wilson	.10	.04
60 Dave Winfield	.75	.30

1986 Topps Tattoos

This set of 24 different tattoo sheets was distributed one sheet (with gum) per pack as a separate issue by Topps (and also by O-Pee-Chee). Each tattoo sheet measures approximately 3 7/16" by 14 1/4" whereas the individual player tattoos are approximately 1 13/16" by 2 3/8". The wrapper advertises 18 tattoos in the pack, which includes eight small (half-size) generic action shots. The players have their names and team names reverse printed beneath their transfers. The 1986 Topps (or O-Pee-Chee) copyright mark is shown at the bottom right. The checklist below lists only the individual player tattoos; they are listed in order of appearance top to bottom on the sheet. Each tattoo sheet is numbered at the top "X of 24."

	Nm-Mt	Ex-Mt
COMPLETE SET (24)	8.00	3.20
*O-PEE-CHEE: SAME VALUE		
1 Dickie Thon	.40	.16
Charlie Leibrandt		
Dave Winfield		
Lee Smith		
Julio Franco		
Keith Hernandez		
Jack Perconte		
Rich Gossage		
2 Dale Murphy	.40	.16
Brian Fisher		
Bret Saberhagen		
Shawon Dunston		
Jesse Barfield		
Moose Haas		
Dennis Eckersley		
Mike Moore		
3 Steve Carlton	.30	.12
Dan Quisenberry		
Bob James		
Bob Brenly		
George Bell		
Jose DeLeon		
Andre Thornton		
Bob Horner		
4 Johnny Ray	2.00	.80
Darrell Evans		
Mike Davis		
Leon Durham		
Harold Baines		
Cal Ripken		
Glenn Hubbard		
Ted Simmons		
5 Jesse Orosco	.30	.12
Rick Dempsey		
John Candelaria		
Tony Pena		
Brook Jacoby		
Gary Matthews		
Ozzie Guillen		
Steve Garvey		
6 Ron Kittle	1.00	.40
Pete Rose		
Sammy Khalifa		
Bruce Bochte		
Scott McGregor		
Mookie Wilson		
George Brett		
Cecil Cooper		
7 Larry Sheets	2.00	.80
John Franco		
Graig Nettles		
Don Mattingly		
Carney Lansford		
Rick Reuschel		
Don Sutton		
Mike Schmidt		
8 Phil Niekro	.75	.30
Ryne Sandberg		
Mike Krukow		
Fred Lynn		
Willie Hernandez		
Pat Tabler		
Ed Nunez		
Cecilio Guante		
9 Chris Codiroli	.40	.16
Glenn Wilson		
Rick Rhoden		
Brett Butler		
Robin Yount		
Dave Parker		
Jim Gantner		
Charlie Hough		
10 Chet Lemon	.40	.16
Mike Smithson		
Ron Darling		
Tom Seaver		
Von Hayes		
Tom Browning		
Bruce Sutter		
Alan Trammell		
11 Rick Mahler	.20	.08
Dave Righetti		
Jay Howell		
Jose Cruz		
Jack Morris		
Tony Armas		
Mike Young		
Rafael Ramirez		
12 Keith Moreland	.10	.04
Alvin Davis		
Doug DeCinces		
John Tudor		
Jim Presley		
Andy Hawkins		
Dennis Lamp		
Mario Soto		
13 Charles Hudson	1.50	.60
Dwight Evans		
Kirby Puckett		
Jody Davis		
Eddie Murray		
Jose Uribe		
Ron Hassey		
Hubie Brooks		
14 LaMarr Hoyt	.20	.08
Brian Downing		
Ron Guidry		
Dan Driessen		
Tony Bernazard		
Garry Maddox		
Phil Bradley		
Bill Buckner		
15 Tito Landrum	.40	.16
Hal McRae		
Joe Carter		
Jeff Leonard		
Tony Fernandez		
Juan Samuel		
Buddy Bell		
Willie Randolph		
16 Scott Garrelts	.75	.30
Dennis Boyd		
Donnie Moore		
Tony Perez		
Vince Coleman		
Alfredo Griffin		
Frank White		
Ozzie Smith		
17 Claudell Washington	.75	.30
Rich Gedman		
Reggie Jackson		
Terry Pendleton		
Mark Salas		
Mike Marshall		
Kent Hrbek		
Tim Raines		
18 Ron Davis	.20	.08
Glenn Davis		
Chris Brown		
Burt Hooton		
Darryl Strawberry		
Tom Brunansky		
Tim Wallach		
Frank Viola		
19 Jack Clark	.20	.08
Toby Harrah		
Larry Parrish		
Mike Scioscia		
Pete O'Brien		
Bill Doran		
Garry Templeton		
Bill Madlock		
20 Dwight Gooden	.75	.30
Andre Dawson		
Roger McDowell		
Oddibe McDowell		
Gary Carter		
Orel Hershiser		
Jim Rice		
Dwayne Murphy		
21 Steve Balboni	.10	.04
Rick Sutcliffe		
Charlie Lea		
Mike Easler		
Steve Sax		
Gary Ward		
Lloyd Moseby		
Willie Wilson		
22 Lance Parrish	.40	.16
Tom Herr		
Bryn Smith		
Kirk Gibson		
Jeff Reardon		
Gorman Thomas		
Wade Boggs		
Dave Concepcion		
23 Dave Stieb	.40	.16
Willie McGee		
Bob Grich		
Paul Molitor		
Pedro Guerrero		
Carlton Fisk		
Mike Scott		
Lou Whitaker		
24 Tony Gwynn	3.00	1.20
Rickey Henderson		
Damaso Garcia		
Nolan Ryan		
Bert Blyleven		
Fernando Valenzuela		
Ben Oglivie		
Phil Garner		

1987 Topps

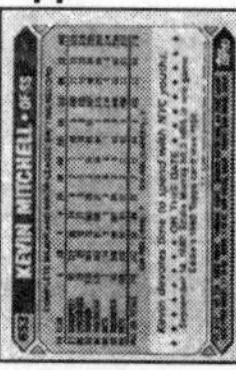

This set consists of 792 standard-size cards. Cards were primarily issued in 17-card wax packs, 50-card rack packs and factory sets. Card fronts feature wood grain borders encasing a color photo (reminiscent of Topps' classic 1962 baseball set). Subsets include Record Breakers (1-7), Turn Back the Clock (311-315), All-Star selections (595-616) and Team Leaders (scattered throughout the set). The manager cards contain a team checklist on back. The key Rookie Cards in this set are Barry Bonds, Bobby Bonilla, Will Clark, Bo Jackson, Wally Joyner, John Kruk, Barry Larkin, Rafael Palmiero, Ruben Sierra, and Devon White.

	Nm-Mt	Ex-Mt
COMPLETE SET (792)	25.00	10.00
COMP.FACT SET (792)	25.00	10.00
COMP.HOBBY SET (792)	40.00	16.00
COMP.X-MAS.SET (792)	40.00	16.00
1 Roger Clemens RB	.25	.10
2 Jim Deshaies RB	.05	.02
3 Dwight Evans RB	.10	.04
4 Davey Lopes RB	.05	.02
5 Dave Righetti RB	.05	.02
6 Ruben Sierra RB	.25	.10
7 Todd Worrell RB	.05	.02
8 Terry Pendleton	.10	.04
9 Jay Tibbs	.05	.02
10 Cecil Cooper	.10	.04
11 Indians Team	.05	.02
(Mound conference)		
12 Jeff Sellers	.05	.02
13 Nick Esasky	.05	.02
14 Dave Stewart	.10	.04
15 Claudell Washington	.05	.02
16 Pat Clements	.05	.02
17 Pete O'Brien	.05	.02
18 Dick Howser MG	.05	.02
19 Matt Young	.05	.02
20 Gary Carter	.15	.06
21 Mark Davis	.05	.02
22 Doug DeCinces	.05	.02
23 Lee Smith	.15	.06
24 Tony Walker	.05	.02
25 Bert Blyleven	.10	.04
26 Greg Brock	.05	.02
27 Joe Cowley	.05	.02
28 Rick Dempsey	.10	.04
29 Jimmy Key	.10	.04
30 Tim Raines	.10	.04
31 Braves Team	.05	.02
(Glenn Hubbard and Rafael Ramirez)		
32 Tim Leary	.05	.02
33 Andy Van Slyke	.10	.04
34 Jose Rijo	.05	.02
35 Sid Bream	.05	.02
36 Eric King	.05	.02
37 Marvell Wynne	.05	.02
38 Dennis Leonard	.05	.02
39 Marty Barrett	.05	.02
40 Dave Righetti	.05	.02
41 Bo Diaz	.05	.02
42 Gary Redus	.05	.02
43 Gene Michael MG	.05	.02
44 Greg Harris	.05	.02
45 Jim Presley	.05	.02
46 Dan Gladden	.05	.02
47 Dennis Powell	.05	.02
48 Wally Backman	.05	.02
49 Terry Harper	.05	.02
50 Dave Smith	.05	.02
51 Mel Hall	.05	.02
52 Keith Atherton	.05	.02
53 Ruppert Jones	.05	.02
54 Bill Dawley	.05	.02
55 Tim Wallach	.05	.02
56 Brewers Team	.05	.02
(Mound conference)		
57 Scott Nielsen	.05	.02
58 Thad Bosley	.05	.02
59 Ken Dayley	.05	.02
60 Tony Pena	.05	.02
61 Bobby Thigpen RC	.25	.10
62 Bobby Meacham	.05	.02
63 Fred Toliver	.05	.02
64 Harry Spilman	.05	.02
65 Tom Browning	.05	.02
66 Marc Sullivan	.05	.02
67 Bill Swift	.05	.02
68 Tony LaRussa MG	.10	.04
69 Lonnie Smith	.05	.02
70 Charlie Hough	.10	.04
71 Mike Aldrete	.05	.02
72 Walt Terrell	.05	.02
73 Dave Anderson	.05	.02
74 Dan Pasqua	.05	.02
75 Ron Darling	.05	.02
76 Rafael Ramirez	.05	.02
77 Bryan Oelkers	.05	.02
78 Tom Foley	.05	.02
79 Juan Nieves	.05	.02
80 Wally Joyner RC	.40	.16
81 Padres Team	.05	.02
(Andy Hawkins and Terry Kennedy)		
82 Rob Murphy	.05	.02
83 Mike Davis	.05	.02
84 Steve Lake	.05	.02
85 Kevin Bass	.05	.02
86 Nate Snell	.05	.02
87 Mark Salas	.05	.02
88 Ed Wojna	.05	.02
89 Ozzie Guillen	.10	.04
90 Dave Stieb	.05	.02
91 Harold Reynolds	.10	.04
92A Urbano Lugo	.15	.06
ERR (no trademark)		
92B Urbano Lugo COR	.05	.02
93 Jim Leyland MG/TC RC*	.25	.10
94 Calvin Schiraldi	.05	.02
95 Oddibe McDowell	.05	.02
96 Frank Williams	.05	.02
97 Glenn Wilson	.05	.02
98 Bill Scherrer	.05	.02
99 Darryl Motley	.05	.02
(Now with Braves on card front)		
100 Steve Garvey	.10	.04
101 Carl Willis RC	.10	.04
102 Paul Zuvella	.05	.02
103 Rick Aguilera	.10	.04
104 Billy Sample	.05	.02
105 Floyd Youmans	.05	.02
106 Blue Jays Team	.05	.02
(George Bell and Jesse Barfield)		
107 John Butcher	.05	.02
108 Jim Gantner UER	.05	.02
(Brewers logo reversed)		
109 R.J. Reynolds	.05	.02
110 John Tudor	.05	.02
111 Alfredo Griffin	.05	.02
112 Alan Ashby	.05	.02
113 Neil Allen	.05	.02
114 Billy Beane	.10	.04
115 Donnie Moore	.05	.02
116 Bill Russell	.05	.02
117 Jim Beattie	.05	.02
118 Bobby Valentine MG	.05	.02
119 Ron Robinson	.05	.02
120 Eddie Murray	.25	.10
121 Kevin Romine	.05	.02
122 Jim Clancy	.05	.02
123 John Kruk RC*	.40	.16
124 Ray Fontenot	.05	.02
125 Bob Brenly	.05	.02
126 Mike Loynd RC	.05	.02
127 Vance Law	.05	.02
128 Checklist 1-132	.05	.02
129 Rick Cerone	.05	.02
130 Dwight Gooden	.15	.06
131 Pirates Team	.05	.02
(Sid Bream and Tony Pena)		
132 Paul Assenmacher	.15	.06
133 Jose Oquendo	.05	.02
134 Rich Yett	.05	.02
135 Mike Easler	.05	.02
136 Ron Romanick	.05	.02
137 Jerry Willard	.05	.02
138 Roy Lee Jackson	.05	.02
139 Devon White RC	.40	.16
140 Bret Saberhagen	.10	.04
141 Herm Winningham	.05	.02
142 Rick Sutcliffe	.10	.04
143 Steve Boros MG	.05	.02
144 Mike Scioscia	.05	.02
145 Charlie Kerfeld	.05	.02
146 Tracy Jones	.05	.02
147 Randy Niemann	.05	.02
148 Dave Collins	.05	.02
149 Ray Searage	.05	.02
150 Wade Boggs	.15	.06
151 Mike LaCoss	.05	.02
152 Toby Harrah	.05	.02
153 Duane Ward RC *	.25	.10
154 Tom O'Malley	.05	.02
155 Eddie Whitson	.05	.02
156 Mariners Team	.05	.02
(Mound conference)		
157 Danny Darwin	.05	.02
158 Tim Teufel	.05	.02
159 Ed Olwine	.05	.02
160 Julio Franco	.10	.04
161 Steve Ontiveros	.05	.02
162 Mike LaValliere RC *	.25	.10
163 Kevin Gross	.05	.02
164 Sammy Khalifa	.05	.02
165 Jeff Reardon	.10	.04
166 Bob Boone	.10	.04
167 Jim Deshaies RC *	.10	.04
168 Lou Piniella MG	.10	.04
169 Ron Washington	.05	.02
170 Bo Jackson RC	1.00	.40
171 Chuck Cary	.05	.02
172 Ron Oester	.05	.02
173 Alex Trevino	.05	.02
174 Henry Cotto	.05	.02
175 Bob Stanley	.05	.02
176 Steve Buechele	.05	.02
177 Keith Moreland	.05	.02
178 Cecil Fielder	.15	.06
179 Bill Wegman	.05	.02
180 Chris Brown	.05	.02
181 Cardinals Team	.05	.02
(Mound conference)		
182 Lee Lacy	.05	.02
183 Andy Hawkins	.05	.02
184 Bobby Bonilla RC	.40	.16
185 Roger McDowell	.05	.02
186 Bruce Benedict	.05	.02
187 Mark Huismann	.05	.02
188 Tony Phillips	.05	.02
189 Joe Hesketh	.05	.02

190 Jim Sundberg .05 .02
191 Charles Hudson .05 .02
192 Cory Snyder .05 .02
193 Roger Craig MG .05 .02
194 Kirk McCaskill .05 .02
195 Mike Pagliarulo .05 .02
196 Randy O'Neal UER .05 .02
(Wrong ML career
W-L totals)
197 Mark Bailey .05 .02
198 Lee Mazzilli .05 .02
199 Mariano Duncan .05 .02
200 Pete Rose .60 .24
201 John Cangelosi .05 .02
202 Ricky Wright .05 .02
203 Mike Kingery RC .10 .04
204 Sammy Stewart .05 .02
205 Graig Nettles .10 .04
206 Twins Team .05 .02
(Frank Viola and
Tim Laudner)
207 George Frazier .05 .02
208 John Shelby .05 .02
209 Rick Schu .05 .02
210 Lloyd Moseby .05 .02
211 John Morris .05 .02
212 Mike Fitzgerald .05 .02
213 Randy Myers RC .40 .16
214 Omar Moreno .05 .02
215 Mark Langston .05 .02
216 B.J. Surhoff RC .40 .16
217 Chris Codiroli .05 .02
218 Sparky Anderson MG .10 .04
219 Cecilio Guante .05 .02
220 Joe Carter .25 .10
221 Vern Ruhle .05 .02
222 Denny Walling .05 .02
223 Charlie Leibrandt .05 .02
224 Wayne Tolleson .05 .02
225 Mike Smithson .05 .02
226 Max Venable .05 .02
227 Jamie Moyer RC .50 .20
228 Curt Wilkerson .05 .02
229 Mike Birkbeck .10 .04
230 Don Baylor .10 .04
231 Giants Team .05 .02
(Bob Brenly and
Jim Gott)
232 Reggie Williams .05 .02
233 Russ Morman .05 .02
234 Pat Sheridan .05 .02
235 Alvin Davis .05 .02
236 Tommy John .10 .04
237 Jim Morrison .05 .02
238 Bill Krueger .05 .02
239 Juan Espino .05 .02
240 Steve Balboni .05 .02
241 Danny Heep .05 .02
242 Rick Mahler .05 .02
243 Whitey Herzog MG .10 .04
244 Dickie Noles .05 .02
245 Willie Upshaw .05 .02
246 Jim Dwyer .05 .02
247 Jeff Reed .05 .02
248 Gene Walter .05 .02
249 Jim Pankovits .05 .02
250 Teddy Higuera .05 .02
251 Rob Wilfong .05 .02
252 Dennis Martinez .10 .04
253 Eddie Milner .05 .02
254 Bob Tewksbury RC * .25 .10
255 Juan Samuel .05 .02
256 Royals Team .15 .06
(George Brett and
Frank White)
257 Bob Forsch .05 .02
258 Steve Yeager .05 .02
259 Mike Greenwell RC .25 .10
260 Vida Blue .10 .04
261 Ruben Sierra RC .40 .16
262 Jim Winn .05 .02
263 Stan Javier .05 .02
264 Checklist 133-264 .05 .02
265 Darrell Evans .10 .04
266 Jeff Hamilton .05 .02
267 Howard Johnson .05 .02
268 Pat Corrales MG .10 .04
269 Cliff Speck .05 .02
270 Jody Davis .05 .02
271 Mike G. Brown .05 .02
272 Andres Galarraga .15 .06
273 Gene Nelson .05 .02
274 Jeff Hearron UER .05 .02
(Duplicate 1986
stat line on back)
275 LaMarr Hoyt .05 .02
276 Jackie Gutierrez .05 .02
277 Juan Agosto .05 .02
278 Gary Pettis .05 .02
279 Dan Plesac .05 .02
280 Jeff Leonard .05 .02
281 Reds Team .25 .10
Pete Rose, Bo Diaz
and Bill Gullickson
282 Jeff Calhoun .05 .02
283 Doug Drabek RC* .25 .10
284 John Moses .05 .02
285 Dennis Boyd .05 .02
286 Mike Woodard .05 .02
287 Dave Von Ohlen .05 .02
288 Tito Landrum .05 .02
289 Bob Kipper .05 .02
290 Leon Durham .05 .02
291 Mitch Williams RC * .25 .10
292 Franklin Stubbs .05 .02
293 Bob Rodgers MG .05 .02
294 Steve Jeltz .05 .02
295 Len Dykstra .15 .06
296 Andres Thomas .05 .02
297 Don Schulze .05 .02
298 Larry Herndon .05 .02
299 Joel Davis .05 .02
300 Reggie Jackson .15 .06
301 Luis Aquino UER .05 .02
(No trademark
never corrected)
302 Bill Schroeder .05 .02
303 Juan Berenguer .05 .02
304 Phil Garner .05 .02
305 John Franco .10 .04
306 Red Sox Team .10 .04
(Tom Seaver,
John McNamara MG,
and Rich Gedman)
307 Lee Guetterman .05 .02
308 Don Slaught .05 .02
309 Mike Young .05 .02
310 Frank Viola .05 .02
311 Rickey Henderson .15 .06
TBC '82
312 Reggie Jackson .10 .04
TBC '77
313 Roberto Clemente .25 .10
TBC '72
314 Carl Yastrzemski UER .25 .10
TBC '67 (Sic, 112
RBI's on back)
315 Maury Wills TBC '62 .10 .04
316 Brian Fisher .05 .02
317 Clint Hurdle .05 .02
318 Jim Fregosi MG .05 .02
319 Greg Swindell RC .25 .10
320 Barry Bonds RC 10.00 4.00
321 Mike Laga .05 .02
322 Chris Bando .05 .02
323 Al Newman .05 .02
324 David Palmer .05 .02
325 Garry Templeton .05 .02
326 Mark Gubicza .05 .02
327 Dale Sveum .05 .02
328 Bob Welch .05 .02
329 Ron Roenicke .05 .02
330 Mike Scott .05 .02
331 Mets Team .15 .06
(Gary Carter and
Darryl Strawberry)
332 Joe Price .05 .02
333 Ken Phelps .05 .02
334 Ed Correa .05 .02
335 Candy Maldonado .05 .02
336 Allan Anderson .05 .02
337 Darrell Miller .05 .02
338 Tim Conroy .05 .02
339 Donnie Hill .05 .02
340 Roger Clemens .50 .20
341 Mike C. Brown .05 .02
342 Bob James .05 .02
343 Hal Lanier MG .05 .02
344A Joe Niekro .05 .02
(Copyright inside
righthand border)
344B Joe Niekro .05 .02
(Copyright outside
righthand border)
345 Andre Dawson .10 .04
346 Shawon Dunston .05 .02
347 Mickey Brantley .05 .02
348 Carmelo Martinez .05 .02
349 Storm Davis .05 .02
350 Keith Hernandez .15 .06
351 Gene Garber .05 .02
352 Mike Felder .05 .02
353 Ernie Camacho .05 .02
354 Jamie Quirk .05 .02
355 Don Carman .05 .02
356 White Sox Team .05 .02
(Mound conference)
357 Steve Fireovid .05 .02
358 Sal Butera .05 .02
359 Doug Corbett .05 .02
360 Pedro Guerrero .05 .02
361 Mark Thurmond .05 .02
362 Luis Quinones .05 .02
363 Jose Guzman .05 .02
364 Randy Bush .05 .02
365 Rick Rhoden .05 .02
366 Mark McGwire 4.00 1.60
367 Jeff Lahti .05 .02
368 John McNamara MG .05 .02
369 Brian Dayett .05 .02
370 Fred Lynn .10 .04
371 Mark Eichhorn .05 .02
372 Jerry Mumphrey .05 .02
373 Jeff Dedmon .05 .02
374 Glenn Hoffman .05 .02
375 Ron Guidry .10 .04
376 Scott Bradley .05 .02
377 John Henry Johnson .05 .02
378 Rafael Santana .05 .02
379 John Russell .05 .02
380 Rich Gossage .10 .04
381 Expos Team .05 .02
(Mound conference)
382 Rudy Law .05 .02
383 Ron Davis .05 .02
384 Johnny Grubb .05 .02
385 Orel Hershiser .10 .04
386 Dickie Thon .05 .02
387 T.R. Bryden .05 .02
388 Geno Petralli .05 .02
389 Jeff D. Robinson .05 .02
390 Gary Matthews .05 .02
391 Jay Howell .05 .02
392 Checklist 265-396 .05 .02
393 Pete Rose MG .15 .06
394 Mike Bielecki .05 .02
395 Damaso Garcia .05 .02
396 Tim Lollar .05 .02
397 Greg Walker .05 .02
398 Brad Havens .05 .02
399 Curt Ford .05 .02
400 George Brett .60 .24
401 Billy Joe Robidoux .05 .02
402 Mike Trujillo .05 .02
403 Jerry Royster .05 .02
404 Doug Sisk .05 .02
405 Brook Jacoby .05 .02
406 Yankees Team .50 .20
(Rickey Henderson and
Don Mattingly)
407 Jim Acker .05 .02
408 John Mizerock .05 .02
409 Milt Thompson .05 .02
410 Fernando Valenzuela .10 .04
411 Darnell Coles .05 .02
412 Eric Davis .15 .06
413 Moose Haas .05 .02
414 Joe Orsulak .05 .02
415 Bobby Witt RC .25 .10
416 Tom Nieto .05 .02
417 Pat Perry .05 .02
418 Dick Williams MG .10 .04
419 Mark Portugal RC * .10 .04
420 Will Clark RC 1.00 .40
421 Jose DeLeon .05 .02
422 Jack Howell .05 .02
423 Jaime Cocanower .05 .02
424 Chris Speier .05 .02
425 Tom Seaver UER .15 .06
Earned Runs amount is wrong
For 86 Red Sox and Career
Also the ERA is wrong for 86 and career
426 Floyd Rayford .05 .02
427 Edwin Nunez .05 .02
428 Bruce Bochy .05 .02
429 Tim Pyznarski .05 .02
430 Mike Schmidt .50 .20
431 Dodgers Team .05 .02
(Mound conference)
432 Jim Slaton .05 .02
433 Ed Hearn .05 .02
434 Mike Fischlin .05 .02
435 Bruce Sutter .05 .02
436 Andy Allanson .05 .02
437 Ted Power .05 .02
438 Kelly Downs RC .10 .04
439 Karl Best .05 .02
440 Willie McGee .10 .04
441 Dave Leiper .05 .02
442 Mitch Webster .05 .02
443 John Felske MG .05 .02
444 Jeff Russell .05 .02
445 Dave Lopes .10 .04
446 Chuck Finley RC .40 .16
447 Bill Almon .05 .02
448 Chris Bosio RC .25 .10
449 Pat Dodson .10 .04
450 Kirby Puckett .25 .10
451 Joe Sambito .05 .02
452 Dave Henderson .05 .02
453 Scott Terry RC .10 .04
454 Luis Salazar .05 .02
455 Mike Boddicker .05 .02
456 A's Team .05 .02
(Mound conference)
457 Len Matuszek .05 .02
458 Kelly Gruber .05 .02
459 Dennis Eckersley .15 .06
460 Darryl Strawberry .15 .06
461 Craig McMurtry .05 .02
462 Scott Fletcher .05 .02
463 Tom Candiotti .05 .02
464 Butch Wynegar .05 .02
465 Todd Worrell .10 .04
466 Kal Daniels .05 .02
467 Randy St.Claire .05 .02
468 G.Bamberger MG .05 .02
469 Mike Diaz .05 .02
470 Dave Dravecky .10 .04
471 Ronn Reynolds .05 .02
472 Bill Doran .05 .02
473 Steve Farr .05 .02
474 Jerry Narron .05 .02
475 Scott Garrelts .05 .02
476 Danny Tartabull .05 .02
477 Ken Howell .05 .02
478 Tim Laudner .05 .02
479 Bob Sebra .05 .02
480 Jim Rice .10 .04
481 Phillies Team .05 .02
(Glenn Wilson
Juan Samuel and
Von Hayes)
482 Daryl Boston .05 .02
483 Dwight Lowry .05 .02
484 Jim Traber .05 .02
485 Tony Fernandez .05 .02
486 Otis Nixon .05 .02
487 Dave Gumpert .05 .02
488 Ray Knight .05 .02
489 Bill Gullickson .05 .02
490 Dale Murphy .25 .10
491 Ron Karkovice RC .25 .10
492 Mike Heath .05 .02
493 Tom Lasorda MG .10 .04
494 Barry Jones .05 .02
495 Gorman Thomas .05 .02
496 Bruce Bochte .05 .02
497 Dale Mohorcic .05 .02
498 Bob Kearney .05 .02
499 Bruce Ruffin RC .10 .04
500 Don Mattingly .60 .24
501 Craig Lefferts .05 .02
502 Dick Schofield .05 .02
503 Larry Andersen .05 .02
504 Mickey Hatcher .05 .02
505 Bryn Smith .05 .02
506 Orioles Team .05 .02
(Mound conference)
507 Dave L. Stapleton .05 .02
508 Scott Bankhead .05 .02
509 Enos Cabell .05 .02
510 Tom Henke .05 .02
511 Steve Lyons .05 .02
512 Dave Magadan RC .25 .10
513 Carmen Castillo .05 .02
514 Orlando Mercado .05 .02
515 Willie Hernandez .05 .02
516 Ted Simmons .10 .04
517 Mario Soto .05 .02
518 Gene Mauch MG .10 .04
519 Curt Young .05 .02
520 Jack Clark .10 .04
521 Rick Reuschel .05 .02
522 Checklist 397-528 .05 .02
523 Earnie Riles .05 .02
524 Bob Shirley .05 .02
525 Phil Bradley .05 .02
526 Roger Mason .05 .02
527 Jim Wohlford .05 .02
528 Ken Dixon .05 .02
529 Alvaro Espinoza RC .10 .04
530 Tony Gwynn .30 .12
531 Astros Team .10 .04
(Yogi Berra conference)
532 Jeff Stone .05 .02
533 Argenis Salazar .05 .02
534 Scott Sanderson .05 .02
535 Tony Armas .05 .02
536 Terry Mulholland RC .25 .10
537 Rance Mulliniks .05 .02
538 Tom Niedenfuer .05 .02
539 Reid Nichols .05 .02
540 Terry Kennedy .05 .02
541 Rafael Belliard RC .25 .10
542 Ricky Horton .05 .02
543 Dave Johnson MG .10 .04
544 Zane Smith .05 .02
545 Buddy Bell .10 .04
546 Mike Morgan .05 .02
547 Rob Deer .05 .02
548 Bill Mooneyham .05 .02
549 Bob Melvin .05 .02
550 Pete Incaviglia RC * .25 .10
551 Frank Wills .05 .02
552 Larry Sheets .05 .02
553 Mike Maddux .05 .02
554 Buddy Biancalana .05 .02
555 Dennis Rasmussen .05 .02
556 Angels Team .05 .02
(Rene Lachemann CO,
Mike Witt, and
Bob Boone)
557 John Cerutti .05 .02
558 Greg Gagne .05 .02
559 Lance McCullers .05 .02
560 Glenn Davis .05 .02
561 Rey Quinones .05 .02
562 Bryan Clutterbuck .05 .02
563 John Stefero .05 .02
564 Larry McWilliams .05 .02
565 Dusty Baker .10 .04
566 Tim Hulett .05 .02
567 Greg Mathews .05 .02
568 Earl Weaver MG .25 .10
569 Wade Rowdon .05 .02
570 Sid Fernandez .05 .02
571 Ozzie Virgil .05 .02
572 Pete Ladd .05 .02
573 Hal McRae .10 .04
574 Manny Lee .05 .02
575 Pat Tabler .05 .02
576 Frank Pastore .05 .02
577 Dann Bilardello .05 .02
578 Billy Hatcher .05 .02
579 Rick Burleson .05 .02
580 Mike Krukow .05 .02
581 Cubs Team .05 .02
(Ron Cey and
Steve Trout)
582 Bruce Berenyi .05 .02
583 Junior Ortiz .05 .02
584 Ron Kittle .05 .02
585 Scott Bailes .05 .02
586 Ben Oglivie .05 .02
587 Eric Plunk .05 .02
588 Wallace Johnson .05 .02
589 Steve Crawford .05 .02
590 Vince Coleman .05 .02
591 Spike Owen .05 .02
592 Chris Welsh .05 .02
593 Chuck Tanner MG .05 .02
594 Rick Anderson .05 .02
595 Keith Hernandez AS .10 .04
596 Steve Sax AS .05 .02
597 Mike Schmidt AS .25 .10
598 Ozzie Smith AS .25 .10
599 Tony Gwynn AS .15 .06
600 Dave Parker AS .05 .02
601 Darryl Strawberry AS .10 .04
602 Gary Carter AS .10 .04
603A D.Gooden AS .15 .06
ERR no trademark
603B D.Gooden AS COR .15 .06
604 F.Valenzuela AS .10 .04
605 Todd Worrell AS .10 .04
606 D.Mattingly AS COR .30 .12
606A Don Mattingly AS 1.00 .40
ERR (no trademark)
607 Tony Bernazard AS .05 .02
608 Wade Boggs AS .10 .04
609 Cal Ripken AS .25 .10
610 Jim Rice AS .05 .02
611 Kirby Puckett AS .15 .06
612 George Bell AS .05 .02
613 Lance Parrish AS UER .10 .04
(Pitcher heading
on back)
614 Roger Clemens AS .25 .10
615 Teddy Higuera AS .05 .02
616 Dave Righetti AS .05 .02
617 Al Nipper .05 .02
618 Tom Kelly MG .05 .02
619 Jerry Reed .05 .02
620 Jose Canseco .50 .20
621 Danny Cox .05 .02
622 Glenn Braggs RC .10 .04
623 Kurt Stillwell .05 .02
624 Tim Burke .05 .02
625 Mookie Wilson .10 .04
626 Joel Skinner .05 .02
627 Ken Oberkfell .05 .02
628 Bob Walk .05 .02
629 Larry Parrish .05 .02
630 John Candelaria .05 .02
631 Tigers Team .05 .02
(Mound conference)
632 Rob Woodward .05 .02
633 Jose Uribe .05 .02
634 Rafael Palmeiro RC 2.00 .80
635 Ken Schrom .05 .02
636 Darren Daulton .15 .06
637 Bip Roberts RC* .25 .10
638 Rich Bordi .05 .02
639 Gerald Perry .05 .02
640 Mark Clear .05 .02
641 Domingo Ramos .05 .02
642 Al Pulido .05 .02
643 Ron Shepherd .05 .02
644 John Denny .05 .02
645 Dwight Evans .10 .04
646 Mike Mason .05 .02
647 Tom Lawless .05 .02
648 Barry Larkin RC 1.00 .40
649 Mickey Tettleton .05 .02
650 Hubie Brooks .05 .02
651 Benny Distefano .05 .02
652 Terry Forster .05 .02
653 Kevin Mitchell RC * .40 .16
654 Checklist 529-660 .10 .04
655 Jesse Barfield .05 .02
656 Rangers Team .05 .02
(Bobby Valentine MG
and Ricky Wright)
657 Tom Waddell .05 .02
658 R.Thompson RC* .25 .10
659 Aurelio Lopez .05 .02
660 Bob Horner .05 .02
661 Lou Whitaker .10 .04
662 Frank DiPino .05 .02
663 Cliff Johnson .05 .02
664 Mike Marshall .05 .02
665 Rod Scurry .05 .02
666 Von Hayes .05 .02
667 Ron Hassey .05 .02
668 Juan Bonilla .05 .02
669 Bud Black .05 .02
670 Jose Cruz .10 .04
671A Ray Soff ERR .05 .02
(No D* before
copyright line)
671B Ray Soff COR .05 .02
(D* before
copyright line)
672 Chili Davis .15 .06
673 Don Sutton .25 .10
674 Bill Campbell .05 .02
675 Ed Romero .05 .02
676 Charlie Moore .05 .02
677 Bob Grich .10 .04
678 Carney Lansford .10 .04
679 Kent Hrbek .10 .04
680 Ryne Sandberg .40 .16
681 George Bell .05 .02
682 Jerry Reuss .05 .02
683 Gary Roenicke .05 .02
684 Kent Tekulve .05 .02
685 Jerry Hairston .05 .02
686 Doyle Alexander .05 .02
687 Alan Trammell .15 .06
688 Juan Beniquez .05 .02
689 Darrell Porter .05 .02
690 Dane Iorg .05 .02
691 Dave Parker .10 .04
692 Frank White .10 .04
693 Terry Puhl .05 .02
694 Phil Niekro .10 .04
695 Chico Walker .05 .02
696 Gary Lucas .05 .02
697 Ed Lynch .05 .02
698 Ernie Whitt .05 .02
699 Ken Landreaux .05 .02
700 Dave Bergman .05 .02
701 Willie Randolph .10 .04
702 Greg Gross .05 .02
703 Dave Schmidt .05 .02
704 Jesse Orosco .05 .02
705 Bruce Hurst .05 .02
706 Rick Manning .05 .02
707 Bob McClure .05 .02
708 Scott McGregor .05 .02
709 Dave Kingman .10 .04
710 Gary Gaetti .10 .04
711 Ken Griffey .10 .04
712 Don Robinson .05 .02
713 Tom Brookens .05 .02
714 Dan Quisenberry .05 .02
715 Bob Dernier .05 .02
716 Rick Leach .05 .02
717 Ed VandeBerg .05 .02
718 Steve Carlton .10 .04
719 Tom Hume .05 .02
720 Richard Dotson .05 .02
721 Tom Herr .05 .02
722 Bob Knepper .05 .02
723 Brett Butler .10 .04
724 Greg Minton .05 .02
725 George Hendrick .05 .02
726 Frank Tanana .05 .02
727 Mike Moore .05 .02
728 Tippy Martinez .05 .02
729 Tom Paciorek .10 .04
730 Eric Show .05 .02
731 Dave Concepcion .10 .04
732 Manny Trillo .05 .02
733 Bill Caudill .05 .02
734 Bill Madlock .10 .04
735 Rickey Henderson .25 .10
736 Steve Bedrosian .05 .02
737 Floyd Bannister .05 .02
738 Jorge Orta .05 .02
739 Chet Lemon .05 .02
740 Rich Gedman .05 .02
741 Paul Molitor .15 .06
742 Andy McGaffigan .05 .02
743 Dwayne Murphy .05 .02
744 Roy Smalley .05 .02
745 Glenn Hubbard .05 .02
746 Bob Ojeda .05 .02
747 Johnny Ray .05 .02
748 Mike Flanagan .05 .02
749 Ozzie Smith .40 .16
750 Steve Trout .05 .02
751 Garth Iorg .05 .02
752 Dan Petry .05 .02
753 Rick Honeycutt .05 .02
754 Dave LaPoint .05 .02
755 Luis Aguayo .05 .02
756 Carlton Fisk .15 .06
757 Nolan Ryan 1.00 .40
758 Tony Bernazard .05 .02
759 Joel Youngblood .05 .02
760 Mike Witt .05 .02
761 Greg Pryor .05 .02
762 Gary Ward .05 .02
763 Tim Flannery .05 .02
764 Bill Buckner .10 .04
765 Kirk Gibson .10 .04
766 Don Aase .05 .02
767 Ron Cey .10 .04
768 Dennis Lamp .05 .02
769 Steve Sax .05 .02
770 Dave Winfield .10 .04
771 Shane Rawley .05 .02
772 Harold Baines .10 .04
773 Robin Yount .40 .16
774 Wayne Krenchicki .05 .02
775 Joaquin Andujar .05 .02
776 Tom Brunansky .05 .02
777 Chris Chambliss .10 .04
778 Jack Morris .10 .04
779 Craig Reynolds .05 .02
780 Andre Thornton .05 .02
781 Atlee Hammaker .05 .02
782 Brian Downing .05 .02

783 Willie Wilson .10 .04
784 Cal Ripken .75 .30
785 Terry Francona .10 .04
786 Jimy Williams MG .05 .02
787 Alejandro Pena .05 .02
788 Tim Stoddard .05 .02
789 Dan Schatzeder .05 .02
790 Julio Cruz .05 .02
791 Lance Parrish .10 .04
792 Checklist 661-792 .05 .02

1987 Topps Tiffany

These 792 standard-size cards were a parallel to the regular Topps issue. These cards feature "glossy" fronts and easy to read backs. These cards are in the same style as the regular Topps issue. This set was printed in Ireland and was issued only in factory set form. Unlike previous years, a significantly higher amount of these cards were produced. Therefore, the values of these cards are a much lower mulitplier to the regular cards than previous years. It is believed that as many as 30,000 of these sets were produced. This increase was probably in response to increased dealer interest.

Nm-Mt Ex-Mt
COMP.FACT.SET (792) 150.00 60.00
*STARS: 2.5X TO 6X BASIC CARDS
*ROOKIES: 4X TO 10X BASIC CARDS

1987 Topps Glossy All-Stars

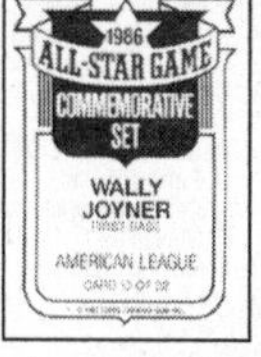

This set of 22 glossy cards was inserted one per rack pack. Players selected for the set are the starting players (plus manager and two pitchers) in the 1986 All-Star Game in Houston. Cards measure the standard size and the backs feature red and blue printing on a white card stock.

Nm-Mt Ex-Mt
COMPLETE SET (22) 5.00 2.00
1 Whitey Herzog MG .10 .04
2 Keith Hernandez .10 .04
3 Ryne Sandberg 1.00 .40
4 Mike Schmidt .50 .20
5 Ozzie Smith 1.00 .40
6 Tony Gwynn 1.00 .40
7 Dale Murphy .20 .08
8 Darryl Strawberry .10 .04
9 Gary Carter .50 .20
10 Dwight Gooden .15 .06
11 Fernando Valenzuela .10 .04
12 Dick Howser MG .05 .02
13 Wally Joyner .10 .04
14 Lou Whitaker .10 .04
15 Wade Boggs .50 .20
16 Cal Ripken 2.00 .80
17 Dave Winfield .20 .08
18 Rickey Henderson .60 .24
19 Kirby Puckett .50 .20
20 Lance Parrish .10 .04
21 Roger Clemens 1.00 .40
22 Teddy Higuera .05 .02

1987 Topps Glossy Send-Ins

Topps issued this set through a mail-in offer explained and advertised on the wax packs. This 60-card set features glossy fronts with each card measuring the standard size. The offer provided your choice of any one of the six 10-card subsets (1-10, 11-20, etc.) for 1.00 plus six of the Special Offer ("Spring Fever Baseball") insert cards, which were found one per wax pack. The last two players (numerically) in each ten-card subset are actually "Hot Prospects." This set is highlighted by an early Barry Bonds card.

Nm-Mt Ex-Mt
COMPLETE SET (60) 25.00 10.00
1 Don Mattingly 2.00 .80
2 Tony Gwynn 1.00 .40
3 Gary Gaetti .30 .12
4 Glenn Davis .20 .08
5 Roger Clemens 2.00 .80
6 Dale Murphy .75 .30
7 Lou Whitaker .30 .12
8 Roger McDowell .20 .08
9 Cory Snyder .20 .08
10 Todd Worrell .30 .12
11 Gary Carter .50 .20
12 Eddie Murray .75 .30
13 Bob Knepper .20 .08
14 Harold Baines .30 .12
15 Jeff Reardon .30 .12
16 Joe Carter .30 .12
17 Dave Parker .30 .12
18 Wade Boggs .50 .20
19 Danny Tartabull .20 .08
20 Jim Deshaies .20 .08
21 Rickey Henderson .75 .30
22 Rob Deer .20 .08
23 Ozzie Smith 1.25 .50
24 Dave Righetti .30 .12
25 Kent Hrbek .30 .12
26 Keith Hernandez .50 .20
27 Don Baylor .30 .12
28 Mike Schmidt 1.50 .60
29 Pete Incaviglia .30 .12
30 Barry Bonds 15.00 6.00
31 George Brett 2.00 .80
32 Darryl Strawberry .50 .20
33 Mike Witt .20 .08
34 Kevin Bass .20 .08
35 Jesse Barfield .20 .08
36 Bob Ojeda .20 .08
37 Cal Ripken 2.50 1.00
38 Vince Coleman .20 .08
39 Wally Joyner .75 .30
40 Robby Thompson .30 .12
41 Pete Rose 2.00 .80
42 Jim Rice .30 .12
43 Tony Bernazard .20 .08
44 Eric Davis .30 .12
45 George Bell .20 .08
46 Hubie Brooks .20 .08
47 Jack Morris .30 .12
48 Tim Raines .30 .12
49 Mark Eichhorn .20 .08
50 Kevin Mitchell .30 .12
51 Dwight Gooden .50 .20
52 Doug DeCinces .20 .08
53 Fernando Valenzuela .30 .12
54 Reggie Jackson .50 .20
55 Johnny Ray .20 .08
56 Mike Pagliarulo .20 .08
57 Kirby Puckett .75 .30
58 Lance Parrish .30 .12
59 Jose Canseco 1.00 .40
60 Greg Mathews .20 .08

1987 Topps Rookies

Inserted in each supermarket jumbo pack is a card from this series of 22 of 1986's best rookies as determined by Topps. Jumbo packs consisted of 100 (regular issue 1987 Topps baseball) cards with a stick of gum plus the insert "Rookie" card. The card fronts are in full color and measure the standard size. The card backs are printed in red and blue on white card stock and are numbered at the bottom essentially by alphabetical order.

Nm-Mt Ex-Mt
COMPLETE SET (22) 12.00 4.80
1 Andy Allanson .25 .10
2 John Cangelosi .25 .10
3 Jose Canseco 2.50 1.00
4 Will Clark 2.50 1.00
5 Mark Eichhorn .25 .10
6 Pete Incaviglia .50 .20
7 Wally Joyner .75 .30
8 Eric King .25 .10
9 Dave Magadan .50 .20
10 John Morris .25 .10
11 Juan Nieves .25 .10
12 Rafael Palmeiro 6.00 2.40
13 Billy Joe Robidoux .25 .10
14 Bruce Ruffin .25 .10
15 Ruben Sierra 1.00 .40
16 Cory Snyder .25 .10
17 Kurt Stillwell .25 .10
18 Dale Sveum .25 .10
19 Danny Tartabull .25 .10
20 Andres Thomas .25 .10
21 Robby Thompson .50 .20
22 Todd Worrell .50 .20

1987 Topps Wax Box Cards

This set of eight cards is really four different sets of two smaller (approximately 2 1/8" by 3") cards which were printed on the side of the wax pack box; these eight cards are lettered A through H and are very similar in design to the Topps regular issue cards. The order of the set is alphabetical by player's name. Complete boxes would be worth an additional 25 percent premium over the prices below. The card backs are done in a newspaper headline style describing something about that player that happened the previous season. The card backs feature blue and yellow ink on gray card stock.

Nm-Mt Ex-Mt
COMPLETE SET (8) 3.00 1.20
A Don Baylor .25 .10
B Steve Carlton .75 .30
C Ron Cey .25 .10
D Cecil Cooper .10 .04
E Rickey Henderson .75 .30
F Jim Rice .25 .10
G Don Sutton .75 .30
H Dave Winfield .75 .30

1987 Topps Traded

This 132-card standard-size Traded set was distributed exclusively in factory set form in a special green and white box through hobby dealers. The card fronts are identical in style to the Topps regular issue except for whiter stock and t-suffixed numbering on back. The cards are ordered alphabetically by player's last name. The key extended Rookie Cards in this set are Ellis Burks, David Cone, Greg Maddux, Fred McGriff and Matt Williams.

Nm-Mt Ex-Mt
COMP.FACT.SET (132) 10.00 4.00
1T Bill Almon .05 .02
2T Scott Bankhead .05 .02
3T Eric Bell .10 .04
4T Juan Beniquez .05 .02
5T Juan Berenguer .05 .02
6T Greg Booker .05 .02
7T Thad Bosley .05 .02
8T Larry Bowa MG .10 .04
9T Greg Brock .05 .02
10T Bob Brower .05 .02
11T Jerry Browne .10 .04
12T Ralph Bryant .05 .02
13T DeWayne Buice .05 .02
14T Ellis Burks XRC .50 .20
15T Ivan Calderon .05 .02
16T Jeff Calhoun .05 .02
17T Casey Candaele .05 .02
18T John Cangelosi .05 .02
19T Steve Carlton .10 .04
20T Juan Castillo .10 .04
21T Rick Cerone .05 .02
22T Ron Cey .10 .04
23T John Christensen .05 .02
24T David Cone XRC .75 .30
25T Chuck Crim .05 .02
26T Storm Davis .05 .02
27T Andre Dawson .10 .04
28T Rick Dempsey .10 .04
29T Doug Drabek .25 .10
30T Mike Dunne .05 .02
31T Dennis Eckersley .15 .06
32T Lee Elia MG .05 .02
33T Brian Fisher .05 .02
34T Terry Francona .10 .04
35T Willie Fraser .10 .04
36T Billy Gardner MG .05 .02
37T Ken Gerhart .05 .02
38T Dan Gladden .05 .02
39T Jim Gott .05 .02
40T Cecilio Guante .05 .02
41T Albert Hall .05 .02
42T Terry Harper .05 .02
43T Mickey Hatcher .05 .02
44T Brad Havens .05 .02
45T Neal Heaton .05 .02
46T Mike Henneman XRC .25 .10
47T Donnie Hill .05 .02
48T Guy Hoffman .05 .02
49T Brian Holton .05 .02
50T Charles Hudson .05 .02
51T Danny Jackson .05 .02
52T Reggie Jackson .15 .06
53T Chris James XRC * .10 .04
54T Dion James .05 .02
55T Stan Jefferson .05 .02
56T Joe Johnson .05 .02
57T Terry Kennedy .05 .02
58T Mike Kingery .10 .04
59T Ray Knight .05 .02
60T Gene Larkin XRC .25 .10
61T Mike LaValliere .25 .10
62T Jack Lazorko .05 .02
63T Terry Leach .05 .02
64T Tim Leary .05 .02
65T Jim Lindeman .10 .04
66T Steve Lombardozzi .05 .02
67T Bill Long .05 .02
68T Barry Lyons .05 .02
69T Shane Mack .05 .02
70T Greg Maddux XRC 5.00 2.00
71T Bill Madlock .10 .04
72T Joe Magrane XRC .10 .04
73T Dave Martinez XRC * .25 .10
74T Fred McGriff .60 .24
75T Mark McLemore .10 .04
76T Kevin McReynolds .05 .02
77T Dave Meads .05 .02
78T Eddie Milner .05 .02
79T Greg Minton .05 .02
80T John Mitchell XRC .10 .04
81T Kevin Mitchell .15 .06
82T Charlie Moore .05 .02
83T Jeff Musselman .05 .02
84T Gene Nelson .05 .02
85T Graig Nettles .10 .04
86T Al Newman .05 .02
87T Reid Nichols .05 .02
88T Tom Niedenfuer .05 .02
89T Joe Niekro .05 .02
90T Tom Nieto .05 .02
91T Matt Nokes XRC .25 .10
92T Dickie Noles .05 .02
93T Pat Pacillo .05 .02
94T Lance Parrish .10 .04
95T Tony Pena .05 .02
96T Luis Polonia XRC .10 .04
97T Randy Ready .05 .02
98T Jeff Reardon .10 .04
99T Gary Redus .05 .02
100T Jeff Reed .05 .02
101T Rick Rhoden .05 .02
102T Cal Ripken Sr. MG .05 .02
103T Wally Ritchie .05 .02
104T Jeff M. Robinson .05 .02
105T Gary Roenicke .05 .02
106T Jerry Royster .05 .02
107T Mark Salas .05 .02
108T Luis Salazar .05 .02
109T Benny Santiago .50 .20
110T Dave Schmidt .05 .02
111T Kevin Seitzer XRC* .25 .10
112T John Shelby .05 .02
113T Steve Shields .05 .02
114T John Smiley XRC .25 .10
115T Chris Speier .05 .02
116T Mike Stanley XRC* .25 .10
117T Terry Steinbach XRC .25 .10
118T Les Straker .05 .02
119T Jim Sundberg .05 .02
120T Danny Tartabull .05 .02
121T Tom Trebelhorn MG .05 .02
122T Dave Valle XRC ** .10 .04
123T Ed VandeBerg .05 .02
124T Andy Van Slyke .10 .04
125T Gary Ward .05 .02
126T Alan Wiggins .05 .02
127T Bill Wilkinson .05 .02
128T Frank Williams .05 .02
129T Matt Williams XRC 1.00 .40
130T Jim Winn .05 .02
131T Matt Young .05 .02
132T Checklist 1T-132T .05 .02

1987 Topps Traded Tiffany

Since the update Tiffany cards were issued in the same quantities as the regular cards, again these cards are not valued as high as a multiplier as the previous years. These 132 standard-size cards parallel the regular cards but have glossy fronts and easy to read backs. These cards were issued in factory set form only. These sets, believed to be issued in the range of 30,000, are among the easiest of the Tiffany sets to find in the secondary market.

Nm-Mt Ex-Mt
COMP.FACT.SET (132) 50.00 20.00
*STARS: ,2X TO 5X BASIC CARDS
*ROOKIES: 2.5X TO 6X BASIC CARDS

1987 Topps Gallery of Champions

These 12 cards, issued in complete set form only, are "metal" versions of regular Topps cards. These 12 players were either 1986 award winners or league leaders. These cards measure approximately 1 14" by 1 3/4" and were issued in aluminum, silver and bronze versions. We have priced the aluminum versions with the bronze valued at 2X to 4X the aluminums and the silvers are 5X to 10X the values listed below. The set is sequenced in alphabetical order.

Nm-Mt Ex-Mt
COMPLETE SET (12) 150.00 60.00
1 Jesse Barfield 5.00 2.00
2 Wade Boggs 20.00 8.00
3 Jose Canseco 30.00 12.00
4 Joe Carter 10.00 4.00
5 Roger Clemens 25.00 10.00
6 Tony Gwynn 25.00 10.00
7 Don Mattingly 25.00 10.00
8 Tim Raines 8.00 3.20
9 Dave Righetti 5.00 2.00
10 Mike Schmidt 20.00 8.00
11 Mike Scott 5.00 2.00
12 Todd Worrell 8.00 3.20

1987 Topps Mini Leaders

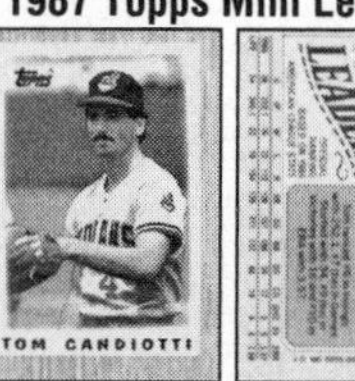

The 1987 Topps Mini set of Major League Leaders features 77 cards of leaders of the various statistical categories for the 1986 season. The cards are numbered on the back and measure approximately 2 5/32" by 3". The card backs are printed in orange and brown on white card stock. They are very similar in design to the Team Leader cards in the 1987 Topps regular issue. The cards were distributed as a separate issue in wax packs of seven for 30 cents. Eleven of the cards were double printed and are hence more plentiful; they are marked DP in the checklist below. The order of the set is alphabetical by player's name within team; the teams themselves are ordered alphabetically by city name within each league.

Nm-Mt Ex-Mt
COMPLETE SET (77) 5.00 2.00
COMMON CARD (1-77) .05 .02
COMMON DP .05 .02
1 Bob Horner DP .05 .02
2 Dale Murphy .20 .08
3 Lee Smith .15 .06
4 Eric Davis .15 .06
5 John Franco .10 .04
6 Dave Parker .10 .04
7 Kevin Bass .05 .02
8 Glenn Davis DP .05 .02
9 Bill Doran DP .05 .02
10 Bob Knepper DP .05 .02
11 Mike Scott .05 .02
12 Dave Smith .05 .02
13 Mariano Duncan .05 .02
14 Orel Hershiser .10 .04
15 Steve Sax DP .05 .02
16 Fernando Valenzuela .10 .04
17 Tim Raines .10 .04
18 Jeff Reardon .10 .04
19 Floyd Youmans .05 .02
20 Gary Carter DP .25 .10
21 Ron Darling .05 .02
22 Sid Fernandez .05 .02
23 Dwight Gooden .10 .04
24 Keith Hernandez .10 .04
25 Bob Ojeda .05 .02
26 Darryl Strawberry .10 .04
27 Steve Bedrosian .05 .02
28 Von Hayes DP .05 .02
29 Juan Samuel .05 .02
30 Mike Schmidt .50 .20
31 Rick Rhoden .05 .02
32 Vince Coleman .05 .02
33 Danny Cox .05 .02
34 Todd Worrell .10 .04
35 Tony Gwynn .75 .30
36 Mike Krukow .05 .02
37 Candy Maldonado .05 .02
38 Don Aase .05 .02
39 Eddie Murray .40 .16
40 Cal Ripken 1.50 .60
41 Wade Boggs .40 .16
42 Roger Clemens .75 .30
43 Bruce Hurst .05 .02
44 Jim Rice .10 .04
45 Wally Joyner .15 .06
46 Donnie Moore .05 .02
47 Gary Pettis .05 .02
48 Mike Witt .05 .02
49 John Cangelosi .05 .02
50 Tom Candiotti .10 .04
51 Joe Carter .15 .06
52 Pat Tabler .05 .02
53 Kirk Gibson DP .10 .04
54 Willie Hernandez .05 .02
55 Jack Morris .10 .04
56 Alan Trammell DP .15 .06
57 George Brett .75 .30
58 Willie Wilson .10 .04
59 Rob Deer .05 .02
60 Teddy Higuera .05 .02
61 Bert Blyleven DP .05 .02
62 Gary Gaetti DP .10 .04
63 Kirby Puckett .40 .16
64 Rickey Henderson .50 .20
65 Don Mattingly .75 .30
66 Dennis Rasmussen .05 .02
67 Dave Righetti .05 .02
68 Jose Canseco .75 .30
69 Dave Kingman .10 .04
70 Phil Bradley .05 .02
71 Mark Langston .05 .02
72 Pete O'Brien .05 .02
73 Jesse Barfield .05 .02
74 George Bell .05 .02
75 Tony Fernandez .10 .04
76 Tom Henke .05 .02
77 Checklist Card .05 .02

1987 Topps Stickers

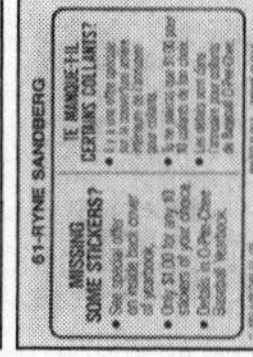

Made in Italy for Topps and O-Pee-Chee by Panini, these 313 stickers measure approximately 2 1/8" by 3" and are numbered on both front and back. The fronts feature white-bordered color player photos. The horizontal backs carry a bilingual ad for O-Pee-Chee. The Topps stickers contain offers on the back to obtain either a trip for four to Spring Training of the team of your choice or a complete set of Topps baseball cards directly from Topps. An album onto which the stickers could be affixed was available at retail stores. The album and the sticker numbering are organized as follows: 1986 Highlights (1-12), 1986 Championship Series (13-18), 1986 World Series (19-25), Houston Astros (26-35), Atlanta Braves (36-45), St. Louis Cardinals (46-55), Chicago Cubs (56-65), Los Angeles Dodgers (66-75), Montreal Expos (76-85), San Francisco Giants (86-95), New York Mets (96-105), San Diego Padres (106-115), Philadelphia Phillies (116-125), Pittsburgh Pirates (126-135), Cincinnati Reds (136-145), Foil All-Stars (146-163), Oakland A's (164-173), California Angels (174-183), Toronto Blue Jays (184-193), Milwaukee Brewers (194-203), Cleveland Indians (204-213), Seattle Mariners (214-223), Baltimore Orioles (224-233), Texas Rangers (234-243), Boston Red Sox (244-253), Kansas City Royals (254-263), Detroit Tigers (264-273), Minnesota Twins (274-283), Chicago White Sox (284-293), New York Yankees (294-303), and Future Stars (304-313). For those stickers featuring more than one player, the other numbers on that sticker are given below in parentheses. There was a variation of this set that was test-marketed by Topps. Its stickers had card backings (precursors of the Super Stars sticker backs) rather than the paper backing Topps had been using in previous years. Apparently the test was successful as both Topps and O-Pee-Chee switched to the home-printed, stiffer-backed stickers the following year.Will Clark and Barry Bonds are featured on stickers during their Rookie Card Year

Nm-Mt Ex-Mt
COMPLETE SET (313) 15.00 6.00
COMMON (1-145, 164-313) .05 .02
COMMON FOIL (146-163) .10 .04
*TOPPS AND OPC: SAME VALUE
1 Jim Deshaies (172) .05 .02
2 Roger Clemens (175) .15 .06
(Top half)
3 Roger Clemens (176) .15 .06
(Bottom half)
4 Dwight Evans (177) .10 .04
5 Dwight Gooden (178) .15 .06
(Top half)
6 Dwight Gooden (180) .15 .06
(Bottom half)
7 Dave Lopes (181) .10 .04
8 Dave Righetti (182) .05 .02
(Top half)
9 Dave Righetti (183) .05 .02
(Bottom half)
10 Ruben Sierra (185) .25 .10
11 Todd Worrell (186) .10 .04
(Top half)
12 Todd Worrell (187) .10 .04
(Bottom half)
13 Len Dykstra LCS .15 .06
14 Gary Carter LCS .10 .04
15 Mike Scott LCS .05 .02
16 Gary Pettis LCS .05 .02
17 Jim Rice LCS .10 .04
18 Marty Barrett LCS .05 .02

19 Bruce Hurst WS .05 .02
20 Dwight Evans WS .10 .04
21 Len Dykstra WS .15 .06
22 Gary Carter WS .10 .04
23 Dave Henderson WS .05 .02
24 Ray Knight WS .05 .02
25 Mets Celebrate WS .10 .04
26 Glenn Davis .05 .02
27 Nolan Ryan (188) 2.00 .80
28 Charlie Kerfeld(189) .05 .02
29 Jose Cruz (190) .10 .04
30 Phil Garner (191) .10 .04
31 Bill Doran (192) .05 .02
32 Bob Knepper (195) .05 .02
33 Denny Walling (196) .05 .02
34 Kevin Bass (197) .05 .02
35 Mike Scott .05 .02
36 Dale Murphy .25 .10
37 Paul Assenmacher .15 .06
(198)
38 Ken Oberkfell (200) .05 .02
39 Andres Thomas (201) .05 .02
40 Gene Garber (202) .05 .02
41 Bob Horner .05 .02
42 Rafael Ramirez (203) .05 .02
43 Rick Mahler (204) .05 .02
44 Omar Moreno (205) .05 .02
45 Dave Palmer (206) .05 .02
46 Ozzie Smith .40 .16
47 Bob Forsch (207) .05 .02
48 Willie McGee (209) .10 .04
49 Tom Herr (210) .05 .02
50 Vince Coleman (211) .05 .02
51 Andy Van Slyke (212) .10 .04
52 Jack Clark (215) .10 .04
53 John Tudor (216) .05 .02
54 Terry Pendleton(217) .10 .04
55 Todd Worrell .10 .04
56 Lee Smith .15 .06
57 Leon Durham (218) .05 .02
58 Jerry Mumphrey (219) .05 .02
59 Shawon Dunston (220) .05 .02
60 Scott Sanderson(221) .05 .02
61 Ryne Sandberg .50 .20
62 Gary Matthews (222) .05 .02
63 Dennis Eckersley .25 .10
(225)
64 Jody Davis (226) .05 .02
65 Keith Moreland (227) .05 .02
66 Mike Marshall (228) .05 .02
67 Bill Madlock (229) .10 .04
68 Greg Brock (230) .05 .02
69 Pedro Guerrero (231) .05 .02
70 Steve Sax .05 .02
71 Rick Honeycutt (232) .05 .02
72 Franklin Stubbs(235) .05 .02
73 Mike Scioscia (236) .05 .02
74 Mariano Duncan (237) .05 .02
75 Fernando Valenzuela .10 .04
76 Hubie Brooks .05 .02
77 Andre Dawson (238) .25 .10
78 Tim Burke (240) .05 .02
79 Floyd Youmans (241) .05 .02
80 Tim Wallach (242) .05 .02
81 Jeff Reardon (243) .10 .04
82 Mitch Webster (244) .05 .02
83 Bryn Smith (245) .05 .02
84 Andres Galarraga .50 .20
(246)
85 Tim Raines .10 .04
86 Chris Brown .05 .02
87 Bob Brenly (247) .05 .02
88 Will Clark (249) 1.50 .60
89 Scott Garrelts (250) .05 .02
90 Jeffrey Leonard(251) .05 .02
91 Robby Thompson (252) .10 .04
92 Mike Krukow (255) .05 .02
93 Danny Gladden (256) .05 .02
94 Candy Maldonado(257) .05 .02
95 Chili Davis .15 .06
96 Dwight Gooden .15 .06
97 Sid Fernandez (258) .05 .02
98 Len Dykstra (259) .15 .06
99 Bob Ojeda (260) .05 .02
100 Wally Backman (261) .05 .02
101 Gary Carter .15 .06
102 Keith Hernandez(262) .10 .04
103 Darryl Strawberry .15 .06
(265)
104 Roger McDowell (266) .05 .02
105 Ron Darling (267) .05 .02
106 Tony Gwynn .75 .30
107 Dave Dravecky (268) .10 .04
108 Terry Kennedy (269) .05 .02
109 Rich Gossage (270) .10 .04
110 Garry Templeton(271) .05 .02
111 Lance McCullers(272) .05 .02
112 Eric Show (275) .05 .02
113 John Kruk (276) .50 .20
114 Tim Flannery (277) .05 .02
115 Steve Garvey .15 .06
116 Mike Schmidt .60 .24
117 Glenn Wilson (278) .05 .02
118 Kent Tekulve (280) .05 .02
119 Gary Redus (281) .05 .02
120 Shane Rawley (282) .05 .02
121 Von Hayes .05 .02
122 Don Carman (283) .05 .02
123 Bruce Ruffin (285) .05 .02
124 Steve Bedrosian(286) .05 .02
125 Juan Samuel (287) .05 .02
126 Sid Bream (288) .05 .02
127 Cecilio Guante (289) .05 .02
128 Rick Reuschel (290) .05 .02
129 Tony Pena (291) .05 .02
130 Rick Rhoden .05 .02
131 Barry Bonds (292) 6.00 2.40
132 Joe Orsulak (295) .05 .02
133 Jim Morrison (296) .05 .02
134 R.J. Reynolds (297) .05 .02
135 Johnny Ray .05 .02
136 Eric Davis .15 .06
137 Tom Browning (298) .05 .02
138 John Franco (300) .10 .04
139 Pete Rose (301) .75 .30
140 Bill Gullickson(302) .05 .02
141 Ron Oester (303) .05 .02
142 Bo Diaz (304) .05 .02
143 Buddy Bell (305) .10 .04
144 Eddie Milner (306) .05 .02
145 Dave Parker .10 .04
146 Kirby Puckett FOIL 1.00 .40
147 Rickey Henderson FOIL .40 .16
148 Wade Boggs FOIL .40 .16
149 Lance Parrish FOIL .15 .06
150 Wally Joyner FOIL .75 .30
151 Cal Ripken FOIL 3.00 1.20
152 Dave Winfield FOIL .40 .16
153 Lou Whitaker FOIL .15 .06
154 Roger Clemens FOIL .60 .24
155 Tony Gwynn FOIL 1.25 .50
156 Ryne Sandberg FOIL .75 .30
157 Keith Hernandez FOIL .15 .06
158 Gary Carter FOIL .25 .10
159 Darryl Strawberry FOIL .20 .08
160 Mike Schmidt FOIL 1.00 .40
161 Dale Murphy FOIL .25 .10
162 Ozzie Smith FOIL .60 .24
163 Dwight Gooden FOIL .25 .10
164 Jose Canseco 1.00 .40
165 Curt Young (307) .05 .02
166 Alfredo Griffin(308) .05 .02
167 Dave Stewart (309) .10 .04
168 Mike Davis (310) .05 .02
169 Bruce Bochte (311) .05 .02
170 Dwayne Murphy (312) .05 .02
171 Carney Lansford(313) .10 .04
172 Joaquin Andujar (1) .05 .02
173 Dave Kingman .10 .04
174 Wally Joyner .50 .20
175 Gary Pettis (2) .05 .02
176 Dick Schofield (3) .05 .02
177 Donnie Moore (4) .05 .02
178 Brian Downing (5) .05 .02
179 Mike Witt .05 .02
180 Bob Boone (6) .10 .04
181 Kirk McCaskill (7) .05 .02
182 Doug DeCinces (8) .05 .02
183 Don Sutton (9) .25 .10
184 Jesse Barfield .05 .02
185 Tom Henke (10) .05 .02
186 Willie Upshaw (11) .05 .02
187 Mark Eichhorn (12) .05 .02
188 Damaso Garcia (27) .05 .02
189 Jim Clancy (28) .05 .02
190 Lloyd Moseby (29) .05 .02
191 Tony Fernandez (30) .05 .02
192 Jimmy Key (31) .15 .06
193 George Bell .05 .02
194 Rob Deer .05 .02
195 Mark Clear (32) .05 .02
196 Robin Yount (33) .25 .10
197 Jim Gantner (34) .05 .02
198 Cecil Cooper (35) .10 .04
199 Teddy Higuera .05 .02
200 Paul Molitor (38) .25 .10
201 Dan Plesac (39) .05 .02
202 Billy Joe Robidoux .05 .02
(40)
203 Earnie Riles (42) .05 .02
204 Ken Schrom (43) .05 .02
205 Pat Tabler (44) .05 .02
206 Mel Hall (45) .05 .02
207 Tony Bernazard (47) .05 .02
208 Joe Carter .25 .10
209 Ernie Camacho (48) .05 .02
210 Julio Franco (49) .10 .04
211 Tom Candiotti (50) .05 .02
212 Brook Jacoby (51) .05 .02
213 Cory Snyder .05 .02
214 Jim Presley .05 .02
215 Mike Moore (52) .05 .02
216 Harold Reynolds (53) .10 .04
217 Scott Bradley (54) .05 .02
218 Matt Young (57) .05 .02
219 Mark Langston (58) .10 .04
220 Alvin Davis (59) .05 .02
221 Phil Bradley (60) .05 .02
222 Ken Phelps (62) .05 .02
223 Danny Tartabull .05 .02
224 Eddie Murray .25 .10
225 Rick Dempsey (63) .05 .02
226 Fred Lynn (64) .10 .04
227 Mike Boddicker (65) .05 .02
228 Don Aase (66) .05 .02
229 Larry Sheets (67) .05 .02
230 Storm Davis (68) .05 .02
231 Lee Lacy (69) .05 .02
232 Jim Traber (71) .05 .02
233 Cal Ripken 2.00 .80
234 Larry Parrish .05 .02
235 Gary Ward (72) .05 .02
236 Pete Incaviglia (73) .10 .04
237 Scott Fletcher (74) .05 .02
238 Greg Harris (77) .05 .02
239 Pete O'Brien .05 .02
240 Charlie Hough (78) .05 .02
241 Don Slaught (79) .05 .02
242 Steve Buechele (80) .05 .02
243 Oddibe McDowell (81) .05 .02
244 Roger Clemens (82) .40 .16
245 Bob Stanley (83) .05 .02
246 Tom Seaver (84) .50 .20
247 Rich Gedman (87) .05 .02
248 Jim Rice .10 .04
249 Dennis Boyd (88) .05 .02
250 Bill Buckner (89) .10 .04
251 Dwight Evans (90) .10 .04
252 Don Baylor (91) .10 .04
253 Wade Boggs .25 .10
254 George Brett .75 .30
255 Steve Farr (92) .05 .02
256 Jim Sundberg (93) .05 .02
257 Dan Quisenberry (94) .05 .02
258 Charlie Leibrandt(97) .05 .02
259 Angel Salazar (98) .05 .02
260 Frank White (99) .10 .04
261 Willie Wilson (100) .10 .04
262 Lonnie Smith (102) .05 .02
263 Steve Balboni .05 .02
264 Darrell Evans .10 .04
265 Johnny Grubb (103) .05 .02
266 Jack Morris (104) .10 .04
267 Lou Whitaker (105) .10 .04
268 Chet Lemon (107) .05 .02
269 Lance Parrish (108) .10 .04
270 Alan Trammell (109) .15 .06
271 Darnell Coles (110) .05 .02
272 Willie Hernandez .05 .02
(111)
273 Kirk Gibson .10 .04
274 Kirby Puckett .60 .24
275 Mike Smithson (112) .05 .02
276 Mickey Hatcher (113) .05 .02
277 Frank Viola (114) .05 .02
278 Bert Blyleven (117) .10 .04
279 Gary Gaetti .10 .04
280 Tom Brunansky (118) .05 .02
281 Kent Hrbek (119) .10 .04
282 Roy Smalley (120) .05 .02
283 Greg Gagne (122) .05 .02
284 Harold Baines .10 .04
285 Ron Hassey (123) .05 .02
286 Floyd Bannister(124) .05 .02
287 Ozzie Guillen (125) .05 .02
288 Carlton Fisk (126) .25 .10
289 Tim Hulett (127) .05 .02
290 Joe Cowley (128) .05 .02
291 Greg Walker (129) .05 .02
292 Neil Allen (131) .05 .02
293 John Cangelosi .05 .02
294 Don Mattingly 1.00 .40
295 Mike Easler (132) .05 .02
296 Rickey Henderson(133) .25 .10
297 Dan Pasqua (134) .05 .02
298 Dave Winfield (137) .25 .10
299 Dave Righetti .05 .02
300 Mike Pagliarulo(138) .05 .02
301 Ron Guidry (139) .10 .04
302 Willie Randolph(140) .10 .04
303 Dennis Rasmussen .05 .02
(141)
304 Jose Canseco (142) 1.00 .40
305 Andres Thomas (143) .05 .02
306 Danny Tartabull(144) .05 .02
307 Robby Thompson (165) .10 .04
308 Pete Incaviglia(166) .10 .04
309 Dale Sveum (167) .05 .02
310 Todd Worrell (168) .10 .04
311 Andy Allanson (169) .05 .02
312 Bruce Ruffin (170) .05 .02
313 Wally Joyner (171) .50 .20
NNO Album 1.00 .40

1988 Topps

This set consists of 792 standard-size cards. The cards were primarily issued in 15-card wax packs, 42-card rack packs and factory sets. Card fronts feature white borders encasing a color photo with team name running across the top and player name diagonally across the bottom. Subsets include Record Breakers (1-7), All-Stars (386-407), Turn Back the Clock (661-665), and Team Leaders (scattered throughout the set). The manager cards contain a team checklist on back. The key Rookie Cards in this set are Ellis Burks, Ken Caminiti, Tom Glavine, and Matt Williams.

	Nm-Mt	Ex-Mt
COMPLETE SET (792)	15.00	6.00
COMP.FACT SET (792)	15.00	6.00
COMP.X-MAS.SET (792)	40.00	16.00

1 Vince Coleman RB .05 .02
2 Don Mattingly RB .30 .12
3 Mark McGwire RB .75 .30
Rookie Homer Record
(No white spot)
3A Mark McGwire RB .20 .08
Rookie Homer Record
(White spot behind
left foot)
4 Eddie Murray RB .15 .06
Switch Home Runs,
Two Straight Games
(No caption on front)
4A Eddie Murray RB .50 .20
Switch Home Runs,
Two Straight Games
(Caption in box
on card front)
5 Phil Niekro .10 .04
Joe Niekro RB
6 Nolan Ryan RB .40 .16
7 Benito Santiago RB .10 .04
8 Kevin Elster .05 .02
9 Andy Hawkins .05 .02
10 Ryne Sandberg .40 .16
11 Mike Young .05 .02
12 Bill Schroeder .05 .02
13 Andres Thomas .05 .02
14 Sparky Anderson MG .10 .04
15 Chili Davis .15 .06
16 Kirk McCaskill .05 .02
17 Ron Oester .05 .02
18A Al Leiter RC ERR .20 .08
(Photo actually
Steve George,
right ear visible)
18B Al Leiter RC COR .50 .20
(Left ear visible)
19 Mark Davidson .05 .02
20 Kevin Gross .05 .02
21 Wade Boggs .10 .04
Spike Owen TL
22 Greg Swindell .05 .02
23 Ken Landreaux .05 .02
24 Jim Deshaies .05 .02
25 Andres Galarraga .10 .04
26 Mitch Williams .05 .02
27 R.J. Reynolds .05 .02
28 Jose Nunez .05 .02
29 Angel Salazar .05 .02
30 Sid Fernandez .05 .02
31 Bruce Bochy .05 .02
32 Mike Morgan .05 .02
33 Rob Deer .05 .02
34 Ricky Horton .05 .02
35 Harold Baines .10 .04
36 Jamie Moyer .20 .08
37 Ed Romero .05 .02
38 Jeff Calhoun .05 .02
39 Gerald Perry .05 .02
40 Orel Hershiser .10 .04
41 Bob Melvin .05 .02
42 Bill Landrum .05 .02
43 Dick Schofield .05 .02
44 Lou Piniella MG .10 .04
45 Kent Hrbek .10 .04
46 Darnell Coles .05 .02
47 Joaquin Andujar .05 .02
48 Alan Ashby .05 .02
49 Dave Clark .05 .02
50 Hubie Brooks .05 .02
51 Eddie Murray .40 .16
Cal Ripken TL
52 Don Robinson .05 .02
53 Curt Wilkerson .05 .02
54 Jim Clancy .05 .02
55 Phil Bradley .05 .02
56 Ed Hearn .05 .02
57 Tim Crews RC .05 .02
58 Dave Magadan .05 .02
59 Danny Cox .05 .02
60 Rickey Henderson .20 .08
61 Mark Knudson .05 .02
62 Jeff Hamilton .05 .02
63 Jimmy Jones .05 .02
64 Ken Caminiti RC .40 .16
65 Leon Durham .05 .02
66 Shane Rawley .05 .02
67 Ken Oberkfell .05 .02
68 Dave Dravecky .10 .04
69 Mike Hart .05 .02
70 Roger Clemens .50 .20
71 Gary Pettis .05 .02
72 Dennis Eckersley .10 .04
73 Randy Bush .05 .02
74 Tom Lasorda MG .20 .08
75 Joe Carter .20 .08
76 Dennis Martinez .10 .04
77 Tom O'Malley .05 .02
78 Dan Petry .05 .02
79 Ernie Whitt .05 .02
80 Mark Langston .05 .02
81 Ron Robinson .05 .02
John Franco TL
82 Darrel Akerfelds .05 .02
83 Jose Oquendo .05 .02
84 Cecilio Guante .05 .02
85 Howard Johnson .05 .02
86 Ron Karkovice .05 .02
87 Mike Mason .05 .02
88 Earnie Riles .05 .02
89 Gary Thurman .05 .02
90 Dale Murphy .20 .08
91 Joey Cora RC .20 .08
92 Len Matuszek .05 .02
93 Bob Sebra .05 .02
94 Chuck Jackson .05 .02
95 Lance Parrish .05 .02
96 Todd Benzinger RC* .05 .02
97 Scott Garrelts .05 .02
98 Rene Gonzales RC .05 .02
99 Chuck Finley .15 .06
100 Jack Clark .10 .04
101 Allan Anderson .05 .02
102 Barry Larkin .20 .08
103 Curt Young .05 .02
104 Dick Williams MG .10 .04
105 Jesse Orosco .05 .02
106 Jim Walewander .05 .02
107 Scott Bailes .05 .02
108 Steve Lyons .05 .02
109 Joel Skinner .05 .02
110 Teddy Higuera .05 .02
111 Hubie Brooks .05 .02
Vance Law TL
112 Les Lancaster .05 .02
113 Kelly Gruber .05 .02
114 Jeff Russell .05 .02
115 Johnny Ray .05 .02
116 Jerry Don Gleaton .05 .02
117 James Steels .05 .02
118 Bob Welch .05 .02
119 Robbie Wine .05 .02
120 Kirby Puckett .20 .08
121 Checklist 1-132 .05 .02
122 Tony Bernazard .05 .02
123 Tom Candiotti .05 .02
124 Ray Knight .05 .02
125 Bruce Hurst .05 .02
126 Steve Jeltz .05 .02
127 Jim Gott .05 .02
128 Johnny Grubb .05 .02
129 Greg Minton .05 .02
130 Buddy Bell .10 .04
131 Don Schulze .05 .02
132 Donnie Hill .05 .02
133 Greg Mathews .05 .02
134 Chuck Tanner MG .10 .04
135 Dennis Rasmussen .05 .02
136 Brian Dayett .05 .02
137 Chris Bosio .05 .02
138 Mitch Webster .05 .02
139 Jerry Browne .05 .02
140 Jesse Barfield .05 .02
141 George Brett .20 .08
Bret Saberhagen TL
142 Andy Van Slyke .10 .04
143 Mickey Tettleton .05 .02
144 Don Gordon .05 .02
145 Bill Madlock .10 .04
146 Donell Nixon .05 .02
147 Bill Buckner .10 .04
148 Carmelo Martinez .05 .02
149 Ken Howell .05 .02
150 Eric Davis .10 .04
151 Bob Knepper .05 .02
152 Jody Reed RC .10 .04
153 John Habyan .05 .02
154 Jeff Stone .05 .02
155 Bruce Sutter .10 .04
156 Gary Matthews .05 .02
157 Atlee Hammaker .05 .02
158 Tim Hulett .05 .02
159 Brad Arnsberg .05 .02
160 Willie McGee .10 .04
161 Bryn Smith .05 .02
162 Mark McLemore .05 .02
163 Dale Mohorcic .05 .02
164 Dave Johnson MG .10 .04
165 Robin Yount .30 .12
166 Rick Rodriguez .05 .02
167 Rance Mulliniks .05 .02
168 Barry Jones .05 .02
169 Ross Jones .05 .02
170 Rich Gossage .10 .04
171 Shawon Dunston .05 .02
Manny Trillo TL
172 Lloyd McClendon RC .05 .02
173 Eric Plunk .05 .02
174 Phil Garner .05 .02
175 Kevin Bass .05 .02
176 Jeff Reed .05 .02
177 Frank Tanana .05 .02
178 Dwayne Henry .05 .02
179 Charlie Puleo .05 .02
180 Terry Kennedy .05 .02
181 David Cone .10 .04
182 Ken Phelps .05 .02
183 Tom Lawless .05 .02
184 Ivan Calderon .05 .02
185 Rick Rhoden .05 .02
186 Rafael Palmeiro .40 .16
187 Steve Kiefer .05 .02
188 John Russell .05 .02
189 Wes Gardner .05 .02
190 Candy Maldonado .05 .02
191 John Cerutti .05 .02
192 Devon White .10 .04
193 Brian Fisher .05 .02
194 Tom Kelly MG .05 .02
195 Dan Quisenberry .05 .02
196 Dave Engle .05 .02
197 Lance McCullers .05 .02
198 Franklin Stubbs .05 .02
199 Dave Meads .05 .02
200 Wade Boggs .15 .06
201 Bobby Valentine MG .05 .02
Pete O'Brien
Pete Incaviglia
Steve Buechele TL
202 Glenn Hoffman .05 .02
203 Fred Toliver .05 .02
204 Paul O'Neill .15 .06
205 Nelson Liriano .05 .02
206 Domingo Ramos .05 .02
207 John Mitchell RC .05 .02
208 Steve Lake .05 .02
209 Richard Dotson .05 .02
210 Willie Randolph .10 .04
211 Frank DiPino .05 .02
212 Greg Brock .05 .02
213 Albert Hall .05 .02
214 Dave Schmidt .05 .02
215 Von Hayes .05 .02
216 Jerry Reuss .05 .02
217 Harry Spilman .05 .02
218 Dan Schatzeder .05 .02
219 Mike Stanley .10 .04
220 Tom Henke .05 .02
221 Rafael Belliard .05 .02
222 Steve Farr .05 .02
223 Stan Jefferson .05 .02
224 Tom Trebelhorn MG .05 .02
225 Mike Scioscia .05 .02
226 Dave Lopes .10 .04
227 Ed Correa .05 .02
228 Wallace Johnson .05 .02
229 Jeff Musselman .05 .02
230 Pat Tabler .05 .02
231 Barry Bonds .50 .20
Bobby Bonilla TL
232 Bob James .05 .02
233 Rafael Santana .05 .02
234 Ken Dayley .05 .02
235 Gary Ward .05 .02
236 Ted Power .05 .02
237 Mike Heath .05 .02
238 Luis Polonia RC* .05 .02
239 Roy Smalley .05 .02
240 Lee Smith .10 .04
241 Damaso Garcia .05 .02
242 Tom Niedenfuer .05 .02
243 Mark Ryal .05 .02
244 Jeff D. Robinson .05 .02
245 Rich Gedman .05 .02
246 Mike Campbell .05 .02
247 Thad Bosley .05 .02
248 Storm Davis .05 .02
249 Mike Marshall .05 .02
250 Nolan Ryan 1.00 .40
251 Tom Foley .05 .02
252 Bob Brower .05 .02
253 Checklist 133-264 .05 .02
254 Lee Elia MG .05 .02
255 Mookie Wilson .10 .04
256 Ken Schrom .05 .02
257 Jerry Royster .05 .02
258 Ed Nunez .05 .02
259 Ron Kittle .05 .02
260 Vince Coleman .05 .02
261 Giants TL .05 .02
(Five players)
262 Drew Hall .05 .02
263 Glenn Braggs .05 .02
264 Les Straker .05 .02
265 Bo Diaz .05 .02
266 Paul Assenmacher .05 .02
267 Billy Bean RC .15 .06
268 Bruce Ruffin .05 .02
269 Ellis Burks RC .40 .16
270 Mike Witt .05 .02
271 Ken Gerhart .05 .02
272 Steve Ontiveros .05 .02
273 Garth Iorg .05 .02
274 Junior Ortiz .05 .02
275 Kevin Seitzer .10 .04
276 Luis Salazar .05 .02
277 Alejandro Pena .05 .02
278 Jose Cruz .05 .02
279 Randy St.Claire .05 .02
280 Pete Incaviglia .05 .02
281 Jerry Hairston .05 .02
282 Pat Perry .05 .02
283 Phil Lombardi .05 .02
284 Larry Bowa MG .05 .02
285 Jim Presley .05 .02
286 Chuck Crim .05 .02
287 Manny Trillo .05 .02
288 Pat Pacillo .05 .02

(Chris Sabo in background of photo)
289 Dave Bergman .05 .02
290 Tony Fernandez .05 .02
291 Billy Hatcher .05 .02
Kevin Bass TL
292 Carney Lansford .10 .04
293 Doug Jones RC .20 .08
294 Al Pedrique .05 .02
295 Bert Blyleven .10 .04
296 Floyd Rayford .05 .02
297 Zane Smith .05 .02
298 Milt Thompson .05 .02
299 Steve Crawford .05 .02
300 Don Mattingly .60 .24
301 Bud Black .05 .02
302 Jose Uribe .05 .02
303 Eric Show .05 .02
304 George Hendrick .05 .02
305 Steve Sax .05 .02
306 Billy Hatcher .05 .02
307 Mike Trujillo .05 .02
308 Lee Mazzilli .05 .02
309 Bill Long .05 .02
310 Tom Herr .05 .02
311 Scott Sanderson .05 .02
312 Joey Meyer .05 .02
313 Bob McClure .05 .02
314 Jimy Williams MG .05 .02
315 Dave Parker .10 .04
316 Jose Rijo .05 .02
317 Tom Nieto .05 .02
318 Mel Hall .05 .02
319 Mike Loynd .05 .02
320 Alan Trammell .15 .06
321 Harold Baines .10 .04
Carlton Fisk TL
322 Vicente Palacios .05 .02
323 Rick Leach .05 .02
324 Danny Jackson .05 .02
325 Glenn Hubbard .05 .02
326 Al Nipper .05 .02
327 Larry Sheets .05 .02
328 Greg Cadaret .05 .02
329 Chris Speier .05 .02
330 Eddie Whitson .05 .02
331 Brian Downing .05 .02
332 Jerry Reed .05 .02
333 Wally Backman .05 .02
334 Dave LaPoint .05 .02
335 Claudell Washington .05 .02
336 Ed Lynch .05 .02
337 Jim Gantner .05 .02
338 Brian Holton UER .05 .02
1987 ERA .389, should be 3.89
339 Kurt Stillwell .05 .02
340 Jack Morris .10 .04
341 Carmen Castillo .05 .02
342 Larry Andersen .05 .02
343 Greg Gagne .05 .02
344 Tony LaRussa MG .10 .04
345 Scott Fletcher .05 .02
346 Vance Law .05 .02
347 Joe Johnson .05 .02
348 Jim Eisenreich .20 .08
349 Bob Walk .05 .02
350 Will Clark .20 .08
351 Red Schoendienst CO .10 .04
Tony Pena TL
352 Bill Ripken RC* .05 .02
353 Ed Olwine .05 .02
354 Marc Sullivan .05 .02
355 Roger McDowell .05 .02
356 Luis Aguayo .05 .02
357 Floyd Bannister .05 .02
358 Rey Quinones .05 .02
359 Tim Stoddard .05 .02
360 Tony Gwynn .30 .12
361 Greg Maddux 1.00 .40
362 Juan Castillo .05 .02
363 Willie Fraser .05 .02
364 Nick Esasky .05 .02
365 Floyd Youmans .05 .02
366 Chet Lemon .05 .02
367 Tim Leary .05 .02
368 Gerald Young .05 .02
369 Greg Harris .05 .02
370 Jose Canseco .20 .08
371 Joe Hesketh .05 .02
372 Matt Williams RC .75 .30
373 Checklist 265-396 .05 .02
374 Doc Edwards MG .05 .02
375 Tom Brunansky .05 .02
376 Bill Wilkinson .05 .02
377 Sam Horn RC .05 .02
378 Todd Frohwirth .05 .02
379 Rafael Ramirez .05 .02
380 Joe Magrane RC* .05 .02
381 Wally Joyner .10 .04
Jack Howell TL
382 Keith A. Miller RC .05 .02
383 Eric Bell .05 .02
384 Neil Allen .05 .02
385 Carlton Fisk .15 .06
386 Don Mattingly AS .30 .12
387 Willie Randolph AS .05 .02
388 Wade Boggs AS .10 .04
389 Alan Trammell AS .05 .02
390 George Bell AS .05 .02
391 Kirby Puckett AS .15 .06
392 Dave Winfield AS .05 .02
393 Matt Nokes AS .05 .02
394 Roger Clemens AS .20 .08
395 Jimmy Key AS .05 .02
396 Tom Henke AS .05 .02
397 Jack Clark AS .10 .04
398 Juan Samuel AS .05 .02
399 Tim Wallach AS .05 .02
400 Ozzie Smith AS .20 .08
401 Andre Dawson AS .05 .02
402 Tony Gwynn AS .15 .06
403 Tim Raines AS .10 .04
404 Benny Santiago AS .10 .04
405 Dwight Gooden AS .15 .06
406 Shane Rawley AS .05 .02
407 Steve Bedrosian AS .05 .02
408 Dion James .05 .02
409 Joel McKeon .05 .02
410 Tony Pena .05 .02
411 Wayne Tolleson .05 .02
412 Randy Myers .15 .06
413 John Christensen .05 .02
414 John McNamara MG .05 .02
415 Don Carman .05 .02
416 Keith Moreland .05 .02
417 Mark Ciardi .05 .02
418 Joel Youngblood .05 .02
419 Scott McGregor .05 .02
420 Wally Joyner .15 .06
421 Ed VandeBerg .05 .02
422 Dave Concepcion .10 .04
423 John Smiley RC* .10 .04
424 Dwayne Murphy .05 .02
425 Jeff Reardon .10 .04
426 Randy Ready .05 .02
427 Paul Kilgus .05 .02
428 John Shelby .05 .02
429 Alan Trammell .05 .02
Kirk Gibson TL
430 Glenn Davis .05 .02
431 Casey Candaele .05 .02
432 Mike Moore .05 .02
433 Bill Pecota RC* .05 .02
434 Rick Aguilera .10 .04
435 Mike Pagliarulo .05 .02
436 Mike Bielecki .05 .02
437 Fred Manrique .05 .02
438 Rob Ducey .05 .02
439 Dave Martinez .05 .02
440 Steve Bedrosian .05 .02
441 Rick Manning .05 .02
442 Tom Bolton .05 .02
443 Ken Griffey .10 .04
444 C.Ripken Sr. MG UER .05 .02
two copyrights
445 Mike Krukow .05 .02
446 Doug DeCinces .05 .02
(Now with Cardinals on card front)
447 Jeff Montgomery RC .20 .08
448 Mike Davis .05 .02
449 Jeff M. Robinson .05 .02
450 Barry Bonds 2.00 .80
451 Keith Atherton .05 .02
452 Willie Wilson .05 .02
453 Dennis Powell .05 .02
454 Marvell Wynne .05 .02
455 Shawn Hillegas .05 .02
456 Dave Anderson .05 .02
457 Terry Leach .05 .02
458 Ron Hassey .05 .02
459 Dave Winfield .05 .02
Willie Randolph TL
460 Ozzie Smith .30 .12
461 Danny Darwin .05 .02
462 Don Slaught .05 .02
463 Fred McGriff .20 .08
464 Jay Tibbs .05 .02
465 Paul Molitor .15 .06
466 Jerry Mumphrey .05 .02
467 Don Aase .05 .02
468 Darren Daulton .10 .04
469 Jeff Dedmon .05 .02
470 Dwight Evans .10 .04
471 Donnie Moore .05 .02
472 Robby Thompson .05 .02
473 Joe Niekro .05 .02
474 Tom Brookens .05 .02
475 Pete Rose MG .50 .20
476 Dave Stewart .10 .04
477 Jamie Quirk .05 .02
478 Sid Bream .05 .02
479 Brett Butler .10 .04
480 Dwight Gooden .15 .06
481 Mariano Duncan .05 .02
482 Mark Davis .05 .02
483 Rod Booker .05 .02
484 Pat Clements .05 .02
485 Harold Reynolds .10 .04
486 Pat Keedy .05 .02
487 Jim Pankovits .05 .02
488 Andy McGaffigan .05 .02
489 Pedro Guerrero .05 .02
Fernando Valenzuela TL
490 Larry Parrish .05 .02
491 B.J. Surhoff .10 .04
492 Doyle Alexander .05 .02
493 Mike Greenwell .05 .02
494 Wally Ritchie .05 .02
495 Eddie Murray .20 .08
496 Guy Hoffman .05 .02
497 Kevin Mitchell .10 .04
498 Bob Boone .10 .04
499 Eric King .05 .02
500 Andre Dawson .10 .04
501 Tim Birtsas .05 .02
502 Dan Gladden .05 .02
503 Junior Noboa .05 .02
504 Bob Rodgers MG .05 .02
505 Willie Upshaw .05 .02
506 John Cangelosi .05 .02
507 Mark Gubicza .05 .02
508 Tim Teufel .05 .02
509 Bill Dawley .05 .02
510 Dave Winfield .10 .04
511 Joel Davis .05 .02
512 Alex Trevino .05 .02
513 Tim Flannery .05 .02
514 Pat Sheridan .05 .02
515 Juan Nieves .05 .02
516 Jim Sundberg .05 .02
517 Ron Robinson .05 .02
518 Greg Gross .05 .02
519 Harold Reynolds .05 .02
Phil Bradley TL
520 Dave Smith .05 .02
521 Jim Dwyer .05 .02
522 Bob Patterson .05 .02
523 Gary Roenicke .05 .02
524 Gary Lucas .05 .02
525 Marty Barrett .05 .02
526 Juan Berenguer .05 .02
527 Steve Henderson .05 .02
528A Checklist 397-528 .15 .06
ERR (455 S. Carlton)
528B Checklist 397-528 .10 .04
COR (455 S. Hillegas)
529 Tim Burke .05 .02
530 Gary Carter .15 .06
531 Rich Yett .05 .02
532 Mike Kingery .05 .02
533 John Farrell RC .05 .02
534 John Wathan MG .05 .02
535 Ron Guidry .10 .04
536 John Morris .05 .02
537 Steve Buechele .05 .02
538 Bill Wegman .05 .02
539 Mike LaValliere .05 .02
540 Bret Saberhagen .10 .04
541 Juan Beniquez .05 .02
542 Paul Noce .05 .02
543 Kent Tekulve .05 .02
544 Jim Traber .05 .02
545 Don Baylor .10 .04
546 John Candelaria .05 .02
547 Felix Fermin .05 .02
548 Shane Mack .05 .02
549 Albert Hall .10 .04
Dale Murphy
Ken Griffey
Dion James TL
550 Pedro Guerrero .05 .02
551 Terry Steinbach .10 .04
552 Mark Thurmond .05 .02
553 Tracy Jones .05 .02
554 Mike Smithson .05 .02
555 Brook Jacoby .05 .02
556 Stan Clarke .05 .02
557 Craig Reynolds .05 .02
558 Bob Ojeda .05 .02
559 Ken Williams RC .05 .02
560 Tim Wallach .05 .02
561 Rick Cerone .05 .02
562 Jim Lindeman .05 .02
563 Jose Guzman .05 .02
564 Frank Lucchesi MG .05 .02
565 Lloyd Moseby .05 .02
566 Charlie O'Brien .05 .02
567 Mike Diaz .05 .02
568 Chris Brown .05 .02
569 Charlie Leibrandt .05 .02
570 Jeffrey Leonard .05 .02
571 Mark Williamson .05 .02
572 Chris James .05 .02
573 Bob Stanley .05 .02
574 Graig Nettles .10 .04
575 Don Sutton .20 .08
576 Tommy Hinzo .05 .02
577 Tom Browning .05 .02
578 Gary Gaetti .10 .04
579 Gary Carter .05 .02
Kevin McReynolds TL
580 Mark McGwire 1.50 .60
581 Tito Landrum .05 .02
582 Mike Henneman RC* .10 .04
583 Dave Valle .05 .02
584 Steve Trout .05 .02
585 Ozzie Guillen .05 .02
586 Bob Forsch .05 .02
587 Terry Puhl .05 .02
588 Jeff Parrett .05 .02
589 Geno Petralli .05 .02
590 George Bell .05 .02
591 Doug Drabek .05 .02
592 Dale Sveum .05 .02
593 Bob Tewksbury .05 .02
594 Bobby Valentine MG .10 .04
595 Frank White .10 .04
596 John Kruk .10 .04
597 Gene Garber .05 .02
598 Lee Lacy .05 .02
599 Calvin Schiraldi .05 .02
600 Mike Schmidt .50 .20
601 Jack Lazorko .05 .02
602 Mike Aldrete .05 .02
603 Rob Murphy .05 .02
604 Chris Bando .05 .02
605 Kirk Gibson .10 .04
606 Moose Haas .05 .02
607 Mickey Hatcher .05 .02
608 Charlie Kerfeld .05 .02
609 Gary Gaetti .10 .04
Kent Hrbek TL
610 Keith Hernandez .15 .06
611 Tommy John .10 .04
612 Curt Ford .05 .02
613 Bobby Thigpen .05 .02
614 Herm Winningham .05 .02
615 Jody Davis .05 .02
616 Jay Aldrich .05 .02
617 Oddibe McDowell .05 .02
618 Cecil Fielder .15 .06
619 Mike Dunne .05 .02
Inconsistent design, black name on front
620 Cory Snyder .05 .02
621 Gene Nelson .05 .02
622 Kal Daniels .05 .02
623 Mike Flanagan .05 .02
624 Jim Leyland MG .10 .04
625 Frank Viola .05 .02
626 Glenn Wilson .05 .02
627 Joe Boever .05 .02
628 Dave Henderson .05 .02
629 Kelly Downs .05 .02
630 Darrell Evans .10 .04
631 Jack Howell .05 .02
632 Steve Shields .05 .02
633 Barry Lyons .05 .02
634 Jose DeLeon .05 .02
635 Terry Pendleton .10 .04
636 Charles Hudson .05 .02
637 Jay Bell RC .40 .16
638 Steve Balboni .05 .02
639 Glenn Braggs .05 .02
Tony Muser CO TL
640 Garry Templeton .05 .02
(Inconsistent design, green border)
641 Rick Honeycutt .05 .02
642 Bob Dernier .05 .02
643 Rocky Childress .05 .02
644 Terry McGriff .05 .02
645 Matt Nokes RC* .05 .02
646 Checklist 529-660 .05 .02
647 Pascual Perez .05 .02
648 Al Newman .05 .02
649 DeWayne Buice .05 .02
650 Cal Ripken .75 .30
651 Mike Jackson RC* .10 .04
652 Bruce Benedict .05 .02
653 Jeff Sellers .05 .02
654 Roger Craig MG .10 .04
655 Len Dykstra .10 .04
656 Lee Guetterman .05 .02
657 Gary Redus .05 .02
658 Tim Conroy .05 .02
(Inconsistent design, name in white)
659 Bobby Meacham .05 .02
660 Rick Reuschel .05 .02
661 Nolan Ryan TBC '83 .50 .20
662 Jim Rice TBC .05 .02
663 Ron Blomberg TBC .05 .02
664 Bob Gibson TBC '68 .25 .10
665 Stan Musial TBC '63 .20 .08
666 Mario Soto .05 .02
667 Luis Quinones .05 .02
668 Walt Terrell .05 .02
669 Lance Parrish .05 .02
Mike Ryan CO TL
670 Dan Plesac .05 .02
671 Tim Laudner .05 .02
672 John Davis .05 .02
673 Tony Phillips .05 .02
674 Mike Fitzgerald .05 .02
675 Jim Rice .10 .04
676 Ken Dixon .05 .02
677 Eddie Milner .05 .02
678 Jim Acker .05 .02
679 Darrell Miller .05 .02
680 Charlie Hough .10 .04
681 Bobby Bonilla .10 .04
682 Jimmy Key .10 .04
683 Julio Franco .05 .02
684 Hal Lanier MG .05 .02
685 Ron Darling .05 .02
686 Terry Francona .05 .02
687 Mickey Brantley .05 .02
688 Jim Winn .05 .02
689 Tom Pagnozzi RC .05 .02
690 Jay Howell .05 .02
691 Dan Pasqua .05 .02
692 Mike Birkbeck .05 .02
693 Benito Santiago .15 .06
694 Eric Nolte .05 .02
695 Shawon Dunston .05 .02
696 Duane Ward .05 .02
697 Steve Lombardozzi .05 .02
698 Brad Havens .05 .02
699 Benito Santiago .10 .04
Tony Gwynn TL
700 George Brett .50 .20
701 Sammy Stewart .05 .02
702 Mike Gallego .05 .02
703 Bob Brenly .05 .02
704 Dennis Boyd .05 .02
705 Juan Samuel .05 .02
706 Rick Mahler .05 .02
707 Fred Lynn .05 .02
708 Gus Polidor .05 .02
709 George Frazier .05 .02
710 Darryl Strawberry .15 .06
711 Bill Gullickson .05 .02
712 John Moses .05 .02
713 Willie Hernandez .05 .02
714 Jim Fregosi MG .05 .02
715 Todd Worrell .10 .04
716 Lenn Sakata .05 .02
717 Jay Baller .05 .02
718 Mike Felder .05 .02
719 Denny Walling .05 .02
720 Tim Raines .10 .04
721 Pete O'Brien .05 .02
722 Manny Lee .05 .02
723 Bob Kipper .05 .02
724 Danny Tartabull .05 .02
725 Mike Boddicker .05 .02
726 Alfredo Griffin .05 .02
727 Greg Booker .05 .02
728 Andy Allanson .05 .02
729 George Bell .10 .04
Fred McGriff TL
730 John Franco .10 .04
731 Rick Schu .05 .02
732 David Palmer .05 .02
733 Spike Owen .05 .02
734 Craig Lefferts .05 .02
735 Kevin McReynolds .05 .02
736 Matt Young .05 .02
737 Butch Wynegar .05 .02
738 Scott Bankhead .05 .02
739 Daryl Boston .05 .02
740 Rick Sutcliffe .10 .04
741 Mike Easler .05 .02
742 Mark Clear .05 .02
743 Larry Herndon .05 .02
744 Whitey Herzog MG .10 .04
745 Bill Doran .05 .02
746 Gene Larkin RC* .05 .02
747 Bobby Witt .05 .02
748 Reid Nichols .05 .02
749 Mark Eichhorn .05 .02
750 Bo Jackson .20 .08
751 Jim Morrison .05 .02
752 Mark Grant .05 .02
753 Danny Heep .05 .02
754 Mike LaCoss .05 .02
755 Ozzie Virgil .05 .02
756 Mike Maddux .05 .02
757 John Marzano .05 .02
758 Eddie Williams RC .10 .04
759 Mark McGwire .75 .30
Jose Canseco TL UER
(two copyrights)
760 Mike Scott .05 .02
761 Tony Armas .05 .02
762 Scott Bradley .05 .02
763 Doug Sisk .05 .02
764 Greg Walker .05 .02
765 Neal Heaton .05 .02
766 Henry Cotto .05 .02
767 Jose Lind RC .05 .02
768 Dickie Noles .05 .02
(Now with Tigers on card front)
769 Cecil Cooper .10 .04
770 Lou Whitaker .10 .04
771 Ruben Sierra .05 .02
772 Sal Butera .05 .02
773 Frank Williams .05 .02
774 Gene Mauch MG .10 .04
775 Dave Stieb .05 .02
776 Checklist 661-792 .05 .02
777 Lonnie Smith .05 .02
778A Keith Comstock ERR 2.00 .80
(White "Padres")
778B Keith Comstock COR .05 .02
(Blue "Padres")
779 Tom Glavine RC 1.50 .60
780 Fernando Valenzuela .10 .04
781 Keith Hughes .05 .02
782 Jeff Ballard .05 .02
783 Ron Roenicke .05 .02
784 Joe Sambito .05 .02
785 Alvin Davis .05 .02
786 Joe Price .05 .02
Inconsistent design, orange team name
787 Bill Almon .05 .02
788 Ray Searage .05 .02
789 Joe Carter .10 .04
Cory Snyder TL
790 Dave Righetti .05 .02
791 Ted Simmons .10 .04
792 John Tudor .05 .02

1988 Topps Tiffany

This was the fifth year that Topps issued a "Tiffany" set. These 792 standard-size cards parallel the regular Topps cards. These cards were issued in factory set form only, produced in Topps Irish facility, and only available through Topps hobby dealers. These cards were again produced in relatively large quantities and the mulitplier value is reduced compared to pre-1987 levels. It is believed that as many as 25,000 of these sets were produced.

Nm-Mt Ex-Mt
COMP.FACT.SET (792) 60.00 24.00
*STARS: 4X TO 10X BASIC CARDS
*ROOKIES: 4X TO 10X BASIC CARDS

1988 Topps Glossy All-Stars

This set of 22 glossy cards was inserted one per rack pack. Players selected for the set are the starting players (plus manager and honorary captain) in the 1987 All-Star Game in Oakland. Cards measure the standard size and the backs feature red and blue printing on a white card stock.

Nm-Mt Ex-Mt
COMPLETE SET (22) 4.00 1.60
1 John McNamara MG .05 .02
2 Don Mattingly 1.00 .40
3 Willie Randolph .10 .04
4 Wade Boggs .50 .20
5 Cal Ripken 2.00 .80
6 George Bell .05 .02
7 Rickey Henderson .75 .30
8 Dave Winfield .40 .16
9 Terry Kennedy .05 .02
10 Bret Saberhagen .10 .04
11 Jim Hunter CAPT .10 .04
12 Dave Johnson MG .10 .04
13 Jack Clark .10 .04
14 Ryne Sandberg 1.00 .40
15 Mike Schmidt .50 .20
16 Ozzie Smith 1.00 .40
17 Eric Davis .10 .04
18 Andre Dawson .20 .08
19 Darryl Strawberry .10 .04
20 Gary Carter .40 .16
21 Mike Scott .05 .02
22 Billy Williams CAPT .10 .04

1988 Topps Glossy Send-Ins

Topps issued this set through a mail-in offer explained and advertised on the wax packs. This 60-card set features glossy fronts with each card measuring the standard size. The offer provided your choice of any one of the six 10-card subsets (1-10, 11-20, etc.) for 1.25 plus six of the Special Offer ("Spring Fever Baseball") insert cards, which were found one per wax pack. One complete set was obtainable by sending 7.50 plus 18 special offer cards. The last two players (numerically) in each ten-card subset are actually "Hot Prospects."

Nm-Mt Ex-Mt
COMPLETE SET (60) 10.00 4.00
1 Andre Dawson .40 .16
2 Jesse Barfield .10 .04
3 Mike Schmidt 1.00 .40
4 Ruben Sierra .20 .08
5 Mike Scott .10 .04
6 Cal Ripken 4.00 1.60
7 Gary Carter .75 .30
8 Kent Hrbek .20 .08
9 Kevin Seitzer .10 .04
10 Mike Henneman .20 .08

11 Don Mattingly 2.00 .80
12 Tim Raines .20 .08
13 Roger Clemens 2.00 .80
14 Ryne Sandberg 1.50 .60
15 Tony Fernandez .20 .08
16 Eric Davis .20 .08
17 Jack Morris .20 .08
18 Tim Wallach .10 .04
19 Mike Dunne .10 .04
20 Mike Greenwell .10 .04
21 Dwight Evans .20 .08
22 Darryl Strawberry .20 .08
23 Cory Snyder .10 .04
24 Pedro Guerrero .10 .04
25 Rickey Henderson 1.25 .50
26 Dale Murphy .40 .16
27 Kirby Puckett .75 .30
28 Steve Bedrosian .10 .04
29 Devon White .20 .08
30 Benito Santiago .20 .08
31 George Bell .10 .04
32 Keith Hernandez .20 .08
33 Dave Stewart .20 .08
34 Dave Parker .20 .08
35 Tom Henke .10 .04
36 Willie McGee .20 .08
37 Alan Trammell .30 .12
38 Tony Gwynn 2.00 .80
39 Mark McGwire 3.00 1.20
40 Joe Magrane .10 .04
41 Jack Clark .20 .08
42 Willie Randolph .20 .08
43 Juan Samuel .10 .04
44 Joe Carter .30 .12
45 Shane Rawley .10 .04
46 Dave Winfield .50 .20
47 Ozzie Smith 2.00 .80
48 Wally Joyner .20 .08
49 B.J. Surhoff .20 .08
50 Ellis Burks .75 .30
51 Wade Boggs .75 .30
52 Howard Johnson .10 .04
53 George Brett 2.00 .80
54 Dwight Gooden .20 .08
55 Jose Canseco 1.00 .40
56 Lee Smith .20 .08
57 Paul Molitor .75 .30
58 Andres Galarraga .40 .16
59 Matt Nokes .10 .04
60 Casey Candaele .10 .04

1988 Topps Rookies

Inserted in each supermarket jumbo pack is a card from this series of 22 of 1987's best rookies as determined by Topps. Jumbo packs consisted of 100 (regular issue 1988 Topps baseball) cards with a stick of gum plus the insert "Rookie" card. The card fronts are in full color and measure the standard size. The card backs are printed in red and blue on white card stock and are numbered at the bottom.

Nm-Mt Ex-Mt
COMPLETE SET (22) 25.00 10.00
1 Bill Ripken .25 .10
2 Ellis Burks 1.00 .40
3 Mike Greenwell .25 .10
4 DeWayne Buice .25 .10
5 Devon White .50 .20
6 Fred Manrique .25 .10
7 Mike Henneman .50 .20
8 Matt Nokes .25 .10
9 Kevin Seitzer .50 .20
10 B.J. Surhoff .50 .20
11 Casey Candaele .25 .10
12 Randy Myers .75 .30
13 Mark McGwire 15.00 6.00
14 Luis Polonia .25 .10
15 Terry Steinbach .50 .20
16 Mike Dunne .25 .10
17 Al Pedrique .25 .10
18 Benito Santiago .75 .30
19 Kelly Downs .25 .10
20 Joe Magrane .25 .10
21 Jerry Browne .25 .10
22 Jeff Musselman .25 .10

1988 Topps Wax Box Cards

The cards in this 16-card set measure the standard size. Cards have essentially the same design as the 1988 Topps regular issue set. The cards were printed on the bottoms of the regular issue wax pack boxes. These 16 cards, "lettered" A through P, are considered a separate set in their own right and are not typically included in a complete set of the regular issue 1988 Topps cards. The value of the panels uncut is slightly greater, perhaps by 25 percent greater, than the value of the individual cards cut up carefully. The card lettering is sequenced alphabetically by player's name.

Nm-Mt Ex-Mt
COMPLETE SET (16) 5.00 2.00
A Don Baylor .20 .08
B Steve Bedrosian .10 .04
C Juan Beniquez .10 .04
D Bob Boone .20 .08
E Darrell Evans .20 .08
F Tony Gwynn 1.25 .50
G John Kruk .20 .08
H Marvell Wynne .10 .04
I Joe Carter .40 .16
J Eric Davis .20 .08
K Howard Johnson .10 .04
L Darryl Strawberry .20 .08
M Rickey Henderson 1.00 .40
N Nolan Ryan 2.50 1.00
O Mike Schmidt .75 .30
P Kent Tekulve .10 .04

1988 Topps Traded

This standard-size 132-card Traded set was distributed exclusively in factory set form in blue and white taped boxes through hobby dealers. The cards are identical in style to the Topps regular issue except for whiter stock and t-suffixed numbering on back. Cards are ordered alphabetically by player's last name. This set generated additional interest upon release due to the inclusion of members of the 1988 U.S. Olympic baseball team. These Olympians are indicated in the checklist below by OLY. The key extended Rookie Cards in this set are Jim Abbott, Roberto Alomar, Brady Anderson, Andy Benes, Jay Buhner, Ron Gant, Mark Grace, Tino Martinez, Charles Nagy, Robin Ventura and Walt Weiss.

Nm-Mt Ex-Mt
COMP.FACT.SET (132) 8.00 3.20
1T Jim Abbott OLY XRC 1.00 .40
2T Juan Agosto .10 .04
3T Luis Alicea XRC .20 .08
4T Roberto Alomar XRC 2.00 .80
5T Brady Anderson XRC .75 .30
6T Jack Armstrong XRC .10 .04
7T Don August .10 .04
8T Floyd Bannister .10 .04
9T Bret Barberie OLY XRC .20 .08
10T Jose Bautista XRC .10 .04
11T Don Baylor .20 .08
12T Tim Belcher .20 .08
13T Buddy Bell .20 .08
14T Andy Benes OLY XRC .50 .20
15T Damon Berryhill XRC .10 .04
16T Bud Black .10 .04
17T Pat Borders XRC .20 .08
18T Phil Bradley .10 .04
19T J.Branson XRC OLY .20 .08
20T Tom Brunansky .10 .04
21T Jay Buhner XRC 1.00 .40
22T Brett Butler .20 .08
23T Jim Campanis OLY .10 .04
24T Sil Campusano .10 .04
25T John Candelaria .10 .04
26T Jose Cecena .10 .04
27T Rick Cerone .10 .04
28T Jack Clark .20 .08
29T Kevin Coffman .10 .04
30T Pat Combs XRC OLY .10 .04
31T Henry Cotto .10 .04
32T Chili Davis .30 .12
33T Mike Davis .10 .04
34T Jose DeLeon .10 .04
35T Richard Dotson .10 .04
36T Cecil Espy .10 .04
37T Tom Filer .10 .04
38T Mike Fiore OLY .10 .04
39T Ron Gant XRC .75 .30
40T Kirk Gibson .50 .20
41T Rich Gossage .20 .08
42T Mark Grace XRC 1.50 .60
43T Alfredo Griffin .10 .04
44T Ty Griffin OLY .10 .04
45T Bryan Harvey XRC .20 .08
46T Ron Hassey .10 .04
47T Ray Hayward .10 .04
48T Dave Henderson .10 .04
49T Tom Herr .10 .04
50T Bob Horner .10 .04
51T Ricky Horton .10 .04
52T Jay Howell .10 .04
53T Glenn Hubbard .10 .04
54T Jeff Innis .10 .04
55T Danny Jackson .10 .04
56T Darrin Jackson XRC* .20 .08
57T Roberto Kelly XRC* .50 .20
58T Ron Kittle .10 .04
59T Ray Knight .10 .04
60T Vance Law .10 .04
61T Jeffrey Leonard .10 .04
62T Mike Macfarlane XRC .10 .04
63T Scotti Madison .10 .04
64T Kirt Manwaring .10 .04
65T M.Marquess OLY CO .10 .04
66T T.Martinez OLY XRC 1.50 .60
67T Billy Masse OLY XRC .10 .04
68T Jack McDowell XRC .50 .20
69T Jack McKeon MG .10 .04
70T Larry McWilliams .10 .04
71T M.Morandini OLY XRC .50 .20
72T Keith Moreland .10 .04
73T Mike Morgan .10 .04
74T C.Nagy OLY XRC .50 .20
75T Al Nipper .10 .04
76T Russ Nixon MG .10 .04
77T Jesse Orosco .10 .04
78T Joe Orsulak .10 .04
79T Dave Palmer .10 .04
80T Mark Parent .10 .04
81T Dave Parker .20 .08
82T Dan Pasqua .10 .04
83T Melido Perez XRC* .10 .04
84T Steve Peters .10 .04
85T Dan Petry .10 .04
86T Gary Pettis .10 .04
87T Jeff Pico .10 .04
88T Jim Poole XRC OLY .20 .08
89T Ted Power .10 .04
90T Rafael Ramirez .10 .04
91T Dennis Rasmussen .10 .04
92T Jose Rijo .10 .04
93T Ernie Riles .10 .04
94T Luis Rivera .10 .04
95T D.Robbins XRC OLY .10 .04
96T Frank Robinson MG .30 .12
97T Cookie Rojas MG .10 .04
98T Chris Sabo XRC .20 .08
99T Mark Salas .10 .04
100T Luis Salazar .10 .04
101T Rafael Santana .10 .04
102T Nelson Santovenia .10 .04
103T Mackey Sasser XRC .10 .04
104T Calvin Schiraldi .10 .04
105T Mike Schooler .10 .04
106T S.Servais XRC OLY .10 .04
107T D.Silvestri XRC OLY .10 .04
108T Don Slaught .10 .04
109T J.Slusarski XRC OLY .10 .04
110T Lee Smith .20 .08
111T Pete Smith XRC* .10 .04
112T Jim Snyder MG .10 .04
113T E.Sprague OLY XRC .50 .20
114T Pete Stanicek .10 .04
115T Kurt Stillwell .10 .04
116T T.Stottlemyre XRC .50 .20
117T Bill Swift .10 .04
118T Pat Tabler .10 .04
119T Scott Terry .10 .04
120T Mickey Tettleton .10 .04
121T Dickie Thon .10 .04
122T Jeff Treadway XRC* .10 .04
123T Willie Upshaw .10 .04
124T R.Ventura OLY XRC 1.50 .60
125T Ron Washington .10 .04
126T Walt Weiss XRC* .50 .20
127T Bob Welch .10 .04
128T David Wells XRC 1.50 .60
129T Glenn Wilson .10 .04
130T Ted Wood XRC OLY .10 .04
131T Don Zimmer MG .20 .08
132T Checklist 1T-132T .10 .04

1988 Topps Traded Tiffany

As a bonus for those dealers who ordered the regular Tiffany sets, they received an equivalent number of Tiffany update sets. These 132 standard-size cards parallel the regular traded issue. Again issued in the Topps Irish facility, these cards feature glossy fronts and easy to read backs. These sets were only issued in complete factory form.

Nm-Mt Ex-Mt
COMP.FACT.SET (132) 60.00 24.00
*STARS: 1.5X TO 4X BASIC CARDS ...
*ROOKIES: 4X TO 10X BASIC CARDS

1988 Topps Big

This set of 264 cards was issued as three separately distributed series of 88 cards each. Cards were distributed in wax packs with seven cards for a suggested retail of 40 cents. These cards are very reminiscent in style of the 1956 Topps card set. The cards measure approximately 2 5/8" by 3 3/4" and are oriented horizontally.

Nm-Mt Ex-Mt
COMPLETE SET (264) 20.00 8.00
1 Paul Molitor 1.00 .40
2 Milt Thompson .05 .02
3 Billy Hatcher .05 .02
4 Mike Witt .05 .02
5 Vince Coleman .05 .02
6 Dwight Evans .10 .04
7 Tim Wallach .05 .02
8 Alan Trammell .15 .06
9 Will Clark 1.00 .40
10 Jeff Reardon .10 .04
11 Dwight Gooden .10 .04
12 Benito Santiago .10 .04
13 Jose Canseco 1.25 .50
14 Dale Murphy .50 .20
15 George Bell .05 .02
16 Ryne Sandberg 1.50 .60
17 Brook Jacoby .05 .02
18 Fernando Valenzuela .10 .04
19 Scott Fletcher .05 .02
20 Eric Davis .10 .04
21 Willie Wilson .05 .02
22 B.J. Surhoff .10 .04
23 Steve Bedrosian .05 .02
24 Dave Winfield .75 .30
25 Bobby Bonilla .10 .04
26 Larry Sheets .05 .02
27 Ozzie Guillen .10 .04
28 Checklist 1-88 .05 .02
29 Nolan Ryan 5.00 2.00
30 Bob Boone .10 .04
31 Tom Herr .05 .02
32 Wade Boggs 1.00 .40
33 Neal Heaton .05 .02
34 Doyle Alexander .05 .02
35 Candy Maldonado .05 .02
36 Kirby Puckett 2.00 .80
37 Gary Carter 1.00 .40
38 Lance McCullers .05 .02
39A Terry Steinbach .15 .06
(Topps logo in black)
39B Terry Steinbach .15 .06
(Topps logo in white)
40 Gerald Perry .05 .02
41 Tom Henke .05 .02
42 Leon Durham .05 .02
43 Cory Snyder .05 .02
44 Dale Sveum .05 .02
45 Lance Parrish .05 .02
46 Steve Sax .05 .02
47 Charlie Hough .10 .04
48 Kal Daniels .05 .02
49 Bo Jackson .25 .10
50 Ron Guidry .10 .04
51 Bill Doran .05 .02
52 Wally Joyner .15 .06
53 Terry Pendleton .10 .04
54 Marty Barrett .05 .02
55 Andres Galarraga .50 .20
56 Larry Herndon .05 .02
57 Kevin Mitchell .10 .04
58 Greg Gagne .05 .02
59 Keith Hernandez .10 .04
60 John Kruk .10 .04
61 Mike LaValliere .05 .02
62 Cal Ripken 5.00 2.00
63 Ivan Calderon .05 .02
64 Alvin Davis .05 .02
65 Luis Polonia .05 .02
66 Robin Yount .50 .20
67 Juan Samuel .05 .02
68 Andres Thomas .05 .02
69 Jeff Musselman .05 .02
70 Jerry Mumphrey .05 .02
71 Joe Carter .25 .10
72 Mike Scioscia .10 .04
73 Pete Incaviglia .05 .02
74 Barry Larkin 1.00 .40
75 Frank White .10 .04
76 Willie Randolph .10 .04
77 Kevin Bass .05 .02
78 Brian Downing .05 .02
79 Willie McGee .10 .04
80 Ellis Burks .75 .30
81 Hubie Brooks .05 .02
82 Darrell Evans .10 .04
83 Robby Thompson .05 .02
84 Kent Hrbek .10 .04
85 Ron Darling .05 .02
86 Stan Jefferson .05 .02
87 Teddy Higuera .05 .02
88 Mike Schmidt .75 .30
89 Barry Bonds 2.50 1.00
90 Jim Presley .05 .02
91 Orel Hershiser .10 .04
92 Jesse Barfield .05 .02
93 Tom Candiotti .05 .02
94 Bret Saberhagen .10 .04
95 Jose Uribe .05 .02
96 Tom Browning .05 .02
97 Johnny Ray .05 .02
98 Mike Morgan .05 .02
99 Lou Whitaker .10 .04
100 Jim Sundberg .05 .02
101 Roger McDowell .05 .02
102 Randy Ready .05 .02
103 Mike Gallego .05 .02
104 Steve Buechele .05 .02
105 Greg Walker .05 .02
106 Jose Lind .05 .02
107 Steve Trout .05 .02
108 Rick Rhoden .05 .02
109 Jim Pankovits .05 .02
110 Ken Griffey .10 .04
111 Danny Cox .05 .02
112 Franklin Stubbs .05 .02
113 Lloyd Moseby .05 .02
114 Mel Hall .05 .02
115 Kevin Seitzer .10 .04
116 Tim Raines .10 .04
117 Juan Castillo .05 .02
118 Roger Clemens 2.50 1.00
119 Mike Aldrete .05 .02
120 Mario Soto .05 .02
121 Jack Howell .05 .02
122 Rick Schu .05 .02
123 Jeff D. Robinson .05 .02
124 Doug Drabek .10 .04
125 Henry Cotto .05 .02
126 Checklist 89-176 .05 .02
127 Gary Gaetti .10 .04
128 Rick Sutcliffe .10 .04
129 Howard Johnson .05 .02
130 Chris Brown .05 .02
131 Dave Henderson .05 .02
132 Curt Wilkerson .05 .02
133 Mike Marshall .05 .02
134 Kelly Gruber .05 .02
135 Julio Franco .10 .04
136 Kurt Stillwell .05 .02
137 Donnie Hill .05 .02
138 Mike Pagliarulo .05 .02
139 Von Hayes .05 .02
140 Mike Scott .05 .02
141 Bob Kipper .05 .02
142 Harold Reynolds .10 .04
143 Bob Brenly .10 .04
144 Dave Concepcion .10 .04
145 Devon White .10 .04
146 Jeff Stone .05 .02
147 Chet Lemon .05 .02
148 Ozzie Virgil .05 .02
149 Todd Worrell .10 .04
150 Mitch Webster .05 .02
151 Rob Deer .05 .02
152 Rich Gedman .05 .02
153 Andre Dawson .50 .20
154 Mike Davis .05 .02
155 Nelson Liriano .05 .02
156 Greg Swindell .05 .02
157 George Brett 1.50 .60
158 Kevin McReynolds .05 .02
159 Brian Fisher .05 .02
160 Mike Kingery .05 .02
161 Tony Gwynn 2.50 1.00
162 Don Baylor .10 .04
163 Jerry Browne .05 .02
164 Dan Pasqua .05 .02
165 Rickey Henderson 1.50 .60
166 Brett Butler .10 .04
167 Nick Esasky .05 .02
168 Kirk McCaskill .05 .02
169 Fred Lynn .05 .02
170 Jack Morris .10 .04
171 Pedro Guerrero .05 .02
172 Dave Stieb .05 .02
173 Pat Tabler .05 .02
174 Floyd Bannister .05 .02
175 Rafael Belliard .05 .02
176 Mark Langston .05 .02
177 Greg Mathews .05 .02
178 Claudell Washington .05 .02
179 Mark McGwire 4.00 1.60
180 Bert Blyleven .10 .04
181 Jim Rice .10 .04
182 Mookie Wilson .10 .04
183 Willie Fraser .05 .02
184 Andy Van Slyke .10 .04
185 Matt Nokes .05 .02
186 Eddie Whitson .05 .02
187 Tony Fernandez .10 .04
188 Rick Reuschel .10 .04
189 Ken Phelps .05 .02
190 Juan Nieves .05 .02
191 Kirk Gibson .25 .10
192 Glenn Davis .05 .02
193 Zane Smith .05 .02
194 Jose DeLeon .05 .02
195 Gary Ward .05 .02
196 Pascual Perez .05 .02
197 Carlton Fisk .75 .30
198 Oddibe McDowell .05 .02
199 Mark Gubicza .05 .02
200 Glenn Hubbard .05 .02
201 Frank Viola .05 .02
202 Jody Reed .10 .04
203 Len Dykstra .10 .04
204 Dick Schofield .05 .02
205 Sid Bream .05 .02
206 Willie Hernandez .05 .02
207 Keith Moreland .05 .02
208 Mark Eichhorn .05 .02
209 Rene Gonzales .05 .02
210 Dave Valle .05 .02
211 Tom Brunansky .05 .02
212 Charles Hudson .05 .02
213 John Farrell .05 .02
214 Jeff Treadway .05 .02
215 Eddie Murray 1.00 .40
216 Checklist 177-264 .05 .02
217 Greg Brock .05 .02
218 John Shelby .05 .02
219 Craig Reynolds .05 .02
220 Dion James .05 .02
221 Carney Lansford .10 .04
222 Juan Berenguer .05 .02
223 Luis Rivera .05 .02
224 Harold Baines .15 .06
225 Shawon Dunston .05 .02
226 Luis Aguayo .05 .02
227 Pete O'Brien .05 .02
228 Ozzie Smith 1.50 .60
229 Don Mattingly 2.50 1.00
230 Danny Tartabull .05 .02
231 Andy Allanson .05 .02
232 John Franco .10 .04
233 Mike Greenwell .05 .02
234 Bob Ojeda .05 .02
235 Chili Davis .15 .06
236 Mike Dunne .05 .02
237 Jim Morrison .05 .02
238 Carmelo Martinez .05 .02
239 Ernie Whitt .05 .02
240 Scott Garrelts .05 .02
241 Mike Moore .05 .02
242 Dave Parker .10 .04
243 Tim Laudner .05 .02
244 Bill Wegman .05 .02
245 Bob Horner .05 .02
246 Rafael Santana .05 .02
247 Alfredo Griffin .05 .02
248 Mark Bailey .05 .02
249 Ron Gant .50 .20
250 Bryn Smith .05 .02
251 Lance Johnson .10 .04
252 Sam Horn .05 .02
253 Darryl Strawberry .10 .04
254 Chuck Finley .15 .06
255 Darnell Coles .05 .02
256 Mike Henneman .10 .04
257 Andy Hawkins .05 .02
258 Jim Clancy .05 .02
259 Atlee Hammaker .05 .02
260 Glenn Wilson .05 .02
261 Larry McWilliams .05 .02
262 Jack Clark .10 .04
263 Walt Weiss .10 .04
264 Gene Larkin .10 .04

1988 Topps Cloth

This 120-card set was actually an "Experimental Issue" produced by Topps and was discarded even though it appeared in the collectors market in a limited way. The set features a color player head photo printed on a thin gauze fabric which supposedly expanded into a sponge when submerged in water. The backs are blank. The cards are unnumbered and checklisted below in alphabetical order.

Nm-Mt Ex-Mt
COMPLETE SET (120) 2000.00 800.00
1 Rick Aguilera 15.00 6.00
2 Andy Allanson 10.00 4.00
3 Tony Armas 10.00 4.00
4 Keith Atherton 10.00 4.00
5 Steve Balboni 10.00 4.00
6 Billy Bean 20.00 8.00
7 Steve Bedrosian AS 10.00 4.00
8 George Bell AS 10.00 4.00
9 Bruce Benedict 10.00 4.00
10 Dave Bergman 10.00 4.00
11 Mike Bielicki 10.00 4.00
12 Bruce Bochy 10.00 4.00
13 Wade Boggs AS 50.00 20.00
14 Greg Booker 10.00 4.00
15 Dennis Boyd 10.00 4.00
16 Dale Murphy TL 25.00 10.00
17 Tim Birtsas 10.00 4.00
18 Tom Browning 10.00 4.00
19 Juan Castillo 10.00 4.00
20 Rick Cerone 10.00 4.00
21 Jack Clark AS 15.00 6.00
22 Mark Clear 10.00 4.00

23 Roger Clemens AS 80.00 32.00
24 Roger Clemens 150.00 60.00
25 Keith Comstock 10.00 4.00
26 Cecil Cooper 15.00 6.00
27 Joey Cora 20.00 8.00
28 Ed Correa 10.00 4.00
29 Mark Davidson 10.00 4.00
30 Davis 10.00 4.00
31 Jeff Dedmon 10.00 4.00
32 Jim Dwyer 10.00 4.00
33 Marshall Edwards 10.00 4.00
34 John Farrell 10.00 4.00
35 Mike Felder 10.00 4.00
36 Curt Ford 10.00 4.00
37 Bob Forsch 10.00 4.00
38 Garcia 10.00 4.00
39 Tom Glavine 100.00 40.00
40 Mark Grant 10.00 4.00
41 Hall 10.00 4.00
42 Jeff Hamilton 10.00 4.00
43 Mike Hart 10.00 4.00
44 Andy Hawkins 10.00 4.00
45 Ed Hearn 10.00 4.00
46 Tom Henke AS 10.00 4.00
47 Whitey Herzog MG 10.00 4.00
48 Shawn Hillegas 10.00 4.00
49 Kent Hrbek 10.00 4.00
Gary Gaetti
50 Charles Hudson 10.00 4.00
51 Dave Johnson 10.00 4.00
52 Ron Karkovice 10.00 4.00
53 Pat Keedy 10.00 4.00
54 Jimmy Key AS 15.00 6.00
55 Steve Kiefer 10.00 4.00
56 Bob Kipper 10.00 4.00
57 Les Lancaster 10.00 4.00
58 Ken Landreaux 10.00 4.00
59 Craig Lefferts 10.00 4.00
60 Jim Leyland MG 10.00 4.00
61 Jose Lind 10.00 4.00
62 Gary Lucas 10.00 4.00
63 Frank Lucchesi MG 10.00 4.00
64 Barry Lyons 10.00 4.00
65 John Marzano 10.00 4.00
66 Gary Matthews 10.00 4.00
67 Don Mattingly AS 150.00 60.00
68 Len Matuszek 10.00 4.00
69 Kurt McCaskill 10.00 4.00
70 Fred McGriff 40.00 16.00
71 Mark McGwire 150.00 60.00
Jose Canseco
72 Joey Meyer 10.00 4.00
73 John Mitchell 10.00 4.00
74 Jeff Montgomery 10.00 4.00
75 Morris 10.00 4.00
76 John Moses 10.00 4.00
77 Tom Nieto 10.00 4.00
78 Matt Nokes 10.00 4.00
79 Charlie O'Brien 10.00 4.00
80 Paul O'Neill 15.00 6.00
81 Ed Olwine 10.00 4.00
82 Steve Ontiveros 10.00 4.00
83 Pat Pacillo 10.00 4.00
84 Tom Pagnozzi 10.00 4.00
85 Jim Pankovitz 10.00 4.00
86 Bill Pecota 10.00 4.00
87 Geno Petralli 10.00 4.00
88 Eric Plunk 10.00 4.00
89 Gus Polidor 10.00 4.00
90 Powell 10.00 4.00
91 Terry Puhl 10.00 4.00
92 Charlie Puleo 10.00 4.00
93 Shane Rawley AS 10.00 4.00
94 Rodriguez 10.00 4.00
95 Gary Roenicke 10.00 4.00
96 Pete Rose MG 100.00 40.00
97 Lenn Sakata 10.00 4.00
98 Joe Sambito 10.00 4.00
99 Juan Samuel AS 10.00 4.00
100 Rafael Santana 10.00 4.00
101 Dan Schatzeder 10.00 4.00
102 Pat Sheridan 10.00 4.00
103 Tommy Shields 10.00 4.00
104 Nelson Simmons 10.00 4.00
105 Doug Sisk 10.00 4.00
106 Joel Skinner 10.00 4.00
107 Ozzie Smith AS 120.00 47.50
108 Chris Speier 10.00 4.00
109 Jim Sundberg 10.00 4.00
110 Don Sutton 50.00 20.00
111 Chuck Tanner MG 10.00 4.00
112 Mickey Tettleton 15.00 6.00
113 Tim Teufel 10.00 4.00
114 Gary Thurman 10.00 4.00
115 Alex Trevino 10.00 4.00
116 Mike Trujillo 10.00 4.00
117 Tim Wallach AS 10.00 4.00
118 Williams 10.00 4.00
119 Dave Winfield AS 40.00 16.00
120 Butch Wynegar 10.00 4.00

1988 Topps Gallery of Champions

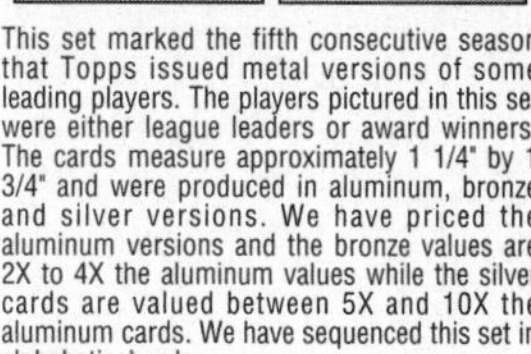

This set marked the fifth consecutive season that Topps issued metal versions of some leading players. The players pictured in this set were either league leaders or award winners. The cards measure approximately 1 1/4" by 1 3/4" and were produced in aluminum, bronze and silver versions. We have priced the aluminum versions and the bronze values are 2X to 4X the aluminum values while the silver cards are valued between 5X and 10X the aluminum cards. We have sequenced this set in alphabetical order.

Nm-Mt Ex-Mt
COMPLETE SET (12) 150.00 60.00
1 Steve Bedrosian 5.00 2.00
2 George Bell 5.00 2.00
3 Wade Boggs 15.00 6.00
4 Jack Clark 5.00 2.00
5 Roger Clemens 30.00 12.00
6 Andre Dawson 10.00 4.00
7 Tony Gwynn 25.00 10.00
8 Mark Langston 5.00 2.00
9 Mark McGwire 40.00 16.00
10 Dave Righetti 5.00 2.00
11 Nolan Ryan 50.00 20.00
12 Benito Santiago 8.00 3.20

1988 Topps Mattingly World

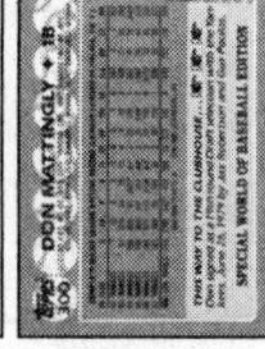

This one-card Special World of Baseball Edition set features a color portrait of Don Mattingly with white borders. The back displays player information and career statistics.

Nm-Mt Ex-Mt
1 Don Mattingly 50.00 20.00

1988 Topps Mini Leaders

The 1988 Topps Mini set of Major League Leaders features 77 cards of leaders of the various statistical categories for the 1987 season. The cards are numbered on the back and measure approximately 2 1/8" by 3". The set numbering is alphabetical by player within team and the teams themselves are in alphabetical order as well. The card backs are printed in blue, red, and yellow on white card stock. The cards were distributed as a separate issue in wax packs.

Nm-Mt Ex-Mt
COMPLETE SET (77) 5.00 2.00
1 Wade Boggs .40 .16
2 Roger Clemens 1.00 .40
3 Dwight Evans .10 .04
4 DeWayne Buice .05 .02
5 Brian Downing .05 .02
6 Wally Joyner .10 .04
7 Ivan Calderon .05 .02
8 Carlton Fisk .40 .16
9 Gary Redus .05 .02
10 Darrell Evans .10 .04
11 Jack Morris .10 .04
12 Alan Trammell .15 .06
13 Lou Whitaker .10 .04
14 Bret Saberhagen .10 .04
15 Kevin Seitzer .05 .02
16 Danny Tartabull .05 .02
17 Willie Wilson .05 .02
18 Teddy Higuera .05 .02
19 Paul Molitor .50 .20
20 Dan Plesac .05 .02
21 Robin Yount .40 .16
22 Kent Hrbek .10 .04
23 Kirby Puckett .50 .20
24 Jeff Reardon .10 .04
25 Frank Viola .05 .02
26 Rickey Henderson .75 .30
27 Don Mattingly 1.00 .40
28 Willie Randolph .10 .04
29 Dave Righetti .05 .02
30 Jose Canseco .50 .20
31 Mark McGwire 1.50 .60
32 Dave Stewart .10 .04
33 Phil Bradley .05 .02
34 Mark Langston .05 .02
35 Harold Reynolds .10 .04
36 Charlie Hough .10 .04
37 George Bell .05 .02
38 Tom Henke .05 .02
39 Jimmy Key .05 .02
40 Dion James .05 .02
41 Dale Murphy .20 .08
42 Zane Smith .05 .02
43 Andre Dawson .20 .08
44 Lee Smith .10 .04
45 Rick Sutcliffe .10 .04
46 Eric Davis .10 .04
47 John Franco .10 .04
48 Dave Parker .10 .04
49 Billy Hatcher .05 .02
50 Nolan Ryan 2.00 .80
51 Mike Scott .05 .02
52 Pedro Guerrero .05 .02
53 Orel Hershiser .10 .04
54 Fernando Valenzuela .10 .04
55 Bob Welch .05 .02
56 Andres Galarraga .20 .08
57 Tim Raines .10 .04
58 Tim Wallach .05 .02
59 Len Dykstra .10 .04
60 Dwight Gooden .10 .04
61 Howard Johnson .05 .02
62 Roger McDowell .05 .02
63 Darryl Strawberry .10 .04
64 Steve Bedrosian .05 .02
65 Shane Rawley .05 .02
66 Juan Samuel .05 .02
67 Mike Schmidt .50 .20
68 Mike Dunne .05 .02
69 Jack Clark .10 .04
70 Vince Coleman .05 .02
71 Willie McGee .10 .04
72 Ozzie Smith .75 .30
73 Todd Worrell .10 .04
74 Tony Gwynn 1.00 .40
75 John Kruk .10 .04
76 Rick Reuschel .05 .02
77 Checklist Card .05 .02

1988 Topps/O-Pee-Chee Sticker Backs

These 67 cards were actually the backs of the 1988 O-Pee-Chee Stickers. In previous years O-Pee-Chee had used a disposable peel-off sticker back. The 1988 Super Star sticker back was actually collectible and attractive. In fact, many collectors felt that the sticker backs were more desirable than the stickers. The white-bordered cards measure approximately 2 1/8" by 3" and have either a red (AL, 1-33) or blue (NL, 34-66) background behind the player's photo. The player's 1987 and career statistics were shown at the bottom of each card. The cards are numbered in the statistics box in small print. Three different front (sticker) combinations exist for each of the 66 players and checklist. The cards were retailed in cellophane wax packs at 25 cents for a stick of gum and five sticker cards.

Nm-Mt Ex-Mt
COMPLETE SET (67) 6.00 2.40
1 Jack Clark .10 .04
2 Andres Galarraga .25 .10
3 Keith Hernandez .10 .04
4 Tom Herr .05 .02
5 Juan Samuel .05 .02
6 Ryne Sandberg .50 .20
7 Terry Pendleton .10 .04
8 Mike Schmidt .50 .20
9 Tim Wallach .05 .02
10 Hubie Brooks .05 .02
11 Shawon Dunston .05 .02
12 Ozzie Smith .40 .16
13 Andre Dawson .25 .10
14 Eric Davis .10 .04
15 Pedro Guerrero .05 .02
16 Tony Gwynn .75 .30
17 Jeffrey Leonard .05 .02
18 Dale Murphy .25 .10
19 Dave Parker .10 .04
20 Tim Raines .10 .04
21 Darryl Strawberry .05 .02
22 Gary Carter .15 .06
23 Jody Davis .05 .02
24 Ozzie Virgil .05 .02
25 Dwight Gooden .10 .04
26 Mike Scott .05 .02
27 Rick Sutcliffe .05 .02
28 Sid Fernandez .05 .02
29 Neal Heaton .05 .02
30 Fernando Valenzuela .10 .04
31 Steve Bedrosian .05 .02
32 John Franco .10 .04
33 Lee Smith .10 .04
34 Wally Joyner .15 .06
35 Don Mattingly .75 .30
36 Mark McGwire 1.25 .50
37 Willie Randolph .10 .04
38 Lou Whitaker .10 .04
39 Frank White .10 .04
40 Wade Boggs .30 .12
41 George Brett .75 .30
42 Paul Molitor .25 .10
43 Tony Fernandez .05 .02
44 Cal Ripken 1.50 .60
45 Alan Trammell .15 .06
46 Jesse Barfield .05 .02
47 George Bell .05 .02
48 Jose Canseco .40 .16
49 Joe Carter .25 .10
50 Dwight Evans .10 .04
51 Rickey Henderson .40 .16
52 Kirby Puckett .40 .16
53 Cory Snyder .05 .02
54 Dave Winfield .25 .10
55 Terry Kennedy .05 .02
56 Matt Nokes .05 .02
57 B.J. Surhoff .10 .04
58 Roger Clemens .75 .30
59 Jack Morris .10 .04
60 Bret Saberhagen .10 .04
61 Ron Guidry .05 .02
62 Bruce Hurst .05 .02
63 Mark Langston .05 .02
64 Tom Henke .05 .02
65 Dan Plesac .05 .02
66 Dave Righetti .05 .02
67 Checklist .05 .02

1988 Topps Revco League Leaders

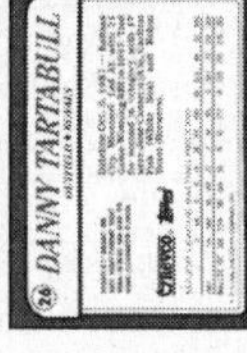

Topps produced this 33-card boxed standard-size set for Revco stores subtitled "League Leaders". The cards feature a high-gloss, full-color photo of the player inside a white border. The card backs are printed in red and black on white card stock. The statistics provided on the card backs cover only two lines, last season and Major League totals.

Nm-Mt Ex-Mt
COMP. FACT SET (33) 5.00 2.00
1 Tony Gwynn 1.00 .40
2 Andre Dawson .20 .08
3 Vince Coleman .05 .02
4 Jack Clark .10 .04
5 Tim Raines .10 .04
6 Tim Wallach .05 .02
7 Juan Samuel .05 .02
8 Nolan Ryan 2.00 .80
9 Rick Sutcliffe .05 .02
10 Kent Tekulve .05 .02
11 Steve Bedrosian .05 .02
12 Orel Hershiser .10 .04
13 Rick Reuschel .05 .02
14 Fernando Valenzuela .10 .04
15 Bob Welch .05 .02
16 Wade Boggs .40 .16
17 Mark McGwire 1.50 .60
18 George Bell .05 .02
19 Harold Reynolds .10 .04
20 Paul Molitor .40 .16
21 Kirby Puckett .40 .16
22 Kevin Seitzer .10 .04
23 Brian Downing .05 .02
24 Dwight Evans .10 .04
25 Willie Wilson .05 .02
26 Danny Tartabull .05 .02
27 Jimmy Key .10 .04
28 Roger Clemens 1.00 .40
29 Dave Stewart .10 .04
30 Mark Eichhorn .05 .02
31 Tom Henke .05 .02
32 Charlie Hough .10 .04
33 Mark Langston .05 .02

1988 Topps Rite-Aid Team MVP's

Topps produced this 33-card boxed standard-size set for Rite Aid Drug and Discount Stores subtitled "Team MVP's". The Rite Aid logo is at the top of every obverse. The cards feature a high-gloss, full-color photo of the player inside a red, white, and blue border. The card backs are printed in blue and black on white card stock. The checklist for the set is found on the back panel of the small collector box. The statistics provided on the card backs cover only two lines, last season and Major League totals.

Nm-Mt Ex-Mt
COMP. FACT SET (33) 4.00 1.60
1 Dale Murphy .20 .08
2 Andre Dawson .20 .08
3 Eric Davis .10 .04
4 Mike Scott .05 .02
5 Pedro Guerrero .05 .02
6 Tim Raines .10 .04
7 Darryl Strawberry .10 .04
8 Mike Schmidt .50 .20
9 Mike Dunne .05 .02
10 Jack Clark .10 .04
11 Tony Gwynn 1.00 .40
12 Will Clark .20 .08
13 Cal Ripken 2.00 .80
14 Wade Boggs .50 .20
15 Wally Joyner .10 .04
16 Harold Baines .10 .04
17 Joe Carter .10 .04
18 Alan Trammell .15 .06
19 Kevin Seitzer .10 .04
20 Paul Molitor .50 .20
21 Kirby Puckett .40 .16
22 Don Mattingly 1.00 .40
23 Mark McGwire 1.50 .60
24 Alvin Davis .05 .02
25 Ruben Sierra .10 .04
26 George Bell .05 .02
27 Jack Morris .10 .04
28 Jeff Reardon .10 .04
29 John Tudor .05 .02
30 Rick Reuschel .05 .02
31 Gary Gaetti .10 .04
32 Jeffrey Leonard .05 .02
33 Frank Viola .05 .02

1988 Topps UK Minis

The 1988 Topps UK (United Kingdom) Mini set of "American Baseball" features 88 cards. The cards measure approximately 2 1/8" by 3". The card backs are printed in blue, red, and yellow on white card stock. The cards were distributed as a separate issue in packs. A custom black and yellow small set box was also available for holding a complete set; the box has a complete checklist on the back panel. The set player numbering is according to alphabetical order.

Nm-Mt Ex-Mt
COMPLETE SET (88) 5.00 2.00
*TIFFANY: 4X BASIC CARDS
1 Harold Baines .10 .04
2 Steve Bedrosian .05 .02
3 George Bell .05 .02
4 Wade Boggs .40 .16
5 Barry Bonds 1.00 .40
6 Bob Boone .10 .04
7 George Brett .75 .30
8 Hubie Brooks .05 .02
9 Ivan Calderon .05 .02
10 Jose Canseco .50 .20
11 Gary Carter .40 .16
12 Joe Carter .10 .04
13 Jack Clark .10 .04
14 Will Clark .40 .16
15 Roger Clemens 1.00 .40
16 Vince Coleman .05 .02
17 Alvin Davis .05 .02
18 Eric Davis .10 .04
19 Glenn Davis .05 .02
20 Andre Dawson .15 .06
21 Mike Dunne .05 .02
22 Dwight Evans .10 .04
23 Tony Fernandez .10 .04
24 John Franco .10 .04
25 Gary Gaetti .10 .04
26 Kirk Gibson .10 .04
27 Dwight Gooden .10 .04
28 Pedro Guerrero .05 .02
29 Tony Gwynn 1.00 .40
30 Billy Hatcher .05 .02
31 Rickey Henderson .75 .30
32 Tom Henke .05 .02
33 Keith Hernandez .10 .04
34 Orel Hershiser .10 .04
35 Teddy Higuera .05 .02
36 Charlie Hough .10 .04
37 Kent Hrbek .10 .04
38 Brook Jacoby .05 .02
39 Dion James .05 .02
40 Wally Joyner .10 .04
41 John Kruk .10 .04
42 Mark Langston .05 .02
43 Jeffrey Leonard .05 .02
44 Candy Maldonado .05 .02
45 Don Mattingly 1.00 .40
46 Willie McGee .10 .04
47 Mark McGwire 1.50 .60
48 Kevin Mitchell .10 .04
49 Paul Molitor .40 .16
50 Jack Morris .10 .04
51 Lloyd Moseby .05 .02
52 Dale Murphy .20 .08
53 Eddie Murray .50 .20
54 Matt Nokes .05 .02
55 Dave Parker .10 .04
56 Larry Parrish .05 .02
57 Kirby Puckett .40 .16
58 Tim Raines .10 .04
59 Willie Randolph .10 .04
60 Harold Reynolds .10 .04
61 Cal Ripken 2.00 .80
62 Nolan Ryan 2.00 .80
63 Bret Saberhagen .10 .04
64 Juan Samuel .05 .02
65 Ryne Sandberg .75 .30
66 Benito Santiago .10 .04
67 Mike Schmidt .50 .20
68 Mike Scott .05 .02
69 Kevin Seitzer .05 .02
70 Larry Sheets .05 .02
71 Ruben Sierra .10 .04
72 Ozzie Smith .75 .30
73 Zane Smith .05 .02
74 Cory Snyder .05 .02
75 Dave Stewart .10 .04
76 Darryl Strawberry .10 .04
77 Rick Sutcliffe .05 .02
78 Danny Tartabull .05 .02
79 Alan Trammell .15 .06
80 Fernando Valenzuela .10 .04
81 Andy Van Slyke .10 .04
82 Frank Viola .05 .02
83 Greg Walker .05 .02
84 Tim Wallach .05 .02
85 Dave Winfield .40 .16
86 Mike Witt .05 .02
87 Robin Yount .40 .16
88 Checklist Card .05 .02

1989 Topps

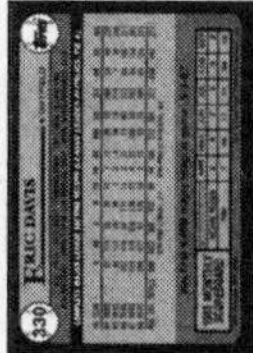

This set consists of 792 standard-size cards. Cards were primarily issued in 15-card wax packs, 42-card rack packs and factory sets. Subsets in the set include Record Breakers (1-7), Turn Back the Clock (661-665), All-Star selections (386-407) and First Draft Picks, Future Stars and Team Leaders (all scattered throughout the set). The manager cards contain a team checklist on back. The key Rookie Cards in this set are Jim Abbott, Sandy Alomar Jr., Brady Anderson, Steve Avery, Andy Benes, Dante Bichette, Craig Biggio, Randy Johnson, Ramon Martinez, Gary Sheffield, John Smoltz, and Robin Ventura.

Nm-Mt Ex-Mt
COMPLETE SET (792) 20.00 8.00
COMP.FACT SET (792) 20.00 8.00
COMP.X-MAS.SET (792) 25.00 10.00
1 George Bell RB .05 .02
Slams 3 HR on
Opening Day
2 Wade Boggs RB .10 .04
3 Gary Carter RB .10 .04

Sets Record for
Career Putouts
4 Andre Dawson RB .05 .02
Logs Double Figures
in HR and SB
5 Orel Hershiser RB .10 .04
Pitches 59
Scoreless Innings
6 Doug Jones RB UER .05 .02
Earns His 15th
Straight Save

Photo actually Chris Codiroli
7 Kevin McReynolds RB .05 .02
Steals 21 Without
Being Caught
8 Dave Eiland .05 .02
9 Tim Teufel .05 .02
10 Andre Dawson .10 .04
11 Bruce Sutter .05 .02
12 Dale Sveum .05 .02
13 Doug Sisk .05 .02
14 Tom Kelly MG .05 .02
15 Robby Thompson .05 .02
16 Ron Robinson .05 .02
17 Brian Downing .05 .02
18 Rick Rhoden .05 .02
19 Greg Gagne .05 .02
20 Steve Bedrosian .05 .02
21 Greg Walker TL .05 .02
22 Tim Crews .05 .02
23 Mike Fitzgerald .05 .02
24 Larry Andersen .05 .02
25 Frank White .10 .04
26 Dale Mohorcic .05 .02
27A Orestes Destrade .10 .04
(F* next to copyright) RC*
27B Orestes Destrade .10 .04
(E*F* next to
copyright) RC*
28 Mike Moore .05 .02
29 Kelly Gruber .05 .02
30 Dwight Gooden .15 .06
31 Terry Francona .10 .04
32 Dennis Rasmussen .05 .02
33 B.J. Surhoff .10 .04
34 Ken Williams .05 .02
35 John Tudor UER .05 .02
(With Red Sox in '84,should be Pirates)
36 Mitch Webster .05 .02
37 Bob Stanley .05 .02
38 Paul Runge .05 .02
39 Mike Maddux .05 .02
40 Steve Sax .05 .02
41 Terry Mulholland .05 .02
42 Jim Eppard .05 .02
43 Guillermo Hernandez .05 .02
44 Jim Snyder MG .05 .02
45 Kal Daniels .05 .02
46 Mark Portugal .05 .02
47 Carney Lansford .10 .04
48 Tim Burke .05 .02
49 Craig Biggio RC .75 .30
50 George Bell .05 .02
51 Mark McLemore TL .05 .02
52 Bob Brenly .05 .02
53 Ruben Sierra .05 .02
54 Steve Trout .05 .02
55 Julio Franco .05 .02
56 Pat Tabler .05 .02
57 Alejandro Pena .05 .02
58 Lee Mazzilli .05 .02
59 Mark Davis .05 .02
60 Tom Brunansky .05 .02
61 Neil Allen .05 .02
62 Alfredo Griffin .05 .02
63 Mark Clear .05 .02
64 Alex Trevino .05 .02
65 Rick Reuschel .05 .02
66 Manny Trillo .05 .02
67 Dave Palmer .05 .02
68 Darrell Miller .05 .02
69 Jeff Ballard .05 .02
70 Mark McGwire 1.00 .40
71 Mike Boddicker .05 .02
72 John Moses .05 .02
73 Pascual Perez .05 .02
74 Nick Leyva MG .05 .02
75 Tom Henke .05 .02
76 Terry Blocker .05 .02
77 Doyle Alexander .05 .02
78 Jim Sundberg .05 .02
79 Scott Bankhead .05 .02
80 Cory Snyder .05 .02
81 Tim Raines TL .10 .04
82 Dave Leiper .05 .02
83 Jeff Blauser .10 .04
84 Bill Bene FDP .05 .02
85 Kevin McReynolds .05 .02
86 Al Nipper .05 .02
87 Larry Owen .05 .02
88 Darryl Hamilton RC * .25 .10
89 Dave LaPoint .05 .02
90 Vince Coleman UER .05 .02
(Wrong birth year)
91 Floyd Youmans .05 .02
92 Jeff Kunkel .05 .02
93 Ken Howell .05 .02
94 Chris Speier .05 .02
95 Gerald Young .05 .02
96 Rick Cerone .05 .02
97 Greg Mathews .05 .02
98 Larry Sheets .05 .02
99 Sherman Corbett .05 .02
100 Mike Schmidt .50 .20
101 Les Straker .05 .02
102 Mike Gallego .05 .02
103 Tim Birtsas .05 .02
104 Dallas Green MG .05 .02
105 Ron Darling .05 .02
106 Willie Upshaw .05 .02
107 Jose DeLeon .05 .02
108 Fred Manrique .05 .02
109 Hipolito Pena .05 .02
110 Paul Molitor .15 .06
111 Eric Davis TL .05 .02
112 Jim Presley .05 .02
113 Lloyd Moseby .05 .02
114 Bob Kipper .05 .02
115 Jody Davis .05 .02
116 Jeff Montgomery .10 .04
117 Dave Anderson .05 .02
118 Checklist 1-132 .05 .02
119 Terry Puhl .05 .02
120 Frank Viola .05 .02
121 Garry Templeton .05 .02
122 Lance Johnson .10 .04
123 Spike Owen .05 .02
124 Jim Traber .05 .02
125 Mike Krukow .05 .02
126 Sid Bream .05 .02
127 Walt Terrell .05 .02
128 Milt Thompson .05 .02
129 Terry Clark .05 .02
130 Gerald Perry .05 .02
131 Dave Otto .05 .02
132 Curt Ford .05 .02
133 Bill Long .05 .02
134 Don Zimmer MG .05 .02
135 Jose Rijo .05 .02
136 Joey Meyer .05 .02
137 Geno Petralli .05 .02
138 Wallace Johnson .05 .02
139 Mike Flanagan .05 .02
140 Shawon Dunston .05 .02
141 Brook Jacoby TL .05 .02
142 Mike Diaz .05 .02
143 Mike Campbell .05 .02
144 Jay Bell .15 .06
145 Dave Stewart .10 .04
146 Gary Pettis .05 .02
147 DeWayne Buice .05 .02
148 Bill Pecota .05 .02
149 Doug Dascenzo .05 .02
150 Fernando Valenzuela .10 .04
151 Terry McGriff .05 .02
152 Mark Thurmond .05 .02
153 Jim Pankovits .05 .02
154 Don Carman .05 .02
155 Marty Barrett .05 .02
156 Dave Gallagher .05 .02
157 Tom Glavine .25 .10
158 Mike Aldrete .05 .02
159 Pat Clements .05 .02
160 Jeffrey Leonard .05 .02
161 G. Olson RC FDP UER .25 .10
Born Scribner, NE,
should be Omaha, NE
162 John Davis .05 .02
163 Bob Forsch .05 .02
164 Hal Lanier MG .05 .02
165 Mike Dunne .05 .02
166 Doug Jennings .05 .02
167 Steve Searcy FS .05 .02
168 Willie Wilson .05 .02
169 Mike Jackson .05 .02
170 Tony Fernandez .05 .02
171 Andres Thomas TL .05 .02
172 Frank Williams .05 .02
173 Mel Hall .05 .02
174 Todd Burns .05 .02
175 John Shelby .05 .02
176 Jeff Parrett .05 .02
177 Monty Fariss FDP .05 .02
178 Mark Grant .05 .02
179 Ozzie Virgil .05 .02
180 Mike Scott .05 .02
181 Craig Worthington .05 .02
182 Bob McClure .05 .02
183 Oddibe McDowell .05 .02
184 John Costello .05 .02
185 Claudell Washington .05 .02
186 Pat Perry .05 .02
187 Darren Daulton .10 .04
188 Dennis Lamp .05 .02
189 Kevin Mitchell .10 .04
190 Mike Witt .05 .02
191 Sil Campusano .05 .02
192 Paul Mirabella .05 .02
193 Sparky Anderson MG .10 .04
UER (553 Salazer)
194 Greg W. Harris RC .10 .04
195 Ozzie Guillen .05 .02
196 Denny Walling .05 .02
197 Neal Heaton .05 .02
198 Danny Heep .05 .02
199 Mike Schooler RC * .10 .04
200 George Brett .60 .24
201 Kelly Gruber TL .05 .02
202 Brad Moore .05 .02
203 Rob Ducey .05 .02
204 Brad Havens .05 .02
205 Dwight Evans .10 .04
206 Roberto Alomar .30 .12
207 Terry Leach .05 .02
208 Tom Pagnozzi .05 .02
209 Jeff Bittiger .05 .02
210 Dale Murphy .25 .10
211 Mike Pagliarulo .05 .02
212 Scott Sanderson .05 .02
213 Rene Gonzales .05 .02
214 Charlie O'Brien .05 .02
215 Kevin Gross .05 .02
216 Jack Howell .05 .02
217 Joe Price .05 .02
218 Mike LaValliere .05 .02
219 Jim Clancy .05 .02
220 Gary Gaetti .10 .04
221 Cecil Espy .05 .02
222 Mark Lewis FDP RC .25 .10
223 Jay Buhner .10 .04
224 Tony LaRussa MG .10 .04
225 Ramon Martinez RC .25 .10
226 Bill Doran .05 .02
227 John Farrell .05 .02
228 Nelson Santovenia .05 .02
229 Jimmy Key .10 .04
230 Ozzie Smith .40 .16
231 Roberto Alomar TL .25 .10
(Gary Carter at plate)
232 Ricky Horton .05 .02
233 Gregg Jefferies FS .10 .04
234 Tom Browning .05 .02
235 John Kruk .10 .04
236 Charles Hudson .05 .02
237 Glenn Hubbard .05 .02
238 Eric King .05 .02
239 Tim Laudner .05 .02
240 Greg Maddux .50 .20
241 Brett Butler .10 .04
242 Ed VandeBerg .05 .02
243 Bob Boone .10 .04
244 Jim Acker .05 .02
245 Jim Rice .10 .04
246 Rey Quinones .05 .02
247 Shawn Hillegas .05 .02
248 Tony Phillips .05 .02
249 Tim Leary .05 .02
250 Cal Ripken .75 .30
251 John Dopson .05 .02
252 Billy Hatcher .05 .02
253 Jose Alvarez RC .10 .04
254 Tom Lasorda MG .25 .10
255 Ron Guidry .10 .04
256 Benny Santiago .10 .04
257 Rick Aguilera .10 .04
258 Checklist 133-264 .05 .02
259 Larry McWilliams .05 .02
260 Dave Winfield .10 .04
261 Tom Brunansky .05 .02
Luis Alicea TL
262 Jeff Pico .05 .02
263 Mike Felder .05 .02
264 Rob Dibble RC * .50 .20
265 Kent Hrbek .10 .04
266 Luis Aquino .05 .02
267 Jeff M. Robinson .05 .02
268 Keith Miller RC .10 .04
269 Tom Bolton .05 .02
270 Wally Joyner .10 .04
271 Jay Tibbs .05 .02
272 Ron Hassey .05 .02
273 Jose Lind .05 .02
274 Mark Eichhorn .05 .02
275 Danny Tartabull UER .05 .02
(Born San Juan, PR
should be Miami, FL)
276 Paul Kilgus .05 .02
277 Mike Davis .05 .02
278 Andy McGaffigan .05 .02
279 Scott Bradley .05 .02
280 Bob Knepper .05 .02
281 Gary Redus .05 .02
282 Cris Carpenter RC * .10 .04
283 Andy Allanson .05 .02
284 Jim Leyland MG .10 .04
285 John Candelaria .05 .02
286 Darrin Jackson .05 .02
287 Juan Nieves .05 .02
288 Pat Sheridan .05 .02
289 Ernie Whitt .05 .02
290 John Franco .10 .04
291 Darryl Strawberry .10 .04
Keith Hernandez
Kevin McReynolds TL
292 Jim Corsi .05 .02
293 Glenn Wilson .05 .02
294 Juan Berenguer .05 .02
295 Scott Fletcher .05 .02
296 Ron Gant .10 .04
297 Oswald Peraza .05 .02
298 Chris James .05 .02
299 Steve Ellsworth .05 .02
300 Darryl Strawberry .15 .06
301 Charlie Leibrandt .05 .02
302 Gary Ward .05 .02
303 Felix Fermin .05 .02
304 Joel Youngblood .05 .02
305 Dave Smith .05 .02
306 Tracy Woodson .05 .02
307 Lance McCullers .05 .02
308 Ron Karkovice .05 .02
309 Mario Diaz .05 .02
310 Rafael Palmeiro .25 .10
311 Chris Bosio .05 .02
312 Tom Lawless .05 .02
313 Dennis Martinez .10 .04
314 Bobby Valentine MG .05 .02
315 Greg Swindell .05 .02
316 Walt Weiss .05 .02
317 Jack Armstrong RC * .25 .10
318 Gene Larkin .05 .02
319 Greg Booker .05 .02
320 Lou Whitaker .10 .04
321 Jody Reed TL .05 .02
322 John Smiley .05 .02
323 Gary Thurman .05 .02
324 Bob Milacki .05 .02
325 Jesse Barfield .05 .02
326 Dennis Boyd .05 .02
327 Mark Lemke RC .25 .10
328 Rick Honeycutt .05 .02
329 Bob Melvin .05 .02
330 Eric Davis .10 .04
331 Curt Wilkerson .05 .02
332 Tony Armas .05 .02
333 Bob Ojeda .05 .02
334 Steve Lyons .05 .02
335 Dave Righetti .05 .02
336 Steve Balboni .05 .02
337 Calvin Schiraldi .05 .02
338 Jim Adduci .05 .02
339 Scott Bailes .05 .02
340 Kirk Gibson .10 .04
341 Jim Deshaies .05 .02
342 Tom Brookens .05 .02
343 Gary Sheffield FS RC 1.50 .60
344 Tom Trebelhorn MG .05 .02
345 Charlie Hough .10 .04
346 Rex Hudler .10 .04
347 John Cerutti .05 .02
348 Ed Hearn .05 .02
349 Ron Jones .05 .02
350 Andy Van Slyke .10 .04
351 Bob Melvin .05 .02
Bill Fahey CO TL
352 Rick Schu .05 .02
353 Marvell Wynne .05 .02
354 Larry Parrish .05 .02
355 Mark Langston .05 .02
356 Kevin Elster .05 .02
357 Jerry Reuss .05 .02
358 Ricky Jordan RC * .25 .10
359 Tommy John .10 .04
360 Ryne Sandberg .40 .16
361 Kelly Downs .05 .02
362 Jack Lazorko .05 .02
363 Rich Yett .05 .02
364 Rob Deer .05 .02
365 Mike Henneman .05 .02
366 Herm Winningham .05 .02
367 Johnny Paredes .05 .02
368 Brian Holton .05 .02
369 Ken Caminiti .10 .04
370 Dennis Eckersley .10 .04
371 Manny Lee .05 .02
372 Craig Lefferts .05 .02
373 Tracy Jones .05 .02
374 John Wathan MG .05 .02
375 Terry Pendleton .10 .04
376 Steve Lombardozzi .05 .02
377 Mike Smithson .05 .02
378 Checklist 265-396 .05 .02
379 Tim Flannery .05 .02
380 Rickey Henderson .25 .10
381 Larry Sheets TL .05 .02
382 John Smoltz RC 1.00 .40
383 Howard Johnson .05 .02
384 Mark Salas .05 .02
385 Von Hayes .05 .02
386 Andres Galarraga AS .05 .02
387 Ryne Sandberg AS .25 .10
388 Bobby Bonilla AS .10 .04
389 Ozzie Smith AS .25 .10
390 Darryl Strawberry AS .10 .04
391 Andre Dawson AS .05 .02
392 Andy Van Slyke AS .05 .02
393 Gary Carter AS .10 .04
394 Orel Hershiser AS .10 .04
395 Danny Jackson AS .05 .02
396 Kirk Gibson AS .10 .04
397 Don Mattingly AS .30 .12
398 Julio Franco AS .05 .02
399 Wade Boggs AS .10 .04
400 Alan Trammell AS .05 .02
401 Jose Canseco AS .10 .04
402 Mike Greenwell AS .05 .02
403 Kirby Puckett AS .15 .06
404 Bob Boone AS .05 .02
405 Roger Clemens AS .25 .10
406 Frank Viola AS .05 .02
407 Dave Winfield AS .05 .02
408 Greg Walker .05 .02
409 Ken Dayley .05 .02
410 Jack Clark .05 .02
411 Mitch Williams .05 .02
412 Barry Lyons .05 .02
413 Mike Kingery .05 .02
414 Jim Fregosi MG .05 .02
415 Rich Gossage .10 .04
416 Fred Lynn .05 .02
417 Mike LaCoss .05 .02
418 Bob Dernier .05 .02
419 Tom Filer .05 .02
420 Joe Carter .15 .06
421 Kirk McCaskill .05 .02
422 Bo Diaz .05 .02
423 Brian Fisher .05 .02
424 Luis Polonia UER .05 .02
(Wrong birthdate)
425 Jay Howell .05 .02
426 Dan Gladden .05 .02
427 Eric Show .05 .02
428 Craig Reynolds .05 .02
429 Greg Gagne TL .05 .02
430 Mark Gubicza .05 .02
431 Luis Rivera .05 .02
432 Chad Kreuter RC .25 .10
433 Albert Hall .05 .02
434 Ken Patterson .05 .02
435 Len Dykstra .10 .04
436 Bobby Meacham .05 .02
437 Andy Benes FDP RC .40 .16
438 Greg Gross .05 .02
439 Frank DiPino .05 .02
440 Bobby Bonilla .10 .04
441 Jerry Reed .05 .02
442 Jose Oquendo .05 .02
443 Rod Nichols .05 .02
444 Moose Stubing MG .05 .02
445 Matt Nokes .05 .02
446 Rob Murphy .05 .02
447 Donell Nixon .05 .02
448 Eric Plunk .05 .02
449 Carmelo Martinez .05 .02
450 Roger Clemens .50 .20
451 Mark Davidson .05 .02
452 Israel Sanchez .05 .02
453 Tom Prince .05 .02
454 Paul Assenmacher .05 .02
455 Johnny Ray .05 .02
456 Tim Belcher .05 .02
457 Mackey Sasser .05 .02
458 Donn Pall .05 .02
459 Dave Valle TL .05 .02
460 Dave Stieb .05 .02
461 Buddy Bell .10 .04
462 Jose Guzman .05 .02
463 Steve Lake .05 .02
464 Bryn Smith .05 .02
465 Mark Grace .25 .10
466 Chuck Crim .05 .02
467 Jim Walewander .05 .02
468 Henry Cotto .05 .02
469 Jose Bautista RC .10 .04
470 Lance Parrish .05 .02
471 Steve Curry .05 .02
472 Brian Harper .05 .02
473 Don Robinson .05 .02
474 Bob Rodgers MG .05 .02
475 Dave Parker .10 .04
476 Jon Perlman .05 .02
477 Dick Schofield .05 .02
478 Doug Drabek .05 .02
479 Mike Macfarlane RC * .25 .10
480 Keith Hernandez .15 .06
481 Chris Brown .05 .02
482 Steve Peters .05 .02
483 Mickey Hatcher .05 .02
484 Steve Shields .05 .02
485 Hubie Brooks .05 .02
486 Jack McDowell .10 .04
487 Scott Lusader .05 .02
488 Kevin Coffman .05 .02
Now with Cubs
489 Mike Schmidt TL .15 .06
490 Chris Sabo RC * .40 .16
491 Mike Birkbeck .05 .02
492 Alan Ashby .05 .02
493 Todd Benzinger .05 .02
494 Shane Rawley .05 .02
495 Candy Maldonado .05 .02
496 Dwayne Henry .05 .02
497 Pete Stanicek .05 .02
498 Dave Valle .05 .02
499 Don Heinkel .05 .02
500 Jose Canseco .25 .10
501 Vance Law .05 .02
502 Duane Ward .05 .02
503 Al Newman .05 .02
504 Bob Walk .05 .02
505 Pete Rose MG .50 .20
506 Kirt Manwaring .05 .02
507 Steve Farr .05 .02
508 Wally Backman .05 .02
509 Bud Black .05 .02
510 Bob Horner .05 .02
511 Richard Dotson .05 .02
512 Donnie Hill .05 .02
513 Jesse Orosco .05 .02
514 Chet Lemon .05 .02
515 Barry Larkin .25 .10
516 Eddie Whitson .05 .02
517 Greg Brock .05 .02
518 Bruce Ruffin .05 .02
519 Willie Randolph TL .05 .02
520 Rick Sutcliffe .10 .04
521 Mickey Tettleton .05 .02
522 Randy Kramer .05 .02
523 Andres Thomas .05 .02
524 Checklist 397-528 .05 .02
525 Chili Davis .10 .04
526 Wes Gardner .05 .02
527 Dave Henderson .05 .02
528 Luis Medina .05 .02
(Lower left front
has white triangle)
529 Tom Foley .05 .02
530 Nolan Ryan 1.00 .40
531 Dave Hengel .05 .02
532 Jerry Browne .05 .02
533 Andy Hawkins .05 .02
534 Doc Edwards MG .05 .02
535 Todd Worrell UER .05 .02
(4 wins in '88,
should be 5)
536 Joel Skinner .05 .02
537 Pete Smith .05 .02
538 Juan Castillo .05 .02
539 Barry Jones .05 .02
540 Bo Jackson .25 .10
541 Cecil Fielder .10 .04
542 Todd Frohwirth .05 .02
543 Damon Berryhill .05 .02
544 Jeff Sellers .05 .02
545 Mookie Wilson .10 .04
546 Mark Williamson .05 .02
547 Mark McLemore .05 .02
548 Bobby Witt .05 .02
549 Jamie Moyer TL .05 .02
550 Orel Hershiser .10 .04
551 Randy Ready .05 .02
552 Greg Cadaret .05 .02
553 Luis Salazar .05 .02
554 Nick Esasky .05 .02
555 Bert Blyleven .10 .04
556 Bruce Fields .05 .02
557 Keith A. Miller .05 .02
558 Dan Pasqua .05 .02
559 Juan Agosto .05 .02
560 Tim Raines .10 .04
561 Luis Aguayo .05 .02
562 Danny Cox .05 .02
563 Bill Schroeder .05 .02
564 Russ Nixon MG .05 .02
565 Jeff Russell .05 .02
566 Al Pedrique .05 .02
567 David Wells UER .10 .04
(Complete Pitching
Recor)
568 Mickey Brantley .05 .02
569 German Jimenez .05 .02
570 Tony Gwynn UER .30 .12
('88 average should
be italicized as
league leader)
571 Billy Ripken .05 .02
572 Atlee Hammaker .05 .02
573 Jim Abbott FDP RC* .50 .20
574 Dave Clark .05 .02
575 Juan Samuel .05 .02
576 Greg Minton .05 .02
577 Randy Bush .05 .02
578 John Morris .05 .02
579 Glenn Davis TL .05 .02
580 Harold Reynolds .10 .04
581 Gene Nelson .05 .02
582 Mike Marshall .05 .02
583 Paul Gibson .05 .02
584 Randy Velarde UER .05 .02
(Signed 1935,
should be 1985)
585 Harold Baines .10 .04
586 Joe Boever .05 .02
587 Mike Stanley .05 .02
588 Luis Alicea RC * .25 .10
589 Dave Meads .05 .02
590 Andres Galarraga .10 .04
591 Jeff Musselman .05 .02
592 John Cangelosi .05 .02
593 Drew Hall .05 .02
594 Jimy Williams MG .05 .02
595 Teddy Higuera .05 .02
596 Kurt Stillwell .05 .02
597 Terry Taylor RC .10 .04
598 Ken Gerhart .05 .02
599 Tom Candiotti .05 .02
600 Wade Boggs .15 .06
601 Dave Dravecky .10 .04
602 Devon White .10 .04
603 Frank Tanana .05 .02
604 Paul O'Neill .15 .06
605A Bob Welch ERR 2.00 .80
(Missing line on back
Complete M.L. Pitching Record
605B Bob Welch COR .05 .02
606 Rick Dempsey .05 .02
607 Willie Ansley FDP RC .10 .04
608 Phil Bradley .05 .02
609 Frank Tanana .05 .02
Alan Trammell
Mike Heath TL
610 Randy Myers .10 .04
611 Don Slaught .05 .02
612 Dan Quisenberry .05 .02

613 Gary Varsho .05 .02
614 Joe Hesketh .05 .02
615 Robin Yount .40 .16
616 Steve Rosenberg .05 .02
617 Mark Parent .05 .02
618 Rance Mulliniks .05 .02
619 Checklist 529-660 .05 .02
620 Barry Bonds 1.25 .50
621 Rick Mahler .05 .02
622 Stan Javier .05 .02
623 Fred Toliver .05 .02
624 Jack McKeon MG .05 .02
625 Eddie Murray .25 .10
626 Jeff Reed .05 .02
627 Greg A. Harris .05 .02
628 Matt Williams .25 .10
629 Pete O'Brien .05 .02
630 Mike Greenwell .05 .02
631 Dave Bergman .05 .02
632 Bryan Harvey RC * .25 .10
633 Daryl Boston .05 .02
634 Marvin Freeman .05 .02
635 Willie Randolph .10 .04
636 Bill Wilkinson .05 .02
637 Carmen Castillo .05 .02
638 Floyd Bannister .05 .02
639 Walt Weiss TL .05 .02
640 Willie McGee .10 .04
641 Curt Young .05 .02
642 Angel Salazar .05 .02
643 Louie Meadows .05 .02
644 Lloyd McClendon .05 .02
645 Jack Morris .10 .04
646 Kevin Bass .05 .02
647 Randy Johnson RC 3.00 1.20
648 Sandy Alomar FS RC .40 .16
649 Stu Cliburn .05 .02
650 Kirby Puckett .25 .10
651 Tom Niedenfuer .05 .02
652 Rich Gedman .05 .02
653 Tommy Barrett .05 .02
654 Whitey Herzog MG .05 .02
655 Dave Magadan .05 .02
656 Ivan Calderon .05 .02
657 Joe Magrane .05 .02
658 R.J. Reynolds .05 .02
659 Al Leiter .25 .10
660 Will Clark .25 .10
661 D.Gooden TBC84 .10 .04
662 Lou Brock TBC79 .10 .04
663 Hank Aaron TBC74 .25 .10
664 Gil Hodges TBC 69 .10 .04
665A Tony Oliva TBC64 2.00 .80
ERR (fabricated card is enlarged version of Oliva's 64T card; Topps copyright missing)
665B Tony Oliva TBC 64 .10 .04
COR (fabricated card)
666 Randy St.Claire .05 .02
667 Dwayne Murphy .05 .02
668 Mike Bielecki .05 .02
669 Orel Hershiser .10 .04
Mike Scioscia TL
670 Kevin Seitzer .05 .02
671 Jim Gantner .05 .02
672 Allan Anderson .05 .02
673 Don Baylor .10 .04
674 Otis Nixon .05 .02
675 Bruce Hurst .05 .02
676 Ernie Riles .05 .02
677 Dave Schmidt .05 .02
678 Dion James .05 .02
679 Willie Fraser .05 .02
680 Gary Carter .15 .06
681 Jeff D. Robinson .05 .02
682 Rick Leach .05 .02
683 Jose Cecena .05 .02
684 Dave Johnson MG .05 .02
685 Jeff Treadway .05 .02
686 Scott Terry .05 .02
687 Alvin Davis .05 .02
688 Zane Smith .05 .02
689A Stan Jefferson .05 .02
(Pink triangle on front bottom left)
689B Stan Jefferson .05 .02
(Violet triangle on front bottom left)
690 Doug Jones .05 .02
691 Roberto Kelly UER .05 .02
(83 Oneonita)
692 Steve Ontiveros .05 .02
693 Pat Borders RC * .25 .10
694 Les Lancaster .05 .02
695 Carlton Fisk .15 .06
696 Don August .05 .02
697A Franklin Stubbs .05 .02
(Team name on front in white)
697B Franklin Stubbs .05 .02
(Team name on front in gray)
698 Keith Atherton .05 .02
699 Al Pedrique TL .05 .02
Tony Gwynn sliding
700 Don Mattingly .60 .24
701 Storm Davis .05 .02
702 Jamie Quirk .05 .02
703 Scott Garrelts .05 .02
704 Carlos Quintana RC .10 .04
705 Terry Kennedy .05 .02
706 Pete Incaviglia .05 .02
707 Steve Jeltz .05 .02
708 Chuck Finley .10 .04
709 Tom Herr .05 .02
710 David Cone .10 .04
711 Candy Sierra .05 .02
712 Bill Swift .05 .02
713 Ty Griffin FDP .05 .02
714 Joe Morgan MG .05 .02
715 Tony Pena .05 .02
716 Wayne Tolleson .05 .02
717 Jamie Moyer .10 .04
718 Glenn Braggs .05 .02
719 Danny Darwin .05 .02
720 Tim Wallach .05 .02
721 Ron Tingley .05 .02
722 Todd Stottlemyre .15 .06
723 Rafael Belliard .05 .02
724 Jerry Don Gleaton .05 .02
725 Terry Steinbach .10 .04
726 Dickie Thon .05 .02
727 Joe Orsulak .05 .02
728 Charlie Puleo .05 .02
729 Steve Buechele TL .05 .02
(Inconsistent design, team name on front surrounded by black, should be white)
730 Danny Jackson .05 .02
731 Mike Young .05 .02
732 Steve Buechele .05 .02
733 Randy Bockus .05 .02
734 Jody Reed .05 .02
735 Roger McDowell .05 .02
736 Jeff Hamilton .05 .02
737 Norm Charlton RC .25 .10
738 Darnell Coles .05 .02
739 Brook Jacoby .05 .02
740 Dan Plesac .05 .02
741 Ken Phelps .05 .02
742 Mike Harkey FS RC .10 .04
743 Mike Heath .05 .02
744 Roger Craig MG .05 .02
745 Fred McGriff .25 .10
746 G.Gonzalez UER .05 .02
Wrong birthdate
747 Wil Tejada .05 .02
748 Jimmy Jones .05 .02
749 Rafael Ramirez .05 .02
750 Bret Saberhagen .10 .04
751 Ken Oberkfell .05 .02
752 Jim Gott .05 .02
753 Jose Uribe .05 .02
754 Bob Brower .05 .02
755 Mike Scioscia .05 .02
756 Scott Medvin .05 .02
757 Brady Anderson RC .50 .20
758 Gene Walter .05 .02
759 Rob Deer TL .05 .02
760 Lee Smith .10 .04
761 Dante Bichette RC .40 .16
762 Bobby Thigpen .05 .02
763 Dave Martinez .05 .02
764 Robin Ventura FDP RC .75 .30
765 Glenn Davis .05 .02
766 Cecilio Guante .05 .02
767 Mike Capel .05 .02
768 Bill Wegman .05 .02
769 Junior Ortiz .05 .02
770 Alan Trammell .15 .06
771 Ron Kittle .05 .02
772 Ron Oester .05 .02
773 Keith Moreland .05 .02
774 Frank Robinson MG .15 .06
775 Jeff Reardon .10 .04
776 Nelson Liriano .05 .02
777 Ted Power .05 .02
778 Bruce Benedict .05 .02
779 Craig McMurtry .05 .02
780 Pedro Guerrero .05 .02
781 Greg Briley .05 .02
782 Checklist 661-792 .05 .02
783 Trevor Wilson RC .10 .04
784 Steve Avery FDP RC .25 .10
785 Ellis Burks .15 .06
786 Melido Perez .05 .02
787 Dave West RC .10 .04
788 Mike Morgan .05 .02
789 Bo Jackson TL .25 .10
790 Sid Fernandez .05 .02
791 Jim Lindeman .05 .02
792 Rafael Santana .05 .02

1989 Topps Tiffany

Again, Topps issed a standard-size "Glossy" parallel to their regular set. These cards, printed in the Topps Irish facility, have 792 standard-size cards and were issued in complete set form only. These cards have a "shiny" front as well as an easy to read back. These cards were issued only through Topps hobby dealers. With the "glut" of the previous two years Tiffany sets in the marketplace, it seems that approximately 15,000 of these sets were produced in 1989.

Nm-Mt Ex-Mt
COMP.FACT.SET (792) 120.00 47.50
*STARS: 5X TO 12X BASIC CARDS
*ROOKIES: 5X TO 12X BASIC CARDS

1989 Topps Batting Leaders

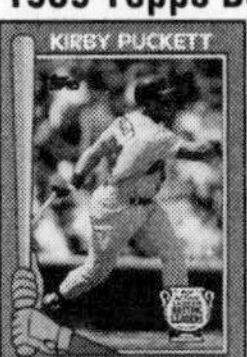

The 1989 Topps Batting Leaders set contains 22 standard-size glossy cards. The fronts are bright red. The set depicts the 22 veterans with the highest lifetime batting averages. The cards were distributed one per Topps blister pack. These blister packs were sold exclusively through K-Mart stores. The cards in the set were numbered by K-Mart essentially in order of highest active career batting average entering the 1989 season.

Nm-Mt Ex-Mt
COMPLETE SET (22) 100.00 40.00
1 Wade Boggs 10.00 4.00
2 Tony Gwynn 20.00 8.00
3 Don Mattingly 20.00 8.00
4 Kirby Puckett 10.00 4.00
5 George Brett 20.00 8.00
6 Pedro Guerrero .50 .20
7 Tim Raines 1.00 .40
8 Keith Hernandez 1.00 .40
9 Jim Rice 1.00 .40
10 Paul Molitor 8.00 3.20
11 Eddie Murray 8.00 3.20
12 Willie McGee 1.00 .40
13 Dave Parker 1.00 .40
14 Julio Franco 1.00 .40
15 Rickey Henderson 12.00 4.80
16 Kent Hrbek 1.00 .40
17 Willie Wilson .50 .20
18 Johnny Ray .50 .20
19 Pat Tabler .50 .20
20 Carney Lansford .50 .20
21 Robin Yount 8.00 3.20
22 Alan Trammell 2.00 .80

1989 Topps Glossy All-Stars

These glossy cards were inserted with Topps rack packs and honor the starting line-ups, managers, and honorary captains of the 1988 National and American League All-Star teams. The standard size cards are very similar in design to what Topps has used since 1984. The backs are printed in red and blue on white card stock.

Nm-Mt Ex-Mt
COMPLETE SET (22) 3.00 1.20
1 Tom Kelly MG .05 .02
2 Mark McGwire 1.25 .50
3 Paul Molitor .40 .16
4 Wade Boggs .30 .12
5 Cal Ripken 1.50 .60
6 Jose Canseco .25 .10
7 Rickey Henderson .60 .24
8 Dave Winfield .40 .16
9 Terry Steinbach .05 .02
10 Frank Viola .05 .02
11 Bobby Doerr CAPT .10 .04
12 Whitey Herzog MG .05 .02
13 Will Clark .20 .08
14 Ryne Sandberg .50 .20
15 Bobby Bonilla .10 .04
16 Ozzie Smith .50 .20
17 Vince Coleman .05 .02
18 Andre Dawson .20 .08
19 Darryl Strawberry .10 .04
20 Gary Carter .40 .16
21 Dwight Gooden .10 .04
22 Willie Stargell CAPT .15 .06

1989 Topps Glossy Send-Ins

The 1989 Topps Glossy Send-In set contains 60 standard-size cards. The fronts have color photos with white borders; the backs are light blue. The cards were distributed through the mail by Topps in six groups of ten cards. The last two cards out of each group of ten are young players or prospects.

Nm-Mt Ex-Mt
COMPLETE SET (60) 10.00 4.00
1 Kirby Puckett .75 .30
2 Eric Davis .20 .08
3 Joe Carter .20 .08
4 Andy Van Slyke .10 .04
5 Wade Boggs .60 .24
6 David Cone .20 .08
7 Kent Hrbek .20 .08
8 Darryl Strawberry .20 .08
9 Jay Buhner .20 .08
10 Ron Gant .20 .08
11 Will Clark .40 .16
12 Jose Canseco .75 .30
13 Juan Samuel .10 .04
14 George Brett 1.50 .60
15 Benito Santiago .20 .08
16 Dennis Eckersley .60 .24
17 Gary Carter .60 .24
18 Frank Viola .10 .04
19 Roberto Alomar 1.50 .60
20 Paul Gibson .10 .04
21 Dave Winfield .60 .24
22 Howard Johnson .10 .04
23 Roger Clemens 1.50 .60
24 Bobby Bonilla .20 .08
25 Alan Trammell .30 .12
26 Kevin McReynolds .10 .04
27 George Bell .10 .04
28 Bruce Hurst .10 .04
29 Mark Grace .75 .30
30 Tim Belcher .10 .04
31 Mike Greenwell .10 .04
32 Glenn Davis .10 .04
33 Gary Gaetti .20 .08
34 Ryne Sandberg 1.50 .60
35 Rickey Henderson 1.00 .40
36 Dwight Evans .20 .08
37 Dwight Gooden .20 .08
38 Robin Yount .60 .24
39 Damon Berryhill .10 .04
40 Chris Sabo .10 .04
41 Mark McGwire 2.50 1.00
42 Ozzie Smith 1.50 .60
43 Paul Molitor .60 .24
44 Andres Galarraga .40 .16
45 Dave Stewart .20 .08
46 Tom Browning .10 .04
47 Cal Ripken 3.00 1.20
48 Orel Hershiser .20 .08
49 Dave Gallagher .10 .04
50 Walt Weiss .10 .04
51 Don Mattingly 1.50 .60
52 Tony Fernandez .10 .04
53 Tim Raines .20 .08
54 Jeff Reardon .20 .08
55 Kirk Gibson .20 .08
56 Jack Clark .10 .04
57 Danny Jackson .10 .04
58 Tony Gwynn 1.50 .60
59 Cecil Espy .10 .04
60 Jody Reed .10 .04

1989 Topps Rookies

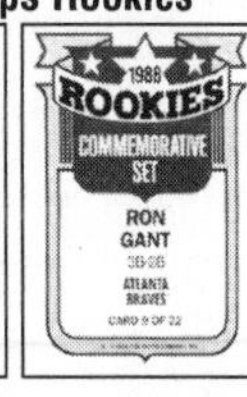

Inserted in each supermarket jumbo pack is a card from this series of 22 of 1988's best rookies as determined by Topps. Jumbo packs consisted of 100 (regular issue 1989 Topps baseball) cards with a stick of gum plus the insert "Rookie" card. The card fronts are in full color and measure the standard size. The card backs are printed in red and blue on white card stock and are numbered at the bottom. The order of the set is alphabetical by player's name.

Nm-Mt Ex-Mt
COMPLETE SET (22) 12.00 4.80
1 Roberto Alomar 2.50 1.00
2 Brady Anderson .75 .30
3 Tim Belcher .25 .10
4 Damon Berryhill .25 .10
5 Jay Buhner 1.00 .40
6 Kevin Elster .25 .10
7 Cecil Espy .25 .10
8 Dave Gallagher .25 .10
9 Ron Gant 1.00 .40
10 Paul Gibson .25 .10
11 Mark Grace 2.00 .80
12 Darrin Jackson .25 .10
13 Gregg Jefferies .50 .20
14 Ricky Jordan .25 .10
15 Al Leiter 1.00 .40
16 Melido Perez .25 .10
17 Chris Sabo .25 .10
18 Nelson Santovenia .25 .10
19 Mackey Sasser .25 .10
20 Gary Sheffield 3.00 1.20
21 Walt Weiss .25 .10
22 David Wells 2.00 .80

1989 Topps Wax Box Cards

The cards in this 16-card set measure the standard size. Cards have essentially the same design as the 1989 Topps regular issue set. The cards were printed on the bottoms of the regular issue wax pack boxes. These 16 cards, "lettered" A through P, are considered a separate set in their own right and are not typically included in a complete set of the regular issue 1989 Topps cards. The order of the set is alphabetical by player's name. The value of the panels uncut is slightly greater, perhaps by 25 percent greater, than the value of the individual cards cut up carefully. The sixteen cards in this set honor players (and one manager) who reached career milestones during the 1988 season.

Nm-Mt Ex-Mt
COMPLETE SET (16) 8.00 3.20
A George Brett 1.00 .40
B Bill Buckner .20 .08
C Darrell Evans .20 .08
D Rich Gossage .20 .08
E Greg Gross .10 .04
F Rickey Henderson .75 .30
G Keith Hernandez .20 .08
H Tom Lasorda MG .40 .16
I Jim Rice .20 .08
J Cal Ripken 2.00 .80
K Nolan Ryan 2.00 .80
L Mike Schmidt .75 .30
M Bruce Sutter .20 .08
N Don Sutton .50 .20
O Kent Tekulve .10 .04
P Dave Winfield .50 .20

1989 Topps Traded

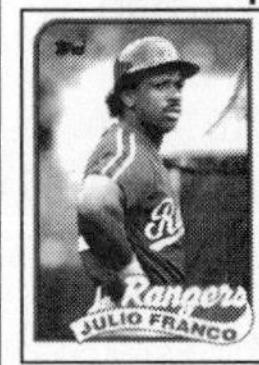

The 1989 Topps Traded set contains 132 standard-size cards. The cards were distributed exclusively in factory set form in red and white taped boxes through hobby dealers. The cards are identical to the 1989 Topps regular issue cards except for whiter stock and t-suffixed numbering on back. Rookie Cards in this set include Ken Griffey Jr., Deion Sanders and Omar Vizquel.

Nm-Mt Ex-Mt
COMP.FACT.SET (132) 15.00 6.00
1T Don Aase .05 .02
2T Jim Abbott .25 .10
3T Kent Anderson .05 .02
4T Keith Atherton .05 .02
5T Wally Backman .05 .02
6T Steve Balboni .05 .02
7T Jesse Barfield .05 .02
8T Steve Bedrosian .05 .02
9T Todd Benzinger .05 .02
10T Geronimo Berroa .05 .02
11T Bert Blyleven .10 .04
12T Bob Boone .10 .04
13T Phil Bradley .05 .02
14T Jeff Brantley RC .25 .10
15T Kevin Brown .25 .10
16T Jerry Browne .05 .02
17T Chuck Cary .05 .02
18T Carmen Castillo .05 .02
19T Jim Clancy .05 .02
20T Jack Clark .05 .02
21T Bryan Clutterbuck .05 .02
22T Jody Davis .05 .02
23T Mike Devereaux .05 .02
24T Frank DiPino .05 .02
25T Benny Distefano .05 .02
26T John Dopson .05 .02
27T Len Dykstra .10 .04
28T Jim Eisenreich .05 .02
29T Nick Esasky .05 .02
30T Alvaro Espinoza .05 .02
31T Darrell Evans UER .10 .04
(Stat headings on back are for a pitcher)
32T Junior Felix RC .10 .04
33T Felix Fermin .05 .02
34T Julio Franco .05 .02
35T Terry Francona .10 .04
36T Cito Gaston MG .10 .04
37T Bob Geren RC UER .05 .02
(Photo actually Mike Fennell)
38T Tom Gordon RC .25 .10
39T Tommy Gregg .05 .02
40T Ken Griffey Sr. .10 .04
41T Ken Griffey Jr. RC 8.00 3.20
42T Kevin Gross .05 .02
43T Lee Guetterman .05 .02
44T Mel Hall .05 .02
45T Erik Hanson RC .25 .10
46T Gene Harris RC .10 .04
47T Andy Hawkins .05 .02
48T Rickey Henderson .25 .10
49T Tom Herr .05 .02
50T Ken Hill RC .25 .10
51T Brian Holman RC * .10 .04
52T Brian Holton .05 .02
53T Art Howe MG .05 .02
54T Ken Howell .05 .02
55T Bruce Hurst .05 .02
56T Chris James .05 .02
57T Randy Johnson 2.00 .80
58T Jimmy Jones .05 .02
59T Terry Kennedy .05 .02
60T Paul Kilgus .05 .02
61T Eric King .05 .02
62T Ron Kittle .05 .02
63T John Kruk .10 .04
64T Randy Kutcher .05 .02
65T Steve Lake .05 .02
66T Mark Langston .05 .02
67T Dave LaPoint .05 .02
68T Rick Leach .05 .02
69T Terry Leach .05 .02
70T Jim Lefebvre MG .05 .02
71T Al Leiter .25 .10
72T Jeffrey Leonard .05 .02
73T Derek Lilliquist RC .10 .04
74T Rick Mahler .05 .02
75T Tom McCarthy .05 .02
76T Lloyd McClendon .05 .02
77T Lance McCullers .05 .02
78T Oddibe McDowell .05 .02
79T Roger McDowell .05 .02
80T Larry McWilliams .05 .02
81T Randy Milligan .05 .02
82T Mike Moore .05 .02
83T Keith Moreland .05 .02
84T Mike Morgan .05 .02
85T Jamie Moyer .10 .04
86T Rob Murphy .05 .02
87T Eddie Murray .25 .10
88T Pete O'Brien .05 .02
89T Gregg Olson .25 .10
90T Steve Ontiveros .05 .02
91T Jesse Orosco .05 .02
92T Spike Owen .05 .02
93T Rafael Palmeiro .25 .10
94T Clay Parker .05 .02
95T Jeff Parrett .05 .02
96T Lance Parrish .05 .02
97T Dennis Powell .05 .02
98T Rey Quinones .05 .02
99T Doug Rader MG .05 .02
100T Willie Randolph .10 .04
101T Shane Rawley .05 .02
102T Randy Ready .05 .02
103T Bip Roberts .10 .04
104T Kenny Rogers RC .50 .20
105T Ed Romero .05 .02
106T Nolan Ryan 1.50 .60
107T Luis Salazar .05 .02
108T Juan Samuel .05 .02
109T Alex Sanchez .05 .02
110T Deion Sanders RC .75 .30
111T Steve Sax .05 .02
112T Rick Schu .05 .02
113T Dwight Smith RC .25 .10
114T Lonnie Smith .05 .02
115T Billy Spiers RC .25 .10
116T Kent Tekulve .05 .02
117T Walt Terrell .05 .02
118T Milt Thompson .05 .02
119T Dickie Thon .05 .02
120T Jeff Torborg MG .05 .02
121T Jeff Treadway .05 .02
122T Omar Vizquel RC .50 .20
123T Jerome Walton .25 .10
124T Gary Ward .05 .02
125T Claudell Washington .05 .02
126T Curt Wilkerson .05 .02
127T Eddie Williams .05 .02
128T Frank Williams .05 .02
129T Ken Williams .05 .02

130T Mitch Williams .05 .02
131T Steve Wilson RC .10 .04
132T Checklist 1T-132T .05 .02

1989 Topps Traded Tiffany

For each set of regular Tiffany cards ordered, dealers received an update set. These 132 standard-size cards update the regular Topps issue. Again, these cards feature "glossy" fronts as well as easy to read backs. This set was issued only in complete form from the company. Again, the Topps Ireland printing facility produced these cards. Again, approximately 15,000 of these sets were produced.

Nm-Mt Ex-Mt
COMP.FACT.SET (132) 120.00 47.50
*STARS: 4X TO 10X BASIC CARDS ....
*ROOKIES: 5X TO 12X BASIC CARDS

1989 Topps Ames 20/20 Club

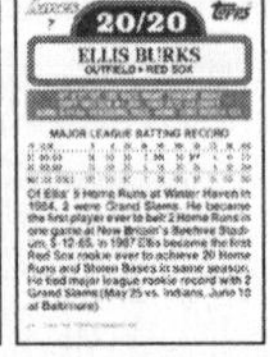

The 1989 (Topps) Ames 20/20 Club set contains 33 standard-size glossy cards. The fronts resemble plaques with gold and silver trim. The vertically oriented backs show career stats. The cards were distributed at Ames department stores as a boxed set. The set was produced by Topps for Ames; the Topps logo is also on the front of each card. The set includes active major leaguers who have had seasons of at least 20 home runs and 20 stolen bases. The backs include lifetime batting records with home run and stolen base totals for their 20/20 years highlighted. The subject list for the set is printed on the back panel of the set's custom box. These numbered cards are ordered alphabetically by player's name.

Nm-Mt Ex-Mt
COMP. FACT SET (33) 5.00 2.00
1 Jesse Barfield .05 .02
2 Kevin Bass .05 .02
3 Don Baylor .10 .04
4 George Bell .05 .02
5 Barry Bonds 1.00 .40
6 Phil Bradley .05 .02
7 Ellis Burks .15 .06
8 Jose Canseco .30 .12
9 Joe Carter .10 .04
10 Kal Daniels .05 .02
11 Eric Davis .10 .04
12 Mike Davis .05 .02
13 Andre Dawson .20 .08
14 Kirk Gibson .10 .04
15 Pedro Guerrero .05 .02
16 Rickey Henderson .60 .24
17 Bo Jackson .20 .08
18 Howard Johnson .05 .02
19 Jeffrey Leonard .05 .02
20 Kevin McReynolds .05 .02
21 Dale Murphy .20 .08
22 Dwayne Murphy .05 .02
23 Dave Parker .10 .04
24 Kirby Puckett .50 .20
25 Juan Samuel .05 .02
26 Ryne Sandberg .50 .20
27 Mike Schmidt .50 .20
28 Darryl Strawberry .10 .04
29 Alan Trammell .15 .06
30 Andy Van Slyke .05 .02
31 Devon White .10 .04
32 Dave Winfield .40 .16
33 Robin Yount .40 .16

1989 Topps Award Winners

This commemorative sheet measures 8 3/4" by 8 1/8" and features the MVP, Cy Young and Rookie of the Year award winners from the AL and the NL. If the cards were cut they would measure the standard size. Fronts feature glossy color player photos with different color inner and outer borders. The player's name and the award he received is listed in a color stripe at the bottom of the card. The backs are blank and unnumbered. The players are checklisted below in alphabetical order. This sheet was included in a blister pack with a complete set of 1990 Topps Stickers.

Nm-Mt Ex-Mt
COMPLETE SET (6) 2.00 .80
1 Mark Davis .10 .04
2 Kevin Mitchell .15 .06
3 Gregg Olson .15 .06
4 Bret Saberhagen .50 .20
5 Jerome Walton .10 .04
6 Robin Yount 2.00 .80

1989 Topps Baseball Talk/LJN

The BB Talk Soundcards include action photos of players, complete player statistics, exclusive specially recorded baseball programs and player autographs. These cards were produced by LJN Toys. The fronts of the cards feature oversized replicas of Topps cards. Card numbers 41, 82, 123 and 164 were issued only with the record player. They might well be tougher to acquire now.

Nm-Mt Ex-Mt
COMPLETE SET (164) 250.00 100.00
1 1975 World Series 2.50 1.00
Game 6
2 1986 World Series 2.00 .80
Game 6
3 1986 A.L. Championship 2.00 .80
Game 5
4 1956 World Series 2.00 .80
Game 5
5 1986 N.L. Championship 2.00 .80
Game 6
6 1969 World Series 2.00 .80
Game 5
7 1984 World Series 2.00 .80
Game 5
8 1988 World Series 2.50 1.00
Game 1
9 Reggie Jackson 4.00 1.60
10 Brooks Robinson 2.50 1.00
11 Billy Williams 2.50 1.00
12 Bobby Thomson 2.00 .80
13 Harmon Killebrew 2.50 1.00
14 Johnny Bench 4.00 1.60
15 Tom Seaver 5.00 2.00
16 Willie Stargell 2.50 1.00
17 Ernie Banks 4.00 1.60
18 Gaylord Perry 2.50 1.00
19 Bill Mazeroski 2.50 1.00
20 Babe Ruth 20.00 8.00
21 Lou Gehrig 12.00 4.80
22 Ty Cobb 8.00 3.20
23 Bob Gibson 2.50 1.00
24 Al Kaline 2.50 1.00
25 Rod Carew 2.50 1.00
26 Lou Brock 2.50 1.00
27 Stan Musial 5.00 2.00
28 Joe L. Morgan 2.50 1.00
29 Willie McCovey 2.50 1.00
30 Duke Snider 2.50 1.00
31 Whitey Ford 2.50 1.00
32 Eddie Mathews 2.50 1.00
33 Carl Yastrzemski 2.50 1.00
34 Pete Rose 5.00 2.00
35 Hank Aaron 8.00 3.20
36 Ralph Kiner 2.50 1.00
37 Steve Carlton 2.50 1.00
38 Roberto Clemente 10.00 4.00
39 Don Drysdale 2.50 1.00
40 Robin Roberts 2.50 1.00
41 Hank Aaron 8.00 3.20
42 Dave Winfield 4.00 1.60
43 Alan Trammell 2.00 .80
44 Darryl Strawberry 1.50 .60
45 Ozzie Smith 8.00 3.20
46 Kirby Puckett 8.00 3.20
47 Will Clark 4.00 1.60
48 Keith Hernandez 1.50 .60
49 Wally Joyner 1.50 .60
50 Mike Scott 1.00 .40
51 Eric Davis 1.50 .60
52 George Brett 10.00 4.00
53 George Bell 1.00 .40
54 Tommy Lasorda MG 2.50 1.00
55 Rickey Henderson 5.00 2.00
56 Robin Yount 5.00 2.00
57 Wade Boggs 5.00 2.00
58 Roger Clemens 10.00 4.00
59 Alvin Davis 1.00 .40
60 Jose Canseco 4.00 1.60
61 Fernando Valenzuela 1.50 .60
62 Tony Gwynn 10.00 4.00
63 Dwight Gooden 1.50 .60
64 Mark McGwire 15.00 6.00
65 Jack Clark 1.00 .40
66 Dale Murphy 2.50 1.00
67 Kirk Gibson 1.50 .60
68 Jack Morris 1.50 .60
69 Ryne Sandberg 8.00 3.20
70 Nolan Ryan 20.00 8.00
71 John Tudor 1.00 .40
72 Mike Schmidt 4.00 1.60
73 Dave Righetti 1.00 .40
74 Pedro Guerrero 1.00 .40
75 Rick Sutcliffe 1.00 .40
76 Gary Carter 4.00 1.60
77 Cal Ripken 20.00 8.00
78 Andre Dawson 2.50 1.00
79 Andy Van Slyke 1.00 .40
80 Tim Raines 1.50 .60
81 Frank Viola 1.00 .40
82 Orel Hershiser 2.50 1.00
83 Rick Reuschel 1.00 .40
84 Willie McGee 1.50 .60
85 Mark Langston 1.00 .40
86 Ron Darling 1.00 .40
87 Gregg Jefferies 1.00 .40
88 Harold Baines 1.50 .60
89 Eddie Murray 5.00 2.00
90 Barry Larkin 2.50 1.00
91 Gary Gaetti 1.50 .60
92 Bret Saberhagen 1.50 .60
93 Roger McDowell 1.00 .40
94 Joe Magrane 1.00 .40
95 Juan Samuel 1.00 .40
96 Bert Blyleven 1.50 .60
97 Kal Daniels 1.00 .40
98 Kevin Bass 1.00 .40
99 Glenn Davis 1.00 .40
100 Steve Sax 1.00 .40
101 Rich Gossage 1.50 .60
102 Roger Craig MG 1.00 .40
103 Carney Lansford 1.00 .40
104 Joe Carter 1.50 .60
105 Bruce Sutter 1.50 .60
106 Barry Bonds 10.00 4.00
107 Danny Jackson 1.00 .40
108 Mike Flanagan 1.00 .40
109 Dwight Evans 1.50 .60
110 Ron Guidry 1.50 .60
111 Bruce Hurst 1.00 .40
112 Jim Rice 1.50 .60
113 Oddibe McDowell 1.00 .40
114 Bobby Bonilla 1.50 .60
115 Bob Welch 1.50 .60
116 Dave Parker 1.50 .60
117 Tim Wallach 1.00 .40
118 Tom Henke 1.00 .40
119 Mike Greenwell 1.00 .40
120 Kevin Seitzer 1.00 .40
121 Randy Myers 1.50 .60
122 Andres Galarraga 2.00 .80
123 Don Mattingly 10.00 4.00
124 Cory Snyder 1.00 .40
125 Mike Witt 1.00 .40
126 Mike LaValliere 1.00 .40
127 Pete Incaviglia 1.00 .40
128 Dennis Eckersley 3.00 1.20
129 Jimmy Key 1.50 .60
130 John Franco 1.50 .60
131 Dan Plesac 1.00 .40
132 Tony LaRussa MG 1.50 .60
133 Hubie Brooks 1.00 .40
134 Chili Davis 1.50 .60
135 Bob Boone 1.50 .60
136 Jeff Reardon 1.50 .60
137 Candy Maldonado 1.00 .40
138 Mike Marshall 1.00 .40
139 Tommy John 1.50 .60
140 Chris Sabo 1.00 .40
141 Vince Coleman 1.00 .40
142 Frank White 1.50 .60
143 Harold Reynolds 1.50 .60
144 Lee Smith 1.50 .60
145 John Kruk 1.50 .60
146 Tony Fernandez 1.50 .60
147 Steve Bedrosian 1.00 .40
148 Benito Santiago 1.50 .60
149 Ozzie Guillen 1.50 .60
150 Gerald Perry 1.00 .40
151 Carlton Fisk 5.00 2.00
152 Tom Brunansky 1.00 .40
153 Paul Molitor 3.00 1.20
154 Todd Worrell 1.00 .40
155 Brett Butler 1.50 .60
156 Sparky Anderson MG 2.00 .80
157 Kent Hrbek 1.50 .60
158 Frank Tanana 1.00 .40
159 Kevin Mitchell 1.00 .40
160 Charlie Hough 1.50 .60
161 Doug Jones 1.00 .40
162 Lou Whitaker 1.50 .60
163 Fred Lynn 1.00 .40
164 Checklist 1.00 .40

1989 Topps Big

The 1989 Topps Big Baseball set contains 330 glossy cards measuring approximately 2 1/2" by 3 3/4". The fronts feature mug shots superimposed on action photos. The horizontally oriented backs have color cartoons and statistics for the player's previous season and total career. Team members for the United States Olympic team were also included in this set. The set was released in three series of 110 cards. The cards were distributed in seven-card packs marked with the series number.

Nm-Mt Ex-Mt
COMPLETE SET (330) 25.00 10.00
1 Orel Hershiser .10 .04
2 Harold Reynolds .10 .04
3 Jody Davis .05 .02
4 Greg Walker .05 .02
5 Barry Bonds 2.00 .80
6 Bret Saberhagen .10 .04
7 Johnny Ray .05 .02
8 Mike Fiore .05 .02
9 Juan Castillo .05 .02
10 Todd Burns .05 .02
11 Carmelo Martinez .05 .02
12 Geno Petralli .05 .02
13 Mel Hall .05 .02
14 Tom Browning .05 .02
15 Fred McGriff .50 .20
16 Kevin Elster .05 .02
17 Tim Leary .05 .02
18 Jim Rice .10 .04
19 Bret Barberie .05 .02
20 Jay Buhner .20 .08
21 Atlee Hammaker .05 .02
22 Lou Whitaker .10 .04
23 Paul Runge .05 .02
24 Carlton Fisk .50 .20
25 Jose Lind .05 .02
26 Mark Gubicza .05 .02
27 Billy Ripken .05 .02
28 Mike Pagliarulo .05 .02
29 Jim Deshaies .05 .02
30 Mark McLemore .10 .04
31 Scott Terry .05 .02
32 Franklin Stubbs .05 .02
33 Don August .05 .02
34 Mark McGwire 3.00 1.20
35 Eric Show .05 .02
36 Cecil Espy .05 .02
37 Ron Tingley .05 .02
38 Mickey Brantley .05 .02
39 Paul O'Neill .10 .04
40 Ed Sprague .15 .06
41 Len Dykstra .10 .04
42 Roger Clemens 2.00 .80
43 Ron Gant .10 .04
44 Dan Pasqua .05 .02
45 Jeff D. Robinson .05 .02
46 George Brett 2.00 .80
47 Bryn Smith .05 .02
48 Mike Marshall .05 .02
49 Doug Robbins .05 .02
50 Don Mattingly 2.00 .80
51 Mike Scott .05 .02
52 Steve Jeltz .05 .02
53 Dick Schofield .05 .02
54 Tom Brunansky .05 .02
55 Gary Sheffield 2.50 1.00
56 Dave Valle .05 .02
57 Carney Lansford .10 .04
58 Tony Gwynn 2.00 .80
59 Checklist 1-110 .05 .02
60 Damon Berryhill .05 .02
61 Jack Morris .10 .04
62 Brett Butler .10 .04
63 Mickey Hatcher .05 .02
64 Bruce Sutter .10 .04
65 Robin Ventura 1.00 .40
66 Junior Ortiz .05 .02
67 Pat Tabler .05 .02
68 Greg Swindell .05 .02
69 Jeff Branson .05 .02
70 Manny Lee .05 .02
71 Dave Magadan .05 .02
72 Rich Gedman .05 .02
73 Tim Raines .10 .04
74 Mike Maddux .05 .02
75 Jim Presley .05 .02
76 Chuck Finley .10 .04
77 Jose Oquendo .05 .02
78 Rob Deer .05 .02
79 Jay Howell .05 .02
80 Terry Steinbach .05 .02
81 Ed Whitson .05 .02
82 Ruben Sierra .10 .04
83 Bruce Benedict .05 .02
84 Fred Manrique .05 .02
85 John Smiley .05 .02
86 Mike Macfarlane .05 .02
87 Rene Gonzales .05 .02
88 Charles Hudson .05 .02
89 Glenn Davis .05 .02
90 Les Straker .05 .02
91 Carmen Castillo .05 .02
92 Tracy Woodson .05 .02
93 Tino Martinez .75 .30
94 Herm Winningham .05 .02
95 Kelly Gruber .05 .02
96 Terry Leach .05 .02
97 Jody Reed .05 .02
98 Nelson Santovenia .05 .02
99 Tony Armas .05 .02
100 Greg Brock .05 .02
101 Dave Stewart .10 .04
102 Roberto Alomar 1.50 .60
103 Jim Sundberg .05 .02
104 Albert Hall .05 .02
105 Steve Lyons .10 .04
106 Sid Bream .05 .02
107 Danny Tartabull .05 .02
108 Rick Dempsey .05 .02
109 Rich Renteria .05 .02
110 Ozzie Smith 1.50 .60
111 Steve Sax .05 .02
112 Kelly Downs .05 .02
113 Larry Sheets .05 .02
114 Andy Benes .20 .08
115 Pete O'Brien .05 .02
116 Kevin McReynolds .05 .02
117 Juan Berenguer .05 .02
118 Billy Hatcher .05 .02
119 Rick Cerone .05 .02
120 Andre Dawson .20 .08
121 Storm Davis .05 .02
122 Devon White .05 .02
123 Alan Trammell .15 .06
124 Vince Coleman .05 .02
125 Al Leiter .20 .08
126 Dale Sveum .05 .02
127 Pete Incaviglia .05 .02
128 Dave Stieb .05 .02
129 Kevin Mitchell .05 .02
130 Dave Schmidt .05 .02
131 Gary Redus .05 .02
132 Ron Robinson .05 .02
133 Darnell Coles .05 .02
134 Benito Santiago .10 .04
135 John Farrell .05 .02
136 Willie Wilson .05 .02
137 Steve Bedrosian .05 .02
138 Don Slaught .05 .02
139 Darryl Strawberry .10 .04
140 Frank Viola .05 .02
141 Dave Silvestri .05 .02
142 Carlos Quintana .05 .02
143 Vance Law .05 .02
144 Dave Parker .10 .04
145 Tim Belcher .05 .02
146 Will Clark 1.00 .40
147 Mark Williamson .05 .02
148 Ozzie Guillen .10 .04
149 Kirk McCaskill .05 .02
150 Pat Sheridan .05 .02
151 Terry Pendleton .10 .04
152 Roberto Kelly .05 .02
153 Joey Meyer .05 .02
154 Mark Grant .05 .02
155 Joe Carter .20 .08
156 Steve Buechele .05 .02
157 Tony Fernandez .10 .04
158 Jeff Reed .05 .02
159 Bobby Bonilla .10 .04
160 Henry Cotto .05 .02
161 Kurt Stillwell .05 .02
162 Mickey Morandini .05 .02
163 Robby Thompson .05 .02
164 Rick Schu .05 .02
165 Stan Jefferson .05 .02
166 Ron Darling .05 .02
167 Kirby Puckett 1.00 .40
168 Bill Doran .05 .02
169 Dennis Lamp .05 .02
170 Ty Griffin .05 .02
171 Ron Hassey .05 .02
172 Dale Murphy .50 .20
173 Andres Galarraga .20 .08
174 Tim Flannery .05 .02
175 Cory Snyder .05 .02
176 Checklist 111-220 .05 .02
177 Tommy Barrett .05 .02
178 Dan Petry .05 .02
179 Billy Masse .05 .02
180 Terry Kennedy .05 .02
181 Joe Orsulak .05 .02
182 Doyle Alexander .05 .02
183 Willie McGee .10 .04
184 Jim Gantner .05 .02
185 Keith Hernandez .10 .04
186 Greg Gagne .05 .02
187 Kevin Bass .05 .02
188 Mark Eichhorn .05 .02
189 Mark Grace 1.00 .40
190 Jose Canseco .50 .20
191 Bobby Witt .05 .02
192 Rafael Santana .05 .02
193 Dwight Evans .10 .04
194 Greg Booker .05 .02
195 Brook Jacoby .05 .02
196 Rafael Belliard .05 .02
197 Candy Maldonado .05 .02
198 Mickey Tettleton .10 .04
199 Barry Larkin .75 .30
200 Frank White .10 .04
201 Wally Joyner .10 .04
202 Chet Lemon .05 .02
203 Joe Magrane .05 .02
204 Glenn Braggs .05 .02
205 Scott Fletcher .05 .02
206 Gary Ward .05 .02
207 Nelson Liriano .05 .02
208 Howard Johnson .05 .02
209 Kent Hrbek .10 .04
210 Ken Caminiti .10 .04
211 Mike Greenwell .05 .02
212 Ryne Sandberg 1.50 .60
213 Joe Slusarski .05 .02
214 Donell Nixon .05 .02
215 Tim Wallach .05 .02
216 John Kruk .10 .04
217 Charles Nagy .15 .06
218 Alvin Davis .05 .02
219 Oswald Peraza .05 .02
220 Mike Schmidt .75 .30
221 Spike Owen .05 .02
222 Mike Smithson .05 .02
223 Dion James .05 .02
224 Ernie Whitt .05 .02
225 Mike Davis .05 .02
226 Gene Larkin .05 .02
227 Pat Combs .05 .02
228 Jack Howell .05 .02
229 Ron Oester .05 .02
230 Paul Gibson .05 .02
231 Mookie Wilson .10 .04
232 Glenn Hubbard .05 .02
233 Shawon Dunston .05 .02
234 Otis Nixon .05 .02
235 Melido Perez .05 .02
236 Jerry Browne .05 .02
237 Rick Rhoden .05 .02
238 Bo Jackson .20 .08
239 Randy Velarde .05 .02
240 Jack Clark .05 .02
241 Wade Boggs .75 .30
242 Lonnie Smith .05 .02
243 Mike Flanagan .05 .02
244 Willie Randolph .10 .04
245 Oddibe McDowell .05 .02
246 Ricky Jordan .05 .02
247 Greg Briley .05 .02
248 Rex Hudler .10 .04
249 Robin Yount .50 .20
250 Lance Parrish .10 .04
251 Chris Sabo .05 .02
252 Mike Henneman .05 .02
253 Gregg Jefferies .05 .02
254 Curt Young .05 .02
255 Andy Van Slyke .05 .02
256 Rod Booker .05 .02
257 Rafael Palmeiro .75 .30
258 Jose Uribe .05 .02
259 Ellis Burks .50 .20
260 John Smoltz .50 .20
261 Tom Foley .05 .02
262 Lloyd Moseby .05 .02
263 Jim Poole .05 .02
264 Gary Gaetti .10 .04
265 Bob Dernier .05 .02
266 Harold Baines .15 .06
267 Tom Candiotti .05 .02
268 Rafael Ramirez .05 .02
269 Bob Boone .10 .04
270 Buddy Bell .10 .04
271 Rickey Henderson 1.25 .50
272 Willie Fraser .05 .02
273 Eric Davis .10 .04
274 Jeff M. Robinson .05 .02
275 Damaso Garcia .05 .02
276 Sid Fernandez .05 .02
277 Stan Javier .05 .02
278 Marty Barrett .05 .02
279 Gerald Perry .05 .02
280 Rob Ducey .05 .02
281 Mike Scioscia .10 .04
282 Randy Bush .05 .02
283 Tom Herr .05 .02
284 Glenn Wilson .05 .02
285 Pedro Guerrero .05 .02
286 Cal Ripken 4.00 1.60
287 Randy Johnson 4.00 1.60
288 Julio Franco .10 .04
289 Ivan Calderon .05 .02
290 Rich Yett .05 .02
291 Scott Servais .05 .02
292 Bill Pecota .05 .02
293 Ken Phelps .05 .02
294 Chili Davis .10 .04
295 Manny Trillo .05 .02
296 Mike Boddicker .05 .02
297 Geronimo Berroa .05 .02
298 Todd Stottlemyre .10 .04
299 Kirk Gibson .10 .04
300 Wally Backman .05 .02
301 Hubie Brooks .05 .02
302 Von Hayes .05 .02
303 Matt Nokes .05 .02

304 Dwight Gooden	.10	.04
305 Walt Weiss	.05	.02
306 Mike LaValliere	.05	.02
307 Cris Carpenter	.05	.02
308 Ted Wood	.05	.02
309 Jeff Russell	.05	.02
310 Dave Gallagher	.05	.02
311 Andy Allanson	.05	.02
312 Craig Reynolds	.05	.02
313 Kevin Seitzer	.05	.02
314 Dave Winfield	.60	.24
315 Andy McGaffigan	.05	.02
316 Nick Esasky	.05	.02
317 Jeff Blauser	.05	.02
318 George Bell	.05	.02
319 Eddie Murray	.75	.30
320 Mark Davidson	.05	.02
321 Juan Samuel	.05	.02
322 Jim Abbott	.20	.08
323 Kal Daniels	.05	.02
324 Mike Brumley	.05	.02
325 Gary Carter	.50	.20
326 Dave Henderson	.05	.02
327 Checklist 221-330	.05	.02
328 Garry Templeton	.05	.02
329 Pat Perry	.05	.02
330 Paul Molitor	.75	.30

1989 Topps Cap'n Crunch

The 1989 Topps Cap'n Crunch set contains 22 standard-size cards. The fronts have red, white and blue borders surrounding "mugshot" photos. The backs are horizontally oriented and show lifetime stats. The team logos have been airbrushed out. Two cards were included (in a cellophane wrapper with a piece of gum) in each specially marked Cap'n Crunch cereal box. The set was not available as a complete set as part of any mail-in offer.

	Nm-Mt	Ex-Mt
COMPLETE SET (22)	12.00	4.80
1 Jose Canseco	1.00	.40
2 Kirk Gibson	.40	.16
3 Orel Hershiser	.40	.16
4 Frank Viola	.20	.08
5 Tony Gwynn	2.00	.80
6 Cal Ripken	4.00	1.60
7 Darryl Strawberry	.40	.16
8 Don Mattingly	2.00	.80
9 George Brett	2.00	.80
10 Andre Dawson	.75	.30
11 Dale Murphy	.75	.30
12 Alan Trammell	.60	.24
13 Eric Davis	.40	.16
14 Jack Clark	.20	.08
15 Eddie Murray	1.00	.40
16 Mike Schmidt	1.00	.40
17 Dwight Gooden	.40	.16
18 Roger Clemens	2.00	.80
19 Will Clark	.75	.30
20 Kirby Puckett	1.00	.40
21 Robin Yount	1.00	.40
22 Mark McGwire	3.00	1.20

1989 Topps Doubleheaders All-Stars

The 1989 Topps Doubleheaders were a novel idea from Topps to capitalize on the interest in rookie cards. The one side of the plastic holder shows a small color photo of the rookie card while the other side shows a photo of the current year Topps card. The holders measure 2" by 2 1/8". The set contains 24 holders, eight starting players, two starting pitchers, one reliever, and one DH from each league. They are unnumbered. Apparently the twelve from each league are considered by Topps as the "best" at each position.

	Nm-Mt	Ex-Mt
COMPLETE SET (24)	20.00	8.00
1 Don Mattingly	4.00	1.60
2 Julio Franco	.50	.20
3 Wade Boggs	2.00	.80
4 Alan Trammell	.75	.30
5 Jose Canseco	1.50	.60
6 Mike Greenwell	.25	.10
7 Kirby Puckett	2.00	.80
8 Carlton Fisk	1.25	.50

The Rookie Card side is a reproduction of his 1972 Topps Card
Cecil Cooper
Mike Garman are also featured on this card

9 Roger Clemens	4.00	1.60
10 Frank Viola	.25	.10
11 Dennis Eckersley	1.50	.60
12 Mark McGwire	6.00	2.40
13 Will Clark	1.00	.40
14 Ryne Sandberg	4.00	1.60
15 Bobby Bonilla	.50	.20
16 Ozzie Smith	4.00	1.60
17 Andre Dawson	1.00	.40
18 Darryl Strawberry	.50	.20
19 Andy Van Slyke	.25	.10
20 Alan Ashby	.25	.10
21 Orel Hershiser	.50	.20
22 Danny Jackson	.25	.10
23 John Franco	.50	.20
24 Kirk Gibson	.50	.20

1989 Topps Doubleheaders Mets/Yankees Test

This set of 24 Doubleheaders, which was test marketed by Topps, and is extremely tough to find, features the New York Mets (1-13) and the New York Yankees (14-24). Each item is a clear plastic stand-up holder containing two mini-reproductions of the player's cards. On one side is the 1989 Topps card, and on the reverse is a reproduction of the rookie card.

	Nm-Mt	Ex-Mt
COMPLETE SET (24)	400.00	160.00
1 Darryl Strawberry	15.00	6.00
2 Gregg Jefferies	10.00	4.00
3 Kevin McReynolds	10.00	4.00
4 Gary Carter	40.00	16.00
5 Dwight Gooden	15.00	6.00
6 David Cone	25.00	10.00
7 Ron Darling	15.00	6.00
8 Keith Hernandez	15.00	6.00
9 Randy Myers	15.00	6.00
10 Howard Johnson	15.00	6.00
11 Tim Teufel	10.00	4.00
12 Len Dykstra	15.00	6.00
13 Mookie Wilson	15.00	6.00
14 Don Mattingly	100.00	40.00
15 Dave Winfield	40.00	16.00
16 Rickey Henderson	75.00	30.00
17 Claudell Washington	10.00	4.00
18 Dave Righetti	15.00	6.00
19 Steve Sax	10.00	4.00
20 Mike Pagliarulo	10.00	4.00
21 Rafael Santana	10.00	4.00
22 Richard Dotson	10.00	4.00
23 Rick Rhoden	10.00	4.00
24 Ken Phelps	10.00	4.00

1989 Topps Gallery of Champions

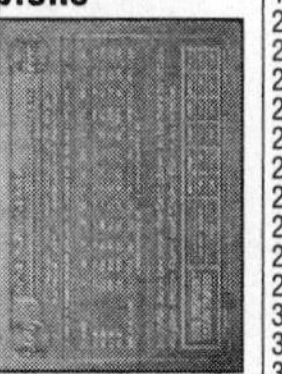

These 12 mini "cards" were produced by Topps and sold in complete set form only. The players selected for this set were either award winners or were league leaders. These approximately 1 1/4" by 1 3/4" cards were printed using either aluminum, bronze or silver. We have priced the aluminum versions of these cards. The bronze versions have a value of between 2X to 4X the aluminums while the silvers have a value between 5X to 10X the aluminum cards. We have sequenced this set in alphabetical order.

	Nm-Mt	Ex-Mt
COMPLETE SET (12)	100.00	40.00
1 Wade Boggs	20.00	8.00
2 Jose Canseco	15.00	6.00
3 Will Clark	20.00	8.00
4 Dennis Eckersley	15.00	6.00
5 John Franco	8.00	3.20
6 Kirk Gibson	8.00	3.20
7 Tony Gwynn	25.00	10.00
8 Orel Hershiser	8.00	3.20
9 Chris Sabo	5.00	2.00
10 Darryl Strawberry	8.00	3.20
11 Frank Viola	5.00	2.00
12 Walt Weiss	5.00	2.00

1989 Topps Heads Up Test

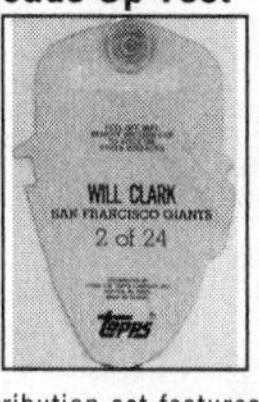

This very limited distribution set features baseball superstars. A large photo of the player's head is featured. These "faces" were released one per pack and the player's name and team are noted on the back.

	Nm-Mt	Ex-Mt
COMPLETE SET (24)	3000.00	1200.00
1 Tony Gwynn	250.00	100.00
2 Will Clark	100.00	40.00
3 Dwight Gooden	50.00	20.00
4 Ricky Jordan	25.00	10.00
5 Ken Griffey Jr.	500.00	200.00
6 Darryl Strawberry	50.00	20.00
7 Frank Viola	25.00	10.00
8 Bo Jackson	50.00	20.00
9 Ryne Sandberg	200.00	80.00
10 Gregg Jefferies	50.00	20.00
11 Wade Boggs	125.00	50.00
12 Ellis Burks	50.00	20.00
13 Gary Sheffield	200.00	80.00
14 Mark McGwire	400.00	160.00
15 Mark Grace	150.00	60.00
16 Jim Abbott	50.00	20.00
17 Ozzie Smith	150.00	60.00
18 Jose Canseco	125.00	50.00
19 Don Mattingly	250.00	100.00
20 Kirby Puckett	125.00	50.00
21 Eric Davis	50.00	20.00
22 Mike Greenwell	25.00	10.00
23 Dale Murphy	75.00	30.00
24 Mike Schmidt	125.00	50.00

1989 Topps Hills Team MVP's

The 1989 Topps Hills Team MVP's set contains 33 glossy standard-size cards. The fronts and backs are yellow, red, white and navy. The horizontally oriented backs are green. The cards were distributed through Hills stores as a boxed set. The set was printed in Ireland. These numbered cards are ordered alphabetically by player's name.

	Nm-Mt	Ex-Mt
COMP. FACT SET (33)	5.00	2.00
1 Harold Baines	.10	.04
2 Wade Boggs	.40	.16
3 George Brett	.75	.30
4 Tom Brunansky	.05	.02
5 Jose Canseco	.30	.12
6 Joe Carter	.15	.06
7 Will Clark	.40	.16
8 Roger Clemens	.75	.30
9 David Cone	.15	.06
10 Glenn Davis	.05	.02
11 Andre Dawson	.20	.08
12 Dennis Eckersley	.40	.16
13 Andres Galarraga	.20	.08
14 Kirk Gibson	.10	.04
15 Mike Greenwell	.05	.02
16 Tony Gwynn	.75	.30
17 Orel Hershiser	.10	.04
18 Danny Jackson	.05	.02
19 Mark Langston	.05	.02
20 Fred McGriff	.40	.16
21 Dale Murphy	.20	.08
22 Eddie Murray	.20	.08
23 Kirby Puckett	.40	.16
24 Johnny Ray	.05	.02
25 Juan Samuel	.05	.02
26 Ruben Sierra	.10	.04
27 Dave Stewart	.10	.04
28 Darryl Strawberry	.10	.04
29 Alan Trammell	.15	.06
30 Andy Van Slyke	.05	.02
31 Frank Viola	.05	.02
32 Dave Winfield	.40	.16
33 Robin Yount	.40	.16

1989 Topps Mini Leaders

The 1989 Topps Mini League Leaders set contains 77 cards measuring approximately 2 1/8" by 3". The fronts have color photos with large white borders. The backs are yellow and feature 1988 and career stats. The cards were distributed in seven-card cello packs. These numbered cards are ordered alphabetically by player within team and the teams themselves are ordered alphabetically.

	Nm-Mt	Ex-Mt
COMPLETE SET (77)	8.00	3.20
1 Dale Murphy	.20	.08
2 Gerald Perry	.05	.02
3 Andre Dawson	.20	.08
4 Greg Maddux	1.25	.50
5 Rafael Palmeiro	.40	.16
6 Tom Browning	.05	.02
7 Kal Daniels	.05	.02
8 Eric Davis	.10	.04
9 John Franco	.10	.04
10 Danny Jackson	.05	.02
11 Barry Larkin	.30	.12
12 Jose Rijo	.05	.02
13 Chris Sabo	.05	.02
14 Nolan Ryan	2.00	.80
15 Mike Scott	.05	.02
16 Gerald Young	.05	.02
17 Kirk Gibson	.10	.04
18 Orel Hershiser	.10	.04
19 Steve Sax	.05	.02
20 John Tudor	.05	.02
21 Hubie Brooks	.05	.02
22 Andres Galarraga	.20	.08
23 Otis Nixon	.05	.02
24 David Cone	.15	.06
25 Sid Fernandez	.05	.02
26 Dwight Gooden	.10	.04
27 Kevin McReynolds	.05	.02
28 Darryl Strawberry	.10	.04
29 Juan Samuel	.05	.02
30 Bobby Bonilla	.05	.02
31 Sid Bream	.05	.02
32 Jim Gott	.05	.02
33 Andy Van Slyke	.05	.02
34 Vince Coleman	.05	.02
35 Jose DeLeon	.05	.02
36 Joe Magrane	.05	.02
37 Ozzie Smith	.75	.30
38 Todd Worrell	.05	.02
39 Tony Gwynn	1.00	.40
40 Brett Butler	.10	.04
41 Will Clark	.40	.16
42 Rick Reuschel	.05	.02
43 Checklist Card	.05	.02
44 Eddie Murray	.50	.20
45 Wade Boggs	.40	.16
46 Roger Clemens	1.00	.40
47 Dwight Evans	.10	.04
48 Mike Greenwell	.05	.02
49 Bruce Hurst	.05	.02
50 Johnny Ray	.05	.02
51 Doug Jones	.05	.02
52 Greg Swindell	.05	.02
53 Gary Pettis	.05	.02
54 George Brett	1.00	.40
55 Mark Gubicza	.05	.02
56 Willie Wilson	.05	.02
57 Teddy Higuera	.05	.02
58 Paul Molitor	.40	.16
59 Robin Yount	.40	.16
60 Allan Anderson	.05	.02
61 Gary Gaetti	.10	.04
62 Kirby Puckett	.50	.20
63 Jeff Reardon	.10	.04
64 Frank Viola	.05	.02
65 Jack Clark	.05	.02
66 Rickey Henderson	.60	.24
67 Dave Winfield	.40	.16
68 Jose Canseco	.40	.16
69 Dennis Eckersley	.40	.16
70 Mark McGwire	1.50	.60
71 Dave Stewart	.10	.04
72 Alvin Davis	.05	.02
73 Mark Langston	.05	.02
74 Harold Reynolds	.10	.04
75 George Bell	.05	.02
76 Tony Fernandez	.10	.04
77 Fred McGriff	.40	.16

1989 Topps/O-Pee-Chee Sticker Backs

These 67 cards were actually the backs of the 1989 O-Pee-Chee Stickers. The white-bordered cards measure approximately 2 1/8" by 3" and have colorful backgrounds behind the cut-out color player photos. Cards 1-33 feature NL players; cards 34-66 feature AL players. The player's name and position appear in a colored banner near the bottom of the photo. Below are player biography and statistics. The cards are numbered at the lower left.

	Nm-Mt	Ex-Mt
COMPLETE SET (67)	6.00	2.40
1 George Brett	.60	.24
2 Don Mattingly	.75	.30
3 Mark McGwire	1.25	.50
4 Julio Franco	.05	.02
5 Harold Reynolds	.05	.02
6 Lou Whitaker	.10	.04
7 Wade Boggs	.30	.12
8 Gary Gaetti	.10	.04
9 Paul Molitor	.25	.10
10 Tony Fernandez	.05	.02
11 Cal Ripken	1.50	.60
12 Alan Trammell	.15	.06
13 Jose Canseco	.40	.16
14 Joe Carter	.10	.04
15 Dwight Evans	.10	.04
16 Mike Greenwell	.05	.02
17 Dave Henderson	.05	.02
18 Rickey Henderson	.40	.16
19 Kirby Puckett	.40	.16
20 Dave Winfield	.30	.12
21 Robin Yount	.25	.10
22 Bob Boone	.10	.04
23 Carlton Fisk	.25	.10
24 Geno Petralli	.05	.02
25 Roger Clemens	.75	.30
26 Mark Gubicza	.05	.02
27 Dave Stewart	.10	.04
28 Teddy Higuera	.05	.02
29 Bruce Hurst	.05	.02
30 Frank Viola	.05	.02
31 Dennis Eckersley	.15	.06
32 Doug Jones	.05	.02
33 Jeff Reardon	.10	.04
34 Will Clark	.25	.10
35 Glenn Davis	.05	.02
36 Andres Galarraga	.25	.10
37 Juan Samuel	.05	.02
38 Ryne Sandberg	.40	.16
39 Steve Sax	.05	.02
40 Bobby Bonilla	.10	.04
41 Howard Johnson	.05	.02
42 Vance Law	.05	.02
43 Shawon Dunston	.05	.02
44 Barry Larkin	.25	.10
45 Ozzie Smith	.40	.16
46 Barry Bonds	.75	.30
47 Eric Davis	.10	.04
48 Andre Dawson	.15	.06
49 Kirk Gibson	.10	.04
50 Tony Gwynn	.60	.24
51 Kevin McReynolds	.05	.02
52 Rafael Palmeiro	.25	.10
53 Darryl Strawberry	.05	.02
54 Andy Van Slyke	.10	.04
55 Gary Carter	.15	.06
56 Mike LaValliere	.05	.02
57 Benito Santiago	.05	.02
58 Dave Cone	.25	.10
59 Dwight Gooden	.10	.04
60 Orel Hershiser	.10	.04
61 Tom Browning	.05	.02
62 Danny Jackson	.05	.02
63 Bob Knepper	.05	.02
64 Mark Davis	.05	.02
65 John Franco	.10	.04
66 Randy Myers	.10	.04
67 Checklist	.05	.02

1989 Topps Ritz Mattingly

This set is actually a sheet of cards all featuring the career of Don Mattingly. The set was produced by Topps for Nabisco (Ritz Crackers) and was available via a send-in offer involving two proofs of purchase of boxes of Ritz Crackers. The uncut sheet is approximately 14" by 10 5/8". Included on the sheet are eight standard sized cards surrounding one large (5 1/8" by 7") card. In each case the Yankee logo has been airbrushed off the card.

	Nm-Mt	Ex-Mt
COMPLETE SET (9)	6.00	2.40
COMMON CARD (1-9)	1.00	.40

1989 Topps UK Minis

The 1989 Topps UK Minis baseball set contains 88 cards measuring approximately 2 1/8" by 3". The fronts are red, white and blue. The backs are yellow and red, and feature 1988 and career stats. The cards were distributed in five-card poly packs. The card set numbering is in alphabetical order by player's name.

	Nm-Mt	Ex-Mt
COMPLETE SET (88)	12.00	4.80
1 Brady Anderson	.30	.12
2 Harold Baines	.20	.08
3 George Bell	.10	.04
4 Wade Boggs	.75	.30
5 Barry Bonds	1.50	.60
6 Bobby Bonilla	.20	.08
7 George Brett	1.50	.60
8 Hubie Brooks	.10	.04
9 Tom Brunansky	.10	.04
10 Jay Buhner	.30	.12
11 Brett Butler	.20	.08
12 Jose Canseco	.50	.20
13 Joe Carter	.20	.08
14 Jack Clark	.10	.04
15 Will Clark	.40	.16
16 Roger Clemens	1.50	.60
17 David Cone	.40	.16
18 Alvin Davis	.10	.04
19 Eric Davis	.20	.08
20 Glenn Davis	.10	.04
21 Andre Dawson	.40	.16
22 Bill Doran	.10	.04
23 Dennis Eckersley	.60	.24
24 Dwight Evans	.20	.08
25 Tony Fernandez	.30	.12
26 Carlton Fisk	.50	.20
27 John Franco	.20	.08
28 Andres Galarraga	.40	.16
29 Ron Gant	.20	.08
30 Kirk Gibson	.20	.08
31 Dwight Gooden	.20	.08
32 Mike Greenwell	.10	.04
33 Mark Gubicza	.10	.04
34 Pedro Guerrero	.10	.04
35 Ozzie Guillen	.20	.08
36 Tony Gwynn	1.50	.60
37 Rickey Henderson	.75	.30
38 Orel Hershiser	.20	.08
39 Teddy Higuera	.10	.04
40 Charlie Hough	.20	.08
41 Kent Hrbek	.20	.08
42 Bruce Hurst	.10	.04
43 Bo Jackson	.40	.16
44 Gregg Jefferies	.10	.04
45 Ricky Jordan	.10	.04
46 Wally Joyner	.20	.08
47 Mark Langston	.10	.04
48 Mike Marshall	.10	.04
49 Don Mattingly	1.50	.60
50 Fred McGriff	.40	.16
51 Mark McGwire	2.50	1.00
52 Kevin McReynolds	.10	.04
53 Paul Molitor	.60	.24
54 Jack Morris	.20	.08
55 Dale Murphy	.40	.16
56 Eddie Murray	.75	.30
57 Pete O'Brien	.10	.04
58 Rafael Palmeiro	.40	.16
59 Gerald Perry	.10	.04
60 Kirby Puckett	1.50	.60
61 Tim Raines	.20	.08
62 Johnny Ray	.10	.04
63 Rick Reuschel	.10	.04
64 Cal Ripken	3.00	1.20
65 Chris Sabo	.10	.04
66 Juan Samuel	.10	.04
67 Ryne Sandberg	1.50	.60
68 Benito Santiago	.20	.08
69 Steve Sax	.10	.04
70 Mike Schmidt	1.00	.40
71 Ruben Sierra	.20	.08
72 Ozzie Smith	1.50	.60
73 Cory Snyder	.10	.04
74 Dave Stewart	.20	.08
75 Darryl Strawberry	.20	.08
76 Greg Swindell	.10	.04

Card		
77 Alan Trammell	.30	.12
78 Fernando Valenzuela	.20	.08
79 Andy Van Slyke	.10	.04
80 Frank Viola	.10	.04
81 Claudell Washington	.10	.04
82 Walt Weiss	.10	.04
83 Lou Whitaker	.20	.08
84 Dave Winfield	.50	.20
85 Mike Witt	.10	.04
86 Gerald Young	.10	.04
87 Robin Yount	.50	.20
88 Checklist Card	.10	.04

1989-90 Topps Senior League

The 1989-90 Topps Senior League baseball set was issued second among the three sets commemorating the first Senior league season. This set was issued in set form in its own box containing all 132 standard-size cards.

	NRMT-MT	NM
COMP. FACT SET (132)	5.00	2.20
1 George Foster	.15	.07
2 Dwight Lowry	.05	.02
3 Bob Jones	.05	.02
4 Clete Boyer MG	.10	.05
5 Rafael Landestoy	.05	.02
6 Bob Shirley	.05	.02
7 Ivan Murrell	.05	.02
8 Jerry White	.05	.02
9 Steve Henderson	.05	.02
10 Marty Castillo	.05	.02
11 Bruce Kison	.05	.02
12 George Hendrick	.10	.05
13 Bernie Carbo	.05	.02
14 Jerry Martin	.05	.02
15 Al Hrabosky	.10	.05
16 Luis Gomez	.05	.02
17 Dick Drago	.05	.02
18 Bobby Ramos	.05	.02
19 Jose Pittman	.05	.02
20 Ike Blessitt	.05	.02
21 Bill Travers	.05	.02
22 Dick Williams MG	.10	.05
23 Randy Lerch	.05	.02
24 Tom Spencer	.05	.02
25 Graig Nettles	.15	.07
26 Jim Gideon	.05	.02
27 Al Bumbry	.05	.02
28 Tom Murphy	.05	.02
29 Rodney Scott	.05	.02
30 Alan Bannister	.05	.02
31 John D'Acquisto	.05	.02
32 Bert Campaneris	.10	.05
33 Bill Lee	.10	.05
34 Jerry Grote	.10	.05
35 Ken Reitz	.05	.02
36 Al Oliver	.10	.05
37 Tim Stoddard	.05	.02
38 Lenny Randle	.05	.02
39 Rick Manning	.05	.02
40 Bobby Bonds	.25	.11
41 Rick Wise	.05	.02
42 Sal Butera	.05	.02
43 Ed Figueroa	.05	.02
44 Ron Washington	.05	.02
45 Elias Sosa	.05	.02
46 Dan Driessen	.05	.02
47 Wayne Nordhagen	.05	.02
48 Vida Blue	.10	.05
49 Butch Hobson	.05	.02
50 Randy Bass	.05	.02
51 Paul Mirabella	.05	.02
52 Steve Kemp	.05	.02
53 Kim Allen	.05	.02
54 Stan Cliburn	.05	.02
55 Derrel Thomas	.05	.02
56 Pete Falcone	.05	.02
57 Willie Aikens	.05	.02
58 Toby Harrah	.10	.05
59 Bob Tolan	.05	.02
60 Rick Waits	.05	.02
61 Jim Morrison	.05	.02
62 Stan Bahnsen	.05	.02
63 Gene Richards	.05	.02
64 Dave Cash	.05	.02
65 Rollie Fingers	.50	.23
66 Butch Benton	.05	.02
67 Tim Ireland	.05	.02
68 Rick Lysander	.05	.02
69 Cesar Cedeno	.10	.05
70 Jim Willoughby	.05	.02
71 Bill Madlock	.15	.07
72 Lee Lacy	.05	.02
73 Milt Wilcox	.05	.02
74 Ron Pruitt	.05	.02
75 Wayne Krenchicki	.05	.02
76 Earl Weaver MG	.50	.23
77 Pedro Borbon	.05	.02
78 Jose Cruz	.10	.05
79 Steve Ontiveros	.05	.02
80 Mike Easler	.05	.02
81 Amos Otis	.10	.05
82 Mickey Mahler	.05	.02
83 Orlando Gonzalez	.05	.02
84 Doug Simunic	.05	.02
85 Felix Millan	.05	.02
86 Garth Iorg	.05	.02
87 Pete Broberg	.05	.02
88 Roy Howell	.05	.02
89 Dave LaRoche	.05	.02
90 Jerry Manuel	.10	.05
91 Tony Scott	.05	.02
92 Larvell Blanks	.05	.02
93 Joaquin Andujar	.10	.05
94 Tito Landrum	.05	.02
95 Joe Sambito	.05	.02
96 Pat Dobson	.05	.02
97 Dan Meyer	.05	.02
98 Clint Hurdle	.10	.05
99 Pete LaCock	.05	.02
100 Bob Galasso	.05	.02
101 Dave Kingman	.25	.11
102 Jon Matlack	.05	.02
103 Larry Harlow	.05	.02
104 Rick Peterson	.05	.02
105 Joe Hicks	.05	.02
106 Bill Campbell	.05	.02
107 Tom Paciorek	.05	.02
108 Ray Burris	.05	.02
109 Ken Landreaux	.05	.02
110 Steve McCatty	.05	.02
111 Ron LeFlore	.10	.05
112 Joe Decker	.05	.02
113 Leon Roberts	.05	.02
114 Doug Corbett	.05	.02
115 Mickey Rivers	.10	.05
116 Dock Ellis	.05	.02
117 Ron Jackson	.05	.02
118 Bob Molinaro	.05	.02
119 Fergie Jenkins	.50	.23
120 U.L. Washington	.05	.02
121 Roy Thomas	.05	.02
122 Hal McRae	.10	.05
123 Juan Eichelberger	.05	.02
124 Gary Rajsich	.05	.02
125 Dennis Leonard	.05	.02
126 Walt Williams	.05	.02
127 Rennie Stennett	.05	.02
128 Jim Bibby	.05	.02
129 Dyar Miller	.05	.02
130 Luis Pujols	.05	.02
131 Juan Beniquez	.05	.02
132 Checklist Card	.05	.02

1990 Topps

The 1990 Topps set contains 792 standard-size cards. Cards were issued primarily in wax packs, rack packs and hobby and retail Christmas factory sets. Card fronts feature various colored borders with the player's name at the bottom and team name at top. Subsets include All-Stars (385-407), Turn Back the Clock (661-665) and Draft Picks (scattered throughout the set). The key Rookie Cards in this set are Juan Gonzalez, Marquis Grissom, Sammy Sosa, Frank Thomas, Larry Walker and Bernie Williams. The Thomas card (414A) was printed without his name on front creating a scarce variation. The card is rarely seen and, for a newer issue, has experienced unprecedented growth as far as value. Be careful when purchasing this card as counterfeits have been produced. A very few cards of President George Bush made their ways into packs. While these cards are supposed to be never issued, a few collectors did receive these cards when opening packs. Since this card is thinly traded, no pricing is provided.

	Nm-Mt	Ex-Mt
COMPLETE SET (792)	20.00	6.00
COMP.FACT.SET (792)	25.00	7.50
COMP.X-MAS.SET (792)	40.00	12.00
1 Nolan Ryan	1.00	.30
2 Nolan Ryan Mets	.50	.15
3 Nolan Ryan Angels	.50	.15
4 Nolan Ryan Astros	.50	.15
5 N.Ryan Rangers UER (Says Texas Stadium rather than Arlington Stadium)	.50	.15
6 Vince Coleman RB	.05	.02
7 Rickey Henderson RB	.15	.04
8 Cal Ripken RB	.25	.07
9 Eric Plunk	.05	.02
10 Barry Larkin	.25	.07
11 Paul Gibson	.05	.02
12 Joe Girardi	.15	.04
13 Mark Williamson	.05	.02
14 Mike Fetters RC	.25	.07
15 Teddy Higuera	.05	.02
16 Kent Anderson	.05	.02
17 Kelly Downs	.05	.02
18 Carlos Quintana	.05	.02
19 Al Newman	.05	.02
20 Mark Gubicza	.05	.02
21 Jeff Torborg MG	.05	.02
22 Bruce Ruffin	.05	.02
23 Randy Velarde	.05	.02
24 Joe Hesketh	.05	.02
25 Willie Randolph	.10	.03
26 Don Slaught	.05	.02
27 Rick Leach	.05	.02
28 Duane Ward	.05	.02
29 John Cangelosi	.05	.02
30 David Cone	.10	.03
31 Henry Cotto	.05	.02
32 John Farrell	.05	.02
33 Greg Walker	.05	.02
34 Tony Fossas	.05	.02
35 Benito Santiago	.10	.03
36 John Costello	.05	.02
37 Domingo Ramos	.05	.02
38 Wes Gardner	.05	.02
39 Curt Ford	.05	.02
40 Jay Howell	.05	.02
41 Matt Williams	.10	.03
42 Jeff M. Robinson	.05	.02
43 Dante Bichette	.25	.07
44 Roger Salkeld FDP RC	.10	.03
45 Dave Parker UER (Born in Jackson, not Calhoun)	.10	.03
46 Rob Dibble	.10	.03
47 Brian Harper	.05	.02
48 Zane Smith	.05	.02
49 Tom Lawless	.05	.02
50 Glenn Davis	.05	.02
51 Doug Rader MG	.05	.02
52 Jack Daugherty	.05	.02
53 Mike LaCoss	.05	.02
54 Joel Skinner	.05	.02
55 Darrell Evans UER (HR total should be 414, not 424)	.10	.03
56 Franklin Stubbs	.05	.02
57 Greg Vaughn	.10	.03
58 Keith Miller	.05	.02
59 Ted Power	.05	.02
60 George Brett	.60	.18
61 Deion Sanders	.25	.07
62 Ramon Martinez	.05	.02
63 Mike Pagliarulo	.05	.02
64 Danny Darwin	.05	.02
65 Devon White	.05	.02
66 Greg Litton	.05	.02
67 Scott Sanderson	.05	.02
68 Dave Henderson	.05	.02
69 Todd Frohwirth	.05	.02
70 Mike Greenwell	.05	.02
71 Allan Anderson	.05	.02
72 Jeff Huson RC	.10	.03
73 Bob Milacki	.05	.02
74 Jeff Jackson FDP RC	.10	.03
75 Doug Jones	.05	.02
76 Dave Valle	.05	.02
77 Dave Bergman	.05	.02
78 Mike Flanagan	.05	.02
79 Ron Kittle	.05	.02
80 Jeff Russell	.05	.02
81 Bob Rodgers MG	.05	.02
82 Scott Terry	.05	.02
83 Hensley Meulens	.05	.02
84 Ray Searage	.05	.02
85 Juan Samuel	.05	.02
86 Paul Kilgus	.05	.02
87 Rick Luecken	.05	.02
88 Glenn Braggs	.05	.02
89 Clint Zavaras	.05	.02
90 Jack Clark	.10	.03
91 Steve Frey	.05	.02
92 Mike Stanley	.05	.02
93 Shawn Hillegas	.05	.02
94 Herm Winningham	.05	.02
95 Todd Worrell	.05	.02
96 Jody Reed	.05	.02
97 Curt Schilling	1.00	.30
98 Jose Gonzalez	.05	.02
99 Rich Monteleone	.05	.02
100 Will Clark	.25	.07
101 Shane Rawley	.05	.02
102 Stan Javier	.05	.02
103 Marvin Freeman	.05	.02
104 Bob Knepper	.05	.02
105 Randy Myers	.10	.03
106 Charlie O'Brien	.05	.02
107 Fred Lynn	.05	.02
108 Rod Nichols	.05	.02
109 Roberto Kelly	.05	.02
110 Tommy Helms MG	.05	.02
111 Ed Whited	.05	.02
112 Glenn Wilson	.05	.02
113 Manny Lee	.05	.02
114 Mike Bielecki	.05	.02
115 Tony Pena	.05	.02
116 Floyd Bannister	.05	.02
117 Mike Sharperson	.05	.02
118 Erik Hanson	.05	.02
119 Billy Hatcher	.05	.02
120 John Franco	.10	.03
121 Robin Ventura	.25	.07
122 Shawn Abner	.05	.02
123 Rich Gedman	.05	.02
124 Dave Dravecky	.10	.03
125 Kent Hrbek	.10	.03
126 Randy Kramer	.05	.02
127 Mike Devereaux	.05	.02
128 Checklist 1	.05	.02
129 Ron Jones	.05	.02
130 Bert Blyleven	.10	.03
131 Matt Nokes	.05	.02
132 Lance Blankenship	.05	.02
133 Ricky Horton	.05	.02
134 E.Cunningham FDP RC	.10	.03
135 Dave Magadan	.05	.02
136 Kevin Brown	.10	.03
137 Marty Pevey	.05	.02
138 Al Leiter	.25	.07
139 Greg Brock	.05	.02
140 Andre Dawson	.10	.03
141 John Hart MG	.05	.02
142 Jeff Wetherby	.05	.02
143 Rafael Belliard	.05	.02
144 Bud Black	.05	.02
145 Terry Steinbach	.05	.02
146 Rob Richie	.05	.02
147 Chuck Finley	.10	.03
148 Edgar Martinez	.15	.04
149 Steve Farr	.05	.02
150 Kirk Gibson	.10	.03
151 Rick Mahler	.05	.02
152 Lonnie Smith	.05	.02
153 Randy Milligan	.05	.02
154 Mike Maddux	.05	.02
155 Ellis Burks	.15	.04
156 Ken Patterson	.05	.02
157 Craig Biggio	.15	.04
158 Craig Lefferts	.05	.02
159 Mike Felder	.05	.02
160 Dave Righetti	.05	.02
161 Harold Reynolds	.10	.03
162 Todd Zeile	.10	.03
163 Phil Bradley	.05	.02
164 Jeff Juden FDP RC	.10	.03
165 Walt Weiss	.05	.02
166 Bobby Witt	.05	.02
167 Kevin Appier	.25	.07
168 Jose Lind	.05	.02
169 Richard Dotson	.05	.02
170 George Bell	.05	.02
171 Russ Nixon MG	.05	.02
172 Tom Lampkin	.05	.02
173 Tim Belcher	.05	.02
174 Jeff Kunkel	.05	.02
175 Mike Moore	.05	.02
176 Luis Quinones	.05	.02
177 Mike Henneman	.05	.02
178 Chris James	.05	.02
179 Brian Holton	.05	.02
180 Tim Raines	.10	.03
181 Juan Agosto	.05	.02
182 Mookie Wilson	.10	.03
183 Steve Lake	.05	.02
184 Danny Cox	.05	.02
185 Ruben Sierra	.05	.02
186 Dave LaPoint	.05	.02
187 Rick Wrona	.05	.02
188 Mike Smithson	.05	.02
189 Dick Schofield	.05	.02
190 Rick Reuschel	.05	.02
191 Pat Borders	.05	.02
192 Don August	.05	.02
193 Andy Benes	.10	.03
194 Glenallen Hill	.05	.02
195 Tim Burke	.05	.02
196 Gerald Young	.05	.02
197 Doug Drabek	.05	.02
198 Mike Marshall	.05	.02
199 Sergio Valdez	.05	.02
200 Don Mattingly	.60	.18
201 Cito Gaston MG	.05	.02
202 Mike Macfarlane	.05	.02
203 Mike Roesler	.05	.02
204 Bob Dernier	.05	.02
205 Mark Davis	.05	.02
206 Nick Esasky	.05	.02
207 Bob Ojeda	.05	.02
208 Brook Jacoby	.05	.02
209 Greg Mathews	.05	.02
210 Ryne Sandberg	.40	.12
211 John Cerutti	.05	.02
212 Joe Orsulak	.05	.02
213 Scott Bankhead	.05	.02
214 Terry Francona	.10	.03
215 Kirk McCaskill	.05	.02
216 Ricky Jordan	.05	.02
217 Don Robinson	.05	.02
218 Wally Backman	.05	.02
219 Donn Pall	.05	.02
220 Barry Bonds	.60	.18
221 Gary Mielke	.05	.02
222 Kurt Stillwell UER (Graduate misspelled as gradute)	.05	.02
223 Tommy Gregg	.05	.02
224 Delino DeShields RC	.25	.07
225 Jim Deshaies	.05	.02
226 Mickey Hatcher	.05	.02
227 Kevin Tapani RC	.25	.07
228 Dave Martinez	.05	.02
229 David Wells	.10	.03
230 Keith Hernandez	.15	.04
231 Jack McKeon MG	.05	.02
232 Darnell Coles	.05	.02
233 Ken Hill	.10	.03
234 Mariano Duncan	.05	.02
235 Jeff Reardon	.10	.03
236 Hal Morris	.05	.02
237 Kevin Ritz	.05	.02
238 Felix Jose	.05	.02
239 Eric Show	.05	.02
240 Mark Grace	.15	.04
241 Mike Krukow	.05	.02
242 Fred Manrique	.05	.02
243 Barry Jones	.05	.02
244 Bill Schroeder	.05	.02
245 Roger Clemens	.50	.15
246 Jim Eisenreich	.05	.02
247 Jerry Reed	.05	.02
248 Dave Anderson	.05	.02
249 Mike (Texas) Smith	.05	.02
250 Jose Canseco	.25	.07
251 Jeff Blauser	.05	.02
252 Otis Nixon	.05	.02
253 Mark Portugal	.05	.02
254 Francisco Cabrera	.05	.02
255 Bobby Thigpen	.05	.02
256 Marvell Wynne	.05	.02
257 Jose DeLeon	.05	.02
258 Barry Lyons	.05	.02
259 Lance McCullers	.05	.02
260 Eric Davis	.10	.03
261 Whitey Herzog MG	.10	.03
262 Checklist 2	.05	.02
263 Mel Stottlemyre Jr.	.05	.02
264 Bryan Clutterbuck	.05	.02
265 Pete O'Brien	.05	.02
266 German Gonzalez	.05	.02
267 Mark Davidson	.05	.02
268 Rob Murphy	.05	.02
269 Dickie Thon	.05	.02
270 Dave Stewart	.10	.03
271 Chet Lemon	.05	.02
272 Bryan Harvey	.05	.02
273 Bobby Bonilla	.10	.03
274 Mauro Gozzo	.05	.02
275 Mickey Tettleton	.05	.02
276 Gary Thurman	.05	.02
277 Lenny Harris	.05	.02
278 Pascual Perez	.05	.02
279 Steve Buechele	.05	.02
280 Lou Whitaker	.10	.03
281 Kevin Bass	.05	.02
282 Derek Lilliquist	.05	.02
283 Joey Belle	.25	.07
284 Mark Gardner RC	.10	.03
285 Willie McGee	.10	.03
286 Lee Guetterman	.05	.02
287 Vance Law	.05	.02
288 Greg Briley	.05	.02
289 Norm Charlton	.05	.02
290 Robin Yount	.40	.12
291 Dave Johnson MG	.05	.02
292 Jim Gott	.05	.02
293 Mike Gallego	.05	.02
294 Craig McMurtry	.05	.02
295 Fred McGriff	.25	.07
296 Jeff Ballard	.05	.02
297 Tommy Herr	.05	.02
298 Dan Gladden	.05	.02
299 Adam Peterson	.05	.02
300 Bo Jackson	.25	.07
301 Don Aase	.05	.02
302 Marcus Lawton	.05	.02
303 Rick Cerone	.05	.02
304 Marty Clary	.05	.02
305 Eddie Murray	.25	.07
306 Tom Niedenfuer	.05	.02
307 Bip Roberts	.05	.02
308 Jose Guzman	.05	.02
309 Eric Yelding	.05	.02
310 Steve Bedrosian	.05	.02
311 Dwight Smith	.05	.02
312 Dan Quisenberry	.05	.02
313 Gus Polidor	.05	.02
314 Donald Harris FDP	.05	.02
315 Bruce Hurst	.05	.02
316 Carney Lansford	.10	.03
317 Mark Guthrie	.05	.02
318 Wallace Johnson	.05	.02
319 Dion James	.05	.02
320 Dave Stieb	.10	.03
321 Joe Morgan MG	.05	.02
322 Junior Ortiz	.05	.02
323 Willie Wilson	.05	.02
324 Pete Harnisch	.05	.02
325 Robby Thompson	.05	.02
326 Tom McCarthy	.05	.02
327 Ken Williams	.05	.02
328 Curt Young	.05	.02
329 Oddibe McDowell	.05	.02
330 Ron Darling	.05	.02
331 Juan Gonzalez RC	1.50	.45
332 Paul O'Neill	.15	.04
333 Bill Wegman	.05	.02
334 Johnny Ray	.05	.02
335 Andy Hawkins	.05	.02
336 Ken Griffey Jr.	.75	.23
337 Lloyd McClendon	.05	.02
338 Dennis Lamp	.05	.02
339 Dave Clark	.05	.02
340 Fernando Valenzuela	.10	.03
341 Tom Foley	.05	.02
342 Alex Trevino	.05	.02
343 Frank Tanana	.05	.02
344 George Canale	.05	.02
345 Harold Baines	.10	.03
346 Jim Presley	.05	.02
347 Junior Felix	.05	.02
348 Gary Wayne	.05	.02
349 Steve Finley	.10	.03
350 Bret Saberhagen	.10	.03
351 Roger Craig MG	.05	.02
352 Bryn Smith	.05	.02
353 Sandy Alomar Jr. (Not listed as Jr. on card front)	.10	.03
354 Stan Belinda RC	.10	.03
355 Marty Barrett	.05	.02
356 Randy Ready	.05	.02
357 Dave West	.05	.02
358 Andres Thomas	.05	.02
359 Jimmy Jones	.05	.02
360 Paul Molitor	.15	.04
361 Randy McCament	.05	.02
362 Damon Berryhill	.05	.02
363 Dan Petry	.05	.02
364 Rolando Roomes	.05	.02
365 Ozzie Guillen	.05	.02
366 Mike Heath	.05	.02
367 Mike Morgan	.05	.02
368 Bill Doran	.05	.02
369 Todd Burns	.05	.02
370 Tim Wallach	.05	.02
371 Jimmy Key	.10	.03
372 Terry Kennedy	.05	.02
373 Alvin Davis	.05	.02
374 Steve Cummings RC	.05	.02
375 Dwight Evans	.10	.03
376 Checklist 3 UER (Higuera misalphabetized in Brewer list)	.05	.02
377 Mickey Weston	.05	.02
378 Luis Salazar	.05	.02
379 Steve Rosenberg	.05	.02
380 Dave Winfield	.10	.03
381 Frank Robinson MG	.15	.04
382 Jeff Musselman	.05	.02
383 John Morris	.05	.02
384 Pat Combs	.05	.02
385 Fred McGriff AS	.10	.03
386 Julio Franco AS	.05	.02
387 Wade Boggs AS	.10	.03
388 Cal Ripken AS	.40	.12
389 Robin Yount AS	.25	.07
390 Ruben Sierra AS	.05	.02
391 Kirby Puckett AS	.15	.04
392 Carlton Fisk AS	.10	.03
393 Bret Saberhagen AS	.05	.02
394 Jeff Ballard AS	.05	.02
395 Jeff Russell AS	.05	.02
396 A.Bartlett Giamatti RC COMM MEM	.25	.07
397 Will Clark AS	.10	.03
398 Ryne Sandberg AS	.25	.07
399 Howard Johnson AS	.05	.02
400 Ozzie Smith AS	.25	.07
401 Kevin Mitchell AS	.05	.02
402 Eric Davis AS	.05	.02
403 Tony Gwynn AS	.15	.04
404 Craig Biggio AS	.10	.03
405 Mike Scott AS	.05	.02
406 Joe Magrane AS	.05	.02
407 Mark Davis AS	.05	.02
408 Trevor Wilson	.05	.02
409 Tom Brunansky	.05	.02
410 Joe Boever	.05	.02
411 Ken Phelps	.05	.02
412 Jamie Moyer	.10	.03
413 Brian DuBois	.05	.02
414A Frank Thomas FDP ERR (Name missing on card front)	400.00	120.00
414B F.Thomas COR RC	1.50	.45
415 Shawon Dunston	.05	.02
416 Dave Johnson (P)	.05	.02
417 Jim Gantner	.05	.02
418 Tom Browning	.05	.02
419 Beau Allred RC	.05	.02
420 Carlton Fisk	.15	.04
421 Greg Minton	.05	.02
422 Pat Sheridan	.05	.02
423 Fred Toliver	.05	.02
424 Jerry Reuss	.05	.02
425 Bill Landrum	.05	.02
426 Jeff Hamilton UER	.05	.02

(Stats say he fanned 197 times in 1987, but he only had 147 at bats)
427 Carmen Castillo .05 .02
428 Steve Davis .05 .02
429 Tom Kelly MG .05 .02
430 Pete Incaviglia .05 .02
431 Randy Johnson .40 .12
432 Damaso Garcia .05 .02
433 Steve Olin RC .25 .07
434 Mark Carreon .05 .02
435 Kevin Seitzer .05 .02
436 Mel Hall .05 .02
437 Les Lancaster .05 .02
438 Greg Myers .05 .02
439 Jeff Parrett .05 .02
440 Alan Trammell .15 .04
441 Bob Kipper .05 .02
442 Jerry Browne .05 .02
443 Cris Carpenter .05 .02
444 Kyle Abbott FDP .05 .02
445 Danny Jackson .05 .02
446 Dan Pasqua .05 .02
447 Atlee Hammaker .05 .02
448 Greg Gagne .05 .02
449 Dennis Rasmussen .05 .02
450 Rickey Henderson .25 .07
451 Mark Lemke .05 .02
452 Luis DeLosSantos .05 .02
453 Jody Davis .05 .02
454 Jeff King .05 .02
455 Jeffrey Leonard .05 .02
456 Chris Gwynn .05 .02
457 Gregg Jefferies .10 .03
458 Bob McClure .05 .02
459 Jim Lefebvre MG .05 .02
460 Mike Scott .05 .02
461 Carlos Martinez .05 .02
462 Denny Walling .05 .02
463 Drew Hall .05 .02
464 Jerome Walton .05 .02
465 Kevin Gross .05 .02
466 Rance Mulliniks .05 .02
467 Juan Nieves .05 .02
468 Bill Ripken .05 .02
469 John Kruk .10 .03
470 Frank Viola .05 .02
471 Mike Brumley .05 .02
472 Jose Uribe .05 .02
473 Joe Price .05 .02
474 Rich Thompson .05 .02
475 Bob Welch .05 .02
476 Brad Komminsk .05 .02
477 Willie Fraser .05 .02
478 Mike LaValliere .05 .02
479 Frank White .10 .03
480 Sid Fernandez .05 .02
481 Garry Templeton .05 .02
482 Steve Carter .05 .02
483 Alejandro Pena .05 .02
484 Mike Fitzgerald .05 .02
485 John Candelaria .05 .02
486 Jeff Treadway .05 .02
487 Steve Searcy .05 .02
488 Ken Oberkfell .05 .02
489 Nick Leyva MG .05 .02
490 Dan Plesac .05 .02
491 Dave Cochrane RC .05 .02
492 Ron Oester .05 .02
493 Jason Grimsley RC .10 .03
494 Terry Puhl .05 .02
495 Lee Smith .10 .03
496 Cecil Espy UER .05 .02
('88 stats have 3 SB's, should be 33)
497 Dave Schmidt .05 .02
498 Rick Schu .05 .02
499 Bill Long .05 .02
500 Kevin Mitchell .05 .02
501 Matt Young .05 .02
502 Mitch Webster .05 .02
503 Randy St.Claire .05 .02
504 Tom O'Malley .05 .02
505 Kelly Gruber .05 .02
506 Tom Glavine .15 .04
507 Gary Redus .05 .02
508 Terry Leach .05 .02
509 Tom Pagnozzi .05 .02
510 Dwight Gooden .15 .04
511 Clay Parker .05 .02
512 Gary Pettis .05 .02
513 Mark Eichhorn .05 .02
514 Andy Allanson .05 .02
515 Len Dykstra .10 .03
516 Tim Leary .05 .02
517 Roberto Alomar .25 .07
518 Bill Krueger .05 .02
519 Bucky Dent MG .05 .02
520 Mitch Williams .05 .02
521 Craig Worthington .05 .02
522 Mike Dunne .05 .02
523 Jay Bell .10 .03
524 Daryl Boston .05 .02
525 Wally Joyner .10 .03
526 Checklist 4 .05 .02
527 Ron Hassey .05 .02
528 Kevin Wickander UER .05 .02
(Monthly scoreboard strikeout total was 2.2, that was his innings pitched total)
529 Greg A. Harris .05 .02
530 Mark Langston .05 .02
531 Ken Caminiti .10 .03
532 Cecilio Guante .05 .02
533 Tim Jones .05 .02
534 Louie Meadows .05 .02
535 John Smoltz .25 .07
536 Bob Geren .05 .02
537 Mark Grant .05 .02
538 Bill Spiers UER .05 .02
(Photo actually George Canale)
539 Neal Heaton .05 .02
540 Danny Tartabull .05 .02
541 Pat Perry .05 .02
542 Darren Daulton .10 .03
543 Nelson Liriano .05 .02
544 Dennis Boyd .05 .02
545 Kevin McReynolds .05 .02
546 Kevin Hickey .05 .02
547 Jack Howell .05 .02
548 Pat Clements .05 .02
549 Don Zimmer MG .05 .02
550 Julio Franco .05 .02
551 Tim Crews .05 .02
552 Mike(Miss.) Smith .05 .02
553 Scott Scudder UER .05 .02
(Cedar Rap1ds)
554 Jay Buhner .10 .03
555 Jack Morris .10 .03
556 Gene Larkin .05 .02
557 Jeff Innis .05 .02
558 Rafael Ramirez .05 .02
559 Andy McGaffigan .05 .02
560 Steve Sax .05 .02
561 Ken Dayley .05 .02
562 Chad Kreuter .05 .02
563 Alex Sanchez .05 .02
564 T.Houston FDP RC .25 .07
565 Scott Fletcher .05 .02
566 Mark Knudson .05 .02
567 Ron Gant .10 .03
568 John Smiley .05 .02
569 Ivan Calderon .05 .02
570 Cal Ripken .75 .23
571 Brett Butler .10 .03
572 Greg W. Harris .05 .02
573 Danny Heep .05 .02
574 Bill Swift .05 .02
575 Lance Parrish .05 .02
576 Mike Dyer RC .05 .02
577 Charlie Hayes .05 .02
578 Joe Magrane .05 .02
579 Art Howe MG .05 .02
580 Joe Carter .10 .03
581 Ken Griffey Sr. .10 .03
582 Rick Honeycutt .05 .02
583 Bruce Benedict .05 .02
584 Phil Stephenson .05 .02
585 Kal Daniels .05 .02
586 Edwin Nunez .05 .02
587 Lance Johnson .05 .02
588 Rick Rhoden .05 .02
589 Mike Aldrete .05 .02
590 Ozzie Smith .40 .12
591 Todd Stottlemyre .10 .03
592 R.J. Reynolds .05 .02
593 Scott Bradley .05 .02
594 Luis Sojo .05 .02
595 Greg Swindell .05 .02
596 Jose DeJesus .05 .02
597 Chris Bosio .05 .02
598 Brady Anderson .10 .03
599 Frank Williams .05 .02
600 Darryl Strawberry .15 .04
601 Luis Rivera .05 .02
602 Scott Garrelts .05 .02
603 Tony Armas .05 .02
604 Ron Robinson .05 .02
605 Mike Scioscia .05 .02
606 Storm Davis .05 .02
607 Steve Jeltz .05 .02
608 Eric Anthony RC .10 .03
609 Sparky Anderson MG .10 .03
610 Pedro Guerrero .05 .02
611 Walt Terrell .05 .02
612 Dave Gallagher .05 .02
613 Jeff Pico .05 .02
614 Nelson Santovenia .05 .02
615 Rob Deer .05 .02
616 Brian Holman .05 .02
617 Geronimo Berroa .05 .02
618 Ed Whitson .05 .02
619 Rob Ducey .05 .02
620 Tony Castillo .05 .02
621 Melido Perez .05 .02
622 Sid Bream .05 .02
623 Jim Corsi .05 .02
624 Darrin Jackson .05 .02
625 Roger McDowell .05 .02
626 Bob Melvin .05 .02
627 Jose Rijo .05 .02
628 Candy Maldonado .05 .02
629 Eric Hetzel .05 .02
630 Gary Gaetti .10 .03
631 John Wetteland .25 .07
632 Scott Lusader .05 .02
633 Dennis Cook .05 .02
634 Luis Polonia .05 .02
635 Brian Downing .05 .02
636 Jesse Orosco .05 .02
637 Craig Reynolds .05 .02
638 Jeff Montgomery .10 .03
639 Tony LaRussa MG .10 .03
640 Rick Sutcliffe .10 .03
641 Doug Strange .05 .02
642 Jack Armstrong .05 .02
643 Alfredo Griffin .05 .02
644 Paul Assenmacher .05 .02
645 Jose Oquendo .05 .02
646 Checklist 5 .05 .02
647 Rex Hudler .05 .02
648 Jim Clancy .05 .02
649 Dan Murphy RC .10 .03
650 Mike Witt .05 .02
651 Rafael Santana .05 .02
652 Mike Boddicker .05 .02
653 John Moses .05 .02
654 Paul Coleman FDP RC .10 .03
655 Gregg Olson .10 .03
656 Mackey Sasser .05 .02
657 Terry Mulholland .05 .02
658 Donell Nixon .05 .02
659 Greg Cadaret .05 .02
660 Vince Coleman .05 .02
661 Dick Howser TBC'85 .05 .02
UER (Seaver's 300th on 7/11/85, should be 8/4/85)
662 Mike Schmidt TBC'80 .25 .07
663 Fred Lynn TBC'75 .05 .02
664 Johnny Bench TBC'70 .15 .04
665 Sandy Koufax TBC'65 .50 .15
666 Brian Fisher .05 .02
667 Curt Wilkerson .05 .02
668 Joe Oliver .05 .02
669 Tom Lasorda MG .25 .07
670 Dennis Eckersley .10 .03
671 Bob Boone .10 .03
672 Roy Smith .05 .02
673 Joey Meyer .05 .02
674 Spike Owen .05 .02
675 Jim Abbott .15 .04
676 Randy Kutcher .05 .02
677 Jay Tibbs .05 .02
678 Kirt Manwaring UER .05 .02
('88 Phoenix stats repeated)
679 Gary Ward .05 .02
680 Howard Johnson .05 .02
681 Mike Schooler .05 .02
682 Dann Bilardello .05 .02
683 Kenny Rogers .10 .03
684 Julio Machado .05 .02
685 Tony Fernandez .05 .02
686 Carmelo Martinez .05 .02
687 Tim Birtsas .05 .02
688 Milt Thompson .05 .02
689 Rich Yett .05 .02
690 Mark McGwire .60 .18
691 Chuck Cary .05 .02
692 Sammy Sosa RC 8.00 2.40
693 Calvin Schiraldi .05 .02
694 Mike Stanton RC .25 .07
695 Tom Henke .05 .02
696 B.J. Surhoff .10 .03
697 Mike Davis .05 .02
698 Omar Vizquel .25 .07
699 Jim Leyland MG .05 .02
700 Kirby Puckett .25 .07
701 Bernie Williams RC 1.00 .30
702 Tony Phillips .05 .02
703 Jeff Brantley .05 .02
704 Chip Hale .05 .02
705 Claudell Washington .05 .02
706 Geno Petralli .05 .02
707 Luis Aquino .05 .02
708 Larry Sheets .05 .02
709 Juan Berenguer .05 .02
710 Von Hayes .05 .02
711 Rick Aguilera .10 .03
712 Todd Benzinger .05 .02
713 Tim Drummond .05 .02
714 Marquis Grissom RC .25 .07
715 Greg Maddux .40 .12
716 Steve Balboni .05 .02
717 Ron Karkovice .05 .02
718 Gary Sheffield .25 .07
719 Wally Whitehurst .05 .02
720 Andres Galarraga .10 .03
721 Lee Mazzilli .05 .02
722 Felix Fermin .05 .02
723 Jeff D. Robinson .05 .02
724 Juan Bell .05 .02
725 Terry Pendleton .10 .03
726 Gene Nelson .05 .02
727 Pat Tabler .05 .02
728 Jim Acker .05 .02
729 Bobby Valentine MG .05 .02
730 Tony Gwynn .30 .09
731 Don Carman .05 .02
732 Ernest Riles .05 .02
733 John Dopson .05 .02
734 Kevin Elster .05 .02
735 Charlie Hough .10 .03
736 Rick Dempsey .05 .02
737 Chris Sabo .05 .02
738 Gene Harris .05 .02
739 Dale Sveum .05 .02
740 Jesse Barfield .05 .02
741 Steve Wilson .05 .02
742 Ernie Whitt .05 .02
743 Tom Candiotti .05 .02
744 Kelly Mann .05 .02
745 Hubie Brooks .05 .02
746 Dave Smith .05 .02
747 Randy Bush .05 .02
748 Doyle Alexander .05 .02
749 Mark Parent UER .05 .02
('87 BA .80, should be .080)
750 Dale Murphy .25 .07
751 Steve Lyons .05 .02
752 Tom Gordon .10 .03
753 Chris Speier .05 .02
754 Bob Walk .05 .02
755 Rafael Palmeiro .15 .04
756 Ken Howell .05 .02
757 Larry Walker RC 1.00 .30
758 Mark Thurmond .05 .02
759 Tom Trebelhorn MG .05 .02
760 Wade Boggs .15 .04
761 Mike Jackson .05 .02
762 Doug Dascenzo .05 .02
763 Dennis Martinez .10 .03
764 Tim Teufel .05 .02
765 Chili Davis .10 .03
766 Brian Meyer .05 .02
767 Tracy Jones .05 .02
768 Chuck Crim .05 .02
769 Greg Hibbard RC .10 .03
770 Cory Snyder .05 .02
771 Pete Smith .05 .02
772 Jeff Reed .05 .02
773 Dave Leiper .05 .02
774 Ben McDonald RC .25 .07
775 Andy Van Slyke .10 .03
776 Charlie Leibrandt .05 .02
777 Tim Laudner .05 .02
778 Mike Jeffcoat .05 .02
779 Lloyd Moseby .05 .02
780 Orel Hershiser .10 .03
781 Mario Diaz .05 .02
782 Jose Alvarez .05 .02
783 Checklist 6 .05 .02
784 Scott Bailes .05 .02
785 Jim Rice .10 .03
786 Eric King .05 .02
787 Rene Gonzales .05 .02
788 Frank DiPino .05 .02
789 John Wathan MG .05 .02
790 Gary Carter .15 .04
791 Alvaro Espinoza .05 .02
792 Gerald Perry .05 .02
XX George Bush PRES

1990 Topps Tiffany

For the seventh year, Topps issued through its hobby dealer network a special "Tiffany" set. These sets which parallel the regular cards consist of 792 standard-size cards. These cards were only issued in complete set form. Since the number of cards produced is similar to the 1989 issue, it is believed that approximately 15,000 of these sets were produced.

Nm-Mt Ex-Mt
COMP.FACT.SET (792) 200.00 60.00
*STARS: 6X TO 15X BASIC CARDS
*ROOKIES: 6X TO 15X BASIC CARDS

1990 Topps Batting Leaders

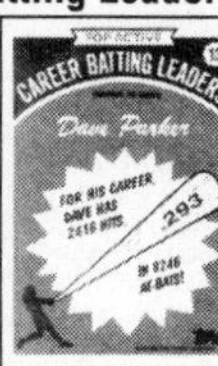

The 1990 Topps Batting Leaders set contains 22 standard-size cards. The front borders are emerald green, and the backs are white, blue and evergreen. This set, like the 1989 set of the same name, depicts the 22 major leaguers with the highest lifetime batting averages (minimum 765 games). The card numbers correspond to the player's rank in terms of career batting average. Many of the photos are the same as those from the 1989 set. The cards were distributed one per special 100-card Topps blister pack available only at K-Mart stores and were produced by Topps. The K-Mart logo does not appear anywhere on the cards themselves, although there is a Topps logo on the front and back of each card.

Nm-Mt Ex-Mt
COMPLETE SET (22) 100.00 30.00
1 Wade Boggs 10.00 3.00
2 Tony Gwynn 20.00 6.00
3 Kirby Puckett 10.00 3.00
4 Don Mattingly 20.00 6.00
5 George Brett 20.00 6.00
6 Pedro Guerrero .50 .15
7 Tim Raines 1.00 .30
8 Paul Molitor 8.00 2.40
9 Jim Rice 1.00 .30
10 Keith Hernandez 1.00 .30
11 Julio Franco 1.00 .30
12 Carney Lansford 1.00 .30
13 Dave Parker 1.00 .30
14 Willie McGee 1.00 .30
15 Robin Yount 8.00 2.40
16 Tony Fernandez 1.00 .30
17 Eddie Murray 8.00 2.40
18 Johnny Ray .50 .15
19 Lonnie Smith .50 .15
20 Phil Bradley .50 .15
21 Rickey Henderson 12.00 3.60
22 Kent Hrbek 1.00 .30

1990 Topps Glossy All-Stars

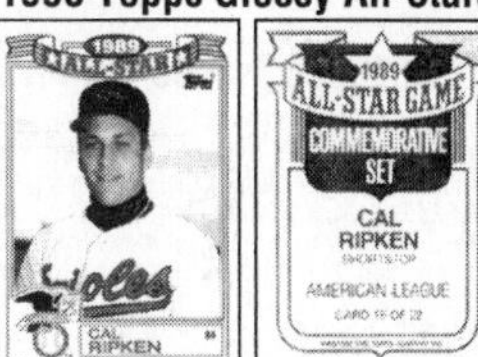

The 1990 Topps Glossy All-Star set contains 22 standard-size glossy cards. The front and back borders are white, and other design elements are red, blue and yellow. This set is almost identical to previous year sets of the same name. One card was included in each 1990 Topps rack pack. The players selected for the set were the starters, managers, and honorary captains in the previous year's All-Star Game.

Nm-Mt Ex-Mt
COMPLETE SET (22) 3.00 .90
1 Tom Lasorda MG .20 .06
2 Will Clark .20 .06
3 Ryne Sandberg .50 .15
4 Howard Johnson .05 .02
5 Ozzie Smith .60 .18
6 Kevin Mitchell .05 .02
7 Eric Davis .10 .03
8 Tony Gwynn .75 .23
9 Benito Santiago .10 .03
10 Rick Reuschel .05 .02
11 Don Drysdale CAPT .15 .04
12 Tony LaRussa MG .05 .02
13 Mark McGwire 1.25 .35
14 Julio Franco .10 .03
15 Wade Boggs .40 .12
16 Cal Ripken 1.50 .45
17 Bo Jackson .20 .06
18 Kirby Puckett .30 .09
19 Ruben Sierra .10 .03
20 Terry Steinbach .05 .02
21 Dave Stewart .10 .03
22 Carl Yastrzemski CAPT .20 .06

1990 Topps Glossy Send-Ins

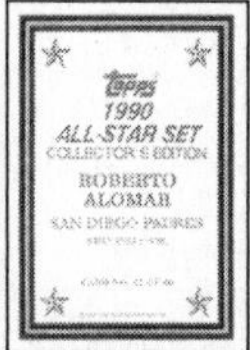

The 1990 Topps Glossy 60 set was issued as a mailaway by Topps for the eighth straight year. This standard-size, 60-card set features two young players among every ten players as Topps again broke down these cards into six series of ten cards each.

Nm-Mt Ex-Mt
COMPLETE SET (60) 12.00 3.60
1 Ryne Sandberg 1.50 .45
2 Nolan Ryan 5.00 1.50
3 Glenn Davis .10 .03
4 Dave Stewart .20 .06
5 Barry Larkin .40 .12
6 Carney Lansford .20 .06
7 Darryl Strawberry .20 .06
8 Steve Sax .10 .03
9 Carlos Martinez .10 .03
10 Gary Sheffield .50 .15
11 Don Mattingly 2.50 .75
12 Mark Grace 1.00 .30
13 Bret Saberhagen .20 .06
14 Mike Scott .10 .03
15 Robin Yount .50 .15
16 Ozzie Smith 1.50 .45
17 Jeff Ballard .10 .03
18 Rick Reuschel .10 .03
19 Greg Briley .10 .03
20 Ken Griffey Jr. 3.00 .90
21 Kevin Mitchell .10 .03
22 Wade Boggs .75 .23
23 Dwight Gooden .20 .06
24 George Bell .10 .03
25 Eric Davis .20 .06
26 Ruben Sierra .20 .06
27 Roberto Alomar .75 .23
28 Gary Gaetti .20 .06
29 Gregg Olson .10 .03
30 Tom Gordon .20 .06
31 Jose Canseco .75 .23
32 Pedro Guerrero .10 .03
33 Joe Carter .20 .06
34 Mike Scioscia .20 .06
35 Julio Franco .20 .06
36 Joe Magrane .10 .03
37 Rickey Henderson 1.00 .30
38 Tim Raines .20 .06
39 Jerome Walton .10 .03
40 Bob Geren .10 .03
41 Andre Dawson .40 .12
42 Mark McGwire 4.00 1.20
43 Howard Johnson .10 .03
44 Bo Jackson .40 .12
45 Shawon Dunston .10 .03
46 Carlton Fisk .50 .15
47 Mitch Williams .10 .03
48 Kirby Puckett .75 .23
49 Craig Worthington .10 .03
50 Jim Abbott .50 .15
51 Cal Ripken 5.00 1.50
52 Will Clark .40 .12
53 Dennis Eckersley .50 .15
54 Craig Biggio .30 .09
55 Fred McGriff .40 .12
56 Tony Gwynn 2.00 .60
57 Mickey Tettleton .20 .06
58 Mark Davis .10 .03
59 Omar Vizquel .40 .12
60 Gregg Jefferies .10 .03

1990 Topps Rookies

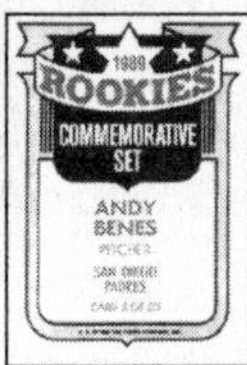

The 1990 Topps Jumbo Rookies set contains 33 standard-size glossy cards. The front and back borders are white, and other design elements are red, blue and yellow. This set is almost identical to previous year sets of the same name except that it contains 33 cards rather than only 22. One card was included in each 1990 Topps "jumbo" pack. The cards are numbered in alphabetical order. Sets of these cards were issued and stamped with various colors so Topps could test for colors of foil stamping.

Nm-Mt Ex-Mt
COMPLETE SET (33) 25.00 7.50
1 Jim Abbott .75 .23
2 Albert Belle 1.00 .30
3 Andy Benes .50 .15
4 Greg Briley .25 .07
5 Kevin Brown .50 .15
6 Mark Carreon .25 .07
7 Mike Devereaux .25 .07
8 Junior Felix .25 .07
9 Bob Geren .25 .07
10 Tom Gordon .50 .15
11 Ken Griffey Jr. 5.00 1.50
12 Pete Harnisch .25 .07
13 Greg W. Harris .25 .07
14 Greg Hibbard .25 .07
15 Ken Hill .25 .07
16 Gregg Jefferies .25 .07
17 Jeff King .25 .07
18 Derek Lilliquist .25 .07
19 Carlos Martinez .25 .07
20 Ramon Martinez .25 .07
21 Bob Milacki .25 .07
22 Gregg Olson .25 .07
23 Donn Pall .25 .07
24 Kenny Rogers .50 .15
25 Gary Sheffield 1.00 .30
26 Dwight Smith .25 .07
27 Billy Spiers .25 .07
28 Omar Vizquel 1.00 .30
29 Jerome Walton .25 .07
30 Dave West .25 .07
31 John Wetteland .50 .15
32 Steve Wilson .25 .07
33 Craig Worthington .25 .07

1990 Topps Wax Box Cards

The 1990 Topps wax box cards comprise four different box bottoms with four cards each, for a total of 16 standard-size cards. The front borders are green. The vertically oriented backs are yellowish green. These cards depict various career milestones achieved during the 1989 season. The card numbers are actually the letters A through P. The card ordering is alphabetical by player's name.

	Nm-Mt	Ex-Mt
COMPLETE SET (16)	8.00	2.40
A Wade Boggs	.50	.15
B George Brett	1.00	.30
C Andre Dawson	.40	.12
D Darrell Evans	.20	.06
E Dwight Gooden	.20	.06
F Rickey Henderson	.75	.23
G Tom Lasorda MG	.30	.09
H Fred Lynn	.10	.03
I Mark McGwire	2.00	.60
J Dave Parker	.20	.06
K Jeff Reardon	.20	.06
L Rick Reuschel	.10	.03
M Jim Rice	.20	.06
N Cal Ripken	2.50	.75
O Nolan Ryan	2.50	.75
P Ryne Sandberg	.50	.15

1990 Topps Traded

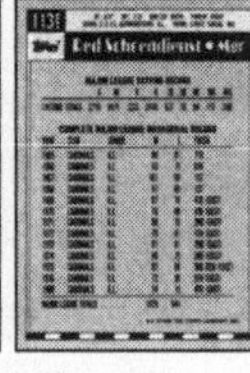

The 1990 Topps Traded Set was the tenth consecutive year Topps issued a 132-card standard-size set at the end of the year. For the first time, Topps not only issued the set in factory set form but also distributed (on a significant basis) the set via seven-card wax packs. Unlike the factory set cards (which feature the whiter paper stock typical of the previous years Traded sets), the wax pack cards feature gray paper stock. Gray and white stock cards are equally valued. This set was arranged alphabetically by player and includes a mix of traded players and rookies for whom Topps did not include a card in the regular set. The key Rookie Cards in this set are Travis Fryman, Todd Hundley and Dave Justice.

	Nm-Mt	Ex-Mt
COMPLETE SET (132)	3.00	.90
COMP.FACT.SET (132)	2.50	.75
1T Darrel Akerfelds	.05	.02
2T Sandy Alomar Jr.	.10	.03
3T Brad Arnsberg	.05	.02
4T Steve Avery	.05	.02
5T Wally Backman	.05	.02
6T Carlos Baerga RC	.25	.07
7T Kevin Bass	.05	.02
8T Willie Blair RC	.10	.03
9T Mike Blowers RC	.25	.07
10T Shawn Boskie RC	.10	.03
11T Daryl Boston	.05	.02
12T Dennis Boyd	.05	.02
13T Glenn Braggs	.05	.02
14T Hubie Brooks	.05	.02
15T Tom Brunansky	.05	.02
16T John Burkett	.05	.02
17T Casey Candaele	.05	.02
18T John Candelaria	.05	.02
19T Gary Carter	.15	.04
20T Joe Carter	.10	.03
21T Rick Cerone	.05	.02
22T Scott Coolbaugh	.05	.02
23T Bobby Cox MG	.10	.03
24T Mark Davis	.05	.02
25T Storm Davis	.05	.02
26T Edgar Diaz	.05	.02
27T Wayne Edwards	.05	.02
28T Mark Eichhorn	.05	.02
29T Scott Erickson RC	.25	.07
30T Nick Esasky	.05	.02
31T Cecil Fielder	.10	.03
32T John Franco	.10	.03
33T Travis Fryman RC	.40	.12
34T Bill Gullickson	.05	.02
35T Darryl Hamilton	.05	.02
36T Mike Harkey	.05	.02
37T Bud Harrelson MG	.05	.02
38T Billy Hatcher	.05	.02
39T Keith Hernandez	.15	.04
40T Joe Hesketh	.05	.02
41T Dave Hollins RC	.25	.07
42T Sam Horn	.05	.02
43T Steve Howard	.05	.02
44T Todd Hundley RC	.25	.07
45T Jeff Huson	.05	.02
46T Chris James	.05	.02
47T Stan Javier	.05	.02
48T Dave Justice RC	.50	.15
49T Jeff Kaiser	.05	.02
50T Dana Kiecker	.05	.02
51T Joe Klink	.05	.02
52T Brent Knackert RC	.10	.03
53T Brad Komminsk	.05	.02
54T Mark Langston	.05	.02
55T Tim Layana	.05	.02
56T Rick Leach	.05	.02
57T Terry Leach	.05	.02
58T Tim Leary	.05	.02
59T Craig Lefferts	.05	.02
60T Charlie Leibrandt	.05	.02
61T Jim Leyritz RC	.25	.07
62T Fred Lynn	.05	.02
63T Kevin Maas RC	.25	.07
64T Shane Mack	.05	.02
65T Candy Maldonado	.05	.02
66T Fred Manrique	.05	.02
67T Mike Marshall	.05	.02
68T Carmelo Martinez	.05	.02
69T John Marzano	.05	.02
70T Ben McDonald	.05	.02
71T Jack McDowell	.05	.02
72T John McNamara MG	.05	.02
73T Orlando Mercado	.05	.02
74T Stump Merrill MG	.05	.02
75T Alan Mills RC	.10	.03
76T Hal Morris	.05	.02
77T Lloyd Moseby	.05	.02
78T Randy Myers	.10	.03
79T Tim Naehring RC	.10	.03
80T Junior Noboa	.05	.02
81T Matt Nokes	.05	.02
82T Pete O'Brien	.05	.02
83T John Olerud RC	.50	.15
84T Greg Olson RC	.10	.03
85T Junior Ortiz	.05	.02
86T Dave Parker	.10	.03
87T Rick Parker	.05	.02
88T Bob Patterson	.05	.02
89T Alejandro Pena	.05	.02
90T Tony Pena	.05	.02
91T Pascual Perez	.05	.02
92T Gerald Perry	.05	.02
93T Dan Petry	.05	.02
94T Gary Pettis	.05	.02
95T Tony Phillips	.05	.02
96T Lou Piniella MG	.10	.03
97T Luis Polonia	.05	.02
98T Jim Presley	.05	.02
99T Scott Radinsky RC	.10	.03
100T Willie Randolph	.10	.03
101T Jeff Reardon	.10	.03
102T Greg Riddoch MG	.05	.02
103T Jeff Robinson	.05	.02
104T Ron Robinson	.05	.02
105T Kevin Romine	.05	.02
106T Scott Ruskin	.05	.02
107T John Russell	.05	.02
108T Bill Sampen	.05	.02
109T Juan Samuel	.05	.02
110T Scott Sanderson	.05	.02
111T Jack Savage	.05	.02
112T Dave Schmidt	.05	.02
113T R.Schoendienst MG	.25	.07
114T Terry Shumpert	.05	.02
115T Matt Sinatro	.05	.02
116T Don Slaught	.05	.02
117T Bryn Smith	.05	.02
118T Lee Smith	.10	.03
119T Paul Sorrento RC	.25	.07
120T Franklin Stubbs UER ('84 says '99 and has the same stats as '89, '83 stats are missing)	.05	.02
121T Russ Swan RC	.10	.03
122T Bob Tewksbury	.05	.02
123T Wayne Tolleson	.05	.02
124T John Tudor	.05	.02
125T Randy Veres	.05	.02
126T Hector Villanueva RC	.10	.03
127T Mitch Webster	.05	.02
128T Ernie Whitt	.05	.02
129T Frank Wills	.05	.02
130T Dave Winfield	.10	.03
131T Matt Young	.05	.02
132T Checklist 1T-132T	.05	.02

1990 Topps Traded Tiffany

Again, one of these sets were issued for each regular Tiffany set produced. These 132 standard-size cards parallel the regular Traded issue and feature Glossy fronts and clearer backs. These cards were issued in complete set form only and were distributed through Topps hobby network. Similar to the regular Topps Tiffany set, it is believed that 15,000 of these sets were produced.

	Nm-Mt	Ex-Mt
COMP.FACT.SET (132)	30.00	9.00
*STARS: 6X TO 15X BASIC CARDS		
*ROOKIES: 6X TO 15X BASIC CARDS		

1990 Topps Ames All-Stars

The 1990 Topps Ames All-Stars set was issued by Topps for the Ames department stores for the second straight year. This standard-size set featured 33 of the leading hitters active in major league baseball.

	Nm-Mt	Ex-Mt
COMP. FACT SET (33)	5.00	1.50
1 Dave Winfield	.40	.12
2 George Brett	.75	.23
3 Jim Rice	.10	.03
4 Dwight Evans	.10	.03
5 Robin Yount	.40	.12
6 Dave Parker	.10	.03
7 Eddie Murray	.40	.12
8 Keith Hernandez	.10	.03
9 Andre Dawson	.20	.06
10 Fred Lynn	.10	.03
11 Dale Murphy	.20	.06
12 Jack Clark	.10	.03
13 Rickey Henderson	.75	.23
14 Paul Molitor	.40	.12
15 Cal Ripken	2.00	.60
16 Wade Boggs	.50	.15
17 Tim Raines	.10	.03
18 Don Mattingly	1.00	.30
19 Kent Hrbek	.10	.03
20 Kirk Gibson	.10	.03
21 Julio Franco	.10	.03
22 George Bell	.10	.03
23 Darryl Strawberry	.10	.03
24 Kirby Puckett	.40	.12
25 Juan Samuel	.05	.02
26 Alvin Davis	.05	.02
27 Joe Carter	.10	.03
28 Eric Davis	.10	.03
29 Jose Canseco	.30	.09
30 Wally Joyner	.05	.02
31 Will Clark	.20	.06
32 Ruben Sierra	.10	.03
33 Danny Tartabull	.05	.02

1990 Topps Big

The 1990 Topps Big set contains 330 cards each measuring a slightly over-sized 2 5/8" by 3 3/4". In 1989 Topps had issued two oversize sets (Bigs and Bowmans), but in 1990 only the Topps Big were issued by Topps as an oversize set. The set was issued in three series of 110 cards. Some dealers believe the third series was distributed in far less quantity than the first two series. An early card of slugger Sammy Sosa was included in this set.

	Nm-Mt	Ex-Mt
COMPLETE SET (330)	25.00	7.50
1 Dwight Evans	.30	.09
2 Kirby Puckett	.75	.23
3 Kevin Gross	.20	.06
4 Ron Hassey	.20	.06
5 Lloyd McClendon	.20	.06
6 Bo Jackson	.75	.23
7 Lonnie Smith	.20	.06
8 Alvaro Espinoza	.20	.06
9 Roberto Alomar	.75	.23
10 Glenn Braggs	.20	.06
11 David Cone	.30	.09
12 Claudell Washington	.20	.06
13 Pedro Guerrero	.20	.06
14 Todd Benzinger	.20	.06
15 Jeff Russell	.20	.06
16 Terry Kennedy	.20	.06
17 Kelly Gruber	.20	.06
18 Alfredo Griffin	.20	.06
19 Mark Grace	.50	.15
20 Dave Winfield	.30	.09
21 Bret Saberhagen	.30	.09
22 Roger Clemens	1.50	.45
23 Bob Walk	.20	.06
24 Dave Magadan	.20	.06
25 Spike Owen	.20	.06
26 Jody Davis	.20	.06
27 Kent Hrbek	.30	.09
28 Mark McGwire	2.00	.60
29 Eddie Murray	.75	.23
30 Paul O'Neill	.50	.15
31 Jose DeLeon	.20	.06
32 Steve Lyons	.20	.06
33 Dan Plesac	.20	.06
34 Jack Howell	.20	.06
35 Greg Briley	.20	.06
36 Andy Hawkins	.20	.06
37 Cecil Espy	.20	.06
38 Rick Sutcliffe	.30	.09
39 Jack Clark	.30	.09
40 Dale Murphy	.75	.23
41 Mike Henneman	.20	.06
42 Rick Honeycutt	.20	.06
43 Willie Randolph	.30	.09
44 Marty Barrett	.20	.06
45 Willie Wilson	.20	.06
46 Wallace Johnson	.20	.06
47 Greg Brock	.20	.06
48 Tom Browning	.20	.06
49 Gerald Young	.20	.06
50 Dennis Eckersley	.30	.09
51 Scott Garrelts	.20	.06
52 Gary Redus	.20	.06
53 Al Newman	.20	.06
54 Daryl Boston	.20	.06
55 Ron Oester	.20	.06
56 Danny Tartabull	.20	.06
57 Gregg Jefferies	.30	.09
58 Tom Foley	.20	.06
59 Robin Yount	1.25	.35
60 Pat Borders	.20	.06
61 Mike Greenwell	.20	.06
62 Shawon Dunston	.20	.06
63 Steve Buechele	.20	.06
64 Dave Stewart	.30	.09
65 Jose Oquendo	.20	.06
66 Ron Gant	.30	.09
67 Mike Scioscia	.20	.06
68 Randy Velarde	.20	.06
69 Von Hayes	.20	.06
70 Tim Wallach	.20	.06
71 Eric Show	.20	.06
72 Eric Davis	.30	.09
73 Mike Gallego	.20	.06
74 Rob Deer	.20	.06
75 Ryne Sandberg	1.25	.35
76 Kevin Seitzer	.20	.06
77 Wade Boggs	.50	.15
78 Greg Gagne	.20	.06
79 John Smiley	.20	.06
80 Ivan Calderon	.20	.06
81 Pete Incaviglia	.20	.06
82 Orel Hershiser	.30	.09
83 Carney Lansford	.30	.09
84 Mike Fitzgerald	.20	.06
85 Don Mattingly	2.00	.60
86 Chet Lemon	.20	.06
87 Rolando Roomes	.20	.06
88 Billy Spiers	.20	.06
89 Pat Tabler	.20	.06
90 Danny Heep	.20	.06
91 Andre Dawson	.30	.09
92 Randy Bush	.20	.06
93 Tony Gwynn	1.00	.30
94 Tom Brunansky	.20	.06
95 Johnny Ray	.20	.06
96 Matt Williams	.30	.09
97 Barry Lyons	.20	.06
98 Jeff Hamilton	.20	.06
99 Tom Glavine	.50	.15
100 Ken Griffey Sr.	.30	.09
101 Tom Henke	.20	.06
102 Dave Righetti	.20	.06
103 Paul Molitor	.50	.15
104 Mike LaValliere	.20	.06
105 Frank White	.30	.09
106 Bob Welch	.20	.06
107 Ellis Burks	.50	.15
108 Andres Galarraga	.30	.09
109 Mitch Williams	.20	.06
110 Checklist 1-110	.20	.06
111 Craig Biggio	.50	.15
112 Dave Stieb	.30	.09
113 Ron Darling	.20	.06
114 Bert Blyleven	.30	.09
115 Dickie Thon	.20	.06
116 Carlos Martinez	.20	.06
117 Jeff King	.20	.06
118 Terry Steinbach	.20	.06
119 Frank Tanana	.20	.06
120 Mark Lemke	.20	.06
121 Chris Sabo	.20	.06
122 Glenn Davis	.20	.06
123 Mel Hall	.20	.06
124 Jim Gantner	.20	.06
125 Benito Santiago	.30	.09
126 Milt Thompson	.20	.06
127 Rafael Palmeiro	.50	.15
128 Barry Bonds	2.00	.60
129 Mike Bielecki	.20	.06
130 Lou Whitaker	.30	.09
131 Bob Ojeda	.20	.06
132 Dion James	.20	.06
133 Dennis Martinez	.30	.09
134 Fred McGriff	.75	.23
135 Terry Pendleton	.30	.09
136 Pat Combs	.20	.06
137 Kevin Mitchell	.20	.06
138 Marquis Grissom	.75	.23
139 Chris Bosio	.20	.06
140 Omar Vizquel	.75	.23
141 Steve Sax	.20	.06
142 Nelson Liriano	.20	.06
143 Kevin Elster	.20	.06
144 Dan Pasqua	.20	.06
145 Dave Smith	.20	.06
146 Craig Worthington	.20	.06
147 Dan Gladden	.20	.06
148 Oddibe McDowell	.20	.06
149 Bip Roberts	.20	.06
150 Randy Ready	.20	.06
151 Dwight Smith	.20	.06
152 Eddie Whitson	.20	.06
153 George Bell	.20	.06
154 Tim Raines	.30	.09
155 Sid Fernandez	.20	.06
156 Henry Cotto	.20	.06
157 Harold Baines	.30	.09
158 Willie McGee	.30	.09
159 Bill Doran	.20	.06
160 Steve Balboni	.20	.06
161 Pete Smith	.20	.06
162 Frank Viola	.20	.06
163 Gary Sheffield	.75	.23
164 Bill Landrum	.20	.06
165 Tony Fernandez	.20	.06
166 Mike Heath	.20	.06
167 Jody Reed	.20	.06
168 Wally Joyner	.30	.09
169 Robby Thompson	.20	.06
170 Ken Caminiti	.30	.09
171 Nolan Ryan	3.00	.90
172 Ricky Jordan	.20	.06
173 Lance Blankenship	.20	.06
174 Dwight Gooden	.50	.15
175 Ruben Sierra	.20	.06
176 Carlton Fisk	.50	.15
177 Garry Templeton	.20	.06
178 Mike Devereaux	.20	.06
179 Mookie Wilson	.30	.09
180 Jeff Blauser	.20	.06
181 Scott Bradley	.20	.06
182 Luis Salazar	.20	.06
183 Rafael Ramirez	.20	.06
184 Vince Coleman	.20	.06
185 Doug Drabek	.20	.06
186 Darryl Strawberry	.50	.15
187 Tim Burke	.20	.06
188 Jesse Barfield	.20	.06
189 Barry Larkin	.75	.23
190 Alan Trammell	.50	.15
191 Steve Lake	.20	.06
192 Derek Lilliquist	.20	.06
193 Don Robinson	.20	.06
194 Kevin McReynolds	.20	.06
195 Melido Perez	.20	.06
196 Jose Lind	.20	.06
197 Eric Anthony	.20	.06
198 B.J. Surhoff	.30	.09
199 John Olerud	1.00	.30
200 Mike Moore	.20	.06
201 Mark Gubicza	.20	.06
202 Phil Bradley	.20	.06
203 Ozzie Smith	1.25	.35
204 Greg Maddux	1.25	.35
205 Julio Franco	.20	.06
206 Tom Herr	.20	.06
207 Scott Fletcher	.20	.06
208 Bobby Bonilla	.30	.09
209 Bob Geren	.20	.06
210 Junior Felix	.20	.06
211 Dick Schofield	.20	.06
212 Jim Deshaies	.20	.06
213 Jose Uribe	.20	.06
214 John Kruk	.30	.09
215 Ozzie Guillen	.20	.06
216 Howard Johnson	.20	.06
217 Andy Van Slyke	.30	.09
218 Tim Laudner	.20	.06
219 Manny Lee	.20	.06
220 Checklist 111-220	.20	.06
221 Cory Snyder	.20	.06
222 Billy Hatcher	.20	.06
223 Bud Black	.20	.06
224 Will Clark	.75	.23
225 Kevin Tapani	.75	.23
226 Mike Pagliarulo	.20	.06
227 Dave Parker	.30	.09
228 Ben McDonald	.20	.06
229 Carlos Baerga	.30	.09
230 Roger McDowell	.20	.06
231 Delino DeShields	.75	.23
232 Mark Langston	.20	.06
233 Wally Backman	.20	.06
234 Jim Eisenreich	.20	.06
235 Mike Schooler	.20	.06
236 Kevin Bass	.20	.06
237 John Farrell	.20	.06
238 Kal Daniels	.20	.06
239 Tony Phillips	.20	.06
240 Todd Stottlemyre	.30	.09
241 Greg Olson	.20	.06
242 Charlie Hough	.30	.09
243 Mariano Duncan	.20	.06
244 Bill Ripken	.20	.06
245 Joe Carter	.30	.09
246 Tim Belcher	.20	.06
247 Roberto Kelly	.20	.06
248 Candy Maldonado	.20	.06
249 Mike Scott	.20	.06
250 Ken Griffey Jr.	3.00	.90
251 Nick Esasky	.20	.06
252 Tom Gordon	.30	.09
253 John Tudor	.20	.06
254 Gary Gaetti	.30	.09
255 Neal Heaton	.20	.06
256 Jerry Browne	.20	.06
257 Jose Rijo	.20	.06
258 Mike Boddicker	.20	.06
259 Brett Butler	.30	.09
260 Andy Benes	.30	.09
261 Kevin Brown	.30	.09
262 Hubie Brooks	.20	.06
263 Randy Milligan	.20	.06
264 John Franco	.30	.09
265 Sandy Alomar Jr.	.30	.09
266 Dave Valle	.20	.06
267 Jerome Walton	.20	.06
268 Bob Boone	.30	.09
269 Ken Howell	.20	.06
270 Jose Canseco	.75	.23
271 Joe Magrane	.20	.06
272 Brian DuBois	.20	.06
273 Carlos Quintana	.20	.06
274 Lance Johnson	.20	.06
275 Steve Bedrosian	.20	.06
276 Brook Jacoby	.20	.06
277 Fred Lynn UER (Pirates logo on card front)	.20	.06
278 Jeff Ballard	.20	.06
279 Otis Nixon	.20	.06
280 Chili Davis	.30	.09
281 Joe Oliver	.20	.06
282 Brian Holman	.20	.06
283 Juan Samuel	.20	.06
284 Rick Aguilera	.30	.09
285 Jeff Reardon	.30	.09
286 Sammy Sosa	10.00	3.00
287 Carmelo Martinez	.20	.06
288 Greg Swindell	.20	.06
289 Erik Hanson	.20	.06
290 Tony Pena	.20	.06
291 Pascual Perez	.20	.06
292 Rickey Henderson	.75	.23
293 Kurt Stillwell	.20	.06
294 Todd Zeile	.30	.09
295 Bobby Thigpen	.20	.06
296 Larry Walker	1.50	.45
297 Rob Murphy	.20	.06
298 Mitch Webster	.20	.06
299 Devon White	.20	.06
300 Len Dykstra	.30	.09
301 Keith Hernandez	.50	.15
302 Gene Larkin	.20	.06
303 Jeffrey Leonard	.20	.06
304 Jim Presley	.20	.06
305 Lloyd Moseby	.20	.06
306 John Smoltz	.75	.23
307 Sam Horn	.20	.06
308 Greg Litton	.20	.06
309 Dave Henderson	.20	.06
310 Mark McLemore	.20	.06
311 Gary Pettis	.20	.06
312 Mark Davis	.20	.06
313 Cecil Fielder	.30	.09
314 Jack Armstrong	.20	.06
315 Alvin Davis	.20	.06
316 Doug Jones	.20	.06
317 Eric Yelding	.20	.06
318 Joe Orsulak	.20	.06
319 Chuck Finley	.30	.09
320 Glenn Wilson	.20	.06
321 Harold Reynolds	.30	.09
322 Teddy Higuera	.20	.06
323 Lance Parrish	.20	.06
324 Bruce Hurst	.20	.06
325 Dave West	.20	.06
326 Kirk Gibson	.30	.09
327 Cal Ripken	2.50	.75
328 Rick Reuschel	.20	.06
329 Jim Abbott	.50	.15
330 Checklist 221-330	.20	.06

1990 Topps Debut '89

The 1990 Topps Major League Debut Set is a 152-card, standard-size set arranged in alphabetical order by player's name. Each card front features the date of the player's first major league appearance. Strangely enough, even though the set commemorates the 1989 Major League debuts, the set was not issued until the 1990 season had almost begun. Key cards in this set include Joey (Albert) Belle,

Juan Gonzalez, Ken Griffey, Jr., David Justice, Deion Sanders and Sammy Sosa (pictured as a member of the Texas Rangers).

	Nm-Mt	Ex-Mt
COMP.FACT.SET (152)	20.00	6.00
1 Jim Abbott	.50	.15
2 Beau Allred	.15	.04
3 Wilson Alvarez	.25	.07
4 Kent Anderson	.15	.04
5 Eric Anthony	.15	.04
6 Kevin Appier	.75	.23
7 Larry Arndt	.15	.04
8 John Barfield	.15	.04
9 Billy Bates	.15	.04
10 Kevin Batiste	.15	.04
11 Blaine Beatty	.15	.04
12 Stan Belinda	.15	.04
13 Juan Bell	.15	.04
14 Joey Belle (Now known as Albert)	.75	.23
15 Andy Benes	.25	.07
16 Mike Benjamin	.15	.04
17 Geronimo Berroa	.15	.04
18 Mike Blowers	.25	.07
19 Brian Brady	.15	.04
20 Francisco Cabrera	.15	.04
21 George Canale	.15	.04
22 Jose Cano	.15	.04
23 Steve Carter	.15	.04
24 Pat Combs	.15	.04
25 Scott Coolbaugh	.15	.04
26 Steve Cummings	.15	.04
27 Pete Dalena	.15	.04
28 Jeff Datz	.15	.04
29 Bobby Davidson	.15	.04
30 Drew Denson	.15	.04
31 Gary DiSarcina	.25	.07
32 Brian DuBois	.15	.04
33 Mike Dyer	.15	.04
34 Wayne Edwards	.15	.04
35 Junior Felix	.15	.04
36 Mike Fetters	.15	.04
37 Steve Finley	.50	.15
38 Darrin Fletcher	.25	.07
39 LaVel Freeman	.15	.04
40 Steve Frey	.15	.04
41 Mark Gardner	.15	.04
42 Joe Girardi	.25	.07
43 Juan Gonzalez	2.50	.75
44 Goose Gozzo	.15	.04
45 Tommy Greene	.15	.04
46 Ken Griffey Jr.	5.00	1.50
47 Jason Grimsley	.15	.04
48 Marquis Grissom	.75	.23
49 Mark Guthrie	.15	.04
50 Chip Hale	.15	.04
51 Jack Hardy	.15	.04
52 Gene Harris	.15	.04
53 Mike Hartley	.15	.04
54 Scott Hemond	.15	.04
55 Xavier Hernandez	.15	.04
56 Eric Hetzel	.15	.04
57 Greg Hibbard	.15	.04
58 Mark Higgins	.15	.04
59 Glenallen Hill	.15	.04
60 Chris Hoiles	.25	.07
61 Shawn Holman	.15	.04
62 Dann Howitt	.15	.04
63 Mike Huff	.15	.04
64 Terry Jorgensen	.15	.04
65 David Justice	1.00	.30
66 Jeff King	.15	.04
67 Matt Kinzer	.15	.04
68 Joe Kraemer	.15	.04
69 Marcus Lawton	.15	.04
70 Derek Lilliquist	.15	.04
71 Scott Little	.15	.04
72 Greg Litton	.15	.04
73 Rick Luecken	.15	.04
74 Julio Machado	.15	.04
75 Tom Magrann	.15	.04
76 Kelly Mann	.15	.04
77 Randy McCament	.15	.04
78 Ben McDonald	.15	.04
79 Chuck McElroy	.15	.04
80 Jeff McKnight	.15	.04
81 Kent Mercker	.15	.04
82 Matt Merullo	.15	.04
83 Hensley Meulens	.15	.04
84 Kevin Mmahat	.15	.04
85 Mike Munoz	.15	.04
86 Dan Murphy	.15	.04
87 Jaime Navarro	.15	.04
88 Randy Nosek	.15	.04
89 John Olerud	1.00	.30
90 Steve Olin	.25	.07
91 Joe Oliver	.15	.04
92 Francisco Oliveras	.15	.04
93 Gregg Olson	.25	.07
94 John Orton	.15	.04
95 Dean Palmer	.50	.15
96 Ramon Pena	.15	.04
97 Jeff Peterek	.15	.04
98 Marty Pevey	.15	.04
99 Rusty Richards	.15	.04
100 Jeff Richardson	.15	.04
101 Rob Richie	.15	.04
102 Kevin Ritz	.15	.04
103 Rosario Rodriguez	.15	.04
104 Mike Roesler	.15	.04
105 Kenny Rogers	.25	.07
106 Bobby Rose	.15	.04
107 Alex Sanchez	.15	.04
108 Deion Sanders	.75	.23
109 Jeff Schaefer	.15	.04
110 Jeff Schulz	.15	.04
111 Mike Schwabe	.15	.04
112 Dick Scott	.15	.04
113 Scott Scudder	.15	.04
114 Rudy Seanez	.15	.04
115 Joe Skalski	.15	.04
116 Dwight Smith	.15	.04
117 Greg Smith	.15	.04
118 Mike Smith	.15	.04
119 Paul Sorrento	.25	.07
120 Sammy Sosa	10.00	3.00
121 Billy Spiers	.15	.04
122 Mike Stanton	.15	.04
123 Phil Stephenson	.15	.04
124 Doug Strange	.15	.04
125 Russ Swan	.15	.04
126 Kevin Tapani	.25	.07
127 Stu Tate	.15	.04
128 Greg Vaughn	.25	.07
129 Robin Ventura	.75	.23
130 Randy Veres	.15	.04
131 Jose Vizcaino	.25	.07
132 Omar Vizquel	.75	.23
133 Larry Walker	1.50	.45
134 Jerome Walton	.15	.04
135 Gary Wayne	.15	.04
136 Lenny Webster	.15	.04
137 Mickey Weston	.15	.04
138 Jeff Wetherby	.15	.04
139 John Wetteland	.50	.15
140 Ed Whited	.15	.04
141 Wally Whitehurst	.15	.04
142 Kevin Wickander	.15	.04
143 Dean Wilkins	.15	.04
144 Dana Williams	.15	.04
145 Paul Wilmet	.15	.04
146 Craig Wilson	.15	.04
147 Matt Winters	.15	.04
148 Eric Yelding	.15	.04
149 Clint Zavaras	.15	.04
150 Todd Zeile	.50	.15
151 Checklist Card	.15	.04
152 Checklist Card	.15	.04

1990 Topps Doubleheaders

The 1990 Topps Double Headers set consists of 72 collectibles. Each Double Header consists of a clear plastic holder that contains a mini-reproduction of the player's 1990 card on one side and a mini-reproduction of his rookie card on the other side. The Double Headers were packaged in a paper pouch to conceal the player's identity prior to purchase. Three different checklists (A, B, and C) are printed on the outside of the packs, with the players listed in alphabetical order, and the double headers are checklisted below in alphabetical order.

	Nm-Mt	Ex-Mt
COMPLETE SET (72)	25.00	7.50
1 Jim Abbott	.50	.15
2 Jeff Ballard	.25	.07
3 George Bell	.25	.07
4 Wade Boggs	2.00	.60
5 Barry Bonds	4.00	1.20
6 Bobby Bonilla	.25	.07
7 Ellis Burks	.50	.15
8 Jose Canseco	1.25	.35
9 Joe Carter	.50	.15
10 Will Clark	1.50	.45
11 Roger Clemens	4.00	1.20
12 Vince Coleman	.25	.07
13 Alvin Davis	.25	.07
14 Eric Davis	.50	.15
15 Glenn Davis	.25	.07
16 Mark Davis	.25	.07
17 Andre Dawson	1.00	.30
18 Shawon Dunston	.25	.07
19 Dennis Eckersley	1.50	.45
20 Sid Fernandez	.25	.07
21 Tony Fernandez	.50	.15
22 Chuck Finley	.25	.07
23 Carlton Fisk	1.50	.45
24 Julio Franco	.50	.15
25 Gary Gaetti	.50	.15
26 Doc Gooden	.50	.15
27 Mark Grace	1.00	.30
28 Mike Greenwell	.25	.07
29 Ken Griffey Jr.	5.00	1.50
30 Pedro Guerrero	.25	.07
31 Tony Gwynn	4.00	1.20
32 Von Hayes	.25	.07
33 Rickey Henderson	3.00	.90
34 Orel Hershiser	.50	.15
35 Bo Jackson	1.00	.30
36 Gregg Jefferies	.25	.07
37 Howard Johnson	.25	.07
38 Ricky Jordan	.25	.07
39 Carney Lansford	.25	.07
40 Barry Larkin	1.50	.45
41 Greg Maddux	5.00	1.50
42 Joe Magrane	.25	.07
43 Don Mattingly	4.00	1.20
44 Fred McGriff	1.00	.30
45 Mark McGwire	6.00	1.80
46 Kevin McReynolds	.25	.07
47 Kevin Mitchell	.25	.07
48 Gregg Olson	.25	.07
49 Kirby Puckett	2.00	.60
50 Rock Raines	.50	.15
51 Harold Reynolds	.50	.15
52 Cal Ripken	8.00	2.40
53 Nolan Ryan	8.00	2.40
54 Bret Saberhagen	.25	.07
55 Ryne Sandberg	3.00	.90
56 Benny Santiago	.50	.15
57 Steve Sax	.25	.07
58 Mike Scioscia	.50	.15
59 Mike Scott	.25	.07
60 Ruben Sierra	.50	.15
61 Lonnie Smith	.25	.07
62 Ozzie Smith	3.00	.90
63 Dave Stewart	.25	.07
64 Darryl Strawberry	.50	.15
65 Greg Swindell	.25	.07
66 Alan Trammell	.75	.23
67 Frank Viola	.25	.07
68 Tim Wallach	.25	.07
69 Jerome Walton	.25	.07
70 Lou Whitaker	.50	.15
71 Mitch Williams	.25	.07
72 Robin Yount	2.00	.60

1990 Topps Gallery of Champions

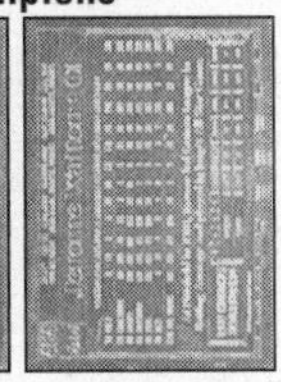

This would be the seventh out of eight consecutive seasons that Topps issued small "metal" versions of some leading players' from their regular issue set. These 12 cards, issued in complete set form only, feature league leaders and award winners. The cards measure approximately 1 1/4" by 1 3/4" and were produced in aluminum, bronze and silver versions. We have valued the aluminum cards, the bronze cards are valued at 2X to 5X the values of the aluminum versions while the silvers are 7X to 15X the aluminums. We have sequenced this set in alphabetical order.

	Nm-Mt	Ex-Mt
COMPLETE SET (12)	125.00	38.00
1 Mark Davis	5.00	1.50
2 Jose DeLeon	5.00	1.50
3 Tony Gwynn	30.00	9.00
4 Fred McGriff	12.00	3.60
5 Kevin Mitchell	5.00	1.50
6 Gregg Olson	5.00	1.50
7 Kirby Puckett	15.00	4.50
8 Jeff Russell	5.00	1.50
9 Nolan Ryan	50.00	15.00
10 Bret Saberhagen	5.00	1.50
11 Jerome Walton	5.00	1.50
12 Robin Yount	15.00	4.50

1990 Topps Heads Up

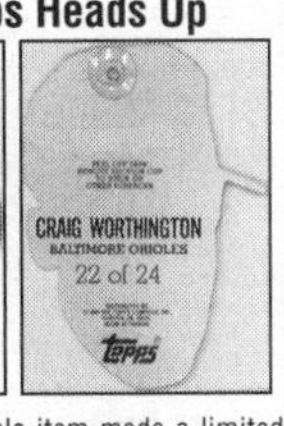

Though this collectible item made a limited appearance in 1989, the 1990 Topps set features 24 different Heads-Up pin-ups. Each item is a die-cut pin-up of a baseball star printed on thick white board, with a suction cup attached to the back. The die-cuts follow the contours of the player's hat and head, and they can be attached to any flat surface. The player's name and number appear on the back. The pin-ups are listed below according to the checklist printed on the back of each wrapper.

	Nm-Mt	Ex-Mt
COMPLETE SET (24)	10.00	3.00
1 Tony Gwynn	1.50	.45
2 Will Clark	.50	.15
3 Doc Gooden	.20	.06
4 Dennis Eckersley	.60	.18
5 Ken Griffey Jr.	2.00	.60
6 Craig Biggio	.30	.09
7 Bret Saberhagen	.10	.03
8 Bo Jackson	.50	.15
9 Ryne Sandberg	.75	.23
10 Gregg Olson	.10	.03
11 John Franco	.20	.06
12 Rafael Palmeiro	.60	.18
13 Gary Sheffield	.60	.18
14 Mark McGwire	2.50	.75
15 Kevin Mitchell	.10	.03
16 Jim Abbott	.20	.06
17 Harold Reynolds	.20	.06
18 Jose Canseco	.50	.15
19 Don Mattingly	1.50	.45
20 Kirby Puckett	.50	.15
21 Tom Gordon	.20	.06
22 Craig Worthington	.10	.03
23 Dwight Smith	.10	.03
24 Jerome Walton	.10	.03

1990 Topps Hills Hit Men

The 1990 Topps Hit Men set is a standard-size 33-card set arranged in order of slugging percentage. The set was produced by Topps for Hills Department stores. Each card in the set has a glossy-coated front.

	Nm-Mt	Ex-Mt
COMP. FACT SET (33)	5.00	1.50
1 Eric Davis	.10	.03
2 Will Clark	.40	.12
3 Don Mattingly	1.00	.30
4 Darryl Strawberry	.10	.03
5 Kevin Mitchell	.05	.02
6 Pedro Guerrero	.05	.02
7 Jose Canseco	.30	.09
8 Jim Rice	.10	.03
9 Danny Tartabull	.05	.02
10 George Brett	1.00	.30
11 Kent Hrbek	.10	.03
12 George Bell	.05	.02
13 Eddie Murray	.40	.12
14 Fred Lynn	.05	.02
15 Andre Dawson	.25	.07
16 Dale Murphy	.25	.07
17 Dave Winfield	.40	.12
18 Jack Clark	.10	.03
19 Wade Boggs	.50	.15
20 Ruben Sierra	.10	.03
21 Dave Parker	.10	.03
22 Glenn Davis	.05	.02
23 Dwight Evans	.10	.03
24 Jesse Barfield	.05	.02
25 Kirk Gibson	.10	.03
26 Alvin Davis	.05	.02
27 Kirby Puckett	.40	.12
28 Joe Carter	.10	.03
29 Carlton Fisk	.40	.12
30 Harold Baines	.15	.04
31 Andres Galarraga	.25	.07
32 Cal Ripken	2.00	.60
33 Howard Johnson	.05	.02

1990 Topps Mini Leaders

The 1990 Topps League Leader Minis is an 88-card set with cards measuring approximately 2 1/8" by 3". The set features players who finished 1989 in the top five in any major hitting or pitching category. This set marked the fifth year that Topps issued their Mini set. The card numbering is alphabetical by player within team and the teams themselves are ordered alphabetically.

	Nm-Mt	Ex-Mt
COMPLETE SET (88)	6.00	1.80
1 Jeff Ballard	.05	.02
2 Phil Bradley	.05	.02
3 Wade Boggs	.50	.15
4 Roger Clemens	1.00	.30
5 Nick Esasky	.05	.02
6 Jody Reed	.05	.02
7 Bert Blyleven	.10	.03
8 Chuck Finley	.10	.03
9 Kirk McCaskill	.05	.02
10 Devon White	.05	.02
11 Ivan Calderon	.05	.02
12 Bobby Thigpen	.05	.02
13 Joe Carter	.10	.03
14 Gary Pettis	.05	.02
15 Tom Gordon	.05	.02
16 Bo Jackson	.25	.07
17 Bret Saberhagen	.10	.03
18 Kevin Seitzer	.05	.02
19 Chris Bosio	.05	.02
20 Paul Molitor	.50	.15
21 Dan Plesac	.05	.02
22 Robin Yount	.40	.12
23 Kirby Puckett	.40	.12
24 Don Mattingly	1.00	.30
25 Steve Sax	.05	.02
26 Storm Davis	.05	.02
27 Dennis Eckersley	.40	.12
28 Rickey Henderson	.60	.18
29 Carney Lansford	.05	.02
30 Mark McGwire	1.50	.45
31 Mike Moore	.05	.02
32 Dave Stewart	.10	.03
33 Alvin Davis	.05	.02
34 Harold Reynolds	.10	.03
35 Mike Schooler	.05	.02
36 Cecil Espy	.05	.02
37 Julio Franco	.10	.03
38 Jeff Russell	.05	.02
39 Nolan Ryan	2.00	.60
40 Ruben Sierra	.10	.03
41 George Bell	.05	.02
42 Tony Fernandez	.10	.03
43 Fred McGriff	.25	.07
44 Dave Stieb	.05	.02
45 Checklist Card	.05	.02
46 Lonnie Smith	.05	.02
47 John Smoltz	.25	.07
48 Mike Bielecki	.05	.02
49 Mark Grace	.50	.15
50 Greg Maddux	1.25	.35
51 Ryne Sandberg	.75	.23
52 Mitch Williams	.05	.02
53 Eric Davis	.10	.03
54 John Franco	.10	.03
55 Glenn Davis	.05	.02
56 Mike Scott	.05	.02
57 Tim Belcher	.05	.02
58 Orel Hershiser	.10	.03
59 Jay Howell	.05	.02
60 Eddie Murray	.50	.15
61 Tim Burke	.05	.02
62 Mark Langston	.05	.02
63 Tim Raines	.10	.03
64 Tim Wallach	.05	.02
65 David Cone	.25	.07
66 Sid Fernandez	.05	.02
67 Howard Johnson	.05	.02
68 Juan Samuel	.05	.02
69 Von Hayes	.05	.02
70 Barry Bonds	1.00	.30
71 Bobby Bonilla	.10	.03
72 Andy Van Slyke	.05	.02
73 Vince Coleman	.05	.02
74 Jose DeLeon	.05	.02
75 Pedro Guerrero	.05	.02
76 Joe Magrane	.05	.02
77 Roberto Alomar	.50	.15
78 Jack Clark	.10	.03
79 Mark Davis	.05	.02
80 Tony Gwynn	1.00	.30
81 Bruce Hurst	.05	.02
82 Eddie Whitson	.05	.02
83 Brett Butler	.10	.03
84 Will Clark	.25	.07
85 Scott Garrelts	.05	.02
86 Kevin Mitchell	.05	.02
87 Rick Reuschel	.05	.02
88 Robby Thompson	.05	.02

1990 Topps Mylar Stickers Test

These six standard-size stickers represent Topps attempt to change their sticker format from the smaller size used throughout the 1980's to a larger item. The test, obviously, did not work as these were never issued as a full set. These stickers are in the same design as the regular 1990 Topps set. As the stickers are unnumbered we have sequenced them in alphabetical order.

	Nm-Mt	Ex-Mt
COMPLETE SET (6)	80.00	24.00
1 Joe Carter	20.00	6.00
2 Shane Mack	10.00	3.00
3 Alan Mills	10.00	3.00
4 Alejandro Pena	10.00	3.00
5 Gerald Perry	10.00	3.00
6 Dave Winfield	40.00	12.00

1990 Topps Sticker Backs

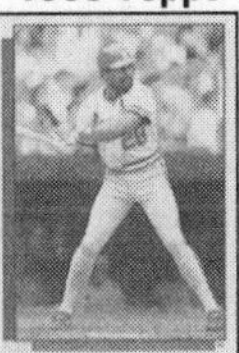

These cards were actually the backs of the 1990 Topps Stickers. The white-bordered cards measure approximately 2 1/8" by 3" and have colored backgrounds behind the cut-out color player action shots. The player's name and position appear in colored lettering within the upper white margin. Cards of AL players have red backgrounds and blue lettering; NL players have blue backgrounds and red lettering. Player biography and statistics appear within a yellowish panel near the bottom of the photo. The cards are numbered at the lower left.

	Nm-Mt	Ex-Mt
COMPLETE SET (67)	15.00	4.50
1 Will Clark	.25	.07
2 Glenn Davis	.05	.02
3 Pedro Guerrero	.05	.02
4 Roberto Alomar	.50	.15
5 Gregg Jefferies	.05	.02
6 Ryne Sandberg	.60	.18
7 Bobby Bonilla	.05	.02
8 Howard Johnson	.05	.02
9 Tim Wallach	.05	.02
10 Shawon Dunston	.05	.02
11 Barry Larkin	.25	.07
12 Ozzie Smith	.75	.23
13 Eric Davis	.10	.03
14 Andre Dawson	.25	.07
15 Tony Gwynn	1.25	.35
16 Von Hayes	.05	.02
17 Kevin Mitchell	.05	.02
18 Rock Raines	.10	.03
19 Lonnie Smith	.05	.02
20 Darryl Strawberry	.05	.02
21 Jerome Walton	.05	.02
22 Craig Biggio	.50	.15
23 Benny Santiago	.05	.02
24 Mike Scioscia	.05	.02
25 Doc Gooden	.10	.03
26 Rick Reuschel	.05	.02
27 Mike Scott	.05	.02
28 Sid Fernandez	.05	.02
29 Mark Langston	.05	.02
30 Joe Magrane	.05	.02
31 Mark Davis	.05	.02
32 Jay Howell	.05	.02
33 Mitch Williams	.05	.02
34 Don Mattingly	1.50	.45
35 Fred McGriff	.25	.07
36 Mark McGwire	2.50	.75
37 Julio Franco	.05	.02
38 Steve Sax	.05	.02
39 Lou Whitaker	.10	.03
40 Wade Boggs	.50	.15
41 Gary Gaetti	.10	.03
42 Carney Lansford	.10	.03
43 Tony Fernandez	.05	.02
44 Cal Ripken	3.00	.90
45 Alan Trammell	.15	.04
46 George Bell	.05	.02
47 Jose Canseco	.50	.15
48 Joe Carter	.10	.03
49 Ken Griffey Jr.	2.50	.75
50 Rickey Henderson	.75	.23
51 Bo Jackson	.25	.07
52 Kirby Puckett	.75	.23
53 Ruben Sierra	.05	.02
54 Robin Yount	.50	.15
55 Carlton Fisk	.40	.12
56 Terry Steinbach	.05	.02
57 Mickey Tettleton	.10	.03
58 Nolan Ryan	3.00	.90
59 Bret Saberhagen	.10	.03
60 Dave Stewart	.10	.03
61 Jeff Ballard	.05	.02
62 Chuck Finley	.10	.03
63 Greg Swindell	.05	.02

64 Dennis Eckersley .15 .04
65 Gregg Olson .05 .02
66 Jeff Russell .05 .02
67 Checklist .05 .02

1990 Topps TV All-Stars

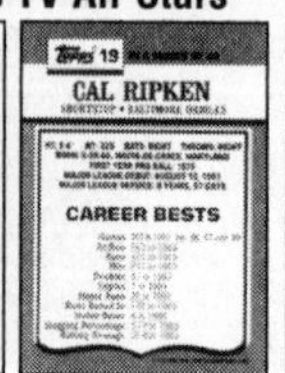

This All-Star team set contains 66 cards measuring the standard size. The fronts feature posed or action color player photos with a high gloss. In block lettering, the words "All-Star" are printed vertically in blue on the left side of the card. The player's name appears in a red plaque below the picture, and white borders round out the card face. The backs are printed in black lettering and have a red and white background. Inside a decal design, biographical information and career bests are superimposed on a blue, pink, and white background. These cards were offered only on television as a complete set for sale through an 800 number.

Nm-Mt Ex-Mt
COMP. FACT. SET (66) 80.00 24.00
1 Mark McGwire 10.00 3.00
2 Julio Franco 1.00 .30
3 Ozzie Guillen 1.00 .30
4 Carney Lansford 1.00 .30
5 Bo Jackson 2.50 .75
6 Kirby Puckett 3.00 .90
7 Ruben Sierra 1.00 .30
8 Carlton Fisk 3.00 .90
9 Nolan Ryan 12.00 3.60
10 Rickey Henderson 5.00 1.50
11 Jose Canseco 3.00 .90
12 Mark Davis .50 .15
13 Dennis Eckersley 3.00 .90
14 Chuck Finley 1.00 .30
15 Bret Saberhagen 1.00 .30
16 Dave Stewart 1.00 .30
17 Don Mattingly 6.00 1.80
18 Steve Sax .50 .15
19 Cal Ripken 12.00 3.60
20 Wade Boggs 3.00 .90
21 George Bell .50 .15
22 Mike Greenwell .50 .15
23 Robin Yount 3.00 .90
24 Mickey Tettleton 1.00 .30
25 Roger Clemens 6.00 1.80
26 Fred McGriff 2.50 .75
27 Jeff Ballard .50 .15
28 Dwight Evans 1.00 .30
29 Paul Molitor 3.00 .90
30 Gregg Olson .50 .15
31 Dan Plesac .50 .15
32 Greg Swindell .50 .15
33 Tony LaRussa MG 1.00 .30
Cito Gaston MG
34 Will Clark 3.00 .90
35 Roberto Alomar 2.50 .75
36 Barry Larkin 2.50 .75
37 Ken Caminiti 1.00 .30
38 Eric Davis 1.00 .30
39 Tony Gwynn 6.00 1.80
40 Kevin Mitchell .50 .15
41 Craig Biggio 2.00 .60
42 Mike Scott .50 .15
43 Joe Carter 1.00 .30
44 Jack Clark 1.00 .30
45 Glenn Davis .50 .15
46 Orel Hershiser 1.00 .30
47 Jay Howell .50 .15
48 Bruce Hurst .50 .15
49 Dave Smith .50 .15
50 Pedro Guerrero .50 .15
51 Ryne Sandberg 6.00 1.80
52 Ozzie Smith 6.00 1.80
53 Howard Johnson .50 .15
54 Von Hayes .50 .15
55 Tim Raines 1.00 .30
56 Darryl Strawberry 1.00 .30
57 Mike LaValliere .50 .15
58 Dwight Gooden 1.00 .30
59 Bobby Bonilla .50 .15
60 Tim Burke .50 .15
61 Sid Fernandez .50 .15
62 Andres Galarraga 2.50 .75
63 Mark Grace 2.50 .75
64 Joe Magrane .50 .15
65 Mitch Williams .50 .15
66 Roger Craig MG and .50 .15
Don Zimmer MG

1990-93 Topps Magazine

These cards were inserted either four or eight cards per issue of Topps magazine. The cards were all issued in perforated form and when separated measured the standard size. The backs are unnumbered with a "TM" prefix. Some cards were issued in every Topps magazine from its inagural issue through the magazine's final issue.

Nm-Mt Ex-Mt
COMPLETE SET (112) 25.00 7.50
1 Dave Staton .10 .03
2 Dan Peltier .10 .03
3 Ken Griffey Jr. 2.50 .75
4 Ruben Sierra .20 .06
5 Bret Saberhagen .20 .06
6 Jerome Walton .10 .03
7 Kevin Mitchell .10 .03
8 Mike Scott .10 .03
9 Bo Jackson .40 .12
10 Nolan Ryan 3.00 .90
11 Will Clark .40 .12
12 Robin Yount .75 .23
13 Joe Morgan .75 .23
14 Jim Palmer .75 .23
15 Ben McDonald .10 .03
16 John Olerud .30 .09
17 Don Mattingly 1.50 .45
18 Eric Davis .30 .09
Barry Larkin
Chris Sabo
19 Jim Abbott .30 .09
20 Sandy Alomar .30 .09
21 Jose Canseco .50 .15
22 Delino DeShields .40 .12
23 Wade Boggs .75 .23
24 Kirby Puckett .50 .15
25 Ryne Sandberg 1.00 .30
26 Roger Clemens 1.50 .45
27 Ken Griffey Jr. 1.00 .30
Ken Griffey Sr.
28 Cecil Fielder .20 .06
29 Steve Avery .10 .03
30 Rickey Henderson 1.00 .30
31 Kevin Maas .10 .03
32 Len Dykstra .20 .06
33 Darryl Strawberry .10 .03
34 Mark McGwire 2.50 .75
35 Matt Williams .30 .09
36 David Justice .40 .12
37 Cincinnati Reds .20 .06
38 Todd Van Poppel .10 .03
39 Jose Offerman .10 .03
40 Alex Fernandez .10 .03
41 Carlton Fisk .75 .23
42 Barry Bonds 1.50 .45
43 Bobby Bonilla .10 .03
44 Bob Welch .10 .03
45 Mo Vaughn .20 .06
46 Tino Martinez .30 .09
47 D.J. Dozier .10 .03
48 Frank Thomas .75 .23
49 Cal Ripken 3.00 .90
50 Dave Winfield .75 .23
51 Dwight Gooden .20 .06
52 Bo Jackson .40 .12
53 Kirk Dressendorfer .10 .03
54 Gary Scott .10 .03
55 Steve Decker .10 .03
56 Ray Lankford .40 .12
57 Ozzie Smith 1.25 .35
58 Joe Carter .20 .06
59 Dave Henderson .10 .03
60 Tony Gwynn 1.50 .45
61 Jeff Bagwell 1.00 .30
62 Scott Erickson .10 .03
63 Pat Kelly .10 .03
64 Orlando Merced .10 .03
65 Andre Dawson .40 .12
66 Reggie Sanders .50 .15
67 Phil Plantier .10 .03
68 Paul Molitor .75 .23
69 Terry Pendleton .20 .06
70 Julio Franco .10 .03
71 Lee Smith .20 .06
72 Minnesota Twins .20 .06
73 Royce Clayton .10 .03
74 Tom Glavine .40 .12
75 Roger Salkeld .10 .03
76 Robin Ventura .40 .12
77 John Goodman .40 .12
As Babe Ruth
78 Jack Morris .20 .06
79 Brien Taylor .10 .03
80 Howard Johnson .10 .03
81 Barry Larkin .40 .12
82 Deion Sanders .40 .12
83 Mike Mussina .50 .15
84 Juan Gonzalez .75 .23
85 Roberto Alomar .40 .12
86 Fred McGriff .30 .09
87 Doug Drabek .10 .03
88 George Brett .75 .23
89 Otis Nixon .20 .06
90 Brady Anderson .40 .12
91 Gary Sheffield .50 .15
92 Dave Fleming .10 .03
93 Jeff Reardon .20 .06
94 Mark McGwire 2.50 .75
95 Larry Walker .30 .09
96 John Kruk .20 .06
97 Carlos Baerga .20 .06
98 Pat Listach .10 .03
99 Toronto Blue Jays .30 .09
100 Eric Karros .20 .06
101 Bret Boone .40 .12
102 Al Martin .10 .03
103 Wil Cordero .10 .03
104 Tim Salmon .40 .12
105 Danny Tartabull .10 .03
106 J.T. Snow .20 .06
107 Mike Piazza 2.00 .60
108 Frank Viola .10 .03
109 Nolan Ryan 3.00 .90
Mets
110 Nolan Ryan 3.00 .90
Angels
111 Nolan Ryan 3.00 .90
Astros
112 Nolan Ryan 3.00 .90
Rangers

1991 Topps

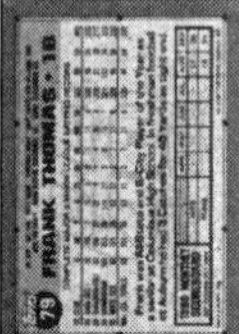

This set marks Topps tenth consecutive year of issuing a 792-card standard-size set. Cards were primarily issued in wax packs, rack packs and factory sets. The fronts feature a full color player photo with a white border. Topps also commemorated their fortieth anniversary by including a "Topps 40" logo on the front and back of each card. Virtually all of the cards have been discovered without the 40th logo on the back. Subsets include Record Breakers (2-8) and All-Stars (386-407). In addition, First Draft Picks and Future Stars subset cards are scattered throughout the set. The key Rookie Cards include Chipper Jones and Brian McRae. As a special promotion Topps inserted (randomly) into their wax packs one of every previous card they ever issued.

Nm-Mt Ex-Mt
COMPLETE SET (792) 20.00 6.00
COMP.FACT.SET (792) 25.00 7.50
1 Nolan Ryan 1.00 .30
2 George Brett RB .30 .09
3 Carlton Fisk RB .10 .03
4 Kevin Maas RB .05 .02
5 Cal Ripken RB .40 .12
6 Nolan Ryan RB .50 .15
7 Ryne Sandberg RB .25 .07
8 Bobby Thigpen RB .05 .02
9 Darrin Fletcher .05 .02
10 Gregg Olson .05 .02
11 Roberto Kelly .05 .02
12 Paul Assenmacher .05 .02
13 Mariano Duncan .05 .02
14 Dennis Lamp .05 .02
15 Von Hayes .05 .02
16 Mike Heath .05 .02
17 Jeff Brantley .05 .02
18 Nelson Liriano .05 .02
19 Jeff D. Robinson .05 .02
20 Pedro Guerrero .10 .03
21 Joe Morgan MG .05 .02
22 Storm Davis .05 .02
23 Jim Gantner .05 .02
24 Dave Martinez .05 .02
25 Tim Belcher .05 .02
26 Luis Sojo UER .05 .02
(Born in Barquisimento,
not Carquis)
27 Bobby Witt .05 .02
28 Alvaro Espinoza .05 .02
29 Bob Walk .05 .02
30 Gregg Jefferies .05 .02
31 Colby Ward .05 .02
32 Mike Simms .05 .02
33 Barry Jones .05 .02
34 Atlee Hammaker .05 .02
35 Greg Maddux .40 .12
36 Donnie Hill .05 .02
37 Tom Bolton .05 .02
38 Scott Bradley .05 .02
39 Jim Neidlinger .05 .02
40 Kevin Mitchell .05 .02
41 Ken Dayley .05 .02
42 Chris Hoiles .05 .02
43 Roger McDowell .05 .02
44 Mike Felder .05 .02
45 Chris Sabo .05 .02
46 Tim Drummond .05 .02
47 Brook Jacoby .05 .02
48 Dennis Boyd .05 .02
49A Pat Borders ERR .25 .07
(40 steals at
Kinston in '86)
49B Pat Borders COR .05 .02
(0 steals at
Kinston in '86)
50 Bob Welch .05 .02
51 Art Howe MG .05 .02
52 Francisco Oliveras .05 .02
53 Mike Sharperson UER .05 .02
(Born in 1961, not 1960)
54 Gary Mielke .05 .02
55 Jeffrey Leonard .05 .02
56 Jeff Parrett .05 .02
57 Jack Howell .05 .02
58 Mel Stottlemyre Jr. .05 .02
59 Eric Yelding .05 .02
60 Frank Viola .10 .03
61 Stan Javier .05 .02
62 Lee Guetterman .05 .02
63 Milt Thompson .05 .02
64 Tom Herr .05 .02
65 Bruce Hurst .05 .02
66 Terry Kennedy .05 .02
67 Rick Honeycutt .05 .02
68 Gary Sheffield .10 .03
69 Steve Wilson .05 .02
70 Ellis Burks .10 .03
71 Jim Acker .05 .02
72 Junior Ortiz .05 .02
73 Craig Worthington .05 .02
74 Shane Andrews RC .25 .07
75 Jack Morris .10 .03
76 Jerry Browne .05 .02
77 Drew Hall .05 .02
78 Geno Petralli .05 .02
79 Frank Thomas .25 .07
80A Fernando Valenzuela .40 .12
ERR (104 earned runs
in '90 tied for
league lead)
80B Fernando Valenzuela .10 .03
COR (104 earned runs
in '90 led league, 20
CG's in 1986 now
italicized)
81 Cito Gaston MG .05 .02
82 Tom Glavine .15 .04
83 Daryl Boston .05 .02
84 Bob McClure .05 .02
85 Jesse Barfield .05 .02
86 Les Lancaster .05 .02
87 Tracy Jones .05 .02
88 Bob Tewksbury .05 .02
89 Darren Daulton .10 .03
90 Danny Tartabull .05 .02
91 Greg Colbrunn RC .25 .07
92 Danny Jackson .05 .02
93 Ivan Calderon .05 .02
94 John Dopson .05 .02
95 Paul Molitor .15 .04
96 Trevor Wilson .05 .02
97A Brady Anderson ERR .40 .12
(September, 2 RBI and
3 hits, should be 3
RBI and 14 hits
97B Brady Anderson COR .10 .03
98 Sergio Valdez .05 .02
99 Chris Gwynn .05 .02
100 Don Mattingly COR .60 .18
(101 hits in 1990)
100A Don Mattingly ERR 2.00 .60
(10 hits in 1990)
101 Rob Ducey .05 .02
102 Gene Larkin .05 .02
103 Tim Costo RC .05 .02
104 Don Robinson .05 .02
105 Kevin McReynolds .05 .02
106 Ed Nunez .05 .02
107 Luis Polonia .05 .02
108 Matt Young .05 .02
109 Greg Riddoch MG .05 .02
110 Tom Henke .05 .02
111 Andres Thomas .05 .02
112 Frank DiPino .05 .02
113 Carl Everett RC .50 .15
114 Lance Dickson RC .10 .03
115 Hubie Brooks .05 .02
116 Mark Davis .05 .02
117 Dion James .05 .02
118 Tom Edens .05 .02
119 Carl Nichols .05 .02
120 Joe Carter .10 .03
121 Eric King .05 .02
122 Paul O'Neill .15 .04
123 Greg A. Harris .05 .02
124 Randy Bush .05 .02
125 Steve Bedrosian .05 .02
126 Bernard Gilkey .05 .02
127 Joe Price .05 .02
128 Travis Fryman .10 .03
(Front has SS
back has SS-3B)
129 Mark Eichhorn .05 .02
130 Ozzie Smith .40 .12
131A Checklist 1 ERR .25 .07
727 Phil Bradley
131B Checklist 1 COR .05 .02
717 Phil Bradley
132 Jamie Quirk .05 .02
133 Greg Briley .05 .02
134 Kevin Elster .05 .02
135 Jerome Walton .05 .02
136 Dave Schmidt .05 .02
137 Randy Ready .05 .02
138 Jamie Moyer .10 .03
139 Jeff Treadway .05 .02
140 Fred McGriff .15 .04
141 Nick Leyva MG .05 .02
142 Curt Wilkerson .05 .02
143 John Smiley .05 .02
144 Dave Henderson .05 .02
145 Lou Whitaker .10 .03
146 Dan Plesac .05 .02
147 Carlos Baerga .05 .02
148 Rey Palacios .05 .02
149 Al Osuna UER .10 .03
(Shown throwing right,
but bio says lefty)
150 Cal Ripken .75 .23
151 Tom Browning .05 .02
152 Mickey Hatcher .05 .02
153 Bryan Harvey .05 .02
154 Jay Buhner .10 .03
155A Dwight Evans ERR .40 .12
(Led league with
162 games in '82)
155B Dwight Evans COR .10 .03
(Tied for lead with
162 games in '82)
156 Carlos Martinez .05 .02
157 John Smoltz .15 .04
158 Jose Uribe .05 .02
159 Joe Boever .05 .02
160 Vince Coleman UER .05 .02
(Wrong birth year,
born 9/22/60)
161 Tim Leary .05 .02
162 Ozzie Canseco .05 .02
163 Dave Johnson .05 .02
164 Edgar Diaz .05 .02
165 Sandy Alomar Jr. .05 .02
166 Harold Baines .10 .03
167A R.Tomlin RC ERR .25 .07
Harriburg
167B R.Tomlin RC COR .10 .03
Harrisburg
168 John Olerud .10 .03
169 Luis Aquino .05 .02
170 Carlton Fisk .15 .04
171 Tony LaRussa MG .05 .02
172 Pete Incaviglia .05 .02
173 Jason Grimsley .05 .02
174 Ken Caminiti .10 .03
175 Jack Armstrong .05 .02
176 John Orton .05 .02
177 Reggie Harris .05 .02
178 Dave Valle .05 .02
179 Pete Harnisch .05 .02
180 Tony Gwynn .30 .09
181 Duane Ward .05 .02
182 Junior Noboa .05 .02
183 Clay Parker .05 .02
184 Gary Green .05 .02
185 Joe Magrane .05 .02
186 Rod Booker .05 .02
187 Greg Cadaret .05 .02
188 Damon Berryhill .05 .02
189 Daryl Irvine .05 .02
190 Matt Williams .10 .03
191 Willie Blair .05 .02
192 Rob Deer .05 .02
193 Felix Fermin .05 .02
194 Xavier Hernandez .05 .02
195 Wally Joyner .10 .03
196 Jim Vatcher .05 .02
197 Chris Nabholz .05 .02
198 R.J. Reynolds .05 .02
199 Mike Hartley .05 .02
200 Darryl Strawberry .15 .04
201 Tom Kelly MG .05 .02
202 Jim Leyritz .05 .02
203 Gene Harris .05 .02
204 Herm Winningham .05 .02
205 Mike Perez RC .10 .03
206 Carlos Quintana .05 .02
207 Gary Wayne .05 .02
208 Willie Wilson .05 .02
209 Ken Howell .05 .02
210 Lance Parrish .10 .03
211 Brian Barnes RC .10 .03
212 Steve Finley .10 .03
213 Frank Wills .05 .02
214 Joe Girardi .05 .02
215 Dave Smith .05 .02
216 Greg Gagne .05 .02
217 Chris Bosio .05 .02
218 Rick Parker .05 .02
219 Jack McDowell .05 .02
220 Tim Wallach .05 .02
221 Don Slaught .05 .02
222 Brian McRae RC .25 .07
223 Allan Anderson .05 .02
224 Juan Gonzalez .25 .07
225 Randy Johnson .30 .09
226 Alfredo Griffin .05 .02
227 Steve Avery UER .05 .02
(Pitched 13 games for
Durham in 1989, not 2)
228 Rex Hudler .05 .02
229 Rance Mulliniks .05 .02
230 Sid Fernandez .05 .02
231 Doug Rader MG .05 .02
232 Jose DeJesus .05 .02
233 Al Leiter .10 .03
234 Scott Erickson .05 .02
235 Dave Parker .10 .03
236A Frank Tanana ERR .25 .07
(Tied for lead with
269 K's in '75)
236B Frank Tanana COR .05 .02
(Led league with
269 K's in '75)
237 Rick Cerone .05 .02
238 Mike Dunne .05 .02
239 Darren Lewis .05 .02
240 Mike Scott .05 .02
241 Dave Clark UER .05 .02
(Career totals 19 HR
and 5 3B, should
be 22 and 3)
242 Mike LaCoss .05 .02
243 Lance Johnson .05 .02
244 Mike Jeffcoat .05 .02
245 Kal Daniels .05 .02
246 Kevin Wickander .05 .02
247 Jody Reed .05 .02
248 Tom Gordon .05 .02
249 Bob Melvin .05 .02
250 Dennis Eckersley .10 .03
251 Mark Lemke .05 .02
252 Mel Rojas .05 .02
253 Garry Templeton .05 .02
254 Shawn Boskie .05 .02
255 Brian Downing .05 .02
256 Greg Hibbard .05 .02
257 Tom O'Malley .05 .02
258 Chris Hammond .05 .02
259 Hensley Meulens .05 .02
260 Harold Reynolds .10 .03
261 Bud Harrelson MG .05 .02
262 Tim Jones .05 .02
263 Checklist 2 .05 .02
264 Dave Hollins .05 .02
265 Mark Gubicza .05 .02
266 Carmelo Castillo .05 .02
267 Mark Knudson .05 .02
268 Tom Brookens .05 .02
269 Joe Hesketh .05 .02
270 Mark McGwire COR .60 .18
(1987 Slugging Pctg.
listed as .618)
270A Mark McGwire ERR 2.00 .60
(1987 Slugging Pctg.
listed as 618)
271 Omar Olivares RC .10 .03
272 Jeff King .05 .02
273 Johnny Ray .05 .02
274 Ken Williams .05 .02
275 Alan Trammell .15 .04
276 Bill Swift .05 .02
277 Scott Coolbaugh .05 .02
278 Alex Fernandez UER .05 .02
(No '90 White Sox stats)
279A Jose Gonzalez ERR .25 .07
(Photo actually
Billy Bean)
279B Jose Gonzalez COR .05 .02
280 Bret Saberhagen .10 .03
281 Larry Sheets .05 .02
282 Don Carman .05 .02
283 Marquis Grissom .05 .02
284 Billy Spiers .05 .02
285 Jim Abbott .15 .04
286 Ken Oberkfell .05 .02
287 Mark Grant .05 .02
288 Derrick May .05 .02
289 Tim Birtsas .05 .02
290 Steve Sax .05 .02
291 John Wathan MG .05 .02
292 Bud Black .05 .02
293 Jay Bell .10 .03
294 Mike Moore .05 .02
295 Rafael Palmeiro .15 .04
296 Mark Williamson .05 .02
297 Manny Lee .05 .02
298 Omar Vizquel .10 .03
299 Scott Radinsky .05 .02
300 Kirby Puckett .25 .07
301 Steve Farr .05 .02
302 Tim Teufel .05 .02
303 Mike Boddicker .05 .02
304 Kevin Reimer .05 .02
305 Mike Scioscia .05 .02
306A Lonnie Smith ERR .40 .12
(136 games in '90)
306B Lonnie Smith COR .05 .02
(135 games in '90)
307 Andy Benes .05 .02
308 Tom Pagnozzi .05 .02
309 Norm Charlton .05 .02
310 Gary Carter .15 .04
311 Jeff Pico .05 .02
312 Charlie Hayes .05 .02
313 Ron Robinson .05 .02
314 Gary Pettis .05 .02
315 Roberto Alomar .25 .07
316 Gene Nelson .05 .02
317 Mike Fitzgerald .05 .02
318 Rick Aguilera .10 .03
319 Jeff McKnight .05 .02
320 Tony Fernandez .05 .02
321 Bob Rodgers MG .05 .02

322 Terry Shumpert .05 .02
323 Cory Snyder .05 .02
324A Ron Kittle ERR .40 .12
(Set another standard ...)
324B Ron Kittle COR .05 .02
(Tied another standard ...)
325 Brett Butler .10 .03
326 Ken Patterson .05 .02
327 Ron Hassey .05 .02
328 Walt Terrell .05 .02
329 Dave Justice UER .10 .03
(Drafted third round on card, should say fourth pick)
330 Dwight Gooden .15 .04
331 Eric Anthony .05 .02
332 Kenny Rogers .10 .03
333 C.Jones FDP RC 4.00 1.20
334 Todd Benzinger .05 .02
335 Mitch Williams .05 .02
336 Matt Nokes .05 .02
337A Keith Comstock ERR .25 .07
(Cubs logo on front)
337B Keith Comstock COR .05 .02
(Mariners logo on front)
338 Luis Rivera .05 .02
339 Larry Walker .25 .07
340 Ramon Martinez .05 .02
341 John Moses .05 .02
342 Mickey Morandini .05 .02
343 Jose Oquendo .05 .02
344 Jeff Russell .05 .02
345 Len Dykstra .10 .03
346 Jesse Orosco .05 .02
347 Greg Vaughn .10 .03
348 Todd Stottlemyre .05 .02
349 Dave Gallagher .05 .02
350 Glenn Davis .05 .02
351 Joe Torre MG .10 .03
352 Frank White .10 .03
353 Tony Castillo .05 .02
354 Sid Bream .05 .02
355 Chili Davis .10 .03
356 Mike Marshall .05 .02
357 Jack Savage .05 .02
358 Mark Parent .05 .02
359 Chuck Cary .05 .02
360 Tim Raines .10 .03
361 Scott Garrelts .05 .02
362 Hector Villenueva .05 .02
363 Rick Mahler .05 .02
364 Dan Pasqua .05 .02
365 Mike Schooler .05 .02
366A Checklist 3 ERR .25 .07
19 Carl Nichols
366B Checklist 3 COR .05 .02
119 Carl Nichols
367 Dave Walsh RC .05 .02
368 Felix Jose .05 .02
369 Steve Searcy .05 .02
370 Kelly Gruber .05 .02
371 Jeff Montgomery .05 .02
372 Spike Owen .05 .02
373 Darrin Jackson .05 .02
374 Larry Casian .05 .02
375 Tony Pena .05 .02
376 Mike Harkey .05 .02
377 Rene Gonzales .05 .02
378A Wilson Alvarez ERR .25 .07
('89 Port Charlotte and '90 Birmingham stat lines omitted)
378B Wilson Alvarez COR .05 .02
Text still says 143 K's in 1988, whereas stats say 134
379 Randy Velarde .05 .02
380 Willie McGee .10 .03
381 Jim Leyland MG .05 .02
382 Mackey Sasser .05 .02
383 Pete Smith .05 .02
384 Gerald Perry .05 .02
385 Mickey Tettleton .05 .02
386 Cecil Fielder AS .05 .02
387 Julio Franco AS .05 .02
388 Kelly Gruber AS .05 .02
389 Alan Trammell AS .10 .03
390 Jose Canseco AS .10 .03
391 Rickey Henderson AS .15 .04
392 Ken Griffey Jr. AS .40 .12
393 Carlton Fisk AS .10 .03
394 Bob Welch AS .05 .02
395 Chuck Finley AS .05 .02
396 Bobby Thigpen AS .05 .02
397 Eddie Murray AS .15 .04
398 Ryne Sandberg AS .25 .07
399 Matt Williams AS .05 .02
400 Barry Larkin AS .10 .03
401 Barry Bonds AS .40 .12
402 Darryl Strawberry AS .10 .03
403 Bobby Bonilla AS .05 .02
404 Mike Scioscia AS .05 .02
405 Doug Drabek AS .05 .02
406 Frank Viola AS .05 .02
407 John Franco AS .05 .02
408 Earnest Riles .05 .02
409 Mike Stanley .05 .02
410 Dave Righetti .10 .03
411 Lance Blankenship .05 .02
412 Dave Bergman .05 .02
413 Terry Mulholland .05 .02
414 Sammy Sosa .50 .15
415 Rick Sutcliffe .10 .03
416 Randy Milligan .05 .02
417 Bill Krueger .05 .02
418 Nick Esasky .05 .02
419 Jeff Reed .05 .02
420 Bobby Thigpen .05 .02
421 Alex Cole .05 .02
422 Rick Reuschel .05 .02
423 Rafael Ramirez UER .05 .02
(Born 1959, not 1958)
424 Calvin Schiraldi .05 .02
425 Andy Van Slyke .10 .03
426 Joe Grahe RC .10 .03
427 Rick Dempsey .05 .02
428 John Barfield .05 .02
429 Stump Merrill MG .05 .02
430 Gary Gaetti .10 .03
431 Paul Gibson .05 .02
432 Delino DeShields .10 .03
433 Pat Tabler .05 .02
434 Julio Machado .05 .02
435 Kevin Maas .05 .02
436 Scott Bankhead .05 .02
437 Doug Dascenzo .05 .02
438 Vicente Palacios .05 .02
439 Dickie Thon .05 .02
440 George Bell .05 .02
441 Zane Smith .05 .02
442 Charlie O'Brien .05 .02
443 Jeff Innis .05 .02
444 Glenn Braggs .05 .02
445 Greg Swindell .05 .02
446 Craig Grebeck .05 .02
447 John Burkett .05 .02
448 Craig Lefferts .05 .02
449 Juan Berenguer .05 .02
450 Wade Boggs .15 .04
451 Neal Heaton .05 .02
452 Bill Schroeder .05 .02
453 Lenny Harris .05 .02
454A Kevin Appier ERR .40 .12
('90 Omaha stat line omitted)
454B Kevin Appier COR .10 .03
455 Walt Weiss .05 .02
456 Charlie Leibrandt .05 .02
457 Todd Hundley .05 .02
458 Brian Holman .05 .02
459 T.Trebelhorn MG UER .05 .02
Pitching and batting columns switched
460 Dave Stieb .05 .02
461 Robin Ventura .10 .03
462 Steve Frey .05 .02
463 Dwight Smith .05 .02
464 Steve Buechele .05 .02
465 Ken Griffey Sr. .10 .03
466 Charles Nagy .10 .03
467 Dennis Cook .05 .02
468 Tim Hulett .05 .02
469 Chet Lemon .05 .02
470 Howard Johnson .05 .02
471 Mike Lieberthal RC .40 .12
472 Kirt Manwaring .05 .02
473 Curt Young .05 .02
474 Phil Plantier RC .10 .03
475 Ted Higuera .05 .02
476 Glenn Wilson .05 .02
477 Mike Fetters .05 .02
478 Kurt Stillwell .05 .02
479 Bob Patterson UER .05 .02
(Has a decimal point between 7 and 9)
480 Dave Magadan .05 .02
481 Eddie Whitson .05 .02
482 Tino Martinez .15 .04
483 Mike Aldrete .05 .02
484 Dave LaPoint .05 .02
485 Terry Pendleton .10 .03
486 Tommy Greene .05 .02
487 Rafael Belliard .05 .02
488 Jeff Manto .05 .02
489 Bobby Valentine MG .05 .02
490 Kirk Gibson .10 .03
491 Kurt Miller RC .05 .02
492 Ernie Whitt .05 .02
493 Jose Rijo .05 .02
494 Chris James .05 .02
495 Charlie Hough .10 .03
496 Marty Barrett .05 .02
497 Ben McDonald .05 .02
498 Mark Salas .05 .02
499 Melido Perez .05 .02
500 Will Clark .25 .07
501 Mike Bielecki .05 .02
502 Carney Lansford .10 .03
503 Roy Smith .05 .02
504 Julio Valera .05 .02
505 Chuck Finley .10 .03
506 Darnell Coles .05 .02
507 Steve Jeltz .05 .02
508 Mike York .05 .02
509 Glenallen Hill .05 .02
510 John Franco .10 .03
511 Steve Balboni .05 .02
512 Jose Mesa .05 .02
513 Jerald Clark .05 .02
514 Mike Stanton .05 .02
515 Alvin Davis .05 .02
516 Karl Rhodes .05 .02
517 Joe Oliver .05 .02
518 Cris Carpenter .05 .02
519 Sparky Anderson MG .10 .03
520 Mark Grace .15 .04
521 Joe Orsulak .05 .02
522 Stan Belinda .05 .02
523 Rodney McCray .05 .02
524 Darrel Akerfelds .05 .02
525 Willie Randolph .10 .03
526A Moises Alou ERR .40 .12
(37 runs in 2 games for '90 Pirates)
526B Moises Alou COR .10 .03
(0 runs in 2 games for '90 Pirates)
527A Checklist 4 ERR .25 .07
105 Keith Miller
719 Kevin McReynolds
527B Checklist 4 COR .05 .02
105 Kevin McReynolds
719 Keith Miller
528 Dennis Martinez .10 .03
529 Marc Newfield RC .10 .03
530 Roger Clemens .50 .15
531 Dave Rohde .05 .02
532 Kirk McCaskill .05 .02
533 Oddibe McDowell .05 .02
534 Mike Jackson .05 .02
535 Ruben Sierra UER .05 .02
(Back reads 100 Runs amd 100 RBI's)
536 Mike Witt .05 .02
537 Jose Lind .05 .02
538 Bip Roberts .05 .02
539 Scott Terry .05 .02
540 George Brett .60 .18
541 Domingo Ramos .05 .02
542 Rob Murphy .05 .02
543 Junior Felix .05 .02
544 Alejandro Pena .05 .02
545 Dale Murphy .25 .07
546 Jeff Ballard .05 .02
547 Mike Pagliarulo .05 .02
548 Jaime Navarro .05 .02
549 John McNamara MG .05 .02
550 Eric Davis .10 .03
551 Bob Kipper .05 .02
552 Jeff Hamilton .05 .02
553 Joe Klink .05 .02
554 Brian Harper .05 .02
555 Turner Ward RC .10 .03
556 Gary Ward .05 .02
557 Wally Whitehurst .05 .02
558 Otis Nixon .05 .02
559 Adam Peterson .05 .02
560 Greg Smith .05 .02
561 Tim McIntosh .05 .02
562 Jeff Kunkel .05 .02
563 Brent Knackert .05 .02
564 Dante Bichette .10 .03
565 Craig Biggio .15 .04
566 Craig Wilson .05 .02
567 Dwayne Henry .05 .02
568 Ron Karkovice .05 .02
569 Curt Schilling .15 .04
570 Barry Bonds .75 .23
571 Pat Combs .05 .02
572 Dave Anderson .05 .02
573 Rich Rodriguez UER .05 .02
(Stats say drafted 4th, but bio says 9th round)
574 John Marzano .05 .02
575 Robin Yount .40 .12
576 Jeff Kaiser .05 .02
577 Bill Doran .05 .02
578 Dave West .05 .02
579 Roger Craig MG .05 .02
580 Dave Stewart .10 .03
581 Luis Quinones .05 .02
582 Marty Clary .05 .02
583 Tony Phillips .05 .02
584 Kevin Brown .10 .03
585 Pete O'Brien .05 .02
586 Fred Lynn .05 .02
587 Jose Offerman UER .05 .02
(Text says he signed 7/24/86, but bio says 1988)
588 Mark Whiten .05 .02
589 Scott Ruskin .05 .02
590 Eddie Murray .25 .07
591 Ken Hill .05 .02
592 B.J. Surhoff .10 .03
593A Mike Walker ERR .25 .07
('90 Canton-Akron stat line omitted)
593B Mike Walker COR .05 .02
594 Rich Garces RC .10 .03
595 Bill Landrum .05 .02
596 Ronnie Walden RC .10 .03
597 Jerry Don Gleaton .05 .02
598 Sam Horn .05 .02
599A Greg Myers ERR .25 .07
('90 Syracuse stat line omitted)
599B Greg Myers COR .05 .02
600 Bo Jackson .25 .07
601 Bob Ojeda .05 .02
602 Casey Candaele .05 .02
603A W.Chamberlain RC ERR .40 .12
Photo actually Louie Meadows
603B Wes Chamberlain RC COR .10 .03
604 Billy Hatcher .05 .02
605 Jeff Reardon .10 .03
606 Jim Gott .05 .02
607 Edgar Martinez .15 .04
608 Todd Burns .05 .02
609 Jeff Torborg MG .05 .02
610 Andres Galarraga .10 .03
611 Dave Eiland .05 .02
612 Steve Lyons .05 .02
613 Eric Show .05 .02
614 Luis Salazar .05 .02
615 Bert Blyleven .10 .03
616 Todd Zeile .05 .02
617 Bill Wegman .05 .02
618 Sil Campusano .05 .02
619 David Wells .10 .03
620 Ozzie Guillen .05 .02
621 Ted Power .05 .02
622 Jack Daugherty .05 .02
623 Jeff Blauser .05 .02
624 Tom Candiotti .05 .02
625 Terry Steinbach .05 .02
626 Gerald Young .05 .02
627 Tim Layana .05 .02
628 Greg Litton .05 .02
629 Wes Gardner .05 .02
630 Dave Winfield .10 .03
631 Mike Morgan .05 .02
632 Lloyd Moseby .05 .02
633 Kevin Tapani .05 .02
634 Henry Cotto .05 .02
635 Andy Hawkins .05 .02
636 Geronimo Pena .05 .02
637 Bruce Ruffin .05 .02
638 Mike Macfarlane .05 .02
639 Frank Robinson MG .15 .04
640 Andre Dawson .10 .03
641 Mike Henneman .05 .02
642 Hal Morris .05 .02
643 Jim Presley .05 .02
644 Chuck Crim .05 .02
645 Juan Samuel .05 .02
646 Andujar Cedeno .05 .02
647 Mark Portugal .05 .02
648 Lee Stevens .05 .02
649 Bill Sampen .05 .02
650 Jack Clark .10 .03
651 Alan Mills .05 .02
652 Kevin Romine .05 .02
653 Anthony Telford .05 .02
654 Paul Sorrento .10 .03
655 Erik Hanson .05 .02
656A Checklist 5 ERR .25 .07
348 Vicente Palacios
381 Jose Lind
537 Mike LaValliere
665 Jim Leyland
656B Checklist 5 ERR .25 .07
433 Vicente Palacios
(Palacios should be 438)
537 Jose Lind
665 Mike LaValliere
381 Jim Leyland
656C Checklist 5 COR .05 .02
438 Vicente Palacios
537 Jose Lind
665 Mike LaValliere
381 Jim Leyland
657 Mike Kingery .05 .02
658 Scott Aldred .05 .02
659 Oscar Azocar .05 .02
660 Lee Smith .10 .03
661 Steve Lake .05 .02
662 Ron Dibble .10 .03
663 Greg Brock .05 .02
664 John Farrell .05 .02
665 Mike LaValliere .05 .02
666 Danny Darwin .05 .02
667 Kent Anderson .05 .02
668 Bill Long .05 .02
669 Lou Piniella MG .10 .03
670 Rickey Henderson .25 .07
671 Andy McGaffigan .05 .02
672 Shane Mack .05 .02
673 Greg Olson UER .05 .02
(6 RBI in '88 at Tidewater and 2 RBI in '87, should be 48 and 15)
674A Kevin Gross ERR .25 .07
(89 BB with Phillies in '88 tied for league lead)
674B Kevin Gross COR .05 .02
(89 BB with Phillies in '88 led league)
675 Tom Brunansky .05 .02
676 Scott Chiamparino .05 .02
677 Billy Ripken .05 .02
678 Mark Davidson .05 .02
679 Bill Bathe .05 .02
680 David Cone .10 .03
681 Jeff Schaefer .05 .02
682 Ray Lankford .05 .02
683 Derek Lilliquist .05 .02
684 Milt Cuyler .05 .02
685 Doug Drabek .05 .02
686 Mike Gallego .05 .02
687A John Cerutti ERR .25 .07
(4.46 ERA in '90)
687B John Cerutti COR .05 .02
(4.76 ERA in '90)
688 Rosario Rodriguez .05 .02
689 John Kruk .10 .03
690 Orel Hershiser .10 .03
691 Mike Blowers .05 .02
692A Efrain Valdez ERR .25 .07
(Born 6/11/66)
692B Efrain Valdez COR .05 .02
(Born 7/11/66 and two lines of text added)
693 Francisco Cabrera .05 .02
694 Randy Veres .05 .02
695 Kevin Seitzer .05 .02
696 Steve Olin .05 .02
697 Shawn Abner .05 .02
698 Mark Guthrie .05 .02
699 Jim Lefebvre MG .05 .02
700 Jose Canseco .25 .07
701 Pascual Perez .05 .02
702 Tim Naehring .05 .02
703 Juan Agosto .05 .02
704 Devon White .05 .02
705 Robby Thompson .05 .02
706A Brad Arnsberg ERR .25 .07
(68.2 IP in '90)
706B Brad Arnsberg COR .05 .02
(62.2 IP in '90)
707 Jim Eisenreich .05 .02
708 John Mitchell .05 .02
709 Matt Sinatro .05 .02
710 Kent Hrbek .10 .03
711 Jose DeLeon .05 .02
712 Ricky Jordan .05 .02
713 Scott Scudder .05 .02
714 Marvell Wynne .05 .02
715 Tim Burke .05 .02
716 Bob Geren .05 .02
717 Phil Bradley .05 .02
718 Steve Crawford .05 .02
719 Keith Miller .05 .02
720 Cecil Fielder .10 .03
721 Mark Lee RC .05 .02
722 Wally Backman .05 .02
723 Candy Maldonado .05 .02
724 David Segui .05 .02
725 Ron Gant .10 .03
726 Phil Stephenson .05 .02
727 Mookie Wilson .10 .03
728 Scott Sanderson .05 .02
729 Don Zimmer MG .10 .03
730 Barry Larkin .25 .07
731 Jeff Gray .05 .02
732 Franklin Stubbs .05 .02
733 Kelly Downs .05 .02
734 John Russell .05 .02
735 Ron Darling .05 .02
736 Dick Schofield .05 .02
737 Tim Crews .05 .02
738 Mel Hall .05 .02
739 Russ Swan .05 .02
740 Ryne Sandberg .40 .12
741 Jimmy Key .10 .03
742 Tommy Gregg .05 .02
743 Bryn Smith .05 .02
744 Nelson Santovenia .05 .02
745 Doug Jones .05 .02
746 John Shelby .05 .02
747 Tony Fossas .05 .02
748 Al Newman .05 .02
749 Greg W. Harris .05 .02
750 Bobby Bonilla .10 .03
751 Wayne Edwards .05 .02
752 Kevin Bass .05 .02
753 Paul Marak UER .05 .02
(Stats say drafted in Jan. but bio says May)
754 Bill Pecota .05 .02
755 Mark Langston .05 .02
756 Jeff Huson .05 .02
757 Mark Gardner .05 .02
758 Mike Devereaux .05 .02
759 Bobby Cox MG .05 .02
760 Benny Santiago .10 .03
761 Larry Andersen .05 .02
762 Mitch Webster .05 .02
763 Dana Kiecker .05 .02
764 Mark Carreon .05 .02
765 Shawon Dunston .05 .02
766 Jeff Robinson .05 .02
767 Dan Wilson RC .25 .07
768 Don Pall .05 .02
769 Tim Sherrill .05 .02
770 Jay Howell .05 .02
771 Gary Redus UER .05 .02
(Born in Tanner, should say Athens)
772 Kent Mercker UER .05 .02
(Born in Indianapolis, should say Dublin, Ohio)
773 Tom Foley .05 .02
774 Dennis Rasmussen .05 .02
775 Julio Franco .10 .03
776 Brent Mayne .05 .02
777 John Candelaria .05 .02
778 Dan Gladden .05 .02
779 Carmelo Martinez .05 .02
780A Randy Myers ERR .40 .12
(15 career losses)
780B Randy Myers COR .05 .02
(19 career losses)
781 Darryl Hamilton .05 .02
782 Jim Deshaies .05 .02
783 Joel Skinner .05 .02
784 Willie Fraser .05 .02
785 Scott Fletcher .05 .02
786 Eric Plunk .05 .02
787 Checklist 6 .05 .02
788 Bob Milacki .05 .02
789 Tom Lasorda MG .25 .07
790 Ken Griffey Jr. .75 .23
791 Mike Benjamin .05 .02
792 Mike Greenwell .05 .02

1991 Topps Desert Shield

These 792 standard-size cards are parallel to the regular Topps issue. These cards were issued in special packs available only to servicepeople serving in the Desert Shield (later to be Desert Storm) campaign. The cards are differentiated by a "Desert Shield" logo in the upper right corner. There were many different types of forgeries created for these cards so some caution is urged in purchasing any expensive cards from the set.

Nm-Mt Ex-Mt
*STARS: 40X TO 100X BASIC CARDS
*ROOKIES: 15X TO 40X BASIC CARDS

1991 Topps Micro

This 792 card set parallels the regular Topps issue. The cards are significantly smaller (slightly larger than a postage stamp) than the regular Topps cards and are valued at a percentage of the regular 1991 Topps cards.

Nm-Mt Ex-Mt
COMP.FACT.SET (792) 15.00 4.50
*STARS: .4X to 1X BASIC CARDS ......

1991 Topps Tiffany

This 792 standard-size set proved to be the final time Topps issued their Tiffany sets. These cards again parallel the regular issue and have "glossy" fronts and easy to read backs. These cards were issued in complete set form only. Since a limited amount of these sets were produced, the multiplier is one of the highest for any of these Topps sets. While no production number is guessed at for these sets, it is perceived in the hobby to be among the shortest printed Tiffany sets.

Nm-Mt Ex-Mt
COMP.FACT.SET (792) 200.00 60.00
*STARS: 12.5X TO 30X BASIC CARDS
*ROOKIES: 6X TO 15X BASIC CARDS

1991 Topps Rookies

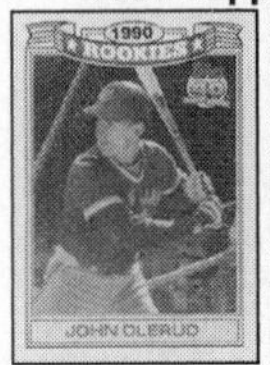

This set contains 33 standard-size cards and were distributed at a rate of one per retail jumbo pack. The front and back borders are white and other design elements are red, blue, and yellow. This set is identical to the previous year's set. Topps also commemorated its 40th anniversary by including a "Topps 40" logo on the front. The cards are unnumbered and checklisted below in alphabetical order.

Nm-Mt Ex-Mt
COMPLETE SET (33) 20.00 6.00
1 Sandy Alomar .50 .15
2 Kevin Appier .50 .15
3 Steve Avery .25 .07
4 Carlos Baerga .50 .15
5 John Burkett .25 .07
6 Alex Cole .25 .07
7 Pat Combs .25 .07
8 Delino DeShields .50 .15
9 Travis Fryman 1.00 .30
10 Marquis Grissom .50 .15
11 Mike Harkey .25 .07

12 Glenallen Hill .25 .07
13 Jeff Huson .25 .07
14 Felix Jose .25 .07
15 Dave Justice 1.50 .45
16 Jim Leyritz .25 .07
17 Kevin Maas .25 .07
18 Ben McDonald .25 .07
19 Kent Mercker .25 .07
20 Hal Morris .25 .07
21 Chris Nabholz .25 .07
22 Tim Naehring .25 .07
23 Jose Offerman .25 .07
24 John Olerud 2.00 .60
25 Scott Radinsky .25 .07
26 Scott Ruskin .25 .07
27 Kevin Tapani .25 .07
28 Frank Thomas 8.00 2.40
29 Randy Tomlin .25 .07
30 Greg Vaughn 1.50 .45
31 Robin Ventura 1.50 .45
32 Larry Walker 1.50 .45
33 Todd Zeile 1.00 .30

1991 Topps Wax Box Cards

Topps again in 1991 issued cards on the bottom of their wax pack boxes. There are four different boxes, each with four cards and a checklist on the side. These standard-size cards have yellow borders rather than the white borders of the regular issue cards, and they have different photos of the players. The backs are printed in pink and blue on gray cardboard stock and feature outstanding achievements of the players. The cards are numbered by letter on the back. The cards have the typical Topps 1991 design on the front of the card. The set was ordered in alphabetical order and lettered A-P.

Nm-Mt Ex-Mt
COMPLETE SET (16) 6.00 1.80
A Bert Blyleven .20 .06
B George Brett 1.00 .30
C Brett Butler .10 .03
D Andre Dawson .50 .15
E Dwight Evans .20 .06
F Carlton Fisk .60 .18
G Alfredo Griffin .10 .03
H Rickey Henderson .60 .18
I Willie McGee .20 .06
J Dale Murphy .50 .15
K Eddie Murray .60 .18
L Dave Parker .20 .06
M Jeff Reardon .20 .06
N Nolan Ryan 2.50 .75
O Juan Samuel .10 .03
P Robin Yount .60 .18

1991 Topps Traded

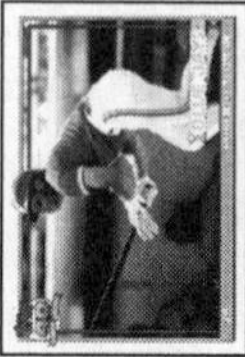
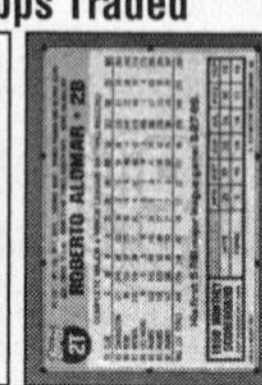

The 1991 Topps Traded set contains 132 standard-size cards. The cards were issued primarily in factory set form through hobby dealers but were also made available on a limited basis in wax packs. The cards in the wax packs (gray backs) and collated factory sets (white backs) are from different card stock. Both versions are valued equally. The card design is identical to the regular issue 1991 Topps cards except for the whiter stock (for factory set cards) and T-suffixed numbering. The set is numbered in alphabetical order. The set includes a Team U.S.A. subset, featuring 25 of America's top collegiate players. The key Rookie Cards in this set are Jeff Bagwell, Jason Giambi, Luis Gonzalez, Charles Johnson and Ivan Rodriguez.

Nm-Mt Ex-Mt
COMPLETE SET (132) 15.00 4.50
COMP.FACT.SET (132) 15.00 4.50
1T Juan Agosto .05 .02
2T Roberto Alomar .25 .07
3T Wally Backman .05 .02
4T Jeff Bagwell RC 1.50 .45
5T Skeeter Barnes .05 .02
6T Steve Bedrosian .05 .02
7T Derek Bell .10 .03
8T George Bell .05 .02
9T Rafael Belliard .05 .02
10T Dante Bichette .10 .03
11T Bud Black .05 .02
12T Mike Boddicker .05 .02
13T Sid Bream .05 .02
14T Hubie Brooks .05 .02
15T Brett Butler .10 .03
16T Ivan Calderon .05 .02
17T John Candelaria .05 .02
18T Tom Candiotti .05 .02
19T Gary Carter .15 .04
20T Joe Carter .10 .03
21T Rick Cerone .05 .02
22T Jack Clark .10 .03
23T Vince Coleman .05 .02
24T Scott Coolbaugh .05 .02
25T Danny Cox .05 .02
26T Danny Darwin .05 .02
27T Chili Davis .10 .03
28T Glenn Davis .05 .02
29T Steve Decker .05 .02
30T Rob Deer .05 .02
31T Rich DeLucia .05 .02
32T John Dettmer USA RC .25 .07
33T Brian Downing .05 .02
34T D.Dreifort USA RC .50 .15
35T K.Dressendorfer RC .05 .02
36T Jim Essian MG .05 .02
37T Dwight Evans .10 .03
38T Steve Farr .05 .02
39T Jeff Fassero RC .25 .07
40T Junior Felix .05 .02
41T Tony Fernandez .05 .02
42T Steve Finley .10 .03
43T Jim Fregosi MG .05 .02
44T Gary Gaetti .10 .03
45T Jason Giambi USA RC 8.00 2.40
46T Kirk Gibson .10 .03
47T Leo Gomez .05 .02
48T Luis Gonzalez RC 1.00 .30
49T Jeff Granger USA RC .25 .07
50T Todd Greene USA RC .50 .15
51T J.Hammonds USA RC .50 .15
52T Mike Hargrove MG .05 .02
53T Pete Harnisch .05 .02
54T Rick Helling RC .50 .15
USA UER
Misspelled Hellings on card back
55T Glenallen Hill .05 .02
56T Charlie Hough .10 .03
57T Pete Incaviglia .05 .02
58T Bo Jackson .25 .07
59T Danny Jackson .05 .02
60T Reggie Jefferson .05 .02
61T C.Johnson USA RC .75 .23
62T Jeff Johnson .05 .02
63T T.Johnson USA RC .25 .07
64T Barry Jones .05 .02
65T Chris Jones RC .10 .03
66T Scott Kamieniecki RC .10 .03
67T Pat Kelly RC .10 .03
68T Darryl Kile .10 .03
69T Chuck Knoblauch .10 .03
70T Bill Krueger .05 .02
71T Scott Leius .05 .02
72T D.Leshnock USA RC .25 .07
73T Mark Lewis .05 .02
74T Candy Maldonado .05 .02
75T J.McDonald USA RC .25 .07
76T Willie McGee .10 .03
77T Fred McGriff .15 .04
78T B.McMillon USA RC .25 .07
79T Hal McRae MG .10 .03
80T D.Melendez USA RC .25 .07
81T Orlando Merced RC .10 .03
82T Jack Morris .10 .03
83T Phil Nevin USA RC 1.00 .30
84T Otis Nixon .05 .02
85T Johnny Oates MG .05 .02
86T Bob Ojeda .05 .02
87T Mike Pagliarulo .05 .02
88T Dean Palmer .10 .03
89T Dave Parker .10 .03
90T Terry Pendleton .10 .03
91T T.Phillips (P) USA RC .25 .07
92T Doug Piatt .05 .02
93T Ron Polk USA CO .25 .07
94T Tim Raines .10 .03
95T Willie Randolph .10 .03
96T Dave Righetti .10 .03
97T Ernie Riles .05 .02
98T C.Roberts USA RC .25 .07
99T Jeff D. Robinson .05 .02
100T Jeff M. Robinson .05 .02
101T Ivan Rodriguez RC 2.00 .60
102T S.Rodriguez USA RC .25 .07
103T Tom Runnells MG .05 .02
104T Scott Sanderson .05 .02
105T Bob Scanlan .05 .02
106T Pete Schourek RC .10 .03
107T Gary Scott .05 .02
108T Paul Shuey USA RC .50 .15
109T Doug Simons .05 .02
110T Dave Smith .05 .02
111T Cory Snyder .05 .02
112T Luis Sojo .05 .02
113T K.Steenstra USA RC .25 .07
114T Darryl Strawberry .15 .04
115T Franklin Stubbs .05 .02
116T Todd Taylor USA RC .25 .07
117T Wade Taylor .05 .02
118T Garry Templeton .05 .02
119T Mickey Tettleton .05 .02
120T Tim Teufel .05 .02
121T Mike Timlin RC .25 .07
122T David Tuttle USA RC .25 .07
123T Mo Vaughn .10 .03
124T Jeff Ware USA RC .25 .07
125T Devon White .05 .02
126T Mark Whiten .05 .02
127T Mitch Williams .05 .02
128T C.Wilson USA RC .25 .07
129T Willie Wilson .05 .02
130T C.Wimmer USA RC .25 .07
131T Ivan Zweig USA RC .25 .07
132T Checklist 1T-132T .05 .02

1991 Topps Traded Tiffany

In the final Tiffany relase, this 132-card standard-size set was released as a parallel issue to the regular Topps Traded issue. These cards were released in very limited quantities and the multiplier for these cards is higher than many previous Tiffany issues. These cards were issued in complete factory set form only. The set is considered to be among the shortest print of the Tiffany run and these cards are rarely seen in the secondary market.

Nm-Mt Ex-Mt
COMP.FACT.SET (132) 200.00 60.00
*STARS: 12.5X TO 30X BASIC CARDS
*ROOKIES: 10X TO 25X BASIC CARDS
*USA ROOKIES: 6X TO 15X BASIC CARDS

1991 Topps Cracker Jack I

This 36-card set is the first of two 36-card series produced by Topps for Cracker Jack, and the cards were inserted inside specially marked packages of Cracker Jack. These cards were the "toy surprise" inside. The cards measure approximately one-fourth standard-size (1 1/4" by 1 3/4") and are frequently referenced as micro-cards. The micro-cards have color player photos with different color borders but are otherwise identical to the corresponding cards in the Topps regular issue. Standard-size cards featuring four micro-cards each were seen at trade shows but were not inserted inside the product. These were apparently test runs or uncut sheets. Although each mini-card is numbered on the back, the numbering of the four cards on any standard-size card is not consecutive.

Nm-Mt Ex-Mt
COMPLETE SET (36) 10.00 3.00
1 Nolan Ryan 2.50 .75
2 Paul Molitor .50 .15
3 Tim Raines .20 .06
4 Frank Viola .10 .03
5 Sandy Alomar Jr. .20 .06
6 Ryne Sandberg 1.00 .30
7 Don Mattingly 1.25 .35
8 Pedro Guerrero .10 .03
9 Jose Rijo .20 .06
10 Jose Canseco .50 .15
11 Dave Parker .20 .06
12 Doug Drabek .10 .03
13 Cal Ripken 2.50 .75
14 Dave Justice .40 .12
15 George Brett 1.00 .30
16 Eric Davis .20 .06
17 Mark Langston .10 .03
18 Rickey Henderson 1.00 .30
19 Barry Bonds 1.25 .35
20 Kevin Maas .10 .03
21 Len Dykstra .20 .06
22 Roger Clemens 1.25 .35
23 Robin Yount .50 .15
24 Mark Grace .40 .12
25 Bo Jackson .40 .12
26 Tony Gwynn 1.25 .35
27 Mark McGwire 2.00 .60
28 Dwight Gooden .20 .06
29 Wade Boggs .50 .15
30 Kevin Mitchell .10 .03
31 Cecil Fielder .20 .06
32 Bobby Thigpen .10 .03
33 Benito Santiago .20 .06
34 Kirby Puckett .50 .15
35 Will Clark .40 .12
36 Ken Griffey Jr. 1.50 .45

1991 Topps Cracker Jack II

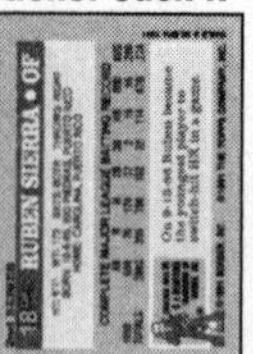

This 36-card set is the second of two different 36-card series produced by Topps for Cracker Jack, and the cards were inserted inside specially marked packages of Cracker Jack. These cards were the "toy surprise" inside. The cards measure approximately one-fourth standard-size (1 1/4" by 1 3/4") and are frequently referenced as micro-cards. The micro-cards have color player photos with different color borders but are otherwise identical to the corresponding cards in the Topps regular issue. Standard-size cards featuring four micro-cards each were seen at trade shows but were not inserted inside the product. These were apparently test runs or uncut sheets. Although each mini-card is numbered on the back, the numbering of the four cards on any standard-size card is not consecutive.

Nm-Mt Ex-Mt
COMPLETE SET (36) 6.00 1.80
1 Eddie Murray .50 .15
2 Carlton Fisk .50 .15
3 Eric Anthony .10 .03
4 Kelly Gruber .10 .03
5 Von Hayes .10 .03
6 Ben McDonald .10 .03
7 Andre Dawson .40 .12
8 Ellis Burks .20 .06
9 Matt Williams .30 .09
10 Dave Stewart .20 .06
11 Barry Larkin .40 .12
12 Chuck Finley .20 .06
13 Shane Andrews .10 .03
14 Bret Saberhagen .20 .06
15 Bobby Bonilla .10 .03
16 Roberto Kelly .10 .03
17 Orel Hershiser .20 .06
18 Ruben Sierra .20 .06
19 Ron Gant .20 .06
20 Frank Thomas .50 .15
21 Tim Wallach .10 .03
22 Gregg Olson .10 .03
23 Shawon Dunston .10 .03
24 Kent Hrbek .20 .06
25 Ramon Martinez .20 .06
26 Alan Trammell .30 .09
27 Ozzie Smith .75 .23
28 Bob Welch .10 .03
29 Chris Sabo .10 .03
30 Steve Sax .10 .03
31 Bip Roberts .10 .03
32 Dave Stieb .10 .03
33 Howard Johnson .10 .03
34 Mike Greenwell .10 .03
35 Delino DeShields .10 .03
36 Alex Fernandez .10 .03

1991 Topps Debut '90

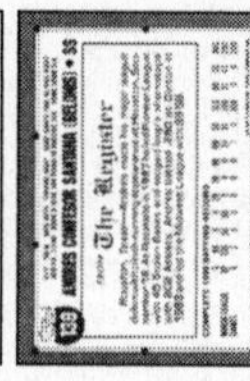

The 1991 Topps Major League Debut Set contains 171 standard-size cards. Although the checklist card is arranged chronologically in order of first major league appearance in 1990, the player cards are arranged alphabetically by the player's last name. Carlos Baerga and Frank Thomas are among the more prominent players featured in this set.

Nm-Mt Ex-Mt
COMP. FACT SET (171) 20.00 6.00
1 Paul Abbott .75 .23
2 Steve Adkins .15 .04
3 Scott Aldred .15 .04
4 Gerald Alexander .15 .04
5 Moises Alou .75 .23
6 Steve Avery .15 .04
7 Oscar Azocar .15 .04
8 Carlos Baerga .15 .04
9 Kevin Baez .15 .04
10 Jeff Baldwin .15 .04
11 Brian Barnes .15 .04
12 Kevin Bearse .15 .04
13 Kevin Belcher .15 .04
14 Mike Bell .15 .04
15 Sean Berry .75 .23
16 Joe Bitker .15 .04
17 Willie Blair .15 .04
18 Brian Bohanon .15 .04
19 Mike Bordick .75 .23
20 Shawn Boskie .15 .04
21 Rod Brewer .15 .04
22 Kevin D. Brown .15 .04
23 Dave Burba .75 .23
24 Jim Campbell .15 .04
25 Ozzie Canseco .15 .04
26 Chuck Carr .15 .04
27 Larry Casian .15 .04
28 Andujar Cedeno .15 .04
29 Wes Chamberlain .15 .04
30 Scott Chiamparino .15 .04
31 Steve Chitren .15 .04
32 Pete Coachman .15 .04
33 Alex Cole .15 .04
34 Jeff Conine .75 .23
35 Scott Cooper .15 .04
36 Milt Cuyler .15 .04
37 Steve Decker .15 .04
38 Rich DeLucia .15 .04
39 Delino DeShields .75 .23
40 Mark Dewey .15 .04
41 Carlos Diaz .15 .04
42 Lance Dickson .15 .04
43 Narciso Elvira .15 .04
44 Luis Encarnacion .15 .04
45 Scott Erickson .15 .04
46 Paul Faries .15 .04
47 Howard Farmer .15 .04
48 Alex Fernandez .15 .04
49 Travis Fryman .75 .23
50 Rich Garces .15 .04
51 Carlos Garcia .15 .04
52 Mike Gardiner .15 .04
53 Bernard Gilkey .15 .04
54 Tom Gilles .15 .04
55 Jerry Goff .15 .04
56 Leo Gomez .15 .04
57 Luis Gonzalez 3.00 .90
58 Joe Grahe .15 .04
59 Craig Grebeck .15 .04
60 Kip Gross .15 .04
61 Eric Gunderson .15 .04
62 Chris Hammond .15 .04
63 Dave Hansen .15 .04
64 Reggie Harris .15 .04
65 Bill Haselman .15 .04
66 Randy Hennis .15 .04
67 Carlos Hernandez .15 .04
68 Howard Hilton .15 .04
69 Dave Hollins .15 .04
70 Darren Holmes .75 .23
71 John Hoover .15 .04
72 Steve Howard .15 .04
73 Thomas Howard .15 .04
74 Todd Hundley .15 .04
75 Daryl Irvine .15 .04
76 Chris Jelic .15 .04
77 Dana Kiecker .15 .04
78 Brent Knackert .15 .04
79 Jimmy Kremers .15 .04
80 Jerry Kutzler .15 .04
81 Ray Lankford .15 .04
82 Tim Layana .15 .04
83 Terry Lee .15 .04
84 Mark Leiter .15 .04
85 Scott Leius .15 .04
86 Mark Leonard .15 .04
87 Darren Lewis .15 .04
88 Scott Lewis .15 .04
89 Jim Leyritz .15 .04
90 Dave Liddell .15 .04
91 Luis Lopez .15 .04
92 Kevin Maas .15 .04
93 Bob MacDonald .15 .04
94 Carlos Maldonado .15 .04
95 Chuck Malone .15 .04
96 Ramon Manon .15 .04
97 Jeff Manto .15 .04
98 Paul Marak .15 .04
99 Tino Martinez 1.50 .45
100 Derrick May .15 .04
101 Brent Mayne .15 .04
102 Paul McClellan .15 .04
103 Rodney McCray .15 .04
104 Tim McIntosh .15 .04
105 Brian McRae .75 .23
106 Jose Melendez .15 .04
107 Orlando Merced .15 .04
108 Alan Mills .15 .04
109 Gino Minutelli .15 .04
110 Mickey Morandini .15 .04
111 Pedro Munoz .15 .04
112 Chris Nabholz .15 .04
113 Tim Naehring .15 .04
114 Charles Nagy .15 .04
115 Jim Neidlinger .15 .04
116 Rafael Novoa .15 .04
117 Jose Offerman .15 .04
118 Omar Olivares .75 .23
119 Javier Ortiz .15 .04
120 Al Osuna .15 .04
121 Rick Parker .15 .04
122 Dave Pavlas .15 .04
123 Geronimo Pena .15 .04
124 Mike Perez .15 .04
125 Phil Plantier .15 .04
126 Jim Poole .15 .04
127 Tom Quinlan .15 .04
128 Scott Radinsky .15 .04
129 Darren Reed .15 .04
130 Karl Rhodes .15 .04
131 Jeff Richardson .15 .04
132 Rich Rodriguez .15 .04
133 Dave Rohde .15 .04
134 Mel Rojas .15 .04
135 Vic Rosario .15 .04
136 Rich Rowland .15 .04
137 Scott Ruskin .15 .04
138 Bill Sampen .15 .04
139 Andres Santana .15 .04
140 David Segui .15 .04
141 Jeff Shaw .15 .04
142 Tim Sherrill .15 .04
143 Terry Shumpert .15 .04
144 Mike Simms .15 .04
145 Daryl Smith .15 .04
146 Luis Sojo .15 .04
147 Steve Springer .15 .04
148 Ray Stephens .15 .04
149 Lee Stevens .15 .04
150 Mel Stottlemyre Jr. .15 .04
151 Glenn Sutko .15 .04
152 Anthony Telford .15 .04
153 Frank Thomas 5.00 1.50
154 Randy Tomlin .15 .04
155 Brian Traxler .15 .04
156 Efrain Valdez .15 .04
157 Rafael Valdez .15 .04
158 Julio Valera .15 .04
159 Jim Vatcher .15 .04
160 Hector Villanueva .15 .04
161 Hector Wagner .15 .04
162 Dave Walsh .15 .04
163 Steve Wapnick .15 .04
164 Colby Ward .15 .04
165 Turner Ward .75 .23
166 Terry Wells .15 .04
167 Mark Whiten .15 .04
168 Mike York .15 .04
169 Cliff Young .15 .04
170 Checklist Card .15 .04
171 Checklist Card .15 .04

1991 Topps East Coast National

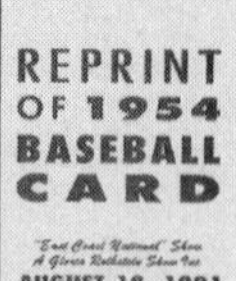

REPRINT
OF 1954
BASEBALL
CARD
AUGUST 16, 1991

This four-card, standard-size set was included in the paid admission for the 1991 East Coast National Show (August 15-18). Each card is a reproduction of the player's first Topps card: Aaron, ('54 Topps) Mantle, ('52 Topps) Musial, ('58 Topps) and Robinson ('57 Topps). In blue print on white, the backs indicate that these cards are reprints. The cards are unnumbered and checklisted below in alphabetical order.

Nm-Mt Ex-Mt
COMPLETE SET (4) 15.00 4.50
1 Hank Aaron 5.00 1.50
2 Mickey Mantle 8.00 2.40
3 Stan Musial 4.00 1.20
4 Frank Robinson 2.50 .75

1991 Topps Gallery of Champions

In what would be the final season for this issue, Topps issued these 12 cards to honor award winners and league leaders. These "metal" cards measure approximately 1 1/4" by 1 3/4" and were made in aluminum, silver and bronze. We have valued the aluminum versions. The bronze cards are worth 2X to 3X the aluminums while the silvers are worth 4X to 6X the aluminum versions. This set, just as all the other Topps Gallery sets, were issued in complete set form only. We have sequenced this set in alphabetical order.

Nm-Mt Ex-Mt
COMPLETE SET (12) 150.00 45.00
1 Sandy Alomar 8.00 2.40
2 Barry Bonds 40.00 12.00
3 George Brett 40.00 12.00
4 Doug Drabek 5.00 1.50
5 Cecil Fielder 8.00 2.40
6 John Franco 8.00 2.40
7 Rickey Henderson 30.00 9.00
8 Dave Justice 15.00 4.50

9 Willie McGee 8.00 2.40
10 Ryne Sandberg 30.00 9.00
11 Bobby Thigpen 5.00 1.50
12 Bob Welch 5.00 1.50

1991 Topps Glossy All-Stars

These 22 glossy standard-size cards were inserted one per Topps rack packs and honor the starting lineup, managers and honorary captains of the 1990 National and American League All-Star teams. This would be the final year that this insert set was issued and the design is similar to what Topps produced each year since 1984.

Nm-Mt Ex-Mt
COMPLETE SET (22) 10.00 3.00
1 Tony LaRussa MG .20 .06
2 Mark McGwire 2.50 .75
3 Steve Sax .10 .03
4 Wade Boggs .50 .15
5 Cal Ripken Jr. 3.00 .90
6 Rickey Henderson .75 .23
7 Ken Griffey, Jr. 2.00 .60
8 Jose Canseco .50 .15
9 Sandy Alomar Jr. .20 .06
10 Bob Welch .10 .03
11 Al Lopez CAPT .20 .06
12 Roger Craig MG .10 .03
13 Will Clark .50 .15
14 Ryne Sandberg .75 .23
15 Chris Sabo .10 .03
16 Ozzie Smith 1.00 .30
17 Kevin Mitchell .10 .03
18 Len Dykstra .20 .06
19 Andre Dawson .50 .15
20 Mike Scioscia .20 .06
21 Jack Armstrong .10 .03
22 Juan Marichal CAPT .30 .09

1991 Topps Ruth

This 11-card set was produced by Topps to commemorate the NBC made-for-television movie about Ruth that aired Sunday, October 6, 1991.

Nm-Mt Ex-Mt
COMPLETE SET (11) 10.00 3.00
1 Babe Ruth-Sunday 1.00 .30
October 6th NBC
2 Babe Ruth 1.00 .30
Stephen Lang as
Babe Ruth
3 Babe Ruth 1.00 .30
Bruce Weitz as
Miller Huggins
4 Babe Ruth 1.00 .30
Lisa Zane as
Claire Ruth
5 Babe Ruth 1.00 .30
Donald Moffat as
Jacob Ruppert
6 Babe Ruth 1.00 .30
Neil McDonough as
Lou Gehrig
7 Babe Ruth 2.00 .60
Pete Rose
as Ty Cobb
8 Babe Ruth 1.50 .45
Rod Carew
Baseball Consultant
9 Babe Ruth 1.00 .30
Ruth and Mgr. Huggins
10 Babe Ruth 1.00 .30
Ruth in Action
11 Babe Ruth 1.00 .30
Babe Calls His Shot

1991 Topps Stand-Ups

These stand-ups were not widely distributed and therefore appear to be a test issue. The stand-ups are packaged in a wrapper that has a checklist on the back. Each stand-up is actually a 2" by 2 1/2" plastic semi-transparent green container filled with sweet-tart type candy. The National League players came in green, the American league players came in red. There are also clear plastic variations for all players which are much tougher.

Nm-Mt Ex-Mt
COMPLETE SET (36) 200.00 60.00
1 Jim Abbott 1.00 .30
2 Sandy Alomar Jr. 2.00 .60
3 Wade Boggs 5.00 1.50
4 Barry Bonds 12.00 3.60
5 Bobby Bonilla 1.00 .30
6 George Brett 10.00 3.00
7 Jose Canseco 5.00 1.50
8 Will Clark 4.00 1.20
9 Roger Clemens 12.00 3.60
10 Eric Davis 2.00 .60
11 Andre Dawson 3.00 .90
12 Len Dykstra 2.00 .60
13 Cecil Fielder 2.00 .60
14 Carlton Fisk 5.00 1.50
15 Dwight Gooden 2.00 .60
16 Mark Grace 4.00 1.20
17 Ken Griffey Jr. 15.00 4.50
18 Tony Gwynn 12.00 3.60
19 Rickey Henderson 8.00 2.40
20 Bo Jackson 4.00 1.20
21 Dave Justice 4.00 1.20
22 Kevin Maas 1.00 .30
23 Ramon Martinez 2.00 .60
24 Don Mattingly 12.00 3.60
25 Ben McDonald 2.00 .60
26 Mark McGwire 20.00 6.00
27 Kevin Mitchell 1.00 .30
28 Cal Ripken 25.00 7.50
29 Nolan Ryan 25.00 7.50
30 Ryne Sandberg 8.00 2.40
31 Ozzie Smith 8.00 2.40
32 Dave Stewart 1.00 .30
33 Darryl Strawberry 2.00 .60
34 Frank Viola 1.00 .30
35 Matt Williams 3.00 .90
36 Robin Yount 5.00 1.50

1991 Topps Triple Headers

These balls feature the players' photo and fascimile autographs. Three players per team are featured. A piece of candy was included in each pack. We have sequenced this set in alphabetical order by league. There are reports that the Chicago Cub and St. Louis Cardinal balls were issued less frequently than other teams. They are noted as SP's below.

Nm-Mt Ex-Mt
COMPLETE SET (26) 120.00 36.00
A1 Ben McDonald 15.00 4.50
Cal Ripken
Gregg Olson
A2 Wade Boggs 8.00 2.40
Mike Greenwell
Roger Clemens
A3 Chuck Finley 4.00 1.20
Dave Winfield
Wally Joyner
A4 Carlton Fisk 15.00 4.50
Robin Ventura
Frank Thomas
A5 Sandy Alomar 2.00 .60
Alex Cole
Mark Lewis
A6 Cecil Fielder 4.00 1.20
Tony Phillips
Alan Trammell
A7 George Brett 8.00 2.40
Danny Tartabull
Bret Saberhagen
A8 Paul Molitor 6.00 1.80
Robin Yount
Greg Vaughn
A9 Scott Erickson 8.00 2.40
Kirby Puckett
Kent Hrbek
A10 Don Mattingly 8.00 2.40
Steve Sax
Willie Randolph
A11 Jose Canseco 6.00 1.80
Dave Henderson
Rickey Henderson
A12 Ken Griffey Jr. 15.00 4.50
Harold Reynolds
Ken Griffey Sr.
A13 Julio Franco 15.00 4.50
Nolan Ryan
Juan Gonzalez
A14 Roberto Alomar 4.00 1.20
Kelly Gruber
Joe Carter
N1 Ron Gant 4.00 1.20
Tom Glavine
David Justice
N2 Ryne Sandberg SP 25.00 7.50
George Bell
Mark Grace
N3 Eric Davis 2.00 .60
Barry Larkin
Chris Sabo
N4 Jeff Bagwell 40.00 12.00
Craig Biggio
Ken Caminiti
N5 Ramon Martinez 4.00 1.20
Eddie Murray
Darryl Strawberry
N6 Delino DeShields 2.00 .60
Dennis Martinez
Ivan Calderon
N7 Vince Coleman 2.00 .60
Dwight Gooden
Howard Johnson
N8 Len Dykstra 4.00 1.20
John Kruk
Dale Murphy
N9 Barry Bonds 2.00 .60
Bobby Bonilla
Andy Van Slyke
N10 Fred McGriff 6.00 1.80
Tony Gwynn
Benito Santiago
N11 Will Clark 6.00 1.80
Kevin Mitchell
Matt Williams
N12 Pedro Guerrero SP 15.00 4.50
Ozzie Smith
Todd Zeile

1991-94 Topps Golden Spikes

From 1991 through 1994, Topps produced a special card for the Golden Spikes award winner that was given away to attendees of the annual United States Baseball Federation luncheon. The USBF sponsors the Golden Spikes award, given to the top amateur baseball player. The unnumbered card backs indicate the player's name, year of award and luncheon date. The card fronts vary -- the 1991 and 1992 cards use slightly altered Topps Major League Debut designs, the 1993 and 1994 cards use slightly altered Topps Traded USA designs.

Nm-Mt Ex-Mt
COMPLETE SET (4) 200.00 60.00
1 Alex Fernandez 40.00 12.00
1991 ML Debut
2 Mike Kelly 20.00 6.00
1992 ML Debut
3 Phil Nevin 50.00 15.00
1993 USA
4 Darren Dreifort 40.00 12.00
1994 USA

1992 Topps Pre-Production Sheet

This 1992 Topps pre-production sample sheet measures approximately 7 3/4" by 10 3/4" and features nine player cards. The sheet is unperforated and if cut, the cards would measure the standard size. The fronts have glossy color action photos on a white card face, with different color borders overlaying the picture. In a horizontal format, the backs have biography and complete Major League statistics. Moreover, some of the backs display pictures of baseball stadiums, if the player's career length permits. The cards are numbered on the back with "1992 Pre-Production Sample" prominent. There are two different types of sheets issued. Either sheet has the same value.

Nm-Mt Ex-Mt
COMPLETE SET (9) 5.00 1.50
3 Shawon Dunston .50 .15
16 Mike Heath .50 .15
18 Todd Frohwirth .50 .15
20 Bip Roberts .50 .15
131 Rob Dibble .50 .15
174 Otis Nixon 1.00 .30
273 Denny Martinez 1.00 .30
325 Brett Butler 1.00 .30
798 Tom Lasorda MG 2.00 .60

1992 Topps Gold Pre-Production Sheet

This 1992 Topps Gold pre-production sample sheet measures approximately 7 3/4" by 10 3/4" and features nine player cards. The sheet is unperforated and if cut, the cards would measure the standard size. The fronts have glossy color action photos on a white card face, with different color borders overlaying the picture. In a horizontal format, the backs have biography and complete Major League statistics. Moreover, some of the backs display pictures of baseball stadiums, if the player's career length permits. The cards are numbered on the back with "1992 Pre-Production Sample" prominent. These sheets have also been seen without gold.

Nm-Mt Ex-Mt
COMPLETE SET (9) 25.00 7.50
1 Nolan Ryan 10.00 3.00
15 Denny Martinez 1.50 .45
20 Bip Roberts 1.00 .30
40 Cal Ripken 10.00 3.00
261 Tom Lasorda MG 2.50 .75
370 Shawon Dunston 1.00 .30
512 Mike Heath 1.00 .30
655 Brett Butler 1.50 .45
757 Rob Dibble 1.00 .30

1992 Topps

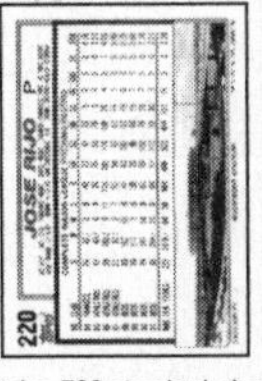

The 1992 Topps set contains 792 standard-size cards. Cards were distributed in plastic wrap packs, jumbo packs, rack packs and factory sets. The fronts have either posed or action color player photos on a white card face. Different color stripes frame the pictures, and the player's name and team name appear in two short color stripes respectively at the bottom. Special subsets included are Record Breakers (2-5), Prospects (58, 126, 179, 473, 551, 591, 618, 656, 676), and All-Stars (386-407). The key Rookie Cards in this set are Shawn Green and Manny Ramirez.

Nm-Mt Ex-Mt
COMPLETE SET (792) 25.00 7.50
COMP.FACT.SET (802) 25.00 7.50
COMP.HOLIDAY (811) 40.00 12.00
1 Nolan Ryan 1.00 .30
2 Ricky Henderson RB .15 .04
Most career SB's
(Some cards have print
marks that show 1.991
on the front)
3 Jeff Reardon RB .05 .02
4 Nolan Ryan RB .50 .15
5 Dave Winfield RB .05 .02
6 Brien Taylor RC .25 .07
7 Jim Olander .05 .02
8 Bryan Hickerson RC .10 .03
9 Jon Farrell RC .10 .03
10 Wade Boggs .15 .04
11 Jack McDowell .05 .02
12 Luis Gonzalez .15 .04
13 Mike Scioscia .05 .02
14 Wes Chamberlain .05 .02
15 Dennis Martinez .10 .03
16 Jeff Montgomery .05 .02
17 Randy Milligan .05 .02
18 Greg Cadaret .05 .02
19 Jamie Quirk .05 .02
20 Bip Roberts .05 .02
21 Buck Rodgers MG .05 .02
22 Bill Wegman .05 .02
23 Chuck Knoblauch .10 .03
24 Randy Myers .05 .02
25 Ron Gant .10 .03
26 Mike Bielecki .05 .02
27 Juan Gonzalez .25 .07
28 Mike Schooler .05 .02
29 Mickey Tettleton .05 .02
30 John Kruk .10 .03
31 Bryn Smith .05 .02
32 Chris Nabholz .05 .02
33 Carlos Baerga .05 .02
34 Jeff Juden .05 .02
35 Dave Righetti .10 .03
36 Scott Ruffcorn RC .10 .03
37 Luis Polonia .05 .02
38 Tom Candiotti .05 .02
39 Greg Olson .05 .02
40 Cal Ripken 2.00 .60
41 Craig Lefferts .05 .02
42 Mike Macfarlane .05 .02
43 Jose Lind .05 .02
44 Rick Aguilera .10 .03
45 Gary Carter .15 .04
46 Steve Farr .05 .02
47 Rex Hudler .05 .02
48 Scott Scudder .05 .02
49 Damon Berryhill .05 .02
50 Ken Griffey Jr. .40 .12
51 Tom Runnells MG .05 .02
52 Juan Bell .05 .02
53 Tommy Gregg .05 .02
54 David Wells .10 .03
55 Rafael Palmeiro .15 .04
56 Charlie O'Brien .05 .02
57 Donn Pall .05 .02
58 Brad Ausmus RC .25 .07
Jim Campanis Jr.
Dave Nilsson
Doug Robbins
59 Mo Vaughn .10 .03
60 Tony Fernandez .05 .02
61 Paul O'Neill .15 .04
62 Gene Nelson .05 .02
63 Randy Ready .05 .02
64 Bob Kipper .05 .02
65 Willie McGee .10 .03
66 Scott Stahoviak RC .10 .03
67 Luis Salazar .05 .02
68 Marvin Freeman .05 .02
69 Kenny Lofton .25 .07
70 Gary Gaetti .10 .03
71 Erik Hanson .05 .02
72 Eddie Zosky .05 .02
73 Brian Barnes .05 .02
74 Scott Leius .05 .02
75 Bret Saberhagen .10 .03
76 Mike Gallego .05 .02
77 Jack Armstrong .05 .02
78 Ivan Rodriguez .25 .07
79 Jesse Orosco .05 .02
80 David Justice .10 .03
81 Ced Landrum .05 .02
82 Doug Simons .05 .02
83 Tommy Greene .05 .02
84 Leo Gomez .05 .02
85 Jose DeLeon .05 .02
86 Steve Finley .10 .03
87 Bob MacDonald .05 .02
88 Darrin Jackson .05 .02
89 Neal Heaton .05 .02
90 Robin Yount .40 .12
91 Jeff Reed .05 .02
92 Lenny Harris .05 .02
93 Reggie Jefferson .05 .02
94 Sammy Sosa .40 .12
95 Scott Bailes .05 .02
96 Tom McKinnon RC .10 .03
97 Luis Rivera .05 .02
98 Mike Harkey .05 .02
99 Jeff Treadway .05 .02
100 Jose Canseco .25 .07
101 Omar Vizquel .10 .03
102 Scott Kamieniecki .05 .02
103 Ricky Jordan .05 .02
104 Jeff Ballard .05 .02
105 Felix Jose .05 .02
106 Mike Boddicker .05 .02
107 Dan Pasqua .05 .02
108 Mike Timlin .05 .02
109 Roger Craig MG .05 .02
110 Ryne Sandberg .40 .12
111 Mark Carreon .05 .02
112 Oscar Azocar .05 .02
113 Mike Greenwell .05 .02
114 Mark Portugal .05 .02
115 Terry Pendleton .10 .03
116 Willie Randolph .10 .03
117 Scott Terry .05 .02
118 Chili Davis .10 .03
119 Mark Gardner .05 .02
120 Alan Trammell .15 .04
121 Derek Bell .10 .03
122 Gary Varsho .05 .02
123 Bob Ojeda .05 .02
124 Shawn Livsey RC .10 .03
125 Chris Hoiles .05 .02
126 Ryan Klesko .25 .07
John Jaha RC
Rico Brogna
Dave Staton
127 Carlos Quintana .05 .02
128 Kurt Stillwell .05 .02
129 Melido Perez .05 .02
130 Alvin Davis .05 .02
131 Checklist 1-132 .05 .02
132 Eric Show .05 .02
133 Rance Mulliniks .05 .02
134 Darryl Kile .10 .03
135 Von Hayes .05 .02
136 Bill Doran .05 .02
137 Jeff D. Robinson .05 .02
138 Monty Fariss .05 .02
139 Jeff Innis .05 .02
140 Mark Grace UER .15 .04
Home Calie., should
be Calif.
141 Jim Leyland MG UER .10 .03
(No closed parenthesis
after East in 1991)
142 Todd Van Poppel .05 .02
143 Paul Gibson .05 .02
144 Bill Swift .05 .02
145 Danny Tartabull .05 .02
146 Al Newman .05 .02
147 Cris Carpenter .05 .02
148 Anthony Young .05 .02
149 Brian Bohanon .05 .02
150 Roger Clemens UER .50 .15
(League leading ERA in
1990 not italicized)
151 Jeff Hamilton .05 .02
152 Charlie Leibrandt .05 .02
153 Ron Karkovice .05 .02
154 Hensley Meulens .05 .02
155 Scott Bankhead .05 .02
156 Manny Ramirez RC 1.50 .45
157 Keith Miller .05 .02
158 Todd Frohwirth .05 .02
159 Darrin Fletcher .05 .02
160 Bobby Bonilla .10 .03
161 Casey Candaele .05 .02
162 Paul Faries .05 .02
163 Dana Kiecker .05 .02
164 Shane Mack .05 .02
165 Mark Langston .05 .02
166 Geronimo Pena .05 .02
167 Andy Allanson .05 .02
168 Dwight Smith .05 .02
169 Chuck Crim .05 .02
170 Alex Cole .05 .02
171 Bill Plummer MG .05 .02
172 Juan Berenguer .05 .02
173 Brian Downing .05 .02
174 Steve Frey .05 .02
175 Orel Hershiser .10 .03
176 Ramon Garcia .05 .02
177 Dan Gladden .05 .02
178 Jim Acker .05 .02
179 Bobby DeJardin .05 .02
Cesar Bernhardt
Armando Moreno
Andy Stankiewicz
180 Kevin Mitchell .05 .02
181 Hector Villanueva .05 .02
182 Jeff Reardon .10 .03
183 Brent Mayne .05 .02
184 Jimmy Jones .05 .02
185 Benito Santiago .10 .03
186 Cliff Floyd RC .75 .23
187 Ernie Riles .05 .02
188 Jose Guzman .05 .02
189 Junior Felix .05 .02
190 Glenn Davis .05 .02
191 Charlie Hough .10 .03
192 Dave Fleming .05 .02
193 Omar Olivares .05 .02
194 Eric Karros .10 .03
195 David Cone .10 .03
196 Frank Castillo .05 .02
197 Glenn Braggs .05 .02
198 Scott Aldred .05 .02
199 Jeff Blauser .05 .02
200 Len Dykstra .10 .03
201 B.Showalter RC MG .25 .07
202 Rick Honeycutt .05 .02
203 Greg Myers .05 .02
204 Trevor Wilson .05 .02
205 Jay Howell .05 .02
206 Luis Sojo .05 .02
207 Jack Clark .10 .03
208 Julio Machado .05 .02
209 Lloyd McClendon .05 .02
210 Ozzie Guillen .05 .02
211 Jeremy Hernandez RC .10 .03
212 Randy Velarde .05 .02
213 Les Lancaster .05 .02
214 Andy Mota .05 .02
215 Rich Gossage .10 .03
216 Brent Gates RC .10 .03
217 Brian Harper .05 .02
218 Mike Flanagan .05 .02
219 Jerry Browne .05 .02
220 Jose Rijo .05 .02
221 Skeeter Barnes .05 .02
222 Jaime Navarro .05 .02
223 Mel Hall .05 .02
224 Bret Barberie .05 .02
225 Roberto Alomar .25 .07
226 Pete Smith .05 .02
227 Daryl Boston .05 .02
228 Eddie Whitson .05 .02
229 Shawn Boskie .05 .02
230 Dick Schofield .05 .02
231 Brian Drahman .05 .02
232 John Smiley .05 .02
233 Mitch Webster .05 .02
234 Terry Steinbach .05 .02
235 Jack Morris .10 .03
236 Bill Pecota .05 .02
237 Jose Hernandez RC .40 .12

238 Greg Litton .05 .02
239 Brian Holman .05 .02
240 Andres Galarraga .10 .03
241 Gerald Young .05 .02
242 Mike Mussina .25 .07
243 Alvaro Espinoza .05 .02
244 Darren Daulton .10 .03
245 John Smoltz .15 .04
246 Jason Pruitt RC .10 .03
247 Chuck Finley .10 .03
248 Jim Gantner .05 .02
249 Tony Fossas .05 .02
250 Ken Griffey Sr. .10 .03
251 Kevin Elster .05 .02
252 Dennis Rasmussen .05 .02
253 Terry Kennedy .05 .02
254 Ryan Bowen .05 .02
255 Robin Ventura .10 .03
256 Mike Aldrete .05 .02
257 Jeff Russell .05 .02
258 Jim Lindeman .05 .02
259 Ron Darling .05 .02
260 Devon White .05 .02
261 Tom Lasorda MG .10 .03
262 Terry Lee .05 .02
263 Bob Patterson .05 .02
264 Checklist 133-264 .05 .02
265 Teddy Higuera .05 .02
266 Roberto Kelly .05 .02
267 Steve Bedrosian .05 .02
268 Brady Anderson .10 .03
269 Ruben Amaro .05 .02
270 Tony Gwynn .30 .09
271 Tracy Jones .05 .02
272 Jerry Don Gleaton .05 .02
273 Craig Grebeck .05 .02
274 Bob Scanlan .05 .02
275 Todd Zeile .05 .02
276 Shawn Green RC 1.50 .45
277 Scott Chiamparino .05 .02
278 Darryl Hamilton .05 .02
279 Jim Clancy .05 .02
280 Carlos Martinez .05 .02
281 Kevin Appier .10 .03
282 John Wehner .05 .02
283 Reggie Sanders .10 .03
284 Gene Larkin .05 .02
285 Bob Welch .05 .02
286 Gilberto Reyes .05 .02
287 Pete Schourek .05 .02
288 Andujar Cedeno .05 .02
289 Mike Morgan .05 .02
290 Bo Jackson .25 .07
291 Phil Garner MG .05 .02
292 Ray Lankford .05 .02
293 Mike Henneman .05 .02
294 Dave Valle .05 .02
295 Alonzo Powell .05 .02
296 Tom Brunansky .05 .02
297 Kevin Brown .10 .03
298 Kelly Gruber .05 .02
299 Charles Nagy .05 .02
300 Don Mattingly .60 .18
301 Kirk McCaskill .05 .02
302 Joey Cora .05 .02
303 Dan Plesac .05 .02
304 Joe Oliver .05 .02
305 Tom Glavine .15 .04
306 Al Shirley RC .10 .03
307 Bruce Ruffin .05 .02
308 Craig Shipley .05 .02
309 Dave Martinez .05 .02
310 Jose Mesa .05 .02
311 Henry Cotto .05 .02
312 Mike LaValliere .05 .02
313 Kevin Tapani .05 .02
314 Jeff Huson .05 .02
(Shows Jose Canseco
sliding into second)
315 Juan Samuel .05 .02
316 Curt Schilling .15 .04
317 Mike Bordick .05 .02
318 Steve Howe .05 .02
319 Tony Phillips .05 .02
320 George Bell .05 .02
321 Lou Piniella MG .10 .03
322 Tim Burke .05 .02
323 Milt Thompson .05 .02
324 Danny Darwin .05 .02
325 Joe Orsulak .05 .02
326 Eric King .05 .02
327 Jay Buhner .10 .03
328 Joel Johnston .05 .02
329 Franklin Stubbs .05 .02
330 Will Clark .25 .07
331 Steve Lake .05 .02
332 Chris Jones .05 .02
333 Pat Tabler .05 .02
334 Kevin Gross .05 .02
335 Dave Henderson .05 .02
336 Greg Anthony RC .10 .03
337 Alejandro Pena .05 .02
338 Shawn Abner .05 .02
339 Tom Browning .05 .02
340 Otis Nixon .05 .02
341 Bob Geren .05 .02
342 Tim Spehr .05 .02
343 John Vander Wal .05 .02
344 Jack Daugherty .05 .02
345 Zane Smith .05 .02
346 Rheal Cormier .05 .02
347 Kent Hrbek .10 .03
348 Rick Wilkins .05 .02
349 Steve Lyons .05 .02
350 Gregg Olson .05 .02
351 Greg Riddoch MG .05 .02
352 Ed Nunez .05 .02
353 Braulio Castillo .05 .02
354 Dave Bergman .05 .02
355 Warren Newson .05 .02
356 Luis Quinones .05 .02
357 Mike Witt .05 .02
358 Ted Wood .05 .02
359 Mike Moore .05 .02
360 Lance Parrish .10 .03
361 Barry Jones .05 .02
362 Javier Ortiz .05 .02
363 John Candelaria .05 .02
364 Glenallen Hill .05 .02
365 Duane Ward .05 .02
366 Checklist 265-396 .05 .02
367 Rafael Belliard .05 .02
368 Bill Krueger .05 .02
369 Steve Whitaker RC .10 .03
370 Shawon Dunston .05 .02
371 Dante Bichette .10 .03
372 Kip Gross .05 .02
373 Don Robinson .05 .02
374 Bernie Williams .15 .04
375 Bert Blyleven .10 .03
376 Chris Donnels .05 .02
377 Bob Zupcic RC .10 .03
378 Joel Skinner .05 .02
379 Steve Chitren .05 .02
380 Barry Bonds .60 .18
381 Sparky Anderson MG .10 .03
382 Sid Fernandez .05 .02
383 Dave Hollins .05 .02
384 Mark Lee .05 .02
385 Tim Wallach .05 .02
386 Will Clark AS .10 .03
387 Ryne Sandberg AS .25 .07
388 Howard Johnson AS .05 .02
389 Barry Larkin AS .10 .03
390 Barry Bonds AS .30 .09
391 Ron Gant AS .05 .02
392 Bobby Bonilla AS .05 .02
393 Craig Biggio AS .10 .03
394 Dennis Martinez AS .05 .02
395 Tom Glavine AS .10 .03
396 Lee Smith AS .05 .02
397 Cecil Fielder AS .05 .02
398 Julio Franco AS .05 .02
399 Wade Boggs AS .10 .03
400 Cal Ripken AS .40 .12
401 Jose Canseco AS .25 .07
402 Joe Carter AS .05 .02
403 Ruben Sierra AS .05 .02
404 Matt Nokes AS .05 .02
405 Roger Clemens AS .25 .07
406 Jim Abbott AS .10 .03
407 Bryan Harvey AS .05 .02
408 Bob Milacki .05 .02
409 Geno Petralli .05 .02
410 Dave Stewart .10 .03
411 Mike Jackson .05 .02
412 Luis Aquino .05 .02
413 Tim Teufel .05 .02
414 Jeff Ware .05 .02
415 Jim Deshaies .05 .02
416 Ellis Burks .10 .03
417 Allan Anderson .05 .02
418 Alfredo Griffin .05 .02
419 Wally Whitehurst .05 .02
420 Sandy Alomar Jr. .05 .02
421 Juan Agosto .05 .02
422 Sam Horn .05 .02
423 Jeff Fassero .05 .02
424 Paul McClellan .05 .02
425 Cecil Fielder .10 .03
426 Tim Raines .10 .03
427 Eddie Taubensee RC .25 .07
428 Dennis Boyd .05 .02
429 Tony LaRussa MG .10 .03
430 Steve Sax .05 .02
431 Tom Gordon .05 .02
432 Billy Hatcher .05 .02
433 Cal Eldred .05 .02
434 Wally Backman .05 .02
435 Mark Eichhorn .05 .02
436 Mookie Wilson .10 .03
437 Scott Servais .05 .02
438 Mike Maddux .05 .02
439 Chico Walker .05 .02
440 Doug Drabek .05 .02
441 Rob Deer .05 .02
442 Dave West .05 .02
443 Spike Owen .05 .02
444 Tyrone Hill RC .10 .03
445 Matt Williams .10 .03
446 Mark Lewis .05 .02
447 David Segui .05 .02
448 Tom Pagnozzi .05 .02
449 Jeff Johnson .05 .02
450 Mark McGwire .60 .18
451 Tom Henke .05 .02
452 Wilson Alvarez .05 .02
453 Gary Redus .05 .02
454 Darren Holmes .05 .02
455 Pete O'Brien .05 .02
456 Pat Combs .05 .02
457 Hubie Brooks .05 .02
458 Frank Tanana .05 .02
459 Tom Kelly MG .05 .02
460 Andre Dawson .10 .03
461 Doug Jones .05 .02
462 Rich Rodriguez .05 .02
463 Mike Simms .05 .02
464 Mike Jeffcoat .05 .02
465 Barry Larkin .25 .07
466 Stan Belinda .05 .02
467 Lonnie Smith .05 .02
468 Greg Harris .05 .02
469 Jim Eisenreich .05 .02
470 Pedro Guerrero .10 .03
471 Jose DeJesus .05 .02
472 Rich Rowland RC .10 .03
473 Frank Bolick .05 .02
Craig Paquette
Tom Redington
Paul Russo UER
(Line around top border)
474 Mike Rossiter RC .10 .03
475 Robby Thompson .05 .02
476 Randy Bush .05 .02
477 Greg Hibbard .05 .02
478 Dale Sveum .05 .02
479 Chito Martinez .05 .02
480 Scott Sanderson .05 .02
481 Tino Martinez .15 .04
482 Jimmy Key .10 .03
483 Terry Shumpert .05 .02
484 Mike Hartley .05 .02
485 Chris Sabo .05 .02
486 Bob Walk .05 .02
487 John Cerutti .05 .02
488 Scott Cooper .05 .02
489 Bobby Cox MG .10 .03
490 Julio Franco .10 .03
491 Jeff Brantley .05 .02
492 Mike Devereaux .05 .02
493 Jose Offerman .05 .02
494 Gary Thurman .05 .02
495 Carney Lansford .10 .03
496 Joe Grahe .05 .02
497 Andy Ashby .05 .02
498 Gerald Perry .05 .02
499 Dave Otto .05 .02
500 Vince Coleman .05 .02
501 Rob Mallicoat .05 .02
502 Greg Briley .05 .02
503 Pascual Perez .05 .02
504 Aaron Sele RC .40 .12
505 Bobby Thigpen .05 .02
506 Todd Benzinger .05 .02
507 Candy Maldonado .05 .02
508 Bill Gullickson .05 .02
509 Doug Dascenzo .05 .02
510 Frank Viola .10 .03
511 Kenny Rogers .10 .03
512 Mike Heath .05 .02
513 Kevin Bass .05 .02
514 Kim Batiste .05 .02
515 Delino DeShields .05 .02
516 Ed Sprague .05 .02
517 Jim Gott .05 .02
518 Jose Melendez .05 .02
519 Hal McRae MG .10 .03
520 Jeff Bagwell .25 .07
521 Joe Hesketh .05 .02
522 Milt Cuyler .05 .02
523 Shawn Hillegas .05 .02
524 Don Slaught .05 .02
525 Randy Johnson .25 .07
526 Doug Piatt .05 .02
527 Checklist 397-528 .05 .02
528 Steve Foster .05 .02
529 Joe Girardi .05 .02
530 Jim Abbott .15 .04
531 Larry Walker .15 .04
532 Mike Huff .05 .02
533 Mackey Sasser .05 .02
534 Benji Gil RC .25 .07
535 Dave Stieb .05 .02
536 Willie Wilson .05 .02
537 Mark Leiter .05 .02
538 Jose Uribe .05 .02
539 Thomas Howard .05 .02
540 Ben McDonald .05 .02
541 Jose Tolentino .05 .02
542 Keith Mitchell .05 .02
543 Jerome Walton .05 .02
544 Cliff Brantley .05 .02
545 Andy Van Slyke .10 .03
546 Paul Sorrento .05 .02
547 Herm Winningham .05 .02
548 Mark Guthrie .05 .02
549 Joe Torre MG .10 .03
550 Darryl Strawberry .15 .04
551 Wilfredo Cordero .25 .07
Chipper Jones
Manny Alexander
Alex Arias UER
(No line around
top border)
552 Dave Gallagher .05 .02
553 Edgar Martinez .15 .04
554 Donald Harris .05 .02
555 Frank Thomas .25 .07
556 Storm Davis .05 .02
557 Dickie Thon .05 .02
558 Scott Garrelts .05 .02
559 Steve Olin .05 .02
560 Rickey Henderson .25 .07
561 Jose Vizcaino .05 .02
562 Wade Taylor .05 .02
563 Pat Borders .05 .02
564 Jimmy Gonzalez RC .10 .03
565 Lee Smith .10 .03
566 Bill Sampen .05 .02
567 Dean Palmer .10 .03
568 Bryan Harvey .05 .02
569 Tony Pena .05 .02
570 Lou Whitaker .10 .03
571 Randy Tomlin .05 .02
572 Greg Vaughn .10 .03
573 Kelly Downs .05 .02
574 Steve Avery UER .05 .02
(Should be 13 games
for Durham in 1989)
575 Kirby Puckett .25 .07
576 Heathcliff Slocumb .05 .02
577 Kevin Seitzer .05 .02
578 Lee Guetterman .05 .02
579 Johnny Oates MG .05 .02
580 Greg Maddux .40 .12
581 Stan Javier .05 .02
582 Vicente Palacios .05 .02
583 Mel Rojas .05 .02
584 Wayne Rosenthal RC .10 .03
585 Lenny Webster .05 .02
586 Rod Nichols .05 .02
587 Mickey Morandini .05 .02
588 Russ Swan .05 .02
589 Mariano Duncan .05 .02
590 Howard Johnson .05 .02
591 Jeromy Burnitz .10 .03
Jacob Brumfield
Alan Cockrell
D.J. Dozier
592 Denny Neagle .10 .03
593 Steve Decker .05 .02
594 Brian Barber RC .10 .03
595 Bruce Hurst .05 .02
596 Kent Mercker .05 .02
597 Mike Magnante RC .10 .03
598 Jody Reed .05 .02
599 Steve Searcy .05 .02
600 Paul Molitor .15 .04
601 Dave Smith .05 .02
602 Mike Fetters .05 .02
603 Luis Mercedes .05 .02
604 Chris Gwynn .05 .02
605 Scott Erickson .05 .02
606 Brook Jacoby .05 .02
607 Todd Stottlemyre .05 .02
608 Scott Bradley .05 .02
609 Mike Hargrove MG .10 .03
610 Eric Davis .10 .03
611 Brian Hunter .05 .02
612 Pat Kelly .05 .02
613 Pedro Munoz .05 .02
614 Al Osuna .05 .02
615 Matt Merullo .05 .02
616 Larry Andersen .05 .02
617 Junior Ortiz .05 .02
618 Cesar Hernandez .05 .02
Steve Hosey
Jeff McNeely
Dan Peltier
619 Danny Jackson .05 .02
620 George Brett .60 .18
621 Dan Gakeler .05 .02
622 Steve Buechele .05 .02
623 Bob Tewksbury .05 .02
624 Shawn Estes RC .25 .07
625 Kevin McReynolds .05 .02
626 Chris Haney .05 .02
627 Mike Sharperson .05 .02
628 Mark Williamson .05 .02
629 Wally Joyner .10 .03
630 Carlton Fisk .15 .04
631 Armando Reynoso RC .25 .07
632 Felix Fermin .05 .02
633 Mitch Williams .05 .02
634 Manuel Lee .05 .02
635 Harold Baines .10 .03
636 Greg Harris .05 .02
637 Orlando Merced .05 .02
638 Chris Bosio .05 .02
639 Wayne Housie .05 .02
640 Xavier Hernandez .05 .02
641 David Howard .05 .02
642 Tim Crews .05 .02
643 Rick Cerone .05 .02
644 Terry Leach .05 .02
645 Deion Sanders .15 .04
646 Craig Wilson .05 .02
647 Marquis Grissom .05 .02
648 Scott Fletcher .05 .02
649 Norm Charlton .05 .02
650 Jesse Barfield .05 .02
651 Joe Slusarski .05 .02
652 Bobby Rose .05 .02
653 Dennis Lamp .05 .02
654 Allen Watson RC .10 .03
655 Brett Butler .10 .03
656 Rudy Pemberton .10 .03
Henry Rodriguez
Lee Tinsley RC
Gerald Williams
657 Dave Johnson .05 .02
658 Checklist 529-660 .05 .02
659 Brian McRae .05 .02
660 Fred McGriff .15 .04
661 Bill Landrum .05 .02
662 Juan Guzman .05 .02
663 Greg Gagne .05 .02
664 Ken Hill .05 .02
665 Dave Haas .05 .02
666 Tom Foley .05 .02
667 Roberto Hernandez .05 .02
668 Dwayne Henry .05 .02
669 Jim Fregosi MG .05 .02
670 Harold Reynolds .10 .03
671 Mark Whiten .05 .02
672 Eric Plunk .05 .02
673 Todd Hundley .05 .02
674 Mo Sanford .05 .02
675 Bobby Witt .05 .02
676 Sam Militello .25 .07
Pat Mahomes RC
Turk Wendell
Roger Salkeld
677 John Marzano .05 .02
678 Joe Klink .05 .02
679 Pete Incaviglia .05 .02
680 Dale Murphy .25 .07
681 Rene Gonzales .05 .02
682 Andy Benes .05 .02
683 Jim Poole .05 .02
684 Trever Miller RC .10 .03
685 Scott Livingstone .05 .02
686 Rich DeLucia .05 .02
687 Harvey Pulliam .05 .02
688 Tim Belcher .05 .02
689 Mark Lemke .05 .02
690 John Franco .10 .03
691 Walt Weiss .05 .02
692 Scott Ruskin .05 .02
693 Jeff King .05 .02
694 Mike Gardiner .05 .02
695 Gary Sheffield .10 .03
696 Joe Boever .05 .02
697 Mike Felder .05 .02
698 John Habyan .05 .02
699 Cito Gaston MG .05 .02
700 Ruben Sierra .05 .02
701 Scott Radinsky .05 .02
702 Lee Stevens .05 .02
703 Mark Wohlers .05 .02
704 Curt Young .05 .02
705 Dwight Evans .10 .03
706 Rob Murphy .05 .02
707 Gregg Jefferies .05 .02
708 Tom Bolton .05 .02
709 Chris James .05 .02
710 Kevin Maas .05 .02
711 Ricky Bones .05 .02
712 Curt Wilkerson .05 .02
713 Roger McDowell .05 .02
714 Pokey Reese RC .25 .07
715 Craig Biggio .15 .04
716 Kirk Dressendorfer .05 .02
717 Ken Dayley .05 .02
718 B.J. Surhoff .10 .03
719 Terry Mulholland .05 .02
720 Kirk Gibson .10 .03
721 Mike Pagliarulo .05 .02
722 Walt Terrell .05 .02
723 Jose Oquendo .05 .02
724 Kevin Morton .05 .02
725 Dwight Gooden .15 .04
726 Kirt Manwaring .05 .02
727 Chuck McElroy .05 .02
728 Dave Burba .05 .02
729 Art Howe MG .05 .02
730 Ramon Martinez .05 .02
731 Donnie Hill .05 .02
732 Nelson Santovenia .05 .02
733 Bob Melvin .05 .02
734 Scott Hatteberg RC .25 .07
735 Greg Swindell .05 .02
736 Lance Johnson .05 .02
737 Kevin Reimer .05 .02
738 Dennis Eckersley .10 .03
739 Rob Ducey .05 .02
740 Ken Caminiti .10 .03
741 Mark Gubicza .05 .02
742 Bill Spiers .05 .02
743 Darren Lewis .05 .02
744 Chris Hammond .05 .02
745 Dave Magadan .05 .02
746 Bernard Gilkey .05 .02
747 Willie Banks .05 .02
748 Matt Nokes .05 .02
749 Jerald Clark .05 .02
750 Travis Fryman .10 .03
751 Steve Wilson .05 .02
752 Billy Ripken .05 .02
753 Paul Assenmacher .05 .02
754 Charlie Hayes .05 .02
755 Alex Fernandez .05 .02
756 Gary Pettis .05 .02
757 Rob Dibble .10 .03
758 Tim Naehring .05 .02
759 Jeff Torborg MG .05 .02
760 Ozzie Smith .40 .12
761 Mike Fitzgerald .05 .02
762 John Burkett .05 .02
763 Kyle Abbott .05 .02
764 Tyler Green RC .10 .03
765 Pete Harnisch .05 .02
766 Mark Davis .05 .02
767 Kal Daniels .05 .02
768 Jim Thome .25 .07
769 Jack Howell .05 .02
770 Sid Bream .05 .02
771 Arthur Rhodes .05 .02
772 Garry Templeton UER .05 .02
(Stat heading in for pitchers)
773 Hal Morris .05 .02
774 Bud Black .05 .02
775 Ivan Calderon .05 .02
776 Doug Henry RC .10 .03
777 John Olerud .10 .03
778 Tim Leary .05 .02
779 Jay Bell .10 .03
780 Eddie Murray .25 .07
781 Paul Abbott .05 .02
782 Phil Plantier .05 .02
783 Joe Magrane .05 .02
784 Ken Patterson .05 .02
785 Albert Belle .10 .03
786 Royce Clayton .05 .02
787 Checklist 661-792 .05 .02
788 Mike Stanton .05 .02
789 Bobby Valentine MG .05 .02
790 Joe Carter .10 .03
791 Danny Cox .05 .02
792 Dave Winfield .10 .03

1992 Topps Gold

Topps produced a 792-card Topps Gold factory set packaged in a foil display box. Only this set contained an additional card of Brien Taylor, numbered 793 and hand signed by him. The production run was 12,000 sets. The Topps Gold cards were also available in regular series packs. According to Topps, on average collectors would find one Topps Gold card in every 36 wax packs, one in every 18 cello packs, one in every 12 rak packs, five per Vending box, one in every six jumbo packs, and ten per regular factory set. The checklist cards in the regular set were replaced with six individual Rookie player cards (131, 264, 366, 527, 658, 787) in the gold set. There were a number of uncorrected errors in the Gold set. Steve Finley (86) has gold band indicating he is Mark Davidson of the Astros. Andujar Cedeno (288) is listed as a member of the New York Yankees. Mike Huff (532) is listed as a member of the Boston Red Sox. Barry Larkin (465) is listed as a member of the Houston Astros but is correctly listed as a member of the Cincinnati Reds on his Gold Winners cards. Typically the individual cards are sold at a multiple of the player's respective value in the regular set.

	Nm-Mt	Ex-Mt
COMPLETE SET (792)	80.00	24.00
COMP.FACT.SET (793)	80.00	24.00
*STARS: 6X TO 15X BASIC CARDS		
*ROOKIES: 4X TO 10X BASIC CARDS		
131 Terry Mathews	.75	.23
264 Rod Beck	.75	.23
366 Tony Perezchica	.75	.23
527 Terry McDaniel	.75	.23
658 John Ramos	.75	.23
787 Brian Williams	.75	.23
793 B. Taylor AU/12000	15.00	4.50

1992 Topps Gold Winners

The 1992 Topps baseball card packs featured "Match-the-Stats" game cards in which the consumer could save "Runs". For 2.00 and every 100 Runs saved in this game, the consumer could receive through a mail-in offer ten Topps Gold cards. These particular Topps Gold cards carry the word "Winner" in gold foil on the card front. The checklist cards in the regular set were replaced with six individual Rookie player cards (131, 264, 366, 527, 658, 787) in the gold set. Typically the individual cards are sold at a multiple of the player's respective value in the regular set. The Gold winner promotion was very popular and the cards are in noticably larger supply than the basic Gold parallels. It did not hurt the supply of Winnner cards collectors could hold their cards up to the light to see which were the correct answers. Later printing of 1992 game cards were fixed so collectors could not cheat to get the answers.

	Nm-Mt	Ex-Mt
COMPLETE SET (792)	40.00	12.00
*STARS: 1.25X TO 3X BASIC CARDS		
*ROOKIES: 1.25X TO 3X BASIC CARDS		
131 Terry Mathews	.15	.04
264 Rod Beck	.15	.04
366 Tony Perezchica	.15	.04
527 Terry McDaniel	.15	.04

658 John Ramos .15 .04
787 Brian Williams .15 .04

1992 Topps Micro

This 804 card parallel set was issued in factory set form only. The set is an exact replica of the regular issue 1992 Topps set (not including the Traded set).The cards, however, measure considerably smaller (1" by 1 3/8") than the regular cards. The set also includes 12 special gold foil parallel mini cards which are listed below. Please refer to the multipliers provided for values on the other singles.

Nm-Mt Ex-Mt
COMP. FACT.SET (804) 15.00 4.50
COMMON GOLD INSERT .10 .03
*STARS: .4X TO 1X BASIC CARDS
G1 Nolan Ryan RB 2.50 .75
G2 Rickey Henderson RB .50 .15
G10 Wade Boggs .50 .15
G50 Ken Griffey Jr. 2.50 .75
G100 Jose Canseco .50 .15
G270 Tony Gwynn 1.25 .35
G300 Don Mattingly 1.25 .35
G380 Barry Bonds .50 .15
G397 Cecil Fielder AS .10 .03
G403 Ruben Sierra AS .10 .03
G460 Andre Dawson .40 .12
G725 Dwight Gooden .20 .06

1992 Topps Traded

The 1992 Topps Traded set comprises 132 standard-size cards. The set was distributed exclusively in factory set form through hobby dealers. As in past editions, the set focuses on promising rookies, new managers, and players who changed teams. The set also includes a Team U.S.A. subset, featuring 25 of America's top college players and the Team U.S.A. coach. Card design is identical to the regular issue 1992 Topps cards except for the T-suffixed numbering. The cards are arranged in alphabetical order by player's last name. The key Rookie Cards in this set are Nomar Garciaparra, Brian Jordan and Jason Varitek.

Nm-Mt Ex-Mt
COMP.FACT.SET (132) 60.00 18.00
1T Willie Adams USA RC .25 .07
2T Jeff Alkire USA RC .25 .07
3T Felipe Alou MG .20 .06
4T Moises Alou .20 .06
5T Ruben Amaro .10 .03
6T Jack Armstrong .10 .03
7T Scott Bankhead .10 .03
8T Tim Belcher .10 .03
9T George Bell .10 .03
10T Freddie Benavides .10 .03
11T Todd Benzinger .10 .03
12T Joe Boever .10 .03
13T Ricky Bones .10 .03
14T Bobby Bonilla .20 .06
15T Hubie Brooks .10 .03
16T Jerry Browne .10 .03
17T Jim Bullinger .10 .03
18T Dave Burba .10 .03
19T Kevin Campbell .10 .03
20T Tom Candiotti .10 .03
21T Mark Carreon .10 .03
22T Gary Carter .30 .09
23T Archi Cianfrocco RC .10 .03
24T Phil Clark .10 .03
25T Chad Curtis RC .40 .12
26T Eric Davis .20 .06
27T Tim Davis USA RC .25 .07
28T Gary DiSarcina .10 .03
29T Darren Dreifort USA .20 .06
30T Mariano Duncan .10 .03
31T Mike Fitzgerald .10 .03
32T John Flaherty .10 .03
33T Darrin Fletcher .10 .03
34T Scott Fletcher .10 .03
35T R.Fraser CO USA RC .25 .07
36T Andres Galarraga .20 .06
37T Dave Gallagher .10 .03
38T Mike Gallego .10 .03
39T Nomar Garciaparra USA RC 50.00 15.00
40T Jason Giambi USA 2.00 .60
41T Danny Gladden .10 .03
42T Rene Gonzales .10 .03
43T Jeff Granger USA .10 .03
44T Rick Greene USA RC .25 .07
45T J.Hammonds USA .20 .06
46T Charlie Hayes .10 .03
47T Von Hayes .10 .03
48T Rick Helling USA .10 .03
49T Butch Henry RC .10 .03
50T Carlos Hernandez .10 .03
51T Ken Hill .10 .03
52T Butch Hobson .10 .03
53T Vince Horsman .10 .03
54T Pete Incaviglia .10 .03
55T Gregg Jefferies .10 .03
56T Charles Johnson USA .20 .06
57T Doug Jones .10 .03
58T Brian Jordan RC 1.50 .45
59T Wally Joyner .20 .06
60T D.Kirkreit USA RC .25 .07
61T Bill Krueger .10 .03
62T Gene Lamont MG .10 .03
63T Jim Lefebvre MG .10 .03
64T Danny Leon .10 .03
65T Pat Listach RC .40 .12
66T Kenny Lofton .50 .15
67T Dave Martinez .10 .03
68T Derrick May .10 .03
69T Kirk McCaskill .10 .03
70T C.McConnell USA RC .25 .07
71T Kevin McReynolds .10 .03
72T Rusty Meacham .10 .03
73T Keith Miller .10 .03
74T Kevin Mitchell .10 .03
75T Jason Moler USA RC .25 .07
76T Mike Morgan .10 .03
77T Jack Morris .20 .06
78T C.Murray USA RC .75 .23
79T Eddie Murray .50 .15
80T Randy Myers .10 .03
81T Denny Neagle .20 .06
82T Phil Nevin USA .30 .09
83T Dave Nilsson .10 .03
84T Junior Ortiz .10 .03
85T Donovan Osborne .10 .03
86T Bill Pecota .10 .03
87T Melido Perez .10 .03
88T Mike Perez .10 .03
89T Hipolito Pichardo RC .10 .03
90T Willie Randolph .20 .06
91T Darren Reed .10 .03
92T Bip Roberts .10 .03
93T Chris Roberts USA .10 .03
94T Steve Rodriguez USA .10 .03
95T Bruce Ruffin .10 .03
96T Scott Ruskin .10 .03
97T Bret Saberhagen .20 .06
98T Rey Sanchez RC .40 .12
99T Steve Sax .10 .03
100T Curt Schilling .30 .09
101T Dick Schofield .10 .03
102T Gary Scott .10 .03
103T Kevin Seitzer .10 .03
104T Frank Seminara RC .10 .03
105T Gary Sheffield .20 .06
106T John Smiley .10 .03
107T Cory Snyder .10 .03
108T Paul Sorrento .10 .03
109T Sammy Sosa 1.50 .45
110T Matt Stairs RC .50 .15
111T Andy Stankiewicz .10 .03
112T Kurt Stillwell .10 .03
113T Rick Sutcliffe .20 .06
114T Bill Swift .10 .03
115T Jeff Tackett .10 .03
116T Danny Tartabull .10 .03
117T Eddie Taubensee .20 .06
118T Dickie Thon .10 .03
119T M.Tucker USA RC .75 .23
120T Scooter Tucker .10 .03
121T Marc Valdes USA RC .25 .07
122T Julio Valera .10 .03
123T J.Varitek USA RC 3.00 .90
124T Ron Villone USA RC .25 .07
125T Frank Viola .20 .06
126T B.J. Wallace USA RC .25 .07
127T Dan Walters .10 .03
128T Craig Wilson USA .10 .03
129T Chris Wimmer USA .10 .03
130T Dave Winfield .20 .06
131T Herm Winningham .10 .03
132T Checklist 1T-132T .10 .03

1992 Topps Traded Gold

This 132 card standard-size set parallels the regular 1992 Topps Traded set. It was only issued through the Topps dealer network. Six thousand of these sets were produced and the only player difference is that Kerry Woodson replaces the checklist card

Nm-Mt Ex-Mt
COMP.FACT.SET (132) 120.00 36.00
*GOLD STARS: 1.5X TO 4X BASIC CARDS
*GOLD RC's: .75X TO 2X BASIC CARDS

1992 Topps Cashen

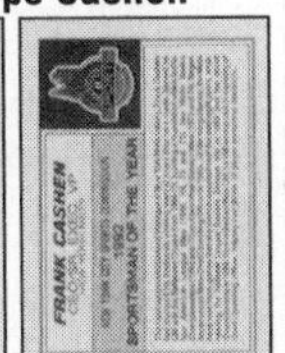

This one-card set was given away at the 1992 New York Sports Commission Luncheon and honors New York Mets General Manager Frank Cashen who was selected as Sportsman of the Year by the Commission.

Nm-Mt Ex-Mt
1 Frank Cashen 5.00 1.50

1992 Topps Dairy Queen Team USA

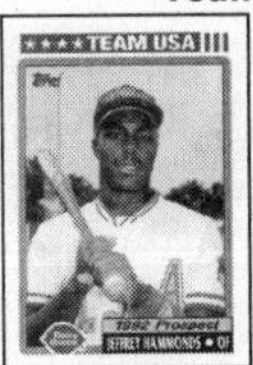

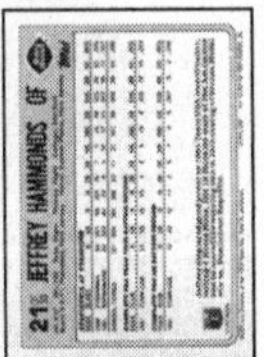

This 33-card standard size set was produced by Topps for Dairy Queen. The set was available in four-card packs with the purchase of a regular-sized sundae in a Team USA helmet during June and July 1992. The set features 16 Team USA players from the 1984 and 1988 teams who are now major league stars as well as 15 1992 Team USA prospects. Completing the set is a 1988 Gold Medal team celebration card and the 1992 Head Coach Ron Fraser.

Nm-Mt Ex-Mt
COMPLETE SET (33) 25.00 7.50
1 Mark McGwire 10.00 3.00
2 Will Clark 2.50 .75
3 John Marzano .25 .07
4 Barry Larkin 2.50 .75
5 Bobby Witt .25 .07
6 Scott Bankhead .25 .07
7 B.J. Surhoff .75 .23
8 Shane Mack .25 .07
9 Jim Abbott .50 .15
10 Ben McDonald .25 .07
11 Robin Ventura 1.00 .30
12 Charles Nagy .25 .07
13 Andy Benes .25 .07
14 Joe Slusarski .25 .07
15 Ed Sprague .25 .07
16 Bret Barberie .25 .07
17 Team USA Strikes Gold .50 .15
18 Jeff Granger .25 .07
19 John Dettmer .25 .07
20 Todd Greene .25 .07
21 Jeffrey Hammonds .50 .15
22 Dan Melendez .25 .07
23 Kennie Steenstra .25 .07
24 Todd Johnson .25 .07
25 Chris Roberts .25 .07
26 Steve Rodriguez .25 .07
27 Charles Johnson 1.00 .30
28 Chris Wimmer .25 .07
29 Tony Phillips P .25 .07
30 Craig Wilson .25 .07
31 Jason Giambi 10.00 3.00
32 Paul Shuey .25 .07
33 Ron Fraser CO .25 .07

1992 Topps Debut '91

The 1991 Topps Debut '91 set contains 194 standard-size cards. The fronts feature a mix of either posed or action glossy color player photos, framed with two color border stripes on a white card face. Future MVP's Jeff Bagwell, Ivan Rodriguez and Mo Vaughn along with Vinny Castilla and Mike Mussina are among the featured players in the set.

Nm-Mt Ex-Mt
COMP.FACT.SET (194) 15.00 4.50
1 Kyle Abbott .25 .07
2 Dana Allison .25 .07
3 Rich Amaral .25 .07
4 Ruben Amaro .25 .07
5 Andy Ashby .25 .07
6 Jim Austin .25 .07
7 Jeff Bagwell 2.00 .60
8 Jeff Banister .25 .07
9 Willie Banks .25 .07
10 Bret Barberie .25 .07
11 Kim Batiste .25 .07
12 Chris Beasley .25 .07
13 Rod Beck .50 .15
14 Derek Bell .50 .15
15 Esteban Beltre .25 .07
16 Freddie Benavides .25 .07
17 Ricky Bones .25 .07
18 Denis Boucher .25 .07
19 Ryan Bowen .25 .07
20 Cliff Brantley .25 .07
21 John Briscoe .25 .07
22 Scott Brosius 2.00 .60
23 Terry Bross .25 .07
24 Jarvis Brown .25 .07
25 Scott Bullett .25 .07
26 Kevin Campbell .25 .07
27 Amalio Carreno .25 .07
28 Matias Carrillo .25 .07
29 Jeff Carter .25 .07
30 Vinny Castilla 2.00 .60
31 Braulio Castillo .25 .07
32 Frank Castillo .25 .07
33 Darrin Chapin .25 .07
34 Mike Christopher .25 .07
35 Mark Clark .50 .15
36 Royce Clayton .25 .07
37 Stu Cole .25 .07
38 Gary Cooper .25 .07
39 Archie Corbin .25 .07
40 Rheal Cormier .25 .07
41 Chris Cron .25 .07
42 Mike Dalton .25 .07
43 Mark Davis .25 .07
44 Francisco de la Rosa .25 .07
45 Chris Donnels .25 .07
46 Brian Drahman .25 .07
47 Tom Drees .25 .07
48 Kirk Dressendorfer .25 .07
49 Bruce Egloff .25 .07
50 Cal Eldred .25 .07
51 Jose Escobar .25 .07
52 Tony Eusebio .50 .15
53 Hector Fajardo .25 .07
54 Monty Fariss .25 .07
55 Jeff Fassero .25 .07
56 Dave Fleming .25 .07
57 Kevin Flora .25 .07
58 Steve Foster .25 .07
59 Dan Gakeler .25 .07
60 Ramon Garcia .25 .07
61 Chris Gardner .25 .07
62 Jeff Gardner .25 .07
63 Chris George .25 .07
64 Ray Giannelli .25 .07
65 Tom Goodwin .25 .07
66 Mark Grater .25 .07
67 Johnny Guzman .25 .07
68 Juan Guzman .25 .07
69 Dave Haas .25 .07
70 Chris Haney .25 .07
71 Shawn Hare .25 .07
72 Donald Harris .25 .07
73 Doug Henry .25 .07
74 Pat Hentgen .25 .07
75 Gil Heredia .50 .15
76 Jeremy Hernandez .25 .07
77 Jose Hernandez 1.00 .30
78 Roberto Hernandez .25 .07
79 Bryan Hickerson .25 .07
80 Milt Hill .25 .07
81 Vince Horsman .25 .07
82 Wayne Housie .25 .07
83 Chris Howard .25 .07
84 David Howard .25 .07
85 Mike Humphreys .25 .07
86 Brian Hunter .25 .07
87 Jim Hunter .25 .07
88 Mike Ignasiak .25 .07
89 Reggie Jefferson .25 .07
90 Jeff Johnson .25 .07
91 Joel Johnston .25 .07
92 Calvin Jones .25 .07
93 Chris Jones .25 .07
94 Stacy Jones .25 .07
95 Jeff Juden .25 .07
96 Scott Kamieniecki .25 .07
97 Eric Karros .50 .15
98 Pat Kelly .25 .07
99 John Kiely .25 .07
100 Darryl Kile .50 .15
101 Wayne Kirby .25 .07
102 Garland Kiser .25 .07
103 Chuck Knoblauch .50 .15
104 Randy Knorr .25 .07
105 Tom Kramer .25 .07
106 Ced Landrum .25 .07
107 Patrick Lennon .25 .07
108 Jim Lewis .25 .07
109 Mark Lewis .25 .07
110 Doug Lindsey .25 .07
111 Scott Livingstone .25 .07
112 Kenny Lofton 1.00 .30
113 Ever Magallanes .25 .07
114 Mike Magnante .25 .07
115 Barry Manuel .25 .07
116 Josias Manzanillo .25 .07
117 Chito Martinez .25 .07
118 Terry Mathews .25 .07
119 Rob Maurer .25 .07
120 Tim Mauser .25 .07
121 Terry McDaniel .25 .07
122 Rusty Meacham .25 .07
123 Luis Mercedes .25 .07
124 Paul Miller .25 .07
125 Keith Mitchell .25 .07
126 Bobby Moore .25 .07
127 Kevin Morton .25 .07
128 Andy Mota .25 .07
129 Jose Mota .25 .07
130 Mike Mussina 2.00 .60
131 Jeff Mutis .25 .07
132 Denny Neagle .50 .15
133 Warren Newson .25 .07
134 Jim Olander .25 .07
135 Erik Pappas .25 .07
136 Jorge Pedre .25 .07
137 Yorkis Perez .25 .07
138 Mark Petkovsek .25 .07
139 Doug Piatt .25 .07
140 Jeff Plympton .25 .07
141 Harvey Pulliam .25 .07
142 John Ramos .25 .07
143 Mike Remlinger .25 .07
144 Laddie Renfroe .25 .07
145 Armando Reynoso .50 .15
146 Arthur Rhodes .25 .07
147 Pat Rice .25 .07
148 Nikco Riesgo .25 .07
149 Carlos Rodriguez .25 .07
150 Ivan Rodriguez 2.00 .60
151 Wayne Rosenthal .25 .07
152 Rico Rossy .25 .07
153 Stan Royer .25 .07
154 Rey Sanchez .50 .15
155 Reggie Sanders .50 .15
156 Mo Sanford .25 .07
157 Bob Scanlan .25 .07
158 Pete Schourek .25 .07
159 Gary Scott .25 .07
160 Tim Scott .25 .07
161 Tony Scruggs .25 .07
162 Scott Servais .25 .07
163 Doug Simons .25 .07
164 Heathcliff Slocumb .25 .07
165 Joe Slusarski .25 .07
166 Tim Spehr .25 .07
167 Ed Sprague .25 .07
168 Jeff Tackett .25 .07
169 Eddie Taubensee .50 .15
170 Wade Taylor .25 .07
171 Jim Thome 2.00 .60
172 Mike Timlin .25 .07
173 Jose Tolentino .25 .07
174 John Vander Wal .25 .07
175 Todd Van Poppel .25 .07
176 Mo Vaughn .50 .15
177 Dave Wainhouse .25 .07
178 Don Wakamatsu .25 .07
179 Bruce Walton .25 .07
180 Kevin Ward .25 .07
181 Dave Weathers .25 .07
182 Eric Wedge .50 .15
183 John Wehner .25 .07
184 Rick Wilkins .25 .07
185 Bernie Williams 1.00 .30
186 Brian Williams .25 .07
187 Ron Witmeyer .25 .07
188 Mark Wohlers .25 .07
189 Ted Wood .25 .07
190 Anthony Young .25 .07
191 Eddie Zosky .25 .07
192 Bob Zupcic .25 .07
193 Checklist 1 .25 .07
194 Checklist 2 .25 .07

1992 Topps Kids

This 132-card standard size set was packaged in seven-card wax packs with a stick of bubble gum. The set numbering is arranged by teams in alphabetical order within division.

Nm-Mt Ex-Mt
COMPLETE SET (132) 12.00 3.60
1 Ryne Sandberg .50 .15
2 Andre Dawson .20 .06
3 George Bell .05 .02
4 Mark Grace .15 .04
5 Shawon Dunston .05 .02
6 Tim Wallach .05 .02
7 Ivan Calderon .05 .02
8 Marquis Grissom .05 .02
9 Delino DeShields .10 .03
10 Dennis Martinez .10 .03
11 Dwight Gooden .10 .03
12 Howard Johnson .05 .02
13 John Franco .10 .03
14 Gregg Jefferies .05 .02
15 Kevin McReynolds .05 .02
16 David Cone .10 .03
17 Len Dykstra .10 .03
18 John Kruk .10 .03
19 Von Hayes .05 .02
20 Mitch Williams .05 .02
21 Barry Bonds 1.00 .30
22 Bobby Bonilla .10 .03
23 Andy Van Slyke .05 .02
24 Doug Drabek .05 .02
25 Ozzie Smith .75 .23
26 Pedro Guerrero .05 .02
27 Todd Zeile .10 .03
28 Lee Smith .10 .03
29 Felix Jose .05 .02
30 Jose DeLeon .05 .02
31 David Justice .20 .06
32 Ron Gant .10 .03
33 Terry Pendleton .05 .02
34 Tom Glavine .20 .06
35 Otis Nixon .05 .02
36 Steve Avery .05 .02
37 Barry Larkin .20 .06
38 Eric Davis .10 .03
39 Chris Sabo .05 .02
40 Rob Dibble .05 .02
41 Paul O'Neill .10 .03
42 Jose Rijo .05 .02
43 Craig Biggio .15 .04
44 Jeff Bagwell .75 .23
45 Ken Caminiti .10 .03
46 Steve Finley .10 .03
47 Darryl Strawberry .10 .03
48 Ramon Martinez .05 .02
49 Brett Butler .10 .03
50 Eddie Murray .20 .06
51 Kal Daniels .05 .02
52 Orel Hershiser .10 .03
53 Tony Gwynn 1.00 .30
54 Benito Santiago .10 .03
55 Fred McGriff .15 .04
56 Bip Roberts .05 .02
57 Tony Fernandez .05 .02
58 Will Clark .20 .06
59 Kevin Mitchell .10 .03
60 Matt Williams .15 .04
61 Willie McGee .10 .03
62 Dave Righetti .05 .02
63 Cal Ripken 2.00 .60
64 Ben McDonald .05 .02
65 Glenn Davis .05 .02
66 Gregg Olson .05 .02
67 Roger Clemens 1.00 .30
68 Wade Boggs .50 .15
69 Mike Greenwell .05 .02
70 Ellis Burks .10 .03
71 Sandy Alomar Jr. .10 .03
72 Greg Swindell .05 .02
73 Albert Belle .10 .03
74 Mark Whiten .05 .02
75 Alan Trammell .15 .04
76 Cecil Fielder .10 .03
77 Lou Whitaker .10 .03
78 Travis Fryman .10 .03
79 Tony Phillips .05 .02
80 Robin Yount .50 .15
81 Paul Molitor .50 .15
82 B.J. Surhoff .10 .03
83 Greg Vaughn .10 .03
84 Don Mattingly 1.00 .30
85 Steve Sax .05 .02
86 Kevin Maas .05 .02
87 Mel Hall .05 .02
88 Roberto Kelly .05 .02
89 Joe Carter .10 .03
90 Roberto Alomar .20 .06
91 Dave Stieb .05 .02
92 Kelly Gruber .05 .02
93 Tom Henke .05 .02
94 Chuck Finley .10 .03
95 Wally Joyner .05 .02
96 Dave Winfield .50 .15
97 Jim Abbott .10 .03
98 Mark Langston .05 .02
99 Frank Thomas .50 .15
100 Ozzie Guillen .10 .03
101 Bobby Thigpen .05 .02
102 Robin Ventura .20 .06
103 Bo Jackson .20 .06
104 Tim Raines .10 .03
105 George Brett .75 .23
106 Danny Tartabull .05 .02
107 Bret Saberhagen .10 .03
108 Brian McRae .10 .03
109 Kirby Puckett .40 .12
110 Scott Erickson .10 .03
111 Kent Hrbek .10 .03
112 Chuck Knoblauch .15 .04
113 Chili Davis .10 .03
114 Rick Aguilera .10 .03
115 Jose Canseco .40 .12
116 Dave Henderson .05 .02
117 Dave Stewart .10 .03
118 Rickey Henderson .75 .23
119 Dennis Eckersley .40 .12

120 Harold Baines .10 .03
121 Mark McGwire 1.50 .45
122 Ken Griffey Jr. 1.25 .35
123 Harold Reynolds .10 .03
124 Erik Hanson .05 .02
125 Edgar Martinez .15 .04
126 Randy Johnson .75 .23
127 Nolan Ryan 2.00 .60
128 Ruben Sierra .10 .03
129 Julio Franco .10 .03
130 Rafael Palmeiro .30 .09
131 Juan Gonzalez .50 .15
132 Checklist Card .05 .02

1992 Topps McDonald's

This 44-card standard-size set was produced by Topps for McDonald's and distributed in the New York, New Jersey, and Connecticut areas. The set was subtitled "McDonald's Baseball's Best". For 99 cents with the purchase of an Extra Value Meal or 1.79 with any other food purchase, the collector received a five-card cello pack. The top card of each pack was always one of eleven different rookies (34-44) randomly packed with four other non-rookie cards.

Nm-Mt Ex-Mt
COMPLETE SET (44) 15.00 4.50
1 Cecil Fielder .20 .06
2 Benny Santiago .20 .06
3 Rickey Henderson 1.25 .35
4 Roberto Alomar .40 .12
5 Ryne Sandberg 1.50 .45
6 George Brett 2.00 .60
7 Terry Pendleton .10 .03
8 Ken Griffey Jr. 2.50 .75
9 Bobby Bonilla .10 .03
10 Roger Clemens 2.00 .60
11 Ozzie Smith 1.50 .45
12 Barry Bonds 2.00 .60
13 Cal Ripken 4.00 1.20
14 Ron Gant .20 .06
15 Carlton Fisk .75 .23
16 Steve Avery .10 .03
17 Robin Yount .75 .23
18 Will Clark .40 .12
19 Kirby Puckett 1.00 .30
20 Jim Abbott .20 .06
21 Barry Larkin .30 .09
22 Jose Canseco .50 .15
23 Howard Johnson .10 .03
24 Nolan Ryan 4.00 1.20
25 Frank Thomas 1.00 .30
26 Danny Tartabull .10 .03
27 Julio Franco .20 .06
28 David Justice .40 .12
29 Joe Carter .20 .06
30 Dale Murphy .40 .12
31 Andre Dawson .40 .12
32 Dwight Gooden .20 .06
33 Bo Jackson .40 .12
34 Jeff Bagwell 1.50 .45
35 Chuck Knoblauch .30 .09
36 Derek Bell .10 .03
37 Jim Thome 1.00 .30
38 Royce Clayton .10 .03
39 Ryan Klesko .50 .15
40 Chito Martinez .10 .03
41 Ivan Rodriguez 1.50 .45
42 Todd Hundley .20 .06
43 Eric Karros .40 .12
44 Todd Van Poppel .10 .03

1993 Topps Pre-Production

These nine pre-production cards were included in the 1992 Topps Holiday set as a special insert set. The cards are standard size and were done in the style of the 1993 Topps baseball cards. The fronts feature color action player photos bordered in white. A team color-coded horizontal bar and two short diagonal bars accent the pictures at the bottom. The backs carry a color close-up photo, biography, statistics, and (where space allows) a summary of the player's outstanding performance during a game. The cards say "1993 Pre-Production Sample" inside a gray in the middle of the card back.

Nm-Mt Ex-Mt
COMPLETE SET (9) 8.00 2.40
1 Robin Yount 1.00 .30
2 Barry Bonds 2.00 .60
11 Eric Karros .50 .15
32 Don Mattingly 2.00 .60
100 Mark McGwire 3.00 .90
150 Frank Thomas 1.00 .30
179 Ken Griffey Jr. 2.50 .75
230 Carlton Fisk 1.00 .30
250 Chuck Knoblauch .25 .07

1993 Topps Pre-Production Sheet

The 1993 Topps Pre-Production sheet was sent out to give collectors a preview of the design of Topps' 1993 regular issue cards. The sheet measures 8" by 11" and features nine standard-size cards. The fronts feature color action player photos with white borders. The player's name appears in a stripe at the bottom of the picture, and this stripe and two short diagonal stripes at the bottom corners of the picture are team color-coded. The backs are colorful and carry a color head shot, biography, complete statistical information, with a career highlight if space permits. A gray circle with the message "1993 Pre-Production Sample: For General Look Only" is superimposed over the statistical section. The cards are all numbered "000" and are therefore checklisted below in alphabetical order.

Nm-Mt Ex-Mt
COMPLETE SET (9) 6.00 1.80
1 Roberto Alomar .75 .23
2 Bobby Bonilla .20 .06
3 Gary Carter 1.00 .30
4 Andre Dawson .75 .23
5 Dave Fleming .20 .06
6 Ken Griffey Jr. 4.00 1.20
7 Pete Incaviglia .20 .06
8 Spike Owen .20 .06
9 Larry Walker .40 .12

1993 Topps

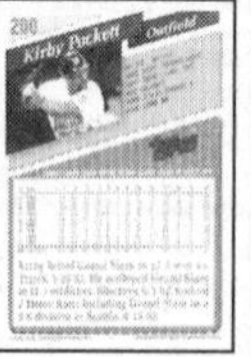

The 1993 Topps baseball set consists of two series, respectively, of 396 and 429 standard-size cards. A Topps Gold card was inserted in every 15-card pack. In addition, hobby and retail factory sets were produced. The fronts feature color action player photos with white borders. The player's name appears in a stripe at the bottom of the picture, and this stripe and two short diagonal stripes at the bottom corners of the picture are team color-coded. The backs are colorful and carry a color head shot, biography, complete statistical information, with a career highlight if space permitted. Cards 401-411 comprise an All-Star subset. Rookie Cards in this set include Jim Edmonds, Derek Jeter and Jason Kendall.

Nm-Mt Ex-Mt
COMPLETE SET (825) 40.00 12.00
COMP.HOBBY.SET (847) 50.00 15.00
COMP.RETAIL.SET (838) 40.00 12.00
COMP. SERIES 1 (396) 20.00 6.00
COMP.SERIES 2 (429) 20.00 6.00
1 Robin Yount .75 .23
2 Barry Bonds 1.25 .35
3 Ryne Sandberg .75 .23
4 Roger Clemens 1.00 .30
5 Tony Gwynn .60 .18
6 Jeff Tackett .10 .03
7 Pete Incaviglia .10 .03
8 Mark Wohlers .10 .03
9 Kent Hrbek .20 .06
10 Will Clark .50 .15
11 Eric Karros .20 .06
12 Lee Smith .20 .06
13 Esteban Beltre .10 .03
14 Greg Briley .10 .03
15 Marquis Grissom .10 .03
16 Dan Plesac .10 .03
17 Dave Hollins .10 .03
18 Terry Steinbach .10 .03
19 Ed Nunez .10 .03
20 Tim Salmon .30 .09
21 Luis Salazar .10 .03
22 Jim Eisenreich .10 .03
23 Todd Stottlemyre .10 .03
24 Tim Naehring .10 .03
25 John Franco .20 .06
26 Skeeter Barnes .10 .03
27 Carlos Garcia .10 .03
28 Joe Orsulak .10 .03
29 Dwayne Henry .10 .03
30 Fred McGriff .30 .09
31 Derek Lilliquist .10 .03
32 Don Mattingly 1.25 .35
33 B.J. Wallace .10 .03
34 Juan Gonzalez .50 .15
35 John Smoltz .30 .09
36 Scott Servais .10 .03
37 Lenny Webster .10 .03
38 Chris James .10 .03
39 Roger McDowell .10 .03
40 Ozzie Smith .75 .23
41 Alex Fernandez .10 .03
42 Spike Owen .10 .03
43 Ruben Amaro .10 .03
44 Kevin Seitzer .10 .03
45 Dave Fleming .10 .03
46 Eric Fox .10 .03
47 Bob Scanlan .10 .03
48 Bert Blyleven .20 .06
49 Brian McRae .10 .03
50 Roberto Alomar .50 .15
51 Mo Vaughn .20 .06
52 Bobby Bonilla .20 .06
53 Frank Tanana .10 .03
54 Mike LaValliere .10 .03
55 Mark McLemore .10 .03
56 Chad Mottola RC .10 .03
57 Norm Charlton .10 .03
58 Jose Melendez .10 .03
59 Carlos Martinez .10 .03
60 Roberto Kelly .10 .03
61 Gene Larkin .10 .03
62 Rafael Belliard .10 .03
63 Al Osuna .10 .03
64 Scott Chiamparino .10 .03
65 Brett Butler .20 .06
66 John Burkett .10 .03
67 Felix Jose .10 .03
68 Omar Vizquel .20 .06
69 John Vander Wal .10 .03
70 Roberto Hernandez .10 .03
71 Ricky Bones .10 .03
72 Jeff Grotewold .10 .03
73 Mike Moore .10 .03
74 Steve Buechele .10 .03
75 Juan Guzman .10 .03
76 Kevin Appier .20 .06
77 Junior Felix .10 .03
78 Greg W. Harris .10 .03
79 Dick Schofield .10 .03
80 Cecil Fielder .20 .06
81 Lloyd McClendon .10 .03
82 David Segui .10 .03
83 Reggie Sanders .20 .06
84 Kurt Stillwell .10 .03
85 Sandy Alomar Jr. .10 .03
86 John Habyan .10 .03
87 Kevin Reimer .10 .03
88 Mike Stanton .10 .03
89 Eric Anthony .10 .03
90 Scott Erickson .10 .03
91 Craig Colbert .10 .03
92 Tom Pagnozzi .10 .03
93 Pedro Astacio .10 .03
94 Lance Johnson .10 .03
95 Larry Walker .30 .09
96 Russ Swan .10 .03
97 Scott Fletcher .10 .03
98 Derek Jeter RC 15.00 4.50
99 Mike Williams .10 .03
100 Mark McGwire 1.25 .35
101 Jim Bullinger .10 .03
102 Brian Hunter .10 .03
103 Jody Reed .10 .03
104 Mike Butcher .10 .03
105 Gregg Jefferies .10 .03
106 Howard Johnson .10 .03
107 John Kiely .10 .03
108 Jose Lind .10 .03
109 Sam Horn .10 .03
110 Barry Larkin .50 .15
111 Bruce Hurst .10 .03
112 Brian Barnes .10 .03
113 Thomas Howard .10 .03
114 Mel Hall .10 .03
115 Robby Thompson .10 .03
116 Mark Lemke .10 .03
117 Eddie Taubensee .10 .03
118 David Hulse RC .10 .03
119 Pedro Munoz .10 .03
120 Ramon Martinez .10 .03
121 Todd Worrell .10 .03
122 Joey Cora .10 .03
123 Moises Alou .20 .06
124 Franklin Stubbs .10 .03
125 Pete O'Brien .10 .03
126 Bob Ayrault .10 .03
127 Carney Lansford .20 .06
128 Kal Daniels .10 .03
129 Joe Grahe .10 .03
130 Jeff Montgomery .10 .03
131 Dave Winfield .20 .06
132 Preston Wilson RC 1.00 .30
133 Steve Wilson .10 .03
134 Lee Guetterman .10 .03
135 Mickey Tettleton .10 .03
136 Jeff King .10 .03
137 Alan Mills .10 .03
138 Joe Oliver .10 .03
139 Gary Gaetti .20 .06
140 Gary Sheffield .20 .06
141 Dennis Cook .10 .03
142 Charlie Hayes .10 .03
143 Jeff Huson .10 .03
144 Kent Mercker .10 .03
145 Eric Young .10 .03
146 Scott Leius .10 .03
147 Bryan Hickerson .10 .03
148 Steve Finley .20 .06
149 Rheal Cormier .10 .03
150 Frank Thomas UER .50 .15
(Categories leading league are italicized but not printed in red)
151 Archi Cianfrocco .10 .03
152 Rich DeLucia .10 .03
153 Greg Vaughn .20 .06
154 Wes Chamberlain .10 .03
155 Dennis Eckersley .20 .06
156 Sammy Sosa .75 .23
157 Gary DiSarcina .10 .03
158 Kevin Koslofski .10 .03
159 Doug Linton .10 .03
160 Lou Whitaker .20 .06
161 Chad McConnell .10 .03
162 Joe Hesketh .10 .03
163 Tim Wakefield .20 .06
164 Leo Gomez .10 .03
165 Jose Rijo .10 .03
166 Tim Scott .10 .03
167 Steve Olin UER .10 .03
(Born 10/4/65 should say 10/10/65)
168 Kevin Maas .10 .03
169 Kenny Rogers .20 .06
170 David Justice .20 .06
171 Doug Jones .10 .03
172 Jeff Reboulet .10 .03
173 Andres Galarraga .20 .06
174 Randy Velarde .10 .03
175 Kirk McCaskill .10 .03
176 Darren Lewis .10 .03
177 Lenny Harris .10 .03
178 Jeff Fassero .10 .03
179 Ken Griffey Jr. .75 .23
180 Darren Daulton .20 .06
181 John Jaha .10 .03
182 Ron Darling .10 .03
183 Greg Maddux .75 .23
184 Damion Easley .10 .03
185 Jack Morris .20 .06
186 Mike Magnante .10 .03
187 John Dopson .10 .03
188 Sid Fernandez .10 .03
189 Tony Phillips .10 .03
190 Doug Drabek .10 .03
191 Sean Lowe RC .10 .03
192 Bob Milacki .10 .03
193 Steve Foster .10 .03
194 Jerald Clark .10 .03
195 Pete Harnisch .10 .03
196 Pat Kelly .10 .03
197 Jeff Frye .10 .03
198 Alejandro Pena .10 .03
199 Junior Ortiz .10 .03
200 Kirby Puckett .50 .15
201 Jose Uribe .10 .03
202 Mike Scioscia .10 .03
203 Bernard Gilkey .10 .03
204 Dan Pasqua .10 .03
205 Gary Carter .30 .09
206 Henry Cotto .10 .03
207 Paul Molitor .30 .09
208 Mike Hartley .10 .03
209 Jeff Parrett .10 .03
210 Mark Langston .10 .03
211 Doug Dascenzo .10 .03
212 Rick Reed .10 .03
213 Candy Maldonado .10 .03
214 Danny Darwin .10 .03
215 Pat Howell .10 .03
216 Mark Leiter .10 .03
217 Kevin Mitchell .10 .03
218 Ben McDonald .10 .03
219 Bip Roberts .10 .03
220 Benny Santiago .20 .06
221 Carlos Baerga .10 .03
222 Bernie Williams .30 .09
223 Roger Pavlik .10 .03
224 Sid Bream .10 .03
225 Matt Williams .20 .06
226 Willie Banks .10 .03
227 Jeff Bagwell .30 .09
228 Tom Goodwin .10 .03
229 Mike Perez .10 .03
230 Carlton Fisk .30 .09
231 John Wetteland .20 .06
232 Tino Martinez .30 .09
233 Rick Greene .10 .03
234 Tim McIntosh .10 .03
235 Mitch Williams .10 .03
236 Kevin Campbell .10 .03
237 Jose Vizcaino .10 .03
238 Chris Donnels .10 .03
239 Mike Boddicker .10 .03
240 John Olerud .20 .06
241 Mike Gardiner .10 .03
242 Charlie O'Brien .10 .03
243 Rob Deer .10 .03
244 Denny Neagle .20 .06
245 Chris Sabo .10 .03
246 Gregg Olson .10 .03
247 Frank Seminara UER .10 .03
(Acquired 12/3/98)
248 Scott Scudder .10 .03
249 Tim Burke .10 .03
250 Chuck Knoblauch .20 .06
251 Mike Bielecki .10 .03
252 Xavier Hernandez .10 .03
253 Jose Guzman .10 .03
254 Cory Snyder .10 .03
255 Orel Hershiser .20 .06
256 Wil Cordero .10 .03
257 Luis Alicea .10 .03
258 Mike Schooler .10 .03
259 Craig Grebeck .10 .03
260 Duane Ward .10 .03
261 Bill Wegman .10 .03
262 Mickey Morandini .10 .03
263 Vince Horsman .10 .03
264 Paul Sorrento .10 .03
265 Andre Dawson .20 .06
266 Rene Gonzales .10 .03
267 Keith Miller .10 .03
268 Derek Bell .10 .03
269 Todd Steverson RC .10 .03
270 Frank Viola .20 .06
271 Wally Whitehurst .10 .03
272 Kurt Knudsen .10 .03
273 Dan Walters .10 .03
274 Rick Sutcliffe .20 .06
275 Andy Van Slyke .20 .06
276 Paul O'Neill .30 .09
277 Mark Whiten .10 .03
278 Chris Nabholz .10 .03
279 Todd Burns .10 .03
280 Tom Glavine .30 .09
281 Butch Henry .10 .03
282 Shane Mack .10 .03
283 Mike Jackson .10 .03
284 Henry Rodriguez .10 .03
285 Bob Tewksbury .10 .03
286 Ron Karkovice .10 .03
287 Mike Gallego .10 .03
288 Dave Cochrane .10 .03
289 Jesse Orosco .10 .03
290 Dave Stewart .20 .06
291 Tommy Greene .10 .03
292 Rey Sanchez .10 .03
293 Rob Ducey .10 .03
294 Brent Mayne .10 .03
295 Dave Stieb .10 .03
296 Luis Rivera .10 .03
297 Jeff Innis .10 .03
298 Scott Livingstone .10 .03
299 Bob Patterson .10 .03
300 Cal Ripken 1.50 .45
301 Cesar Hernandez .10 .03
302 Randy Myers .10 .03
303 Brook Jacoby .10 .03
304 Melido Perez .10 .03
305 Rafael Palmeiro .30 .09
306 Damon Berryhill .10 .03
307 Dan Serafini RC .10 .03
308 Darryl Kile .20 .06
309 J.T. Bruett .10 .03
310 Dave Righetti .20 .06
311 Jay Howell .10 .03
312 Geronimo Pena .10 .03
313 Greg Hibbard .10 .03
314 Mark Gardner .10 .03
315 Edgar Martinez .30 .09
316 Dave Nilsson .10 .03
317 Kyle Abbott .10 .03
318 Willie Wilson .10 .03
319 Paul Assenmacher .10 .03
320 Tim Fortugno .10 .03
321 Rusty Meacham .10 .03
322 Pat Borders .10 .03
323 Mike Greenwell .10 .03
324 Willie Randolph .20 .06
325 Bill Gullickson .10 .03
326 Gary Varsho .10 .03
327 Tim Hulett .10 .03
328 Scott Ruskin .10 .03
329 Mike Maddux .10 .03
330 Danny Tartabull .10 .03
331 Kenny Lofton .20 .06
332 Geno Petralli .10 .03
333 Otis Nixon .10 .03
334 Jason Kendall RC .75 .23
335 Mark Portugal .10 .03
336 Mike Pagliarulo .10 .03
337 Kirt Manwaring .10 .03
338 Bob Ojeda .10 .03
339 Mark Clark .10 .03
340 John Kruk .20 .06
341 Mel Rojas .10 .03
342 Erik Hanson .10 .03
343 Doug Henry .10 .03
344 Jack McDowell .10 .03
345 Harold Baines .20 .06
346 Chuck McElroy .10 .03
347 Luis Sojo .10 .03
348 Andy Stankiewicz .10 .03
349 Hipolito Pichardo .10 .03
350 Joe Carter .20 .06
351 Ellis Burks .20 .06
352 Pete Schourek .10 .03
353 Buddy Groom .10 .03
354 Jay Bell .20 .06
355 Brady Anderson .20 .06
356 Freddie Benavides .10 .03
357 Phil Stephenson .10 .03
358 Kevin Wickander .10 .03
359 Mike Stanley .10 .03
360 Ivan Rodriguez .50 .15
361 Scott Bankhead .10 .03
362 Luis Gonzalez .20 .06
363 John Smiley .10 .03
364 Trevor Wilson .10 .03
365 Tom Candiotti .10 .03
366 Craig Wilson .10 .03
367 Steve Sax .10 .03
368 Delino DeShields .10 .03
369 Jaime Navarro .10 .03
370 Dave Valle .10 .03
371 Mariano Duncan .10 .03
372 Rod Nichols .10 .03
373 Mike Morgan .10 .03
374 Julio Valera .10 .03
375 Wally Joyner .20 .06
376 Tom Henke .10 .03
377 Herm Winningham .10 .03
378 Orlando Merced .10 .03
379 Mike Munoz .10 .03
380 Todd Hundley .10 .03
381 Mike Flanagan .10 .03
382 Tim Belcher .10 .03
383 Jerry Browne .10 .03
384 Mike Benjamin .10 .03
385 Jim Leyritz .10 .03
386 Ray Lankford .10 .03
387 Devon White .10 .03
388 Jeremy Hernandez .10 .03
389 Brian Harper .10 .03
390 Wade Boggs .30 .09
391 Derrick May .10 .03
392 Travis Fryman .20 .06
393 Ron Gant .20 .06
394 Checklist 1-132 .10 .03
395 CL 133-264 UER .10 .03
Eckerlsey
396 Checklist 265-396 .10 .03
397 George Brett 1.25 .35
398 Bobby Witt .10 .03
399 Daryl Boston .10 .03
400 Bo Jackson .50 .15
401 Fred McGriff .30 .09
Frank Thomas AS
402 Ryne Sandberg .50 .15
Carlos Baerga AS
403 Gary Sheffield .20 .06
Edgar Martinez AS
404 Barry Larkin .20 .06
Travis Fryman AS
405 Andy Van Slyke .50 .15
Ken Griffey Jr. AS
406 Larry Walker .30 .09
Kirby Puckett AS
407 Barry Bonds .60 .18
Joe Carter AS
408 Darren Daulton .20 .06
Brian Harper AS
409 Greg Maddux .50 .15
Roger Clemens AS
410 Tom Glavine .20 .06
Dave Fleming AS
411 Lee Smith .20 .06
Dennis Eckersley AS
412 Jamie McAndrew .10 .03
413 Pete Smith .10 .03
414 Juan Guerrero .10 .03
415 Todd Frohwirth .10 .03
416 Randy Tomlin .10 .03
417 B.J. Surhoff .20 .06
418 Jim Gott .10 .03
419 Mark Thompson RC .10 .03
420 Kevin Tapani .10 .03
421 Curt Schilling .30 .09
422 J.T. Snow RC .50 .15
423 Ryan Klesko .20 .06
Ivan Cruz
Bubba Smith
Larry Sutton RC
424 John Valentin .10 .03
425 Joe Girardi .10 .03
426 Nigel Wilson .10 .03
427 Bob MacDonald .10 .03
428 Todd Zeile .10 .03
429 Milt Cuyler .10 .03
430 Eddie Murray .50 .15
431 Rich Amaral .10 .03
432 Pete Young .10 .03
433 Roger Bailey RC .10 .03
Tom Schmidt
434 Jack Armstrong .10 .03
435 Willie McGee .20 .06
436 Greg W. Harris .10 .03
437 Chris Hammond .10 .03
438 Ritchie Moody RC .10 .03
439 Bryan Harvey .10 .03
440 Ruben Sierra .10 .03
441 Don Lemon .10 .03
Todd Pridy RC
442 Kevin McReynolds .10 .03
443 Terry Leach .10 .03
444 David Nied .10 .03
445 Dale Murphy .50 .15
446 Luis Mercedes .10 .03
447 Keith Shepherd RC .10 .03

448 Ken Caminiti .20 .06
449 Jim Austin .10 .03
450 Darryl Strawberry .30 .09
451 Ramon Caraballo .25 .07
Jon Shave RC
Brent Gates
Quinton McCracken
452 Bob Wickman .10 .03
453 Victor Cole .10 .03
454 John Johnstone RC .10 .03
455 Chili Davis .20 .06
456 Scott Taylor .10 .03
457 Tracy Woodson .10 .03
458 David Wells .20 .06
459 Derek Wallace RC .10 .03
460 Randy Johnson .50 .15
461 Steve Reed RC .10 .03
462 Felix Fermin .10 .03
463 Scott Aldred .10 .03
464 Greg Colbrunn .10 .03
465 Tony Fernandez .10 .03
466 Mike Felder .10 .03
467 Lee Stevens .10 .03
468 Matt Whiteside RC .10 .03
469 Dave Hansen .10 .03
470 Rob Dibble .20 .06
471 Dave Gallagher .10 .03
472 Chris Gwynn .10 .03
473 Dave Henderson .10 .03
474 Ozzie Guillen .10 .03
475 Jeff Reardon .20 .06
476 Mark Voisard .10 .03
Will Scalzitti RC
477 Jimmy Jones .10 .03
478 Greg Cadaret .10 .03
479 Todd Pratt RC .10 .03
480 Pat Listach .10 .03
481 Ryan Luzinski RC .10 .03
482 Darren Reed .10 .03
483 Brian Griffiths RC .10 .03
484 John Wehner .10 .03
485 Glenn Davis .10 .03
486 Eric Wedge RC .10 .03
487 Jesse Hollins .10 .03
488 Manuel Lee .10 .03
489 Scott Fredrickson RC .10 .03
490 Omar Olivares .10 .03
491 Shawn Hare .10 .03
492 Tom Lampkin .10 .03
493 Jeff Nelson .10 .03
494 Kevin Young .10 .03
Adell Davenport
Eduardo Perez
Lou Lucca RC
495 Ken Hill .10 .03
496 Reggie Jefferson .10 .03
497 Matt Petersen .10 .03
Willie Brown RC
498 Bud Black .10 .03
499 Chuck Crim .10 .03
500 Jose Canseco .50 .15
501 Johnny Oates MG .20 .06
Bobby Cox MG
502 Butch Hobson MG .10 .03
Jim Lefebvre MG
503 Buck Rodgers MG .20 .06
Tony Perez MG
504 Gene Lamont MG .20 .06
Don Baylor MG
505 Mike Hargrove MG .20 .06
Rene Lachemann MG
506 Sparky Anderson MG .20 .06
Art Howe MG
507 Hal McRae MG .20 .06
Tom Lasorda MG
508 Phil Garner MG .20 .06
Felipe Alou MG
509 Tom Kelly MG .10 .03
Jeff Torborg MG
510 Buck Showalter MG .20 .06
Jim Fregosi MG
511 Tony LaRussa MG .20 .06
Jim Leyland MG
512 Lou Piniella MG .20 .06
Joe Torre MG
513 Kevin Kennedy MG .10 .03
Jim Riggleman MG
514 Cito Gaston MG .20 .06
Dusty Baker MG
515 Greg Swindell .10 .03
516 Alex Arias .10 .03
517 Bill Pecota .10 .03
518 Benji Grigsby RC UER .10 .03
(Misspelled Bengi
on card front)
519 David Howard .10 .03
520 Charlie Hough .20 .06
521 Kevin Flora .10 .03
522 Shane Reynolds .10 .03
523 Doug Bochtler RC .10 .03
524 Chris Hoiles .10 .03
525 Scott Sanderson .10 .03
526 Mike Sharperson .10 .03
527 Mike Fetters .10 .03
528 Paul Quantrill .10 .03
529 Dave Silvestri .50 .15
Chipper Jones
Benji Gil
Jeff Patzke
530 Sterling Hitchcock RC .25 .07
531 Joe Millette .10 .03
532 Tom Brunansky .10 .03
533 Frank Castillo .10 .03
534 Randy Knorr .10 .03
535 Jose Oquendo .10 .03
536 Dave Haas .10 .03
537 Jason Hutchins RC .10 .03
Ryan Turner
538 Jimmy Baron RC .10 .03
539 Kerry Woodson .10 .03
540 Ivan Calderon .10 .03
541 Denis Boucher .10 .03
542 Royce Clayton .10 .03
543 Reggie Williams .10 .03
544 Steve Decker .10 .03
545 Dean Palmer .20 .06
546 Hal Morris .10 .03
547 Ryan Thompson .10 .03
548 Lance Blankenship .10 .03
549 Hensley Meulens .10 .03
550 Scott Radinsky .10 .03
551 Eric Young .10 .03
552 Jeff Blauser .10 .03
553 Andujar Cedeno .10 .03
554 Arthur Rhodes .10 .03
555 Terry Mulholland .10 .03
556 Darryl Hamilton .10 .03
557 Pedro Martinez 1.00 .30
558 Ryan Whitman RC .10 .03
Mark Skeels
559 Jamie Arnold RC .10 .03
560 Zane Smith .10 .03
561 Matt Nokes .10 .03
562 Bob Zupcic .10 .03
563 Shawn Boskie .10 .03
564 Mike Timlin .10 .03
565 Jerald Clark .10 .03
566 Rod Brewer .10 .03
567 Mark Carreon .10 .03
568 Andy Benes .10 .03
569 Shawn Barton RC .10 .03
570 Tim Wallach .10 .03
571 Dave Mlicki .10 .03
572 Trevor Hoffman .20 .06
573 John Patterson .10 .03
574 De Shawn Warren RC .10 .03
575 Monty Fariss .10 .03
576 Darrell Sherman .30 .09
Damon Buford
Cliff Floyd
Michael Moore
577 Tim Costo .10 .03
578 Dave Magadan .10 .03
579 Neil Garret .10 .03
Jason Bates RC
580 Walt Weiss .10 .03
581 Chris Haney .10 .03
582 Shawn Abner .10 .03
583 Marvin Freeman .10 .03
584 Casey Candaele .10 .03
585 Ricky Jordan .10 .03
586 Jeff Tabaka RC .10 .03
587 Manny Alexander .10 .03
588 Mike Trombley .10 .03
589 Carlos Hernandez .10 .03
590 Cal Eldred .10 .03
591 Alex Cole .10 .03
592 Phil Plantier .10 .03
593 Brett Merriman RC .10 .03
594 Jerry Nielsen .10 .03
595 Shawon Dunston .10 .03
596 Jimmy Key .20 .06
597 Gerald Perry .10 .03
598 Rico Brogna .10 .03
599 Clemente Nunez .10 .03
Daniel Robinson
600 Bret Saberhagen .20 .06
601 Craig Shipley .10 .03
602 Henry Mercedes .10 .03
603 Jim Thome .50 .15
604 Rod Beck .10 .03
605 Chuck Finley .20 .06
606 J. Owens RC .10 .03
607 Dan Smith .10 .03
608 Bill Doran .10 .03
609 Lance Parrish .20 .06
610 Dennis Martinez .20 .06
611 Tom Gordon .10 .03
612 Byron Mathews RC .10 .03
613 Joel Adamson RC .10 .03
614 Brian Williams .10 .03
615 Steve Avery .10 .03
616 Matt Mieske .10 .03
Tracy Sanders
Midre Cummings RC
Ryan Freeburg
617 Craig Lefferts .10 .03
618 Tony Pena .10 .03
619 Billy Spiers .10 .03
620 Todd Benzinger .10 .03
621 Mike Kotarski .10 .03
Greg Boyd RC
622 Ben Rivera .10 .03
623 Al Martin .10 .03
624 Sam Militello UER .10 .03
(Profile says drafted
in 1988, bio says
drafted in 1990)
625 Rick Aguilera .10 .03
626 Dan Gladden .10 .03
627 Andres Berumen RC .10 .03
628 Kelly Gruber .10 .03
629 Cris Carpenter .10 .03
630 Mark Grace .30 .09
631 Jeff Brantley .10 .03
632 Chris Widger RC .25 .07
633 Three Russians UER .10 .03
Rudolf Razjigaev
Eugneyi Puchkov
Ilya Bogatyrev
Bogatyrev is a shortstop,
card has pitching header
634 Mo Sanford .10 .03
635 Albert Belle .20 .06
636 Tim Teufel .10 .03
637 Greg Myers .10 .03
638 Brian Bohanon .10 .03
639 Mike Bordick .10 .03
640 Dwight Gooden .30 .09
641 Pat Leahy .10 .03
Gavin Baugh RC
642 Milt Hill .10 .03
643 Luis Aquino .10 .03
644 Dante Bichette .20 .06
645 Bobby Thigpen .10 .03
646 Rich Scheid RC .10 .03
647 Brian Sackinsky RC .10 .03
648 Ryan Hawblitzel .10 .03
649 Tom Marsh .10 .03
650 Terry Pendleton .20 .06
651 Rafael Bournigal .10 .03
652 Dave West .10 .03
653 Steve Hosey .10 .03
654 Gerald Williams .10 .03
655 Scott Cooper .10 .03
656 Gary Scott .10 .03
657 Mike Harkey .10 .03
658 Jeromy Burnitz .10 .03
Melvin Nieves
Rich Becker
Shon Walker RC
659 Ed Sprague .10 .03
660 Alan Trammell .30 .09
661 Garvin Alston RC .10 .03
Michael Case
662 Donovan Osborne .10 .03
663 Jeff Gardner .10 .03
664 Calvin Jones .10 .03
665 Darrin Fletcher .10 .03
666 Glenallen Hill .10 .03
667 Jim Rosenbohm RC .10 .03
668 Scott Lewis .10 .03
669 Kip Yaughn RC .10 .03
670 Julio Franco .20 .06
671 Dave Martinez .10 .03
672 Kevin Bass .10 .03
673 Todd Van Poppel .10 .03
674 Mark Gubicza .10 .03
675 Tim Raines .20 .06
676 Rudy Seanez .10 .03
677 Charlie Leibrandt .10 .03
678 Randy Milligan .10 .03
679 Kim Batiste .10 .03
680 Craig Biggio .30 .09
681 Darren Holmes .10 .03
682 John Candelaria .10 .03
683 Jerry Stafford .10 .03
Eddie Christian RC
684 Pat Mahomes .10 .03
685 Bob Walk .10 .03
686 Russ Springer .10 .03
687 Tony Sheffield RC .10 .03
688 Dwight Smith .10 .03
689 Eddie Zosky .10 .03
690 Bien Figueroa .10 .03
691 Jim Tatum RC .10 .03
692 Chad Kreuter .10 .03
693 Rich Rodriguez .10 .03
694 Shane Turner .10 .03
695 Kent Bottenfield .10 .03
696 Jose Mesa .10 .03
697 Darrell Whitmore RC .10 .03
698 Ted Wood .10 .03
699 Chad Curtis .10 .03
700 Nolan Ryan 2.00 .60
701 Mike Piazza 1.50 .45
Brook Fordyce
Carlos Delgado
Donnie Leshnock
702 Tim Pugh RC .10 .03
703 Jeff Kent .50 .15
704 Jon Goodrich .10 .03
Danny Figueroa RC
705 Bob Welch .10 .03
706 S.Clinkscales RC .10 .03
707 Donn Pall .10 .03
708 Greg Olson .10 .03
709 Jeff Juden .10 .03
710 Mike Mussina .50 .15
711 Scott Chiamparino .10 .03
712 Stan Javier .10 .03
713 John Doherty .10 .03
714 Kevin Gross .10 .03
715 Greg Gagne .10 .03
716 Steve Cooke .10 .03
717 Steve Farr .10 .03
718 Jay Buhner .20 .06
719 Butch Henry .10 .03
720 David Cone .20 .06
721 Rick Wilkins .10 .03
722 Chuck Carr .10 .03
723 Kenny Felder RC .10 .03
724 Guillermo Velasquez .10 .03
725 Billy Hatcher .10 .03
726 Mike Veneziale RC .10 .03
Ken Kendrena
727 Jonathan Hurst .10 .03
728 Steve Frey .10 .03
729 Mark Leonard .10 .03
730 Charles Nagy .10 .03
731 Donald Harris .10 .03
732 Travis Buckley RC .10 .03
733 Tom Browning .10 .03
734 Anthony Young .10 .03
735 Steve Shifflett .10 .03
736 Jeff Russell .10 .03
737 Wilson Alvarez .10 .03
738 Lance Painter RC .10 .03
739 Dave Weathers .10 .03
740 Len Dykstra .20 .06
741 Mike Devereaux .10 .03
742 Rene Arocha .25 .07
Alan Embree
Brien Taylor
Tim Crabtree
743 Dave Landaker RC .10 .03
744 Chris George .10 .03
745 Eric Davis .20 .06
746 Mark Strittmatter .10 .03
Lamarr Rogers RC
747 Carl Willis .10 .03
748 Stan Belinda .10 .03
749 Scott Kamieniecki .10 .03
750 Rickey Henderson .50 .15
751 Eric Hillman .10 .03
752 Pat Hentgen .10 .03
753 Jim Corsi .10 .03
754 Brian Jordan .20 .06
755 Bill Swift .10 .03
756 Mike Henneman .10 .03
757 Harold Reynolds .20 .06
758 Sean Berry .10 .03
759 Charlie Hayes .10 .03
760 Luis Polonia .10 .03
761 Darrin Jackson .10 .03
762 Mark Lewis .10 .03
763 Rob Maurer .10 .03
764 Willie Greene .10 .03
765 Vince Coleman .10 .03
766 Todd Revenig .10 .03
767 Rich Ireland RC .10 .03
768 Mike Macfarlane .10 .03
769 Francisco Cabrera .10 .03
770 Robin Ventura .20 .06
771 Kevin Ritz .10 .03
772 Chito Martinez .10 .03
773 Cliff Brantley .10 .03
774 Curt Leskanic RC .10 .03
775 Chris Bosio .10 .03
776 Jose Offerman .10 .03
777 Mark Guthrie .10 .03
778 Don Slaught .10 .03
779 Rich Monteleone .10 .03
780 Jim Abbott .30 .09
781 Jack Clark .20 .06
782 Reynol Mendoza .10 .03
Dan Roman RC
783 Heathcliff Slocumb .10 .03
784 Jeff Branson .10 .03
785 Kevin Brown .20 .06
786 Mike Christopher .10 .03
Ken Ryan
Aaron Taylor
Gus Gandarillas RC
787 Mike Matthews RC .10 .03
788 Mackey Sasser .10 .03
789 Jeff Conine UER .20 .06
No inclusion of 1990
RBI stats in career total
790 George Bell .10 .03
791 Pat Rapp .10 .03
792 Joe Boever .10 .03
793 Jim Poole .10 .03
794 Andy Ashby .30 .09
795 Deion Sanders .30 .09
796 Scott Brosius .20 .06
797 Brad Pennington .10 .03
798 Greg Blosser .10 .03
799 Jim Edmonds RC 1.50 .45
800 Shawn Jeter .10 .03
801 Jesse Levis .10 .03
802 Phil Clark UER .10 .03
(Word "a" is missing in
sentence beginning
with "In 1992 ...")
803 Ed Pierce RC .10 .03
804 Jose Valentin RC .25 .07
805 Terry Jorgensen .10 .03
806 Mark Hutton .10 .03
807 Troy Neel .10 .03
808 Bret Boone .30 .09
809 Cris Colon .10 .03
810 Domingo Martinez RC .10 .03
811 Javier Lopez .30 .09
812 Matt Walbeck RC .10 .03
813 Dan Wilson .20 .06
814 Scooter Tucker .10 .03
815 Billy Ashley .10 .03
816 Tim Laker RC .10 .03
817 Bobby Jones .20 .06
818 Brad Brink .10 .03
819 William Pennyfeather .10 .03
820 Stan Royer .10 .03
821 Doug Brocail .10 .03
822 Kevin Rogers .10 .03
823 Checklist 397-540 .10 .03
824 Checklist 541-691 .10 .03
825 Checklist 692-825 .10 .03

1993 Topps Gold

Several insertion schemes were devised for these 825 standard-size cards. Gold cards were inserted one per wax pack, three per rack pack, five per jumbo pack, and ten per factory set. The cards are identical to the regular-issue 1993 Topps baseball cards except that the gold-foil Topps Gold logo appears in an upper corner, and the team color-coded stripe at the bottom of the front, which carried the player's name, has been replaced with an embossed gold-foil stripe. The checklist cards (394-396, 823-825) have been replaced by player cards.

Nm-Mt Ex-Mt
COMP.GOLD SET (825) 60.00 18.00
COMP.SERIES 1 (396) 40.00 12.00
COMP.SERIES 2 (429) 25.00 7.50
COMMON (1G-825G) .30 .09
*STARS: 1X TO 2.5X BASIC CARDS ...
*ROOKIES: 1.25X TO 3X BASIC CARDS
394 Bernardo Brito .25 .07
395 Jim McNamara .25 .07
396 Rich Sauveur .25 .07
823 Keith Brown .25 .07
824 Russ McGinnis .25 .07
825 Mike Walker UER .25 .07
(Card has 1993 Mariner
stats, should be 1992)

1993 Topps Inaugural Marlins

These 825-card standard-size sets were issued by Topps to commemorate the debut seasons of the Colorado Rockies and Florida Marlins. Gold foil Marlins or Rockies logos distinguish these from regular issue cards. These cards were only issued in factory set form. 5,000 Rockies sets and 4,000 Marlins sets were initially printed, but each team had the option of receiving a maximum of 10,000 sets. The Rockies sets were distributed through the four team-owned stores and at Mile High Stadium. The Marlins sets were distributed through FMI and Joe Robbie Stadium.

Nm-Mt Ex-Mt
COMP.FACT.SET (825) 100.00 30.00
*STARS: 2.5X TO 6X BASIC CARDS ...
*ROOKIES: 2.5X TO 6X BASIC CARDS

1993 Topps Inaugural Rockies

Similar to the Marlins set. This was a 1993 set with the Rockies logo imprinted on the card. They were only issued in factory set form. They were distributed through four Rockie owned stores and at Mile High Stadium. They are valued slightly less than the Marlins card as 1,000 more sets of Rockies were produced

Nm-Mt Ex-Mt
COMP.FACT.SET (825) 100.00 30.00
*STARS: 2.5X TO 6X BASIC CARDS ...
*ROOKIES: 2.5X TO 6X BASIC CARDS

1993 Topps Micro

This set was only issued in factory set form. It was issued as a 837 card set with the regular 825 card as well as a special 12 card prism

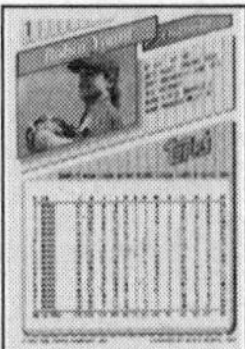

insert set. The cards measure 1" by 1 3/8" which is approximately 40 percent of the regular card size. Only the Prism inserts are listed below. Please refer to the multiplier for values on the other other cards. This was the final year Topps issued the Micro factory set.

Nm-Mt Ex-Mt
COMP. FACT. SET (837) 20.00 6.00
COMMON PRISM INSERT .10 .03
*MICRO: .4X TO 1X BASIC CARDS .....
P1 Robin Yount .50 .15
P20 Tim Salmon .40 .12
P32 Don Mattingly 1.25 .35
P50 Roberto Alomar .40 .12
P150 Frank Thomas 1.00 .30
P155 Dennis Eckersley .20 .06
P179 Ken Griffey Jr. 2.50 .75
P200 Kirby Puckett 1.00 .30
P397 George Brett 1.00 .30
P426 Nigel Wilson .10 .03
P444 David Nied .10 .03
P700 Nolan Ryan 2.50 .75

1993 Topps Black Gold

Topps Black Gold cards 1-22 were randomly inserted in series I packs while card numbers 23-44 were featured in series II packs. They were also inserted three per factory set. In the packs, the cards were inserted one evrery 72 hobby or retail packs; one every 12 jumbo packs and one every 24 rack packs. Hobbyists could obtain the set by collecting individual random insert cards or receive 11, 22, or 44 Black Gold cards by mail when they sent in special "You've Just Won" cards, which were randomly inserted in packs. Series I packs featured three different "You've Just Won" cards, entitling the holder to receive Group A (cards 1-11), Group B (cards 12-22), or Groups A and B (Cards 1-22). In a similar fashion, four "You've Just Won" cards were inserted in series II packs and entitled the holder to receive Group C (23-33), Group D (34-44), Groups C and D (23-44), or Groups A-D (1-44). By returning the "You've Just Won" card with 1.50 for postage and handling, the collector received not only the Black Gold cards won but also a special "You've Just Won" card and a congratulatory letter informing the collector that his/her name has been entered into a drawing for one of 500 uncut sheets of all 44 Topps Black Gold cards in a leatherette frame. These standard-size cards feature different color player photos than either the 1993 Topps regular issue or the Topps Gold issue. The player pictures are cut out and superimposed on a black gloss background. Inside white borders, gold refractory foil edges the top and bottom of the card face. On a black-and-gray pinstripe pattern inside white borders, the horizontal backs have a a second cut out player photo and a player profile on a blue panel. The player's name appears in gold foil lettering on a blue-and-gray geometric shape. The first 22 cards are National Leaguers while the second 22 cards are American Leaguers. Winner cards C and D were both originally produced erroneously and later corrected; the error versions show the players from Winner A and B on the respective fronts of Winner cards Cand D. There is no value difference in the variations at this time. The winner cards were redeemable until January 31, 1994.

Nm-Mt Ex-Mt
COMPLETE SET (44) 10.00 3.00
COMPLETE SERIES 1 (22) 4.00 1.20
COMPLETE SERIES 2 (22) 6.00 1.80
1 Barry Bonds 2.00 .60
2 Will Clark .75 .23
3 Darren Daulton .30 .09
4 Andre Dawson .30 .09
5 Delino DeShields .15 .04
6 Tom Glavine .50 .15
7 Marquis Grissom .15 .04
8 Tony Gwynn 1.00 .30
9 Eric Karros .30 .09
10 Ray Lankford .15 .04
11 Barry Larkin .75 .23
12 Greg Maddux 1.25 .35
13 Fred McGriff .50 .15
14 Joe Oliver .15 .04
15 Terry Pendleton .30 .09
16 Bip Roberts .15 .04
17 Ryne Sandberg 1.25 .35
18 Gary Sheffield .30 .09
19 Lee Smith .30 .09
20 Ozzie Smith 1.25 .35
21 Andy Van Slyke .30 .09
22 Larry Walker .50 .15
23 Roberto Alomar .75 .23
24 Brady Anderson .30 .09
25 Carlos Baerga .15 .04
26 Joe Carter .30 .09
27 Roger Clemens 1.50 .45

28 Mike Devereaux .15 .04
29 Dennis Eckersley .30 .09
30 Cecil Fielder .30 .09
31 Travis Fryman .30 .09
32 Juan Gonzalez UER .75 .23
(No copyright or licensing on card)
33 Ken Griffey Jr. 1.25 .35
34 Brian Harper .15 .04
35 Pat Listach .15 .04
36 Kenny Lofton .30 .09
37 Edgar Martinez .50 .15
38 Jack McDowell .15 .04
39 Mark McGwire 2.00 .60
40 Kirby Puckett .75 .23
41 Mickey Tettleton .15 .04
42 Frank Thomas UER .75 .23
(No copyright or licensing on card)
43 Robin Ventura .30 .09
44 Dave Winfield .30 .09

1993 Topps Traded

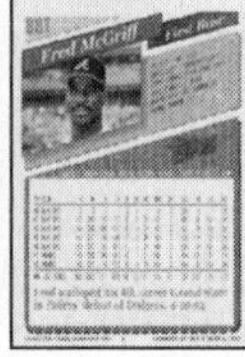

This 132-card standard-size set focuses on promising rookies, new managers, free agents, and players who changed teams. The set also includes 22 members of Team USA. The set has the same design on the front as the regular 1993 Topps issue. The backs are also the same design and carry a head shot, biography, stats, and career highlights. Rookie Cards in this set include Todd Helton.

Nm-Mt Ex-Mt
COMP.FACT.SET (132) 40.00 12.00
1T Barry Bonds 1.25 .35
2T Rich Renteria .10 .03
3T Aaron Sele .10 .03
4T C.Loewer USA RC .25 .07
5T Erik Pappas .10 .03
6T Greg McMichael RC .25 .07
7T Freddie Benavides .10 .03
8T Kirk Gibson .20 .06
9T Tony Fernandez .10 .03
10T Jay Gainer RC .25 .07
11T Orestes Destrade .10 .03
12T A.J. Hinch USA RC .50 .15
13T Bobby Munoz .10 .03
14T Tom Henke .10 .03
15T Rob Butler .10 .03
16T Gary Wayne .10 .03
17T David McCarty .10 .03
18T Walt Weiss .10 .03
19T Todd Helton USA RC 30.00 9.00
20T Mark Whiten .10 .03
21T Ricky Gutierrez .10 .03
22T D.Hermanson USA RC .50 .15
23T Sherman Obando RC .25 .07
24T Mike Piazza 1.25 .35
25T Jeff Russell .10 .03
26T Jason Bere .10 .03
27T Jack Voigt RC .25 .07
28T Chris Bosio .10 .03
29T Phil Hiatt .10 .03
30T M.Beaumont USA RC .25 .07
31T Andres Galarraga .20 .06
32T Greg Swindell .10 .03
33T Vinny Castilla .20 .06
34T P.Clougherty RC USA .25 .07
35T Greg Briley .10 .03
36T Dallas Green MG .10 .03
Davey Johnson MG
37T Tyler Green .10 .03
38T Craig Paquette .10 .03
39T Danny Sheaffer RC .25 .07
40T Jim Converse RC .25 .07
41T Terry Harvey USA RC .25 .07
42T Phil Plantier .10 .03
43T Doug Saunders RC .25 .07
44T Benny Santiago .20 .06
45T Dante Powell USA RC .25 .07
46T Jeff Parrett .10 .03
47T Wade Boggs .30 .09
48T Paul Molitor .30 .09
49T Turk Wendell .10 .03
50T David Wells .20 .06
51T Gary Sheffield .20 .06
52T Kevin Young .20 .06
53T Nelson Liriano .10 .03
54T Greg Maddux .75 .23
55T Derek Bell .10 .03
56T Matt Turner RC .25 .07
57T C.Nelson RC USA .25 .07
58T Mike Hampton .20 .06
59T Troy O'Leary RC .50 .15
60T Benji Gil .10 .03
61T Mitch Lyden RC .25 .07
62T J.T. Snow .50 .15
63T Damon Buford .10 .03
64T Gene Harris .10 .03
65T Randy Myers .10 .03
66T Felix Jose .10 .03
67T Todd Dunn USA RC .25 .07
68T Jimmy Key .20 .06
69T Pedro Castellano .10 .03
70T Mark Merila USA RC .25 .07
71T Rich Rodriguez .10 .03
72T Matt Mieske .10 .03
73T Pete Incaviglia .10 .03
74T Carl Everett .20 .06
75T Jim Abbott .30 .09
76T Luis Aquino .10 .03
77T Rene Arocha .20 .06
78T Jon Shave .10 .03
79T Todd Walker USA RC 2.00 .60
80T Jack Armstrong .10 .03
81T Jeff Richardson .10 .03
82T Blas Minor .10 .03
83T Dave Winfield .20 .06
84T Paul O'Neill .30 .09
85T Steve Reich USA RC .25 .07
86T Chris Hammond .10 .03
87T Hilly Hathaway RC .25 .07
88T Fred McGriff .30 .09
89T Dave Telgheder RC .25 .07
90T Richie Lewis RC .25 .07
91T Brent Gates .10 .03
92T Andre Dawson .20 .06
93T Andy Barkett USA RC .25 .07
94T Doug Drabek .10 .03
95T Joe Klink .10 .03
96T Willie Blair .10 .03
97T D.Graves USA RC .50 .15
98T Pat Meares RC .50 .15
99T Mike Lansing RC .50 .15
100T Marcos Armas RC .25 .07
101T D.Grass RC USA .25 .07
102T Chris Jones .10 .03
103T Ken Ryan RC .25 .07
104T Ellis Burks .20 .06
105T Roberto Kelly .10 .03
106T Dave Magadan .10 .03
107T Paul Wilson USA RC .50 .15
108T Rob Natal .10 .03
109T Paul Wagner .10 .03
110T Jeromy Burnitz .20 .06
111T Monty Fariss .10 .03
112T Kevin Mitchell .10 .03
113T Scott Pose RC .25 .07
114T Dave Stewart .20 .06
115T R.Johnson USA RC .25 .07
116T Armando Reynoso .10 .03
117T Geronimo Berroa .10 .03
118T Woody Williams RC 1.50 .45
119T Tim Bogar RC .25 .07
120T Bob Scafa USA RC .25 .07
121T Henry Cotto .10 .03
122T Gregg Jefferies .10 .03
123T Norm Charlton .10 .03
124T B.Wagner USA RC .25 .07
125T David Cone .20 .06
126T Daryl Boston .10 .03
127T Tim Wallach .10 .03
128T Mike Martin USA RC .25 .07
129T John Cummings RC .25 .07
130T Ryan Bowen .10 .03
131T John Powell USA RC .25 .07
132T Checklist 1-132 .10 .03

1993 Topps Commanders of the Hill

This 30-card standard-size set issued by Topps features pitchers of the American and National Leagues. The cards were available for an additional 25 cents per pack with the purchase of a fountain coke at military installation snack bars and food courts only, through the PX/BX. Each pack contained five cards.

Nm-Mt Ex-Mt
COMPLETE SET (30) 10.00 3.00
1 Dennis Eckersley .50 .15
2 Mike Mussina .50 .15
3 Roger Clemens 2.00 .60
4 Jim Abbott .20 .06
5 Jack McDowell .10 .03
6 Charles Nagy .10 .03
7 Bill Gullickson .10 .03
8 Kevin Appier .20 .06
9 Bill Wegman .10 .03
10 John Smiley .10 .03
11 Melido Perez .10 .03
12 Dave Stewart .20 .06
13 Dave Fleming .10 .03
14 Kevin Brown .30 .09
15 Juan Guzman .10 .03
16 Randy Johnson .75 .23
17 Greg Maddux 2.50 .75
18 Tom Glavine .50 .15
19 Greg Maddux 2.50 .75
20 Jose Rijo .10 .03
21 Pete Harnisch .10 .03
22 Tom Candiotti .20 .06
23 Denny Martinez .20 .06
24 Sid Fernandez .10 .03
25 Curt Schilling .50 .15
26 Doug Drabek .10 .03
27 Bob Tewksbury .10 .03
28 Andy Benes .10 .03
29 Bill Swift .10 .03
30 John Smoltz .30 .09

1993 Topps Full Shots

Issued as one-card inserts in retail re-packs containing a pack each of 1993 Topps Series I and II, and in specially marked jumbo boxes of 1993 Bowman, these 21 cards measure approximately 3 1/2" by 5" and feature on their fronts white-bordered color player action photos. In contrast to many of the oversized cards offered by other baseball card manufacturers, Full Shots were unique cards rather than enlarged versions of existing cards.

Nm-Mt Ex-Mt
COMPLETE SET (21) 40.00 12.00
1 Frank Thomas 2.00 .60
2 Ken Griffey Jr. 5.00 1.50
3 Barry Bonds 4.00 1.20
4 Juan Gonzalez 2.00 .60
5 Roberto Alomar 1.50 .45
6 Mike Piazza 5.00 1.50
7 Tony Gwynn 4.00 1.20
8 Jeff Bagwell 2.00 .60
9 Tim Salmon 1.50 .45
10 John Olerud 1.00 .30
11 Cal Ripken 8.00 2.40
12 David McCarty .50 .15
13 Darren Daulton .75 .23
14 Carlos Baerga .75 .23
15 Roger Clemens 4.00 1.20
16 John Kruk .75 .23
17 Barry Larkin 1.50 .45
18 Gary Sheffield 2.00 .60
19 Tom Glavine 2.00 .60
20 Andres Galarraga 1.50 .45
21 Fred McGriff 1.00 .30

1993 Topps Magazine Jumbo Rookie Cards

This set was inserted in the last four issues of Topps Magazine. When removed from the magazine the cards measure 5" by 7". The players featured autographed 100 of these cards: 50 for subscriber copies and 50 for newstand issues. The cards are all reprinted version of earlier Topps cards. The original Rookie Card year is noted after the player's name

Nm-Mt Ex-Mt
COMPLETE SET (4) 5.00 1.50
1 Dennis Eckersley .50 .15
1976
2 Dave Winfield 1.00 .30
1974
3 George Brett 1.50 .45
1975
4 Nolan Ryan 3.00 .90
1968

1993 Topps Nikon House

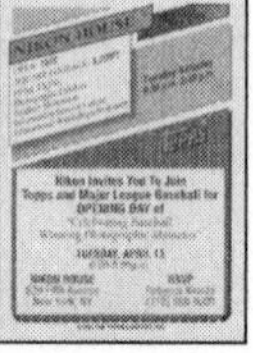

This one-card set commemorates the opening day of the Celebrating Baseball photographic show at Nikon House Photo Gallery on April 13, 1993. The front features a photo of a baseball player batting inside a baseball park. The back displays information about the photo gallery and the Baseball photo show.

Nm-Mt Ex-Mt
1 Batter in Major League Park 3.00 .90

1993 Topps Postcards

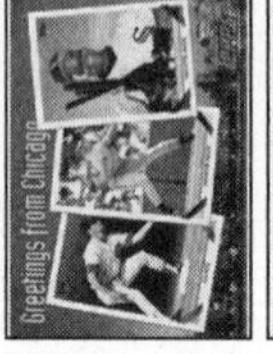

This three-card set is a promotional issue produced by Topps and features a preview of the cards in the 1993 regular Topps set as well as Topps Stadium Club Series II and Series III. Each card displays three different card fronts from the same set. The backs have a postcard format. The cards are unnumbered.

Nm-Mt Ex-Mt
COMPLETE SET (3) 10.00 3.00
1 Topps Regular Issue 4.00 1.20
Ryne Sandberg
Robin Ventura
Frank Thomas
2 Topps Stadium Club 3.00 .90
Walt Weiss
Alex Cole
Benny Santiago
3 Topps Stadium Club 3.00 .90
Benny Santiago
Walt Weiss
Alex Cole

1994 Topps Pre-Production

This nine-card standard-size set was issued by Topps for hobby dealers to preview the 1994 Topps regular-issue series. The back of each card is identical to the player's regular issue 1994 Topps card back except for a diagonal white box across the statistics stating "PRE-PRODUCTION SAMPLE Design and Photo Selection Subject To Change." These cards were also issued in some of the 1993 Topps factory sets. The factory set versions are worth about the same as the hobby versions. There is both a horizontal and vertical version of Ryan.

Nm-Mt Ex-Mt
COMPLETE SET (9) 8.00 2.40
2 Barry Bonds 1.50 .45
6 Jeff Tackett .25 .07
34 Juan Gonzalez 1.25 .35
225 Matt Williams .75 .23
294 Carlos Quintana .25 .07
331 Kenny Lofton .50 .15
390 Wade Boggs 1.00 .30
397 George Brett 1.50 .45
700 Nolan Ryan 3.00 .90

1994 Topps

These 792 standard-size cards were issued in two series of 396. Two types of factory sets were also issued. One features the 792 basic cards, ten Topps Gold, three Black Gold and three Finest Pre-Production cards for a total of 808. The other factory set (Bakers Dozen) includes the 792 basic cards, ten Topps Gold, three Black Gold, ten 1995 Topps Pre-Production cards and a sample pack of three special Topps cards for a total of 818. The standard cards feature glossy color player photos with white borders on the fronts. The player's name is in white cursive lettering at the bottom left, with the team name and player's position printed on a team color-coded bar. There is an inner multicolored border along the left side that extends obliquely across the bottom. The horizontal backs carry an action shot of the player with biography, statistics and highlights. Subsets include Draft Picks (201-210/739-762), All-Stars (384-394) and Stat Twins (601-609). Rookie Cards include Billy Wagner.

Nm-Mt Ex-Mt
COMPLETE SET (792) 50.00 15.00
COMP.FACT.SET (808) 60.00 18.00
COMP.BAKER SET (818) 60.00 18.00
COMP. SERIES 1 (396) 25.00 7.50
COMP. SERIES 2 (396) 25.00 7.50
1 Mike Piazza 1.00 .30
2 Bernie Williams .30 .09
3 Kevin Rogers .10 .03
4 Paul Carey .10 .03
5 Ozzie Guillen .10 .03
6 Derrick May .10 .03
7 Jose Mesa .10 .03
8 Todd Hundley .10 .03
9 Chris Haney .10 .03
10 John Olerud .20 .06
11 Andujar Cedeno .10 .03
12 John Smiley .10 .03
13 Phil Plantier .10 .03
14 Willie Banks .10 .03
15 Jay Bell .20 .06
16 Doug Henry .10 .03
17 Lance Blankenship .10 .03
18 Greg W. Harris .10 .03
19 Scott Livingstone .10 .03
20 Bryan Harvey .10 .03
21 Wil Cordero .10 .03
22 Roger Pavlik .10 .03
23 Mark Lemke .10 .03
24 Jeff Nelson .10 .03
25 Todd Zeile .10 .03
26 Billy Hatcher .10 .03
27 Joe Magrane .10 .03
28 Tony Longmire .10 .03
29 Omar Daal .10 .03
30 Kirt Manwaring .10 .03
31 Melido Perez .10 .03
32 Tim Hulett .10 .03
33 Jeff Schwarz .10 .03
34 Nolan Ryan 2.00 .60
35 Jose Guzman .10 .03
36 Felix Fermin .10 .03
37 Jeff Innis .10 .03
38 Brett Mayne .10 .03
39 Huck Flener RC .10 .03
40 Jeff Bagwell .30 .09
41 Kevin Wickander .10 .03
42 Ricky Gutierrez .10 .03
43 Pat Mahomes .10 .03
44 Jeff King .10 .03
45 Cal Eldred .10 .03
46 Craig Paquette .10 .03
47 Richie Lewis .10 .03
48 Tony Phillips .10 .03
49 Armando Reynoso .10 .03
50 Moises Alou .20 .06
51 Manuel Lee .10 .03
52 Otis Nixon .10 .03
53 Billy Ashley .10 .03
54 Mark Whiten .10 .03
55 Jeff Russell .10 .03
56 Chad Curtis .10 .03
57 Kevin Stocker .10 .03
58 Mike Jackson .10 .03
59 Matt Nokes .10 .03
60 Chris Bosio .10 .03
61 Damon Buford .10 .03
62 Tim Belcher .10 .03
63 Glenallen Hill .10 .03
64 Bill Wertz .10 .03
65 Eddie Murray .50 .15
66 Tom Gordon .10 .03
67 Alex Gonzalez .10 .03
68 Eddie Taubensee .10 .03
69 Jacob Brumfield .10 .03
70 Andy Benes .10 .03
71 Rich Becker .10 .03
72 Steve Cooke .10 .03
73 Billy Spiers .10 .03
74 Scott Brosius .20 .06
75 Alan Trammell .30 .09
76 Luis Aquino .10 .03
77 Jerald Clark .10 .03
78 Mel Rojas .10 .03
79 Billy Masse .10 .03
Stanton Cameron
Tim Clark
Craig McClure RC
80 Jose Canseco .50 .15
81 Greg McMichael .10 .03
82 Brian Turang RC .10 .03
83 Tom Urbani .10 .03
84 Garret Anderson .50 .15
85 Tony Pena .10 .03
86 Ricky Jordan .10 .03
87 Jim Gott .10 .03
88 Pat Kelly .10 .03
89 Bud Black .10 .03
90 Robin Ventura .20 .06
91 Rick Sutcliffe .20 .06
92 Jose Bautista .10 .03
93 Bob Ojeda .10 .03
94 Phil Hiatt .10 .03
95 Tim Pugh .10 .03
96 Randy Knorr .10 .03
97 Todd Jones .10 .03
98 Ryan Thompson .10 .03
99 Tim Mauser .10 .03
100 Kirby Puckett .50 .15
101 Mark Dewey .10 .03
102 B.J. Surhoff .20 .06
103 Sterling Hitchcock .10 .03
104 Alex Arias .10 .03
105 David Wells .20 .06
106 Daryl Boston .10 .03
107 Mike Stanton .10 .03
108 Gary Redus .10 .03
109 Delino DeShields .10 .03
110 Lee Smith .20 .06
111 Greg Litton .10 .03
112 Frankie Rodriguez .10 .03
113 Russ Springer .10 .03
114 Mitch Williams .10 .03
115 Eric Karros .20 .06
116 Jeff Brantley .10 .03
117 Jack Voigt .10 .03
118 Jason Bere .10 .03
119 Kevin Roberson .10 .03
120 Jimmy Key .20 .06
121 Reggie Jefferson .10 .03
122 Jeromy Burnitz .20 .06
123 Billy Brewer .10 .03
124 Willie Canate .10 .03
125 Greg Swindell .10 .03
126 Hal Morris .10 .03
127 Brad Ausmus .10 .03
128 George Tsamis .10 .03
129 Denny Neagle .20 .06
130 Pat Listach .10 .03
131 Steve Karsay .10 .03
132 Bret Barberie .10 .03
133 Mark Leiter .10 .03
134 Greg Colbrunn .10 .03
135 David Nied .10 .03
136 Dean Palmer .20 .06
137 Steve Avery .10 .03
138 Bill Haselman .10 .03
139 Tripp Cromer .10 .03
140 Frank Viola .20 .06
141 Rene Gonzales .10 .03
142 Curt Schilling .30 .09
143 Tim Wallach .10 .03
144 Bobby Munoz .10 .03
145 Brady Anderson .20 .06
146 Rod Beck .10 .03
147 Mike LaValliere .10 .03
148 Greg Hibbard .10 .03
149 Kenny Lofton .20 .06
150 Dwight Gooden .30 .09
151 Greg Gagne .10 .03
152 Ray McDavid .10 .03
153 Chris Donnels .10 .03
154 Dan Wilson .10 .03
155 Todd Stottlemyre .10 .03
156 David McCarty .10 .03
157 Paul Wagner .10 .03
158 Orlando Miller 1.50 .45
Brandon Wilson
Derek Jeter
Mike Neal
159 Mike Fetters .10 .03
160 Scott Lydy .10 .03
161 Darrell Whitmore .10 .03
162 Bob MacDonald .10 .03
163 Vinny Castilla .20 .06
164 Denis Boucher .10 .03
165 Ivan Rodriguez .50 .15
166 Ron Gant .20 .06
167 Tim Davis .10 .03
168 Steve Dixon .10 .03
169 Scott Fletcher .10 .03
170 Terry Mulholland .10 .03
171 Greg Myers .10 .03
172 Brett Butler .20 .06
173 Bob Wickman .10 .03
174 Dave Martinez .10 .03
175 Fernando Valenzuela .20 .06
176 Craig Grebeck .10 .03
177 Shawn Boskie .10 .03
178 Albie Lopez .10 .03
179 Butch Huskey .10 .03
180 George Brett 1.25 .35
181 Juan Guzman .10 .03
182 Eric Anthony .10 .03
183 Rob Dibble .20 .06
184 Craig Shipley .10 .03
185 Kevin Tapani .10 .03
186 Marcus Moore .10 .03
187 Graeme Lloyd .10 .03
188 Mike Bordick .10 .03
189 Chris Hammond .10 .03
190 Cecil Fielder .20 .06
191 Curt Leskanic .10 .03
192 Lou Frazier .10 .03
193 Steve Dreyer RC .10 .03
194 Javier Lopez .20 .06
195 Edgar Martinez .30 .09
196 Allen Watson .10 .03
197 John Flaherty .10 .03
198 Kurt Stillwell .10 .03
199 Danny Jackson .10 .03
200 Cal Ripken 1.50 .45
201 Mike Bell FDP RC .10 .03
202 Alan Benes FDP RC .25 .07
203 Matt Farner FDP RC .10 .03
204 Jeff Granger .10 .03
205 B.Kieschnick FDP RC .25 .07
206 Jeremy Lee FDP RC .10 .03
207 C.Peterson FDP RC .10 .03
208 Alan Rice FDP RC .10 .03
209 Billy Wagner FDP RC .50 .15

210 Kelly Wunsch FDP RC .25 .07
211 Tom Candiotti .10 .03
212 Domingo Jean .10 .03
213 John Burkett .10 .03
214 George Bell .10 .03
215 Dan Plesac .10 .03
216 Manny Ramirez .30 .09
217 Mike Maddux .10 .03
218 Kevin McReynolds .10 .03
219 Pat Borders .10 .03
220 Doug Drabek .10 .03
221 Larry Luebbers RC .10 .03
222 Trevor Hoffman .20 .06
223 Pat Meares .10 .03
224 Danny Miceli .10 .03
225 Greg Vaughn .20 .06
226 Scott Hemond .10 .03
227 Pat Rapp .10 .03
228 Kirk Gibson .20 .06
229 Lance Painter .10 .03
230 Larry Walker .30 .09
231 Benji Gil .10 .03
232 Mark Wohlers .10 .03
233 Rich Amaral .10 .03
234 Eric Pappas .10 .03
235 Scott Cooper .10 .03
236 Mike Butcher .10 .03
237 Curtis Pride .50 .15
Shawn Green
Mark Sweeney
Eddie Davis
238 Kim Batiste .10 .03
239 Paul Assenmacher .10 .03
240 Will Clark .50 .15
241 Jose Offerman .10 .03
242 Todd Frohwirth .10 .03
243 Tim Raines .20 .06
244 Rick Wilkins .10 .03
245 Bret Saberhagen .20 .06
246 Thomas Howard .10 .03
247 Stan Belinda .10 .03
248 Rickey Henderson .50 .15
249 Brian Williams .10 .03
250 Barry Larkin .50 .15
251 Jose Valentin .10 .03
252 Lenny Webster .10 .03
253 Blas Minor .10 .03
254 Tim Teufel .10 .03
255 Bobby Witt .10 .03
256 Walt Weiss .10 .03
257 Chad Kreuter .10 .03
258 Roberto Mejia .10 .03
259 Cliff Floyd .20 .06
260 Julio Franco .20 .06
261 Rafael Belliard .10 .03
262 Marc Newfield .10 .03
263 Gerald Perry .10 .03
264 Ken Ryan .10 .03
265 Chili Davis .20 .06
266 Dave West .10 .03
267 Royce Clayton .10 .03
268 Pedro Martinez .50 .15
269 Mark Hutton .10 .03
270 Frank Thomas .50 .15
271 Brad Pennington .10 .03
272 Mike Harkey .10 .03
273 Sandy Alomar Jr. .10 .03
274 Dave Gallagher .10 .03
275 Wally Joyner .20 .06
276 Ricky Trlicek .10 .03
277 Al Osuna .10 .03
278 Pokey Reese .10 .03
279 Kevin Higgins .10 .03
280 Rick Aguilera .10 .03
281 Orlando Merced .10 .03
282 Mike Mohler .10 .03
283 John Jaha .10 .03
284 Robb Nen .20 .06
285 Travis Fryman .20 .06
286 Mark Thompson .10 .03
287 Mike Lansing .10 .03
288 Craig Lefferts .10 .03
289 Damon Berryhill .10 .03
290 Randy Johnson .50 .15
291 Jeff Reed .10 .03
292 Danny Darwin .10 .03
293 J.T. Snow .20 .06
294 Tyler Green .10 .03
295 Chris Hoiles .10 .03
296 Roger McDowell .10 .03
297 Spike Owen .10 .03
298 Salomon Torres .10 .03
299 Wilson Alvarez .10 .03
300 Ryne Sandberg .75 .23
301 Derek Lilliquist .10 .03
302 Howard Johnson .10 .03
303 Greg Cadaret .10 .03
304 Pat Hentgen .10 .03
305 Craig Biggio .30 .09
306 Scott Service .10 .03
307 Melvin Nieves .10 .03
308 Mike Trombley .10 .03
309 Carlos Garcia .10 .03
310 Robin Yount UER .75 .23
(listed with 111 triples in
1988; should be 11)
311 Marcos Armas .10 .03
312 Rich Rodriguez .10 .03
313 Justin Thompson .10 .03
314 Danny Sheaffer .10 .03
315 Ken Hill .10 .03
316 Chad Ogea .10 .03
Duff Brumley
Terrell Wade RC
Chris Michalak
317 Cris Carpenter .10 .03
318 Jeff Blauser .10 .03
319 Ted Power .10 .03
320 Ozzie Smith .75 .23
321 John Dopson .10 .03
322 Chris Turner .10 .03
323 Pete Incaviglia .10 .03
324 Alan Mills .10 .03
325 Jody Reed .10 .03
326 Rich Monteleone .10 .03
327 Mark Carreon .10 .03
328 Donn Pall .10 .03
329 Matt Walbeck .10 .03
330 Charles Nagy .10 .03
331 Jeff McKnight .10 .03
332 Jose Lind .10 .03
333 Mike Timlin .10 .03
334 Doug Jones .10 .03
335 Kevin Mitchell .10 .03
336 Luis Lopez .10 .03
337 Shane Mack .10 .03
338 Randy Tomlin .10 .03
339 Matt Mieske .10 .03
340 Mark McGwire 1.25 .35
341 Nigel Wilson .10 .03
342 Danny Gladden .10 .03
343 Mo Sanford .10 .03
344 Sean Berry .10 .03
345 Kevin Brown .20 .06
346 Greg Olson .10 .03
347 Dave Magadan .10 .03
348 Rene Arocha .10 .03
349 Carlos Quintana .10 .03
350 Jim Abbott .30 .09
351 Gary DiSarcina .10 .03
352 Ben Rivera .10 .03
353 Carlos Hernandez .10 .03
354 Darren Lewis .10 .03
355 Harold Reynolds .20 .06
356 Scott Ruffcorn .10 .03
357 Mark Gubicza .10 .03
358 Paul Sorrento .10 .03
359 Anthony Young .10 .03
360 Mark Grace .30 .09
361 Rob Butler .10 .03
362 Kevin Bass .10 .03
363 Eric Helfand .10 .03
364 Derek Bell .10 .03
365 Scott Erickson .10 .03
366 Al Martin .10 .03
367 Ricky Bones .10 .03
368 Jeff Branson .10 .03
369 Luis Ortiz .75 .23
David Bell RC
Jason Giambi
George Arias
370 Benito Santiago .20 .06
(See also 379)
371 John Doherty .10 .03
372 Joe Girardi .10 .03
373 Tim Scott .10 .03
374 Marvin Freeman .10 .03
375 Deion Sanders .30 .09
376 Roger Salkeld .10 .03
377 Bernard Gilkey .10 .03
378 Tony Fossas .10 .03
379 Mark McLemore UER .10 .03
(Card number is 370)
380 Darren Daulton .20 .06
381 Chuck Finley .20 .06
382 Mitch Webster .10 .03
383 Gerald Williams .10 .03
384 Frank Thomas AS .30 .09
Fred McGriff AS
385 Roberto Alomar AS .20 .06
Robby Thompson AS
386 Wade Boggs AS .20 .06
Matt Williams AS
387 Cal Ripken AS .50 .15
Jeff Blauser AS
388 Ken Griffey Jr. AS .50 .15
Len Dykstra AS
389 Juan Gonzalez AS .30 .09
David Justice AS
390 George Belle AS .60 .18
Bobby Bonds AS
391 Mike Stanley AS .50 .15
Mike Piazza AS
392 Jack McDowell AS .30 .09
Greg Maddux AS
393 Jimmy Key AS .20 .06
Tom Glavine AS
394 Jeff Montgomery AS .10 .03
Randy Myers AS
395 Checklist 1-198 .10 .03
396 Checklist 199-396 .10 .03
397 Tim Salmon .30 .09
398 Todd Benzinger .10 .03
399 Frank Castillo .10 .03
400 Ken Griffey Jr. .75 .23
401 John Kruk .20 .06
402 Dave Telgheder .10 .03
403 Gary Gaetti .20 .06
404 Jim Edmonds .30 .09
405 Don Slaught .10 .03
406 Jose Oquendo .10 .03
407 Bruce Ruffin .10 .03
408 Phil Clark .10 .03
409 Joe Klink .10 .03
410 Lou Whitaker .20 .06
411 Kevin Seitzer .10 .03
412 Darrin Fletcher .10 .03
413 Kenny Rogers .20 .06
414 Bill Pecota .10 .03
415 Dave Fleming .10 .03
416 Luis Alicea .10 .03
417 Paul Quantrill .10 .03
418 Damion Easley .10 .03
419 Wes Chamberlain .10 .03
420 Harold Baines .20 .06
421 Scott Radinsky .10 .03
422 Rey Sanchez .10 .03
423 Junior Ortiz .10 .03
424 Jeff Kent .20 .06
425 Brian McRae .10 .03
426 Ed Sprague .10 .03
427 Tom Edens .10 .03
428 Willie Greene .10 .03
429 Bryan Hickerson .10 .03
430 Dave Winfield .20 .06
431 Pedro Astacio .10 .03
432 Mike Gallego .10 .03
433 Dave Burba .10 .03
434 Bob Walk .10 .03
435 Darryl Hamilton .10 .03
436 Vince Horsman .10 .03
437 Bob Natal .10 .03
438 Mike Henneman .10 .03
439 Willie Blair .10 .03
440 Dennis Martinez .20 .06
441 Dan Peltier .10 .03
442 Tony Tarasco .10 .03
443 John Cummings .10 .03
444 Geronimo Pena .10 .03
445 Aaron Sele .10 .03
446 Stan Javier .10 .03
447 Mike Williams .10 .03
448 Greg Pirkl .10 .03
Roberto Petagine
D.J.Boston
Shawn Wooten RC
449 Jim Poole .10 .03
450 Carlos Baerga .10 .03
451 Bob Scanlan .10 .03
452 Lance Johnson .10 .03
453 Eric Hillman .10 .03
454 Keith Miller .10 .03
455 Dave Stewart .20 .06
456 Pete Harnisch .10 .03
457 Roberto Kelly .10 .03
458 Tim Worrell .10 .03
459 Pedro Munoz .10 .03
460 Orel Hershiser .20 .06
461 Randy Velarde .10 .03
462 Trevor Wilson .10 .03
463 Jerry Goff .10 .03
464 Bill Wegman .10 .03
465 Dennis Eckersley .20 .06
466 Jeff Conine .20 .06
467 Joe Boever .10 .03
468 Dante Bichette .20 .06
469 Jeff Shaw .10 .03
470 Rafael Palmeiro .30 .09
471 Phil Leftwich RC .10 .03
472 Jay Buhner .20 .06
473 Bob Tewksbury .10 .03
474 Tim Naehring .10 .03
475 Tom Glavine .30 .09
476 Dave Hollins .10 .03
477 Arthur Rhodes .10 .03
478 Joey Cora .10 .03
479 Mike Morgan .10 .03
480 Albert Belle .20 .06
481 John Franco .20 .06
482 Hipolito Pichardo .10 .03
483 Duane Ward .10 .03
484 Luis Gonzalez .20 .06
485 Joe Oliver .10 .03
486 Wally Whitehurst .10 .03
487 Mike Benjamin .10 .03
488 Eric Davis .20 .06
489 Scott Kamieniecki .10 .03
490 Kent Hrbek .20 .06
491 John Hope RC .10 .03
492 Jesse Orosco .10 .03
493 Troy Neel .10 .03
494 Ryan Bowen .10 .03
495 Mickey Tettleton .10 .03
496 Chris Jones .10 .03
497 John Wetteland .20 .06
498 David Hulse .10 .03
499 Greg Maddux .75 .23
500 Bo Jackson .50 .15
501 Donovan Osborne .10 .03
502 Mike Greenwell .10 .03
503 Steve Frey .10 .03
504 Jim Eisenreich .10 .03
505 Robby Thompson .10 .03
506 Leo Gomez .10 .03
507 Dave Staton .10 .03
508 Wayne Kirby .10 .03
509 Tim Bogar .10 .03
510 David Cone .20 .06
511 Devon White .10 .03
512 Xavier Hernandez .10 .03
513 Tim Costo .10 .03
514 Gene Harris .10 .03
515 Jack McDowell .10 .03
516 Kevin Gross .10 .03
517 Scott Leius .10 .03
518 Lloyd McClendon .10 .03
519 Alex Diaz RC .10 .03
520 Wade Boggs .30 .09
521 Bob Welch .10 .03
522 Henry Cotto .10 .03
523 Mike Moore .10 .03
524 Tim Laker .10 .03
525 Andres Galarraga .20 .06
526 Jamie Moyer .20 .06
527 Norberto Martin .10 .03
Ruben Santana
Jason Hardtke
Chris Sexton RC
528 Sid Bream .10 .03
529 Erik Hanson .10 .03
530 Ray Lankford .10 .03
531 Rob Deer .10 .03
532 Rod Correia .10 .03
533 Roger Mason .10 .03
534 Mike Devereaux .10 .03
535 Jeff Montgomery .10 .03
536 Dwight Smith .10 .03
537 Jeremy Hernandez .10 .03
538 Ellis Burks .20 .06
539 Bobby Jones .10 .03
540 Paul Molitor .30 .09
541 Jeff Juden .10 .03
542 Chris Sabo .10 .03
543 Larry Casian .10 .03
544 Jeff Gardner .10 .03
545 Ramon Martinez .10 .03
546 Paul O'Neill .30 .09
547 Steve Hosey .10 .03
548 Dave Nilsson .10 .03
549 Ron Darling .10 .03
550 Matt Williams .20 .06
551 Jack Armstrong .10 .03
552 Bill Krueger .10 .03
553 Freddie Benavides .10 .03
554 Jeff Fassero .10 .03
555 Chuck Knoblauch .20 .06
556 Guillermo Velasquez .10 .03
557 Joel Johnston .10 .03
558 Tom Lampkin .10 .03
559 Todd Van Poppel .10 .03
560 Gary Sheffield .20 .06
561 Skeeter Barnes .10 .03
562 Darren Holmes .10 .03
563 John Vander Wal .10 .03
564 Mike Ignasiak .10 .03
565 Fred McGriff .30 .09
566 Luis Polonia .10 .03
567 Mike Perez .10 .03
568 John Valentin .10 .03
569 Mike Felder .10 .03
570 Tommy Greene .10 .03
571 David Segui .10 .03
572 Roberto Hernandez .10 .03
573 Steve Wilson .10 .03
574 Willie McGee .20 .06
575 Randy Myers .10 .03
576 Darrin Jackson .10 .03
577 Eric Plunk .10 .03
578 Mike Macfarlane .10 .03
579 Doug Brocail .10 .03
580 Steve Finley .20 .06
581 John Roper .10 .03
582 Danny Cox .10 .03
583 Chip Hale .10 .03
584 Scott Bullett .10 .03
585 Kevin Reimer .10 .03
586 Brent Gates .10 .03
587 Matt Turner .10 .03
588 Rich Rowland .10 .03
589 Kent Bottenfield .10 .03
590 Marquis Grissom .10 .03
591 Doug Strange .10 .03
592 Jay Howell .10 .03
593 Omar Vizquel .20 .06
594 Rheal Cormier .10 .03
595 Andre Dawson .20 .06
596 Hilly Hathaway .10 .03
597 Todd Pratt .10 .03
598 Mike Mussina .50 .15
599 Alex Fernandez .10 .03
600 Don Mattingly 1.25 .35
601 Frank Thomas MOG .30 .09
602 Ryne Sandberg MOG .50 .15
603 Wade Boggs MOG .20 .06
604 Cal Ripken MOG .75 .23
605 Barry Bonds MOG .60 .18
606 Ken Griffey Jr. MOG .50 .15
607 Kirby Puckett MOG .30 .09
608 Darren Daulton MOG .10 .03
609 Paul Molitor MOG .20 .06
610 Terry Steinbach .10 .03
611 Todd Worrell .10 .03
612 Jim Thome .50 .15
613 Chuck McElroy .10 .03
614 John Habyan .10 .03
615 Sid Fernandez .10 .03
616 Eddie Zambrano .10 .03
Glenn Murray
Chad Mottola
Jermaine Allensworth RC
617 Steve Bedrosian .10 .03
618 Rob Ducey .10 .03
619 Tom Browning .10 .03
620 Tony Gwynn .60 .18
621 Carl Willis .10 .03
622 Kevin Young .10 .03
623 Rafael Novoa .10 .03
624 Jerry Browne .10 .03
625 Charlie Hough .20 .06
626 Chris Gomez .10 .03
627 Steve Reed .10 .03
628 Kirk Rueter .20 .06
629 Matt Whiteside .10 .03
630 David Justice .20 .06
631 Brad Holman .10 .03
632 Brian Jordan .20 .06
633 Scott Bankhead .10 .03
634 Torey Lovullo .10 .03
635 Len Dykstra .20 .06
636 Ben McDonald .10 .03
637 Steve Howe .10 .03
638 Jose Vizcaino .10 .03
639 Bill Swift .10 .03
640 Darryl Strawberry .30 .09
641 Steve Farr .10 .03
642 Tom Kramer .10 .03
643 Joe Orsulak .10 .03
644 Tom Henke .10 .03
645 Joe Carter .20 .06
646 Ken Caminiti .20 .06
647 Reggie Sanders .20 .06
648 Andy Ashby .20 .06
649 Derek Parks .10 .03
650 Andy Van Slyke .20 .06
651 Juan Bell .10 .03
652 Roger Smithberg .10 .03
653 Chuck Carr .10 .03
654 Bill Gullickson .10 .03
655 Charlie Hayes .10 .03
656 Chris Nabholz .10 .03
657 Karl Rhodes .10 .03
658 Pete Smith .10 .03
659 Bret Boone .20 .06
660 Gregg Jefferies .10 .03
661 Bob Zupcic .10 .03
662 Steve Sax .10 .03
663 Mariano Duncan .10 .03
664 Jeff Tackett .10 .03
665 Mark Langston .10 .03
666 Steve Buechele .10 .03
667 Candy Maldonado .10 .03
668 Woody Williams .20 .06
669 Tim Wakefield .20 .06
670 Danny Tartabull .10 .03
671 Charlie O'Brien .10 .03
672 Felix Jose .10 .03
673 Bobby Ayala .10 .03
674 Scott Servais .10 .03
675 Roberto Alomar .50 .15
676 Pedro A.Martinez RC .10 .03
677 Eddie Guardado .20 .06
678 Mark Lewis .10 .03
679 Jaime Navarro .10 .03
680 Ruben Sierra .10 .03
681 Rick Renteria .10 .03
682 Storm Davis .10 .03
683 Cory Snyder .10 .03
684 Ron Karkovice .10 .03
685 Juan Gonzalez .50 .15
686 Chris Howard .30 .09
Carlos Delgado
Jason Kendall
Paul Bako
687 John Smoltz .30 .09
688 Brian Dorsett .10 .03
689 Omar Olivares .10 .03
690 Mo Vaughn .20 .06
691 Joe Grahe .10 .03
692 Mickey Morandini .10 .03
693 Tino Martinez .30 .09
694 Brian Barnes .10 .03
695 Mike Stanley .10 .03
696 Mark Clark .10 .03
697 Dave Hansen .10 .03
698 Willie Wilson .10 .03
699 Pete Schourek .10 .03
700 Barry Bonds 1.25 .35
701 Kevin Appier .20 .06
702 Tony Fernandez .10 .03
703 Darryl Kile .20 .06
704 Archi Cianfrocco .10 .03
705 Jose Rijo .10 .03
706 Brian Harper .10 .03
707 Zane Smith .10 .03
708 Dave Henderson .10 .03
709 Angel Miranda UER .10 .03
(no Topps logo on back)
710 Orestes Destrade .10 .03
711 Greg Gohr .10 .03
712 Eric Young .10 .03
713 Todd Williams .10 .03
Ron Watson
Kirk Bullinger
Mike Welch
714 Tim Spehr .10 .03
715 Hank Aaron 715 HR .50 .15
716 Nate Minchey .10 .03
717 Mike Blowers .10 .03
718 Kent Mercker .10 .03
719 Tom Pagnozzi .10 .03
720 Roger Clemens 1.00 .30
721 Eduardo Perez .10 .03
722 Milt Thompson .10 .03
723 Gregg Olson .10 .03
724 Kirk McCaskill .10 .03
725 Sammy Sosa .75 .23
726 Alvaro Espinoza .10 .03
727 Henry Rodriguez .10 .03
728 Jim Leyritz .10 .03
729 Steve Scarsone .10 .03
730 Bobby Bonilla .20 .06
731 Chris Gwynn .10 .03
732 Al Leiter .20 .06
733 Bip Roberts .10 .03
734 Mark Portugal .10 .03
735 Terry Pendleton .20 .06
736 Dave Valle .10 .03
737 Paul Kilgus .10 .03
738 Greg A. Harris .10 .03
739 Jon Ratliff DP RC .10 .03
740 Kirk Presley DP RC .10 .03
741 Josue Estrada DP RC .10 .03
742 Wayne Gomes DP RC .10 .03
743 Pat Watkins DP RC .10 .03
744 Jamey Wright DP RC .25 .07
745 Jay Powell DP RC .10 .03
746 Ryan McGuire DP RC .10 .03
747 Marc Barcelo DP RC .10 .03
748 Sloan Smith DP RC .10 .03
749 John Wasdin DP RC .10 .03
750 Marc Vlades DP .10 .03
751 Dan Ehler DP RC .10 .03
752 Andre King DP RC .10 .03
753 Greg Keagle DP RC .10 .03
754 Jason Myers DP RC .10 .03
755 Dax Winslett DP RC .10 .03
756 Casey Whitten DP RC .10 .03
757 Tony Fuduric DP RC .10 .03
758 Greg Norton DP RC .25 .07
759 Jeff D'Amico DP RC .25 .07
760 Ryan Hancock DP RC .10 .03
761 David Cooper DP RC .10 .03
762 Kevin Orie DP RC .10 .03
763 John O'Donoghue .10 .03
Mike Oquist
764 Cory Bailey RC .10 .03
Scott Hatteberg
765 Mark Holzemer .10 .03
Paul Swingle RC
766 James Baldwin .10 .03
Rod Bolton
767 Jerry Di Poto .25 .07
Julian Tavarez RC
768 Danny Bautista .10 .03
Sean Bergman
769 Bob Hamelin .10 .03
Joe Vitiello
770 Mark Kiefer .10 .03
Troy O'Leary
771 Denny Hocking .10 .03
Oscar Munoz RC
772 Russ Davis .10 .03
Brien Taylor
773 Kyle Abbott RC .25 .07
Miguel Jimenez
774 Kevin King .10 .03
Eric Plantenberg RC
775 Jon Shave .10 .03
Desi Wilson
776 Domingo Cedeno .10 .03
Paul Spoljaric
777 Chipper Jones .50 .15
Ryan Klesko
778 Steve Trachsel .10 .03
Turk Wendell
779 Johnny Ruffin .10 .03
Jerry Spradlin RC
780 Jason Bates .10 .03
John Burke
781 Carl Everett .20 .06
Dave Weathers
782 Gary Mota .10 .03
James Mouton
783 Raul Mondesi .20 .06
Ben Van Ryn
784 Gabe White .20 .06
Rondell White
785 Brook Fordyce .20 .06
Bill Pulsipher
786 Kevin Foster RC .10 .03
Gene Schall
787 Rich Aude RC .10 .03
Midre Cummings
788 Brian Barber .10 .03
Rich Batchelor
789 Brian Johnson RC .10 .03
Scott Sanders
790 Ricky Faneyte .10 .03
J.R. Phillips

791 Checklist 3 .10 .03
792 Checklist 4 .10 .03

1994 Topps Gold

The 1994 Topps Gold set is parallel to the basic issue. They were inserted one per wax or mini pack, two per mini jumbo, three per rack pack, four per jumbo, five per jumbo rack and ten per factory set. The only difference between the Gold issue and the basic cards is gold foil on the player's name and the Topps logo. As in previous Gold Sets, player cards (cards 395-96 and 791-92) replace the Checklist cards.

Nm-Mt Ex-Mt
COMPLETE SET (792) 80.00 24.00
COMP.SERIES 1 (396) 40.00 12.00
COMP.SERIES 2 (396) 40.00 12.00
*STARS: 1.5X to 4X BASIC CARDS ...
*ROOKIES: 1.25X to 3X BASIC CARDS
395 Bill Brennan .40 .12
396 Jeff Bronkey .40 .12
791 Mike Cook .40 .12
792 Dan Pasqua .40 .12

1994 Topps Spanish

Issued in complete factory set form only, these 792 standard-size cards parallel the regular Topps issue. These cards have the same front photos but are billingual. The factory set also contains the Topps Spanish Legends 10-card set. That set which is entitled "Topps Legends" features retired Latin players.

Nm-Mt Ex-Mt
COMP. FACT.SET (802) 125.00 38.00
COMPLETE SET (792) 120.00 36.00
SPANISH LEG. SET (10) 5.00 1.50
COMMON CARD (1-792) .20 .06
COM.LEGENDS (L1-L10) .25 .07
*STARS: 3X to 6X BASIC CARDS ...
L1 Felipe Alou .75 .23
L2 Ruben Amaro .25 .07
L3 Luis Aparicio 1.00 .30
L4 Rod Carew 1.00 .30
L5 Chico Carrasquel .50 .15
L6 Orlando Cepeda 1.00 .30
L7 Juan Marichal 1.00 .30
L8 Minnie Minoso .75 .23
L9 Cookie Rojas .25 .07
L10 Luis Tiant .50 .15

1994 Topps Black Gold

Randomly inserted one in every 72 packs, this 44-card standard-size set was issued in two series of 22. Cards were also issued three per 1994 Topps factory set. Collectors had a chance, through redemption cards to receive all or part of the set. There are seven Winner redemption cards for a total 51 cards associated with this set. The set is considered complete with the 44 player cards. Card fronts feature color player action photos. The player's name at bottom and the team name at top are screened in gold foil. The backs contain a player photo and statistical rankings. The winner cards were redeemable until January 31, 1995

Nm-Mt Ex-Mt
COMPLETE SET (44) 25.00 7.50
COMPLETE SERIES 1 (22) 15.00 4.50
COMPLETE SERIES 2 (22) 10.00 3.00
1 Roberto Alomar 1.00 .30
2 Carlos Baerga .20 .06
3 Albert Belle .40 .12
4 Joe Carter .40 .12
5 Cecil Fielder .40 .12
6 Travis Fryman .40 .12
7 Juan Gonzalez 1.00 .30
8 Ken Griffey Jr. 1.50 .45
9 Chris Hoiles .20 .06
10 Randy Johnson 1.00 .30
11 Kenny Lofton .40 .12
12 Jack McDowell .20 .06
13 Paul Molitor .60 .18
14 Jeff Montgomery .20 .06
15 John Olerud .40 .12
16 Rafael Palmeiro .60 .18
17 Kirby Puckett 1.00 .30
18 Cal Ripken 3.00 .90
19 Tim Salmon .60 .18
20 Mike Stanley .20 .06
21 Frank Thomas 1.00 .30
22 Robin Ventura .40 .12
23 Jeff Bagwell .60 .18
24 Jay Bell .40 .12
25 Craig Biggio .60 .18
26 Jeff Blauser .20 .06
27 Barry Bonds 2.50 .75
28 Darren Daulton .40 .12
29 Len Dykstra .40 .12
30 Andres Galarraga .40 .12
31 Ron Gant .40 .12
32 Tom Glavine .60 .18
33 Mark Grace .60 .18
34 Marquis Grissom .20 .06
35 Gregg Jefferies .20 .06
36 David Justice .40 .12
37 John Kruk .40 .12
38 Greg Maddux 1.50 .45
39 Fred McGriff .60 .18
40 Randy Myers .20 .06
41 Mike Piazza 2.00 .60
42 Sammy Sosa 1.50 .45
43 Robby Thompson .20 .06
44 Matt Williams .40 .12
A Winner A 1-11 .20 .06
B Winner B 12-22 .20 .06
C Winner C 23-33 .20 .06
D Winner D 34-44 .20 .06
AB Winner AB 1-22 .20 .06
CD Winner CD 23-44 .20 .06
ABCD Winner ABCD 1-44 .20 .06

1994 Topps Traded

This set consists of 132 standard-size cards featuring traded players in their new uniforms, rookies and draft choices. Factory sets consisted of 140 cards including a set of eight Topps Finest cards. Card fronts feature a player photo with the player's name, team and position at the bottom. The horizontal backs have a player photo to the left with complete career statisics and highlights. Rookie Cards include Rusty Greer, Ben Grieve, Paul Konerko Terrence Long and Chan Ho Park.

Nm-Mt Ex-Mt
COMP.FACT.SET (140) 40.00 12.00
1T Paul Wilson .10 .03
2T Bill Taylor RC 1.00 .30
3T Dan Wilson .10 .03
4T Mark Smith .10 .03
5T Toby Borland RC .25 .07
6T Dave Clark .10 .03
7T Dennis Martinez .20 .06
8T Dave Gallagher .10 .03
9T Josias Manzanillo .10 .03
10T Brian Anderson RC 1.00 .30
11T Damon Berryhill .10 .03
12T Alex Cole .10 .03
13T Jacob Shumate RC .25 .07
14T Oddibe McDowell .10 .03
15T Willie Banks .10 .03
16T Jerry Browne .10 .03
17T Donnie Elliott .10 .03
18T Ellis Burks .20 .06
19T Chuck McElroy .10 .03
20T Luis Polonia .10 .03
21T Brian Harper .10 .03
22T Mark Portugal .10 .03
23T Dave Henderson .10 .03
24T Mark Acre RC .25 .07
25T Julio Franco .20 .06
26T Darren Hall RC .25 .07
27T Eric Anthony .10 .03
28T Sid Fernandez .10 .03
29T Rusty Greer RC 1.50 .45
30T Riccardo Ingram RC .25 .07
31T Gabe White .10 .03
32T Tim Belcher .10 .03
33T Terrence Long RC 2.50 .75
34T Mark Dalesandro RC .25 .07
35T Mike Kelly .10 .03
36T Jack Morris .20 .06
37T Jeff Brantley .10 .03
38T Larry Barnes RC .25 .07
39T Brian R. Hunter .10 .03
40T Otis Nixon .10 .03
41T Bret Wagner .10 .03
42T Pedro Martinez TR .50 .15
Delino Deshields
43T Heathcliff Slocumb .10 .03
44T Ben Grieve RC 1.50 .45
45T John Hudek RC .25 .07
46T Shawon Dunston .10 .03
47T Greg Colbrunn .10 .03
48T Joey Hamilton .10 .03
49T Marvin Freeman .10 .03
50T Terry Mulholland .10 .03
51T Keith Mitchell .10 .03
52T Dwight Smith .10 .03
53T Shawn Boskie .10 .03
54T Kevin Witt RC 1.00 .30
55T Ron Gant .20 .06
56T Trenidad Hubbard RC 10.00 3.00
Jason Schmidt RC
Larry Sutton
Stephen Larkin RC
57T Jody Reed .10 .03
58T Rick Helling .10 .03
59T John Powell .10 .03
60T Eddie Murray .50 .15
61T Joe Hall RC .25 .07
62T Jorge Fabregas .10 .03
63T Mike Mordecai RC .25 .07
64T Ed Vosberg .10 .03
65T Rickey Henderson .50 .15
66T Tim Grieve RC .25 .07
67T Jon Lieber .10 .03
68T Chris Howard .10 .03
69T Matt Walbeck .10 .03
70T Chan Ho Park RC 2.50 .75
71T Bryan Eversgerd RC .25 .07
72T John Dettmer .10 .03
73T Erik Hanson .10 .03
74T Mike Thurman RC .25 .07
75T Bobby Ayala .10 .03
76T Rafael Palmeiro .30 .09
77T Bret Boone .20 .06
78T Paul Shuey .10 .03
79T Kevin Foster RC .25 .07
80T Dave Magadan .10 .03
81T Bip Roberts .10 .03
82T Howard Johnson .10 .03
83T Xavier Hernandez .10 .03
84T Ross Powell RC .25 .07
85T Doug Million RC .25 .07
86T Geronimo Berroa .10 .03
87T Mark Farris RC .25 .07
88T Butch Henry .10 .03
89T Junior Felix .10 .03
90T Bo Jackson .50 .15
91T Hector Carrasco .10 .03
92T Charlie O'Brien .10 .03
93T Omar Vizquel .20 .06
94T David Segui .10 .03
95T Dustin Hermanson .20 .06
96T Gar Finnvold RC .25 .07
97T Dave Stevens .10 .03
98T Corey Pointer RC .25 .07
99T Felix Fermin .10 .03
100T Lee Smith .20 .06
101T Reid Ryan RC 1.00 .30
102T Bobby Munoz .10 .03
103T Deion Sanders TR .30 .09
Roberto Kelly
104T Turner Ward .10 .03
105T W.VanLandingham RC .25 .07
106T Vince Coleman .10 .03
107T Stan Javier .10 .03
108T Darrin Jackson .10 .03
109T C.J. Nitkowski RC .25 .07
110T Anthony Young .10 .03
111T Kurt Miller .10 .03
112T Paul Konerko RC 4.00 1.20
113T Walt Weiss .10 .03
114T Daryl Boston .10 .03
115T Will Clark .50 .15
116T Matt Smith RC .25 .07
117T Mark Leiter .10 .03
118T Gregg Olson .10 .03
119T Tony Pena .10 .03
120T Jose Vizcaino .10 .03
121T Rick White RC .25 .07
122T Rich Rowland .10 .03
123T Jeff Reboulet .10 .03
124T Greg Hibbard .10 .03
125T Chris Sabo .10 .03
126T Doug Jones .10 .03
127T Tony Fernandez .10 .03
128T Carlos Reyes RC .25 .07
129T Kevin L.Brown RC 1.00 .30
130T Ryne Sandberg 1.25 .35
Farewell
131T Ryne Sandberg 1.25 .35
Farewell
132T Checklist 1-132 .10 .03

1994 Topps Traded Finest Inserts

Each Topps Traded factory set contained a complete eight card set of Finest Inserts. These cards are numbered separately and designed differently from the base cards. Each Finest Insert features a action shot of a player set against purple chrome background. The set highlights the top performers midway through the 1994 season, detailing their performances through July. The cards are numbered on back "X of 8".

Nm-Mt Ex-Mt
COMPLETE SET (8) 5.00 1.50
1 Greg Maddux .75 .23
2 Mike Piazza 1.00 .30
3 Matt Williams .20 .06
4 Raul Mondesi .20 .06
5 Ken Griffey Jr. .75 .23
6 Kenny Lofton .20 .06
7 Frank Thomas .50 .15
8 Manny Ramirez .30 .09

1994 Topps Porcelain Promo

Manufactured by R and N China Co. and licensed by Topps, this porcelain promo was issued to herald the March 1994 release of the porcelain version of the 1994 Topps I set. The porcelain promo is actually reproduced from the 1993 Topps set (number 700, Nolan Ryan) and the design is identical to that card, aside from having rounded corners and carrying the manufacturer's name and production number at the bottom of the back. The promo was issued in its own box, which also contained a wooden stand for the card and a small certificate of limited issue.

Nm-Mt Ex-Mt
700 Nolan Ryan 30.00 9.00

1994 Topps Superstar Samplers

Sold only in retail outlets, each 1994 Topps Baker's Dozen factory set included a cello-wrapped three-card sampler of a MLB player. Each player is represented by a Bowman, a Finest, and a Stadium Club card. These cards are identical to their regular issue counterparts except for a special "Topps Superstar Sampler" emblem on their backs. The prices listed below are for all three cards; the Finest card represents 50 percent of the value, while the Bowman or Stadium Club card are worth 25 percent each of the value. We have sequenced each player in alphabetical order.

Nm-Mt Ex-Mt
COMPLETE SET (135) 1000.00 300.00
COMMON BAG (1-45) 6.00 1.80
1 Roberto Alomar 20.00 6.00
2 Carlos Baerga 10.00 3.00
3 Jeff Bagwell 30.00 9.00
4 Albert Belle 10.00 3.00
5 Barry Bonds 50.00 15.00
6 Bobby Bonilla 10.00 3.00
7 Jose Canseco 25.00 7.50
8 Joe Carter 10.00 3.00
9 Will Clark 20.00 6.00
10 Roger Clemens 50.00 15.00
11 Darren Daulton 10.00 3.00
12 Len Dykstra 6.00 1.80
13 Cecil Fielder 10.00 3.00
14 Cliff Floyd 10.00 3.00
15 Andres Galarraga 20.00 6.00
16 Tom Glavine 25.00 7.50
17 Juan Gonzalez 25.00 7.50
18 Mark Grace 15.00 4.50
19 Ken Griffey Jr. 60.00 18.00
20 Marquis Grissom 10.00 3.00
21 Tony Gwynn 50.00 15.00
22 Gregg Jefferies 6.00 1.80
23 Randy Johnson 30.00 9.00
24 David Justice 20.00 6.00
25 Barry Larkin 20.00 6.00
26 Greg Maddux 60.00 18.00
27 Don Mattingly 50.00 15.00
28 Jack McDowell 6.00 1.80
29 Fred McGriff 15.00 4.50
30 Paul Molitor 25.00 7.50
31 Raul Mondesi 15.00 4.50
32 John Olerud 15.00 4.50
33 Rafael Palmeiro 20.00 6.00
34 Mike Piazza 50.00 15.00
35 Kirby Puckett 25.00 7.50
36 Manny Ramirez 30.00 9.00
37 Cal Ripken 100.00 30.00
38 Tim Salmon 20.00 6.00
39 Ryne Sandberg 40.00 12.00
40 Gary Sheffield 25.00 7.50
41 Frank Thomas 30.00 9.00
42 Andy Van Slyke 6.00 1.80
43 Mo Vaughn 10.00 3.00
44 Larry Walker 20.00 6.00
45 Matt Williams 15.00 4.50

1995 Topps Pre-Production

Each 1994 Topps Baker's Dozen Factory set included a cello bag containing nine pre-production cards as well as one Spectralite version of one of those cards. The standard-size cards feature on their fronts color photos with ragged white borders and the player's name stamped in gold foil. The horizontal backs carry a color closeup photo, biography, major league batting or pitching record, and statistical highlights. The cards are easily distinguished from their regular issue counterparts not only by the "PP" number prefix but also by the words "Pre-Production Sample" printed across the 1994 stat line.

Nm-Mt Ex-Mt
COMPLETE SET (9) 8.00 2.40
*SPECTRALITE: 3X BASIC CARDS ...
PP1 Larry Walker 1.00 .30
PP2 Mike Piazza 2.50 .75
PP3 Greg Vaughn .50 .15
PP4 Sandy Alomar .50 .15
PP5 Travis Fryman .50 .15
PP6 Ken Griffey Jr. 2.50 .75
PP7 Mike Devereaux .25 .07
PP8 Roberto Hernandez .50 .15
PP9 Alex Fernandez .25 .07

1995 Topps

These 660 standard-size cards feature color action player photos with white borders on the fronts. This set was released in two series. The first series contained 396 cards while the second series had 264 cards. Cards were distributed in 11-card packs (SRP $1.29), jumbo packs and factory sets. One "Own The Game" instant winner card has been inserted in every 120 packs. Rookie cards in this set include Rey Ordonez. Due to the 1994 baseball strike, it was publicly announced that production for this set was the lowest print run since 1966.

Nm-Mt Ex-Mt
COMPLETE SET (660) 80.00 24.00
COMP.HOBBY SET (677) 120.00 36.00
COMP.RETAIL SET (677) 120.00 36.00
COMP.SERIES 1 (396) 40.00 12.00
COMP.SERIES 2 (264) 40.00 12.00
1 Frank Thomas .75 .23
2 Mickey Morandini .15 .04
3 Babe Ruth 100th B-Day 2.00 .60
4 Scott Cooper .15 .04
5 David Cone .30 .09
6 Jacob Shumate .15 .04
7 Trevor Hoffman .30 .09
8 Shane Mack .15 .04
9 Delino DeShields .15 .04
10 Matt Williams .30 .09
11 Sammy Sosa 1.25 .35
12 Gary DiSarcina .15 .04
13 Kenny Rogers .30 .09
14 Jose Vizcaino .15 .04
15 Lou Whitaker .30 .09
16 Ron Darling .15 .04
17 Dave Nilsson .15 .04
18 Chris Hammond .15 .04
19 Sid Bream .15 .04
20 Denny Martinez .30 .09
21 Orlando Merced .15 .04
22 John Wetteland .30 .09
23 Mike Devereaux .15 .04
24 Rene Arocha .15 .04
25 Jay Buhner .30 .09
26 Darren Holmes .15 .04
27 Hal Morris .15 .04
28 Brian Buchanan RC .15 .04
29 Keith Miller .15 .04
30 Paul Molitor .50 .15
31 Dave West .15 .04
32 Tony Tarasco .15 .04
33 Scott Sanders .15 .04
34 Eddie Zambrano .15 .04
35 Ricky Bones .15 .04
36 John Valentin .15 .04
37 Kevin Tapani .15 .04
38 Tim Wallach .15 .04
39 Darren Lewis .15 .04
40 Travis Fryman .30 .09
41 Mark Leiter .15 .04
42 Jose Bautista .15 .04
43 Pete Smith .15 .04
44 Bret Barberie .15 .04
45 Dennis Eckersley .30 .09
46 Ken Hill .15 .04
47 Chad Ogea .15 .04
48 Pete Harnisch .15 .04
49 James Baldwin .15 .04
50 Mike Mussina .75 .23
51 Al Martin .15 .04
52 Mark Thompson .15 .04
53 Matt Smith .15 .04
54 Joey Hamilton .15 .04
55 Edgar Martinez .50 .15
56 John Smiley .15 .04
57 Rey Sanchez .15 .04
58 Mike Timlin .15 .04
59 Ricky Bottalico .15 .04
60 Jim Abbott .50 .15
61 Mike Kelly .15 .04
62 Brian Jordan .30 .09
63 Ken Ryan .15 .04
64 Matt Mieske .15 .04
65 Rick Aguilera .15 .04
66 Ismael Valdes .15 .04
67 Royce Clayton .15 .04
68 Junior Felix .15 .04
69 Harold Reynolds .30 .09
70 Juan Gonzalez .75 .23
71 Kelly Stinnett .15 .04
72 Carlos Reyes .15 .04
73 Dave Weathers .15 .04
74 Mel Rojas .15 .04
75 Doug Drabek .15 .04
76 Charles Nagy .15 .04
77 Tim Raines .30 .09
78 Midre Cummings .15 .04
79 Gene Schall .15 .04
Scott Talanoa
Harold Williams
Ray Brown RC
80 Rafael Palmeiro .50 .15
81 Charlie Hayes .15 .04
82 Ray Lankford .15 .04
83 Tim Davis .15 .04
84 C.J. Nitkowski .15 .04
85 Andy Ashby .15 .04
86 Gerald Williams .15 .04
87 Terry Shumpert .15 .04
88 Heathcliff Slocumb .15 .04
89 Domingo Cedeno .15 .04
90 Mark Grace .50 .15
91 Brad Woodall RC .15 .04
92 Gar Finnvold .15 .04
93 Jaime Navarro .15 .04
94 Carlos Hernandez .15 .04
95 Mark Langston .15 .04
96 Chuck Carr .15 .04
97 Mike Gardiner .15 .04
98 Dave McCarty .15 .04
99 Cris Carpenter .15 .04
100 Barry Bonds 2.00 .60
101 David Segui .15 .04
102 Scott Brosius .30 .09
103 Mariano Duncan .15 .04
104 Kenny Lofton .30 .09
105 Ken Caminiti .30 .09
106 Darrin Jackson .15 .04
107 Jim Poole .15 .04
108 Wil Cordero .15 .04
109 Danny Miceli .15 .04
110 Walt Weiss .15 .04
111 Tom Pagnozzi .15 .04
112 Terrence Long .30 .09
113 Bret Boone .30 .09
114 Daryl Boston .15 .04
115 Wally Joyner .30 .09
116 Rob Butler .15 .04
117 Rafael Belliard .15 .04
118 Luis Lopez .15 .04
119 Tony Fossas .15 .04
120 Len Dykstra .30 .09
121 Mike Morgan .15 .04
122 Denny Hocking .15 .04
123 Kevin Gross .15 .04
124 Todd Benzinger .15 .04
125 John Doherty .15 .04
126 Eduardo Perez .15 .04
127 Dan Smith .15 .04
128 Joe Orsulak .15 .04
129 Brent Gates .15 .04
130 Jeff Conine .30 .09
131 Doug Henry .15 .04
132 Paul Sorrento .15 .04
133 Mike Hampton .30 .09
134 Tim Spehr .15 .04
135 Julio Franco .30 .09
136 Mike Dyer .15 .04
137 Chris Sabo .15 .04
138 Rheal Cormier .15 .04
139 Paul Konerko .30 .09
140 Dante Bichette .30 .09
141 Chuck McElroy .15 .04
142 Mike Stanley .15 .04
143 Bob Hamelin .15 .04
144 Tommy Greene .15 .04
145 John Smoltz .50 .15
146 Ed Sprague .15 .04
147 Ray McDavid .15 .04
148 Otis Nixon .15 .04
149 Turk Wendell .15 .04
150 Chris James .15 .04
151 Derek Parks .15 .04
152 Jose Offerman .15 .04

153 Tony Clark .15 .04
154 Chad Curtis .15 .04
155 Mark Portugal .15 .04
156 Bill Pulsipher .15 .04
157 Troy Neel .15 .04
158 Dave Winfield .30 .09
159 Bill Wegman .15 .04
160 Benito Santiago .30 .09
161 Jose Mesa .15 .04
162 Luis Gonzalez .30 .09
163 Alex Fernandez .15 .04
164 Freddie Benavides .15 .04
165 Ben McDonald .15 .04
166 Blas Minor .15 .04
167 Bret Wagner .15 .04
168 Mac Suzuki .15 .04
169 Roberto Mejia .15 .04
170 Wade Boggs .50 .15
171 Pokey Reese .15 .04
172 Hipolito Pichardo .15 .04
173 Kim Batiste .15 .04
174 Darren Hall .15 .04
175 Tom Glavine .50 .15
176 Phil Plantier .15 .04
177 Chris Howard .15 .04
178 Karl Rhodes .15 .04
179 LaTroy Hawkins .15 .04
180 Raul Mondesi .30 .09
181 Jeff Reed .15 .04
182 Milt Cuyler .15 .04
183 Jim Edmonds .30 .09
184 Hector Fajardo .15 .04
185 Jeff Kent .30 .09
186 Wilson Alvarez .15 .04
187 Geronimo Berroa .15 .04
188 Billy Spiers .15 .04
189 Derek Lilliquist .15 .04
190 Craig Biggio .50 .15
191 Roberto Hernandez .15 .04
192 Bob Natal .15 .04
193 Bobby Ayala .15 .04
194 Travis Miller RC .15 .04
195 Bob Tewksbury .15 .04
196 Rondell White .30 .09
197 Steve Cooke .15 .04
198 Jeff Branson .15 .04
199 Derek Jeter 2.00 .60
200 Tim Salmon .50 .15
201 Steve Frey .15 .04
202 Kent Mercker .15 .04
203 Randy Johnson .75 .23
204 Todd Worrell .15 .04
205 Mo Vaughn .30 .09
206 Howard Johnson .15 .04
207 John Wasdin .15 .04
208 Eddie Williams .15 .04
209 Tim Belcher .15 .04
210 Jeff Montgomery .15 .04
211 Kirt Manwaring .15 .04
212 Ben Grieve .30 .09
213 Pat Hentgen .15 .04
214 Shawon Dunston .15 .04
215 Mike Greenwell .15 .04
216 Alex Diaz .15 .04
217 Pat Mahomes .15 .04
218 Dave Hansen .15 .04
219 Kevin Rogers .15 .04
220 Cecil Fielder .30 .09
221 Andrew Lorraine .15 .04
222 Jack Armstrong .15 .04
223 Todd Hundley .15 .04
224 Mark Acre .15 .04
225 Darrell Whitmore .15 .04
226 Randy Milligan .15 .04
227 Wayne Kirby .15 .04
228 Darryl Kile .30 .09
229 Bob Zupcic .15 .04
230 Jay Bell .30 .09
231 Dustin Hermanson .15 .04
232 Harold Baines .30 .09
233 Alan Benes .15 .04
234 Felix Fermin .15 .04
235 Ellis Burks .30 .09
236 Jeff Brantley .15 .04
237 Brian Hunter .25 .07
Jose Malave
Karim Garcia RC
Shane Pullen
238 Matt Nokes .15 .04
239 Ben Rivera .15 .04
240 Joe Carter .30 .09
241 Jeff Granger .15 .04
242 Terry Pendleton .30 .09
243 Melvin Nieves .15 .04
244 Frankie Rodriguez .15 .04
245 Darryl Hamilton .15 .04
246 Brooks Kieschnick .15 .04
247 Todd Hollandsworth .15 .04
248 Joe Rosselli .15 .04
249 Bill Gullickson .15 .04
250 Chuck Knoblauch .30 .09
251 Kurt Miller .15 .04
252 Bobby Jones .15 .04
253 Lance Blankenship .15 .04
254 Matt Whiteside .15 .04
255 Darrin Fletcher .15 .04
256 Eric Plunk .15 .04
257 Shane Reynolds .15 .04
258 Norberto Martin .15 .04
259 Mike Thurman .15 .04
260 Andy Van Slyke .30 .09
261 Dwight Smith .15 .04
262 Allen Watson .15 .04
263 Dan Wilson .15 .04
264 Brent Mayne .15 .04
265 Bip Roberts .15 .04
266 Sterling Hitchcock .15 .04
267 Alex Gonzalez .15 .04
268 Greg Harris .15 .04
269 Ricky Jordan .15 .04
270 Johnny Ruffin .15 .04
271 Mike Stanton .15 .04
272 Rich Rowland .15 .04
273 Steve Trachsel .15 .04
274 Pedro Munoz .15 .04
275 Ramon Martinez .15 .04
276 Dave Henderson .15 .04
277 Chris Gomez .15 .04
278 Joe Grahe .15 .04
279 Rusty Greer .30 .09
280 John Franco .30 .09
281 Mike Bordick .15 .04
282 Jeff D'Amico .15 .04
283 Dave Magadan .15 .04
284 Tony Pena .15 .04
285 Greg Swindell .15 .04
286 Doug Million .15 .04
287 Gabe White .30 .09
288 Trey Beamon .15 .04
289 Arthur Rhodes .15 .04
290 Juan Guzman .15 .04
291 Jose Oquendo .15 .04
292 Willie Blair .15 .04
293 Eddie Taubensee .15 .04
294 Steve Howe .15 .04
295 Greg Maddux 1.25 .35
296 Mike Macfarlane .15 .04
297 Curt Schilling .50 .15
298 Phil Clark .15 .04
299 Woody Williams .15 .04
300 Jose Canseco .75 .23
301 Aaron Sele .15 .04
302 Carl Willis .15 .04
303 Steve Buechele .15 .04
304 Dave Burba .15 .04
305 Orel Hershiser .30 .09
306 Damion Easley .15 .04
307 Mike Henneman .15 .04
308 Josias Manzanillo .15 .04
309 Kevin Seitzer .15 .04
310 Ruben Sierra .15 .04
311 Bryan Harvey .15 .04
312 Jim Thome .75 .23
313 Ramon Castro RC .25 .07
314 Lance Johnson .15 .04
315 Marquis Grissom .15 .04
316 Terrell Wade .15 .04
Juan Acevedo
Matt Arrandale
Eddie Priest RC
317 Paul Wagner .15 .04
318 Jamie Moyer .30 .09
319 Todd Zeile .15 .04
320 Chris Bosio .15 .04
321 Steve Reed .15 .04
322 Erik Hanson .15 .04
323 Luis Polonia .15 .04
324 Ryan Klesko .30 .09
325 Kevin Appier .30 .09
326 Jim Eisenreich .15 .04
327 Randy Knorr .15 .04
328 Craig Shipley .15 .04
329 Tim Naehring .15 .04
330 Randy Myers .15 .04
331 Alex Cole .15 .04
332 Jim Gott .15 .04
333 Mike Jackson .15 .04
334 John Flaherty .15 .04
335 Chili Davis .30 .09
336 Benji Gil .15 .04
337 Jason Jacome .15 .04
338 Stan Javier .15 .04
339 Mike Fetters .15 .04
340 Rich Renteria .15 .04
341 Kevin Witt .15 .04
342 Scott Servais .15 .04
343 Craig Grebeck .15 .04
344 Kirk Rueter .30 .09
345 Don Slaught .15 .04
346 Armando Benitez .30 .09
347 Ozzie Smith 1.25 .35
348 Mike Blowers .15 .04
349 Armando Reynoso .15 .04
350 Barry Larkin .75 .23
351 Mike Williams .15 .04
352 Scott Kamieniecki .15 .04
353 Gary Gaetti .30 .09
354 Todd Stottlemyre .15 .04
355 Fred McGriff .50 .15
356 Tim Mauser .15 .04
357 Chris Gwynn .15 .04
358 Frank Castillo .15 .04
359 Jeff Reboulet .15 .04
360 Roger Clemens 1.50 .45
361 Mark Carreon .15 .04
362 Chad Kreuter .15 .04
363 Mark Farris .15 .04
364 Bob Welch .15 .04
365 Dean Palmer .30 .09
366 Jeromy Burnitz .30 .09
367 B.J. Surhoff .30 .09
368 Mike Butcher .15 .04
369 Brad Clontz .15 .04
Steve Phoenix
Scott Gentile
Bucky Buckles RC
370 Eddie Murray .75 .23
371 Orlando Miller .15 .04
372 Ron Karkovice .15 .04
373 Richie Lewis .15 .04
374 Lenny Webster .15 .04
375 Jeff Tackett .15 .04
376 Tom Urbani .15 .04
377 Tino Martinez .50 .15
378 Mark Dewey .15 .04
379 Charles O'Brien .15 .04
380 Terry Mulholland .15 .04
381 Thomas Howard .15 .04
382 Chris Haney .15 .04
383 Billy Hatcher .15 .04
384 Jeff Bagwell AS .50 .15
Frank Thomas AS
385 Bret Boone AS .30 .09
Carlos Baerga AS
386 Matt Williams AS .30 .09
Wade Boggs AS
387 Wil Cordero AS .75 .23
Cal Ripken AS
388 Barry Bonds AS 1.00 .30
Ken Griffey AS
389 Tony Gwynn AS .30 .09
Albert Belle AS
390 Dante Bichette AS .50 .15
Kirby Puckett AS
391 Mike Piazza AS .75 .23
Mike Stanley AS
392 Greg Maddux AS .75 .23
David Cone AS
393 Danny Jackson AS .15 .04
Jimmy Key AS
394 John Franco AS .15 .04
Lee Smith AS
395 Checklist 1-198 .15 .04
396 Checklist 199-396 .15 .04
397 Ken Griffey Jr. 1.25 .35
398 Rick Heiserman RC .15 .04
399 Don Mattingly 2.00 .60
400 Henry Rodriguez .15 .04
401 Lenny Harris .15 .04
402 Ryan Thompson .15 .04
403 Darren Oliver .15 .04
404 Omar Vizquel .30 .09
405 Jeff Bagwell .50 .15
406 Doug Webb RC .15 .04
407 Todd Van Poppel .15 .04
408 Leo Gomez .15 .04
409 Mark Whiten .15 .04
410 Pedro A.Martinez .15 .04
411 Reggie Sanders .30 .09
412 Kevin Foster .15 .04
413 Danny Tartabull .15 .04
414 Jeff Blauser .15 .04
415 Mike Magnante .15 .04
416 Tom Candiotti .15 .04
417 Rod Beck .15 .04
418 Jody Reed .15 .04
419 Vince Coleman .15 .04
420 Danny Jackson .15 .04
421 Ryan Nye RC .15 .04
422 Larry Walker .50 .15
423 Russ Johnson DP .15 .04
424 Pat Borders .15 .04
425 Lee Smith .30 .09
426 Paul O'Neill .50 .15
427 Devon White .30 .09
428 Jim Bullinger .15 .04
429 Greg Hansell .15 .04
Brian Sackinsky
Carey Paige
Rob Welch RC
430 Steve Avery .15 .04
431 Tony Gwynn 1.00 .30
432 Pat Meares .15 .04
433 Bill Swift .15 .04
434 David Wells .30 .09
435 John Briscoe .15 .04
436 Roger Pavlik .15 .04
437 Jayson Peterson RC .15 .04
438 Roberto Alomar .75 .23
439 Billy Brewer .15 .04
440 Gary Sheffield .30 .09
441 Lou Frazier .15 .04
442 Terry Steinbach .15 .04
443 Jay Payton RC .50 .15
444 Jason Bere .15 .04
445 Denny Neagle .30 .09
446 Andres Galarraga .30 .09
447 Hector Carrasco .15 .04
448 Bill Risley .15 .04
449 Andy Benes .15 .04
450 Jim Leyritz .15 .04
451 Jose Oliva .15 .04
452 Greg Vaughn .30 .09
453 Rich Monteleone .15 .04
454 Tony Eusebio .15 .04
455 Chuck Finley .30 .09
456 Kevin Brown .30 .09
457 Joe Boever .15 .04
458 Bobby Munoz .15 .04
459 Bret Saberhagen .30 .09
460 Kurt Abbott .15 .04
461 Bobby Witt .15 .04
462 Cliff Floyd .30 .09
463 Mark Clark .15 .04
464 Andujar Cedeno .15 .04
465 Marvin Freeman .15 .04
466 Mike Piazza 1.25 .35
467 Willie Greene .15 .04
468 Pat Kelly .15 .04
469 Carlos Delgado .30 .09
470 Willie Banks .15 .04
471 Matt Walbeck .15 .04
472 Mark McGwire 2.00 .60
473 M.Christensen RC .15 .04
474 Alan Trammell .50 .15
475 Tom Gordon .15 .04
476 Greg Colbrunn .15 .04
477 Darren Daulton .30 .09
478 Albie Lopez .30 .09
479 Robin Ventura .30 .09
480 Eddie Perez RC .25 .07
Jason Kendall
Einar Diaz
Bret Hemphill
481 Bryan Eversgerd .15 .04
482 Dave Fleming .15 .04
483 Scott Livingstone .15 .04
484 Pete Schourek .15 .04
485 Bernie Williams .50 .15
486 Mark Lemke .15 .04
487 Eric Karros .30 .09
488 Scott Ruffcorn .15 .04
489 Billy Ashley .15 .04
490 Rico Brogna .15 .04
491 John Burkett .15 .04
492 Cade Gaspar RC .15 .04
493 Jorge Fabregas .15 .04
494 Greg Gagne .15 .04
495 Doug Jones .15 .04
496 Troy O'Leary .15 .04
497 Pat Rapp .15 .04
498 Butch Henry .15 .04
499 John Olerud .30 .09
500 John Hudek .15 .04
501 Jeff King .15 .04
502 Bobby Bonilla .30 .09
503 Albert Belle .30 .09
504 Rick Wilkins .15 .04
505 John Jaha .15 .04
506 Nigel Wilson .15 .04
507 Sid Fernandez .15 .04
508 Deion Sanders .50 .15
509 Gil Heredia .15 .04
510 Scott Elarton RC .25 .07
511 Melido Perez .15 .04
512 Greg McMichael .15 .04
513 Rusty Meacham .15 .04
514 Shawn Green .30 .09
515 Carlos Garcia .15 .04
516 Dave Stevens .15 .04
517 Eric Young .15 .04
518 Omar Daal .15 .04
519 Kirk Gibson .30 .09
520 Spike Owen .15 .04
521 Jacob Cruz RC .30 .09
522 Sandy Alomar Jr. .15 .04
523 Steve Bedrosian .15 .04
524 Ricky Gutierrez .15 .04
525 Dave Veres .15 .04
526 Gregg Jefferies .15 .04
527 Jose Valentin .15 .04
528 Robb Nen .30 .09
529 Jose Rijo .15 .04
530 Sean Berry .15 .04
531 Mike Gallego .15 .04
532 Roberto Kelly .15 .04
533 Kevin Stocker .15 .04
534 Kirby Puckett .75 .23
535 Chipper Jones .75 .23
536 Russ Davis .15 .04
537 Jon Lieber .15 .04
538 Trey Moore RC .15 .04
539 Joe Girardi .15 .04
540 Quilvio Veras .25 .07
Arquimedez Pozo
Miguel Cairo RC
Jason Camilli
541 Tony Phillips .15 .04
542 Brian Anderson .15 .04
543 Ivan Rodriguez .75 .23
544 Jeff Cirillo .15 .04
545 Joey Cora .15 .04
546 Chris Hoiles .15 .04
547 Bernard Gilkey .15 .04
548 Mike Lansing .15 .04
549 Jimmy Key .30 .09
550 Mark Wohlers .15 .04
551 Chris Clemons RC .15 .04
552 Vinny Castilla .30 .09
553 Mark Guthrie .15 .04
554 Mike Lieberthal .30 .09
555 Tommy Davis RC .15 .04
556 Robby Thompson .15 .04
557 Danny Bautista .15 .04
558 Will Clark .75 .23
559 Rickey Henderson .75 .23
560 Todd Jones .15 .04
561 Jack McDowell .15 .04
562 Carlos Rodriguez .15 .04
563 Mark Eichhorn .15 .04
564 Jeff Nelson .15 .04
565 Eric Anthony .15 .04
566 Randy Velarde .15 .04
567 Javier Lopez .30 .09
568 Kevin Mitchell .15 .04
569 Steve Karsay .15 .04
570 Brian Meadows RC .15 .04
571 Rey Ordonez RC .50 .15
Mike Metcalfe
Kevin Orie
Ray Holbert
572 John Kruk .30 .09
573 Scott Leius .15 .04
574 John Patterson .15 .04
575 Kevin Brown .30 .09
576 Mike Moore .15 .04
577 Manny Ramirez .30 .09
578 Jose Lind .15 .04
579 Derrick May .15 .04
580 Cal Eldred .15 .04
581 David Bell 2.00 .60
Joel Chelmis
Lino Diaz
Aaron Boone RC
582 J.T. Snow .30 .09
583 Luis Sojo .15 .04
584 Moises Alou .30 .09
585 Dave Clark .15 .04
586 Dave Hollins .15 .04
587 Nomar Garciaparra 2.50 .75
588 Cal Ripken 2.50 .75
589 Pedro Astacio .15 .04
590 J.R. Phillips .15 .04
591 Jeff Frye .15 .04
592 Bo Jackson .75 .23
593 Steve Ontiveros .15 .04
594 David Nied .15 .04
595 Brad Ausmus .15 .04
596 Carlos Baerga .15 .04
597 James Mouton .15 .04
598 Ozzie Guillen .15 .04
599 Ozzie Timmons .25 .07
Curtis Goodwin
Johnny Damon
Jeff Abbott RC
600 Yorkis Perez .15 .04
601 Rich Rodriguez .15 .04
602 Mark McLemore .15 .04
603 Jeff Fassero .15 .04
604 John Roper .15 .04
605 Mark Johnson RC .25 .07
606 Wes Chamberlain .15 .04
607 Felix Jose .15 .04
608 Tony Longmire .15 .04
609 Duane Ward .15 .04
610 Brett Butler .30 .09
611 W.VanLandingham .15 .04
612 Mickey Tettleton .15 .04
613 Brady Anderson .30 .09
614 Reggie Jefferson .15 .04
615 Mike Kingery .15 .04
616 Derek Bell .15 .04
617 Scott Erickson .15 .04
618 Bob Wickman .15 .04
619 Phil Leftwich .15 .04
620 David Justice .30 .09
621 Paul Wilson .15 .04
622 Pedro Martinez .75 .23
623 Terry Mathews .15 .04
624 Brian McRae .15 .04
625 Bruce Ruffin .15 .04
626 Steve Finley .30 .09
627 Ron Gant .30 .09
628 Rafael Bournigal .15 .04
629 Darryl Strawberry .50 .15
630 Luis Alicea .15 .04
631 Mark Smith .15 .04
Scott Klingenbeck
632 Cory Bailey .15 .04
Scott Hatteberg
633 Todd Greene .30 .09
Troy Percival
634 Rod Bolton .15 .04
Olmedo Saenz
635 Steve Kline .15 .04
Herb Perry
636 Sean Bergman .15 .04
Shannon Penn
637 Joe Randa .15 .04
Joe Vitiello
638 Jose Mercedes .15 .04
Duane Singleton
639 Marc Barcelo .15 .04
Marty Cordova
640 Andy Pettitte .30 .09
Ruben Rivera
641 Willie Adams .15 .04
Scott Spiezio
642 Eddy Diaz RC .15 .04
Desi Relaford
643 Terrell Lowery .15 .04
Jon Shave
644 Angel Martinez .15 .04
Paul Spoljaric
645 Tony Graffanino .15 .04
Damon Hollins
646 Darron Cox .15 .04
Doug Glanville
647 Tim Belk .15 .04
Pat Watkins
648 Rod Pedraza .15 .04
Phil Schneider
649 Vic Darensbourg .15 .04
Marc Valdes
650 Rick Huisman .15 .04
Roberto Petagine
651 Roger Cedeno .25 .07
Ron Coomer RC
652 Shane Andrews .25 .07
Carlos Perez RC
653 Jason Isringhausen .30 .09
Chris Roberts
654 Wayne Gomes .15 .04
Kevin Jordan
655 Esteban Loiaza .30 .09
Steve Pegues
656 Terry Bradshaw .15 .04
John Frascatore
657 Andres Berumen .15 .04
Bryce Florie
658 Dan Carlson .15 .04
Keith Williams
659 Checklist .15 .04
660 Checklist .15 .04

1995 Topps Cyberstats

The 396-card Cyberstats insert set was issued one per pack and three per jumbo pack. Each 1995 Topps series had 198 Cyberstat cards. The idea was to present prorated statistics for the 1994 strike shortened season. The photos on front are the same as the basic issue. The difference is that the photo is given a glossy or metallic finish. The backs contain yearly and career statistics, including the prorated 1994 numbers.

	Nm-Mt	Ex-Mt
COMPLETE SET (396)	60.00	18.00
COMP.SERIES 1 (198)	25.00	7.50
COMP.SERIES 2 (198)	40.00	12.00

*STARS: 1X TO 2.5X BASIC CARDS ...

1995 Topps Cyber Season in Review

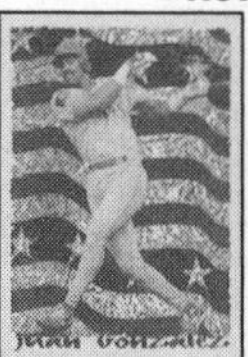
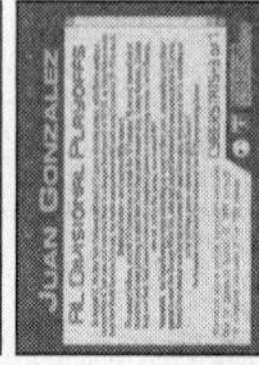

This seven-card set was distributed exclusively in 1995 Topps hobby factory sets. It continues the Cyberstats insert theme used in the regular issue product, which presented "what if" statistics to fill in the strike-shortened 1994 season. The Season in Review cards commemorate projected accomplishments including Barry Bonds' 61 home runs and Kenny Lofton's World Series MVP.

	Nm-Mt	Ex-Mt
COMPLETE SET (7)	5.00	1.50
1 Barry Bonds	2.50	.75
2 Jose Canseco	1.25	.35
3 Juan Gonzalez	1.25	.35
4 Fred McGriff	.75	.23
5 Carlos Baerga	.50	.15
6 Ryan Klesko	.75	.23
7 Kenny Lofton	.75	.23

1995 Topps Finest Inserts

This 15-card standard-size set was inserted one every 36 Topps series two packs. This set featured the top 15 players in total bases from the 1994 season. The fronts feature a player photo, with his team identification and name on the bottom of the card. The horizontal backs feature another player photo along with a breakdown of how many of each type of hit each player got on the way to their season total. The set is sequenced in order of how they finished in the majors for the 1994 season.

	Nm-Mt	Ex-Mt
COMPLETE SET (15)	60.00	18.00
1 Jeff Bagwell	3.00	.90
2 Albert Belle	2.00	.60
3 Ken Griffey Jr.	8.00	2.40
4 Frank Thomas	5.00	1.50
5 Matt Williams	2.00	.60
6 Dante Bichette	2.00	.60
7 Barry Bonds	12.00	3.60
8 Moises Alou	2.00	.60
9 Andres Galarraga	2.00	.60
10 Kenny Lofton	2.00	.60
11 Rafael Palmeiro	3.00	.90
12 Tony Gwynn	6.00	1.80
13 Kirby Puckett	5.00	1.50
14 Jose Canseco	5.00	1.50
15 Jeff Conine	2.00	.60

1995 Topps League Leaders

Randomly inserted in jumbo packs at a rate of one in three and retail packs at a rate of one in six, this 50-card standard-size set showcases those that were among league leaders in various categories. Card fronts feature a player photo with a black background. The player's name appears in gold foil at the bottom and the category with which he led the league or was among the leaders is in yellow letters up the right side. The backs contain various graphs and where the player placed among the leaders.

	Nm-Mt	Ex-Mt
COMPLETE SET (50)	50.00	15.00
COMPLETE SERIES 1 (25)	20.00	6.00
COMPLETE SERIES 2 (25)	30.00	9.00
LL1 Albert Belle	.60	.18
LL2 Kevin Mitchell	.30	.09
LL3 Wade Boggs	1.00	.30
LL4 Tony Gwynn	2.00	.60
LL5 Moises Alou	.60	.18
LL6 Andres Galarraga	.60	.18
LL7 Matt Williams	.60	.18
LL8 Barry Bonds	4.00	1.20
LL9 Frank Thomas	1.50	.45
LL10 Jose Canseco	1.50	.45
LL11 Jeff Bagwell	1.00	.30
LL12 Kirby Puckett	1.50	.45
LL13 Julio Franco	.60	.18
LL14 Albert Belle	.60	.18
LL15 Fred McGriff	1.00	.30
LL16 Kenny Lofton	.60	.18
LL17 Otis Nixon	.30	.09
LL18 Brady Anderson	.60	.18
LL19 Deion Sanders	1.00	.30
LL20 Chuck Carr	.30	.09
LL21 Pat Hentgen	.30	.09
LL22 Andy Benes	.30	.09
LL23 Roger Clemens	3.00	.90
LL24 Greg Maddux	2.50	.75
LL25 Pedro Martinez	.30	.09
LL26 Paul O'Neill	1.00	.30
LL27 Jeff Bagwell	1.00	.30
LL28 Frank Thomas	1.50	.45
LL29 Hal Morris	.30	.09
LL30 Kenny Lofton	.60	.18
LL31 Ken Griffey Jr.	2.50	.75
LL32 Jeff Bagwell	1.00	.30
LL33 Albert Belle	.60	.18
LL34 Fred McGriff	1.00	.30
LL35 Cecil Fielder	.60	.18
LL36 Matt Williams	.60	.18
LL37 Joe Carter	.60	.18
LL38 Dante Bichette	.60	.18
LL39 Frank Thomas	1.50	.45
LL40 Mike Piazza	2.50	.75
LL41 Craig Biggio	1.00	.30
LL42 Vince Coleman	.30	.09
LL43 Marquis Grissom	.30	.09
LL44 Chuck Knoblauch	.60	.18
LL45 Darren Lewis	.30	.09
LL46 Randy Johnson	1.50	.45
LL47 Jose Rijo	.30	.09
LL48 Chuck Finley	.60	.18
LL49 Bret Saberhagen	.60	.18
LL50 Kevin Appier	.60	.18

1995 Topps Opening Day

This 10-card standard-size set was inserted into all retail factory sets. The borderless fronts feature the player's photo set against a prismatic star background and the player's name on the bottom. In the lower right, the player's opening day highlight is mentioned and there is an "Opening Day" verbiage and logo in the upper right. The horizontal back has a player photo, description of the player's opening day as well as a line score for the player.

	Nm-Mt	Ex-Mt
COMPLETE SET (10)	30.00	9.00
1 Kevin Appier	.50	.15
2 Dante Bichette	1.00	.30
3 Ken Griffey Jr.	20.00	6.00
4 Todd Hundley	1.00	.30
5 John Jaha	.50	.15
6 Fred McGriff	1.50	.45
7 Raul Mondesi	2.00	.60
8 Manny Ramirez	5.00	1.50
9 Danny Tartabull	.50	.15
10 Devon White	1.00	.30

1995 Topps Traded

This set contains 165 standard-size cards and was sold in 11-card packs for $1.29. The set features rookies, draft picks and players who had been traded. The fronts contain a photo with a white border. The backs have a player picture in a scoreboard and his statistics and information. Subsets featured are: At the Break (1T-10T) and All-Stars (156T-164T). Rookie Cards in this set include Michael Barrett, Carlos Beltran, Ben Davis, Hideo Nomo and Richie Sexson.

	Nm-Mt	Ex-Mt
COMPLETE SET (165)	40.00	12.00
1T Frank Thomas ATB	.60	.18
2T Ken Griffey Jr. ATB	1.00	.30
3T Barry Bonds ATB	1.25	.35
4T Albert Belle ATB	.40	.12
5T Cal Ripken ATB	1.50	.45
6T Mike Piazza ATB	1.00	.30
7T Tony Gwynn ATB	.60	.18
8T Jeff Bagwell ATB	.40	.12
9T Mo Vaughn ATB	.20	.06
10T Matt Williams ATB	.20	.06
11T Ray Durham	.40	.12
12T Juan LeBron	2.00	.60
Card pictures Carlos Beltran instead of Juan LeBron RC		
13T Shawn Green	.40	.12
14T Kevin Gross	.20	.06
15T Jon Nunnally	.20	.06
16T Brian Maxcy RC	.25	.07
17T Mark Kiefer	.20	.06
18T Carlos Beltran UER	15.00	4.50
Card pictures Juan LeBron instead of Carlos Beltran RC.		
19T Mike Mimbs RC	.25	.07
20T Larry Walker	.60	.18
21T Chad Curtis	.20	.06
22T Jeff Barry	.20	.06
23T Joe Oliver	.20	.06
24T Tomas Perez RC	.25	.07
25T Michael Barrett RC	1.50	.45
26T Brian McRae	.20	.06
27T Derek Bell	.20	.06
28T Ray Durham	.40	.12
29T Todd Williams	.20	.06
30T Ryan Jaroncyk RC	.25	.07
31T Todd Steverson	.20	.06
32T Mike Devereaux	.20	.06
33T Rheal Cormier	.20	.06
34T Benny Santiago	.40	.12
35T Bobby Higginson RC	1.00	.30
36T Jack McDowell	.20	.06
37T Mike Macfarlane	.20	.06
38T Tony McKnight RC	.25	.07
39T Brian Hunter	.20	.06
40T Hideo Nomo RC	3.00	.90
41T Brett Butler	.40	.12
42T Donovan Osborne	.20	.06
43T Scott Karl	.20	.06
44T Tony Phillips	.20	.06
45T Marty Cordova	.20	.06
46T Dave Mlicki	.20	.06
47T Bronson Arroyo RC	.25	.07
48T John Burkett	.20	.06
49T J.D. Smart RC	.25	.07
50T Mickey Tettleton	.20	.06
51T Todd Stottlemyre	.20	.06
52T Mike Perez	.20	.06
53T Terry Mulholland	.20	.06
54T Edgardo Alfonzo	.40	.12
55T Zane Smith	.20	.06
56T Jacob Brumfield	.20	.06
57T Andujar Cedeno	.20	.06
58T Jose Parra	.20	.06
59T Manny Alexander	.20	.06
60T Tony Tarasco	.20	.06
61T Orel Hershiser	.40	.12
62T Tim Scott	.20	.06
63T Felix Rodriguez RC	.50	.15
64T Ken Hill	.20	.06
65T Marquis Grissom	.20	.06
66T Lee Smith	.40	.12
67T Jason Bates	.20	.06
68T Felipe Lira	.20	.06
69T Alex Hernandez RC	.25	.07
70T Tony Fernandez	.20	.06
71T Scott Radinsky	.20	.06
72T Jose Canseco	1.00	.30
73T Mark Grudzielanek RC	1.00	.30
74T Ben Davis RC	.50	.15
75T Jim Abbott	.60	.18
76T Roger Bailey	.20	.06
77T Gregg Jefferies	.20	.06
78T Erik Hanson	.20	.06
79T Brad Radke RC	2.00	.60
80T Jaime Navarro	.20	.06
81T John Wetteland	.40	.12
82T Chad Fonville RC	.25	.07
83T John Mabry	.20	.06
84T Glenallen Hill	.20	.06
85T Ken Caminiti	.40	.12
86T Tom Goodwin	.20	.06
87T Darren Bragg	.20	.06
88T Pat Ahearne	.25	.07
Gary Rath		
Larry Wimberly		
Robbie Bell RC		
89T Jeff Russell	.20	.06
90T Dave Gallagher	.20	.06
91T Steve Finley	.40	.12
92T Vaughn Eshelman	.20	.06
93T Kevin Jarvis	.20	.06
94T Mark Gubicza	.20	.06
95T Tim Wakefield	.40	.12
96T Bob Tewksbury	.20	.06
97T Sid Roberson RC	.25	.07
98T Tom Henke	.20	.06
99T Michael Tucker	.20	.06
100T Jason Bates	.20	.06
101T Otis Nixon	.20	.06
102T Mark Whiten	.20	.06
103T Dilson Torres RC	.25	.07
104T Melvin Bunch RC	.25	.07
105T Terry Pendleton	.40	.12
106T Corey Jenkins RC	.25	.07
107T Glenn Dishman RC	.25	.07
Rob Grable		
108T Reggie Taylor RC	.50	.15
109T Curtis Goodwin	.20	.06
110T David Cone	.40	.12
111T Antonio Osuna	.20	.06
112T Paul Shuey	.20	.06
113T Doug Jones	.20	.06
114T Mark McLemore	.20	.06
115T Kevin Ritz	.20	.06
116T John Kruk	.40	.12
117T Trevor Wilson	.20	.06
118T Jerald Clark	.20	.06
119T Julian Tavarez	.20	.06
120T Tim Pugh	.20	.06
121T Todd Zeile	.20	.06
122T Mark Sweeney UER	5.00	1.50
George Arias		
Richie Sexson RC		
Brian Schneider		
123T Bobby Witt	.20	.06
124T Hideo Nomo	1.00	.30
125T Joey Cora	.20	.06
126T Jim Scharrer RC	.25	.07
127T Paul Quantrill	.20	.06
128T Chipper Jones ROY	.60	.18
129T Kenny James RC	.25	.07
130T Lyle Mouton	.60	.18
Mariano Rivera		
131T Tyler Green	.20	.06
132T Brad Clontz	.20	.06
133T Jon Nunnally	.20	.06
134T Dave Magadan	.20	.06
135T Al Leiter	.40	.12
136T Bret Barberie	.20	.06
137T Bill Swift	.20	.06
138T Scott Cooper	.20	.06
139T Roberto Kelly	.20	.06
140T Charlie Hayes	.20	.06
141T Pete Harnisch	.20	.06
142T Rich Amaral	.20	.06
143T Rudy Seanez	.20	.06
144T Pat Listach	.20	.06
145T Quilvio Veras	.20	.06
146T Jose Olmeda RC	.25	.07
147T Roberto Petagine	.20	.06
148T Kevin Brown	.40	.12
149T Phil Plantier	.20	.06
150T Carlos Perez	.40	.12
151T Pat Borders	.20	.06
152T Tyler Green	.20	.06
153T Stan Belinda	.20	.06
154T Dave Stewart	.40	.12
155T Andre Dawson	.40	.12
156T Frank Thomas AS	.60	.18
Fred McGriff UER		
(McGriff's team shown aş Blue Jays)		
157T Carlos Baerga AS	.40	.12
Craig Biggio		
158T Wade Boggs AS	.40	.12
Matt Williams		
159T Cal Ripken AS	1.00	.30
Ozzie Smith		
160T Ken Griffey Jr. AS	1.00	.30
Tony Gwynn		
161T Albert Belle AS	1.25	.35
Barry Bonds		
162T Kirby Puckett	.60	.18
Len Dykstra		
163T Ivan Rodriguez AS	1.00	.30
Mike Piazza		
164T Randy Johnson AS	1.25	.35
Hideo Nomo		
165T Checklist	.20	.06

1995 Topps Traded Proofs

Little is known about these cards, the one sample we have has a photo of Shawn Green used on his 1995 Topps Traded card but the back is the one used in the regular 1995 Topps set. There may be more cards so all additional information is appreciated.

	Nm-Mt	Ex-Mt
NNO Shawn Green	10.00	3.00

1995 Topps Traded Power Boosters

This 10-card standard-size set was inserted in packs at a rate of one in 36. The set is comprised of parallel cards for the first 10 cards of the regular Topps Traded set which was the "At the Break" subset. The cards are done on extra-thick stock. The fronts have an action photo on a "Power Boosted" background, which is similar to diffraction technology, with the words "at the break" on the left side. The backs have a head shot and player information including his mid-season statistics for 1995 and previous years.

	Nm-Mt	Ex-Mt
COMPLETE SET (10)	80.00	24.00
1 Frank Thomas	10.00	3.00
2 Ken Griffey Jr.	15.00	4.50
3 Barry Bonds	20.00	6.00
4 Albert Belle	6.00	1.80
5 Cal Ripken	25.00	7.50
6 Mike Piazza	15.00	4.50
7 Tony Gwynn	10.00	3.00
8 Jeff Bagwell	6.00	1.80
9 Mo Vaughn	3.00	.90
10 Matt Williams	3.00	.90

1995 Topps Legends of the '60s Medallions

These 12 bronze medallions feature some of the best players of the 60's, duplicating the regular issue Topps cards from various years. This was a special offering for Topps Stadium Club members. One medallion was issued each month; the issue price was $39.95 per card.

	Nm-Mt	Ex-Mt
COMPLETE SET (12)	500.00	150.00
1 Willie Mays	50.00	15.00
2 Hank Aaron	50.00	15.00
3 Bob Gibson	40.00	12.00
4 Don Drysdale	40.00	12.00
5 Frank Robinson	40.00	12.00
6 Carl Yastrzemski	40.00	12.00
7 Willie McCovey	40.00	12.00
8 Roberto Clemente	50.00	15.00
9 Juan Marichal	40.00	12.00
10 Brooks Robinson	40.00	12.00
11 Harmon Killebrew	40.00	12.00
12 Billy Williams	40.00	12.00

1996 Topps

This set consists of 440 standard-size cards. These cards were issued in 12-card foil packs with a suggested retail price of $1.29. The fronts feature full-color photos surrounded by a white background. Information on the backs includes a player photo, season and career stats and text. First series subsets include Star Power (1-6, 8-12), Draft Picks (13-26), AAA Stars (101-104), and Future Stars (210-219). A special Mickey Mantle card was issued as card number 7 (his uniform number) and became the last card to be issued as card number 7 in the Topps brand set. Rookie Cards in this set include Sean Casey, Geoff Jenkins and Daryle Ward.

	Nm-Mt	Ex-Mt
COMPLETE SET (440)	40.00	12.00
COMP.HOBBY SET (449)	40.00	12.00
COMP.CEREAL SET (444)	80.00	24.00
COMP.SERIES 1 (220)	20.00	6.00
COMP.SERIES 2 (220)	20.00	6.00
COMMON CARD (1-440)	.20	.06
COMMON RC	.25	.07
1 Tony Gwynn STP	.30	.09
2 Mike Piazza STP	.50	.15
3 Greg Maddux STP	.50	.15
4 Jeff Bagwell STP	.20	.06
5 Larry Walker STP	.20	.06
6 Barry Larkin STP	.30	.09
7 Mickey Mantle	4.00	1.20
8 Tom Glavine STP UER	.20	.06
Won 21 games in June 95		
9 Craig Biggio STP	.20	.06
10 Barry Bonds STP	.50	.15
11 H.Slocumb STP	.20	.06
12 Matt Williams STP	.20	.06
13 Todd Helton	1.00	.30
14 Mark Redman	.40	.12
15 Michael Barrett	.40	.12
16 Ben Davis	.25	.07
17 Juan LeBron	.25	.07
18 Tony McKnight	.25	.07
19 Ryan Jaroncyk	.25	.07
20 Corey Jenkins	.25	.07
21 Jim Scharrer	.25	.07
22 Mark Bellhorn RC	.40	.12
23 Jarrod Washburn RC	1.00	.30
24 Geoff Jenkins RC	1.25	.35
25 Sean Casey RC	2.00	.60
26 Brett Tomko RC	.40	.12
27 Tony Fernandez	.20	.06
28 Rich Becker	.20	.06
29 Andujar Cedeno	.20	.06
30 Paul Molitor	.30	.09
31 Brent Gates	.20	.06
32 Glenallen Hill	.20	.06
33 Mike Macfarlane	.20	.06
34 Manny Alexander	.20	.06
35 Todd Zeile	.20	.06
36 Joe Girardi	.20	.06
37 Tony Tarasco	.20	.06
38 Tim Belcher	.20	.06
39 Tom Goodwin	.20	.06
40 Orel Hershiser	.20	.06
41 Tripp Cromer	.20	.06
42 Sean Bergman	.20	.06
43 Troy Percival	.20	.06
44 Kevin Stocker	.20	.06
45 Albert Belle	.20	.06
46 Tony Eusebio	.20	.06
47 Sid Roberson	.20	.06
48 Todd Hollandsworth	.20	.06
49 Mark Wohlers	.20	.06
50 Kirby Puckett	.50	.15
51 Darren Holmes	.20	.06
52 Ron Karkovice	.20	.06
53 Al Martin	.20	.06
54 Pat Rapp	.20	.06
55 Mark Grace	.30	.09
56 Greg Gagne	.20	.06
57 Stan Javier	.20	.06
58 Scott Sanders	.20	.06
59 J.T. Snow	.20	.06
60 David Justice	.20	.06
61 Royce Clayton	.20	.06
62 Kevin Foster	.20	.06
63 Tim Naehring	.20	.06
64 Orlando Miller	.20	.06
65 Mike Mussina	.50	.15
66 Jim Eisenreich	.20	.06
67 Felix Fermin	.20	.06
68 Bernie Williams	.30	.09
69 Robb Nen	.20	.06
70 Ron Gant	.20	.06
71 Felipe Lira	.20	.06
72 Jacob Brumfield	.20	.06
73 John Mabry	.20	.06
74 Mark Carreon	.20	.06
75 Carlos Baerga	.20	.06
76 Jim Dougherty	.20	.06
77 Ryan Thompson	.20	.06
78 Scott Leius	.20	.06
79 Roger Pavlik	.20	.06
80 Gary Sheffield	.20	.06
81 Julian Tavarez	.20	.06
82 Andy Ashby	.20	.06
83 Mark Lemke	.20	.06
84 Omar Vizquel	.20	.06
85 Darren Daulton	.20	.06
86 Mike Lansing	.20	.06
87 Rusty Greer	.20	.06
88 Dave Stevens	.20	.06
89 Jose Offerman	.20	.06
90 Tom Henke	.20	.06
91 Troy O'Leary	.20	.06
92 Michael Tucker	.20	.06
93 Marvin Freeman	.20	.06
94 Alex Diaz	.20	.06
95 John Wetteland	.20	.06
96 Cal Ripken 2131	2.00	.60
97 Mike Mimbs	.20	.06
98 Bobby Higginson	.20	.06
99 Edgardo Alfonzo	.20	.06
100 Frank Thomas	.50	.15
101 Steve Gibralter	.20	.06
Bob Abreu		
102 Brian Givens	.25	.07
T.J. Mathews		
103 Chris Pritchett	.25	.07
Trenidad Hubbard		
104 Eric Owens	.25	.07
Butch Huskey		
105 Doug Drabek	.20	.06
106 Tomas Perez	.20	.06
107 Mark Leiter	.20	.06
108 Joe Oliver	.20	.06
109 Tony Castillo	.20	.06
110 Checklist (1-110)	.20	.06
111 Kevin Seitzer	.20	.06
112 Pete Schourek	.20	.06
113 Sean Berry	.20	.06
114 Todd Stottlemyre	.20	.06
115 Joe Carter	.20	.06
116 Jeff King	.20	.06
117 Dan Wilson	.20	.06
118 Kurt Abbott	.20	.06
119 Lyle Mouton	.20	.06
120 Jose Rijo	.20	.06
121 Curtis Goodwin	.20	.06
122 Jose Valentin	.20	.06
123 Ellis Burks	.20	.06
124 David Cone	.20	.06
125 Eddie Murray	.50	.15
126 Brian Jordan	.20	.06
127 Darrin Fletcher	.20	.06
128 Curt Schilling	.30	.09
129 Ozzie Guillen	.20	.06
130 Kenny Rogers	.20	.06
131 Tom Pagnozzi	.20	.06
132 Garret Anderson	.20	.06
133 Bobby Jones	.20	.06
134 Chris Gomez	.20	.06
135 Mike Stanley	.20	.06
136 Hideo Nomo	.50	.15
137 Jon Nunnally	.20	.06
138 Tim Wakefield	.20	.06
139 Steve Finley	.20	.06
140 Ivan Rodriguez	.50	.15
141 Quilvio Veras	.20	.06
142 Mike Fetters	.20	.06
143 Mike Greenwell	.20	.06
144 Bill Pulsipher	.20	.06
145 Mark McGwire	1.25	.35
146 Frank Castillo	.20	.06
147 Greg Vaughn	.20	.06
148 Pat Hentgen	.20	.06
149 Walt Weiss	.20	.06
150 Randy Johnson	.50	.15
151 David Segui	.20	.06
152 Benji Gil	.20	.06
153 Tom Candiotti	.20	.06
154 Geronimo Berroa	.20	.06
155 John Franco	.20	.06
156 Jay Bell	.20	.06
157 Mark Gubicza	.20	.06
158 Hal Morris	.20	.06
159 Wilson Alvarez	.20	.06
160 Derek Bell	.20	.06
161 Ricky Bottalico	.20	.06
162 Bret Boone	.20	.06
163 Brad Radke	.20	.06
164 John Valentin	.20	.06
165 Steve Avery	.20	.06
166 Mark McLemore	.20	.06
167 Danny Jackson	.20	.06
168 Tino Martinez	.30	.09
169 Shane Reynolds	.20	.06
170 Terry Pendleton	.20	.06
171 Jim Edmonds	.20	.06
172 Esteban Loaiza	.20	.06
173 Ray Durham	.20	.06
174 Carlos Perez	.20	.06
175 Raul Mondesi	.20	.06
176 Steve Ontiveros	.20	.06
177 Chipper Jones	.50	.15
178 Otis Nixon	.20	.06
179 John Burkett	.20	.06
180 Gregg Jefferies	.20	.06
181 Denny Martinez	.20	.06
182 Ken Caminiti	.20	.06
183 Doug Jones	.20	.06
184 Brian McRae	.20	.06
185 Don Mattingly	1.25	.35
186 Mel Rojas	.20	.06
187 Marty Cordova	.20	.06
188 Vinny Castilla	.20	.06
189 John Smoltz	.30	.09
190 Travis Fryman	.20	.06
191 Chris Hoiles	.20	.06
192 Chuck Finley	.20	.06
193 Ryan Klesko	.20	.06

194 Alex Fernandez .20 .06
195 Dante Bichette .20 .06
196 Eric Karros .20 .06
197 Roger Clemens 1.00 .30
198 Randy Myers .20 .06
199 Tony Phillips .20 .06
200 Cal Ripken 1.50 .45
201 Rod Beck .20 .06
202 Chad Curtis .20 .06
203 Jack McDowell .20 .06
204 Gary Gaetti .20 .06
205 Ken Griffey Jr. .75 .23
206 Ramon Martinez .20 .06
207 Jeff Kent .20 .06
208 Brad Ausmus .20 .06
209 Devon White .20 .06
210 Jason Giambi .50 .15
211 Nomar Garciaparra .75 .23
212 Billy Wagner .20 .06
213 Todd Greene .20 .06
214 Paul Wilson .20 .06
215 Johnny Damon .20 .06
216 Alan Benes .20 .06
217 Karim Garcia .20 .06
218 Dustin Hermanson .20 .06
219 Derek Jeter 1.25 .35
220 Checklist (111-220) .20 .06
221 Kirby Puckett STP .30 .09
222 Cal Ripken STP .75 .23
223 Albert Belle STP .20 .06
224 Randy Johnson STP .30 .09
225 Wade Boggs STP .20 .06
226 Carlos Baerga STP .20 .06
227 Ivan Rodriguez STP .30 .09
228 Mike Mussina STP .30 .09
229 Frank Thomas STP .30 .09
230 Ken Griffey Jr. STP .50 .15
231 Jose Mesa STP .20 .06
232 Matt Morris RC 2.00 .60
233 Craig Wilson RC .50 .15
234 Alvie Shepherd .25 .07
235 Randy Winn RC .75 .23
236 David Yocum RC .25 .07
237 Jason Brester RC .25 .07
238 Shane Monahan RC .25 .07
239 Brian McNichol RC .25 .07
240 Reggie Taylor .25 .07
241 Garrett Long .25 .07
242 Jonathan Johnson .25 .07
243 Jeff Liefer RC .25 .07
244 Brian Powell .25 .07
245 Brian Buchanan RC .25 .07
246 Mike Piazza .75 .23
247 Edgar Martinez .30 .09
248 Chuck Knoblauch .20 .06
249 Andres Galarraga .20 .06
250 Tony Gwynn .60 .18
251 Lee Smith .20 .06
252 Sammy Sosa .75 .23
253 Jim Thome .50 .15
254 Frank Rodriguez .20 .06
255 Charlie Hayes .20 .06
256 Bernard Gilkey .20 .06
257 John Smiley .20 .06
258 Brady Anderson .20 .06
259 Rico Brogna .20 .06
260 Kirt Manwaring .20 .06
261 Len Dykstra .20 .06
262 Tom Glavine .30 .09
263 Vince Coleman .20 .06
264 John Olerud .20 .06
265 Orlando Merced .20 .06
266 Kent Mercker .20 .06
267 Terry Steinbach .20 .06
268 Brian L. Hunter .20 .06
269 Jeff Fassero .20 .06
270 Jay Buhner .20 .06
271 Jeff Brantley .20 .06
272 Tim Raines .20 .06
273 Jimmy Key .20 .06
274 Mo Vaughn .20 .06
275 Andre Dawson .20 .06
276 Jose Mesa .20 .06
277 Brett Butler .20 .06
278 Luis Gonzalez .20 .06
279 Steve Sparks .20 .06
280 Chili Davis .20 .06
281 Carl Everett .20 .06
282 Jeff Cirillo .20 .06
283 Thomas Howard .20 .06
284 Paul O'Neill .30 .09
285 Pat Meares .20 .06
286 Mickey Tettleton .20 .06
287 Rey Sanchez .20 .06
288 Bip Roberts .20 .06
289 Roberto Alomar .50 .15
290 Ruben Sierra .20 .06
291 John Flaherty .20 .06
292 Bret Saberhagen .20 .06
293 Barry Larkin .50 .15
294 Sandy Alomar Jr. .20 .06
295 Ed Sprague .20 .06
296 Gary DiSarcina .20 .06
297 Marquis Grissom .20 .06
298 John Frascatore .20 .06
299 Will Clark .50 .15
300 Barry Bonds 1.25 .35
301 Ozzie Smith UER .75 .23
Padres is listed as Padre
302 Dave Nilsson .20 .06
303 Pedro Martinez .50 .15
304 Joey Cora .20 .06
305 Rick Aguilera .20 .06
306 Craig Biggio .30 .09
307 Jose Vizcaino .20 .06
308 Jeff Montgomery .20 .06
309 Moises Alou .20 .06
310 Robin Ventura .20 .06
311 David Wells .20 .06
312 Delino DeShields .20 .06
313 Trevor Hoffman .20 .06
314 Andy Benes .20 .06
315 Deion Sanders .30 .09
316 Jim Bullinger .20 .06
317 John Jaha .20 .06
318 Greg Maddux .75 .23
319 Tim Salmon .30 .09
320 Ben McDonald .20 .06
321 Sandy Martinez .20 .06
322 Dan Miceli .20 .06
323 Wade Boggs .30 .09
324 Ismael Valdes .20 .06
325 Juan Gonzalez .50 .15
326 Charles Nagy .20 .06
327 Ray Lankford .20 .06
328 Mark Portugal .20 .06
329 Bobby Bonilla .20 .06
330 Reggie Sanders .20 .06
331 Jamie Brewington RC .25 .07
332 Aaron Sele .20 .06
333 Pete Harnisch .20 .06
334 Cliff Floyd .20 .06
335 Cal Eldred .20 .06
336 Jason Bates .20 .06
337 Tony Clark .20 .06
338 Jose Herrera .20 .06
339 Alex Ochoa .20 .06
340 Mark Loretta .20 .06
341 Donne Wall .20 .06
342 Jason Kendall .20 .06
343 Shannon Stewart .20 .06
344 Brooks Kieschnick .20 .06
345 Chris Snopek .20 .06
346 Ruben Rivera .20 .06
347 Jeff Suppan .20 .06
348 Phil Nevin .20 .06
349 John Wasdin .20 .06
350 Jay Payton .20 .06
351 Tim Crabtree .20 .06
352 Rick Krivda .20 .06
353 Bob Wolcott .20 .06
354 Jimmy Haynes .20 .06
355 Herb Perry .20 .06
356 Ryne Sandberg .75 .23
357 Harold Baines .20 .06
358 Chad Ogea .20 .06
359 Lee Tinsley .20 .06
360 Matt Williams .20 .06
361 Randy Velarde .20 .06
362 Jose Canseco .50 .15
363 Larry Walker .30 .09
364 Kevin Appier .20 .06
365 Darryl Hamilton .20 .06
366 Jose Lima .20 .06
367 Javy Lopez .20 .06
368 Dennis Eckersley .20 .06
369 Jason Isringhausen .20 .06
370 Mickey Morandini .20 .06
371 Scott Cooper .20 .06
372 Jim Abbott .30 .09
373 Paul Sorrento .20 .06
374 Chris Hammond .20 .06
375 Lance Johnson .20 .06
376 Kevin Brown .20 .06
377 Luis Alicea .20 .06
378 Andy Pettitte .30 .09
379 Dean Palmer .20 .06
380 Jeff Bagwell .30 .09
381 Jaime Navarro .20 .06
382 Rondell White .20 .06
383 Erik Hanson .20 .06
384 Pedro Munoz .20 .06
385 Heathcliff Slocumb .20 .06
386 Wally Joyner .20 .06
387 Bob Tewksbury .20 .06
388 David Bell .20 .06
389 Fred McGriff .30 .09
390 Mike Henneman .20 .06
391 Robby Thompson .20 .06
392 Norm Charlton .20 .06
393 Cecil Fielder .20 .06
394 Benito Santiago .20 .06
395 Rafael Palmeiro .30 .09
396 Ricky Bones .20 .06
397 Rickey Henderson .50 .15
398 C.J. Nitkowski .20 .06
399 Shawon Dunston .20 .06
400 Manny Ramirez .20 .06
401 Bill Swift .20 .06
402 Chad Fonville .20 .06
403 Joey Hamilton .20 .06
404 Alex Gonzalez .20 .06
405 Roberto Hernandez .20 .06
406 Jeff Blauser .20 .06
407 LaTroy Hawkins .20 .06
408 Greg Colbrunn .20 .06
409 Todd Hundley .20 .06
410 Glenn Dishman .20 .06
411 Joe Vitiello .20 .06
412 Todd Worrell .20 .06
413 Wil Cordero .20 .06
414 Ken Hill .20 .06
415 Carlos Garcia .20 .06
416 Bryan Rekar .20 .06
417 Shawn Green .20 .06
418 Tyler Green .20 .06
419 Mike Blowers .20 .06
420 Kenny Lofton .20 .06
421 Denny Neagle .20 .06
422 Jeff Conine .20 .06
423 Mark Langston .20 .06
424 Steve Cox .40 .12
Jesse Ibarra
Derrek Lee
Ron Wright RC
425 Jim Bonnici .40 .12
Billy Owens
Richie Sexson
Daryle Ward RC
426 Kevin Jordan .25 .07
Bobby Morris
Desi Relaford
Adam Riggs RC
427 Tim Harkrider .25 .07
Rey Ordonez
Neifi Perez
Enrique Wilson
428 Bartolo Colon .20 .06
Doug Million
Rafael Orellano
Ray Ricken
429 Jeff D'Amico .25 .07
Marty Janzen RC
Gary Rath
Clint Sodowsky
430 Matt Drews .25 .07
Rich Hunter RC
Matt Ruebel
Bret Wagner
431 Jaime Bluma .25 .07
David Coggin
Steve Montgomery
Brandon Reed RC
432 Mike Figga 1.25 .35
Raul Ibanez
Paul Konerko
Julio Mosquera
433 Brian Barber .20 .06
Marc Kroon
Marc Valdes
Don Wengert
434 George Arias .50 .15
Chris Haas RC
Scott Rolen
Scott Spiezio
435 Brian Banks 2.00 .60
Vladimir Guerrero
Andruw Jones
Billy McMillon
436 Roger Cedeno 1.00 .30
Derrick Gibson
Ben Grieve
Shane Spencer RC
437 Anton French .25 .07
Demond Smith
DaRond Stovall RC
Keith Williams
438 Michael Coleman RC .40 .12
Jacob Cruz
Richard Hidalgo
Charles Peterson
439 Trey Beamon .20 .06
Yamil Benitez
Jermaine Dye
Angel Echevarria
440 Checklist .20 .06
F7 M.Mantle Last Day 5.00 1.50
NNO Mickey Mantle TRIB 3.00 .90
Promotes the Mantle Foundation
Black and White Photo

1996 Topps Classic Confrontations

These cards were inserted at a rate of one in every five-card Series one retail pack sold at Walmart. The first ten cards showcase hitters, while the last five cards feature pitchers. Inside white borders, the fronts show player cutouts on a brownish rock background featuring a shadow image of the player. The player's name is gold foil stamped across the bottom. The horizontal backs of the hitters' cards are aqua and present headshots and statistics. The backs of the pitchers cards are purple and present the same information.

	Nm-Mt	Ex-Mt
COMPLETE SET (15)	6.00	1.80
CC1 Ken Griffey Jr.	.60	.18
CC2 Cal Ripken	1.25	.35
CC3 Edgar Martinez	.25	.07
CC4 Kirby Puckett	.40	.12
CC5 Frank Thomas	.40	.12
CC6 Barry Bonds	1.00	.30
CC7 Reggie Sanders	.15	.04
CC8 Andres Galarraga	.15	.04
CC9 Tony Gwynn	.50	.15
CC10 Mike Piazza	.60	.18
CC11 Randy Johnson	.40	.12
CC12 Mike Mussina	.40	.12
CC13 Roger Clemens	.75	.23
CC14 Tom Glavine	.25	.07
CC15 Greg Maddux	.60	.18

1996 Topps Mantle

Randomly inserted in Series one packs at a rate of one in nine hobby packs, one in six retail packs and one in two jumbo packs; these cards are reprints of the original Mickey Mantle cards issued from 1951 through 1969. The fronts look the same except for a commemorative stamp, while the backs clearly state that they are "Mickey Mantle Commemorative" cards and have a 1996 copyright date. These cards honor Yankee great Mickey Mantle, who passed away in August 1995 after a gallant battle against cancer. Based on evidence from an uncut sheet auctioned off at the 1996 Kit Young Hawaii Trade Show, some collectors/dealers believe that cards 15 through 19 were slightly shorter printed in relation to the other 14 cards.

	Nm-Mt	Ex-Mt
COMPLETE SET (19)	120.00	36.00
COMMON MANTLE (3-14)	8.00	2.40
COM.MANTLE SP (15-19)	10.00	3.00

SER.1 ODDS 1:9 HOB, 1:6 RET, 1:2 JUM
FOUR PER CEREAL FACT.SET
CARDS 15-19 SHORTPRINTED BY 20%
*'51-'53 CASE: 3X TO 6X BASIC
ONE CASE PER SER.2 HOB/JUM/VEND CASE
*'51-'53 FINEST: .5X TO 1X BASIC
FINEST SER.2 ODDS 1:18 RET, 1:12 ANCO
*'51-'53 REF: 2.5X TO 5X BASIC
REF.SER.2 ODDS 1:96 HOB, 1:144 RET
*'51-'53 RDMP: 1X TO 2X BASIC
RDMP.SER.2 ODDS 1:72 ANCO, 1:108 RET
1 Mickey Mantle 30.00 9.00
1951 Bowman
2 Mickey Mantle 30.00 9.00
1952 Topps

1996 Topps Masters of the Game

Cards from this 20-card standard-size set were randomly inserted into first-series hobby packs at a rate of one in 18. In addition, every factory set contained two Masters of the Game cards. The cards are numbered with a "MG" prefix in the lower left corner.

	Nm-Mt	Ex-Mt
COMPLETE SET (20)	30.00	9.00
1 Dennis Eckersley	1.00	.30
2 Denny Martinez	1.00	.30
3 Eddie Murray	2.50	.75
4 Paul Molitor	1.50	.45
5 Ozzie Smith	4.00	1.20
6 Rickey Henderson	2.50	.75
7 Tim Raines	1.00	.30
8 Lee Smith	1.00	.30
9 Cal Ripken	8.00	2.40
10 Chili Davis	1.00	.30
11 Wade Boggs	1.50	.45
12 Tony Gwynn	3.00	.90
13 Don Mattingly	6.00	1.80
14 Bret Saberhagen	1.00	.30
15 Kirby Puckett	2.50	.75
16 Joe Carter	1.00	.30
17 Roger Clemens	5.00	1.50
18 Barry Bonds	6.00	1.80
19 Greg Maddux	4.00	1.20
20 Frank Thomas	2.50	.75

1996 Topps Mystery Finest

Randomly inserted in first-series packs at a rate of one in 36 hobby and retail packs and one in eight jumbo packs, this 26-card standard-size set features a bit of a mystery. The fronts have opaque coating that must be removed before the player can be identified. After the opaque coating is removed, the fronts feature a player photo surrounded by silver borders. The backs feature a choice of players along with a corresponding mystery finest trivia fact. Some of these cards were also issued with refractor fronts.

	Nm-Mt	Ex-Mt
COMPLETE SET (26)	120.00	36.00

*REF: 1.25X TO 3X BASIC MYSTERY FINEST
REF.SER.1 ODDS 1:216 HOB/RET, 1:36 JUM

	Nm-Mt	Ex-Mt
M1 Hideo Nomo	5.00	1.50
M2 Greg Maddux	8.00	2.40
M3 Randy Johnson	5.00	1.50
M4 Chipper Jones	5.00	1.50
M5 Marty Cordova	2.00	.60
M6 Garret Anderson	2.00	.60
M7 Cal Ripken	15.00	4.50
M8 Kirby Puckett	5.00	1.50
M9 Tony Gwynn	6.00	1.80
M10 Manny Ramirez	2.00	.60
M11 Jim Edmonds	2.00	.60
M12 Mike Piazza	8.00	2.40
M13 Barry Bonds	12.00	3.60
M14 Raul Mondesi	2.00	.60
M15 Sammy Sosa	8.00	2.40
M16 Ken Griffey Jr.	8.00	2.40
M17 Albert Belle	2.00	.60
M18 Dante Bichette	2.00	.60
M19 Mo Vaughn	2.00	.60
M20 Jeff Bagwell	3.00	.90
M21 Frank Thomas	5.00	1.50
M22 Hideo Nomo	5.00	1.50
M23 Cal Ripken	15.00	4.50
M24 Mike Piazza	8.00	2.40
M25 Ken Griffey Jr.	8.00	2.40
M26 Frank Thomas	5.00	1.50

1996 Topps Power Boosters

Randomly inserted into packs, these cards are a metallic version of 25 of the first 26 cards from the basic Topps set. Card numbers 1-6 and 8-12 were issued at a rate of one every 36 first series retail packs, while numbers 13-26 were issued in hobby packs at a rate of one in 36. Inserted in place of two basic cards, they are printed on 28 point stock and the fronts have prismatic foil printing. Card number 7, which is Mickey Mantle in the regular set, was not issued in a Power Booster form. A first year card of Sean Casey highlights this set.

	Nm-Mt	Ex-Mt
COMP. STAR POWER SET (11)	50.00	15.00
COMMON (1-6/8-12)	1.00	.30
COMP. DRAFT PICKS SET (14)	100.00	30.00
COMMON (12-26)	2.00	.60
1 Tony Gwynn	6.00	1.80
2 Mike Piazza	8.00	2.40
3 Greg Maddux	8.00	2.40
4 Jeff Bagwell	3.00	.90
5 Larry Walker	3.00	.90
6 Barry Larkin	5.00	1.50
8 Tom Glavine	3.00	.90
9 Craig Biggio	3.00	.90
10 Barry Bonds	12.00	3.60
11 Heathcliff Slocumb	2.00	.60
12 Matt Williams	2.00	.60
13 Todd Helton	10.00	3.00
14 Mark Redman	5.00	1.50
15 Michael Barrett	5.00	1.50
16 Ben Davis	2.00	.60
17 Juan LeBron	2.00	.60
18 Tony McKnight	2.00	.60
19 Ryan Jaroncyk	2.00	.60
20 Corey Jenkins	2.00	.60
21 Jim Scharrer	2.00	.60
22 Mark Bellhorn	5.00	1.50
23 Jarrod Washburn	10.00	3.00
24 Geoff Jenkins	15.00	4.50
25 Sean Casey	20.00	6.00
26 Brett Tomko	5.00	1.50

1996 Topps Profiles

Randomly inserted into Series one and two packs at a rate of one in 12 hobby and retail packs, one in six jumbo packs and one in eight ANCO packs;, this 20-card standard-size set features 10 players from each league. One card from the first series and two from the second series were also included in all Topps factory sets. Topps spokesmen Kirby Puckett (AL) and Tony Gwynn (NL) give opinions on players within their league. The fronts feature a player photo set against a silver-foil background. The player's name is on the bottom. A photo of either Gwynn or Puckett as well as the words "Profiles by ..." is on the right. The backs feature a player photo, some career data as well as Gwynn's or Puckett's opinion about the featured player. The cards are numbered with either an "AL or NL" prefix on the back depending on the player's league. The cards are sequenced in alphabetical order within league.

	Nm-Mt	Ex-Mt
COMPLETE SET (40)	40.00	12.00
COMPLETE SERIES 1 (20)	30.00	9.00
COMPLETE SERIES 2 (20)	10.00	3.00
AL1 Roberto Alomar	1.25	.35
AL2 Carlos Baerga	.50	.15
AL3 Albert Belle	.50	.15
AL4 Cecil Fielder	.50	.15
AL5 Ken Griffey Jr.	2.00	.60
AL6 Randy Johnson	1.25	.35
AL7 Paul O'Neill	.75	.23
AL8 Cal Ripken	4.00	1.20
AL9 Frank Thomas	1.25	.35
AL10 Mo Vaughn	.50	.15
AL11 Jay Buhner	.50	.15
AL12 Marty Cordova	.50	.15
AL13 Jim Edmonds	.50	.15
AL14 Juan Gonzalez	1.25	.35
AL15 Kenny Lofton	.50	.15
AL16 Edgar Martinez	.75	.23
AL17 Don Mattingly	3.00	.90
AL18 Mark McGwire	3.00	.90
AL19 Rafael Palmeiro	.75	.23
AL20 Tim Salmon	.75	.23
NL1 Jeff Bagwell	.75	.23
NL2 Derek Bell	.50	.15
NL3 Barry Bonds	3.00	.90
NL4 Greg Maddux	2.00	.60
NL5 Fred McGriff	.75	.23
NL6 Raul Mondesi	.50	.15
NL7 Mike Piazza	2.00	.60
NL8 Reggie Sanders	.50	.15
NL9 Sammy Sosa	2.00	.60
NL10 Larry Walker	.75	.23
NL11 Dante Bichette	.50	.15
NL12 Andres Galarraga	.50	.15
NL13 Ron Gant	.50	.15
NL14 Tom Glavine	.75	.23
NL15 Chipper Jones	1.25	.35
NL16 David Justice	.50	.15
NL17 Barry Larkin	1.25	.35
NL18 Hideo Nomo	1.25	.35
NL19 Gary Sheffield	.50	.15
NL20 Matt Williams	.50	.15

1996 Topps Road Warriors

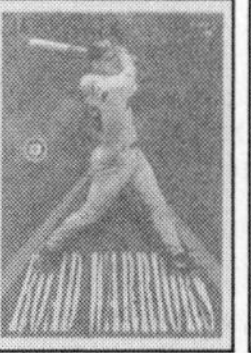

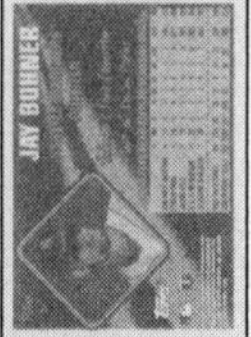

This 20-card set was inserted only into Series two WalMart packs at a rate of one per pack and featured leading hitters of the majors. The set is sequenced in alphabetical order.

	Nm-Mt	Ex-Mt
COMPLETE SET (20)	12.00	3.60
RW1 Derek Bell	.40	.12
RW2 Albert Belle	.40	.12
RW3 Craig Biggio	.60	.18
RW4 Barry Bonds	2.50	.75
RW5 Jay Buhner	.40	.12
RW6 Jim Edmonds	.40	.12
RW7 Gary Gaetti	.40	.12
RW8 Ron Gant	.40	.12
RW9 Edgar Martinez	.60	.18
RW10 Tino Martinez	.60	.18
RW11 Mark McGwire	2.50	.75
RW12 Mike Piazza	1.50	.45
RW13 Manny Ramirez	.40	.12
RW14 Tim Salmon	.60	.18
RW15 Reggie Sanders	.40	.12
RW16 Frank Thomas	1.00	.30
RW17 John Valentin	.40	.12
RW18 Mo Vaughn	.40	.12
RW19 Robin Ventura	.40	.12
RW20 Matt Williams	.40	.12

1996 Topps Wrecking Crew

Randomly inserted in Series two hobby packs at a rate of one in 18, this 15-card set honors some of the hottest home run producers in the League. One card from this set was also inserted into Topps Hobby Factory sets. The cards feature color action player photos with foil stamping.

	Nm-Mt	Ex-Mt
COMPLETE SET (15)	60.00	18.00
WC1 Jeff Bagwell	3.00	.90
WC2 Albert Belle	2.00	.60
WC3 Barry Bonds	12.00	3.60
WC4 Jose Canseco	5.00	1.50
WC5 Joe Carter	2.00	.60
WC6 Cecil Fielder	2.00	.60
WC7 Ron Gant	2.00	.60
WC8 Juan Gonzalez	5.00	1.50
WC9 Ken Griffey Jr.	8.00	2.40
WC10 Fred McGriff	3.00	.90
WC11 Mark McGwire	12.00	3.60
WC12 Mike Piazza	8.00	2.40
WC13 Frank Thomas	5.00	1.50
WC14 Mo Vaughn	2.00	.60
WC15 Matt Williams	2.00	.60

1996 Topps Bronze League Leaders

This six-card set features color action player images on a background of silver rays, sealed to a bed of solid bronze, and silk-screened with the player's league leading 1995 stats plus career numbers. Only 2,000 of this set was produced.

	Nm-Mt	Ex-Mt
COMPLETE SET (6)	100.00	30.00
1 Barry Larkin	15.00	4.50
2 Greg Maddux	25.00	7.50
3 Hideo Nomo	20.00	6.00
4 Mo Vaughn	10.00	3.00
5 Randy Johnson	20.00	6.00
6 Marty Cordova	10.00	3.00

1996 Topps Mantle Ceramic

This eight-card set features reprints of the original Mickey Mantle cards issued from 1951 through 1969 and are printed on a ceramic card stock. The fronts look the same as the original cards, while the backs state that they were manufactured by R and N China Co. under license from the Topps Company and have a 1996 copyright date. Only 1000 of each card was reproduced and are sequentially numbered. These cards honor Yankee great Mickey Mantle, who passed away in August 1995 after a gallant battle against cancer. The cards are checklisted below according to the year they were originally produced.

	Nm-Mt	Ex-Mt
COMPLEE SET (8)	200.00	60.00
COMMON CARD (1-8)	25.00	7.50
1 Mickey Mantle	30.00	9.00
1951 Bowman		
2 Mickey Mantle	40.00	12.00
1952 Topps		

1996-97 Topps Members Only 55

This 55-card set features color player photos of Topps' selection of 50 (numbers 1-50) top American and National League players. The set includes five Finest Cards (numbers 51-55) which represent Topps' selection of the top rookies from 1997. The backs carry information

about the player. Each card displays the "Member Only" gold foil stamp.

	Nm-Mt	Ex-Mt
COMP. FACT SET (55)	20.00	6.00
1 Brady Anderson	.20	.06
2 Carlos Baerga	.20	.06
3 Jeff Bagwell	.75	.23
4 Albert Belle	.20	.06
5 Dante Bichette	.20	.06
6 Craig Biggio	.30	.09
7 Wade Boggs	.75	.23
8 Barry Bonds	1.50	.45
9 Jay Buhner	.20	.06
10 Ellis Burks	.20	.06
11 Ken Caminiti	.20	.06
12 Jose Canseco	.50	.15
13 Joe Carter	.20	.06
14 Roger Clemens	1.50	.45
15 Jeff Conine	.10	.03
16 Andres Galarraga	.40	.12
17 Ron Gant	.10	.03
18 Juan Gonzalez	.40	.12
19 Mark Grace	.30	.09
20 Ken Griffey Jr.	2.00	.60
21 Tony Gwynn	1.50	.45
22 Pat Hentgen	.20	.06
23 Todd Hollandsworth	.10	.03
24 Todd Hundley	.20	.06
25 Derek Jeter	3.00	.90
26 Randy Johnson	.75	.23
27 Chipper Jones	1.50	.45
28 Ryan Klesko	.20	.06
29 Chuck Knoblauch	.30	.09
30 Barry Larkin	.40	.12
31 Kenny Lofton	.30	.09
32 Greg Maddux	2.00	.60
33 Mark McGwire	2.50	.75
34 Paul Molitor	.60	.18
35 Raul Mondesi	.30	.09
36 Hideo Nomo	.75	.23
37 Rafael Palmeiro	.40	.12
38 Mike Piazza	2.00	.60
39 Manny Ramirez	.75	.23
40 Cal Ripken	3.00	.90
41 Ivan Rodriguez	.75	.23
42 Tim Salmon	.30	.09
43 Gary Sheffield	.50	.15
44 John Smoltz	.40	.12
45 Sammy Sosa	1.50	.45
46 Frank Thomas	1.00	.30
47 Jim Thome	.50	.15
48 Mo Vaughn	.20	.06
49 Bernie Williams	.40	.12
50 Matt Williams	.30	.09
51 Darin Erstad	1.00	.30
52 Vladimir Guerrero	1.50	.45
53 Andruw Jones	.75	.23
54 Scott Rolen	.50	.15
55 Todd Walker	.10	.03

1996 Topps Team Topps

Parallel cards from nine selected teams were issued by Topps in 1996 and distributed in team set form to commemorate their superior performances in 1995. The team sets were issued with the "Big Topps cards" in special packaging for retail stores. Each team set carried an SRP of $4.99. Please note, alphabetical prefixes have been added to the card numbers below for easier checklisting purposes. The actual cards do not carry these prefixes. The Cubs, Orioles, Rangers, White Sox and Yankees cards carry a "Team Topps" logo on each card front. The four other teams carry logos on the card fronts as follows: Braves - "World Champions", Dodgers - "35 Seasons", Indians - "1995 American League Champions" and Mariners - "1995 AL West Champions". It's interesting to note that a parallel version of star first basemen Sean Casey's Rookie Card was included within the Indians team set.

	Nm-Mt	Ex-Mt
COMPLETE SET (150)	100.00	30.00
B3 Greg Maddux STAR	3.00	.90
B8 Tom Glavine STAR	1.25	.35
B12 Jim Scharrer	.25	.07
B49 Mark Wohlers	.25	.07
B60 David Justice	1.00	.30
B83 Mark Lemke	.25	.07
B165 Steve Avery	.25	.07
B177 Chipper Jones	3.00	.90
B189 John Smoltz	.50	.15
B193 Ryan Klesko	.50	.15
B262 Tom Glavine	1.25	.35
B266 Kent Mercker	.25	.07
B297 Marquis Grissom	.25	.07
B318 Greg Maddux	3.00	.90
B367 Javy Lopez	.50	.15
B389 Fred McGriff	.75	.23
B406 Jeff Blauser	.25	.07
C35 Todd Zeile	.50	.15
C55 Mark Grace	1.00	.30
C62 Kevin Foster	.25	.07
C146 Frank Castillo	.25	.07
C184 Brian McRae	.25	.07
C198 Randy Myers	.25	.07
C239 Brian McNichol	.25	.07
C252 Sammy Sosa	2.50	.75
C278 Luis Gonzalez	1.00	.30
C287 Rey Sanchez	.25	.07
C316 Jim Bullinger	.25	.07
C344 Brooks Kieschnick	.25	.07
C356 Ryne Sandberg	1.25	.35
C381 Jaime Navarro	.25	.07
C399 Shawon Dunston	.25	.07
D2 Mike Piazza UER	3.00	.90
Basic card front, Star Power subset back		
D48 Todd Hollandsworth	.25	.07
D89 Jose Offerman	.25	.07
D136 Hideo Nomo	1.25	.35
D153 Tom Candiotti	.50	.15
D175 Raul Mondesi	.50	.15
D196 Eric Karros	.50	.15
D206 Ramon Martinez	.25	.07
D217 Karim Garcia	1.00	.30
D236 David Yocum	.25	.07
D246 M.Piazza STAR UER	3.00	.90
Star Power subset front, basic issue card back		
D277 Brett Butler	.50	.15
D312 Delino DeShields	.50	.15
D324 Ismael Valdes	.25	.07
D402 Chad Fonville	.25	.07
D412 Todd Worrell	.25	.07
I25 Sean Casey	5.00	1.50
I40 Orel Hershiser	.50	.15
I45 Albert Belle	.50	.15
I75 Carlos Baerga	.50	.15
I81 Julian Tavarez	.25	.07
I84 Omar Vizquel	1.00	.30
I125 Eddie Murray	1.25	.35
I181 Denny Martinez	.50	.15
I223 Albert Belle STAR	.50	.15
I226 Carlos Baerga STAR	.50	.15
I231 Jose Mesa STAR	.50	.15
I253 Jim Thome	1.00	.30
I276 Jose Mesa	.50	.15
I294 Sandy Alomar Jr.	.50	.15
I326 Charles Nagy	.25	.07
I355 Herb Perry	.25	.07
I358 Chad Ogea	.25	.07
I373 Paul Sorrento	.25	.07
I400 Manny Ramirez	1.25	.35
I414 Ken Hill	.25	.07
I420 Kenny Lofton	.75	.23
M38 Tim Belcher	.25	.07
M67 Felix Fermin	.25	.07
M94 Alex Diaz	.25	.07
M117 Dan Wilson	.25	.07
M150 Randy Johnson	1.25	.35
M168 Tino Martinez	.50	.15
M205 Ken Griffey Jr.	3.00	.90
M224 R.Johnson STAR	1.25	.35
M230 K.Griffey Jr. STAR	3.00	.90
M238 Shane Monahan	.25	.07
M247 Edgar Martinez	.75	.23
M263 Vince Coleman	.25	.07
M270 Jay Buhner	.50	.15
M304 Joey Cora	.25	.07
M314 Andy Benes	.25	.07
M353 Bob Wolcott	.25	.07
M392 Norm Charlton	.25	.07
M419 Mike Blowers	.25	.07
O34 Manny Alexander	.25	.07
O65 M.Mussina STAR UER	1.00	.30
Star Power card front, basic issue card back		
O96 Cal Ripken 2131	5.00	1.50
O121 Curtis Goodwin	.25	.07
O183 Doug Jones	.25	.07
O191 Chris Hoiles	.25	.07
O200 Cal Ripken	5.00	1.50
O222 Cal Ripken STAR	5.00	1.50
O228 M.Mussina UER	1.00	.30
Basic issue card front, Star Power subset card back		
O234 Alvie Shepherd	.25	.07
O258 Brady Anderson	.50	.15
O320 Ben McDonald	.25	.07
O329 Bobby Bonilla	.25	.07
O352 Rick Krivda	.25	.07
O354 Jimmy Haynes	.25	.07
O357 Harold Baines	.50	.15
O376 Kevin Brown	.75	.23
O395 Rafael Palmeiro	1.00	.30
R79 Roger Pavlik	.25	.07
R87 Rusty Greer	.50	.15
R130 Kenny Rogers	.25	.07
R140 Ivan Rodriguez	1.25	.35
R152 Benji Gil	.25	.07
R166 Mark McLemore	.50	.15
R178 Otis Nixon	.25	.07
R227 I.Rodriguez STAR	1.25	.35
R242 Jonathan Johnson	.25	.07
R286 Mickey Tettleton	.25	.07
R299 Will Clark	1.00	.30
R325 Juan Gonzalez	1.25	.35
R379 Dean Palmer	.50	.15
R387 Bob Tewksbury	.25	.07
W52 Ron Karkovice	.25	.07
W100 Frank Thomas	2.00	.60
W119 Lyle Mouton	.25	.07
W129 Ozzie Guillen	.50	.15
W159 Wilson Alvarez	.25	.07
W173 Ray Durham	.50	.15
W194 Alex Fernandez	.25	.07
W229 F.Thomas STAR	2.00	.60
W243 Jeff Liefer	.25	.07
W272 Tim Raines	.50	.15
W310 Robin Ventura	1.00	.30
W345 Chris Snopek	.25	.07
W375 Lance Johnson	.25	.07
W405 Roberto Hernandez	.25	.07
Y7 Mickey Mantle	10.00	3.00
Y27 Tony Fernandez	.50	.15
Y68 Bernie Williams	1.00	.30
Y95 John Wetteland	.50	.15
Y124 David Cone	.75	.23
Y135 Mike Stanley	.25	.07
Y185 Don Mattingly	2.50	.75
Y203 Jack McDowell	.25	.07
Y219 Derek Jeter	5.00	1.50
Y225 Wade Boggs STAR	1.25	.35
Y245 Brian Buchanan	.25	.07
Y273 Jimmy Key	.50	.15
Y284 Paul O'Neill	1.00	.30
Y290 Ruben Sierra	.50	.15
Y323 Wade Boggs	1.25	.35
Y346 Ruben Rivera	.25	.07
Y361 Randy Velarde	.25	.07
Y378 Andy Pettitte	.50	.15

1996 Topps Team Topps Big

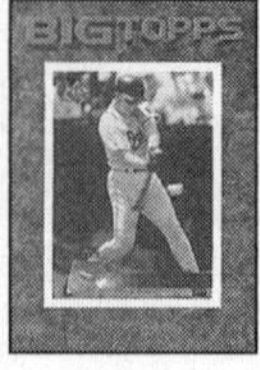

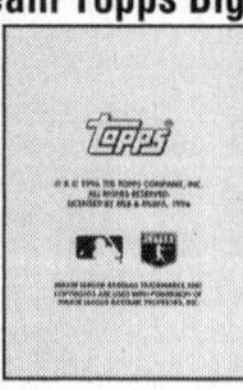

This nine-card set measures approximately 3 1/2" by 5" and was distributed only by Walmart. One star player card was packed with each Team Topps set. The fronts feature oversized photos of the Topps cards. The cards are unnumbered and checklisted below in alphabetical order.

	Nm-Mt	Ex-Mt
COMPLETE SET (9)	20.00	6.00
1 Albert Belle	.50	.15
2 Juan Gonzalez	1.25	.35
3 Ken Griffey Jr.	3.00	.90
4 Derek Jeter	5.00	1.50
5 Greg Maddux	3.00	.90
6 Hideo Nomo	1.25	.35
7 Cal Ripken	5.00	1.50
8 Ryne Sandberg	1.25	.35
9 Frank Thomas	1.25	.35

1996 Topps 22K Mantle

This standard-size was issued by Topps seemingly as part of a series of cards honoring retired greats. The cards are exact replicas of already issued cards and it is believed that there might be more cards so any additions to this checklist is appreciated. The back has serial numbering and mentions that Topps copywrited this card in 1996

	Nm-Mt	Ex-Mt
1 Mickey Mantle	20.00	6.00

1997 Topps

This 495-card set was primarily distributed in first and second series 11-card packs with a suggested retail price of $1.29. In addition, eight-card retail packs, 40-card jumbo packs and 504-card factory sets (containing the complete 495-card set plus a random selection of eight insert cards and one hermetically sealed Willie Mays or Mickey Mantle Reprint insert) were made available. The card fronts feature a color action player photo with a gloss coating and a spot matte finish on the outside border with gold foil stamping. The backs carry another player photo, player information and statistics. The set includes the following subsets: Season Highlights (100-104, 462-466), Prospects (200-207, 487-494), the first ever expansion team cards of the Arizona Diamondbacks (249-251,468-469 and the Tampa Bay Devil Rays (252-253, 470-472) and Draft Picks (269-274, 477-483). Card 42 is a special Jackie Robinson tribute card commemorating the 50th anniversary of his contribution to baseball history and numbered for his Dodgers uniform number. Card number 7 does not exist because it was retired in honor of Mickey Mantle. Card number 84 does not exist because Mike Fetters' card was incorrectly numbered 61. Card number 277 does not exist because Chipper Jones' card was incorrectly numbered 276. Rookie Cards include Kris Benson and Eric Chavez. The Derek Jeter autograph card found at the end of our checklist was seeded one every 576 second series packs.

	Nm-Mt	Ex-Mt
COMPLETE SET (495)	80.00	24.00
COMP.SERIES 1 (275)	40.00	12.00
COMP.SERIES 2 (220)	40.00	12.00
1 Barry Bonds	1.25	.35
2 Tom Pagnozzi	.20	.06
3 Terrell Wade	.20	.06
4 Jose Valentin	.20	.06
5 Mark Clark	.20	.06
6 Brady Anderson	.20	.06
8 Wade Boggs	.30	.09
9 Scott Stahoviak	.20	.06
10 Andres Galarraga	.20	.06
11 Steve Avery	.20	.06
12 Rusty Greer	.20	.06
13 Derek Jeter	1.25	.35
14 Ricky Bottalico	.20	.06
15 Andy Ashby	.20	.06
16 Paul Shuey	.20	.06
17 F.P. Santangelo	.20	.06
18 Royce Clayton	.20	.06
19 Mike Mohler	.20	.06
20 Mike Piazza	.75	.23
21 Jaime Navarro	.20	.06
22 Billy Wagner	.20	.06
23 Mike Timlin	.20	.06
24 Garret Anderson	.20	.06
25 Ben McDonald	.20	.06
26 Mel Rojas	.20	.06
27 John Burkett	.20	.06
28 Jeff King	.20	.06
29 Reggie Jefferson	.20	.06
30 Kevin Appier	.20	.06
31 Felipe Lira	.20	.06
32 Kevin Tapani	.20	.06
33 Mark Portugal	.20	.06
34 Carlos Garcia	.20	.06
35 Joey Cora	.20	.06
36 David Segui	.20	.06
37 Mark Grace	.30	.09
38 Erik Hanson	.20	.06
39 Jeff D'Amico	.20	.06
40 Jay Buhner	.20	.06
41 B.J. Surhoff	.20	.06
42 Jackie Robinson TRIB	2.00	.60
43 Roger Pavlik	.20	.06
44 Hal Morris	.20	.06
45 Mariano Duncan	.20	.06
46 Harold Baines	.20	.06
47 Jorge Fabregas	.20	.06
48 Jose Herrera	.20	.06
49 Jeff Cirillo	.20	.06
50 Tom Glavine	.30	.09
51 Pedro Astacio	.20	.06
52 Mark Gardner	.20	.06
53 Arthur Rhodes	.20	.06
54 Troy O'Leary	.20	.06
55 Bip Roberts	.20	.06
56 Mike Lieberthal	.20	.06
57 Shane Andrews	.20	.06
58 Scott Karl	.20	.06
59 Gary DiSarcina	.20	.06
60 Andy Pettitte	.30	.09
61 Kevin Elster	.20	.06
61B Mike Fetters UER	.20	.06
Card was intended as number 84		
62 Mark McGwire	1.25	.35
63 Dan Wilson	.20	.06
64 Mickey Morandini	.20	.06
65 Chuck Knoblauch	.20	.06
66 Tim Wakefield	.20	.06
67 Raul Mondesi	.20	.06
68 Todd Jones	.20	.06
69 Albert Belle	.20	.06
70 Trevor Hoffman	.20	.06
71 Eric Young	.20	.06
72 Robert Perez	.20	.06
73 Butch Huskey	.20	.06
74 Brian McRae	.20	.06
75 Jim Edmonds	.20	.06
76 Mike Henneman	.20	.06
77 Frank Rodriguez	.20	.06
78 Danny Tartabull	.20	.06
79 Robb Nen	.20	.06
80 Reggie Sanders	.20	.06
81 Ron Karkovice	.20	.06
82 Benito Santiago	.20	.06
83 Mike Lansing	.20	.06
85 Craig Biggio	.30	.09
86 Mike Bordick	.20	.06
87 Ray Lankford	.20	.06
88 Charles Nagy	.20	.06
89 Paul Wilson	.20	.06
90 John Wetteland	.20	.06
91 Tom Candiotti	.20	.06
92 Carlos Delgado	.20	.06
93 Derek Bell	.20	.06
94 Mark Lemke	.20	.06
95 Edgar Martinez	.30	.09
96 Rickey Henderson	.50	.15
97 Greg Myers	.20	.06
98 Jim Leyritz	.20	.06
99 Mark Johnson	.20	.06
100 Dwight Gooden HL	.20	.06
101 Al Leiter HL	.20	.06
102 John Mabry HL	.20	.06
103 Alex Ochoa HL	.20	.06
104 Mike Piazza HL	.50	.15
105 Jim Thome	.50	.15
106 Ricky Otero	.20	.06
107 Jamey Wright	.20	.06
108 Frank Thomas	.50	.15
109 Jody Reed	.20	.06
110 Orel Hershiser	.20	.06
111 Terry Steinbach	.20	.06
112 Mark Loretta	.20	.06
113 Turk Wendell	.20	.06
114 Marvin Benard	.20	.06
115 Kevin Brown	.20	.06
116 Robert Person	.20	.06
117 Joey Hamilton	.20	.06
118 Francisco Cordova	.20	.06
119 John Smiley	.20	.06
120 Travis Fryman	.20	.06
121 Jimmy Key	.20	.06
122 Tom Goodwin	.20	.06
123 Mike Greenwell	.20	.06
124 Juan Gonzalez	.50	.15
125 Pete Harnisch	.20	.06
126 Roger Cedeno	.20	.06
127 Ron Gant	.20	.06
128 Mark Langston	.20	.06
129 Tim Crabtree	.20	.06
130 Greg Maddux	.75	.23
131 W.VanLandingham	.20	.06
132 Wally Joyner	.20	.06
133 Randy Myers	.20	.06
134 John Valentin	.20	.06
135 Bret Boone	.20	.06
136 Bruce Ruffin	.20	.06
137 Chris Snopek	.20	.06
138 Paul Molitor	.30	.09
139 Mark McLemore	.20	.06
140 Rafael Palmeiro	.30	.09
141 Herb Perry	.20	.06
142 Luis Gonzalez	.20	.06
143 Doug Drabek	.20	.06
144 Ken Ryan	.20	.06
145 Todd Hundley	.20	.06
146 Ellis Burks	.20	.06
147 Ozzie Guillen	.20	.06
148 Rich Becker	.20	.06
149 Sterling Hitchcock	.20	.06
150 Bernie Williams	.30	.09
151 Mike Stanley	.20	.06
152 Roberto Alomar	.50	.15
153 Jose Mesa	.20	.06
154 Steve Trachsel	.20	.06
155 Alex Gonzalez	.20	.06

156 Troy Percival .20 .06
157 John Smoltz .20 .09
158 Pedro Martinez .50 .15
159 Jeff Conine .20 .06
160 Bernard Gilkey .20 .06
161 Jim Eisenreich .20 .06
162 Mickey Tettleton .20 .06
163 Justin Thompson .20 .06
164 Jose Offerman .20 .06
165 Tony Phillips .20 .06
166 Ismael Valdes .20 .06
167 Ryne Sandberg UER .75 .23
Card has him with 252 homers in 1996
168 Matt Mieske .20 .06
169 Geronimo Berroa .20 .06
170 Otis Nixon .20 .06
171 John Mabry .20 .06
172 Shawon Dunston .20 .06
173 Omar Vizquel .20 .06
174 Chris Hoiles .20 .06
175 Dwight Gooden .30 .09
176 Wilson Alvarez .20 .06
177 Todd Hollandsworth .20 .06
178 Roger Salkeld .20 .06
179 Rey Sanchez .20 .06
180 Rey Ordonez .20 .06
181 Denny Martinez .20 .06
182 Ramon Martinez .20 .06
183 Dave Nilsson .20 .06
184 Marquis Grissom .20 .06
185 Randy Velarde .20 .06
186 Ron Coomer .20 .06
187 Tino Martinez .30 .09
188 Jeff Brantley .20 .06
189 Steve Finley .20 .06
190 Andy Benes .20 .06
191 Terry Adams .20 .06
192 Mike Blowers .20 .06
193 Russ Davis .20 .06
194 Darryl Hamilton .20 .06
195 Jason Kendall .20 .06
196 Johnny Damon .20 .06
197 Dave Martinez .20 .06
198 Mike Macfarlane .20 .06
199 Norm Charlton .20 .06
200 Doug Million RC .25 .07
Damian Moss
Bobby Rodgers
201 Geoff Jenkins .20 .06
Raul Ibanez
Mike Cameron
202 Sean Casey .20 .06
Jim Bonnici
Dmitri Young
203 Jed Hansen .20 .06
Homer Bush
Felipe Crespo
204 Kevin Orie .20 .06
Gabe Alvarez
Aaron Boone
205 Ben Davis .20 .06
Kevin Brown
Bobby Estalella
206 Billy McMillon RC .40 .12
Bubba Trammell
Dante Powell
207 Jarrod Washburn .20 .06
Marc Wilkins RC
Glendon Rusch
208 Brian Hunter .20 .06
209 Jason Giambi .50 .15
210 Henry Rodriguez .20 .06
211 Edgar Renteria .20 .06
212 Edgardo Alfonzo .20 .06
213 Fernando Vina .20 .06
214 Shawn Green .20 .06
215 Ray Durham .20 .06
216 Joe Randa .20 .06
217 Armando Reynoso .20 .06
218 Eric Davis .20 .06
219 Bob Tewksbury .20 .06
220 Jacob Cruz .20 .06
221 Glenallen Hill .20 .06
222 Gary Gaetti .20 .06
223 Donne Wall .20 .06
224 Brad Clontz .20 .06
225 Marty Janzen .20 .06
226 Todd Worrell .20 .06
227 John Franco .20 .06
228 David Wells .20 .06
229 Gregg Jefferies .20 .06
230 Tim Naehring .20 .06
231 Thomas Howard .20 .06
232 Roberto Hernandez .20 .06
233 Kevin Ritz .20 .06
234 Julian Tavarez .20 .06
235 Ken Hill .20 .06
236 Greg Gagne .20 .06
237 Bobby Chouinard .20 .06
238 Joe Carter .20 .06
239 Jermaine Dye .20 .06
240 Antonio Osuna .20 .06
241 Julio Franco .20 .06
242 Mike Grace .20 .06
243 Aaron Sele .20 .06
244 David Justice .20 .06
245 Sandy Alomar Jr. .20 .06
246 Jose Canseco .50 .15
247 Paul O'Neill .30 .09
248 Sean Berry .20 .06
249 Nick Bierbrodt .25 .07
Kevin Sweeney RC
250 Larry Rodriguez RC .25 .07
Vladimir Nunez RC
251 Ron Hartman .25 .07
David Hayman RC
252 Alex Sanchez .40 .12
Matthew Quatraro RC
253 Ronni Seberino RC .25 .07
Pablo Ortego RC
254 Rex Hudler .20 .06
255 Orlando Miller .20 .06
256 Mariano Rivera .30 .09
257 Brad Radke .20 .06
258 Bobby Higginson .20 .06
259 Jay Bell .20 .06
260 Mark Grudzielanek .20 .06
261 Lance Johnson .20 .06
262 Ken Caminiti .20 .06
263 J.T. Snow .20 .06
264 Gary Sheffield .20 .06
265 Darrin Fletcher .20 .06
266 Eric Owens .20 .06
267 Luis Castillo .20 .06
268 Scott Rolen .30 .09
269 Todd Noel .25 .07
John Oliver RC
270 Robert Stratton RC .40 .12
Corey Lee RC
271 Gil Meche RC 4.00 1.20
Matt Halloran RC
272 Eric Milton RC .75 .23
Dee Brown RC
273 Josh Garrett .25 .07
Chris Reitsma RC
274 A.J.Zapp RC .40 .12
Jason Marquis
275 Checklist .20 .06
276 Checklist .20 .06
277 Chipper Jones UER .50 .15
incorrectly numbered 276
278 Orlando Merced .20 .06
279 Ariel Prieto .20 .06
280 Al Leiter .20 .06
281 Pat Meares .20 .06
282 Darryl Strawberry .30 .09
283 Jamie Moyer .20 .06
284 Scott Servais .20 .06
285 Delino DeShields .20 .06
286 Danny Graves .20 .06
287 Gerald Williams .20 .06
288 Todd Greene .20 .06
289 Rico Brogna .20 .06
290 Derrick Gibson .20 .06
291 Joe Girardi .20 .06
292 Darren Lewis .20 .06
293 Nomar Garciaparra .75 .23
294 Greg Colbrunn .20 .06
295 Jeff Bagwell .30 .09
296 Brent Gates .20 .06
297 Jose Vizcaino .20 .06
298 Alex Ochoa .20 .06
299 Sid Fernandez .20 .06
300 Ken Griffey Jr. .75 .23
301 Chris Gomez .20 .06
302 Wendell Magee .20 .06
303 Darren Oliver .20 .06
304 Mel Nieves .20 .06
305 Sammy Sosa .75 .23
306 George Arias .20 .06
307 Jack McDowell .20 .06
308 Stan Javier .20 .06
309 Kimera Bartee .20 .06
310 James Baldwin .20 .06
311 Rocky Coppinger .20 .06
312 Keith Lockhart .20 .06
313 C.J. Nitkowski .20 .06
314 Allen Watson .20 .06
315 Darryl Kile .20 .06
316 Amaury Telemaco .20 .06
317 Jason Isringhausen .20 .06
318 Manny Ramirez .20 .06
319 Terry Pendleton .20 .06
320 Tim Salmon .30 .09
321 Eric Karros .20 .06
322 Mark Whiten .20 .06
323 Rick Krivda .20 .06
324 Brett Butler .20 .06
325 Randy Johnson .50 .15
326 Eddie Taubensee .20 .06
327 Mark Leiter .20 .06
328 Kevin Gross .20 .06
329 Ernie Young .20 .06
330 Pat Hentgen .20 .06
331 Rondell White .20 .06
332 Bobby Witt .20 .06
333 Eddie Murray .50 .15
334 Tim Raines .20 .06
335 Jeff Fassero .20 .06
336 Chuck Finley .20 .06
337 Willie Adams .20 .06
338 Chan Ho Park .20 .06
339 Jay Powell .20 .06
340 Ivan Rodriguez .50 .15
341 Jermaine Allensworth .20 .06
342 Jay Payton .20 .06
343 T.J. Mathews .20 .06
344 Tony Batista .20 .06
345 Ed Sprague .20 .06
346 Jeff Kent .20 .06
347 Scott Erickson .20 .06
348 Jeff Suppan .20 .06
349 Pete Schourek .20 .06
350 Kenny Lofton .20 .06
351 Alan Benes .20 .06
352 Fred McGriff .30 .09
353 Charlie O'Brien .20 .06
354 Darren Bragg .20 .06
355 Alex Fernandez .20 .06
356 Al Martin .20 .06
357 Bob Wells .20 .06
358 Chad Mottola .20 .06
359 Devon White .20 .06
360 David Cone .20 .06
361 Bobby Jones .20 .06
362 Scott Sanders .20 .06
363 Karim Garcia .20 .06
364 Kirt Manwaring .20 .06
365 Chili Davis .20 .06
366 Mike Hampton .20 .06
367 Chad Ogea .20 .06
368 Curt Schilling .30 .09
369 Phil Nevin .20 .06
370 Roger Clemens 1.00 .30
371 Willie Greene .20 .06
372 Kenny Rogers .20 .06
373 Jose Rijo .20 .06
374 Bobby Bonilla .20 .06
375 Mike Mussina .50 .15
376 Curtis Pride .20 .06
377 Todd Walker .20 .06
378 Jason Bere .20 .06
379 Heathcliff Slocumb .20 .06
380 Dante Bichette .20 .06
381 Carlos Baerga .20 .06
382 Livan Hernandez .20 .06
383 Jason Schmidt .20 .06
384 Kevin Stocker .20 .06
385 Matt Williams .20 .06
386 Bartolo Colon .20 .06
387 Will Clark .50 .15
388 Dennis Eckersley .20 .06
389 Brooks Kieschnick .20 .06
390 Ryan Klesko .20 .06
391 Mark Carreon .20 .06
392 Tim Worrell .20 .06
393 Dean Palmer .20 .06
394 Wil Cordero .20 .06
395 Javy Lopez .20 .06
396 Rich Aurilia .20 .06
397 Greg Vaughn .20 .06
398 Vinny Castilla .20 .06
399 Jeff Montgomery .20 .06
400 Cal Ripken 1.50 .45
401 Walt Weiss .20 .06
402 Brad Ausmus .20 .06
403 Ruben Rivera .20 .06
404 Mark Wohlers .20 .06
405 Rick Aguilera .20 .06
406 Tony Clark .20 .06
407 Lyle Mouton .20 .06
408 Bill Pulsipher .20 .06
409 Jose Rosado .20 .06
410 Tony Gwynn .60 .18
411 Cecil Fielder .20 .06
412 John Flaherty .20 .06
413 Lenny Dykstra .20 .06
414 Ugueth Urbina .20 .06
415 Brian Jordan .20 .06
416 Bob Abreu .20 .06
417 Craig Paquette .20 .06
418 Sandy Martinez .20 .06
419 Jeff Blauser .20 .06
420 Barry Larkin .50 .15
421 Kevin Seitzer .20 .06
422 Tim Belcher .20 .06
423 Paul Sorrento .20 .06
424 Cal Eldred .20 .06
425 Robin Ventura .20 .06
426 John Olerud .20 .06
427 Bob Wolcott .20 .06
428 Matt Lawton .20 .06
429 Rod Beck .20 .06
430 Shane Reynolds .20 .06
431 Mike James .20 .06
432 Steve Wojciechowski .20 .06
433 Vladimir Guerrero .50 .15
434 Dustin Hermanson .20 .06
435 Marty Cordova .20 .06
436 Marc Newfield .20 .06
437 Todd Stottlemyre .20 .06
438 Jeffrey Hammonds .20 .06
439 Dave Stevens .20 .06
440 Hideo Nomo .50 .15
441 Mark Thompson .20 .06
442 Mark Lewis .20 .06
443 Quinton McCracken .20 .06
444 Cliff Floyd .20 .06
445 Denny Neagle .20 .06
446 John Jaha .20 .06
447 Mike Sweeney .20 .06
448 John Wasdin .20 .06
449 Chad Curtis .20 .06
450 Mo Vaughn .20 .06
451 Donovan Osborne .20 .06
452 Ruben Sierra .20 .06
453 Michael Tucker .20 .06
454 Kurt Abbott .20 .06
455 Andruw Jones UER .20 .06
Birthdate is incorrectly listed
as 1-22-67, should be 1-22-77
456 Shannon Stewart .20 .06
457 Scott Brosius .20 .06
458 Juan Guzman .20 .06
459 Ron Villone .20 .06
460 Moises Alou .20 .06
461 Larry Walker .30 .09
462 Eddie Murray SH .30 .09
463 Paul Molitor SH .20 .06
464 Hideo Nomo SH .20 .06
465 Barry Bonds SH .50 .15
466 Todd Hundley SH .20 .06
467 Rheal Cormier .20 .06
468 Jason Conti RC .25 .07
Jhensy Sandoval
469 Rod Barajas .40 .12
Jackie Rexrode RC
470 Cedric Bowers RC .40 .12
Jared Sandberg RC
471 Chei Gunner RC .25 .07
Paul Wilder
472 Mike Decelle .25 .07
Marcus McCain RC
473 Todd Zeile .20 .06
474 Neifi Perez .20 .06
475 Jeromy Burnitz .20 .06
476 Trey Beamon .20 .06
477 Braden Looper RC .40 .12
John Patterson
478 Danny Peoples .40 .12
Jake Westbrook RC
479 Eric Chavez 2.00 .60
Adam Eaton RC
480 Joe Lawrence RC .40 .12
Pete Tucci
481 Kris Benson .40 .12
Billy Koch RC
482 John Nicholson .25 .07
Andy Prater RC
483 Mark Johnson RC .40 .12
Mark Kotsay
484 Armando Benitez .20 .06
485 Mike Matheny .20 .06
486 Jeff Reed .20 .06
487 Mark Bellhorn .20 .06
Russ Johnson
Enrique Wilson
488 Ben Grieve .20 .06
Richard Hidalgo
Scott Morgan RC
489 Paul Konerko .20 .06
Derrek Lee UER
spelled Derek on back
Ron Wright
490 Wes Helms RC 4.00 1.20
Bill Mueller
Brad Seitzer
491 Jeff Abbott .20 .06
Shane Monahan
Edgard Velazquez
492 Jimmy Anderson RC .25 .07
Ron Blazier
Gerald Witasick
493 Darin Blood .20 .06
Heath Murray
Carl Pavano
494 Nelson Figueroa RC .40 .12
Mark Redman
Mike Villano
495 Checklist .20 .06
496 Checklist .20 .06
NNO Derek Jeter AU 120.00 36.00

1997 Topps All-Stars

Randomly inserted in Series one hobby and retail packs at a rate of one in 18 and one in every six jumbo packs, this 22-card set printed on rainbow foilboard features the top 11 players from each league and from each position as voted by the Topps Sports Department. The fronts carry a photo of a "first team" all-star player while the backs carry a different photo of that player alongside the "second team" and "third team" selections. Only the "first team" players are checklisted listed below.

	Nm-Mt	Ex-Mt
COMPLETE SET (22)	25.00	7.50
AS1 Ivan Rodriguez	1.50	.45
AS2 Todd Hundley	.60	.18
AS3 Frank Thomas	1.50	.45
AS4 Andres Galarraga	.60	.18
AS5 Chuck Knoblauch	.60	.18
AS6 Eric Young	.60	.18
AS7 Jim Thome	1.50	.45
AS8 Chipper Jones	1.50	.45
AS9 Cal Ripken	5.00	1.50
AS10 Barry Larkin	1.50	.45
AS11 Albert Belle	.60	.18
AS12 Barry Bonds	4.00	1.20
AS13 Ken Griffey Jr.	2.50	.75
AS14 Ellis Burks	.60	.18
AS15 Juan Gonzalez	1.50	.45
AS16 Gary Sheffield	.60	.18
AS17 Andy Pettitte	1.00	.30
AS18 Tom Glavine	1.00	.30
AS19 Pat Hentgen	.60	.18
AS20 John Smoltz	1.00	.30
AS21 Roberto Hernandez	.60	.18
AS22 Mark Wohlers	.60	.18

1997 Topps Awesome Impact

Randomly inserted in second series 11-card retail packs at a rate of 1:18, cards from this 20-card set feature a selection of top young stars and prospects. Each card front features a color player action shot cut out against a silver prismatic background.

	Nm-Mt	Ex-Mt
COMPLETE SET (20)	100.00	30.00
AI1 Jaime Bluma	3.00	.90
AI2 Tony Clark	3.00	.90
AI3 Jermaine Dye	3.00	.90
AI4 Nomar Garciaparra	12.00	3.60
AI5 Vladimir Guerrero	8.00	2.40
AI6 Todd Hollandsworth	3.00	.90
AI7 Derek Jeter	20.00	6.00
AI8 Andruw Jones	3.00	.90
AI9 Chipper Jones	8.00	2.40
AI10 Jason Kendall	3.00	.90
AI11 Brooks Kieschnick	3.00	.90
AI12 Alex Ochoa	3.00	.90
AI13 Rey Ordonez	3.00	.90
AI14 Neifi Perez	3.00	.90
AI15 Edgar Renteria	3.00	.90
AI16 Mariano Rivera	5.00	1.50
AI17 Ruben Rivera	3.00	.90
AI18 Scott Rolen	5.00	1.50
AI19 Billy Wagner	3.00	.90
AI20 Todd Walker	3.00	.90

1997 Topps Hobby Masters

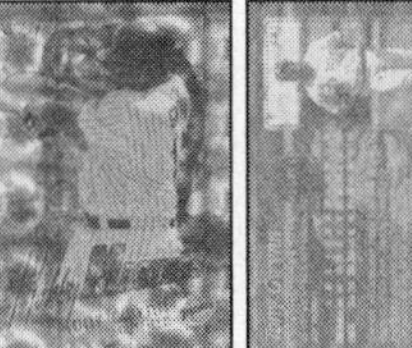

Randomly inserted in first and second series hobby packs at a rate of one in 36, cards from this 10-card set honor twenty players picked by hobby dealers from across the country as their all-time favorites. Cards 1-10 were issued in first series packs and 11-20 in second series. Printed on 28-point diffraction foilboard, one card replaces two regular cards when inserted in packs. The fronts feature borderless color player photos on a background of the player's profile. The backs carry player information.

	Nm-Mt	Ex-Mt
COMPLETE SET (20)	80.00	24.00
COMPLETE SERIES 1 (10)	40.00	12.00
COMPLETE SERIES 2 (10)	40.00	12.00
HM1 Ken Griffey Jr.	6.00	1.80
HM2 Cal Ripken	12.00	3.60
HM3 Greg Maddux	6.00	1.80
HM4 Albert Belle	1.50	.45
HM5 Tony Gwynn	5.00	1.50
HM6 Jeff Bagwell	2.50	.75
HM7 Randy Johnson	4.00	1.20
HM8 Raul Mondesi	1.50	.45
HM9 Juan Gonzalez	4.00	1.20
HM10 Kenny Lofton	1.50	.45
HM11 Frank Thomas	4.00	1.20
HM12 Mike Piazza	6.00	1.80
HM13 Chipper Jones	4.00	1.20
HM14 Brady Anderson	1.50	.45
HM15 Ken Caminiti	1.50	.45
HM16 Barry Bonds	10.00	3.00
HM17 Mo Vaughn	1.50	.45
HM18 Derek Jeter	10.00	3.00
HM19 Sammy Sosa	6.00	1.80
HM20 Andres Galarraga	1.50	.45

1997 Topps Inter-League Finest

Randomly inserted in Series one hobby and retail packs at a rate of one in 36 and jumbo packs at a rate of one in 10; this 14-card set features top individual match-ups from inter-league rivalries. One player from each major league team is represented on each side of this double-sided set with a color photo and is covered with the patented Finest clear protector.

	Nm-Mt	Ex-Mt
COMPLETE SET (14)	60.00	18.00
*REF.: 1X TO 2.5X BASIC INTER-LG...		
REF.SER.1 ODDS 1:216 HOB/RET, 1:56 JUM		
ILM1 Mark McGwire / Barry Bonds	10.00	3.00
ILM2 Tim Salmon / Mike Piazza	6.00	1.80
ILM3 Ken Griffey Jr. / Dante Bichette	6.00	1.80
ILM4 Juan Gonzalez / Tony Gwynn	5.00	1.50
ILM5 Frank Thomas / Sammy Sosa	6.00	1.80
ILM6 Albert Belle / Barry Larkin	1.50	.45
ILM7 Johnny Damon / Brian Jordan	1.50	.45
ILM8 Paul Molitor / Jeff King	2.50	.75
ILM9 John Jaha / Jeff Bagwell	2.50	.75
ILM10 Bernie Williams / Todd Hundley	2.50	.75
ILM11 Joe Carter / Henry Rodriguez	1.50	.45
ILM12 Cal Ripken / Gregg Jefferies	12.00	3.60
ILM13 Mo Vaughn / Chipper Jones	4.00	1.20
ILM14 Travis Fryman / Gary Sheffield	1.50	.45

1997 Topps Mantle

Randomly inserted at the rate of one in 12 Series one hobby/retail packs and one every three jumbo packs, this 16-card set features authentic reprints of Topps Mickey Mantle cards that were not reprinted last year. Each card is stamped with the commemorative gold foil logo.

	Nm-Mt	Ex-Mt
COMPLETE SET (16)	100.00	30.00
COMMON (21-36)	8.00	2.40
COMMON FINEST (21-36)	8.00	2.40
FINEST SER.2 1:24 HOB/RET, 1:6 JUM		
COMMON REF. (21-36)	30.00	9.00
REF.SER.2 1:216 HOB/RET,1:60 JUM.		

1997 Topps Mays

Randomly inserted at the rate of one in eight first series hobby/retail packs and one every two jumbo packs; cards from this 27-card set feature reprints of both the Topps and Bowman vintage Mays cards. Each card front is highlighted by a special commemorative gold foil stamp. Randomly inserted in first series hobby packs only (at the rate of one in 2,400) are personally signed cards. A special 4 1/4" by 5 3/4" jumbo reprint of the 1952 Topps Willie Mays card was made available exclusively in special series one Wal-Mart boxes. Each box (shaped much like a cereal box) contained ten eight-card retail packs and the aforementioned jumbo card and retailed for $10.

	Nm-Mt	Ex-Mt
COMPLETE SET (27)	100.00	30.00
COMMON MAYS (3-27)	4.00	1.20
COMMON FINEST (1-27)	4.00	1.20
*'51-'52 FINEST: .4X TO 1X BASIC MAYS REPRINTS		
FINEST SER.2 1:20 HOB/RET,1:4 JUM		
COMMON REF. (1-27)	10.00	3.00
*'51-'52 REF: 1X TO 2.5X BASIC MAYS REPRINTS		
REF.SER.2 1:180 HOB/RET,1:48 JUM.		
1 Willie Mays 1951 Bowman	8.00	2.40
2 Willie Mays 1952 Topps	6.00	1.80
J261 W.Mays 1952 Jumbo	6.00	1.80

1997 Topps Mays Autographs

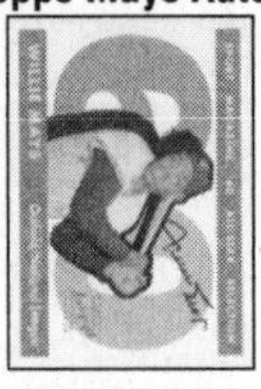

Acording to Topps, Mays signed about 65 each of the following cards: 51B, 52T, 53T, 55B, 55T, 57T, 58T, 60T, 60T AS, 61T, 61T AS, 63T, 64T, 65T, 66T, 69T, 70T, 72T, 73T. The cards all have a "Certified Topps Autograph" stamp on them.

	Nm-Mt	Ex-Mt
COMMON CARD (1953-1958)	120.00	36.00
COMMON CARD (1960-1973)	120.00	36.00
1 Willie Mays 1951 Bowman	200.00	60.00
2 Willie Mays 1952 Topps	200.00	60.00

1997 Topps Season's Best

This 25-card set was randomly inserted into Topps Series two packs at a rate of one every six hobby/retail packs and one per jumbo pack; this set features five top players from each of the following five statistical categories: Leading Looters (top base stealers), Bleacher Reachers (top home run hitters), Hill Toppers (most wins), Number Crunchers (most RBI's), Kings of Swings (top slugging percentages). The fronts display color player photos printed on prismatic illusion foilboard. The backs carry another player photo and statistics.

	Nm-Mt	Ex-Mt
COMPLETE SET (25)	25.00	7.50
SB1 Tony Gwynn	2.50	.75
SB2 Frank Thomas	2.00	.60
SB3 Ellis Burks	.75	.23
SB4 Paul Molitor	1.25	.35
SB5 Chuck Knoblauch	.75	.23
SB6 Mark McGwire	5.00	1.50
SB7 Brady Anderson	.75	.23
SB8 Ken Griffey Jr.	3.00	.90
SB9 Albert Belle	.75	.23
SB10 Andres Galarraga	.75	.23
SB11 Andres Galarraga	.75	.23
SB12 Albert Belle	.75	.23
SB13 Juan Gonzalez	2.00	.60
SB14 Mo Vaughn	.75	.23
SB15 Rafael Palmeiro	1.25	.35
SB16 John Smoltz	1.25	.35
SB17 Andy Pettitte	1.25	.35
SB18 Pat Hentgen	.75	.23
SB19 Mike Mussina	2.00	.60
SB20 Andy Benes	.75	.23
SB21 Kenny Lofton	.75	.23
SB22 Tom Goodwin	.75	.23
SB23 Otis Nixon	.75	.23
SB24 Eric Young	.75	.23
SB25 Lance Johnson	.75	.23

1997 Topps Sweet Strokes

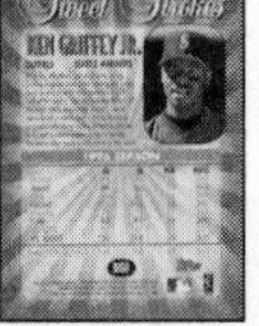

This 15-card retail only set was randomly inserted in series one retail packs at a rate of one in 12. Printed on Rainbow foilboard, the set features color photos of some of Baseball's top hitters.

	Nm-Mt	Ex-Mt
COMPLETE SET (15)	40.00	12.00
SS1 Roberto Alomar	2.50	.75
SS2 Jeff Bagwell	1.50	.45
SS3 Albert Belle	1.00	.30
SS4 Barry Bonds	6.00	1.80
SS5 Mark Grace	1.50	.45
SS6 Ken Griffey Jr.	4.00	1.20
SS7 Tony Gwynn	3.00	.90
SS8 Chipper Jones	2.50	.75
SS9 Edgar Martinez	1.50	.45
SS10 Mark McGwire	6.00	1.80
SS11 Rafael Palmeiro	1.50	.45
SS12 Mike Piazza	4.00	1.20
SS13 Gary Sheffield	1.00	.30
SS14 Frank Thomas	2.50	.75
SS15 Mo Vaughn	1.00	.30

1997 Topps Team Timber

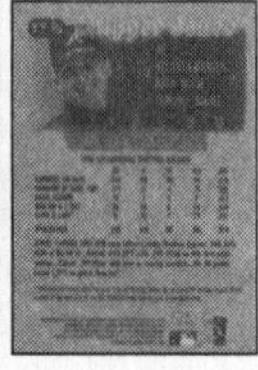

Randomly inserted into all second series hobby/retail packs at a rate of 1:36 and second series Hobby Collector (jumbo) packs at a rate of 1:8, cards from this 16-card set highlight a selection of baseball's top sluggers. Each card features a simulated wood-grain stock, but the fronts are UV-coated, making the cards bow noticeably.

	Nm-Mt	Ex-Mt
COMPLETE SET (16)	40.00	12.00
TT1 Ken Griffey Jr.	4.00	1.20
TT2 Ken Caminiti	1.00	.30
TT3 Bernie Williams	1.50	.45
TT4 Jeff Bagwell	1.50	.45
TT5 Frank Thomas	2.50	.75
TT6 Andres Galarraga	1.00	.30
TT7 Barry Bonds	6.00	1.80
TT8 Rafael Palmeiro	1.50	.45
TT9 Brady Anderson	1.00	.30
TT10 Juan Gonzalez	2.50	.75
TT11 Mo Vaughn	1.00	.30
TT12 Mark McGwire	6.00	1.80
TT13 Gary Sheffield	1.00	.30
TT14 Albert Belle	1.00	.30
TT15 Chipper Jones	2.50	.75
TT16 Mike Piazza	4.00	1.20

1997 Topps 22k Gold

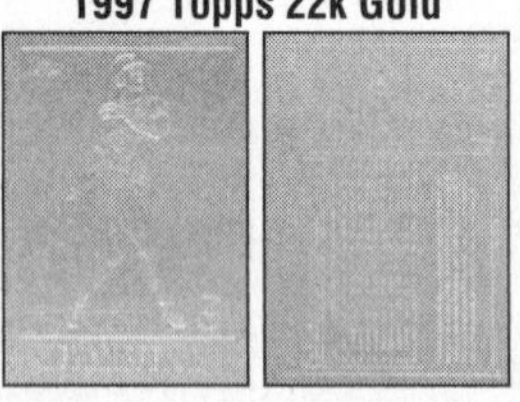

This one-card set is an embossed 22 karat gold foil replica of the 1997 Topps regular Ken Griffey Jr. card. Only a limited number of this set were produced and are serially numbered. Each card is packed in a protective display holder.

	Nm-Mt	Ex-Mt
1 Ken Griffey Jr.	30.00	9.00

1998 Topps Pre-Production

This six-card set was a preview of the 1998 Topps set and features color action player photos in gold borders with gold foil printing. The backs carry another player photo with player information and career statistics with white borders.

	Nm-Mt	Ex-Mt
COMPLETE SET (6)	8.00	2.40
PP1 Carlos Baerga	.40	.12
PP2 Jeff Bagwell	1.00	.30
PP3 Marquis Grissom	.40	.12
PP4 Derek Jeter	4.00	1.20
PP5 Randy Johnson	1.00	.30
PP6 Mike Piazza	3.00	.90

1998 Topps

This 503-card set was distributed in two separate series: 282 cards in first series and 221 cards in second series. 11-card packs carried a suggested retail price of $1.29. Cards were also distributed in Home Team Advantage jumbo packs and hobby, retail and Christmas factory sets. Card fronts feature color action player photos printed on 16 pt. stock with player information and career statistics on the back. Card number 7 was permanently retired in 1996 to honor Mickey Mantle. Series one contains the following subsets: Draft Picks (245-249), Prospects (250-259), Season Highlights (265-269), Interleague (270-274) Checklists (275-276) and World Series (277-283). Series two contains Season Highlights (474-478), Interleague (479-483), Prospects (484-495/498-501) and Checklists (502-503). Rookie Cards of note include Ryan Anderson, Michael Cuddyer, Jack Cust and Troy Glaus. This set also features Topps long-awaited first regular-issue Alex Rodriguez card (504). The superstar shortstop was left out of all Topps sets for the first four years of his career due to a problem between Topps and Rodriguez's agent Scott Boras. Finally, as part of an agreement with the Baseball Hall of Fame, Topps produced commemorative admission tickets featuring Roberto Clemente memorabilia from the Hall in the form of a Topps card. These were the standard admission tickets for the shrine, and were also included one per case in 1998 Topps series two baseball.

	Nm-Mt	Ex-Mt
COMPLETE SET (503)	80.00	24.00
COMP.HOBBY SET (511)	100.00	30.00
COMP.RETAIL SET (511)	100.00	30.00
COMP.SERIES 1 (282)	40.00	12.00
COMP.SERIES 2 (221)	40.00	12.00
1 Tony Gwynn	.60	.18
2 Larry Walker	.30	.09
3 Billy Wagner	.20	.06
4 Denny Neagle	.20	.06
5 Vladimir Guerrero	.50	.15
6 Kevin Brown	.30	.09
8 Mariano Rivera	.30	.09
9 Tony Clark	.20	.06
10 Deion Sanders	.30	.09
11 Francisco Cordova	.20	.06
12 Matt Williams	.20	.06
13 Carlos Baerga	.20	.06
14 Mo Vaughn	.20	.06
15 Bobby Witt	.20	.06
16 Matt Stairs	.20	.06
17 Chan Ho Park	.20	.06
18 Mike Bordick	.20	.06
19 Michael Tucker	.20	.06
20 Frank Thomas	.50	.15
21 Roberto Clemente	1.00	.30
22 Dmitri Young	.20	.06
23 Steve Trachsel	.20	.06
24 Jeff Kent	.20	.06
25 Scott Rolen	.30	.09
26 John Thomson	.20	.06
27 Joe Vitiello	.20	.06
28 Eddie Guardado	.20	.06
29 Charlie Hayes	.20	.06
30 Juan Gonzalez	.50	.15
31 Garret Anderson	.20	.06
32 John Jaha	.20	.06
33 Omar Vizquel	.20	.06
34 Brian Hunter	.20	.06
35 Jeff Bagwell	.30	.09
36 Mark Lemke	.20	.06
37 Doug Glanville	.20	.06
38 Dan Wilson	.20	.06
39 Steve Cooke	.20	.06
40 Chili Davis	.20	.06
41 Mike Cameron	.20	.06
42 F.P. Santangelo	.20	.06
43 Brad Ausmus	.20	.06
44 Gary DiSarcina	.20	.06
45 Pat Hentgen	.20	.06
46 Wilton Guerrero	.20	.06
47 Devon White	.20	.06
48 Danny Patterson	.20	.06
49 Pat Meares	.20	.06
50 Rafael Palmeiro	.30	.09
51 Mark Gardner	.20	.06
52 Jeff Blauser	.20	.06
53 Dave Hollins	.20	.06
54 Carlos Garcia	.20	.06
55 Ben McDonald	.20	.06
56 John Mabry	.20	.06
57 Trevor Hoffman	.20	.06
58 Tony Fernandez	.20	.06
59 Rich Loiselle	.20	.06
60 Mark Leiter	.20	.06
61 Pat Kelly	.20	.06
62 John Flaherty	.20	.06
63 Roger Bailey	.20	.06
64 Tom Gordon	.20	.06
65 Ryan Klesko	.20	.06
66 Darryl Hamilton	.20	.06
67 Jim Eisenreich	.20	.06
68 Butch Huskey	.20	.06
69 Mark Grudzielanek	.20	.06
70 Marquis Grissom	.20	.06
71 Mark McLemore	.20	.06
72 Gary Gaetti	.20	.06
73 Greg Gagne	.20	.06
74 Lyle Mouton	.20	.06
75 Jim Edmonds	.20	.06
76 Shawn Green	.20	.06
77 Greg Vaughn	.20	.06
78 Terry Adams	.20	.06
79 Kevin Polcovich	.20	.06
80 Troy O'Leary	.20	.06
81 Jeff Shaw	.20	.06
82 Rich Becker	.20	.06
83 David Wells	.20	.06
84 Steve Karsay	.20	.06
85 Charles Nagy	.20	.06
86 B.J. Surhoff	.20	.06
87 Jamey Wright	.20	.06
88 James Baldwin	.20	.06
89 Edgardo Alfonzo	.20	.06
90 Jay Buhner	.20	.06
91 Brady Anderson	.20	.06
92 Scott Servais	.20	.06
93 Edgar Renteria	.20	.06
94 Mike Lieberthal	.20	.06
95 Rick Aguilera	.20	.06
96 Walt Weiss	.20	.06
97 Deivi Cruz	.20	.06
98 Kurt Abbott	.20	.06
99 Henry Rodriguez	.20	.06
100 Mike Piazza	.75	.23
101 Bill Taylor	.20	.06
102 Todd Zeile	.20	.06
103 Rey Ordonez	.20	.06
104 Willie Greene	.20	.06
105 Tony Womack	.20	.06
106 Mike Sweeney	.20	.06
107 Jeffrey Hammonds	.20	.06
108 Kevin Orie	.20	.06
109 Alex Gonzalez	.20	.06
110 Jose Canseco	.50	.15
111 Paul Sorrento	.20	.06
112 Joey Hamilton	.20	.06
113 Brad Radke	.20	.06
114 Steve Avery	.20	.06
115 Esteban Loaiza	.20	.06
116 Stan Javier	.20	.06
117 Chris Gomez	.20	.06
118 Royce Clayton	.20	.06
119 Orlando Merced	.20	.06
120 Kevin Appier	.20	.06
121 Mel Nieves	.20	.06
122 Joe Girardi	.20	.06
123 Rico Brogna	.20	.06
124 Kent Mercker	.20	.06
125 Manny Ramirez	.20	.06
126 Jeromy Burnitz	.20	.06
127 Kevin Foster	.20	.06
128 Matt Morris	.20	.06
129 Jason Dickson	.20	.06
130 Tom Glavine	.30	.09
131 Wally Joyner	.20	.06
132 Rick Reed	.20	.06
133 Todd Jones	.20	.06
134 Dave Martinez	.20	.06
135 Sandy Alomar Jr.	.20	.06
136 Mike Lansing	.20	.06
137 Sean Berry	.20	.06
138 Doug Jones	.20	.06
139 Todd Stottlemyre	.20	.06
140 Jay Bell	.20	.06
141 Jaime Navarro	.20	.06
142 Chris Hoiles	.20	.06
143 Joey Cora	.20	.06
144 Scott Spiezio	.20	.06
145 Joe Carter	.20	.06
146 Jose Guillen	.20	.06
147 Damion Easley	.20	.06
148 Lee Stevens	.20	.06
149 Alex Fernandez	.20	.06
150 Randy Johnson	.50	.15
151 J.T. Snow	.20	.06
152 Chuck Finley	.20	.06
153 Bernard Gilkey	.20	.06
154 David Segui	.20	.06
155 Dante Bichette	.20	.06
156 Kevin Stocker	.20	.06
157 Carl Everett	.20	.06
158 Jose Valentin	.20	.06
159 Pokey Reese	.20	.06
160 Derek Jeter	1.25	.35
161 Roger Pavlik	.20	.06
162 Mark Wohlers	.20	.06
163 Ricky Bottalico	.20	.06
164 Ozzie Guillen	.20	.06
165 Mike Mussina	.50	.15
166 Gary Sheffield	.20	.06
167 Hideo Nomo	.50	.15
168 Mark Grace	.30	.09
169 Aaron Sele	.20	.06
170 Darryl Kile	.20	.06
171 Shawn Estes	.20	.06
172 Vinny Castilla	.20	.06
173 Ron Coomer	.20	.06
174 Jose Rosado	.20	.06
175 Kenny Lofton	.20	.06
176 Jason Giambi	.50	.15
177 Hal Morris	.20	.06
178 Darren Bragg	.20	.06
179 Orel Hershiser	.20	.06
180 Ray Lankford	.20	.06
181 Hideki Irabu	.20	.06
182 Kevin Young	.20	.06
183 Javy Lopez	.20	.06
184 Jeff Montgomery	.20	.06
185 Mike Holtz	.20	.06
186 George Williams	.20	.06
187 Cal Eldred	.20	.06
188 Tom Candiotti	.20	.06
189 Glenallen Hill	.20	.06
190 Brian Giles	.20	.06
191 Dave Mlicki	.20	.06
192 Garrett Stephenson	.20	.06
193 Jeff Frye	.20	.06
194 Joe Oliver	.20	.06
195 Bob Hamelin	.20	.06
196 Luis Sojo	.20	.06
197 LaTroy Hawkins	.20	.06
198 Kevin Elster	.20	.06
199 Jeff Reed	.20	.06
200 Dennis Eckersley	.20	.06
201 Bill Mueller	.20	.06
202 Russ Davis	.20	.06
203 Armando Benitez	.20	.06
204 Quilvio Veras	.20	.06
205 Tim Naehring	.20	.06
206 Quinton McCracken	.20	.06
207 Raul Casanova	.20	.06
208 Matt Lawton	.20	.06
209 Luis Alicea	.20	.06
210 Luis Gonzalez	.20	.06
211 Allen Watson	.20	.06
212 Gerald Williams	.20	.06
213 David Bell	.20	.06
214 Todd Hollandsworth	.20	.06
215 Wade Boggs	.30	.09
216 Jose Mesa	.20	.06
217 Jamie Moyer	.20	.06
218 Darren Daulton	.20	.06
219 Mickey Morandini	.20	.06
220 Rusty Greer	.20	.06
221 Jim Bullinger	.20	.06
222 Jose Offerman	.20	.06
223 Matt Karchner	.20	.06
224 Woody Williams	.20	.06
225 Mark Loretta	.20	.06
226 Mike Hampton	.20	.06
227 Willie Adams	.20	.06
228 Scott Hatteberg	.20	.06
229 Rich Amaral	.20	.06
230 Terry Steinbach	.20	.06
231 Glendon Rusch	.20	.06
232 Bret Boone	.20	.06
233 Robert Person	.20	.06
234 Jose Hernandez	.20	.06
235 Doug Drabek	.20	.06
236 Jason McDonald	.20	.06
237 Chris Widger	.20	.06
238 Tom Martin	.20	.06
239 Dave Burba	.20	.06
240 Pete Rose Jr.	.20	.06
241 Bobby Ayala	.20	.06
242 Tim Wakefield	.20	.06
243 Dennis Springer	.20	.06
244 Tim Belcher	.20	.06
245 Jon Garland Geoff Goetz	.20	.06
246 Glenn Davis Lance Berkman	.40	.12
247 Vernon Wells Aaron Akin	.40	.12
248 Adam Kennedy Jason Romano	.20	.06
249 Jason Dellaero Troy Cameron	.20	.06
250 Alex Sanchez Jared Sandberg	.20	.06
251 Pablo Ortega James Manias	.20	.06
252 Jason Conti RC Mike Stoner	.20	.06
253 John Patterson Larry Rodriguez	.20	.06
254 Adrian Beltre Ryan Minor RC Aaron Boone	.30	.09
255 Ben Grieve Brian Buchanan Dermal Brown	.20	.06
256 Kerrry Wood Carl Pavano Gil Meche	.60	.18
257 David Ortiz Daryle Ward Richie Sexson	.30	.09
258 Randy Winn Juan Encarnacion Andrew Vessel	.20	.06
259 Kris Benson Travis Smith Courtney Duncan RC	.20	.06
260 Chad Hermansen Brent Butler Warren Morris RC	.20	.06
261 Ben Davis Eli Marrero Ramon Hernandez	.20	.06
262 Eric Chavez Russell Branyan Russ Johnson	.40	.12
263 Todd Dunwoody RC John Barnes Ryan Jackson	.20	.06
264 Matt Clement Roy Halladay Brian Fuentes RC	.30	.09
265 Randy Johnson SH	.30	.09
266 Kevin Brown SH	.20	.06
267 Ricardo Rincon SH Francisco Cordova	.20	.06
268 N.Garciaparra SH	.50	.15
269 Tino Martinez SH	.20	.06
270 Chuck Knoblauch IL	.20	.06
271 Pedro Martinez IL	.30	.09
272 Denny Neagle IL	.20	.06
273 Juan Gonzalez IL	.30	.09
274 Andres Galarraga IL	.20	.06
275 Checklist	.20	.06
276 Checklist	.20	.06
277 Moises Alou WS	.20	.06
278 Sandy Alomar Jr. WS	.20	.06
279 Gary Sheffield WS	.20	.06
280 Matt Williams WS	.20	.06
281 Livan Hernandez WS	.20	.06
282 Chad Ogea WS	.20	.06
283 Marlins Champs	.20	.06
284 Tino Martinez	.30	.09
285 Roberto Alomar	.50	.15
286 Jeff King	.20	.06
287 Brian Jordan	.20	.06
288 Darin Erstad	.20	.06
289 Ken Caminiti	.20	.06
290 Jim Thome	.50	.15
291 Paul Molitor	.30	.09
292 Ivan Rodriguez	.50	.15
293 Bernie Williams	.30	.09
294 Todd Hundley	.20	.06
295 Andres Galarraga	.20	.06
296 Greg Maddux	.75	.23
297 Edgar Martinez	.30	.09
298 Ron Gant	.20	.06
299 Derek Bell	.20	.06
300 Roger Clemens	1.00	.30
301 Rondell White	.20	.06
302 Barry Larkin	.50	.15
303 Robin Ventura	.20	.06
304 Jason Kendall	.20	.06
305 Chipper Jones	.50	.15
306 John Franco	.20	.06
307 Sammy Sosa	.75	.23
308 Troy Percival	.20	.06
309 Chuck Knoblauch	.20	.06
310 Ellis Burks	.20	.06
311 Al Martin	.20	.06
312 Tim Salmon	.30	.09
313 Moises Alou	.20	.06
314 Lance Johnson	.20	.06
315 Justin Thompson	.20	.06
316 Will Clark	.50	.15
317 Barry Bonds	1.25	.35
318 Craig Biggio	.30	.09
319 John Smoltz	.30	.09
320 Cal Ripken	1.50	.45
321 Ken Griffey Jr.	.75	.23
322 Paul O'Neill	.30	.09
323 Todd Helton	.30	.09
324 John Olerud	.20	.06
325 Mark McGwire	1.25	.35
326 Jose Cruz Jr.	.20	.06
327 Jeff Cirillo	.20	.06
328 Dean Palmer	.20	.06
329 John Wetteland	.20	.06
330 Steve Finley	.20	.06
331 Albert Belle	.20	.06
332 Curt Schilling	.30	.09
333 Raul Mondesi	.20	.06
334 Andruw Jones	.20	.06
335 Nomar Garciaparra	.75	.23
336 David Justice	.20	.06
337 Andy Pettitte	.30	.09
338 Pedro Martinez	.50	.15

339 Travis Miller .20 .06
340 Chris Stynes .20 .06
341 Gregg Jefferies .20 .06
342 Jeff Fassero .20 .06
343 Craig Counsell .20 .06
344 Wilson Alvarez .20 .06
345 Bip Roberts .20 .06
346 Kelvim Escobar .20 .06
347 Mark Bellhorn .20 .06
348 Cory Lidle RC .40 .12
349 Fred McGriff .30 .09
350 Chuck Carr .20 .06
351 Bob Abreu .20 .06
352 Juan Guzman .20 .06
353 Fernando Vina .20 .06
354 Andy Benes .20 .06
355 Dave Nilsson .20 .06
356 Bobby Bonilla .20 .06
357 Ismael Valdes .20 .06
358 Carlos Perez .20 .06
359 Kirk Rueter .20 .06
360 Bartolo Colon .20 .06
361 Mel Rojas .20 .06
362 Johnny Damon .20 .06
363 Geronimo Berroa .20 .06
364 Reggie Sanders .20 .06
365 Jermaine Allensworth .20 .06
366 Orlando Cabrera .20 .06
367 Jorge Fabregas .20 .06
368 Scott Stahoviak .20 .06
369 Ken Cloude .20 .06
370 Donovan Osborne .20 .06
371 Roger Cedeno .20 .06
372 Neifi Perez .20 .06
373 Chris Holt .20 .06
374 Cecil Fielder .20 .06
375 Marty Cordova .20 .06
376 Tom Goodwin .20 .06
377 Jeff Suppan .20 .06
378 Jeff Brantley .20 .06
379 Mark Langston .20 .06
380 Shane Reynolds .20 .06
381 Mike Fetters .20 .06
382 Todd Greene .20 .06
383 Ray Durham .20 .06
384 Carlos Delgado .20 .06
385 Jeff D'Amico .20 .06
386 Brian McRae .20 .06
387 Alan Benes .20 .06
388 Heathcliff Slocumb .20 .06
389 Eric Young .20 .06
390 Travis Fryman .20 .06
391 David Cone .20 .06
392 Otis Nixon .20 .06
393 Jeremi Gonzalez .20 .06
394 Jeff Juden .20 .06
395 Jose Vizcaino .20 .06
396 Ugueth Urbina .20 .06
397 Ramon Martinez .20 .06
398 Robb Nen .20 .06
399 Harold Baines .20 .06
400 Delino DeShields .20 .06
401 John Burkett .20 .06
402 Sterling Hitchcock .20 .06
403 Mark Clark .20 .06
404 Terrell Wade .20 .06
405 Scott Brosius .20 .06
406 Chad Curtis .20 .06
407 Brian Johnson .20 .06
408 Roberto Kelly .20 .06
409 Dave Dellucci RC .20 .06
410 Michael Tucker .20 .06
411 Mark Kotsay .20 .06
412 Mark Lewis .20 .06
413 Ryan McGuire .20 .06
414 Shawon Dunston .20 .06
415 Brad Rigby .20 .06
416 Scott Erickson .20 .06
417 Bobby Jones .20 .06
418 Darren Oliver .20 .06
419 John Smiley .20 .06
420 T.J. Mathews .20 .06
421 Dustin Hermanson .20 .06
422 Mike Timlin .20 .06
423 Willie Blair .20 .06
424 Manny Alexander .20 .06
425 Bob Tewksbury .20 .06
426 Pete Schourek .20 .06
427 Reggie Jefferson .20 .06
428 Ed Sprague .20 .06
429 Jeff Conine .20 .06
430 Roberto Hernandez .20 .06
431 Tom Pagnozzi .20 .06
432 Jaret Wright .20 .06
433 Livan Hernandez .20 .06
434 Andy Ashby .20 .06
435 Todd Dunn .20 .06
436 Bobby Higginson .20 .06
437 Rod Beck .20 .06
438 Jim Leyritz .20 .06
439 Matt Williams .20 .06
440 Brett Tomko .20 .06
441 Joe Randa .20 .06
442 Chris Carpenter .20 .06
443 Dennis Reyes .20 .06
444 Al Leiter .20 .06
445 Jason Schmidt .20 .06
446 Ken Hill .20 .06
447 Shannon Stewart .20 .06
448 Enrique Wilson .20 .06
449 Fernando Tatis .20 .06
450 Jimmy Key .20 .06
451 Darrin Fletcher .20 .06
452 John Valentin .20 .06
453 Kevin Tapani .20 .06
454 Eric Karros .20 .06
455 Jay Bell .20 .06
456 Walt Weiss .20 .06
457 Devon White .20 .06
458 Carl Pavano .20 .06
459 Mike Lansing .20 .06
460 John Flaherty .20 .06
461 Richard Hidalgo .20 .06
462 Quinton McCracken .20 .06
463 Karim Garcia .20 .06
464 Miguel Cairo .20 .06
465 Edwin Diaz .20 .06
466 Bobby Smith .20 .06
467 Yamil Benitez .20 .06
468 Rich Butler .20 .06
469 Ben Ford RC .20 .06
470 Bubba Trammell .20 .06
471 Brent Brede .20 .06
472 Brooks Kieschnick .20 .06
473 Carlos Castillo .20 .06
474 Brad Radke SH .20 .06
475 Roger Clemens SH .50 .15
476 Curt Schilling SH .20 .06
477 John Olerud SH .20 .06
478 Mark McGwire SH .60 .18
479 Mike Piazza .50 .15
Ken Griffey Jr. IL
480 Jeff Bagwell .30 .09
Frank Thomas IL
481 Chipper Jones .30 .09
Nomar Garciaparra IL
482 Larry Walker .30 .09
Juan Gonzalez IL
483 Gary Sheffield .20 .06
Tino Martinez IL
484 Derrick Gibson .20 .06
Michael Coleman
Norm Hutchins
485 Braden Looper .20 .06
Cliff Politte
Brian Rose
486 Eric Milton .20 .06
Jason Marquis
Corey Lee
487 A.J.Hinch .50 .15
Mark Osborne
Robert Fick RC
488 Aramis Ramirez .30 .09
Alex Gonzalez
Sean Casey
489 Donnie Bridges .30 .09
Tim Drew RC
490 Ntema Ndungidi RC .30 .09
Darnell McDonald
491 Ryan Anderson RC .30 .09
Mark Mangum
492 J.J.Davis 1.50 .45
Troy Glaus RC
493 Jayson Werth RC .30 .09
Dan Reichert
494 John Curtice RC .50 .15
Michael Cuddyer RC
495 Jack Cust RC .30 .09
Jason Standridge
496 Brian Anderson .20 .06
497 Tony Saunders .20 .06
498 Vladimir Nunez .20 .06
Jhensy Sandoval
499 Brad Penny .30 .09
Nick Bierbrodt
500 Dustin Carr .20 .06
Luis Cruz RC
501 Cedric Bowers .20 .06
Marcus McCain
502 Checklist .20 .06
503 Checklist .20 .06
504 Alex Rodriguez 2.00 .60

1998 Topps Minted in Cooperstown

Randomly inserted in first and second series packs at the rate of one in eight, this 503 card set is a parallel version of the base set. The set is distinguished by the special "Minted in Cooperstown" logo stamped on each card. Similar to the regular set, card number 7 does not exist.

Nm-Mt Ex-Mt
*STARS: 5X TO 12X BASIC CARDS
*ROOKIES: 6X TO 15X BASIC CARDS

1998 Topps Inaugural Devil Rays

This 503 card set was issued by Topps only in factory set form. Just as for the teams which began play in 1993, special sets with a Devil Rays logo was issued. The sets were sold only through retail outlets. These sets apparently did not sell well enough at the stadium and were later closed out to one of the home shopping networks. The logo is in gold foil and is in the middle of the card.

Nm-Mt Ex-Mt
COMP.FACT.SET (503) 120.00 36.00
*STARS: 1.5X TO 4X BASIC CARDS
*ROOKIES: 2.5X TO 6X BASIC CARDS

1998 Topps Inaugural Diamondbacks

Similar to the Devil Rays set, Topps issued a factory set with the Diamond Backs logo to honor the first season the Arizona Diamondbacks played. The sets were issued in factory form and were only available through the Diamondback retail outlet.

Nm-Mt Ex-Mt
COMP.FACT.SET (503) 120.00 36.00
*STARS: 1.5X TO 4X BASIC CARDS
*ROOKIES: 2.5X TO 6X BASIC CARDS

1998 Topps Baby Boomers

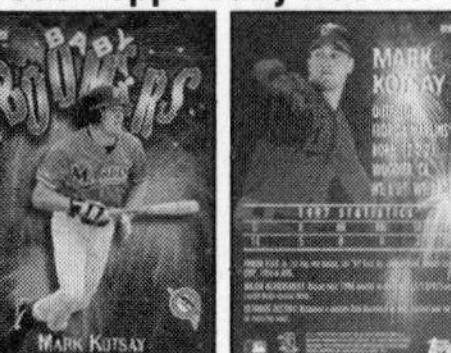

Randomly inserted in retail packs only at the rate of one in 36, this 15-card set features color photos of young players who have already made their mark in the game dispite less than three years in the majors.

Nm-Mt Ex-Mt
COMPLETE SET (15) 50.00 15.00
BB1 Derek Jeter 12.00 3.60
BB2 Scott Rolen 3.00 .90
BB3 Nomar Garciaparra 8.00 2.40
BB4 Jose Cruz Jr. 2.00 .60
BB5 Darin Erstad 2.00 .60
BB6 Todd Helton 3.00 .90
BB7 Tony Clark 2.00 .60
BB8 Jose Guillen 2.00 .60
BB9 Andruw Jones 2.00 .60
BB10 Vladimir Guerrero 5.00 1.50
BB11 Mark Kotsay 2.00 .60
BB12 Todd Greene 2.00 .60
BB13 Andy Pettitte 3.00 .90
BB14 Justin Thompson 2.00 .60
BB15 Alan Benes 2.00 .60

1998 Topps Clemente

Randomly inserted in first and second series packs at the rate of one in 18, cards from this 19-card set honor the memory of Roberto Clemente on the 25th anniversary of his untimely death with conventional reprints of his Topps cards. All odd numbered cards were seeded in first series packs. All even numbered cards were seeded in second series packs.

Nm-Mt Ex-Mt
COMPLETE SET (19) 120.00 36.00
COMPLETE SERIES 1 (10) 60.00 18.00
COMPLETE SERIES 2 (9) 60.00 18.00
COMMON CARD (2-19) 8.00 2.40
1 Roberto Clemente 1955 15.00 4.50

1998 Topps Clemente Memorabilia Madness

As a major promotion for 1998 Topps series one, Topps created 46 different Roberto Clemente exchange cards for a total of 854 prizes. All 46 prizes (including the quantity available of each prize) is detailed explicitly in the listings below. The quantity is noted immediately after the prize. All 854 exchange cards looked identical to each other on front and almost identical to each other on back. Card fronts feature a blue, purple and white dot matrix head shot of Clemente surrounded by burgundy borders. Card backs featured extensive guidelines and rules for the exchange program. The only difference for each card were the few sentences on back detailing which specific prize each of the 46 different cards could be exchanged for. Lucky collectors that got their hands on these scarce exchange cards had until August 31st, 1998 to redeem their prizes. Odds for pulling one of these cards was approximately 1:3,708 hobby packs and approximately 1:1,020 hobby collector packs. Prices for almost all of these exchange cards have been excluded due to scarcity and lack of market information.

Nm-Mt Ex-Mt
COMMON CARD (1-46) 80.00 24.00
NNO Wild Card 1.00 .30

1998 Topps Clemente Sealed

Each 1998 Topps hobby factory set contained one of 19 different hermetically sealed Roberto Clemente reprint cards. The actual cards are identical to standard Clemente reprints available in 1998 Topps packs. The difference in these special cards is the clear plastic seal entirely encasing the card. Each seal is stamped with a gold foil logo on the card back stating "Factory Topps Seal 1998".

Nm-Mt Ex-Mt
*SEALED: .4X TO 1X BASIC CLEMENTE

1998 Topps Clemente Tribute

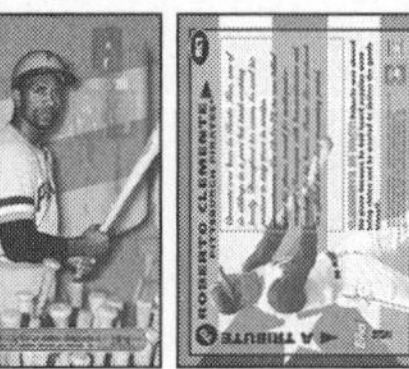

Randomly inserted in packs at the rate of one in 12, this five-card set honors the memory of Roberto Clemente on the 25th anniversary of his untimely death and features color photos printed on mirror foilboard on newly designed cards.

Nm-Mt Ex-Mt
COMPLETE SET (5) 8.00 2.40
COMMON (RC1-RC5) 2.00 .60

1998 Topps Clout Nine

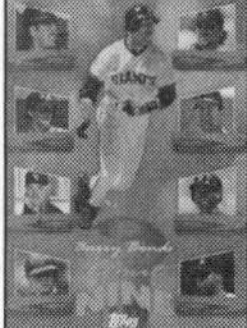

Randomly inserted in Topps Series two packs at the rate of one in 72, this nine-card set features color photos of the top players statiscally at each of the nine playing positions.

Nm-Mt Ex-Mt
COMPLETE SET (9) 40.00 12.00
C1 Edgar Martinez 4.00 1.20
C2 Mike Piazza 10.00 3.00
C3 Frank Thomas 6.00 1.80
C4 Craig Biggio 4.00 1.20
C5 Vinny Castilla 2.50 .75
C6 Jeff Blauser 2.50 .75
C7 Barry Bonds 15.00 4.50
C8 Ken Griffey Jr. 10.00 3.00
C9 Larry Walker 4.00 1.20

1998 Topps Etch-A-Sketch

Randomly inserted in Topps Series one packs at the rate of one in 36, this nine-card set features drawings by artist George Vlosich III of some of baseball's hottest superstars using an Etch A Sketch as a canvas.

Nm-Mt Ex-Mt
COMPLETE SET (9) 30.00 9.00
ES1 Albert Belle 1.25 .35
ES2 Barry Bonds 8.00 2.40
ES3 Ken Griffey Jr. 5.00 1.50
ES4 Greg Maddux 5.00 1.50
ES5 Hideo Nomo 3.00 .90
ES6 Mike Piazza 5.00 1.50
ES7 Cal Ripken 10.00 3.00
ES8 Frank Thomas 3.00 .90
ES9 Mo Vaughn 1.25 .35

1998 Topps Flashback

Randomly inserted in Topps Series one packs at the rate of one in 72, these two-sided cards of top players feature photographs of how they looked "then" as rookies on one side and how they look "now" as stars on the other.

Nm-Mt Ex-Mt
COMPLETE SET (10) 80.00 24.00
FB1 Barry Bonds 20.00 6.00
FB2 Ken Griffey Jr. 12.00 3.60
FB3 Paul Molitor 5.00 1.50
FB4 Randy Johnson 8.00 2.40
FB5 Cal Ripken 25.00 7.50
FB6 Tony Gwynn 10.00 3.00
FB7 Kenny Lofton 3.00 .90
FB8 Gary Sheffield 3.00 .90
FB9 Deion Sanders 5.00 1.50
FB10 Brady Anderson 3.00 .90

1998 Topps Focal Points

Randomly inserted in Topps Series two hobby packs only at the rate of one in 36, this 15-card set features color photos of current superstars with a special focus on the skills that have put them at the top.

Nm-Mt Ex-Mt
COMPLETE SET (15) 80.00 24.00
FP1 Juan Gonzalez 5.00 1.50
FP2 Nomar Garciaparra 8.00 2.40
FP3 Jose Cruz Jr. 2.00 .60
FP4 Cal Ripken 15.00 4.50
FP5 Ken Griffey Jr. 8.00 2.40
FP6 Ivan Rodriguez 5.00 1.50
FP7 Larry Walker 3.00 .90
FP8 Barry Bonds 12.00 3.60
FP9 Roger Clemens 10.00 3.00
FP10 Frank Thomas 5.00 1.50
FP11 Chuck Knoblauch 2.00 .60
FP12 Mike Piazza 8.00 2.40
FP13 Greg Maddux 8.00 2.40
FP14 Vladimir Guerrero 5.00 1.50
FP15 Andruw Jones 2.00 .60

1998 Topps HallBound

Randomly inserted in Topps Series one hobby packs only at the rate of one in 36, this 15-card set features color photos of top stars who are bound for the Hall of Fame printed on foil mirrorboard cards.

Nm-Mt Ex-Mt
COMPLETE SET (15) 80.00 24.00
HB1 Paul Molitor 3.00 .90
HB2 Tony Gwynn 6.00 1.80
HB3 Wade Boggs 3.00 .90
HB4 Roger Clemens 10.00 3.00
HB5 Dennis Eckersley 2.00 .60
HB6 Cal Ripken 15.00 4.50
HB7 Greg Maddux 8.00 2.40
HB8 Rickey Henderson 3.00 .90
HB9 Ken Griffey Jr. 8.00 2.40
HB10 Frank Thomas 5.00 1.50
HB11 Mark McGwire 12.00 3.60
HB12 Barry Bonds 12.00 3.60
HB13 Mike Piazza 8.00 2.40
HB14 Juan Gonzalez 5.00 1.50
HB15 Randy Johnson 5.00 1.50

1998 Topps Milestones

Randomly inserted in Topps Series two retail packs only at the rate of one in 36, this ten-card set features color photos of players with the ability to set new records in the sport.

Nm-Mt Ex-Mt
COMPLETE SET (10) 50.00 15.00
MS1 Barry Bonds 10.00 3.00
MS2 Roger Clemens 8.00 2.40
MS3 Dennis Eckersley 1.50 .45
MS4 Juan Gonzalez 4.00 1.20
MS5 Ken Griffey Jr. 6.00 1.80
MS6 Tony Gwynn 5.00 1.50
MS7 Greg Maddux 6.00 1.80
MS8 Mark McGwire 10.00 3.00
MS9 Cal Ripken 12.00 3.60
MS10 Frank Thomas 4.00 1.20

1998 Topps Mystery Finest

Randomly inserted in first series packs at the rate of one in 36, this 20-card set features color action player photos which showcase five of the 1997 season's most intriguing inter-league matchups.

Nm-Mt Ex-Mt
COMPLETE SET (20) 80.00 24.00
*REFRACTOR: 1X TO 2.5X BASIC MYS.FIN.
REFRACTOR SER.1 STATED ODDS: 1:144
ILM1 Chipper Jones 5.00 1.50
ILM2 Cal Ripken 15.00 4.50
ILM3 Greg Maddux 8.00 2.40
ILM4 Rafael Palmeiro 3.00 .90
ILM5 Todd Hundley 2.00 .60
ILM6 Derek Jeter 12.00 3.60
ILM7 John Olerud 2.00 .60
ILM8 Tino Martinez 3.00 .90
ILM9 Larry Walker 3.00 .90
ILM10 Ken Griffey Jr. 8.00 2.40
ILM11 Andres Galarraga 2.00 .60
ILM12 Randy Johnson 5.00 1.50
ILM13 Mike Piazza 8.00 2.40
ILM14 Jim Edmonds 2.00 .60
ILM15 Eric Karros 2.00 .60
ILM16 Tim Salmon 3.00 .90
ILM17 Sammy Sosa 8.00 2.40
ILM18 Frank Thomas 5.00 1.50
ILM19 Mark Grace 3.00 .90
ILM20 Albert Belle 2.00 .60

1998 Topps Mystery Finest Bordered

Randomly inserted in Topps Series two packs at the rate of one in 36, this 20-card set features bordered color player photos of current hot players.

	Nm-Mt	Ex-Mt
COMPLETE SET (20)	100.00	30.00
*BORDERED REF: .75X TO 2X BORDERED		
BORDERED REF.SER.2 ODDS 1:108...		
*BORDERLESS: .6X TO 1.5X BORDERED		
BORDERLESS SER.2 ODDS 1:72		
*BORDERLESS REF: 1.25X TO 3X BORDERED		
BORDERLESS REF.SER.2 ODDS 1:288		
M1 Nomar Garciaparra	8.00	2.40
M2 Chipper Jones	5.00	1.50
M3 Scott Rolen	3.00	.90
M4 Albert Belle	2.00	.60
M5 Mo Vaughn	2.00	.60
M6 Jose Cruz Jr.	2.00	.60
M7 Mark McGwire	12.00	3.60
M8 Derek Jeter	12.00	3.60
M9 Tony Gwynn	6.00	1.80
M10 Frank Thomas	5.00	1.50
M11 Tino Martinez	3.00	.90
M12 Greg Maddux	8.00	2.40
M13 Juan Gonzalez	5.00	1.50
M14 Larry Walker	3.00	.90
M15 Mike Piazza	8.00	2.40
M16 Cal Ripken	15.00	4.50
M17 Jeff Bagwell	3.00	.90
M18 Andruw Jones	2.00	.60
M19 Barry Bonds	12.00	3.60
M20 Ken Griffey Jr.	8.00	2.40

1998 Topps Rookie Class

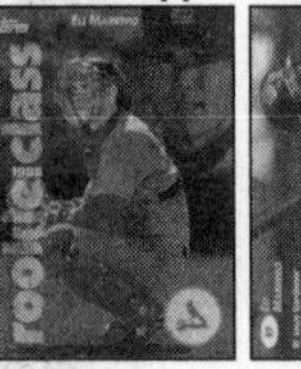

Randomly inserted in Topps Series two packs at the rate of one in 12, this 10-card set features color photos of top young stars with less than one year's playing time in the Majors. The backs carry player information.

	Nm-Mt	Ex-Mt
COMPLETE SET (10)	6.00	1.80
R1 Travis Lee	.75	.23
R2 Richard Hidalgo	.75	.23
R3 Todd Helton	1.25	.35
R4 Paul Konerko	.75	.23
R5 Mark Kotsay	.75	.23
R6 Derrek Lee	.75	.23
R7 Eli Marrero	.75	.23
R8 Fernando Tatis	.75	.23
R9 Juan Encarnacion	.75	.23
R10 Ben Grieve	.75	.23

1998 Topps Fruit Roll-Ups

This eight-card set measures approximately 1 1/2" by 2" and were found on boxes of specially marked 38-pack Betty Crocker Fruit Roll-ups. The fronts of these perforated cards feature color action player photos with a thin red border. The backs are blank. The cards are unnumbered and checklisted below in alphabetical order.

	Nm-Mt	Ex-Mt
COMPLETE SET (8)	20.00	6.00
1 Tony Gwynn	2.50	.75
2 Derek Jeter	5.00	1.50
3 Kenny Lofton	.50	.15
4 Mark McGwire	4.00	1.20
5 Mike Piazza	3.00	.90
6 Cal Ripken	5.00	1.50
7 Ivan Rodriguez	1.25	.35
8 Frank Thomas	1.25	.35

1999 Topps Pre-Production

Distributed in six-card cello packs to wholesale hobby and retail accounts in October 1998, these cards were intended to preview the upcoming 1999 Topps series one release. The cards are identical in design to basic issue 1999 Topps cards except for the "PP" based numbering on back.

	Nm-Mt	Ex-Mt
COMPLETE SET (6)	10.00	3.00
PP1 Roger Clemens	2.50	.75
PP2 Sammy Sosa	2.50	.75
PP3 Derek Jeter	5.00	1.50
PP4 Walt Weiss	.25	.07
PP5 Darin Erstad	1.00	.30
PP6 Jason Kendall	.75	.23

1999 Topps

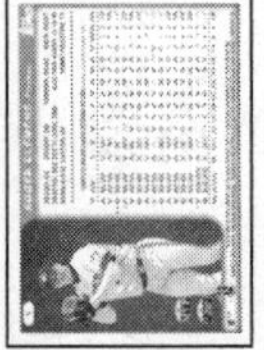

The 1999 Topps set consisted of 462 standard-size cards. Each 11 card pack carried a suggested retail price of $1.29 per pack. Cards were also distributed in 40-card Home Team advantage jumbo packs, hobby, retail and Christmas factory sets. The Mark McGwire number 220 card was issued in 70 different varieties to honor his record setting season. The Sammy Sosa number 461 card was issued in 66 different varieties to honor his 1998 season. Basic sets are considered complete with any one of the 70 McGwire and 66 Sosa variations. A.J. Burnett, Pat Burrell, and Alex Escobar are the most notable Rookie Cards in the set. Card number 7 was not issued as Topps continues to honor the memory of Mickey Mantle. The Christmas factory set contains one Nolan Ryan finest reprint card as an added bonus, while the hobby and retail factory sets just contained the regular sets in a factory box.

	Nm-Mt	Ex-Mt
COMPLETE SET (462)	80.00	24.00
COMP.HOBBY SET (462)	80.00	24.00
COMP.X-MAS SET (463)	80.00	24.00
COMP. SERIES 1 (241)	40.00	12.00
COMP. SERIES 2 (221)	40.00	12.00
COMP.MAC HR SET (70)	400.00	120.00
COMP.SOSA HR SET (66)	200.00	60.00
1 Roger Clemens	1.00	.30
2 Andres Galarraga	.20	.06
3 Scott Brosius	.20	.06
4 John Flaherty	.20	.06
5 Jim Leyritz	.20	.06
6 Ray Durham	.20	.06
8 Jose Vizcaino	.20	.06
9 Will Clark	.50	.15
10 David Wells	.20	.06
11 Jose Guillen	.20	.06
12 Scott Hatteberg	.20	.06
13 Edgardo Alfonzo	.20	.06
14 Mike Bordick	.20	.06
15 Manny Ramirez	.20	.06
16 Greg Maddux	.75	.23
17 David Segui	.20	.06
18 Darryl Strawberry	.30	.09
19 Brad Radke	.20	.06
20 Kerry Wood	.50	.15
21 Matt Anderson	.20	.06
22 Derrek Lee	.20	.06
23 Mickey Morandini	.20	.06
24 Paul Konerko	.20	.06
25 Travis Lee	.20	.06
26 Ken Hill	.20	.06
27 Kenny Rogers	.20	.06
28 Paul Sorrento	.20	.06
29 Quilvio Veras	.20	.06
30 Todd Walker	.20	.06
31 Ryan Jackson	.20	.06
32 John Olerud	.20	.06
33 Doug Glanville	.20	.06
34 Nolan Ryan	2.00	.60
35 Ray Lankford	.20	.06
36 Mark Loretta	.20	.06
37 Jason Dickson	.20	.06
38 Sean Bergman	.20	.06
39 Quinton McCracken	.20	.06
40 Bartolo Colon	.20	.06
41 Brady Anderson	.20	.06
42 Chris Stynes	.20	.06
43 Jorge Posada	.30	.09
44 Justin Thompson	.20	.06
45 Johnny Damon	.20	.06
46 Armando Benitez	.20	.06
47 Brant Brown	.20	.06
48 Charlie Hayes	.20	.06
49 Darren Dreifort	.20	.06
50 Juan Gonzalez	.50	.15
51 Chuck Knoblauch	.20	.06
52 Todd Helton	.30	.09
53 Rick Reed	.20	.06
54 Chris Gomez	.20	.06
55 Gary Sheffield	.20	.06
56 Rod Beck	.20	.06
57 Rey Sanchez	.20	.06
58 Garret Anderson	.20	.06
59 Jimmy Haynes	.20	.06
60 Steve Woodard	.20	.06
61 Rondell White	.20	.06
62 Vladimir Guerrero	.50	.15
63 Eric Karros	.20	.06
64 Russ Davis	.20	.06
65 Mo Vaughn	.20	.06
66 Sammy Sosa	.75	.23
67 Troy Percival	.20	.06
68 Kenny Lofton	.20	.06
69 Bill Taylor	.20	.06
70 Mark McGwire	1.25	.35
71 Roger Cedeno	.20	.06
72 Javy Lopez	.20	.06
73 Damion Easley	.20	.06
74 Andy Pettitte	.30	.09
75 Tony Gwynn	.60	.18
76 Ricardo Rincon	.20	.06
77 F.P. Santangelo	.20	.06
78 Jay Bell	.20	.06
79 Scott Servais	.20	.06
80 Jose Canseco	.50	.15
81 Roberto Hernandez	.20	.06
82 Todd Dunwoody	.20	.06
83 John Wetteland	.20	.06
84 Mike Caruso	.20	.06
85 Derek Jeter	1.25	.35
86 Aaron Sele	.20	.06
87 Jose Lima	.20	.06
88 Ryan Christenson	.20	.06
89 Jeff Cirillo	.20	.06
90 Jose Hernandez	.20	.06
91 Mark Kotsay	.20	.06
92 Darren Bragg	.20	.06
93 Albert Belle	.20	.06
94 Matt Lawton	.20	.06
95 Pedro Martinez	.50	.15
96 Greg Vaughn	.20	.06
97 Neifi Perez	.20	.06
98 Gerald Williams	.20	.06
99 Derek Bell	.20	.06
100 Ken Griffey Jr.	.75	.23
101 David Cone	.20	.06
102 Brian Johnson	.20	.06
103 Dean Palmer	.20	.06
104 Javier Valentin	.20	.06
105 Trevor Hoffman	.20	.06
106 Butch Huskey	.20	.06
107 Dave Martinez	.20	.06
108 Billy Wagner	.20	.06
109 Shawn Green	.20	.06
110 Ben Grieve	.20	.06
111 Tom Goodwin	.20	.06
112 Jaret Wright	.20	.06
113 Aramis Ramirez	.20	.06
114 Dmitri Young	.20	.06
115 Hideki Irabu	.20	.06
116 Roberto Kelly	.20	.06
117 Jeff Fassero	.20	.06
118 Mark Clark UER	.20	.06
1997 and Career Victory totals are wrong		
119 Jason McDonald	.20	.06
120 Matt Williams	.20	.06
121 Dave Burba	.20	.06
122 Bret Saberhagen	.20	.06
123 Deivi Cruz	.20	.06
124 Chad Curtis	.20	.06
125 Scott Rolen	.30	.09
126 Lee Stevens	.20	.06
127 J.T. Snow	.20	.06
128 Rusty Greer	.20	.06
129 Brian Meadows	.20	.06
130 Jim Edmonds	.20	.06
131 Ron Gant	.20	.06
132 A.J. Hinch UER	.20	.06
Photo is a reverse negative		
133 Shannon Stewart	.20	.06
134 Brad Fullmer	.20	.06
135 Cal Eldred	.20	.06
136 Matt Walbeck	.20	.06
137 Carl Everett	.20	.06
138 Walt Weiss	.20	.06
139 Fred McGriff	.30	.09
140 Darin Erstad	.20	.06
141 Dave Nilsson	.20	.06
142 Eric Young	.20	.06
143 Dan Wilson	.20	.06
144 Jeff Reed	.20	.06
145 Brett Tomko	.20	.06
146 Terry Steinbach	.20	.06
147 Seth Greisinger	.20	.06
148 Pat Meares	.20	.06
149 Livan Hernandez	.20	.06
150 Jeff Bagwell	.30	.09
151 Bob Wickman	.20	.06
152 Omar Vizquel	.20	.06
153 Eric Davis	.20	.06
154 Larry Sutton	.20	.06
155 Magglio Ordonez	.20	.06
156 Eric Milton	.20	.06
157 Darren Lewis	.20	.06
158 Rick Aguilera	.20	.06
159 Mike Lieberthal	.20	.06
160 Robb Nen	.20	.06
161 Brian Giles	.20	.06
162 Jeff Brantley	.20	.06
163 Gary DiSarcina	.20	.06
164 John Valentin	.20	.06
165 David Dellucci	.20	.06
166 Chan Ho Park	.20	.06
167 Masato Yoshii	.20	.06
168 Jason Schmidt	.20	.06
169 LaTroy Hawkins	.20	.06
170 Bret Boone	.20	.06
171 Jerry DiPoto	.20	.06
172 Mariano Rivera	.30	.09
173 Mike Cameron	.20	.06
174 Scott Erickson	.20	.06
175 Charles Johnson	.20	.06
176 Bobby Jones	.20	.06
177 Francisco Cordova	.20	.06
178 Todd Jones	.20	.06
179 Jeff Montgomery	.20	.06
180 Mike Mussina	.50	.15
181 Bob Abreu	.20	.06
182 Ismael Valdes	.20	.06
183 Andy Fox	.20	.06
184 Woody Williams	.20	.06
185 Denny Neagle	.20	.06
186 Jose Valentin	.20	.06
187 Darrin Fletcher	.20	.06
188 Gabe Alvarez	.20	.06
189 Eddie Taubensee	.20	.06
190 Edgar Martinez	.30	.09
191 Jason Kendall	.20	.06
192 Darryl Kile	.20	.06
193 Jeff King	.20	.06
194 Rey Ordonez	.20	.06
195 Andruw Jones	.20	.06
196 Tony Fernandez	.20	.06
197 Jamey Wright	.20	.06
198 B.J. Surhoff	.20	.06
199 Vinny Castilla	.20	.06
200 David Wells HL	.20	.06
201 Mark McGwire HL	.60	.18
202 Sammy Sosa HL	.50	.15
203 Roger Clemens HL	.50	.15
204 Kerry Wood HL	.30	.09
205 Lance Berkman	.40	.12
Mike Frank		
Gabe Kapler		
206 Alex Escobar RC	.40	.12
Ricky Ledee		
Mike Stoner		
207 Peter Bergeron RC	.40	.12
Jeremy Giambi		
George Lombard		
208 Michael Barrett	.25	.07
Ben Davis		
Robert Fick		
209 Pat Cline	.25	.07
Ramon Hernandez		
Jayson Werth		
210 Bruce Chen	.25	.07
Chris Enochs		
Ryan Anderson		
211 Mike Lincoln	.25	.07
Octavio Dotel		
Brad Penny		
212 Chuck Abbott RC	.25	.07
Brent Butler		
Danny Klassen		
213 Chris C.Jones	.40	.12
Jeff Urban RC		
214 Arturo McDowell RC	.40	.12
Tony Torcato		
215 Josh McKinley RC	.40	.12
Jason Tyner		
216 Matt Burch	.40	.12
Seth Etheron RC		
UER back Etherton		
217 Mamon Tucker RC	.40	.12
Rick Elder		
218 J.M.Gold	.40	.12
Ryan Mills RC		
219 Adam Brown	.40	.12
Choo Freeman RC		
220A Mark McGwire HR 1	40.00	12.00
220B Mark McGwire HR 2	15.00	4.50
220C Mark McGwire HR 3	15.00	4.50
220D Mark McGwire HR 4	15.00	4.50
220E Mark McGwire HR 5	15.00	4.50
220F Mark McGwire HR 6	15.00	4.50
220G Mark McGwire HR 7	15.00	4.50
220H Mark McGwire HR 8	15.00	4.50
220I Mark McGwire HR 9	15.00	4.50
220J M.McGwire HR 10	15.00	4.50
220K M.McGwire HR 11	15.00	4.50
220L M.McGwire HR 12	15.00	4.50
220M M.McGwire HR 13	15.00	4.50
220N M.McGwire HR 14	15.00	4.50
220O M.McGwire HR 15	15.00	4.50
220P M.McGwire HR 16	15.00	4.50
220Q M.McGwire HR 17	15.00	4.50
220R M.McGwire HR 18	15.00	4.50
220S M.McGwire HR 19	15.00	4.50
220T M.McGwire HR 20	15.00	4.50
220U M.McGwire HR 21	15.00	4.50
220V M.McGwire HR 22	15.00	4.50
220W M.McGwire HR 23	15.00	4.50
220X M.McGwire HR 24	15.00	4.50
220Y M.McGwire HR 25	15.00	4.50
220Z M.McGwire HR 26	15.00	4.50
220AA M.McGwire HR 27	15.00	4.50
220AB M.McGwire HR 28	15.00	4.50
220AC M.McGwire HR 29	15.00	4.50
220AD M.McGwire HR 30	15.00	4.50
220AE M.McGwire HR 31	15.00	4.50
220AF M.McGwire HR 32	15.00	4.50
220AG M.McGwire HR 33	15.00	4.50
220AH M.McGwire HR 34	15.00	4.50
220AI M.McGwire HR 35	15.00	4.50
220AJ M.McGwire HR 36	15.00	4.50
220AK M.McGwire HR 37	15.00	4.50
220AL M.McGwire HR 38	15.00	4.50
220AM M.McGwire HR 39	15.00	4.50
220AN M.McGwire HR 40	15.00	4.50
220AO M.McGwire HR 41	15.00	4.50
220AP M.McGwire HR 42	15.00	4.50
220AQ M.McGwire HR 43	15.00	4.50
220AR M.McGwire HR 44	15.00	4.50
220AS M.McGwire HR 45	15.00	4.50
220AT M.McGwire HR 46	15.00	4.50
220AU M.McGwire HR 47	15.00	4.50
220AV M.McGwire HR 48	15.00	4.50
220AW M.McGwire HR 49	15.00	4.50
220AX M.McGwire HR 50	15.00	4.50
220AY M.McGwire HR 51	15.00	4.50
220AZ M.McGwire HR 52	15.00	4.50
220BB M.McGwire HR 53	15.00	4.50
220CC M.McGwire HR 54	15.00	4.50
220DD M.McGwire HR 55	15.00	4.50
220EE M.McGwire HR 56	15.00	4.50
220FF M.McGwire HR 57	15.00	4.50
220GG M.McGwire HR 58	15.00	4.50
220HH M.McGwire HR 59	15.00	4.50
220II M.McGwire HR 60	15.00	4.50
220JJ M.McGwire HR 61	30.00	9.00
220KK M.McGwire HR 62	40.00	12.00
220LL M.McGwire HR 63	15.00	4.50
220MM M.McGwire HR 64	15.00	4.50
220NN M.McGwire HR 65	15.00	4.50
220OO M.McGwire HR 66	15.00	4.50
220PP M.McGwire HR 67	15.00	4.50
220QQ M.McGwire HR 68	15.00	4.50
220RR M.McGwire HR 69	15.00	4.50
220SS M.McGwire HR 70	80.00	24.00
221 Larry Walker LL	.20	.06
222 Bernie Williams LL	.20	.06
223 Mark McGwire LL	.60	.18
224 Ken Griffey Jr. LL	.50	.15
225 Sammy Sosa LL	.50	.15
226 Juan Gonzalez LL	.30	.09
227 Dante Bichette LL	.20	.06
228 Alex Rodriguez LL	.50	.15
229 Sammy Sosa LL	.50	.15
230 Derek Jeter LL	.60	.18
231 Greg Maddux LL	.50	.15
232 Roger Clemens LL	.50	.15
233 Ricky Ledee WS	.20	.06
234 Chuck Knoblauch WS	.20	.06
235 Bernie Williams WS	.20	.06
236 Tino Martinez WS	.20	.06
237 Orl. Hernandez WS	.20	.06
238 Scott Brosius WS	.20	.06
239 Andy Pettitte WS	.20	.06
240 Mariano Rivera WS	.20	.06
241 Checklist 1	.20	.06
242 Checklist 2	.20	.06
243 Tom Glavine	.30	.09
244 Andy Benes	.20	.06
245 Sandy Alomar Jr.	.20	.06
246 Wilton Guerrero	.20	.06
247 Alex Gonzalez	.20	.06
248 Roberto Alomar	.50	.15
249 Ruben Rivera	.20	.06
250 Eric Chavez	.20	.06
251 Ellis Burks	.20	.06
252 Richie Sexson	.20	.06
253 Steve Finley	.20	.06
254 Dwight Gooden	.30	.09
255 Dustin Hermanson	.20	.06
256 Kirk Rueter	.20	.06
257 Steve Trachsel	.20	.06
258 Gregg Jefferies	.20	.06
259 Matt Stairs	.20	.06
260 Shane Reynolds	.20	.06
261 Gregg Olson	.20	.06
262 Kevin Tapani	.20	.06
263 Matt Morris	.20	.06
264 Carl Pavano	.20	.06
265 Nomar Garciaparra	.75	.23
266 Kevin Young	.20	.06
267 Rick Helling	.20	.06
268 Matt Franco	.20	.06
269 Brian McRae	.20	.06
270 Cal Ripken	1.50	.45
271 Jeff Abbott	.20	.06
272 Tony Batista	.20	.06
273 Bill Simas	.20	.06
274 Brian Hunter	.20	.06
275 John Franco	.20	.06
276 Devon White	.20	.06
277 Rickey Henderson	.50	.15
278 Chuck Finley	.20	.06
279 Mike Blowers	.20	.06
280 Mark Grace	.30	.09
281 Randy Winn	.20	.06
282 Bobby Bonilla	.20	.06
283 David Justice	.20	.06
284 Shane Monahan	.20	.06
285 Kevin Brown	.30	.09
286 Todd Zeile	.20	.06
287 Al Martin	.20	.06
288 Troy O'Leary	.20	.06
289 Darryl Hamilton	.20	.06
290 Tino Martinez	.30	.09
291 David Ortiz	.20	.06
292 Tony Clark	.20	.06
293 Ryan Minor	.20	.06
294 Mark Leiter	.20	.06
295 Wally Joyner	.20	.06
296 Cliff Floyd	.20	.06
297 Shawn Estes	.20	.06
298 Pat Hentgen	.20	.06
299 Scott Elarton	.20	.06
300 Alex Rodriguez	.75	.23
301 Ozzie Guillen	.20	.06
302 Hideo Nomo	.50	.15
303 Ryan McGuire	.20	.06
304 Brad Ausmus	.20	.06
305 Alex Gonzalez	.20	.06
306 Brian Jordan	.20	.06
307 John Jaha	.20	.06
308 Mark Grudzielanek	.20	.06
309 Juan Guzman	.20	.06
310 Tony Womack	.20	.06
311 Dennis Reyes	.20	.06
312 Marty Cordova	.20	.06
313 Ramiro Mendoza	.20	.06
314 Robin Ventura	.20	.06
315 Rafael Palmeiro	.30	.09
316 Ramon Martinez	.20	.06
317 Pedro Astacio	.20	.06
318 Dave Hollins	.20	.06
319 Tom Candiotti	.20	.06
320 Al Leiter	.20	.06
321 Rico Brogna	.20	.06
322 Reggie Jefferson	.20	.06
323 Bernard Gilkey	.20	.06
324 Jason Giambi	.50	.15
325 Craig Biggio	.30	.09
326 Troy Glaus	.30	.09
327 Delino DeShields	.20	.06
328 Fernando Vina	.20	.06
329 John Smoltz	.30	.09
330 Jeff Kent	.20	.06
331 Roy Halladay	.20	.06
332 Andy Ashby	.20	.06
333 Tim Wakefield	.20	.06
334 Roger Clemens	1.00	.30
335 Bernie Williams	.30	.09
336 Desi Relaford	.20	.06
337 John Burkett	.20	.06
338 Mike Hampton	.20	.06
339 Royce Clayton	.20	.06
340 Mike Piazza	.75	.23
341 Jeremi Gonzalez	.20	.06
342 Mike Lansing	.20	.06
343 Jamie Moyer	.20	.06
344 Ron Coomer	.20	.06
345 Barry Larkin	.50	.15
346 Fernando Tatis	.20	.06
347 Chili Davis	.20	.06
348 Bobby Higginson	.20	.06
349 Hal Morris	.20	.06
350 Larry Walker	.30	.09
351 Carlos Guillen	.20	.06
352 Miguel Tejada	.20	.06
353 Travis Fryman	.20	.06
354 Jarrod Washburn	.20	.06
355 Chipper Jones	.50	.15
356 Todd Stottlemyre	.20	.06
357 Henry Rodriguez	.20	.06
358 Eli Marrero	.20	.06
359 Alan Benes	.20	.06
360 Tim Salmon	.30	.09
361 Luis Gonzalez	.20	.06
362 Scott Spiezio	.20	.06
363 Chris Carpenter	.20	.06
364 Bobby Howry	.20	.06
365 Raul Mondesi	.20	.06
366 Ugueth Urbina	.20	.06
367 Tom Evans	.20	.06
368 Kerry Ligtenberg RC	.25	.07
369 Adrian Beltre	.20	.06
370 Ryan Klesko	.20	.06
371 Wilson Alvarez	.20	.06
372 John Thomson	.20	.06
373 Tony Saunders	.20	.06
374 Dave Mlicki	.20	.06
375 Ken Caminiti	.20	.06
376 Jay Buhner	.20	.06
377 Bill Mueller	.20	.06
378 Jeff Blauser	.20	.06
379 Edgar Renteria	.20	.06
380 Jim Thome	.50	.15
381 Joey Hamilton	.20	.06
382 Calvin Pickering	.20	.06
383 Marquis Grissom	.20	.06
384 Omar Daal	.20	.06
385 Curt Schilling	.30	.09
386 Jose Cruz Jr.	.20	.06
387 Chris Widger	.20	.06
388 Pete Harnisch	.20	.06
389 Charles Nagy	.20	.06
390 Tom Gordon	.20	.06
391 Bobby Smith	.20	.06
392 Derrick Gibson	.20	.06
393 Jeff Conine	.20	.06
394 Carlos Perez	.20	.06
395 Barry Bonds	1.25	.35
396 Mark McLemore	.20	.06
397 Juan Encarnacion	.20	.06
398 Wade Boggs	.30	.09
399 Ivan Rodriguez	.50	.15
400 Moises Alou	.20	.06
401 Jeromy Burnitz	.20	.06
402 Sean Casey	.20	.06

403 Jose Offerman .20 .06
404 Joe Fontenot .20 .06
405 Kevin Millwood .20 .06
406 Lance Johnson .20 .06
407 Richard Hidalgo .20 .06
408 Mike Jackson .20 .06
409 Brian Anderson .20 .06
410 Jeff Shaw .20 .06
411 Preston Wilson .20 .06
412 Todd Hundley .20 .06
413 Jim Parque .20 .06
414 Justin Baughman .20 .06
415 Dante Bichette .20 .06
416 Paul O'Neill .30 .09
417 Miguel Cairo .20 .06
418 Randy Johnson .50 .15
419 Jesus Sanchez .20 .06
420 Carlos Delgado .20 .06
421 Ricky Ledee .20 .06
422 Orlando Hernandez .20 .06
423 Frank Thomas .50 .15
424 Pokey Reese .20 .06
425 Carlos Lee .40 .12
Mike Lowell
Kit Pellow RC
426 Michael Cuddyer .25 .07
Mark DeRosa
Jerry Hairston Jr.
427 Marlon Anderson .25 .07
Ron Belliard
Orlando Cabrera
428 Micah Bowie .40 .12
Phil Norton RC
Randy Wolf
429 Jack Cressend RC .25 .07
Jason Rakers
John Rocker
430 Ruben Mateo .25 .07
Scott Morgan
Mike Zywica RC
431 Jason LaRue .25 .07
Matt LeCroy
Mitch Meluskey
432 Gabe Kapler .25 .07
Armando Rios
Fernando Seguignol
433 Adam Kennedy .25 .07
Mickey Lopez RC
Jackie Rexrode
434 Jose Fernandez RC .25 .07
Jeff Liefer
Chris Truby
435 Corey Koskie 1.25 .35
Doug Mientkiewicz RC
Damon Minor
436 Roosevelt Brown RC .40 .12
Dernell Stenson
Vernon Wells
437 A.J. Burnett RC .75 .23
Billy Koch
John Nicholson
438 Matt Belisle .40 .12
Matt Roney RC
439 Austin Kearns 3.00 .90
Chris George RC
440 Nate Bump RC .50 .15
Nate Cornejo
441 Brad Lidge .50 .15
Mike Nannini RC
442 Matt Holliday .40 .12
Jeff Winchester RC
443 Adam Everett .40 .12
Chip Ambres RC
444 Pat Burrell 2.50 .75
Eric Valent RC
445 Roger Clemens SK .50 .15
446 Kerry Wood SK .30 .09
447 Curt Schilling SK .20 .06
448 Randy Johnson SK .30 .09
449 Pedro Martinez SK .30 .09
450 Jeff Bagwell AT .50 .15
Andres Galarraga
Mark McGwire
451 John Olerud AT .20 .06
Jim Thome
Tino Martinez
452 Alex Rodriguez AT .60 .18
Nomar Garciaparra
Derek Jeter
453 Vinny Castilla AT .30 .09
Chipper Jones
Scott Rolen
454 Sammy Sosa AT .50 .15
Ken Griffey Jr.
Juan Gonzalez
455 Barry Bonds AT .50 .15
Manny Ramirez
Larry Walker
456 Frank Thomas AT .50 .15
Tim Salmon
David Justice
457 Travis Lee AT .20 .06
Todd Helton
Ben Grieve
458 Vladimir Guerrero AT .20 .06
Greg Vaughn
Bernie Williams
459 Mike Piazza AT .50 .15
Ivan Rodriguez
Jason Kendall
460 Roger Clemens AT .50 .15
Kerry Wood
Greg Maddux
461A Sammy Sosa HR 1 20.00 6.00
461B Sammy Sosa HR 2 8.00 2.40
461C Sammy Sosa HR 3 8.00 2.40
461D Sammy Sosa HR 4 8.00 2.40
461E Sammy Sosa HR 5 8.00 2.40
461F Sammy Sosa HR 6 8.00 2.40
461G Sammy Sosa HR 7 8.00 8.75
461H Sammy Sosa HR 8 8.00 2.40
461I Sammy Sosa HR 9 8.00 2.40
461J Sammy Sosa HR 10 8.00 2.40
461K Sammy Sosa HR 11 8.00 2.40
461L Sammy Sosa HR 12 8.00 2.40
461M Sammy Sosa HR 13 8.00 2.40
461N Sammy Sosa HR 14 8.00 2.40
461O Sammy Sosa HR 15 8.00 2.40
461P Sammy Sosa HR 16 8.00 2.40
461Q Sammy Sosa HR 17 8.00 2.40
461R Sammy Sosa HR 18 8.00 2.40
461S Sammy Sosa HR 19 8.00 2.40
461T Sammy Sosa HR 20 8.00 2.40
461U Sammy Sosa HR 21 8.00 2.40
461V Sammy Sosa HR 22 8.00 2.40
461W Sammy Sosa HR 23 8.00 2.40
461X Sammy Sosa HR 24 8.00 2.40
461Y Sammy Sosa HR 25 8.00 2.40
461Z Sammy Sosa HR 26 8.00 2.40
461AA S.Sosa HR 27 8.00 2.40
461AB S.Sosa HR 28 8.00 2.40
461AC S.Sosa HR 29 8.00 2.40
461AD S.Sosa HR 30 8.00 2.40
461AE S.Sosa HR 31 8.00 2.40
461AF S.Sosa HR 32 8.00 2.40
461AG S.Sosa HR 33 8.00 2.40
461AH S.Sosa HR 34 8.00 2.40
461AI S.Sosa HR 35 8.00 2.40
461AJ S.Sosa HR 36 8.00 2.40
461AK S.Sosa HR 37 8.00 2.40
461AL S.Sosa HR 38 8.00 2.40
461AM S.Sosa HR 39 8.00 2.40
461AN S.Sosa HR 40 8.00 2.40
461AO S.Sosa HR 41 8.00 2.40
461AP S.Sosa HR 42 8.00 2.40
461AR S.Sosa HR 43 8.00 2.40
461AS S.Sosa HR 44 8.00 2.40
461AT S.Sosa HR 45 8.00 2.40
461AU S.Sosa HR 46 8.00 2.40
461AV S.Sosa HR 47 8.00 2.40
461AW S.Sosa HR 48 8.00 2.40
461AX S.Sosa HR 49 8.00 2.40
461AY S.Sosa HR 50 8.00 2.40
461AZ S.Sosa HR 51 8.00 2.40
461BB S.Sosa HR 52 8.00 2.40
461CC S.Sosa HR 53 8.00 2.40
461DD S.Sosa HR 54 8.00 2.40
461EE S.Sosa HR 55 8.00 2.40
461FF S.Sosa HR 56 8.00 2.40
461GG S.Sosa HR 57 8.00 2.40
461HH S.Sosa HR 58 8.00 2.40
461II S.Sosa HR 59 8.00 2.40
461JJ S.Sosa HR 60 8.00 2.40
461KK S.Sosa HR 61 20.00 6.00
461LL S.Sosa HR 62 25.00 7.50
461MM S.Sosa HR 63 10.00 3.00
461NN S.Sosa HR 64 10.00 3.00
461OO S.Sosa HR 65 10.00 3.00
461PP S.Sosa HR 66 30.00 9.00
462 Checklist .20 .06
463 Checklist .20 .06

1999 Topps MVP Promotion

This is a partial parallel to the regular Topps set. Draft pick and Prospect cards were not included in series one but were included in series two. The front of the card features the same photo as the basic issue card but is adorned with a bold gold foil MVP Promotion logo. The back features contest guidelines for the Topps MVP Promotion. If the featured player was awarded player of the week status (as determined by Topps) his card was then redeemable at season's end for a special set of all the weekly winners. Only 100 of each MVP Promotion card was produced. Stated odds were as follows: series 1 hobby packs 1:515, series 1 Home Team Advantage packs 1:142 and series 2 hobby packs 1:504, Series 2 Home Team Advantage 1:139 and series 2 retail 1:504. The exchange deadline to redeem winning cards was December 31st, 1999. Winning prize cards were mailed out between February 15th, 2000 and April 30th, 2000. The winning cards were the following numbers (which correspond to the regular Topps set): 35, 52. 70, 96, 101, 125, 127, 139, 159, 198, 248, 265, 290, 292, 300, 315, 340, 346, 350, 352, 355, 360, 365, 416, and 418. Since Topps destroyed these Winner exchange cards once they received them, they're in noticeably shorter supply than other cards from this set. Despite this fact, no noticeable premiums in secondary trading levels have been detected for these cards.

Nm-Mt Ex-Mt
*STARS: 20X TO 50X BASIC CARDS..
*ROOKIES: 12.5X TO 30X BASIC CARDS
35 Ray Lankford W 10.00 3.00
52 Todd Helton W 15.00 4.50
70 Mark McGwire W 60.00 18.00
96 Greg Vaughn W 10.00 3.00
101 David Cone W 10.00 3.00
125 Scott Rolen W 15.00 4.50
127 J.T. Snow W 10.00 3.00
139 Fred McGriff W 15.00 4.50
159 Mike Lieberthal W 10.00 3.00
198 B.J. Surhoff W 10.00 3.00
248 Roberto Alomar W 25.00 7.50
265 Nomar Garciaparra W 40.00 12.00
290 Tino Martinez W 15.00 4.50
292 Tony Clark W 10.00 3.00
300 Alex Rodriguez W 40.00 12.00
315 Rafael Palmeiro W 15.00 4.50
340 Mike Piazza W 40.00 12.00
346 Fernando Tatis W 10.00 3.00
350 Larry Walker W 15.00 4.50
352 Miguel Tejada W 10.00 3.00
355 Chipper Jones W 25.00 7.50
360 Tim Salmon W 15.00 4.50
365 Raul Mondesi W 10.00 3.00
416 Paul O'Neill W 15.00 4.50
418 Randy Johnson W 25.00 7.50

1999 Topps MVP Promotion Exchange

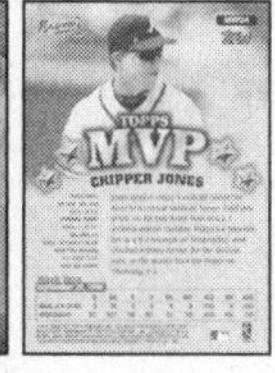

This 25-card set was available only to those lucky collectors who obtained one of the twenty-five winning player cards from the 1999 Topps MVP Promotion parallel set. Each week, throughout the 1999 season, Topps named a new Player of the Week, and that player's Topps MVP Promotion parallel card was made redeemable for this 25-card set. The deadline to exchange the winning cards was December 31st, 1999. The exchange cards shipped out in mid-February, 2000.

Nm-Mt Ex-Mt
COMP.FACT.SET (25) 50.00 15.00
MVP1 Raul Mondesi 1.50 .45
MVP2 Tim Salmon 2.50 .75
MVP3 Fernando Tatis 1.50 .45
MVP4 Larry Walker 2.50 .75
MVP5 Fred McGriff 2.50 .75
MVP6 Nomar Garciaparra 6.00 1.80
MVP7 Rafael Palmeiro 2.50 .75
MVP8 Randy Johnson 4.00 1.20
MVP9 Mike Lieberthal 1.50 .45
MVP10 B.J. Surhoff 1.50 .45
MVP11 Todd Helton 2.50 .75
MVP12 Tino Martinez 2.50 .75
MVP13 Scott Rolen 2.50 .75
MVP14 Mike Piazza 6.00 1.80
MVP15 David Cone 1.50 .45
MVP16 Tony Clark 1.50 .45
MVP17 Roberto Alomar 4.00 1.20
MVP18 Miguel Tejada 1.50 .45
MVP19 Alex Rodriguez 6.00 1.80
MVP20 J.T. Snow 1.50 .45
MVP21 Ray Lankford 1.50 .45
MVP22 Greg Vaughn 1.50 .45
MVP23 Paul O'Neill 2.50 .75
MVP24 Chipper Jones 4.00 1.20
MVP25 Mark McGwire 10.00 3.00

1999 Topps Oversize

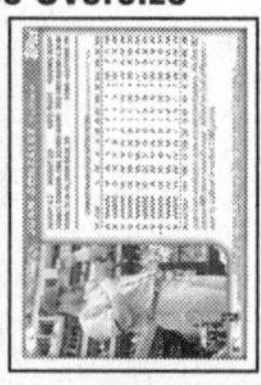

Inserted one per Home Team Advantage and one per Hobby box, these cards feature sixteen of the leading players in an oversize version. The photos are the same as the regular Topps cards. We have numbered the cards with A and B prefixes to denote series one versus series two distribution, although Topps decided to number each series 1 through 8.

Nm-Mt Ex-Mt
COMPLETE SERIES 1 (8) 15.00 4.50
COMPLETE SERIES 2 (8) 15.00 4.50
A1 Roger Clemens 3.00 .90
A2 Greg Maddux 2.50 .75
A3 Kerry Wood 1.50 .45
A4 Juan Gonzalez 1.50 .45
A5 Sammy Sosa 2.50 .75
A6 Mark McGwire 4.00 1.20
A7 Ken Griffey Jr. 2.50 .75
A8 Ben Grieve .60 .18
B1 Nomar Garciaparra 2.50 .75
B2 Cal Ripken 5.00 1.50
B3 Alex Rodriguez 2.50 .75
B4 Mike Piazza 2.50 .75
B5 Larry Walker 1.00 .30
B6 Chipper Jones 1.50 .45
B7 Barry Bonds 4.00 1.20
B8 Frank Thomas 1.50 .45

1999 Topps All-Matrix

This 30-card insert set consists of three thematic subsets (Club 40 are numbers 1-13, '99 Rookie Rush are number's 14-23 and Club K are numbers 24-30). All 30-cards feature silver foil dot-matrix technology. Cards were seeded exclusively into series 2 packs as follows: 1:18 hobby, 1:18 retail and 1:5 Home Team Advantage.

Nm-Mt Ex-Mt
COMPLETE SET (30) 80.00 24.00
AM1 Mark McGwire 10.00 3.00
AM2 Sammy Sosa 6.00 1.80
AM3 Ken Griffey Jr. 6.00 1.80
AM4 Greg Vaughn 1.50 .45
AM5 Albert Belle 1.50 .45
AM6 Vinny Castilla 1.50 .45
AM7 Jose Canseco 4.00 1.20
AM8 Juan Gonzalez 4.00 1.20
AM9 Manny Ramirez 1.50 .45
AM10 Andres Galarraga 1.50 .45
AM11 Rafael Palmeiro 2.50 .75
AM12 Alex Rodriguez 6.00 1.80
AM13 Mo Vaughn 1.50 .45
AM14 Eric Chavez 1.50 .45
AM15 Gabe Kapler 3.00 .90
AM16 Calvin Pickering 1.50 .45
AM17 Ruben Mateo 2.00 .60
AM18 Roy Halladay 1.50 .45
AM19 Jeremy Giambi 1.50 .45
AM20 Alex Gonzalez 1.50 .45
AM21 Ron Belliard 2.00 .60
AM22 Marlon Anderson 2.00 .60
AM23 Carlos Lee 3.00 .90
AM24 Kerry Wood 4.00 1.20
AM25 Roger Clemens 8.00 2.40
AM26 Curt Schilling 2.50 .75
AM27 Kevin Brown 2.50 .75
AM28 Randy Johnson 4.00 1.20
AM29 Pedro Martinez 4.00 1.20
AM30 Orlando Hernandez 1.50 .45

1999 Topps All-Topps Mystery Finest

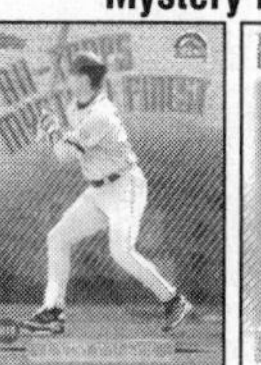

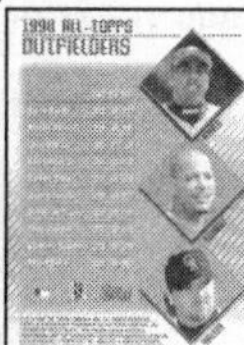
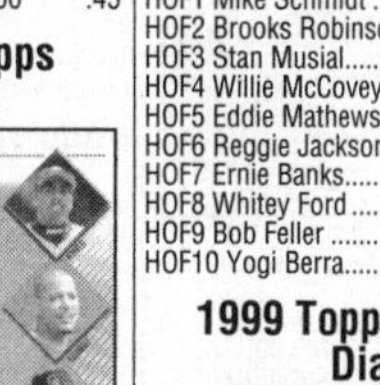

Randomly inserted in Topps Series two packs at the the rate of one in 36, this 33-card set features 11 three-player positional parallels of the All-Topps subset printed using Finest technology. All three players are printed on the back, but the collector has to peel off the opaque protector to reveal who is on the front.

Nm-Mt Ex-Mt
COMPLETE SET (33) 250.00 75.00
*REFRACTORS: 1X TO 2.5X BASIC ATMF
SER.2 REF.ODDS 1:144 HOB/RET, 1:32 HTA
M1 Jeff Bagwell 5.00 1.50
M2 Andres Galarraga 3.00 .90
M3 Mark McGwire 20.00 6.00
M4 John Olerud 3.00 .90
M5 Jim Thome 8.00 2.40
M6 Tino Martinez 5.00 1.50
M7 Alex Rodriguez 12.00 3.60
M8 Nomar Garciaparra 12.00 3.60
M9 Derek Jeter 20.00 6.00
M10 Vinny Castilla 3.00 .90
M11 Chipper Jones 8.00 2.40
M12 Scott Rolen 5.00 1.50
M13 Sammy Sosa 12.00 3.60
M14 Ken Griffey Jr. 12.00 3.60
M15 Juan Gonzalez 8.00 2.40
M16 Barry Bonds 20.00 6.00
M17 Manny Ramirez 3.00 .90
M18 Larry Walker 5.00 1.50
M19 Frank Thomas 8.00 2.40
M20 Tim Salmon 5.00 1.50
M21 Dave Justice 3.00 .90
M22 Travis Lee 3.00 .90
M23 Todd Helton 5.00 1.50
M24 Ben Grieve 3.00 .90
M25 Vladimir Guerrero 8.00 2.40
M26 Greg Vaughn 3.00 .90
M27 Bernie Williams 5.00 1.50
M28 Mike Piazza 12.00 3.60
M29 Ivan Rodriguez 8.00 2.40
M30 Jason Kendall 3.00 .90
M31 Roger Clemens 15.00 4.50
M32 Kerry Wood 8.00 2.40
M33 Greg Maddux 12.00 3.60

1999 Topps Autographs

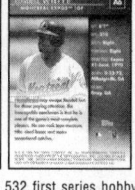

Inserted one in every 532 first series hobby packs, one in every 146 first series Home Team Advantage packs,d one in every 501 second series hobby packs and one in every 138 second seriesHome Team Advantage packs, these cards feature an assortment of young and old players affixing their signature to these cards. Cards A1-A8 were distributed exclusively in first series packs and cards A9-A16 were distributed exclusively in second series packs. The fronts feature a player photo with the authentic autograph on the bottom.

Nm-Mt Ex-Mt
A1 Roger Clemens 100.00 30.00
A2 Chipper Jones 40.00 12.00
A3 Scott Rolen 25.00 7.50
A4 Alex Rodriguez 100.00 30.00
A5 Andres Galarraga 15.00 4.50
A6 Rondell White 15.00 4.50
A7 Ben Grieve 15.00 4.50
A8 Troy Glaus 25.00 7.50
A9 Moises Alou 15.00 4.50
A10 Barry Bonds 175.00 52.50
A11 Vladimir Guerrero 40.00 12.00
A12 Andruw Jones 25.00 7.50
A13 Darin Erstad 15.00 4.50
A14 Shawn Green 15.00 4.50
A15 Eric Chavez 15.00 4.50
A16 Pat Burrell 30.00 9.00

1999 Topps Hall of Fame Collection

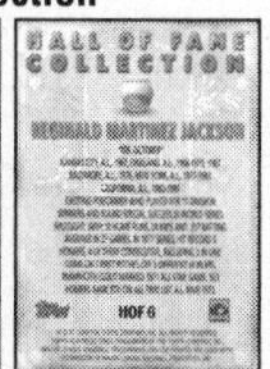

This 10 card set features Hall of Famers with photos of the plaques and a silhoutted photo. These cards were inserted one every 12 hobby packs and one every three HTA packs.

Nm-Mt Ex-Mt
COMPLETE SET (10) 20.00 6.00
HOF1 Mike Schmidt 4.00 1.20
HOF2 Brooks Robinson 2.00 .60
HOF3 Stan Musial 3.00 .90
HOF4 Willie McCovey 2.00 .60
HOF5 Eddie Mathews 2.00 .60
HOF6 Reggie Jackson 2.00 .60
HOF7 Ernie Banks 2.00 .60
HOF8 Whitey Ford 2.00 .60
HOF9 Bob Feller 2.00 .60
HOF10 Yogi Berra 2.00 .60

1999 Topps Lords of the Diamond

This die-cut insert set was inserted one every 18 hobby packs and one every five HTA packs. The words "Lords of the Diamond" are printed on the top while the players name is at the bottom. The middle of the card has the players photo.

Nm-Mt Ex-Mt
COMPLETE SET (15) 50.00 15.00
LD1 Ken Griffey Jr. 4.00 1.20
LD2 Chipper Jones 2.50 .75
LD3 Sammy Sosa 4.00 1.20
LD4 Frank Thomas 2.50 .75
LD5 Mark McGwire 6.00 1.80
LD6 Jeff Bagwell 1.50 .45
LD7 Alex Rodriguez 4.00 1.20
LD8 Juan Gonzalez 2.50 .75
LD9 Barry Bonds 6.00 1.80
LD10 Nomar Garciaparra 4.00 1.20
LD11 Darin Erstad 1.00 .30
LD12 Tony Gwynn 3.00 .90
LD13 Andres Galarraga 1.00 .30
LD14 Mike Piazza 4.00 1.20
LD15 Greg Maddux 4.00 1.20

1999 Topps New Breed

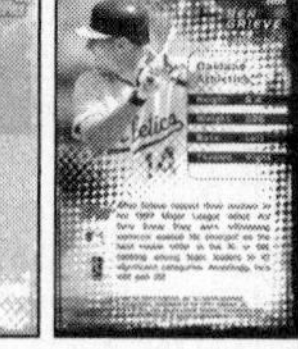

Fifteen of the young stars of the game are featured in this insert set. The cards were seeded into the 99 Topps packs at a rate of one every 18 hobby packs and one every five HTA packs.

Nm-Mt Ex-Mt
COMPLETE SET (15) 25.00 7.50
NB1 Darin Erstad .75 .23
NB2 Brad Fullmer .75 .23
NB3 Kerry Wood 2.00 .60
NB4 Nomar Garciaparra 3.00 .90
NB5 Travis Lee .75 .23
NB6 Scott Rolen 1.25 .35
NB7 Todd Helton 1.25 .35
NB8 Vladimir Guerrero 2.00 .60
NB9 Derek Jeter 5.00 1.50
NB10 Alex Rodriguez 3.00 .90
NB11 Ben Grieve .75 .23
NB12 Andruw Jones .75 .23
NB13 Paul Konerko .75 .23
NB14 Aramis Ramirez .75 .23
NB15 Adrian Beltre .75 .23

1999 Topps Picture Perfect

This 10 card insert set was inserted one every eight hobby packs and one every two HTA packs. These cards all contain a minor, very difficult to determine mistake and part of the charm is to figure out what the error is in the card.

Nm-Mt Ex-Mt
COMPLETE SET (10) 15.00 4.50
P1 Ken Griffey Jr. 1.50 .45
P2 Kerry Wood 1.00 .30
P3 Pedro Martinez 1.00 .30
P4 Mark McGwire 2.50 .75
P5 Greg Maddux 1.50 .45
P6 Sammy Sosa 1.50 .45
P7 Greg Vaughn .40 .12
P8 Juan Gonzalez 1.00 .30
P9 Jeff Bagwell .60 .18
P10 Derek Jeter 2.50 .75

1999 Topps Power Brokers

This 20 card set features leading baseball players. They were inserted at a seeded rate of

one every 36 hobby/retail packs and one every eight HTA packs.

	Nm-Mt	Ex-Mt
COMPLETE SET (20)	120.00	36.00
*REFRACTORS: 1X TO 2.5X BASIC BROKERS		
SER.1 REF.ODDS 1:144 HOB/RET, 1:32 HTA		
PB1 Mark McGwire	12.00	3.60
PB2 Andres Galarraga	2.00	.60
PB3 Ken Griffey Jr.	8.00	2.40
PB4 Sammy Sosa	8.00	2.40
PB5 Juan Gonzalez	5.00	1.50
PB6 Alex Rodriguez	8.00	2.40
PB7 Frank Thomas	5.00	1.50
PB8 Jeff Bagwell	3.00	.90
PB9 Vinny Castilla	2.00	.60
PB10 Mike Piazza	8.00	2.40
PB11 Greg Vaughn	2.00	.60
PB12 Barry Bonds	12.00	3.60
PB13 Mo Vaughn	2.00	.60
PB14 Jim Thome	5.00	1.50
PB15 Larry Walker	3.00	.90
PB16 Chipper Jones	5.00	1.50
PB17 Nomar Garciaparra	8.00	2.40
PB18 Manny Ramirez	2.00	.60
PB19 Roger Clemens	10.00	3.00
PB20 Kerry Wood	5.00	1.50

1999 Topps Record Numbers

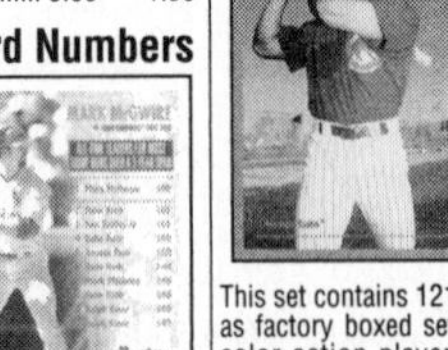

Randomly inserted in Series two hobby and retail packs at the rate of one in eight and HTA packs at a rate of one in two, this 10-card set features action color photos of record-setting players with silver foil highlights.

	Nm-Mt	Ex-Mt
COMPLETE SET (10)	15.00	4.50
RN1 Mark McGwire	2.50	.75
RN2 Mike Piazza	1.50	.45
RN3 Curt Schilling	.60	.18
RN4 Ken Griffey Jr.	1.50	.45
RN5 Sammy Sosa	1.50	.45
RN6 Nomar Garciaparra	1.50	.45
RN7 Kerry Wood	1.00	.30
RN8 Roger Clemens	2.00	.60
RN9 Cal Ripken	3.00	.90
RN10 Mark McGwire	2.50	.75

1999 Topps Record Numbers Gold

Randomly seeded in series two packs, these scarce gold-foiled cards parallel the more common "silver-foiled" Record Numbers inserts. The print run for each card was based upon the statistic specified on the card. Erroneous stated odds for these Gold cards were unfortunately printed on all series two wrappers. According to sources at Topps the correct pack odds are as follows: RN1 1:151,320 hob, 1:38,016 HTA, 1:138,567 ret, RN2 1:28,317 hob, 1:7,797 HTA, 1:28,340 ret, RN3 1:32,134 hob, 1:8,848 HTA, 1:32,160 ret, RN4 1:29,288 hob, 1:8,064 HTA, 1:29,312 ret, RN5 1:907,920 hob, 1:133,056 HTA, 1:1,524,420 ret, RN6 1:605,280 hob, 1:88,704 HTA, 1:1,016,280 ret, RN7 1:907,920 hob, 1:133,056 HTA, 1:1,524,420 ret, RN8 1:907,920 hob, 1:133,056 HTA, 1:1,524,420 ret, RN9 1:3891 hob, 1:1069 HTA, 1:3888 ret, RN10 1:63,312 hob, 1:17,741 HTA, 1:63,510 ret.

	Nm-Mt	Ex-Mt
RN1 Mark McGwire/70	100.00	30.00
RN2 Mike Piazza/362	15.00	4.50
RN3 Curt Schilling/319	10.00	3.00
RN4 Ken Griffey Jr./350	20.00	6.00
RN5 Sammy Sosa/20		
RN6 N.Garciaparra/30	120.00	36.00
RN7 Kerry Wood/20		
RN8 Roger Clemens/20		
RN9 Cal Ripken/2632	15.00	4.50
RN10 Mark McGwire/162	40.00	12.00

1999 Topps Ryan

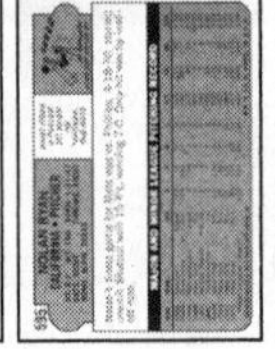

These cards reflect the Nolan Ryan Reprints of earlier Topps cards featuring the pitcher known for "Texas Heat". These cards are replicas of Ryan's cards and have a commemorative sticker placed on them as well. The cards were seeded one every 18 hobby/retail packs and one every five HTA packs. Odd-numbered cards (i.e. 1, 3, 5 etc.) were distributed in first series packs and even numbered cards were distributed in second series packs.

	Nm-Mt	Ex-Mt
COMPLETE SET (27)	80.00	24.00
COMPLETE SERIES 1 (14)	40.00	12.00
COMPLETE SERIES 2 (13)	40.00	12.00
COMMON CARD (1-27)	5.00	1.50
1 Nolan Ryan 1968	10.00	3.00

1999 Topps Ryan Autographs

Nolan Ryan signed a selection of all 27 cards for this reprint set. The autographed cards were issued one every 4,250 series one hobby packs, one in every 5,007 series two hobby packs and one every 1,176 series one HTA packs.

	Nm-Mt	Ex-Mt
COMMON CARD (1-13)	200.00	60.00
COMMON CARD (14-27)	150.00	45.00
1 Nolan Ryan 1968	300.00	90.00

1999 Topps Traded

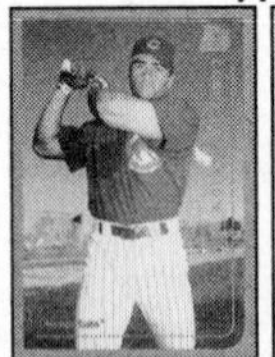

This set contains 121 cards and was distributed as factory boxed sets only. The fronts feature color action player photo. The backs carry player information. Rookie Cards include Sean Burroughs, Josh Hamilton, Corey Patterson and Alfonso Soriano.

	Nm-Mt	Ex-Mt
COMP.FACT.SET (122)	40.00	12.00
COMPLETE SET (121)	25.00	7.50
T1 Seth Etherton	.20	.06
T2 Mark Harriger RC	.25	.07
T3 Matt Wise RC	.25	.07
T4 Carlos E. Hernandez RC	.25	.07
T5 Julio Lugo RC	.25	.07
T6 Mike Nannini	.20	.06
T7 Justin Bowles RC	.25	.07
T8 Mark Mulder RC	2.50	.75
T9 Roberto Vaz RC	.25	.07
T10 Felipe Lopez RC	.25	.07
T11 Matt Belisle	.30	.09
T12 Micah Bowie	.20	.06
T13 Ruben Quevedo RC	.25	.07
T14 Jose Garcia RC	.25	.07
T15 David Kelton RC	.40	.12
T16 Phil Norton	.20	.06
T17 Corey Patterson RC	2.50	.75
T18 Ron Walker RC	.25	.07
T19 Paul Hoover RC	.25	.07
T20 Ryan Rupe RC	.25	.07
T21 J.D. Closser RC	.25	.07
T22 Rob Ryan RC	.25	.07
T23 Steve Colyer RC	.25	.07
T24 Bubba Crosby RC	.60	.18
T25 Luke Prokopec RC	.25	.07
T26 Matt Blank RC	.25	.07
T27 Josh McKinley	.20	.06
T28 Nate Bump	.20	.06
T29 G.Chiaramonte RC	.25	.07
T30 Arturo McDowell	.20	.06
T31 Tony Torcato	.20	.06
T32 Dave Roberts RC	.40	.12
T33 C.C. Sabathia RC	.60	.18
T34 Sean Spencer RC	.25	.07
T35 Chip Ambres	.20	.06
T36 A.J. Burnett	.60	.18
T37 Mo Bruce RC	.25	.07
T38 Jason Tyner	.20	.06
T39 Mamon Tucker	.20	.06
T40 Sean Burroughs RC	2.00	.60
T41 Kevin Eberwein RC	.25	.07
T42 Junior Herndon RC	.25	.07
T43 Bryan Wolff RC	.25	.07
T44 Pat Burrell	2.00	.60
T45 Eric Valent	.20	.06
T46 Carlos Pena RC	.60	.18
T47 Mike Zywica	.20	.06
T48 Adam Everett	.20	.06
T49 Juan Pena RC	.25	.07
T50 Adam Dunn RC	5.00	1.50
T51 Austin Kearns	2.50	.75
T52 Jacobo Sequea RC	.25	.07
T53 Choo Freeman	.20	.06
T54 Jeff Winchester	.20	.06
T55 Matt Burch	.20	.06
T56 Chris George	.20	.06
T57 Scott Mullen RC	.25	.07
T58 Kit Pellow	.20	.06
T59 Mark Quinn RC	.25	.07
T60 Nate Cornejo	.40	.12
T61 Ryan Mills	.20	.06
T62 Kevin Beirne RC	.25	.07
T63 Kip Wells RC	.40	.12
T64 Juan Rivera RC	.40	.12
T65 Alfonso Soriano RC	5.00	1.50
T66 Josh Hamilton RC	.60	.18
T67 Josh Girdley RC	.25	.07
T68 Kyle Snyder RC	.25	.07
T69 Mike Paradis RC	.25	.07
T70 Jason Jennings RC	.40	.12
T71 David Walling RC	.25	.07
T72 Omar Ortiz RC	.25	.07
T73 Jay Gehrke RC	.25	.07
T74 Casey Burns RC	.25	.07
T75 Carl Crawford RC	1.25	.35
T76 Reggie Sanders	.20	.06
T77 Will Clark	.50	.15
T78 David Wells	.20	.06
T79 Paul Konerko	.20	.06
T80 Armando Benitez	.20	.06
T81 Brant Brown	.20	.06
T82 Mo Vaughn	.20	.06
T83 Jose Canseco	.50	.15
T84 Albert Belle	.20	.06
T85 Dean Palmer	.20	.06
T86 Greg Vaughn	.20	.06
T87 Mark Clark	.20	.06
T88 Pat Meares	.20	.06
T89 Eric Davis	.20	.06
T90 Brian Giles	.20	.06
T91 Jeff Brantley	.20	.06
T92 Bret Boone	.20	.06
T93 Ron Gant	.20	.06
T94 Mike Cameron	.20	.06
T95 Charles Johnson	.20	.06
T96 Denny Neagle	.20	.06
T97 Brian Hunter	.20	.06
T98 Jose Hernandez	.20	.06
T99 Rick Aguilera	.20	.06
T100 Tony Batista	.20	.06
T101 Roger Cedeno	.20	.06
T102 C.Gubanich RC	.25	.07
T103 Tim Belcher	.20	.06
T104 Bruce Aven	.20	.06
T105 Brian Daubach RC	.25	.07
T106 Ed Sprague	.20	.06
T107 Michael Tucker	.20	.06
T108 Homer Bush	.20	.06
T109 Armando Reynoso	.20	.06
T110 Brook Fordyce	.20	.06
T111 Matt Mantei	.20	.06
T112 Dave Mlicki	.20	.06
T113 Kenny Rogers	.20	.06
T114 Livan Hernandez	.20	.06
T115 Butch Huskey	.20	.06
T116 David Segui	.20	.06
T117 Darryl Hamilton	.20	.06
T118 Terry Mulholland	.20	.06
T119 Randy Velarde	.20	.06
T120 Bill Taylor	.20	.06
T121 Kevin Appier	.20	.06

1999 Topps Traded Autographs

Inserted one per factory box set, this 75-card set features autographed parallel version of the first 75 cards of the basic 1999 Topps Traded set. The card fronts have a light faded image on the base to accentuate the signature.

	Nm-Mt	Ex-Mt
COMPLETE SET (75)	1000.00	300.00
T1 Seth Etherton	10.00	3.00
T2 Mark Harriger	10.00	3.00
T3 Matt Wise	10.00	3.00
T4 Carlos E. Hernandez	10.00	3.00
T5 Julio Lugo	10.00	3.00
T6 Mike Nannini	10.00	3.00
T7 Justin Bowles	10.00	3.00
T8 Mark Mulder	40.00	12.00
T9 Roberto Vaz	10.00	3.00
T10 Felipe Lopez	10.00	3.00
T11 Matt Belisle	10.00	3.00
T12 Micah Bowie	5.00	1.50
T13 Ruben Quevedo	10.00	3.00
T14 Jose Garcia	10.00	3.00
T15 David Kelton	15.00	4.50
T16 Phil Norton	10.00	3.00
T17 Corey Patterson	80.00	24.00
T18 Ron Walker	5.00	1.50
T19 Paul Hoover	10.00	3.00
T20 Ryan Rupe	10.00	3.00
T21 J.D. Closser	10.00	3.00
T22 Rob Ryan	5.00	1.50
T23 Steve Colyer	10.00	3.00
T24 Bubba Crosby	25.00	7.50
T25 Luke Prokopec	10.00	3.00
T26 Matt Blank	10.00	3.00
T27 Josh McKinley	10.00	3.00
T28 Nate Bump	10.00	3.00
T29 G.Chiaramonte	5.00	1.50
T30 Arturo McDowell	10.00	3.00
T31 Tony Torcato	10.00	3.00
T32 Dave Roberts	15.00	4.50
T33 C.C. Sabathia	40.00	12.00
T34 Sean Spencer	5.00	1.50
T35 Chip Ambres	10.00	3.00
T36 A.J. Burnett	25.00	7.50
T37 Mo Bruce	5.00	1.50
T38 Jason Tyner	10.00	3.00
T39 Mamon Tucker	10.00	3.00
T40 Sean Burroughs	50.00	15.00
T41 Kevin Eberwein	10.00	3.00
T42 Junior Herndon	10.00	3.00
T43 Bryan Wolff	10.00	3.00
T44 Pat Burrell	50.00	15.00
T45 Eric Valent	10.00	3.00
T46 Carlos Pena	25.00	7.50
T47 Mike Zywica	10.00	3.00
T48 Adam Everett	10.00	3.00
T49 Juan Pena	10.00	3.00
T50 Adam Dunn	120.00	36.00
T51 Austin Kearns	60.00	18.00
T52 Jacobo Sequea	10.00	3.00
T53 Choo Freeman	10.00	3.00
T54 Jeff Winchester	10.00	3.00
T55 Matt Burch	10.00	3.00
T56 Chris George	10.00	3.00
T57 Scott Mullen	5.00	1.50
T58 Kit Pellow	5.00	1.50
T59 Mark Quinn	10.00	3.00
T60 Nate Cornejo	15.00	4.50
T61 Ryan Mills	10.00	3.00
T62 Kevin Beirne	10.00	3.00
T63 Kip Wells	15.00	4.50
T64 Juan Rivera	15.00	4.50
T65 Alfonso Soriano	150.00	45.00
T66 Josh Hamilton	25.00	7.50
T67 Josh Girdley	10.00	3.00
T68 Kyle Snyder	10.00	3.00
T69 Mike Paradis	10.00	3.00
T70 Jason Jennings	15.00	4.50
T71 David Walling	5.00	1.50
T72 Omar Ortiz	10.00	3.00
T73 Jay Gehrke	10.00	3.00
T74 Casey Burns	10.00	3.00
T75 Carl Crawford	25.00	7.50

2000 Topps Pre-Production

This three card set was issued in a sealed cello pack to dealers and hobby media several weeks prior to the products release. The cards have a "PP" prefix so they can be differentiated from the regular cards.

	Nm-Mt	Ex-Mt
COMPLETE SET (3)	3.00	.90
PP1 Brady Anderson	1.00	.30
PP2 Jason Kendall	1.00	.30
PP3 Ryan Klesko	1.00	.30

2000 Topps

This 478 card set was issued in two separate series. The first series (containing cards 1-239) was released in December, 1999. The second series (containing cards 240-479) was released in April, 2000. The cards were issued in various formats including an eleven card hobby or retail pack with an SRP of $1.29 and a 40 card HomeTeam Advantage jumbo pack. Cards 1-200 and 240-440 are individual player cards with subsets as follows: Prospects (201-208/441-448), Draft Picks (209-220/449-455), Season Highlights (217-221/456-460), Post Season Highlights (222-228), 20th Century's Best (229-235/468-474), Magic Moments (236-240/475-479) and League Leaders (461-467). After the success Topps had with the multiple versions of Mark McGwire 220 and Sammy Sosa 461 in 1999, they made five versions each of the Magic Moments cards this year. Each Magic Moment variation featured different gold foil text on front commemorating a specific achievement in the featured player's career. Please note, that basic hand-collected sets are considered complete with the inclusion of any one of each of these Magic Moment cards. A reprint of the 1985 Mark McGwire Rookie Card was inserted one every 36 hobby and retail first series packs and one every eight HTA first series packs. Card number 7 was not issued as Topps continues to honor the memory of Mickey Mantle who wore that number during his career. Players with notable Rookie Cards in this set include Rick Asadoorian, Vince Faison, B.J. Garbe, Ben Sheets and Barry Zito.

	Nm-Mt	Ex-Mt
COMPLETE SET (478)	50.00	15.00
COMP.HOBBY SET (478)	50.00	15.00
COMP. SERIES 1 (239)	25.00	7.50
COMP. SERIES 2 (240)	25.00	7.50
MCGWIRE MM SET (5)	12.00	3.60
AARON MM SET (5)	10.00	3.00
RIPKEN MM SET (5)	15.00	4.50
BOGGS MM SET (5)	3.00	.90
GWYNN MM SET (5)	6.00	1.80
GRIFFEY MM SET (5)	8.00	2.40
BONDS MM SET (5)	12.00	3.60
SOSA MM SET (5)	8.00	2.40
JETER MM SET (5)	12.00	3.60
A.ROD MM SET (5)	8.00	2.40
1 Mark McGwire	1.25	.35
2 Tony Gwynn	.60	.18
3 Wade Boggs	.30	.09
4 Cal Ripken	1.50	.45
5 Matt Williams	.20	.06
6 Jay Buhner	.20	.06
8 Jeff Conine	.20	.06
9 Todd Greene	.20	.06
10 Mike Lieberthal	.20	.06
11 Steve Avery	.20	.06
12 Bret Saberhagen	.20	.06
13 Magglio Ordonez	.20	.06
14 Brad Radke	.20	.06
15 Derek Jeter	1.25	.35
16 Javy Lopez	.20	.06
17 Russ Davis	.20	.06
18 Armando Benitez	.20	.06
19 B.J. Surhoff	.20	.06
20 Darryl Kile	.20	.06
21 Mark Lewis	.20	.06
22 Mike Williams	.20	.06
23 Mark McLemore	.20	.06
24 Sterling Hitchcock	.20	.06
25 Darin Erstad	.20	.06
26 Ricky Gutierrez	.20	.06
27 John Jaha	.20	.06
28 Homer Bush	.20	.06
29 Darrin Fletcher	.20	.06
30 Mark Grace	.30	.09
31 Fred McGriff	.30	.09
32 Omar Daal	.20	.06
33 Eric Karros	.20	.06
34 Orlando Cabrera	.20	.06
35 J.T. Snow	.20	.06
36 Luis Castillo	.20	.06
37 Rey Ordonez	.20	.06
38 Bob Abreu	.20	.06
39 Warren Morris	.20	.06
40 Juan Gonzalez	.50	.15
41 Mike Lansing	.20	.06
42 Chili Davis	.20	.06
43 Dean Palmer	.20	.06
44 Hank Aaron	.75	.23
45 Jeff Bagwell	.30	.09
46 Jose Valentin	.20	.06
47 Shannon Stewart	.20	.06
48 Kent Bottenfield	.20	.06
49 Jeff Shaw	.20	.06
50 Sammy Sosa	.75	.23
51 Randy Johnson	.50	.15
52 Benny Agbayani	.20	.06
53 Dante Bichette	.20	.06
54 Pete Harnisch	.20	.06
55 Frank Thomas	.50	.15
56 Jorge Posada	.30	.09
57 Todd Walker	.20	.06
58 Juan Encarnacion	.20	.06
59 Mike Sweeney	.20	.06
60 Pedro Martinez	.50	.15
61 Lee Stevens	.20	.06
62 Brian Giles	.20	.06
63 Chad Ogea	.20	.06
64 Ivan Rodriguez	.50	.15
65 Roger Cedeno	.20	.06
66 David Justice	.20	.06
67 Steve Trachsel	.20	.06
68 Eli Marrero	.20	.06
69 Dave Nilsson	.20	.06
70 Ken Caminiti	.20	.06
71 Tim Raines	.20	.06
72 Brian Jordan	.20	.06
73 Jeff Blauser	.20	.06
74 Bernard Gilkey	.20	.06
75 John Flaherty	.20	.06
76 Brent Mayne	.20	.06
77 Jose Vidro	.20	.06
78 David Bell	.20	.06
79 Bruce Aven	.20	.06
80 John Olerud	.20	.06
81 Pokey Reese	.20	.06
82 Woody Williams	.20	.06
83 Ed Sprague	.20	.06
84 Joe Girardi	.20	.06
85 Barry Larkin	.50	.15
86 Mike Caruso	.20	.06
87 Bobby Higginson	.20	.06
88 Roberto Kelly	.20	.06
89 Edgar Martinez	.30	.09
90 Mark Kotsay	.20	.06
91 Paul Sorrento	.20	.06
92 Eric Young	.20	.06
93 Carlos Delgado	.20	.06
94 Troy Glaus	.30	.09
95 Ben Grieve	.20	.06
96 Jose Lima	.20	.06
97 Garret Anderson	.20	.06
98 Luis Gonzalez	.20	.06
99 Carl Pavano	.20	.06
100 Alex Rodriguez	.75	.23
101 Preston Wilson	.20	.06
102 Ron Gant	.20	.06
103 Brady Anderson	.20	.06
104 Rickey Henderson	.50	.15
105 Gary Sheffield	.20	.06
106 Mickey Morandini	.20	.06
107 Jim Edmonds	.20	.06
108 Kris Benson	.20	.06
109 Adrian Beltre	.20	.06
110 Alex Fernandez	.20	.06
111 Dan Wilson	.20	.06
112 Mark Clark	.20	.06
113 Greg Vaughn	.20	.06
114 Neifi Perez	.20	.06
115 Paul O'Neill	.30	.09
116 Jermaine Dye	.20	.06
117 Todd Jones	.20	.06
118 Terry Steinbach	.20	.06
119 Greg Norton	.20	.06
120 Curt Schilling	.30	.09
121 Todd Zeile	.20	.06
122 Edgardo Alfonzo	.20	.06
123 Ryan McGuire	.20	.06
124 Rich Aurilia	.20	.06
125 John Smoltz	.30	.09
126 Bob Wickman	.20	.06
127 Richard Hidalgo	.20	.06
128 Chuck Finley	.20	.06
129 Billy Wagner	.20	.06
130 Todd Hundley	.20	.06
131 Dwight Gooden	.30	.09
132 Russ Ortiz	.20	.06
133 Mike Lowell	.20	.06
134 Reggie Sanders	.20	.06
135 John Valentin	.20	.06
136 Brad Ausmus	.20	.06
137 Chad Kreuter	.20	.06
138 David Cone	.20	.06
139 Brook Fordyce	.20	.06
140 Roberto Alomar	.50	.15
141 Charles Nagy	.20	.06
142 Brian Hunter	.20	.06
143 Mike Mussina	.50	.15
144 Robin Ventura	.30	.09
145 Kevin Brown	.30	.09
146 Pat Hentgen	.20	.06
147 Ryan Klesko	.20	.06
148 Derek Bell	.20	.06
149 Andy Sheets	.20	.06
150 Larry Walker	.30	.09
151 Scott Williamson	.20	.06
152 Jose Offerman	.20	.06
153 Doug Mientkiewicz	.20	.06
154 John Snyder RC	.40	.12
155 Sandy Alomar Jr.	.20	.06
156 Joe Nathan	.20	.06
157 Lance Johnson	.20	.06
158 Odalis Perez	.20	.06
159 Hideo Nomo	.50	.15
160 Steve Finley	.20	.06
161 Dave Martinez	.20	.06
162 Matt Walbeck	.20	.06
163 Bill Spiers	.20	.06
164 Fernando Tatis	.20	.06
165 Kenny Lofton	.20	.06
166 Paul Byrd	.20	.06
167 Aaron Sele	.20	.06
168 Eddie Taubensee	.20	.06
169 Reggie Jefferson	.20	.06

170 Roger Clemens 1.00 .30
171 Francisco Cordova .20 .06
172 Mike Bordick .20 .06
173 Wally Joyner .20 .06
174 Marvin Benard .20 .06
175 Jason Kendall .20 .06
176 Mike Stanley .20 .06
177 Chad Allen .20 .06
178 Carlos Beltran .20 .06
179 Deivi Cruz .20 .06
180 Chipper Jones .50 .15
181 Vladimir Guerrero .50 .15
182 Dave Burba .20 .06
183 Tom Goodwin .20 .06
184 Brian Daubach .20 .06
185 Jay Bell .20 .06
186 Roy Halladay .20 .06
187 Miguel Tejada .20 .06
188 Armando Rios .20 .06
189 Fernando Vina .20 .06
190 Eric Davis .20 .06
191 Henry Rodriguez .20 .06
192 Joe McEwing .20 .06
193 Jeff Kent .20 .06
194 Mike Jackson .20 .06
195 Mike Morgan .20 .06
196 Jeff Montgomery .20 .06
197 Jeff Zimmerman .20 .06
198 Tony Fernandez .20 .06
199 Jason Giambi .50 .15
200 Jose Canseco .50 .15
201 Alex Gonzalez .20 .06
202 Jack Cust .40 .12
Mike Colangelo
Dee Brown
203 Felipe Lopez .50 .15
Alfonso Soriano
Pablo Ozuna
204 Erubiel Durazo .50 .15
Pat Burrell
Nick Johnson
205 John Sneed RC .40 .12
Kip Wells
Matt Blank
206 Josh Kalinowski .40 .12
Michael Tejera
Chris Mears RC
207 Roosevelt Brown .40 .12
Corey Patterson
Lance Berkman
208 Kit Pellow .40 .12
Kevin Barker
Russ Branyan
209 B.J. Garbe .50 .15
Larry Bigbie RC
210 Eric Munson .40 .12
Bobby Bradley RC
211 Josh Girdley .40 .12
Kyle Snyder
212 Chance Caple RC .40 .12
Jason Jennings
213 Ryan Christianson 2.00 .60
Brett Myers RC
214 Jason Stumm .40 .12
Rob Purvis RC
215 David Walling .40 .12
Mike Paradis
216 Omar Ortiz .40 .12
Jay Gehrke
217 David Cone HL .20 .06
218 Jose Jimenez HL .20 .06
219 Chris Singleton HL .20 .06
220 Fernando Tatis HL .20 .06
221 Todd Helton HL .20 .06
222 Kevin Millwood DIV .20 .06
223 Todd Pratt DIV .20 .06
224 Orl.Hernandez DIV .20 .06
225 Pedro Martinez DIV .30 .09
226 Tom Glavine LCS .20 .06
227 Bernie Williams LCS .20 .06
228 Mariano Rivera WS .20 .06
229 Tony Gwynn 20CB .60 .18
230 Wade Boggs 20CB .30 .09
231 Lance Johnson CB .20 .06
232 Mark McGwire 20CB 1.25 .35
233 R.Henderson 20CB .50 .15
234 R.Henderson 20CB .50 .15
235 Roger Clemens 20CB 1.00 .30
236A M.McGwire MM 3.00 .90
1st HR
236B M.McGwire MM 3.00 .90
1987 ROY
236C M.McGwire MM 3.00 .90
62nd HR
236D M.McGwire MM 3.00 .90
70th HR
236E M.McGwire MM 3.00 .90
500th HR
237A H.Aaron MM 2.00 .60
1st Career HR
237B H.Aaron MM 2.00 .60
1957 MVP
237C H.Aaron MM 2.00 .60
3000th Hit
237D H.Aaron MM 2.00 .60
715th HR
237E H.Aaron MM 2.00 .60
755th HR
238A C.Ripken MM 4.00 1.20
1982 ROY
238B C.Ripken MM 4.00 1.20
1991 MVP
238C C.Ripken MM 4.00 1.20
2131 Game
238D C.Ripken MM 4.00 1.20
Streak Ends
238E C.Ripken MM 4.00 1.20
400th HR
239A W.Boggs MM .75 .23
1983 Batting
239B W.Boggs MM .75 .23
1988 Batting
239C W.Boggs MM .75 .23
2000th Hit
239D W.Boggs MM .75 .23
1996 Champs
239E W.Boggs MM .75 .23
3000th Hit
240A T.Gwynn MM 1.50 .45
1984 Batting
240B T.Gwynn MM 1.50 .45
1984 NLCS
240C T.Gwynn MM 1.50 .45
1995 Batting
240D T.Gwynn MM 1.50 .45
1998 NLCS
240E T.Gwynn MM 1.50 .45
3000th Hit
241 Tom Glavine .30 .09
242 David Wells .20 .06
243 Kevin Appier .20 .06
244 Troy Percival .20 .06
245 Ray Lankford .20 .06
246 Marquis Grissom .20 .06
247 Randy Winn .20 .06
248 Miguel Batista .20 .06
249 Darren Dreifort .20 .06
250 Barry Bonds 1.25 .35
251 Harold Baines .20 .06
252 Cliff Floyd .20 .06
253 Freddy Garcia .20 .06
254 Kenny Rogers .20 .06
255 Ben Davis .20 .06
256 Charles Johnson .20 .06
257 Bubba Trammell .20 .06
258 Desi Relaford .20 .06
259 Al Martin .20 .06
260 Andy Pettitte .30 .09
261 Carlos Lee .20 .06
262 Matt Lawton .20 .06
263 Andy Fox .20 .06
264 Chan Ho Park .20 .06
265 Billy Koch .20 .06
266 Dave Roberts .20 .06
267 Carl Everett .20 .06
268 Orel Hershiser .20 .06
269 Trot Nixon .30 .09
270 Rusty Greer .20 .06
271 Will Clark .50 .15
272 Quilvio Veras .20 .06
273 Rico Brogna .20 .06
274 Devon White .20 .06
275 Tim Hudson .30 .09
276 Mike Hampton .20 .06
277 Miguel Cairo .20 .06
278 Darren Oliver .20 .06
279 Jeff Cirillo .20 .06
280 Al Leiter .20 .06
281 Shane Andrews .20 .06
282 Carlos Febles .20 .06
283 Pedro Astacio .20 .06
284 Juan Guzman .20 .06
285 Orlando Hernandez .20 .06
286 Paul Konerko .20 .06
287 Tony Clark .20 .06
288 Aaron Boone .20 .06
289 Ismael Valdes .20 .06
290 Moises Alou .20 .06
291 Kevin Tapani .20 .06
292 John Franco .20 .06
293 Todd Zeile .20 .06
294 Jason Schmidt .20 .06
295 Johnny Damon .20 .06
296 Scott Brosius .20 .06
297 Travis Fryman .20 .06
298 Jose Vizcaino .20 .06
299 Eric Chavez .20 .06
300 Mike Piazza .75 .23
301 Matt Clement .20 .06
302 Cristian Guzman .20 .06
303 C.J. Nitkowski .20 .06
304 Michael Tucker .20 .06
305 Brett Tomko .20 .06
306 Mike Lansing .20 .06
307 Eric Owens .20 .06
308 Livan Hernandez .20 .06
309 Rondell White .20 .06
310 Todd Stottlemyre .20 .06
311 Chris Carpenter .20 .06
312 Ken Hill .20 .06
313 Mark Loretta .20 .06
314 John Rocker .20 .06
315 Richie Sexson .20 .06
316 Ruben Mateo .20 .06
317 Joe Randa .20 .06
318 Mike Sirotka .20 .06
319 Jose Rosado .20 .06
320 Matt Mantei .20 .06
321 Kevin Millwood .20 .06
322 Gary DiSarcina .20 .06
323 Dustin Hermanson .20 .06
324 Mike Stanton .20 .06
325 Kirk Rueter .20 .06
326 Damian Miller RC .40 .12
327 Doug Glanville .20 .06
328 Scott Rolen .30 .09
329 Ray Durham .20 .06
330 Butch Huskey .20 .06
331 Mariano Rivera .30 .09
332 Darren Lewis .20 .06
333 Mike Timlin .20 .06
334 Mark Grudzielanek .20 .06
335 Mike Cameron .20 .06
336 Kelvim Escobar .20 .06
337 Bret Boone .20 .06
338 Mo Vaughn .20 .06
339 Craig Biggio .30 .09
340 Michael Barrett .20 .06
341 Marlon Anderson .20 .06
342 Bobby Jones .20 .06
343 John Halama .20 .06
344 Todd Ritchie .20 .06
345 Chuck Knoblauch .20 .06
346 Rick Reed .20 .06
347 Kelly Stinnett .20 .06
348 Tim Salmon .30 .09
349 A.J. Hinch .20 .06
350 Jose Cruz Jr. .20 .06
351 Roberto Hernandez .20 .06
352 Edgar Renteria .20 .06
353 Jose Hernandez .20 .06
354 Brad Fullmer .20 .06
355 Trevor Hoffman .20 .06
356 Troy O'Leary .20 .06
357 Justin Thompson .20 .06
358 Kevin Young .20 .06
359 Hideki Irabu .20 .06
360 Jim Thome .50 .15
361 Steve Karsay .20 .06
362 Octavio Dotel .20 .06
363 Omar Vizquel .20 .06
364 Raul Mondesi .20 .06
365 Shane Reynolds .20 .06
366 Bartolo Colon .20 .06
367 Chris Widger .20 .06
368 Gabe Kapler .20 .06
369 Bill Simas .20 .06
370 Tino Martinez .30 .09
371 John Thomson .20 .06
372 Delino DeShields .20 .06
373 Carlos Perez .20 .06
374 Eddie Perez .20 .06
375 Jeromy Burnitz .20 .06
376 Jimmy Haynes .20 .06
377 Travis Lee .20 .06
378 Darryl Hamilton .20 .06
379 Jamie Moyer .20 .06
380 Alex Gonzalez .20 .06
381 John Wetteland .20 .06
382 Vinny Castilla .20 .06
383 Jeff Suppan .20 .06
384 Jim Leyritz .20 .06
385 Robb Nen .20 .06
386 Wilson Alvarez .20 .06
387 Andres Galarraga .20 .06
388 Mike Remlinger .20 .06
389 Geoff Jenkins .20 .06
390 Matt Stairs .20 .06
391 Bill Mueller .20 .06
392 Mike Lowell .20 .06
393 Andy Ashby .20 .06
394 Ruben Rivera .20 .06
395 Todd Helton .30 .09
396 Bernie Williams .30 .09
397 Royce Clayton .20 .06
398 Manny Ramirez .20 .06
399 Kerry Wood .50 .15
400 Ken Griffey Jr. .75 .23
401 Enrique Wilson .20 .06
402 Joey Hamilton .20 .06
403 Shawn Estes .20 .06
404 Ugueth Urbina .20 .06
405 Albert Belle .20 .06
406 Rick Helling .20 .06
407 Steve Parris .20 .06
408 Eric Milton .20 .06
409 Dave Mlicki .20 .06
410 Shawn Green .20 .06
411 Jaret Wright .20 .06
412 Tony Womack .20 .06
413 Vernon Wells .20 .06
414 Ron Belliard .20 .06
415 Ellis Burks .20 .06
416 Scott Erickson .20 .06
417 Rafael Palmeiro .30 .09
418 Damion Easley .20 .06
419 Jamey Wright .20 .06
420 Corey Koskie .20 .06
421 Bobby Howry .20 .06
422 Ricky Ledee .20 .06
423 Dmitri Young .20 .06
424 Sidney Ponson .20 .06
425 Greg Maddux .75 .23
426 Jose Guillen .20 .06
427 Jon Lieber .20 .06
428 Andy Benes .20 .06
429 Randy Velarde .20 .06
430 Sean Casey .20 .06
431 Torii Hunter .20 .06
432 Ryan Rupe .20 .06
433 David Segui .20 .06
434 Todd Pratt .20 .06
435 Nomar Garciaparra .75 .23
436 Denny Neagle .20 .06
437 Ron Coomer .20 .06
438 Chris Singleton .20 .06
439 Tony Batista .20 .06
440 Andruw Jones .20 .06
441 Aubrey Huff .20 .06
Sean Burroughs
Adam Piatt
442 Rafael Furcal .40 .12
Travis Dawkins
Jason Dellaero
443 Mike Lamb RC .40 .12
Joe Crede
Wilton Veras
444 Julio Zuleta RC .40 .12
Jorge Toca
Dernell Stenson
445 Garry Maddux Jr. RC .40 .12
Gary Matthews Jr.
Tim Raines Jr.
446 Mark Mulder .50 .15
C.C. Sabathia
Matt Riley
447 Scott Downs RC .40 .12
Chris George
Matt Belisle
448 Doug Mirabelli .40 .12
Ben Petrick
Jayson Werth
449 Josh Hamilton .40 .12
Corey Myers RC
450 Ben Christensen RC .40 .12
Richard Stahl RC
451 Ben Sheets RC 3.00 .90
Barry Zito
452 Kurt Ainsworth .75 .23
Ty Howington RC
453 Vince Faison RC .40 .12
Rick Asadoorian
454 Keith Reed RC .40 .12
Jeff Heaverlo
455 Mike MacDougal .50 .15
Brad Baker RC
456 Mark McGwire SH .60 .18
457 Cal Ripken SH .75 .23
458 Wade Boggs SH .20 .06
459 Tony Gwynn SH .30 .09
460 Jesse Orosco SH .20 .06
461 Larry Walker .30 .09
Nomar Garciaparra LL
462 Ken Griffey Jr. .50 .15
Mark McGwire LL
463 Manny Ramirez .50 .15
Mark McGwire LL
464 Pedro Martinez .30 .09
Randy Johnson LL
465 Pedro Martinez .30 .09
Randy Johnson LL
466 Derek Jeter .50 .15
Luis Gonzalez LL
467 Larry Walker .20 .06
Manny Ramirez LL
468 Tony Gwynn 20CB .60 .18
469 Mark McGwire 20CB 1.25 .35
470 Frank Thomas 20CB .50 .15
471 Harold Baines 20CB .20 .06
472 Roger Clemens 20CB 1.00 .30
473 John Franco 20CB .20 .06
474 John Franco 20CB .20 .06
475A K.Griffey Jr. MM 2.00 .60
350th HR
475B K.Griffey Jr. MM 2.00 .60
1997 MVP
475C K.Griffey Jr. MM 2.00 .60
HR Dad
475D K.Griffey Jr. MM 2.00 .60
1992 AS MVP
475E K.Griffey Jr. MM 2.00 .60
50 HR 1997
476A B.Bonds MM 3.00 .90
400HR/400SB
476B B.Bonds MM 3.00 .90
40HR/40SB
476C B.Bonds MM 3.00 .90
1993 MVP
476D B.Bonds MM 3.00 .90
1990 MVP
476E B.Bonds MM 3.00 .90
1992 MVP
477A S.Sosa MM 2.00 .60
20 HR June
477B S.Sosa MM 2.00 .60
66 HR 1998
477C S.Sosa MM 2.00 .60
60 HR 1999
477D S.Sosa MM 2.00 .60
1998 MVP
477E S.Sosa MM HR's 2.00 .60
61/62
478A D.Jeter MM 3.00 .90
1996 ROY
478B D.Jeter MM 3.00 .90
Wins 1999 WS
478C D.Jeter MM 3.00 .90
Wins 1998 WS
478D D.Jeter MM 3.00 .90
Wins 1996 WS
478E D.Jeter MM 3.00 .90
17 GM Hit Streak
479A A.Rodriguez MM 2.00 .60
40HR/40SB
479B A.Rodriguez MM 2.00 .60
100th HR
479C A.Rodriguez MM 2.00 .60
1996 POY
479D A.Rodriguez MM 2.00 .60
Wins 1 Million
479E A.Rodriguez MM 2.00 .60
1996 Batting Leader
NNO M. McGwire 85 Reprint 5.00 1.50

2000 Topps 20th Century Best Sequential

Inserted into first series hobby packs at an overall rate of one in 869 and one in 239 HTA packs, and into series two hobby packs at one in 362 and one in 100 HTA packs, these cards parallel the Century's Best subset within the base 2000 Topps set (cards 229-235/468-474). These insert cards, unlike the regular cards, feature "CB" prefixed numbering on back and have dramatic sparkling foil-coated fronts. Each card is sequentially numbered to the featured players highlighted career statistic.

	Nm-Mt	Ex-Mt
CB1 T.Gwynn AVG/339	60.00	18.00
CB2 W.Boggs 2B/578	30.00	9.00
CB3 L.Johnson 3B/117	60.00	18.00
CB4 M.McGwire HR/522	50.00	15.00
CB5 Rickey Henderson SB/1334	25.00	7.50
CB6 Rickey Henderson RUN/2103	20.00	6.00
CB7 R.Clemens WIN/247	100.00	30.00
CB8 Tony Gwynn HIT/3067	25.00	7.50
CB9 Mark McGwire SLG/587	60.00	18.00
CB10 Frank Thomas OBP/440	25.00	7.50
CB11 Harold Baines RBI/1583	15.00	4.50
CB12 Roger Clemens K's/3316	40.00	12.00
CB13 John Franco ERA/264	30.00	9.00
CB14 John Franco SV/416	20.00	6.00

2000 Topps Home Team Advantage

These cards were distributed exclusively in a 479-card factory set. Each set contained the 478-card base issue 2000 Topps set plus one Hank Aaron Chrome Reprint card. All of the base cards within Home Team Advantage factory sets were stamped with a special "HTA" gold foil logo on the card front. Oddly, cards 222-228 (Divisional Playoffs), 229-235 (20th Century's Best), 236-240 (Magic Moments), 461-467 (League Leaders) and 468-474 (20th Century Best) did NOT feature the gold-foil HTA tag. Thus, those cards are identical to basic issue Topps cards and are not included within our checklist for this set (though they are included within the complete factory set).

	Nm-Mt	Ex-Mt
COMP.FACT.SET (479)	80.00	24.00
*HTA: .75X TO 2X BASIC CARDS		

2000 Topps MVP Promotion

Inserted one in every 510 first series hobby and retail packs and one in every 140 first series HTA packs, this set is an almost complete parallel of the regular Topps set. The cards in the first series parallel cards number 1 through 201 and second series parallels cards 241-440. Card numbers 7 and 44 were never produced for this set. Each MVP Promotion parallel card has a prominent gold foil MVP logo on the front and contest rules and guidelines on back. Only 100 of each of these cards were printed and a new winner was announced each week throughout the 2000 season as Topps selected their top player of the week. Winning cards could be redeemed for a complete set of exchnage cards featuring every weekly winning player. Winning cards were verified through either calling 1-888-Go-Topps or checking on the Topps web site prior to the deadline. The exchange deadline for these cards was December 31st, 2000. The winning cards were the following numbers (in correspondence with the basic issue 2000 Topps card): 13, 15, 45, 50, 53, 55, 60, 72, 87, 90, 93, 107, 109, 116, 148, 165, 180, 199, 250, 271, 350, 395, 398, 403 and 427. Since Topps destroyed these Winner exchange cards once they received them, they're in noticeably shorter supply than other cards from this set. Despite this fact, no noticeable premiums in secondary trading levels have been detected for these cards.

	Nm-Mt	Ex-Mt
*STARS: 30X TO 60X BASIC CARDS		
13 Magglio Ordonez W	12.00	3.60
15 Derek Jeter W	80.00	24.00
45 Jeff Bagwell W	20.00	6.00
50 Sammy Sosa W	50.00	15.00
53 Dante Bichette W	12.00	3.60
55 Frank Thomas W	30.00	9.00
60 Pedro Martinez W	30.00	9.00
72 Brian Jordan W	12.00	3.60
87 Bobby Higginson W	12.00	3.60
90 Mark Kotsay W	12.00	3.60
93 Carlos Delgado W	12.00	3.60
107 Jim Edmonds W	12.00	3.60
109 Adrian Beltre W	12.00	3.60
116 Jermaine Dye W	12.00	3.60
148 Derek Bell W	12.00	3.60
165 Kenny Lofton W	12.00	3.60
180 Chipper Jones W	30.00	9.00
199 Jason Giambi W	30.00	9.00
250 Barry Bonds W	80.00	24.00
271 Will Clark W	30.00	9.00
350 Jose Cruz Jr. W	12.00	3.60
395 Todd Helton W	20.00	6.00
398 Manny Ramirez W	12.00	3.60
403 Shawn Estes W	12.00	3.60
427 Jon Lieber W	12.00	3.60

2000 Topps MVP Promotion Exchange

This 25-card set was available only to those lucky collectors who obtained one of the twenty-five winning player cards from the 2000 Topps MVP Promotion parallel set. Each week, throughout the 2000 season, Topps named a new Player of the Week, and that player's Topps MVP Promotion parallel card was made redeemable for this 25-card set. The deadline to exchange the winning cards was 12/31/00.

	Nm-Mt	Ex-Mt
COMPLETE SET (25)	50.00	15.00
MVP1 Pedro Martinez	4.00	1.20
MVP2 Jim Edmonds	1.50	.45
MVP3 Derek Bell	1.50	.45
MVP4 Jermaine Dye	1.50	.45
MVP5 Jose Cruz Jr.	1.50	.45
MVP6 Todd Helton	2.50	.75
MVP7 Brian Jordan	1.50	.45
MVP8 Shawn Estes	1.50	.45
MVP9 Dante Bichette	1.50	.45
MVP10 Carlos Delgado	1.50	.45
MVP11 Bobby Higginson	1.50	.45
MVP12 Mark Kotsay	1.50	.45
MVP13 Magglio Ordonez	1.50	.45
MVP14 Jon Lieber	1.50	.45
MVP15 Frank Thomas	4.00	1.20
MVP16 Manny Ramirez	1.50	.45
MVP17 Sammy Sosa	6.00	1.80
MVP18 Will Clark	4.00	1.20
MVP19 Jeff Bagwell	2.50	.75
MVP20 Derek Jeter	10.00	3.00
MVP21 Adrian Beltre	1.50	.45
MVP22 Kenny Lofton	1.50	.45
MVP23 Barry Bonds	10.00	3.00
MVP24 Jason Giambi	4.00	1.20
MVP25 Chipper Jones	4.00	1.20

2000 Topps Oversize

Each 2000 Topps hobby and Home Team Advantage box has one of these cards as a chiptopper. A chiptopper is a card that lies on top of the packs within the sealed box. These cards are exact parallels of their corresponding base issue card except, of course, for their larger size (3" by 5") and 1-8 numbering on back. Please note, for checklisting purposes, we've added "A" and "B" prefixes to each card number to signify which cards were seeded in first versus second series packs.

	Nm-Mt	Ex-Mt
COMPLETE SERIES 1 (8)	20.00	6.00
COMPLETE SERIES 2 (8)	15.00	4.50
A1 Mark McGwire	3.00	.90
A2 Hank Aaron	2.00	.60
A3 Derek Jeter	3.00	.90
A4 Sammy Sosa	2.00	.60
A5 Alex Rodriguez	2.00	.60
A6 Chipper Jones	1.25	.35
A7 Cal Ripken	4.00	1.20
A8 Pedro Martinez	1.25	.35
B1 Barry Bonds	3.00	.90
B2 Orlando Hernandez	.50	.15
B3 Mike Piazza	2.00	.60
B4 Manny Ramirez	.50	.15
B5 Ken Griffey Jr.	2.00	.60
B6 Rafael Palmeiro	.75	.23
B7 Greg Maddux	2.00	.60
B8 Nomar Garciaparra	2.00	.60

2000 Topps 21st Century

Inserted one every 18 first series hobby and retail packs and one every five first series HTA packs, these 10 cards feature players who are among those expected to be among the best players in the first part of the 21st century.

	Nm-Mt	Ex-Mt
COMPLETE SET (10)	10.00	3.00
C1 Ben Grieve	.40	.12
C2 Alex Gonzalez	.40	.12
C3 Derek Jeter	2.50	.75
C4 Sean Casey	.40	.12
C5 Nomar Garciaparra	1.50	.45
C6 Alex Rodriguez	1.50	.45
C7 Scott Rolen	.60	.18
C8 Andruw Jones	.40	.12
C9 Vladimir Guerrero	1.00	.30
C10 Todd Helton	.60	.18

2000 Topps Aaron

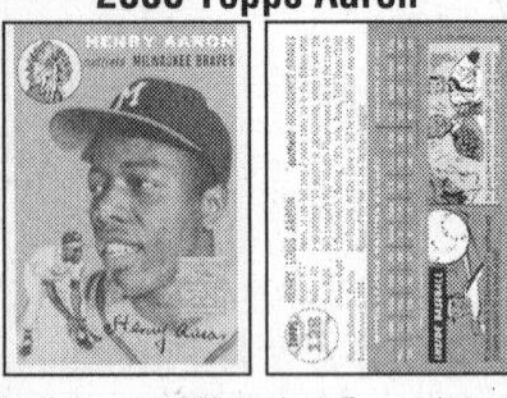

For their year 2000 product, Topps chose to reprint cards of All-Time Home Run King, Hank Aaron. The cards were inserted one every 18 hobby and retail pack and one every five HTA packs in both first and second series. The even year cards were released in the first series and the odd year cards were issued in the second series. Each card can be easily detected from the original cards issued from the 1950-70s by the large gold foil logo on front and the glossy card stock.

	Nm-Mt	Ex-Mt
COMMON CARD (1-23)	5.00	1.50
1 Hank Aaron 1954	10.00	3.00

2000 Topps Aaron Autographs

Due to the fact that Topps could not obtain actual signed Hank Aaron cards prior to pack out for first series in December, 2000 - Topps inserted into first series packs at a rate of one in 4361 hobby and retail and 1 in 1199 first series HTA packs exchange cards of which were redeemable (prior to the May 31st, 2000 deadline) for a signed Hank Aaron Reprint card. The 12 exchange cards distributed in series one were redeemable exclusively for specific even year Reprint cards. The 11 odd year Autographs were obtained by Topps well in time for the second series release in April, 2000 and thus those actual autographed cards were seeded directly into the series two packs.

	Nm-Mt	Ex-Mt
COMMON CARD (2-23)	200.00	60.00
1 Hank Aaron 1954	250.00	75.00

2000 Topps All-Star Rookie Team

Randomly inserted into packs at one in 36 HOB/RET packs and one in eight HTA packs, this 10-card insert set features players that had break-through seasons their first year. Card backs carry a "RT" prefix.

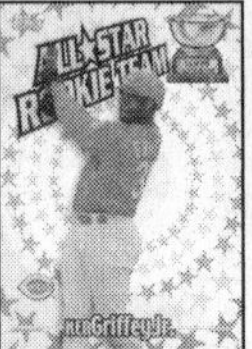

	Nm-Mt	Ex-Mt
COMPLETE SET (10)	25.00	7.50
RT1 Mark McGwire	5.00	1.50
RT2 Chuck Knoblauch	.75	.23
RT3 Chipper Jones	2.00	.60
RT4 Cal Ripken	6.00	1.80
RT5 Manny Ramirez	.75	.23
RT6 Jose Canseco	2.00	.60
RT7 Ken Griffey Jr.	3.00	.90
RT8 Mike Piazza	3.00	.90
RT9 Dwight Gooden	1.25	.35
RT10 Billy Wagner UER	.75	.23

Les Cain's name is spelled Less

2000 Topps All-Topps

Inserted one every 12 first series hobby and retail packs and one every three first series HTA packs, this set features 10 star National Leaguers, 10 star American Leaguers, and a comparision to Hall of Famers at their respective position. Each card is printed on silver foil-board with select metalization. The National League players were issued in series one, while the American League players were issued in series two.

	Nm-Mt	Ex-Mt
COMPLETE SET (20)	20.00	6.00
COMPLETE N.L.(10)	10.00	3.00
COMPLETE A.L. (10)	10.00	3.00
AT1 Greg Maddux	1.50	.45
AT2 Mike Piazza	1.50	.45
AT3 Mark McGwire	2.50	.75
AT4 Craig Biggio	.60	.18
AT5 Chipper Jones	1.00	.30
AT6 Barry Larkin	1.00	.30
AT7 Barry Bonds	2.50	.75
AT8 Andruw Jones	.40	.12
AT9 Sammy Sosa	1.50	.45
AT10 Larry Walker	.60	.18
AT11 Pedro Martinez	1.00	.30
AT12 Ivan Rodriguez	1.00	.30
AT13 Rafael Palmeiro	.60	.18
AT14 Roberto Alomar	1.00	.30
AT15 Cal Ripken	3.00	.90
AT16 Derek Jeter	2.50	.75
AT17 Albert Belle	.40	.12
AT18 Ken Griffey Jr.	1.50	.45
AT19 Manny Ramirez	.40	.12
AT20 Jose Canseco	1.00	.30

2000 Topps Autographs

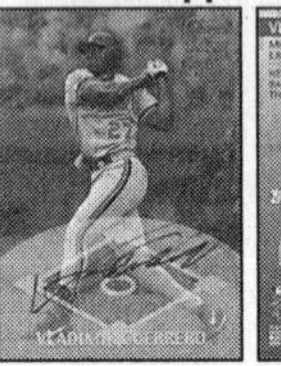

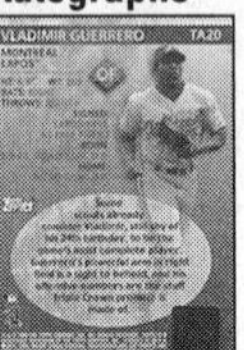

Inserted at various level of difficulty, these players signed autographs for the 2000 Topps product. Group A players were inserted one every 7589 first series hobby and retail packs and one every 2087 first series HTA packs. Group A players were issued at a rate of one in every 5840 second series hobby and retail packs, and one every 1607 HTA packs. Group B players were inserted one every 4553 first series hobby and retail packs and one every 1252 first series HTA packs. Group B players were inserted at a rate of one every 2337 second series hobby and retail packs, and one every 643 HTA packs. Group C players were inserted one every 1518 first series hobby and retail packs and one every 417 first series HTA packs. Group C players were inserted one every 1169 second series hobby and retail packs, and one in every 321 HTA packs. Group D players were inserted one every 911 first series hobby and retails packs and one every 250 first series HTA packs. Group D players were inserted one in every 701 second series hobby and retail packs, and one in every 193 HTA packs. Group E autographs were issued one every 1138 first series hobby and retail packs and one every 313 first series HTA packs. Group E players were inserted one in every 1754 second series hobby and retail packs, and one in every 482 HTA packs. Originally intended to be a straight numerical run of TA1-TA15 for series one, cards TA 4 (Sean Casey) and TA 15 (Carlos Beltran) were dropped and replaced with TA 20 (Vladimir Guerrero) and TA 27 (Mike Sweeney).

	Nm-Mt	Ex-Mt
TA1 Alex Rodriguez A	120.00	36.00
TA2 Tony Gwynn A	80.00	24.00
TA3 Vinny Castilla B	25.00	7.50
TA4 Sean Casey B	40.00	12.00
TA5 Shawn Green C	25.00	7.50
TA6 Rey Ordonez C	15.00	4.50
TA7 Matt Lawton C	15.00	4.50
TA8 Tony Womack C	15.00	4.50
TA9 Gabe Kapler D	15.00	4.50
TA10 Pat Burrell D	25.00	7.50
TA11 Preston Wilson D	25.00	7.50
TA12 Troy Glaus D	40.00	12.00
TA13 Carlos Beltran D	25.00	7.50
TA14 Josh Girdley E	15.00	4.50
TA15 B.J. Garbe E	15.00	4.50
TA16 Derek Jeter A	150.00	45.00
TA17 Cal Ripken A	200.00	60.00
TA18 Ivan Rodriguez B	50.00	15.00
TA19 Rafael Palmeiro B	60.00	18.00
TA20 Vladimir Guerrero B	60.00	18.00
TA21 Raul Mondesi C	25.00	7.50
TA22 Scott Rolen C	40.00	12.00
TA23 Billy Wagner C	40.00	12.00
TA24 Fernando Tatis C	15.00	4.50
TA25 Ruben Mateo D	15.00	4.50
TA26 Carlos Febles D	15.00	4.50
TA27 Mike Sweeney D	25.00	7.50
TA28 Alex Gonzalez D	15.00	4.50
TA29 Miguel Tejada D	25.00	7.50
TA30 Josh Hamilton E	15.00	4.50

2000 Topps Combos

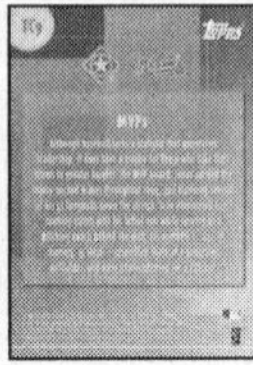

Randomly inserted into packs at one in 18 hobby and retail packs, and one in every five HTA packs, this 10-card insert set showcases player groupings unified by a common theme, such as Home Run Kings, and features artist renderings of each player reminiscent of Topps' classic 1959 set. Card backs carry a "TC" prefix.

	Nm-Mt	Ex-Mt
COMPLETE SET (10)	25.00	7.50
TC1 Roberto Alomar Manny Ramirez Kenny Lofton Jim Thome	1.50	.45
TC2 Tom Glavine Greg Maddux John Smoltz	3.00	.90
TC3 Derek Jeter Bernie Williams Tino Martinez	4.00	1.20
TC4 Ivan Rodriguez Mike Piazza	2.50	.75
TC5 Nomar Garciaparra Alex Rodriguez Derek Jeter	2.50	.75
TC6 Sammy Sosa Mark McGwire	3.00	.90
TC7 Pedro Martinez Randy Johnson	1.50	.45
TC8 Barry Bonds Ken Griffey Jr.	4.00	1.20
TC9 Chipper Jones Ivan Rodriguez	1.50	.45
TC10 Cal Ripken Tony Gwynn Wade Boggs	1.50	.45

2000 Topps Hands of Gold

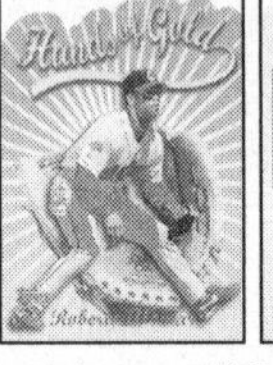

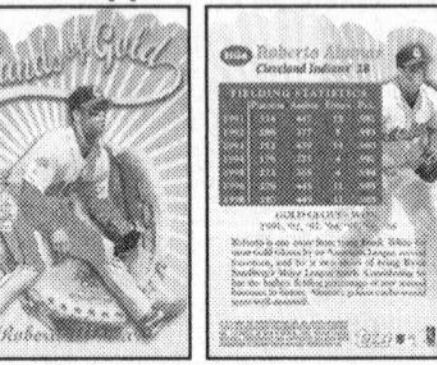

Inserted on every 18 first series hobby and retail packs and one every five first series HTA packs, this seven card set features players who have won at least five Gold Gloves. Each card is foil-stamped, die-cut and specially embossed.

	Nm-Mt	Ex-Mt
COMPLETE SET (7)	8.00	2.40
HG1 Barry Bonds	2.50	.75
HG2 Ivan Rodriguez	1.00	.30
HG3 Ken Griffey Jr.	1.50	.45
HG4 Roberto Alomar	1.00	.30
HG5 Tony Gwynn	1.25	.35
HG6 Omar Vizquel	.40	.12
HG7 Greg Maddux	1.50	.45

2000 Topps Own the Game

Randomly inserted into series two hobby and retail packs at a rate one in every 12, and one in every three series two HTA packs, this 30-card insert set features the top statistical leaders in major league baseball. Card backs carry an "OTG" prefix.

	Nm-Mt	Ex-Mt
COMPLETE SET (30)	50.00	15.00
OTG1 Derek Jeter	5.00	1.50
OTG2 B.J. Surhoff	.75	.23
OTG3 Luis Gonzalez	.75	.23
OTG4 Manny Ramirez	.75	.23
OTG5 Rafael Palmeiro	1.25	.35
OTG6 Mark McGwire	5.00	1.50
OTG7 Mark McGwire	5.00	1.50
OTG8 Sammy Sosa	3.00	.90
OTG9 Ken Griffey Jr.	3.00	.90
OTG10 Larry Walker	1.25	.35
OTG11 Nomar Garciaparra	3.00	.90
OTG12 Derek Jeter	5.00	1.50
OTG13 Larry Walker	1.25	.35
OTG14 Mark McGwire	5.00	1.50
OTG15 Manny Ramirez	.75	.23
OTG16 Pedro Martinez	2.00	.60
OTG17 Randy Johnson	2.00	.60
OTG18 Kevin Millwood	.75	.23
OTG19 Randy Johnson	2.00	.60
OTG20 Pedro Martinez	2.00	.60
OTG21 Kevin Brown	1.25	.35
OTG22 Chipper Jones	2.00	.60
OTG23 Ivan Rodriguez	2.00	.60
OTG24 Mariano Rivera	1.25	.35
OTG25 Scott Williamson	.75	.23
OTG26 Carlos Beltran	.75	.23
OTG27 Randy Johnson	2.00	.60
OTG28 Pedro Martinez	2.00	.60
OTG29 Sammy Sosa	3.00	.90
OTG30 Manny Ramirez	.75	.23

2000 Topps Perennial All-Stars

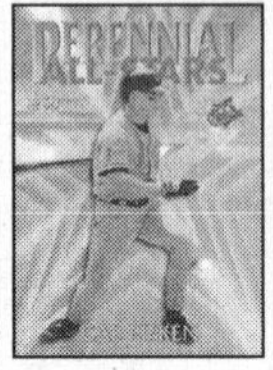

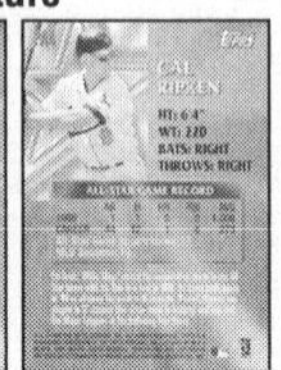

This set is inserted into first series hobby and retail packs at a rate of one in 18 and first series HTA packs at a rate of one every five packs. These 10 cards feature players who consistently achieve All-Star recognition.

	Nm-Mt	Ex-Mt
COMPLETE SET (10)	20.00	6.00
PA1 Ken Griffey Jr.	1.50	.45
PA2 Derek Jeter	2.50	.75
PA3 Sammy Sosa	1.50	.45
PA4 Cal Ripken	3.00	.90
PA5 Mike Piazza	1.50	.45
PA6 Nomar Garciaparra	1.50	.45
PA7 Jeff Bagwell	.60	.18
PA8 Barry Bonds	2.50	.75
PA9 Alex Rodriguez	1.50	.45
PA10 Mark McGwire	2.50	.75

2000 Topps Power Players

Inserted into hobby and retail first series packs at a rate of one in eight and first series HTA packs at a rate one every other pack, this set features 20 of the best sluggers in baseball.

	Nm-Mt	Ex-Mt
COMPLETE SET (20)	25.00	7.50
P1 Juan Gonzalez	1.00	.30
P2 Ken Griffey Jr.	1.50	.45
P3 Mark McGwire	2.50	.75
P4 Nomar Garciaparra	1.50	.45
P5 Barry Bonds	2.50	.75
P6 Mo Vaughn	.40	.12
P7 Larry Walker	.60	.18
P8 Alex Rodriguez	1.50	.45
P9 Jose Canseco	1.00	.30
P10 Jeff Bagwell	.60	.18
P11 Manny Ramirez	.40	.12
P12 Albert Belle	.40	.12
P13 Frank Thomas	1.00	.30
P14 Mike Piazza	1.50	.45
P15 Chipper Jones	1.00	.30
P16 Sammy Sosa	1.50	.45
P17 Vladimir Guerrero	1.00	.30
P18 Scott Rolen	.60	.18
P19 Raul Mondesi	.40	.12
P20 Derek Jeter	2.50	.75

2000 Topps Stadium Relics

Exclusively inserted into first series HTA jumbo packs at a rate of one in 165 first series packs, and one in every 135 second series HTA packs, these cards feature a piece of a major league stadium (mostly infield bases) as well as a photo and an autograph of the featured superstar who played there. Among the venerable ballparks included in this set are Wrigley Field, Fenway Park and Yankee Stadium.

	Nm-Mt	Ex-Mt
SR1 Don Mattingly	150.00	45.00
SR2 Carl Yastrzemski	120.00	36.00
SR3 Ernie Banks	100.00	30.00
SR4 Johnny Bench	100.00	30.00
SR5 Willie Mays	200.00	60.00
SR6 Mike Schmidt	120.00	36.00
SR7 Lou Brock	80.00	24.00
SR8 Al Kaline	100.00	30.00
SR9 Paul Molitor	80.00	24.00
SR10 Eddie Mathews	100.00	30.00

2000 Topps Limited

These parallel cards were issued exclusively in factory set form (an attractive black box with a glossy teal overlay) and offered collectors the chance to get an upgraded premium version of the basic 2000 Topps. Each factory set contained a total of 619 cards including the complete 478 card basic Topps set plus the following insert sets: 21st Century Topps, Aaron Reprints, All-Star Rookie Team, All-Topps, Combos, Hands of Gold, Own the Game, Perennial All-Stars, Power Players and the Mark McGwire 1985 Reprint. Collectors received only one of five different variations of the Magic Moments subset cards (236-240/475-479) per factory set. Each card has thick gloss and features a "Limited Edition" gold foil stamp on front. Stated print run was originally 6000 serial numbered sets but actual production turned out to be 4,000 sets (with only 800 copies of each of the Magic Moments variation subset cards). Each factory box is serial numbered x/4000 but the individual cards are not numbered in any way. The sets were distributed in late September, 2000.

	Nm-Mt	Ex-Mt
COMP.FACT.SET (619)	200.00	60.00
COMPLETE SET (478)	100.00	30.00

*STARS: 2.5X TO 6X BASIC CARDS ...
*ROOKIES: 3X TO 8X BASIC CARDS ..
*MAGIC MOMENTS: 1.25X TO 3X BASIC MM

2000 Topps Limited 21st Century

These inserts were seeded at one complete set per sealed Topps Limited factory set. This is a complete parallel of the 21st Century insert that is found in 2000 Topps, and can be easily distinguished by the thicker card stock, glossy finish, and the words "Limited Edition" stamped in gold lettering on each card. Please note that only 4000 sets were produced.

	Nm-Mt	Ex-Mt
COMPLETE SET (10)	25.00	7.50

*LIMITED: 1X TO 2.5X TOPPS 21ST CENT.

2000 Topps Limited Aaron

These inserts were seeded at one complete set per sealed Topps Limited factory set. This is a complete parallel of the Aaron insert that is found in 2000 Topps, and can be easily distinguished by the thicker card stock, glossy finish, and the words "Limited Edition" stamped in gold lettering on each card. Please note that only 4000 sets were produced.

	Nm-Mt	Ex-Mt
COMPLETE SET (23)	80.00	24.00
*LIMITED: .3X TO .8X TOPPS AARON		
1 Hank Aaron 1954	10.00	3.00

2000 Topps Limited All-Star Rookie Team

These inserts were seeded at one complete set per sealed Topps Limited factory set. This is a complete parallel of the All-Star Rookie Team insert that is found in 2000 Topps, and can be easily distinguished by the thicker card stock, glossy finish, and the words "Limited Edition" stamped in gold lettering on each card. Please note that only 4000 sets were produced.

	Nm-Mt	Ex-Mt
COMPLETE SET (10)	30.00	9.00

*LIMITED: .5X TO 1.2X TOPPS AS ROOK.

2000 Topps Limited All-Topps

These inserts were seeded at one complete set per sealed Topps Limited factory set. This is a complete parallel of the All-Topps insert that is found in 2000 Topps, and can be easily distinguished by the thicker card stock, glossy finish, and the words "Limited Edition" stamped in gold lettering on each card. Please note that only 4000 sets were produced.

	Nm-Mt	Ex-Mt
COMPLETE SET (20)	40.00	12.00

*LIMITED: 1X TO 2.5X TOPPS ALL-TOPPS

2000 Topps Limited Combos

These inserts were seeded at one complete set per sealed Topps Limited factory set. This is a complete parallel of the Combos insert that is found in 2000 Topps, and can be easily distinguished by the thicker card stock, glossy finish, and the words "Limited Edition" stamped in gold lettering on each card. Please note that only 4000 sets were produced.

	Nm-Mt	Ex-Mt
COMPLETE SET (10)	50.00	15.00

*LIMITED: .75X TO 2X TOPPS COMBOS

2000 Topps Limited Hands of Gold

These inserts were seeded at one complete set per sealed Topps Limited factory set. This is a complete parallel of the Hands of Gold insert that is found in 2000 Topps, and can be easily distinguished by the thicker card stock, glossy finish, and the words "Limited Edition" stamped in gold lettering on each card. Please note that only 4000 sets were produced.

	Nm-Mt	Ex-Mt
COMPLETE SET (7)	15.00	4.50

*LIMITED: 1X TO 2.5X TOPPS HANDS

2000 Topps Limited Own the Game

These inserts were seeded at one complete set per sealed Topps Limited factory set. This is a complete parallel of the Own the Game insert that is found in 2000 Topps, and can be easily distinguished by the thicker card stock, glossy finish, and the words "Limited Edition" stamped in gold lettering on each card. Please note that only 4000 sets were produced.

Nm-Mt Ex-Mt
COMPLETE SET (30) 60.00 18.00
*LIMITED: .5X TO 1.2X TOPPS OTG ...

2000 Topps Limited Perennial All-Stars

These inserts were seeded at one complete set per sealed Topps Limited factory set. This is a complete parallel of the Perennial All-Stars insert that is found in 2000 Topps, and can be easily distinguished by the thicker card stock, glossy finish, and the words "Limited Edition" stamped in gold lettering on each card. Please note that only 4000 sets were produced.

Nm-Mt Ex-Mt
COMPLETE SET (10) 40.00 12.00
*LIMITED: 1X TO 2.5X TOPPS PER.AS

2000 Topps Limited Power Players

These inserts were seeded at one complete set per sealed Topps Limited factory set. This is a complete parallel of the Power Players insert that is found in 2000 Topps, and can be easily distinguished by the thicker card stock, glossy finish, and the words "Limited Edition" stamped in gold lettering on each card. Please note that only 4000 sets were produced.

Nm-Mt Ex-Mt
COMPLETE SET (20) 50.00 15.00
*LIMITED: 1X TO 2.5X TOPPS POWER

2000 Topps Traded

The 2000 Topps Traded sets were released in October, 2000 and featured a 135-card base set, and one additional autograph card. The set carried a suggested retail price of $29.99. Please note that each card in the base set carried a "T" prefix before the card number. Topps announced that due to the unavailability of certain players previously scheduled to sign autographs, Topps will include a small quantity of autographed cards from the 2000 Topps Baseball Rookies/Traded set into its 2000 Bowman Baseball Draft Picks and Prospects set. Notable Rookie Cards include Cristian Guerrero and J.R. House.

Nm-Mt Ex-Mt
COMP.FACT.SET (136) 40.00 12.00
COMPLETE SET (135) 25.00 7.50
T1 Mike MacDougal .50 .15
T2 Andy Tracy RC .30 .09
T3 Brandon Phillips RC 1.00 .30
T4 Brandon Inge RC .30 .09
T5 Robbie Morrison RC .30 .09
T6 Josh Pressley RC .30 .09
T7 Todd Moser RC .30 .09
T8 Rob Purvis .30 .09
T9 Chance Caple .30 .09
T10 Ben Sheets .75 .23
T11 Russ Jacobson RC .30 .09
T12 Brian Cole RC .30 .09
T13 Brad Baker .30 .09
T14 Alex Cintron RC 1.50 .45
T15 Lyle Overbay RC .50 .15
T16 Mike Edwards RC .30 .09
T17 Sean McGowan RC .30 .09
T18 Jose Molina .20 .06
T19 Marcos Castillo RC .30 .09
T20 Josue Espada RC .30 .09
T21 Alex Gordon RC .30 .09
T22 Rob Pugmire RC .30 .09
T23 Jason Stumm .30 .09
T24 Ty Howington .30 .09
T25 Brett Myers 1.50 .45
T26 Maicer Izturis RC .30 .09
T27 John McDonald .20 .06
T28 W.Rodriguez RC .30 .09
T29 Carlos Zambrano RC 2.00 .60
T30 Alejandro Diaz RC .30 .09
T31 Geraldo Guzman RC .30 .09
T32 J.R. House RC .30 .09
T33 Elvin Nina RC .30 .09
T34 Juan Pierre RC 1.50 .45
T35 Ben Johnson RC .30 .09
T36 Jeff Bailey RC .30 .09
T37 Miguel Olivo RC .30 .09
T38 F.Rodriguez RC 1.50 .45
T39 Tony Pena Jr. RC .30 .09
T40 Miguel Cabrera RC 20.00 6.00
T41 Asdrubal Oropeza RC .30 .09
T42 Junior Zamora RC .30 .09
T43 Jovanny Cedeno RC .30 .09
T44 John Sneed .30 .09
T45 Josh Kalinowski .30 .09
T46 Mike Young RC 2.50 .75
T47 Rico Washington RC .30 .09
T48 Chad Durbin RC .30 .09
T49 Junior Brignac RC .30 .09
T50 Carlos Hernandez RC .30 .09
T51 Cesar Izturis RC .30 .09
T52 Oscar Salazar RC .30 .09
T53 Pat Strange RC .30 .09
T54 Rick Asadoorian .30 .09
T55 Keith Reed .30 .09
T56 Leo Estrella RC .30 .09
T57 Wascar Serrano RC .30 .09
T58 Richard Gomez RC .30 .09
T59 Ramon Santiago RC .30 .09
T60 Jovanny Sosa RC .30 .09
T61 Aaron Rowand RC .30 .09
T62 Junior Guerrero RC .30 .09
T63 Luis Terrero RC .30 .09
T64 Brian Sanches RC .30 .09
T65 Scott Sobkowiak RC .30 .09
T66 Gary Majewski RC .30 .09
T67 Barry Zito 2.00 .60
T68 Ryan Christianson .30 .09
T69 Cristian Guerrero RC .30 .09
T70 T.De La Rosa RC .30 .09
T71 Andrew Beinbrink RC .30 .09
T72 Ryan Knox RC .30 .09
T73 Alex Graman RC .30 .09
T74 Juan Guzman RC .30 .09
T75 Ruben Salazar RC .30 .09
T76 Luis Matos RC 1.50 .45
T77 Tony Mota RC .30 .09
T78 Doug Davis .20 .06
T79 Ben Christensen .30 .09
T80 Mike Lamb .30 .09
T81 Adrian Gonzalez RC 1.50 .45
T82 Mike Stodolka RC .30 .09
T83 Adam Johnson RC .30 .09
T84 Matt Wheatland RC .30 .09
T85 Corey Smith RC .50 .15
T86 Rocco Baldelli RC 8.00 2.40
T87 Keith Bucktrot RC .30 .09
T88 Adam Wainwright RC 1.25 .35
T89 Scott Thorman RC .50 .15
T90 Tripper Johnson RC .50 .15
T91 Jim Edmonds .30 .09
T92 Masato Yoshii .20 .06
T93 Adam Kennedy .20 .06
T94 Darryl Kile .30 .09
T95 Mark McLemore .20 .06
T96 Ricky Gutierrez .20 .06
T97 Juan Gonzalez .75 .23
T98 Melvin Mora .30 .09
T99 Dante Bichette .30 .09
T100 Lee Stevens .20 .06
T101 Roger Cedeno .20 .06
T102 John Olerud .30 .09
T103 Eric Young .20 .06
T104 Mickey Morandini .20 .06
T105 Travis Lee .20 .06
T106 Greg Vaughn .30 .09
T107 Todd Zeile .30 .09
T108 Chuck Finley .30 .09
T109 Ismael Valdes .20 .06
T110 Reggie Sanders .30 .09
T111 Pat Hentgen .20 .06
T112 Ryan Klesko .30 .09
T113 Derek Bell .20 .06
T114 Hideo Nomo .75 .23
T115 Aaron Sele .20 .06
T116 Fernando Vina .30 .09
T117 Wally Joyner .30 .09
T118 Brian Hunter .20 .06
T119 Joe Girardi .20 .06
T120 Omar Daal .20 .06
T121 Brook Fordyce .20 .06
T122 Jose Valentin .20 .06
T123 Curt Schilling .50 .15
T124 B.J. Surhoff .30 .09
T125 Henry Rodriguez .20 .06
T126 Mike Bordick .20 .06
T127 David Justice .30 .09
T128 Charles Johnson .30 .09
T129 Will Clark .75 .23
T130 Dwight Gooden .50 .15
T131 David Segui .20 .06
T132 Denny Neagle .30 .09
T133 Jose Canseco .75 .23
T134 Bruce Chen .20 .06
T135 Jason Bere .20 .06

2000 Topps Traded Autographs

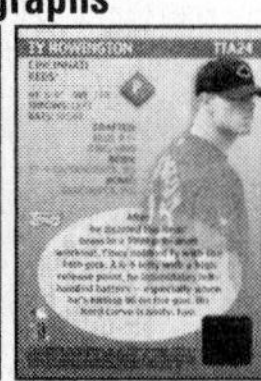

Randomly inserted into 2000 Topps Traded sets at a rate of one per sealed factory set, this 80-card set features autographed cards of some of the Major League's most talented prospects. Card backs carry a "TTA" prefix.

Nm-Mt Ex-Mt
TTA1 Mike MacDougal 12.00 3.60
TTA2 Andy Tracy 5.00 1.50
TTA3 Brandon Phillips 20.00 6.00
TTA4 Brandon Inge 8.00 2.40
TTA5 Robbie Morrison 5.00 1.50
TTA6 Josh Pressley 5.00 1.50
TTA7 Todd Moser 5.00 1.50
TTA8 Rob Purvis 8.00 2.40
TTA9 Chance Caple 8.00 2.40
TTA10 Ben Sheets 20.00 6.00
TTA11 Russ Jacobson 5.00 1.50
TTA12 Brian Cole 8.00 2.40
TTA13 Brad Baker 8.00 2.40
TTA14 Alex Cintron 25.00 7.50
TTA15 Lyle Overbay 12.00 3.60
TTA16 Mike Edwards 5.00 1.50
TTA17 Sean McGowan 5.00 1.50
TTA18 Jose Molina 5.00 1.50
TTA19 Marcos Castillo 5.00 1.50
TTA20 Josue Espada 5.00 1.50
TTA21 Alex Gordon 8.00 2.40
TTA22 Rob Pugmire 5.00 1.50
TTA23 Jason Stumm 8.00 2.40
TTA24 Ty Howington 8.00 2.40
TTA25 Brett Myers 40.00 12.00
TTA26 Maicer Izturis 5.00 1.50
TTA27 John McDonald 5.00 1.50
TTA28 Wilfredo Rodriguez 8.00 2.40
TTA29 Carlos Zambrano 40.00 12.00
TTA30 Alejandro Diaz 5.00 1.50
TTA31 Geraldo Guzman 5.00 1.50
TTA32 J.R. House 8.00 2.40
TTA33 Elvin Nina 5.00 1.50
TTA34 Juan Pierre 25.00 7.50
TTA35 Ben Johnson 8.00 2.40
TTA36 Jeff Bailey 5.00 1.50
TTA37 Miguel Olivo 8.00 2.40
TTA38 F.Rodriguez 40.00 12.00
TTA39 Tony Pena Jr. 8.00 2.40
TTA40 Miguel Cabrera 325.00 100.00
TTA41 Asdrubal Oropeza 8.00 2.40
TTA42 Junior Zamora 5.00 1.50
TTA43 Jovanny Cedeno 8.00 2.40
TTA44 John Sneed 5.00 1.50
TTA45 Josh Kalinowski 8.00 2.40
TTA46 Mike Young 50.00 15.00
TTA47 Rico Washington 5.00 1.50
TTA48 Chad Durbin 5.00 1.50
TTA49 Junior Brignac 5.00 1.50
TTA50 Carlos Hernandez 8.00 2.40
TTA51 Cesar Izturis 8.00 2.40
TTA52 Oscar Salazar 8.00 2.40
TTA53 Pat Strange 8.00 2.40
TTA54 Rick Asadoorian 8.00 2.40
TTA55 Keith Reed 8.00 2.40
TTA56 Leo Estrella 5.00 1.50
TTA57 Wascar Serrano 8.00 2.40
TTA58 Richard Gomez 5.00 1.50
TTA59 Ramon Santiago 8.00 2.40
TTA60 Jovanny Sosa 8.00 2.40
TTA61 Aaron Rowand 8.00 2.40
TTA62 Junior Guerrero 5.00 1.50
TTA63 Luis Terrero 8.00 2.40
TTA64 Brian Sanches 5.00 1.50
TTA65 Scott Sobkowiak 5.00 1.50
TTA66 Gary Majewski 5.00 1.50
TTA67 Barry Zito 50.00 15.00
TTA68 Ryan Christianson 8.00 2.40
TTA69 Cristian Guerrero 8.00 2.40
TTA70 Tomas De La Rosa 5.00 1.50
TTA71 Andrew Beinbrink 8.00 2.40
TTA72 Ryan Knox 5.00 1.50
TTA73 Alex Graman 5.00 1.50
TTA74 Juan Guzman 5.00 1.50
TTA75 Ruben Salazar 8.00 2.40
TTA76 Luis Matos 25.00 7.50
TTA77 Tony Mota 5.00 1.50
TTA78 Doug Davis 5.00 1.50
TTA79 Ben Christensen 8.00 2.40
TTA80 Mike Lamb 8.00 2.40

2001 Topps Press Release Jumbos

This eight-card set was released to hobby dealers and members of the media to promote the 2001 Topps baseball product. These gigantic cards measure 9" by 12 1/2" and feature legendary players like Nolan Ryan and Mark McGwire. These cards are not numbered and are listed below in alphabetical order.

Nm-Mt Ex-Mt
COMPLETE SET (8) 25.00 7.50
1 Title Card 1.00 .30
2 Topps Checklist 1.00 .30
3 Hank Aaron 4.00 1.20
4 Johnny Bench 3.00 .90
5 Bob Gibson 2.00 .60
Pedro Martinez
6 Mark McGwire 6.00 1.80
7 Nolan Ryan 8.00 2.40
8 Mike Schmidt 3.00 .90

2001 Topps

The 2001 Topps set featured 790 cards and was issued over two series. The set looks to bring back some of the heritage that Topps established in the past by bringing back Manager cards, dual-player prospect cards, and the 2000 season highlight cards. Notable Rookie Cards include Hee Seop Choi. Please note that some cards have been discovered with nothing printed on front but blank white except for the players name and 50th Topps anniversary logo printed in Gold. Factory sets include five special cards inserted specifically in those sets. Card number 7 was not issued as Topps continued to honor the memory of Mickey Mantle.

Nm-Mt Ex-Mt
COMPLETE SET (790) 80.00 24.00
COMP.FACT.BLUE SET (795) 100.00 30.00
COMP.SERIES 1 (405) 40.00 12.00
COMP. SERIES 2 (385) 40.00 12.00
COMMON (1-6/8-791) .20 .06
COMMON (352-376/727-751) .25 .07
1 Cal Ripken 1.50 .45
2 Chipper Jones .50 .15
3 Roger Cedeno .20 .06
4 Garret Anderson .20 .06
5 Robin Ventura .20 .06
6 Daryle Ward .20 .06
7 Does Not Exist
8 Craig Paquette .20 .06
9 Phil Nevin .20 .06
10 Jermaine Dye .20 .06
11 Chris Singleton .20 .06
12 Mike Stanton .20 .06
13 Brian Hunter .20 .06
14 Mike Redmond .20 .06
15 Jim Thome .50 .15
16 Brian Jordan .20 .06
17 Joe Girardi .20 .06
18 Steve Woodard .20 .06
19 Dustin Hermanson .20 .06
20 Shawn Green .20 .06
21 Todd Stottlemyre .20 .06
22 Dan Wilson .20 .06
23 Todd Pratt .20 .06
24 Derek Lowe .20 .06
25 Juan Gonzalez .50 .15
26 Clay Bellinger .20 .06
27 Jeff Fassero .20 .06
28 Pat Meares .20 .06
29 Eddie Taubensee .20 .06
30 Paul O'Neill .30 .09
31 Jeffrey Hammonds .20 .06
32 Pokey Reese .20 .06
33 Mike Mussina .50 .15
34 Rico Brogna .20 .06
35 Jay Buhner .20 .06
36 Steve Cox .20 .06
37 Quilvio Veras .20 .06
38 Marquis Grissom .20 .06
39 Shigetoshi Hasegawa .20 .06
40 Shane Reynolds .20 .06
41 Adam Piatt .20 .06
42 Luis Polonia .20 .06
43 Brook Fordyce .20 .06
44 Preston Wilson .20 .06
45 Ellis Burks .20 .06
46 Armando Rios .20 .06
47 Chuck Finley .20 .06
48 Dan Plesac .20 .06
49 Shannon Stewart .20 .06
50 Mark McGwire 1.25 .35
51 Mark Loretta .20 .06
52 Gerald Williams .20 .06
53 Eric Young .20 .06
54 Peter Bergeron .20 .06
55 Dave Hansen .20 .06
56 Arthur Rhodes .20 .06
57 Bobby Jones .20 .06
58 Matt Clement .20 .06
59 Mike Benjamin .20 .06
60 Pedro Martinez .50 .15
61 Jose Canseco .50 .15
62 Matt Anderson .20 .06
63 Torii Hunter .20 .06
64 Carlos Lee UER .20 .06
1999 Charlotte Games Played are wrong
65 David Cone .20 .06
66 Rey Sanchez .20 .06
67 Eric Chavez .20 .06
68 Rick Helling .20 .06
69 Manny Alexander .20 .06
70 John Franco .20 .06
71 Mike Bordick .20 .06
72 Andres Galarraga .20 .06
73 Jose Cruz Jr. .20 .06
74 Mike Matheny .20 .06
75 Randy Johnson .50 .15
76 Richie Sexson .20 .06
77 Vladimir Nunez .20 .06
78 Harold Baines .20 .06
79 Aaron Boone .20 .06
80 Darin Erstad .20 .06
81 Alex Gonzalez .20 .06
82 Gil Heredia .20 .06
83 Shane Andrews .20 .06
84 Todd Hundley .20 .06
85 Bill Mueller .20 .06
86 Mark McLemore .20 .06
87 Scott Spiezio .20 .06
88 Kevin McGlinchy .20 .06
89 Bubba Trammell .20 .06
90 Manny Ramirez .20 .06
91 Mike Lamb .20 .06
92 Scott Karl .20 .06
93 Brian Buchanan .20 .06
94 Chris Turner .20 .06
95 Mike Sweeney .20 .06
96 John Wetteland .20 .06
97 Rob Bell .20 .06
98 Pat Rapp .20 .06
99 John Burkett .20 .06
100 Derek Jeter 1.25 .35
101 J.D. Drew .20 .06
102 Jose Offerman .20 .06
103 Rick Reed .20 .06
104 Will Clark .50 .15
105 Rickey Henderson .50 .15
106 Dave Berg .20 .06
107 Kirk Rueter .20 .06
108 Lee Stevens .20 .06
109 Jay Bell .20 .06
110 Fred McGriff .30 .09
111 Julio Zuleta .20 .06
112 Brian Anderson .20 .06
113 Orlando Cabrera .20 .06
114 Alex Fernandez .20 .06
115 Derek Bell .20 .06
116 Eric Owens .20 .06
117 Brian Bohanon .20 .06
118 Dennys Reyes .20 .06
119 Mike Stanley .20 .06
120 Jorge Posada .30 .09
121 Rich Becker .20 .06
122 Paul Konerko .20 .06
123 Mike Remlinger .20 .06
124 Travis Lee .20 .06
125 Ken Caminiti .20 .06
126 Kevin Barker .20 .06
127 Paul Quantrill .20 .06
128 Ozzie Guillen .20 .06
129 Kevin Tapani .20 .06
130 Mark Johnson .20 .06
131 Randy Wolf .20 .06
132 Michael Tucker .20 .06
133 Darren Lewis .20 .06
134 Joe Randa .20 .06
135 Jeff Cirillo .20 .06
136 David Ortiz .20 .06
137 Herb Perry .20 .06
138 Jeff Nelson .20 .06
139 Chris Stynes .20 .06
140 Johnny Damon .20 .06
141 Jeff Reboulet .20 .06
142 Jason Schmidt .20 .06
143 Charles Johnson .20 .06
144 Pat Burrell .20 .06
145 Gary Sheffield .20 .06
146 Tom Glavine .30 .09
147 Jason Isringhausen .20 .06
148 Chris Carpenter .20 .06
149 Jeff Suppan .20 .06
150 Ivan Rodriguez .50 .15
151 Luis Sojo .20 .06
152 Ron Villone .20 .06
153 Mike Sirotka .20 .06
154 Chuck Knoblauch .20 .06
155 Jason Kendall .20 .06
156 Dennis Cook .20 .06
157 Bobby Estalella .20 .06
158 Jose Guillen .20 .06
159 Thomas Howard .20 .06
160 Carlos Delgado .20 .06
161 Benji Gil .20 .06
162 Tim Bogar .20 .06
163 Kevin Elster .20 .06
164 Einar Diaz .20 .06
165 Andy Benes .20 .06
166 Adrian Beltre .20 .06
167 David Bell .20 .06
168 Turk Wendell .20 .06
169 Pete Harnisch .20 .06
170 Roger Clemens 1.00 .30
171 Scott Williamson .20 .06
172 Kevin Jordan .20 .06
173 Brad Penny .20 .06
174 John Flaherty .20 .06
175 Troy Glaus .30 .09
176 Kevin Appier .20 .06
177 Walt Weiss .20 .06
178 Tyler Houston .20 .06
179 Michael Barrett .20 .06
180 Mike Hampton .20 .06
181 Francisco Cordova .20 .06
182 Mike Jackson .20 .06
183 David Segui .20 .06
184 Carlos Febles .20 .06
185 Roy Halladay .20 .06
186 Seth Etherton .20 .06
187 Charlie Hayes .20 .06
188 Fernando Tatis .20 .06
189 Steve Trachsel .20 .06
190 Livan Hernandez .20 .06
191 Joe Oliver .20 .06
192 Stan Javier .20 .06
193 B.J. Surhoff .20 .06
194 Rob Ducey .20 .06
195 Barry Larkin .50 .15
196 Danny Patterson .20 .06
197 Bobby Howry .20 .06
198 Dmitri Young .20 .06
199 Brian Hunter .20 .06
200 Alex Rodriguez .75 .23
201 Hideo Nomo .50 .15
202 Luis Alicea .20 .06
203 Warren Morris .20 .06
204 Antonio Alfonseca .20 .06
205 Edgardo Alfonzo .20 .06
206 Mark Grudzielanek .20 .06
207 Fernando Vina .20 .06
208 Willie Greene .20 .06
209 Homer Bush .20 .06
210 Jason Giambi .50 .15
211 Mike Morgan .20 .06
212 Steve Karsay .20 .06
213 Matt Lawton .20 .06
214 Wendell Magee Jr. .20 .06
215 Rusty Greer .20 .06
216 Keith Lockhart .20 .06
217 Billy Koch .20 .06
218 Todd Hollandsworth .20 .06
219 Raul Ibanez .20 .06
220 Tony Gwynn .60 .18
221 Carl Everett .20 .06
222 Hector Carrasco .20 .06
223 Jose Valentin .20 .06
224 Deivi Cruz .20 .06
225 Bret Boone .20 .06
226 Kurt Abbott .20 .06
227 Melvin Mora .20 .06
228 Danny Graves .20 .06
229 Jose Jimenez .20 .06
230 James Baldwin .20 .06
231 C.J. Nitkowski .20 .06
232 Jeff Zimmerman .20 .06
233 Mike Lowell .20 .06
234 Hideki Irabu .20 .06
235 Greg Vaughn .20 .06
236 Omar Daal .20 .06
237 Darren Dreifort .20 .06
238 Gil Meche .20 .06
239 Damian Jackson .20 .06
240 Frank Thomas .50 .15
241 Travis Miller .20 .06
242 Jeff Frye .20 .06
243 Dave Magadan .20 .06
244 Luis Castillo .20 .06
245 Bartolo Colon .20 .06
246 Steve Kline .20 .06
247 Shawon Dunston .20 .06
248 Rick Aguilera .20 .06
249 Omar Olivares .20 .06
250 Craig Biggio .30 .09
251 Scott Schoeneweis .20 .06
252 Dave Veres .20 .06
253 Ramon Martinez .20 .06
254 Jose Vidro .20 .06
255 Todd Helton .30 .09
256 Greg Norton .20 .06
257 Jacque Jones .20 .06
258 Jason Grimsley .20 .06
259 Dan Reichert .20 .06
260 Robb Nen .20 .06
261 Mark Clark .20 .06
262 Scott Hatteberg .20 .06

263 Doug Brocail .20 .06
264 Mark Johnson .20 .06
265 Eric Davis .20 .06
266 Terry Shumpert .20 .06
267 Kevin Millar .20 .06
268 Ismael Valdes .20 .06
269 Richard Hidalgo .20 .06
270 Randy Velarde .20 .06
271 Bengie Molina .20 .06
272 Tony Womack .20 .06
273 Enrique Wilson .20 .06
274 Jeff Brantley .20 .06
275 Rick Ankiel .20 .06
276 Terry Mulholland .20 .06
277 Ron Belliard .20 .06
278 Terrence Long .20 .06
279 Alberto Castillo .20 .06
280 Royce Clayton .20 .06
281 Joe McEwing .20 .06
282 Jason McDonald .20 .06
283 Ricky Bottalico .20 .06
284 Keith Foulke .20 .06
285 Brad Radke .20 .06
286 Gabe Kapler .20 .06
287 Pedro Astacio .20 .06
288 Armando Reynoso .20 .06
289 Darryl Kile .20 .06
290 Reggie Sanders .20 .06
291 Esteban Yan .20 .06
292 Joe Nathan .20 .06
293 Jay Payton .20 .06
294 Francisco Cordero .20 .06
295 Gregg Jefferies .20 .06
296 LaTroy Hawkins .20 .06
297 Jeff Tam RC .40 .12
298 Jacob Cruz .20 .06
299 Chris Holt .20 .06
300 Vladimir Guerrero .50 .15
301 Marvin Benard .20 .06
302 Alex Ramirez .20 .06
303 Mike Williams .20 .06
304 Sean Bergman .20 .06
305 Juan Encarnacion .20 .06
306 Russ Davis .20 .06
307 Hanley Frias .20 .06
308 Ramon Hernandez .20 .06
309 Matt Walbeck .20 .06
310 Bill Spiers .20 .06
311 Bob Wickman .20 .06
312 Sandy Alomar Jr. .20 .06
313 Eddie Guardado .20 .06
314 Shane Halter .20 .06
315 Geoff Jenkins .20 .06
316 Brian Meadows .20 .06
317 Damian Miller .20 .06
318 Darrin Fletcher .20 .06
319 Rafael Furcal .20 .06
320 Mark Grace .30 .09
321 Mark Mulder .20 .06
322 Joe Torre MG .20 .06
323 Bobby Cox MG .20 .06
324 Mike Scioscia MG .20 .06
325 Mike Hargrove MG .20 .06
326 Jimy Williams MG .20 .06
327 Jerry Manuel MG .20 .06
328 Buck Showalter MG .20 .06
329 Charlie Manuel MG .20 .06
330 Don Baylor MG .20 .06
331 Phil Garner MG .20 .06
332 Jack McKeon MG .20 .06
333 Tony Muser MG .20 .06
334 Buddy Bell MG .20 .06
335 Tom Kelly MG .20 .06
336 John Boles MG .20 .06
337 Art Howe MG .20 .06
338 Larry Dierker MG .20 .06
339 Lou Piniella MG .20 .06
340 Davey Johnson MG .20 .06
341 Larry Rothschild MG .20 .06
342 Davey Lopes MG .20 .06
343 Johnny Oates MG .20 .06
344 Felipe Alou MG .20 .06
345 Jim Fregosi MG .20 .06
346 Bobby Valentine MG .20 .06
347 Terry Francona MG .20 .06
348 Gene Lamont MG .20 .06
349 Tony LaRussa MG .20 .06
350 Bruce Bochy MG .20 .06
351 Dusty Baker MG .20 .06
352 Adrian Gonzalez .40 .12
Adam Johnson
353 Matt Wheatland .25 .07
Bryan Digby
354 Tripper Johnson .25 .07
Scott Thorman
355 Phil Dumatrait .40 .12
Adam Wainwright
356 Scott Heard .40 .12
David Parrish RC
357 Rocco Baldelli 2.00 .60
Mark Folsom RC
358 Dominic Rich RC .40 .12
Aaron Herr
359 Mike Stodolka .40 .12
Sean Burnett
360 Derek Thompson .25 .07
Corey Smith
361 Danny Borrell RC .40 .12
Jason Bourgeois RC
362 Chin-Feng Chen .40 .12
Corey Patterson
Josh Hamilton
363 Ryan Anderson .75 .23
Barry Zito
C.C. Sabathia
364 Scott Sobkowiak .40 .12
David Walling
Ben Sheets
365 Ty Howington .25 .07
Josh Kalinowski
Josh Girdley
366 Hee Seop Choi RC 3.00 .90
Aaron McNeal
Jason Hart
367 Bobby Bradley .40 .12
Kurt Ainsworth
Chin-Hui Tsao
368 Mike Glendenning .25 .07
Kenny Kelly
Juan Silvestri
369 J.R. House .25 .07
Ramon Castro
Ben Davis
370 Chance Caple 1.25 .35
Rafael Soriano RC
Pasqual Coco
371 Travis Hafner RC 1.25 .35
Eric Munson
Bucky Jacobsen
372 Jason Conti .40 .12
Chris Wakeland
Brian Cole
373 Scott Seabol .40 .12
Aubrey Huff
Joe Crede
374 Adam Everett .25 .07
Jose Ortiz
Keith Ginter
375 Carlos Hernandez .25 .07
Geraldo Guzman
Adam Eaton
376 Bobby Kielty .25 .07
Milton Bradley
Juan Rivera
377 Mark McGwire GM .60 .18
378 Don Larsen GM .20 .06
379 Bobby Thomson GM .20 .06
380 Bill Mazeroski GM .20 .06
381 Reggie Jackson GM .30 .09
382 Kirk Gibson GM .20 .06
383 Roger Maris GM .50 .15
384 Cal Ripken GM .75 .23
385 Hank Aaron GM .50 .15
386 Joe Carter GM .20 .06
387 Cal Ripken SH 1.50 .45
388 Randy Johnson SH .30 .09
389 Ken Griffey Jr. SH .75 .23
390 Troy Glaus SH .30 .09
391 Kazuhiro Sasaki SH .20 .06
392 Sammy Sosa LL .30 .09
Troy Glaus
393 Todd Helton LL .20 .06
Edgar Martinez
394 Todd Helton LL .50 .15
Nomar Garicaparra
395 Barry Bonds LL .50 .15
Jason Giambi
396 Todd Helton LL .20 .06
Manny Ramirez
397 Todd Helton LL .20 .06
Darin Erstad
398 Kevin Brown LL .30 .09
Pedro Martinez
399 Randy Johnson LL .30 .09
Pedro Martinez
400 Will Clark HL .50 .15
401 New York Mets HL .50 .15
402 New York Yankees HL .75 .23
403 Seattle Mariners HL .20 .06
404 Mike Hampton HL .20 .06
405 New York Yankees HL 1.00 .30
406 N.Y. Yankees Champs 2.00 .60
407 Jeff Bagwell .30 .09
408 Brant Brown .20 .06
409 Brad Fullmer .20 .06
410 Dean Palmer .20 .06
411 Greg Zaun .20 .06
412 Jose Vizcaino .20 .06
413 Jeff Abbott .20 .06
414 Travis Fryman .20 .06
415 Mike Cameron .20 .06
416 Matt Mantei .20 .06
417 Alan Benes .20 .06
418 Mickey Morandini .20 .06
419 Troy Percival .20 .06
420 Eddie Perez .20 .06
421 Vernon Wells .20 .06
422 Ricky Gutierrez .20 .06
423 Carlos Hernandez .20 .06
424 Chan Ho Park .20 .06
425 Armando Benitez .20 .06
426 Sidney Ponson .20 .06
427 Adrian Brown .20 .06
428 Ruben Mateo .20 .06
429 Alex Ochoa .20 .06
430 Jose Rosado .20 .06
431 Masato Yoshii .20 .06
432 Corey Koskie .20 .06
433 Andy Pettitte .30 .09
434 Brian Daubach .20 .06
435 Sterling Hitchcock .20 .06
436 Timo Perez .20 .06
437 Shawn Estes .20 .06
438 Tony Armas Jr. .20 .06
439 Danny Bautista .20 .06
440 Randy Winn .20 .06
441 Wilson Alvarez .20 .06
442 Rondell White .20 .06
443 Jeromy Burnitz .20 .06
444 Kelvim Escobar .20 .06
445 Paul Bako .20 .06
446 Javier Vazquez .20 .06
447 Eric Gagne .30 .09
448 Kenny Lofton .20 .06
449 Mark Kotsay .20 .06
450 Jamie Moyer .20 .06
451 Delino DeShields .20 .06
452 Rey Ordonez .20 .06
453 Russ Ortiz .20 .06
454 Dave Burba .20 .06
455 Eric Karros .20 .06
456 Felix Martinez .20 .06
457 Tony Batista .20 .06
458 Bobby Higginson .20 .06
459 Jeff D'Amico .20 .06
460 Shane Spencer .20 .06
461 Brent Mayne .20 .06
462 Glendon Rusch .20 .06
463 Chris Gomez .20 .06
464 Jeff Shaw .20 .06
465 Damon Buford .20 .06
466 Mike DiFelice .20 .06
467 Jimmy Haynes .20 .06
468 Billy Wagner .20 .06
469 A.J. Hinch .20 .06
470 Gary DiSarcina .20 .06
471 Tom Lampkin .20 .06
472 Adam Eaton .20 .06
473 Brian Giles .20 .06
474 John Thomson .20 .06
475 Cal Eldred .20 .06
476 Ramiro Mendoza .20 .06
477 Scott Sullivan .20 .06
478 Scott Rolen .30 .09
479 Todd Ritchie .20 .06
480 Pablo Ozuna .20 .06
481 Carl Pavano .20 .06
482 Matt Morris .20 .06
483 Matt Stairs .20 .06
484 Tim Belcher .20 .06
485 Lance Berkman .20 .06
486 Brian Meadows .20 .06
487 Bob Abreu .20 .06
488 John VanderWal .20 .06
489 Donnie Sadler .20 .06
490 Damion Easley .20 .06
491 David Justice .20 .06
492 Ray Durham .20 .06
493 Todd Zeile .20 .06
494 Desi Relaford .20 .06
495 Cliff Floyd .20 .06
496 Scott Downs .20 .06
497 Barry Bonds 1.25 .35
498 Jeff D'Amico .20 .06
499 Octavio Dotel .20 .06
500 Kent Mercker .20 .06
501 Craig Grebeck .20 .06
502 Roberto Hernandez .20 .06
503 Matt Williams .20 .06
504 Bruce Aven .20 .06
505 Brett Tomko .20 .06
506 Kris Benson .20 .06
507 Neifi Perez .20 .06
508 Alfonso Soriano .30 .09
509 Keith Osik .20 .06
510 Matt Franco .20 .06
511 Steve Finley .20 .06
512 Olmedo Saenz .20 .06
513 Esteban Loaiza .20 .06
514 Adam Kennedy .20 .06
515 Scott Elarton .20 .06
516 Moises Alou .20 .06
517 Bryan Rekar .20 .06
518 Darryl Hamilton .20 .06
519 Osvaldo Fernandez .20 .06
520 Kip Wells .20 .06
521 Bernie Williams .30 .09
522 Mike Darr .20 .06
523 Marlon Anderson .20 .06
524 Derrek Lee .20 .06
525 Ugueth Urbina .20 .06
526 Vinny Castilla .20 .06
527 David Wells .20 .06
528 Jason Marquis .20 .06
529 Orlando Palmeiro .20 .06
530 Carlos Perez .20 .06
531 J.T. Snow .20 .06
532 Al Leiter .20 .06
533 Jimmy Anderson .20 .06
534 Brett Laxton .20 .06
535 Butch Huskey .20 .06
536 Orlando Hernandez .20 .06
537 Maggio Ordonez .20 .06
538 Willie Blair .20 .06
539 Kevin Sefcik .20 .06
540 Chad Curtis .20 .06
541 John Halama .20 .06
542 Andy Fox .20 .06
543 Juan Guzman .20 .06
544 Frank Menechino RC .20 .06
545 Raul Mondesi .20 .06
546 Tim Salmon .20 .06
547 Ryan Rupe .20 .06
548 Jeff Reed .20 .06
549 Mike Mordecai .20 .06
550 Jeff Kent .20 .06
551 Wiki Gonzalez .20 .06
552 Kenny Rogers .20 .06
553 Kevin Young .20 .06
554 Brian Johnson .20 .06
555 Tom Goodwin .20 .06
556 Tony Clark UER .20 .06
0 games, 208 At-Bats
557 Mac Suzuki .20 .06
558 Brian Moehler .20 .06
559 Jim Parque .20 .06
560 Mariano Rivera .30 .09
561 Trot Nixon .30 .09
562 Mike Mussina .50 .15
563 Nelson Figueroa .20 .06
564 Alex Gonzalez .20 .06
565 Benny Agbayani .20 .06
566 Ed Sprague .20 .06
567 Scott Erickson .20 .06
568 Abraham Nunez .20 .06
569 Jerry DiPoto .20 .06
570 Sean Casey .20 .06
571 Wilton Veras .20 .06
572 Joe Mays .20 .06
573 Bill Simas .20 .06
574 Doug Glanville .20 .06
575 Scott Sauerbeck .20 .06
576 Ben Davis .20 .06
577 Jesus Sanchez .20 .06
578 Ricardo Rincon .20 .06
579 John Olerud .20 .06
580 Curt Schilling .30 .09
581 Alex Cora .20 .06
582 Pat Hentgen .20 .06
583 Javy Lopez .20 .06
584 Ben Grieve .20 .06
585 Frank Castillo .20 .06
586 Kevin Stocker .20 .06
587 Mark Sweeney .20 .06
588 Ray Lankford .20 .06
589 Turner Ward .20 .06
590 Felipe Crespo .20 .06
591 Omar Vizquel .20 .06
592 Mike Lieberthal .20 .06
593 Ken Griffey Jr. .75 .23
594 Troy O'Leary .20 .06
595 Dave Mlicki .20 .06
596 Manny Ramirez .20 .06
597 Mike Lansing .20 .06
598 Rich Aurilia .20 .06
599 Russell Branyan .20 .06
600 Russ Johnson .20 .06
601 Greg Colbrunn .20 .06
602 Andruw Jones .20 .06
603 Henry Blanco .20 .06
604 Jarrod Washburn .20 .06
605 Tony Eusebio .20 .06
606 Aaron Sele .20 .06
607 Charles Nagy .20 .06
608 Ryan Klesko .30 .09
609 Dante Bichette .20 .06
610 Bill Haselman .20 .06
611 Jerry Spradlin .20 .06
612 A. Rodriguez Rangers .75 .23
613 Jose Silva .20 .06
614 Darren Oliver .20 .06
615 Pat Mahomes .20 .06
616 Roberto Alomar .50 .15
617 Edgar Renteria .20 .06
618 Jon Lieber .20 .06
619 John Rocker .20 .06
620 Miguel Tejada .20 .06
621 Mo Vaughn .20 .06
622 Jose Lima .20 .06
623 Kerry Wood .50 .15
624 Mike Timlin .20 .06
625 Wil Cordero .20 .06
626 Albert Belle .20 .06
627 Bobby Jones .20 .06
628 Doug Mirabelli .20 .06
629 Jason Tyner .20 .06
630 Andy Ashby .20 .06
631 Jose Hernandez .20 .06
632 Devon White .20 .06
633 Ruben Rivera .20 .06
634 Steve Parris .20 .06
635 David McCarty .20 .06
636 Jose Canseco .50 .15
637 Todd Walker .20 .06
638 Stan Spencer .30 .09
639 Wayne Gomes .20 .06
640 Freddy Garcia .20 .06
641 Jeremy Giambi .20 .06
642 Luis Lopez .20 .06
643 John Smoltz .30 .09
644 Kelly Stinnett .20 .06
645 Kevin Brown .20 .06
646 Wilton Guerrero .20 .06
647 Al Martin .20 .06
648 Woody Williams .20 .06
649 Brian Rose .20 .06
650 Rafael Palmeiro .30 .09
651 Pete Schourek .20 .06
652 Kevin Jarvis .20 .06
653 Mark Redman .20 .06
654 Ricky Ledee .20 .06
655 Larry Walker .30 .09
656 Paul Byrd .20 .06
657 Jason Bere .20 .06
658 Rick White .20 .06
659 Calvin Murray .20 .06
660 Greg Maddux .75 .23
661 Ron Gant .20 .06
662 Eli Marrero .20 .06
663 Graeme Lloyd .20 .06
664 Trevor Hoffman .20 .06
665 Nomar Garciaparra .75 .23
666 Glenallen Hill .20 .06
667 Matt LeCroy .20 .06
668 Justin Thompson .20 .06
669 Brady Anderson .20 .06
670 Miguel Batista .20 .06
671 Erubiel Durazo .20 .06
672 Kevin Millwood .20 .06
673 Mitch Meluskey .20 .06
674 Luis Gonzalez .20 .06
675 Edgar Martinez .30 .09
676 Robert Person .20 .06
677 Benito Santiago .20 .06
678 Todd Jones .20 .06
679 Tino Martinez .30 .09
680 Carlos Beltran .20 .06
681 Gabe White .20 .06
682 Bret Saberhagen .20 .06
683 Jeff Conine .20 .06
684 Jaret Wright .20 .06
685 Bernard Gilkey .20 .06
686 Garrett Stephenson .20 .06
687 Jamey Wright .20 .06
688 Sammy Sosa .75 .23
689 John Jaha .20 .06
690 Ramon Martinez .20 .06
691 Robert Fick .20 .06
692 Eric Milton .20 .06
693 Denny Neagle .20 .06
694 Ron Coomer .20 .06
695 John Valentin .20 .06
696 Placido Polanco .20 .06
697 Tim Hudson .20 .06
698 Marty Cordova .20 .06
699 Chad Kreuter .20 .06
700 Frank Catalanotto .20 .06
701 Tim Wakefield .20 .06
702 Jim Edmonds .20 .06
703 Michael Tucker .20 .06
704 Cristian Guzman .20 .06
705 Joey Hamilton .20 .06
706 Mike Piazza .75 .23
707 Dave Martinez .20 .06
708 Mike Hampton .20 .06
709 Bobby Bonilla .20 .06
710 Juan Pierre .20 .06
711 John Parrish .20 .06
712 Kory DeHaan .20 .06
713 Brian Tollberg .20 .06
714 Chris Truby .20 .06
715 Emil Brown .20 .06
716 Ryan Dempster .20 .06
717 Rich Garces .20 .06
718 Mike Myers .20 .06
719 Luis Ordaz .20 .06
720 Kazuhiro Sasaki .20 .06
721 Mark Quinn .20 .06
722 Ramon Ortiz .20 .06
723 Kerry Ligtenberg .20 .06
724 Rolando Arrojo .20 .06
725 Tsuyoshi Shinjo RC 1.00 .30
726 Ichiro Suzuki RC 15.00 4.50
727 Roy Oswalt .50 .15
Pat Strange
Jon Rauch
728 Phil Wilson RC 1.25 .35
Jake Peavy RC
Darwin Cubillan RC
729 Steve Smyth RC .40 .12
Mike Bynum
Nathan Haynes
730 Michael Cuddyer .25 .07
Joe Lawrence
Choo Freeman
731 Carlos Pena .25 .07
Larry Barnes
DeWayne Wise
732 Travis Dawkins .40 .12
Erick Almonte
Felipe Lopez
733 Alex Escobar .25 .07
Eric Valent
Brad Wilkerson
734 Toby Hall .25 .07
Rod Barajas
Jeff Goldbach
735 Jason Romano .40 .12
Marcus Giles
Pablo Ozuna
736 Dee Brown .40 .12
Jack Cust
Vernon Wells
737 David Espinosa .40 .12
Luis Montanez RC
738 Anthony Pluta RC .50 .15
Justin Wayne RC
739 Josh Axelson RC .40 .12
Carmen Cali RC
740 Shaun Boyd RC .40 .12
Chris Morris RC
741 Tommy Arko RC .40 .12
Dan Moylan RC
742 Luis Cotto RC .40 .12
Luis Escobar
743 Brandon Mims RC .40 .12
Blake Williams RC
744 Chris Russ RC .40 .12
Bryan Edwards
745 Joe Torres .25 .07
Ben Diggins
746 Hugh Quattlebaum RC .50 .15
Edwin Encarnacion RC
747 Brian Bass RC .40 .12
Odannis Ayala RC
748 Jason Kaanoi .25 .07
Michael Matthews RC UER
name misspelled Mathews
749 Stuart McFarland RC .40 .12
Adam Sterrett RC
750 David Krynzel 1.00 .30
Grady Sizemore
751 Keith Bucktrot .25 .07
Dane Sardinha
752 Anaheim Angels TC .20 .06
753 Ariz. Diamondbacks TC .20 .06
754 Atlanta Braves TC .20 .06
755 Baltimore Orioles TC .20 .06
756 Boston Red Sox TC .20 .06
757 Chicago Cubs TC .20 .06
758 Chicago White Sox TC .20 .06
759 Cincinnati Reds TC .20 .06
760 Cleveland Indians TC .20 .06
761 Colorado Rockies TC .20 .06
762 Detroit Tigers TC .20 .06
763 Florida Marlins TC .20 .06
764 Houston Astros TC .20 .06
765 K.C. Royals TC .20 .06
766 L.A. Dodgers TC .20 .06
767 Milw. Brewers TC .20 .06
768 Minnesota Twins TC .20 .06
769 Montreal Expos TC .20 .06
770 New York Mets TC .20 .06
771 New York Yankees TC 1.00 .30
772 Oakland Athletics TC .20 .06
773 Phil. Phillies TC .20 .06
774 Pittsburgh Pirates TC .20 .06
775 San Diego Padres TC .20 .06
776 San Francisco Giants TC .20 .06
777 Seattle Mariners TC .20 .06
778 St. Louis Cardinals TC .20 .06
779 T.B. Devil Rays TC .20 .06
780 Texas Rangers TC .20 .06
781 Toronto Blue Jays TC .20 .06
782 Bucky Dent GM .20 .06
783 Jackie Robinson GM .30 .09
784 Roberto Clemente GM .60 .18
785 Nolan Ryan GM .75 .23
786 Kerry Wood GM .30 .09
787 Rickey Henderson GM .20 .06
788 Lou Brock GM .30 .09
789 David Wells GM .20 .06
790 Andruw Jones GM .20 .06
791 Carlton Fisk GM .20 .06
TK Bo Jackson 120.00 36.00
Deion Sanders Bat
NNO Bobby Thomson 50.00 15.00
Ralph Branca
1991 Bowman Autograph

2001 Topps Employee

Topps created as a special bonus for their employees, a "parallel" set of the 2001 Topps set with a special employee logo embossed on the card. It is believed approximately 150 of these sets were produced.

Nm-Mt Ex-Mt
*STARS 5X TO 10X BASIC CARDS .....

2001 Topps Gold

Randomly inserted into first series packs at a rate of 1:17 Hobby/Retail and 1:4 HTA and second series packs at a rate of 1:14 Hobby/Retail and 1:3 HTA, this 790-card set is a complete parallel of the 2001 Topps base set. These cards were produced with a special gold-foil border on front and were individually serial numbered to 2001 on back. Please note that card number 7 does not exist.

Nm-Mt Ex-Mt
*STARS: 10X TO 25X BASIC CARDS ..
*PROSPECTS 352-376/725/751: 4X TO 10X
*ROOKIES 352-376/725-751: 4X TO 10X

2001 Topps Home Team Advantage

This factory-sealed 790-card set was issued exclusively to Topps network of Home Team Advantage baseball card shops. The sets were packaged in attractive gold foil boxes and each card features a distinctive "HTA" foil stamp on front.

Nm-Mt Ex-Mt
COMP.HTA.GOLD SET (790) ... 120.00 36.00
*HTA: .75X TO 2X BASIC CARDS

2001 Topps Limited

These attractive cards parallel the basic 2001 Topps set. The product was distributed exclusively in factory set format. Each set contained the 790-card basic set plus five Topps Archives Reserve Future Rookie Reprints chrome inserts wrapped together in a plastic cello pack. The sets were distributed through hobby dealers in attractive wood boxes and carried a suggested retail price of $173. Each Topps Limited card was printed on 20 pt. stock paper featuring glossy fronts and backs and a "Limited Edition" gold foil logo on front. Though the cards lack individual serial-numbering, Topps announced production at 3,805 sets. Each set states that total on the bottom of the wooden box.

Nm-Mt Ex-Mt
COMP.FACT.SET (790) 200.00 60.00
*STARS: 2X TO 5X BASIC CARDS
*ROOKIES: 1.25X TO 3X BASIC CARDS

2001 Topps A Look Ahead

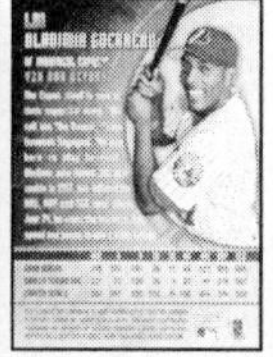

Randomly inserted into packs at 1:25 Hobby/Retail and 1:5 HTA, this 10-card insert takes a look a players that are on their way to Cooperstown. Card backs carry a "LA" prefix.

Nm-Mt Ex-Mt
COMPLETE SET (10) 30.00 9.00
LA1 Vladimir Guerrero 2.50 .75
LA2 Derek Jeter 6.00 1.80
LA3 Todd Helton 1.50 .45
LA4 Alex Rodriguez 4.00 1.20
LA5 Ken Griffey Jr. 4.00 1.20
LA6 Nomar Garciaparra 4.00 1.20
LA7 Chipper Jones 2.50 .75
LA8 Ivan Rodriguez 2.50 .75
LA9 Pedro Martinez 2.50 .75
LA10 Rick Ankiel 1.00 .30

2001 Topps A Tradition Continues

Randomly inserted into packs at 1:17 Hobby/Retail and 1:5 HTA, this 30-card insert features players that look to carry the tradition of Major League Baseball well into the 21st century. Card backs carry a "TRC" prefix.

Nm-Mt Ex-Mt
COMPLETE SET (30) 100.00 30.00
TRC1 Chipper Jones 3.00 .90
TRC2 Cal Ripken 10.00 3.00
TRC3 Mike Piazza 5.00 1.50
TRC4 Ken Griffey Jr. 5.00 1.50
TRC5 Randy Johnson 3.00 .90
TRC6 Derek Jeter 8.00 2.40
TRC7 Scott Rolen 2.00 .60
TRC8 Nomar Garciaparra 5.00 1.50
TRC9 Roberto Alomar 3.00 .90
TRC10 Greg Maddux 5.00 1.50
TRC11 Ivan Rodriguez 3.00 .90
TRC12 Jeff Bagwell 2.00 .60
TRC13 Alex Rodriguez 5.00 1.50
TRC14 Pedro Martinez 3.00 .90
TRC15 Sammy Sosa 5.00 1.50
TRC16 Jim Edmonds 1.25 .35
TRC17 Mo Vaughn 1.25 .35
TRC18 Barry Bonds 8.00 2.40
TRC19 Larry Walker 2.00 .60
TRC20 Mark McGwire 8.00 2.40
TRC21 Vladimir Guerrero 3.00 .90
TRC22 Andruw Jones 1.25 .35
TRC23 Todd Helton 2.00 .60
TRC24 Kevin Brown 1.25 .35
TRC25 Tony Gwynn 4.00 1.20
TRC26 Manny Ramirez 1.25 .35
TRC27 Roger Clemens 6.00 1.80
TRC28 Frank Thomas 3.00 .90
TRC29 Shawn Green 1.25 .35
TRC30 Jim Thome 3.00 .90

2001 Topps Base Hit

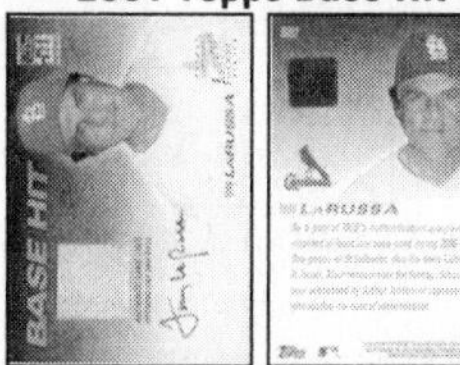

Inserted in series two packs at a rate of one in 1,1462 hobby or retail packs and one in 325 HTA packs, these 28 cards features managers along with a game-used memorabilia piece.

Nm-Mt Ex-Mt
BH1 Mike Scioscia 60.00 18.00
BH2 Larry Dierker 50.00 15.00
BH3 Art Howe 50.00 15.00
BH4 Jim Fregosi 50.00 15.00
BH5 Bobby Cox 60.00 18.00
BH6 Davey Lopes 60.00 18.00
BH7 Tony LaRussa 60.00 18.00
BH8 Don Baylor 60.00 18.00
BH9 Larry Rothschild 50.00 15.00
BH10 Buck Showalter 50.00 15.00
BH11 Davey Johnson 60.00 18.00
BH12 Felipe Alou 60.00 18.00
BH13 Charlie Manuel 50.00 15.00
BH14 Lou Piniella 60.00 18.00
BH15 John Boles 50.00 15.00
BH16 Bobby Valentine 60.00 18.00
BH17 Mike Hargrove 60.00 18.00
BH18 Bruce Bochy 50.00 15.00
BH19 Terry Francona 50.00 15.00
BH20 Gene Lamont 50.00 15.00
BH21 Johnny Oates 50.00 15.00
BH22 Jimy Williams 50.00 15.00
BH23 Jack McKeon 50.00 15.00
BH24 Buddy Bell 60.00 18.00
BH25 Tony Muser 50.00 15.00
BH26 Phil Garner 50.00 15.00
BH27 Tom Kelly 50.00 15.00
BH28 Jerry Manuel 50.00 15.00

2001 Topps Before There Was Topps

Issued in series two packs at a rate of one in 25 hobby/retail packs and one in five HTA packs; these 10 cards feature superstars who concluded their career before Topps started their dominance of the card market.

Nm-Mt Ex-Mt
COMPLETE SET (10) 40.00 12.00
BT1 Lou Gehrig 6.00 1.80
BT2 Babe Ruth 10.00 3.00
BT3 Cy Young 3.00 .90
BT4 Walter Johnson 3.00 .90
BT5 Ty Cobb 5.00 1.50
BT6 Rogers Hornsby 3.00 .90
BT7 Honus Wagner 3.00 .90
BT8 Christy Mathewson 3.00 .90
BT9 Grover Alexander 3.00 .90
BT10 Joe DiMaggio 6.00 1.80

2001 Topps Combos

Randomly inserted into packs at a rate of 1:12 Hobby/Retail and 1:4 HTA, this 20-card insert set pairs up players that have put up similar statistics throughout their carriers. Card backs carry a "TC" prefix. Instead of having photographs, these cards feature drawings of the featured players.

Nm-Mt Ex-Mt
COMPLETE SET (20) 60.00 18.00
COMPLETE SERIES 1 (10) 30.00 9.00
COMPLETE SERIES 2 (10) 30.00 9.00
TC1 Derek Jeter 5.00 1.50
Yogi Berra
Whitey Ford
Don Mattingly
Reggie Jackson
TC2 Chipper Jones 1.50 .45
Mike Schmidt
TC3 Brooks Robinson 4.00 1.20
Cal Ripken
TC4 Bob Gibson 1.50 .45
Pedro Martinez
TC5 Ivan Rodriguez 1.50 .45
Johnny Bench
TC6 Ernie Banks 2.50 .75
Alex Rodriguez
TC7 Joe Morgan 1.50 .45
Ken Griffey Jr.
Barry Larkin
Johnny Bench
TC8 Vladmir Guerrero 1.50 .45
Roberto Clemente
TC9 Ken Griffey Jr. 2.00 .60
Hank Aaron
TC10 Casey Stengel MG 1.50 .45
Joe Torre MG
TC11 Kevin Brown 3.00 .90
Sandy Koufax
Don Drysdale UER
Card states the Dodgers swept the 1965 World Series
They won the Series in 7 games
TC12 Mark McGwire 4.00 1.20
Sammy Sosa
Roger Maris
Babe Ruth
TC13 Ted Williams 3.00 .90
Carl Yastrzemski
Nomar Garciaparra
TC14 Greg Maddux 2.50 .75
Roger Clemens
Cy Young
TC15 Tony Gwynn 3.00 .90
Ted Williams
TC16 Cal Ripken 5.00 1.50
Lou Gehrig
TC17 Sandy Koufax 5.00 1.50
Randy Johnson
Warren Spahn
Steve Carlton
TC18 Mike Piazza 2.00 .60
Josh Gibson
TC19 Barry Bonds 4.00 1.20
Willie Mays
TC20 Jackie Robinson 2.00 .60
Larry Doby

2001 Topps Golden Anniversary

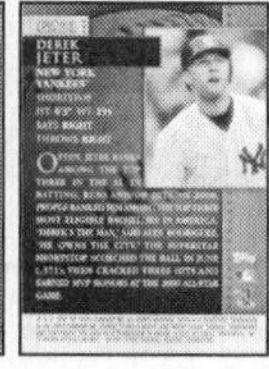

Randomly inserted into packs at 1:10 Hobby/Retail and 1:1 HTA, this 50-card insert celibrates Topp's 50th Anniversary by taking a look at some of the all-time greats. Card backs carry a "GA" prefix.

Nm-Mt Ex-Mt
COMPLETE SET (50) 80.00 24.00
GA1 Hank Aaron 5.00 1.50
GA2 Ernie Banks 2.50 .75
GA3 Mike Schmidt 5.00 1.50
GA4 Willie Mays 5.00 1.50
GA5 Johnny Bench 2.50 .75
GA6 Tom Seaver 1.50 .45
GA7 Frank Robinson 1.50 .45
GA8 Sandy Koufax 8.00 2.40
GA9 Bob Gibson 1.50 .45
GA10 Ted Williams 6.00 1.80
GA11 Cal Ripken 8.00 2.40
GA12 Tony Gwynn 3.00 .90
GA13 Mark McGwire 6.00 1.80
GA14 Ken Griffey Jr. 4.00 1.20
GA15 Greg Maddux 4.00 1.20
GA16 Roger Clemens 5.00 1.50
GA17 Barry Bonds 6.00 1.80
GA18 Rickey Henderson 2.50 .75
GA19 Mike Piazza 4.00 1.20
GA20 Jose Canseco 2.50 .75
GA21 Derek Jeter 6.00 1.80
GA22 N.Garciaparra UER 4.00 1.20
Card has incorrect bat and throw information
Garciaparra bats and throws righthanded
GA23 Alex Rodriguez 4.00 1.20
GA24 Sammy Sosa 4.00 1.20
GA25 Ivan Rodriguez 2.50 .75
GA26 Vladimir Guerrero 2.50 .75
GA27 Chipper Jones 2.50 .75
GA28 Jeff Bagwell 1.50 .45
GA29 Pedro Martinez 2.50 .75
GA30 Randy Johnson 2.50 .75
GA31 Pat Burrell 1.00 .30
GA32 Josh Hamilton 1.00 .30
GA33 Ryan Anderson 1.00 .30
GA34 Corey Patterson 1.00 .30
GA35 Eric Munson 1.00 .30
GA36 Sean Burroughs 1.00 .30
GA37 C.C. Sabathia 1.00 .30
GA38 Chin-Feng Chen 1.00 .30
GA39 Barry Zito 2.50 .75
GA40 Adrian Gonzalez 1.00 .30
GA41 Mark McGwire 6.00 1.80
GA42 Nomar Garciaparra 4.00 1.20
GA43 Todd Helton 1.50 .45
GA44 Matt Williams 1.00 .30
GA45 Troy Glaus 1.50 .45
GA46 Geoff Jenkins 1.00 .30
GA47 Frank Thomas 2.50 .75
GA48 Mo Vaughn 1.00 .30
GA49 Barry Larkin 2.50 .75
GA50 J.D. Drew 1.00 .30

2001 Topps Golden Anniversary Autographs

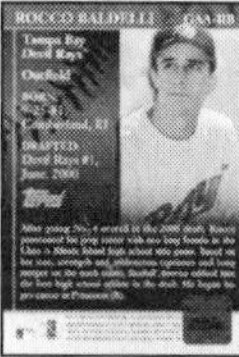

Randomly inserted into packs, this 98-card insert features authentic autographs of both modern day and former greats. Card backs carry a "GAA" prefix followed by the players initials. Please note that the Andy Pafko, Lou Brock, Rafael Furcal and Todd Zeile cards all packed out in series one packs as exchange cards with a redemption deadline of November 30th, 2001. In addition, Carlos Silva, Eddy Furniss, Phil Merrell and Carlos Silva packed out as exchange cards in series two packs with a redemption deadline of April 30th, 2003.

Nm-Mt Ex-Mt
GAA-AG A.Gonzalez G 15.00 4.50
GAA-AH Aaron Herr I2 10.00 3.00
GAA-AJ A. Johnson G1-I2 10.00 3.00
GAA-AO Augie Ojeda B2 15.00 4.50
GAA-AP Andy Pafko C1 40.00 12.00
GAA-BB Barry Bonds B2 300.00 90.00
GAA-BE Brian Esposito I2 10.00 3.00
GAA-BG Bob Gibson C2 60.00 18.00
GAA-BK Bobby Kielty I2 10.00 3.00
GAA-BO Ben Oglivie D2 15.00 4.50
GAA-BR B.Robinson B 120.00 36.00
GAA-BT Brian Tollberg I2 10.00 3.00
GAA-CC Chris Clapinski I2 10.00 3.00
GAA-CD Chad Durbin I2 10.00 3.00
GAA-CE Carl Erskine D2 25.00 7.50
GAA-CJ Chipper Jones B1 120.00 36.00
GAA-CL Colby Lewis I2 10.00 3.00
GAA-CR Chris Richard I2 10.00 3.00
GAA-CS Carlos Silva I2 10.00 3.00
GAA-CY C. Yastrzemski C2 100.00 30.00
GAA-DA Dick Allen C1 40.00 12.00
GAA-DA Denny Abreu I2 10.00 3.00
GAA-DG Dick Groat D2 25.00 7.50
GAA-DT D. Thompson I2 10.00 3.00
GAA-EB Ernie Banks B1 120.00 36.00
GAA-EB Eric Byrnes I2 10.00 3.00
GAA-EF Eddy Furniss I2 10.00 3.00
GAA-EM Eric Munson G2 10.00 3.00
GAA-ER E. Ramirez I2 10.00 3.00
GAA-GB George Bell D2 15.00 4.50
GAA-GG G. Guzman I2 10.00 3.00
GAA-GM G. Matthews Jr. D2 15.00 4.50
GAA-GS G. Sizemore I2 40.00 12.00
GAA-GT G.Templeton C 15.00 4.50
GAA-HA Hank Aaron B1 250.00 75.00
GAA-JB Johnny Bench C2 100.00 30.00
GAA-JC Jorge Cantu I2 10.00 3.00
GAA-JL John Lackey I2 10.00 3.00
GAA-JM J. Marquis G1 10.00 3.00
GAA-JR Joe Rudi C1 25.00 7.50
GAA-JR Juan Rincon I2 10.00 3.00
GAA-JS Juan Salas I2 10.00 3.00
GAA-JV Jose Vidro F1 20.00 6.00
GAA-JW Justin Wayne H2 15.00 4.50
GAA-KG Kevin Gregg B2 15.00 4.50
GAA-KH Ken Holtzman D2 15.00 4.50
GAA-KT Kent Tekulve D2 15.00 4.50
GAA-LB Lou Brock B1 80.00 24.00
GAA-LM L. Montanez H2 10.00 3.00
GAA-LR Luis Rivas I2 10.00 3.00
GAA-MB M. Bradley G2 10.00 3.00
GAA-MC Mike Cuellar C1 15.00 4.50
GAA-MG M. Glendenning I2 10.00 3.00
GAA-ML Matt Lawton F2 15.00 4.50
GAA-ML Mike Lamb G1 10.00 3.00
GAA-MO M.Ordonez B 50.00 15.00
GAA-MS Mike Schmidt B1 150.00 45.00
GAA-MS Mike Sweeney F2 20.00 6.00
GAA-MS Mike Stodolka I2 10.00 3.00
GAA-MW M.Wheatland G 10.00 3.00
GAA-MW M. Wenner I2 10.00 3.00
GAA-NG Nick Green I2 10.00 3.00
GAA-NJ Neil Jenkins I2 10.00 3.00
GAA-NR Nolan Ryan A2 300.00 90.00
GAA-PB Pat Burrell G1 15.00 4.50
GAA-PM Phil Merrell I2 10.00 3.00
GAA-RA Rick Ankiel D1 15.00 4.50
GAA-RB R. Baldelli G1-I2 60.00 18.00
GAA-RC Rod Carew B1 80.00 24.00
GAA-RF Rafael Furcal G1 15.00 4.50
GAA-RJ R. Jackson A2 200.00 60.00
GAA-RS Ron Swoboda C1 25.00 7.50
GAA-SH Scott Heard G1 10.00 3.00
GAA-SK Sandy Koufax A1 400.00 120.00
GAA-SM Stan Musial A2 200.00 60.00
GAA-SR Scott Rolen F2 30.00 9.00
GAA-ST Scott Thorman I2 10.00 3.00
GAA-TA Tony Alvarez I2 10.00 3.00
GAA-TH Todd Helton B2 50.00 15.00
GAA-TJ T. Johnson I2 10.00 3.00
GAA-TS Tom Seaver A2 150.00 45.00
GAA-VL Vernon Law C1 15.00 4.50
GAA-WD Willie Davis D2 15.00 4.50
GAA-WF Whitey Ford C2 60.00 18.00
GAA-WH W.Hernandez C 15.00 4.50
GAA-WM Willie Mays A1 300.00 90.00
GAA-WW Wilbur Wood D2 15.00 4.50
GAA-YB Yogi Berra B1 120.00 36.00
GAA-YH Yamid Haad I2 10.00 3.00
GAA-YT Y. Torrealba I2 10.00 3.00
GAA-CCS Corey Smith I2 10.00 3.00
GAA-GHB George Brett A2 300.00 90.00
GAA-JDD J.D. Drew E2 25.00 7.50
GAA-MAB Mike Bynum I2 10.00 3.00
GAA-MFL M. Lockwood I2 10.00 3.00
GAA-MJS M. Stodolka G1 10.00 3.00
GAA-MJW M. Wheatland I2 10.00 3.00
GAA-TDLR T. De la Rosa I2 10.00 3.00

2001 Topps Hit Parade

Issued in retail packs at odds of one in 2,607 these six cards feature players who have achieved major career milestones along with a piece of memorabilia.

Nm-Mt Ex-Mt
HP1 Reggie Jackson 60.00 18.00
HP2 Dave Winfield 60.00 18.00
HP3 Eddie Murray 60.00 18.00
HP4 Rickey Henderson 60.00 18.00
HP5 Robin Yount 80.00 24.00
HP6 Carl Yastrzemski 100.00 30.00

2001 Topps King of Kings

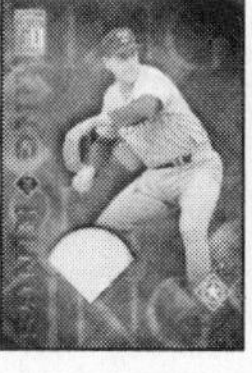

Randomly inserted into packs at 1:2056 Hobby/Retail and 1:457 HTA, this four-card insert features game-used memorabilia from Nolan Ryan, Rickey Henderson, and Hank Aaron. Please note that a special fourth card containing game-used memorabila of all three were inserted into HTA packs at 1:8903. Card backs carry a "KKG" prefix.

Nm-Mt Ex-Mt
KKR1 Hank Aaron 80.00 24.00
KKR2 Nolan Ryan 100.00 30.00
KKR3 Rickey Henderson 40.00 12.00
KKR4 Mark McGwire B 120.00 36.00
KKR5 Bob Gibson A 40.00 12.00
KKR6 Nolan Ryan B 100.00 30.00
KKGE Hank Aaron 400.00 120.00
Nolan Ryan
Rickey Henderson
KKLE2 Mark Mcgwire 600.00 180.00
Bob Gibson
Nolan Ryan

2001 Topps Noteworthy

Inserted in hobby/retail packs at a rate of one in eight and HTA packs at a rate of one per pack; this 50-card set feature a mix of active and retired players who achieved significant feats during their career.

Nm-Mt Ex-Mt
COMPLETE SET (50) 80.00 24.00
TN1 Mark McGwire 4.00 1.20
TN2 Derek Jeter 4.00 1.20
TN3 Sammy Sosa 2.50 .75
TN4 Todd Helton 1.00 .30
TN5 Alex Rodriguez 2.50 .75
TN6 Chipper Jones 1.50 .45
TN7 Barry Bonds 4.00 1.20
TN8 Ken Griffey Jr. 2.50 .75
TN9 Nomar Garciaparra 2.50 .75
TN10 Frank Thomas 1.50 .45
TN11 Randy Johnson 1.50 .45
TN12 Cal Ripken 5.00 1.50
TN13 Mike Piazza 2.50 .75
TN14 Ivan Rodriguez 1.50 .45
TN15 Jeff Bagwell 1.00 .30
TN16 Vladimir Guerrero 1.50 .45
TN17 Greg Maddux 2.50 .75
TN18 Tony Gwynn 2.00 .60
TN19 Larry Walker 1.00 .30
TN20 Juan Gonzalez 1.50 .45
TN21 Scott Rolen 1.00 .30
TN22 Jason Giambi 1.50 .45
TN23 Jeff Kent 1.00 .30
TN24 Pat Burrell 1.00 .30
TN25 Pedro Martinez 1.50 .45
TN26 Willie Mays 4.00 1.20
TN27 Whitey Ford 1.00 .30
TN28 Jackie Robinson 2.00 .60
TN29 Ted Williams UER 5.00 1.50
Card has wrong year for his last at-bat
TN30 Babe Ruth 8.00 2.40
TN31 Warren Spahn 1.00 .30
TN32 Nolan Ryan 6.00 1.80
TN33 Yogi Berra 1.50 .45
TN34 Mike Schmidt 4.00 1.20
TN35 Steve Carlton 1.00 .30
TN36 Brooks Robinson 1.50 .45
TN37 Bob Gibson 1.00 .30
TN38 Reggie Jackson 1.00 .30
TN39 Johnny Bench 1.00 .30
TN40 Ernie Banks 1.50 .45
TN41 Eddie Mathews 1.50 .45
TN42 Don Mattingly 5.00 1.50
TN43 Duke Snider 1.00 .30
TN44 Hank Aaron 4.00 1.20
TN45 Roberto Clemente 5.00 1.50
TN46 Harmon Killebrew 1.50 .45
TN47 Frank Robinson 1.00 .30
TN48 Stan Musial 3.00 .90
TN49 Lou Brock 1.00 .30
TN50 Joe Morgan 1.00 .30

2001 Topps Originals

Randomly inserted into packs at different rates depening which series these cards were inserted in, this ten-card insert set features game-used jersey cards of players like Roberto Clemente and Carl Yastrzemski. Please note that the Willie Mays card is actually a game-used jacket.

Nm-Mt Ex-Mt
SER.1 STATED ODDS 1:1172 H/R, 1:260 HTA
SER.2 STATED ODDS 1:1023 H/R, 1:227 HTA
1 Roberto Clemente 55 100.00 30.00
2 Carl Yastrzemski 60 40.00 12.00
3 Mike Schmidt 73 40.00 12.00
4 Wade Boggs 83 25.00 7.50
5 Chipper Jones 91 25.00 7.50
6 Willie Mays 52 50.00 15.00
7 Lou Brock 62 25.00 7.50
8 Dave Parker 74 15.00 4.50
9 Barry Bonds 86 50.00 15.00
10 Alex Rodriguez 98 40.00 12.00

2001 Topps Team Topps Legends Autographs

These signed cards were inserted into various 2001-2003 Topps products. As these cards were inserted into different products and some were exchange cards. Most players in this set were featured on reprinted versions of their classic Topps "rookie" and "final" cards. The checklist was originally comprised of cards TT1-TT50 (with each player having an R and F suffix (i.e. Willie Mays is featured on TT1F with his 1973 card and TT1R with his 1952 card). In late 2002 and throughout 2003, additional players were added to the set with checklist numbering outside of the TT1-TT50 schematic. The numbering for these late additions was based on player's initials (i.e. Lou Brock's card is TT-LB) and only reprints of their rookie-year cards were produced.

Nm-Mt Ex-Mt
RANDOM INSERTS IN 01-03 TOPPS BRANDS
TOPPS AMER.PIE EXCH.DEADLINE 11/01/03
TOPPS GALLERY EXCH.DEADLINE 06/30/03
02 TOPPS EXCH.DEADLINE 12/01/03.
TT1F Willie Mays 73 120.00 36.00
T'02-TA'02/A
TT1R Willie Mays 52 150.00 45.00
AP
TT2F Hank Aaron 76
TT2R Hank Aaron 54
TT3F Stan Musial 63
TT3R Stan Musial 58 AS 80.00 24.00
TT4F Ernie Banks 71
TT4R Ernie Banks 54
TT5F Yogi Berra 65
TT5R Yogi Berra 52
TT6F Whitey Ford 67 25.00 7.50
TT/A-T10'02
TT6R Whitey Ford 53 25.00 7.50
T'02/F-TA'02/B
TT7F Nolan Ryan 94
TT7R Nolan Ryan 68 200.00 60.00
T206'02/A-TA'02/A
TT8F Carl Yastrzemski 83 50.00 15.00
TT8R Carl Yastrzemski 60 60.00 18.00
AP-T'02/A-TA'02/B-T10'02
TT9F Brooks Robinson 77
TT9R Brooks Robinson 57 50.00 15.00
TT10F Frank Robinson 75 25.00 7.50
BH5-TH'02/2
TT10R Frank Robinson 57 40.00 12.00
GL-T'02/A-TA'02/B
TT11F Tom Seaver 87
TT11R Tom Seaver 67 60.00 18.00
TA'02/A
TT12F Duke Snider 64
TT12R Duke Snider 52 40.00 12.00
TT13F Warren Spahn 65 40.00 12.00
BH1-TT-T'02/B-TA'02/B
TT13R Warren Spahn 52 40.00 12.00
AP-BB/A-TT/C
TT14F Johnny Bench 83 50.00 15.00
TT14R Johnny Bench 68 80.00 24.00
AP
TT15F Reggie Jackson 87
TT15R Reggie Jackson 69 80.00 24.00
AP-TA'02/A
TT16F Al Kaline 74
TT16R Al Kaline 54 50.00 15.00
TT17F Willie McCovey 80
TT17R Willie McCovey 60
TT18F Bob Gibson 75 25.00 7.50
AP'02
TT18R Bob Gibson 59 40.00 12.00
AP-BB/A-T'02/A
TT19F Mike Schmidt 89
TT19R Mike Schmidt 73 100.00 30.00
TT20F Harmon Killebrew 75
TT20R Harmon Killebrew 55 60.00 18.00
TT21F Bob Feller 56
TT21R Bob Feller 52 BH2 25.00 7.50
TT23F Gil McDougald 60 15.00 4.50
GL-TA'02/B
TT23R Gil McDougald 52 15.00 4.50
BB/B
TT24F Jimmy Piersall 67
TT24R Jimmy Piersall 56
TT25F Luis Tiant 83 15.00 4.50
GL EXCH
TT25R Luis Tiant 65 15.00 4.50
AP-BB/B-'02 TA/B
TT26F Minnie Minoso 64
TT26R Minnie Minoso 52
TT27F Andy Pafko 59 15.00 4.50
GL
TT27R Andy Pafko 52 15.00 4.50
BB/B-BH/3-GL
TT28F Herb Score 62 15.00 4.50
BB/B-GL-TT/B
TT28R Herb Score 56 15.00 4.50
BB/B-TA'02/B
TT29F Bill Skowron 67 15.00 4.50
TT29R Bill Skowron 54 15.00 4.50
AP-BB/A-T206'02/C
TT30F Maury Wills 72
TT30R Maury Wills 67
TT31F Clete Boyer 71 15.00 4.50
TA'02/B
TT31R Clete Boyer 57 15.00 4.50
AP-BB/B
TT32F Hank Bauer 61
TT32R Hank Bauer 52
TT33F Vida Blue 87 15.00 4.50
T'02/C/TR
TT33R Vida Blue 70 15.00 4.50
AP-T206'02/B-TH'02/4
TT34F Don Larsen 65
TT34R Don Larsen 56 15.00 4.50
TT35F Joe Pepitone 73 10.00 3.00
TT/A
TT35R Joe Pepitone 62 10.00 3.00
AP
TT36F Enos Slaughter 59 25.00 7.50
BH4-TT/A
TT36R Enos Slaughter 52 25.00 7.50
TAR'02
TT37F Tug McGraw 85 25.00 7.50
BB/B
TT37R Tug McGraw 65 40.00 12.00
AP-BB/B-TT/B
TT38F Fergie Jenkins 84
TT38R Fergie Jenkins 66 15.00 4.50
TT39F Willie Hernandez 89
TT39R Willie Hernandez 78
TT40F Gaylord Perry 83
TT40R Gaylord Perry 62 15.00 4.50
TT41F Carlton Fisk 93
TT41R Carlton Fisk 72
TT42F Kirk Gibson 95
TT42R Kirk Gibson 81
TT43F Bobby Thomson 60 15.00 4.50
TT-TH'02/3
TT43R Bobby Thomson 52 15.00 4.50
AP-TT/D-T'02/B-T10'02
TT44F Juan Marichal 74
TT44R Juan Marichal 61
TT45F Dom DiMaggio 53
TT45R Dom DiMaggio 52
TT46F Robin Roberts 66 T'02/E 25.00 7.50
TT46R Robin Roberts 52
TT47F Frank Howard 73 15.00 4.50
TT/A-TH'02/1
TT47R Frank Howard 60 15.00 4.50
AP-T'02/D-TA'02/B
TT48F Bobby Richardson 66 15.00 4.50
TT/A-T'02/B-T10'02
TT48R Bobby Richardson 57 15.00 4.50
AP-BB/B
TT49F Tony Kubek 65
TT49R Tony Kubek 57 60.00 18.00
AP-TA/B
TT50F Mickey Lolich 80 15.00 4.50
TT/A
TT50R Mickey Lolich 64 15.00 4.50
AP-T'02/C-TA'02/B-TH'02/1
TT51RF Ralph Branca 52 15.00 4.50
TT/D-T'02/E
TT-GC Gary Carter 75 15.00 4.50
TT-GG Goose Gossage 73 15.00 4.50
TAR'02
TT-GN Craig Nettles 69 15.00 4.50
02 'TAR
TT-JB Jim Bunning 65 25.00 7.50
TT-JM Joe Morgan 65 40.00 12.00
TT-JP Jim Palmer 66 15.00 4.50
TAR '02
TT-JS Johnny Sain 52 15.00 4.50
TT-LA Luis Aparicio 56 15.00 4.50
TT-LB Lou Brock 62 40.00 12.00
TT-PB Paul Blair 65 10.00 3.00
TT-RY Robin Yount 75 80.00 24.00
TT-VL Vern Law 52 15.00 4.50

2001 Topps Through the Years Reprints

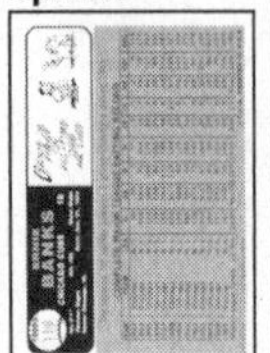

Randomly inserted into packs at 1:8 Hobby/Retail and 1:1 HTA, this 50-card set takes a look at some of the best players to every make it onto a Topps trading card.

Nm-Mt Ex-Mt
COMPLETE SET (50) 120.00 36.00
1 Yogi Berra '57 3.00 .90
2 Roy Campanella '56 3.00 .90
3 Willie Mays '53 5.00 1.50
4 Andy Pafko '52 3.00 .90
5 Jackie Robinson '52 5.00 1.50
6 Stan Musial '59 4.00 1.20
7 Duke Snider '56 3.00 .90
8 Warren Spahn '56 3.00 .90
9 Ted Williams '54 UER 10.00 3.00
Williams is spelled William
Also wrong birthdate
10 Eddie Mathews '55 3.00 .90
11 Willie McCovey '60 3.00 .90
12 Frank Robinson '69 3.00 .90
13 Ernie Banks '66 3.00 .90
14 Hank Aaron '65 5.00 1.50
15 Sandy Koufax '61 6.00 1.80
16 Bob Gibson '68 3.00 .90
17 Harmon Killebrew '67 3.00 .90
18 Whitey Ford '64 3.00 .90
19 Roberto Clemente '63 8.00 2.40
20 Juan Marichal '62 3.00 .90
21 Johnny Bench '70 3.00 .90
22 Willie Stargell '73 3.00 .90
23 Joe Morgan '74 3.00 .90
24 Carl Yastrzemski '71 4.00 1.20
25 Reggie Jackson '76 3.00 .90
26 Tom Seaver '78 3.00 .90
27 Steve Carlton '77 3.00 .90
28 Jim Palmer '79 3.00 .90
29 Rod Carew '72 3.00 .90
30 George Brett '75 8.00 2.40
31 Roger Clemens '85 6.00 1.80
32 Don Mattingly '84 10.00 3.00
33 Ryne Sandberg '89 5.00 1.50
34 Mike Schmidt '81 5.00 1.50
35 Cal Ripken '82 10.00 3.00
36 Tony Gwynn '83 4.00 1.20
37 Ozzie Smith '87 3.00 .90
38 Wade Boggs '88 3.00 .90
39 Nolan Ryan '80 6.00 1.80
40 Robin Yount '86 5.00 1.50
41 Mark McGwire '99 6.00 1.80
42 Ken Griffey Jr. '92 4.00 1.20
43 Sammy Sosa '99 4.00 1.20
44 Alex Rodriguez '98 4.00 1.20
45 Barry Bonds '94 6.00 1.80
46 Mike Piazza '95 4.00 1.20
47 Chipper Jones '91 3.00 .90
48 Greg Maddux '96 4.00 1.20
49 Nomar Garciaparra '97 4.00 1.20
50 Derek Jeter '93 8.00 2.40

2001 Topps What Could Have Been

Inserted at a rate of one in 25 hobby/retail packs or one in five HTA packs, these 10 cards feature stars of the Negro leagues who never got to play in the majors while they were at their peak.

Nm-Mt Ex-Mt
COMPLETE SET (10) 25.00 7.50
WCB1 Josh Gibson 5.00 1.50
WCB2 Satchel Paige 3.00 .90
WCB3 Buck Leonard 2.00 .60
WCB4 James Bell 3.00 .90
WCB5 Rube Foster 3.00 .90
WCB6 Martin DiHigo 2.00 .60
WCB7 William Johnson 2.00 .60
WCB8 Mule Suttles 2.00 .60
WCB9 Ray Dandridge 2.00 .60
WCB10 John Lloyd 2.00 .60

2001 Topps Traded

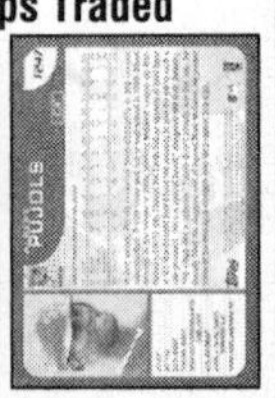

The 2001 Topps Traded product was released in October 2001, and features a 265-card base set. The 2001 Topps Traded and the 2001 Topps Chrome Traded were combined and sold together. Each pack contained eight 2001 Topps Traded and two 2001 Topps Chrome Traded cards for a total of ten cards in each pack. The 265-card set is broken down as follows: 99 cards highlighting player deals made during the 2000 off-season and 2001 season; 60 future stars who have never appeared alone on a Topps card; 55 rookies who make their premiere on a Topps card; six managers (T145-T150) who've either switched teams or were newly hired for the 2001 season and 45 traded repints (T100 through T144) of rookie cards featured in past Topps Traded sets. The packs carried a 3.00 per pack SRP and came 24 packs to a box.

Nm-Mt Ex-Mt
COMPLETE SET (265) 80.00 24.00
COMMON (T1-T99/T145-T265) .40 .12
COMMON (100-144) 1.00 .30
T1 Sandy Alomar Jr. .40 .12
T2 Kevin Appier .50 .15
T3 Brad Ausmus .40 .12
T4 Derek Bell .40 .12
T5 Bret Boone .50 .15
T6 Rico Brogna .40 .12
T7 Ellis Burks .50 .15
T8 Ken Caminiti .50 .15
T9 Roger Cedeno .40 .12
T10 Royce Clayton .40 .12
T11 Enrique Wilson .40 .12
T12 Rheal Cormier .40 .12
T13 Eric Davis .50 .15
T14 Shawon Dunston .40 .12
T15 Andres Galarraga .50 .15
T16 Tom Gordon .40 .12
T17 Mark Grace .75 .23
T18 Jeffrey Hammonds .40 .12
T19 Dustin Hermanson .40 .12
T20 Quinton McCracken .40 .12
T21 Todd Hundley .40 .12
T22 Charles Johnson .50 .15
T23 Marquis Grissom .40 .12
T24 Jose Mesa .40 .12
T25 Brian Boehringer .40 .12
T26 John Rocker .40 .12
T27 Jeff Frye .40 .12
T28 Reggie Sanders .50 .15
T29 David Segui .40 .12
T30 Mike Sirotka .40 .12
T31 Fernando Tatis .40 .12
T32 Steve Trachsel .40 .12
T33 Ismael Valdes .40 .12
T34 Randy Velarde .40 .12
T35 Ryan Kohlmeier .40 .12
T36 Mike Bordick .50 .15
T37 Kent Bottenfield .40 .12
T38 Pat Rapp .40 .12
T39 Jeff Nelson .40 .12
T40 Ricky Bottalico .40 .12
T41 Luke Prokopec .40 .12
T42 Hideo Nomo 1.25 .35
T43 Bill Mueller .50 .15
T44 Roberto Kelly .40 .12
T45 Chris Holt .40 .12
T46 Mike Jackson .40 .12
T47 Devon White .40 .12
T48 Gerald Williams .40 .12
T49 Eddie Taubensee .40 .12
T50 Brian Hunter UER .40 .12
Brian R Hunter pictured
Brian L Hunter stats
T51 Nelson Cruz .40 .12
T52 Jeff Fassero .40 .12
T53 Bubba Trammell .40 .12
T54 Bo Porter .40 .12
T55 Greg Norton .40 .12
T56 Benito Santiago .50 .15
T57 Ruben Rivera .40 .12
T58 Dee Brown .40 .12
T59 Jose Canseco UER 1.25 .35
2000 strikeout totals are wrong
T60 Chris Michalak .40 .12
T61 Tim Worrell .40 .12
T62 Matt Clement .50 .15
T63 Bill Pulsipher .40 .12
T64 Troy Brohawn RC .40 .12
T65 Mark Kotsay .40 .12
T66 Jimmy Rollins .50 .15
T67 Shea Hillenbrand .50 .15
T68 Ted Lilly .40 .12
T69 Jermaine Dye .50 .15
T70 Jerry Hairston Jr. .40 .12
T71 John Mabry .40 .12
T72 Kurt Abbott .40 .12
T73 Eric Owens .40 .12
T74 Jeff Brantley .40 .12
T75 Roy Oswalt .75 .23
T76 Doug Mientkiewicz .50 .15
T77 Rickey Henderson 1.25 .35
T78 Jason Grimsley .40 .12
T79 Christian Parker RC .40 .12
T80 Donne Wall .40 .12
T81 Alex Arias .40 .12
T82 Willis Roberts .40 .12
T83 Ryan Minor .40 .12
T84 Jason LaRue .40 .12
T85 Ruben Sierra .40 .12
T86 Johnny Damon .50 .15
T87 Juan Gonzalez 1.25 .35
T88 C.C. Sabathia .50 .15
T89 Tony Batista .50 .15
T90 Jay Witasick .40 .12
T91 Brent Abernathy .40 .12
T92 Paul LoDuca .50 .15
T93 Wes Helms .40 .12
T94 Mark Wohlers .40 .12
T95 Rob Bell .40 .12
T96 Tim Redding .40 .12
T97 Bud Smith RC .40 .12
T98 Adam Dunn .50 .15
T99 Ichiro Suzuki 10.00 3.00
Albert Pujols ROY
T100 Carlton Fisk 81 1.25 .35
T101 Tim Raines 81 1.00 .30
T102 Juan Marichal 74 1.00 .30
T103 Dave Winfield 81 1.00 .30
T104 Reggie Jackson 82 1.25 .35
T105 Cal Ripken 82 6.00 1.80
T106 Ozzie Smith 82 3.00 .90
T107 Tom Seaver 83 1.25 .35
T108 Lou Piniella 74 1.00 .30
T109 Dwight Gooden 84 1.25 .35
T110 Bret Saberhagen 84 1.00 .30
T111 Gary Carter 85 1.00 .30
T112 Jack Clark 85 1.00 .30
T113 R. Henderson 85 2.00 .60
T114 Barry Bonds 86 5.00 1.50
T115 Bobby Bonilla 86 1.00 .30
T116 Jose Canseco 86 2.00 .60
T117 Will Clark 86 2.00 .60
T118 Andres Galarraga 86 1.00 .30
T119 Bo Jackson 86 2.00 .60
T120 Wally Joyner 86 1.00 .30
T121 Ellis Burks 87 1.00 .30
T122 David Cone 87 1.00 .30
T123 Greg Maddux 87 3.00 .90
T124 Willie Randolph 76 1.00 .30
T125 Dennis Eckersley 87 1.00 .30
T126 Matt Williams 87 1.00 .30
T127 Joe Morgan 81 1.00 .30
T128 Fred McGriff 87 1.25 .35
T129 Roberto Alomar 88 2.00 .60
T130 Lee Smith 88 1.00 .30
T131 David Wells 88 1.00 .30
T132 Ken Griffey Jr. 89 3.00 .90
T133 Deion Sanders 89 1.25 .35
T134 Nolan Ryan 89 4.00 1.20
T135 David Justice 90 1.00 .30
T136 Joe Carter 91 1.00 .30
T137 Jack Morris 92 1.00 .30
T138 Mike Piazza 93 3.00 .90
T139 Barry Bonds 93 5.00 1.50
T140 Terrence Long 94 1.00 .30
T141 Ben Grieve 94 1.00 .30
T142 Richie Sexson 95 1.00 .30
George Arias
Mark Sweeney
Brian Schneider
T143 Sean Burroughs 99 1.00 .30
T144 Alfonso Soriano 99 1.25 .35
T145 Bob Boone MG .50 .15
T146 Larry Bowa MG .50 .15
T147 Bob Brenly MG .40 .12
T148 Buck Martinez MG .40 .12
T149 L. McClendon MG .40 .12
T150 Jim Tracy MG .40 .12
T151 Jared Abruzzo RC .40 .12
T152 Kurt Ainsworth .40 .12
T153 Willie Bloomquist .50 .15
T154 Ben Broussard .40 .12
T155 Bobby Bradley .40 .12
T156 Mike Bynum .40 .12
T157 A.J. Hinch .40 .12
T158 Ryan Christianson .40 .12
T159 Carlos Silva .40 .12
T160 Joe Crede .40 .12
T161 Jack Cust .40 .12
T162 Ben Diggins .40 .12
T163 Phil Dumatrait .40 .12
T164 Alex Escobar .40 .12
T165 Miguel Olivo .40 .12
T166 Chris George .40 .12
T167 Marcus Giles .50 .15
T168 Keith Ginter .40 .12
T169 Josh Girdley .40 .12
T170 Tony Alvarez .40 .12
T171 Scott Seabol .40 .12
T172 Josh Hamilton .40 .12
T173 Jason Hart .40 .12
T174 Israel Alcantara .40 .12
T175 Jake Peavy 1.00 .30
T176 Stubby Clapp RC .40 .12
T177 D'Angelo Jimenez .40 .12
T178 Nick Johnson .50 .15
T179 Ben Johnson .40 .12
T180 Larry Bigbie .40 .12
T181 Allen Levrault .40 .12
T182 Felipe Lopez .40 .12
T183 Sean Burnett .50 .15
T184 Nick Neugebauer .40 .12
T185 Austin Kearns .50 .15
T186 Corey Patterson .50 .15
T187 Carlos Pena .40 .12
T188 R. Rodriguez RC .40 .12
T189 Juan Rivera .40 .12
T190 Grant Roberts .40 .12
T191 Adam Pettyjohn RC .40 .12
T192 Jared Sandberg .40 .12
T193 Xavier Nady .50 .15
T194 Dane Sardinha .40 .12
T195 Shawn Sonnier .40 .12
T196 Rafael Soriano 1.50 .45
T197 Brian Specht RC .40 .12
T198 Aaron Myette .40 .12
T199 Juan Uribe RC .40 .12
T200 Jayson Werth .40 .12
T201 Brad Wilkerson .40 .12
T202 Horacio Estrada .40 .12
T203 Joel Pineiro 1.25 .35
T204 Matt LeCroy .40 .12
T205 Michael Coleman .40 .12
T206 Ben Sheets .50 .15
T207 Eric Byrnes .40 .12
T208 Sean Burroughs .50 .15
T209 Ken Harvey .40 .12
T210 Travis Hafner 1.50 .45
T211 Erick Almonte .40 .12
T212 Jason Belcher RC .40 .12
T213 Wilson Betemit RC .40 .12
T214 Hank Blalock RC 5.00 1.50
T215 Danny Borrell .40 .12
T216 John Buck RC .60 .18
T217 Freddie Bynum RC .40 .12
T218 Noel Devarez RC .40 .12
T219 Juan Diaz RC .40 .12
T220 Felix Diaz RC .40 .12
T221 Josh Fogg RC .40 .12
T222 Matt Ford RC .40 .12
T223 Scott Heard .40 .12
T224 Ben Hendrickson RC .40 .12
T225 Cody Ross RC .40 .12
T226 A. Hernandez RC .40 .12
T227 Alfredo Amezaga RC .60 .18
T228 Bob Keppel RC .60 .18
T229 Ryan Madson RC .60 .18
T230 Octavio Martinez RC .40 .12
T231 Hee Seop Choi 3.00 .90
T232 Thomas Mitchell .40 .12
T233 Luis Montanez .40 .12
T234 Andy Morales RC .40 .12
T235 Justin Morneau RC 3.00 .90
T236 Toe Nash RC .40 .12
T237 V. Pascucci RC .40 .12
T238 Roy Smith RC .40 .12
T239 Antonio Perez RC .40 .12
T240 Chad Petty RC .40 .12
T241 Steve Smyth .40 .12
T242 Jose Reyes RC 5.00 1.50
T243 Eric Reynolds RC .40 .12
T244 Dominic Rich .40 .12
T245 J. Richardson RC .40 .12
T246 Ed Rogers RC .40 .12
T247 Albert Pujols RC 30.00 9.00
T248 Esix Snead RC .40 .12
T249 Luis Torres RC .40 .12
T250 Matt White RC .40 .12
T251 Blake Williams .40 .12
T252 Chris Russ .40 .12
T253 Joe Kennedy RC .40 .12
T254 Jeff Randazzo RC .40 .12
T255 Beau Hale RC .40 .12
T256 Brad Hennessey RC .40 .12
T257 Jake Gautreau RC .40 .12
T258 Jeff Mathis RC 2.00 .60
T259 Aaron Heilman RC 1.00 .30
T260 B. Sardinha RC .60 .18
T261 Irvin Guzman RC 2.50 .75
T262 Gabe Gross RC .60 .18
T263 J.D. Martin RC .40 .12
T264 Chris Smith RC .40 .12
T265 Kenny Baugh RC .40 .12

2001 Topps Traded Gold

This set is a parallel to the 2001 Topps Traded set. Inserted into the 2001 Topps Traded at a rate of one in three, these cards are serial numbered to 2001 have have a gold foil border.

Nm-Mt Ex-Mt
*STARS: 4X TO 10X BASIC CARDS
*REPRINTS: 1.5X TO 4X BASIC
*ROOKIES: 1.5X TO 4X BASIC

2001 Topps Traded Autographs

Inserted at a rate of one in 626, these cards share the same design as the 2001 Topps Golden Anniversary Autographs. The only difference is the front bottom of the card reads "Golden Anniversary Traded Star". The cards carry a 'TTA' prefix.

Nm-Mt Ex-Mt
TTA-JD Johnny Damon 20.00 6.00
TTA-MM Mike Mussina 40.00 12.00

2001 Topps Traded Dual Relics

Inserted at a rate of one in 376, these cards highlight a player who has switched teams and feature a swatch of game-used jersey from both his former and current teams. The cards carry a 'TRR' prefix.

	Nm-Mt	Ex-Mt
TTR-BG Ben Grieve EXCH	15.00	4.50
TTR-DH D. Hermanson	15.00	4.50
TTR-FT Fernando Tatis	15.00	4.50
TTR-MR Manny Ramirez	15.00	4.50

2001 Topps Traded Farewell Dual Relic

Inserted at a rate of one in 4693, this card features bat pieces from both Cal Ripken and Tony Gwynn and is a farewell tribute to both players. The card carries a 'FR' prefix.

	Nm-Mt	Ex-Mt
FR-RG Cal Ripken Tony Gwynn	120.00	36.00

2001 Topps Traded Hall of Fame Bat Relic

Inserted at a rate of one in 2796, this card features bat pieces from both Kirby Puckett and Dave Winfield and commemorates their entrance in Cooperstown. The card carries a 'HFR' prefix.

	Nm-Mt	Ex-Mt
HFR-PW Kirby Puckett Dave Winfield	50.00	15.00

2001 Topps Traded Relics

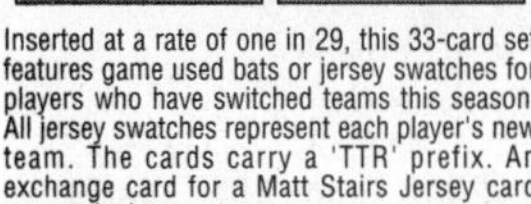

Inserted at a rate of one in 29, this 33-card set features game used bats or jersey swatches for players who have switched teams this season. All jersey swatches represent each player's new team. The cards carry a 'TTR' prefix. An exchange card for a Matt Stairs Jersey card was packed out.

	Nm-Mt	Ex-Mt
TTR-AG A. Galarraga Bat	10.00	3.00
TTR-BB Bobby Bonilla Bat	10.00	3.00
TTR-BB Bret Boone Jsy	10.00	3.00
TTR-BM Bill Mueller Jsy	10.00	3.00
TTR-CJ C. Johnson Jsy	10.00	3.00
TTR-DB Derek Bell Bat	10.00	3.00
TTR-DN Denny Neagle Jsy	10.00	3.00
TTR-DW David Wells Jsy	10.00	3.00
TTR-ED Eric Davis Bat	10.00	3.00
TTR-EW E. Wilson Bat	10.00	3.00
TTR-FM Fred McGriff Bat	15.00	4.50
TTR-GW G. Williams Bat	10.00	3.00
TTR-HR Hideo Nomo Jsy	50.00	15.00
TTR-JC Jose Canseco Bat	15.00	4.50
TTR-JD J. Damon Bat	10.00	3.00
TTR-JG Juan Gonzalez Bat	15.00	4.50
TTR-JH J. Hammonds Jsy	10.00	3.00
TTR-KC Ken Caminiti Bat	10.00	3.00
TTR-KS K. Stinnett Bat SP	10.00	3.00
TTR-MG Mark Grace Bat	15.00	4.50
TTR-MG M. Grissom Bat	10.00	3.00
TTR-MH M. Hampton Jsy	10.00	3.00
TTR-MS M. Stairs Jsy EXCH	10.00	3.00
TTR-NP Neifi Perez Bat	10.00	3.00
TTR-RB Rico Brogna Jsy	10.00	3.00
TTR-RG Ron Gant Bat	10.00	3.00
TTR-RS Ruben Sierra Bat	10.00	3.00
TTR-SA S. Alomar Jr. Bat	10.00	3.00
TTR-TH Todd Hundley Jsy	10.00	3.00
TTR-TR Tim Raines Jsy	10.00	3.00
TTR-JD1 J. Dye Bat SP	10.00	3.00
TTR-ROC R. Cedeno Jsy	10.00	3.00
TTR-RSC R. Clayton Bat	10.00	3.00

2001 Topps Traded Rookie Relics

Inserted at a rate of one in 91, this 18-card set features bat pieces or jersey swatches for rookies. The cards carry a 'TRR' prefix. An exchange card for the Ed Rogers Bat card was seeded into packs.

	Nm-Mt	Ex-Mt
TRR-AB Angel Berroa Jsy	10.00	3.00
TRR-AP A. Pujols Bat SP	40.00	12.00
TRR-BO Bill Ortega Jsy	8.00	2.40
TRR-ER E.Rogers Bat SP EXCH	10.00	3.00
TRR-HC H. Cota Jsy	8.00	2.40
TRR-JL Jason Lane Jsy	10.00	3.00
TRR-JS Jae Seo Jsy	8.00	2.40
TRR-JS Jamal Strong Jsy	8.00	2.40
TRR-JV Jose Valverde Jsy	10.00	3.00
TRR-JY Jason Young Jsy	8.00	2.40
TRR-NC Nate Cornejo Jsy	8.00	2.40
TRR-NN N. Neugebauer Jsy	8.00	2.40
TRR-PF P. Feliz Jsy SP	8.00	2.40
TRR-RS Richard Stahl Jsy	8.00	2.40
TRR-SB S. Burroughs Jsy	8.00	2.40
TRR-TS T. Shinjo Bat SP	15.00	4.50
TRR-WB W. Betemit Bat	8.00	2.40
TRR-WR Wilkin Ruan Jsy	8.00	2.40

2001 Topps Traded Who Would Have Thought

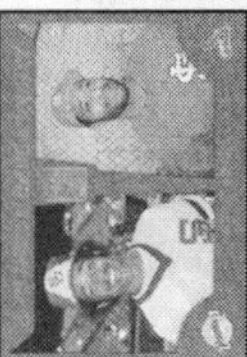

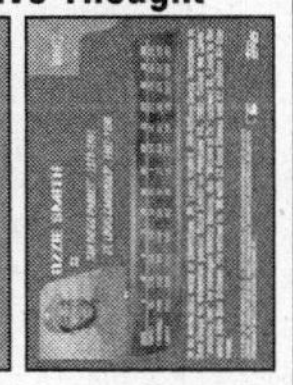

Inserted at a rate of one in eight, this 20-card set portrays players who fans thought would never be traded. The cards carry a 'WWHT' prefix.

	Nm-Mt	Ex-Mt
COMPLETE SET (20)	40.00	12.00
WWHT1 Nolan Ryan	6.00	1.80
WWHT2 Ozzie Smith	4.00	1.20
WWHT3 Tom Seaver	1.50	.45
WWHT4 Steve Carlton	1.50	.45
WWHT5 Reggie Jackson	1.50	.45
WWHT6 Frank Robinson	1.50	.45
WWHT7 Keith Hernandez	1.50	.45
WWHT8 Andre Dawson	1.50	.45
WWHT9 Lou Brock	1.50	.45
WWHT10 D. Eckersley	1.50	.45
WWHT11 Dave Winfield	1.50	.45
WWHT12 Rod Carew	1.50	.45
WWHT13 Willie Randolph	1.50	.45
WWHT14 Dwight Gooden	1.50	.45
WWHT15 Carlton Fisk	1.50	.45
WWHT16 Dale Murphy	2.50	.75
WWHT17 Paul Molitor	1.50	.45
WWHT18 Gary Carter	1.50	.45
WWHT19 Wade Boggs	1.50	.45
WWHT20 Willie Mays	5.00	1.50

2002 Topps Promos

This three card set was issued in a sealed cello pack to dealers and hobby media several weeks prior to the products release. The cards have a "P" prefix so they can be differentiated from the regular cards.

	Nm-Mt	Ex-Mt
COMPLETE SET (3)	3.00	.90
P1 Sammy Sosa	2.00	.60
P2 Jason Giambi	1.00	.30
P3 Curt Schilling	1.00	.30

2002 Topps

The complete set of 2002 Topps consists of 718 cards issued in two separate series. The first series of 364 cards was distributed in November, 2001 and the second series of 354 cards followed up in April, 2002. Please note, the first series is numbered 1-365, but card number seven does not exist (the number was "retired" in 1996 by Topps to honor Mickey Mantle). Similar to the 1999 McGwire and Sosa home run cards, Barry Bonds is featured on card number 365 with 73 different versions to commemorate each of the homers he smashed during the 2001 season. The first series set is considered complete with any "one" of these variations. The cards were issued either in 10 card hobby/retail packs with an SRP of $1.29 or 37 card HTA packs with an SRP of $5 per pack. The hobby packs were issued 36 to a box and 12 boxes to a case. The HTA packs were issued 12 to a box and eight to a case. Cards numbered 277-305 feature managers; cards numbered 307-325/671-690 feature leading prospects; cards numbered 326-331/691-695 feature 2001 draft picks; cards numbered 332-336 feature leading highlights of the 2001 season; cards numbered 337-348 feature league leaders; cards numbered 349-356 feature the eight teams which made the playoffs; cards numbered 357-364 feature major league baseball's stirring tribute to the events of September 11, 2001; cards 641-670 feature Team Cards; 696-713 are Gold Glove subsets, 714-715 are Cy Young subsets, 716-717 are MVP subsets and 718-719 are Rookie of the Year subsets. Notable Rookie Cards include Joe Mauer and Kazhuisa Ishii. Also, Topps repurchased more than 21,000 actual vintage Topps cards and randomly seeded them into packs as follows - Ser.1 Home Team Advantage 1:169, ser.1 retail 1:tbd, ser.2 hobby 1:431, ser.2 Home Team Advantage 1:113 and ser.2 retail 1:331. Brown-boxed hobby factory sets were issued in May, 2002 containing the full 718-card basic set and five Topps Archives Reprints inserts. Green-boxed retail factory sets were issued in late August, 2002 containing the full 718-card basic set and cards 1-5 of a 10-card Draft Picks set.

	Nm-Mt	Ex-Mt
COMPLETE SET (718)	80.00	24.00
COMP.FACT.BROWN SET (723)	80.00	24.00
COMP.FACT.GREEN SET (723)	80.00	24.00
COMP. SERIES 1 (365)	40.00	12.00
COMPLETE SERIES 2 (354)	40.00	12.00
COMMON CARD (1-6/8-719)	.20	.06
COMMON (307-331)	.50	.15
COMMON CARD (332-364)	.50	.15
1 Pedro Martinez	.50	.15
2 Mike Stanton	.20	.06
3 Brad Penny	.20	.06
4 Mike Matheny	.20	.06
5 Johnny Damon	.20	.06
6 Bret Boone	.20	.06
7 Does Not Exist		
8 Chris Truby	.20	.06
9 B.J. Surhoff	.20	.06
10 Mike Hampton	.20	.06
11 Juan Pierre	.20	.06
12 Mark Buehrle	.20	.06
13 Bob Abreu	.20	.06
14 David Cone	.20	.06
15 Aaron Sele UER Card lists him as being born in New Mexico He was born in Minnesota	.20	.06
16 Fernando Tatis	.20	.06
17 Bobby Jones	.20	.06
18 Rick Helling	.20	.06
19 Dmitri Young	.20	.06
20 Mike Mussina UER Career win total is wrong	.50	.15
21 Mike Sweeney	.20	.06
22 Cristian Guzman	.20	.06
23 Ryan Kohlmeier	.20	.06
24 Adam Kennedy	.20	.06
25 Larry Walker	.30	.09
26 Eric Davis UER 2000 Stolen Base totals are wrong	.20	.06
27 Jason Tyner	.20	.06
28 Eric Young	.20	.06
29 Jason Marquis	.20	.06
30 Luis Gonzalez	.20	.06
31 Kevin Tapani	.20	.06
32 Orlando Cabrera	.20	.06
33 Marty Cordova UER Career homer total, 1003	.20	.06
34 Brad Ausmus	.20	.06
35 Livan Hernandez	.20	.06
36 Alex Gonzalez	.20	.06
37 Edgar Renteria	.20	.06
38 Bengie Molina	.20	.06
39 Frank Menechino	.20	.06
40 Rafael Palmeiro	.30	.09
41 Brad Fullmer	.20	.06
42 Julio Zuleta	.20	.06
43 Darren Dreifort	.20	.06
44 Trot Nixon	.30	.09
45 Trevor Hoffman	.20	.06
46 Vladimir Nunez	.20	.06
47 Mark Kotsay	.20	.06
48 Kenny Rogers	.20	.06
49 Ben Petrick	.20	.06
50 Jeff Bagwell	.30	.09
51 Juan Encarnacion	.20	.06
52 Ramiro Mendoza	.20	.06
53 Brian Meadows	.20	.06
54 Chad Curtis	.20	.06
55 Aramis Ramirez	.20	.06
56 Mark McLemore	.20	.06
57 Dante Bichette	.20	.06
58 Scott Schoeneweis	.20	.06
59 Jose Cruz Jr.	.20	.06
60 Roger Clemens	1.00	.30
61 Jose Guillen	.20	.06
62 Darren Oliver	.20	.06
63 Chris Reitsma	.20	.06
64 Jeff Abbott	.20	.06
65 Robin Ventura	.20	.06
66 Denny Neagle	.20	.06
67 Al Martin	.20	.06
68 Benito Santiago	.20	.06
69 Roy Oswalt	.20	.06
70 Juan Gonzalez	.50	.15
71 Garret Anderson	.20	.06
72 Bobby Bonilla	.20	.06
73 Danny Bautista	.20	.06
74 J.T. Snow	.20	.06
75 Derek Jeter	1.25	.35
76 John Olerud	.20	.06
77 Kevin Appier	.20	.06
78 Phil Nevin	.20	.06
79 Sean Casey	.20	.06
80 Troy Glaus	.30	.09
81 Joe Randa	.20	.06
82 Jose Valentin	.20	.06
83 Ricky Bottalico	.20	.06
84 Todd Zeile	.20	.06
85 Barry Larkin	.50	.15
86 Bob Wickman	.20	.06
87 Jeff Shaw	.20	.06
88 Greg Vaughn	.20	.06
89 Fernando Vina	.20	.06
90 Mark Mulder	.20	.06
91 Paul Bako	.20	.06
92 Aaron Boone	.20	.06
93 Esteban Loaiza	.20	.06
94 Richie Sexson	.20	.06
95 Alfonso Soriano	.30	.09
96 Tony Womack	.20	.06
97 Paul Shuey	.20	.06
98 Melvin Mora	.20	.06
99 Tony Gwynn	.60	.18
100 Vladimir Guerrero	.50	.15
101 Keith Osik	.20	.06
102 Bud Smith	.20	.06
103 Scott Williamson	.20	.06
104 Daryle Ward	.20	.06
105 Doug Mientkiewicz	.20	.06
106 Stan Javier	.20	.06
107 Russ Ortiz	.20	.06
108 Wade Miller	.20	.06
109 Luke Prokopec	.20	.06
110 Andruw Jones UER Careel SB total, 1442	.20	.06
111 Ron Coomer	.20	.06
112 Dan Wilson UER Career SB total, 1245	.20	.06
113 Luis Castillo	.20	.06
114 Derek Bell	.20	.06
115 Gary Sheffield	.20	.06
116 Ruben Rivera	.20	.06
117 Paul O'Neill	.30	.09
118 Craig Paquette	.20	.06
119 Kelvin Escobar	.20	.06
120 Brad Radke	.20	.06
121 Jorge Fabregas	.20	.06
122 Randy Winn	.20	.06
123 Tom Goodwin	.20	.06
124 Jaret Wright	.20	.06
125 Manny Ramirez	.20	.06
126 Al Leiter	.20	.06
127 Ben Davis	.20	.06
128 Frank Catalanotto	.20	.06
129 Jose Cabrera	.20	.06
130 Magglio Ordonez	.20	.06
131 Jose Macias	.20	.06
132 Ted Lilly	.20	.06
133 Chris Holt	.20	.06
134 Eric Milton	.20	.06
135 Shannon Stewart	.20	.06
136 Omar Olivares	.20	.06
137 David Segui	.20	.06
138 Jeff Nelson	.20	.06
139 Matt Williams	.20	.06
140 Ellis Burks	.20	.06
141 Jason Bere	.20	.06
142 Jimmy Haynes	.20	.06
143 Ramon Hernandez	.20	.06
144 Craig Counsell UER Card pictures Greg Colbrunn Some vital stats are wrong as well	.20	.06
145 John Smoltz	.30	.09
146 Homer Bush	.20	.06
147 Quilvio Veras	.20	.06
148 Esteban Yan	.20	.06
149 Ramon Ortiz	.20	.06
150 Carlos Delgado	.20	.06
151 Lee Stevens	.20	.06
152 Wil Cordero	.20	.06
153 Mike Bordick	.20	.06
154 John Flaherty	.20	.06
155 Omar Daal	.20	.06
156 Todd Ritchie	.20	.06
157 Carl Everett	.20	.06
158 Scott Sullivan	.20	.06
159 Deivi Cruz	.20	.06
160 Albert Pujols UER Placido Polanco pictured on back	1.00	.30
161 Royce Clayton	.20	.06
162 Jeff Suppan	.20	.06
163 C.C. Sabathia	.20	.06
164 Jimmy Rollins	.20	.06
165 Rickey Henderson	.50	.15
166 Rey Ordonez	.20	.06
167 Shawn Estes	.20	.06
168 Reggie Sanders	.20	.06
169 Jon Lieber	.20	.06
170 Armando Benitez	.20	.06
171 Mike Remlinger	.20	.06
172 Billy Wagner	.20	.06
173 Troy Percival	.20	.06
174 Devon White	.20	.06
175 Ivan Rodriguez	.50	.15
176 Dustin Hermanson	.20	.06
177 Brian Anderson	.20	.06
178 Graeme Lloyd	.20	.06
179 Russel Branyan	.20	.06
180 Bobby Higginson	.20	.06
181 Alex Gonzalez	.20	.06
182 John Franco	.20	.06
183 Sidney Ponson	.20	.06
184 Jose Mesa	.20	.06
185 Todd Hollandsworth	.20	.06
186 Kevin Young	.20	.06
187 Tim Wakefield	.20	.06
188 Craig Biggio	.30	.09
189 Jason Isringhausen	.20	.06
190 Mark Quinn	.20	.06
191 Glendon Rusch	.20	.06
192 Damian Miller	.20	.06
193 Sandy Alomar Jr.	.20	.06
194 Scott Brosius	.20	.06
195 Dave Martinez	.20	.06
196 Danny Graves	.20	.06
197 Shea Hillenbrand	.20	.06
198 Jimmy Anderson	.20	.06
199 Travis Lee	.20	.06
200 Randy Johnson	.50	.15
201 Carlos Beltran	.20	.06
202 Jerry Hairston	.20	.06
203 Jesus Sanchez	.20	.06
204 Eddie Taubensee	.20	.06
205 David Wells	.20	.06
206 Russ Davis	.20	.06
207 Michael Barrett	.20	.06
208 Marquis Grissom	.20	.06
209 Byung-Hyun Kim	.20	.06
210 Hideo Nomo	.50	.15
211 Ryan Rupe	.20	.06
212 Ricky Gutierrez	.20	.06
213 Darryl Kile	.20	.06
214 Rico Brogna	.20	.06
215 Terrence Long	.20	.06
216 Mike Jackson	.20	.06
217 Jamey Wright	.20	.06
218 Adrian Beltre	.20	.06
219 Benny Agbayani	.20	.06
220 Chuck Knoblauch	.20	.06
221 Randy Wolf	.20	.06
222 Andy Ashby	.20	.06
223 Corey Koskie	.20	.06
224 Roger Cedeno	.20	.06
225 Ichiro Suzuki	.75	.23
226 Keith Foulke	.20	.06
227 Ryan Minor	.20	.06
228 Shawon Dunston	.20	.06
229 Alex Cora	.20	.06
230 Jeromy Burnitz	.20	.06
231 Mark Grace	.30	.09
232 Aubrey Huff	.20	.06
233 Jeffrey Hammonds	.20	.06
234 Olmedo Saenz	.20	.06
235 Brian Jordan	.20	.06
236 Jeremy Giambi	.20	.06
237 Joe Girardi	.20	.06
238 Eric Gagne	.30	.09
239 Masato Yoshii	.20	.06
240 Greg Maddux	.75	.23
241 Bryan Rekar	.20	.06
242 Ray Durham	.20	.06
243 Torii Hunter	.20	.06
244 Derrek Lee	.20	.06
245 Jim Edmonds	.20	.06
246 Einar Diaz	.20	.06
247 Brian Bohanon	.20	.06
248 Ron Belliard	.20	.06
249 Mike Lowell	.20	.06
250 Sammy Sosa	.75	.23
251 Richard Hidalgo	.20	.06
252 Bartolo Colon	.20	.06
253 Jorge Posada	.30	.09
254 LaTroy Hawkins	.20	.06
255 Paul LoDuca	.20	.06
256 Carlos Febles	.20	.06
257 Nelson Cruz	.20	.06
258 Edgardo Alfonzo	.20	.06
259 Joey Hamilton	.20	.06
260 Cliff Floyd	.20	.06
261 Wes Helms	.20	.06
262 Jay Bell	.20	.06
263 Mike Cameron	.20	.06
264 Paul Konerko	.20	.06
265 Jeff Kent	.20	.06
266 Robert Fick	.20	.06
267 Allen Levrault	.20	.06
268 Placido Polanco	.20	.06
269 Marlon Anderson	.20	.06
270 Mariano Rivera	.30	.09
271 Chan Ho Park	.20	.06
272 Jose Vizcaino	.20	.06
273 Jeff D'Amico	.20	.06
274 Mark Gardner	.20	.06
275 Travis Fryman	.20	.06
276 Darren Lewis	.20	.06
277 Bruce Bochy MG	.20	.06
278 Jerry Manuel MG	.20	.06
279 Bob Brenly MG	.20	.06
280 Don Baylor MG	.20	.06
281 Davey Lopes MG	.20	.06
282 Jerry Narron MG	.20	.06
283 Tony Muser MG	.20	.06
284 Hal McRae MG	.20	.06
285 Bobby Cox MG	.20	.06
286 Larry Dierker MG	.20	.06
287 Phil Garner MG	.20	.06
288 Joe Kerrigan MG	.20	.06
289 Bobby Valentine MG	.20	.06
290 Dusty Baker MG	.20	.06
291 Lloyd McClendon MG	.20	.06
292 Mike Scioscia MG	.20	.06
293 Buck Martinez MG	.20	.06
294 Larry Bowa MG	.20	.06
295 Tony LaRussa MG	.20	.06
296 Jeff Torborg MG	.20	.06
297 Tom Kelly MG	.20	.06
298 Mike Hargrove MG	.20	.06
299 Art Howe MG	.20	.06
300 Lou Piniella MG	.20	.06
301 Charlie Manuel MG	.20	.06
302 Buddy Bell MG	.20	.06
303 Tony Perez MG	.20	.06
304 Bob Boone MG	.20	.06
305 Joe Torre MG	.50	.15
306 Jim Tracy MG	.20	.06
307 Jason Lane PROS	.50	.15
308 Chris George PROS	.50	.15
309 Hank Blalock PROS UER Bio has him throwing lefty	1.00	.30
310 Joe Borchard PROS	.50	.15
311 Marlon Byrd PROS	.50	.15
312 R. Cabrera PROS RC	.50	.15
313 F. Sanchez PROS RC	.50	.15
314 S. Wiggins PROS RC	.50	.15
315 J. Maule PROS RC	.50	.15
316 D. Cesar PROS RC	.50	.15
317 Boof Bonser PROS	.50	.15
318 J. Tolentino PROS RC	.50	.15
319 Earl Snyder PROS RC	.50	.15
320 T. Wade PROS RC	.50	.15
321 N. Calzado PROS RC	.50	.15
322 Eric Glaser PROS RC	.50	.15
323 C. Kuzmic PROS RC	.50	.15
324 Nic Jackson PROS RC	.50	.15
325 Mike Rivera PROS	.50	.15
326 Jason Bay PROS RC	1.25	.35
327 Chris Smith DP	.50	.15
328 Jake Gautreau DP	.50	.15
329 Gabe Gross DP	.50	.15
330 Kenny Baugh DP	.50	.15
331 J.D. Martin DP	.50	.15
332 Barry Bonds HL 500th Homer	1.25	.35
333 Rickey Henderson HL Sets record for career walks	.50	.15
334 Bud Smith HL	.50	.15
335 R. Henderson HL 3000	.50	.15
336 Barry Bonds HL 73 homers in a season	1.25	.35
337 Ichiro Suzuki Jason Giambi	.50	.15

2002 Topps

Roberto Alomar LL
338 Alex Rodriguez .50 .15
Ichiro Suzuki
Bret Boone LL
339 Alex Rodriguez .50 .15
Jim Thome
Rafael Palmeiro LL
340 Bret Boone .50 .15
Juan Gonzalez
Alex Rodriguez LL
341 Freddy Garcia .50 .15
Mike Mussina
Joe Mays LL
342 Hideo Nomo .50 .15
Mike Mussina
Roger Clemens LL
343 Larry Walker .50 .15
Todd Helton
Moises Alou
Lance Berkman LL
344 Sammy Sosa .50 .15
Todd Helton
Barry Bonds LL
345 Barry Bonds .50 .15
Sammy Sosa
Luis Gonzalez LL
346 Sammy Sosa .50 .15
Todd Helton
Luis Gonzalez LL
347 Randy Johnson .50 .15
Curt Schilling
John Burkett LL
348 Randy Johnson .50 .15
Curt Schilling
Chan Ho Park LL
349 Seattle Mariners PB .50 .15
350 Oakland Athletics PB .50 .15
351 New York Yankees PB .50 .15
352 Cleveland Indians PB .50 .15
353 Ariz. Diamondbacks PB .50 .15
354 Atlanta Braves PB .50 .15
355 St. Louis Cardinals PB .50 .15
356 Houston Astros PB .50 .15
357 Ariz.Diamondbacks .50 .15
Colorado Rockies UWS
358 Mike Piazza UWS .50 .15
359 Braves-Phillies UWS .50 .15
360 Curt Schilling UWS .50 .15
361 Roger Clemens .50 .15
Lee Mazzilli UWS
362 Sammy Sosa UWS .50 .15
363 Tom Lampkin .50 .15
Ichiro Suzuki
Bret Boone UWS
364 Barry Bonds .50 .15
Jeff Bagwell UWS
365 Barry Bonds HR 1 15.00 4.50
365 Barry Bonds HR 2 10.00 3.00
365 Barry Bonds HR 3 10.00 3.00
365 Barry Bonds HR 4 10.00 3.00
365 Barry Bonds HR 5 10.00 3.00
365 Barry Bonds HR 6 10.00 3.00
365 Barry Bonds HR 7 10.00 3.00
365 Barry Bonds HR 8 10.00 3.00
365 Barry Bonds HR 9 10.00 3.00
365 Barry Bonds HR 10 10.00 3.00
365 Barry Bonds HR 11 10.00 3.00
365 Barry Bonds HR 12 10.00 3.00
365 Barry Bonds HR 13 10.00 3.00
365 Barry Bonds HR 14 10.00 3.00
365 Barry Bonds HR 15 10.00 3.00
365 Barry Bonds HR 16 10.00 3.00
365 Barry Bonds HR 17 10.00 3.00
365 Barry Bonds HR 18 10.00 3.00
365 Barry Bonds HR 19 10.00 3.00
365 Barry Bonds HR 20 10.00 3.00
365 Barry Bonds HR 21 10.00 3.00
365 Barry Bonds HR 22 10.00 3.00
365 Barry Bonds HR 23 10.00 3.00
365 Barry Bonds HR 24 10.00 3.00
365 Barry Bonds HR 25 10.00 3.00
365 Barry Bonds HR 26 10.00 3.00
365 Barry Bonds HR 27 10.00 3.00
365 Barry Bonds HR 28 10.00 3.00
365 Barry Bonds HR 29 10.00 3.00
365 Barry Bonds HR 30 10.00 3.00
365 Barry Bonds HR 31 10.00 3.00
365 Barry Bonds HR 32 UER 10.00 3.00
No pitcher is listed on this card
365 Barry Bonds HR 33 10.00 3.00
365 Barry Bonds HR 34 10.00 3.00
365 Barry Bonds HR 35 10.00 3.00
365 Barry Bonds HR 36 10.00 3.00
365 Barry Bonds HR 37 10.00 3.00
365 Barry Bonds HR 38 10.00 3.00
365 Barry Bonds HR 39 10.00 3.00
365 Barry Bonds HR 40 10.00 3.00
365 Barry Bonds HR 41 10.00 3.00
365 Barry Bonds HR 42 10.00 3.00
365 Barry Bonds HR 43 10.00 3.00
365 Barry Bonds HR 44 10.00 3.00
365 Barry Bonds HR 45 10.00 3.00
365 Barry Bonds HR 46 10.00 3.00
365 Barry Bonds HR 47 10.00 3.00
365 Barry Bonds HR 48 10.00 3.00
365 Barry Bonds HR 49 10.00 3.00
365 Barry Bonds HR 50 10.00 3.00
365 Barry Bonds HR 51 10.00 3.00
365 Barry Bonds HR 52 10.00 3.00
365 Barry Bonds HR 53 10.00 3.00
365 Barry Bonds HR 54 10.00 3.00
365 Barry Bonds HR 55 10.00 3.00
365 Barry Bonds HR 56 10.00 3.00
365 Barry Bonds HR 57 10.00 3.00
365 Barry Bonds HR 58 10.00 3.00
365 Barry Bonds HR 59 10.00 3.00
365 Barry Bonds HR 60 10.00 3.00
365 Barry Bonds HR 61 15.00 4.50
365 Barry Bonds HR 62 10.00 3.00
365 Barry Bonds HR 63 10.00 3.00
365 Barry Bonds HR 64 10.00 3.00
365 Barry Bonds HR 65 10.00 3.00
365 Barry Bonds HR 66 10.00 3.00
365 Barry Bonds HR 67 10.00 3.00
365 Barry Bonds HR 68 10.00 3.00
365 Barry Bonds HR 69 10.00 3.00
365 Barry Bonds HR 70 25.00 7.50
365 Barry Bonds HR 71 10.00 3.00
365 Barry Bonds HR 72 10.00 3.00
365 Barry Bonds HR 73 60.00 18.00
366 Pat Meares .20 .06
367 Mike Lieberthal .20 .06
368 Larry Bigbie .20 .06
369 Ron Gant .20 .06
370 Moises Alou .20 .06
371 Chad Kreuter .20 .06
372 Willis Roberts .20 .06
373 Toby Hall .20 .06
374 Miguel Batista .20 .06
375 John Burkett .20 .06
376 Cory Lidle .20 .06
377 Nick Neugebauer .20 .06
378 Jay Payton .20 .06
379 Steve Karsay .20 .06
380 Eric Chavez .20 .06
381 Kelly Stinnett .20 .06
382 Jarrod Washburn .20 .06
383 Rick White .20 .06
384 Jeff Conine .20 .06
385 Fred McGriff .30 .09
386 Marvin Benard .20 .06
387 Joe Crede .20 .06
388 Dennis Cook .20 .06
389 Rick Reed .20 .06
390 Tom Glavine .30 .09
391 Rondell White .20 .06
392 Matt Morris .20 .06
393 Pat Rapp .20 .06
394 Robert Person .20 .06
395 Omar Vizquel .20 .06
396 Jeff Cirillo .20 .06
397 Dave Mlicki .20 .06
398 Jose Ortiz .20 .06
399 Ryan Dempster .20 .06
400 Curt Schilling .30 .09
401 Peter Bergeron .20 .06
402 Kyle Lohse .20 .06
403 Craig Wilson UER .20 .06
Homer totals are wrong
404 David Justice .20 .06
405 Darin Erstad .20 .06
406 Jose Mercedes .20 .06
407 Carl Pavano .20 .06
408 Albie Lopez .20 .06
409 Alex Ochoa .20 .06
410 Chipper Jones .50 .15
411 Tyler Houston .20 .06
412 Dean Palmer .20 .06
413 Damian Jackson .20 .06
414 Josh Towers .20 .06
415 Rafael Furcal .20 .06
416 Mike Morgan .20 .06
417 Herb Perry .20 .06
418 Mike Sirotka .20 .06
419 Mark Wohlers .20 .06
420 Nomar Garciaparra .75 .23
421 Felipe Lopez .20 .06
422 Joe McEwing .20 .06
423 Jacque Jones .20 .06
424 Julio Franco .20 .06
425 Frank Thomas .50 .15
426 So Taguchi RC .75 .23
427 Kazuhisa Ishii RC 1.50 .45
428 D'Angelo Jimenez .20 .06
429 Chris Stynes .20 .06
430 Kerry Wood .50 .15
431 Chris Singleton .20 .06
432 Erubiel Durazo .20 .06
433 Matt Lawton .20 .06
434 Bill Mueller .20 .06
435 Jose Canseco .50 .15
436 Ben Grieve .20 .06
437 Terry Mulholland .20 .06
438 David Bell .20 .06
439 A.J. Pierzynski .20 .06
440 Adam Dunn .20 .06
441 Jon Garland .20 .06
442 Jeff Fassero .20 .06
443 Julio Lugo .20 .06
444 Carlos Guillen .20 .06
445 Orlando Hernandez .20 .06
446 Mark Loretta UER .20 .06
Photo is Curtis Leskanic
447 Scott Spiezio .20 .06
448 Kevin Millwood .20 .06
449 Jamie Moyer .20 .06
450 Todd Helton .30 .09
451 Todd Walker .20 .06
452 Jose Lima .20 .06
453 Brook Fordyce .20 .06
454 Aaron Rowand .20 .06
455 Barry Zito .30 .09
456 Eric Owens .20 .06
457 Charles Nagy .20 .06
458 Raul Ibanez .20 .06
459 Joe Mays .20 .06
460 Jim Thome .50 .15
461 Adam Eaton .20 .06
462 Felix Martinez .20 .06
463 Vernon Wells .20 .06
464 Donnie Sadler .20 .06
465 Tony Clark .20 .06
466 Jose Hernandez .20 .06
467 Ramon Martinez .20 .06
468 Rusty Greer .20 .06
469 Rod Barajas .20 .06
470 Lance Berkman .20 .06
471 Brady Anderson .20 .06
472 Pedro Astacio .20 .06
473 Shane Halter .20 .06
474 Bret Prinz .20 .06
475 Edgar Martinez .30 .09
476 Steve Trachsel .20 .06
477 Gary Matthews Jr. .20 .06
478 Ismael Valdes .20 .06
479 Juan Uribe .20 .06
480 Shawn Green .20 .06
481 Kirk Rueter .20 .06
482 Damion Easley .20 .06
483 Chris Carpenter .20 .06
484 Kris Benson .20 .06
485 Antonio Alfonseca .20 .06
486 Kyle Farnsworth .20 .06
487 Brandon Lyon .20 .06
488 Hideki Irabu .20 .06
489 David Ortiz .20 .06
490 Mike Piazza .75 .23
491 Derek Lowe .20 .06
492 Chris Gomez .20 .06
493 Mark Johnson .20 .06
494 John Rocker .20 .06
495 Eric Karros .20 .06
496 Bill Haselman .20 .06
497 Dave Veres .20 .06
498 Pete Harnisch .20 .06
499 Tomokazu Ohka .20 .06
500 Barry Bonds 1.25 .35
501 David Dellucci .20 .06
502 Wendell Magee .20 .06
503 Tom Gordon .20 .06
504 Javier Vazquez .20 .06
505 Ben Sheets .20 .06
506 Wilton Guerrero .20 .06
507 John Halama .20 .06
508 Mark Redman .20 .06
509 Jack Wilson .20 .06
510 Bernie Williams .30 .09
511 Miguel Cairo .20 .06
512 Denny Hocking .20 .06
513 Tony Batista .20 .06
514 Mark Grudzielanek .20 .06
515 Jose Vidro .20 .06
516 Sterling Hitchcock .20 .06
517 Billy Koch .20 .06
518 Matt Clement .20 .06
519 Bruce Chen .20 .06
520 Roberto Alomar .50 .15
521 Orlando Palmeiro .20 .06
522 Steve Finley .20 .06
523 Danny Patterson .20 .06
524 Terry Adams .20 .06
525 Tino Martinez .30 .09
526 Tony Armas Jr. .20 .06
527 Geoff Jenkins .20 .06
528 Kerry Robinson .20 .06
529 Corey Patterson .20 .06
530 Brian Giles .20 .06
531 Jose Jimenez .20 .06
532 Joe Kennedy .20 .06
533 Armando Rios .20 .06
534 Osvaldo Fernandez .20 .06
535 Ruben Sierra .20 .06
536 Octavio Dotel .20 .06
537 Luis Sojo .20 .06
538 Brent Butler .20 .06
539 Pablo Ozuna .20 .06
540 Freddy Garcia .20 .06
541 Chad Durbin .20 .06
542 Orlando Merced .20 .06
543 Michael Tucker .20 .06
544 Roberto Hernandez .20 .06
545 Pat Burrell .20 .06
546 A.J. Burnett .20 .06
547 Bubba Trammell .20 .06
548 Scott Elarton .20 .06
549 Mike Darr .20 .06
550 Ken Griffey Jr. .75 .23
551 Ugueth Urbina .20 .06
552 Todd Jones .20 .06
553 Delino Deshields .20 .06
554 Adam Piatt .20 .06
555 Jason Kendall .20 .06
556 Hector Ortiz .20 .06
557 Turk Wendell .20 .06
558 Rob Bell .20 .06
559 Sun Woo Kim .20 .06
560 Raul Mondesi .20 .06
561 Brent Abernathy .20 .06
562 Seth Etherton .20 .06
563 Shawn Wooten .20 .06
564 Jay Buhner .20 .06
565 Andres Galarraga .20 .06
566 Shane Reynolds .20 .06
567 Rod Beck .20 .06
568 Dee Brown .20 .06
569 Pedro Feliz .20 .06
570 Ryan Klesko .20 .06
571 John Vander Wal UER .20 .06
Home Run Total in 1999 was 64
572 Nick Bierbrodt .20 .06
573 Joe Nathan .20 .06
574 James Baldwin .20 .06
575 J.D. Drew .20 .06
576 Greg Colbrunn .20 .06
577 Doug Glanville .20 .06
578 Brandon Duckworth .20 .06
579 Shawn Chacon .20 .06
580 Rich Aurilia .20 .06
581 Chuck Finley .20 .06
582 Abraham Nunez .20 .06
583 Kenny Lofton .20 .06
584 Brian Daubach .20 .06
585 Miguel Tejada .20 .06
586 Nate Cornejo .20 .06
587 Kazuhiro Sasaki .20 .06
588 Chris Richard .20 .06
589 Armando Reynoso .20 .06
590 Tim Hudson .20 .06
591 Neifi Perez .20 .06
592 Steve Cox .20 .06
593 Henry Blanco .20 .06
594 Ricky Ledee .20 .06
595 Tim Salmon .30 .09
596 Luis Rivas .20 .06
597 Jeff Zimmerman .20 .06
598 Matt Stairs .20 .06
599 Preston Wilson .20 .06
600 Mark McGwire 1.25 .35
601 Timo Perez UER .20 .06
Biographical Information is that of Aaron Rowand's
602 Matt Anderson .20 .06
603 Todd Hundley .20 .06
604 Rick Ankiel .20 .06
605 Tsuyoshi Shinjo .20 .06
606 Woody Williams .20 .06
607 Jason LaRue .20 .06
608 Carlos Lee .20 .06
609 Russ Johnson .20 .06
610 Scott Rolen .30 .09
611 Brent Mayne .20 .06
612 Darrin Fletcher .20 .06
613 Ray Lankford .20 .06
614 Troy O'Leary .20 .06
615 Javier Lopez .20 .06
616 Randy Velarde .20 .06
617 Vinny Castilla .20 .06
618 Milton Bradley .20 .06
619 Ruben Mateo .20 .06
620 Jason Giambi Yankees .50 .15
621 Andy Benes .20 .06
622 Joe Mauer RC 5.00 1.50
623 Andy Pettitte .30 .09
624 Jose Offerman .20 .06
625 Mo Vaughn .20 .06
626 Steve Sparks .20 .06
627 Mike Matthews .20 .06
628 Robb Nen .20 .06
629 Kip Wells .20 .06
630 Kevin Brown .20 .06
631 Arthur Rhodes .20 .06
632 Gabe Kapler .20 .06
633 Jermaine Dye .20 .06
634 Josh Beckett .30 .09
635 Pokey Reese .20 .06
636 Benji Gil .20 .06
637 Marcus Giles .20 .06
638 Julian Tavarez .20 .06
639 Jason Schmidt .20 .06
640 Alex Rodriguez .75 .23
641 Anaheim Angels TC .20 .06
642 Arizona Diamondbacks TC .30 .09
643 Atlanta Braves TC .20 .06
644 Baltimore Orioles TC .20 .06
645 Boston Red Sox TC .20 .06
646 Chicago Cubs TC .20 .06
647 Chicago White Sox TC .20 .06
648 Cincinnati Reds TC .20 .06
649 Cleveland Indians TC .20 .06
650 Colorado Rockies TC .20 .06
651 Detroit Tigers TC .20 .06
652 Florida Marlins TC .20 .06
653 Houston Astros TC .20 .06
654 Kansas City Royals TC .20 .06
655 Los Angeles Dodgers TC .20 .06
656 Milwaukee Brewers TC .20 .06
657 Minnesota Twins TC .20 .06
658 Montreal Expos TC .20 .06
659 New York Mets TC .20 .06
660 New York Yankees TC .50 .15
661 Oakland Athletics TC .20 .06
662 Philadelphia Phillies TC .20 .06
663 Pittsburgh Pirates TC .20 .06
664 San Diego Padres TC .20 .06
665 San Francisco Giants TC .20 .06
666 Seattle Mariners TC .30 .09
667 St. Louis Cardinals TC .20 .06
668 T.B. Devil Rays TC .20 .06
669 Texas Rangers TC .20 .06
670 Toronto Blue Jays TC .20 .06
671 Juan Cruz PROS .50 .15
672 Kevin Cash PROS RC .50 .15
673 Jimmy Gobble PROS RC 1.25 .35
674 Mike Hill PROS RC .50 .15
675 T.Buchholz PROS RC .50 .15
676 Bill Hall PROS .50 .15
677 B.Roneberg PROS RC .50 .15
678 R.Huffman PROS RC .50 .15
679 Chris Tritle PROS RC .50 .15
680 Nate Espy PROS RC .50 .15
681 Nick Alvarez PROS RC .50 .15
682 Jason Botts PROS RC .50 .15
683 Ryan Gripp PROS RC .50 .15
684 Dan Phillips PROS RC .50 .15
685 Pablo Arias PROS RC .50 .15
686 J.Rodriguez PROS RC .50 .15
687 Rich Harden PROS RC 4.00 1.20
688 Neal Frendling PROS RC .50 .15
689 Rich Thompson PROS RC .50 .15
690 G.Montalbano PROS RC .50 .15
691 Len Dinardo DP RC .50 .15
692 Ryan Raburn DP RC .50 .15
693 Josh Barfield DP RC 2.50 .75
694 David Bacani DP RC .50 .15
695 Dan Johnson DP RC .50 .15
696 Mike Mussina GG .30 .09
697 Ivan Rodriguez GG .50 .15
698 Doug Mientkiewicz GG .20 .06
699 Roberto Alomar GG .30 .09
700 Eric Chavez GG .20 .06
701 Omar Vizquel GG .20 .06
702 Mike Cameron GG .20 .06
703 Torii Hunter GG .20 .06
704 Ichiro Suzuki GG .50 .15
705 Greg Maddux GG .50 .15
706 Brad Ausmus GG .20 .06
707 Todd Helton GG .20 .06
708 Fernando Vina GG .20 .06
709 Scott Rolen GG .20 .06
710 Orlando Cabrera GG .20 .06
711 Andruw Jones GG .20 .06
712 Jim Edmonds GG .20 .06
713 Larry Walker GG .20 .06
714 Roger Clemens CY .50 .15
715 Randy Johnson CY .30 .09
716 Ichiro Suzuki MVP .50 .15
717 Barry Bonds MVP .50 .15
718 Ichiro Suzuki ROY .50 .15
719 Albert Pujols ROY .50 .15

2002 Topps Gold

Inserted one per 19 first series hobby packs, one per 15 first series retail packs, one per 5 first series HTA packs, one per 12 second series hobby packs, one per 9 second series retail packs and one per three second series HTA packs, this set parallels cards 1-330 and 366-695 of the 2002 Topps set. Each card features bold, gold-foil borders on front and 2002 serial-numbered sets were produced.

Nm-Mt Ex-Mt
*GOLD 1-306/366-670: 8X TO 20X BASIC
*GOLD 307-330/671-695: 3X TO 8X BASIC
*GOLD 426-427: 2X TO 5X BASIC

2002 Topps Home Team Advantage

This is a parallel to the Topps set. Each of these cards, which were available only in the blue factory sets have the words "Home Team Advantage" stamped on them.

Nm-Mt Ex-Mt
COMP.FACT.SET (685) 70.00 21.00
*HTA: .75X TO 2X BASIC
*BONDS HR 70: .2X TO .5X BASIC HR 70

2002 Topps Limited

This 790 card factory set was issued in October, 2002. It had a SRP of $150 and parallels the regular Topps set except for the reprinting of all 73 Barry Bonds 365 cards. These cards can be differentiated from the regular cards by their "glossy" finish on the front.

Nm-Mt Ex-Mt
COMP.FACT.SET (790) 200.00 60.00
*LTD STARS: 2X TO 5X BASIC CARDS
*307-331/426-427/622/671-695: 1.5X TO 4X
*BONDS HR: .2X TO .5X BASIC BONDS HR

2002 Topps 1952 Reprints

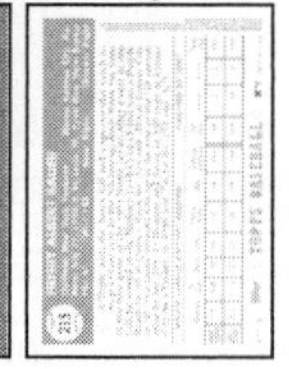

Inserted at a rate of one in 25 hobby, one in five HTA packs and one in 16 retail packs, these nineteen reprint cards feature players who participated in the 1952 World Series which was won by the New York Yankees.

Nm-Mt Ex-Mt
COMPLETE SET (19) 50.00 15.00
COMPLETE SERIES 1 (9) 25.00 7.50
COMPLETE SERIES 2 (10) 25.00 7.50
52R-1 Roy Campanella 5.00 1.50
52R-2 Duke Snider 4.00 1.20
52R-3 Carl Erskine 4.00 1.20
52R-4 Andy Pafko 4.00 1.20
52R-5 Johnny Mize 4.00 1.20
52R-6 Billy Martin 5.00 1.50
52R-7 Phil Rizzuto 5.00 1.50
52R-8 Gil McDougald 4.00 1.20
52R-9 Allie Reynolds 4.00 1.20
52R-10 Jackie Robinson 5.00 1.50
52R-11 Preacher Roe 4.00 1.20
52R-12 Gil Hodges 5.00 1.50
52R-13 Billy Cox 4.00 1.20
52R-14 Yogi Berra 5.00 1.50
52R-15 Gene Woodling 4.00 1.20
52R-16 Johnny Sain 4.00 1.20
52R-17 Ralph Houk 4.00 1.20
52R-18 Joe Collins 4.00 1.20
52R-19 Hank Bauer 4.00 1.20

2002 Topps 1952 Reprints Autographs

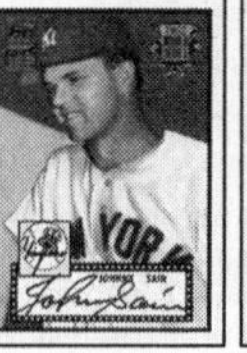

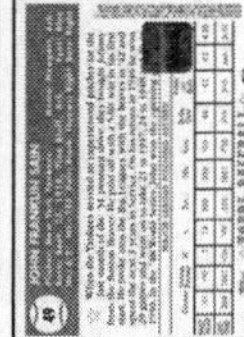

Inserted in series one packs at a rate of one in 10,268 hobby packs, one in 2826 HTA packs and one in 8,005 retail packs and series two packs at a rate of 1:7524 hobby, one in 1985 HTA packs and one in 5839 retail packs these eleven cards feature signed copies of the 1952 reprints. Phil Rizzuto did not return his cards in time for inclusion in this product and those cards could be redeemed until December 1st, 2003. Due to scarcity, no pricing is provided for these cards. These cards were released in different series and we have notated that information next to the player's name in our checklist.

Nm-Mt Ex-Mt
AP-A Andy Pafko S1 80.00 24.00
CE-A Carl Erskine S1 100.00 30.00
DS-A Duke Snider S1 150.00 45.00
GM-A Gil McDougald S1 100.00 30.00
HB-A Hank Bauer S2
JB-A Joe Black S1 100.00 30.00
JS-A Johnny Sain S2
PR-A Preacher Roe S2
PR-A Phil Rizzuto S1 150.00 45.00
RH-A Ralph Houk S2
YB-A Yogi Berra S2

2002 Topps 1952 World Series Highlights

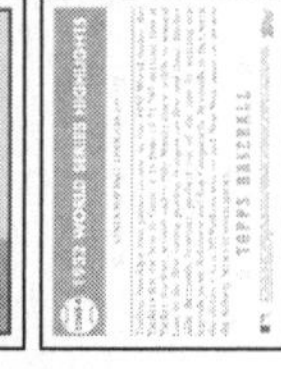

Inserted in first and second series packs at a rate of one in 25 hobby, one in five HTA and one in 16 retail packs, these eleven cards feature highlights of the 1952 World Series. Next to the card, we have notated whether they were released in the first or second series.

Nm-Mt Ex-Mt
COMPLETE SET (7) 10.00 3.00
COMPLETE SERIES 1 (3) 4.00 1.20
COMPLETE SERIES 2 (4) 6.00 1.80
52WS-1 Dodgers Line Up 1 2.00 .60
52WS-2 Billy Martin's Homer 2 2.00 .60
52WS-3 Dodgers Celebrate 1 2.00 .60
52WS-4 Yanks Slip Dodgers 2 2.00 .60
52WS-5 Carl Erskine 1 2.00 .60
52WS-6 Casey Stengel MG 2.00 .60
Allie Reynolds 2
52WS-7 Allie Reynolds 2.00 .60
Relieves Ed Lopat 2

2002 Topps 5-Card Stud Aces Relics

Inserted into second series packs at a rate of one in 1180 hobby, one in 293 HTA and one in 966 retail, these five cards feature some of the best pitchers in baseball along with a game jersey swatch "relic".

	Nm-Mt	Ex-Mt
5A-GM Greg Maddux Jsy	40.00	12.00
5A-MH Mike Hampton Jsy	15.00	4.50
5A-MM Mark Mulder Jsy	15.00	4.50
5A-PM Pedro Martinez Jsy	25.00	7.50
5A-RJ Randy Johnson Jsy	25.00	7.50

2002 Topps 5-Card Stud Deuces are Wild Relics

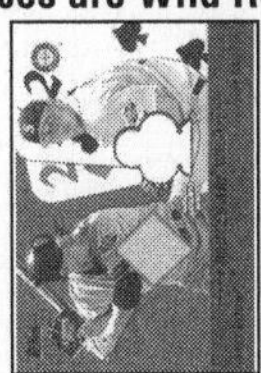

Inserted into second series packs at an overall rate of one in 1962 hobby, one in 487 HTA and one in 1609 retail, these five cards feature memorabilia game bat and game jersey relics from two of the stars from the same team. These cards were issued in different odds depending on which series they were from and we have notated which group next to the card in the checklist.

	Nm-Mt	Ex-Mt
SER.2 A ODDS 1:3078 H, 1:796 HTA, 1:2422 R		
SER.2 B ODDS 1:5410 H, 1:1254 HTA, 1:4827 R		
5D-BG Bret Boone Jsy	25.00	7.50
Freddy Garcia Jsy A		
5D-BK Barry Bonds Jsy	50.00	15.00
Jeff Kent Jsy A		
5D-JG Randy Johnson Jsy	40.00	12.00
Luis Gonzalez Bat B		
5D-TA Jim Thome Jsy	40.00	12.00
Roberto Alomar Bat B		
5D-WH Larry Walker Bat	40.00	12.00
Todd Helton Bat B		

2002 Topps 5-Card Stud Jack of All Trades Relics

Inserted into second series packs at an overall rate of one in 1350 Hobby packs, one in 333 HTA packs and one on 1119 retail packs, these five cards feature some of the best five-tool players in the field along with a game-used memorabilia relic from their career. These cards were issued at different odds depending on the player and we have notated that information in our checklist.

	Nm-Mt	Ex-Mt
5J-AJ Andruw Jones A	15.00	4.50
5J-BB Barry Bonds A	40.00	12.00
5J-BW Bernie Williams A	25.00	7.50
5J-IR Ivan Rodriguez A	25.00	7.50
5J-RO Roberto Alomar B		

2002 Topps 5-Card Stud Kings of the Clubhouse Relics

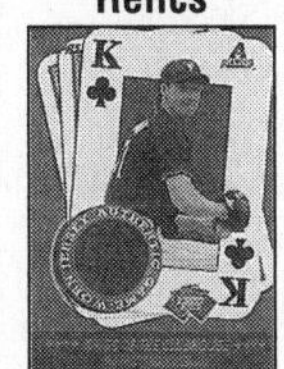

Inserted into packs at an overall rate of one in 1449 hobby packs, one in 334 HTA packs and one in 1119 retail packs, these five cards feature some of the most effective and highly driven clubhouse leaders along with a game-used memorabilia relic from their career. Depending on the player, these cards were issued in two groups and we have notated that information in our checklist.

	Nm-Mt	Ex-Mt
SER.2 A ODDS 1:1570 H, 1:358 HTA, 1:1211 R		
SER.2B ODDS 1:18883 H,1:4943 HTA,1:14736 R		
5K-EM Edgar Martinez A	25.00	7.50
5K-PO Paul O'Neill B		
5K-RJ Randy Johnson A	25.00	7.50
5K-TG Tom Glavine A	25.00	7.50
5K-TH Todd Helton A	25.00	7.50

2002 Topps 5-Card Stud Three of a Kind Relics

Inserted into packs at an overall rate of one in 2039 Hobby packs, one in 524 HTA packs and one in retail 1609 packs, these five cards feature memorabilia relics from three stars from the same team. Depending on the card, these cards were issued as part of two groups, and we have notated that information next to the card in our checklist

	Nm-Mt	Ex-Mt
SER.2 A ODDS 1:3078 H, 1:796 HTA, 1:2422 R		
SER.2 B ODDS 1:6043 H, 1:1532 HTA, 1:4827 R		
5TBDB A.J. Burnett	80.00	24.00
Ryan Dempster		
Josh Beckett A		
5TFBJ Rafael Furcal	60.00	18.00
Wilson Betemit		
Andruw Jones B		
5TLOC Carlos Lee	80.00	24.00
Magglio Ordonez		
Jose Canseco B		
5TPSW Jorge Posada	80.00	24.00
Alfonso Soriano		
Bernie Williams B		
5TSPA Tsuyoshi Shinjo	80.00	24.00
Mike Piazza		
Edgardo Alfonzo A		

2002 Topps All-World Team

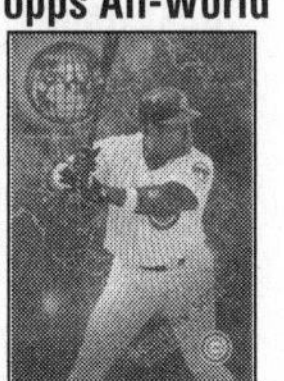

Inserted into second series packs at a rate of one in 12 packs and one in 4 HTA packs, these 25 cards feature an international mix of upper-echelon stars. These cards are extremely thick as well.

	Nm-Mt	Ex-Mt
COMPLETE SET (25)	60.00	18.00
AW-1 Ichiro Suzuki	3.00	.90
AW-2 Barry Bonds	5.00	1.50
AW-3 Pedro Martinez	2.00	.60
AW-4 Juan Gonzalez	2.00	.60
AW-5 Larry Walker	1.50	.45
AW-6 Sammy Sosa	3.00	.90
AW-7 Mariano Rivera	1.50	.45
AW-8 Vladimir Guerrero	2.00	.60
AW-9 Alex Rodriguez	3.00	.90
AW-10 Albert Pujols	4.00	1.20
AW-11 Luis Gonzalez	1.50	.45
AW-12 Ken Griffey Jr.	3.00	.90
AW-13 Kazuhiro Sasaki	1.50	.45
AW-14 Bob Abreu	1.50	.45
AW-15 Todd Helton	1.50	.45
AW-16 Nomar Garciaparra	3.00	.90
AW-17 Miguel Tejada	1.50	.45
AW-18 Roger Clemens	4.00	1.20
AW-19 Mike Piazza	3.00	.90
AW-20 Carlos Delgado	1.50	.45
AW-21 Derek Jeter	5.00	1.50
AW-22 Hideo Nomo	2.00	.60
AW-23 Randy Johnson	2.00	.60
AW-24 Ivan Rodriguez	2.00	.60
AW-25 Chan Ho Park	1.50	.45

2002 Topps Autographs

Inserted at varying odds, these 40 cards feature authentic autographs. Alex Rodriguez, Barry Bonds and Xavier Nady did not return their cards in time for series one packout, thus exchange cards were seeded into packs. Those cards could be redeemed until December 1st, 2003. First series cards have a numerical card number on back (i.e. TA-1) and series two cards have card numbering based on player's initials (i.e. TA-AB).

	Nm-Mt	Ex-Mt
SER.1 A 1:15,402 H, 1:4256 HTA, 1:12,008 R		
SER.2 A 1:10,071 H, 1:2404, 1:7702 R		
SER.1 B 1:49,599 H, 1:12,312 HTA, 1:46,944 R		
SER.2 B 1:1867 H, 1:487 HTA, 1:1449 R		
SER.1 C 1:4104 H, 1:1130 HTA, 1:3238 R		
SER.2 C 1:10,071 H, 1:2646 HTA, 1:7702 R		
SER.1 D 1:9853 H, 1:2714 HTA, 1:7284 R		
SER.2 D 1:1885 H, 1:496 HTA, 1:1449 R		
SER.1 E 1:4104 H, 1:1130 HTA, 1:3238 R		
SER.2 E 1:5023 H, 1:1323 HTA, 1:3851 R		
SER.1 F 1:985 H, 1:271 HTA, 1:776 R.		
SER.2 F 1:940 H, 1:247 HTA, 1:725 R.		
SER.2 G 1:3017 H, 1:794 HTA, 1:2327 R		
NO A1/B1 PRICING DUE TO SCARCITY		
TA-1 Carlos Delgado B1		
TA-2 Ivan Rodriguez A1		
TA-3 Miguel Tejada C1	25.00	7.50
TA-4 Geoff Jenkins E1	15.00	4.50
TA-5 Johnny Damon A1	30.00	9.00
TA-6 Tim Hudson C1	30.00	9.00
TA-7 Terrence Long E1	15.00	4.50
TA-8 Gabe Kapler C1	15.00	4.50
TA-9 Magglio Ordonez C1	25.00	7.50
TA-10 Barry Bonds A1		
TA-11 Pat Burrell C1	25.00	7.50
TA-12 Mike Mussina A1		
TA-13 Eric Valent F1	10.00	3.00
TA-14 Xavier Nady F1	10.00	3.00
TA-15 Cristian Guerrero F1	10.00	3.00
TA-16 Ben Sheets F1	15.00	4.50
TA-17 Corey Patterson C1	25.00	7.50
TA-18 Carlos Pena F1	10.00	3.00
TA-19 Alex Rodriguez	120.00	36.00
D1/A2 EXCH		
TA-AB Adrian Beltre B2	30.00	9.00
TA-AE Alex Escobar F2	15.00	4.50
TA-BG Brian Giles B2	30.00	9.00
TA-BW Brad Wilkerson G2	10.00	3.00
TA-BGR Ben Grieve B2	30.00	9.00
TA-CF Cliff Floyd C2	25.00	7.50
TA-CG Cristian Guzman B2	30.00	9.00
TA-JD Jermaine Dye D2	25.00	7.50
TA-JH Josh Hamilton E2	15.00	4.50
TA-JO Jose Ortiz D2	15.00	4.50
TA-JR Jimmy Rollins D2	25.00	7.50
TA-JW Justin Wayne D2	15.00	4.50
TA-KG Keith Ginter F2	10.00	3.00
TA-MS Mike Sweeney B2	30.00	9.00
TA-NJ Nick Johnson F2	15.00	4.50
TA-RF Rafael Furcal B2	30.00	9.00
TA-RK Ryan Klesko B2	30.00	9.00
TA-RO Roy Oswalt F2	15.00	4.50
TA-RP Rafael Palmeiro A2	60.00	18.00
TA-RS Richie Sexson B2	30.00	9.00
TA-TG Troy Glaus A2	60.00	18.00

2002 Topps Coaches Collection Relics

Inserted at overall odds of one in 236 retail packs, these 26 cards feature memorabilia from either a coach or a manager currently involved in major league baseball. The Billy Williams jersey card was not available when these cards were packed and that card could be redeemed until April 30th, 2004.

	Nm-Mt	Ex-Mt
SER.2 BAT ODDS 1:404 RETAIL		
SER.2 UNIFORM ODDS 1:565 RETAIL		
CC-AH Art Howe Bat	15.00	4.50
CC-AT Alan Trammell Bat	50.00	15.00
CC-BB Bruce Bochy Bat	15.00	4.50
CC-BM Buck Martinez Bat	15.00	4.50
CC-BV Bobby Valentine Bat	25.00	7.50
CC-BW Billy Williams Jsy	25.00	7.50
CC-BBE Buddy Bell Bat	25.00	7.50
CC-BBR Bob Brenly Bat	25.00	7.50
CC-DB Dusty Baker Bat	25.00	7.50
CC-DL Davey Lopes Bat	25.00	7.50
CC-DBA Don Baylor Bat	25.00	7.50
CC-EH Elrod Hendricks Bat	15.00	4.50
CC-EM Eddie Murray Bat	60.00	18.00
CC-FW Frank White Bat	25.00	7.50
CC-HM Hal McRae Jsy	10.00	3.00
CC-JT Joe Torre Jsy	15.00	4.50
CC-KG Ken Griffey Sr. Jsy	10.00	3.00
CC-LB Larry Bowa Bat	25.00	7.50
CC-LP Lance Parrish Bat	25.00	7.50
CC-MH Mike Hargrove Bat	25.00	7.50
CC-MS Mike Scioscia Bat	25.00	7.50
CC-MW Mookie Wilson Bat	25.00	7.50
CC-PG Phil Garner Bat	15.00	4.50
CC-PM Paul Molitor Bat	50.00	15.00
CC-TP Tony Perez Jsy	10.00	3.00
CC-WR Willie Randolph Bat	25.00	7.50

2002 Topps Draft Picks

This 10-card set was distributed in two separate cello-wrapped five-card packets. Cards 1-5 were distributed in late August, 2002 as a bonus in green-boxed 2002 Topps retail factory sets. Cards 6-10 were distributed in November, 2002 within 2002 Topps Holiday factory sets. The cards are designed in the same manner as the Draft Picks and Prospects subsets from the basic 2002 Topps set and feature a selection of players chosen in the 2002 MLB Draft.

	Nm-Mt	Ex-Mt
COMPLETE SET (10)	50.00	15.00
COMP.SERIES 1 SET (5)	25.00	7.50
COMP.SERIES 2 SET (5)	25.00	7.50
1 Scott Moore	8.00	2.40
2 Val Majewski	8.00	2.40
3 Brian Slocum	5.00	1.50
4 Chris Gruler	8.00	2.40
5 Mark Schramek	8.00	2.40
6 Joe Saunders	8.00	2.40
7 Jeff Francis	5.00	1.50
8 Royce Ring	8.00	2.40
9 Greg Miller	15.00	4.50
10 Brandon Weeden	5.00	1.50

2002 Topps East Meets West

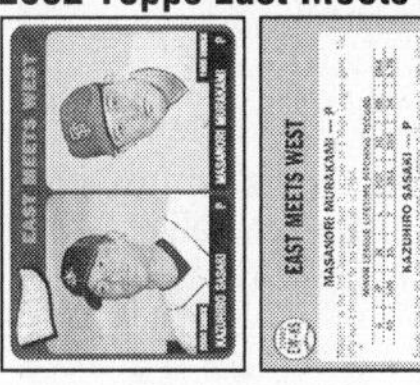

Issued at a rate of one in 24, these eight cards feature Masanori Murakami along with eight other Japanese players who have also played in the major leagues.

	Nm-Mt	Ex-Mt
COMPLETE SET (8)	15.00	4.50
EWHI Hideki Irabu	2.00	.60
Masanori Murakami		
EWHN Hideo Nomo	2.00	.60
Masanori Murakami		
EWKS Kazuhiro Sasaki	2.00	.60
Masanori Murakami		
EWMS Mac Suzuki	2.00	.60
Masanori Murakami		
EWMY Masato Yoshii	2.00	.60
Masanori Murakami		
EWSH S. Hasagawa	2.00	.60
Masanori Murakami		
EWTO Tomo Ohka	2.00	.60
Masanori Murakami		
EWTS Tsuyoshi Shinjo	2.00	.60
Masanori Murakami		

2002 Topps East Meets West Relics

Inserted in packs at different odds depending on whether it is a bat or jersey card, these three cards feature game-used relics from Japanese born players.

	Nm-Mt	Ex-Mt
SR1 BAT 1:12296 H,1:3380 HTA,1:9606 R		
SER.1 JSY 1:3419 H, 1:939 HTA, 1:2685 R		
EWR-HN Hideo Nomo Jsy	50.00	15.00
EWR-KS K. Sasaki Jsy	25.00	7.50
EWR-TS T. Shinjo Bat	25.00	7.50

2002 Topps Ebbets Field Seat Relics

Inserted at a rate of one in 9,116 hobby packs, one in 2516 HTA packs and one in 7,222 retail packs, these nine cards feature not only the player but a slice of a seat used at Brooklyn's Ebbetts Field.

	Nm-Mt	Ex-Mt
EFR-AP Andy Pafko	150.00	45.00
EFR-BC Billy Cox	150.00	45.00
EFR-CF Carl Furillo	150.00	45.00
EFR-DS Duke Snider	200.00	60.00
EFR-GH Gil Hodges	200.00	60.00
EFR-JB Joe Black	150.00	45.00
EFR-JR Jackie Robinson	250.00	75.00
EFR-RC Roy Campanella	200.00	60.00
EFR-PWR Pee Wee Reese	200.00	60.00

2002 Topps Ebbets Field/Yankee Stadium Seat Dual Relics

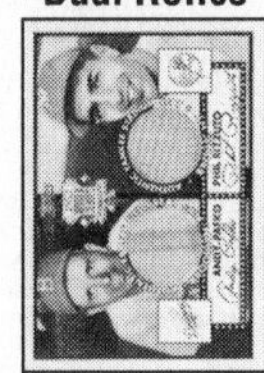

Featuring a slice of a seat from both Ebbetts Field and from Yankee Stadium, these cards feature a selection of leading players from the 1952 World Series paired up with actual pieces of stadium seats taken from the historic Ebbets Field and Yankee Stadium ballparks. The Snider/Berra card was inserted at a rate of one in 86,070 series one hobby packs and the Rizzuto/Pafko card was inserted ata rate of one in 59,511 series two hobby packs. Only 52 copies of each card were produced. Both cards were intended to be hand-numbered (i.e. 1/52, 2/52 etc.) but due to production errors only the Snider/Berra card packed out as such.

	Nm-Mt	Ex-Mt
RP Phil Rizzuto		
Andy Pafko		
SB Duke Snider		
Yogi Berra		

2002 Topps Ebbets Field/Yankee Stadium Seat Dual Relics Autographs

Inserted into first series packs at stated odds of one in 15,670 HTA packs and second series packs at a rate of one in 11,908 HTA packs, these cards feature a stadium seat along with an autograph of both featured players on these cards. Each card was issued to 25 serial numbered sets and due to market scarcity, no pricing is provided. The Rizzuto/Pafko card from series two was seeded into packs as an exchange card with a deadline of April 30th, 2004.

	Nm-Mt	Ex-Mt
RP Phil Rizzuto		
Andy Pafko 2		
SB Duke Snider		
Yogi Berra 1		

2002 Topps Hall of Fame Vintage BuyBacks AutoProofs

In one of the most ambitious efforts put forth by a manufacturer in hobby history, Topps went into the secondary market and bought more than 3,500 vintage Topps cards (including an amazing selection from the 1950's and 1960's) featuring almost two dozen Hall of Famers (including stars such as Nolan Ryan, Yogi Berra and Carl Yastrzemski) for this far-reaching AutoProofs promotion. In most cases, 100 count lots of each vintage card were used (a staggering figure considering the scarcity of many of the 1950's and 1960's cards) with a few of the more common cards from the early 1980's tallying 200 or 300 count lots. After repurchase, each card was signed by the featured athlete, serial-numbered to a specific amount (exact print runs provided in our checklist) and affixed with a Topps hologram of authenticity on back. The cards were distributed across many 2002 Topps products - starting off with 2002 Topps series one baseball in November, 2001. Odds for finding these cards in packs is as follows: series 1 - 1:2341 hobby and 1:1841 retail; series 2 - 1:2341 hobby, 1:tbd retail.

	Nm-Mt	Ex-Mt
BR17 B.Robinson 82 KM/200	60.00	18.00
EW10 Earl Weaver 87/100	25.00	7.50
FJ33 F.Jenkins 84/100	25.00	7.50
GP26 G.Perry 82/100	25.00	7.50
GP29 G.Perry 83/100	25.00	7.50
GP30 G.Perry 83 SV/200	25.00	7.50
OC2 Orl Cepeda 82 KM/200	25.00	7.50
RF15 R.Fingers 81/300	25.00	7.50
RF16 R.Fingers 81 LL/100	25.00	7.50
RF18 R.Fingers 82/100	25.00	7.50
RF19 Rollie Fingers 82 IA/200	25.00	7.50
RF21 Rollie Fingers 82 KM/300	25.00	7.50
RF22 Rollie Fingers 83/200	25.00	7.50
RF24 Rollie Fingers 84/200	25.00	7.50
RF27 R.Fingers 85/300	25.00	7.50
RF28 Rollie Fingers 86/100	25.00	7.50
SC7 S.Carlton 84 LL V/100	40.00	12.00
SC8 Steve Carlton 85/200	40.00	12.00
SC10 Steve Carlton 87/200	40.00	12.00

2002 Topps Hobby Masters

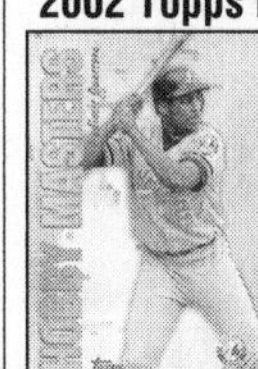

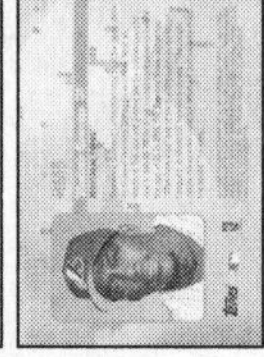

Inserted at a rate of one in 25 hobby and one in 16 retail packs, these 20 cards feature some of the leading players in the game.

	Nm-Mt	Ex-Mt
COMPLETE SET (20)	80.00	24.00
HM1 Mark McGwire	8.00	2.40
HM2 Derek Jeter	8.00	2.40
HM3 Chipper Jones	3.00	.90
HM4 Roger Clemens	6.00	1.80
HM5 Vladimir Guerrero	3.00	.90
HM6 Ichiro Suzuki	5.00	1.50
HM7 Todd Helton	3.00	.90
HM8 Alex Rodriguez	5.00	1.50
HM9 Albert Pujols	6.00	1.80
HM10 Sammy Sosa	5.00	1.50
HM11 Ken Griffey Jr.	5.00	1.50
HM12 Randy Johnson	3.00	.90

HM13 Nomar Garciaparra 5.00 1.50
HM14 Ivan Rodriguez 3.00 .90
HM15 Manny Ramirez 3.00 .90
HM16 Barry Bonds 8.00 2.40
HM17 Mike Piazza 5.00 1.50
HM18 Pedro Martinez 3.00 .90
HM19 Jeff Bagwell 3.00 .90
HM20 Luis Gonzalez 3.00 .90

2002 Topps Like Father Like Son Relics

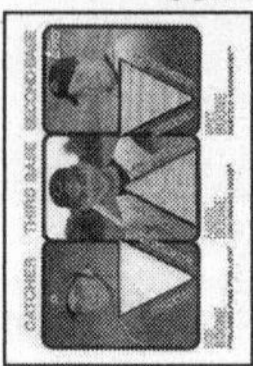
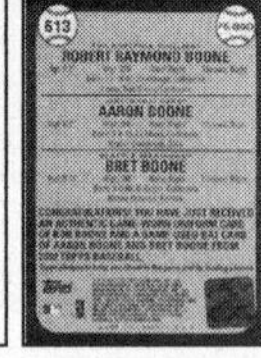

These combination memorabilia cards feature famous baseball families with two generations of fathers and sons. The card designs are each based upon the original Topps design of the father's rookie card season (aka The Boone Family card features a 1973 Topps style to honor the year Bob Boone had his Rookie Card issued). The cards were seeded exclusively into retail packs at a rate of 1:1304.

Nm-Mt Ex-Mt
FS-AL Sandy Alomar Sr. Bat 80.00 24.00
Sandy Alomar Jr. Bat
Roberto Alomar Bat
FS-BE Yogi Berra Jsy 80.00 24.00
Dale Berra Jsy
FS-BON Bobby Bonds 120.00 36.00
Barry Bonds
FS-BOO Bob Boone Jsy 80.00 24.00
Aaron Boone Jsy
Bret Boone Bat
FS-CR Jose Cruz Sr. 80.00 24.00
Jose Cruz Jr.

2002 Topps Own the Game

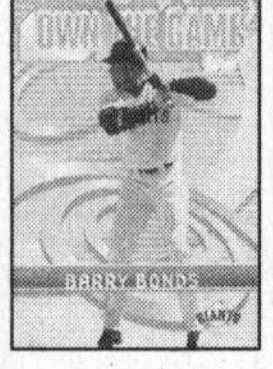

Issued at a rate of one in 12 hobby packs and one in eight retail packs, these 30 cards feature players who are among the league leaders for their position.

Nm-Mt Ex-Mt
COMPLETE SET (30) 40.00 12.00
OG1 Moises Alou 1.00 .30
OG2 Roberto Alomar 2.50 .75
OG3 Luis Gonzalez 1.00 .30
OG4 Bret Boone 1.00 .30
OG5 Barry Bonds 6.00 1.80
OG6 Jim Thome 2.50 .75
OG7 Jimmy Rollins 1.00 .30
OG8 Cristian Guzman 1.00 .30
OG9 Lance Berkman 1.00 .30
OG10 Mike Sweeney 1.00 .30
OG11 Rich Aurilia 1.00 .30
OG12 Ichiro Suzuki 4.00 1.20
OG13 Luis Gonzalez 1.00 .30
OG14 Ichiro Suzuki 4.00 1.20
OG15 Jimmy Rollins 1.00 .30
OG16 Roger Cedeno 1.00 .30
OG17 Barry Bonds 6.00 1.80
OG18 Jim Thome 2.50 .75
OG19 Curt Schilling 1.50 .45
OG20 Roger Clemens 5.00 1.50
OG21 Curt Schilling 1.50 .45
OG22 Brad Radke 1.00 .30
OG23 Greg Maddux 4.00 1.20
OG24 Mark Mulder 1.00 .30
OG25 Jeff Shaw 1.00 .30
OG26 Mariano Rivera 1.50 .45
OG27 Randy Johnson 2.50 .75
OG28 Pedro Martinez 2.50 .75
OG29 John Burkett 1.00 .30
OG30 Tim Hudson 1.00 .30

2002 Topps Prime Cuts Autograph Relics

Inserted into first series packs at a rate of one in 88,678 hobby and one in 24,624 HTA and second series packs at one in 8927 hobby and one in 2360 HTA packs, these eight cards feature both a memorabilia relic from the player's career as well as their autograph. Cards from series one were issued to a stated print run of 60 serial numbered sets while cards from series two were issued to a stated print run of 50 serial numbered sets. We have notated next to the players name which series the card was issued in.

Nm-Mt Ex-Mt
NO PRICING DUE TO SCARCITY
PCA-AE Alex Escobar S2
PCA-BB Barry Bonds S1
PCA-JH Josh Hamilton S2
PCA-NJ Nick Johnson S2
PCA-TH Toby Hall S2
PCA-WB Wilson Betemit S2
PCA-XN Xavier Nady S2
PCA-CPE Carlos Pena S2

2002 Topps Prime Cuts Barrel Relics

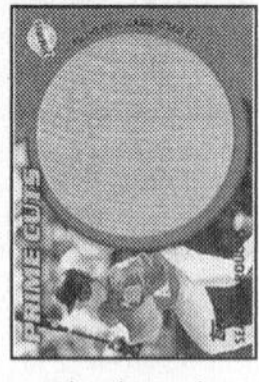

Inserted in second series packs at a rate of one in 7824 hobby packs and one in 2063 HTA packs, these eight cards feature a piece from the selected player bat barrel. These cards were issued to a stated print run of 50 serial numbered sets.

Nm-Mt Ex-Mt
NO PRICING DUE TO SCARCITY
PCA-AD Adam Dunn
PCA-AG Alexis Gomez
PCA-AR Aaron Rowand
PCA-CP Corey Patterson
PCA-JC Joe Crede
PCA-MG Marcus Giles
PCA-RS Ruben Salazar
PCA-SB Sean Burroughs

2002 Topps Prime Cuts Pine Tar Relics

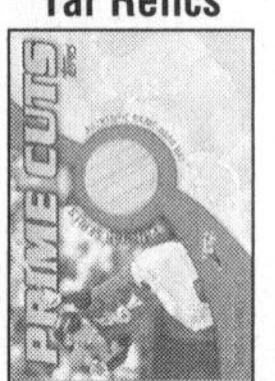

Inserted in packs at stated odds of one in 4,420 hobby packs and one in 1214 HTA packs for first series packs and one in 1043 hobby and one in 275 HTA packs for second series packs, these 20 cards feature pieces from the pine tar section of the player's bat. We have notated which series the player was issued in next to his name in our checklist. These cards have a stated print run of 200 serial numbered sets.

Nm-Mt Ex-Mt
PCP-AD Adam Dunn 2 25.00 7.50
PCP-AE Alex Escobar 2 25.00 7.50
PCP-AG Alexis Gomez 2 25.00 7.50
PCP-AP Albert Pujols 1 60.00 18.00
PCP-AR Aaron Rowand 2 25.00 7.50
PCP-BB Barry Bonds 1 80.00 24.00
PCP-CP Corey Patterson 2 25.00 7.50
PCP-JC Joe Crede 2 25.00 7.50
PCP-JH Josh Hamilton 2 25.00 7.50
PCP-LG Luis Gonzalez 1 25.00 7.50
PCP-MG Marcus Giles 2 25.00 7.50
PCP-NJ Nick Johnson 2 25.00 7.50
PCP-RS Ruben Salazar 2 25.00 7.50
PCP-SB Sean Burroughs 2 25.00 7.50
PCP-TG Tony Gwynn 1 50.00 15.00
PCP-TH Todd Helton 1 40.00 12.00
PCP-TH Toby Hall 2 25.00 7.50
PCP-WB Wilson Betemit 2 25.00 7.50
PCP-XN Xavier Nady 2 25.00 7.50
PCP-CPE Carlos Pena 2 25.00 7.50

2002 Topps Prime Cuts Trademark Relics

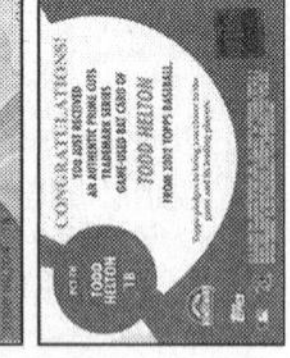

Issued in first series packs at a rate of one in 8,868 hobby and one in 2428 HTA packs and second series packs at a rate of one in 2087 hobby and one in 549 HTA packs, these cards feature a slice of bat taken from the trademark section of a game used bat. Only 100 serial numbered copies of each card were produced. First and second series distribution information is detailed after the player's name in our set checklist.

Nm-Mt Ex-Mt
PCT-AD Adam Dunn 2 40.00 12.00
PCT-AE Alex Escobar 2 40.00 12.00
PCT-AG Alexis Gomez 2 40.00 12.00
PCT-AP Albert Pujols 1 100.00 30.00
PCT-AR Aaron Rowand 2 40.00 12.00
PCT-BB Barry Bonds 1 120.00 36.00
PCT-CP Corey Patterson 2 40.00 12.00
PCT-JC Joe Crede 2 40.00 12.00
PCT-JH Josh Hamilton 2 40.00 12.00
PCT-LG Luis Gonzalez 1 40.00 12.00
PCT-MG Marcus Giles 2 40.00 12.00
PCT-NJ Nick Johnson 2 40.00 12.00
PCT-RS Ruben Salazar 2 40.00 12.00
PCT-SB Sean Burroughs 2 40.00 12.00
PCT-TG Tony Gwynn 1 80.00 24.00
PCT-TH Todd Helton 1 60.00 18.00
PCT-TH Toby Hall 2 40.00 12.00
PCT-WB Wilson Betemit 2 40.00 12.00
PCT-XN Xavier Nady 2 40.00 12.00
PCT-CPE Carlos Pena 2 40.00 12.00

2002 Topps Ring Masters

Issued at a rate of one in 25 hobby packs and one in 16 retail packs, these 10 cards feature players who have earned World Series rings in their career.

Nm-Mt Ex-Mt
COMPLETE SET (10) 25.00 7.50
RM1 Derek Jeter 5.00 1.50
RM2 Mark McGwire 5.00 1.50
RM3 Mariano Rivera 1.50 .45
RM4 Gary Sheffield 1.50 .45
RM5 Al Leiter 1.50 .45
RM6 Chipper Jones 2.00 .60
RM7 Roger Clemens 4.00 1.20
RM8 Greg Maddux 3.00 .90
RM9 Roberto Alomar 2.00 .60
RM10 Paul O'Neill 1.50 .45

2002 Topps Summer School Battery Mates Relics

Issued at a rate of one in 4,4401 hobby packs and one in 3,477 retail packs, these two cards feature a pitcher and catcher from the same team.

Nm-Mt Ex-Mt
BM-LP Al Leiter 40.00 12.00
Mike Piazza
BM-ML Greg Maddux 40.00 12.00
Javy Lopez

2002 Topps Summer School Heart of the Order Relics

Issued at an overall rate of one in 4,247 hobby packs and one in 3,325 retail packs, these four cards feature relics from three key players from a team's lineup.

Nm-Mt Ex-Mt
SER.1 A 1:8,220 H, 1:2253 HTA, 1:6452 R
SER.1 B 1:8,778 H, 1:2411 HTA, 1:6862 R
HTO-ARB Bob Abreu 80.00 24.00
Scott Rolen
Pat Burrell A
HTO-KBA Jeff Kent 100.00 30.00
Barry Bonds
Rich Aurilia A
HTO-OWM Paul O'Neill 80.00 24.00
Bernie Williams
Tino Martinez
HTO-TGA Jim Thome 80.00 24.00
Juan Gonzalez
Roberto Alomar

2002 Topps Summer School Hit and Run Relics

Issued at an overall rate of one in 4,241 hobby packs and one in 3,325 HTA packs, these three cards feature relics from some of the leading young stars in baseball.

Nm-Mt Ex-Mt
SER.1 A 1:24591 H, 1:6760 HTA, 1:19649 R
SER.1 B 1:12296 H, 1:3380 HTA, 1:9606 R
SER.1 C 1:8788 H, 1:2411 HTA, 1:6862 R
HRR-DE Darin Erstad 15.00 4.50
UER BAT B
Name spelled Darrin on front
HRR-JD J.Damon Bat A 15.00 4.50
HRR-RF R.Furcal Jsy C 15.00 4.50

2002 Topps Summer School Turn Two Relics

Issued at a rate of one in 4,401 hobby packs and one in 3,477 retail packs, these two cards

feature relics from two of the best double play combination in baseball's history.

Nm-Mt Ex-Mt
TTR-TW Alan Trammell 50.00 15.00
Lou Whitaker
TTR-VA Omar Vizquel 50.00 15.00
Roberto Alomar

2002 Topps Summer School Two Bagger Relics

Issued at an overall rate of one in 3,733 hobby packs and one in 2,941 retail packs, these three cards feature game-used relics from leading hitters in the game.

Nm-Mt Ex-Mt
SER.1 A 1:4401 H, 1:1210 HTA, 1:3477 R
SER.1 B 1:24591 H,1:6760 HTA,1:19649 R
2B-SR Scott Rolen Jsy A 25.00 7.50
2B-TG Tony Gwynn Bat B 40.00 12.00
2B-TH Todd Helton Jsy A 25.00 7.50

2002 Topps Yankee Stadium Seat Relics

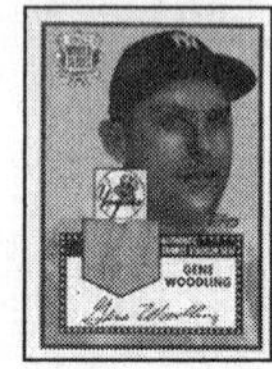

Inserted into second series packs at a stated rate of one in 579 Hobby, one in 1472 HTA and one in 4313 Retail, these nine cards feature retired Yankee greats along with a piece of a seat used in the originaly Yankee Stadium.

Nm-Mt Ex-Mt
YSR-AR Allie Reynolds 150.00 45.00
YSR-BM Billy Martin 200.00 60.00
YSR-GM Gil McDougald 150.00 45.00
YSR-GW Gene Woodling 150.00 45.00
YSR-HB Hank Bauer 150.00 45.00
YSR-JC Joe Collins 150.00 45.00
YSR-JM Johnny Mize 150.00 45.00
YSR-PR Phil Rizzuto 200.00 60.00
YSR-YB Yogi Berra 200.00 60.00

2002 Topps Traded

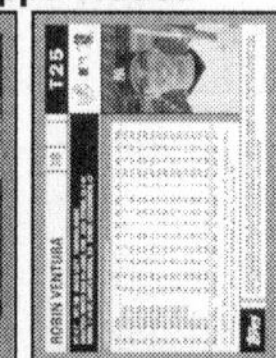

This 275 card set was released in October, 2002. These cards were issued in 10 card hobby packs which were issued 24 packs to a box and 12 boxes to a case with an SRP of $3 per pack. In addition, this product was also issued in 35 count HTA packs. Cards numbered 1 to 100 were issued one per pack. Cards from previous traded sets were repurchased by Topps and were issued at a stated rate of one in 24 Hobby and Retail Packs and one in 10 HTA packs. However, there is no way of being able to identify that these cards are anything but original cards as no marking or stamping is on these cards.

Nm-Mt Ex-Mt
COMPLETE SET (275) 180.00 55.00
COMMON CARD (T1-T110) 1.50 .45
COMMON CARD (T111-T275) .40 .12
T1 Jeff Weaver 1.50 .45
T2 Jay Powell 1.50 .45
T3 Alex Gonzalez 1.50 .45
T4 Jason Isringhausen 1.50 .45
T5 Tyler Houston 1.50 .45
T6 Ben Broussard 1.50 .45
T7 Chuck Knoblauch 1.50 .45
T8 Brian L. Hunter 1.50 .45
T9 Dustan Mohr 1.50 .45
T10 Eric Hinske 1.50 .45
T11 Roger Cedeno 1.50 .45
T12 Eddie Perez 1.50 .45
T13 Jeromy Burnitz 1.50 .45
T14 Bartolo Colon 1.50 .45
T15 Rick Helling 1.50 .45
T16 Dan Plesac 1.50 .45
T17 Scott Strickland 1.50 .45
T18 Antonio Alfonseca 1.50 .45
T19 Ricky Gutierrez 1.50 .45
T20 John Valentin 1.50 .45
T21 Raul Mondesi 1.50 .45
T22 Ben Davis 1.50 .45
T23 Nelson Figueroa 1.50 .45
T24 Earl Snyder 1.50 .45
T25 Robin Ventura 1.50 .45
T26 Jimmy Haynes 1.50 .45
T27 Kenny Kelly 1.50 .45
T28 Morgan Ensberg 1.50 .45
T29 Reggie Sanders 1.50 .45
T30 Shigetoshi Hasegawa 1.50 .45
T31 Mike Timlin 1.50 .45
T32 Russell Branyan 1.50 .45
T33 Alan Embree 1.50 .45
T34 D'Angelo Jimenez 1.50 .45
T35 Kent Mercker 1.50 .45
T36 Jesse Orosco 1.50 .45
T37 Gregg Zaun 1.50 .45
T38 Reggie Taylor 1.50 .45
T39 Andres Galarraga 1.50 .45
T40 Chris Truby 1.50 .45
T41 Bruce Chen 1.50 .45
T42 Darren Lewis 1.50 .45
T43 Ryan Kohlmeier 1.50 .45
T44 John McDonald 1.50 .45
T45 Omar Daal 1.50 .45
T46 Matt Clement 1.50 .45
T47 Glendon Rusch 1.50 .45
T48 Chan Ho Park 1.50 .45
T49 Benny Agbayani 1.50 .45
T50 Juan Gonzalez 4.00 1.20
T51 Carlos Baerga 1.50 .45
T52 Tim Raines 1.50 .45
T53 Kevin Appier 1.50 .45
T54 Marty Cordova 1.50 .45
T55 Jeff D'Amico 1.50 .45
T56 Dmitri Young 1.50 .45
T57 Roosevelt Brown 1.50 .45
T58 Dustin Hermanson 1.50 .45
T59 Jose Rijo 1.50 .45
T60 Todd Ritchie 1.50 .45
T61 Lee Stevens 1.50 .45
T62 Placido Polanco 1.50 .45
T63 Eric Young 1.50 .45
T64 Chuck Finley 1.50 .45
T65 Dicky Gonzalez 1.50 .45
T66 Jose Macias 1.50 .45
T67 Gabe Kapler 1.50 .45
T68 Sandy Alomar Jr. 1.50 .45
T69 Henry Blanco 1.50 .45
T70 Julian Tavarez 1.50 .45
T71 Paul Bako 1.50 .45
T72 Scott Rolen 2.50 .75
T73 Brian Jordan 1.50 .45
T74 Rickey Henderson 4.00 1.20
T75 Kevin Mench 1.50 .45
T76 Hideo Nomo 4.00 1.20
T77 Jeremy Giambi 1.50 .45
T78 Brad Fullmer 1.50 .45
T79 Carl Everett 1.50 .45
T80 David Wells 1.50 .45
T81 Aaron Sele 1.50 .45
T82 Todd Hollandsworth 1.50 .45
T83 Vicente Padilla 1.50 .45
T84 Kenny Lofton 1.50 .45
T85 Corky Miller 1.50 .45
T86 Josh Fogg 1.50 .45
T87 Cliff Floyd 1.50 .45
T88 Craig Paquette 1.50 .45
T89 Jay Payton 1.50 .45
T90 Carlos Pena 1.50 .45
T91 Juan Encarnacion 1.50 .45
T92 Rey Sanchez 1.50 .45
T93 Ryan Dempster 1.50 .45
T94 Mario Encarnacion 1.50 .45
T95 Jorge Julio 1.50 .45
T96 John Mabry 1.50 .45
T97 Todd Zeile 1.50 .45
T98 Johnny Damon 1.50 .45
T99 Deivi Cruz 1.50 .45
T100 Gary Sheffield 1.50 .45
T101 Ted Lilly 1.50 .45
T102 Todd Van Poppel 1.50 .45
T103 Shawn Estes 1.50 .45
T104 Cesar Izturis 1.50 .45
T105 Ron Coomer 1.50 .45
T106 Grady Little MG RC 1.50 .45
T107 Jimy Williams MG 1.50 .45
T108 Tony Pena MG 1.50 .45
T109 Frank Robinson MG 2.50 .75
T110 Ron Gardenhire MG 1.50 .45
T111 Dennis Tankersley .40 .12
T112 Alejandro Cadena RC .40 .12
T113 Justin Reid RC .40 .12
T114 Nate Field RC .40 .12
T115 Rene Reyes RC .40 .12
T116 Nelson Castro RC .40 .12
T117 Miguel Olivo .40 .12
T118 David Espinosa .40 .12
T119 Chris Bootcheck RC .40 .12
T120 Rob Henkel RC .40 .12
T121 Steve Bechler RC .40 .12
T122 Mark Outlaw RC .40 .12
T123 Henry Pichardo RC .40 .12
T124 Michael Floyd RC .40 .12
T125 Richard Lane RC .40 .12
T126 Pete Zamora RC .40 .12
T127 Javier Colina .40 .12
T128 Greg Sain RC .40 .12
T129 Ronnie Merrill .40 .12
T130 Gavin Floyd RC 2.00 .60
T131 Josh Bonifay RC .40 .12
T132 Tommy Marx RC .40 .12
T133 Gary Cates Jr. RC .40 .12
T134 Neal Cotts RC 1.50 .45
T135 Angel Berroa .40 .12
T136 Elio Serrano RC .40 .12
T137 J.J. Putz RC .40 .12
T138 Ruben Gotay RC .40 .12
T139 Eddie Rogers .40 .12
T140 Wily Mo Pena .40 .12
T141 Tyler Yates RC .75 .23
T142 Colin Young RC .40 .12
T143 Chance Caple .40 .12
T144 Ben Howard RC .40 .12
T145 Ryan Bukvich RC .40 .12
T146 Cliff Bartosh RC .40 .12
T147 Brandon Claussen 1.00 .30
T148 Cristian Guerrero .40 .12
T149 Derrick Lewis .40 .12
T150 Eric Miller RC .40 .12

T151 Justin Huber RC 1.00 .30
T152 Adrian Gonzalez .40 .12
T153 Brian West RC .40 .12
T154 Chris Baker RC .40 .12
T155 Drew Henson .40 .12
T156 Scott Hairston RC 1.50 .45
T157 Jason Simontacchi RC .40 .12
T158 Jason Arnold RC 1.00 .30
T159 Brandon Phillips .40 .12
T160 Adam Roller RC .40 .12
T161 Scotty Layfield RC .40 .12
T162 Freddie Money RC .40 .12
T163 Noochie Varner RC .40 .12
T164 Terrance Hill RC .40 .12
T165 Jeremy Hill RC .40 .12
T166 Carlos Cabrera RC .40 .12
T167 Jose Morban RC .40 .12
T168 Kevin Frederick RC .40 .12
T169 Mark Teixeira 1.00 .30
T170 Brian Rogers .40 .12
T171 Anastacio Martinez RC .40 .12
T172 Bobby Jenks RC 1.25 .35
T173 David Gil RC .40 .12
T174 Andres Torres .40 .12
T175 James Barrett RC .40 .12
T176 Jimmy Journell .40 .12
T177 Brett Kay RC .40 .12
T178 Jason Young RC .40 .12
T179 Mark Hamilton RC .40 .12
T180 Jose Bautista RC .75 .23
T181 Blake McGinley RC .40 .12
T182 Ryan Mottl RC .40 .12
T183 Jeff Austin RC .40 .12
T184 Xavier Nady .40 .12
T185 Kyle Kane RC .40 .12
T186 Travis Foley RC .40 .12
T187 Nathan Kaup RC .40 .12
T188 Eric Cyr .40 .12
T189 Josh Cisneros RC .40 .12
T190 Brad Nelson RC 1.25 .35
T191 Clint Weibl RC .40 .12
T192 Ron Calloway RC .40 .12
T193 Jung Bong .40 .12
T194 Rolando Viera RC .40 .12
T195 Jason Bulger RC .40 .12
T196 Chone Figgins RC .40 .12
T197 Jimmy Alvarez RC .40 .12
T198 Joel Crump RC .40 .12
T199 Ryan Doumit RC .50 .15
T200 Demetrius Heath RC .40 .12
T201 John Ennis RC .40 .12
T202 Doug Sessions RC .40 .12
T203 Clinton Hosford RC .40 .12
T204 Chris Narveson RC .40 .12
T205 Ross Peeples RC .40 .12
T206 Alex Requena RC .40 .12
T207 Matt Erickson RC .40 .12
T208 Brian Forystek RC .40 .12
T209 Dewon Brazelton .40 .12
T210 Nathan Haynes .40 .12
T211 Jack Cust .40 .12
T212 Jesse Foppert RC 1.50 .45
T213 Jesus Cota RC .40 .12
T214 Juan M. Gonzalez RC .40 .12
T215 Tim Kalita RC .40 .12
T216 Manny Delcarmen RC .40 .12
T217 Jim Kavourias RC .40 .12
T218 C.J. Wilson RC .40 .12
T219 Edwin Yan RC .40 .12
T220 Andy Van Hekken .40 .12
T221 Michael Cuddyer .40 .12
T222 Jeff Verplancke RC .40 .12
T223 Mike Wilson RC .40 .12
T224 Corwin Malone RC .40 .12
T225 Chris Snelling RC 1.00 .30
T226 Joe Rogers RC .40 .12
T227 Jason Bay 1.25 .35
T228 Ezequiel Astacio RC .40 .12
T229 Joey Hammond RC .40 .12
T230 Chris Duffy RC .40 .12
T231 Mark Prior 3.00 .90
T232 Hansel Izquierdo RC .40 .12
T233 Franklyn German RC .40 .12
T234 Alexis Gomez .40 .12
T235 Jorge Padilla RC .40 .12
T236 Ryan Snare RC .40 .12
T237 Deivis Santos .40 .12
T238 Taggert Bozied RC 1.50 .45
T239 Mike Peeples RC .40 .12
T240 Ronald Acuna RC .40 .12
T241 Koyie Hill .40 .12
T242 Garrett Guzman RC .40 .12
T243 Ryan Church RC .50 .15
T244 Tony Fontana RC .40 .12
T245 Keto Anderson RC .40 .12
T246 Brad Bouras RC .40 .12
T247 Jason Dubois RC 1.50 .45
T248 Angel Guzman RC 4.00 1.20
T249 Joel Hanrahan RC .75 .23
T250 Joe Jiannetti RC .40 .12
T251 Sean Pierce RC .40 .12
T252 Jake Mauer RC .40 .12
T253 Marshall McDougall RC .40 .12
T254 Edwin Almonte RC .40 .12
T255 Shawn Riggans RC .40 .12
T256 Steven Shell RC .40 .12
T257 Kevin Hooper RC .40 .12
T258 Michael Frick RC .40 .12
T259 Travis Chapman RC .40 .12
T260 Tim Hummel RC .40 .12
T261 Adam Morrissey RC .40 .12
T262 Dontrelle Willis RC 8.00 2.40
T263 Justin Sherrod RC .40 .12
T264 Gerald Smiley RC .40 .12
T265 Tony Miller RC .40 .12
T266 Nolan Ryan WW 2.50 .75
T267 Reggie Jackson WW .60 .18
T268 Steve Garvey WW .60 .18
T269 Wade Boggs WW .60 .18
T270 Sammy Sosa WW 1.50 .45
T271 Curt Schilling WW .60 .18
T272 Mark Grace WW .60 .18
T273 Jason Giambi WW 1.00 .30
T274 Ken Griffey Jr. WW 1.50 .45
T275 Roberto Alomar WW 1.00 .30

2002 Topps Traded Gold

Inserted at a stated rate of one in three hobby and retail and one per HTA pack, this is a parallel of the 2002 Topps Traded set. Each card has "gold" borders and were issued to a stated print run of 2002 serial numbered sets.

Nm-Mt Ex-Mt
*GOLD 1-110: .6X TO 1.5X BASIC
*GOLD 111-275: 2.5X TO 6X BASIC
*GOLD RC'S 111-275: 1.5X TO 4X BASIC RC'S

2002 Topps Traded Farewell Relic

Inserted at a stated rate of one in 590 Hobby, one in 169 HTA and in 595 Retail packs, this one card set features one-time MVP Jose Canseco along with a game-used bat piece from his career. Canseco had announced his retirement during the 2002 season in an failed attempt to return to the majors.

Nm-Mt Ex-Mt
FW-JC Jose Canseco Bat 15.00 4.50

2002 Topps Traded Hall of Fame Relic

Inserted at a stated rate of one in 1533 Hobby Packs, one in 439 HTA packs and one in 1574 Retail packs, this one card set features Ozzie Smith along with a game-used bat piece from his career. Ozzie Smith was inducted into the HOF in 2002.

Nm-Mt Ex-Mt
HOF-OS Ozzie Smith Bat 30.00 9.00

2002 Topps Traded Signature Moves

Inserted at overall odds of one in 91 Hobby or Retail packs and one in 26 HTA packs, these 26 cards feature a mix of basically prospects along with a couple of stars who moved to new teams for 2002 and signed these cards for inclusion in the Topps Traded set. Since there were nine different insertion odds for these cards we have notated both the insertion odds for each group along with which group the player belong to.

Nm-Mt Ex-Mt
A ODDS 1:15,292 H, 1:4288 HTA, 1:22,032 R
B ODDS 1:3846 H, 1:1105 HTA, 1:3840 R
C ODDS 1:6147 H, 1:1778 HTA, 1:6418 R
D ODDS 1:1917 H, 1:548 HTA, 1:1953 R
E ODDS 1:341 H, 1:97 HTA, 1:342 R...
F ODDS 1:2247 H, 1:645 HTA, 1:2261 R
G ODDS 1:568 H, 1:162 HTA, 1:571 R
GROUP H ODDS 1:256 H/R, 1:73 HTA
I ODDS 1:1023 H, 1:293 HTA, 1:1025 R
OVERALL ODDS 1:91 HOB/RET, 1:26 HTA
AC Antoine Cameron D 15.00 4.50
AM Andy Morales H 8.00 2.40
BB Boof Bonser E 10.00 3.00
BC Brandon Claussen E 25.00 7.50
CS Chris Smith G 8.00 2.40
CU Chase Utley E 25.00 7.50
CW Corwin Malone H 10.00 3.00
DT Dennis Tankersley F 10.00 3.00
FJ Forrest Johnson E 10.00 3.00
JD Johnny Damon B 25.00 7.50
JD Jeff DaVanon I 8.00 2.40
JM Jake Mauer G 10.00 3.00
JM Justin Morneau H 15.00 4.50
JP Juan Pena E 10.00 3.00
JS Juan Silvestre D 10.00 3.00
JW Justin Wayne E 10.00 3.00
KI Kazuhisa Ishii A 50.00 15.00
MC Matt Cooper E 10.00 3.00
MO Moises Alou B 15.00 4.50
MT Marcus Thames G 8.00 2.40
RA Roberto Alomar C 40.00 12.00
RH Ryan Hannaman E 10.00 3.00
RM Ramon Moreta H 10.00 3.00
TB Tony Blanco E 10.00 3.00
TL Todd Linden H 20.00 6.00
VD Victor Diaz H 15.00 4.50

2002 Topps Traded Tools of the Trade Dual Relics

Inserted at overall odds of one in 539 Hobby, one in 155 HTA and one in 542 Retail packs, these three cards feature two game-used relics from the featured players. As these cards were issued in different insertion ratios, we have

notated that information as to the player's specific group next to their name in our checklist.

Nm-Mt Ex-Mt
A ODDS 1:3407 H, 1:972 HTA, 1:3672 R
B ODDS 1:639 H, 1:183 HTA, 1:642 R
DTRR-CP Chan Ho Park B 15.00 4.50
DTRR-HN Hideo Nomo A 50.00 15.00
DTRR-MO Moises Alou B 15.00 4.50

2002 Topps Traded Tools of the Trade Relics

Inserted at overall odds for bats of one in 34 Hobby and Retail and one in 10 HTA and for jerseys at one in 426 Hobby, one in 122 HTA and one in 427 retail, these 35 cards feature players who switched teams for the 2002 season along with a game-used memorabilia piece. We have notated in our checklist what type of memorabilia piece on each player's card. In addition, since the bat cards were inserted at three different odds, we have notated that information as to the card's group next to their name in our checklist.

Nm-Mt Ex-Mt
BAT A 1:1203 H, 1:344 HTA, 1:1224 R
BAT B 1:1807 H, 1:517 HTA, 1:1836 R
BAT C 1:35 H/R, 1:10 HTA
AB Roberto Alomar Bat C 10.00 3.00
AG Andres Galarraga Bat C 8.00 2.40
BF Brad Fullmer Bat C 8.00 2.40
BJ Brian Jordan Bat C 8.00 2.40
CE Carl Everett Bat C 8.00 2.40
CK Chuck Knoblauch Bat C 8.00 2.40
CP Carlos Pena Bat A 10.00 3.00
DB David Bell Bat C 8.00 2.40
DJ Dave Justice Bat C 8.00 2.40
EY Eric Young Bat C 8.00 2.40
GS Gary Sheffield Bat C 8.00 2.40
HB Rickey Henderson Bat C 10.00 3.00
JBU Jeromy Burnitz Bat C 8.00 2.40
JCI Jeff Cirillo Bat B 8.00 2.40
JDB Johnny Damon Bat C 8.00 2.40
JG Juan Gonzalez Jsy 10.00 3.00
JP Josh Phelps Jsy 8.00 2.40
JV John Vander Wal Bat C 8.00 2.40
KL Kenny Lofton Bat C 8.00 2.40
MA Moises Alou Bat C 8.00 2.40
MLB Matt Lawton Bat C 8.00 2.40
MT Michael Tucker Bat C 8.00 2.40
MVB Mo Vaughn Bat C 8.00 2.40
MVJ Mo Vaughn Jsy 8.00 2.40
PP Placido Polanco Bat A 10.00 3.00
RS Reggie Sanders Bat C 8.00 2.40
RV Robin Ventura Bat C 8.00 2.40
RW Rondell White Bat C 8.00 2.40
SI Ruben Sierra Bat C 8.00 2.40
SR Scott Rolen Bat A 25.00 7.50
TC Tony Clark Bat C 8.00 2.40
TM Tino Martinez Bat C 10.00 3.00
TR Tim Raines Bat C 8.00 2.40
TS Tsuyoshi Shinjo Bat C 8.00 2.40
VC Vinny Castilla Bat C 8.00 2.40

2003 Topps Promos

This three card set was issued in a sealed cello pack to dealers and hobby media several weeks prior to the products release. The cards have a "PP" prefix so they can be differentiated from the regular cards.

Nm-Mt Ex-Mt
COMPLETE SET (3) 5.00 1.50
PP1 Albert Pujols 2.00 .60
PP2 Josh Beckett 2.00 .60
PP3 Nomar Garciaparra 2.00 .60

2003 Topps

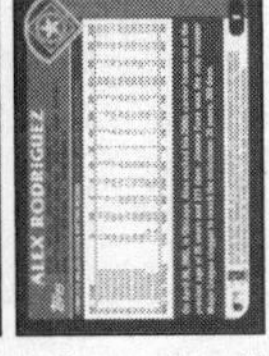

The first series of 366 cards was released in November, 2002. The second series of 354 cards were released in April, 2003. The set was issued either in 10 card hobby packs or 36 card HTA packs. The regular packs were issued 36 packs to a box and 12 boxes to a case with an SRP of $1.59. The HTA packs were issued 12 packs to a box and eight boxes to a case with an SRP of $5 per pack. The following subsets were issued in the first series: 262 through 291 basically featured current managers, cards numbered 292 through 321 featured players in their first year on a Topps card, cards numbered 322 through 331 featured two players who were expected to be major rookies during the 2003 season, cards numbered 332 through 336 honored players who achieved major feats during 2002, cards numbered 337 through 352 featured league leaders, cards 354 and 355 had post season highlights and cards 356 through 367 honored the best players in the American League. Second series subsets included Team Checklists (630-659); Draft Picks (660-674); Prospects (675-684); Award Winners (685-708) All-Stars (709-719) and World Series (720-721). As has been Topps tradition since 1997, there was no card number 7 issued in honor of the memory of Mickey Mantle.

Nm-Mt Ex-Mt
COMPLETE SET (720) 80.00 24.00
COMPLETE SERIES 1 (366) 40.00 12.00
COMPLETE SERIES 2 (354) 40.00 12.00
COMMON CARD (1-6/8-721) .20 .06
COMMON (292-331/660-684) .50 .15
1 Alex Rodriguez .75 .23
2 Dan Wilson .20 .06
3 Jimmy Rollins .20 .06
4 Jermaine Dye .20 .06
5 Steve Karsay .20 .06
6 Timo Perez .20 .06
7 Does Not Exist
8 Jose Vidro .20 .06
9 Eddie Guardado .20 .06
10 Mark Prior 1.00 .30
11 Curt Schilling .30 .09
12 Dennis Cook .20 .06
13 Andruw Jones .20 .06
14 David Segui .20 .06
15 Trot Nixon .30 .09
16 Kerry Wood .50 .15
17 Magglio Ordonez .20 .06
18 Jason LaRue .20 .06
19 Danys Baez .20 .06
20 Todd Helton .30 .09
21 Denny Neagle .20 .06
22 Dave Mlicki .20 .06
23 Roberto Hernandez .20 .06
24 Odalis Perez .20 .06
25 Nick Neugebauer .20 .06
26 David Ortiz .20 .06
27 Andres Galarraga .20 .06
28 Edgardo Alfonzo .20 .06
29 Chad Bradford .20 .06
30 Jason Giambi .50 .15
31 Brian Giles .20 .06
32 Deivi Cruz .20 .06
33 Robb Nen .20 .06
34 Jeff Nelson .20 .06
35 Edgar Renteria .20 .06
36 Aubrey Huff .20 .06
37 Brandon Duckworth .20 .06
38 Juan Gonzalez .50 .15
39 Sidney Ponson .20 .06
40 Eric Hinske .20 .06
41 Kevin Appier .20 .06
42 Danny Bautista .20 .06
43 Javier Lopez .20 .06
44 Jeff Conine .20 .06
45 Carlos Baerga .20 .06
46 Ugueth Urbina .20 .06
47 Mark Buehrle .20 .06
48 Aaron Boone .20 .06
49 Jason Simontacchi .20 .06
50 Sammy Sosa .75 .23
51 Jose Jimenez .20 .06
52 Bobby Higginson .20 .06
53 Luis Castillo .20 .06
54 Orlando Merced .20 .06
55 Brian Jordan .20 .06
56 Eric Young .20 .06
57 Bobby Kielty .20 .06
58 Luis Rivas .20 .06
59 Brad Wilkerson .20 .06
60 Roberto Alomar .50 .15
61 Roger Clemens 1.00 .30
62 Scott Hatteberg .20 .06
63 Andy Ashby .20 .06
64 Mike Williams .20 .06
65 Ron Gant .20 .06
66 Benito Santiago .20 .06
67 Bret Boone .20 .06
68 Matt Morris .20 .06
69 Troy Glaus .30 .09
70 Austin Kearns .20 .06
71 Jim Thome .50 .15
72 Rickey Henderson .50 .15
73 Luis Gonzalez .20 .06
74 Brad Fullmer .20 .06
75 Herbert Perry .20 .06
76 Randy Wolf .20 .06
77 Miguel Tejada .20 .06
78 Jimmy Anderson .20 .06
79 Ramon Martinez .20 .06
80 Ivan Rodriguez .50 .15
81 John Flaherty .20 .06
82 Shannon Stewart .20 .06
83 Orlando Palmeiro .20 .06
84 Rafael Furcal .20 .06
85 Kenny Rogers .20 .06
86 Terry Adams .20 .06
87 Mo Vaughn .20 .06
88 Jose Cruz Jr. .20 .06
89 Mike Matheny .20 .06
90 Alfonso Soriano .30 .09
91 Orlando Cabrera .20 .06
92 Jeffrey Hammonds .20 .06
93 Hideo Nomo .50 .15
94 Carlos Febles .20 .06
95 Billy Wagner .20 .06
96 Alex Gonzalez .20 .06
97 Todd Zeile .20 .06
98 Omar Vizquel .20 .06
99 Jose Rijo .20 .06
100 Ichiro Suzuki .75 .23
101 Steve Cox .20 .06
102 Hideki Irabu .20 .06
103 Roy Halladay .20 .06
104 David Eckstein .20 .06
105 Greg Maddux .75 .23
106 Jay Gibbons .20 .06
107 Travis Driskill .20 .06
108 Fred McGriff .30 .09
109 Frank Thomas .50 .15
110 Shawn Green .20 .06
111 Ruben Quevedo .20 .06
112 Jacque Jones .20 .06
113 Tomo Ohka .20 .06
114 Joe McEwing .20 .06
115 Ramiro Mendoza .20 .06
116 Mark Mulder .20 .06
117 Mike Lieberthal .20 .06
118 Jack Wilson .20 .06
119 Randall Simon .20 .06
120 Bernie Williams .30 .09
121 Marvin Benard .20 .06
122 Jamie Moyer .20 .06
123 Andy Benes .20 .06
124 Tino Martinez .30 .09
125 Esteban Yan .20 .06
126 Juan Uribe .20 .06
127 Jason Isringhausen .20 .06
128 Chris Carpenter .20 .06
129 Mike Cameron .20 .06
130 Gary Sheffield .20 .06
131 Geronimo Gil .20 .06
132 Brian Daubach .20 .06
133 Corey Patterson .20 .06
134 Aaron Rowand .20 .06
135 Chris Reitsma .20 .06
136 Bob Wickman .20 .06
137 Cesar Izturis .20 .06
138 Jason Jennings .20 .06
139 Brandon Inge .20 .06
140 Larry Walker .30 .09
141 Ramon Santiago .20 .06
142 Vladimir Nunez .20 .06
143 Jose Vizcaino .20 .06
144 Mark Quinn .20 .06
145 Michael Tucker .20 .06
146 Darren Dreifort .20 .06
147 Ben Sheets .20 .06
148 Corey Koskie .20 .06
149 Tony Armas Jr. .20 .06
150 Kazuhisa Ishii .20 .06
151 Al Leiter .20 .06
152 Steve Trachsel .20 .06
153 Mike Stanton .20 .06
154 David Justice .20 .06
155 Marlon Anderson .20 .06
156 Jason Kendall .20 .06
157 Brian Lawrence .20 .06
158 J.T. Snow .20 .06
159 Edgar Martinez .30 .09
160 Pat Burrell .20 .06
161 Kerry Robinson .20 .06
162 Greg Vaughn .20 .06
163 Carl Everett .20 .06
164 Vernon Wells .20 .06
165 Jose Mesa .20 .06
166 Troy Percival .20 .06
167 Erubiel Durazo .20 .06
168 Jason Marquis .20 .06
169 Jerry Hairston Jr. .20 .06
170 Vladimir Guerrero .50 .15
171 Byung-Hyun Kim .20 .06
172 Marcus Giles .20 .06
173 Johnny Damon .20 .06
174 Jon Lieber .20 .06
175 Terrence Long .20 .06
176 Sean Casey .20 .06
177 Adam Dunn .20 .06
178 Juan Pierre .20 .06
179 Wendell Magee .20 .06
180 Barry Zito .30 .09
181 Aramis Ramirez .20 .06
182 Pokey Reese .20 .06
183 Jeff Kent .20 .06
184 Russ Ortiz .20 .06
185 Ruben Sierra .20 .06
186 Brent Abernathy .20 .06
187 Ismael Valdes UER .20 .06
Card does not include 2002 Rangers stats
188 Tom Wilson .20 .06
189 Craig Counsell .20 .06
190 Mike Mussina .50 .15
191 Ramon Hernandez .20 .06
192 Adam Kennedy .20 .06
193 Tony Womack .20 .06
194 Wes Helms .20 .06
195 Tony Batista .20 .06
196 Rolando Arrojo .20 .06
197 Kyle Farnsworth .20 .06
198 Gary Bennett .20 .06
199 Scott Sullivan .20 .06
200 Albert Pujols 1.00 .30
201 Kirk Rueter .20 .06
202 Phil Nevin .20 .06
203 Kip Wells .20 .06
204 Ron Coomer .20 .06
205 Jeromy Burnitz .20 .06
206 Kyle Lohse .20 .06
207 Mike DeJean .20 .06
208 Paul Lo Duca .20 .06
209 Carlos Beltran .20 .06
210 Roy Oswalt .20 .06
211 Mike Lowell .20 .06
212 Robert Fick .20 .06
213 Todd Jones .20 .06
214 C.C. Sabathia .20 .06
215 Danny Graves .20 .06
216 Todd Hundley .20 .06
217 Tim Wakefield .20 .06
218 Derek Lowe .20 .06
219 Kevin Millwood .20 .06
220 Jorge Posada .30 .09
221 Bobby J. Jones .20 .06
222 Carlos Guillen .20 .06
223 Fernando Vina .20 .06
224 Ryan Rupe .20 .06
225 Kelvim Escobar .20 .06
226 Ramon Ortiz .20 .06
227 Junior Spivey .20 .06
228 Juan Cruz .20 .06
229 Melvin Mora .20 .06
230 Lance Berkman .20 .06
231 Brent Butler .20 .06
232 Shane Halter .20 .06
233 Derrek Lee .20 .06
234 Matt Lawton .20 .06
235 Chuck Knoblauch .20 .06
236 Eric Gagne .30 .09

237 Alex Sanchez .20 .06
238 Denny Hocking .20 .06
239 Eric Milton .20 .06
240 Rey Ordonez .20 .06
241 Orlando Hernandez .20 .06
242 Robert Person .20 .06
243 Sean Burroughs .20 .06
244 Jeff Cirillo .20 .06
245 Mike Lamb .20 .06
246 Jose Valentin .20 .06
247 Ellis Burks .20 .06
248 Shawn Chacon .20 .06
249 Josh Beckett .30 .09
250 Nomar Garciaparra .75 .23
251 Craig Biggio .30 .09
252 Joe Randa .20 .06
253 Mark Grudzielanek .20 .06
254 Glendon Rusch .20 .06
255 Michael Barrett .20 .06
256 Omar Daal .20 .06
257 Elmer Dessens .20 .06
258 Wade Miller .20 .06
259 Adrian Beltre .20 .06
260 Vicente Padilla .20 .06
261 Kazuhiro Sasaki .20 .06
262 Mike Scioscia MG .20 .06
263 Bobby Cox MG .20 .06
264 Mike Hargrove MG .20 .06
265 Grady Little MG RC .20 .06
266 Alex Gonzalez UER .20 .06
2002 stats are listed as all zero's
267 Jerry Manuel MG .20 .06
268 Bob Boone MG .20 .06
269 Joel Skinner MG .20 .06
270 Clint Hurdle MG .20 .06
271 Miguel Batista UER .20 .06
All 2002 Stats are 0's
272 Bob Brenly MG .20 .06
273 Jeff Torborg MG .20 .06
274 Jimmy Williams MG UER .20 .06
Career managerial record is wrong
275 Tony Pena MG .20 .06
276 Jim Tracy MG .20 .06
277 Jerry Royster MG .20 .06
278 Ron Gardenhire MG .20 .06
279 Frank Robinson MG .30 .09
280 John Halama .20 .06
281 Joe Torre MG .30 .09
282 Art Howe MG .20 .06
283 Larry Bowa MG .20 .06
284 Lloyd McClendon MG .20 .06
285 Bruce Bochy MG .20 .06
286 Dusty Baker MG .20 .06
287 Lou Piniella MG .20 .06
288 Tony LaRussa MG .20 .06
289 Todd Walker .20 .06
290 Jerry Narron MG .20 .06
291 Carlos Tosca MG .20 .06
292 Chris Duncan FY RC .50 .15
293 Franklin Gutierrez FY RC 2.00 .60
294 Adam LaRoche FY .50 .15
295 Manuel Ramirez FY RC .50 .15
296 Il Kim FY RC .50 .15
297 Wayne Lydon FY RC .50 .15
298 Daryl Clark FY RC .50 .15
299 Sean Pierce FY .50 .15
300 Andy Marte FY RC 2.50 .75
301 Matthew Peterson FY RC .50 .15
302 Gonzalo Lopez FY RC .50 .15
303 Bernie Castro FY RC .50 .15
304 Cliff Lee FY .50 .15
305 Jason Perry FY RC .75 .23
306 Jaime Bubela FY RC .50 .15
307 Alexis Rios FY 1.25 .35
308 Brendan Harris FY RC .50 .15
309 R.Nivar-Martinez FY RC .75 .23
310 Terry Tiffee FY RC .50 .15
311 Kevin Youkilis FY RC 1.50 .45
312 Ruddy Lugo FY RC .50 .15
313 C.J. Wilson FY .50 .15
314 Mike McNutt FY RC .50 .15
315 Jeff Clark FY RC .50 .15
316 Mark Malaska FY RC .50 .15
317 Doug Waechter FY RC .50 .15
318 Derell McCall FY RC .50 .15
319 Scott Tyler FY RC .50 .15
320 Craig Brazell FY RC .50 .15
321 Walter Young FY .50 .15
322 Marlon Byrd .50 .15
Jorge Padilla FS
323 Chris Snelling .50 .15
Shin-Soo Choo FS
324 Hank Blalock .50 .15
Mark Teixeira FS
325 Josh Hamilton .50 .15
Carl Crawford FS
326 Orlando Hudson .50 .15
Josh Phelps FS
327 Jack Cust .50 .15
Rene Reyes FS
328 Angel Berroa .50 .15
Alexis Gomez FS
329 Michael Cuddyer .50 .15
Michael Restovich FS
330 Juan Rivera .50 .15
Marcus Thames FS
331 Brandon Puffer .50 .15
Jung Bong FS
332 Mike Cameron SH .20 .06
333 Shawn Green SH .20 .06
334 Oakland A's SH .20 .06
335 Jason Giambi SH .30 .09
336 Derek Lowe SH .20 .06
337 Manny Ramirez .50 .15
Mike Sweeney
Bernie Williams LL
338 Alfonso Soriano .30 .09
Alex Rodriguez
Derek Jeter LL
339 Alex Rodriguez .50 .15
Jim Thome
Rafael Palmeiro LL
340 Alex Rodriguez .50 .15
Magglio Ordonez
Miguel Tejada LL
341 Pedro Martinez .30 .09
Derek Lowe
Barry Zito LL
342 Pedro Martinez .50 .15
Roger Clemens
Mike Mussina LL
343 Larry Walker .50 .15
Vladimir Guerrero
Todd Helton LL
344 Sammy Sosa .50 .15
Albert Pujols
Shawn Green LL
345 Sammy Sosa .50 .15
Lance Berkman
Shawn Green LL
346 Lance Berkman .20 .06
Albert Pujols
Pat Burrell LL
347 Randy Johnson .30 .09
Greg Maddux
Tom Glavine LL
348 Randy Johnson .30 .09
Curt Schilling
Kerry Wood LL
349 Francisco Rodriguez .20 .06
Darin Erstad
Tim Salmon
AL Division Series
350 Minnesota Twins .30 .09
St. Louis Cardinals
AL and NL Division Series
351 Anaheim Angels .30 .09
San Francisco Giants
AL and NL Division Series
352 Jim Edmonds .30 .09
Scott Rolen
NL Division Series
353 Adam Kennedy ALCS .20 .06
354 J.T. Snow WS .30 .09
355 David Bell NLCS .30 .09
356 Jason Giambi AS .30 .09
357 Alfonso Soriano AS .20 .06
358 Alex Rodriguez AS .50 .15
359 Eric Chavez AS .20 .06
360 Torii Hunter AS .20 .06
361 Bernie Williams AS .20 .06
362 Garret Anderson AS .20 .06
363 Jorge Posada AS .20 .06
364 Derek Lowe AS .20 .06
365 Barry Zito AS .20 .06
366 Manny Ramirez AS .20 .06
367 Mike Scioscia AS .20 .06
368 Francisco Rodriguez .20 .06
369 Chris Hammond .20 .06
370 Chipper Jones .50 .15
371 Chris Singleton .20 .06
372 Cliff Floyd .20 .06
373 Bobby Hill .20 .06
374 Antonio Osuna .20 .06
375 Barry Larkin .50 .15
376 Charles Nagy .20 .06
377 Denny Stark .20 .06
378 Dean Palmer .20 .06
379 Eric Owens .20 .06
380 Randy Johnson .50 .15
381 Jeff Suppan .20 .06
382 Eric Karros .20 .06
383 Luis Vizcaino .20 .06
384 Johan Santana .20 .06
385 Javier Vazquez .20 .06
386 John Thomson .20 .06
387 Nick Johnson .20 .06
388 Mark Ellis .20 .06
389 Doug Glanville .20 .06
390 Ken Griffey Jr. .75 .23
391 Bubba Trammell .20 .06
392 Livan Hernandez .20 .06
393 Desi Relaford .20 .06
394 Eli Marrero .20 .06
395 Jared Sandberg .20 .06
396 Barry Bonds 1.25 .35
397 Esteban Loaiza .20 .06
398 Aaron Sele .20 .06
399 Geoff Blum .20 .06
400 Derek Jeter 1.25 .35
401 Eric Byrnes .20 .06
402 Mike Timlin .20 .06
403 Mark Kotsay .20 .06
404 Rich Aurilia .20 .06
405 Joel Pineiro .20 .06
406 Chuck Finley .20 .06
407 Bengie Molina .20 .06
408 Steve Finley .20 .06
409 Julio Franco .20 .06
410 Marty Cordova .20 .06
411 Shea Hillenbrand .20 .06
412 Mark Bellhorn .20 .06
413 Jon Garland .20 .06
414 Reggie Taylor .20 .06
415 Milton Bradley .20 .06
416 Carlos Pena .20 .06
417 Andy Fox .20 .06
418 Brad Ausmus .20 .06
419 Brent Mayne .20 .06
420 Paul Quantrill .20 .06
421 Carlos Delgado .20 .06
422 Kevin Mench .20 .06
423 Joe Kennedy .20 .06
424 Mike Crudale .20 .06
425 Mark McLemore .20 .06
426 Bill Mueller .20 .06
427 Rob Mackowiak .20 .06
428 Ricky Ledee .20 .06
429 Ted Lilly .20 .06
430 Sterling Hitchcock .20 .06
431 Scott Strickland .20 .06
432 Damion Easley .20 .06
433 Torii Hunter .20 .06
434 Brad Radke .20 .06
435 Geoff Jenkins .20 .06
436 Paul Byrd .20 .06
437 Morgan Ensberg .20 .06
438 Mike Maroth .20 .06
439 Mike Hampton .20 .06
440 Adam Hyzdu .20 .06
441 Vance Wilson .20 .06
442 Todd Ritchie .20 .06
443 Tom Gordon .20 .06
444 John Burkett .20 .06
445 Rodrigo Lopez .20 .06
446 Tim Spooneybarger .20 .06
447 Quinton Mccracken .20 .06
448 Tim Salmon .30 .09
449 Jarrod Washburn .20 .06
450 Pedro Martinez .50 .15
451 Dustan Mohr .20 .06
452 Julio Lugo .20 .06
453 Scott Stewart .20 .06
454 Armando Benitez .20 .06
455 Raul Mondesi .20 .06
456 Robin Ventura .20 .06
457 Bobby Abreu .20 .06
458 Josh Fogg .20 .06
459 Ryan Klesko .20 .06
460 Tsuyoshi Shinjo .20 .06
461 Jim Edmonds .20 .06
462 Cliff Politte .20 .06
463 Chan Ho Park .20 .06
464 John Mabry .20 .06
465 Woody Williams .20 .06
466 Jason Michaels .20 .06
467 Scott Schoeneweis .20 .06
468 Brian Anderson .20 .06
469 Brett Tomko .20 .06
470 Scott Erickson .20 .06
471 Kevin Millar .20 .06
472 Danny Wright .20 .06
473 Jason Schmidt .20 .06
474 Scott Williamson .20 .06
475 Einar Diaz .20 .06
476 Jay Payton .20 .06
477 Juan Acevedo .20 .06
478 Ben Grieve .20 .06
479 Raul Ibanez .20 .06
480 Richie Sexson .20 .06
481 Rick Reed .20 .06
482 Pedro Astacio .20 .06
483 Adam Piatt .20 .06
484 Bud Smith .20 .06
485 Tomas Perez .20 .06
486 Adam Eaton .20 .06
487 Rafael Palmeiro .30 .09
488 Jason Tyner .20 .06
489 Scott Rolen .30 .09
490 Randy Winn .20 .06
491 Ryan Jensen .20 .06
492 Trevor Hoffman .20 .06
493 Craig Wilson .20 .06
494 Jeremy Giambi .20 .06
495 Daryle Ward .20 .06
496 Shane Spencer .20 .06
497 Andy Pettitte .30 .09
498 John Franco .20 .06
499 Felipe Lopez .20 .06
500 Mike Piazza .75 .23
501 Cristian Guzman .20 .06
502 Jose Hernandez .20 .06
503 Octavio Dotel .20 .06
504 Brad Penny .20 .06
505 Dave Veres .20 .06
506 Ryan Dempster .20 .06
507 Joe Crede .20 .06
508 Chad Hermansen .20 .06
509 Gary Matthews Jr. .20 .06
510 Matt Franco .20 .06
511 Ben Weber .20 .06
512 Dave Berg .20 .06
513 Michael Young .20 .06
514 Frank Catalanotto .20 .06
515 Darin Erstad .20 .06
516 Matt Williams .20 .06
517 B.J. Surhoff .20 .06
518 Kerry Ligtenberg .20 .06
519 Mike Bordick .20 .06
520 Arthur Rhodes .20 .06
521 Joe Girardi .20 .06
522 D'Angelo Jimenez .20 .06
523 Paul Konerko .20 .06
524 Jose Macias .20 .06
525 Joe Mays .20 .06
526 Marquis Grissom .20 .06
527 Neifi Perez .20 .06
528 Preston Wilson .20 .06
529 Jeff Weaver .20 .06
530 Eric Chavez .20 .06
531 Placido Polanco .20 .06
532 Matt Mantei .20 .06
533 James Baldwin .20 .06
534 Toby Hall .20 .06
535 Brendan Donnelly .20 .06
536 Benji Gil .20 .06
537 Damian Moss .20 .06
538 Jorge Julio .20 .06
539 Matt Clement .20 .06
540 Brian Moehler .20 .06
541 Lee Stevens .20 .06
542 Jimmy Haynes .20 .06
543 Terry Mulholland .20 .06
544 Dave Roberts .20 .06
545 J.C. Romero .20 .06
546 Bartolo Colon .20 .06
547 Roger Cedeno .20 .06
548 Mariano Rivera .30 .09
549 Billy Koch .20 .06
550 Manny Ramirez .20 .06
551 Travis Lee .20 .06
552 Oliver Perez .20 .06
553 Tim Worrell .20 .06
554 Rafael Soriano .20 .06
555 Damian Miller .20 .06
556 John Smoltz .30 .09
557 Willis Roberts .20 .06
558 Tim Hudson .20 .06
559 Moises Alou .20 .06
560 Gary Glover .20 .06
561 Corky Miller .20 .06
562 Ben Broussard .20 .06
563 Gabe Kapler .20 .06
564 Chris Woodward .20 .06
565 Paul Wilson .20 .06
566 Todd Hollandsworth .20 .06
567 So Taguchi .20 .06
568 John Olerud .20 .06
569 Reggie Sanders .20 .06
570 Jake Peavy .20 .06
571 Kris Benson .20 .06
572 Todd Pratt .20 .06
573 Ray Durham .20 .06
574 Boomer Wells .20 .06
575 Chris Widger .20 .06
576 Shawn Wooten .20 .06
577 Tom Glavine .30 .09
578 Antonio Alfonseca .20 .06
579 Keith Foulke .20 .06
580 Shawn Estes .20 .06
581 Mark Grace .30 .09
582 Dmitri Young .20 .06
583 A.J. Burnett .20 .06
584 Richard Hidalgo .20 .06
585 Mike Sweeney .20 .06
586 Alex Cora .20 .06
587 Matt Stairs .20 .06
588 Doug Mientkiewicz .20 .06
589 Fernando Tatis .20 .06
590 David Weathers .20 .06
591 Cory Lidle .20 .06
592 Dan Plesac .20 .06
593 Jeff Bagwell .30 .09
594 Steve Sparks .20 .06
595 Sandy Alomar Jr. .20 .06
596 John Lackey .20 .06
597 Rick Helling .20 .06
598 Mark DeRosa .20 .06
599 Carlos Lee .20 .06
600 Garret Anderson .20 .06
601 Vinny Castilla .20 .06
602 Ryan Drese .20 .06
603 LaTroy Hawkins .20 .06
604 David Bell .20 .06
605 Freddy Garcia .20 .06
606 Miguel Cairo .20 .06
607 Scott Spiezio .20 .06
608 Mike Remlinger .20 .06
609 Tony Graffanino .20 .06
610 Russell Branyan .20 .06
611 Chris Magruder .20 .06
612 Jose Contreras RC 1.50 .45
613 Carl Pavano .20 .06
614 Kevin Brown .20 .06
615 Tyler Houston .20 .06
616 A.J. Pierzynski .20 .06
617 Tony Fiore .20 .06
618 Peter Bergeron .20 .06
619 Rondell White .20 .06
620 Brett Myers .20 .06
621 Kevin Young .20 .06
622 Kenny Lofton .20 .06
623 Ben Davis .20 .06
624 J.D. Drew .20 .06
625 Chris Gomez .20 .06
626 Karim Garcia .20 .06
627 Ricky Gutierrez .20 .06
628 Mark Redman .20 .06
629 Juan Encarnacion .20 .06
630 Anaheim Angels TC .30 .09
631 Ariz.Diamondbacks TC .20 .06
632 Atlanta Braves TC .20 .06
633 Baltimore Orioles TC .20 .06
634 Boston Red Sox TC .20 .06
635 Chicago Cubs TC .20 .06
636 Chicago White Sox TC .20 .06
637 Cincinnati Reds TC .20 .06
638 Cleveland Indians TC .20 .06
639 Colorado Rockies TC .20 .06
640 Detroit Tigers TC .20 .06
641 Florida Marlins TC .20 .06
642 Houston Astros TC .20 .06
643 Kansas City Royals TC .20 .06
644 Los Angeles Dodgers TC .20 .06
645 Milwaukee Brewers TC .20 .06
646 Minnesota Twins TC .20 .06
647 Montreal Expos TC .20 .06
648 New York Mets TC .20 .06
649 New York Yankees TC .30 .09
650 Oakland Athletics TC .20 .06
651 Philadelphia Phillies TC .20 .06
652 Pittsburgh Pirates TC .20 .06
653 San Diego Padres TC .20 .06
654 San Francisco Giants TC .20 .06
655 Seattle Mariners TC .20 .06
656 St. Louis Cardinals TC .20 .06
657 T.B. Devil Rays TC .20 .06
658 Texas Rangers TC .20 .06
659 Toronto Blue Jays TC .20 .06
660 Bryan Bullington DP RC 1.50 .45
661 Jeremy Guthrie DP RC .50 .15
662 Joey Gomes DP RC .50 .15
663 E.Bastida-Martinez DP RC .50 .15
664 Brian Wright DP RC .50 .15
665 B.J. Upton DP .75 .23
666 Jeff Francis DP .50 .15
667 Drew Meyer DP .50 .15
668 Jeremy Hermida DP .50 .15
669 Khalil Greene DP .50 .15
670 Darrell Rasner DP RC .50 .15
671 Cole Hamels DP .75 .23
672 James Loney DP .50 .15
673 Sergio Santos DP .50 .15
674 Jason Pridie DP .50 .15
675 Brandon Phillips .50 .15
Victor Martinez
676 Hee Seop Choi .50 .15
Nic Jackson
677 Dontrelle Willis .75 .23
Jason Stokes
678 Chad Tracy .50 .15
Lyle Overbay
679 Joe Borchard .50 .15
Corwin Malone
680 Joe Mauer .75 .23
Justin Morneau
681 Drew Henson .50 .15
Brandon Claussen
682 Chase Utley .50 .15
Gavin Floyd
683 Taggert Bozied .50 .15
Xavier Nady
684 Aaron Heilman .50 .15
Jose Reyes
685 Kenny Rogers AW .20 .06
686 Bengie Molina AW .20 .06
687 John Olerud AW .20 .06
688 Bret Boone AW .20 .06
689 Eric Chavez AW .20 .06
690 Alex Rodriguez AW .50 .15
691 Darin Erstad AW .20 .06
692 Ichiro Suzuki AW .50 .15
693 Torii Hunter AW .20 .06
694 Greg Maddux AW .50 .15
695 Brad Ausmus AW .20 .06
696 Todd Helton AW .20 .06
697 Fernando Vina AW .20 .06
698 Scott Rolen AW .20 .06
699 Edgar Renteria AW .20 .06
700 Andruw Jones AW .20 .06
701 Larry Walker AW .20 .06
702 Jim Edmonds AW .20 .06
703 Barry Zito AW .20 .06
704 Randy Johnson AW .30 .09
705 Miguel Tejada AW .20 .06
706 Barry Bonds AW .60 .18
707 Eric Hinske AW .20 .06
708 Jason Jennings AW .20 .06
709 Todd Helton AS .20 .06
710 Jeff Kent AS .20 .06
711 Edgar Renteria AS .20 .06
712 Scott Rolen AS .20 .06
713 Barry Bonds AS .60 .18
714 Sammy Sosa AS .50 .15
715 Vladimir Guerrero AS .30 .09
716 Mike Piazza AS .50 .15
717 Curt Schilling AS .20 .06
718 Randy Johnson AS .30 .09
719 Bobby Cox AS .20 .06
720 Anaheim Angels WS .30 .09
721 Anaheim Angels WS .50 .15

2003 Topps Black

Inserted at a stated rate of one in 16 HTA series one packs and one in 10 HTA series 2 packs, this is a partial parallel to the Topps set. Only cards numbered from 1 through 331 were printed (though card number 7 does not exist, thus 330 cards comprise the series one set). However, the second series was issued in complete parallel form. These cards were issued to a stated print run of 52 serial numbered sets.

Nm-Mt Ex-Mt
*BLACK 1-291/368-659/685-721: 20X TO 50X
*BLACK 292-331/660-684: 12.5X TO 30X
*BLACK RC 292-331/612/660-684: 10X TO 25X

2003 Topps Box Bottoms

These cards were issued as a four-card sheet on the bottom of first and second series Home Team Advantage boxes. The sheets were not perforated, but did include dotted lines between each card indicating where the cards should be cut if they were to be separated. The cards are identical parallels to the basic issue 2003 Topps cards (including the same checklist numbers on the card backs). The key difference is the readily noticeable plain cardboard stock used for these Box Bottom parallels as averse to the high gloss card stock used for the basic issue cards.

Nm-Mt Ex-Mt
*BOX BOTTOM CARDS: 1X TO 2.5X BASIC
1 Alex Rodriguez 1 2.00 .60
10 Mark Prior 4 2.50 .75
11 Curt Schilling 1 .75 .23
20 Todd Helton 1 .75 .23
50 Sammy Sosa 2 2.00 .60
73 Luis Gonzalez 1 .50 .15
77 Miguel Tejada 4 .50 .15
80 Ivan Rodriguez 4 1.25 .35
90 Alfonso Soriano 2 .75 .23
150 Kazuhisa Ishii 2 .50 .15
160 Pat Burrell 4 .50 .15
177 Adam Dunn 3 .50 .15
180 Barry Zito 3 .75 .23
200 Albert Pujols 2 2.50 .75
230 Lance Berkman 3 .50 .15
250 Nomar Garciaparra 3 2.00 .60
368 Francisco Rodriguez 5 .50 .15
370 Chipper Jones 8 1.25 .35
380 Randy Johnson 8 1.25 .35
387 Nick Johnson 7 .50 .15
390 Ken Griffey Jr. 6 2.00 .60
396 Barry Bonds 5 3.00 .90
433 Torii Hunter 5 .50 .15
450 Pedro Martinez 6 1.25 .35
489 Scott Rolen 8 .75 .23
500 Mike Piazza 6 2.00 .60
530 Eric Chavez 6 .50 .15
550 Manny Ramirez 7 .50 .15
558 Tim Hudson 7 .50 .15
585 Mike Sweeney 8 .50 .15
593 Jeff Bagwell 5 .75 .23
600 Garret Anderson 7 .50 .15

2003 Topps Gold

Inserted at a stated rate of one in 16 first series hobby packs and one in five first series HTA packs, this is a partial parallel to the first series set. For the first series, nly cards numbered from 1 through 331 were printed. The second series was issued in its totality for this parallel. The second series cards were also issued at a stated rate of one in seven hobby packs, one in two HTA packs and one in five retail packs. All gold cards were issued to a stated print run of 2003 serial numbered sets.

Nm-Mt Ex-Mt
*GOLD 1-291/368-659/685-721: 6X TO 15X
*GOLD: 292-331/660-684: 3X TO 8X..
*GOLD RC's: 292-331/612/660-684: 3X TO 8X

2003 Topps Trademark Variations

Inserted into first series packs at a stated rate of one in 8852 hobby and one in 2665 HTA and series two packs at a rate of one in 4487 Hobby, one in 1277 HTA and one in 3763 retail packs, this is a partial parallel to the 2003 Topps set. These cards can be differentiated as the "Topps" logo on the card front is one the company used in the 1960's and 1970's. Cards numbered between 1 and 324 were seeded into first series packs and cards numbered between 368 and 600 were in second series packs.

Nm-Mt Ex-Mt
1 Alex Rodriguez
10 Mark Prior
11 Curt Schilling
20 Todd Helton
30 Jason Giambi
50 Sammy Sosa
61 Roger Clemens
73 Luis Gonzalez
77 Miguel Tejada
80 Ivan Rodriguez
90 Alfonso Soriano
100 Ichiro Suzuki
130 Gary Sheffield

150 Kazuhisa Ishii
160 Pat Burrell
170 Vladimir Guerrero
177 Adam Dunn
180 Barry Zito
200 Albert Pujols
230 Lance Berkman
250 Nomar Garciaparra
300 Andy Marte FY
321 Walter Young FY
322 Marlon Byrd
Jorge Padilla FS
324 Hank Blalock
Mark Teixeira FS
368 Francisco Rodriguez
370 Chipper Jones
380 Randy Johnson
387 Nick Johnson
390 Ken Griffey Jr.
396 Barry Bonds
400 Derek Jeter
421 Carlos Delgado
433 Torii Hunter
450 Pedro Martinez
461 Jim Edmonds
489 Scott Rolen
500 Mike Piazza
515 Darin Erstad
530 Eric Chavez
550 Manny Ramirez
558 Tim Hudson
585 Mike Sweeney
593 Jeff Bagwell
600 Garret Anderson

2003 Topps All-Stars

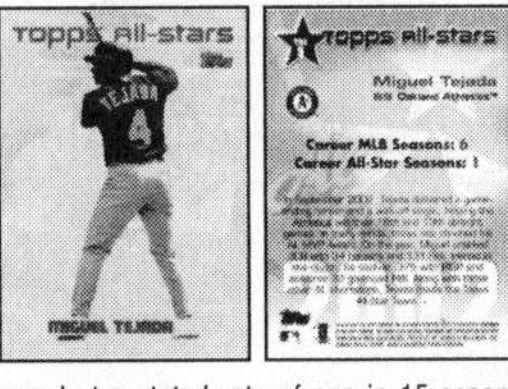

Issued at a stated rate of one in 15 second series hobby packs and one in five second series HTA packs, this 20 card set features most of the leading players in baseball.

	Nm-Mt	Ex-Mt
COMPLETE SET (20)	50.00	15.00
1 Alfonso Soriano	2.00	.60
2 Barry Bonds	6.00	1.80
3 Ichiro Suzuki	4.00	1.20
4 Alex Rodriguez	4.00	1.20
5 Miguel Tejada	2.00	.60
6 Nomar Garciaparra	4.00	1.20
7 Jason Giambi	2.50	.75
8 Manny Ramirez	2.00	.60
9 Derek Jeter	6.00	1.80
10 Garret Anderson	2.00	.60
11 Barry Zito	2.00	.60
12 Sammy Sosa	4.00	1.20
13 Adam Dunn	2.00	.60
14 Vladimir Guerrero	2.50	.75
15 Mike Piazza	4.00	1.20
16 Shawn Green	2.00	.60
17 Luis Gonzalez	2.00	.60
18 Todd Helton	2.00	.60
19 Torii Hunter	2.00	.60
20 Curt Schilling	2.00	.60

2003 Topps Autographs

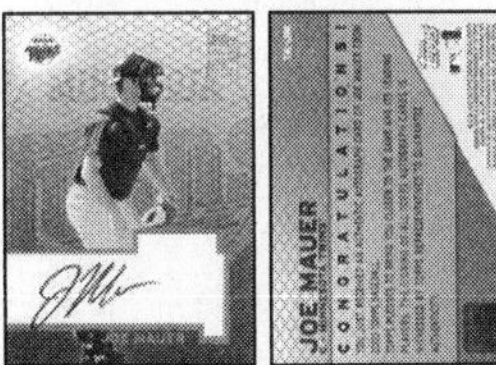

Issued at varying stated odds, these 38 cards feature a mix of prospect and starts who signed cards for inclusion in the 2003 Topps product. A couple of players did not return their cards in time for inclusion in packs and these cards could be redeemed until November 30, 2004.

	Nm-Mt	Ex-Mt
GROUP A1 SER.1 1:8910 H, 1: 2533 HTA		
GROUP B1 SER.1 1:24,710 H, 1:7037 HTA		
GROUP C1 SER.1 1:11,097 H, 1:3167 HTA		
GROUP D1 SER.1 1:20,144 H, 1:5758 HTA		
GROUP E1 SER.1 1:11,730 H, 1:3333 HTA		
GROUP F1 SER.1 1:2209 H, 1:395 HTA		
GROUP G1 SER.1 1:3471 H, 1:460 HTA		
GROUP A2 1:31,408 H, 1:8808 HTA, 1:26,208 R		
GROUP B2 1:5188 H, 1:1460 HTA, 1:4368 R		
GROUP C2 1:864 H, 1:232 HTA, 1:708 R		
GROUP D2 1:790 H, 1:214 HTA, 1:647 R		
AJ Andruw Jones A1		
AK1 Austin Kearns F1	15.00	4.50
AK2 Austin Kearns C2	15.00	4.50
AP Albert Pujols B2	150.00	45.00
AS Alfonso Soriano A1		
BH Brad Hawpe D2	15.00	4.50
BS Ben Sheets E1	15.00	4.50
BU B.J. Upton D2	25.00	7.50
BZ Barry Zito C2	50.00	15.00
CE Clint Everts D2	15.00	4.50
CF Cliff Floyd C2	25.00	7.50
DE Darin Erstad B1 EXCH	25.00	7.50
DW Dontrelle Willis D2	50.00	15.00
EC Eric Chavez A1	40.00	12.00
EH Eric Hinske C2	15.00	4.50
EM Eric Milton C1	15.00	4.50
HB Hank Blalock F1	25.00	7.50
JB Josh Beckett C2	50.00	15.00
JDM J.D. Martin G1	10.00	3.00
JL Jason Lane G1	10.00	3.00
JM Joe Mauer F1	25.00	7.50
JPH Josh Phelps C2	15.00	4.50
JV Jose Vidro C2	15.00	4.50
LB Lance Berkman A2	40.00	12.00
MB Mark Buehrle C1	25.00	7.50
MO Magglio Ordonez B2	25.00	7.50
MP Mark Prior F1	100.00	30.00
MTE Mark Teixeira F1	25.00	7.50
MTH Marcus Thames G1	10.00	3.00
MT1 Miguel Tejada A1	40.00	12.00
MT2 Miguel Tejada C2	25.00	7.50
NN Nick Neugebauer D1	15.00	4.50
OH Orlando Hudson G1	10.00	3.00
PK Paul Konerko C2	25.00	7.50
PL1 Paul Lo Duca F1	15.00	4.50
PL2 Paul Lo Duca C2	25.00	7.50
SR Scott Rolen A1 EXCH	60.00	18.00
TH Torii Hunter C2	25.00	7.50

2003 Topps Blue Backs

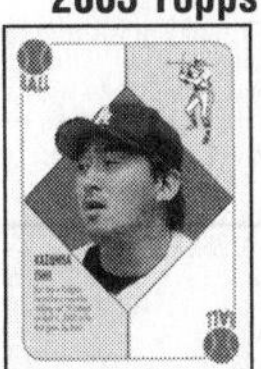

Issued in the style of the 1951 Topps Blue Back set, these 40 cards were inserted into first series packs at a stated rate of one in 12 hobby packs and one in four HTA packs.

	Nm-Mt	Ex-Mt
BB1 Albert Pujols	4.00	1.20
BB2 Ichiro Suzuki	3.00	.90
BB3 Sammy Sosa	3.00	.90
BB4 Kazuhisa Ishii	2.00	.60
BB5 Alex Rodriguez	3.00	.90
BB6 Derek Jeter	5.00	1.50
BB7 Vladimir Guerrero	2.00	.60
BB8 Ken Griffey Jr.	3.00	.90
BB9 Jason Giambi	2.00	.60
BB10 Todd Helton	2.00	.60
BB11 Mike Piazza	3.00	.90
BB12 Nomar Garciaparra	3.00	.90
BB13 Chipper Jones	2.00	.60
BB14 Ivan Rodriguez	2.00	.60
BB15 Luis Gonzalez	2.00	.60
BB16 Pat Burrell	2.00	.60
BB17 Mark Prior	4.00	1.20
BB18 Adam Dunn	2.00	.60
BB19 Jeff Bagwell	2.00	.60
BB20 Austin Kearns	2.00	.60
BB21 Alfonso Soriano	2.00	.60
BB22 Jim Thome	2.00	.60
BB23 Bernie Williams	2.00	.60
BB24 Pedro Martinez	2.00	.60
BB25 Lance Berkman	2.00	.60
BB26 Randy Johnson	2.00	.60
BB27 Rafael Palmeiro	2.00	.60
BB28 Richie Sexson	2.00	.60
BB29 Troy Glaus	2.00	.60
BB30 Shawn Green	2.00	.60
BB31 Larry Walker	2.00	.60
BB32 Eric Hinske	2.00	.60
BB33 Andruw Jones	2.00	.60
BB34 Barry Bonds	5.00	1.50
BB35 Curt Schilling	2.00	.60
BB36 Greg Maddux	3.00	.90
BB37 Jimmy Rollins	2.00	.60
BB38 Eric Chavez	2.00	.60
BB39 Scott Rolen	2.00	.60
BB40 Mike Sweeney	2.00	.60

2003 Topps Draft Picks

	MINT	NRMT
COMPLETE SERIES 1 (5)	25.00	11.00
COMPLETE SERIES 2 (5)	25.00	11.00
1-5 ISSUED IN RETAIL SETS		
6-10 DISTRIBUTED IN HOLIDAY SETS		
1 Brandon Wood	8.00	3.60
2 Ryan Wagner	8.00	3.60
3 Sean Rodriguez	6.00	2.70
4 Chris Lubanski	8.00	3.60
5 Chad Billingsley	5.00	2.20
6 Javi Herrera	5.00	2.20
7 Brian McFall	5.00	2.20
8 Nick Markakis	8.00	3.60
9 Adam Miller	5.00	2.20
10 Daric Barton	8.00	3.60

2003 Topps Farewell to Riverfront Stadium Relics

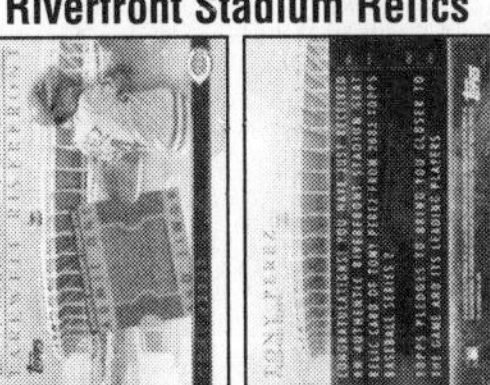

Issued at a stated rate of one in 37 second series HTA packs, this 10 card set featured leading current and retired Cincinnati Reds players since 1970 as well as a piece of Riverfront Stadium.

	Nm-Mt	Ex-Mt
AD Adam Dunn	25.00	7.50
AK Austin Kearns	25.00	7.50
BL Barry Larkin	25.00	7.50
DC Dave Concepcion	25.00	7.50
JB Johnny Bench	40.00	12.00
JM Joe Morgan	25.00	7.50
KG Ken Griffey Jr.	25.00	7.50
PO Paul O'Neill	25.00	7.50
TP Tony Perez	25.00	7.50
TS Tom Seaver	25.00	7.50

2003 Topps First Year Player Bonus

Issued as five card bonus "packs" these 10 cards featured players in their first year on a Topps card. Cards number 1 through 5 were issued in a sealed clear cello pack within the "red" hobby factory sets while cards number 6-10 were issued in the "blue" Sears/JC Penney factory sets.

	Nm-Mt	Ex-Mt
COMP.HOBBY SET (5)		
1 Ismael Castro		
2 Branden Florence		
3 Michael Garciaparra		
4 Hanley Ramirez		
5 Pete LaForest		
6 Rajai Davis		
7 Gary Schneidmiller		
8 Corey Shafer		
9 Thomari Story-Harden		
10 Bryan Grace		

2003 Topps Flashback

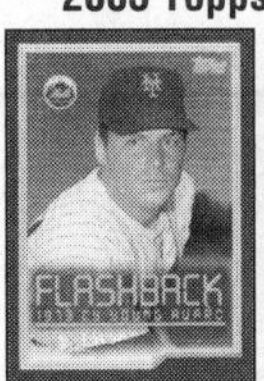
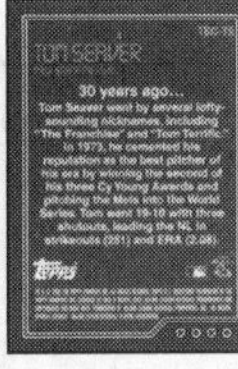

This set, featuring basically retired players, was inserted at a stated rate of one in 12 HTA first series packs. Only Mike Piazza and Randy Johnson were active at the time this set was issued.

	Nm-Mt	Ex-Mt
AR Al Rosen	5.00	1.50
BM Bill Madlock	5.00	1.50
CY Carl Yastrzemski	12.00	3.60
DM Dale Murphy	6.00	1.80
EM Eddie Mathews	6.00	1.80
GB George Brett	15.00	4.50
HK Harmon Killebrew	6.00	1.80
JP Jim Palmer	5.00	1.50
LD Lenny Dykstra	5.00	1.50
MP Mike Piazza	10.00	3.00
NR Nolan Ryan	15.00	4.50
RJ Randy Johnson	6.00	1.80
RR Robin Roberts	5.00	1.50
TS Tom Seaver	5.00	1.50
WS Warren Spahn	5.00	1.50

2003 Topps Hit Parade

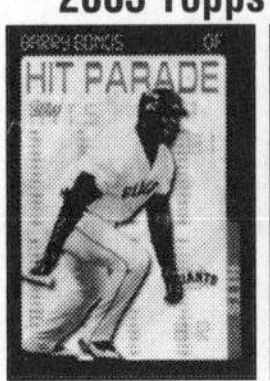

Issued at a stated rate of one in 15 hobby packs, one in 5 HTA packs and one in 10 retail packs, this 30 card set feature active players in the top 10 of home runs, runs batted in or hits.

	Nm-Mt	Ex-Mt
COMPLETE SET (30)	60.00	18.00
1 Barry Bonds	5.00	1.50
2 Sammy Sosa	3.00	.90
3 Rafael Palmeiro	2.00	.60
4 Fred McGriff	2.00	.60
5 Ken Griffey Jr.	3.00	.90
6 Juan Gonzalez	2.00	.60
7 Andres Galarraga	2.00	.60
8 Jeff Bagwell	2.00	.60
9 Frank Thomas	2.00	.60
10 Matt Williams	2.00	.60
11 Barry Bonds	5.00	1.50
12 Rafael Palmeiro	2.00	.60
13 Fred McGriff	2.00	.60
14 Andres Galarraga	2.00	.60
15 Ken Griffey Jr.	3.00	.90
16 Sammy Sosa	3.00	.90
17 Jeff Bagwell	2.00	.60
18 Juan Gonzalez	2.00	.60
19 Frank Thomas	2.00	.60
20 Matt Williams	2.00	.60
21 Rickey Henderson	2.00	.60
22 Rafael Palmeiro	2.00	.60
23 Roberto Alomar	2.00	.60
24 Barry Bonds	5.00	1.50
25 Mark Grace	2.00	.60
26 Fred McGriff	2.00	.60
27 Julio Franco	2.00	.60
28 Craig Biggio	2.00	.60
29 Andres Galarraga	2.00	.60
30 Barry Larkin	2.00	.60

2003 Topps Hobby Masters

Inserted into first series packs at stated odds of one in 18 Hobby packs and one in six HTA packs, these 20 cards feature some of the most popular players in the hobby.

	Nm-Mt	Ex-Mt
COMPLETE SET (20)	40.00	12.00
HM1 Ichiro Suzuki	3.00	.90
HM2 Kazuhisa Ishii	2.00	.60
HM3 Derek Jeter	5.00	1.50
HM4 Sammy Sosa	3.00	.90
HM5 Alex Rodriguez	3.00	.90
HM6 Mike Piazza	3.00	.90
HM7 Chipper Jones	2.00	.60
HM8 Vladimir Guerrero	2.00	.60
HM9 Nomar Garciaparra	3.00	.90
HM10 Todd Helton	2.00	.60
HM11 Jason Giambi	2.00	.60
HM12 Ken Griffey Jr.	3.00	.90
HM13 Albert Pujols	4.00	1.20
HM14 Ivan Rodriguez	2.00	.60
HM15 Mark Prior	4.00	1.20
HM16 Adam Dunn	2.00	.60
HM17 Randy Johnson	2.00	.60
HM18 Barry Bonds	5.00	1.50
HM19 Alfonso Soriano	2.00	.60
HM20 Pat Burrell	2.00	.60

2003 Topps Own the Game

Inserted into first series packs at stated odds of one in 12 hobby and one in four HTA, these 30 cards feature players who put up big numbers during the 2002 season.

	Nm-Mt	Ex-Mt
OG1 Ichiro Suzuki	3.00	.90
OG2 Todd Helton	2.00	.60
OG3 Larry Walker	2.00	.60
OG4 Mike Sweeney	2.00	.60
OG5 Sammy Sosa	3.00	.90
OG6 Lance Berkman	2.00	.60
OG7 Alex Rodriguez	3.00	.90
OG8 Jim Thome	2.00	.60
OG9 Shawn Green	2.00	.60
OG10 Nomar Garciaparra	3.00	.90
OG11 Miguel Tejada	2.00	.60
OG12 Jason Giambi	2.00	.60
OG13 Magglio Ordonez	2.00	.60
OG14 Manny Ramirez	2.00	.60
OG15 Alfonso Soriano	2.00	.60
OG16 Johnny Damon	2.00	.60
OG17 Derek Jeter	5.00	1.50
OG18 Albert Pujols	4.00	1.20
OG19 Luis Castillo	2.00	.60
OG20 Barry Bonds	5.00	1.50
OG21 Garret Anderson	2.00	.60
OG22 Jimmy Rollins	2.00	.60
OG23 Curt Schilling	2.00	.60
OG24 Barry Zito	2.00	.60
OG25 Randy Johnson	2.00	.60
OG26 Tom Glavine	2.00	.60
OG27 Roger Clemens	4.00	1.20
OG28 Pedro Martinez	2.00	.60
OG29 Derek Lowe	2.00	.60
OG30 John Smoltz	2.00	.60

2003 Topps Prime Cuts Relics

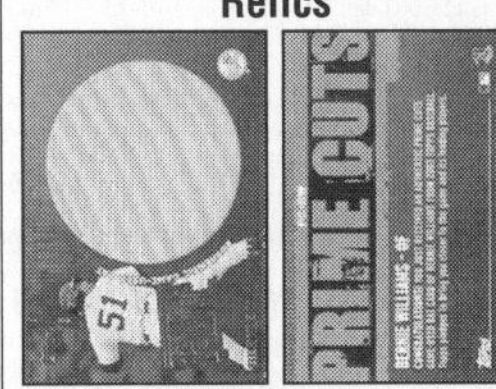

Inserted into first series packs at a stated rate of one in 37,066 hobby packs and one in 5067 HTA packs and second series packs at a rate of one in 116,208 hobby, one in 1480 HTA and one in 4368 retail packs, these 31 cards featured game-used bat pieces taken from the barrel of the bat. Each of these cards were issued to a stated print run of 50 serial numbered sets.

	Nm-Mt	Ex-Mt
AD1 Adam Dunn 1	50.00	15.00
AD2 Adam Dunn 2	50.00	15.00
AP Albert Pujols 1	120.00	36.00
AR1 Alex Rodriguez 1	80.00	24.00
AR2 Alex Rodriguez 2	80.00	24.00
AS Alfonso Soriano 2	80.00	24.00
BBO Barry Bonds 2	120.00	36.00
BW Bernie Williams 1	80.00	24.00
CD Carlos Delgado 2	50.00	15.00
EC Eric Chavez 2	50.00	15.00
EM Edgar Martinez 2	80.00	24.00
FT Frank Thomas 1	80.00	24.00
HB Hank Blalock 2	80.00	24.00
IR Ivan Rodriguez 1	80.00	24.00
JG Juan Gonzalez 1	80.00	24.00
JP Jorge Posada 2	80.00	24.00
LB Lance Berkman 1	50.00	15.00
LG Luis Gonzalez 2	50.00	15.00
MP Mike Piazza 1	80.00	24.00
MP Mark Prior 2	120.00	36.00
MV Mo Vaughn 1	50.00	15.00
NG1 Nomar Garciaparra 1	100.00	30.00
NG2 Nomar Garciaparra 2	100.00	30.00
RA1 Roberto Alomar 1	80.00	24.00
RA2 Roberto Alomar 2	80.00	24.00
RH Rickey Henderson 2	80.00	24.00
RJ Randy Johnson 2	80.00	24.00
RP Rafael Palmeiro 2	80.00	24.00
TG Tony Gwynn 2	80.00	24.00
TH Todd Helton 1	80.00	24.00
TM Tino Martinez 2	80.00	24.00

2003 Topps Prime Cuts Autograph Relics

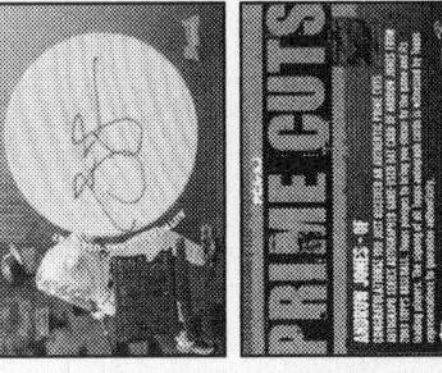

Inserted into first series packs at stated odds of one in 27,661 hobby and one in 7,917 HTA packs or second series packs at stated odds of one in 232,416 hobb packs, one in 8808 HTA packs or one in 28,598 retail packs, these ten cards feature players who signed the relics cut from the barrel of the bat they used in a game. These cards were issued to a stated print run of 50 serial numbered sets.

	Nm-Mt	Ex-Mt
AJ Andruw Jones 1	150.00	45.00
AP Albert Pujols 2		
CJ Chipper Jones 1	200.00	60.00
DE Darin Erstad 1		
EC Eric Chavez 1	150.00	45.00
LB Lance Berkman 2	150.00	45.00
MO Magglio Ordonez 2	150.00	45.00
MT Miguel Tejada 1	150.00	45.00
RP Rafael Palmeiro 1		
SR Scott Rolen 1		

2003 Topps Prime Cuts Pine Tar Relics

Inserted into first series packs at a stated rate of one in 9266 hobby packs and one in 1267 HTA packs and second series packs at a rate of one in 4288 hobby, one in 587 HTA and one in 928 retail, these 42 cards featured game-used bat pieces taken from the handle of the bat. Each of these cards were issued to a stated print run of 200 serial numbered sets.

	Nm-Mt	Ex-Mt
AD1 Adam Dunn 1	25.00	7.50
AD2 Adam Dunn 2	25.00	7.50
AJ Andruw Jones 1	25.00	7.50
AP1 Albert Pujols 1	60.00	18.00
AP2 Albert Pujols 2	60.00	18.00
AR1 Alex Rodriguez 1	40.00	12.00
AR2 Alex Rodriguez 2	40.00	12.00
AS1 Alfonso Soriano 1	40.00	12.00
AS2 Alfonso Soriano 2	40.00	12.00
BBO Barry Bonds 2	60.00	18.00
BW Bernie Williams 1	40.00	12.00
CD Carlos Delgado 2	25.00	7.50
CJ Chipper Jones 1	40.00	12.00
DE Darin Erstad 1	25.00	7.50
EC1 Eric Chavez 1	25.00	7.50
EC2 Eric Chavez 2	25.00	7.50
EM Edgar Martinez 2	40.00	12.00
FT Frank Thomas 1	40.00	12.00
HB Hank Blalock 2	40.00	12.00
IR Ivan Rodriguez 1	40.00	12.00
JG Juan Gonzalez 1	40.00	12.00
JP Jorge Posada 2	40.00	12.00
LB1 Lance Berkman 1	25.00	7.50
LB2 Lance Berkman 2	25.00	7.50
LG Luis Gonzalez 2	25.00	7.50
MO Magglio Ordonez 2	25.00	7.50
MP Mike Piazza 1	40.00	12.00
MP Mark Prior 2	60.00	18.00
MT Miguel Tejada 1	25.00	7.50
MV Mo Vaughn 1	25.00	7.50
NG1 Nomar Garciaparra 1	50.00	15.00
NG2 Nomar Garciaparra 2	50.00	15.00
RA1 Roberto Alomar 1	40.00	12.00
RA2 Roberto Alomar 2	40.00	12.00
RH Rickey Henderson 2	40.00	12.00
RJ Randy Johnson 2	40.00	12.00
RP1 Rafael Palmeiro 1	40.00	12.00
RP2 Rafael Palmeiro 2	40.00	12.00
SR Scott Rolen 1	40.00	12.00
TG Tony Gwynn 2	40.00	12.00
TH Todd Helton 1	40.00	12.00
TM Tino Martinez 2	40.00	12.00

2003 Topps Prime Cuts Trademark Relics

Inserted into first series packs at a stated rate of one in 18,533 hobby packs and one in 2533 HTA packs or second series packs at a rate of one in 12,912 hobby, one in 881 HTA or one in 1857 retail; these 42 cards featured game-used bat pieces taken from the middle of the bat. Each of these cards were issued to a stated print run of 100 serial numbered sets.

	Nm-Mt	Ex-Mt
AD1 Adam Dunn 1	40.00	12.00

AD2 Adam Dunn 2 40.00 12.00
AJ Andruw Jones 1 40.00 12.00
AP1 Albert Pujols 1 100.00 30.00
AP2 Albert Pujols 2 100.00 30.00
AR1 Alex Rodriguez 1 60.00 18.00
AR2 Alex Rodriguez 2 60.00 18.00
AS1 Alfonso Soriano 1 50.00 15.00
AS2 Alfonso Soriano 2 50.00 15.00
BBO Barry Bonds 2 100.00 30.00
BW Bernie Williams 1 50.00 15.00
CD Carlos Delgado 2 40.00 12.00
CJ Chipper Jones 1 50.00 15.00
DE Darin Erstad 1 40.00 12.00
EC1 Eric Chavez 1 40.00 12.00
EC2 Eric Chavez 2 40.00 12.00
EM Edgar Martinez 2 50.00 15.00
FT Frank Thomas 1 50.00 15.00
HB Hank Blalock 2 50.00 15.00
IR Ivan Rodriguez 1 50.00 15.00
JG Juan Gonzalez 1 50.00 15.00
JP Jorge Posada 2 50.00 15.00
LB1 Lance Berkman 1 40.00 12.00
LB2 Lance Berkman 2 40.00 12.00
LG Luis Gonzalez 2 40.00 12.00
MO Maggio Ordonez 2 40.00 12.00
MP Mike Piazza 1 80.00 24.00
MP Mark Prior 2 100.00 30.00
MT Miguel Tejada 1 40.00 12.00
MV Mo Vaughn 1 40.00 12.00
NG1 Nomar Garciaparra 1 80.00 24.00
NG2 Nomar Garciaparra 2 80.00 24.00
RA1 Roberto Alomar 1 50.00 15.00
RA2 Roberto Alomar 2 50.00 15.00
RH Rickey Henderson 2 50.00 15.00
RJ Randy Johnson 2 50.00 15.00
RP1 Rafael Palmeiro 1 50.00 15.00
RP2 Rafael Palmeiro 2 50.00 15.00
SR Scott Rolen 1 50.00 15.00
TG Tony Gwynn 2 50.00 15.00
TH Todd Helton 1 50.00 15.00
TM Tino Martinez 2 50.00 15.00

2003 Topps Record Breakers

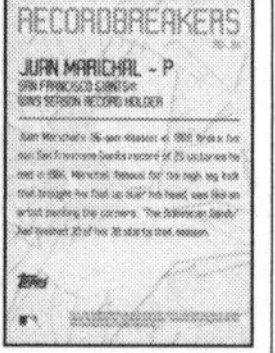

Inserted into packs at a stated rate of one in six hobby, one in two HTA and one in four retail, these 101 cards feature a mix of active and retired players who hold some sort of season, team, league or major league record.

Nm-Mt Ex-Mt
COMPLETE SET (100) 120.00 36.00
COMPLETE SERIES 1 (50) 60.00 18.00
COMPLETE SERIES 2 (50) 60.00 18.00
AG Andres Galarraga 1 1.50 .45
AR1 Alex Rodriguez 1 2.50 .75
AR2 Alex Rodriguez 2 2.50 .75
BB1 Barry Bonds 1 4.00 1.20
BB2 Barry Bonds 2 4.00 1.20
BF Bob Feller 2 1.50 .45
BG Bob Gibson 1 1.50 .45
CB Craig Biggio 2 1.50 .45
CD1 Carlos Delgado 1 1.50 .45
CD2 Carlos Delgado 2 1.50 .45
CF Cliff Floyd 1 1.50 .45
CJ Chipper Jones 1 1.50 .45
CK Chuck Klein 1 1.50 .45
CS Curt Schilling 1 1.50 .45
DE Darin Erstad 2 1.50 .45
DG Dwight Gooden 2 2.00 .60
DM Don Mattingly 1 5.00 1.50
EM Edgar Martinez 2 1.50 .45
EM Eddie Mathews 1 2.00 .60
FJ Fergie Jenkins 1 1.50 .45
FM Fred McGriff 1 1.50 .45
FR1 Frank Robinson 1 2.00 .60
FR2 Frank Robinson 2 2.00 .60
FT Frank Thomas 2 1.50 .45
GA Garret Anderson 2 1.50 .45
GB1 George Brett 1 5.00 1.50
GB2 George Brett 2 5.00 1.50
GF1 George Foster 1 1.50 .45
GF2 George Foster 2 1.50 .45
GM Greg Maddux 2 2.50 .75
GS Gary Sheffield 1 1.50 .45
HG Hank Greenberg 1 2.00 .60
HK Harmon Killebrew 1 2.00 .60
HW Hack Wilson 1 2.00 .60
IS Ichiro Suzuki 2 2.50 .75
JB1 Jeff Bagwell 1 1.50 .45
JB2 Jeff Bagwell 2 1.50 .45
JD Johnny Damon 2 1.50 .45
JG Jason Giambi 1 1.50 .45
JK Jeff Kent 2 1.50 .45
JME Jose Mesa 2 1.50 .45
JM1 Juan Marichal 1 1.50 .45
JM2 Juan Marichal 2 1.50 .45
JO John Olerud 1 1.50 .45
JP Jim Palmer 2 1.50 .45
JR Jim Rice 2 1.50 .45
JS John Smoltz 2 1.50 .45
JT Jim Thome 2 1.50 .45
KG1 Ken Griffey Jr. 1 2.50 .75
KG2 Ken Griffey Jr. 2 2.50 .75
LA Luis Aparicio 2 1.50 .45
LBR1 Lou Brock 1 2.00 .60
LBR2 Lou Brock 2 2.00 .60
LB1 Lance Berkman 1 1.50 .45
LB2 Lance Berkman 2 1.50 .45
LC Luis Castillo 1 1.50 .45
LD Lenny Dykstra 2 1.50 .45
LG1 Luis Gonzalez 1 1.50 .45
LG2 Luis Gonzalez 2 1.50 .45
LW Larry Walker 2 1.50 .45
MP Mike Piazza 1 2.50 .75
MR Manny Ramirez 2 1.50 .45
MS Mike Sweeney 1 1.50 .45
MSC Mike Schmidt 1 4.00 1.20
NG Nomar Garciaparra 2 2.50 .75
NR Nolan Ryan 1 5.00 1.50
PM Pedro Martinez 1 1.50 .45
PM Paul Molitor 2 2.00 .60
PW Preston Wilson 1 1.50 .45
RA Roberto Alomar 2 1.50 .45
RC Roger Clemens 1 3.00 .90
RCA Rod Carew 1 2.00 .60
RG Ron Guidry 1 1.50 .45
RH1 Rickey Henderson 1 1.50 .45
RH2 Rickey Henderson 2 1.50 .45
RJ1 Randy Johnson 1 1.50 .45
RJ2 Randy Johnson 2 1.50 .45
RP Rafael Palmeiro 1 1.50 .45
RS1 Richie Sexson 1 1.50 .45
RS2 Richie Sexson 2 1.50 .45
RY1 Robin Yount 1 3.00 .90
RY2 Robin Yount 2 3.00 .90
SG1 Shawn Green 1 1.50 .45
SG2 Shawn Green 2 1.50 .45
SS1 Sammy Sosa 1 2.50 .75
SS2 Sammy Sosa 2 2.50 .75
TG Troy Glaus 1 1.50 .45
TG1 Tony Gwynn 1 2.50 .75
TG2 Tony Gwynn 2 2.50 .75
TH1 Todd Helton 1 1.50 .45
TH2 Todd Helton 2 1.50 .45
TK Ted Kluszewski 2 2.00 .60
TR Tim Raines 2 1.50 .45
TS1 Tom Seaver 1 2.00 .60
TS2 Tom Seaver 2 2.00 .60
VG1 Vladimir Guerrero 1 1.50 .45
VG2 Vladimir Guerrero 2 1.50 .45
WB Wade Boggs 2 2.00 .60
WM Willie Mays 2 5.00 1.50
WS Willie Stargell 2 2.00 .60

2003 Topps Record Breakers Autographs

This 19 card set partially parallels the Record Breaker insert set. Most of the cards, except for Luis Gonzalez, were inserted into first series packs at a stated rate of one in 6941 hobby packs and one in 1178 HTA packs. The second series cards were issued at a stated rate of one in 2218 hobby, one in 634 HTA and one in 1850 retail packs.

Nm-Mt Ex-Mt
GROUP A1 SER.1 1:6941 H, 1:1178 HTA
GROUP B1 SER.1 1:34,320 H, 1:9744 HTA
GROUP 2 SER.2 1:2218 H, 1:634 HTA, 1:1850 R
CF Cliff Floyd A1 25.00 7.50
CJ Chipper Jones A1 80.00 24.00
DM Don Mattingly 2 200.00 60.00
FJ Fergie Jenkins A1 40.00 12.00
GF George Foster 2 40.00 12.00
HK Harmon Killebrew A1 80.00 24.00
JM Juan Marichal 2 60.00 18.00
LA Luis Aparicio 2 40.00 12.00
LB Lance Berkman 2 40.00 12.00
LBR Lou Brock 2 60.00 18.00
LG Luis Gonzalez B1 40.00 12.00
MS Mike Schmidt A1 120.00 36.00
RP Rafael Palmeiro A1 80.00 24.00
RS Richie Sexson A1 40.00 12.00
RY Robin Yount A1 80.00 24.00
SG Shawn Green A1
SW Mike Sweeney A1 40.00 12.00
TG Troy Glaus A1
WM Willie Mays 2 150.00 45.00

2003 Topps Record Breakers Relics

This 40 card set partially parallels the Record Breaker insert set. These cards, depending on the group they belonged to, were inserted into first and second series packs at different rates and we have noted all that information in our headers.

Nm-Mt Ex-Mt
BAT A1 SER.1 ODDS 1:13,528 H, 1:4872 HTA
BAT B1 SER.1 ODDS 1:9058 H, 1:1689 HTA
BAT C1 SER.1 ODDS 1:743 H, 1:90 HTA
UNI A1 SER.1 ODDS 1:6178 H, 1:700 HTA
UNI B1 SER.1 ODDS 1:355 H, 1:51 HTA
BAT 2 SER.2 ODDS 1:191 H, 1:59 HTA
UNI A2 SER.2 ODDS 1:5235, 1:400 HTA
UNI B2 SER.2 ODDS 1:418, 1:176 HTA
UNI C2 SER.2 ODDS 1:1151, 1:87 HTA
AR1 Alex Rodriguez Uni B1 15.00 4.50
AR2 Alex Rodriguez Uni B2 15.00 4.50
CD1 Carlos Delgado Uni B1 10.00 3.00
CD2 Carlos Delgado Uni B2 10.00 3.00
CJ Chipper Jones Uni B1 15.00 4.50
DE Darin Erstad Uni A2 10.00 3.00
DG Dwight Gooden Uni B2 15.00 4.50
DM Don Mattingly Bat C1 40.00 12.00
EM Edgar Martinez Bat 2 15.00 4.50
FR1 Frank Robinson Bat C1 15.00 4.50
FR2 Frank Robinson Bat 2 15.00 4.50
FT Frank Thomas Bat 2 15.00 4.50
GB1 George Brett Bat C1 25.00 7.50
GB2 George Brett Bat 2 25.00 7.50
HG Hank Greenberg Bat B1 40.00 12.00
HW Hack Wilson Bat A1 50.00 15.00
JB Jeff Bagwell Uni B1 15.00 4.50
JR Jim Rice Uni B2 10.00 3.00
LBE Lance Berkman Bat C1 10.00 3.00
LC Luis Castillo Bat C1 10.00 3.00
LG Luis Gonzalez Bat 2 10.00 3.00
LGO Luis Gonzalez Uni B1 10.00 3.00
MP Mike Piazza Bat C1 25.00 7.50
MS Mike Sweeney Bat C1 10.00 3.00
NR Nolan Ryan Uni A1 50.00 15.00
NRA Nolan Ryan Uni C2 40.00 12.00
PM Pedro Martinez Uni B1 15.00 4.50
RH Rickey Henderson Bat C1 15.00 4.50
RHO Rogers Hornsby Bat 2 40.00 12.00
RS Richie Sexson Uni C2 10.00 3.00
RY1 Robin Yount Uni B1 15.00 4.50
RY2 Robin Yount Bat 2 15.00 4.50
SG Shawn Green Uni B1 10.00 3.00
TG Tony Gwynn 2B Bat 2 15.00 4.50
TG2 Tony Gwynn Avg Bat 2 15.00 4.50
TH1 Todd Helton Uni B1 15.00 4.50
TH2 Todd Helton Uni B2 15.00 4.50
TK Ted Kluszewski Bat 2 15.00 4.50
TR Tim Raines Bat 2 10.00 3.00
WB Wade Boggs Bat 2 15.00 4.50

2003 Topps Record Breakers Nolan Ryan

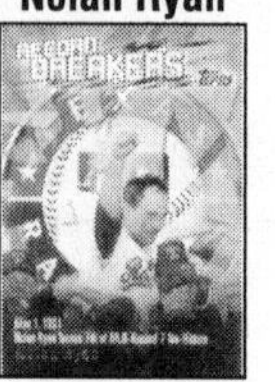

Inserted at a stated rate of one in two HTA packs, this seven card set features all-time strikeout king Nolan Ryan. Each of these cards commemorate one of his record setting seven no-hitters.

Nm-Mt Ex-Mt
COMPLETE SET (7) 60.00 18.00
COMMON CARD (NR1-NR7) 10.00 3.00

2003 Topps Record Breakers Nolan Ryan Autographs

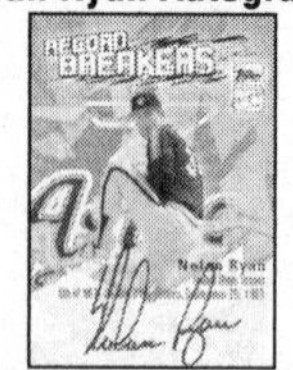

Inserted at a stated rate of one in 1894 HTA packs, this three card set honors Nolan Ryan and the teams he tossed no-hitters for.

Nm-Mt Ex-Mt
COMMON CARD 250.00 75.00

2003 Topps Red Backs

Inserted in second series packs at a stated rate of one in 12 hobby and one in eight retail; this 40-card set features leading players in the style of the 1951 Topps Red Back set.

Nm-Mt Ex-Mt
COMPLETE SET (40) 100.00 30.00
1 Nomar Garciaparra 4.00 1.20
2 Ichiro Suzuki 4.00 1.20
3 Alex Rodriguez 4.00 1.20
4 Sammy Sosa 4.00 1.20
5 Barry Bonds 6.00 1.80
6 Vladimir Guerrero 2.50 .75
7 Derek Jeter 6.00 1.80
8 Miguel Tejada 2.00 .60
9 Alfonso Soriano 2.00 .60
10 Manny Ramirez 2.00 .60
11 Adam Dunn 2.00 .60
12 Jason Giambi 2.50 .75
13 Mike Piazza 4.00 1.20
14 Scott Rolen 2.00 .60
15 Shawn Green 2.00 .60
16 Randy Johnson 2.50 .75
17 Todd Helton 2.00 .60
18 Garret Anderson 2.00 .60
19 Curt Schilling 2.00 .60
20 Albert Pujols 5.00 1.50
21 Chipper Jones 2.50 .75
22 Luis Gonzalez 2.00 .60
23 Mark Prior 5.00 1.50
24 Jim Thome 2.50 .75
25 Ivan Rodriguez 2.50 .75
26 Torii Hunter 2.00 .60
27 Lance Berkman 2.00 .60
28 Troy Glaus 2.00 .60
29 Andruw Jones 2.00 .60
30 Barry Zito 2.00 .60
31 Jeff Bagwell 2.00 .60
32 Magglio Ordonez 2.00 .60
33 Pat Burrell 2.00 .60
34 Mike Sweeney 2.00 .60
35 Rafael Palmeiro 2.00 .60
36 Larry Walker 2.00 .60
37 Carlos Delgado 2.00 .60
38 Brian Giles 2.00 .60
39 Pedro Martinez 2.50 .75
40 Greg Maddux 4.00 1.20

2003 Topps Turn Back the Clock Autographs

This five card set was inserted at a stated rate of one in 134 HTA packs except for Bill Madlock who signed fewer cards and his card was inserted at a stated rate of one in 268 HTA packs.

Nm-Mt Ex-Mt
GROUP A SER.1 ODDS 1:134 HTA
GROUP B SER.1 ODDS 1:268 HTA
BM Bill Madlock B 15.00 4.50
DM Dale Murphy A 40.00 12.00
HK Harmon Killebrew A
JP Jim Palmer A 20.00 6.00
LD Lenny Dykstra A 20.00 6.00

2003 Topps Traded

This 275 card-set was released in October, 2003. The set was issued in 10 card packs with an $3 SRP which came 24 packs to a box and 12 boxes to a case. Cards numbered 1 through 115 feature veterans who were traded while cards 116 through 120 feature managers. Cards numbered 121 through 165 featured prospects and cards 166 through 275 feature Rookie Cards. All of these cards were issued with a "T" prefix.

MINT NRMT
COMPLETE SET (275) 50.00 22.00
COMMON CARD (T1-T120) .20 .09
COMMON CARD (121-165) .40 .18
T1 Juan Pierre .20 .09
T2 Mark Grudzielanek .20 .09
T3 Tanyon Sturtze .20 .09
T4 Greg Vaughn .20 .09
T5 Greg Myers .20 .09
T6 Randall Simon .20 .09
T7 Todd Hundley .20 .09
T8 Marlon Anderson .20 .09
T9 Jeff Reboulet .20 .09
T10 Alex Sanchez .20 .09
T11 Mike Rivera .20 .09
T12 Todd Walker .20 .09
T13 Ray King .20 .09
T14 Shawn Estes .20 .09
T15 Gary Matthews Jr. .20 .09
T16 Jaret Wright .20 .09
T17 Edgardo Alfonzo .20 .09
T18 Omar Daal .20 .09
T19 Ryan Rupe .20 .09
T20 Tony Clark .20 .09
T21 Jeff Suppan .20 .09
T22 Mike Stanton .20 .09
T23 Ramon Martinez .20 .09
T24 Armando Rios .20 .09
T25 Johnny Estrada .20 .09
T26 Joe Girardi .20 .09
T27 Ivan Rodriguez .50 .23
T28 Robert Fick .20 .09
T29 Rick White .20 .09
T30 Robert Person .20 .09
T31 Alan Benes .20 .09
T32 Chris Carpenter .20 .09
T33 Chris Widger .20 .09
T34 Travis Hafner .20 .09
T35 Mike Venafro .20 .09
T36 Jon Lieber .20 .09
T37 Orlando Hernandez .20 .09
T38 Aaron Myette .20 .09
T39 Paul Bako .20 .09
T40 Erubiel Durazo .20 .09
T41 Mark Guthrie .20 .09
T42 Steve Avery .20 .09
T43 Damian Jackson .20 .09
T44 Rey Ordonez .20 .09
T45 John Flaherty .20 .09
T46 Byung-Hyun Kim .20 .09
T47 Tom Goodwin .20 .09
T48 Elmer Dessens .20 .09
T49 Al Martin .20 .09
T50 Gene Kingsale .20 .09
T51 Lenny Harris .20 .09
T52 David Ortiz .20 .09
T53 Jose Lima .20 .09
T54 Mike Difelice .20 .09
T55 Jose Hernandez .20 .09
T56 Todd Zeile .20 .09
T57 Roberto Hernandez .20 .09
T58 Albie Lopez .20 .09
T59 Roberto Alomar .50 .23
T60 Russ Ortiz .20 .09
T61 Brian Daubach .20 .09
T62 Carl Everett .20 .09
T63 Jeromy Burnitz .20 .09
T64 Mark Bellhorn .20 .09
T65 Ruben Sierra .20 .09
T66 Mike Fetters .20 .09
T67 Armando Benitez .20 .09
T68 Deivi Cruz .20 .09
T69 Jose Cruz Jr. .20 .09
T70 Jeremy Fikac .20 .09
T71 Jeff Kent .20 .09
T72 Andres Galarraga .20 .09
T73 Rickey Henderson .50 .23
T74 Royce Clayton .20 .09
T75 Troy O'Leary .20 .09
T76 Ron Coomer .20 .09
T77 Greg Colbrunn .20 .09
T78 Wes Helms .20 .09
T79 Kevin Millwood .20 .09
T80 Damion Easley .20 .09
T81 Bobby Kielty .20 .09
T82 Keith Osik .20 .09
T83 Ramiro Mendoza .20 .09
T84 Shea Hillenbrand .20 .09
T85 Shannon Stewart .20 .09
T86 Eddie Perez .20 .09
T87 Ugueth Urbina .20 .09
T88 Orlando Palmeiro .20 .09
T89 Graeme Lloyd .20 .09
T90 John Vander Wal .20 .09
T91 Gary Bennett .20 .09
T92 Shane Reynolds .20 .09
T93 Steve Parris .20 .09
T94 Julio Lugo .20 .09
T95 John Halama .20 .09
T96 Carlos Baerga .20 .09
T97 Jim Parque .20 .09
T98 Mike Williams .20 .09
T99 Fred McGriff .30 .14
T100 Kenny Rogers .20 .09
T101 Matt Herges .20 .09
T102 Jay Bell .20 .09
T103 Esteban Yan .20 .09
T104 Eric Owens .20 .09
T105 Aaron Fultz .20 .09
T106 Rey Sanchez .20 .09
T107 Jim Thome .50 .23
T108 Aaron Boone .20 .09
T109 Raul Mondesi .20 .09
T110 Kenny Lofton .20 .09
T111 Jose Guillen .20 .09
T112 Aramis Ramirez .20 .09
T113 Sidney Ponson .20 .09
T114 Scott Williamson .20 .09
T115 Robin Ventura .20 .09
T116 Dusty Baker MG .20 .09
T117 Felipe Alou MG .20 .09
T118 Buck Showalter MG .20 .09
T119 Jack McKeon MG .20 .09
T120 Art Howe MG .20 .09
T121 Bobby Crosby PROS .60 .25
T122 Adrian Gonzalez PROS .40 .18
T123 Kevin Cash PROS .40 .18
T124 Shin-Soo Choo PROS .40 .18
T125 Chin-Feng Chen PROS 1.00 .45
T126 Miguel Cabrera PROS 1.50 .70
T127 Jason Young PROS .40 .18
T128 Alex Herrera PROS .40 .18
T129 Jason Dubois PROS .40 .18
T130 Jeff Mathis PROS .40 .18
T131 Casey Kotchman PROS .60 .25
T132 Ed Rogers PROS .40 .18
T133 Wilson Betemit PROS .40 .18
T134 Jim Kavourias PROS .40 .18
T135 Taylor Buchholz PROS .40 .18
T136 Adam LaRoche PROS .60 .25
T137 D.McPherson PROS .60 .25
T138 Jesus Cota PROS .40 .18
T139 Clint Nageotte PROS .40 .18
T140 Boof Bonser PROS .40 .18
T141 Walter Young PROS .40 .18
T142 Joe Crede PROS .40 .18
T143 Denny Bautista PROS .40 .18
T144 Victor Diaz PROS .40 .18
T145 Chris Narveson PROS .40 .18
T146 Gabe Gross PROS .40 .18
T147 Jimmy Journell PROS .40 .18
T148 Rafael Soriano PROS .40 .18
T149 Jerome Williams PROS .40 .18
T150 Aaron Cook PROS .40 .18
T151 An. Martinez PROS .40 .18
T152 Scott Hairston PROS .40 .18
T153 John Buck PROS .40 .18
T154 Ryan Ludwick PROS .40 .18
T155 Chris Bootcheck PROS .40 .18
T156 John Rheinecker PROS .40 .18
T157 Jason Lane PROS .40 .18
T158 Shelley Duncan PROS .40 .18
T159 Adam Wainwright PROS .40 .18
T160 Jason Arnold PROS .40 .18
T161 Jonny Gomes PROS .40 .18
T162 James Loney PROS .60 .25
T163 Mike Fontenot PROS .40 .18
T164 Khalil Greene PROS .60 .25
T165 Sean Burnett PROS .40 .18
T166 David Martinez FY RC .40 .18
T167 Felix Pie FY RC 2.50 1.10
T168 Joe Valentine FY RC .40 .18
T169 Brandon Webb FY RC 2.00 .90
T170 Matt Diaz FY RC .75 .35
T171 Lew Ford FY RC .50 .23
T172 Jeremy Griffiths FY RC .50 .23
T173 Matt Hensley FY RC .40 .18
T174 Charlie Manning FY RC .40 .18
T175 Elizardo Ramirez FY RC 1.00 .45
T176 Greg Aquino FY RC .40 .18
T177 Felix Sanchez FY RC .40 .18
T178 Kelly Shoppach FY RC 1.25 .55
T179 Bubba Nelson FY RC .75 .35
T180 Mike O'Keefe FY RC .40 .18
T181 Hanley Ramirez FY RC 1.50 .70
T182 T.Wellemeyer FY RC .50 .23
T183 Dustin Moseley FY RC .50 .23
T184 Eric Crozier FY RC .50 .23
T185 Ryan Shealy FY RC .75 .35
T186 Jer. Bonderman FY RC 1.00 .45
T187 T.Story-Harden FY RC .40 .18
T188 Dusty Brown FY RC .50 .23
T189 Rob Hammock FY RC .50 .23
T190 Jorge Piedra FY RC .50 .23
T191 Chris De La Cruz FY RC .40 .18
T192 Eli Whiteside FY RC .40 .18
T193 Jason Kubel FY RC .50 .23
T194 Jon Schuerholz FY RC .40 .18
T195 St. Randolph FY RC .40 .18
T196 Andy Sisco FY RC 1.25 .55
T197 Sean Smith FY RC .50 .23
T198 Jon-Mark Sprowl FY RC .75 .35

T199 Matt Kata FY RC .75 .35
T200 Robinson Cano FY RC .50 .23
T201 Nook Logan FY RC .40 .18
T202 Ben Francisco FY RC .50 .23
T203 Arnie Munoz FY RC .40 .18
T204 Ozzie Chavez FY RC .40 .18
T205 Eric Riggs FY RC .50 .23
T206 Beau Kemp FY RC .40 .18
T207 Travis Wong FY RC .50 .23
T208 Dustin Yount FY RC .75 .35
T209 Brian McCann FY RC .75 .35
T210 Wilton Reynolds FY RC .50 .23
T211 Matt Bruback FY RC .40 .18
T212 Andrew Brown FY RC .40 .18
T213 Edgar Gonzalez FY RC .40 .18
T214 Eider Torres FY RC .40 .18
T215 Aquilino Lopez FY RC .40 .18
T216 Bobby Basham FY RC .75 .35
T217 Tim Olson FY RC .50 .23
T218 Nathan Panther FY RC .75 .35
T219 Bryan Grace FY RC .40 .18
T220 Dusty Gomon FY RC .75 .35
T221 Wil Ledezma FY RC .40 .18
T222 Josh Willingham FY RC 1.25 .55
T223 David Cash FY RC .40 .18
T224 Oscar Villarreal FY RC .40 .18
T225 Jeff Duncan FY RC .50 .23
T226 Kade Johnson FY RC .40 .18
T227 L.Steidlmayer FY RC .40 .18
T228 Brandon Watson FY RC .40 .18
T229 Jose Morales FY RC .40 .18
T230 Mike Gallo FY RC .40 .18
T231 Tyler Adamczyk FY RC .40 .18
T232 Adam Stern FY RC .40 .18
T233 Brennan King FY RC .40 .18
T234 Dan Haren FY RC 1.00 .45
T235 Mi. Hernandez FY RC .40 .18
T236 Ben Fritz FY RC .40 .18
T237 Clay Hensley FY RC .40 .18
T238 Tyler Johnson FY RC .40 .18
T239 Pete LaForest FY RC .50 .23
T240 Tyler Martin FY RC .40 .18
T241 J.D. Durbin FY RC .75 .35
T242 Shane Victorino FY RC .40 .18
T243 Rajai Davis FY RC .50 .23
T244 Ismael Castro FY RC .40 .18
T245 C.Wang FY RC 1.50 .70
T246 Travis Ishikawa FY RC .50 .23
T247 Corey Shafer FY RC .50 .23
T248 G.Schneidmiller FY RC .40 .18
T249 Dave Pember FY RC .40 .18
T250 Keith Stamler FY RC .40 .18
T251 Tyson Graham FY RC .40 .18
T252 Ryan Cameron FY RC .40 .18
T253 E.Eckenstahler FY RC .40 .18
T254 Ma. Peterson FY RC .40 .18
T255 D. McGowan FY RC 1.00 .45
T256 Pr. Redman FY RC .40 .18
T257 Haj Turay FY RC .50 .23
T258 Carlos Guzman FY RC .50 .23
T259 Matt DeMarco FY RC .40 .18
T260 Derek Michaelis FY RC .50 .23
T261 Brian Burgamy FY RC .40 .18
T262 Jay Sitzman FY RC .40 .18
T263 Chris Fallon FY RC .40 .18
T264 Mike Adams FY RC .40 .18
T265 Clint Barmes FY RC .50 .23
T266 Eric Reed FY RC .75 .35
T267 Willie Eyre FY RC .40 .18
T268 Carlos Duran FY RC .40 .18
T269 Nick Trzesniak FY RC .40 .18
T270 Ferdin Tejeda FY RC .40 .18
T271 Mi. Garciaparra FY RC 1.00 .45
T272 Michael Hinckley FY RC .75 .35
T273 Br. Florence FY RC .40 .18
T274 Trent Oeltjen FY RC .50 .23
T275 Mike Neu FY RC .40 .18

2003 Topps Traded Gold

MINT NRMT
*GOLD 1-120: 5X TO 12X BASIC
*GOLD 121-165: 2.5X TO 6X BASIC
*GOLD 166-275: 1.5X TO 4X BASIC
STATED ODDS 1:2 HOB/RET, 1:1 HTA
STATED PRINT RUN 2003 SERIAL #'d SETS

2003 Topps Traded Future Phenoms Relics

MINT NRMT
GROUP A ODDS 1:2330 HOB/RET, 1:669 HTA
GROUP B ODDS 1:505 HOB/RET, 1:144 HTA
GROUP C ODDS 1:101 HOB/RET, 1:29 HTA
BP Brandon Phillips Bat B 8.00 3.60
CC Chin-Feng Chen Jsy C 25.00 11.00
CDC Carl Crawford Bat C 8.00 3.60
CS Chris Snelling Bat C 8.00 3.60
HB Hank Blalock Bat C 10.00 4.50
JM Justin Morneau Bat C 8.00 3.60
JT Joe Thurston Jsy C 8.00 3.60
MB Marlon Byrd Bat C 8.00 3.60
MR Michael Restovich Bat B 8.00 3.60
MT Mark Teixeira Bat B 10.00 4.50
RB Rocco Baldelli Bat B 15.00 6.75
TAH Trey Hodges Jsy C 8.00 3.60
TH Travis Hafner Bat C 8.00 3.60
WB Wilson Betemit Bat C 8.00 3.60
WPB Willie Bloomquist Bat A 15.00 6.75

2003 Topps Traded Hall of Fame Relics

MINT NRMT
STATED ODDS 1:1009 HOB/RET, 1:289 HTA

EM Eddie Murray Bat 25.00 11.00
GC Gary Carter Uni 15.00 6.75

2003 Topps Traded Hall of Fame Dual Relic

MINT NRMT
STATED ODDS 1:2015 HOB/RET, 1:578 HTA
CM Gary Carter Uni 30.00 13.50
Eddie Murray Bat

2003 Topps Traded Signature Moves Autographs

MINT NRMT
GROUP A ODDS 1:280 HOB/RET, 1:80 HTA
GROUP B ODDS 1:114 HOB/RET, 1:33 HTA
BC Bartolo Colon A 15.00 6.75
BU B.J. Upton B 25.00 11.00
CF Cliff Floyd A 15.00 6.75
DB David Bell A 15.00 6.75
EA Erick Almonte B 10.00 4.50
ER Elizardo Ramirez B 15.00 6.75
FP Felix Pie B 40.00 18.00
IR Robert Fick A 15.00 6.75
JB Joe Borchard B 15.00 6.75
JC Jose Cruz Jr. A 15.00 6.75
JF Jesse Foppert B 15.00 6.75
JG Joey Gomes B 10.00 4.50
JJC Jack Cust A 10.00 4.50
JL James Loney B 25.00 11.00
JR Jose Reyes B 25.00 11.00
JS Jason Stokes A 25.00 11.00
KG Khalil Greene A 25.00 11.00
MT Mark Teixeira A 25.00 11.00
VM Victor Martinez B 15.00 6.75
WY Walter Young B 10.00 4.50

2003 Topps Traded Team Topps Blue Chips Autographs

MINT NRMT
STATED ODDS 1:631
SEE 03 TEAM TOPPS BLUE CHIP FOR PRICES

2003 Topps Traded Transactions Bat Relics

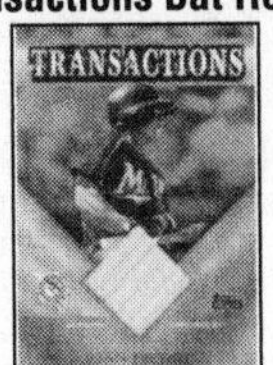

MINT NRMT
GROUP A ODDS 1:168 HOB/RET, 1:48 HTA
GROUP B ODDS 1:78 HOB/RET, 1:22 HTA
AG Andres Galarraga A 8.00 3.60
CF Cliff Floyd B 8.00 3.60
DB David Bell B 8.00 3.60
EA Edgardo Alfonzo B 8.00 3.60
ED Erubiel Durazo B 8.00 3.60
EK Eric Karros B 10.00 4.50
FL Felipe Lopez A 8.00 3.60
FM Fred McGriff B 10.00 4.50
JC Jose Cruz Jr. B 8.00 3.60
JG Jeremy Giambi A 8.00 3.60
JK Jeff Kent B 8.00 3.60
JP Juan Pierre B 8.00 3.60
JT Jim Thome A 10.00 4.50
KL Kenny Lofton A 15.00 6.75
KM Kevin Millar B 15.00 6.75
PW Preston Wilson A 8.00 3.60
RD Ray Durham A 8.00 3.60
RF Robert Fick A 8.00 3.60
RO Rey Ordonez B 8.00 3.60
RS Ruben Sierra A 8.00 3.60
RW Rondell White B 8.00 3.60
SH Tsuyoshi Shinjo B 8.00 3.60
SS Shane Spencer A 8.00 3.60
TG Tom Glavine A 10.00 4.50
TZ Todd Zeile A 8.00 3.60

2003 Topps Traded Transactions Dual Relics

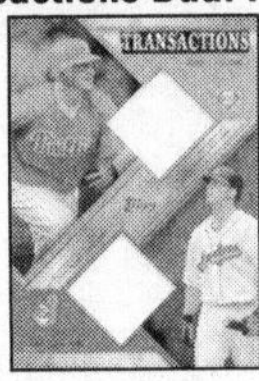

MINT NRMT
STATED ODDS 1:421 HOB/RET, 1:120 HTA
IR Ivan Rodriguez Marlins-Rgr.. 20.00 9.00
JT Jim Thome Phils-Indians 20.00 9.00
KM Kevin Millwood Phils-Braves 15.00 6.75

2004 Topps

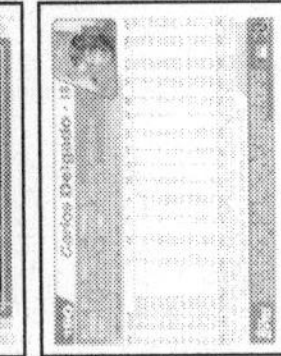

This 366-card standard-size first series was released in November, 2003. The cards were issued in 10-card hobby or retail packs with an $1.59 SRP which came 36 packs to a box and 12 boxes to a case. In addition, these cards were also issued in 35-card HTA packs with an $5 SRP which came 12 packs to a box and 8 boxes to a case. Please note that insert cards were issued in different rates in retail packs as they were in hobby packs. In addition, to continuing honoring the memory of Mickey Mantle, there was no card number 7 issued in this set. Both cards numbered 267 and 274 are numbered as 267 and thus no card number 274 exists. Please note the following subsets were issued: Managers (268-296); First Year Cards (297-326); Future Stars (327-331); Highlights (332-336); League Leaders (337-348); Post-Season Play (349-355); American League All-Stars (356-367).

MINT NRMT
COMPLETE SERIES 1 (366) 35.00 16.00
COMMON CARD (1-6/8-366) .20 .09
COMMON CARD (297-326) .50 .23
COMMON CARD (327-331) .50 .23
1 Jim Thome .50 .23
2 Reggie Sanders .20 .09
3 Mark Kotsay .20 .09
4 Edgardo Alfonzo .20 .09
5 Ben Davis .20 .09
6 Mike Matheny .20 .09
8 Marlon Anderson .20 .09
9 Chan Ho Park .20 .09
10 Ichiro Suzuki .75 .35
11 Kevin Millwood .20 .09
12 Bengie Molina .20 .09
13 Tom Glavine .30 .14
14 Junior Spivey .20 .09
15 Marcus Giles .20 .09
16 David Segui .20 .09
17 Kevin Millar .20 .09
18 Corey Patterson .20 .09
19 Aaron Rowand .20 .09
20 Derek Jeter 1.25 .55
21 Jason LaRue .20 .09
22 Chris Hammond .20 .09
23 Jay Payton .20 .09
24 Bobby Higginson .20 .09
25 Lance Berkman .20 .09
26 Juan Pierre .20 .09
27 Brent Mayne .20 .09
28 Fred McGriff .30 .14
29 Richie Sexson .20 .09
30 Tim Hudson .20 .09
31 Mike Piazza .75 .35
32 Brad Radke .20 .09
33 Jeff Weaver .20 .09
34 Ramon Hernandez .20 .09
35 David Bell .20 .09
36 Craig Wilson .20 .09
37 Jake Peavy .20 .09
38 Tim Worrell .20 .09
39 Gil Meche .20 .09
40 Albert Pujols 1.00 .45
41 Michael Young .20 .09
42 Josh Phelps .20 .09
43 Brendan Donnelly .20 .09
44 Steve Finley .20 .09
45 John Smoltz .30 .14
46 Jay Gibbons .20 .09
47 Trot Nixon .30 .14
48 Carl Pavano .20 .09
49 Frank Thomas .50 .23
50 Mark Prior 1.00 .45
51 Danny Graves .20 .09
52 Milton Bradley UER .20 .09
53 Jose Jimenez .20 .09
54 Shane Halter .20 .09
55 Mike Lowell .20 .09
56 Geoff Blum .20 .09
57 Michael Tucker UER .20 .09
Dee Brown pictured
58 Paul Lo Duca .20 .09
59 Vicente Padilla .20 .09
60 Jacque Jones .20 .09
61 Fernando Tatis .20 .09
62 Ty Wigginton .20 .09
63 Pedro Astacio .20 .09
64 Andy Pettitte .30 .14
65 Terrence Long .20 .09
66 Cliff Floyd .20 .09
67 Mariano Rivera .30 .14
68 Carlos Silva .20 .09
69 Marlon Byrd .20 .09
70 Mark Mulder .20 .09
71 Kerry Ligtenberg .20 .09
72 Carlos Guillen .20 .09
73 Fernando Vina .20 .09
74 Lance Carter .20 .09
75 Hank Blalock .20 .09
76 Jimmy Rollins .20 .09
77 Francisco Rodriguez .20 .09
78 Javy Lopez .20 .09
79 Jerry Hairston Jr. .20 .09
80 Andruw Jones .20 .09
81 Rodrigo Lopez .20 .09
82 Johnny Damon .20 .09
83 Hee Seop Choi .20 .09
84 Miguel Olivo .20 .09
85 Jon Garland .20 .09
86 Matt Lawton .20 .09
87 Juan Uribe .20 .09
88 Steve Sparks .20 .09
89 Tim Spooneybarger .20 .09
90 Jose Vidro .20 .09
91 Luis Rivas .20 .09
92 Hideo Nomo .50 .23
93 Javier Vazquez .20 .09
94 Al Leiter .20 .09
95 Darren Dreifort .20 .09
96 Alex Cintron .20 .09
97 Zach Day .20 .09
98 Jorge Posada .30 .14
99 John Halama .20 .09
100 Alex Rodriguez .75 .35
101 Orlando Palmeiro .20 .09
102 Dave Berg .20 .09
103 Brad Fullmer .20 .09
104 Mike Hampton .20 .09
105 Willis Roberts .20 .09
106 Ramiro Mendoza .20 .09
107 Juan Cruz .20 .09
108 Esteban Loaiza .20 .09
109 Russell Branyan .20 .09
110 Todd Helton .30 .14
111 Braden Looper .20 .09
112 Octavio Dotel .20 .09
113 Mike MacDougal .20 .09
114 Cesar Izturis .20 .09
115 Johan Santana .20 .09
116 Jose Contreras .20 .09
117 Placido Polanco .20 .09
118 Jason Phillips .20 .09
119 Adam Eaton .20 .09
120 Vernon Wells .20 .09
121 Ben Grieve .20 .09
122 Randy Winn .20 .09
123 Ismael Valdes .20 .09
124 Eric Owens .20 .09
125 Curt Schilling .30 .14
126 Russ Ortiz .20 .09
127 Mark Buehrle .20 .09
128 Danys Baez .20 .09
129 Dmitri Young .20 .09
130 Kazuhisa Ishii .20 .09
131 A.J. Pierzynski .20 .09
132 Michael Barrett .20 .09
133 Joe McEwing .20 .09
134 Alex Cora .20 .09
135 Tom Wilson .20 .09
136 Carlos Zambrano .20 .09
137 Brett Tomko .20 .09
138 Shigetoshi Hasegawa .20 .09
139 Jarrod Washburn .20 .09
140 Greg Maddux .75 .35
141 Craig Counsell .20 .09
142 Reggie Taylor .20 .09
143 Omar Vizquel .20 .09
144 Alex Gonzalez .20 .09
145 Billy Wagner .20 .09
146 Brian Jordan .20 .09
147 Wes Helms .20 .09
148 Kyle Lohse .20 .09
149 Timo Perez .20 .09
150 Jason Giambi .50 .23
151 Erubiel Durazo .20 .09
152 Mike Lieberthal .20 .09
153 Jason Kendall .20 .09
154 Xavier Nady .20 .09
155 Kirk Rueter .20 .09
156 Mike Cameron .20 .09
157 Miguel Cairo .20 .09
158 Woody Williams .20 .09
159 Toby Hall .20 .09
160 Bernie Williams .30 .14
161 Darin Erstad .20 .09
162 Matt Mantei .20 .09
163 Geronimo Gil .20 .09
164 Bill Mueller .20 .09
165 Damian Miller .20 .09
166 Tony Graffanino .20 .09
167 Sean Casey .20 .09
168 Brandon Phillips .20 .09
169 Mike Remlinger .20 .09
170 Adam Dunn .20 .09
171 Carlos Lee .20 .09
172 Juan Encarnacion .20 .09
173 Angel Berroa .20 .09
174 Desi Relaford .20 .09
175 Paul Quantrill .20 .09
176 Ben Sheets .20 .09
177 Eddie Guardado .20 .09
178 Rocky Biddle .20 .09
179 Mike Stanton .20 .09
180 Eric Chavez .20 .09
181 Jason Michaels .20 .09
182 Terry Adams .20 .09
183 Kip Wells .20 .09
184 Brian Lawrence .20 .09
185 Bret Boone .20 .09
186 Tino Martinez .30 .14
187 Aubrey Huff .20 .09
188 Kevin Mench .20 .09
189 Tim Salmon .30 .14
190 Carlos Delgado .20 .09
191 John Lackey .20 .09
192 Oscar Villarreal .20 .09
193 Luis Matos .20 .09
194 Derek Lowe .20 .09
195 Mark Grudzielanek .20 .09
196 Tom Gordon .20 .09
197 Matt Clement .20 .09
198 Byung-Hyun Kim .20 .09
199 Brandon Inge .20 .09
200 Nomar Garciaparra .75 .35
201 Antonio Osuna .20 .09
202 Jose Mesa .20 .09
203 Bo Hart .20 .09
204 Jack Wilson .20 .09
205 Ray Durham .20 .09
206 Freddy Garcia .20 .09
207 J.D. Drew .20 .09
208 Einar Diaz .20 .09
209 Roy Halladay .20 .09
210 David Eckstein UER .20 .09
Adam Kennedy pictured
211 Jason Marquis .20 .09
212 Jorge Julio .20 .09
213 Tim Wakefield .20 .09
214 Moises Alou .20 .09
215 Bartolo Colon .20 .09
216 Jimmy Haynes .20 .09
217 Preston Wilson .20 .09
218 Luis Castillo .20 .09
219 Richard Hidalgo .20 .09
220 Manny Ramirez .20 .09
221 Mike Mussina .50 .23
222 Randy Wolf .20 .09
223 Kris Benson .20 .09
224 Ryan Klesko .20 .09
225 Rich Aurilia .20 .09
226 Kelvim Escobar .20 .09
227 Francisco Cordero .20 .09
228 Kazuhiro Sasaki .20 .09
229 Danny Bautista .20 .09
230 Rafael Furcal .20 .09
231 Travis Driskill .20 .09
232 Kyle Farnsworth .20 .09
233 Jose Valentin .20 .09
234 Felipe Lopez .20 .09
235 C.C. Sabathia .20 .09
236 Brad Penny .20 .09
237 Brad Ausmus .20 .09
238 Raul Ibanez .20 .09
239 Adrian Beltre .20 .09
240 Rocco Baldelli .50 .23
241 Orlando Hudson .20 .09
242 Dave Roberts .20 .09
243 Doug Mientkiewicz .20 .09
244 Brad Wilkerson .20 .09
245 Scott Strickland .20 .09
246 Ryan Franklin .20 .09
247 Chad Bradford .20 .09
248 Gary Bennett .20 .09
249 Jose Cruz Jr. .20 .09
250 Jeff Kent .20 .09
251 Josh Beckett .30 .14
252 Ramon Ortiz .20 .09
253 Miguel Batista .20 .09
254 Jung Bong .20 .09
255 Deivi Cruz .20 .09
256 Alex Gonzalez .20 .09
257 Shawn Chacon .20 .09
258 Runelvys Hernandez .20 .09
259 Joe Mays .20 .09
260 Eric Gagne .30 .14
261 Dustan Mohr .20 .09
262 Tomokazu Ohka .20 .09
263 Eric Byrnes .20 .09
264 Frank Catalanotto .20 .09
265 Cristian Guzman .20 .09
266 Orlando Cabrera .20 .09
267A Juan Castro .20 .09
267B M.Scioscia MG UER 274 .20 .09
268 Bob Brenly MG .20 .09
269 Bobby Cox MG .20 .09
270 Mike Hargrove MG .20 .09
271 Grady Little MG .20 .09
272 Dusty Baker MG .20 .09
273 Jerry Manuel MG .20 .09
275 Eric Wedge MG .20 .09
276 Clint Hurdle MG .20 .09
277 Alan Trammell MG .30 .14
278 Jack McKeon MG .20 .09
279 Jimy Williams MG .20 .09
280 Tony Pena MG .20 .09
281 Jim Tracy MG .20 .09
282 Ned Yost MG .20 .09
283 Ron Gardenhire MG .20 .09
284 Frank Robinson MG .30 .14
285 Art Howe MG .20 .09
286 Joe Torre MG .30 .14
287 Ken Macha MG .20 .09
288 Larry Bowa MG .20 .09
289 Lloyd McClendon MG .20 .09
290 Bruce Bochy MG .20 .09
291 Felipe Alou MG .20 .09
292 Bob Melvin MG .20 .09
293 Tony LaRussa MG .20 .09
294 Lou Piniella MG .20 .09
295 Buck Showalter MG .20 .09
296 Carlos Tosca MG .20 .09
297 Anthony Acevedo FY RC 1.25 .55
298 Anthony Lerew FY RC .50 .23
299 Blake Hawksworth FY RC .75 .35
300 Brayan Pena FY RC .50 .23
301 Casey Myers FY RC .50 .23
302 Craig Ansman FY RC .50 .23
303 David Murphy FY RC 1.50 .70
304 Dave Crouthers FY RC .50 .23
305 Dioner Navarro FY RC 1.50 .70
306 Donald Levinski FY RC .50 .23
307 Jesse Roman FY RC .50 .23
308 Sung Jung FY RC 1.25 .55
309 Jon Knott FY RC .50 .23
310 Josh Labandeira FY RC .50 .23
311 Kenny Perez FY RC .50 .23
312 Khalid Ballouli FY RC .50 .23
313 Kyle Davies FY RC .75 .35
314 Marcus McBeth FY RC .50 .23
315 Matt Creighton FY RC .75 .35
316 Chris O'Riordan FY RC .50 .23
317 Mike Gosling FY RC .50 .23

318 Nic Ungs FY RC .50 .23
319 Omar Falcon FY RC .50 .23
320 Rodney Choy Foo FY RC .50 .23
321 Tim Frend FY RC 2.00 .90
322 Todd Self FY RC .50 .23
323 Tydus Meadows FY RC .50 .23
324 Yadier Molina FY RC .50 .23
325 Zach Duke FY RC .50 .23
326 Zach Miner FY RC .50 .23
327 Bernie Castro .50 .23
Khalil Greene FS
328 Ryan Madson .50 .23
Elizardo Ramirez FS
329 Rich Harden .50 .23
Bobby Crosby FS
330 Zack Greinke .50 .23
Jimmy Gobble FS
331 Bobby Jenks .50 .23
Casey Kotchman FS
332 Sammy Sosa HL .50 .23
333 Kevin Millwood HL .20 .09
334 Rafael Palmeiro HL .20 .09
335 Roger Clemens HL .50 .23
336 Eric Gagne HL .20 .09
337 Bill Mueller .50 .23
Manny Ramirez
Derek Jeter
AL Batting Avg LL
338 Vernon Wells .50 .23
Ichiro Suzuki
Michael Young
AL Hits LL
339 Alex Rodriguez .50 .23
Frank Thomas
Carlos Delgado
AL Home Runs LL
340 Carlos Delgado .50 .23
Alex Rodriguez
Bret Boone
AL RBI's LL
341 Pedro Martinez .30 .14
Tim Hudson
Esteban Loaiza
AL ERA LL
342 Esteban Loaiza .30 .14
Pedro Martinez
Roy Halladay
AL Strikeouts LL
343 Albert Pujols .50 .23
Todd Helton
Edgar Renteria
NL Batting Avg LL
344 Albert Pujols .50 .23
Todd Helton
Juan Pierre
NL Hits LL
345 Jim Thome .30 .14
Richie Sexson
Javy Lopez
NL Home Runs LL
346 Preston Wilson .30 .14
Gary Sheffield
Jim Thome
NL RBI's LL
347 Jason Schmidt .50 .23
Kevin Brown
Mark Prior
NL ERA LL
348 Kerry Wood .50 .23
Mark Prior
Javier Vazquez
NL Strikeouts LL
349 Roger Clemens .50 .23
David Wells ALDS
350 Kerry Wood .50 .23
Mark Prior NLDS
351 Josh Beckett .50 .23
Miguel Cabrera
Ivan Rodriguez NLCS
352 Jason Giambi .50 .23
Mariano Rivera
Aaron Boone ALCS
353 Derek Lowe .50 .23
Ivan Rodriguez AL/NLDS
354 Pedro Martinez .50 .23
Jorge Posada
Roger Clemens ALCS
355 Juan Pierre WS .20 .09
356 Carlos Delgado AS .20 .09
357 Bret Boone AS .20 .09
358 Alex Rodriguez AS .50 .23
359 Bill Mueller AS .20 .09
360 Vernon Wells AS .20 .09
361 Garret Anderson AS .20 .09
362 Magglio Ordonez AS .20 .09
363 Jorge Posada AS .20 .09
364 Roy Halladay AS .20 .09
365 Andy Pettitte AS .20 .09
366 Frank Thomas AS .30 .14
367 Jody Gerut AS .20 .09

2004 Topps Black

MINT NRMT
*BLACK 1-296: 20X TO 50X BASIC
*BLACK 297-326: 10X TO 25X BASIC
*BLACK 327-331: 12.5X TO 30X BASIC
SERIES 1 ODDS 1:13 HTA
STATED PRINT RUN 53 SERIAL #'d SETS
CARDS 7 AND 274 DO NOT EXIST
SCIOSCIA AND J.CASTRO NUMBERED 267

2004 Topps Box Bottoms

The player list in our checklist has the player's name as well as what sheet his card is located on. Sheets 1-4 were issued on the bottom of first series HTA boxes and sheets 5-8 on second series.

MINT NRMT
*BOX BOTTOM CARDS: 1X TO 2.5X BASIC
ONE 4-CARD SHEET PER HTA BOX
1 Jim Thome 3 1.25 .55
25 Lance Berkman 3 .50 .23
31 Mike Piazza 1 2.00 .90
40 Albert Pujols 3 2.50 1.10
50 Mark Prior 4 2.50 1.10
75 Hank Blalock 4 .50 .23
80 Andruw Jones 1 .50 .23
100 Alex Rodriguez 1 2.00 .90
110 Todd Helton 2 .75 .35

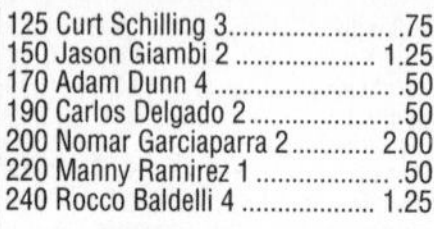

125 Curt Schilling 3 .75 .35
150 Jason Giambi 2 1.25 .55
170 Adam Dunn 4 .50 .23
190 Carlos Delgado 2 .50 .23
200 Nomar Garciaparra 2 2.00 .90
220 Manny Ramirez 1 .50 .23
240 Rocco Baldelli 4 1.25 .55

2004 Topps Gold

MINT NRMT
*GOLD 1-296: 6X TO 15X BASIC
*GOLD 297-326: 3X TO 8X BASIC
*GOLD 327-331: 3X TO 8X BASIC
SERIES 1 ODDS 1:11 HOB, 1:3 HTA, 1:10 RET
STATED PRINT RUN 2004 SERIAL #'d SETS
CARDS 7 AND 274 DO NOT EXIST
SCIOSCIA AND J.CASTRO NUMBERED 267

2004 Topps 1st Edition

MINT NRMT
*1ST ED 1-296: 1.25X TO 3X BASIC
*1ST ED 297-RC'S: X TO X BASIC
*1ST ED 327-331: 1.25X TO 3X BASIC
DISTRIBUTED IN 1ST EDITION BOXES
CARDS 7 AND 274 DO NOT EXIST
SCIOSCIA AND J.CASTRO NUMBERED 267

2004 Topps All-Star Stitches Jersey Relics

MINT NRMT
SERIES 1 ODDS 1:137 HOB/RET, 1:39 HTA
AB Aaron Boone 10.00 4.50
AJ Andruw Jones 10.00 4.50
AR Alex Rodriguez 15.00 6.75
BD Brendan Donnelly 10.00 4.50
BW Billy Wagner 10.00 4.50
CE Carl Everett 10.00 4.50
EG Eddie Guardado 10.00 4.50
EGA Eric Gagne 10.00 4.50
EL Esteban Loaiza 10.00 4.50
EM Edgar Martinez 10.00 4.50
ER Edgar Renteria 10.00 4.50
HB Hank Blalock 10.00 4.50
JL Javy Lopez 10.00 4.50
JM Jamie Moyer 10.00 4.50
JP Jorge Posada 10.00 4.50
JS Jason Schmidt 10.00 4.50
JV Jose Vidro 10.00 4.50
KF Keith Foulke 10.00 4.50
KW Kerry Wood 10.00 4.50
ML Mike Lowell 10.00 4.50
MM Mark Mulder 10.00 4.50
MMO Melvin Mora 10.00 4.50
NG Nomar Garciaparra 15.00 6.75
PL Paul Lo Duca 10.00 4.50
PW Preston Wilson 10.00 4.50
RF Rafael Furcal 10.00 4.50
RH Ramon Hernandez 10.00 4.50
RO Russ Ortiz 10.00 4.50
RW Randy Wolf 10.00 4.50
RWH Rondell White 10.00 4.50
SH Shigetoshi Hasegawa 10.00 4.50
SR Scott Rolen 10.00 4.50
TG Troy Glaus 10.00 4.50
TH Todd Helton 10.00 4.50
VW Vernon Wells 10.00 4.50
WW Woody Williams 10.00 4.50

2004 Topps American Treasures Presidential Signatures

Randomly inserted into packs, this set features a "cut" signature from each of the United State Presidents. Each of these cards feature the cut signature against a United States flag background while the back features an informational blurb about that president.

MINT NRMT
SER.1 ODDS 1:175,770 HOBBY, 1:52,080 HTA
SER.1 ODDS 1:138,240 RETAIL
STATED PRINT RUN 1 SERIAL #'d SET
NO PRICING DUE TO SCARCITY
AJ Andrew Jackson
AJO Andrew Johnson
AL Abraham Lincoln
BC Bill Clinton
BH Benjamin Harrison
CA Chester A. Arthur
CC Calvin Coolidge
DE Dwight D. Eisenhower
FP Franklin Pierce
FR Franklin D. Roosevelt
GB George W. Bush
GC Grover Cleveland
GF Gerald Ford
GHB George H.W. Bush
GW George Washington
HH Herbert Hoover
HT Harry S. Truman
JA John Adams
JB James Buchanan
JC Jimmy Carter
JG James Garfield
JK John F. Kennedy
JM James Madison
JMO James Monroe
JP James K. Polk
JQA John Quincy Adams
JT John Tyler
LJ Lyndon B. Johnson
MF Millard Fillmore
MV Martin Van Buren
RH Rutherford B. Hayes
RN Richard Nixon
RR Ronald Reagan
TJ Thomas Jefferson
TR Theodore Roosevelt
UG Ulysses S. Grant
WH Warren Harding
WHH William H. Harrison
WM William McKinley
WT William Howard Taft
WW Woodrow Wilson
ZT Zachary Taylor

2004 Topps American Treasures Presidential Signatures Dual

This card is similar to the basic American Treasures Presidential Cut Signatures but feature two signatures from George H. Bush and his son George W. Bush. Only one copy of the card was produced and it was seeded exclusively into first series Home Team Advantage packs. Pricing is unavailable due to scarcity.

Nm-Mt Ex-Mt
SERIES 1 ODDS 1:208,320 HTA
STATED PRINT RUN 1 SERIAL #'d CARD
NO PRICING DUE TO SCARCITY
GB2 George H.W. Bush
George W. Bush

2004 Topps Autographs

Please note Josh Beckett, Mike Lowell and Mark Prior did not return their cards in time for inclusion in first series packs and the exchange date for these cards was November 30th, 2005. Cards issued in first series packs carry a "1" and cards from series 2 carry a "2" after their group seeding notes within our checklist.

MINT NRMT
SER.1 B 1:7362 H, 1:1911 HTA, 1:7472 R
SER.1 C 1:10,900 H, 1:2741 HTA, 1:11,059 R
SER.1 D 1:1053 H, 1:273 HTA, 1:1055 R
SER.1 E 1:6278 H, 1:1640 HTA, 1:6284 R
SER.1 F 1:1229 H, 1:318 HTA, 1:1229 R
SER.1 G 1:2340 H, 1:668 HTA, 1:1881 R
SER.1 H 1:1167 H, 1:351 HTA, 1:1229 R
AK Austin Kearns B1 15.00 6.75
BS Benito Santiago D1 30.00 13.50
BU B.J. Upton F1 15.00 6.75
CF Cliff Floyd D1 15.00 6.75
EH Eric Hinske H1 8.00 3.60
ER Elizardo Ramirez H1 10.00 4.50
HB Hank Blalock D1 25.00 11.00
JB Josh Beckett B1 EXCH 40.00 18.00
JG Jay Gibbons A1 15.00 6.75
JP1 Josh Phelps G1 8.00 3.60
JV Jose Vidro F1 10.00 4.50
KG Khalil Greene H1 15.00 6.75
ML Mike Lowell F1 EXCH 10.00 4.50
MO Magglio Ordonez F1 25.00 11.00
MP Mark Prior D1 EXCH 120.00 55.00
MS Mike Sweeney D1 15.00 6.75
MT Mark Teixeira D1 15.00 6.75
PK Paul Konerko G1 10.00 4.50
PL Paul Lo Duca E1 15.00 6.75
TH Torii Hunter C1 15.00 6.75
VM Victor Martinez D1 15.00 6.75

2004 Topps Derby Digs Jersey Relics

MINT NRMT
SERIES 1 ODDS 1:585 H, 1:167 HTA, 1:586 R
AP Albert Pujols 25.00 11.00
BB Bret Boone 10.00 4.50
CD Carlos Delgado 10.00 4.50
GA Garret Anderson 10.00 4.50
JE Jim Edmonds 10.00 4.50
JG Jason Giambi 15.00 6.75
RS Richie Sexson 10.00 4.50

2004 Topps Fall Classic Program Covers

MINT NRMT
COMPLETE SERIES 1 (48) 120.00 55.00
COMMON CARD 4.00 1.80
SERIES 1 ODDS 1:12 HOB/RET, 1:4 HTA
EVEN YEARS DISTRIBUTED IN SERIES 1

2004 Topps Hobby Masters

MINT NRMT
COMPLETE SET (20) 40.00 18.00
SERIES 1 ODDS 1:12 HOBBY, 1:4 HTA
1 Albert Pujols 4.00 1.80
2 Mark Prior 4.00 1.80
3 Alex Rodriguez 3.00 1.35
4 Nomar Garciaparra 3.00 1.35
5 Barry Bonds 5.00 2.20
6 Sammy Sosa 3.00 1.35
7 Alfonso Soriano 2.00 .90
8 Ichiro Suzuki 3.00 1.35
9 Derek Jeter 5.00 2.20
10 Jim Thome 2.00 .90
11 Jason Giambi 2.00 .90
12 Mike Piazza 3.00 1.35
13 Barry Zito 2.00 .90
14 Randy Johnson 2.00 .90
15 Adam Dunn 2.00 .90
16 Vladimir Guerrero 2.00 .90
17 Gary Sheffield 2.00 .90
18 Carlos Delgado 2.00 .90
19 Chipper Jones 2.00 .90
20 Dontrelle Willis 2.00 .90

2004 Topps Own the Game

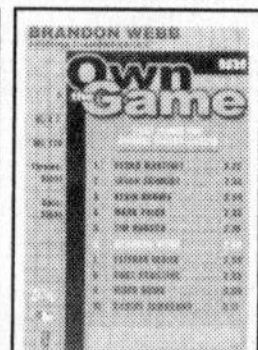

MINT NRMT
COMPLETE SET (30) 60.00 27.00
SERIES 1 ODDS 1:18 HOB/RET, 1:6 HTA
1 Jim Thome 2.00 .90
2 Albert Pujols 4.00 1.80
3 Alex Rodriguez 3.00 1.35
4 Barry Bonds 5.00 2.20
5 Ichiro Suzuki 3.00 1.35
6 Derek Jeter 5.00 2.20
7 Nomar Garciaparra 3.00 1.35
8 Alfonso Soriano 2.00 .90
9 Gary Sheffield 2.00 .90
10 Jason Giambi 2.00 .90
11 Todd Helton 2.00 .90
12 Garret Anderson 2.00 .90
13 Carlos Delgado 2.00 .90
14 Manny Ramirez 2.00 .90
15 Richie Sexson 2.00 .90
16 Vernon Wells 2.00 .90
17 Preston Wilson 2.00 .90
18 Frank Thomas 2.00 .90
19 Shawn Green 2.00 .90
20 Rafael Furcal 2.00 .90
21 Juan Pierre 2.00 .90
22 Javy Lopez 2.00 .90
23 Edgar Renteria 2.00 .90
24 Mark Prior 4.00 1.80
25 Pedro Martinez 2.00 .90
26 Kerry Wood 2.00 .90
27 Curt Schilling 2.00 .90
28 Roy Halladay 2.00 .90
29 Eric Gagne 2.00 .90
30 Brandon Webb 2.00 .90

2004 Topps Team Topps Legends Autographs

MINT NRMT
ISSUED IN VARIOUS 03-04 TOPPS BRANDS
SER.1 ODDS 1:1399 H, 1:421 HTA, 1:1494 R
01 APARICIO/CARTER AU'S DIST.IN 04 PACKS
SEE 01 TOPPS FOR APARICIO/CARTER PRICES
AD Andre Dawson
BC Bert Campaneris
BP Boog Powell 15.00 6.75
CE Carl Erskine
DE Dwight Evans 25.00 11.00
DJ Davey Johnson 10.00 4.50
JP Johnny Podres
JP Jim Piersall
JR Joe Rudi 15.00 6.75
LD Lenny Dykstra
NR Nolan Ryan
SA Sparky Anderson 15.00 6.75
SG Steve Garvey 15.00 6.75
WM Willie Mays

2004 Topps World Series Highlights

MINT NRMT
COMPLETE SET (30) 30.00 13.50
SERIES 1 ODDS 1:18 HOB/RET, 1:6 HTA
BM Bill Mazeroski 1 2.50 1.10
BR Brooks Robinson 1 2.50 1.10
CF Carlton Fisk 1 2.50 1.10
CY Carl Yastrzemski 1 4.00 1.80
DL Don Larsen 1 2.50 1.10
JP1 Jim Palmer 1 2.50 1.10
KG Kirk Gibson 1 2.50 1.10
KP Kirby Puckett 1 2.50 1.10
LB Lou Brock 1 2.50 1.10
MS Mike Schmidt 1 5.00 2.20
RJ Reggie Jackson 1 2.50 1.10
RY Robin Yount 1 4.00 1.80
SM Stan Musial 1 4.00 1.80
TS Tom Seaver 1 2.50 1.10
WM1 Willie Mays 1 5.00 2.20

2004 Topps World Series Highlights Autographs

MINT NRMT
BM Bill Mazeroski 1 40.00 18.00
BR Brooks Robinson 1 40.00 18.00
CF Carlton Fisk 1 80.00 36.00
DL Don Larsen 1 25.00 11.00
HK Harmon Killebrew 1 40.00 18.00
JP1 Jim Palmer 1 25.00 11.00
KG Kirk Gibson 1 40.00 18.00
LB Lou Brock 1 40.00 18.00
MS Mike Schmidt 1 60.00 27.00
RY Robin Yount 1 50.00 22.00

1952 Topps Advertising Panels

These three card strips feature a regular 1952 Topps card and ad information on the back. These cards are not numbered in the traditional sense. Any additions to this list or any Advertising Panel list is obviously very appreciated

NM Ex
COMPLETE SET 200.00 100.00
1 Bob Mahoney 100.00 50.00
Robin Roberts
Sid Hudson
2 Bob Wellman 50.00 25.00
Lou Kretlow
Ray Scarborough
3 Wally Westlake 50.00 25.00
Dizzy Trout
Irv Noren
4 Eddie Joost 50.00 25.00
Willie Jones
Gordon Goldsberry

1953 Topps Advertising Panels

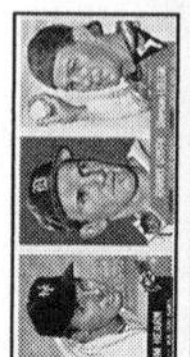

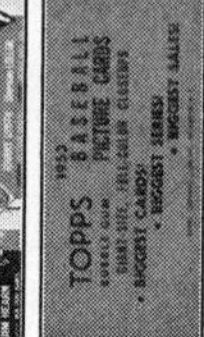

These three card strips feature a regular 53 Topps card on the front and advertising information on the back.

NM Ex
COMPLETE SET 600.00 300.00
1 Johnny Mize 100.00 50.00
Clem Kosorek
Toby Atwell
2 Jim Hearn 50.00 25.00
Johnny Groth
Sherm Lollar
3 Mickey Mantle 500.00 250.00
Johnny Wyrostek
Sal Yvars

1955 Topps Advertising Panels

These panels feature regular 1955 Topps cards on the front and advertising information on the back.

NM Ex
COMPLETE SET 300.00 150.00
1 Danny Schell 50.00 25.00
Jake Thies
Howie Pollet
2 Jackie Robinson 250.00 125.00
Bill Taylor
Curt Roberts

1956 Topps Advertising Panels

These panels feature regular 1956 Topps cards on the front and advertising information on the back.

NM Ex
COMPLETE SET 50.00 25.00
1 Johnny O'Brien...................... 50.00 25.00
Harvey Haddix
Frank House

1957 Topps Advertising Panels

Issued in three card strips to promote the upcoming 1957 Topps set, these three card panels are somewhat different in that the backs of these cards were composites of other cards as well as an advertisment for Topps/Bazooka bubble gum.

NM Ex
COMPLETE SET 200.00 100.00
1 Dick Williams 60.00 30.00
Brooks Lawrence
Lou Skizas
2 Jim Piersall 150.00 75.00
Pee Wee Reese
Harvey Kuenn

1959 Topps Advertising Panels

The fronts of these cards feature standard 1959 Topps cards while the backs feature cards of either Nellie Fox or Ted Kluszewski.

NM Ex
COMPLETE SET 800.00 400.00
1 Don McMahon....................... 50.00 25.00
Red Wilson
Bob Boyd
2 Joe Pignatano 50.00 25.00
Sam Jones
Jack Urban
3 Billy Hunter 50.00 25.00
Chuck Stobbs
Carl Sawatski
4 Vito Valentinelli 50.00 25.00
Ken Lehman
Ed Bouchee
5 Mel Roach 100.00 50.00
Brooks Lawrence
Warren Spahn
6 Harvey Kuenn 50.00 25.00
Alex Grammas
Bob Cerv
7 Bob Cerv 500.00 250.00
Jim Bolger
Mickey Mantle

1960 Topps Advertising Panels

These panels were issued to promote the upcoming Topps set. The fronts feature standard 1960 Topps cards while the backs feature advertising information.

NM Ex
COMPLETE SET 400.00 160.00
1 Wayne Terwillger.................... 50.00 20.00
Kent Hadley
Faye Throneberry
2 Hank Foiles 50.00 20.00
Hobie Landrith
Hal Smith
3 Cal McLish 300.00 120.00
Hal Smith
Ernie Banks
Jim Grant
Al Kaline
Jerry Casale
Milt Pappas
Wally Moon

1961 Topps Advertising Panels

Used to promote the upcoming Topps sets; these fronts show standard 1961 Topps cards on the front with advertising information on the back.

NM Ex
COMPLETE SET 200.00 80.00
1 Dan Dobbek........................... 50.00 20.00
Russ Nixon
1960 NL Pitching Leaders
2 Jack Kralick 50.00 20.00
Dick Stigman
Joe Christopher
3 Ed Roebuck 50.00 20.00
Bob Schmidt
Zoilo Versalles
4 Lindy Shows Larry 50.00 20.00
Johnny Blanchard
Johnny Kucks

1962 Topps Advertising Panels

These panels feature standard 1962 Topps cards on the front as well as a Roger Maris card back.

NM Ex
COMPLETE SET 100.00 40.00
1 AL Home Run Leaders 50.00 20.00
Barney Schultz
Carl Sawatski
2 NL Strikeout Leaders............. 50.00 20.00
Carroll Hardy
Carl Sawatski

1963 Topps Advertising Panels

This Panel features regular 1963 Topps cards on the front and a Stan Musial ad/endorsement on the back.

NM Ex
COMPLETE SET 100.00 40.00
1 Hoyt Wilhelm 100.00 40.00
Don Lock
Bob Duliba

1964 Topps Advertising Panels

These panels, which were used to promote the 1964 Topps set; feature standard 1964 Topps cards on the front and a Mickey Mantle card back.

NM Ex
COMPLETE SET 150.00 60.00
1 Walt Alston 80.00 32.00
Bill Henry
Vada Pinson
2 Jimmie Hall 50.00 20.00
Ernie Broglio
A.L. ERA Leaders
3 Carl Willey 50.00 20.00
White Sox Rookies
Bob Friend

1966 Topps Advertising Panels

This panel was issued to preview the 1966 Topps baseball set. As is traditional for these panels, they were issued in three card strips.

NM Ex
1 Sandy Koufax 250.00 100.00
Jim Fregosi
Don Mossi

1967 Topps Advertising Panels

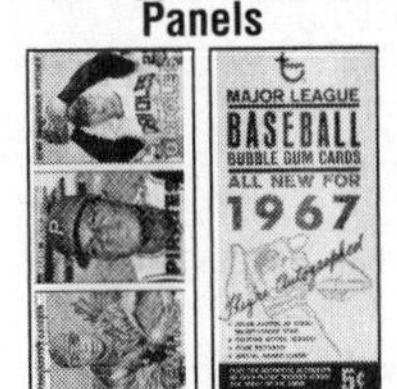

Described as a salesman's sample; the front of this panel features standard 1967 Topps cards on the front and advertising information on the back

NM Ex
COMPLETE SET 50.00 20.00
1 Earl Battey 50.00 20.00
Manny Mota
Gene Brabender

2003 Topps 205

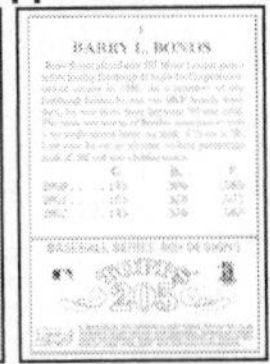

This 165 card series one set was released in July, 2003. The 175 card series two set was released several months later in February, 204. These cards were issued in eight-card packs which came 20 packs to a box and 10 boxes to a case. Cards number 1 through 120 feature veterans. Please note that 15 of these cards were issued with variations and we have notated the differences in these cards in our checklist. Cards number 121 through 130 feature propsects who were about ready to jump into the majors. Cards numbered 131 through 144 feature some players in their first year of cards. Card number number 145 features Louis Sockalexis who was supposedly the player the Cleveland Indians named their team in honor of. (This supposition has been buttressed by recently redisovered newspaper clippings from 1897). Cards numbered 146 to 150 feature various "reprints" of some of the tougher T-205 cards. Also randomly inserted in packs were cards featuring "repurchased" tobacco cards. Those cards were inserted at a stated rate of one in 336 for 1st series cards and one in 295 for second series cards. The second series featured the following subsets: T205 Reprints from cards 151 through 154, retired players from card 155 through 160; prospects from cards 161 through 169. First year players from cards 170 through 192. In addition, 10 players had 2 variations in the second series and we have notated this information along with some players who were issued in shorter quantity we have put an SP next to that player's name.

Nm-Mt Ex-Mt
COMPLETE SERIES 1 (165) 40.00 12.00
COMPLETE SERIES 2 (175) 100.00 30.00
COMP.SERIES 2 w/o SP's (155) 40.00 12.00
COM (1-130/161-169/193-315) .... .50 .15
COMMON (131-145/170-192)....... .50 .15
COMMON (146-150) .... 1.00 .30
COMMON SP .... 2.00 .60
SERIES 2 SP STATED ODDS 1:5.........
1A Barry Bonds w/Cap .... 3.00 .90
1B Barry Bonds w/Helmet .... 3.00 .90
2 Bret Boone .... .50 .15
3A Albert Pujols Clear Logo .... 2.50 .75
3B Albert Pujols White Logo .... 2.50 .75
4 Carl Crawford .... .50 .15
5 Bartolo Colon .... .50 .15
6 Cliff Floyd .... .50 .15
7 John Olerud................................. .50 .15
8A Jason Giambi Full Jkt............. 1.25 .35
8B Jason Giambi Partial Jkt .... 1.25 .35
9 Edgardo Alfonzo .... .50 .15
10 Ivan Rodriguez .... 1.25 .35
11 Jim Edmonds .... .50 .15
12A Mike Piazza Orange.............. 2.00 .60
12B Mike Piazza Yellow............... 2.00 .60
13 Greg Maddux........................... 2.00 .60
14 Jose Vidro .... .50 .15
15A Vlad Guerrero Clear Logo..... 1.25 .35
15B V.Guerrero White Logo .... 1.25 .35
16 Bernie Williams .... .75 .23
17 Roger Clemens......................... 2.50 .75
18A Miguel Tejada Blue.................. .50 .15
18B Miguel Tejada Green .... .50 .15
19 Carlos Delgado.......................... .50 .15
20A Alfonso Soriano w/Bat .... .75 .23
20B Alf. Soriano Sunglasses .... .75 .23
21 Bobby Cox MG .... .50 .15
22 Mike Scioscia............................. .50 .15
23 John Smoltz .... .75 .23
24 Luis Gonzalez .... .50 .15
25 Shawn Green.............................. .50 .15
26 Raul Ibanez .... .50 .15
27 Andruw Jones .... .50 .15
28 Josh Beckett............................... .75 .23
29 Derek Lowe .... .50 .15
30 Todd Helton................................ .75 .23
31 Barry Larkin............................. 1.25 .35
32 Jason Jennings .... .50 .15
33 Darin Erstad .... .50 .15
34 Magglio Ordonez......................... .50 .15
35 Mike Sweeney .... .50 .15
36 Kazuhisa Ishii .... .50 .15
37 Ron Gardenhire MG .... .50 .15
38 Tim Hudson................................ .50 .15
39 Tim Salmon................................ .75 .23
40A Pat Burrell Black Bat .... .50 .15
40B Pat Burrell Brown Bat.............. .50 .15
41 Manny Ramirez .... .50 .15
42 Nick Johnson .... .50 .15
43 Tom Glavine .... .75 .23
44 Mark Mulder................................ .50 .15
45 Brian Jordan................................ .50 .15
46 Rafael Palmeiro .... .75 .23
47 Vernon Wells............................... .50 .15
48 Bob Brenly MG .... .50 .15
49 C.C. Sabathia.............................. .50 .15
50A A.Rodriguez Look Ahead...... 2.00 .60
50B A.Rodriguez Look Away .... 2.00 .60
51A Sammy Sosa Head Duck...... 2.00 .60
51B Sammy Sosa Head Left........ 2.00 .60
52 Paul Konerko.............................. .50 .15
53 Craig Biggio................................ .75 .23
54 Moises Alou .... .50 .15
55 Johnny Damon............................ .50 .15
56 Torii Hunter .... .50 .15
57 Omar Vizquel.............................. .50 .15
58 Orlando Hernandez..................... .50 .15
59 Barry Zito .... .75 .23
60 Lance Berkman .... .50 .15
61 Carlos Beltran............................. .50 .15
62 Edgar Renteria............................ .50 .15
63 Ben Sheets .... .50 .15
64 Doug Mientkiewicz .... .50 .15
65 Troy Glaus.................................. .75 .23
66 Preston Wilson............................ .50 .15
67 Kerry Wood .... 1.25 .35
68 Frank Thomas .... 1.25 .35
69 Jimmy Rollins .... .50 .15
70 Brian Giles.................................. .50 .15
71 Bobby Higginson......................... .50 .15
72 Larry Walker................................ .75 .23
73 Randy Johnson .... 1.25 .35
74 Tony LaRussa MG...................... .50 .15
75A Derek Jeter w/Gold Trim ...... 3.00 .90
75B D.Jeter w/o Gold Trim.......... 3.00 .90
76 Bobby Abreu .... .50 .15
77A A.Dunn Closed Mouth .... .50 .15
77B Adam Dunn Open Mouth .... .50 .15
78 Ryan Klesko .... .50 .15
79 Francisco Rodriguez................... .50 .15
80 Scott Rolen .... .75 .23
81 Roberto Alomar....................... 1.25 .35
82 Joe Torre MG .... .75 .23
83 Jim Thome............................... 1.25 .35
84 Kevin Millwood............................ .50 .15
85 J.T. Snow .... .50 .15
86 Trevor Hoffman........................... .50 .15
87 Jay Gibbons .... .50 .15
88A Mark Prior New Logo........... 2.50 .75
88B Mark Prior Old Logo .... 2.50 .75
89 Rich Aurilia.................................. .50 .15
90 Chipper Jones .... 1.25 .35
91 Richie Sexson .... .50 .15
92 Gary Sheffield............................. .50 .15
93 Pedro Martinez........................ 1.25 .35
94 Rodrigo Lopez............................ .50 .15
95 Al Leiter...................................... .50 .15
96 Jorge Posada .... .75 .23
97 Luis Castillo................................ .50 .15
98 Aubrey Huff .... .50 .15
99 A.J. Pierzynski............................ .50 .15
100A I.Suzuki Look Ahead .... 2.00 .60
100B Ichiro Suzuki Look Right.... 2.00 .60
101 Eric Chavez............................... .50 .15
102 Brett Myers .... .50 .15
103 Jason Kendall............................ .50 .15
104 Jeff Kent.................................... .50 .15
105 Eric Hinske .... .50 .15
106 Jacque Jones .... .50 .15
107 Phil Nevin.................................. .50 .15
108 Roy Oswalt................................ .50 .15
109 Curt Schilling............................. .75 .23
110A N.Garciaparra w/Gold Trim 2.00 .60
110B N.Garciaparra w/o Gold Trim 2.00 .60
111 Garret Anderson........................ .50 .15
112 Eric Gagne................................. .75 .23
113 Javier Vazquez........................... .50 .15
114 Jeff Bagwell............................... .75 .23
115 Mike Lowell .... .50 .15
116 Carlos Pena .... .50 .15
117 Ken Griffey Jr. .... 2.00 .60
118 Tony Batista .... .50 .15
119 Edgar Martinez .... .75 .23
120 Austin Kearns............................ .50 .15
121 Jason Stokes PROS .... 1.25 .35
122 Jose Reyes PROS..................... .75 .23
123 Rocco Baldelli PROS .... 2.00 .60
124 Joe Borchard PROS .... .50 .15
125 Joe Mauer PROS................... 1.25 .35
126 Gavin Floyd PROS .... .50 .15
127 Mark Teixeira PROS .... .75 .23
128 Jeremy Guthrie PROS .... .50 .15
129 B.J. Upton PROS.................. 1.25 .35
130 Khalil Greene PROS.................. .75 .23
131 Hanley Ramirez FY RC.......... 2.00 .60
132 Andy Marte FY RC................. 3.00 .90
133 J.D. Durbin FY RC .... 1.00 .30
134 Jason Kubel FY RC................ 1.00 .30
135 Craig Brazell FY RC .... .60 .18
136 Bryan Bullington FY RC .... 2.00 .60
137 Jose Contreras FY RC .... 2.00 .60
138 Brian Burgamy FY RC.............. .50 .15
139 E.Bastida-Martinez FY RC....... .50 .15
140 Joey Gomes FY RC.................. .50 .15
141 Ismael Castro FY RC .... .60 .18
142 Travis Wong FY RC .... .60 .18
143 Mi.Garciaparra FY RC........... 1.25 .35
144 Arnaldo Munoz FY RC .... .50 .15
145 Louis Sockalexis FY XRC......... .50 .15
146 Richard Hoblitzell REP .... 1.00 .30
147 George Graham REP .... 1.00 .30
148 Hal Chase REP .... 1.00 .30
149 John McGraw REP .... 1.50 .45
150 Bobby Wallace REP .... 1.00 .30
151 David Shean REP .... 1.00 .30
152 Richard Hoblitzell REP SP .... 2.00 .60
153 Hal Chase REP .... 1.00 .30
154 Hooks Wiltse REP .... 1.00 .30
155 George Brett RET 4.00 1.20
156 Willie Mays RET .... 3.00 .90
157 Honus Wagner RET SP 10.00 3.00
158 Nolan Ryan RET 4.00 1.20
159 Reggie Jackson RET............. 1.50 .45
160 Mike Schmidt RET................. 3.00 .90
161 Josh Barfield PROS................. .75 .23
162 Grady Sizemore PROS .... .75 .23
163 Justin Morneau PROS............. .50 .15
164 Laynce Nix PROS .... 1.25 .35
165 Zack Greinke PROS .... 1.25 .35
166 Victor Martinez PROS.............. .50 .15
167 Jeff Mathis PROS .... .50 .15
168 Casey Kotchman PROS .... .75 .23
169 Gabe Gross PROS .... .50 .15
170 Edwin Jackson FY RC........... 3.00 .90
171 Delmon Young FY SP RC ... 10.00 3.00
172 Eric Duncan FY SP RC.......... 4.00 1.20
173 Brian Snyder FY SP RC .... 2.00 .60
174 Chris Lubanski FY SP RC 4.00 1.20
175 Ryan Harvey FY SP RC......... 6.00 1.80
176 Nick Markakis FY SP RC....... 3.00 .90
177 Chad Billingsley FY SP RC.... 2.50 .75
178 Elizardo Ramirez FY RC........ 1.25 .35
179 Ben Francisco FY RC .... .60 .18
180 Franklin Gutierrez FY SP RC . 5.00 1.50
181 Aaron Hill FY SP RC 4.00 1.20
182 Kevin Correia FY RC .... .50 .15
183 Kelly Shoppach FY RC.......... 1.50 .45
184 Felix Pie FY SP RC................ 6.00 1.80
185 Adam Loewen FY SP RC 5.00 1.50
186 Danny Garcia FY RC .... .50 .15
187 Rickie Weeks FY SP RC........ 8.00 2.40
188 Robby Hammock FY SP RC . 2.00 .60
189 Ryan Wagner FY SP RC .... 3.00 .90
190 Matt Kata FY SP RC.............. 2.00 .60
191 Bo Hart FY SP RC................. 4.00 1.20
192 Brandon Webb FY SP RC 5.00 1.50
193 Bengie Molina .... .50 .15
194 Junior Spivey .... .50 .15
195 Gary Sheffield........................... .50 .15
196 Jason Johnson.......................... .50 .15
197 David Ortiz................................ .50 .15
198 Roberto Alomar..................... 1.25 .35
199 Wily Mo Pena............................ .50 .15
200 Sammy Sosa .... 2.00 .60
201 Jay Payton................................ .50 .15
202 Dmitri Young............................. .50 .15
203 Derrek Lee................................ .50 .15
204A Jeff Bagwell w/Hat .... .75 .23
204B Jeff Bagwell w/o Hat .... .75 .23
205 Runelvys Hernandez................. .50 .15
206 Kevin Brown.............................. .50 .15
207 Wes Helms................................ .50 .15
208 Eddie Guardado........................ .50 .15
209 Orlando Cabrera .... .50 .15
210 Alfonso Soriano......................... .75 .23
211 Ty Wigginton............................. .50 .15
212A Rich Harden Look Left .... .75 .23
212B Rich Harden Look Right........ .75 .23
213 Mike Lieberthal.......................... .50 .15
214 Brian Giles................................ .50 .15
215 Jason Schmidt .... .50 .15
216 Jamie Moyer .... .50 .15
217 Matt Morris .... .50 .15
218 Victor Zambrano .... .50 .15
219 Roy Halladay .... .50 .15
220 Mike Hampton........................... .50 .15
221 Kevin Millar .... .50 .15
222 Hideo Nomo .... 1.25 .35
223 Milton Bradley .... .50 .15
224 Jose Guillen.............................. .50 .15
225 Derek Jeter .... 3.00 .90
226 Rondell White........................... .50 .15
227A Hank Blalock Blue Jsy .... .75 .23
227B Hank Blalock White Jsy .... .75 .23
228 Shigetoshi Hasegawa .... .50 .15
229 Mike Mussina...................... 1.25 .35
230 Cristian Guzman .... .50 .15
231A Todd Helton Blue .... .75 .23
231B Todd Helton Green .... .75 .23
232 Kenny Lofton............................ .50 .15
233 Carl Everett.............................. .50 .15
234 Shea Hillenbrand .... .50 .15
235 Brad Fullmer............................. .50 .15
236 Bernie Williams .... .75 .23
237 Vicente Padilla.......................... .50 .15
238 Tim Worrell .... .50 .15
239 Juan Gonzalez .... 1.25 .35
240 Ichiro Suzuki .... 2.00 .60
241 Aaron Boone .... .50 .15
242 Shannon Stewart...................... .50 .15
243A Barry Zito Blue .... .75 .23
243B Barry Zito Green................... .75 .23
244 Reggie Sanders .... .50 .15
245 Scott Podsednik .... 1.25 .35
246 Miguel Cabrera.................... 2.00 .60
247 Angel Berroa .... .50 .15
248 Carlos Zambrano...................... .50 .15
249 Marlon Byrd .... .50 .15
250 Mark Prior .... 2.50 .75
251 Esteban Loaiza .... .50 .15
252 David Eckstein.......................... .50 .15
253 Alex Cintron.............................. .50 .15
254 Melvin Mora .... .50 .15
255 Russ Ortiz .... .50 .15
256 Carlos Lee .... .50 .15
257 Tino Martinez .... .75 .23
258 Randy Wolf .... .50 .15
259 Jason Phillips............................ .50 .15
260 Vladimir Guerrero................. 1.25 .35
261 Brad Wilkerson......................... .50 .15
262 Ivan Rodriguez .... 1.25 .35
263 Matt Lawton .... .50 .15
264 Adam Dunn .... .50 .15
265 Joe Borowski............................ .50 .15
266 Jody Gerut............................... .50 .15
267 Alex Rodriguez .... 2.00 .60
268 Brendan Donnelly..................... .50 .15
269A Randy Johnson Grey......... 1.25 .35
269B Randy Johnson Pink .... 1.25 .35
270 Nomar Garciaparra............. 2.00 .60
271 Javy Lopez .... .50 .15
272 Travis Hafner............................ .50 .15
273 Juan Pierre............................... .50 .15
274 Morgan Ensberg....................... .50 .15
275 Albert Pujols....................... 2.50 .75
276 Jason LaRue .... .50 .15
277 Paul Lo Duca............................ .50 .15
278 Andy Pettitte............................. .75 .23
279 Mike Piazza .... 2.00 .60
280A Jim Thome Blue .... 1.25 .35
280B Jim Thome Green............. 1.25 .35
281 Marquis Grissom...................... .50 .15
282 Woody Williams .... .50 .15
283A Curt Schilling Look Ahead.... .75 .23
283B Curt Schilling Look Right ..... .75 .23
284A Chipper Jones Blue .... 1.25 .35
284B Chipper Jones Yellow........ 1.25 .35
285 Deivi Cruz................................. .50 .15
286 Johnny Damon.......................... .50 .15
287 Chin-Hui Tsao .... .50 .15
288 Alex Gonzalez .... .50 .15
289 Billy Wagner.............................. .50 .15
290 Jason Giambi .... 1.25 .35
291 Keith Foulke.............................. .50 .15
292 Jerome Williams .... .50 .15
293 Livan Hernandez....................... .50 .15
294 Aaron Guiel .... .50 .15
295 Randall Simon........................... .50 .15
296 Byung-Hyun Kim .... .50 .15
297 Jorge Julio .... .50 .15
298 Miguel Batista .... .50 .15
299 Rafael Furcal .... .50 .15
300A Dontrelle Willis No Smile ... 1.25 .35
300B Dontrelle Willis Smile SP ... 2.50 .75
301 Alex Sanchez............................ .50 .15
302 Shawn Chacon .... .50 .15
303 Matt Clement............................. .50 .15
304 Luis Matos .... .50 .15
305 Steve Finley.............................. .50 .15
306 Marcus Giles .... .50 .15
307 Boomer Wells............................ .50 .15
308 Jeromy Burnitz.......................... .50 .15
309 Mike MacDougal .... .50 .15
310 Mariano Rivera.......................... .75 .23
311 Adrian Beltre .... .50 .15
312 Mark Loretta.............................. .50 .15
313 Ugueth Urbina........................... .50 .15
314 Bill Mueller .... .50 .15
315 Johan Santana.......................... .50 .15
NNO Vintage Buyback ....

2003 Topps 205 American Beauty

Nm-Mt Ex-Mt
*AMER.BTY: 1.25X TO 3X BASIC........
RANDOM INSERTS IN PACKS ....
*AMER.BTY PURPLE: 4X TO 10X BASIC
PURPLE CARDS ARE 10% OF PRINT RUN
CL: 1/20/50/51/100/146-150..............

2003 Topps 205 Bazooka Blue

Nm-Mt Ex-Mt
SERIES 2 STATED ODDS 1:2744 PACKS
SERIES 2 STATED ODDS 1:208 MINI BOXES
STATED PRINT RUN 1 SET ....
NO PRICING DUE TO SCARCITY.........

2003 Topps 205 Bazooka Red

Nm-Mt Ex-Mt
SERIES 1 STATED ODDS 1:1573 PACKS
SERIES 2 STATED ODDS 1:691 PACKS
SERIES 2 STATED ODDS 1:52 MINI BOXES
SERIES 1 STATED PRINT RUN 5 SETS
SERIES 2 STATED PRINT RUN 4 SETS
NO PRICING DUE TO SCARCITY.........

2003 Topps 205 Brooklyn

Nm-Mt Ex-Mt
*BROOKLYN C 1-130: .75X TO 2X BASIC
*BROOKLYN U 1-130: 1.25X TO 3X BASIC
*BROOKLYN U 131-144: 1.25X TO 3X BASIC
*BROOKLYN R 1-130: 2X TO 5X BASIC
*BROOKLYN R 131-144: 2X TO 5X BASIC
BROOKLYN 5 PRINT RUN 5 SETS
NO BROOKLYN 5 PRICING DUE TO SCARCITY
1-150 RANDOM INSERTS IN SER.1 PACKS
SEE BECKETT.COM FOR C/U/R/5 SCHEMATIC
SCHEMATIC IS IN OPG SUBSCRIPTION AREA
*BROOKLYN 151-315: 2X TO 5X BASIC
*BROOKLYN 151-315: 1X TO 2.5X BASIC SP
151-315 SERIES 2 STATED ODDS 1:12
151-315 STATED PRINT RUN 205 SETS
151-315 ARE NOT SERIAL-NUMBERED
151-315 PRINT RUN PROVIDED BY TOPPS

2003 Topps 205 Brooklyn Exclusive Pose

Nm-Mt Ex-Mt
*BROOKLYN EP: 1X TO 2.5X POLAR EP
OVERALL BROOKLYN SERIES 2 ODDS 1:12
STATED PRINT RUN 205 SETS
CARDS ARE NOT SERIAL-NUMBERED
PRINT RUN PROVIDED BY TOPPS

2003 Topps 205 Cycle

Nm-Mt Ex-Mt
*CYCLE 121-145: 1.25X TO 3X BASIC
RANDOM INSERTS IN PACKS
*CYCLE PURPLE 121-130: 4X TO 10X BASIC
*CYCLE PURPLE 131-145: 3X TO 8X BASIC
PURPLE CARDS ARE 10% OF PRINT RUN

2003 Topps 205 Drum

Nm-Mt Ex-Mt
*DRUM: 2X TO 5X BASIC
*DRUM: 1X TO 2.5X BASIC SP
RANDOM INSERTS IN PACKS

2003 Topps 205 Drum Exclusive Pose

Nm-Mt Ex-Mt
*DRUM EP: 1X TO 2.5X POLAR EP
RANDOM INSERTS IN SERIES 2 PACKS

2003 Topps 205 Honest

Nm-Mt Ex-Mt
*HONEST: 1.25X TO 3X BASIC
RANDOM INSERTS IN PACKS
*HONEST PURPLE: 4X TO 10X BASIC
PURPLE CARDS ARE 10% OF PRINT RUN
CL: 1/3/8/12/15/18/20/40/50/51/75/77/88
CL: 100/110

2003 Topps 205 Piedmont

Nm-Mt Ex-Mt
*PIEDMONT: 1.25X TO 3X BASIC
RANDOM INSERTS IN PACKS
*PIEDMONT PURPLE: 4X TO 10X BASIC
PURPLE CARDS ARE 10% OF PRINT RUN
CL: 2-19/21-49/

2003 Topps 205 Polar Bear

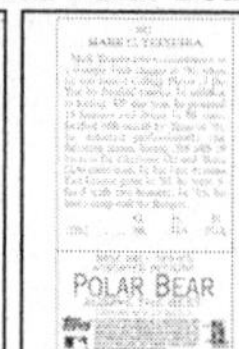

Nm-Mt Ex-Mt
*POLAR BEAR: .75X TO 2X BASIC
*POLAR BEAR: .4X TO 1X BASIC SP
RANDOM INSERTS IN PACKS

2003 Topps 205 Polar Bear Exclusive Pose

Nm-Mt Ex-Mt
RANDOM INSERTS IN SERIES 2 PACKS
316 Willie Mays EP 6.00 1.80
317 Delmon Young EP 10.00 3.00
318 Rickie Weeks EP 8.00 2.40
319 Ryan Wagner EP 3.00 .90
320 Brandon Webb EP 5.00 1.50
321 Chris Lubanski EP 4.00 1.20
322 Ryan Harvey EP 6.00 1.80
323 Nick Markakis EP 3.00 .90
324 Chad Billingsley EP 2.50 .75
325 Aaron Hill EP 4.00 1.20
326 Brian Snyder EP 2.00 .60
327 Eric Duncan EP 4.00 1.20
328 Sammy Sosa EP 4.00 1.20
329 Alfonso Soriano EP 2.00 .60
330 Ichiro Suzuki EP 4.00 1.20
331 Alex Rodriguez EP 4.00 1.20
332 Nomar Garciaparra EP 4.00 1.20
333 Albert Pujols EP 5.00 1.50
334 Jim Thome EP 2.50 .75
335 Dontrelle Willis EP 2.50 .75

2003 Topps 205 Sovereign

Nm-Mt Ex-Mt
*SOVEREIGN: 1.25X TO 3X BASIC
*SOVEREIGN: .6X TO 1.5X BASIC SP
RANDOM INSERTS IN PACKS
*SOV.GREEN: 2.5X TO 6X BASIC
*SOV.GREEN: 1.25X TO 3X BASIC SP
SOV.GREEN CARDS ARE 25% OF PRINT RUN

2003 Topps 205 Sovereign Exclusive Pose

Nm-Mt Ex-Mt
*SOVEREIGN EP: .6X TO 1.5X POLAR EP
RANDOM INSERTS IN SERIES 2 PACKS
*SOV.GREEN EP: 1.25X TO 3X POLAR EP
SOV.GREEN CARDS ARE 25% OF PRINT RUN

2003 Topps 205 Sweet Caporal

Nm-Mt Ex-Mt
*SWEET CAP: 1.25X TO 3X BASIC
RANDOM INSERTS IN PACKS
*SWEET CAP PURPLE: 4X TO 10X BASIC
PURPLE CARDS ARE 10% OF PRINT RUN
CL: 70-99/101-120

2003 Topps 205 Autographs

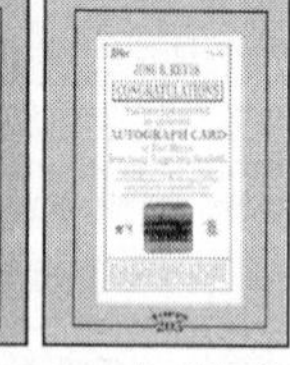

These cards feature autographs of leading players. These cards were inserted at varying odds and we have noted what group the player belongs to in our checklist. Though lacking serial numbering, representatives at Topps publicly announced only 50 copies of Hank Aaron's card were produced - making it, by far, the scarcest card in this set.

Nm-Mt Ex-Mt
SER.1 GROUP A1 ODDS 1:2434
SER.1 GROUP B1 ODDS 1:608
SER.1 GROUP C1 ODDS 1:1460
SER.1 GROUP D1 ODDS 1:122
SER.2 GROUP A2 ODDS 1:5816
SER.2 GROUP B2 ODDS 1:646
SER.2 GROUP C2 ODDS 1:49
A2 STATED PRINT RUN 50 CARDS
A2 IS NOT SERIAL-NUMBERED
A2 PRINT RUN PROVIDED BY TOPPS
CF Cliff Floyd B1 20.00 6.00
DW Dontrelle Willis C2 25.00 7.50
ED Eric Duncan C2 25.00 7.50
FP Felix Pie C2 25.00 7.50
HA Hank Aaron A2 SP/50
JR Jose Reyes D1 25.00 7.50
JW Jerome Williams B2 25.00 7.50
LB Lance Berkman B1 25.00 7.50
LC Luis Castillo C2 15.00 4.50
MB Marlon Byrd D1 15.00 4.50
MO Magglio Ordonez C1 25.00 7.50
MS Mike Sweeney B1 25.00 7.50
PL Paul Lo Duca D1 15.00 4.50
RH Rich Harden C2 25.00 7.50
RWA Ryan Wagner C2 20.00 6.00
SR Scott Rolen A1 40.00 12.00
TH Torii Hunter D1 15.00 4.50

2003 Topps 205 Relics

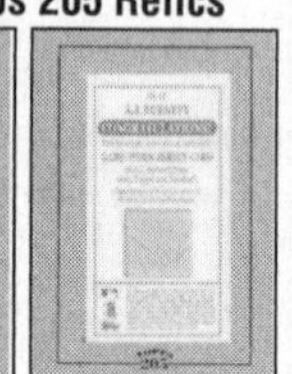

Randomly inserted into packs, these 43 cards feature game-used memorabilia pieces of the featured players. Please note that many of these cards were inserted in different rates and we have noted both the insert ratio as well as the group the player belongs to in our checklisting information.

Nm-Mt Ex-Mt
COM.UNI A1/RELIC A2 15.00 4.50
COM.BAT B-D1/UNI E1/RELIC B2 10.00 3.00
COMMON BAT E-H1/UNI F-M1 8.00 2.40
SER.1 BAT GROUP A1 ODDS 1:1216
SER.1 BAT GROUP B1 ODDS 1:972
SER.1 BAT GROUP C1 ODDS 1:270
SER.1 BAT GROUP D1 ODDS 1:365
SER.1 BAT GROUP E1 ODDS 1:561
SER.1 BAT GROUP F1 ODDS 1:486
SER.1 BAT GROUP G1 ODDS 1:91
SER.1 BAT GROUP H1 ODDS 1:203
SER.1 UNI GROUP A1 ODDS 1:4884
SER.1 UNI GROUP B1 ODDS 1:456
SER.1 UNI GROUP C1 ODDS 1:1460
SER.1 UNI GROUP D1 ODDS 1:1216
SER.1 UNI GROUP E1 ODDS 1:973
SER.1 UNI GROUP F1 ODDS 1:608
SER.1 UNI GROUP G1 ODDS 1:61
SER.1 UNI GROUP H1 ODDS 1:183
SER.1 UNI GROUP I1 ODDS 1:83
SER.1 UNI GROUP J1 ODDS 1:324
SER.1 UNI GROUP K1 ODDS 1:317
SER.1 UNI GROUP L1 ODDS 1:243
SER.1 UNI GROUP M1 ODDS 1:221
SER.2 RELIC GROUP A ODDS 1:79
SER.2 RELIC GROUP B ODDS 1:16
AB A.J. Burnett Jsy G1 8.00 2.40
AD Adam Dunn Bat G1 8.00 2.40
AJ Andruw Jones Jsy B2 UER 15.00 4.50
Chipper Jones is pictured
AL Al Leiter Jsy I1 8.00 2.40
APB Albert Pujols Bat A2 25.00 7.50
AP1 Albert Pujols Uni E1 20.00 6.00
AP2 Albert Pujols Hat A2 25.00 7.50
ARA Aramis Ramirez Bat B2 10.00 3.00
AR1 Alex Rodriguez Jsy H1 15.00 4.50
AR2 Alex Rodriguez Bat B2 15.00 4.50
AS1 Alfonso Soriano Uni G1 10.00 3.00
AS2 Alfonso Soriano Bat A2 20.00 6.00
BB1 Barry Bonds Uni B1 25.00 7.50
BB2 Bret Boone Bat A2 15.00 4.50
BD Brandon Duckworth Jsy B2 10.00 3.00
BG1 Brian Giles Bat G1 8.00 2.40
BG2 Brian Giles Bat A2 15.00 4.50
BP Brad Penny Jsy B2 10.00 3.00
BW1 Bernie Williams Bat D1 15.00 4.50
BW2 Bernie Williams Jsy A2 20.00 6.00
BZ Barry Zito Jsy K1 10.00 3.00
CB Craig Biggio Uni B2 15.00 4.50
CD Carlos Delgado Jsy B2 10.00 3.00
CG Cristian Guzman Jsy B2 10.00 3.00
CJB Chipper Jones Bat A2 20.00 6.00
CP Corey Patterson Bat A2 15.00 4.50
CS1 Curt Schilling Jsy B1 15.00 4.50
CS2 Curt Schilling Bat B2 15.00 4.50
DE Darin Erstad Uni A2 15.00 4.50
DL Derek Lowe Hat A1 15.00 4.50
DW Dontrelle Willis Uni B2 15.00 4.50
EC Eric Chavez Bat G1 8.00 2.40
EG Eric Gagne Jsy G1 10.00 3.00
EMA Edgar Martinez Jsy B2 15.00 4.50
EMU Eddie Murray Bat A2 25.00 7.50
FM Fred McGriff Bat B2 15.00 4.50
FR Frank Robinson Bat A2 20.00 6.00
FT Frank Thomas Jsy B2 15.00 4.50
GA Garret Anderson Uni L1 8.00 2.40
GB George Brett Jsy A2 40.00 12.00
GC Gary Carter Bat A2 20.00 6.00
GM1 Greg Maddux Jsy B1 15.00 4.50
GM2 Greg Maddux Bat A2 20.00 6.00
GS Gary Sheffield Bat B2 10.00 3.00
HB Hank Blalock Bat B2 15.00 4.50
IR Ivan Rodriguez Bat A2 20.00 6.00
JB1 Jeff Bagwell Uni G1 10.00 3.00
JB2 Jeff Bagwell Bat A2 20.00 6.00
JC Jose Canseco Bat B2 15.00 4.50
JD Johnny Damon Bat B1 10.00 3.00
JE Jim Edmonds Jsy A2 15.00 4.50
JG Jason Giambi Bat A2 20.00 6.00
JGI Jeremy Giambi Jsy B2 10.00 3.00
JGO Juan Gonzalez Bat B2 15.00 4.50
JJ Jason Jennings Jsy G1 8.00 2.40
JK Jeff Kent Bat C1 10.00 3.00
JO John Olerud Jsy B2 10.00 3.00
JP Jorge Posada Bat A2 20.00 6.00
JS John Smoltz Jsy B1 15.00 4.50
JT Jim Thome Bat F1 10.00 3.00
KB Kevin Brown Jsy B2 10.00 3.00
KI Kazuhisa Ishii Jsy I1 8.00 2.40
KL1 Kenny Lofton Bat G1 8.00 2.40
KL2 Kenny Lofton Uni B2 10.00 3.00
LB Lance Berkman Bat C1 10.00 3.00
LC Luis Castillo Jsy G1 8.00 2.40
LG1 Luis Gonzalez Jsy J1 8.00 2.40
LG2 Luis Gonzalez Bat A2 15.00 4.50
LW Larry Walker Jsy B2 15.00 4.50
MC Mike Cameron Jsy B2 10.00 3.00
MG Mark Grace Bat A2 20.00 6.00
MGR Marquis Grissom Bat B2 10.00 3.00
MM Mark Mulder Uni A2 15.00 4.50
MO Magglio Ordonez Jsy M1 8.00 2.40
MP1 Mike Piazza Bat C1 15.00 4.50
MP2 Mike Piazza Bat A2 20.00 6.00
MR Manny Ramirez Bat H1 8.00 2.40
MSC Mike Schmidt Bat A2 30.00 9.00
MSW Mike Sweeney Bat H1 8.00 2.40
MTE Miguel Tejada Bat B2 10.00 3.00
MTI Mark Teixeira Bat B2 15.00 4.50
MV Mo Vaughn Jsy I1 8.00 2.40
NG1 Nomar Garciaparra Jsy G1 15.00 4.50
NG2 Nomar Garciaparra Bat A2 20.00 6.00
NJ Nick Johnson Bat D1 10.00 3.00
NR Nolan Ryan Uni A2 60.00 18.00
PM1 Pedro Martinez Jsy F1 10.00 3.00
PM2 Pedro Martinez Jsy A2 20.00 6.00
PO Paul O'Neill Uni B2 15.00 4.50
RA1 Roberto Alomar Bat G1 10.00 3.00
RA2 Roberto Alomar Uni B2 15.00 4.50
RBB Rocco Baldelli Bat B2 15.00 4.50
RBJ Rocco Baldelli Jsy B2 15.00 4.50
RC Roger Clemens Uni A2 20.00 6.00
RF1 Rafael Furcal Bat E1 8.00 2.40
RF2 Rafael Furcal Bat A2 15.00 4.50
RH Rickey Henderson Bat B2 15.00 4.50
RJ1 Randy Johnson Jsy C1 15.00 4.50
RJ2 Randy Johnson Jsy A2 20.00 6.00
RO Roy Oswalt Jsy I1 8.00 2.40
RP1 Rafael Palmeiro Jsy H1 10.00 3.00
RP2 Rafael Palmeiro Bat A2 20.00 6.00
RV Robin Ventura Bat B2 10.00 3.00
SB Sean Burroughs Bat B2 10.00 3.00
SR1 Scott Rolen Bat A1 15.00 4.50
SR2 Scott Rolen Uni A2 20.00 6.00
SS Sammy Sosa Jsy A2 20.00 6.00
SST Shannon Stewart Bat B2 10.00 3.00
TG Troy Glaus Uni A2 20.00 6.00
TH Todd Helton Jsy D1 15.00 4.50
TM Tino Martinez Bat B2 15.00 4.50
TP Troy Percival Uni G1 8.00 2.40
TS Tsuyoshi Shinjo Bat B2 10.00 3.00
VG Vladimir Guerrero Bat A2 20.00 6.00
VW Vernon Wells Jsy A2 15.00 4.50
WB Wade Boggs Bat A2 20.00 6.00

2003 Topps 205 Team Topps Legends Autographs

Nm-Mt Ex-Mt
SER.1 GROUP A1 ODDS 1:1461
SER.1 GROUP B1 ODDS 1:2433
SER.1 GROUP C1 ODDS 1:609
SER.2 STATED ODDS 1:20,581
SEE 2001 TOPPS TEAM TOPPS FOR PRICING
SEE 2003 TOPPS TEAM TOPPS FOR PRICING

2003 Topps 205 Triple Folder Polar Bear

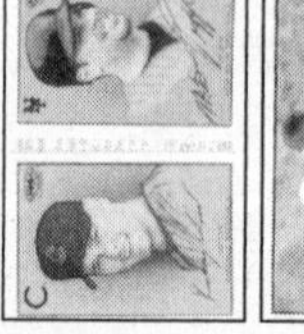

Nm-Mt Ex-Mt
COMPLETE SET (100) 50.00 15.00
COMPLETE SERIES 1 (50) 25.00 7.50
COMPLETE SERIES 2 (50) 25.00 7.50
ONE PER PACK
*BROOKLYN: 3X TO 8X BASIC
SERIES 1 BROOKLYN ODDS 1:72
SERIES 2 BROOKLYN ODDS 1:29
TF1 Barry Bonds 2.50 .75
Jason LaRue
TF2 Alfonso Soriano 2.50 .75
Derek Jeter
TF3 Alex Rodriguez 1.50 .45
Miguel Tejada
TF4 Nomar Garciaparra 2.50 .75
Derek Jeter
TF5 Omar Vizquel 1.50 .45
Alex Rodriguez
TF6 Paul Konerko 1.00 .30
Omar Vizquel
TF7 Paul Konerko 1.00 .30
Magglio Ordonez
TF8 Doug Mientkiewicz 1.00 .30
Darin Erstad
TF9 Jason Kendall 1.00 .30
Jimmy Rollins
TF10 Shawn Green 1.00 .30
Roberto Alomar
TF11 Derek Jeter 2.50 .75
Roberto Alomar
TF12 Bobby Abreu 1.00 .30
Luis Castillo
TF13 Randy Johnson 1.00 .30
Curt Schilling
TF14 Mike Piazza 1.50 .45
Kerry Wood
TF15 Roger Clemens 2.00 .60
Jorge Posada
TF16 Ichiro Suzuki 1.50 .45
Ryan Klesko
TF17 Alfonso Soriano 1.00 .30
Chipper Jones
TF18 Barry Bonds 2.50 .75
Nick Johnson
TF19 Chipper Jones 1.00 .30
Andruw Jones
TF20 Bobby Abreu 1.00 .30
Paul Konerko
TF21 Rafael Palmeiro 1.50 .45
Alex Rodriguez
TF22 Eric Hinske 1.00 .30
Carlos Delgado
TF23 Nomar Garciaparra 1.50 .45
Jay Gibbons
TF24 Mike Piazza 1.50 .45
Luis Gonzalez
TF25 J.T. Snow 1.00 .30
Vladimir Guerrero
TF26 Jason Giambi 1.00 .30
Bernie Williams
TF27 Miguel Tejada 1.00 .30
Richie Sexson
TF28 Doug Mientkiewicz 1.00 .30
Jimmy Rollins
TF29 Eric Chavez 2.50 .75
Derek Jeter
TF30 Alfonso Soriano 1.00 .30
Bret Boone
TF31 Chipper Jones 1.50 .45
Mike Piazza
TF32 Ichiro Suzuki 1.50 .45
Bret Boone
TF33 Bobby Abreu 1.50 .45
Mike Piazza
TF34 Jimmy Rollins 1.00 .30
Pat Burell
TF35 Ichiro Suzuki 1.50 .45
Miguel Tejada
TF36 Jason LaRue 2.50 .75
Barry Bonds
TF37 Derek Jeter 2.50 .75
Alfonso Soriano
TF38 Miguel Tejada 1.50 .45
Alex Rodriguez
TF39 Derek Jeter 2.50 .75
Nomar Garciaparra
TF40 Alex Rodriguez 1.50 .45
Omar Vizquel
TF41 Curt Schilling 1.00 .30
Randy Johnson
TF42 Jorge Posada 2.00 .60
Roger Clemens
TF43 Ryan Klesko 1.50 .45
Ichiro Suzuki
TF44 Nick Johnson 2.50 .75
Barry Bonds
TF45 Alex Rodriguez 1.50 .45
Rafael Palmeiro
TF46 Vladimir Guerrero 1.00 .30
J.T. Snow
TF47 Derek Jeter 2.50 .75
Eric Chavez
TF48 Bret Boone 1.50 .45
Ichiro Suzuki
TF49 Mike Piazza 1.50 .45
Bobby Abreu
TF50 Miguel Tejada 1.50 .45
Ichiro Suzuki
TF51 Juan Pierre 1.00 .30
Jim Thome
TF52 Kevin Millwood 1.00 .30
Jim Thome
TF53 Hank Blalock 1.00 .30
Jorge Posada
TF54 Deivi Cruz 1.00 .30
Hank Blalock
TF55 Rafael Furcal 1.00 .30
Ty Wigginton
TF56 Jim Thome 1.50 .45
Nomar Garciaparra
TF57 Craig Biggio 1.00 .30
Jason Giambi
TF58 Aaron Boone 1.00 .30
Jason Giambi
TF59 Jason Giambi 1.00 .30
Bernie Williams
TF60 Cristian Guzman 1.00 .30
Jody Gerut
TF61 Todd Helton 1.00 .30
Jose Reyes
TF62 Derek Jeter 2.50 .75
Hank Blalock
TF63 Mike Piazza 1.50 .45
Jimmy Rollins
TF64 Bernie Williams 2.50 .75
Derek Jeter
TF65 Andruw Jones 1.00 .30
Rafael Furcal
TF66 Mike Piazza 1.50 .45
Andruw Jones
TF67 Mike Piazza 1.50 .45
Cliff Floyd
TF68 Jason Kendall 2.00 .60
Albert Pujols
TF69 Nomar Garciaparra 1.50 .45
Manny Ramirez
TF70 Jorge Posada 1.50 .45
Alex Rodriguez
TF71 Derek Jeter 2.50 .75
Alex Rodriguez
TF72 Mike Sweeney 1.50 .45
Alex Rodriguez
TF73 Marquis Grissom 1.00 .30
Ivan Rodriguez
TF74 Jason Phillips 1.00 .30
Gary Sheffield
TF75 Chipper Jones 1.00 .30
Gary Sheffield
TF76 Junior Spivey 1.00 .30
Gary Sheffield
TF77 Al Leiter 1.50 .45
Ichiro Suzuki
TF78 Jose Vidro 1.00 .30
Jim Thome
TF79 Jimmy Rollins 1.00 .30
Paul Lo Duca
TF80 Alex Rodriguez 1.50 .45
Rafael Palmeiro
TF81 Albert Pujols 2.00 .60
Jim Edmonds
TF82 Eric Chavez 1.00 .30
Mike Sweeney
TF83 Cristian Guzman 1.00 .30
Jimmy Rollins
TF84 Alfonso Soriano 1.00 .30
Bernie Williams
TF85 Ichiro Suzuki 2.00 .60
Derek Jeter
TF86 Jimmy Rollins 1.00 .30
Derrek Lee
TF87 Shawn Green 1.00 .30
Paul Lo Duca
TF88 Carlos Delgado 1.00 .30
Jorge Posada
TF89 Dmitri Young 1.00 .30
C.C. Sabathia
TF90 Dontrelle Willis 1.00 .30
Shawn Chacon
TF91 Edgar Martinez 1.50 .45
Alex Rodriguez
TF92 Edgar Martinez 1.00 .30
Carlos Delgado
TF93 Edgar Martinez 1.00 .30
Esteban Loaiza
TF94 Roy Halladay 1.00 .30
C.C. Sabathia
TF95 Ichiro Suzuki 1.50 .45
Albert Pujols
TF96 Ichiro Suzuki 1.50 .45
Shigetoshi Hasegawa
TF97 Geoff Jenkins 1.00 .30
Aaron Boone
TF98 Nomar Garciaparra 1.50 .45
Alfonso Soriano
TF99 Jorge Posada 1.00 .30
Alfonso Soriano
TF100 Vernon Wells 1.00 .30
Garret Anderson

2003 Topps 205 Triple Folder Autographs

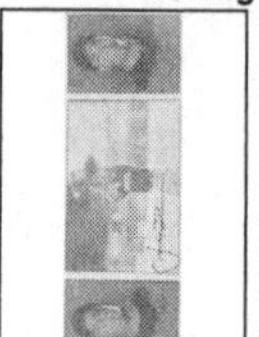

Nm-Mt Ex-Mt
SERIES 2 STATED ODDS 1:355 HOBBY
STATED PRINT RUN 205 SETS
CARDS ARE NOT SERIAL-NUMBERED
PRINT RUN PROVIDED BY TOPPS
DW Dontrelle Willis 50.00 15.00
JW Jerome Williams 40.00 12.00
RH Rich Harden 50.00 15.00
RW Ryan Wagner 50.00 15.00

2003 Topps 205 World Series Line-Ups

Nm-Mt Ex-Mt
SERIES 2 ODDS 1:27,440 PACKS
SERIES 2 ODDS 1:1960 MINI BOXES
STATED PRINT RUN 1 SET
NO PRICING DUE TO SCARCITY
AL1 David Wells
AL2 Jorge Posada
AL3 Nick Johnson
AL4 Alfonso Soriano
AL5 Aaron Boone
AL6 Derek Jeter
AL7 Juan Rivera
AL8 Bernie Williams
AL9 Karim Garcia
AL10 Jason Giambi
NL1 Brad Penny
NL2 Ivan Rodriguez
NL3 Derrek Lee
NL4 Luis Castillo
NL5 Mike Lowell
NL6 Alex Gonzalez
NL7 Miguel Cabrera
NL8 Juan Pierre
NL9 Juan Encarnacion
NL10 Jeff Conine

2002 Topps 206 Olbermann Promos

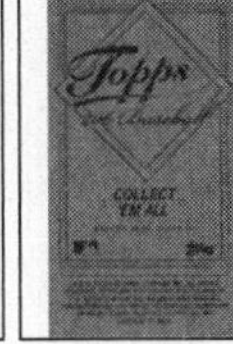

This five card set, issued exclusively through Beckett Sports Collectibles Vintage magazine, featured famed television sports announcer and noted card collector Keith Olbermann. These five cards feature Olbermann in a variety of poses similar to poses of the old tobacco cards.

	Nm-Mt	Ex-Mt
COMPLETE SET	5.00	1.50
COMMON CARD	1.00	.30

2002 Topps 206

Issued in three separate series this 526-card set featured a mix of veterans, rookies and retired greats in the general style of the classic T-206 set issued more than 90 years prior. Series one consists of cards 1-180 and went live in February, 2002, series two consists of cards 181-307 - including 96 variations - and went live in early August, 2002 and series three consists of cards 308-456 - including 15 variations and a total of 55 short prints seeded at a rate of one per pack - and went live in January, 2003. Each pack contained eight cards with an SRP of $4. Packs were issued 20 per box and each case had 10 boxes. The following subsets were issued as part of the set: Prospects (131-140/261-270/399-418); First Year Players (141-155/271-285/419-432), Retired Stars (156-170/286-298/433-448) and Reprints (171-180/299-307/449-456). The First Year Player subset cards 141-155 and 277-285 were inserted at stated odds of one in two packs making them short-prints in comparison to other cards in the set. According to press release notes, Topps purchased more than 4,000 original Tobacco cards and also randomly inserted those in packs. They created a "holder" for these smaller cards inside the standard-size cards of the Topps 206 set. Stated pack odds for these "repurchased" Tobacco cards was 1:110 for series one, 1:179 for series two and 1:101 for series three.

	Nm-Mt	Ex-Mt
COMPLETE SET (525)	220.00	65.00
COMPLETE SERIES 1 (180)	60.00	18.00
COMPLETE SERIES 2 (180)	60.00	18.00
COMPLETE SERIES 3 (165)	100.00	30.00
COM(1-140/181-260/308-418)	.50	.15
COMMON (141-155/271-285)	1.00	.30
COMMON RC (308-418)	.50	.15
COMMON SP (308-398)	2.00	.60
COMMON FYP SP (	1.00	.30
COMMON RET SP (433-447)	2.00	.60
1 Vladimir Guerrero	1.25	.35
2 Sammy Sosa	2.00	.60
3 Garret Anderson	.50	.15
4 Rafael Palmeiro	.75	.23
5 Juan Gonzalez	1.25	.35
6 John Smoltz	.75	.23
7 Mark Mulder	.50	.15
8 Jon Lieber	.50	.15
9 Greg Maddux	2.00	.60
10 Moises Alou	.50	.15
11 Joe Randa	.50	.15
12 Bobby Abreu	.50	.15
13 Juan Pierre	.50	.15
14 Kerry Wood	1.25	.35
15 Craig Biggio	.75	.23
16 Curt Schilling	.75	.23
17 Brian Jordan	.50	.15
18 Edgardo Alfonzo	.50	.15
19 Darren Dreifort	.50	.15
20 Todd Helton	.75	.23
21 Ramon Ortiz	.50	.15
22 Ichiro Suzuki	2.00	.60
23 Jimmy Rollins	.50	.15
24 Darin Erstad	.50	.15
25 Shawn Green	.50	.15
26 Tino Martinez	.75	.23
27 Bret Boone	.50	.15
28 Alfonso Soriano	.75	.23
29 Chan Ho Park	.50	.15
30 Roger Clemens	2.50	.75
31 Cliff Floyd	.50	.15
32 Johnny Damon	.50	.15
33 Frank Thomas	1.25	.35
34 Barry Bonds	3.00	.90
35 Luis Gonzalez	.50	.15
36 Carlos Lee	.50	.15
37 Roberto Alomar	1.25	.35
38 Carlos Delgado	.50	.15
39 Nomar Garciaparra	2.00	.60
40 Jason Kendall	.50	.15
41 Scott Rolen	.75	.23
42 Tom Glavine	.75	.23
43 Ryan Klesko	.50	.15
44 Brian Giles	.50	.15
45 Bud Smith	.50	.15
46 Charles Nagy	.50	.15
47 Tony Gwynn	1.50	.45
48 C.C. Sabathia UER Credited with incorrect victory total in 2001	.50	.15
49 Frank Catalanotto	.50	.15
50 Jerry Hairston	.50	.15
51 Jeromy Burnitz	.50	.15
52 David Justice	.50	.15
53 Bartolo Colon	.50	.15
54 Andres Galarraga	.50	.15
55 Jeff Weaver	.50	.15
56 Terrence Long	.50	.15
57 Tsuyoshi Shinjo	.50	.15
58 Barry Zito	.75	.23
59 Mariano Rivera	.75	.23
60 John Olerud	.50	.15
61 Randy Johnson	1.25	.35
62 Kenny Lofton	.50	.15
63 Jermaine Dye	.50	.15
64 Troy Glaus	.75	.23
65 Larry Walker	.75	.23
66 Hideo Nomo	1.25	.35
67 Mike Mussina	1.25	.35
68 Paul LoDuca	.50	.15
69 Magglio Ordonez	.50	.15
70 Paul O'Neill	.75	.23
71 Sean Casey	.50	.15
72 Lance Berkman	.50	.15
73 Adam Dunn	.50	.15
74 Aramis Ramirez	.50	.15
75 Rafael Furcal	.50	.15
76 Gary Sheffield	.50	.15
77 Todd Hollandsworth	.50	.15
78 Chipper Jones	1.25	.35
79 Bernie Williams	.75	.23
80 Richard Hidalgo	.50	.15
81 Eric Chavez	.50	.15
82 Mike Piazza	2.00	.60
83 J.D. Drew	.50	.15
84 Ken Griffey Jr.	2.00	.60
85 Joe Kennedy	.50	.15
86 Joel Pineiro	.50	.15
87 Josh Towers	.50	.15
88 Andruw Jones	.50	.15
89 Carlos Beltran	.50	.15
90 Mike Cameron	.50	.15
91 Albert Pujols	2.50	.75
92 Alex Rodriguez	2.00	.60
93 Omar Vizquel	.50	.15
94 Juan Encarnacion	.50	.15
95 Jeff Bagwell	.75	.23
96 Jose Canseco	1.25	.35
97 Ben Sheets	.50	.15
98 Mark Grace	.75	.23
99 Mike Sweeney	.50	.15
100 Mark McGwire	3.00	.90
101 Ivan Rodriguez	1.25	.35
102 Rich Aurilia	.50	.15
103 Cristian Guzman	.50	.15
104 Roy Oswalt	.50	.15
105 Tim Hudson	.50	.15
106 Brent Abernathy	.50	.15
107 Mike Hampton	.50	.15
108 Miguel Tejada	.50	.15
109 Bobby Higginson	.50	.15
110 Edgar Martinez	.75	.23
111 Jorge Posada	.75	.23
112 Jason Giambi Yankees	1.25	.35
113 Pedro Astacio	.50	.15
114 Kazuhiro Sasaki	.50	.15
115 Preston Wilson	.50	.15
116 Jason Bere	.50	.15
117 Mark Quinn	.50	.15
118 Pokey Reese	.50	.15
119 Derek Jeter	3.00	.90
120 Shannon Stewart	.50	.15
121 Jeff Kent	.50	.15
122 Jeremy Giambi	.50	.15
123 Pat Burrell	.50	.15
124 Jim Edmonds	.50	.15
125 Mark Buehrle	.50	.15
126 Kevin Brown	.50	.15
127 Raul Mondesi	.50	.15
128 Pedro Martinez	1.25	.35
129 Jim Thome	1.25	.35
130 Russ Ortiz	.50	.15
131 Br.Duckworth PROS	.50	.15
132 Ryan Jamison PROS	.50	.15
133 Brandon Inge PROS	.50	.15
134 Felipe Lopez PROS	.50	.15
135 Jason Lane PROS	.50	.15
136 F.Johnson PROS RC	.50	.15
137 Greg Nash PROS	.50	.15
138 Covelli Crisp PROS	.50	.15
139 Nick Neugebauer PROS	.50	.15
140 Dustan Mohr PROS	.50	.15
141 Freddy Sanchez FYP RC	1.00	.30
142 Justin Backsmeyer FYP RC	1.00	.30
143 Jorge Julio FYP	1.00	.30
144 Ryan Mottl FYP RC	1.00	.30
145 Chris Tritle FYP RC	1.00	.30
146 Noochie Varner FYP RC	1.00	.30
147 Brian Rogers FYP	1.00	.30
148 Michael Hill FYP RC	1.00	.30
149 Luis Pineda FYP	1.00	.30
150 Rich Thompson FYP RC	1.00	.30
151 Bill Hall FYP	1.00	.30
152 Juan Dominguez FYP RC	4.00	1.20
153 Justin Woodrow FYP	1.00	.30
154 Nic Jackson FYP RC	1.00	.30
155 Layunce Nix FYP RC	8.00	2.40
156 Hank Aaron RET	5.00	1.50
157 Ernie Banks RET	2.50	.75
158 Johnny Bench RET	2.50	.75
159 George Brett RET	6.00	1.80
160 Carlton Fisk RET	1.50	.45
161 Bob Gibson RET	1.50	.45
162 Reggie Jackson RET	1.50	.45
163 Don Mattingly RET	6.00	1.80
164 Kirby Puckett RET	2.50	.75
165 Frank Robinson RET	1.50	.45
166 Nolan Ryan RET	6.00	1.80
167 Tom Seaver RET	1.50	.45
168 Mike Schmidt RET	5.00	1.50
169 Dave Winfield RET	1.00	.30
170 Carl Yastrzemski RET	3.00	.90
171 Frank Chance REP	1.00	.30
172 Ty Cobb REP	5.00	1.50
173 Sam Crawford REP	1.00	.30
174 Johnny Evers REP	1.00	.30
175 John McGraw REP	2.50	.75
176 Eddie Plank REP	2.50	.75
177 Tris Speaker REP	2.50	.75
178 Joe Tinker REP	1.00	.30
179 H.Wagner Orange REP	8.00	2.40
180 Cy Young REP	2.50	.75
181 Javier Vazquez	.50	.15
182A Mark Mulder Green Jsy	.50	.15
182B Mark Mulder White Jsy	.50	.15
183A R.Clemens Blue Jsy	2.50	.75
183B R.Clemens Pinstripes	2.50	.75
184 Kazuhisa Ishii RC	1.50	.45
185 Roberto Alomar	1.25	.35
186 Lance Berkman	.50	.15
187A A.Dunn Arms Folded	.50	.15
187B Adam Dunn w/Bat	.50	.15
188A Aramis Ramirez w/Bat	.50	.15
188B Aramis Ramirez w/o Bat	.50	.15
189 Chuck Knoblauch	.50	.15
190 Nomar Garciaparra	2.00	.60
191 Brad Penny	.50	.15
192A Gary Sheffield w/Bat	.50	.15
192B Gary Sheffield w/o Bat	.50	.15
193 Alfonso Soriano	.75	.23
194 Andruw Jones	.50	.15
195A R.Johnson Black Jsy	1.25	.35
195B R.Johnson Purple Jsy	1.25	.35
196A C.Patterson Blue Jsy	.50	.15
196B C.Patterson Pinstripes	.50	.15
197 Milton Bradley	.50	.15
198A J.Damon Blue Jsy/Cap	.50	.15
198B J.Damon Blue Jsy/Hlmt	.50	.15
198C J.Damon White Jsy	.50	.15
199A Paul Lo Duca Blue Jsy	.50	.15
199B Paul Lo Duca White Jsy	.50	.15
200A Albert Pujols Red Jsy	2.50	.75
200B Albert Pujols Running	2.50	.75
200C Albert Pujols w/Bat	2.50	.75
201 Scott Rolen	.75	.23
202A J.D. Drew Running	.50	.15
202B J.D. Drew w/Bat	.50	.15
202C J.D. Drew White Jsy	.50	.15
203 Vladimir Guerrero	1.25	.35
204A Jason Giambi Blue Jsy	1.25	.35
204B Jason Giambi Grey Jsy	1.25	.35
204C Jason Giambi Pinstripes	1.25	.35
205A Moises Alou Grey Jsy	.50	.15
205B Moises Alou Pinstripes	.50	.15
206A Mag. Ordonez Signing	.50	.15
206B Magglio Ordonez w/Bat	.50	.15
207 Carlos Febles	.50	.15
208 So Taguchi RC	.75	.23
209A Raf. Palmeiro One Hand	.75	.23
209B Raf. Palmeiro Two Hands	.75	.23
210 David Wells	.50	.15
211 Orlando Cabrera	.50	.15
212 Sammy Sosa	2.00	.60
213 Armando Benitez	.50	.15
214 Wes Helms	.50	.15
215A Mar. Rivera Arms Folded	.75	.23
215B Mar. Rivera Holding Ball	.75	.23
216 Jimmy Rollins	.50	.15
217 Matt Lawton	.50	.15
218A Shawn Green w/Bat	.50	.15
218B Shawn Green w/o Bat	.50	.15
219A Bernie Williams w/Bat	.75	.23
219B Bernie Williams w/o Bat	.75	.23
220A Bret Boone Blue Jsy	.50	.15
220B Bret Boone White Jsy	.50	.15
221A Alex Rodriguez Blue Jsy	2.00	.60
221B Alex Rodriguez One Hand	2.00	.60
221C Alex Rodriguez Two Hands	2.00	.60
222 Roger Cedeno	.50	.15
223 Marty Cordova	.50	.15
224 Fred McGriff	.75	.23
225A Chipper Jones Batting	1.25	.35
225B Chipper Jones Running	1.25	.35
226 Kerry Wood	1.25	.35
227A Larry Walker Grey Jsy	.75	.23
227B Larry Walker Purple Jsy	.75	.23
228 Robin Ventura	.50	.15
229 Robert Fick	.50	.15
230A Tino Martinez Black Glove	.75	.23
230B Tino Martinez Throwing	.75	.23
230C Tino Martinez w/Bat	.75	.23
231 Ben Petrick	.50	.15
232 Neifi Perez	.50	.15
233 Pedro Martinez	1.25	.35
234A Brian Jordan Grey Jsy	.50	.15
234B Brian Jordan White Jsy	.50	.15
235 Freddy Garcia	.50	.15
236A Derek Jeter Batting	3.00	.90
236B Derek Jeter Blue Jsy	3.00	.90
236C Derek Jeter Kneeling	3.00	.90
237 Ben Grieve	.50	.15
238A Barry Bonds Black Jsy	3.00	.90
238B B.Bonds w/Wrist Band	3.00	.90
238C B.Bonds w/o Wrist Band	3.00	.90
239 Luis Gonzalez	.50	.15
240 Shane Halter	.50	.15
241A Brian Giles Black Jsy	.50	.15
241B Brian Giles Grey Jsy	.50	.15
242 Bud Smith	.50	.15
243 Richie Sexson	.50	.15
244A Barry Zito Green Jsy	.75	.23
244B Barry Zito White Jsy	.75	.23
245 Eric Milton	.50	.15
246A Ivan Rodriguez Blue Jsy	1.25	.35
246B I.Rodriguez Grey Jsy	1.25	.35
246C I.Rodriguez White Jsy	1.25	.35
247 Toby Hall	.50	.15
248A Mike Piazza Black Jsy	2.00	.60
248B Mike Piazza Grey Jsy	2.00	.60
249 Ruben Sierra	.50	.15
250A Tsuyoshi Shinjo Cap	.50	.15
250B Tsuyoshi Shinjo Helmet	.50	.15
251A Jer. Dye Green Jsy	.50	.15
251B Jermaine Dye White Jsy	.50	.15
252 Roy Oswalt	.50	.15
253 Todd Helton	.75	.23
254 Adrian Beltre	.50	.15
255 Doug Mientkiewicz	.50	.15
256A Ichiro Suzuki Blue Jsy	2.00	.60
256B Ichiro Suzuki w/Bat	2.00	.60
256C Ichiro Suzuki White Jsy	2.00	.60
257A C.C. Sabathia Blue Jsy	.50	.15
257B C.C. Sabathia White Jsy	.50	.15
258 Paul Konerko	.50	.15
259 Ken Griffey Jr.	2.00	.60
260A Jeromy Burnitz w/Bat	.50	.15
260B Jeromy Burnitz w/o Bat	.50	.15
261 Hank Blalock PROS	1.25	.35
262 Mark Prior PROS	2.50	.75
263 Josh Beckett PROS	.75	.23
264 Carlos Pena PROS	.50	.15
265 Sean Burroughs PROS	.50	.15
266 Austin Kearns PROS	.50	.15
267 Chin-Hui Tsao PROS	.50	.15
268 Dewon Brazelton PROS	.50	.15
269 J.D. Martin PROS	.50	.15
270 Marlon Byrd PROS	.50	.15
271 Joe Mauer FYP RC	5.00	1.50
272 Jason Botts FYP RC	1.00	.30
273 Mauricio Lara FYP RC	1.00	.30
274 Jonny Gomes FYP RC	1.25	.35
275 Gavin Floyd FYP RC	2.50	.75
276 Alex Requena FYP RC	1.00	.30
277 Jimmy Gobble FYP RC	1.50	.45
278 Chris Duffy FYP RC	1.00	.30
279 Colt Griffin FYP RC	1.25	.35
280 Ryan Church FYP RC	1.00	.30
281 Beltran Perez FYP RC	1.00	.30
282 Clint Nageotte FYP RC	1.25	.35
283 Justin Schuda FYP RC	1.00	.30
284 Scott Hairston FYP RC	2.00	.60
285 Mario Ramos FYP RC	1.00	.30
286 Tom Seaver White Sox RET	1.50	.45
286 Tom Seaver Mets RET	1.50	.45
287 H.Aaron White Jsy RET	5.00	1.50
287 H.Aaron Blue Jsy RET	5.00	1.50
288 Mike Schmidt RET	5.00	1.50
289A R.Yount Blue Jsy RET	4.00	1.20
289B R.Yount P'stripes RET	4.00	1.20
290 Joe Morgan RET	1.00	.30
291 Frank Robinson RET	1.50	.45
292A Reggie Jackson A's RET	1.50	.45
292B Reggie Jackson Yanks RET	1.50	.45
293A Nolan Ryan Astros RET	6.00	1.80
293B N.Ryan Rangers RET	6.00	1.80
294 Dave Winfield RET	1.00	.30
295 Willie Mays RET	5.00	1.50
296 Brooks Robinson RET	2.50	.75
297A Mark McGwire A's RET	6.00	1.80
297B M.McGwire Cards RET	6.00	1.80
298 Honus Wagner RET	2.50	.75
299A Sherry Magee REP	1.00	.30
299B Sherry Magie UER REP	1.00	.30
300 Frank Chance REP	1.00	.30
301A Joe Doyle NY REP	1.00	.30
301B Joe Doyle NY Nat'l REP	1.00	.30
302 John McGraw REP	2.50	.75
303 Jimmy Collins REP	1.00	.30
304 Buck Herzog REP	1.00	.30
305 Sam Crawford REP	1.00	.30
306 Cy Young REP	2.50	.75
307 Honus Wagner Blue REP	8.00	2.40
308A A.Rodriguez Blue Jsy SP	4.00	1.20
308B A.Rodriguez White Jsy	2.00	.60
309 Vernon Wells	.50	.15
310A B.Bonds w/Elbow Pad	3.00	.90
310B B.Bonds w/o Elbow Pad SP	6.00	1.80
311 Vicente Padilla	.50	.15
312A A.Soriano w/Wristband	.75	.23
312B A.Soriano w/o Wristband SP	2.00	.60
313 Mike Piazza	2.00	.60
314 Jacque Jones	.50	.15
315 Shawn Green SP	2.00	.60
316 Paul Byrd	.50	.15
317 Lance Berkman	.50	.15
318 Larry Walker	.75	.23
319 Ken Griffey Jr. SP	4.00	1.20
320 Shea Hillenbrand	.50	.15
321 Jay Gibbons	.50	.15
322 Andruw Jones	.50	.15
323 Luis Gonzalez SP	2.00	.60
324 Garret Anderson	.50	.15
325 Roy Halladay	.50	.15
326 Randy Winn	.50	.15
327 Matt Morris	.50	.15
328 Robb Nen	.50	.15
329 Trevor Hoffman	.50	.15
330 Kip Wells	.50	.15
331 Orlando Hernandez	.50	.15
332 Rey Ordonez	.50	.15
333 Torii Hunter	.50	.15
334 Geoff Jenkins	.50	.15
335 Eric Karros	.50	.15
336 Mike Lowell	.50	.15
337 Nick Johnson	.50	.15
338 Randall Simon	.50	.15
339 Ellis Burks	.50	.15
340A S.Sosa Blue Jsy SP	4.00	1.20
340B Sammy Sosa White Jsy	2.00	.60
341 Pedro Martinez	1.25	.35
342 Junior Spivey	.50	.15
343 Vinny Castilla	.50	.15
344 Randy Johnson SP	2.50	.75
345 Chipper Jones SP	2.50	.75
346 Orlando Hudson	.50	.15
347 Albert Pujols SP	5.00	1.50
348 Rondell White	.50	.15
349 Vladimir Guerrero	1.25	.35
350A Mark Prior Red SP	5.00	1.50
350B Mark Prior Yellow	2.50	.75
351 Eric Gagne	.75	.23
352 Todd Zeile	.50	.15
353 Manny Ramirez SP	2.00	.60
354 Kevin Millwood	.50	.15
355 Troy Percival	.50	.15
356A Jason Giambi Batting SP	2.50	.75
356B Jason Giambi Throwing	1.25	.35
357 Bartolo Colon	.50	.15
358 Jeremy Giambi	.50	.15
359 Jose Cruz Jr.	.50	.15
360A I.Suzuki Blue Jsy SP	4.00	1.20
360B I.Suzuki White Jsy	2.00	.60
361 Eddie Guardado	.50	.15
362 Ivan Rodriguez	1.25	.35
363 Carl Crawford	.50	.15
364 Jason Simontacchi RC	.75	.23
365 Kenny Lofton	.50	.15
366 Raul Mondesi	.50	.15
367 A.J. Pierzynski	.50	.15
368 Ugueth Urbina	.50	.15
369 Rodrigo Lopez	.50	.15
370A N.Garciaparra One Bat SP	4.00	1.20
370B N.Garciaparra Two Bats	2.00	.60
371 Craig Counsell	.50	.15
372 Barry Larkin	1.25	.35
373 Carlos Pena	.50	.15
374 Luis Castillo	.50	.15
375 Raul Ibanez	.50	.15
376 Kazuhisa Ishii SP	2.50	.75
377 Derek Lowe	.50	.15
378 Curt Schilling	.75	.23
379 Jim Thome Phillies	1.25	.35
380A Derek Jeter Blue SP	6.00	1.80
380B Derek Jeter Seats	3.00	.90
381 Pat Burrell	.50	.15
382 Jamie Moyer	.50	.15
383 Eric Hinske	.50	.15
384 Scott Rolen	.75	.23
385 Miguel Tejada SP	2.00	.60
386 Andy Pettitte	.75	.23
387 Mike Lieberthal	.50	.15
388 Al Leiter	.50	.15
389 Todd Helton SP	2.00	.60
390A Adam Dunn Bat SP	2.00	.60
390B Adam Dunn Glove	.50	.15
391 Cliff Floyd	.50	.15
392 Tim Salmon	.75	.23
393 Joe Torre MG	.75	.23
394 Bobby Cox MG	.50	.15
395 Tony LaRussa MG	.50	.15
396 Art Howe MG	.50	.15
397 Bob Brenly MG	.50	.15
398 Ron Gardenhire MG	.50	.15
399 Mike Cuddyer PROS	.50	.15
400 Joe Mauer PROS	5.00	1.50
401 Mark Teixeira PROS	1.25	.35
402 Hee Seop Choi PROS	.75	.23
403 Angel Berroa PROS	.50	.15
404 Jesse Foppert PROS RC	2.00	.60
405 Bobby Crosby PROS	1.25	.35
406 Jose Reyes PROS	1.25	.35
407 C.Kotchman PROS RC	3.00	.90
408 Aaron Heilman PROS	.50	.15
409 Adrian Gonzalez PROS	.50	.15
410 Delwyn Young PROS RC	2.00	.60
411 Brett Myers PROS	.50	.15
412 Justin Huber PROS RC	1.25	.35
413 Drew Henson PROS	.50	.15
414 T.Bozied PROS RC	2.00	.60
415 Dontrelle Willis PROS RC	6.00	1.80
416 Rocco Baldelli PROS	2.50	.75
417 Jason Stokes PROS RC	5.00	1.50
418 Brandon Phillips PROS	.50	.15
419 Jake Blalock FYP RC	2.50	.75
420 Micah Schilling FYP RC	1.00	.30
421 Denard Span FYP RC	1.00	.30
422A J.Loney Red FYP RC	4.00	1.20
422B J.Loney w/Sky FYP RC	4.00	1.20
423A W.Bankston Blue FYP RC	2.00	.60
423B W.Bankston w/Sky FYP RC	2.00	.60
424 Jeremy Hermida FYP RC	3.00	.90
425 C.Granderson FYP RC	1.25	.35
426A J.Pridie Red FYP RC	1.50	.45
426B J.Pridie w/Sky FYP RC	1.50	.45
427 Larry Broadway FYP RC	2.00	.60
428A K.Greene Green FYP RC	4.00	1.20
428B K.Greene Red FYP RC	4.00	1.20
429 Joey Votto FYP RC	1.00	.30
430A B.Upton Grey FYP RC	6.00	1.80
430B B.Upton w/People FYP RC	6.00	1.80
431A S.Santos Gold FYP RC	2.50	.75
431B S.Santos Grey FYP RC	2.50	.75
432 Brian Dopirak FYP RC	2.00	.60
433 Ozzie Smith RET SP	4.00	1.20
434 Wade Boggs RET SP	2.50	.75
435 Yogi Berra RET SP	4.00	1.20
436 Al Kaline RET SP	4.00	1.20
437 Robin Roberts RET SP	2.00	.60
438 Rob. Clemente RET SP	8.00	2.40
439 Gary Carter RET SP	2.50	.75
440 Fergie Jenkins RET SP	2.00	.60
441 Orlando Cepeda RET SP	2.00	.60
442 Rod Carew RET SP	2.50	.75
443 Ha. Killebrew RET SP	4.00	1.20
444 Duke Snider RET SP	2.50	.75
445 Stan Musial RET SP	6.00	1.80
446 Hank Greenberg RET SP	4.00	1.20
447 Lou Brock RET SP	2.50	.75
448 Jim Palmer RET	1.00	.30
449 John McGraw REP	1.00	.30
450 Mordecai Brown REP	1.00	.30
451 Christy Mathewson REP	1.50	.45
452 Sam Crawford REP	1.00	.30
453 Bill O'Hara REP	1.00	.30
454 Joe Tinker REP	1.00	.30
455 Nap Lajoie REP	1.50	.45
456 Honus Wagner Red REP	8.00	2.40
NNO Repurchased Tobacco Card		

2002 Topps 206 American Beauty

Inserted into third series packs as a stated rate of one in 15,316 these five cards were issued with the very scarce American Beauty back. These cards were issued to a stated print run of five sets so no pricing is provided due to scarcity.

	Nm-Mt	Ex-Mt
308 A.Rodriguez White Jsy		
310 B.Bonds w/Elbow Pad		
312 A.Soriano w/Wristband		
370 N.Garciaparra Two Bats		
456 Honus Wagner Red REP		

2002 Topps 206 Bazooka

This quasi-parallel skip-numbered set was inserted at stated odds of one 1185 first series packs, one in 1989 second series packs and one in 825 third series packs. Though the cards are not serial-numbered in any manner, officials at Topps did publicly release a statement verifying that only 30 copies of each card were produced. This set was limited to 15 key players from each series of the 206 set making the set complete at 45 cards. These cards feature a "Bazooka" back, which is the only back on these parallel cards which was not a tobacco producer during the original tobacco card era. Due to market scarcity, no pricing is currently provided.

	Nm-Mt	Ex-Mt
22 Ichiro Suzuki Portrait		
23 Jimmy Rollins		
34 Barry Bonds		
47 Tony Gwynn		

57 Tsuyoshi Shinjo
73 Adam Dunn
91 Albert Pujols
100 Mark McGwire
104 Roy Oswalt
112 Jason Giambi Yankees
119 Derek Jeter
131 Brandon Duckworth PROS
154 Nic Jackson FYP
166 Nolan Ryan RET
172 Ty Cobb REP
185 Roberto Alomar
190 Nomar Garciaparra
203 Vladimir Guerrero
212 Sammy Sosa
221B A.Rodriguez One Hand
233 Pedro Martinez
244B Barry Zito White Jsy
248A Mike Piazza Black Jsy
253 Todd Helton
259 Ken Griffey Jr.
262 Mark Prior Blue PROS
271 Joe Mauer FYP
288 Mike Schmidt RET
306 Cy Young REP
307 Honus Wagner Blue REP
308 A.Rodriguez White Jsy
310 B.Bonds w/Elbow Pad
312 A.Soriano w/Wristband
315 Shawn Green
337 Nick Johnson
350 Mark Prior Yellow
360 Ichiro Suzuki White Jsy
381 Pat Burrell
385 Miguel Tejada
393 Joe Torre MG
413 Drew Henson PROS
430 B.J. Upton Grey FYP
438 Roberto Clemente RET
454 Joe Tinker REP
456 Honus Wagner Red REP

2002 Topps 206 Carolina Brights

Randomly inserted in second series packs and using the "Carolina Brights" backs, these cards parallel the Topps 206 second series cards.

Nm-Mt Ex-Mt
*CAROLINA 181-270: 3X TO 8X BASIC
*CAROLINA RC's 181-270: 1X TO 2.5X
*CAROLINA 271-285: 1.25X TO 3X BASIC
*CAROLINA 286-307: 2X TO 5X BASIC

2002 Topps 206 Cycle

Randomly inserted in first series packs and using the "Cycle" backs, this is a complete parallel of the Topps 206 first series.

Nm-Mt Ex-Mt
*CYCLE 1-140: 5X TO 12X BASIC CARDS
*CYCLE 141-155: 1.25X TO 3X BASIC
*CYCLE 156-180: 3X TO 8X BASIC

2002 Topps 206 Drum

Issued at a stated rate of one in 3711 third series packs, these five cards feature "Drum" backs. These cards have a stated print run of 20 sets and no pricing is provided due to market scarcity.

Nm-Mt Ex-Mt
324 Garret Anderson
356 Jason Giambi Batting
360 I.Suzuki White Jsy
390 Adam Dunn Glove
400 Joe Mauer PROS

2002 Topps 206 Lenox

Issued at a stated rate of one in 7422 third series packs, these five cards feature "Lenox" backs. These cards have a stated print run of 10 sets and no pricing is provided due to market scarcity.

Nm-Mt Ex-Mt
308 A.Rodriguez Blue Jsy
340 Sammy Sosa White Jsy
349 Vladimir Guerrero
353 Manny Ramirez
416 Rocco Baldelli PROS

2002 Topps 206 Piedmont Black

Randomly inserted in second series packs and using the "Piedmont" backs, these cards parallel the Topps 206 second series cards. The words on the back are in black ink and thus these cards are called Piedmont Black

Nm-Mt Ex-Mt
*P'MONT.BLACK 181-270: 1.5X TO 4X BASIC
*P'MONT.BLACK RC's 181-270: .5X TO 1.2X
*P'MONT.BLACK 271-285: .6X TO 1.5X
*P'MONT.BLACK 286-307: 1X TO 2.5X

2002 Topps 206 Piedmont Red

Randomly inserted in second series packs and using the "Piedmont" backs, these cards parallel the Topps 206 second series cards. The words on the back are in black ink and thus these cards are called Piedmont Red.

Nm-Mt Ex-Mt
*P'MONT.RED 181-270: 3X TO 8X BASIC
*P'MONT.RED RC's 181-270: 1X TO 2.5X
*P'MONT.RED 271-285: 1.25X TO 3X
*P'MONT.RED 286-307: 2X TO 5X BASIC

2002 Topps 206 Polar Bear

Randomly inserted into approximately two out of every three packs and using the "Polar Bear" backs, this is a complete parallel of the Topps 206 set. Cards 1-180 were distributed in first series packs, 181-307 in second series packs and 308-456 in third series packs. The set is actually complete at 525 cards, but the checklist runs from 1-307 with 96 variations intermingled within.

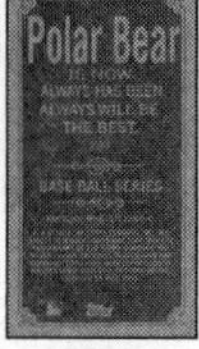

Nm-Mt Ex-Mt
*POLAR 1-140/181-270/308-418: 1.25X TO 3X
*RC 1-140/181-270/308-418: .5X TO 1.2X
*FYP 141-155/271-285: .5X TO 1.2X
*SP 308-418: .6X TO 1.5X SP
*FYP 419-432: .5X TO 1.2X
*RT/RP 156-180/286-307/448-456: .75X TO 2X
*RET 443-447: .75X TO 2X

2002 Topps 206 Sweet Caporal Black

Randomly inserted into packs, this is a parallel to the T206 third series. These cards have the words "Sweet Caporal" in black on the back.

Nm-Mt Ex-Mt
*BLACK 308-418: 2.5X TO 6X BASIC
*BLACK SP 308-418: 1.25X TO 3X BASIC
*BLACK RC 308-418: 1X TO 2.5X BASIC
*BLACK 419-432: 1.25X TO 3X BASIC
*BLACK 433-447: .75X TO 2X BASIC
*BLACK 448-456: 1.5X TO 4X BASIC

2002 Topps 206 Sweet Caporal Blue

Randomly inserted into packs, this is a parallel to the T206 third series. These cards have the words "Sweet Caporal" in blue on the back.

Nm-Mt Ex-Mt
*BLUE 308-418: 2X TO 5X BASIC
*BLUE SP 308-418: 1X TO 2.5X BASIC
*BLUE RC 308-418: .75X TO 2X BASIC
*BLUE 419-432: 1X TO 2.5X BASIC
*BLUE 433-447: .6X TO 1.5X BASIC
*BLUE 448-456: 1.25X TO 3X BASIC

2002 Topps 206 Sweet Caporal Red

Randomly inserted into packs, this is a parallel to the T206 third series. These cards have the words "Sweet Caporal" in blue on the back.

Nm-Mt Ex-Mt
*RED 308-418: 1.5X TO 4X BASIC
*RED SP 308-418: .75X TO 2X BASIC
*RED RC 308-418: .6X TO 1.5X BASIC
*RED 419-432: .75X TO 2X BASIC
*RED 433-447: .5X TO 1.2X BASIC
*RED 448-456: 1X TO 2.5X BASIC

2002 Topps 206 Tolstoi

Randomly inserted in first series packs and using the "Tolstoi" backs, this is a complete parallel of the Topps 206 first series.

Nm-Mt Ex-Mt
*TOLSTOI 1-140: 1.5X TO 4X BASIC
*TOLSTOI 141-155: .4X TO 1X BASIC
*TOLSTOI 156-180: 1X TO 2.5X BASIC

2002 Topps 206 Tolstoi Red

Randomly inserted in packs and using the "Tolstoi" backs, this is a complete parallel of the Topps 206 first series. These cards are differentiated from the more common Tolstoi backs as the color on the back is red. These cards were printed at a stated rate of 25 percent of the total Tolstoi run.

Nm-Mt Ex-Mt
*TOLSTOI RED 1-140: 3X TO 8X BASIC
*TOLSTOI RED 141-155: .6X TO 1.5X BASIC
*TOLSTOI RED 156-180: 2X TO 5X BASIC

2002 Topps 206 Uzit

Randomly inserted into packs, this is a parallel to the T206 third series. These cards have "Uzit" on the back.

Nm-Mt Ex-Mt
*UZIT 308-418: 3X TO 8X BASIC
*UZIT SP 308-418: 1.5X TO 4X BASIC
*UZIT RC 308-418: 1.5X TO 4X BASIC
*UZIT 419-432: 1.5X TO 4X BASIC
*UZIT 433-447: 1X TO 2.5X BASIC
*UZIT 448-456: 2X TO 5X BASIC

2002 Topps 206 Autographs

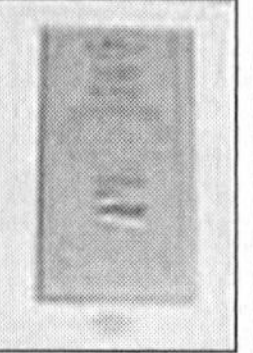

Inserted at an overall stated rate of one in 41 series one packs, one in 55 series two packs and varying group specific odds in series three packs (see details below), these cards feature a mix of young players and veteran stars who autographed cards for the T206 product.

Nm-Mt Ex-Mt
SER.1 GROUP A1 ODDS 1:1067
SER.1 GROUP B1 ODDS 1:1122
SER.1 GROUP C1 ODDS 1:532
SER.1 GROUP D1 ODDS 1:444
SER.1 GROUP E1 ODDS 1:532
SER.1 GROUP F1 ODDS 1:121
SER.1 GROUP G1 ODDS 1:118
SER.2 GROUP A2 ODDS 1:511
SER.2 GROUP B2 ODDS 1:893
SER.2 GROUP C2 ODDS 1:1557
SER.2 GROUP D2 ODDS 1:106
SER.2 GROUP E2 ODDS 1:638
SER.2 GROUP F2 ODDS 1:596
SER.2 GROUP G2 ODDS 1:526
SER.3 GROUP A3 ODDS 1:810
SER.3 GROUP B3 ODDS 1:442
SER.3 GROUP C3 ODDS 1:411
SER.3 GROUP D3 ODDS 1:393
SER.3 GROUP E3 ODDS 1:393
SER.3 GROUP F3 ODDS 1:384
SER.3 GROUP G3 ODDS 1:383
AP Albert Pujols A2 150.00 45.00
AR Alex Rodriguez A1 150.00 45.00
BB Barry Bonds A1 200.00 60.00
BG Brian Giles G1 15.00 4.50
BI Brandon Inge D1 15.00 4.50
BS Ben Sheets E2 15.00 4.50
BSM Bud Smith B2 15.00 4.50
BZ Barry Zito D1 40.00 12.00
CG Cristian Guzman G1 15.00 4.50
CT Chris Tritle G2 15.00 4.50
DB Dewon Brazelton D2 10.00 3.00
DE David Eckstein G3 10.00 3.00
DH Drew Henson D3 20.00 6.00
EC Eric Chavez A2 30.00 9.00
FJ Forrest Johnson F1 10.00 3.00
FL Felipe Lopez C1 15.00 4.50
GF Gavin Floyd D2 25.00 7.50
GN Greg Nash F1 10.00 3.00
HB Hank Blalock D2 20.00 6.00
JC Jose Cruz Jr. A3 25.00 7.50
JD Johnny Damon B2 25.00 7.50
JDM J.D. Martin D2 10.00 3.00
JE Jim Edmonds C1 30.00 9.00
JJ Jorge Julio F1 10.00 3.00
JM Joe Mauer D2 60.00 18.00
JR Jimmy Rollins G1 15.00 4.50
JV Jose Vidro B3 15.00 4.50
KI Kazuhisa Ishii A2 60.00 18.00
LB Lance Berkman A2 30.00 9.00
LG Luis Gonzalez C2 25.00 7.50
MA Moises Alou A2 15.00 4.50
MB Milton Bradley C3 15.00 4.50
MB Marlon Byrd D2 15.00 4.50
ML Mike Lamb F3 10.00 3.00
MO Maggilo Ordonez E1 20.00 6.00
MP Mark Prior D2 100.00 30.00
MT Marcus Thames E3 10.00 3.00
RC Roger Clemens B1 150.00 45.00
RJ Ryan Jamison F1 10.00 3.00
RS Richie Sexson F2 15.00 4.50
SR Scott Rolen A2 40.00 12.00
ST So Taguchi A2 40.00 12.00

2002 Topps 206 Relics

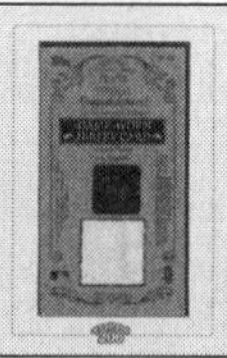

Issued in first series packs at overall stated odds of one in 11 and second series packs at overall stated odds of one in 12 and third series packs at various odds, these 109 cards feature either a bat sliver or a jersey/uniform swatch. Representatives at Topps announced that only 25 copies of the Honus Wagner blue Bat and Honus Wagner Red Bat and 100 copies of the Ty Cobb Bat card (both seeded into second series packs) were produced. Please note, all first series Relics feature light yellow frames (surrounding the mini-sized card), all second series Relics feature light blue frames and third series Relics feature light pink frames.

Nm-Mt Ex-Mt
SER.1 BAT GROUP A1 ODDS 1:166
SER.1 BAT GROUP B1 ODDS 1:1780
SER.2 BAT GROUP A2 ODDS 1:35,217
SER.2 BAT GROUP B2 ODDS 1:8991
SER.2 BAT GROUP C2 ODDS 1:2097
SER.2 BAT GROUP D2 ODDS 1:75
SER.2 BAT GROUP E2 ODDS 1:1377
SER.2 BAT GROUP F2 ODDS 1:893
SER.2 BAT GROUP G2 ODDS 1:248
SER.2 BAT GROUP H2 ODDS 1:319
SER.2 BAT GROUP I2 ODDS 1:447
SER.2 BAT OVERALL ODDS 1:40
SER.3 BAT GROUP A3 ODDS 1:15,316
SER.3 BAT GROUP B3 ODDS 1:390
SER.3 BAT GROUP C3 ODDS 1:370
SER.3 BAT GROUP D3 ODDS 1:34
SER.3 BAT GROUP E3 ODDS 1:187
SER.3 BAT GROUP F3 ODDS 1:185
SER.1 UNI GROUP A1 ODDS 1:15
SER.1 UNI GROUP B1 ODDS 1:74
SER.2 UNI GROUP A2 ODDS 1:372
SER.2 UNI GROUP B2 ODDS 1:27
SER.2 UNI GROUP C2 ODDS 1:62
SER.2 UNI GROUP D2 ODDS 1:447
SER.2 UNI OVERALL ODDS 1:18
SER.3 UNI GROUP A3 ODDS 1:247
SER.3 UNI GROUP B3 ODDS 1:185
SER.3 UNI GROUP C3 ODDS 1:62
SER.3 UNI GROUP D3 ODDS 1:187
SER.3 UNI GROUP E3 ODDS 1:27
SER.3 UNI GROUP F3 ODDS 1:176
AB A.J. Burnett Jsy B2 8.00 2.40
AD2 Adam Dunn Bat D2 15.00 4.50
AD3 Adam Dunn Bat C3 15.00 4.50
AJ1 Andruw Jones Jsy A1 8.00 2.40
AJ2 Andruw Jones Jsy C2 8.00 2.40
AJ3 Andruw Jones Uni E3 8.00 2.40
AP1 Albert Pujols Bat A1 20.00 6.00
AP2 Albert Pujols Jsy B2 20.00 6.00
AP3 Albert Pujols Bat D3 20.00 6.00
ARA Aramis Ramirez Bat D2 15.00 4.50
AR2 Alex Rodriguez Bat D2 20.00 6.00
AR3 Alex Rodriguez Bat D3 15.00 4.50
AS1 Alfonso Soriano Bat A1 15.00 4.50
AS2 Alfonso Soriano Bat I2 10.00 3.00
AS3 Alfonso Soriano Bat D3 10.00 3.00
BB1 Barry Bonds Jsy A1 25.00 7.50
BB2 Barry Bonds Uni C2 25.00 7.50
BD Brandon Duckworth Jsy B2 8.00 2.40
BH Buck Herzog Bat G2 40.00 12.00
BL Barry Larkin Jsy B2 15.00 4.50
BP Brad Penny Jsy B2 8.00 2.40
BW1 Bernie Williams Jsy A1 10.00 3.00
BW2 Bernie Williams Jsy B2 10.00 3.00
BW3 Bernie Williams Uni A3 15.00 4.50
BZ1 Barry Zito Jsy A1 10.00 3.00
BZ3 Barry Zito Uni C3 10.00 3.00
CB Craig Biggio Jsy B1 10.00 3.00
CD Carlos Delgado Jsy A1 8.00 2.40
CF1 Cliff Floyd Jsy A1 8.00 2.40
CF2 Cliff Floyd Jsy B2 8.00 2.40
CG Cristian Guzman Jsy B2 8.00 2.40
CJ1 Chipper Jones Jsy A1 15.00 4.50
CJ2 Chipper Jones Jsy B2 15.00 4.50
CJ3 Chipper Jones Uni B3 15.00 4.50
CL Carlos Lee Jsy A1 8.00 2.40
CP Corey Patterson Bat F3 8.00 2.40
CS2 Curt Schilling Bat D2 15.00 4.50
CS3 Curt Schilling Bat D3 10.00 3.00
DE Darin Erstad Jsy B2 8.00 2.40
DM Doug Mientkiewicz Uni D3 8.00 2.40
EC2 Eric Chavez Bat H2 8.00 2.40
EC3 Eric Chavez Uni E3 8.00 2.40
EM1 Edgar Martinez Jsy A1 10.00 3.00
EM2 Edgar Martinez Jsy B2 10.00 3.00
FM Fred McGriff Bat D2 15.00 4.50
FT1 Frank Thomas Jsy A1 15.00 4.50
FT2 Frank Thomas Jsy B2 15.00 4.50
FT3 Frank Thomas Uni C3 15.00 4.50
GM1 Greg Maddux Jsy A1 15.00 4.50
GM2 Greg Maddux Jsy C2 15.00 4.50
GS2 Gary Sheffield Bat D2 15.00 4.50
GS3 Gary Sheffield Bat B3 15.00 4.50
HW1 H.Wagner Orange Bat B1 500.00 150.00
HW2 H.Wagner Blue Bat A2 SP/25
HW3 H.Wagner Red Bat A3 SP/25
IR1 Ivan Rodriguez Jsy A1 15.00 4.50
IR2 Ivan Rodriguez Uni A2 15.00 4.50
IR3 Ivan Rodriguez Bat D3 15.00 4.50
JB1 Jeff Bagwell Jsy A1 10.00 3.00
JB2 Jeff Bagwell Uni C2 10.00 3.00
JB3 Jeff Bagwell Bat D3 10.00 3.00
JD Johnny Damon Bat D2 15.00 4.50
JE1 Jim Edmonds Jsy A1 8.00 2.40
JE3 Jim Edmonds Uni F3 8.00 2.40
JG Juan Gonzalez Bat D2 20.00 6.00
JH Josh Hamilton Bat D2 10.00 3.00
JJ Jason Jennings Jsy B2 8.00 2.40
JK Jeff Kent Uni B2 8.00 2.40
JO1 John Olerud Jsy A1 8.00 2.40
JO2 John Olerud Jsy B2 8.00 2.40
JT Joe Tinker Bat G2 60.00 18.00
JW Jeff Weaver Jsy A1 8.00 2.40
KB Kevin Brown Jsy B2 8.00 2.40
KL Kenny Lofton Jsy B1 8.00 2.40
LG Luis Gonzalez Uni E3 8.00 2.40
LW1 Larry Walker Jsy A1 10.00 3.00
LW2 Larry Walker Jsy B2 10.00 3.00
MC Mike Cameron Jsy A1 8.00 2.40
MG Mark Grace Bat D2 15.00 4.50
MO Maggilo Ordonez Jsy A1 8.00 2.40
MP1 Mike Piazza Jsy A1 15.00 4.50
MP2 Mike Piazza Uni C2 15.00 4.50
MP3 Mike Piazza Uni C3 15.00 4.50
MT2 Miguel Tejada Bat H2 8.00 2.40
MT3 Miguel Tejada Uni E3 8.00 2.40
MV2 Mo Vaughn Bat D2 15.00 4.50
MV3 Mo Vaughn Uni E3 8.00 2.40
MW Matt Williams Jsy B2 8.00 2.40
NG Nomar Garciaparra Bat C3 20.00 6.00
NJ Nick Johnson Bat E3 8.00 2.40
PB Pat Burrell Bat B3 15.00 4.50
PM Pedro Martinez Uni A3 20.00 6.00
PO Paul O'Neill Jsy A1 10.00 3.00
PW Preston Wilson Jsy B2 8.00 2.40
RA1 Roberto Alomar Jsy A1 15.00 4.50
RA2 Roberto Alomar Bat D2 20.00 6.00
RA3 Roberto Alomar Bat D3 15.00 4.50
RD Ryan Dempster Jsy B2 8.00 2.40
RH2 Rickey Henderson Bat D2 20.00 6.00
RH3 Rickey Henderson Bat D3 15.00 4.50
RJ1 Randy Johnson Jsy A1 15.00 4.50
RJ2 Randy Johnson Jsy C2 15.00 4.50
RJ3 Randy Johnson Uni A3 20.00 6.00
RP2 Rafael Palmeiro Jsy B2 10.00 3.00
RP3 Rafael Palmeiro Uni B3 10.00 3.00
RV Robin Ventura Bat D2 15.00 4.50
SB Sean Burroughs Bat D2 15.00 4.50
SC Sam Crawford Bat A1 60.00 18.00
SCR Sam Crawford Bat C2 60.00 18.00
SG1 Shawn Green Jsy A1 8.00 2.40
SG2 Shawn Green Jsy C2 8.00 2.40
SR Scott Rolen Bat D3 10.00 3.00
SS Shannon Stewart Bat A1 15.00 4.50
TC Ty Cobb Bat B2 SP/100 500.00 150.00
TL Travis Lee Bat D2 10.00 3.00
TM1 Tino Martinez Jsy A1 10.00 3.00
TM2 Tino Martinez Bat D2 15.00 4.50
WB Wilson Betemit Bat D3 8.00 2.40
BBO1 Bret Boone Jsy B1 8.00 2.40
BBO2 Bret Boone Jsy D2 8.00 2.40
CHP Chan Ho Park Bat A1 15.00 4.50
JCA Jose Canseco Bat A1 20.00 6.00
JCO Jimmy Collins Bat F2 60.00 18.00
JEV1 Johnny Evers Jsy A1 60.00 18.00
JEV2 Johnny Evers Bat G2 60.00 18.00
JMA Joe Mays Jsy B2 8.00 2.40
JMC1 John McGraw Bat A1 80.00 24.00
JMC2 John McGraw Bat E2 80.00 24.00
JTH1 Jim Thome Jsy A1 15.00 4.50
JTH2 Jim Thome Bat D2 20.00 6.00
JTH3 Jim Thome Uni C3 15.00 4.50
TGL1 Tom Glavine Jsy A1 10.00 3.00
TGL2 Tom Glavine Jsy A2 10.00 3.00
TGW1 Tony Gwynn Jsy A1 15.00 4.50
TGW2 Tony Gwynn Jsy B2 15.00 4.50
TGW3 Tony Gwynn Uni E3 15.00 4.50
THA Toby Hall Jsy B2 8.00 2.40
THE1 Todd Helton Jsy A1 10.00 3.00
THE2 Todd Helton Jsy C2 10.00 3.00
THE3 Todd Helton Uni E3 10.00 3.00
TSH2 Tsuyoshi Shinjo Bat D2 15.00 4.50
TSH3 Tsuyoshi Shinjo Bat D3 8.00 2.40
TSP Tris Speaker Bat A1 100.00 30.00
JAGI Jason Giambi Jsy A1 15.00 4.50
JEGI Jeremy Giambi Jsy A1 8.00 2.40

2002 Topps 206 Team 206 Series 1

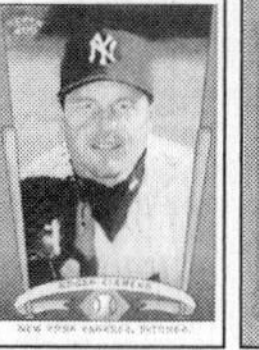

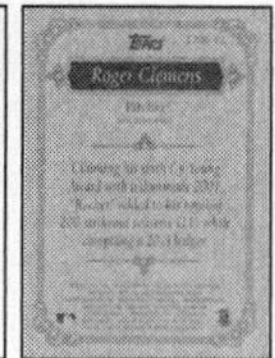

Inserted at an approximate rate of one per pack (only not in a pack when an autograph or relic card was inserted), these 20 cards feature the leading players from the 206 first series in a more modern design.

Nm-Mt Ex-Mt
COMPLETE SET (20) 15.00 4.50
T206-1 Barry Bonds 2.50 .75
T206-2 Ivan Rodriguez 1.00 .30
T206-3 Luis Gonzalez .50 .15
T206-4 Jason Giambi Yankees 1.00 .30
T206-5 Pedro Martinez 1.00 .30
T206-6 Larry Walker .60 .18
T206-7 Bob Abreu .50 .15
T206-8 Derek Jeter 2.50 .75
T206-9 Bret Boone .50 .15
T206-10 Mike Piazza 1.50 .45
T206-11 Alex Rodriguez 1.50 .45
T206-12 Roger Clemens 2.00 .60
T206-13 Albert Pujols 2.00 .60
T206-14 Randy Johnson 1.00 .30
T206-15 Sammy Sosa 1.50 .45
T206-16 Cristian Guzman .50 .15
T206-17 Shawn Green .50 .15
T206-18 Curt Schilling .60 .18
T206-19 Ichiro Suzuki 1.50 .45
T206-20 Chipper Jones 1.00 .30

2002 Topps 206 Team 206 Series 2

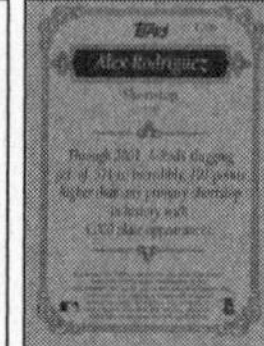

Inserted at an approximate rate of one per pack (only not in a pack when an autograph or relic card was inserted), these 20 cards feature the leading players from the 206 second series in a more modern design.

Nm-Mt Ex-Mt
COMPLETE SET (25) 15.00 4.50
T206-1 Alex Rodriguez 1.50 .45
T206-2 Sammy Sosa 1.50 .45
T206-3 Jason Giambi 1.00 .30
T206-4 Nomar Garciaparra 1.50 .45
T206-5 Ichiro Suzuki 1.50 .45
T206-6 Chipper Jones 1.00 .30
T206-7 Derek Jeter 2.50 .75
T206-8 Barry Bonds 2.50 .75
T206-9 Mike Piazza 1.50 .45
T206-10 Randy Johnson 1.00 .30
T206-11 Shawn Green .50 .15
T206-12 Todd Helton .60 .18
T206-13 Luis Gonzalez .50 .15
T206-14 Albert Pujols 2.00 .60
T206-15 Curt Schilling .60 .18
T206-16 Scott Rolen .60 .18
T206-17 Ivan Rodriguez 1.00 .30
T206-18 Roberto Alomar 1.00 .30
T206-19 Cristian Guzman .50 .15
T206-20 Bret Boone .50 .15
T206-21 Barry Zito .60 .18
T206-22 Larry Walker .60 .18
T206-23 Eric Chavez .50 .15
T206-24 Roger Clemens 2.00 .60
T206-25 Pedro Martinez 1.00 .30

2002 Topps 206 Team 206 Series 3

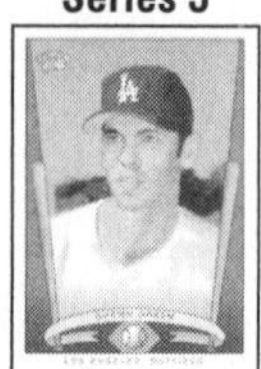

Inserted at an approximate rate of one per pack (only not in a pack when an autograph or relic card was inserted), these 30 cards feature the leading players from the 206 third series in a more modern design.

Nm-Mt Ex-Mt
COMPLETE SET (30) 15.00 4.50
1 Ichiro Suzuki 1.50 .45
2 Kazuhisa Ishii .50 .15
3 Alex Rodriguez 1.50 .45
4 Mark Prior 2.00 .60
5 Derek Jeter 2.50 .75
6 Sammy Sosa 1.50 .45
7 Nomar Garciaparra 1.50 .45
8 Mike Piazza 1.50 .45
9 Jason Giambi 1.00 .30
10 Vladimir Guerrero 1.00 .30
11 Curt Schilling .60 .18
12 Jim Thome Phillies 1.00 .30
13 Adam Dunn .50 .15
14 Albert Pujols 2.00 .60
15 Pat Burrell .50 .15

	Nm-Mt	Ex-Mt
16 Chipper Jones	1.00	.30
17 Randy Johnson	1.00	.30
18 Todd Helton	.60	.18
19 Luis Gonzalez	.50	.15
20 Alfonso Soriano	.60	.18
21 Shawn Green	.50	.15
22 Pedro Martinez	1.00	.30
23 Lance Berkman	.50	.15
24 Ivan Rodriguez	1.00	.30
25 Larry Walker	.60	.18
26 Andruw Jones	.50	.15
27 Ken Griffey Jr.	1.50	.45
28 Manny Ramirez	.50	.15
29 Barry Bonds	2.50	.75
30 Miguel Tejada	.50	.15

2003 Topps All-Time Fan Favorites

This 150-card set was released in May, 2003. This set was issued in six card packs with an $3 SRP which came 24 packs to a box and eight boxes to a case. These cards were issued in different styles with photos purporting to be from that era in which the faux card was issued. While most of the photos are close to the era they are supposed to be from, some photos such as the 64 Brooks Robinson design and the 54 Tom Lasorda are obviously not from the correct time period. The Monte Irvin card was issued in equal quantities with or without the facsmile autograph. A set is considered complete with only one of the Irvin cards. A notable card in this set is the first mainstream card of legendary broadcaster Ernie Harwell who was the Tigers announcers for more than 30 years.

	Nm-Mt	Ex-Mt
COMPLETE SET (150)	50.00	15.00
1 Willie Mays	3.00	.90
2 Whitey Ford	1.00	.30
3 Stan Musial	2.50	.75
4 Paul Blair	.60	.18
5 Harold Reynolds	.60	.18
6 Bob Friend	.60	.18
7 Rod Carew	1.00	.30
8 Kirk Gibson	.60	.18
9 Graig Nettles	.60	.18
10 Ozzie Smith	2.50	.75
11 Tony Perez	.60	.18
12 Tim Wallach	.60	.18
13 Bert Campaneris	.60	.18
14 Cory Snyder	.60	.18
15 Dave Parker	.60	.18
16 Darrell Evans	.60	.18
17 Joe Pepitone	.60	.18
18 Don Sutton	.60	.18
19 Dale Murphy	1.50	.45
20 George Brett	4.00	1.20
21 Carlton Fisk	1.00	.30
22 Bob Watson	.60	.18
23 Wally Joyner	.60	.18
24 Paul Molitor	1.00	.30
25 Keith Hernandez	1.00	.30
26 Jerry Koosman	.60	.18
27 George Bell	.60	.18
28 Boog Powell	1.00	.30
29 Bruce Sutter	.60	.18
30 Ernie Banks	1.50	.45
31 Steve Lyons	.60	.18
32 Earl Weaver	.60	.18
33 Dave Stieb	.60	.18
34 Alan Trammell	1.00	.30
35 Bret Saberhagen	.60	.18
36 J.R. Richard	.60	.18
37 Mickey Rivers	.60	.18
38 Juan Marichal	.60	.18
39 Gaylord Perry	.60	.18
40 Don Mattingly	4.00	1.20
41 Bob Grich	.60	.18
42 Steve Sax	.60	.18
43 Sparky Anderson	.60	.18
44 Luis Aparicio	.60	.18
45 Fergie Jenkins	.60	.18
46 Jim Palmer	.60	.18
47 Howard Johnson	.60	.18
48 Dwight Evans	.60	.18
49 Bill Buckner	.60	.18
50 Cal Ripken	5.00	1.50
51 Jose Cruz	.60	.18
52 Tony Oliva	.60	.18
53 Bobby Richardson	.60	.18
54 Luis Tiant	.60	.18
55 Warren Spahn	1.00	.30
56 Phil Rizzuto	1.00	.30
57 Eric Davis	.60	.18
58 Vida Blue	.60	.18
59 Steve Balboni	.60	.18
60 Mike Schmidt	3.00	.90
61 Ken Griffey Sr.	.60	.18
62 Jim Abbott	1.00	.30
63 Whitey Herzog	.60	.18
64 Rich Gossage	.60	.18
65 Tony Armas	.60	.18
66 Bill Skowron	1.00	.30
67 Don Newcombe	.60	.18
68 Bill Madlock	.60	.18
69 Lance Parrish	.60	.18
70 Reggie Jackson	1.00	.30
71 Willie Wilson	.60	.18
72 Terry Pendleton	.60	.18
73 Jim Piersall	.60	.18
74 George Foster	.60	.18
75 Bob Horner	.60	.18
76 Chris Sabo	.60	.18
77 Fred Lynn	.60	.18
78 Jim Rice	.60	.18
79 Maury Wills	.60	.18
80 Yogi Berra	1.50	.45
81 Johnny Sain	1.00	.30
82 Tom Lasorda	.60	.18
83 Bill Mazeroski	1.00	.30
84 John Kruk	.60	.18
85 Bob Feller	1.00	.30
86 Frank Robinson	1.00	.30
87 Red Schoendienst	.60	.18
88 Gary Carter	1.00	.30
89 Andre Dawson	.60	.18
90 Tim McCarver	.60	.18
91 Robin Yount	2.50	.75
92 Phil Niekro	.60	.18
93 Joe Morgan	.60	.18
94 Darren Daulton	.60	.18
95 Bobby Thomson	.60	.18
96 Alvin Davis	.60	.18
97 Robin Roberts	1.00	.30
98 Kirby Puckett	1.50	.45
99 Jack Clark	.60	.18
100 Hank Aaron	3.00	.90
101 Orlando Cepeda	.60	.18
102 Vern Law	.60	.18
103 Cecil Cooper	.60	.18
104 Don Larsen	1.00	.30
105 Mario Mendoza	.60	.18
106 Tony Gwynn	2.00	.60
107 Ernie Harwell	.60	.18
108A Monte Irvin	.60	.18
108B Monte Irvin NO AU ERR	.60	.18
109 Tommy John	.60	.18
110 Rollie Fingers	.60	.18
111 Johnny Podres	.60	.18
112 Jeff Reardon	.60	.18
113 Buddy Bell	.60	.18
114 Dwight Gooden	1.00	.30
115 Garry Templeton	.60	.18
116 Johnny Bench	1.50	.45
117 Joe Rudi	.60	.18
118 Ron Guidry	.60	.18
119 Vince Coleman	.60	.18
120 Al Kaline	1.50	.45
121 Carl Yastrzemski	2.50	.75
122 Hank Bauer	.60	.18
123 Mark Fidrych	.60	.18
124 Paul O'Neill	1.00	.30
125 Ron Cey	.60	.18
126 Willie McGee	.60	.18
127 Harmon Killebrew	1.50	.45
128 Dave Concepcion	.60	.18
129 Harold Baines	.60	.18
130 Lou Brock	1.00	.30
131 Lee Smith	.60	.18
132 Willie McCovey	.60	.18
133 Steve Garvey	.60	.18
134 Kent Tekulve	.60	.18
135 Tom Seaver	1.00	.30
136 Bo Jackson	1.50	.45
137 Walt Weiss	.60	.18
138 Brook Jacoby	.60	.18
139 Dennis Eckersley	.60	.18
140 Duke Snider	1.00	.30
141 Lenny Dykstra	.60	.18
142 Greg Luzinski	.60	.18
143 Jim Bunning	.60	.18
144 Jose Canseco	1.50	.45
145 Ron Santo	1.00	.30
146 Bert Blyleven	.60	.18
147 Wade Boggs	1.00	.30
148 Brooks Robinson	1.50	.45
149 Ray Knight	.60	.18
150 Nolan Ryan	4.00	1.20

2003 Topps All-Time Fan Favorites Chrome Refractors

Inserted at a stated rate of one in 18, this is a parallel to the basic set. These cards were produced using the Topps Chrome technology and were issued to a stated print run of 299 serial numbered sets.

	Nm-Mt	Ex-Mt
*CHROME REF: 3X TO 8X BASIC		

2003 Topps All-Time Fan Favorites Archives Autographs

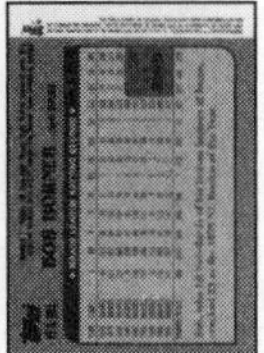

This 165-card set was issued at different odds depending on what group the player belonged to. Please note that exchange cards with a redemption deadline of April 30th, 2005, were seeded into packs for the following players: Dave Concepcion, Bob Feller, Tug McGraw, Paul O'Neill and Kirby Puckett. In addition, exchange cards were produced for a small percentage of Eric Davis cards (though the bulk of his real autographs did make pack out).

	Nm-Mt	Ex-Mt
GROUP A STATED ODDS 1:218		
GROUP B STATED ODDS 1:759		
GROUP C STATED ODDS 1:116		
GROUP D STATED ODDS 1:45		
GROUP E STATED ODDS 1:87		
GROUP F STATED ODDS 1:1028		
GROUP G STATED ODDS 1:838		
GROUP H STATED ODDS 1:818		
GROUP I STATED ODDS 1:796		
GROUP J STATED ODDS 1:111		
GROUP K STATED ODDS 1:759		
GROUP L STATED ODDS 1:744		
AD Alvin Davis D	10.00	3.00
ADA Andre Dawson A	60.00	18.00
AK Al Kaline A	150.00	45.00
AO Al Oliver D	10.00	3.00
AT Alan Trammell C	40.00	12.00
BB Bert Blyleven D	15.00	4.50
BBE Buddy Bell C	15.00	4.50
BBI Buddy Biancalana D	10.00	3.00
BBU Bill Buckner C	15.00	4.50
BC Bert Campaneris E	10.00	3.00
BF Bob Feller C EXCH	25.00	7.50
BFR Bob Friend D	10.00	3.00
BGR Bob Grich D	10.00	3.00
BH Bob Horner J	10.00	3.00
BJ Bo Jackson A	150.00	45.00
BJA Brook Jacoby E	10.00	3.00
BL Bill Lee D	10.00	3.00
BMA Bill Madlock D	10.00	3.00
BMZ Bill Mazeroski A	100.00	30.00
BP Boog Powell D	15.00	4.50
BRO Brooks Robinson A	150.00	45.00
BS Bill Skowron D	15.00	4.50
BSA Bret Saberhagen A	60.00	18.00
BSU Bruce Sutter C	15.00	4.50
BT Bobby Thomson A	60.00	18.00
BW Bob Watson C	15.00	4.50
CC Cecil Cooper E	10.00	3.00
CF Carlton Fisk A	100.00	30.00
CL Carney Lansford C	15.00	4.50
CLE Chet Lemon D	10.00	3.00
CN Cory Snyder C	15.00	4.50
CR Cal Ripken A	300.00	90.00
CS Chris Sabo H	10.00	3.00
CSP Chris Speier C	15.00	4.50
CY Carl Yastrzemski A	200.00	60.00
DC Dave Concepcion A EXCH	60.00	18.00
DD Darren Daulton C	25.00	7.50
DDE Doug DeCinces C	15.00	4.50
DE Darrell Evans D	10.00	3.00
DEC Dennis Eckersley A	60.00	18.00
DEV Dwight Evans A	60.00	18.00
DG Dwight Gooden A	100.00	30.00
DL Don Larsen D	15.00	4.50
DM Dale Murphy A	150.00	45.00
DN Don Newcombe A	60.00	18.00
DON Don Mattingly A	150.00	45.00
DP Dave Parker A	60.00	18.00
DS Dave Stieb C	15.00	4.50
DSN Duke Snider A	100.00	30.00
DSU Don Sutton A	60.00	18.00
EB Ernie Banks A	150.00	45.00
ED Eric Davis I	15.00	4.50
EH Ernie Harwell C	60.00	18.00
EW Earl Weaver D	15.00	4.50
FJ Fergie Jenkins C	15.00	4.50
FL Fred Lynn A	60.00	18.00
FR Frank Robinson A	100.00	30.00
GB George Bell D	10.00	3.00
GBR George Brett A	250.00	75.00
GC Gary Carter A	100.00	30.00
GF George Foster D	10.00	3.00
GL Greg Luzinski C	15.00	4.50
GN Graig Nettles D	15.00	4.50
GP Gaylord Perry B	25.00	7.50
GT Garry Templeton C	15.00	4.50
HA Hank Aaron A	300.00	90.00
HB Hank Bauer A	60.00	18.00
HBA Harold Baines C	15.00	4.50
HJ Howard Johnson K	10.00	3.00
HK Harmon Killebrew A	150.00	45.00
HR Harold Reynolds A	60.00	18.00
JA Jim Abbott D	15.00	4.50
JB Jim Bunning A	100.00	30.00
JBE Johnny Bench A	250.00	75.00
JC Jack Clark B	25.00	7.50
JCA Joe Carter A	60.00	18.00
JCR Jose Cruz D	10.00	3.00
JK Jerry Koosman F	25.00	7.50
JKR John Kruk A	100.00	30.00
JM Joe Morgan A	60.00	18.00
JMA Juan Marichal A	100.00	30.00
JMO John Montefusco D	10.00	3.00
JOS Jose Canseco A	150.00	45.00
JP Jim Palmer A	100.00	30.00
JPE Joe Pepitone E	10.00	3.00
JR J.R. Richard E	10.00	3.00
JRE Jeff Reardon D	10.00	3.00
JRI Jim Rice A	100.00	30.00
JRU Joe Rudi E	10.00	3.00
KG Ken Griffey Sr. A	60.00	18.00
KGI Kirk Gibson A	60.00	18.00
KH Keith Hernandez A	100.00	30.00
KM Kevin Mitchell L	10.00	3.00
KP Kirby Puckett A EXCH	80.00	24.00
KS Kevin Seitzer D	10.00	3.00
KT Kent Tekulve C	15.00	4.50
LA Luis Aparicio D	25.00	7.50
LB Lou Brock A	100.00	30.00
LD Lenny Dykstra G	10.00	3.00
LDU Leon Durham D	10.00	3.00
LP Lance Parrish D	10.00	3.00
LS Lee Smith J	10.00	3.00
LT Luis Tiant A	60.00	18.00
MCG Willie McGee A	60.00	18.00
MF Mark Fidrych J	15.00	4.50
MI Monte Irvin A	100.00	30.00
MM Mario Mendoza E	10.00	3.00
MP Mike Pagliarulo E	10.00	3.00
MR Mickey Rivers E	10.00	3.00
MS Mike Schmidt A	250.00	75.00
MW Maury Wills E	10.00	3.00
NR Nolan Ryan A	300.00	90.00
OC Orlando Cepeda A	60.00	18.00
OS Ozzie Smith A	150.00	45.00
PB Paul Blair J	10.00	3.00
PM Paul Molitor A	100.00	30.00
PN Phil Niekro A	60.00	18.00
PO Paul O'Neill A EXCH	60.00	18.00
PR Phil Rizzuto A	100.00	30.00
RCA Rod Carew A	100.00	30.00
RCE Ron Cey D	10.00	3.00
RD Rob Dibble C	25.00	7.50
RDA Ron Darling C	15.00	4.50
RF Rollie Fingers A	60.00	18.00
RG Rich Gossage A	60.00	18.00
RGU Ron Guidry C	25.00	7.50
RJ Reggie Jackson A	150.00	45.00
RK Ralph Kiner A	100.00	30.00
RKI Ron Kittle D	10.00	3.00
RR Robin Roberts B	25.00	7.50
RS Red Schoendienst C	15.00	4.50
RSA Ron Santo D	25.00	7.50
RY Ray Knight J	10.00	3.00
RYO Robin Yount A	150.00	45.00
SA Sparky Anderson A	60.00	18.00
SB Steve Balboni E	10.00	3.00
SG Steve Garvey B	40.00	12.00
SL Steve Lyons C	15.00	4.50
SM Stan Musial A	200.00	60.00
SS Steve Sax D	10.00	3.00
SY Steve Yeager E	10.00	3.00
TA Tony Armas D	10.00	3.00
TG Tony Gwynn A	150.00	45.00
TH Tom Herr D	10.00	3.00
TJ Tommy John B	15.00	4.50
TL Tom Lasorda A	60.00	18.00
TM Tim McCarver A	60.00	18.00
TMC Tug McGraw D EXCH	25.00	7.50
TP Terry Pendleton B	15.00	4.50
TPE Tony Perez A	100.00	30.00
TSE Tom Seaver A	100.00	30.00
TW Tim Wallach E	10.00	3.00
VB Vida Blue C	15.00	4.50
VC Vince Coleman J	10.00	3.00
WB Wade Boggs A	100.00	30.00
WF Whitey Ford A	100.00	30.00
WH Whitey Herzog C	25.00	7.50
WHE Willie Hernandez D	10.00	3.00
WJ Wally Joyner J	10.00	3.00
WM Willie Mays A	300.00	90.00
WMC Willie McCovey A	100.00	30.00
WS Warren Spahn D	40.00	12.00
WW Walt Weiss D	10.00	3.00
WWI Willie Wilson A	60.00	18.00
YB Yogi Berra A	120.00	36.00

2003 Topps All-Time Fan Favorites Best Seat in the House Relics

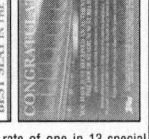

Inserted at a stated rate of one in 13 special relic packs, these five cards feature a group of stars from a team along with a piece of a set from a now retired ballpark.

	Nm-Mt	Ex-Mt
BS1 Brooks Robinson Frank Robinson Jim Palmer	25.00	7.50
BS2 Bob Grich Rod Carew Wally Joyner	25.00	7.50
BS3 Dave Parker Kent Tekulve Willie Stargell Phil Garner	25.00	7.50
BS4 Paul Molitor Robin Yount Rollie Fingers	40.00	12.00
BS5 Bob Horner Dale Murphy Phil Niekro	25.00	7.50

2003 Topps All-Time Fan Favorites Relics

Issued one per special "relic" box-topper pack, these 43 cards feature players from the basic set along with a game-used memorabilia piece.

	Nm-Mt	Ex-Mt
ADA Andre Dawson Bat	10.00	3.00
AT Alan Trammell Bat	15.00	4.50
BFR Bob Friend Jsy	10.00	3.00
BH Bob Horner Bat	10.00	3.00
BJ Bo Jackson Bat	25.00	7.50
BR Bobby Richardson Bat	15.00	4.50
CF Curt Flood Bat	10.00	3.00
CS Chris Sabo Bat	10.00	3.00
DEC Dennis Eckersley Uni	10.00	3.00
DM Dale Murphy Bat	25.00	7.50
DON Don Mattingly Bat	40.00	12.00
DP Dave Parker Bat	10.00	3.00
FL Fred Lynn Bat	10.00	3.00
GBR George Brett Uni	30.00	9.00
GC Gary Carter Bat	15.00	4.50
GF George Foster Bat	10.00	3.00
GL Greg Luzinski Bat	10.00	3.00
HBA Harold Baines Bat	15.00	4.50
HR Harold Reynolds Bat	10.00	3.00
JCR Jose Cruz Bat	10.00	3.00
JM Joe Morgan Bat	10.00	3.00
JOS Jose Canseco Bat	15.00	4.50
JRI Jim Rice Bat	10.00	3.00
JRU Joe Rudi Bat	10.00	3.00
KGI Kirk Gibson Bat	10.00	3.00
KH Keith Hernandez Bat	15.00	4.50
KM Kevin Mitchell Bat	10.00	3.00
KP Kirby Puckett Bat	25.00	7.50
LD Lenny Dykstra Bat	10.00	3.00
LP Lance Parrish Bat	15.00	4.50
MCG Willie McGee Bat	15.00	4.50
MS Mike Schmidt Bat	30.00	9.00
MW Maury Wills Bat	10.00	3.00
NC Norm Cash Jsy	50.00	15.00
PO Paul O'Neill Bat	15.00	4.50
RCA Rod Carew Bat	15.00	4.50
RDA Ron Darling Jsy	10.00	3.00
SG Steve Garvey Bat	10.00	3.00
TMC Tug McGraw Jsy	10.00	3.00
VC Vince Coleman Bat	10.00	3.00
WHE Willie Hernandez Jsy	10.00	3.00
WJ Wally Joyner Bat	10.00	3.00
WS Willie Stargell Bat	15.00	4.50

2003 Topps All-Time Fan Favorites Don Zimmer AutoProofs

Inserted at a stated rate of one in 4971, these 13 cards feature authentic signed versions of Don Zimmer's cards issued between 1955 and 1978. We have notated the print run next to the player's name in our checklist and note that due to market scarcity there is no pricing.

	Nm-Mt	Ex-Mt
1 Don Zimmer 55 Bow/1		
2 Don Zimmer 55/5		
3 Don Zimmer 56/9		
4 Don Zimmer 58/5		
5 Don Zimmer 59/17		
6 Don Zimmer 60/14		
7 Don Zimmer 61/24		
8 Don Zimmer 62/1		
9 Don Zimmer 63/29		
10 Don Zimmer 64/14		
11 Don Zimmer 65/14		
12 Don Zimmer 73 MG/3		
13 Don Zimmer 78 MG/11		

2001 Topps American Pie

This 150-card set captured the essence of America at the height of the Baby Boomers Era of the '60s and '70s. Cards 1-115 features major leaguers, 116-140 features historic events and 141-150 features American icons of the '60s and '70s. The cards were issued in five card packs with an SRP of $4.00/pack. These packs were issued 24 to a box.

	Nm-Mt	Ex-Mt
COMPLETE SET (150)	40.00	12.00
1 Al Kaline	1.25	.35
2 Al Oliver	.50	.15
3 Andre Dawson	.50	.15
4 Bert Blyleven	.50	.15
5 Bill Buckner	.50	.15
6 Bill Mazeroski	.75	.23
7 Bob Gibson	.75	.23
8 Bill Freehan	.50	.15
9 Bobby Grich	.50	.15
10 Bobby Murcer	.50	.15
11 Bobby Richardson	.50	.15
12 Boog Powell	.75	.23
13 Brooks Robinson	1.25	.35
14 Carl Yastrzemski	2.00	.60
15 Carlton Fisk	.75	.23
16 Clete Boyer	.30	.09
17 Curt Flood	.50	.15
18 Dale Murphy	1.25	.35
19 Tony Conigliaro	.75	.23
20 Dave Parker	.50	.15
21 Dave Winfield	.50	.15
22 Dick Allen	.50	.15
23 Dick Groat	.50	.15
24 Don Drysdale	1.25	.35
25 Don Sutton	.50	.15
26 Dwight Evans	.50	.15
27 Eddie Mathews	1.25	.35
28 Elston Howard	.75	.23
29 Frank Howard	.50	.15
30 Frank Robinson	.75	.23
31 Fred Lynn	.50	.15
32 Gary Carter	.75	.23
33 Gaylord Perry	.50	.15
34 Norm Cash	.50	.15
35 George Brett	3.00	.90
36 George Foster	.50	.15
37 Goose Gossage	.50	.15
38 Graig Nettles	.50	.15
39 Greg Luzinski	.50	.15
40 Hank Aaron	2.50	.75
41 Harmon Killebrew	1.25	.35
42 Jack Clark	.50	.15
43 Jack Morris	.50	.15
44 Jim Wynn	.50	.15
45 Jim Kaat	.50	.15
46 Jim Palmer	.50	.15
47 Joe Pepitone	.30	.09
48 Joe Rudi	.50	.15
49 Johnny Bench	1.25	.35
50 Juan Marichal	.50	.15
51 Keith Hernandez	.75	.23
52 Bucky Dent	.50	.15
53 Lou Brock	.75	.23
54 Ron Cey	.50	.15
55 Luis Aparicio	.50	.15
56 Luis Tiant	.50	.15
57 Mark Fidrych	.50	.15
58 Maury Wills	.50	.15
59 Mickey Lolich	.50	.15
60 Mickey Rivers	.30	.09
61 Mike Schmidt	2.50	.75
62 Moose Skowron	.50	.15
63 Nolan Ryan	3.00	.90
64 Orlando Cepeda	.50	.15

65 Ozzie Smith 2.00 .60
66 Phil Niekro .50 .15
67 Reggie Jackson .75 .23
68 Reggie Smith .50 .15
69 Rico Carty .30 .09
70 Roberto Clemente 3.00 .90
71 Robin Yount 2.00 .60
72 Roger Maris 2.00 .60
73 Rollie Fingers .50 .15
74 Ron Guidry .50 .15
75 Ron Santo .75 .23
76 Ron Swoboda .50 .15
77 Sal Bando .50 .15
78 Sam McDowell .50 .15
79 Steve Carlton .50 .15
80 Thurman Munson 1.50 .45
81 Tim McCarver .50 .15
82 Tom Seaver .75 .23
83 Mike Cuellar .50 .15
84 Tony Kubek .75 .23
85 Tommy John .50 .15
86 Tony Perez .50 .15
87 Tug McGraw .50 .15
88 Vida Blue .50 .15
89 Warren Spahn .75 .23
90 Whitey Ford .75 .23
91 Willie Mays 2.50 .75
92 Willie McCovey .50 .15
93 Willie Stargell .75 .23
94 Yogi Berra 1.25 .35
95 Stan Musial 2.00 .60
96 Jim Piersall .50 .15
97 Duke Snider .75 .23
98 Bruce Sutter .50 .15
99 Dave Concepcion .50 .15
100 Darrell Evans .50 .15
101 Dennis Eckersley .50 .15
102 Hoyt Wilhelm .50 .15
103 Minnie Minoso .50 .15
104 Don Newcombe .50 .15
105 Richie Ashburn .75 .23
106 Alan Trammell .75 .23
107 Jim Hunter .75 .23
108 Lou Whitaker .50 .15
109 Johnny Podres .50 .15
110 Denny Martinez .50 .15
111 Willie Horton .50 .15
112 Dean Chance .30 .09
113 Fergie Jenkins .50 .15
114 Cecil Cooper .50 .15
115 Rick Reuschel .30 .09
116 Civil Rights .30 .09
117 Bay of Pigs .30 .09
118 Cuban Missile Crisis .30 .09
119 N.Y. World's Fair .30 .09
120 Atomic Bomb .30 .09
Test Ban Treaty
121 John F. Kennedy 1.25 .35
Assassination
122 Lyndon Johnson .30 .09
123 The Motown Sound .30 .09
124 British Music Invasion .50 .15
125 U.S.Troops .30 .09
in Vietnam
126 Space Race .30 .09
127 Robert F. Kennedy .50 .15
128 Peace Movement .30 .09
129 Man On The Moon .50 .15
130 Woodstock .30 .09
131 Flower Power .30 .09
132 Women's Lib .30 .09
133 Vietnam Cease Fire .30 .09
134 U.S. Gas Shortage .30 .09
135 Watergate .50 .15
136 Nixon Resigns .50 .15
137 Bicentennial .30 .09
138 Disco .30 .09
139 Three Mile Island .30 .09
140 Iran Hostage Crisis .30 .09
141 John F. Kennedy 2.00 .60
142 Marilyn Monroe 2.00 .60
143 Elvis Presley 2.00 .60
144 Jimi Hendrix 1.25 .35
145 Arthur Ashe .50 .15
146 Richard Nixon .50 .15
147 James Dean 1.25 .35
148 Janis Joplin .50 .15
149 Frank Sinatra 1.25 .35
150 Malcolm X .50 .15

2001 Topps American Pie Decade Leaders

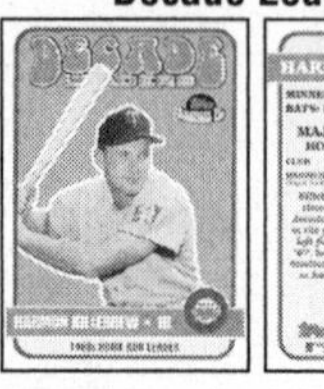

Inserted at a rate of one in 12, this 10-card set features players who led the Majors in different categories for the entire decades of the '60's and '70's. These cards contained a 'DL' prefix in the numbering.

Nm-Mt Ex-Mt
COMPLETE SET (10) 30.00 9.00
DL1 Willie Stargell 1.50 .45
DL2 Harmon Killebrew 2.50 .75
DL3 Johnny Bench 2.50 .75
DL4 Hank Aaron 5.00 1.50
DL5 Rod Carew 1.50 .45
DL6 Roberto Clemente 6.00 1.80
DL7 Nolan Ryan 6.00 1.80
DL8 Bob Gibson 1.50 .45
DL9 Jim Palmer 1.50 .45
DL10 Juan Marichal 1.50 .45

2001 Topps American Pie Entertainment Star Autographs

Inserted at a rate of one in 1,071, this three card set features T.V. personalities who've

signed original Topps non-sports cards from the 60's and '70's. Many different cards were signed by each person, but all carry equal value. Each card displays a sequentially numbered Topps "Genuine Issue" sticker.

Nm-Mt Ex-Mt
1 Danny Bonaduce 80.00 24.00
2 Lou Ferrigno 120.00 36.00
3 Adam West 100.00 30.00

2001 Topps American Pie Profiles in Courage

Inserted at a rate of one in eight, this 20-card set profiled major leaguers who possessed unparalleled tenacity. The cards carry a 'PIC' prefix. The term "Profiles in Courage" comes from a book authored by John F. Kennedy before he became President.

Nm-Mt Ex-Mt
COMPLETE SET (20) 50.00 15.00
PIC1 Roger Maris 4.00 1.20
PIC2 Lou Brock 2.00 .60
PIC3 Brooks Robinson 3.00 .90
PIC4 Carl Yastrzemski 4.00 1.20
PIC5 Mike Schmidt 6.00 1.80
PIC6 Hank Aaron 6.00 1.80
PIC7 Tom Seaver 2.00 .60
PIC8 Willie Mays 6.00 1.80
PIC9 Graig Nettles 1.50 .45
PIC10 Frank Robinson 2.00 .60
PIC11 Rollie Fingers 1.50 .45
PIC12 Tony Perez 1.50 .45
PIC13 George Brett 8.00 2.40
PIC14 Robin Yount 5.00 1.50
PIC15 Nolan Ryan 8.00 2.40
PIC16 Warren Spahn 2.00 .60
PIC17 Johnny Bench 3.00 .90
PIC18 Vida Blue 1.50 .45
PIC19 Roberto Clemente 8.00 2.40
PIC20 Thurman Munson 4.00 1.20

2001 Topps American Pie Relics

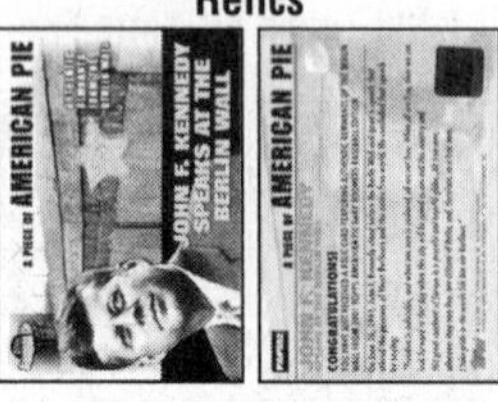

Inserted at a rate of one in 29, this four card set featured memorabilia from pop culture icons of the '60's and '70's. The cards carry a 'PAPM' prefix.

Nm-Mt Ex-Mt
PAPM1 F. Sinatra Jacket 50.00 15.00
PAPM2 John F. Kennedy 20.00 6.00
Berlin Wall
PAPM3 E. Presley Jacket 150.00 45.00
PAPM4 Janis Joplin Dress 80.00 24.00

2001 Topps American Pie Rookie Reprint Relics

Inserted at a rate of one in 116, this 20-card set featured jersey swatches and bat pieces inserted into the players' reprinted rookie cards. The cards carry a 'BBRR' prefix.

Nm-Mt Ex-Mt
BBRR-AD A.Dawson Bat 15.00 4.50
BBRR-AO Al Oliver Jsy 15.00 4.50
BBRR-BG Bobby Grich Jsy 15.00 4.50
BBRR-BM B.Murcer Bat 25.00 7.50
BBRR-BP Boog Powell Bat 25.00 7.50
BBRR-DE D.Eckersley Bat 15.00 4.50
BBRR-DS Don Sutton Jsy 15.00 4.50
BBRR-DW D.Winfield Bat 15.00 4.50
BBRR-GB G.Brett Jsy 40.00 12.00
BBRR-GC Gary Carter Bat 25.00 7.50
BBRR-JB J. Bench Bat 25.00 7.50
BBRR-JK Jim Kaat Bat 15.00 4.50
BBRR-JM Joe Morgan Jsy 15.00 4.50
BBRR-MF M. Fidrych Jsy 15.00 4.50
BBRR-OS Ozzie Smith Bat 25.00 7.50
BBRR-RJ R. Jackson Jsy 25.00 7.50
BBRR-RY R. Yount Jsy 25.00 7.50
BBRR-SC S. Carlton Bat 15.00 4.50
BBRR-TM T. McCarver Bat 15.00 4.50
BBRR-TM T.Munson Jsy 40.00 12.00

2001 Topps American Pie Timeless Classics Relics

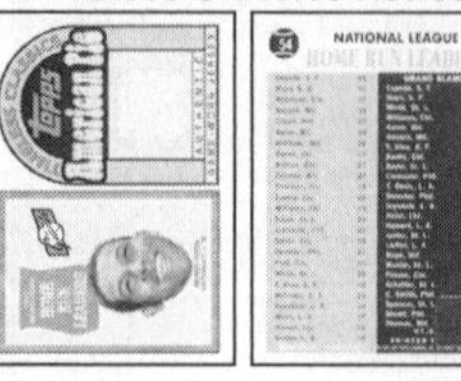

Inserted at a rate of one in 80, this 45-card set contains game-used bat or game-used uniform reprint leader cards depicting ballplayers who led the league during some of the game's most memorable seasons. The cards carry a 'BBTC' prefix.

Nm-Mt Ex-Mt
BBTC1 S.McDowell 66 Jsy 15.00 4.50
BBTC2 S.McDowell 70 Jsy 15.00 4.50
BBTC3 F.Howard 60 Jsy 15.00 4.50
BBTC4 Dick Groat 61 Bat 15.00 4.50
BBTC5 R.Maris 62 Bat 60.00 18.00
BBTC6 O.Cepeda 62 Jsy 15.00 4.50
BBTC7 Willie Mays 63 Jsy 50.00 15.00
BBTC8 Carl Yastrzemski 40.00 12.00
64 Jsy
BBTC9 R.Clemente 65 Bat 80.00 24.00
BBTC10 Harmon Killebrew 25.00 7.50
65 Bat
BBTC11 Brooks Robinson 25.00 7.50
65 Jsy
BBTC12 W. Mays 66 Jsy 50.00 15.00
BBTC13 T. Conigliaro 66 Jsy 25.00 7.50
BBTC14 F.Robinson 66 Jsy 25.00 7.50
BBTC15 Carl Yastrzemski 40.00 12.00
68 HR Jsy
BBTC16 Carl Yastrzemski 40.00 12.00
68 RBI Jsy
BBTC17 Carl Yastrzemski 40.00 12.00
68 BA Jsy
BBTC18 H.Aaron 66 Bat 50.00 15.00
BBTC19 F.Howard 69 Bat 15.00 4.50
BBTC20 Carl Yastrzemski 40.00 12.00
69 Bat
BBTC21 Willie McCovey 15.00 4.50
70 Jsy
BBTC22 Rico Carty 71 Bat 15.00 4.50
BBTC23 F.Howard 71 Bat 15.00 4.50
BBTC24 J.Bench 71 Bat 25.00 7.50
BBTC25 W.Stargell 72 Bat 25.00 7.50
BBTC26 S.Carlton 73 Jsy 15.00 4.50
BBTC27 N.Cash 62 Jsy 25.00 7.50
BBTC28 R.Jackson 74 Jsy 25.00 7.50
BBTC29 W.Stargell 74 Jsy 25.00 7.50
BBTC30 Mike Schmidt 40.00 12.00
75 Jsy
BBTC31 Mike Schmidt 40.00 12.00
76 Jsy
BBTC32 M. Rivers 76 Bat 15.00 4.50
BBTC33 T. Seaver 77 Jsy 25.00 7.50
BBTC34 G. Brett 77 Bat 40.00 12.00
BBTC35 G. Foster 77 Bat 15.00 4.50
BBTC36 G. Nettles 77 Bat 15.00 4.50
BBTC37 N. Ryan 77 Jsy 60.00 18.00
BBTC38 N. Ryan 79 Jsy 60.00 18.00
BBTC39 D. Parker 78 Bat 15.00 4.50
BBTC40 G. Foster 78 Bat 15.00 4.50
BBTC41 Dick Allen 78 Bat 15.00 4.50
BBTC42 D.Parker 79 Bat 15.00 4.50
BBTC43 Fred Lynn 80 Jsy 15.00 4.50
BBTC44 Keith Hernandez 25.00 7.50
80 Bat
BBTC45 D. Winfield 80 Bat 15.00 4.50

2001 Topps American Pie Woodstock Relics

Inserted at an overall rate of one in 138, this 25 card set featured 24 game used bat cards and one card featuring mud from Yasgur's farm. Yasgur's farm was the location of the Woodstock festival in 1969. The odds for bat cards were one in 167, while the odds for the mud was one in 806.

Nm-Mt Ex-Mt
BBWM-BB B. Buckner Bat 15.00 4.50
BBWM-BF Bill Freehan Bat 15.00 4.50
BBWM-BR Brooks Robinson 25.00 7.50
Bat
BBWM-CF Carlton Fisk Bat 25.00 7.50
BBWM-CY Carl Yastrzemski 40.00 12.00
Bat
BBWM-DE Dw. Evans Bat 15.00 4.50
BBWM-DG Dick Groat Bat 15.00 4.50
BBWM-DS D. Snider Bat 25.00 7.50
BBWM-DW Dave Winfield 15.00 4.50
Bat
BBWM-FL Fred Lynn Bat 15.00 4.50
BBWM-FR Frank Robinson 25.00 7.50
Bat
BBWM-GB G. Brett Bat 40.00 12.00
BBWM-JP J. Piersall Bat 15.00 4.50
BBWM-JR Joe Rudi Bat 15.00 4.50
BBWM-JW Jim Wynn Bat 15.00 4.50
BBWM-MW M. Wills Bat 15.00 4.50
BBWM-OC O. Cepeda Bat 15.00 4.50
BBWM-RJ R. Jackson Bat 25.00 7.50
BBWM-RY R. Yount Bat 25.00 7.50
BBWM-SM S. Musial Bat 50.00 15.00
BBWM-TK Ted Kluszewski 25.00 7.50
Bat
BBWM-TP Tony Perez Bat 15.00 4.50
BBWM-WM W. Mays Bat 50.00 15.00
BBWM-WS Woodstock 15.00 4.50
BBWM-WS Willie Stargell 25.00 7.50
Bat

2002 Topps American Pie

This set was released in May, 2002. These cards were issued in seven card packs with a $4 SRP and were issued 24 packs to a box and 10 boxes to a case. This set has an eclectic mix between baseball players and celebrities and events of the past.

Nm-Mt Ex-Mt
COMPLETE SET (150) 40.00 12.00
1 Warren Spahn .75 .23
2 Reggie Jackson .75 .23
3 Bill Mazeroski .75 .23
4 Carl Yastrzemski 2.00 .60
5 Whitey Ford .75 .23
6 Ralph Houk .50 .15
7 Rod Carew .75 .23
8 Kirk Gibson .50 .15
9 Bobby Thomson .50 .15
10 Don Newcombe .50 .15
11 Gaylord Perry .50 .15
12 Bruce Sutter .50 .15
13 Bob Gibson .75 .23
14 Brooks Robinson 1.25 .35
15 Steve Carlton .50 .15
16 Robin Yount 2.00 .60
17 Ernie Banks 1.25 .35
18 Lou Brock .75 .23
19 Al Kaline 1.25 .35
20 Carlton Fisk .75 .23
21 Frank Robinson .75 .23
22 Bobby Bonds .50 .15
23 Andre Dawson .50 .15
24 Goose Gossage .50 .15
25 Fred Lynn .50 .15
26 Keith Hernandez .75 .23
27 Rollie Fingers .50 .15
28 Juan Marichal .50 .15
29 Maury Wills .50 .15
30 Dave Winfield .50 .15
31 Frank Howard .50 .15
32 Tony Gwynn 1.50 .45
33 Jim Palmer .50 .15
34 Mike Schmidt 2.50 .75
35 Bo Jackson 1.25 .35
36 Ferguson Jenkins .50 .15
37 Bobby Richardson .50 .15
38 Harmon Killebrew 1.25 .35
39 Monte Irvin .50 .15
40 Jim Abbott .75 .23
41 Wade Boggs .75 .23
42 Jackie Robinson 1.50 .45
43 Ralph Branca .50 .15
44 Minnie Minoso .50 .15
45 Tug McGraw .50 .15
46 Willie Mays 2.50 .75
47 Nolan Ryan 3.00 .90
48 Duke Snider .75 .23
49 Tom Seaver .75 .23
50 Casey Stengel .75 .23
51 D-Day .50 .15
52 Gulf War .50 .15
53 Vietnam War .50 .15
54 Korean War .50 .15
55 Secret Service .50 .15
56 Crayons .50 .15
57 Hoover Dam .50 .15
58 Penicillin .50 .15
59 Polio Vaccine .50 .15
60 Empire State Building .50 .15
61 Television .50 .15
62 Duke Ellington .75 .23
63 Voyager Mission .50 .15
64 Space Shuttle .50 .15
65 Ellis Island .50 .15
66 Statue Of Liberty .50 .15
67 Battle Of The Bulge .50 .15
68 Battle Of Midway .50 .15
69 Iwo Jima .50 .15
70 Panama Canal .50 .15
71 Charles Lindbergh .50 .15
Spirit Of St. Louis
72 Civil Rights .50 .15
We Shall Overcome
73 Space Race .50 .15
74 Alaska Pipeline .50 .15
75 Teddy Bear .50 .15
76 Seabiscuit .50 .15
77 Bazooka Joe .50 .15
78 Mt. Rushmore .50 .15
79 Yellowstone Park .50 .15
80 Niagara Falls .50 .15
81 Grand Canyon .50 .15
82 Hoola Hoop .50 .15
83 George Patton .75 .23
84 Florence Griffith Joyner .50 .15
85 Amelia Earhart .50 .15
86 Glen Miller .50 .15
87 Rick Monday .50 .15
88 Buzz Aldrin .50 .15
89 Rosa Parks .50 .15
90 Edward R. Murrow .50 .15
91 Susan B. Anthony .50 .15
92 Bobby Kennedy .50 .15
93 Gloria Steinem .50 .15
94 Hank Greenberg 1.25 .35
95 Jimmy Doolittle .50 .15
96 Thurgood Marshall .50 .15
97 Ernest Hemingway 1.25 .35
98 Henry Ford .75 .23
99 Wright Brothers .50 .15
100 Thomas Edison .50 .15
101 Albert Einstein 1.25 .35
102 Will Rogers .50 .15
103 George Gershwin .50 .15
104 Irving Berlin .50 .15
105 Frank Lloyd Wright .50 .15
106 Howard Hughes .75 .23
107 George M. Cohan .50 .15
108 Jack Kerouac .75 .23
109 Harry Houdini .75 .23
110 Helen Keller .50 .15
111 John McCain .50 .15
112 Andrew Carnegie .50 .15
113 Sandra Day O'Connor .50 .15
114 Brooklyn Bridge .50 .15
115 Douglas MacArthur .75 .23
116 Elvis Presley 2.00 .60
117 George Burns .50 .15
118 Judy Garland 1.25 .35
119 Buddy Holly .50 .15
120 Don McLean .50 .15
121 Marilyn Monroe 2.00 .60
122 Humphrey Bogart 1.50 .45
123 Gary Cooper .75 .23
124 The Andrews Sisters .50 .15
125 Jim Thorpe 1.25 .35
126 Joe Louis 1.25 .35
127 Jesse Owens .75 .23
128 Kate Smith .50 .15
129 W.C. Fields .50 .15
130 Bette Davis .75 .23
131 Jayne Mansfield .75 .23
132 William McKinley .50 .15
133 Teddy Roosevelt 1.25 .35
134 William Taft .50 .15
135 Woodrow Wilson .50 .15
136 Warren Harding .50 .15
137 Calvin Coolidge .50 .15
138 Herbert Hoover .50 .15
139 Franklin D. Roosevelt .75 .23
140 Harry Truman .75 .23
141 Dwight Eisenhower .75 .23
142 John F. Kennedy 2.00 .60
143 Lyndon B. Johnson .75 .23
144 Richard Nixon .75 .23
145 Gerald Ford .75 .23
146 Jimmy Carter .75 .23
147 Ronald Reagan .75 .23
148 George H.W. Bush .50 .15
149 Bill Clinton 2.00 .60
150 George W. Bush 2.50 .75

2002 Topps American Pie First Pitch Seat Relics

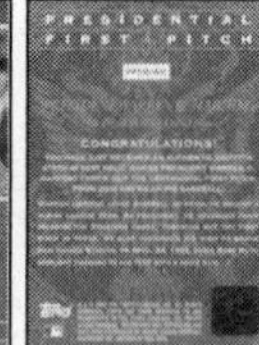

Inserted into packs at stated odds of one in 32 hobby and 1:56 retail, these cards feature pictures of presidents along with seats from a ball park in which they threw out a first pitch of a game.

Nm-Mt Ex-Mt
BC Bill Clinton 50.00 15.00
CC Calvin Coolidge 15.00 4.50
DE Dwight Eisenhower 25.00 7.50
FDR Franklin D. Roosevelt 25.00 7.50
GF Gerald Ford 25.00 7.50
GHWB George H.W. Bush 15.00 4.50
GWB George W. Bush 60.00 18.00
HH Herbert Hoover 15.00 4.50
HT Harry Truman 25.00 7.50
JFK John F. Kennedy 60.00 18.00
RN Richard Nixon 25.00 7.50
RR Ronald Reagan 25.00 7.50
WH Warren Harding 15.00 4.50
WT William Taft 15.00 4.50
WW Woodrow Wilson 15.00 4.50
LBJ Lyndon B. Johnson 25.00 7.50

2002 Topps American Pie Piece of American Pie

Inserted at different odds depending on the memorabilia item, these cards feature a cut swatch from an clothing item worn by a famous celebrity.

Nm-Mt Ex-Mt
H.BOGART SCARF ODDS 1:1074 H, 1:1930 R
G.BURNS COAT ODDS 1:680 H, 1:1218 R
G.COOPER SCARF ODDS 1:414 H, 1:739 R
B.DAVIS JACKET ODDS 1:680 H, 1:1218 R
J.GARLAND SCARF ODDS 1:680 H, 1:1218 R
J.MANSFIELD PANTS ODDS 1:680 H, 11218 R
M.MONROE DRESS ODDS 1:684 H, 1:1221 R
E.PRESLEY COAT ODDS 1:684 H, 1:1221 R
E.PRESLEY SHIRT ODDS 1:684 H, 1:1221 R
R.REAGAN WALL ODDS 1:675 H, 1:1218 R
BD Bette Davis Jacket 80.00 24.00
EP Elvis Presley Shirt 150.00 45.00
EP2 Elvis Presley Coat 150.00 45.00
GB George Burns Coat 60.00 18.00
GC Gary Cooper Scarf 60.00 18.00

HB H.Bogart Scarf 120.00 36.00
JD Judy Garland Scarf 80.00 24.00
JM Jayne Mansfield Shirt 100.00 30.00
MM Marilyn Monroe Dress 300.00 90.00
RR Ronald Reagan Wall 60.00 18.00

2002 Topps American Pie Sluggers Blue

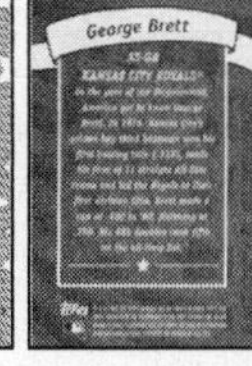

Inserted one per pack, these 25 cards feature famous sluggers born in America. These cards came in four different colored borders: Blue, Gold, Red and Silver. All four colors were produced in equal quantities.

	Nm-Mt	Ex-Mt
COMPLETE SET (25)	50.00	15.00
*RED/GOLD/SILVER: EQUAL VALUE		
1 Rod Carew	2.50	.75
2 Brooks Robinson	4.00	1.20
3 Mike Schmidt	8.00	2.40
4 Carlton Fisk	2.50	.75
5 Reggie Jackson	2.50	.75
6 Carl Yastrzemski	6.00	1.80
7 Kirk Gibson	1.50	.45
8 Al Kaline	4.00	1.20
9 Frank Robinson	2.50	.75
10 Fred Lynn	1.50	.45
11 Dave Winfield	1.50	.45
12 Harmon Killebrew	4.00	1.20
13 Monte Irvin	1.50	.45
14 Willie Mays	8.00	2.40
15 Duke Snider	2.50	.75
16 George Foster	1.50	.45
17 Joe Carter	1.50	.45
18 Eddie Mathews	4.00	1.20
19 George Brett	10.00	3.00
20 Frank Howard	1.50	.45
21 Andre Dawson	1.50	.45
22 Ted Kluszewski	2.50	.75
23 Ryne Sandberg	6.00	1.80
24 Jack Clark	1.50	.45
25 Cecil Cooper	1.50	.45

2002 Topps American Pie Through the Year Relics

These 26 cards feature various memorabilia items from retired players career. These cards were inserted at differening odds depending on what type of memorabilia was attached to the card. All the cards in this set have a "TTY" prefix.

	Nm-Mt	Ex-Mt
BAT STATED ODDS 1:211 H, 1:377 R		
JERSEY STATED ODDS 1:32 H, 1:58 R		
UNIFORM STATED ODDS 1:60 H, 1:107 R		
AD Andre Dawson Bat	15.00	4.50
AL Al Oliver Jsy	15.00	4.50
BB Bill Buckner Jsy	15.00	4.50
CY Carl Yastrzemski Jsy	40.00	12.00
DA Dick Allen Bat	15.00	4.50
DM Don Mattingly Bat	50.00	15.00
DP Dave Parker Jsy	15.00	4.50
DS Darryl Strawberry Bat	25.00	7.50
DW Dave Winfield Bat	15.00	4.50
EM Eddie Mathews Uni.	25.00	7.50
FR Frank Robinson Jsy	20.00	6.00
GP Gaylord Perry Uniform	15.00	4.50
JA Jim Abbott Jsy	20.00	6.00
JB Johnny Bench Uniform	25.00	7.50
JC Jack Clark Jsy	15.00	4.50
JK Jim Kaat Uniform	15.00	4.50
JM Joe Morgan Jsy	15.00	4.50
JR Joe Rudi Jsy	15.00	4.50
MM Minnie Minoso Jsy	15.00	4.50
NR Nolan Ryan Uniform	50.00	15.00
RM Rick Monday Jsy	15.00	4.50
TM Thurman Munson Bat	40.00	12.00
TS Tom Seaver Jsy	20.00	6.00
WB Wade Boggs Jsy	20.00	6.00
WM Willie Mays Uniform	40.00	12.00
WS Willie Stargell Uniform	20.00	6.00

1991 Topps Archives 1953

The 1953 Topps Archive set is a reprint of the original 274-card 1953 Topps set. The only card missing from the reprint set is that of Billy Loes (174), who did not give Topps permission to reprint his card. Moreover, the set has been extended by 57 cards, with cards honoring Mrs. Eleanor Engle, Hoyt Wilhelm (who had already been included in the set as card number 151), 1953 HOF inductees Dizzy Dean and Al Simmons, and "prospect" Hank Aaron. Although the original cards measured 2 5/8" by 3 3/4", the reprint cards measure the modern standard size. Production quantities were supposedly limited to not more than 18,000 cases.

	Nm-Mt	Ex-Mt
COMPLETE SET (330)	60.00	18.00
COMMON CARD (1-220)	.15	.04
COMMON (221-280)	.25	.07
COMMON (281-337)	.30	.09
1 Jackie Robinson	6.00	1.80
2 Luke Easter	.30	.09
3 George Crowe	.15	.04
4 Ben Wade	.15	.04
5 Joe Dobson	.15	.04
6 Sam Jones	.15	.04
7 Bob Borkowski	.15	.04
8 Clem Koshorek	.15	.04
9 Joe Collins	.30	.09
10 Smoky Burgess	.30	.09
11 Sal Yvars	.15	.04
12 Howie Judson	.15	.04
13 Conrado Marrero	.15	.04
14 Clem Labine	.50	.15
15 Bobo Newsom	.30	.09
16 Peanuts Lowrey	.15	.04
17 Billy Hitchcock	.15	.04
18 Ted Lepcio	.15	.04
19 Mel Parnell	.15	.04
20 Hank Thompson	.15	.04
21 Billy Johnson	.15	.04
22 Howie Fox	.15	.04
23 Toby Atwell	.15	.04
24 Ferris Fain	.15	.04
25 Ray Boone	.15	.04
26 Dale Mitchell	.30	.09
27 Roy Campanella	.75	.23
28 Eddie Pellagrini	.15	.04
29 Hal Jeffcoat	.15	.04
30 Willard Nixon	.15	.04
31 Ewell Blackwell	.30	.09
32 Clyde Vollmer	.15	.04
33 Bob Kennedy	.15	.04
34 George Shuba	.15	.04
35 Irv Noren	.15	.04
36 Johnny Groth	.15	.04
37 Eddie Mathews	.75	.23
38 Jim Hearn	.15	.04
39 Eddie Miksis	.15	.04
40 John Lipon	.15	.04
41 Enos Slaughter	.30	.09
42 Gus Zernial	.30	.09
43 Gil McDougald	.30	.09
44 Ellis Kinder	.15	.04
45 Grady Hatton	.15	.04
46 Johnny Klippstein	.15	.04
47 Bubba Church	.15	.04
48 Bob Del Greco	.15	.04
49 Faye Throneberry	.15	.04
50 Chuck Dressen MG	.15	.04
51 Frank Campos	.15	.04
52 Ted Gray	.15	.04
53 Sherm Lollar	.30	.09
54 Bob Feller	.50	.15
55 Maurice McDermott	.15	.04
56 Gerry Staley	.15	.04
57 Carl Scheib	.15	.04
58 George Metkovich	.15	.04
59 Karl Drews	.15	.04
60 Cloyd Boyer	.15	.04
61 Early Wynn	.50	.15
62 Monte Irvin	.30	.09
63 Gus Niarhos	.15	.04
64 Dave Philley	.15	.04
65 Earl Harrist	.15	.04
66 Minnie Minoso	.30	.09
67 Roy Sievers	.30	.09
68 Del Rice	.15	.04
69 Dick Brodowski	.15	.04
70 Ed Yuhas	.15	.04
71 Tony Bartirome	.15	.04
72 Fred Hutchinson	.30	.09
73 Eddie Robinson	.15	.04
74 Joe Rossi	.15	.04
75 Mike Garcia	.30	.09
76 Pee Wee Reese	.75	.23
77 Johnny Mize	.30	.09
78 Red Schoendienst	.30	.09
79 Johnny Wyrostek	.15	.04
80 Jim Hegan	.15	.04
81 Joe Black	.30	.09
82 Mickey Mantle	20.00	6.00
83 Howie Pollet	.15	.04
84 Bob Hooper	.15	.04
85 Bobby Morgan	.15	.04
86 Billy Martin	.50	.15
87 Ed Lopat	.30	.09
88 Willie Jones	.15	.04
89 Chuck Stobbs	.15	.04
90 Hank Edwards	.15	.04
91 Ebba St.Claire	.15	.04
92 Paul Minner	.15	.04
93 Hal Rice	.15	.04
94 Bill Kennedy	.15	.04
95 Willard Marshall	.15	.04
96 Virgil Trucks	.15	.04
97 Don Kolloway	.15	.04
98 Cal Abrams	.15	.04
99 Dave Madison	.15	.04
100 Bill Miller	.15	.04
101 Ted Wilks	.15	.04
102 Connie Ryan	.15	.04
103 Joe Astroth	.15	.04
104 Yogi Berra	2.50	.75
105 Joe Nuxhall	.30	.09
106 Johnny Antonelli	.30	.09
107 Danny O'Connell	.15	.04
108 Bob Porterfield	.15	.04
109 Alvin Dark	.30	.09
110 Herman Wehmeier	.15	.04
111 Hank Sauer	.30	.09
112 Ned Garver	.15	.04
113 Jerry Priddy	.15	.04
114 Phil Rizzuto	.75	.23
115 George Spencer	.15	.04
116 Frank Smith	.15	.04
117 Sid Gordon	.15	.04
118 Gus Bell	.30	.09
119 Johnny Sain	.30	.09
120 Davey Williams	.15	.04
121 Walt Dropo	.15	.04
122 Elmer Valo	.15	.04
123 Tommy Byrne	.15	.04
124 Sibby Sisti	.15	.04
125 Dick Williams	.30	.09
126 Bill Connelly	.15	.04
127 Clint Courtney	.15	.04
128 Wilmer Mizell	.30	.09
129 Keith Thomas	.15	.04
130 Turk Lown	.15	.04
131 Harry Byrd	.15	.04
132 Tom Morgan	.15	.04
133 Gil Coan	.15	.04
134 Rube Walker	.15	.04
135 Al Rosen	.30	.09
136 Ken Heintzelman	.15	.04
137 John Rutherford	.15	.04
138 George Kell	.50	.15
139 Sammy White	.15	.04
140 Tommy Glaviano	.15	.04
141 Allie Reynolds	.75	.23
142 Vic Wertz	.30	.09
143 Billy Pierce	.30	.09
144 Bob Schultz	.15	.04
145 Harry Dorish	.15	.04
146 Granny Hamner	.30	.09
147 Warren Spahn	.50	.15
148 Mickey Grasso	.15	.04
149 Dom DiMaggio	.75	.23
150 Harry Simpson	.15	.04
151 Hoyt Wilhelm	.30	.09
152 Bob Adams	.15	.04
153 Andy Seminick	.30	.09
154 Dick Groat	.30	.09
155 Dutch Leonard	.15	.04
156 Jim Rivera	.15	.04
157 Bob Addis	.15	.04
158 Johnny Logan	.30	.09
159 Wayne Terwilliger	.15	.04
160 Bob Young	.15	.04
161 Vern Bickford	.15	.04
162 Ted Kluszewski	.50	.15
163 Fred Hatfield	.15	.04
164 Frank Shea	.15	.04
165 Billy Hoeft	.15	.04
166 Billy Hunter	.15	.04
167 Art Schult	.15	.04
168 Willard Schmidt	.15	.04
169 Dizzy Trout	.15	.04
170 Bill Werle	.15	.04
171 Bill Glynn	.15	.04
172 Rip Repulski	.15	.04
173 Preston Ward	.15	.04
174 Billy Loes (Not printed)		
175 Ron Kline	.15	.04
176 Don Hoak	.15	.04
177 Jim Dyck	.15	.04
178 Jim Waugh	.15	.04
179 Gene Hermanski	.15	.04
180 Virgil Stallcup	.15	.04
181 Al Zarilla	.15	.04
182 Bobby Hofman	.15	.04
183 Stu Miller	.15	.04
184 Hal Brown	.15	.04
185 Jim Pendleton	.15	.04
186 Charlie Bishop	.15	.04
187 Jim Fridley	.15	.04
188 Andy Carey	.30	.09
189 Ray Jablonski	.15	.04
190 Dixie Walker CO	.30	.09
191 Ralph Kiner	.50	.15
192 Wally Westlake	.15	.04
193 Mike Clark	.15	.04
194 Eddie Kazak	.15	.04
195 Ed McGhee	.15	.04
196 Bob Keegan	.15	.04
197 Del Crandall	.30	.09
198 Forrest Main	.15	.04
199 Marion Fricano	.15	.04
200 Gordon Goldsberry	.15	.04
201 Paul LaPalme	.15	.04
202 Carl Sawatski	.15	.04
203 Cliff Fannin	.15	.04
204 Dick Bokelman	.15	.04
205 Vern Benson	.15	.04
206 Ed Bailey	.15	.04
207 Whitey Ford	.50	.15
208 Jim Wilson	.15	.04
209 Jim Greengrass	.15	.04
210 Bob Cerv	.15	.04
211 J.W. Porter	.15	.04
212 Jack Dittmer	.15	.04
213 Ray Scarborough	.15	.04
214 Bill Bruton	.15	.04
215 Gene Conley	.15	.04
216 Jim Hughes	.15	.04
217 Murray Wall	.15	.04
218 Les Fusselman	.15	.04
219 Pete Runnels UER (Photo actually Don Johnson)	.30	.09
220 Satchel Paige UER (Misspelled Satchell on card front)	.75	.23
221 Bob Milliken	.25	.07
222 Vic Janowicz	.50	.15
223 Johnny O'Brien	.50	.15
224 Lou Sleater	.25	.07
225 Bobby Shantz	.50	.15
226 Ed Erautt	.25	.07
227 Morrie Martin	.25	.07
228 Hal Newhouser	.75	.23
229 Rocky Krsnich	.25	.07
230 Johnny Lindell	.25	.07
231 Solly Hemus	.25	.07
232 Dick Kokos	.25	.07
233 Al Aber	.25	.07
234 Ray Murray	.25	.07
235 John Hetki	.25	.07
236 Harry Perkowski	.25	.07
237 Bud Podbielan	.25	.07
238 Cal Hogue	.25	.07
239 Jim Delsing	.25	.07
240 Fred Marsh	.25	.07
241 Al Sima	.25	.07
242 Charlie Silvera	.50	.15
243 Carlos Bernier	.25	.07
244 Willie Mays	12.00	3.60
245 Bill Norman CO	.25	.07
246 Roy Face	.50	.15
247 Mike Sandlock	.25	.07
248 Gene Stephens	.25	.07
249 Eddie O'Brien	.50	.15
250 Bob Wilson	.25	.07
251 Sid Hudson	.25	.07
252 Hank Foiles	.25	.07
253 Does not exist		
254 Preacher Roe	.50	.15
255 Dixie Howell	.25	.07
256 Les Peden	.25	.07
257 Bob Boyd	.25	.07
258 Jim Gilliam	.50	.15
259 Roy McMillan	.50	.15
260 Sam Calderone	.25	.07
261 Does not exist		
262 Bob Oldis	.25	.07
263 Johnny Podres	.50	.15
264 Gene Woodling	.50	.15
265 Jackie Jensen	.50	.15
266 Bob Cain	.25	.07
267 Does not exist		
268 Does not exist		
269 Duane Pillette	.25	.07
270 Vern Stephens	.50	.15
271 Does not exist		
272 Bill Antonello	.25	.07
273 Harvey Haddix	.50	.15
274 John Riddle	.25	.07
275 Does not exist		
276 Ken Raffensberger	.25	.07
277 Don Lund	.25	.07
278 Willie Miranda	.25	.07
279 Joe Coleman	.25	.07
280 Milt Bolling	.25	.07
281 Jimmie Dykes MG	.50	.15
282 Ralph Houk	.50	.15
283 Frank Thomas	.50	.15
284 Bob Lemon	1.25	.35
285 Joe Adcock	.50	.15
286 Jimmie Piersall	.50	.15
287 Mickey Vernon	.50	.15
288 Robin Roberts	.50	.15
289 Rogers Hornsby MG	.75	.23
290 Hank Bauer	.50	.15
291 Hoot Evers	.30	.09
292 Whitey Lockman	.50	.15
293 Ralph Branca	.50	.15
294 Wally Post	.50	.15
295 Phil Cavarretta MG	.50	.15
296 Gil Hodges	1.25	.35
297 Roy Smalley	.30	.09
298 Bob Friend	.50	.15
299 Dusty Rhodes	.30	.09
300 Eddie Stanky	.30	.09
301 Harvey Kuenn	.50	.15
302 Marty Marion	.30	.09
303 Sal Maglie	.50	.15
304 Lou Boudreau MG	.50	.15
305 Carl Furillo	.75	.23
306 Bobo Holloman	.30	.09
307 Steve O'Neill MG	.30	.09
308 Carl Erskine	.75	.23
309 Leo Durocher MG	.50	.15
310 Lew Burdette	.50	.15
311 Richie Ashburn	.75	.23
312 Hoyt Wilhelm	.50	.15
313 Bucky Harris MG	.50	.15
314 Joe Garagiola	.50	.15
315 Johnny Pesky	.50	.15
316 Fred Haney MG	.30	.09
317 Hank Aaron	10.00	3.00
318 Curt Simmons	.50	.15
319 Ted Williams	10.00	3.00
320 Don Newcombe	.50	.15
321 Charlie Grimm MG	.50	.15
322 Paul Richards MG	.50	.15
323 Wes Westrum	.30	.09
324 Vern Law	.30	.09
325 Casey Stengel MG	1.25	.35
326 Dizzy Dean and Al Simmons (1953 HOF Inductees)	.75	.23
327 Duke Snider	.50	.15
328 Bill Rigney	.50	.15
329 Al Lopez MG	.50	.15
330 Bobby Thomson	.50	.15
331 Nellie Fox	.75	.23
332 Eleanor Engle	.50	.15
333 Larry Doby	.50	.15
334 Billy Goodman	.50	.15
335 Checklist 1-140	.30	.09
336 Checklist 141-280	.30	.09
337 Checklist 281-337	.30	.09

1994 Topps Archives 1954

The 1954 Archives set includes 248 reprint cards from the original set, plus eight specially created prospect cards (Roberto Clemente, Harmon Killebrew, Bob Grim, Camilo Pascual, Herb Score, Elston Howard, Bill Virdon, and Don Zimmer). No factory sets were sold. Randomly inserted were 1,954 redemption cards good for actual 1954 Topps cards; 1,954 Hank Aaron autographed gold cards; and 1,954 redemption cards for full sets of ToppsGold Archives cards. Each 12-card pack contains 11 Archives cards plus one ToppsGold Archives card. A random insert card replaced the gold card in every 2,210 packs. Ted Williams' card numbers 1 and 250, as well as a new Mickey Mantle's card number 259, were issued as inserts in the 1994 Upper Deck All-Time Heroes series.

	Nm-Mt	Ex-Mt
COMPLETE SET (256)	100.00	30.00
COMMON CARD (2-249)	.15	.04
COMMON (251-258)	.15	.04
1 Not Issued		
2 Gus Zernial	.30	.09
3 Monte Irvin	.30	.09
4 Hank Sauer	.30	.09
5 Ed Lopat	.30	.09
6 Pete Runnels	.30	.09
7 Ted Kluszewski	.50	.15
8 Bobby Young	.15	.04
9 Harvey Haddix	.30	.09
10 Jackie Robinson	4.00	1.20
11 Paul Smith	.15	.04
12 Del Crandall	.30	.09
13 Billy Martin	.50	.15
14 Preacher Roe	.30	.09
15 Al Rosen	.30	.09
16 Vic Janowicz	.30	.09
17 Phil Rizzuto	.75	.23
18 Walt Dropo	.15	.04
19 Johnny Lipon	.15	.04
20 Warren Spahn	.50	.15
21 Bobby Shantz	.30	.09
22 Jim Greengrass	.15	.04
23 Luke Easter	.30	.09
24 Granny Hamner	.30	.09
25 Harvey Kuenn	.30	.09
26 Ray Jablonski	.15	.04
27 Ferris Fain	.15	.04
28 Paul Minner	.15	.04
29 Jim Hegan	.15	.04
30 Ed Mathews	.75	.23
31 Johnny Klippstein	.15	.04
32 Duke Snider	.50	.15
33 Johnny Schmitz	.15	.04
34 Jim Rivera	.15	.04
35 Jim Gilliam	.30	.09
36 Hoyt Wilhelm	.30	.09
37 Whitey Ford	.50	.15
38 Eddie Stanky MG	.30	.09
39 Sherm Lollar	.30	.09
40 Mel Parnell	.15	.04
41 Willie Jones	.15	.04
42 Don Mueller	.15	.04
43 Dick Groat	.30	.09
44 Ned Garver	.15	.04
45 Richie Ashburn	.50	.15
46 Ken Raffensberger	.15	.04
47 Ellis Kinder	.15	.04
48 Billy Hunter	.15	.04
49 Ray Murray	.15	.04
50 Yogi Berra	1.50	.45
51 Johnny Lindell	.15	.04
52 Vic Power	.15	.04
53 Jack Dittmer	.15	.04
54 Vern Stephens	.30	.09
55 Phil Cavarretta MG	.30	.09
56 Willie Miranda	.15	.04
57 Luis Aloma	.15	.04
58 Bob Wilson	.15	.04
59 Gene Conley	.15	.04
60 Frank Baumholtz	.15	.04
61 Bob Cain	.15	.04
62 Eddie Robinson	.15	.04
63 Johnny Pesky	.30	.09
64 Hank Thompson	.15	.04
65 Bob Swift	.15	.04
66 Ted Lepcio	.15	.04
67 Jim Willis	.15	.04
68 Sammy Calderone	.15	.04
69 Bud Podbielan	.15	.04
70 Larry Doby	.30	.09
71 Frank Smith	.15	.04
72 Preston Ward	.15	.04
73 Wayne Terwilliger	.15	.04
74 Bill Taylor	.15	.04
75 Fred Haney MG	.15	.04
76 Bob Scheffing CO	.15	.04
77 Ray Boone	.15	.04
78 Ted Kazanski	.15	.04
79 Andy Pafko	.30	.09
80 Jackie Jensen	.30	.09
81 Dave Hoskins	.15	.04
82 Milt Bolling	.15	.04
83 Joe Collins	.30	.09
84 Dick Cole	.15	.04
85 Bob Turley	.30	.09
86 Billy Herman CO	.30	.09
87 Roy Face	.30	.09
88 Matt Batts	.15	.04
89 Howie Pollet	.15	.04
90 Willie Mays	5.00	1.50
91 Bob Oldis	.15	.04
92 Wally Westlake	.15	.04
93 Sid Hudson	.15	.04
94 Ernie Banks	3.00	.90
95 Hal Rice	.15	.04
96 Charlie Silvera	.30	.09
97 Jerry Lane	.15	.04
98 Joe Black	.30	.09
99 Bob Hofman	.15	.04
100 Bob Keegan	.15	.04
101 Gene Woodling	.30	.09
102 Gil Hodges	.75	.23
103 Jim Lemon	.15	.04
104 Mike Sandlock	.15	.04
105 Andy Carey	.30	.09
106 Dick Kokos	.15	.04
107 Duane Pillette	.15	.04
108 Thornton Kipper	.15	.04
109 Bill Bruton	.15	.04
110 Harry Dorish	.15	.04
111 Jim Delsing	.15	.04
112 Bill Renna	.15	.04
113 Bob Boyd	.15	.04
114 Dean Stone	.15	.04
115 Rip Repulski	.15	.04
116 Steve Bilko	.15	.04
117 Solly Hemus	.15	.04
118 Carl Scheib	.15	.04
119 Johnny Antonelli	.30	.09
120 Roy McMillan	.30	.09
121 Clem Labine	.50	.15
122 Johnny Logan	.30	.09
123 Bobby Adams	.15	.04
124 Marion Fricano	.15	.04
125 Harry Perkowski	.15	.04
126 Ben Wade	.15	.04

127 Steve O'Neill MG .15 .04
128 Henry Aaron 6.00 1.80
129 Forrest Jacobs .15 .04
130 Hank Bauer .30 .09
131 Reno Bertoia .15 .04
132 Tom Lasorda .50 .15
133 Del Baker CO .15 .04
134 Cal Hogue .15 .04
135 Joe Presko .15 .04
136 Connie Ryan .15 .04
137 Wally Moon .30 .09
138 Bob Borkowski .15 .04
139 Ed O'Brien .30 .09
Johnny O'Brien
140 Tom Wright .15 .04
141 Joe Jay .15 .04
142 Tom Poholsky .15 .04
143 Rollie Hemsley CO .15 .04
144 Bill Werle .15 .04
145 Elmer Valo .15 .04
146 Don Johnson .15 .04
147 John Riddle CO .15 .04
148 Bob Trice .15 .04
149 Jim Robertson .15 .04
150 Dick Kryhoski .15 .04
151 Alex Grammas .15 .04
152 Mike Blyzka .15 .04
153 Rube Walker .15 .04
154 Mike Fornieles .15 .04
155 Bob Kennedy .15 .04
156 Joe Coleman .15 .04
157 Don Lenhardt .15 .04
158 Peanuts Lowrey .15 .04
159 Dave Philley .15 .04
160 Red Kress CO .15 .04
161 John Hetki .15 .04
162 Herman Wehmeier .15 .04
163 Frank House .15 .04
164 Stu Miller .15 .04
165 Jim Pendleton .15 .04
166 Johnny Podres .30 .09
167 Don Lund .15 .04
168 Morrie Martin .15 .04
169 Jim Hughes .15 .04
170 Dusty Rhodes .15 .04
171 Leo Kiely .15 .04
172 Hal Brown .15 .04
173 Jack Harshman .15 .04
174 Tom Qualters .15 .04
175 Frank Leja .15 .04
176 Bob Keely .15 .04
177 Bob Milliken .15 .04
178 Bill Glynn .15 .04
179 Gair Allie .15 .04
180 Wes Westrum .15 .04
181 Mel Roach .15 .04
182 Chuck Harmon .15 .04
183 Earle Combs CO .75 .23
184 Ed Bailey .15 .04
185 Chuck Stobbs .15 .04
186 Karl Olson .15 .04
187 Heinie Manush CO .75 .23
188 Dave Jolly .15 .04
189 Bob Ross .15 .04
190 Ray Herbert .15 .04
191 Dick Schofield .15 .04
192 Cot Deal CO .15 .04
193 Johnny Hopp CO .15 .04
194 Bill Sarni .15 .04
195 Bill Consolo .15 .04
196 Stan Jok .15 .04
197 Schoolboy Rowe CO .30 .09
198 Carl Sawatski .15 .04
199 Rocky Nelson .15 .04
200 Larry Jansen .15 .04
201 Al Kaline 3.00 .90
202 Bob Purkey .15 .04
203 Harry Brecheen CO .15 .04
204 Angel Scull .15 .04
205 Johnny Sain .30 .09
206 Ray Crone .15 .04
207 Tom Oliver CO .15 .04
208 Grady Hatton .15 .04
209 Charlie Thompson .15 .04
210 Bob Buhl .15 .04
211 Don Hoak .15 .04
212 Mickey Micelotta .15 .04
213 John Fitzpatrick CO .15 .04
214 Arnold Portocarrero .15 .04
215 Ed McGhee .15 .04
216 Al Sima .15 .04
217 Paul Schreiber CO .15 .04
218 Fred Marsh .15 .04
219 Charlie Kress .15 .04
220 Ruben Gomez .15 .04
221 Dick Brodowski .15 .04
222 Bill Wilson .15 .04
223 Joe Haynes CO .15 .04
224 Dick Weik .15 .04
225 Don Liddle .15 .04
226 Jehosie Heard .15 .04
227 Buster Mills CO .15 .04
228 Gene Hermanski .15 .04
229 Bob Talbot .15 .04
230 Bob Kuzava .15 .04
231 Roy Smalley .15 .04
232 Lou Limmer .15 .04
233 Augie Galan .15 .04
234 Jerry Lynch .15 .04
235 Vern Law .15 .04
236 Paul Penson .15 .04
237 Mike Ryba .15 .04
238 Al Aber .15 .04
239 Bill Skowron .50 .15
240 Sam Mele .15 .04
241 Bob Miller .15 .04
242 Curt Roberts .15 .04
243 Ray Blades CO .15 .04
244 Leroy Wheat .15 .04
245 Roy Sievers .30 .09
246 Howie Fox .15 .04
247 Eddie Mayo CO .15 .04
248 Al Smith .15 .04
249 Wilmer Mizell .30 .09
250 Not Issued
251 Roberto Clemente 10.00 3.00
252 Bob Grim .15 .04
253 Elston Howard .50 .15
254 Harmon Killebrew .75 .23
255 Camilo Pascual .15 .04
256 Herb Score .30 .09
257 Bill Virdon .30 .09
258 Don Zimmer .30 .09
NNO Hank Aaron AU 150.00 45.00
NNO0 Gold Redem. Card Exp. 3.50 1.05

1994 Topps Archives 1954 Gold

This set parallels the 1994 Topps Archives 1954 reprint series. It has the same design as the regular issue reprint, except that the team logo and the facsimile autograph are gold-foil stamped on the fronts.

Nm-Mt Ex-Mt
*STARS: 1.5X TO 4X BASIC CARDS ...

1995 Topps Archives Brooklyn Dodgers

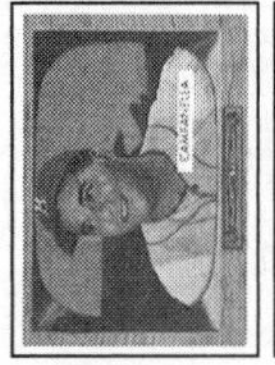

This 165-card set measures the standard size and is a single series release. The set honors the Brooklyn Dodger teams of 1952-1956 and consists of 127 reprints of Topps and Bowman cards produced during that time. The cards "that never were" have been created for the players not featured on Topps and Bowman cards and replicate the design of the card for the year the player would have been pictured. Cards numbered 117-120 commemorate the four games the Dodgers won for the 1955 World Series Championship. Though the cards are numbered as they were originally issued, Topps renumbered them as a complete set and they are checklisted accordingly. Some dealers believe that cards numbered from 111 through 165 were printed in shorter supply than other cards in this set. A very limited amount of signed Sandy Koufax cards (number 102 and number 146) were signed and randomly inserted into packs.

Nm-Mt Ex-Mt
COMPLETE SET (165) 100.00 30.00
1 Andy Pafko .50 .15
2 Wayne Terwilliger .25 .07
3 Billy Loes .50 .15
4 Gil Hodges 1.25 .35
5 Duke Snider .75 .23
6 Jim Russell .25 .07
7 Chris Van Cuyk .25 .07
8 Preacher Roe .50 .15
9 Johnny Schmitz .25 .07
10 Bud Podbielan .25 .07
11 Phil Haugstad .25 .07
12 Clyde King .25 .07
13 Billy Cox .50 .15
14 Rocky Bridges .25 .07
15 Carl Erskine .75 .23
16 Erv Palica .25 .07
17 Ralph Branca .50 .15
18 Jackie Robinson 2.00 .60
19 Roy Campanella 1.25 .35
20 Rube Walker .25 .07
21 Johnny Rutherford .25 .07
22 Joe Black .50 .15
23 George Shuba .25 .07
24 Pee Wee Reese 1.25 .35
25 Clem Labine .75 .23
26 Bobby Morgan .25 .07
27 Cookie Lavagetto CO .25 .07
28 Chuck Dressen MG .25 .07
29 Ben Wade .25 .07
30 Rocky Nelson .25 .07
31 Billy Herman CO .50 .15
32 Jake Pitler CO .25 .07
33 Dick Williams .50 .15
34 Cal Abrams .25 .07
35 Carl Furillo .75 .23
36 Don Newcombe .50 .15
37 Jackie Robinson 2.00 .60
38 Ben Wade .25 .07
39 Clem Labine .75 .23
40 Roy Campanella 1.25 .35
41 George Shuba .25 .07
42 Chuck Dressen MG .25 .07
43 Pee Wee Reese 1.25 .35
44 Joe Black .50 .15
45 Bobby Morgan .25 .07
46 Dick Williams .50 .15
47 Rube Walker .25 .07
48 Johnny Rutherford .25 .07
49 Billy Loes .50 .15
50 Don Hoak .25 .07
51 Jim Hughes .25 .07
52 Bob Milliken .25 .07
53 Preacher Roe .50 .15
54 Dixie Howell .25 .07
55 Junior Gilliam .75 .23
56 Johnny Podres .50 .15
57 Bill Antonello .25 .07
58 Ralph Branca .50 .15
59 Gil Hodges 1.25 .35
60 Carl Furillo .75 .23
61 Carl Erskine .75 .23
62 Don Newcombe .50 .15
63 Duke Snider .75 .23
64 Billy Cox .50 .15
65 Russ Meyer .25 .07
66 Jackie Robinson 2.00 .60
67 Preacher Roe .50 .15
68 Duke Snider .75 .23
69 Junior Gilliam .75 .23
70 Billy Herman CO .50 .15
71 Joe Black .50 .15
72 Gil Hodges 1.25 .35
73 Clem Labine .75 .23
74 Ben Wade .25 .07
75 Tom Lasorda .75 .23
76 Rube Walker .25 .07
77 Johnny Podres .50 .15
78 Jim Hughes .25 .07
79 Bob Milliken .25 .07
80 Charlie Thompson .25 .07
81 Don Hoak .25 .07
82 Roberto Clemente 4.00 1.20
83 Don Zimmer .50 .15
84 Roy Campanella 1.25 .35
85 Billy Cox .50 .15
86 Carl Erskine .75 .23
87 Carl Furillo .75 .23
88 Don Newcombe .50 .15
89 Pee Wee Reese 1.25 .35
90 George Shuba .25 .07
91 Junior Gilliam .75 .23
92 Billy Herman CO .50 .15
93 Johnny Podres .50 .15
94 Don Hoak .25 .07
95 Jackie Robinson 2.00 .60
96 Jim Hughes .25 .07
97 Bob Borkowski .50 .15
98 Sandy Amoros .25 .07
99 Karl Spooner .50 .15
100 Don Zimmer .25 .07
101 Rube Walker .25 .07
102 Bob Milliken 4.00 1.20
103 Sandy Koufax .50 .15
104 Joe Black .75 .23
105 Clem Labine 1.25 .35
106 Gil Hodges .25 .07
107 Ed Roebuck .25 .07
108 Bert Hamrik .75 .23
109 Duke Snider .75 .23
110 Bob Borkowski .25 .07
111 Roger Craig .50 .15
112 Don Drysdale 1.25 .35
113 Dixie Howell .25 .07
114 Frank Kellert .25 .07
115 Tom Lasorda .75 .23
116 Chuck Templeton .25 .07
117 Jackie Robinson WS .75 .23
118 Gil Hodges WS 1.25 .35
119 Duke Snider WS .75 .23
120 Johnny Podres WS 1.25 .35
121 Don Hoak .25 .07
122 Roy Campanella 1.25 .35
123 Pee Wee Reese 1.25 .35
124 Bob Darnell .25 .07
125 Don Zimmer .50 .15
126 George Shuba .25 .07
127 Johnny Podres .50 .15
128 Junior Gilliam .75 .23
129 Don Newcombe .50 .15
130 Jim Hughes .25 .07
131 Gil Hodges 1.25 .35
132 Carl Furillo .75 .23
133 Carl Erskine .75 .23
134 Erv Palica .25 .07
135 Russ Meyer .25 .07
136 Billy Loes .50 .15
137 Walt Moryn .25 .07
138 Chico Fernandez .25 .07
139 Charlie Neal .25 .07
140 Ken Lehman .25 .07
141 Walter Alston MG .75 .23
142 Jackie Robinson 2.00 .60
143 Sandy Amoros .50 .15
144 Ed Roebuck .25 .07
145 Roger Craig .50 .15
146 Sandy Koufax 2.00 .60
147 Karl Spooner .25 .07
148 Don Zimmer .50 .15
149 Roy Campanella 1.25 .35
150 Gil Hodges 1.25 .35
151 Duke Snider .75 .23
152 Team Card .75 .23
153 Johnny Podres .50 .15
154 Don Bessent .25 .07
155 Carl Furillo .75 .23
156 Randy Jackson .25 .07
157 Carl Erskine .75 .23
158 Don Newcombe .50 .15
159 Pee Wee Reese 1.25 .35
160 Billy Loes .50 .15
161 Junior Gilliam .75 .23
162 Clem Labine .75 .23
163 Charlie Neal .25 .07
164 Rube Walker .25 .07
165 Checklist .25 .07
AU103 Sandy Koufax 103AU 800.00 240.00
AU146 Sandy Koufax 146 AU 800.00 240.00

2001 Topps Archives

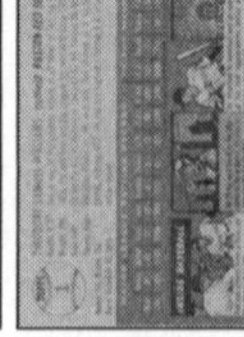

Issued in two series of 225 cards, this 450 card set features some of the first and last cards of retired superstars and other retired star players. The cards were issued in eight card packs with an SRP of $4. These packs were issued 20 packs to a box and eight boxes to a case. A very annoying feature of this set was the checklist numbers were so small that it was very difficult to tell what the number of the card was if a collector was trying to build a set.

Nm-Mt Ex-Mt
COMPLETE SET (450) 160.00 47.50
COMP. SERIES 1 (225) 80.00 24.00
COMP. SERIES 2 (225) 80.00 24.00
1 Johnny Antonelli 52 1.00 .30
2 Yogi Berra 52 UER 2.50 .75
Berra's first card was 51 Topps Red Back
3 Dom DiMaggio 52 UER 1.00 .30
His first Topps card is 1951 Red Back
4 Carl Erskine 52 1.00 .30
5 Larry Doby 52 1.00 .30
6 Monte Irvin 52 1.00 .30
7 Vernon Law 52 1.00 .30
8 Eddie Mathews 52 2.50 .75
9 Willie Mays 52 5.00 1.50
10 Gil McDougald 52 1.00 .30
11 Andy Pafko 52 1.50 .45
12 Phil Rizzuto 52 2.50 .75
13 Preacher Roe 52 UER 1.00 .30
His first Topps card is 51 Topps Red Back
14 Hank Sauer 52 UER 1.00 .30
His first Topps card is 51 Topps Blue Back
15 Bobby Shantz 52 1.00 .30
16 Enos Slaughter 52 1.00 .30
His first Topps card is 51 Topps Blue Back
17 Warren Spahn 52 UER 1.50 .45
His First Topps card was 1951 Topps Red Back
18 Mickey Vernon 52 UER 1.00 .30
His First Topps Card was 1951 Topps Blue Back
19 Early Wynn 52 UER 1.00 .30
His first Topps card is a 1951 Topps Red Back
20 Gaylord Perry 62 1.00 .30
21 Johnny Podres 53 1.00 .30
22 Ernie Banks 54 2.50 .75
23 Moose Skowron 54 1.00 .30
24 Harmon Killebrew 55 2.50 .75
25 Ted Williams 54 6.00 1.80
26 Jimmy Piersall 56 1.00 .30
27 Frank Thomas 56 1.00 .30
28 Bill Mazeroski 57 2.50 .75
29 Bobby Richardson 57 1.00 .30
30 Frank Robinson 57 1.50 .45
31 Stan Musial 58 4.00 1.20
32 Johnny Callison 59 1.00 .30
33 Bob Gibson 59 1.50 .45
34 Frank Howard 60 1.00 .30
35 Willie McCovey 60 1.00 .30
36 Carl Yastrzemski 60 4.00 1.20
37 Jim Maloney 61 1.00 .30
38 Ron Santo 61 1.50 .45
39 Lou Brock 62 1.50 .45
40 Tim McCarver 62 1.00 .30
41 Joe Pepitone 62 .50 .15
42 Boog Powell 62 1.50 .45
43 Bill Freehan 63 1.00 .30
44 Dick Allen 64 1.00 .30
45 Willie Horton 64 .50 .15
46 Mickey Lolich 64 1.00 .30
47 Wilbur Wood 64 .50 .15
48 Bert Campaneris 65 1.00 .30
49 Rod Carew 67 1.50 .45
50 Luis Aparicio 56 1.00 .30
51 Joe Morgan 65 1.00 .30
52 Luis Tiant 65 1.00 .30
53 Bobby Murcer 66 1.00 .30
54 Don Sutton 66 1.00 .30
55 Ken Holtzman 67 .50 .15
56 Reggie Smith 67 1.00 .30
57 Hal McRae 68 1.00 .30
58 Roy White 68 UER 1.00 .30
His Rookie Card is 66 Topps
59 Reggie Jackson 69 1.50 .45
60 Graig Nettles 69 1.00 .30
61 Joe Rudi 69 1.00 .30
62 Vida Blue 70 1.00 .30
63 Darrell Evans 70 1.00 .30
64 David Concepcion 71 1.00 .30
65 Bobby Grich 71 1.00 .30
66 Greg Luzinski 71 1.00 .30
67 Ron Cey 72 1.00 .30
68 George Hendrick 72 .50 .15
69 Dwight Evans 73 1.50 .45
70 Gary Matthews 73 .50 .15
71 Mike Schmidt 73 6.00 1.80
72 Jim Kaat 60 1.00 .30
73 Dave Winfield 74 1.00 .30
74 Gary Carter 75 2.50 .75
75 Dennis Eckersley 76 1.00 .30
76 Kent Tekulve 76 1.00 .30
77 Andre Dawson 77 1.50 .45
78 Denny Martinez 77 1.00 .30
79 Bruce Sutter 77 1.00 .30
80 Jack Morris 78 1.00 .30
81 Ozzie Smith 80 5.00 1.50
82 Lee Smith 82 1.00 .30
83 Don Mattingly 84 8.00 2.40
84 Joe Carter 85 1.00 .30
85 Kirby Puckett 85 2.50 .75
86 Joe Adcock 52 1.00 .30
87 Gus Bell 52 UER .50 .15
His first Topps card is 1951 Topps Red Back
88 Roy Campanella 52 2.50 .75
89 Jackie Jensen 52 1.00 .30
90 Johnny Mize 52 1.50 .45
91 Allie Reynolds 52 1.00 .30
92 Al Rosen 52 UER 1.00 .30
His first Topps card is a 1951 Topps Red Back
93 Hal Newhouser 53 1.00 .30
94 Harvey Kuenn 54 1.00 .30
95 Nellie Fox 56 2.50 .75
96 Elston Howard 56 1.50 .45
97 Sal Maglie 57 1.00 .30
98 Roger Maris 58 4.00 1.20
99 Norm Cash 60 UER 1.00 .30
His Rookie Card was in 1959 Topps
100 Thurman Munson 70 3.00 .90
101 Roy Campanella 57 UER 2.50 .75
His first Topps card is in 1952
102 Larry Doby 59 1.00 .30
103 Dom Dimaggio 53 1.00 .30
104 Johnny Mize 53 1.00 .30
105 Allie Reynolds 53 1.00 .30
106 Preacher Roe 54 1.00 .30
107 Hal Newhouser 55 .50 .15
108 Monte Irvin 56 1.00 .30
109 Carl Erskine 59 1.00 .30
110 Enos Slaughter 59 1.00 .30
111 Gil McDougald 60 1.00 .30
112 Andy Pafko 59 1.00 .30
113 Sal Maglie 59 .50 .15
114 Johnny Antonelli 61 .50 .15
115 Phil Rizzuto 61 1.50 .45
116 Yogi Berra 62 2.50 .75
117 Jim Wynn 77 .50 .15
118 Mickey Vernon 63 .50 .15
119 Gus Bell 64 .50 .15
120 Ted Williams 58 4.00 1.20
121 Frank Thomas 65 .50 .15
122 Bobby Richardson 66 1.00 .30
123 Gaylord Perry 83 1.00 .30
124 Vernon Law 67 .50 .15
125 Jimmy Piersall 67 .50 .15
126 Moose Skowron 67 1.00 .30
127 Joe Adcock 63 .50 .15
128 Johnny Podres 69 1.00 .30
129 Ernie Banks 71 2.50 .75
130 Jim Maloney 72 .50 .15
131 Johnny Callison 73 .50 .15
132 Eddie Mathews 68 1.50 .45
133 Joe Pepitone 73 .50 .15
134 Warren Spahn 65 1.50 .45
135 Bill Mazeroski 72 1.50 .45
136 Norm Cash 74 1.00 .30
137 Bob Gibson 75 1.50 .45
138 Harmon Killebrew 75 2.50 .75
139 Frank Robinson 75 1.50 .45
140 Ron Santo 75 1.00 .30
141 Hank Sauer 59 .50 .15
142 Bobby Shantz 64 .50 .15
143 Nellie Fox 65 1.50 .45
144 Elston Howard 68 1.50 .45
145 Jackie Jensen 61 1.00 .30
146 Al Rosen 56 1.00 .30
147 Dick Allen 76 .50 .15
148 Bill Freehan 77 1.00 .30
149 Boog Powell 77 1.00 .30
150 Lou Brock 79 UER 1.50 .45
Header for stats on back is for a pitcher
Brock was an outfielder
151 Rod Carew 86 1.50 .45
152 Wilbur Wood 79 .50 .15
153 Thurman Munson 79 2.50 .75
154 Ken Holtzman 80 .50 .15
155 Willie Horton 80 .50 .15
156 Mickey Lolich 80 .50 .15
157 Tim McCarver 80 .50 .15
158 Willie McCovey 80 1.00 .30
159 Roy White 80 .50 .15
160 Bobby Murcer 83 1.00 .30
161 Joe Rudi 83 .50 .15
162 Reggie Smith 83 .50 .15
163 Luis Tiant 83 .50 .15
164 Bert Campaneris 84 .50 .15
165 Frank Howard 73 .50 .15
166 Harvey Kuenn 66 .50 .15
167 Greg Luzinski 85 .50 .15
168 Luis Aparicio 74 1.00 .30
169 Willie Mays 73 3.00 .90
170 Roger Maris 68 2.50 .75
171 Vida Blue 87 .50 .15
172 Bobby Grich 87 .50 .15
173 Reggie Jackson 87 1.50 .45
174 Hal McRae 87 .50 .15
175 Carl Yastrzemski 83 2.50 .75
176 David Concepcion 88 .50 .15
177 Ron Cey 87 .50 .15
178 George Hendrick 88 .50 .15
179 Gary Matthews 88 .50 .15
180 Stan Musial 63 2.50 .75
181 Graig Nettles 88 .50 .15
182 Don Sutton 88 1.00 .30
183 Kent Tekulve 88 .50 .15
184 Bruce Sutter 89 1.00 .30
185 Darrell Evans 90 .50 .15
186 Mike Schmidt 89 2.50 .75
187 Jim Kaat 83 .50 .15
188 Dwight Evans 92 1.00 .30
189 Gary Carter 93 1.50 .45
190 Jack Morris 94 .50 .15
191 Joe Morgan 85 1.00 .30
192 Dave Winfield 95 1.00 .30
193 Andre Dawson 96 1.00 .30
194 Lee Smith 96 .50 .15
195 Ozzie Smith 96 4.00 1.20
196 Denny Martinez 97 .50 .15
197 Don Mattingly 96 4.00 1.20
198 Joe Carter 98 1.00 .30
199 Dennis Eckersley 98 1.00 .30
200 Kirby Puckett 96 2.50 .75
201 Walter Alston MG 56 1.00 .30
202 Casey Stengel MG 60 1.00 .30
203 S. Anderson MG 71 1.00 .30
204 T. Lasorda MG 88 1.00 .30
205 Whitey Herzog MG 88 .50 .15
206 AL HR Leaders 70 1.00 .30
Harmon Killebrew
Frank Howard
Reggie Jackson
207 NL HR Leaders 68 1.00 .30
Hank Aaron
Jim Wynn
Ron Santo
Willie McCovey
208 AL HR Leaders 67 2.50 .75
Brooks Robinson
Harmon Killebrew
Boog Powell
209 AL Batting Leaders 65 1.00 .30
Tony Oliva
Brooks Robinson
Elston Howard
210 NL HR Leaders 64 1.00 .30
Hank Aaron
Willie McCovey
Willie Mays
Orlando Cepeda
211 NL HR Leaders 63 1.00 .30
Hank Aaron
Frank Robinson
Willie Mays
Ernie Banks
Orlando Cepeda
212 AL HR Leaders 68 2.50 .75
Carl Yastrzemski
Harmon Killebrew
Frank Howard
213 Ernie Banks 59 Thrill 2.50 .75
214 Hank Aaron 59 Thrill 3.00 .90
215 Willie Mays 59 Thrill 3.00 .90
216 Al Kaline 59 Thrill 2.50 .75
217 Stan Musial 59 Thrill 2.50 .75
218 Duke Snider 59 Thrill 1.50 .45
219 The Champs 67 2.50 .75
Frank Robinson
Hank Bauer MG

Brooks Robinson UER
All Cards have a 1965 Leaders Back
220 Pride of the NL 63 2.50 .75
Willie Mays
Stan Musial
221 Whitey Ford WS 63 1.50 .45
222 Jerry Koosman WS 70 .50 .15
223 Bob Gibson WS 65 1.50 .45
224 Gil Hodges WS 60 1.50 .45
225 R. Jackson WS 78 1.50 .45
226 Hank Bauer 52 1.00 .30
227 Ralph Branca 52 1.00 .30
228 Joe Garagiola 52 1.00 .30
229 Bob Feller 52 1.50 .45
230 Dick Groat 52 1.00 .30
231 George Kell 52 1.50 .45
232 Bob Boone 73 1.00 .30
233 Minnie Minoso 52 1.00 .30
234 Billy Pierce 52 1.00 .30
235 Robin Roberts 52 1.00 .30
236 Johnny Sain 52 1.00 .30
237 Red Schoendienst 52 1.00 .30
238 Curt Simmons 52 1.00 .30
239 Duke Snider 52 1.50 .45
240 Bobby Thomson 52 1.50 .45
241 Hoyt Wilhelm 52 1.50 .45
242 Roy Face 53 1.00 .30
243 Ralph Kiner 53 1.00 .30
244 Hank Aaron 54 6.00 1.80
245 Al Kaline 54 2.50 .75
246 Don Larsen 56 2.50 .75
247 Tug McGraw 65 1.00 .30
248 Don Newcombe 56 1.50 .45
249 Herb Score 56 1.00 .30
250 Clete Boyer 57 1.00 .30
251 Lindy McDaniel 57 .50 .15
252 Brooks Robinson 57 2.50 .75
253 Orlando Cepeda 58 1.00 .30
254 Larry Bowa 70 1.00 .30
255 Mike Cuellar 59 1.00 .30
256 Jim Perry 59 1.00 .30
257 Dave Parker 74 1.00 .30
258 Maury Wills 60 1.00 .30
259 Willie Davis 61 .50 .15
260 Juan Marichal 61 1.00 .30
261 Jim Bouton 62 1.00 .30
262 Dean Chance 62 1.00 .30
263 Sam McDowell 62 1.00 .30
264 Whitey Ford 53 1.50 .45
265 Bob Uecker 62 1.50 .45
266 Willie Stargell 63 1.50 .45
267 Rico Carty 64 1.00 .30
268 Tommy John 64 1.00 .30
269 Phil Niekro 64 1.00 .30
270 Paul Blair 65 1.00 .30
271 Steve Carlton 65 3.00 .90
272 Jim Lonborg 65 1.00 .30
273 Tony Perez 65 1.00 .30
274 Ron Swoboda 65 1.00 .30
275 Fergie Jenkins 66 1.00 .30
276 Jim Palmer 66 1.00 .30
277 Sal Bando 67 1.00 .30
278 Tom Seaver 67 4.00 1.20
279 Johnny Bench 68 4.00 1.20
280 Nolan Ryan 68 6.00 1.80
281 Rollie Fingers 69 1.00 .30
282 Sparky Lyle 69 1.00 .30
283 Al Oliver 69 1.00 .30
284 Bob Watson 69 1.00 .30
285 Bill Buckner 70 1.00 .30
286 Bert Blyleven 71 1.50 .45
287 George Foster 71 1.00 .30
288 Al Hrabosky 71 .50 .15
289 Cecil Cooper 72 1.00 .30
290 Carlton Fisk 72 1.50 .45
291 Mickey Rivers 72 1.00 .30
292 Goose Gossage 73 1.00 .30
293 Rick Reuschel 73 1.00 .30
294 Bucky Dent 74 1.00 .30
295 Frank Tanana 74 1.00 .30
296 George Brett 75 8.00 2.40
297 Keith Hernandez 75 1.50 .45
298 Fred Lynn 75 1.00 .30
299 Robin Yount 75 5.00 1.50
300 Ron Guidry 76 1.00 .30
301 Jack Clark 77 1.00 .30
302 Mark Fidrych 77 1.00 .30
303 Dale Murphy 77 2.50 .75
304 Willie Hernandez 78 .50 .15
305 Lou Whitaker 78 1.00 .30
306 Kirk Gibson 81 1.50 .45
307 Wade Boggs 83 1.50 .45
308 Ryne Sandberg 83 6.00 1.80
309 Orel Hershiser 85 1.00 .30
310 Jimmy Key 85 1.00 .30
311 Richie Ashburn 52 1.50 .45
312 Smoky Burgess 52 1.00 .30
313 Gil Hodges 52 2.50 .75
314 Ted Kluszewski 52 1.50 .45
315 Pee Wee Reese 52 2.50 .75
316 Jackie Robinson 52 3.00 .90
317 Jim Wynn 64 .50 .15
318 Satchel Paige 53 4.00 1.20
319 Roberto Clemente 55 6.00 1.80
320 Carl Furillo 56 1.00 .30
321 Don Drysdale 57 2.50 .75
322 Curt Flood 58 1.00 .30
323 Bob Allison 59 1.00 .30
324 Tony Conigliaro 64 1.00 .30
325 Dan Quisenberry 80 1.00 .30
326 Ralph Branca 52 .50 .15
327 Bob Feller 53 1.50 .45
328 Satchel Paige 53 4.00 1.20
329 George Kell 58 1.50 .45
330 Pee Wee Reese 58 1.50 .45
331 Bobby Thomson 60 1.00 .30
332 Carl Furillo 60 .50 .15
333 Hank Bauer 61 .50 .15
334 Herb Score 62 .50 .15
335 Richie Ashburn 63 1.50 .45
336 Billy Pierce 64 .50 .15
337 Duke Snider 64 1.50 .45
338 Early Wynn 62 .50 .15
339 Robin Roberts 66 1.00 .30
340 Dick Groat 67 .50 .15
341 Curt Simmons 67 .50 .15
342 Bob Uecker 67 1.50 .45
343 Smoky Burgess 67 .50 .15
344 Jim Bouton 68 .50 .15
345 Roy Face 69 .50 .15
346 Don Drysdale 69 2.50 .75
347 Bob Allison 70 .50 .15
348 Clete Boyer 71 .50 .15
349 Dean Chance 71 .50 .15
350 Tony Conigliaro 71 .50 .15
351 Curt Flood 71 .50 .15
352 Hoyt Wilhelm 72 1.00 .30
353 Ron Swoboda 73 .50 .15
354 Roberto Clemente 73 4.00 1.20
355 Tug McGraw 85 .50 .15
356 Orlando Cepeda 74 1.00 .30
357 Joe Garagiola 52 .50 .15
358 Juan Marichal 74 1.00 .30
359 Sam McDowell 74 .50 .15
360 Johnny Sain 55 .50 .15
361 Ted Kluszewski 61 1.00 .30
362 Al Kaline 74 2.50 .75
363 Lindy McDaniel 75 .50 .15
364 Don Newcombe 60 1.00 .30
365 Jim Perry 75 .50 .15
366 Hank Aaron 76 4.00 1.20
367 Don Larsen 65 1.00 .30
368 Mike Cuellar 77 .50 .15
369 Willie Davis 77 .50 .15
370 Ralph Kiner 53 1.00 .30
371 Minnie Minoso 64 1.00 .30
372 Larry Bowa 85 .50 .15
373 Brooks Robinson 77 1.50 .45
374 Bob Boone 90 .50 .15
375 Jim Lonborg 79 .50 .15
376 Paul Blair 80 .50 .15
377 Rico Carty 80 .50 .15
378 Sal Bando 81 .50 .15
379 Mark Fidrych 81 .50 .15
380 Al Hrabosky 82 .50 .15
381 Willie Stargell 82 1.50 .45
382 Johnny Bench 83 2.50 .75
383 Dave Parker 81 .50 .15
384 Sparky Lyle 83 .50 .15
385 Fergie Jenkins 84 1.00 .30
386 Jim Palmer 84 1.00 .30
387 Whitey Ford 67 1.50 .45
388 Tony Perez 86 1.00 .30
389 Mickey Rivers 85 .50 .15
390 Bob Watson 85 .50 .15
391 Rollie Fingers 86 1.00 .30
392 George Foster 86 .50 .15
393 Al Oliver 86 .50 .15
394 Tom Seaver 87 1.50 .45
395 Maury Wills 72 .50 .15
396 Steve Carlton 87T 1.00 .30
397 Cecil Cooper 88 .50 .15
398 Bill Buckner 88 .50 .15
399 Phil Niekro 87 1.00 .30
400 Red Schoendienst 62 1.00 .30
401 Ron Guidry 89 .50 .15
402 Willie Hernandez 89 .50 .15
403 Tommy John 89 .50 .15
404 Gil Hodges 63 2.50 .75
405 Bucky Dent 84 .50 .15
406 Keith Hernandez 90 1.00 .30
407 Dan Quisenberry 90 .50 .15
408 Fred Lynn 91 .50 .15
409 Rick Reuschel 91 .50 .15
410 Jackie Robinson 56 3.00 .90
411 Goose Gossage 92 .50 .15
412 Bert Blyleven 93 1.00 .30
413 Jack Clark 93 .50 .15
414 Carlton Fisk 93 1.50 .45
415 Dale Murphy 93 1.50 .45
416 Frank Tanana 93 .50 .15
417 George Brett 94 5.00 1.50
418 Robin Yount 94 4.00 1.20
419 Kirk Gibson 95 1.00 .30
420 Lou Whitaker 95 .50 .15
421 R. Sandberg 97 UER 5.00 1.50
Card lists 1996 homers as 252
422 Jimmy Key 98 .50 .15
423 Nolan Ryan 94 4.00 1.20
424 Wade Boggs 00 1.00 .30
425 Orel Hershiser 00 .50 .15
426 Billy Martin MG 84 1.00 .30
427 Ralph Houk MG 62 1.00 .30
428 Chuck Tanner MG 72 .50 .15
429 Earl Weaver MG 71 1.00 .30
430 Leo Durocher MG 52 1.00 .30
431 AL HR Leaders 60 1.00 .30
Tony Conigliaro
Norm Cash
Willie Horton
432 NL HR Leaders 60 2.50 .75
Ernie Banks
Hank Aaron
Eddie Mathews
Ken Boyer
433 AL Batting Leaders 62 1.00 .30
Norm Cash
Elston Howard
Al Kaline
Jimmy Piersall
434 Leading Firemen 79 .50 .15
Goose Gossage
Rollie Fingers
435 Strikeout Leaders 77 1.50 .45
Nolan Ryan
Tom Seaver
436 HR Leaders 74 1.00 .30
Reggie Jackson
Willie Stargell
437 RBI Leaders 73 1.50 .45
Johnny Bench
Dick Allen
438 Roger Maris 2.50 .75
Blasts 61st 62
439 Carl Yastrzemski 2.50 .75
World Series Game Two 68
440 Nolan Ryan RB 78 4.00 1.20
441 Baltimore Orioles 70 1.00 .30
442 Tony Perez RB 86 .50 .15
443 Steve Carlton RB 84 .50 .15
444 Wade Boggs RB 89 .50 .15
445 Andre Dawson RB 89 1.00 .30
446 Whitey Ford WS 62 1.50 .45
447 Hank Aaron WS 59 4.00 1.20
448 Bob Gibson WS 69 1.50 .45
449 R.Clemente WS 72 4.00 1.20
450 Brooks Robinson 1.50 .45
Orioles/WS 71

2001 Topps Archives Autographs

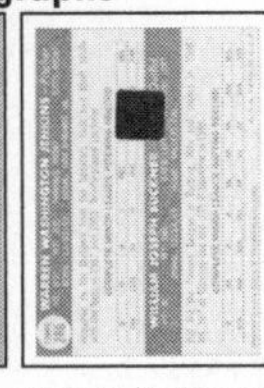

Inserted at overall odds of one in 20, these 159 cards feature the players signing their reprint cards. The set is checklisted TAA1-TAA170 but 11 cards do not exist as follows: 9, 15, 47, 72, 82, 84, 95, 105, 109, 159 and 161. The only first series exchange card was Keith Hernandez but unfortunately, Topps was unable to fulfill the card and sent collectors an array of other signed cards. The series two exchange card subjects were Juan Marichal, Jack Morris, Billy Pierce, Boog Powell, Ron Santo, Enos Slaughter, Ozzie Smith, Reggie Smith, Don Sutton, Bob Uecker, Jim Wynn and Robin Yount. Of these players, Juan Marichal, Ozzie Smith and Reggie Smith did not return any cards. The series one exchange date was April 30th, 2002 . The series two exchange deadline was exactly one year later - April 30th, 2003.

Nm-Mt Ex-Mt
SER.1 GROUP A ODDS 1:3049
SER.2 GROUP A ODDS 1:2904
SER.1 GROUP B ODDS 1:872
SER.2 GROUP B ODDS 1:480
SER.1 GROUP C ODDS 1:697
SER.2 GROUP C ODDS 1:4782
SER.1 GROUP D ODDS 1:122
SER.2 GROUP D ODDS 1:662
SER.1 GROUP E ODDS 1:26
SER.2 GROUP E ODDS 1:209
SER.1 GROUP F ODDS 1:6097
SER.2 GROUP F ODDS 1:1455
SER.2 GROUP G ODDS 1:320
SER.2 GROUP H ODDS 1:412
SER.2 GROUP I ODDS 1:192
SER.2 GROUP J ODDS 1:38
SER.2 GROUP K ODDS 1:329
TAA1 Johnny Antonelli E1 15.00 4.50
TAA2 Hank Bauer E1 25.00 7.50
TAA3 Yogi Berra A2 SP/50 250.00 75.00
TAA4 Ralph Branca E1 25.00 7.50
TAA5 Dom DiMaggio E1 40.00 12.00
TAA6 Joe Garagiola E1 40.00 12.00
TAA7 Carl Erskine D1 30.00 9.00
TAA8 Bob Feller E1 25.00 7.50
TAA9 Does Not Exist
TAA10 Dick Groat D1 30.00 9.00
TAA11 Monte Irvin E1 25.00 7.50
TAA12 George Kell E1 25.00 7.50
TAA13 Vernon Law E1 15.00 4.50
TAA14 Bob Boone E1 15.00 4.50
TAA15 Does Not Exist
TAA16 W.Mays A2 SP/50 400.00 120.00
TAA17 Gil McDougald E1 25.00 7.50
TAA18 Minnie Minoso E1 25.00 7.50
TAA19 Andy Pafko D2 25.00 7.50
TAA20 Billy Pierce E2 10.00 3.00
TAA21 P. Rizzuto B2 SP/200 120.00 36.00
TAA22 Robin Roberts C1 50.00 15.00
TAA23 Preacher Roe E1 25.00 7.50
TAA24 Johnny Sain E1 15.00 4.50
TAA25 Hank Sauer E1 15.00 4.50
TAA26 R. Schoendienst E1 15.00 4.50
TAA27 Bobby Shantz E1 15.00 4.50
TAA28 Curt Simmons E1 15.00 4.50
TAA29 Enos Slaughter E2 40.00 12.00
TAA30 Duke Snider B1 100.00 30.00
TAA31 Warren Spahn C2 100.00 30.00
TAA32 B.Thomson E1 25.00 7.50
TAA33 Mickey Vernon B2 15.00 4.50
TAA34 Hoyt Wilhelm D1 50.00 15.00
TAA35 Jim Wynn E2 10.00 3.00
TAA36 Roy Face E1 15.00 4.50
TAA37 Gaylord Perry C2 60.00 18.00
TAA38 Ralph Kiner B1 60.00 18.00
TAA39 Johnny Podres E2 15.00 4.50
TAA40 H.Aaron A2 SP/50 400.00 120.00
TAA41 E.Banks A2 SP/50 250.00 75.00
TAA42 Al Kaline B1 150.00 45.00
TAA43 Moose Skowron E1 15.00 4.50
TAA44 D.Larsen A1 SP/50 150.00 45.00
TAA45 H.Killebrew B1 150.00 45.00
TAA46 Tug McGraw E1 40.00 12.00
TAA47 Does Not Exist
TAA48 Don Newcombe E1 15.00 4.50
TAA49 Jim Piersall E2 15.00 4.50
TAA50 Herb Score E1 15.00 4.50
TAA51 Frank Thomas E1 15.00 4.50
TAA52 Clete Boyer D1 20.00 6.00
TAA53 Bill Mazeroski C2 60.00 18.00
TAA54 Lindy McDaniel E1 15.00 4.50
TAA55 B. Richardson E2 15.00 4.50
TAA56 B. Robinson A SP/50 250.00 75.00
TAA57 Frank Robinson B1 150.00 45.00
TAA58 Orlando Cepeda B1 60.00 18.00
TAA59 S. Musial A1 SP/50 300.00 90.00
TAA60 Larry Bowa D1 30.00 9.00
TAA61 Johnny Callison E2 10.00 3.00
TAA62 Mike Cuellar D1 20.00 6.00
TAA63 B. Gibson A1 SP/50 200.00 60.00
TAA64 Jim Perry E2 10.00 3.00
TAA65 Frank Howard E1 15.00 4.50
TAA66 Dave Parker E1 15.00 4.50
TAA67 Willie McCovey D2 100.00 30.00
TAA68 Maury Wills E1 15.00 4.50
TAA69 C. Yastrzemski F1 200.00 60.00
TAA70 Willie Davis E1 15.00 4.50
TAA71 Jim Maloney E2 10.00 3.00
TAA72 Does Not Exist
TAA73 Ron Santo E2 40.00 12.00
TAA74 Jim Bouton D1 30.00 9.00
TAA75 L. Brock A2 SP/50 200.00 60.00
TAA76 Dean Chance E1 15.00 4.50
TAA77 Tim McCarver 80.00 24.00
B2 SP/200
TAA78 Sam McDowell D1 20.00 6.00
TAA79 Joe Pepitone E1 15.00 4.50
TAA80 Whitey Ford F1 100.00 30.00
TAA81 Boog Powell E2 25.00 7.50
TAA82 Does Not Exist
TAA83 Bill Freehan D2 15.00 4.50
TAA84 Does Not Exist
TAA85 Dick Allen B2 40.00 12.00
TAA86 Rico Carty E1 15.00 4.50
TAA87 Willie Horton E2 10.00 3.00
TAA88 Tommy John E1 15.00 4.50
TAA89 Mickey Lolich E2 15.00 4.50
TAA90 Phil Niekro D1 30.00 9.00
TAA91 Wilbur Wood E1 15.00 4.50
TAA92 Paul Blair E1 15.00 4.50
TAA93 B. Campaneris E2 15.00 4.50
TAA94 Steve Carlton D1 50.00 15.00
TAA95 Does Not Exist
TAA96 Jim Lonborg E1 15.00 4.50
TAA97 Luis Aparicio B1 60.00 18.00
TAA98 Tony Perez D1 50.00 15.00
TAA99 J. Morgan B2 SP/200 80.00 24.00
TAA100 Ron Swoboda D1 30.00 9.00
TAA101 Luis Tiant E2 15.00 4.50
TAA102 Fergie Jenkins D1 30.00 9.00
TAA103 Bobby Murcer D2 60.00 18.00
TAA104 Jim Palmer B1 100.00 30.00
TAA105 Does Not Exist
TAA106 Sal Bando E2 15.00 4.50
TAA107 Ken Holtzman B1 40.00 12.00
TAA108 T.Seaver A2 SP/50 200.00 60.00
TAA109 Does Not Exist
TAA110 J.Bench A1 SP/50 250.00 75.00
TAA111 Hal McRae E2 10.00 3.00
TAA112 Nolan Ryan A2 300.00 90.00
TAA113 Roy White D2 15.00 4.50
TAA114 Rollie Fingers C1 30.00 9.00
TAA115 R.Jackson A2 SP/50 250.00 75.00
TAA116 Sparky Lyle E1 15.00 4.50
TAA117 Graig Nettles D2 25.00 7.50
TAA118 Al Oliver E1 15.00 4.50
TAA119 Joe Rudi B2 15.00 4.50
TAA120 Bob Watson E1 15.00 4.50
TAA121 Vida Blue E2 10.00 3.00
TAA122 Bill Buckner E1 15.00 4.50
TAA123 Darrell Evans E1 15.00 4.50
TAA124 Bert Blyleven D1 30.00 9.00
TAA125 D.Concepcion D2 25.00 7.50
TAA126 George Foster E1 15.00 4.50
TAA127 Bobby Grich E1 15.00 4.50
TAA128 Al Hrabosky E1 15.00 4.50
TAA129 Greg Luzinski D1 30.00 9.00
TAA130 Cecil Cooper E1 15.00 4.50
TAA131 Ron Cey E2 10.00 3.00
TAA132 Carlton Fisk B1 100.00 30.00
TAA133 G.Hendrick E2 10.00 3.00
TAA134 Mickey Rivers E1 15.00 4.50
TAA135 Dwight Evans D2 25.00 7.50
TAA136 Rich Gossage E1 15.00 4.50
TAA137 G. Matthews B2 15.00 4.50
TAA138 Rick Reuschel E1 15.00 4.50
TAA139 Mike Schmidt 300.00 90.00
A1 SP/50
TAA140 Bucky Dent D1 30.00 9.00
TAA141 Jim Kaat B2 25.00 7.50
TAA142 Frank Tanana E1 15.00 4.50
TAA143 Dave Winfield 120.00 36.00
B2 SP/200
TAA144 G.Brett A1 SP/50 300.00 90.00
TAA145 G.Carter B2 SP/200 120.00 36.00
TAA146 Keith Hernandez D1
TAA147 Fred Lynn C1 30.00 9.00
TAA148 R.Yount B2 SP/200 175.00 52.50
TAA149 Dennis Eckersley 80.00 24.00
B2 SP/200
TAA150 Ron Guidry E2 15.00 4.50
TAA151 Kent Tekulve D1 20.00 6.00
TAA152 Jack Clark E1 15.00 4.50
TAA153 A.Dawson B2 SP/200 80.00 24.00
TAA154 Mark Fidrych E1 15.00 4.50
TAA155 Dennis Martinez 50.00 15.00
B2 SP/200
TAA156 Dale Murphy C1 80.00 24.00
TAA157 Bruce Sutter D2 25.00 7.50
TAA158 W.Hernandez D2 15.00 4.50
TAA159 Does Not Exist
TAA160 Lou Whitaker D2 25.00 7.50
TAA161 Does Not Exist
TAA162 Kirk Gibson E1 25.00 7.50
TAA163 Lee Smith D2 25.00 7.50
TAA164 Wade Boggs B1 100.00 30.00
TAA165 Ryne Sandberg 150.00 45.00
B2 SP/200
TAA166 Don Mattingly D1 120.00 36.00
TAA167 J.Carter B2 SP/200 50.00 15.00
TAA168 Orel Hershiser D2 40.00 12.00
TAA169 Kirby Puckett A2 100.00 30.00
TAA170 Jimmy Key C1 50.00 15.00

2001 Topps Archives AutoProofs

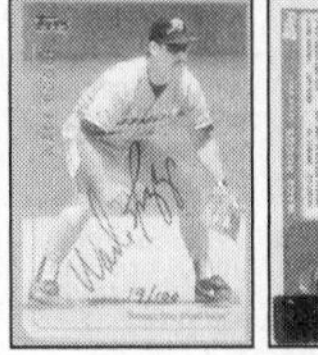

Inserted at a rate of one in 2,444 in series one and one in 2,391 in series two these 10 cards feature players signing their actual cards. Each of these cards are serial numbered to 100. Willie McCovey and Willie Mays were both first series exchange cards with a redemption deadline of April 30th, 2002. Carlton Fisk, Robin Roberts and Hoyt Wilhelm were series two exchange cards with a redemption deadline of April 30th, 2003.

Nm-Mt Ex-Mt
1 Wade Boggs 99 S1 80.00 24.00
2 Carlton Fisk 93 S2 100.00 30.00
3 Willie Mays 73 S1 200.00 60.00
4 Willie McCovey 80 S1 80.00 24.00
5 J.Palmer 82/84 EXCH S1 60.00 18.00
6 Robin Roberts 66 S2 80.00 24.00
7 Duke Snider 64 S2 80.00 24.00
8 Warren Spahn 65 S2 80.00 24.00
9 Hoyt Wilhelm 63 S2 60.00 18.00
10 Carl Yastrzemski 83 S1 150.00 45.00

2001 Topps Archives Bucks

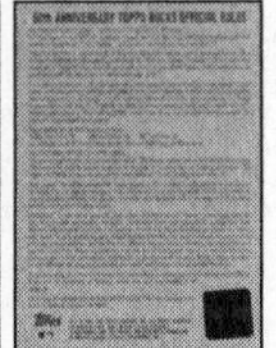

Randomly inserted in packs, these three cards issued in the style of the old Baseball Bucks were good for money toward Topps 50th anniversary merchandise.

Nm-Mt Ex-Mt
TB1 Willie Mays $1 10.00 3.00
TB2 Roberto Clemente $5 25.00 7.50
TB3 Jackie Robinson $10 25.00 7.50

2001 Topps Archives Future Rookie Reprints

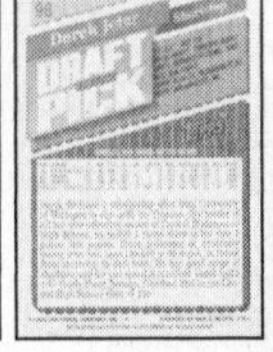

Issued five per sealed Topps factory and HTA sets, these 20 cards feature Rookie Card reprints of today's leading players.

Nm-Mt Ex-Mt
COMPLETE SET (20) 50.00 15.00
1 Barry Bonds 87 8.00 2.40
2 Chipper Jones 91 3.00 .90
3 Cal Ripken 82 10.00 3.00
4 Shawn Green 92 1.25 .35
5 Frank Thomas 90 3.00 .90
6 Derek Jeter 93 8.00 2.40
7 Geoff Jenkins 96 1.25 .35
8 Jim Edmonds 93 1.25 .35
9 Bernie Williams 90 2.00 .60
10 Sammy Sosa 90 5.00 1.50
11 Rickey Henderson 80 3.00 .90
12 Calvin Reese 92 1.25 .35
13 Randy Johnson 89 3.00 .90
14 Juan Gonzalez 90 3.00 .90
15 Gary Sheffield 89 1.25 .35
16 Manny Ramirez 92 1.25 .35
17 Pokey Reese 92 1.25 .35
18 Preston Wilson 93 1.25 .35
19 Jay Payton 95 1.25 .35
20 Rafael Palmeiro 87 2.00 .60

2001 Topps Archives Rookie Reprint Bat Relics

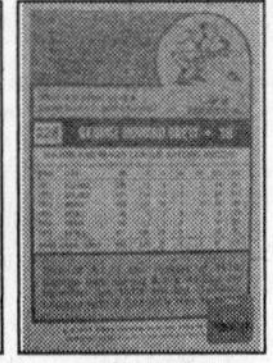

Inserted in series one packs at a rate of one in 1,356 and second series packs at a rate of one in 1,1307 these six cards feature not only the rookie reprint but also a game used bat slice.

Nm-Mt Ex-Mt
TARR1 Johnny Bench 40.00 12.00
TARR2 George Brett 80.00 24.00
TARR3 Fred Lynn 25.00 7.50
TARR4 Reggie Jackson 40.00 12.00
TARR5 Mike Schmidt 80.00 24.00
TARR6 Willie Stargell 40.00 12.00

2002 Topps Archives

This 200 card set was released in early April, 2002. These cards were issued in eight card packs which were issued in 20 pack boxes and were packed eight boxes to a case. The packs had an SRP of $4 per pack. This set was subtitled "Best Years" and it featured a reprint of the player's Topps card from their best year in the majors. Interestingly, Topps changed the backs of most of the cards to include the stats from that selected year. Also, in many of the cards, the text was changed to reflect the best year rather than using the original verbiage.

Nm-Mt Ex-Mt
COMPLETE SET (200) 100.00 30.00
1 Willie Mays 62 5.00 1.50
2 Dale Murphy 83 2.50 .75

3 Dave Winfield 79 1.00 .30
4 Roger Maris 61 4.00 1.20
5 Ron Cey 77 1.00 .30
6 Lee Smith 91 1.00 .30
7 Len Dykstra 93 1.00 .30
8 Ray Fosse 70 1.00 .30
9 Warren Spahn 57 1.50 .45
10 Herb Score 56 1.00 .30
11 Jim Wynn 74 1.00 .30
12 Sam McDowell 70 1.00 .30
13 Fred Lynn 79 1.00 .30
14 Yogi Berra 54 2.50 .75
15 Ron Santo 64 1.50 .45
16 Alvin Dark 53 1.00 .30
17 Bill Buckner 85 1.00 .30
18 Rollie Fingers 81 1.00 .30
19 Tony Gwynn 97 3.00 .90
20 Red Schoendienst 53 1.00 .30
21 Gaylord Perry 72 1.00 .30
22 Jose Cruz 83 1.00 .30
23 Dennis Martinez 91 1.00 .30
24 Dave McNally 68 1.00 .30
25 Norm Cash 61 1.00 .30
26 Ted Kluszewski 54 UER 1.50 .45
Card has Yogi Berra's stats on back
27 Rick Reuschel 77 1.00 .30
28 Bruce Sutter 77 1.00 .30
29 Don Larsen 56 1.50 .45
30 Claudell Washington 82 1.00 .30
31 Luis Aparicio 60 1.00 .30
32 Clete Boyer 62 1.00 .30
33 Goose Gossage 77 1.00 .30
34 Ray Knight 79 1.00 .30
35 Roy Campanella 53 2.50 .75
36 Tug McGraw 71 1.00 .30
37 Bob Lemon 52 1.00 .30
38 Willie Stargell 71 1.50 .45
39 Roberto Clemente 66 5.00 1.50
40 Jim Fregosi 70 1.00 .30
41 Reggie Smith 77 1.00 .30
42 Dave Parker 78 1.00 .30
43 Darrell Evans 73 1.00 .30
44 Ryne Sandberg 90 4.00 1.20
45 Manny Mota 72 1.00 .30
46 Dennis Eckersley 92 1.00 .30
47 Nellie Fox 59 1.50 .45
48 Gil Hodges 54 2.50 .75
49 Reggie Jackson 69 1.50 .45
50 Bobby Shantz 52 1.00 .30
51 Cecil Cooper 80 1.00 .30
52 Jim Kaat 66 1.00 .30
53 George Hendrick 80 1.00 .30
54 Johnny Podres 61 1.00 .30
55 Bob Gibson 68 1.50 .45
56 Vern Law 60 1.00 .30
57 Joe Adcock 56 1.00 .30
58 Jack Clark 87 1.00 .30
59 Bill Mazeroski 60 1.50 .45
60 Carl Yastrzemski 67 4.00 1.20
61 Bobby Murcer 71 1.00 .30
62 Davey Johnson 73 1.00 .30
63 Jim Palmer 75 1.00 .30
64 Roy Face 59 1.00 .30
65 Dean Chance 64 1.00 .30
66 Moose Skowron 60 1.50 .45
67 Dwight Evans 87 1.00 .30
68 Kirk Gibson 88 1.00 .30
69 Sal Bando 69 1.00 .30
70 Mike Schmidt 80 5.00 1.50
71 Bo Jackson 89 2.50 .75
72 Chris Chambliss 76 1.00 .30
73 Fergie Jenkins 71 1.00 .30
74 Brooks Robinson 64 2.50 .75
75 Bobby Richardson 62 1.00 .30
76 Duke Snider 54 1.50 .45
77 Allie Reynolds 52 1.50 .45
78 Harmon Killebrew 66 2.50 .75
79 Steve Carlton 72 1.00 .30
80 Bert Blyleven 73 1.00 .30
81 Phil Niekro 69 1.00 .30
82 Lew Burdette 56 1.00 .30
83 Hoyt Wilhelm 64 1.00 .30
84 Curt Flood 65 1.00 .30
85 Willie Hernandez 84 1.00 .30
86 Robin Yount 82 4.00 1.20
87 Robin Roberts 52 1.00 .30
88 Whitey Ford 61 1.50 .45
89 Tony Oliva 64 1.00 .30
90 Don Newcombe 56 1.00 .30
91 Al Oliver 82 1.00 .30
92 Mike Cuellar 69 1.00 .30
93 Mike Scott 86 1.00 .30
94 Dick Allen 66 1.00 .30
95 Jimmy Piersall 56 1.00 .30
96 Bill Freehan 68 1.00 .30
97 Willie Horton 65 1.00 .30
98 Bob Friend 60 1.00 .30
99 Ken Holtzman 73 1.00 .30
100 Rico Carty 70 1.00 .30
101 Gil McDougald 56 1.00 .30
102 Lee May 69 1.00 .30
103 Joe Pepitone 64 1.00 .30
104 Gene Tenace 75 1.00 .30
105 Gary Carter 85 1.50 .45
106 Tim McCarver 67 1.00 .30
107 Ernie Banks 58 2.50 .75
108 George Foster 77 1.00 .30
109 Lou Brock 74 1.50 .45
110 Dick Groat 60 1.00 .30
111 Graig Nettles 77 1.00 .30
112 Boog Powell 69 1.50 .45
113 Joe Carter 86 1.00 .30
114 Juan Marichal 66 1.00 .30
115 Larry Doby 54 1.00 .30
116 Fernando Valenzuela 86 1.00 .30
117 Luis Tiant 68 1.00 .30
118 Early Wynn 59 1.00 .30
119 Bill Madlock 75 1.00 .30
120 Eddie Mathews 53 2.50 .75
121 George Brett 80 6.00 1.80
122 Al Kaline 55 2.50 .75
123 Frank Howard 69 1.00 .30
124 Mickey Lolich 71 1.00 .30
125 Kirby Puckett 88 2.50 .75
126 Bob Cerv 58 1.00 .30
127 Will Clark 89 2.50 .75
128 Vida Blue 71 1.00 .30
129 Kevin Mitchell 89 1.00 .30
130 Bucky Dent 80 1.00 .30
131 Tom Seaver 69 1.50 .45
132 Jerry Koosman 76 1.00 .30
133 Orlando Cepeda 61 1.00 .30
134 Nolan Ryan 73 6.00 1.80
135 Tony Kubek 60 1.50 .45
136 Don Drysdale 62 2.50 .75
137 Paul Blair 69 1.00 .30
138 Elston Howard 63 1.50 .45
139 Joe Rudi 74 1.00 .30
140 Tommie Agee 70 1.00 .30
141 Richie Ashburn 58 1.50 .45
142 Jim Bunning 65 1.00 .30
143 Hank Sauer 52 1.00 .30
144 Greg Luzinski 77 1.00 .30
145 Ron Guidry 78 1.00 .30
146 Rod Carew 77 1.50 .45
147 Andre Dawson 87 1.00 .30
148 Keith Hernandez 79 1.50 .45
149 Carlton Fisk 77 1.50 .45
150 Cleon Jones 69 1.00 .30
151 Don Mattingly 85 6.00 1.80
152 Vada Pinson 63 1.00 .30
153 Ozzie Smith 87 4.00 1.20
154 Dave Concepcion 79 1.00 .30
155 Al Rosen 53 1.00 .30
156 Tommy John 68 1.00 .30
157 Bob Ojeda 86 1.00 .30
158 Frank Robinson 66 1.50 .45
159 Darryl Strawberry 87 1.50 .45
160 Bobby Bonds 73 1.50 .45
161 Bert Campaneris 70 1.00 .30
162 Catfish Hunter 74 1.50 .45
163 Bud Harrelson 70 1.00 .30
164 Dwight Gooden 85 1.50 .45
165 Wade Boggs 87 1.50 .45
166 Joe Morgan 76 1.00 .30
167 Ron Swoboda 67 1.00 .30
168 Hank Aaron 57 5.00 1.50
169 Steve Garvey 77 1.00 .30
170 Mickey Rivers 77 1.00 .30
171 Johnny Bench 70 2.50 .75
172 Ralph Terry 62 1.00 .30
173 Billy Pierce 56 1.00 .30
174 Thurman Munson 76 3.00 .90
175 Don Sutton 72 1.00 .30
176 Sparky Anderson 84 MG 1.00 .30
177 Gil Hodges 69 MG 2.50 .75
178 Davey Johnson 86 MG 1.00 .30
179 Frank Robinson 89 MG 1.50 .45
180 Red Schoendienst 67 MG 1.00 .30
181 Roger Maris 61 AS 4.00 1.20
182 Willie Mays 62 AS 5.00 1.50
183 Luis Aparicio 60 AS 1.00 .30
184 Nellie Fox 59 AS 1.50 .45
185 Ernie Banks 58 AS 2.50 .75
186 Orlando Cepeda 62 AS 1.00 .30
187 Whitey Ford 61 AS 1.50 .45
188 Bob Gibson 69 AS 1.50 .45
189 Bill Mazeroski 59 AS 1.50 .45
190 Hank Aaron 58 AS 5.00 1.50
191 1971 AL HR Leaders 1.00 .30
Frank Howard
Harmon Killebrew
Carl Yastrzemski
192 1962 NL HR Leaders 1.50 .45
Orlando Cepeda
Frank Robinson
Willie Mays
193 1967 NL RBI Leaders 2.50 .75
Hank Aaron
Roberto Clemente
Dick Allen
194 1970 NL Win Leaders 1.00 .30
Tom Seaver
Phil Niekro
Fergie Jenkins
Juan Marichal
195 1976 AL ERA Leaders 1.00 .30
Jim Palmer
Catfish Hunter
Dennis Eckersley
196 Hank Aaron 76 HL 5.00 1.50
197 Brooks Robinson 78 HL 2.50 .75
198 Tom Seaver 70 HL 1.00 .30
199 Jim Palmer 71 HL 1.00 .30
200 Lou Brock 75 HL 1.50 .45

2002 Topps Archives Autographs

Issued at overall stated odds of one in 22 hobby packs and 1:22 retail packs, these 59 cards feature many of the players featured in the 2002 Topps Archives set. Since there were so many groups that the different players belong to 12 different groups. We have notated the group that these players belong to next to their name in our checklist.

Nm-Mt Ex-Mt
GROUP A ODDS 1:19,803 HOB, 1:20,040 RET
GROUP B ODDS 1:12,872 HOB, 1:13,360 RET
GROUP C ODDS 1:11,193 HOB, 1:11,451 RET
GROUP D ODDS 1:8045 HOB, 1:8016 RET
GROUP E ODDS 1:753 HOB, 1:756 RET
GROUP F ODDS 1:3387 HOB, 1:3340 RET
GROUP G ODDS 1:1355 HOB, 1:1359 RET
GROUP H ODDS 1:1129 HOB, 1:1129 RET
GROUP K ODDS 1:748 HOB, 1:749 RET
GROUP L ODDS 1:45 HOB, 1:45 RET..
TAA-AD Alvin Dark 53 J 20.00 6.00
TAA-AK Al Kaline 55 E 150.00 45.00
TAA-BB Bobby Bonds 73 J 30.00 9.00
TAA-BC Bert Campaneris 70 L 15.00 4.50
TAA-BD Bucky Dent 80 J 20.00 6.00
TAA-BH Bud Harrelson 70 L 15.00 4.50
TAA-BJ Bo Jackson 89 F
TAA-BP Billy Pierce 56 J 15.00 4.50
TAA-BS Bruce Sutter 77 J 20.00 6.00
TAA-CC Chris Chambliss 76 J 20.00 6.00
TAA-DA Dick Allen 66 J 30.00 9.00
TAA-DG Dwight Gooden 85 G
TAA-DM Dave McNally 68 L 20.00 6.00
TAA-DN Don Newcombe 56 I 20.00 6.00
TAA-DP Dave Parker 78 H 20.00 6.00
TAA-DS Duke Snider 54 E
TAA-DW Dave Winfield 79 D
TAA-EB Ernie Banks 58 E 150.00 45.00
TAA-FJ Fergie Jenkins 71 J 20.00 6.00
TAA-FL Fred Lynn 79 J 20.00 6.00
TAA-GB George Brett 80 E 300.00 90.00
TAA-GC Gary Carter 85 E
TAA-GF George Foster 77 L 20.00 6.00
TAA-GH Willie Hernandez 84 L 15.00 4.50
TAA-GL Greg Luzinski 77 J 20.00 6.00
TAA-GP Gaylord Perry 72 J 20.00 6.00
TAA-HA Hank Aaron 57 E 250.00 75.00
TAA-HK Harmon Killebrew 69 E
TAA-HW Hoyt Wilhelm 64 L 20.00 6.00
TAA-JF Jim Fregosi 70 I 15.00 4.50
TAA-JK Jim Kaat 66 J 20.00 6.00
TAA-JP Jim Palmer 75 E
TAA-JR Joe Rudi 74 J 20.00 6.00
TAA-KH Keith Hernandez 79 J 50.00 15.00
TAA-KM Kevin Mitchell 89 J 20.00 6.00
TAA-KP Kirby Puckett 88 A
TAA-LB Lew Burdette 56 L 20.00 6.00
TAA-LD Len Dykstra 94 J 20.00 6.00
TAA-LS Lee Smith 91 H 20.00 6.00
TAA-MR Mickey Rivers 77 L 15.00 4.50
TAA-MS Mike Schmidt 80 B
TAA-RS Ron Santo 64 L 30.00 9.00
TAA-RT Ralph Terry 62 J 30.00 9.00
TAA-RY Robin Yount 82 C 100.00 30.00
TAA-SB Sal Bando 69 L 20.00 6.00
TAA-SG Steve Garvey 77 J 20.00 6.00
TAA-TJ Tommy John 68 L 20.00 6.00
TAA-TO Tony Oliva 64 J 40.00 12.00
TAA-BPO Boog Powell 69 J 30.00 9.00
TAA-BRO B.Robinson 64 E 150.00 45.00
TAA-DEV Darrell Evans 73 J 20.00 6.00
TAA-DGR Dick Groat 60 L 20.00 6.00
TAA-JBU Jim Bunning 65 L 30.00 9.00
TAA-JCR Jose Cruz 83 K 20.00 6.00
TAA-JKO Jerry Koosman 76 G
TAA-JPI Jimmy Piersall 56 J 20.00 6.00
TAA-JPO Johnny Podres 61 J 20.00 6.00
TAA-RCE Ron Cey 77 L 20.00 6.00
TAA-RSM Reggie Smith 77 L 20.00 6.00

2002 Topps Archives AutoProofs

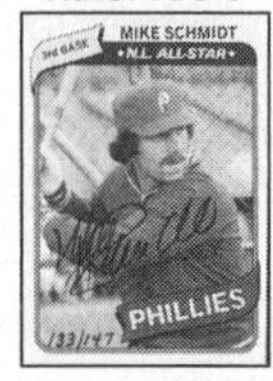

Randomly inserted into 1:616 hobby packs and 1:617 retail packs, these 10 cards feature original Topps cards which were repurchased by Topps on the secondary market and then signed by the featured player. Since each player signed a different amount of cards, we have notated those stated print runs next to the players name in our checklist. Cards with a print run of 40 or fewer are not priced due to market scarcity.

Nm-Mt Ex-Mt
GROUP A ODDS 1:128,720 H, 1:80,160 R
GROUP B ODDS 1:42,907 H, 1:40,080 R
GROUP C ODDS 1:17,163 H, 1:16,032 R
GROUP D ODDS 1:5254 H, 1:5344 R..
GROUP E ODDS 1:8305 H, 1:8016 R..
GROUP F ODDS 1:7151 H, 1:7287 R..
GROUP G ODDS 1:6436 H, 1:6680 R..
GROUP H ODDS 1:4597 H, 1:4453 R..
GROUP I ODDS 1:3731 H, 1:3817 R...
GROUP J ODDS 1:2258 H, 1:2290 R..
NO PRICING ON QTY 16 OR LESS
1 Gary Carter 85 E/80 50.00 15.00
2 Jose Cruz 83 F/95 40.00 12.00
3 Steve Garvey 77 A/5
4 Bo Jackson 89 J/300 60.00 18.00
5 Kevin Mitchell 89 D/65 40.00 12.00
6 Kirby Puckett 88 D/65 100.00 30.00
7 Mike Schmidt 80 H/147 120.00 36.00
8 Ozzie Smith 87 G/105 100.00 30.00
9 Darryl Strawberry 87 I/181 60.00 18.00
10 Dave Winfield 79 B/16
11 Robin Yount 82 C/39 150.00 45.00

2002 Topps Archives Bat Relics

Randomly inserted into hobby and retail packs, these 19 cards feature players from the Archives set along a game-used bat piece. Players in group A were inserted at stated odds of one in 106 while players in group B were inserted at stated odds of one in 282. We have notated what group each player is part of in our checklist.

Nm-Mt Ex-Mt
TBR-AD Andre Dawson 87 A 15.00 4.50
TBR-BF Bill Freehan 68 A 15.00 4.50
TBR-BR Brooks Robinson 64 A 25.00 7.50
TBR-CY Carl Yastrzemski 67 B 40.00 12.00
TBR-DE Dwight Evans 87 A 15.00 4.50
TBR-DM Don Mattingly 85 A 50.00 15.00
TBR-DP Dave Parker 78 A 15.00 4.50
TBR-GB George Brett 80 A 40.00 12.00
TBR-GC Gary Carter 85 A 20.00 6.00
TBR-JB Johnny Bench 70 A 25.00 7.50
TBR-JC Joe Carter 86 A 15.00 4.50
TBR-JM Joe Morgan 76 B 15.00 4.50
TBR-NC Norm Cash 61 A 15.00 4.50
TBR-RJ Reggie Jackson 69 A 20.00 6.00
TBR-RM Roger Maris 61 A 60.00 18.00
TBR-RS Ron Santo 64 A 20.00 6.00
TBR-RY Robin Yount 82 B 25.00 7.50
TBR-WH Willie Horton 65 A 15.00 4.50
TBR-WS Willie Stargell 71 A 20.00 6.00

2002 Topps Archives Reprints

Issued at a stated rate of five per sealed 2002 Topps Factory set, these 10 cards feature reprints of first Topps cards of some of the leading superstars in baseball.

Nm-Mt Ex-Mt
COMPLETE SET (10) 25.00 7.50
1 Alex Rodriguez 98 3.00 .90
2 Jason Giambi 94 2.00 .60
3 Pedro Martinez 93 2.00 .60
4 Ichiro Suzuki 01 3.00 .90
5 Jeff Bagwell 91 2.00 .60
6 Ivan Rodriguez 91 2.00 .60
7 Mike Piazza 93 3.00 .90
8 Nomar Garciaparra 95 3.00 .90
9 Ken Griffey Jr. 89 3.00 .90
10 Albert Pujols 01 4.00 1.20

2002 Topps Archives Seat Relics

Randomly inserted into hobby and retail packs, these 19 cards feature a player from the Archives set along with a piece of a seat from a ballpark they played in. There were three different groups of players and they were inserted at odds ranging from one in 80 packs to one in 1636 packs.

Nm-Mt Ex-Mt
GROUP A ODDS 1:1629 HOB, 1:1636 RET
GROUP B ODDS 1:80 HOB, 1:80 RET .
GROUP C ODDS 1:1160 HOB, 1:1162 RET
TSR-BL Bob Lemon 52 B 15.00 4.50
TSR-DP Dave Parker 78 B 15.00 4.50
TSR-DS Duke Snider 54 B 20.00 6.00
TSR-EB Ernie Banks 58 B 25.00 7.50
TSR-EM Eddie Mathews 53 B 25.00 7.50
TSR-HS Herb Score 56 B 15.00 4.50
TSR-JB Jim Bunning 65 B 15.00 4.50
TSR-JC Joe Carter 86 B 15.00 4.50
TSR-JP Jim Palmer 75 B 15.00 4.50
TSR-ML Mickey Lolich 71 B 15.00 4.50
TSR-NF Nellie Fox 59 B 20.00 6.00
TSR-RA Richie Ashburn 58 B 20.00 6.00
TSR-RC Rod Carew 77 B 20.00 6.00
TSR-RG Ron Guidry 78 C 15.00 4.50
TSR-SA Sparky Anderson 84 B 15.00 4.50
TSR-SM Sam McDowell 70 B 15.00 4.50
TSR-TK Ted Kluszewski 54 B 20.00 6.00
TSR-WS Warren Spahn 57 B 20.00 6.00
TSR-YB Yogi Berra 54 A 25.00 7.50

2002 Topps Archives Uniform Relics

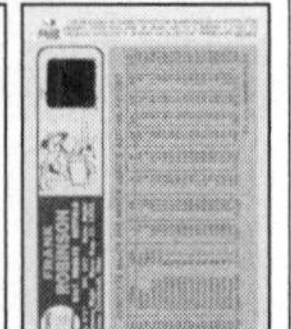

Inserted into hobby and retail packs at stated odds of one in 28, these 20 cards feature players from the Archives set along with a game-worn uniform swatch of that player.

Nm-Mt Ex-Mt
TUR-BB Bobby Bonds 73 15.00 4.50
TUR-DC Dave Concepcion 79 15.00 4.50
TUR-DE Dennis Eckersley 92 15.00 4.50
TUR-DM Dale Murphy 83 25.00 7.50
TUR-DS Don Sutton 72 15.00 4.50
TUR-DW Dave Winfield 79 15.00 4.50
TUR-FL Fred Lynn 79 15.00 4.50
TUR-FR Frank Robinson 66 20.00 6.00
TUR-GB George Brett 80 40.00 12.00
TUR-GP Gaylord Perry 72 15.00 4.50
TUR-KP Kirby Puckett 88 25.00 7.50
TUR-NR Nolan Ryan 73 50.00 15.00
TUR-OC Orlando Cepeda 61 15.00 4.50
TUR-OS Ozzie Smith 87 25.00 7.50
TUR-PN Phil Niekro 69 15.00 4.50
TUR-RS Ryne Sandberg 90 40.00 12.00
TUR-SA Sparky Anderson 84 15.00 4.50
TUR-SG Steve Garvey 77 15.00 4.50
TUR-WB Wade Boggs 87 20.00 6.00
TUR-WC Will Clark 89 25.00 7.50

2001 Topps Archives Reserve

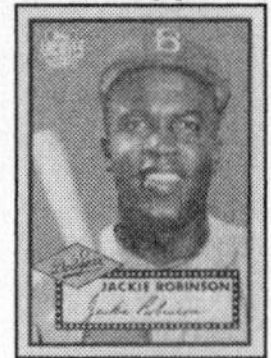

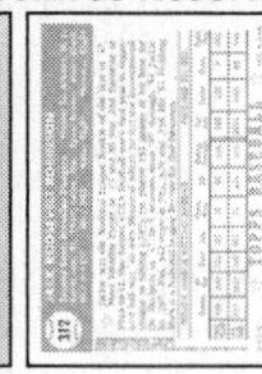

This 100 card set was issued in five card packs. These five card packs were issued in special display boxes which included one signed baseball per sealed box. These sealed boxes were issued six boxes to a case. The boxes (ball plus packs) had an SPR of $100 per box.

Nm-Mt Ex-Mt
COMPLETE SET (100) 100.00 30.00
1 Joe Adcock 52 1.50 .45
2 Brooks Robinson 57 4.00 1.20
3 Luis Aparicio 56 1.50 .45
4 Richie Ashburn 52 2.50 .75
5 Hank Bauer 52 1.50 .45
6 Johnny Bench 68 6.00 1.80
7 Wade Boggs 83 2.50 .75
8 Moose Skowron 54 1.50 .45
9 George Brett 75 12.00 3.60
10 Lou Brock 62 2.50 .75
11 Roy Campanella 52 4.00 1.20
12 Willie Hernandez 78 1.50 .45
13 Steve Carlton 65 5.00 1.50
14 Gary Carter 75 4.00 1.20
15 Hoyt Wilhelm 52 2.50 .75
16 Orlando Cepeda 58 1.50 .45
17 Roberto Clemente 55 8.00 2.40
18 Dale Murphy 77 4.00 1.20
19 Dave Concepcion 71 1.50 .45
20 Dom DiMaggio 52 1.50 .45
21 Larry Doby 52 1.50 .45
22 Don Drysdale 57 4.00 1.20
23 Dennis Eckersley 76 1.50 .45
24 Bob Feller 52 2.50 .75
25 Rollie Fingers 69 1.50 .45
26 Carlton Fisk 72 2.50 .75
27 Nellie Fox 56 2.50 .75
28 Mickey Rivers 72 1.50 .45
29 Tommy John 64 1.50 .45
30 Johnny Sain 52 1.50 .45
31 Keith Hernandez 75 2.50 .75
32 Gil Hodges 52 4.00 1.20
33 Elston Howard 56 2.50 .75
34 Frank Howard 60 1.50 .45
35 Bob Gibson 59 2.50 .75
36 Fergie Jenkins 66 1.50 .45
37 Jackie Jensen 52 1.50 .45
38 Al Kaline 54 4.00 1.20
39 Harmon Killebrew 55 4.00 1.20
40 Ralph Kiner 53 1.50 .45
41 Dick Groat 52 1.50 .45
42 Don Larsen 56 4.00 1.20
43 Ralph Branca 52 1.50 .45
44 Mickey Lolich 64 1.50 .45
45 Juan Marichal 61 1.50 .45
46 Roger Maris 58 5.00 1.50
47 Bobby Thomson 52 2.50 .75
48 Eddie Mathews 52 4.00 1.20
49 Don Mattingly 84 12.00 3.60
50 Willie McCovey 60 1.50 .45
51 Gil McDougald 52 1.50 .45
52 Tug McGraw 65 1.50 .45
53 Billy Pierce 52 1.50 .45
54 Minnie Minoso 52 1.50 .45
55 Johnny Mize 52 2.50 .75
56 Roy Face 53 1.50 .45
57 Joe Morgan 65 1.50 .45
58 Thurman Munson 70 5.00 1.50
59 Stan Musial 58 5.00 1.50
60 Phil Niekro 64 1.50 .45
61 Paul Blair 65 1.50 .45
62 Andy Pafko 52 2.50 .75
63 Satchel Paige 53 6.00 1.80
64 Tony Perez 65 1.50 .45
65 Sal Bando 67 1.50 .45
66 Jimmy Piersall 56 1.50 .45
67 Kirby Puckett 85 4.00 1.20
68 Phil Rizzuto 52 4.00 1.20
69 Robin Roberts 52 1.50 .45
70 Jackie Robinson 52 5.00 1.50
71 Ryne Sandberg 83 12.00 3.60
72 Mike Schmidt 73 10.00 3.00
73 Red Schoendienst 52 1.50 .45
74 Herb Score 56 1.50 .45
75 Enos Slaughter 52 1.50 .45
76 Ozzie Smith 80 8.00 2.40
77 Warren Spahn 52 2.50 .75
78 Don Sutton 66 1.50 .45
79 Luis Tiant 65 1.50 .45
80 Ted Kluszewski 52 2.50 .75
81 Whitey Ford 53 2.50 .75
82 Maury Wills 60 1.50 .45
83 Dave Winfield 74 1.50 .45
84 Early Wynn 52 1.50 .45
85 Carl Yastrzemski 60 5.00 1.50
86 Robin Yount 75 8.00 2.40
87 Bob Allison 59 1.50 .45
88 Clete Boyer 57 1.50 .45
89 Reggie Jackson 69 2.50 .75
90 Yogi Berra 52 4.00 1.20
91 Willie Mays 52 8.00 2.40
92 Jim Palmer 66 1.50 .45
93 Pee Wee Reese 52 4.00 1.20
94 Frank Robinson 57 2.50 .75
95 Boog Powell 62 2.50 .75
96 Willie Stargell 63 2.50 .75
97 Nolan Ryan 68 10.00 3.00
98 Tom Seaver 67 6.00 1.80
99 Duke Snider 52 2.50 .75
100 Bill Mazeroski 57 4.00 1.20

2001 Topps Archives Reserve Autographed Baseballs

Issued one per sealed box, these 30 players signed baseballs for inclusion in this product. Each player signed an amount of ball between 100 and 1000 and we have included that

information next to the player's name.

	Nm-Mt	Ex-Mt
1 Johnny Bench/100	100.00	30.00
2 Paul Blair/1000	20.00	6.00
3 Clete Boyer/1000	25.00	7.50
4 Ralph Branca/400	30.00	9.00
5 Roy Face/1000	25.00	7.50
6 Bob Feller/1000	30.00	9.00
7 Whitey Ford/100	80.00	24.00
8 Bob Gibson/1000	40.00	12.00
9 Dick Groat/1000	25.00	7.50
10 Frank Howard/1000	25.00	7.50
11 Reggie Jackson/100	100.00	30.00
12 Don Larsen/100	40.00	12.00
13 Mickey Lolich/500	25.00	7.50
14 Willie Mays/100	200.00	60.00
15 Gil McDougald/500	30.00	9.00
16 Tug McGraw/1000	30.00	9.00
17 Minnie Minoso/1000	25.00	7.50
18 Andy Pafko/500	25.00	7.50
19 Joe Pepitone/1000	20.00	6.00
20 Robin Roberts/1000	30.00	9.00
21 Frank Robinson/100	60.00	18.00
22 Nolan Ryan/100	200.00	60.00
23 Herb Score/500	25.00	7.50
24 Tom Seaver/100	100.00	30.00
25 Moose Skowron/1000	30.00	9.00
26 Warren Spahn/100	80.00	24.00
27 Bobby Thomson/400	30.00	9.00
28 Luis Tiant/500	25.00	7.50
29 Carl Yastrzemski/100	120.00	36.00
30 Maury Wills/1000	25.00	7.50

2001 Topps Archives Reserve Future Rookie Reprints

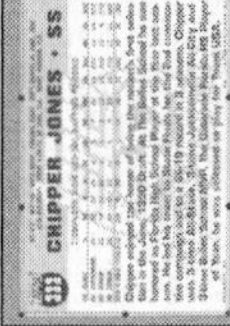

Issued five per Topps Limited factory set, these 20 cards are reprints of the featured players rookie card.

	Nm-Mt	Ex-Mt
COMPLETE SET (20)	120.00	36.00
1 Barry Bonds 87	15.00	4.50
2 Chipper Jones 91	6.00	1.80
3 Cal Ripken 82	25.00	7.50
4 Shawn Green 92	2.50	.75
5 Frank Thomas 90	6.00	1.80
6 Derek Jeter 93	20.00	6.00
7 Geoff Jenkins 96	2.50	.75
8 Jim Edmonds 93	2.50	.75
9 Bernie Williams 90	4.00	1.20
10 Sammy Sosa 90	10.00	3.00
11 Rickey Henderson 80	6.00	1.80
12 Tony Gwynn 83	8.00	2.40
13 Randy Johnson 89	6.00	1.80
14 Juan Gonzalez 90	6.00	1.80
15 Gary Sheffield 89	2.50	.75
16 Manny Ramirez 92	2.50	.75
17 Pokey Reese 92	2.50	.75
18 Preston Wilson 93	2.50	.75
19 Jay Payton 95	2.50	.75
20 Rafael Palmeiro 87	4.00	1.20

2001 Topps Archives Reserve Rookie Reprint Autographs

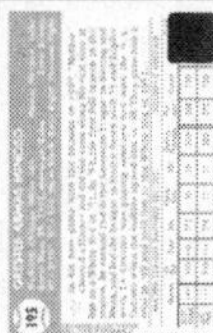

Inserted one per 10 packs, these 27 cards feature autographs of the players rookie reprint card. Each player signed a different amount of cards and those are notated by groups A, B or C in our checklist. Cards 15, 20, 22, 24, 28, 30, 31, and 35 do not exist. Willie Mays did not return his cards in time for inclusion in the packout. Those cards could be redeemed until July 31, 2003.

	Nm-Mt	Ex-Mt
ARA1 Willie Mays C	175.00	52.50
ARA2 Whitey Ford B	60.00	18.00
ARA3 Nolan Ryan A	200.00	60.00
ARA4 Carl Yastrzemski B	120.00	36.00
ARA5 Frank Robinson B	50.00	15.00
ARA6 Tom Seaver A	120.00	36.00
ARA7 Warren Spahn A	80.00	24.00
ARA8 Johnny Bench A	120.00	36.00
ARA9 Reggie Jackson A	120.00	36.00
ARA10 Bob Gibson B	50.00	15.00
ARA11 Bob Feller D	25.00	7.50
ARA12 Gil McDougald A	25.00	7.50
ARA13 Luis Tiant A	20.00	6.00
ARA14 Minnie Minoso D	20.00	6.00
ARA16 Herb Score B	20.00	6.00
ARA17 Moose Skowron C	25.00	7.50
ARA18 Maury Wills D	20.00	6.00
ARA19 Clete Boyer A	20.00	6.00
ARA21 Don Larsen A	25.00	7.50
ARA23 Tug McGraw C	30.00	9.00
ARA25 Robin Roberts C	25.00	7.50
ARA26 Frank Howard A	20.00	6.00
ARA27 Mickey Lolich D	20.00	6.00
ARA29 Tommy John C	20.00	6.00
ARA32 Dick Groat D	20.00	6.00
ARA33 Roy Face D	20.00	6.00
ARA34 Paul Blair D	15.00	4.50

2001 Topps Archives Reserve Rookie Reprint Relics

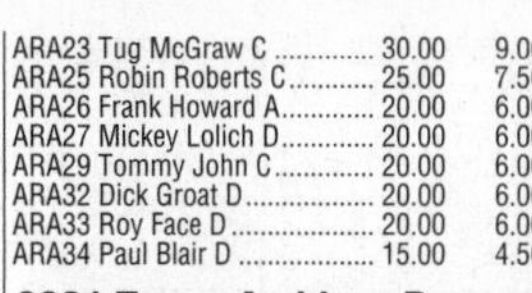

Issued at a rate of one in 10 packs, these 51 cards feature not only a rookie reprint of the featured player but also a memorabilia piece relating to their career.

	Nm-Mt	Ex-Mt
ARR1 B.Robinson Jsy	25.00	7.50
ARR2 Tony Conigliaro Jsy	25.00	7.50
ARR3 Frank Howard Jsy	15.00	4.50
ARR4 Don Sutton Jsy	15.00	4.50
ARR5 F.Jenkins Jsy	15.00	4.50
ARR6 Frank Robinson Jsy	25.00	7.50
ARR7 Don Mattingly Jsy	40.00	12.00
ARR8 Willie Stargell Jsy	25.00	7.50
ARR9 Moose Skowron Jsy	25.00	7.50
ARR10 Fred Lynn Jsy	15.00	4.50
ARR11 George Brett Jsy	40.00	12.00
ARR12 Nolan Ryan Jsy	50.00	15.00
ARR13 O.Cepeda Jsy	15.00	4.50
ARR14 R.Jackson Jsy	25.00	7.50
ARR15 Steve Carlton Jsy	15.00	4.50
ARR16 Tom Seaver Jsy	25.00	7.50
ARR17 T. Munson Jsy	40.00	12.00
ARR18 Yogi Berra Jsy	25.00	7.50
ARR19 W. McCovey Jsy	15.00	4.50
ARR20 Robin Yount Jsy	25.00	7.50
ARR21 Al Kaline Bat	25.00	7.50
ARR22 C. Yastrzemski Bat	40.00	12.00
ARR23 Carlton Fisk Bat	25.00	7.50
ARR24 Dale Murphy Bat	25.00	7.50
ARR25 Dave Winfield Bat	15.00	4.50
ARR26 Dick Groat Bat	15.00	4.50
ARR27 Dom DiMaggio Bat	25.00	7.50
ARR28 Don Mattingly Bat	40.00	12.00
ARR29 Gary Carter Bat	25.00	7.50
ARR30 George Kell Bat	25.00	7.50
ARR31 H. Killebrew Bat	25.00	7.50
ARR32 Jackie Jensen Bat	25.00	7.50
ARR33 J. Robinson Bat	100.00	30.00
ARR34 Jim Piersall Bat	15.00	4.50
ARR35 Joe Adcock Bat	15.00	4.50
ARR36 Joe Carter Bat	15.00	4.50
ARR37 Johnny Mize Bat	25.00	7.50
ARR38 Kirk Gibson Bat	15.00	4.50
ARR39 Mickey Vernon Bat	15.00	4.50
ARR40 Mike Schmidt Bat	40.00	12.00
ARR41 R. Sandberg Bat	40.00	12.00
ARR42 Ozzie Smith Bat	25.00	7.50
ARR43 T.Kluszewski Bat	25.00	7.50
ARR44 Wade Boggs Bat	25.00	7.50
ARR45 Willie Mays Bat	100.00	30.00
ARR46 Duke Snider Bat	25.00	7.50
ARR47 Harvey Kuenn Bat	15.00	4.50
ARR48 Robin Yount Bat	25.00	7.50
ARR49 R.Schoendienst Bat	15.00	4.50
ARR50 Elston Howard Bat	25.00	7.50
ARR51 Bob Allison Bat	15.00	4.50

2002 Topps Archives Reserve

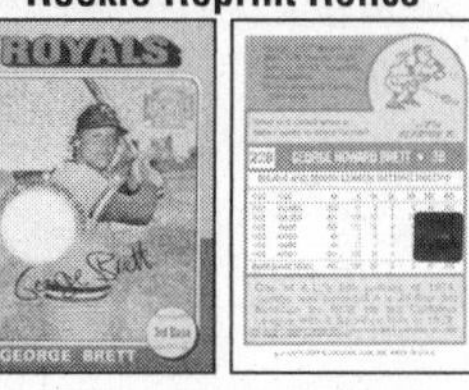

This 100 card set was released in June, 2002. This 100 card set was issued in four card packs which came 10 packs to a box and four boxes to a case. Each box also contined an autographed baseball.

	Nm-Mt	Ex-Mt
COMPLETE SET (100)	150.00	45.00
1 Lee Smith 91	1.50	.45
2 Gaylord Perry 72	1.50	.45
3 Al Oliver 82	1.50	.45
4 Goose Gossage 77	1.50	.45
5 Bill Madlock 75	1.50	.45
6 Rod Carew 77	2.50	.75
7 Fred Lynn 79	1.50	.45
8 Frank Robinson 66	2.50	.75
9 Al Kaline 55	4.00	1.20
10 Len Dykstra 93	1.50	.45
11 Carlton Fisk 77	2.50	.75
12 Nellie Fox 59	2.50	.75
13 Reggie Jackson 69	2.50	.75
14 Bob Gibson 68	2.50	.75
15 Bill Buckner 85	1.50	.45
16 Harmon Killebrew 69	4.00	1.20
17 Gary Carter 85	2.50	.75
18 Dave Winfield 79	1.50	.45
19 Ozzie Smith 87	6.00	1.80
20 Dwight Evans 87	1.50	.45
21 Dave Concepcion 79	1.50	.45
22 Joe Morgan 76	1.50	.45
23 Clete Boyer 62	1.50	.45
24 Will Clark 89	4.00	1.20
25 Lee May 69	1.50	.45
26 Kevin Mitchell 89	1.50	.45
27 Roger Maris 61	6.00	1.80
28 Mickey Lolich 71	1.50	.45
29 Luis Aparicio 60	1.50	.45
30 George Foster 77	1.50	.45
31 Don Mattingly 85	10.00	3.00
32 Fernando Valenzuela 86	1.50	.45
33 Bobby Bonds 73	1.50	.45
34 Jim Palmer 75	1.50	.45
35 Dennis Eckersley 92	1.50	.45
36 Kirby Puckett 88	4.00	1.20
37 Jose Cruz 83	1.50	.45
38 Richie Ashburn 58	2.50	.75
39 Whitey Ford 61	2.50	.75
40 Robin Roberts 52	1.50	.45
41 Don Newcombe 56	1.50	.45
42 Roy Campanella 53	4.00	1.20
43 Dennis Martinez 91	1.50	.45
44 Larry Doby 54	1.50	.45
45 Steve Garvey 77	1.50	.45
46 Thurman Munson 76	5.00	1.50
47 Dale Murphy 83	4.00	1.20
48 Moose Skowron 60	2.50	.75
49 Tom Seaver 69	2.50	.75
50 Orlando Cepeda 61	1.50	.45
51 Graig Nettles 77	1.50	.45
52 Willie Stargell 71	2.50	.75
53 Yogi Berra 54	4.00	1.20
54 Steve Carlton 72	1.50	.45
55 Don Sutton 72	1.50	.45
56 Brooks Robinson 64	4.00	1.20
57 Vida Blue 71	1.50	.45
58 Rollie Fingers 81	1.50	.45
59 Jim Bunning 65	1.50	.45
60 Nolan Ryan 73	10.00	3.00
61 Hank Aaron 57	8.00	2.40
62 Fergie Jenkins 71	1.50	.45
63 Andre Dawson 87	1.50	.45
64 Ernie Banks 58	4.00	1.20
65 Early Wynn 59	1.50	.45
66 Duke Snider 54	2.50	.75
67 Red Schoendienst 53	1.50	.45
68 Don Drysdale 62	4.00	1.20
69 Catfish Hunter 74	2.50	.75
70 George Brett 80	10.00	3.00
71 Elston Howard 63	2.50	.75
72 Wade Boggs 87	2.50	.75
73 Keith Hernandez 79	2.50	.75
74 Billy Pierce 56	1.50	.45
75 Ted Kluszewski 54	2.50	.75
76 Carl Yastrzemski 67	6.00	1.80
77 Bert Blyleven 73	1.50	.45
78 Tony Oliva 64	1.50	.45
79 Joe Carter 86	1.50	.45
80 Johnny Bench 70	4.00	1.20
81 Tony Gwynn 97	5.00	1.50
82 Mike Schmidt 80	8.00	2.40
83 Phil Niekro 69	1.50	.45
84 Juan Marichal 66	1.50	.45
85 Eddie Mathews 53	4.00	1.20
86 Boog Powell 69	2.50	.75
87 Dwight Gooden 85	2.50	.75
88 Darryl Strawberry 87	2.50	.75
89 Roberto Clemente 66	10.00	3.00
90 Ryne Sandberg 90	8.00	2.40
91 Jack Clark 87	1.50	.45
92 Willie Mays 62	8.00	2.40
93 Ron Guidry 78	1.50	.45
94 Kirk Gibson 88	1.50	.45
95 Lou Brock 74	2.50	.75
96 Robin Yount 82	6.00	1.80
97 Bill Mazeroski 60	2.50	.75
98 Dave Parker 78	1.50	.45
99 Hoyt Wilhelm 64	1.50	.45
100 Warren Spahn 57	2.50	.75

2002 Topps Archives Reserve Autographed Baseballs

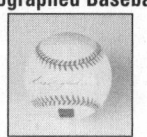

Inserted one per Archives Reserve box, these 21 autographed baseballs feature authentic signatures from some of baseball's best all-time players. Since the players signed a different amount of cards, we have notated that information next to their name in our checklist.

	Nm-Mt	Ex-Mt
1 Luis Aparicio/1600	25.00	7.50
2 Ernie Banks/50		
3 Yogi Berra/100	120.00	36.00
4 Lou Brock/400	50.00	15.00
5 Jim Bunning/500	50.00	15.00
6 Gary Carter/500	50.00	15.00
7 Goose Gossage/500	30.00	9.00
8 Fergie Jenkins/1000	25.00	7.50
9 Al Kaline/250	100.00	30.00
10 Harmon Killebrew/250	100.00	30.00
11 Willie Mays/50		
12 Joe Morgan/250	50.00	15.00
13 Graig Nettles/1600	25.00	7.50
14 Jim Palmer/400	30.00	9.00
15 Gaylord Perry/500	30.00	9.00
16 Brooks Robinson/500	60.00	18.00
17 Mike Schmidt/250	120.00	36.00
18 Duke Snider/100	100.00	30.00
19 Dave Winfield/1650	40.00	12.00
20 Robin Yount/250	100.00	30.00
NNO Auto Ball Exchange Card	50.00	15.00

2002 Topps Archives Reserve Autographs

Inserted at overall stated odds of one in 15 hobby and one in 203 retail, these 17 cards feature the players signed the Archives reserve "reprint" of their key year card. Since the players all signed at a different rate based on their "group", we have listed their group affiliation next to their name in our checklist.

	Nm-Mt	Ex-Mt
GROUP A ODDS 1:1077 RET		
GROUP B ODDS 1:1421 RET		
GROUP C ODDS 1:947 RET		
GROUP D ODDS 1:1421 RET		
GROUP E ODDS 1:718 RET		
TRA-AK Al Kaline 55 C	60.00	18.00
TRA-BR Brooks Robinson 64 B	30.00	9.00
TRA-DS Duke Snider 54 A	80.00	24.00
TRA-EB Ernie Banks 58 A	100.00	30.00
TRA-FJ Fergie Jenkins 71 E	15.00	4.50
TRA-GC Gary Carter 85 B	30.00	9.00
TRA-GN Graig Nettles 77 D	15.00	4.50
TRA-GP Gaylord Perry 72 C	20.00	6.00
TRA-HK Harmon Killebrew 69 C	60.00	18.00
TRA-JM Joe Morgan 76 B	30.00	9.00
TRA-LA Luis Aparicio 60 D	20.00	6.00
TRA-LB Lou Brock 74 B	30.00	9.00
TRA-LS Lee Smith 91 E	15.00	4.50
TRA-MS Mike Schmidt 80 A	120.00	36.00
TRA-RY Robin Yount 82 A	120.00	36.00
TRA-WM Willie Mays 62 A	150.00	45.00
TRA-YB Yogi Berra 54 A	100.00	30.00

2002 Topps Archives Reserve Bat Relics

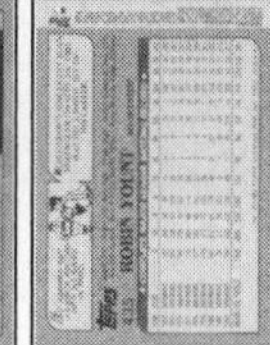

Inserted at stated odds of one in 22 hobby packs, these 10 cards feature not only the player's "best card" but also a game-used bat piece from each player. The players belonged to different groups in terms of scarcity and we have put that information next to their name in our checklist.

	Nm-Mt	Ex-Mt
TRR-CF Carlton Fisk 77 B	15.00	4.50
TRR-DW Dave Winfield 79 C	15.00	4.50
TRR-OC Orlando Cepeda 61 B	15.00	4.50
TRR-RM Roger Maris 61 A	100.00	30.00
TRR-TM Thurman Munson 76 B	40.00	12.00
TRR-CYB Carl Yastrzemski 67 B	30.00	9.00
TRR-DMB Don Mattingly 85 B	40.00	12.00
TRR-EMB Eddie Mathews 53 B	20.00	6.00
TRR-GBB George Brett 80 B	25.00	7.50
TRR-HAB Hank Aaron 57 B	40.00	12.00

2002 Topps Archives Reserve Uniform Relics

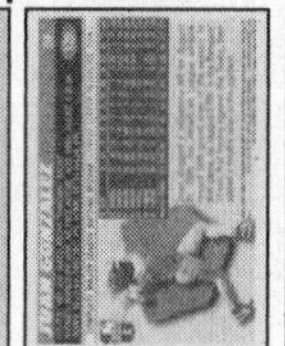

Inserted at stated odds of one in seven hobby packs, these 15 cards feature not only the player's "best card" but also a game-used bat piece from each player. The players belonged to different groups in terms of scarcity and we have put that information next to their name in our checklist.

	Nm-Mt	Ex-Mt
BR Brooks Robinson 64 Uni D	15.00	4.50
EB Ernie Banks 58 Uni C	25.00	7.50
GC Gary Carter 85 Jsy C	20.00	6.00
JB Johnny Bench 70 Uni D	15.00	4.50
JM Juan Marichal 66 Jsy A	20.00	6.00
KP Kirby Puckett 88 Jsy D	15.00	4.50
NF Nellie Fox 59 Uni C	20.00	6.00
NR Nolan Ryan 73 Jsy D	40.00	12.00
RS Red Schoendienst 53 Jsy B	15.00	4.50
RY Robin Yount 82 Uni D	15.00	4.50
TG Tony Gwynn 97 Jsy D	20.00	6.00
WB Wade Boggs 87 Jsy D	15.00	4.50
WC Will Clark 89 Jsy C	25.00	7.50
WM Willie Mays 62 Uni C	50.00	15.00
WS Willie Stargell 71 Uni D	15.00	4.50

1996 Topps Chrome

The 1996 Topps Chrome set was issued in one series totalling 165 cards and features a selection of players from the 1996 Topps regular set. The four-card packs retailed for $3.00 each. Each chromium card is a replica of its regular version with the exception of the Topps Chrome logo replacing the traditional logo. Included in the set is a Mickey Mantle number 7 Commemorative card and a Cal Ripken Tribute card.

	Nm-Mt	Ex-Mt
COMPLETE SET (165)	50.00	15.00
1 Tony Gwynn STP	1.25	.35
2 Mike Piazza STP	2.00	.60
3 Greg Maddux STP	2.00	.60
4 Jeff Bagwell STP	.75	.23
5 Larry Walker STP	.75	.23
6 Barry Larkin STP	.75	.23
7 Mickey Mantle COMM	10.00	3.00
8 Tom Glavine STP	.75	.23
9 Craig Biggio STP	.75	.23
10 Barry Bonds STP	2.00	.60
11 H.Slocumb STP	.75	.23
12 Matt Williams STP	.75	.23
13 Todd Helton	4.00	1.20
14 Paul Molitor	1.25	.35
15 Glenallen Hill	.75	.23
16 Troy Percival	.75	.23
17 Albert Belle	.75	.23
18 Mark Wohlers	.75	.23
19 Kirby Puckett	2.00	.60
20 Mark Grace	1.25	.35
21 J.T. Snow	.75	.23
22 David Justice	.75	.23
23 Mike Mussina	2.00	.60
24 Bernie Williams	1.25	.35
25 Ron Gant	.75	.23
26 Carlos Baerga	.75	.23
27 Gary Sheffield	.75	.23
28 Cal Ripken 2131	6.00	1.80
29 Frank Thomas	2.00	.60
30 Kevin Seitzer	.75	.23
31 Joe Carter	.75	.23
32 Jeff King	.75	.23
33 David Cone	.75	.23
34 Eddie Murray	2.00	.60
35 Brian Jordan	.75	.23
36 Garret Anderson	.75	.23
37 Hideo Nomo	2.00	.60
38 Steve Finley	.75	.23
39 Ivan Rodriguez	2.00	.60
40 Quilvio Veras	.75	.23
41 Mark McGwire	5.00	1.50
42 Greg Vaughn	.75	.23
43 Randy Johnson	2.00	.60
44 David Segui	.75	.23
45 Derek Bell	.75	.23
46 John Valentin	.75	.23
47 Steve Avery	.75	.23
48 Tino Martinez	1.25	.35
49 Shane Reynolds	.75	.23
50 Jim Edmonds	.75	.23
51 Raul Mondesi	.75	.23
52 Chipper Jones	2.00	.60
53 Gregg Jefferies	.75	.23
54 Ken Caminiti	.75	.23
55 Brian McRae	.75	.23
56 Don Mattingly	5.00	1.50
57 Marty Cordova	.75	.23
58 Vinny Castilla	.75	.23
59 John Smoltz	1.25	.35
60 Travis Fryman	.75	.23
61 Ryan Klesko	.75	.23
62 Alex Fernandez	.75	.23
63 Dante Bichette	.75	.23
64 Eric Karros	.75	.23
65 Roger Clemens	4.00	1.20
66 Randy Myers	.75	.23
67 Cal Ripken	6.00	1.80
68 Rod Beck	.75	.23
69 Jack McDowell	.75	.23
70 Ken Griffey Jr.	3.00	.90
71 Ramon Martinez	.75	.23
72 Jason Giambi	2.00	.60
73 Nomar Garciaparra FS	3.00	.90
74 Billy Wagner	.75	.23
75 Todd Greene	.75	.23
76 Paul Wilson	.75	.23
77 Johnny Damon	.75	.23
78 Alan Benes	.75	.23
79 Karim Garcia FS	.75	.23
80 Derek Jeter FS	5.00	1.50
81 Kirby Puckett STP	1.25	.35
82 Cal Ripken STP	3.00	.90
83 Albert Belle STP	.75	.23
84 Randy Johnson STP	1.25	.35
85 Wade Boggs STP	.75	.23
86 Carlos Baerga STP	.75	.23
87 Ivan Rodriguez STP	1.25	.35
88 Mike Mussina STP	1.25	.35
89 Frank Thomas STP	1.25	.35
90 Ken Griffey Jr. STP	2.00	.60
91 Jose Mesa STP	.75	.23
92 Matt Morris RC	6.00	1.80
93 Mike Piazza	3.00	.90
94 Edgar Martinez	1.25	.35
95 Chuck Knoblauch	.75	.23
96 Andres Galarraga	.75	.23
97 Tony Gwynn	2.50	.75
98 Lee Smith	.75	.23
99 Sammy Sosa	3.00	.90
100 Jim Thome	2.00	.60
101 Bernard Gilkey	.75	.23
102 Brady Anderson	.75	.23
103 Rico Brogna	.75	.23
104 Len Dykstra	.75	.23
105 Tom Glavine	1.25	.35
106 John Olerud	.75	.23
107 Terry Steinbach	.75	.23
108 Brian Hunter	.75	.23
109 Jay Buhner	.75	.23
110 Mo Vaughn	.75	.23
111 Jose Mesa	.75	.23
112 Brett Butler	.75	.23
113 Chili Davis	.75	.23
114 Paul O'Neill	1.25	.35
115 Roberto Alomar	2.00	.60
116 Barry Larkin	2.00	.60
117 Marquis Grissom	.75	.23
118 Will Clark	2.00	.60
119 Barry Bonds	5.00	1.50
120 Ozzie Smith	3.00	.90
121 Pedro Martinez	2.00	.60
122 Craig Biggio	1.25	.35
123 Moises Alou	.75	.23
124 Robin Ventura	.75	.23
125 Greg Maddux	3.00	.90
126 Tim Salmon	1.25	.35
127 Wade Boggs	1.25	.35
128 Ismael Valdes	.75	.23

Card	Nm-Mt	Ex-Mt
129 Juan Gonzalez	2.00	.60
130 Ray Lankford	.75	.23
131 Bobby Bonilla	.75	.23
132 Reggie Sanders	.75	.23
133 Alex Ochoa	.75	.23
134 Mark Loretta	.75	.23
135 Jason Kendall	.75	.23
136 Brooks Kieschnick	.75	.23
137 Chris Snopek	.75	.23
138 Ruben Rivera NOW	.75	.23
139 Jeff Suppan	.75	.23
140 John Wasdin	.75	.23
141 Jay Payton	.75	.23
142 Rick Krivda	.75	.23
143 Jimmy Haynes	.75	.23
144 Ryne Sandberg	3.00	.90
145 Matt Williams	.75	.23
146 Jose Canseco	2.00	.60
147 Larry Walker	1.25	.35
148 Kevin Appier	.75	.23
149 Javy Lopez	.75	.23
150 Dennis Eckersley	.75	.23
151 Jason Isringhausen	.75	.23
152 Dean Palmer	.75	.23
153 Jeff Bagwell	1.25	.35
154 Rondell White	.75	.23
155 Wally Joyner	.75	.23
156 Fred McGriff	1.25	.35
157 Cecil Fielder	.75	.23
158 Rafael Palmeiro	1.25	.35
159 Rickey Henderson	2.00	.60
160 Shawon Dunston	.75	.23
161 Manny Ramirez	.75	.23
162 Alex Gonzalez	.75	.23
163 Shawn Green	.75	.23
164 Kenny Lofton	.75	.23
165 Jeff Conine	.75	.23

1996 Topps Chrome Refractors

Randomly inserted at the rate of one in every 12 packs, this 165-card set is parallel to the regular Chrome set. The difference in design is the refractive quality of the cards.

	Nm-Mt	Ex-Mt
*STARS: 2.5X TO 6X BASIC CARDS ...		
*ROOKIES: 1.5X TO 4X BASIC CARDS		

1996 Topps Chrome Masters of the Game

Randomly inserted in packs at a rate of one in 12, this 20-card set honors players who are masters of their playing positions. The fronts feature color action photography with brilliant color metallization.

Card	Nm-Mt	Ex-Mt
COMPLETE SET (20)	60.00	18.00
*REF: 1X TO 2.5X BASIC CHR.MASTERS		
REF.STATED ODDS 1:36 HOBBY		
1 Dennis Eckersley	2.00	.60
2 Denny Martinez	2.00	.60
3 Eddie Murray	5.00	1.50
4 Paul Molitor	3.00	.90
5 Ozzie Smith	8.00	2.40
6 Rickey Henderson	5.00	1.50
7 Tim Raines	2.00	.60
8 Lee Smith	2.00	.60
9 Cal Ripken	15.00	4.50
10 Chili Davis	2.00	.60
11 Wade Boggs	3.00	.90
12 Tony Gwynn	6.00	1.80
13 Don Mattingly	12.00	3.60
14 Bret Saberhagen	2.00	.60
15 Kirby Puckett	5.00	1.50
16 Joe Carter	2.00	.60
17 Roger Clemens	10.00	3.00
18 Barry Bonds	12.00	3.60
19 Greg Maddux	8.00	2.40
20 Frank Thomas	5.00	1.50

1996 Topps Chrome Wrecking Crew

Randomly inserted in packs at a rate of one in 24, this 15-card set features baseball's top hitters and is printed in color action photography with brilliant color metallization.

Card	Nm-Mt	Ex-Mt
COMPLETE SET (15)	80.00	24.00
*REF: 1X TO 2.5X BASIC CHR.WRECKING		
REF.STATED ODDS 1:72 HOBBY		
WC1 Jeff Bagwell	4.00	1.20
WC2 Albert Belle	2.50	.75
WC3 Barry Bonds	15.00	4.50
WC4 Jose Canseco	6.00	1.80
WC5 Joe Carter	2.50	.75
WC6 Cecil Fielder	2.50	.75
WC7 Ron Gant	2.50	.75
WC8 Juan Gonzalez	6.00	1.80
WC9 Ken Griffey Jr.	10.00	3.00
WC10 Fred McGriff	4.00	1.20
WC11 Mark McGwire	15.00	4.50
WC12 Mike Piazza	10.00	3.00
WC13 Frank Thomas	6.00	1.80
WC14 Mo Vaughn	2.50	.75
WC15 Matt Williams	2.50	.75

1997 Topps Chrome

The 1997 Topps Chrome set was issued in one series totalling 165 cards and was distributed in four-card packs with a suggested retail price of $3.00. Using Chromium technology to highlight the cards, this set features a metalized version of the cards of some of the best players from the 1997 regular Topps Series one and two. An attractive 8 1/2" by 11" chrome promo sheet was sent to dealers advertising this set.

Card	Nm-Mt	Ex-Mt
COMPLETE SET (165)	50.00	15.00
1 Barry Bonds	5.00	1.50
2 Jose Valentin	.75	.23
3 Brady Anderson	.75	.23
4 Wade Boggs	1.25	.35
5 Andres Galarraga	.75	.23
6 Rusty Greer	.75	.23
7 Derek Jeter	5.00	1.50
8 Ricky Bottalico	.75	.23
9 Mike Piazza	3.00	.90
10 Garret Anderson	.75	.23
11 Jeff King	.75	.23
12 Kevin Appier	.75	.23
13 Mark Grace	1.25	.35
14 Jeff D'Amico	.75	.23
15 Jay Buhner	.75	.23
16 Hal Morris	.75	.23
17 Harold Baines	.75	.23
18 Jeff Cirillo	.75	.23
19 Tom Glavine	1.25	.35
20 Andy Pettitte	1.25	.35
21 Mark McGwire	5.00	1.50
22 Chuck Knoblauch	.75	.23
23 Raul Mondesi	.75	.23
24 Albert Belle	.75	.23
25 Trevor Hoffman	.75	.23
26 Eric Young	.75	.23
27 Brian McRae	.75	.23
28 Jim Edmonds	.75	.23
29 Robb Nen	.75	.23
30 Reggie Sanders	.75	.23
31 Mike Lansing	.75	.23
32 Craig Biggio	1.25	.35
33 Ray Lankford	.75	.23
34 Charles Nagy	.75	.23
35 Paul Wilson	.75	.23
36 John Wetteland	.75	.23
37 Derek Bell	.75	.23
38 Edgar Martinez	1.25	.35
39 Rickey Henderson	2.00	.60
40 Jim Thome	2.00	.60
41 Frank Thomas	2.00	.60
42 Jackie Robinson	5.00	1.50
43 Terry Steinbach	.75	.23
44 Kevin Brown	.75	.23
45 Joey Hamilton	.75	.23
46 Travis Fryman	.75	.23
47 Juan Gonzalez	2.00	.60
48 Ron Gant	.75	.23
49 Greg Maddux	3.00	.90
50 Wally Joyner	.75	.23
51 John Valentin	.75	.23
52 Bret Boone	.75	.23
53 Paul Molitor	1.25	.35
54 Rafael Palmeiro	1.25	.35
55 Todd Hundley	.75	.23
56 Ellis Burks	.75	.23
57 Bernie Williams	1.25	.35
58 Roberto Alomar	2.00	.60
59 Jose Mesa	.75	.23
60 Troy Percival	.75	.23
61 John Smoltz	1.25	.35
62 Jeff Conine	.75	.23
63 Bernard Gilkey	.75	.23
64 Mickey Tettleton	.75	.23
65 Justin Thompson	.75	.23
66 Tony Phillips	.75	.23
67 Ryne Sandberg	3.00	.90
68 Geronimo Berroa	.75	.23
69 Todd Hollandsworth	.75	.23
70 Rey Ordonez	.75	.23
71 Marquis Grissom	.75	.23
72 Tino Martinez	1.25	.35
73 Steve Finley	.75	.23
74 Andy Benes	.75	.23
75 Jason Kendall	.75	.23
76 Johnny Damon	.75	.23
77 Jason Giambi	2.00	.60
78 Henry Rodriguez	.75	.23
79 Edgar Renteria	.75	.23
80 Ray Durham	.75	.23
81 Gregg Jefferies	.75	.23
82 Roberto Hernandez	.75	.23
83 Joe Carter	.75	.23
84 Jermaine Dye	.75	.23
85 Julio Franco	.75	.23
86 David Justice	.75	.23
87 Jose Canseco	2.00	.60
88 Paul O'Neill	1.25	.35
89 Mariano Rivera	1.25	.35
90 Bobby Higginson	.75	.23
91 Mark Grudzielanek	.75	.23
92 Lance Johnson	.75	.23
93 Ken Caminiti	.75	.23
94 Gary Sheffield	.75	.23
95 Luis Castillo	.75	.23
96 Scott Rolen	1.25	.35
97 Chipper Jones	2.00	.60
98 Darryl Strawberry	1.25	.35
99 Nomar Garciaparra	3.00	.90
100 Jeff Bagwell	1.25	.35
101 Ken Griffey Jr.	3.00	.90
102 Sammy Sosa	3.00	.90
103 Jack McDowell	.75	.23
104 James Baldwin	.75	.23
105 Rocky Coppinger	.75	.23
106 Manny Ramirez	.75	.23
107 Tim Salmon	1.25	.35
108 Eric Karros	.75	.23
109 Brett Butler	.75	.23
110 Randy Johnson	2.00	.60
111 Pat Hentgen	.75	.23
112 Rondell White	.75	.23
113 Eddie Murray	2.00	.60
114 Ivan Rodriguez	2.00	.60
115 Jermaine Allensworth	.75	.23
116 Ed Sprague	.75	.23
117 Kenny Lofton	.75	.23
118 Alan Benes	.75	.23
119 Fred McGriff	1.25	.35
120 Alex Fernandez	.75	.23
121 Al Martin	.75	.23
122 Devon White	.75	.23
123 David Cone	.75	.23
124 Karim Garcia	.75	.23
125 Chili Davis	.75	.23
126 Roger Clemens	4.00	1.20
127 Bobby Bonilla	.75	.23
128 Mike Mussina	2.00	.60
129 Todd Walker	.75	.23
130 Dante Bichette	.75	.23
131 Carlos Baerga	.75	.23
132 Matt Williams	.75	.23
133 Will Clark	2.00	.60
134 Dennis Eckersley	.75	.23
135 Ryan Klesko	.75	.23
136 Dean Palmer	.75	.23
137 Javy Lopez	.75	.23
138 Greg Vaughn	.75	.23
139 Vinny Castilla	.75	.23
140 Cal Ripken	6.00	1.80
141 Ruben Rivera	.75	.23
142 Mark Wohlers	.75	.23
143 Tony Clark	.75	.23
144 Jose Rosado	.75	.23
145 Tony Gwynn	2.50	.75
146 Cecil Fielder	.75	.23
147 Brian Jordan	.75	.23
148 Bob Abreu	.75	.23
149 Barry Larkin	2.00	.60
150 Robin Ventura	.75	.23
151 John Olerud	.75	.23
152 Rod Beck	.75	.23
153 Vladimir Guerrero	2.00	.60
154 Marty Cordova	.75	.23
155 Todd Stottlemyre	.75	.23
156 Hideo Nomo	2.00	.60
157 Denny Neagle	.75	.23
158 John Jaha	.75	.23
159 Mo Vaughn	.75	.23
160 Andruw Jones	.75	.23
161 Moises Alou	.75	.23
162 Larry Walker	1.25	.35
163 Eddie Murray SH	1.25	.35
164 Paul Molitor SH	.75	.23
165 Checklist	.75	.23

1997 Topps Chrome Refractors

Randomly inserted in packs at a rate of one in 12, this 165-card set is a parallel version of the regular Topps Chrome set and is similar in design. The difference is found in the refractive quality of the cards.

	Nm-Mt	Ex-Mt
*STARS: 2.5X TO 6X BASE CARDS		

1997 Topps Chrome All-Stars

Randomly inserted in packs at a rate of one in 24, this 22-card set features color player photos printed on rainbow foilboard. The set showcases the top three players from each position from both the American and National leagues as voted on by the Topps Sports Department.

Card	Nm-Mt	Ex-Mt
COMPLETE SET (22)	100.00	30.00
*REF: 1X TO 2.5X BASIC CHROME AS		
REFRACTOR STATED ODDS 1:72		
AS1 Ivan Rodriguez	6.00	1.80
AS2 Todd Hundley	2.50	.75
AS3 Frank Thomas	6.00	1.80
AS4 Andres Galarraga	2.50	.75
AS5 Chuck Knoblauch	2.50	.75
AS6 Eric Young	2.50	.75
AS7 Jim Thome	6.00	1.80
AS8 Chipper Jones	6.00	1.80
AS9 Cal Ripken	20.00	6.00
AS10 Barry Larkin	6.00	1.80
AS11 Albert Belle	2.50	.75
AS12 Barry Bonds	15.00	4.50
AS13 Ken Griffey Jr.	10.00	3.00
AS14 Ellis Burks	2.50	.75
AS15 Juan Gonzalez	6.00	1.80
AS16 Gary Sheffield	2.50	.75
AS17 Andy Pettitte	4.00	1.20
AS18 Tom Glavine	4.00	1.20
AS19 Pat Hentgen	2.50	.75
AS20 John Smoltz	4.00	1.20
AS21 Roberto Hernandez	2.50	.75
AS22 Mark Wohlers	2.50	.75

1997 Topps Chrome Diamond Duos

Randomly inserted in packs at a rate of one in 36, this 10-card set features color player photos of two superstar teammates on double sided chromium cards.

Card	Nm-Mt	Ex-Mt
COMPLETE SET (10)	50.00	15.00
*REF.: 1X TO 2.5X BASIC DIAM.DUOS		
REFRACTOR STATED ODDS 1:108		
DD1 Chipper Jones / Andruw Jones	5.00	1.50
DD2 Derek Jeter / Bernie Williams	12.00	3.60
DD3 Ken Griffey Jr. / Jay Buhner	8.00	2.40
DD4 Kenny Lofton / Manny Ramirez	2.00	.60
DD5 Jeff Bagwell / Craig Biggio	3.00	.90
DD6 Juan Gonzalez / Ivan Rodriguez	5.00	1.50
DD7 Cal Ripken / Brady Anderson	15.00	4.50
DD8 Mike Piazza / Hideo Nomo	8.00	2.40
DD9 Andres Galarraga / Dante Bichette	2.00	.60
DD10 Frank Thomas / Albert Belle	5.00	1.50

1997 Topps Chrome Season's Best

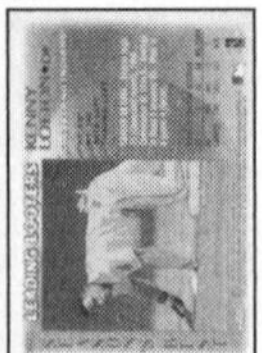

Randomly inserted in packs at a rate of one in 18, this 25-card set features color player photos of the five top players from five statistical categories: most steals (Leading Looters), most home runs (Bleacher Reachers), most wins (Hill Toppers), most RBIs (Number Crunchers), and best slugging percentage (Kings of Swing).

Card	Nm-Mt	Ex-Mt
COMPLETE SET (25)	60.00	18.00
*REF: 1X TO 2.5X BASIC SEAS.BEST .		
REFRACTOR STATED ODDS 1:54		
1 Tony Gwynn	6.00	1.80
2 Frank Thomas	5.00	1.50
3 Ellis Burks	2.00	.60
4 Paul Molitor	3.00	.90
5 Chuck Knoblauch	2.00	.60
6 Mark McGwire	12.00	3.60
7 Brady Anderson	2.00	.60
8 Ken Griffey Jr.	8.00	2.40
9 Albert Belle	2.00	.60
10 Andres Galarraga	2.00	.60
11 Andres Galarraga	2.00	.60
12 Albert Belle	2.00	.60
13 Juan Gonzalez	5.00	1.50
14 Mo Vaughn	2.00	.60
15 Rafael Palmeiro	3.00	.90
16 John Smoltz	3.00	.90
17 Andy Pettitte	3.00	.90
18 Pat Hentgen	2.00	.60
19 Mike Mussina	5.00	1.50
20 Andy Benes	2.00	.60
21 Kenny Lofton	2.00	.60
22 Tom Goodwin	2.00	.60
23 Otis Nixon	2.00	.60
24 Eric Young	2.00	.60
25 Lance Johnson	2.00	.60

1997 Topps Chrome Jumbos

This six-card set contains jumbo versions of the six featured players' regular Topps Chrome cards and measures approximately 3 3/4" by 5 1/4". One of these cards was found in a special box with five Topps Chrome packs issued through Wal-Mart. The cards are numbered according to their corresponding number in the regular set.

Card	Nm-Mt	Ex-Mt
COMPLETE SET (6)	15.00	4.50
9 Mike Piazza	3.00	.90
94 Gary Sheffield	1.25	.35
97 Chipper Jones	2.50	.75
101 Ken Griffey Jr.	3.00	.90
102 Sammy Sosa	2.50	.75
140 Cal Ripken Jr.	5.00	1.50

1998 Topps Chrome

The 1998 Topps Chrome set was issued in two separate series of 282 and 221 cards respectively with design and content paralleling the base 1998 Topps set. Four-card packs carried a suggested retail price of $3 each. Card fronts feature color action player photos printed wtih Chromium technology on metalized cards. The backs carry player information. As is tradition with Topps sets since 1996, card number seven was excluded from the set in honor of Mickey Mantle. Subsets are as follows: Prospects/Draft Picks (245-264/484-501), Season Highlights (265-269/474-478), Inter-League (270-274/479-483), Checklists (275-276/502-503) and World Series (277-283). After four years of being excluded from Topps products, superstar Alex Rodriguez finally made his Topps debut as card number 504. Notable Rookie Cards include Ryan Anderson, Michael Cuddyer, Jack Cust and Troy Glaus.

Card	Nm-Mt	Ex-Mt
COMPLETE SET (503)	150.00	45.00
COMP. SERIES 1 (282)	80.00	24.00
COMP. SERIES 2 (221)	80.00	24.00
1 Tony Gwynn	2.50	.75
2 Larry Walker	1.25	.35
3 Billy Wagner	.75	.23
4 Denny Neagle	.75	.23
5 Vladimir Guerrero	2.00	.60
6 Kevin Brown	1.25	.35
8 Mariano Rivera	1.25	.35
9 Tony Clark	.75	.23
10 Deion Sanders	1.25	.35
11 Francisco Cordova	.75	.23
12 Matt Williams	.75	.23
13 Carlos Baerga	.75	.23
14 Mo Vaughn	.75	.23
15 Bobby Witt	.75	.23
16 Matt Stairs	.75	.23
17 Chan Ho Park	.75	.23
18 Mike Bordick	.75	.23
19 Michael Tucker	.75	.23
20 Frank Thomas	2.00	.60
21 Roberto Clemente	5.00	1.50
22 Dmitri Young	.75	.23
23 Steve Trachsel	.75	.23
24 Jeff Kent	.75	.23
25 Scott Rolen	1.25	.35
26 John Thomson	.75	.23
27 Joe Vitiello	.75	.23
28 Eddie Guardado	.75	.23
29 Charlie Hayes	.75	.23
30 Juan Gonzalez	2.00	.60
31 Garret Anderson	.75	.23
32 John Jaha	.75	.23
33 Omar Vizquel	.75	.23
34 Brian Hunter	.75	.23
35 Jeff Bagwell	1.25	.35
36 Mark Lemke	.75	.23
37 Doug Glanville	.75	.23
38 Dan Wilson	.75	.23
39 Steve Cooke	.75	.23
40 Chili Davis	.75	.23
41 Mike Cameron	.75	.23
42 F.P. Santangelo	.75	.23
43 Brad Ausmus	.75	.23
44 Gary DiSarcina	.75	.23
45 Pat Hentgen	.75	.23
46 Wilton Guerrero	.75	.23
47 Devon White	.75	.23
48 Danny Patterson	.75	.23
49 Pat Meares	.75	.23
50 Rafael Palmeiro	1.25	.35
51 Mark Gardner	.75	.23
52 Jeff Blauser	.75	.23
53 Dave Hollins	.75	.23
54 Carlos Garcia	.75	.23
55 Ben McDonald	.75	.23
56 John Mabry	.75	.23
57 Trevor Hoffman	.75	.23
58 Tony Fernandez	.75	.23
59 Rich Loiselle RC	.75	.23
60 Mark Leiter	.75	.23
61 Pat Kelly	.75	.23
62 John Flaherty	.75	.23
63 Roger Bailey	.75	.23
64 Tom Gordon	.75	.23
65 Ryan Klesko	.75	.23
66 Darryl Hamilton	.75	.23
67 Jim Eisenreich	.75	.23
68 Butch Huskey	.75	.23
69 Mark Grudzielanek	.75	.23
70 Marquis Grissom	.75	.23
71 Mark McLemore	.75	.23
72 Gary Gaetti	.75	.23
73 Greg Gagne	.75	.23
74 Lyle Mouton	.75	.23
75 Jim Edmonds	.75	.23
76 Shawn Green	.75	.23
77 Greg Vaughn	.75	.23
78 Terry Adams	.75	.23
79 Kevin Polcovich	.75	.23
80 Troy O'Leary	.75	.23
81 Jeff Shaw	.75	.23
82 Rich Becker	.75	.23
83 David Wells	.75	.23
84 Steve Karsay	.75	.23
85 Charles Nagy	.75	.23
86 B.J. Surhoff	.75	.23
87 Jamey Wright	.75	.23
88 James Baldwin	.75	.23
89 Edgardo Alfonzo	.75	.23
90 Jay Buhner	.75	.23
91 Brady Anderson	.75	.23
92 Scott Servais	.75	.23
93 Edgar Renteria	.75	.23
94 Mike Lieberthal	.75	.23
95 Rick Aguilera	.75	.23
96 Walt Weiss	.75	.23
97 Deivi Cruz	.75	.23
98 Kurt Abbott	.75	.23
99 Henry Rodriguez	.75	.23
100 Mike Piazza	3.00	.90
101 Billy Taylor	.75	.23
102 Todd Zeile	.75	.23
103 Rey Ordonez	.75	.23
104 Willie Greene	.75	.23
105 Tony Womack	.75	.23
106 Mike Sweeney	.75	.23
107 Jeffrey Hammonds	.75	.23
108 Kevin Orie	.75	.23
109 Alex Gonzalez	.75	.23
110 Jose Canseco	2.00	.60
111 Paul Sorrento	.75	.23
112 Joey Hamilton	.75	.23
113 Brad Radke	.75	.23

114 Steve Avery .75 .23
115 Esteban Loaiza .75 .23
116 Stan Javier .75 .23
117 Chris Gomez .75 .23
118 Royce Clayton .75 .23
119 Orlando Merced .75 .23
120 Kevin Appier .75 .23
121 Mel Nieves .75 .23
122 Joe Girardi .75 .23
123 Rico Brogna .75 .23
124 Kent Mercker .75 .23
125 Manny Ramirez .75 .23
126 Jeromy Burnitz .75 .23
127 Kevin Foster .75 .23
128 Matt Morris .75 .23
129 Jason Dickson .75 .23
130 Tom Glavine 1.25 .35
131 Wally Joyner .75 .23
132 Rick Reed .75 .23
133 Todd Jones .75 .23
134 Dave Martinez .75 .23
135 Sandy Alomar Jr. .75 .23
136 Mike Lansing .75 .23
137 Sean Berry .75 .23
138 Doug Jones .75 .23
139 Todd Stottlemyre .75 .23
140 Jay Bell .75 .23
141 Jaime Navarro .75 .23
142 Chris Hoiles .75 .23
143 Joey Cora .75 .23
144 Scott Spiezio .75 .23
145 Joe Carter .75 .23
146 Jose Guillen .75 .23
147 Damion Easley .75 .23
148 Lee Stevens .75 .23
149 Alex Fernandez .75 .23
150 Randy Johnson 2.00 .60
151 J.T. Snow .75 .23
152 Chuck Finley .75 .23
153 Bernard Gilkey .75 .23
154 David Segui .75 .23
155 Dante Bichette .75 .23
156 Kevin Stocker .75 .23
157 Carl Everett .75 .23
158 Jose Valentin .75 .23
159 Pokey Reese .75 .23
160 Derek Jeter 5.00 1.50
161 Roger Pavlik .75 .23
162 Mark Wohlers .75 .23
163 Ricky Bottalico .75 .23
164 Ozzie Guillen .75 .23
165 Mike Mussina 2.00 .60
166 Gary Sheffield .75 .23
167 Hideo Nomo 2.00 .60
168 Mark Grace 1.25 .35
169 Aaron Sele .75 .23
170 Darryl Kile .75 .23
171 Shawn Estes .75 .23
172 Vinny Castilla .75 .23
173 Ron Coomer .75 .23
174 Jose Rosado .75 .23
175 Kenny Lofton .75 .23
176 Jason Giambi 2.00 .60
177 Hal Morris .75 .23
178 Darren Bragg .75 .23
179 Orel Hershiser .75 .23
180 Ray Lankford .75 .23
181 Hideki Irabu .75 .23
182 Kevin Young .75 .23
183 Javy Lopez .75 .23
184 Jeff Montgomery .75 .23
185 Mike Holtz .75 .23
186 George Williams .75 .23
187 Cal Eldred .75 .23
188 Tom Candiotti .75 .23
189 Glenallen Hill .75 .23
190 Brian Giles .75 .23
191 Dave Mlicki .75 .23
192 Garrett Stephenson .75 .23
193 Jeff Frye .75 .23
194 Joe Oliver .75 .23
195 Bob Hamelin .75 .23
196 Luis Sojo .75 .23
197 LaTroy Hawkins .75 .23
198 Kevin Elster .75 .23
199 Jeff Reed .75 .23
200 Dennis Eckersley .75 .23
201 Bill Mueller .75 .23
202 Russ Davis .75 .23
203 Armando Benitez .75 .23
204 Quilvio Veras .75 .23
205 Tim Naehring .75 .23
206 Quinton McCracken .75 .23
207 Raul Casanova .75 .23
208 Matt Lawton .75 .23
209 Luis Alicea .75 .23
210 Luis Gonzalez .75 .23
211 Allen Watson .75 .23
212 Gerald Williams .75 .23
213 David Bell .75 .23
214 Todd Hollandsworth .75 .23
215 Wade Boggs 1.25 .35
216 Jose Mesa .75 .23
217 Jamie Moyer .75 .23
218 Darren Daulton .75 .23
219 Mickey Morandini .75 .23
220 Rusty Greer .75 .23
221 Jim Bullinger .75 .23
222 Jose Offerman .75 .23
223 Matt Karchner .75 .23
224 Woody Williams .75 .23
225 Mark Loretta .75 .23
226 Mike Hampton .75 .23
227 Willie Adams .75 .23
228 Scott Hatteberg .75 .23
229 Rich Amaral .75 .23
230 Terry Steinbach .75 .23
231 Glendon Rusch .75 .23
232 Bret Boone .75 .23
233 Robert Person .75 .23
234 Jose Hernandez .75 .23
235 Doug Drabek .75 .23
236 Jason McDonald .75 .23
237 Chris Widger .75 .23
238 Tom Martin .75 .23
239 Dave Burba .75 .23
240 Pete Rose Jr. RC .75 .23
241 Bobby Ayala .75 .23
242 Tim Wakefield .75 .23
243 Dennis Springer .75 .23
244 Tim Belcher .75 .23
245 Jon Garland 1.00 .30
Geoff Goetz
246 Glenn Davis 1.25 .35
Lance Berkman
247 Vernon Wells 1.25 .35
Aaron Akin
248 Adam Kennedy 1.00 .30
Jason Romano
249 Jason Dellaero 1.00 .30
Troy Cameron
250 Alex Sanchez 1.00 .30
Jared Sandberg
251 Pablo Ortega 1.00 .30
James Manias
252 Jason Conti RC 1.00 .30
Mike Stoner
253 John Patterson 1.00 .30
Larry Rodriguez
254 Adrian Beltre 1.00 .30
Ryan Minor RC
Aaron Boone
255 Ben Grieve 1.00 .30
Brian Buchanan
Dermal Brown
256 Kerrry Wood 2.00 .60
Carl Pavano
Gil Meche
257 David Ortiz 1.00 .30
Daryle Ward
Richie Sexson
258 Randy Winn 1.00 .30
Juan Encarnacion
Andrew Vessel
259 Kris Benson 1.00 .30
Travis Smith
Courtney Duncan RC
260 Chad Hermansen RC 1.00 .30
Brent Butler
Warren Morris
261 Ben Davis 1.00 .30
Eli Marrero
Ramon Hernandez
262 Eric Chavez 1.25 .35
Russell Branyan
Russ Johnson
263 Todd Dunwoody RC 1.00 .30
John Barnes
Ryan Jackson
264 Matt Clement 1.00 .30
Roy Halladay
Brian Fuentes RC
265 Randy Johnson SH 1.25 .35
266 Kevin Brown SH .75 .23
267 Ricardo Rincon SH .75 .23
268 N.Garciaparra SH 2.00 .60
269 Tino Martinez SH .75 .23
270 Chuck Knoblauch IL .75 .23
271 Pedro Martinez IL 1.25 .35
272 Denny Neagle IL .75 .23
273 Juan Gonzalez IL 1.25 .35
274 Andres Galarraga IL .75 .23
275 Checklist .75 .23
276 Checklist .75 .23
277 Moises Alou WS .75 .23
278 Sandy Alomar Jr. WS .75 .23
279 Gary Sheffield WS .75 .23
280 Matt Williams WS .75 .23
281 Livan Hernandez WS .75 .23
282 Chad Ogea WS .75 .23
283 Marlins Champs .75 .23
284 Tino Martinez 1.25 .35
285 Roberto Alomar 2.00 .60
286 Jeff King .75 .23
287 Brian Jordan .75 .23
288 Darin Erstad .75 .23
289 Ken Caminiti .75 .23
290 Jim Thome 2.00 .60
291 Paul Molitor 1.25 .35
292 Ivan Rodriguez 2.00 .60
293 Bernie Williams 1.25 .35
294 Todd Hundley .75 .23
295 Andres Galarraga .75 .23
296 Greg Maddux 3.00 .90
297 Edgar Martinez 1.25 .35
298 Ron Gant .75 .23
299 Derek Bell .75 .23
300 Roger Clemens 4.00 1.20
301 Rondell White .75 .23
302 Barry Larkin 2.00 .60
303 Robin Ventura .75 .23
304 Jason Kendall .75 .23
305 Chipper Jones 2.00 .60
306 John Franco .75 .23
307 Sammy Sosa 3.00 .90
308 Troy Percival .75 .23
309 Chuck Knoblauch .75 .23
310 Ellis Burks .75 .23
311 Al Martin .75 .23
312 Tim Salmon 1.25 .35
313 Moises Alou .75 .23
314 Lance Johnson .75 .23
315 Justin Thompson .75 .23
316 Will Clark 2.00 .60
317 Barry Bonds 5.00 1.50
318 Craig Biggio 1.25 .35
319 John Smoltz 1.25 .35
320 Cal Ripken 6.00 1.80
321 Ken Griffey Jr. 3.00 .90
322 Paul O'Neill 1.25 .35
323 Todd Helton 1.25 .35
324 John Olerud .75 .23
325 Mark McGwire 5.00 1.50
326 Jose Cruz Jr. .75 .23
327 Jeff Cirillo .75 .23
328 Dean Palmer .75 .23
329 John Wetteland .75 .23
330 Steve Finley .75 .23
331 Albert Belle .75 .23
332 Curt Schilling 1.25 .35
333 Raul Mondesi .75 .23
334 Andruw Jones .75 .23
335 Nomar Garciaparra 3.00 .90
336 David Justice .75 .23
337 Andy Pettitte 1.25 .35
338 Pedro Martinez 2.00 .60
339 Travis Miller .75 .23
340 Chris Stynes .75 .23
341 Gregg Jefferies .75 .23
342 Jeff Fassero .75 .23
343 Craig Counsell .75 .23
344 Wilson Alvarez .75 .23
345 Bip Roberts .75 .23
346 Kelvim Escobar .75 .23
347 Mark Bellhorn .75 .23
348 Cory Lidle RC 1.25 .35
349 Fred McGriff 1.25 .35
350 Chuck Carr .75 .23
351 Bob Abreu .75 .23
352 Juan Guzman .75 .23
353 Fernando Vina .75 .23
354 Andy Benes .75 .23
355 Dave Nilsson .75 .23
356 Bobby Bonilla .75 .23
357 Ismael Valdes .75 .23
358 Carlos Perez .75 .23
359 Kirk Rueter .75 .23
360 Bartolo Colon .75 .23
361 Mel Rojas .75 .23
362 Johnny Damon .75 .23
363 Geronimo Berroa .75 .23
364 Reggie Sanders .75 .23
365 Jermaine Allensworth .75 .23
366 Orlando Cabrera .75 .23
367 Jorge Fabregas .75 .23
368 Scott Stahoviak .75 .23
369 Ken Cloude .75 .23
370 Donovan Osborne .75 .23
371 Roger Cedeno .75 .23
372 Neifi Perez .75 .23
373 Chris Holt .75 .23
374 Cecil Fielder .75 .23
375 Marty Cordova .75 .23
376 Tom Goodwin .75 .23
377 Jeff Suppan .75 .23
378 Jeff Brantley .75 .23
379 Mark Langston .75 .23
380 Shane Reynolds .75 .23
381 Mike Fetters .75 .23
382 Todd Greene .75 .23
383 Ray Durham .75 .23
384 Carlos Delgado .75 .23
385 Jeff D'Amico .75 .23
386 Brian McRae .75 .23
387 Alan Benes .75 .23
388 Heathcliff Slocumb .75 .23
389 Eric Young .75 .23
390 Travis Fryman .75 .23
391 David Cone .75 .23
392 Otis Nixon .75 .23
393 Jeremi Gonzalez .75 .23
394 Jeff Juden .75 .23
395 Jose Vizcaino .75 .23
396 Ugueth Urbina .75 .23
397 Ramon Martinez .75 .23
398 Robb Nen .75 .23
399 Harold Baines .75 .23
400 Delino DeShields .75 .23
401 John Burkett .75 .23
402 Sterling Hitchcock .75 .23
403 Mark Clark .75 .23
404 Terrell Wade .75 .23
405 Scott Brosius .75 .23
406 Chad Curtis .75 .23
407 Brian Johnson .75 .23
408 Roberto Kelly .75 .23
409 Dave Dellucci RC .75 .23
410 Michael Tucker .75 .23
411 Mark Kotsay .75 .23
412 Mark Lewis .75 .23
413 Ryan McGuire .75 .23
414 Shawon Dunston .75 .23
415 Brad Rigby .75 .23
416 Scott Erickson .75 .23
417 Bobby Jones .75 .23
418 Darren Oliver .75 .23
419 John Smiley .75 .23
420 T.J. Mathews .75 .23
421 Dustin Hermanson .75 .23
422 Mike Timlin .75 .23
423 Willie Blair .75 .23
424 Manny Alexander .75 .23
425 Bob Tewksbury .75 .23
426 Pete Schourek .75 .23
427 Reggie Jefferson .75 .23
428 Ed Sprague .75 .23
429 Jeff Conine .75 .23
430 Roberto Hernandez .75 .23
431 Tom Pagnozzi .75 .23
432 Jaret Wright .75 .23
433 Livan Hernandez .75 .23
434 Andy Ashby .75 .23
435 Todd Dunn .75 .23
436 Bobby Higginson .75 .23
437 Rod Beck .75 .23
438 Jim Leyritz .75 .23
439 Matt Williams .75 .23
440 Brett Tomko .75 .23
441 Joe Randa .75 .23
442 Chris Carpenter .75 .23
443 Dennis Reyes .75 .23
444 Al Leiter .75 .23
445 Jason Schmidt .75 .23
446 Ken Hill .75 .23
447 Shannon Stewart .75 .23
448 Enrique Wilson .75 .23
449 Fernando Tatis .75 .23
450 Jimmy Key .75 .23
451 Darrin Fletcher .75 .23
452 John Valentin .75 .23
453 Kevin Tapani .75 .23
454 Eric Karros .75 .23
455 Jay Bell .75 .23
456 Walt Weiss .75 .23
457 Devon White .75 .23
458 Carl Pavano .75 .23
459 Mike Lansing .75 .23
460 John Flaherty .75 .23
461 Richard Hidalgo .75 .23
462 Quinton McCracken .75 .23
463 Karim Garcia .75 .23
464 Miguel Cairo .75 .23
465 Edwin Diaz .75 .23
466 Bobby Smith .75 .23
467 Yamil Benitez .75 .23
468 Rich Butler RC .75 .23
469 Ben Ford RC .75 .23
470 Bubba Trammell .75 .23
471 Brent Brede .75 .23
472 Brooks Kieschnick .75 .23
473 Carlos Castillo .75 .23
474 Brad Radke SH .75 .23
475 Roger Clemens SH 2.00 .60
476 Curt Schilling SH .75 .23
477 John Olerud SH .75 .23
478 Mark McGwire SH 2.50 .75
479 Mike Piazza IL 2.00 .60
Ken Griffey Jr.
480 Jeff Bagwell 1.25 .35
Frank Thomas
481 Chipper Jones 1.25 .35
Nomar Garciaparra IL
482 Larrry Walker IL 1.25 .35
Juan Gonzalez IL
483 Gary Sheffield IL .75 .23
Tino Martinez IL
484 Derrick Gibson 1.00 .30
Michael Coleman
Norm Hutchins
485 Braden Looper 1.00 .30
Cliff Politte
Brian Rose
486 Eric Milton 1.00 .30
Jason Marquis
Corey Lee
487 A.J.Hinch 2.00 .60
Mark Osborne RC
Robert Fick
488 Aramis Ramirez 1.00 .30
Alex Gonzalez
Sean Casey
489 Donnie Bridges 1.00 .30
Tim Drew RC
490 Ntema Ndungidi RC 1.00 .30
Darnell McDonald
491 Ryan Anderson RC 1.00 .30
Mark Mangum
492 J.J.Davis 8.00 2.40
Troy Glaus RC
493 Jayson Werth RC 1.00 .30
Dan Reichert
494 John Curtice RC 1.50 .45
Michael Cuddyer RC
495 Jack Cust RC 1.00 .30
Jason Standridge
496 Brian Anderson 1.00 .30
497 Tony Saunders 1.00 .30
498 Vladimir Nunez 1.00 .30
Jhensy Sandoval
499 Brad Penny 1.00 .30
Nick Bierbrodt
500 Dustin Carr 1.00 .30
Luis Cruz RC
501 Cedric Bowers 1.00 .30
Marcus McCain
502 Checklist .75 .23
503 Checklist .75 .23
504 Alex Rodriguez 4.00 1.20

1998 Topps Chrome Refractors

Randomly inserted in first and second series packs at the rate of one in 12, this set is parallel to the base set and is similar in design. The difference is found in the refractive quality of the cards.

Nm-Mt Ex-Mt
*STARS: 2.5X TO 6X BASIC CARDS ...
*ROOKIES: 1.25X TO 3X BASIC ....

1998 Topps Chrome Baby Boomers

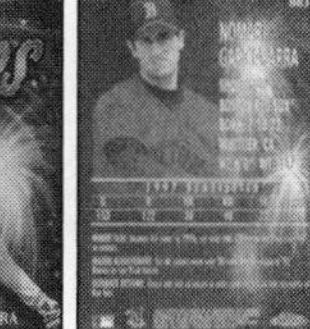

Randomly inserted in first series packs at the rate of one in 24, this 15 card set features color action photos printed on metalized cards with Chromium technology of young players who have already made their mark in the game with less than three years in the majors.

Nm-Mt Ex-Mt
COMPLETE SET (15) 80.00 24.00
*REF: .75X TO 2X BASIC CHR.BOOMERS
REFRACTOR SER.1 STATED ODDS 1:72
BB1 Derek Jeter 15.00 4.50
BB2 Scott Rolen 4.00 1.20
BB3 Nomar Garciaparra 10.00 3.00
BB4 Jose Cruz Jr. 2.50 .75
BB5 Darin Erstad 2.50 .75
BB6 Todd Helton 4.00 1.20
BB7 Tony Clark 2.50 .75
BB8 Jose Guillen 2.50 .75
BB9 Andruw Jones 2.50 .75
BB10 Vladimir Guerrero 6.00 1.80
BB11 Mark Kotsay 2.50 .75
BB12 Todd Greene 2.50 .75
BB13 Andy Pettitte 4.00 1.20
BB14 Justin Thompson 2.50 .75
BB15 Alan Benes 2.50 .75

1998 Topps Chrome Clout Nine

Randomly seeded at a rate of one in 24 second series packs, cards from this nine-card set feature a selection of the league's top sluggers. The cards are a straight parallel of the previously released 1998 Topps Clout 9 set, except of course for the Chromium stock fronts.

Nm-Mt Ex-Mt
COMPLETE SET (9) 60.00 18.00
*REF: .75X TO 2X BASIC CHR.CLOUT
REFRACTOR SER.2 STATED ODDS 1:72
C1 Edgar Martinez 4.00 1.20
C2 Mike Piazza 10.00 3.00
C3 Frank Thomas 6.00 1.80
C4 Craig Biggio 4.00 1.20
C5 Vinny Castilla 2.50 .75
C6 Jeff Blauser 2.50 .75
C7 Barry Bonds 15.00 4.50
C8 Ken Griffey Jr. 10.00 3.00
C9 Larry Walker 4.00 1.20

1998 Topps Chrome Flashback

Randomly inserted in first series packs at the rate of one in 24, this 10-card set features two-sided cards with color action photos of top players printed on metalized cards with Chromium technology. One side displays how they looked "then" as rookies, while the other side shows how they look "now" as stars.

Nm-Mt Ex-Mt
COMPLETE SET (10) 80.00 24.00
*REF: .75X TO 2X BASIC CHR.FLASHBACK
REFRACTOR SER.1 STATED ODDS 1:72
FB1 Barry Bonds 15.00 4.50
FB2 Ken Griffey Jr. 10.00 3.00
FB3 Paul Molitor 4.00 1.20
FB4 Randy Johnson 6.00 1.80
FB5 Cal Ripken 20.00 6.00
FB6 Tony Gwynn 8.00 2.40
FB7 Kenny Lofton 2.50 .75
FB8 Gary Sheffield 2.50 .75
FB9 Deion Sanders 4.00 1.20
FB10 Brady Anderson 2.50 .75

1998 Topps Chrome HallBound

Randomly inserted in first series packs at the rate of one in 24, this 15-card set features color photos printed on metalized cards with Chromium technology of top stars who are bound for the Hall of Fame in Cooperstown, New York.

Nm-Mt Ex-Mt
COMPLETE SET (15) 150.00 45.00
*REF: .75X TO 2X BASIC HALLBOUND
REFRACTOR SER.1 STATED ODDS 1:72
HB1 Paul Molitor 5.00 1.50
HB2 Tony Gwynn 10.00 3.00
HB3 Wade Boggs 5.00 1.50
HB4 Roger Clemens 15.00 4.50
HB5 Dennis Eckersley 3.00 .90
HB6 Cal Ripken 25.00 7.50
HB7 Greg Maddux 12.00 3.60
HB8 Rickey Henderson 5.00 1.50
HB9 Ken Griffey Jr. 12.00 3.60
HB10 Frank Thomas 8.00 2.40
HB11 Mark McGwire 20.00 6.00
HB12 Barry Bonds 20.00 6.00
HB13 Mike Piazza 12.00 3.60
HB14 Juan Gonzalez 8.00 2.40
HB15 Randy Johnson 8.00 2.40

1998 Topps Chrome Milestones

Randomly seeded at a rate of one in every 24 second series packs, these 10 cards feature a selection of veteran stars that achieved specific career milestones in 1997. The cards are a straight parallel from the previously released 1998 Topps Milestones inserts except, of course, for the Chromium finish on the fronts.

Nm-Mt Ex-Mt
COMPLETE SET (10) 120.00 36.00
*REF: .75X TO 2X BASIC CHR.MILE ...
REFRACTOR SER.2 STATED ODDS 1:72
MS1 Barry Bonds 12.00 3.60
MS2 Roger Clemens 10.00 3.00
MS3 Dennis Eckersley 2.00 .60

MS4 Juan Gonzalez 5.00 1.50
MS5 Ken Griffey Jr. 8.00 2.40
MS6 Tony Gwynn 6.00 1.80
MS7 Greg Maddux 8.00 2.40
MS8 Mark McGwire 12.00 3.60
MS9 Cal Ripken 15.00 4.50
MS10 Frank Thomas 5.00 1.50

1998 Topps Chrome Rookie Class

Randomly seeded at a rate of one in 12 second series packs, cards from this 10-card set feature a selection of the league's top rookies for 1998. The cards are a straight parallel of the previously released 1998 Topps Rookie Class set, except of course for the Chromium stock fronts.

	Nm-Mt	Ex-Mt
COMPLETE SET (10)	20.00	6.00
*REF: .75X TO 2X BASIC CHR.RK.CLASS		
REFRACTOR SER.2 STATED ODDS 1:24		
R1 Travis Lee	2.00	.60
R2 Richard Hidalgo	2.00	.60
R3 Todd Helton	3.00	.90
R4 Paul Konerko	2.00	.60
R5 Mark Kotsay	2.00	.60
R6 Derrek Lee	2.00	.60
R7 Eli Marrero	2.00	.60
R8 Fernando Tatis	2.00	.60
R9 Juan Encarnacion	2.00	.60
R10 Ben Grieve	2.00	.60

1999 Topps Chrome

The 1999 Topps Chrome set totaled 462 cards (though is numbered 1-463 - card number 7 was never issued in honor of Mickey Mantle). The product was distributed in first and second series four-card packs each carrying a suggested retail price of $3. The first series cards were 1-6/8-242, second series cards 243-463. The card fronts feature action color player photos. The backs carry player information. The set contains the following subsets: Season Highlights (200-204), Prospects (205-212/425-437), Draft Picks (213-219/438-444), League Leaders (221-232), World Series (233-240), Strikeout Kings (445-449), All-Topps (450-460) and four Checklist Cards (241-242/462-463). The Mark McGwire Home Run Record Breaker card (220) was released in 70 different variations highlighting every home run that he hit in 1998. The Sammy Sosa Home Run Parade card (461) was issued in 66 different variations. A 462 card set of 1999 Topps Chrome is considered complete with any version of the McGwire 220 and Sosa 461. Rookie Cards of note include Pat Burrell and Alex Escobar

	Nm-Mt	Ex-Mt
COMPLETE SET (462)	120.00	36.00
COMP. SERIES 1 (241)	60.00	18.00
COMP. SERIES 2 (221)	60.00	18.00
COMMON (1-6/8-463)	.50	.15
COMMON (205-212/425-437)	1.00	.30
1 Roger Clemens	4.00	1.20
2 Andres Galarraga	.75	.23
3 Scott Brosius	.75	.23
4 John Flaherty	.50	.15
5 Jim Leyritz	.50	.15
6 Ray Durham	.75	.23
8 Jose Vizcaino	.50	.15
9 Will Clark	2.00	.60
10 David Wells	.75	.23
11 Jose Guillen	.50	.15
12 Scott Hatteberg	.50	.15
13 Edgardo Alfonzo	.75	.23
14 Mike Bordick	.50	.15
15 Manny Ramirez	.75	.23
16 Greg Maddux	3.00	.90
17 David Segui	.50	.15
18 Darryl Strawberry	1.25	.35
19 Brad Radke	.75	.23
20 Kerry Wood	2.00	.60
21 Matt Anderson	.50	.15
22 Derrek Lee	.75	.23
23 Mickey Morandini	.50	.15
24 Paul Konerko	.75	.23
25 Travis Lee	.50	.15
26 Ken Hill	.50	.15
27 Kenny Rogers	.75	.23
28 Paul Sorrento	.50	.15
29 Quilvio Veras	.50	.15
30 Todd Walker	.75	.23
31 Ryan Jackson	.50	.15
32 John Olerud	.75	.23
33 Doug Glanville	.50	.15
34 Nolan Ryan	6.00	1.80
35 Ray Lankford	.50	.15
36 Mark Loretta	.50	.15
37 Jason Dickson	.50	.15
38 Sean Bergman	.50	.15
39 Quinton McCracken	.50	.15
40 Bartolo Colon	.75	.23
41 Brady Anderson	.75	.23
42 Chris Stynes	.50	.15
43 Jorge Posada	1.25	.35
44 Justin Thompson	.50	.15
45 Johnny Damon	.75	.23
46 Armando Benitez	.50	.15
47 Brant Brown	.50	.15
48 Charlie Hayes	.50	.15
49 Darren Dreifort	.50	.15
50 Juan Gonzalez	2.00	.60
51 Chuck Knoblauch	.75	.23
52 Todd Helton	1.25	.35
53 Rick Reed	.50	.15
54 Chris Gomez	.50	.15
55 Gary Sheffield	.75	.23
56 Rod Beck	.50	.15
57 Rey Sanchez	.50	.15
58 Garret Anderson	.75	.23
59 Jimmy Haynes	.50	.15
60 Steve Woodard	.50	.15
61 Rondell White	.75	.23
62 Vladimir Guerrero	2.00	.60
63 Eric Karros	.75	.23
64 Russ Davis	.50	.15
65 Mo Vaughn	.75	.23
66 Sammy Sosa	3.00	.90
67 Troy Percival	.75	.23
68 Kenny Lofton	.75	.23
69 Bill Taylor	.50	.15
70 Mark McGwire	5.00	1.50
71 Roger Cedeno	.50	.15
72 Javy Lopez	.75	.23
73 Damion Easley	.50	.15
74 Andy Pettitte	1.25	.35
75 Tony Gwynn	2.50	.75
76 Ricardo Rincon	.50	.15
77 F.P. Santangelo	.50	.15
78 Jay Bell	.75	.23
79 Scott Servais	.50	.15
80 Jose Canseco	2.00	.60
81 Roberto Hernandez	.50	.15
82 Todd Dunwoody	.50	.15
83 John Wetteland	.75	.23
84 Mike Caruso	.50	.15
85 Derek Jeter	5.00	1.50
86 Aaron Sele	.50	.15
87 Jose Lima	.50	.15
88 Ryan Christenson	.50	.15
89 Jeff Cirillo	.50	.15
90 Jose Hernandez	.50	.15
91 Mark Kotsay	.50	.15
92 Darren Bragg	.50	.15
93 Albert Belle	.75	.23
94 Matt Lawton	.50	.15
95 Pedro Martinez	2.00	.60
96 Greg Vaughn	.75	.23
97 Neifi Perez	.50	.15
98 Gerald Williams	.50	.15
99 Derek Bell	.50	.15
100 Ken Griffey Jr.	3.00	.90
101 David Cone	.75	.23
102 Brian Johnson	.50	.15
103 Dean Palmer	.75	.23
104 Javier Valentin	.50	.15
105 Trevor Hoffman	.75	.23
106 Butch Huskey	.50	.15
107 Dave Martinez	.50	.15
108 Billy Wagner	.75	.23
109 Shawn Green	.75	.23
110 Ben Grieve	.50	.15
111 Tom Goodwin	.50	.15
112 Jaret Wright	.50	.15
113 Aramis Ramirez	.75	.23
114 Dmitri Young	.75	.23
115 Hideki Irabu	.50	.15
116 Roberto Kelly	.50	.15
117 Jeff Fassero	.50	.15
118 Mark Clark	.50	.15
119 Jason McDonald	.50	.15
120 Matt Williams	.75	.23
121 Dave Burba	.50	.15
122 Bret Saberhagen	.75	.23
123 Deivi Cruz	.50	.15
124 Chad Curtis	.50	.15
125 Scott Rolen	1.25	.35
126 Lee Stevens	.50	.15
127 J.T. Snow	.75	.23
128 Rusty Greer	.75	.23
129 Brian Meadows	.50	.15
130 Jim Edmonds	.75	.23
131 Ron Gant	.75	.23
132 A.J. Hinch	.50	.15
133 Shannon Stewart	.75	.23
134 Brad Fullmer	.50	.15
135 Cal Eldred	.50	.15
136 Matt Walbeck	.50	.15
137 Carl Everett	.75	.23
138 Walt Weiss	.50	.15
139 Fred McGriff	1.25	.35
140 Darin Erstad	.75	.23
141 Dave Nilsson	.50	.15
142 Eric Young	.50	.15
143 Dan Wilson	.50	.15
144 Jeff Reed	.50	.15
145 Brett Tomko	.50	.15
146 Terry Steinbach	.50	.15
147 Seth Greisinger	.50	.15
148 Pat Meares	.50	.15
149 Livan Hernandez	.50	.15
150 Jeff Bagwell	1.25	.35
151 Bob Wickman	.50	.15
152 Omar Vizquel	.75	.23
153 Eric Davis	.75	.23
154 Larry Sutton	.50	.15
155 Magglio Ordonez	.75	.23
156 Eric Milton	.50	.15
157 Darren Lewis	.50	.15
158 Rick Aguilera	.50	.15
159 Mike Lieberthal	.50	.15
160 Robb Nen	.50	.15
161 Brian Giles	.75	.23
162 Jeff Brantley	.50	.15
163 Gary DiSarcina	.50	.15
164 John Valentin	.50	.15
165 Dave Dellucci	.50	.15
166 Chan Ho Park	.75	.23
167 Masato Yoshii	.50	.15
168 Jason Schmidt	.75	.23
169 LaTroy Hawkins	.50	.15
170 Bret Boone	.75	.23
171 Jerry DiPoto	.50	.15
172 Mariano Rivera	1.25	.35
173 Mike Cameron	.75	.23
174 Scott Erickson	.50	.15
175 Charles Johnson	.75	.23
176 Bobby Jones	.50	.15
177 Francisco Cordova	.50	.15
178 Todd Jones	.50	.15
179 Jeff Montgomery	.50	.15
180 Mike Mussina	2.00	.60
181 Bob Abreu	.75	.23
182 Ismael Valdes	.50	.15
183 Andy Fox	.50	.15
184 Woody Williams	.50	.15
185 Denny Neagle	.50	.15
186 Jose Valentin	.50	.15
187 Darrin Fletcher	.50	.15
188 Gabe Alvarez	.50	.15
189 Eddie Taubensee	.50	.15
190 Edgar Martinez	1.25	.35
191 Jason Kendall	.75	.23
192 Darryl Kile	.75	.23
193 Jeff King	.50	.15
194 Rey Ordonez	.50	.15
195 Andruw Jones	.75	.23
196 Tony Fernandez	.50	.15
197 Jamey Wright	.50	.15
198 B.J. Surhoff	.75	.23
199 Vinny Castilla	.75	.23
200 David Wells HL	.50	.15
201 Mark McGwire HL	2.50	.75
202 Sammy Sosa HL	2.00	.60
203 Roger Clemens HL	2.00	.60
204 Kerry Wood HL	1.25	.35
205 Gabe Kapler / Lance Berkman / Mike Frank	1.00	.30
206 Alex Escobar RC / Ricky Ledee / Mike Stoner	1.00	.30
207 Peter Bergeron RC / Jeremy Giambi / George Lombard	1.00	.30
208 Michael Barrett / Ben Davis / Robert Fick	1.00	.30
209 Jayson Werth / Ramon Hernandez / Pat Cline	1.00	.30
210 Ryan Anderson / Bruce Chen / Chris Enochs	1.00	.30
211 Brad Penny / Octavio Dotel / Mike Lincoln	1.00	.30
212 Chuck Abbott RC / Brent Butler / Danny Klassen	1.00	.30
213 Chris C.Jones / Jeff Urban RC	1.00	.30
214 Arturo McDowell RC / Tony Torcato	1.00	.30
215 Josh McKinley RC / Jason Tyner	1.00	.30
216 Matt Burch / Seth Etheron RC	1.00	.30
217 Mamon Tucker RC / Rick Elder	1.00	.30
218 J.M.Gold / Ryan Mills RC	1.00	.30
219 Andy Brown / Choo Freeman RC	1.00	.30
220A Mark McGwire HR 1	50.00	15.00
220B Mark McGwire HR 2	30.00	9.00
220C Mark McGwire HR 3	30.00	9.00
220D Mark McGwire HR 4	30.00	9.00
220E Mark McGwire HR 5	30.00	9.00
220F Mark McGwire HR 6	30.00	9.00
220G Mark McGwire HR 7	30.00	9.00
220H Mark McGwire HR 8	30.00	9.00
220I Mark McGwire HR 9	30.00	9.00
220J M.McGwire HR 10	30.00	9.00
220K M.McGwire HR 11	30.00	9.00
220L M.McGwire HR 12	30.00	9.00
220M M.McGwire HR 13	30.00	9.00
220N M.McGwire HR 14	30.00	9.00
220O M.McGwire HR 15	30.00	9.00
220P M.McGwire HR 16	30.00	9.00
220Q M.McGwire HR 17	30.00	9.00
220R M.McGwire HR 18	30.00	9.00
220S M.McGwire HR 19	30.00	9.00
220T M.McGwire HR 20	30.00	9.00
220U M.McGwire HR 21	30.00	9.00
220V M.McGwire HR 22	30.00	9.00
220W M.McGwire HR 23	30.00	9.00
220X M.McGwire HR 24	30.00	9.00
220Y M.McGwire HR 25	30.00	9.00
220Z M.McGwire HR 26	30.00	9.00
220AA M.McGwire HR 27	30.00	9.00
220AB M.McGwire HR 28	30.00	9.00
220AC M.McGwire HR 29	30.00	9.00
220AD M.McGwire HR 30	30.00	9.00
220AE M.McGwire HR 31	30.00	9.00
220AF M.McGwire HR 32	30.00	9.00
220AG M.McGwire HR 33	30.00	9.00
220AH M.McGwire HR 34	30.00	9.00
220AI M.McGwire HR 35	30.00	9.00
220AJ M.McGwire HR 36	30.00	9.00
220AK M.McGwire HR 37	30.00	9.00
220AL M.McGwire HR 38	30.00	9.00
220AM M.McGwire HR 39	30.00	9.00
220AN M.McGwire HR 40	30.00	9.00
220AO M.McGwire HR 41	30.00	9.00
220AP M.McGwire HR 42	30.00	9.00
220AQ M.McGwire HR 43	30.00	9.00
220AR M.McGwire HR 44	30.00	9.00
220AS M.McGwire HR 45	30.00	9.00
220AT M.McGwire HR 46	30.00	9.00
220AU M.McGwire HR 47	30.00	9.00
220AV M.McGwire HR 48	30.00	9.00
220AW M.McGwire HR 49	30.00	9.00
220AX M.McGwire HR 50	30.00	9.00
220AY M.McGwire HR 51	30.00	9.00
220AZ M.McGwire HR 52	30.00	9.00
220BB M.McGwire HR 53	30.00	9.00
220CC M.McGwire HR 54	30.00	9.00
220DD M.McGwire HR 55	30.00	9.00
220EE M.McGwire HR 56	30.00	9.00
220FF M.McGwire HR 57	30.00	9.00
220GG M.McGwire HR 58	30.00	9.00
220HH M.McGwire HR 59	30.00	9.00
220II M.McGwire HR 60	30.00	9.00
220JJ M.McGwire HR 61	50.00	15.00
220KK M.McGwire HR 62	80.00	24.00
220LL M.McGwire HR 63	50.00	15.00
220MM M.McGwire HR 64	50.00	15.00
220NN M.McGwire HR 65	50.00	15.00
220OO M.McGwire HR 66	50.00	15.00
220PP M.McGwire HR 67	50.00	15.00
220QQ M.McGwire HR 68	50.00	15.00
220RR M.McGwire HR 69	50.00	15.00
220SS M.McGwire HR 70	150.00	45.00
221 Larry Walker LL	.75	.23
222 Bernie Williams LL	.75	.23
223 Mark McGwire LL	2.50	.75
224 Ken Griffey Jr. LL	2.00	.60
225 Sammy Sosa LL	2.00	.60
226 Juan Gonzalez LL	1.25	.35
227 Dante Bichette LL	.50	.15
228 Alex Rodriguez LL	2.00	.60
229 Sammy Sosa LL	2.00	.60
230 Derek Jeter LL	2.50	.75
231 Greg Maddux LL	2.00	.60
232 Roger Clemens LL	2.00	.60
233 Ricky Ledee WS	.50	.15
234 Chuck Knoblauch WS	.50	.15
235 Bernie Williams WS	.75	.23
236 Tino Martinez WS	.75	.23
237 Orl. Hernandez WS	.50	.15
238 Scott Brosius WS	.50	.15
239 Andy Pettitte WS	.75	.23
240 Mariano Rivera WS	.75	.23
241 Checklist	.50	.15
242 Checklist	.50	.15
243 Tom Glavine	1.25	.35
244 Andy Benes	.50	.15
245 Sandy Alomar Jr.	.50	.15
246 Wilton Guerrero	.50	.15
247 Alex Gonzalez	.50	.15
248 Roberto Alomar	2.00	.60
249 Ruben Rivera	.50	.15
250 Eric Chavez	.75	.23
251 Ellis Burks	.75	.23
252 Richie Sexson	.75	.23
253 Steve Finley	.75	.23
254 Dwight Gooden	1.25	.35
255 Dustin Hermanson	.50	.15
256 Kirk Rueter	.50	.15
257 Steve Trachsel	.50	.15
258 Gregg Jefferies	.50	.15
259 Matt Stairs	.50	.15
260 Shane Reynolds	.50	.15
261 Gregg Olson	.50	.15
262 Kevin Tapani	.50	.15
263 Matt Morris	.75	.23
264 Carl Pavano	.50	.15
265 Nomar Garciaparra	3.00	.90
266 Kevin Young	.75	.23
267 Rick Helling	.50	.15
268 Matt Franco	.50	.15
269 Brian McRae	.50	.15
270 Cal Ripken	6.00	1.80
271 Jeff Abbott	.50	.15
272 Tony Batista	.75	.23
273 Bill Simas	.50	.15
274 Brian Hunter	.50	.15
275 John Franco	.75	.23
276 Devon White	.50	.15
277 Rickey Henderson	2.00	.60
278 Chuck Finley	.75	.23
279 Mike Blowers	.50	.15
280 Mark Grace	1.25	.35
281 Randy Winn	.50	.15
282 Bobby Bonilla	.75	.23
283 David Justice	.75	.23
284 Shane Monahan	.50	.15
285 Kevin Brown	1.25	.35
286 Todd Zeile	.75	.23
287 Al Martin	.50	.15
288 Troy O'Leary	.50	.15
289 Darryl Hamilton	.50	.15
290 Tino Martinez	1.25	.35
291 David Ortiz	.75	.23
292 Tony Clark	.50	.15
293 Ryan Minor	.50	.15
294 Mark Leiter	.50	.15
295 Wally Joyner	.75	.23
296 Cliff Floyd	.75	.23
297 Shawn Estes	.50	.15
298 Pat Hentgen	.50	.15
299 Scott Elarton	.50	.15
300 Alex Rodriguez	3.00	.90
301 Ozzie Guillen	.50	.15
302 Hideo Nomo	2.00	.60
303 Ryan McGuire	.50	.15
304 Brad Ausmus	.50	.15
305 Alex Gonzalez	.50	.15
306 Brian Jordan	.75	.23
307 John Jaha	.50	.15
308 Mark Grudzielanek	.50	.15
309 Juan Guzman	.50	.15
310 Tony Womack	.50	.15
311 Dennis Reyes	.50	.15
312 Marty Cordova	.50	.15
313 Ramiro Mendoza	.50	.15
314 Robin Ventura	.75	.23
315 Rafael Palmeiro	1.25	.35
316 Ramon Martinez	.50	.15
317 Pedro Astacio	.50	.15
318 Dave Hollins	.50	.15
319 Tom Candiotti	.50	.15
320 Al Leiter	.75	.23
321 Rico Brogna	.50	.15
322 Reggie Jefferson	.50	.15
323 Bernard Gilkey	.50	.15
324 Jason Giambi	2.00	.60
325 Craig Biggio	1.25	.35
326 Troy Glaus	1.25	.35
327 Delino DeShields	.50	.15
328 Fernando Vina	.75	.23
329 John Smoltz	1.25	.35
330 Jeff Kent	.75	.23
331 Roy Halladay	.75	.23
332 Andy Ashby	.50	.15
333 Tim Wakefield	.75	.23
334 Roger Clemens	4.00	1.20
335 Bernie Williams	1.25	.35
336 Desi Relaford	.50	.15
337 John Burkett	.50	.15
338 Mike Hampton	.75	.23
339 Royce Clayton	.50	.15
340 Mike Piazza	3.00	.90
341 Jeremi Gonzalez	.50	.15
342 Mike Lansing	.50	.15
343 Jamie Moyer	.75	.23
344 Ron Coomer	.50	.15
345 Barry Larkin	2.00	.60
346 Fernando Tatis	.50	.15
347 Chili Davis	.75	.23
348 Bobby Higginson	.75	.23
349 Hal Morris	.50	.15
350 Larry Walker	1.25	.35
351 Carlos Guillen	.50	.15
352 Miguel Tejada	.75	.23
353 Travis Fryman	.75	.23
354 Jarrod Washburn	.75	.23
355 Chipper Jones	2.00	.60
356 Todd Stottlemyre	.50	.15
357 Henry Rodriguez	.50	.15
358 Eli Marrero	.50	.15
359 Alan Benes	.50	.15
360 Tim Salmon	1.25	.35
361 Luis Gonzalez	.75	.23
362 Scott Spiezio	.50	.15
363 Chris Carpenter	.50	.15
364 Bobby Howry	.50	.15
365 Raul Mondesi	.75	.23
366 Ugueth Urbina	.50	.15
367 Tom Evans	.50	.15
368 Kerry Ligtenberg RC	.75	.23
369 Adrian Beltre	.75	.23
370 Ryan Klesko	.75	.23
371 Wilson Alvarez	.50	.15
372 John Thomson	.50	.15
373 Tony Saunders	.50	.15
374 Dave Mlicki	.50	.15
375 Ken Caminiti	.75	.23
376 Jay Buhner	.75	.23
377 Bill Mueller	.75	.23
378 Jeff Blauser	.50	.15
379 Edgar Renteria	.75	.23
380 Jim Thome	2.00	.60
381 Joey Hamilton	.50	.15
382 Calvin Pickering	.50	.15
383 Marquis Grissom	.50	.15
384 Omar Daal	.50	.15
385 Curt Schilling	1.25	.35
386 Jose Cruz Jr.	.75	.23
387 Chris Widger	.50	.15
388 Pete Harnisch	.50	.15
389 Charles Nagy	.50	.15
390 Tom Gordon	.50	.15
391 Bobby Smith	.50	.15
392 Derrick Gibson	.50	.15
393 Jeff Conine	.75	.23
394 Carlos Perez	.50	.15
395 Barry Bonds	5.00	1.50
396 Mark McLemore	.50	.15
397 Juan Encarnacion	.50	.15
398 Wade Boggs	1.25	.35
399 Ivan Rodriguez	2.00	.60
400 Moises Alou	.75	.23
401 Jeromy Burnitz	.75	.23
402 Sean Casey	.75	.23
403 Jose Offerman	.50	.15
404 Joe Fontenot	.50	.15
405 Kevin Millwood	.75	.23
406 Lance Johnson	.50	.15
407 Richard Hidalgo	.75	.23
408 Mike Jackson	.50	.15
409 Brian Anderson	.50	.15
410 Jeff Shaw	.50	.15
411 Preston Wilson	.75	.23
412 Todd Hundley	.50	.15
413 Jim Parque	.50	.15
414 Justin Baughman	.50	.15
415 Dante Bichette	.75	.23
416 Paul O'Neill	1.25	.35
417 Miguel Cairo	.50	.15
418 Randy Johnson	2.00	.60
419 Jesus Sanchez	.50	.15
420 Carlos Delgado	.75	.23
421 Ricky Ledee	.50	.15
422 Orlando Hernandez	.75	.23
423 Frank Thomas	2.00	.60
424 Pokey Reese	.50	.15
425 Carlos Lee / Mike Lowell / Kit Pellow RC	1.00	.30
426 Michael Cuddyer / Mark DeRosa / Jerry Hairston Jr.	1.00	.30
427 Marlon Anderson / Ron Belliard / Orlando Cabrera	1.00	.30
428 Micah Bowie / Phil Norton RC / Randy Wolf	1.00	.30
429 Jack Cressend RC / Jason Rakers / John Rocker	1.00	.30
430 Ruben Mateo / Scott Morgan / Mike Zywica RC	1.00	.30
431 Jason LaRue / Matt LeCroy / Mitch Meluskey	1.00	.30
432 Gabe Kapler / Armando Rios / Fernando Seguignol	1.00	.30
433 Adam Kennedy / Mickey Lopez RC / Jackie Rexrode	1.00	.30
434 Jose Fernandez RC / Jeff Liefer / Chris Truby	1.00	.30
435 Corey Koskie / Doug Mientkiewicz RC / Damon Minor	2.50	.75
436 Roosevelt Brown RC / Dernell Stenson / Vernon Wells	1.00	.30
437 A.J. Burnett RC / Billy Koch / John Nicholson	2.00	.60
438 Matt Belisle / Matt Roney RC	1.00	.30
439 Austin Kearns / Chris George RC	6.00	1.80
440 Nate Bump RC / Nate Cornejo	1.50	.45
441 Brad Lidge / Mike Nannini RC	1.50	.45
442 Matt Holliday / Jeff Winchester RC	1.00	.30

443 Adam Everett 1.00 .30
Chip Ambres RC
444 Pat Burrell 5.00 1.50
Eric Valent RC
445 Roger Clemens SK 2.00 .60
446 Kerry Wood SK 1.25 .35
447 Curt Schilling SK .75 .23
448 Randy Johnson SK 1.25 .35
449 Pedro Martinez SK 1.25 .35
450 Jeff Bagwell AT 2.00 .60
Andres Galarraga
Mark McGwire
451 John Olerud AT .75 .23
Jim Thome
Tino Martinez
452 Alex Rodriguez AT 2.50 .75
Nomar Garciaparra
Derek Jeter
453 Vinny Castilla AT 1.25 .35
Chipper Jones
Scott Rolen
454 Sammy Sosa AT 2.00 .60
Ken Griffey Jr.
Juan Gonzalez
455 Barry Bonds AT 2.00 .60
Manny Ramirez
Larry Walker
456 Frank Thomas AT 2.00 .60
Tim Salmon
David Justice
457 Travis Lee AT .75 .23
Todd Helton
Ben Grieve
458 Vladimir Guerrero AT .75 .23
Greg Vaughn
Bernie Williams
459 Mike Piazza AT 2.00 .60
Ivan Rodriguez
Jason Kendall
460 Roger Clemens AT 2.00 .60
Kerry Wood
Greg Maddux
461A Sammy Sosa HR 1 25.00 7.50
461B Sammy Sosa HR 2 15.00 4.50
461C Sammy Sosa HR 3 15.00 4.50
461D Sammy Sosa HR 4 15.00 4.50
461E Sammy Sosa HR 5 15.00 4.50
461F Sammy Sosa HR 6 15.00 4.50
461G Sammy Sosa HR 7 15.00 4.50
461H Sammy Sosa HR 8 15.00 4.50
461I Sammy Sosa HR 9 15.00 4.50
461J Sammy Sosa HR 10 15.00 4.50
461K Sammy Sosa HR 11 15.00 4.50
461L Sammy Sosa HR 12 15.00 4.50
461M Sammy Sosa HR 13 15.00 4.50
461N Sammy Sosa HR 14 15.00 4.50
461O Sammy Sosa HR 15 15.00 4.50
461P Sammy Sosa HR 16 15.00 4.50
461Q Sammy Sosa HR 17 15.00 4.50
461R Sammy Sosa HR 18 15.00 4.50
461S Sammy Sosa HR 19 15.00 4.50
461T Sammy Sosa HR 20 15.00 4.50
461U Sammy Sosa HR 21 15.00 4.50
461V Sammy Sosa HR 22 15.00 4.50
461W Sammy Sosa HR 23 15.00 4.50
461X Sammy Sosa HR 24 15.00 4.50
461Y Sammy Sosa HR 25 15.00 4.50
461Z Sammy Sosa HR 26 15.00 4.50
461AA S.Sosa HR 27 15.00 4.50
461AB S.Sosa HR 28 15.00 4.50
461AC S.Sosa HR 29 15.00 4.50
461AD S.Sosa HR 30 15.00 4.50
461AE S.Sosa HR 31 15.00 4.50
461AF S.Sosa HR 32 15.00 4.50
461AG S.Sosa HR 33 15.00 4.50
461AH S.Sosa HR 34 15.00 4.50
461AI S.Sosa HR 35 15.00 4.50
461AJ S.Sosa HR 36 15.00 4.50
461AK S.Sosa HR 37 15.00 4.50
461AL S.Sosa HR 38 15.00 4.50
461AM S.Sosa HR 39 15.00 4.50
461AN S.Sosa HR 40 15.00 4.50
461AO S.Sosa HR 41 15.00 4.50
461AP S.Sosa HR 42 15.00 4.50
461AR S.Sosa HR 43 15.00 4.50
461AS S.Sosa HR 44 15.00 4.50
461AT S.Sosa HR 45 15.00 4.50
461AU S.Sosa HR 46 15.00 4.50
461AV S.Sosa HR 47 15.00 4.50
461AW S.Sosa HR 48 15.00 4.50
461AX S.Sosa HR 49 15.00 4.50
461AY S.Sosa HR 50 15.00 4.50
461AZ S.Sosa HR 51 15.00 4.50
461BB S.Sosa HR 52 15.00 4.50
461CC S.Sosa HR 53 15.00 4.50
461DD S.Sosa HR 54 15.00 4.50
461EE S.Sosa HR 55 15.00 4.50
461FF S.Sosa HR 56 15.00 4.50
461GG S.Sosa HR 57 15.00 4.50
461HH S.Sosa HR 58 15.00 4.50
461II S.Sosa HR 59 15.00 4.50
461JJ S.Sosa HR 60 15.00 4.50
461KK S.Sosa HR 61 25.00 7.50
461LL S.Sosa HR 62 40.00 12.00
461MM S.Sosa HR 63 25.00 7.50
461NN S.Sosa HR 64 25.00 7.50
461OO S.Sosa HR 65 25.00 7.50
461PP S.Sosa HR 66 80.00 24.00
462 Checklist .50 .15
463 Checklist .50 .15

1999 Topps Chrome Refractors

Randomly inserted in packs at the rate of one in 12, this 462-card set is parallel to the base set and is similar in design. The difference is found in the refractive quality of the card. It's estimated that only around 15 to 25 of each McGwire number 220 refractor was produced.

Nm-Mt Ex-Mt
*STARS: 2.5X TO 6X BASIC CARDS
*ROOKIES: 1.5X TO 4X BASIC CARDS
MCGWIRE 220 HR 1 250.00 75.00
MCGWIRE 220 HR 2-60 120.00 36.00
MCGWIRE 220 HR 61 200.00 60.00
MCGWIRE 220 HR 62 300.00 90.00
MCGWIRE 220 HR 63-69 120.00 36.00
MCGWIRE 220 HR 70 400.00 120.00
SOSA 461 HR 1 80.00 24.00
SOSA 461 HR 2-60 40.00 12.00
SOSA 461 HR 61 60.00 18.00
SOSA 461 HR 62 100.00 30.00
SOSA 461 HR 63-65 40.00 12.00
SOSA 461 HR 66 150.00 45.00

1999 Topps Chrome All-Etch

Randomly inserted in Series two packs at the rate of one in six, this 30-card set features color player photos printed on All-Etch technology. A refractive parallel version of this set was also produced with an insertion rate of 1:24 packs.

Nm-Mt Ex-Mt
COMPLETE SET (30) 100.00 30.00
*REFRACTORS: .75X TO 2X BASIC ALL-ETCH
SER.2 REFRACTOR ODDS 1:24
AE1 Mark McGwire 12.00 3.60
AE2 Sammy Sosa 8.00 2.40
AE3 Ken Griffey Jr. 8.00 2.40
AE4 Greg Vaughn 2.00 .60
AE5 Albert Belle 2.00 .60
AE6 Vinny Castilla 2.00 .60
AE7 Jose Canseco 5.00 1.50
AE8 Juan Gonzalez 5.00 1.50
AE9 Manny Ramirez 2.00 .60
AE10 Andres Galarraga 2.00 .60
AE11 Rafael Palmeiro 3.00 .90
AE12 Alex Rodriguez 8.00 2.40
AE13 Mo Vaughn 2.00 .60
AE14 Eric Chavez 2.00 .60
AE15 Gabe Kapler 2.50 .75
AE16 Calvin Pickering 1.25 .35
AE17 Ruben Mateo 2.50 .75
AE18 Roy Halladay 2.00 .60
AE19 Jeremy Giambi 1.25 .35
AE20 Alex Gonzalez 1.25 .35
AE21 Ron Belliard 2.50 .75
AE22 Marlon Anderson 2.50 .75
AE23 Carlos Lee 2.50 .75
AE24 Kerry Wood 5.00 1.50
AE25 Roger Clemens 10.00 3.00
AE26 Curt Schilling 3.00 .90
AE27 Kevin Brown 3.00 .90
AE28 Randy Johnson 5.00 1.50
AE29 Pedro Martinez 5.00 1.50
AE30 Orlando Hernandez 2.00 .60

1999 Topps Chrome Early Road to the Hall

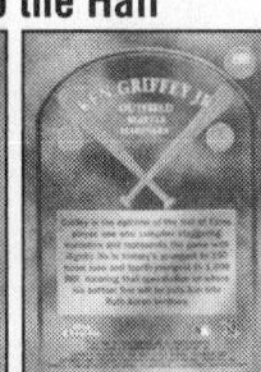

Randomly inserted in Series one packs at the rate of one in 12, this 10-card set features color photos of ten players with less than 10 years in the Majors but are already headed towards the Hall of Fame in Cooperstown, New York.

Nm-Mt Ex-Mt
COMPLETE SET (10) 60.00 18.00
*REFRACTORS: 3X TO 8X BASIC ROAD
SER.1 REFRACTOR ODDS 1:944 HOBBY
REF.PRINT RUN 100 SERIAL #'d SETS
ER1 Nomar Garciaparra 8.00 2.40
ER2 Derek Jeter 12.00 3.60
ER3 Alex Rodriguez 8.00 2.40
ER4 Juan Gonzalez 5.00 1.50
ER5 Ken Griffey Jr. 8.00 2.40
ER6 Chipper Jones 5.00 1.50
ER7 Vladimir Guerrero 5.00 1.50
ER8 Jeff Bagwell 3.00 .90
ER9 Ivan Rodriguez 5.00 1.50
ER10 Frank Thomas 5.00 1.50

1999 Topps Chrome Fortune 15

Randomly inserted into Series two packs at the rate of one in 12, this 15-card set features color photos of the League's most elite veteran and rookie players. A refractor parallel version of this set was also produced with an insertion rate of 1:627 packs and sequentially numnbered to 100.

Nm-Mt Ex-Mt
COMPLETE SET (15) 100.00 30.00
*REFRACTORS: 4X TO 8X BASIC FORT.15
SER.2 REFRACTOR ODDS 1:627
REF.PRINT RUN 100 SERIAL #'d SETS
FF1 Alex Rodriguez 8.00 2.40
FF2 Nomar Garciaparra 8.00 2.40
FF3 Derek Jeter 12.00 3.60
FF4 Troy Glaus 3.00 .90
FF5 Ken Griffey Jr. 8.00 2.40
FF6 Vladimir Guerrero 5.00 1.50
FF7 Kerry Wood 5.00 1.50
FF8 Eric Chavez 2.00 .60
FF9 Greg Maddux 8.00 2.40
FF10 Mike Piazza 8.00 2.40
FF11 Sammy Sosa 8.00 2.40
FF12 Mark McGwire 12.00 3.60
FF13 Ben Grieve 1.25 .35
FF14 Chipper Jones 5.00 1.50
FF15 Manny Ramirez 2.00 .60

1999 Topps Chrome Lords of the Diamond

Randomly inserted in Series one packs at the rate of one in eight, this 15-card set features color photos of some of the true masters of the ballfield. A refractive parallel version of this set was also produced with an insertion rate of 1:24.

Nm-Mt Ex-Mt
COMPLETE SET (15) 50.00 15.00
*REFRACTORS: .6X TO 1.5X BASIC LORDS
SER.1 REFRACTOR ODDS 1:24
LD1 Ken Griffey Jr. 4.00 1.20
LD2 Chipper Jones 2.50 .75
LD3 Sammy Sosa 4.00 1.20
LD4 Frank Thomas 2.50 .75
LD5 Mark McGwire 6.00 1.80
LD6 Jeff Bagwell 1.50 .45
LD7 Alex Rodriguez 4.00 1.20
LD8 Juan Gonzalez 2.50 .75
LD9 Barry Bonds 6.00 1.80
LD10 Nomar Garciaparra 4.00 1.20
LD11 Darin Erstad 1.00 .30
LD12 Tony Gwynn 3.00 .90
LD13 Andres Galarraga 1.00 .30
LD14 Mike Piazza 4.00 1.20
LD15 Greg Maddux 4.00 1.20

1999 Topps Chrome New Breed

Randomly inserted in Series one packs at the rate of one in 24, this 15-card set features color photos of some of today's young stars in Major League Baseball. A refractive parallel version of this set was also produced with an insertion rate of 1:72.

Nm-Mt Ex-Mt
COMPLETE SET (15) 100.00 30.00
*REFRACTORS: .6X TO 1.5X BASIC BREED
SER.1 REFRACTOR ODDS 1:72
NB1 Darin Erstad 3.00 .90
NB2 Brad Fullmer 2.00 .60
NB3 Kerry Wood 8.00 2.40
NB4 Nomar Garciaparra 12.00 3.60
NB5 Travis Lee 2.00 .60
NB6 Scott Rolen 5.00 1.50
NB7 Todd Helton 5.00 1.50
NB8 Vladimir Guerrero 8.00 2.40
NB9 Derek Jeter 20.00 6.00
NB10 Alex Rodriguez 12.00 3.60
NB11 Ben Grieve 2.00 .60
NB12 Andruw Jones 3.00 .90
NB13 Paul Konerko 3.00 .90
NB14 Aramis Ramirez 3.00 .90
NB15 Adrian Beltre 3.00 .90

1999 Topps Chrome Record Numbers

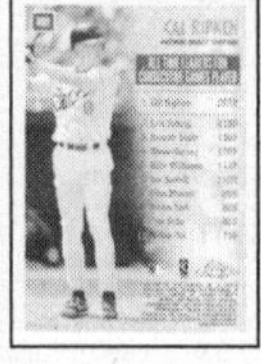

Randomly inserted in Series two packs at the rate of one in 36, this 10-card set features color photos of top Major League record-setters. A refractive parallel version of this set was also produced with an insertion rate of 1:144.

Nm-Mt Ex-Mt
COMPLETE SET (10) 150.00 45.00
*REFRACTORS: .75X TO 2X BASIC REC.NUM.
SER.2 REFRACTOR ODDS 1:144
RN1 Mark McGwire 20.00 6.00
RN2 Mike Piazza 12.00 3.60
RN3 Curt Schilling 5.00 1.50
RN4 Ken Griffey Jr. 12.00 3.60
RN5 Sammy Sosa 12.00 3.60
RN6 Nomar Garciaparra 12.00 3.60
RN7 Kerry Wood 8.00 2.40
RN8 Roger Clemens 15.00 4.50
RN9 Cal Ripken 25.00 7.50
RN10 Mark McGwire 20.00 6.00

1999 Topps Chrome Traded

This 121-card set features color photos on Chromium cards of 46 of the most notable transactions of the 1999 season and 75 newcomers accented with the Topps "Rookie Card" logo. The set was distributed only in factory boxes. Due to a very late ship date (January, 2000) this set caused some commotion in the hobby as to its status as a 1999 or 2000 product. Notable Rookie Cards include Josh Hamilton and Corey Patterson.

Nm-Mt Ex-Mt
COMP.FACT SET (121) 80.00 24.00
T1 Seth Etherton .60 .18
T2 Mark Harriger RC .50 .15
T3 Matt Wise RC .50 .15
T4 Carlos E. Hernandez RC .75 .23
T5 Julio Lugo RC .75 .23
T6 Mike Nannini .60 .18
T7 Justin Bowles RC .50 .15
T8 Mark Mulder RC 8.00 2.40
T9 Roberto Vaz RC .50 .15
T10 Felipe Lopez RC .75 .23
T11 Matt Belisle 1.00 .30
T12 Micah Bowie .40 .12
T13 Ruben Quevedo RC .75 .23
T14 Jose Garcia RC .50 .15
T15 David Kelton RC 1.25 .35
T16 Phil Norton .40 .12
T17 Corey Patterson RC 8.00 2.40
T18 Ron Walker RC .50 .15
T19 Paul Hoover RC .50 .15
T20 Ryan Rupe RC .75 .23
T21 J.D. Closser RC .75 .23
T22 Rob Ryan RC .50 .15
T23 Steve Colyer RC .75 .23
T24 Bubba Crosby RC 2.00 .60
T25 Luke Prokopec RC .75 .23
T26 Matt Blank RC .50 .15
T27 Josh McKinley .60 .18
T28 Nate Bump .50 .15
T29 G.Chiaramonte RC .50 .15
T30 Arturo McDowell .60 .18
T31 Tony Torcato .60 .18
T32 Dave Roberts RC 1.25 .35
T33 C.C. Sabathia RC 2.00 .60
T34 Sean Spencer RC .50 .15
T35 Chip Ambres 1.50 .45
T36 A.J. Burnett 1.50 .45
T37 Mo Bruce RC .50 .15
T38 Jason Tyner .60 .18
T39 Mamon Tucker .60 .18
T40 Sean Burroughs RC 6.00 1.80
T41 Kevin Eberwein RC .75 .23
T42 Junior Herndon RC .75 .23
T43 Bryan Wolff RC .50 .15
T44 Pat Burrell 5.00 1.50
T45 Eric Valent .75 .23
T46 Carlos Pena RC 2.00 .60
T47 Mike Zywica .40 .12
T48 Adam Everett .60 .18
T49 Juan Pena RC .50 .15
T50 Adam Dunn RC 10.00 3.00
T51 Austin Kearns 6.00 1.80
T52 Jacobo Sequea RC .75 .23
T53 Choo Freeman .60 .18
T54 Jeff Winchester .60 .18
T55 Matt Burch .50 .15
T56 Chris George .60 .18
T57 Scott Mullen RC .50 .15
T58 Kit Pellow .50 .15
T59 Mark Quinn RC .75 .23
T60 Nate Cornejo 1.25 .35
T61 Ryan Mills .60 .18
T62 Kevin Beirne RC .75 .23
T63 Kip Wells RC 1.25 .35
T64 Juan Rivera RC 2.50 .75
T65 Alfonso Soriano RC 15.00 4.50
T66 Josh Hamilton RC 2.00 .60
T67 Josh Girdley RC .75 .23
T68 Kyle Snyder RC .75 .23
T69 Mike Paradis RC .75 .23
T70 Jason Jennings RC 1.25 .35
T71 David Walling RC .75 .23
T72 Omar Ortiz RC .50 .15
T73 Jay Gehrke RC .50 .15
T74 Casey Burns RC .50 .15
T75 Carl Crawford RC 4.00 1.20
T76 Reggie Sanders .60 .18
T77 Will Clark 1.50 .45
T78 David Wells .60 .18
T79 Paul Konerko .60 .18
T80 Armando Benitez .40 .12
T81 Brant Brown .40 .12
T82 Mo Vaughn .60 .18
T83 Jose Canseco 1.50 .45
T84 Albert Belle .60 .18
T85 Dean Palmer .60 .18
T86 Greg Vaughn .60 .18
T87 Mark Clark .40 .12
T88 Pat Meares .40 .12
T89 Eric Davis .60 .18
T90 Brian Giles .60 .18
T91 Jeff Brantley .40 .12
T92 Bret Boone .60 .18
T93 Ron Gant .60 .18
T94 Mike Cameron .60 .18
T95 Charles Johnson .60 .18
T96 Denny Neagle .40 .12
T97 Brian Hunter .40 .12
T98 Jose Hernandez .40 .12
T99 Rick Aguilera .40 .12
T100 Tony Batista .60 .18
T101 Roger Cedeno .40 .12
T102 C.Gubanich RC .50 .15
T103 Tim Belcher .40 .12
T104 Bruce Aven .40 .12
T105 Brian Daubach RC .75 .23
T106 Ed Sprague .40 .12
T107 Michael Tucker .40 .12
T108 Homer Bush .40 .12
T109 Armando Reynoso .40 .12
T110 Brook Fordyce .40 .12
T111 Matt Mantei .40 .12
T112 Dave Mlicki .40 .12
T113 Kenny Rogers .60 .18
T114 Livan Hernandez .40 .12
T115 Butch Huskey .40 .12
T116 David Segui .40 .12
T117 Darryl Hamilton .40 .12
T118 Terry Mulholland .40 .12
T119 Randy Velarde .40 .12
T120 Bill Taylor .40 .12
T121 Kevin Appier .60 .18

2000 Topps Chrome

These cards parallel the regular Topps set and are issued using Topps' Chromium technology and color metallization. The first series product was released in February, 2000 and second series in May, 2000. Four card packs for each series carried an SRP of $3.00. Similar to the regular set, no card number 7 was issued and a Mark McGwire rookie reprint card was also inserted into packs. Also, like the base Topps set all of the Magic Moments subset cards (235-239 and 475-479) are available in five variations - each detailing a different highlight in the featured player's career. The base Chrome set is considered complete with any of the Magic Moments variations (for each player). Notable Rookie Cards include Rick Asadoorian, Ben Sheets and Barry Zito.

Nm-Mt Ex-Mt
COMPLETE SET (478) 160.00 47.50
COMP. SERIES 1 (240) 80.00 24.00
COMP. SERIES 2 (240) 80.00 24.00
MCGWIRE MM SET (5) 50.00 15.00
AARON MM SET (5) 40.00 12.00
RIPKEN MM SET (5) 60.00 18.00
BOGGS MM SET (5) 12.00 3.60
GWYNN MM SET (5) 25.00 7.50
GRIFFEY MM SET (5) 30.00 9.00
BONDS MM SET (5) 50.00 15.00
SOSA MM SET (5) 30.00 9.00
JETER MM SET (5) 50.00 15.00
A.ROD MM SET (5) 40.00 12.00
1 Mark McGwire 5.00 1.50
2 Tony Gwynn 2.50 .75
3 Wade Boggs 1.25 .35
4 Cal Ripken 6.00 1.80
5 Matt Williams .75 .23
6 Jay Buhner .75 .23
7 Does Not Exist
8 Jeff Conine .75 .23
9 Todd Greene .75 .23
10 Mike Lieberthal .75 .23
11 Steve Avery .75 .23
12 Bret Saberhagen .75 .23
13 Magglio Ordonez .75 .23
14 Brad Radke .75 .23
15 Derek Jeter 5.00 1.50
16 Javy Lopez .75 .23
17 Russ Davis .75 .23
18 Armando Benitez .75 .23
19 B.J. Surhoff .75 .23
20 Darryl Kile .75 .23
21 Mark Lewis .75 .23
22 Mike Williams .75 .23
23 Mark McLemore .75 .23
24 Sterling Hitchcock .75 .23
25 Darin Erstad .75 .23
26 Ricky Gutierrez .75 .23
27 John Jaha .75 .23
28 Homer Bush .75 .23
29 Darrin Fletcher .75 .23
30 Mark Grace 1.25 .35
31 Fred McGriff 1.25 .35
32 Omar Daal .75 .23
33 Eric Karros .75 .23
34 Orlando Cabrera .75 .23
35 J.T. Snow .75 .23
36 Luis Castillo .75 .23
37 Rey Ordonez .75 .23
38 Bob Abreu .75 .23
39 Warren Morris .75 .23
40 Juan Gonzalez 2.00 .60
41 Mike Lansing .75 .23
42 Chili Davis .75 .23
43 Dean Palmer .75 .23
44 Hank Aaron 4.00 1.20
45 Jeff Bagwell 1.25 .35
46 Jose Valentin .75 .23
47 Shannon Stewart .75 .23
48 Kent Bottenfield .75 .23
49 Jeff Shaw .75 .23
50 Sammy Sosa 3.00 .90
51 Randy Johnson 2.00 .60
52 Benny Agbayani .75 .23
53 Dante Bichette .75 .23
54 Pete Harnisch .75 .23
55 Frank Thomas 2.00 .60
56 Jorge Posada 1.25 .35
57 Todd Walker .75 .23
58 Juan Encarnacion .75 .23
59 Mike Sweeney .75 .23
60 Pedro Martinez 2.00 .60
61 Lee Stevens .75 .23
62 Brian Giles .75 .23
63 Chad Ogea .75 .23
64 Ivan Rodriguez 2.00 .60
65 Roger Cedeno .75 .23
66 David Justice .75 .23
67 Steve Trachsel .75 .23

68 Eli Marrero .75 .23
69 Dave Nilsson .75 .23
70 Ken Caminiti .75 .23
71 Tim Raines .75 .23
72 Brian Jordan .75 .23
73 Jeff Blauser .75 .23
74 Bernard Gilkey .75 .23
75 John Flaherty .75 .23
76 Brent Mayne .75 .23
77 Jose Vidro .75 .23
78 David Bell .75 .23
79 Bruce Aven .75 .23
80 John Olerud .75 .23
81 Pokey Reese .75 .23
82 Woody Williams .75 .23
83 Ed Sprague .75 .23
84 Joe Girardi .75 .23
85 Barry Larkin 2.00 .60
86 Mike Caruso .75 .23
87 Bobby Higginson .75 .23
88 Roberto Kelly .75 .23
89 Edgar Martinez 1.25 .35
90 Mark Kotsay .75 .23
91 Paul Sorrento .75 .23
92 Eric Young .75 .23
93 Carlos Delgado .75 .23
94 Troy Glaus 1.25 .35
95 Ben Grieve .75 .23
96 Jose Lima .75 .23
97 Garret Anderson .75 .23
98 Luis Gonzalez .75 .23
99 Carl Pavano .75 .23
100 Alex Rodriguez 3.00 .90
101 Preston Wilson .75 .23
102 Ron Gant .75 .23
103 Brady Anderson .75 .23
104 Rickey Henderson 2.00 .60
105 Gary Sheffield .75 .23
106 Mickey Morandini .75 .23
107 Jim Edmonds .75 .23
108 Kris Benson .75 .23
109 Adrian Beltre .75 .23
110 Alex Fernandez .75 .23
111 Dan Wilson .75 .23
112 Mark Clark .75 .23
113 Greg Vaughn .75 .23
114 Neifi Perez .75 .23
115 Paul O'Neill 1.25 .35
116 Jermaine Dye .75 .23
117 Todd Jones .75 .23
118 Terry Steinbach .75 .23
119 Greg Norton .75 .23
120 Curt Schilling 1.25 .35
121 Todd Zeile .75 .23
122 Edgardo Alfonzo .75 .23
123 Ryan McGuire .75 .23
124 Rich Aurilia .75 .23
125 John Smoltz 1.25 .35
126 Bob Wickman .75 .23
127 Richard Hidalgo .75 .23
128 Chuck Finley .75 .23
129 Billy Wagner .75 .23
130 Todd Hundley .75 .23
131 Dwight Gooden 1.25 .35
132 Russ Ortiz .75 .23
133 Mike Lowell .75 .23
134 Reggie Sanders .75 .23
135 John Valentin .75 .23
136 Brad Ausmus .75 .23
137 Chad Kreuter .75 .23
138 David Cone .75 .23
139 Brook Fordyce .75 .23
140 Roberto Alomar 2.00 .60
141 Charles Nagy .75 .23
142 Brian Hunter .75 .23
143 Mike Mussina 2.00 .60
144 Robin Ventura 1.25 .35
145 Kevin Brown 1.25 .35
146 Pat Hentgen .75 .23
147 Ryan Klesko .75 .23
148 Derek Bell .75 .23
149 Andy Sheets .75 .23
150 Larry Walker .75 .23
151 Scott Williamson .75 .23
152 Jose Offerman .75 .23
153 Doug Mientkiewicz .75 .23
154 John Snyder RC 1.00 .30
155 Sandy Alomar Jr. .75 .23
156 Joe Nathan .75 .23
157 Lance Johnson .75 .23
158 Odalis Perez .75 .23
159 Hideo Nomo 2.00 .60
160 Steve Finley .75 .23
161 Dave Martinez .75 .23
162 Matt Walbeck .75 .23
163 Bill Spiers .75 .23
164 Fernando Tatis .75 .23
165 Kenny Lofton .75 .23
166 Paul Byrd .75 .23
167 Aaron Sele .75 .23
168 Eddie Taubensee .75 .23
169 Reggie Jefferson .75 .23
170 Roger Clemens 4.00 1.20
171 Francisco Cordova .75 .23
172 Mike Bordick .75 .23
173 Wally Joyner .75 .23
174 Marvin Benard .75 .23
175 Jason Kendall .75 .23
176 Mike Stanley .75 .23
177 Chad Allen .75 .23
178 Carlos Beltran .75 .23
179 Deivi Cruz .75 .23
180 Chipper Jones 2.00 .60
181 Vladimir Guerrero 2.00 .60
182 Dave Burba .75 .23
183 Tom Goodwin .75 .23
184 Brian Daubach .75 .23
185 Jay Bell .75 .23
186 Roy Halladay .75 .23
187 Miguel Tejada .75 .23
188 Armando Rios .75 .23
189 Fernando Vina .75 .23
190 Eric Davis .75 .23
191 Henry Rodriguez .75 .23
192 Joe McEwing .75 .23
193 Jeff Kent .75 .23
194 Mike Jackson .75 .23
195 Mike Morgan .75 .23
196 Jeff Montgomery .75 .23
197 Jeff Zimmerman .75 .23
198 Tony Fernandez .75 .23
199 Jason Giambi 2.00 .60
200 Jose Canseco 2.00 .60
201 Alex Gonzalez .75 .23
202 Jack Cust 1.00 .30
Mike Colangelo
Dee Brown
203 Felipe Lopez 2.00 .60
Alfonso Soriano
Pablo Ozuna
204 Erubiel Durazo 2.50 .75
Pat Burrell
Nick Johnson
205 John Sneed RC 1.00 .30
Kip Wells
Matt Blank
206 Josh Kalinowski 1.50 .45
Michael Tejera
Chris Mears RC
207 Roosevelt Brown 1.50 .45
Corey Patterson
Lance Berkman
208 Kit Pellow 1.00 .30
Kevin Barker
Russ Branyan
209 B.J. Garbe 2.50 .75
Larry Bigbie RC
210 Eric Munson 1.50 .45
Bobby Bradley RC
211 Josh Girdley 1.00 .30
Kyle Snyder
212 Chance Caple RC 1.50 .45
Jason Jennings
213 Ryan Christianson 8.00 2.40
Brett Myers RC
214 Jason Stumm 1.50 .45
Rob Purvis RC
215 David Walling 1.50 .45
Mike Paradis
216 Omar Ortiz 1.00 .30
Jay Gehrke
217 David Cone HL .75 .23
218 Jose Jimenez HL .75 .23
219 Chris Singleton HL .75 .23
220 Fernando Tatis HL .75 .23
221 Todd Helton HL .75 .23
222 Kevin Millwood DIV .75 .23
223 Todd Pratt DIV .75 .23
224 Orl. Hernandez DIV .75 .23
225 Pedro Martinez DIV 1.25 .35
226 Tom Glavine LCS .75 .23
227 Bernie Williams LCS .75 .23
228 Mariano Rivera WS .75 .23
229 Tony Gwynn 20CB 2.50 .75
230 Wade Boggs 20CB 1.25 .35
231 Lance Johnson CB .75 .23
232 Mark McGwire 20CB 5.00 1.50
233 R.Henderson 20CB 2.00 .60
234 R.Henderson 20CB 2.00 .60
235 Roger Clemens 20CB 4.00 1.20
236A Mark McGwire MM 12.00 3.60
1st HR
236B Mark McGwire MM 12.00 3.60
1987 ROY
236C Mark McGwire MM 12.00 3.60
62nd HR
236D Mark McGwire MM 12.00 3.60
70th HR
236E Mark McGwire MM 12.00 3.60
500th HR
237A Hank Aaron MM 10.00 3.00
1st Career HR
237B Hank Aaron MM 10.00 3.00
1957 MVP
237C Hank Aaron MM 10.00 3.00
3000th Hit
237D Hank Aaron MM 10.00 3.00
715th HR
237E Hank Aaron 10.00 3.00
MM 755th HR
238A Cal Ripken MM 15.00 4.50
1982 ROY
238B Cal Ripken MM 15.00 4.50
1991 MVP
238C Cal Ripken MM 15.00 4.50
2131 Game
238D Cal Ripken MM 15.00 4.50
Streak Ends
238E Cal Ripken MM 15.00 4.50
400th HR
239A Wade Boggs MM 3.00 .90
1983 Batting
239B Wade Boggs MM 3.00 .90
1988 Batting
239C Wade Boggs MM 3.00 .90
2000th Hit
239D Wade Boggs MM 3.00 .90
1996 Champs
239E Wade Boggs MM 3.00 .90
3000th Hit
240A Tony Gwynn MM 6.00 1.80
1984 Batting
240B Tony Gwynn MM 6.00 1.80
1984 NLCS
240C Tony Gwynn MM 6.00 1.80
1995 Batting
240D Tony Gwynn MM 6.00 1.80
1998 NLCS
240E Tony Gwynn MM 6.00 1.80
3000th Hit
241 Tom Glavine 1.25 .35
242 David Wells .75 .23
243 Kevin Appier .75 .23
244 Troy Percival .75 .23
245 Ray Lankford .75 .23
246 Marquis Grissom .75 .23
247 Randy Winn .75 .23
248 Miguel Batista .75 .23
249 Darren Dreifort .75 .23
250 Barry Bonds 4.00 1.20
251 Harold Baines .75 .23
252 Cliff Floyd .75 .23
253 Freddy Garcia .75 .23
254 Kenny Rogers .75 .23
255 Ben Davis .75 .23
256 Charles Johnson .75 .23
257 Bubba Trammell .75 .23
258 Desi Relaford .75 .23
259 Al Martin .75 .23
260 Andy Pettitte 1.25 .35
261 Carlos Lee .75 .23
262 Matt Lawton .75 .23
263 Andy Fox .75 .23
264 Chan Ho Park .75 .23
265 Billy Koch .75 .23
266 Dave Roberts .75 .23
267 Carl Everett .75 .23
268 Orel Hershiser .75 .23
269 Trot Nixon 1.25 .35
270 Rusty Greer .75 .23
271 Will Clark 2.00 .60
272 Quilvio Veras .75 .23
273 Rico Brogna .75 .23
274 Devon White .75 .23
275 Tim Hudson 1.25 .35
276 Mike Hampton .75 .23
277 Miguel Cairo .75 .23
278 Darren Oliver .75 .23
279 Jeff Cirillo .75 .23
280 Al Leiter .75 .23
281 Shane Andrews .75 .23
282 Carlos Febles .75 .23
283 Pedro Astacio .75 .23
284 Juan Guzman .75 .23
285 Orlando Hernandez .75 .23
286 Paul Konerko .75 .23
287 Tony Clark .75 .23
288 Aaron Boone .75 .23
289 Ismael Valdes .75 .23
290 Moises Alou .75 .23
291 Kevin Tapani .75 .23
292 John Franco .75 .23
293 Todd Zeile .75 .23
294 Jason Schmidt .75 .23
295 Johnny Damon .75 .23
296 Scott Brosius .75 .23
297 Travis Fryman .75 .23
298 Jose Vizcaino .75 .23
299 Eric Chavez .75 .23
300 Mike Piazza 3.00 .90
301 Matt Clement .75 .23
302 Cristian Guzman .75 .23
303 C.J. Nitkowski .75 .23
304 Michael Tucker .75 .23
305 Brett Tomko .75 .23
306 Mike Lansing .75 .23
307 Eric Owens .75 .23
308 Livan Hernandez .75 .23
309 Rondell White .75 .23
310 Todd Stottlemyre .75 .23
311 Chris Carpenter .75 .23
312 Ken Hill .75 .23
313 Mark Loretta .75 .23
314 John Rocker .75 .23
315 Richie Sexson .75 .23
316 Ruben Mateo .75 .23
317 Joe Randa .75 .23
318 Mike Sirotka .75 .23
319 Jose Rosado .75 .23
320 Matt Mantei .75 .23
321 Kevin Millwood .75 .23
322 Gary DiSarcina .75 .23
323 Dustin Hermanson .75 .23
324 Mike Stanton .75 .23
325 Kirk Rueter .75 .23
326 Damian Miller RC 2.00 .60
327 Doug Glanville .75 .23
328 Scott Rolen 1.25 .35
329 Ray Durham .75 .23
330 Butch Huskey .75 .23
331 Mariano Rivera 1.25 .35
332 Darren Lewis .75 .23
333 Mike Timlin .75 .23
334 Mark Grudzielanek .75 .23
335 Mike Cameron .75 .23
336 Kelvim Escobar .75 .23
337 Bret Boone .75 .23
338 Mo Vaughn .75 .23
339 Craig Biggio 1.25 .35
340 Michael Barrett .75 .23
341 Marlon Anderson .75 .23
342 Bobby Jones .75 .23
343 John Halama .75 .23
344 Todd Ritchie .75 .23
345 Chuck Knoblauch .75 .23
346 Rick Reed .75 .23
347 Kelly Stinnett .75 .23
348 Tim Salmon 1.25 .35
349 A.J. Hinch .75 .23
350 Jose Cruz Jr. .75 .23
351 Roberto Hernandez .75 .23
352 Edgar Renteria .75 .23
353 Jose Hernandez .75 .23
354 Brad Fullmer .75 .23
355 Trevor Hoffman .75 .23
356 Troy O'Leary .75 .23
357 Justin Thompson .75 .23
358 Kevin Young .75 .23
359 Hideki Irabu .75 .23
360 Jim Thome 2.00 .60
361 Steve Karsay .75 .23
362 Octavio Dotel .75 .23
363 Omar Vizquel .75 .23
364 Raul Mondesi .75 .23
365 Shane Reynolds .75 .23
366 Bartolo Colon .75 .23
367 Chris Widger .75 .23
368 Gabe Kapler .75 .23
369 Bill Simas .75 .23
370 Tino Martinez 1.25 .35
371 John Thomson .75 .23
372 Delino DeShields .75 .23
373 Carlos Perez .75 .23
374 Eddie Perez .75 .23
375 Jeromy Burnitz .75 .23
376 Jimmy Haynes .75 .23
377 Travis Lee .75 .23
378 Darryl Hamilton .75 .23
379 Jamie Moyer .75 .23
380 Alex Gonzalez .75 .23
381 John Wetteland .75 .23
382 Vinny Castilla .75 .23
383 Jeff Suppan .75 .23
384 Jim Leyritz .75 .23
385 Robb Nen .75 .23
386 Wilson Alvarez .75 .23
387 Andres Galarraga .75 .23
388 Mike Remlinger .75 .23
389 Geoff Jenkins .75 .23
390 Matt Stairs .75 .23
391 Bill Mueller .75 .23
392 Mike Lowell .75 .23
393 Andy Ashby .75 .23
394 Ruben Rivera .75 .23
395 Todd Helton 1.25 .35
396 Bernie Williams 1.25 .35
397 Royce Clayton .75 .23
398 Manny Ramirez .75 .23
399 Kerry Wood 2.00 .60
400 Ken Griffey Jr. 3.00 .90
401 Enrique Wilson .75 .23
402 Joey Hamilton .75 .23
403 Shawn Estes .75 .23
404 Ugueth Urbina .75 .23
405 Albert Belle .75 .23
406 Rick Helling .75 .23
407 Steve Parris .75 .23
408 Eric Milton .75 .23
409 Dave Mlicki .75 .23
410 Shawn Green .75 .23
411 Jaret Wright .75 .23
412 Tony Womack .75 .23
413 Vernon Wells .75 .23
414 Ron Belliard .75 .23
415 Ellis Burks .75 .23
416 Scott Erickson .75 .23
417 Rafael Palmeiro 1.25 .35
418 Damion Easley .75 .23
419 Jamey Wright .75 .23
420 Corey Koskie .75 .23
421 Bobby Howry .75 .23
422 Ricky Ledee .75 .23
423 Dmitri Young .75 .23
424 Sidney Ponson .75 .23
425 Greg Maddux 3.00 .90
426 Jose Guillen .75 .23
427 Jon Lieber .75 .23
428 Andy Benes .75 .23
429 Randy Velarde .75 .23
430 Sean Casey .75 .23
431 Torii Hunter .75 .23
432 Ryan Rupe .75 .23
433 David Segui .75 .23
434 Todd Pratt .75 .23
435 Nomar Garciaparra 3.00 .90
436 Denny Neagle .75 .23
437 Ron Coomer .75 .23
438 Chris Singleton .75 .23
439 Tony Batista .75 .23
440 Andruw Jones .75 .23
441 Aubrey Huff .75 .23
Sean Burroughs
Adam Piatt
442 Rafael Furcal 1.50 .45
Travis Dawkins
Jason Dellaero
443 Mike Lamb RC 1.50 .45
Joe Crede
Wilton Veras
444 Julio Zuleta RC 1.50 .45
Jorge Toca
Dernell Stenson
445 Garry Maddox Jr. RC 1.00 .30
Gary Matthews Jr.
Tim Raines Jr.
446 Mark Mulder 2.50 .75
C.C. Sabathia
Matt Riley
447 Scott Downs RC 1.00 .30
Chris George
Matt Belisle
448 Doug Mirabelli 1.00 .30
Ben Petrick
Jayson Werth
449 Josh Hamilton 1.50 .45
Corey Myers RC
450 Ben Christensen RC 1.50 .45
Richard Stahl
451 Ben Sheets RC 10.00 3.00
Barry Zito RC
452 Kurt Ainsworth 4.00 1.20
Ty Howington RC
453 Vince Faison RC 1.50 .45
Rick Asadoorian
454 Keith Reed RC 1.50 .45
Jeff Heaverlo
455 Mike MacDougal 2.50 .75
Brad Baker RC
456 Mark McGwire SH 2.50 .75
457 Cal Ripken SH 3.00 .90
458 Wade Boggs SH .75 .23
459 Tony Gwynn SH 1.25 .35
460 Jesse Orosco SH .75 .23
461 Larry Walker 1.25 .35
Nomar Garciaparra LL
462 Ken Griffey Jr. 2.00 .60
Mark McGwire LL
463 Manny Ramirez 2.00 .60
Mark McGwire LL
464 Pedro Martinez 1.25 .35
Randy Johnson LL
465 Pedro Martinez 1.25 .35
Randy Johnson LL
466 Derek Jeter 2.00 .60
Luis Gonzalez LL
467 Larry Walker .75 .23
Manny Ramirez LL
468 Tony Gwynn 20CB 2.50 .75
469 Mark McGwire 20CB 5.00 1.50
470 Frank Thomas 20CB 2.00 .60
471 Harold Baines 20CB .75 .23
472 Roger Clemens 20CB 4.00 1.20
473 John Franco 20CB .75 .23
474 John Franco 20CB .75 .23
475A Ken Griffey Jr. MM 8.00 2.40
350th HR
475B Ken Griffey Jr. MM 8.00 2.40
1997 MVP
475C Ken Griffey Jr. MM 8.00 2.40
HR Dad
475D Ken Griffey Jr. MM 8.00 2.40
1992 AS MVP
475E Ken Griffey Jr. MM 8.00 2.40
50 HR 1997
476A Barry Bonds MM 12.00 3.60
400HR/400SB
476B Barry Bonds MM 12.00 3.60
40HR/40SB
476C Barry Bonds MM 12.00 3.60
1993 MVP
476D Barry Bonds MM 12.00 3.60
1990 MVP
476E Barry Bonds MM 12.00 3.60
1992 MVP
477A Sammy Sosa 8.00 2.40
MM 20 HR June
477B Sammy Sosa MM 8.00 2.40
66 HR 1998
477C Sammy Sosa MM 8.00 2.40
60 HR 1999
477D Sammy Sosa MM 8.00 2.40
1998 MVP
477E Sammy Sosa MM 8.00 2.40
HR's 61/62
478A Derek Jeter MM 12.00 3.60
1996 ROY
478B Derek Jeter MM 12.00 3.60
Wins 1999 WS
478C Derek Jeter MM 12.00 3.60
Wins 1998 WS
478D Derek Jeter MM 12.00 3.60
Wins 1996 WS
478E Derek Jeter MM 12.00 3.60
17 GM Hit Streak
479A Alex Rodriguez MM 10.00 3.00
40HR/40SB
479B Alex Rodriguez MM 10.00 3.00
100th HR
479C Alex Rodriguez 10.00 3.00
MM 1996 POY
479D Alex Rodriguez 10.00 3.00
MM Wins 1 Million
479E Alex Rodriguez MM 10.00 3.00
1996 Batting Leader
NNO M.McGwire 85 Reprint 8.00 2.40

2000 Topps Chrome Refractors

These cards which parallel the regular Topps Chrome set were issued at a rate of one in 12 packs. The Mark McGwire rookie reprint card was issued at a rate of one in 12,116 first series packs and are serial numbered to 70.

Nm-Mt Ex-Mt
*STARS: 2.5X TO 6X BASIC CARDS ...
*PROSPECTS 202-216: 2.5X TO 6X BASIC
*ROOKIES 202-216: 2X TO 5X BASIC.
*PROSPECTS 441-455: 2.5X TO 6X BASIC
*ROOKIES 441-455: 2X TO 5X BASIC.
MCGWIRE MM SET (5) 150.00 45.00
MCGWIRE MM (236A-236E) 40.00 12.00
AARON MM SET (5) 120.00 36.00
AARON MM (237A-237E) 30.00 9.00
RIPKEN MM SET (5) 200.00 60.00
RIPKEN MM (238A-238E) 50.00 15.00
BOGGS MM SET (5) 40.00 12.00
BOGGS MM (239A-239E) 10.00 3.00
GWYNN MM SET (5) 80.00 24.00
GWYNN MM (240A-240E) 20.00 6.00
GRIFFEY MM SET (5) 100.00 30.00
GRIFFEY MM (475A-475E) 25.00 7.50
BONDS MM SET (5) 150.00 45.00
BONDS MM (476A-476E) 40.00 12.00
SOSA MM SET (5) 100.00 30.00
SOSA MM (477A-477E) 25.00 7.50
JETER MM SET (5) 150.00 45.00
JETER MM (478A-478E) 40.00 12.00
A.ROD MM SET (5) 120.00 36.00
A.ROD MM (479A-479E) 30.00 9.00

2000 Topps Chrome 21st Century

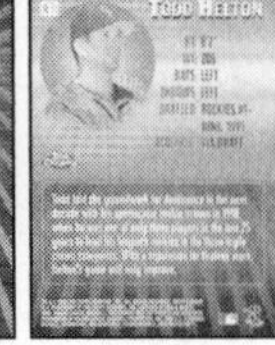

Inserted at a rate of one in 16, this 10 cards feature players who are expected to be the best in the first part of the 21st century. Card backs carry a "C" prefix.

Nm-Mt Ex-Mt
COMPLETE SET (10) 40.00 12.00
*REF: 1X TO 2.5X BASIC 21ST CENT..
SER.1 REFRACTOR ODDS 1:80..........
C1 Ben Grieve 1.50 .45
C2 Alex Gonzalez 1.50 .45
C3 Derek Jeter 10.00 3.00
C4 Sean Casey 1.50 .45
C5 Nomar Garciaparra 6.00 1.80
C6 Alex Rodriguez 6.00 1.80
C7 Scott Rolen 2.50 .75
C8 Andruw Jones 1.50 .45
C9 Vladimir Guerrero 4.00 1.20
C10 Todd Helton 2.50 .75

2000 Topps Chrome All-Star Rookie Team

Randomly inserted into packs at one in 16, this 10-card insert set features players that made the All-Star game their rookie season. Card backs carry a "RT" prefix.

Nm-Mt Ex-Mt
COMPLETE SET (10) 50.00 15.00
*REF: 1X TO 2.5X BASIC ASR TEAM ..
REFRACTOR STATED ODDS 1:80 ....
RT1 Mark McGwire 10.00 3.00
RT2 Chuck Knoblauch 1.50 .45
RT3 Chipper Jones 4.00 1.20
RT4 Cal Ripken 12.00 3.60
RT5 Manny Ramirez 1.50 .45

RT6 Jose Canseco 4.00 1.20
RT7 Ken Griffey Jr. 6.00 1.80
RT8 Mike Piazza 6.00 1.80
RT9 Dwight Gooden 2.50 .75
RT10 Billy Wagner 1.50 .45

2000 Topps Chrome All-Topps

Inserted at a rate of one in 32 first and second series packs, these 10 cards feature the best players in the American and National Leagues. National League cards 91-10) were distributed in series one and American league (11-20) in series two. Card backs carry an "AT" prefix.

Nm-Mt Ex-Mt
COMPLETE SET (20) 160.00 47.50
COMPLETE N.L. (10) 80.00 24.00
COMPLETE A.L.(10) 80.00 24.00
*REFRACTORS: 1X TO 2.5X BASIC ALL NL
REFRACTOR ODDS 1:160
AT1 Greg Maddux 10.00 3.00
AT2 Mike Piazza 10.00 3.00
AT3 Mark McGwire 15.00 4.50
AT4 Craig Biggio 4.00 1.20
AT5 Chipper Jones 6.00 1.80
AT6 Barry Larkin 6.00 1.80
AT7 Barry Bonds 12.00 3.60
AT8 Andruw Jones 2.50 .75
AT9 Sammy Sosa 10.00 3.00
AT10 Larry Walker 2.50 .75
AT11 Pedro Martinez 6.00 1.80
AT12 Ivan Rodriguez 6.00 1.80
AT13 Rafael Palmeiro 4.00 1.20
AT14 Roberto Alomar 6.00 1.80
AT15 Cal Ripken 20.00 6.00
AT16 Derek Jeter 15.00 4.50
AT17 Albert Belle 2.50 .75
AT18 Ken Griffey Jr. 10.00 3.00
AT19 Manny Ramirez 2.50 .75
AT20 Jose Canseco 6.00 1.80

2000 Topps Chrome Allegiance

This Topps Chrome exclusive set features 20 players who have spent their entire career with just one team. The Allegiance cards were issued at a rate of one in 16 and have a "TA" prefix.

Nm-Mt Ex-Mt
COMPLETE SET (20) 120.00 36.00
*REF: 4X TO 10X BASIC ALLEGIANCE
SER.1 REFRACTOR ODDS 1:424 HOBBY
REFRACTOR PRINT RUN 100 SERIAL #'d SETS
TA1 Derek Jeter 15.00 4.50
TA2 Ivan Rodriguez 6.00 1.80
TA3 Alex Rodriguez 10.00 3.00
TA4 Cal Ripken 20.00 6.00
TA5 Mark Grace 4.00 1.20
TA6 Tony Gwynn 8.00 2.40
TA7 Tom Glavine 4.00 1.20
TA8 Frank Thomas 6.00 1.80
TA9 Manny Ramirez 2.50 .75
TA10 Barry Larkin 6.00 1.80
TA11 Bernie Williams 4.00 1.20
TA12 Eric Karros 2.50 .75
TA13 Vladimir Guerrero 6.00 1.80
TA14 Craig Biggio 4.00 1.20
TA15 Nomar Garciaparra 10.00 3.00
TA16 Andruw Jones 2.50 .75
TA17 Jim Thome 6.00 1.80
TA18 Scott Rolen 4.00 1.20
TA19 Chipper Jones 6.00 1.80
TA20 Ken Griffey Jr. 10.00 3.00

2000 Topps Chrome Combos

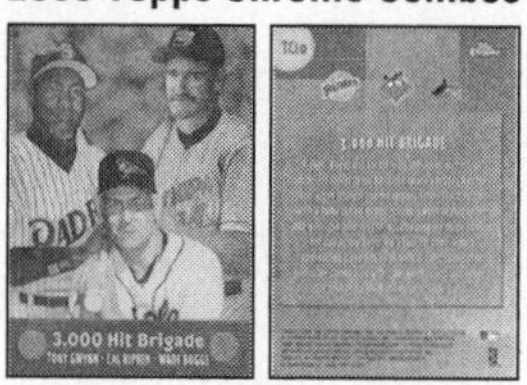

Randomly inserted into series two packs at one in 16, this 10-card insert features a variety of player combinations, such as the 1999 MVP's. Card backs carry a "TC" prefix.

Nm-Mt Ex-Mt
COMPLETE SET (10) 80.00 24.00
*REFRACTORS: 1X TO 2.5X BASIC COMBO
REFRACTOR ODDS 1:80
TC1 Roberto Alomar 1.50 .45
Manny Ramirez
Kenny Lofton
Jim Thome
TC2 Tom Glavine 6.00 1.80
Greg Maddux
John Smoltz
TC3 Derek Jeter 10.00 3.00
Bernie Williams
Tino Martinez
TC4 Ivan Rodriguez 6.00 1.80
Mike Piazza
TC5 Nomar Garciaparra 10.00 3.00
Alex Rodriguez
Derek Jeter
TC6 Sammy Sosa 10.00 3.00
Mark McGwire
TC7 Pedro Martinez 4.00 1.20
Randy Johnson
TC8 Barry Bonds 6.00 1.80
Ken Griffey Jr.
TC9 Chipper Jones 4.00 1.20
Ivan Rodriguez
TC10 Cal Ripken 12.00 3.60
Tony Gwynn
Wade Boggs

2000 Topps Chrome Kings

Randomly inserted into series two packs at one in 32, this 10-card insert features some of the greatest players in major league baseball. Card backs carry a "CK" prefix.

Nm-Mt Ex-Mt
COMPLETE SET (10) 80.00 24.00
CK1 Mark McGwire 15.00 4.50
CK2 Sammy Sosa 10.00 3.00
CK3 Ken Griffey Jr. 10.00 3.00
CK4 Mike Piazza 10.00 3.00
CK5 Alex Rodriguez 10.00 3.00
CK6 Manny Ramirez 2.50 .75
CK7 Barry Bonds 12.00 3.60
CK8 Nomar Garciaparra 10.00 3.00
CK9 Chipper Jones 6.00 1.80
CK10 Vladimir Guerrero 6.00 1.80

2000 Topps Chrome Kings Refractors

Randomly inserted into series two packs at one in 514, this 10-card insert is a complete parallel of the Chrome Kings insert. Each card was produced using Topps' "refractor" technology. Please note that each card was serial numbered to the amount of homeruns that the individual players had after the 1999 season. Production runs are listed below. Card backs carry a "CK" prefix.

Nm-Mt Ex-Mt
COMPLETE SET (10) 300.00 90.00
CK1 Mark McGwire/522 30.00 9.00
CK2 Sammy Sosa/366 25.00 7.50
CK3 Ken Griffey Jr./398 25.00 7.50
CK4 Mike Piazza/240 25.00 7.50
CK5 Alex Rodriguez/148 50.00 15.00
CK6 Manny Ramirez/198 10.00 3.00
CK7 Barry Bonds/445 25.00 7.50
CK8 N.Garciaparra/96 50.00 15.00
CK9 Chipper Jones/153 20.00 6.00
CK10 V.Guerrero/92 40.00 12.00

2000 Topps Chrome New Millennium Stars

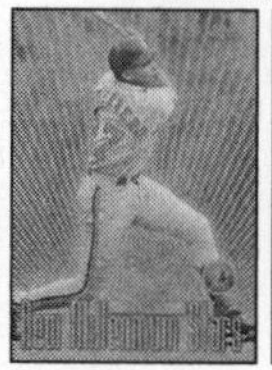
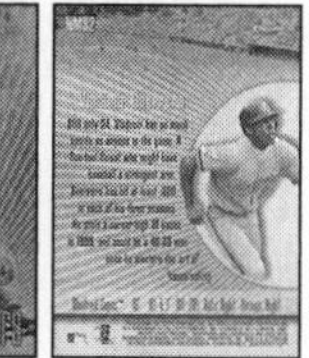

Randomly inserted into series two packs at one in 32, this 10-card insert features some of the major league's hottest young talent. Card backs carry a "NMS" prefix.

Nm-Mt Ex-Mt
COMPLETE SET (10) 40.00 12.00
*REFRACTORS: 1X TO 2.5X BASIC MILL.
SER.2 REFRACTOR ODDS 1:160
NMS1 Nomar Garciaparra 10.00 3.00
NMS2 Vladimir Guerrero 6.00 1.80
NMS3 Sean Casey 2.50 .75
NMS4 Richie Sexson 2.50 .75
NMS5 Todd Helton 4.00 1.20
NMS6 Carlos Beltran 2.50 .75
NMS7 Kevin Millwood 2.50 .75
NMS8 Ruben Mateo 2.50 .75
NMS9 Pat Burrell 8.00 2.40
NMS10 Alfonso Soriano 2.50 .75

2000 Topps Chrome Own the Game

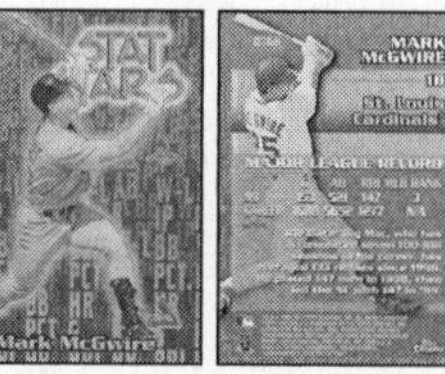

Randomly inserted into series two packs at one in 11, this 30-card insert features players that are amoung the major league's statistical leaders year after year. Card backs carry an "OTG" prefix.

Nm-Mt Ex-Mt
COMPLETE SET (30) 200.00 60.00
*REFRACTORS: 1X TO 2.5X BASIC OWN
SER.2 REFRACTOR ODDS 1:55
OTG1 Derek Jeter 15.00 4.50
OTG2 B.J. Surhoff 2.50 .75
OTG3 Luis Gonzalez 2.50 .75
OTG4 Manny Ramirez 2.50 .75
OTG5 Rafael Palmeiro 4.00 1.20
OTG6 Mark McGwire 15.00 4.50
OTG7 Mark McGwire 15.00 4.50
OTG8 Sammy Sosa 10.00 3.00
OTG9 Ken Griffey Jr. 10.00 3.00
OTG10 Larry Walker 2.50 .75
OTG11 Nomar Garciaparra 10.00 3.00
OTG12 Derek Jeter 15.00 4.50
OTG13 Larry Walker 2.50 .75
OTG14 Mark McGwire 15.00 4.50
OTG15 Manny Ramirez 2.50 .75
OTG16 Pedro Martinez 6.00 1.80
OTG17 Randy Johnson 6.00 1.80
OTG18 Kevin Millwood 2.50 .75
OTG19 Randy Johnson 6.00 1.80
OTG20 Pedro Martinez 6.00 1.80
OTG21 Kevin Brown 4.00 1.20
OTG22 Chipper Jones 6.00 1.80
OTG23 Ivan Rodriguez 6.00 1.80
OTG24 Mariano Rivera 4.00 1.20
OTG25 Scott Williamson 2.50 .75
OTG26 Carlos Beltran 2.50 .75
OTG27 Randy Johnson 6.00 1.80
OTG28 Pedro Martinez 6.00 1.80
OTG29 Sammy Sosa 10.00 3.00
OTG30 Manny Ramirez 2.50 .75

2000 Topps Chrome Power Players

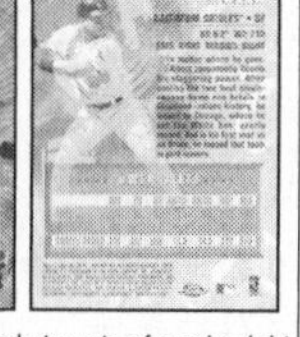

This 20 card set, issued at a rate of one in eight packs, features players who are the leading power hitters in the majors. Card backs carry a "P" prefix.

Nm-Mt Ex-Mt
COMPLETE SET (20) 100.00 30.00
*REFRACTORS: 1X TO 2.5X BASIC POWER
SER.1 REFRACTOR ODDS 1:40
P1 Juan Gonzalez 4.00 1.20
P2 Ken Griffey Jr. 6.00 1.80
P3 Mark McGwire 10.00 3.00
P4 Nomar Garciaparra 6.00 1.80
P5 Barry Bonds 8.00 2.40
P6 Mo Vaughn 1.50 .45
P7 Larry Walker 1.50 .45
P8 Alex Rodriguez 6.00 1.80
P9 Jose Canseco 4.00 1.20
P10 Jeff Bagwell 2.50 .75
P11 Manny Ramirez 1.50 .45
P12 Albert Belle 1.50 .45
P13 Frank Thomas 4.00 1.20
P14 Mike Piazza 6.00 1.80
P15 Chipper Jones 4.00 1.20
P16 Sammy Sosa 6.00 1.80
P17 Vladimir Guerrero 4.00 1.20
P18 Scott Rolen 2.50 .75
P19 Raul Mondesi 1.50 .45
P20 Derek Jeter 10.00 3.00

2000 Topps Chrome Traded

The 2000 Topps Chrome Traded set was released in late November, 2000 and features a 135-card base set. The set is an exact parallel of the Topps Traded set.This set was produced using Topps' chrome technology. Please note that card backs carry a "T" prefix. Each set came with 135 cards and carried a $99.99 suggested retail price. Notable Rookie Cards include Cristian Guerrero and J.R. House.

Nm-Mt Ex-Mt
COMP.FACT.SET (135) 70.00 21.00
T1 Mike MacDougal 1.00 .30
T2 Andy Tracy RC .50 .15
T3 Brandon Phillips RC 2.00 .60
T4 Brandon Inge RC .75 .23
T5 Robbie Morrison RC .50 .15
T6 Josh Pressley RC .75 .23
T7 Todd Moser RC .50 .15
T8 Rob Purvis .75 .23
T9 Chance Caple .75 .23
T10 Ben Sheets 2.00 .60
T11 Russ Jacobson RC .50 .15
T12 Brian Cole RC .75 .23
T13 Brad Baker .75 .23
T14 Alex Cintron RC 3.00 .90
T15 Lyle Overbay RC 1.00 .30
T16 Mike Edwards RC .50 .15
T17 Sean McGowan RC .50 .15
T18 Jose Molina .50 .15
T19 Marcos Castillo RC .75 .23
T20 Josue Espada RC .50 .15
T21 Alex Gordon RC .75 .23
T22 Rob Pugmire RC .75 .23
T23 Jason Stumm .75 .23
T24 Ty Howington .75 .23
T25 Brett Myers 3.00 .90
T26 Maicer Izturis RC .75 .23
T27 John McDonald .50 .15
T28 W.Rodriguez RC .75 .23
T29 Carlos Zambrano RC 4.00 1.20
T30 Alejandro Diaz RC .75 .23
T31 Geraldo Guzman RC .50 .15
T32 J.R. House RC .75 .23
T33 Elvin Nina RC .50 .15
T34 Juan Pierre RC 6.00 1.80
T35 Ben Johnson RC .75 .23
T36 Jeff Bailey RC .50 .15
T37 Miguel Olivo RC .75 .23
T38 F.Rodriguez RC 3.00 .90
T39 Tony Pena Jr. RC .75 .23
T40 Miguel Cabrera RC 50.00 15.00
T41 Asdrubal Oropeza RC .75 .23
T42 Junior Zamora RC .75 .23
T43 Jovanny Cedeno RC .75 .23
T44 John Sneed .75 .23
T45 Josh Kalinowski .75 .23
T46 Mike Young RC 5.00 1.50
T47 Rico Washington RC .75 .23
T48 Chad Durbin RC .50 .15
T49 Junior Brignac RC .75 .23
T50 Carlos Hernandez RC .75 .23
T51 Cesar Izturis RC .75 .23
T52 Oscar Salazar RC .75 .23
T53 Pat Strange RC .75 .23
T54 Rick Asadoorian .75 .23
T55 Keith Reed .75 .23
T56 Leo Estrella RC .50 .15
T57 Wascar Serrano RC .75 .23
T58 Richard Gomez RC .50 .15
T59 Ramon Santiago RC .75 .23
T60 Jovanny Sosa RC .75 .23
T61 Aaron Rowand RC .75 .23
T62 Junior Guerrero RC .75 .23
T63 Luis Terrero RC .75 .23
T64 Brian Sanches RC .75 .23
T65 Scott Sobkowiak RC .50 .15
T66 Gary Majewski RC .75 .23
T67 Barry Zito 4.00 1.20
T68 Ryan Christianson .75 .23
T69 Cristian Guerrero RC .75 .23
T70 T.De La Rosa RC .50 .15
T71 Andrew Beinbrink RC .50 .15
T72 Ryan Knox RC .50 .15
T73 Alex Graman RC .50 .15
T74 Juan Guzman RC .75 .23
T75 Ruben Salazar RC .75 .23
T76 Luis Matos RC 3.00 .90
T77 Tony Mota RC .50 .15
T78 Doug Davis .50 .15
T79 Ben Christensen 1.25 .35
T80 Mike Lamb .75 .23
T81 Adrian Gonzalez RC 3.00 .90
T82 Mike Stodolka RC .75 .23
T83 Adam Johnson RC .75 .23
T84 Matt Wheatland RC .50 .15
T85 Corey Smith RC 1.00 .30
T86 Rocco Baldelli RC 15.00 4.50
T87 Keith Bucktrot RC .50 .15
T88 Adam Wainwright RC 3.00 .90
T89 Scott Thorman RC 1.00 .30
T90 Tripper Johnson RC 1.00 .30
T91 Jim Edmonds .75 .23
T92 Masato Yoshii .50 .15
T93 Adam Kennedy .50 .15
T94 Darryl Kile .75 .23
T95 Mark McLemore .50 .15
T96 Ricky Gutierrez .50 .15
T97 Juan Gonzalez 2.00 .60
T98 Melvin Mora .75 .23
T99 Dante Bichette .75 .23
T100 Lee Stevens .50 .15
T101 Roger Cedeno .50 .15
T102 John Olerud .75 .23
T103 Eric Young .50 .15
T104 Mickey Morandini .50 .15
T105 Travis Lee .50 .15
T106 Greg Vaughn .75 .23
T107 Todd Zeile .75 .23
T108 Chuck Finley .75 .23
T109 Ismael Valdes .50 .15
T110 Reggie Sanders .75 .23
T111 Pat Hentgen .50 .15
T112 Ryan Klesko .75 .23
T113 Derek Bell .50 .15
T114 Hideo Nomo 2.00 .60
T115 Aaron Sele .50 .15
T116 Fernando Vina .75 .23
T117 Wally Joyner .75 .23
T118 Brian Hunter .50 .15
T119 Joe Girardi .50 .15
T120 Omar Daal .50 .15
T121 Brook Fordyce .50 .15
T122 Jose Valentin .50 .15
T123 Curt Schilling 1.25 .35
T124 B.J. Surhoff .75 .23
T125 Henry Rodriguez .50 .15
T126 Mike Bordick .50 .15
T127 David Justice .75 .23
T128 Charles Johnson .75 .23
T129 Will Clark 2.00 .60
T130 Dwight Gooden 1.25 .35
T131 David Segui .50 .15
T132 Denny Neagle .75 .23
T133 Jose Canseco 2.00 .60
T134 Bruce Chen .50 .15
T135 Jason Bere .50 .15

2001 Topps Chrome

The 2001 Topps Chrome product was released in two separate series. The first series shipped in February 2001, and features a 331-card base set produced with Topps' special chrome technology. This set parallels the regular 2001 Topps base set in card design and photography but card numbering differs due to the fact that the manufacturer decided to select only the best 331 cards of the 405 card basic Topps set to be featured in this upgraded Chrome product. Each Topps Chrome pack contains four cards, and carried a suggested retail price of $2.99. Please note, card number 7 does not exist. The number was retired in Topps and Topps Chrome brands back in 1996 in honor of Yankees legend Mickey Mantle. Notable Rookie Cards include Hee Seop Choi.

Nm-Mt Ex-Mt
COMPLETE SET (661) 300.00 90.00
COMP. SERIES 1 (331) 150.00 45.00
COMP. SERIES 2 (330) 150.00 45.00
1 Cal Ripken 6.00 1.80
2 Chipper Jones 2.00 .60
3 Roger Cedeno .50 .15
4 Garret Anderson .75 .23
5 Robin Ventura .75 .23
6 Daryle Ward .50 .15
7 Does Not Exist
8 Phil Nevin .75 .23
9 Jermaine Dye .75 .23
10 Chris Singleton .50 .15
11 Mike Redmond .50 .15
12 Jim Thome 2.00 .60
13 Brian Jordan .75 .23
14 Dustin Hermanson .50 .15
15 Shawn Green .75 .23
16 Todd Stottlemyre .50 .15
17 Dan Wilson .50 .15
18 Derek Lowe .75 .23
19 Juan Gonzalez 2.00 .60
20 Pat Meares .50 .15
21 Paul O'Neill 1.25 .35
22 Jeffrey Hammonds .50 .15
23 Pokey Reese .50 .15
24 Mike Mussina 2.00 .60
25 Rico Brogna .50 .15
26 Jay Buhner .75 .23
27 Steve Cox .50 .15
28 Quilvio Veras .50 .15
29 Marquis Grissom .50 .15
30 Shigetoshi Hasegawa .75 .23
31 Shane Reynolds .50 .15
32 Adam Piatt .50 .15
33 Preston Wilson .75 .23
34 Ellis Burks .75 .23
35 Armando Rios .50 .15
36 Chuck Finley .75 .23
37 Shannon Stewart .75 .23
38 Mark McGwire 5.00 1.50
39 Gerald Williams .50 .15
40 Eric Young .50 .15
41 Peter Bergeron .50 .15
42 Arthur Rhodes .50 .15
43 Bobby Jones .50 .15
44 Matt Clement .75 .23
45 Pedro Martinez 2.00 .60
46 Jose Canseco 2.00 .60
47 Matt Anderson .50 .15
48 Torii Hunter .75 .23
49 Carlos Lee .75 .23
50 Eric Chavez .75 .23
51 Rick Helling .50 .15
52 John Franco .75 .23
53 Mike Bordick .75 .23
54 Andres Galarraga .75 .23
55 Jose Cruz Jr. .75 .23
56 Mike Matheny .50 .15
57 Randy Johnson 2.00 .60
58 Richie Sexson .75 .23
59 Vladimir Nunez .50 .15
60 Aaron Boone .75 .23
61 Darin Erstad .75 .23
62 Alex Gonzalez .50 .15
63 Gil Heredia .50 .15
64 Shane Andrews .50 .15
65 Todd Hundley .50 .15
66 Bill Mueller .75 .23
67 Mark McLemore .50 .15
68 Scott Spiezio .50 .15
69 Kevin McGlinchy .50 .15
70 Manny Ramirez .75 .23
71 Mike Lamb .50 .15
72 Brian Buchanan .50 .15
73 Mike Sweeney .75 .23
74 John Wetteland .75 .23
75 Rob Bell .50 .15
76 John Burkett .50 .15
77 Derek Jeter 5.00 1.50
78 J.D. Drew .75 .23
79 Jose Offerman .50 .15
80 Rick Reed .50 .15
81 Will Clark 2.00 .60
82 Rickey Henderson 2.00 .60
83 Kirk Rueter .50 .15
84 Lee Stevens .50 .15
85 Jay Bell .75 .23
86 Fred McGriff 1.25 .35
87 Julio Zuleta .50 .15
88 Brian Anderson .50 .15
89 Orlando Cabrera .50 .15
90 Alex Fernandez .50 .15
91 Derek Bell .50 .15
92 Eric Owens .50 .15
93 Dennys Reyes .50 .15
94 Mike Stanley .50 .15
95 Jorge Posada 1.25 .35
96 Paul Konerko .75 .23
97 Mike Remlinger .50 .15
98 Travis Lee .50 .15
99 Ken Caminiti .75 .23
100 Kevin Barker .50 .15
101 Ozzie Guillen .50 .15
102 Randy Wolf .75 .23
103 Michael Tucker .50 .15
104 Darren Lewis .50 .15
105 Joe Randa .50 .15
106 Jeff Cirillo .50 .15
107 David Ortiz .75 .23
108 Herb Perry .50 .15

109 Jeff Nelson .50 .15
110 Chris Stynes .50 .15
111 Johnny Damon .75 .23
112 Jason Schmidt .75 .23
113 Charles Johnson .50 .15
114 Pat Burrell .75 .23
115 Gary Sheffield .75 .23
116 Tom Glavine 1.25 .35
117 Jason Isringhausen .50 .15
118 Chris Carpenter .50 .15
119 Jeff Suppan .50 .15
120 Ivan Rodriguez 2.00 .60
121 Luis Sojo .50 .15
122 Ron Villone .50 .15
123 Mike Sirotka .50 .15
124 Chuck Knoblauch .75 .23
125 Jason Kendall .75 .23
126 Bobby Estalella .50 .15
127 Jose Guillen .50 .15
128 Carlos Delgado .75 .23
129 Benji Gil .50 .15
130 Einar Diaz .50 .15
131 Andy Benes .50 .15
132 Adrian Beltre .75 .23
133 Roger Clemens 4.00 1.20
134 Scott Williamson .50 .15
135 Brad Penny .50 .15
136 Troy Glaus 1.25 .35
137 Kevin Appier .75 .23
138 Walt Weiss .50 .15
139 Michael Barrett .50 .15
140 Mike Hampton .75 .23
141 Francisco Cordova .50 .15
142 David Segui .50 .15
143 Carlos Febles .50 .15
144 Roy Halladay .75 .23
145 Seth Etherton .50 .15
146 Fernando Tatis .50 .15
147 Livan Hernandez .50 .15
148 B.J. Surhoff .75 .23
149 Barry Larkin 2.00 .60
150 Bobby Howry .50 .15
151 Dmitri Young .75 .23
152 Brian Hunter .50 .15
153 A.Rodriguez Rangers 3.00 .90
154 Hideo Nomo 2.00 .60
155 Warren Morris .50 .15
156 Antonio Alfonseca .50 .15
157 Edgardo Alfonzo .75 .23
158 Mark Grudzielanek .50 .15
159 Fernando Vina .75 .23
160 Homer Bush .50 .15
161 Jason Giambi 2.00 .60
162 Steve Karsay .50 .15
163 Matt Lawton .50 .15
164 Rusty Greer .75 .23
165 Billy Koch .50 .15
166 Todd Hollandsworth .50 .15
167 Raul Ibanez .50 .15
168 Tony Gwynn 2.50 .75
169 Carl Everett .75 .23
170 Hector Carrasco .50 .15
171 Jose Valentin .50 .15
172 Deivi Cruz .50 .15
173 Bret Boone .75 .23
174 Melvin Mora .50 .15
175 Danny Graves .50 .15
176 Jose Jimenez .50 .15
177 James Baldwin .50 .15
178 C.J. Nitkowski .50 .15
179 Jeff Zimmerman .50 .15
180 Mike Lowell .75 .23
181 Hideki Irabu .50 .15
182 Greg Vaughn .75 .23
183 Omar Daal .50 .15
184 Darren Dreifort .50 .15
185 Gil Meche .75 .23
186 Damian Jackson .50 .15
187 Frank Thomas 2.00 .60
188 Luis Castillo .75 .23
189 Bartolo Colon .75 .23
190 Craig Biggio 1.25 .35
191 Scott Schoeneweis .50 .15
192 Dave Veres .50 .15
193 Ramon Martinez .50 .15
194 Jose Vidro .75 .23
195 Todd Helton 1.25 .35
196 Greg Norton .50 .15
197 Jacque Jones .75 .23
198 Jason Grimsley .50 .15
199 Dan Reichert .50 .15
200 Robb Nen .75 .23
201 Scott Hatteberg .50 .15
202 Terry Shumpert .50 .15
203 Kevin Millar .75 .23
204 Ismael Valdes .50 .15
205 Richard Hidalgo .75 .23
206 Randy Velarde .50 .15
207 Bengie Molina .50 .15
208 Tony Womack .50 .15
209 Enrique Wilson .50 .15
210 Jeff Brantley .50 .15
211 Rick Ankiel .50 .15
212 Terry Mulholland .50 .15
213 Ron Belliard .50 .15
214 Terrence Long .75 .23
215 Alberto Castillo .50 .15
216 Royce Clayton .50 .15
217 Joe McEwing .50 .15
218 Jason McDonald .50 .15
219 Ricky Bottalico .50 .15
220 Keith Foulke .50 .15
221 Brad Radke .75 .23
222 Gabe Kapler .50 .15
223 Pedro Astacio .50 .15
224 Armando Reynoso .50 .15
225 Darryl Kile .75 .23
226 Reggie Sanders .75 .23
227 Esteban Yan .50 .15
228 Joe Nathan .50 .15
229 Jay Payton .50 .15
230 Francisco Cordero .50 .15
231 Gregg Jefferies .50 .15
232 LaTroy Hawkins .50 .15
233 Jacob Cruz .50 .15
234 Chris Holt .50 .15
235 Vladimir Guerrero 2.00 .60
236 Marvin Benard .50 .15
237 Alex Ramirez .50 .15
238 Mike Williams .50 .15
239 Sean Bergman .50 .15
240 Juan Encarnacion .50 .15
241 Russ Davis .50 .15
242 Ramon Hernandez .50 .15
243 Sandy Alomar Jr. .50 .15
244 Eddie Guardado .75 .23
245 Shane Halter .50 .15
246 Geoff Jenkins .75 .23
247 Brian Meadows .50 .15
248 Damian Miller .50 .15
249 Darrin Fletcher .50 .15
250 Rafael Furcal .75 .23
251 Mark Grace 1.25 .35
252 Mark Mulder .75 .23
253 Joe Torre MG .75 .23
254 Bobby Cox MG .75 .23
255 Mike Scioscia MG .50 .15
256 Mike Hargrove MG .50 .15
257 Jimy Williams MG .50 .15
258 Jerry Manuel MG .50 .15
259 Charlie Manuel MG .50 .15
260 Don Baylor MG .75 .23
261 Phil Garner MG .50 .15
262 Tony Muser MG .50 .15
263 Buddy Bell MG .75 .23
264 Tom Kelly MG .50 .15
265 John Boles MG .50 .15
266 Art Howe MG .50 .15
267 Larry Dierker MG .50 .15
268 Lou Piniella MG .75 .23
269 Larry Rothschild MG .50 .15
270 Davey Lopes MG .75 .23
271 Johnny Oates MG .50 .15
272 Felipe Alou MG .50 .15
273 Bobby Valentine MG .50 .15
274 Tony LaRussa MG .50 .15
275 Bruce Bochy MG .50 .15
276 Dusty Baker MG .75 .23
277 Adrian Gonzalez 1.50 .45
Adam Johnson
278 Matt Wheatland 1.00 .30
Bryan Digby
279 Tripper Johnson 1.00 .30
Scott Thorman
280 Phil Dumatrait 1.50 .45
Adam Wainwright
281 Scott Heard 1.50 .45
David Parrish RC
282 Rocco Baldelli 8.00 2.40
Mark Folsom
283 Dominic Rich RC 1.50 .45
Aaron Herr
284 Mike Stodolka 1.50 .45
Sean Burnett
285 Derek Thompson 1.00 .30
Corey Smith
286 Danny Borrell 1.50 .45
Jason Bourgeois RC
287 Chin-Feng Chen 1.50 .45
Corey Patterson
Josh Hamilton
288 Ryan Anderson 3.00 .90
Barry Zito
C.C. Sabathia
289 Scott Sobkowiak 1.50 .45
David Walling
Ben Sheets
290 Ty Howington 1.00 .30
Josh Kalinowski
Josh Girdley
291 Hee Seop Choi 10.00 3.00
Aaron McNeal
Jason Hart
292 Bobby Bradley 1.50 .45
Kurt Ainsworth
Chin-Hui Tsao
293 Mike Glendenning 1.00 .30
Kenny Kelly
Juan Silvestre
294 J.R. House 1.00 .30
Ramon Castro
Ben Davis
295 Chance Caple 5.00 1.50
Rafael Soriano
Pasqual Coco
296 Travis Hafner RC 5.00 1.50
Eric Munson
Bucky Jacobsen
297 Jason Conti 1.50 .45
Chris Wakeland
Brian Cole
298 Scott Seabol 1.50 .45
Aubrey Huff
Joe Crede
299 Adam Everett 1.00 .30
Jose Ortiz
Keith Ginter
300 Carlos Hernandez 1.00 .30
Geraldo Guzman
Adam Eaton
301 Bobby Kielty 1.00 .30
Milton Bradley
Juan Rivera
302 Mark McGwire GM 2.50 .75
303 Don Larsen GM .75 .23
304 Bobby Thomson GM .75 .23
305 Bill Mazeroski GM .75 .23
306 Reggie Jackson GM 1.25 .35
307 Kirk Gibson GM .75 .23
308 Roger Maris GM 2.00 .60
309 Cal Ripken GM 3.00 .90
310 Hank Aaron GM 2.00 .60
311 Joe Carter GM .75 .23
312 Cal Ripken SH 3.00 .90
313 Randy Johnson SH 1.25 .35
314 Ken Griffey Jr. SH 2.00 .60
315 Troy Glaus SH 1.25 .35
316 Kazuhiro Sasaki SH .75 .23
317 Sammy Sosa 1.25 .35
Troy Glaus LL
318 Todd Helton .75 .23
Edgar Martinez LL
319 Todd Helton 2.00 .60
Nomar Garicaparra LL
320 Barry Bonds 2.00 .60
Jason Giambi LL
321 Todd Helton 1.25 .35
Manny Ramirez LL
322 Todd Helton .75 .23
Darin Erstad LL
323 Kevin Brown 1.25 .35
Pedro Martinez LL
324 Randy Johnson 1.25 .35
Pedro Martinez LL
325 Will Clark HL 2.00 .60
326 New York Mets HL 2.00 .60
327 New York Yankees HL 3.00 .90
328 Seattle Mariners HL .75 .23
329 Mike Hampton HL .75 .23
330 New York Yankees HL 4.00 1.20
331 N.Y. Yankees Champs 8.00 2.40
332 Jeff Bagwell 1.25 .35
333 Andy Pettitte 1.25 .35
334 Tony Armas Jr. .50 .15
335 Jeromy Burnitz .75 .23
336 Javier Vazquez .75 .23
337 Eric Karros .75 .23
338 Brian Giles .75 .23
339 Scott Rolen 1.25 .35
340 David Justice .75 .23
341 Ray Durham .75 .23
342 Todd Zeile .75 .23
343 Cliff Floyd .75 .23
344 Barry Bonds 5.00 1.50
345 Matt Williams .75 .23
346 Steve Finley .75 .23
347 Scott Elarton .50 .15
348 Bernie Williams 1.25 .35
349 David Wells .75 .23
350 J.T. Snow .75 .23
351 Al Leiter .75 .23
352 Magglio Ordonez .75 .23
353 Raul Mondesi .75 .23
354 Tim Salmon 1.25 .35
355 Jeff Kent .75 .23
356 Mariano Rivera 1.25 .35
357 John Olerud .75 .23
358 Javy Lopez .75 .23
359 Ben Grieve .50 .15
360 Ray Lankford .50 .15
361 Ken Griffey Jr. 3.00 .90
362 Rich Aurilia .75 .23
363 Andruw Jones .75 .23
364 Ryan Klesko .75 .23
365 Roberto Alomar 2.00 .60
366 Miguel Tejada .75 .23
367 Mo Vaughn .75 .23
368 Albert Belle .75 .23
369 Jose Canseco 2.00 .60
370 Kevin Brown .75 .23
371 Rafael Palmeiro 1.25 .35
372 Mark Redman .50 .15
373 Larry Walker 1.25 .35
374 Greg Maddux 3.00 .90
375 Nomar Garciaparra 3.00 .90
376 Kevin Millwood .75 .23
377 Edgar Martinez 1.25 .35
378 Sammy Sosa 3.00 .90
379 Tim Hudson .75 .23
380 Jim Edmonds .75 .23
381 Mike Piazza 3.00 .90
382 Brant Brown .50 .15
383 Brad Fullmer .50 .15
384 Alan Benes .50 .15
385 Mickey Morandini .50 .15
386 Troy Percival .75 .23
387 Eddie Perez .50 .15
388 Vernon Wells .75 .23
389 Ricky Gutierrez .50 .15
390 Rondell White .75 .23
391 Kelvim Escobar .50 .15
392 Tony Batista .75 .23
393 Jimmy Haynes .50 .15
394 Billy Wagner .75 .23
395 A.J. Hinch .50 .15
396 Matt Morris .75 .23
397 Lance Berkman .75 .23
398 Jeff D'Amico .50 .15
399 Octavio Dotel .50 .15
400 Olmedo Saenz .50 .15
401 Esteban Loaiza .75 .23
402 Adam Kennedy .50 .15
403 Moises Alou .75 .23
404 Orlando Palmeiro .50 .15
405 Kevin Young .50 .15
406 Tom Goodwin .50 .15
407 Mac Suzuki .50 .15
408 Pat Hentgen .50 .15
409 Kevin Stocker .50 .15
410 Mark Sweeney .50 .15
411 Tony Eusebio .50 .15
412 Edgar Renteria .75 .23
413 John Rocker .50 .15
414 Jose Lima .50 .15
415 Kerry Wood 2.00 .60
416 Mike Timlin .50 .15
417 Jose Hernandez .50 .15
418 Jeremy Giambi .50 .15
419 Luis Lopez .50 .15
420 Mitch Meluskey .50 .15
421 Garrett Stephenson .50 .15
422 Jamey Wright .50 .15
423 John Jaha .50 .15
424 Placido Polanco .50 .15
425 Marty Cordova .50 .15
426 Joey Hamilton .50 .15
427 Travis Fryman .75 .23
428 Mike Cameron .75 .23
429 Matt Mantei .50 .15
430 Chan Ho Park .75 .23
431 Shawn Estes .50 .15
432 Danny Bautista .50 .15
433 Wilson Alvarez .50 .15
434 Kenny Lofton .75 .23
435 Russ Ortiz .75 .23
436 Dave Burba .50 .15
437 Felix Martinez .50 .15
438 Jeff Shaw .50 .15
439 Mike DiFelice .50 .15
440 Roberto Hernandez .50 .15
441 Bryan Rekar .50 .15
442 Ugueth Urbina .50 .15
443 Vinny Castilla .75 .23
444 Carlos Perez .50 .15
445 Juan Guzman .50 .15
446 Ryan Rupe .50 .15
447 Mike Mordecai .50 .15
448 Ricardo Rincon .50 .15
449 Curt Schilling 1.25 .35
450 Alex Cora .50 .15
451 Turner Ward .50 .15
452 Omar Vizquel .75 .23
453 Russ Branyan .50 .15
454 Russ Johnson .50 .15
455 Greg Colbrunn .50 .15
456 Charles Nagy .50 .15
457 Wil Cordero .50 .15
458 Jason Tyner .50 .15
459 Devon White .50 .15
460 Kelly Stinnett .50 .15
461 Wilton Guerrero .50 .15
462 Jason Bere .50 .15
463 Calvin Murray .50 .15
464 Miguel Batista .50 .15
466 Luis Gonzalez .75 .23
467 Jaret Wright .50 .15
468 Chad Kreuter .50 .15
469 Armando Benitez .75 .23
470 Erubiel Durazo .50 .15
470 Sidney Ponson .50 .15
471 Adrian Brown .50 .15
472 Sterling Hitchcock .50 .15
473 Timo Perez .50 .15
474 Jamie Moyer .75 .23
475 Delino DeShields .50 .15
476 Glendon Rusch .50 .15
477 Chris Gomez .50 .15
478 Adam Eaton .50 .15
479 Pablo Ozuna .50 .15
480 Bob Abreu .75 .23
481 Kris Benson .50 .15
482 Keith Osik .50 .15
483 Darryl Hamilton .50 .15
484 Marlon Anderson .50 .15
485 Jimmy Anderson .50 .15
486 John Halama .50 .15
487 Nelson Figueroa .50 .15
488 Alex Gonzalez .50 .15
489 Benny Agbayani .50 .15
490 Ed Sprague .50 .15
491 Scott Erickson .50 .15
492 Doug Glanville .50 .15
493 Jesus Sanchez .50 .15
494 Mike Lieberthal .75 .23
495 Aaron Sele .50 .15
496 Pat Mahomes .50 .15
497 Ruben Rivera .50 .15
498 Wayne Gomes .50 .15
499 Freddy Garcia .75 .23
500 Al Martin .50 .15
501 Woody Williams .50 .15
502 Paul Byrd .50 .15
503 Rick White .50 .15
504 Trevor Hoffman .75 .23
505 Brady Anderson .75 .23
506 Robert Person .50 .15
507 Jeff Conine .75 .23
508 Chris Truby .50 .15
509 Emil Brown .50 .15
510 Ryan Dempster .50 .15
511 Ruben Mateo .50 .15
512 Alex Ochoa .50 .15
513 Jose Rosado .50 .15
514 Masato Yoshii .50 .15
515 Brian Daubach .50 .15
516 Jeff D'Amico .50 .15
517 Brent Mayne .50 .15
518 John Thomson .50 .15
519 Todd Ritchie .50 .15
520 John VanderWal .50 .15
521 Neifi Perez .50 .15
522 Chad Curtis .50 .15
523 Kenny Rogers .75 .23
524 Trot Nixon 1.25 .35
525 Sean Casey .75 .23
526 Wilton Veras .50 .15
527 Troy O'Leary .50 .15
528 Dante Bichette .75 .23
529 Jose Silva .50 .15
530 Darren Oliver .50 .15
531 Steve Parris .50 .15
532 David McCarty .50 .15
533 Todd Walker .75 .23
534 Brian Rose .50 .15
535 Pete Schourek .50 .15
536 Ricky Ledee .50 .15
537 Justin Thompson .50 .15
538 Benito Santiago .75 .23
539 Carlos Beltran .75 .23
540 Gabe White .50 .15
541 Bret Saberhagen .75 .23
542 Ramon Martinez .50 .15
543 John Valentin .50 .15
544 Frank Catalanotto .50 .15
545 Tim Wakefield .75 .23
546 Michael Tucker .50 .15
547 Juan Pierre .75 .23
548 Rich Garces .50 .15
549 Luis Ordaz .50 .15
550 Jerry Spradlin .50 .15
551 Corey Koskie .75 .23
552 Cal Eldred .50 .15
553 Alfonso Soriano 1.25 .35
554 Kip Wells .50 .15
555 Orlando Hernandez .75 .23
556 Bill Simas .50 .15
557 Jim Parque .50 .15
558 Joe Mays .50 .15
559 Tim Belcher .50 .15
560 Shane Spencer .75 .23
561 Glenallen Hill .50 .15
562 Matt LeCroy .50 .15
563 Tino Martinez 1.25 .35
564 Eric Milton .50 .15
565 Ron Coomer .50 .15
566 Cristian Guzman .75 .23
567 Kazuhiro Sasaki .75 .23
568 Mark Quinn .50 .15
569 Eric Gagne 1.25 .35
570 Kerry Ligtenberg .50 .15
571 Rolando Arrojo .50 .15
572 Jon Lieber .50 .15
573 Jose Vizcaino .50 .15
574 Jeff Abbott .50 .15
575 Carlos Hernandez .50 .15
576 Scott Sullivan .50 .15
577 Matt Stairs .50 .15
578 Tom Lampkin .50 .15
579 Donnie Sadler .50 .15
580 Desi Relaford .50 .15
581 Scott Downs .50 .15
582 Mike Mussina 2.00 .60
583 Ramon Ortiz .50 .15
584 Mike Myers .50 .15
585 Frank Castillo .50 .15
586 Manny Ramirez .75 .23
587 Alex Rodriguez 3.00 .90
588 Andy Ashby .50 .15
589 Felipe Crespo .50 .15
590 Bobby Bonilla .75 .23
591 Denny Neagle .50 .15
592 Dave Martinez .50 .15
593 Mike Hampton .75 .23
594 Gary DiSarcina .50 .15
595 Tsuyoshi Shinjo RC 4.00 1.20
596 Albert Pujols RC 50.00 15.00
597 Roy Oswalt 2.00 .60
Pat Strange
Jon Rauch
598 Phil Wilson RC 5.00 1.50
Jake Peavy RC
Darwin Cubillan RC
599 Nathan Haynes 1.50 .45
Steve Smyth RC
Mike Bynum
600 Joe Lawrence 1.00 .30
Choo Freeman
Michael Cuddyer
601 Larry Barnes 1.00 .30
DeWayne Wise
Carlos Pena
602 Feilpe Lopez 1.50 .45
Gookie Dawkins
Eric Almonte RC
603 Brad Wilkerson 1.00 .30
Alex Escobar
Eric Valent
604 Jeff Goldbach 1.00 .30
Toby Hall
Rod Barajas
605 Marcus Giles 1.50 .45
Pablo Ozuna
Jason Romano
606 Vernon Wells 1.50 .45
Jack Cust
Dee Brown
607 Luis Montanez RC 1.50 .45
David Espinosa
608 Anthony Pluta RC 2.00 .60
Justin Wayne RC
609 Josh Axelson RC 1.50 .45
Carmen Cali RC
610 Shaun Boyd RC 1.50 .45
Chris Morris RC
611 Dan Moylan RC 1.50 .45
Tommy Arko RC
612 Luis Cotto RC 1.50 .45
Luis Escobar
613 Blake Williams RC 1.50 .45
Brandon Mims RC
614 Chris Russ RC 1.50 .45
Bryan Edwards
615 Joe Torres 1.00 .30
Ben Diggins
616 Hugh Quattlebaum RC 2.00 .60
Edwin Encarnacion RC
617 Brian Bass RC 1.50 .45
Odannis Ayala RC
618 Jason Kaanoi 1.00 .30
Michael Matthews RC UER
name misspelled Mathews
619 Stuart McFarland RC 1.50 .45
Adam Sterrett RC
620 David Krynzel 4.00 1.20
Grady Sizemore
621 Keith Bucktrot 1.00 .30
Dane Sardinha
622 Anaheim Angels TC .75 .23
623 Ariz. Diamondbacks TC .75 .23
624 Atlanta Braves TC .75 .23
625 Baltimore Orioles TC .75 .23
626 Boston Red Sox TC .75 .23
627 Chicago Cubs TC .75 .23
628 Chicago White Sox TC .75 .23
629 Cincinnati Reds TC .75 .23
630 Cleveland Indians TC .75 .23
631 Colorado Rockies TC .75 .23
632 Detroit Tigers TC .75 .23
633 Florida Marlins TC .75 .23
634 Houston Astros TC .75 .23
635 K.C. Royals TC .75 .23
636 L.A. Dodgers TC .75 .23
637 Milw. Brewers TC .75 .23
638 Minnesota Twins TC .75 .23
639 Montreal Expos TC .75 .23
640 New York Mets TC .75 .23
641 New York Yankees TC 4.00 1.20
642 Oakland Athletics TC .75 .23
643 Phil. Phillies TC .75 .23
644 Pittsburgh Pirates TC .75 .23
645 San Diego Padres TC .75 .23
646 S.F. Giants TC .75 .23
647 Seattle Mariners TC .75 .23
648 St. Louis Cardinals TC .75 .23
649 T. Bay Devil Rays TC .75 .23
650 Texas Rangers TC .75 .23
651 Toronto Blue Jays TC .75 .23
652 Bucky Dent GM .50 .15
653 Jackie Robinson GM 1.25 .35
654 Roberto Clemente GM 2.50 .75
655 Nolan Ryan GM 3.00 .90
656 Kerry Wood GM 1.25 .35
657 Rickey Henderson GM 2.00 .60
658 Lou Brock GM 1.25 .35
659 David Wells GM .50 .15
660 Andruw Jones GM .50 .15
661 Carlton Fisk GM .75 .23

2001 Topps Chrome Retrofractors

Randomly inserted into packs at one in 12, this 661-card set is a complete parallel set of the 2001 Topps Chrome base set. Please note that these cards were produced with Topps Refractor technology.

Nm-Mt Ex-Mt
*STARS: 2.5X TO 6X BASIC CARDS ...
*PROSPECTS 277-301/595-621: 2X TO 5X
*ROOKIES 277-301/595-621: 2X TO 5X

2001 Topps Chrome Before There Was Topps

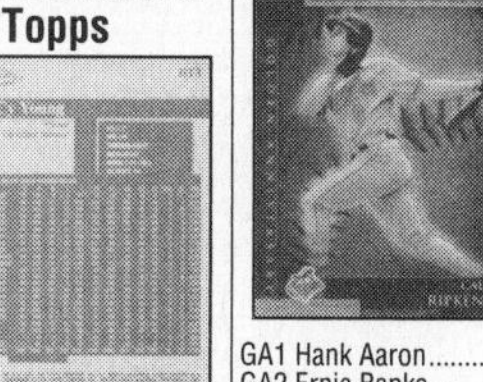

This set parallels the regular Before There Was Topps insert cards. These cards were inserted at a rate of one in 20 2001 Topps Chrome series two hobby/retail packs.

	Nm-Mt	Ex-Mt
COMPLETE SET (10)	80.00	24.00
*REFRACTORS: 1.25X TO 3X BASIC BEFORE		
SER.2 REFRACTOR ODDS 1:200 HOB/RET		
BT1 Lou Gehrig	12.00	3.60
BT2 Babe Ruth	20.00	6.00
BT3 Cy Young	6.00	1.80
BT4 Walter Johnson	6.00	1.80
BT5 Ty Cobb	10.00	3.00
BT6 Rogers Hornsby	6.00	1.80
BT7 Honus Wagner	6.00	1.80
BT8 Christy Mathewson	6.00	1.80
BT9 Grover Alexander	6.00	1.80
BT10 Joe DiMaggio	12.00	3.60

2001 Topps Chrome Combos

Randomly insert into packs at 1:12 Hobby/Retail and 1:4 HTA, this 10-card insert pairs up players that have put up similar statistics throughout their careers. Card backs carry a "TC" prefix. Please note that these cards feature Topps' special chrome technology.

	Nm-Mt	Ex-Mt
COMPLETE SET (20)	120.00	36.00
COMPLETE SERIES 1 (10)	60.00	18.00
COMPLETE SERIES 2 (10)	60.00	18.00
*REFRACTORS: 1.5X TO 4X BASIC COMBO		
REFRACTOR ODDS 1:120 H/R		
TC1 Derek Jeter	10.00	3.00
Yogi Berra		
Whitey Ford		
Don Mattingly		
Reggie Jackson		
TC2 Chipper Jones	3.00	.90
Mike Schmidt		
TC3 Brooks Robinson	8.00	2.40
Cal Ripken		
TC4 Bob Gibson	3.00	.90
Pedro Martinez		
TC5 Ivan Rodriguez	3.00	.90
Johnny Bench		
TC6 Ernie Banks	5.00	1.50
Alex Rodriguez		
TC7 Joe Morgan	3.00	.90
Ken Griffey Jr.		
Barry Larkin		
Johnny Bench		
TC8 Vladimir Guerrero	3.00	.90
Roberto Clemente		
TC9 Ken Griffey Jr.	5.00	1.50
Hank Aaron		
TC10 Casey Stengel MG	3.00	.90
Joe Torre		
TC11 Kevin Brown	6.00	1.80
Sandy Koufax		
Don Drysdale UER		
Card states the Dodgers swept the 1965 World Series		
They won the Series in 7 games		
TC12 Mark McGwire	8.00	2.40
Sammy Sosa		
Roger Maris		
Babe Ruth		
TC13 Ted Williams	5.00	1.50
Carl Yastrzemski		
Nomar Garciaparra		
TC14 Greg Maddux	5.00	1.50
Roger Clemens		
Cy Young		
TC15 Tony Gwynn	6.00	1.80
Ted Williams		
TC16 Cal Ripken	10.00	3.00
Lou Gehrig		
TC17 Sandy Koufax	10.00	3.00
Randy Johnson		
Warren Spahn		
Steve Carlton		
TC18 Mike Piazza	4.00	1.20
Josh Gibson		
TC19 Barry Bonds	8.00	2.40
Willie Mays		
TC20 Jackie Robinson	4.00	1.20
Larry Doby		

2001 Topps Chrome Golden Anniversary

Randomly inserted into packs at 1:10 Hobby/Retail, this 50-card insert celibrates Topp's 50th Anniversary by taking a look at some of the all-time greats. Card backs carry a "GA" prefix. Please note that these cards feature Topps' special chrome technology.

	Nm-Mt	Ex-Mt
COMPLETE SET (50)	300.00	90.00
*REFRACTORS: 1.5X TO 4X BASIC ANNV.		
SER.1 REFRACTOR ODDS 1:100		
GA1 Hank Aaron	10.00	3.00
GA2 Ernie Banks	5.00	1.50
GA3 Mike Schmidt	10.00	3.00
GA4 Willie Mays	10.00	3.00
GA5 Johnny Bench	5.00	1.50
GA6 Tom Seaver	3.00	.90
GA7 Frank Robinson	3.00	.90
GA8 Sandy Koufax	15.00	4.50
GA9 Bob Gibson	3.00	.90
GA10 Ted Williams	12.00	3.60
GA11 Cal Ripken	15.00	4.50
GA12 Tony Gwynn	6.00	1.80
GA13 Mark McGwire	12.00	3.60
GA14 Ken Griffey Jr.	8.00	2.40
GA15 Greg Maddux	8.00	2.40
GA16 Roger Clemens	10.00	3.00
GA17 Barry Bonds	12.00	3.60
GA18 Rickey Henderson	5.00	1.50
GA19 Mike Piazza	8.00	2.40
GA20 Jose Canseco	5.00	1.50
GA21 Derek Jeter	12.00	3.60
GA22 Nomar Garciaparra	8.00	2.40
GA23 Alex Rodriguez	8.00	2.40
GA24 Sammy Sosa	8.00	2.40
GA25 Ivan Rodriguez	5.00	1.50
GA26 Vladimir Guerrero	5.00	1.50
GA27 Chipper Jones	5.00	1.50
GA28 Jeff Bagwell	3.00	.90
GA29 Pedro Martinez	5.00	1.50
GA30 Randy Johnson	5.00	1.50
GA31 Pat Burrell	2.00	.60
GA32 Josh Hamilton	2.00	.60
GA33 Ryan Anderson	2.00	.60
GA34 Corey Patterson	2.00	.60
GA35 Eric Munson	2.00	.60
GA36 Sean Burroughs	2.00	.60
GA37 C.C. Sabathia	2.00	.60
GA38 Chin-Feng Chen	2.00	.60
GA39 Barry Zito	5.00	1.50
GA40 Adrian Gonzalez	2.00	.60
GA41 Mark McGwire	12.00	3.60
GA42 Nomar Garciaparra	8.00	2.40
GA43 Todd Helton	3.00	.90
GA44 Matt Williams	2.00	.60
GA45 Troy Glaus	3.00	.90
GA46 Geoff Jenkins	2.00	.60
GA47 Frank Thomas	5.00	1.50
GA48 Mo Vaughn	2.00	.60
GA49 Barry Larkin	5.00	1.50
GA50 J.D. Drew	2.00	.60

2001 Topps Chrome King Of Kings

Randomly inserted into packs at 1:5,157 series one hobby and 1:5,209 series one retail and 1:6383 series two hobby and 1:6,520 series two retail, this seven-card insert features game-used memorabilia from major superstars. Please note that a special fourth card containing game-used memorabilia of all three were inserted into Hobby packs at 1:59,220. Card backs carry a "KKR" prefix.

	Nm-Mt	Ex-Mt
KKR1 Hank Aaron	120.00	36.00
KKR2 Nolan Ryan Rangers	200.00	60.00
KKR3 Rickey Henderson	50.00	15.00
KKR4 Does Not Exist		
KKR5 Bob Gibson	50.00	15.00
KKR6 Nolan Ryan Angels	200.00	60.00
KKGE Hank Aaron		
Nolan Ryan		
Rickey Henderson		

2001 Topps Chrome King Of Kings Refractors

This insert is a complete parallel of the Chrome King of Kings insert set produced with Topps patented refractor technology. The first three cards were randomly inserted exclusively into first series hobby packs at 1:16,920. Cards 5 and 6 were randomly seeded exclusively into second series hobby packs at a rate of 1:23,022. Card number 4 in the set (intended to feature Mark McGwire) was never produced. Only ten of each card was printed and each is hand-numbered in thein blue pen on back. Please note that a special "Golden Edition" card containing game-used memorabilia of Aaron, Ryan and Henderson was inserted into first series hobby packs at a rate of 1:212,169. Only 5 copies of this card were produced. Card backs carry a "KKR" prefix. Due to scarcity, no pricing is provided.

	Nm-Mt	Ex-Mt
KKR1 Hank Aaron/10		
KKR2 Nolan Ryan Rangers/10		
KKR3 Rickey Henderson/10		
KKR4 Does Not Exist		
KKR5 Bob Gibson/10		
KKR6 Nolan Ryan Angels/10		
KKGE Hank Aaron		
Nolan Ryan		
Rickey Henderson/5		

2001 Topps Chrome Originals

Randomly inserted into Hobby packs at 1:1783 and Retail packs at 1:1788, this ten-card insert features game-used jersey cards of players like Roberto Clemente and Carl Yastrzemski produced with Topps patented chrome technology.

	Nm-Mt	Ex-Mt
1 Roberto Clemente	200.00	60.00
2 Carl Yastrzemski	100.00	30.00
3 Mike Schmidt	100.00	30.00
4 Wade Boggs	40.00	12.00
5 Chipper Jones	60.00	18.00
6 Willie Mays		
7 Lou Brock	40.00	12.00
8 Dave Parker	25.00	7.50
9 Barry Bonds	120.00	36.00
10 Alex Rodriguez	80.00	24.00

2001 Topps Chrome Past to Present

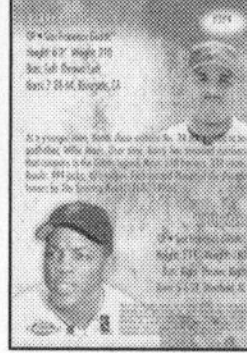

Randomly insert into packs at 1:18 Hobby/Retail, this 10-card insert pairs up players that have put up similar statistics throughout their careers. Card backs carry a "PTP" prefix. Please note that these cards feature Topps' special chrome technology.

	Nm-Mt	Ex-Mt
COMPLETE SET (10)	60.00	18.00
*REFRACTORS: 1.5X TO 4X BASIC PAST		
SER.1 REFRACTOR ODDS 1:180		
PTP1 Phil Rizzuto	12.00	3.60
Derek Jeter		
PTP2 Warren Spahn	8.00	2.40
Greg Maddux		
PTP3 Yogi Berra	10.00	3.00
Jorge Posada		
PTP4 Willie Mays	20.00	6.00
Barry Bonds		
PTP5 Red Schoendienst	4.00	1.20
Fernando Vina		
PTP6 Duke Snider	4.00	1.20
Shawn Green		
PTP7 Bob Feller	4.00	1.20
Bartolo Colon		
PTP8 Johnny Mize	4.00	1.20
Tino Martinez		
PTP9 Larry Doby	4.00	1.20
Manny Ramirez		
PTP10 Eddie Mathews	5.00	1.50
Chipper Jones		

2001 Topps Chrome Through the Years Reprints

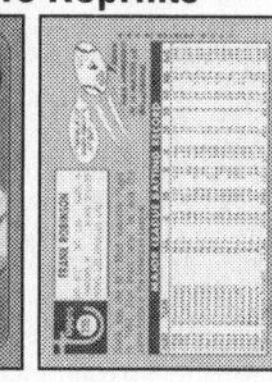

Randomly inserted into packs at 1:10 Hobby/Retail, this 50-card set takes a look at some of the best players to every make it onto a Topps trading card. Please note that these cards were produced with Topps chrome technology.

	Nm-Mt	Ex-Mt
COMPLETE SET (50)	300.00	90.00
*REFRACTORS: 1.5X TO 4X BASIC THROUGH		
SER.1 REFRACTOR ODDS 1:100		
1 Yogi Berra 57	6.00	1.80
2 Roy Campanella 56	6.00	1.80
3 Willie Mays 53	10.00	3.00
4 Andy Pafko 52	6.00	1.80
5 Jackie Robinson 52	10.00	3.00
6 Stan Musial 59	8.00	2.40
7 Duke Snider 56	5.00	1.50
8 Warren Spahn 56	5.00	1.50
9 Ted Williams 54	20.00	6.00
10 Eddie Mathews 55	6.00	1.80
11 Willie McCovey 60	5.00	1.50
12 Frank Robinson 69	5.00	1.50
13 Ernie Banks 66	6.00	1.80
14 Hank Aaron 65	10.00	3.00
15 Sandy Koufax 61	12.00	3.60
16 Bob Gibson 68	5.00	1.50
17 Harmon Killebrew 67	6.00	1.80
18 Whitey Ford 64	5.00	1.50
19 Roberto Clemente 63	15.00	4.50
20 Juan Marichal 61	5.00	1.50
21 Johnny Bench 70	6.00	1.80
22 Willie Stargell 73	5.00	1.50
23 Joe Morgan 74	5.00	1.50
24 Carl Yastrzemski 71	8.00	2.40
25 Reggie Jackson 76	5.00	1.50
26 Tom Seaver 78	5.00	1.50
27 Steve Carlton 77	5.00	1.50
28 Jim Palmer 79	5.00	1.50
29 Rod Carew 72	5.00	1.50
30 George Brett 75	20.00	6.00
31 Roger Clemens 85	12.00	3.60
32 Don Mattingly 84	20.00	6.00
33 Ryne Sandberg 89	10.00	3.00
34 Mike Schmidt 81	10.00	3.00
35 Cal Ripken 82	20.00	6.00
36 Tony Gwynn 83	8.00	2.40
37 Ozzie Smith 87	10.00	3.00
38 Wade Boggs 88	5.00	1.50
39 Nolan Ryan 80	15.00	4.50
40 Robin Yount 86	10.00	3.00
41 Mark McGwire 99	12.00	3.60
42 Ken Griffey Jr. 92	8.00	2.40
43 Sammy Sosa 90	8.00	2.40
44 Alex Rodriguez 98	8.00	2.40
45 Barry Bonds 94	12.00	3.60
46 Mike Piazza 95	8.00	2.40
47 Chipper Jones 91	6.00	1.80
48 Greg Maddux 96	8.00	2.40
49 Nomar Garciaparra 97	8.00	2.40
50 Derek Jeter 93	15.00	4.50

2001 Topps Chrome What Could Have Been

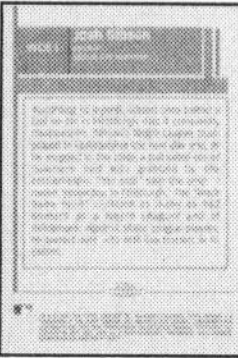

Inserted a rate of one in 30 hobby/retail packs, these 10 cards parallel the regular What Could Have Been retail set.

	Nm-Mt	Ex-Mt
COMPLETE SET (10)	40.00	12.00
*REFRACTORS: 1.5X TO 4X BASIC WHAT		
SER.2 REFRACTOR ODDS 1:300 HOB/RET		
WCB1 Josh Gibson	10.00	3.00
WCB2 Satchel Paige	4.00	1.20
WCB3 Buck Leonard	4.00	1.20
WCB4 James Bell	4.00	1.20
WCB5 Rube Foster	4.00	1.20
WCB6 Martin DiHigo	4.00	1.20
WCB7 William Johnson	4.00	1.20
WCB8 Mule Suttles	4.00	1.20
WCB9 Ray Dandridge	4.00	1.20
WCB10 John Lloyd	4.00	1.20

2001 Topps Chrome Traded

This set is a parallel to the 2001 Topps Traded set. Inserted into the 2001 Topps Traded at a rate of two per pack, these cards feature the patented "Chrome" technology which Topps uses.

	Nm-Mt	Ex-Mt
COMPLETE SET (266)	120.00	36.00
COMMON (1-99/145-266)	.75	.23
COMMON (100-144)	1.25	.35
T1 Sandy Alomar Jr.	.75	.23
T2 Kevin Appier	1.25	.35
T3 Brad Ausmus	.75	.23
T4 Derek Bell	.75	.23
T5 Bret Boone	1.25	.35
T6 Rico Brogna	.75	.23
T7 Ellis Burks	1.25	.35
T8 Ken Caminiti	1.25	.35
T9 Roger Cedeno	.75	.23
T10 Royce Clayton	.75	.23
T11 Enrique Wilson	.75	.23
T12 Rheal Cormier	.75	.23
T13 Eric Davis	1.25	.35
T14 Shawon Dunston	.75	.23
T15 Andres Galarraga	1.25	.35
T16 Tom Gordon	.75	.23
T17 Mark Grace	2.00	.60
T18 Jeffrey Hammonds	.75	.23
T19 Dustin Hermanson	.75	.23
T20 Quinton McCracken	.75	.23
T21 Todd Hundley	.75	.23
T22 Charles Johnson	1.25	.35
T23 Marquis Grissom	.75	.23
T24 Jose Mesa	.75	.23
T25 Brian Boehringer	.75	.23
T26 John Rocker	.75	.23
T27 Jeff Frye	.75	.23
T28 Reggie Sanders	1.25	.35
T29 David Segui	.75	.23
T30 Mike Sirotka	.75	.23
T31 Fernando Tatis	.75	.23
T32 Steve Trachsel	.75	.23
T33 Ismael Valdes	.75	.23
T34 Randy Velarde	.75	.23
T35 Ryan Kohlmeier	.75	.23
T36 Mike Bordick	1.25	.35
T37 Kent Bottenfield	.75	.23
T38 Pat Rapp	.75	.23
T39 Jeff Nelson	.75	.23
T40 Ricky Bottalico	.75	.23
T41 Luke Prokopec	.75	.23
T42 Hideo Nomo	3.00	.90
T43 Bill Mueller	1.25	.35
T44 Roberto Kelly	.75	.23
T45 Chris Holt	.75	.23
T46 Mike Jackson	.75	.23
T47 Devon White	.75	.23
T48 Gerald Williams	.75	.23
T49 Eddie Taubensee	.75	.23
T50 Brian Hunter UER	.75	.23
Brian R Hunter pictured		
Brian L Hunter stats		
T51 Nelson Cruz	.75	.23
T52 Jeff Fassero	.75	.23
T53 Bubba Trammell	.75	.23
T54 Bo Porter	.75	.23
T55 Greg Norton	.75	.23
T56 Benito Santiago	1.25	.35
T57 Ruben Rivera	.75	.23
T58 Dee Brown	.75	.23
T59 Jose Canseco	3.00	.90
T60 Chris Michalak	.75	.23
T61 Tim Worrell	.75	.23
T62 Matt Clement	1.25	.35
T63 Bill Pulsipher	.75	.23
T64 Troy Brohawn RC	1.00	.30
T65 Mark Kotsay	.75	.23
T66 Jimmy Rollins	1.25	.35
T67 Shea Hillenbrand	1.25	.35
T68 Ted Lilly	.75	.23
T69 Jermaine Dye	1.25	.35
T70 Jerry Hairston Jr.	.75	.23
T71 John Mabry	.75	.23
T72 Kurt Abbott	.75	.23
T73 Eric Owens	.75	.23
T74 Jeff Brantley	.75	.23
T75 Roy Oswalt	2.00	.60
T76 Doug Mientkiewicz	1.25	.35
T77 Rickey Henderson	3.00	.90
T78 Jason Grimsley	.75	.23
T79 Christian Parker RC	1.00	.30
T80 Donne Wall	.75	.23
T81 Alex Arias	.75	.23
T82 Willis Roberts	.75	.23
T83 Ryan Minor	.75	.23
T84 Jason LaRue	.75	.23
T85 Ruben Sierra	.75	.23
T86 Johnny Damon	1.25	.35
T87 Juan Gonzalez	3.00	.90
T88 C.C. Sabathia	1.25	.35
T89 Tony Batista	1.25	.35
T90 Jay Witasick	.75	.23
T91 Brent Abernathy	.75	.23
T92 Paul LoDuca	1.25	.35
T93 Wes Helms	.75	.23
T94 Mark Wohlers	.75	.23
T95 Rob Bell	.75	.23
T96 Tim Redding	.75	.23
T97 Bud Smith RC	1.00	.30
T98 Adam Dunn	1.25	.35
T99 Ichiro Suzuki	15.00	4.50
Albert Pujols ROY		
T100 Carlton Fisk 81	2.00	.60
T101 Tim Raines 81	1.25	.35
T102 Juan Marichal 74	1.25	.35
T103 Dave Winfield 81	1.25	.35
T104 Reggie Jackson 82	2.00	.60
T105 Cal Ripken 82	10.00	3.00
T106 Ozzie Smith 82	5.00	1.50
T107 Tom Seaver 83	2.00	.60
T108 Lou Piniella 74	1.25	.35
T109 Dwight Gooden 84	2.00	.60
T110 Bret Saberhagen 84	1.25	.35
T111 Gary Carter 85	1.25	.35
T112 Jack Clark 85	1.25	.35
T113 Rickey Henderson 85	3.00	.90
T114 Barry Bonds 86	8.00	2.40
T115 Bobby Bonilla 86	1.25	.35
T116 Jose Canseco 86	3.00	.90
T117 Will Clark 86	3.00	.90
T118 Andres Galarraga 86	1.25	.35
T119 Bo Jackson 86	3.00	.90
T120 Wally Joyner 86	1.25	.35
T121 Ellis Burks 87	1.25	.35
T122 David Cone 87	1.25	.35
T123 Greg Maddux 87	5.00	1.50
T124 Willie Randolph 76	1.25	.35
T125 Dennis Eckersley 87	1.25	.35
T126 Matt Williams 87	1.25	.35
T127 Joe Morgan 81	1.25	.35
T128 Fred McGriff 87	2.00	.60
T129 Roberto Alomar 88	3.00	.90
T130 Lee Smith 88	1.25	.35
T131 David Wells 88	1.25	.35
T132 Ken Griffey Jr. 89	5.00	1.50
T133 Deion Sanders 89	2.00	.60
T134 Nolan Ryan 89	8.00	2.40
T135 David Justice 90	1.25	.35
T136 Joe Carter 91	1.25	.35
T137 Jack Morris 92	1.25	.35
T138 Mike Piazza 93	5.00	1.50
T139 Barry Bonds 93	8.00	2.40
T140 Terrence Long 94	1.25	.35
T141 Ben Grieve 94	1.25	.35
T142 Richie Sexson 95	1.25	.35
George Arias		
Mark Sweeney		
Brian Schneider		
T143 Sean Burroughs 99	1.25	.35
T144 Alfonso Soriano 99	2.00	.60
T145 Bob Boone MG	1.25	.35
T146 Larry Bowa MG	1.25	.35
T147 Bob Brenly MG	.75	.23
T148 Buck Martinez MG	.75	.23
T149 L. McClendon MG	.75	.23
T150 Jim Tracy MG	.75	.23
T151 Jared Abruzzo RC	1.00	.30
T152 Kurt Ainsworth	.75	.23
T153 Willie Bloomquist	1.25	.35
T154 Ben Broussard	.75	.23
T155 Bobby Bradley	.75	.23
T156 Mike Bynum	.75	.23
T157 A.J. Hinch	.75	.23
T158 Ryan Christianson	.75	.23
T159 Carlos Silva	.75	.23
T160 Joe Crede	.75	.23
T161 Jack Cust	.75	.23
T162 Ben Diggins	.75	.23
T163 Phil Dumatrait	.75	.23
T164 Alex Escobar	.75	.23
T165 Miguel Olivo	.75	.23
T166 Chris George	.75	.23
T167 Marcus Giles	1.25	.35
T168 Keith Ginter	.75	.23
T169 Josh Girdley	.75	.23
T170 Tony Alvarez	.75	.23
T171 Scott Seabol	.75	.23

T172 Josh Hamilton .75 .23
T173 Jason Hart .75 .23
T174 Israel Alcantara .75 .23
T175 Jake Peavy 4.00 1.20
T176 Stubby Clapp RC 1.00 .30
T177 D'Angelo Jimenez .75 .23
T178 Nick Johnson 1.25 .35
T179 Ben Johnson .75 .23
T180 Larry Bigbie .75 .23
T181 Allen Levrault .75 .23
T182 Felipe Lopez .75 .23
T183 Sean Burnett 1.25 .35
T184 Nick Neugebauer .75 .23
T185 Austin Kearns 1.25 .35
T186 Corey Patterson 1.25 .35
T187 Carlos Pena .75 .23
T188 R. Rodriguez RC 1.00 .30
T189 Juan Rivera .75 .23
T190 Grant Roberts .75 .23
T191 Adam Pettyjohn RC 1.00 .30
T192 Jared Sandberg .75 .23
T193 Xavier Nady 1.25 .35
T194 Dane Sardinha .75 .23
T195 Shawn Sonnier .75 .23
T196 Rafael Soriano 4.00 1.20
T197 Brian Specht RC 1.00 .30
T198 Aaron Myette .75 .23
T199 Juan Uribe RC 1.00 .30
T200 Jayson Werth .75 .23
T201 Brad Wilkerson .75 .23
T202 Horacio Estrada .75 .23
T203 Joel Pineiro 3.00 .90
T204 Matt LeCroy .75 .23
T205 Michael Coleman .75 .23
T206 Ben Sheets 1.25 .35
T207 Eric Byrnes .75 .23
T208 Sean Burroughs 1.25 .35
T209 Ken Harvey .75 .23
T210 Travis Hafner 4.00 1.20
T211 Erick Almonte 1.00 .30
T212 Jason Belcher RC 1.00 .30
T213 Wilson Betemit RC 1.00 .30
T214 Hank Blalock RC 15.00 4.50
T215 Danny Borrell 1.00 .30
T216 John Buck RC 2.00 .60
T217 Freddie Bynum RC 1.00 .30
T218 Noel Devarez RC 1.00 .30
T219 Juan Diaz RC 1.00 .30
T220 Felix Diaz RC 1.00 .30
T221 Josh Fogg RC 1.00 .30
T222 Matt Ford RC 1.00 .30
T223 Scott Heard .75 .23
T224 Ben Hendrickson RC 1.00 .30
T225 Cody Ross RC 1.00 .30
T226 A. Hernandez RC 1.00 .30
T227 Alfredo Amezaga RC 2.00 .60
T228 Bob Keppel RC 2.00 .60
T229 Ryan Madson RC 2.00 .60
T230 Octavio Martinez RC 1.00 .30
T231 Hee Seop Choi 10.00 3.00
T232 Thomas Mitchell .75 .23
T233 Luis Montanez 1.00 .30
T234 Andy Morales RC 1.00 .30
T235 Justin Morneau RC 10.00 3.00
T236 Toe Nash RC 1.00 .30
T237 V. Pascucci RC 1.00 .30
T238 Roy Smith RC 1.00 .30
T239 Antonio Perez RC 1.00 .30
T240 Chad Petty RC 1.00 .30
T241 Steve Smyth 1.00 .30
T242 Jose Reyes RC 15.00 4.50
T243 Eric Reynolds RC 1.00 .30
T244 Dominic Rich 1.00 .30
T245 J. Richardson RC 1.00 .30
T246 Ed Rogers RC 1.00 .30
T247 Albert Pujols 40.00 12.00
T248 Esix Snead RC 1.00 .30
T249 Luis Torres RC 1.00 .30
T250 Matt White RC 1.00 .30
T251 Blake Williams 1.00 .30
T252 Chris Russ 1.00 .30
T253 Joe Kennedy RC 1.00 .30
T254 Jeff Randazzo RC 1.00 .30
T255 Beau Hale RC 1.00 .30
T256 Brad Hennessey RC 1.00 .30
T257 Jake Gautreau RC 1.00 .30
T258 Jeff Mathis RC 6.00 1.80
T259 Aaron Heilman RC 3.00 .90
T260 B. Sardinha RC 2.00 .60
T261 Irvin Guzman RC 8.00 2.40
T262 Gabe Gross RC 2.00 .60
T263 J.D. Martin RC 1.00 .30
T264 Chris Smith RC 1.00 .30
T265 Kenny Baugh RC 1.00 .30
T266 Ichiro Suzuki RC 25.00 7.50

2001 Topps Chrome Traded Retrofractors

This set is a parallel to the 2001 Topps Chrome Traded set. Inserted into the 2001 Topps Traded at a rate of one in 12, these cards feature grayback card stock with refractor technology on the front.

Nm-Mt Ex-Mt
*STARS: 1.5X TO 4X BASIC CARDS ...
*REPRINTS: 1X TO 2.5X BASIC ....
*ROOKIES: 1.5X TO 4X BASIC ....

2002 Topps Chrome

This product's first series, consisting of cards 1-6 and 8-331, was released in late January, 2002. The second series, consisting of cards 366-695, was released in early June, 2002. Both first and second series packs contained four cards and carried an SRP of $3. Sealed boxes contained 24 packs. The set parallels the 2002 Topps set except, of course, for the upgraded chrome card stock. Unlike the 1999 Topps Chrome product, featuring 70 variations of Mark McGwire's Home Run record card, the 2002 first series product did not include different variations of the Barry Bonds Home Run record cards. Please note, that just as in the basic 2002 Topps set there is no card number 7 as it is still retired in honor of Mickey Mantle. In addition, the foil-coated subset cards from the basic Topps set (cards 332-365 and 696-719) were NOT replicated for this Chrome set, thus it's considered complete at 660 cards. Notable Rookie Cards include Kazuhisa Ishii and Joe Mauer.

Nm-Mt Ex-Mt
COMPLETE SET (660) 300.00 90.00
COMPLETE SERIES 1 (330) 150.00 45.00
COMPLETE SERIES 2 (330) 150.00 45.00
COMMON (1-331/366-695) .50 .15
COMMON (307-326/671-690) 1.50 .45
COMMON (327-331/691-695) 1.50 .45
1 Pedro Martinez 2.50 .75
2 Mike Stanton .50 .15
3 Brad Penny .50 .15
4 Mike Matheny .50 .15
5 Johnny Damon 1.00 .30
6 Bret Boone 1.00 .30
7 Does Not Exist
8 Chris Truby .50 .15
9 B.J. Surhoff 1.00 .30
10 Mike Hampton 1.00 .30
11 Juan Pierre 1.00 .30
12 Mark Buehrle 1.00 .30
13 Bob Abreu 1.00 .30
14 David Cone 1.00 .30
15 Aaron Sele .50 .15
16 Fernando Tatis .50 .15
17 Bobby Jones .50 .15
18 Rick Helling .50 .15
19 Dmitri Young 1.00 .30
20 Mike Mussina 2.50 .75
21 Mike Sweeney 1.00 .30
22 Cristian Guzman 1.00 .30
23 Ryan Kohlmeier .50 .15
24 Adam Kennedy .50 .15
25 Larry Walker 1.50 .45
26 Eric Davis 1.00 .30
27 Jason Tyner .50 .15
28 Eric Young .50 .15
29 Jason Marquis .50 .15
30 Luis Gonzalez 1.00 .30
31 Kevin Tapani .50 .15
32 Orlando Cabrera .50 .15
33 Marty Cordova .50 .15
34 Brad Ausmus .50 .15
35 Livan Hernandez .50 .15
36 Alex Gonzalez .50 .15
37 Edgar Renteria 1.00 .30
38 Bengie Molina .50 .15
39 Frank Menechino .50 .15
40 Rafael Palmeiro 1.50 .45
41 Brad Fullmer .50 .15
42 Julio Zuleta .50 .15
43 Darren Dreifort .50 .15
44 Trot Nixon 1.50 .45
45 Trevor Hoffman 1.00 .30
46 Vladimir Nunez .50 .15
47 Mark Kotsay .50 .15
48 Kenny Rogers 1.00 .30
49 Ben Petrick .50 .15
50 Jeff Bagwell 1.50 .45
51 Juan Encarnacion .50 .15
52 Ramiro Mendoza .50 .15
53 Brian Meadows .50 .15
54 Chad Curtis .50 .15
55 Aramis Ramirez 1.00 .30
56 Mark McLemore .50 .15
57 Dante Bichette 1.00 .30
58 Scott Schoeneweis .50 .15
59 Jose Cruz Jr. 1.00 .30
60 Roger Clemens 5.00 1.50
61 Jose Guillen .50 .15
62 Darren Oliver .50 .15
63 Chris Reitsma .50 .15
64 Jeff Abbott .50 .15
65 Robin Ventura 1.00 .30
66 Denny Neagle .50 .15
67 Al Martin .50 .15
68 Benito Santiago 1.00 .30
69 Roy Oswalt 1.00 .30
70 Juan Gonzalez 2.50 .75
71 Garret Anderson 1.00 .30
72 Bobby Bonilla 1.00 .30
73 Danny Bautista .50 .15
74 J.T. Snow 1.00 .30
75 Derek Jeter 6.00 1.80
76 John Olerud 1.00 .30
77 Kevin Appier 1.00 .30
78 Phil Nevin 1.00 .30
79 Sean Casey 1.00 .30
80 Troy Glaus 1.50 .45
81 Joe Randa .50 .15
82 Jose Valentin .50 .15
83 Ricky Bottalico .50 .15
84 Todd Zeile 1.00 .30
85 Barry Larkin 2.50 .75
86 Bob Wickman .50 .15
87 Jeff Shaw .50 .15
88 Greg Vaughn 1.00 .30
89 Fernando Vina 1.00 .30
90 Mark Mulder 1.00 .30
91 Paul Bako .50 .15
92 Aaron Boone 1.00 .30
93 Esteban Loaiza 1.00 .30
94 Richie Sexson 1.00 .30
95 Alfonso Soriano 1.50 .45
96 Tony Womack .50 .15
97 Paul Shuey .50 .15
98 Melvin Mora .50 .15
99 Tony Gwynn 3.00 .90
100 Vladimir Guerrero 2.50 .75
101 Keith Osik .50 .15
102 Bud Smith .50 .15
103 Scott Williamson .50 .15
104 Daryle Ward .50 .15
105 Doug Mientkiewicz 1.00 .30
106 Stan Javier .50 .15
107 Russ Ortiz 1.00 .30
108 Wade Miller 1.00 .30
109 Luke Prokopec .50 .15
110 Andruw Jones 1.00 .30
111 Ron Coomer .50 .15
112 Dan Wilson .50 .15
113 Luis Castillo 1.00 .30
114 Derek Bell .50 .15
115 Gary Sheffield 1.00 .30
116 Ruben Rivera .50 .15
117 Paul O'Neill 1.50 .45
118 Craig Paquette .50 .15
119 Kelvim Escobar .50 .15
120 Brad Radke 1.00 .30
121 Jorge Fabregas .50 .15
122 Randy Winn .50 .15
123 Tom Goodwin .50 .15
124 Jaret Wright .50 .15
125 Barry Bonds HR 73 40.00 12.00
126 Al Leiter .50 .15
127 Ben Davis .50 .15
128 Frank Catalanotto .50 .15
129 Jose Cabrera .50 .15
130 Maggio Ordonez 1.00 .30
131 Jose Macias .50 .15
132 Ted Lilly .50 .15
133 Chris Holt .50 .15
134 Eric Milton .50 .15
135 Shannon Stewart 1.00 .30
136 Omar Olivares .50 .15
137 David Segui .50 .15
138 Jeff Nelson .50 .15
139 Matt Williams 1.00 .30
140 Ellis Burks 1.00 .30
141 Jason Bere .50 .15
142 Jimmy Haynes .50 .15
143 Ramon Hernandez .50 .15
144 Craig Counsell .50 .15
145 John Smoltz 1.50 .45
146 Homer Bush .50 .15
147 Quilvio Veras .50 .15
148 Esteban Yan .50 .15
149 Ramon Ortiz .50 .15
150 Carlos Delgado 1.00 .30
151 Lee Stevens .50 .15
152 Wil Cordero .50 .15
153 Mike Bordick 1.00 .30
154 John Flaherty .50 .15
155 Omar Daal .50 .15
156 Todd Ritchie .50 .15
157 Carl Everett 1.00 .30
158 Scott Sullivan .50 .15
159 Deivi Cruz .50 .15
160 Albert Pujols 5.00 1.50
161 Royce Clayton .50 .15
162 Jeff Suppan .50 .15
163 C.C. Sabathia 1.00 .30
164 Jimmy Rollins 1.00 .30
165 Rickey Henderson 2.50 .75
166 Rey Ordonez .50 .15
167 Shawn Estes .50 .15
168 Reggie Sanders 1.00 .30
169 Jon Lieber .50 .15
170 Armando Benitez 1.00 .30
171 Mike Remlinger .50 .15
172 Billy Wagner 1.00 .30
173 Troy Percival 1.00 .30
174 Devon White .50 .15
175 Ivan Rodriguez 2.50 .75
176 Dustin Hermanson .50 .15
177 Brian Anderson .50 .15
178 Graeme Lloyd .50 .15
179 Russell Branyan .50 .15
180 Bobby Higginson 1.00 .30
181 Alex Gonzalez .50 .15
182 John Franco 1.00 .30
183 Sidney Ponson 1.00 .30
184 Jose Mesa .50 .15
185 Todd Hollandsworth .50 .15
186 Kevin Young .50 .15
187 Tim Wakefield 1.00 .30
188 Craig Biggio 1.50 .45
189 Jason Isringhausen 1.00 .30
190 Mark Quinn .50 .15
191 Glendon Rusch .50 .15
192 Damian Miller .50 .15
193 Sandy Alomar Jr. .50 .15
194 Scott Brosius 1.00 .30
195 Dave Martinez .50 .15
196 Danny Graves .50 .15
197 Shea Hillenbrand 1.00 .30
198 Jimmy Anderson .50 .15
199 Travis Lee .50 .15
200 Randy Johnson 2.50 .75
201 Carlos Beltran 1.00 .30
202 Jerry Hairston .50 .15
203 Jesus Sanchez .50 .15
204 Eddie Taubensee .50 .15
205 David Wells 1.00 .30
206 Russ Davis .50 .15
207 Michael Barrett .50 .15
208 Marquis Grissom .50 .15
209 Byung-Hyun Kim 1.00 .30
210 Hideo Nomo 2.50 .75
211 Ryan Rupe .50 .15
212 Ricky Gutierrez .50 .15
213 Darryl Kile 1.00 .30
214 Rico Brogna .50 .15
215 Terrence Long 1.00 .30
216 Mike Jackson .50 .15
217 Jamey Wright .50 .15
218 Adrian Beltre 1.00 .30
219 Benny Agbayani .50 .15
220 Chuck Knoblauch 1.00 .30
221 Randy Wolf 1.00 .30
222 Andy Ashby .50 .15
223 Corey Koskie 1.00 .30
224 Roger Cedeno .50 .15
225 Ichiro Suzuki 4.00 1.20
226 Keith Foulke .50 .15
227 Ryan Minor .50 .15
228 Shawon Dunston .50 .15
229 Alex Cora .50 .15
230 Jeromy Burnitz 1.00 .30
231 Mark Grace 1.50 .45
232 Aubrey Huff 1.00 .30
233 Jeffrey Hammonds .50 .15
234 Olmedo Saenz .50 .15
235 Brian Jordan 1.00 .30
236 Jeremy Giambi .50 .15
237 Joe Girardi .50 .15
238 Eric Gagne 1.50 .45
239 Masato Yoshii .50 .15
240 Greg Maddux 4.00 1.20
241 Bryan Rekar .50 .15
242 Ray Durham 1.00 .30
243 Torii Hunter 1.00 .30
244 Derrek Lee 1.00 .30
245 Jim Edmonds 1.00 .30
246 Einar Diaz .50 .15
247 Brian Bohanon .50 .15
248 Ron Belliard .50 .15
249 Mike Lowell 1.00 .30
250 Sammy Sosa 4.00 1.20
251 Richard Hidalgo 1.00 .30
252 Bartolo Colon 1.00 .30
253 Jorge Posada 1.50 .45
254 Latroy Hawkins .50 .15
255 Paul LoDuca 1.00 .30
256 Carlos Febles .50 .15
257 Nelson Cruz .50 .15
258 Edgardo Alfonzo 1.00 .30
259 Joey Hamilton .50 .15
260 Cliff Floyd 1.00 .30
261 Wes Helms .50 .15
262 Jay Bell 1.00 .30
263 Mike Cameron 1.00 .30
264 Paul Konerko 1.00 .30
265 Jeff Kent 1.00 .30
266 Robert Fick 1.00 .30
267 Allen Levrault .50 .15
268 Placido Polanco .50 .15
269 Marlon Anderson .50 .15
270 Mariano Rivera 1.50 .45
271 Chan Ho Park 1.00 .30
272 Jose Vizcaino .50 .15
273 Jeff D'Amico .50 .15
274 Mark Gardner .50 .15
275 Travis Fryman 1.00 .30
276 Darren Lewis .50 .15
277 Bruce Bochy MG .50 .15
278 Jerry Manuel MG .50 .15
279 Bob Brenly MG .50 .15
280 Don Baylor MG 1.00 .30
281 Davey Lopes MG 1.00 .30
282 Jerry Narron MG .50 .15
283 Tony Muser MG .50 .15
284 Hal McRae MG 1.00 .30
285 Bobby Cox MG .50 .15
286 Larry Dierker MG .50 .15
287 Phil Garner MG .50 .15
288 Joe Kerrigan MG .50 .15
289 Bobby Valentine MG .50 .15
290 Dusty Baker MG 1.00 .30
291 Lloyd McClendon MG .50 .15
292 Mike Scioscia MG .50 .15
293 Buck Martinez MG .50 .15
294 Larry Bowa MG 1.00 .30
295 Tony LaRussa MG 1.00 .30
296 Jeff Torborg MG .50 .15
297 Tom Kelly MG .50 .15
298 Mike Hargrove MG .50 .15
299 Art Howe MG .50 .15
300 Lou Piniella MG 1.00 .30
301 Charlie Manuel MG .50 .15
302 Buddy Bell MG 1.00 .30
303 Tony Perez MG 1.00 .30
304 Bob Boone MG 1.00 .30
305 Joe Torre MG 2.50 .75
306 Jim Tracy MG .50 .15
307 Jason Lane PROS 1.50 .45
308 Chris George PROS 1.50 .45
309 Hank Blalock PROS 4.00 1.20
310 Joe Borchard PROS 1.50 .45
311 Marlon Byrd PROS 1.50 .45
312 Ray. Cabrera PROS RC 1.50 .45
313 Fr. Sanchez PROS RC 1.50 .45
314 Scott Wiggins PROS RC 1.50 .45
315 Jason Maule PROS RC 1.50 .45
316 Dionys Cesar PROS RC 1.50 .45
317 Boof Bonser PROS 1.50 .45
318 Juan Tolentino PROS RC 1.50 .45
319 Earl Snyder PROS RC 1.50 .45
320 Travis Wade PROS RC 1.50 .45
321 Nap. Calzado PROS RC 1.50 .45
322 Eric Glaser PROS 1.50 .45
323 Craig Kuzmic PROS RC 1.50 .45
324 Nic Jackson PROS RC 1.50 .45
325 Mike Rivera PROS 1.50 .45
326 Jason Bay PROS RC 6.00 1.80
327 Chris Smith DP 1.50 .45
328 Jake Gautreau DP 1.50 .45
329 Gabe Gross DP 1.50 .45
330 Kenny Baugh DP 1.50 .45
331 J.D. Martin DP 1.50 .45
366 Pat Meares .50 .15
367 Mike Lieberthal 1.00 .30
368 Larry Bigbie .50 .15
369 Ron Gant 1.00 .30
370 Moises Alou 1.00 .30
371 Chad Kreuter .50 .15
372 Willis Roberts .50 .15
373 Toby Hall .50 .15
374 Miguel Batista .50 .15
375 John Burkett .50 .15
376 Cory Lidle .50 .15
377 Nick Neugebauer .50 .15
378 Jay Payton .50 .15
379 Steve Karsay .50 .15
380 Eric Chavez 1.00 .30
381 Kelly Stinnett .50 .15
382 Jarrod Washburn 1.00 .30
383 Rick White .50 .15
384 Jeff Conine 1.00 .30
385 Fred McGriff 1.50 .45
386 Marvin Benard .50 .15
387 Joe Crede .50 .15
388 Dennis Cook .50 .15
389 Rick Reed .50 .15
390 Tom Glavine 1.50 .45
391 Rondell White 1.00 .30
392 Matt Morris 1.00 .30
393 Pat Rapp .50 .15
394 Robert Person .50 .15
395 Omar Vizquel 1.00 .30
396 Jeff Cirillo .50 .15
397 Dave Mlicki .50 .15
398 Jose Ortiz .50 .15
399 Ryan Dempster .50 .15
400 Curt Schilling 1.50 .45
401 Peter Bergeron .50 .15
402 Kyle Lohse .50 .15
403 Craig Wilson .50 .15
404 David Justice 1.00 .30
405 Darin Erstad 1.00 .30
406 Jose Mercedes .50 .15
407 Carl Pavano .50 .15
408 Albie Lopez .50 .15
409 Alex Ochoa .50 .15
410 Chipper Jones 2.50 .75
411 Tyler Houston .50 .15
412 Dean Palmer 1.00 .30
413 Damian Jackson .50 .15
414 Josh Towers .50 .15
415 Rafael Furcal 1.00 .30
416 Mike Morgan .50 .15
417 Herb Perry .50 .15
418 Mike Sirotka .50 .15
419 Mark Wohlers .50 .15
420 Nomar Garciaparra 4.00 1.20
421 Felipe Lopez .50 .15
422 Joe McEwing .50 .15
423 Jacque Jones 1.00 .30
424 Julio Franco 1.00 .30
425 Frank Thomas 2.50 .75
426 So Taguchi RC 2.50 .75
427 Kazuhisa Ishii RC 5.00 1.50
428 D'Angelo Jimenez .50 .15
429 Chris Stynes .50 .15
430 Kerry Wood 2.50 .75
431 Chris Singleton .50 .15
432 Erubiel Durazo .50 .15
433 Matt Lawton .50 .15
434 Bill Mueller 1.00 .30
435 Jose Canseco 2.50 .75
436 Ben Grieve .50 .15
437 Terry Mulholland .50 .15
438 David Bell .50 .15
439 A.J. Pierzynski 1.00 .30
440 Adam Dunn 1.00 .30
441 Jon Garland .50 .15
442 Jeff Fassero .50 .15
443 Julio Lugo .50 .15
444 Carlos Guillen .50 .15
445 Orlando Hernandez 1.00 .30
446 Mark Loretta .50 .15
447 Scott Spiezio .50 .15
448 Kevin Millwood 1.00 .30
449 Jamie Moyer 1.00 .30
450 Todd Helton 1.50 .45
451 Todd Walker 1.00 .30
452 Jose Lima .50 .15
453 Brook Fordyce .50 .15
454 Aaron Rowand .50 .15
455 Barry Zito 1.50 .45
456 Eric Owens .50 .15
457 Charles Nagy .50 .15
458 Raul Ibanez .50 .15
459 Joe Mays .50 .15
460 Jim Thome 2.50 .75
461 Adam Eaton .50 .15
462 Felix Martinez .50 .15
463 Vernon Wells 1.00 .30
464 Donnie Sadler .50 .15
465 Tony Clark .50 .15
466 Jose Hernandez .50 .15
467 Ramon Martinez .50 .15
468 Rusty Greer 1.00 .30
469 Rod Barajas .50 .15
470 Lance Berkman 1.00 .30
471 Brady Anderson 1.00 .30
472 Pedro Astacio .50 .15
473 Shane Halter .50 .15
474 Bret Prinz .50 .15
475 Edgar Martinez 1.50 .45
476 Steve Trachsel .50 .15
477 Gary Matthews Jr. .50 .15
478 Ismael Valdes .50 .15
479 Juan Uribe .50 .15
480 Shawn Green 1.00 .30
481 Kirk Rueter .50 .15
482 Damion Easley .50 .15
483 Chris Carpenter .50 .15
484 Kris Benson .50 .15
485 Antonio Alfonseca .50 .15
486 Kyle Farnsworth .50 .15
487 Brandon Lyon .50 .15
488 Hideki Irabu .50 .15
489 David Ortiz 1.00 .30
490 Mike Piazza 4.00 1.20
491 Derek Lowe 1.00 .30
492 Chris Gomez .50 .15
493 Mark Johnson .50 .15
494 John Rocker .50 .15
495 Eric Karros 1.00 .30
496 Bill Haselman .50 .15
497 Dave Veres .50 .15
498 Pete Harnisch .50 .15
499 Tomokazu Ohka .50 .15
500 Barry Bonds 6.00 1.80
501 David Dellucci .50 .15
502 Wendell Magee .50 .15
503 Tom Gordon .50 .15
504 Javier Vazquez 1.00 .30
505 Ben Sheets 1.00 .30
506 Wilton Guerrero .50 .15
507 John Halama .50 .15
508 Mark Redman .50 .15
509 Jack Wilson .50 .15
510 Bernie Williams 1.50 .45
511 Miguel Cairo .50 .15
512 Denny Hocking .50 .15
513 Tony Batista 1.00 .30
514 Mark Grudzielanek .50 .15
515 Jose Vidro 1.00 .30
516 Sterling Hitchcock .50 .15
517 Billy Koch .50 .15
518 Matt Clement 1.00 .30
519 Bruce Chen .50 .15
520 Roberto Alomar 2.50 .75
521 Orlando Palmeiro .50 .15
522 Steve Finley 1.00 .30
523 Danny Patterson .50 .15
524 Terry Adams .50 .15
525 Tino Martinez 1.50 .45
526 Tony Armas Jr. UER .50 .15
Career stats do not include pre-2001
527 Geoff Jenkins 1.00 .30
528 Kerry Robinson .50 .15
529 Corey Patterson 1.00 .30
530 Brian Giles 1.00 .30
531 Jose Jimenez .50 .15
532 Joe Kennedy .50 .15
533 Armando Rios .50 .15
534 Osvaldo Fernandez .50 .15
535 Ruben Sierra .50 .15

Card	Nm-Mt	Ex-Mt
536 Octavio Dotel	.50	.15
537 Luis Sojo	.50	.15
538 Brent Butler	.50	.15
539 Pablo Ozuna	.50	.15
540 Freddy Garcia	1.00	.30
541 Chad Durbin	.50	.15
542 Orlando Merced	.50	.15
543 Michael Tucker	.50	.15
544 Roberto Hernandez	.50	.15
545 Pat Burrell	1.00	.30
546 A.J. Burnett	.50	.15
547 Bubba Trammell	.50	.15
548 Scott Elarton	.50	.15
549 Mike Darr	.50	.15
550 Ken Griffey Jr.	4.00	1.20
551 Ugueth Urbina	.50	.15
552 Todd Jones	.50	.15
553 Delino Deshields	.50	.15
554 Adam Piatt	.50	.15
555 Jason Kendall	1.00	.30
556 Hector Ortiz	.50	.15
557 Turk Wendell	.50	.15
558 Rob Bell	.50	.15
559 Sun Woo Kim	.50	.15
560 Raul Mondesi	1.00	.30
561 Brent Abernathy	.50	.15
562 Seth Etherton	.50	.15
563 Shawn Wooten	.50	.15
564 Jay Buhner	1.00	.30
565 Andres Galarraga	1.00	.30
566 Shane Reynolds	.50	.15
567 Rod Beck	.50	.15
568 Dee Brown	.50	.15
569 Pedro Feliz	.50	.15
570 Ryan Klesko	1.00	.30
571 John Vander Wal	.50	.15
572 Nick Bierbrodt	.50	.15
573 Joe Nathan	.50	.15
574 James Baldwin	.50	.15
575 J.D. Drew	1.00	.30
576 Greg Colbrunn	.50	.15
577 Doug Glanville	.50	.15
578 Brandon Duckworth	.50	.15
579 Shawn Chacon	.50	.15
580 Rich Aurilia	1.00	.30
581 Chuck Finley	1.00	.30
582 Abraham Nunez	.50	.15
583 Kenny Lofton	1.00	.30
584 Brian Daubach	.50	.15
585 Miguel Tejada	1.00	.30
586 Nate Cornejo	.50	.15
587 Kazuhiro Sasaki	1.00	.30
588 Chris Richard	.50	.15
589 Armando Reynoso	.50	.15
590 Tim Hudson	1.00	.30
591 Neifi Perez	.50	.15
592 Steve Cox	.50	.15
593 Henry Blanco	.50	.15
594 Ricky Ledee	.50	.15
595 Tim Salmon	1.50	.45
596 Luis Rivas	.50	.15
597 Jeff Zimmerman	.50	.15
598 Matt Stairs	.50	.15
599 Preston Wilson	1.00	.30
600 Mark McGwire	6.00	1.80
601 Timo Perez	.50	.15
602 Matt Anderson	.50	.15
603 Todd Hundley	.50	.15
604 Rick Ankiel	.50	.15
605 Tsuyoshi Shinjo	1.00	.30
606 Woody Williams	.50	.15
607 Jason LaRue	.50	.15
608 Carlos Lee	1.00	.30
609 Russ Johnson	.50	.15
610 Scott Rolen	1.50	.45
611 Brent Mayne	.50	.15
612 Darrin Fletcher	.50	.15
613 Ray Lankford	.50	.15
614 Troy O'Leary	.50	.15
615 Javier Lopez	1.00	.30
616 Randy Velarde	.50	.15
617 Vinny Castilla	1.00	.30
618 Milton Bradley	1.00	.30
619 Ruben Mateo	.50	.15
620 Jason Giambi Yankees	2.50	.75
621 Andy Benes	.50	.15
622 Joe Mauer RC	15.00	4.50
623 Andy Pettitte	1.50	.45
624 Jose Offerman	.50	.15
625 Mo Vaughn	1.00	.30
626 Steve Sparks	.50	.15
627 Mike Matthews	.50	.15
628 Robb Nen	1.00	.30
629 Kip Wells	.50	.15
630 Kevin Brown	1.00	.30
631 Arthur Rhodes	.50	.15
632 Gabe Kapler	.50	.15
633 Jermaine Dye	1.00	.30
634 Josh Beckett	1.50	.45
635 Pokey Reese	.50	.15
636 Benji Gil	.50	.15
637 Marcus Giles	1.00	.30
638 Julian Tavarez	.50	.15
639 Jason Schmidt	1.00	.30
640 Alex Rodriguez	4.00	1.20
641 Anaheim Angels TC	1.00	.30
642 Ariz. Diamondbacks TC	1.50	.45
643 Atlanta Braves TC	1.00	.30
644 Baltimore Orioles TC	1.00	.30
645 Boston Red Sox TC	1.00	.30
646 Chicago Cubs TC	1.00	.30
647 Chicago White Sox TC	1.00	.30
648 Cincinnati Reds TC	1.00	.30
649 Cleveland Indians TC	1.00	.30
650 Colorado Rockies TC	1.00	.30
651 Detroit Tigers TC	1.00	.30
652 Florida Marlins TC	1.00	.30
653 Houston Astros TC	1.00	.30
654 Kansas City Royals TC	1.00	.30
655 Los Angeles Dodgers TC	1.00	.30
656 Milwaukee Brewers TC	1.00	.30
657 Minnesota Twins TC	1.00	.30
658 Montreal Expos TC	1.00	.30
659 New York Mets TC	1.00	.30
660 New York Yankees TC	2.50	.75
661 Oakland Athletics TC	1.00	.30
662 Philadelphia Phillies TC	1.00	.30
663 Pittsburgh Pirates TC	1.00	.30
664 San Diego Padres TC	1.00	.30
665 San Francisco Giants TC	1.00	.30
666 Seattle Mariners TC	1.50	.45
667 St. Louis Cardinals TC	1.00	.30
668 T.B. Devil Rays TC	1.00	.30
669 Texas Rangers TC	1.00	.30
670 Toronto Blue Jays TC	1.00	.30
671 Juan Cruz PROS	1.50	.45
672 Kevin Cash PROS RC	1.50	.45
673 Jimmy Gobble PROS RC	6.00	1.80
674 Mike Hill PROS RC	1.50	.45
675 T.Buchholz PROS RC	2.50	.75
676 Bill Hall PROS	1.50	.45
677 B.Roneberg PROS RC	1.50	.45
678 R.Huffman PROS RC	1.50	.45
679 Chris Tritle PROS RC	1.50	.45
680 Nate Espy PROS	1.50	.45
681 Nick Alvarez PROS RC	1.50	.45
682 Jason Botts PROS RC	1.50	.45
683 Ryan Gripp PROS RC	1.50	.45
684 Dan Phillips PROS RC	1.50	.45
685 Pablo Arias PROS RC	1.50	.45
686 J.Rodriguez PROS RC	1.50	.45
687 Rich Harden PROS RC	10.00	3.00
688 Neal Frendling PROS RC	1.50	.45
689 R.Thompson PROS RC	1.50	.45
690 G.Montalbano PROS RC	2.50	.75
691 Len Dinardo DP RC	1.50	.45
692 Ryan Raburn DP RC	1.50	.45
693 Josh Barfield DP RC	10.00	3.00
694 David Bacani DP RC	1.50	.45
695 Dan Johnson DP RC	2.50	.75

2002 Topps Chrome Black Refractors

Issued in second series hobby packs at a stated rate of one in 21, these cards parallel the 2002 Topps Chrome set. Black Refractors can be differentiated from the regular cards by their black borders. In addition, each card was serial-numbered to 50 in thin gold foil on the card back.

	Nm-Mt	Ex-Mt
*BLACK: 6X TO 15X BASIC CARDS		
*BLACK 307-331/671-695: 4X TO 10X BASIC		
125 Barry Bonds HR 73		

2002 Topps Chrome Gold Refractors

Inserted into first and second series packs at stated odds of one in four, these cards parallel the 2002 Topps Chrome set. The cards can be differentiated by their striking gold borders and refractive sheen on front.

	Nm-Mt	Ex-Mt
*GOLD: 2X TO 5X BASIC		
*GOLD 307-331/671-695: 1.5X TO 4X BASIC		

2002 Topps Chrome 1952 Reprints

Issued in packs at stated odds of one in eight, these nineteen reprint cards feature players who participated in the 1952 World Series which was won by the New York Yankees.

	Nm-Mt	Ex-Mt
COMPLETE SET (19)	50.00	15.00
COMPLETE SERIES 1 (9)	25.00	7.50
COMPLETE SERIES 2 (10)	25.00	7.50
*REF: .75X TO 2X BASIC 52 REPRINTS		
52R-1 Roy Campanella	5.00	1.50
52R-2 Duke Snider	4.00	1.20
52R-3 Carl Erskine	4.00	1.20
52R-4 Andy Pafko	4.00	1.20
52R-5 Johnny Mize	4.00	1.20
52R-6 Billy Martin	5.00	1.50
52R-7 Phil Rizzuto	5.00	1.50
52R-8 Gil McDougald	4.00	1.20
52R-9 Allie Reynolds	4.00	1.20
52R-10 Jackie Robinson	6.00	1.80
52R-11 Preacher Roe	4.00	1.20
52R-12 Gil Hodges	5.00	1.50
52R-13 Billy Cox	4.00	1.20
52R-14 Yogi Berra	5.00	1.50
52R-15 Gene Woodling	4.00	1.20
52R-16 Johnny Sain	4.00	1.20
52R-17 Ralph Houk	4.00	1.20
52R-18 Joe Collins	4.00	1.20
52R-19 Hank Bauer	4.00	1.20

2002 Topps Chrome 5-Card Stud Aces Relics

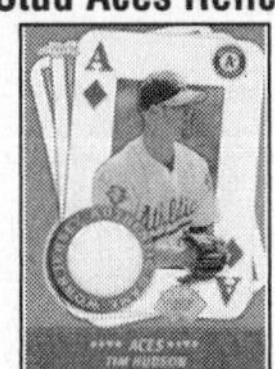

Inserted in second series packs at a stated rate of one in 140, these five cards feature leading pitchers along with a game-worn jersey swatch.

	Nm-Mt	Ex-Mt
5A-AL Al Leiter Jsy	15.00	4.50
5A-BZ Barry Zito Jsy	20.00	6.00
5A-CS Curt Schilling Jsy	20.00	6.00
5A-KB Kevin Brown Jsy	15.00	4.50
5A-TH Tim Hudson Jsy	15.00	4.50

2002 Topps Chrome 5-Card Stud Deuces are Wild Relics

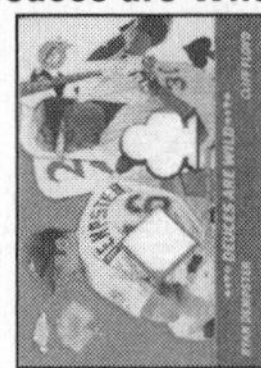

Inserted in second series packs at an overall stated rate of one in 428, these three cards feature teammates as well as a piece of game-used memorabilia from each player.

	Nm-Mt	Ex-Mt
SER.2 BAT ODDS 1:1098		
SER.2 UNIFORM ODDS 1:704		
5D-BT Bernie Williams Bat Tino Martinez Bat		
5D-CA Chipper Jones Bat Andruw Jones Bat		
5D-RC Ryan Dempster Uni Cliff Floyd Uni	15.00	4.50

2002 Topps Chrome 5-Card Stud Jack of all Trades Relics

Inserted in second series packs at a stated rate of one in 428, these three cards feature players who have all five tools along with a piece of game-used memorabilia of that player.

	Nm-Mt	Ex-Mt
SER.2 BAT ODDS 1:1098		
SER.2 JERSEY ODDS 1:704		
5J-AR Alex Rodriguez Bat		
5J-CJ Chipper Jones Jsy	25.00	7.50
5J-MO Magglio Ordonez Bat		

2002 Topps Chrome 5-Card Stud Kings of the Clubhouse Relics

Inserted in second series packs at a stated rate of one in 303, these three cards feature three of the best team leaders along with a piece of game-used memorabilia from the featured player.

	Nm-Mt	Ex-Mt
SER.2 BAT ODDS 1:2204		
SER.2 JERSEY ODDS 1:704		
SER.2 UNIFORM ODDS 1:704		
5K-AR Alex Rodriguez Bat		
5K-JB Jeff Bagwell Uniform	20.00	6.00
5K-TG Tony Gwynn Jsy	30.00	9.00

2002 Topps Chrome 5-Card Stud Three of a Kind Relics

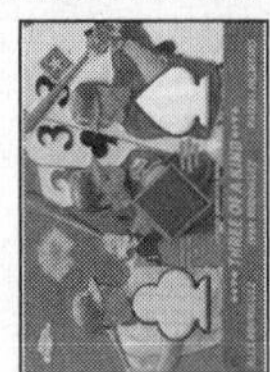

Inserted into second series packs at a stated rate of one in 689, these three cards feature a group of three teammates along with a piece of game-used memorabilia from each player.

	Nm-Mt	Ex-Mt
5TAIR Alex Rodriguez Bat Ivan Rodriguez Jsy Rafael Palmeiro Uni	80.00	24.00
5TBEJ Bret Boone Bat Edgar Martinez Bat John Olerud Bat	80.00	24.00
5TJCL Jeff Bagwell Uni Craig Biggio Bat Lance Berkman Bat	80.00	24.00

2002 Topps Chrome Summer School Like Father Like Son Relics

Issued in packs at stated odds of one in 790, this card features memorabilia from Preston and Mookie Wilson.

	Nm-Mt	Ex-Mt
FSC-WI Preston Wilson Mookie Wilson	15.00	4.50

2002 Topps Chrome Summer School Battery Mates Relics

Inserted at overall odds of one in 349, these two cards feature memorabilia from a pitcher and catcher from the same team. The Hampton/Petrick card was seeded at a rate of 1:716 and the Glavine/Lopez at 1:681.

	Nm-Mt	Ex-Mt
BMC-GL Tom Glavine Javier Lopez B	25.00	7.50
BMC-HP Mike Hampton Ben Petrick A UER Card has two jersey swatches on it	15.00	4.50

2002 Topps Chrome Summer School Top of the Order Relics

Inserted into packs at an overall rate of one in 106, these 12 cards featured players who lead off for their teams along with a memorabilia piece. Uniforms (a.k.a. pants), jerseys and bats were utilized for this set. Bat cards were seeded into five different groups at the following ratios: Group A 1:1383, Group B 1:1538, Group C 1:3170, Group D 1:2902, Group E 1:2544. Jersey cards were seeded into two groups as follows: Group A 1:790 and Group B 1:659. Uniform cards were seeded into three groups as follows: Group A 1:920, Group B 1:651 and Group C 1:614.

	Nm-Mt	Ex-Mt
TOC-BA Benny Agbayani Uni C	15.00	4.50
TOC-CB Craig Biggio Uni A	25.00	7.50
TOC-CK Chuck Knoblauch Bat E	15.00	4.50
TOC-JD Johnny Damon Bat B	15.00	4.50
TOC-JK Jason Kendall Bat D	15.00	4.50
TOC-JP Juan Pierre Bat A	15.00	4.50
TOC-KL Kenny Lofton Uni B	15.00	4.50
TOC-PB Peter Bergeron Jsy A	15.00	4.50
TOC-PL Paul LoDuca Bat A	15.00	4.50
TOC-RF Rafael Furcal Bat C	15.00	4.50
TOC-RH R.Henderson Bat B	25.00	7.50
TOC-SS Shannon Stewart Jsy B	15.00	4.50

2002 Topps Chrome Traded

Inserted at a stated rate of two per 2002 Topps Traded Hobby or Retail Pack and sever per 2002 Topps Traded HTA pack, this is a complete parallel of the 2002 Topps Traded set. Unlike the regular Topps Traded set, all cards are printed in equal quantities.

Card	Nm-Mt	Ex-Mt
COMPLETE SET (275)	120.00	36.00
T1 Jeff Weaver	.50	.15
T2 Jay Powell	.50	.15
T3 Alex Gonzalez	.50	.15
T4 Jason Isringhausen	.75	.23
T5 Tyler Houston	.50	.15
T6 Ben Broussard	.50	.15
T7 Chuck Knoblauch	.75	.23
T8 Brian L. Hunter	.50	.15
T9 Dustan Mohr	.50	.15
T10 Eric Hinske	.50	.15
T11 Roger Cedeno	.50	.15
T12 Eddie Perez	.50	.15
T13 Jeromy Burnitz	.75	.23
T14 Bartolo Colon	.75	.23
T15 Rick Helling	.50	.15
T16 Dan Plesac	.50	.15
T17 Scott Strickland	.50	.15
T18 Antonio Alfonseca	.50	.15
T19 Ricky Gutierrez	.50	.15
T20 John Valentin	.50	.15
T21 Raul Mondesi	.75	.23
T22 Ben Davis	.50	.15
T23 Nelson Figueroa	.50	.15
T24 Earl Snyder	.50	.15
T25 Robin Ventura	.75	.23
T26 Jimmy Haynes	.50	.15
T27 Kenny Kelly	.50	.15
T28 Morgan Ensberg	.75	.23
T29 Reggie Sanders	.75	.23
T30 Shigetoshi Hasegawa	.75	.23
T31 Mike Timlin	.50	.15
T32 Russell Branyan	.50	.15
T33 Alan Embree	.50	.15
T34 D'Angelo Jimenez	.50	.15
T35 Kent Mercker	.50	.15
T36 Jesse Orosco	.50	.15
T37 Gregg Zaun	.50	.15
T38 Reggie Taylor	.50	.15
T39 Andres Galarraga	.75	.23
T40 Chris Truby	.50	.15
T41 Bruce Chen	.50	.15
T42 Darren Lewis	.50	.15
T43 Ryan Kohlmeier	.50	.15
T44 John McDonald	.50	.15
T45 Omar Daal	.50	.15
T46 Matt Clement	.75	.23
T47 Glendon Rusch	.50	.15
T48 Chan Ho Park	.75	.23
T49 Benny Agbayani	.50	.15
T50 Juan Gonzalez	2.00	.60
T51 Carlos Baerga	.50	.15
T52 Tim Raines	.75	.23
T53 Kevin Appier	.75	.23
T54 Marty Cordova	.50	.15
T55 Jeff D'Amico	.50	.15
T56 Dmitri Young	.75	.23
T57 Roosevelt Brown	.50	.15
T58 Dustin Hermanson	.50	.15
T59 Jose Rijo	.50	.15
T60 Todd Ritchie	.50	.15
T61 Lee Stevens	.50	.15
T62 Placido Polanco	.50	.15
T63 Eric Young	.50	.15
T64 Chuck Finley	.75	.23
T65 Dicky Gonzalez	.50	.15
T66 Jose Macias	.50	.15
T67 Gabe Kapler	.50	.15
T68 Sandy Alomar Jr.	.50	.15
T69 Henry Blanco	.50	.15
T70 Julian Tavarez	.50	.15
T71 Paul Bako	.50	.15
T72 Scott Rolen	1.25	.35
T73 Brian Jordan	.75	.23
T74 Rickey Henderson	2.00	.60
T75 Kevin Mench	.50	.15
T76 Hideo Nomo	2.00	.60
T77 Jeremy Giambi	.50	.15
T78 Brad Fullmer	.50	.15
T79 Carl Everett	.75	.23
T80 David Wells	.75	.23
T81 Aaron Sele	.50	.15
T82 Todd Hollandsworth	.50	.15
T83 Vicente Padilla	.50	.15
T84 Kenny Lofton	.75	.23
T85 Corky Miller	.50	.15
T86 Josh Fogg	.50	.15
T87 Cliff Floyd	.75	.23
T88 Craig Paquette	.50	.15
T89 Jay Payton	.50	.15
T90 Carlos Pena	.50	.15
T91 Juan Encarnacion	.50	.15
T92 Rey Sanchez	.50	.15
T93 Ryan Dempster	.50	.15
T94 Mario Encarnacion	.50	.15
T95 Jorge Julio	.50	.15
T96 John Mabry	.50	.15
T97 Todd Zeile	.75	.23
T98 Johnny Damon	.75	.23
T99 Deivi Cruz	.50	.15
T100 Gary Sheffield	.75	.23
T101 Ted Lilly	.50	.15
T102 Todd Van Poppel	.50	.15
T103 Shawn Estes	.50	.15
T104 Cesar Izturis	.50	.15
T105 Ron Coomer	.50	.15
T106 Grady Little MG RC	.50	.15
T107 Jimy Williams MGR	.50	.15
T108 Tony Pena MGR	.50	.15
T109 Frank Robinson MGR	1.25	.35
T110 Ron Gardenhire MGR	.50	.15
T111 Dennis Tankersley	.50	.15
T112 Alejandro Cadena RC	1.00	.30
T113 Justin Reid RC	1.00	.30
T114 Nate Field RC	1.00	.30
T115 Rene Reyes RC	1.00	.30
T116 Nelson Castro RC	1.00	.30
T117 Miguel Olivo	.50	.15
T118 David Espinosa	.50	.15
T119 Chris Bootcheck RC	1.00	.30
T120 Rob Henkel RC	1.00	.30
T121 Steve Bechler RC	1.00	.30
T122 Mark Outlaw RC	1.00	.30
T123 Henry Pichardo RC	1.00	.30
T124 Michael Floyd RC	1.00	.30
T125 Richard Lane RC	1.00	.30
T126 Pete Zamora RC	1.00	.30
T127 Javier Colina	.50	.15
T128 Greg Sain RC	1.00	.30
T129 Ronnie Merrill	.50	.15
T130 Gavin Floyd RC	5.00	1.50
T131 Josh Bonifay RC	1.00	.30
T132 Tommy Marx RC	1.00	.30
T133 Gary Cates Jr. RC	1.00	.30
T134 Neal Cotts RC	4.00	1.20
T135 Angel Berroa	.75	.23
T136 Elio Serrano RC	1.00	.30
T137 J.J. Putz RC	1.00	.30
T138 Ruben Gotay RC	1.00	.30
T139 Eddie Rogers	.50	.15
T140 Wily Mo Pena	.50	.15
T141 Tyler Yates RC	2.00	.60
T142 Colin Young RC	.75	.23
T143 Chance Caple	.50	.15
T144 Ben Howard RC	1.00	.30
T145 Ryan Bukvich RC	1.00	.30
T146 Cliff Bartosh RC	1.00	.30
T147 Brandon Claussen	2.00	.60

T148 Cristian Guerrero .50 .15
T149 Derrick Lewis .50 .15
T150 Eric Miller RC 1.00 .30
T151 Justin Huber RC 2.50 .75
T152 Adrian Gonzalez .75 .23
T153 Brian West RC 1.00 .30
T154 Chris Baker RC 1.00 .30
T155 Drew Henson .75 .23
T156 Scott Hairston RC 4.00 1.20
T157 Jason Simontacchi RC 1.00 .30
T158 Jason Arnold RC 2.50 .75
T159 Brandon Phillips .50 .15
T160 Adam Roller RC 1.00 .30
T161 Scotty Layfield RC 1.00 .30
T162 Freddie Money RC 1.00 .30
T163 Noochie Varner RC 1.00 .30
T164 Terrance Hill RC 1.00 .30
T165 Jeremy Hill RC 1.00 .30
T166 Carlos Cabrera RC 1.00 .30
T167 Jose Morban RC 1.00 .30
T168 Kevin Frederick RC 1.00 .30
T169 Mark Teixeira 2.00 .60
T170 Brian Rogers .50 .15
T171 Anastacio Martinez RC 1.00 .30
T172 Bobby Jenks RC 3.00 .90
T173 David Gil RC 1.00 .30
T174 Andres Torres .50 .15
T175 James Barrett RC 1.00 .30
T176 Jimmy Journell .50 .15
T177 Brett Kay RC 1.00 .30
T178 Jason Young RC 1.00 .30
T179 Mark Hamilton RC 1.00 .30
T180 Jose Bautista RC 2.00 .60
T181 Blake McGinley RC 1.00 .30
T182 Ryan Mottl RC 1.00 .30
T183 Jeff Austin RC 1.00 .30
T184 Xavier Nady .50 .15
T185 Kyle Kane RC 1.00 .30
T186 Travis Foley RC 1.00 .30
T187 Nathan Kaup RC 1.00 .30
T188 Eric Cyr .50 .15
T189 Josh Cisneros RC 1.00 .30
T190 Brad Nelson RC 3.00 .90
T191 Clint Weibl RC 1.00 .30
T192 Ron Calloway RC 1.00 .30
T193 Jung Bong .50 .15
T194 Rolando Viera RC 1.00 .30
T195 Jason Bulger RC 1.00 .30
T196 Chone Figgins RC 1.00 .30
T197 Jimmy Alvarez RC 1.00 .30
T198 Joel Crump RC 1.00 .30
T199 Ryan Doumit RC 1.25 .35
T200 Demetrius Heath RC 1.00 .30
T201 John Ennis RC 1.00 .30
T202 Doug Sessions RC 1.00 .30
T203 Clinton Hosford RC 1.00 .30
T204 Chris Narveson RC 1.00 .30
T205 Ross Peeples RC 1.00 .30
T206 Alex Requena RC 1.00 .30
T207 Matt Erickson RC 1.00 .30
T208 Brian Forystek RC 1.00 .30
T209 Dewon Brazelton .50 .15
T210 Nathan Haynes .50 .15
T211 Jack Cust .50 .15
T212 Jesse Foppert RC 4.00 1.20
T213 Jesus Cota RC 1.00 .30
T214 Juan M. Gonzalez RC 1.00 .30
T215 Tim Kalita RC 1.00 .30
T216 Manny Delcarmen RC 1.00 .30
T217 Jim Kavourias RC 1.00 .30
T218 C.J. Wilson RC 1.00 .30
T219 Edwin Yan RC 1.00 .30
T220 Andy Van Hekken .50 .15
T221 Michael Cuddyer .50 .15
T222 Jeff Verplancke RC 1.00 .30
T223 Mike Wilson RC 1.00 .30
T224 Corwin Malone RC 1.00 .30
T225 Chris Snelling RC 2.50 .75
T226 Joe Rogers RC 1.00 .30
T227 Jason Bay 3.00 .90
T228 Ezequiel Astacio RC 1.00 .30
T229 Joey Hammond RC 1.00 .30
T230 Chris Duffy RC 1.00 .30
T231 Mark Prior 4.00 1.20
T232 Hansel Izquierdo RC 1.00 .30
T233 Franklyn German RC 1.00 .30
T234 Alexis Gomez .50 .15
T235 Jorge Padilla RC 1.00 .30
T236 Ryan Snare RC 1.00 .30
T237 Deivis Santos .50 .15
T238 Taggert Bozied RC 4.00 1.20
T239 Mike Peeples RC 1.00 .30
T240 Ronald Acuna RC 1.00 .30
T241 Koyie Hill .50 .15
T242 Garrett Guzman RC 1.00 .30
T243 Ryan Church RC 1.25 .35
T244 Tony Fontana RC 1.00 .30
T245 Keto Anderson RC 1.00 .30
T246 Brad Bouras RC 1.00 .30
T247 Jason Dubois RC 4.00 1.20
T248 Angel Guzman RC 10.00 3.00
T249 Joel Hanrahan RC 2.00 .60
T250 Joe Jiannetti RC 1.00 .30
T251 Sean Pierce RC 1.00 .30
T252 Jake Mauer RC 1.00 .30
T253 Marshall McDougall RC 1.00 .30
T254 Edwin Almonte RC 1.00 .30
T255 Shawn Riggans RC 1.00 .30
T256 Steven Shell RC 1.00 .30
T257 Kevin Hooper RC 1.00 .30
T258 Michael Frick RC 1.00 .30
T259 Travis Chapman RC 1.00 .30
T260 Tim Hummel RC 1.00 .30
T261 Adam Morrissey RC 1.00 .30
T262 Dontrelle Willis RC 15.00 4.50
T263 Justin Sherrod RC 1.00 .30
T264 Gerald Smiley RC 1.00 .30
T265 Tony Miller RC 1.00 .30
T266 Nolan Ryan WW 5.00 1.50
T267 Reggie Jackson WW 1.25 .35
T268 Steve Garvey WW .75 .23
T269 Wade Boggs WW 1.25 .35
T270 Sammy Sosa WW 3.00 .90
T271 Curt Schilling WW 1.25 .35
T272 Mark Grace WW 1.25 .35
T273 Jason Giambi WW 2.00 .60
T274 Ken Griffey Jr. WW 3.00 .90
T275 Roberto Alomar WW 2.00 .60

2002 Topps Chrome Traded Black Refractors

Inserted at a stated rate of one in 56 Topps Traded hobby or retail packs and one in 16 HTA packs, this is a parallel of the Topps Chrome Traded set. These cards can be differentiated from the regular cards by their black borders and are printed to a stated print run of 100 serial numbered sets.

Nm-Mt Ex-Mt
*BLACK REF: 5X TO 12X BASIC
*BLACK REF RC'S: 5X TO 12X BASIC RC'S

2002 Topps Chrome Traded Refractors

nserted at a stated rate of one in 12 Topps Traded packs, this is a parallel of the Topps Chrome Traded set. These cards can be differentiated from the regular cards by their "refractive" sheen and are notated as refractors on the back of the card.

Nm-Mt Ex-Mt
*REF: 2X TO 5X BASIC
*REF RC'S: 1.5X TO 4X BASIC RC'S
STATED ODDS 1:12 HOB/RET, 1:12 HTA

2003 Topps Chrome

The first series of 2003 Topps Chrome was released in January, 2003. These cards were issued in four card packs which came 24 packs to a box and 10 boxes to a case with an SRP of $3 per pack. Cards numbered 201 through 220 feature players in their first year of Topps cards. The second series, which also consisted of 220 cards, was released in May, 2003. Cards number 421 through 430 were draft pick cards while cards 431 through 440 were two player prospect cards.

Nm-Mt Ex-Mt
COMPLETE SET (440) 200.00 60.00
COMPLETE SERIES 1 (220) 100.00 30.00
COMPLETE SERIES 2 (220) 100.00 30.00
COMMON (1-200/221-420) 1.00 .30
COMMON (201-220/421-440) 1.50 .45
1 Alex Rodriguez 4.00 1.20
2 Eddie Guardado 1.00 .30
3 Curt Schilling 1.50 .45
4 Andruw Jones 1.00 .30
5 Magglio Ordonez 1.00 .30
6 Todd Helton 1.50 .45
7 Odalis Perez 1.00 .30
8 Edgardo Alfonzo 1.00 .30
9 Eric Hinske 1.00 .30
10 Danny Bautista 1.00 .30
11 Sammy Sosa 4.00 1.20
12 Roberto Alomar 2.50 .75
13 Roger Clemens 5.00 1.50
14 Austin Kearns 1.00 .30
15 Luis Gonzalez 1.00 .30
16 Mo Vaughn 1.00 .30
17 Alfonso Soriano 1.50 .45
18 Orlando Cabrera 1.00 .30
19 Hideo Nomo 2.50 .75
20 Omar Vizquel 1.00 .30
21 Greg Maddux 4.00 1.20
22 Fred McGriff 1.50 .45
23 Frank Thomas 2.50 .75
24 Shawn Green 1.00 .30
25 Jacque Jones 1.00 .30
26 Bernie Williams 1.50 .45
27 Corey Patterson 1.00 .30
28 Cesar Izturis 1.00 .30
29 Larry Walker 1.50 .45
30 Darren Dreifort 1.00 .30
31 Al Leiter 1.00 .30
32 Jason Marquis 1.00 .30
33 Sean Casey 1.00 .30
34 Craig Counsell 1.00 .30
35 Albert Pujols 5.00 1.50
36 Kyle Lohse 1.00 .30
37 Paul Lo Duca 1.00 .30
38 Roy Oswalt 1.00 .30
39 Danny Graves 1.00 .30
40 Kevin Millwood 1.00 .30
41 Lance Berkman 1.00 .30
42 Denny Hocking 1.00 .30
43 Jose Valentin 1.00 .30
44 Josh Beckett 1.50 .45
45 Nomar Garciaparra 4.00 1.20
46 Craig Biggio 1.50 .45
47 Omar Daal 1.00 .30
48 Jimmy Rollins 1.00 .30
49 Jermaine Dye 1.00 .30
50 Edgar Renteria 1.00 .30
51 Brandon Duckworth 1.00 .30
52 Luis Castillo 1.00 .30
53 Andy Ashby 1.00 .30
54 Mike Williams 1.00 .30
55 Benito Santiago 1.00 .30
56 Bret Boone 1.00 .30
57 Randy Wolf 1.00 .30
58 Ivan Rodriguez 2.50 .75
59 Shannon Stewart 1.00 .30
60 Jose Cruz Jr. 1.00 .30
61 Billy Wagner 1.00 .30
62 Alex Gonzalez 1.00 .30
63 Ichiro Suzuki 4.00 1.20
64 Joe McEwing 1.00 .30
65 Mark Mulder 1.00 .30
66 Mike Cameron 1.00 .30
67 Corey Koskie 1.00 .30
68 Marlon Anderson 1.00 .30
69 Jason Kendall 1.00 .30
70 J.T. Snow 1.00 .30
71 Edgar Martinez 1.50 .45
72 Vernon Wells 1.00 .30
73 Vladimir Guerrero 2.50 .75
74 Adam Dunn 1.00 .30
75 Barry Zito 1.50 .45
76 Jeff Kent 1.00 .30
77 Russ Ortiz 1.00 .30
78 Phil Nevin 1.00 .30
79 Carlos Beltran 1.00 .30
80 Mike Lowell 1.00 .30
81 Bob Wickman 1.00 .30
82 Junior Spivey 1.00 .30
83 Melvin Mora 1.00 .30
84 Derrek Lee 1.00 .30
85 Chuck Knoblauch 1.00 .30
86 Eric Gagne 1.50 .45
87 Orlando Hernandez 1.00 .30
88 Robert Person 1.00 .30
89 Elmer Dessens 1.00 .30
90 Wade Miller 1.00 .30
91 Adrian Beltre 1.00 .30
92 Kazuhiro Sasaki 1.00 .30
93 Timo Perez 1.00 .30
94 Jose Vidro 1.00 .30
95 Geronimo Gil 1.00 .30
96 Trot Nixon 1.50 .45
97 Denny Neagle 1.00 .30
98 Roberto Hernandez 1.00 .30
99 David Ortiz 1.00 .30
100 Robb Nen 1.00 .30
101 Sidney Ponson 1.00 .30
102 Kevin Appier 1.00 .30
103 Javier Lopez 1.00 .30
104 Jeff Conine 1.00 .30
105 Mark Buehrle 1.00 .30
106 Jason Simontacchi 1.00 .30
107 Jose Jimenez 1.00 .30
108 Brian Jordan 1.00 .30
109 Brad Wilkerson 1.00 .30
110 Scott Hatteberg 1.00 .30
111 Matt Morris 1.00 .30
112 Miguel Tejada 1.00 .30
113 Rafael Furcal 1.00 .30
114 Steve Cox 1.00 .30
115 Roy Halladay 1.00 .30
116 David Eckstein 1.00 .30
117 Tomo Ohka 1.00 .30
118 Jack Wilson 1.00 .30
119 Randall Simon 1.00 .30
120 Jamie Moyer 1.00 .30
121 Andy Benes 1.00 .30
122 Tino Martinez 1.50 .45
123 Esteban Yan 1.00 .30
124 Jason Isringhausen 1.00 .30
125 Chris Carpenter 1.00 .30
126 Aaron Rowand 1.00 .30
127 Brandon Inge 1.00 .30
128 Jose Vizcaino 1.00 .30
129 Jose Mesa 1.00 .30
130 Troy Percival 1.00 .30
131 Jon Lieber 1.00 .30
132 Brian Giles 1.00 .30
133 Aaron Boone 1.00 .30
134 Bobby Higginson 1.00 .30
135 Luis Rivas 1.00 .30
136 Troy Glaus 1.50 .45
137 Jim Thome 2.50 .75
138 Ramon Martinez 1.00 .30
139 Jay Gibbons 1.00 .30
140 Mike Lieberthal 1.00 .30
141 Juan Uribe 1.00 .30
142 Gary Sheffield 1.00 .30
143 Ramon Santiago 1.00 .30
144 Ben Sheets 1.00 .30
145 Tony Armas Jr. 1.00 .30
146 Kazuhisa Ishii 1.00 .30
147 Erubiel Durazo 1.00 .30
148 Jerry Hairston Jr. 1.00 .30
149 Byung-Hyun Kim 1.00 .30
150 Marcus Giles 1.00 .30
151 Johnny Damon 1.00 .30
152 Terrence Long 1.00 .30
153 Juan Pierre 1.00 .30
154 Aramis Ramirez 1.00 .30
155 Brent Abernathy 1.00 .30
156 Ismael Valdes 1.00 .30
157 Mike Mussina 2.50 .75
158 Ramon Hernandez 1.00 .30
159 Adam Kennedy 1.00 .30
160 Tony Womack 1.00 .30
161 Tony Batista 1.00 .30
162 Kip Wells 1.00 .30
163 Jeromy Burnitz 1.00 .30
164 Todd Hundley 1.00 .30
165 Tim Wakefield 1.00 .30
166 Derek Lowe 1.00 .30
167 Jorge Posada 1.50 .45
168 Ramon Ortiz 1.00 .30
169 Brent Butler 1.00 .30
170 Shane Halter 1.00 .30
171 Matt Lawton 1.00 .30
172 Alex Sanchez 1.00 .30
173 Eric Milton 1.00 .30
174 Vicente Padilla 1.00 .30
175 Steve Karsay 1.00 .30
176 Mark Prior 5.00 1.50
177 Kerry Wood 2.50 .75
178 Jason LaRue 1.00 .30
179 Danys Baez 1.00 .30
180 Nick Neugebauer 1.00 .30
181 Andres Galarraga 1.00 .30
182 Jason Giambi 2.50 .75
183 Aubrey Huff 1.00 .30
184 Juan Gonzalez 2.50 .75
185 Ugueth Urbina 1.00 .30
186 Rickey Henderson 2.50 .75
187 Brad Fullmer 1.00 .30
188 Todd Zeile 1.00 .30
189 Jason Jennings 1.00 .30
190 Vladimir Nunez 1.00 .30
191 David Justice 1.00 .30
192 Brian Lawrence 1.00 .30
193 Pat Burrell 1.00 .30
194 Pokey Reese 1.00 .30
195 Robert Fick 1.00 .30
196 C.C. Sabathia 1.00 .30
197 Fernando Vina 1.00 .30
198 Sean Burroughs 1.00 .30
199 Ellis Burks 1.00 .30
200 Joe Randa 1.00 .30
201 Chris Duncan FY RC 1.50 .45
202 Franklin Gutierrez FY RC 6.00 1.80
203 Adam LaRoche FY 1.50 .45
204 Manuel Ramirez FY RC 2.50 .75
205 Il Kim FY RC 1.50 .45
206 Daryl Clark FY RC 2.50 .75
207 Sean Pierce FY 1.50 .45
208 Andy Marte FY RC 8.00 2.40
209 Bernie Castro FY RC 1.50 .45
210 Jason Perry FY RC 2.50 .75
211 Jaime Bubela FY RC 1.50 .45
212 Alexis Rios FY 4.00 1.20
213 Brendan Harris FY RC 2.50 .75
214 R.Nivar-Martinez FY RC 2.50 .75
215 Terry Tiffee FY RC 2.50 .75
216 Kevin Youkilis FY RC 5.00 1.50
217 Derell McCall FY RC 1.50 .45
218 Scott Tyler FY RC 2.50 .75
219 Craig Brazell FY RC 2.50 .75
220 Walter Young FY 1.50 .45
221 Francisco Rodriguez 1.00 .30
222 Chipper Jones 2.50 .75
223 Chris Singleton 1.00 .30
224 Cliff Floyd 1.00 .30
225 Bobby Hill 1.00 .30
226 Antonio Osuna 1.00 .30
227 Barry Larkin 2.50 .75
228 Dean Palmer 1.00 .30
229 Eric Owens 1.00 .30
230 Randy Johnson 2.50 .75
231 Jeff Suppan 1.00 .30
232 Eric Karros 1.00 .30
233 Johan Santana 1.00 .30
234 Javier Vazquez 1.00 .30
235 John Thomson 1.00 .30
236 Nick Johnson 1.00 .30
237 Mark Ellis 1.00 .30
238 Doug Glanville 1.00 .30
239 Ken Griffey Jr. 4.00 1.20
240 Bubba Trammell 1.00 .30
241 Livan Hernandez 1.00 .30
242 Desi Relaford 1.00 .30
243 Eli Marrero 1.00 .30
244 Jared Sandberg 1.00 .30
245 Barry Bonds 6.00 1.80
246 Aaron Sele 1.00 .30
247 Derek Jeter 6.00 1.80
248 Eric Byrnes 1.00 .30
249 Rich Aurilia 1.00 .30
250 Joel Pineiro 1.00 .30
251 Chuck Finley 1.00 .30
252 Bengie Molina 1.00 .30
253 Steve Finley 1.00 .30
254 Marty Cordova 1.00 .30
255 Shea Hillenbrand 1.00 .30
256 Milton Bradley 1.00 .30
257 Carlos Pena 1.00 .30
258 Brad Ausmus 1.00 .30
259 Carlos Delgado 1.00 .30
260 Kevin Mench 1.00 .30
261 Joe Kennedy 1.00 .30
262 Mark McLemore 1.00 .30
263 Bill Mueller 1.00 .30
264 Ricky Ledee 1.00 .30
265 Ted Lilly 1.00 .30
266 Sterling Hitchcock 1.00 .30
267 Scott Strickland 1.00 .30
268 Damion Easley 1.00 .30
269 Torii Hunter 1.00 .30
270 Brad Radke 1.00 .30
271 Geoff Jenkins 1.00 .30
272 Paul Byrd 1.00 .30
273 Morgan Ensberg 1.00 .30
274 Mike Maroth 1.00 .30
275 Mike Hampton 1.00 .30
276 Flash Gordon 1.00 .30
277 John Burkett 1.00 .30
278 Rodrigo Lopez 1.00 .30
279 Tim Spooneybarger 1.00 .30
280 Quinton McCracken 1.00 .30
281 Tim Salmon 1.50 .45
282 Jarrod Washburn 1.00 .30
283 Pedro Martinez 2.50 .75
284 Julio Lugo 1.00 .30
285 Armando Benitez 1.00 .30
286 Raul Mondesi 1.00 .30
287 Robin Ventura 1.00 .30
288 Bobby Abreu 1.00 .30
289 Josh Fogg 1.00 .30
290 Ryan Klesko 1.00 .30
291 Tsuyoshi Shinjo 1.00 .30
292 Jim Edmonds 1.00 .30
293 Chan Ho Park 1.00 .30
294 John Mabry 1.00 .30
295 Woody Williams 1.00 .30
296 Scott Schoeneweis 1.00 .30
297 Brian Anderson 1.00 .30
298 Brett Tomko 1.00 .30
299 Scott Erickson 1.00 .30
300 Kevin Millar 1.00 .30
301 Danny Wright 1.00 .30
302 Jason Schmidt 1.00 .30
303 Scott Williamson 1.00 .30
304 Einar Diaz 1.00 .30
305 Jay Payton 1.00 .30
306 Juan Acevedo 1.00 .30
307 Ben Grieve 1.00 .30
308 Raul Ibanez 1.00 .30
309 Richie Sexson 1.00 .30
310 Rick Reed 1.00 .30
311 Pedro Astacio 1.00 .30
312 Bud Smith 1.00 .30
313 Tomas Perez 1.00 .30
314 Rafael Palmeiro 1.50 .45
315 Jason Tyner 1.00 .30
316 Scott Rolen 1.50 .45
317 Randy Winn 1.00 .30
318 Ryan Jensen 1.00 .30
319 Trevor Hoffman 1.00 .30
320 Craig Wilson 1.00 .30
321 Jeremy Giambi 1.00 .30
322 Andy Pettitte 1.50 .45
323 John Franco 1.00 .30
324 Felipe Lopez 1.00 .30
325 Mike Piazza 4.00 1.20
326 Cristian Guzman 1.00 .30
327 Jose Hernandez 1.00 .30
328 Octavio Dotel 1.00 .30
329 Brad Penny 1.00 .30
330 Dave Veres 1.00 .30
331 Ryan Dempster 1.00 .30
332 Joe Crede 1.00 .30
333 Chad Hermansen 1.00 .30
334 Gary Matthews Jr. 1.00 .30
335 Frank Catalanotto 1.00 .30
336 Darin Erstad 1.00 .30
337 Matt Williams 1.00 .30
338 B.J. Surhoff 1.00 .30
339 Kerry Ligtenberg 1.00 .30
340 Mike Bordick 1.00 .30
341 Joe Girardi 1.00 .30
342 D'Angelo Jimenez 1.00 .30
343 Paul Konerko 1.00 .30
344 Joe Mays 1.00 .30
345 Marquis Grissom 1.00 .30
346 Neifi Perez 1.00 .30
347 Preston Wilson 1.00 .30
348 Jeff Weaver 1.00 .30
349 Eric Chavez 1.00 .30
350 Placido Polanco 1.00 .30
351 Matt Mantei 1.00 .30
352 James Baldwin 1.00 .30
353 Toby Hall 1.00 .30
354 Benji Gil 1.00 .30
355 Damian Moss 1.00 .30
356 Jorge Julio 1.00 .30
357 Matt Clement 1.00 .30
358 Lee Stevens 1.00 .30
359 Dave Roberts 1.00 .30
360 J.C. Romero 1.00 .30
361 Bartolo Colon 1.00 .30
362 Roger Cedeno 1.00 .30
363 Mariano Rivera 1.50 .45
364 Billy Koch 1.00 .30
365 Manny Ramirez 1.00 .30
366 Travis Lee 1.00 .30
367 Oliver Perez 1.00 .30
368 Tim Worrell 1.00 .30
369 Damian Miller 1.00 .30
370 John Smoltz 1.50 .45
371 Willis Roberts 1.00 .30
372 Tim Hudson 1.00 .30
373 Moises Alou 1.00 .30
374 Corky Miller 1.00 .30
375 Ben Broussard 1.00 .30
376 Gabe Kapler 1.00 .30
377 Chris Woodward 1.00 .30
378 Todd Hollandsworth 1.00 .30
379 So Taguchi 1.00 .30
380 John Olerud 1.00 .30
381 Reggie Sanders 1.00 .30
382 Jake Peavy 1.00 .30
383 Kris Benson 1.00 .30
384 Ray Durham 1.00 .30
385 Boomer Wells 1.00 .30
386 Tom Glavine 1.50 .45
387 Antonio Alfonseca 1.00 .30
388 Keith Foulke 1.00 .30
389 Shawn Estes 1.00 .30
390 Mark Grace 1.50 .45
391 Dmitri Young 1.00 .30
392 A.J. Burnett 1.00 .30
393 Richard Hidalgo 1.00 .30
394 Mike Sweeney 1.00 .30
395 Doug Mientkiewicz 1.00 .30
396 Cory Lidle 1.00 .30
397 Jeff Bagwell 1.50 .45
398 Steve Sparks 1.00 .30
399 Sandy Alomar Jr. 1.00 .30
400 John Lackey 1.00 .30
401 Rick Helling 1.00 .30
402 Carlos Lee 1.00 .30
403 Garret Anderson 1.00 .30
404 Vinny Castilla 1.00 .30
405 David Bell 1.00 .30
406 Freddy Garcia 1.00 .30
407 Scott Spiezio 1.00 .30
408 Russell Branyan 1.00 .30
409 Jose Contreras RC 4.00 1.20
410 Kevin Brown 1.00 .30
411 Tyler Houston 1.00 .30
412 A.J. Pierzynski 1.00 .30
413 Peter Bergeron 1.00 .30
414 Brett Myers 1.00 .30
415 Kenny Lofton 1.00 .30
416 Ben Davis 1.00 .30
417 J.D. Drew 1.00 .30
418 Ricky Gutierrez 1.00 .30
419 Mark Redman 1.00 .30
420 Juan Encarnacion 1.00 .30
421 Bryan Bullington DP RC 5.00 1.50
422 Jeremy Guthrie DP 1.50 .45
423 Joey Gomes DP RC 1.50 .45
424 E.Bastida-Martinez DP RC 1.50 .45
425 Brian Wright DP RC 1.50 .45
426 B.J. Upton DP 2.50 .75
427 Jeff Francis DP 1.50 .45
428 Jeremy Hermida DP 1.50 .45
429 Khalil Greene DP 1.50 .45
430 Darrell Rasner DP RC 1.50 .45
431 Brandon Phillips 1.50 .45
Victor Martinez
432 Hee Seop Choi 1.50 .45
Nic Jackson
433 Dontrelle Willis 2.50 .75
Jason Stokes
434 Chad Tracy 1.50 .45
Lyle Overbay
435 Joe Borchard 1.50 .45
Corwin Malone
436 Joe Mauer 2.50 .75
Justin Morneau
437 Drew Henson 1.50 .45
Brandon Claussen
438 Chase Utley 1.50 .45
Gavin Floyd
439 Taggert Bozied 1.50 .45
Xavier Nady
440 Aaron Heilman 1.50 .45
Jose Reyes

2003 Topps Chrome Black Refractors

Issued at a stated rate of one in 20 for first series cards and one in 17 for second series cards, this is a parallel to the Topps Chrome set. These cards have black borders and were issued to a stated print run of 199 serial numbered sets.

Nm-Mt Ex-Mt
*BLACK 1-200/221-420: 2X TO 5X
*BLACK 201-220/409/421-440: 2.5X TO 6X

2003 Topps Chrome Gold Refractors

Issued at a stated rate of one in eight for first series cards and two in eight for second series cards, this is a parallel to the Topps Chrome set. These cards have gold borders and were issued to a stated print run of 449 serial numbered sets.

Nm-Mt Ex-Mt
*GOLD 1-200/221-420: 1.25X TO 3X..
*GOLD 201-220/409/421-440: 1.5X TO 4X

2003 Topps Chrome Refractors

Issued at a stated rate of one in five, this is a parallel to the Topps Chrome set. These cards use the patented Topps Chrome technology and were issued to a stated print run of 699 serial numbered sets.

Nm-Mt Ex-Mt
*REF 1-200/201-420: 1X TO 2.5X.......
*REF 201-220/409/421-440: 1.25X TO 3X

2003 Topps Chrome Silver Refractors

Nm-Mt Ex-Mt
*SILVER REF 221-420: 1.25X TO 3X BASIC
*SILVER REF 421-440: 1.5X TO 4X BASIC
ONE PER SER.2 RETAIL EXCH.CARD .
CARDS WERE ONLY PRODUCED FOR SER.2

2003 Topps Chrome Uncirculated X-Fractors

Issued at a box-topper, this is a parallel to the Topps Chrome set. Each of these cards were issued in a special case and each of these cards were issued to a stated print run of 50 serial numbered sets for first series cards and a stated print run of 57 serial numbered cards for second series cards.

Nm-Mt Ex-Mt
*X-FRACT 1-200/221-420: 4X TO 10X
*X-FRACT 201-220/409/421-440: 5X TO 12X

2003 Topps Chrome Blue Backs Relics

Randomly inserted into packs, these 20 cards are authentic game-used memorabilia attached to a card which was in 1951 Blue Back design. These cards were issued in three different odds and we have notated those odds as well as what group the player belonged to in our checklist.

Nm-Mt Ex-Mt
BAT ODDS 1:236 HOB/RET...............
UNI GROUP A ODDS 1:69 HOB/RET ...
UNI GROUP B ODDS 1:662 HOB/RET .
AD Adam Dunn Uni B............... 15.00 4.50
AP Albert Pujols Uni A............ 25.00 7.50
AR Alex Rodriguez Bat 25.00 7.50
AS Alfonso Soriano Bat............ 15.00 4.50
BW Bernie Williams Bat........... 15.00 4.50
EC Eric Chavez Uni A.............. 10.00 3.00
FT Frank Thomas Uni A............ 15.00 4.50
JB Josh Beckett Uni A............. 10.00 3.00
JBA Jeff Bagwell Uni A............ 10.00 3.00
JR Jimmy Rollins Uni A........... 10.00 3.00
KW Kerry Wood Uni A.............. 15.00 4.50
LB Lance Berkman Bat............. 15.00 4.50
MO Magglio Ordonez Uni A....... 10.00 3.00
MP Mike Piazza Uni A.............. 20.00 6.00
NG Nomar Garciaparra Bat........ 25.00 7.50
NJ Nick Johnson Bat............... 15.00 4.50
PK Paul Konerko Uni A............ 10.00 3.00
RA Roberto Alomar Bat............ 20.00 6.00
SG Shawn Green Uni A............ 10.00 3.00
TS Tsuyoshi Shinjo Bat............ 15.00 4.50

2003 Topps Chrome Record Breakers Relics

Randomly inserted into packs, these 40 cards feature a mix of active and retired players along with a game-used memorabilia piece. These cards were issued in a few different group and we have notated that information next to the player's name in our checklist.

Nm-Mt Ex-Mt
BAT 1 ODDS 1:364 HOB/RET.............
BAT 2 ODDS 1:131 HOB/RET.............
UNI GROUP A1 ODDS 1:413 HOB/RET
UNI GROUP B1 ODDS 1:50 HOB/RET .
UNI GROUP A2 ODDS 1:1707 HOB/RET
UNI GROUP B2 ODDS 1:127 HOB/RET
AR1 Alex Rodriguez Uni B1....... 15.00 4.50
AR2 Alex Rodriguez Bat 2......... 15.00 4.50
BB Barry Bonds Walks Uni B2... 25.00 7.50
BB2 Barry Bonds Slg Uni B2 ..... 25.00 7.50
BB3 Barry Bonds Bat 2............ 25.00 7.50
CB Craig Biggio Uni B1 .... 10.00 3.00
CD Carlos Delgado Uni B1......... 10.00 3.00
CF Cliff Floyd Bat 1.................. 10.00 3.00
DE Darin Erstad Bat 2.............. 10.00 3.00
DLE Dennis Eckersley Uni A2..... 15.00 4.50
DM Don Mattingly Bat 2............ 40.00 12.00
FT Frank Thomas Uni B1 .... 15.00 4.50
HK Harmon Killebrew Uni B1 ..... 25.00 7.50
HR Harold Reynolds Bat 2......... 10.00 3.00
JB1 Jeff Bagwell Slg Uni B1 ...... 10.00 3.00
JB2 Jeff Bagwell RBI Uni B2 ..... 10.00 3.00
JC Jose Canseco Bat 2............. 15.00 4.50
JG Juan Gonzalez Uni B1 .... 15.00 4.50
JM Joe Morgan Bat 1 .... 10.00 3.00
JS John Smoltz Uni B2............. 10.00 3.00
KS Kazuhiro Sasaki Uni B1........ 10.00 3.00
LB Lou Brock Bat 1 .... 20.00 6.00
LG1 Luis Gonzalez RBI Bat 1..... 10.00 3.00
LG2 Luis Gonzalez Avg Bat 2..... 10.00 3.00
LW Larry Walker Bat 1 .... 15.00 4.50
MP Mike Piazza Uni B1.............. 20.00 6.00
MR Manny Ramirez Bat 2.......... 10.00 3.00
MS Mike Schmidt Uni A1 .... 40.00 12.00
PM Paul Molitor Bat 2............... 15.00 4.50
RC Rod Carew Avg Bat 2........... 15.00 4.50
RC2 Rod Carew Hits Bat 2......... 15.00 4.50
RH1 R.Henderson A's Bat 1 .... 15.00 4.50
RH2 R.Henderson Yanks Bat 2.. 15.00 4.50
RJ1 Randy Johnson ERA Uni B1 15.00 4.50
RJ2 Randy Johnson Wins Uni B2 15.00 4.50
RY Robin Yount Uni B1............. 25.00 7.50
SM Stan Musial Uni A1 .... 50.00 15.00
SS Sammy Sosa Bat 2 .... 20.00 6.00
TH Todd Helton Bat 1 .... 15.00 4.50
TS Tom Seaver Uni B2.............. 20.00 6.00

2003 Topps Chrome Red Backs Relics

Randomly inserted into packs, these 20 cards are authentic game-used memorabilia attached to a card which was in 1951 Red Back design. These cards were issued in three different odds and we have notated those odds as well as what group the player belonged to in our checklist.

Nm-Mt Ex-Mt
SERIES 2 BAT A ODDS 1:342 HOB/RET
SERIES 2 BAT B ODDS 1:383 HOB/RET
SERIES 2 JERSEY ODDS 1:49 HOB/RET
AD Adam Dunn Jsy 10.00 3.00
AJ Andruw Jones Jsy.............. 10.00 3.00
AP Albert Pujols Bat B............. 20.00 6.00
AR Alex Rodriguez Jsy............. 15.00 4.50
AS Alfonso Soriano Bat A......... 15.00 4.50
CJ Chipper Jones Jsy.............. 15.00 4.50
CS Curt Schilling Jsy.............. 10.00 3.00
GA Garrett Anderson Bat A....... 15.00 4.50
JB Jeff Bagwell Jsy 10.00 3.00
MP Mike Piazza Jsy................. 15.00 4.50
MR Manny Ramirez Bat B 10.00 3.00
MS Mike Sweeney Jsy.............. 10.00 3.00
NG Nomar Garciaparra Bat A..... 25.00 7.50
PB Pat Burrell Bat A 15.00 4.50
PM Pedro Martinez Jsy 15.00 4.50
RA Roberto Alomar Jsy............ 15.00 4.50
RJ Randy Johnson Jsy............. 15.00 4.50
SR Scott Rolen Bat A 15.00 4.50
TH Todd Helton Jsy................. 15.00 4.50
TKH Torii Hunter Jsy............... 10.00 3.00

2003 Topps Chrome Traded

These cards were issued at a stated rate of two per 2003 Topps Traded pack. Cards numbered 1 through 115 feature veterans who were traded while cards 116 through 120 feature managers. Cards numbered 121 through 165 featured prospects and cards 166 through 275 feature Rookie Cards. All of these cards were issued with a "T" prefix.

MINT NRMT
COMPLETE SET (275)............ 120.00 55.00
COMMON CARD (1-120)............ .75 .35
COMMON CARD (121-165).......... 1.00 .45
COMMON CARD (166-275).......... 1.00 .45
2 PER 2003 TOPPS TRADED HOBBY PACK
2 PER 2003 TOPPS TRADED HTA PACK
2 PER 2003 TOPPS TRADED RETAIL PACK
T1 Juan Pierre........................ .75 .35
T2 Mark Grudzielanek............... .75 .35
T3 Tanyon Sturtze .... .75 .35
T4 Greg Vaughn .... .75 .35
T5 Greg Myers .... .75 .35
T6 Randall Simon..................... .75 .35
T7 Todd Hundley...................... .75 .35
T8 Marlon Anderson.................. .75 .35
T9 Jeff Reboulet....................... .75 .35
T10 Alex Sanchez.................... .75 .35
T11 Mike Rivera .... .75 .35
T12 Todd Walker....................... .75 .35
T13 Ray King............................ .75 .35
T14 Shawn Estes...................... .75 .35
T15 Gary Matthews Jr................ .75 .35
T16 Jaret Wright .... .75 .35
T17 Edgardo Alfonzo.................. .75 .35
T18 Omar Daal .... .75 .35
T19 Ryan Rupe.......................... .75 .35
T20 Tony Clark........................... .75 .35
T21 Jeff Suppan .... .75 .35
T22 Mike Stanton .... .75 .35
T23 Ramon Martinez................... .75 .35
T24 Armando Rios .... .75 .35
T25 Johnny Estrada .... .75 .35
T26 Joe Girardi.......................... .75 .35
T27 Ivan Rodriguez .... 2.00 .90
T28 Robert Fick.......................... .75 .35
T29 Rick White........................... .75 .35
T30 Robert Person...................... .75 .35
T31 Alan Benes .... .75 .35
T32 Chris Carpenter .... .75 .35
T33 Chris Widger .... .75 .35
T34 Travis Hafner...................... .75 .35
T35 Mike Venafro....................... .75 .35
T36 Jon Lieber .... .75 .35
T37 Orlando Hernandez............... .75 .35
T38 Aaron Myette....................... .75 .35
T39 Paul Bako .... .75 .35
T40 Erubiel Durazo..................... .75 .35
T41 Mark Guthrie .... .75 .35
T42 Steve Avery .... .75 .35
T43 Damian Jackson .... .75 .35
T44 Rey Ordonez........................ .75 .35
T45 John Flaherty....................... .75 .35
T46 Byung-Hyun Kim .... .75 .35
T47 Tom Goodwin....................... .75 .35
T48 Elmer Dessens .... .75 .35
T49 Al Martin .... .75 .35
T50 Gene Kingsale .... .75 .35
T51 Lenny Harris......................... .75 .35
T52 David Ortiz........................... .75 .35
T53 Jose Lima............................. .75 .35
T54 Mike Difelice......................... .75 .35
T55 Jose Hernandez.................... .75 .35
T56 Todd Zeile .... .75 .35
T57 Roberto Hernandez .... .75 .35
T58 Albie Lopez........................... .75 .35
T59 Roberto Alomar.................... 2.00 .90
T60 Russ Ortiz .... .75 .35
T61 Brian Daubach...................... .75 .35
T62 Carl Everett.......................... .75 .35
T63 Jeromy Burnitz..................... .75 .35
T64 Mark Bellhorn....................... .75 .35
T65 Ruben Sierra .... .75 .35
T66 Mike Fetters......................... .75 .35
T67 Armando Benitez................... .75 .35
T68 Deivi Cruz............................ .75 .35
T69 Jose Cruz Jr. .... .75 .35
T70 Jeremy Fikac .... .75 .35
T71 Jeff Kent.............................. .75 .35
T72 Andres Galarraga.................. .75 .35
T73 Rickey Henderson .... 2.00 .90
T74 Royce Clayton .... .75 .35
T75 Troy O'Leary......................... .75 .35
T76 Ron Coomer.......................... .75 .35
T77 Greg Colbrunn....................... .75 .35
T78 Wes Helms............................ .75 .35
T79 Kevin Millwood...................... .75 .35
T80 Damion Easley....................... .75 .35
T81 Bobby Kielty .... .75 .35
T82 Keith Osik............................. .75 .35
T83 Ramiro Mendoza.................... .75 .35
T84 Shea Hillenbrand .... .75 .35
T85 Shannon Stewart.................... .75 .35
T86 Eddie Perez .... .75 .35
T87 Ugueth Urbina .... .75 .35
T88 Orlando Palmeiro .... .75 .35
T89 Graeme Lloyd......................... .75 .35
T90 John Vander Wal..................... .75 .35
T91 Gary Bennett .... .75 .35
T92 Shane Reynolds .... .75 .35
T93 Steve Parris............................ .75 .35
T94 Julio Lugo .... .75 .35
T95 John Halama .... .75 .35
T96 Carlos Baerga.......................... .75 .35
T97 Jim Parque .... .75 .35
T98 Mike Williams........................... .75 .35
T99 Fred McGriff........................... 1.25 .55
T100 Kenny Rogers........................ .75 .35
T101 Matt Herges........................... .75 .35
T102 Jay Bell.................................. .75 .35
T103 Esteban Yan .... .75 .35
T104 Eric Owens .... .75 .35
T105 Aaron Fultz............................ .75 .35
T106 Rey Sanchez........................... .75 .35
T107 Jim Thome .... 2.00 .90
T108 Aaron Boone .... .75 .35
T109 Raul Mondesi .... .75 .35
T110 Kenny Lofton.......................... .75 .35
T111 Jose Guillen........................... .75 .35
T112 Aramis Ramirez...................... .75 .35
T113 Sidney Ponson .... .75 .35
T114 Scott Williamson..................... .75 .35
T115 Robin Ventura .... .75 .35
T116 Dusty Baker MG .... .75 .35
T117 Felipe Alou MG........................ .75 .35
T118 Buck Showalter MG.................. .75 .35
T119 Jack McKeon MG .... .75 .35
T120 Art Howe MG............................ .75 .35
T121 Bobby Crosby PROS .... 1.50 .70
T122 Adrian Gonzalez PROS .... 1.00 .45
T123 Kevin Cash PROS .... 1.00 .45
T124 Shin-Soo Choo PROS .... 1.00 .45
T125 Chin-Feng Chen PROS 2.50 1.10
T126 Miguel Cabrera PROS.......... 4.00 1.80
T127 Jason Young PROS .... 1.00 .45
T128 Alex Herrera PROS............... 1.00 .45
T129 Jason Dubois PROS .... 1.00 .45
T130 Jeff Mathis PROS.................. 1.00 .45
T131 Casey Kotchman PROS .... 1.50 .70
T132 Ed Rogers PROS.................... 1.00 .45
T133 Wilson Betemit PROS............ 1.00 .45
T134 Jim Kavourias PROS.............. 1.00 .45
T135 Taylor Buchholz PROS .... 1.00 .45
T136 Adam LaRoche PROS............. 1.50 .70
T137 D.McPherson PROS .... 1.50 .70
T138 Jesus Cota PROS .... 1.00 .45
T139 Clint Nageotte PROS .... 1.00 .45
T140 Boof Bonser PROS................. 1.00 .45
T141 Walter Young PROS .... 1.00 .45
T142 Joe Crede PROS.................... 1.00 .45
T143 Denny Bautista PROS............ 1.00 .45
T144 Victor Diaz PROS .... 1.00 .45
T145 Chris Narveson PROS .... 1.00 .45
T146 Gabe Gross PROS .... 1.00 .45
T147 Jimmy Journell PROS........ 1.00 .45
T148 Rafael Soriano PROS .... 1.00 .45
T149 Jerome Williams PROS...... 1.00 .45
T150 Aaron Cook PROS .... 1.00 .45
T151 An. Martinez PROS............. 1.00 .45
T152 Scott Hairston PROS.......... 1.00 .45
T153 John Buck PROS................ 1.00 .45
T154 Ryan Ludwick PROS .... 1.00 .45
T155 Chris Bootcheck PROS...... 1.00 .45
T156 John Rheinecker PROS ..... 1.00 .45
T157 Jason Lane PROS.............. 1.00 .45
T158 Shelley Duncan PROS .... 1.00 .45
T159 Adam Wainwright PROS .... 1.00 .45
T160 Jason Arnold PROS........... 1.00 .45
T161 Jonny Gomes PROS.......... 1.00 .45
T162 James Loney PROS........... 1.50 .70
T163 Mike Fontenot PROS .... 1.00 .45
T164 Khalil Greene PROS........... 1.50 .70
T165 Sean Burnett PROS........... 1.00 .45
T166 David Martinez FY RC........ 1.00 .45
T167 Felix Pie FY RC................. 6.00 2.70
T168 Joe Valentine FY RC.......... 1.00 .45
T169 Brandon Webb FY RC........ 5.00 2.20
T170 Matt Diaz FY RC............... 2.00 .90
T171 Lew Ford FY RC................ 1.25 .55
T172 Jeremy Griffiths FY RC...... 1.25 .55
T173 Matt Hensley FY RC.......... 1.00 .45
T174 Charlie Manning FY RC ..... 1.00 .45
T175 Elizardo Ramirez FY RC.... 2.50 1.10
T176 Greg Aquino FY RC........... 1.00 .45
T177 Felix Sanchez FY RC......... 1.00 .45
T178 Kelly Shoppach FY RC........ 3.00 1.35
T179 Bubba Nelson FY RC......... 2.00 .90
T180 Mike O'Keefe FY RC.......... 1.00 .45
T181 Hanley Ramirez FY RC....... 4.00 1.80
T182 T.Wellemeyer FY RC.......... 1.25 .55
T183 Dustin Moseley FY RC....... 1.25 .55
T184 Eric Crozier FY RC............ 1.25 .55
T185 Ryan Shealy FY RC........... 2.00 .90
T186 Jer. Bonderman FY RC....... 2.50 1.10
T187 T.Story-Harden FY RC........ 1.00 .45
T188 Dusty Brown FY RC........... 1.00 .45
T189 Rob Hammock FY RC......... 1.25 .55
T190 Jorge Piedra FY RC .... 1.25 .55
T191 Chris De La Cruz FY RC..... 1.00 .45
T192 Eli Whiteside FY RC........... 1.00 .45
T193 Jason Kubel FY RC............ 1.25 .55
T194 Jon Schuerholz FY RC....... 1.00 .45
T195 St. Randolph FY RC........... 1.00 .45
T196 Andy Sisco FY RC............. 3.00 1.35
T197 Sean Smith FY RC............. 1.25 .55
T198 Jon-Mark Sprowl FY RC...... 2.00 .90
T199 Matt Kata FY RC................ 2.00 .90
T200 Robinson Cano FY RC .... 1.25 .55
T201 Nook Logan FY RC............ 1.00 .45
T202 Ben Francisco FY RC .... 1.25 .55
T203 Arnie Munoz FY RC .... 1.00 .45
T204 Ozzie Chavez FY RC.......... 1.00 .45
T205 Eric Riggs FY RC............... 1.25 .55
T206 Beau Kemp FY RC .... 1.00 .45
T207 Travis Wong FY RC .... 1.25 .55
T208 Dustin Yount FY RC .... 2.00 .90
T209 Brian McCann FY RC.......... 2.00 .90
T210 Wilton Reynolds FY RC ...... 1.25 .55
T211 Matt Bruback FY RC .... 1.00 .45
T212 Andrew Brown FY RC......... 1.00 .45
T213 Edgar Gonzalez FY RC....... 1.00 .45
T214 Eider Torres FY RC............ 1.00 .45
T215 Aquilino Lopez FY RC......... 1.00 .45
T216 Bobby Basham FY RC .... 2.00 .90
T217 Tim Olson FY RC............... 1.25 .55
T218 Nathan Panther FY RC........ 2.00 .90
T219 Bryan Grace FY RC............ 1.00 .45
T220 Dusty Gomon FY RC .... 2.00 .90
T221 Wil Ledezma FY RC........... 1.00 .45
T222 Josh Willingham FY RC....... 3.00 1.35
T223 David Cash FY RC .... 1.00 .45
T224 Oscar Villarreal FY RC........ 1.00 .45
T225 Jeff Duncan FY RC .... 1.25 .55
T226 Kade Johnson FY RC .... 1.00 .45
T227 L.Steidlmayer FY RC.......... 1.00 .45
T228 Brandon Watson FY RC....... 1.00 .45
T229 Jose Morales FY RC........... 1.00 .45
T230 Mike Gallo FY RC............... 1.00 .45
T231 Tyler Adamczyk FY RC .... 1.00 .45
T232 Adam Stern FY RC............. 1.00 .45
T233 Brennan King FY RC........... 1.00 .45
T234 Dan Haren FY RC............... 2.50 1.10
T235 Mi. Hernandez FY RC .... 1.00 .45
T236 Ben Fritz FY RC .... 1.00 .45
T237 Clay Hensley FY RC........... 1.00 .45
T238 Tyler Johnson FY RC.......... 1.00 .45
T239 Pete LaForest FY RC.......... 1.25 .55
T240 Tyler Martin FY RC .... 1.00 .45
T241 J.D. Durbin FY RC .... 2.00 .90
T242 Shane Victorino FY RC .... 1.00 .45
T243 Rajai Davis FY RC.............. 1.25 .55
T244 Ismael Castro FY RC .... 1.00 .45
T245 C.Wang FY RC 4.00 1.80
T246 Travis Ishikawa FY RC........ 1.25 .55
T247 Corey Shafer FY RC........... 1.25 .55
T248 G.Schneidmiller FY RC .... 1.00 .45
T249 Dave Pember FY RC........... 1.00 .45
T250 Keith Stamler FY RC........... 1.00 .45
T251 Tyson Graham FY RC......... 1.00 .45
T252 Ryan Cameron FY RC .... 1.00 .45
T253 Eric Eckenstahler FY........... 1.00 .45
T254 Ma. Peterson FY RC .... 1.00 .45
T255 Dustin McGowan FY RC...... 2.50 1.10
T256 Pr. Redman FY RC .... 1.00 .45
T257 Haj Turay FY RC................ 1.25 .55
T258 Carlos Guzman FY RC .... 1.25 .55
T259 Matt DeMarco FY RC .... 1.00 .45
T260 Derek Michaelis FY RC........ 1.25 .55
T261 Brian Burgamy FY RC......... 1.00 .45
T262 Jay Sitzman FY RC............ 1.00 .45
T263 Chris Fallon FY RC............. 1.00 .45
T264 Mike Adams FY RC............. 1.00 .45
T265 Clint Barmes FY RC .... 1.25 .55
T266 Eric Reed FY RC .... 2.00 .90
T267 Willie Eyre FY RC............... 1.00 .45
T268 Carlos Duran FY RC........... 1.00 .45
T269 Nick Trzesniak FY RC .... 1.00 .45
T270 Ferdin Tejeda FY RC .... 1.00 .45
T271 Mi. Garciaparra FY RC 2.50 1.10
T272 Michael Hinckley FY RC....... 2.00 .90
T273 Br. Florence FY RC .... 1.00 .45
T274 Trent Oeltjen FY RC .... 1.25 .55
T275 Mike Neu FY RC................. 1.00 .45

2003 Topps Chrome Traded Refractors

MINT NRMT
*REF 1-120: 2X TO 5X BASIC ....
*REF 121-165: 1.5X TO 4X BASIC ......
*REF 166-275: 1.5X TO 4X BASIC ......
STATED ODDS 1:12 HOB/RET, 1:4 HTA

2003 Topps Chrome Traded Uncirculated X-Fractors

MINT NRMT
ONE PER TOPPS TRADED HTA BOX...
STATED PRINT RUN 25 SERIAL #'d SETS
NO PRICING DUE TO SCARCITY........

2004 Topps Chrome

This 233 card standard-size set was released in January, 2004. This set was issued in four-card packs with an $3 SRP which came 20 packs to a box and 10 boxes to a case. The first 210 cards of this set are veterans while the final 23 cards of the set feature first year cards. Please note that cards 221 through 233 were autographed by the featured players and those cards were issued to a stated rate of one in 21.

Nm-Mt Ex-Mt
COMP.SERIES 1 w/o SP's (220) 80.00 24.00
COMMON CARD (1-210).......... 1.50 .30
COMMON CARD (211-220)........ 1.50 .45
COMMON CARD (221-233)....... 15.00 4.50
1 Jim Thome .... 2.50 .75
2 Reggie Sanders...................... 1.00 .30
3 Mark Kotsay.......................... 1.00 .30
4 Edgardo Alfonzo.................... 1.00 .30
5 Tim Wakefield .... 1.00 .30
6 Moises Alou .... 1.00 .30
7 Jorge Julio .... 1.00 .30
8 Bartolo Colon .... 1.00 .30
9 Chan Ho Park .... 1.00 .30
10 Ichiro Suzuki 4.00 1.20
11 Kevin Millwood.................... 1.00 .30
12 Preston Wilson.................... 1.00 .30
13 Tom Glavine .... 1.50 .45
14 Junior Spivey .... 1.00 .30
15 Marcus Giles .... 1.00 .30
16 David Segui........................ 1.00 .30
17 Kevin Millar .... 1.00 .30
18 Corey Patterson.................. 1.00 .30
19 Aaron Rowand.................... 1.00 .30
20 Derek Jeter........................ 6.00 1.80
21 Luis Castillo........................ 1.00 .30
22 Manny Ramirez .... 1.00 .30
23 Jay Payton.......................... 1.00 .30
24 Bobby Higginson................. 1.00 .30
25 Lance Berkman .... 1.00 .30
26 Juan Pierre......................... 1.00 .30
27 Mike Mussina...................... 2.50 .75
28 Fred McGriff........................ 1.50 .45
29 Richie Sexson .... 1.00 .30
30 Tim Hudson......................... 1.00 .30
31 Mike Piazza 4.00 1.20
32 Brad Radke......................... 1.00 .30
33 Jeff Weaver .... 1.00 .30
34 Ramon Hernandez................ 1.00 .30
35 David Bell .... 1.00 .30
36 Randy Wolf .... 1.00 .30
37 Jake Peavy .... 1.00 .30
38 Tim Worrell .... 1.00 .30
39 Gil Meche .... 1.00 .30
40 Albert Pujols....................... 5.00 1.50
41 Michael Young .... 1.00 .30
42 Josh Phelps......................... 1.00 .30
43 Brendan Donnelly................. 1.00 .30
44 Steve Finley......................... 1.00 .30
45 John Smoltz......................... 1.50 .45
46 Jay Gibbons .... 1.00 .30
47 Trot Nixon .... 1.50 .45
48 Carl Pavano.......................... 1.00 .30
49 Frank Thomas .... 2.50 .75
50 Mark Prior............................ 5.00 1.50
51 Danny Graves....................... 1.00 .30
52 Milton Bradley....................... 1.00 .30
53 Kris Benson.......................... 1.00 .30
54 Ryan Klesko .... 1.00 .30
55 Mike Lowell.......................... 1.00 .30
56 Geoff Blum .... 1.00 .30
57 Michael Tucker...................... 1.00 .30
58 Paul Lo Duca........................ 1.00 .30
59 Vicente Padilla...................... 1.00 .30
60 Jacque Jones .... 1.00 .30
61 Fernando Tatis...................... 1.00 .30
62 Ty Wigginton......................... 1.00 .30
63 Rich Aurilia........................... 1.00 .30
64 Andy Pettitte......................... 1.50 .45
65 Terrence Long .... 1.00 .30
66 Cliff Floyd .... 1.00 .30
67 Mariano Rivera...................... 1.50 .45
68 Kelvim Escobar .... 1.00 .30
69 Marlon Byrd .... 1.00 .30
70 Mark Mulder......................... 1.00 .30
71 Francisco Cordero................. 1.00 .30
72 Carlos Guillen....................... 1.00 .30
73 Fernando Vina .... 1.00 .30
74 Lance Carter......................... 1.00 .30
75 Hank Blalock .... 1.00 .30
76 Jimmy Rollins .... 1.00 .30
77 Francisco Rodriguez.............. 1.00 .30
78 Javy Lopez .... 1.00 .30
79 Jerry Hairston Jr. .... 1.00 .30
80 Andruw Jones .... 1.00 .30
81 Rodrigo Lopez....................... 1.00 .30
82 Johnny Damon...................... 1.00 .30
83 Hee Seop Choi...................... 1.00 .30
84 Kazuhiro Sasaki.................... 1.00 .30

85 Danny Bautista 1.00 .30
86 Matt Lawton 1.00 .30
87 Juan Uribe 1.00 .30
88 Rafael Furcal 1.00 .30
89 Kyle Farnsworth 1.00 .30
90 Jose Vidro 1.00 .30
91 Luis Rivas 1.00 .30
92 Hideo Nomo 2.50 .75
93 Javier Vazquez 1.00 .30
94 Al Leiter 1.00 .30
95 Jose Valentin 1.00 .30
96 Alex Cintron 1.00 .30
97 Zach Day 1.00 .30
98 Jorge Posada 1.50 .45
99 C.C. Sabathia 1.00 .30
100 Alex Rodriguez 4.00 1.20
101 Brad Penny 1.00 .30
102 Brad Ausmus 1.00 .30
103 Raul Ibanez 1.00 .30
104 Mike Hampton 1.00 .30
105 Adrian Beltre 1.00 .30
106 Ramiro Mendoza 1.00 .30
107 Rocco Baldelli 2.50 .75
108 Esteban Loaiza 1.00 .30
109 Russell Branyan 1.00 .30
110 Todd Helton 1.50 .45
111 Braden Looper 1.00 .30
112 Octavio Dotel 1.00 .30
113 Mike MacDougal 1.00 .30
114 Cesar Izturis 1.00 .30
115 Johan Santana 1.00 .30
116 Jose Contreras 1.00 .30
117 Placido Polanco 1.00 .30
118 Jason Phillips 1.00 .30
119 Orlando Hudson 1.00 .30
120 Vernon Wells 1.00 .30
121 Ben Grieve 1.00 .30
122 Dave Roberts 1.00 .30
123 Ismael Valdes 1.00 .30
124 Eric Owens 1.00 .30
125 Curt Schilling 1.50 .45
126 Russ Ortiz 1.00 .30
127 Mark Buehrle 1.00 .30
128 Doug Mientkiewicz 1.00 .30
129 Dmitri Young 1.00 .30
130 Kazuhisa Ishii 1.00 .30
131 A.J. Pierzynski 1.00 .30
132 Brad Wilkerson 1.00 .30
133 Joe McEwing 1.00 .30
134 Alex Cora 1.00 .30
135 Jose Cruz Jr. 1.00 .30
136 Carlos Zambrano 1.00 .30
137 Jeff Kent 1.00 .30
138 Shigetoshi Hasegawa 1.00 .30
139 Jarrod Washburn 1.00 .30
140 Greg Maddux 4.00 1.20
141 Josh Beckett 1.50 .45
142 Miguel Batista 1.00 .30
143 Omar Vizquel 1.00 .30
144 Alex Gonzalez 1.00 .30
145 Billy Wagner 1.00 .30
146 Brian Jordan 1.00 .30
147 Wes Helms 1.00 .30
148 Deivi Cruz 1.00 .30
149 Alex Gonzalez 1.00 .30
150 Jason Giambi 2.50 .75
151 Erubiel Durazo 1.00 .30
152 Mike Lieberthal 1.00 .30
153 Jason Kendall 1.00 .30
154 Xavier Nady 1.00 .30
155 Kirk Rueter 1.00 .30
156 Mike Cameron 1.00 .30
157 Miguel Cairo 1.00 .30
158 Woody Williams 1.00 .30
159 Toby Hall 1.00 .30
160 Bernie Williams 1.50 .45
161 Darin Erstad 1.00 .30
162 Matt Mantei 1.00 .30
163 Shawn Chacon 1.00 .30
164 Bill Mueller 1.00 .30
165 Damian Miller 1.00 .30
166 Tony Graffanino 1.00 .30
167 Sean Casey 1.00 .30
168 Brandon Phillips 1.00 .30
169 Runelvys Hernandez 1.00 .30
170 Adam Dunn 1.00 .30
171 Carlos Lee 1.00 .30
172 Juan Encarnacion 1.00 .30
173 Angel Berroa 1.00 .30
174 Desi Relaford 1.00 .30
175 Joe Mays 1.00 .30
176 Ben Sheets 1.00 .30
177 Eddie Guardado 1.00 .30
178 Rocky Biddle 1.00 .30
179 Eric Gagne 1.50 .45
180 Eric Chavez 1.00 .30
181 Jason Michaels 1.00 .30
182 Dustan Mohr 1.00 .30
183 Kip Wells 1.00 .30
184 Brian Lawrence 1.00 .30
185 Bret Boone 1.00 .30
186 Tino Martinez 1.50 .45
187 Aubrey Huff 1.00 .30
188 Kevin Mench 1.00 .30
189 Tim Salmon 1.50 .45
190 Carlos Delgado 1.00 .30
191 John Lackey 1.00 .30
192 Eric Byrnes 1.00 .30
193 Luis Matos 1.00 .30
194 Derek Lowe 1.00 .30
195 Mark Grudzielanek 1.00 .30
196 Tom Gordon 1.00 .30
197 Matt Clement 1.00 .30
198 Byung-Hyun Kim 1.00 .30
199 Brandon Inge 1.00 .30
200 Nomar Garciaparra 4.00 1.20
201 Frank Catalanotto 1.00 .30
202 Cristian Guzman 1.00 .30
203 Bo Hart 1.00 .30
204 Jack Wilson 1.00 .30
205 Ray Durham 1.00 .30
206 Freddy Garcia 1.00 .30
207 J.D. Drew 1.00 .30
208 Orlando Cabrera 1.00 .30
209 Roy Halladay 1.00 .30
210 David Eckstein 1.00 .30
211 Omar Falcon FY RC 1.50 .45
212 Todd Self FY RC 1.50 .45
213 David Murphy FY RC 5.00 1.50
214 Dioner Navarro FY RC 5.00 1.50
215 Marcus McBeth FY RC 1.50 .45
216 Chris O'Riordan FY RC 1.50 .45
217 Rodney Choy Foo FY RC 2.50 .75
218 Tim Frend FY RC 6.00 1.80
219 Yadier Molina FY RC 2.50 .75
220 Zach Duke FY RC 2.50 .75
221 Anthony Lerew FY AU RC 20.00 6.00
222 Blake Hawksworth FY AU RC 25.00 7.50
223 Brayan Pena FY AU RC 15.00 4.50
224 Craig Ansman FY AU RC 25.00 7.50
225 Jon Knott FY AU RC 20.00 6.00
226 Josh Labandeira FY AU RC 15.00 4.50
227 Khalid Ballouli FY AU RC 15.00 4.50
228 Kyle Davies FY AU RC 25.00 7.50
229 Matt Creighton FY AU RC 25.00 7.50
230 Mike Gosling FY AU RC 15.00 4.50
231 Nic Ungs FY AU RC 15.00 4.50
232 Zach Miner FY AU RC 20.00 6.00
233 Donald Levinski FY AU RC 15.00 4.50

2004 Topps Chrome Black Refractors

Nm-Mt Ex-Mt
*1-210 BLACK: 1.5X TO 4X BASIC
*211-220 BLACK: 2X TO 5X BASIC
1-220 SERIES 1 ODDS 1:10 H, 1:20 R
221-233 SERIES 1 ODDS 1:1527 H, 1:2480 R
221-233 PRINT RUN 25 SERIAL #'d SETS
221-233 NO PRICING DUE TO SCARCITY

2004 Topps Chrome Gold Refractors

Nm-Mt Ex-Mt
*GOLD 1-210: 1.25X TO 3X BASIC
*GOLD 211-220: 1.5X TO 4X BASIC
1-220 SERIES 1 ODDS 1:5 H, 1:10 R
221-233 SERIES 1 ODDS 1:759 H, 1:1208 R
221-233 PRINT RUN 50 SERIAL #'d SETS

2004 Topps Chrome Red X-Fractors

Nm-Mt Ex-Mt
*RED XF 1-210: 3X TO 8X BASIC
*RED XF 211-220: 4X TO 10X BASIC
1-220 ONE PER PARALLEL HOT PACK
ONE HOT PACK PER SER.1 HOBBY BOX
1-220 STATED PRINT RUN 63 SETS
1-220 ARE NOT SERIAL-NUMBERED
1-220 PRINT RUN PROVIDED BY TOPPS
221-233 SERIES 1 ODDS 1:21,371 HOBBY
221-233 PRINT RUN 1 SERIAL #'d SET
221-233 NO PRICING DUE TO SCARCITY

2004 Topps Chrome Refractors

Nm-Mt Ex-Mt
*REF 1-210: 1X TO 2.5X BASIC
*REF 211-220: 1.25X TO 3X BASIC
1-220 SERIES 1 ODDS 1:4 H/R
*REF 221-233: .75X TO 2X BASIC
221-233 SERIES 1 ODDS 1:380 H, 1:597 R
221-233 PRINT RUN 100 SERIAL #'d SETS

2004 Topps Chrome Fashionably Great Relics

Nm-Mt Ex-Mt
ONE RELIC PER SER.1 GU HOBBY PACK
GROUP A 1:59 SER.1 RETAIL
GROUP B 1:107 SER.1 RETAIL
AD Adam Dunn Jsy A 8.00 2.40
AJ Andruw Jones Uni A 8.00 2.40
AP Albert Pujols Jsy A 25.00 7.50
AR Alex Rodriguez Uni A 15.00 4.50
BM Brett Myers Jsy A 8.00 2.40
BW Billy Wagner Jsy B 8.00 2.40
CB Craig Biggio Uni A 10.00 3.00
CD Carlos Delgado Jsy A 8.00 2.40
CF Cliff Floyd Jsy A 8.00 2.40
CJ Chipper Jones Uni A 10.00 3.00
CS Curt Schilling Jsy A 10.00 3.00
DL Derek Lowe Uni B 8.00 2.40
EC Eric Chavez Uni B 8.00 2.40
FG Freddy Garcia Jsy A 8.00 2.40
FM Fred McGriff Jsy A 10.00 3.00
FT Frank Thomas Uni A 10.00 3.00
HB Hank Blalock Jsy A 8.00 2.40
IR Ivan Rodriguez Uni B 10.00 3.00
JB Jeff Bagwell Uni A 10.00 3.00
JBO Joe Borchard Jsy A 8.00 2.40
JO John Olerud Jsy A 8.00 2.40
JR Juan Rivera Jsy A 8.00 2.40
JS John Smoltz Uni A 10.00 3.00
JV Jose Vidro Jsy A 8.00 2.40
KB Kevin Brown Jsy B 8.00 2.40
MM Mark Mulder Uni A 8.00 2.40
MP Mike Piazza Uni A 15.00 4.50
MR Manny Ramirez Uni A 8.00 2.40
MS Mike Sweeney Uni A 8.00 2.40
NG Nomar Garciaparra Uni B 15.00 4.50
PM Pedro Martinez Jsy A 10.00 3.00
RP Rafael Palmeiro Jsy A 10.00 3.00
SS Sammy Sosa Jsy A 15.00 4.50
TH Tim Hudson Uni B 8.00 2.40
THO Trevor Hoffman Uni A 8.00 2.40
VW Vernon Wells Jsy B 8.00 2.40
WP Wily Mo Pena Jsy A 8.00 2.40

2004 Topps Chrome Handle With Care Bat Knob Relics

Nm-Mt Ex-Mt
STATED PRINT RUN 5 SERIAL #'d SETS

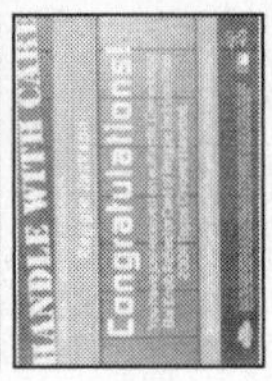

1 OF 1 PRINT RUN 1 SERIAL #'d SET.
NO PRICING DUE TO SCARCITY
RANDOM IN SERIES 1 HOBBY RELIC PACKS
AK Al Kaline
AP Albert Pujols
AR Alex Rodriguez
AS Alfonso Soriano
BR Brooks Robinson
CF Carlton Fisk
CY Carl Yastrzemski
FR Frank Robinson
GB George Brett
HK Harmon Killebrew
JB Johnny Bench
JG Jason Giambi
JT Jim Thome
LB Lance Berkman
LBR Lou Brock
LG Luis Gonzalez
MT Miguel Tejada
NG Nomar Garciaparra
PM Paul Molitor
RJ Reggie Jackson
RY Robin Yount
TH Torii Hunter
WB Wade Boggs
WM Willie Mays
WS Willie Stargell

2004 Topps Cracker Jack

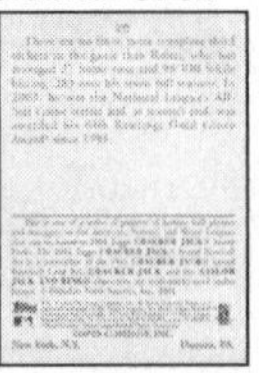

This 250 card set was released in April, 2004. The set was issued in nine-card packs which came 20 packs to a box and 10 boxes to a case. Please note that many cards in this set were issued in shorter supply than others (we have notated those cards with an SP) or have variation poses. In addition, to mirror the original Cracker Jack set the managers of the 2003 World Series were included as well as the Marlins Owner, Jeffrey Loria. In addition, to acknowledge the late trade of Alex Rodriguez to the Yankees a Rodriguez card in a Yankee uniform was a late addition to this set and was issued without a card number. In addition, 550 original cracker jacks were inserted into packs, those cards were issued at a stated rate of one in 2598 hobby and one in 3084 retail packs.

Nm-Mt Ex-Mt
COMPLETE SET (250) 200.00 60.00
COMP.SET w/o SP's (200) 40.00 12.00
COMMON CARD .40 .12
COMMON SP 4.00 1.20
COMMON SP RC 4.00 1.20
SP STATED ODDS 1:3
SP CL: 229B/232/236A-236B
1 Jose Reyes SP 5.00 1.50
2 Edgar Renteria .40 .12
3A Albert Pujols Portrait 2.00 .60
3B Albert Pujols Swinging SP 8.00 2.40
4 Garret Anderson .40 .12
5 Bobby Abreu .40 .12
6 Andruw Jones .40 .12
7 Jeff Kent .40 .12
8 Magglio Ordonez .40 .12
9 Kris Benson .40 .12
10 Luis Gonzalez .40 .12
11 Corey Patterson .40 .12
12 Connie Mack MG .40 .12
13 Vernon Wells SP 4.00 1.20
14 Jim Edmonds .40 .12
15 Bret Boone .40 .12
16 Travis Lee .40 .12
17 Alex Rodriguez Yanks SP 10.00 3.00
18 Erubiel Durazo .40 .12
19 Brett Myers .40 .12
20 Scott Rolen SP 5.00 1.50
21 Paul Lo Duca .40 .12
22 Geoff Jenkins .40 .12
23 Charles Comiskey .40 .12
24 Cliff Floyd .40 .12
25A Jim Thome Batting 1.00 .30
25B Jim Thome Fielding SP 5.00 1.50
26 Russ Ortiz .40 .12
27 Bill Mueller .40 .12
28 Kenny Lofton .40 .12
29 Jay Gibbons .40 .12
30 Ken Griffey Jr. 1.50 .45
31 Jeff Bagwell .60 .18
32 Jose Lima .40 .12
33 Brad Radke .40 .12
34 Ramon Hernandez .40 .12
35 Brian Giles SP 4.00 1.20
36 Jeremy Bonderman .40 .12
37 Jerome Williams .40 .12
38 Rafael Palmeiro .60 .18
39 Scott Podsednik 1.00 .30
40 Rafael Furcal .40 .12
41 Roy Oswalt .40 .12
42 Orlando Hudson .40 .12
43 Todd Helton .60 .18
44 Kerry Wood 1.00 .30
45 Tom Glavine .60 .18
46 David Eckstein .40 .12
47 Trot Nixon .60 .18
48 Preston Wilson .40 .12
49 Bernie Williams .60 .18
50 Eric Gagne SP 5.00 1.50
51 Ichiro Suzuki SP 6.00 1.80
52 Juan Gonzalez 1.00 .30
53 Torii Hunter .40 .12
54 Bartolo Colon .40 .12
55A Dick Hoblitzel ERR .40 .12
55B Dick Hoblitzell COR .40 .12
56 Al Leiter .40 .12
57 Johnny Damon .40 .12
58 Larry Walker .60 .18
59 Brian Jordan .40 .12
60 Richie Sexson SP 4.00 1.20
61 Orlando Cabrera .40 .12
62 Jason Phillips .40 .12
63 Phil Nevin .40 .12
64 John Olerud .40 .12
65 Miguel Tejada .40 .12
66A Nap La Joie ERR 1.00 .30
66B Nap Lajoie COR 1.00 .30
67 C.C. Sabathia .40 .12
68 Ty Wigginton .40 .12
69 Troy Glaus .60 .18
70 Mike Piazza 1.50 .45
71 Craig Biggio .60 .18
72 Cristian Guzman .40 .12
73 Dmitri Young .40 .12
74 Roger Clemens 2.00 .60
75 Runelvys Hernandez .40 .12
76 Nomar Garciaparra 1.50 .45
77 Mark Mulder .40 .12
78 Derek Lowe .40 .12
79 Paul Konerko .40 .12
80A Sammy Sosa SP 6.00 1.80
80B Felix Pie SP 5.00 1.50
81 Vladimir Guerrero 1.00 .30
82 Xavier Nady .40 .12
83 Joel Pineiro .40 .12
84 Chipper Jones 1.00 .30
85 Manny Ramirez .40 .12
86A Burt Shotten ERR .40 .12
86B Burt Shotton COR .40 .12
87 Raul Ibanez SP 4.00 1.20
88 Eric Chavez .40 .12
89 Frank Catalanotto .40 .12
90 Dontrelle Willis .40 .12
91 Roy Halladay .40 .12
92 Jermaine Dye .40 .12
93 Jason Kendall .40 .12
94 Jacque Jones .40 .12
95A Gary Sheffield Braves .40 .12
95B Gary Sheffield Yanks SP 5.00 1.50
96 Mike Lieberthal .40 .12
97 Adam Dunn .40 .12
98 Carl Crawford .40 .12
99 Reggie Sanders .40 .12
100 Mark Prior SP 8.00 2.40
101 Luis Matos .40 .12
102 Barry Zito .60 .18
103 Randy Johnson 1.00 .30
104A Kevin Brown .40 .12
104B Edwin Jackson SP 5.00 1.50
105 Pat Burrell .40 .12
106 Steve Finley .40 .12
107 Moises Alou .40 .12
108 David Ortiz SP 4.00 1.20
109 Austin Kearns SP 4.00 1.20
110 Carlos Beltran .40 .12
111 Shawn Green .40 .12
112 Javier Vazquez .40 .12
113 Hideo Nomo 1.00 .30
114 Kazuhisa Ishii .40 .12
115 Corey Koskie .40 .12
116 Kevin Millwood .40 .12
117 Randy Wolf .40 .12
118 Darin Erstad .40 .12
119 Fernando Vina .40 .12
120 Pedro Martinez 1.00 .30
121 Melvin Mora .40 .12
122 Carl Everett .40 .12
123 Matt Morris .40 .12
124 Greg Maddux 1.50 .45
125 Jason Schmidt .40 .12
126 Mark Teixeira SP 4.00 1.20
127 Randy Winn .40 .12
128 Rich Aurilia .40 .12
129 Vicente Padilla .40 .12
130 Tim Hudson .40 .12
131 Marlon Byrd .40 .12
132 Jae Weong Seo .40 .12
133 Branch Rickey MG .40 .12
134 A.J. Pierzynski .40 .12
135 Ryan Klesko .40 .12
136 Eric Hinske .40 .12
137 Mike Cameron .40 .12
138 Roberto Alomar 1.00 .30
139 Jarrod Washburn .40 .12
140A Curt Schilling D'backs .60 .18
140B Curt Schilling Sox SP 5.00 1.50
141 Omar Vizquel .40 .12
142 Mike Sweeney .40 .12
143 Wade Miller .40 .12
144 Jose Vidro .40 .12
145 Rich Harden SP 4.00 1.20
146 Eric Munson .40 .12
147 Lance Berkman .40 .12
148 Mark Buehrle .40 .12
149 Carlos Delgado .40 .12
150 Sean Burroughs .40 .12
151 Kevin Millar .40 .12
152 Frank Thomas 1.00 .30
153 Adrian Beltre .40 .12
154 Shannon Stewart .40 .12
155 Johan Santana .40 .12
156 Edgardo Alfonzo .40 .12
157 Jose Cruz Jr. .40 .12
158 Sidney Ponson .40 .12
159 Edgar Martinez .60 .18
160 Jamie Moyer .40 .12
161 Tony Batista .40 .12
162 Wes Helms .40 .12
163 Brandon Webb SP 4.00 1.20
164 Gil Meche .40 .12
165 Marcus Giles SP 4.00 1.20
166 Angel Berroa SP 4.00 1.20
167 Rocco Baldelli SP 5.00 1.50
168 Michael Young .40 .12
169 Esteban Loaiza .40 .12
170 Casey Blake .40 .12
171 Jody Gerut .40 .12
172 Bo Hart SP 4.00 1.20
173 Kelvim Escobar .40 .12
174 Aaron Guiel .40 .12
175 Javy Lopez SP 4.00 1.20
176 Aubrey Huff .40 .12
177 Hank Blalock .40 .12
178 Edwin Jackson .60 .18
179 Delmon Young SP 5.00 1.50
180 Bobby Jenks .40 .12
181 Felix Pie .60 .18
182 Jeremy Reed SP 4.00 1.20
183 Aaron Hill .40 .12
184 Casey Kotchman SP 4.00 1.20
185 Grady Sizemore .60 .18
186 Joe Mauer SP 5.00 1.50
187 Ryan Harvey .60 .18
188 Neal Cotts .40 .12
189 Victor Martinez .40 .12
190 Rene Reyes .40 .12
191 Eric Duncan .40 .12
192 B.J. Upton SP 5.00 1.50
193 Khalil Greene SP 4.00 1.20
194 Bobby Crosby .60 .18
195 Rickie Weeks SP 5.00 1.50
196 Zack Greinke SP 5.00 1.50
197 Laynce Nix .40 .12
198 Vito Chiaravalloti SP RC 4.00 1.20
199 Estee Harris RC .50 .15
200 Jon Knott SP RC 5.00 1.50
201 Dioner Navarro RC 1.50 .45
202 Craig Ansman RC .75 .23
203 Travis Blackley RC 1.50 .45
204 Yadier Molina RC .75 .23
205 Rodney Choy Foo RC .75 .23
206 Kyle Sleeth SP RC 6.00 1.80
207 Jeff Allison RC 2.00 .60
208 Josh Labandeira RC .50 .15
209 Lastings Milledge SP RC 8.00 2.40
210 Rudy Guillen SP RC 5.00 1.50
211 Blake Hawksworth SP RC 5.00 1.50
212 David Aardsma RC 1.25 .35
213 Shawn Hill RC .75 .23
214 Erick Aybar SP RC 5.00 1.50
215 Ervin Santana RC 2.00 .60
216 Tim Stauffer SP RC 5.00 1.50
217 Merkin Valdez RC 2.00 .60
218 Jack McKeon MG .40 .12
219 Jeff Conine .40 .12
220 Josh Beckett SP 5.00 1.50
221 Luis Castillo .40 .12
222 Mike Lowell .40 .12
223 Juan Pierre .40 .12
224A Ivan Rodriguez Marlins 1.00 .30
224B Ivan Rodriguez Tigers SP 5.00 1.50
225 A.J. Burnett .40 .12
226 Miguel Cabrera SP 5.00 1.50
227 Jeffrey Loria .40 .12
228 Joe Torre MG .60 .18
229A Jason Giambi Portrait 1.00 .30
229B Jason Giambi Fielding SP 5.00 1.50
230 Aaron Boone .40 .12
231 Jose Contreras .40 .12
232 Derek Jeter SP 10.00 3.00
233 Ruben Sierra .40 .12
234 Mike Mussina 1.00 .30
235 Mariano Rivera .60 .18
236A Jorge Posada SP 5.00 1.50
236B Dioner Navarro SP 5.00 1.50
237 Alfonso Soriano .60 .18
NNO Alex Rodriguez Yanks 4.00 1.20
VB Vintage Buyback

2004 Topps Cracker Jack Mini

Nm-Mt Ex-Mt
COMP.SET w/o SP's (200) 80.00 24.00
*MINI: .75X TO 2X BASIC
*MINI: .75X TO 2X BASIC RC
*MINI SP: .6X TO 1.5X BASIC SP
*MINI SP: .5X TO 1.2X BASIC SP RC
MINI STATED ODDS ONE PER PACK
MINI SP STATED ODDS 1:20
SP'S ARE SAME AS IN BASIC SET

2004 Topps Cracker Jack Mini Autographs

Luis Castillo did not return his cards in time for pack-out and those cards could be redeemed until March 31, 2006.

Nm-Mt Ex-Mt
STATED ODDS 1:258 HOBBY/RETAIL.
SHEFFIELD PRINT RUN 50 CARDS
SHEFFIELD IS NOT SERIAL NUMBERED
SHEFFIELD INFO PROVIDED BY TOPPS
95 Gary Sheffield SP/50
112 Javier Vazquez 40.00 12.00
163 Brandon Webb 20.00 6.00
165 Marcus Giles 20.00 6.00
221 Luis Castillo EXCH 10.00 3.00
226 Miguel Cabrera 40.00 12.00

2004 Topps Cracker Jack Mini Blue

Nm-Mt Ex-Mt
*BLUE: 4X TO 10X BASIC
*BLUE: 2.5X TO 6X BASIC RC
*BLUE SP: 1.25X TO 3X BASIC SP
*BLUE SP: 1X TO 2.5X BASIC SP RC
BLUE STATED ODDS 1:10
BLUE SP STATED ODDS 1:60
SP'S ARE SAME AS IN BASIC SET

2004 Topps Cracker Jack Mini White

Nm-Mt Ex-Mt
STATED ODDS 1:6189 HOB, 1:6413 RET
STATED PRINT RUN 1 SET
CARDS ARE NOT SERIAL-NUMBERED
PRINT RUN INFO PROVIDED BY TOPPS
NO PRICING DUE TO SCARCITY

2004 Topps Cracker Jack Stickers

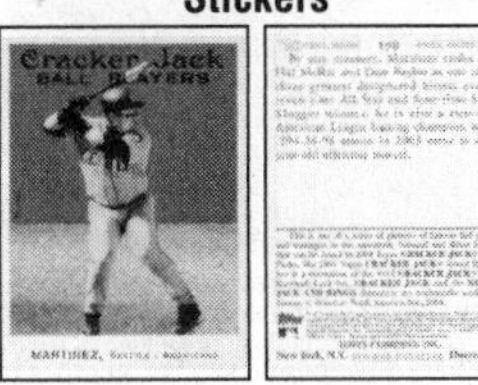
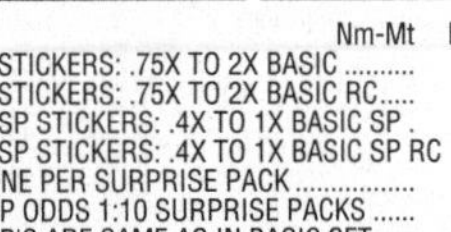

Nm-Mt Ex-Mt
*STICKERS: .75X TO 2X BASIC
*STICKERS: .75X TO 2X BASIC RC
*SP STICKERS: .4X TO 1X BASIC SP
*SP STICKERS: .4X TO 1X BASIC SP RC
ONE PER SURPRISE PACK
SP ODDS 1:10 SURPRISE PACKS
SP'S ARE SAME AS IN BASIC SET

2004 Topps Cracker Jack 1-2-3 Strikes You're Out Relics

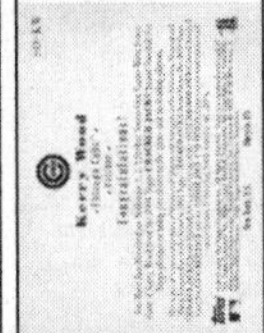

Nm-Mt Ex-Mt
GROUP A 1:5045 H, 1:5310 R SURPRISE
GROUP B 1:103 H, 1:109 R SURPRISE
GROUP C 1:177 H, 1:202 R SURPRISE
GROUP D 1:157 H, 1:191 R SURPRISE
BM Brett Myers Jsy C 8.00 2.40
BW Billy Wagner Jsy B 8.00 2.40
BZ Barry Zito Jsy B 10.00 3.00
CCS C.C. Sabathia Jsy C 8.00 2.40
CS Curt Schilling Jsy A 20.00 6.00
DL Derek Lowe Jsy B 8.00 2.40
EG Eric Gagne Jsy C 10.00 3.00
HN Hideo Nomo Jsy B 10.00 3.00
JB Josh Beckett Uni B 10.00 3.00
JS John Smoltz Jsy D 10.00 3.00
KB Kevin Brown Uni B 8.00 2.40
KM Kevin Millwood Jsy D 8.00 2.40
KW Kerry Wood Jsy C 10.00 3.00
MAM Mark Mulder Uni D 8.00 2.40
MM Mike Mussina Uni A 20.00 6.00
PM Pedro Martinez Jsy B 10.00 3.00
RH Rich Harden Jsy B 8.00 2.40
RJ Randy Johnson Jsy B 10.00 3.00

2004 Topps Cracker Jack Secret Surprise Signatures

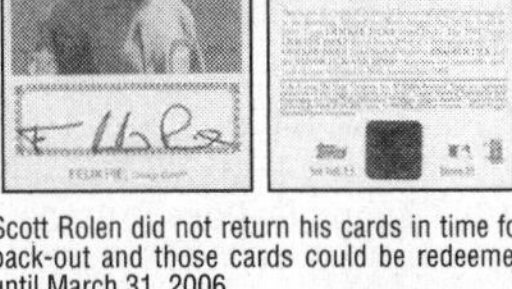

Scott Rolen did not return his cards in time for pack-out and those cards could be redeemed until March 31, 2006.

Nm-Mt Ex-Mt
GROUP A 1:1448 H, 1:1657 R SURPRISE
GROUP B 1:451 H, 1:524 R SURPRISE
GROUP C 1:323 H, 1:368 R SURPRISE
GROUP D 1:372 H, 1:404 R SURPRISE
AH Aubrey Huff B 15.00 4.50
BG Brian Giles D 15.00 4.50
CF Cliff Floyd B 15.00 4.50
DM Dustin McGowan B 15.00 4.50
DW Dontrelle Willis A 25.00 7.50
FP Felix Pie C 25.00 7.50
JW Jerome Williams A 25.00 7.50
ML Mike Lamb C 10.00 3.00
MV Merkin Valdez B 25.00 7.50
SP Scott Podsednik D 25.00 7.50
SR Scott Rolen C EXCH 25.00 7.50

2004 Topps Cracker Jack Take Me Out to the Ballgame Relics

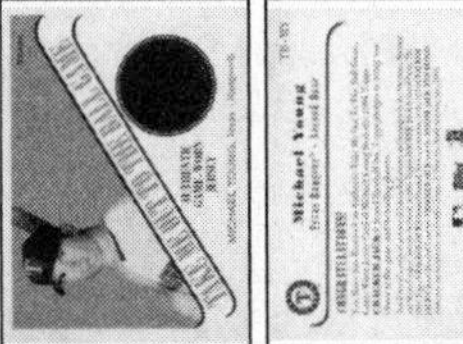

Nm-Mt Ex-Mt
GROUP A 1:654 SURPRISE
GROUP B 1:645 H, 1:645 R SURPRISE
GROUP C 1:152 H, 1:194 R SURPRISE
GROUP D 1:131 H, 1:223 R SURPRISE
GROUP E 1:99 H, 1:125 R SURPRISE.
GROUP F 1:201 H, 1:264 R SURPRISE
GROUP G 1:211 H, 1:297 R SURPRISE
GROUP H 1:190 H, 1:226 R SURPRISE
GROUP I 1:126 H, 1:154 R SURPRISE
GROUP J 1:149 H, 1:189 R SURPRISE
GROUP K 1:89 H, 1:93 R SURPRISE
AB Angel Berroa Bat I 8.00 2.40
AD Adam Dunn Jsy C 8.00 2.40
AP Albert Pujols Uni G 15.00 4.50
AP2 Albert Pujols Bat C 15.00 4.50
AR Alex Rodriguez Jsy H 10.00 3.00
AR2 A.Rodriguez Yanks Bat C 20.00 6.00
AS Alfonso Soriano Uni G 10.00 3.00
AS2 Alfonso Soriano Bat A 15.00 4.50
BA Bob Abreu Jsy E 8.00 2.40
BB1 Bret Boone Bat C 8.00 2.40
BB2 Bret Boone Jsy K 8.00 2.40
CB Craig Biggio Jsy E 10.00 3.00
CJ Chipper Jones Jsy K 10.00 3.00
EC Eric Chavez Uni F 8.00 2.40
GA Garrett Anderson Bat B 10.00 3.00
HB Hank Blalock Bat C 8.00 2.40
IR Ivan Rodriguez Bat D 10.00 3.00
JB Jeff Bagwell Uni E 10.00 3.00
JE Jim Edmonds Jsy E 8.00 2.40
JGA Jason Giambi Jsy C 10.00 3.00
JGH Jason Giambi Uni F 10.00 3.00
JL Javy Lopez Jsy E 8.00 2.40
JL2 Javy Lopez Bat A 10.00 3.00
JR Jose Reyes Jsy D 10.00 3.00
JRO Jimmy Rollins Jsy E 8.00 2.40
JT Jim Thome Jsy I 10.00 3.00
KW Kerry Wood Jsy G 10.00 3.00
LB Lance Berkman Bat F 8.00 2.40
LB2 Lance Berkman Jsy K 8.00 2.40
LG Luis Gonzalez Jsy B 10.00 3.00
LW Larry Walker Jsy J 10.00 3.00
MA Moises Alou Jsy J 8.00 2.40
MC Miguel Cabrera Bat H 10.00 3.00
MCT Mark Teixeira Jsy I 8.00 2.40
MG Marcus Giles Jsy E 8.00 2.40
MP Mike Piazza Jsy F 10.00 3.00
MR Manny Ramirez Uni C 8.00 2.40
MS Mike Sweeney Jsy A 10.00 3.00
MT Miguel Tejada Bat K 8.00 2.40
MY Michael Young Jsy D 8.00 2.40
NG Nomar Garciaparra Jsy B 15.00 4.50
NG2 Nomar Garciaparra Bat A 15.00 4.50
PB Pat Burrell Jsy E 8.00 2.40
PL Paul Lo Duca Uni D 8.00 2.40
RB Rocco Baldelli Bat H 10.00 3.00
RF Rafael Furcal Jsy J 8.00 2.40
SG Shawn Green Uni D 8.00 2.40
SG2 Shawn Green Bat C 8.00 2.40
SS Sammy Sosa Bat D 15.00 4.50
SS2 Sammy Sosa Jsy E 15.00 4.50
TG Troy Glaus Jsy I 10.00 3.00
TH Todd Helton Jsy K 10.00 3.00
TKH Torii Hunter Jsy B 10.00 3.00
VW Vernon Wells Jsy D 8.00 2.40

2004 Topps Cracker Jack Team Topps Legends Autographs

Nm-Mt Ex-Mt
STATED ODDS 1:755,000 HOBBY
SEE 04 TOPPS TEAM TOPPS FOR PRICING

1995 Topps D3

Manufactured by Topps, this set consists of 59 three-dimension standard-size cards of better players. Utilizing uncluttered fronts, the player's name is at the top with the set logo toward bottom right. The backs offer a small photo with statistical breakdowns in areas such as Home, Away, Day, Night, etc. A second series was planned for this issue but was never issued due to lack of consumer interest. Promo cards featuring Greg Gagne and Tim Bogar were distributed to dealers and hobby media to preview the set.

Nm-Mt Ex-Mt
COMPLETE SET (59) 15.00 4.50
1 David Justice .30 .09
2 Cal Ripken 2.50 .75
3 Ruben Sierra .15 .04
4 Roberto Alomar .75 .23
5 Denny Martinez .30 .09
6 Todd Zeile .15 .04
7 Albert Belle .30 .09
8 Chuck Knoblauch .30 .09
9 Roger Clemens 1.50 .45
10 Cal Eldred .15 .04
11 Dennis Eckersley .30 .09
12 Andy Benes .15 .04
13 Moises Alou .30 .09
14 Andres Galarraga .30 .09
15 Jim Thome .75 .23
16 Tim Salmon .50 .15
17 Carlos Garcia .15 .04
18 Scott Leius .15 .04
19 Jeff Montgomery .15 .04
20 Brian Anderson .15 .04
21 Will Clark .75 .23
22 Bobby Bonilla .30 .09
23 Mike Stanley .15 .04
24 Barry Bonds 2.00 .60
25 Jeff Conine .30 .09
26 Paul O'Neill .50 .15
27 Mike Piazza 1.25 .35
28 Tom Glavine .50 .15
29 Jim Edmonds .30 .09
30 Lou Whitaker .30 .09
31 Jeff Frye .15 .04
32 Ivan Rodriguez .75 .23
33 Bret Boone .30 .09
34 Mike Greenwell .15 .04
35 Mark Grace .50 .15
36 Darren Lewis .15 .04
37 Don Mattingly 2.00 .60
38 Jose Rijo .15 .04
39 Robin Ventura .30 .09
40 Bob Hamelin .15 .04
41 Tim Wallach .15 .04
42 Tony Gwynn 1.00 .30
43 Ken Griffey Jr. 1.25 .35
44 Doug Drabek .15 .04
45 Rafael Palmeiro .50 .15
46 Dean Palmer .30 .09
47 Bip Roberts .15 .04
48 Barry Larkin .75 .23
49 Dave Nilsson .15 .04
50 Wil Cordero .15 .04
51 Travis Fryman .30 .09
52 Chuck Carr .15 .04
53 Rey Sanchez .15 .04
54 Walt Weiss .15 .04
55 Joe Carter .30 .09
56 Len Dykstra .30 .09
57 Orlando Merced .15 .04
58 Ozzie Smith 1.25 .35
59 Chris Gomez .15 .04
PB1 Greg Gagne 1.00 .30
Baseball Promo
TB1 Tim Bogar 1.00 .30
Baseball Promo

1995 Topps D3 Zone

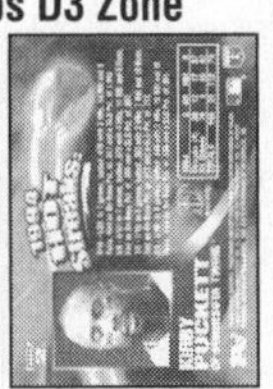

This three-dimensional, six-card set was inserted in Topps D3 packs. They were inserted one in three hobby packs and one in six retail packs. The 3D front has a player photo surrounded by baseballs. The player's name is at the top with the set logo at the bottom. Horizontal backs offer a small player photo and a synopsis of various hot streaks in 1994. Cards are numbered with a "DIII" prefix.

Nm-Mt Ex-Mt
COMPLETE SET (6) 5.00 1.50
1 Frank Thomas 1.00 .30
2 Kirby Puckett 1.00 .30
3 Jeff Bagwell 1.00 .30
4 Fred McGriff 1.00 .30
5 Raul Mondesi 1.00 .30
6 Kenny Lofton 1.00 .30

1995 Topps Embossed

This 140-card standard-size set was issued by Topps. The cards were issued in six-card packs with five regular cards and one parallel Golden Idols card in each pack. The suggested retail price of the packs was $3 with 24 packs per box. Each case contained four boxes. Cards 97-120 are a subset dedicated to active players who have won major awards. The cards are embossed on both sides. The fronts have an embossed player photo surrounded by a gray border. In addition, the TMB (Topps Embossed) logo is in an upper corner and the player's name at the bottom. The horizontal backs have an embossed player photo on the left, while vital statistics, seasonal and career statistics and some interesting facts about the player are on the right.

Nm-Mt Ex-Mt
COMPLETE SET (140) 25.00 7.50
1 Kenny Lofton .30 .09
2 Gary Sheffield .30 .09
3 Hal Morris .15 .04
4 Cliff Floyd .30 .09
5 Pat Hentgen .15 .04
6 Tony Gwynn 1.00 .30
7 Jose Valentin .15 .04
8 Jason Bere .15 .04
9 Jeff Kent .30 .09
10 John Valentin .15 .04
11 Brian Anderson .15 .04
12 Deion Sanders .50 .15
13 Ryan Thompson .15 .04
14 Ruben Sierra .15 .04
15 Jay Bell .30 .09
16 Chuck Carr .15 .04
17 Brent Gates .15 .04
18 Bret Boone .30 .09
19 Paul Molitor .50 .15
20 Chili Davis .30 .09
21 Ryan Klesko .30 .09
22 Will Clark .75 .23
23 Greg Vaughn .30 .09
24 Moises Alou .30 .09
25 Ray Lankford .15 .04
26 Jose Rijo .15 .04
27 Bobby Jones .15 .04
28 Rick Wilkins .15 .04
29 Cal Eldred .15 .04
30 Juan Gonzalez .75 .23
31 Royce Clayton .15 .04
32 Bryan Harvey .15 .04
33 Dave Nilsson .15 .04
34 Chris Hoiles .15 .04
35 David Nied .15 .04
36 Javier Lopez .30 .09
37 Tim Wallach .15 .04
38 Bobby Bonilla .30 .09
39 Danny Tartabull .15 .04
40 Andy Benes .15 .04
41 Dean Palmer .30 .09
42 Chris Gomez .15 .04
43 Kevin Appier .30 .09
44 Brady Anderson .30 .09
45 Alex Fernandez .15 .04
46 Roberto Kelly .15 .04
47 Dave Hollins .15 .04
48 Chuck Finley .30 .09
49 Wade Boggs .50 .15
50 Travis Fryman .30 .09
51 Ken Griffey Jr. 1.25 .35
52 John Olerud .30 .09
53 Delino DeShields .15 .04
54 Ivan Rodriguez .75 .23
55 Tommy Greene .15 .04
56 Tom Pagnozzi .15 .04
57 Bip Roberts .15 .04
58 Luis Gonzalez .30 .09
59 Rey Sanchez .15 .04
60 Ken Ryan .15 .04
61 Darren Daulton .30 .09
62 Rick Aguilera .30 .09
63 Wally Joyner .30 .09
64 Mike Greenwell .15 .04
65 Jay Buhner .30 .09
66 Craig Biggio .50 .15
67 Charles Nagy .15 .04
68 Devon White .15 .04
69 Randy Johnson .75 .23
70 Shawon Dunston .15 .04
71 Kirby Puckett .75 .23
72 Paul O'Neill .50 .15
73 Tino Martinez .50 .15
74 Carlos Garcia .15 .04
75 Ozzie Smith 1.25 .35
76 Cecil Fielder .30 .09
77 Mike Stanley .15 .04
78 Lance Johnson .15 .04
79 Tony Phillips .15 .04
80 Bobby Munoz .15 .04
81 Kevin Tapani .15 .04
82 W.VanLandingham .15 .04
83 Dante Bichette .30 .09
84 Tom Candiotti .15 .04
85 Wil Cordero .15 .04
86 Jeff Conine .30 .09
87 Joey Hamilton .15 .04
88 Mark Whiten .15 .04
89 Jeff Montgomery .15 .04
90 Andres Galarraga .30 .09
91 Roberto Alomar .75 .23
92 Orlando Merced .15 .04
93 Mike Mussina .75 .23
94 Pedro Martinez .75 .23
95 Carlos Baerga .15 .04
96 Steve Trachsel .15 .04
97 Lou Whitaker .30 .09
98 David Cone .30 .09
99 Chuck Knoblauch .30 .09
100 Frank Thomas .75 .23
101 David Justice .30 .09
102 Raul Mondesi .30 .09
103 Rickey Henderson .75 .23
104 Doug Drabek .15 .04
105 Sandy Alomar Jr. .15 .04
106 Roger Clemens 1.50 .45
107 Mark McGwire 2.00 .60
108 Tim Salmon .50 .15
109 Greg Maddux 1.25 .35
110 Mike Piazza 1.25 .35
111 Tom Glavine .50 .15
112 Walt Weiss .15 .04
113 Cal Ripken 2.50 .75
114 Eddie Murray .75 .23
115 Don Mattingly 2.00 .60
116 Ozzie Guillen .15 .04
117 Bob Hamelin .15 .04
118 Jeff Bagwell .50 .15
119 Eric Karros .30 .09
120 Barry Bonds 2.00 .60
121 Mickey Tettleton .15 .04
122 Mark Langston .15 .04
123 Robin Ventura .30 .09
124 Bret Saberhagen .30 .09
125 Albert Belle .30 .09
126 Rafael Palmeiro .50 .15
127 Fred McGriff .50 .15
128 Jimmy Key .30 .09
129 Barry Larkin .75 .23
130 Tim Raines .30 .09
131 Len Dykstra .30 .09
132 Todd Zeile .15 .04
133 Joe Carter .30 .09
134 Matt Williams .30 .09
135 Terry Steinbach .15 .04
136 Manny Ramirez .30 .09
137 John Wetteland .30 .09
138 Rod Beck .15 .04
139 Mo Vaughn .30 .09
140 Darren Lewis .15 .04

1995 Topps Embossed Golden Idols

This 140-card parallel set was inserted one per Embossed pack. The only difference between these and the regular cards is the gold foil surrounding the front borders.

Nm-Mt Ex-Mt
COMPLETE SET (140) 120.00 36.00
*STARS: 1.5X TO 4X BASIC CARDS

2001 Topps Fusion

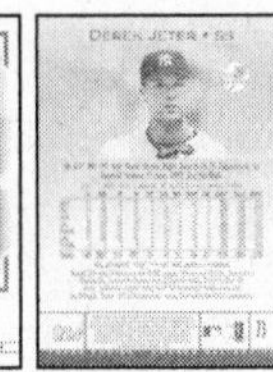

The 2001 Topps Fusion product was released in March, 2001 and featured a 250-card base set that fused many of the Topps' Brand names all into one product. The product included cards from Bowman's Best=BB, Finest=FIN, Gold Label=GL, Stadium Club=SC, and Topps Gallery=GAL. Each pack contained five cards and carried a suggested retail price of $4.00 per pack.

Nm-Mt Ex-Mt
COMPLETE SET (250) 200.00 60.00
1 Albert Belle BB .75 .23
2 Albert Belle FIN .75 .23
3 Albert Belle GAL .75 .23
4 Nick Bierbrodt GL .40 .12
5 A. Rodriguez Rangers SC 2.00 .60
6 A. Rodriguez Rangers BB 2.00 .60
7 A.Rodriguez Rangers FIN 2.00 .60
8 A.Rodriguez Rangers GAL 2.00 .60
9 Eric Munson GL .40 .12
10 Barry Bonds SC 3.00 .90
11 Andruw Jones BB .50 .15
12 Antonio Alfonseca FIN .50 .15
13 Andres Galarraga GAL .50 .15
14 Joe Crede GL .40 .12
15 Barry Larkin SC 1.25 .35
16 Barry Bonds BB 3.00 .90
17 Barry Bonds FIN 3.00 .90
18 Andruw Jones GAL .50 .15
19 C.C. Sabathia GL .50 .15
20 Bobby Higginson SC .50 .15
21 Barry Larkin BB 1.25 .35
22 Ben Grieve FIN .40 .12
23 Barry Bonds GAL 3.00 .90
24 Corey Patterson GL .50 .15
25 Carlos Delgado SC .50 .15
26 Bernie Williams BB .75 .23
27 Brian Giles FIN .50 .15
28 Barry Larkin GAL 1.25 .35
29 Travis Dawkins GL .40 .12
30 Chipper Jones SC 1.25 .35
31 Brian Giles BB .50 .15
32 Carlos Delgado FIN .50 .15
33 Ben Grieve GAL .40 .12
34 Geoff Goetz GL .40 .12
35 Cristian Guzman SC .50 .15
36 Cal Ripken BB 4.00 1.20
37 Chipper Jones FIN 1.25 .35
38 Bernie Williams GAL .75 .23
39 Pablo Ozuna GL .40 .12
40 Vinny Castilla SC .50 .15
41 Carlos Delgado BB .50 .15
42 Craig Biggio FIN .75 .23
43 Cal Ripken GAL 4.00 1.20
44 Tim Redding GL .40 .12
45 Darin Erstad SC .50 .15
46 Chipper Jones BB 1.25 .35
47 Darin Erstad FIN .50 .15
48 Carlos Delgado GAL .50 .15
49 Josh Hamilton GL .40 .12
50 Derek Jeter SC 3.00 .90
51 Darin Erstad BB .50 .15
52 Dean Palmer FIN .50 .15
53 Chipper Jones GAL 1.25 .35
54 Chin-Feng Chen GL .50 .15
55 Edgar Martinez SC .75 .23
56 Derek Jeter BB 3.00 .90
57 Derek Jeter FIN 3.00 .90
58 Craig Biggio GAL .75 .23
59 Keith Ginter GL .40 .12
60 Edgardo Alfonzo SC .50 .15
61 Edgar Martinez BB .75 .23
62 Edgardo Alfonzo FIN .50 .15
63 David Justice GAL .50 .15
64 Roy Oswalt GL .75 .23
65 Eric Karros SC .50 .15
66 Edgardo Alfonzo BB .50 .15
67 Frank Thomas FIN 1.50 .45
68 Dean Palmer GAL .50 .15
69 Alfonso Soriano GL .75 .23
70 Fernando Vina SC .50 .15
71 Frank Thomas BB 1.50 .45
72 Garret Anderson FIN .50 .15
73 Derek Jeter GAL 3.00 .90
74 Bobby Bradley GL .40 .12
75 Frank Thomas SC 1.50 .45
76 Gary Sheffield BB .50 .15
77 Geoff Jenkins FIN .50 .15
78 Edgar Martinez GAL .75 .23
79 Nick Johnson GL .50 .15
80 Fred McGriff SC .75 .23
81 Geoff Jenkins BB .50 .15
82 Greg Maddux FIN 2.00 .60
83 Edgardo Alfonzo GAL .50 .15
84 Hee Seop Choi GL RC 6.00 1.80
85 Garret Anderson SC .50 .15
86 Greg Maddux BB 2.00 .60
87 Ivan Rodriguez FIN 1.25 .35
88 Eric Karros GAL .50 .15
89 Scott Seabol GL .40 .12
90 Ivan Rodriguez SC 1.25 .35
91 Ivan Rodriguez BB 1.25 .35
92 J.D. Drew FIN .50 .15
93 Frank Thomas GAL 1.50 .45
94 Ryan Anderson GL .40 .12
95 Jason Giambi SC 1.25 .35
96 Jason Giambi BB 1.25 .35
97 Jason Kendall FIN .50 .15
98 Gary Sheffield GAL .50 .15
99 Milton Bradley GL .50 .15
100 Jason Kendall SC .50 .15
101 Jason Kendall BB .50 .15
102 Jeff Bagwell FIN .75 .23
103 Greg Maddux GAL 2.00 .60
104 Sean Burroughs GL .50 .15
105 Jay Bell SC .50 .15
106 Jeff Bagwell BB .75 .23
107 J. Hammonds FIN .40 .12
108 Ivan Rodriguez GAL 1.25 .35
109 Ben Petrick GL .40 .12
110 Jeff Bagwell SC .75 .23
111 Jeff Cirillo BB .40 .12

Card	Nm-Mt	Ex-Mt
112 Jermaine Dye FIN	.50	.15
113 J.T. Snow GAL	.50	.15
114 Ben Davis GL	.40	.12
115 Jeff Cirillo SC	.40	.12
116 Jeff Kent BB	.50	.15
117 Jeromy Burnitz FIN	.50	.15
118 Jay Bell GAL	.50	.15
119 Jason Hart GL	.40	.12
120 Jeff Kent SC	.50	.15
121 Jermaine Dye BB	.50	.15
122 John Olerud FIN	.50	.15
123 Jeff Bagwell GAL	.75	.23
124 Jeff Segar GL RC	.75	.23
125 Jeromy Burnitz SC	.50	.15
126 Jeromy Burnitz BB	.50	.15
127 Johnny Damon FIN	.50	.15
128 Jim Edmonds GAL	.50	.15
129 Tim Christman GL RC	.75	.23
130 Jim Thome SC	1.25	.35
131 Jim Edmonds BB	.50	.15
132 Jorge Posada FIN	.75	.23
133 Jim Thome GAL	1.25	.35
134 Danny Borrell GL RC	.75	.23
135 Johnny Damon SC	.50	.15
136 Jim Thome BB	1.25	.35
137 Jose Vidro FIN	.50	.15
138 Ken Griffey Jr. GAL	2.00	.60
139 Sean Burnett GL	.50	.15
140 Larry Walker SC	.75	.23
141 Jose Vidro BB	.50	.15
142 Ken Griffey Jr. FIN	2.00	.60
143 Larry Walker GAL	.75	.23
144 Robert Keppel GL RC	1.00	.30
145 Luis Castillo SC	.50	.15
146 Ken Griffey Jr. BB	2.00	.60
147 Kevin Brown FIN	.50	.15
148 Manny Ramirez GAL	.50	.15
149 David Parrish GL RC	.75	.23
150 Manny Ramirez SC	.50	.15
151 Kevin Brown BB	.50	.15
152 Luis Castillo FIN	.50	.15
153 Mark Grace GAL	.75	.23
154 Mike Jacobs GL	.75	.23
155 Mark Grace SC	.75	.23
156 Larry Walker BB	.75	.23
157 Magglio Ordonez FIN	.50	.15
158 Mark McGwire GAL	3.00	.90
159 Adam Johnson GL	.40	.12
160 Mark McGwire SC	3.00	.90
161 Magglio Ordonez BB	.50	.15
162 Mark McGwire FIN	3.00	.90
163 Matt Williams GAL	.50	.15
164 Oscar Ramirez GL RC	.75	.23
165 Mike Piazza SC	2.00	.60
166 Manny Ramirez BB	.50	.15
167 Mike Piazza FIN	2.00	.60
168 Mike Mussina GAL	1.25	.35
169 Odannis Ayala GL RC	.75	.23
170 Mike Sweeney SC	.50	.15
171 Mark McGwire BB	3.00	.90
172 N. Garciaparra FIN	2.00	.60
173 Mike Piazza GAL	2.00	.60
174 J.R. House GL	.40	.12
175 Neifi Perez SC	.40	.12
176 Mike Piazza BB	2.00	.60
177 Pedro Martinez FIN	1.25	.35
178 Mo Vaughn GAL	.50	.15
179 Shawn Fagan GL RC	.75	.23
180 N.Garciaparra SC	2.00	.60
181 Mo Vaughn BB	.50	.15
182 Rafael Palmeiro FIN	.75	.23
183 N.Garciaparra GAL	2.00	.60
184 Chris Bass GL RC	.75	.23
185 Raul Mondesi SC	.50	.15
186 N.Garciaparra BB	2.00	.60
187 Randy Johnson FIN	1.25	.35
188 Omar Vizquel GAL	.75	.23
189 Erick Almonte GL RC	.75	.23
190 Ray Durham SC	.50	.15
191 Pedro Martinez BB	1.25	.35
192 Robb Nen FIN	.50	.15
193 Pedro Martinez GAL	1.25	.35
194 Luis Montanez GL RC	.75	.23
195 Ray Lankford SC	.40	.12
196 Rafael Palmeiro BB	.75	.23
197 Roberto Alomar FIN	1.25	.35
198 Rafael Palmeiro GAL	.75	.23
199 Chad Petty GL RC	.75	.23
200 Richard Hidalgo SC	.50	.15
201 Randy Johnson BB	1.25	.35
202 Robin Ventura FIN	.50	.15
203 Randy Johnson GAL	1.25	.35
204 Derek Thompson GL	.40	.12
205 Sammy Sosa SC	2.00	.60
206 Roberto Alomar BB	1.25	.35
207 Sammy Sosa FIN	2.00	.60
208 Raul Mondesi GAL	.50	.15
209 Scott Heard GL	.40	.12
210 Scott Rolen SC	.75	.23
211 Sammy Sosa BB	2.00	.60
212 Scott Rolen FIN	.75	.23
213 Roberto Alomar GAL	1.25	.35
214 Dominic Rich GL RC	.75	.23
215 Sean Casey SC	.50	.15
216 Scott Rolen BB	.75	.23
217 Sean Casey FIN	.50	.15
218 Robin Ventura GAL	.50	.15
219 William Smith GL RC	.75	.23
220 Tim Salmon SC	.75	.23
221 Sean Casey BB	.50	.15
222 Shannon Stewart FIN	.50	.15
223 Sammy Sosa GAL	2.00	.60
224 Joel Pineiro GL	1.25	.35
225 Tino Martinez SC	.75	.23
226 Shawn Green BB	.50	.15
227 Shawn Green FIN	.50	.15
228 Scott Rolen GAL	.75	.23
229 Greg Morrison GL RC	.75	.23
230 Tony Gwynn SC	1.50	.45
231 Todd Helton BB	.75	.23
232 Steve Finley FIN	.50	.15
233 Scott Williamson GAL	.40	.12
234 Talmadge Nunnari GL	.40	.12
235 Tony Womack SC	.40	.12
236 Tony Batista BB	.50	.15
237 Tim Salmon FIN	.50	.15
238 Shawn Green GAL	.50	.15
239 C. Villalobos GL RC	.75	.23
240 Troy Glaus SC	.75	.23
241 Troy Glaus BB	.75	.23
242 Todd Helton FIN	.75	.23
243 Tim Salmon GAL	.75	.23
244 M. Scutaro GL RC	.75	.23
245 Troy O'Leary SC	.40	.12
246 Vladimir Guerrero BB	1.25	.35
247 Vladimir Guerrero FIN	1.25	.35
248 V. Guerrero GAL	1.25	.35
249 Horacio Estrada GL	.40	.12
250 Vladimir Guerrero SC	1.25	.35

2001 Topps Fusion Autographs

Randomly inserted into packs, this 37-card insert features authentic autographs from some of the best names in Major League Baseball. Included in the set are Chipper Jones, Alex Rodriguez, and Ivan Rodriguez. Please note that there were seven tiers of autographs, and are listed as follows: Group A 1:151 H/R, Group B 1:1227 H; 1:1235 R, Group C 1:164 H/R, Group D 1:109 H/R, Group E 1:246 H/R, Group F 1:447 H/R, and Group G 1:65 H; 1:66 R. Card backs carry a "FA" prefix.

Card	Nm-Mt	Ex-Mt
FA1 Rafael Furcal FIN D	15.00	4.50
FA2 Mike Lamb GAL D	10.00	3.00
FA3 Jason Marquis BB D	10.00	3.00
FA4 Milton Bradley SC D	15.00	4.50
FA5 Barry Zito GL D	30.00	9.00
FA6 Derrek Lee SC F	15.00	4.50
FA7 Corey Patterson BB A	15.00	4.50
FA8 Josh Hamilton GAL A	10.00	3.00
FA9 Sean Burroughs GL A	15.00	4.50
FA10 Jason Hart FIN A	10.00	3.00
FA11 Luis Montanez GL G	15.00	4.50
FA12 Robert Keppel SC G	25.00	7.50
FA13 Blake Williams FIN G	15.00	4.50
FA14 Phil Wilson BB G	10.00	3.00
FA15 Jake Peavy GAL G	25.00	7.50
FA16 Alex Rodriguez BB C	100.00	30.00
FA17 Ivan Rodriguez GL C	30.00	9.00
FA18 Don Larsen BB E	25.00	7.50
FA19 Todd Helton SC C	25.00	7.50
FA20 C. Delgado FIN B	15.00	4.50
FA21 Geoff Jenkins GAL C	15.00	4.50
FA22 Willie Stargell GAL E	40.00	12.00
FA23 F. Robinson FIN E	40.00	12.00
FA24 Warren Spahn GL E	50.00	15.00
FA25 H. Killebrew SC E	40.00	12.00
FA26 Chipper Jones BB C	40.00	12.00
FA27 Chipper Jones FIN C	40.00	12.00
FA28 C.Jones GAL C	40.00	12.00
FA29 Chipper Jones GL C	40.00	12.00
FA30 Chipper Jones SC C	40.00	12.00
FA31 R. Baldelli GAL G	40.00	12.00
FA32 Keith Ginter GAL G	10.00	3.00
FA33 J.R. House GAL G	10.00	3.00
FA34 Alex Cabrera GAL G	10.00	3.00
FA35 Tony Alvarez GAL G	10.00	3.00
FA36 Pablo Ozuna GAL G	10.00	3.00
FA37 Juan Salas GAL G	10.00	3.00

2001 Topps Fusion Double Feature

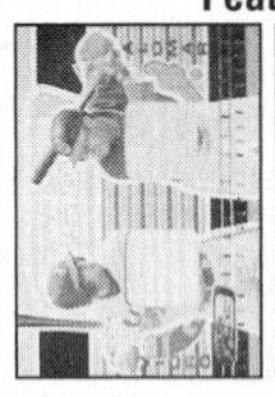

Randomly inserted into packs, this 11-card insert set features dual-player game-used Bat and Jersey cards. The game-used bat cards can be found in packs at a rate of 1:491 Hobby; and 1:492 Retail. The game-jersey cards were inserted in three different tiers as follows: Group A 1:1964 H; 1:1998 R, Group B 1:6531 H; 1:6584 R, and Group C 1:10068 H; 1:10656 R. Card backs carry a "DF" prefix.

Card	Nm-Mt	Ex-Mt
DF1 Ivan Rodriguez Rickey Henderson Bat	25.00	7.50
DF2 John Smoltz Tom Glavine Bat	25.00	7.50
DF3 Willie Stargell Frank Thomas Bat	25.00	7.50
DF4 Carlos Delgado Todd Helton Jsy A	25.00	7.50
DF5 Adrian Gonzalez Pat Burrell Bat	15.00	4.50
DF6 Jose Vidro Roberto Alomar Bat	25.00	7.50
DF7 Chipper Jones Robin Ventura Bat	25.00	7.50
DF8 J.D. Drew Matt Lawton Bat	15.00	4.50
DF9 Josh Hamilton Chin-Feng Chen Jsy B	40.00	12.00
DF10 Rafael Furcal Miguel Tejada Bat	15.00	4.50
DF11 Josh Beckett Ryan Anderson Jsy C	25.00	7.50

2001 Topps Fusion Feature

Randomly inserted into packs, this 22-card insert set features game-used bat and jersey cards of many of today's top players. Game-used bat cards were inserted into packs at 1:82 Hob/Ret. Game-used Jerseys were inserted into

packs in four different tiers as follows: Group A 1:327 Hob/Ret, Group B 1:1313 H; 1:1332 R, Group C 1:1405 H; 1:1411 R, Group D 1:4931 H; 1:5328 R. Card backs carry a "F" prefix.

Card	Nm-Mt	Ex-Mt
F1 Ivan Rodriguez Bat	15.00	4.50
F2 Rickey Henderson Bat	15.00	4.50
F3 John Smoltz Bat	15.00	4.50
F4 Tom Glavine Bat	15.00	4.50
F5 Willie Stargell Bat	15.00	4.50
F6 Frank Thomas Bat	15.00	4.50
F7 Carlos Delgado Jsy A	10.00	3.00
F8 Todd Helton Jsy A	15.00	4.50
F9 Adrian Gonzalez Bat	10.00	3.00
F10 Pat Burrell Bat	10.00	3.00
F11 Jose Vidro Bat	10.00	3.00
F12 Roberto Alomar Bat	15.00	4.50
F13 Chipper Jones Bat	15.00	4.50
F14 Robin Ventura Bat	10.00	3.00
F15 J.D. Drew Bat	10.00	3.00
F16 Matt Lawton Bat	10.00	3.00
F17 Josh Hamilton Jsy C	10.00	3.00
F18 Chin-Feng Chen Jsy B	40.00	12.00
F19 Rafael Furcal Bat	10.00	3.00
F20 Miguel Tejada Bat	10.00	3.00
F21 Josh Beckett Jsy C	15.00	4.50
F22 Ryan Anderson Jsy D	10.00	3.00

1996 Topps Gallery

The 1996 Topps Gallery set was issued in one series totalling 180 cards. The eight-card packs retailed for $3.00 each. The set is divided into five themes: Classics (1-90), New Editions (91-108), Modernists (109-126), Futurists (127-144) and Masters (145-180). Each theme features a different design on front, but the bulk of the set has full-bleed, color action shots. A Mickey Mantle Masterpiece was inserted into these packs at a rate of one every 48 packs. It is priced at the bottom of these listings.

Card	Nm-Mt	Ex-Mt
COMPLETE SET (180)	40.00	12.00
1 Tom Glavine	.75	.23
2 Carlos Baerga	.50	.15
3 Dante Bichette	.50	.15
4 Mark Langston	.50	.15
5 Ray Lankford	.50	.15
6 Moises Alou	.50	.15
7 Marquis Grissom	.50	.15
8 Ramon Martinez	.50	.15
9 Steve Finley	.50	.15
10 Todd Hundley	.50	.15
11 Brady Anderson	.50	.15
12 John Valentin	.50	.15
13 Heathcliff Slocumb	.50	.15
14 Ruben Sierra	.50	.15
15 Jeff Conine	.50	.15
16 Jay Buhner	.50	.15
17 Sammy Sosa	2.00	.60
18 Doug Drabek	.50	.15
19 Jose Mesa	.50	.15
20 Jeff King	.50	.15
21 Mickey Tettleton	.50	.15
22 Jeff Montgomery	.50	.15
23 Alex Fernandez	.50	.15
24 Greg Vaughn	.50	.15
25 Chuck Finley	.50	.15
26 Terry Steinbach	.50	.15
27 Rod Beck	.50	.15
28 Jack McDowell	.50	.15
29 Mark Wohlers	.50	.15
30 Len Dykstra	.50	.15
31 Bernie Williams	.75	.23
32 Travis Fryman	.50	.15
33 Jose Canseco	1.25	.35
34 Ken Caminiti	.50	.15
35 Devon White	.50	.15
36 Bobby Bonilla	.50	.15
37 Paul Sorrento	.50	.15
38 Ryne Sandberg	2.00	.60
39 Derek Bell	.50	.15
40 Bobby Jones	.50	.15
41 J.T. Snow	.50	.15
42 Denny Neagle	.50	.15
43 Tim Wakefield	.50	.15
44 Andres Galarraga	.50	.15
45 David Segui	.50	.15
46 Lee Smith	.50	.15
47 Mel Rojas	.50	.15
48 John Franco	.50	.15
49 Pete Schourek	.50	.15
50 John Wetteland	.50	.15
51 Paul Molitor	.75	.23
52 Ivan Rodriguez	1.25	.35
53 Chris Hoiles	.50	.15
54 Mike Greenwell	.50	.15
55 Orel Hershiser	.50	.15
56 Brian McRae	.50	.15
57 Geronimo Berroa	.50	.15
58 Craig Biggio	.75	.23
59 David Justice	.50	.15
60 Lance Johnson	.50	.15
61 Andy Ashby	.50	.15
62 Randy Myers	.50	.15
63 Gregg Jefferies	.50	.15
64 Kevin Appier	.50	.15
65 Rick Aguilera	.50	.15
66 Shane Reynolds	.50	.15
67 John Smoltz	.75	.23
68 Ron Gant	.50	.15
69 Eric Karros	.50	.15
70 Jim Thome	1.25	.35
71 Terry Pendleton	.50	.15
72 Kenny Rogers	.50	.15
73 Robin Ventura	.50	.15
74 Dave Nilsson	.50	.15
75 Brian Jordan	.50	.15
76 Glenallen Hill	.50	.15
77 Greg Colbrunn	.50	.15
78 Roberto Alomar	1.25	.35
79 Rickey Henderson	1.25	.35
80 Carlos Garcia	.50	.15
81 Dean Palmer	.50	.15
82 Mike Stanley	.50	.15
83 Hal Morris	.50	.15
84 Wade Boggs	.75	.23
85 Chad Curtis	.50	.15
86 Roberto Hernandez	.50	.15
87 John Olerud	.50	.15
88 Frank Castillo	.50	.15
89 Rafael Palmeiro	.75	.23
90 Trevor Hoffman	.50	.15
91 Marty Cordova	.50	.15
92 Hideo Nomo	1.25	.35
93 Johnny Damon	.50	.15
94 Bill Pulsipher	.50	.15
95 Garret Anderson	.50	.15
96 Ray Durham	.50	.15
97 Ricky Bottalico	.50	.15
98 Carlos Perez	.50	.15
99 Troy Percival	.50	.15
100 Chipper Jones	1.25	.35
101 Esteban Loaiza	.50	.15
102 John Mabry	.50	.15
103 Jon Nunnally	.50	.15
104 Andy Pettitte	.75	.23
105 Lyle Mouton	.50	.15
106 Jason Isringhausen	.50	.15
107 Brian L.Hunter	.50	.15
108 Quilvio Veras	.50	.15
109 Jim Edmonds	.50	.15
110 Ryan Klesko	.50	.15
111 Pedro Martinez	1.25	.35
112 Joey Hamilton	.50	.15
113 Vinny Castilla	.50	.15
114 Alex Gonzalez	.50	.15
115 Raul Mondesi	.50	.15
116 Rondell White	.50	.15
117 Dan Miceli	.50	.15
118 Tom Goodwin	.50	.15
119 Bret Boone	.50	.15
120 Shawn Green	.50	.15
121 Jeff Cirillo	.50	.15
122 Rico Brogna	.50	.15
123 Chris Gomez	.50	.15
124 Ismael Valdes	.50	.15
125 Javy Lopez	.50	.15
126 Manny Ramirez	.50	.15
127 Paul Wilson	.50	.15
128 Billy Wagner	.50	.15
129 Eric Owens	.50	.15
130 Todd Greene	.50	.15
131 Karim Garcia	.50	.15
132 Jimmy Haynes	.50	.15
133 Michael Tucker	.50	.15
134 John Wasdin	.50	.15
135 Brooks Kieschnick	.50	.15
136 Alex Ochoa	.50	.15
137 Ariel Prieto	.50	.15
138 Tony Clark	.50	.15
139 Mark Loretta	.50	.15
140 Rey Ordonez	.50	.15
141 Chris Snopek	.50	.15
142 Roger Cedeno	.50	.15
143 Derek Jeter	3.00	.90
144 Jeff Suppan	.50	.15
145 Greg Maddux	2.00	.60
146 Ken Griffey Jr.	2.00	.60
147 Tony Gwynn	1.50	.45
148 Darren Daulton	.50	.15
149 Will Clark	1.25	.35
150 Mo Vaughn	.50	.15
151 Reggie Sanders	.50	.15
152 Kirby Puckett	1.25	.35
153 Paul O'Neill	.75	.23
154 Tim Salmon	.75	.23
155 Mark McGwire	3.00	.90
156 Barry Bonds	3.00	.90
157 Albert Belle	.50	.15
158 Edgar Martinez	.75	.23
159 Mike Mussina	1.25	.35
160 Cecil Fielder	.50	.15
161 Kenny Lofton	.50	.15
162 Randy Johnson	1.25	.35
163 Juan Gonzalez	1.25	.35
164 Jeff Bagwell	.75	.23
165 Joe Carter	.50	.15
166 Mike Piazza	2.00	.60
167 Eddie Murray	1.25	.35
168 Cal Ripken	4.00	1.20
169 Barry Larkin	1.25	.35
170 Chuck Knoblauch	.50	.15
171 Chili Davis	.50	.15
172 Fred McGriff	.75	.23
173 Matt Williams	.50	.15
174 Roger Clemens	2.50	.75
175 Frank Thomas	1.25	.35
176 Dennis Eckersley	.50	.15
177 Gary Sheffield	.50	.15
178 David Cone	.50	.15
179 Larry Walker	.75	.23
180 Mark Grace	.75	.23
NNO M. Mantle Masterpiece	20.00	6.00

1996 Topps Gallery Players Private Issue

Randomly inserted in packs at a rate of one in 12, this 180-card parallel is foil stamped. The backs are sequentially numbered 0-999, with the first 100 cards (numbers 0-99) sent to the players and the balance inserted in packs. Topps released a statement at the end of the 1996 season, claiming that they destroyed 400 sets.

	Nm-Mt	Ex-Mt
*STARS: 6X TO 15X BASIC CARDS		
*ROOKIES: 5X TO 12X BASIC CARDS		

1996 Topps Gallery Expressionists

Randomly inserted in packs at a rate of one in 24, this 20-card set features leaders printed on triple foil stamped and texture embossed cards. Card backs contain a second photo and narrative about the player.

Card	Nm-Mt	Ex-Mt
COMPLETE SET (20)	80.00	24.00
1 Mike Piazza	8.00	2.40
2 J.T. Snow	2.00	.60
3 Ken Griffey Jr.	8.00	2.40
4 Kirby Puckett	5.00	1.50
5 Carlos Baerga	2.00	.60
6 Chipper Jones	5.00	1.50
7 Hideo Nomo	5.00	1.50
8 Mark McGwire	12.00	3.60
9 Gary Sheffield	2.00	.60
10 Randy Johnson	5.00	1.50
11 Ray Lankford	2.00	.60
12 Sammy Sosa	8.00	2.40
13 Denny Martinez	2.00	.60
14 Jose Canseco	5.00	1.50
15 Tony Gwynn	6.00	1.80
16 Edgar Martinez	3.00	.90
17 Reggie Sanders	2.00	.60
18 Andres Galarraga	2.00	.60
19 Albert Belle	2.00	.60
20 Barry Larkin	5.00	1.50

1996 Topps Gallery Photo Gallery

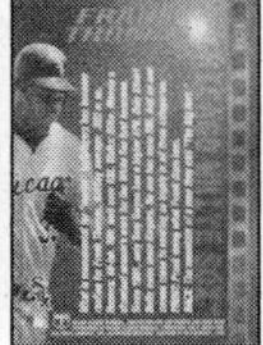

Randomly inserted in packs at a rate of one in 30, this 15-card set features top photography chronicling baseball's biggest stars and greatest moments from last year. Each double foil stamped card is printed on 24 pt. stock with customized designs to accentuate the photography.

Card	Nm-Mt	Ex-Mt
COMPLETE SET (15)	80.00	24.00
PG1 Eddie Murray	6.00	1.80
PG2 Randy Johnson	6.00	1.80
PG3 Cal Ripken	20.00	6.00
PG4 Bret Boone	2.50	.75
PG5 Frank Thomas	6.00	1.80
PG6 Jeff Conine	2.50	.75
PG7 Johnny Damon	2.50	.75
PG8 Roger Clemens	12.00	3.60
PG9 Albert Belle	2.50	.75
PG10 Ken Griffey Jr.	10.00	3.00
PG11 Kirby Puckett	6.00	1.80
PG12 David Justice	2.50	.75
PG13 Bobby Bonilla	2.50	.75
PG14 Colorado Rockies	2.50	.75
PG15 Atlanta Braves	2.50	.75

1997 Topps Gallery Promos

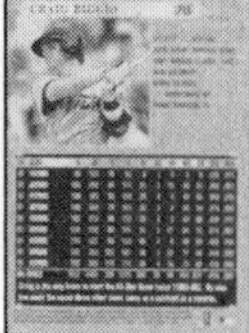

This four-card set was distributed as a promotion for the 1997 Topps Gallery set and features color player pictures in four different frame designs with a player portrait, biographical, and career statistics on the backs.

Card	Nm-Mt	Ex-Mt
COMPLETE SET (4)	10.00	3.00
PP1 Andruw Jones	2.50	.75
PP2 Derek Jeter	6.00	1.80
PP3 Mike Piazza	4.00	1.20
PP4 Craig Biggio	1.00	.30

1997 Topps Gallery

The 1997 Topps Gallery set was issued in one series totalling 180 cards. The eight-card packs retailed for $4.00 each. This hobby only set is divided into four themes: Veterans, Prospects, Rising Stars and Young Stars. Printed on 24-point card stock with a high-gloss film and etch stamped with one or more foils, each theme features a different design on front with a variety of informative statistics and revealing player text on the back.

Nm-Mt Ex-Mt
COMPLETE SET (180) 50.00 15.00
1 Paul Molitor .75 .23
2 Devon White .50 .15
3 Andres Galarraga .50 .15
4 Cal Ripken 4.00 1.20
5 Tony Gwynn 1.50 .45
6 Mike Stanley .50 .15
7 Orel Hershiser .50 .15
8 Jose Canseco 1.25 .35
9 Chili Davis .50 .15
10 Harold Baines .50 .15
11 Rickey Henderson 1.25 .35
12 Darryl Strawberry .75 .23
13 Todd Worrell .50 .15
14 Cecil Fielder .50 .15
15 Gary Gaetti .50 .15
16 Bobby Bonilla .50 .15
17 Will Clark 1.25 .35
18 Kevin Brown .50 .15
19 Tom Glavine .75 .23
20 Wade Boggs .75 .23
21 Edgar Martinez .75 .23
22 Lance Johnson .50 .15
23 Gregg Jefferies .50 .15
24 Bip Roberts .50 .15
25 Tony Phillips .50 .15
26 Greg Maddux 2.00 .60
27 Mickey Tettleton .50 .15
28 Terry Steinbach .50 .15
29 Ryne Sandberg 2.00 .60
30 Wally Joyner .50 .15
31 Joe Carter .50 .15
32 Ellis Burks .50 .15
33 Fred McGriff .75 .23
34 Barry Larkin 1.25 .35
35 John Franco .50 .15
36 Rafael Palmeiro .75 .23
37 Mark McGwire 3.00 .90
38 Ken Caminiti .50 .15
39 David Cone .50 .15
40 Julio Franco .50 .15
41 Roger Clemens 2.50 .75
42 Barry Bonds 3.00 .90
43 Dennis Eckersley .50 .15
44 Eddie Murray 1.25 .35
45 Paul O'Neill .75 .23
46 Craig Biggio .75 .23
47 Roberto Alomar 1.25 .35
48 Mark Grace .75 .23
49 Matt Williams .50 .15
50 Jay Buhner .50 .15
51 John Smoltz .75 .23
52 Randy Johnson 1.25 .35
53 Ramon Martinez .50 .15
54 Curt Schilling .75 .23
55 Gary Sheffield .75 .23
56 Jack McDowell .50 .15
57 Brady Anderson .50 .15
58 Dante Bichette .50 .15
59 Ron Gant .50 .15
60 Alex Fernandez .50 .15
61 Moises Alou .50 .15
62 Travis Fryman .50 .15
63 Dean Palmer .50 .15
64 Todd Hundley .50 .15
65 Jeff Brantley .50 .15
66 Bernard Gilkey .50 .15
67 Geronimo Berroa .50 .15
68 John Wetteland .50 .15
69 Robin Ventura .50 .15
70 Ray Lankford .50 .15
71 Kevin Appier .50 .15
72 Larry Walker .75 .23
73 Juan Gonzalez 1.25 .35
74 Jeff King .50 .15
75 Greg Vaughn .50 .15
76 Steve Finley .50 .15
77 Brian McRae .50 .15
78 Paul Sorrento .50 .15
79 Ken Griffey Jr. 2.00 .60
80 Omar Vizquel .50 .15
81 Jose Mesa .50 .15
82 Albert Belle .50 .15
83 Glenallen Hill .50 .15
84 Sammy Sosa 2.00 .60
85 Andy Benes .50 .15
86 David Justice .50 .15
87 Marquis Grissom .50 .15
88 John Olerud .50 .15
89 Tino Martinez .75 .23
90 Frank Thomas 1.25 .35
91 Raul Mondesi .50 .15
92 Steve Trachsel .50 .15
93 Jim Edmonds .50 .15
94 Rusty Greer .50 .15
95 Joey Hamilton .50 .15
96 Ismael Valdes .50 .15
97 Dave Nilsson .50 .15
98 John Jaha .50 .15
99 Alex Gonzalez .50 .15
100 Javy Lopez .50 .15
101 Ryan Klesko .50 .15
102 Tim Salmon .75 .23
103 Bernie Williams .75 .23
104 Roberto Hernandez .50 .15
105 Chuck Knoblauch .50 .15
106 Mike Lansing .50 .15
107 Vinny Castilla .50 .15
108 Reggie Sanders .50 .15
109 Mo Vaughn .50 .15
110 Rondell White .50 .15
111 Ivan Rodriguez 1.25 .35
112 Mike Mussina 1.25 .35
113 Carlos Baerga .50 .15
114 Jeff Conine .50 .15
115 Jim Thome 1.25 .35
116 Manny Ramirez .50 .15
117 Kenny Lofton .50 .15
118 Wilson Alvarez .50 .15
119 Eric Karros .50 .15
120 Robb Nen .50 .15
121 Mark Wohlers .50 .15
122 Ed Sprague .50 .15
123 Pat Hentgen .50 .15
124 Juan Guzman .50 .15
125 Derek Bell .50 .15
126 Jeff Bagwell .75 .23
127 Eric Young .50 .15
128 John Valentin .50 .15
129 Al Martin UER .50 .15
Picture of Javy Lopez
130 Trevor Hoffman .50 .15
131 Henry Rodriguez .50 .15
132 Pedro Martinez 1.25 .35
133 Mike Piazza 2.00 .60
134 Brian Jordan .50 .15
135 Jose Valentin .50 .15
136 Jeff Cirillo .50 .15
137 Chipper Jones 1.25 .35
138 Ricky Bottalico .50 .15
139 Hideo Nomo 1.25 .35
140 Troy Percival .50 .15
141 Rey Ordonez .50 .15
142 Edgar Renteria .50 .15
143 Luis Castillo .50 .15
144 Vladimir Guerrero 1.25 .35
145 Jeff D'Amico .50 .15
146 Andruw Jones .50 .15
147 Darin Erstad .50 .15
148 Bob Abreu .50 .15
149 Carlos Delgado .50 .15
150 Jamey Wright .50 .15
151 Nomar Garciaparra 2.00 .60
152 Jason Kendall .50 .15
153 Jermaine Allensworth .50 .15
154 Scott Rolen .75 .23
155 Rocky Coppinger .50 .15
156 Paul Wilson .50 .15
157 Garret Anderson .50 .15
158 Mariano Rivera .75 .23
159 Ruben Rivera .50 .15
160 Andy Pettitte .75 .23
161 Derek Jeter 3.00 .90
162 Neifi Perez .50 .15
163 Ray Durham .50 .15
164 James Baldwin .50 .15
165 Marty Cordova .50 .15
166 Tony Clark .50 .15
167 Michael Tucker .50 .15
168 Mike Sweeney .50 .15
169 Johnny Damon .50 .15
170 Jermaine Dye .50 .15
171 Alex Ochoa .50 .15
172 Jason Isringhausen .50 .15
173 Mark Grudzielanek .50 .15
174 Jose Rosado .50 .15
175 Todd Hollandsworth .50 .15
176 Alan Benes .50 .15
177 Jason Giambi 1.25 .35
178 Billy Wagner .50 .15
179 Justin Thompson .50 .15
180 Todd Walker .50 .15

1997 Topps Gallery Player's Private Issue

Randomly inserted in packs at a rate of one in 12, this 180-card set is a foil-stamped parallel version of the regular Topps Gallery set, limited to 250, with some of the cards sent to the players. The cards are spot UV coated on the photo only to allow for autographing.

Nm-Mt Ex-Mt
*STARS: 6X TO 15X BASIC CARDS ....

1997 Topps Gallery Gallery of Heroes

Randomly inserted in packs at a rate of one in 36, this 10-card set features color player photos designed to command the attention paid to works hanging in art museums. The backs carry player information.

Nm-Mt Ex-Mt
COMPLETE SET (10) 150.00 45.00
GH1 Derek Jeter 25.00 7.50
GH2 Chipper Jones 10.00 3.00
GH3 Frank Thomas 10.00 3.00
GH4 Ken Griffey Jr. 15.00 4.50
GH5 Cal Ripken 30.00 9.00
GH6 Mark McGwire 25.00 7.50
GH7 Mike Piazza 15.00 4.50
GH8 Jeff Bagwell 6.00 1.80
GH9 Tony Gwynn 12.00 3.60
GH10 Mo Vaughn 4.00 1.20

1997 Topps Gallery Peter Max Serigraphs

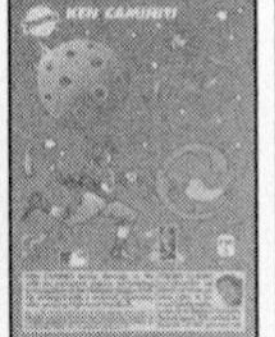

Randomly inserted in packs at a rate of one in 24, this 10-card set features painted renditions of ten superstars by the artist, Peter Max. The backs carry his commentary about the player.

Nm-Mt Ex-Mt
COMPLETE SET (10) 80.00 24.00
*AUTOS: 8X TO 20X BASIC SERIGRAPHS
AUTOS RANDOM INSERTS IN PACKS
AUTOS PRINT RUN 40 SERIAL #'d SETS
AU'S SIGNED BY MAX BENEATH UV COATING
1 Derek Jeter 12.00 3.60
2 Albert Belle 2.00 .60
3 Ken Caminiti 2.00 .60
4 Chipper Jones 5.00 1.50
5 Ken Griffey Jr. 8.00 2.40
6 Frank Thomas 5.00 1.50
7 Cal Ripken 15.00 4.50
8 Mark McGwire 12.00 3.60
9 Barry Bonds 12.00 3.60
10 Mike Piazza 8.00 2.40

1997 Topps Gallery Photo Gallery

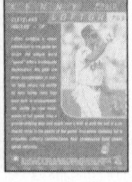

Randomly inserted in packs at a rate of one in 24, this 16-card set features color photos of some of baseball's hottest stars and their most memorable moments. Each card is enhanced by customized designs and double foil-stamping.

Nm-Mt Ex-Mt
COMPLETE SET (16) 100.00 30.00
PG1 John Wetteland 2.50 .75
PG2 Paul Molitor 4.00 1.20
PG3 Eddie Murray 6.00 1.80
PG4 Ken Griffey Jr. 10.00 3.00
PG5 Chipper Jones 6.00 1.80
PG6 Derek Jeter 15.00 4.50
PG7 Frank Thomas 6.00 1.80
PG8 Mark McGwire 15.00 4.50
PG9 Kenny Lofton 2.50 .75
PG10 Gary Sheffield 2.50 .75
PG11 Mike Piazza 10.00 3.00
PG12 Vinny Castilla 2.50 .75
PG13 Andres Galarraga 2.50 .75
PG14 Andy Pettitte 4.00 1.20
PG15 Robin Ventura 2.50 .75
PG16 Barry Larkin 6.00 1.80

1998 Topps Gallery

The 1998 Topps Gallery hobby-only set was issued in one series totalling 150 cards. The six-card packs retailed for $3.00 each. The set is divided by five subset groupings: Expressionists, Exhibitionists, Impressions, Portraits and Permanent Collection. Each theme features a different design with informative stats and text on each player.

Nm-Mt Ex-Mt
COMPLETE SET (150) 50.00 15.00
1 Andruw Jones .50 .15
2 Fred McGriff .75 .23
3 Wade Boggs .75 .23
4 Pedro Martinez 1.25 .35
5 Matt Williams .50 .15
6 Wilson Alvarez .50 .15
7 Henry Rodriguez .50 .15
8 Jay Bell .50 .15
9 Marquis Grissom .50 .15
10 Darryl Kile .50 .15
11 Chuck Knoblauch .50 .15
12 Kenny Lofton .50 .15
13 Quinton McCracken .50 .15
14 Andres Galarraga .50 .15
15 Brian Jordan .50 .15
16 Mike Lansing .50 .15
17 Travis Fryman .50 .15
18 Tony Saunders .50 .15
19 Moises Alou .50 .15
20 Travis Lee .50 .15
21 Garret Anderson .50 .15
22 Ken Caminiti .50 .15
23 Pedro Astacio .50 .15
24 Ellis Burks .50 .15
25 Albert Belle .50 .15
26 Alan Benes .50 .15
27 Jay Buhner .50 .15
28 Derek Bell .50 .15
29 Jeromy Burnitz .50 .15
30 Kevin Appier .50 .15
31 Jeff Cirillo .50 .15
32 Bernard Gilkey .50 .15
33 David Cone .50 .15
34 Jason Dickson .50 .15
35 Jose Cruz Jr. .50 .15
36 Marty Cordova .50 .15
37 Ray Durham .50 .15
38 Jaret Wright .50 .15
39 Billy Wagner .50 .15
40 Roger Clemens 2.50 .75
41 Juan Gonzalez 1.25 .35
42 Jeremi Gonzalez .50 .15
43 Mark Grudzielanek .50 .15
44 Tom Glavine .75 .23
45 Barry Larkin 1.25 .35
46 Lance Johnson .50 .15
47 Bobby Higginson .50 .15
48 Mike Mussina 1.25 .35
49 Al Martin .50 .15
50 Mark McGwire 3.00 .90
51 Todd Hundley .50 .15
52 Ray Lankford .50 .15
53 Jason Kendall .50 .15
54 Javy Lopez .50 .15
55 Ben Grieve .50 .15
56 Randy Johnson 1.25 .35
57 Jeff King .50 .15
58 Mark Grace .75 .23
59 Rusty Greer .50 .15
60 Greg Maddux 2.00 .60
61 Jeff Kent .50 .15
62 Rey Ordonez .50 .15
63 Hideo Nomo 1.25 .35
64 Charles Nagy .50 .15
65 Rondell White .50 .15
66 Todd Helton .75 .23
67 Jim Thome 1.25 .35
68 Denny Neagle .50 .15
69 Ivan Rodriguez 1.25 .35
70 Vladimir Guerrero 1.25 .35
71 Jorge Posada .75 .23
72 J.T. Snow .50 .15
73 Reggie Sanders .50 .15
74 Scott Rolen .75 .23
75 Robin Ventura .50 .15
76 Mariano Rivera .75 .23
77 Cal Ripken 4.00 1.20
78 Justin Thompson .50 .15
79 Mike Piazza 2.00 .60
80 Kevin Brown .75 .23
81 Sandy Alomar Jr. .50 .15
82 Craig Biggio .75 .23
83 Vinny Castilla .50 .15
84 Eric Young .50 .15
85 Bernie Williams .75 .23
86 Brady Anderson .50 .15
87 Bobby Bonilla .50 .15
88 Tony Clark .50 .15
89 Dan Wilson .50 .15
90 John Wetteland .50 .15
91 Barry Bonds 3.00 .90
92 Chan Ho Park .50 .15
93 Carlos Delgado .50 .15
94 David Justice .50 .15
95 Chipper Jones 1.25 .35
96 Shawn Estes .50 .15
97 Jason Giambi 1.25 .35
98 Ron Gant .50 .15
99 John Olerud .50 .15
100 Frank Thomas 1.25 .35
101 Jose Guillen .50 .15
102 Brad Radke .50 .15
103 Troy Percival .50 .15
104 John Smoltz .75 .23
105 Edgardo Alfonzo .50 .15
106 Dante Bichette .50 .15
107 Larry Walker .75 .23
108 John Valentin .50 .15
109 Roberto Alomar 1.25 .35
110 Mike Cameron .50 .15
111 Eric Davis .50 .15
112 Johnny Damon .50 .15
113 Darin Erstad .50 .15
114 Omar Vizquel .50 .15
115 Derek Jeter 3.00 .90
116 Tony Womack .50 .15
117 Edgar Renteria .50 .15
118 Raul Mondesi .50 .15
119 Tony Gwynn 1.50 .45
120 Ken Griffey Jr. 2.00 .60
121 Jim Edmonds .50 .15
122 Brian Hunter .50 .15
123 Neifi Perez .50 .15
124 Dean Palmer .50 .15
125 Alex Rodriguez 2.00 .60
126 Tim Salmon .75 .23
127 Curt Schilling .75 .23
128 Kevin Orie .50 .15
129 Andy Pettitte .75 .23
130 Gary Sheffield .50 .15
131 Jose Rosado .50 .15
132 Manny Ramirez .50 .15
133 Rafael Palmeiro .75 .23
134 Sammy Sosa 2.00 .60
135 Jeff Bagwell .75 .23
136 Delino DeShields .50 .15
137 Ryan Klesko .50 .15
138 Mo Vaughn .50 .15
139 Steve Finley .50 .15
140 Nomar Garciaparra 2.00 .60
141 Paul Molitor .75 .23
142 Pat Hentgen .50 .15
143 Eric Karros .50 .15
144 Bobby Jones .50 .15
145 Tino Martinez .75 .23
146 Matt Morris .50 .15
147 Livan Hernandez .50 .15
148 Edgar Martinez .75 .23
149 Paul O'Neill .75 .23
150 Checklist .50 .15

1998 Topps Gallery Gallery Proofs

Randomly inserted in packs at a rate of one in 34, this 150-card set is a parallel to the Topps Gallery base set. The set is sequentially numbered to 125.

Nm-Mt Ex-Mt
*STARS: 10X TO 25X BASIC CARDS ..

1998 Topps Gallery Player's Private Issue

Randomly inserted in packs at a rate of one in 17, this 150-card set is a parallel to the Topps Gallery base set. The set is sequentially numbered to 250.

Nm-Mt Ex-Mt
*STARS: 5X TO 12X BASIC CARDS ....

1998 Topps Gallery Player's Private Issue Auction

Seeded at a rate of one per pack, these standard-sized cards loosely parallel the far more scarce Player's Private Issue cards. Two glaring differences, however, are readily apparent: 1) The Auction cards are printed on thin paper stock (compared to the thick 20 pt board for PPI cards) and 2) The Auction card backs contain rules and guidelines for the auction promotion (compared to the normal statistics and player photo on the PPI cards). Collectors who obtained Auction cards were supposed to "bid" on a selection of ten different pieces of framed artwork (one for each of the following players: J.Gonzalez, M.McGwire, C.Ripken, M.Piazza, C.Jones, F.Thomas, D.Jeter, K.Griffey Jr., A.Rodriguez and N.Garciaparra). Bidding points were available in 25, 50, 75 and 100 point increments detailed at the top right corner of each Auction card back. Point totals were doubled, however, when the player featured on the Auction card was the same player actually being bid on. The auction period ran from July 4th, 1998 through October 16th, 1998. During that time period, collectors had to mail in their accumulated bid points and specify which of the ten pieces they were bidding upon. An "800" number was available for collectors to check upon the status of the current high bid, allowing them the opportunity to submit additional bid points prior to the October 16th closing date. Winners were notified 30 days after the closing date.

Nm-Mt Ex-Mt
COMPLETE SET (150) 100.00 30.00
*STARS: .75X TO 2X BASIC CARDS ...

1998 Topps Gallery Awards Gallery

Randomly inserted in packs at a rate of one in 24, this 10-card set honors the achievements of the majors top stars.

Nm-Mt Ex-Mt
COMPLETE SET (10) 60.00 18.00
AG1 Ken Griffey Jr. 10.00 3.00
AG2 Larry Walker 4.00 1.20
AG3 Roger Clemens 12.00 3.60
AG4 Pedro Martinez 6.00 1.80
AG5 Nomar Garciaparra 10.00 3.00
AG6 Scott Rolen 4.00 1.20
AG7 Frank Thomas 6.00 1.80
AG8 Tony Gwynn 8.00 2.40
AG9 Mark McGwire 15.00 4.50
AG10 Livan Hernandez 2.50 .75

1998 Topps Gallery Gallery of Heroes

Randomly inserted in packs at a rate of one in 24, this 15-card set is an insert to the Topps Gallery base set. The fronts feature a translucent stain-glass design that helps showcase some of today's high performance players.

Nm-Mt Ex-Mt
COMPLETE SET (15) 150.00 45.00
*JUMBOS: .3X TO .8X BASIC HEROES
ONE JUMBO PER HOBBY BOX..........
GH1 Ken Griffey Jr. 12.00 3.60
GH2 Derek Jeter 20.00 6.00
GH3 Barry Bonds 20.00 6.00
GH4 Alex Rodriguez 12.00 3.60
GH5 Frank Thomas 8.00 2.40
GH6 Nomar Garciaparra 12.00 3.60
GH7 Mark McGwire 20.00 6.00
GH8 Mike Piazza 12.00 3.60
GH9 Cal Ripken 25.00 7.50
GH10 Jose Cruz Jr. 3.00 .90
GH11 Jeff Bagwell 5.00 1.50
GH12 Chipper Jones 8.00 2.40
GH13 Juan Gonzalez 8.00 2.40
GH14 Hideo Nomo 8.00 2.40
GH15 Greg Maddux 12.00 3.60

1998 Topps Gallery Photo Gallery

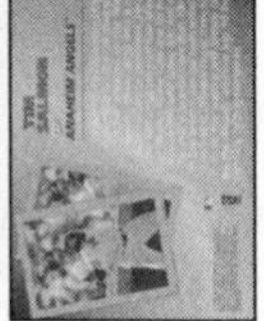

Randomly inserted in packs at a rate of one in 24, this 10-card set features a selection of top stars in riveting game action.

Nm-Mt Ex-Mt
COMPLETE SET (10) 80.00 24.00
PG1 Alex Rodriguez 10.00 3.00
PG2 Frank Thomas 6.00 1.80
PG3 Derek Jeter 15.00 4.50
PG4 Cal Ripken 20.00 6.00

Card	Nm-Mt	Ex-Mt
PG5 Ken Griffey Jr.	10.00	3.00
PG6 Mike Piazza	10.00	3.00
PG7 Nomar Garciaparra	10.00	3.00
PG8 Tim Salmon	4.00	1.20
PG9 Jeff Bagwell	4.00	1.20
PG10 Barry Bonds	15.00	4.50

1999 Topps Gallery Previews

This three-card standard-size set was released to preview the 1999 Topps Gallery set. The set features a regular design as well as a couple of the subsets involved in this set.

	Nm-Mt	Ex-Mt
COMPLETE SET (3)	5.00	1.50
PP1 Scott Rolen	2.00	.60
PP2 A.Galarrraga MAS	1.50	.45
PP3 Brad Fullmer ART	1.00	.30

1999 Topps Gallery

The 1999 Topps Gallery set was issued in one series totalling 150 cards and was distributed in six-card packs for a suggested retail price of $3. The set features 100 veteran stars and 50 subset cards finely crafted and printed on 24-pt. stock, with serigraph textured frame, etched foil stamping, and spot UV finish. The set contains the following subsets: Masters (101-115), Artisans (116-127), and Apprentices (128-150). Rookie Cards inlcude Pat Burrell, Nick Johnson and Alfonso Soriano.

	Nm-Mt	Ex-Mt
COMPLETE SET (150)	50.00	15.00
COMP.SET w/o SP's (100)	25.00	7.50
COMMON CARD (1-100)	.30	.09
COMMON (101-150)	.75	.23
1 Mark McGwire	2.00	.60
2 Jim Thome	.75	.23
3 Bernie Williams	.50	.15
4 Larry Walker	.50	.15
5 Juan Gonzalez	.75	.23
6 Ken Griffey Jr.	1.25	.35
7 Raul Mondesi	.30	.09
8 Sammy Sosa	1.25	.35
9 Greg Maddux	1.25	.35
10 Jeff Bagwell	.50	.15
11 Vladimir Guerrero	.75	.23
12 Scott Rolen	.50	.15
13 Nomar Garciaparra	1.25	.35
14 Mike Piazza	1.25	.35
15 Travis Lee	.30	.09
16 Carlos Delgado	.30	.09
17 Darin Erstad	.30	.09
18 David Justice	.30	.09
19 Cal Ripken	2.50	.75
20 Derek Jeter	2.00	.60
21 Tony Clark	.30	.09
22 Barry Larkin	.75	.23
23 Greg Vaughn	.30	.09
24 Jeff Kent	.30	.09
25 Wade Boggs	.50	.15
26 Andres Galarraga	.30	.09
27 Ken Caminiti	.30	.09
28 Jason Kendall	.30	.09
29 Todd Helton	.50	.15
30 Chuck Knoblauch	.30	.09
31 Roger Clemens	1.50	.45
32 Jeromy Burnitz	.30	.09
33 Javy Lopez	.30	.09
34 Roberto Alomar	.75	.23
35 Eric Karros	.30	.09
36 Ben Grieve	.30	.09
37 Eric Davis	.30	.09
38 Rondell White	.30	.09
39 Dmitri Young	.30	.09
40 Ivan Rodriguez	.75	.23
41 Paul O'Neill	.50	.15
42 Jeff Cirillo	.30	.09
43 Kerry Wood	.75	.23
44 Albert Belle	.30	.09
45 Frank Thomas	.75	.23
46 Manny Ramirez	.30	.09
47 Tom Glavine	.50	.15
48 Mo Vaughn	.30	.09
49 Jose Cruz Jr.	.30	.09
50 Sandy Alomar Jr.	.30	.09
51 Edgar Martinez	.50	.15
52 John Olerud	.30	.09
53 Todd Walker	.30	.09
54 Tim Salmon	.50	.15
55 Derek Bell	.30	.09
56 Matt Williams	.30	.09
57 Alex Rodriguez	1.25	.35
58 Rusty Greer	.30	.09
59 Vinny Castilla	.30	.09
60 Jason Giambi	.75	.23
61 Mark Grace	.50	.15
62 Jose Canseco	.75	.23
63 Gary Sheffield	.30	.09
64 Brad Fullmer	.30	.09
65 Trevor Hoffman	.30	.09
66 Mark Kotsay	.30	.09
67 Mike Mussina	.75	.23
68 Johnny Damon	.30	.09
69 Tino Martinez	.50	.15
70 Curt Schilling	.50	.15
71 Jay Buhner	.30	.09
72 Kenny Lofton	.30	.09
73 Randy Johnson	.75	.23
74 Kevin Brown	.50	.15
75 Brian Jordan	.30	.09
76 Craig Biggio	.50	.15
77 Barry Bonds	2.00	.60
78 Tony Gwynn	1.00	.30
79 Jim Edmonds	.30	.09
80 Shawn Green	.30	.09
81 Todd Hundley	.30	.09
82 Cliff Floyd	.30	.09
83 Jose Guillen	.30	.09
84 Dante Bichette	.30	.09
85 Moises Alou	.30	.09
86 Chipper Jones	.75	.23
87 Ray Lankford	.30	.09
88 Fred McGriff	.50	.15
89 Rod Beck	.30	.09
90 Dean Palmer	.30	.09
91 Pedro Martinez	.75	.23
92 Andruw Jones	.30	.09
93 Robin Ventura	.30	.09
94 Ugueth Urbina	.30	.09
95 Orlando Hernandez	.30	.35
96 Sean Casey	.30	.09
97 Denny Neagle	.30	.09
98 Troy Glaus	.50	.15
99 John Smoltz	.50	.15
100 Al Leiter	.30	.09
101 Ken Griffey Jr. MAS	2.50	.75
102 Frank Thomas MAS	1.50	.45
103 Mark McGwire MAS	4.00	1.20
104 Sammy Sosa MAS	2.50	.75
105 Chipper Jones MAS	1.50	.45
106 Alex Rodriguez MAS	2.50	.75
107 N.Garciaparra MAS	2.50	.75
108 Juan Gonzalez MAS	1.50	.45
109 Derek Jeter MAS	4.00	1.20
110 Mike Piazza MAS	2.50	.75
111 Barry Bonds MAS	4.00	1.20
112 Tony Gwynn MAS	2.00	.40
113 Cal Ripken MAS	5.00	1.50
114 Greg Maddux MAS	2.50	.75
115 Roger Clemens MAS	3.00	.90
116 Brad Fullmer ART	.75	.23
117 Kerry Wood ART	1.50	.45
118 Ben Grieve ART	.75	.23
119 Todd Helton ART	1.00	.30
120 Kevin Millwood ART	.75	.23
121 Sean Casey ART	.75	.23
122 V.Guerrero ART	1.50	.45
123 Travis Lee ART	.75	.23
124 Troy Glaus ART	1.00	.30
125 Bartolo Colon ART	.75	.23
126 Andruw Jones ART	.75	.23
127 Scott Rolen ART	1.00	.30
128 A.Soriano APP RC	8.00	2.40
129 Nick Johnson APP RC	2.50	.75
130 Matt Belisle APP RC	.75	.23
131 Jorge Toca APP RC	.75	.23
132 Masao Kida APP RC	.75	.23
133 Carlos Pena APP RC	1.50	.45
134 Adrian Beltre APP	.75	.23
135 Eric Chavez APP	.75	.23
136 Carlos Beltran APP	.75	.23
137 Alex Gonzalez APP	.75	.23
138 Ryan Anderson APP	.75	.23
139 Ruben Mateo APP	.75	.23
140 Bruce Chen APP	.75	.23
141 Pat Burrell APP RC	5.00	1.50
142 Michael Barrett APP	.75	.23
143 Carlos Lee APP	.75	.23
144 Mark Mulder APP RC	5.00	1.50
145 C.Freeman APP RC	.75	.23
146 Gabe Kapler APP	.75	.23
147 J.Encarnacion APP	.75	.23
148 Jeremy Giambi APP	.75	.23
149 Jason Tyner APP RC	.75	.23
150 George Lombard APP	.75	.23

1999 Topps Gallery Player's Private Issue

Randomly inserted in packs at the rate of one in 17, this 150-card set is parallel to the base set with a "Players Private Issue" foil stamp and sequentially numbered to 250.

Nm-Mt Ex-Mt

*STARS 1-100: 8X TO 20X BASIC CARDS
*MASTERS 101-115: 4X TO 10X BASIC
*ARTISANS 116-127: ,3X TO 8X BASIC
*APPRENTICES 128-150: 3X TO 8X BASIC
*APP.RC'S 128-150: 2X TO 5X BASIC

1999 Topps Gallery Autographs

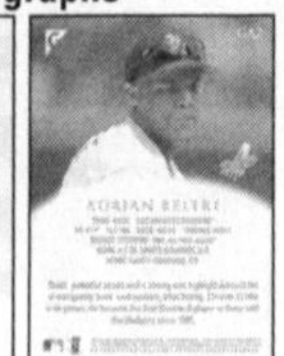

Randomly inserted into packs at the rate of one in 209, this three-card set features color photos of three of baseball's top prospects printed on 24-point stock with the "Topps Certified Autograph" foil stamp logo.

	Nm-Mt	Ex-Mt
GA1 Troy Glaus	20.00	6.00
GA2 Adrian Beltre	15.00	4.50
GA3 Eric Chavez	15.00	4.50

1999 Topps Gallery Awards Gallery

Randomly inserted into packs at the rate of one in 12, this 10-card set features color photos of the game's HR Champs, Cy Young award winners, RBI Leaders, MVP winnners, and Rookies of the year from 1998.

	Nm-Mt	Ex-Mt
COMPLETE SET (10)	30.00	9.00
AG1 Kerry Wood	3.00	.90
AG2 Ben Grieve	1.25	.35
AG3 Roger Clemens	6.00	1.80
AG4 Tom Glavine	2.00	.60
AG5 Juan Gonzalez	3.00	.90
AG6 Sammy Sosa	5.00	1.50
AG7 Ken Griffey Jr.	5.00	1.50
AG8 Mark McGwire	8.00	2.40
AG9 Bernie Williams	2.00	.60
AG10 Larry Walker	2.00	.60

1999 Topps Gallery Exhibitions

Randomly inserted in packs at the rate of one in 48, this 20-card set features color photos of top players printed on textured 24-point card stock with the look and feel of brushstrokes on canvas.

	Nm-Mt	Ex-Mt
COMPLETE SET (20)	200.00	60.00
E1 Sammy Sosa	12.00	3.60
E2 Mark McGwire	20.00	6.00
E3 Greg Maddux	12.00	3.60
E4 Roger Clemens	15.00	4.50
E5 Ben Grieve	3.00	.90
E6 Kerry Wood	8.00	2.40
E7 Ken Griffey Jr.	12.00	3.60
E8 Tony Gwynn	10.00	3.00
E9 Cal Ripken	25.00	7.50
E10 Frank Thomas	8.00	2.40
E11 Jeff Bagwell	5.00	1.50
E12 Derek Jeter	20.00	6.00
E13 Alex Rodriguez	12.00	3.60
E14 Nomar Garciaparra	12.00	3.60
E15 Manny Ramirez	3.00	.90
E16 Vladimir Guerrero	8.00	2.40
E17 Darin Erstad	3.00	.90
E18 Scott Rolen	5.00	1.50
E19 Mike Piazza	12.00	3.60
E20 Andres Galarraga	3.00	.90

1999 Topps Gallery Gallery of Heroes

Randomly inserted into packs at the rate of one in 24, this 10-card set features some of the game's top players depicted on clear Polycarbonate stock simulating the appearance of stained glass.

	Nm-Mt	Ex-Mt
COMPLETE SET (10)	80.00	24.00
GH1 Mark McGwire	12.00	3.60
GH2 Sammy Sosa	8.00	2.40
GH3 Ken Griffey Jr.	8.00	2.40
GH4 Mike Piazza	8.00	2.40
GH5 Derek Jeter	12.00	3.60
GH6 Nomar Garciaparra	8.00	2.40
GH7 Kerry Wood	5.00	1.50
GH8 Ben Grieve	2.00	.60
GH9 Chipper Jones	5.00	1.50
GH10 Alex Rodriguez	8.00	2.40

1999 Topps Gallery Heritage

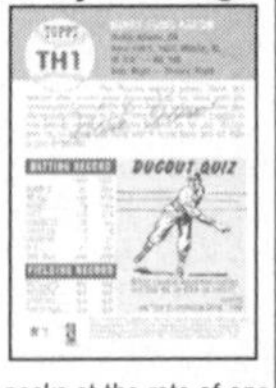

Randomly inserted into packs at the rate of one in 12, this 20-card set features color photos of legendary stars printed on 24-point conventional card stock depicting the 1953 Topps design. This was one of the most popular insert sets issued in 1999 as hobbyists responded well to the gorgeous 1953 retro art. Interestingly, the back of the Aaron card was written as if it were 1953 while the modern players were written about their current accomplishments.

	Nm-Mt	Ex-Mt
COMPLETE SET (20)	250.00	75.00
*PROOFS: .4X TO 1X BASIC HERITAGE		
PROOFS STATED ODDS 1:48		
TH1 Hank Aaron	30.00	9.00
TH2 Ben Grieve	8.00	2.40
TH3 Nomar Garciaparra	25.00	7.50
TH4 Roger Clemens	30.00	9.00
TH5 Travis Lee	8.00	2.40
TH6 Tony Gwynn	20.00	6.00
TH7 Alex Rodriguez	25.00	7.50
TH8 Ken Griffey Jr.	25.00	7.50
TH9 Derek Jeter	40.00	12.00
TH10 Sammy Sosa	25.00	7.50
TH11 Scott Rolen	10.00	3.00
TH12 Chipper Jones	15.00	4.50
TH13 Cal Ripken	50.00	15.00
TH14 Kerry Wood	15.00	4.50
TH15 Barry Bonds	40.00	12.00
TH16 Juan Gonzalez	15.00	4.50
TH17 Mike Piazza	25.00	7.50
TH18 Greg Maddux	25.00	7.50
TH19 Frank Thomas	15.00	4.50
TH20 Mark McGwire	50.00	15.00

1999 Topps Gallery Heritage Postcards

This seven-card postcard-sized set was issued by Topps in 1999. The set features superstar players painted by James Fiorentino.

	Nm-Mt	Ex-Mt
COMPLETE SET (7)	50.00	15.00
1 Mark McGwire	8.00	2.40
2 Sammy Sosa	5.00	1.50
3 Roger Clemens	5.00	1.50
4 Mike Piazza	6.00	1.80
5 Cal Ripken	10.00	3.00
6 Derek Jeter	10.00	3.00
7 Ken Griffey Jr.	6.00	1.80

2000 Topps Gallery Pre-Production

This three card set was issued in a sealed cello pack to dealers and hobby media several weeks prior to the products release. The cards have a "PP" prefix so they can be differentiated from the regular cards.

	Nm-Mt	Ex-Mt
COMPLETE SET (3)	8.00	2.40
PP1 Derek Jeter	4.00	1.20
PP2 Mark McGwire	3.00	.90
PP3 Josh Hamilton	1.00	.30

2000 Topps Gallery

The 2000 Topps Gallery product was released in early June, 2000 as a 150-card set. The set features 100 player cards, a 20-card Masters of the Game subset, and a 30-card Students of the Game subset. Please note that cards 101-150 were issued at a rate of one per pack. Each pack contained six cards and carried a suggested retail price of $3.00. Notable Rookie Cards include Bobby Bradley.

	Nm-Mt	Ex-Mt
COMPLETE SET (150)	100.00	30.00
COMP.SET w/o SP's (100)	25.00	7.50
COMMON CARD (1-100)	.30	.09
COMMON (101-150)	1.00	.30
1 Nomar Garciaparra	1.25	.35
2 Kevin Millwood	.30	.09
3 Jay Bell	.30	.09
4 Rusty Greer	.30	.09
5 Bernie Williams	.50	.15
6 Barry Larkin	.75	.23
7 Carlos Beltran	.30	.09
8 Damion Easley	.30	.09
9 Magglio Ordonez	.30	.09
10 Matt Williams	.30	.09
11 Shannon Stewart	.30	.09
12 Ray Lankford	.30	.09
13 Vinny Castilla	.30	.09
14 Miguel Tejada	.30	.09
15 Craig Biggio	.50	.15
16 Chipper Jones	.75	.23
17 Albert Belle	.30	.09
18 Doug Glanville	.30	.09
19 Brian Giles	.30	.09
20 Shawn Green	.30	.09
21 Bret Boone	.30	.09
22 Luis Gonzalez	.30	.09
23 Carlos Delgado	.30	.09
24 J.D. Drew	.30	.09
25 Ivan Rodriguez	.75	.23
26 Tino Martinez	.50	.15
27 Erubiel Durazo	.30	.09
28 Scott Rolen	.50	.15
29 Gary Sheffield	.30	.09
30 Manny Ramirez	.30	.09
31 Luis Castillo	.30	.09
32 Fernando Tatis	.30	.09
33 Darin Erstad	.30	.09
34 Tim Hudson	.50	.15
35 Sammy Sosa	1.25	.35
36 Jason Kendall	.30	.09
37 Todd Walker	.30	.09
38 Orlando Hernandez	.30	.09
39 Pokey Reese	.30	.09
40 Mike Piazza	1.25	.35
41 B.J. Surhoff	.30	.09
42 Tony Gwynn	1.00	.30
43 Kevin Brown	.30	.09
44 Preston Wilson	.30	.09
45 Kenny Lofton	.30	.09
46 Rondell White	.30	.09
47 Frank Thomas	.75	.23
48 Neifi Perez	.30	.09
49 Edgardo Alfonzo	.15	.04
50 Ken Griffey Jr.	1.25	.35
51 Barry Bonds	2.00	.60
52 Brian Jordan	.30	.09
53 Raul Mondesi	.30	.09
54 Troy Glaus	.50	.15
55 Curt Schilling	.50	.15
56 Mike Mussina	.75	.23
57 Brian Daubach	.30	.09
58 Roger Clemens	1.50	.45
59 Carlos Febles	.30	.09
60 Todd Helton	.50	.15
61 Mark Grace	.50	.15
62 Randy Johnson	.75	.23
63 Jeff Bagwell	.50	.15
64 Tom Glavine	.50	.15
65 Adrian Beltre	.30	.09
66 Rafael Palmeiro	.50	.15
67 Paul O'Neill	.50	.15
68 Robin Ventura	.30	.09
69 Ray Durham	.30	.09
70 Mark McGwire	2.00	.60
71 Greg Vaughn	.30	.09
72 Javy Lopez	.30	.09
73 Ryan Klesko	.30	.09
74 Mike Lieberthal	.30	.09
75 Cal Ripken	2.50	.75
76 Juan Gonzalez	.75	.23
77 Sean Casey	.30	.09
78 Jermaine Dye	.30	.09
79 John Olerud	.30	.09
80 Jose Canseco	.75	.23
81 Eric Karros	.30	.09
82 Roberto Alomar	.75	.23
83 Ben Grieve	.30	.09
84 Greg Maddux	1.25	.35
85 Pedro Martinez	.75	.23
86 Tony Clark	.30	.09
87 Richie Sexson	.30	.09
88 Cliff Floyd	.30	.09
89 Eric Chavez	.30	.09
90 Andruw Jones	.30	.09
91 Vladimir Guerrero	.75	.23
92 Alex Gonzalez	.30	.09
93 Jim Thome	.75	.23
94 Bob Abreu	.30	.09
95 Derek Jeter	2.00	.60
96 Larry Walker	.50	.15
97 Mike Hampton	.30	.09
98 Mo Vaughn	.30	.09
99 Jason Giambi	.75	.23
100 Alex Rodriguez	1.25	.35
101 Mark McGwire MAS	4.00	1.20
102 Sammy Sosa MAS	2.50	.75
103 Alex Rodriguez MAS	2.50	.75
104 Derek Jeter MAS	4.00	1.20
105 Greg Maddux MAS	2.50	.75
106 Jeff Bagwell MAS	1.25	.35
107 N.Garciaparra MAS	2.50	.75
108 Mike Piazza MAS	2.50	.75
109 Pedro Martinez MAS	2.00	.60
110 Chipper Jones MAS	2.00	.60
111 Randy Johnson MAS	2.00	.60
112 Barry Bonds MAS	4.00	1.20
113 Ken Griffey Jr. MAS	2.50	.75
114 Manny Ramirez MAS	1.00	.30
115 Ivan Rodriguez MAS	2.00	.60
116 Juan Gonzalez MAS	2.00	.60
117 V.Guerrero MAS	2.00	.60
118 Tony Gwynn MAS	2.00	.60
119 Larry Walker MAS	1.25	.35
120 Cal Ripken MAS	5.00	1.50
121 Josh Hamilton SG	1.00	.30
122 Corey Patterson SG	1.25	.35
123 Pat Burrell SG	1.25	.35
124 Nick Johnson SG	1.00	.30
125 Adam Piatt SG	1.00	.30
126 Rick Ankiel SG	1.00	.30
127 A.J. Burnett SG	1.00	.30
128 Ben Petrick SG	1.00	.30
129 Rafael Furcal SG	1.00	.30
130 Alfonso Soriano SG	2.00	.60
131 Dee Brown SG	1.00	.30
132 Ruben Mateo SG	1.00	.30
133 Pablo Ozuna SG	1.00	.30
134 S.Burroughs SG UER	1.25	.35
Eric Munson's bio on back		
135 Mark Mulder SG	1.25	.35
136 Jason Jennings SG	1.00	.30
137 Eric Munson SG	1.00	.30
138 Vernon Wells SG	1.00	.30
139 Brett Myers SG RC	4.00	1.20
140 B.Christensen SG RC	1.00	.30
141 Bobby Bradley SG RC	1.00	.30
142 Ruben Salazar SG RC	1.00	.30
143 R.Christianson SG RC	1.00	.30
144 Corey Myers SG RC	1.00	.30
145 Aaron Rowand SG RC	1.00	.30
146 Julio Zuleta SG RC	1.00	.30
147 Kurt Ainsworth SG RC	2.00	.60
148 Scott Downs SG RC	1.00	.30
149 Larry Bigbie SG RC	1.25	.35
150 Chance Caple SG RC	1.00	.30

2000 Topps Gallery Player's Private Issue

Randomly inserted into packs at one in 20, this 150-card set is a complete parallel of the Topps Gallery base set. Each card in the set is individually serial numbered to 250. The cards are serial numbered in gold foil on the back of the cards.

Nm-Mt Ex-Mt

*STARS 1-100: 6X TO 15X BASIC CARDS
*MASTERS 101-120: 3X TO 8X BASIC
*STUDENTS 121-138: 1.5X TO 4X BASIC
*STUDENTS RC's 139-150: 2X TO 5X BASIC

2000 Topps Gallery Autographs

Randomly inserted into packs at one in 153, this insert set features autographed cards from five of the major league's top prospects. Card backs are numbered using the players initials.

	Nm-Mt	Ex-Mt
BP Ben Petrick	10.00	3.00
CP Corey Patterson	25.00	7.50
RA Rick Ankiel	10.00	3.00

RM Ruben Mateo 10.00 3.00
VW Vernon Wells 15.00 4.50

2000 Topps Gallery Exhibits

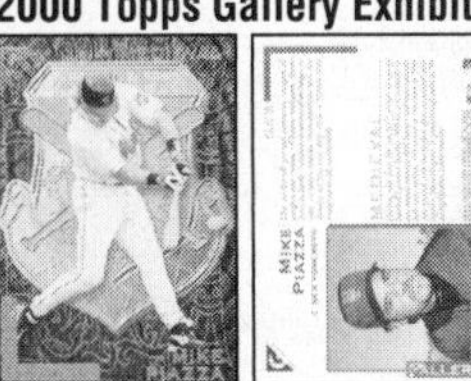

Randomly inserted into packs at one in 18, this 30-card insert captures some of baseball's best on canvas texturing. Card backs carry a "GE" prefix.

	Nm-Mt	Ex-Mt
COMPLETE SET (30)	300.00	90.00
GE1 Mark McGwire	20.00	6.00
GE2 Jeff Bagwell	5.00	1.50
GE3 Mike Piazza	12.00	3.60
GE4 Alex Rodriguez	12.00	3.60
GE5 Nomar Garciaparra	12.00	3.60
GE6 Ivan Rodriguez	8.00	2.40
GE7 Chipper Jones	8.00	2.40
GE8 Cal Ripken	25.00	7.50
GE9 Tony Gwynn	10.00	3.00
GE10 Jose Canseco	8.00	2.40
GE11 Albert Belle	3.00	.90
GE12 Greg Maddux	12.00	3.60
GE13 Barry Bonds	20.00	6.00
GE14 Ken Griffey Jr.	12.00	3.60
GE15 Juan Gonzalez	8.00	2.40
GE16 Rickey Henderson	20.00	6.00
GE17 Craig Biggio	5.00	1.50
GE18 Vladimir Guerrero	8.00	2.40
GE19 Rey Ordonez	10.00	3.00
GE20 Roberto Alomar	8.00	2.40
GE21 Derek Jeter	20.00	6.00
GE22 Manny Ramirez	3.00	.90
GE23 Shawn Green	3.00	.90
GE24 Sammy Sosa	12.00	3.60
GE25 Larry Walker	5.00	1.50
GE26 Pedro Martinez	8.00	2.40
GE27 Randy Johnson	8.00	2.40
GE28 Pat Burrell	4.00	1.20
GE29 Josh Hamilton	3.00	.90
GE30 Corey Patterson	4.00	1.20

2000 Topps Gallery Gallery of Heroes

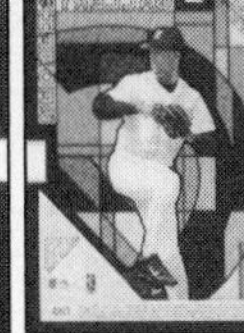

Randomly inserted into packs at one in 24, this insert features ten celestial superstars on clear, die-cut polycarbonate stock, creating a stained glass effect. Card backs carry a "GH" prefix.

	Nm-Mt	Ex-Mt
COMPLETE SET (10)	80.00	24.00
GH1 Alex Rodriguez	8.00	2.40
GH2 Chipper Jones	5.00	1.50
GH3 Pedro Martinez	5.00	1.50
GH4 Sammy Sosa	8.00	2.40
GH5 Mark McGwire	12.00	3.60
GH6 Nomar Garciaparra	8.00	2.40
GH7 Vladimir Guerrero	5.00	1.50
GH8 Ken Griffey Jr.	8.00	2.40
GH9 Mike Piazza	8.00	2.40
GH10 Derek Jeter	12.00	3.60

2000 Topps Gallery Heritage

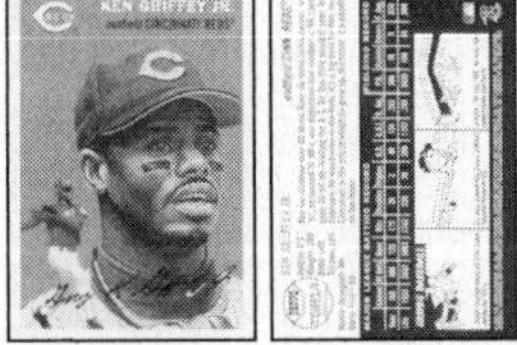

Randomly inserted into packs at one in 12, this 20-card insert set was influenced by the 1954 Topps set, the set features many of baseball's elite players as illustrated artist renderings. Card backs carry a "TGH" prefix.

	Nm-Mt	Ex-Mt
COMPLETE SET (20)	150.00	45.00
*PROOFS: .6X TO 1.5X BASIC HERITAGE		
PROOFS STATED ODDS 1:27		
TGH1 Mark McGwire	25.00	7.50
TGH2 Sammy Sosa	15.00	4.50
TGH3 Greg Maddux	15.00	4.50
TGH4 Mike Piazza	15.00	4.50
TGH5 Ivan Rodriguez	10.00	3.00
TGH6 Manny Ramirez	4.00	1.20
TGH7 Jeff Bagwell	6.00	1.80
TGH8 Sean Casey	4.00	1.20
TGH9 Orlando Hernandez	4.00	1.20
TGH10 Randy Johnson	10.00	3.00
TGH11 Pedro Martinez	10.00	3.00
TGH12 Vladimir Guerrero	10.00	3.00
TGH13 Shawn Green	4.00	1.20
TGH14 Ken Griffey Jr.	15.00	4.50
TGH15 Alex Rodriguez	15.00	4.50
TGH16 Nomar Garciaparra	15.00	4.50
TGH17 Derek Jeter	25.00	7.50
TGH18 Tony Gwynn	12.00	3.60
TGH19 Chipper Jones	10.00	3.00
TGH20 Cal Ripken	30.00	9.00

2000 Topps Gallery Proof Positive

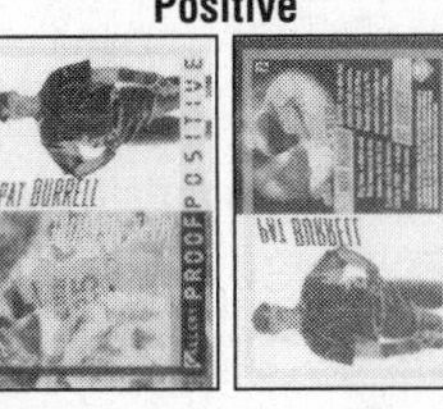

Randomly insert into packs at one in 48, these ten cards couple one master of the game with one student of the game by way of positive and negative photography. Card backs carry a "P" prefix.

	Nm-Mt	Ex-Mt
COMPLETE SET (10)	100.00	30.00
P1 Ken Griffey Jr. / Ruben Mateo	10.00	3.00
P2 Derek Jeter / Alfonso Soriano	15.00	4.50
P3 Mark McGwire / Pat Burrell	15.00	4.50
P4 Pedro Martinez / A.J.Burnett	6.00	1.80
P5 Alex Rodriguez / Rafael Furcal	10.00	3.00
P6 Sammy Sosa / Corey Patterson	10.00	3.00
P7 Randy Johnson / Rick Ankiel	6.00	1.80
P8 Chipper Jones / Adam Piatt	6.00	1.80
P9 Nomar Garciparra / Pablo Ozuna	10.00	3.00
P10 Mike Piazza / Eric Munson	10.00	3.00

2001 Topps Gallery

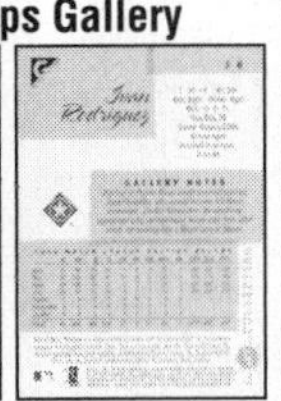

This 150 card set was issued in six card packs with an SRP of $3. The packs were issued 24 packs to a box with eight boxes to a case. Cards numbered 102-150 were short printed in these ratios: Prospects from 102-141 were issued one every 2.5 packs, rookies from 102-141 were issued one every 3.5 packs and cards numbered 142-150 were issued one every five packs. Card number 50 was supposedly only available to people who could show their dealers that that was the only card they were missing for the set. However, a retail version of that card was issued so many collectors did not get to share in the surprise of finding out the missing card was Willie Mays. In addition, a special Ichiro card was randomly included in packs, these cards were good for either an American or a Japanese version of what would become card number 151. The deadline to receive the Mays HTA version was October 24th, 2001 while the Ichiro exchange deadline was June 30th, 2003.

	Nm-Mt	Ex-Mt
COMPLETE SET (150)	80.00	24.00
COMP.SET w/o SP's (100)	40.00	12.00
COMMON (1-49/51-101)	.50	.15
COMMON (102-150)	3.00	.90
1 Darin Erstad	.50	.15
2 Chipper Jones	1.25	.35
3 Nomar Garciaparra	2.00	.60
4 Fernando Vina	.50	.15
5 Bartolo Colon	.50	.15
6 Bobby Higginson	.50	.15
7 Antonio Alfonseca	.50	.15
8 Mike Sweeney	.50	.15
9 Kevin Brown	.50	.15
10 Jose Vidro	.50	.15
11 Derek Jeter	3.00	.90
12 Jason Giambi	1.25	.35
13 Pat Burrell	.50	.15
14 Jeff Kent	.50	.15
15 Alex Rodriguez	2.00	.60
16 Rafael Palmeiro	.75	.23
17 Garret Anderson	.50	.15
18 Brad Fullmer	.50	.15
19 Doug Glanville	.50	.15
20 Mark Quinn	.50	.15
21 Mo Vaughn	.50	.15
22 Andruw Jones	.50	.15
23 Pedro Martinez	1.25	.35
24 Ken Griffey Jr.	2.00	.60
25 Roberto Alomar	1.25	.35
26 Dean Palmer	.50	.15
27 Jeff Bagwell	.75	.23
28 Jermaine Dye	.50	.15
29 Chan Ho Park	.50	.15
30 Vladimir Guerrero	1.25	.35
31 Bernie Williams	.75	.23
32 Ben Grieve	.50	.15
33 Jason Kendall	.50	.15
34 Barry Bonds	3.00	.90
35 Jim Edmonds	.50	.15
36 Ivan Rodriguez	1.25	.35
37 Javy Lopez	.50	.15
38 J.T. Snow	.50	.15
39 Erubiel Durazo	.50	.15
40 Terrence Long	.50	.15
41 Tim Salmon	.75	.23
42 Greg Maddux	2.00	.60
43 Sammy Sosa	2.00	.60
44 Sean Casey	.50	.15
45 Jeff Cirillo	.50	.15
46 Juan Gonzalez	1.25	.35
47 Richard Hidalgo	.50	.15
48 Shawn Green	.50	.15
49 Jeromy Burnitz	.50	.15
50 Willie Mays HTA N.Y. Giants	15.00	4.50
50 Willie Mays RETAIL S.F. Giants	40.00	12.00
51 David Justice	.50	.15
52 Tim Hudson	.50	.15
53 Brian Giles	.50	.15
54 Robb Nen	.50	.15
55 Fernando Tatis	.50	.15
56 Tony Batista	.50	.15
57 Pokey Reese	.50	.15
58 Ray Durham	.50	.15
59 Greg Vaughn	.50	.15
60 Kazuhiro Sasaki	.50	.15
61 Troy Glaus	.75	.23
62 Rafael Furcal	.50	.15
63 Magglio Ordonez	.50	.15
64 Jim Thome	1.25	.35
65 Todd Helton	.75	.23
66 Preston Wilson	.50	.15
67 Moises Alou	.50	.15
68 Gary Sheffield	.50	.15
69 Geoff Jenkins	.50	.15
70 Mike Piazza	2.00	.60
71 Jorge Posada	.75	.23
72 Bobby Abreu	.50	.15
73 Phil Nevin	.50	.15
74 John Olerud	.50	.15
75 Mark McGwire	3.00	.90
76 Jose Cruz Jr.	.50	.15
77 David Segui	.50	.15
78 Neifi Perez	.50	.15
79 Omar Vizquel	.50	.15
80 Rick Ankiel	.50	.15
81 Randy Johnson	1.25	.35
82 Albert Belle	.50	.15
83 Frank Thomas	1.25	.35
84 Manny Ramirez	.50	.15
85 Larry Walker	.75	.23
86 Luis Castillo	.50	.15
87 Johnny Damon	.50	.15
88 Adrian Beltre	.50	.15
89 Cristian Guzman	.50	.15
90 Jay Payton	.50	.15
91 Miguel Tejada	.50	.15
92 Scott Rolen	.75	.23
93 Ryan Klesko	.50	.15
94 Edgar Martinez	.75	.23
95 Fred McGriff	.75	.23
96 Carlos Delgado	.50	.15
97 Barry Zito	1.25	.35
98 Mike Lieberthal	.50	.15
99 Trevor Hoffman	.50	.15
100 Gabe Kapler	.50	.15
101 Edgardo Alfonzo	.50	.15
102 Corey Patterson	3.00	.90
103 Alfonso Soriano	.75	.23
104 Keith Ginter	3.00	.90
105 Keith Reed	3.00	.90
106 Nick Johnson	3.00	.90
107 Carlos Pena	3.00	.90
108 Vernon Wells	3.00	.90
109 Roy Oswalt	3.00	.90
110 Alex Escobar	3.00	.90
111 Adam Everett	3.00	.90
112 Jimmy Rollins	3.00	.90
113 Marcus Giles	3.00	.90
114 Jack Cust	3.00	.90
115 Chin-Feng Chen	3.00	.90
116 Pablo Ozuna	3.00	.90
117 Ben Sheets	3.00	.90
118 Adrian Gonzalez	3.00	.90
119 Ben Davis	3.00	.90
120 Eric Valent	3.00	.90
121 Scott Heard	3.00	.90
122 David Parrish RC	3.00	.90
123 Sean Burnett	3.00	.90
124 Derek Thompson	3.00	.90
125 Tim Christman RC	3.00	.90
126 Mike Jacobs RC	3.00	.90
127 Luis Montanez RC	3.00	.90
128 Chris Bass RC	3.00	.90
129 Will Smith RC	3.00	.90
130 Justin Wayne RC	3.00	.90
131 Shawn Fagan RC	3.00	.90
132 Chad Petty RC	3.00	.90
133 J.R. House	3.00	.90
134 Joel Pineiro	4.00	1.20
135 Albert Pujols RC	30.00	9.00
136 Carmen Cali RC	3.00	.90
137 Steve Smyth RC	3.00	.90
138 John Lackey	3.00	.90
139 Bob Keppel RC	3.00	.90
140 Dominic Rich RC	3.00	.90
141 Josh Hamilton	3.00	.90
142 Nolan Ryan	6.00	1.80
143 Tom Seaver	3.00	.90
144 Reggie Jackson	3.00	.90
145 Johnny Bench	4.00	1.20
146 Warren Spahn	3.00	.90
147 Brooks Robinson	4.00	1.20
148 Carl Yastrzemski	5.00	1.50
149 Al Kaline	4.00	1.20
150 Bob Feller	3.00	.90
151A I. Suzuki English RC	25.00	7.50
151B I.Suzuki Japan RC	25.00	7.50

2001 Topps Gallery Press Plates

Randomly inserted into packs at one in 1347, this 150-card insert is a complete parallel of the base set. The set features the actual press plates used to make all of the 150-card base set. There are four colored press plates inserted for each player: black, cyan, magenta, and yellow.

Nm-Mt Ex-Mt

NO PRICING DUE TO SCARCITY

2001 Topps Gallery Autographs

Inserted at overall odds of one in 232, these six cards feature cards signed by active professionals. All of these cards are all also the special painted cards for this product. Rick Ankiel did not return his cards in time for inclusion in this product. Those cards were redeemable until June 30, 2003.

	Nm-Mt	Ex-Mt
GROUP A STATED ODDS 1:1066		
GROUP B STATED ODDS 1:1144		
GROUP C STATED ODDS 1:400		
GA-AG Adrian Gonzalez B	20.00	6.00
GA-AR Alex Rodriguez A	150.00	45.00
GA-BB Barry Bonds A	200.00	60.00
GA-IR Ivan Rodriguez A	80.00	24.00
GA-PB Pat Burrell C	20.00	6.00
GA-RA R. Ankiel C EXCH	20.00	6.00

2001 Topps Gallery Bucks

Issued at a rate of one in 102, this "Buck" was good for $5 towards purchase of Topps Memorabilia.

	Nm-Mt	Ex-Mt
1 Johnny Bench $5	5.00	1.50

2001 Topps Gallery Heritage

Inserted one per 12 packs, these 12 cards feature a mix of active and retired players in the design Topps used for their 1965 set.

	Nm-Mt	Ex-Mt
COMPLETE SET (10)	60.00	18.00
GH1 Todd Helton	3.00	.90
GH2 Greg Maddux	8.00	2.40
GH3 Pedro Martinez	5.00	1.50
GH4 Orlando Cepeda	3.00	.90
GH5 Willie McCovey	3.00	.90
GH6 Ken Griffey Jr.	8.00	2.40
GH7 Alex Rodriguez	8.00	2.40
GH8 Derek Jeter	12.00	3.60
GH9 Mark McGwire	12.00	3.60
GH10 Vladimir Guerrero	5.00	1.50

2001 Topps Gallery Heritage Game Jersey

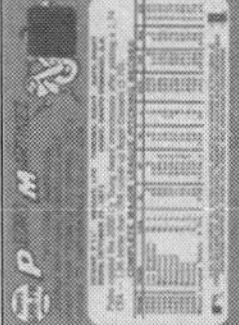

Inserted at a rate of one in 133 packs, these five cards feature pieces of game-worn uniforms along with the Gallery Heritage design.

	Nm-Mt	Ex-Mt
GHR-GM Greg Maddux	25.00	7.50
GHR-MR Mystery Jersey	1.00	.30
GHR-OC Orlando Cepeda	15.00	4.50
GHR-PM Pedro Martinez	25.00	7.50
GHR-VG Vladimir Guerrero	25.00	7.50
GHR-WM Willie McCovey	15.00	4.50

2001 Topps Gallery Heritage Game Jersey Autographs

Issued at a rate of one in 16,313 these two cards feature not only the Heritage design and a game-worn jersey piece but they also feature an autograph by the featured player. Orlando Cepeda did not return his cards in time for inclusion in this set so those cards were redeemable until June 30, 2003. These cards

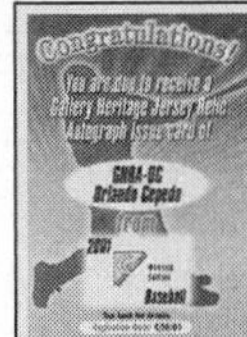

are serial numbered to 25.

Nm-Mt Ex-Mt

GHRA-OC Orlando Cepeda
GHRA-WM W.McCovey

2001 Topps Gallery Originals Game Bat

Issued at a rate of one per 133 packs these 15 cards feature game-used bat cards from 15 leading active hitters today. These cards display the genuine issue sticker. Sammy Sosa and Jason Giambi were the two players made available through the Mystery Exchange redemption cards.

	Nm-Mt	Ex-Mt
GR-AG Adrian Gonzalez	10.00	3.00
GR-AJ Andruw Jones	10.00	3.00
GR-BW Bernie Williams	15.00	4.50
GR-DE Darin Erstad	10.00	3.00
GR-JD Jermaine Dye	10.00	3.00
GR-JG Jason Giambi	15.00	4.50
GR-JK Jason Kendall	10.00	3.00
GR-JFK Jeff Kent	10.00	3.00
GR-MR1 Mystery Relic	1.00	.30
GR-MR2 Mystery Relic	1.00	.30
GR-PR Pokey Reese	10.00	3.00
GR-PW Preston Wilson	10.00	3.00
GR-RA Roberto Alomar	15.00	4.50
GR-RP Rafael Palmeiro	15.00	4.50
GR-RV Robin Ventura	10.00	3.00
GR-SG Shawn Green	10.00	3.00
GR-SS Sammy Sosa	25.00	7.50

2001 Topps Gallery Star Gallery

Issued at a rate of one in eight, these 10 cards feature some of the most popular players in the game.

	Nm-Mt	Ex-Mt
COMPLETE SET (10)	40.00	12.00
SG1 Vladimir Guerrero	2.50	.75
SG2 Alex Rodriguez	4.00	1.20
SG3 Derek Jeter	6.00	1.80
SG4 Nomar Garciaparra	4.00	1.20
SG5 Ken Griffey Jr.	4.00	1.20
SG6 Mark McGwire	6.00	1.80
SG7 Chipper Jones	2.50	.75
SG8 Sammy Sosa	4.00	1.20
SG9 Barry Bonds	6.00	1.80
SG10 Mike Piazza	4.00	1.20

2002 Topps Gallery

This 200 card set was released in June, 2002. The set was issued in five-card packs, with an SRP of $3, which came packaged 24 packs to a box and eight boxes to a case. The first 150 cards of this set featured veterans while cards 1511 through 190 featured rookies and cards 191-200 featured retired stars.

	Nm-Mt	Ex-Mt
COMPLETE SET (200)	100.00	30.00
COMMON CARD (1-150)	.50	.15
COMMON CARD (151-190)	1.00	.30
COMMON CARD (191-200)	2.00	.60
1 Jason Giambi	1.25	.35
2 Mark Grace	.75	.23
3 Bret Boone	.50	.15
4 Antonio Alfonseca	.50	.15
5 Kevin Brown	.50	.15
6 Cristian Guzman	.50	.15
7 Magglio Ordonez	.50	.15
8 Luis Gonzalez	.50	.15
9 Jorge Posada	.75	.23
10 Roberto Alomar	1.25	.35
11 Mike Sweeney	.50	.15
12 Jeff Kent	.50	.15
13 Matt Morris	.50	.15

14 Alfonso Soriano .75 .23
15 Adam Dunn .50 .15
16 Neifi Perez .50 .15
17 Todd Walker .50 .15
18 J.D. Drew .50 .15
19 Eric Chavez .50 .15
20 Alex Rodriguez 2.00 .60
21 Ray Lankford .50 .15
22 Roger Cedeno .50 .15
23 Chipper Jones 1.25 .35
24 Josh Beckett .75 .23
25 Mike Piazza 2.00 .60
26 Freddy Garcia .50 .15
27 Todd Helton .75 .23
28 Tino Martinez .75 .23
29 Kazuhiro Sasaki .50 .15
30 Curt Schilling .75 .23
31 Mark Buehrle .50 .15
32 John Olerud .50 .15
33 Brad Radke .50 .15
34 Steve Sparks .50 .15
35 Jason Tyner .50 .15
36 Jeff Shaw .50 .15
37 Mariano Rivera .75 .23
38 Russ Ortiz .50 .15
39 Richard Hidalgo .50 .15
40 Carl Everett .50 .15
41 John Burkett .50 .15
42 Tim Hudson .50 .15
43 Mike Hampton .50 .15
44 Orlando Cabrera .50 .15
45 Barry Zito .75 .23
46 C.C. Sabathia .50 .15
47 Chan Ho Park .50 .15
48 Tom Glavine .75 .23
49 Aramis Ramirez .50 .15
50 Lance Berkman .50 .15
51 Al Leiter .50 .15
52 Phil Nevin .50 .15
53 Javier Vazquez .50 .15
54 Troy Glaus .75 .23
55 Tsuyoshi Shinjo .50 .15
56 Albert Pujols 2.50 .75
57 John Smoltz .75 .23
58 Derek Jeter 3.00 .90
59 Robb Nen .50 .15
60 Jason Kendall .50 .15
61 Eric Gagne .75 .23
62 Vladimir Guerrero 1.25 .35
63 Corey Patterson .50 .15
64 Rickey Henderson 1.25 .35
65 Jack Wilson .50 .15
66 Jason LaRue .50 .15
67 Sammy Sosa 2.00 .60
68 Ken Griffey Jr. 2.00 .60
69 Randy Johnson 1.25 .35
70 Nomar Garciaparra 2.00 .60
71 Ivan Rodriguez 1.25 .35
72 J.T. Snow .50 .15
73 Darryl Kile .50 .15
74 Andruw Jones .50 .15
75 Brian Giles .50 .15
76 Pedro Martinez 1.25 .35
77 Jeff Bagwell .75 .23
78 Rafael Palmeiro .75 .23
79 Ryan Dempster .50 .15
80 Jeff Cirillo .50 .15
81 Geoff Jenkins .50 .15
82 Brandon Duckworth .50 .15
83 Roger Clemens 2.50 .75
84 Fred McGriff .75 .23
85 Hideo Nomo 1.25 .35
86 Larry Walker .75 .23
87 Sean Casey .50 .15
88 Trevor Hoffman .50 .15
89 Robert Fick .50 .15
90 Armando Benitez .50 .15
91 Jeromy Burnitz .50 .15
92 Bernie Williams .75 .23
93 Carlos Delgado .50 .15
94 Troy Percival .50 .15
95 Nate Cornejo .50 .15
96 Derrek Lee .50 .15
97 Jose Ortiz .50 .15
98 Brian Jordan .50 .15
99 Jose Cruz Jr. .50 .15
100 Ichiro Suzuki 2.00 .60
101 Jose Mesa .50 .15
102 Tim Salmon .75 .23
103 Bud Smith .50 .15
104 Paul LoDuca .50 .15
105 Juan Pierre .50 .15
106 Ben Grieve .50 .15
107 Russell Branyan .50 .15
108 Bob Abreu .50 .15
109 Moises Alou .50 .15
110 Richie Sexson .50 .15
111 Jerry Hairston Jr. .50 .15
112 Marlon Anderson .50 .15
113 Juan Gonzalez 1.25 .35
114 Craig Biggio .75 .23
115 Carlos Beltran .50 .15
116 Eric Milton .50 .15
117 Cliff Floyd .50 .15
118 Rich Aurilia .50 .15
119 Adrian Beltre .50 .15
120 Jason Bere .50 .15
121 Darin Erstad .50 .15
122 Ben Sheets .50 .15
123 Johnny Damon .50 .15
124 Jimmy Rollins .50 .15
125 Shawn Green .50 .15
126 Greg Maddux 2.00 .60
127 Mark Mulder .50 .15
128 Bartolo Colon .50 .15
129 Shannon Stewart .50 .15
130 Ramon Ortiz .50 .15
131 Kerry Wood 1.25 .35
132 Ryan Klesko .50 .15
133 Preston Wilson .50 .15
134 Roy Oswalt .50 .15
135 Rafael Furcal .75 .23
136 Eric Karros .50 .15
137 Nick Neugebauer .50 .15
138 Doug Mientkiewicz .50 .15
139 Paul Konerko .50 .15
140 Bobby Higginson .50 .15
141 Garret Anderson .50 .15
142 Wes Helms .50 .15
143 Brent Abernathy .50 .15
144 Scott Rolen .75 .23
145 Dmitri Young .50 .15
146 Jim Thome 1.25 .35
147 Raul Mondesi .50 .15
148 Pat Burrell .50 .15
149 Gary Sheffield .50 .15
150 Miguel Tejada .50 .15
151 Brandon Inge PROS 1.00 .30
152 Carlos Pena PROS 1.00 .30
153 Jason Lane PROS 1.00 .30
154 Nathan Haynes PROS 1.00 .30
155 Hank Blalock PROS 2.50 .75
156 Juan Cruz PROS 1.00 .30
157 Morgan Ensberg PROS 1.00 .30
158 Sean Burroughs PROS 1.00 .30
159 Ed Rogers PROS 1.00 .30
160 Nick Johnson PROS 1.00 .30
161 Orlando Hudson PROS 1.00 .30
162 A.Martinez PROS RC 1.00 .30
163 Jeremy Affeldt PROS 1.00 .30
164 Brandon Claussen PROS 2.50 .75
165 Deivis Santos PROS 1.00 .30
166 Mike Rivera PROS 1.00 .30
167 Carlos Silva PROS 1.00 .30
168 Val Pascucci PROS 1.00 .30
169 Xavier Nady PROS 1.00 .30
170 David Espinosa PROS 1.00 .30
171 Dan Phillips FYP RC 1.00 .30
172 Tony Fontana FYP RC 1.00 .30
173 Juan Silvestre FYP 1.00 .30
174 Henry Pichardo FYP RC 1.00 .30
175 Pablo Arias FYP RC 1.00 .30
176 Brett Roneberg FYP RC 1.00 .30
177 Chad Qualls FYP RC 1.00 .30
178 Greg Sain FYP RC 1.00 .30
179 Rene Reyes FYP RC 1.00 .30
180 So Taguchi FYP RC 1.50 .45
181 Dan Johnson FYP RC 1.50 .45
182 J.Backsmeyer FYP RC 1.00 .30
183 J.M. Gonzalez FYP RC 1.00 .30
184 Jason Ellison FYP RC 1.00 .30
185 Kazuhisa Ishii FYP RC 4.00 1.20
186 Joe Mauer FYP RC 8.00 2.40
187 James Shanks FYP RC 1.00 .30
188 Kevin Cash FYP RC 1.00 .30
189 J.J. Trujillo FYP RC 1.00 .30
190 Jorge Padilla FYP RC 1.00 .30
191 Nolan Ryan RET 6.00 1.80
192 George Brett RET 6.00 1.80
193 Ryne Sandberg RET 5.00 1.50
194 Robin Yount RET 4.00 1.20
195 Tom Seaver RET 2.00 .60
196 Mike Schmidt RET 5.00 1.50
197 Frank Robinson RET 2.00 .60
198 Harmon Killebrew RET 2.50 .75
199 Kirby Puckett RET 2.50 .75
200 Don Mattingly RET 6.00 1.80

2002 Topps Gallery Veteran Variation 1

Inserted at stated odds of one in 24, these 10 cards feature the most important players from the Gallery set featuring a variation from the regular issue cards. Since these were not announced until after the product went live, we have put the information about the variation next to the player's name.

Nm-Mt Ex-Mt
1 Jason Giambi Solid Blue 6.00 1.80
20 Alex Rodriguez Grey Jsy 10.00 3.00
25 Mike Piazza Black Jsy 10.00 3.00
27 Todd Helton Solid Blue 4.00 1.20
56 Albert Pujols Red Hat 12.00 3.60
58 Derek Jeter Solid Blue 15.00 4.50
67 Sammy Sosa Black Bat 10.00 3.00
71 Ivan Rodriguez Blue Jsy 6.00 1.80
76 Pedro Martinez Red Shirt 6.00 1.80
100 Ichiro Suzuki Empty Dugout 10.00 3.00

2002 Topps Gallery Autographs

Issued at overall stated odds of one in 240, these 10 cards feature players who have added their signature to these painted cards. The players belong to three different groups and we have put that information about their group next to their name in our checklist.

Nm-Mt Ex-Mt
GROUP A ODDS 1:815 HOB/RET
GROUP B ODDS 1:1017 HOB, 1:1023 RET
GROUP C ODDS 1:509 HOB/RET
GA-BBO Bret Boone A 25.00 7.50
GA-JD J.D. Drew B 25.00 7.50
GA-JL Jason Lane C 10.00 3.00
GA-JP Jorge Posada A 50.00 15.00
GA-JS Juan Silvestre C 10.00 3.00
GA-LB Lance Berkman A 25.00 7.50
GA-LG Luis Gonzalez B 25.00 7.50
GA-MO Magglio Ordonez A 25.00 7.50
GA-SG Shawn Green A 25.00 7.50

2002 Topps Gallery Bucks

Inserted at stated odds of one in 27, this $5 buck could be used for redemption towards purchasing original Topps Gallery artwork.

Nm-Mt Ex-Mt
NNO Nolan Ryan $5 8.00 2.40

2002 Topps Gallery Heritage

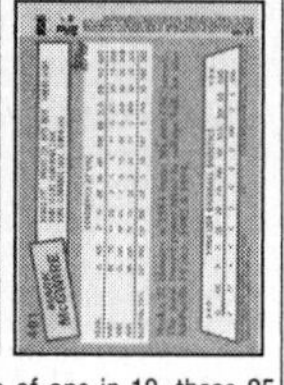

Inserted at stated odds of one in 12, these 25 cards feature drawings of players in the style of their Topps rookie card. We have put the year of the players "Topps" rookie card next to their name in our checklist.

Nm-Mt Ex-Mt
COMPLETE SET (25) 120.00 36.00
GH-AK Al Kaline 54 5.00 1.50
GH-AR Alex Rodriguez 98 8.00 2.40
GH-BR Brooks Robinson 57 5.00 1.50
GH-BBO Bret Boone 93 3.00 .90
GH-CJ Chipper Jones 91 5.00 1.50
GH-CY Carl Yastrzemski 60 8.00 2.40
GH-GM Greg Maddux 87 8.00 2.40
GH-JG Jason Giambi 91 5.00 1.50
GH-KG Ken Griffey Jr. 89 8.00 2.40
GH-LG Luis Gonzalez 91 3.00 .90
GH-MM Mark McGwire 85 15.00 4.50
GH-MP Mike Piazza 93 8.00 2.40
GH-MS Mike Schmidt 73 10.00 3.00
GH-NR Nolan Ryan 68 12.00 3.60
GH-PM Pedro Martinez 93 5.00 1.50
GH-RA Roberto Alomar 88 5.00 1.50
GH-RC Roger Clemens 85 10.00 3.00
GH-RJ Reggie Jackson 69 3.00 .90
GH-RY Robin Yount 75 8.00 2.40
GH-SG Shawn Green 92 3.00 .90
GH-SM Stan Musial 58 8.00 2.40
GH-SS Sammy Sosa 90 8.00 2.40
GH-TG Tony Gwynn 83 6.00 1.80
GH-TS Tom Seaver 67 3.00 .90
GH-TSH Tsuyoshi Shinjo 01 3.00 .90

2002 Topps Gallery Heritage Autographs

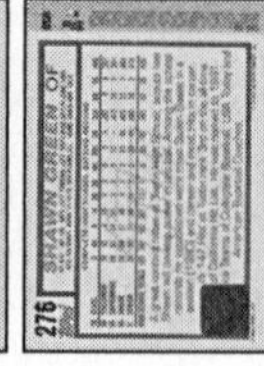

Inserted at stated odds of one in 13,595 hobby and one in 14,064 retail, these three cards feature authentic autographs of the featured players. These cards have a stated print run of 25 serial numbered sets and due to market scarcity, no pricing is provided for these cards.

Nm-Mt Ex-Mt
GHA-LG Luis Gonzalez 91
GHA-SG Shawn Green 92
GHA-BBO Bret Boone 93

2002 Topps Gallery Heritage Uniform Relics

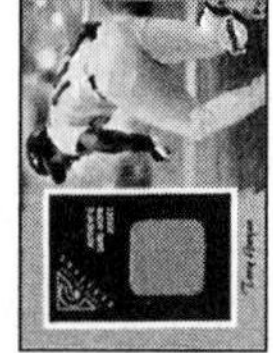

Inserted in packs at an overall stated rate of one in 85, these nine cards are a partial parallel to the Heritage insert set. Each card contains not only the player's photo but also a game-worn uniform piece. The players were broken up into two groups and we have notated the groups the player belonged to as well as their stated odds in our set information.

Nm-Mt Ex-Mt
GROUP A ODDS 1:106 HOB/RET
GROUP B ODDS 1:424 HOB/RET
GHR-AR Alex Rodriguez 98 A 20.00 6.00
GHR-CJ Chipper Jones 91 B 15.00 4.50
GHR-GM Greg Maddux 87 A 15.00 4.50
GHR-LG Luis Gonzalez 91 A 10.00 3.00
GHR-MP Mike Piazza 93 A 15.00 4.50
GHR-PM Pedro Martinez 93 A 15.00 4.50
GHR-TG Tony Gwynn 83 A 15.00 4.50
GHR-TS Tsuyoshi Shinjo 01 A 10.00 3.00
GHR-BBO Bret Boone 93 A 10.00 3.00

2002 Topps Gallery Original Bat Relics

Inserted at overall stated odds of one in 169, these 15 cards feature not only the player's photo featured but also a game-used bat piece.

Nm-Mt Ex-Mt
GO-AJ Andruw Jones 10.00 3.00
GO-AP Albert Pujols 40.00 12.00
GO-AR Alex Rodriguez 15.00 4.50
GO-AS Alfonso Soriano 15.00 4.50
GO-BW Bernie Williams 15.00 4.50
GO-BBO Bret Boone 10.00 3.00
GO-CD Carlos Delgado 10.00 3.00

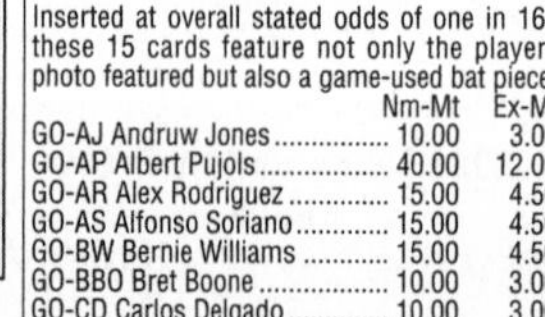

GO-CJ Chipper Jones 15.00 4.50
GO-JC Jose Canseco 15.00 4.50
GO-JG Juan Gonzalez 15.00 4.50
GO-LG Luis Gonzalez 10.00 3.00
GO-MP Mike Piazza 25.00 7.50
GO-TG Tony Gwynn 20.00 6.00
GO-TH Todd Helton 15.00 4.50
GO-TM Tino Martinez 15.00 4.50

2003 Topps Gallery

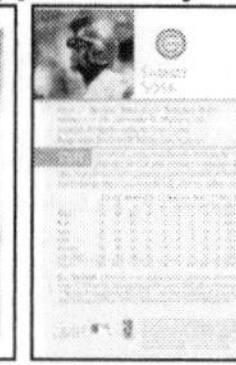

This 200 card set was released in August, 2003. These cards were issued in four card packs with an $5 SRP which came 20 packs to a box and eight boxes to a case. Cards numbered 1 through 150 featured veterans while cards 151 through 167 featured first year cards, cards 168 through 190 featured leading prospects and cards numbered 191 through 200 featured legendary retired players. In addition, 20 variations (seeded at a stated rate of one in 20) were also included in this set.

MINT NRMT
COMP.SET w/o SP's (200) 100.00 45.00
COMMON (1-150/168-190) .50 .23
COMMON CARD (151-167) .60 .25
VARIATION STATED ODDS 1:20
COMMON CARD (191-200) 1.25 .55
1 Jason Giambi 1.25 .55
1A Jason Giambi Blue Jsy 5.00 2.20
2 Miguel Tejada .50 .23
3 Mike Lieberthal .50 .23
4 Jason Kendall .50 .23
5 Robb Nen .50 .23
6 Freddy Garcia .50 .23
7 Scott Rolen .75 .35
8 Boomer Wells .50 .23
9 Rafael Palmeiro .75 .35
10 Garret Anderson .50 .23
11 Curt Schilling .75 .35
12 Greg Maddux 2.00 .90
13 Rodrigo Lopez .50 .23
14 Nomar Garciaparra 2.00 .90
14A N.Garciaparra Btg Glv 8.00 3.60
15 Kerry Wood 1.25 .55
16 Frank Thomas 1.25 .55
17 Ken Griffey Jr. 2.00 .90
18 Jim Thome 1.25 .55
19 Todd Helton .75 .35
20 Lance Berkman .50 .23
21 Robert Fick .50 .23
22 Kevin Brown .50 .23
23 Richie Sexson .50 .23
24 Eddie Guardado .50 .23
25 Vladimir Guerrero 1.25 .55
26 Mike Piazza 2.00 .90
27 Bernie Williams .75 .35
28 Eric Chavez .50 .23
29 Jimmy Rollins .50 .23
30 Ichiro Suzuki 2.00 .90
30A I.Suzuki Black Sleeve 8.00 3.60
31 J.D. Drew .50 .23
32 Nick Johnson .50 .23
33 Shannon Stewart .50 .23
34 Tim Salmon .75 .35
35 Andruw Jones .50 .23
36 Jay Gibbons .50 .23
37 Johnny Damon .50 .23
38 Fred McGriff .75 .35
39 Carlos Lee .50 .23
40 Adam Dunn .50 .23
40A Adam Dunn Red Sleeve 5.00 2.20
41 Jason Jennings .50 .23
42 Mike Lowell .50 .23
43 Mike Sweeney .50 .23
44 Shawn Green .50 .23
45 Doug Mientkiewicz .50 .23
46 Bartolo Colon .50 .23
47 Edgardo Alfonzo .50 .23
48 Roger Clemens 2.50 1.10
49 Randy Wolf .50 .23
50 Alex Rodriguez 2.00 .90
50A Alex Rodriguez Red Shirt 8.00 3.60
51 Vernon Wells .50 .23
52 Kenny Lofton .50 .23
53 Mariano Rivera .75 .35
54 Brian Jordan .50 .23
55 Roberto Alomar 1.25 .55
56 Carlos Pena .50 .23
57 Moises Alou .50 .23
58 John Smoltz .75 .35
59 Adam Kennedy .50 .23
60 Randy Johnson 1.25 .55
61 Mark Buehrle .50 .23
62 C.C. Sabathia .50 .23
63 Craig Biggio .75 .35
64 Eric Karros .50 .23
65 Jose Vidro .50 .23
66 Tim Hudson .50 .23
67 Trevor Hoffman .50 .23
68 Bret Boone .50 .23
69 Carl Crawford .50 .23
70 Derek Jeter 3.00 1.35
71 Troy Percival .50 .23
72 Gary Sheffield .50 .23
73 Rickey Henderson 1.25 .55
74 Paul Konerko .50 .23
75 Larry Walker .75 .35
76 Pat Burrell .50 .23
77 Brian Giles .50 .23
78 Jeff Kent .50 .23
79 Kazuhiro Sasaki .50 .23
80 Chipper Jones 1.25 .55
81 Darin Erstad .50 .23
82 Sean Casey .50 .23
83 Luis Gonzalez .50 .23
84 Roy Oswalt .50 .23
85 Dustan Mohr .50 .23
86 Al Leiter .50 .23
87 Mike Mussina 1.25 .55
88 Vicente Padilla .50 .23
89 Rich Aurilia .50 .23
90 Albert Pujols 2.50 1.10
91 John Olerud .50 .23
92 Ivan Rodriguez 1.25 .55
93 Eric Hinske .50 .23
94 Phil Nevin .50 .23
95 Barry Zito .75 .35
96 Armando Benitez .50 .23
97 Torii Hunter .50 .23
98 Paul Lo Duca .50 .23
99 Preston Wilson .50 .23
100 Sammy Sosa 2.00 .90
100A Sammy Sosa Black Bat 8.00 3.60
101 Jarrod Washburn .50 .23
102 Steve Finley .50 .23
103 Cliff Floyd .50 .23
104 Mark Prior 2.50 1.10
105 Austin Kearns .50 .23
106 Jeff Bagwell .75 .35
107 A.J. Pierzynski .50 .23
108 Pedro Martinez 1.25 .55
109 Orlando Cabrera .50 .23
110 Raul Mondesi .50 .23
111 Russ Ortiz .50 .23
112 Ruben Sierra .50 .23
113 Tino Martinez .75 .35
114 Manny Ramirez .50 .23
115 Troy Glaus .75 .35
116 Magglio Ordonez .50 .23
117 Omar Vizquel .50 .23
118 Carlos Beltran .50 .23
119 Jose Hernandez .50 .23
120 Javier Vazquez .50 .23
121 Jorge Posada .75 .35
122 Aramis Ramirez .50 .23
123 Jason Schmidt .50 .23
124 Jamie Moyer .50 .23
125 Jim Edmonds .50 .23
126 Aubrey Huff .50 .23
127 Carlos Delgado .50 .23
128 Junior Spivey .50 .23
129 Tom Glavine .75 .35
130 Marty Cordova .50 .23
131 Derek Lowe .50 .23
132 Ellis Burks .50 .23
133 Barry Bonds 3.00 1.35
134 Josh Beckett .75 .35
135 Raul Ibanez .50 .23
136 Kazuhisa Ishii .50 .23
137 Geoff Jenkins .50 .23
138 Eric Milton .50 .23
139 Mo Vaughn .50 .23
140 Mark Mulder .50 .23
141 Bobby Abreu .50 .23
142 Ryan Klesko .50 .23
143 Tsuyoshi Shinjo .50 .23
144 Jose Mesa .50 .23
145 Shea Hillenbrand .50 .23
146 Edgar Renteria .50 .23
147 Juan Gonzalez 1.25 .55
148 Edgar Martinez .75 .35
149 Matt Morris .50 .23
150 Alfonso Soriano .75 .35
150A Alfonso Soriano No Pad 5.00 2.20
151 Bryan Bullington FY RC 3.00 1.35
151A B.Bullington Red Back FY 6.00 2.70
152 Andy Marte FY RC 5.00 2.20
152A A.Marte No Necklace FY 10.00 4.50
153 Brendan Harris FY RC 1.00 .45
154 Juan Camacho FY RC .60 .25
155 Byron Gettis FY RC .60 .25
156 Daryl Clark FY RC 1.00 .45
157 J.D. Durbin FY RC 1.50 .70
158 Craig Brazell FY RC 1.00 .45
158A Craig Brazell Black Jsy 5.00 2.20
159 Jason Kubel FY RC 1.50 .70
160 Br. Roberson FY RC .60 .25
161 Jose Contreras FY RC 3.00 1.35
162 Hanley Ramirez FY RC 3.00 1.35
163 Jaime Bubela FY RC .60 .25
164 Chris Duncan FY RC .60 .25
165 Tyler Johnson FY RC .60 .25
166 Joey Gomes FY RC .60 .25
167 Ben Francisco FY RC 1.00 .45
168 Adam LaRoche PROS .75 .35
169 Tommy Whiteman PROS .50 .23
170 Trey Hodges PROS .50 .23
171 Fr. Rodriguez PROS .50 .23
172 Jason Arnold PROS .50 .23
173 Brett Myers PROS .50 .23
174 Rocco Baldelli PROS 3.00 1.35
175 Adrian Gonzalez PROS .50 .23
176 Dontrelle Willis PROS 1.25 .55
177 Walter Young PROS .50 .23
178 Marlon Byrd PROS .50 .23
179 Aaron Heilman PROS .50 .23
180 Casey Kotchman PROS .75 .35
181 Miguel Cabrera PROS 3.00 1.35
182 Hee Seop Choi PROS .50 .23
183 Drew Henson PROS .50 .23
184 Jose Reyes PROS .75 .35
185 Michael Cuddyer PROS .50 .23
186 Brandon Phillips PROS .50 .23
187 Victor Martinez PROS .50 .23
188 Joe Mauer PROS 1.25 .55
189 Hank Blalock PROS .75 .35
190 Mark Teixeira PROS .75 .35
191 Willie Mays RET 4.00 1.80
192 George Brett RET 5.00 2.20
193 Tony Gwynn RET 2.50 1.10
194 Carl Yastrzemski RET 3.00 1.35
195 Nolan Ryan RET 5.00 2.20
196 Reggie Jackson RET 1.25 .55
197 Mike Schmidt RET 4.00 1.80
198 Cal Ripken RET 6.00 2.70

199 Don Mattingly RET	5.00	2.20
200 Tom Seaver RET	1.25	.55

2003 Topps Gallery Artist's Proofs

	MINT	NRMT
COMPLETE SET (200)		
*AP 1-150/168-190: .75X TO 2X BASIC		
*AP 151-167: .75X TO 2X BASIC		
*AP 191-200: 1X TO 2.5X BASIC		
ONE PER PACK		
AP'S FEATURE SILVER HOLO-FOIL		

2003 Topps Gallery Press Plates

	MINT	NRMT
RANDOM INSERTS IN PACKS		
STATED PRINT RUN 4 SERIAL #'d SETS		
NO PRICING DUE TO SCARCITY		

2003 Topps Gallery Bucks

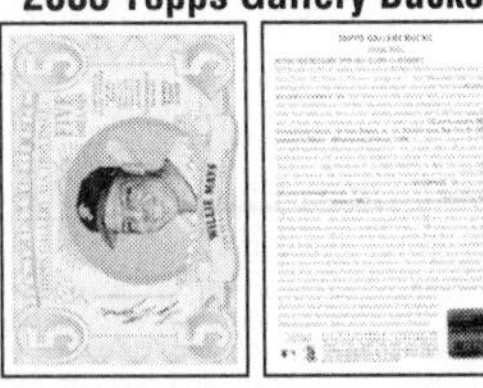

Inserted at a stated rate of one in 41, this one "card" insert set featured a photo of Willie Mays along with a $5 gift certificate good for Topps product.

	MINT	NRMT
5 Willie Mays $5	5.00	2.20

2003 Topps Gallery Currency Collection Coin Relics

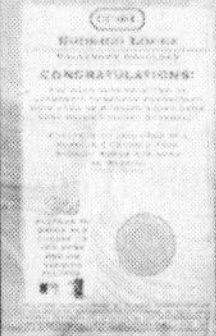

Inserted in each hobby box as a "box-topper" these 25 cards feature players from throughout the world along with a coin from their homeland.

	MINT	NRMT
AJ Andruw Jones	8.00	3.60
AP Albert Pujols	20.00	9.00
AS Alfonso Soriano	8.00	3.60
BA Bobby Abreu	8.00	3.60
BC Bartolo Colon	8.00	3.60
ER Edgar Renteria	8.00	3.60
FR Francisco Rodriguez	8.00	3.60
HC Hee Seop Choi	8.00	3.60
HN Hideo Nomo	10.00	4.50
IS Ichiro Suzuki	15.00	6.75
JR Jose Reyes	8.00	3.60
KI Kazuhisa Ishii	8.00	3.60
KS Kazuhiro Sasaki	8.00	3.60
LW Larry Walker	8.00	3.60
MO Magglio Ordonez	8.00	3.60
MR Manny Ramirez	8.00	3.60
MRI Mariano Rivera	8.00	3.60
OC Orlando Cabrera	8.00	3.60
OV Omar Vizquel	8.00	3.60
PM Pedro Martinez	10.00	4.50
RL Rodrigo Lopez	8.00	3.60
RM Raul Mondesi	8.00	3.60
SS Sammy Sosa	15.00	6.75
VG Vladimir Guerrero	10.00	4.50
VP Vicente Padilla	8.00	3.60

2003 Topps Gallery Heritage

	MINT	NRMT
STATED ODDS 1:10		
AD Adam Dunn	3.00	1.35
AS Alfonso Soriano	5.00	2.20
BW Bernie Williams	5.00	2.20
CY Carl Yastrzemski	8.00	3.60
DJ Derek Jeter	12.00	5.50
DS Duke Snider	5.00	2.20
GB George Brett	10.00	4.50
HK Harmon Killebrew	5.00	2.20
HN Hideo Nomo	5.00	2.20
IR Ivan Rodriguez	5.00	2.20
IS Ichiro Suzuki	8.00	3.60
JC Jose Canseco	5.00	2.20
JT Jim Thome	5.00	2.20
KP Kirby Puckett	5.00	2.20
KR Jerry Koosman Nolan Ryan	15.00	6.75
MT Miguel Tejada	3.00	1.35
NG Nomar Garciaparra	8.00	3.60
RC Roger Clemens	10.00	4.50
RH Rickey Henderson	5.00	2.20
RJ Randy Johnson	5.00	2.20
SG Shawn Green	3.00	1.35
TG Tom Glavine	5.00	2.20
TGW Tony Gwynn	6.00	2.70
WB Wade Boggs	5.00	2.20
WM Willie Mays	10.00	4.50

2003 Topps Gallery Heritage Autograph Relics

Randomly inserted into packs, these four cards feature not only a game-used memorabilia piece but also an authentic autograph of the featured player. Each of these cards were issued to a stated print run of 25 copies and no pricing is available due to market scarcity.

	MINT	NRMT
NO PRICING DUE TO SCARCITY		
GB George Brett Bat		
KP Kirby Puckett Bat		
TG Tony Gwynn Jsy		
WB Wade Boggs Uni		

2003 Topps Gallery Heritage Relics

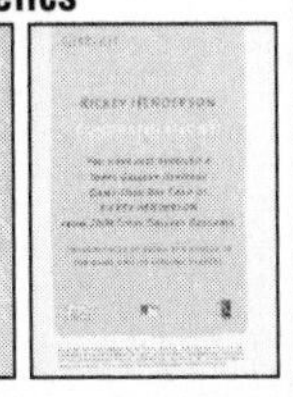

Inserted at varying odds depending what group the card belonged to, this 10 card set featured game-used memorabilia pieces of the featured player.

	MINT	NRMT
GROUP A ODDS 1:141		
GROUP B ODDS 1:67		
GB George Brett Bat A	25.00	11.00
HK Harmon Killebrew Bat A	25.00	11.00
HN Hideo Nomo Jsy A	15.00	6.75
JC Jose Canseco Bat B	10.00	4.50
KP Kirby Puckett Bat A	15.00	6.75
RC Roger Clemens Jsy A	15.00	6.75
RH Rickey Henderson Bat B	10.00	4.50
SG Shawn Green Jsy B	8.00	3.60
TG Tony Gwynn Jsy B	15.00	6.75
WB Wade Boggs Uni B	10.00	4.50

2003 Topps Gallery Originals Bat Relics

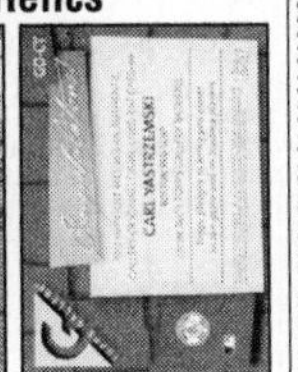

	MINT	NRMT
GROUP A ODDS 1:131		
GROUP B ODDS 1:81		
GROUP C ODDS 1:15		
AD Adam Dunn C	8.00	3.60
AJ Andruw Jones C	8.00	3.60
AP Albert Pujols B	20.00	9.00
AR Alex Rodriguez C	15.00	6.75
AS Alfonso Soriano B	10.00	4.50
BB Bret Boone C	8.00	3.60
BW Bernie Williams C	10.00	4.50
CJ Chipper Jones C	10.00	4.50
CY Carl Yastrzemski A	20.00	9.00
DH Drew Henson B	8.00	3.60
FT Frank Thomas C	10.00	4.50
GS Gary Sheffield C	8.00	3.60
IR Ivan Rodriguez C	10.00	4.50
JM Joe Mauer A	15.00	6.75
JT Jim Thome C	10.00	4.50
LB Lance Berkman C	8.00	3.60
LG Luis Gonzalez A	10.00	4.50
MA Moises Alou B	8.00	3.60
MO Magglio Ordonez C	8.00	3.60
MP Mike Piazza C	15.00	6.75
MR Manny Ramirez C	8.00	3.60
MT Miguel Tejada A	10.00	4.50
NG Nomar Garciaparra B	15.00	6.75
RA Roberto Alomar C	10.00	4.50
RH Rickey Henderson C	10.00	4.50
RP Rafael Palmeiro C	10.00	4.50
SG Shawn Green B	8.00	3.60
TG Tony Gwynn C	10.00	4.50
TH Todd Helton C	10.00	4.50
THU Torii Hunter A	10.00	4.50

2003 Topps Gallery HOF

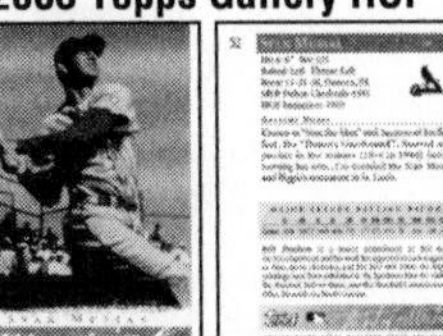

This set was released in April, 2003. Each card in the set was actually issued in different versions, some of each were easy to identify and others had far more subtle differences. This set was issued in five card packs with an $5 SRP. The packs were issued in 20 pack boxes which came six boxes to a case.

	Nm-Mt	Ex-Mt
COMPLETE SET (74)	40.00	12.00
COMMON CARD (1-74)	.75	.23
COMMON VARIATION (1-74)	1.50	.45
1 Willie Mays Bleachers	3.00	.90
1B Willie Mays Gold	6.00	1.80
2 Al Kaline Stripes	1.50	.45
2B Al Kaline No Stripes	3.00	.90
3 Hank Aaron Black Hat	3.00	.90
3B Hank Aaron Blue Hat	6.00	1.80
4 Carl Yastrzemski Black Ltr	2.50	.75
4B Carl Yastrzemski Red Ltr	5.00	1.50
5 Luis Aparicio Wood Bat	.75	.23
5B Luis Aparicio Black Bat	1.50	.45
6 Sam Crawford Grey Uni	.75	.23
6B Sam Crawford Navy Uni	1.50	.45
7 Tom Lasorda Trees	.75	.23
7B Tom Lasorda Red	1.50	.45
8 John McGraw MG No Logo	.75	.23
8B J.McGraw MG NY Logo	1.50	.45
9 Edd Roush White C	.75	.23
9B Edd Roush Red C	1.50	.45
10 Reggie Jackson Grass	1.00	.30
10B Reggie Jackson Red	2.00	.60
11 Catfish Hunter Yellow Jsy	1.00	.30
11B Catfish Hunter White Jsy	2.00	.60
12 Rob. Clemente White Uni	4.00	1.20
12B Rob. Clemente Yellow Uni	8.00	2.40
13 Eddie Collins Grey Uni	.75	.23
13B Eddie Collins Navy Uni	1.50	.45
14 Frankie Frisch Olive	.75	.23
14B Frankie Frisch Blue	1.50	.45
15 Nolan Ryan Leather Glv	4.00	1.20
15B Nolan Ryan Black Glv	8.00	2.40
16 Brooks Robinson Yellow	1.50	.45
16B Brooks Robinson Green	3.00	.90
17 Phil Niekro Black Hat	.75	.23
17B Phil Niekro Blue Hat	1.50	.45
18 Joe Cronin Blue Sleeve	.75	.23
18B Joe Cronin White Sleeve	1.50	.45
19 Joe Tinker White Hat	.75	.23
19B Joe Tinker Blue Hat	1.50	.45
20 Johnny Bench Day	1.50	.45
20B Johnny Bench Night	3.00	.90
21 Harry Heilmann Day	.75	.23
21B Harry Heilmann Night	1.50	.45
22 Ernie Harwell BRD Red Tie	.75	.23
22B Ernie Harwell BRD Blue Tie	1.50	.45
23 Warren Spahn Patch	1.00	.30
23B Warren Spahn No Patch	2.00	.60
24 George Kelly Blue Bill	.75	.23
24B George Kelly Red Bill	1.50	.45
25 Phil Rizzuto Bleachers	1.00	.30
25B Phil Rizzuto Green	2.00	.60
26 Robin Roberts Day	.75	.23
26B Robin Roberts Night	1.50	.45
27 Ozzie Smith Red Sleeve	2.50	.75
27B Ozzie Smith Blue Sleeve	5.00	1.50
28 Jim Palmer White Hat	.75	.23
28B Jim Palmer Black Hat	1.50	.45
29 Duke Snider No Patch	1.00	.30
29B Duke Snider Flag Patch	2.00	.60
30 Bob Feller White Uni	1.00	.30
30B Bob Feller Grey Uni	2.00	.60
31 Buck Leonard Bleachers	.75	.23
31B Buck Leonard Red	1.50	.45
32 Kirby Puckett Wood Bat	1.50	.45
32B Kirby Puckett Black Bat	3.00	.90
33 Monte Irvin Black Sleeve	.75	.23
33B Monte Irvin White Sleeve	1.50	.45
34 Chuck Klein Black Socks	.75	.23
34B Chuck Klein Red Socks	1.50	.45
35 Willie Stargell Yellow Uni	1.00	.30
35B Willie Stargell White Uni	2.00	.60
36 Juan Marichal Ballpark	.75	.23
36B Juan Marichal Gold	1.50	.45
37 Lou Brock Day	1.00	.30
37B Lou Brock Night	2.00	.60
38 Bucky Harris Black W	.75	.23
38B Bucky Harris Red W	1.50	.45
39 Bobby Doerr Ballpark	.75	.23
39B Bobby Doerr Red	1.50	.45
40 Lee MacPhail Blue Tie	.75	.23
40B Lee MacPhail Red Tie	1.50	.45
41 H.Manush Grey Sleeve	.75	.23
41B H.Manush Navy Sleeve	1.50	.45
42 George Brett Patch	4.00	1.20
42B George Brett No Patch	8.00	2.40
43 Harmon Killebrew Blue Hat	1.50	.45
43B Har. Killebrew Red Hat	3.00	.90
44 Whitey Ford Day	1.00	.30
44B Whitey Ford Night	2.00	.60
45 Eddie Mathews Day	1.50	.45
45B Eddie Mathews Night	3.00	.90
46 Gaylord Perry Leather Glv	.75	.23
46B Gaylord Perry Black Glv	1.50	.45
47 Red Schoendienst Stripes	.75	.23
47B R.Schoendienst No Stripes	1.50	.45
48 Earl Weaver MG Day	.75	.23
48B Earl Weaver MG Night	1.50	.45
49 Joe Morgan Day	.75	.23
49B Joe Morgan Night	1.50	.45
50 Mike Schmidt Grey Uni	3.00	.90
50B Mike Schmidt White Uni	6.00	1.80
51 Willie McCovey Wood Bat	.75	.23
51B Willie McCovey Black Bat	1.50	.45
52 Stan Musial Day	2.50	.75
52B Stan Musial Night	5.00	1.50
53 Don Sutton Ballpark	.75	.23
53B Don Sutton Gray	1.50	.45
54 Hank Greenberg w/Player	1.50	.45
54B H.Greenberg No Player	3.00	.90
55 Robin Yount w/Player	2.50	.75
55B Robin Yount No Player	5.00	1.50
56 Tom Seaver Leather Glv	1.00	.30
56B Tom Seaver Black Glv	2.00	.60
57 Tony Perez Wood Bat	.75	.23
57B Tony Perez Black Bat	1.50	.45
58 George Sisler w/Ad	.75	.23
58B George Sisler No Ad	1.50	.45
59 Jim Bottomley White Hat	.75	.23
59B Jim Bottomley Red Hat	1.50	.45
60 Yogi Berra Leather Chest	1.50	.45
60B Yogi Berra Navy Chest	3.00	.90
61 Fred Lindstrom Blue Bill	.75	.23
61B Fred Lindstrom Red Bill	1.50	.45
62 Napoleon Lajoie White Uni	1.50	.45
62B Nap. Lajoie Navy Uni	3.00	.90
63 Frank Robinson Wood Bat	1.00	.30
63B Fr. Robinson Black Bat	2.00	.60
64 Carlton Fisk Red Ltr	1.00	.30
64B Carlton Fisk Black Ltr	2.00	.60
65 Orlando Cepeda Blue Sky	.75	.23
65B Orlando Cepeda Sunset	1.50	.45
66 Fergie Jenkins Leather Glv	.75	.23
66B Fergie Jenkins Black Glv	1.50	.45
67 Ernie Banks Day	1.50	.45
67B Ernie Banks Night	3.00	.90
68 Bill Mazeroski No Sleeves	1.00	.30
68B Bill Mazeroski w/Sleeves	2.00	.60
69 Jim Bunning Grey Uni	.75	.23
69B Jim Bunning White Uni	1.50	.45
70 Rollie Fingers Day	.75	.23
70B Rollie Fingers Night	1.50	.45
71 Jimmie Foxx Black Sleeve	1.50	.45
71B Ji. Foxx White Sleeve	3.00	.90
72 Rod Carew Red Btg Glv	1.00	.30
72B Rod Carew Blue Btg Glv	2.00	.60
73 Sparky Anderson Blue Sky	.75	.23
73B Sparky Anderson Yellow	1.50	.45
74 George Kell Red D	.75	.23
74B George Kell White D	1.50	.45

2003 Topps Gallery HOF Artist's Proofs

Inserted in packs at a rate of one per for basic cards and one in 20 for variations cards, this is a complete parallel of the Topps Gallery set. The Artist Proof cards can be differentiated by the presence of silver foil and those are also much heavier than the regular cards.

	Nm-Mt	Ex-Mt
*ARTIST'S PROOFS: .75X TO 2X BASIC		
*VARIATIONS: 2X TO 5X BASIC VAR .		

2003 Topps Gallery HOF Accent Mark Autographs

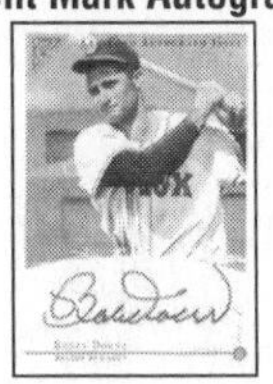

Issued at various odds depending on who signed the cards, these six cards featured authentic autographs of the featured HOFer. Each person signed a different amount of cards and we have notated the group of the signed card next to their name in our checklist.

	Nm-Mt	Ex-Mt
GROUP A ODDS 1:3446		
GROUP B ODDS 1:2074		
GROUP C ODDS 1:1483		
GROUP D ODDS 1:1149		
GROUP E ODDS 1:941		
GROUP F ODDS 1:545		
ARTIST'S PROOFS ODDS 1:1723		
ARTIST'S PROOFS PRINT RUN 25 #'d SETS		
NO AP PRICING DUE TO SCARCITY		
AP'S FEATURE SILVER HOLO-FOIL		
BD Bobby Doerr B	40.00	12.00
LM Lee MacPhail D	40.00	12.00
RR Robin Roberts E	40.00	12.00
RS Red Schoendienst C	40.00	12.00
WS Warren Spahn F	30.00	9.00
YB Yogi Berra A	80.00	24.00

2003 Topps Gallery HOF ARTifact Relics

Inserted in packs at differing rates depending on what group the relic belongs to, this is a 57-card insert set featuring game-used relic pieces of various Hall of Famers. We have notated next to the player's name both the relic piece as well as what group the relic piece belonged to.

	Nm-Mt	Ex-Mt
BAT GROUP A ODDS 1:1812		
BAT GROUP B ODDS 1:469		
BAT GROUP C ODDS 1:242		
BAT GROUP D ODDS 1:111		
BAT GROUP E ODDS 1:96		
BAT GROUP F ODDS 1:28		
BAT GROUP G ODDS 1:62		
JSY/UNI GROUP A ODDS 1:1812		
JSY/UNI GROUP B ODDS 1:2353		
JSY/UNI GROUP C ODDS 1:728		
JSY/UNI GROUP D ODDS 1:151		
JSY/UNI GROUP E ODDS 1:145		
ARTIST'S PROOFS BAT ODDS 1:345		
ARTIST'S PROOFS JSY/UNI ODDS 1:967		
ARTIST'S PROOFS PRINT RUN 25 #'d SETS		
NO AP PRICING DUE TO SCARCITY		
AP'S FEATURE SILVER HOLO-FOIL		
AK Al Kaline Bat F	15.00	4.50
BD Bobby Doerr Jsy D	10.00	3.00
BH Bucky Harris Bat F	15.00	4.50
BR Babe Ruth Bat B	180.00	55.00
BRO Brooks Robinson Bat D	20.00	6.00
CF Carlton Fisk Bat G	15.00	4.50
CK Chuck Klein Bat F	15.00	4.50
CY Carl Yastrzemski Bat F	20.00	6.00
DS Duke Snider Bat F	15.00	4.50
DSU Don Sutton Bat D	10.00	3.00
EB Ernie Banks Uni B	40.00	12.00
EC Eddie Collins Bat B	30.00	9.00
EM Eddie Mathews Jsy A		
ER Edd Roush Bat B	30.00	9.00
FF Frankie Frisch Bat E	15.00	4.50
FR Frank Robinson Bat G	15.00	4.50
GB George Brett Jsy D	30.00	9.00
GK George Kelly Bat D	20.00	6.00
GP Gaylord Perry Uni E	10.00	3.00
GS George Sisler Bat F	15.00	4.50
HA Hank Aaron Bat F	25.00	7.50
HG Hank Greenberg Bat D	40.00	12.00
HH Harry Heilmann Bat B	20.00	6.00
HK Harmon Killebrew Jsy E	20.00	6.00
HM Heinie Manush Bat B	20.00	6.00
HW Honus Wagner Bat A		
HWI Hoyt Wilhelm Uni D	10.00	3.00
JB Jim Bottomley Bat E	15.00	4.50
JBE Johnny Bench Bat G	15.00	4.50
JF Jimmie Foxx Bat A		
JM Joe Morgan Bat E	10.00	3.00
JP Jim Palmer Jsy A		
JR Jackie Robinson Bat C	50.00	15.00
JT Joe Tinker Bat E	25.00	7.50
KP Kirby Puckett Bat E	20.00	6.00
LA Luis Aparicio Bat A		
LB Lou Brock Bat A		
LG Lou Gehrig Bat C	150.00	45.00
MS Mike Schmidt Uni E	30.00	9.00
NR Nolan Ryan Bat C	60.00	18.00
OC Orlando Cepeda Bat F	10.00	3.00
OS Ozzie Smith Bat E	20.00	6.00
PN Phil Niekro Uni D	10.00	3.00
PW Paul Waner Bat C	25.00	7.50
RCA Rod Carew Jsy E	15.00	4.50
RJ Reggie Jackson Bat F	15.00	4.50
RY Robin Yount Bat F	20.00	6.00
SA Sparky Anderson Uni A		
SC Sam Crawford Bat D	25.00	7.50
SM Stan Musial Bat D	30.00	9.00
TC Ty Cobb Bat C	120.00	36.00
TLA Tom Lasorda Jsy A		
TP Tony Perez Bat F	10.00	3.00
TS Tom Seaver Bat C	20.00	6.00
WM Willie Mays Jsy C	50.00	15.00
WMC Willie McCovey Bat F	10.00	3.00
WS Willie Stargell Jsy C	20.00	6.00

2003 Topps Gallery HOF ARTifact Relics Autographs

Inserted at different rates depending on which group the player belonged to, these 11 cards feature not only a game-used relic piece of the featured player but also an authentic autograph. We have notated next to the player's name not only what type of memorabilia piece but also what group the card belongs to.

	Nm-Mt	Ex-Mt
GROUP A ODDS 1:3446		
GROUP B ODDS 1:691		
GROUP C ODDS 1:691		
ARTIST'S PROOFS ODDS 1:941		
ARTIST'S PROOFS PRINT RUN 25 #'d SETS		
NO AP PRICING DUE TO SCARCITY		
AP'S FEATURE SILVER HOLO-FOIL		
AK Al Kaline Bat C	100.00	30.00
BD Bobby Doerr Jsy C	50.00	15.00
BRO Brooks Robinson Bat C	80.00	24.00
DS Duke Snider Bat B	80.00	24.00
HK Harmon Killebrew Jsy B	80.00	24.00
JM Joe Morgan Bat B	50.00	15.00
JP Jim Palmer Jsy A		
MS Mike Schmidt Uni B		
OC Orlando Cepeda Bat B		
RS Red Schoendienst Jsy A		
RY Robin Yount Bat A		

2003 Topps Gallery HOF Currency Connection Coin Relics

Issued as a box topper, these 12 cards feature not only a player but an authentic coin from a key point in their career.

	Nm-Mt	Ex-Mt
STATED ODDS ONE PER BOX		
BF B.Feller 1945 Dime B	25.00	7.50
BR B.Ruth 1916 Dime A	80.00	24.00
EB E.Banks 1958 Penny B	25.00	7.50
HG H.Greenberg 1945 Nickel B	25.00	7.50
JR J.Robinson 1946 Dime B	30.00	9.00
LG L.Gehrig 1938 Nickel A	40.00	12.00
OC O.Cepeda 1958 Penny B	15.00	4.50
SM S.Musial 1943 Penny B	40.00	12.00
TC T.Cobb 1909 Penny A	50.00	15.00
WM W.Mays 1958 Penny B	25.00	7.50
WMA W.Mays 1954 Nickel B	25.00	7.50
WMC W.McCovey 1959 Penny B	15.00	4.50

2003 Topps Gallery HOF Paint by Number Patch Relics

Inserted into packs at a stated rate of one in 1037, these 14 cards feature prime patch swatches of game-worn jerseys on specially designed art cards. These cards were issued to a stated print run of 25 serial numbered sets and no pricing is available due to market scarcity.

Nm-Mt Ex-Mt
CH Catfish Hunter
CY Carl Yastrzemski
DS Don Sutton
EM Eddie Mathews
FJ Fergie Jenkins
GB George Brett
HK Harmon Killebrew
JP Jim Palmer
MS Mike Schmidt
NR Nolan Ryan
OS Ozzie Smith
RY Robin Yount
TL Tom Lasorda
WM Willie McCovey

1998 Topps Gold Label Pre-Production

These three cards were distributed to wholesale dealer and retail accounts in a three-card cello. The cards were intended to preview the upcoming Topps Gold Label product and were ditributed around October, 1998. They're very similar in design to basic issue Gold Label Class 1 cards except for the PP numbering on back.

Nm-Mt Ex-Mt
COMPLETE SET (3) 6.00 1.80
PP1 Vinny Castilla .50 .15
PP2 Ken Griffey Jr. 3.00 .90
PP3 Mike Piazza 3.00 .90

1998 Topps Gold Label Class 1

This 150 standard-size set was issued in many different confusing versions. The basic Class 1 set is a gold set featuring fielding poses in the background. The SRP of these packs were $3 each and the packs contained three cards wiith 24 packs in a box and 8 boxes in a case. The HTA packs contained five cards and the SRP packs on those packs were $5, keeping both packs at $1 per card.

Nm-Mt Ex-Mt
COMP.GOLD SET (100) 50.00 15.00
1 Kevin Brown .75 .23
2 Greg Maddux 2.00 .60
3 Albert Belle .50 .15
4 Andres Galarraga .50 .15
5 Craig Biggio .75 .23
6 Matt Williams .50 .15
7 Derek Jeter 3.00 .90
8 Randy Johnson 1.25 .35
9 Jay Bell .50 .15
10 Jim Thome 1.25 .35
11 Roberto Alomar 1.25 .35
12 Tom Glavine .75 .23
13 Reggie Sanders .50 .15
14 Tony Gwynn 1.50 .45
15 Mark McGwire 3.00 .90
16 Jeromy Burnitz .50 .15
17 Andruw Jones .50 .15
18 Jay Buhner .50 .15
19 Robin Ventura .50 .15
20 Jeff Bagwell .75 .23
21 Roger Clemens 2.50 .75
22 Masato Yoshii RC .75 .23
23 Travis Fryman .50 .15
24 Rafael Palmeiro .75 .23
25 Alex Rodriguez 2.00 .60
26 Sandy Alomar Jr. .50 .15
27 Chipper Jones 1.25 .35
28 Rusty Greer .50 .15
29 Cal Ripken 4.00 1.20
30 Tony Clark .50 .15
31 Derek Bell .50 .15
32 Fred McGriff .75 .23
33 Paul O'Neill .75 .23
34 Moises Alou .50 .15
35 Henry Rodriguez .50 .15
36 Steve Finley .50 .15
37 Marquis Grissom .50 .15
38 Jason Giambi 1.25 .35
39 Javy Lopez .50 .15
40 Damion Easley .50 .15
41 Mariano Rivera .75 .23
42 Mo Vaughn .50 .15
43 Mike Mussina 1.25 .35
44 Jason Kendall .50 .15
45 Pedro Martinez 1.25 .35
46 Frank Thomas 1.25 .35
47 Jim Edmonds .50 .15
48 Hideki Irabu .50 .15
49 Eric Karros .50 .15
50 Juan Gonzalez 1.25 .35
51 Ellis Burks .50 .15
52 Dean Palmer .50 .15
53 Scott Rolen .75 .23
54 Raul Mondesi .50 .15
55 Quinton McCracken .50 .15
56 John Olerud .50 .15
57 Ken Caminiti .50 .15
58 Brian Jordan .50 .15
59 Wade Boggs .75 .23
60 Mike Piazza 2.00 .60
61 Darin Erstad .50 .15
62 Curt Schilling .75 .23
63 David Justice .50 .15
64 Kenny Lofton .50 .15
65 Barry Bonds 3.00 .90
66 Ray Lankford .50 .15
67 Brian Hunter .50 .15
68 Chuck Knoblauch .50 .15
69 Vinny Castilla .50 .15
70 Vladimir Guerrero 1.25 .35
71 Tim Salmon .75 .23
72 Larry Walker .75 .23
73 Paul Molitor .75 .23
74 Barry Larkin 1.25 .35
75 Edgar Martinez .75 .23
76 Bernie Williams .75 .23
77 Dante Bichette .50 .15
78 Nomar Garciaparra 2.00 .60
79 Ben Grieve .50 .15
80 Ivan Rodriguez 1.25 .35
81 Todd Helton .75 .23
82 Ryan Klesko .50 .15
83 Sammy Sosa 2.00 .60
84 Travis Lee .50 .15
85 Jose Cruz Jr. .50 .15
86 Mark Kotsay .50 .15
87 Richard Hidalgo .50 .15
88 Rondell White .50 .15
89 Greg Vaughn .50 .15
90 Gary Sheffield .50 .15
91 Paul Konerko .50 .15
92 Mark Grace .75 .23
93 Kevin Millwood RC 2.00 .60
94 Manny Ramirez .50 .15
95 Tino Martinez .75 .23
96 Brad Fullmer .50 .15
97 Todd Walker .50 .15
98 Carlos Delgado .50 .15
99 Kerry Wood 1.25 .35
100 Ken Griffey Jr. 2.00 .60

1998 Topps Gold Label Class 1 Black

The black parallel versions of these cards were issued one every eight packs.

Nm-Mt Ex-Mt
*CLASS 1 BLACK: 3X TO 8X CLASS 1 GOLD

1998 Topps Gold Label Class 1 Red

The red parallel versions of these cards were issued one every 99 packs and are serial numbered to 100.

Nm-Mt Ex-Mt
*CLASS 1 RED STARS: 8X TO 20X CLASS 1 GOLD
CLASS 1 RED RC'S: 8X TO 20X CLASS 1

1998 Topps Gold Label Class 1 One to One

This parallel was randomly issued in packs, and only one of these cards were produced. No pricing on any of the Gold Label star One of Ones (actually nine since each color version in each class has a one of one) is provided due to scarcity.

Nm-Mt Ex-Mt
STATED PRINT RUN 1 SERIAL #'d SET
BLACK, GOLD AND RED VERSIONS EXIST

1998 Topps Gold Label Class 2

The gold class 2 cards were issued one every two packs. Each player is featured in a running pose in the background. The class 2 cards were printed in a sparkling silver text on the front.

Nm-Mt Ex-Mt
COMP.GOLD SET (100) 150.00 45.00
*CLASS 2 GOLD: 1X TO 2.5X CLASS 1 GOLD

1998 Topps Gold Label Class 2 Black

The black class 2 parallel versions of these cards were issued one every 16 packs.

Nm-Mt Ex-Mt
*CLASS 2 BLACK: 4X TO 10X CLASS 1 GOLD

1998 Topps Gold Label Class 2 Red

The red class 2 parallel versions of these cards were issued one every 198 packs. These cards have a stated print run of 50 sets.

Nm-Mt Ex-Mt
*CLASS 2 STARS: 5X TO 12X CLASS 2
*CLASS 2 RC'S: 5X TO 12X CLASS 2 .

1998 Topps Gold Label Class 2 One to One

This parallel was randomly issued in packs, and only one of these cards were produced. Due to scarcity, no pricing is provided.

Nm-Mt Ex-Mt
STATED PRINT RUN 1 SERIAL #'d SET
BLACK, GOLD AND RED VERSIONS EXIST

1998 Topps Gold Label Class 3

The gold class 3 cards were issued one every four packs. Each player is featured in a hitting pose (except for pitchers) in the background. These cards feature sparkling gold text on the front.

Nm-Mt Ex-Mt
COMMON GOLD (1-100) 2.00 .60
*CLASS 3 GOLD: 1.5X TO 4X CLASS 1 GOLD

1998 Topps Gold Label Class 3 Black

The black class 3 parallel versions of these cards were issued one every 32 packs.

Nm-Mt Ex-Mt
*CLASS 3 BLACK: 8X TO 20X CLASS 1 GOLD

1998 Topps Gold Label Class 3 Red

The red class 3 parallel versions of these cards were issued one every 396 packs and are serially numbered to 25.

Nm-Mt Ex-Mt
*CLASS 3 RED STARS: 5X TO 12X CLASS 3
CLASS 3 RED RC'S: 25X TO 60X CLASS 3

1998 Topps Gold Label Class 3 One to One

This parallel was randomly issued in packs, and only one of these cards were produced. Due to scarcity, no pricing is provided.

Nm-Mt Ex-Mt
STATED PRINT RUN 1 SERIAL #'d SET
BLACK, GOLD AND RED VERSIONS EXIST

1998 Topps Gold Label Home Run Race

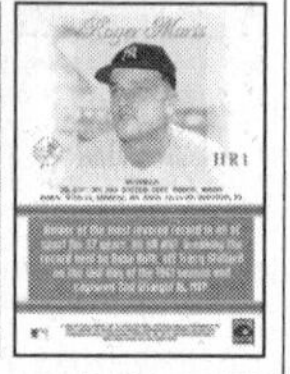

Inserted specially into the Gold Label HTA packs at a rate on one in 12, these cards feature Roger Maris and the three players who chased his legend during the summer of 1998. A large photo of Roger Maris is also looking over each player's shoulders. These cards were also issued in three different colors,

Nm-Mt Ex-Mt
COMPLETE SET (4) 30.00 9.00
*BLACK HR: 1.25X TO 3X GOLD HR...
BLACK HR STATED ODDS 1:48
*RED HR: 8X TO 20X GOLD HR
RED HR STATED ODDS 1:4055 HTA...
RED HR STATED PRINT RUN 61 SETS
HR1 Roger Maris 8.00 2.40
HR2 Mark McGwire 12.00 3.60
HR3 Ken Griffey Jr. 8.00 2.40
HR4 Sammy Sosa 8.00 2.40

1999 Topps Gold Label Class 1

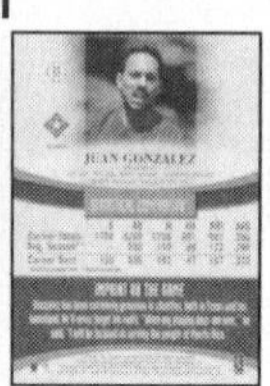

This 100-card set was distributed in four-card packs with a suggested retail price of $3.99. The set features color action player photos printed with spectral reflective rainbow technology on 35-point card stock. Three different versions of the cards were produced each having the same foreground player photo but a different background photo. This Class 1 set carried a Fielding background player photo or a Set Position photo for pitchers.

Nm-Mt Ex-Mt
COMP.GOLD SET (100) 40.00 12.00
1 Mike Piazza 2.00 .60
2 Andres Galarraga .50 .15
3 Mark Grace .75 .23
4 Tony Clark .50 .15
5 Jim Thome 1.25 .35
6 Tony Gwynn 1.50 .45
7 Kelly Dransfeldt RC .50 .15
8 Eric Chavez .50 .15
9 Brian Jordan .50 .15
10 Todd Hundley .50 .15
11 Rondell White .50 .15
12 Dmitri Young .50 .15
13 Jeff Kent .50 .15
14 Derek Bell .50 .15
15 Todd Helton .75 .23
16 Chipper Jones 1.25 .35
17 Albert Belle .50 .15
18 Barry Larkin 1.25 .35
19 Dante Bichette .50 .15
20 Gary Sheffield .50 .15
21 Cliff Floyd .50 .15
22 Derek Jeter 3.00 .90
23 Jason Giambi 1.25 .35
24 Ray Lankford .50 .15
25 Alex Rodriguez 2.00 .60
26 Ruben Mateo .50 .15
27 Wade Boggs .75 .23
28 Carlos Delgado .50 .15
29 Tim Salmon .75 .23
30 Alfonso Soriano RC 8.00 2.40
31 Javy Lopez .50 .15
32 Jason Kendall .50 .15
33 Nick Johnson RC 2.00 .60
34 A.J. Burnett RC 1.25 .35
35 Troy Glaus .75 .23
36 Pat Burrell RC 4.00 1.20
37 Jeff Cirillo .50 .15
38 David Justice .50 .15
39 Ivan Rodriguez 1.25 .35
40 Bernie Williams .75 .23
41 Jay Buhner .50 .15
42 Mo Vaughn .50 .15
43 Randy Johnson 1.25 .35
44 Pedro Martinez 1.25 .35
45 Larry Walker .75 .23
46 Todd Walker .50 .15
47 Roberto Alomar 1.25 .35
48 Kevin Brown .75 .23
49 Mike Mussina 1.25 .35
50 Tom Glavine .75 .23
51 Curt Schilling .75 .23
52 Ken Caminiti .50 .15
53 Brad Fullmer .50 .15
54 Bobby Seay RC .50 .15
55 Orlando Hernandez .50 .15
56 Sean Casey .50 .15
57 Al Leiter .50 .15
58 Sandy Alomar Jr. .50 .15
59 Mark Kotsay .50 .15
60 Matt Williams .50 .15
61 Raul Mondesi .50 .15
62 Joe Crede RC 5.00 1.50
63 Jim Edmonds .50 .15
64 Jose Cruz Jr. .50 .15
65 Juan Gonzalez 1.25 .35
66 Sammy Sosa 2.00 .60
67 Cal Ripken 4.00 1.20
68 Vinny Castilla .50 .15
69 Craig Biggio .75 .23
70 Mark McGwire 3.00 .90
71 Greg Vaughn .50 .15
72 Greg Maddux 2.00 .60
73 Paul O'Neill .75 .23
74 Scott Rolen .75 .23
75 Ben Grieve .50 .15
76 Vladimir Guerrero 1.25 .35
77 John Olerud .50 .15
78 Eric Karros .50 .15
79 Jeromy Burnitz .50 .15
80 Jeff Bagwell .75 .23
81 Kenny Lofton .50 .15
82 Manny Ramirez .50 .15
83 Andruw Jones .50 .15
84 Travis Lee .50 .15
85 Darin Erstad .50 .15
86 Nomar Garciaparra 2.00 .60
87 Frank Thomas 1.25 .35
88 Moises Alou .50 .15
89 Tino Martinez .75 .23
90 Carlos Pena RC 1.25 .35
91 Shawn Green .50 .15
92 Rusty Greer .50 .15
93 Matt Belisle RC .50 .15
94 Adrian Beltre .50 .15
95 Roger Clemens 2.50 .75
96 John Smoltz .75 .23
97 Mark Mulder RC 4.00 1.20
98 Kerry Wood 1.25 .35
99 Barry Bonds 3.00 .90
100 Ken Griffey Jr. 2.00 .60

1999 Topps Gold Label Class 1 Black

Randomly inserted in retail packs at the rate of one in 12 and HTA packs at a rate of one in eight, this 100-card set is parallel to the Class 1 base set and is distinguished by the Black "Topps Gold Label" foil stamp on each card.

Nm-Mt Ex-Mt
*CLASS 1 BLACK: 1.5X TO 4X C1 GOLD
*C1 BLACK RC'S: .75X TO 2X C1 GOLD
*C1 BLACK CREDE: .5X TO 1.2X C1 GOLD

1999 Topps Gold Label Class 1 Red

Randomly inserted into retail packs at the rate of one in 148 and HTA packs at a rate of one in 118, this 100-card set is parallel to the Class 1 base set and features a red foil stamp. Only 100 sequentially numbered sets were produced.

Nm-Mt Ex-Mt
*CLASS 1 RED STARS: 8X TO 20X CLASS 1 GOLD
*CLASS 1 RED RC'S: 4X TO 10X C1 GOLD
*CLASS 1 RED CREDE: 2.5X TO 6X C1 GOLD

1999 Topps Gold Label Class 2

Randomly inserted in packs at the rate of one in four retail and 1:2 HTA, this 100-card set is parallel to the Class 1 set and features a Running background player photo or a Wind-Up photo for pitchers.

Nm-Mt Ex-Mt
*CLASS 2 GOLD: .75X TO 2X CLASS 1 GOLD

1999 Topps Gold Label Class 2 Black

Randomly inserted in retail packs at the rate of one in 24 and HTA packs at a rate on one in 16, this 100-card set is parallel to the Class 2 regular parallel set and is distinguished by the Black "Topps Gold Label" foil stamp on each card.

Nm-Mt Ex-Mt
*C2 BLACK: 1.5X TO 4X C2 GOLD
*C2 BLACK RC'S: .75X TO 2X C2 GOLD
*C2 BLACK CREDE: .6X TO 1.5X C2 GOLD

1999 Topps Gold Label Class 2 Red

Randomly inserted into retail packs at the rate of one in 296 and HTA packs at a rate of one in 237, this 100-card set is parallel to the Class 2 regular set and features a red foil stamp. Only 50 sequentially numbered sets were produced.

Nm-Mt Ex-Mt
*C2 RED: 6X TO 15X C2 GOLD
*C2 RED RC'S: 5X TO 12X C2 GOLD ..
*C2 RED CREDE: 4X TO 10X C2 GOLD

1999 Topps Gold Label Class 3

Randomly inserted in hobby packs at the rate of one in eight and HTA packs at the rate of one in four, this 100-card set is parallel to the Class 1 set and features a Hitting background player photo or a Throwing photo for pitchers.

Nm-Mt Ex-Mt
*CLASS 3 GOLD: 1.5X TO 4X CLASS 1 GOLD

1999 Topps Gold Label Class 3 Black

Randomly inserted in packs at the rate of one in 48, this 100-card set is parallel to the Class 3 regualr parallel set and is distinguished by the Black "Topps Gold Label" foil stamp on each card.

Nm-Mt Ex-Mt
*C3 BLACK: 1.5X TO 4X C3 GOLD
*C3 BLACK RC'S: .75X TO 2X C3 GOLD
*C3 BLACK CREDE: .6X TO 1.5X C3 GOLD

1999 Topps Gold Label Class 3 Red

Randomly inserted into packs at the rate of one in 591, this 100-card set is parallel to the Class 3 regular set and features a red foil stamp. Only 25 sequentially numbered sets were produced.

Nm-Mt Ex-Mt
*C3 RED: 6X TO 15X C3 GOLD

1999 Topps Gold Label One to One

Nine different "one of one" parallels were produced for each Class (1, 2 or 3) and color (Black, Gold or Red) of every Topps Gold Label base issue card. The cards were seeded into packs at a rate of 1:1,587 retail and 1:1,271 Home Team Advantage jumbos. No pricing is available on star cards due to scarcity.

Nm-Mt Ex-Mt
NINE VERSIONS OF EACH CARD EXIST

1999 Topps Gold Label Race to Aaron

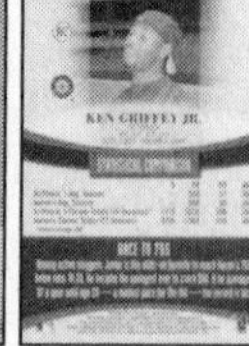

Randomly inserted into packs at the rate of one in 20 retail packs and 1:12 HTA, this 10-card set features color photos in the foreground of ten contemporary players chasing two of baseball legend Hank Aaron's all-time records: his career home run record and his RBI record. A silhouetted photo of Hank Aaron appears on each card in the background. Two parallel sets were also produced: a Black parallel set with an insertion rate of 1:80 retail packs and 1:48 HTA, and a 44 serial- numbered Red parallel set with a 1:3343 retail pack insertion rate and 1:2695 HTA.

Nm-Mt Ex-Mt
COMPLETE SET (10) 60.00 18.00
*BLACK: 1X TO 2.5X BASIC RACE TO AARON
BLACK ODDS 1:80 RETAIL, 1:48 HTA.
*RED: 8X TO 20X BASIC RACETO AARON
RED ODDS 1:3343 RETAIL, 1:2695 HTA
RED PRINT RUN 44 SERIAL #'d SETS
AARON ONE TO ONE PARALLELS EXIST
1 TO 1'S NOT PRICED DUE TO SCARCITY
RA1 Mark McGwire 10.00 3.00
RA2 Ken Griffey Jr. 6.00 1.80
RA3 Alex Rodriguez 6.00 1.80
RA4 Vladimir Guerrero 4.00 1.20
RA5 Albert Belle 1.50 .45
RA6 Nomar Garciaparra 6.00 1.80
RA7 Ken Griffey Jr. 6.00 1.80
RA8 Alex Rodriguez 6.00 1.80
RA9 Juan Gonzalez 4.00 1.20
RA10 Barry Bonds 10.00 3.00

2000 Topps Gold Label Pre-Production

This three card set was issued in a sealed cello pack to dealers and hobby media several weeks prior to the products release. The cards have a "PP" prefix so they can be differentiated from the regular cards. All three cards feature Derek Jeter on them.

Nm-Mt Ex-Mt
COMPLETE SET (3) 8.00 2.40
COMMON CARD (PP1-PP3) 3.00 .90

2000 Topps Gold Label Class 1

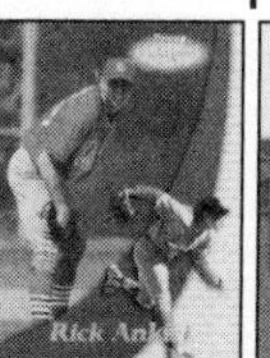

The 2000 Topps Gold Label product was released in June, 2000 as a 100-card base set. Please note that there are three classes of the base. The class 1 version (1-100) features each player in a hitting stance, the class 2 version (1-100) features each player in a fielding stance, and the class 3 version features each player running. There is also a gold parallel of each class that is individually serial numbered to 100. An uncut sheet of 2000 Topps Gold Label that was autographed by Derek Jeter (numbered to 1000) was also given to lucky collectors who collected all the letters to spell G-O-L-D-L-A-B-E-L. Each pack contained five cards and carried a suggested retail price of $2.99. Notable Rookie Cards include Rick Asadoorian and Bobby Bradley.

	Nm-Mt	Ex-Mt
COMPLETE SET (100)	60.00	18.00
1 Sammy Sosa	2.00	.60
2 Greg Maddux	2.00	.60
3 Mark Quinn	.50	.15
4 Rondell White	.50	.15
5 Fernando Tatis	.50	.15
6 Troy Glaus	.75	.23
7 Nick Johnson	.50	.15
8 Albert Belle	.50	.15
9 Scott Rolen	.75	.23
10 Rafael Palmeiro	.75	.23
11 Tony Gwynn	1.50	.45
12 Kevin Brown	.50	.15
13 Roberto Alomar	1.25	.35
14 John Olerud	.50	.15
15 Rick Ankiel	.50	.15
16 Chipper Jones	1.25	.35
17 Craig Biggio	.75	.23
18 Mark Mulder	.75	.23
19 Carlos Delgado	.50	.15
20 Alex Gonzalez	.50	.15
21 Gabe Kapler	.50	.15
22 Derek Jeter	3.00	.90
23 Carlos Beltran	.50	.15
24 Todd Helton	.75	.23
25 Mark McGwire	3.00	.90
26 Ben Grieve	.50	.15
27 Rafael Furcal	.50	.15
28 Vernon Wells	.50	.15
29 Greg Vaughn	.50	.15
30 Vladimir Guerrero	1.25	.35
31 Mike Piazza	2.00	.60
32 Roger Clemens	2.50	.75
33 Barry Larkin	1.25	.35
34 Pedro Martinez	1.25	.35
35 Matt Williams	.50	.15
36 Mo Vaughn	.50	.15
37 Tim Hudson	.25	.07
38 Andruw Jones	.50	.15
39 Vinny Castilla	.50	.15
40 Frank Thomas	1.25	.35
41 Pokey Reese	.50	.15
42 Corey Patterson	.75	.23
43 Jeromy Burnitz	.50	.15
44 Preston Wilson	.50	.15
45 Juan Gonzalez	1.25	.35
46 Brian Giles	.50	.15
47 Todd Walker	.50	.15
48 Maggio Ordonez	.50	.15
49 Alfonso Soriano	1.25	.35
50 Ken Griffey Jr.	2.00	.60
51 Michael Barrett	.50	.15
52 Shawn Green	.50	.15
53 Erubiel Durazo	.50	.15
54 Adam Piatt	.50	.15
55 Pat Burrell	.75	.23
56 Mike Mussina	1.25	.35
57 Bernie Williams	.75	.23
58 Sean Casey	.50	.15
59 Randy Johnson	1.25	.35
60 Jeff Bagwell	.75	.23
61 Eric Chavez	.50	.15
62 Josh Hamilton	.50	.15
63 A.J. Burnett	.50	.15
64 Jim Thome	1.25	.35
65 Raul Mondesi	.50	.15
66 Jason Kendall	.50	.15
67 Mike Lieberthal	.50	.15
68 Robin Ventura	.50	.15
69 Ivan Rodriguez	1.25	.35
70 Larry Walker	.75	.23
71 Eric Munson	.50	.15
72 Brian Jordan	.50	.15
73 Edgardo Alfonzo	.50	.15
74 Curt Schilling	.75	.23
75 Nomar Garciaparra	2.00	.60
76 Mark Grace	.75	.23
77 Shannon Stewart	.50	.15
78 J.D. Drew	.50	.15
79 Jack Cust	.50	.15
80 Cal Ripken	4.00	1.20
81 Bob Abreu	.50	.15
82 Ruben Mateo	.50	.15
83 Orlando Hernandez	.50	.15
84 Kris Benson	.50	.15
85 Barry Bonds	3.00	.90
86 Manny Ramirez	.50	.15
87 Jose Canseco	1.25	.35
88 Sean Burroughs	.75	.23
89 Kevin Millwood	.50	.15
90 Alex Rodriguez	2.00	.60
91 Brett Myers RC	2.50	.75
92 Rick Asadoorian RC	.50	.15
93 Ben Christensen RC	.50	.15
94 Bobby Bradley RC	.50	.15
95 Chris Wakeland RC	.50	.15
96 Brad Baisley RC	.50	.15
97 Aaron McNeal RC	.50	.15
98 Aaron Rowand RC	.50	.15
99 Scott Downs RC	.50	.15
100 Michael Tejera RC	.50	.15
NNO D.Jeter AU Sheet/40 EXCH		

2000 Topps Gold Label Class 1 Gold

Randomly inserted into packs, this 100-card insert is a complete parallel of the Class 1 base set. Each card in this set is individually serial numbered to 100.

	Nm-Mt	Ex-Mt
*STARS: 8X TO 20X BASIC CARDS....		
*ROOKIES: 6X TO 15X BASIC CARDS		

2000 Topps Gold Label Class 2

Randomly inserted into packs, this 100-card insert is a complete parallel of the Class 1 base set. Please note that Class 2 cards feature each player in a fielding stance.

	Nm-Mt	Ex-Mt
COMPLETE SET (100)	60.00	18.00
*CLASS 2: .4X TO 1X CLASS 1		

2000 Topps Gold Label Class 2 Gold

Randomly inserted into packs, this 100-card insert is a complete parallel of the Class 2 base set. Each card in this set is individually serial numbered to 100.

	Nm-Mt	Ex-Mt
*STARS: 8X TO 20X BASIC CARDS....		
*ROOKIES: 6X TO 15X BASIC CARDS		

2000 Topps Gold Label Class 3

Randomly inserted into packs, this 100-card insert is a complete parallel of the Class 1 base set. Please note that Class 3 cards feature each player in a running motion.

	Nm-Mt	Ex-Mt
COMPLETE SET (100)	60.00	18.00
*CLASS 3: .4X TO 1X CLASS 1		

2000 Topps Gold Label Class 3 Gold

Randomly inserted into packs, this 100-card insert is a complete parallel of the Class 3 base set. Each card in this set is individually serial numbered to 100.

	Nm-Mt	Ex-Mt
*STARS: 8X TO 20X BASIC CARDS....		
*ROOKIES: 6X TO 15X BASIC CARDS		

2000 Topps Gold Label Bullion

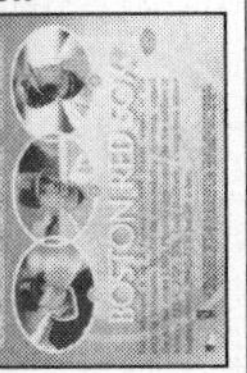

Randomly inserted into packs at one in 32, this 10-card insert features three teammates on each card superimposed over their team logo. Card backs carry a "B" prefix.

	Nm-Mt	Ex-Mt
ONE TO ONE RANDOM INSERT IN PACKS		
ONE TO ONE PRINT RUN 1 SERIAL #'d SET		
ONE TO ONE NO PRICING DUE TO SCARCITY		
B1 Jim Thome / Manny Ramirez / Roberto Alomar	3.00	.90
B2 Derek Jeter / Orlando Hernandez / Bernie Williams	20.00	6.00
B3 Chipper Jones / Andruw Jones / Greg Maddux	12.00	3.60
B4 Alex Rodriguez / Jay Buhner / John Olerud	12.00	3.60
B5 Nomar Garciaparra / Pedro Martinez / Brian Daubach	12.00	3.60
B6 Mark McGwire / J.D. Drew / Rick Ankiel	20.00	6.00
B7 Sammy Sosa / Mark Grace / Kerry Wood	12.00	3.60
B8 Ken Griffey Jr. / Sean Casey / Barry Larkin	12.00	3.60
B9 Mike Piazza / Edgardo Alfonzo / Robin Ventura	12.00	3.60
B10 Randy Johnson / Matt Williams / Erubiel Durazo	8.00	2.40

2000 Topps Gold Label End of the Rainbow

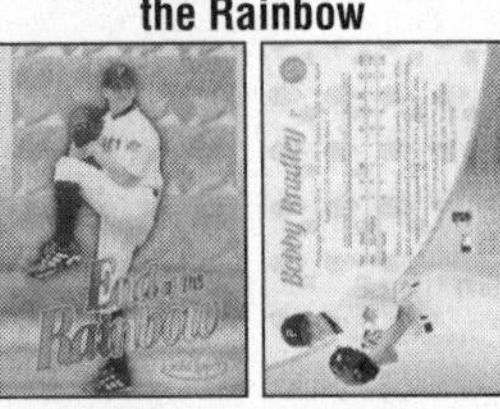

Randomly inserted into packs at one in seven, this insert features 15 of the major league's top prospects. Card backs carry an "ER" prefix.

	Nm-Mt	Ex-Mt
COMPLETE SET (15)	25.00	7.50
ONE TO ONE RANDOM INSERT IN PACKS		
ONE TO ONE PRINT RUN 1 SERIAL #'d SET		
ONE TO ONE NO PRICING DUE TO SCARCITY		
ER1 Pat Burrell	1.50	.45
ER2 Corey Patterson	1.50	.45
ER3 Josh Hamilton	1.00	.30
ER4 Eric Munson	1.00	.30
ER5 Sean Burroughs	1.50	.45
ER6 Jack Cust	1.00	.30
ER7 Rafael Furcal	1.00	.30
ER8 Ruben Salazar	1.00	.30
ER9 Brett Myers	3.00	.90
ER10 Bobby Bradley	1.00	.30
ER11 Nick Johnson	1.00	.30
ER12 Scott Downs	1.00	.30
ER13 Choo Freeman	2.50	.75
ER14 Brad Baisley	1.00	.30
ER15 A.J. Burnett	1.00	.30

2000 Topps Gold Label Prospector's Dream

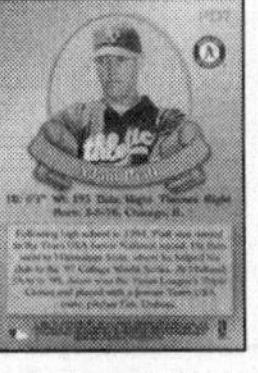

Randomly inserted into packs at one in 16, this 10-card insert features players whose major league accomplishments continue to fulfill their early career potential and aspirations. Card backs carry a "PD" prefix.

	Nm-Mt	Ex-Mt
ONE TO ONE RANDOM INSERTS IN PACKS		
ONE TO ONE PRINT RUN 1 SERIAL #'d SET		
ONE TO ONE NO PRICING DUE TO SCARCITY		
PD1 Mark McGwire	12.00	3.60
PD2 Alex Rodriguez	8.00	2.40
PD3 Nomar Garciaparra	8.00	2.40
PD4 Pat Burrell	3.00	.90
PD5 Todd Helton	3.00	.90
PD6 Derek Jeter	12.00	3.60
PD7 Adam Piatt	2.00	.60
PD8 Chipper Jones	5.00	1.50
PD9 Shawn Green	2.00	.60
PD10 Josh Hamilton	2.00	.60

2000 Topps Gold Label The Treasury

Randomly inserted into packs at one in 13, this 25-card insert features the game's most precious resources. Card backs carry a "T" prefix.

	Nm-Mt	Ex-Mt
ONE TO ONE RANDOM INSERTS IN PACKS		
ONE TO ONE PRINT RUN 1 SERIAL #'d SET		
ONE TO ONE NO PRICING DUE TO SCARCITY		
T1 Ken Griffey Jr.	10.00	3.00
T2 Derek Jeter	15.00	4.50
T3 Chipper Jones	6.00	1.80
T4 Manny Ramirez	2.50	.75
T5 Nomar Garciaparra	10.00	3.00
T6 Sammy Sosa	10.00	3.00
T7 Cal Ripken	20.00	6.00
T8 Alex Rodriguez	10.00	3.00
T9 Mike Piazza	10.00	3.00
T10 Pedro Martinez	6.00	1.80
T11 Vladimir Guerrero	6.00	1.80
T12 Jeff Bagwell	4.00	1.20
T13 Shawn Green	2.50	.75
T14 Greg Maddux	10.00	3.00
T15 Mark McGwire	15.00	4.50
T16 Josh Hamilton	2.50	.75
T17 Corey Patterson	4.00	1.20
T18 Dee Brown	2.50	.75
T19 Rafael Furcal	2.50	.75
T20 Pat Burrell	4.00	1.20
T21 Alfonso Soriano	6.00	1.80
T22 Adam Piatt	2.50	.75
T23 A.J. Burnett	2.50	.75
T24 Mark Mulder	4.00	1.20
T25 Ruben Mateo	2.50	.75

2001 Topps Gold Label Class 1

This 115 card set was released in May, 2001. The set was issued in five card packs with an SRP of $5. The packs were issued 24 to a box and four boxes to a case. The rookie/prospect cards were short printed and were issued at a rate of one in 87 packs and were also serial numbered to 999.

	Nm-Mt	Ex-Mt
COMPLETE SET (115)	200.00	60.00
COMP.SET w/o SP's (100)	50.00	15.00
COMMON CARD (1-115)	.50	.15
COMMON SP	10.00	3.00
1 Adrian Beltre	.50	.15
2 Danny Borrell SP RC	10.00	3.00
3 Albert Belle	.50	.15
4 Jay Buhner	.50	.15
5 Alex Rodriguez	2.00	.60
6 Andruw Jones	.50	.15
7 Antonio Alfonseca	.50	.15
8 Barry Bonds	3.00	.90
9 Barry Larkin	1.25	.35
10 Ben Grieve	.50	.15
11 Ben Molina	.50	.15
12 Bernie Williams	.75	.23
13 Bobby Abreu	.50	.15
14 Bobby Higginson	.50	.15
15 Brad Fullmer	.50	.15
16 Brian Giles	.50	.15
17 Cal Ripken	4.00	1.20
18 Carlos Delgado	.50	.15
19 Chad Petty SP RC	10.00	3.00
20 Charles Johnson	.50	.15
21 Chipper Jones	1.25	.35
22 Cristian Guzman	.50	.15
23 Darin Erstad	.50	.15
24 David Justice	.50	.15
25 David Segui	.50	.15
26 Derek Jeter	3.00	.90
27 Edgar Martinez	.75	.23
28 Edgardo Alfonzo	.50	.15
29 Fernando Tatis	.50	.15
30 Eric Karros	.50	.15
31 Eric Munson	.50	.15
32 Eric Young	.50	.15
33 Frank Thomas	1.25	.35
34 Fernando Vina	.50	.15
35 Garret Anderson	.50	.15
36 Gary Sheffield	.50	.15
37 Geoff Jenkins	.50	.15
38 Greg Maddux	2.00	.60
39 Ivan Rodriguez	1.25	.35
40 J.D. Drew	.50	.15
41 J.R. House SP	10.00	3.00
42 J.T. Snow	.50	.15
43 Jason Giambi	1.25	.35
44 Jason Kendall	.50	.15
45 Jay Payton	.50	.15
46 Jeff Bagwell	.75	.23
47 Jeff Cirillo	.50	.15
48 Jeff Kent	.50	.15
49 Chan Ho Park	.50	.15
50 Jermaine Dye	.50	.15
51 Jeromy Burnitz	.50	.15
52 Jim Edmonds	.50	.15
53 Jim Thome	1.25	.35
54 John Olerud	.50	.15
55 Johnny Damon	.50	.15
56 Jorge Posada	.75	.23
57 Jose Cruz Jr.	.50	.15
58 Jose Vidro	.50	.15
59 Josh Hamilton	.50	.15
60 Juan Gonzalez	1.25	.35
61 Juan Uribe	10.00	3.00
62 Justin Wayne SP RC	10.00	3.00
63 Kazuhiro Sasaki	.50	.15
64 Ken Griffey Jr.	2.00	.60
65 Kevin Brown	.50	.15
66 Kevin Young	.50	.15
67 Larry Walker	.75	.23
68 Luis Castillo	.50	.15
69 Steve Finley	.50	.15
70 Magglio Ordonez	.50	.15
71 Manny Ramirez	.50	.15
72 Mark McGwire	3.00	.90
73 Mark Quinn	.50	.15
74 Miguel Tejada	.50	.15
75 Mike Piazza	2.00	.60
76 Mike Sweeney	.50	.15
77 Mo Vaughn	.50	.15
78 Moises Alou	.50	.15
79 Nomar Garciaparra	2.00	.60
80 Pat Burrell	.50	.15
81 Paul Konerko	.50	.15
82 Pedro Martinez	1.25	.35
83 Phil Nevin	.50	.15
84 Preston Wilson	.50	.15
85 Rafael Furcal	.50	.15
86 Todd Zeile	.50	.15
87 Randy Johnson	1.25	.35
88 Travis Lee	.50	.15
89 Carl Everett	.50	.15
90 Quilvio Veras	.50	.15
91 Rick Ankiel	.50	.15
92 Rick Brosseau SP RC	10.00	3.00
93 Robert Keppel SP RC	10.00	3.00
94 Roberto Alomar	1.25	.35
95 Ryan Klesko	.50	.15
96 Sammy Sosa	2.00	.60
97 Scott Heard SP	10.00	3.00
98 Scott Rolen	.75	.23
99 Sean Casey	.50	.15
100 Shawn Green	.50	.15
101 Terrence Long	.50	.15
102 Tim Salmon	.75	.23
103 Todd Helton	.75	.23
104 Tom Glavine	.75	.23
105 Tony Batista	.50	.15
106 Travis Baptist SP RC	10.00	3.00
107 Troy Glaus	.75	.23
108 Victor Hall SP RC	10.00	3.00
109 Vladimir Guerrero	1.25	.35
110 Tim Hudson	.50	.15
111 Brian Roberts SP RC	10.00	3.00
112 Virgil Chevalier SP RC	10.00	3.00
113 F. Rodney SP RC	10.00	3.00
114 Paul Phillips SP RC	10.00	3.00
115 Cesar Bolivar SP RC	10.00	3.00

2001 Topps Gold Label Class 1 Gold

This is a parallel to the Class I cards of Topps Gold Label. The veteran cards are serial numbered to 999 and inserted at a rate of 1:13 while the SP cards are serial numbered to 99 and inserted at a rate of 1:883.

	Nm-Mt	Ex-Mt
*STARS: 2.5X TO 6X BASIC CARDS...		
*SP'S: .75X TO 2X BASIC SP'S		

2001 Topps Gold Label Class 2

This is a parallel to the Topps Gold Label set. These cards were issued at a rate of one in seven for the veterans and one in 125 for the rookies. The rookie cards are also serial numbered to 699.

	Nm-Mt	Ex-Mt
*STARS: 1.25X TO 3X CLASS 1..........		
*SP'S: .4X TO 1X CLASS 1 SP'S.........		

2001 Topps Gold Label Class 2 Gold

This is a parallel to the Topps Gold Label set. These cards were issued at a rate of one in 19 for the veterans and one in 1,271 for the rookies. The rookie cards are also serial numbered to 69.

	Nm-Mt	Ex-Mt
*STARS: 3X TO 8X BASIC CLASS 1....		
*SP'S: 1X TO 2.5X BASIC SP'S		

2001 Topps Gold Label Class 3

This is a parallel to the Topps Gold Label set. These cards were issued at a rate of one in 20 for the veterans and one in 292 for the rookies. The rookie cards are also serial numbered to 299.

	Nm-Mt	Ex-Mt
*STARS: 3X TO 8X CLASS 1		
*SP'S: .75X TO 1.5X CLASS 1 SP'S....		

2001 Topps Gold Label Class 3 Gold

This is a parallel to the Topps Gold Label set. These cards were issued at a rate of one in 44 for the veterans and one in 3,051 for the rookies. The veteran cards are serial numbered to 299 whie the rookie cards are also serial numbered to 29.

	Nm-Mt	Ex-Mt
*STARS: 5X TO 12X BASIC CLASS 1..		
*SP'S: 1.25X TO 3X BASIC SP'S		

2001 Topps Gold Label Gold Fixtures

Inserted at a rate of one in 374, these 10 cards feature players who have becomed imbedded into baseball's history.

	Nm-Mt	Ex-Mt
COMPLETE SET (10)	300.00	90.00
GF1 Alex Rodriguez	30.00	9.00
GF2 Mark McGwire	40.00	12.00
GF3 Derek Jeter	40.00	12.00
GF4 Nomar Garciaparra	25.00	7.50
GF5 Chipper Jones	15.00	4.50
GF6 Sammy Sosa	25.00	7.50
GF7 Ken Griffey Jr.	25.00	7.50
GF8 Carlos Delgado	15.00	4.50
GF9 Frank Thomas	15.00	4.50
GF10 Barry Bonds	40.00	12.00

2001 Topps Gold Label MLB Award Ceremony Relics

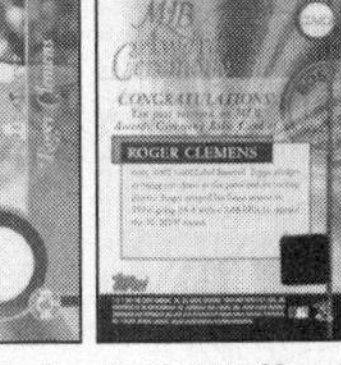

Inserted at a rate of one in 24, these 88 cards feature relics from players who have been recognized as the best in what they do. Relic cards of Mark McGwire and Hideo Nomo highlight this set.

	Nm-Mt	Ex-Mt
AB1 Albert Belle RBI Bat	10.00	3.00
AB2 Albert Belle HR Bat	10.00	3.00
AG1 A.Galarraga BTG Bat	10.00	3.00
AG2 A.Galarraga HR Bat	10.00	3.00
AR A.Rodriguez BTG Bat	20.00	6.00
BB1 Barry Bonds HR Bat	30.00	9.00
BB2 Barry Bonds MVP Jsy	30.00	9.00
BB3 Barry Bonds RBI Bat	30.00	9.00
BG Ben Grieve ROY Jsy	10.00	3.00
BL Barry Larkin MVP Bat	15.00	4.50
BW B. Williams BTG Bat	15.00	4.50
CB Carlos Beltran ROY Bat	10.00	3.00
CJ C. Jones MVP Jsy	15.00	4.50
CK C. Knoblauch ROY Bat	10.00	3.00
CR1 Cal Ripken ROY Jsy	50.00	15.00
CR2 Cal Ripken MVP Jsy	50.00	15.00
DB1 D. Bichette HR Bat	10.00	3.00
DB2 D. Bichette RBI Bat	10.00	3.00
DG Dwight Gooden CY Jsy	15.00	4.50
DJ1 Derek Jeter ROY Bat	30.00	9.00
DJ2 D. Jeter WS MVP Bat	30.00	9.00
DS1 D.Strawberry HR Bat	15.00	4.50
DS2 D.Strawberry ROY Jsy	15.00	4.50
EM1 E.Martinez BTG Bat	15.00	4.50
EM2 E.Martinez RBI Bat	15.00	4.50
FM Fred McGriff HR Bat	15.00	4.50
FT1 F. Thomas BTG Bat	15.00	4.50
FT2 F. Thomas MVP Jsy	15.00	4.50
GM Greg Maddux CY Jsy	15.00	4.50
GS Gary Sheffield BTG Bat	10.00	3.00
HN Hideo Nomo ROY Jsy	40.00	12.00
IR I. Rodriguez MVP Jsy	15.00	4.50
JB1 Jeff Bagwell ROY Bat	15.00	4.50

JB2 Jeff Bagwell MVP Bat 15.00 4.50
JB3 Jeff Bagwell RBI Bat 15.00 4.50
JC1 Jose Canseco HR Bat 15.00 4.50
JC2 J. Canseco MVP Bat 15.00 4.50
JC3 Jose Canseco RBI Bat 15.00 4.50
JC4 J.Canseco ROY Jsy 15.00 4.50
JG Jason Giambi MVP Bat 15.00 4.50
JG1 Juan Gonzalez HR Bat 15.00 4.50
JG2 J. Gonzalez MVP Jsy 15.00 4.50
JG3 J. Gonzalez RBI Bat 15.00 4.50
JK Jeff Kent MVP Bat 10.00 3.00
JO John Olerud BTG Bat 10.00 3.00
JS John Smoltz CY Jsy 15.00 4.50
JW J.Wetteland WS MVP Jsy 10.00 3.00
KG1 K.Griffey Jr. HR Bat 20.00 6.00
KG2 K.Griffey Jr. MVP Jsy 20.00 6.00
KG3 K.Griffey Jr. RBI Bat 20.00 6.00
KS K.Sasaki ROY Jsy 10.00 3.00
LW1 L. Walker BTG Bat 15.00 4.50
LW2 Larry Walker HR Bat 15.00 4.50
LW3 L. Walker MVP Jsy 15.00 4.50
MC M. Cordova ROY Bat 10.00 3.00
MM1 M. McGwire HR Bat 80.00 24.00
MM2 M. McGwire ROY Jsy 80.00 24.00
MP Mike Piazza ROY Bat 15.00 4.50
MV1 Mo Vaughn MVP Jsy 10.00 3.00
MV2 Mo Vaughn RBI Bat 10.00 3.00
MW1 M. Williams HR Bat 10.00 3.00
MW2 M. Williams RBI Bat 10.00 3.00
NG1 N. Garciaparra BTG Bat 20.00 6.00
NG2 N.Garciaparra ROY Jsy 20.00 6.00
PM Pedro Martinez CY Jsy 15.00 4.50
PO Paul O'Neill BTG Bat 15.00 4.50
RC1 R.Clemens CY Jsy 25.00 7.50
RC2 R.Clemens MVP Jsy 25.00 7.50
RF Rafael Furcal ROY Bat 10.00 3.00
RH R.Henderson MVP Jsy 15.00 4.50
RJ Randy Johnson CY Jsy 15.00 4.50
RM R.Mondesi ROY Bat 10.00 3.00
SA Sandy Alomar ROY Bat 10.00 3.00
SB S.Brosius WS MVP Bat 10.00 3.00
SR Scott Rolen ROY Jsy 15.00 4.50
SS1 Sammy Sosa HR Bat 20.00 6.00
SS2 S.Sosa MVP Jsy 20.00 6.00
SS3 Sammy Sosa RBI Bat 20.00 6.00
TG Troy Glaus HR Bat 15.00 4.50
TH1 Todd Helton BTG Bat 15.00 4.50
TH2 Todd Helton RBI Bat 15.00 4.50
TS Tim Salmon ROY Jsy 15.00 4.50
WC Will Clark RBI Bat 15.00 4.50
DJU D. Justice ROY Jsy 10.00 3.00
TGL1 Tom Glavine CY Jsy 15.00 4.50
TGL2 T. Glavine WS MVP Jsy 15.00 4.50
TGW T. Gwynn BTG Bat 15.00 4.50
THO T.Hollandsworth ROY Bat 10.00 3.00

2002 Topps Gold Label

This 200 card set was issued in May, 2002. This set was issued in four card packs which came 18 packs to a box and eight boxes to a case. These packs had an SRP of $3 per pack.

Nm-Mt Ex-Mt
COMPLETE SET (200) 100.00 30.00
1 Alex Rodriguez 2.00 .60
2 Derek Jeter 3.00 .90
3 Luis Gonzalez .50 .15
4 Troy Glaus .75 .23
5 Albert Pujols 2.50 .75
6 Lance Berkman .50 .15
7 J.D. Drew .50 .15
8 Chipper Jones 1.25 .35
9 Miguel Tejada .50 .15
10 Randy Johnson 1.25 .35
11 Mike Cameron .50 .15
12 Brian Giles .50 .15
13 Roger Cedeno .50 .15
14 Kerry Wood 1.25 .35
15 Ken Griffey Jr. 2.00 .60
16 Carlos Lee .50 .15
17 Todd Helton .75 .23
18 Gary Sheffield .50 .15
19 Richie Sexson .50 .15
20 Vladimir Guerrero 1.25 .35
21 Bobby Higginson .50 .15
22 Roger Clemens 2.50 .75
23 Barry Zito .75 .23
24 Juan Pierre .50 .15
25 Pedro Martinez 1.25 .35
26 Sean Casey .50 .15
27 David Segui .50 .15
28 Jose Garcia RC .75 .23
29 Curt Schilling .75 .23
30 Bernie Williams .75 .23
31 Ben Grieve .50 .15
32 Hideo Nomo 1.25 .35
33 Aramis Ramirez .50 .15
34 Cristian Guzman .50 .15
35 Rich Aurilia .50 .15
36 Greg Maddux 2.00 .60
37 Eric Chavez .50 .15
38 Shawn Green .50 .15
39 Luis Rivas .50 .15
40 Maggio Ordonez .50 .15
41 Jose Vidro .50 .15
42 Mariano Rivera .75 .23
43 Chris Tritle RC .75 .23
44 C.C. Sabathia .50 .15
45 Larry Walker .75 .23
46 Raul Mondesi .50 .15
47 Kevin Brown .50 .15
48 Jeff Bagwell .75 .23
49 Earl Snyder RC .75 .23
50 Jason Giambi 1.25 .35
51 Ichiro Suzuki 2.00 .60
52 Andruw Jones .50 .15
53 Ivan Rodriguez 1.25 .35
54 Jim Edmonds .50 .15
55 Preston Wilson .50 .15
56 Greg Vaughn .50 .15
57 Jon Lieber .50 .15
58 Justin Sherrod RC .75 .23
59 Marcus Giles .50 .15
60 Roberto Alomar 1.25 .35
61 Pat Burrell .50 .15
62 Doug Mientkiewicz .50 .15
63 Mark Mulder .50 .15
64 Mike Hampton .50 .15
65 Adam Dunn .50 .15
66 Moises Alou .50 .15
67 Jose Cruz Jr. .50 .15
68 Derek Bell .50 .15
69 Sammy Sosa 2.00 .60
70 Joe Mays .50 .15
71 Phil Nevin .50 .15
72 Edgardo Alfonzo .50 .15
73 Barry Bonds 3.00 .90
74 Edgar Martinez .75 .23
75 Juan Encarnacion .50 .15
76 Jason Tyner .50 .15
77 Edgar Renteria .50 .15
78 Bret Boone .50 .15
79 Scott Rolen .75 .23
80 Nomar Garciaparra 2.00 .60
81 Frank Thomas 1.25 .35
82 Roy Oswalt .50 .15
83 Tsuyoshi Shinjo .50 .15
84 Ben Sheets .50 .15
85 Hank Blalock 1.25 .35
86 Carlos Delgado .50 .15
87 Tim Hudson .50 .15
88 Alfonso Soriano .75 .23
89 Michael Hill RC .75 .23
90 Jim Thome 1.25 .35
91 Craig Biggio .75 .23
92 Ryan Klesko .50 .15
93 Geoff Jenkins .50 .15
94 Matt Morris .50 .15
95 Jorge Posada .75 .23
96 Cliff Floyd .50 .15
97 Jimmy Rollins .50 .15
98 Mike Sweeney .50 .15
99 Frank Catalanotto .50 .15
100 Mike Piazza 2.00 .60
101 Mark Quinn .50 .15
102 Torii Hunter .50 .15
103 Lee Stevens .50 .15
104 Byung-Hyun Kim .50 .15
105 Freddy Sanchez RC .75 .23
106 David Cone .50 .15
107 Jerry Hairston Jr. .50 .15
108 Kyle Farnsworth .50 .15
109 Rafael Furcal .50 .15
110 Bartolo Colon .50 .15
111 Juan Rivera .50 .15
112 Kevin Young .50 .15
113 Chris Narveson RC 1.25 .35
114 Richard Hidalgo .50 .15
115 Andy Pettitte .75 .23
116 Darin Erstad .50 .15
117 Corey Koskie .50 .15
118 So Taguchi RC 1.25 .35
119 Derrek Lee .50 .15
120 Sean Burroughs .50 .15
121 Paul Konerko .50 .15
122 Ross Peeples RC .75 .23
123 Terrence Long .50 .15
124 John Smoltz .75 .23
125 Brandon Duckworth .50 .15
126 Luis Maza .50 .15
127 Morgan Ensberg .50 .15
128 Eric Valent .50 .15
129 Shannon Stewart .50 .15
130 D'Angelo Jimenez .50 .15
131 Jeff Cirillo .50 .15
132 Jack Cust .50 .15
133 Dmitri Young .50 .15
134 Darryl Kile .50 .15
135 Reggie Sanders .50 .15
136 Marlon Byrd .50 .15
137 Napoleon Calzado RC .75 .23
138 Javy Lopez .50 .15
139 Orlando Cabrera .50 .15
140 Mike Mussina 1.25 .35
141 Josh Beckett .75 .23
142 Kazuhiro Sasaki .50 .15
143 Jermaine Dye .50 .15
144 Carlos Beltran .50 .15
145 Trevor Hoffman .50 .15
146 Kazuhisa Ishii RC 3.00 .90
147 Alex Gonzalez .50 .15
148 Marty Cordova .50 .15
149 Kevin Deaton RC .75 .23
150 Toby Hall .50 .15
151 Rafael Palmeiro .75 .23
152 John Olerud .50 .15
153 David Eckstein .50 .15
154 Doug Glanville .50 .15
155 Johnny Damon .50 .15
156 Javier Vazquez .50 .15
157 Jason Bay RC 3.00 .90
158 Robb Nen .50 .15
159 Rafael Soriano .50 .15
160 Placido Polanco .50 .15
161 Garret Anderson .50 .15
162 Aaron Boone .50 .15
163 Mike Lieberthal .50 .15
164 Joe Mauer RC 8.00 2.40
165 Matt Lawton .50 .15
166 Juan Tolentino RC .75 .23
167 Alex Gonzalez .50 .15
168 Steve Finley .50 .15
169 Troy Percival .50 .15
170 Bud Smith .50 .15
171 Freddy Garcia .50 .15
172 Ray Lankford .50 .15
173 Tim Redding .50 .15
174 Ryan Dempster .50 .15
175 Travis Lee .50 .15
176 Jeff Kent .50 .15
177 Ramon Hernandez .50 .15
178 Carl Everett .50 .15
179 Tom Glavine .75 .23
180 Juan Gonzalez 1.25 .35
181 Nick Johnson .50 .15
182 Mike Lowell .50 .15
183 Al Leiter .50 .15
184 Jason Maule RC .75 .23
185 Wilson Betemit .50 .15
186 Tino Martinez .75 .23
187 Jason Standridge .50 .15
188 Mike Peeples RC .75 .23
189 Jason Kendall .50 .15
190 Fred McGriff .75 .23
191 John Rodriguez RC .75 .23
192 Brett Roneberg RC .75 .23
193 Marlyn Tisdale RC .75 .23
194 J.T. Snow .50 .15
195 Craig Kuzmic RC .75 .23
196 Cory Lidle .50 .15
197 Alex Cintron .50 .15
198 Fernando Vina .50 .15
199 Austin Kearns .50 .15
200 Paul LoDuca .50 .15

2002 Topps Gold Label Class 1 Gold

Inserted in packs at a stated rate of one in seven these cards parallel the Class 1 set. They are printed to a stated print run of 500 serial numbered sets.

Nm-Mt Ex-Mt
*CLASS 1 GOLD: 2.5X TO 6X BASIC...
*CLASS 1 GOLD RC'S: 1X TO 2.5X BASIC

2002 Topps Gold Label Class 2 Platinum

Inserted in packs at a stated rate of one in 13 these cards parallel the Class 1 set. They are printed to a stated print run of 250 serial numbered sets.

Nm-Mt Ex-Mt
*CLASS 2 PLAT: 4X TO 10X BASIC ....
*CLASS 2 PLAT RC'S: 1.5X TO 4X BASIC

2002 Topps Gold Label Class 3 Titanium

Inserted in packs at a stated rate of one in 33 these cards parallel the Class 1 set. They are printed to a stated print run of 100 serial numbered sets.

Nm-Mt Ex-Mt
*CLASS 3 TITAN: 6X TO 15X BASIC ...
*CLASS 3 TITAN RC'S: 2.5X TO 6X BASIC

2002 Topps Gold Label Major League Moments Relics Gold

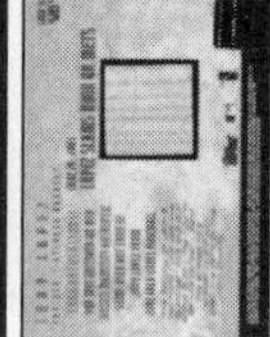

Inserted at a stated rate of one in 245 hobby, 1:678 retail for bats and one in 306 hobby, 1:844 retail for jerseys, these cards feature current players and honoring their shining baseball moment.

Nm-Mt Ex-Mt
*PLATINUM BAT: .6X TO 1.5X BASIC BAT
*PLATINUM JSY: .5X TO 1.2X BASIC JSY
PLATINUM BAT ODDS 1:613 H, 1:1707 R
PLATINUM JSY ODDS 1:460 H, 1:1280: R
*TITANIUM BAT: 1X TO 2.5X BASIC BAT
*TITANIUM JSY: .75X TO 2X BASIC JSY
TITANIUM BAT ODDS 1:1228 H, 1:3435 R
TITANIUM JSY ODDS 1:920 H, 1:2560 R
AR Alex Rodriguez Bat 20.00 6.00
BB1 Bret Boone Bat 10.00 3.00
BB2 Bret Boone Jsy 10.00 3.00
BLB Barry Bonds Jsy 25.00 7.50
CD Carlos Delgado Bat 10.00 3.00
CL Carlos Lee Bat 10.00 3.00
JL Javy Lopez Bat 10.00 3.00
MO Magglio Ordonez Bat 10.00 3.00
RP1 Rafael Palmeiro Bat 15.00 4.50
RP2 Rafael Palmeiro Bat 15.00 4.50
TG Tony Gwynn Jsy 15.00 4.50
TH Toby Hall Bat 10.00 3.00

2002 Topps Gold Label MLB Awards Ceremony Relics Gold

Inserted at a stated rate of one in 32 for Bat cards and one in 38 for Jersey cards, these 94 cards feature a mix of active and retired stars who won an major award during their career.

Nm-Mt Ex-Mt
*PLATINUM BAT: .6X TO 1.5X GOLD BAT
*PLATINUM JSY: .5X TO 1.2X GOLD JSY
PLATINUM BAT ODDS 1:79 HOB, 1:217 RET
PLATINUM JSY ODDS 1:57 HOB, 1:159 RET
*TITANIUM BAT: 1X TO 2.5X GOLD BAT
*TITANIUM JSY: .75X TO 2X GOLD JSY
TITANIUM BAT ODDS 1:158 HOB, 1:435 RET
TITANIUM JSY ODDS 1:115 HOB, 1:317 RET
AB Al Bumbry ROY Bat 10.00 3.00
AEP Andy Pettitte LC MVP Jsy 15.00 4.50
AO Al Oliver RBI Bat 10.00 3.00
AP Albert Pujols ROY Bat 20.00 6.00
AR Alex Rodriguez HR Bat 15.00 4.50
BB Bill Buckner BTG Jsy 10.00 3.00
BB1 Barry Bonds MVP Uni 25.00 7.50
BB2 Barry Bonds HR Uni 25.00 7.50
BFW B.Williams LC MVP Jsy 15.00 4.50
BLB Barry Bonds AS MVP Bat 10.00 3.00
BM1 Bill Madlock AS MVP Jsy 10.00 3.00
BM2 Bill Madlock BTG Bat 10.00 3.00
BR Brooks Robinson MVP Bat 15.00 4.50
BRB Bret Boone RBI Bat 10.00 3.00
BRB2 Bret Boone RBI Bat 10.00 3.00
BS Bret Saberhagen CY Jsy 10.00 3.00
BW Billy Williams ROY Bat 10.00 3.00
CC Craig Counsell LC MVP Bat 10.00 3.00
CF Carlton Fisk ROY Bat 15.00 4.50
CY1 Carl Yastrzemski MVP Bat 40.00 12.00
CY2 Carl Yastrzemski BTG Bat 40.00 12.00
DA Dick Allen ROY Bat 15.00 4.50
DB Don Baylor MVP Bat 10.00 3.00
DC D.Concepcion AS MVP Bat 10.00 3.00
DE Dennis Eckersley CY Jsy 10.00 3.00
DJ David Justice ROY Bat 10.00 3.00
DM Don Mattingly MVP Bat 50.00 15.00
DM1 Dale Murphy MVP Bat
DM2 Dale Murphy HR Bat
DP1 Dave Parker MVP Bat 15.00 4.50
DP2 Dave Parker RBI Bat 15.00 4.50
DP3 Dave Parker AS MVP Bat 15.00 4.50
DP4 Dave Parker BTG Bat 15.00 4.50
DS1 Darryl Strawberry HR Bat 15.00 4.50
DS2 Darryl Strawberry ROY Bat 15.00 4.50
DW Dave Winfield RBI Bat 10.00 3.00
EB Ernie Banks MVP Jacket 25.00 7.50
EM1 Eddie Murray RBI Uni 15.00 4.50
EM2 Eddie Murray ROY Bat 15.00 4.50
FM Fred McGriff AS MVP Bat 15.00 4.50
FR Frank Robinson MVP Bat 15.00 4.50
FV Fernando Valenzuela ROY Bat 10.00 3.00
FW Frank White LC MVP Jsy 10.00 3.00
GB1 George Brett MVP Bat 40.00 12.00
GB2 George Brett LC MVP Bat 40.00 12.00
GC Gary Carter RBI Bat 15.00 4.50
GF George Foster HR Bat 10.00 3.00
GL Greg Luzinski RBI Bat 10.00 3.00
HS Hank Sauer MVP Bat 10.00 3.00
JB Johnny Bench WS MVP Bat 15.00 4.50
JL Javy Lopez LC MVP Jsy 10.00 3.00
JM Joe Morgan MVP Bat 10.00 3.00
JS John Smoltz CY Jsy 15.00 4.50
JT Joe Torre MVP Uni 15.00 4.50
KG Ken Griffey Sr. AS MVP Bat 10.00 3.00
KH Keith Hernandez MVP Bat 15.00 4.50
KHG Kirk Gibson MVP Bat 10.00 3.00
KM1 Kevin Mitchell MVP Bat 10.00 3.00
KM2 Kevin Mitchell HR Bat 10.00 3.00
KP1 Kirby Puckett LC MVP Jsy 15.00 4.50
KP2 Kirby Puckett AS MVP Bat 15.00 4.50
KP3 Kirby Puckett BTG Bat 15.00 4.50
LP Lou Piniella ROY Bat 10.00 3.00
LW Larry Walker BTG Bat 15.00 4.50
MH Mike Hargrove ROY Bat 10.00 3.00
MP Mike Piazza AS MVP Bat 15.00 4.50
MR M.Rivera WS MVP Jsy 15.00 4.50
MW Maury Wills MVP Jsy 10.00 3.00
NC Norm Cash BTG Bat 25.00 7.50
PM Paul Molitor WS MVP Bat 15.00 4.50
RA Roberto Alomar AS MVP Bat 15.00 4.50
RAC Rico Carty BTG Bat 10.00 3.00
RCC Ron Cey WS MVP Bat 10.00 3.00
RC1 Rod Carew ROY Bat 15.00 4.50
RC2 Rod Carew BTG Bat 15.00 4.50
RH R Henderson LC MVP Jsy 15.00 4.50
RJ Randy Johnson CY Jsy 15.00 4.50
RJ1 Reggie Jackson MVP Bat 15.00 4.50
RJ2 R.Jackson WS MVP Bat 15.00 4.50
RS Ryne Sandberg MVP Bat
RWC Roger Clemens CY Uni 25.00 7.50
RY Robin Yount MVP Bat 25.00 7.50
SA Sandy Alomar AS MVP Bat 10.00 3.00
SG1 Steve Garvey MVP Uni 15.00 4.50
SG2 Steve Garvey AS MVP Bat 15.00 4.50
TG1 Tony Gwynn BTG Bat 15.00 4.50
TG2 Tony Gwynn BTG Jsy 15.00 4.50
TK2 Ted Kluszewski HR Bat 15.00 4.50
TP Tony Perez AS MVP Bat 10.00 3.00
TR Tim Raines AS MVP Bat 10.00 3.00
WB Wade Boggs BTG Bat 15.00 4.50
WC Will Clark LC MVP Bat 15.00 4.50
WS Willie Stargell MVP Bat 15.00 4.50
YB Yogi Berra MVP Jsy 15.00 4.50

2000 Topps HD

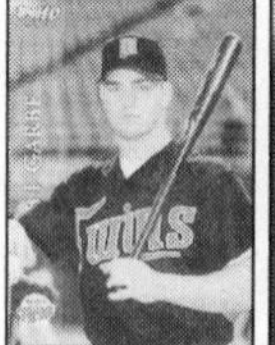

This 100-card set was issued in four card packs with a SRP of $3.99 per pack. This set was issued on 50 point card stock and has hyper-color technology. Cards numbered from 89 through 100 features rookie players. Notable Rookie Cards include Bobby Bradley.

Nm-Mt Ex-Mt
COMPLETE SET (100) 50.00 15.00
1 Derek Jeter 4.00 1.20
2 Andruw Jones .60 .18
3 Ben Grieve .60 .18
4 Carlos Beltran .60 .18
5 Randy Johnson 1.50 .45
6 Javy Lopez .60 .18
7 Gary Sheffield .60 .18
8 John Olerud .60 .18
9 Vinny Castilla .60 .18
10 Barry Larkin 1.50 .45
11 Tony Clark .60 .18
12 Roberto Alomar 1.50 .45
13 Brian Jordan .60 .18
14 Wade Boggs 1.00 .30
15 Carlos Febles .60 .18
16 Alfonso Soriano 1.50 .45
17 A.J. Burnett .60 .18
18 Matt Williams .60 .18
19 Alex Gonzalez .60 .18
20 Larry Walker 1.00 .30
21 Jeff Bagwell 1.00 .30
22 Al Leiter .60 .18
23 Ken Griffey Jr. 2.50 .75
24 Ruben Mateo .60 .18
25 Mark Grace 1.00 .30
26 Carlos Delgado .60 .18
27 Vladimir Guerrero 1.50 .45
28 Kenny Lofton .60 .18
29 Rusty Greer .60 .18
30 Pedro Martinez 1.50 .45
31 Todd Helton 1.00 .30
32 Ray Lankford .60 .18
33 Jose Canseco 1.50 .45
34 Raul Mondesi .60 .18
35 Mo Vaughn .60 .18
36 Eric Chavez .60 .18
37 Manny Ramirez .60 .18
38 Jason Kendall .60 .18
39 Mike Mussina 1.50 .45
40 Dante Bichette .60 .18
41 Troy Glaus 1.00 .30
42 Rickey Henderson 1.50 .45
43 Pablo Ozuna .60 .18
44 Michael Barrett .60 .18
45 Tony Gwynn 2.00 .60
46 John Smoltz 1.00 .30
47 Rafael Palmeiro 1.00 .30
48 Curt Schilling 1.00 .30
49 Todd Walker .60 .18
50 Greg Vaughn .60 .18
51 Orlando Hernandez .60 .18
52 Jim Thome 1.50 .45
53 Pat Burrell 1.00 .30
54 Tim Salmon 1.00 .30
55 Tom Glavine 1.00 .30
56 Travis Lee .60 .18
57 Gabe Kapler .60 .18
58 Greg Maddux 2.50 .75
59 Scott Rolen 1.00 .30
60 Cal Ripken 5.00 1.50
61 Preston Wilson .60 .18
62 Ivan Rodriguez 1.50 .45
63 Johnny Damon .60 .18
64 Bernie Williams 1.00 .30
65 Barry Bonds 4.00 1.20
66 Sammy Sosa 2.50 .75
67 Robin Ventura 1.00 .30
68 Tony Fernandez .60 .18
69 Jay Bell .60 .18
70 Mark McGwire 4.00 1.20
71 Jeromy Burnitz .60 .18
72 Chipper Jones 1.50 .45
73 Josh Hamilton .60 .18
74 Darin Erstad .60 .18
75 Alex Rodriguez 2.50 .75
76 Sean Casey .60 .18
77 Tino Martinez 1.00 .30
78 Juan Gonzalez 1.50 .45
79 Cliff Floyd .60 .18
80 Craig Biggio 1.00 .30
81 Shawn Green .60 .18
82 Adrian Beltre .60 .18
83 Mike Piazza 2.50 .75
84 Nomar Garciaparra 2.50 .75
85 Kevin Brown 1.00 .30
86 Roger Clemens 3.00 .90
87 Frank Thomas 1.50 .45
88 Albert Belle .60 .18
89 Erubiel Durazo .60 .18
90 David Walling .60 .18
91 John Sneed RC .60 .18
92 Larry Bigbie RC 1.50 .45
93 B.J. Garbe RC 1.00 .30
94 Bobby Bradley RC 1.00 .30
95 Ryan Christianson RC 1.00 .30
96 Jay Gehrke .60 .18
97 Jason Stumm RC 1.00 .30
98 Brett Myers RC 5.00 1.50
99 Chance Caple RC 1.00 .30
100 Corey Myers RC 1.00 .30

2000 Topps HD Platinum

This set is a parallel to the regular Topps HD set. The cards, inserted into packs at a rate of one in 44, are treated with platinum metallic ink and are serial numbered to 99.

Nm-Mt Ex-Mt
*STARS: 8X TO 20X BASIC CARDS ....
*ROOKIES: 4X TO 10X BASIC CARDS

2000 Topps HD Autographs

Inserted into the HD packs were autographs of Derek Jeter and an exchange card for Cal Ripken. The Jeter cards were inserted one every 859 packs and the Ripken exchange cards were inserted one every 4386 packs. The deadline for the Ripken exchange card was June 30th, 2000.

Nm-Mt Ex-Mt
HDA1 Derek Jeter 120.00 36.00
HDA2 Cal Ripken 300.00 90.00

2000 Topps HD Ballpark Figures

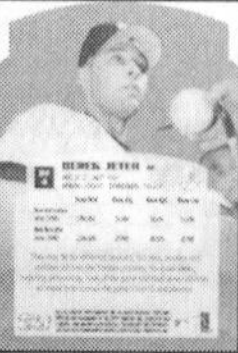

Inserted one every 11 packs, these 10 cards feature collector favorites. These cards are printed on a high definition stock and feature a baseball field-designed die cut.

	Nm-Mt	Ex-Mt
COMPLETE SET (10)	60.00	18.00
BF1 Mark McGwire	10.00	3.00
BF2 Ken Griffey Jr.	6.00	1.80
BF3 Nomar Garciaparra	6.00	1.80
BF4 Derek Jeter	10.00	3.00
BF5 Sammy Sosa	6.00	1.80
BF6 Mike Piazza	6.00	1.80
BF7 Juan Gonzalez	4.00	1.20
BF8 Larry Walker	2.50	.75
BF9 Ben Grieve	1.50	.45
BF10 Barry Bonds	10.00	3.00

2000 Topps HD Clearly Refined

Inserted one every 20 packs, this 10 card set features rising prospects who are expected to make an impact in the majors during the 2000 season.

	Nm-Mt	Ex-Mt
COMPLETE SET (10)	25.00	7.50
CR1 Alfonso Soriano	6.00	1.80
CR2 Ruben Mateo	2.50	.75
CR3 Josh Hamilton	2.50	.75
CR4 Chad Hermansen	2.50	.75
CR5 Ryan Anderson	6.00	1.80
CR6 Nick Johnson	2.50	.75
CR7 Octavio Dotel	2.50	.75
CR8 Peter Bergeron	2.50	.75
CR9 Adam Piatt	2.50	.75
CR10 Pat Burrell	4.00	1.20

2000 Topps HD Image

Inserted one every 10 packs, this 10-card set features players who are known for their hitting.

	Nm-Mt	Ex-Mt
COMPLETE SET (10)	150.00	45.00
HDI1 Sammy Sosa	15.00	4.50
HDI2 Mark McGwire	25.00	7.50
HDI3 Derek Jeter	25.00	7.50
HDI4 Albert Belle	4.00	1.20
HDI5 Vladimir Guerrero	10.00	3.00
HDI6 Ken Griffey Jr.	15.00	4.50
HDI7 Mike Piazza	15.00	4.50
HDI8 Alex Rodriguez	15.00	4.50
HDI9 Barry Bonds	25.00	7.50
HDI10 Nomar Garciaparra	15.00	4.50

2000 Topps HD On the Cutting Edge

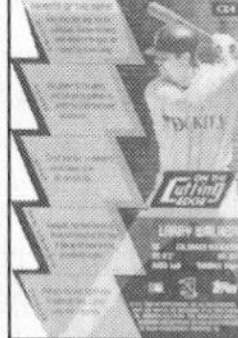

inserted one every 22 packs, this 10-card set feature players who are considered to have all five tools needed for superstardom. The cards are intricately die-cut and the corners are very sharp when pulled from the packs.

	Nm-Mt	Ex-Mt
COMPLETE SET (10)	100.00	30.00
CE1 Andruw Jones	2.50	.75
CE2 Nomar Garciaparra	10.00	3.00
CE3 Barry Bonds	15.00	4.50
CE4 Larry Walker	4.00	1.20
CE5 Vladimir Guerrero	6.00	1.80
CE6 Jeff Bagwell	4.00	1.20
CE7 Derek Jeter	15.00	4.50
CE8 Sammy Sosa	10.00	3.00
CE9 Alex Rodriguez	10.00	3.00
CE10 Ken Griffey Jr.	10.00	3.00

2001 Topps HD

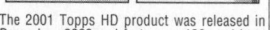

The 2001 Topps HD product was released in December, 2000 and features a 120-card base set. The base set is broken into tiers as follows: Base Veterans and Rookies (1-100), and a Superstar subset (101-120) that was inserted at one in sx packs. Each pack contained four-cards and carried a suggested retail price of $3.99.

	Nm-Mt	Ex-Mt
COMPLETE SET (120)	200.00	60.00
COMP.SET w/o SP's (100)	80.00	24.00
COMMON CARD (1-100)	.60	.18
COMMON (101-120)	3.00	.90
1 Derek Jeter	4.00	1.20
2 Magglio Ordonez	.60	.18
3 Eric Munson	.60	.18
4 Jermaine Dye	.60	.18
5 Larry Walker	1.00	.30
6 Pokey Reese	.60	.18
7 Pedro Martinez	1.50	.45
8 Rafael Palmeiro	1.00	.30
9 Jason Kendall	.60	.18
10 Mike Lieberthal	.60	.18
11 Ryan Klesko	.60	.18
12 Cal Ripken	5.00	1.50
13 Mike Piazza	2.50	.75
14 Adam Sterrett RC	.60	.18
15 John Olerud	.60	.18
16 Manny Ramirez	.60	.18
17 Chad Petty RC	.60	.18
18 Vladimir Guerrero	1.50	.45
19 Kevin Brown	.60	.18
20 Luis Cotto RC	.60	.18
21 Josh Hamilton	.60	.18
22 Mark Grace	1.00	.30
23 Mark McGwire	4.00	1.20
24 Jeromy Burnitz	.60	.18
25 Andruw Jones	.60	.18
26 Raul Mondesi	.60	.18
27 Stuart McFarland RC	.60	.18
28 Craig Biggio	1.00	.30
29 Troy Glaus	1.00	.30
30 Carlos Delgado	.60	.18
31 Rafael Furcal	.60	.18
32 J.D. Drew	.60	.18
33 Corey Patterson	.60	.18
34 Gary Sheffield	.60	.18
35 Jeff Kent	.60	.18
36 Alex Rodriguez	2.50	.75
37 Edgardo Alfonzo	.60	.18
38 Jeff Segar RC	.60	.18
39 Bob Abreu	.60	.18
40 Brian Giles	.60	.18
41 Jason Smith RC	.60	.18
42 Mo Vaughn	.60	.18
43 Pat Burrell	.60	.18
44 Barry Larkin	1.50	.45
45 Carlos Beltran	.60	.18
46 Eric Mosley RC	.60	.18
47 Alfonso Soriano	1.00	.30
48 Tim Salmon	1.00	.30
49 Jason Giambi	1.50	.45
50 Greg Maddux	2.50	.75
51 Randy Johnson	1.50	.45
52 Jose Vidro	.60	.18
53 Edgar Martinez	1.00	.30
54 Albert Belle	.60	.18
55 Ivan Rodriguez	1.50	.45
56 Sean Casey	.60	.18
57 Jorge Posada	1.00	.30
58 Preston Wilson	.60	.18
59 Paul Konerko	.60	.18
60 Todd Helton	1.00	.30
61 Dominic Rich RC	.60	.18
62 Tony Gwynn	2.00	.60
63 Bernie Williams	1.00	.30
64 Anthony Brewer RC	.60	.18
65 Shawn Green	.60	.18
66 Jeff Bagwell	1.00	.30
67 Jose Cruz Jr.	.60	.18
68 Darin Erstad	.60	.18
69 Jim Edmonds	.60	.18
70 Frank Thomas	1.50	.45
71 Ryan Anderson	.60	.18
72 Scott Rolen	1.00	.30
73 Jeff Cirillo	.60	.18
74 Chris Bass RC	.60	.18
75 William Smith RC	.60	.18
76 Trot Nixon	1.00	.30
77 Bobby Bradley	.60	.18
78 Odannis Ayala RC	.60	.18
79 Jim Thome	1.50	.45
80 Sammy Sosa	2.50	.75
81 Geoff Jenkins	.60	.18
82 Ben Grieve	.60	.18
83 Andres Galarraga	.60	.18
84 Rick Ankiel	.60	.18
85 Barry Bonds	4.00	1.20
86 Alex Gonzalez	.60	.18
87 Sean Burroughs	.60	.18
88 Nomar Garciaparra	2.50	.75
89 Ken Griffey Jr.	2.50	.75
90 Tim Hudson	.60	.18
91 Chipper Jones	1.50	.45
92 Matt Williams	.60	.18
93 Roberto Alomar	1.50	.45
94 Adrian Gonzalez	.60	.18
95 Juan Gonzalez	1.50	.45
96 Brian Bass RC	.60	.18
97 Rick Brosseau RC	.60	.18
98 Mariano Rivera	1.00	.30
99 James Baldwin	.60	.18
100 Dean Palmer	.60	.18
101 Pedro Martinez SS	3.00	.90
102 Randy Johnson SS	3.00	.90
103 Greg Maddux SS	6.00	1.80
104 Sammy Sosa SS	6.00	1.80
105 Mark McGwire SS	10.00	3.00
106 Ivan Rodriguez SS	3.00	.90
107 Mike Piazza SS	6.00	1.80
108 Chipper Jones SS	3.00	.90
109 Vladimir Guerrero SS	3.00	.90
110 Alex Rodriguez SS	6.00	1.80
111 Ken Griffey Jr. SS	6.00	1.80
112 Cal Ripken SS	12.00	3.60
113 Derek Jeter SS	10.00	3.00
114 Barry Bonds SS	10.00	3.00
115 N.Garciaparra SS	6.00	1.80
116 Jeff Bagwell SS	1.00	.30
117 Todd Helton SS	3.00	.90
118 Darin Erstad SS	3.00	.90
119 Shawn Green SS	3.00	.90
120 Roberto Alomar SS	3.00	.90

2001 Topps HD Platinum

Randomly seeded at a rate of 1:18, these Platinum cards parallel the base HD set. Each Platinum parallel features an upgraded Chromium coating on the card front. In addition, each card is serial numbered to 199.

Nm-Mt Ex-Mt

*STARS 1-100: 4X TO 10X BASIC CARDS
*YNG.STARS 1-100: 4X TO 10X BASIC CARDS
*ROOKIES 1-100: 2X TO 5X BASIC CARDS
*SS 101-120: 1.5X TO 4X BASIC CARDS

2001 Topps HD 20-20

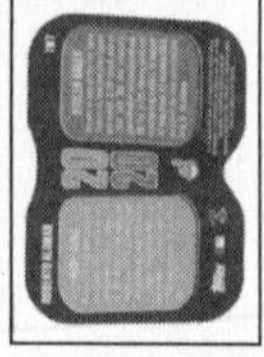

Randomly inserted into packs at one in 12, this 10-card insert features players that are capable of hitting 20 homeruns and stealing 20 bases in the same season. Card backs carry a "TW" prefix.

	Nm-Mt	Ex-Mt
COMPLETE SET (10)	30.00	9.00
TW1 Barry Bonds	6.00	1.80
TW2 Chipper Jones	2.50	.75
TW3 Ken Griffey Jr.	4.00	1.20
TW4 Alex Rodriguez	4.00	1.20
TW5 Ivan Rodriguez	2.50	.75
TW6 Sammy Sosa	4.00	1.20
TW7 Roberto Alomar	2.50	.75
TW8 Larry Walker	1.50	.45
TW9 Shawn Green	1.50	.45
TW10 Jeff Bagwell	1.50	.45

2001 Topps HD Clear Autographs

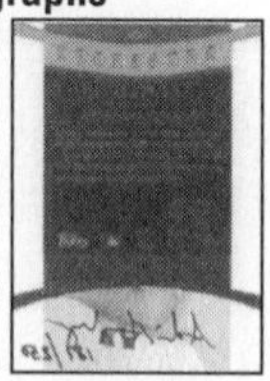

Randomly inserted into packs at one in 431, this four-card set features authentic autographs from some of the hottest young players in the Major Leagues. Please note that these cards are clear. Card backs carry a "HDA" prefix. Please note that Todd Helton packed out as an exchange card and must have been redeemed by 12/31/01.

	Nm-Mt	Ex-Mt
HDA1 Todd Helton	40.00	12.00
HDA2 Rick Ankiel	25.00	7.50
HDA3 Mark Quinn	25.00	7.50
HDA4 Adrian Gonzalez	25.00	7.50

2001 Topps HD Clear Jerseys

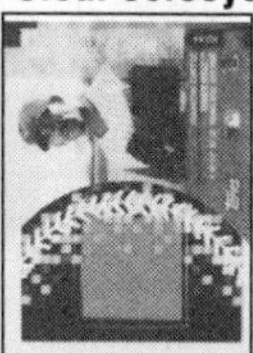

Randomly inserted into packs at one in 108, this eight-card set features authentic game-used jersey swatches from some of the hottest young players in the Major Leagues. Please note that these cards are clear. Card backs carry a "HDCR" prefix. Please note that Ramon Hernandez and Jay Payton both packed out as exchange cards with a redemption deadline of 12/31/01.

	Nm-Mt	Ex-Mt
HDCR1 Grant Roberts	10.00	3.00
HDCR2 Vernon Wells	15.00	4.50
HDCR3 Travis Dawkins	10.00	3.00
HDCR4 Ramon Ortiz	10.00	3.00
HDCR5 Steve Finley	15.00	4.50
HDCR6 Ramon Hernandez	10.00	3.00
HDCR7 Jay Payton	10.00	3.00
HDCR8 Jeromy Burnitz	15.00	4.50

2001 Topps HD Game Defined

Randomly inserted into packs at one in 24, this 10-card insert features players that define how the game is played. Card backs carry a "GD" prefix.

	Nm-Mt	Ex-Mt
COMPLETE SET (10)	80.00	24.00
*ALUMINUM: .75X TO 2X BASIC GAME.DEF		
ALUMINUM STATED ODDS 1:72		
GD1 Ken Griffey Jr.	8.00	2.40
GD2 Derek Jeter	12.00	3.60
GD3 Sammy Sosa	8.00	2.40
GD4 Mark McGwire	12.00	3.60
GD5 Todd Helton	5.00	1.50
GD6 Mike Piazza	8.00	2.40
GD7 Chipper Jones	5.00	1.50
GD8 Vladimir Guerrero	5.00	1.50
GD9 Alex Rodriguez	8.00	2.40
GD10 Nomar Garciaparra	8.00	2.40

2001 Topps HD Images of Excellence

Randomly inserted into packs at one in eight, this 10-card insert features Hall of Fame players from the past. Card backs carry an "IE" prefix.

	Nm-Mt	Ex-Mt
COMPLETE SET (10)	60.00	18.00
*ALUMINUM: .75X TO 2X BASIC IMAGES		
ALUMINUM STATED ODDS 1:24		
IE1 Willie Mays	8.00	2.40
IE2 Reggie Jackson	5.00	1.50
IE3 Ernie Banks	5.00	1.50
IE4 Hank Aaron	10.00	3.00
IE5 Ted Williams	12.00	3.60
IE6 Mike Schmidt	10.00	3.00
IE7 Tom Seaver	5.00	1.50
IE8 Johnny Bench	5.00	1.50
IE9 George Brett	12.00	3.60
IE10 Nolan Ryan	12.00	3.60

2001 Topps Heritage Pre-Production

This three-card set was released prior to the release of 2001 Topps Heritage to dealers and members of the hobby media. The three cards packed out with the media release in a three-card cello pack. Please note that these cards carry a "PP" prefix.

	Nm-Mt	Ex-Mt
COMPLETE SET (3)	4.00	1.20
PP1 Kevin Brown	1.00	.30
PP2 Andres Galarraga	1.00	.30
PP3 Roger Clemens	2.50	.75

2001 Topps Heritage

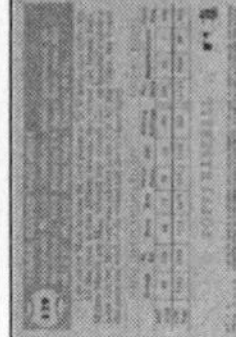

The 2001 Topps Heritage product was released in February 2001. Each pack contained eight cards and carried a $1.99 SRP. The base set features 407 cards. Please note that all low series cards 1-80, feature both red and black back variations and are in shorter supply than mid-series cards 81-310. Also, high series cards 311-407 are short-printed with an announced seeding ratio of 1:2 packs. Finally, the following mid-series cards were erroneously printed exclusively in black back format: 103, 159, 171, 176, 179, 188, 201, 212, 224 and 241. All told, a master set of all red and black variations consists of 487-cards (397 red backs and 90 black backs). Most collectors in pursuit of a 407-card complete set typically intermingle red and black back cards.

	Nm-Mt	Ex-Mt
COMP.MASTER SET (487)	400.00	120.00
COMPLETE SET (407)	300.00	90.00
COMP.SET w/o SP's (230)	60.00	18.00
COMMON CARD (81-310)	.50	.15
COMMON CARD (1-80)	2.50	.75
COMMON (311-407)	5.00	1.50
1 Kris Benson	2.50	.75
1 Kris Benson Black	2.50	.75
2 Brian Jordan	2.50	.75
2 Brian Jordan Black	2.50	.75
3 Fernando Vina	2.50	.75
3 Fernando Vina Black	2.50	.75
4 Mike Sweeney	2.50	.75
4 Mike Sweeney Black	2.50	.75
5 Rafael Palmeiro	2.50	.75
5 Rafael Palmeiro Black	2.50	.75
6 Paul O'Neill	2.50	.75
6 Paul O'Neill Black	2.50	.75
7 Todd Helton	2.50	.75
7 Todd Helton Black	2.50	.75
8 Ramiro Mendoza	2.50	.75
8 Ramiro Mendoza Black	2.50	.75
9 Kevin Millwood	2.50	.75
9 Kevin Millwood Black	2.50	.75
10 Chuck Knoblauch	2.50	.75
10 Chuck Knoblauch Black	2.50	.75
11 Derek Jeter	10.00	3.00
11 Derek Jeter Black	10.00	3.00
12 A.Rodriguez Rangers	6.00	1.80
12 A.Rod Black Rangers	6.00	1.80
13 Geoff Jenkins	2.50	.75
13 Geoff Jenkins Black	2.50	.75
14 David Justice	2.50	.75
14 David Justice Black	2.50	.75
15 David Cone	2.50	.75
15 David Cone Black	2.50	.75
16 Andres Galarraga	2.50	.75
16 Andres Galarraga Black	2.50	.75
17 Garret Anderson	2.50	.75
17 Garret Anderson Black	2.50	.75
18 Roger Cedeno	2.50	.75
18 Roger Cedeno Black	2.50	.75
19 Randy Velarde	2.50	.75
19 Randy Velarde Black	2.50	.75
20 Carlos Delgado	2.50	.75
20 Carlos Delgado Black	2.50	.75
21 Quilvio Veras	2.50	.75
21 Quilvio Veras Black	2.50	.75
22 Jose Vidro	2.50	.75
22 Jose Vidro Black	2.50	.75
23 Corey Patterson	2.50	.75
23 Corey Patterson Black	2.50	.75
24 Jorge Posada	2.50	.75
24 Jorge Posada Black	2.50	.75
25 Eddie Perez	2.50	.75
25 Eddie Perez Black	2.50	.75
26 Jack Cust	2.50	.75
26 Jack Cust Black	2.50	.75
27 Sean Burroughs	2.50	.75
27 Sean Burroughs Black	2.50	.75
28 Randy Wolf	2.50	.75
28 Randy Wolf Black	2.50	.75
29 Mike Lamb	2.50	.75
29 Mike Lamb Black	2.50	.75
30 Rafael Furcal	2.50	.75
30 Rafael Furcal Black	2.50	.75
31 Barry Bonds	10.00	3.00
31 Barry Bonds Black	10.00	3.00
32 Tim Hudson	2.50	.75
32 Tim Hudson Black	2.50	.75
33 Tom Glavine	2.50	.75
33 Tom Glavine Black	2.50	.75
34 Javy Lopez	2.50	.75
34 Javy Lopez Black	2.50	.75
35 Aubrey Huff	2.50	.75
35 Aubrey Huff Black	2.50	.75
36 Wally Joyner	2.50	.75
36 Wally Joyner Black	2.50	.75
37 Magglio Ordonez	2.50	.75
37 Magglio Ordonez Black	2.50	.75
38 Matt Lawton	2.50	.75
38 Matt Lawton Black	2.50	.75
39 Mariano Rivera	2.50	.75
39 Mariano Rivera Black	2.50	.75
40 Andy Ashby	2.50	.75
40 Andy Ashby Black	2.50	.75
41 Mark Buehrle	2.50	.75
41 Mark Buehrle Black	2.50	.75
42 Esteban Loaiza	2.50	.75
42 Esteban Loaiza Black	2.50	.75
43 Mark Redman	2.50	.75
43 Mark Redman Black	2.50	.75
44 Mark Quinn	2.50	.75
44 Mark Quinn Black	2.50	.75
45 Tino Martinez	2.50	.75
45 Tino Martinez Black	2.50	.75
46 Joe Mays	2.50	.75
46 Joe Mays Black	2.50	.75
47 Walt Weiss	2.50	.75
47 Walt Weiss Black	2.50	.75
48 Roger Clemens	8.00	2.40
48 Roger Clemens Black	8.00	2.40
49 Greg Maddux	6.00	1.80
49 Greg Maddux Black	6.00	1.80
50 Richard Hidalgo	2.50	.75
50 Richard Hidalgo Black	2.50	.75
51 Orlando Hernandez	2.50	.75
51 O.Hernandez Black	2.50	.75
52 Chipper Jones	4.00	1.20
52 Chipper Jones Black	4.00	1.20
53 Ben Grieve	2.50	.75
53 Ben Grieve Black	2.50	.75
54 Jimmy Haynes	2.50	.75
54 Jimmy Haynes Black	2.50	.75
55 Ken Caminiti	2.50	.75
55 Ken Caminiti Black	2.50	.75
56 Tim Salmon	2.50	.75
56 Tim Salmon Black	2.50	.75
57 Andy Pettitte	2.50	.75
57 Andy Pettitte Black	2.50	.75
58 Darin Erstad	2.50	.75
58 Darin Erstad Black	2.50	.75
59 Marquis Grissom	2.50	.75
59 Marquis Grissom Black	2.50	.75
60 Raul Mondesi	2.50	.75
60 Raul Mondesi Black	2.50	.75
61 Bengie Molina	2.50	.75
61 Bengie Molina Black	2.50	.75
62 Miguel Tejada	2.50	.75
62 Miguel Tejada Black	2.50	.75
63 Jose Cruz Jr.	2.50	.75
63 Jose Cruz Jr. Black	2.50	.75
64 Billy Koch	2.50	.75
64 Billy Koch Black	2.50	.75
65 Troy Glaus	2.50	.75
65 Troy Glaus Black	2.50	.75
66 Cliff Floyd	2.50	.75
66 Cliff Floyd Black	2.50	.75
67 Tony Batista	2.50	.75
67 Tony Batista Black	2.50	.75
68 Jeff Bagwell	2.50	.75
68 Jeff Bagwell Black	2.50	.75
69 Billy Wagner	2.50	.75
69 Billy Wagner Black	2.50	.75
70 Eric Chavez	2.50	.75
70 Eric Chavez Black	2.50	.75
71 Troy Percival	2.50	.75
71 Troy Percival Black	2.50	.75
72 Andruw Jones	2.50	.75
72 Andruw Jones Black	2.50	.75
73 Shane Reynolds	2.50	.75
73 Shane Reynolds Black	2.50	.75
74 Barry Zito	4.00	1.20
74 Barry Zito Black	4.00	1.20
75 Roy Halladay	2.50	.75
75 Roy Halladay Black	2.50	.75
76 David Wells	2.50	.75
76 David Wells Black	2.50	.75
77 Jason Giambi	4.00	1.20
77 Jason Giambi Black	4.00	1.20
78 Scott Elarton	2.50	.75
78 Scott Elarton Black	2.50	.75
79 Moises Alou	2.50	.75

79 Moises Alou Black 2.50 .75
80 Adam Piatt 2.50 .75
80 Adam Piatt Black 2.50 .75
81 Wilton Veras .50 .15
82 Darryl Kile .60 .18
83 Johnny Damon .60 .18
84 Tony Armas Jr. .50 .15
85 Ellis Burks .60 .18
86 Jamey Wright .50 .15
87 Jose Vizcaino .50 .15
88 Bartolo Colon .60 .18
89 Carmen Cali RC .60 .18
90 Kevin Brown .60 .18
91 Josh Hamilton .50 .15
92 Jay Buhner .60 .18
93 Scott Pratt RC .60 .18
94 Alex Cora .50 .15
95 Luis Montanez RC .60 .18
96 Dmitri Young .60 .18
97 J.T. Snow .60 .18
98 Damion Easley .50 .15
99 Greg Norton .50 .15
100 Matt Wheatland .50 .15
101 Chin-Feng Chen .60 .18
102 Tony Womack .50 .15
103 Adam Kennedy Black .50 .15
104 J.D. Drew .60 .18
105 Carlos Febles .50 .15
106 Jim Thome 1.50 .45
107 Danny Graves .50 .15
108 Dave Mlicki .50 .15
109 Ron Coomer .50 .15
110 James Baldwin .50 .15
111 Shaun Boyd RC .60 .18
112 Brian Bohanon .50 .15
113 Jacque Jones .60 .18
114 Alfonso Soriano 1.00 .30
115 Tony Clark .50 .15
116 Terrence Long .60 .18
117 Todd Hundley .50 .15
118 Kazuhiro Sasaki .60 .18
119 Brian Sellier RC .60 .18
120 John Olerud .60 .18
121 Javier Vazquez .60 .18
122 Sean Burnett .60 .18
123 Matt LeCroy .50 .15
124 Erubiel Durazo .50 .15
125 Juan Encarnacion .50 .15
126 Pablo Ozuna .50 .15
127 Russ Ortiz .60 .18
128 David Segui .50 .15
129 Mark McGwire 4.00 1.20
130 Mark Grace 1.00 .30
131 Fred McGriff 1.00 .30
132 Carl Pavano .50 .15
133 Derek Thompson .50 .15
134 Shawn Green .60 .18
135 B.J. Surhoff .60 .18
136 Michael Tucker .50 .15
137 Jason Isringhausen .50 .15
138 Eric Milton .50 .15
139 Mike Stodolka .50 .15
140 Milton Bradley .60 .18
141 Curt Schilling 1.00 .30
142 Sandy Alomar Jr. .50 .15
143 Brent Mayne .50 .15
144 Todd Jones .50 .15
145 Charles Johnson .60 .18
146 Dean Palmer .60 .18
147 Masato Yoshii .50 .15
148 Edgar Renteria .60 .18
149 Joe Randa .50 .15
150 Adam Johnson .50 .15
151 Greg Vaughn .60 .18
152 Adrian Beltre .60 .18
153 Glenallen Hill .50 .15
154 David Parrish RC .60 .18
155 Neifi Perez .50 .15
156 Pete Harnisch .50 .15
157 Paul Konerko .60 .18
158 Dennys Reyes .50 .15
159 Jose Lima Black .50 .15
160 Eddie Taubensee .50 .15
161 Miguel Cairo .50 .15
162 Jeff Kent .60 .18
163 Dustin Hermanson .50 .15
164 Alex Gonzalez .50 .15
165 Hideo Nomo 1.50 .45
166 Sammy Sosa 2.50 .75
167 C.J. Nitkowski .50 .15
168 Cal Eldred .50 .15
169 Jeff Abbott .50 .15
170 Jim Edmonds .60 .18
171 Mark Mulder Black .60 .18
172 Dominic Rich RC .60 .18
173 Ray Lankford .50 .15
174 Danny Borrell RC .60 .18
175 Rick Aguilera .50 .15
176 S.Stewart Black .60 .18
177 Steve Finley .60 .18
178 Jim Parque .50 .15
179 Kevin Appier Black .60 .18
180 Adrian Gonzalez .60 .18
181 Tom Goodwin .50 .15
182 Kevin Tapani .50 .15
183 Fernando Tatis .50 .15
184 Mark Grudzielanek .50 .15
185 Ryan Anderson .50 .15
186 Jeffrey Hammonds .50 .15
187 Corey Koskie .60 .18
188 Brad Fullmer Black .50 .15
189 Rey Sanchez .50 .15
190 Michael Barrett .50 .15
191 Rickey Henderson 1.50 .45
192 Jermaine Dye .60 .18
193 Scott Brosius .60 .18
194 Matt Anderson .50 .15
195 Brian Buchanan .50 .15
196 Derrek Lee .60 .18
197 Larry Walker 1.00 .30
198 Dan Moylan RC .60 .18
199 Vinny Castilla .60 .18
200 Ken Griffey Jr. 2.50 .75
201 Matt Stairs Black .50 .15
202 Ty Howington .50 .15
203 Andy Benes .50 .15
204 Luis Gonzalez .60 .18
205 Brian Moehler .50 .15
206 Harold Baines .60 .18
207 Pedro Astacio .50 .15
208 Cristian Guzman .60 .18
209 Kip Wells .50 .15
210 Frank Thomas 1.50 .45
211 Jose Rosado .50 .15
212 Vernon Wells Black .60 .18
213 Bobby Higginson .60 .18
214 Juan Gonzalez 1.50 .45
215 Omar Vizquel .60 .18
216 Bernie Williams 1.00 .30
217 Aaron Sele .50 .15
218 Shawn Estes .50 .15
219 Roberto Alomar 1.50 .45
220 Rick Ankiel .50 .15
221 Josh Kalinowski .50 .15
222 David Bell .50 .15
223 Keith Foulke .50 .15
224 Craig Biggio Black 1.00 .30
225 Josh Axelson RC .60 .18
226 Scott Williamson .50 .15
227 Ron Belliard .50 .15
228 Chris Singleton .50 .15
229 Alex Serrano RC .60 .18
230 Deivi Cruz .50 .15
231 Eric Munson .50 .15
232 Luis Castillo .60 .18
233 Edgar Martinez 1.00 .30
234 Jeff Shaw .50 .15
235 Jeromy Burnitz .60 .18
236 Richie Sexson .60 .18
237 Will Clark 1.50 .45
238 Ron Villone .50 .15
239 Kerry Wood 1.50 .45
240 Rich Aurilia .60 .18
241 Mo Vaughn Black .60 .18
242 Travis Fryman .60 .18
243 M. Ramirez Red Sox .60 .18
244 Chris Stynes .50 .15
245 Ray Durham .60 .18
246 Juan Uribe RC .60 .18
247 Juan Guzman .50 .15
248 Lee Stevens .50 .15
249 Devon White .60 .18
250 Kyle Lohse RC 1.50 .45
251 Bryan Wolff .50 .15
252 Matt Galante RC .60 .18
253 Eric Young .50 .15
254 Freddy Garcia .60 .18
255 Jay Bell .60 .18
256 Steve Cox .50 .15
257 Torii Hunter .60 .18
258 Jose Canseco 1.50 .45
259 Brad Ausmus .50 .15
260 Jeff Cirillo .50 .15
261 Brad Penny .50 .15
262 Antonio Alfonseca .50 .15
263 Russ Branyan .50 .15
264 Chris Morris RC .60 .18
265 John Lackey .50 .15
266 Justin Wayne RC 1.00 .30
267 Brad Radke .60 .18
268 Todd Stottlemyre .50 .15
269 Mark Loretta .50 .15
270 Matt Williams .60 .18
271 Kenny Lofton .60 .18
272 Jeff D'Amico .50 .15
273 Jamie Moyer .60 .18
274 Darren Dreifort .50 .15
275 Denny Neagle .50 .15
276 Orlando Cabrera .50 .15
277 Chuck Finley .60 .18
278 Miguel Batista .60 .18
279 Carlos Beltran .60 .18
280 Eric Karros .60 .18
281 Mark Kotsay .50 .15
282 Ryan Dempster .50 .15
283 Barry Larkin 1.50 .45
284 Jeff Suppan .50 .15
285 Gary Sheffield .60 .18
286 Jose Valentin .50 .15
287 Robb Nen .60 .18
288 Chan Ho Park .60 .18
289 John Halama .50 .15
290 Steve Smyth RC .60 .18
291 Gerald Williams .50 .15
292 Preston Wilson .60 .18
293 Victor Hall RC .60 .18
294 Ben Sheets .60 .18
295 Eric Davis .60 .18
296 Kirk Rueter .50 .15
297 Chad Petty RC .60 .18
298 Kevin Millar .60 .18
299 Marvin Benard .50 .15
300 Vladimir Guerrero 1.50 .45
301 Livan Hernandez .50 .15
302 Travis Baptist RC .50 .15
303 Bill Mueller .60 .18
304 Mike Cameron .60 .18
305 Randy Johnson 1.50 .45
306 Alan Mahaffey RC .50 .15
307 Timo Perez UER .50 .15
No facsimile autograph on card
308 Pokey Reese .50 .15
309 Ryan Rupe .50 .15
310 Carlos Lee .60 .18
311 Doug Glanville SP 5.00 1.50
312 Jay Payton SP 5.00 1.50
313 Troy O'Leary SP 5.00 1.50
314 Francisco Cordero SP 5.00 1.50
315 Rusty Greer SP 5.00 1.50
316 Cal Ripken SP 25.00 7.50
317 Ricky Ledee SP 5.00 1.50
318 Brian Daubach SP 5.00 1.50
319 Robin Ventura SP 5.00 1.50
320 Todd Zeile SP 5.00 1.50
321 Francisco Cordova SP 5.00 1.50
322 Henry Rodriguez SP 5.00 1.50
323 Pat Meares SP 5.00 1.50
324 Glendon Rusch SP 5.00 1.50
325 Keith Osik SP 5.00 1.50
326 Robert Keppel SP RC 8.00 2.40
327 Bobby Jones SP 5.00 1.50
328 Alex Ramirez SP 5.00 1.50
329 Robert Person SP 5.00 1.50
330 Ruben Mateo SP 5.00 1.50
331 Rob Bell SP 5.00 1.50
332 Carl Everett SP 5.00 1.50
333 Jason Schmidt SP 5.00 1.50
334 Scott Rolen SP 8.00 2.40
335 Jimmy Anderson SP 5.00 1.50
336 Bret Boone SP 5.00 1.50
337 Delino DeShields SP 5.00 1.50
338 Trevor Hoffman SP 5.00 1.50
339 Bob Abreu SP 5.00 1.50
340 Mike Williams SP 5.00 1.50
341 Mike Hampton SP 5.00 1.50
342 John Wetteland SP 5.00 1.50
343 Scott Erickson SP 5.00 1.50
344 Enrique Wilson SP 5.00 1.50
345 Tim Wakefield SP 5.00 1.50
346 Mike Lowell SP 5.00 1.50
347 Todd Pratt SP 5.00 1.50
348 Brook Fordyce SP 5.00 1.50
349 Benny Agbayani SP 5.00 1.50
350 Gabe Kapler SP 5.00 1.50
351 Sean Casey SP 5.00 1.50
352 Darren Oliver SP 5.00 1.50
353 Todd Ritchie SP 5.00 1.50
354 Kenny Rogers SP 5.00 1.50
355 Jason Kendall SP 5.00 1.50
356 John Vander Wal SP 5.00 1.50
357 Ramon Martinez SP 5.00 1.50
358 Edgardo Alfonzo SP 5.00 1.50
359 Phil Nevin SP 5.00 1.50
360 Albert Belle SP 5.00 1.50
361 Ruben Rivera SP 5.00 1.50
362 Pedro Martinez SP 8.00 2.40
363 Derek Lowe SP 5.00 1.50
364 Pat Burrell SP 5.00 1.50
365 Mike Mussina SP 8.00 2.40
366 Brady Anderson SP 5.00 1.50
367 Darren Lewis SP 5.00 1.50
368 Sidney Ponson SP 5.00 1.50
369 Adam Eaton SP 5.00 1.50
370 Eric Owens SP 5.00 1.50
371 Aaron Boone SP 5.00 1.50
372 Matt Clement SP 5.00 1.50
373 Derek Bell SP 5.00 1.50
374 Trot Nixon SP 8.00 2.40
375 Travis Lee SP 5.00 1.50
376 Mike Benjamin SP 5.00 1.50
377 Jeff Zimmerman SP 5.00 1.50
378 Mike Lieberthal SP 5.00 1.50
379 Rick Reed SP 5.00 1.50
380 N.Garciaparra SP 12.00 3.60
381 Omar Daal SP 5.00 1.50
382 Ryan Klesko SP 5.00 1.50
383 Rey Ordonez SP 5.00 1.50
384 Kevin Young SP 5.00 1.50
385 Rick Helling SP 5.00 1.50
386 Brian Giles SP 5.00 1.50
387 Tony Gwynn SP 10.00 3.00
388 Ed Sprague SP 5.00 1.50
389 J.R. House SP 5.00 1.50
390 Scott Hatteberg SP 5.00 1.50
391 John Valentin SP 5.00 1.50
392 Melvin Mora SP 5.00 1.50
393 Royce Clayton SP 5.00 1.50
394 Jeff Fassero SP 5.00 1.50
395 Manny Alexander SP 5.00 1.50
396 John Franco SP 5.00 1.50
397 Luis Alicea SP 5.00 1.50
398 Ivan Rodriguez SP 8.00 2.40
399 Kevin Jordan SP 5.00 1.50
400 Jose Offerman SP 5.00 1.50
401 Jeff Conine SP 5.00 1.50
402 Seth Etherton SP 5.00 1.50
403 Mike Bordick SP 5.00 1.50
404 Al Leiter SP 5.00 1.50
405 Mike Piazza SP 12.00 3.60
406 Armando Benitez SP 5.00 1.50
407 Warren Morris SP 5.00 1.50
NNO 1952 Card Redemption EXCH
NNO Replica Hat-Jsy EXCH

2001 Topps Heritage Chrome

Randomly inserted into packs at one in 25 Hob/Ret, this 110-card insert is a partial parallel of the 2001 Topps Heritage base set. Each card was produced using Topps Chrome technology. Please note that each card is also individually serial numbered to 552.

Nm-Mt Ex-Mt
STATED ODDS 1:25 HOB/RET
STATED PRINT RUN 552 SERIAL #'d SETS
CP1 Cal Ripken 50.00 15.00
CP2 Jim Thome 15.00 4.50
CP3 Derek Jeter 40.00 12.00
CP4 Andres Galarraga 8.00 2.40
CP5 Carlos Delgado 8.00 2.40
CP6 Roberto Alomar 15.00 4.50
CP7 Tom Glavine 10.00 3.00
CP8 Gary Sheffield 8.00 2.40
CP9 Mo Vaughn 8.00 2.40
CP10 Preston Wilson 8.00 2.40
CP11 Mike Mussina 15.00 4.50
CP12 Greg Maddux 25.00 7.50
CP13 Ivan Rodriguez 15.00 4.50
CP14 Al Leiter 8.00 2.40
CP15 Seth Etherton 8.00 2.40
CP16 Edgardo Alfonzo 8.00 2.40
CP17 Richie Sexson 8.00 2.40
CP18 Andruw Jones 8.00 2.40
CP19 Bartolo Colon 8.00 2.40
CP20 Darin Erstad 8.00 2.40
CP21 Kevin Brown 8.00 2.40
CP22 Mike Sweeney 8.00 2.40
CP23 Mike Piazza 25.00 7.50
CP24 Rafael Palmeiro 10.00 3.00
CP25 Terrence Long 8.00 2.40
CP26 Kazuhiro Sasaki 8.00 2.40
CP27 John Olerud 8.00 2.40
CP28 Mark McGwire 40.00 12.00
CP29 Fred McGriff 10.00 3.00
CP30 Todd Helton 10.00 3.00
CP31 Curt Schilling 10.00 3.00
CP32 Alex Rodriguez 25.00 7.50
CP33 Jeff Kent 8.00 2.40
CP34 Pat Burrell 8.00 2.40
CP35 Jim Edmonds 8.00 2.40
CP36 Mark Mulder 8.00 2.40
CP37 Troy Glaus 10.00 3.00
CP38 Jay Payton 8.00 2.40
CP39 Jermaine Dye 8.00 2.40
CP40 Larry Walker 10.00 3.00
CP41 Ken Griffey Jr. 25.00 7.50
CP42 Jeff Bagwell 10.00 3.00
CP43 Rick Ankiel 8.00 2.40
CP44 Mark Redman 8.00 2.40
CP45 Edgar Martinez 10.00 3.00
CP46 Mike Hampton 8.00 2.40
CP47 Manny Ramirez 8.00 2.40
CP48 Ray Durham 8.00 2.40
CP49 Rafael Furcal 8.00 2.40
CP50 Sean Casey 8.00 2.40
CP51 Jose Canseco 15.00 4.50
CP52 Barry Bonds 40.00 12.00
CP53 Tim Hudson 8.00 2.40
CP54 Barry Zito 15.00 4.50
CP55 Chuck Finley 8.00 2.40
CP56 Magglio Ordonez 8.00 2.40
CP57 David Wells 8.00 2.40
CP58 Jason Giambi 15.00 4.50
CP59 Tony Gwynn 20.00 6.00
CP60 Vladimir Guerrero 15.00 4.50
CP61 Randy Johnson 15.00 4.50
CP62 Bernie Williams 10.00 3.00
CP63 Craig Biggio 10.00 3.00
CP64 Jason Kendall 8.00 2.40
CP65 Pedro Martinez 15.00 4.50
CP66 Mark Quinn 8.00 2.40
CP67 Frank Thomas 15.00 4.50
CP68 Nomar Garciaparra 25.00 7.50
CP69 Brian Giles 8.00 2.40
CP70 Shawn Green 8.00 2.40
CP71 Roger Clemens 30.00 9.00
CP72 Sammy Sosa 25.00 7.50
CP73 Juan Gonzalez 15.00 4.50
CP74 Orlando Hernandez 8.00 2.40
CP75 Chipper Jones 15.00 4.50
CP76 Josh Hamilton 8.00 2.40
CP77 Adam Johnson 8.00 2.40
CP78 Shaun Boyd 8.00 2.40
CP79 Alfonso Soriano 10.00 3.00
CP80 Derek Thompson 8.00 2.40
CP81 Adrian Gonzalez 8.00 2.40
CP82 Ryan Anderson 8.00 2.40
CP83 Corey Patterson 8.00 2.40
CP84 J.R. House 8.00 2.40
CP85 Sean Burroughs 8.00 2.40
CP86 Bryan Wolff 8.00 2.40
CP87 John Lackey 8.00 2.40
CP88 Ben Sheets 8.00 2.40
CP89 Timo Perez 8.00 2.40
CP90 Robert Keppel 10.00 3.00
CP91 Luis Montanez 8.00 2.40
CP92 Sean Burnett 8.00 2.40
CP93 Justin Wayne 10.00 3.00
CP94 Eric Munson 8.00 2.40
CP95 Steve Smyth 8.00 2.40
CP96 Matt Galante 8.00 2.40
CP97 Carmen Cali 8.00 2.40
CP98 Brian Sellier 8.00 2.40
CP99 David Parrish 8.00 2.40
CP100 Danny Borrell 8.00 2.40
CP101 Chad Petty 8.00 2.40
CP102 Dominic Rich 8.00 2.40
CP103 Josh Axelson 8.00 2.40
CP104 Alex Serrano 8.00 2.40
CP105 Juan Uribe 8.00 2.40
CP106 Travis Baptist 8.00 2.40
CP107 Alan Mahaffey 8.00 2.40
CP108 Kyle Lohse 10.00 3.00
CP109 Victor Hall 8.00 2.40
CP110 Scott Pratt 8.00 2.40

2001 Topps Heritage Autographs

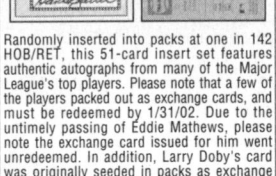

Randomly inserted into packs at one in 142 HOB/RET, this 51-card insert set features authentic autographs from many of the Major League's top players. Please note that a few of the players packed out as exchange cards, and must be redeemed by 1/31/02. Due to the untimely passing of Eddie Mathews, please note the exchange card issued for him went unredeemed. In addition, Larry Doby's card was originally seeded in packs as exchange cards (of which carried a January 31st, 2002 deadline).

Nm-Mt Ex-Mt
THAAH Aubrey Huff 50.00 15.00
THAAP Andy Pafko 80.00 24.00
THAAR Alex Rodriguez 200.00 60.00
THABB Barry Bonds 300.00 90.00
THABS Bobby Shantz 50.00 15.00
THABT Bobby Thomson 100.00 30.00
THACD Carlos Delgado 50.00 15.00
THACF Cliff Floyd 50.00 15.00
THACJ Chipper Jones 120.00 36.00
THACP Corey Patterson 50.00 15.00
THACS Curt Simmons 50.00 15.00
THADD Dom DiMaggio 120.00 36.00
THADG Dick Groat 50.00 15.00
THADS Duke Snider 150.00 45.00
THAEM Eddie Mathews EXCH .50 .15
THAES Enos Slaughter 100.00 30.00
THAFV Fernando Vina 50.00 15.00
THAGJ Geoff Jenkins 50.00 15.00
THAGM Gil McDougald 60.00 18.00
THAHB Hank Bauer 100.00 30.00
THAHS Hank Sauer 50.00 15.00
THAHW Hoyt Wilhelm 100.00 30.00
THAJG Joe Garagiola 80.00 24.00
THAJM Joe Mays 30.00 9.00
THAJS Johnny Sain 50.00 15.00
THAJV Jose Vidro 50.00 15.00
THAKB Kris Benson 30.00 9.00
THALD Larry Doby 150.00 45.00
THAMB Mark Buehrle 50.00 15.00
THAMI Monte Irvin 60.00 18.00
THAML Mike Lamb 30.00 9.00
THAML Matt Lawton 30.00 9.00
THAMM Minnie Minoso 100.00 30.00
THAMO Magglio Ordonez 50.00 15.00
THAMQ Mark Quinn 30.00 9.00
THAMR Mark Redman 30.00 9.00
THAMS Mike Sweeney 50.00 15.00
THAMV Mickey Vernon 50.00 15.00
THANG N.Garciaparra 200.00 60.00
THAPR Preacher Roe 120.00 36.00
THAPFR Phil Rizzuto 120.00 36.00
THARH Richard Hidalgo 50.00 15.00
THARR Robin Roberts 100.00 30.00
THARS Red Schoendienst 50.00 15.00
THARW Randy Wolf 50.00 15.00
THASPB Sean Burroughs 50.00 15.00
THATG Tom Glavine 100.00 30.00
THATH Todd Helton 60.00 18.00
THATL Terrence Long 50.00 15.00
THAVL Vernon Law 50.00 15.00
THAWM Willie Mays 250.00 75.00
THAWS Warren Spahn 120.00 36.00

2001 Topps Heritage Autographs Red Ink

Randomly inserted into packs at 1:545 Hobby and 1:546 Retail, this 52-card insert set is a complete parallel of the Heritage Autographs signed in red ink. Please note that each of these cards are individually serial numbered to 52. Also note that a few of the players packed out as exchange cards, and must be redeemed by 1/31/02. Tdue to his untimely death, the Eddie Mathews exchange card went unredeemed. The Willie Mays autograph cards come with or without serial numbering.

Nm-Mt Ex-Mt
*RED INK: .6X TO 1.2X BASIC BLUE INK AUTO'S

2001 Topps Heritage AutoProofs

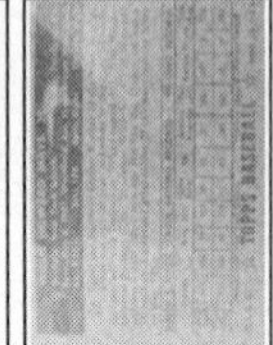

Randomly inserted at approximately 1 in every 5749 boxes, this card is an actual 1952 Topps Willie Mays card that was bought from the Topps Company, then individually autographed by Willie Mays, and distributed into packs. Please note that each card is individually serial numbered to 25.

Nm-Mt Ex-Mt
AP1 Willie Mays '52T AU/25

2001 Topps Heritage Classic Renditions

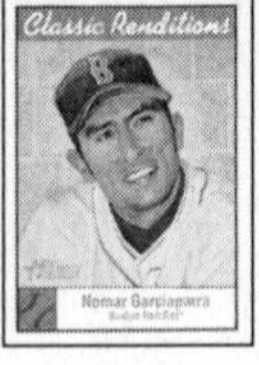

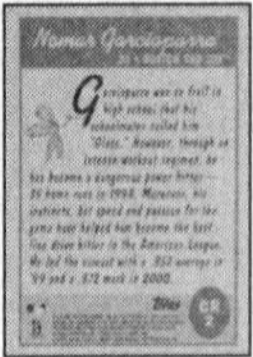

Randomly inserted into packs at one in 5 Hobby, and one in 9 Retail, this 10-card insert set features artist drawn sketches of some of the best modern day ballplayers. Card backs carry a "CR" prefix.

Nm-Mt Ex-Mt
COMPLETE SET (10) 20.00 6.00
CR1 Mark McGwire 4.00 1.20
CR2 Nomar Garciaparra 2.50 .75
CR3 Barry Bonds 4.00 1.20
CR4 Sammy Sosa 2.50 .75
CR5 Chipper Jones 1.50 .45
CR6 Pat Burrell 1.00 .30
CR7 Frank Thomas 1.50 .45
CR8 Manny Ramirez 1.00 .30
CR9 Derek Jeter 4.00 1.20
CR10 Ken Griffey Jr. 2.50 .75

2001 Topps Heritage Classic Renditions Autograph

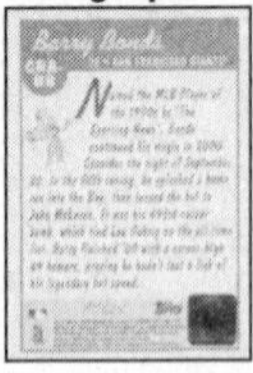

Randomly inserted into packs at one in 19,710 Hobby, and 1:20,926 Retail, this three-card insert set is a partial parallel of the Classic Renditions insert. Each of these cards have been autographed by the given player and are individually serial numbered to 25. Due to market scarcity, no pricing is provided.

Nm-Mt Ex-Mt
CRA-BB Barry Bonds
CRA-CJ Chipper Jones
CRA-NG Nomar Garciaparra

2001 Topps Heritage Clubhouse Collection

Randomly inserted into packs, this 22-card insert features game-used memorabilia cards from past and present stars. Included in the set are game-used bat and jersey cards. Please note that a numbered of the players have autographed 25 of each of these cards. Also note that a few of the cards packed out as exchange cards, and must have been redeemed

by 01/31/02. Common Bat cards were inserted at a rate of 1:590 and Jersey cards at 1:798 Hobby/1:799 Retail. Dual Bat cards were inserted at 1:5701 Hobby/1:5772 Retail. Dual Jersey cards were inserted into packs at 1:28,744 Hobby/1:29,820 Retail. Autographed Bat cards were inserted at 1:19,710 Hobby/1:20,928 Retail, and Autographed Jerseys at 1:62,714 Hobby/1:83,712 Retail. Exchange cards - with a deadline of Janury 31st, 2002 - were seeded into packs for the following cards: Eddie Mathews Bat, Duke Snider Bat AU and Willie Mays Bat AU.

	Nm-Mt	Ex-Mt
BB Barry Bonds Bat	80.00	24.00
CJ Chipper Jones Bat	50.00	15.00
DS Duke Snider Bat	50.00	15.00
EM Eddie Mathews Bat	50.00	15.00
FT Frank Thomas Jsy	50.00	15.00
FV Fernando Vina Bat	40.00	12.00
MM Minnie Minoso Jsy	40.00	12.00
RA Richie Ashburn Bat	50.00	15.00
RS Red Schoendienst Bat	40.00	12.00
SG Shawn Green Bat	40.00	12.00
SR Scott Rolen Bat	50.00	15.00
WM Willie Mays Bat	150.00	45.00
ADS Duke Snider Bat AU/25		
AMM Minnie Minoso Jsy AU/25		
ARS Red Schoendienst Bat AU/25		
AWM Willie Mays Bat AU/25		
DSSG Duke Snider Shawn Green Bat/52	200.00	60.00
EMCJ Eddie Mathews Chipper Jones Bat/52	150.00	45.00
MMFT Minnie Minoso Frank Thomas Jsy/52	150.00	45.00
RASR Richie Ashburn Scott Rolen Bat/52	200.00	60.00
RSFV Red Schoendienst Fernando Vina Bat/52	150.00	45.00
WMBB Willie Mays Barry Bonds Bat/52	300.00	90.00

2001 Topps Heritage Grandstand Glory

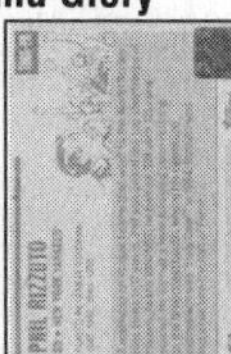

Randomly inserted into packs at 1:211 Hobby/Retail, this seven-card insert set features a swatch of original stadium seating. Card backs carry the player's initials as numbering.

	Nm-Mt	Ex-Mt
JR Jackie Robinson	50.00	15.00
NF Nellie Fox	25.00	7.50
PR Phil Rizzuto	40.00	12.00
RA Richie Ashburn	25.00	7.50
RR Robin Roberts	25.00	7.50
WM Willie Mays	80.00	24.00
YB Yogi Berra	40.00	12.00

2001 Topps Heritage New Age Performers

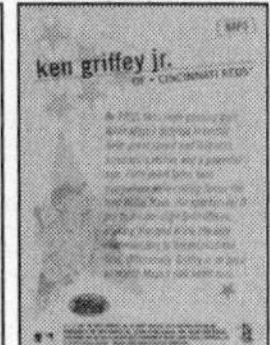

Randomly inserted into packs at 1:8 Hobby, 1:15 Retail, this 15-card insert set features players that have become the superstars of the future. Card backs carry a "NAP" prefix.

	Nm-Mt	Ex-Mt
COMPLETE SET (15)	50.00	15.00
NAP1 Mike Piazza	4.00	1.20
NAP2 Sammy Sosa	4.00	1.20
NAP3 Alex Rodriguez	4.00	1.20
NAP4 Barry Bonds	6.00	1.80
NAP5 Ken Griffey Jr.	4.00	1.20
NAP6 Chipper Jones	2.50	.75
NAP7 Randy Johnson	2.50	.75
NAP8 Derek Jeter	6.00	1.80
NAP9 Nomar Garciaparra	4.00	1.20
NAP10 Mark McGwire	6.00	1.80
NAP11 Jeff Bagwell	2.50	.75
NAP12 Pedro Martinez	2.50	.75
NAP13 Todd Helton	2.50	.75
NAP14 Vladimir Guerrero	2.50	.75
NAP15 Greg Maddux	4.00	1.20

2001 Topps Heritage Then and Now

Randomly inserted into Hobby packs at 1:8 and Retail packs at 1:15, this 10-card set pairs up

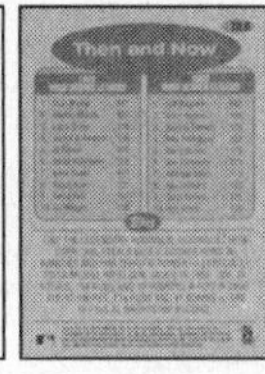

modern day heroes with players from the past that compare statistically. Card backs carry a "TH" prefix.

	Nm-Mt	Ex-Mt
COMPLETE SET (10)	30.00	9.00
TH1 Yogi Berra Mike Piazza	3.00	.90
TH2 Duke Snider Sammy Sosa	3.00	.90
TH3 Willie Mays Ken Griffey Jr.	4.00	1.20
TH4 Phil Rizzuto Derek Jeter	5.00	1.50
TH5 Pee Wee Reese Nomar Garciaparra	3.00	.90
TH6 Jackie Robinson Alex Rodriguez	3.00	.90
TH7 Johnny Mize Mark McGwire	5.00	1.50
TH8 Bob Feller Pedro Martinez	2.00	.60
TH9 Robin Roberts Greg Maddux	3.00	.90
TH10 Warren Spahn Randy Johnson	2.00	.60

2001 Topps Heritage Time Capsule

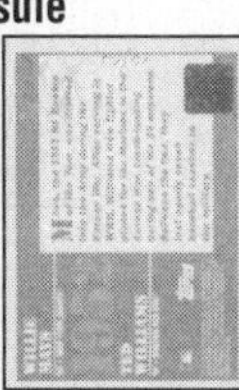

This unique set features swatches of fabric taken from actual combat uniforms from the 1952 Korean War. It's important to note that though these cards do indeed feature patches of vintage Korean War uniforms, they were not worn by the athlete featured on the card. Stated odds for the four single-player cards was 1:369. Unlike the other cards in this set, the lone dual-player Willie Mays-Ted Williams card is hand-numbered on back. Only 52 copies of this card were produced, and each is marked by hand on back in black pen "X/52". The stated odds for this dual-player card is 1:28,744 packs.

	Nm-Mt	Ex-Mt
DN Don Newcombe	25.00	7.50
TW Ted Williams UER Card says 525 career homers, Williams hit 521	120.00	36.00
WF Whitey Ford	40.00	12.00
WM Willie Mays	100.00	30.00
WMTW Willie Mays Ted Williams/52	400.00	120.00

2002 Topps Heritage

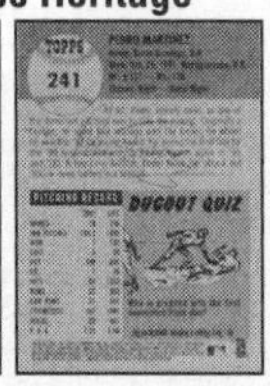

Issued in early February 2002, this set was the second year that Topps used their Heritage brand and achieved success in the secondary market. These cards were issued in eight card packs which were packed 24 to a box and had a SRP of $3 per pack. The set consists of 440 cards with seven short prints among the low numbers as well as all cards from 364 through 446 as short prints. Those cards were all inserted at a rate of one in two packs. In addition, there was an unannounced variation in which 10 cards were printed in both day and night versions. The night versions were also inserted into packs at a rate of one in two.

	Nm-Mt	Ex-Mt
COMPLETE SET (440)	250.00	75.00
COMP.SET w/o SP's (350)	80.00	24.00
COMMON CARD (1-363)	.50	.15
COMMON SP (364-446)	5.00	1.50
1 Ichiro Suzuki SP	12.00	3.60
2 Darin Erstad	.60	.18
3 Rod Beck	.60	.18
4 Doug Mientkiewicz	.60	.18
5 Mike Sweeney	.60	.18
6 Roger Clemens	3.00	.90
7 Jason Tyner	.50	.15
8 Alex Gonzalez	.50	.15
9 Eric Young	.50	.15
10 Randy Johnson	1.50	.45
10N Randy Johnson Night SP	8.00	2.40
11 Aaron Sele	.50	.15
12 Tony Clark	.50	.15
13 C.C. Sabathia	.60	.18
14 Melvin Mora	.50	.15
15 Tim Hudson	.60	.18
16 Ben Petrick	.50	.15
17 Tom Glavine	1.00	.30
18 Jason Lane	.50	.15
19 Larry Walker	1.00	.30
20 Mark Mulder	.60	.18
21 Steve Finley	.60	.18
22 Bengie Molina	.50	.15
23 Rob Bell	.50	.15
24 Nathan Haynes	.50	.15
25 Rafael Furcal	.60	.18
25N Rafael Furcal Night SP	5.00	1.50
26 Mike Mussina	1.50	.45
27 Paul LoDuca	.60	.18
28 Torii Hunter	.60	.18
29 Carlos Lee	.60	.18
30 Jimmy Rollins	.60	.18
31 Arthur Rhodes	.50	.15
32 Ivan Rodriguez	1.50	.45
33 Wes Helms	.50	.15
34 Cliff Floyd	.60	.18
35 Julian Tavarez	.50	.15
36 Mark McGwire	4.00	1.20
37 Chipper Jones SP	8.00	2.40
38 Denny Neagle	.50	.15
39 Odalis Perez	.50	.15
40 Antonio Alfonseca	.50	.15
41 Edgar Renteria	.60	.18
42 Troy Glaus	1.00	.30
43 Scott Brosius	.60	.18
44 Abraham Nunez	.50	.15
45 Jamey Wright	.50	.15
46 Bobby Bonilla	.60	.18
47 Ismael Valdes	.50	.15
48 Chris Reitsma	.50	.15
49 Neifi Perez	.50	.15
50 Juan Cruz	.50	.15
51 Kevin Brown	.60	.18
52 Ben Grieve	.50	.15
53 Alex Rodriguez SP	12.00	3.60
54 Charles Nagy	.50	.15
55 Reggie Sanders	.60	.18
56 Nelson Figueroa	.50	.15
57 Felipe Lopez	.50	.15
58 Bill Ortega	.50	.15
59 Jeffrey Hammonds	.60	.18
60 Johnny Estrada	.60	.18
61 Bob Wickman	.50	.15
62 Doug Glanville	.50	.15
63 Jeff Cirillo	.50	.15
63N Jeff Cirillo Night SP	5.00	1.50
64 Corey Patterson	.60	.18
65 Aaron Myette	.50	.15
66 Magglio Ordonez	.60	.18
67 Ellis Burks	.60	.18
68 Miguel Tejada	.60	.18
69 John Olerud	.60	.18
69N John Olerud Night SP	5.00	1.50
70 Greg Vaughn	.60	.18
71 Andy Pettitte	1.00	.30
72 Mike Matheny	.50	.15
73 Brandon Duckworth	.50	.15
74 Scott Schoeneweis	.50	.15
75 Mike Lowell	.60	.18
76 Einar Diaz	.50	.15
77 Tino Martinez	1.00	.30
78 Matt Williams	.60	.18
79 Jason Young RC	1.00	.30
80 Nate Cornejo	.50	.15
81 Andres Galarraga	.60	.18
82 Bernie Williams SP	8.00	2.40
83 Ryan Klesko	.60	.18
84 Dan Wilson	.50	.15
85 Henry Pichardo RC	1.00	.30
86 Ray Durham	.60	.18
87 Omar Daal	.50	.15
88 Derrek Lee	.60	.18
89 Al Leiter	.60	.18
90 Darrin Fletcher	.50	.15
91 Josh Beckett	1.00	.30
92 Johnny Damon	.60	.18
92N Johnny Damon Night SP	5.00	1.50
93 Abraham Nunez	.50	.15
94 Ricky Ledee	.50	.15
95 Richie Sexson	.60	.18
96 Adam Kennedy	.50	.15
97 Raul Mondesi	.60	.18
98 John Burkett	.60	.18
99 Ben Sheets	.60	.18
99N Ben Sheets Night SP	5.00	1.50
100 Preston Wilson	.60	.18
100N Pr. Wilson Night SP	5.00	1.50
101 Boof Bonser	.50	.15
102 Shigetoshi Hasegawa	.60	.18
103 Carlos Febles	.50	.15
104 Jorge Posada SP	8.00	2.40
105 Michael Tucker	.50	.15
106 Roberto Hernandez	.60	.18
107 John Rodriguez RC	1.00	.30
108 Danny Graves	.50	.15
109 Rich Aurilia	.60	.18
110 Jon Lieber	.50	.15
111 Tim Hummel RC	1.00	.30
112 J.T. Snow	.60	.18
113 Kris Benson	.50	.15
114 Derek Jeter	4.00	1.20
115 John Franco	.60	.18
116 Matt Stairs	.50	.15
117 Ben Davis	.50	.15
118 Darryl Kile	.60	.18
119 Mike Peeples RC	1.00	.30
120 Kevin Tapani	.50	.15
121 Armando Benitez	.60	.18
122 Damian Miller	.50	.15
123 Jose Jimenez	.50	.15
124 Pedro Astacio	.50	.15
125 Marlyn Tisdale RC	1.00	.30
126 Deivi Cruz	.50	.15
127 Paul O'Neill	1.00	.30
128 Jermaine Dye	.60	.18
129 Marcus Giles	.60	.18
130 Mark Loretta	.50	.15
131 Garret Anderson	.60	.18
132 Todd Ritchie	.50	.15
133 Joe Crede	.50	.15
134 Kevin Millwood	.60	.18
135 Shane Reynolds	.50	.15
136 Mark Grace	1.00	.30
137 Shannon Stewart	.60	.18
138 Nick Neugebauer	.50	.15
139 Nic Jackson RC	1.00	.30
140 Robb Nen UER Name spelled Rob on front	.60	.18
141 Dmitri Young	.60	.18
142 Kevin Appier	.60	.18
143 Jack Cust	.50	.15
144 Andres Torres	.50	.15
145 Frank Thomas	1.50	.45
146 Jason Kendall	.60	.18
147 Greg Maddux	2.50	.75
148 David Justice	.60	.18
149 Hideo Nomo	1.50	.45
150 Bret Boone	.60	.18
151 Wade Miller	.60	.18
152 Jeff Kent	.60	.18
153 Scott Williamson	.50	.15
154 Julio Lugo	.50	.15
155 Bobby Higginson	.60	.18
156 Geoff Jenkins	.60	.18
157 Darren Dreifort	.50	.15
158 Freddy Sanchez RC	1.00	.30
159 Bud Smith	.50	.15
160 Phil Nevin	.60	.18
161 Cesar Izturis	.50	.15
162 Sean Casey	.60	.18
163 Jose Ortiz	.50	.15
164 Brent Abernathy	.50	.15
165 Kevin Young	.50	.15
166 Daryle Ward	.50	.15
167 Trevor Hoffman	.60	.18
168 Rondell White	.60	.18
169 Kip Wells	.50	.15
170 John Vander Wal	.50	.15
171 Jose Lima	.50	.15
172 Wilton Guerrero	.50	.15
173 Aaron Dean RC	1.00	.30
174 Rick Helling	.50	.15
175 Juan Pierre	.60	.18
176 Jay Bell	.60	.18
177 Craig House	.50	.15
178 David Bell	.50	.15
179 Pat Burrell	.60	.18
180 Eric Gagne	1.00	.30
181 Adam Pettyjohn	.50	.15
182 Ugueth Urbina	.50	.15
183 Peter Bergeron	.50	.15
184 Adrian Gonzalez UER Birthdate is wrong	.60	.18
184N Adrian Gonzalez Night SP UER Birthdate is wrong	5.00	1.50
185 Damion Easley	.50	.15
186 Gookie Dawkins	.50	.15
187 Matt Lawton	.50	.15
188 Frank Catalanotto	.50	.15
189 David Wells	.60	.18
190 Roger Cedeno	.50	.15
191 Brian Giles	.60	.18
192 Julio Zuleta	.50	.15
193 Timo Perez	.50	.15
194 Billy Wagner	.60	.18
195 Craig Counsell	.50	.15
196 Bart Miadich	.50	.15
197 Gary Sheffield	.60	.18
198 Richard Hidalgo	.60	.18
199 Juan Uribe	.50	.15
200 Curt Schilling	1.00	.30
201 Javy Lopez	.60	.18
202 Jimmy Haynes	.50	.15
203 Jim Edmonds	.60	.18
204 Pokey Reese	.50	.15
204N Pokey Reese Night SP	5.00	1.50
205 Matt Clement	.60	.18
206 Dean Palmer	.60	.18
207 Nick Johnson	.60	.18
208 Nate Espy RC	1.00	.30
209 Pedro Feliz	.50	.15
210 Aaron Rowand	.50	.15
211 Masato Yoshii	.50	.15
212 Jose Cruz Jr.	.60	.18
213 Paul Byrd	.50	.15
214 Mark Phillips RC	1.00	.30
215 Benny Agbayani	.50	.15
216 Frank Menechino	.50	.15
217 John Flaherty	.50	.15
218 Brian Boehringer	.50	.15
219 Todd Hollandsworth	.50	.15
220 Sammy Sosa SP	12.00	3.60
221 Steve Sparks	.50	.15
222 Homer Bush	.50	.15
223 Mike Hampton	.60	.18
224 Bobby Abreu	.60	.18
225 Barry Larkin	1.50	.45
226 Ryan Rupe	.50	.15
227 Bubba Trammell	.50	.15
228 Todd Zeile	.60	.18
229 Jeff Shaw	.50	.15
230 Alex Ochoa	.50	.15
231 Orlando Cabrera	.50	.15
232 Jeremy Giambi	.50	.15
233 Tomo Ohka	.50	.15
234 Luis Castillo	.60	.18
235 Chris Holt	.50	.15
236 Shawn Green	.60	.18
237 Sidney Ponson	.60	.18
238 Lee Stevens	.50	.15
239 Hank Blalock	1.50	.45
240 Randy Winn	.50	.15
241 Pedro Martinez	1.50	.45
242 Vinny Castilla	.60	.18
243 Steve Karsay	.50	.15
244 Barry Bonds SP	20.00	6.00
245 Jason Bere	.50	.15
246 Scott Rolen	1.00	.30
246N Scott Rolen Night SP	8.00	2.40
247 Ryan Kohlmeier	.50	.15
248 Kerry Wood	1.50	.45
249 Aramis Ramirez	.60	.18
250 Lance Berkman	.60	.18
251 Omar Vizquel	.60	.18
252 Juan Encarnacion	.50	.15
253 Does Not Exist		
254 David Segui	.50	.15
255 Brian Anderson	.50	.15
256 Jay Payton	.50	.15
257 Mark Grudzielanek	.50	.15
258 Jimmy Anderson	.50	.15
259 Eric Valent	.50	.15
260 Chad Durbin	.50	.15
261 Does Not Exist		
262 Alex Gonzalez	.50	.15
263 Scott Dunn	.50	.15
264 Scott Elarton	.50	.15
265 Tom Gordon	.50	.15
266 Moises Alou	.60	.18
267 Does Not Exist		
268 Does Not Exist		
269 Mark Buehrle	.60	.18
270 Jerry Hairston	.50	.15
271 Does Not Exist		
272 Luke Prokopec	.50	.15
273 Graeme Lloyd	.50	.15
274 Bret Prinz	.50	.15
275 Does Not Exist		
276 Chris Carpenter	.50	.15
277 Ryan Minor	.50	.15
278 Jeff D'Amico	.50	.15
279 Raul Ibanez	.50	.15
280 Joe Mays	.50	.15
281 Livan Hernandez	.50	.15
282 Robin Ventura	.60	.18
283 Gabe Kapler	.50	.15
284 Tony Batista	.60	.18
285 Ramon Hernandez	.50	.15
286 Craig Paquette	.50	.15
287 Mark Kotsay	.50	.15
288 Mike Lieberthal	.60	.18
289 Joe Borchard	.60	.18
290 Cristian Guzman	.60	.18
291 Craig Biggio	1.00	.30
292 Joaquin Benoit	.50	.15
293 Ken Caminiti	.60	.18
294 Sean Burroughs	.60	.18
295 Eric Karros	.60	.18
296 Eric Chavez	.60	.18
297 LaTroy Hawkins	.50	.15
298 Alfonso Soriano	1.00	.30
299 John Smoltz	1.00	.30
300 Adam Dunn	.60	.18
301 Ryan Dempster	.50	.15
302 Travis Hafner	.60	.18
303 Russell Branyan	.50	.15
304 Dustin Hermanson	.50	.15
305 Jim Thome	1.50	.45
306 Carlos Beltran	.60	.18
307 Jason Botts RC	1.00	.30
308 David Cone	.60	.18
309 Ivanon Coffie	.50	.15
310 Brian Jordan	.60	.18
311 Todd Walker	.60	.18
312 Jeromy Burnitz	.60	.18
313 Tony Armas Jr.	.50	.15
314 Jeff Conine	.60	.18
315 Todd Jones	.50	.15
316 Roy Oswalt	.60	.18
317 Aubrey Huff	.60	.18
318 Josh Fogg	.50	.15
319 Jose Vidro	.60	.18
320 Jace Brewer	.50	.15
321 Mike Redmond	.50	.15
322 Noochie Varner RC	1.00	.30
323 Russ Ortiz	.60	.18
324 Edgardo Alfonzo	.60	.18
325 Ruben Sierra	.50	.15
326 Calvin Murray	.50	.15
327 Marlon Anderson	.50	.15
328 Albie Lopez	.50	.15
329 Chris Gomez	.50	.15
330 Fernando Tatis	.50	.15
331 Stubby Clapp	.50	.15
332 Rickey Henderson	1.50	.45
333 Brad Radke	.60	.18
334 Brent Mayne	.50	.15
335 Cory Lidle	.50	.15
336 Edgar Martinez	1.00	.30
337 Aaron Boone	.60	.18
338 Jay Witasick	.50	.15
339 Benito Santiago	.60	.18
340 Jose Mercedes	.50	.15
341 Fernando Vina	.60	.18
342 A.J. Pierzynski	.60	.18
343 Jeff Bagwell	1.00	.30
344 Brian Bohanon	.50	.15
345 Adrian Beltre	.60	.18
346 Troy Percival	.60	.18
347 Napoleon Calzado RC	1.00	.30
348 Ruben Rivera	.50	.15
349 Rafael Soriano	.60	.18
350 Damian Jackson	.50	.15
351 Joe Randa	.50	.15
352 Chan Ho Park	.60	.18
353 Dante Bichette	.60	.18
354 Bartolo Colon	.60	.18
355 Jason Bay RC	1.50	.45
356 Shea Hillenbrand	.60	.18
357 Matt Morris	.60	.18
358 Brad Penny	.50	.15
359 Mark Quinn	.50	.15
360 Marquis Grissom	.50	.15
361 Henry Blanco	.50	.15
362 Billy Koch	.50	.15
363 Mike Cameron	.60	.18
364 Albert Pujols SP	15.00	4.50
365 Paul Konerko SP	5.00	1.50
366 Eric Milton SP	5.00	1.50
367 Nick Bierbrodt SP	5.00	1.50
368 Rafael Palmeiro SP	8.00	2.40
369 Jorge Padilla SP RC	5.00	1.50
370 Jason Giambi Yankees SP Stats on back are Jeremy Giambi's	20.00	6.00
371 Mike Piazza SP	12.00	3.60
372 Alex Cora SP	5.00	1.50
373 Todd Helton SP	8.00	2.40
374 Juan Gonzalez SP	8.00	2.40
375 Mariano Rivera SP	8.00	2.40
376 Jason LaRue SP	5.00	1.50
377 Tony Gwynn SP	10.00	3.00
378 Wilson Betemit SP	5.00	1.50
379 J.J. Trujillo SP RC	5.00	1.50
380 Brad Ausmus SP	5.00	1.50
381 Chris George SP	5.00	1.50
382 Jose Canseco SP	8.00	2.40
383 Ramon Ortiz SP	5.00	1.50
384 John Rocker SP	5.00	1.50
385 Rey Ordonez SP	5.00	1.50
386 Ken Griffey Jr. SP	12.00	3.60
387 Juan Pena SP	5.00	1.50
388 Michael Barrett SP	5.00	1.50
389 J.D. Drew SP	5.00	1.50
390 Corey Koskie SP	5.00	1.50
391 Vernon Wells SP	5.00	1.50
392 Juan Tolentino SP RC	5.00	1.50

393 Luis Gonzalez SP.......... 5.00 1.50
394 Terrence Long SP.......... 5.00 1.50
395 Travis Lee SP.......... 5.00 1.50
396 Earl Snyder SP RC.......... 5.00 1.50
397 Nomar Garciaparra SP.......... 12.00 3.60
398 Jason Schmidt SP.......... 5.00 1.50
399 David Espinosa SP.......... 5.00 1.50
400 Steve Green SP.......... 5.00 1.50
401 Jack Wilson SP.......... 5.00 1.50
402 Chris Tritle SP RC.......... 5.00 1.50
403 Angel Berroa SP.......... 5.00 1.50
404 Josh Towers SP.......... 5.00 1.50
405 Andruw Jones SP.......... 5.00 1.50
406 Brent Butler SP.......... 5.00 1.50
407 Craig Kuzmic SP.......... 5.00 1.50
408 Derek Bell SP.......... 5.00 1.50
409 Eric Glaser SP RC.......... 5.00 1.50
410 Joel Pineiro SP.......... 5.00 1.50
411 Alexis Gomez SP.......... 5.00 1.50
412 Mike Rivera SP.......... 5.00 1.50
413 Shawn Estes SP.......... 5.00 1.50
414 Milton Bradley SP.......... 5.00 1.50
415 Carl Everett SP.......... 5.00 1.50
416 Kazuhiro Sasaki SP.......... 5.00 1.50
417 Tony Fontana SP RC.......... 5.00 1.50
418 Josh Pearce SP.......... 5.00 1.50
419 Gary Matthews Jr. SP.......... 5.00 1.50
420 Raymond Cabrera SP RC.......... 5.00 1.50
421 Joe Kennedy SP.......... 5.00 1.50
422 Jason Maule SP RC.......... 5.00 1.50
423 Casey Fossum SP.......... 5.00 1.50
424 Christian Parker SP.......... 5.00 1.50
425 Laynce Nix SP RC.......... 30.00 9.00
426 Byung-Hyun Kim SP.......... 5.00 1.50
427 Freddy Garcia SP.......... 5.00 1.50
428 Herbert Perry SP.......... 5.00 1.50
429 Jason Marquis SP.......... 5.00 1.50
430 Sandy Alomar Jr. SP.......... 5.00 1.50
431 Roberto Alomar SP.......... 8.00 2.40
432 Tsuyoshi Shinjo SP.......... 5.00 1.50
433 Tim Wakefield SP.......... 5.00 1.50
434 Robert Fick SP.......... 5.00 1.50
435 Vladimir Guerrero SP.......... 8.00 2.40
436 Jose Mesa SP.......... 5.00 1.50
437 Scott Spiezio SP.......... 5.00 1.50
438 Jose Hernandez SP.......... 5.00 1.50
439 Jose Acevedo SP.......... 5.00 1.50
440 Brian West SP RC.......... 5.00 1.50
441 Barry Zito SP.......... 8.00 2.40
442 Luis Maza SP.......... 5.00 1.50
443 Marlon Byrd SP.......... 5.00 1.50
444 A.J. Burnett SP.......... 5.00 1.50
445 Dee Brown SP.......... 5.00 1.50
446 Carlos Delgado SP.......... 5.00 1.50
NNO 1953 Repurchased EXCH..........

2002 Topps Heritage Chrome

Inserted into packs at stated odds of one in 29, these 100 cards feature the "Chrome" technology and have a stated print run of 553 copies.

Nm-Mt Ex-Mt
STATED ODDS 1:29..........
STATED PRINT RUN 553 SERIAL #'d SETS
THC1 Darin Erstad.......... 8.00 2.40
THC2 Doug Mientkiewicz.......... 8.00 2.40
THC3 Mike Sweeney.......... 8.00 2.40
THC4 Roger Clemens.......... 25.00 7.50
THC5 C.C. Sabathia.......... 8.00 2.40
THC6 Tim Hudson.......... 8.00 2.40
THC7 Jason Lane.......... 8.00 2.40
THC8 Larry Walker.......... 8.00 2.40
THC9 Mark Mulder.......... 8.00 2.40
THC10 Mike Mussina.......... 12.00 3.60
THC11 Paul LoDuca.......... 8.00 2.40
THC12 Jimmy Rollins.......... 8.00 2.40
THC13 Ivan Rodriguez.......... 12.00 3.60
THC14 Mark McGwire.......... 30.00 9.00
THC15 Edgar Renteria.......... 8.00 2.40
THC16 Scott Brosius.......... 8.00 2.40
THC17 Juan Cruz.......... 8.00 2.40
THC18 Kevin Brown.......... 8.00 2.40
THC19 Charles Nagy.......... 8.00 2.40
THC20 Bill Ortega.......... 8.00 2.40
THC21 Corey Patterson.......... 8.00 2.40
THC22 Magglio Ordonez.......... 8.00 2.40
THC23 Brandon Duckworth.......... 8.00 2.40
THC24 Scott Schoeneweis.......... 8.00 2.40
THC25 Tino Martinez.......... 8.00 2.40
THC26 Jason Young.......... 8.00 2.40
THC27 Nate Cornejo.......... 8.00 2.40
THC28 Ryan Klesko.......... 8.00 2.40
THC29 Omar Daal.......... 8.00 2.40
THC30 Raul Mondesi.......... 8.00 2.40
THC31 Boof Bonser.......... 8.00 2.40
THC32 Rich Aurilia.......... 8.00 2.40
THC33 Jon Lieber.......... 8.00 2.40
THC34 Tim Hummel.......... 8.00 2.40
THC35 J.T. Snow.......... 8.00 2.40
THC36 Derek Jeter.......... 30.00 9.00
THC37 Darryl Kile.......... 8.00 2.40
THC38 Armando Benitez.......... 8.00 2.40
THC39 Marlyn Tisdale.......... 8.00 2.40
THC40 Shannon Stewart.......... 8.00 2.40
THC41 Nic Jackson.......... 8.00 2.40
THC42 Robb Nen UER.......... 8.00 2.40
First name misspelled Rob
THC43 Dmitri Young.......... 8.00 2.40
THC44 Greg Maddux.......... 20.00 6.00
THC45 Hideo Nomo.......... 12.00 3.60
THC46 Bret Boone.......... 8.00 2.40
THC47 Wade Miller.......... 8.00 2.40
THC48 Jeff Kent.......... 8.00 2.40
THC49 Freddy Sanchez.......... 8.00 2.40
THC50 Bud Smith.......... 8.00 2.40
THC51 Sean Casey.......... 8.00 2.40
THC52 Brent Abernathy.......... 8.00 2.40
THC53 Trevor Hoffman.......... 8.00 2.40
THC54 Aaron Dean.......... 8.00 2.40
THC55 Juan Pierre.......... 8.00 2.40
THC56 Pat Burrell.......... 8.00 2.40
THC57 Gookie Dawkins.......... 8.00 2.40
THC58 Roger Cedeno.......... 8.00 2.40
THC59 Brian Giles.......... 8.00 2.40
THC60 Jim Edmonds.......... 8.00 2.40
THC61 Dean Palmer.......... 8.00 2.40
THC62 Nick Johnson.......... 8.00 2.40
THC63 Nate Espy.......... 8.00 2.40
THC64 Aaron Rowand.......... 8.00 2.40
THC65 Mark Phillips.......... 10.00 3.00
THC66 Mike Hampton.......... 8.00 2.40
THC67 Bobby Abreu.......... 8.00 2.40
THC68 Alex Ochoa.......... 8.00 2.40
THC69 Shawn Green.......... 8.00 2.40
THC70 Hank Blalock.......... 8.00 2.40
THC71 Pedro Martinez.......... 12.00 3.60
THC72 Ryan Kohlmeier.......... 8.00 2.40
THC73 Kerry Wood.......... 12.00 3.60
THC74 Aramis Ramirez.......... 8.00 2.40
THC75 Lance Berkman.......... 8.00 2.40
THC76 Scott Dunn.......... 8.00 2.40
THC77 Moises Alou.......... 8.00 2.40
THC78 Mark Buehrle.......... 8.00 2.40
THC79 Jerry Hairston.......... 8.00 2.40
THC80 Joe Borchard.......... 8.00 2.40
THC81 Cristian Guzman.......... 8.00 2.40
THC82 Sean Burroughs.......... 8.00 2.40
THC83 Alfonso Soriano.......... 8.00 2.40
THC84 Adam Dunn.......... 8.00 2.40
THC85 Jim Thome.......... 12.00 3.60
THC86 Jason Botts.......... 8.00 2.40
THC87 Jeromy Burnitz.......... 8.00 2.40
THC88 Roy Oswalt.......... 8.00 2.40
THC89 Russ Ortiz.......... 8.00 2.40
THC90 Marlon Anderson.......... 8.00 2.40
THC91 Stubby Clapp.......... 8.00 2.40
THC92 Rickey Henderson.......... 12.00 3.60
THC93 Brad Radke.......... 8.00 2.40
THC94 Jeff Bagwell.......... 8.00 2.40
THC95 Troy Percival.......... 8.00 2.40
THC96 Napoleon Calzado.......... 8.00 2.40
THC97 Joe Randa.......... 8.00 2.40
THC98 Chan Ho Park.......... 8.00 2.40
THC99 Jason Bay.......... 12.00 3.60
THC100 Mark Quinn.......... 8.00 2.40

2002 Topps Heritage Classic Renditions

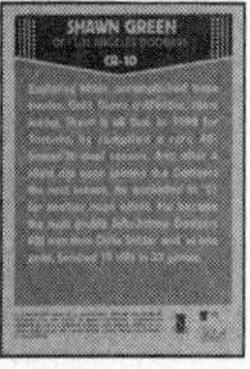

Inserted into packs at stated odds of one in 12, these 10 cards show how current players might look like if they played in their 1953 team uniforms. These cards are printed on grayback paper stock.

Nm-Mt Ex-Mt
COMPLETE SET (10).......... 20.00 6.00
CR1 Kerry Wood.......... 2.50 .75
CR2 Brian Giles.......... 2.00 .60
CR3 Roger Cedeno.......... 2.00 .60
CR4 Jason Giambi.......... 2.50 .75
CR5 Albert Pujols.......... 5.00 1.50
CR6 Mark Buehrle.......... 2.00 .60
CR7 Cristian Guzman.......... 2.00 .60
CR8 Jimmy Rollins.......... 2.00 .60
CR9 Jim Thome.......... 2.50 .75
CR10 Shawn Green.......... 2.00 .60

2002 Topps Heritage Classic Renditions Autographs

Partially paralleling the Classic Rendition set, these three cards were all autographed by the player and have a stated print run of 25 sets. Due to market scarcity, no pricing is provided for these cards.

Nm-Mt Ex-Mt
CRABG Brian Giles..........
CRACG Cristian Guzman..........
CRAJR Jimmy Rollins..........

2002 Topps Heritage Clubhouse Collection

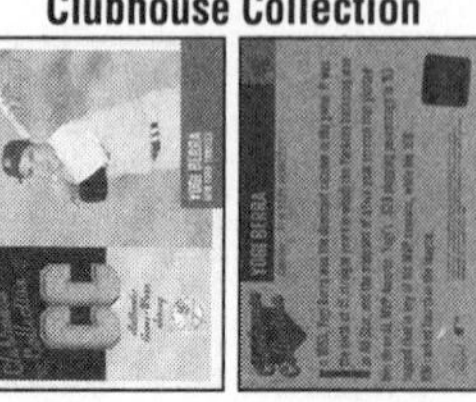

Inserted into packs at a rate for jersey cards of one in 332 and bat cards at a rate of one in 498, these 12 cards feature a mix of active and retired players with a memorabilia swatch.

Nm-Mt Ex-Mt
CCAD Alvin Dark Bat.......... 25.00 7.50
CCBB Barry Bonds Bat.......... 80.00 24.00
CCCP Corey Patterson Bat.......... 25.00 7.50
CCEM Eddie Mathews Jsy.......... 40.00 12.00
CCGK George Kell Jsy.......... 40.00 12.00
CCGM Greg Maddux Jsy.......... 40.00 12.00
CCHS Hank Sauer Bat.......... 25.00 7.50
CCJP Jorge Posada Bat.......... 40.00 12.00
CCNG Nomar Garciaparra Bat.......... 50.00 15.00
CCRA Rich Aurilia Bat.......... 25.00 7.50
CCWM Willie Mays Bat.......... 100.00 30.00
CCYB Yogi Berra Jsy.......... 40.00 12.00

2002 Topps Heritage Clubhouse Collection Autographs

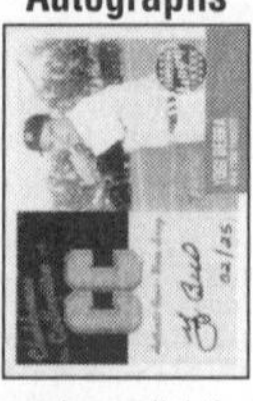

These four cards parallel the Clubhouse Collection insert set. These cards feature autographs from the noted players are are serial numbered to 25. Due to market scarcity, no pricing is provided for these players.

Nm-Mt Ex-Mt
CCAAD Alvin Dark Bat..........
CCAGK George Kell Jsy..........
CCAWM Willie Mays Bat..........
CCAYB Yogi Berra Jsy..........

2002 Topps Heritage Clubhouse Collection Duos

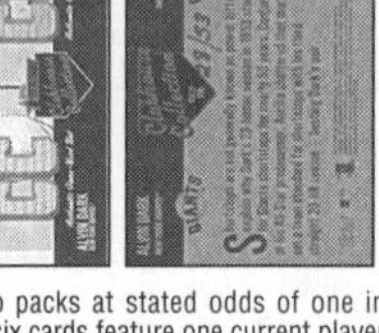

Inserted into packs at stated odds of one in 5016, these six cards feature one current player and one 1953 franchise alum from that same team with a relic from each player. These cards have a stated print run of 53 serial numbered sets. Due to market scarcity, no pricing is provided for these cards.

Nm-Mt Ex-Mt
CC2BP Yogi Berra Jsy.......... 150.00 45.00
Jorge Posada Bat
CC2DA Alvin Dark Bat.......... 100.00 30.00
Rich Aurilia Bat
CC2KR George Kell Jsy.......... 150.00 45.00
Nomar Garciaparra Bat
CC2MB Willie Mays Bat.......... 250.00 75.00
Barry Bonds Bat UER
Card states Bonds is Mays' godfather
It is the other way around
CC2SM Eddie Mathews Jsy.......... 200.00 60.00
Greg Maddux Jsy
CC2SP Hank Sauer Bat.......... 100.00 30.00
Corey Patterson Bat

2002 Topps Heritage Grandstand Glory

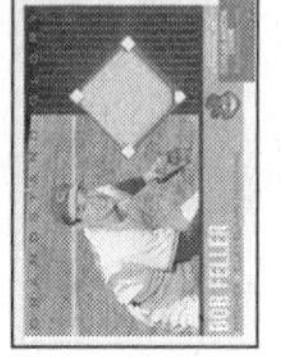

Inserted into packs at different rates depending on which grop the player is from, these 12 cards feature retired 1950's players along with an authentic relic from an historic 1950's stadium.

Nm-Mt Ex-Mt
GROUP A STATED ODDS 1:4115..........
GROUP B STATED ODDS 1:531..........
GROUP C STATED ODDS 1:1576..........
GROUP D STATED ODDS 1:370..........
GROUP E STATED ODDS 1:483..........
GGBF Bob Feller E.......... 25.00 7.50
GGBM Billy Martin B.......... 50.00 15.00
GGBP Billy Pierce B.......... 20.00 6.00
GGBS Bobby Shantz D.......... 20.00 6.00
GGEW Early Wynn E.......... 25.00 7.50
GGHN Hal Newhouser B.......... 25.00 7.50
GGHS Hank Sauer C.......... 20.00 6.00
GGRC Roy Campanella D.......... 40.00 12.00
GGSP Satchel Paige A.......... 60.00 18.00
GGTK Ted Kluszewski E.......... 40.00 12.00
GGWF Whitey Ford D..........
GGWS Warren Spahn D.......... 25.00 7.50

2002 Topps Heritage New Age Performers

Inserted into packs at stated odds of one in 15, these 15 cards feature powerhouse players whose accomplishments have cemented their names in major league history.

Nm-Mt Ex-Mt
COMPLETE SET (15).......... 50.00 15.00
NA1 Luis Gonzalez.......... 2.00 .60
NA2 Mark McGwire.......... 6.00 1.80
NA3 Barry Bonds.......... 6.00 1.80
NA4 Ken Griffey Jr.......... 4.00 1.20
NA5 Ichiro Suzuki.......... 4.00 1.20
NA6 Sammy Sosa.......... 4.00 1.20
NA7 Andruw Jones.......... 2.00 .60
NA8 Derek Jeter.......... 6.00 1.80
NA9 Todd Helton.......... 2.00 .60
NA10 Alex Rodriguez.......... 4.00 1.20
NA11 Jason Giambi Yankees.......... 2.50 .75
NA12 Bret Boone.......... 2.00 .60
NA13 Roberto Alomar.......... 2.50 .75
NA14 Albert Pujols.......... 5.00 1.50
NA15 Vladimir Guerrero.......... 2.50 .75

2002 Topps Heritage Real One Autographs

Inserted into packs at different odds depending on which group the player belongs to, this 28 card set features a mix of authentic autographs between active players and those who were active in the 1953 season. Please note that the group whiche each player belongs to is listed next to their name in our checklist.

Nm-Mt Ex-Mt
GROUP 1 STATED ODDS 1:346..........
GROUP 2 STATED ODDS 1:6363..........
GROUP 3 STATED ODDS 1:4908..........
GROUP 4 STATED ODDS 1:3196..........
GROUP 5 STATED ODDS 1:498..........
RO-AC Andy Carey 1.......... 40.00 12.00
RO-AD Alvin Dark 1.......... 60.00 18.00
RO-AR Al Rosen 1.......... 80.00 24.00
RO-ARO Alex Rodriguez 2.......... 150.00 45.00
RO-ASC Al Schoendienst 1.......... 60.00 18.00
RO-BF Bob Feller 1.......... 80.00 24.00
RO-BG Brian Giles 5.......... 25.00 7.50
RO-BS Bobby Shantz 1.......... 60.00 18.00
RO-CG Cristian Guzman 5.......... 25.00 7.50
RO-DD Dom DiMaggio 1.......... 80.00 24.00
RO-ES Enos Slaughter 1.......... 80.00 24.00
RO-GK George Kell 1.......... 60.00 18.00
RO-GM Gil McDougald 1.......... 80.00 24.00
RO-HW Hoyt Wilhelm 1.......... 60.00 18.00
RO-JB Joe Black 1.......... 60.00 18.00
RO-JE Jim Edmonds 4.......... 50.00 15.00
RO-JP John Podres 1.......... 60.00 18.00
RO-MI Monte Irvin 1.......... 80.00 24.00
RO-OM Minnie Minoso 1.......... 60.00 18.00
RO-PR Phil Rizzuto 1.......... 80.00 24.00
RO-PRO Preacher Roe 1.......... 60.00 18.00
RO-RB Ray Boone 1.......... 60.00 18.00
RO-RF Roy Face 1.......... 60.00 18.00
RO-RCL Roger Clemens 3.......... 150.00 45.00
RO-WF Whitey Ford 1.......... 80.00 24.00
RO-WM Willie Mays 1.......... 200.00 60.00
RO-WS Warren Spahn 1.......... 100.00 30.00
RO-YB Yogi Berra 1.......... 100.00 30.00

2002 Topps Heritage Real One Autographs Red Ink

These cards parallel the "Real One Autograph" insert set. These cards are signed in red ink and were inserted at stated odds of one in 306 and are serial numbered to 53 signed copies.

Nm-Mt Ex-Mt
*RED INK: .75X TO 1.5X BASIC AUTOS

2002 Topps Heritage Then and Now

Inserted into packs at stated odds of one in 15, these 10 cards feature a 1953 player as well as a current stand-out. These cards offer statistical comparisions in major stat categories and are printed in greyback paper stock.

Nm-Mt Ex-Mt
COMPLETE SET (10).......... 30.00 9.00
TN1 Eddie Mathews.......... 6.00 1.80
Barry Bonds
TN2 Al Rosen.......... 4.00 1.20
Alex Rodriguez
TN3 Carl Furillo.......... 2.00 .60
Larry Walker
TN4 Minnie Minoso.......... 4.00 1.20
Ichiro Suzuki
TN5 Richie Ashburn.......... 2.00 .60
Rich Aurilia
TN6 Al Rosen.......... 2.00 .60
Bret Boone
TN7 Duke Snider.......... 4.00 1.20
Sammy Sosa
TN8 Al Rosen.......... 4.00 1.20
Alex Rodriguez
TN9 Robin Roberts.......... 2.50 .75
Randy Johnson
TN10 Billy Pierce.......... 2.50 .75
Hideo Nomo

2003 Topps Heritage

This 430-card set, which was designed to honor the 1954 Topps set, was released in February, 2003. These cards were issued in five card packs with an $3 SRP. These packs were issued in 24 pack boxes which came eight boxes to a case. In addition, many cards in the set were issued in two varieties. A few cards were issued featuring either a logo used today or a scarcer version in which the logo was used in the 1954 set. In addition, some cards were printed with either the originally designed version or a black background. The black background version is the tougher of the two versions of each card. A few cards between 1 and 363 were produced in less quantities and all cards from 364 on up were short printed as well. In a nod to the 1954 set, Alex Rodriguez had both cards 1 and 250; just as Ted Williams had in the original 1954 Topps set.

Nm-Mt Ex-Mt
COMPLETE SET (450).......... 350.00 105.00
COMP.SET w/o SP's (350).......... 80.00 24.00
COMMON CARD.......... .50 .15
COMMON RC.......... 1.00 .30
COMMON SP.......... 5.00 1.50
COMMON SP RC.......... 5.00 1.50
1A Alex Rodriguez Red.......... 2.50 .75
1B Alex Rodriguez Black SP.......... 12.00 3.60
2 Jose Cruz Jr.......... .60 .18
3 Ichiro Suzuki SP.......... 12.00 3.60
4 Rich Aurilia.......... .60 .18
5 Trevor Hoffman.......... .60 .18
6A Brian Giles New Logo.......... .60 .18
6B Brian Giles Old Logo SP.......... 5.00 1.50
7A Albert Pujols Orange.......... 3.00 .90
7B Albert Pujols Black SP.......... 15.00 4.50
8 Vicente Padilla.......... .50 .15
9 Bobby Crosby.......... 1.00 .30
10A Derek Jeter New Logo.......... 4.00 1.20
10B Derek Jeter Old Logo SP.......... 15.00 4.50
11A Pat Burrell New Logo.......... .60 .18
11B Pat Burrell Old Logo SP.......... 5.00 1.50
12 Armando Benitez.......... .60 .18
13 Javier Vazquez.......... .60 .18
14 Justin Morneau.......... .60 .18
15 Doug Mientkiewicz.......... .60 .18
16 Kevin Brown.......... .60 .18
17 Alexis Gomez.......... .50 .15
18A Lance Berkman Blue.......... .60 .18
18B Lance Berkman Black SP.......... 5.00 1.50
19 Adrian Gonzalez.......... .60 .18
20A Todd Helton Green.......... 1.00 .30
20B Todd Helton Black SP.......... 8.00 2.40
21 Carlos Pena.......... .50 .15
22 Matt Lawton.......... .50 .15
23 Elmer Dessens.......... .50 .15
24 Hee Seop Choi.......... .60 .18
25 Chris Duncan SP RC.......... 5.00 1.50
26 Ugueth Urbina.......... .50 .15
27A Rodrigo Lopez New Logo.......... .50 .15
27B Ro. Lopez Old Logo SP.......... 5.00 1.50
28 Damian Moss.......... .50 .15
29 Steve Finley.......... .60 .18
30A Sammy Sosa New Logo.......... 2.50 .75
30B S.Sosa Old Logo SP.......... 12.00 3.60
31 Kevin Cash.......... .50 .15
32 Kenny Rogers.......... .60 .18
33 Ben Grieve.......... .50 .15
34 Jason Simontacchi.......... .50 .15
35 Shin-Soo Choo.......... .60 .18
36 Freddy Garcia.......... .60 .18
37 Jesse Foppert.......... .60 .18
38 Tony LaRussa MG.......... .60 .18
39 Mark Kotsay.......... .50 .15
40 Barry Zito.......... 1.00 .30
41 Josh Fogg.......... .50 .15
42 Marlon Byrd.......... .60 .18
43 Marcus Thames.......... .50 .15
44 Al Leiter.......... .60 .18
45 Michael Barrett.......... .50 .15
46 Jake Peavy.......... .60 .18
47 Dustan Mohr.......... .50 .15
48 Alex Sanchez.......... .50 .15
49 Chin-Feng Chen.......... .60 .18
50A Kazuhisa Ishii Blue.......... .60 .18
50B Kazuhisa Ishii Black SP.......... 5.00 1.50
51 Carlos Beltran.......... .60 .18
52 Franklin Gutierrez RC.......... 3.00 .90
53 Miguel Cabrera.......... 2.50 .75
54 Roger Clemens.......... 3.00 .90
55 Juan Cruz.......... .50 .15
56 Jason Young.......... .50 .15
57 Alex Herrera.......... .50 .15
58 Aaron Boone.......... .60 .18
59 Mark Buehrle.......... .60 .18
60 Larry Walker.......... 1.00 .30
61 Morgan Ensberg.......... .50 .15
62 Barry Larkin.......... 1.50 .45
63 Joe Borchard.......... .60 .18
64 Jason Dubois.......... .60 .18
65 Shea Hillenbrand.......... .60 .18
66 Jay Gibbons.......... .60 .18
67 Vinny Castilla.......... .60 .18
68 Jeff Mathis.......... .60 .18
69 Curt Schilling.......... 1.00 .30
70 Garret Anderson.......... .60 .18
71 Josh Phelps.......... .50 .15
72 Chan Ho Park.......... .60 .18
73 Edgar Renteria.......... .60 .18
74 Kazuhiro Sasaki.......... .60 .18
75 Lloyd McClendon MG.......... .50 .15
76 Jon Lieber.......... .50 .15
77 Rolando Viera.......... .50 .15
78 Jeff Conine.......... .60 .18
79 Kevin Millwood.......... .60 .18
80A Randy Johnson Green.......... 1.50 .45
80B Randy Johnson Black SP.......... 12.00 3.60
81 Troy Percival.......... .60 .18
82 Cliff Floyd.......... .60 .18
83 Tony Graffanino.......... .50 .15
84 Austin Kearns.......... .60 .18

85 Manuel Ramirez SP RC 8.00 2.40
86 Jim Tracy MG .... .50 .15
87 Rondell White .... .60 .18
88 Trot Nixon .... 1.00 .30
89 Carlos Lee .... .60 .18
90 Mike Lowell .... .60 .18
91 Raul Ibanez .... .50 .15
92 Ricardo Rodriguez .... .50 .15
93 Ben Sheets .... .60 .18
94 Jason Perry SP RC 8.00 2.40
95 Mark Teixeira .... 1.00 .30
96 Brad Fullmer .... .50 .15
97 Casey Kotchman .... 1.00 .30
98 Craig Counsell .... .50 .15
99 Jason Marquis .... .50 .15
100A N.Garciaparra New Logo .... 2.50 .75
100B N.Garciaparra Old Logo SP 12.00 3.60
101 Ed Rogers .... .50 .15
102 Wilson Betemit .... .50 .15
103 Wayne Lydon RC .... 1.00 .30
104 Jack Cust .... .50 .15
105 Derrek Lee .... .60 .18
106 Jim Kavourias .... .50 .15
107 Joe Randa .... .50 .15
108 Taylor Buchholz .... .50 .15
109 Gabe Kapler .... .50 .15
110 Preston Wilson .... .60 .18
111 Craig Biggio .... 1.00 .30
112 Paul Lo Duca .... .60 .18
113 Eddie Guardado .... .60 .18
114 Andres Galarraga .... 1.00 .30
115 Edgardo Alfonzo .... .60 .18
116 Robin Ventura .... .60 .18
117 Jeremy Giambi .... .50 .15
118 Ray Durham .... .60 .18
119 Mariano Rivera .... 1.00 .30
120 Jimmy Rollins .... .60 .18
121 Dennis Tankersley .... .50 .15
122 Jason Schmidt .... .60 .18
123 Bret Boone .... .60 .18
124 Josh Hamilton .... .50 .15
125 Scott Rolen .... 1.00 .30
126 Steve Cox .... .50 .15
127 Larry Bowa MG .... .60 .18
128 Adam LaRoche SP 8.00 2.40
129 Ryan Klesko .... .60 .18
130 Tim Hudson .... .60 .18
131 Brandon Claussen .... .60 .18
132 Craig Brazell SP RC 8.00 2.40
133 Grady Little MG .... .50 .15
134 Jarrod Washburn .... .60 .18
135 Lyle Overbay .... .50 .15
136 John Burkett .... .50 .15
137 Daryl Clark RC .... 1.00 .30
138 Kirk Rueter .... .50 .15
139A Joe Mauer .... 1.50 .45
Jake Mauer Green
139B Joe Mauer 8.00 2.40
Jake Mauer Black SP
140 Troy Glaus .... 1.00 .30
141 Trey Hodges SP 5.00 1.50
142 Dallas McPherson .... 1.00 .30
143 Art Howe MG .... .50 .15
144 Jesus Cota .... .50 .15
145 J.R. House .... .50 .15
146 Reggie Sanders .... .60 .18
147 Clint Nageotte .... .60 .18
148 Jim Edmonds .... .60 .18
149 Carl Crawford .... .60 .18
150A Mike Piazza Blue .... 2.50 .75
150B Mike Piazza Black SP 12.00 3.60
151 Seung Song .... .50 .15
152 Roberto Hernandez .... .50 .15
153 Marquis Grissom .... .50 .15
154 Billy Wagner .... .60 .18
155 Josh Beckett .... 1.00 .30
156A R.Simon New Logo .... .50 .15
156B R.Simon Old Logo SP 5.00 1.50
157 Ben Broussard .... .50 .15
158 Russell Branyan .... .50 .15
159 Frank Thomas .... 1.50 .45
160 Alex Escobar .... .50 .15
161 Mark Bellhorn .... .50 .15
162 Melvin Mora .... .50 .15
163 Andruw Jones .... .60 .18
164 Danny Bautista .... .50 .15
165 Ramon Ortiz .... .50 .15
166 Wily Mo Pena .... .50 .15
167 Jose Jimenez .... .50 .15
168 Mark Redman .... .50 .15
169 Angel Berroa .... .60 .18
170 Andy Marte SP RC 15.00 4.50
171 Juan Gonzalez .... 1.50 .45
172 Fernando Vina .... .50 .15
173 Joel Pineiro .... .60 .18
174 Boof Bonser .... .50 .15
175 Bernie Castro SP RC 5.00 1.50
176 Bobby Cox MG .... .50 .15
177 Jeff Kent .... .60 .18
178 Oliver Perez .... .60 .18
179 Chase Utley .... .60 .18
180 Mark Mulder .... .60 .18
181 Bobby Abreu .... .60 .18
182 Ramiro Mendoza .... .50 .15
183 Aaron Heilman .... .50 .15
184 A.J. Pierzynski .... .60 .18
185 Eric Gagne .... 1.00 .30
186 Kirk Saarloos .... .50 .15
187 Ron Gardenhire MG .... .50 .15
188 Dmitri Young .... .60 .18
189 Todd Zeile .... .60 .18
190A Jim Thome New Logo .... 1.50 .45
190B Jim Thome Old Logo SP 8.00 2.40
191 Cliff Lee .... .60 .18
192 Matt Morris .... .60 .18
193 Robert Fick .... .60 .18
194 C.C. Sabathia .... .60 .18
195 Alexis Rios .... 2.50 .75
196 D'Angelo Jimenez .... .50 .15
197 Edgar Martinez .... 1.00 .30
198 Robb Nen .... .60 .18
199 Taggert Bozied .... 1.00 .30
200 Vladimir Guerrero SP 8.00 2.40
201 Walter Young SP 5.00 1.50
202 Brendan Harris RC .... 1.00 .30
203 Mike Hargrove MG .... .50 .15
204 Vernon Wells .... .60 .18
205 Hank Blalock .... 1.00 .30
206 Mike Cameron .... .60 .18
207 Tony Batista .... .60 .18
208 Matt Williams .... .60 .18
209 Tony Womack .... .50 .15
210 R.Nivar-Martinez RC .... 1.00 .30
211 Aaron Sele .... .50 .15
212 Mark Grace .... 1.00 .30
213 Joe Crede .... .50 .15
214 Ryan Dempster .... .50 .15
215 Omar Vizquel .... .60 .18
216 Juan Pierre .... .60 .18
217 Denny Bautista .... .50 .15
218 Chuck Knoblauch .... .60 .18
219 Eric Karros .... .60 .18
220 Victor Diaz .... .60 .18
221 Jacque Jones .... .60 .18
222 Jose Vidro .... .60 .18
223 Joe McEwing .... .50 .15
224 Nick Johnson .... .60 .18
225 Eric Chavez .... .60 .18
226 Jose Mesa .... .50 .15
227 Aramis Ramirez .... .60 .18
228 John Lackey .... .60 .18
229 David Bell .... .60 .18
230 John Olerud .... .60 .18
231 Tino Martinez .... 1.00 .30
232 Randy Winn .... .50 .15
233 Todd Hollandsworth .... .50 .15
234 Ruddy Lugo RC .... 1.00 .30
235 Carlos Delgado .... .60 .18
236 Chris Narveson .... .50 .15
237 Tim Salmon .... 1.00 .30
238 Orlando Palmeiro .... .50 .15
239 Jeff Clark SP RC 5.00 1.50
240 Byung-Hyun Kim .... .60 .18
241 Mike Remlinger .... .50 .15
242 Johnny Damon .... .60 .18
243 Corey Patterson .... .60 .18
244 Paul Konerko .... .60 .18
245 Danny Graves .... .50 .15
246 Ellis Burks .... .60 .18
247 Gavin Floyd .... .60 .18
248 Jaime Bubela RC .... 1.00 .30
249 Sean Burroughs .... .60 .18
250 Alex Rodriguez SP 12.00 3.60
251 Gabe Gross .... .60 .18
252 Rafael Palmeiro .... 1.00 .30
253 Dewon Brazelton .... .50 .15
254 Jimmy Journell .... .50 .15
255 Rafael Soriano .... .50 .15
256 Jerome Williams .... .60 .18
257 Xavier Nady .... .50 .15
258 Mike Williams .... .50 .15
259 Randy Wolf .... .60 .18
260A Miguel Tejada Orange .... .60 .18
260B Miguel Tejada Black SP 5.00 1.50
261 Juan Rivera .... .50 .15
262 Rey Ordonez .... .50 .15
263 Bartolo Colon .... .60 .18
264 Eric Milton .... .50 .15
265 Jeffrey Hammonds .... .50 .15
266 Odalis Perez .... .50 .15
267 Mike Sweeney .... .60 .18
268 Richard Hidalgo .... .60 .18
269 Alex Gonzalez .... .50 .15
270 Aaron Cook .... .50 .15
271 Earl Snyder .... .50 .15
272 Todd Walker .... .60 .18
273 Aaron Rowand .... .60 .18
274 Matt Clement .... .60 .18
275 Anastacio Martinez .... .50 .15
276 Mike Bordick .... .60 .18
277 John Smoltz .... 1.00 .30
278 Scott Hairston .... .60 .18
279 David Eckstein .... .60 .18
280 Shannon Stewart .... .60 .18
281 Carl Everett .... .60 .18
282 Aubrey Huff .... .60 .18
283 Mike Mussina .... 1.50 .45
284 Ruben Sierra .... .50 .15
285 Russ Ortiz .... .50 .15
286 Brian Lawrence .... .50 .15
287 Kip Wells .... .50 .15
288 Placido Polanco .... .50 .15
289 Ted Lilly .... .50 .15
290 Andy Pettitte .... 1.00 .30
291 John Buck .... .50 .15
292 Orlando Cabrera .... .50 .15
293 Cristian Guzman .... .50 .15
294 Ruben Quevedo .... .50 .15
295 Cesar Izturis .... .50 .15
296 Ryan Ludwick .... .50 .15
297 Roy Oswalt .... .60 .18
298 Jason Stokes .... 1.50 .45
299 Mike Hampton .... .60 .18
300 Pedro Martinez .... 1.50 .45
301 Nic Jackson .... .50 .15
302A Mag. Ordonez New Logo .... .60 .18
302B Mag. Ordonez Old Logo SP 5.00 1.50
303 Manny Ramirez .... .60 .18
304 Jorge Julio .... .50 .15
305 Javy Lopez .... .60 .18
306 Roy Halladay .... .60 .18
307 Kevin Mench .... .50 .15
308 Jason Isringhausen .... .60 .18
309 Carlos Guillen .... .50 .15
310 Tsuyoshi Shinjo .... .60 .18
311 Phil Nevin .... .60 .18
312 Pokey Reese .... .50 .15
313 Jorge Padilla .... .50 .15
314 Jermaine Dye .... .60 .18
315 David Wells .... .60 .18
316 Mo Vaughn .... .60 .18
317 Bernie Williams .... 1.00 .30
318 Michael Restovich .... .50 .15
319 Jose Hernandez .... .50 .15
320 Richie Sexson .... .60 .18
321 Daryle Ward .... .50 .15
322 Luis Castillo .... .50 .15
323 Rene Reyes .... .50 .15
324 Victor Martinez .... .60 .18
325A Adam Dunn New Logo .... .60 .18
325B Adam Dunn Old Logo SP ... 5.00 1.50
326 Corwin Malone .... .50 .15
327 Kerry Wood .... 1.50 .45
328 Rickey Henderson .... 1.50 .45
329 Marty Cordova .... .50 .15
330 Greg Maddux .... 2.50 .75
331 Miguel Batista .... .50 .15
332 Chris Bootcheck .... .50 .15
333 Carlos Baerga .... .50 .15
334 Antonio Alfonseca .... .50 .15
335 Shane Halter .... .50 .15
336 Juan Encarnacion .... .50 .15
337 Tom Gordon .... .50 .15
338 Hideo Nomo .... 1.50 .45
339 Torii Hunter .... .60 .18
340A Alfonso Soriano Yellow .... 1.00 .30
340B Alf. Soriano Black SP 8.00 2.40
341 Roberto Alomar .... 1.50 .45
342 David Justice .... .60 .18
343 Mike Lieberthal .... .60 .18
344 Jeff Weaver .... .50 .15
345 Timo Perez .... .50 .15
346 Travis Lee .... .50 .15
347 Sean Casey .... .60 .18
348 Willie Harris .... .50 .15
349 Derek Lowe .... .60 .18
350 Tom Glavine .... 1.00 .30
351 Eric Hinske .... .50 .15
352 Rocco Baldelli .... 2.50 .75
353 J.D. Drew .... .60 .18
354 Jamie Moyer .... .60 .18
355 Todd Linden .... .60 .18
356 Benito Santiago .... .60 .18
357 Brad Baker .... .50 .15
358 Alex Gonzalez .... .50 .15
359 Brandon Duckworth .... .50 .15
360 John Rheinecker .... 1.00 .30
361 Orlando Hernandez .... .60 .18
362 Pedro Astacio .... .50 .15
363 Brad Wilkerson .... .50 .15
364 David Ortiz SP 5.00 1.50
365 Geoff Jenkins SP 5.00 1.50
366 Brian Jordan SP 5.00 1.50
367 Paul Byrd SP 5.00 1.50
368 Jason Lane SP 5.00 1.50
369 Jeff Bagwell SP 8.00 2.40
370 Bobby Higginson SP 5.00 1.50
371 Juan Uribe SP 5.00 1.50
372 Lee Stevens SP 5.00 1.50
373 Jimmy Haynes SP 5.00 1.50
374 Jose Valentin SP 5.00 1.50
375 Ken Griffey Jr. SP 12.00 3.60
376 Barry Bonds SP 20.00 6.00
377 Gary Matthews Jr. SP 5.00 1.50
378 Gary Sheffield SP 5.00 1.50
379 Rick Helling SP 5.00 1.50
380 Junior Spivey SP 5.00 1.50
381 Francisco Rodriguez SP 5.00 1.50
382 Chipper Jones SP 8.00 2.40
383 Orlando Hudson SP 5.00 1.50
384 Ivan Rodriguez SP 8.00 2.40
385 Chris Snelling SP 5.00 1.50
386 Kenny Lofton SP 5.00 1.50
387 Eric Cyr SP 5.00 1.50
388 Jason Kendall SP 5.00 1.50
389 Marlon Anderson SP 5.00 1.50
390 Billy Koch SP 5.00 1.50
391 Shelley Duncan SP 5.00 1.50
392 Jose Reyes SP 8.00 2.40
393 Fernando Tatis SP 5.00 1.50
394 Michael Cuddyer SP 5.00 1.50
395 Mark Prior SP 15.00 4.50
396 Dontrelle Willis SP 8.00 2.40
397 Jay Payton SP 5.00 1.50
398 Brandon Phillips SP 5.00 1.50
399 Dustin Moseley SP RC 8.00 2.40
400 Jason Giambi SP 8.00 2.40
401 John Mabry SP 5.00 1.50
402 Ron Gant SP 5.00 1.50
403 J.T. Snow SP 5.00 1.50
404 Jeff Cirillo SP 5.00 1.50
405 Darin Erstad SP 5.00 1.50
406 Luis Gonzalez SP 5.00 1.50
407 Marcus Giles SP 5.00 1.50
408 Brian Daubach SP 5.00 1.50
409 Moises Alou SP 5.00 1.50
410 Raul Mondesi SP 5.00 1.50
411 Adrian Beltre SP 5.00 1.50
412 A.J. Burnett SP 5.00 1.50
413 Jason Jennings SP 5.00 1.50
414 Edwin Almonte SP 5.00 1.50
415 Fred McGriff SP 8.00 2.40
416 Tim Raines Jr. SP 5.00 1.50
417 Rafael Furcal SP 5.00 1.50
418 Erubiel Durazo SP 5.00 1.50
419 Drew Henson SP 5.00 1.50
420 Kevin Appier SP 5.00 1.50
421 Chad Tracy SP 5.00 1.50
422 Adam Wainwright SP 5.00 1.50
423 Choo Freeman SP 5.00 1.50
424 Sandy Alomar Jr. SP 5.00 1.50
425 Corey Koskie SP 5.00 1.50
426 Jeromy Burnitz SP 5.00 1.50
427 Jorge Posada SP 8.00 2.40
428 Jason Arnold SP 5.00 1.50
429 Brett Myers SP 5.00 1.50
430 Shawn Green SP 5.00 1.50

2003 Topps Heritage Chrome

Inserted at a stated rate of one in eight, this is a partial parallel to the basic Topps Heritage set. These cards feature Topps special Chrome technology and were printed to a stated print run of 1954 serial numbered sets.

Nm-Mt Ex-Mt
STATED ODDS 1:8
STATED PRINT RUN 1954 SERIAL #'d SETS
THC1 Alex Rodriguez 12.00 3.60
THC2 Ichiro Suzuki 12.00 3.60
THC3 Brian Giles 5.00 1.50
THC4 Albert Pujols 15.00 4.50
THC5 Derek Jeter 20.00 6.00
THC6 Pat Burrell 5.00 1.50
THC7 Lance Berkman 5.00 1.50
THC8 Todd Helton 5.00 1.50
THC9 Chris Duncan 5.00 1.50
THC10 Rodrigo Lopez 5.00 1.50
THC11 Sammy Sosa 12.00 3.60
THC12 Barry Zito 5.00 1.50
THC13 Marlon Byrd 5.00 1.50
THC14 Al Leiter 5.00 1.50
THC15 Kazuhisa Ishii 5.00 1.50
THC16 Franklin Gutierrez 12.00 3.60
THC17 Roger Clemens 15.00 4.50
THC18 Mark Buehrle 5.00 1.50
THC19 Larry Walker 5.00 1.50
THC20 Curt Schilling 5.00 1.50
THC21 Garret Anderson 5.00 1.50
THC22 Randy Johnson 8.00 2.40
THC23 Cliff Floyd 5.00 1.50
THC24 Austin Kearns 5.00 1.50
THC25 Manuel Ramirez 5.00 1.50
THC26 Raul Ibanez 5.00 1.50
THC27 Jason Perry 8.00 2.40
THC28 Mark Teixeira 5.00 1.50
THC29 Nomar Garciaparra 12.00 3.60
THC30 Wayne Lydon 5.00 1.50
THC31 Preston Wilson 5.00 1.50
THC32 Paul Lo Duca 5.00 1.50
THC33 Edgardo Alfonzo 5.00 1.50
THC34 Jeremy Giambi 5.00 1.50
THC35 Mariano Rivera 5.00 1.50
THC36 Jimmy Rollins 5.00 1.50
THC37 Bret Boone 5.00 1.50
THC38 Scott Rolen 5.00 1.50
THC39 Adam LaRoche 5.00 1.50
THC40 Tim Hudson 5.00 1.50
THC41 Craig Brazell 8.00 2.40
THC42 Daryl Clark 8.00 2.40
THC43 Joe Mauer 10.00 3.00
Jake Mauer
THC44 Troy Glaus 5.00 1.50
THC45 Trey Hodges 5.00 1.50
THC46 Carl Crawford 5.00 1.50
THC47 Mike Piazza 12.00 3.60
THC48 Josh Beckett 5.00 1.50
THC49 Randall Simon 5.00 1.50
THC50 Frank Thomas 8.00 2.40
THC51 Andruw Jones 5.00 1.50
THC52 Andy Marte 15.00 4.50
THC53 Bernie Castro 5.00 1.50
THC54 Jim Thome 8.00 2.40
THC55 Alexis Rios 12.00 3.60
THC56 Vladimir Guerrero 8.00 2.40
THC57 Walter Young 5.00 1.50
THC58 Hank Blalock 5.00 1.50
THC59 Ramon Nivar-Martinez 8.00 2.40
THC60 Jacque Jones 5.00 1.50
THC61 Nick Johnson 5.00 1.50
THC62 Ruddy Lugo 5.00 1.50
THC63 Carlos Delgado 5.00 1.50
THC64 Jeff Clark 5.00 1.50
THC65 Johnny Damon 5.00 1.50
THC66 Jaime Bubela 5.00 1.50
THC67 Alex Rodriguez 12.00 3.60
THC68 Rafael Palmeiro 5.00 1.50
THC69 Miguel Tejada 5.00 1.50
THC70 Bartolo Colon 5.00 1.50
THC71 Mike Sweeney 5.00 1.50
THC72 John Smoltz 5.00 1.50
THC73 Shannon Stewart 5.00 1.50
THC74 Mike Mussina 8.00 2.40
THC75 Roy Oswalt 5.00 1.50
THC76 Pedro Martinez 8.00 2.40
THC77 Magglio Ordonez 5.00 1.50
THC78 Manny Ramirez 5.00 1.50
THC79 David Wells 5.00 1.50
THC80 Richie Sexson 5.00 1.50
THC81 Adam Dunn 5.00 1.50
THC82 Greg Maddux 12.00 3.60
THC83 Alfonso Soriano 5.00 1.50
THC84 Roberto Alomar 8.00 2.40
THC85 Derek Lowe 5.00 1.50
THC86 Tom Glavine 5.00 1.50
THC87 Jeff Bagwell 5.00 1.50
THC88 Ken Griffey Jr. 12.00 3.60
THC89 Barry Bonds 20.00 6.00
THC90 Gary Sheffield 5.00 1.50
THC91 Chipper Jones 8.00 2.40
THC92 Orlando Hudson 5.00 1.50
THC93 Jose Cruz Jr. 5.00 1.50
THC94 Mark Prior 15.00 4.50
THC95 Jason Giambi 8.00 2.40
THC96 Luis Gonzalez 5.00 1.50
THC97 Drew Henson 5.00 1.50
THC98 Cristian Guzman 5.00 1.50
THC99 Shawn Green 5.00 1.50
THC100 Jose Vidro 5.00 1.50

2003 Topps Heritage Chrome Refractors

Randomly inserted into packs, this is a parallel version of the Chrome insert set. These cards feature Topps' special refractive process and were issued to a stated print run of 554 serial numbered sets.

Nm-Mt Ex-Mt
*CHR.REF: 4X TO 10X BASIC ....
*REFRACTOR: .75X TO 2X CHROME RC YR
RANDOM INSERTS IN PACKS ....
STATED PRINT RUN 554 SERIAL #'d SETS

2003 Topps Heritage Clubhouse Collection Relics

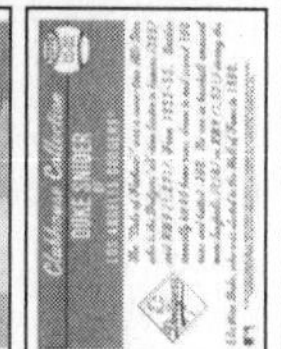

Inserted at different odds depending on the relic, these 12 cards feature a mix of active and retire players and various game-used relics used during their career.

Nm-Mt Ex-Mt
BAT A STATED ODDS 1:2569 ....
BAT B STATED ODDS 1:2506 ....
BAT C STATED ODDS 1:2464 ....
BAT D STATED ODDS 1:1989 ....
UNI A STATED ODDS 1:4223 ....
UNI B STATED ODDS 1:1207 ....
UNI C STATED ODDS 1:921 ....
UNI D STATED ODDS 1:171 ....
AD Adam Dunn Uni D 15.00 4.50
AK Al Kaline Bat D 30.00 9.00
AP Albert Pujols Uni D 20.00 6.00
AR Alex Rodriguez Uni D 20.00 6.00
CJ Chipper Jones Uni D 15.00 4.50
DS Duke Snider Uni A 40.00 12.00
EB Ernie Banks Bat C 30.00 9.00
EM Eddie Mathews Bat B 30.00 9.00
JG Jim Gilliam Uni B 15.00 4.50
KW Kerry Wood Uni D 15.00 4.50
SG Shawn Green Uni C 15.00 4.50
WM Willie Mays Bat A 50.00 15.00

2003 Topps Heritage Clubhouse Collection Autograph Relics

Inserted in packs at a stated rate of one in 15,424, these four cards feature not only a game used relic from the featured player but also an authentic autograph. These cards were issued to a stated print run of 25 serial numbered sets and no pricing is provided due to market scarcity.

Nm-Mt Ex-Mt
AK Al Kaline Bat ....
DS Duke Snider Uni ....
EB Ernie Banks Bat ....
WM Willie Mays Bat ....

2003 Topps Heritage Clubhouse Collection Dual Relics

Issued at a stated rate of one in 9.521, these three cards feature game-used relics from both a legendary player and a current star of the same franchise. These cards were issued to a stated print run of 54 serial numbered sets.

Nm-Mt Ex-Mt
BW Ernie Banks Bat ....
Kerry Wood Uni
MJ Eddie Mathews Bat ....
Chipper Jones Uni
SG Duke Snider Uni ....
Shawn Green Uni

2003 Topps Heritage Flashbacks

Inserted at a stated rate of one in 12, these 10 cards feature thrilling moments from the 1954 season.

Nm-Mt Ex-Mt
COMPLETE SET 10) 20.00 6.00
F1 Willie Mays 5.00 1.50
F2 Yogi Berra .... 2.50 .75
F3 Ted Kluszewski .... 2.00 .60
F4 Stan Musial 4.00 1.20
F5 Hank Aaron 5.00 1.50
F6 Duke Snider .... 2.00 .60
F7 Richie Ashburn .... 2.00 .60
F8 Robin Roberts .... 2.00 .60
F9 Mickey Vernon .... 2.00 .60
F10 Don Larsen .... 2.00 .60

2003 Topps Heritage Flashbacks Autographs

Inserted at a stated rate of one in 65,384 this card features an authentic autograph of Willie Mays. This card was issued to a stated print run of 25 serial numbered cards and no pricing is available due to market scarcity.

Nm-Mt Ex-Mt
WM Willie Mays

2003 Topps Heritage Grandstand Glory Stadium Relics

Inserted at different odds depending on the group, these 12 cards feature a player photo

along with a seat relic from any of nine historic ballparks involved in their career.

Nm-Mt Ex-Mt
GROUP A ODDS 1:2804
GROUP B ODDS 1:514
GROUP C ODDS 1:1446
GROUP D ODDS 1:1356
GROUP E ODDS 1:654
GROUP F ODDS 1:214
AK Al Kaline F 20.00 6.00
AP Andy Pafko F 10.00 3.00
DG Dick Groat D 15.00 4.50
DS Duke Snider A 25.00 7.50
EB Ernie Banks C 25.00 7.50
EM Eddie Mathews F 15.00 4.50
PR Phil Rizzuto E 20.00 6.00
RA Richie Ashburn B 20.00 6.00
TK Ted Kluszewski B 20.00 6.00
WM Willie Mays B 40.00 12.00
WS Warren Spahn F 15.00 4.50
YB Yogi Berra E 25.00 7.50

2003 Topps Heritage New Age Performers

Issued at a stated rate of one in 15, these 15 cards feature prominent active players who have taken the game of baseball to new levels.

Nm-Mt Ex-Mt
NA1 Mike Piazza 4.00 1.20
NA2 Ichiro Suzuki 4.00 1.20
NA3 Derek Jeter 6.00 1.80
NA4 Alex Rodriguez 4.00 1.20
NA5 Sammy Sosa 4.00 1.20
NA6 Jason Giambi 2.50 .75
NA7 Vladimir Guerrero 2.50 .75
NA8 Albert Pujols 5.00 1.50
NA9 Todd Helton 2.00 .60
NA10 Nomar Garciaparra 4.00 1.20
NA11 Randy Johnson 2.50 .75
NA12 Jim Thome 2.50 .75
NA13 Barry Bonds 6.00 1.80
NA14 Miguel Tejada 2.00 .60
NA15 Alfonso Soriano 2.00 .60

2003 Topps Heritage Real One Autographs

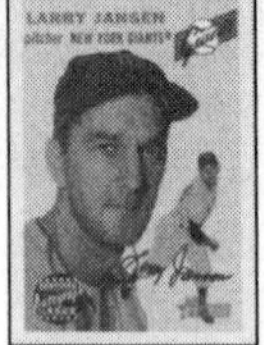
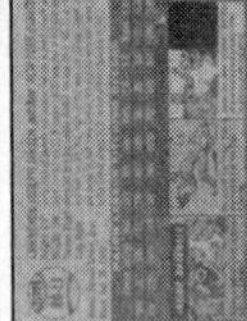

Inserted at various odds depending on what group the player belonged to, these cards feature authentic autographs from the featured player. Topps made an effort to secure autographs from every person who was still living that was in the 1954 Topps set. Hank Aaron, Yogi Berra and Johnny Sain did not return their cards in time for inclusion in this set and a collector could redeem these cards until February 28, 2005.

Nm-Mt Ex-Mt
RETIRED ODDS 1:188
ACTIVE A ODDS 1:6168
ACTIVE B ODDS 1:1540
ACTIVE C ODDS 1:2802
AK Al Kaline 100.00 30.00
AP Andy Pafko 40.00 12.00
BR Bob Ross 25.00 7.50
BS Bill Skowron 40.00 12.00
BSH Bobby Shantz 40.00 12.00
BT Bob Talbot 25.00 7.50
BWE Bill Werle 25.00 7.50
CH Cal Hogue 25.00 7.50
CK Charlie Kress 25.00 7.50
CS Carl Scheib 25.00 7.50
DG Dick Groat 40.00 12.00
DK Dick Kryhoski 25.00 7.50
DL Don Lenhardt 25.00 7.50
DLU Don Lund 25.00 7.50
DS Duke Snider 100.00 30.00
EB Ernie Banks 120.00 36.00
EM Eddie Mayo 25.00 7.50
GH Gene Hermanski 25.00 7.50
HA Hank Aaron EXCH 250.00 75.00
HB Hank Bauer 40.00 12.00
JC Jose Cruz Jr. B 25.00 7.50
JP Joe Presko 25.00 7.50
JPO Johnny Podres 40.00 12.00
JR Jimmy Rollins C 25.00 7.50
JS Johnny Sain EXCH 40.00 12.00
JV Jose Vidro B 25.00 7.50
JW Jim Willis 25.00 7.50
LB Lance Berkman A 40.00 12.00
LJ Larry Jansen 40.00 12.00
LW Leroy Wheat 25.00 7.50
MB Matt Batts 25.00 7.50
MBL Mike Blyzka 25.00 7.50
MI Monte Irvin 60.00 18.00
MM Mickey Micelotta 25.00 7.50
MS Mike Sandlock 25.00 7.50
PP Paul Penson 25.00 7.50
PR Phil Rizzuto 60.00 18.00
PRO Preacher Roe 40.00 12.00
RF Roy Face 40.00 12.00
RM Ray Murray 25.00 7.50
TL Tom Lasorda 100.00 30.00
VL Vern Law 40.00 12.00
WF Whitey Ford 60.00 18.00
WM Willie Mays 200.00 60.00
YB Yogi Berra EXCH 100.00 30.00

2003 Topps Heritage Real One Autographs Red Ink

Inserted at a stated rate of one in 696, this is a parallel to the Real One Autographs insert set. These cards featured autographs in red ink and were issued to a stated print run of 54 serial numbered sets. Just as with the regular issue, Hank Aaron, Yogi Berra and Johnny Sain did not return their cards in time for inclusion in this set and those redemption cards could be redeemed until February 28, 2005.

Nm-Mt Ex-Mt
*RED INK: 1X TO 2X BASIC RETIRED
*RED INK: .75X TO 1.5X BASIC ACTIVE A
*RED INK: .75X TO 1.5X BASIC ACTIVE B
*RED INK: .75X TO 1.5X BASIC ACTIVE C

2003 Topps Heritage Team Topps Legends Autographs

Nm-Mt Ex-Mt
GROUP A STATED ODDS 1:3085
GROUP B STATED ODDS 1:1028

2003 Topps Heritage Then and Now

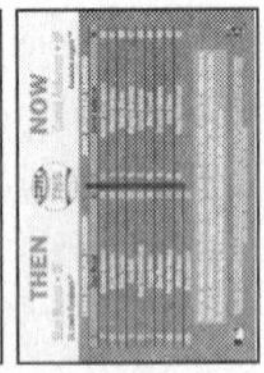

Issued at a stated rate of one in 15, these 10 cards feature an 1954 star along with a current standout. The backs compare 10 league leaders of 1954 to the league leaders of 2002. Interestingly enough, Ted Kluszewski and Alex Rodriguez are on both the first two cards in this set.

Nm-Mt Ex-Mt
COMPLETE SET (10) 30.00 9.00
TN1 Ted Kluszewski 4.00 1.20
Alex Rodriguez HR
TN2 Ted Kluszewski 4.00 1.20
Alex Rodriguez RBI
TN3 Willie Mays 6.00 1.80
Barry Bonds Batting
TN4 Don Mueller 2.00 .60
Alfonso Soriano
TN5 Stan Musial 4.00 1.20
Garret Anderson
TN6 Minnie Minoso 2.00 .60
Johnny Damon
TN7 Willie Mays 6.00 1.80
Barry Bonds Slugging
TN8 Duke Snider 4.00 1.20
Alex Rodriguez
TN9 Robin Roberts 2.50 .75
Randy Johnson
TN10 Johnny Antonelli 2.50 .75
Pedro Martinez

2004 Topps Heritage

This 495 card set was released in February, 2004. As this was the fourth year this set was issued, the cards were designed in the style of the 1955 Topps set. This set was issued in eight card packs which came 24 packs to a box and eight boxes to a case. This set features a mix of cards printed to standard amounts as well as various Short Prints and then even some variation short prints. Any type of short printed card was issued to a stated rate of one in two. We have delineated in our checklist what the various variations are. In addition, all cards from 398 through 475 are SP's.

Nm-Mt Ex-Mt
COMPLETE SET (495) 500.00 150.00
COMP.SET w/o SP's (385) 50.00 15.00
SP STATED ODDS 1:2
1A Jim Thome Fielding 1.50 .45
1B Jim Thome Hitting SP 8.00 2.40
2 Nomar Garciaparra SP 10.00 3.00
3 Aramis Ramirez .60 .18
4 Rafael Palmeiro SP 8.00 2.40
5 Danny Graves .50 .15
6 Casey Blake .50 .15
7 Juan Uribe .50 .15
8A Dmitri Young New Logo .60 .18
8B Dmitri Young Old Logo SP 5.00 1.50
9 Billy Wagner .60 .18
10A Jason Giambi Swinging 1.50 .45
10B Jason Giambi Btg Stance SP 8.00 2.40
11 Carlos Beltran .60 .18
12 Chad Hermansen .50 .15
13 B.J. Upton 1.00 .30
14 Dustan Mohr .50 .15
15 Endy Chavez .50 .15
16 Cliff Floyd .60 .18
17 Bernie Williams 1.00 .30
18 Eric Chavez .60 .18
19 Chase Utley .60 .18
20 Randy Johnson 1.50 .45
21 Vernon Wells .60 .18
22 Juan Gonzalez 1.50 .45
23 Joe Kennedy .50 .15
24 Bengie Molina .50 .15
25 Carlos Lee .60 .18
26 Horacio Ramirez .50 .15
27 Anthony Acevedo RC 1.25 .35
28 Sammy Sosa SP 10.00 3.00
29 Jon Garland .50 .15
30A Adam Dunn Fielding .60 .18
30B Adam Dunn Hitting SP 5.00 1.50
31 Aaron Rowand .50 .15
32 Jody Gerut .60 .18
33 Chin-Hui Tsao .60 .18
34 Alex Sanchez .50 .15
35 A.J. Burnett .50 .15
36 Brad Ausmus .50 .15
37 Blake Hawksworth RC 1.00 .30
38 Francisco Rodriguez .60 .18
39 Alex Cintron .50 .15
40A Chipper Jones Pointing 1.50 .45
40B Chipper Jones Fielding SP 8.00 2.40
41 Deivi Cruz .50 .15
42 Bill Mueller .60 .18
43 Joe Borowski .50 .15
44 Jimmy Haynes .50 .15
45 Mark Loretta .50 .15
46 Jerome Williams .60 .18
47 Gary Sheffield Yanks SP 8.00 2.40
48 Richard Hidalgo .60 .18
49A Jason Kendall New Logo .60 .18
49B Jason Kendall Old Logo SP 5.00 1.50
50 Ichiro Suzuki SP 10.00 3.00
51 Jim Edmonds .60 .18
52 Frank Catalanotto .50 .15
53 Jose Contreras .60 .18
54 Mo Vaughn .60 .18
55 Brendan Donnelly .50 .15
56 Luis Gonzalez .60 .18
57 Robert Fick .60 .18
58 Laynce Nix .60 .18
59 Johnny Damon .60 .18
60A Magglio Ordonez Running .60 .18
60B Magglio Ordonez Hitting SP 5.00 1.50
61 Matt Clement .60 .18
62 Ryan Ludwick .50 .15
63 Luis Castillo .60 .18
64 Dave Crouthers RC 1.00 .30
65 Dave Berg .50 .15
66 Kyle Davies RC 1.00 .30
67 Tim Salmon 1.00 .30
68 Marcus Giles .60 .18
69 Marty Cordova .50 .15
70A Todd Helton White Jsy 1.00 .30
70B Todd Helton Purple Jsy SP 8.00 2.40
71 Jeff Kent .60 .18
72 Michael Tucker .50 .15
73 Cesar Izturis .50 .15
74 Paul Quantrill .50 .15
75 Conor Jackson RC 1.50 .45
76 Placido Polanco .50 .15
77 Adam Eaton .50 .15
78 Ramon Hernandez .60 .18
79 Edgardo Alfonzo .60 .18
80 Dioner Navarro RC 1.50 .45
81 Woody Williams .60 .18
82 Rey Ordonez .50 .15
83 Randy Winn .50 .15
84 Casey Myers RC 1.00 .30
85A R.Choy Foo New Logo RC 1.00 .30
85B R.Choy Foo Old Logo SP 8.00 2.40
86 Ray Durham .60 .18
87 Sean Burroughs .60 .18
88 Tim Frend RC 2.00 .60
89 Shigetoshi Hasegawa .60 .18
90 Jeffrey Allison RC 2.00 .60
91 Orlando Hudson .50 .15
92 Matt Creighton SP RC 8.00 2.40
93 Tim Worrell .50 .15
94 Kris Benson .50 .15
95 Mike Lieberthal .60 .18
96 David Wells .60 .18
97 Jason Phillips .50 .15
98 Bobby Cox MGR .50 .15
99 Johan Santana .60 .18
100A Alex Rodriguez Hitting 2.50 .75
100B Alex Rodriguez Throwing SP 10.00 3.00
101 John Vander Wal .50 .15
102 Orlando Cabrera .50 .15
103 Hideo Nomo 1.50 .45
104 Todd Walker .60 .18
105 Jason Johnson .50 .15
106 Matt Mantei .50 .15
107 Jarrod Washburn .60 .18
108 Preston Wilson .60 .18
109 Carl Pavano .50 .15
110 Geoff Blum .50 .15
111 Eric Gagne 1.00 .30
112 Geoff Jenkins .60 .18
113 Joe Torre MGR 1.00 .30
114 Jon Knott RC 1.00 .30
115 Hank Blalock .60 .18
116 John Olerud .60 .18
117A Pat Burrell New Logo .50 .15
117B Pat Burrell Old Logo SP 5.00 1.50
118 Aaron Boone .60 .18
119 Zach Day .50 .15
120A Frank Thomas New Logo 1.50 .45
120B Frank Thomas Old Logo SP 8.00 2.40
121 Kyle Farnsworth .50 .15
122 Derek Lowe .60 .18
123 Zach Miner SP RC 8.00 2.40
124 Matthew Moses SP RC 10.00 3.00
125 Jesse Roman RC 1.00 .30
126 Josh Phelps .50 .15
127 Nic Ungs RC 1.00 .30
128 Dan Haren .60 .18
129 Kirk Rueter .50 .15
130 Jack McKeon MGR .60 .18
131 Keith Foulke .60 .18
132 Garrett Stephenson .50 .15
133 Wes Helms .50 .15
134 Raul Ibanez .50 .15
135 Morgan Ensberg .50 .15
136 Jay Payton .60 .18
137 Billy Koch .50 .15
138 Mark Grudzielanek .50 .15
139 Rodrigo Lopez .50 .15
140 Corey Patterson .60 .18
141 Troy Percival .60 .18
142 Shea Hillenbrand .60 .18
143 Brad Fullmer .60 .18
144 Ricky Nolasco RC 1.00 .30
145 Mark Teixeira .60 .18
146 Tydus Meadows RC 1.00 .30
147 Toby Hall .50 .15
148 Orlando Palmeiro .50 .15
149 Khalid Ballouli RC 1.00 .30
150 Grady Little MGR .50 .15
151 David Eckstein .50 .15
152 Kenny Perez RC 1.00 .30
153 Ben Grieve .50 .15
154 Ismael Valdes .50 .15
155 Bret Boone .60 .18
156 Jesse Foppert .60 .18
157 Vicente Padilla .60 .18
158 Bobby Abreu .60 .18
159 Scott Hatteberg .50 .15
160 Carlos Quentin RC 1.25 .35
161 Anthony Lerew RC 1.00 .30
162 Lance Carter .50 .15
163 Robb Nen .60 .18
164 Zach Duke SP RC 8.00 2.40
165 Xavier Nady .50 .15
166 Kip Wells .50 .15
167 Kevin Millwood .60 .18
168 Jon Lieber .50 .15
169 Jose Reyes 1.00 .30
170 Eric Byrnes .50 .15
171 Paul Konerko .60 .18
172 Chris Lubanski .60 .18
173 Jae Weong Seo .50 .15
174 Corey Koskie .60 .18
175 Tim Stauffer RC 1.00 .30
176 John Lackey .50 .15
177 Danny Bautista .50 .15
178 Shane Reynolds .50 .15
179 Jorge Julio .50 .15
180A Manny Ramirez New Logo .60 .18
180B Manny Ramirez Old Logo SP 5.00 1.50
181 Alex Gonzalez .50 .15
182A Moises Alou New Logo .60 .18
182B Moises Alou Old Logo SP 5.00 1.50
183 Mark Buehrle .60 .18
184 Carlos Guillen .50 .15
185 Nate Cornejo .50 .15
186 Billy Traber .50 .15
187 Jason Jennings .50 .15
188 Eric Munson .50 .15
189 Braden Looper .50 .15
190 Juan Encarnacion .60 .18
191 Dusty Baker MGR .60 .18
192 Travis Lee .50 .15
193 Miguel Cairo .50 .15
194 Rich Aurilia SP 5.00 1.50
195 Tom Gordon .50 .15
196 Freddy Garcia .60 .18
197 Brian Lawrence .50 .15
198 Jorge Posada SP 8.00 2.40
199 Javier Vazquez .60 .18
200A Albert Pujols New Logo 3.00 .90
200B Albert Pujols Old Logo SP 12.00 3.60
201 Victor Zambrano .50 .15
202 Eli Marrero .60 .18
203 Joel Pineiro .60 .18
204 Rondell White .60 .18
205 Craig Ansman RC 1.00 .30
206 Michael Young .60 .18
207 Carlos Baerga .50 .15
208 Andruw Jones .60 .18
209 Jerry Hairston Jr. .50 .15
210 Shawn Green SP 5.00 1.50
211 Ron Gardenhire MGR .50 .15
212 Darin Erstad .60 .18
213A Brandon Webb Glove Chest .60 .18
213B Brandon Webb Glove Out SP 5.00 1.50
214 Greg Maddux 2.50 .75
215 Reed Johnson .50 .15
216 John Thomson .50 .15
217 Tino Martinez 1.00 .30
218 Mike Cameron .50 .15
219 Edgar Martinez 1.00 .30
220 Eric Young .50 .15
221 Reggie Sanders .60 .18
222 Randy Wolf .60 .18
223 Erubiel Durazo .60 .18
224 Mike Mussina 1.50 .45
225 Tom Glavine 1.00 .30
226 Troy Glaus 1.00 .30
227 Oscar Villarreal .50 .15
228 David Segui .50 .15
229 Jeff Suppan .60 .18
230 Kenny Lofton .60 .18
231 Esteban Loaiza .60 .18
232 Felipe Lopez .50 .15
233 Matt Lawton .50 .15
234 Mark Bellhorn .50 .15
235 Wil Ledezma .50 .15
236 Todd Hollandsworth .50 .15
237 Octavio Dotel .50 .15
238 Darren Dreifort .50 .15
239 Paul Lo Duca .60 .18
240 Richie Sexson .60 .18
241 Doug Mientkiewicz .60 .18
242 Luis Rivas .50 .15
243 Claudio Vargas .50 .15
244 Mark Ellis .50 .15
245 Brett Myers .60 .18
246 Jake Peavy .60 .18
247 Marquis Grissom .50 .15
248 Armando Benitez .50 .15
249 Ryan Franklin .50 .15
250A Alfonso Soriano Throwing 1.00 .30
250B Alfonso Soriano Fielding SP 8.00 2.40
251 Tim Hudson .60 .18
252 Shannon Stewart .60 .18
253 A.J. Pierzynski .60 .18
254 Runelvys Hernandez .50 .15
255 Roy Oswalt .60 .18
256 Shawn Chacon .50 .15
257 Tony Graffanino .50 .15
258 Tim Wakefield .60 .18
259 Damian Miller .50 .15
260 Joe Crede .50 .15
261 Jason LaRue .50 .15
262 Jose Jimenez .50 .15
263 Juan Pierre .60 .18
264 Wade Miller .60 .18
265 Odalis Perez .50 .15
266 Eddie Guardado .60 .18
267 Rocky Biddle .50 .15
268 Jeff Nelson .50 .15
269 Terrence Long .60 .18
270 Ramon Ortiz .50 .15
271 Raul Mondesi .60 .18
272 Ugueth Urbina .50 .15
273 Jeromy Burnitz .60 .18
274 Brad Radke .60 .18
275 Jose Vidro .60 .18
276 Bobby Jenks .60 .18
277 Ty Wigginton .50 .15
278 Jose Guillen .60 .18
279 Delmon Young 1.50 .45
280 Brian Giles .60 .18
281 Jason Schmidt .60 .18
282 Nick Markakis .60 .18
283 Felipe Alou MGR .60 .18
284 Carl Crawford .60 .18
285 Neifi Perez .50 .15
286 Miguel Tejada .60 .18
287 Victor Martinez .60 .18
288 Adam Kennedy .50 .15
289 Kerry Ligtenberg .50 .15
290 Scott Williamson .50 .15
291 Tony Womack .50 .15
292 Travis Hafner .60 .18
293 Bobby Crosby .60 .18
294 Chad Billingsley .60 .18
295 Russ Ortiz .60 .18
296 John Burkett .50 .15
297 Carlos Zambrano .60 .18
298 Randall Simon .50 .15
299 Juan Castro .50 .15
300 Mike Lowell .60 .18
301 Fred McGriff 1.00 .30
302 Glendon Rusch .50 .15
303 Sung Jung RC 1.25 .35
304 Rocco Baldelli 1.50 .45
305 Fernando Vina .50 .15
306 Gil Meche .60 .18
307 Jose Cruz Jr. .60 .18
308 Bernie Castro .50 .15
309 Scott Spiezio .50 .15
310 Paul Byrd .50 .15
311A Jay Gibbons New Logo .60 .18
311B Jay Gibbons Old Logo SP 5.00 1.50
312 Trot Nixon 1.00 .30
313 Chris O'Riordan RC 1.00 .30
314 Julio Lugo .50 .15
315 Ben Davis .50 .15
316 Mike Williams .50 .15
317 Trevor Hoffman .60 .18
318 Andy Pettitte 1.00 .30
319 Orlando Hernandez .60 .18
320 Juan Rivera .50 .15
321 Elizardo Ramirez .60 .18
322 Junior Spivey .50 .15
323 Tony Batista .60 .18
324 Mike Remlinger .50 .15
325 Alex Gonzalez .50 .15
326 Aaron Hill .60 .18
327 Steve Finley .60 .18
328 Vinny Castilla .60 .18
329 Eric Duncan .60 .18
330 Mike Gosling RC 1.00 .30
331 Eric Hinske .50 .15
332 Scott Rolen 1.00 .30
333 Benito Santiago .60 .18
334 Jimmy Gobble .60 .18
335 Bobby Higginson .60 .18
336 Kelvim Escobar .50 .15
337 Mike DeJean .50 .15
338 Sidney Ponson .60 .18
339 Todd Self RC 1.00 .30
340 Jeff Cirillo .50 .15
341 Jimmy Rollins .60 .18
342A Barry Zito White Jsy 1.00 .30
342B Barry Zito Green Jsy SP 8.00 2.40
343 Felix Pie 1.00 .30
344 Matt Morris .60 .18
345 Kazuhiro Sasaki .60 .18
346 Jack Wilson .50 .15
347 Nick Johnson .50 .15
348 Wil Cordero .50 .15
349 Ryan Madson .50 .15
350 Torii Hunter .60 .18
351 Andy Ashby .50 .15
352 Aubrey Huff .60 .18
353 Brad Lidge .60 .18
354 Derrek Lee .60 .18
355 Yadier Molina RC 1.00 .30
356 Paul Wilson .50 .15
357 Omar Vizquel .60 .18
358 Rene Reyes .50 .15
359 Marlon Anderson .50 .15
360 Bobby Kielty .50 .15
361A Ryan Wagner New Logo .50 .15
361B Ryan Wagner Old Logo SP 5.00 1.50
362 Justin Morneau .60 .18
363 Shane Spencer .50 .15
364 David Bell .50 .15
365 Matt Stairs .50 .15
366 Joe Borchard .60 .18
367 Mark Redman .50 .15
368 Dave Roberts .50 .15
369 Desi Relaford .50 .15
370 Rich Harden .60 .18
371 Fernando Tatis .50 .15
372 Eric Karros .60 .18
373 Eric Milton .60 .18
374 Mike Sweeney .60 .18
375 Brian Daubach .50 .15
376 Brian Snyder .50 .15
377 Chris Reitsma .50 .15
378 Kyle Lohse .50 .15
379 Livan Hernandez .50 .15
380 Robin Ventura .60 .18
381 Jacque Jones .60 .18
382 Danny Kolb .50 .15
383 Casey Kotchman .60 .18
384 Cristian Guzman .60 .18

385 Josh Beckett 1.00 .30
386 Khalil Greene .60 .18
387 Greg Myers .50 .15
388 Francisco Cordero .50 .15
389 Donald Levinski RC 1.00 .30
390 Roy Halladay .60 .18
391 J.D. Drew .60 .18
392 Jamie Moyer .60 .18
393 Ken Macha MGR .50 .15
394 Jeff Davanon .50 .15
395 Matt Kata .60 .18
396 Jack Cust .50 .15
397 Mike Timlin .50 .15
398 Zack Greinke SP 8.00 2.40
399 Byung-Hyun Kim SP 5.00 1.50
400 Kazuhisa Ishii SP 5.00 1.50
401 Brayan Pena SP RC 5.00 1.50
402 Garret Anderson SP 5.00 1.50
403 Kyle Sleeth SP RC 10.00 3.00
404 Javy Lopez SP 5.00 1.50
405 Damian Moss SP 5.00 1.50
406 David Ortiz SP 5.00 1.50
407 Pedro Martinez SP 8.00 2.40
408 Hee Seop Choi SP 5.00 1.50
409 Carl Everett SP 5.00 1.50
410 Dontrelle Willis SP 5.00 1.50
411 Ryan Harvey SP 8.00 2.40
412 Russell Branyan SP 5.00 1.50
413 Milton Bradley SP 5.00 1.50
414 Marcus McBeth SP RC 5.00 1.50
415 Carlos Pena SP 5.00 1.50
416 Ivan Rodriguez SP 8.00 2.40
417 Craig Biggio SP 8.00 2.40
418 Angel Berroa SP 5.00 1.50
419 Brian Jordan SP 5.00 1.50
420 Scott Podsednik SP 8.00 2.40
421 Omar Falcon SP RC 5.00 1.50
422 Joe Mays SP 5.00 1.50
423 Brad Wilkerson SP 5.00 1.50
424 Al Leiter SP 5.00 1.50
425 Derek Jeter SP 15.00 4.50
426 Mark Mulder SP 5.00 1.50
427 Marlon Byrd SP 5.00 1.50
428 David Murphy SP RC 8.00 2.40
429 Phil Nevin SP 5.00 1.50
430 J.T. Snow SP 5.00 1.50
431 Brad Sullivan SP RC 8.00 2.40
432 Bo Hart SP 5.00 1.50
433 Josh Labandeira SP RC 5.00 1.50
434 Chan Ho Park SP 5.00 1.50
435 Carlos Delgado SP 5.00 1.50
436 Curt Schilling Sox SP 8.00 2.40
437 John Smoltz SP 8.00 2.40
438 Luis Matos SP 5.00 1.50
439 Mark Prior SP 12.00 3.60
440 Roberto Alomar SP 8.00 2.40
441 Coco Crisp SP 5.00 1.50
442 Austin Kearns SP 5.00 1.50
443 Larry Walker SP 8.00 2.40
444 Neal Cotts SP 5.00 1.50
445 Jeff Bagwell SP 8.00 2.40
446 Adrian Beltre SP 5.00 1.50
447 Grady Sizemore SP 8.00 2.40
448 Keith Ginter SP 5.00 1.50
449 Vladimir Guerrero SP 8.00 2.40
450 Lyle Overbay SP 5.00 1.50
451 Rafael Furcal SP 5.00 1.50
452 Melvin Mora SP 5.00 1.50
453 Kerry Wood SP 8.00 2.40
454 Jose Valentin SP 5.00 1.50
455 Ken Griffey Jr. SP 10.00 3.00
456 Brandon Phillips SP 5.00 1.50
457 Miguel Cabrera SP 8.00 2.40
458 Edwin Jackson SP 8.00 2.40
459 Eric Owens SP 5.00 1.50
460 Miguel Batista SP 5.00 1.50
461 Mike Hampton SP 5.00 1.50
462 Kevin Millar SP 5.00 1.50
463 Bartolo Colon SP 5.00 1.50
464 Sean Casey SP 5.00 1.50
465 C.C. Sabathia SP 5.00 1.50
466 Rickie Weeks SP 8.00 2.40
467 Brad Penny SP 5.00 1.50
468 Mike MacDougal SP 5.00 1.50
469 Kevin Brown SP 5.00 1.50
470 Lance Berkman SP 5.00 1.50
471 Ben Sheets SP 5.00 1.50
472 Mariano Rivera SP 8.00 2.40
473 Mike Piazza SP 10.00 3.00
474 Ryan Klesko SP 5.00 1.50
475 Edgar Renteria SP 5.00 1.50

2004 Topps Heritage Chrome

Nm-Mt Ex-Mt
STATED ODDS 1:7
STATED PRINT RUN 1955 SERIAL #'d SETS
1 Sammy Sosa 10.00 3.00
2 Nomar Garciaparra 10.00 3.00
3 Ichiro Suzuki 10.00 3.00
4 Rafael Palmeiro 6.00 1.80
5 Carlos Delgado 5.00 1.50
6 Troy Glaus 6.00 1.80
7 Jay Gibbons 5.00 1.50
8 Frank Thomas 6.00 1.80
9 Pat Burrell 5.00 1.50
10 Albert Pujols 12.00 3.60
11 Brandon Webb 5.00 1.50
12 Chipper Jones 6.00 1.80
13 Magglio Ordonez 6.00 1.80
14 Adam Dunn 5.00 1.50
15 Todd Helton 6.00 1.80
16 Jason Giambi 6.00 1.80
17 Alfonso Soriano 6.00 1.80
18 Barry Zito 6.00 1.80
19 Jim Thome 6.00 1.80
20 Alex Rodriguez 10.00 3.00
21 Hee Seop Choi 5.00 1.50
22 Pedro Martinez 6.00 1.80
23 Kerry Wood 6.00 1.80
24 Bartolo Colon 5.00 1.50
25 Austin Kearns 5.00 1.50
26 Ken Griffey Jr. 10.00 3.00
27 Coco Crisp 5.00 1.50
28 Larry Walker 6.00 1.80
29 Ivan Rodriguez 6.00 1.80
30 Dontrelle Willis 5.00 1.50
31 Miguel Cabrera 6.00 1.80
32 Jeff Bagwell 6.00 1.80
33 Lance Berkman 5.00 1.50
34 Shawn Green 5.00 1.50
35 Kevin Brown 5.00 1.50
36 Vladimir Guerrero 6.00 1.80
37 Mike Piazza 10.00 3.00
38 Derek Jeter 15.00 4.50
39 John Smoltz 6.00 1.80
40 Mark Prior 12.00 3.60
41 Gary Sheffield Yanks 6.00 1.80
42 Curt Schilling Sox 6.00 1.80
43 Randy Johnson 6.00 1.80
44 Luis Gonzalez 5.00 1.50
45 Andruw Jones 5.00 1.50
46 Greg Maddux 10.00 3.00
47 Tony Batista 5.00 1.50
48 Esteban Loaiza 5.00 1.50
49 Chin-Hui Tsao 5.00 1.50
50 Mike Lowell 5.00 1.50
51 Jeff Kent 5.00 1.50
52 Richie Sexson 5.00 1.50
53 Torii Hunter 5.00 1.50
54 Jose Vidro 5.00 1.50
55 Jose Reyes 6.00 1.80
56 Jimmy Rollins 5.00 1.50
57 Bret Boone 5.00 1.50
58 Rocco Baldelli 6.00 1.80
59 Hank Blalock 5.00 1.50
60 Rickie Weeks 6.00 1.80
61 Rodney Choy Foo 5.00 1.50
62 Zach Miner 5.00 1.50
63 Brayan Pena 5.00 1.50
64 David Murphy 6.00 1.80
65 Matt Creighton 5.00 1.50
66 Kyle Sleeth 8.00 2.40
67 Matthew Moses 8.00 2.40
68 Josh Labandeira 5.00 1.50
69 Grady Sizemore 6.00 1.80
70 Edwin Jackson 6.00 1.80
71 Marcus McBeth 5.00 1.50
72 Brad Sullivan 5.00 1.50
73 Zach Duke 5.00 1.50
74 Omar Falcon 5.00 1.50
75 Conor Jackson 6.00 1.80
76 Carlos Quentin 5.00 1.50
77 Craig Ansman 5.00 1.50
78 Mike Gosling 5.00 1.50
79 Kyle Davies 5.00 1.50
80 Anthony Lerew 5.00 1.50
81 Sung Jung 5.00 1.50
82 Dave Crouthers 5.00 1.50
83 Kenny Perez 5.00 1.50
84 Jeffrey Allison 8.00 2.40
85 Nic Ungs 5.00 1.50
86 Donald Levinski 5.00 1.50
87 Anthony Acevedo 5.00 1.50
88 Todd Self 5.00 1.50
89 Tim Frend 8.00 2.40
90 Tydus Meadows 5.00 1.50
91 Khalid Ballouli 5.00 1.50
92 Dioner Navarro 6.00 1.80
93 Casey Myers 5.00 1.50
94 Jon Knott 5.00 1.50
95 Tim Stauffer 5.00 1.50
96 Ricky Nolasco 5.00 1.50
97 Blake Hawksworth 5.00 1.50
98 Jesse Roman 5.00 1.50
99 Yadier Molina 5.00 1.50
100 Chris O'Riordan 5.00 1.50
101 Cliff Floyd 5.00 1.50
102 Nick Johnson 5.00 1.50
103 Edgar Martinez 6.00 1.80
104 Brett Myers 5.00 1.50
105 Francisco Rodriguez 5.00 1.50
106 Scott Rolen 6.00 1.80
107 Mark Teixeira 5.00 1.50
108 Miguel Tejada 5.00 1.50
109 Vernon Wells 5.00 1.50
110 Jerome Williams 5.00 1.50

2004 Topps Heritage Chrome Black Refractors

Nm-Mt Ex-Mt
*BLACK REF: 3X TO 6X CHROME
*BLACK REF: 4X TO 8X CHROME RC YR
STATED ODDS 1:251
STATED PRINT RUN 55 SERIAL #'d SETS

2004 Topps Heritage Chrome Refractors

Nm-Mt Ex-Mt
*REFRACTOR: .6X TO 1.5X CHROME
*REFRACTOR: .75X TO 2X CHROME RC YR
STATED ODDS 1:25
STATED PRINT RUN 555 SERIAL #'d SETS

2004 Topps Heritage Clubhouse Collection Relics

Nm-Mt Ex-Mt
GROUP A ODDS 1:3037
GROUP B ODDS 1:4142
GROUP C ODDS 1:138
GROUP D ODDS 1:92
GROUP A STATED PRINT RUN 100 SETS
GROUP A PRINT RUN PROVIDED BY TOPPS
GROUP A ARE NOT SERIAL-NUMBERED
AD Adam Dunn Jsy D 8.00 2.40
AJ Andruw Jones Jsy C 8.00 2.40
AK Al Kaline Bat A 50.00 15.00
AP Albert Pujols Uni C 15.00 4.50
AR Alex Rodriguez Jsy C 10.00 3.00
AS Alfonso Soriano Uni D 10.00 3.00
BA Bobby Abreu Jsy D 8.00 2.40
BB Bret Boone Jsy D 8.00 2.40
BM Brett Myers Jsy D 8.00 2.40
BZ Barry Zito Uni C 10.00 3.00
CJ Chipper Jones Jsy D 10.00 3.00
CS C.C. Sabathia Jsy D 8.00 2.40
DS Duke Snider Bat A 40.00 12.00
EC Eric Chavez Uni D 8.00 2.40
EG Eric Gagne Uni D 10.00 3.00
FM Fred McGriff Bat C 10.00 3.00
GM Greg Maddux Jsy C 15.00 4.50
GS Gary Sheffield Uni D 8.00 2.40
HB Hank Blalock Jsy D 8.00 2.40
HK Harmon Killebrew Jsy C 25.00 7.50
IR Ivan Rodriguez Bat C 10.00 3.00
JD Johnny Damon Uni D 8.00 2.40
JG Jason Giambi Uni D 10.00 3.00
JL Javy Lopez Jsy D 8.00 2.40
JR Jimmy Rollins Jsy D 8.00 2.40
JRE Jose Reyes Jsy D 10.00 3.00
JS John Smoltz Jsy C 10.00 3.00
JT Jim Thome Bat D 10.00 3.00
KB Kevin Brown Uni D 8.00 2.40
KI Kazuhisa Ishii Uni D 8.00 2.40
KW Kerry Wood Jsy D 10.00 3.00
LB Lance Berkman Jsy C 8.00 2.40
LG Luis Gonzalez Jsy D 8.00 2.40
MG Marcus Giles Jsy C 8.00 2.40
MM Mark Mulder Uni D 8.00 2.40
MR Manny Ramirez Jsy C 8.00 2.40
MS Mike Sweeney Jsy D 8.00 2.40
MT Miguel Tejada Uni D 8.00 2.40
MTB Miguel Tejada Bat C 8.00 2.40
MTE Mark Teixeira Jsy D 8.00 2.40
NG Nomar Garciaparra Uni C 15.00 4.50
PL Paul Lo Duca Uni C 8.00 2.40
PM Pedro Martinez Jsy D 10.00 3.00
RB Rocco Baldelli Jsy D 10.00 3.00
RC Roger Clemens Uni D 15.00 4.50
RF Rafael Furcal Jsy D 8.00 2.40
RJ Randy Johnson Jsy C 10.00 3.00
SG Shawn Green Uni C 8.00 2.40
SM Stan Musial Bat A 60.00 18.00
SR Scott Rolen Uni B 10.00 3.00
SRB Scott Rolen Bat C 10.00 3.00
SS Sammy Sosa Jsy C 15.00 4.50
TG Troy Glaus Uni C 10.00 3.00
TH Tim Hudson Uni D 8.00 2.40
THU Torii Hunter Bat C 8.00 2.40
VW Vernon Wells Jsy C 8.00 2.40
WM Willie Mays Uni A 100.00 30.00
YB Yogi Berra Jsy A 50.00 15.00

2004 Topps Heritage Clubhouse Collection Autograph Relics

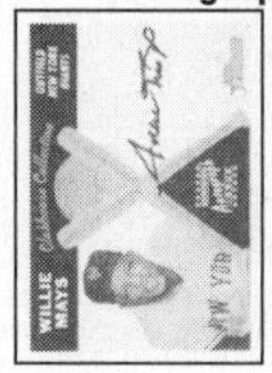

Nm-Mt Ex-Mt
STATED ODDS 1:15,186
STATED PRINT RUN 25 SERIAL #'d SETS
NO PRICING DUE TO SCARCITY
AK Al Kaline Bat
DS Duke Snider Bat
EB Ernie Banks Uni
WM Willie Mays Uni

2004 Topps Heritage Clubhouse Collection Dual Relics

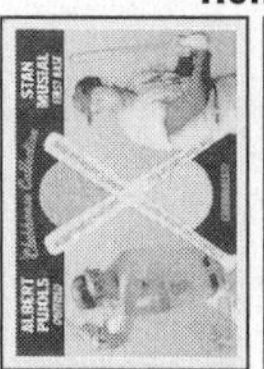

Nm-Mt Ex-Mt
STATED ODDS 1:9244
STATED PRINT RUN 55 SERIAL #'d SETS
BC Yogi Berra Uni 150.00 45.00
Roger Clemens Uni
GS Shawn Green Jsy 150.00 45.00
Duke Snider Uni
MP Albert Pujols Jsy 250.00 75.00
Stan Musial Uni

2004 Topps Heritage Doubleheader

Nm-Mt Ex-Mt
ONE PER SEALED HOBBY BOX
VINTAGE D-HEADERS RANDOMLY SEEDED
1-2 Alex Rodriguez 8.00 2.40
Nomar Garciaparra
3-4 Ichiro Suzuki 10.00 3.00
Albert Pujols
5-6 Sammy Sosa 12.00 3.60
Derek Jeter
7-8 Jim Thome 8.00 2.40
Adam Dunn
9-10 Jason Giambi 8.00 2.40
Ivan Rodriguez
11-12 Todd Helton 8.00 2.40
Luis Gonzalez
13-14 Jeff Bagwell 8.00 2.40
Lance Berkman
15-16 Alfonso Soriano 8.00 2.40
Dontrelle Willis
17-18 Mark Prior 10.00 3.00
Vladimir Guerrero
19-20 Mike Piazza 10.00 3.00
Roger Clemens
21-22 Randy Johnson 8.00 2.40
Curt Schilling
23-24 Gary Sheffield 8.00 2.40
Pedro Martinez
25-26 Carlos Delgado 5.00 1.50
Jimmy Rollins
27-28 Andruw Jones 8.00 2.40
Chipper Jones
29-30 Rocco Baldelli 8.00 2.40
Hank Blalock
NNO Vintage Buyback

2004 Topps Heritage Flashbacks

Nm-Mt Ex-Mt
COMPLETE SET (10) 15.00 4.50
STATED ODDS 1:12
F1 Duke Snider 3.00 .90
F2 Johnny Podres 2.00 .60
F3 Don Newcombe 2.00 .60
F4 Al Kaline 3.00 .90
F5 Willie Mays 5.00 1.50
F6 Stan Musial 4.00 1.20
F7 Harmon Killebrew 3.00 .90
F8 Herb Score 2.00 .60
F9 Whitey Ford 3.00 .90
F10 Robin Roberts 2.00 .60

2004 Topps Heritage Flashbacks Autographs

Nm-Mt Ex-Mt
STATED ODDS 1:30,373
STATED PRINT RUN 25 SERIAL #'d SETS
NO PRICING DUE TO SCARCITY
AK Al Kaline
NPS Don Newcombe
Johnny Podres
Duke Snider

2004 Topps Heritage Grandstand Glory Stadium Seat Relics

Nm-Mt Ex-Mt
GROUP A ODDS 1:27,731
GROUP A ODDS 1:606
GROUP A STATED PRINT RUN 55 CARDS
GROUP A PRINT RUN PROVIDED BY TOPPS
GROUP A IS NOT SERIAL-NUMBERED
AK Al Kaline B 25.00 7.50
HK Harmon Killebrew B 25.00 7.50
SM Stan Musial B 40.00 12.00
WM Willie Mays A 150.00 45.00
WS Warren Spahn B 20.00 6.00
YB Yogi Berra B 25.00 7.50

2004 Topps Heritage New Age Performers

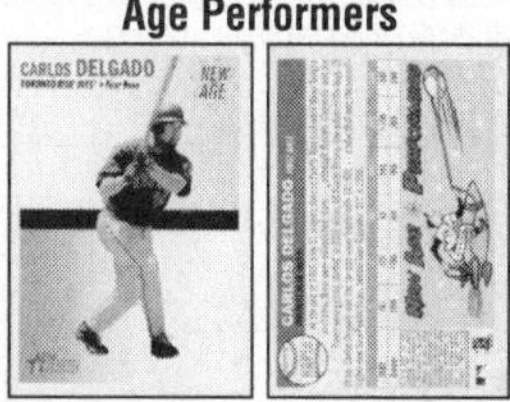

Nm-Mt Ex-Mt
COMPLETE SET (15) 30.00 9.00
STATED ODDS 1:15
NA1 Jason Giambi 2.50 .75
NA2 Ichiro Suzuki 4.00 1.20
NA3 Alex Rodriguez 4.00 1.20
NA4 Alfonso Soriano 2.00 .60
NA5 Albert Pujols 5.00 1.50
NA6 Nomar Garciaparra 4.00 1.20
NA7 Mark Prior 5.00 1.50
NA8 Derek Jeter 6.00 1.80
NA9 Sammy Sosa 4.00 1.20
NA10 Carlos Delgado 2.00 .60
NA11 Jim Thome 2.50 .75
NA12 Todd Helton 2.00 .60
NA13 Gary Sheffield 2.00 .60
NA14 Vladimir Guerrero 2.50 .75
NA15 Josh Beckett 2.00 .60

2004 Topps Heritage Real One Autographs

These autograph cards feature a mix of players who are active today; players who had cards in the 1955 Topps set and Stan Musial signing cards as if he were in the 1955 set. Scott Rolen did not return his cards in time for pack out and those exchange cards could be redeemed until February 28, 2006.

Nm-Mt Ex-Mt
STATED ODDS 1:230
STATED PRINT RUN 200 SETS
PRINT RUN INFO PROVIDED BY TOPPS
BASIC AUTOS ARE NOT SERIAL-NUMBERED
*RED INK: .75X TO 1.5X RETIRED
*RED INK MAYS: 1.25X TO 2X BASIC MAYS
*RED INK: .75X TO 1.5X ACTIVE
RED INK ODDS 1:835
RED INK PRINT RUN 55 #'d SETS
RED INK ALSO CALLED SPECIAL EDITION
EXCHANGE DEADLINE 02/28/06
AH Aubrey Huff 40.00 12.00
AK Al Kaline 100.00 30.00
BB Bob Borkowski 50.00 15.00
BC Billy Consolo 60.00 18.00
BG Bill Glynn 50.00 15.00
BK Bob Kline 50.00 15.00
BM Bob Milliken 50.00 15.00
BW Bill Wilson 50.00 15.00
CF Cliff Floyd 40.00 12.00
DN Don Newcombe 60.00 18.00
DP Duane Pillette 50.00 15.00
DS Duke Snider 100.00 30.00
DW Dontrelle Willis 50.00 15.00
EB Ernie Banks 120.00 36.00
FS Frank Smith 50.00 15.00
GA Gair Allie 50.00 15.00
HE Harry Elliott 50.00 15.00
HK Harmon Killebrew 100.00 30.00
HP Harry Perkowski 50.00 15.00
HV Corky Valentine 50.00 15.00
JG Johnny Gray 50.00 15.00
JP Jim Pearce 50.00 15.00
JPO Johnny Podres 60.00 18.00
LL Lou Limmer 60.00 18.00
ML Mike Lowell 40.00 12.00
MO Magglio Ordonez 40.00 12.00
SK Steve Kraly 60.00 18.00
SM Stan Musial 120.00 36.00
SR Scott Rolen EXCH 50.00 15.00
TK Thornton Kipper 50.00 15.00
TW Tom Wright 50.00 15.00
VT Jake Thies 50.00 15.00
WM Willie Mays 200.00 60.00
YB Yogi Berra 100.00 30.00

2004 Topps Heritage Team Topps Legends Autographs

Nm-Mt Ex-Mt
STATED ODDS 1:505
SEE 04 TOPPS TEAM TOPPS FOR PRICING

2004 Topps Heritage Then and Now

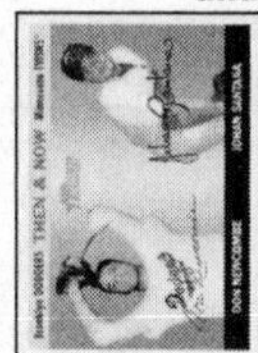

Nm-Mt Ex-Mt
COMPLETE SET (6) 10.00 3.00
STATED ODDS 1:15
TN1 Willie Mays 5.00 1.50
Jim Thome
TN2 Al Kaline 5.00 1.50
Albert Pujols
TN3 Duke Snider 3.00 .90
Carlos Delgado
TN4 Robin Roberts 2.00 .60
Roy Halladay
TN5 Don Newcombe 2.00 .60
Johan Santana
TN6 Herb Score 3.00 .90
Kerry Wood

1996 Topps Laser

The 1996 Topps Laser contains 128 regular cards that are found on one of four perfected designs. Every card is etch foil-stamped and laser-cut. The four-card packs retailed for $5.00 each.

Nm-Mt Ex-Mt
COMPLETE SET (128) 80.00 24.00
COMPLETE SERIES 1 (64) 40.00 12.00

COMPLETE SERIES 2 (64) 40.00 12.00
1 Moises Alou 1.00 .30
2 Derek Bell 1.00 .30
3 Joe Carter 1.00 .30
4 Jeff Conine 1.00 .30
5 Darren Daulton 1.00 .30
6 Jim Edmonds 1.00 .30
7 Ron Gant 1.00 .30
8 Juan Gonzalez 2.50 .75
9 Brian Jordan 1.00 .30
10 Ryan Klesko 1.00 .30
11 Paul Molitor 1.50 .45
12 Tony Phillips 1.00 .30
13 Manny Ramirez 1.00 .30
14 Sammy Sosa 4.00 1.20
15 Devon White 1.00 .30
16 Bernie Williams 1.50 .45
17 Garrett Anderson 1.00 .30
18 Jay Bell 1.00 .30
19 Craig Biggio 1.50 .45
20 Bobby Bonilla 1.00 .30
21 Ken Caminiti 1.00 .30
22 Shawon Dunston 1.00 .30
23 Mark Grace 1.50 .45
24 Gregg Jefferies 1.00 .30
25 Jeff King 1.00 .30
26 Javy Lopez 1.00 .30
27 Edgar Martinez 1.50 .45
28 Dean Palmer 1.00 .30
29 J.T. Snow 1.00 .30
30 Mike Stanley 1.00 .30
31 Terry Steinbach 1.00 .30
32 Robin Ventura 1.00 .30
33 Roberto Alomar 2.50 .75
34 Jeff Bagwell 1.50 .45
35 Dante Bichette 1.00 .30
36 Wade Boggs 1.50 .45
37 Barry Bonds 6.00 1.80
38 Jose Canseco 2.50 .75
39 Vinny Castilla 1.00 .30
40 Will Clark 2.50 .75
41 Marty Cordova 1.00 .30
42 Ken Griffey Jr. 4.00 1.20
43 Tony Gwynn 3.00 .90
44 Rickey Henderson 2.50 .75
45 Chipper Jones 2.50 .75
46 Mark McGwire 6.00 1.80
47 Brian McRae 1.00 .30
48 Ryne Sandberg 4.00 1.20
49 Andy Ashby 1.00 .30
50 Alan Benes 1.00 .30
51 Andy Benes 1.00 .30
52 Roger Clemens 5.00 1.50
53 Doug Drabek 1.00 .30
54 Dennis Eckersley 1.00 .30
55 Tom Glavine 1.50 .45
56 Randy Johnson 2.50 .75
57 Mark Langston 1.00 .30
58 Denny Martinez 1.00 .30
59 Jack McDowell 1.00 .30
60 Hideo Nomo 2.50 .75
61 Shane Reynolds 1.00 .30
62 John Smoltz 1.50 .45
63 Paul Wilson 1.00 .30
64 Mark Wohlers 1.00 .30
65 Shawn Green 1.00 .30
66 Marquis Grissom 1.00 .30
67 Dave Hollins 1.00 .30
68 Todd Hundley 1.00 .30
69 David Justice 1.00 .30
70 Eric Karros 1.00 .30
71 Ray Lankford 1.00 .30
72 Fred McGriff 1.50 .45
73 Hal Morris 1.00 .30
74 Eddie Murray 2.50 .75
75 Paul O'Neill 1.50 .45
76 Rey Ordonez 1.00 .30
77 Reggie Sanders 1.00 .30
78 Gary Sheffield 1.00 .30
79 Jim Thome 2.50 .75
80 Rondell White 1.00 .30
81 Travis Fryman 1.00 .30
82 Derek Jeter 6.00 1.80
83 Chuck Knoblauch 1.00 .30
84 Barry Larkin 2.50 .75
85 Tino Martinez 1.50 .45
86 Raul Mondesi 1.00 .30
87 John Olerud 1.00 .30
88 Rafael Palmeiro 1.50 .45
89 Mike Piazza 4.00 1.20
90 Cal Ripken 8.00 2.40
91 Ivan Rodriguez 2.50 .75
92 Frank Thomas 2.50 .75
93 John Valentin 1.00 .30
94 Mo Vaughn 1.00 .30
95 Quilvio Veras 1.00 .30
96 Matt Williams 1.00 .30
97 Brady Anderson 1.00 .30
98 Carlos Baerga 1.00 .30
99 Albert Belle 1.00 .30
100 Jay Buhner 1.00 .30
101 Johnny Damon 1.00 .30
102 Chili Davis 1.00 .30
103 Ray Durham 1.00 .30
104 Len Dykstra 1.00 .30
105 Cecil Fielder 1.00 .30
106 Andres Galarraga 1.00 .30
107 Brian L.Hunter 1.00 .30
108 Kenny Lofton 1.00 .30
109 Kirby Puckett 2.50 .75
110 Tim Salmon 1.50 .45
111 Greg Vaughn 1.00 .30
112 Larry Walker 1.50 .45
113 Rick Aguilera 1.00 .30
114 Kevin Appier 1.00 .30
115 Kevin Brown 1.00 .30
116 David Cone 1.00 .30
117 Alex Fernandez 1.00 .30

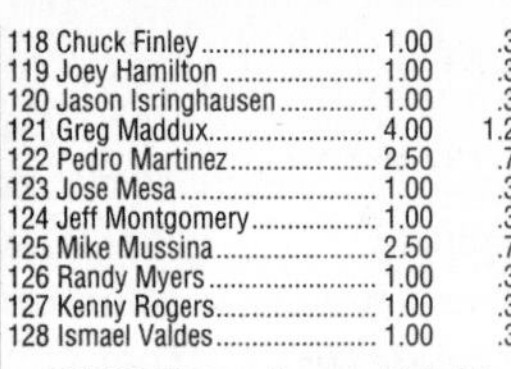

118 Chuck Finley 1.00 .30
119 Joey Hamilton 1.00 .30
120 Jason Isringhausen 1.00 .30
121 Greg Maddux 4.00 1.20
122 Pedro Martinez 2.50 .75
123 Jose Mesa 1.00 .30
124 Jeff Montgomery 1.00 .30
125 Mike Mussina 2.50 .75
126 Randy Myers 1.00 .30
127 Kenny Rogers 1.00 .30
128 Ismael Valdes 1.00 .30

1996 Topps Laser Bright Spots

Randomly inserted in packs at a rate of one in 20, this 16-card set highlights top young star players. The cards are printed on etched silver and gold diffraction foil.

Nm-Mt Ex-Mt
COMPLETE SERIES 1 (8) 25.00 7.50
COMPLETE SERIES 2 (8) 35.00 10.50
1 Brian L.Hunter 2.00 .60
2 Derek Jeter 12.00 3.60
3 Jason Kendall 2.00 .60
4 Brooks Kieschnick 2.00 .60
5 Rey Ordonez 2.00 .60
6 Jason Schmidt 2.00 .60
7 Chris Snopek 2.00 .60
8 Bob Wolcott 2.00 .60
9 Alan Benes 2.00 .60
10 Marty Cordova 2.00 .60
11 Jimmy Haynes 2.00 .60
12 Todd Hollandsworth 2.00 .60
13 Derek Jeter 12.00 3.60
14 Chipper Jones 5.00 1.50
15 Hideo Nomo 5.00 1.50
16 Paul Wilson 2.00 .60

1996 Topps Laser Power Cuts

Randomly inserted in packs at a rate of one in 40, this 16-card set features baseball's biggest bats on laser-cut stock polished off with etched silver and gold diffraction foil.

Nm-Mt Ex-Mt
COMPLETE SERIES 1 (8) 25.00 7.50
COMPLETE SERIES 2 (8) 30.00 9.00
1 Albert Belle 2.00 .60
2 Jay Buhner 2.00 .60
3 Fred McGriff 3.00 .90
4 Mike Piazza 8.00 2.40
5 Tim Salmon 3.00 .90
6 Frank Thomas 5.00 1.50
7 Mo Vaughn 2.00 .60
8 Matt Williams 2.00 .60
9 Jeff Bagwell 3.00 .90
10 Barry Bonds 12.00 3.60
11 Jose Canseco 5.00 1.50
12 Cecil Fielder 2.00 .60
13 Juan Gonzalez 5.00 1.50
14 Ken Griffey Jr. 8.00 2.40
15 Sammy Sosa 8.00 2.40
16 Larry Walker 3.00 .90

1996 Topps Laser Stadium Stars

Randomly inserted in packs at a rate of one in 60, this 16-card set features the best and the brightest stars of the baseball diamond. Each highly detailed, laser-sculpted cover folds back to reveal striated silver and gold etched diffraction foil on every card.

Nm-Mt Ex-Mt
COMPLETE SERIES 1 (8) 80.00 24.00
COMPLETE SERIES 2 (8) 60.00 18.00
1 Carlos Baerga 3.00 .90
2 Barry Bonds 20.00 6.00
3 Andres Galarraga 3.00 .90
4 Ken Griffey Jr. 12.00 3.60
5 Barry Larkin 8.00 2.40
6 Raul Mondesi 3.00 .90
7 Kirby Puckett 8.00 2.40
8 Cal Ripken 25.00 7.50
9 Will Clark 8.00 2.40
10 Roger Clemens 15.00 4.50
11 Tony Gwynn 10.00 3.00
12 Randy Johnson 8.00 2.40
13 Kenny Lofton 3.00 .90
14 Edgar Martinez 5.00 1.50
15 Ryne Sandberg 12.00 3.60
16 Frank Thomas 8.00 2.40

1998 Topps Opening Day

This 165-card set is a parallel version of basic 1998 Topps cards and features 110 cards from Series 1 and 55 cards from Series 2. Cards were issued in special retail seven-card "Opening Day" packs carrying an SRP of $0.99. The cards are an exact parallel of the 1998 Topps base cards except, of course, for the bold Opening Day foil logo on front and the different numbering on back.

Nm-Mt Ex-Mt
COMPLETE SET (165) 50.00 15.00
*OPEN.DAY: .75X TO 2X BASIC TOPPS
ISSUED IN OPENING DAY PACKS

1999 Topps Opening Day

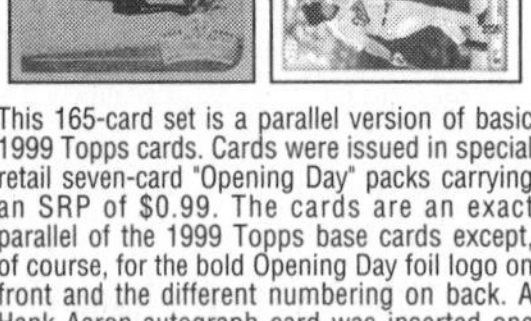

This 165-card set is a parallel version of basic 1999 Topps cards. Cards were issued in special retail seven-card "Opening Day" packs carrying an SRP of $0.99. The cards are an exact parallel of the 1999 Topps base cards except, of course, for the bold Opening Day foil logo on front and the different numbering on back. A Hank Aaron autograph card was inserted one every 29,462 packs.

Nm-Mt Ex-Mt
COMPLETE SET (165) 40.00 12.00
*OPEN.DAY: .75X TO 2X BASIC TOPPS
ISSUED IN OPENING DAY PACKS
AARON AUTO STATED ODDS 1:29,642
1 Hank Aaron 2.50 .75
NNO Hank Aaron AU 200.00 60.00

1999 Topps Opening Day Oversize

Randomly inserted one per retail box of 1999 Topps Opening Day base set, this three-card set features color player photos printed on 4 1/2" by 3 1/4" cards.

Nm-Mt Ex-Mt
COMPLETE SET (3) 8.00 2.40
1 Sammy Sosa 2.00 .60
2 Mark McGwire 3.00 .90
3 Ken Griffey Jr. 2.00 .60

2000 Topps Opening Day

The Topps Opening Day set was released in March, 2000 as a retail only 165-card set that featured 153 player cards, 10 Memorable Moments, 1 Hank Aaron 1954 reprint, and 1 checklist. Each pack contained seven cards and carried a suggested retail price of .99.

Nm-Mt Ex-Mt
COMPLETE SET (165) 40.00 12.00
*OPEN.DAY: .75X TO 2X BASIC TOPPS
ISSUED IN OPENING DAY PACKS
UER 110 AARON '54 REPRINT #'d 128
NO MM VARIATIONS IN OPENING DAY

2000 Topps Opening Day Autographs

Randomly inserted in packs, this insert set features autographs of five major league players. There were three levels of autographs. Level A were inserted into packs at one in 4207, Level B were inserted at one in 48074, Level C were inserted at one in 6280. Card backs carry an "ODA" prefix.

Nm-Mt Ex-Mt
ODA1 Edgardo Alfonzo A 40.00 12.00
ODA2 Wade Boggs A 80.00 24.00
ODA3 Robin Ventura A 40.00 12.00
ODA4 Josh Hamilton B 25.00 7.50
ODA5 Vernon Wells C 40.00 12.00

2001 Topps Opening Day

The 2001 Topps Opening Day product packed out in early March, 2001 and offers a 165-card base set. The base set features 150 Veteran players (1-150), four Prospects (151-154), 10 Golden Moments cards (155-164), and one checklist card (165). Each pack contained seven cards, and carries a suggested retail price of 1.99.

Nm-Mt Ex-Mt
COMPLETE SET (165) 40.00 12.00
*OPEN.DAY: .75X TO 2X BASIC TOPPS
ISSUED IN OPENING DAY PACKS

2001 Topps Opening Day Autographs

Randomly inserted into packs, this 4-card insert set features authentic autographs from four of the Major League's top players. The set is broken down into four groups: Group A is Chipper Jones (1:31,680), Group B is Todd Helton (1:15,020), Group C is Magglio Ordonez (1:10,004), and Group D is Corey Patterson (1:5,940). Card backs carry an "ODA" prefix followed by the player's initials.

Nm-Mt Ex-Mt
ODA-CJ Chipper Jones A 120.00 36.00
ODA-CP Corey Patterson D 30.00 9.00
ODA-MO Magglio Ordonez C 30.00 9.00
ODA-TH Todd Helton B 50.00 15.00

2001 Topps Opening Day Stickers

Randomly inserted into packs at approximately one in two, this 30-card insert features stickers of all 30 Major League Franchises. Card backs are not numbered and are listed below in alphabetical order for convenience.

Nm-Mt Ex-Mt
COMPLETE SET (30) 6.00 1.80
COMMON TEAM (1-30) .25 .07

2002 Topps Opening Day

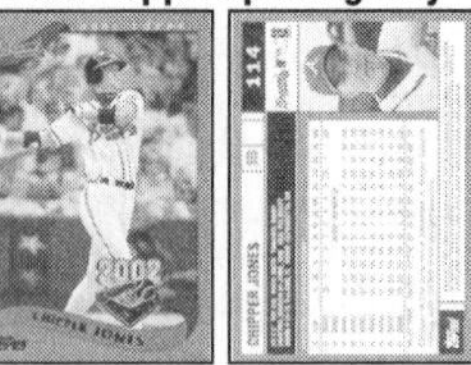

Released in early 2002, this 165 card set, which was issued in seven-card packs is a partial parallel of the 2002 Topps set. These cards all have an opening day logo on the front. The Barry Bonds card issued at card numbered 73 only featured the 73 home run logo. Unlike the regular set, this was the only version of that card issued.

Nm-Mt Ex-Mt
COMPLETE SET (165) 40.00 12.00
*OPEN.DAY: .75X TO X2 BASIC TOPPS
ISSUED IN OPENING DAY PACKS

2002 Topps Opening Day Autographs

Randomly inserted into packs, these three cards feature autographs of players in the Opening Day set. These cards were all inserted at differening odds and we have notated that information next to the player's name.

Nm-Mt Ex-Mt
GROUP A STATED ODDS 1:6069
GROUP B STATED ODDS 1:3036
GROUP C STATED ODDS 1:2014
ODA-BS Ben Sheets B
ODA-GJ Geoff Jenkins A
ODA-NJ Nick Johnson C

2003 Topps Opening Day

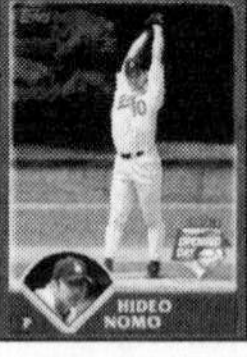

This 165-card set was issued in February, 2003. These cards were issued in six card packs which came 22 packs to a box and 20 boxes to a case. These cards can be notated by the special Topps Opening Day logo printed on the front.

Nm-Mt Ex-Mt
COMPLETE SET (165) 40.00 12.00
*OPEN.DAY: .75X TO 2X BASIC TOPPS
ISSUED IN OPENING DAY PACKS

2003 Topps Opening Day Stickers

Issued one per pack, these 72 cards partially parallel the Opening Day set. Each of the fronts is designed exactly as the basic 2003 Topps card.

Nm-Mt Ex-Mt
*OD STICKERS: 1.5X TO 4X BASIC TOPPS
ONE PER PACK

2003 Topps Opening Day Autographs

Inserted at different odds depending on which group the players were assigned to, these cards feature authentic autographs of the featured players.

Nm-Mt Ex-Mt
GROUP A ODDS 1:10,623
GROUP B ODDS 1:3539
GROUP C ODDS 1:2654
JDO Johnny Damon B 25.00 7.50
LBO Lance Berkman A 40.00 12.00
RFO Rafael Furcal C 25.00 7.50

2004 Topps Opening Day

This 165-card set, which is a mini-parallel to the basic Topps set was released in February, 2004. The set was issued in six card packs which came 36 packs to a box and 20 boxes to a case. Each of these cards have a special "Opening Day" logo embossed on them.

Nm-Mt Ex-Mt
COMPLETE SET (165) 40.00 12.00
*OPEN.DAY 1-165: .75X TO 2X BASIC TOPPS
ISSUED IN OPENING DAY PACKS

2004 Topps Opening Day Autographs

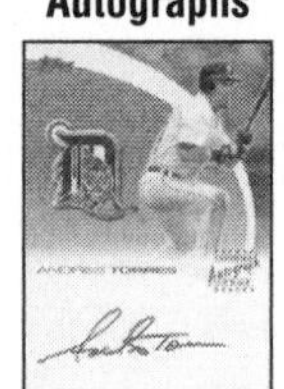

Nm-Mt Ex-Mt
STATED ODDS 1:629
AT Andres Torres 15.00 4.50
DW Dontrelle Willis 40.00 12.00
JD Jeff Duncan
JW Jerome Williams 25.00 7.50
RH Rich Harden 40.00 12.00
RW Ryan Wagner 25.00 7.50

2002 Topps Pristine

This 210 card set was issued in October, 2002. This set was issued in eight card packs with an $40 SRP which came five packs to a box and six boxes to a case. The first 140 cards feature active veterans stars while cards 141-150

feature retired greats and cards numbered 151-210 feature three different versions of each rookie. Each rookie has a common version, a uncommon version which has a print run of 1999 serial numbered sets and a rare version which has a stated print run of 799 serial numbered sets.

	Nm-Mt	Ex-Mt
COMMON CARD (1-140)	1.50	.45
COMMON CARD (141-150)	2.50	.75
COMMON C CARD (151-210)	1.50	.45
COMMON U CARD (151-210)	3.00	.90
COMMON R CARD (151-210)	6.00	1.80
1 Alex Rodriguez	6.00	1.80
2 Carlos Delgado	1.50	.45
3 Jimmy Rollins	1.50	.45
4 Jason Kendall	1.50	.45
5 John Olerud	1.50	.45
6 Albert Pujols	8.00	2.40
7 Curt Schilling	2.50	.75
8 Gary Sheffield	1.50	.45
9 Johnny Damon	1.50	.45
10 Ichiro Suzuki	6.00	1.80
11 Pat Burrell	1.50	.45
12 Garret Anderson	1.50	.45
13 Andruw Jones	1.50	.45
14 Kerry Wood	4.00	1.20
15 Kenny Lofton	1.50	.45
16 Adam Dunn	1.50	.45
17 Juan Pierre	1.50	.45
18 Josh Beckett	2.50	.75
19 Roy Oswalt	1.50	.45
20 Derek Jeter	10.00	3.00
21 Jose Vidro	1.50	.45
22 Richie Sexson	1.50	.45
23 Mike Sweeney	1.50	.45
24 Jeff Kent	1.50	.45
25 Jason Giambi	4.00	1.20
26 Bret Boone	1.50	.45
27 J.D. Drew	1.50	.45
28 Shannon Stewart	1.50	.45
29 Miguel Tejada	1.50	.45
30 Barry Bonds	10.00	3.00
31 Randy Johnson	4.00	1.20
32 Pedro Martinez	4.00	1.20
33 Magglio Ordonez	1.50	.45
34 Todd Helton	2.50	.75
35 Craig Biggio	2.50	.75
36 Shawn Green	1.50	.45
37 Vladimir Guerrero	4.00	1.20
38 Mo Vaughn	1.50	.45
39 Alfonso Soriano	2.50	.75
40 Barry Zito	2.50	.75
41 Aramis Ramirez	1.50	.45
42 Ryan Klesko	1.50	.45
43 Ruben Sierra	1.50	.45
44 Tino Martinez	2.50	.75
45 Toby Hall	1.50	.45
46 Ivan Rodriguez	4.00	1.20
47 Raul Mondesi	1.50	.45
48 Carlos Pena	1.50	.45
49 Darin Erstad	1.50	.45
50 Sammy Sosa	6.00	1.80
51 Bartolo Colon	1.50	.45
52 Robert Fick	1.50	.45
53 Cliff Floyd	1.50	.45
54 Brian Jordan	1.50	.45
55 Torii Hunter	1.50	.45
56 Roberto Alomar	4.00	1.20
57 Roger Clemens	8.00	2.40
58 Mark Mulder	1.50	.45
59 Brian Giles	1.50	.45
60 Mike Piazza	6.00	1.80
61 Rich Aurilia	1.50	.45
62 Freddy Garcia	1.50	.45
63 Jim Edmonds	1.50	.45
64 Eric Hinske	1.50	.45
65 Vicente Padilla	1.50	.45
66 Javier Vazquez	1.50	.45
67 Cristian Guzman	1.50	.45
68 Paul Lo Duca	1.50	.45
69 Bobby Abreu	1.50	.45
70 Nomar Garciaparra	6.00	1.80
71 Troy Glaus	2.50	.75
72 Chipper Jones	4.00	1.20
73 Scott Rolen	2.50	.75
74 Lance Berkman	1.50	.45
75 C.C. Sabathia	1.50	.45
76 Bernie Williams	2.50	.75
77 Rafael Palmeiro	2.50	.75
78 Phil Nevin	1.50	.45
79 Kazuhiro Sasaki	1.50	.45
80 Eric Chavez	1.50	.45
81 Jorge Posada	2.50	.75
82 Edgardo Alfonzo	1.50	.45
83 Geoff Jenkins	1.50	.45
84 Preston Wilson	1.50	.45
85 Jim Thome	4.00	1.20
86 Frank Thomas	4.00	1.20
87 Jeff Bagwell	2.50	.75
88 Greg Maddux	6.00	1.80
89 Mark Prior	8.00	2.40
90 Larry Walker	2.50	.75
91 Luis Gonzalez	1.50	.45
92 Tim Hudson	1.50	.45
93 Tsuyoshi Shinjo	1.50	.45
94 Juan Gonzalez	4.00	1.20
95 Shea Hillenbrand	1.50	.45
96 Paul Konerko	1.50	.45
97 Tom Glavine	2.50	.75
98 Marty Cordova	1.50	.45
99 Moises Alou	1.50	.45
100 Ken Griffey Jr.	6.00	1.80
101 Hank Blalock	4.00	1.20
102 Matt Morris	1.50	.45
103 Robb Nen	1.50	.45
104 Mike Cameron	1.50	.45
105 Mark Buehrle	1.50	.45
106 Sean Burroughs	1.50	.45
107 Orlando Cabrera	1.50	.45
108 Jeromy Burnitz	1.50	.45
109 Juan Uribe	1.50	.45
110 Eric Milton	1.50	.45
111 Carlos Lee	1.50	.45
112 Jose Mesa	1.50	.45
113 Morgan Ensberg	1.50	.45
114 Derek Lowe	1.50	.45
115 Juan Cruz	1.50	.45
116 Mike Lieberthal	1.50	.45
117 Armando Benitez	1.50	.45
118 Vinny Castilla	1.50	.45
119 Russ Ortiz	1.50	.45
120 Mike Lowell	1.50	.45
121 Corey Patterson	1.50	.45
122 Mike Mussina	4.00	1.20
123 Rafael Furcal	1.50	.45
124 Mark Grace	2.50	.75
125 Ben Sheets	1.50	.45
126 John Smoltz	2.50	.75
127 Fred McGriff	2.50	.75
128 Nick Johnson	1.50	.45
129 J.T. Snow	1.50	.45
130 Jeff Cirillo	1.50	.45
131 Trevor Hoffman	1.50	.45
132 Kevin Brown	1.50	.45
133 Mariano Rivera	2.50	.75
134 Marlon Anderson	1.50	.45
135 Al Leiter	1.50	.45
136 Doug Mientkiewicz	1.50	.45
137 Eric Karros	1.50	.45
138 Bobby Higginson	1.50	.45
139 Sean Casey	1.50	.45
140 Troy Percival	1.50	.45
141 Willie Mays	8.00	2.40
142 Carl Yastrzemski	6.00	1.80
143 Stan Musial	6.00	1.80
144 Harmon Killebrew	4.00	1.20
145 Mike Schmidt	8.00	2.40
146 Duke Snider	2.50	.75
147 Brooks Robinson	4.00	1.20
148 Frank Robinson	2.50	.75
149 Nolan Ryan	10.00	3.00
150 Reggie Jackson	2.50	.75
151 Joe Mauer C RC	12.00	3.60
152 Joe Mauer U	25.00	7.50
153 Joe Mauer R	50.00	15.00
154 Colt Griffin C RC	2.50	.75
155 Colt Griffin U	5.00	1.50
156 Colt Griffin R	10.00	3.00
157 Jason Simontacchi C RC	1.50	.45
158 Jason Simontacchi U	3.00	.90
159 Jason Simontacchi R	6.00	1.80
160 Casey Kotchman C RC	6.00	1.80
161 Casey Kotchman U	12.00	3.60
162 Casey Kotchman R	25.00	7.50
163 Greg Sain C RC	1.50	.45
164 Greg Sain U	3.00	.90
165 Greg Sain R	6.00	1.80
166 David Wright C RC	5.00	1.50
167 David Wright U	10.00	3.00
168 David Wright R	20.00	6.00
169 Scott Hairston C RC	4.00	1.20
170 Scott Hairston U	8.00	2.40
171 Scott Hairston R	15.00	4.50
172 Rolando Viera C RC	1.50	.45
173 Rolando Viera U	3.00	.90
174 Rolando Viera R	6.00	1.80
175 Tyrell Godwin C RC	1.50	.45
176 Tyrell Godwin U	3.00	.90
177 Tyrell Godwin R	6.00	1.80
178 Jesus Cota C RC		
179 Jesus Cota U	3.00	.90
180 Jesus Cota R	6.00	1.80
181 Dan Johnson C RC	2.00	.60
182 Dan Johnson U	4.00	1.20
183 Dan Johnson R	8.00	2.40
184 Mario Ramos C RC	1.50	.45
185 Mario Ramos U	3.00	.90
186 Mario Ramos R	6.00	1.80
187 Jason Dubois C RC	4.00	1.20
188 Jason Dubois U	8.00	2.40
189 Jason Dubois R	15.00	4.50
190 Jonny Gomes C RC	2.50	.75
191 Jonny Gomes U	6.00	1.80
192 Jonny Gomes R	12.00	3.60
193 Chris Snelling C RC	2.50	.75
194 Chris Snelling U	5.00	1.50
195 Chris Snelling R	10.00	3.00
196 Hansel Izquierdo C RC	1.50	.45
197 Hansel Izquierdo U	3.00	.90
198 Hansel Izquierdo R	6.00	1.80
199 So Taguchi C RC	2.00	.60
200 So Taguchi U	4.00	1.20
201 So Taguchi R	8.00	2.40
202 Kazuhisa Ishii C RC	3.00	.90
203 Kazuhisa Ishii U	6.00	1.80
204 Kazuhisa Ishii R	12.00	3.60
205 Jorge Padilla C RC	1.50	.45
206 Jorge Padilla U	3.00	.90
207 Jorge Padilla R	6.00	1.80
208 Earl Snyder C RC	1.50	.45
209 Earl Snyder U	3.00	.90
210 Earl Snyder R	6.00	1.80

2002 Topps Pristine Gold Refractors

Inserted one per hobby box, this is a parallel of the regular set. Each card has a stated print run of 70 serial numbered sets.

Nm-Mt Ex-Mt

*GOLD 1-140: 2.5X TO 6X BASIC
*GOLD 141-150: 2.5X TO 6X BASIC
*GOLD C 151-210: .4X TO .10X BASIC C
*GOLD U 151-210: 2X TO 5X BASIC U
*GOLD R 151-210: 1X TO 2.5X BASIC R

2002 Topps Pristine Refractors

Issued at different odds depending on the card number, these cards parallel the regular pristine set. The veterans and retired players were issued to a stated print run of 149 serial numbered sets. The rookie cards were issued to stated print runs of 1999 for the common versions, 799 for the uncommon versions and 149 for the rare version.

Nm-Mt Ex-Mt

*REFRACTORS 1-140: 1.5X TO 4X
*REFRACTORS 141-150: 1.5X TO 4X
1-150 STATED ODDS 1:4
*REFRACTORS C 151-210: .75X TO 2X
COMMON 151-210 STATED ODDS 1:2
*REFRACTORS U 151-210: .75X TO 2X
UNCOMMON 151-210 STATED ODDS 1:5
*REFRACTORS R 151-210: .6X TO 1.5X
RARE 151-210 STATED ODDS 1:27

2002 Topps Pristine Fall Memories

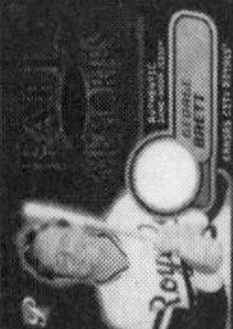

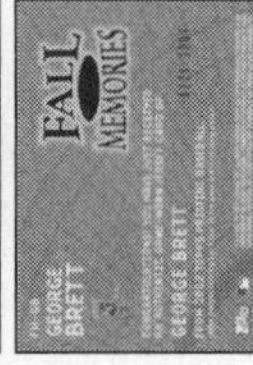

Issued at different odds depending on which group the insert card belonged to, these cards feature players who had participated in post-season play and a piece of game-used memorabilia pertaining to that player. We have listed the stated print run information for that player as well as what type of memorabilia next to the player's name in our checklist.

	Nm-Mt	Ex-Mt
GROUP A ODDS 1:21		
GROUP B ODDS 1:8		
GROUP C ODDS 1:49		
GROUP A PRINT RUN 425 SERIAL #'d SETS		
GROUP B PRINT RUN 1000 SERIAL #'d SETS		
GROUP C PRINT RUN 1600 SERIAL #'d SETS		
AJ Andruw Jones Uni B	8.00	2.40
AS Alfonso Soriano Bat B	10.00	3.00
BB Barry Bonds Bat A	40.00	12.00
BW Bernie Williams Bat B	10.00	3.00
CJ Chipper Jones Bat A	15.00	4.50
CS Curt Schilling Jsy B	10.00	3.00
EM Eddie Murray Bat A	15.00	4.50
GB George Brett Jsy B	25.00	7.50
GS Gary Sheffield Bat C	8.00	2.40
JB Johnny Bench Jsy B	15.00	4.50
JP Jorge Posada Bat B	10.00	3.00
KP Kirby Puckett Bat A	15.00	4.50
LG Luis Gonzalez Bat B	8.00	2.40
MG Mark Grace Bat A	15.00	4.50
RJ Reggie Jackson Bat A	15.00	4.50
SG Shawn Green Bat A	15.00	4.50
TG Tom Glavine Jsy B	10.00	3.00
TH Todd Helton Jsy B	10.00	3.00
TM Tino Martinez Bat A	15.00	4.50
WM Willie Mays Jsy A	40.00	12.00

2002 Topps Pristine In the Gap

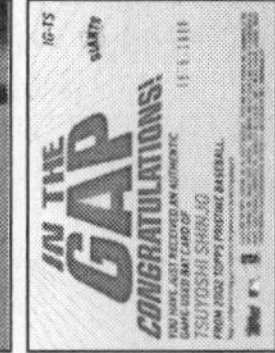

Inserted at a stated rate of one in 12 for group A cards and one in five for group B cards, these 30 cards feature players along with a game-used memorabilia piece. We have notated next to the player's name not only what type of memorabilia but also what grouping they belonged to.

	Nm-Mt	Ex-Mt
GROUP A PRINT RUN 425 SERIAL #'d SETS		
GROUP B PRINT RUN 1000 SERIAL #'d SETS		
AD Adam Dunn Jsy B	8.00	2.40
AJ Andruw Jones Jsy B	8.00	2.40
AP Albert Pujols Uni B	20.00	6.00
AR Alex Rodriguez Bat A	15.00	4.50
ARA Aramis Ramirez Bat A	10.00	3.00
AS Alfonso Soriano Bat A	15.00	4.50
BB Bret Boone Bat B	8.00	2.40
BBO Barry Bonds Uni B	30.00	9.00
BW Bernie Williams Bat A	15.00	4.50
CD Carlos Delgado Bat A	10.00	3.00
DE Darin Erstad Bat A	10.00	3.00
EC Eric Chavez Bat A	10.00	3.00
IR Ivan Rodriguez Bat A	15.00	4.50
JE Jim Edmonds Jsy B	8.00	2.40
JK Jeff Kent Jsy B	8.00	2.40
LB Lance Berkman Bat A	10.00	3.00
LW Larry Walker Jsy B	10.00	3.00
MP Mike Piazza Bat A	15.00	4.50
NG Nomar Garciaparra Bat A	15.00	4.50
PL Paul Lo Duca Bat A	10.00	3.00
PW Preston Wilson Jsy B	8.00	2.40
RA Roberto Alomar Bat B	15.00	4.50
RH Rickey Henderson Bat A	15.00	4.50
RK Ryan Klesko Bat A	10.00	3.00
RP Rafael Palmeiro Bat A	15.00	4.50
TG Tony Gwynn Jsy B	15.00	4.50
TH Todd Helton Bat B	10.00	3.00
TS Tsuyoshi Shinjo Bat B	8.00	2.40
WB Wade Boggs Uni B	10.00	3.00
WBE Wilson Betemit Bat B	8.00	2.40

2002 Topps Pristine Patches

Inserted at stated odds of one in 126, these 25 cards feature game-used patches of the featured player. Each of these cards were issued to a stated print run of 25 serial numbered sets and no pricing is provided due to scarcity.

	Nm-Mt	Ex-Mt
AD Adam Dunn		
AJ Andruw Jones		
AP Albert Pujols		
AR Alex Rodriguez		
BB Bret Boone		
BBO Barry Bonds		
CD Carlos Delgado		
CJ Chipper Jones		
CS Curt Schilling		
DM Don Mattingly		
EC Eric Chavez		
FT Frank Thomas		
GB George Brett		
GM Greg Maddux		
KS Kazuhiro Sasaki		
LW Larry Walker		
MP Mike Piazza		
NG Nomar Garciaparra		
PM Pedro Martinez		
RP Rafael Palmeiro		
SR Scott Rolen		
TG Tony Gwynn		
TGL Tom Glavine		
TH Todd Helton		
WB Wade Boggs		

2002 Topps Pristine Personal Endorsements

Inserted at different odds depending on the group the player belonged to, these cards feature authentic player autographs on a clear acrylic like card surface. We have notated what group the player belongs to next to their name in our checklist.

	Nm-Mt	Ex-Mt
GROUP A ODDS 1:396		
GROUP B ODDS 1:63		
GROUP C ODDS 1:79		
GROUP D ODDS 1:33		
GROUP E ODDS 1:9		
GROUP F ODDS 1:53		
AP Albert Pujols A	100.00	30.00
BB Barry Bonds E	175.00	52.50
BS Ben Sheets B	20.00	6.00
CG Cristian Guzman C	15.00	4.50
CK Casey Kotchman E	25.00	7.50
CM Corwin Malone E	10.00	3.00
DB Dewon Brazelton D	15.00	4.50
GF Gavin Floyd D	25.00	7.50
IG Irvin Guzman E	15.00	4.50
JD Johnny Damon B	20.00	6.00
JL Jason Lane E	10.00	3.00
JR Jimmy Rollins C	15.00	4.50
JS Juan Silvestre E	10.00	3.00
KB Kenny Baugh F	10.00	3.00
KI Kazuhisa Ishii A	40.00	12.00
LB Lance Berkman B	20.00	6.00
MT Marcus Thames E	10.00	3.00
NN Nick Neugebauer E	10.00	3.00
OH Orlando Hudson D	15.00	4.50
RA Roberto Alomar B	40.00	12.00
ST So Taguchi B	30.00	9.00

2002 Topps Pristine Popular Demand

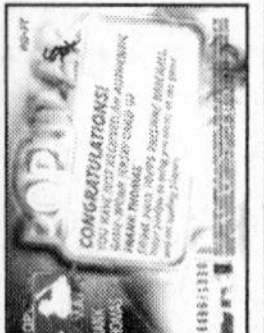

Inserted at a stated print run of one in four, these 20 cards feature some of the leading players in the game along with a game-used memorabilia piece. Each card was issued to a stated print run of 1000 serial numbered sets.

	Nm-Mt	Ex-Mt
AD Adam Dunn Jsy	8.00	2.40
AP Albert Pujols Jsy	20.00	6.00
AR Alex Rodriguez Bat	15.00	4.50
BB Bret Boone Jsy	8.00	2.40
BBO Barry Bonds Uni	30.00	9.00
CD Carlos Delgado Uni	8.00	2.40
CJ Chipper Jones Jsy	15.00	4.50
CS Curt Schilling Jsy	10.00	3.00
DM Don Mattingly Jsy	40.00	12.00
FT Frank Thomas Jsy	15.00	4.50
IR Ivan Rodriguez Uni	15.00	4.50
JB Jeff Bagwell Jsy	10.00	3.00
LW Larry Walker Jsy	10.00	3.00
MP Mike Piazza Jsy	15.00	4.50
NG Nomar Garciaparra Bat	15.00	4.50
RA Roberto Alomar Jsy	15.00	4.50
SG Shawn Green Jsy	8.00	2.40
TG Tony Gwynn Jsy	15.00	4.50
TH Todd Helton Jsy	10.00	3.00
WB Wade Boggs Jsy	10.00	3.00

2002 Topps Pristine Portions

Issued at different odds depending on which group the insert card belonged to, these cards feature some leading players along with a piece of game-used memorabilia pertaining to that player. We have listed the stated print run information for that player as well as what type of memorabilia next to the player's name in our checklist.

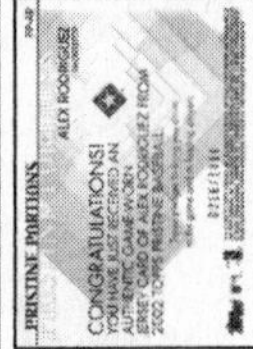

	Nm-Mt	Ex-Mt
GROUP A ODDS 1:21		
GROUP B ODDS 1:4		
GROUP C ODDS 1:33		
GROUP A PRINT RUN 425 SERIAL #'d SETS		
GROUP B PRINT RUN 1000 SERIAL #'d SETS		
GROUP C PRINT RUN 2400 SERIAL #'d SETS		
AD Adam Dunn Bat B	8.00	2.40
AP Albert Pujols Uni B	20.00	6.00
AR Alex Rodriguez Jsy B	15.00	4.50
BB Bret Boone Jsy B	8.00	2.40
BBO Barry Bonds Uni C	20.00	6.00
CB Craig Biggio Jsy B	10.00	3.00
CD Carlos Delgado Jsy B	8.00	2.40
CF Cliff Floyd Jsy B	8.00	2.40
CG Cristian Guzman Jsy B	8.00	2.40
EM Edgar Martinez Bat A	15.00	4.50
GM Greg Maddux Jsy A	15.00	4.50
IR Ivan Rodriguez Bat A	15.00	4.50
JB Jeff Bagwell Uni A	15.00	4.50
JP Jorge Posada Bat A	15.00	4.50
KS Kazuhiro Sasaki Jsy A	15.00	4.50
LB Lance Berkman Bat A	15.00	4.50
LD Paul Lo Duca Jsy B	8.00	2.40
MM Mike Mussina Uni B	15.00	4.50
MO Magglio Ordonez Jsy B	8.00	2.40
MP Mike Piazza Bat A	15.00	4.50
NG Nomar Garciaparra Jsy B	15.00	4.50
NJ Nick Johnson Bat B	8.00	2.40
NR Nolan Ryan Uni B	50.00	15.00
RA Roberto Alomar Bat A	15.00	4.50
RD Ryan Dempster Jsy B	8.00	2.40
RF Rafael Furcal Jsy B	8.00	2.40
RP Rafael Palmeiro Jsy B	10.00	3.00
TH Todd Helton Jsy B	10.00	3.00

2003 Topps Pristine

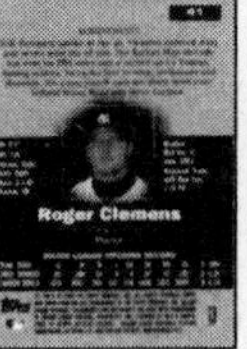

This 190 card pack was issued in special eight-card packs, which actually came as a few packs within a large pack. Each pack contained a mix of cards from the base set as well as an encased special. In the basic set, cards numbered 1 through 95 featured veterans, cards numbered 96 through 100 featured retired greats and cards 101 through 190 featured rookies. Each of the rookies were issued in three forms as "Common", "Uncommon" or "Rare". The "Uncommon" rookies were issued to a stated print run of 1499 serial numbered sets while the "rare" rookies were issued to a stated print run of 499 serial numbered sets.

	MINT	NRMT
COMMON CARD (1-100)	1.50	.70
COMMON C (101-190)	1.50	.70
C 101-190 APPX. 2X EASIER THAN 1-100		
COMMON U (101-190)	3.00	1.35
UNCOMMON 101-190 STATED ODDS 1:2		
UNCOMMON PRINT 1499 SERIAL #'d SETS		
COMMON R (101-190)	6.00	2.70
RARE 101-190 STATED ODDS 1:6		
RARE PRINT RUN 499 SERIAL #'d SETS		
1 Pedro Martinez	4.00	1.80
2 Derek Jeter	10.00	4.50
3 Alex Rodriguez	6.00	2.70
4 Miguel Tejada	1.50	.70
5 Nomar Garciaparra	6.00	2.70
6 Austin Kearns	1.50	.70
7 Jose Vidro	1.50	.70
8 Bret Boone	1.50	.70
9 Scott Rolen	2.50	1.10
10 Mike Sweeney	1.50	.70
11 Jason Schmidt	1.50	.70
12 Alfonso Soriano	2.50	1.10
13 Tim Hudson	1.50	.70
14 A.J. Pierzynski	1.50	.70
15 Lance Berkman	1.50	.70
16 Frank Thomas	4.00	1.80
17 Gary Sheffield	1.50	.70
18 Jarrod Washburn	1.50	.70
19 Hideo Nomo	4.00	1.80
20 Barry Zito	2.50	1.10
21 Kevin Millwood	1.50	.70
22 Matt Morris	1.50	.70
23 Carl Crawford	1.50	.70
24 Carlos Delgado	1.50	.70
25 Mike Piazza	6.00	2.70
26 Brad Radke	1.50	.70
27 Richie Sexson	1.50	.70
28 Kevin Brown	1.50	.70
29 Carlos Beltran	1.50	.70
30 Curt Schilling	2.50	1.10
31 Chipper Jones	4.00	1.80
32 Paul Konerko	1.50	.70
33 Larry Walker	2.50	1.10
34 Jeff Bagwell	2.50	1.10
35 Jason Giambi	4.00	1.80
36 Mark Mulder	1.50	.70
37 Vicente Padilla	1.50	.70
38 Kris Benson	1.50	.70
39 Bernie Williams	2.50	1.10
40 Jim Thome	4.00	1.80
41 Roger Clemens	8.00	3.60
42 Roberto Alomar	4.00	1.80

43 Torii Hunter 1.50 .70
44 Bobby Abreu 1.50 .70
45 Jeff Kent 1.50 .70
46 Roy Oswalt 1.50 .70
47 Bartolo Colon 1.50 .70
48 Greg Maddux 6.00 2.70
49 Tom Glavine 2.50 1.10
50 Sammy Sosa 6.00 2.70
51 Ichiro Suzuki 6.00 2.70
52 Mark Prior 8.00 3.60
53 Manny Ramirez 1.50 .70
54 Andruw Jones 1.50 .70
55 Randy Johnson 4.00 1.80
56 Garret Anderson 1.50 .70
57 Roy Halladay 1.50 .70
58 Rafael Palmeiro 2.50 1.10
59 Rocco Baldelli 6.00 2.70
60 Albert Pujols 8.00 3.60
61 Edgar Renteria 1.50 .70
62 John Olerud 1.50 .70
63 Rich Aurilia 1.50 .70
64 Ryan Klesko 1.50 .70
65 Brian Giles 1.50 .70
66 Eric Chavez 1.50 .70
67 Jorge Posada 2.50 1.10
68 Cliff Floyd 1.50 .70
69 Vladimir Guerrero 4.00 1.80
70 Cristian Guzman 1.50 .70
71 Raul Ibanez 1.50 .70
72 Paul Lo Duca 1.50 .70
73 A.J. Burnett 1.50 .70
74 Ken Griffey Jr. 6.00 2.70
75 Mark Buehrle 1.50 .70
76 Moises Alou 1.50 .70
77 Adam Dunn 1.50 .70
78 Tony Batista 1.50 .70
79 Troy Glaus 2.50 1.10
80 Luis Gonzalez 1.50 .70
81 Shea Hillenbrand 1.50 .70
82 Kerry Wood 4.00 1.80
83 Magglio Ordonez 1.50 .70
84 Omar Vizquel 1.50 .70
85 Bobby Higginson 1.50 .70
86 Mike Lowell 1.50 .70
87 Runelvys Hernandez 1.50 .70
88 Shawn Green 1.50 .70
89 Erubiel Durazo 1.50 .70
90 Pat Burrell 1.50 .70
91 Todd Helton 2.50 1.10
92 Jim Edmonds 1.50 .70
93 Aubrey Huff 1.50 .70
94 Eric Hinske 1.50 .70
95 Barry Bonds 10.00 4.50
96 Willie Mays 8.00 3.60
97 Bo Jackson 4.00 1.80
98 Carl Yastrzemski 6.00 2.70
99 Don Mattingly 10.00 4.50
100 Gary Carter 2.50 1.10
101 Jose Contreras C RC 4.00 1.80
102 Jose Contreras U 8.00 3.60
103 Jose Contreras R 15.00 6.75
104 Dan Haren C RC 2.50 1.10
105 Dan Haren U 5.00 2.20
106 Dan Haren R 10.00 4.50
107 Michel Hernandez C RC 1.50 .70
108 Michel Hernandez U 3.00 1.35
109 Michel Hernandez R 6.00 2.70
110 Bobby Basham C RC 2.00 .90
111 Bobby Basham U 4.00 1.80
112 Bobby Basham R 8.00 3.60
113 Bryan Bullington C RC 4.00 1.80
114 Bryan Bullington U 8.00 3.60
115 Bryan Bullington R 15.00 6.75
116 Bernie Castro C RC 1.50 .70
117 Bernie Castro U 3.00 1.35
118 Bernie Castro R 6.00 2.70
119 Chien-Ming Wang C RC 4.00 1.80
120 Chien-Ming Wang U 8.00 3.60
121 Chien-Ming Wang R 15.00 6.75
122 Eric Crozier C RC 2.00 .90
123 Eric Crozier U 4.00 1.80
124 Eric Crozier R 8.00 3.60
125 Mi. Garciaparra C RC 2.50 1.10
126 Michael Garciaparra U 5.00 2.20
127 Michael Garciaparra R 10.00 4.50
128 Joey Gomes C RC 1.50 .70
129 Joey Gomes U 3.00 1.35
130 Joey Gomes R 6.00 2.70
131 Wil Ledezma C RC 1.50 .70
132 Wil Ledezma U 3.00 1.35
133 Wil Ledezma R 6.00 2.70
134 Branden Florence C RC 1.50 .70
135 Branden Florence U 3.00 1.35
136 Branden Florence R 6.00 2.70
137 Jeremy Bonderman C RC 2.50 1.10
138 Jeremy Bonderman U 5.00 2.20
139 Jeremy Bonderman R 10.00 4.50
140 Travis Ishikawa C RC 2.00 .90
141 Travis Ishikawa U 4.00 1.80
142 Travis Ishikawa R 8.00 3.60
143 Ben Francisco C RC 2.00 .90
144 Ben Francisco U 4.00 1.80
145 Ben Francisco R 8.00 3.60
146 Jason Kubel C RC 2.00 .90
147 Jason Kubel U 4.00 1.80
148 Jason Kubel R 8.00 3.60
149 Tyler Martin C RC 1.50 .70
150 Tyler Martin U 3.00 1.35
151 Tyler Martin R 6.00 2.70
152 Jason Perry C RC 2.50 1.10
153 Jason Perry U 5.00 2.20
154 Jason Perry R 10.00 4.50
155 Ryan Shealy C RC 2.00 .90
156 Ryan Shealy U 4.00 1.80
157 Ryan Shealy R 8.00 3.60
158 Hanley Ramirez C RC 4.00 1.80
159 Hanley Ramirez U 8.00 3.60
160 Hanley Ramirez R 15.00 6.75
161 Rajai Davis C RC 2.00 .90
162 Rajai Davis U 4.00 1.80
163 Rajai Davis R 8.00 3.60
164 Gary Schneidmiller C RC 1.50 .70
165 Gary Schneidmiller U 3.00 1.35
166 Gary Schneidmiller R 6.00 2.70
167 Haj Turay C RC 2.00 .90
168 Haj Turay U 4.00 1.80
169 Haj Turay R 8.00 3.60
170 Kevin Youkilis C RC 4.00 1.80
171 Kevin Youkilis U 8.00 3.60
172 Kevin Youkilis R 15.00 6.75
173 Shane Bazzell C RC 1.50 .70
174 Shane Bazzell U 3.00 1.35
175 Shane Bazzell R 6.00 2.70
176 Elizardo Ramirez C RC 2.50 1.10
177 Elizardo Ramirez U 5.00 2.20
178 Elizardo Ramirez R 10.00 4.50
179 Robinson Cano C RC 2.00 .90
180 Robinson Cano U 4.00 1.80
181 Robinson Cano R 8.00 3.60
182 Nook Logan C RC 1.50 .70
183 Nook Logan U 3.00 1.35
184 Nook Logan R 6.00 2.70
185 Dustin McGowan C RC 2.50 1.10
186 Dustin McGowan U 5.00 2.20
187 Dustin McGowan R 10.00 4.50
188 Ryan Howard C RC 2.50 1.10
189 Ryan Howard U 5.00 2.20
190 Ryan Howard R 10.00 4.50

2003 Topps Pristine Gold Refractors

MINT NRMT
*GOLD 1-95: 2.5X TO 6X BASIC
*GOLD 96-100: 2.5X TO 6X BASIC
*GOLD C 101-190: 4X TO 10X BASIC C
*GOLD U 101-190: 2X TO 5X BASIC U
*GOLD R 101-190: 1X TO 2.5X BASIC R
ONE PER SEALED HOBBY BOX
STATED PRINT RUN 69 SERIAL #'d SETS

2003 Topps Pristine Plates

MINT NRMT
STATED ODDS 1:83
STATED PRINT RUN 4 SETS
BLACK, CYAN, MAGENTA AND YELLOW EXIST
NO PRICING DUE TO SCARCITY

2003 Topps Pristine Refractors

MINT NRMT
*REFRACTORS 1-95: 2X TO 5X BASIC
*REFRACTORS 96-100: 2X TO 5X BASIC
REFRACTORS 1-100 ODDS 1:8
REFRACTORS 1-100 PRINT RUN 99 #'d SETS
*REFRACTORS C 101-190: .75X TO 2X
COMMON 101-190 RANDOM IN PACKS
COMMON 101-190 PRINT RUN 1599 #'d SETS
*REFRACTORS U 101-190: .75X TO 2X
UNCOMMON 101-190 ODDS 1:6
UNCOMMON 101-190 PRINT 499 #'d SETS
*REFRACTORS R 101-190: .75X TO 2X
RARE 101-190 ODDS 1:27
RARE 101-190 PRINT RUN 99 #'d SETS

2003 Topps Pristine Bonds Jersey Relics

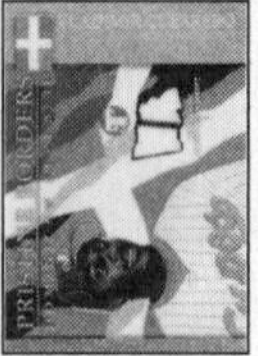

MINT NRMT
REFRACTOR ODDS 1:787
REFRACTOR PRINT RUN 25 SERIAL #'d SETS
NO REFRACTOR PRICING DUE TO SCARCITY
BB Barry Bonds BB 40.00 18.00
GG Barry Bonds GG 40.00 18.00
HR Barry Bonds HR 40.00 18.00
MVP Barry Bonds MVP 40.00 18.00

2003 Topps Pristine Bonds Dual Relics

MINT NRMT
REFRACTOR STATED ODDS 1:787
REFRACTOR PRINT RUN 25 SERIAL #'d SETS
NO REFRACTOR PRICING DUE TO SCARCITY
BJ Barry Bonds Jsy 50.00 22.00
Randy Johnson Jsy
BM Willie Mays Bat 120.00 55.00
Barry Bonds Jsy
BR Alex Rodriguez Jsy 50.00 22.00
Barry Bonds Jsy
BT Miguel Tejada Bat 50.00 22.00
Barry Bonds Bat

2003 Topps Pristine Bomb Squad Relics

MINT NRMT
GROUP A ODDS 1:3
GROUP B ODDS 1:5
GROUP C ODDS 1:9
REFRACTOR ODDS 1:59
REFRACTOR PRINT RUN 25 SERIAL #'d SETS
NO REFRACTOR PRICING DUE TO SCARCITY
AD Adam Dunn Jsy A 8.00 3.60
AJ Andruw Jones Bat B 10.00 4.50
AP1 Albert Pujols Bat A 20.00 9.00
AP2 Albert Pujols Uni B 25.00 11.00
AR1 Alex Rodriguez Bat C 10.00 4.50
AR2 Alex Rodriguez Jsy A 10.00 4.50
AS Alfonso Soriano Uni A 10.00 4.50
BB Barry Bonds Jsy B 25.00 11.00
CC Carl Crawford Bat C 8.00 3.60
CF Cliff Floyd Bat B 10.00 4.50
CJ Chipper Jones Bat B 15.00 6.75
DE1 Darin Erstad Uni B 10.00 4.50
DE2 Darin Erstad Jsy B 10.00 4.50
EC1 Eric Chavez Gray Uni A 8.00 3.60
EC2 Eric Chavez White Uni A 8.00 3.60
FT Frank Thomas Bat C 10.00 4.50
GA1 Garret Anderson Bat A 8.00 3.60
GA2 Garret Anderson Uni B 10.00 4.50
GB1 George Brett Jsy A 25.00 11.00
GB2 George Brett Bat B 30.00 13.50
GC Gary Carter Bat C 10.00 4.50
GS Gary Sheffield Bat A 8.00 3.60
HB Hank Blalock Bat B 15.00 6.75
JAG Juan Gonzalez Jsy B 15.00 6.75
JB Johnny Bench Bat A 10.00 4.50
JG Jason Giambi Bat A 10.00 4.50
JK Jeff Kent Bat B 10.00 4.50
JRB Jeff Bagwell Bat B 15.00 6.75
JT Jim Thome Bat B 15.00 6.75
LB1 Lance Berkman Jsy C 8.00 3.60
LB2 Lance Berkman Bat C 8.00 3.60
LG Luis Gonzalez Jsy B 10.00 4.50
MO Magglio Ordonez Jsy A 8.00 3.60
MO1 Moises Alou Uni A 8.00 3.60
MO2 Moises Alou Bat B 10.00 4.50
MP Mike Piazza Jsy B 15.00 6.75
MR Manny Ramirez Bat A 8.00 3.60
MS1 Mike Schmidt Bat A 20.00 9.00
MS2 Mike Schmidt Uni A 20.00 9.00
MT Miguel Tejada Bat B 10.00 4.50
NG1 Nomar Garciaparra Bat B 15.00 6.75
NG2 Nomar Garciaparra Jsy B 15.00 6.75
RH Rickey Henderson Bat B 15.00 6.75
RP Rafael Palmeiro Jsy B 15.00 6.75
SG Shawn Green Bat B 10.00 4.50
SS1 Sammy Sosa Bat B 15.00 6.75
SS2 Sammy Sosa Jsy A 15.00 6.75
TG1 Troy Glaus Bat A 10.00 4.50
TG2 Troy Glaus Uni B 15.00 6.75
TH Todd Helton Bat B 15.00 6.75
TS Tim Salmon Uni B 15.00 6.75
VG1 Vladimir Guerrero Jsy A 10.00 4.50
VG2 Vladimir Guerrero Bat A 10.00 4.50

2003 Topps Pristine Borders Relics

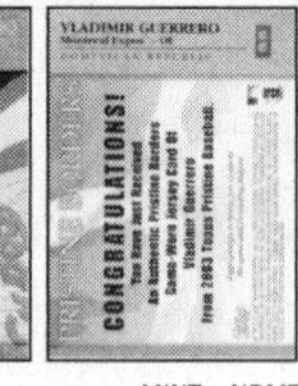

MINT NRMT
REFRACTOR ODDS 1:210
REFRACTOR PRINT RUN 25 SERIAL #'d SETS
NO REFRACTOR PRICING DUE TO SCARCITY
AJ Andruw Jones Uni 10.00 4.50
AP Albert Pujols Jsy 20.00 9.00
AS Alfonso Soriano Bat 10.00 4.50
BW Bernie Williams Bat 10.00 4.50
CC Chin Feng Chen Jsy 40.00 18.00
CG Cristian Guzman Bat 8.00 3.60
IR Ivan Rodriguez Bat 10.00 4.50
KI Kazuhisa Ishii Jsy 8.00 3.60
MO Magglio Ordonez Jsy 8.00 3.60
MR Manny Ramirez Jsy 8.00 3.60
MT Miguel Tejada Bat 8.00 3.60
PM Pedro Martinez Jsy 10.00 4.50
SS Sammy Sosa Jsy 15.00 6.75
TS Tsuyoshi Shinjo Bat 8.00 3.60
VG Vladimir Guerrero Jsy 10.00 4.50

2003 Topps Pristine Corners Relics

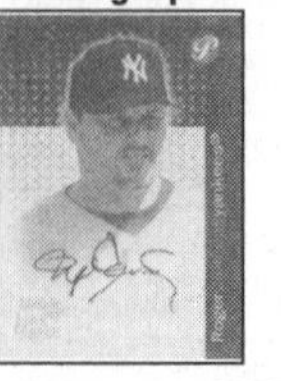

MINT NRMT
STATED ODDS 1:12
REFRACTOR ODDS 1:285
REFRACTOR PRINT RUN 25 SERIAL #'d SETS
NO REFRACTOR PRICING DUE TO SCARCITY
AS Edgardo Alfonzo Bat 10.00 4.50
J.T. Snow Bat
BK Sean Burroughs Jsy 10.00 4.50
Ryan Klesko Bat
BM Adrian Beltre Bat 15.00 6.75
Fred McGriff Bat
BT David Bell Bat 15.00 6.75
Jim Thome Bat
CD Eric Chavez Bat 10.00 4.50
Erubiel Durazo Bat
GS Troy Glaus Jsy 15.00 6.75
Scott Speizio Jsy
KM Corey Koskie Bat 15.00 6.75
Doug Mientkiewicz Bat
RM Scott Rolen Bat 25.00 11.00
Tino Martinez Bat
TP Mark Teixeira Bat 15.00 6.75
Rafael Palmeiro Bat
VG Robin Ventura Bat 15.00 6.75
Jason Giambi Bat
WG Matt Williams Bat 15.00 6.75
Mark Grace Bat

2003 Topps Pristine Factor Bat Relics

MINT NRMT
STATED ODDS 1:9
REFRACTOR ODDS 1:210
REFRACTOR PRINT RUN 25 SERIAL #'d SETS
NO REFRACTOR PRICING DUE TO SCARCITY
AD Adam Dunn 8.00 3.60
AR Alex Rodriguez 10.00 4.50
AS Alfonso Soriano 10.00 4.50
DE Darin Erstad 8.00 3.60
JG Jason Giambi 10.00 4.50
LB Lance Berkman 8.00 3.60
MO Magglio Ordonez 8.00 3.60
MP Mike Piazza 15.00 6.75
MR Manny Ramirez 8.00 3.60
NG Nomar Garciaparra 15.00 6.75
SS Sammy Sosa 15.00 6.75
TG Troy Glaus 10.00 4.50
TH Todd Helton 10.00 4.50
TKH Torii Hunter 8.00 3.60
VG Vladimir Guerrero 10.00 4.50

2003 Topps Pristine Mini

MINT NRMT
VETERAN STATED ODDS 1:8
ROOKIE STATED ODDS 1:16
AK Austin Kearns V 3.00 1.35
AR Alex Rodriguez V 10.00 4.50
AS Alfonso Soriano V 4.00 1.80
BB Barry Bonds V 15.00 6.75
BC Bernie Castro R 3.00 1.35
BG Brian Giles V 3.00 1.35
BPB Bryan Bullington R 12.00 5.50
BWB Bobby Basham R 6.00 2.70
CW Chien-Ming Wang R 12.00 5.50
DH Dan Haren R 8.00 3.60
DJ Derek Jeter V 15.00 6.75
DM Dustin McGowan R 8.00 3.60
EC Eric Chavez V 3.00 1.35
ELC Eric Crozier R 4.00 1.80
ER Elizardo Ramirez R 8.00 3.60
IS Ichiro Suzuki V 10.00 4.50
JB Jeremy Bonderman R 8.00 3.60
JC Jose Contreras R 12.00 5.50
JG Jason Giambi V 6.00 2.70
JJK Jason Kubel R 6.00 2.70
JK Jeff Kent V 3.00 1.35
JT Jim Thome V 6.00 2.70
KY Kevin Youkilis R 12.00 5.50
MH Michel Hernandez R 3.00 1.35
MJP Mike Piazza V 10.00 4.50
MO Magglio Ordonez V 3.00 1.35
MP Mark Prior V 12.00 5.50
MT Miguel Tejada V 3.00 1.35
NG Nomar Garciaparra V 10.00 4.50
NL Nook Logan R 3.00 1.35
RB Rocco Baldelli V 10.00 4.50
RC Roger Clemens V 12.00 5.50
RD Rajai Davis R 4.00 1.80
RH Ryan Howard R 8.00 3.60
RJC Robinson Cano R 4.00 1.80
RS Ryan Shealy R 6.00 2.70
SS Sammy Sosa V 10.00 4.50
TM Tyler Martin R 3.00 1.35
VG Vladimir Guerrero V 6.00 2.70
WL Wil Ledezma R 3.00 1.35

2003 Topps Pristine Mini Autograph

MINT NRMT
STATED ODDS 1:636
STATED PRINT RUN 100 CARDS
PRINT RUN INFO PROVIDED BY TOPPS
CARD IS NOT SERIAL-NUMBERED
RC Roger Clemens 150.00 70.00

2003 Topps Pristine Personal Endorsements

MINT NRMT
STATED ODDS 1:5
GOLD STATED ODDS 1:184
GOLD PRINT RUN 25 SERIAL #'d SETS
NO GOLD PRICING DUE TO SCARCITY

AB Andrew Brown 10.00 4.50
BM Brett Myers 15.00 6.75
DE David Eckstein 10.00 4.50
FS Felix Sanchez 10.00 4.50
FV Fernando Vina 15.00 6.75
JG Jay Gibbons 15.00 6.75
JP Josh Phelps 10.00 4.50
KH Ken Harvey 10.00 4.50
KS Kelly Shoppach 20.00 9.00
LF Lew Ford 15.00 6.75
ML Mike Lowell 15.00 6.75
MS Mike Sweeney 15.00 6.75
PK Paul Konerko 15.00 6.75
RJH Rich Harden 25.00 11.00
RYC Ryan Church 10.00 4.50
SR Scott Rolen 25.00 11.00
VM Victor Martinez 15.00 6.75

2003 Topps Pristine Primary Elements Patch Relics

MINT NRMT
STATED ODDS 1:45
STATED PRINT RUN 50 SETS
CARDS ARE NOT SERIAL-NUMBERED
PRINT RUN INFO PROVIDED BY TOPPS
NO PRICING DUE TO SCARCITY
REFRACTOR ODDS 1:224
REFRACTOR PRINT RUN 10 SERIAL #'d SETS
NO REFRACTOR PRICING DUE TO SCARCITY
AD Adam Dunn
AJ Andruw Jones
AP Albert Pujols
AR Alex Rodriguez
BB Barry Bonds
BRB Bret Boone
BZ Barry Zito
CD Carlos Delgado
CJ Chipper Jones
CR Cal Ripken
CS Curt Schilling
EC Eric Chavez
EG Eric Gagne
GM Greg Maddux
JB Jeff Bagwell
KI Kazuhisa Ishii
LB Lance Berkman
LG Luis Gonzalez
MM Mark Mulder
MO Magglio Ordonez
MP Mike Piazza
MR Manny Ramirez
MRO Moises Alou
MT Miguel Tejada
NG Nomar Garciaparra
PK Paul Konerko
PM Pedro Martinez
RJ Randy Johnson
RO Roy Oswalt
RP Rafael Palmeiro
SG Shawn Green
SS Sammy Sosa
TG Tony Gwynn
TH Todd Helton
TKH Torii Hunter

2001 Topps Reserve

Issued in August, 2001, this 151 card set was issued in special boxes which included a signed baseball of a rookie/prospect and 10 packs. Cards numbered 101-151 were short printed. Cards numbered 101-145 and 151 were available at a rate of one in five hobby packs and one in 52 retail packs. Cards numbered 146-150 were inserted at a rate of one in 54 retail packs. Cards numbered 101-145 had a print run of 945 serial number sets, cards numbered 146-150 had a print run of 1170 sets and card number 151 had a print run of 1500 sets.

Nm-Mt Ex-Mt
COMP.SET w/o SP's (100) 100.00 30.00
COMMON CARD (1-100) 1.00 .30
COMMON (101-151) 8.00 2.40
1 Darin Erstad 1.00 .30
2 Moises Alou 1.00 .30
3 Tony Batista 1.00 .30
4 Andruw Jones 1.00 .30
5 Edgar Renteria 1.00 .30
6 Eric Young 1.00 .30
7 Steve Finley 1.00 .30
8 Adrian Beltre 1.00 .30

Card	Nm-Mt	Ex-Mt
9 Vladimir Guerrero	2.50	.75
10 Barry Bonds	6.00	1.80
11 Juan Gonzalez	2.50	.75
12 Jay Buhner	1.00	.30
13 Luis Castillo	1.00	.30
14 Cal Ripken	8.00	2.40
15 Bob Abreu	1.00	.30
16 Ivan Rodriguez	2.50	.75
17 Nomar Garciaparra	4.00	1.20
18 Todd Helton	1.50	.45
19 Bobby Higginson	1.00	.30
20 Jorge Posada	1.50	.45
21 Tim Salmon	1.50	.45
22 Jason Giambi	2.50	.75
23 Jose Cruz Jr.	1.00	.30
24 Chipper Jones	2.50	.75
25 Jim Edmonds	1.00	.30
26 Gerald Williams	1.00	.30
27 Randy Johnson	2.50	.75
28 Gary Sheffield	1.00	.30
29 Jeff Kent	1.00	.30
30 Jim Thome	2.50	.75
31 John Olerud	1.00	.30
32 Cliff Floyd	1.00	.30
33 Mike Lowell	1.00	.30
34 Phil Nevin	1.00	.30
35 Scott Rolen	1.50	.45
36 Alex Rodriguez	4.00	1.20
37 Ken Griffey Jr.	4.00	1.20
38 Neifi Perez	1.00	.30
39 Cristian Guzman	1.00	.30
40 Mariano Rivera	1.50	.45
41 Troy Glaus	1.50	.45
42 Johnny Damon	1.00	.30
43 Rafael Furcal	1.00	.30
44 Jeromy Burnitz	1.00	.30
45 Mark McGwire	6.00	1.80
46 Fred McGriff	1.50	.45
47 Matt Williams	1.00	.30
48 Kevin Brown	1.00	.30
49 J.T. Snow	1.00	.30
50 Kenny Lofton	1.00	.30
51 Al Martin	1.00	.30
52 Antonio Alfonseca	1.00	.30
53 Edgardo Alfonzo	1.00	.30
54 Ryan Klesko	1.00	.30
55 Pat Burrell	1.00	.30
56 Rafael Palmeiro	1.50	.45
57 Sean Casey	1.00	.30
58 Jeff Cirillo	1.00	.30
59 Ray Durham	1.00	.30
60 Derek Jeter	6.00	1.80
61 Jeff Bagwell	1.50	.45
62 Carlos Delgado	1.00	.30
63 Tom Glavine	1.50	.45
64 Richie Sexson	1.00	.30
65 J.D. Drew	1.00	.30
66 Ben Grieve	1.00	.30
67 Mark Grace	1.50	.45
68 Shawn Green	1.00	.30
69 Robb Nen	1.00	.30
70 Omar Vizquel	1.00	.30
71 Edgar Martinez	1.50	.45
72 Preston Wilson	1.00	.30
73 Mike Piazza	4.00	1.20
74 Tony Gwynn	3.00	.90
75 Jason Kendall	1.00	.30
76 Manny Ramirez	1.00	.30
77 Pokey Reese	1.00	.30
78 Mike Sweeney	1.00	.30
79 Magglio Ordonez	1.00	.30
80 Bernie Williams	1.50	.45
81 Richard Hidalgo	1.00	.30
82 Brad Fullmer	1.00	.30
83 Greg Maddux	4.00	1.20
84 Geoff Jenkins	1.00	.30
85 Sammy Sosa	4.00	1.20
86 Luis Gonzalez	1.00	.30
87 Eric Karros	1.00	.30
88 Jose Vidro	1.00	.30
89 Rich Aurilia	1.00	.30
90 Roberto Alomar	2.50	.75
91 Mike Cameron	1.00	.30
92 Mike Mussina	2.50	.75
93 Barry Zito	2.50	.75
94 Mike Lieberthal	1.00	.30
95 Brian Giles	1.00	.30
96 Pedro Martinez	2.50	.75
97 Barry Larkin	2.50	.75
98 Jermaine Dye	1.00	.30
99 Frank Thomas	2.50	.75
100 David Justice	1.00	.30
101 Gary Johnson RC	8.00	2.40
102 Matt Ford RC	8.00	2.40
103 Albert Pujols RC	60.00	18.00
104 Brad Cresse	8.00	2.40
105 V. Pascucci RC	8.00	2.40
106 Bob Keppel RC	10.00	3.00
107 Luis Torres RC	8.00	2.40
108 Tony Blanco RC	10.00	3.00
109 Ronnie Corona RC	8.00	2.40
110 Phil Wilson RC	8.00	2.40
111 John Buck RC	10.00	3.00
112 Jim Journell RC	8.00	2.40
113 Victor Hall RC	8.00	2.40
114 Jeff Andra RC	8.00	2.40
115 Greg Nash RC	8.00	2.40
116 Travis Hafner RC	15.00	4.50
117 Casey Fossum RC	8.00	2.40
118 Miguel Olivo	8.00	2.40
119 Elpidio Guzman RC	8.00	2.40
120 Jason Belcher RC	8.00	2.40
121 Esix Snead RC	8.00	2.40
122 Joe Thurston RC	10.00	3.00
123 Rafael Soriano RC	15.00	4.50
124 Ed Rogers RC	8.00	2.40
125 Omar Beltre RC	8.00	2.40
126 Brett Gray RC	8.00	2.40
127 Deivi Mendez RC	8.00	2.40
128 Freddie Bynum RC	8.00	2.40
129 David Krynzel	8.00	2.40
130 Blake Williams RC	8.00	2.40
131 R. Abercrombie RC	8.00	2.40
132 Miguel Villilo RC	8.00	2.40
133 Ryan Madson RC	8.00	2.40
134 Matt Thompson RC	8.00	2.40
135 Mark Burnett RC	8.00	2.40
136 Andy Beal RC	8.00	2.40
137 Ryan Ludwick RC	8.00	2.40
138 Roberto Miniel RC	8.00	2.40
139 Steve Smyth RC	8.00	2.40
140 Ben Washburn RC	8.00	2.40
141 Marvin Seale RC	8.00	2.40
142 Reggie Griggs RC	8.00	2.40
143 Seung Song RC	10.00	3.00
144 Chad Petty RC	8.00	2.40
145 Noel Devarez RC	8.00	2.40
146 Matt Butler RC	8.00	2.40
147 Brett Evert RC	8.00	2.40
148 Cesar Izturis	8.00	2.40
149 Troy Farnsworth RC	8.00	2.40
150 Brian Schmitt RC	8.00	2.40
151 Ichiro Suzuki RC	50.00	15.00

2001 Topps Reserve Rookie Autographs

Inserted in retail packs, these 50 cards feature autographs from rookie/prospects in the Topps Reserve product. Cards numbered 1-45 have a stated print run of 160 sets while cards numbered 46-50 have a stated print run of 330 set. Group A cards were inserted at a rate of one in 155 while Group B cards were inserted at a rate of one in 252. Overall, the odds of getting an autograph card was one in 96 retail packs. These cards have a "TRA" prefix.

Card	Nm-Mt	Ex-Mt
TRA-1 Gary Johnson A	12.00	3.60
TRA-2 Matt Ford A	12.00	3.60
TRA-3 Albert Pujols A	150.00	45.00
TRA-4 Brad Cresse A	12.00	3.60
TRA-5 V. Pascucci A	12.00	3.60
TRA-6 Bob Keppel A	15.00	4.50
TRA-7 Luis Torres A	12.00	3.60
TRA-8 Tony Blanco A	15.00	4.50
TRA-9 Ronnie Corona A	12.00	3.60
TRA-10 Phil Wilson A	12.00	3.60
TRA-11 John Buck A	15.00	4.50
TRA-12 Jim Journell A	12.00	3.60
TRA-13 Victor Hall A	12.00	3.60
TRA-14 Jeff Andra A	12.00	3.60
TRA-15 Greg Nash A	12.00	3.60
TRA-16 Travis Hafner A	25.00	7.50
TRA-17 Casey Fossum A	12.00	3.60
TRA-18 Miguel Olivo A	12.00	3.60
TRA-19 Elpidio Guzman A	12.00	3.60
TRA-20 Jason Belcher A	12.00	3.60
TRA-21 Esix Snead A	12.00	3.60
TRA-22 Joe Thurston A	20.00	6.00
TRA-23 Rafael Soriano A	25.00	7.50
TRA-24 Ed Rogers A	12.00	3.60
TRA-25 Omar Beltre A	12.00	3.60
TRA-26 Brett Gray A	12.00	3.60
TRA-27 Deivi Mendez A	12.00	3.60
TRA-28 Freddie Bynum A	12.00	3.60
TRA-29 David Krynzel A	12.00	3.60
TRA-30 Blake Williams A	12.00	3.60
TRA-31 R. Abercrombie A	12.00	3.60
TRA-32 Miguel Villilo A	12.00	3.60
TRA-33 Ryan Madson A	12.00	3.60
TRA-34 Matt Thompson A	12.00	3.60
TRA-35 Mark Burnett A	12.00	3.60
TRA-36 Andy Beal A	12.00	3.60
TRA-37 Ryan Ludwick A	12.00	3.60
TRA-38 Roberto Miniel A	12.00	3.60
TRA-39 Steve Smyth A	12.00	3.60
TRA-40 Ben Washburn A	12.00	3.60
TRA-41 Marvin Seale A	12.00	3.60
TRA-42 Reggie Griggs A	12.00	3.60
TRA-43 Seung Song A	20.00	6.00
TRA-44 Chad Petty A	12.00	3.60
TRA-45 Noel Devarez A	12.00	3.60
TRA-46 Matt Butler B	12.00	3.60
TRA-47 Brett Evert B	12.00	3.60
TRA-48 Cesar Izturis B	12.00	3.60
TRA-49 Troy Farnsworth B	12.00	3.60
TRA-50 Brian Schmitt B	12.00	3.60

2001 Topps Reserve Rookie Autographs PSA Graded

Inserted one per hobby box, these cards were graded by PSA and included in the Topps Reserve product. 555 of each card was produced as a cumulative print run. The mystery exchange card had an exchange deadline of July 31, 2003.

Card	Nm-Mt	Ex-Mt
101 G.Johnson Mint	20.00	6.00
101 G.Johnson NmMt	12.00	3.60
102 M.Ford Mint	20.00	6.00
102 M.Ford NmMt	12.00	3.60
103 A.Pujols NmMt	150.00	45.00
104 B.Cresse Mint	20.00	6.00
104 B.Cresse NmMt	12.00	3.60
105 V.Pascucci Mint	20.00	6.00
105 V.Pascucci NmMt	12.00	3.60
106 B.Keppel Mint	20.00	6.00
106 B.Keppel NmMt	12.00	3.60
107 L.Torres Mint	20.00	6.00
107 L.Torres NmMt	12.00	3.60
108 T.Blanco NmMt	15.00	4.50
109 R.Corona Mint	20.00	6.00
109 R.Corona NmMt	12.00	3.60
110 P.Wilson NmMt	20.00	6.00
111 J.Buck NmMt	15.00	4.50
112 J.Journell NmMt	12.00	3.60
113 V.Hall Mint	20.00	6.00
113 V.Hall NmMt	12.00	3.60
114 J.Andra NmMt	20.00	6.00
115 G.Nash Mint	20.00	6.00
115 G.Nash NmMt	12.00	3.60
116 T.Hafner Mint	30.00	9.00
116 T.Hafner NmMt	20.00	6.00
117 C.Fossum Mint	20.00	6.00
117 C.Fossum NmMt	12.00	3.60
118 M.Olivo NmMt	12.00	3.60
119 E.Guzman Mint	20.00	6.00
119 E.Guzman NmMt	12.00	3.60
120 J.Belcher Mint	20.00	6.00
120 J.Belcher NmMt	12.00	3.60
121 E.Snead NmMt	12.00	3.60
122 J.Thurston Mint	30.00	9.00
122 J.Thurston NmMt	20.00	6.00
123 R.Soriano Mint	40.00	12.00
123 R.Soriano NmMt	25.00	7.50
124 E.Rogers Mint	20.00	6.00
124 E.Rogers NmMt	12.00	3.60
125 O.Beltre Mint	20.00	6.00
125 O.Beltre NmMt	12.00	3.60
126 B.Gray Mint	20.00	6.00
126 B.Gray NmMt	12.00	3.60
127 D.Mendez Mint	20.00	6.00
127 D.Mendez NmMt	12.00	3.60
128 F.Bynum Mint	20.00	6.00
128 F.Bynum NmMt	12.00	3.60
129 D.Krynzel Mint	20.00	6.00
129 D.Krynzel NmMt	12.00	3.60
130 B.Williams Mint	20.00	6.00
130 B.Williams NmMt	12.00	3.60
131 R.Abercrombie Mint	20.00	6.00
131 R.Abercrombie NmMt	12.00	3.60
132 M.Villilo Mint	20.00	6.00
132 M.Villilo NmMt	12.00	3.60
133 R.Madson NmMt	12.00	3.60
134 M.Thompson Mint	20.00	6.00
134 M.Thompson NmMt	12.00	3.60
135 M.Burnett Mint	20.00	6.00
135 M.Burnett NmMt	12.00	3.60
136 A.Beal Mint	20.00	6.00
136 A.Beal NmMt	12.00	3.60
137 R.Ludwick Mint	20.00	6.00
137 R.Ludwick NmMt	12.00	3.60
138 R.Miniel Mint	20.00	6.00
138 R.Miniel NmMt	12.00	3.60
139 S.Smyth Mint	20.00	6.00
139 S.Smyth NmMt	12.00	3.60
140 B.Washburn Mint	20.00	6.00
140 B.Washburn NmMt	12.00	3.60
141 M.Seale Mint	20.00	6.00
141 M.Seale NmMt	12.00	3.60
142 R.Griggs Mint	20.00	6.00
142 R.Griggs NmMt	12.00	3.60
143 S.Song Mint	30.00	9.00
143 S.Song NmMt	20.00	6.00
144 C.Petty Mint	20.00	6.00
144 C.Petty NmMt	12.00	3.60
145 N.Devarez Mint	20.00	6.00
145 N.Devarez NmMt	12.00	3.60
NNO Mystery Exchange	.50	.15

2001 Topps Reserve Game Bats

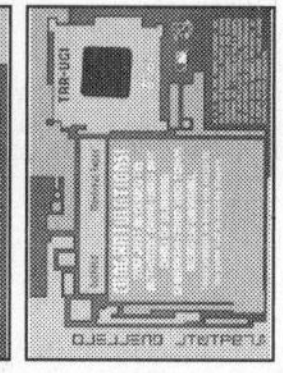

Randomly inserted in packs, these 14 cards feature bat relic cards from some of the leading hitters in the game.

Card	Nm-Mt	Ex-Mt
TRR-BW Bernie Williams	15.00	4.50
TRR-DE Darin Erstad	15.00	4.50
TRR-JB Jeff Bagwell	15.00	4.50
TRR-MP Mike Piazza	25.00	7.50
TRR-NG N.Garciaparra	40.00	12.00
TRR-VG Vladimir Guerrero	15.00	4.50
TRR-ARI Alex Rodriguez	25.00	7.50
TRR-BBI Barry Bonds	40.00	12.00
TRR-CDI Carlos Delgado	15.00	4.50
TRR-CJI Chipper Jones	15.00	4.50
TRR-IRI Ivan Rodriguez	15.00	4.50
TRR-JEI Jim Edmonds	10.00	3.00
TRR-RFI Rafael Furcal	10.00	3.00
TRR-TGI Tony Gwynn	15.00	4.50

2001 Topps Reserve Game Jerseys

Randomly inserted in packs, these 20 cards feature game-worn uniform relics from some of the leading players in the game.

Card	Nm-Mt	Ex-Mt
TRR-AR Alex Rodriguez	25.00	7.50
TRR-BB Barry Bonds	30.00	9.00
TRR-CD Carlos Delgado	10.00	3.00
TRR-CJ Chipper Jones	15.00	4.50
TRR-DJ David Justice	10.00	3.00
TRR-FT Frank Thomas	15.00	4.50
TRR-GM Greg Maddux	15.00	4.50
TRR-IR Ivan Rodriguez	15.00	4.50
TRR-JE Jim Edmonds	10.00	3.00
TRR-JG Juan Gonzalez	15.00	4.50
TRR-NP N.Garciaparra	20.00	6.00
TRR-PM Pedro Martinez	15.00	4.50
TRR-RA Roberto Alomar	15.00	4.50
TRR-RJ Randy Johnson	15.00	4.50
TRR-RP Rafael Palmeiro	15.00	4.50
TRR-SG Shawn Green	10.00	3.00
TRR-SR Scott Rolen	15.00	4.50
TRR-TG Tony Gwynn	15.00	4.50
TRR-TH Todd Helton	15.00	4.50
TRR-VG Vladimir Guerrero	15.00	4.50

2001 Topps Reserve Rookie Baseballs

Inserted at a rate of one per box, these 45 baseballs were signed by the feature rookie/prospect. The Fernando Cabrera and Felix Lugo cards were only available in retail packs as an exchange. These signed balls were redeemable until July 31, 2003.

Card	Nm-Mt	Ex-Mt
1 Reggie Abercrombie	20.00	6.00
2 Jeff Andra	20.00	6.00
3 Andy Beal	20.00	6.00
4 Omar Beltre	20.00	6.00
5 Tony Blanco	25.00	7.50
6 Mark Burnett	20.00	6.00
7 Freddie Bynum	20.00	6.00
8 Fernando Cabrera	20.00	6.00
9 Ronnie Corona	20.00	6.00
10 Brad Cresse	20.00	6.00
11 Noel Devarez	20.00	6.00
12 Matt Ford	20.00	6.00
13 Casey Fossum	20.00	6.00
14 Brett Gray	20.00	6.00
15 Reggie Griggs	20.00	6.00
16 Elpidio Guzman	20.00	6.00
17 Travis Hafner	40.00	12.00
18 Victor Hall	20.00	6.00
19 Gary Johnson	20.00	6.00
20 Jim Journell	20.00	6.00
21 Bob Keppel	25.00	7.50
22 David Krynzel	20.00	6.00
23 Ryan Ludwick	20.00	6.00
24 Felix Lugo	20.00	6.00
25 Ryan Madson	20.00	6.00
26 Deivi Mendez	20.00	6.00
27 Roberto Miniel	20.00	6.00
28 Greg Nash	20.00	6.00
29 Miguel Olivo	20.00	6.00
30 Valentino Pascucci	20.00	6.00
31 Chad Petty	20.00	6.00
32 Albert Pujols	300.00	90.00
33 Ed Rogers	20.00	6.00
34 Marvin Seale	20.00	6.00
35 Steve Smyth	20.00	6.00
36 Esix Snead	20.00	6.00
37 Seung Song	25.00	7.50
38 Rafael Soriano	40.00	12.00
39 Matt Thompson	20.00	6.00
40 Joe Thurston	25.00	7.50
41 Luis Torres	20.00	6.00
42 Miguel Villilo	20.00	6.00
43 Ben Washburn	20.00	6.00
44 Blake Williams	20.00	6.00
45 Phil Wilson	20.00	6.00

2002 Topps Reserve

This 150 card set was released in late July, 2002. These cards were issued in five card packs which came 10 packs to a box and six boxes in a case. Each box also contained a autographed mini-helmet as an inducement to purchase the box. Cards number 1-135 featured veteran stars while cards 136 through 150 featured Rookie Cards which had a stated print run of 999 serial numbered sets.

Card	Nm-Mt	Ex-Mt
COMP.SET w/o SP's (135)	100.00	30.00
COMMON CARD (1-135)	1.00	.30
COMMON CARD (136-150)	8.00	2.40
1 Alex Rodriguez	4.00	1.20
2 Tsuyoshi Shinjo	1.00	.30
3 Craig Biggio	1.50	.45
4 Troy Glaus	1.50	.45
5 Mike Rivera	1.00	.30
6 Curt Schilling	1.50	.45
7 Garret Anderson	1.00	.30
8 Ben Sheets	1.00	.30
9 Todd Helton	1.50	.45
10 Paul Konerko	1.00	.30
11 Sammy Sosa	4.00	1.20
12 Bud Smith	1.00	.30
13 Jeff Bagwell	1.50	.45
14 Albert Pujols	5.00	1.50
15 Jose Vidro	1.00	.30
16 Carlos Delgado	1.00	.30
17 Torii Hunter	1.00	.30
18 Jerry Hairston	1.00	.30
19 Troy Percival	1.00	.30
20 Vladimir Guerrero	2.50	.75
21 Geoff Jenkins	1.00	.30
22 Carlos Pena	1.00	.30
23 Juan Gonzalez	2.50	.75
24 Raul Mondesi	1.00	.30
25 Jimmy Rollins	1.00	.30
26 Mariano Rivera	1.50	.45
27 Jorge Posada	1.50	.45
28 Magglio Ordonez	1.00	.30
29 Roberto Alomar	2.50	.75
30 Randy Johnson	2.50	.75
31 Xavier Nady	1.00	.30
32 Terrence Long	1.00	.30
33 Chipper Jones	2.50	.75
34 Rich Aurilia	1.00	.30
35 Aramis Ramirez	1.00	.30
36 Jim Thome	2.50	.75
37 Bret Boone	1.00	.30
38 Angel Berroa	1.00	.30
39 Jeff Conine	1.00	.30
40 Cliff Floyd	1.00	.30
41 Pedro Martinez	2.50	.75
42 J.D. Drew	1.00	.30
43 Kazuhiro Sasaki	1.00	.30
44 Jon Rauch	1.00	.30
45 Orlando Hudson	1.00	.30
46 Scott Rolen	1.50	.45
47 Rafael Furcal	1.00	.30
48 Brad Penny	1.00	.30
49 Miguel Tejada	1.00	.30
50 Orlando Cabrera	1.00	.30
51 Bob Abreu	1.00	.30
52 Darin Erstad	1.00	.30
53 Edgar Martinez	1.50	.45
54 Ben Grieve	1.00	.30
55 Shawn Green	1.00	.30
56 Ivan Rodriguez	2.50	.75
57 Josh Beckett	1.50	.45
58 Ray Durham	1.00	.30
59 Jason Hart	1.00	.30
60 Nathan Haynes	1.00	.30
61 Jason Giambi	2.50	.75
62 Eric Chavez	1.00	.30
63 Matt Morris	1.00	.30
64 Lance Berkman	1.00	.30
65 Jeff Kent	1.00	.30
66 Andruw Jones	1.00	.30
67 Brian Giles	1.00	.30
68 Morgan Ensberg	1.00	.30
69 Pat Burrell	1.00	.30
70 Ken Griffey Jr.	4.00	1.20
71 Carlos Beltran	1.00	.30
72 Ichiro Suzuki	4.00	1.20
73 Larry Walker	1.50	.45
74 J.J. Putz RC	1.00	.30
75 Mike Piazza	4.00	1.20
76 Rafael Palmeiro	1.50	.45
77 Mark Prior	5.00	1.50
78 Toby Hall	1.00	.30
79 Pokey Reese	1.00	.30
80 Mike Mussina	2.50	.75
81 Omar Vizquel	1.00	.30
82 Shannon Stewart	1.00	.30
83 Jeromy Burnitz	1.00	.30
84 Bernie Williams	1.50	.45
85 C.C. Sabathia	1.00	.30
86 Mike Hampton	1.00	.30
87 Kevin Brown	1.00	.30
88 Juan Cruz	1.00	.30
89 Jeff Weaver	1.00	.30
90 Jason Lane	1.00	.30
91 Adam Dunn	1.00	.30
92 Jose Cruz Jr.	1.00	.30
93 Marlon Anderson	1.00	.30
94 Jeff Cirillo	1.00	.30
95 Mark Buehrle	1.00	.30
96 Austin Kearns	1.00	.30
97 Tim Hudson	1.00	.30
98 Brian Jordan	1.00	.30
99 Phil Nevin	1.00	.30
100 Barry Bonds	6.00	1.80
101 Derek Jeter	6.00	1.80
102 Javier Vazquez	1.00	.30
103 Jason Kendall	1.00	.30
104 Jim Edmonds	1.00	.30
105 Kenny Kelly	1.00	.30
106 Juan Pena	1.00	.30
107 Mark Grace	1.50	.45
108 Roger Clemens	5.00	1.50
109 Barry Zito	1.50	.45
110 Greg Vaughn	1.00	.30
111 Greg Maddux	4.00	1.20
112 Richie Sexson	1.00	.30
113 Jermaine Dye	1.00	.30
114 Kerry Wood	2.50	.75
115 Matt Lawton	1.00	.30
116 Sean Casey	1.00	.30
117 Gary Sheffield	1.00	.30
118 Preston Wilson	1.00	.30
119 Cristian Guzman	1.00	.30
120 Mike Sweeney	1.00	.30
121 Neifi Perez	1.00	.30
122 Paul LoDuca	1.00	.30
123 Luis Gonzalez	1.00	.30
124 Ryan Klesko	1.00	.30
125 Alfonso Soriano	1.50	.45
126 Bobby Higginson	1.00	.30
127 Juan Pierre	1.00	.30
128 Moises Alou	1.00	.30
129 Roy Oswalt	1.00	.30
130 Nomar Garciaparra	4.00	1.20
131 Fred McGriff	1.50	.45
132 Edgardo Alfonzo	1.00	.30
133 Johnny Damon	1.00	.30
134 Dewon Brazelton	1.00	.30
135 Mark Mulder	1.00	.30
136 So Taguchi FYP RC	10.00	3.00
137 Mario Ramos FYP RC	10.00	3.00
138 Dan Johnson FYP RC	10.00	3.00
139 Hansel Izquierdo FYP RC	8.00	2.40
140 Kazuhisa Ishii FYP RC	12.00	3.60
141 Jon Switzer FYP RC	8.00	2.40
142 Chris Tritle FYP RC	8.00	2.40
143 Chris Snelling FYP RC	10.00	3.00
144 Chone Figgins FYP RC	8.00	2.40
145 Dan Phillips FYP RC	8.00	2.40
146 John Rodriguez FYP RC	8.00	2.40
147 Colt Griffin FYP RC	10.00	3.00
148 Jonny Gomes FYP RC	10.00	3.00
149 Josh Barfield FYP RC	15.00	4.50
150 Joe Mauer FYP RC	30.00	9.00

2002 Topps Reserve Parallel

Inserted in packs at stated odds of one in 12, this is a parallel to the basic Reserve set. These cards are also printed to a stated print run of 150 serial numbered sets.

Nm-Mt Ex-Mt
*PARALLEL 1-135: 1.5X TO 4X BASIC
*PARALLEL 136-150: .6X TO 1.5X BASIC

2002 Topps Reserve Autograph Mini-Helmets

Topps got eighteen major league stars to sign Riddell mini-helmets. The helmets were inserted exclusively into hobby boxes at a rate of one per box. Each helmet is serial-numbered to either 225 (for group A), 475 (for group B) or 975 (for group C) on the outside back portion of the item. Oddly, the wrappers and boxes contradict one another when referencing the grouping manner these helmets were distributed in. Our checklist follows the groups detailed on the boxes (groups A-C). Please note, the wrapper confusingly references groups A-D in an effort to intermingle the scarce gold Autograph Mini-Helmets (of which feature gold ink signatures and are each serial-numbered to 25). For ease of use, we've transferred the wrapper stated odds to match the box. For example, the box lists Todd Helton and Luis Gonzalez as group A yet the wrapper references them as group B. In this instance, we've listed the wrapper odds for Helton and Gonzalez as group A to match up the checklist provided on the box.

Nm-Mt Ex-Mt
GROUP A ODDS 1:285
GROUP B ODDS 1:39
GROUP C ODDS 1:14
ODDS ARE PER PACK NOT PER BOX .
GROUP A PRINT RUN 225 SERIAL #'d SETS
GROUP B PRINT RUN 475 SERIAL #'d SETS
GROUP C PRINT RUN 975 SERIAL #'d SETS
1 Roberto Alomar C 50.00 15.00
2 Moises Alou C 25.00 7.50
3 Lance Berkman C 25.00 7.50
4 Bret Boone B 30.00 9.00
5 Eric Chavez B 30.00 9.00
6 Adam Dunn C 40.00 12.00
7 Cliff Floyd C 25.00 7.50
8 Troy Glaus B 50.00 15.00
9 Luis Gonzalez A 40.00 12.00
10 Todd Helton A 50.00 15.00
11 Maggio Ordonez C 25.00 7.50
12 Rafael Palmeiro B 60.00 18.00
13 Albert Pujols B 150.00 45.00
14 Alex Rodriguez B 150.00 45.00
15 Scott Rolen C 40.00 12.00
16 Jimmy Rollins C 25.00 7.50
17 Alfonso Soriano B 60.00 18.00
18 Barry Zito C 50.00 15.00

2002 Topps Reserve Baseball Relics

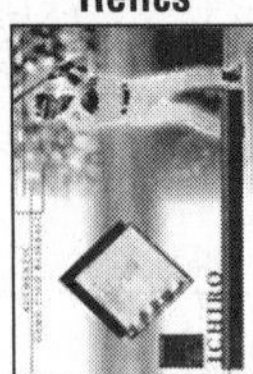

Issued at stated odds of one in 1761, these two cards feature cut up baseballs used in games by the featured players. Each card is printed to a stated print run of 100 serial numbered sets.

Nm-Mt Ex-Mt
AR Alex Rodriguez
I Ichiro Suzuki

2002 Topps Reserve Bat Relics

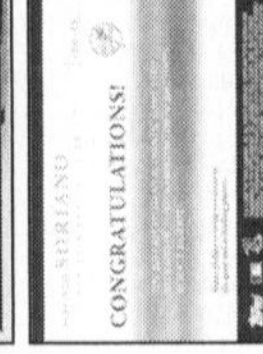

Inserted at overall stated odds of one in 12, these 20 cards feature game-used bat pieces from the featured player. These cards were inserted in packs at different odds depending on the featured player. We have listed each of the odds in our set information and put the group id for the player next to their name in our checklist.

Nm-Mt Ex-Mt
GROUP A ODDS 1:1563
GROUP B ODDS 1:1180
GROUP C ODDS 1:61
GROUP D ODDS 1:219
GROUP E ODDS 1:31
GROUP F ODDS 1:179
GROUP G ODDS 1:135
GROUP H ODDS 1:46
AJ Andruw Jones E 10.00 3.00
AP Albert Pujols F 15.00 4.50
AR Alex Rodriguez E 15.00 4.50
AS Alfonso Soriano E 10.00 3.00
BB Barry Bonds A 30.00 9.00
BW Bernie Williams E 10.00 3.00
CD Carlos Delgado C 10.00 3.00
CJ Chipper Jones C 10.00 3.00
FT Frank Thomas E 10.00 3.00
IR Ivan Rodriguez E 10.00 3.00
JB Jeff Bagwell E 10.00 3.00
JG Juan Gonzalez D 10.00 3.00
LG Luis Gonzalez C 10.00 3.00
MP Mike Piazza H 15.00 4.50
RA Roberto Alomar B 15.00 4.50
RH Rickey Henderson C 10.00 3.00
RP Rafael Palmeiro C 10.00 3.00
TG Tony Gwynn H 15.00 4.50
TM Tino Martinez C 10.00 3.00
TS Tsuyoshi Shinjo G 10.00 3.00

2002 Topps Reserve Patch Relics

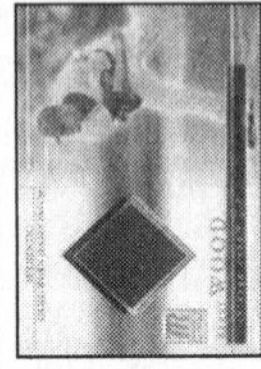
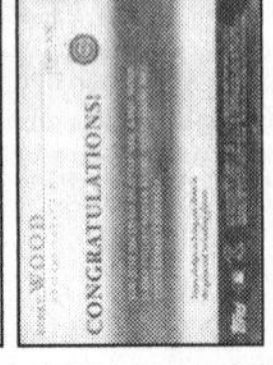

Inserted in packs at stated odds of one in 668, these 21 cards feature game worn uniform patches. These cards are serial numbered to a stated print run of 25 serial numbered sets and there is no pricing due to market scarcity.

Nm-Mt Ex-Mt
AJ Andruw Jones
BB Barry Bonds
CD Carlos Delgado
CJ Chipper Jones
CS Curt Schilling
DE Darin Erstad
FT Frank Thomas
GM Greg Maddux
IR Ivan Rodriguez
JG Juan Gonzalez
KS Kazuhiro Sasaki
KW Kerry Wood
LG Luis Gonzalez
MO Magglio Ordonez
MP Mike Piazza
PM Pedro Martinez
RJ Randy Johnson
RP Rafael Palmeiro
SR Scott Rolen
TG Tony Gwynn
TH Todd Helton

2002 Topps Reserve Uniform Relics

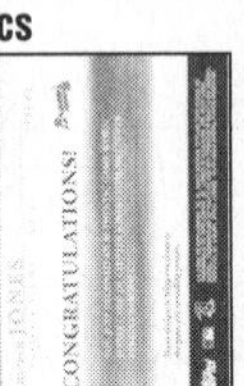

Inserted at overall stated odds of one in five, these 24 cards feature game-worn uniform swatches of the featured player. These cards were issued at differing odds depending on which group and we have included those odds in our set information. Our checklist also includes the information of what group the specific card belongs to.

Nm-Mt Ex-Mt
GROUP A ODDS 1:376
GROUP B ODDS 1:179
GROUP C ODDS 1:10
GROUP D ODDS 1:14
GROUP E ODDS 1:16
AJ Andruw Jones D 10.00 3.00
AP Albert Pujols E 15.00 4.50
AR Alex Rodriguez C 15.00 4.50
BB Barry Bonds E 25.00 7.50
BBO Bret Boone C 10.00 3.00
CJ Chipper Jones C 10.00 3.00
CS Curt Schilling E 10.00 3.00
DE Darin Erstad D 10.00 3.00
FT Frank Thomas C 10.00 3.00
GM Greg Maddux C 15.00 4.50
IR Ivan Rodriguez D 10.00 3.00
KS Kazuhiro Sasaki C 10.00 3.00
KW Kerry Wood E 10.00 3.00
LG Luis Gonzalez C 10.00 3.00
MM Mark Mulder C 10.00 3.00
MO Maggio Ordonez D 10.00 3.00
MP Mike Piazza C 15.00 4.50
NG Nomar Garciaparra D 15.00 4.50
PM Pedro Martinez A 15.00 4.50
RJ Randy Johnson B 10.00 3.00
RP Rafael Palmeiro C 10.00 3.00
SR Scott Rolen C 10.00 3.00
TG Tony Gwynn E 15.00 4.50
TH Todd Helton C 10.00 3.00

2003 Topps Retired Signature

This 110-card set was released in July, 2003. The set was issued in five card packs with an $30 SRP which came five packs to a box and six boxes to a case.

MINT NRMT
COMPLETE SET (110) 200.00 90.00
1 Willie Mays 6.00 2.70
2 Tony Perez 1.25 .55
3 Tom Seaver 2.00 .90
4 Johnny Bench 3.00 1.35
5 Rod Carew 2.00 .90

6 Red Schoendienst 1.25 .55
7 Phil Rizzuto 2.00 .90
8 Ozzie Smith 5.00 2.20
9 Maury Wills 1.25 .55
10 Hank Aaron 6.00 2.70
11 Jim Palmer 1.25 .55
12 Jose Cruz Sr. 1.25 .55
13 Dave Parker 1.25 .55
14 Don Sutton 1.25 .55
15 Brooks Robinson 3.00 1.35
16 Bo Jackson 3.00 1.35
17 Andre Dawson 1.25 .55
18 Fergie Jenkins 1.25 .55
19 George Foster 1.25 .55
20 George Brett 8.00 3.60
21 Jerry Koosman 1.25 .55
22 John Kruk 1.25 .55
23 Kent Tekulve 1.25 .55
24 Lee Smith 1.25 .55
25 Nolan Ryan 8.00 3.60
26 Paul O'Neill 1.25 .55
27 Rich Gossage 1.25 .55
28 Ron Santo 1.25 .55
29 Tom Lasorda 1.25 .55
30 Tony Gwynn 4.00 1.80
31 Vida Blue 1.25 .55
32 Whitey Herzog 1.25 .55
33 Willie McGee 1.25 .55
34 Bill Mazeroski 1.25 .55
35 Al Kaline 3.00 1.35
36 Bobby Richardson 1.25 .55
37 Carlton Fisk 2.00 .90
38 Darrell Evans 1.25 .55
39 Dave Concepcion 1.25 .55
40 Cal Ripken 10.00 4.50
41 Dwight Evans 1.25 .55
42 Earl Weaver 1.25 .55
43 Fred Lynn 1.25 .55
44 Greg Luzinski 1.25 .55
45 Duke Snider 2.00 .90
46 Hank Bauer 1.25 .55
47 Jim Rice 1.25 .55
48 Johnny Sain 1.25 .55
49 Lenny Dykstra 1.25 .55
50 Mike Schmidt 6.00 2.70
51 Orlando Cepeda 1.25 .55
52 Ralph Kiner 1.25 .55
53 Robin Roberts 1.25 .55
54 Ron Guidry 1.25 .55
55 Steve Garvey 1.25 .55
56 Tony Oliva 1.25 .55
57 Whitey Ford 2.00 .90
58 Willie McCovey 2.00 .90
59 Phil Niekro 1.25 .55
60 Stan Musial 5.00 2.20
61 Rollie Fingers 1.25 .55
62 Robin Yount 5.00 2.20
63 Alan Trammell 2.00 .90
64 Bill Buckner 1.25 .55
65 Bob Feller 2.00 .90
66 Bruce Sutter 1.25 .55
67 Dale Murphy 3.00 1.35
68 Dennis Eckersley 1.25 .55
69 Don Newcombe 1.25 .55
70 Don Mattingly 8.00 3.60
71 Dwight Gooden 2.00 .90
72 Frank Robinson 2.00 .90
73 Gary Carter 2.00 .90
74 Graig Nettles 1.25 .55
75 Harmon Killebrew 3.00 1.35
76 Jim Bunning 1.25 .55
77 Joe Morgan 1.25 .55
78 Joe Rudi 1.25 .55
79 Jose Canseco 3.00 1.35
80 Ernie Banks 3.00 1.35
81 Luis Aparicio 1.25 .55
82 Luis Tiant 1.25 .55
83 Mark Fidrych 1.25 .55
84 Kirk Gibson 1.25 .55
85 Lou Brock 2.00 .90
86 Juan Marichal 1.25 .55
87 Monte Irvin 1.25 .55
88 Paul Molitor 2.00 .90
89 Tommy John 1.25 .55
90 Warren Spahn 2.00 .90
91 Wade Boggs 2.00 .90
92 Reggie Jackson 2.00 .90
93 Kirby Puckett 3.00 1.35
94 Boog Powell 2.00 .90
95 Carl Yastrzemski 5.00 2.20
96 Bobby Thomson 1.25 .55
97 Bill Skowron 1.25 .55
98 Bill Madlock 1.25 .55
99 Sparky Anderson 1.25 .55
100 Yogi Berra 3.00 1.35
101 Bobby Doerr 1.25 .55
102 Gaylord Perry 1.25 .55
103 George Kell 1.25 .55
104 Harold Reynolds 1.25 .55
105 Joe Carter 1.25 .55
106 Johnny Podres 1.25 .55
107 Ron Cey 1.25 .55
108 Tim McCarver 1.25 .55
109 Tug McGraw 1.25 .55
110 Don Larsen 1.25 .55

2003 Topps Retired Signature Black

MINT NRMT
*BLACK: 2.5X TO 6X BASIC
STATED ODDS 1:8
STATED PRINT RUN 99 SERIAL #'d SETS

2003 Topps Retired Signature Chrome Autographs

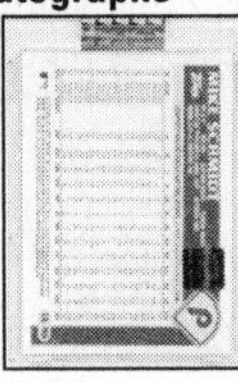

Inserted at a stated rate of one per pack, these 120 cards feature signatures from some of the most famous retired players. These cards were signed in different ratios and we have notated the insert odds as well as what group the player belonged to in our checklist.

MINT NRMT
ONE AUTOGRAPH PER PACK
A-B PRINT RUNS PROVIDED BY TOPPS
GROUPS A-B ARE NOT SERIAL-NUMBERED
NO GROUP A PRICING DUE TO SCARCITY
AD Andre Dawson D 20.00 9.00
AK Al Kaline C 100.00 45.00
AT Alan Trammell E 15.00 6.75
BB Bert Blyleven F 10.00 4.50
BBU Bill Buckner C 30.00 13.50
BD Bobby Doerr C 50.00 22.00
BF Bob Feller F 15.00 6.75
BGR Bobby Grich C 30.00 13.50
BH Bob Horner C 50.00 22.00
BJ Bo Jackson C 100.00 45.00
BM Bill Madlock G 10.00 4.50
BMA Bill Mazeroski C 60.00 27.00
BP Boog Powell G 15.00 6.75
BR Bobby Richardson G 10.00 4.50
BRO Brooks Robinson B/75 150.00 70.00
BS Bill Skowron G 15.00 6.75
BSA Bret Saberhagen C 50.00 22.00
BSU Bruce Sutter E 10.00 4.50
BT Bobby Thomson D 20.00 9.00
BW Bob Watson C 30.00 13.50
CF Carlton Fisk C 60.00 27.00
CR Cal Ripken A/25
CY Carl Yastrzemski C 150.00 70.00
DE Darrell Evans F 10.00 4.50
DEC Dennis Eckersley C 60.00 27.00
DEV Dwight Evans B/78 150.00 70.00
DG Dwight Gooden C 60.00 27.00
DL Don Larsen G 15.00 6.75
DM Dale Murphy C 100.00 45.00
DN Don Newcombe C 30.00 13.50
DON Don Mattingly B/81 250.00 110.00
DP Dave Parker C 50.00 22.00
DS Dave Stieb C 50.00 22.00
DSN Duke Snider B/75 150.00 70.00
DSU Don Sutton C 50.00 22.00
EB Ernie Banks A/24
EW Earl Weaver G 10.00 4.50
FJ Fergie Jenkins D 20.00 9.00
FL Fred Lynn C 50.00 22.00
FR Frank Robinson C 80.00 36.00
GB George Brett A/25
GC Gary Carter B/77 150.00 70.00
GF George Foster G 10.00 4.50
GK George Kell C 50.00 22.00
GL Greg Luzinski D 20.00 9.00
GN Graig Nettles G 15.00 6.75
GP Gaylord Perry C 30.00 13.50
HA Hank Aaron A/30
HB Harold Baines F 10.00 4.50
HBA Hank Bauer C 50.00 22.00
HK Harmon Killebrew B/76 150.00 70.00
HR Harold Reynolds C 30.00 13.50
JA Jim Abbott E 15.00 6.75
JB Jim Bunning B/76 150.00 70.00
JBE Johnny Bench C 80.00 36.00
JC Joe Carter C 50.00 22.00
JCA Jose Canseco C 60.00 27.00
JCR Jose Cruz Sr. D 15.00 6.75
JK Jerry Koosman C 30.00 13.50
JKR John Kruk C 50.00 22.00
JM Joe Morgan C 50.00 22.00
JMA Juan Marichal C 50.00 22.00
JP Jim Palmer C 60.00 27.00
JPI Jim Piersall G 15.00 6.75
JPO Johnny Podres G 10.00 4.50
JR Jim Rice C 60.00 27.00
JRU Joe Rudi F 10.00 4.50
KG Kirk Gibson C 50.00 22.00
KGR Ken Griffey Sr. C 50.00 22.00
KP Kirby Puckett B/75
KT Kent Tekulve C 30.00 13.50
LA Luis Aparicio G 15.00 6.75
LB Lou Brock B/76 150.00 70.00
LD Lenny Dykstra D 20.00 9.00
LP Lance Parrish G 10.00 4.50
LS Lee Smith E 10.00 4.50
LT Luis Tiant G 10.00 4.50
MF Mark Fidrych D 20.00 9.00
MI Monte Irvin C 60.00 27.00
MS Mike Schmidt B/83 200.00 90.00
MW Maury Wills F 10.00 4.50
NR Nolan Ryan B/77 300.00 135.00
OC Orlando Cepeda B/75 150.00 70.00
OS Ozzie Smith C 100.00 45.00
PM Paul Molitor C 60.00 27.00
PN Phil Niekro D 20.00 9.00
PO Paul O'Neill C 60.00 27.00
PR Phil Rizzuto B/77 150.00 70.00
RCA Rod Carew C 80.00 36.00
RCE Ron Cey F 10.00 4.50
RF Rollie Fingers C 50.00 22.00
RG Rich Gossage C 30.00 13.50
RGU Ron Guidry D 20.00 9.00
RJ Reggie Jackson C 100.00 45.00
RK Ralph Kiner B/80 150.00 70.00
RR Robin Roberts C 60.00 27.00
RS Red Schoendienst B/83 150.00 70.00
RSA Ron Santo G 15.00 6.75
RY Robin Yount A/25
SA Sparky Anderson C 30.00 13.50
SG Steve Garvey D 20.00 9.00
SM Stan Musial A/28
TG Tony Gwynn A/25
TJ Tommy John C 30.00 13.50
TL Tom Lasorda B/76 150.00 70.00
TM Tim McCarver C 50.00 22.00
TMC Tug McGraw D 50.00 22.00
TO Tony Oliva C 50.00 22.00
TP Tony Perez C 50.00 22.00
TPE Terry Pendleton D 15.00 6.75
TS Tom Seaver C 60.00 27.00
VB Vida Blue E 10.00 4.50
WB Wade Boggs B/77 150.00 70.00
WF Whitey Ford C 60.00 27.00
WH Whitey Herzog D 15.00 6.75
WM Willie Mays A/25
WMC Willie McCovey C 80.00 36.00
WMG Willie McGee D 20.00 9.00
WS Warren Spahn F 40.00 18.00
YB Yogi Berra A/25

2003 Topps Retired Signature Chrome Refractor Autographs

MINT NRMT
STATED ODDS 1:27
STATED PRINT RUN 25 SERIAL #'d SETS
NO PRICING DUE TO SCARCITY

1997 Topps Screenplays

The 1997 Topps Screenplays set was issued in one series totalling 20 cards and distributed in one-card packs with a suggested retail price of 9.99. Each card displays 24 frames of actual game footage with the help of Kodak's revolutionary Kodamotion technology. The cards have a dura clear back. Each card is individually packaged in a fold metal finish collectible tin that resembles a movie reel canister and features a full-color image of the player inside.The tin contains a display stand for it and the card and includes player info, bio, and stats. The cards are unnumbered and checklisted below in alphabetical order.

Nm-Mt Ex-Mt
COMPLETE SET (20) 80.00 24.00
1 Jeff Bagwell 3.00 .90
2 Albert Belle 2.00 .60
3 Barry Bonds 12.00 3.60
4 Andres Galarraga 2.00 .60
5 Nomar Garciaparra 8.00 2.40
6 Juan Gonzalez 5.00 1.50
7 Ken Griffey Jr. 8.00 2.40
8 Tony Gwynn 6.00 1.80
9 Derek Jeter 12.00 3.60
10 Randy Johnson 5.00 1.50
11 Andruw Jones 2.00 .60
12 Chipper Jones 5.00 1.50
13 Kenny Lofton 2.00 .60
14 Mark McGwire 12.00 3.60
15 Paul Molitor 3.00 .90
16 Hideo Nomo 5.00 1.50
17 Cal Ripken 15.00 4.50
18 Sammy Sosa 8.00 2.40
19 Frank Thomas 5.00 1.50
20 Jim Thome 5.00 1.50

1997 Topps Screenplays Tins

After the protective cover which hid the player's identity is removed, there remains a photo of the player on the front of the tin. These tins are considered collectible in their own right and are valued as a small percentage of the regular "Screenplays" card.

Nm-Mt Ex-Mt
*TINS: .075 TO .2X OF SCREENPLAYS

1997 Topps Screenplays Premium Series

This six-card limited production set features six top stars from the regular base set in additional action shots. The cards were seeded at a rate of 1:21 packs. The cards are unnumbered and checklisted below in alphabetical order.

Nm-Mt Ex-Mt
COMPLETE SET (6) 100.00 30.00
1 Ken Griffey Jr. 20.00 6.00
2 Chipper Jones 10.00 3.00
3 Mike Piazza 20.00 6.00
4 Cal Ripken 40.00 12.00
5 Frank Thomas 10.00 3.00
6 Larry Walker 10.00 3.00

2003 Topps Shoebox

This 96-card standard-size set was issued by Topps in a special factory box along with a framed strip of a card from each decade from the 1950's through the 1980's. These reprint cards, usually based on the style of the player's rookie year, feature the original Topps design but also have a "Shoe Box Collection" logo embossed on the card. Sadly, like many of the Topps reprint issues, the numbering is in very small print on the bottom of the card.

	MINT	NRMT
COMP.FACT SET (96)	100.00	45.00
1 Willie Mays	5.00	2.20
2 Monte Irvin	1.00	.45
3 Bill Mazeroski	1.00	.45
4 Phil Rizzuto	2.00	.90
5 Hank Sauer	.25	.11
6 Hank Bauer	.50	.23
7 Ted Kluszewski	.75	.35
8 Robin Roberts	1.00	.45
9 Red Schoendienst	1.00	.45
10 Bob Feller	1.50	.70
11 Duke Snider	2.00	.90
12 Bobby Thomson	.50	.23
13 Hoyt Wilhelm	1.00	.45
14 John Podres	.50	.23
15 Whitey Ford	2.00	.90
16 Ralph Kiner	1.50	.70
17 Harmon Killebrew	2.00	.90
18 Luis Aparicio	1.00	.45
19 Bobby Richardson	.75	.35
20 Don Newcombe	.50	.23
21 Frank Robinson	2.00	.90
22 Brooks Robinson	2.00	.90
23 Stan Musial	4.00	1.80
24 Orlando Cepeda	1.00	.45
25 Willie McCovey	1.00	.45
26 Maury Wills	.75	.35
27 Carl Yastrzemski	1.00	.45
28 Juan Marichal	1.00	.45
29 Boog Powell	.75	.35
30 Willie Stargell	1.00	.45
31 Bert Campaneris	.50	.23
32 Tug McGraw	.50	.23
33 Joe Morgan	1.50	.70
34 Tony Perez	1.00	.45
35 Luis Tiant	.50	.23
36 Fergie Jenkins	1.00	.45
37 Jim Palmer	1.50	.70
38 Rod Carew	1.50	.70
39 Tom Seaver	2.50	1.10
40 Nolan Ryan	10.00	4.50
41 Rollie Fingers	1.00	.45
42 Reggie Jackson	2.50	1.10
43 Gaylord Perry	1.00	.45
44 Al Oliver	.50	.23
45 Lou Brock	1.00	.45
46 Johnny Bench	1.50	.70
47 Paul Blair	.25	.11
48 Phil Niekro	1.00	.45
49 Bill Buckner	.50	.23
50 Darrell Evans	.50	.23
51 Bert Blyleven	.50	.23
52 Dave Concepcion	.50	.23
53 George Foster	.50	.23
54 Bob Grich	.25	.11
55 Greg Luzinski	.50	.23
56 Ron Cey	.50	.23
57 Cecil Cooper	.25	.11
58 Carlton Fisk	1.50	.70
59 Mickey Rivers	.50	.23
60 Dwight Evans	.50	.23
61 Rich Gossage	.75	.35
62 Mike Schmidt	2.00	.90
63 Dave Parker	.50	.23
64 Gary Carter	1.50	.70
65 Robin Yount	1.50	.70
66 Dennis Eckersley	1.50	.70
67 Ron Guidry	.75	.35
68 Jack Clark	.50	.23
69 Andre Dawson	.75	.35
70 Mark Fidrych	.75	.35
Used the League Leader Card		
71 Bruce Sutter	.50	.23
72 Willie Hernandez	.25	.11
73 Ozzie Smith	2.50	1.10
74 Kirk Gibson	.50	.23
75 Don Mattingly	5.00	2.20
76 Joe Carter	.50	.23
77 Kirby Puckett	2.00	.90
78 Dale Murphy	.75	.35
79 Keith Hernandez	.50	.23
80 Tony Armas	.25	.11
81 Walt Weiss	.25	.11
82 Bill Madlock	.50	.23
83 Bo Jackson	.75	.35
84 Buddy Bell	.25	.11
85 Dwight Gooden	.50	.23
86 Eric Davis	.50	.23
87 George Bell	.25	.11
88 Harold Reynolds	.50	.23
89 Jim Rice	.75	.35
90 Ken Griffey	.50	.23
91 Lee Smith	.50	.23
92 Jose Canseco	.75	.35
93 Alan Trammell	.75	.35
94 Paul O'Neill	.50	.23
95 Paul Molitor	2.00	.90
96 Lance Parrish	.50	.23

1997 Topps Stars Promos

This three-card set features borderless color action photos of three top players printed on textured cards with six rows of stars running down one side of the front. The backs carry another player photo with player information and career statistics.

	Nm-Mt	Ex-Mt
COMPLETE SET (3)	6.00	1.80
PP1 Larry Walker	1.00	.30
PP2 Roger Clemens	3.00	.90
PP3 Frank Thomas	2.00	.60

1997 Topps Stars

The 1997 Topps Stars set was issued in one series totalling 125 cards and was distributed in seven-card packs with a suggested retail

price of $3. A checklisted card was added to every fifth pack as an extra card. The set was available exclusively to Home Team Advantage members and features color player photos printed on super-thick, 20-point stock with matte gold foil stamping and a textured matte laminate and spot UV coating. The backs carry another photo of the same player with biographical information and career statistics. Rookie cards include Kris Benson, Lance Berkman, Vernon Wells and Kerry Wood.

	Nm-Mt	Ex-Mt
COMPLETE SET (125)	30.00	9.00
1 Larry Walker	.50	.15
2 Tino Martinez	.50	.15
3 Cal Ripken	2.50	.75
4 Ken Griffey Jr.	1.25	.35
5 Chipper Jones	.75	.23
6 David Justice	.30	.09
7 Mike Piazza	1.25	.35
8 Jeff Bagwell	.50	.15
9 Ron Gant	.30	.09
10 Sammy Sosa	1.25	.35
11 Tony Gwynn	1.00	.30
12 Carlos Baerga	.30	.09
13 Frank Thomas	.75	.23
14 Moises Alou	.30	.09
15 Barry Larkin	.75	.23
16 Ivan Rodriguez	.75	.23
17 Greg Maddux	1.25	.35
18 Jim Edmonds	.30	.09
19 Jose Canseco	.75	.23
20 Rafael Palmeiro	.50	.15
21 Paul Molitor	.50	.15
22 Kevin Appier	.30	.09
23 Raul Mondesi	.30	.09
24 Lance Johnson	.30	.09
25 Edgar Martinez	.50	.15
26 Andres Galarraga	.30	.09
27 Mo Vaughn	.30	.09
28 Ken Caminiti	.30	.09
29 Cecil Fielder	.30	.09
30 Harold Baines	.30	.09
31 Roberto Alomar	.75	.23
32 Shawn Estes	.30	.09
33 Tom Glavine	.50	.15
34 Dennis Eckersley	.30	.09
35 Manny Ramirez	.30	.09
36 John Olerud	.30	.09
37 Juan Gonzalez	.75	.23
38 Chuck Knoblauch	.30	.09
39 Albert Belle	.30	.09
40 Vinny Castilla	.30	.09
41 John Smoltz	.50	.15
42 Barry Bonds	2.00	.60
43 Randy Johnson	.75	.23
44 Brady Anderson	.30	.09
45 Jeff Blauser	.30	.09
46 Craig Biggio	.50	.15
47 Jeff Conine	.30	.09
48 Marquis Grissom	.30	.09
49 Mark Grace	.50	.15
50 Roger Clemens	1.50	.45
51 Mark McGwire	2.00	.60
52 Fred McGriff	.50	.15
53 Gary Sheffield	.30	.09
54 Bobby Jones	.30	.09
55 Eric Young	.30	.09
56 Robin Ventura	.30	.09
57 Wade Boggs	.50	.15
58 Joe Carter	.30	.09
59 Ryne Sandberg	1.25	.35
60 Matt Williams	.30	.09
61 Todd Hundley	.30	.09
62 Dante Bichette	.30	.09
63 Chili Davis	.30	.09
64 Kenny Lofton	.30	.09
65 Jay Buhner	.30	.09
66 Will Clark	.75	.23
67 Travis Fryman	.30	.09
68 Pat Hentgen	.30	.09
69 Ellis Burks	.30	.09
70 Mike Mussina	.75	.23
71 Hideo Nomo	.75	.23
72 Sandy Alomar Jr.	.30	.09
73 Bobby Bonilla	.30	.09
74 Rickey Henderson	.75	.23
75 David Cone	.30	.09
76 Terry Steinbach	.30	.09
77 Pedro Martinez	.75	.23
78 Jim Thome	.75	.23
79 Rod Beck	.30	.09
80 Randy Myers	.30	.09
81 Charles Nagy	.30	.09
82 Mark Wohlers	.30	.09
83 Paul O'Neill	.50	.15
84 Curt Schilling	.50	.15
85 Joey Cora	.30	.09
86 John Franco	.30	.09
87 Kevin Brown	.30	.09
88 Benito Santiago	.30	.09
89 Ray Lankford	.30	.09
90 Bernie Williams	.50	.15
91 Jason Dickson	.30	.09
92 Jeff Cirillo	.30	.09
93 Nomar Garciaparra	1.25	.35
94 Mariano Rivera	.50	.15
95 Javy Lopez	.30	.09
96 Tony Womack RC	.75	.23
97 Jose Rosado	.30	.09
98 Denny Neagle	.30	.09
99 Darryl Kile	.30	.09
100 Justin Thompson	.30	.09
101 Juan Encarnacion	.30	.09
102 Brad Fullmer	.30	.09
103 Kris Benson RC	1.00	.30
104 Todd Helton	.75	.23
105 Paul Konerko	.30	.09
106 Travis Lee RC	.75	.23
107 Todd Greene	.30	.09
108 Mark Kotsay RC	.75	.23
109 Carl Pavano	.30	.09
110 Kerry Wood RC	15.00	4.50
111 Jason Romano RC	.75	.23
112 Geoff Goetz RC	.50	.15
113 Scott Hodges RC	.75	.23
114 Aaron Akin RC	.50	.15
115 Vernon Wells RC	6.00	1.80
116 Chris Stowe RC	.50	.15
117 Brett Caradonna RC	.50	.15
118 Adam Kennedy RC	1.50	.45
119 Jayson Werth RC	.75	.23
120 Glenn Davis RC	.50	.15
121 Troy Cameron RC	.75	.23
122 J.J. Davis RC	.75	.23
123 Jason Dellaero RC	.50	.15
124 Jason Standridge RC	.75	.23
125 Lance Berkman RC	6.00	1.80
NNO Checklist	.30	.09

1997 Topps Stars Always Mint

Randomly inserted in packs at the rate of one in 12, this 125-card set is parallel to the base set and is printed on double-chromed paper stock.

	Nm-Mt	Ex-Mt
*ALWAYS: 4X TO 10X BASIC		
*ALWAYS: 2X TO 5X BASIC RC'S		

1997 Topps Stars '97 All-Stars

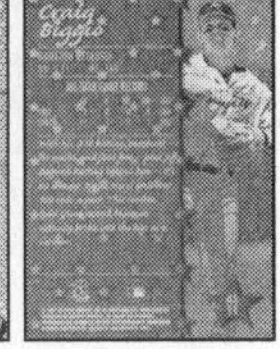

Randomly inserted in packs at the rate of one in 24, this 20-card set features color photos of players who represented their league in the 1997 All-Star Game in Cleveland and are printed on embossed uniluster.

	Nm-Mt	Ex-Mt
COMPLETE SET (20)	300.00	90.00
AS1 Greg Maddux	25.00	7.50
AS2 Randy Johnson	15.00	4.50
AS3 Tino Martinez	10.00	3.00
AS4 Jeff Bagwell	10.00	3.00
AS5 Ivan Rodriguez	15.00	4.50
AS6 Mike Piazza	25.00	7.50
AS7 Cal Ripken	50.00	15.00
AS8 Ken Caminiti	6.00	1.80
AS9 Tony Gwynn	20.00	6.00
AS10 Edgar Martinez	10.00	3.00
AS11 Craig Biggio	10.00	3.00
AS12 Roberto Alomar	15.00	4.50
AS13 Larry Walker	10.00	3.00
AS14 Brady Anderson	6.00	1.80
AS15 Barry Bonds	40.00	12.00
AS16 Ken Griffey Jr.	25.00	7.50
AS17 Ray Lankford	6.00	1.80
AS18 Paul O'Neill	10.00	3.00
AS19 Jeff Blauser	6.00	1.80
AS20 Sandy Alomar	6.00	1.80

1997 Topps Stars All-Star Memories

Randomly inserted in packs at the rate of one in 24, this 10-card set features color photos printed on laser-cut foilboard of the best performing all-star players.

	Nm-Mt	Ex-Mt
COMPLETE SET (10)	60.00	18.00
ASM1 Cal Ripken	20.00	6.00
ASM2 Jeff Conine	2.50	.75
ASM3 Mike Piazza	10.00	3.00
ASM4 Randy Johnson	6.00	1.80
ASM5 Ken Griffey Jr.	10.00	3.00
ASM6 Fred McGriff	4.00	1.20
ASM7 Moises Alou	2.50	.75
ASM8 Hideo Nomo	6.00	1.80
ASM9 Larry Walker	4.00	1.20
ASM10 Sandy Alomar	2.50	.75

1997 Topps Stars Future All-Stars

Randomly inserted in packs at the rate of one in 12, this 15-card set features color photos printed on prismatic rainbow diffraction foilboard of players who are candidates to be next year's all-stars.

	Nm-Mt	Ex-Mt
COMPLETE SET (15)	40.00	12.00
FAS1 Derek Jeter	12.00	3.60
FAS2 Andruw Jones	2.00	.60
FAS3 Vladimir Guerrero	4.00	1.20
FAS4 Scott Rolen	2.50	.75
FAS5 Jose Guillen	2.00	.60
FAS6 Jose Cruz Jr.	5.00	1.50
FAS7 Darin Erstad	2.00	.60
FAS8 Tony Clark	1.00	.30
FAS9 Scott Spiezio	1.00	.30
FAS10 Kevin Orie	1.00	.30
FAS11 Pokey Reese	1.00	.30
FAS12 Billy Wagner	2.00	.60
FAS13 Matt Morris	2.00	.60
FAS14 Jeremi Gonzalez	1.00	.30
FAS15 Hideki Irabu	2.00	.60

1997 Topps Stars Rookie Reprints

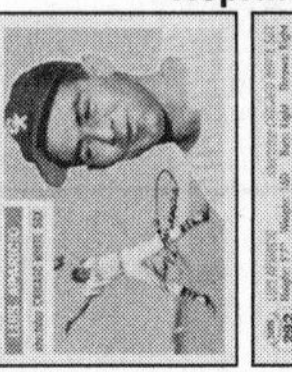

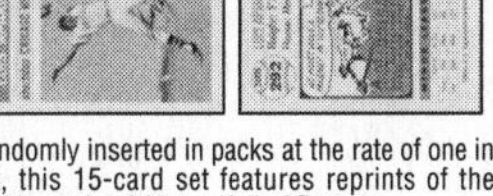

Randomly inserted in packs at the rate of one in six, this 15-card set features reprints of the rookie cards of 15 top Hall of Famers.

	Nm-Mt	Ex-Mt
COMPLETE SET (15)	50.00	15.00
1 Luis Aparicio	4.00	1.20
2 Richie Ashburn	4.00	1.20
3 Jim Bunning	4.00	1.20
4 Bob Feller	4.00	1.20
5 Rollie Fingers	4.00	1.20
6 Monte Irvin	4.00	1.20
7 Al Kaline	8.00	2.40
8 Ralph Kiner	4.00	1.20
9 Eddie Mathews	8.00	2.40
10 Hal Newhouser	4.00	1.20
11 Gaylord Perry	4.00	1.20
12 Robin Roberts	4.00	1.20
13 Brooks Robinson	6.00	1.80
14 Enos Slaughter	4.00	1.20
15 Earl Weaver	4.00	1.20

1997 Topps Stars Rookie Reprint Autographs

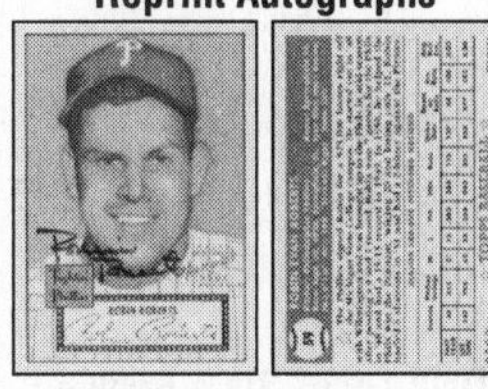

Randomly inserted in packs at the rate of one in 30, this 14-card set is an autographed parallel version of the regular Topps Stars Rookie Reprint set. The Topps Certified Issue Autograph stamp is printed on each card. Card No. 2 was supposed to be Richie Ashburn but he passed away before being able to sign his cards so this card does not exist. This set is one of the more noteworthy issues from the late 1990's in that it started the popular trend of reprinted card autographed Rookie Cards heavily used by Topps for several years thereafter.

	Nm-Mt	Ex-Mt
1 Luis Aparicio	25.00	7.50
3 Jim Bunning	40.00	12.00
4 Bob Feller	40.00	12.00
5 Rollie Fingers	25.00	7.50
6 Monte Irvin	40.00	12.00
7 Al Kaline	50.00	15.00
8 Ralph Kiner	25.00	7.50
9 Eddie Mathews	80.00	24.00
10 Hal Newhouser	100.00	30.00
11 Gaylord Perry	25.00	7.50
12 Robin Roberts	40.00	12.00
13 Brooks Robinson	50.00	15.00
14 Enos Slaughter	40.00	12.00
15 Earl Weaver	25.00	7.50

1998 Topps Stars Pre-Production

These six cards were issued to dealers and hobby media in July, 1998 to preview the (then) upcoming 1998 Topps Stars product. The cards are similar in design to standard 1998 Topps Stars cards except for the PP based card numbering and serial numbered stamp "000/000" on back.

	Nm-Mt	Ex-Mt
COMPLETE SET (6)	6.00	1.80
PP1 Mike Piazza	3.00	.90
PP2 Darin Erstad	1.00	.30
PP3 Vinny Castilla	.50	.15
PP4 Craig Biggio	.75	.23
PP5 Ivan Rodriguez	1.25	.35
PP6 Pedro Martinez	1.00	.30

1998 Topps Stars

Distributed in six-card packs, this 150-card set features color action player photos printed on 20 pt. stock with red foil highlights, luminous diffraction, matte gold foil stamping, textured matte laminate, and spot UV coating. The pictured players are also grouped into five tool categories of baseball: Arm Strength, Hit for Average, Hit for Power, Defense, and Speed. A checklist card was added to every fifth pack as an extra card.

	Nm-Mt	Ex-Mt
COMP.RED SET (150)	80.00	24.00
1 Greg Maddux	3.00	.90
2 Darryl Kile	.75	.23
3 Rod Beck	.75	.23
4 Ellis Burks	.75	.23
5 Gary Sheffield	.75	.23
6 David Ortiz	.75	.23
7 Marquis Grissom	.75	.23
8 Tony Womack	.75	.23
9 Mike Mussina	2.00	.60
10 Bernie Williams	1.25	.35
11 Andy Benes	.75	.23
12 Rusty Greer	.75	.23
13 Carlos Delgado	.75	.23
14 Jim Edmonds	.75	.23
15 Raul Mondesi	.75	.23
16 Andres Galarraga	.75	.23
17 Wade Boggs	1.25	.35
18 Paul O'Neill	1.25	.35
19 Edgar Renteria	.75	.23
20 Tony Clark	.75	.23
21 Vladimir Guerrero	2.00	.60
22 Moises Alou	.75	.23
23 Bernard Gilkey	.75	.23
24 Lance Johnson	.75	.23
25 Ben Grieve	.75	.23
26 Sandy Alomar Jr.	.75	.23
27 Ray Durham	.75	.23
28 Shawn Estes	.75	.23
29 David Segui	.75	.23
30 Javy Lopez	.75	.23
31 Steve Finley	.75	.23
32 Rey Ordonez	.75	.23
33 Derek Jeter	5.00	1.50
34 Henry Rodriguez	.75	.23
35 Mo Vaughn	.75	.23
36 Richard Hidalgo	.75	.23
37 Omar Vizquel	.75	.23
38 Johnny Damon	.75	.23
39 Brian Hunter	.75	.23
40 Matt Williams	.75	.23
41 Chuck Finley	.75	.23
42 Jeromy Burnitz	.75	.23
43 Livan Hernandez	.75	.23
44 Delino DeShields	.75	.23
45 Charles Nagy	.75	.23
46 Scott Rolen	1.25	.35
47 Neifi Perez	.75	.23
48 John Wetteland	.75	.23
49 Eric Milton	.75	.23
50 Mike Piazza	3.00	.90
51 Cal Ripken	6.00	1.80
52 Mariano Rivera	1.25	.35
53 Butch Huskey	.75	.23
54 Quinton McCracken	.75	.23
55 Jose Cruz Jr.	.75	.23
56 Brian Jordan	.75	.23
57 Hideo Nomo	2.00	.60
58 Masato Yoshii RC	1.25	.35
59 Cliff Floyd	.75	.23
60 Jose Guillen	.75	.23
61 Jeff Shaw	.75	.23
62 Edgar Martinez	1.25	.35
63 Rondell White	.75	.23
64 Hal Morris	.75	.23
65 Barry Larkin	2.00	.60
66 Eric Young	.75	.23
67 Ray Lankford	.75	.23
68 Derek Bell	.75	.23
69 Charles Johnson	.75	.23
70 Robin Ventura	.75	.23
71 Chuck Knoblauch	.75	.23
72 Kevin Brown	1.25	.35
73 Jose Valentin	.75	.23
74 Jay Buhner	.75	.23
75 Tony Gwynn	2.50	.75
76 Andy Pettitte	1.25	.35
77 Edgardo Alfonzo	.75	.23
78 Kerry Wood	2.00	.60
79 Darin Erstad	.75	.23
80 Paul Konerko	.75	.23
81 Jason Kendall	.75	.23
82 Tino Martinez	1.25	.35
83 Brad Radke	.75	.23
84 Jeff King	.75	.23
85 Travis Lee	.75	.23
86 Jeff Kent	.75	.23
87 Trevor Hoffman	.75	.23
88 David Cone	.75	.23
89 Jose Canseco	2.00	.60
90 Juan Gonzalez	2.00	.60
91 Todd Hundley	.75	.23
92 John Valentin	.75	.23
93 Sammy Sosa	3.00	.90
94 Jason Giambi	2.00	.60
95 Chipper Jones	2.00	.60
96 Jeff Blauser	.75	.23
97 Brad Fullmer	.75	.23
98 Derrek Lee	.75	.23
99 Denny Neagle	.75	.23
100 Ken Griffey Jr.	3.00	.90
101 David Justice	.75	.23
102 Tim Salmon	1.25	.35
103 J.T. Snow	.75	.23
104 Fred McGriff	1.25	.35
105 Brady Anderson	.75	.23
106 Larry Walker	1.25	.35
107 Jeff Cirillo	.75	.23
108 Andruw Jones	.75	.23
109 Manny Ramirez	.75	.23
110 Justin Thompson	.75	.23
111 Vinny Castilla	.75	.23
112 Chan Ho Park	.75	.23
113 Mark Grudzielanek	.75	.23
114 Mark Grace	1.25	.35
115 Ken Caminiti	.75	.23

116 Ryan Klesko .75 .23
117 Rafael Palmeiro 1.25 .35
118 Pat Hentgen .75 .23
119 Eric Karros .75 .23
120 Randy Johnson 2.00 .60
121 Roberto Alomar 2.00 .60
122 John Olerud .75 .23
123 Paul Molitor 1.25 .35
124 Dean Palmer .75 .23
125 Nomar Garciaparra 3.00 .90
126 Curt Schilling 1.25 .35
127 Jay Bell .75 .23
128 Craig Biggio 1.25 .35
129 Marty Cordova .75 .23
130 Ivan Rodriguez 2.00 .60
131 Todd Helton 1.25 .35
132 Jim Thome 2.00 .60
133 Albert Belle .75 .23
134 Mike Lansing .75 .23
135 Mark McGwire 5.00 1.50
136 Roger Clemens 4.00 1.20
137 Tom Glavine 1.25 .35
138 Ron Gant .75 .23
139 Alex Rodriguez 3.00 .90
140 Jeff Bagwell 1.25 .35
141 John Smoltz 1.25 .35
142 Kenny Lofton .75 .23
143 Dante Bichette .75 .23
144 Pedro Martinez 2.00 .60
145 Barry Bonds 5.00 1.50
146 Travis Fryman .75 .23
147 Bobby Jones .75 .23
148 Bobby Higginson .75 .23
149 Reggie Sanders .75 .23
150 Frank Thomas 2.00 .60

1998 Topps Stars Bronze

Randomly inserted one in every pack, this 150-card set is a parallel version of the base set and is distinguished by bronze foil highlights. Only 9799 sets were produced and are serially numbered.

Nm-Mt Ex-Mt
COMPLETE SET (150) 80.00 24.00
*BRONZE: SAME VALUE AS RED

1998 Topps Stars Gold

Randomly inserted in packs at the rate of one in two, this 150-card set is a parallel version of the base set and is distinguished by gold foil highlights. Only 2299 of this set were produced and serially numbered.

Nm-Mt Ex-Mt
COMPLETE SET (150) 300.00 90.00
*STARS: 1.25X TO 3X BASIC CARDS.

1998 Topps Stars Gold Rainbow

Randomly inserted in packs at the rate of one in 46, this 150-card set is a parallel version of the base set and is distinguished by its foil highlights. Only 99 sets were produced and and serially numbered.

Nm-Mt Ex-Mt
*STARS: 4X TO 10X BASIC CARDS

1998 Topps Stars Silver

Randomly inserted in packs, this 150-card set is a parallel version of the base set and is distinguished by silver foil highlights. Only 4399 of this set were produced and serially numbered.

Nm-Mt Ex-Mt
COMPLETE SET (150) 200.00 60.00
*STARS: .75X TO 2X BASIC CARDS

1998 Topps Stars Galaxy Bronze

Randomly inserted in packs at the rate of one in 818, this 10-card set features color images of players who possess all five of the tools of Baseball printed on a star galaxy background with bronze foil highlights. Only 100 of each card were produced and are sequentially numbered.

Nm-Mt Ex-Mt
COMPLETE SET (10) 400.00 120.00
*SILVER: .5X TO 1.2X BRONZE
SILVER STATED ODDS 1:910
SILVER PRINT RUN 75 SERIAL #'d SETS
*GOLD: .6X TO 1.5X BRONZE
GOLD STATED ODDS 1:1364
GOLD PRINT RUN 50 SERIAL #'d SETS
GOLD RAINBOW STATED ODDS 1:13643
GOLD RBW.PRINT RUN 5 SERIAL #'d SETS
GOLD RBW.NO PRICING DUE TO SCARCITY
G1 Barry Bonds 80.00 24.00
G2 Jeff Bagwell 20.00 6.00
G3 Nomar Garciaparra 50.00 15.00
G4 Chipper Jones 30.00 9.00
G5 Ken Griffey Jr. 50.00 15.00
G6 Sammy Sosa 50.00 15.00
G7 Larry Walker 20.00 6.00
G8 Alex Rodriguez 50.00 15.00
G9 Craig Biggio 20.00 6.00
G10 Raul Mondesi 12.00 3.60

1998 Topps Stars Luminaries Bronze

Randomly inserted in packs at the rate of one in 545, this 15-card insert set features color photos of three of the top players from each of

the five tools of Baseball with bronze foil highlights. Only 100 of each card were produced and are sequentially numbered.

Nm-Mt Ex-Mt
COMPLETE SET (15) 400.00 120.00
*SILVER: .5X TO 1.2X BRONZE
SILVER STATED ODDS 1:606
SILVER PRINT RUN 75 SERIAL #'d SETS
*GOLD: .6X TO 1.5X BRONZE
GOLD STATED ODDS 1:910
GOLD PRINT RUN 50 SERIAL #'d SETS
GOLD RAINBOW STATED ODDS 1:9095
GOLD RBW.PRINT RUN 5 SERIAL #'d SETS
GOLD RBW.NO PRICING DUE TO SCARCITY
L1 Ken Griffey Jr. 40.00 12.00
L2 Mark McGwire 60.00 18.00
L3 Juan Gonzalez 25.00 7.50
L4 Tony Gwynn 30.00 9.00
L5 Frank Thomas 25.00 7.50
L6 Mike Piazza 40.00 12.00
L7 Chuck Knoblauch 10.00 3.00
L8 Kenny Lofton 10.00 3.00
L9 Barry Bonds 60.00 18.00
L10 Matt Williams 10.00 3.00
L11 Raul Mondesi 10.00 3.00
L12 Ivan Rodriguez 25.00 7.50
L13 Alex Rodriguez 40.00 12.00
L14 Nomar Garciaparra 40.00 12.00
L15 Ken Caminiti 10.00 3.00

1998 Topps Stars Rookie Reprints

Randomly inserted in packs at the rate of one in 24, this five-card set features reprints of Topps rookie cards of five Hall of Famers.

Nm-Mt Ex-Mt
COMPLETE SET (5) 40.00 12.00
1 Johnny Bench 8.00 2.40
2 Whitey Ford 5.00 1.50
3 Joe Morgan 5.00 1.50
4 Mike Schmidt 12.00 3.60
5 Carl Yastrzemski 10.00 3.00

1998 Topps Stars Rookie Reprints Autographs

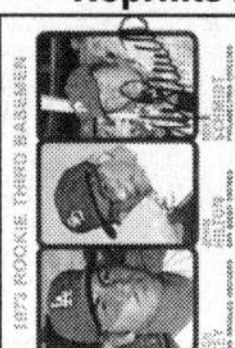

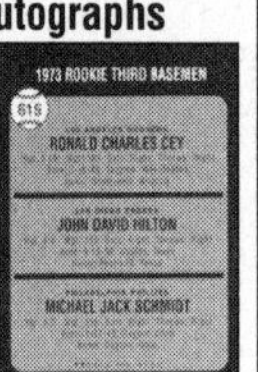

Randomly inserted in packs at the rate of one in 327, this five-card set is an autographed parallel version to the Topps Stars Rookie Reprints set. Each card carries the Certified Autograph Issue stamp.

Nm-Mt Ex-Mt
1 Johnny Bench 80.00 24.00
2 Whitey Ford 50.00 15.00
3 Joe Morgan 50.00 15.00
4 Mike Schmidt 100.00 30.00
5 Carl Yastrzemski 100.00 30.00

1998 Topps Stars Supernovas Bronze

Randomly inserted in packs at the rate of one in 818, this 10-card set features color images of players who dramatically excel in one or possess all five tools of Baseball printed on a star background with bronze foil highlights. Only 100 of each card were produced and are sequentially numbered.

Nm-Mt Ex-Mt
COMPLETE SET (10) 150.00 45.00
*SILVER: .5X TO 1.2X BRONZE
SILVER STATED ODDS 1:910
SILVER PRINT RUN 75 SERIAL #'d SETS
*GOLD: .6X TO 1.5X BRONZE
GOLD STATED ODDS 1:1364
GOLD PRINT RUN 50 SERIAL #'d SETS
GOLD RAINBOW STATED ODDS 1:13643
GOLD RBW.PRINT RUN 5 SERIAL #'d SETS
GOLD RBW.NO PRICING DUE TO SCARCITY
S1 Ben Grieve 12.00 3.60
S2 Travis Lee 12.00 3.60
S3 Todd Helton 20.00 6.00
S4 Adrian Beltre 12.00 3.60
S5 Derrek Lee 12.00 3.60
S6 David Ortiz 12.00 3.60
S7 Brad Fullmer 12.00 3.60
S8 Mark Kotsay 12.00 3.60
S9 Paul Konerko 12.00 3.60
S10 Kerry Wood 30.00 9.00

1999 Topps Stars Pre-Production

This five-card set was issued to preview the (then) upcoming 1999 Topps Stars product. The cards are similar in design to the cards in the regular set except for the "PP" before each card's number.

Nm-Mt Ex-Mt
COMPLETE SET (5) 8.00 2.40
PP1 Paul O'Neill No Star 2.00 .60
PP2 V.Castilla One Star 1.00 .30
PP3 Darin Erstad Two Star 2.00 .60
PP4 K.Wood Three Star 2.00 .60
PP5 C.Jones Four Star 3.00 .90

1999 Topps Stars

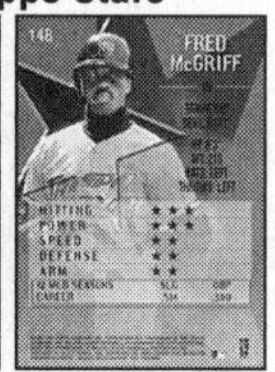

The 1999 Topps Stars set was issued in one series for a total of 180 cards and distributed in six-card packs with a suggested retail price of $3. The set features action color player photos printed on 20-point card stock with foil-stamping, flood gloss, and metallic inks. The backs carry five-star player evaluation. The set features the following subsets: Luminaries (151-170) and Supernovas (171-180). Rookie Cards include Pat Burrell, Alex Escobar, Nick Johnson and Alfonso Soriano.

Nm-Mt Ex-Mt
COMPLETE SET (180) 50.00 15.00
1 Ken Griffey Jr. 2.00 .60
2 Chipper Jones 1.25 .35
3 Mike Piazza 2.00 .60
4 Nomar Garciaparra 2.00 .60
5 Derek Jeter 3.00 .90
6 Frank Thomas 1.25 .35
7 Ben Grieve .50 .15
8 Mark McGwire 3.00 .90
9 Sammy Sosa 2.00 .60
10 Alex Rodriguez 2.00 .60
11 Troy Glaus .75 .23
12 Eric Chavez .50 .15
13 Kerry Wood 1.25 .35
14 Barry Bonds 3.00 .90
15 Vladimir Guerrero 1.25 .35
16 Albert Belle .50 .15
17 Juan Gonzalez 1.25 .35
18 Roger Clemens 2.50 .75
19 Ruben Mateo .50 .15
20 Cal Ripken 4.00 1.20
21 Darin Erstad .50 .15
22 Jeff Bagwell .75 .23
23 Roy Halladay .50 .15
24 Todd Helton .75 .23
25 Michael Barrett .50 .15
26 Manny Ramirez .50 .15
27 Fernando Seguignol .50 .15
28 Pat Burrell RC 3.00 .90
29 Andruw Jones .50 .15
30 Randy Johnson 1.25 .35
31 Jose Canseco 1.25 .35
32 Brad Fullmer .50 .15
33 Alex Escobar RC .50 .15
34 Alfonso Soriano RC 8.00 2.40
35 Larry Walker .75 .23
36 Matt Clement .50 .15
37 Mo Vaughn .50 .15
38 Bruce Chen .50 .15
39 Travis Lee .50 .15
40 Adrian Beltre .50 .15
41 Alex Gonzalez .50 .15
42 Jason Tyner RC .50 .15
43 George Lombard .50 .15
44 Scott Rolen .75 .23
45 Mark Mulder RC 3.00 .90
46 Gabe Kapler .50 .15
47 Choo Freeman RC .50 .15
48 Tony Gwynn 1.50 .45
49 A.J. Burnett RC 1.00 .30
50 Matt Belisle RC .50 .15
51 Greg Maddux 2.00 .60
52 John Smoltz .75 .23
53 Mark Grace .75 .23
54 Wade Boggs .75 .23
55 Bernie Williams .75 .23
56 Pedro Martinez 1.25 .35
57 Barry Larkin 1.25 .35
58 Orlando Hernandez .50 .15
59 Jason Kendall .50 .15
60 Mark Kotsay .50 .15
61 Jim Thome 1.25 .35
62 Gary Sheffield .50 .15
63 Preston Wilson .50 .15
64 Rafael Palmeiro .75 .23
65 David Wells .50 .15
66 Shawn Green .50 .15
67 Tom Glavine .75 .23
68 Jeromy Burnitz .50 .15
69 Kevin Brown .75 .23
70 Rondell White .50 .15
71 Roberto Alomar 1.25 .35
72 Cliff Floyd .50 .15
73 Craig Biggio .75 .23
74 Greg Vaughn .50 .15
75 Ivan Rodriguez 1.25 .35
76 Vinny Castilla .50 .15
77 Todd Walker .50 .15
78 Paul Konerko .50 .15
79 Andy Brown RC .50 .15
80 Todd Hundley .50 .15
81 Dmitri Young .50 .15
82 Tony Clark .50 .15
83 Nick Johnson RC 1.50 .45
84 Mike Caruso .50 .15
85 David Ortiz .50 .15
86 Matt Williams .50 .15
87 Raul Mondesi .50 .15
88 Kenny Lofton .50 .15
89 Miguel Tejada .50 .15
90 Dante Bichette .50 .15
91 Jorge Posada .75 .23
92 Carlos Beltran .50 .15
93 Carlos Delgado .50 .15
94 Javy Lopez .50 .15
95 Aramis Ramirez .50 .15
96 Neifi Perez .50 .15
97 Marlon Anderson .50 .15
98 David Cone .50 .15
99 Moises Alou .50 .15
100 John Olerud .50 .15
101 Tim Salmon .75 .23
102 Jason Giambi 1.25 .35
103 Sandy Alomar Jr. .50 .15
104 Curt Schilling .75 .23
105 Andres Galarraga .50 .15
106 Rusty Greer .50 .15
107 Bobby Seay RC .50 .15
108 Eric Young .50 .15
109 Brian Jordan .50 .15
110 Eric Davis .50 .15
111 Will Clark 1.25 .35
112 Andy Ashby .50 .15
113 Edgardo Alfonzo .50 .15
114 Paul O'Neill .75 .23
115 Denny Neagle .50 .15
116 Eric Karros .50 .15
117 Ken Caminiti .50 .15
118 Garret Anderson .50 .15
119 Todd Stottlemyre .50 .15
120 David Justice .50 .15
121 Francisco Cordova .50 .15
122 Robin Ventura .50 .15
123 Mike Mussina 1.25 .35
124 Hideki Irabu .50 .15
125 Justin Thompson .50 .15
126 Mariano Rivera .75 .23
127 Delino DeShields .50 .15
128 Steve Finley .50 .15
129 Jose Cruz Jr. .50 .15
130 Ray Lankford .50 .15
131 Jim Edmonds .50 .15
132 Charles Johnson .50 .15
133 Al Leiter .50 .15
134 Jose Offerman .50 .15
135 Eric Milton .50 .15
136 Dean Palmer .50 .15
137 Johnny Damon .50 .15
138 Andy Pettitte .75 .23
139 Ray Durham .50 .15
140 Ugueth Urbina .50 .15
141 Marquis Grissom .50 .15
142 Ryan Klesko .50 .15
143 Brady Anderson .50 .15
144 Bobby Higginson .50 .15
145 Chuck Knoblauch .50 .15
146 Rickey Henderson 1.25 .35
147 Kevin Millwood .50 .15
148 Fred McGriff .75 .23
149 Damion Easley .50 .15
150 Tino Martinez .75 .23
151 Greg Maddux LUM 1.25 .35
152 Scott Rolen LUM .50 .15
153 Pat Burrell LUM 1.00 .30
154 Roger Clemens LUM 1.25 .35
155 Albert Belle LUM .50 .15
156 Troy Glaus LUM .50 .15
157 Cal Ripken LUM 2.00 .60
158 Alfonso Soriano LUM 3.00 .90
159 Manny Ramirez LUM .50 .15
160 Eric Chavez LUM .50 .15
161 Kerry Wood LUM .75 .23
162 Tony Gwynn LUM .75 .23
163 Barry Bonds LUM 1.25 .35
164 Ruben Mateo LUM .50 .15
165 Todd Helton LUM .50 .15
166 Darin Erstad LUM .50 .15
167 Jeff Bagwell LUM .50 .15
168 Juan Gonzalez LUM .75 .23
169 Mo Vaughn LUM .50 .15
170 V.Guerrero LUM .75 .23
171 N.Garciaparra SUP 1.25 .35
172 Derek Jeter SUP 1.50 .45
173 Alex Rodriguez SUP 1.25 .35
174 Ben Grieve SUP .50 .15
175 Mike Piazza SUP 1.25 .35
176 Chipper Jones SUP .75 .23
177 Frank Thomas SUP .75 .23
178 Ken Griffey Jr. SUP 1.25 .35
179 Sammy Sosa SUP 1.25 .35
180 Mark McGwire SUP 1.50 .45

1999 Topps Stars Foil

Randomly inserted into packs at the rate of one in 15, this 180-card set is parallel to the base se, printed on heavy 20-point card stock treated with silver select metallization, and sequentially numbered to 299. This numbering is quite off is that it lacks gold foil. Instead, the cards are simply embossed with the serial number on back, making it easy to miss.

Nm-Mt Ex-Mt
*STARS: 3X TO 8X BASIC CARDS
*ROOKIES: 1.5X TO 4X BASIC CARDS

1999 Topps Stars One Star

Inserted two per pack, this 100-card set features the game's top stars from the 150 veterans pictured on the base cards and printed with dark silver metallic inks and foil stamping. The backs outline the player's career highlights.

Nm-Mt Ex-Mt
COMPLETE SET (100) 40.00 12.00
1 Ken Griffey Jr. 1.50 .45
2 Chipper Jones 1.00 .30
3 Mike Piazza 1.50 .45
4 Nomar Garciaparra 1.50 .45
5 Derek Jeter 2.50 .75
6 Frank Thomas 1.00 .30
7 Ben Grieve .40 .12
8 Mark McGwire 2.50 .75
9 Sammy Sosa 1.50 .45
10 Alex Rodriguez 1.50 .45
11 Troy Glaus .60 .18
12 Eric Chavez .40 .12
13 Kerry Wood 1.00 .30
14 Barry Bonds 2.50 .75
15 Vladimir Guerrero 1.00 .30
16 Albert Belle .40 .12
17 Juan Gonzalez 1.00 .30
18 Roger Clemens 2.00 .60
19 Ruben Mateo .40 .12
20 Cal Ripken 3.00 .90
21 Darin Erstad .40 .12
22 Jeff Bagwell .60 .18
23 Roy Halladay .40 .12
24 Todd Helton .60 .18
25 Michael Barrett .40 .12
26 Manny Ramirez .40 .12
27 Fernando Seguignol .40 .12
28 Pat Burrell 2.00 .60
29 Andruw Jones .40 .12
30 Randy Johnson 1.00 .30
31 Jose Canseco 1.00 .30
32 Brad Fullmer .40 .12
33 Alex Escobar .30 .09
34 Alfonso Soriano 6.00 1.80
35 Larry Walker .60 .18
36 Matt Clement .40 .12
37 Mo Vaughn .40 .12
38 Bruce Chen .40 .12
39 Travis Lee .40 .12
40 Adrian Beltre .40 .12
41 Alex Gonzalez .40 .12
42 Jason Tyner .40 .12
43 George Lombard .40 .12
44 Scott Rolen .60 .18
45 Mark Mulder 2.50 .75
46 Gabe Kapler .40 .12
47 Choo Freeman .40 .12
48 Tony Gwynn 1.25 .35
49 A.J. Burnett .75 .23
50 Matt Belisle .40 .12
51 Greg Maddux 1.50 .45
52 John Smoltz .60 .18
53 Mark Grace .60 .18
54 Wade Boggs .60 .18
55 Bernie Williams .60 .18
56 Pedro Martinez 1.00 .30
57 Barry Larkin 1.00 .30
58 Orlando Hernandez .40 .12
59 Jason Kendall .40 .12
60 Mark Kotsay .40 .12
61 Jim Thome 1.00 .30
62 Gary Sheffield .40 .12
63 Preston Wilson .40 .12
64 Rafael Palmeiro .60 .18
65 David Wells .40 .12
66 Shawn Green .40 .12
67 Tom Glavine .60 .18
68 Jeromy Burnitz .40 .12
69 Kevin Brown .60 .18
70 Rondell White .40 .12
71 Roberto Alomar 1.00 .30
72 Cliff Floyd .40 .12
73 Craig Biggio .60 .18
74 Greg Vaughn .40 .12
75 Ivan Rodriguez 1.00 .30
76 Vinny Castilla .40 .12
77 Todd Walker .40 .12
78 Paul Konerko .40 .12
79 Andy Brown .40 .12
80 Todd Hundley .40 .12
81 Dmitri Young .40 .12
82 Tony Clark .40 .12
83 Nick Johnson 1.00 .30
84 Mike Caruso .40 .12
85 David Ortiz .40 .12
86 Matt Williams .40 .12
87 Raul Mondesi .40 .12
88 Kenny Lofton .40 .12
89 Miguel Tejada .40 .12
90 Dante Bichette .40 .12
91 Jorge Posada .60 .18
92 Carlos Beltran .40 .12
93 Carlos Delgado .40 .12
94 Javy Lopez .40 .12
95 Aramis Ramirez .40 .12
96 Neifi Perez .40 .12
97 Marlon Anderson .40 .12
98 David Cone .40 .12
99 Moises Alou .40 .12
100 John Olerud .40 .12

1999 Topps Stars One Star Foil

This 100-card set is parallel to the regular insert set and serially numbered to 249.

Nm-Mt Ex-Mt
*STARS: 5X TO 12X BASIC ONE STAR
*ROOKIES: 2.5X TO 6X BASIC ONE STAR

1999 Topps Stars Two Star

Inserted one per pack, this 50-card set features color photos of the game's top players printed with light gold metallic inks and foil stamping. The backs carry the player 1998 season highlights.

Nm-Mt Ex-Mt
COMPLETE SET (50) 30.00 9.00
1 Ken Griffey Jr. 1.50 .45
2 Chipper Jones 1.00 .30
3 Mike Piazza 1.50 .45
4 Nomar Garciaparra 1.50 .45
5 Derek Jeter 2.50 .75
6 Frank Thomas 1.00 .30
7 Ben Grieve .40 .12
8 Mark McGwire 2.50 .75
9 Sammy Sosa 1.50 .45
10 Alex Rodriguez 1.50 .45
11 Troy Glaus .60 .18
12 Eric Chavez .40 .12
13 Kerry Wood 1.00 .30
14 Barry Bonds 2.50 .75

15 Vladimir Guerrero 1.00 .30
16 Albert Belle .40 .12
17 Juan Gonzalez 1.00 .30
18 Roger Clemens 2.00 .60
19 Ruben Mateo .40 .12
20 Cal Ripken 3.00 .90
21 Darin Erstad .40 .12
22 Jeff Bagwell .60 .18
23 Roy Halladay .40 .12
24 Todd Helton .60 .18
25 Michael Barrett .40 .12
26 Manny Ramirez .40 .12
27 Fernando Seguignol .40 .12
28 Pat Burrell 2.00 .60
29 Andruw Jones .40 .12
30 Randy Johnson 1.00 .30
31 Jose Canseco 1.00 .30
32 Brad Fullmer .40 .12
33 Alex Escobar .30 .09
34 Alfonso Soriano 6.00 1.80
35 Larry Walker .60 .18
36 Matt Clement .40 .12
37 Mo Vaughn .40 .12
38 Bruce Chen .40 .12
39 Travis Lee .40 .12
40 Adrian Beltre .40 .12
41 Alex Gonzalez .40 .12
42 Jason Tyner .40 .12
43 George Lombard .40 .12
44 Scott Rolen .60 .18
45 Mark Mulder 2.50 .75
46 Gabe Kapler .40 .12
47 Choo Freeman .40 .12
48 Tony Gwynn 1.25 .35
49 A.J. Burnett .75 .23
50 Matt Belisle .40 .12

1999 Topps Stars Two Star Foil

Randomly inserted in packs at the rate of one in 82, this 50-card set is a gold select metallization parallel version of the regular insert set. Only 199 serial-numbered sets were produced.

Nm-Mt Ex-Mt
*STARS: 6X TO 15X BASIC TWO STAR
*ROOKIES: 4X TO 10X BASIC TWO STAR

1999 Topps Stars Three Star

Randomly inserted in packs at the rate of one in five, this 20-card set features color photos of the hottest stars in the game printed with refractive silver foil stamping along with gold metallic inks. The backs carry "Star Qualities" text indicating exactly what makes the player shine.

Nm-Mt Ex-Mt
COMPLETE SET (20) 50.00 15.00
*FOIL STARS: 8X TO 20X THREE STAR
FOIL STATED ODDS 1:410
FOIL PRINT RUN 99 SERIAL #'d SETS
1 Ken Griffey Jr. 2.50 .75
2 Chipper Jones 1.50 .45
3 Mike Piazza 2.50 .75
4 Nomar Garciaparra 2.50 .75
5 Derek Jeter 4.00 1.20
6 Frank Thomas 1.50 .45
7 Ben Grieve .60 .18
8 Mark McGwire 4.00 1.20
9 Sammy Sosa 2.50 .75
10 Alex Rodriguez 2.50 .75
11 Troy Glaus 1.00 .30
12 Eric Chavez .60 .18
13 Kerry Wood 1.50 .45
14 Barry Bonds 4.00 1.20
15 Vladimir Guerrero 1.50 .45
16 Albert Belle .60 .18
17 Juan Gonzalez 1.50 .45
18 Roger Clemens 3.00 .90
19 Ruben Mateo .60 .18
20 Cal Ripken 5.00 1.50

1999 Topps Stars Three Star Foil

Randomly inserted in packs at the rate of one in 410, this 20-card set is a gold select metallization parallel version of the regular insert set and sequentially numbered to 99.

Nm-Mt Ex-Mt
*STARS: 6X TO 15X BASIC THREE STAR

1999 Topps Stars Four Star

Randomly inserted in packs at the rate of one in 10, this 10-card set features color action photos of top rank players printed using dark gold metallic inks and refractive foil stamping on the fronts. The backs carry the player's honors and accolades.

Nm-Mt Ex-Mt
COMPLETE SET (10) 40.00 12.00
*FOIL: 12.5X TO 30X BASIC FOUR STAR
FOIL STATED ODDS 1:1650
FOIL PRINT RUN 49 SERIAL #'d SETS
1 Ken Griffey Jr. 2.50 .75
2 Chipper Jones 1.50 .45
3 Mike Piazza 2.50 .75
4 Nomar Garciaparra 2.50 .75
5 Derek Jeter 4.00 1.20
6 Frank Thomas 1.50 .45
7 Ben Grieve .60 .18
8 Mark McGwire 4.00 1.20
9 Sammy Sosa 2.50 .75
10 Alex Rodriguez 2.50 .75

1999 Topps Stars Four Star Foil

Randomly inserted in packs at the rate of one in 1650, this 10-card set is a gold select metallization parallel version of the regular insert set. Only 49 serial-numbered sets were produced.

Nm-Mt Ex-Mt
*STARS: 8X TO 20X BASIC FOUR STAR

1999 Topps Stars Bright Futures

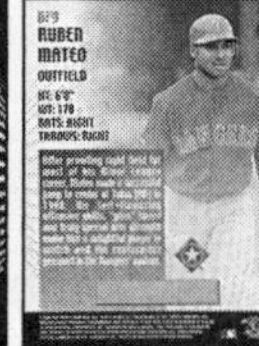

Randomly inserted in packs at the rate of one in 41, this 10-card set features action color photos of top rising prospects with foil stamping and sequentially numbered to 1999.

Nm-Mt Ex-Mt
COMPLETE SET (10) 40.00 12.00
*FOIL: 3X TO 8X BASIC BR.FUTURES
FOIL ODDS 1:2702
FOIL PRINT RUN 30 SERIAL #'d SETS
BF1 Troy Glaus 5.00 1.50
BF2 Eric Chavez 3.00 .90
BF3 Adrian Beltre 3.00 .90
BF4 Michael Barrett 3.00 .90
BF5 Gabe Kapler 3.00 .90
BF6 Alex Gonzalez 3.00 .90
BF7 Matt Clement 3.00 .90
BF8 Pat Burrell 6.00 1.80
BF9 Ruben Mateo 3.00 .90
BF10 Alfonso Soriano 10.00 3.00

1999 Topps Stars Galaxy

Randomly inserted in packs at the rate of one in 41, this 10-card set features color action photos of top MLB stars printed with a foil stamp and sequentially numbered to 1999. Each card is serial numbered of 1999 on back.

Nm-Mt Ex-Mt
COMPLETE SET (10) 100.00 30.00
*FOIL: 4X TO 10X BASIC GALAXY
FOIL ODDS 1:2702
FOIL PRINT RUN 30 SERIAL #'d SETS
G1 Mark McGwire 15.00 4.50
G2 Roger Clemens 12.00 3.60
G3 Nomar Garciaparra 10.00 3.00
G4 Alex Rodriguez 10.00 3.00
G5 Kerry Wood 6.00 1.80
G6 Ben Grieve 2.50 .75
G7 Derek Jeter 15.00 4.50
G8 Vladimir Guerrero 6.00 1.80
G9 Ken Griffey Jr. 10.00 3.00
G10 Sammy Sosa 10.00 3.00

1999 Topps Stars Rookie Reprints

These five cards are reprints of famous vintage Rookie Cards issued by Topps from an era gone by. The cards are very detailed replicas of the actual vintage issues except, of course, for the modern era high end white card stock, glossy coatings and standard 2 1/2" by 3 1/2" size (the real Banks and Berra RC's were not made with those dimensions). The cards were randomly seeded into packs at a rate of 1:65. A total of 2,500 serial numbered sets were produced.

Nm-Mt Ex-Mt
COMPLETE SET (5) 80.00 24.00
1 Frank Robinson 15.00 4.50
2 Ernie Banks 20.00 6.00
3 Yogi Berra 20.00 6.00
4 Bob Gibson 15.00 4.50
5 Tom Seaver 15.00 4.50

1999 Topps Stars Rookie Reprints Autographs

These autographed cards are parallel issues to the more common Rookie Reprints inserts. Each card has been signed by the athlete and stamped as a "Topps Certified Autograph Issue". The cards are randomly seeded into packs at a rate of 1:406 except for the Ernie Banks card of which is seeded at 1:812. Judging from analysis of the total product print run, it appears that each athlete signed approximately 500 cards - except for Banks of whom it appears signed around 1,000 cards.

Nm-Mt Ex-Mt
1 Frank Robinson 40.00 12.00
2 Ernie Banks DP 80.00 24.00
3 Yogi Berra 60.00 18.00
4 Bob Gibson 40.00 12.00
5 Tom Seaver 40.00 12.00

2000 Topps Stars Pre-Production

This five-card set was distributed to dealers and hobby media in a sealed cello wrap bag several weeks prior to the release of 2000 Topps Stars to preview the product. The cards can be distinguished from their basic issue counterparts by their "PP" prefixed numbering.

Nm-Mt Ex-Mt
COMPLETE SET (5) 8.00 2.40
PP1 Bob Gibson 1.00 .30
PP2 Alex Rodriguez 3.00 .90
PP3 Sammy Sosa 2.50 .75
PP4 Pat Burrell 2.00 .60
PP5 Rick Asadoorian .50 .15

2000 Topps Stars

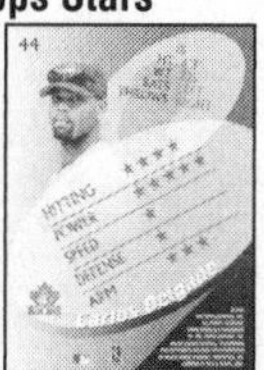

The 2000 Topps Stars product was released in July, 2000 and featured a 200-card base set. The base set was broken into tiers as follows: 135 Base Veterans (1-135), 15 Rookies (136-150), 50 Spotlights (151-200). Each pack contained six cards and carried a suggested retail price of $3.00. Notable Rookie Cards include Jose Ortiz (his first licensed Rookie Card on the market), Rick Asadoorian and Bobby Bradley.

Nm-Mt Ex-Mt
COMPLETE SET (200) 50.00 15.00
1 Vladimir Guerrero 1.25 .35
2 Eric Karros .50 .15
3 Omar Vizquel .50 .15
4 Ken Griffey Jr. 2.00 .60
5 Preston Wilson .50 .15
6 Albert Belle .50 .15
7 Ryan Klesko .50 .15
8 Bob Abreu .50 .15
9 Warren Morris .40 .12
10 Rafael Palmeiro .75 .23
11 Nomar Garciaparra 2.00 .60
12 Dante Bichette .50 .15
13 Jeff Cirillo .40 .12
14 Carlos Beltran .50 .15
15 Tony Clark .40 .12
16 Ray Durham .50 .15
17 Mark McGwire 3.00 .90
18 Jim Thome 1.25 .35
19 Todd Walker .50 .15
20 Richie Sexson .50 .15
21 Adrian Beltre .50 .15
22 Jay Bell .50 .15
23 Craig Biggio .75 .23
24 Ben Grieve .40 .12
25 Greg Maddux 2.00 .60
26 Fernando Tatis .40 .12
27 Jeromy Burnitz .50 .15
28 Vinny Castilla .50 .15
29 Mark Grace .75 .23
30 Derek Jeter 3.00 .90
31 Larry Walker .75 .23
32 Ivan Rodriguez 1.25 .35
33 Curt Schilling .75 .23
34 Mike Lamb RC .50 .15
35 Kevin Brown .50 .15
36 Andruw Jones .50 .15
37 Chris Mears RC .50 .15
38 Bartolo Colon .50 .15
39 Edgardo Alfonzo .50 .15
40 Brady Anderson .50 .15
41 Andres Galarraga .50 .15
42 Scott Rolen .75 .23
43 Manny Ramirez .50 .15
44 Carlos Delgado .50 .15
45 David Cone .50 .15
46 Carl Everett .50 .15
47 Chipper Jones 1.25 .35
48 Barry Bonds 3.00 .90
49 Dean Palmer .50 .15
50 Frank Thomas 1.25 .35
51 Paul O'Neill .75 .23
52 Mo Vaughn .50 .15
53 Todd Helton .75 .23
54 Jason Giambi 1.25 .35
55 Brian Jordan .50 .15
56 Luis Gonzalez .50 .15
57 Alex Rodriguez 2.00 .60
58 J.D. Drew .50 .15
59 Javy Lopez .50 .15
60 Tony Gwynn 1.50 .45
61 Jason Kendall .50 .15
62 Pedro Martinez 1.25 .35
63 Matt Williams .50 .15
64 Gary Sheffield .50 .15
65 Roberto Alomar 1.25 .35
66 Lyle Overbay RC .75 .23
67 Jeff Bagwell .75 .23
68 Tim Hudson .75 .23
69 Sammy Sosa 2.00 .60
70 Keith Reed RC .50 .15
71 Robin Ventura .50 .15
72 Cal Ripken 4.00 1.20
73 Alex Gonzalez .40 .12
74 Aaron McNeal RC .50 .15
75 Mike Lieberthal .50 .15
76 Brian Giles .50 .15
77 Kevin Millwood .50 .15
78 Troy O'Leary .40 .12
79 Raul Mondesi .50 .15
80 John Olerud .50 .15
81 David Justice .50 .15
82 Erubiel Durazo .40 .12
83 Shawn Green .50 .15
84 Tino Martinez .75 .23
85 Greg Vaughn .50 .15
86 Tom Glavine .75 .23
87 Jose Canseco 1.25 .35
88 Kenny Lofton .50 .15
89 Brian Daubach .40 .12
90 Mike Piazza 2.00 .60
91 Randy Johnson 1.25 .35
92 Pokey Reese .40 .12
93 Troy Glaus .75 .23
94 Kerry Wood 1.25 .35
95 Sean Casey .50 .15
96 Magglio Ordonez .50 .15
97 Bernie Williams .75 .23
98 Juan Gonzalez 1.25 .35
99 Barry Larkin 1.25 .35
100 Orlando Hernandez .50 .15
101 Roger Clemens 2.50 .75
102 Bob Gibson .75 .23
103 Gary Carter .75 .23
104 Willie Stargell .75 .23
105 Joe Morgan .50 .15
106 Brooks Robinson 1.25 .35
107 Ozzie Smith 2.00 .60
108 Carl Yastrzemski 2.00 .60
109 Al Kaline 1.25 .35
110 Frank Robinson .75 .23
111 Lance Berkman .50 .15
112 Adam Piatt .40 .12
113 Vernon Wells .50 .15
114 Rafael Furcal .50 .15
115 Rick Ankiel .40 .12
116 Corey Patterson .75 .23
117 Josh Hamilton .40 .12
118 Jack Cust .40 .12
119 Josh Girdley .40 .12
120 Pablo Ozuna .40 .12
121 Sean Burroughs .75 .23
122 Pat Burrell .75 .23
123 Chad Hermansen .40 .12
124 Ruben Mateo .40 .12
125 Ben Petrick .40 .12
126 Dee Brown .40 .12
127 Eric Munson .40 .12
128 Ruben Salazar RC .50 .15
129 Kip Wells .40 .12
130 Alfonso Soriano 1.25 .35
131 Mark Mulder .75 .23
132 Roosevelt Brown .40 .12
133 Nick Johnson .50 .15
134 Kyle Snyder .40 .12
135 David Walling .40 .12
136 Geraldo Guzman RC .50 .15
137 John Sneed RC .50 .15
138 Ben Christensen RC .50 .15
139 Corey Myers RC .50 .15
140 Jose Ortiz RC .50 .15
141 Ryan Christianson RC .50 .15
142 Brett Myers RC 3.00 .90
143 Bobby Bradley RC .50 .15
144 Rick Asadoorian RC .50 .15
145 Julio Zuleta RC .50 .15
146 Ty Howington RC .50 .15
147 Josh Kalinowski RC .50 .15
148 B.J. Garbe RC .50 .15
149 Scott Downs RC .50 .15
150 Dan Wright RC .50 .15
151 Jeff Bagwell SPOT .50 .15
152 V.Guerrero SPOT .75 .23
153 Mike Piazza SPOT 1.25 .35
154 Juan Gonzalez SPOT .75 .23
155 Ivan Rodriguez SPOT .75 .23
156 Manny Ramirez SPOT .75 .23
157 Sammy Sosa SPOT 1.25 .35
158 Chipper Jones SPOT .75 .23
159 Shawn Green SPOT .40 .12
160 Ken Griffey Jr. SPOT 1.25 .35
161 Cal Ripken SPOT 2.00 .60
162 N.Garciaparra SPOT 1.25 .35
163 Derek Jeter SPOT 1.50 .45
164 Barry Bonds SPOT 1.50 .45
165 Greg Maddux SPOT 1.25 .35
166 Mark McGwire SPOT 1.50 .45
167 Roberto Alomar SPOT .75 .23
168 Alex Rodriguez SPOT 1.25 .35
169 Randy Johnson SPOT .75 .23
170 Tony Gwynn SPOT .75 .23
171 Pedro Martinez SPOT .75 .23
172 Bob Gibson SPOT .50 .15
173 Gary Carter SPOT .50 .15
174 Willie Stargell SPOT .50 .15
175 Joe Morgan SPOT .40 .12
176 B.Robinson SPOT .75 .23
177 Ozzie Smith SPOT 1.25 .35
178 C.Yastrzemski SPOT 1.25 .35
179 Al Kaline SPOT .75 .23
180 Frank Robinson SPOT .50 .15
181 Adam Piatt SPOT .40 .12
182 Alfonso Soriano SPOT .50 .15
183 Corey Patterson SPOT .50 .15
184 Vernon Wells SPOT .40 .12
185 Pat Burrell SPOT .50 .15
186 Mark Mulder SPOT .50 .15
187 Eric Munson SPOT .40 .12
188 Rafael Furcal SPOT .40 .12
189 Rick Ankiel SPOT .40 .12
190 Ruben Mateo SPOT .40 .12
191 S.Burroughs SPOT .50 .15
192 Josh Hamilton SPOT .40 .12
193 Brett Myers SPOT 1.50 .45
194 B.Christensen SPOT .50 .15
195 Ty Howington SPOT .50 .15
196 R.Asadoorian SPOT .50 .15
197 J.Kalinowski SPOT .50 .15
198 Corey Myers SPOT .50 .15
199 R.Christianson SPOT .50 .15
200 John Sneed SPOT .50 .15

2000 Topps Stars Metallic Blue

Randomly inserted into packs, this 200-card set is a complete parallel of the 2000 Topps Stars base set that features a metallic blue foil lettering. The set is broken into two tiers as follows: Veterans (1-150) inserted one in 26, individually serial numbered to 299, Subset cards (151-200) inserted at one in 232, individually serial numbered to 99.

Nm-Mt Ex-Mt
COMMON CARD (1-150) 2.00 .60
*STARS 1-150: 3X TO 8X BASIC CARDS
*ROOKIES 1-150: 2.5X TO 6X BASIC CARDS
COMMON (151-200) 4.00 1.20
*STARS 151-180: 10X TO 25X BASIC
*ROOKIES 193-200: 8X TO 20X BASIC

2000 Topps Stars All-Star Authority

Randomly inserted into packs at one in 13, this 14-card insert features players that make the all-star team on a regular basis. Card backs carry an "AS" prefix.

Nm-Mt Ex-Mt
COMPLETE SET (14) 60.00 18.00
AS1 Mark McGwire 6.00 1.80
AS2 Sammy Sosa 4.00 1.20
AS3 Ken Griffey Jr. 4.00 1.20
AS4 Cal Ripken 8.00 2.40
AS5 Tony Gwynn 3.00 .90
AS6 Barry Bonds 6.00 1.80
AS7 Mike Piazza 4.00 1.20
AS8 Pedro Martinez 2.50 .75
AS9 Chipper Jones 2.50 .75
AS10 Manny Ramirez 1.00 .30
AS11 Alex Rodriguez 4.00 1.20
AS12 Derek Jeter 6.00 1.80
AS13 Nomar Garciaparra 4.00 1.20
AS14 Roberto Alomar 2.50 .75

2000 Topps Stars Autographs

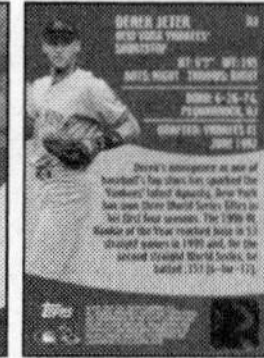

Randomly inserted into packs, this 13-card insert features autographed cards of past and present Major League stars. Please note that there are two tiers in this autograph set: Group A were inserted at a rate of one in 382, and Group B were inserted at a rate of one in 1636. Please note that these cards were numbered using the player's initials.

Nm-Mt Ex-Mt
AK Al Kaline B 60.00 18.00
BG Bob Gibson A 40.00 12.00
BR Brooks Robinson B 60.00 18.00
CY Carl Yastrzemski B 120.00 36.00
DJ Derek Jeter A 120.00 36.00
FR Frank Robinson B 50.00 15.00
GC Gary Carter B 50.00 15.00
JM Joe Morgan B 40.00 12.00
KM Kevin Millwood A 15.00 4.50
OS Ozzie Smith A 80.00 24.00
RA Rick Ankiel A 15.00 4.50
RF Rafael Furcal A 15.00 4.50
WS Willie Stargell B 50.00 15.00

2000 Topps Stars Game Gear Bats

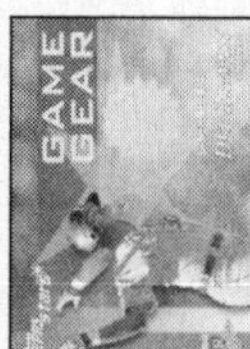

Randomly inserted into packs, this 10-card insert features game-used bat cards of Major League prospects. Please note that there are three tiers in this bat set: Group A were inserted at a rate of one in 2289, and Group B were inserted at a rate of one in 1353, and Group C were inserted at one in 175. Card backs carry a "GGB" prefix. Chipper Jones and Mark Quinn were seeded into packs as exchange cards with a redemption deadline of May 30th, 2001.

Nm-Mt Ex-Mt
GGB1 Rafael Furcal C 10.00 3.00
GGB2 Sean Burroughs B 15.00 4.50
GGB3 Corey Patterson B 15.00 4.50
GGB4 Chipper Jones B 15.00 4.50
GGB5 Vernon Wells C 10.00 3.00
GGB6 Mark Quinn B 8.00 2.40
GGB7 Eric Munson C 8.00 2.40
GGB8 Ben Petrick B 8.00 2.40
GGB9 Dee Brown A 8.00 2.40
GGB10 Lance Berkman C 10.00 3.00

2000 Topps Stars Game Gear Jerseys

Randomly inserted into packs at one in 382, this three-card insert features game-used jersey cards of Kevin Millwood, Brad Penny and J.D. Drew. Please note that the Brad Penny was an exchange card with a deadline of 05/30/01. Card backs carry a "GGJ" prefix.

	Nm-Mt	Ex-Mt
GGJ1 Kevin Millwood	10.00	3.00
GGJ2 Brad Penny	10.00	3.00
GGJ3 J.D. Drew	10.00	3.00

2000 Topps Stars Progression

Randomly inserted into packs at one in 13, this nine-card insert set features a past star, a modern star, and a future star on each card. Card backs carry a "P" prefix.

	Nm-Mt	Ex-Mt
COMPLETE SET (9)	50.00	15.00
P1 Bob Gibson Pedro Martinez Rick Ankiel	3.00	.90
P2 Gary Carter Mike Piazza Ben Petrick	5.00	1.50
P3 Willie Stargell Mark McGwire Pat Burrell	8.00	2.40
P4 Joe Morgan Roberto Alomar Ruben Salazar	3.00	.90
P5 Brooks Robinson Chipper Jones Sean Burroughs	3.00	.90
P6 Ozzie Smith Derek Jeter Rafael Furcal	8.00	2.40
P7 Carl Yastrzemski Barry Bonds Josh Hamilton	8.00	2.40
P8 Al Kaline Ken Griffey Jr. Ruben Mateo	5.00	1.50
P9 Frank Robinson Manny Ramirez Corey Patterson	1.25	.35

2000 Topps Stars Walk of Fame

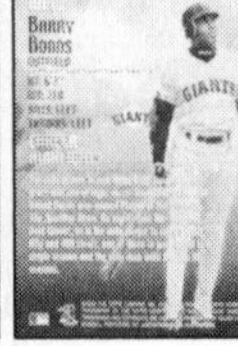

Randomly inserted into packs at one in eight, this 15-card insert features players that are on their way to the Hall of Fame. Card backs carry a "WF" prefix.

	Nm-Mt	Ex-Mt
COMPLETE SET (15)	50.00	15.00
WF1 Cal Ripken	6.00	1.80
WF2 Ken Griffey Jr.	3.00	.90
WF3 Mark McGwire	5.00	1.50
WF4 Sammy Sosa	3.00	.90
WF5 Alex Rodriguez	3.00	.90
WF6 Derek Jeter	5.00	1.50
WF7 Nomar Garciaparra	3.00	.90
WF8 Chipper Jones	2.00	.60
WF9 Manny Ramirez	.75	.23
WF10 Mike Piazza	3.00	.90
WF11 Vladimir Guerrero	2.00	.60
WF12 Barry Bonds	5.00	1.50
WF13 Tony Gwynn	2.50	.75
WF14 Roberto Alomar	2.00	.60
WF15 Pedro Martinez	2.00	.60

2001 Topps Stars

The 2001 Topps Stars product was released in June, 2001 and featured a 200-card base set that was broken into tiers as follows: Base Veterans (1-150), and Prospects/Rookies (151-200). Each pack contained six cards, and carried a suggested retail price of $3.00.

	Nm-Mt	Ex-Mt
COMPLETE SET (200)	50.00	15.00
1 Darin Erstad	.50	.15
2 Luis Gonzalez	.50	.15
3 Rafael Furcal	.50	.15
4 Dante Bichette	.50	.15
5 Sammy Sosa	2.00	.60
6 Ken Griffey Jr.	2.00	.60
7 Jim Thome	1.25	.35
8 Bobby Higginson	.50	.15
9 Cliff Floyd	.50	.15
10 Lance Berkman	.50	.15
11 Eric Karros	.50	.15
12 Jeromy Burnitz	.50	.15
13 Jose Vidro	.50	.15
14 Benny Agbayani	.40	.12
15 Jorge Posada	.75	.23
16 Ramon Hernandez	.40	.12
17 Jason Kendall	.50	.15
18 Jeff Kent	.50	.15
19 John Olerud	.50	.15
20 Al Martin	.40	.12
21 Gerald Williams	.40	.12
22 Gabe Kapler	.40	.12
23 Carlos Delgado	.50	.15
24 Mariano Rivera	.75	.23
25 Javy Lopez	.50	.15
26 Paul Konerko	.50	.15
27 Daryle Ward	.40	.12
28 Mike Lieberthal	.50	.15
29 Tom Goodwin	.40	.12
30 Garret Anderson	.50	.15
31 Steve Finley	.50	.15
32 Brian Jordan	.50	.15
33 Nomar Garciaparra	2.00	.60
34 Ray Durham	.50	.15
35 Sean Casey	.50	.15
36 Kenny Lofton	.50	.15
37 Dean Palmer	.50	.15
38 Jeff Bagwell	.75	.23
39 Mike Sweeney	.50	.15
40 Adrian Beltre	.50	.15
41 Richie Sexson	.50	.15
42 Vladimir Guerrero	1.25	.35
43 Derek Jeter	3.00	.90
44 Miguel Tejada	.50	.15
45 Doug Glanville	.40	.12
46 Brian Giles	.50	.15
47 Marvin Benard	.40	.12
48 Edgar Martinez	.75	.23
49 Edgar Renteria	.50	.15
50 Fred McGriff	.75	.23
51 Ivan Rodriguez	1.25	.35
52 Brad Fullmer	.40	.12
53 Antonio Alfonseca	.40	.12
54 Tom Glavine	.75	.23
55 Warren Morris	.40	.12
56 Johnny Damon	.50	.15
57 Dmitri Young	.50	.15
58 Mo Vaughn	.50	.15
59 Randy Johnson	1.25	.35
60 Greg Maddux	2.00	.60
61 Carl Everett	.50	.15
62 Magglio Ordonez	.50	.15
63 Pokey Reese	.40	.12
64 Todd Helton	.75	.23
65 Preston Wilson	.50	.15
66 Richard Hidalgo	.50	.15
67 Jermaine Dye	.50	.15
68 Gary Sheffield	.50	.15
69 Geoff Jenkins	.50	.15
70 Edgardo Alfonzo	.50	.15
71 Paul O'Neill	.75	.23
72 Terrence Long	.50	.15
73 Bob Abreu	.50	.15
74 Kevin Young	.40	.12
75 J.T. Snow	.50	.15
76 Alex Rodriguez	2.00	.60
77 Jim Edmonds	.50	.15
78 Mark McGwire	3.00	.90
79 Tony Batista	.50	.15
80 Darrin Fletcher	.40	.12
81 Robb Nen	.50	.15
82 Jose Offerman	.40	.12
83 Travis Fryman	.50	.15
84 Joe Randa	.40	.12
85 Omar Vizquel	.50	.15
86 Tim Salmon	.75	.23
87 Andruw Jones	.50	.15
88 Albert Belle	.50	.15
89 Manny Ramirez	.50	.15
90 Frank Thomas	1.25	.35
91 Barry Larkin	1.25	.35
92 Neifi Perez	.40	.12
93 Luis Castillo	.50	.15
94 Moises Alou	.50	.15
95 Mark Quinn	.40	.12
96 Kevin Brown	.50	.15
97 Cristian Guzman	.50	.15
98 Mike Piazza	2.00	.60
99 Bernie Williams	.75	.23
100 Jason Giambi	1.25	.35
101 Scott Rolen	.75	.23
102 Phil Nevin	.50	.15
103 Rich Aurilia	.50	.15
104 Mike Cameron	.50	.15
105 Fernando Vina	.50	.15
106 Greg Vaughn	.50	.15
107 Jose Cruz Jr.	.50	.15
108 Raul Mondesi	.50	.15
109 Ben Molina	.40	.12
110 Pedro Martinez	1.25	.35
111 Todd Hollandsworth	.40	.12
112 Jacque Jones	.50	.15
113 Rickey Henderson	1.25	.35
114 Troy Glaus	.75	.23
115 Chipper Jones	1.25	.35
116 Delino DeShields	.40	.12
117 Eric Young	.40	.12
118 Jose Valentin	.40	.12
119 Roberto Alomar	1.25	.35
120 Jeff Cirillo	.40	.12
121 Mike Lowell	.50	.15
122 Julio Lugo	.40	.12
123 Shawn Green	.50	.15
124 Marquis Grissom	.40	.12
125 Matt Lawton	.40	.12
126 Jay Payton	.40	.12
127 David Justice	.50	.15
128 Eric Chavez	.50	.15
129 Pat Burrell	.50	.15
130 Ryan Klesko	.50	.15
131 Barry Bonds	3.00	.90
132 Jay Buhner	.50	.15
133 J.D. Drew	.50	.15
134 Rafael Palmeiro	.75	.23
135 Shannon Stewart	.50	.15
136 Juan Gonzalez	1.25	.35
137 Tony Womack	.40	.12
138 Carlos Lee	.50	.15
139 Derrek Lee	.50	.15
140 Ben Grieve	.40	.12
141 Ron Belliard	.40	.12
142 Stan Musial	2.00	.60
143 Ernie Banks	1.25	.35
144 Jim Palmer	.50	.15
145 Tony Perez	.50	.15
146 Duke Snider	.75	.23
147 Rod Carew	.75	.23
148 Warren Spahn	.75	.23
149 Yogi Berra	1.50	.45
150 Juan Marichal	.50	.15
151 Eric Munson	.40	.12
152 Carlos Pena	.40	.12
153 Joe Crede	.40	.12
154 Ryan Anderson	.40	.12
155 Milton Bradley	.50	.15
156 Sean Burroughs	.50	.15
157 Corey Patterson	.50	.15
158 C.C. Sabathia	.50	.15
159 Ben Petrick	.40	.12
160 Aubrey Huff	.50	.15
161 Gookie Dawkins	.40	.12
162 Ben Sheets	.50	.15
163 Pablo Ozuna	.40	.12
164 Eric Valent	.40	.12
165 Rod Barajas	.40	.12
166 Chin-Feng Chen	.50	.15
167 Josh Hamilton	.40	.12
168 Keith Ginter	.40	.12
169 Vernon Wells	.50	.15
170 Dernell Stenson	.40	.12
171 Alfonso Soriano	.75	.23
172 Jason Marquis	.40	.12
173 Nick Johnson	.50	.15
174 Adam Everett	.40	.12
175 Jimmy Rollins	.50	.15
176 Ben Diggins	.40	.12
177 John Lackey	.40	.12
178 Scott Heard	.40	.12
179 Brian Hitchcox RC	.60	.18
180 Odannis Ayala RC	.60	.18
181 Scott Pratt RC	.60	.18
182 Greg Runser RC	.60	.18
183 Chris Russ RC	.60	.18
184 Derek Thompson	.40	.12
185 Jason Jones RC	.60	.18
186 Dominic Rich RC	.60	.18
187 Chad Petty RC	.60	.18
188 Steve Smyth RC	.60	.18
189 Bryan Hebson RC	.60	.18
190 Danny Borrell RC	.60	.18
191 Bob Keppel RC	1.00	.30
192 Justin Wayne RC	1.00	.30
193 R. Abercrombie RC	.60	.18
194 Travis Baptist RC	.60	.18
195 Shawn Fagan RC	.60	.18
196 Jose Reyes RC	8.00	2.40
197 Chris Bass RC	.60	.18
198 Albert Pujols RC	40.00	12.00
199 Luis Cotto RC	.60	.18
200 Jake Peavy RC	2.50	.75

2001 Topps Stars Elimination

Randomly inserted into packs at one in 72, this insert set is actually a partial parallel of the 2001 Topps Stars base set. These cards are serial numbered to 100, and offer the collector a chance at winning two tickets to the 2002 All-Star Game. Winning cards must be exchanged by 10/19/01.

Nm-Mt Ex-Mt

*STARS: 6X TO 15X BASIC CARDS....

2001 Topps Stars Gold

Randomly inserted into packs at one in 9, this insert set is actually a complete parallel of the 2001 Topps Stars base set. These cards are serial numbered to 499, and feature a special gold-foil stamping on the card fronts.

Nm-Mt Ex-Mt

*STARS: 2X TO 5X BASIC CARDS......
*ROOKIES: 1.5X TO 4X BASIC CARDS

2001 Topps Stars Onyx

Randomly inserted into packs at one in 48, this insert set is actually a complete parallel of the 2001 Topps Stars base set. These cards are serial numbered to 99, and feature a special onyx-foil stamping on the card fronts.

Nm-Mt Ex-Mt

*STARS: 8X TO 20X BASIC CARDS....
*ROOKIES: 5X TO 12X BASIC CARDS

2001 Topps Stars Autographs

Randomly inserted into packs at one in 353, this insert set features 13 authentic autographs from award winning superstars. Card backs carry a "TSA" prefix followed by the player's initials. Exchange cards with a redemption deadline of April 30th, 2003 were seeded into packs for Ernie Banks, Yogi Berra, Rod Carew, Todd Helton, Juan Marichal, Tony Perez and Duke Snider.

	Nm-Mt	Ex-Mt
TSA-CD Carlos Delgado	25.00	7.50
TSA-DS Duke Snider	40.00	12.00
TSA-EB Ernie Banks	50.00	15.00
TSA-EM Eric Munson	15.00	4.50
TSA-IR Ivan Rodriguez	50.00	15.00
TSA-JM Juan Marichal	25.00	7.50
TSA-JP Jim Palmer	25.00	7.50
TSA-RC Rod Carew	40.00	12.00
TSA-SM Stan Musial	100.00	30.00
TSA-TH Todd Helton	40.00	12.00
TSA-TP Tony Perez	25.00	7.50
TSA-WS Warren Spahn	50.00	15.00
TSA-YB Yogi Berra	50.00	15.00

2001 Topps Stars Game Gear Autographs

Randomly inserted into packs, this five-card insert set features authentic swatches of memorabilia plus an authentic autograph from some of the younger talent in the Major Leagues. Card backs carry a "TSR" prefix followed by the player's initials. Please note that cards featuring a swatch of jersey were inserted at 1:19288, cards containing bat were inserted at 1:12240. Each card is individually serial numbered to 25. Due to market scarcity, no pricing is provided. Exchange cards wiith a redemption deadline of April 30th, 2003 were seeded into packs for Barry Bonds, Todd Helton and Corey Patterson.

Nm-Mt Ex-Mt

TSRABB Barry Bonds Jsy
TSRACP Cory Patterson Bat
TSRARF Rafael Furcal Bat
TSRATH Todd Helton Jsy
TSRATL Terrence Long Bat

2001 Topps Stars Game Gear Bats

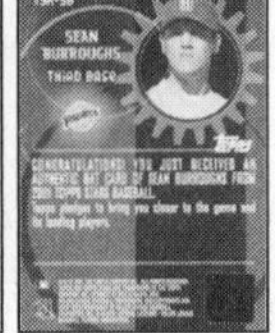

Randomly inserted into packs at one in 187, this insert set features swatches of actual game-used bats. Card backs carry a "TSR" prefix followed by the player's initials.

	Nm-Mt	Ex-Mt
TSRAB Adrian Beltre A	10.00	3.00
TSRAK Adam Kennedy A	10.00	3.00
TSRAP Adam Piatt A	10.00	3.00
TSRBD Ben Davis A	10.00	3.00
TSRCP Corey Patterson B	10.00	3.00
TSRED Erubiel Durazo A	10.00	3.00
TSREM Eric Munson A	10.00	3.00
TSRFL Felipe Lopez A	10.00	3.00
TSRFS F. Seguignol A	10.00	3.00
TSRGL George Lombard A	10.00	3.00
TSRGM G.Matthews Jr. A	10.00	3.00
TSRJE J.Encarnacion A	10.00	3.00
TSRJDD J.D. Drew A	10.00	3.00
TSRLB Lance Berkman A	10.00	3.00
TSRMC M. Cuddyer A	10.00	3.00
TSRNP Neifi Perez A	10.00	3.00
TSRRF Rafael Furcal B	10.00	3.00
TSRRS Richie Sexson A	10.00	3.00
TSRSB Sean Burroughs A	10.00	3.00
TSRSR Scott Rolen A	15.00	4.50
TSRTL Terrence Long B	10.00	3.00

2001 Topps Stars Game Gear Jerseys

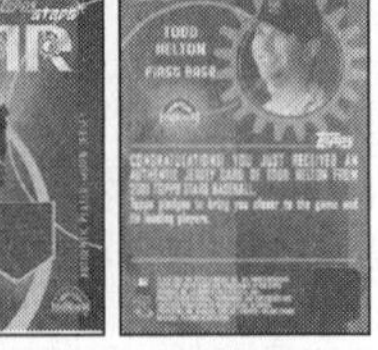

Randomly inserted into packs at one in 61, this insert set features swatches of actual game-used jerseys. Card backs carry a "TSR" prefix followed by the player's initials.

	Nm-Mt	Ex-Mt
TSR-AJ Andruw Jones A	10.00	3.00
TSR-BB Barry Bonds B	30.00	9.00
TSR-CJ Chipper Jones A	15.00	4.50
TSR-EA E. Alfonzo A	10.00	3.00
TSR-EM Edgar Martinez A	15.00	4.50
TSR-FT Frank Thomas A	15.00	4.50
TSR-JV Jose Vidro A	10.00	3.00
TSR-LC Luis Castillo A	10.00	3.00
TSR-MO M. Ordonez A	10.00	3.00
TSR-MP Mike Piazza A	20.00	6.00
TSR-RA Roberto Alomar A	15.00	4.50
TSR-SS Sammy Sosa A	20.00	6.00
TSR-TG Tony Gwynn A	15.00	4.50
TSR-TH Todd Helton B	15.00	4.50
TSR-SHS S. Stewart A	10.00	3.00

2001 Topps Stars Player's Choice Awards

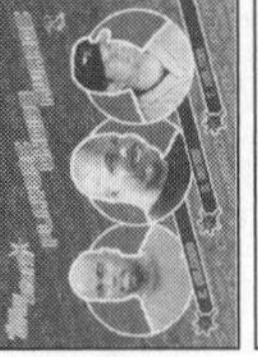

Inserted at a rate of one in 12, these 10 cards feature the three nominees for various honors at the MLBPA Player's Choice Award ceremony.

	Nm-Mt	Ex-Mt
COMPLETE SET (10)	30.00	9.00
PCA1 Barry Bonds Todd Helton Carlos Delgado	8.00	2.40
PCA2 Eric Davis Gary Sheffield Turk Wendell	1.25	.35
PCA3 Carlos Delgado Alex Rodriguez Frank Thomas	5.00	1.50
PCA4 Pedro Martinez David Wells Andy Pettitte	2.00	.60
PCA5 Kazuhiro Sasaki Mark Quinn Terrence Long	1.25	.35
PCA6 Frank Thomas Jay Buhner Bobby Higginson	3.00	.90
PCA7 Todd Helton Barry Bonds Jeff Kent	8.00	2.40
PCA8 Randy Johnson Tom Glavine Greg Maddux	5.00	1.50
PCA9 Rafael Furcal Rick Ankiel Jay Payton	1.25	.35
PCA10 Andres Galarraga Moises Alou Jeff D'Amico	1.25	.35

2001 Topps Stars Player's Choice Awards Relics

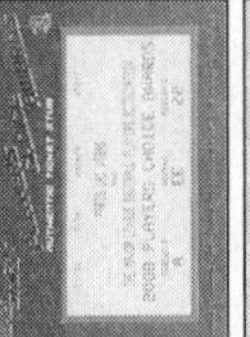
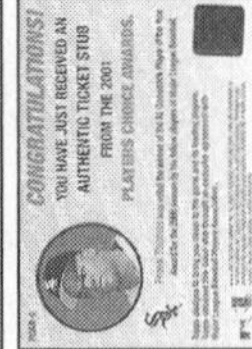

Inserted at a rate of one in 1,530 packs, these 10 cards feature pieces of memorabilia from 10 of the players nominated for various Player's Choice awards.

	Nm-Mt	Ex-Mt
PCAR1 Carlos Delgado	20.00	6.00
PCAR2 Eric Davis	20.00	6.00
PCAR3 Carlos Delgado	20.00	6.00
PCAR4 Pedro Martinez	30.00	9.00
PCAR5 Terrence Long	20.00	6.00
PCAR6 Frank Thomas	30.00	9.00
PCAR7 Todd Helton	30.00	9.00
PCAR8 Randy Johnson	30.00	9.00
PCAR9 Rafael Furcal	20.00	6.00
PCAR10 Andres Galarraga	20.00	6.00

2001 Topps Stars Progression

Randomly inserted into packs at one in 8, each card in the set features three players that are very similar statistically. Card backs carry a "P" prefix.

	Nm-Mt	Ex-Mt
COMPLETE SET (9)	15.00	4.50
P1 Ernie Banks Alex Rodriguez Alfonso Soriano	2.50	.75
P2 Yogi Berra Ivan Rodriguez Ramon Hernandez	1.50	.45
P3 Tony Perez Carlos Delgado Eric Munson	1.50	.45
P4 Rod Carew Roberto Alomar Jose Ortiz	1.50	.45
P5 Stan Musial Darin Erstad Alex Escobar	2.50	.75
P6 Jim Palmer Kevin Brown Kurt Ainsworth	1.50	.45
P7 Duke Snider Jim Edmonds Vernon Wells	1.50	.45

P8 Warren Spahn 1.50 .45
Randy Johnson
Ryan Anderson
P9 Juan Marichal 1.50 .45
Bartolo Colon
Bobby Bradley

1998 Topps Stars 'N Steel

The 1998 Topps Stars 'N Steel set was issued in one series totalling 44 cards and was distributed in three-card tri-fold packs with a suggested retail price of $9.99. The fronts feature color action player photos printed using Serillustion technology on .25 gauge metal stock. The backs carry player information.

Nm-Mt Ex-Mt
COMPLETE SET (44) 150.00 45.00
1 Roberto Alomar 6.00 1.80
2 Jeff Bagwell 4.00 1.20
3 Albert Belle 2.50 .75
4 Dante Bichette 2.50 .75
5 Barry Bonds 15.00 4.50
6 Jay Buhner 2.50 .75
7 Ken Caminiti 2.50 .75
8 Vinny Castilla 2.50 .75
9 Roger Clemens 12.00 3.60
10 Jose Cruz Jr. 2.50 .75
11 Andres Galarraga 2.50 .75
12 Nomar Garciaparra 10.00 3.00
13 Juan Gonzalez 6.00 1.80
14 Mark Grace 4.00 1.20
15 Ken Griffey Jr. 10.00 3.00
16 Tony Gwynn 8.00 2.40
17 Todd Hundley 2.50 .75
18 Derek Jeter 15.00 4.50
19 Randy Johnson 6.00 1.80
20 Andruw Jones 2.50 .75
21 Chipper Jones 6.00 1.80
22 David Justice 2.50 .75
23 Ray Lankford 2.50 .75
24 Barry Larkin 6.00 1.80
25 Kenny Lofton 2.50 .75
26 Greg Maddux 10.00 3.00
27 Edgar Martinez 4.00 1.20
28 Tino Martinez 4.00 1.20
29 Mark McGwire 15.00 4.50
30 Paul Molitor 4.00 1.20
31 Rafael Palmeiro 4.00 1.20
32 Mike Piazza 10.00 3.00
33 Manny Ramirez 2.50 .75
34 Cal Ripken 20.00 6.00
35 Ivan Rodriguez 6.00 1.80
36 Scott Rolen 4.00 1.20
37 Tim Salmon 4.00 1.20
38 Gary Sheffield 2.50 .75
39 Sammy Sosa 10.00 3.00
40 Frank Thomas 6.00 1.80
41 Jim Thome 6.00 1.80
42 Mo Vaughn 2.50 .75
43 Larry Walker 4.00 1.20
44 Bernie Williams 4.00 1.20

1998 Topps Stars 'N Steel Gold

Randomly inserted in packs at the rate of one in 12, this 44-card set is parallel to the base set and is distinguished by its gold foil highlights.

Nm-Mt Ex-Mt
*STARS: 1X TO 2.5X BASIC CARDS ...

1998 Topps Stars 'N Steel Gold Holographic

Randomly inserted in packs at the rate of one in 40, this 44-card set is parallel to the base set and is distinguished by its gold holographic foil highlights.

Nm-Mt Ex-Mt
*STARS: 3X TO 8X BASIC CARDS ......

1999 Topps Stars 'N Steel

The 1999 Topps Stars 'N Steel set was issued in one series totalling 44 cards and was distributed in three-card tri-fold packs with a suggested retail price of $9.99. The fronts feature color action player photos printed using Serillusion technology and bonded to 25-gauge metal with a silver border.

Nm-Mt Ex-Mt
COMPLETE SET (44) 80.00 24.00
1 Kerry Wood 4.00 1.20
2 Ben Grieve 2.00 .60
3 Chipper Jones 4.00 1.20
4 Alex Rodriguez 6.00 1.80
5 Mo Vaughn 2.00 .60
6 Bernie Williams 2.50 .75
7 Juan Gonzalez 4.00 1.20
8 Vinny Castilla 2.00 .60
9 Tony Gwynn 5.00 1.50
10 Manny Ramirez 2.00 .60
11 Raul Mondesi 2.00 .60
12 Roger Clemens 8.00 2.40
13 Darin Erstad 2.00 .60
14 Barry Bonds 10.00 3.00
15 Cal Ripken 12.00 3.60
16 Barry Larkin 4.00 1.20
17 Scott Rolen 2.50 .75
18 Albert Belle 2.00 .60
19 Craig Biggio 2.50 .75
20 Tony Clark 2.00 .60
21 Mark McGwire 10.00 3.00
22 Andres Galarraga 2.00 .60
23 Kenny Lofton 2.00 .60
24 Pedro Martinez 4.00 1.20
25 Paul O'Neill 2.50 .75
26 Ken Griffey Jr. 6.00 1.80
27 Travis Lee 2.00 .60
28 Tim Salmon 2.50 .75
29 Frank Thomas 4.00 1.20
30 Larry Walker 2.50 .75
31 Moises Alou 2.00 .60
32 Vladimir Guerrero 4.00 1.20
33 Ivan Rodriguez 4.00 1.20
34 Derek Jeter 10.00 3.00
35 Greg Vaughn 2.00 .60
36 Gary Sheffield 2.00 .60
37 Carlos Delgado 2.00 .60
38 Greg Maddux 6.00 1.80
39 Sammy Sosa 6.00 1.80
40 Mike Piazza 6.00 1.80
41 Nomar Garciaparra 6.00 1.80
42 Dante Bichette 2.00 .60
43 Jeff Bagwell 2.50 .75
44 Jim Thome 4.00 1.20

1999 Topps Stars 'N Steel Gold

Randomly inserted in packs at the rate of one in 12, this 44-card set is parallel to the base set and is distinguished by its gold foil highlights and gold border.

Nm-Mt Ex-Mt
*STARS: 1.25X TO 3X BASIC CARDS .

1999 Topps Stars 'N Steel Gold Domed Holographic

Randomly inserted in packs at the rate of one in 24, this 44-card set is parallel to the base set and is distinguished by its holographic gold domed design including a thick latyer of glass like coating.

Nm-Mt Ex-Mt
*STARS: 3X TO 6X BASIC CARDS ......

2000 Topps Subway Series

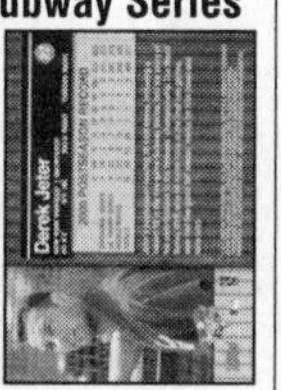

This 100 card standard-size set was issued by Topps to honor the first World Series played between two teams from NY since 1956. The sets were issued in a special box and included one "Fan-Fare Token" card inserted per set. A couple different tokens have been discovered for some players in this set. There is no value difference for whatever token in in this card. Please note that the complete rosters were included for each team as well as various cards featuring post-season highlights.

Nm-Mt Ex-Mt
COMP.FACT SET (101) 150.00 45.00
COMPLETE SET (100) 25.00 7.50
1 Mike Piazza 2.50 .75
2 Jay Payton .40 .12
3 Edgardo Alfonzo .60 .18
4 Todd Pratt .40 .12
5 Todd Zeile .60 .18
6 Mike Bordick .40 .12
7 Robin Ventura .60 .18
8 Benny Agbayani .40 .12
9 Timo Perez .60 .18
10 Kurt Abbott .40 .12
11 Matt Franco .40 .12
12 Bubba Trammell .40 .12
13 Darryl Hamilton .40 .12
14 Lenny Harris .40 .12
15 Joe McEwing .40 .12
16 Mike Hampton .60 .18
17 Al Leiter .60 .18
18 Rick Reed .40 .12
19 Bobby Jones .40 .12
20 Glendon Rusch .40 .12
21 Armando Benitez .60 .18
22 John Franco .60 .18
23 Rick White .40 .12
24 Dennis Cook .40 .12
25 Turk Wendell .40 .12
26 Bobby Valentine MG .40 .12
27 Derek Jeter 4.00 1.20
28 Chuck Knoblauch .60 .18
29 Tino Martinez 1.00 .30
30 Jorge Posada 1.00 .30
31 Luis Sojo .40 .12
32 Scott Brosius .60 .18
33 Chris Turner .40 .12
34 Bernie Williams 1.00 .30
35 David Justice .60 .18
36 Paul O'Neill 1.00 .30
37 Glenallen Hill .40 .12
38 Jose Vizcaino .40 .12
39 Luis Polonia .40 .12
40 Clay Bellinger .40 .12
41 Orlando Hernandez .60 .18
42 Roger Clemens 3.00 .90
43 Andy Pettitte 1.00 .30
44 Denny Neagle .40 .12
45 Dwight Gooden 1.00 .30
46 David Cone .60 .18
47 Mariano Rivera 1.00 .30
48 Jeff Nelson .40 .12
49 Mike Stanton .40 .12
50 Jason Grimsley .40 .12
51 Jose Canseco 1.50 .45
52 Joe Torre MG .60 .18
53 Edgardo Alfonzo .60 .18
54 Darryl Hamilton .40 .12
55 John Franco .60 .18
56 Benny Agbayani .40 .12
57 Bobby Jones .40 .12
58 New York Mets .60 .18
59 Bobby Valentine MG .60 .18
60 Mike Piazza 2.50 .75
61 Armando Benitez .60 .18
62 Mike Piazza 2.50 .75
63 Mike Piazza 2.50 .75
64 Todd Zeile .60 .18
65 Timo Perez .60 .18
66 Timo Perez .60 .18
67 Mike Hampton .60 .18
68 Andy Pettitte 1.00 .30
69 Tino Martinez 1.00 .30
70 Joe Torre MG .60 .18
71 New York Yankees .60 .18
72 Orlando Hernandez .60 .18
73 Bernie Williams 1.00 .30
74 Andy Pettitte 1.00 .30
75 Mariano Rivera 1.00 .30
76 New York Yankees .60 .18
77 Roger Clemens 3.00 .90
78 Derek Jeter 4.00 1.20
79 David Justice .60 .18
80 Mariano Rivera 1.00 .30
81 Tino Martinez 1.00 .30
82 New York Yankees .60 .18
83 Jorge Posada 1.00 .30
84 Chuck Knoblauch .60 .18
85 Jose Vizcaino .40 .12
86 Roger Clemens 3.00 .90
87 Mike Piazza 2.50 .75
88 Clay Bellinger .40 .12
89 Robin Ventura .60 .18
90 Benny Agbayani .40 .12
91 Orlando Hernandez .60 .18
92 Derek Jeter 4.00 1.20
93 Mike Piazza 2.50 .75
94 Mariano Rivera 1.00 .30
95 Derek Jeter 4.00 1.20
96 Luis Sojo .40 .12
97 New York Yankees .60 .18
98 Mike Hampton .60 .18
99 David Justice .60 .18
100 Derek Jeter 4.00 1.20
NNO New York Yankees
Promo card

2000 Topps Subway Series FanFare Tokens

Issued one per Topps Subway Series factory set, these cards featured the player photo next to an New York City subway token. The token embedded in the card were used by the MTA (Metropolitan Transportation Authority) in approximately 1953. These cards became very heavily sought after soon after release and have continued to be popular for their unique design.

Nm-Mt Ex-Mt
SSR1 Timo Perez 50.00 15.00
SSR2 Edgardo Alfonzo 50.00 15.00
SSR3 Mike Piazza 150.00 45.00
SSR4 Robin Ventura 50.00 15.00
SSR5 Todd Zeile 50.00 15.00
SSR6 Benny Agbayani 40.00 12.00
SSR7 Jay Payton 40.00 12.00
SSR8 Mike Bordick 40.00 12.00
SSR9 Matt Franco 40.00 12.00
SSR10 Mike Hampton 50.00 15.00
SSR11 Al Leiter 50.00 15.00
SSR12 Rick Reed 40.00 12.00
SSR13 Bobby Jones 40.00 12.00
SSR14 Glendon Rusch 40.00 12.00
SSR15 Darryl Hamilton 40.00 12.00
SSR16 Turk Wendell 40.00 12.00
SSR17 John Franco 50.00 15.00
SSR18 Armando Benitez 50.00 15.00
SSR19 Chuck Knoblauch 50.00 15.00
SSR20 Derek Jeter 250.00 75.00
SSR21 David Justice 50.00 15.00
SSR22 Bernie Williams 80.00 24.00
SSR23 Jorge Posada 80.00 24.00
SSR24 Paul O'Neill 80.00 24.00
SSR25 Tino Martinez 80.00 24.00
SSR26 Luis Sojo 40.00 12.00
SSR27 Scott Brosius 50.00 15.00
SSR28 Jose Canseco 80.00 24.00
SSR29 Orlando Hernandez 50.00 15.00
SSR30 Roger Clemens 200.00 60.00
SSR31 Andy Pettitte 80.00 24.00
SSR32 Denny Neagle 40.00 12.00
SSR33 David Cone 50.00 15.00
SSR34 Jeff Nelson 40.00 12.00
SSR35 Mike Stanton 40.00 12.00
SSR36 Mariano Rivera 80.00 24.00

1998 Topps SuperChrome

The 1998 Topps SuperChrome set was issued in one series totalling 36 cards. The 3-card packs retail for $4.99 each. The fronts feature color player photos surrounded by a white four-sided border. The player's name and team are written along the bottom of the card.

Nm-Mt Ex-Mt
COMPLETE SET (36) 40.00 12.00
1 Tony Gwynn 1.50 .45
2 Larry Walker .75 .23
3 Vladimir Guerrero 1.25 .35
4 Mo Vaughn .50 .15
5 Frank Thomas 1.25 .35
6 Barry Larkin 1.25 .35
7 Scott Rolen .75 .23
8 Juan Gonzalez 1.25 .35
9 Jeff Bagwell .75 .23
10 Ryan Klesko .50 .15
11 Mike Piazza 2.00 .60
12 Randy Johnson 1.25 .35
13 Derek Jeter 3.00 .90
14 Gary Sheffield .50 .15
15 Hideo Nomo 1.25 .35
16 Tino Martinez .75 .23
17 Ivan Rodriguez 1.25 .35
18 Bernie Williams .75 .23
19 Greg Maddux 2.00 .60
20 Roger Clemens 2.50 .75
21 Roberto Clemente 2.50 .75
22 Chipper Jones 1.25 .35
23 Sammy Sosa 2.00 .60
24 Tony Clark .50 .15
25 Barry Bonds 3.00 .90
26 Craig Biggio .75 .23
27 Cal Ripken 4.00 1.20
28 Ken Griffey Jr. 2.00 .60
29 Todd Helton .75 .23
30 Mark McGwire 3.00 .90
31 Jose Cruz Jr. .50 .15
32 Albert Belle .50 .15
33 Andruw Jones .50 .15
34 Nomar Garciaparra 2.00 .60
35 Andy Pettitte .75 .23
36 Alex Rodriguez 2.00 .60

1998 Topps SuperChrome Refractors

Randomly inserted in packs at a rate of one in 12, this 36-card set is a parallel to the Topps SuperChrome base set.

Nm-Mt Ex-Mt
*STARS: 5X TO 12X BASIC CARDS ....

1999 Topps SuperChrome

This 36-card set was distributed in three-card packs with a suggested retail price of $4.99. The fronts feature color action player photos printed on large cards that measure approximately 4 1/8" by 5 3/4". The backs carry player information.

Nm-Mt Ex-Mt
COMPLETE SET (36) 80.00 24.00
1 Roger Clemens 4.00 1.20
2 Andres Galarraga .75 .23
3 Manny Ramirez .75 .23
4 Greg Maddux 3.00 .90
5 Kerry Wood 2.00 .60
6 Travis Lee .75 .23
7 Nolan Ryan 8.00 2.40
8 Juan Gonzalez 2.00 .60
9 Vladimir Guerrero 2.00 .60
10 Sammy Sosa 3.00 .90
11 Mark McGwire 5.00 1.50
12 Javy Lopez .75 .23
13 Tony Gwynn 2.50 .75
14 Derek Jeter 5.00 1.50
15 Albert Belle .75 .23
16 Pedro Martinez 2.00 .60
17 Greg Vaughn .75 .23
18 Ken Griffey Jr. 3.00 .90
19 Ben Grieve .75 .23
20 Vinny Castilla .75 .23
21 Moises Alou .75 .23
22 Barry Bonds 5.00 1.50
23 Nomar Garciaparra 3.00 .90
24 Chipper Jones 2.00 .60
25 Mike Piazza 3.00 .90
26 Alex Rodriguez 3.00 .90
27 Ivan Rodriguez 2.00 .60
28 Frank Thomas 2.00 .60
29 Larry Walker 1.25 .35
30 Troy Glaus 1.25 .35
31 David Wells HL .75 .23
32 Roger Clemens HL 2.00 .60
33 Kerry Wood HL 1.25 .35
34 Mark McGwire HR 70 25.00 7.50
35 Sammy Sosa HR 66 10.00 3.00
36 Scott Brosius WS .75 .23

1999 Topps SuperChrome Refractors

Randomly inserted in packs at the rate of one in 12, this 36-card set is a refractive parallel version of the base set.

Nm-Mt Ex-Mt
*STARS: 2X TO 5X BASIC CARDS ......

2002 Topps Super Teams

This 147 card set was released in January, 2002. This set feature players from memorable world championship teams of the past. For each team featured, the first card honored the manager of that team while the last card had an art drawing of several of that team's stars.

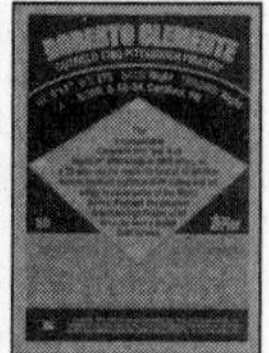

These cards were issued in seven card packs with an SRP of $4 per pack. These cards were issued 20 packs to a box and 10 boxes to a case. A "gold" super pack was included in each box. These packs featured cards from the same team.

Nm-Mt Ex-Mt
COMPLETE SET (146) 50.00 15.00
1 Leo Durocher MG 1.00 .30
2 Whitey Lockman .60 .18
3 Alvin Dark .60 .18
4 Monte Irvin .60 .18
5 Willie Mays 3.00 .90
6 Wes Westrum .40 .12
7 Johnny Antonelli .40 .12
8 Sal Maglie .60 .18
9 Dusty Rhodes .40 .12
10 Davey Williams .40 .12
11 Hoyt Wilhelm .60 .18
12 Don Mueller .40 .12
13 Dusty Rhodes .40 .12
14 Willie Mays 1.00 .30
Monte Irvin
Dusty Rhodes
15 Walt Alston MG .60 .18
16 Gil Hodges 1.50 .45
17 Jim Gilliam .60 .18
18 Pee Wee Reese 1.50 .45
19 Jackie Robinson 2.00 .60
20 Duke Snider 1.00 .30
21 Carl Furillo .60 .18
22 Roy Campanella 1.50 .45
23 Don Newcombe .60 .18
24 Don Hoak .40 .12
25 Johnny Podres .60 .18
26 Clem Labine .60 .18
27 Johnny Podres .60 .18
28 Pee Wee Reese 1.00 .30
Jackie Robinson
Duke Snider
29 Fred Haney MG .40 .12
30 Joe Adcock .60 .18
31 Frank Torre .40 .12
32 Red Schoendienst .60 .18
33 Johnny Logan .60 .18
34 Eddie Mathews 1.50 .45
35 Hank Aaron 3.00 .90
36 Andy Pafko .60 .18
37 Wes Covington .40 .12
38 Lew Burdette .60 .18
39 Warren Spahn 1.00 .30
40 Del Crandall .40 .12
41 Lew Burdette .60 .18
42 Warren Spahn 1.50 .45
Eddie Mathews
Hank Aaron
43 Danny Murtaugh MG .40 .12
44 Dick Stuart .40 .12
45 Bill Mazeroski 1.00 .30
46 Dick Groat .60 .18
47 Don Hoak .40 .12
48 Gino Cimoli .40 .12
49 Bill Virdon .40 .12
50 Roberto Clemente 4.00 1.20
51 Smoky Burgess .60 .18
52 Bob Friend .40 .12
53 Vernon Law .60 .18
54 Roy Face .60 .18
55 Harvey Haddix .40 .12
56 Bill Mazeroski 1.00 .30
57 Roberto Clemente 2.00 .60
Bill Mazeroski
Dick Groat
58 Ralph Houk MG .60 .18
59 Moose Skowron .60 .18
60 Bobby Richardson .60 .18
61 Tony Kubek 1.00 .30
62 Clete Boyer .40 .12
63 Yogi Berra 1.50 .45
64 Bob Cerv .40 .12
65 Roger Maris 2.50 .75
66 Elston Howard 1.00 .30
67 Whitey Ford 1.00 .30
68 Ralph Terry .40 .12
69 Johnny Blanchard .40 .12
70 Whitey Ford 1.00 .30
71 Yogi Berra 1.50 .45
Roger Maris
Elston Howard
Moose Skowron
72 Red Schoendienst MG .60 .18
73 Orlando Cepeda .60 .18
74 Julian Javier .40 .12
75 Dal Maxvill .40 .12
76 Mike Shannon .60 .18
77 Lou Brock 1.00 .30
78 Roger Maris 2.50 .75
79 Curt Flood .60 .18
80 Tim McCarver .60 .18
81 Steve Carlton .60 .18
82 Bob Gibson 1.00 .30
83 Nelson Briles .40 .12
84 Bobby Tolan .40 .12
85 Bob Gibson 1.00 .30
86 Bob Gibson .60 .18
Steve Carlton
Orlando Cepeda
Lou Brock
87 Gil Hodges MG 1.50 .45
88 Ed Kranepool .40 .12
89 Buddy Harrelson .40 .12
90 Wayne Garrett .40 .12
91 Cleon Jones .40 .12
92 Tommie Agee .60 .18
93 Ron Swoboda .60 .18
94 Al Weis .40 .12
95 Jerry Grote .40 .12

96 Tom Seaver............................ 1.00 .30
97 Jerry Koosman........................ .60 .18
98 Tug McGraw............................ .60 .18
99 Nolan Ryan............................ 4.00 1.20
100 Donn Clendenon..................... .40 .12
101 Tom Seaver.......................... 1.50 .45
Jerry Koosman
Tug McGraw
Nolan Ryan
102 Earl Weaver MG..................... .60 .18
103 Boog Powell......................... 1.00 .30
104 Davey Johnson...................... .60 .18
105 Mark Belanger...................... .40 .12
106 Brooks Robinson.................. 1.50 .45
107 Don Buford.......................... .40 .12
108 Paul Blair............................. .40 .12
109 Frank Robinson..................... 1.00 .30
110 Dick Hall.............................. .40 .12
111 Jim Palmer........................... .60 .18
112 Mike Cuellar......................... .60 .18
113 Dave McNally........................ .60 .18
114 Andy Etchebarren.................. .40 .12
115 Brooks Robinson.................. 1.50 .45
116 Dick Hall.............................. .60 .18
Jim Palmer
Mike Cuellar
Dave McNally
117 Alvin Dark MG...................... .60 .18
118 Gene Tenace......................... .60 .18
119 Dick Green........................... .40 .12
120 Bert Campaneris.................... .60 .18
121 Sal Bando............................. .60 .18
122 Reggie Jackson.................... 1.00 .30
123 Joe Rudi............................... .60 .18
124 Claudell Washington............. .40 .12
125 Ray Fosse............................. .40 .12
126 Vida Blue.............................. .60 .18
127 Rollie Fingers....................... .60 .18
128 Catfish Hunter...................... 1.00 .30
129 Ken Holtzman....................... .60 .18
130 Rollie Fingers....................... .60 .18
131 Catfish Hunter...................... 1.00 .30
Sal Bando
Reggie Jackson
Rollie Fingers
132 Davey Johnson MG................ .60 .18
133 Keith Hernandez................... 1.00 .30
134 Wally Backman...................... .40 .12
135 Rafael Santana...................... .40 .12
136 Ray Knight............................ .60 .18
137 Len Dykstra.......................... .60 .18
138 Darryl Strawberry................. 1.00 .30
139 Kevin Mitchell....................... .40 .12
140 Dwight Gooden..................... 1.00 .30
141 Bob Ojeda............................. .40 .12
142 Sid Fernandez....................... .60 .18
143 Ron Darling........................... .60 .18
144 Gary Carter........................... 1.00 .30
145 Ray Knight............................. .60 .18
146 Darryl Strawberry................. 1.00 .30
Dwight Gooden
Keith Hernandez
NNO Repurchased Vintage EXCH........

2002 Topps Super Teams Retrofractors

Issued one per pack, these cards parallel the Topps Super Team set. Each card is serial numbered to the year in which the team won the World Series.

Nm-Mt Ex-Mt
*RETROFRACTORS: 1.5X TO 4X BASIC
1-14 GIANTS SERIAL #'d TO 1954.....
CARDS 15-30 DODGERS SERIAL #'d to 1955
CARDS 29-45 BRAVES SERIAL #'d to 1957
CARDS 43-60 PIRATES SERIAL #'d to 1960
CARDS 58-75 YANKEES SERIAL #'d to 1961
72-86 CARDINALS SERIAL #'d TO 1967
87-101 METS SERIAL #'d TO 1969.....
102-116 ORIOLES SERIAL #'d TO 1970
117-131 A'S SERIAL #'d TO 1974.....
131-146 METS SERIAL #'d TO 1986...

2002 Topps Super Teams A View To A Thrill Relics

Inserted into packs at overall stated odds of one in 30, these 18 cards feature a player along with a seat relice from that player's home stadium. These cards were inserted into packs in two different ratios and we have notated that in our checklist.

Nm-Mt Ex-Mt
GROUP 1 STATED ODDS 1:124..........
GROUP 2 STATED ODDS 1:39............
VT-BG Bob Gibson 2.................. 15.00 4.50
VT-BM Bill Mazeroski 1.............. 15.00 4.50
VT-BP Boog Powell 2.................. 15.00 4.50
VT-BR Brooks Robinson 2.......... 20.00 6.00
VT-DS Duke Snider 1................. 15.00 4.50
VT-EM Eddie Mathews 2............ 20.00 6.00
VT-FR Frank Robinson 2............ 15.00 4.50
VT-HA Hank Aaron 2................. 30.00 9.00
VT-JP Jim Palmer 2.................. 15.00 4.50
VT-LB Lew Burdette 2.............. 15.00 4.50
VT-RC Roberto Clemente 1........ 60.00 18.00
VT-RS Red Schoendienst 2........ 15.00 4.50
VT-RMB R.Maris Cardinals 2..... 25.00 7.50
VT-RMY R.Maris Yankees 1....... 50.00 15.00
VT-WF Whitey Ford 1................ 15.00 4.50
VT-WM Willie Mays 1................ 40.00 12.00
VT-WS Warren Spahn 2............. 15.00 4.50
VT-YB Yogi Berra 1.................. 20.00 6.00

2002 Topps Super Teams A View To A Thrill Relics Autographs

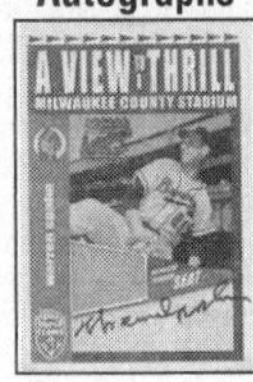

Inserted into packs at stated odds of one in 735, these five cards parallel the A View to a Thrill Relic insert set. These cards are autographed by the player and we have notated the stated print runs next to the player's name. Note that the amount of cards each player signed is related to the year that the player was on a World Series champion.

Nm-Mt Ex-Mt
VT-BGA Bob Gibson/67............ 80.00 24.00
VT-DSA Duke Snider/55.......... 100.00 30.00
VT-WFA Whitey Ford/61.......... 100.00 30.00
VT-WMA Willie Mays/54.......... 150.00 45.00
VT-WSA Warren Spahn/57........ 80.00 24.00

2002 Topps Super Teams Autographs

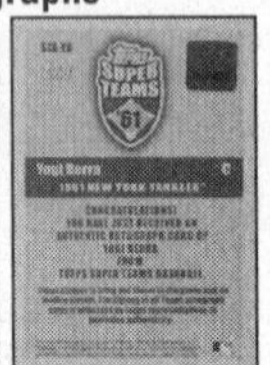

Inserted into packs at stated odds of one in 19, these 18 cards feature authentic autographs of some of the players in the Super Teams set. Please note that each player is assigned a group depending on how many autographs they signed and we have noted which group they belong to next to their name in our checklist.

Nm-Mt Ex-Mt
GROUP A STATED ODDS 1:28...........
GROUP B STATED ODDS 1:75...........
GROUP C STATED ODDS 1:441.........
GROUP D STATED ODDS 1:1441.......
GROUP E STATED ODDS 1:432.........
STA-AP Andy Pafko A............... 15.00 4.50
STA-BR Bobby Richardson B...... 25.00 7.50
STA-CB Clete Boyer B.............. 20.00 6.00
STA-HW Hoyt Wilhelm A........... 15.00 4.50
STA-JP Jim Palmer C............... 25.00 7.50
STA-MI Monte Irvin B.............. 25.00 7.50
STA-MS Moose Skowron B........ 25.00 7.50
STA-NR Nolan Ryan E............. 150.00 45.00
STA-RJ Reggie Jackson E......... 80.00 24.00
STA-SC Steve Carlton C........... 30.00 9.00
STA-TK Tony Kubek D............. 50.00 15.00
STA-TM Tug McGraw A............ 25.00 7.50
STA-TS Tom Seaver E.............. 50.00 15.00
STA-VB Vida Blue A................ 15.00 4.50
STA-WS Warren Spahn B.......... 30.00 9.00
STA-YB Yogi Berra E.............. 80.00 24.00
STA-BRO Brooks Robinson B.... 30.00 9.00
STA-JPO Johnny Podres A........ 15.00 4.50

2002 Topps Super Teams AutoProofs

Randomly inserted into packs, these seven cards feature authentic signed original signed cards of some of the players in the Super Teams set. Players in group one signed at stated odds of one in 2162 and players in group two signed at stated odds of one in 5404. Please note that the print runs for all signed cards is next to the player's name in our checklist.

Nm-Mt Ex-Mt
BG67 Bob Gibson 67 TC/10 G2..........
BG68 Bob Gibson 68 WS/10 G2..........
BR70 Brooks Robinson 70/25 G1.........
BR71 Brooks Robinson 71 TC/10 G2..
KH86 Keith Hernandez 86/25 G1........
LB68 Lou Brock 68 WS/10 G2...........
RJ74 Reggie Jackson 74/25 G1.........

2002 Topps Super Teams Classic Combos Relics

Inserted into packs at stated odds one in 865, these five cards feature two teammates along with a relic related to each player.

Nm-Mt Ex-Mt
CC-AJ Tommy Agee.................. 50.00 15.00
Cleon Jones
CC-JR Reggie Jackson............. 50.00 15.00
Joe Rudi
CC-RR Frank Robinson............. 50.00 15.00
Brooks Robinson
CC-SK Tom Seaver.................. 50.00 15.00
Jerry Koosman
CC-SRBK Moose Skowron....... 100.00 30.00
Bobby Richardson
Clete Boyer
Tony Kubek

2002 Topps Super Teams Relics

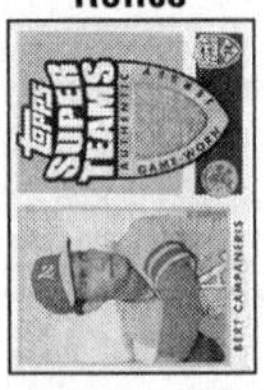

Inserted into packs at overall rates of one in 46, these 48 cards feature a memorabilia relic of the featured player. Each player either has a bat sliver or a jersey swatch in addition to their picture

Nm-Mt Ex-Mt
BAT GROUP 1 ODDS 1:393..................
BAT GROUP 2 ODDS 1:103..................
BAT GROUP 3 ODDS 1:1081................
BAT OVERALL ODDS 1:76....................
JACKET ODDS 1:721...........................
UNIFORM/JSY GROUP 1 ODDS 1:865
UNIFORM/JSY GROUP 2 ODDS 1:66..
UNIFORM/JSY GROUP 3 ODDS 1:180
UNIFORM/JSY OVERALL ODDS 1:46..
BAT GROUP 1 PRINT RUN 50 SETS...
BAT GROUP 2 PRINT RUN 100 SETS.
BAT GROUP 3 PRINT RUN 200 CARDS
BAT CARDS ARE NOT SERIAL-NUMBERED
BAT PRINT RUNS PROVIDED BY TOPPS
STR-AP Andy Pafko Bat 2......... 15.00 4.50
STR-BC Bert Campaneris Jsy 2. 15.00 4.50
STR-BF Bob Friend Jsy 3......... 10.00 3.00
STR-BR B.Richardson Bat 1...... 30.00 9.00
STR-CB Clete Boyer Bat 1........ 25.00 7.50
STR-CJ Cleon Jones Bat 1........ 25.00 7.50
STR-CW C.Washington Bat 2.... 10.00 3.00
STR-DC Del Crandall Bat 2....... 15.00 4.50
STR-DG Dwight Gooden Jsy 2.. 25.00 7.50
STR-DH Don Hoak Bat 2........... 10.00 3.00
STR-DJ Davey Johnson Bat 2... 15.00 4.50
STR-DM Dave McNally Jsy 2..... 15.00 4.50
STR-DS Darryl Strawberry Bat 2 25.00 7.50
STR-EK Ed Kranepool Jsy 3...... 15.00 4.50
STR-FR Frank Robinson Bat 1... 30.00 9.00
STR-GC Gary Carter Jsy 2........ 25.00 7.50
STR-JA Joe Adcock Bat............ 15.00 4.50
STR-JK Jerry Koosman Jsy 1.... 15.00 4.50
STR-JR Joe Rudi Bat 1............. 25.00 7.50
STR-KM Kevin Mitchell Bat 2.... 15.00 4.50
STR-LB Lew Burdette Jsy 2...... 15.00 4.50
STR-LD Len Dykstra Bat 2........ 15.00 4.50
STR-MB Mark Belanger Bat 2.... 15.00 4.50
STR-MC Mike Cuellar Jsy 2...... 15.00 4.50
STR-MS Moose Skowron Bat 1. 30.00 9.00
STR-NR Nolan Ryan Bat 2....... 100.00 30.00
STR-OC Orlando Cepeda Bat 2.. 15.00 4.50
STR-PB Paul Blair Bat 2........... 10.00 3.00
STR-RD Ron Darling Jsy 2....... 15.00 4.50
STR-RF Ray Fosse Bat 2.......... 15.00 4.50
STR-RH Ralph Houk Uni 2........ 15.00 4.50
STR-RJ Reggie Jackson Bat 1... 30.00 9.00
STR-RK Ray Knight Bat 2......... 15.00 4.50
STR-RS Red Schoendienst Bat 2 15.00 4.50
STR-SB Smoky Burgess Bat 2.. 15.00 4.50
STR-TA Tommie Agee Bat 1...... 25.00 7.50
STR-TK Tony Kubek Bat 1........ 30.00 9.00
STR-TM Tug McGraw Jsy 2...... 15.00 4.50
STR-TS Tom Seaver Bat 1........ 20.00 6.00
STR-WG Wayne Garrett Bat 2... 10.00 3.00
STR-BCE Bob Cerv Bat 2.......... 15.00 4.50
STR-BRO B.Robinson Bat 1...... 40.00 12.00
STR-EKU Ed Kranepool Uni 2.... 15.00 4.50
STR-GCB Gary Carter Bat 2...... 20.00 6.00
STR-GCI Gino Cimoli Bat 2....... 15.00 4.50
STR-GCJ Gary Carter Jacket..... 25.00 7.50
STR-SBB Sal Bando Bat 3......... 15.00 4.50
STR-SBJ Sal Bando Jsy 2........ 15.00 4.50

2002 Topps Super Teams Teammates

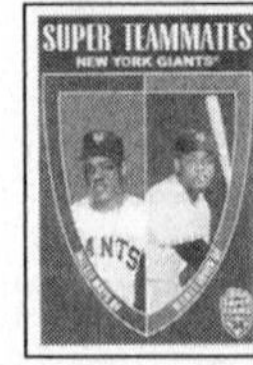

Inserted into packs at a stated rate of one in 10, these five cards honor teammates from five of the teams in this set.

Nm-Mt Ex-Mt
ST-BG Lou Brock....................... 4.00 1.20
Bob Gibson
ST-FB Whitey Ford.................... 4.00 1.20
Yogi Berra
ST-MI Willie Mays...................... 4.00 1.20
Monte Irvin
ST-RR Brooks Robinson............ 4.00 1.20
Frank Robinson
ST-SRBK Moose Skowron.......... 4.00 1.20
Bobby Richardson
Clete Boyer
Tony Kubek

2002 Topps Super Teams Teammates Autographs

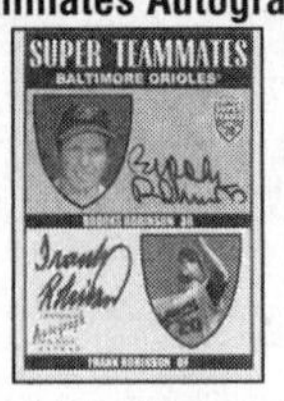

This set parallels the Teammates insert set. These five cards were inserted into packs at stated odds of one in 865 and are serial numbered to 50. The cards featuring Lou Brock and Bob Gibson were not returned in time for inclusion into packs and they could be redeemed until January 1, 2004.

Nm-Mt Ex-Mt
BGA Lou Brock......................... 120.00 36.00
Bob Gibson
FBA Whitey Ford...................... 200.00 60.00
Yogi Berra
MIA Willie Mays....................... 200.00 60.00
Monte Irvin
RRA Brooks Robinson............. 150.00 45.00
Frank Robinson
SRBKA Moose Skowron.......... 250.00 75.00
Bobby Richardson
Clete Boyer
Tony Kubek

2002 Topps Ten

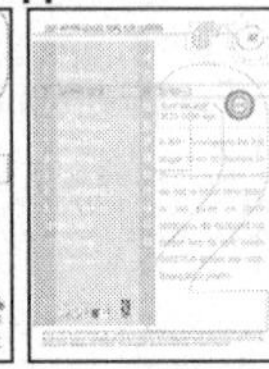

This 200 card set was issued in March, 2002. These cards were issued in seven card packs issued 24 packs to a box and 12 boxes per case with a SRP of $1.95 per pack. There were 10 cards selected by Topps in 19 different categories as well 10 prospect cards to finish the set.

Nm-Mt Ex-Mt
COMPLETE SET (200)............... 80.00 24.00
COMMON CARD (1-190)................ .30 .09
COMMON CARD (191-200).......... 1.00 .30
1 Ichiro Suzuki HITS.................. 1.25 .35
2 Rich Aurilia HITS...................... .30 .09
3 Bret Boone HITS....................... .30 .09
4 Juan Pierre HITS...................... .30 .09
5 Shannon Stewart HITS.............. .30 .09
6 Alex Rodriguez HITS................ 1.25 .35
7 Luis Gonzalez HITS.................. .30 .09
8 Todd Helton HITS..................... .50 .15
9 Garret Anderson HITS.............. .30 .09
10 Albert Pujols HITS................. 1.50 .45
11 Lance Berkman 2B.................. .30 .09
12 Todd Helton 2B....................... .50 .15
13 Jeff Kent 2B............................ .30 .09
14 Bob Abreu 2B.......................... .30 .09
15 Jason Giambi 2B...................... .75 .23
16 Albert Pujols 2B..................... 1.50 .45
17 Mike Sweeney 2B..................... .30 .09
18 Vladimir Guerrero 2B............... .75 .23
19 Cliff Floyd 2B.......................... .30 .09
20 Shannon Stewart 2B................. .30 .09
21 Cristian Guzman 3B................. .30 .09
22 Roberto Alomar 3B.................. .75 .23
23 Carlos Beltran 3B.................... .30 .09
24 Jimmy Rollins 3B..................... .30 .09
25 Roger Cedeno 3B..................... .30 .09
26 Juan Pierre 3B......................... .30 .09
27 Juan Uribe 3B.......................... .30 .09
28 Luis Castillo 3B....................... .30 .09
29 Ray Durham 3B........................ .30 .09
30 Mark McLemore 3B.................. .30 .09
31 Barry Bonds HR..................... 2.00 .60
32 Sammy Sosa HR.................... 1.25 .35
33 Luis Gonzalez HR.................... .30 .09
34 Alex Rodriguez HR................. 1.25 .35
35 Shawn Green HR...................... .30 .09
36 Todd Helton HR........................ .50 .15
37 Jim Thome HR.......................... .75 .23
38 Rafael Palmeiro HR.................. .50 .15
39 Richie Sexson HR..................... .30 .09
40 Phil Nevin HR........................... .30 .09
41 Troy Glaus HR.......................... .50 .15
42 Sammy Sosa RBI................... 1.25 .35
43 Todd Helton RBI....................... .50 .15
44 Luis Gonzalez RBI.................... .30 .09
45 Bret Boone RBI........................ .30 .09
46 Juan Gonzalez RBI................... .75 .23
47 Barry Bonds RBI.................... 2.00 .60
48 Alex Rodriguez RBI............... 1.25 .35
49 Jeff Bagwell RBI...................... .50 .15
50 Albert Pujols RBI................... 1.50 .45
51 Phil Nevin RBI.......................... .30 .09
52 Ichiro Suzuki AVG.................. 1.25 .35
53 Larry Walker AVG.................... .50 .15
54 Jason Giambi AVG.................... .75 .23
55 Roberto Alomar AVG................ .75 .23
56 Todd Helton AVG...................... .50 .15
57 Moises Alou AVG...................... .30 .09
58 Lance Berkman AVG................. .30 .09
59 Bret Boone AVG....................... .30 .09
60 Frank Catalanotto AVG............. .30 .09
61 Chipper Jones AVG.................. .75 .23
62 Barry Bonds SLG................... 2.00 .60
63 Sammy Sosa SLG................... 1.25 .35
64 Luis Gonzalez SLG................... .30 .09
65 Todd Helton SLG...................... .50 .15
66 Larry Walker SLG..................... .50 .15
67 Jason Giambi SLG.................... .75 .23
68 Jim Thome SLG........................ .75 .23
69 Alex Rodriguez SLG............... 1.25 .35
70 Lance Berkman SLG................. .30 .09
71 Albert Pujols SLG.................. 1.50 .45
72 Ichiro Suzuki SB.................... 1.25 .35
73 Roger Cedeno SB..................... .30 .09
74 Juan Pierre SB......................... .30 .09
75 Jimmy Rollins SB...................... .30 .09
76 Alfonso Soriano SB.................. .50 .15
77 Mark McLemore SB.................. .30 .09
78 Chuck Knoblauch SB................ .30 .09
79 Vladimir Guerrero SB............... .75 .23
80 Bob Abreu SB.......................... .30 .09
81 Mike Cameron SB..................... .30 .09
82 Sammy Sosa RUNS................ 1.25 .35
83 Alex Rodriguez RUNS............. 1.25 .35
84 Todd Helton RUNS.................... .50 .15
85 Barry Bonds RUNS................. 2.00 .60
86 Luis Gonzalez RUNS................. .30 .09
87 Ichiro Suzuki RUNS................ 1.25 .35
88 Jeff Bagwell RUNS................... .50 .15
89 Cliff Floyd RUNS...................... .30 .09
90 Shawn Green RUNS.................. .30 .09
91 Craig Biggio RUNS.................... .50 .15
92 Juan Pierre K/AB...................... .30 .09
93 Fernando Vina K/AB................. .30 .09
94 Paul LoDuca K/AB.................... .30 .09
95 Mark Grace K/AB..................... .50 .15
96 Eric Young K/AB....................... .30 .09
97 Placido Polanco K/AB............... .30 .09
98 Jason Kendall K/AB.................. .30 .09
99 Ichiro Suzuki K/AB................. 1.25 .35
100 Orlando Cabrera K/AB............ .30 .09
101 Rey Sanchez K/AB................. .30 .09
102 Ichiro Suzuki AS VOTE......... 1.25 .35
103 Edgar Martinez AS VOTE........ .50 .15
104 Bret Boone AS VOTE.............. .30 .09
105 Barry Bonds AS VOTE.......... 2.00 .60
106 Ivan Rodriguez AS VOTE......... .75 .23
107 Mike Piazza AS VOTE........... 1.25 .35
108 Sammy Sosa AS VOTE.......... 1.25 .35
109 John Olerud AS VOTE............ .30 .09
110 Roberto Alomar AS VOTE........ .75 .23
111 Roberto Alomar AS APP......... .75 .23
112 Mark McGwire AS APP.......... 2.00 .60
113 Barry Larkin AS APP.............. .75 .23
114 Ken Griffey Jr. AS APP......... 1.25 .35
115 Rickey Henderson AS APP...... .75 .23
116 Barry Bonds AS APP............. 2.00 .60
117 Ivan Rodriguez AS APP........... .75 .23
118 Mike Piazza AS APP.............. 1.25 .35
119 Roger Clemens AS APP......... 1.50 .45
120 Randy Johnson AS APP........... .75 .23
121 Albert Pujols ROY................ 1.50 .45
122 Ichiro Suzuki ROY................ 1.25 .35
123 Roy Oswalt ROY..................... .30 .09
124 C.C. Sabathia ROY.................. .30 .09
125 Jimmy Rollins ROY.................. .30 .09
126 Alfonso Soriano ROY............... .50 .15
127 David Eckstein ROY................. .30 .09
128 Adam Dunn ROY...................... .30 .09
129 Bud Smith ROY....................... .30 .09
130 Tsuyoshi Shinjo ROY.............. .30 .09
131 Matt Morris WINS................... .30 .09
132 Curt Schilling WINS................ .50 .15
133 Randy Johnson WINS.............. .75 .23
134 Mark Mulder WINS................. .30 .09
135 Roger Clemens WINS........... 1.50 .45
136 Jon Lieber WINS..................... .30 .09
137 Jamie Moyer WINS.................. .30 .09
138 Freddy Garcia WINS................ .30 .09
139 Tim Hudson WINS................... .30 .09
140 C.C. Sabathia WINS................ .30 .09
141 Randy Johnson ERA................ .75 .23
142 Curt Schilling ERA.................. .50 .15
143 John Burkett ERA................... .30 .09
144 Freddy Garcia ERA.................. .30 .09
145 Greg Maddux ERA................ 1.25 .35
146 Darryl Kile ERA...................... .30 .09
147 Mike Mussina ERA.................. .75 .23
148 Joe Mays ERA........................ .30 .09
149 Matt Morris ERA..................... .30 .09
150 Russ Ortiz ERA...................... .30 .09
151 Randy Johnson K.................... .75 .23
152 Curt Schilling K...................... .50 .15
153 Hideo Nomo K........................ .75 .23
154 Chan Ho Park K...................... .30 .09
155 Kerry Wood K......................... .75 .23
156 Mike Mussina K...................... .75 .23
157 Roger Clemens K.................. 1.50 .45
158 Javier Vazquez K.................... .30 .09
159 Barry Zito K........................... .50 .15
160 Bartolo Colon K...................... .30 .09
161 Mariano Rivera SV.................. .50 .15
162 Robb Nen SV.......................... .30 .09
163 Kazuhiro Sasaki SV................. .30 .09
164 Armando Benitez SV............... .30 .09
165 Trevor Hoffman SV................. .30 .09
166 Jeff Shaw SV......................... .30 .09
167 Keith Foulke SV...................... .30 .09
168 Jose Mesa SV........................ .30 .09
169 Troy Percival SV.................... .30 .09
170 Billy Wagner SV..................... .30 .09
171 Pat Burrell AST...................... .30 .09
172 Raul Mondesi AST.................. .30 .09
173 Gary Sheffield AST................. .30 .09
174 Carlos Beltran AST................. .30 .09
175 Vladimir Guerrero AST............. .75 .23
176 Torii Hunter AST.................... .30 .09
177 Jeromy Burnitz AST................ .30 .09
178 Tim Salmon AST..................... .50 .15
179 Jim Edmonds AST.................. .30 .09
180 Tsuyoshi Shinjo AST.............. .30 .09
181 Greg Maddux GLV................ 1.25 .35
182 Roberto Alomar GLV............... .75 .23
183 Ken Griffey Jr. GLV.............. 1.25 .35
184 Ivan Rodriguez GLV................ .75 .23
185 Omar Vizquel GLV.................. .30 .09
186 Barry Bonds GLV.................. 2.00 .60
187 Devon White GLV.................... .30 .09
188 J.T. Snow GLV........................ .30 .09
189 Larry Walker GLV.................... .50 .15
190 Robin Ventura GLV.................. .30 .09
191 Mark Phillips PROS RC.......... 4.00 1.20
192 Clint Nageotte PROS RC....... 2.50 .75
193 Mauricio Lara PROS RC........ 1.00 .30
194 Nic Jackson PROS RC........... 1.00 .30
195 Chris Tritle PROS RC............ 1.00 .30

Card	Nm-Mt	Ex-Mt
196 Ryan Gripp PROS RC	1.00	.30
197 Greg Montalbano PROS RC	1.50	.45
198 Noochie Varner PROS RC	1.00	.30
199 Nick Alvarez PROS RC	1.00	.30
200 Craig Kuzmic PROS RC	1.00	.30

2002 Topps Ten Die Cuts

Inserted at stated odds at one in four, this is a parallel to the 2002 Topps Ten set. The difference with these cards and the regular cards is that these cards are die cut.

Nm-Mt Ex-Mt
*DIE CUTS 1-190: 2X TO 5X BASIC ....
*DIE CUTS 191-200: 2X TO 5X BASIC

2002 Topps Ten Autographs

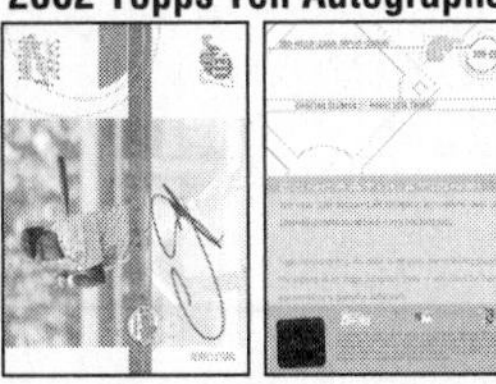

Inserted at overall odds of one in 67, these 10 cards feature signed cards from players featured in the Topps Ten set. As the autographs were inserted in differing odds based on what group the player belonged to, we have notated that group next to the player's name in our checklist.

Card	Nm-Mt	Ex-Mt
GROUP A STATED ODDS 1:1928		
GROUP B STATED ODDS 1:123		
GROUP C STATED ODDS 1:539		
GROUP D STATED ODDS 1:617		
TTA-BB Barry Bonds B	175.00	52.50
TTA-BZ Barry Zito B	25.00	7.50
TTA-CF Cliff Floyd D	15.00	4.50
TTA-CG Cristian Guzman C	15.00	4.50
TTA-JE Jim Edmonds B	20.00	6.00
TTA-JR Jimmy Rollins B	20.00	6.00
TTA-LG Luis Gonzalez B	20.00	6.00
TTA-RC Roger Clemens A	100.00	30.00
TTA-RO Roy Oswalt B	20.00	6.00
TTA-BBO Bret Boone B	20.00	6.00

2002 Topps Ten Relics

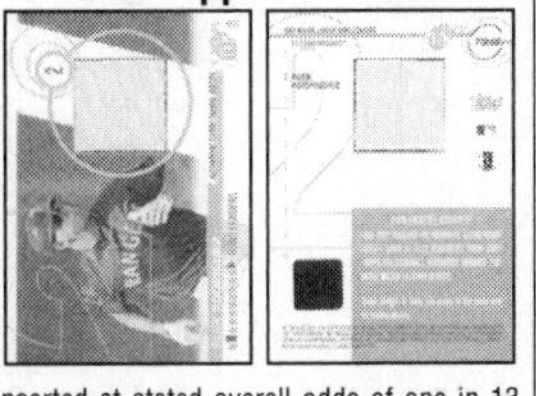

Inserted at stated overall odds of one in 13, these 65 cards feature either game-used bat or game-worn jersey from players featured in the Topps Ten set. As both the jersey and bat cards were inserted at differing rates, we have notated those groups these cards belong to in our checklist.

Card	Nm-Mt	Ex-Mt
BAT GROUP A 1:108		
BAT GROUP B 1:108		
BAT GROUP C 1:80		
BAT GROUP D 1:539		
BAT GROUP E 1:216		
UNIFORM GROUP A 1:34		
UNIFORM GROUP B 1:120		
TTR-AB Armando Benitez Jsy A	10.00	3.00
TTR-AP Albert Pujols Bat A	25.00	7.50
TTR-AR Alex Rodriguez Jsy A	15.00	4.50
TTR-AS Alfonso Soriano Bat B	15.00	4.50
TTR-BA Bob Abreu Bat A	15.00	4.50
TTR-BB Bret Boone Bat E	15.00	4.50
TTR-BC Bartolo Colon Jsy A	10.00	3.00
TTR-BW Billy Wagner Jsy B	10.00	3.00
TTR-BZ Barry Zito Jsy B	15.00	4.50
TTR-CB Craig Biggio Jsy A	15.00	4.50
TTR-CF Cliff Floyd Bat C	10.00	3.00
TTR-CG Cristian Guzman Bat A	15.00	4.50
TTR-CJ Chipper Jones Bat B	15.00	4.50
TTR-CK Chuck Knoblauch Bat B	10.00	3.00
TTR-CP Chan Ho Park Jsy A	10.00	3.00
TTR-CS Curt Schilling Jsy A	15.00	4.50
TTR-DW Devon White Bat A	15.00	4.50
TTR-EM Edgar Martinez Jsy A	15.00	4.50
TTR-FG Freddy Garcia Jsy A	10.00	3.00
TTR-FV Fernando Vina Bat A	15.00	4.50
TTR-GA Garret Anderson Bat A	15.00	4.50
TTR-GM Greg Maddux Jsy A	20.00	6.00
TTR-GS Gary Sheffield Jsy A	10.00	3.00
TTR-JB John Burkett Jsy A	10.00	3.00
TTR-JE Jim Edmonds Bat B	10.00	3.00
TTR-JG Juan Gonzalez Bat B	15.00	4.50
TTR-JK Jason Kendall Jsy A	10.00	3.00
TTR-JO John Olerud Jsy A	10.00	3.00
TTR-JP Juan Pierre Jsy A	10.00	3.00
TTR-JS J.T. Snow Bat B	10.00	3.00
TTR-JT Jim Thome Bat A	20.00	6.00
TTR-LB Lance Berkman Bat A	20.00	6.00
TTR-LC Luis Castillo Bat A	15.00	4.50
TTR-LG Luis Gonzalez Bat C	15.00	4.50
TTR-LW Larry Walker Bat C	15.00	4.50
TTR-MA Moises Alou Bat C	10.00	3.00
TTR-MC Mike Cameron Bat A	15.00	4.50
TTR-MG Mark Grace Bat A	20.00	6.00
TTR-MM Mark McLemore Bat A	15.00	4.50
TTR-MP Mike Piazza Jsy A	25.00	7.50
TTR-MS Mike Sweeney Bat A	15.00	4.50
TTR-OV Omar Vizquel Bat A	15.00	4.50
TTR-PL Paul LoDuca Bat C	10.00	3.00
TTR-PN Phil Nevin Bat A	15.00	4.50
TTR-PP Placido Polanco Bat A	15.00	4.50
TTR-RA Roberto Alomar Bat C	15.00	4.50
TTR-RC Roger Cedeno Bat B	10.00	3.00
TTR-RD Ray Durham Bat B	10.00	3.00
TTR-RJ Randy Johnson Jsy A	20.00	6.00
TTR-RM Raul Mondesi Bat A	15.00	4.50
TTR-RP Rafael Palmeiro Jsy B	15.00	4.50
TTR-RS Richie Sexson Bat B	10.00	3.00
TTR-RV Robin Ventura Bat A	15.00	4.50
TTR-SG Shawn Green Bat D	15.00	4.50
TTR-SS Shannon Stewart Bat C	10.00	3.00
TTR-TH Todd Helton Bat C	15.00	4.50
TTR-TH Trevor Hoffman Jsy A	10.00	3.00
TTR-TH Torii Hunter Bat A	15.00	4.50
TTR-TS Tim Salmon Bat B	10.00	3.00
TTR-TS Tsuyoshi Shinjo Bat A	15.00	4.50
TTR-BAB Barry Bonds Jsy A	25.00	7.50
TTR-CBE Carlos Beltran Bat C	10.00	3.00
TTR-JBA Jeff Bagwell Jsy A	15.00	4.50
TTR-JBU Jeromy Burnitz Jsy A	10.00	3.00
TTR-JEK Jeff Kent Jsy A	10.00	3.00

1998 Topps Tek Pre-Production

These three cards were distributed to dealers around September, 1998 to preview the upcoming release of 1998 Topps Tek baseball. In truth, 90 different versions of each card were created - all featuring a different background. However, since there's no simple way to catalog the variances in backgrounds, we've listed only the basic checklist. Each card parallels the regular issue Tek format except for the word "pre-production" that runs diagonally across the card number on back.

Card	Nm-Mt	Ex-Mt
COMPLETE SET (3)	8.00	2.40
13 Mark McGwire	5.00	1.50
21 Roger Clemens	3.00	.90
76 Raul Mondesi	.50	.15

1998 Topps Tek

The 1998 Topps Tek set consists of 90 standard size cards. The four-card packs retailed for a suggested price of $5 each. The card fronts present a brand-new way to collect, as each card is marked by not only a player number, but also a pattern number. The backs feature a player head shot along with his expected achievements in the coming years. The set was released in October, 1998. Notable Rookie Cards include Troy Glaus.

Card	Nm-Mt	Ex-Mt
COMPLETE SET (90)	100.00	30.00
1 Ben Grieve	1.00	.30
2 Kerry Wood	2.50	.75
3 Barry Bonds	6.00	1.80
4 John Olerud	1.00	.30
5 Ivan Rodriguez	2.50	.75
6 Frank Thomas	2.50	.75
7 Bernie Williams	1.50	.45
8 Dante Bichette	1.00	.30
9 Alex Rodriguez	4.00	1.20
10 Tom Glavine	1.50	.45
11 Eric Karros	1.00	.30
12 Craig Biggio	1.50	.45
13 Mark McGwire	6.00	1.80
14 Derek Jeter	6.00	1.80
15 Nomar Garciaparra	4.00	1.20
16 Brady Anderson	1.00	.30
17 Vladimir Guerrero	2.50	.75
18 David Justice	1.00	.30
19 Chipper Jones	2.50	.75
20 Jim Edmonds	1.00	.30
21 Roger Clemens	5.00	1.50
22 Mark Kotsay	1.00	.30
23 Tony Gwynn	3.00	.90
24 Todd Walker	1.00	.30
25 Tino Martinez	1.50	.45
26 Andruw Jones	1.00	.30
27 Sandy Alomar Jr.	1.00	.30
28 Sammy Sosa	4.00	1.20
29 Gary Sheffield	1.00	.30
30 Ken Griffey Jr.	4.00	1.20
31 Aramis Ramirez	1.00	.30
32 Curt Schilling	1.50	.45
33 Robin Ventura	1.00	.30
34 Larry Walker	1.50	.45
35 Darin Erstad	1.00	.30
36 Todd Dunwoody	1.00	.30
37 Paul O'Neill	1.50	.45
38 Vinny Castilla	1.00	.30
39 Randy Johnson	2.50	.75
40 Rafael Palmeiro	1.50	.45
41 Pedro Martinez	2.50	.75
42 Derek Bell	1.00	.30
43 Carlos Delgado	1.00	.30
44 Matt Williams	1.00	.30
45 Kenny Lofton	1.00	.30
46 Edgar Renteria	1.00	.30
47 Albert Belle	1.00	.30
48 Jeromy Burnitz	1.00	.30
49 Adrian Beltre	1.00	.30
50 Greg Maddux	4.00	1.20
51 Cal Ripken	8.00	2.40
52 Jason Kendall	1.00	.30
53 Ellis Burks	1.00	.30
54 Paul Molitor	1.50	.45
55 Moises Alou	1.00	.30
56 Raul Mondesi	1.00	.30
57 Barry Larkin	2.50	.75
58 Tony Clark	1.00	.30
59 Travis Lee	1.00	.30
60 Juan Gonzalez	2.50	.75
61 Troy Glaus RC	5.00	1.50
62 Jose Cruz Jr.	1.00	.30
63 Paul Konerko	1.00	.30
64 Edgar Martinez	1.50	.45
65 Javy Lopez	1.00	.30
66 Manny Ramirez	1.00	.30
67 Roberto Alomar	2.50	.75
68 Ken Caminiti	1.00	.30
69 Todd Helton	1.50	.45
70 Chuck Knoblauch	1.00	.30
71 Kevin Brown	1.50	.45
72 Tim Salmon	1.50	.45
73 Orlando Hernandez RC	1.50	.45
74 Jeff Bagwell	1.50	.45
75 Brian Jordan	1.00	.30
76 Derrek Lee	1.00	.30
77 Brad Fullmer	1.00	.30
78 Mark Grace	1.50	.45
79 Jeff King	1.00	.30
80 Mike Mussina	2.50	.75
81 Jay Buhner	1.00	.30
82 Quinton McCracken	1.00	.30
83 A.J. Hinch	1.00	.30
84 Richard Hidalgo	1.00	.30
85 Andres Galarraga	1.00	.30
86 Mike Piazza	4.00	1.20
87 Mo Vaughn	1.00	.30
88 Scott Rolen	1.50	.45
89 Jim Thome	2.50	.75
90 Ray Lankford	1.00	.30

1998 Topps Tek Diffractors

The 1998 Topps Tek Diffractors set consists of 90 cards and is a parallel to the 1998 Topps Tek Diffractors base set. The cards are randomly inserted in packs at a rate of one in six.

Nm-Mt Ex-Mt
*STARS: 2X TO 5X BASIC CARDS ......
*ROOKIES: 2X TO 5X BASIC CARDS ..

1999 Topps Tek Pre-Production

This three-card standard-size set was issued to promote the second year of Topps Tek. The cards have the same design as the regular Topps Tek cards will have but are differentiated by having a "PP" prefix before the card number.

Card	Nm-Mt	Ex-Mt
COMPLETE SET (3)	5.00	1.50
PP1A Derek Jeter	3.00	.90
PP2A Moises Alou	1.00	.30
PP3A Tony Clark	1.00	.30

1999 Topps Tek

The 1999 Topps Tek set was issued in one series for a total of 90 cards and distributed in four-card packs with a suggested retail price of $5. The set features color photos of 45 different players each with a Version A and a Version B which are differentiated by design and uniform printed on 30 different background patterns. The card backs carry the player's headshot and technical merit achievements. Notable Rookie Cards include Pat Burrell.

Card	Nm-Mt	Ex-Mt
COMPLETE SET (90)	100.00	30.00
1A Ben Grieve	.75	.23
2A Andres Galarraga	.75	.23
3A Travis Lee	.75	.23
4A Larry Walker	1.25	.35
5A Ken Griffey Jr.	3.00	.90
6A Sammy Sosa	3.00	.90
7A Mark McGwire	5.00	1.50
8A Roberto Alomar	2.00	.60
9A Wade Boggs	1.25	.35
10A Troy Glaus	1.25	.35
11A Craig Biggio	1.25	.35
12A Kerry Wood	2.00	.60
13A Vladimir Guerrero	2.00	.60
14A Albert Belle	.75	.23
15A Mike Piazza	3.00	.90
16A Chipper Jones	2.00	.60
17A Randy Johnson	2.00	.60
18A Adrian Beltre	.75	.23
19A Barry Bonds	5.00	1.50
20A Jim Thome	2.00	.60
21A Greg Vaughn	.75	.23
22A Scott Rolen	1.25	.35
23A Ivan Rodriguez	2.00	.60
24A Derek Jeter	5.00	1.50
25A Cal Ripken	6.00	1.80
26A Mark Grace	1.25	.35
27A Bernie Williams	1.25	.35
28A Darin Erstad	.75	.23
29A Eric Chavez	.75	.23
30A Tom Glavine	1.25	.35
31A Jeff Bagwell	1.25	.35
32A Manny Ramirez	.75	.23
33A Tino Martinez	1.25	.35
34A Todd Helton	1.25	.35
35A Jason Kendall	.75	.23
36A Pat Burrell RC	4.00	1.20
37A Tony Gwynn	2.50	.75
38A Nomar Garciaparra	3.00	.90
39A Frank Thomas	2.00	.60
40A Orlando Hernandez	.75	.23
41A Juan Gonzalez	2.00	.60
42A Alex Rodriguez	3.00	.90
43A Greg Maddux	3.00	.90
44A Mo Vaughn	.75	.23
45A Roger Clemens	4.00	1.20

1999 Topps Tek Gold

Randomly inserted in packs at the rate of one in 15, this set is a gold parallel version of the base set and each card is sequentially numbered to 10.

Nm-Mt Ex-Mt
*STARS: 8X TO 20X BASIC CARDS ....
*ROOKIES: 8X TO 20X BASIC CARDS

1999 Topps Tek Fantastek Phenoms

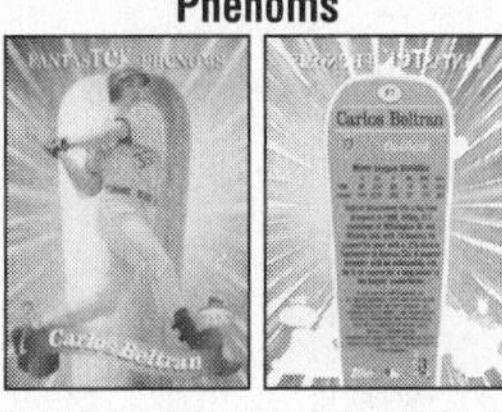

Randomly inserted in packs at the rate of one in 18, this 10-card set features color photos of young prospects printed on transparent plastic card stock.

Card	Nm-Mt	Ex-Mt
COMPLETE SET (10)	30.00	9.00
F1 Eric Chavez	2.50	.75
F2 Troy Glaus	4.00	1.20
F3 Pat Burrell	8.00	2.40
F4 Alex Gonzalez	2.50	.75
F5 Carlos Lee	2.50	.75
F6 Ruben Mateo	2.50	.75
F7 Carlos Beltran	2.50	.75
F8 Adrian Beltre	2.50	.75
F9 Bruce Chen	2.50	.75
F10 Ryan Anderson	2.50	.75

1999 Topps Tek Teknicians

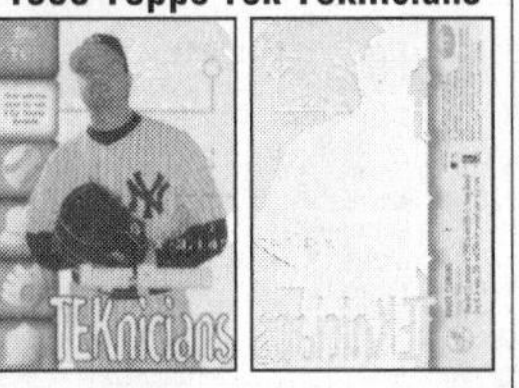

Randomly inserted in packs at the rate of one in 18, this 10-card set features color photos of top stars printed on clear card stock utilizing eye-catching metallic inks.

Card	Nm-Mt	Ex-Mt
COMPLETE SET (10)	80.00	24.00
T1 Ken Griffey Jr.	8.00	2.40
T2 Mark McGwire	12.00	3.60
T3 Kerry Wood	5.00	1.50
T4 Ben Grieve	2.00	.60
T5 Sammy Sosa	8.00	2.40
T6 Derek Jeter	12.00	3.60
T7 Alex Rodriguez	8.00	2.40
T8 Roger Clemens	10.00	3.00
T9 Nomar Garciaparra	8.00	2.40
T10 Vladimir Guerrero	5.00	1.50

2000 Topps Tek

The 2000 Tops Tek product was released in July,2000 as a 45-card base set. The set features 40 player cards (1-40), and five short-printed rookie cards (41-45). Please note that there are 20 variations of the 45-card base set. Variations 16-20 feature an assortment of colors. Each variation of the rookie subset is short-printed to 2000 serial numbered sets. Notable Rookie Cards include Rick Asadoorian.

Card	Nm-Mt	Ex-Mt
COMPLETE SET (45)	50.00	15.00
COMMON CARD (1-40)	.50	.15
COMMON ROOK.(41-45)	.75	.23
1 Mike Piazza	2.00	.60
2 Chipper Jones	1.25	.35
3 Juan Gonzalez	1.25	.35
4 Ivan Rodriguez	1.25	.35
5 Cal Ripken	4.00	1.20
6 A.J. Burnett	.50	.15
7 Jim Thome	1.25	.35
8 Mo Vaughn	.50	.15
9 Andruw Jones	.50	.15
10 Mark McGwire	3.00	.90
11 Jose Canseco	1.25	.35
12 Shawn Green	.50	.15
13 Barry Bonds	3.00	.90
14 Bernie Williams	.75	.23
15 Manny Ramirez	.50	.15
16 Greg Maddux	2.00	.60
17 Carlos Beltran	.50	.15
18 Pedro Martinez	1.25	.35
19 Jeff Bagwell	.75	.23
20 Sammy Sosa	2.00	.60
21 J.D. Drew	.50	.15
22 Randy Johnson	1.25	.35
23 Larry Walker	.75	.23
24 Frank Thomas	1.25	.35
25 Orlando Hernandez	.50	.15
26 Scott Rolen	.75	.23
27 Tony Gwynn	1.50	.45
28 Rick Ankiel	.50	.15
29 Roberto Alomar	1.25	.35
30 Ken Griffey Jr.	2.00	.60
31 Vladimir Guerrero	1.25	.35
32 Derek Jeter	3.00	.90
33 Nomar Garciaparra	2.00	.60
34 Alex Rodriguez	2.00	.60
35 Sean Casey	.50	.15
36 Adam Piatt	.50	.15
37 Corey Patterson	.75	.23
38 Josh Hamilton	.50	.15
39 Pat Burrell	.75	.23
40 Eric Munson	.50	.15
41 Ruben Salazar 1-5 RC	.75	.23
41 Ruben Salazar 6-10 RC	.75	.23
41 R.Salazar 11-15 RC	.75	.23
42 John Sneed 1-5 RC	.75	.23
42 John Sneed 6-10 RC	.75	.23
42 John Sneed 11-15 RC	.75	.23
43 Josh Girdley 1-5	.75	.23
43 Josh Girdley 6-10	.75	.23
43 Josh Girdley 11-15	.75	.23
44 Brett Myers 1-5 RC	3.00	.90
44 Brett Myers 6-10 RC	3.00	.90
44 Brett Myers 11-15 RC	3.00	.90
45 R.Asadoorian 1-5 RC	.75	.23
45 R.Asadoorian 6-10 RC	.75	.23
45 R.Asadoorian 11-15 RC	.75	.23

2000 Topps Tek Color

Randomly inserted into packs, this 45-card insert is a complete parallel of the Topps Tek base set. Please note that there are 20 different variations of the 45-card base set. Variations 16-20 feature an assortment of colors. Each variation of the rookie subset is short-printed to 2000 serial numbered sets. Pattern 16 cards are purple, pattern 17 are red, pattern 18 are yellow, pattern 19 are green, and pattern 20 are blue.

Nm-Mt Ex-Mt
*COLOR 1-40: 2X TO 5X BASIC 1-40..
*COLOR 41-45: .4X TO 1X BASIC 41-45

2000 Topps Tek Gold

Randomly inserted into packs, this 45-card insert is a complete parallel of the Topps Tek base set. Each card is die-cut and remastered in gold. Please note that 10 serial numbered sets were produced for all 20 variations of the original base set.

Nm-Mt Ex-Mt
*STARS 1-40: 15X TO 40X BASIC CARDS
*ROOKIES 41-45: 6X TO 15X BASIC CARDS

2000 Topps Tek Architeks

Randomly inserted into packs at one in five, this 18-card insert features players that are the foundation of their teams. Card backs carry an "A" prefix.

Card	Nm-Mt	Ex-Mt
COMPLETE SET (18)	50.00	15.00
A1 Nomar Garciaparra	3.00	.90
A2 Derek Jeter	5.00	1.50
A3 Chipper Jones	2.00	.60
A4 Vladimir Guerrero	2.00	.60
A5 Mark McGwire	5.00	1.50
A6 Ken Griffey Jr.	3.00	.90
A7 Mike Piazza	3.00	.90
A8 Jeff Bagwell	1.25	.35
A9 Larry Walker	1.25	.35
A10 Manny Ramirez	.75	.23
A11 Alex Rodriguez	3.00	.90
A12 Sammy Sosa	3.00	.90
A13 Shawn Green	.75	.23
A14 Juan Gonzalez	2.00	.60
A15 Barry Bonds	5.00	1.50
A16 Pedro Martinez	2.00	.60
A17 Cal Ripken	6.00	1.80
A18 Ivan Rodriguez	2.00	.60

2000 Topps Tek Dramatek Performers

Randomly inserted into packs at one in ten, this nine-card insert set features players that have a flair for the dramatics. Card backs carry a "DP" prefix.

Card	Nm-Mt	Ex-Mt
COMPLETE SET (9)	30.00	9.00
DP1 Mark McGwire	5.00	1.50
DP2 Sammy Sosa	3.00	.90
DP3 Ken Griffey Jr.	3.00	.90
DP4 Nomar Garciaparra	3.00	.90
DP5 Chipper Jones	2.00	.60
DP6 Mike Piazza	3.00	.90
DP7 Alex Rodriguez	3.00	.90
DP8 Derek Jeter	5.00	1.50
DP9 Vladimir Guerrero	2.00	.60

2000 Topps Tek Tektonics

Randomly inserted into packs at one in 30, this 9-card insert features the major league's top clutch hitters. Card backs carry a "TT" prefix.

Card	Nm-Mt	Ex-Mt
COMPLETE SET (9)	120.00	36.00
TT1 Derek Jeter	15.00	4.50
TT2 Mark McGwire	15.00	4.50
TT3 Ken Griffey Jr.	10.00	3.00
TT4 Mike Piazza	10.00	3.00

Card	Nm-Mt	Ex-Mt
TT5 Alex Rodriguez	10.00	3.00
TT6 Chipper Jones	6.00	1.80
TT7 Nomar Garciaparra	10.00	3.00
TT8 Sammy Sosa	10.00	3.00
TT9 Cal Ripken	20.00	6.00

2002 Topps Total Pre-Production

This three-card set was distributed in complete set form within a sealed, clear-plastic cello wrapper to dealers and hobby media in April, 2002 to preview the upcoming Topps Total baseball product.

	Nm-Mt	Ex-Mt
COMPLETE SET (3)	2.00	.60
PP1 Barry Bonds	1.00	.30
PP2 Ichiro Suzuki	1.00	.30
PP3 Hank Blalock	.50	.15

2002 Topps Total

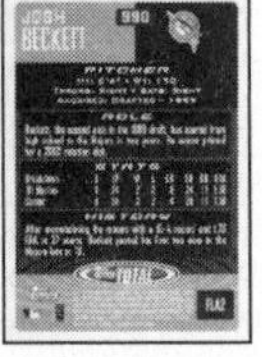

This 990 card set was issued in June, 2002. These cards were issued in 10 card packs which came 36 packs to a box and six boxes to a case. Each card was numbered not only in a numerical sequence but also in a team sequence.

	Nm-Mt	Ex-Mt
COMPLETE SET (990)	150.00	45.00
1 Joe Mauer RC	5.00	1.50
2 Derek Jeter	2.00	.60
3 Shawn Green	.30	.09
4 Vladimir Guerrero	.75	.23
5 Mike Piazza	1.25	.35
6 Brandon Duckworth	.20	.06
7 Aramis Ramirez	.30	.09
8 Josh Barfield RC	2.50	.75
9 Troy Glaus	.50	.15
10 Sammy Sosa	1.25	.35
11 Rod Barajas	.20	.06
12 Tsuyoshi Shinjo	.30	.09
13 Larry Bigbie	.20	.06
14 Tino Martinez	.50	.15
15 Craig Biggio	.50	.15
16 Anastacio Martinez RC	.40	.12
17 John McDonald	.20	.06
18 Kyle Kane RC	.25	.07
19 Aubrey Huff	.30	.09
20 Juan Cruz	.20	.06
21 Doug Creek	.20	.06
22 Luther Hackman	.20	.06
23 Rafael Furcal	.30	.09
24 Andres Torres	.30	.09
25 Jason Giambi	.75	.23
26 Jose Paniagua	.20	.06
27 Jose Offerman	.20	.06
28 Alex Arias	.20	.06
29 J.M. Gold	.20	.06
30 Jeff Bagwell	.50	.15
31 Brent Cookson	.20	.06
32 Kelly Wunsch	.20	.06
33 Larry Walker	.50	.15
34 Luis Gonzalez	.30	.09
35 John Franco	.30	.09
36 Roy Oswalt	.30	.09
37 Tom Glavine	.50	.15
38 C.C. Sabathia	.30	.09
39 Jay Gibbons	.30	.09
40 Wilson Betemit	.20	.06
41 Tony Armas Jr.	.20	.06
42 Mo Vaughn	.30	.09
43 Gerard Oakes RC	.40	.12
44 Dmitri Young	.30	.09
45 Tim Salmon	.50	.15
46 Barry Zito	.50	.15
47 Adrian Gonzalez	.30	.09
48 Joe Davenport	.20	.06
49 Adrian Hernandez	.20	.06
50 Randy Johnson	.75	.23
52 Adam Pettyjohn	.20	.06
53 Alex Escobar	.20	.06
54 Stevenson Agosto RC	.25	.07
55 Omar Daal	.20	.06
56 Mike Buddie	.20	.06
57 Dave Williams	.20	.06
58 Marquis Grissom	.20	.06
59 Pat Burrell	.30	.09
60 Mark Prior	2.50	.75
61 Mike Bynum	.20	.06
62 Mike Hill RC	.40	.12
63 Brandon Backe RC	.40	.12
64 Dan Wilson	.20	.06
65 Nick Johnson	.30	.09
66 Jason Grimsley	.20	.06
67 Russ Johnson	.20	.06
68 Todd Walker	.30	.09
69 Kyle Farnsworth	.20	.06
70 Ben Broussard	.20	.06
71 Garrett Guzman RC	.40	.12
72 Terry Mulholland	.20	.06
73 Tyler Houston	.20	.06
74 Jace Brewer	.20	.06
75 Chris Baker RC	.40	.12
76 Frank Catalanotto	.20	.06
77 Mike Redmond	.20	.06
78 Matt Wise	.20	.06
79 Fernando Vina	.30	.09
80 Kevin Brown	.30	.09
81 Grant Balfour	.20	.06
82 Clint Nageotte RC	1.00	.30
83 Jeff Tam	.20	.06
84 Steve Trachsel	.20	.06
85 Tomo Ohka	.20	.06
86 Keith McDonald	.20	.06
87 Jose Ortiz	.20	.06
88 Rusty Greer	.30	.09
89 Jeff Suppan	.20	.06
90 Moises Alou	.30	.09
91 Juan Encarnacion	.20	.06
92 Tyler Yates RC	.75	.23
93 Scott Strickland	.20	.06
94 Brent Butler	.20	.06
95 Jon Rauch	.20	.06
96 Brian Mallette RC	.25	.07
97 Joe Randa	.20	.06
98 Cesar Crespo	.20	.06
99 Felix Rodriguez	.20	.06
100 Chipper Jones	.75	.23
101 Victor Martinez	.30	.09
102 Danny Graves	.20	.06
103 Brandon Berger	.20	.06
104 Carlos Garcia	.20	.06
105 Alfonso Soriano	.50	.15
106 Allan Simpson RC	.25	.07
107 Brad Thomas	.20	.06
108 Devon White	.20	.06
109 Scott Chiasson	.20	.06
110 Cliff Floyd	.30	.09
111 Scott Williamson	.20	.06
112 Julio Zuleta	.20	.06
113 Terry Adams	.20	.06
114 Zach Day	.20	.06
115 Ben Grieve	.20	.06
116 Mark Ellis	.20	.06
117 Bobby Jenks RC	1.25	.35
118 LaTroy Hawkins	.20	.06
119 Tim Raines Jr.	.20	.06
120 Juan Uribe	.20	.06
121 Bob Scanlan	.20	.06
122 Brad Nelson RC	1.25	.35
123 Adam Johnson	.20	.06
124 Raul Casanova	.20	.06
125 Jeff D'Amico	.20	.06
126 Aaron Cook RC	.40	.12
127 Alan Benes	.20	.06
128 Mark Little	.20	.06
129 Randy Wolf	.30	.09
130 Phil Nevin	.30	.09
131 Guillermo Mota	.20	.06
132 Nick Neugebauer	.20	.06
133 Pedro Borbon Jr.	.20	.06
134 Doug Mientkiewicz	.30	.09
135 Edgardo Alfonzo	.30	.09
136 Dustan Mohr	.20	.06
137 Dan Reichert	.20	.06
138 Dewon Brazelton	.20	.06
139 Orlando Cabrera	.20	.06
140 Todd Hollandsworth	.20	.06
141 Darren Dreifort	.20	.06
142 Jose Valentin	.20	.06
143 Josh Kalinowski	.20	.06
144 Randy Keisler	.20	.06
145 Bret Boone	.30	.09
146 Roosevelt Brown	.20	.06
147 Brent Abernathy	.20	.06
148 Jorge Julio	.20	.06
149 Alex Gonzalez	.20	.06
150 Juan Pierre	.30	.09
151 Roger Cedeno	.20	.06
152 Javier Vazquez	.30	.09
153 Armando Benitez	.20	.06
154 Dave Burba	.20	.06
155 Brad Penny	.20	.06
156 Ryan Jensen	.20	.06
157 Jeromy Burnitz	.30	.09
158 Matt Childers RC	.40	.12
159 Wilmy Caceres	.20	.06
160 Roger Clemens	1.50	.45
161 Jamie Cerda RC	.40	.12
162 Jason Christiansen	.20	.06
163 Pokey Reese	.20	.06
164 Ivanon Coffie	.20	.06
165 Joaquin Benoit	.20	.06
166 Mike Matheny	.20	.06
167 Eric Cammack	.20	.06
168 Alex Graman	.20	.06
169 Brook Fordyce	.20	.06
170 Mike Lieberthal	.30	.09
171 Giovanni Carrara	.20	.06
172 Antonio Perez	.20	.06
173 Fernando Tatis	.20	.06
174 Jason Bay RC	1.25	.35
175 Jason Botts RC	.40	.12
176 Danys Baez	.20	.06
177 Shea Hillenbrand	.30	.09
178 Jack Cust	.20	.06
179 Clay Bellinger	.20	.06
180 Roberto Alomar	.75	.23
181 Graeme Lloyd	.20	.06
182 Clint Weibl RC	.25	.07
183 Royce Clayton	.20	.06
184 Ben Davis	.20	.06
185 Brian Adams RC	.25	.07
186 Jack Wilson	.20	.06
187 David Coggin	.20	.06
188 Derrick Turnbow	.20	.06
189 Vladimir Nunez	.20	.06
190 Mariano Rivera	.50	.15
191 Wilson Guzman	.20	.06
192 Michael Barrett	.20	.06
193 Corey Patterson	.30	.09
194 Luis Sojo	.20	.06
195 Scott Elarton	.20	.06
196 Charles Thomas RC	.40	.12
197 Ricky Bottalico	.20	.06
198 Wilfredo Rodriguez	.20	.06
199 Ricardo Rincon	.20	.06
200 John Smoltz	.50	.15
201 Travis Miller	.20	.06
202 Ben Weber	.20	.06
203 T.J. Tucker	.20	.06
204 Terry Shumpert	.20	.06
205 Bernie Williams	.50	.15
206 Russ Ortiz	.30	.09
207 Nate Rolison	.20	.06
208 Jose Cruz Jr.	.30	.09
209 Bill Ortega	.20	.06
210 Carl Everett	.30	.09
211 Luis Lopez	.20	.06
212 Brian Wolfe RC	.40	.12
213 Doug Davis	.20	.06
214 Troy Mattes	.20	.06
215 Al Leiter	.30	.09
216 Joe Mays	.20	.06
217 Bobby Smith	.20	.06
218 J.J. Trujillo RC	.40	.12
219 Hideo Nomo	.75	.23
220 Jimmy Rollins	.30	.09
221 Bobby Seay	.20	.06
222 Mike Thurman	.20	.06
223 Bartolo Colon	.30	.09
224 Jesus Sanchez	.20	.06
225 Ray Durham	.30	.09
226 Juan Diaz	.20	.06
227 Lee Stevens	.20	.06
228 Ben Howard RC	.40	.12
229 James Mouton	.20	.06
230 Paul Quantrill	.20	.06
231 Randy Knorr	.20	.06
232 Abraham Nunez	.20	.06
233 Mike Fetters	.20	.06
234 Mario Encarnacion	.20	.06
235 Jeremy Fikac	.20	.06
236 Travis Lee	.20	.06
237 Bob File	.20	.06
238 Pete Harnisch	.20	.06
239 Randy Galvez RC	.40	.12
240 Geoff Goetz	.20	.06
241 Gary Glover	.20	.06
242 Troy Percival	.30	.09
243 Len Dinardo RC	.40	.12
244 Jonny Gomes RC	1.00	.30
245 Jesus Medrano RC	.40	.12
246 Rey Ordonez	.20	.06
247 Juan Gonzalez	.75	.23
248 Jose Guillen	.20	.06
249 Franklyn German RC	.40	.12
250 Mike Mussina	.75	.23
251 Ugueth Urbina	.20	.06
252 Melvin Mora	.20	.06
253 Gerald Williams	.20	.06
254 Jared Sandberg	.20	.06
255 Darrin Fletcher	.20	.06
256 A.J. Pierzynski	.30	.09
257 Lenny Harris	.20	.06
258 Blaine Neal	.20	.06
259 Denny Neagle	.20	.06
260 Jason Hart	.20	.06
261 Henry Mateo	.20	.06
262 Rheal Cormier	.20	.06
263 Luis Terrero	.20	.06
264 Shigetoshi Hasegawa	.30	.09
265 Bill Haselman	.20	.06
266 Scott Hatteberg	.20	.06
267 Adam Hyzdu	.20	.06
268 Mike Williams	.20	.06
269 Marlon Anderson	.20	.06
270 Bruce Chen	.20	.06
271 Eli Marrero	.20	.06
272 Jimmy Haynes	.20	.06
273 Bronson Arroyo	.20	.06
274 Kevin Jordan	.20	.06
275 Rick Helling	.20	.06
276 Mark Loretta	.20	.06
277 Dustin Hermanson	.20	.06
278 Pablo Ozuna	.20	.06
279 Keto Anderson RC	.40	.12
280 Jermaine Dye	.30	.09
281 Will Smith	.20	.06
282 Brian Daubach	.20	.06
283 Eric Hinske	.30	.09
284 Joe Jiannetti RC	.40	.12
285 Chan Ho Park	.30	.09
286 Curtis Legendre RC	.40	.12
287 Jeff Reboulet	.20	.06
288 Scott Rolen	.50	.15
289 Chris Richard	.20	.06
290 Eric Chavez	.30	.09
291 Scot Shields	.20	.06
292 Donnie Sadler	.20	.06
293 Dave Veres	.20	.06
294 Craig Counsell	.20	.06
295 Armando Reynoso	.20	.06
296 Kyle Lohse	.20	.06
297 Arthur Rhodes	.20	.06
298 Sidney Ponson	.30	.09
299 Trevor Hoffman	.30	.09
300 Kerry Wood	.75	.23
301 Danny Bautista	.20	.06
302 Scott Sauerbeck	.20	.06
303 Johnny Estrada	.20	.06
304 Mike Timlin	.20	.06
305 Orlando Hernandez	.30	.09
306 Tony Clark	.20	.06
307 Tomas Perez	.20	.06
308 Marcus Giles	.30	.09
309 Mike Bordick	.30	.09
310 Jorge Posada	.50	.15
311 Jason Conti	.20	.06
312 Kevin Millar	.30	.09
313 Paul Shuey	.20	.06
314 Jake Mauer RC	.40	.12
315 Luke Hudson	.30	.09
316 Angel Berroa	.30	.09
317 Fred Bastardo RC	.40	.12
318 Shawn Estes	.20	.06
319 Andy Ashby	.20	.06
320 Ryan Klesko	.30	.09
321 Kevin Appier	.30	.09
322 Juan Pena	.20	.06
323 Alex Herrera	.20	.06
324 Robb Nen	.30	.09
325 Orlando Hudson	.20	.06
326 Lyle Overbay	.20	.06
327 Ben Sheets	.30	.09
328 Mike DiFelice	.20	.06
329 Pablo Arias RC	.40	.12
330 Mike Sweeney	.30	.09
331 Rick Ankiel	.20	.06
332 Tomas De La Rosa	.20	.06
333 Kazuhisa Ishii RC	1.50	.45
334 Jose Reyes	.75	.23
335 Jeremy Giambi	.20	.06
336 Jose Mesa	.20	.06
337 Ralph Roberts RC	.40	.12
338 Jose Nunez	.20	.06
339 Curt Schilling	.50	.15
340 Sean Casey	.30	.09
341 Bob Wells	.20	.06
342 Carlos Beltran	.30	.09
343 Alexis Gomez	.20	.06
344 Brandon Claussen	.75	.23
345 Buddy Groom	.20	.06
346 Mark Phillips RC	.75	.23
347 Francisco Cordova	.20	.06
348 Joe Oliver	.20	.06
349 Danny Patterson	.20	.06
350 Joel Pineiro	.30	.09
351 J.R. House	.20	.06
352 Benny Agbayani	.20	.06
353 Jose Vidro	.30	.09
354 Reed Johnson RC	.50	.15
355 Mike Lowell	.30	.09
356 Scott Schoeneweis	.20	.06
357 Brian Jordan	.30	.09
358 Steve Finley	.30	.09
359 Randy Choate	.20	.06
360 Jose Lima	.20	.06
361 Miguel Olivo	.20	.06
362 Kenny Rogers	.30	.09
363 David Justice	.30	.09
364 Brandon Knight	.20	.06
365 Joe Kennedy	.20	.06
366 Eric Valent	.20	.06
367 Nelson Cruz	.20	.06
368 Brian Giles	.30	.09
369 Charles Gipson RC	.25	.07
370 Juan Pena	.20	.06
371 Mark Redman	.20	.06
372 Billy Koch	.20	.06
373 Ted Lilly	.20	.06
374 Craig Paquette	.20	.06
375 Kevin Jarvis	.20	.06
376 Scott Erickson	.20	.06
377 Josh Paul	.20	.06
378 Darwin Cubillan	.20	.06
379 Nelson Figueroa	.20	.06
380 Darin Erstad	.30	.09
381 Jeremy Hill RC	.40	.12
382 Elvin Nina	.20	.06
383 David Wells	.30	.09
384 Jay Caligiuri RC	.40	.12
385 Freddy Garcia	.30	.09
386 Damian Miller	.20	.06
387 Bobby Higginson	.30	.09
388 Alejandro Giron RC	.40	.12
389 Ivan Rodriguez	.75	.23
390 Ed Rogers	.20	.06
391 Andy Benes	.20	.06
392 Matt Blank	.20	.06
393 Ryan Vogelsong	.20	.06
394 Kelly Ramos RC	.25	.07
395 Eric Karros	.30	.09
396 Bobby J. Jones	.20	.06
397 Omar Vizquel	.30	.09
398 Matt Perisho	.20	.06
399 Delino DeShields	.20	.06
400 Carlos Hernandez	.20	.06
401 Derrek Lee	.30	.09
402 Kirk Rueter	.20	.06
403 David Wright RC	2.00	.60
404 Paul LoDuca	.30	.09
405 Brian Schneider	.20	.06
406 Milton Bradley	.30	.09
407 Daryle Ward	.20	.06
408 Cody Ransom	.20	.06
409 Fernando Rodney	.20	.06
410 John Suomi RC	.40	.12
411 Joe Girardi	.20	.06
412 Demetrius Heath RC	.40	.12
413 John Foster RC	.40	.12
414 Doug Glanville	.20	.06
415 Ryan Kohlmeier	.20	.06
416 Mike Matthews	.20	.06
417 Craig Wilson	.20	.06
418 Jay Witasick	.20	.06
419 Jay Payton	.20	.06
420 Andruw Jones	.30	.09
421 Benji Gil	.20	.06
422 Jeff Liefer	.20	.06
423 Kevin Young	.20	.06
424 Richie Sexson	.30	.09
425 Cory Lidle	.20	.06
426 Shane Halter	.20	.06
427 Jesse Foppert RC	1.50	.45
428 Jose Molina	.20	.06
429 Nick Alvarez RC	.40	.12
430 Brian L. Hunter	.20	.06
431 Cliff Bartosh RC	.40	.12
432 Junior Spivey	.20	.06
433 Eric Good RC	.40	.12
434 Chin-Feng Chen	.30	.09
435 T.J. Mathews	.20	.06
436 Rich Rodriguez	.20	.06
437 Bobby Abreu	.30	.09
438 Joe McEwing	.20	.06
439 Michael Tucker	.20	.06
440 Preston Wilson	.30	.09
441 Mike MacDougal	.20	.06
442 Shannon Stewart	.30	.09
443 Bob Howry	.20	.06
444 Mike Benjamin	.20	.06
445 Erik Hiljus	.20	.06
446 Ryan Gripp RC	.40	.12
447 Jose Vizcaino	.20	.06
448 Shawn Wooten	.20	.06
449 Steve Kent RC	.40	.12
450 Ramiro Mendoza	.20	.06
451 Jake Westbrook	.20	.06
452 Joe Lawrence	.20	.06
453 Jae Seo	.20	.06
454 Ryan Fry RC	.40	.12
455 Darren Lewis	.20	.06
456 Brad Wilkerson	.20	.06
457 Gustavo Chacin RC	.40	.12
458 Adrian Brown	.20	.06
459 Mike Cameron	.30	.09
460 Bud Smith	.20	.06
461 Derrick Lewis	.20	.06
462 Derek Lowe	.30	.09
463 Matt Williams	.30	.09
464 Jason Jennings	.20	.06
465 Albie Lopez	.20	.06
466 Felipe Lopez	.20	.06
467 Luke Allen	.20	.06
468 Brian Anderson	.20	.06
469 Matt Riley	.20	.06
470 Ryan Dempster	.20	.06
471 Matt Ginter	.20	.06
472 David Ortiz	.30	.09
473 Cole Barthel RC	.40	.12
474 Damian Jackson	.20	.06
475 Andy Van Hekken	.20	.06
476 Doug Brocail	.20	.06
477 Denny Hocking	.20	.06
478 Sean Douglass	.20	.06
479 Eric Owens	.20	.06
480 Ryan Ludwick	.20	.06
481 Todd Pratt	.20	.06
482 Aaron Sele	.20	.06
483 Edgar Renteria	.30	.09
484 Raymond Cabrera RC	.40	.12
485 Brandon Lyon	.20	.06
486 Chase Utley	.50	.15
487 Robert Fick	.30	.09
488 Wilfredo Cordero	.20	.06
489 Octavio Dotel	.20	.06
490 Paul Abbott	.20	.06
491 Jason Kendall	.30	.09
492 Jarrod Washburn	.30	.09
493 Dane Sardinha	.20	.06
494 Jung Bong	.20	.06
495 J.D. Drew	.30	.09
496 Jason Schmidt	.30	.09
497 Mike Magnante	.20	.06
498 Jorge Padilla RC	.40	.12
499 Eric Gagne	.50	.15
500 Todd Helton	.50	.15
501 Jeff Weaver	.20	.06
502 Alex Sanchez	.20	.06
503 Ken Griffey Jr.	1.25	.35
504 Abraham Nunez	.20	.06
505 Reggie Sanders	.30	.09
506 Casey Kotchman RC	2.50	.75
507 Jim Mann	.20	.06
508 Matt LeCroy	.20	.06
509 Frank Castillo	.20	.06
510 Geoff Jenkins	.30	.09
511 Jayson Durocher RC	.25	.07
512 Ellis Burks	.30	.09
513 Aaron Fultz	.20	.06
514 Hiram Bocachica	.20	.06
515 Nate Espy RC	.40	.12
516 Placido Polanco	.20	.06
517 Kerry Ligtenberg	.20	.06
518 Doug Nickle	.20	.06
519 Ramon Ortiz	.20	.06
520 Greg Swindell	.20	.06
521 J.J. Davis	.20	.06
522 Sandy Alomar Jr.	.20	.06
523 Chris Carpenter	.20	.06
524 Vance Wilson	.20	.06
525 Nomar Garciaparra	1.25	.35
526 Jim Mecir	.20	.06
527 Taylor Buchholz RC	.50	.15
528 Brent Mayne	.20	.06
529 John Rodriguez RC	.40	.12
530 David Segui	.20	.06
531 Nate Cornejo	.20	.06
532 Gil Heredia	.20	.06
533 Esteban Loaiza	.30	.09
534 Pat Mahomes	.20	.06
535 Matt Morris	.30	.09
536 Todd Stottlemyre	.20	.06
537 Brian Lesher	.20	.06
538 Arturo McDowell	.20	.06
539 Felix Diaz	.20	.06
540 Mark Mulder	.30	.09
541 Kevin Frederick RC	.40	.12
542 Andy Fox	.20	.06
543 Dionys Cesar RC	.25	.07
544 Justin Miller	.20	.06
545 Keith Osik	.20	.06
546 Shane Reynolds	.20	.06
547 Mike Myers	.20	.06
548 Raul Chavez RC	.25	.07
549 Joe Nathan	.20	.06
550 Ryan Anderson	.20	.06
551 Jason Marquis	.20	.06
552 Marty Cordova	.20	.06
553 Kevin Tapani	.20	.06
554 Jimmy Anderson	.20	.06
555 Pedro Martinez	.75	.23
556 Rocky Biddle	.20	.06
557 Alex Ochoa	.20	.06
558 D'Angelo Jimenez	.20	.06
559 Wilkin Ruan	.20	.06
560 Terrence Long	.30	.09
561 Mark Lukasiewicz	.20	.06
562 Jose Santiago	.20	.06
563 Brad Fullmer	.20	.06
564 Corky Miller	.20	.06
565 Matt White	.20	.06
566 Mark Grace	.50	.15
567 Raul Ibanez	.20	.06
568 Josh Towers	.20	.06
569 Juan M. Gonzalez RC	.40	.12
570 Brian Buchanan	.20	.06
571 Ken Harvey	.20	.06
572 Jeffrey Hammonds	.20	.06
573 Wade Miller	.30	.09
574 Elpidio Guzman	.20	.06
575 Kevin Olsen	.20	.06
576 Austin Kearns	.30	.09
577 Tim Kalita RC	.40	.12
578 David Dellucci	.20	.06
579 Alex Gonzalez	.20	.06
580 Joe Orloski RC	.40	.12
581 Gary Matthews Jr.	.20	.06
582 Ryan Mills	.20	.06
583 Erick Almonte	.20	.06
584 Jeremy Affeldt	.20	.06
585 Chris Tritle RC	.40	.12
586 Michael Cuddyer	.20	.06
587 Kris Foster	.20	.06
588 Russell Branyan	.20	.06
589 Darren Oliver	.20	.06
590 Freddie Money RC	.40	.12
591 Carlos Lee	.30	.09
592 Tim Wakefield	.30	.09
593 Bubba Trammell	.20	.06
594 John Koronka RC	.40	.12
595 Geoff Blum	.20	.06
596 Darryl Kile	.30	.09
597 Neifi Perez	.20	.06
598 Torii Hunter	.30	.09
599 Luis Castillo	.30	.09
600 Mark Buehrle	.30	.09

601 Jeff Zimmerman .20 .06
602 Mike DeJean .20 .06
603 Julio Lugo .20 .06
604 Chad Hermansen .20 .06
605 Keith Foulke .20 .06
606 Lance Davis .20 .06
607 Jeff Austin RC .40 .12
608 Brandon Inge .20 .06
609 Orlando Merced .20 .06
610 Johnny Damon .30 .09
611 Doug Henry .20 .06
612 Adam Kennedy .20 .06
613 Wiki Gonzalez .20 .06
614 Brian West RC .40 .12
615 Andy Pettitte .50 .15
616 Chone Figgins RC .40 .12
617 Matt Lawton .20 .06
618 Paul Rigdon .20 .06
619 Keith Lockhart .20 .06
620 Tim Redding .20 .06
621 John Parrish .20 .06
622 Homer Bush .20 .06
623 Todd Greene .20 .06
624 David Eckstein .20 .06
625 Greg Montalbano RC .50 .15
626 Joe Beimel .20 .06
627 Adrian Beltre .30 .09
628 Charles Nagy .20 .06
629 Cristian Guzman .30 .09
630 Toby Hall .20 .06
631 Jose Hernandez .20 .06
632 Jose Macias .30 .09
633 Jaret Wright .20 .06
634 Steve Parris .20 .06
635 Gene Kingsale .20 .06
636 Tim Worrell .20 .06
637 Billy Martin .20 .06
638 Jovanny Cedeno .20 .06
639 Curtis Leskanic .20 .06
640 Tim Hudson .30 .09
641 Juan Castro .20 .06
642 Rafael Soriano .30 .09
643 Juan Rincon .20 .06
644 Mark DeRosa .20 .06
645 Carlos Pena .20 .06
646 Robin Ventura .30 .09
647 Odalis Perez .20 .06
648 Damion Easley .20 .06
649 Benito Santiago .30 .09
650 Alex Rodriguez 1.25 .35
651 Aaron Rowand .20 .06
652 Alex Cora .20 .06
653 Bobby Kielty .20 .06
654 Jose Rodriguez RC .40 .12
655 Herbert Perry .20 .06
656 Jeff Urban .20 .06
657 Paul Bako .20 .06
658 Shane Spencer .20 .06
659 Pat Hentgen .20 .06
660 Jeff Kent .30 .09
661 Mark McLemore .20 .06
662 Chuck Knoblauch .30 .09
663 Blake Stein .20 .06
664 Brett Roneberg RC .40 .12
665 Josh Phelps .20 .06
666 Byung-Hyun Kim .30 .09
667 Dave Martinez .20 .06
668 Mike Maroth .20 .06
669 Shawn Chacon .20 .06
670 Billy Wagner .30 .09
671 Luis Alicea .20 .06
672 Sterling Hitchcock .20 .06
673 Adam Piatt .20 .06
674 Ryan Franklin .20 .06
675 Luke Prokopec .20 .06
676 Alfredo Amezaga .20 .06
677 Gookie Dawkins .20 .06
678 Eric Byrnes .20 .06
679 Barry Larkin .75 .23
680 Albert Pujols 1.50 .45
681 Edwards Guzman .20 .06
682 Jason Bere .20 .06
683 Adam Everett .20 .06
684 Greg Colbrunn .20 .06
685 Brandon Puffer RC .40 .12
686 Mark Kotsay .20 .06
687 Willie Bloomquist .30 .09
688 Hank Blalock .75 .23
689 Travis Hafner .30 .09
690 Lance Berkman .30 .09
691 Joe Crede .20 .06
692 Chuck Finley .20 .06
693 John Grabow .20 .06
694 Randy Winn .20 .06
695 Mike James .20 .06
696 Kris Benson .20 .06
697 Bret Prinz .20 .06
698 Jeff Williams .20 .06
699 Eric Munson .20 .06
700 Mike Hampton .30 .09
701 Ramon E. Martinez .20 .06
702 Hansel Izquierdo RC .40 .12
703 Nathan Haynes .20 .06
704 Eddie Taubensee .20 .06
705 Esteban German .20 .06
706 Ross Gload .20 .06
707 Matt Merricks RC .40 .12
708 Chris Piersoll RC .25 .07
709 Seth Greisinger .20 .06
710 Ichiro Suzuki 1.25 .35
711 Cesar Izturis .20 .06
712 Brad Cresse .20 .06
713 Carl Pavano .20 .06
714 Steve Sparks .20 .06
715 Dennis Tankersley .20 .06
716 Kelvim Escobar .20 .06
717 Jason LaRue .20 .06
718 Corey Koskie .30 .09
719 Vinny Castilla .30 .09
720 Tim Drew .20 .06
721 Chin-Hui Tsao .30 .09
722 Paul Byrd .20 .06
723 Alex Cintron .30 .09
724 Orlando Palmeiro .20 .06
725 Ramon Hernandez .20 .06
726 Mark Johnson .20 .06
727 B.J. Ryan .20 .06
728 Wendell Magee .20 .06
729 Michael Coleman .20 .06
730 Mario Ramos RC .50 .15
731 Mike Stanton .20 .06
732 Dee Brown .20 .06
733 Brad Ausmus .20 .06
734 Napoleon Calzado RC .40 .12
735 Woody Williams .20 .06
736 Paxton Crawford .20 .06
737 Jason Karnuth .20 .06
738 Michael Restovich .20 .06
739 Ramon Castro .20 .06
740 Magglio Ordonez .30 .09
741 Tom Gordon .20 .06
742 Mark Grudzielanek .20 .06
743 Jaime Moyer .30 .09
744 Marlyn Tisdale RC .40 .12
745 Steve Kline .20 .06
746 Adam Eaton .20 .06
747 Eric Glaser RC .40 .12
748 Sean DePaula .20 .06
749 Greg Norton .20 .06
750 Steve Reed .20 .06
751 Ricardo Aramboles .20 .06
752 Matt Mantei .20 .06
753 Gene Stechschulte .20 .06
754 Chuck McElroy .20 .06
755 Barry Bonds 2.00 .60
756 Matt Anderson .20 .06
757 Yorvit Torrealba .20 .06
758 Jason Standridge .20 .06
759 Desi Relaford .20 .06
760 Jolbert Cabrera .20 .06
761 Chris George .20 .06
762 Erubiel Durazo .20 .06
763 Paul Konerko .30 .09
764 Tike Redman .20 .06
765 Chad Ricketts RC .25 .07
766 Roberto Hernandez .20 .06
767 Mark Lewis .20 .06
768 Livan Hernandez .20 .06
769 Carlos Brackley RC .40 .12
770 Kazuhiro Sasaki .30 .09
771 Bill Hall .20 .06
772 Nelson Castro RC .40 .12
773 Eric Milton .20 .06
774 Tom Davey .20 .06
775 Todd Ritchie .20 .06
776 Seth Etherton .20 .06
777 Chris Singleton .20 .06
778 Robert Averette RC .25 .07
779 Robert Person .20 .06
780 Fred McGriff .50 .15
781 Richard Hidalgo .30 .09
782 Kris Wilson .20 .06
783 John Rocker .20 .06
784 Justin Kaye .20 .06
785 Glendon Rusch .20 .06
786 Greg Vaughn .30 .09
787 Mike Lamb .20 .06
788 Greg Myers .20 .06
789 Nate Field RC .40 .12
790 Jim Edmonds .30 .09
791 Olmedo Saenz .20 .06
792 Jason Johnson .20 .06
793 Mike Lincoln .20 .06
794 Todd Coffey RC .40 .12
795 Jesus Sanchez .20 .06
796 Aaron Myette .20 .06
797 Tony Womack .20 .06
798 Chad Kreuter .20 .06
799 Brady Clark .20 .06
800 Adam Dunn .30 .09
801 Jacque Jones .30 .09
802 Kevin Millwood .30 .09
803 Mike Rivera .20 .06
804 Jim Thome .75 .23
805 Jeff Conine .30 .09
806 Elmer Dessens .20 .06
807 Randy Velarde .20 .06
808 Carlos Delgado .30 .09
809 Steve Karsay .20 .06
810 Casey Fossum .20 .06
811 J.C. Romero .20 .06
812 Chris Truby .20 .06
813 Tony Graffanino .20 .06
814 Wascar Serrano .20 .06
815 Delvin James .20 .06
816 Pedro Feliz .20 .06
817 Damian Rolls .20 .06
818 Scott Linebrink .20 .06
819 Rafael Palmeiro .50 .15
820 Javy Lopez .30 .09
821 Larry Barnes .20 .06
822 Brian Lawrence .20 .06
823 Scotty Layfield RC .40 .12
824 Jeff Cirillo .20 .06
825 Willis Roberts .20 .06
826 Rich Harden RC 4.00 1.20
827 Chris Snelling RC 1.00 .30
828 Gary Sheffield .30 .09
829 Jeff Heaverlo .20 .06
830 Matt Clement .30 .09
831 Rich Garces .20 .06
832 Rondell White .30 .09
833 Henry Pichardo RC .40 .12
834 Aaron Boone .30 .09
835 Ruben Sierra .20 .06
836 Deivis Santos .20 .06
837 Tony Batista .30 .09
838 Rob Bell .20 .06
839 Frank Thomas .75 .23
840 Jose Silva .20 .06
841 Dan Johnson RC .50 .15
842 Steve Cox .20 .06
843 Jose Acevedo .20 .06
844 Jay Bell .30 .09
845 Mike Sirotka .20 .06
846 Garret Anderson .30 .09
847 James Shanks RC .40 .12
848 Trot Nixon .50 .15
849 Keith Ginter .20 .06
850 Tim Spooneybarger .20 .06
851 Matt Stairs .20 .06
852 Chris Stynes .20 .06
853 Marvin Benard .20 .06
854 Raul Mondesi .30 .09
855 Jeremy Owens .20 .06
856 Jon Garland .20 .06
857 Mitch Meluskey .20 .06
858 Chad Durbin .20 .06
859 John Burkett .20 .06
860 Jon Switzer RC .40 .12
861 Peter Bergeron .20 .06
862 Jesus Colome .20 .06
863 Todd Hundley .20 .06
864 Ben Petrick .20 .06
865 So Taguchi RC .50 .15
866 Ryan Drese .20 .06
867 Mike Trombley .20 .06
868 Rick Reed .20 .06
869 Mark Teixeira .75 .23
870 Corey Thurman RC .40 .12
871 Brian Roberts .20 .06
872 Mike Timlin .20 .06
873 Chris Reitsma .20 .06
874 Jeff Fassero .20 .06
875 Carlos Valderrama .20 .06
876 John Lackey .20 .06
877 Travis Fryman .30 .09
878 Ismael Valdes .20 .06
879 Rick White .20 .06
880 Edgar Martinez .50 .15
881 Dean Palmer .30 .09
882 Matt Allegra RC .40 .12
883 Greg Sain RC .40 .12
884 Carlos Silva .20 .06
885 Jose Valverde RC .50 .15
886 Dernell Stenson .20 .06
887 Todd Van Poppel .20 .06
888 Wes Anderson .20 .06
889 Bill Mueller .30 .09
890 Morgan Ensberg .30 .09
891 Marcus Thames .20 .06
892 Adam Walker RC .40 .12
893 John Halama .20 .06
894 Frank Menechino .20 .06
895 Greg Maddux 1.25 .35
896 Gary Bennett .20 .06
897 Mauricio Lara RC .40 .12
898 Mike Young .30 .09
899 Travis Phelps .20 .06
900 Rich Aurilia .30 .09
901 Henry Blanco .20 .06
902 Carlos Febles .20 .06
903 Scott MacRae .20 .06
904 Lou Merloni .20 .06
905 Dicky Gonzalez .20 .06
906 Jeff DaVanon .20 .06
907 A.J. Burnett .20 .06
908 Einar Diaz .20 .06
909 Julio Franco .30 .09
910 John Olerud .30 .09
911 Mark Hamilton RC .40 .12
912 David Riske .20 .06
913 Jason Tyner .20 .06
914 Britt Reames .20 .06
915 Vernon Wells .30 .09
916 Eddie Perez .20 .06
917 Edwin Almonte RC .40 .12
918 Enrique Wilson .20 .06
919 Chris Gomez .20 .06
920 Jayson Werth .20 .06
921 Jeff Nelson .20 .06
922 Freddy Sanchez RC .40 .12
923 John Vander Wal .20 .06
924 Chad Qualls RC .40 .12
925 Gabe White .20 .06
926 Chad Harville .20 .06
927 Ricky Gutierrez .20 .06
928 Carlos Guillen .20 .06
929 B.J. Surhoff .30 .09
930 Chris Woodward .20 .06
931 Ricardo Rodriguez .20 .06
932 Jimmy Gobble RC 1.25 .35
933 Jon Lieber .20 .06
934 Craig Kuzmic RC .40 .12
935 Eric Young .30 .09
936 Greg Zaun .20 .06
937 Miguel Batista .20 .06
938 Danny Wright .30 .09
939 Todd Zeile .30 .09
940 Chad Zerbe .20 .06
941 Jason Young RC .40 .12
942 Ronnie Belliard .20 .06
943 John Ennis RC .40 .12
944 John Flaherty .20 .06
945 Jerry Hairston Jr. .20 .06
946 Al Levine .20 .06
947 Antonio Alfonseca .20 .06
948 Brian Moehler .20 .06
949 Calvin Murray .20 .06
950 Nick Bierbrodt .20 .06
951 Sun Woo Kim .20 .06
952 Noochie Varner RC .40 .12
953 Luis Rivas .20 .06
954 Donnie Bridges .20 .06
955 Ramon Vazquez .20 .06
956 Luis Garcia .20 .06
957 Mark Quinn .20 .06
958 Armando Rios .20 .06
959 Chad Fox .20 .06
960 Hee Seop Choi .50 .15
961 Turk Wendell .20 .06
962 Adam Roller RC .40 .12
963 Grant Roberts .20 .06
964 Ben Molina .20 .06
965 Juan Rivera .20 .06
966 Matt Kinney .20 .06
967 Rod Beck .30 .09
968 Xavier Nady .20 .06
969 Masato Yoshii .20 .06
970 Miguel Tejada .30 .09
971 Danny Kolb .20 .06
972 Mike Remlinger .20 .06
973 Ray Lankford .20 .06
974 Ryan Minor .20 .06
975 J.T. Snow .30 .09
976 Brad Radke .30 .09
977 Jason Lane .20 .06
978 Jamey Wright .20 .06
979 Tom Goodwin .20 .06
980 Erik Bedard .20 .06
981 Gabe Kapler .20 .06
982 Brian Reith .20 .06
983 Nic Jackson RC .40 .12
984 Kurt Ainsworth .20 .06
985 Jason Isringhausen .20 .06
986 Willie Harris .20 .06
987 David Cone .30 .09
988 Bob Wickman .20 .06
989 Wes Helms .20 .06
990 Josh Beckett .50 .15

2002 Topps Total Award Winners

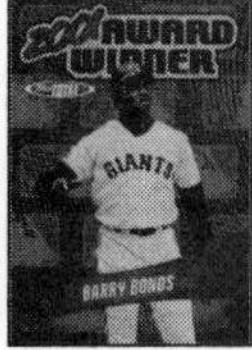

Issued at a stated rate of one in six, these 30 cards honored players who have won major awards during their career.

	Nm-Mt	Ex-Mt
COMPLETE SET (30)	40.00	12.00
AW1 Ichiro Suzuki	3.00	.90
AW2 Albert Pujols	4.00	1.20
AW3 Barry Bonds	5.00	1.50
AW4 Ichiro Suzuki	3.00	.90
AW5 Randy Johnson	2.00	.60
AW6 Roger Clemens	4.00	1.20
AW7 Jason Giambi A's	2.00	.60
AW8 Bret Boone	.75	.23
AW9 Troy Glaus	1.25	.35
AW10 Alex Rodriguez	3.00	.90
AW11 Juan Gonzalez	2.00	.60
AW12 Ichiro Suzuki	3.00	.90
AW13 Jorge Posada	1.25	.35
AW14 Edgar Martinez	1.25	.35
AW15 Todd Helton	1.25	.35
AW16 Jeff Kent	.75	.23
AW17 Albert Pujols	4.00	1.20
AW18 Rich Aurilia	.75	.23
AW19 Barry Bonds	5.00	1.50
AW20 Luis Gonzalez	.75	.23
AW21 Sammy Sosa	3.00	.90
AW22 Mike Piazza	3.00	.90
AW23 Mike Hampton	.75	.23
AW24 Ruben Sierra	.75	.23
AW25 Matt Morris	.75	.23
AW26 Curt Schilling	1.25	.35
AW27 Alex Rodriguez	3.00	.90
AW28 Barry Bonds	5.00	1.50
AW29 Jim Thome	2.00	.60
AW30 Barry Bonds	5.00	1.50

2002 Topps Total Production

Issued at a stated rate of one in 12, these 10 cards feature players who are among the best in the game in producing large offensive numbers.

	Nm-Mt	Ex-Mt
COMPLETE SET (10)	20.00	6.00
TP1 Alex Rodriguez	3.00	.90
TP2 Barry Bonds	5.00	1.50
TP3 Ichiro Suzuki	3.00	.90
TP4 Edgar Martinez	1.25	.35
TP5 Jason Giambi	2.00	.60
TP6 Todd Helton	1.25	.35
TP7 Nomar Garciaparra	3.00	.90
TP8 Vladimir Guerrero	2.00	.60
TP9 Sammy Sosa	3.00	.90
TP10 Chipper Jones	2.00	.60

2002 Topps Total Team Checklists

Seeded at a rate of approximately two in every three packs, these 30 cards feature team checklists for the 990-card Topps Total set. The card fronts are identical to the corresponding basic issue Topps Total cards. But the card backs feature a checklist of players (unlike basic issue cards of which feature statistics and career information on the specific player pictured on front). In addition, unlike basic issue Topps Total cards, these Team Checklist cards do not feature glossy coating on front and back.

	Nm-Mt	Ex-Mt
COMPLETE SET (30)	10.00	3.00
TTC1 Troy Glaus	.30	.09
TTC2 Randy Johnson	.50	.15
TTC3 Chipper Jones	.50	.15
TTC4 Scott Erickson	.20	.06
TTC5 Nomar Garciaparra	.75	.23
TTC6 Sammy Sosa	.75	.23
TTC7 Magglio Ordonez	.20	.06
TTC8 Ken Griffey Jr.	.75	.23
TTC9 Jim Thome	.50	.15
TTC10 Todd Helton	.30	.09
TTC11 Bobby Higginson	.20	.06
TTC12 Josh Beckett	.30	.09
TTC13 Jeff Bagwell	.30	.09
TTC14 Mike Sweeney	.20	.06
TTC15 Shawn Green	.20	.06
TTC16 Geoff Jenkins	.20	.06
TTC17 Cristian Guzman	.20	.06
TTC18 Vladimir Guerrero	.50	.15
TTC19 Mike Piazza	.75	.23
TTC20 Derek Jeter	1.25	.35
TTC21 Eric Chavez	.20	.06
TTC22 Pat Burrell	.20	.06
TTC23 Brian Giles	.20	.06
TTC24 Phil Nevin	.20	.06
TTC25 Ichiro Suzuki	.75	.23
TTC26 Barry Bonds	1.25	.35
TTC27 J.D. Drew	.20	.06
TTC28 Carlos Delgado	.20	.06
TTC29 Toby Hall	.20	.06
TTC30 Alex Rodriguez		

2002 Topps Total Topps

Inserted in packs at a stated rate of one in three, these 50 cards feature some of the leading players in the game.

	Nm-Mt	Ex-Mt
COMPLETE SET (50)	50.00	15.00
TT1 Roberto Alomar	2.00	.60
TT2 Moises Alou	.75	.23
TT3 Jeff Bagwell	1.25	.35
TT4 Lance Berkman	.75	.23
TT5 Barry Bonds	5.00	1.50
TT6 Bret Boone	.75	.23
TT7 Kevin Brown	.75	.23
TT8 Eric Chavez	.75	.23
TT9 Roger Clemens	4.00	1.20
TT10 Carlos Delgado	.75	.23
TT11 Cliff Floyd	.75	.23
TT12 Nomar Garciaparra	3.00	.90
TT13 Jason Giambi	2.00	.60
TT14 Brian Giles	.75	.23
TT15 Troy Glaus	1.25	.35
TT16 Tom Glavine	1.25	.35
TT17 Luis Gonzalez	.75	.23
TT18 Juan Gonzalez	2.00	.60
TT19 Shawn Green	.75	.23
TT20 Ken Griffey Jr.	3.00	.90
TT21 Vladimir Guerrero	2.00	.60
TT22 Jorge Posada	1.25	.35
TT23 Todd Helton	1.25	.35
TT24 Tim Hudson	.75	.23
TT25 Derek Jeter	5.00	1.50
TT26 Randy Johnson	2.00	.60
TT27 Andruw Jones	.75	.23
TT28 Chipper Jones	2.00	.60
TT29 Jeff Kent	.75	.23
TT30 Greg Maddux	3.00	.90
TT31 Edgar Martinez	1.25	.35
TT32 Pedro Martinez	2.00	.60
TT33 Magglio Ordonez	.75	.23
TT34 Rafael Palmeiro	1.25	.35
TT35 Mike Piazza	3.00	.90
TT36 Albert Pujols	4.00	1.20
TT37 Aramis Ramirez	.75	.23
TT38 Mariano Rivera	1.25	.35
TT39 Alex Rodriguez	3.00	.90
TT40 Ivan Rodriguez	2.00	.60
TT41 Curt Schilling	1.25	.35
TT42 Gary Sheffield	.75	.23
TT43 Sammy Sosa	3.00	.90
TT44 Ichiro Suzuki	3.00	.90
TT45 Miguel Tejada	.75	.23
TT46 Frank Thomas	2.00	.60
TT47 Jim Thome	2.00	.60
TT48 Larry Walker	1.25	.35
TT49 Bernie Williams	1.25	.35
TT50 Kerry Wood	2.00	.60

2003 Topps Total

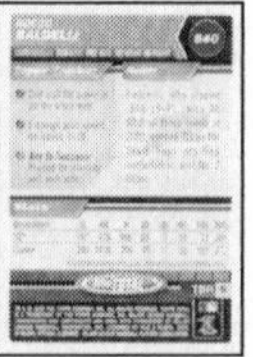

For the second straight year, Topps issued this 990 card set which was designed to be a comprehensive look at who was in the majors at the time of issue. This set was released in May, 2003. This set was issued in 10 card packs with an 99 cent SRP which came 36 packs to a box and 6 boxes to a case.

	Nm-Mt	Ex-Mt
COMPLETE SET (990)	200.00	60.00
COMMON CARD (1-990)	.20	.06
COMMON RC	.25	.07
1 Brent Abernathy	.20	.06
2 Bobby Hill	.20	.06
3 Victor Martinez	.30	.09
4 Chip Ambres	.20	.06
5 Matt Anderson	.20	.06
6 Ricardo Aramboles	.20	.06
7 Carlos Pena	.20	.06
8 Aaron Guiel	.20	.06
9 Luke Allen	.20	.06
10 Francisco Rodriguez	.30	.09
11 Jason Marquis	.20	.06
12 Edwin Almonte	.20	.06
13 Grant Balfour	.20	.06
14 Adam Piatt	.20	.06
15 Andy Phillips	.20	.06
16 Adrian Beltre	.30	.09
17 Brandon Backe	.20	.06
18 Dave Berg	.20	.06
19 Brett Myers	.30	.09
20 Brian Meadows	.20	.06
21 Chin-Feng Chen	.30	.09

2003 Topps Total Silver

22 Blake Williams .20 .06
23 Josh Bard .20 .06
24 Josh Beckett .50 .15
25 Tommy Whiteman .20 .06
26 Matt Childers .20 .06
27 Adam Everett .20 .06
28 Mike Bordick .30 .09
29 Antonio Alfonseca .20 .06
30 Doug Creek .20 .06
31 J.D. Drew .30 .09
32 Milton Bradley .30 .09
33 David Wells .30 .09
34 Vance Wilson .20 .06
35 Jeff Fassero .20 .06
36 Sandy Alomar .20 .06
37 Ryan Vogelsong .20 .06
38 Roger Clemens 1.50 .45
39 Juan Gonzalez .75 .23
40 Dustin Hermanson .20 .06
41 Andy Ashby .20 .06
42 Adam Hyzdu .20 .06
43 Ben Broussard .20 .06
44 Ryan Klesko .30 .09
45 Chris Buglovsky FY RC .40 .12
46 Bud Smith .20 .06
47 Aaron Boone .30 .09
48 Cliff Floyd .30 .09
49 Alex Cora .20 .06
50 Curt Schilling .50 .15
51 Michael Cuddyer .20 .06
52 Joe Valentine FY RC .40 .12
53 Carlos Guillen .20 .06
54 Angel Berroa .30 .09
55 Eli Marrero .20 .06
56 A.J. Burnett .20 .06
57 Oliver Perez .20 .06
58 Matt Morris .30 .09
59 Valerio De Los Santos .20 .06
60 Austin Kearns .30 .09
61 Darren Dreifort .20 .06
62 Jason Standridge .20 .06
63 Carlos Silva .20 .06
64 Moises Alou .30 .09
65 Jason Anderson .20 .06
66 Russell Branyan .20 .06
67 B.J. Ryan .20 .06
68 Cory Aldridge .20 .06
69 Ellis Burks .30 .09
70 Troy Glaus .50 .15
71 Kelly Wunsch .20 .06
72 Brad Wilkerson .20 .06
73 Jayson Durocher .20 .06
74 Tony Fiore .20 .06
75 Brian Giles .30 .09
76 Billy Wagner .30 .09
77 Neifi Perez .20 .06
78 Jose Valverde .20 .06
79 Brent Butler .20 .06
80 Mario Ramos .20 .06
81 Kerry Robinson .20 .06
82 Brent Mayne .20 .06
83 Sean Casey .30 .09
84 Danys Baez .20 .06
85 Chase Utley .30 .09
86 Jared Sandberg .20 .06
87 Terrence Long .30 .09
88 Kevin Walker .20 .06
89 Royce Clayton .20 .06
90 Shea Hillenbrand .30 .09
91 Brad Lidge .20 .06
92 Shawn Chacon .20 .06
93 Kenny Rogers .30 .09
94 Chris Snelling .30 .09
95 Omar Vizquel .30 .09
96 Joe Borchard .30 .09
97 Matt Belisle .20 .06
98 Steve Smyth .20 .06
99 Raul Mondesi .30 .09
100 Chipper Jones .75 .23
101 Victor Alvarez .20 .06
102 J.M. Gold .20 .06
103 Willis Roberts .20 .06
104 Eddie Guardado .30 .09
105 Brad Voyles .20 .06
106 Bronson Arroyo .20 .06
107 Juan Castro .20 .06
108 Dan Plesac .20 .06
109 Ramon Castro .20 .06
110 Tim Salmon .50 .15
111 Gene Kingsale .20 .06
112 J.D. Closser .20 .06
113 Mark Buehrle .30 .09
114 Steve Karsay .20 .06
115 Cristian Guerrero .20 .06
116 Brad Ausmus .20 .06
117 Cristian Guzman .30 .09
118 Dan Wilson .20 .06
119 Jake Westbrook .20 .06
120 Manny Ramirez .30 .09
121 Jason Giambi .75 .23
122 Bob Wickman .20 .06
123 Aaron Cook .20 .06
124 Alfredo Amezaga .20 .06
125 Corey Thurman .20 .06
126 Brandon Puffer .20 .06
127 Hee Seop Choi .30 .09
128 Javier Vazquez .30 .09
129 Carlos Valderrama .20 .06
130 Jerome Williams .30 .09
131 Wilson Betemit .20 .06
132 Luke Prokopec .20 .06
133 Esteban Yan .20 .06
134 Brandon Berger .20 .06
135 Bill Hall .20 .06
136 LaTroy Hawkins .20 .06
137 Nate Cornejo .20 .06
138 Jim Mecir .20 .06
139 Joe Crede .20 .06
140 Andres Galarraga .30 .09
141 Reggie Sanders .20 .06
142 Joey Eischen .20 .06
143 Mike Timlin .20 .06
144 Jose Cruz Jr. .30 .09
145 Wes Helms .20 .06
146 Brian Roberts .20 .06
147 Bret Prinz .20 .06
148 Brian Hunter .20 .06
149 Chad Hermansen .20 .06
150 Andruw Jones .30 .09
151 Kurt Ainsworth .20 .06
152 Cliff Bartosh .20 .06
153 Kyle Lohse .20 .06
154 Brian Jordan .30 .09
155 Coco Crisp .20 .06
156 Tomas Perez .20 .06
157 Keith Foulke .20 .06
158 Chris Carpenter .20 .06
159 Mike Remlinger .20 .06
160 Dewon Brazelton .20 .06
161 Brook Fordyce .20 .06
162 Rusty Greer .30 .09
163 Scott Downs .20 .06
164 Jason Dubois .30 .09
165 David Coggin .20 .06
166 Mike DeJean .20 .06
167 Carlos Hernandez .20 .06
168 Matt Williams .30 .09
169 Rheal Cormier .20 .06
170 Duaner Sanchez .20 .06
171 Craig Counsell .20 .06
172 Edgar Martinez .50 .15
173 Zack Greinke .75 .23
174 Pedro Feliz .20 .06
175 Randy Choate .20 .06
176 Jon Garland .20 .06
177 Keith Ginter .20 .06
178 Carlos Febles .20 .06
179 Kerry Wood .75 .23
180 Jack Cust .20 .06
181 Koyie Hill .20 .06
182 Ricky Gutierrez .20 .06
183 Ben Grieve .20 .06
184 Scott Eyre .20 .06
185 Jason Isringhausen .30 .09
186 Gookie Dawkins .20 .06
187 Roberto Alomar .75 .23
188 Eric Junge .20 .06
189 Carlos Beltran .30 .09
190 Denny Hocking .20 .06
191 Jason Schmidt .30 .09
192 Cory Lidle .20 .06
193 Rob Mackowiak .20 .06
194 Charlton Jimerson RC .40 .12
195 Darin Erstad .30 .09
196 Jason Davis .20 .06
197 Luis Castillo .30 .09
198 Juan Encarnacion .20 .06
199 Jeffrey Hammonds .20 .06
200 Nomar Garciaparra 1.25 .35
201 Ryan Christianson .20 .06
202 Robert Person .20 .06
203 Damian Moss .20 .06
204 Chris Richard .20 .06
205 Todd Hundley .20 .06
206 Paul Bako .20 .06
207 Adam Kennedy .20 .06
208 Scott Hatteberg .20 .06
209 Andy Pratt .20 .06
210 Ken Griffey Jr. 1.25 .35
211 Chris George .20 .06
212 Lance Niekro .20 .06
213 Greg Colbrunn .20 .06
214 Herbert Perry .20 .06
215 Cody Ransom .20 .06
216 Craig Biggio .50 .15
217 Miguel Batista .20 .06
218 Alex Escobar .20 .06
219 Willie Harris .20 .06
220 Scott Strickland .20 .06
221 Felix Rodriguez .20 .06
222 Torii Hunter .30 .09
223 Tyler Houston .20 .06
224 Darrell May .20 .06
225 Benito Santiago .30 .09
226 Ryan Dempster .20 .06
227 Andy Fox .20 .06
228 Jung Bong .20 .06
229 Jose Macias .20 .06
230 Shannon Stewart .30 .09
231 Buddy Groom .20 .06
232 Eric Valent .20 .06
233 Scott Schoenweis .20 .06
234 Corey Hart .30 .09
235 Brett Tomko .20 .06
236 Shane Bazzell RC .40 .12
237 Tim Hummel .20 .06
238 Matt Stairs .20 .06
239 Pete Munro .20 .06
240 Ismael Valdes .20 .06
241 Brian Fuentes .20 .06
242 Cesar Izturis .20 .06
243 Mark Bellhorn .20 .06
244 Geoff Jenkins .30 .09
245 Derek Jeter 2.00 .60
246 Anderson Machado .20 .06
247 Dave Roberts .20 .06
248 Jaime Cerda .20 .06
249 Woody Williams .20 .06
250 Vernon Wells .30 .09
251 Jon Lieber .20 .06
252 Franklyn German .20 .06
253 David Segui .20 .06
254 Freddy Garcia .30 .09
255 James Baldwin .20 .06
256 Tony Alvarez .20 .06
257 Walter Young .20 .06
258 Alex Herrera .20 .06
259 Robert Fick .30 .09
260 Rob Bell .20 .06
261 Ben Petrick .20 .06
262 Dee Brown .20 .06
263 Mike Bacsik .20 .06
264 Corey Patterson .30 .09
265 Marvin Benard .20 .06
266 Eddie Rogers .20 .06
267 Elio Serrano .20 .06
268 D'Angelo Jimenez .20 .06
269 Adam Johnson .20 .06
270 Gregg Zaun .20 .06
271 Nick Johnson .30 .09
272 Geoff Goetz .20 .06
273 Ryan Drese .20 .06
274 Eric Dubose .20 .06
275 Barry Zito .50 .15
276 Mike Crudale .20 .06
277 Paul Byrd .20 .06
278 Eric Gagne .50 .15
279 Aramis Ramirez .30 .09
280 Ray Durham .30 .09
281 Tony Graffanino .20 .06
282 Jeremy Guthrie .20 .06
283 Erik Bedard .20 .06
284 Vince Faison .20 .06
285 Bobby Kielty .20 .06
286 Francis Beltran .20 .06
287 Alexis Gomez .20 .06
288 Vladimir Guerrero .75 .23
289 Kevin Appier .30 .09
290 Gil Meche .20 .06
291 Marquis Grissom .20 .06
292 John Burkett .20 .06
293 Vinny Castilla .30 .09
294 Tyler Walker .20 .06
295 Shane Halter .20 .06
296 Geronimo Gil .20 .06
297 Eric Hinske .20 .06
298 Adam Dunn .30 .09
299 Mike Kinkade .20 .06
300 Mark Prior 1.50 .45
301 Corey Koskie .30 .09
302 David Dellucci .20 .06
303 Todd Helton .50 .15
304 Greg Miller .20 .06
305 Delvin James .20 .06
306 Humberto Cota .20 .06
307 Aaron Harang .20 .06
308 Jeremy Hill .20 .06
309 Billy Koch .20 .06
310 Brandon Claussen .30 .09
311 Matt Ginter .20 .06
312 Jason Lane .20 .06
313 Ben Weber .20 .06
314 Alan Benes .20 .06
315 Matt Walbeck .20 .06
316 Danny Graves .20 .06
317 Jason Johnson .20 .06
318 Jason Grimsley .20 .06
319 Steve Kline .20 .06
320 Johnny Damon .30 .09
321 Jay Gibbons .30 .09
322 J.J. Putz .20 .06
323 Stephen Randolph RC .40 .12
324 Bobby Higginson .30 .09
325 Kazuhisa Ishii .30 .09
326 Carlos Lee .30 .09
327 J.R. House .20 .06
328 Mark Loretta .20 .06
329 Mike Matheny .20 .06
330 Ben Diggins .20 .06
331 Seth Etherton .20 .06
332 Eli Whiteside FY RC .40 .12
333 Juan Rivera .20 .06
334 Jeff Conine .30 .09
335 John McDonald .20 .06
336 Erik Hiljus .20 .06
337 David Eckstein .20 .06
338 Jeff Bagwell .50 .15
339 Matt Holliday .20 .06
340 Jeff Liefer .20 .06
341 Greg Myers .20 .06
342 Scott Sauerbeck .20 .06
343 Omar Infante .20 .06
344 Ryan Langerhans .20 .06
345 Abraham Nunez .20 .06
346 Mike MacDougal .20 .06
347 Travis Phelps .20 .06
348 Terry Shumpert .20 .06
349 Alex Rodriguez 1.25 .35
350 Bobby Seay .20 .06
351 Ichiro Suzuki 1.25 .35
352 Brandon Inge .20 .06
353 Jack Wilson .20 .06
354 John Ennis .20 .06
355 Jamal Strong .20 .06
356 Jason Jennings .20 .06
357 Jeff Kent .30 .09
358 Scott Chiasson .20 .06
359 Jeremy Griffiths RC .50 .15
360 Paul Konerko .30 .09
361 Jeff Austin .20 .06
362 Todd Van Poppel .20 .06
363 Sun Woo Kim .20 .06
364 Jerry Hairston Jr. .20 .06
365 Tony Torcato .20 .06
366 Arthur Rhodes .20 .06
367 Jose Jimenez .20 .06
368 Matt LeCroy .20 .06
369 Curtis Leskanic .20 .06
370 Ramon Vazquez .20 .06
371 Joe Randa .20 .06
372 John Franco .30 .09
373 Bobby Estalella .20 .06
374 Craig Wilson .20 .06
375 Michael Young .30 .09
376 Mark Ellis .20 .06
377 Joe Mauer .75 .23
378 Checklist 1 .20 .06
379 Jason Kendall .30 .09
380 Checklist 2 .20 .06
381 Alex Gonzalez .20 .06
382 Tom Gordon .20 .06
383 John Buck .20 .06
384 Shigetoshi Hasegawa .30 .09
385 Scott Stewart .20 .06
386 Luke Hudson .20 .06
387 Todd Jones .20 .06
388 Fred McGriff .50 .15
389 Mike Sweeney .30 .09
390 Marlon Anderson .20 .06
391 Terry Adams .20 .06
392 Mark DeRosa .20 .06
393 Doug Mientkiewicz .30 .09
394 Miguel Cairo .20 .06
395 Jamie Moyer .30 .09
396 Jose Leon .20 .06
397 Matt Clement .30 .09
398 Bengie Molina .20 .06
399 Marcus Thames .20 .06
400 Nick Bierbrodt .20 .06
401 Tim Kalita .20 .06
402 Corwin Malone .20 .06
403 Jesse Orosco .20 .06
404 Brandon Phillips .20 .06
405 Eric Cyr .20 .06
406 Jason Michaels .20 .06
407 Julio Lugo .20 .06
408 Gabe Kapler .20 .06
409 Mark Mulder .30 .09
410 Adam Eaton .20 .06
411 Ken Harvey .20 .06
412 Jolbert Cabrera .20 .06
413 Eric Milton .20 .06
414 Josh Hall RC .50 .15
415 Bob File .20 .06
416 Brett Evert .20 .06
417 Ron Chiavacci .20 .06
418 Jorge De La Rosa .20 .06
419 Quinton McCracken .20 .06
420 Luther Hackman .20 .06
421 Gary Knotts .20 .06
422 Kevin Brown .30 .09
423 Jeff Cirillo .20 .06
424 Damaso Marte .20 .06
425 Chan Ho Park .30 .09
426 Nathan Haynes .20 .06
427 Matt Lawton .20 .06
428 Mike Stanton .20 .06
429 Bernie Williams .50 .15
430 Kevin Jarvis .20 .06
431 Joe McEwing .20 .06
432 Mark Kotsay .20 .06
433 Juan Cruz .20 .06
434 Russ Ortiz .30 .09
435 Jeff Nelson .20 .06
436 Alan Embree .20 .06
437 Miguel Tejada .30 .09
438 Kirk Saarloos .20 .06
439 Cliff Lee .30 .09
440 Ryan Ludwick .20 .06
441 Derrek Lee .30 .09
442 Bobby Abreu .30 .09
443 Dustan Mohr .20 .06
444 Nook Logan RC .40 .12
445 Seth McClung .20 .06
446 Miguel Olivo .20 .06
447 Henry Blanco .20 .06
448 Seung Song .20 .06
449 Kris Wilson .20 .06
450 Xavier Nady .20 .06
451 Corky Miller .20 .06
452 Jim Thome .75 .23
453 George Lombard .20 .06
454 Rey Ordonez .20 .06
455 Deivis Santos .20 .06
456 Mike Myers .20 .06
457 Edgar Renteria .30 .09
458 Braden Looper .20 .06
459 Guillermo Mota .20 .06
460 Scott Rolen .50 .15
461 Lance Berkman .30 .09
462 Jeff Heaverlo .20 .06
463 Ramon Hernandez .20 .06
464 Jason Simontacchi .20 .06
465 So Taguchi .30 .09
466 Dave Veres .20 .06
467 Shane Loux .20 .06
468 Rodrigo Lopez .20 .06
469 Bubba Trammell .20 .06
470 Scott Sullivan .20 .06
471 Mike Mussina .75 .23
472 Ramon Ortiz .20 .06
473 Lyle Overbay .20 .06
474 Mike Lowell .30 .09
475 Al Martin .20 .06
476 Larry Bigbie .20 .06
477 Rey Sanchez .20 .06
478 Magglio Ordonez .30 .09
479 Rondell White .30 .09
480 Jay Witasick .20 .06
481 Jimmy Rollins .30 .09
482 Mike Maroth .20 .06
483 Alejandro Machado .20 .06
484 Nick Neugebauer .20 .06
485 Victor Zambrano .20 .06
486 Travis Lee .20 .06
487 Bobby Bradley .20 .06
488 Marcus Giles .30 .09
489 Steve Trachsel .20 .06
490 Derek Lowe .30 .09
491 Hideo Nomo .75 .23
492 Brad Hawpe .30 .09
493 Jesus Medrano .20 .06
494 Rick Ankiel .20 .06
495 Pasqual Coco .20 .06
496 Michael Barrett .20 .06
497 Joe Beimel .20 .06
498 Marty Cordova .20 .06
499 Aaron Sele .20 .06
500 Sammy Sosa 1.25 .35
501 Ivan Rodriguez .75 .23
502 Keith Osik .20 .06
503 Hank Blalock .50 .15
504 Hiram Bocachica .20 .06
505 Junior Spivey .20 .06
506 Edgardo Alfonzo .30 .09
507 Alex Graman .20 .06
508 J.J. Davis .20 .06
509 Roger Cedeno .20 .06
510 Joe Roa .20 .06
511 Wily Mo Pena .20 .06
512 Eric Munson .30 .09
513 Arnie Munoz RC .40 .12
514 Albie Lopez .20 .06
515 Andy Pettitte .50 .15
516 Jim Edmonds .30 .09
517 Jeff Davanon .20 .06
518 Aaron Myette .20 .06
519 C.C. Sabathia .30 .09
520 Gerardo Garcia .20 .06
521 Brian Schneider .20 .06
522 Wes Obermueller .20 .06
523 John Mabry .20 .06
524 Casey Fossum .20 .06
525 Toby Hall .20 .06
526 Denny Neagle .20 .06
527 Willie Bloomquist .30 .09
528 A.J. Pierzynski .30 .09
529 Bartolo Colon .30 .09
530 Chad Harville .20 .06
531 Blaine Neal .20 .06
532 Luis Terrero .20 .06
533 Reggie Taylor .20 .06
534 Melvin Mora .20 .06
535 Tino Martinez .50 .15
536 Peter Bergeron .20 .06
537 Jorge Padilla .20 .06
538 Oscar Villarreal RC .40 .12
539 David Weathers .20 .06
540 Mike Lamb .20 .06
541 Greg Norton .20 .06
542 Michael Tucker .20 .06
543 Ben Kozlowski .20 .06
544 Alex Sanchez .20 .06
545 Trey Lunsford .20 .06
546 Abraham Nunez .20 .06
547 Mike Lincoln .20 .06
548 Orlando Hernandez .30 .09
549 Kevin Mench .20 .06
550 Garret Anderson .30 .09
551 Kyle Farnsworth .20 .06
552 Kevin Olsen .20 .06
553 Joel Pineiro .30 .09
554 Jorge Julio .20 .06
555 Jose Mesa .20 .06
556 Jorge Posada .50 .15
557 Jose Ortiz .20 .06
558 Mike Tonis .20 .06
559 Gabe White .20 .06
560 Rafael Furcal .30 .09
561 Matt Franco .20 .06
562 Trey Hodges .20 .06
563 Esteban German .20 .06
564 Josh Fogg .20 .06
565 Fernando Tatis .20 .06
566 Alex Cintron .30 .09
567 Grant Roberts .20 .06
568 Gene Stechschulte .20 .06
569 Rafael Palmeiro .50 .15
570 Mike Hampton .30 .09
571 Ben Davis .20 .06
572 Dean Palmer .30 .09
573 Jerrod Riggan .20 .06
574 Nate Frese .20 .06
575 Josh Phelps .20 .06
576 Freddie Bynum .20 .06
577 Morgan Ensberg .20 .06
578 Juan Rincon .20 .06
579 Kazuhiro Sasaki .30 .09
580 Yorvit Torrealba .20 .06
581 Tim Wakefield .30 .09
582 Sterling Hitchcock .20 .06
583 Craig Paquette .20 .06
584 Kevin Millwood .30 .09
585 Damian Rolls .20 .06
586 Brad Baisley .20 .06
587 Kyle Snyder .20 .06
588 Paul Quantrill .20 .06
589 Trot Nixon .50 .15
590 J.T. Snow .30 .09
591 Kevin Young .20 .06
592 Tomo Ohka .20 .06
593 Brian Boehringer .20 .06
594 Danny Patterson .20 .06
595 Jeff Tam .20 .06
596 Anastacio Martinez .20 .06
597 Rod Barajas .20 .06
598 Octavio Dotel .20 .06
599 Jason Tyner .20 .06
600 Gary Sheffield .30 .09
601 Ruben Quevedo .20 .06
602 Jay Payton .20 .06
603 Mo Vaughn .30 .09
604 Pat Burrell .30 .09
605 Fernando Vina .20 .06
606 Wes Anderson .20 .06
607 Alex Gonzalez .20 .06
608 Ted Lilly .20 .06
609 Nick Punto .20 .06
610 Ryan Madson .20 .06
611 Odalis Perez .20 .06
612 Chris Woodward .20 .06
613 John Olerud .30 .09
614 Brad Cresse .20 .06
615 Chad Zerbe .20 .06
616 Brad Penny .20 .06
617 Barry Larkin .75 .23
618 Brandon Duckworth .20 .06
619 Brad Radke .30 .09
620 Troy Brohawn .20 .06
621 Juan Pierre .30 .09
622 Rick Reed .20 .06
623 Omar Daal .20 .06
624 Jose Hernandez .20 .06
625 Greg Maddux 1.25 .35
626 Henry Mateo .20 .06
627 Kip Wells .20 .06
628 Kevin Cash .20 .06
629 Wil Ledezma FY RC .40 .12
630 Luis Gonzalez .30 .09
631 Jason Conti .20 .06
632 Ricardo Rincon .20 .06
633 Mike Bynum .20 .06
634 Mike Redmond .20 .06
635 Chance Caple .20 .06
636 Chris Widger .20 .06
637 Michael Restovich .20 .06
638 Mark Grudzielanek .20 .06
639 Brandon Larson .20 .06
640 Rocco Baldelli 1.25 .35
641 Javy Lopez .30 .09
642 Rene Reyes .20 .06
643 Orlando Merced .20 .06
644 Jason Phillips .30 .09
645 Luis Ugueto .20 .06
646 Ron Calloway .20 .06
647 Josh Paul .20 .06
648 Todd Greene .20 .06
649 Joe Girardi .20 .06
650 Todd Ritchie .20 .06
651 Kevin Millar .30 .09
652 Shawn Wooten .20 .06
653 David Riske .20 .06
654 Luis Rivas .20 .06
655 Roy Halladay .30 .09
656 Travis Driskill .20 .06
657 Ricky Ledee .20 .06
658 Timo Perez .20 .06
659 Fernando Rodney .20 .06
660 Trevor Hoffman .30 .09
661 Pat Hentgen .30 .09
662 Bret Boone .30 .09
663 Ryan Jensen .20 .06
664 Ricardo Rodriguez .20 .06
665 Jeremy Lambert .20 .06
666 Troy Percival .30 .09
667 Jon Rauch .20 .06
668 Mariano Rivera .50 .15
669 Jason LaRue .20 .06
670 J.C. Romero .20 .06
671 Cody Ross .20 .06
672 Eric Byrnes .20 .06
673 Paul Lo Duca .30 .09
674 Brad Fullmer .20 .06
675 Cliff Politte .20 .06
676 Justin Miller .20 .06

677 Nic Jackson .20 .06
678 Kris Benson .20 .06
679 Carl Sadler .20 .06
680 Joe Nathan .20 .06
681 Julio Santana .20 .06
682 Wade Miller .30 .09
683 Josh Pearce .20 .06
684 Tony Armas Jr. .20 .06
685 Al Leiter .30 .09
686 Raul Ibanez .20 .06
687 Danny Bautista .20 .06
688 Travis Hafner .30 .09
689 Carlos Zambrano .30 .09
690 Pedro Martinez .75 .23
691 Ramon Santiago .20 .06
692 Felipe Lopez .20 .06
693 David Ross .20 .06
694 Chone Figgins .20 .06
695 Antonio Osuna .20 .06
696 Jay Powell .20 .06
697 Ryan Church .20 .06
698 Alexis Rios 1.25 .35
699 Tanyon Sturtze .20 .06
700 Turk Wendell .20 .06
701 Richard Hidalgo .30 .09
702 Joe Mays .20 .06
703 Jorge Sosa .20 .06
704 Eric Karros .30 .09
705 Steve Finley .30 .09
706 Sean Smith FY RC .50 .15
707 Jeremy Giambi .20 .06
708 Scott Hodges .20 .06
709 Vicente Padilla .20 .06
710 Erubiel Durazo .20 .06
711 Aaron Rowand .20 .06
712 Dennis Tankersley .20 .06
713 Rick Bauer .20 .06
714 Tim Olson FY RC .50 .15
715 Jeff Urban .20 .06
716 Steve Sparks .20 .06
717 Glendon Rusch .20 .06
718 Ricky Stone .20 .06
719 Benji Gil .20 .06
720 Pete Walker .20 .06
721 Tim Worrell .20 .06
722 Michael Tejera .20 .06
723 David Kelton .20 .06
724 Britt Reames .20 .06
725 John Stephens .20 .06
726 Mark McLemore .20 .06
727 Jeff Zimmerman .20 .06
728 Checklist 3 .20 .06
729 Andres Torres .20 .06
730 Checklist 4 .20 .06
731 Johan Santana .30 .09
732 Dane Sardinha .20 .06
733 Rodrigo Rosario .20 .06
734 Frank Thomas .75 .23
735 Tom Glavine .50 .15
736 Doug Mirabelli .20 .06
737 Juan Uribe .20 .06
738 Ryan Anderson .20 .06
739 Sean Burroughs .30 .09
740 Eric Chavez .30 .09
741 Enrique Wilson .20 .06
742 Elmer Dessens .20 .06
743 Marlon Byrd .30 .09
744 Brendan Donnelly .20 .06
745 Gary Bennett .20 .06
746 Roy Oswalt .30 .09
747 Andy Van Hekken .20 .06
748 Jesus Colome .20 .06
749 Erick Almonte .20 .06
750 Frank Catalanotto .20 .06
751 Kenny Lofton .30 .09
752 Carlos Delgado .30 .09
753 Ryan Franklin .20 .06
754 Wilkin Ruan .20 .06
755 Kelvim Escobar .20 .06
756 Tim Drew .20 .06
757 Jarrod Washburn .30 .09
758 Runelvys Hernandez .20 .06
759 Cory Vance .20 .06
760 Doug Glanville .20 .06
761 Ryan Rupe .20 .06
762 Jermaine Dye .20 .06
763 Mike Cameron .30 .09
764 Scott Erickson .20 .06
765 Richie Sexson .30 .09
766 Jose Vidro .30 .09
767 Brian West .20 .06
768 Shawn Estes .20 .06
769 Brian Tallet .20 .06
770 Larry Walker .50 .15
771 Josh Hamilton .20 .06
772 Orlando Hudson .20 .06
773 Justin Morneau .30 .09
774 Ryan Bukvich .20 .06
775 Mike Gonzalez .20 .06
776 Tsuyoshi Shinjo .30 .09
777 Matt Mantei .20 .06
778 Jimmy Journell .20 .06
779 Brian Lawrence .20 .06
780 Mike Lieberthal .30 .09
781 Scott Mullen .20 .06
782 Zach Day .20 .06
783 John Thomson .20 .06
784 Ben Sheets .30 .09
785 Damon Minor .20 .06
786 Jose Valentin .20 .06
787 Armando Benitez .30 .09
788 Jamie Walker .20 .06
789 Preston Wilson .30 .09
790 Josh Wilson .20 .06
791 Phil Nevin .30 .09
792 Roberto Hernandez .20 .06
793 Mike Williams .20 .06
794 Jake Peavy .30 .09
795 Paul Shuey .20 .06
796 Chad Bradford .20 .06
797 Bobby Jenks .30 .09
798 Sean Douglass .20 .06
799 Damian Miller .20 .06
800 Mark Wohlers .20 .06
801 Ty Wigginton .30 .09
802 Alfonso Soriano .50 .15
803 Randy Johnson .75 .23
804 Placido Polanco .20 .06
805 Drew Henson .30 .09
806 Tony Womack .20 .06
807 Pokey Reese .20 .06
808 Albert Pujols 1.50 .45
809 Henri Stanley .20 .06
810 Mike Rivera .20 .06
811 John Lackey .20 .06
812 Brian Wright FY RC .40 .12
813 Eric Good .20 .06
814 Dernell Stenson .20 .06
815 Kirk Rueter .20 .06
816 Todd Zeile .20 .06
817 Brad Thomas .20 .06
818 Shawn Sedlacek .20 .06
819 Garrett Stephenson .20 .06
820 Mark Teixeira .50 .15
821 Tim Hudson .30 .09
822 Mike Koplove .20 .06
823 Chris Reitsma .20 .06
824 Rafael Soriano .20 .06
825 Ugueth Urbina .20 .06
826 Lance Carter .20 .06
827 Colin Young .20 .06
828 Pat Strange .20 .06
829 Juan Pena .20 .06
830 Joe Thurston .20 .06
831 Shawn Green .30 .09
832 Pedro Astacio .20 .06
833 Danny Wright .20 .06
834 Wes O'Brien FY RC .40 .12
835 Luis Lopez .20 .06
836 Randall Simon .20 .06
837 Jaret Wright .20 .06
838 Jayson Werth .20 .06
839 Endy Chavez .20 .06
840 Checklist 5 .20 .06
841 Chad Paronto .20 .06
842 Randy Winn .20 .06
843 Sidney Ponson .30 .09
844 Robin Ventura .30 .09
845 Rich Aurilia .30 .09
846 Joaquin Benoit .20 .06
847 Barry Bonds 2.00 .60
848 Carl Crawford .30 .09
849 Jeromy Burnitz .30 .09
850 Orlando Cabrera .20 .06
851 Luis Vizcaino .20 .06
852 Randy Wolf .30 .09
853 Todd Walker .30 .09
854 Jeremy Affeldt .20 .06
855 Einar Diaz .20 .06
856 Carl Everett .30 .09
857 Wiki Gonzalez .20 .06
858 Mike Paradis .20 .06
859 Travis Harper .20 .06
860 Mike Piazza 1.25 .35
861 Will Ohman .20 .06
862 Eric Young .20 .06
863 Jason Grabowski .20 .06
864 Rett Johnson RC .50 .15
865 Aubrey Huff .30 .09
866 John Smoltz .50 .15
867 Mickey Callaway .20 .06
868 Joe Kennedy .20 .06
869 Tim Redding .20 .06
870 Colby Lewis .20 .06
871 Salomon Torres .20 .06
872 Marco Scutaro .20 .06
873 Tony Batista .30 .09
874 Dmitri Young .30 .09
875 Scott Williamson .20 .06
876 Scott Spiezio .20 .06
877 John Webb .20 .06
878 Jose Acevedo .20 .06
879 Kevin Orie .20 .06
880 Jacque Jones .30 .09
881 Ben Francisco FY RC .50 .15
882 Bobby Basham FY RC .75 .23
883 Corey Shafer FY RC .50 .15
884 J.D. Durbin FY RC .75 .23
885 Chien-Ming Wang FY RC 1.50 .45
886 Adam Stern FY RC .40 .12
887 Wayne Lydon FY RC .40 .12
888 Derell McCall FY RC .40 .12
889 Jon Nelson FY RC .50 .15
890 Willie Eyre FY RC .40 .12
891 R.Nivar-Martinez FY RC .75 .23
892 Adrian Myers FY RC .25 .07
893 Jamie Athas FY RC .40 .12
894 Ismael Castro FY RC .50 .15
895 David Martinez FY RC .40 .12
896 Terry Tiffee FY RC .50 .15
897 Nathan Panther FY RC .75 .23
898 Kyle Roat FY RC .40 .12
899 Kason Gabbard FY RC .40 .12
900 Hanley Ramirez FY RC 1.50 .45
901 Bryan Grace FY RC .40 .12
902 B.J. Barns FY RC .40 .12
903 Greg Bruso FY RC .40 .12
904 Mike Neu FY RC .40 .12
905 Dustin Yount FY RC .75 .23
906 Shane Victorino FY RC .40 .12
907 Brian Burgamy FY RC .40 .12
908 Beau Kemp FY RC .40 .12
909 David Corrente FY RC .40 .12
910 Dexter Cooper FY RC .40 .12
911 Chris Colton FY RC .40 .12
912 David Cash FY RC .40 .12
913 Bernie Castro FY RC .40 .12
914 Luis Hodge FY RC .40 .12
915 Jeff Clark FY RC .40 .12
916 Jason Kubel FY RC .75 .23
917 T.J. Bohn FY RC .40 .12
918 Luke Steidlmayer FY RC .40 .12
919 Matthew Peterson FY RC .40 .12
920 Darrell Rasner FY RC .40 .12
921 Scott Tyler FY RC .50 .15
922 G.Schneidmiller FY RC .40 .12
923 Gregor Blanco FY RC .40 .12
924 Ryan Cameron FY RC .40 .12
925 Wilfredo Rodriguez FY .20 .06
926 Rajai Davis FY RC .50 .15
927 E.Bastida-Martinez FY RC .40 .12
928 Chris Duncan FY RC .40 .12
929 Dave Pember FY RC .40 .12
930 Branden Florence FY RC .40 .12
931 Eric Eckenstahler FY .20 .06
932 Hong-Chih Kuo FY RC .75 .23
933 Il Kim FY RC .40 .12
934 Mi. Garciaparra FY RC 1.00 .30
935 Kip Bouknight FY RC .50 .15
936 Gary Harris FY RC .40 .12
937 Derry Hammond FY RC .40 .12
938 Joey Gomes FY RC .40 .12
939 Donnie Hood FY RC .50 .15
940 Clay Hensley FY RC .40 .12
941 David Pahucki FY RC .40 .12
942 Wilton Reynolds FY RC .40 .12
943 Michael Hinckley FY RC .75 .23
944 Josh Willingham FY RC 1.25 .35
945 Pete LaForest FY RC .50 .15
946 Pete Smart FY RC .40 .12
947 Jay Sitzman FY RC .40 .12
948 Mark Malaska FY RC .40 .12
949 Mike Gallo FY RC .40 .12
950 Matt Diaz FY RC .75 .23
951 Brennan King FY RC .40 .12
952 Ryan Howard FY RC 1.00 .30
953 Daryl Clark FY RC .50 .15
954 Dayton Buller FY RC .40 .12
955 Rylan Reed FY RC .40 .12
956 Chris Booker FY .20 .06
957 Brandon Watson FY RC .40 .12
958 Matt DeMarco FY RC .40 .12
959 Doug Waechter FY RC .50 .15
960 Callix Crabbe FY RC .50 .15
961 Jairo Garcia FY RC .40 .12
962 Jason Perry FY RC .75 .23
963 Eric Riggs FY RC .50 .15
964 Travis Ishikawa FY RC .50 .15
965 Simon Pond FY RC .75 .23
966 Manuel Ramirez FY RC .50 .15
967 Tyler Johnson FY RC .40 .12
968 Jaime Bubela FY RC .40 .12
969 Haj Turay FY RC .50 .15
970 Tyson Graham FY RC .40 .12
971 David DeJesus FY RC .75 .23
972 Franklin Gutierrez FY RC 2.00 .60
973 Craig Brazell FY RC .50 .15
974 Keith Stamler FY RC .40 .12
975 Jemel Spearman FY RC .40 .12
976 Ozzie Chavez FY RC .40 .12
977 Nick Trzesniak FY RC .40 .12
978 Bill Simon FY RC .40 .12
979 Matthew Hagen FY RC .75 .23
980 Chris Kroski FY RC .40 .12
981 Prentice Redman FY RC .40 .12
982 Kevin Randel FY RC .40 .12
983 Tho. Story-Harden FY RC .40 .12
984 Brian Shackelford FY RC .40 .12
985 Mike Adams FY RC .40 .12
986 Brian McCann FY RC .75 .23
987 Mike McNutt FY RC .40 .12
988 Aron Weston FY RC .40 .12
989 Dustin Moseley FY RC .50 .15
990 Bryan Bullington FY RC 1.50 .45

2003 Topps Total Silver

Nm-Mt Ex-Mt
*SILVER: 1X TO 2.5X BASIC
*SILVER RC'S: 1X TO 2.5X BASIC
STATED ODDS 1:1

2003 Topps Total Award Winners

Nm-Mt Ex-Mt
COMPLETE SET (30) 40.00 12.00
STATED ODDS 1:12
AW1 Barry Zito 1.25 .35
AW2 Randy Johnson 2.00 .60
AW3 Miguel Tejada .75 .23
AW4 Barry Bonds 5.00 1.50
AW5 Sammy Sosa 3.00 .90
AW6 Barry Bonds 5.00 1.50
AW7 Mike Piazza 3.00 .90
AW8 Todd Helton 1.25 .35
AW9 Jeff Kent .75 .23
AW10 Edgar Renteria .75 .23
AW11 Scott Rolen 1.25 .35
AW12 Vladimir Guerrero 2.00 .60
AW13 Mike Hampton .75 .23
AW14 Jason Giambi 2.00 .60
AW15 Alfonso Soriano 1.25 .35
AW16 Alex Rodriguez 3.00 .90
AW17 Eric Chavez .75 .23
AW18 Jorge Posada 1.25 .35
AW19 Bernie Williams 1.25 .35
AW20 Magglio Ordonez .75 .23
AW21 Garret Anderson .75 .23
AW22 Manny Ramirez .75 .23
AW23 Jason Jennings .75 .23
AW24 Eric Hinske .75 .23
AW25 Billy Koch .75 .23
AW26 John Smoltz 1.25 .35
AW27 Alex Rodriguez 3.00 .90
AW28 Barry Bonds 5.00 1.50
AW29 Tony La Russa MG .75 .23
AW30 Mike Scioscia MG .75 .23

2003 Topps Total Production

Nm-Mt Ex-Mt
COMPLETE SET (10) 20.00 6.00
STATED ODDS 1:18
TP1 Barry Bonds 5.00 1.50
TP2 Manny Ramirez .75 .23
TP3 Albert Pujols 4.00 1.20
TP4 Jason Giambi 2.00 .60
TP5 Magglio Ordonez .75 .23
TP6 Lance Berkman .75 .23
TP7 Todd Helton 1.25 .35
TP8 Miguel Tejada .75 .23
TP9 Sammy Sosa 3.00 .90
TP10 Alex Rodriguez 3.00 .90

2003 Topps Total Signatures

Nm-Mt Ex-Mt
STATED ODDS 1:176
TS-BP Brandon Phillips 10.00 3.00
TS-EM Eli Marrero 10.00 3.00
TS-MB Marlon Byrd 15.00 4.50
TS-MT Marcus Thames 10.00 3.00
TS-TT Tony Torcato 10.00 3.00

2003 Topps Total Team Checklists

Nm-Mt Ex-Mt
COMPLETE SET (30) 10.00 3.00
RANDOM INSERTS IN PACKS
1 Troy Glaus .30 .09
2 Randy Johnson .50 .15
3 Greg Maddux .75 .23
4 Jay Gibbons .20 .06
5 Nomar Garciaparra .75 .23
6 Sammy Sosa .75 .23
7 Paul Konerko .20 .06
8 Ken Griffey Jr. .75 .23
9 Omar Vizquel .20 .06
10 Todd Helton .30 .09
11 Carlos Pena .20 .06
12 Mike Lowell .20 .06
13 Lance Berkman .20 .06
14 Mike Sweeney .20 .06
15 Shawn Green .20 .06
16 Richie Sexson .20 .06
17 Torii Hunter .20 .06
18 Vladimir Guerrero .50 .15
19 Mike Piazza .75 .23
20 Jason Giambi .50 .15
21 Eric Chavez .20 .06
22 Jim Thome .50 .15
23 Brian Giles .20 .06
24 Ryan Klesko .20 .06
25 Barry Bonds 1.25 .35
26 Ichiro Suzuki .75 .23
27 Albert Pujols 1.00 .30
28 Carl Crawford .20 .06
29 Alex Rodriguez .75 .23
30 Carlos Delgado .20 .06

2003 Topps Total Team Logo Stickers

Nm-Mt Ex-Mt
COMPLETE SET (3) 5.00 1.50
STATED ODDS 1:24
1 Anaheim Angels 2.00 .60
Arizona Diamondbacks
Atlanta Braves
Baltimore Orioles
Boston Red Sox
Chicago Cubs
Chicago White Sox
Cincinnati Reds
Cleveland Indians
Colorado Rockies
2 Detroit Tigers 2.00 .60
Florida Marlins
Houston Astros
Kansas City Royals
Los Angeles Dodgers
Milwaukee Brewers
Minnesota Twins
Montreal Expos
New York Mets
New York Yankees
3 Oakland Athletics 2.00 .60
Philadelphia Phillies
Pittsburgh Pirates
San Diego Padres
San Francisco Giants
Seattle Mariners
St. Louis Cardinals
Tampa Bay Devil Rays
Texas Rangers
Toronto Blue Jays

2003 Topps Total Topps

Nm-Mt Ex-Mt
COMPLETE SET (50) 50.00 15.00
STATED ODDS 1:7
TT1 Ichiro Suzuki 4.00 1.20
TT2 Alex Rodriguez 4.00 1.20
TT3 Barry Bonds 6.00 1.80
TT4 Jason Giambi 2.50 .75
TT5 Troy Glaus 1.50 .45
TT6 Greg Maddux 4.00 1.20
TT7 Albert Pujols 5.00 1.50

TT8 Randy Johnson 2.50 .75
TT9 Chipper Jones 2.50 .75
TT10 Magglio Ordonez 1.00 .30
TT11 Jim Thome 2.50 .75
TT12 Jeff Kent 1.00 .30
TT13 Curt Schilling 1.50 .45
TT14 Alfonso Soriano 1.50 .45
TT15 Rafael Palmeiro 1.50 .45
TT16 Carlos Delgado 1.00 .30
TT17 Torii Hunter 1.00 .30
TT18 Pat Burrell 1.00 .30
TT19 Adam Dunn 1.00 .30
TT20 Roberto Alomar 2.50 .75
TT21 Eric Chavez 1.00 .30
TT22 Derek Jeter 6.00 1.80
TT23 Nomar Garciaparra 4.00 1.20
TT24 Lance Berkman 1.00 .30
TT25 Jim Edmonds 1.00 .30
TT26 Todd Helton 1.50 .45
TT27 Sammy Sosa 4.00 1.20
TT28 Phil Nevin 1.00 .30
TT29 Andruw Jones 1.00 .30
TT30 Barry Zito 1.50 .45
TT31 Richie Sexson 1.00 .30
TT32 Ken Griffey Jr. 4.00 1.20
TT33 Gary Sheffield 1.00 .30
TT34 Shawn Green 1.00 .30
TT35 Mike Sweeney 1.00 .30
TT36 Mike Lowell 1.00 .30
TT37 Larry Walker 1.00 .30
TT38 Manny Ramirez 1.00 .30
TT39 Miguel Tejada 1.00 .30
TT40 Mike Piazza 4.00 1.20
TT41 Scott Rolen 1.50 .45
TT42 Brian Giles 1.00 .30
TT43 Garret Anderson 1.00 .30
TT44 Vladimir Guerrero 2.50 .75
TT45 Bartolo Colon 1.00 .30
TT46 Jorge Posada 1.50 .45
TT47 Ivan Rodriguez 2.50 .75
TT48 Ryan Klesko 1.00 .30
TT49 Jose Vidro 1.00 .30
TT50 Pedro Martinez 2.50 .75

2001 Topps Tribute

This hobby-only product was released in mid-December 2001, and featured a 90-card base set that honors Hall of Fame caliber players like Babe Ruth and Mickey Mantle. Each pack contained four-cards, and carried a suggested retail price of 40.00.

Nm-Mt Ex-Mt
COMPLETE SET (90) 250.00 75.00
1 Pee Wee Reese 6.00 1.80
2 Babe Ruth 20.00 6.00
3 Ralph Kiner 5.00 1.50
4 Brooks Robinson 6.00 1.80
5 Don Sutton 5.00 1.50
6 Carl Yastrzemski 10.00 3.00
7 Roger Maris 10.00 3.00
8 Andre Dawson 5.00 1.50
9 Luis Aparicio 5.00 1.50
10 Wade Boggs 5.00 1.50
11 Johnny Bench 6.00 1.80
12 Ernie Banks 6.00 1.80
13 Thurman Munson 10.00 3.00
14 Harmon Killebrew 6.00 1.80
15 Ted Kluszewski 5.00 1.50
16 Bob Feller 5.00 1.50
17 Mike Schmidt 12.00 3.60
18 Warren Spahn 5.00 1.50
19 Jim Palmer 5.00 1.50
20 Don Mattingly 15.00 4.50
21 Willie Mays 12.00 3.60
22 Gil Hodges 6.00 1.80
23 Juan Marichal 5.00 1.50
24 Robin Yount 10.00 3.00
25 Nolan Ryan Angels 15.00 4.50
26 Dave Winfield 5.00 1.50
27 Hank Greenberg 6.00 1.80
28 Honus Wagner 8.00 2.40
29 Nolan Ryan Rangers 15.00 4.50
30 Phil Niekro 5.00 1.50
31 Robin Roberts 5.00 1.50
32 Casey Stengel Yankees 5.00 1.50
33 Willie McCovey 5.00 1.50
34 Roy Campanella 6.00 1.80
35 Rollie Fingers A's 5.00 1.50
36 Tom Seaver 5.00 1.50
37 Jackie Robinson 8.00 2.40
38 Hank Aaron Braves 12.00 3.60
39 Bob Gibson 5.00 1.50
40 Carlton Fisk Red Sox 5.00 1.50
41 Hank Aaron Brewers 12.00 3.60
42 George Brett 15.00 4.50
43 Orlando Cepeda 5.00 1.50
44 Red Schoendienst 5.00 1.50
45 Don Drysdale 6.00 1.80
46 Mel Ott 6.00 1.80
47 Casey Stengel Mets 6.00 1.80
48 Al Kaline 6.00 1.80
49 Reggie Jackson 5.00 1.50
50 Tony Perez 5.00 1.50
51 Ozzie Smith 10.00 3.00

52 Billy Martin 5.00 1.50
53 Bill Dickey 5.00 1.50
54 Catfish Hunter 5.00 1.50
55 Duke Snider 5.00 1.50
56 Dale Murphy 6.00 1.80
57 Bobby Doerr 5.00 1.50
58 Earl Averill UER 5.00 1.50
Card pictures Earl Averill Jr.
59 Carlton Fisk White Sox 5.00 1.50
60 Tom Lasorda 5.00 1.50
61 Lou Gehrig 12.00 3.60
62 Enos Slaughter 5.00 1.50
63 Jim Bunning 5.00 1.50
64 Rollie Fingers Brewers 5.00 1.50
65 Frank Robinson Reds 5.00 1.50
66 Earl Weaver 5.00 1.50
67 Eddie Mathews 6.00 1.80
68 Kirby Puckett 6.00 1.80
69 Phil Rizzuto 6.00 1.80
70 Lou Brock 5.00 1.50
71 Walt Alston 5.00 1.50
72 Billy Pierce 5.00 1.50
73 Joe Morgan 5.00 1.50
74 Roberto Clemente 15.00 4.50
75 Whitey Ford 5.00 1.50
76 Richie Ashburn 5.00 1.50
77 Elston Howard 5.00 1.50
78 Gary Carter 5.00 1.50
79 Carl Hubbell 5.00 1.50
80 Yogi Berra 6.00 1.80
81 Ken Boyer 5.00 1.50
82 Nolan Ryan Astros 15.00 4.50
83 Bill Mazeroski 5.00 1.50
84 Dizzy Dean 6.00 1.80
85 Nellie Fox 5.00 1.50
86 Stan Musial 10.00 3.00
87 Steve Carlton 5.00 1.50
88 Willie Stargell 5.00 1.50
89 Hal Newhouser 5.00 1.50
90 Frank Robinson Orioles 5.00 1.50
NNO Mickey Mantle
PSA Redemption
NNO Mickey Mantle
Buyback EXCH
NNO Jackie Robinson
Buyback EXCH
NNO Ted Williams
Buyback EXCH

2001 Topps Tribute Dual Relics

This two-card set features relic cards of Casey Stengel and Frank Robinson. Each card was issued at 1:860 packs.

Nm-Mt Ex-Mt
CS-YM Casey Stengel 120.00 36.00
FR-RO Frank Robinson 120.00 36.00

2001 Topps Tribute Franchise Figures Relics

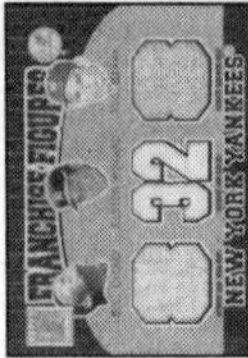

This 19-card set features relic cards of franchise players from teams past. Please note that these cards were broken into two groups: Group A were inserted at a rate of 1:106, while, Group B were inserted at 1:34. Card backs carry a "RM" prefix.

Nm-Mt Ex-Mt
AL Walt Alston Jsy 80.00 24.00
Tommy Lasorda Jsy A
CD Gary Carter 80.00 24.00
Andre Dawson B
FY Carlton Fisk 150.00 45.00
Carl Yastrzemski A
JM Reggie Jackson 200.00 60.00
Billy Martin A
KG Al Kaline 150.00 45.00
Hank Greenberg A
MM Thurman Munson Jsy 250.00 75.00
Don Mattingly Jsy A
PK Kirby Puckett 120.00 36.00
Harmon Killebrew A
RG Babe Ruth 800.00 240.00
Lou Gehrig A
RR Brooks Robinson Bat 120.00 36.00
Frank Robinson Uni A
AFF Luis Aparicio 120.00 36.00
Nellie Fox
Carlton Fisk A
HDB Bill Dickey Jsy 200.00 60.00
Elston Howard Bat
Yogi Berra Jsy A
HSS Gil Hodges 150.00 45.00
Casey Stengel
Tom Seaver A
MCS Bill Mazeroski 250.00 75.00
Roberto Clemente
Willie Stargell A
MMA Dale Murphy 200.00 60.00
Eddie Mathews
Hank Aaron A
MMC Willie Mays Jsy 200.00 60.00
Willie McCovey Bat
Orlando Cepeda Jsy A
RSC Pee Wee Reese 200.00 60.00
Duke Snider
Roy Campanella A
SAC Mike Schmidt Jsy 150.00 45.00
Richie Ashburn Bat
Steve Carlton Uni A
BPKRM Johnny Bench 150.00 45.00
Tony Perez
Ted Kluszewski
Frank Robinson
Joe Morgan A
SBSM Ozzie Smith 150.00 45.00
Lou Brock
Red Schoendienst
Stan Musial A

2001 Topps Tribute Game Bat Relics

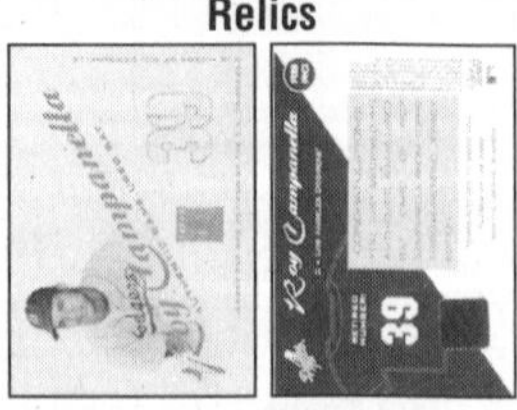

This 31-card set features bat relic cards of classic players like George Brett and Hank Aaron. Please note that these cards were broken into two groups: Group 1 were inserted at a rate of 1:2, while, Group 2 were inserted at 1:35. Card backs carry a "RB" prefix.

Nm-Mt Ex-Mt
BAT LOGO AND STENCIL CUT-OUT SAME QTY
BAT LOGO AND STENCIL CUT-OUT SAME VALUE
RBAK Al Kaline 1 30.00 9.00
RBBM Billy Martin 1 30.00 9.00
RBBR Babe Ruth 2 200.00 60.00
RBBRO B.Robinson 1 30.00 9.00
RBCFR C.Fisk Red Sox 1 30.00 9.00
RBCFW C.Fisk W.Sox 1 30.00 9.00
RBCS Casey Stengel 1 30.00 9.00
RBCY Carl Yastrzemski 1 40.00 12.00
RBDM Don Mattingly 1 50.00 15.00
RBFRR F.Robinson Reds 1 30.00 9.00
RBGB George Brett 1 50.00 15.00
RBGH Gil Hodges 1 30.00 9.00
RBHA H.Aaron Braves 1 60.00 18.00
RBHAB Hank Aaron Brewers 1 60.00 18.00
RBHG Hank Greenberg 1 60.00 18.00
RBHK Harmon Killebrew 1 30.00 9.00
RBHW Honus Wagner 1 150.00 45.00
RBJR Jackie Robinson 1
RBKB Ken Boyer 1 20.00 6.00
RBLA Luis Aparicio 1 20.00 6.00
RBLB Lou Brock 1 30.00 9.00
RBLG Lou Gehrig 1 150.00 45.00
RBOS Ozzie Smith 1 30.00 9.00
RBPWR P.W.Reese 1 30.00 9.00
RBRA Richie Ashburn 1 30.00 9.00
RBRC Roy Campanella 1 30.00 9.00
RBRCL R.Clemente 1 100.00 30.00
RBRJ Reggie Jackson 1 30.00 9.00
RBRM Roger Maris 1 60.00 18.00
RBTM T.Munson 1 40.00 12.00
RBWM Willie McCovey 1 20.00 6.00

2001 Topps Tribute Game Patch-Number Relics

This 23-card set features swatches of actual game-used jersey patches. These cards were issued into packs at 1:61. Card backs carry a "RPN" prefix.

Nm-Mt Ex-Mt
RPNBD Bill Dickey 120.00 36.00
RPNBDO Bobby Doerr 120.00 36.00
RPNCY Carl Yastrzemski 250.00 75.00
RPNDM Don Mattingly 400.00 120.00
RPNDW Dave Winfield 120.00 36.00
RPNEM Eddie Mathews 200.00 60.00
RPNGB George Brett 400.00 120.00
RPNHK Harmon Killebrew 200.00 60.00
RPNJB Johnny Bench 200.00 60.00
RPNJM Juan Marichal 120.00 36.00
RPNJP Jim Palmer 120.00 36.00
RPNKB Kirby Puckett 200.00 60.00
RPNLB Lou Brock 150.00 45.00
RPNMS Mike Schmidt 300.00 90.00
RPNNRA N.Ryan Angels 500.00 150.00
RPNNRH N.Ryan Astros 500.00 150.00
RPNNRR Nolan Ryan Rgr 500.00 150.00
RPNRS Red Schoendienst 120.00 36.00
RPNRY Robin Yount 250.00 75.00
RPNTL Tom Lasorda 120.00 36.00
RPNWA Walt Alston 120.00 36.00
RPNWB Wade Boggs 150.00 45.00
RPNYB Yogi Berra 200.00 60.00

2001 Topps Tribute Game Worn Relics

This 39-card set features swatches of actual game-used jerseys. These cards were issued into packs in two different groups: Group 1 (1:282), and Group 2 (1:13) packs. Card backs carry a "RJ" prefix.

Nm-Mt Ex-Mt
RJ-BD Bill Dickey 5 30.00 9.00
RJ-BDO Bobby Doerr 2 30.00 9.00
RJ-CS Casey Stengel 5 30.00 9.00

RJ-CY C.Yastrzemski White 3 50.00 15.00
RJ-CYA C.Yastrzemski Gray 3 50.00 15.00
RJ-DD Dizzy Dean Uni 4 50.00 15.00
RJ-DM Don Mattingly 2 60.00 18.00
RJ-DW Dave Winfield 2 20.00 6.00
RJ-EB E.Banks White 2 30.00 9.00
RJ-EM Eddie Mathews 2 30.00 9.00
RJ-EBA E.Banks Gray 2 30.00 9.00
RJ-FR Frank Robinson 2 30.00 9.00
RJ-GB George Brett 2 50.00 15.00
RJ-HK H.Killebrew 2 30.00 9.00
RJ-JB J.Bench White 2 30.00 9.00
RJ-JP Jim Palmer White 2 20.00 6.00
RJ-JR Jackie Robinson 1 250.00 75.00
RJ-JBE Johnny Bench Gray 2 30.00 9.00
RJ-JMG Juan Marichal 2 20.00 6.00
RJ-JPA Jim Palmer Gray 2 20.00 6.00
RJ-KP Kirby Puckett 2 30.00 9.00
RJ-LB Lou Brock 2 30.00 9.00
RJ-MSB M.Schmidt Blue 2 60.00 18.00
RJ-MSW M.Schmidt White 2 60.00 18.00
RJ-NF Nellie Fox 2 30.00 9.00
RJ-NRA N.Ryan Angels 2 100.00 30.00
RJ-NRH N.Ryan Astros 2 100.00 30.00
RJ-NRR N.Ryan Rangers 2 100.00 30.00
RJ-RS R.Schoendienst 2 20.00 6.00
RJ-RY Robin Yount 2 30.00 9.00
RJ-SC Steve Carlton 2 20.00 6.00
RJ-SM Stan Musial 2 80.00 24.00
RJ-TL Tom Lasorda 4 20.00 6.00
RJ-WA Walt Alston 4 20.00 6.00
RJ-WB Wade Boggs 2 30.00 9.00
RJ-WMF W.Mays Gray 2 100.00 30.00
RJ-WMW W.Mays White 2 100.00 30.00
RJ-WST Willie Stargell 2 30.00 9.00
RJ-YB Yogi Berra 2 30.00 9.00

2001 Topps Tribute Tri-Relic

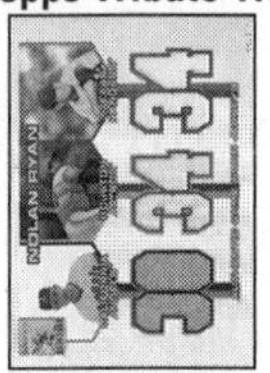

This one-card set features a tri-relic card of Nolan Ryan. This card was issued at 1:1292. Card backs carry a "NR" prefix.

Nm-Mt Ex-Mt
NR-AAR Nolan Ryan

2002 Topps Tribute

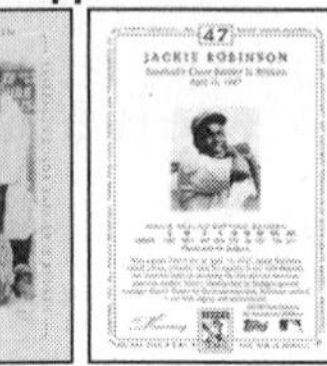

This 90 card set was released in November, 2002. These cards were issued in five card packs which came six packs to a box and four boxes to a case. Each of these packs had an SRP of $50 per pack.

Nm-Mt Ex-Mt
COMPLETE SET (90) 120.00 36.00
1 Hank Aaron 10.00 3.00
2 Rogers Hornsby 5.00 1.50
3 Bobby Thomson 4.00 1.20
4 Eddie Collins 4.00 1.20
5 Joe Carter 4.00 1.20
6 Jim Palmer 4.00 1.20
7 Willie Mays 10.00 3.00
8 Willie Stargell 4.00 1.20
9 Vida Blue 4.00 1.20
10 Whitey Ford 4.00 1.20
11 Bob Gibson 4.00 1.20
12 Nellie Fox 5.00 1.50
13 Napoleon Lajoie 5.00 1.50
14 Frankie Frisch 4.00 1.20
15 Nolan Ryan 12.00 3.60
16 Brooks Robinson 5.00 1.50
17 Kirby Puckett 5.00 1.50
18 Fergie Jenkins 4.00 1.20
19 Edd Roush 4.00 1.20
20 Honus Wagner 8.00 2.40
21 Richie Ashburn 4.00 1.20
22 Bob Feller 4.00 1.20
23 Joe Morgan 4.00 1.20
24 Orlando Cepeda 4.00 1.20
25 Steve Garvey 4.00 1.20
26 Hank Greenberg 5.00 1.50
27 Stan Musial 8.00 2.40
28 Sam Crawford 4.00 1.20
29 Jim Rice 4.00 1.20
30 Hack Wilson 4.00 1.20
31 Lou Brock 4.00 1.20
32 Mickey Vernon 4.00 1.20
33 Chuck Klein 4.00 1.20
34 Tony Gwynn 6.00 1.80
35 Duke Snider 4.00 1.20
36 Ryne Sandberg 10.00 3.00
37 Johnny Bench 5.00 1.50
38 Sam Rice 4.00 1.20
39 Lou Gehrig 10.00 3.00
40 Robin Yount 8.00 2.40
41 Don Sutton 4.00 1.20
42 Jim Bottomley 4.00 1.20
43 Billy Herman 4.00 1.20
44 Zach Wheat 4.00 1.20
45 Juan Marichal 4.00 1.20
46 Bert Blyleven 4.00 1.20
47 Jackie Robinson 6.00 1.80
48 Gil Hodges 4.00 1.20
49 Mike Schmidt 12.00 3.60
50 Dale Murphy 5.00 1.50
51 Phil Rizzuto 4.00 1.20
52 Ty Cobb 8.00 2.40
53 Andre Dawson 4.00 1.20
54 Fred Lindstrom 4.00 1.20
55 Roy Campanella 5.00 1.50
56 Don Larsen 4.00 1.20
57 Harry Heilmann 4.00 1.20
58 Catfish Hunter 4.00 1.20
59 Frank Robinson 4.00 1.20
60 Bill Mazeroski 4.00 1.20
61 Roger Maris 8.00 2.40
62 Dave Winfield 4.00 1.20
63 Warren Spahn 4.00 1.20
64 Babe Ruth 15.00 4.50
65 Ernie Banks 5.00 1.50
66 Wade Boggs 4.00 1.20
67 Carl Yastrzemski 8.00 2.40
68 Ron Santo 4.00 1.20
69 Dennis Martinez 4.00 1.20
70 Yogi Berra 5.00 1.50
71 Paul Waner 4.00 1.20
72 George Brett 12.00 3.60
73 Eddie Mathews 5.00 1.50
74 Bill Dickey 4.00 1.20
75 Carlton Fisk 4.00 1.20
76 Thurman Munson 8.00 2.40
77 Reggie Jackson 4.00 1.20
78 Phil Niekro 4.00 1.20
79 Luis Aparicio 4.00 1.20
80 Steve Carlton 4.00 1.20
81 Tris Speaker 4.00 1.20
82 Johnny Mize 4.00 1.20
83 Tom Seaver 4.00 1.20
84 Heinie Manush 4.00 1.20
85 Tommy John 4.00 1.20
86 Joe Cronin 4.00 1.20
87 Don Mattingly 12.00 3.60
88 Kirk Gibson 4.00 1.20
89 Bo Jackson 5.00 1.50
90 Mel Ott 5.00 1.50

2002 Topps Tribute First Impressions

Inserted into packs at a stated rate of one in 16, this is a parallel to the Topps Tribute set. Each of these cards were printed to a stated print run which matched the player's major league debut season. For those players who debuted in 1925 or before, no pricing is provided due to market scarcity.

Nm-Mt Ex-Mt
1 Hank Aaron/54 60.00 18.00
2 Rogers Hornsby/15
3 Bobby Thomson/46 30.00 9.00
4 Eddie Collins/6
5 Joe Carter/83 15.00 4.50
6 Jim Palmer/65 25.00 7.50
7 Willie Mays/51 60.00 18.00
8 Willie Stargell/62 25.00 7.50
9 Vida Blue/69 20.00 6.00
10 Whitey Ford/50 30.00 9.00
11 Bob Gibson/59 25.00 7.50
12 Nellie Fox/47 50.00 15.00
13 Napoleon Lajoie/96 20.00 6.00
14 Frankie Frisch/19
15 Nolan Ryan/66 60.00 18.00
16 Brooks Robinson/55 30.00 9.00
17 Kirby Puckett/84 20.00 6.00
18 Fergie Jenkins/65 25.00 7.50
19 Edd Roush/13
20 Honus Wagner/97 30.00 9.00
21 Richie Ashburn/48 30.00 9.00
22 Bob Feller/36 30.00 9.00
23 Joe Morgan/63 25.00 7.50
24 Orlando Cepeda/58 25.00 7.50
25 Steve Garvey/69 20.00 6.00
26 Hank Greenberg/30 50.00 15.00
27 Stan Musial/41 60.00 18.00
28 Sam Crawford/99 15.00 4.50
29 Jim Rice/74 20.00 6.00
30 Hack Wilson/23
31 Lou Brock/61 25.00 7.50
32 Mickey Vernon/39 30.00 9.00
33 Chuck Klein/28 40.00 12.00
34 Tony Gwynn/82 25.00 7.50
35 Duke Snider/47 30.00 9.00
36 Ryne Sandberg/81 60.00 18.00
37 Johnny Bench/67 25.00 7.50
38 Sam Rice/15
39 Lou Gehrig/23
40 Robin Yount/74 40.00 12.00
41 Don Sutton/66 20.00 6.00
42 Jim Bottomley/22
43 Billy Herman/31 40.00 12.00
44 Zach Wheat/9
45 Juan Marichal/60 25.00 7.50
46 Bert Blyleven/70 20.00 6.00
47 Jackie Robinson/47 50.00 15.00
48 Gil Hodges/43 30.00 9.00
49 Mike Schmidt/72 60.00 18.00
50 Dale Murphy/76 50.00 15.00
51 Phil Rizzuto/41 30.00 9.00
52 Ty Cobb/5
53 Andre Dawson/76 20.00 6.00
54 Fred Lindstrom/24
55 Roy Campanella/48 40.00 12.00
56 Don Larsen/53 25.00 7.50
57 Harry Heilmann/14
58 Catfish Hunter/65 25.00 7.50
59 Frank Robinson/56 25.00 7.50
60 Bill Mazeroski/56 25.00 7.50
61 Roger Maris/57 50.00 15.00
62 Dave Winfield/73 20.00 6.00
63 Warren Spahn/42 30.00 9.00
64 Babe Ruth/14
65 Ernie Banks/53 30.00 9.00
66 Wade Boggs/82 15.00 4.50
67 Carl Yastrzemski/61 50.00 15.00
68 Ron Santo/60 25.00 7.50
69 Dennis Martinez/76 20.00 6.00
70 Yogi Berra/46 40.00 12.00
71 Paul Waner/26 40.00 12.00
72 George Brett/73 60.00 18.00
73 Eddie Mathews/52 50.00 15.00
74 Bill Dickey/28 40.00 12.00
75 Carlton Fisk/69 20.00 6.00
76 Thurman Munson/69 40.00 12.00
77 Reggie Jackson/67 20.00 6.00
78 Phil Niekro/64 25.00 7.50
79 Luis Aparicio/56 25.00 7.50
80 Steve Carlton/65 25.00 7.50
81 Tris Speaker/7
82 Johnny Mize/36 30.00 9.00
83 Tom Seaver/67 20.00 6.00
84 Heinie Manush/23
85 Tommy John/63 25.00 7.50
86 Joe Cronin/26 40.00 12.00
87 Don Mattingly/82 50.00 15.00
88 Kirk Gibson/79 20.00 6.00
89 Bo Jackson/86 20.00 6.00
90 Mel Ott/26 50.00 15.00

2002 Topps Tribute Lasting Impressions

Inserted into packs at a stated rate of one in 13, this is a parallel to the Topps Tribute set. Each of these cards were printed to a stated print run which matched the player's major league final season. For those players who retired in 1925 or before (or 2001 or later), no pricing is provided due to market scarcity.

Nm-Mt Ex-Mt
1 Hank Aaron/76 50.00 15.00
2 Rogers Hornsby/37 40.00 12.00
3 Bobby Thomson/60 25.00 7.50
4 Eddie Collins/30 40.00 12.00
5 Joe Carter/98 15.00 4.50
6 Jim Palmer/84 15.00 4.50
7 Willie Mays/73 50.00 15.00
8 Willie Stargell/82 15.00 4.50
9 Vida Blue/86 15.00 4.50
10 Whitey Ford/67 20.00 6.00
11 Bob Gibson/75 20.00 6.00
12 Nellie Fox/65 50.00 15.00
13 Napoleon Lajoie/16
14 Frankie Frisch/37 30.00 9.00
15 Nolan Ryan/93 50.00 15.00
16 Brooks Robinson/77 25.00 7.50
17 Kirby Puckett/95 20.00 6.00
18 Fergie Jenkins/83 15.00 4.50
19 Edd Roush/31 40.00 12.00
20 Honus Wagner/17
21 Richie Ashburn/62 25.00 7.50
22 Bob Feller/56 25.00 7.50
23 Joe Morgan/84 15.00 4.50
24 Orlando Cepeda/74 20.00 6.00
25 Steve Garvey/87 15.00 4.50
26 Hank Greenberg/47 40.00 12.00
27 Stan Musial/63 50.00 15.00
28 Sam Crawford/17
29 Jim Rice/89 15.00 4.50
30 Hack Wilson/34 40.00 12.00
31 Lou Brock/79 20.00 6.00
32 Mickey Vernon/60 25.00 7.50
33 Chuck Klein/44 30.00 9.00
34 Tony Gwynn/1
35 Duke Snider/64 25.00 7.50
36 Ryne Sandberg/97 60.00 18.00
37 Johnny Bench/83 20.00 6.00
38 Sam Rice/34 40.00 12.00
39 Lou Gehrig/39 80.00 24.00
40 Robin Yount/93 40.00 12.00
41 Don Sutton/88 15.00 4.50
42 Jim Bottomley/37 30.00 9.00
43 Billy Herman/47 30.00 9.00
44 Zach Wheat/27 40.00 12.00
45 Juan Marichal/75 20.00 6.00
46 Bert Blyleven/92 15.00 4.50
47 Jackie Robinson/56 40.00 12.00
48 Gil Hodges/63 25.00 7.50
49 Mike Schmidt/89 60.00 18.00
50 Dale Murphy/93 50.00 15.00
51 Phil Rizzuto/56 25.00 7.50
52 Ty Cobb/28 80.00 24.00
53 Andre Dawson/96 15.00 4.50
54 Fred Lindstrom/36 30.00 9.00
55 Roy Campanella/57 30.00 9.00
56 Don Larsen/67 20.00 6.00
57 Harry Heilmann/32 40.00 12.00
58 Catfish Hunter/79 20.00 6.00
59 Frank Robinson/76 20.00 6.00
60 Bill Mazeroski/72 20.00 6.00
61 Roger Maris/68 40.00 12.00
62 Dave Winfield/95 15.00 4.50
63 Warren Spahn/65 25.00 7.50
64 Babe Ruth/35 80.00 24.00
65 Ernie Banks/71 25.00 7.50
66 Wade Boggs/99 15.00 4.50
67 Carl Yastrzemski/83 30.00 9.00
68 Ron Santo/74 20.00 6.00
69 Dennis Martinez/98 15.00 4.50
70 Yogi Berra/65 30.00 9.00
71 Paul Waner/45 30.00 9.00
72 George Brett/93 60.00 18.00
73 Eddie Mathews/68 50.00 15.00
74 Bill Dickey/46 30.00 9.00
75 Carlton Fisk/93 15.00 4.50
76 Thurman Munson/79 40.00 12.00
77 Reggie Jackson/87 15.00 4.50
78 Phil Niekro/87 15.00 4.50
79 Luis Aparicio/73 20.00 6.00
80 Steve Carlton/88 15.00 4.50
81 Tris Speaker/28 40.00 12.00
82 Johnny Mize/53 25.00 7.50
83 Tom Seaver/86 15.00 4.50
84 Heinie Manush/39 30.00 9.00
85 Tommy John/89 15.00 4.50
86 Joe Cronin/45 30.00 9.00
87 Don Mattingly/95 50.00 15.00
88 Kirk Gibson/95 15.00 4.50
89 Bo Jackson/94 20.00 6.00
90 Mel Ott/47 40.00 12.00

2002 Topps Tribute The Catch Dual Relic

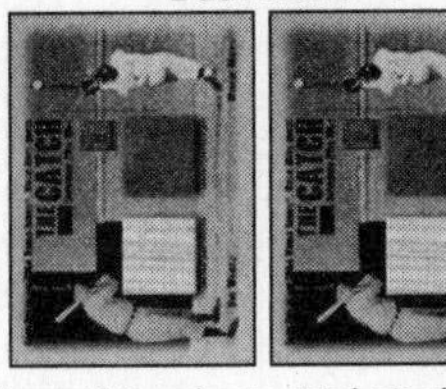

Inserted into packs at a stated rate of one in 1023, this card features relics from players involved in Willie Mays' legendary catch during the 1954 World Series when he ran down a well hit ball by Vic Wertz.

	Nm-Mt	Ex-Mt
MW Vic Wertz Bat	300.00	90.00
Willie Mays Glove		

2002 Topps Tribute The Catch Dual Relic Jersey Number

This is a parallel to the "Catch" insert card. This card was issued to a stated print run of 24 serial numbered set to match Willie Mays jersey number. Due to market scarcity, no pricing is provided for this card.

	Nm-Mt	Ex-Mt
MW Vic Wertz Bat		
Willie Mays Glove		

2002 Topps Tribute The Catch Dual Relic Season

This is a parallel to the "Catch" insert card. This card was issued to a stated print run of 54 serial numbered set to the season that this sensational catch was made in.

	Nm-Mt	Ex-Mt
MW Vic Wertz Bat		
Willie Mays Glove		

2002 Topps Tribute Marks of Excellence Autograph

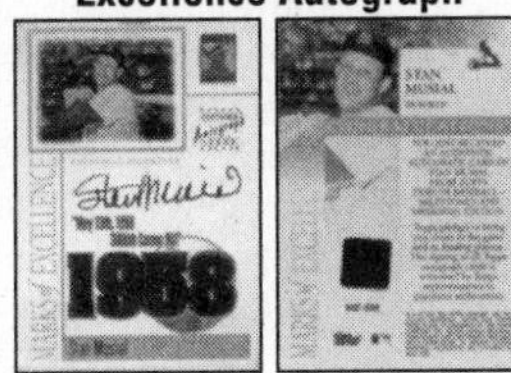

Inserted into packs at a stated rate of one in 61, these six cards feature players who signed cards honoring their signature moment.

	Nm-Mt	Ex-Mt
DL Don Larsen	50.00	15.00
LB Lou Brock	50.00	15.00
MS Mike Schmidt	120.00	36.00
SC Steve Carlton	50.00	15.00
SM Stan Musial	120.00	36.00
WS Warren Spahn	80.00	24.00

2002 Topps Tribute Marks of Excellence Autograph Relics

Inserted in packs at a stated rate of one in 61, these six cards feature game-used memorabilia pieces honoring players and their signature moment.

	Nm-Mt	Ex-Mt
BR Brooks Robinson Bat	80.00	24.00
DM Don Mattingly Jsy	150.00	45.00
DS Duke Snider Uni	80.00	24.00
FJ Fergie Jenkins Jsy	50.00	15.00
JP Jim Palmer Uni	50.00	15.00
RY Robin Yount Uni	80.00	24.00

2002 Topps Tribute Matching Marks Dual Relics

Inserted into packs at an overall stated rate of one in 11, these 22 cards feature two players and a game-used memorabilia piece from each of them.

	Nm-Mt	Ex-Mt
GROUP A ODDS 1:134		
GROUP B ODDS 1:368		
GROUP C ODDS 1:123		
GROUP D ODDS 1:43		
GROUP E ODDS 1:105		
GROUP F ODDS 1:82		
GROUP G ODDS 1:31		
AR Hank Aaron Bat	400.00	120.00
Babe Ruth Bat A		
BB Wade Boggs Jsy	50.00	15.00
George Brett Jsy C		
BF Johnny Bench Bat	60.00	18.00
Carlton Fisk Bat A		
BM Vida Blue Jsy	15.00	4.50
Dennis Martinez Jsy G		
BMA George Brett Jsy	200.00	60.00
Don Mattingly Jsy A		
BS Bert Blyleven Jsy	20.00	6.00
Don Sutton Jsy C		
GA Hank Greenberg Bat	120.00	36.00
Richie Ashburn Bat A		
GH Steve Garvey Bat	25.00	7.50
Gil Hodges Bat D		
JS Fergie Jenkins Jsy	50.00	15.00
Tom Seaver Jsy B		
MA Willie Mays Uni	250.00	75.00
Hank Aaron Bat A		
NS Phil Niekro Uni	20.00	6.00
Tom Seaver Uni G		
PJ Jim Palmer Jsy	25.00	7.50
Tommy John Jsy D		
RJ Frank Robinson Uni	60.00	18.00
Reggie Jackson Bat A		
RS Nolan Ryan Jsy	150.00	45.00
Tom Seaver Jsy A		
SB Tris Speaker Bat	120.00	36.00
George Brett Bat A		
SBA Ron Santo Bat	25.00	7.50
Ernie Banks Bat D		
SM Duke Snider Bat	100.00	30.00
Willie Mays Uni A		
SR Willie Stargell Uni	20.00	6.00
Jim Rice Uni E		
WY Dave Winfield Bat	40.00	12.00
Carl Yastrzemski Bat D		
WYO Dave Winfield Uni	20.00	6.00
Robin Yount Uni F		
YK Carl Yastrzemski Bat	100.00	30.00
Chuck Klein Bat A		
YP Robin Yount Uni	80.00	24.00
Kirby Puckett Uni A		

2002 Topps Tribute Memorable Materials

Inserted into packs at different rates depending on what group and game-used memorabilia piece, these 22 cards feature players from the tribute set as well as a memorabilia piece. We have notated next to the player's name what group this memorabilia piece belongs to.

	Nm-Mt	Ex-Mt
BAT GROUP A ODDS 1:11,592		
BAT GROUP B ODDS 1:6		
JSY/UNI GROUP A ODDS 1:246		
JSY/UNI GROUP B ODDS 1:12		
BJ Bo Jackson Jsy B	25.00	7.50
BM Bill Mazeroski Uni B	20.00	6.00
BT Bobby Thomson Bat B	20.00	6.00
CF Carlton Fisk Bat B	25.00	7.50
CK Chuck Klein Bat B	40.00	12.00
CY Carl Yastrzemski Uni B	30.00	9.00
DM Don Mattingly Jsy B	50.00	15.00
GB George Brett Jsy B	50.00	15.00
HA Hank Aaron Bat B	50.00	15.00
HW Hack Wilson Bat B	50.00	15.00
JC Joe Carter Bat B	20.00	6.00
JM Joe Morgan Bat B	20.00	6.00
JR Jackie Robinson Bat B	60.00	18.00
KG Kirk Gibson Bat B	20.00	6.00
KP Kirby Puckett Bat B	40.00	12.00
LG Lou Gehrig Bat A		
NR Nolan Ryan Jsy A	50.00	15.00
PR Phil Rizzuto Bat B	25.00	7.50
RC Roy Campanella Bat B	40.00	12.00
RJ Reggie Jackson Bat B	25.00	7.50
RM Roger Maris Bat B	80.00	24.00
TM Thurman Munson Bat B	50.00	15.00

2002 Topps Tribute Memorable Materials Jersey Number

Inserted into packs at a different rate depending on whether it is a bat or a uniform piece, this is a parallel to the Memorable Materials insert set. Each of these cards are issued to a stated print run matching the uniform number that the player wore during his career. For cards with less than 40 cards printed, no pricing is provided due to market scarcity.

	Nm-Mt	Ex-Mt
BAT STATED ODDS 1:208		
JSY/UNI STATED ODDS 1:644		
BJ Bo Jackson Jsy/16		
BM Bill Mazeroski Uni/9		
BT Bobby Thomson Bat/23		
CF Carlton Fisk Bat/27		
CK Chuck Klein Bat/1		
CY Carl Yastrzemski Uni/27 UER		
Yaz jersey number is actually 8		
DM Don Mattingly Jsy/23		
GB George Brett Jsy/5		
HA Hank Aaron Bat/44	120.00	36.00
HW Hack Wilson Bat/1		
JC Joe Carter Bat/29		
JM Joe Morgan Bat/8		
JR Jackie Robinson Bat/42	150.00	45.00
KG Kirk Gibson Bat/23		
KP Kirby Puckett Bat/34		
LG Lou Gehrig Bat/4		
NR Nolan Ryan Jsy/34		
PR Phil Rizzuto Bat/10		
RC Roy Campanella Bat/39		
RJ Reggie Jackson Bat/44	60.00	18.00
RM Roger Maris Bat/9		
TM Thurman Munson Bat/15		

2002 Topps Tribute Memorable Materials Season

Inserted into packs at a different rate depending on whether it is a bat or a uniform piece, this is a parallel to the Memorable Materials insert set. Each of these cards are issued to a stated print run matching the most memorable season that the player had during his career. For cards with less than 40 cards printed, no pricing is provided due to market scarcity.

	Nm-Mt	Ex-Mt
BAT STATED ODDS 1:72		
JSY/UNI STATED ODDS 1:152		
BJ Bo Jackson Jsy/89	80.00	24.00
BM Bill Mazeroski Uni/60	40.00	12.00
BT Bobby Thomson Bat/51	40.00	12.00
CF Carlton Fisk Bat/75	40.00	12.00
CK Chuck Klein Bat/33		
CY Carl Yastrzemski Uni/75 UER	50.00	15.00
Card commemorates 1967 season		
DM Don Mattingly Jsy/87	80.00	24.00
GB George Brett Jsy/83	80.00	24.00
HA Hank Aaron Bat/74	80.00	24.00
HW Hack Wilson Bat/30		
JC Joe Carter Bat/93	30.00	9.00
JM Joe Morgan Bat/76	30.00	9.00
JR Jackie Robinson Bat/47	120.00	36.00
KG Kirk Gibson Bat/88	30.00	9.00
KP Kirby Puckett Bat/91	60.00	18.00
LG Lou Gehrig Bat/39		
NR Nolan Ryan Jsy/91	80.00	24.00
PR Phil Rizzuto Bat/50	50.00	15.00
RC Roy Campanella Bat/55	80.00	24.00
RJ Reggie Jackson Bat/77	40.00	12.00
RM Roger Maris Bat/61	150.00	45.00
TM Thurman Munson Bat/76	80.00	24.00

2002 Topps Tribute Milestone Materials

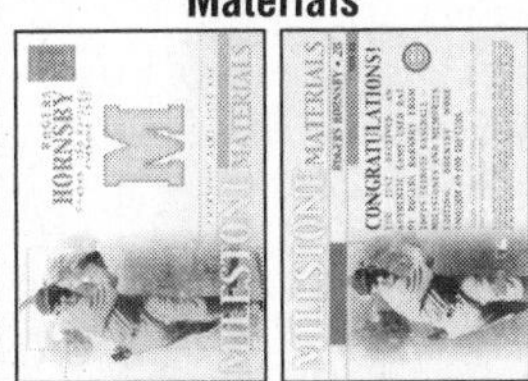

Inserted at different stated odds depending on whether it is a bat or a jersey/uniform piece, these 50 cards feature game-used memorabilia from the feature player's career.

	Nm-Mt	Ex-Mt
BAT STATED ODDS 1:4		
JSY/UNI STATED ODDS 1:5		
AD Andre Dawson Jsy	15.00	4.50
BD Bill Dickey Uni	25.00	7.50
BF Bob Feller Bat	25.00	7.50
BG Bob Gibson Uni	20.00	6.00
BH Billy Herman Uni	15.00	4.50
BR Babe Ruth Bat	150.00	45.00
BRO Brooks Robinson Bat	25.00	7.50
CH Catfish Hunter Jsy	20.00	6.00
DM Dale Murphy Jsy	25.00	7.50
DS Duke Snider Uni	20.00	6.00
EB Ernie Banks Uni	25.00	7.50
EC Eddie Collins Bat	40.00	12.00
EM Eddie Mathews Jsy	25.00	7.50
ER Edd Roush Bat	40.00	12.00
FF Frankie Frisch Bat	25.00	7.50
FL Fred Lindstrom Uni	25.00	7.50
FR Frank Robinson Bat	25.00	7.50
HH Harry Heilmann Bat	25.00	7.50
HM Heinie Manush Bat	40.00	12.00
HW Honus Wagner Bat	150.00	45.00
JB Johnny Bench Jsy	25.00	7.50
JBO Jim Bottomley Bat	25.00	7.50
JC Joe Cronin Bat	25.00	7.50
JM Johnny Mize Uni	20.00	6.00
JMA Juan Marichal Jsy	15.00	4.50
JP Jim Palmer Uni	15.00	4.50
LA Luis Aparicio Bat	20.00	6.00
LG Lou Gehrig Bat	200.00	60.00
MO Mel Ott Bat	60.00	18.00
MV Mickey Vernon Bat	20.00	6.00
NF Nellie Fox Uni	25.00	7.50
NL Napoleon Lajoie Bat	80.00	24.00
NR Nolan Ryan Jsy	50.00	15.00
OC Orlando Cepeda Jsy	15.00	4.50
PW Paul Waner Bat	40.00	12.00
RH Rogers Hornsby Bat	60.00	18.00
RJ Reggie Jackson Jsy	20.00	6.00
RS Ryne Sandberg Bat	40.00	12.00
RY Robin Yount Uni	25.00	7.50
SC Sam Crawford Bat	25.00	7.50
SR Sam Rice Bat	25.00	7.50
TC Ty Cobb Bat	150.00	45.00
TS Tom Seaver Jsy	20.00	6.00
TSP Tris Speaker Bat	80.00	24.00
WB Wade Boggs Uni	20.00	6.00
WF Whitey Ford Uni	20.00	6.00
WM Willie Mays Uni	50.00	15.00
WS Willie Stargell Uni	20.00	6.00
YB Yogi Berra Jsy	25.00	7.50
ZW Zach Wheat Bat	40.00	12.00

2002 Topps Tribute Milestone Materials Jersey Number

Inserted into packs at a different rate depending on whether it is a bat or a uniform piece, this is a parallel to the Milestone Materials insert set. Each of these cards are issued to a stated print run matching the uniform number that the player wore during his career. For cards with less than 40 cards printed, no pricing is provided due to market scarcity.

	Nm-Mt	Ex-Mt
BAT STATED ODDS 1:443		
JSY/UNI STATED ODDS 1:148		
AD Andre Dawson Jsy/8		
BD Bill Dickey Uni/8		
BF Bob Feller Bat/19		
BG Bob Gibson Uni/45	50.00	15.00
BH Billy Herman Uni/2		
BR Babe Ruth Bat/3		
BRO Brooks Robinson Bat/5		
CH Catfish Hunter Jsy/27		
DM Dale Murphy Jsy/3		
DS Duke Snider Uni/4		
EB Ernie Banks Uni/14		
EC Eddie Collins Bat/1		
EM Eddie Mathews Jsy/41	60.00	18.00
ER Edd Roush Bat/1		
FF Frankie Frisch Bat/3		
FL Fred Lindstrom Uni/3		
FR Frank Robinson Bat/20		
HH Harry Heilmann Bat/1		
HM Heinie Manush Bat/3		
HW Honus Wagner Bat/33		
JB Johnny Bench Jsy/5		
JBO Jim Bottomley Bat/4		
JC Joe Cronin Bat/4		
JM Johnny Mize Uni/36		
JMA Juan Marichal Jsy/27		
JP Jim Palmer Uni/22		
LA Luis Aparicio Bat/11		
LG Lou Gehrig Bat/4		
MO Mel Ott Bat/4		
MV Mickey Vernon Bat/3		
NF Nellie Fox Uni/2		
NL Napoleon Lajoie Bat/1		
NR Nolan Ryan Jsy/34		
OC Orlando Cepeda Jsy/30		
PW Paul Waner Bat/9		
RH Rogers Hornsby Bat/9		
RJ Reggie Jackson Jsy/44	50.00	15.00
RS Ryne Sandberg Bat/23		
RY Robin Yount Uni/19		
SC Sam Crawford Bat/1		
SR Sam Rice Bat/1		
TC Ty Cobb Bat/1		
TS Tom Seaver Jsy/41	50.00	15.00
TSP Tris Speaker Bat/1		
WB Wade Boggs Uni/26		
WF Whitey Ford Uni/16		
WM Willie Mays Uni/24		
WS Willie Stargell Uni/8		
YB Yogi Berra Jsy/8		
ZW Zach Wheat Bat/1		

2002 Topps Tribute Milestone Materials Season

Inserted into packs at a different rate depending on whether it is a bat or a uniform piece, this is a parallel to the Memorable Materials insert set. Each of these cards are issued to a stated print run matching the most memorable season that the player had during his career. For cards with less than 40 cards printed, no pricing is provided due to market scarcity.

	Nm-Mt	Ex-Mt
BAT STATED ODDS 1:73		
JSY/UNI STATED ODDS 1:41		
AD Andre Dawson Jsy/95	30.00	9.00
BD Bill Dickey Uni/46	60.00	18.00
BF Bob Feller Bat/54	60.00	18.00
BG Bob Gibson Uni/74	40.00	12.00
BH Billy Herman Uni/47	40.00	12.00
BR Babe Ruth Bat/34		
BRO Brooks Robinson Bat/74	50.00	15.00
CH Catfish Hunter Jsy/79	40.00	12.00
DM Dale Murphy Jsy/91	50.00	15.00
DS Duke Snider Uni/63	50.00	15.00
EB Ernie Banks Uni/70	50.00	15.00
EC Eddie Collins Bat/25		
EM Eddie Mathews Jsy/67	50.00	15.00
ER Edd Roush Bat/31		
FF Frankie Frisch Bat/35		
FL Fred Lindstrom Uni/36		
FR Frank Robinson Bat/71	50.00	15.00
HH Harry Heilmann Bat/32		
HM Heinie Manush Bat/39		
HW Honus Wagner Bat/14		
JB Johnny Bench Jsy/80	50.00	15.00
JBO Jim Bottomley Bat/36		
JC Joe Cronin Bat/45	60.00	18.00
JM Johnny Mize Uni/50	50.00	15.00
JMA Juan Marichal Jsy/71	30.00	9.00
JP Jim Palmer Uni/82	30.00	9.00
LA Luis Aparicio Bat/73	40.00	12.00
LG Lou Gehrig Bat/37		
MO Mel Ott Bat/45	150.00	45.00
MV Mickey Vernon Bat/56	50.00	15.00
NF Nellie Fox Uni/41	100.00	30.00
NL Napoleon Lajoie Bat/14		
NR Nolan Ryan Jsy/89	100.00	30.00
OC Orlando Cepeda Jsy/73	30.00	9.00
PW Paul Waner Bat/42	100.00	30.00
RH Rogers Hornsby Bat/37		
RJ Reggie Jackson Jsy/84	40.00	12.00
RS Ryne Sandberg Bat/93	80.00	24.00
RY Robin Yount Uni/92	80.00	24.00
SC Sam Crawford Bat/16		
SR Sam Rice Bat/34		
TC Ty Cobb Bat/27		
TS Tom Seaver Jsy/81	40.00	12.00
TSP Tris Speaker Bat/25		
WB Wade Boggs Uni/99	40.00	12.00
WF Whitey Ford Uni/62	50.00	15.00
WM Willie Mays Uni/69	100.00	30.00
WS Willie Stargell Uni/80	40.00	12.00
YB Yogi Berra Jsy/61	60.00	18.00
ZW Zach Wheat Bat/25		

2002 Topps Tribute Pastime Patches

Inserted into packs at a stated overall rate of one in 92, these 12 cards feature game-worn patch relic cards of these baseball legends.

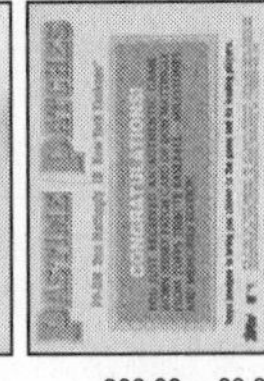

	Nm-Mt	Ex-Mt
*LOGO PATCHES: 2.5X VALUE		
GROUP A ODDS 1:184		
GROUP B ODDS 1:184		
OVERALL ODDS 1:92		
BD Bill Dickey B	150.00	45.00
CY Carl Yastrzemski B	200.00	60.00
DM Don Mattingly A	200.00	60.00
DW Dave Winfield A	150.00	45.00
EM Eddie Mathews A	150.00	45.00
GB George Brett A	200.00	60.00
JB Johnny Bench B	150.00	45.00
JP Jim Palmer B	150.00	45.00
KP Kirby Puckett B	150.00	45.00
RY Robin Yount B	150.00	45.00
WB Wade Boggs B	150.00	45.00
NRR Nolan Ryan B	250.00	75.00

2002 Topps Tribute Signature Cuts

Inserted into packs at a stated rate of one in 9936, these four cards feature cut autographs of four of baseball's most legendary figures. According to Topps, each of these cards were issued to a print run of two cards.

	Nm-Mt	Ex-Mt
BR Babe Ruth		
JR Jackie Robinson		
LG Lou Gehrig		
TC Ty Cobb		

2003 Topps Tribute Contemporary

This 110 card set was released in August, 2003. These cards were issued in five card packs with an $50 SRP which came six packs to a box and four boxes to a case. Cards numbered 1-90 feature veterans and cards 91-100 feature rookies. Cards numbered 101 through 110 also feature rookies, but those cards are signed and were issued to a stated print run of 499 serial numbered sets and these cards were inserted at a stated rate of one in seven. Jose Contreras did not return his cards in time for inclusion in this product and those cards could be redeemed until August 31, 2005.

	MINT	NRMT
COMMON CARD (1-90)	2.00	.90
COMMON CARD (91-100)	2.00	.90
COMMON CARD (101-110)	15.00	6.75
1 Jim Thome	4.00	1.80
2 Edgardo Alfonzo	2.00	.90
3 Edgar Martinez	2.50	1.10
4 Scott Rolen	4.00	1.80
5 Eric Hinske	2.00	.90
6 Mark Mulder	2.00	.90
7 Jason Giambi	4.00	1.80
8 Bernie Williams	2.50	1.10
9 Cliff Floyd	2.00	.90
10 Ichiro Suzuki	6.00	2.70
11 Pat Burrell	2.00	.90
12 Garret Anderson	2.00	.90
13 Gary Sheffield	2.00	.90
14 Johnny Damon	2.00	.90
15 Kerry Wood	4.00	1.80
16 Bartolo Colon	2.00	.90
17 Adam Dunn	2.00	.90
18 Omar Vizquel	2.00	.90
19 Todd Helton	2.50	1.10
20 Nomar Garciaparra	6.00	2.70
21 A.J. Burnett	2.00	.90
22 Craig Biggio	2.50	1.10
23 Carlos Beltran	2.00	.90
24 Kazuhisa Ishii	2.00	.90
25 Vladimir Guerrero	4.00	1.80
26 Roberto Alomar	4.00	1.80
27 Roger Clemens	8.00	3.60
28 Tim Hudson	2.00	.90
29 Brian Giles	2.00	.90
30 Barry Bonds	10.00	4.50
31 Jim Edmonds	2.00	.90
32 Rafael Palmeiro	2.50	1.10
33 Francisco Rodriguez	2.00	.90
34 Andruw Jones	2.00	.90
35 Shea Hillenbrand	2.00	.90
36 Moises Alou	2.00	.90
37 Luis Gonzalez	2.00	.90
38 Darin Erstad	2.00	.90
39 John Smoltz	2.50	1.10
40 Derek Jeter	10.00	4.50
41 Aubrey Huff	2.00	.90
42 Eric Chavez	2.00	.90
43 Doug Mientkiewicz	2.00	.90
44 Lance Berkman	2.00	.90
45 Josh Beckett	2.50	1.10
46 Austin Kearns	2.00	.90

47 Frank Thomas 4.00 1.80
48 Pedro Martinez 4.00 1.80
49 Tim Salmon 2.00 .90
50 Alex Rodriguez 6.00 2.70
51 Ryan Klesko 2.00 .90
52 Tom Glavine 2.50 1.10
53 Shawn Green 2.00 .90
54 Jeff Kent 2.00 .90
55 Carlos Pena 2.00 .90
56 Paul Konerko 2.00 .90
57 Troy Glaus 2.50 1.10
58 Manny Ramirez 2.00 .90
59 Jason Jennings 2.00 .90
60 Randy Johnson 4.00 1.80
61 Ivan Rodriguez 4.00 1.80
62 Roy Oswalt 2.00 .90
63 Kevin Brown 2.00 .90
64 Jose Vidro 2.00 .90
65 Jorge Posada 2.50 1.10
66 Mike Piazza 6.00 2.70
67 Bret Boone 2.00 .90
68 Carlos Delgado 2.00 .90
69 Jimmy Rollins 2.00 .90
70 Alfonso Soriano 2.50 1.10
71 Greg Maddux 6.00 2.70
72 Mark Prior 8.00 3.60
73 Jeff Bagwell 2.50 1.10
74 Richie Sexson 2.00 .90
75 Sammy Sosa 6.00 2.70
76 Curt Schilling 2.50 1.10
77 Mike Sweeney 2.00 .90
78 Torii Hunter 2.00 .90
79 Larry Walker 2.50 1.10
80 Miguel Tejada 2.00 .90
81 Rich Aurilia 2.00 .90
82 Bobby Abreu 2.00 .90
83 Phil Nevin 2.00 .90
84 Rodrigo Lopez 2.00 .90
85 Chipper Jones 4.00 1.80
86 Ken Griffey Jr. 6.00 2.70
87 Mike Lowell 2.00 .90
88 Magglio Ordonez 2.00 .90
89 Barry Zito 2.50 1.10
90 Albert Pujols 8.00 3.60
91 Corey Shafer FY RC 3.00 1.35
92 Dan Haren FY RC 4.00 1.80
93 Jeremy Bonderman FY RC 4.00 1.80
94 Branden Florence FY RC 2.00 .90
95 E.Bastida-Martinez FY RC 2.00 .90
96 Brian Wright FY RC 2.00 .90
97 Elizardo Ramirez FY RC 4.00 1.80
98 Mi.Garciaparra FY RC 4.00 1.80
99 Clay Hensley FY RC 2.00 .90
100 Bobby Basham FY RC 3.00 1.35
101 J.Contreras FY AU RC EXCH 40.00 18.00
102 Br. Bullington FY AU RC 30.00 13.50
103 Joey Gomes FY AU RC 15.00 6.75
104 Craig Brazell FY AU RC 15.00 6.75
105 Andy Marte FY AU RC 80.00 36.00
106 Han. Ramirez FY AU RC 30.00 13.50
107 Ryan Shealy FY AU RC 15.00 6.75
108 Daryl Clark FY AU RC 15.00 6.75
109 Tyler Johnson FY AU RC 15.00 6.75
110 Ben Francisco FY AU RC 15.00 6.75

2003 Topps Tribute Contemporary Gold

MINT NRMT
RANDOM INSERTS IN PACKS
STATED PRINT RUN 25 SERIAL #'d SETS
NO PRICING DUE TO SCARCITY
CONTRERAS EXCH.DEADLINE 08/31/05

2003 Topps Tribute Contemporary Red

MINT NRMT
*RED 1-90: .6X TO 1.5X BASIC CARDS
*RED 91-100: .75X TO 2X BASIC CARDS
1-100 PRINT RUN 225 SERIAL #'d SETS
*RED 101-110: .6X TO 1.5X BASIC
101-110 PRINT RUN 99 SERIAL #'d SETS
RANDOM INSERTS IN PACKS

2003 Topps Tribute Contemporary Bonds Tribute Relics

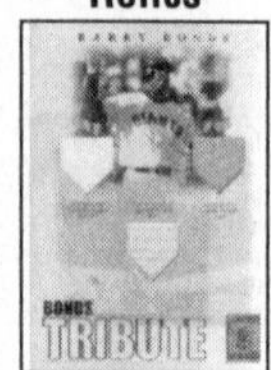

MINT NRMT
*RED BONDS: .6X TO 1.5X BASIC BONDS
RED BONDS PRINT RUN 50 #'d SETS
GOLD BONDS PRINT RUN 1 #'d SET
NO GOLD PRICING DUE TO SCARCITY
RANDOM INSERTS IN PACKS
DB Barry Bonds Bat-Jsy 50.00 22.00
SB Barry Bonds Jsy 40.00 18.00
TB Barry Bonds Bat-Cap-Jsy 80.00 36.00

2003 Topps Tribute Contemporary Bonds Tribute 40-40 Club Relics

MINT NRMT
RANDOM INSERTS IN PACKS
NO GOLD PRICING DUE TO SCARCITY
CBR Jose Canseco Uni 80.00 36.00
Barry Bonds Uni
Alex Rodriguez Uni
CBRG Jose Canseco Uni
Barry Bonds Uni
Alex Rodriguez Uni Gold/1
CBRR Jose Canseco Uni 120.00 55.00
Barry Bonds Uni
Alex Rodriguez Uni Red/50

2003 Topps Tribute Contemporary Bonds Tribute 600 HR Club Relics

MINT NRMT
*RED 600: .6X TO 1.5X BASIC
RED 600 PRINT RUN 50 SERIAL #'d SETS
GOLD PRINT RUN 1 SERIAL #'d SET
NO GOLD PRICING DUE TO SCARCITY
RANDOM INSERTS IN PACKS
BB Barry Bonds Bat 40.00 18.00
BR Babe Ruth Bat 150.00 70.00
HA Hank Aaron Bat 40.00 18.00
WM Willie Mays Uni 50.00 22.00

2003 Topps Tribute Contemporary Bonds Tribute 600 HR Club Double Relics

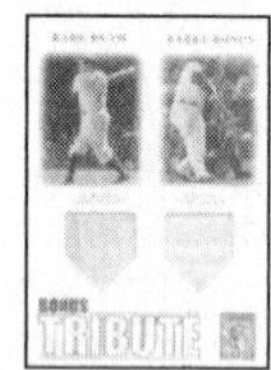

MINT NRMT
*RED 600 DOUBLE: .6X TO 1.5X BASIC
RED 600 DOUBLE PRINT RUN 50 #'d SETS
GOLD 600 DOUBLE PRINT 1 SERIAL #'d SET
NO GOLD PRICING DUE TO SCARCITY
RANDOM INSERTS IN PACKS
BM Barry Bonds Bat 100.00 45.00
Willie Mays Uni
RB Babe Ruth Bat 200.00 90.00
Barry Bonds Bat
BA Barry Bonds Bat 80.00 36.00
Hank Aaron Bat

2003 Topps Tribute Contemporary Bonds Tribute 600 HR Club Quad Relics

MINT NRMT
RANDOM INSERTS IN PACKS
PRINT RUNS B/WN 1-50 COPIES PER
NO GOLD/RED PRICING DUE TO SCARCITY
HR Babe Ruth Bat 600.00 275.00
Willie Mays Uni
Hank Aaron Bat
Barry Bonds Bat/50
HR-G Babe Ruth Bat
Willie Mays Uni
Hank Aaron Bat
Barry Bonds Bat Gold/1
HR-R Babe Ruth Bat
Willie Mays Uni
Hank Aaron Bat
Barry Bonds Bat Red/25

2003 Topps Tribute Contemporary Matching Marks Dual Relics

MINT NRMT
*RED MARKS: .6X TO 1.5X BASIC
RED MARKS PRINT RUN 50 SERIAL #'d SETS
GOLD MARKS PRINT RUN 1 SERIAL #'d SET
NO GOLD PRICING DUE TO SCARCITY
RANDOM INSERTS IN PACKS
AP Roberto Alomar Bat 15.00 6.75
Rafael Palmeiro Bat
BG Jeff Bagwell Uni 15.00 6.75
Juan Gonzalez Bat
BP Barry Bonds Bat 40.00 18.00
Rafael Palmeiro Bat
GR Nomar Garciaparra Jsy 25.00 11.00
Alex Rodriguez Jsy
HR Rickey Henderson Bat 15.00 6.75
Manny Ramirez Bat
MG Fred McGriff Bat 15.00 6.75
Juan Gonzalez Bat
MP Fred McGriff Bat 15.00 6.75
Rafael Palmeiro Bat
PA Rafael Palmeiro Bat 15.00 6.75
Roberto Alomar Uni
PH Rafael Palmeiro Bat 15.00 6.75
Rickey Henderson Bat
PS Rafael Palmeiro Uni 25.00 11.00
Sammy Sosa Bat
RP Manny Ramirez Jsy 25.00 11.00
Mike Piazza Uni
SB Sammy Sosa Bat 20.00 9.00
Jeff Bagwell Uni
SG Alfonso Soriano Uni 15.00 6.75
Vladimir Guerrero Bat

2003 Topps Tribute Contemporary Memorable Materials Relics

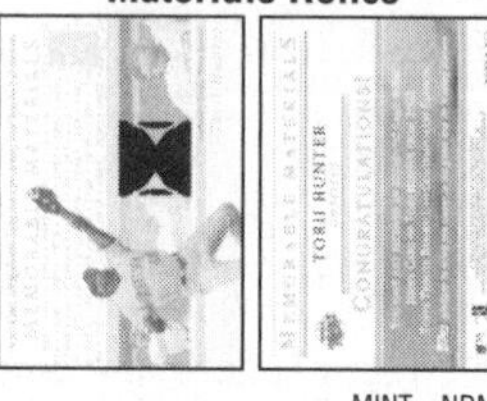

MINT NRMT
*RED MEM: .6X TO 1.5X BASIC
RED MEM PRINT RUN 50 SERIAL #'d SETS
GOLD MEM PRINT RUN 1 SERIAL #'d SET
NO GOLD PRICING DUE TO SCARCITY
RANDOM INSERTS IN PACKS
AJ Andruw Jones Jsy 10.00 4.50
AP Albert Pujols Jsy 25.00 11.00
AR Alex Rodriguez Jsy 20.00 9.00
AS Alfonso Soriano Uni 15.00 6.75
BB Barry Bonds Jsy 40.00 18.00
CR Cal Ripken Bat 50.00 22.00
GM Greg Maddux Jsy 15.00 6.75
JG Jason Giambi Jsy 15.00 6.75
JG2 Jason Giambi Bat 15.00 6.75
KW Kerry Wood Jsy 15.00 6.75
LG Luis Gonzalez Bat 10.00 4.50
MT Miguel Tejada Bat 10.00 4.50
RH Rickey Henderson Uni 15.00 6.75
SG Shawn Green Jsy 10.00 4.50
SS Sammy Sosa Bat 20.00 9.00
SS2 Sammy Sosa Jsy 20.00 9.00
TG Troy Glaus Uni 15.00 6.75
TH Torii Hunter Jsy 10.00 4.50
VG Vladimir Guerrero Bat 15.00 6.75

2003 Topps Tribute Contemporary Milestone Materials Relics

MINT NRMT
*RED MILE: .6X TO 1.5X BASIC
RED MILE PRINT RUN 50 SERIAL #'d SETS
GOLD PRINT RUN 1 SERIAL #'d SET
NO GOLD PRICING DUE TO SCARCITY
RANDOM INSERTS IN PACKS
AR Alex Rodriguez Jsy 20.00 9.00
BB1 Barry Bonds 1500 RBI Uni 25.00 11.00
BB2 Barry Bonds 1500 Runs Uni 25.00 11.00
BB3 Barry Bonds 2000 Hits Uni 25.00 11.00
BB4 Barry Bonds 500 2B Uni 25.00 11.00
BB5 Barry Bonds 600 HR Uni 25.00 11.00
CJ Chipper Jones Jsy 15.00 6.75
FM1 Fred McGriff Cubs Bat 10.00 4.50
FM2 Fred McGriff 2000 Hits Bat 10.00 4.50
FM3 Fred McGriff 400 HR Bat 10.00 4.50
FT Frank Thomas Jsy 15.00 6.75
JB1 Jeff Bagwell Jsy 10.00 4.50
JB2 Jeff Bagwell Uni 10.00 4.50
JG1 Juan Gonzalez Indians Bat 10.00 4.50
JG2 Juan Gonzalez Rgr Bat 10.00 4.50
MP1 Mike Piazza Bat 15.00 6.75
MP2 Mike Piazza Uni 15.00 6.75
MR1 Manny Ramirez Bat 8.00 3.60
MR2 Manny Ramirez Jsy 8.00 3.60
NG Nomar Garciaparra Jsy 25.00 11.00
RA Roberto Alomar Uni 15.00 6.75
RH1 R.Henderson Mets Bat 10.00 4.50
RH2 R.Henderson Sox Bat 10.00 4.50
RH3 R.Henderson A's Bat 10.00 4.50
RH4 R.Henderson 3000 Hits Bat 10.00 4.50
RH5 R.Henderson 500 2B Bat 10.00 4.50
RP1 R.Palmeiro 1500 RBI Jsy 10.00 4.50
RP2 R.Palmeiro 2500 Hits Bat 10.00 4.50
RP3 R.Palmeiro 500 HR Uni 10.00 4.50
RP4 R.Palmeiro 500 2B Bat 10.00 4.50
SS1 Sammy Sosa 1250 RBI Jsy 15.00 6.75
SS2 Sammy Sosa 2000 Hits Jsy 15.00 6.75
SS3 Sammy Sosa Bat 15.00 6.75
TH Todd Helton Jsy 15.00 6.75
VG Vladimir Guerrero Bat 15.00 6.75

2003 Topps Tribute Contemporary Modern Marks Autographs

Inserted at a stated rate of one in 19, these nine cards feature authentic autographs from current major leaguers.

MINT NRMT
STATED ODDS 1:19
*RED MARKS: .5X TO 1.2X BASIC
RED MARKS STATED ODDS 1:38
RED MARKS PRINT RUN 99 SERIAL #'d SETS
GOLD MARKS STATED ODDS 1:149
GOLD MARKS PRINT RUN 25 SERIAL #'d SETS
NO GOLD PRICING DUE TO SCARCITY
CF Cliff Floyd 15.00 6.75
EH Eric Hinske 15.00 6.75
LB Lance Berkman 15.00 6.75
MO Magglio Ordonez 20.00 9.00
MS Mike Sweeney 15.00 6.75
PK Paul Konerko 15.00 6.75
PL Paul Lo Duca 15.00 6.75
RC Roger Clemens 150.00 70.00
TH Torii Hunter 15.00 6.75

2003 Topps Tribute Contemporary Perennial All-Star Relics

MINT NRMT
*RED AS: .6X TO 1.5X BASIC
RED AS PRINT RUN 50 SERIAL #'d SETS
GOLD AS PRINT RUN 1 SERIAL #'d SET
NO GOLD PRICING DUE TO SCARCITY
RANDOM INSERTS IN PACKS
AR Alex Rodriguez Jsy 20.00 9.00
BB Barry Bonds Uni 25.00 11.00
BS Benito Santiago Bat 10.00 4.50
BW Bernie Williams Bat 15.00 6.75
CB Craig Biggio Uni 15.00 6.75
CJ Chipper Jones Jsy 15.00 6.75
CS Curt Schilling Jsy 15.00 6.75
EM Edgar Martinez Bat 15.00 6.75
FT Frank Thomas Bat 15.00 6.75
GM Greg Maddux Jsy 15.00 6.75
GS Gary Sheffield Bat 10.00 4.50
IR Ivan Rodriguez Bat 15.00 6.75
JS John Smoltz Uni 15.00 6.75
LW Larry Walker Bat 15.00 6.75
MM Mike Mussina Uni 15.00 6.75
MP Mike Piazza Bat 15.00 6.75
MR Manny Ramirez Bat 10.00 4.50
PM Pedro Martinez Jsy 15.00 6.75
RA Roberto Alomar Bat 15.00 6.75
RC Roger Clemens Uni 20.00 9.00
RH Rickey Henderson Bat 15.00 6.75
SS Sammy Sosa Bat 20.00 9.00

2003 Topps Tribute Contemporary Performance Double Relics

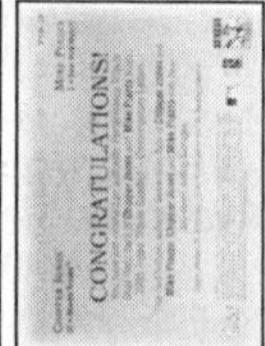

MINT NRMT
*RED DOUBLE: .6X TO 1.5X BASIC
RED DOUBLE PRINT RUN 50 #'d SETS
GOLD DOUBLE PRINT RUN 1 #'d SET
NO GOLD PRICING DUE TO SCARCITY
RANDOM INSERTS IN PACKS
BJ Barry Bonds Uni 25.00 11.00
Chipper Jones Bat
CM Roger Clemens Uni 40.00 18.00
Greg Maddux Jsy
GG Luis Gonzalez Bat 15.00 6.75
Troy Glaus Uni
JP Chipper Jones Bat 20.00 9.00
Mike Piazza Bat
MM Pedro Martinez Jsy 20.00 9.00
Greg Maddux Uni
PR Mike Piazza Uni 20.00 9.00
Ivan Rodriguez Bat
PS Mike Piazza Bat 20.00 9.00
Benito Santiago Bat
PW Albert Pujols Jsy 25.00 11.00
Kerry Wood Jsy
RG Alex Rodriguez Jsy 40.00 18.00
Nomar Garciaparra Jsy
RR Cal Ripken Bat 60.00 27.00
Alex Rodriguez Jsy
RT Alex Rodriguez Jsy 20.00 9.00
Miguel Tejada Bat
SA Alfonso Soriano Uni 15.00 6.75
Roberto Alomar Uni
SG Sammy Sosa Bat 20.00 9.00
Juan Gonzalez Bat
ZJ Barry Zito Uni 15.00 6.75
Randy Johnson Uni

2003 Topps Tribute Contemporary Performance Triple Relics

MINT NRMT
*RED TRIPLE: .6X TO 1.5X BASIC
RED TRIPLE PRINT RUN 50 #'d SETS
GOLD TRIPLE PRINT RUN 1 #'d SET
NO GOLD PRICING DUE TO SCARCITY
RANDOM INSERTS IN PACKS
BMP Barry Bonds Uni 40.00 18.00
Fred McGriff Bat
Rafael Palmeiro Jsy
CMJ Roger Clemens Uni 40.00 18.00
Greg Maddux Jsy
Randy Johnson Jsy
RPH Manny Ramirez Jsy 40.00 18.00
Mike Piazza Uni
Rickey Henderson Bat
SPM Sammy Sosa Bat 30.00 13.50
Rafael Palmeiro Bat
Fred McGriff Bat
STB Sammy Sosa Jsy 30.00 13.50
Frank Thomas Jsy
Jeff Bagwell Jsy

2003 Topps Tribute Contemporary Team Double Relics

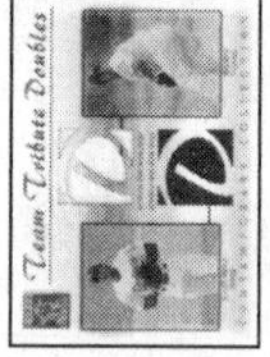

MINT NRMT
*RED DOUBLE: .6X TO 1.5X BASIC
RED DOUBLE PRINT RUN 50 SERIAL #'d SETS
GOLD DOUBLE PRINT RUN 1 #'d SET
NO GOLD PRICING DUE TO SCARCITY
RANDOM INSERTS IN PACKS
BB Craig Biggio Jsy 15.00 6.75
Jeff Bagwell Uni
GR Nomar Garciaparra Jsy 25.00 11.00
Manny Ramirez Jsy
IN Kazuhisa Ishii Jsy 40.00 18.00
Hideo Nomo Jsy
MS Greg Maddux Jsy 50.00 22.00
John Smoltz Jsy
RP Alex Rodriguez Jsy 20.00 9.00
Rafael Palmeiro Bat
WH Larry Walker Jsy 15.00 6.75
Todd Helton Jsy

2003 Topps Tribute Contemporary Team Triple Relics

MINT NRMT
*RED TRIPLE: .6X TO 1.5X BASIC
RED TRIPLE PRINT RUN 50 SERIAL #'d SETS
GOLD PRINT RUN 1 SERIAL #'d SET
NO GOLD PRICING DUE TO SCARCITY
RANDOM INSERTS IN PACKS
ASP Moises Alou Bat 30.00 13.50
Sammy Sosa Jsy
Corey Patterson Bat
BBB Craig Biggio Uni 25.00 11.00
Lance Berkman Bat
Jeff Bagwell Uni
CTM Eric Chavez Uni 25.00 11.00
Miguel Tejada Jsy
Mark Mulder Uni
GRM Nomar Garciaparra Jsy 40.00 18.00
Manny Ramirez Jsy
Pedro Martinez Jsy
HZM Tim Hudson Uni 25.00 11.00
Barry Zito Uni
Mark Mulder Uni
JSJ Andruw Jones Jsy 30.00 13.50
Gary Sheffield Bat
Chipper Jones Jsy
MHM Joe Mauer Bat 30.00 13.50
Torii Hunter Jsy
Doug Mientkiewicz Bat
MOB Edgar Martinez Jsy 25.00 11.00
John Olerud Bat
Bret Boone Jsy

PER Albert Pujols Bat 40.00 18.00
Jim Edmonds Jsy
Scott Rolen Bat
RBT Alex Rodriguez Bat 30.00 13.50
Hank Blalock Bat
Mark Teixeira Bat
RGP Alex Rodriguez Jsy 30.00 13.50
Juan Gonzalez Bat
Rafael Palmeiro Jsy
SGV Alfonso Soriano Bat 30.00 13.50
Jason Giambi Bat
Robin Ventura Bat
TBB Jim Thome Jsy 30.00 13.50
Marlon Byrd Jsy
Pat Burrell Jsy
TOK Frank Thomas Jsy 30.00 13.50
Magglio Ordonez Jsy
Paul Konerko Jsy

2003 Topps Tribute Contemporary Tribute to the Stars Dual Relics

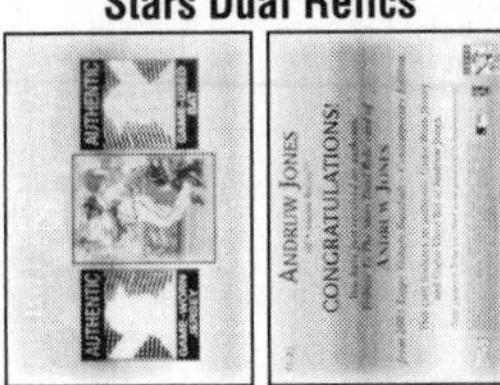

MINT NRMT
*RED DUAL: .6X TO 1.5X BASIC
RED DUAL PRINT RUN 50 #'d SETS
GOLD DUAL PRINT RUN 1 SERIAL #'d SET
NO GOLD PRICING DUE TO SCARCITY
RANDOM INSERTS IN PACKS
AD Adam Dunn Bat-Jsy 15.00 6.75
AJ Andruw Jones Bat-Jsy 15.00 6.75
AP Albert Pujols Bat-Uni 40.00 18.00
AR Alex Rodriguez Bat-Jsy 30.00 13.50
AS Alfonso Soriano Bat-Uni 15.00 6.75
BB Barry Bonds Bat-Uni 50.00 22.00
CJ Chipper Jones Bat-Jsy 15.00 6.75
EC Eric Chavez Bat-Uni 15.00 6.75
FT Frank Thomas Bat-Jsy 15.00 6.75
GA Garret Anderson Bat-Uni 15.00 6.75
GM Greg Maddux Bat-Uni 20.00 9.00
JT Jim Thome Bat-Jsy 15.00 6.75
LB Lance Berkman Bat-Jsy 15.00 6.75
LW Larry Walker Bat-Jsy 15.00 6.75
MP Mike Piazza Bat-Uni 20.00 9.00
NG Nomar Garciaparra Bat-Jsy 40.00 18.00
PB Pat Burrell Bat-Jsy 15.00 6.75
RA Roberto Alomar Bat-Uni 15.00 6.75
RH Rickey Henderson Bat-Uni 15.00 6.75
RP Rafael Palmeiro Bat-Jsy 15.00 6.75
SS Sammy Sosa Bat-Jsy 25.00 11.00
TG Troy Glaus Bat-Uni 15.00 6.75
TH Todd Helton Bat-Jsy 15.00 6.75
VG Vladimir Guerrero Bat-Jsy 15.00 6.75
THU Torii Hunter Bat-Jsy 15.00 6.75

2003 Topps Tribute Contemporary Tribute to the Stars Patchworks Dual Relics

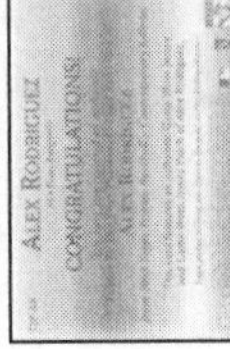

MINT NRMT
STATED ODDS 1:34
STATED PRINT RUN 50 SERIAL #'d SETS
AP Albert Pujols 100.00 45.00
AR Alex Rodriguez 60.00 27.00
AR2 Alex Rodriguez Blue 60.00 27.00
BB Barry Bonds 100.00 45.00
CJ Chipper Jones 40.00 18.00
CS Curt Schilling 40.00 18.00
FT Frank Thomas 40.00 18.00
GM Greg Maddux 50.00 22.00
JB Jeff Bagwell 40.00 18.00
KW Kerry Wood 40.00 18.00
LG Luis Gonzalez 25.00 11.00
MR Manny Ramirez 25.00 11.00
NG Nomar Garciaparra 50.00 22.00
PM Pedro Martinez 40.00 18.00
RJ Randy Johnson 40.00 18.00
RP Rafael Palmeiro 40.00 18.00
SG Shawn Green 25.00 11.00
SS Sammy Sosa 50.00 22.00
TH Todd Helton 40.00 18.00
THU Torii Hunter 25.00 11.00

2003 Topps Tribute Contemporary World Series Relics

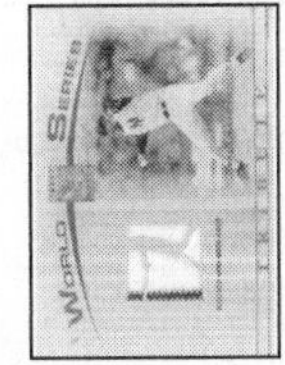

MINT NRMT
*RED WS: .6X TO 1.5X BASIC
RED WS PRINT RUN 50 SERIAL #'d SETS
GOLD WS PRINT RUN 1 SERIAL #'d SET
NO GOLD PRICING DUE TO SCARCITY
RANDOM INSERTS IN PACKS
MR Mariano Rivera Jsy 15.00 6.75
TG Troy Glaus Uni 15.00 6.75

2003 Topps Tribute Contemporary World Series Double Relics

MINT NRMT
*RED WS DOUBLE: .6X TO 1.5X BASIC
RED WS DOUBLE PRINT RUN 50 #'d SETS
GOLD WS DOUBLE PRINT RUN 1 #'d SET
NO GOLD PRICING DUE TO SCARCITY
RANDOM INSERTS IN PACKS
BG Barry Bonds Uni 40.00 18.00
Troy Glaus Uni
LP John Lackey Uni 10.00 4.50
Troy Percival Uni
PC Mike Piazza Bat 40.00 18.00
Roger Clemens Uni
PP Jorge Posada Bat 25.00 11.00
Andy Pettitte Jsy
SJ Curt Schilling Jsy 15.00 6.75
Randy Johnson Jsy
WG Bernie Williams Bat 15.00 6.75
Luis Gonzalez Bat
WO Bernie Williams Bat 15.00 6.75
Paul O'Neill Bat

2003 Topps Tribute Contemporary World Series Triple Relics

MINT NRMT
*RED WS TRIPLE: .6X TO 1.5X BASIC
RED WS TRIPLE PRINT RUN 50 #'d SETS
GOLD WS TRIPLE PRINT RUN 1 #'d SET
NO GOLD PRICING DUE TO SCARCITY
RANDOM INSERTS IN PACKS
EGS Darin Erstad Uni 25.00 11.00
Troy Glaus Uni
Tim Salmon Uni
LGP John Lackey Uni 25.00 11.00
Troy Glaus Bat
Troy Percival Uni

2003 Topps Tribute Perennial All-Star

This 50 card set was released in February, 2003. These cards were issued in five card packs with an $50 SRP. These packs were issued in six pack boxes which came four boxes to a case. Cards honored players who made at least five trips to the All-Star game during their career.

Nm-Mt Ex-Mt
COMPLETE SET (50) 100.00 30.00
1 Willie Mays 10.00 3.00
2 Don Mattingly 12.00 3.60
3 Hoyt Wilhelm 4.00 1.20
4 Hank Aaron 10.00 3.00
5 Hank Greenberg 5.00 1.50
6 Johnny Bench 5.00 1.50
7 Duke Snider 4.00 1.20
8 Carl Yastrzemski 8.00 2.40
9 Jim Palmer 4.00 1.20
10 Roberto Clemente 12.00 3.60
11 Mike Schmidt 10.00 3.00
12 Joe Cronin 4.00 1.20
13 Lou Brock 4.00 1.20
14 Orlando Cepeda 4.00 1.20
15 Bill Mazeroski 4.00 1.20
16 Whitey Ford 4.00 1.20
17 Rod Carew 4.00 1.20
18 Joe Morgan 4.00 1.20
19 Luis Aparicio 4.00 1.20
20 Nolan Ryan 12.00 3.60
21 Bobby Doerr 4.00 1.20
22 Dale Murphy 5.00 1.50
23 Bob Feller 4.00 1.20
24 Paul Molitor 4.00 1.20
25 Tom Seaver 4.00 1.20
26 Ozzie Smith 8.00 2.40
27 Stan Musial 8.00 2.40
28 Willie McCovey 4.00 1.20
29 Gary Carter 4.00 1.20
30 Reggie Jackson 4.00 1.20
31 Gaylord Perry 4.00 1.20
32 George Brett 12.00 3.60
33 Robin Roberts 4.00 1.20
34 Wade Boggs 4.00 1.20
35 Cal Ripken 15.00 4.50
36 Carlton Fisk 4.00 1.20
37 Al Kaline 5.00 1.50
38 Kirby Puckett 5.00 1.50
39 Phil Rizzuto 4.00 1.20
40 Willie Stargell 4.00 1.20
41 Harmon Killebrew 5.00 1.50
42 Red Schoendienst 4.00 1.20
43 Tony Gwynn 6.00 1.80
44 Ralph Kiner 4.00 1.20
45 Yogi Berra 5.00 1.50
46 Catfish Hunter 4.00 1.20
47 Frank Robinson 4.00 1.20
48 Ernie Banks 5.00 1.50
49 Warren Spahn 4.00 1.20
50 Brooks Robinson 5.00 1.50

2003 Topps Tribute Perennial All-Star Gold

This is a parallel to the Topps Tribute set. These cards were issued at different rates depending on what group the card was issued from. We have notated that information next to the player's name in our checklist.

Nm-Mt Ex-Mt
*GOLD p/r 81-86: 1.5X TO 4X BASIC
*GOLD p/r 66-80: 2X TO 5X BASIC
*GOLD p/r 51-65: 2.5X TO 6X BASIC
*GOLD p/r 36-50: 3X TO 8X BASIC
*GOLD p/r 26-35: 4X TO 10X BASIC
GROUP A ODDS 1:106
GROUP B ODDS 1:49
GROUP C ODDS 1:38

2003 Topps Tribute Perennial All-Star Relics

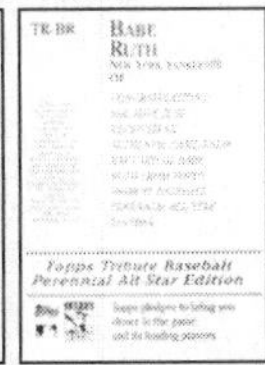

This 65-card insert set was inserted at various odds depending on what type of relic and what group the card belonged to. We have notated the group, the odds for the group as well as the relic in our checklist.

Nm-Mt Ex-Mt
BAT GROUP A ODDS 1:556
BAT GROUP B ODDS 1:
BAT GROUP C ODDS 1:276
BAT GROUP D ODDS 1:61
BAT GROUP E ODDS 1:158
BAT GROUP F ODDS 1:23
BAT GROUP G ODDS 1:111
BAT GROUP H ODDS 1:46
BAT GROUP I ODDS 1:85
BAT GROUP J ODDS 1:16
BAT GROUP K ODDS 1:18
BAT GROUP L ODDS 1:31
BAT GROUP M ODDS 1:50
BAT GROUP N ODDS 1:46
BAT GROUP O ODDS 1:21
BAT GROUP P ODDS 1:37
JSY/UNI GROUP A ODDS 1:368
JSY/UNI GROUP B ODDS 1:148
JSY/UNI GROUP C ODDS 1:92
JSY/UNI GROUP D ODDS 1:185
JSY/UNI GROUP E ODDS 1:69
JSY/UNI GROUP F ODDS 1:55
JSY/UNI GROUP G ODDS 1:79
JSY/UNI GROUP H ODDS 1:61
JSY/UNI GROUP I ODDS 1:55
JSY/UNI GROUP J ODDS 1:25
JSY/UNI GROUP K ODDS 1:46
JSY/UNI GROUP L ODDS 1:43
JSY/UNI GROUP M ODDS 1:21
JSY/UNI GROUP N ODDS 1:8
JSY/UNI GROUP O ODDS 1:29
JSY/UNI GROUP P ODDS 1:10
AD Andre Dawson Bat F 20.00 6.00
AK Al Kaline Bat E 30.00 9.00
BD Bobby Doerr Jsy N 15.00 4.50
BF Bob Feller Bat I 20.00 6.00
BM Bill Mazeroski Uni C 25.00 7.50
BR Babe Ruth Bat J 180.00 55.00
BRO Brooks Robinson Bat J 25.00 7.50
CF Carlton Fisk Bat J 20.00 6.00
CH Catfish Hunter Jsy B 25.00 7.50
CRB Cal Ripken Bat P 40.00 12.00
CY Carl Yastrzemski Jsy E 40.00 12.00
DD Dizzy Dean Uni E 50.00 15.00
DM Dale Murphy Jsy A 50.00 15.00
DMA Don Mattingly Jsy L 40.00 12.00
DN Don Newcombe Bat K 15.00 4.50
DSN Duke Snider Bat F 25.00 7.50
EB Ernie Banks Bat M 20.00 6.00
EM Eddie Mathews Jsy K 20.00 6.00
FR Frank Robinson Uni G 20.00 6.00
GB George Brett Jsy M 30.00 9.00
GC Gary Carter Jsy I 20.00 6.00
HA Hank Aaron Bat O 40.00 12.00
HG Hank Greenberg Bat D 50.00 15.00
HK Harmon Killebrew Jsy J 20.00 6.00
HW Honus Wagner Bat B 180.00 55.00
HWI Hoyt Wilhelm Uni N 15.00 4.50
JBE Johnny Bench Uni F 30.00 9.00
JCR Joe Cronin Bat N 15.00 4.50
JF Jimmie Foxx Bat F 50.00 15.00
JMI Johnny Mize Uni D 20.00 6.00
JMO Joe Morgan Bat K 15.00 4.50
JP Jim Palmer Uni N 15.00 4.50
JR Jackie Robinson Bat L 50.00 15.00
KP Kirby Puckett Jsy N 20.00 6.00
LA Luis Aparicio Bat C 20.00 6.00
LB Lou Brock Bat A 30.00 9.00
LBU Lou Brock Uni H 20.00 6.00
LG Lou Gehrig Bat F 150.00 45.00
MO Mel Ott Bat D 30.00 9.00
MS Mike Schmidt Uni P 20.00 6.00
NL Nap Lajoie Bat D 80.00 24.00
NR Nolan Ryan Rangers Uni O 40.00 12.00
NRA Nolan Ryan Astros Jsy F 50.00 15.00
OC Orlando Cepeda Jsy C 20.00 6.00
OS Ozzie Smith Uni J 20.00 6.00
PM Paul Molitor Bat K 20.00 6.00
PR Phil Rizzuto Bat H 25.00 7.50
RC Roberto Clemente Bat L 60.00 18.00
RCA Roy Campanella Bat F 25.00 7.50
RH Rogers Hornsby Bat G 50.00 15.00
RJ Reggie Jackson Bat O 20.00 6.00
ROD Rod Carew Jsy N 20.00 6.00
RS Red Schoendienst Bat H 15.00 4.50
SM Stan Musial Bat J 40.00 12.00
TC Ty Cobb Bat F 120.00 36.00
TG Tony Gwynn Jsy P 15.00 4.50
TM Thurman Munson Jsy M 30.00 9.00
TS Tris Speaker Bat A 100.00 30.00
TSE Tom Seaver Jsy A 30.00 9.00
WB Wade Boggs Uni C 25.00 7.50
WF Whitey Ford Uni B 25.00 7.50
WM Willie Mays Bat K 40.00 12.00
WMC Willie McCovey Bat J 15.00 4.50
WST Willie Stargell Uni B 25.00 7.50
YB Yogi Berra Jsy A 50.00 15.00

2003 Topps Tribute Perennial All-Star Patch Relics

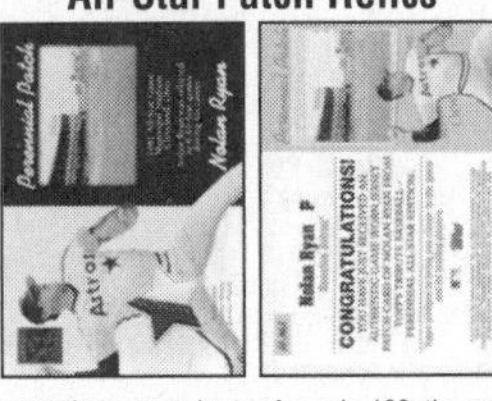

Inserted at a stated rate of one in 123, these 15 cards feature premium relics from prestigious retired talents. These game-worn uniform patch relic cards display a unique design featuring the player, his relic and the site of an All-Star appearance. These cards were issued to a stated print run of 30 serial numbered sets.

Nm-Mt Ex-Mt
CR Cal Ripken 300.00 90.00
CY Carl Yastrzemski 200.00 60.00
DMU Dale Murphy 150.00 45.00
GB George Brett 250.00 75.00
GC Gary Carter 80.00 24.00
HK Harmon Killebrew 150.00 45.00
JM Joe Morgan 50.00 15.00
MS Mike Schmidt 250.00 75.00
NR Nolan Ryan Rangers 250.00 75.00
NRA Nolan Ryan Astros 250.00 75.00
OS Ozzie Smith 200.00 60.00
TG Tony Gwynn 150.00 45.00
WB Wade Boggs 80.00 24.00
WM Willie McCovey 50.00 15.00
WS Willie Stargell 80.00 24.00

2003 Topps Tribute Perennial All-Star Signing

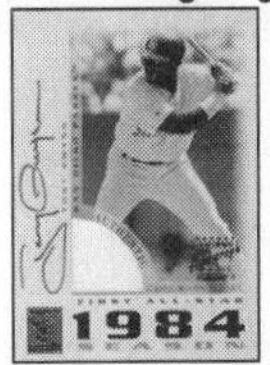

Issued at a stated rate of one in 34, these cards feature not only a game-used relic from the player's career but also an authentic signature of the featured player.

Nm-Mt Ex-Mt
GOLD STATED ODDS 1:201
GOLD PRINT RUN 25 SERIAL #'d SETS
NO GOLD PRICING DUE TO SCARCITY
AD Andre Dawson Bat 40.00 12.00
AK Al Kaline Bat 80.00 24.00
DM Dale Murphy Jsy 80.00 24.00
DMA Don Mattingly Jsy 120.00 36.00
DSN Duke Snider Bat 80.00 24.00
GC Gary Carter Jsy 60.00 18.00
JP Jim Palmer Uni 40.00 12.00
LB Lou Brock Bat 60.00 18.00
MS Mike Schmidt Uni 120.00 36.00
OC Orlando Cepeda Jsy 40.00 12.00
TG Tony Gwynn Jsy 100.00 30.00

2003 Topps Tribute Perennial All-Star 1st Class Cut Relics

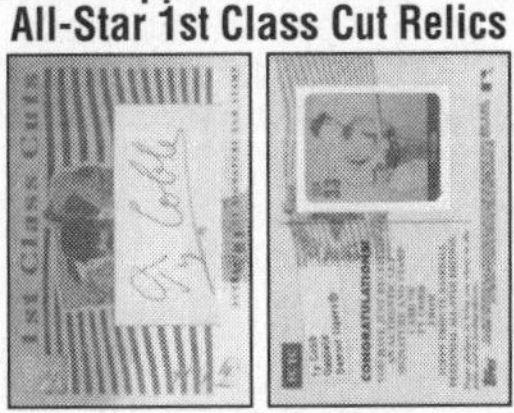

Inserted at a stated rate of one in 7461, these seven cards feature autograph cuts from among the most legendary figures in the game. On back each card is an authentic USPS stamp of the featured player. Each of these cards was issued to a stated print run of one serial numbered set.

Nm-Mt Ex-Mt
BR Babe Ruth
DD Dizzy Dean
HW Honus Wagner
JR Jackie Robinson
LG Lou Gehrig
TC Ty Cobb
TS Tris Speaker

2003 Topps Tribute Perennial All-Star Memorable Match-Up Relics

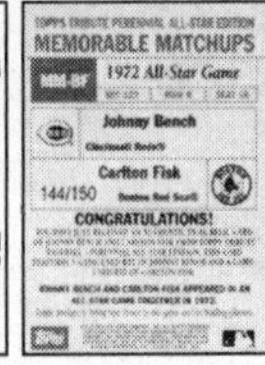

Issued at a stated rate of one in 41, these 10 cards feature two all stars who appeared in the same all-star game along with a game-used relic from each of their career. These cards were issued to a stated print run of 150 serial numbered sets.

Nm-Mt Ex-Mt
GOLD STATED ODDS 1:245
GOLD PRINT RUN 25 SERIAL #'d SETS
NO GOLD PRICING DUE TO SCARCITY
BF Johnny Bench Bat 60.00 18.00
Carlton Fisk Bat
BG Wade Boggs Bat 60.00 18.00
Tony Gwynn Bat
BS George Brett Jsy 120.00 36.00
Mike Schmidt Uni
CM Gary Carter Jsy 80.00 24.00
Don Mattingly Jsy
KA Harmon Killebrew Jsy 120.00 36.00
Hank Aaron Bat
MJ Willie Mays Bat 100.00 30.00
Reggie Jackson Bat
PG Kirby Puckett Bat 60.00 18.00
Tony Gwynn Bat
YB Carl Yastrzemski Jsy 80.00 24.00
Johnny Bench Bat
YBR Carl Yastrzemski Jsy 60.00 18.00
Lou Brock Bat

2003 Topps Tribute World Series

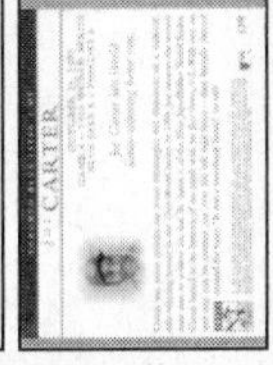

This 150 card set was released in October, 2003. The set was issued in four card packs with an $50 SRP which came six packs to a box and four boxes to a case. Cards numbered 1 through 130 feature players from a year in which their team participated in a World Series while cards 131 through 150 is a Fall Classic sub set featuring key moments in World Series history.

MINT NRMT
COMMON CARD (1-130) 4.00 1.80
COMMON CARD (131-150) 4.00 1.80
1 Willie Mays 54 10.00 4.50
2 Gary Carter 86 4.00 1.80
3 Yogi Berra 47 5.00 2.20
4 Dennis Eckersley 88 4.00 1.80
5 Willie McCovey 62 4.00 1.80
6 Willie Stargell 71 4.00 1.80
7 Mike Schmidt 80 10.00 4.50
8 Robin Yount 82 8.00 3.60
9 Bucky Harris 24 4.00 1.80
10 Carl Yastrzemski 67 8.00 3.60
11 Lenny Dykstra 86 4.00 1.80
12 Boog Powell 66 4.00 1.80
13 Bill Lee 75 4.00 1.80
14 Lou Brock 64 4.00 1.80
15 Bob Friend 60 4.00 1.80
16 Hank Greenberg 34 5.00 2.20
17 Maury Wills 59 4.00 1.80
18 Tom Lasorda 77 4.00 1.80
19 Moose Skowron 55 4.00 1.80
20 Frank Robinson 61 4.00 1.80
21 Rollie Fingers 72 4.00 1.80
22 Doug DeCinces 79 4.00 1.80
23 Eric Davis 90 4.00 1.80
24 Johnny Podres 53 4.00 1.80
25 Darrell Evans 84 4.00 1.80
26 Ron Cey 74 4.00 1.80
27 Ray Knight 86 4.00 1.80
28 Don Larsen 55 4.00 1.80
29 Harold Baines 90 4.00 1.80
30 Brooks Robinson 66 5.00 2.20
31 Wade Boggs 86 4.00 1.80
32 Joe Morgan 72 4.00 1.80
33 Kirk Gibson 84 4.00 1.80
34 Tommy John 77 4.00 1.80
35 Monte Irvin 51 4.00 1.80
36 Goose Gossage 78 4.00 1.80
37 Tug McGraw 73 4.00 1.80
38 Walt Weiss 88 4.00 1.80
39 Bill Madlock 79 4.00 1.80
40 Juan Marichal 62 4.00 1.80
41 Willie McGee 82 4.00 1.80
42 Joe Cronin 33 4.00 1.80
43 Paul Blair 66 4.00 1.80
44 Norm Cash 59 4.00 1.80
45 Ken Griffey 75 4.00 1.80
46 Bret Saberhagen 85 4.00 1.80
47 Don Sutton 74 4.00 1.80
48 Kirby Puckett 87 5.00 2.20
49 Keith Hernandez 82 4.00 1.80
50 George Brett 80 12.00 5.50
51 Bobby Richardson 57 4.00 1.80

52 Jose Canseco 88 5.00 2.20
53 Greg Luzinski 80 4.00 1.80
54 Bill Mazeroski 60 4.00 1.80
55 Red Schoendienst 46 4.00 1.80
56 Graig Nettles 76 4.00 1.80
57 Jerry Koosman 69 4.00 1.80
58 Tony Perez 70 4.00 1.80
59 Jim Rice 86 4.00 1.80
60 Duke Snider 49 4.00 1.80
61 David Justice 91 4.00 1.80
62 Johnny Sain 48 4.00 1.80
63 Chuck Klein 35 4.00 1.80
64 Sparky Anderson 70 4.00 1.80
65 Alan Trammell 84 4.00 1.80
66 Willie Wilson 80 4.00 1.80
67 Hoyt Wilhelm 54 4.00 1.80
68 Joe Pepitone 63 4.00 1.80
69 Darren Daulton 93 4.00 1.80
70 Tom Seaver 69 4.00 1.80
71 Catfish Hunter 72 4.00 1.80
72 Tim McCarver 64 4.00 1.80
73 Dave Parker 79 4.00 1.80
74 Earl Weaver 69 4.00 1.80
75 Ted Kluszewski 59 4.00 1.80
76 John Kruk 93 4.00 1.80
77 Dwight Evans 75 4.00 1.80
78 Ron Darling 86 4.00 1.80
79 Tony Oliva 65 4.00 1.80
80 Johnny Bench 70 5.00 2.20
81 Sam Crawford 07 4.00 1.80
82 Steve Yeager 74 4.00 1.80
83 Paul Molitor 82 4.00 1.80
84 Bert Campaneris 72 4.00 1.80
85 Mickey Rivers 76 4.00 1.80
86 Vince Coleman 87 4.00 1.80
87 Kent Tekulve 79 4.00 1.80
88 Dwight Gooden 86 4.00 1.80
89 Whitey Herzog 82 4.00 1.80
90 Whitey Ford 50 4.00 1.80
91 Warren Spahn 48 4.00 1.80
92 Fred Lynn 75 4.00 1.80
93 Joe Tinker 06 4.00 1.80
94 Bill Buckner 74 4.00 1.80
95 Bob Feller 48 4.00 1.80
96 Hank Bauer 49 4.00 1.80
97 Joe Rudi 72 4.00 1.80
98 Steve Sax 81 4.00 1.80
99 Bruce Sutter 82 4.00 1.80
100 Nolan Ryan 69 12.00 5.50
101 Bobby Thomson 51 4.00 1.80
102 Bob Watson 81 4.00 1.80
103 Vida Blue 72 4.00 1.80
104 Robin Roberts 50 4.00 1.80
105 Orlando Cepeda 62 4.00 1.80
106 Jim Bottomley 26 4.00 1.80
107 Heinie Manush 33 4.00 1.80
108 Jim Gilliam 53 4.00 1.80
109 Dave Concepcion 70 4.00 1.80
110 Al Kaline 68 5.00 2.20
111 Howard Johnson 84 4.00 1.80
112 Phil Rizzuto 41 4.00 1.80
113 Steve Garvey 74 4.00 1.80
114 George Foster 72 4.00 1.80
115 Carlton Fisk 75 4.00 1.80
116 Don Newcombe 49 4.00 1.80
117 Lance Parrish 84 4.00 1.80
118 Reggie Jackson 73 4.00 1.80
119 Luis Aparicio 59 4.00 1.80
120 Jim Palmer 66 4.00 1.80
121 Ron Guidry 77 4.00 1.80
122 Frankie Frisch 21 4.00 1.80
123 Chet Lemon 84 4.00 1.80
124 Cecil Cooper 75 4.00 1.80
125 Harmon Killebrew 65 5.00 2.20
126 Luis Tiant 75 4.00 1.80
127 John McGraw 05 4.00 1.80
128 Paul O'Neill 90 4.00 1.80
129 Jack Clark 85 4.00 1.80
130 Stan Musial 42 8.00 3.60
131 Mike Schmidt FC 10.00 4.50
132 Kirby Puckett FC 5.00 2.20
133 Carlton Fisk FC 4.00 1.80
134 Bill Mazeroski FC 4.00 1.80
135 Johnny Podres FC 4.00 1.80
136 Robin Yount FC 8.00 3.60
137 David Justice FC 4.00 1.80
138 Bobby Thomson FC 4.00 1.80
139 Joe Carter FC 4.00 1.80
140 Reggie Jackson FC 4.00 1.80
141 Kirk Gibson FC 4.00 1.80
142 Whitey Ford FC 4.00 1.80
143 Don Larsen FC 4.00 1.80
144 Duke Snider FC 4.00 1.80
145 Carl Yastrzemski FC 8.00 3.60
146 Johnny Bench FC 5.00 2.20
147 Lou Brock FC 4.00 1.80
148 Ted Kluszewski FC 4.00 1.80
149 Jim Palmer FC 4.00 1.80
150 Willie Mays FC 10.00 4.50

2003 Topps Tribute World Series Gold

MINT NRMT
*GOLD 1-130: 1.5X TO 4X BASIC
*GOLD 131-150: 1.5X TO 4X BASIC
RANDOM INSERTS IN PACKS
STATED PRINT RUN 100 SERIAL #'d SETS

2003 Topps Tribute World Series Fall Classic Cuts

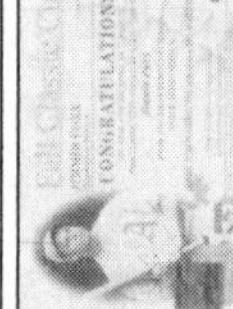

MINT NRMT
STATED ODDS 1:3437
STATED PRINT RUN 1 SERIAL #'d SET
NO PRICING DUE TO SCARCITY
BR Babe Ruth
HG Hank Greenberg
HW Honus Wagner
JF Jimmie Foxx
JR Jackie Robinson
LG Lou Gehrig
MO Mel Ott
RM Roger Maris
TC Ty Cobb
TM Thurman Munson

2003 Topps Tribute World Series Memorable Match-Up Relics

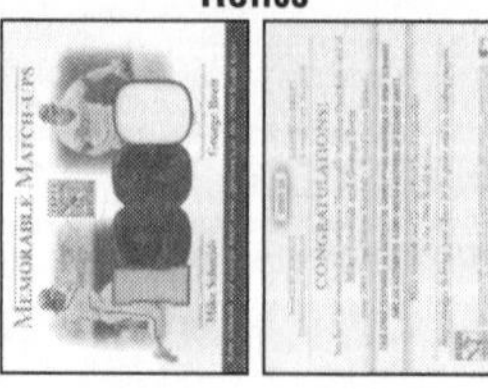

MINT NRMT
STATED ODDS 1:28
PRINT RUNS B/WN 9-88 COPIES PER
NO PRICING ON QTY OF 19 OR LESS.
AM Sparky Anderson Uni 25.00 11.00
Billy Martin Uni/76
AS Luis Aparicio Bat 50.00 22.00
Duke Snider Bat/59
CR Eddie Collins Bat
Edd Roush Bat/19
EG Dennis Eckersley Uni 50.00 22.00
Kirk Gibson Bat/88
FS Whitey Ford Uni 80.00 36.00
Duke Snider Bat/52
GF Hank Greenberg Bat 150.00 70.00
Frankie Frisch Bat/34
GK Hank Greenberg Bat 150.00 70.00
Chuck Klein Bat/35
KB Al Kaline Uni 80.00 36.00
Lou Brock Bat/68
MF Bill Mazeroski Jsy 80.00 36.00
Whitey Ford Uni/64
PR Phil Rizzuto Bat 150.00 70.00
Willie Mays Uni/51
RBE Brooks Robinson Bat 50.00 22.00
Johnny Bench Bat/70
RS Frank Robinson Bat 50.00 22.00
Tom Seaver Uni/69
SB Mike Schmidt Uni 100.00 45.00
George Brett Uni/80
SP Willie Stargell Bat 40.00 18.00
Jim Palmer Jsy/79
SRI Mike Schmidt Uni 150.00 70.00
Cal Ripken Uni/83
SY Ozzie Smith Bat 80.00 36.00
Robin Yount Jsy/82
TG Alan Trammell Jsy 80.00 36.00
Tony Gwynn Bat/84
WB Mookie Wilson Bat 50.00 22.00
Bill Buckner Jsy/86
WC Honus Wagner Bat
Ty Cobb Bat/9

2003 Topps Tribute World Series Pastime Patches

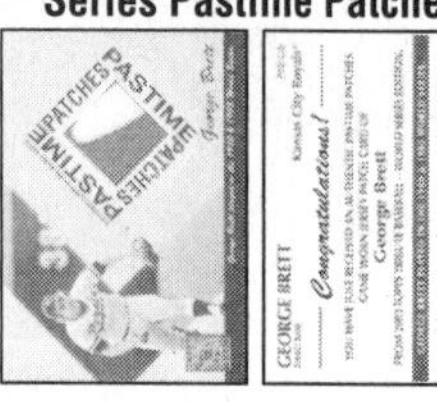

MINT NRMT
STATED ODDS 1:146
STATED PRINT RUN 15 SERIAL #'d SETS
NO PRICING DUE TO SCARCITY
AK Al Kaline
AT Alan Trammell
CH Catfish Hunter
CR Cal Ripken
CY Carl Yastrzemski
DE Dennis Eckersley
DP Dave Parker
DS Don Sutton
GB George Brett
JC Jose Canseco
JP Jim Palmer
JR Jim Rice
MS Mike Schmidt
MSK Moose Skowron
RY Robin Yount

2003 Topps Tribute World Series Signature Relics

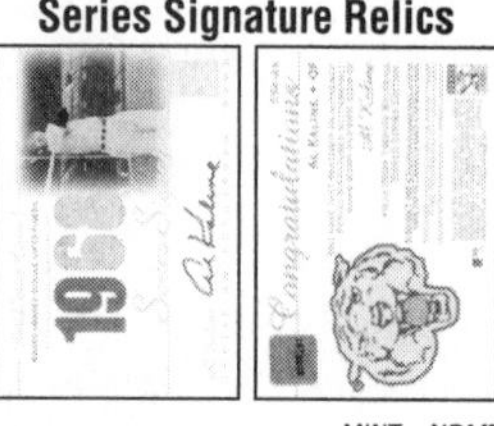

MINT NRMT
GROUP A ODDS 1:218
GROUP B ODDS 1:94
GROUP C ODDS 1:9
GROUP D ODDS 1:12
GOLD STATED ODDS 1:88
GOLD PRINT RUN 25 SERIAL #'d SETS
NO GOLD PRICING DUE TO SCARCITY
AK Al Kaline Uni C 50.00 22.00
AT Alan Trammell Jsy C 40.00 18.00
BR Brooks Robinson Bat A 120.00 55.00
DJ David Justice Uni B 50.00 22.00
DN Don Newcombe Bat A 50.00 22.00
EW Earl Weaver Jsy D 25.00 11.00
JC Joe Carter Bat C 25.00 11.00
JP Jim Palmer Jsy D 40.00 18.00
KG Kirk Gibson Bat C 40.00 18.00
MS Moose Skowron Bat C 25.00 11.00
MW Maury Wills Jsy D 25.00 11.00
MWI Mookie Wilson Bat B 40.00 18.00
SA Sparky Anderson Uni C 25.00 11.00
SG Steve Garvey Bat C 25.00 11.00
WF Whitey Ford Uni C 60.00 27.00

2003 Topps Tribute World Series Subway Fan Fare Tokens

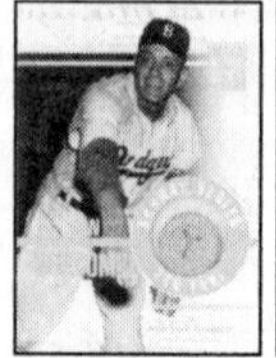

MINT NRMT
ONE PER BOX
BM Billy Martin 15.00 6.75
DJ David Justice 10.00 4.50
DL Don Larsen 10.00 4.50
DN Don Newcombe 10.00 4.50
DS Duke Snider 15.00 6.75
HB Hank Bauer 10.00 4.50
JP Johnny Podres 10.00 4.50
MS Moose Skowron 10.00 4.50
PO Paul O'Neill 15.00 6.75
PR Phil Rizzuto 15.00 6.75
WF Whitey Ford 15.00 6.75
YB Yogi Berra 20.00 9.00

2003 Topps Tribute World Series Team Tribute Relics

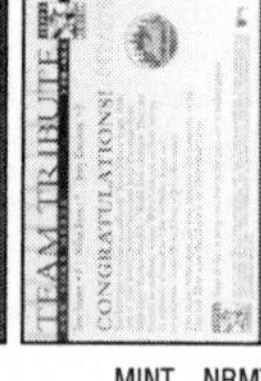

MINT NRMT
GROUP A ODDS 1:436
GROUP B ODDS 1:7
GROUP A PRINT RUN 25 SERIAL #'d SETS
GROUP B PRINT RUN 275 SERIAL #'d SETS
NO GROUP A PRICING DUE TO SCARCITY
CM Orlando Cepeda Bat 30.00 13.50
Juan Marichal Uni B
CPM Dave Concepcion Bat 50.00 22.00
Tony Perez Uni
Joe Morgan Uni B
CYG Ron Cey Bat 30.00 13.50
Steve Yeager Bat
Steve Garvey Bat B
EC Dennis Eckersley Jsy 25.00 11.00
Jose Canseco Jsy B
FB Whitey Ford Uni
Yogi Berra Jsy A
FPG George Foster Bat 40.00 18.00
Tony Perez Uni
Ken Griffey Sr. Bat B
GB Lou Gehrig Bat
Babe Ruth Bat A
GT Kirk Gibson Bat 40.00 18.00
Alan Trammell Jsy B
HCD Keith Hernandez Bat 40.00 18.00
Gary Carter Uni
Lenny Dykstra Bat B
HJ Catfish Hunter Jsy 30.00 13.50
Reggie Jackson Bat B
KCA Al Kaline Uni 40.00 18.00
Norm Cash Bat B
MM Willie Mays Uni 80.00 36.00
Willie McCovey Bat B
OSD Paul O'Neill Bat 40.00 18.00
Chris Sabo Bat
Eric Davis Bat B
SB Bret Saberhagen Jsy 50.00 22.00
George Brett Bat B
SMC Ozzie Smith Uni 60.00 27.00
Willie McGee Bat
Vince Coleman Bat B
SPM Willie Stargell Bat 40.00 18.00
Dave Parker Jsy
Bill Madlock Bat B
SR Moose Skowron Bat
Bobby Richardson Bat A
SRK Tom Seaver Uni 80.00 36.00
Nolan Ryan Bat
Jerry Koosman Jsy B
TA Alan Trammell Jsy 25.00 11.00
Sparky Anderson Uni B
YLK Carl Yastrzemski Jsy 50.00 22.00
Fred Lynn Jsy
Carlton Fisk Bat B
YM Robin Yount Jsy 40.00 18.00
Paul Molitor Bat B

2003 Topps Tribute World Series Tribute Relics

MINT NRMT
GROUP A ODDS 1:41
GROUP B ODDS 1:3
GROUP A PRINT RUN 50 SERIAL #'d SETS
GROUP B PRINT RUN 425 SERIAL #'d SETS
GOLD STATED ODDS 1:25
GOLD PRINT RUN 25 SERIAL #'d SETS

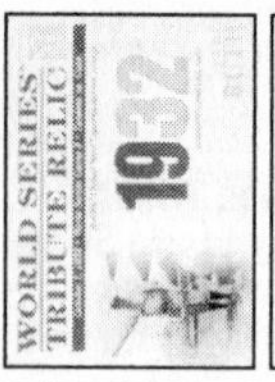
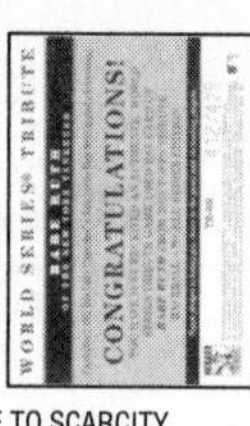

NO GOLD PRICING DUE TO SCARCITY
BH Bucky Harris Bat B 15.00 6.75
BM Bill Mazeroski Uni B 15.00 6.75
BMA Billy Martin Uni B 15.00 6.75
BR Babe Ruth Bat B 150.00 70.00
BT Bobby Thomson Bat B 10.00 4.50
CF Carlton Fisk Bat-Wall B 50.00 22.00
CH Catfish Hunter Jsy B 15.00 6.75
CK Chuck Klein Bat B 15.00 6.75
CR Cal Ripken Uni B 50.00 22.00
CY Carl Yastrzemski Jsy B 40.00 18.00
ER Edd Roush Bat A 50.00 22.00
FF Frankie Frisch Bat B 25.00 11.00
FR Frank Robinson Bat B 15.00 6.75
GB George Brett Uni B 40.00 18.00
HA Hank Aaron Bat A 60.00 27.00
HB Hank Bauer Bat A 50.00 22.00
HG Hank Greenberg Bat A 80.00 36.00
HK Harmon Killebrew Uni B 25.00 11.00
HM Heinie Manush Bat A 50.00 22.00
HW Honus Wagner Bat A 200.00 90.00
JB Jim Bottomley Bat A 50.00 22.00
JBE Johnny Bench Uni B 25.00 11.00
JC Jose Canseco Jsy B 15.00 6.75
JF Jimmie Foxx Bat A 120.00 55.00
JM Juan Marichal Uni B 10.00 4.50
JR Jackie Robinson Bat B 50.00 22.00
JT Joe Tinker Bat B 30.00 13.50
KP Kirby Puckett Bat B 25.00 11.00
LB Lou Brock Bat B 15.00 6.75
LG Lou Gehrig Bat A 250.00 110.00
MS Mike Schmidt Uni B 25.00 11.00
NC Norm Cash Jsy A 50.00 22.00
OC Orlando Cepeda Bat A 50.00 22.00
OS Ozzie Smith Uni B 25.00 11.00
RC Roberto Clemente Bat A 150.00 70.00
RH Rogers Hornsby Bat B 40.00 18.00
RJ Reggie Jackson Bat B 15.00 6.75
RM Roger Maris Bat A 100.00 45.00
RS Red Schoendienst Bat B 15.00 6.75
RY Robin Yount Jsy B 25.00 11.00
SC Sam Crawford Bat A 50.00 22.00
SM Stan Musial Bat B 40.00 18.00
TC Ty Cobb Uni B 120.00 55.00
TG Tony Gwynn Uni B 25.00 11.00
TK Ted Kluszewski Uni B 15.00 6.75
TM Thurman Munson Bat B 30.00 13.50
TS Tom Seaver Uni B 15.00 6.75
TSP Tris Speaker Bat A 120.00 55.00
WB Wade Boggs Bat B 15.00 6.75
WM Willie Mays Uni B 50.00 22.00
WMC Willie McCovey Uni B 15.00 6.75
WS Willie Stargell Uni A 50.00 22.00
YB Yogi Berra Uni B 25.00 11.00

2003 Topps Tribute World Series Tribute Autograph Relics

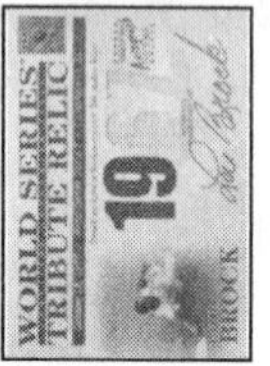

MINT NRMT
STATED ODDS 1:55
GOLD STATED ODDS 1:163
GOLD PRINT RUN 25 SERIAL #'d SETS
NO GOLD PRICING DUE TO SCARCITY
BM Bill Mazeroski Jsy 60.00 27.00
BT Bobby Thomson Bat 40.00 18.00
CF Carlton Fisk Bat-Wall 150.00 70.00
HK Harmon Killebrew Uni 100.00 45.00
JC Jose Canseco Jsy 100.00 45.00
LB Lou Brock Bat 60.00 27.00
MS Mike Schmidt Uni 120.00 55.00
WM Willie Mays Uni 350.00 160.00

2000 Topps Honus Wagner Reprint

This card, which was originally distributed at FanFest, promoted the then upcoming auction of the T-206 Honus Wagner in the best known condition. The front shows a reprinted photo of the Wagner card, while the back has detailed information about the then upcoming auction.

Nm-Mt Ex-Mt
1 Honus Wagner 1.00 .30

1976 Towne Club Discs

This set, also is another version of the 76 Crane Discs. These discs have the Towne Club back and are a multiple of the Crane issue.

NM Ex
COMPLETE SET (70) 25.00 10.00

1 Hank Aaron 3.00 1.20
2 Johnny Bench 2.00 .80
3 Vida Blue .30 .12
4 Larry Bowa .30 .12
5 Lou Brock 2.00 .80
6 Jeff Burroughs .15 .06
7 John Candelaria .15 .06
8 Jose Cardenal .15 .06
9 Rod Carew 2.00 .80
10 Steve Carlton 2.00 .80
11 Dave Cash .15 .06
12 Cesar Cedeno .30 .12
13 Ron Cey .30 .12
14 Carlton Fisk 4.00 1.60
15 Tito Fuentes .15 .06
16 Steve Garvey 2.00 .80
17 Ken Griffey .30 .12
18 Don Gullett .15 .06
19 Willie Horton .15 .06
20 Al Hrabosky .15 .06
21 Catfish Hunter 3.00 1.20
22A Reggie Jackson 10.00 4.00
Oakland Athletics
22B Reggie Jackson 3.00 1.20
Baltimore Orioles
23 Randy Jones .15 .06
24 Jim Kaat .60 .24
25 Don Kessinger .15 .06
26 Dave Kingman .60 .24
27 Jerry Koosman .30 .12
28 Mickey Lolich .30 .12
29 Greg Luzinski .60 .24
30 Fred Lynn .60 .24
31 Bill Madlock .30 .12
32A Carlos May 2.00 .80
Chicago White Sox
32B Carlos May .15 .06
New York Yankees
33 John Mayberry .15 .06
34 Bake McBride .15 .06
35 Doc Medich .15 .06
36A Andy Messersmith 2.00 .80
Los Angeles Dodgers
36B Andy Messersmith .15 .06
Atlanta Braves
37 Rick Monday .15 .06
38 John Montefusco .15 .06
39 Jerry Morales .15 .06
40 Joe Morgan 3.00 1.20
41 Thurman Munson 2.00 .80
42 Bobby Murcer .60 .24
43 Al Oliver .60 .24
44 Jim Palmer 3.00 1.20
45 Dave Parker 1.00 .40
46 Tony Perez 2.00 .80
47 Jerry Reuss .15 .06
48 Brooks Robinson 3.00 1.20
49 Frank Robinson 3.00 1.20
50 Steve Rogers .15 .06
51 Pete Rose 4.00 1.60
52 Nolan Ryan 8.00 3.20
53 Manny Sanguillen .15 .06
54 Mike Schmidt 5.00 2.00
55 Tom Seaver 4.00 1.60
56 Ted Simmons .60 .24
57 Reggie Smith .30 .12
58 Willie Stargell 3.00 1.20
59 Rusty Staub .60 .24
60 Rennie Stennett .15 .06
61 Don Sutton 3.00 1.20
62A Andre Thornton 2.00 .80
Chicago Cubs
62B Andre Thornton .15 .06
Montreal Expos
63 Luis Tiant .60 .24
64 Joe Torre 1.00 .40
65 Mike Tyson .15 .06
66 Bob Watson .30 .12
67 Wilbur Wood .15 .06
68 Jimmy Wynn .15 .06
69 Carl Yastrzemski 3.00 1.20
70 Richie Zisk .15 .06

1987 Toys R Us Rookies

Topps produced this 33-card standard-size boxed set for Toys'R'Us stores. The set is subtitled "Baseball Rookies" and features predominantly younger players. The cards feature a high-gloss, full-color photo of the player inside a black border. The card backs are printed in orange and blue on white card stock. The set numbering is in alphabetical order by player's name. This set is highlighted by an early Barry Bonds card.

Nm-Mt Ex-Mt
COMP. FACT SET (33) 30.00 12.00
1 Andy Allanson .15 .06
2 Paul Assenmacher .15 .06
3 Scott Bailes .15 .06
4 Barry Bonds 25.00 10.00
5 Jose Canseco .75 .30
6 John Cerutti .15 .06
7 Will Clark 1.50 .60
8 Kal Daniels .15 .06
9 Jim Deshaies .15 .06
10 Mark Eichhorn .15 .06
11 Ed Hearn .15 .06

12 Pete Incaviglia .25 .10
13 Bo Jackson 1.50 .60
14 Wally Joyner .60 .24
15 Charlie Kerfeld .15 .06
16 Eric King .15 .06
17 John Kruk .60 .24
18 Barry Larkin 1.50 .60
19 Mike LaValliere .15 .06
20 Greg Mathews .15 .06
21 Kevin Mitchell .25 .10
22 Dan Plesac .15 .06
23 Bruce Ruffin .15 .06
24 Ruben Sierra .75 .30
25 Cory Snyder .15 .06
26 Kurt Stillwell .15 .06
27 Dale Sveum .15 .06
28 Danny Tartabull .15 .06
29 Andres Thomas .15 .06
30 Robby Thompson .25 .10
31 Jim Traber .15 .06
32 Mitch Williams .25 .10
33 Todd Worrell .25 .10

1988 Toys'R'Us Rookies

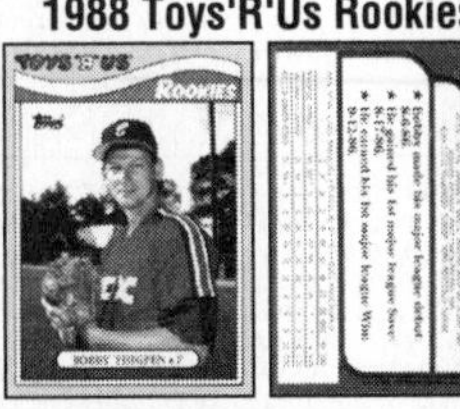

Topps produced this 33-card boxed standard-size set for Toys'R'Us stores. The set is subtitled "Baseball Rookies" and features predominantly younger players. The cards feature a high-gloss, full-color photo of the player inside a blue border. The card backs are printed in pink and blue on white card stock. The checklist for the set is found on the back panel of the small collector box. The statistics provided on the card backs cover only three lines, Minor League totals, last season, and Major League totals. The set numbering is in alphabetical order by player's name.

Nm-Mt Ex-Mt
COMP. FACT SET (33) 6.00 2.40
1 Todd Benzinger .05 .02
2 Bob Brower .05 .02
3 Jerry Browne .05 .02
4 DeWayne Buice .05 .02
5 Ellis Burks .50 .20
6 Ken Caminiti .75 .30
7 Casey Candaele .05 .02
8 Dave Cone .30 .12
9 Kelly Downs .05 .02
10 Mike Dunne .05 .02
11 Ken Gerhart .05 .02
12 Mike Greenwell .05 .02
13 Mike Henneman .10 .04
14 Sam Horn .05 .02
15 Joe Magrane .05 .02
16 Fred Manrique .05 .02
17 John Marzano .05 .02
18 Fred McGriff .75 .30
19 Mark McGwire 3.00 1.20
20 Jeff Musselman .05 .02
21 Randy Myers .20 .08
22 Matt Nokes .05 .02
23 Al Pedrique .05 .02
24 Luis Polonia .05 .02
25 Billy Ripken .05 .02
26 Benito Santiago .10 .04
27 Kevin Seitzer .05 .02
28 John Smiley .05 .02
29 Mike Stanley .05 .02
30 Terry Steinbach .05 .02
31 B.J. Surhoff .10 .04
32 Bobby Thigpen .05 .02
33 Devon White .05 .02

1989 Toys'R'Us Rookies

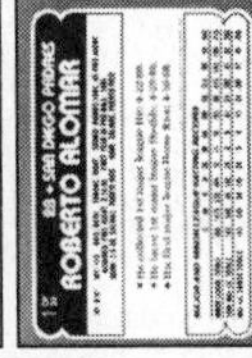

The 1989 Toys'R'Us Rookies set contains 33 standard-size glossy cards. The fronts are yellow and magenta. The horizontally oriented backs are sky blue and red, and feature 1988 and career stats. The cards were distributed through Toys'R'Us stores as a boxed set. The subjects are numbered alphabetically. The set checklist is printed on the back panel of the set's custom box.

Nm-Mt Ex-Mt
COMP. FACT SET (33) 4.00 1.60
1 Roberto Alomar .75 .30
2 Brady Anderson .20 .08
3 Tim Belcher .05 .02
4 Damon Berryhill .05 .02
5 Jay Buhner .20 .08
6 Sherman Corbett .05 .02
7 Kevin Elster .05 .02
8 Cecil Espy .05 .02
9 Dave Gallagher .05 .02
10 Ron Gant .10 .04
11 Paul Gibson .05 .02
12 Mark Grace .75 .30
13 Bryan Harvey .05 .02
14 Darrin Jackson .05 .02
15 Gregg Jefferies .05 .02
16 Ron Jones .05 .02
17 Ricky Jordan .05 .02
18 Roberto Kelly .05 .02
19 Al Leiter .20 .08
20 Jack McDowell .05 .02
21 Melido Perez .05 .02
22 Jeff Pico .05 .02
23 Jody Reed .05 .02
24 Chris Sabo .05 .02
25 Nelson Santovenia .05 .02
26 Mackey Sasser .05 .02
27 Mike Schooler .05 .02
28 Gary Sheffield 1.00 .40
29 Pete Smith .05 .02
30 Pete Stanicek .05 .02
31 Jeff Treadway .05 .02
32 Walt Weiss .05 .02
33 Dave West .05 .02

1990 Toys R Us Rookies

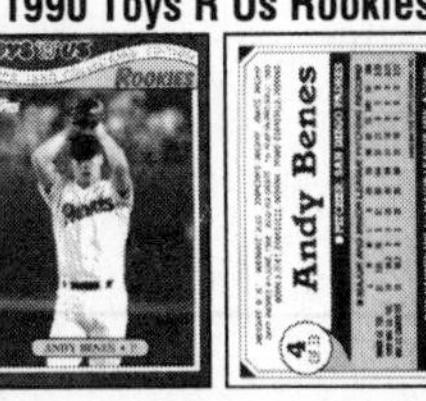

The 1990 Toys'R'Us Rookies set is a 33-card standard-size set of young prospects issued by Topps. For the fourth consecutive year Topps issued a rookie set for Toys'R'Us. There are several players in the set which were on Topps cards for the second time in 1990, i.e., not rookies even for the Topps Company. These players included Gregg Jefferies and Gregg Olson. This set might be more appropriately called the Young Stars set. The cards are numbered, with the numbering being essentially in alphabetical order by player's name. The set checklist is printed on the back panel of the set's custom box.

Nm-Mt Ex-Mt
COMP. FACT SET (33) 6.00 1.80
1 Jim Abbott .25 .07
2 Eric Anthony .05 .02
3 Joey Belle 1.00 .30
4 Andy Benes .05 .02
5 Greg Briley .05 .02
6 Kevin Brown .20 .06
7 Mark Carreon .05 .02
8 Mike Devereaux .05 .02
9 Junior Felix .05 .02
10 Mark Gardner .05 .02
11 Bob Geren .05 .02
12 Tom Gordon .15 .04
13 Ken Griffey Jr. 3.00 .90
14 Pete Harnisch .05 .02
15 Ken Hill .05 .02
16 Gregg Jefferies .05 .02
17 Derek Lilliquist .05 .02
18 Carlos Martinez .05 .02
19 Ramon Martinez .05 .02
20 Bob Milacki .05 .02
21 Gregg Olson .05 .02
22 Kenny Rogers .10 .03
23 Alex Sanchez .05 .02
24 Gary Sheffield .40 .12
25 Dwight Smith .05 .02
26 Billy Spiers .05 .02
27 Greg Vaughn .20 .06
28 Robin Ventura .20 .06
29 Jerome Walton .05 .02
30 Dave West .05 .02
31 John Wetteland .20 .06
32 Craig Worthington .05 .02
33 Todd Zeile .10 .03

1991 Toys'R'Us Rookies

For the fifth year in a row this 33-card standard-size set was produced by Topps for Toys'R'Us, and the sponsor's logo adorns the top of the card front. The front design features glossy color action player photos with yellow borders on a black card face. The words "Topps 1991 Collectors' Edition" appear in a yellow stripe above the picture. The horizontally oriented backs are printed in brown and yellow, and present biographical information, career highlights, and statistics.

Nm-Mt Ex-Mt
COMP. FACT SET (33) 4.00 1.20
1 Sandy Alomar Jr. .10 .03
2 Kevin Appier .10 .03
3 Steve Avery .05 .02
4 Carlos Baerga .10 .03
5 Alex Cole .05 .02
6 Pat Combs .05 .02
7 Delino DeShields .05 .02
8 Travis Fryman .20 .06
9 Marquis Grissom .10 .03
10 Mike Harkey .05 .02
11 Glenallen Hill .05 .02
12 Jeff Huson .05 .02
13 Felix Jose .05 .02
14 Dave Justice .30 .09
15 Dana Kiecker .05 .02
16 Kevin Maas .05 .02
17 Ben McDonald .05 .02
18 Brian McRae .05 .02
19 Kent Mercker .05 .02
20 Hal Morris .05 .02
21 Chris Nabholz .05 .02
22 Tim Naehring .05 .02
23 Jose Offerman .05 .02
24 John Olerud .30 .09
25 Scott Radinsky .05 .02
26 Bill Sampen .05 .02
27 Frank Thomas 1.00 .30
28 Randy Tomlin .05 .02
29 Greg Vaughn .30 .09
30 Robin Ventura .30 .09
31 Larry Walker .30 .09
32 Wally Whitehurst .05 .02
33 Todd Zeile .10 .03

1993 Toys'R'Us

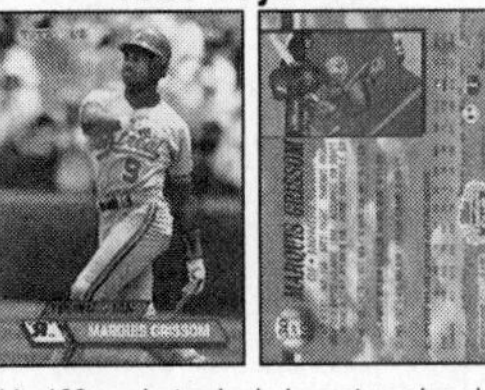

This 100-card standard-size set produced by Topps Stadium Club for Toys'R'Us features 100 young stars, rookie stars, and future stars. The cards carry glossy, full-bleed color photos with the Toys'R'Us logo in an upper corner. In silver lettering on a blue bar near the bottom of the photo, are the words Future Star, Rookie Star, or Young Star. The player's name is printed on a red bar below. The horizontal backs display a player close-up superimposed on a blue sky with clouds background. Also included are player biography, statistics and some career highlights. The cards were distributed through Toys'R'Us in a molded plastic box designed to resemble a store. 7,500 cases of this product was produced.

Nm-Mt Ex-Mt
COMPLETE SET (100) 8.00 2.40
1 Ken Griffey Jr. 2.00 .60
2 Chad Curtis .05 .02
3 Mike Bordick .05 .02
4 Ryan Klesko .15 .04
5 Pat Listach .05 .02
6 Jim Bullinger .05 .02
7 Tim Laker .05 .02
8 Mike Devereaux .05 .02
9 Kevin Young .05 .02
10 John Valentin .05 .02
11 Pat Mahomes .05 .02
12 Todd Hundley .15 .04
13 Roberto Alomar .20 .06
14 David Justice .20 .06
15 Mike Perez .05 .02
16 Royce Clayton .05 .02
17 Ryan Thompson .05 .02
18 Dave Hollins .05 .02
19 Brien Taylor .05 .02
20 Melvin Nieves .05 .02
21 Rheal Cormier .05 .02
22 Mike Piazza 1.50 .45
23 Larry Walker .20 .06
24 Tim Wakefield .15 .04
25 Tim Costo .05 .02
26 Pedro Munoz .05 .02
27 Reggie Sanders .05 .02
28 Arthur Rhodes .05 .02
29 Scott Cooper .05 .02
30 Marquis Grissom .10 .03
31 Dave Nilsson .05 .02
32 John Patterson .05 .02
33 Ivan Rodriguez .50 .15
34 Andy Stankiewicz .05 .02
35 Bret Boone .20 .06
36 Gerald Williams .05 .02
37 Mike Mussina .20 .06
38 Henry Rodriguez .05 .02
39 Chuck Knoblauch .20 .06
40 Bob Wickman .05 .02
41 Donovan Osborne .05 .02
42 Mike Timlin .05 .02
43 Damion Easley .10 .03
44 Pedro Astacio .05 .02
45 David Segui .10 .03
46 Willie Greene .05 .02
47 Mike Trombley .05 .02
48 Bernie Williams .20 .06
49 Eric Anthony .05 .02
50 Tim Naehring .05 .02
51 Carlos Baerga .05 .02
52 Brady Anderson .10 .03
53 Mo Vaughn .20 .06
54 Willie Banks .05 .02
55 Mark Wohlers .05 .02
56 Jeff Bagwell .50 .15
57 Frank Seminara .05 .02
58 Robin Ventura .10 .03
59 Alan Embree .05 .02
60 Rey Sanchez .05 .02
61 Delino DeShields .05 .02
62 Todd Van Poppel .05 .02
63 Eric Karros .15 .04
64 Gary Sheffield .25 .07
65 Dan Wilson .10 .03
66 Frank Thomas .75 .23
67 Tim Salmon .20 .06
68 Dan Smith .05 .02
69 Kenny Lofton .15 .04
70 Carlos Garcia .05 .02
71 Scott Livingstone .05 .02
72 Sam Militello .05 .02
73 Juan Guzman .05 .02
74 Greg Colbrunn .05 .02
75 David Hulse .05 .02
76 Rusty Meacham .05 .02
77 Dave Fleming .05 .02
78 Rene Arocha .05 .02
79 Derrick May .05 .02
80 Cal Eldred .05 .02
81 Bernard Gilkey .05 .02
82 Deion Sanders .20 .06
83 Reggie Jefferson .05 .02
84 Jeff Kent .20 .06
85 Juan Gonzalez .50 .15
86 Billy Ashley .05 .02
87 Travis Fryman .10 .03
88 Roberto Hernandez .10 .03
89 Hipolito Pichardo .05 .02
90 Wilfredo Cordero .05 .02
91 John Jaha .05 .02
92 Javier Lopez .25 .07
93 Derek Bell .05 .02
94 Jeff Juden .05 .02
95 Steve Avery .05 .02
96 Moises Alou .10 .03
97 Brian Jordan .10 .03
98 Brian Williams .05 .02
99 Bob Zupcic .05 .02
100 Ray Lankford .10 .03

1993 Toys'R'Us Master Photos

This 12-card set of Stadium Club Master Photos was a bonus insert in the 1993 Toys'R'Us 100-card factory set. The photo cards measure approximately 5" by 7" with wide white borders with an inner prismatic gold-foil border. An action photo of the player is below a large colorful Toys 'R' Us logo with the words "Master Photo." The backs are blank, except for copyright symbols, licensing information, and MLBPA logo. The cards are unnumbered and checklisted below in alphabetical order.

Nm-Mt Ex-Mt
COMPLETE SET (12) 4.00 1.20
1 Moises Alou .20 .06
2 Eric Anthony .10 .03
3 Carlos Baerga .10 .03
4 Willie Greene .10 .03
5 Ken Griffey Jr. 1.50 .45
6 Marquis Grissom .20 .06
7 Chuck Knoblauch .40 .12
8 Scott Livingstone .10 .03
9 Sam Militello .10 .03
10 Ivan Rodriguez .50 .15
11 Gary Sheffield .50 .15
12 Frank Thomas .75 .23

1993 Treadway Boy Scouts of America

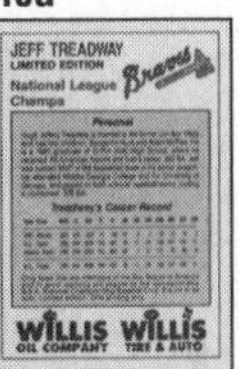

This single standard-size card was distributed by the Flint River Council of the Boy Scouts of America (Griffin, Georgia) to boys who were in scouting as of October 1992. Only 7,000 were produced. The front features a color action photo of Jeff Treadway. The card has black borders. Hot pink lettering sets off the player's name at the bottom and the words "Collector's Edition" at the top. The phrase "Official B.S.A. Baseball Card" is printed in blue just above the player's head. The Flint River Council logo appears in the bottom right corner. The back is white and displays a light blue panel containing personal and career information. Sponsor logos appear at the bottom. The player's name, team logo and the words "Limited Edition" and "National League Champs" are at the top. The bottom has advertisements for Willis Oil Company and Willis Tire and Auto.

Nm-Mt Ex-Mt
1 Jeff Treadway 2.00 .60

1992 Triple Play Previews

This eight-card standard-size set was issued by Donruss to preview the design of the 264-card 1992 Donruss Triple Play set. The front design and player photos are identical to those in the regular issue set; the only difference is the numbering and the word "preview" appearing across the bottom of the backs.

Nm-Mt Ex-Mt
COMPLETE SET (8) 120.00 36.00
1 Ken Griffey Jr. 50.00 15.00
2 Darryl Strawberry 5.00 1.50
3 Andy Van Slyke 8.00 2.40
4 Don Mattingly 40.00 12.00
5 Gary Carter 5.00 1.50
Steve Finley
Awesome Action
6 Frank Thomas 20.00 6.00
7 Kirby Puckett 15.00 4.50
8 David Cone 5.00 1.50
John Franco
Jeff Innis
Fun at the Ballpark

1992 Triple Play

The 1992 Triple Play set contains 264 standard-size cards. Cards were distributed in 15-card foil packs and jumbo packs. Each 15-card foil pack came with one rub off game card. The Triple Play set was created especially for children ages 5-12, featuring bright color borders, player quotes, fun facts. Subsets include Little Hotshots (picturing some players when they were kids) and Awesome Action.

Nm-Mt Ex-Mt
COMPLETE SET (264) 10.00 3.00

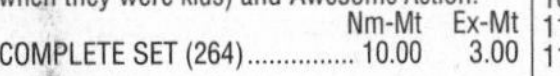

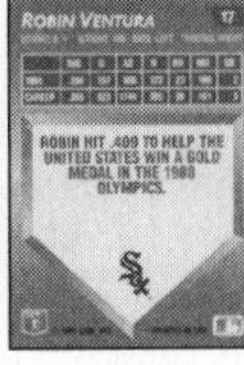

1 SkyDome .10 .03
2 Tom Foley .10 .03
3 Scott Erickson .10 .03
4 Matt Williams .20 .06
5 David Valle .10 .03
6 Andy Van Slyke LH .10 .03
7 Tom Glavine .30 .09
8 Kevin Appier .20 .06
9 Pedro Guerrero .20 .06
10 Terry Steinbach .10 .03
11 Terry Mulholland .10 .03
12 Mike Boddicker .10 .03
13 Gregg Olson .10 .03
14 Tim Burke .10 .03
15 Candy Maldonado .10 .03
16 Orlando Merced .10 .03
17 Robin Ventura .20 .06
18 Eric Anthony .10 .03
19 Greg Maddux .75 .23
20 Erik Hanson .10 .03
21 Bobby Ojeda .10 .03
22 Nolan Ryan 1.50 .45
23 Dave Righetti .20 .06
24 Reggie Jefferson .10 .03
25 Jody Reed .10 .03
26 Steve Finley and .20 .06
Gary Carter AA
27 Chili Davis .20 .06
28 Hector Villanueva .10 .03
29 Cecil Fielder .20 .06
30 Hal Morris .10 .03
31 Barry Larkin .50 .15
32 Bobby Thigpen .10 .03
33 Andy Benes .10 .03
34 Harold Baines .20 .06
35 David Cone .20 .06
36 Mark Langston .10 .03
37 Bryan Harvey .10 .03
38 John Kruk .20 .06
39 Scott Sanderson .10 .03
40 Lonnie Smith .10 .03
41 Rex Hudler AA .10 .03
42 George Bell .10 .03
43 Steve Finley .20 .06
44 Mickey Tettleton .10 .03
45 Robby Thompson .10 .03
46 Pat Kelly .10 .03
47 Marquis Grissom .10 .03
48 Tony Pena .10 .03
49 Alex Cole .10 .03
50 Steve Buechele .10 .03
51 Ivan Rodriguez .50 .15
52 John Smiley .10 .03
53 Gary Sheffield .20 .06
54 Greg Olson .10 .03
55 Ramon Martinez .10 .03
56 B.J. Surhoff .20 .06
57 Bruce Hurst .10 .03
58 Todd Stottlemyre .10 .03
59 Brett Butler .20 .06
60 Glenn Davis .10 .03
61 Glenn Braggs and .10 .03
Kirt Manwaring AA
62 Lee Smith .20 .06
63 Rickey Henderson .50 .15
64 Fun at the Ballpark .20 .06
Dave Cone
Jeff Innis
John Franco
65 Rick Aguilera .20 .06
66 Kevin Elster .10 .03
67 Dwight Evans .20 .06
68 Andujar Cedeno .10 .03
69 Brian McRae .10 .03
70 Benito Santiago .20 .06
71 Randy Johnson .50 .15
72 Roberto Kelly .10 .03
73 Juan Samuel AA .10 .03
74 Alex Fernandez .10 .03
75 Felix Jose .10 .03
76 Brian Harper .10 .03
77 Scott Sanderson LH .10 .03
78 Ken Caminiti .20 .06
79 Mo Vaughn .20 .06
80 Roger McDowell .10 .03
81 Robin Yount .75 .23
82 Dave Magadan .10 .03
83 Julio Franco .20 .06
84 Roberto Alomar .50 .15
85 Steve Avery .10 .03
86 Travis Fryman .20 .06
87 Fred McGriff .30 .09
88 Dave Stewart .20 .06
89 Larry Walker .30 .09
90 Chris Sabo .10 .03
91 Chuck Finley .20 .06
92 Dennis Martinez .20 .06
93 Jeff Johnson .10 .03
94 Len Dykstra .20 .06
95 Mark Whiten .10 .03
96 Wade Taylor .10 .03
97 Lance Dickson .10 .03
98 Kevin Tapani .10 .03
99 Luis Polonia and .10 .03
Tony Phillips AA
100 Milt Cuyler .10 .03
101 Willie McGee .20 .06
102 Tony Fernandez AA .10 .03
103 Albert Belle .20 .06
104 Todd Hundley .10 .03
105 Ben McDonald .10 .03
106 Doug Drabek .10 .03
107 Tim Raines .20 .06
108 Joe Carter .20 .06
109 Reggie Sanders .20 .06
110 John Olerud .20 .06
111 Darren Lewis .10 .03

112 Juan Gonzalez .50 .15
113 Andre Dawson AA .10 .03
114 Mark Grace .30 .09
115 George Brett 1.25 .35
116 Barry Bonds 1.25 .35
117 Lou Whitaker .20 .06
118 Jose Oquendo .10 .03
119 Lee Stevens .10 .03
120 Phil Plantier .10 .03
121 Matt Merullo AA .10 .03
122 Greg Vaughn .20 .06
123 Royce Clayton .10 .03
124 Bob Welch .20 .06
125 Juan Samuel .10 .03
126 Ron Gant .20 .06
127 Edgar Martinez .30 .09
128 Andy Ashby .10 .03
129 Jack McDowell .10 .03
130 Dave Henderson and .10 .03
Jerry Browne AA
131 Leo Gomez .10 .03
132 Checklist 1-88 .10 .03
133 Phillie Phanatic RC .20 .06
134 Bret Barberie .10 .03
135 Kent Hrbek .20 .06
136 Hall of Fame .10 .03
137 Omar Vizquel .20 .06
138 The Famous Chicken .20 .06
139 Terry Pendleton .20 .06
140 Jim Eisenreich .10 .03
141 Todd Zeile .20 .06
142 Todd Van Poppel .10 .03
143 Darren Daulton .20 .06
144 Mike Macfarlane .10 .03
145 Luis Mercedes .10 .03
146 Trevor Wilson .10 .03
147 Dave Stieb .20 .06
148 Andy Van Slyke .20 .06
149 Carlton Fisk .30 .09
150 Craig Biggio .30 .09
151 Joe Girardi .10 .03
152 Ken Griffey Jr. .75 .23
153 Jose Offerman .10 .03
154 Bobby Witt .10 .03
155 Will Clark .50 .15
156 Steve Olin .10 .03
157 Greg W. Harris .10 .03
158 Dale Murphy LH .30 .09
159 Don Mattingly 1.25 .35
160 Shawon Dunston .10 .03
161 Bill Gullickson .10 .03
162 Paul O'Neill .30 .09
163 Norm Charlton .10 .03
164 Bo Jackson .50 .15
165 Tony Fernandez .10 .03
166 Dave Henderson .10 .03
167 Dwight Gooden .30 .09
168 Junior Felix .10 .03
169 Lance Parrish .20 .06
170 Pat Combs .10 .03
171 Chuck Knoblauch .20 .06
172 John Smoltz .30 .09
173 Wrigley Field .20 .06
174 Andre Dawson .20 .06
175 Pete Harnisch .10 .03
176 Alan Trammell .30 .09
177 Kirk Dressendorfer .10 .03
178 Matt Nokes .10 .03
179 Wil Cordero .10 .03
180 Scott Cooper .10 .03
181 Glenallen Hill .10 .03
182 John Franco .20 .06
183 Rafael Palmeiro .30 .09
184 Jay Bell .20 .06
185 Bill Wegman .10 .03
186 Deion Sanders .30 .09
187 Darryl Strawberry .30 .09
188 Jaime Navarro .10 .03
189 Darrin Jackson .10 .03
190 Eddie Zosky .10 .03
191 Mike Scioscia .10 .03
192 Chito Martinez .10 .03
193 Pat Kelly and .10 .03
Ron Tingley AA
194 Ray Lankford .10 .03
195 Dennis Eckersley .20 .06
196 Ivan Calderon and .10 .03
Mike Maddux AA
197 Shane Mack .10 .03
198 Checklist 89-176 .10 .03
199 Cal Ripken 1.50 .45
200 Jeff Bagwell .50 .15
201 Dave Howard .10 .03
202 Kirby Puckett .50 .15
203 Harold Reynolds .20 .06
204 Jim Abbott .30 .09
205 Mark Lewis .10 .03
206 Frank Thomas .50 .15
207 Rex Hudler .10 .03
208 Vince Coleman .10 .03
209 Delino DeShields .10 .03
210 Luis Gonzalez .30 .09
211 Wade Boggs .30 .09
212 Orel Hershiser .20 .06
213 Cal Eldred .10 .03
214 Jose Canseco .50 .15
215 Jose Guzman .10 .03
216 Roger Clemens 1.00 .30
217 David Justice .20 .06
218 Tony Phillips .10 .03
219 Tony Gwynn .60 .18
220 Mitch Williams .10 .03
221 Bill Sampen .10 .03
222 Billy Hatcher .10 .03
223 Gary Gaetti .20 .06
224 Tim Wallach .10 .03
225 Kevin Maas .10 .03
226 Kevin Brown .20 .06
227 Sandy Alomar Jr. .10 .03
228 John Habyan .10 .03
229 Ryne Sandberg .75 .23
230 Greg Gagne .10 .03
231 Autographs .60 .18
(Mark McGwire)
232 Mike LaValliere .10 .03
233 Mark Gubicza .10 .03
234 Lance Parrish LH .10 .03
235 Carlos Baerga .10 .03
236 Howard Johnson .10 .03
237 Mike Mussina .50 .15
238 Ruben Sierra .10 .03
239 Lance Johnson .10 .03
240 Devon White .10 .03
241 Dan Wilson .10 .03
242 Kelly Gruber .10 .03
243 Brett Butler LH .10 .03
244 Ozzie Smith .75 .23
245 Chuck McElroy .10 .03
246 Shawn Boskie .10 .03
247 Mark Davis .10 .03
248 Bill Landrum .10 .03
249 Frank Tanana .20 .06
250 Darryl Hamilton .10 .03
251 Gary DiSarcina .10 .03
252 Mike Greenwell .10 .03
253 Cal Ripken LH .75 .23
254 Paul Molitor .30 .09
255 Tim Teufel .10 .03
256 Chris Hoiles .10 .03
257 Rob Dibble .20 .06
258 Sid Bream .10 .03
259 Tino Martinez .30 .09
260 Dale Murphy .50 .15
261 Greg Hibbard .10 .03
262 Mark McGwire 1.25 .35
263 Oriole Park .10 .03
264 Checklist 177-264 .10 .03

1992 Triple Play Gallery

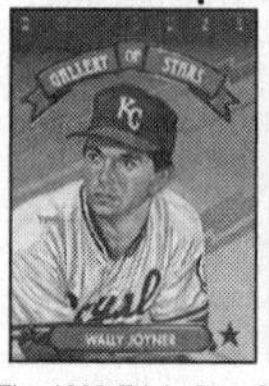

The 1992 Triple Play Gallery of Stars was an insert to the 1992 Triple Play baseball set. Randomly inserted into foil packs, the first six cards feature top players who changed teams in 1992 in their new uniforms. The second six cards were inserted one per jumbo pack. Each group of six cards is sequenced in alphabetical order. On bright-colored backgrounds, the fronts display color player portraits by noted sports artist Dick Perez.

	Nm-Mt	Ex-Mt
COMPLETE FOIL SET (6)	2.50	.75
COMP. JUMBO (6)	12.00	3.60
GS1 Bobby Bonilla	.50	.15
GS2 Wally Joyner	.50	.15
GS3 Jack Morris	.50	.15
GS4 Steve Sax	.50	.15
GS5 Danny Tartabull	.50	.15
GS6 Frank Viola	.50	.15
GS7 Jeff Bagwell	1.25	.35
GS8 Ken Griffey Jr.	2.50	.75
GS9 Dave Justice	.50	.15
GS10 Ryan Klesko	.50	.15
GS11 Cal Ripken	5.00	1.50
GS12 Frank Thomas	1.25	.35

1993 Triple Play Previews

This 12-card set was issued by Donruss to preview the design of the 264-card 1993 Donruss Triple Play set. The front design and player photos are identical to those in the regular issue with the exception of the word "Preview" printed on the card.

	Nm-Mt	Ex-Mt
COMPLETE SET (12)	150.00	45.00
1 Ken Griffey Jr.	40.00	12.00
2 Roberto Alomar	10.00	3.00
3 Cal Ripken	50.00	15.00
4 Eric Karros	6.00	1.80
5 Cecil Fielder	4.00	1.20
6 Gary Sheffield	12.00	3.60
7 Darren Daulton	4.00	1.20
8 Andy Van Slyke	2.00	.60
9 Dennis Eckersley	12.00	3.60
10 Ryne Sandberg	20.00	6.00
11 Mark Grace	10.00	3.00
12 David Segui Luis Polonia Awesome Action	2.00	.60

1993 Triple Play

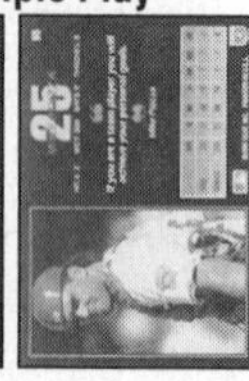

The 1993 Triple Play baseball set consists of 264 standard-size cards. Approximately eight players from each of the 28 teams is represented in the set. Each pack also included one of thirty Triple Play Action Baseball game cards. Scattered throughout the set are seven Little Hotshot (11, 77, 97, 143, 209, 229, 245) and eight Awesome Action (12, 61, 64, 68, 144, 193, 196, 200) cards. There are no key Rookie Cards in this set, however the set does feature the first card of President Bill Clinton.

	Nm-Mt	Ex-Mt
COMPLETE SET (264)	10.00	3.00
1 Ken Griffey Jr.	.75	.23
2 Roberto Alomar	.50	.15
3 Cal Ripken	1.50	.45
4 Eric Karros	.20	.06
5 Cecil Fielder	.20	.06
6 Gary Sheffield	.20	.06
7 Darren Daulton	.20	.06
8 Andy Van Slyke	.20	.06
9 Dennis Eckersley	.20	.06
10 Ryne Sandberg	.75	.23
11 Mark Grace LH	.20	.06

12 David Segui and .10 .03
Luis Polonia AA
13 Mike Mussina .50 .15
14 Vince Coleman .10 .03
15 Rafael Belliard .10 .03
16 Ivan Rodriguez .50 .15
17 Eddie Taubensee .10 .03
18 Cal Eldred .10 .03
19 Rick Wilkins .10 .03
20 Edgar Martinez .30 .09
21 Brian McRae .10 .03
22 Darren Holmes .10 .03
23 Mark Whiten .10 .03
24 Todd Zeile .20 .06
25 Scott Cooper .10 .03
26 Frank Thomas .50 .15
27 Wil Cordero .10 .03
28 Juan Guzman .10 .03
29 Pedro Astacio .10 .03
30 Steve Avery .10 .03
31 Barry Larkin .50 .15
32 Bill Clinton 1.50 .45
33 Scott Erickson .10 .03
34 Mike Devereaux .10 .03
35 Tino Martinez .30 .09
36 Brent Mayne .10 .03
37 Tim Salmon .30 .09
38 Dave Hollins .10 .03
39 Royce Clayton .10 .03
40 Shawon Dunston .10 .03
41 Eddie Murray .50 .15
42 Larry Walker .30 .09
43 Jeff Bagwell .30 .09
44 Milt Cuyler .10 .03
45 Mike Bordick .20 .06
46 Mike Greenwell .10 .03
47 Steve Sax .10 .03
48 Chuck Knoblauch .20 .06
49 Charles Nagy .10 .03
50 Tim Wakefield .20 .06
51 Tony Gwynn .60 .18
52 Rob Dibble .20 .06
53 Mickey Morandini .10 .03
54 Steve Hosey .10 .03
55 Mike Piazza .60 .18
56 Bill Wegman .10 .03
57 Kevin Maas .10 .03
58 Gary DiSarcina .10 .03
59 Travis Fryman .20 .06
60 Ruben Sierra .10 .03
61 Ken Caminiti AA .10 .03
62 Brian Jordan .20 .06
63 Scott Chiamparino .10 .03
64 George Brett and .60 .18
Mike Bordick AA
65 Carlos Garcia .10 .03
66 Checklist .10 .03
67 John Smoltz .30 .09
68 Mark McGwire and .60 .18
Brian Harper AA
69 Kurt Stillwell .10 .03
70 Chad Curtis .10 .03
71 Rafael Palmeiro .30 .09
72 Kevin Young .10 .03
73 Glenn Davis .10 .03
74 Dennis Martinez .20 .06
75 Sam Militello .10 .03
76 Mike Morgan .10 .03
77 Frank Thomas LH .30 .09
78 Staying Fit .10 .03
79 Steve Buechele .10 .03
80 Carlos Baerga .10 .03
81 Robby Thompson .10 .03
82 Kirk McCaskill .10 .03
83 Lee Smith .20 .06
84 Gary Scott .10 .03
85 Tony Pena .10 .03
86 Howard Johnson .10 .03
87 Mark McGwire 1.25 .35
88 Bip Roberts .10 .03
89 Devon White .10 .03
90 John Franco .20 .06
91 Tom Browning .10 .03
92 Mickey Tettleton .10 .03
93 Jeff Conine .20 .06
94 Albert Belle .20 .06
95 Fred McGriff .30 .09
96 Nolan Ryan 1.50 .45
97 Paul Molitor LH .20 .06
98 Juan Bell .10 .03
99 Dave Fleming .10 .03
100 Craig Biggio .30 .09
101A Andy Stankiewicz .10 .03
Name on front in white
101B Andy Stankiewicz .10 .03
Name on front in red
102 Delino DeShields .10 .03
103 Damion Easley .10 .03
104 Kevin McReynolds .10 .03
105 David Nied .10 .03
106 Rick Sutcliffe .20 .06
107 Will Clark .50 .15
108 Tim Raines .20 .06
109 Eric Anthony .10 .03
110 Mike LaValliere .10 .03
111 Dean Palmer .20 .06
112 Eric Davis .20 .06
113 Damon Berryhill .10 .03
114 Felix Jose .10 .03
115 Ozzie Guillen .10 .03
116 Pat Listach .10 .03
117 Tom Glavine .30 .09
118 Roger Clemens 1.00 .30
119 Dave Henderson .10 .03
120 Don Mattingly 1.25 .35
121 Orel Hershiser .20 .06
122 Ozzie Smith .75 .23
123 Joe Carter .20 .06
124 Bret Saberhagen .20 .06
125 Mitch Williams .10 .03
126 Jerald Clark .10 .03
127 Mile High Stadium .20 .06
128 Kent Hrbek .20 .06
129 Equipment .30 .09
Curt Schilling
130 Gregg Jefferies .10 .03
131 John Orton .10 .03
132 Checklist .10 .03
133 Bret Boone .30 .09
134 Pat Borders .10 .03
135 Gregg Olson .10 .03
136 Brett Butler .20 .06
137 Rob Deer .10 .03
138 Darrin Jackson .10 .03
139 John Kruk .20 .06
140 Jay Bell .20 .06
141 Bobby Witt .10 .03
142 Dan Plesac .10 .03
Randy Myers
Jose Guzman
New Cubs
143 Wade Boggs LH .20 .06
144 Ken Lofton AA .10 .03
145 Ben McDonald .10 .03
146 Dwight Gooden .30 .09
147 Terry Pendleton .20 .06
148 Julio Franco .20 .06
149 Ken Caminiti .20 .06
150 Greg Vaughn .20 .06
151 Sammy Sosa .75 .23
152 David Valle .10 .03
153 Wally Joyner .20 .06
154 Dante Bichette .20 .06
155 Mark Lewis .10 .03
156 Bob Tewksbury .10 .03
157 Billy Hatcher .10 .03
158 Jack McDowell .10 .03
159 Marquis Grissom .10 .03
160 Jack Morris .20 .06
161 Ramon Martinez .10 .03
162 Deion Sanders .30 .09
163 Tim Belcher .10 .03
164 Mascots .10 .03
Pirate Parrot
165 Scott Leius .10 .03
166 Brady Anderson .20 .06
167 Randy Johnson .50 .15
168 Mark Gubicza .10 .03
169 Chuck Finley .20 .06
170 Terry Mulholland .10 .03
171 Matt Williams .20 .06
172 Dwight Smith .10 .03
173 Bobby Bonilla .20 .06
174 Ken Hill .10 .03
175 Doug Jones .10 .03
176 Tony Phillips .10 .03
177 Terry Steinbach .10 .03
178 Frank Viola .20 .06
179 Robin Ventura .20 .06
180 Shane Mack .10 .03
181 Kenny Lofton .20 .06
182 Jeff King .10 .03
183 Tim Teufel .10 .03
184 Chris Sabo .10 .03
185 Len Dykstra .20 .06
186 Trevor Wilson .10 .03
187 Darryl Strawberry .30 .09
188 Robin Yount .75 .23
189 Bob Wickman .10 .03
190 Luis Polonia .10 .03
191 Alan Trammell .30 .09
192 Bob Welch .20 .06
193 Omar Vizquel AA .10 .03
194 Tom Pagnozzi .10 .03
195 Bret Barberie .10 .03
196 Mike Scioscia AA .10 .03
197 Randy Tomlin .10 .03
198 Checklist .10 .03
199 Ron Gant .20 .06
200 Roberto Alomar AA .20 .06
201 Andy Benes .10 .03
202 Pirates Pepper .10 .03
203 Steve Finley .20 .06
204 Steve Olin .10 .03
205 Chris Hoiles .10 .03
206 John Wetteland .20 .06
207 Danny Tartabull .10 .03
208 Bernard Gilkey .10 .03
209 Tom Glavine LH .20 .06
210 Benito Santiago .20 .06
211 Mark Grace .30 .09
212 Glenallen Hill .10 .03
213 Jeff Brantley .10 .03
214 George Brett 1.25 .35
215 Mark Lemke .10 .03
216 Ron Karkovice .10 .03
217 Tom Brunansky .10 .03
218 Todd Hundley .10 .03
219 Rickey Henderson .50 .15
220 Joe Oliver .10 .03
221 Juan Gonzalez .50 .15
222 John Olerud .20 .06
223 Hal Morris .10 .03
224 Lou Whitaker .20 .06
225 Bryan Harvey .10 .03
226 Mike Gallego .10 .03
227 Willie McGee .20 .06
228 Jose Oquendo .10 .03
229 Darren Daulton LH .10 .03
230 Curt Schilling .30 .09
231 Jay Buhner .20 .06
232 Doug Drabek .10 .03
Greg Swindell
New Astros
233 Jaime Navarro .10 .03
234 Kevin Appier .20 .06
235 Mark Langston .10 .03
236 Jeff Montgomery .10 .03
237 Joe Girardi .10 .03
238 Ed Sprague .10 .03
239 Dan Walters .10 .03
240 Kevin Tapani .10 .03
241 Pete Harnisch .10 .03
242 Al Martin .10 .03
243 Jose Canseco .50 .15
244 Moises Alou .20 .06
245 Mark McGwire LH .60 .18
246 Luis Rivera .10 .03
247 George Bell .10 .03
248 B.J. Surhoff .20 .06
249 David Justice .20 .06
250 Brian Harper .10 .03
251 Sandy Alomar Jr. .10 .03
252 Kevin Brown .20 .06
253 Tim Wallach .10 .03
Todd Worrell
Jody Reed
New Dodgers
254 Ray Lankford .10 .03
255 Derek Bell .10 .03
256 Joe Grahe .10 .03
257 Charlie Hayes .10 .03
258 Wade Boggs .30 .09
Jim Abbott
New Yankees
259A Joe Robbie Stadium .20 .06
ERR (Misnumbered 129)
259B Joe Robbie Stadium .20 .06
COR
260 Kirby Puckett .50 .15
261 Jay Bell .10 .03
Fun at the Ballpark
262 Bill Swift .10 .03
263 Roger McDowell .10 .03
Fun at the Ballpark
264 Checklist .10 .03

1993 Triple Play Action

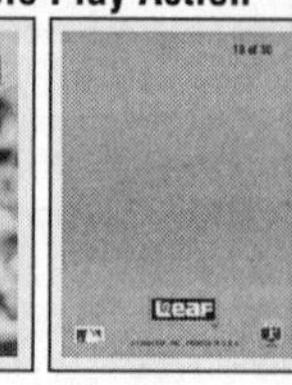

The 1993 Triple Play Action set was inserted one per pack of Triple Play. The cards were designed to serve as a game card with a scratch-off section inside beside a baseball diamond design. The cards are printed on a lighter weight card stock. When unfolded the cards measure approximately 5" by 3 1/2", however when folded they measure the standard size.

	Nm-Mt	Ex-Mt
COMPLETE SET (30)	10.00	3.00
1 Andy Van Slyke	.25	.07
2 Bobby Bonilla	.25	.07
3 Ozzie Smith	1.00	.30
4 Ryne Sandberg	1.00	.30
5 Darren Daulton	.25	.07
6 Larry Walker	.40	.12
7 Eric Karros	.25	.07
8 Barry Larkin	.60	.18
9 Deion Sanders	.40	.12
10 Gary Sheffield	.25	.07
11 Will Clark	.60	.18
12 Jeff Bagwell	.40	.12
13 Roberto Alomar	.60	.18
14 Roger Clemens	1.25	.35
15 Cecil Fielder	.25	.07
16 Robin Yount	1.00	.30
17 Cal Ripken	2.00	.60
18 Carlos Baerga	.15	.04
19 Don Mattingly	1.50	.45
20 Kirby Puckett	.60	.18
21 Frank Thomas	.60	.18
22 Juan Gonzalez	.60	.18
23 Mark McGwire	1.50	.45
24 Ken Griffey Jr.	1.00	.30
25 Wally Joyner	.25	.07
26 Chad Curtis	.15	.04
27 Rockies vs. Marlins	.15	.04
28 Juan Guzman	.15	.04
29 David Justice	.25	.07
30 Joe Carter	.25	.07

1993 Triple Play Gallery

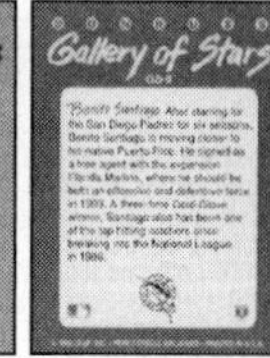

A one per pack insert in 1993 Triple Play jumbo packs, these ten standard-size cards have fronts that feature color player portraits by noted sports artist Dick Perez. The cards are numbered on the back with a "GS" prefix.

	Nm-Mt	Ex-Mt
COMPLETE SET (10)	20.00	6.00
GS1 Barry Bonds	10.00	3.00
GS2 Andre Dawson	1.50	.45
GS3 Wade Boggs	2.50	.75
GS4 Greg Maddux	8.00	2.40
GS5 Dave Winfield	1.50	.45
GS6 Paul Molitor	2.50	.75
GS7 Jim Abbott	2.50	.75
GS8 J.T. Snow	4.00	1.20
GS9 Benito Santiago	1.50	.45
GS10 David Nied	1.00	.30

1993 Triple Play League Leaders

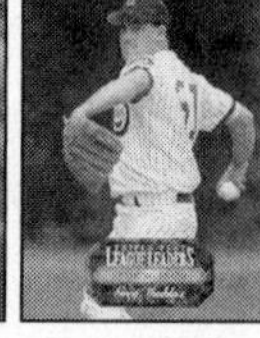

Randomly inserted in magazine distributor packs only, the six standard-size cards comprising this set feature borderless color action player shots on both sides. The cards are numbered on the American League side with an "L" prefix.

	Nm-Mt	Ex-Mt
COMPLETE SET (6)	20.00	6.00
L1 Barry Bonds Dennis Eckersley	10.00	3.00
L2 Greg Maddux	6.00	1.80

Dennis Eckersley
L3 Eric Karros 1.50 .45
Pat Listach
L4 Fred McGriff 4.00 1.20
Juan Gonzalez
L5 Darren Daulton 1.50 .45
Cecil Fielder
L6 Gary Sheffield 2.50 .75
Edgar Martinez

1993 Triple Play Nicknames

Randomly inserted in foil packs only, this ten-card standard-size set is a new insert set featuring popular player's nicknames.

Nm-Mt Ex-Mt
COMPLETE SET (10) 20.00 6.00
1 Frank Thomas 2.00 .60
Big Hurt
2 Roger Clemens 4.00 1.20
Rocket
3 Ryne Sandberg 4.00 1.20
Ryno
4 Will Clark 2.00 .60
Thrill
5 Ken Griffey Jr. 3.00 .90
Junior
6 Dwight Gooden 1.25 .35
Dr. K
7 Nolan Ryan 6.00 1.80
Express
8 Deion Sanders 1.25 .35
Prime Time
9 Ozzie Smith 3.00 .90
Wizard
10 Fred McGriff 1.25 .35
Crime Dog

1994 Triple Play Promos

These ten standard-size promos feature on their fronts color player-action shots that are borderless, except at the bottom, where the player's name appears within a colored stripe. The "Promotional Sample" disclaimer is stenciled obliquely across the front and back.

Nm-Mt Ex-Mt
COMPLETE SET (10) 15.00 4.50
1 Juan Gonzalez 1.00 .30
2 Frank Thomas 1.25 .35
3 Barry Bonds 2.50 .75
4 Ken Griffey Jr. 3.00 .90
5 Paul Molitor .75 .23
6 Mike Piazza 2.50 .75
7 Tim Salmon .75 .23
8 Lenny Dykstra .25 .07
9 Don Mattingly 2.50 .75
10 Greg Maddux 3.00 .90

1994 Triple Play

The 1994 Triple Play set consists of 300 standard-size cards, featuring ten players from each team along with a 17-card Rookie Review set. Triple Play game cards, reedemable for various prizes, were inserted one per pack.

Nm-Mt Ex-Mt
COMPLETE SET (300) 25.00 7.50
1 Mike Bordick .20 .06
2 Dennis Eckersley .20 .06
3 Brent Gates .10 .03
4 Rickey Henderson .50 .15
5 Mark McGwire 1.25 .35
6 Troy Neel .10 .03
7 Craig Paquette .10 .03
8 Ruben Sierra .10 .03
9 Terry Steinbach .10 .03
10 Bobby Witt .10 .03
11 Chad Curtis .10 .03
12 Chili Davis .20 .06
13 Gary DiSarcina .10 .03
14 Damion Easley .10 .03
15 Chuck Finley .20 .06
16 Joe Grahe .10 .03
17 Mark Langston .10 .03
18 Eduardo Perez .10 .03
19 Tim Salmon .30 .09
20 J.T. Snow .20 .06
21 Jeff Bagwell .30 .09
22 Craig Biggio .30 .09
23 Ken Caminiti .20 .06
24 Andujar Cedeno .10 .03
25 Doug Drabek .10 .03
26 Steve Finley .20 .06
27 Luis Gonzalez .20 .06
28 Pete Harnisch .10 .03
29 Darryl Kile .20 .06
30 Mitch Williams .10 .03
31 Roberto Alomar .50 .15
32 Joe Carter .20 .06
33 Juan Guzman .10 .03
34 Pat Hentgen .10 .03
35 Paul Molitor .30 .09
36 John Olerud .20 .06
37 Ed Sprague .10 .03
38 Dave Stewart .20 .06
39 Duane Ward .10 .03
40 Devon White .10 .03
41 Steve Avery .10 .03
42 Jeff Blauser .10 .03
43 Ron Gant .20 .06
44 Tom Glavine .30 .09
45 David Justice .20 .06
46 Greg Maddux .75 .23
47 Fred McGriff .30 .09
48 Terry Pendleton .20 .06
49 Deion Sanders .30 .09
50 John Smoltz .30 .09
51 Ricky Bones .10 .03
52 Cal Eldred .10 .03
53 Darryl Hamilton .10 .03
54 John Jaha .10 .03
55 Pat Listach .10 .03
56 Jaime Navarro .10 .03
57 Dave Nilsson .10 .03
58 B.J. Surhoff .20 .06
59 Greg Vaughn .20 .06
60 Robin Yount .75 .23
61 Bernard Gilkey .10 .03
62 Gregg Jefferies .10 .03
63 Brian Jordan .20 .06
64 Ray Lankford .10 .03
65 Tom Pagnozzi .10 .03
66 Ozzie Smith .75 .23
67 Bob Tewksbury .10 .03
68 Allen Watson .10 .03
69 Mark Whiten .10 .03
70 Todd Zeile .20 .06
71 Steve Buechele .10 .03
72 Mark Grace .30 .09
73 Jose Guzman .10 .03
74 Derrick May .10 .03
75 Mike Morgan .10 .03
76 Randy Myers .20 .06
77 Ryne Sandberg .75 .23
78 Sammy Sosa .75 .23
79 Jose Vizcaino .10 .03
80 Rick Wilkins .10 .03
81 Pedro Astacio .10 .03
82 Brett Butler .20 .06
83 Delino DeShields .10 .03
84 Orel Hershiser .20 .06
85 Eric Karros .20 .06
86 Ramon Martinez .10 .03
87 Jose Offerman .10 .03
88 Mike Piazza .75 .23
89 Darryl Strawberry .30 .09
90 Tim Wallach .10 .03
91 Moises Alou .20 .06
92 Wil Cordero .10 .03
93 Jeff Fassero .10 .03
94 Darrin Fletcher .10 .03
95 Marquis Grissom .10 .03
96 Ken Hill .10 .03
97 Mike Lansing .10 .03
98 Kirk Rueter .20 .06
99 Larry Walker .30 .09
100 John Wetteland .20 .06
101 Rod Beck .10 .03
102 Barry Bonds 1.25 .35
103 John Burkett .10 .03
104 Royce Clayton .10 .03
105 Darren Lewis .10 .03
106 Kirt Manwaring .10 .03
107 Willie McGee .20 .06
108 Bill Swift .10 .03
109 Robby Thompson .10 .03
110 Matt Williams .20 .06
111 Sandy Alomar Jr. .10 .03
112 Carlos Baerga .10 .03
113 Albert Belle .20 .06
114 Wayne Kirby .10 .03
115 Kenny Lofton .20 .06
116 Jose Mesa .10 .03
117 Eddie Murray .50 .15
118 Charles Nagy .10 .03
119 Paul Sorrento .10 .03
120 Jim Thome .50 .15
121 Rich Amaral .10 .03
122 Eric Anthony .10 .03
123 Mike Blowers .10 .03
124 Chris Bosio .10 .03
125 Jay Buhner .20 .06
126 Dave Fleming .10 .03
127 Ken Griffey Jr. .75 .23
128 Randy Johnson .50 .15
129 Edgar Martinez .30 .09
130 Tino Martinez .30 .09
131 Bret Barberie .10 .03
132 Ryan Bowen .10 .03
133 Chuck Carr .10 .03
134 Jeff Conine .20 .06
135 Orestes Destrade .10 .03
136 Chris Hammond .10 .03
137 Bryan Harvey .10 .03
138 Dave Magadan .10 .03
139 Benito Santiago .20 .06
140 Gary Sheffield .20 .06
141 Bobby Bonilla .20 .06
142 Jeromy Burnitz .20 .06
143 Dwight Gooden .30 .09
144 Todd Hundley .10 .03
145 Bobby Jones .10 .03
146 Jeff Kent .20 .06
147 Joe Orsulak .10 .03
148 Bret Saberhagen .20 .06
149 Pete Schourek .10 .03
150 Ryan Thompson .10 .03
151 Brady Anderson .20 .06
152 Harold Baines .20 .06
153 Mike Devereaux .10 .03
154 Chris Hoiles .10 .03
155 Ben McDonald .10 .03
156 Mark McLemore .10 .03
157 Mike Mussina .50 .15
158 Rafael Palmeiro .30 .09
159 Cal Ripken 1.50 .45
160 Chris Sabo .10 .03
161 Brad Ausmus .10 .03
162 Derek Bell .10 .03
163 Andy Benes .10 .03
164 Doug Brocail .10 .03
165 Archi Cianfrocco .10 .03
166 Ricky Gutierrez .10 .03
167 Tony Gwynn .60 .18
168 Gene Harris .10 .03
169 Pedro Martinez RC .10 .03
170 Phil Plantier .10 .03
171 Darren Daulton .20 .06
172 Mariano Duncan .10 .03
173 Lenny Dykstra .20 .06
174 Tommy Greene .10 .03
175 Dave Hollins .10 .03
176 Danny Jackson .10 .03
177 John Kruk .20 .06
178 Terry Mulholland .10 .03
179 Curt Schilling .30 .09
180 Kevin Stocker .10 .03
181 Jay Bell .20 .06
182 Steve Cooke .10 .03
183 Carlos Garcia .10 .03
184 Joel Johnston .10 .03
185 Jeff King .10 .03
186 Al Martin .10 .03
187 Orlando Merced .10 .03
188 Don Slaught .10 .03
189 Andy Van Slyke .20 .06
190 Kevin Young .10 .03
191 Kevin Brown .20 .06
192 Jose Canseco .50 .15
193 Will Clark .50 .15
194 Juan Gonzalez .50 .15
195 Tom Henke .10 .03
196 David Hulse .10 .03
197 Dean Palmer .20 .06
198 Roger Pavlik .10 .03
199 Ivan Rodriguez .50 .15
200 Kenny Rogers .20 .06
201 Roger Clemens 1.00 .30
202 Scott Cooper .10 .03
203 Andre Dawson .20 .06
204 Mike Greenwell .10 .03
205 Billy Hatcher .10 .03
206 Jeff Russell .10 .03
207 Aaron Sele .10 .03
208 John Valentin .10 .03
209 Mo Vaughn .20 .06
210 Frank Viola .20 .06
211 Rob Dibble .20 .06
212 Willie Greene .10 .03
213 Roberto Kelly .10 .03
214 Barry Larkin .50 .15
215 Kevin Mitchell .10 .03
216 Hal Morris .10 .03
217 Joe Oliver .10 .03
218 Jose Rijo .10 .03
219 Reggie Sanders .20 .06
220 John Smiley .10 .03
221 Dante Bichette .20 .06
222 Ellis Burks .20 .06
223 Andres Galarraga .20 .06
224 Joe Girardi .10 .03
225 Charlie Hayes .10 .03
226 Darren Holmes .10 .03
227 Howard Johnson .10 .03
228 Roberto Mejia .10 .03
229 David Nied .10 .03
230 Armando Reynoso .10 .03
231 Kevin Appier .20 .06
232 David Cone .20 .06
233 Greg Gagne .10 .03
234 Tom Gordon .10 .03
235 Felix Jose .10 .03
236 Wally Joyner .20 .06
237 Jose Lind .10 .03
238 Brian McRae .10 .03
239 Mike Macfarliane .10 .03
240 Jeff Montgomery .10 .03
241 Eric Davis .20 .06
242 John Doherty .10 .03
243 Cecil Fielder .20 .06
244 Travis Fryman .20 .06
245 Bill Gullickson .10 .03
246 Mike Henneman .10 .03
247 Tony Phillips .10 .03
248 Mickey Tettleton .10 .03
249 Alan Trammell .30 .09
250 Lou Whitaker .20 .06
251 Rick Aguilera .20 .06
252 Scott Erickson .10 .03
253 Kent Hrbek .20 .06
254 Chuck Knoblauch .20 .06
255 Shane Mack .10 .03
256 Dave McCarty .10 .03
257 Pat Meares .10 .03
258 Kirby Puckett .50 .15
259 Kevin Tapani .10 .03
260 Dave Winfield .20 .06
261 Wilson Alvarez .10 .03
262 Jason Bere .10 .03
263 Alex Fernandez .10 .03
264 Ozzie Guillen .10 .03
265 Roberto Hernandez .10 .03
266 Lance Johnson .10 .03
267 Jack McDowell .10 .03
268 Tim Raines .20 .06
269 Frank Thomas .50 .15
270 Robin Ventura .20 .06
271 Jim Abbott .30 .09
272 Wade Boggs .30 .09
273 Mike Gallego .10 .03
274 Pat Kelly .10 .03
275 Jimmy Key .20 .06
276 Don Mattingly 1.25 .35
277 Paul O'Neill .30 .09
278 Mike Stanley .10 .03
279 Danny Tartabull .10 .03
280 Bernie Williams .30 .09
281 Chipper Jones .50 .15
282 Ryan Klesko .20 .06
283 Javier Lopez .20 .06
284 Jeffrey Hammonds .10 .03
285 Jeff McNeely .10 .03
286 Manny Ramirez .30 .09
287 Billy Ashley .10 .03
288 Raul Mondesi .20 .06
289 Cliff Floyd .20 .06
290 Rondell White .20 .06
291 Steve Karsay .10 .03
292 Midre Cummings .10 .03
293 Salomon Torres .10 .03
294 J.R. Phillips .10 .03
295 Marc Newfield .10 .03
296 Carlos Delgado .30 .09
297 Butch Huskey .10 .03
298 Checklist .10 .03
299 Checklist .10 .03
300 Checklist .10 .03

1994 Triple Play Bomb Squad

Randomly inserted in regular (one in 18) and jumbo (one in eight) packs, this ten-card standard-size set focuses on the top home run hitters in the majors.

Nm-Mt Ex-Mt
COMPLETE SET (10) 15.00 4.50
1 Frank Thomas 2.00 .60
2 Cecil Fielder .75 .23
3 Juan Gonzalez 2.00 .60
4 Barry Bonds 5.00 1.50
5 David Justice .75 .23
6 Fred McGriff 1.25 .35
7 Ron Gant .75 .23
8 Ken Griffey Jr. 3.00 .90
9 Albert Belle .75 .23
10 Matt Williams .75 .23

1994 Triple Play Medalists

Randomly inserted in regular (one in 12) and jumbo packs (one in six), this 15-card standard-size set features the top three players in each league at their position.

Nm-Mt Ex-Mt
COMPLETE SET (15) 20.00 6.00
1 Chris Hoiles .75 .23
Mickey Tettleton
Brian Harper
2 Darren Daulton .75 .23
Rick Wilkins
Kirt Manwaring
3 Frank Thomas 2.00 .60
Rafael Palmeiro
John Olerud
4 Mark Grace 1.25 .35
Fred McGriff
Jeff Bagwell
5 Roberto Alomar 2.00 .60
Carlos Baerga
Lou Whitaker
6 Ryne Sandberg 4.00 1.20
Craig Biggio
Roggie Thompson
7 Tony Fernandez 6.00 1.80
Cal Ripken
Alan Trammell
8 Barry Larkin 2.00 .60
Jay Bell
Jeff Blauser
9 Robin Ventura 1.25 .35
Travis Fryman
Wade Boggs
10 Terry Pendleton .75 .23
Dave Hollins
Gary Sheffield
11 Ken Griffey Jr. 3.00 .90
Kirby Puckett
Albert Belle
12 Barry Bonds 5.00 1.50
Andy Van Slyke
Len Dykstra
13 Jack McDowell 2.00 .60
Kevin Brown
Randy Johnson
14 Greg Maddux 3.00 .90
Jose Rijo
Bill Swift
15 Paul Molitor 1.25 .35
Dave Winfield
Harold Baines

1994 Triple Play Nicknames

Randomly inserted in regular (one in 36) and jumbo packs (one in 12), this eight-card standard-size set features players with a photo depicting the team name and mascot in the background.

Nm-Mt Ex-Mt
COMPLETE SET (8) 40.00 12.00
1 Cecil Fielder 2.00 .60
2 Ryne Sandberg 10.00 3.00
3 Gary Sheffield 2.00 .60
4 Joe Carter 2.00 .60
5 John Olerud 2.00 .60
6 Cal Ripken 15.00 4.50
7 Mark McGwire 12.00 3.60
8 Gregg Jefferies 2.00 .60

1996 Tropicana Hall of Fame Chips

These chips, all have a $5 demoniation and are numbered 1 of 1000. The fronts have a player photo while the back have a photo of the Tropicana casino. Since these are unnumbered, we have sequenced them in alphabetical order.

Nm-Mt Ex-Mt
COMPLETE SET 30.00 9.00
1 Ernie Banks 10.00 3.00
2 Brooks Robinson 10.00 3.00
3 Willie Stargell 10.00 3.00

1867 Troy Haymakers CdV's

These six cards represent one of the earliest known team sets. The Troy Haymakers were among the best known traveling squads of the tme. These photos were taken at a studio in Lansingburg, N.Y. Since these cards are unnumbered, we have sequenced them in alphabetical order.

Ex-Mt VG
COMPLETE SET 12000.00 6000.00
1 Thomas Abrams 2000.00 1000.00
2 William Craver 2000.00 1000.00
3 Steve King 2000.00 1000.00
4 Michael McAtee 2000.00 1000.00
5 Peter McKeon 2000.00 1000.00
6 Andrew McQuide 2000.00 1000.00

1986 True Value

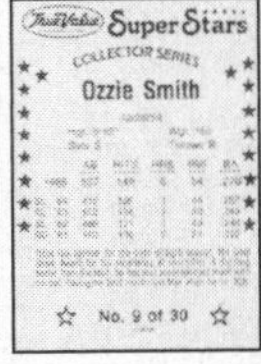

The 1986 True Value set consists of 30 cards, each measuring 2 1/2" by 3 1/2", which were printed as panels of four although one of the cards in the panel only pictures a featured product. The complete panel measures approximately 10 3/8" by 3 1/2". The True Value logo is in the upper left corner of the obverse of each card. Supposedly the cards were distributed to customers purchasing 5.00 or more at the store. Cards are frequently found with perforations intact and still in the closed form where only the top card in the folded panel is visible. The card number appears at the bottom of the reverse. Team logos have been surgically removed (airbrushed) from the photos.

Nm-Mt Ex-Mt
COMPLETE SET (30) 10.00 4.00
1 Pedro Guerrero .10 .04
2 Steve Garvey .20 .08
3 Eddie Murray .75 .30
4 Pete Rose .75 .30
5 Don Mattingly 1.50 .60
6 Fernando Valenzuela .20 .08
7 Jim Rice .20 .08
8 Kirk Gibson .20 .08
9 Ozzie Smith 1.25 .50
10 Dale Murphy .40 .16
11 Robin Yount .75 .30
12 Tom Seaver .75 .30
13 Reggie Jackson .75 .30
14 Ryne Sandberg 1.50 .60
15 Bruce Sutter .20 .08
16 Gary Carter .75 .30
17 George Brett 1.50 .60
18 Rick Sutcliffe .10 .04
19 Dave Stieb .10 .04
20 Buddy Bell .10 .04
21 Alvin Davis .10 .04
22 Cal Ripken 3.00 1.20
23 Bill Madlock .10 .04
24 Kent Hrbek .20 .08
25 Lou Whitaker .20 .08
26 Nolan Ryan 3.00 1.20
27 Dwayne Murphy .10 .04
28 Mike Schmidt .75 .30
29 Andre Dawson .60 .24
30 Wade Boggs 1.50 .60

1989 TV Sports Mailbags

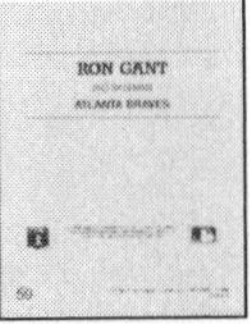

This 140-card set features glossy 8" by 10" color player photos and was distributed in packs with four pictures to a pack at the suggested retail price of $4.95. The backs carry the player's name, playing position, and team name.

Nm-Mt Ex-Mt
COMPLETE SET (140) 75.00 30.00
1 Darryl Strawberry .50 .20
2 Ron Darling .25 .10

3 Dwight Gooden .50 .20
4 Keith Hernandez .50 .20
5 Kevin McReynolds .25 .10
6 David Cone .75 .30
7 Randy Myers .25 .10
8 Gregg Jefferies .25 .10
9 Andy Van Slyke .25 .10
10 Bobby Bonilla .50 .20
11 Doug Drabek .25 .10
12 Barry Bonds 2.50 1.00
13 Tim Raines .25 .10
14 Andres Galarraga 1.00 .40
15 Hubie Brooks .25 .10
16 Tim Wallach .25 .10
17 Mark Grace 1.00 .40
18 Ryne Sandberg 2.00 .80
19 Shawon Dunston .25 .10
20 Mitch Webster .25 .10
21 Andre Dawson 1.00 .40
22 Damon Berryhill .25 .10
23 Greg Maddux 3.00 1.20
24 Vance Law .25 .10
25 Ozzie Smith 2.50 1.00
26 Tom Brunansky .25 .10
27 Pedro Guerrero .25 .10
28 Vince Coleman .25 .10
29 Juan Samuel .25 .10
30 Von Hayes .25 .10
31 Ricky Jordan .25 .10
32 Mike Schmidt 1.25 .50
33 Kirk Gibson .75 .30
34 Orel Hershiser .50 .20
35 Mike Marshall .25 .10
36 Mike Scioscia .50 .20
37 Eric Davis .50 .20
38 Chris Sabo .25 .10
39 Barry Larkin 1.00 .40
40 Danny Jackson .25 .10
41 Tom Browning .25 .10
42 Kal Daniels .25 .10
43 John Franco .50 .20
44 Paul O'Neill 1.00 .40
45 Tony Gwynn 2.50 1.00
46 Benito Santiago .50 .20
47 Roberto Alomar 2.00 .80
48 John Kruk .50 .20
49 Will Clark 1.50 .60
50 Rick Reuschel .25 .10
51 Kevin Mitchell .25 .10
52 Robby Thompson .25 .10
53 Mike Scott .25 .10
54 Glenn Davis .25 .10
55 Billy Hatcher .25 .10
56 Gerald Young .25 .10
57 Gerald Perry .25 .10
58 Dale Murphy .75 .30
59 Ron Gant .75 .30
60 Jody Davis .25 .10
61 Mike Greenwell .25 .10
62 Ellis Burks .50 .20
63 Roger Clemens 2.50 1.00
64 Wade Boggs 1.00 .40
65 Dwight Evans .50 .20
66 Marty Barrett .25 .10
67 Mike Boddicker .25 .10
68 Lee Smith .50 .20
69 Alan Trammell .75 .30
70 Matt Nokes .25 .10
71 Jack Morris .50 .20
72 Jeff Robinson .25 .10
73 Paul Molitor 1.25 .50
74 Robin Yount 1.25 .50
75 Ted Higuera .25 .10
76 Jim Gantner .25 .10
77 Fred McGriff 1.00 .40
78 Dave Stieb .25 .10
79 George Bell .25 .10
80 Tony Fernandez .25 .10
81 Dave Winfield 1.00 .40
82 Don Mattingly 2.50 1.00
83 Rickey Henderson 1.50 .60
84 Dave Righetti .25 .10
85 Joe Carter .75 .30
86 Mel Hall .25 .10
87 Cory Snyder .25 .10
88 Greg Swindell .25 .10
89 Cal Ripken 5.00 2.00
90 Brady Anderson 1.00 .40
91 Larry Sheets .25 .10
92 Billy Ripken .25 .10
93 Jose Canseco 1.00 .40
94 Walt Weiss .25 .10
95 Dave Stewart .25 .10
96 Dennis Eckersley 1.25 .50
97 Terry Steinbach .25 .10
98 Mark McGwire 4.00 1.60
99 Carney Lansford .25 .10
100 Dave Henderson .25 .10
101 Kent Hrbek .25 .10
102 Kirby Puckett 1.25 .50
103 Frank Viola .25 .10
104 Gary Gaetti .50 .20
105 George Brett 2.50 1.00
106 Kevin Seitzer .25 .10
107 Danny Tartabull .25 .10
108 Bo Jackson 1.00 .40
109 Wally Joyner .50 .20
110 Devon White .25 .10
111 Johnny Ray .25 .10
112 Mike Witt .25 .10
113 Harold Baines .50 .20
114 Ozzie Guillen .50 .20
115 Bobby Thigpen .25 .10
116 Dan Pasqua .25 .10
117 Ruben Sierra .50 .20
118 Pete Incaviglia .25 .10
119 Charlie Hough .25 .10
120 Scott Fletcher .25 .10
121 Mark Langston .25 .10
122 Alvin Davis .25 .10
123 Harold Reynolds .50 .20
124 Jay Buhner 1.00 .40
125 Jose Canseco 1.00 .40
126 Wade Boggs 1.25 .50
127 Rickey Henderson 1.50 .60
128 Mike Greenwell .25 .10
129 Darryl Strawberry .50 .20
130 Tony Gwynn 2.50 1.00
131 Will Clark 1.50 .60
132 Vince Coleman .25 .10
133 Jose Canseco 1.25 .50
134 Frank Viola .25 .10
135 Orel Hershiser .50 .20
136 Kirk Gibson .75 .30
137 Mark McGwire 4.00 1.60
138 Benito Santiago .50 .20
139 Chris Sabo .25 .10
140 Walt Weiss .25 .10

1992 TV Sports Mailbag/Photo File 500 Home Run Club

This 15-piece set features horizontal, blank-backed, oversized (10" X 8") cards.They are color action shots (except Ruth, Ott, and Foxx, which are black-and-white) on left side. Player's name, biography, teams, and key home run information are printed on the right side. The cards are unnumbered and checklisted below in alphabetical order.

Nm-Mt Ex-Mt
COMPLETE SET (15) 30.00 9.00
1 Hank Aaron 4.00 1.20
2 Ernie Banks 2.00 .60
3 Jimmie Foxx 2.00 .60
4 Reggie Jackson 2.50 .75
5 Harmon Killebrew 1.50 .45
6 Mickey Mantle 5.00 1.50
7 Eddie Mathews 1.50 .45
8 Willie Mays 4.00 1.20
9 Willie McCovey 1.50 .45
10 Mel Ott 1.50 .45
11 Frank Robinson 1.50 .45
12 Babe Ruth 5.00 1.50
13 Mike Schmidt 2.00 .60
14 Ted Williams 4.00 1.20
15 Header card 1.00 .30

1961 Twins Universal Match Corp.

The Farmers and Mechanics Savings Bank of Minneapolis sponsored this issue produced by the Universal Match Corp. of Minneapolis, MN. Each cover carries a player photo on the outside and a brief bio for each player appears on the covers inside. Players are shown wearing Washington Senators hats. Complete matchbooks carry a fifty percent premium.

NM Ex
COMPLETE SET (13) 100.00 40.00
1 Bob Allison 12.00 4.80
2 Earl Battey 8.00 3.20
3 Reno Bertoia 8.00 3.20
4 Billy Gardner 8.00 3.20
5 Lenny Green 8.00 3.20
6 Jim Kaat 15.00 6.00
(With Twins cap)
7 Harmon Killebrew 20.00 8.00
8 Jack Kralick 8.00 3.20
(With Twins cap)
9 Cookie Lavagetto MG 12.00 4.80
10 Jim Lemon 8.00 3.20
11 Camilo Pascual 8.00 3.20
12 Pedro Ramos 8.00 3.20
13 Zoilo Versalles 12.00 4.80
(With Twins cap)

1961 Twins Peter's Meats

The cards in this 26 card set measure 3 1/2" by 4 5/8". The 1961 Peter's Meats set of full color numbered cards depicts Minnesota Twins players only. The individual cards served as partial packaging for various meat products and are blank backed and heavily waxed. Complete boxes are sometimes available and are valued approximately 50 percent more than single cards. The catalog designation is F173.

NM Ex
COMPLETE SET (26) 600.00 240.00
1 Zoilo Versalles 30.00 12.00
2 Ed Lopat CO 20.00 8.00
3 Pedro Ramos 15.00 6.00
4 Chuck Stobbs 15.00 6.00
5 Don Mincher 20.00 8.00
6 Jack Kralick 15.00 6.00
7 Jim Kaat 80.00 32.00
8 Hal Naragon 15.00 6.00
9 Don Lee 15.00 6.00
10 Cookie Lavagetto CO 20.00 8.00
11 Pete Whisenant 15.00 6.00
12 Elmer Valo 15.00 6.00
13 Ray Moore 15.00 6.00
14 Billy Gardner 15.00 6.00
15 Lenny Green 15.00 6.00
16 Sam Mele MG 15.00 6.00
17 Jim Lemon 15.00 6.00
18 Harmon Killebrew 200.00 80.00
19 Paul Giel 15.00 6.00
20 Reno Bertoia 15.00 6.00
21 Clyde McCullough CO 15.00 6.00
22 Earl Battey 15.00 6.00
23 Camilo Pascual 20.00 8.00
24 Dan Dobbek 15.00 6.00
25 Jose Valdivielso 15.00 6.00
26 Billy Consolo 15.00 6.00

1961 Twins Postcards

These postcards, most of which measure 4" by 5" and are in black and white and are blank-backed, feature members of the 1961 Minnesota Twins, the first year they were in Minnesota. These cards have black and white photograph along with a fascimile autograph. A couple of cards measure 5" by 4" instead. Since these cards are not numbered, we have sequenced them in alphabetical order. Some collectors refer to these as the type 1 postcards for the Twins.

NM Ex
COMPLETE SET 100.00 40.00
1 Bob Allison 3.00 1.20
2 Floyd Baker CO 3.00 1.20
3 Earl Battey 3.00 1.20
4 Reno Bertoia 3.00 1.20
5 Fred Bruckbauer 3.00 1.20
6 Billy Consolo 3.00 1.20
7 Dan Dobbek 3.00 1.20
8 Billy Gardner 3.00 1.20
9 Lenny Green 3.00 1.20
10 Calvin Griffith PRES 3.00 1.20
11 Ron Henry 3.00 1.20
12 Jim Kaat 6.00 2.40
13 Harmon Killebrew 12.00 4.80
14 Jack Kralick 3.00 1.20
15 Cookie Lavagetto MG 3.00 1.20
16 Don Lee 3.00 1.20
17 Jim Lemon 3.00 1.20
18 Ed Lopat CO 3.00 1.20
19 Clyde McCullough CO 3.00 1.20
20 Sam Mele CO 3.00 1.20
21 Don Mincher 3.00 1.20
22 Ray Moore 3.00 1.20
23 Hal Naragon 3.00 1.20
24 Ed Palmquist 3.00 1.20
25 Camilo Pascual 4.00 1.60
26 Bill Pleis 3.00 1.20
27 Pedro Ramos 3.00 1.20
28 Ted Sadowski 3.00 1.20
29 Lee Stange 3.00 1.20
30 Chuck Stobbs 3.00 1.20
31 Jose Valdivielso 3.00 1.20
32 Elmer Valo 3.00 1.20
33 Zoilo Versalles 4.00 1.60

1961-62 Twins Cloverleaf Dairy

These large (3 3/4" by 7 3/4") cards are unnumbered; they made up the side of a Cloverleaf Dairy milk carton. Cards still on the carton are valued double the listed price below. The last two digits of the year of issue for each player is given in parentheses. However those players appearing both (BOTH) years are indistinguishable (as to which year they were produced) when cut from the carton. There were 16 cards produced in 1961 and 24 cards produced in 1962. These unnumbered cards are sequenced in alphabetical order. The catalog designation for this set is F103.

NM Ex
COMPLETE SET (31) 800.00 325.00
1 Bernie Allen 62 25.00 10.00
2 George Banks 62 25.00 10.00
3 Earl Battey BOTH 20.00 8.00
4 Joe Bonikowski 62 25.00 10.00
5 Billy Gardner 61 30.00 12.00
6 Paul Giel 61 25.00 10.00
7 John Goryl 62 25.00 10.00
8 Lenny Green BOTH 20.00 8.00
9 Jim Kaat BOTH 40.00 16.00
10 Harmon Killebrew 61 150.00 60.00
11 Jack Kralick BOTH 20.00 8.00
12 Don Lee 61 25.00 10.00
13 Jim Lemon BOTH 20.00 8.00
14 Manager/Coaches 62 25.00 10.00
15 Georges Maranda 62 25.00 10.00
16 Orlando Martinez 62 25.00 10.00
17 Don Mincher BOTH 25.00 10.00
18 Ray Moore 62 25.00 10.00
19 Hal Naragon 62 25.00 10.00
20 Camilo Pascual BOTH 25.00 10.00
21 Vic Power 62 25.00 10.00
22 Pedro Ramos 61 30.00 12.00
23 Rich Rollins 62 30.00 12.00
24 Theodore Sadowski 62 25.00 10.00
25 Albert Stange 62 25.00 10.00
26 Dick Stigman 62 25.00 10.00
27 Chuck Stobbs 61 30.00 12.00
28 Bill Tuttle BOTH 20.00 8.00
29 Jose Valdivielso 61 25.00 10.00
30 Zoilo Versalles BOTH 25.00 10.00
31 Gerald Zimmerman 62 25.00 10.00

1962 Twins Jay Publishing

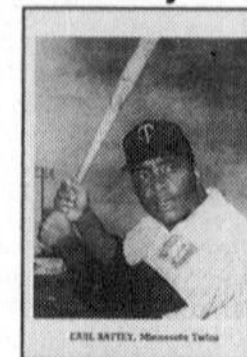

This 12-card set of the Minnesota Twins measures approximately 5" by 7". The fronts feature black-and-white posed player photos with the player's and team name printed below in the white border. These cards were packaged 12 to a packet. The backs are blank. The cards are unnumbered and checklisted below in alphabetical order.

NM Ex
COMPLETE SET (12) 40.00 16.00
1 Bob Allison 4.00 1.60
2 Earl Battey 2.50 1.00
3 Lenny Green 2.50 1.00
4 Jim Kaat 5.00 2.00
5 Harmon Killebrew 12.00 4.80
6 John Kralick 2.50 1.00
7 Don Lee 2.50 1.00
8 Jim Lemon 2.50 1.00
9 Sam Mele MG 2.50 1.00
10 Camilo Pascual 3.00 1.20
11 Jose Valdivielso 2.50 1.00
12 Zoilo Versalles 4.00 1.60

1963 Twins Jay Publishing

This 12-card set of the Minnesota Twins measures approximately 5" by 7". The fronts feature black-and-white posed player photos with the player's and team name printed below in the white border. These cards were packaged 12 to a packet. The backs are blank. The cards are unnumbered and checklisted below in alphabetical order.

NM Ex
COMPLETE SET (12) 30.00 12.00
1 Bernie Allen 2.00 .80
2 Bob Allison 2.00 .80
3 Earl Battey 2.00 .80
4 Jim Kaat 4.00 1.60
5 Harmon Killebrew 12.00 4.80
6 Jack Kralick 2.00 .80
7 Jim Lemon 2.00 .80
8 Sam Mele MG 2.00 .80
9 Camilo Pascual 2.50 1.00
10 Vic Power 2.00 .80
11 Rich Rollins 2.50 1.00
12 Zolio Versalles 2.50 1.00

1963 Twins Volpe

Sponsored by Western Oil and Fuel Company, these 24 portraits of the 1963 Minnesota Twins by noted artist Nicholas Volpe measure approximately 8 1/2" by 11". Each white-bordered color reproduction of pastel chalk on bordered color reproduction features a larger portrait and a smaller action drawing. The player's name appears in black lettering within the white margin at bottom, and also as a white fascimile autograph on the black background. The white back carries the player's name, position and biography at the top, followed below by career highlights and statistics. Artist information and the sponsor's logo at the bottom round out the backs. The drawings are unnumbered and checklisted in alphabetical order.

NM Ex
COMPLETE SET (24) 200.00 80.00
1 Bernie Allen 8.00 3.20
2 Bob Allison 10.00 4.00
3 George Banks 8.00 3.20
4 Earl Battey 10.00 4.00
5 Bill Dailey 8.00 3.20
6 John Goryl 8.00 3.20
7 Lenny Green 8.00 3.20
8 Jimmie Hall 8.00 3.20
9 Jim Kaat 15.00 6.00
10 Harmon Killebrew 25.00 10.00
11 Sam Mele MG 10.00 4.00
12 Don Mincher 10.00 4.00
13 Ray Moore 8.00 3.20
14 Camilio Pascual 10.00 4.00
15 Jim Perry 12.00 4.80
16 Bill Pleis 8.00 3.20
17 Vic Power 10.00 4.00
18 Gary Roggenburk 8.00 3.20
19 Jim Roland 8.00 3.20
20 Rich Rollins 10.00 4.00
21 Lee Stange 8.00 3.20
22 Dick Stigman 8.00 3.20
23 Zoilo Versalles 10.00 4.00
24 Jerry Zimmerman 8.00 3.20

1964 Twins Jay Publishing

The 1964 Twins Jay set consists of 12 cards produced by Jay Publishing. The Henry and Oliva cards establish the year of the set, since 1964 was Henry's last year and Oliva's first year with the Twins. The cards measure approximately 5" by 7" and are printed on photographic paper stock. The white fronts feature a black-and-white player portrait with the player's name and the team name below. The backs are blank. The cards are packaged 12 to a packet. The cards are unnumbered and checklisted below in alphabetical order.

NM Ex
COMPLETE SET (12) 35.00 14.00
1 Bob Allison 3.00 1.20
2 Earl Battey 2.00 .80
3 Jim Grant 2.00 .80
4 Jimmie Hall 2.00 .80
5 Ron Henry 2.00 .80
6 Jim Kaat 4.00 1.60
7 Harmon Killebrew 12.00 4.80
8 Tony Oliva 4.00 1.60
9 Camilo Pascual 2.50 1.00
10 Rich Rollins 2.00 .80
11 Dick Stigman 2.00 .80
12 Zorro Versalles 2.50 1.00

1964 Twins Volpe

This 15 drawings, which measure 8" by 11", feature members of the 1964 Minnesota Twins. The fronts feature two drawings of the players while the backs have biographical information, a blurb about the player as well as career statistics. Since these are unnumbered, we have sequenced them in alphabetical order.

NM Ex
COMPLETE SET 150.00 60.00
1 Bernie Allen 8.00 3.20
2 Bob Allison 10.00 4.00
3 Earl Battey 8.00 3.20
4 Bill Dailey 8.00 3.20
5 Jim Hall 8.00 3.20
6 Jim Kaat 15.00 6.00
7 Harmon Killebrew 25.00 10.00
8 Don Mincher 10.00 4.00
9 Tony Oliva 20.00 8.00
10 Camilo Pascual 10.00 4.00
11 Bill Pleis 8.00 3.20
12 Jim Roland 8.00 3.20
13 Rich Rollins 8.00 3.20
14 Dick Stigman 8.00 3.20
15 Zoilo Versalles 8.00 3.20

1965 Twins Jay Publishing

This 12-card set of the Minnesota Twins measures approximately 5" by 7". The fronts feature black-and-white posed player photos with the player's and team name printed below in the white border. These cards were packaged 12 to a packet. The backs are blank. The cards are unnumbered and checklisted below in alphabetical order.

NM Ex
COMPLETE SET (12) 30.00 12.00
1 Bernie Allen 2.00 .80
2 Bob Allison 3.00 1.20
3 Earl Battey 2.00 .80
4 Bill Dailey 2.00 .80
5 Jim Kaat 4.00 1.60
6 Harmon Killebrew 12.00 4.80
7 Sam Mele MG 2.50 1.00
8 Camilo Pascual 3.00 1.20
9 Vic Power 2.00 .80
10 Rich Rollins 2.00 .80
11 Dick Stigman 2.00 .80
12 Zoilo Versalles 2.50 1.00

1965 Twins Postcards

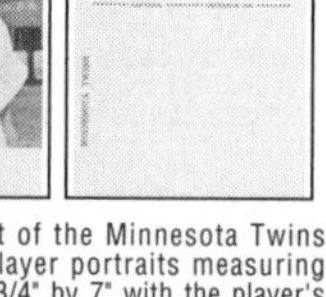

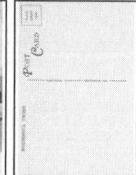

This 10-card set of the Minnesota Twins features color player portraits measuring approximately 4 3/4" by 7" with the player's name in the wide bottom margin. The backs display a postcard format. The cards are unnumbered and checklisted below in alphabetical order.

NM Ex
COMPLETE SET (10) 100.00 40.00
1 Bob Allison 10.00 4.00
2 Earl Battey 8.00 3.20
3 Jimmie Hall 8.00 3.20
4 Jim Kaat 15.00 6.00
5 Harmon Killebrew 25.00 10.00
6 Sam Mele MG 8.00 3.20
7 Tony Oliva 15.00 6.00
8 Camilo Pascual 10.00 4.00
9 Rich Rollins 8.00 3.20
10 Zoilo Versalles 10.00 4.00

1966 Twins Fairway Grocery

This 17-card set features 8" by 10" color player portraits of the Minnesota Twins with player information and statistics on the backs. The cards are unnumbered and checklisted below in alphabetical order.

	NM	Ex
COMPLETE SET (17)	100.00	40.00
1 Bernie Allen	5.00	2.00
2 Bob Allison	8.00	3.20
3 Earl Battey	5.00	2.00
4 Jim Grant	6.00	2.40
5 Jimmie Hall	5.00	2.00
6 Jim Kaat	8.00	3.20
7 Harmon Killebrew	20.00	8.00
8 Jim Merritt	5.00	2.00
9 Don Mincher	5.00	2.00
10 Tony Oliva	10.00	4.00
11 Camilo Pascual	6.00	2.40
12 Jim Perry	6.00	2.40
13 Frank Quilici	5.00	2.00
14 Rich Rollins	6.00	2.40
15 Sandy Valdespino	5.00	2.00
16 Zoilo Versalles	6.00	2.40
17 Al Worthington	5.00	2.00

1967 Twins Team Issue

This 26-card set of the 1967 Minnesota Twins measures approximately 4" by 5" and features black-and-white facsimile autographed player portraits with white borders. The backs are blank. The cards are unnumbered and checklisted below in alphabetical order. A card of Rod Carew is featured in his Rookie Card year.

	NM	Ex
COMPLETE SET (26)	60.00	24.00
1 Bob Allison	2.50	1.00
2 Earl Battey	2.00	.80
3 Rod Carew	15.00	6.00
4 Dean Chance Pitching	2.50	1.00
5 Dean Chance Portrait	2.50	1.00
6 Ron Clark	2.00	.80
7 Harmon Killebrew	10.00	4.00
8 Ron Kline	2.00	.80
9 Jim Lemon CO	2.00	.80
10 Billy Martin CO	4.00	1.60
11 Jim Merritt	2.00	.80
12 Tony Oliva Portrait	4.00	1.60
13 Tony Oliva Batting	4.00	1.60
14 Jim Ollom	2.00	.80
15 Jim Perry	2.50	1.00
16 Frank Quilici	2.00	.80
17 Rich Reese	2.00	.80
18 Jim Roland	2.00	.80
19 Rich Rollins	2.00	.80
20 Cesar Tovar	2.00	.80
21 Cesar Tovar Closeup	2.00	.80
22 Ted Uhlaender	2.00	.80
23 Sandy Valdespino	2.00	.80
24 Zoilo Versalles	2.50	1.00
25 Early Wynn CO	4.00	1.60
26 Jerry Zimmerman	2.00	.80

1969 Twins Team Issue Color

This 13-card set of the Minnesota Twins measures approximately 7" by 8 3/4" with the fronts featuring white-bordered color player photos. The player's name and team is printed in black in the white margin below the picture. The backs are blank. The cards are unnumbered and checklisted below in alphabetical order.

	NM	Ex
COMPLETE SET (13)	60.00	24.00
1 Bob Allison	4.00	1.60
2 Leo Cardenas	4.00	1.60
3 Rod Carew	10.00	4.00
4 Dean Chance	4.00	1.60
5 Jim Kaat	5.00	2.00
6 Harmon Killebrew	8.00	3.20
7 Billy Martin MG	8.00	3.20
8 Tony Oliva	6.00	2.40
9 Ron Perranoski	3.00	1.20
10 Jim Perry	4.00	1.60
11 Rich Reese	3.00	1.20
12 Cesar Tovar	4.00	1.60
13 Ted Uhlaender	3.00	1.20

1970 Twins Super Valu

This 12-card set features color player drawings in white borders and measures approximately 7 3/4" by 9 3/8". The cards feature both an action player drawing and a head drawing with a facsimile autograph. The player's name is printed in the bottom margin. The backs are blank. The cards are unnumbered and checklisted below in alphabetical order.

	NM	Ex
COMPLETE SET (12)	50.00	20.00
1 Brant Alyea	3.00	1.20
2 Leo Cardenas	3.00	1.20
3 Rod Carew	15.00	6.00
4 Jim Kaat	4.00	1.60
5 Harmon Killebrew	10.00	4.00
6 George Mitterwald	3.00	1.20
7 Tony Oliva	6.00	2.40
8 Ron Perranoski	4.00	1.60
9 Jim Perry	5.00	2.00
10 Rich Reese	3.00	1.20
11 Luis Tiant	6.00	2.40
12 Cesar Tovar	3.00	1.20

1970 Twins Team Issue

This 14-card set features black-and-white player portraits with white borders and a facsimile autograph printed on the front. The backs are blank. The cards are unnumbered and checklisted below in alphabetical order.

	NM	Ex
COMPLETE SET (14)	15.00	6.00
1 Brant Alyea	1.00	.40
2 Steve Barber	1.00	.40
3 Frank Crosetti CO	2.00	.80
4 Marv Grissom CO	1.00	.40
5 Minnie Mendoza	1.00	.40
6 Paul Ratliff	1.00	.40
7 Rich Reese	1.00	.40
8 Bill Rigney MG	1.00	.40
9 Bob Rodgers CO	1.00	.40
10 Luis Tiant	2.50	1.00
11 Cesar Tovar	1.00	.40
12 Stan Williams	1.00	.40
13 Bill Zepp	1.00	.40
14 Metropolitan Stadium	1.00	.40

1972 Twins Team Issue

This 25-card set of the Minnesota Twins features black-and-white player portraits in white borders with facsimile autographs and measures approximately 4" by 5 1/8". The backs are blank. The cards are unnumbered and checklisted below in alphabetical order.

	NM	Ex
COMPLETE SET (25)	75.00	30.00
1 Bert Blyleven	6.00	2.40
2 Steve Braun	3.00	1.20
3 Ray Corbin	3.00	1.20
4 Rick Dempsey	5.00	2.00
5 Bob Gebhard	3.00	1.20
6 Wayne Granger	3.00	1.20
7 Jim Kaat	6.00	2.40
8 Harmon Killebrew	10.00	4.00
9 Dave Laroche	3.00	1.20
10 George Mitterwald	3.00	1.20
11 Dan Monzon	3.00	1.20
12 Vern Morgan CO	3.00	1.20
13 Jim Nettles	3.00	1.20
14 Tom Norton	3.00	1.20
15 Tony Oliva	6.00	2.40
16 Jim Perry	5.00	2.00
17 Frank Quilici	3.00	1.20
18 Rich Reese	3.00	1.20
19 Phil Roof	3.00	1.20
20 Ralph Rowe CO	3.00	1.20
21 Eric Soderholm	3.00	1.20
22 Danny Thompson	3.00	1.20
23 Cesar Tovar	4.00	1.60
24 Dick Woodson	3.00	1.20
25 Al Worthington CO	3.00	1.20

1975 Twins Postcards

This 24-card set of the Minnesota Twins features player photos on postcard-size cards. The cards are unnumbered and checklisted below in alphabetical order.

	NM	Ex
COMPLETE SET (24)	12.00	4.80
1 Vic Albury	.50	.20
2 Bert Blyleven	1.50	.60
3 Glenn Borgmann	.50	.20
4 Steve Braun	.50	.20
5 Steve Brye	.50	.20
6 Bill Campbell	.50	.20
7 Rod Carew	4.00	1.60
8 Ray Corbin	.50	.20
9 Bobby Darwin	.50	.20
10 Joe Decker	.50	.20
11 Dan Ford	.50	.20
12 Dave Goltz	.50	.20
13 Luis Gomez	.50	.20
14 Larry Hisle	.75	.30
15 Craig Kusick	.50	.20
16 Tom Lundstedt	.50	.20
17 Vern Morgan CO	.50	.20
18 Tony Oliva	1.00	.40
19 Frank Quilici MG	.50	.20
20 Phil Roof	.50	.20
21 Ralph Rowe CO	.50	.20
22 Eric Soderholm	.50	.20
23 Lee Stange CO	.50	.20
24 Jerry Terrell	.50	.20

1975 Twins Team Issue

These photos feature members of the 1975 Minnesota Twins. They are unnumbered and we have sequenced them in alphabetical order.

	NM	Ex
COMPLETE SET	25.00	10.00
1 Vic Albury	1.00	.40
2 Bert Blyleven	2.50	1.00
3 Glen Borgmann	1.00	.40
4 Lyman Bostock	2.50	1.00
5 Steve Braun	1.00	.40
6 John Briggs	1.00	.40
7 Steve Brye	1.00	.40
8 Tom Burgmeier	1.00	.40
9 Bill Butler	1.00	.40
10 Bill Campbell	1.00	.40
11 Ray Corbin	1.00	.40
12 Joe Decker	1.00	.40
13 Dan Ford	1.00	.40
14 Dave Goltz	1.00	.40
15 Luis Gomez	1.00	.40
16 Larry Hisle	1.00	.40
17 Jim Hughes	1.00	.40
18 Tom Johnson	1.00	.40
19 Craig Kusick	1.00	.40
20 Tom Lundstedt	1.00	.40
21 Tony Oliva	2.50	1.00
22 Frank Quilici MG	1.00	.40
23 Phil Roof	1.00	.40
24 Eric Soderholm	1.00	.40
25 Lee Strange	1.00	.40
26 Jerry Terrell	1.00	.40
27 Danny Thompson	1.00	.40
28 Mark Wiley	1.00	.40

1976 Twins Postcards

This 18-card set of the Minnesota Twins features player photos on postcard-size cards. The cards are unnumbered and checklisted below in alphabetical order.

	NM	Ex
COMPLETE SET (18)	10.00	4.00
1 Bert Blyleven	1.50	.60
2 Lyman Bostock	1.00	.40
3 Steve Brye	.50	.20
4 Bill Campbell	.50	.20
5 Rod Carew	4.00	1.60
6 Mike Cubbage	.50	.20
7 Dan Ford	.50	.20
8 Dave Goltz	.50	.20
9 Larry Hisle	.50	.20
10 Craig Kusick	.50	.20
11 Dave McKay	.50	.20
12 Bob Randall	.50	.20
13 Pete Redfern	.50	.20
14 Phil Roof	.50	.20
15 Bill Singer	.50	.20
16 Roy Smalley	.50	.20
17 Jerry Terrell	.50	.20
18 Danny Thompson	.50	.20

1978 Twins Frisz

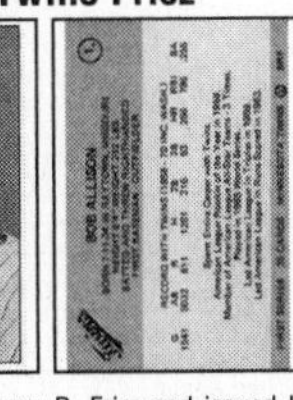

Manufactured by Barry R. Frisz and issued by the Twins in two 25-card series, these cards measure approximately 2 1/2" by 3 3/4" and feature on their fronts white-bordered posed color photos of retired Twins players. The white and gray horizontal back carries the player's name, biography, position, statistics, and career highlights. The cards are numbered on the back.

	NM	Ex
COMPLETE SET (50)	25.00	10.00
1 Bob Allison	1.50	.60
2 Earl Battey	.50	.20
3 Dave Boswell	.50	.20
4 Dean Chance	1.50	.60
5 Jim Grant	1.00	.40
6 Calvin Griffith PRES	.50	.20
7 Jimmie Hall	.50	.20
8 Harmon Killebrew	2.50	1.00
9 Jim Lemon	.50	.20
10 Billy Martin MG	1.50	.60
11 Gene Mauch MG	.75	.30
12 Sam Mele MG	.50	.20
13 Metropolitan Stadium	1.50	.60
14 Don Mincher	.50	.20
15 Tony Oliva	1.00	.40
16 Camilo Pascual	.75	.30
17 Jim Perry	.50	.20
18 Frank Quilici MG	.50	.20
19 Rich Reese	.50	.20
20 Bill Rigney MG	.50	.20
21 Cesar Tovar	.75	.30
22 Zoilo Versalles	.75	.30
23 Al Worthington	.50	.20
24 Jerry Zimmerman	.50	.20
25 Checklist 1-25	.50	.20
26 Bernie Allen	.50	.20
27 Leo Cardenas	1.00	.40
28 Ray Corbin	.50	.20
29 Joe Decker	.50	.20
30 Johnny Goryl	.50	.20
31 Tom Hall	.50	.20
32 Bill Hands	.50	.20
33 Jim Holt	.50	.20
34 Randy Hundley	1.00	.40
35 Jerry Kindall	.50	.20
36 Johnny Klippstein	.50	.20
37 Jack Kralick	.50	.20
38 Jim Merritt	.50	.20
39 Joe Nossek	.50	.20
40 Ron Perranoski	.75	.30
41 Bill Pleis	.50	.20
42 Rick Renick	.50	.20
43 Jim Roland	.50	.20
44 Lee Stange	.50	.20
45 Dick Stigman	.50	.20
46 Danny Thompson	.50	.20
47 Ted Uhlaender	.50	.20
48 Sandy Valdespino	.75	.30
49 Dick Woodson	.50	.20
50 Checklist 25-50	.50	.20

1978 Twins Frisz Postcards

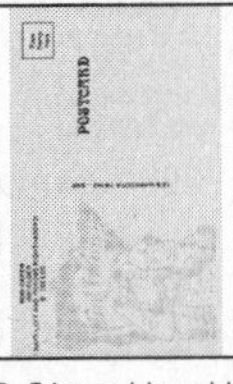

Manufactured by Barry R. Frisz and issued by the Twins, these 25 postcards measure 3 1/2" by 5 1/2" and feature on their fronts borderless color posed-on-field photos of then-current Twins. The back carries the player's name, position, and height and weight at the upper left. Below is a ghosted cartoon logo that carries the words "Win, Twins." The year of the set appears in the vertical lettering bisecting the postcard. The postcards are unnumbered and checklisted below in alphabetical order.

	NM	Ex
COMPLETE SET (25)	20.00	8.00
1 Glenn Adams	.75	.30
2 Glenn Borgmann	.75	.30
3 Rod Carew	4.00	1.60
4 Rich Chiles	.75	.30
5 Mike Cubbage	.75	.30
6 Roger Erickson	.75	.30
7 Dan Ford	.75	.30
8 Dave Goltz	.75	.30
9 Dave Johnson	.75	.30
10 Tom Johnson	.75	.30
11 Craig Kusick	.75	.30
12 Jose Morales	.75	.30
13 Willie Norwood	.75	.30
14 Hosken Powell	.75	.30
15 Bob Randall	.75	.30
16 Pete Redfern	.75	.30
17 Bombo Rivera	.75	.30
18 Gary Serum	.75	.30
19 Roy Smalley	1.50	.60
20 Greg Thayer	.75	.30
21 Paul Thormodsgard	.75	.30
22 Rob Wilfong	.75	.30
23 Larry Wolfe	.75	.30
24 Butch Wynegar	.75	.30
25 Geoff Zahn	.75	.30

1979 Twins Frisz Postcards

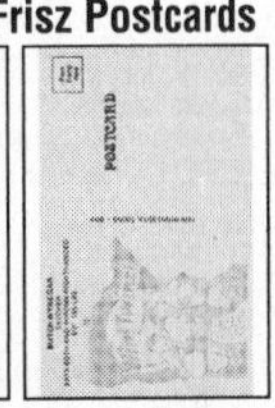

Manufactured by Barry R. Frisz and issued by the Twins, these 30 postcards measure 3 1/2" by 5 1/2" and feature on their fronts borderless color posed-on-field photos of then-current Twins. The back carries the player's name, position, and height and weight at the upper left. Below is a ghosted cartoon logo that carries the words "Win, Twins." The year of the set appears in the vertical lettering bisecting the postcard. The postcards are unnumbered and checklisted below in alphabetical order.

	NM	Ex
COMPLETE SET (30)	15.00	6.00
1 Glenn Adams	.50	.20
2 Glenn Borgmann	.50	.20
3 John Castino	.50	.20
4 Mike Cubbage	.50	.20
5 Dave Edwards	.50	.20
6 Roger Erickson	.50	.20
7 Dave Goltz	.50	.20
8 John Goryl CO	.50	.20
9 Paul Hartzell	.50	.20
10 Jeff Holly	.50	.20
11 Ron Jackson	.50	.20
12 Jerry Koosman	1.50	.60
13 Karl Kuehl CO	.50	.20
14 Craig Kusick	.50	.20
15 Ken Landreaux	.50	.20
16 Mike Marshall	1.00	.40
17 Gene Mauch MG	1.00	.40
18 Jose Morales	.50	.20
19 Willie Norwood	.50	.20
20 Camilo Pascual CO	1.00	.40
21 Hosken Powell	.50	.20
22 Bobby Randall	.50	.20
23 Pete Redfern	.50	.20
24 Bombo Rivera	.50	.20
25 Gary Serum	.50	.20
26 Roy Smalley	1.00	.40
27 Rob Wilfong	.50	.20
28 Butch Wynegar	.50	.20
29 Geoff Zahn	.50	.20
30 Jerry Zimmerman CO	.50	.20

1980 Twins Postcards

This 33-card set features photos of the 1980 Minnesota Twins on postcard-size cards. A facsimile autograph is printed on some of the cards. The cards are unnumbered and checklisted below in alphabetical order.

	NM	Ex
COMPLETE SET (33)	15.00	6.00
1 Glenn Adams	.50	.20
2 Sal Butera	.50	.20
3 John Castino	.50	.20
4 Doug Corbett	.50	.20
5 Mike Cubbage	.50	.20
6 Dave Edwards	.50	.20
7 Roger Erickson	.50	.20
8 Terry Felton	.50	.20
9 Danny Goodwin	.50	.20
10 Johnny Goryl CO	.50	.20
11 Darrell Jackson	.50	.20
12 Ron Jackson	.50	.20
13 Harmon Killebrew CO	3.00	1.20
14 Jerry Koosman	1.00	.40
15 Karl Kuehl CO	.50	.20
16 Ken Landreaux	.50	.20
17 Pete Mackanin	.50	.20
18 Mike Marshall	.75	.30
19 Gene Mauch MG	.50	.20
20 Jose Morales	.50	.20
21 Willie Norwood	.50	.20
22 Camilo Pascual CO	.75	.30
23 Hosken Powell	.50	.20
24 Bobby Randall CO	.50	.20
25 Pete Redfern	.50	.20
26 Bombo Rivera	.50	.20
27 Roy Smalley	.50	.20
28 Rich Sofield	.50	.20
29 John Verhoeven	.50	.20
30 Rob Wilfong	.50	.20
31 Butch Wynegar	.50	.20
32 Geoff Zahn	.50	.20
33 Jerry Zimmerman CO	.50	.20

1981 Twins Postcards

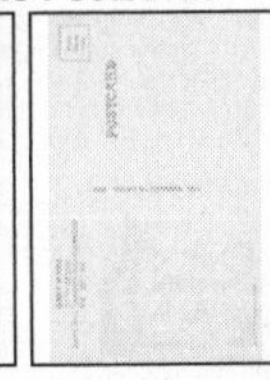

This 33-card set of the Minnesota Twins measures approximately 3 1/2" by 5 7/16" and features borderless color player photos with a facsimile autograph. The backs display a postcard format. The cards are unnumbered and checklisted below in alphabetical order.

	Nm-Mt	Ex-Mt
COMPLETE SET (33)	12.00	4.80
1 Glenn Adams	.50	.20
2 Fernando Arroyo	.50	.20
3 Chuck Baker	.50	.20
4 Sal Butera	.50	.20
5 John Castino	.50	.20
6 Don Cooper	.50	.20
7 Doug Corbett	.50	.20
8 Dave Engle	.50	.20
9 Roger Erickson	.50	.20
10 Billy Gardner CO	.50	.20
11 Danny Goodwin	.50	.20
12 Johnny Goryl MG	.50	.20
13 Mickey Hatcher	.50	.20
14 Darrell Jackson	.50	.20
15 Ron Jackson	.50	.20
16 Greg Johnston	.50	.20
17 Jerry Koosman	1.00	.40
18 Karl Kuehl CO	.50	.20
19 Pete Mackanin	.50	.20
20 Jack O'Connor	.50	.20
21 Johnny Podres CO	.75	.30
22 Hosken Powell	.50	.20
23 Pete Redfern	.50	.20
24 Roy Smalley	.50	.20
25 Ray Smith	.50	.20
26 Rick Sofield	.50	.20
27 Rick Stelmaszek CO	.50	.20
28 John Verhoeven	.50	.20
29 Gary Ward	.50	.20
30 Rob Wilfong	.50	.20
31 Al Williams	.50	.20
32 Butch Wynegar	.50	.20
33 Metropolitan Stadium	.50	.20

1982 Twins Postcards

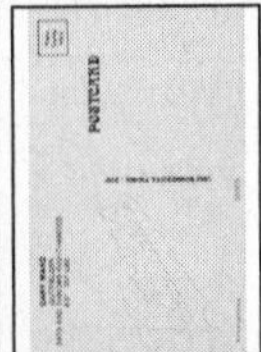

This 34-postcard set features the 1982 Minnesota Twins Baseball Team and features borderless color player photos with a simulated autograph. The backs display a postcard format. The cards are unnumbered and checklisted below in alphabetical order.

	Nm-Mt	Ex-Mt
COMPLETE SET (34)	10.00	4.00
1 Fernando Arroyo	.25	.10
2 Sal Butera	.25	.10
3 Bobby Castillo	.25	.10
4 John Castino	.25	.10
5 Doug Corbett	.25	.10
6 Ron Davis	.25	.10
7 Jim Eisenreich	1.00	.40
8 Dave Engle	.25	.10
9 Roger Erickson	.25	.10
10 Lenny Faedo	.25	.10
11 Terry Felton	.25	.10
12 Gary Gaetti	2.50	1.00
13 Billy Gardner MG	.25	.10
14 Mickey Hatcher	.25	.10
15 Brad Havens	.25	.10
16 Kent Hrbek	2.00	.80
17 Darrell Jackson	.25	.10
18 Randy Johnson	.25	.10
19 Karl Kuehl CO	.25	.10
20 Jim Lemon CO	.25	.10
21 Bobby Mitchell	.25	.10
22 Jack O'Connor	.25	.10
23 Johnny Podres CO	.50	.20
24 Pete Redfern	.25	.10
25 Rick Stelmaszek CO	.25	.10

26 Jesus Vega .25 .10
27 Gary Ward .25 .10
28 Ron Washington .25 .10
29 Rob Wilfong .25 .10
30 Al Williams .25 .10
31 Butch Wynegar .25 .10
32 Metrodome .25 .10
Outside view
33 Metrodome .25 .10
Inside view
34 Team Picture .25 .10

1983 Twins Team Issue

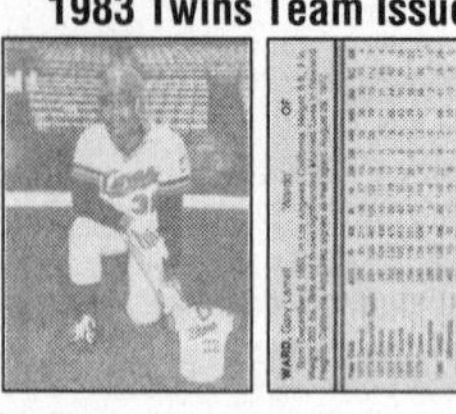

This 36-card set measures the standard size. The fronts feature borderless color player photos with a miniature representation of the player's jersey superimposed on the picture at the bottom. On a white background, biographical information and statistics are printed in red and blue.

Nm-Mt Ex-Mt
COMPLETE SET (36) 6.00 2.40
1 John Castino .10 .04
2 Jim Eisenreich .75 .30
3 Ray Smith .10 .04
4 Scott Ullger .10 .04
5 Gary Gaetti 1.50 .60
6 Mickey Hatcher .25 .10
7 Bobby Mitchell .10 .04
8 Len Faedo .10 .04
9 Kent Hrbek .75 .30
10 Tim Laudner .10 .04
11 Frank Viola .75 .30
12 Bryan Oelkers .10 .04
13 Rick Lysander .10 .04
14 Dave Engle .10 .04
15 Len Whitehouse .10 .04
16 Pete Filson .10 .04
17 Tom Brunansky .25 .10
18 Randy Bush .10 .04
19 Brad Havens .10 .04
20 Al Williams .10 .04
21 Gary Ward .10 .04
22 Jack O'Connor .10 .04
23 Robert Castillo .10 .04
24 Ron Washington .10 .04
25 Ron Davis .10 .04
26 Tom Kelly CO .25 .10
27 Billy Gardner MG .10 .04
28 Rich Stelmaszek CO .10 .04
29 Jim Lemon CO .10 .04
30 Johnny Podres CO .25 .10
31 Tim Laudner .50 .20
Jim Eisenreich
Kent Hrbek
32 Ray Smith .10 .04
Dave Engle
Tim Laudner
33 Tom Brunansky .25 .10
Gary Gaetti
Gary Ward
Kent Hrbek
34 Tom Kelly CO .10 .04
Rick Stelmaszek CO
Billy Gardner MG
Jim Lemon CO
Johnny Podres CO
35 Team Photo .10 .04
36 Metrodome CL .10 .04

1984 Twins Postcards

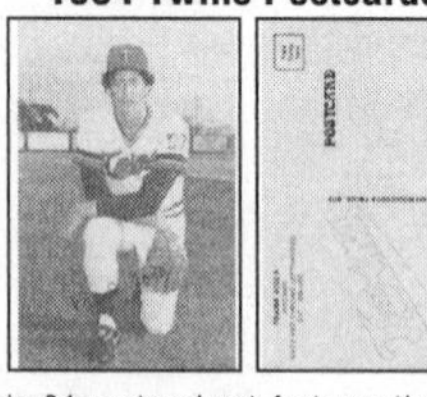

This 34-postcard set features the 1984 Minnesota Twins Baseball Team and features borderless color player photos with a simulated autograph. The backs display a postcard format. The cards are unnumbered and checklisted below in alphabetical order.

Nm-Mt Ex-Mt
COMPLETE SET (34) 10.00 4.00
1 Darrell Brown .25 .10
2 Tom Brunansky .50 .20
3 Randy Bush .25 .10
4 John Butcher .25 .10
5 Bobby Castillo .25 .10
6 John Castino .25 .10
7 Keith Comstock .25 .10
8 Ron Davis .25 .10
9 Jim Eisenreich 1.00 .40
10 Dave Engle .25 .10
11 Lenny Faedo .25 .10
12 Pete Filson .25 .10
13 Gary Gaetti 1.00 .40
14 Billy Gardner .25 .10
15 Mickey Hatcher .25 .10
16 Kent Hrbek .50 .20
17 Houston Jimenez .25 .10
18 Tim Laudner .25 .10
19 Tom Kelly CO .50 .20
20 Jim Lemon CO .25 .10
21 Dave Meier .25 .10
22 Larry Pashnick .25 .10
23 Johnny Podres CO .50 .20
24 Jeff Reed .25 .10
25 Ken Schrom .25 .10
26 Mike Smithson .25 .10
27 Rick Stelmaszek .25 .10
28 Tim Teufel .50 .20
29 Frank Viola .75 .30
30 Mike Walters .25 .10
31 Ron Washington .25 .10
32 Al Williams .25 .10
33 Metrodome .25 .10
34 Team Picture .25 .10

1984 Twins Team Issue

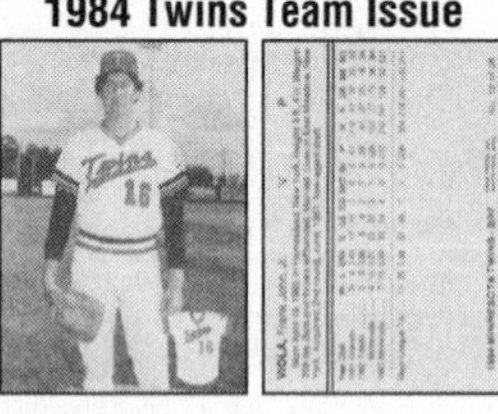

This 36-card set features borderless color player photos of the Minnesota Twins with a small jersey replica in the bottom right displaying the player's jersey number. The backs carry player information and statistics.

Nm-Mt Ex-Mt
COMPLETE SET (36) 6.00 2.40
1 John Castino .10 .04
2 Jim Eisenreich .50 .20
3 Houston Jimenez .10 .04
4 Dave Meier .10 .04
5 Gary Gaetti .75 .30
6 Mickey Hatcher .10 .04
7 Jeff Reed .10 .04
8 Tim Teufel .10 .04
9 Lenny Faedo .10 .04
10 Kent Hrbek .25 .10
11 Tim Laudner .10 .04
12 Frank Viola .50 .20
13 Ken Schrom .10 .04
14 Larry Pashnick .10 .04
15 Dave Engle .10 .04
16 Keith Comstock .10 .04
17 Pete Filson .10 .04
18 Tom Brunansky .25 .10
19 Randy Bush .10 .04
20 Darrell Brown .10 .04
21 Al Williams .10 .04
22 Mike Walters .10 .04
23 John Butcher .10 .04
24 Bobby Castillo .10 .04
25 Ron Washington .10 .04
26 Ron Davis .10 .04
27 Tom Kelly CO .25 .10
28 Billy Gardner MG .10 .04
29 Rick Stelmaszek CO .10 .04
30 Jim Lemon CO .10 .04
31 Johnny Podres CO .25 .10
32 Mike Smithson .10 .04
33 Harmon Killebrew 1.00 .40
34 Twins Team Picture .10 .04
35 Twins Logo Card .10 .04
36 Metrodome CL .10 .04

1985 Twins Postcards

This 33-card set features photos of the Minnesota Twins on postcard-size cards. The All-Star Game logo appears in the upper right. The cards are unnumbered and checklisted below in alphabetical order. Kirby Puckett appears in his Rookie Card year.

Nm-Mt Ex-Mt
COMPLETE SET (33) 20.00 8.00
1 Tom Brunansky .75 .30
2 Randy Bush .50 .20
3 John Butcher .50 .20
4 Andre David .50 .20
5 Ron Davis .50 .20
6 Dave Engle .50 .20
7 Alvaro Espinoza .50 .20
8 Pete Filson .50 .20
9 Gary Gaetti 1.00 .40
10 Greg Gagne .50 .20
11 Billy Gardner MG .50 .20
12 Mickey Hatcher .50 .20
13 Kent Hrbek .75 .30
14 Tom Kelly CO .50 .20
15 Tom Klawitter .50 .20
16 Tim Laudner .50 .20
17 Rick Lysander .50 .20
18 Dave Meier .50 .20
19 Tony Oliva CO 1.50 .60
20 Johnny Podres CO .75 .30
21 Kirby Puckett 5.00 2.00
22 Mark Salas .50 .20
23 Ken Schrom .50 .20
24 Roy Smalley .50 .20
25 Mike Smithson .50 .20
26 Rick Stelmaszek CO .50 .20
27 Mike Stenhouse .50 .20
28 Tim Teufel .50 .20
29 Frank Viola .75 .30
30 Curt Wardle .50 .20
31 Ron Washington .50 .20
32 Len Whitehouse .50 .20
33 Rich Yett .50 .20

1985 Twins 7-Eleven

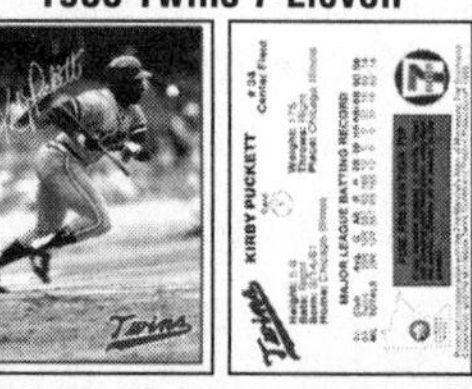

This 13-card set of Minnesota Twins was produced and distributed by the Twins in conjunction with the 7-Eleven stores and the Fire Marshall's Association. The cards measure approximately 2 1/2" by 3 1/2" and are in full color. Supposedly 20,000 sets of cards were distributed during the promotion which began on June 2nd and lasted throughout the month of July. The card backs have some statistics and a fire safety tip. The set features an early Kirby Puckett card.

Nm-Mt Ex-Mt
COMPLETE SET (13) 12.00 4.80
1 Kirby Puckett 5.00 2.00
2 Frank Viola .75 .30
3 Mickey Hatcher .50 .20
4 Kent Hrbek 1.00 .40
5 John Butcher .50 .20
6 Roy Smalley .75 .30
7 Tom Brunansky .75 .30
8 Ron Davis .50 .20
9 Gary Gaetti 1.50 .60
10 Tim Teufel .50 .20
11 Mike Smithson .50 .20
12 Tim Laudner .50 .20
NNO Checklist Card .50 .20

1985 Twins Team Issue

This 36-card set measures the standard size. The fronts feature borderless color player photos with a miniature representation of the player's jersey superimposed on the picture at the lower right corner. The "1985 All-Star Game" logo in the lower left corner rounds out the card face. On a white background, the horizontally oriented backs carry biographical information and statistics printed in red and blue. Kirby Puckett appears in his Rookie Card year.

Nm-Mt Ex-Mt
COMPLETE SET (36) 6.00 2.40
1 Alvaro Espinoza .10 .04
2 Roy Smalley .25 .10
3 Tony Oliva CO .50 .20
4 Dave Meier .10 .04
5 Gary Gaetti .75 .30
6 Mickey Hatcher .25 .10
7 Jeff Reed .10 .04
8 Tim Teufel .10 .04
9 Mark Salas .10 .04
10 Kent Hrbek .50 .20
11 Tim Laudner .10 .04
12 Frank Viola .50 .20
13 Ken Schrom .10 .04
14 Rick Lysander .10 .04
15 Dave Engle .10 .04
16 Andre David .10 .04
17 Len Whitehouse .10 .04
18 Pete Filson .10 .04
19 Tom Brunansky .25 .10
20 Randy Bush .10 .04
21 Greg Gagne .10 .04
22 John Butcher .10 .04
23 Mike Stenhouse .10 .04
24 Kirby Puckett 1.50 .60
25 Tom Klawitter .10 .04
26 Curt Wardle .10 .04
27 Rich Yett .10 .04
28 Ron Washington .10 .04
29 Ron Davis .10 .04
30 Tom Kelly CO .25 .10
31 Bill Gardner MG .10 .04
32 Rick Stelmaszek CO .10 .04
33 Johnny Podres CO .25 .10
34 Mike Smithson .10 .04
35 All-Star Game Logo .10 .04
36 Twins Logo/Checklist .10 .04

1986 Twins Greats TCMA

This 12-card standard-size set features some of the best Minnesota Twins from their first 25 seasons. These cards have player photos on the front and player information on the back.

Nm-Mt Ex-Mt
COMPLETE SET (12) 5.00 2.00
1 Harmon Killebrew 1.00 .40
2 Rod Carew 1.50 .60
3 Zoilo Versalles .25 .10
4 Cesar Tovar .25 .10
5 Bob Allison .50 .20
6 Larry Hisle .25 .10
7 Tony Oliva .75 .30
8 Earl Battey .25 .10
9 Jim Perry .50 .20
10 Jim Kaat .75 .30
11 Al Worthington .25 .10
12 Sam Mele MG .25 .10

1986 Twins Team Issue

These cards feature members of the 1986 Minnesota Twins. Players, coaches and the manager are included in this set. The 25th anniversary logo is in the upper right hand corner of each card.

Nm-Mt Ex-Mt
COMPLETE SET (36) 6.00 2.40
1 Chris Pittaro .10 .04
2 Steve Lombardozzi .10 .04
3 Roy Smalley .25 .10
4 Tony Oliva CO .50 .20
5 Gary Gaetti .75 .30
6 Mickey Hatcher .25 .10
7 Jeff Reed .10 .04
8 Mark Salas .10 .04
9 Kent Hrbek .50 .20
10 Tim Laudner .10 .04
11 Frank Viola .25 .10
12 Dennis Burtt .10 .04
13 Alex Sanchez .10 .04
14 Roy Smith .10 .04
15 Billy Beane .10 .04
16 Pete Filson .10 .04
17 Tom Brunansky .25 .10
18 Randy Bush .10 .04
19 Frank Eufemia .10 .04
20 Mark Davidson .10 .04
21 Bert Blyleven .50 .20
22 Greg Gagne .25 .10
23 John Butcher .10 .04
24 Kirby Puckett 1.25 .50
25 Bill Latham .10 .04
26 Ron Washington .10 .04
27 Ron Davis .10 .04
28 Tom Kelly CO .25 .10
29 Dick Such CO .10 .04
30 Rick Stelmaszek CO .10 .04
31 Ray Miller MG .10 .04
32 Wayne Terwilliger CO .10 .04
33 Mike Smithson .10 .04
34 Al Woods .10 .04
35 Team Photo .25 .10
36 Twins Logo/Checklist .10 .04

1987 Twins Postcards

This 32-card set features photos of the 1987 Minnesota Twins on postcard-size cards. The cards are unnumbered and checklisted below in alphabetical order.

Nm-Mt Ex-Mt
COMPLETE SET (32) 15.00 6.00
1 Keith Atherton .50 .20
2 Juan Berenguer .50 .20
3 Bert Blyleven 1.00 .40
4 Tom Brunansky .75 .30
5 Randy Bush .50 .20
6 Mark Davidson .50 .20
7 George Frazier .50 .20
8 Gary Gaetti 1.00 .40
9 Greg Gagne .50 .20
10 Dan Gladden .50 .20
11 Kent Hrbek .75 .30
12 Tom Kelly MG .75 .30
13 Joe Klink .50 .20
14 Tim Laudner .50 .20
15 Steve Lombardozzi .50 .20
16 Al Newman .50 .20
17 Tom Nieto .50 .20
18 Tony Oliva CO 1.00 .40
19 Mark Portugal .50 .20
20 Kirby Puckett 1.50 .60
21 Jeff Reardon .75 .30
22 Rick Renick CO .50 .20
23 Mark Salas .50 .20
24 Roy Smalley .75 .30
25 Mike Smithson .50 .20
26 Rick Stelmaszek CO .50 .20
27 Dick Such CO .50 .20
28 Les Straker .50 .20
29 Wayne Terwilliger CO .50 .20
30 Frank Viola .75 .30
31 Team Photo .50 .20
32 Team Logo .50 .20

1987 Twins Team Issue

This 33-card standard-size set features borderless color player photos of the 1987 Minnesota Twins World Championship Team. There are two versions of this set. One features the 1987 World Championship Logo, the other does not. We have priced the version with the logo which was pulled from circulation shortly after released. The backs carry player information and season statistics. The cards were pulled from distribution after a dispute with the Commissioner's office.

Nm-Mt Ex-Mt
COMPLETE SET (33) 40.00 16.00
1 Steve Lombardozzi 1.00 .40
2 Roy Smalley 1.00 .40
3 Tony Oliva CO 2.50 1.00
4 Greg Gagne 1.00 .40
5 Gary Gaetti 2.50 1.00
6 Gene Larkin 1.50 .60
7 Tom Kelly MG 2.00 .80
8 Kent Hrbek 1.00 .40
9 Tim Laudner 1.00 .40
10 Frank Viola 1.50 .60
11 Les Straker 1.00 .40
12 Don Baylor 2.00 .80
13 George Frazier 1.00 .40
14 Keith Atherton 1.00 .40
15 Tom Brunansky 1.50 .60
16 Randy Bush 1.00 .40
17 Al Newman 1.00 .40
18 Mark Davidson 1.00 .40
19 Bert Blyleven 2.00 .80
20 Dan Schatzeder 1.00 .40
21 Dan Gladden 1.00 .40
22 Sal Butera 1.00 .40
23 Kirby Puckett 10.00 4.00
24 Joe Niekro 1.50 .60
25 Juan Berenguer 1.00 .40
26 Jeff Reardon 1.50 .60
27 Dick Such CO 1.00 .40
28 Rick Stelmaszek CO 1.00 .40
29 Rick Renick CO 1.00 .40
30 Wayne Terwilliger CO 1.00 .40
31 1987 Team Photo 1.00 .40
32 Twins Championship Logo 1.00 .40
33 Twins Logo/Checklist 1.00 .40

1988 Twins Master Bread Discs

Master Bread introduced a set of 12 discs produced in conjunction with the Major League Baseball Players Association and Mike Schechter Associates. The set commemorates the Minnesota Twins' World Championship the year before and features only Twins players. A single disc was inserted inside each loaf of bread. The discs are numbered on the back and have a medium blue border on the front. Discs are approximately 2 3/4" in diameter. The disc backs contain very sparse personal or statistical information about the player and are printed in blue on white stock.

Nm-Mt Ex-Mt
COMPLETE SET (12) 8.00 3.20
1 Bert Blyleven 1.00 .40
2 Frank Viola 1.00 .40
3 Juan Berenguer .50 .20
4 Jeff Reardon .75 .30
5 Tim Laudner .50 .20
6 Steve Lombardozzi .50 .20
7 Randy Bush .50 .20
8 Kirby Puckett 2.50 1.00
9 Gary Gaetti .75 .30
10 Kent Hrbek 1.50 .60
11 Greg Gagne .50 .20
12 Tom Brunansky .50 .20

1988 Twins Smokey Colorgrams

These cards are actually pages of a booklet featuring members of the Minnesota Twins and Smokey's fire safety tips. The booklet has 12 pages each containing a black and white photo card (approximately 2 1/2" by 3 3/4") and a black and white player caricature (oversized head) postcard (approximately 3 3/4" by 5 5/8"). The cards are unnumbered but they have biographical information and a fire-prevention cartoon on the back of the card.

Nm-Mt Ex-Mt
COMPLETE SET (12) 15.00 6.00
1 Frank Viola 1.50 .60
2 Gary Gaetti 2.00 .80
3 Kent Hrbek 1.50 .60
4 Jeff Reardon 1.50 .60
5 Gene Larkin 1.00 .40
6 Bert Blyleven 1.50 .60
7 Tim Laudner 1.00 .40
8 Greg Gagne 1.25 .50
9 Randy Bush 1.00 .40
10 Dan Gladden 1.00 .40
11 Al Newman 1.00 .40
12 Kirby Puckett 5.00 2.00

1992 Twins Photos

These photos feature members of the 1991 World Champion Minnesota Twins.

Nm-Mt Ex-Mt
COMPLETE SET 10.00 3.00
1 Tom Kelly MG .25 .07
2 Minnesota Twins .25 .07
3 Terry Crowley CO .25 .07
4 Ron Gardenhire CO .25 .07
5 Tony Oliva CO 1.00 .30
6 Dick Such CO .25 .07
7 Wayne Terrwilliger CO .25 .07
8 Rick Aguilera .50 .15
9 Steve Bedrosian .25 .07
10 Allen Anderson .25 .07
11 Randy Bush .25 .07
12 Chili Davis .75 .23
13 Scott Erickson .75 .23
14 Dan Gladden .25 .07
15 Brian Harper .25 .07
16 Greg Gagne .25 .07
17 Chuck Knoblauch 1.00 .30
18 Terry Leach .25 .07
19 Gene Larkin .25 .07
20 Kent Hrbek .75 .23
21 Al Newman .25 .07
22 Shane Mack .25 .07
23 Jack Morris 1.00 .30
24 Scott Leius .25 .07
25 Junior Ortiz .25 .07
26 Kevin Tapani .25 .07
27 Kirby Puckett 1.50 .45
28 Carl Willis .25 .07
29 Gene Larkin WS .25 .07

2003 Twins Team Issue

These cards feature photographs taken by Barry Colla. Each of these photos feature a full color photo of the player surrounded by blue borders. Each of these photos are have numbers ending in 03.

MINT NRMT
COMPLETE SET 10.00 4.50
73 Cristian Guzman .75 .35
74 Torii Hunter 1.50 .70
75 Corey Koskie .75 .35
76 Joe Mauer 3.00 1.35
77 Doug Mientkiewicz 1.00 .45
78 A.J. Pierzynski .75 .35
79 Kirby Puckett 2.00 .90
80 Brad Radke .75 .35
81 J.C. Romero .75 .35
82 Johan Santana .75 .35
83 T.C. (The Bear Mascot) .50 .23

1994 U.S. Department of Transportation

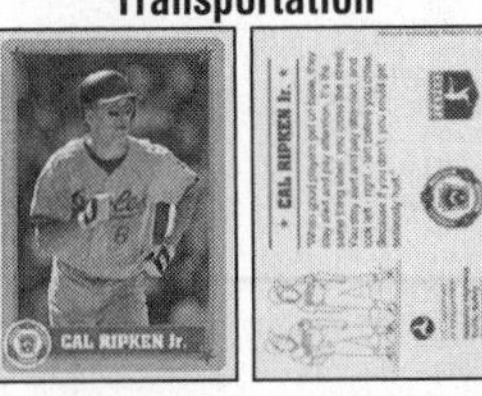

These strip of three cards was co-sponsored by the U.S. Department of Transportation and the National Highway Traffic Safety Administration. The cards were reportedly given out at the Little League World Series. The 8" by 3 1/2" strip is not perforated, but if the cards were cut along the dotted lines, they would measure the standard size. The cards are unnumbered and checklisted below in alphabetical order.

Nm-Mt Ex-Mt
COMPLETE SET (6) 15.00 4.50
1 Mike Piazza 4.00 1.20
2 Cal Ripken 6.00 1.80
3 Mo Vaughn 1.50 .45
4 Orel Hershiser 1.50 .45
5 Don Mattingly 3.00 .90
6 Mike Mussina 2.50 .75

1991 U.S. Game Systems Baseball Legends

These cards feature leading all time greats. Each player is given one card (Ace, Queen, etc.) in all four suits. This set was issued in its own card box and we have used 1 for Ace, 11 for Jacks, 12 for Queens and 13 for Kings.

Nm-Mt Ex-Mt
COMP. FACT SET (56) 5.00 1.50
1C Ty Cobb .50 .15
1D Ty Cobb .50 .15
1H Ty Cobb .50 .15
1S Ty Cobb .50 .15
2C Babe Ruth .75 .23
2D Babe Ruth .75 .23
2H Babe Ruth .75 .23
2S Babe Ruth .75 .23
3C Lou Gehrig .50 .15
3D Lou Gehrig .50 .15
3H Lou Gehrig .50 .15
3S Lou Gehrig .50 .15
4C Hank Aaron .50 .15
4D Hank Aaron .50 .15
4H Hank Aaron .50 .15
4S Hank Aaron .50 .15
5C Satchel Paige .30 .09
5D Satchel Paige .30 .09
5H Satchel Paige .30 .09
5S Satchel Paige .30 .09
6C Jimmie Foxx .20 .06
6D Jimmie Foxx .20 .06
6H Jimmie Foxx .20 .06
6S Jimmie Foxx .20 .06
7C Rogers Hornsby .20 .06
7D Rogers Hornsby .20 .06
7H Rogers Hornsby .20 .06
7S Rogers Hornsby .20 .06
8C Stan Musial .50 .15
8D Stan Musial .50 .15
8H Stan Musial .50 .15
8S Stan Musial .50 .15
9C Walter Johnson .20 .06
9D Walter Johnson .20 .06
9H Walter Johnson .20 .06
9S Walter Johnson .20 .06
10C Honus Wagner .20 .06
10D Honus Wagner .20 .06
10H Honus Wagner .20 .06
10S Honus Wagner .20 .06
11C Roberto Clemente .50 .15
11D Roberto Clemente .50 .15
11H Roberto Clemente .50 .15
11S Roberto Clemente .50 .15
12C Christy Mathewson .20 .06
12D Christy Mathewson .20 .06
12H Christy Mathewson .20 .06
12S Christy Mathewson .20 .06
13A Cy Young .20 .06
13C Cy Young .20 .06
13D Cy Young .20 .06
13H Cy Young .20 .06
NNO Title Card .10 .03

1990 U.S. Playing Cards All-Stars

Thse 56 playing standard-size cards have rounded corners and feature color posed and action player photos on white-bordered fronts. The cards are checklisted in playing card order by suits and assigned numbers to aces (1), jacks (11), queens (12), and kings (13). A limited Silver Series parallel set was produced distinguished from the regular set by the silver foil on the cards' edges.

Nm-Mt Ex-Mt
COMP. FACT SET (56) 6.00 1.80
1C Bob Welch .05 .02
1D Frank Viola .05 .02
1H Ramon Martinez .05 .02
1S Roger Clemens 1.00 .30
2C Lance Parrish .05 .02
2D Greg Olson .05 .02
2H Mike Scioscia .10 .03
2S Sandy Alomar .10 .03
3C Bret Saberhagen .05 .02
3D Dennis Martinez .10 .03
3H Jeff Brantley .10 .03
3S Randy Johnson .50 .15
4C Gregg Olson .05 .02
4D Roberto Alomar .25 .07
4H Ryne Sandberg .50 .15
4S Steve Sax .05 .02
5C Brook Jacoby .05 .02
5D Tim Wallach .05 .02
5H Chris Sabo .05 .02
5S Kelly Gruber .05 .02
6C Ozzie Guillen .10 .03
6D Barry Larkin .25 .07
6H Ozzie Smith .75 .23
6S Cal Ripken 2.00 .60
7C Ellis Burks .15 .04
7D Neal Heaton .05 .02
7H John Franco .10 .03
7S Doug Jones .05 .02
8C Dennis Eckersley .40 .12
8D Dave Smith .05 .02
8H Matt Williams .15 .04
8S Kirby Puckett .50 .15
9C Bobby Thigpen .05 .02
9D Lenny Dykstra .05 .02
9H Andre Dawson .15 .04
9S Chuck Finley .10 .03
10C Dave Stieb .05 .02
10D Shawon Dunston .05 .02
10H Benito Santiago .10 .03
10S Alan Trammell .15 .04
11C Wade Boggs .50 .15
11D Tony Gwynn 1.00 .30
11H Bobby Bonilla .05 .02
11S Ken Griffey Jr. 1.25 .35
12C George Bell .05 .02
12D Will Clark .40 .12
12H Kevin Mitchell .05 .02
12S Dave Parker .05 .02
13C Rickey Henderson .50 .15
13D Barry Bonds 1.00 .30
13H Darryl Strawberry .10 .03
13S Cecil Fielder .10 .03
JKO Jack Armstrong .05 .02
JKO Julio Franco .10 .03
WCO Mark McGwire 1.00 .30
Jose Canseco
WCO Rob Dibble .05 .02
Randy Myers

1991 U.S. Playing Cards All-Stars

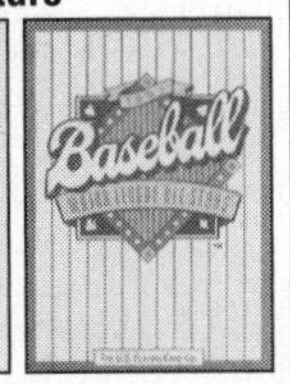

Thse 56 playing standard-size cards have rounded corners and feature color posed and action player photos on white-bordered fronts. The cards are checklisted in playing card order by suits and assigned numbers to aces (1), jacks (11), queens (12), and kings (13). A limited Silver Series parallel set was produced distinguished from the regular set by the silver foil on the cards' edges.

Nm-Mt Ex-Mt
COMP. FACT SET (56) 6.00 1.80
1C Tony Gwynn 1.00 .30
1D Ken Griffey Jr. 1.00 .30
1H Jack Morris .10 .03
1S Tom Glavine .40 .12
2C Paul O'Neill .25 .07
2D Carlton Fisk .50 .15
2H Ozzie Guillen .10 .03
2S Eddie Murray .50 .15
3C John Smiley .05 .02
3D Scott Sanderson .05 .02
3H Jack McDowell .05 .02
3S Pete Harnisch .05 .02
4C Howard Johnson .05 .02
4D Kirby Puckett .50 .15
4H Joe Carter .15 .04
4S John Kruk .10 .03
5C Mike Morgan .05 .02
5D Jeff Reardon .05 .02
5H Mark Langston .05 .02
5S Tom Browning .05 .02
6C Barry Larkin .25 .07
6D Rafael Palmeiro .25 .07
6H Julio Franco .10 .03
6S George Bell .05 .02
7C Frank Viola .05 .02
7D Bryan Harvey .05 .02
7H Rick Aguilera .10 .03
7S Dennis Martinez .10 .03
8C Juan Samuel .05 .02
8D Jimmy Key .05 .02
8H Paul Molitor .40 .12
8S Brett Butler .05 .02
9C Craig Biggio .15 .04
9D Harold Baines .05 .02
9H Ruben Sierra .10 .03
9S Felix Jose .05 .02
10C Lee Smith .10 .03
10D Dennis Eckersley .40 .12
10H Roger Clemens 1.00 .30
10S Rob Dibble .05 .02
11C Andre Dawson .25 .07
11D Sandy Alomar .05 .02
11H Rickey Henderson .75 .23
11S Benito Santiago .10 .03
12C Chris Sabo .05 .02
12D Cecil Fielder .10 .03
12H Roberto Alomar .25 .07
12S Ryne Sandberg .60 .18
13C Ivan Calderon .05 .02
13D Cal Ripken 2.00 .60
13H Dave Henderson .05 .02
13S Ozzie Smith .60 .18
JKO Bobby Bonilla .05 .02
JKO Danny Tartabull .05 .02
WCO Wade Boggs .40 .12
WCO Will Clark .25 .07

1992 U.S. Playing Cards All-Stars

Thse 54 playing standard-size cards have rounded corners and feature color posed and action player photos on white-bordered fronts. The cards are checklisted in playing card order by suits and assigned numbers to aces (1), jacks (11), queens (12), and kings (13).

Nm-Mt Ex-Mt
COMP. FACT SET (54) 5.00 1.50
1C Jose Canseco .50 .15
1D Julio Franco .10 .03
1H Cecil Fielder .10 .03
1S Denny Martinez .10 .03
2C Chili Davis .10 .03
2D Danny Tartabull .05 .02
2H Juan Gonzalez UER .50 .15
Card spelled Gonzales
2S Mike Moore .05 .02
3C Mickey Tettleton .05 .02
3D Tony Gwynn 1.00 .30
3H Andre Dawson .30 .09
3S Nolan Ryan 2.00 .60
4C Danny Tartabull .05 .02
4D Frank Thomas .50 .15
4H Ron Gant .10 .03
4S Jim Abbott .05 .02
5C Fred McGriff .20 .06
5D Hal Morris .05 .02
5H Fred McGriff .20 .06
5S Bill Wegman .05 .02
6C Andre Dawson .30 .09
6D Kirby Puckett .50 .15
6H Joe Carter .10 .03
6S Mike Morgan .05 .02
7C Frank Thomas .50 .15
7D Terry Pendleton .05 .02
7H Frank Thomas .50 .15
7S Jose DeLeon .05 .02
8C Ron Gant .05 .02
8D Rafael Palmeiro .30 .09
8H Cal Ripken Jr UER 2.00 .60
Spelled Ripkin
8S Pete Harnisch .05 .02
9C Joe Carter .05 .02
9D Cal Ripken Jr UER 2.00 .60
Spelled Ripkin
9H Ruben Sierra .10 .03
9S Tom Candiotti .05 .02
10C Matt Williams .20 .06
10D Paul Molitor .40 .12
10H Barry Bonds 1.00 .30
10S Roger Clemens 1.00 .30
11C Cal Ripken Jr UER 2.00 .60
Spelled Ripkin
11D Ken Griffey Jr 1.00 .30
11H Will Clark .30 .09
11S Tim Belcher .05 .02
12C Howard Johnson .05 .02
12D Willie Randolph .10 .03
12H Howard Johnson .05 .02
12S Tom Glavine .40 .12
13C Cecil Fielder .10 .03
13D Wade Boggs .60 .18
13H Jose Canseco .40 .12
13S Jose Rijo .05 .02
JKA Roger Clemens 1.00 .30
JKN Tom Glavine .40 .12

1993 U.S. Playing Cards Aces

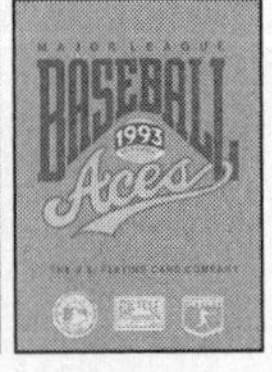

This 55-card standard-size set features the top 13 players in four categories according to suits: lowest ERA's, (spades) Most Stolen Bases, (hearts) Most Home Runs, (clubs) and Highest Batting Average (diamonds). Since this set is similar to a playing card set, the set is checklisted as if it were a playing card deck. In the checklist C means Clubs, D means Diamonds, H means Hearts, S means Spades, and JK means Joker. The cards are checklisted in playing order by suits and numbers are assigned to Aces, (1) Jacks, (11) Queens, (12) and Kings (13). The Jokers, Wild Card, and the title card are unnumbered and listed at the end. A few players signed some limited cards for this set. Due to market scarcity, those cards are unpriced but more information is greatly appreciated.

Nm-Mt Ex-Mt
COMP. FACT SET (56) 6.00 1.80
1C Juan Gonzalez .40 .12
1D Edgar Martinez .15 .04
1H Marquis Grissom .10 .03
1S Bill Swift .05 .02
2C Dave Hollins .05 .02
2D Roberto Alomar .25 .07
2H Chad Curtis .05 .02
2S Tom Glavine .40 .12
3C Darren Daulton .10 .03
3D Terry Pendleton .05 .02
3H Ozzie Smith .75 .23
3S Sid Fernandez .05 .02
4C Ken Griffey Jr. 1.00 .30
4D Carlos Baerga .10 .03
4H Bip Roberts .05 .02
4S Greg Swindell .05 .02
5C Rob Deer .05 .02
5D Shane Mack .05 .02
5H Steve Finley .10 .03
5S Juan Guzman .05 .02
6C Mickey Tettleton .05 .02
6D Tony Gwynn 1.00 .30
6H Tim Raines .10 .03
6S Jose Rijo .05 .02
7C Gary Sheffield .40 .12
7D Paul Molitor .40 .12
7H Delino DeShields .05 .02
7S Mike Morgan .05 .02
8C Joe Carter .15 .04
8D Frank Thomas .50 .15
8H Rickey Henderson .60 .18
8S Mike Mussina .25 .07
9C Albert Belle .10 .03
9D Bip Roberts .05 .02
9H Roberto Alomar .25 .07
9S Dennis Martinez .10 .03
10C Barry Bonds 1.00 .30
10D John Kruk .05 .02
10H Luis Polonia .05 .02
10S Kevin Appier .05 .02
11C Fred McGriff .15 .04
11D Andy Van Slyke .05 .02
11H Brady Anderson .10 .03
11S Roger Clemens 1.00 .30
12C Cecil Fielder .10 .03
12D Kirby Puckett .50 .15
12H Pat Listach .05 .02
12S Curt Schilling .40 .12
13C Mark McGwire 1.50 .45
13D Gary Sheffield .40 .12
13H Kenny Lofton .40 .12
13S Greg Maddux 1.25 .35
WCO Cal Ripken 2.00 .60
JKO American League Logo .05 .02
WCOA Cal Ripken AU
AU1 Terry Pendleton AU
3 Diamonds Auto
AU2 Fred McGriff AU
Jack of Clubs autographed
NNO Title Card .05 .02

1993 U.S. Playing Cards Rookies

These 56 playing cards from the Bicycle Sports Collection feature outstanding 1992 rookies. The set is checklisted in playing card order by suits and assigned numbers to Aces (1), Jacks (11), Queens (12), Kings (13), and Jokers (JK).

Nm-Mt Ex-Mt
COMP. FACT SET (56) 5.00 1.50
1C Kenny Lofton .75 .23
1D Dave Fleming .05 .02
1H Pat Listach .05 .02
1S Eric Karros .50 .15
2C Eric Fox .05 .02
2D Reggie Jefferson .05 .02
2H Pat Mahomes .05 .02
2S Butch Henry .05 .02
3C Mark Wohlers .05 .02
3D Anthony Young .05 .02
3H Greg Colbrunn .05 .02
3S Wilfredo Cordero .05 .02
4C John Patterson .05 .02
4D Kevin Koslofski .05 .02
4H Dan Walters .05 .02
4S Pedro Astacio .05 .02
5C Eric Young .10 .03
5D Brian Williams .05 .02
5H John Vander Wal .05 .02
5S Derek Bell .05 .02
6C Arthur Rhodes .05 .02
6D Brian Jordan .40 .12
6H Jeff Branson .05 .02
6S David Nied .05 .02
7C Jeff Frye .05 .02
7D John Doherty .05 .02
7H Monty Fariss .05 .02
7S Jeff Kent 1.00 .30
8C Scott Servais .05 .02
8D Lenny Webster .05 .02
8H Rey Sanchez .05 .02
8S David Haas .05 .02
9C Ruben Amaro .05 .02
9D Roberto Hernandez .25 .07
9H Robert Wickman .05 .02
9S Eddie Taubensee .05 .02
10C Reggie Sanders .10 .03
10D Frank Seminara .05 .02
10H Derrick May .05 .02
10S Royce Clayton .05 .02
11C Alan Mills .05 .02
11D Scott Cooper .05 .02
11H Donovan Osborne .05 .02
11S Moises Alou .25 .07
12C Bob Zupcic .05 .02
12D Andy Stankiewicz .05 .02
12H Scott Livingstone .05 .02
12S Rusty Meacham .05 .02
13C Cal Eldred .05 .02
13D Tim Wakefield .15 .04
13H Gary DiSarcina .05 .02
13S Chad Curtis .05 .02
JK Pat Listach AL ROY .05 .02
NNO Alphabetical Checklist .05 .02

1994 U.S. Playing Cards Aces

These 56 playing standard-size cards have rounded corners, and feature borderless color posed and action player photos on their fronts. The set is checklisted in playing card order by suits and assigned numbers to aces (1), jacks (11), queens (12), and kings (13).

Nm-Mt Ex-Mt
COMP. FACT SET (56) 6.00 1.80
1C Barry Bonds 1.00 .30
1D Andres Galarraga .25 .07
1H Kenny Lofton .15 .04
1S Greg Maddux 1.25 .35
2C Phil Plantier .05 .02
2D John Kruk .05 .02
2H Brett Butler .05 .02
2S Tom Candiotti .05 .02
3C Bobby Bonilla .10 .03
3D Frank Thomas .50 .15
3H Eric Young .10 .03
3S Jimmy Key .05 .02
4C Mike Piazza 1.25 .35
4D Mike Piazza 1.25 .35
4H Delino DeShields .05 .02
4S Jack McDowell .05 .02
5C Ron Gant .10 .03
5D Jeff Bagwell .50 .15
5H Darren Lewis .05 .02
5S John Burkett .05 .02
6C Rafael Palmeiro .25 .07
6D Carlos Baerga .10 .03
6H Gregg Jefferies .05 .02
6S Tom Glavine .40 .12
7C Fred McGriff .15 .04
7D Mark Grace .25 .07
7H Otis Nixon .05 .02
7S Pete Harnisch .05 .02
8C Matt Williams .10 .03
8D Kenny Lofton .15 .04
8H Chad Curtis .05 .02
8S Wilson Alvarez .05 .02
9C Albert Belle .10 .03
9D Roberto Alomar .25 .07
9H Rickey Henderson .60 .18
9S Steve Avery .05 .02
10C David Justice .25 .07
10D Paul Molitor .40 .12
10H Marquis Grissom .10 .03
10S Bill Swift .05 .02
11C Frank Thomas .50 .15
11D Barry Bonds 1.00 .30
11H Luis Polonia .05 .02
11S Mark Portugal .05 .02
12C Ken Griffey Jr. 1.00 .30
12D Gregg Jefferies .05 .02
12H Roberto Alomar .25 .07
12S Kevin Appier .05 .02
13C Juan Gonzalez .40 .12
13D John Olerud .10 .03
13H Chuck Carr .05 .02
13S Jose Rijo .05 .02
NNO Featured Players .05 .02

1994 U.S. Playing Cards Rookies

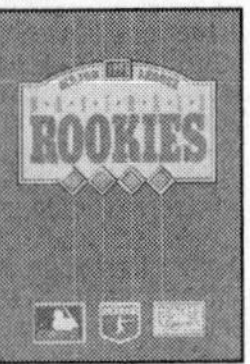

These 56 playing standard-size cards have rounded corners, and feature color posed and action player photos on their white-bordered fronts. The set is checklisted in playing card order by suits and assigned numbers to aces (1), jacks (11), queens (12), and kings (13).

Nm-Mt Ex-Mt
COMP. FACT SET (56) 5.00 1.50
1C Mike Piazza 1.50 .45
1D Chuck Carr .05 .02
1H Kevin Stocker .05 .02
1S Greg McMichael .05 .02
2C Vinny Castilla .25 .07
2D Jeff McNeely .05 .02
2H Alex Arias .05 .02
2S Paul Quantrill .10 .03
3C Wil Cordero .05 .02
3D Joe Kmak .05 .02

3H Carlos Garcia .05 .02
3S Steve Reed .05 .02
4C Ryan Thompson .05 .02
4D Phil Hiatt .05 .02
4H Erik Pappas .05 .02
4S Trevor Hoffman .25 .07
5C Craig Paquette .05 .02
5D Brent Gates .05 .02
5H Al Martin .05 .02
5S Tim Pugh .05 .02
6C Carlos Garcia .05 .02
6D Wil Cordero .05 .02
6H Tim Salmon .50 .15
6S Angel Miranda .05 .02
7C Jeff Conine .10 .03
7D Al Martin .05 .02
7H Mike Lansing .05 .02
7S Steve Cooke .05 .02
8C Bret Boone .25 .07
8D Wayne Kirby .05 .02
8H Rich Amaral .05 .02
8S Aaron Sele .05 .02
9C Jeromy Burnitz .25 .07
9D Lou Frazier .05 .02
9H Brent Gates .05 .02
9S Kirk Rueter .05 .02
10C J.T. Snow .25 .07
10D Carlos Garcia .05 .02
10H David Hulse .05 .02
10S Rene Arocha .05 .02
11C Al Martin .05 .02
11D Rich Amaral .05 .02
11H Troy Neel .05 .02
11S Pedro Martinez .75 .23
12C Troy Neel .05 .02
12D Mike Lansing .05 .02
12H Jeff Conine .10 .03
12S Armando Reynoso .05 .02
13C Tim Salmon .50 .15
13D David Hulse .05 .02
13H Mike Piazza 1.50 .45
13S Jason Bere .05 .02
JK Mike Piazza NL ROY .75 .23
JK Tim Salmon AL ROY .25 .07
NNO Rookie Qualification .05 .02

1995 U.S. Playing Cards Aces

This 52 standard-size card set features leading major league players. The fronts of these rounded-corner cards feature borderless full-color posed and action player shots while the backs have the 1995 Major League Baseball Aces design on a silver and black background. The team logo appears in the lower left of each picture. The player's name and position appear in a reddish-brown stripe to the right of the team logo. Since this set is similar to a playing card set, the set is checklisted as if it were a playing card deck. In the checklist C means Clubs, D means Diamonds, H means Hearts and S means Spades. The cards are checklisted in playing order by suits and numbers are assigned to Aces (1), Jacks (11), Queens (12) and Kings (13).

Nm-Mt Ex-Mt
COMP. FACT SET (52) 6.00 1.80
1C Matt Williams .15 .04
1D Tony Gwynn .75 .23
1H Kenny Lofton .15 .04
1S Greg Maddux 1.25 .35
2C Joe Carter .15 .04
2D Gregg Jefferies .05 .02
2H Brian McRae .05 .02
2S Steve Trachsel .05 .02
3C Dante Bichette .10 .03
3D Kevin Mitchell .05 .02
3H Alex Cole .05 .02
3S Randy Johnson .60 .18
4C Cecil Fielder .10 .03
4D Will Clark .25 .07
4H Barry Bonds 1.00 .30
4S Bobby Jones .05 .02
5C Kevin Mitchell .05 .02
5D Hal Morris .05 .02
5H Darren Lewis .05 .02
5S Jose Rijo .05 .02
6C Andres Galarraga .25 .07
6D Moises Alou .10 .03
6H Brady Anderson .10 .03
6S Mike Mussina .25 .07
7C Jose Canseco .40 .12
7D Paul Molitor .40 .12
7H Chuck Carr .05 .02
7S Shane Reynolds .05 .02
8C Fred McGriff .15 .04
8D Wade Boggs .60 .18
8H Chuck Knoblauch .25 .07
8S Jeff Fassero .05 .02
9C Albert Belle .10 .03
9D Kenny Lofton .15 .04
9H Marquis Grissom .10 .03
9S David Cone .10 .03
10C Barry Bonds 1.00 .30
10D Frank Thomas .50 .15
10H Deion Sanders .25 .07
10S Roger Clemens 1.00 .30
11C Frank Thomas .50 .15
11D Albert Belle .10 .03
11H Craig Biggio .15 .04
11S Doug Drabek .05 .02
12C Jeff Bagwell .50 .15
12D Paul O'Neill .10 .03
12H Otis Nixon .05 .02
12S Bret Saberhagen .05 .02
13C Ken Griffey Jr. 1.50 .45
13D Jeff Bagwell .50 .15
13H Vince Coleman .05 .02
13S Steve Ontiveros .05 .02

2000 U.S. Playing Card All Century Team

This 52 card set, issued in a playing card format, featured members of the All Century Team. We have sequenced these cards in playing card order by suit and assigned numbers to aces (1), jacks (11), queens (12) and kings (13).

Nm-Mt Ex-Mt
COMP.FACT SET
1C Willie Keeler .05 .02
1D Eddie Collins .15 .04
1H Bob Gibson .20 .06
1S Babe Ruth 1.00 .30
2C Bob Feller .10 .03
2D Robin Roberts .10 .03
2H Whitey Ford .20 .06
2S Satchel Paige .20 .06
3C Luke Appling .10 .03
3D Honus Wagner .50 .15
3H Christy Mathewson .50 .15
3S Willie McCovey .20 .06
4C Dizzy Dean .20 .06
4D Warren Spahn .15 .04
4H Ralph Kiner .10 .03
4S Joe Morgan .15 .04
5C Johnny Bench .20 .06
5D Mickey Mantle 1.00 .30
5H Juan Marichal .20 .06
5S Mel Ott .40 .12
6C Lou Brock .10 .03
6D Brooks Robinson .10 .03
6H Lefty Grove .20 .06
6S Jim Palmer .15 .04
7C Joe Cronin .10 .03
7D Hank Aaron .75 .23
7H Carl Hubbell .10 .03
7S Frank Robinson .20 .06
8C Mickey Cochrane .10 .03
8D Rollie Fingers .10 .03
8H Al Kaline .20 .06
8S Mike Schmidt .40 .12
9C Rod Carew .30 .09
9D Dennis Eckersley .15 .04
9H Rogers Hornsby .40 .12
9S George Sisler .10 .03
10C Bill Dickey .15 .04
10D Ty Cobb .75 .23
10H Harmon Killebrew .20 .06
10S Al Simmons .10 .03
11C Josh Gibson .50 .15
11D Joe Medwick .10 .03
11H Walter Johnson .50 .15
11S Cy Young .50 .15
12C Lou Gehrig .75 .23
12D Ernie Banks .40 .12
12H Jimmie Foxx .50 .15
12S Ozzie Smith .50 .15
13C Jackie Robinson 1.00 .30
13D Grover Alexander .40 .12
13H Carlton Fisk .20 .06
13S Tris Speaker .20 .06

1995 UC3

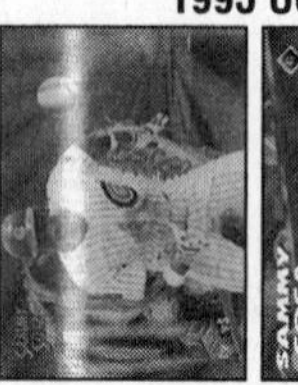

This 147-card standard-size set was issued by Pinnacle Brands. The cards were issued in 16-box cases with 36 packs per box and five cards per pack. The fronts feature a mix of horizontal and vertical designs. The player's photo is shown against a computer generated background. According to Pinnacle, this is the first set issued as an all-3D product. The key Rookie Card in this set is Hideo Nomo.

Nm-Mt Ex-Mt
COMPLETE SET (147) 20.00 6.00
1 Frank Thomas .75 .23
2 Wil Cordero .15 .04
3 John Olerud .30 .09
4 Deion Sanders .30 .09
5 Mike Mussina .75 .23
6 Mo Vaughn .30 .09
7 Will Clark .75 .23
8 Chili Davis .30 .09
9 Jimmy Key .30 .09
10 John Valentin .15 .04
11 Tony Tarasco .15 .04
12 Alan Trammell .50 .15
13 David Cone .30 .09
14 Tim Salmon .30 .09
15 Danny Tartabull .15 .04
16 Aaron Sele .15 .04
17 Alex Fernandez .15 .04
18 Barry Bonds 2.00 .60
19 Andres Galarraga .30 .09
20 Don Mattingly 2.00 .60
21 Kevin Appier .30 .09
22 Paul Molitor .50 .15
23 Omar Vizquel .30 .09
24 Andy Benes .15 .04
25 Rafael Palmeiro .50 .15
26 Barry Larkin .75 .23
27 Bernie Williams .50 .15
28 Gary Sheffield .30 .09
29 Wally Joyner .30 .09
30 Wade Boggs .50 .15
31 Rico Brogna .15 .04
32 Ken Caminiti .30 .09
33 Kirby Puckett .75 .23
34 Bobby Bonilla .30 .09
35 Hal Morris .15 .04
36 Moises Alou .30 .09
37 Jim Thome .75 .23
38 Chuck Knoblauch .30 .09
39 Mike Piazza 1.25 .35
40 Travis Fryman .30 .09
41 Rickey Henderson .75 .23
42 Jack McDowell .15 .04
43 Carlos Baerga .15 .04
44 Gregg Jefferies .15 .04
45 Kirk Gibson .30 .09
46 Bret Saberhagen .30 .09
47 Cecil Fielder .30 .09
48 Manny Ramirez .30 .09
49 Marquis Grissom .15 .04
50 Dave Winfield .30 .09
51 Mark McGwire 2.00 .60
52 Dennis Eckersley .30 .09
53 Robin Ventura .30 .09
54 Ryan Klesko .30 .09
55 Jeff Bagwell .50 .15
56 Ozzie Smith 1.25 .35
57 Brian McRae .15 .04
58 Albert Belle .30 .09
59 Darren Daulton .30 .09
60 Jose Canseco .75 .23
61 Greg Maddux 1.25 .35
62 Ben McDonald .15 .04
63 Lenny Dykstra .30 .09
64 Randy Johnson .75 .23
65 Fred McGriff .50 .15
66 Ray Lankford .15 .04
67 Dave Justice .30 .09
68 Paul O'Neill .50 .15
69 Tony Gwynn 1.00 .30
70 Matt Williams .30 .09
71 Dante Bichette .30 .09
72 Craig Biggio .50 .15
73 Ken Griffey Jr. 1.25 .35
74 Juan Gonzalez .75 .23
75 Cal Ripken 2.50 .75
76 Jay Bell .30 .09
77 Joe Carter .30 .09
78 Roberto Alomar .75 .23
79 Mark Langston .15 .04
80 Dave Hollins .15 .04
81 Tom Glavine .50 .15
82 Ivan Rodriguez .75 .23
83 Mark Whiten .15 .04
84 Raul Mondesi .30 .09
85 Kenny Lofton .30 .09
86 Ruben Sierra .15 .04
87 Mark Grace .50 .15
88 Royce Clayton .15 .04
89 Billy Ashley .15 .04
90 Larry Walker .50 .15
91 Sammy Sosa 1.25 .35
92 Jason Bere .15 .04
93 Bob Hamelin .15 .04
94 Greg Vaughn .30 .09
95 Roger Clemens 1.50 .45
96 Scott Ruffcorn .15 .04
97 Hideo Nomo RC 2.00 .60
98 Michael Tucker .15 .04
99 J.R. Phillips .15 .04
100 Roberto Petagine .15 .04
101 Chipper Jones .75 .23
102 Armando Benitez .30 .09
103 Orlando Miller .15 .04
104 Carlos Delgado .30 .09
105 Jeff Cirillo .15 .04
106 Shawn Green .30 .09
107 Joe Randa .15 .04
108 Vaughn Eshelman .15 .04
109 Frank Rodriguez .15 .04
110 Russ Davis .15 .04
111 Todd Hollandsworth .15 .04
112 Mark Grudzielanek RC .50 .15
113 Jose Oliva .15 .04
114 Ray Durham .30 .09
115 Alex Rodriguez 2.00 .60
116 Alex Gonzalez .15 .04
117 Midre Cummings .15 .04
118 Marty Cordova .15 .04
119 John Mabry .15 .04
120 Jason Jacome .15 .04
121 Joe Vitiello .15 .04
122 Charles Johnson .30 .09
123 Cal Ripken ID 1.25 .35
124 Ken Griffey Jr. ID .75 .23
125 Frank Thomas ID .50 .15
126 Mike Piazza ID .75 .23
127 Matt Williams ID .15 .04
128 Barry Bonds ID 1.00 .30
129 Greg Maddux ID .75 .23
130 Randy Johnson ID .50 .15
131 Albert Belle ID .30 .09
132 Will Clark ID .30 .09
133 Tony Gwynn ID .50 .15
134 Manny Ramirez ID .30 .09
135 Raul Mondesi ID .15 .04
136 Mo Vaughn ID .15 .04
137 Mark McGwire ID 1.00 .30
138 Kirby Puckett ID .50 .15
139 Don Mattingly ID 1.00 .30
140 Carlos Baerga ID .15 .04
141 Roger Clemens ID .75 .23
142 Fred McGriff ID .30 .09
143 Kenny Lofton ID .15 .04
144 Jeff Bagwell ID .30 .09
145 Larry Walker ID .50 .15
146 Joe Carter ID .15 .04
147 Rafael Palmeiro ID .30 .09

1995 UC3 Artist's Proofs

This 147-card standard-size set is a parallel to the regular UC3 set. These cards were inserted one per 36-pack UC3 box. The only difference between these and the regular UC3 cards is the words "Artist's Proof" in a circle in a bottom corner.

Nm-Mt Ex-Mt
*STARS: 8X TO 20X BASIC CARDS
*ROOKIES: 6X TO 15X BASIC CARDS

1995 UC3 Clear Shots

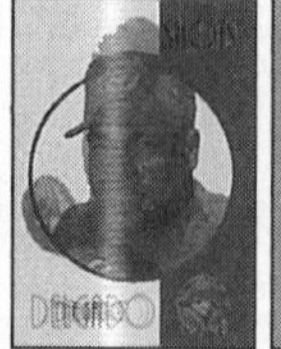

This 12-card standard-size set was inserted approximately one in every 24 packs. The backs are opaque, but do have the card number in the upper left corner with a "CS" prefix.

Nm-Mt Ex-Mt
COMPLETE SET (12) 40.00 12.00
CS1 Alex Rodriguez 12.00 3.60
CS2 Shawn Green 2.50 .75
CS3 Hideo Nomo 6.00 1.80
CS4 Charles Johnson 2.50 .75
CS5 Orlando Miller 1.50 .45
CS6 Billy Ashley 1.50 .45
CS7 Carlos Delgado 2.50 .75
CS8 Cliff Floyd 2.50 .75
CS9 Chipper Jones 5.00 1.50
CS10 Alex Gonzalez 1.50 .45
CS11 J.R. Phillips 1.50 .45
CS12 Michael Tucker 1.50 .45
PCS8 Cliff Floyd 1.00 .30
Promo
PCS10 Alex Gonzalez 1.00 .30
Promo

1995 UC3 Cyclone Squad

This 20-card standard-size set was inserted approximately one in every four packs. The cards are numbered in the upper left with a "CS" prefix.

Nm-Mt Ex-Mt
COMPLETE SET (20) 20.00 6.00
CS1 Frank Thomas 1.00 .30
CS2 Ken Griffey Jr. 1.50 .45
CS3 Jeff Bagwell .60 .18
CS4 Cal Ripken 3.00 .90
CS5 Barry Bonds 2.50 .75
CS6 Mike Piazza 1.50 .45
CS7 Matt Williams .40 .12
CS8 Kirby Puckett 1.00 .30
CS9 Jose Canseco 1.00 .30
CS10 Will Clark 1.00 .30
CS11 Don Mattingly 2.50 .75
CS12 Albert Belle .40 .12
CS13 Tony Gwynn 1.25 .35
CS14 Raul Mondesi .40 .12
CS15 Bobby Bonilla .40 .12
CS16 Rafael Palmeiro .60 .18
CS17 Fred McGriff .60 .18
CS18 Tim Salmon .60 .18
CS19 Kenny Lofton .40 .12
CS20 Joe Carter .40 .12

1995 UC3 In Motion

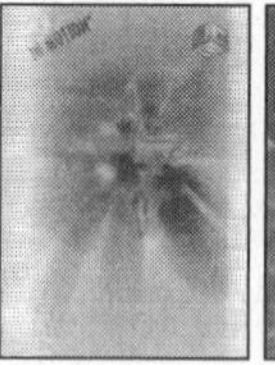
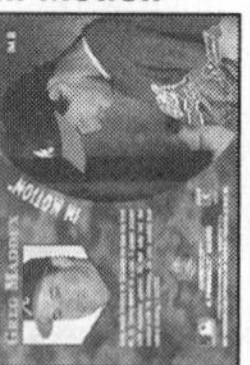

This 10-card standard-size set was inserted approximately one in every 18 packs. The cards are numbered with an "IM" prefix in the upper right corner.

Nm-Mt Ex-Mt
COMPLETE SET (10) 30.00 9.00
IM1 Cal Ripken 6.00 1.80
IM2 Ken Griffey Jr. 3.00 .90
IM3 Frank Thomas 2.00 .60
IM4 Mike Piazza 3.00 .90
IM5 Barry Bonds 5.00 1.50
IM6 Matt Williams .75 .23
IM7 Kirby Puckett 2.00 .60
IM8 Greg Maddux 3.00 .90
IM9 Don Mattingly 5.00 1.50
IM10 Will Clark 2.00 .60

1997 UD3

This 60-card standard-size super premium set was released by Upper Deck exclusively to retail outlets in mid-April,1997. Packs carried a suggested retail price of $3.99. Each pack contained three cards, one from each of the subsets. Boxes contained 24 packs. The set is broken up into three distinct 20-card subsets: Homerun Heroes (1-20) featuring Electric Wood technology, Pro-Motion (21-40) featuring Light F/X technology and Future Impact (41-60) featuring Cel Chrome technology.

Nm-Mt Ex-Mt
COMPLETE SET (60) 40.00 12.00
1 Mark McGwire 4.00 1.20
2 Brady Anderson .60 .18
3 Ken Griffey Jr. 2.50 .75
4 Albert Belle .60 .18
5 Andres Galarraga .60 .18
6 Juan Gonzalez 1.50 .45
7 Jay Buhner .60 .18
8 Mo Vaughn .60 .18
9 Barry Bonds 4.00 1.20
10 Gary Sheffield .60 .18
11 Todd Hundley .60 .18
12 Ellis Burks .60 .18
13 Ken Caminiti .60 .18
14 Vinny Castilla .60 .18
15 Sammy Sosa 2.50 .75
16 Frank Thomas 1.50 .45
17 Rafael Palmeiro 1.00 .30
18 Mike Piazza 2.50 .75
19 Matt Williams .60 .18
20 Eddie Murray 1.50 .45
21 Roger Clemens 3.00 .90
22 Tim Salmon 1.00 .30
23 Robin Ventura .60 .18
24 Ron Gant .60 .18
25 Cal Ripken 5.00 1.50
26 Bernie Williams 1.00 .30
27 Hideo Nomo 1.50 .45
28 Ivan Rodriguez 1.50 .45
29 John Smoltz 1.00 .30
30 Paul Molitor 1.00 .30
31 Greg Maddux 2.50 .75
32 Raul Mondesi .60 .18
33 Roberto Alomar 1.50 .45
34 Barry Larkin 1.50 .45
35 Tony Gwynn 2.00 .60
36 Jim Thome 1.50 .45
37 Kenny Lofton .60 .18
38 Jeff Bagwell 1.00 .30
39 Ozzie Smith 2.50 .75
40 Kirby Puckett 1.50 .45
41 Andruw Jones .60 .18
42 Vladimir Guerrero 1.50 .45
43 Edgar Renteria .60 .18
44 Luis Castillo .60 .18
45 Darin Erstad .60 .18
46 Nomar Garciaparra 2.50 .75
47 Todd Greene .60 .18
48 Jason Kendall .60 .18
49 Rey Ordonez .60 .18
50 Alex Rodriguez 2.50 .75
51 Manny Ramirez .60 .18
52 Todd Walker .60 .18
53 Ruben Rivera .60 .18
54 Andy Pettitte 1.00 .30
55 Derek Jeter 4.00 1.20
56 Todd Hollandsworth .60 .18
57 Rocky Coppinger .60 .18
58 Scott Rolen 1.00 .30
59 Jermaine Dye .60 .18
60 Chipper Jones 1.50 .45

1997 UD3 Generation Next

Randomly seeded into one in every 11 packs, cards from this 20-card set feature a selection of the game's top prospects. The horizontal card fronts feature a full-color cut-out player photo set against a metallized background with another picture of the player in action. Card backs include 1996 season statistics, a rarity for insert issues.

Nm-Mt Ex-Mt
COMPLETE SET (20) 100.00 30.00
GN1 Alex Rodriguez 12.00 3.60
GN2 Vladimir Guerrero 8.00 2.40
GN3 Luis Castillo 3.00 .90
GN4 Rey Ordonez 3.00 .90
GN5 Andruw Jones 3.00 .90
GN6 Darin Erstad 3.00 .90
GN7 Edgar Renteria 3.00 .90
GN8 Jason Kendall 3.00 .90
GN9 Jermaine Dye 3.00 .90
GN10 Chipper Jones 8.00 2.40
GN11 Rocky Coppinger 3.00 .90
GN12 Andy Pettitte 5.00 1.50
GN13 Todd Greene 3.00 .90
GN14 Todd Hollandsworth 3.00 .90
GN15 Derek Jeter 20.00 6.00
GN16 Ruben Rivera 3.00 .90
GN17 Todd Walker 3.00 .90
GN18 Nomar Garciaparra 12.00 3.60
GN19 Scott Rolen 5.00 1.50
GN20 Manny Ramirez 3.00 .90

1997 UD3 Marquee Attraction

Randomly seed into one in every 144 packs, cards from this 10-card set feature a selection of the game's top veteran stars. Horizontal card fronts feature a small color action player photo set against a bold diamond-shaped holographic image of the player. Card backs feature silver foil, statistics, another photo and text.

Nm-Mt Ex-Mt
COMPLETE SET (10) 150.00 45.00
MA1 Ken Griffey Jr. 20.00 6.00
MA2 Mark McGwire 30.00 9.00
MA3 Juan Gonzalez 12.00 3.60
MA4 Barry Bonds 30.00 9.00
MA5 Frank Thomas 12.00 3.60
MA6 Albert Belle 5.00 1.50
MA7 Mike Piazza 20.00 6.00
MA8 Cal Ripken 40.00 12.00
MA9 Mo Vaughn 5.00 1.50
MA10 Alex Rodriguez 20.00 6.00

1997 UD3 Superb Signatures

Randomly seeded into one in every 1,500 packs, cards from this four-card set feature

actual autographs from some of baseball's top stars. Horizontal wood-cel card fronts feature a rectangular clear plastic player photo, statistics on height, weight, date of birth and hometown, plus of course a real autograph at the base of the card. Card backs feature text congratulating the bearer of the card plus the signature of Upper Deck's president Brian Burr.

	Nm-Mt	Ex-Mt
1 Ken Caminiti	40.00	12.00
2 Ken Griffey Jr.	200.00	60.00
3 Vladimir Guerrero	80.00	24.00
4 Derek Jeter	250.00	75.00

1998 UD3

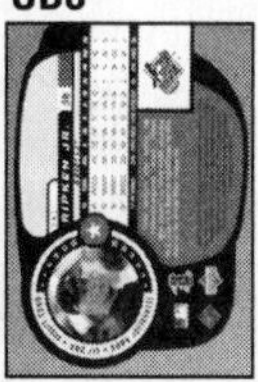

The 1998 UD3 set (made by Upper Deck) consists of 270 cards. The three-card packs retailed for a suggested price of $3.99 each. The set contains the subsets: Future Impact-Light FX (1-30) seeded 1:12, Power Corps-Light FX (31-60) seeded 1:1, The Establishment-Light FX (61-90) seeded 1:6, Future Impact-Embossed (91-120) seeded 1:6, Power Corps-Embossed (121-150) seeded 1:4, The Establishment-Embossed (151-180) seeded 1:1, Future Impact-Rainbow (181-210) seeded 1:1, Power Corps-Rainbow (211-240) seeded 1:12, and The Establishment-Rainbow (241-270) seeded 1:24. A Ken Griffey Jr. Power Corps Embossed Sample card was distributed to dealers prior to release. The card is easily differentiated by the bold red "SAMPLE" text running diagonally across it's back.

	Nm-Mt	Ex-Mt
COMP.FUTURE SET (30)	60.00	18.00
COMMON (1-30)	1.50	.45
COMP.POWER FX (30)	30.00	9.00
COMMON (31-60)	.50	.15
COMP.EST.FX SET (30)	50.00	15.00
COMMON EST.FX (61-90)	1.25	.35
COMP.FUTURE EMB. (30)	40.00	12.00
COMMON (91-120)	1.00	.30
COMP.POWER EMB.(30)	50.00	15.00
COMMON (121-150)	.75	.23
COMP.EST.EMB.SET (30)	15.00	4.50
COMMON (151-180)	.40	.12
COMP.FUTURE RBW. (30)	20.00	6.00
COMMON (181-210)	.50	.15
COMP.POWER RBW.(30)	100.00	30.00
COMMON (211-240)	2.00	.60
COMP.EST.RBW.SET (30)	120.00	36.00
COMMON (241-270)	3.00	.90
1 Travis Lee FF	1.50	.45
2 A.J. Hinch FF	1.50	.45
3 Mike Caruso FF	1.50	.45
4 Miguel Tejada FF	2.50	.75
5 Brad Fullmer FF	1.50	.45
6 Eric Milton FF	1.50	.45
7 Mark Kotsay FF	1.50	.45
8 Darin Erstad FF	1.50	.45
9 Magglio Ordonez FF	8.00	2.40
10 Ben Grieve FF	1.50	.45
11 Brett Tomko FF	1.50	.45
12 Mike Kinkade FF	4.00	1.20
13 Rolando Arrojo FF	4.00	1.20
14 Todd Helton FF	2.50	.75
15 Scott Rolen FF	2.50	.75
16 Bruce Chen FF	1.50	.45
17 Daryle Ward FF	1.50	.45
18 Jaret Wright FF	1.50	.45
19 Sean Casey FF	1.50	.45
20 Paul Konerko FF	1.50	.45
21 Kerry Wood FF	4.00	1.20
22 Russell Branyan FF	1.50	.45
23 Gabe Alvarez FF	1.50	.45
24 Juan Encarnacion FF	1.50	.45
25 Andruw Jones FF	1.50	.45
26 Vladimir Guerrero FF	4.00	1.20
27 Eli Marrero FF	1.50	.45
28 Matt Clement FF	1.50	.45
29 Gary Matthews Jr. FF	4.00	1.20
30 Derrek Lee FF	1.50	.45
31 Ken Caminiti PF	.50	.15
32 Gary Sheffield PF	.50	.15
33 Jay Buhner PF	.50	.15
34 Ryan Klesko PF	.50	.15
35 Nomar Garciaparra PF	2.00	.60
36 Vinny Castilla PF	.50	.15
37 Tony Clark PF	.50	.15
38 Sammy Sosa PF	2.00	.60
39 Tino Martinez PF	.75	.23
40 Mike Piazza PF	2.00	.60
41 Manny Ramirez PF	.50	.15
42 Larry Walker PF	.75	.23
43 Jose Cruz Jr. PF	.50	.15
44 Matt Williams PF	.50	.15
45 Frank Thomas PF	1.25	.35
46 Jim Edmonds PF	.50	.15
47 Raul Mondesi PF	.50	.15
48 Alex Rodriguez PF	2.00	.60
49 Albert Belle PF	.50	.15
50 Mark McGwire PF	3.00	.90
51 Tim Salmon PF	.75	.23
52 Andres Galarraga PF	.50	.15
53 Jeff Bagwell PF	.75	.23
54 Jim Thome PF	1.25	.35
55 Barry Bonds PF	3.00	.90
56 Carlos Delgado PF	.50	.15
57 Mo Vaughn PF	.50	.15
58 Chipper Jones PF	1.25	.35
59 Juan Gonzalez PF	1.25	.35
60 Ken Griffey Jr. PF	2.00	.60
61 David Cone EF	1.25	.35
62 Hideo Nomo EF	3.00	.90
63 Edgar Martinez EF	2.00	.60
64 Fred McGriff EF	2.00	.60
65 Cal Ripken EF	10.00	3.00
66 Todd Hundley EF	1.25	.35
67 Barry Larkin EF	3.00	.90
68 Dennis Eckersley EF	1.25	.35
69 Randy Johnson EF	3.00	.90
70 Paul Molitor EF	2.00	.60
71 Eric Karros EF	1.25	.35
72 Rafael Palmeiro EF	2.00	.60
73 Chuck Knoblauch EF	1.25	.35
74 Ivan Rodriguez EF	3.00	.90
75 Greg Maddux EF	5.00	1.50
76 Dante Bichette EF	1.25	.35
77 Brady Anderson EF	1.25	.35
78 Craig Biggio EF	2.00	.60
79 Derek Jeter EF	8.00	2.40
80 Roger Clemens EF	6.00	1.80
81 Roberto Alomar EF	3.00	.90
82 Wade Boggs EF	2.00	.60
83 Charles Johnson EF	1.25	.35
84 Mark Grace EF	2.00	.60
85 Kenny Lofton EF	1.25	.35
86 Mike Mussina EF	3.00	.90
87 Pedro Martinez EF	3.00	.90
88 Curt Schilling EF	2.00	.60
89 Bernie Williams EF	2.00	.60
90 Tony Gwynn EF	4.00	1.20
91 Travis Lee FE	1.00	.30
92 A.J. Hinch FE	1.00	.30
93 Mike Caruso FE	1.00	.30
94 Miguel Tejada FE	1.50	.45
95 Brad Fullmer FE	1.00	.30
96 Eric Milton FE	1.00	.30
97 Mark Kotsay FE	1.00	.30
98 Darin Erstad FE	1.00	.30
99 Magglio Ordonez FE	5.00	1.50
100 Ben Grieve FE	1.00	.30
101 Brett Tomko FE	1.00	.30
102 Mike Kinkade FE	2.50	.75
103 Rolando Arrojo FE	2.50	.75
104 Todd Helton FE	1.50	.45
105 Scott Rolen FE	1.50	.45
106 Bruce Chen FE	1.00	.30
107 Daryle Ward FE	1.00	.30
108 Jaret Wright FE	1.00	.30
109 Sean Casey FE	1.00	.30
110 Paul Konerko FE	1.00	.30
111 Kerry Wood FE	2.50	.75
112 Russell Branyan FE	1.00	.30
113 Gabe Alvarez FE	1.00	.30
114 Juan Encarnacion FE	1.00	.30
115 Andruw Jones FE	1.00	.30
116 Vladimir Guerrero FE	2.50	.75
117 Eli Marrero FE	1.00	.30
118 Matt Clement FE	1.00	.30
119 Gary Matthews Jr. FE	2.50	.75
120 Derrek Lee FE	1.00	.30
121 Ken Caminiti PE	.75	.23
122 Gary Sheffield PE	.75	.23
123 Jay Buhner PE	.75	.23
124 Ryan Klesko PE	.75	.23
125 Nomar Garciaparra PE	3.00	.90
126 Vinny Castilla PE	.75	.23
127 Tony Clark PE	.75	.23
128 Sammy Sosa PE	3.00	.90
129 Tino Martinez PE	1.25	.35
130 Mike Piazza PE	3.00	.90
131 Manny Ramirez PE	.75	.23
132 Larry Walker PE		
133 Jose Cruz Jr. PE	.75	.23
134 Matt Williams PE	.75	.23
135 Frank Thomas PE	2.00	.60
136 Jim Edmonds PE	.75	.23
137 Raul Mondesi PE	.75	.23
138 Alex Rodriguez PE	3.00	.90
139 Albert Belle PE	.75	.23
140 Mark McGwire PE	5.00	1.50
141 Tim Salmon PE	1.25	.35
142 Andres Galarraga PE	.75	.23
143 Jeff Bagwell PE	1.25	.35
144 Jim Thome PE	2.00	.60
145 Barry Bonds PE	5.00	1.50
146 Carlos Delgado PE	.75	.23
147 Mo Vaughn PE	.75	.23
148 Chipper Jones PE	2.00	.60
149 Juan Gonzalez PE	2.00	.60
150 Ken Griffey Jr. PE	3.00	.90
151 David Cone EE	.40	.12
152 Hideo Nomo EE	1.00	.30
153 Edgar Martinez EE	.60	.18
154 Fred McGriff EE	.60	.18
155 Cal Ripken EE	3.00	.90
156 Todd Hundley EE	.40	.12
157 Barry Larkin EE	1.00	.30
158 Dennis Eckersley EE	.40	.12
159 Randy Johnson EE	1.00	.30
160 Paul Molitor EE	.60	.18
161 Eric Karros EE	.40	.12
162 Rafael Palmeiro EE	.60	.18
163 Chuck Knoblauch EE	.40	.12
164 Ivan Rodriguez EE	1.00	.30
165 Greg Maddux EE	1.50	.45
166 Dante Bichette EE	.40	.12
167 Brady Anderson EE	.40	.12
168 Craig Biggio EE	.60	.18
169 Derek Jeter EE	2.50	.75
170 Roger Clemens EE	2.00	.60
171 Roberto Alomar EE	1.00	.30
172 Wade Boggs EE	.60	.18
173 Charles Johnson EE	.40	.12
174 Mark Grace EE	.60	.18
175 Kenny Lofton EE	.40	.12
176 Mike Mussina EE	1.00	.30
177 Pedro Martinez EE	1.00	.30
178 Curt Schilling EE	.60	.18
179 Bernie Williams EE	.60	.18
180 Tony Gwynn EE	1.25	.35
181 Travis Lee FR	.50	.15
182 A.J. Hinch FR	.50	.15
183 Mike Caruso FR	.50	.15
184 Miguel Tejada FR	.75	.23
185 Brad Fullmer FR	.50	.15
186 Eric Milton FR	.50	.15
187 Mark Kotsay FR	.50	.15
188 Darin Erstad FR	.50	.15
189 M.Ordonez FR RC	2.50	.75
190 Ben Grieve FR	.50	.15
191 Brett Tomko FR	.50	.15
192 Mike Kinkade FR RC	.50	.15
193 Rolando Arrojo FR RC	.50	.15
194 Todd Helton FR	.75	.23
195 Scott Rolen FR	.75	.23
196 Bruce Chen FR	.50	.15
197 Daryle Ward FR	.50	.15
198 Jaret Wright FR	.50	.15
199 Sean Casey FR	.50	.15
200 Paul Konerko FR	.50	.15
201 Kerry Wood FR	1.25	.35
202 Russell Branyan FR	.50	.15
203 Gabe Alvarez FR	.50	.15
204 Juan Encarnacion FR	.50	.15
205 Andruw Jones FR	.50	.15
206 Vladimir Guerrero FR	1.25	.35
207 Eli Marrero FR	.50	.15
208 Matt Clement FR	.50	.15
209 G.Matthews Jr. FR RC	.50	.15
210 Derrek Lee FR	.50	.15
211 Ken Caminiti PR	2.00	.60
212 Gary Sheffield PR	2.00	.60
213 Jay Buhner PR	2.00	.60
214 Ryan Klesko PR	2.00	.60
215 N.Garciaparra PR	8.00	2.40
216 Vinny Castilla PR	2.00	.60
217 Tony Clark PR	2.00	.60
218 Sammy Sosa PR	8.00	2.40
219 Tino Martinez PR	3.00	.90
220 Mike Piazza PR	8.00	2.40
221 Manny Ramirez PR	2.00	.60
222 Larry Walker PR	3.00	.90
223 Jose Cruz Jr. PR	2.00	.60
224 Matt Williams PR	2.00	.60
225 Frank Thomas PR	5.00	1.50
226 Jim Edmonds PR	2.00	.60
227 Raul Mondesi PR	2.00	.60
228 Alex Rodriguez PR	8.00	2.40
229 Albert Belle PR	2.00	.60
230 Mark McGwire PR	12.00	3.60
231 Tim Salmon PR	3.00	.90
232 Andres Galarraga PR	2.00	.60
233 Jeff Bagwell PR	3.00	.90
234 Jim Thome PR	5.00	1.50
235 Barry Bonds PR	12.00	3.60
236 Carlos Delgado PR	2.00	.60
237 Mo Vaughn PR	2.00	.60
238 Chipper Jones PR	5.00	1.50
239 Juan Gonzalez PR	5.00	1.50
240 Ken Griffey Jr. PR	8.00	2.40
241 David Cone ER	3.00	.90
242 Hideo Nomo ER	8.00	2.40
243 Edgar Martinez ER	5.00	1.50
244 Fred McGriff ER	5.00	1.50
245 Cal Ripken ER	25.00	7.50
246 Todd Hundley ER	3.00	.90
247 Barry Larkin ER	8.00	2.40
248 Dennis Eckersley ER	3.00	.90
249 Randy Johnson ER	8.00	2.40
250 Paul Molitor ER	5.00	1.50
251 Eric Karros ER	3.00	.90
252 Rafael Palmeiro ER	5.00	1.50
253 Chuck Knoblauch ER	3.00	.90
254 Ivan Rodriguez ER	8.00	2.40
255 Greg Maddux ER	12.00	3.60
256 Dante Bichette ER	3.00	.90
257 Brady Anderson ER	3.00	.90
258 Craig Biggio ER	5.00	1.50
259 Derek Jeter ER	20.00	6.00
260 Roger Clemens ER	15.00	4.50
261 Roberto Alomar ER	8.00	2.40
262 Wade Boggs ER	5.00	1.50
263 Charles Johnson ER	3.00	.90
264 Mark Grace ER	5.00	1.50
265 Kenny Lofton ER	3.00	.90
266 Mike Mussina ER	8.00	2.40
267 Pedro Martinez ER	8.00	2.40
268 Curt Schilling ER	5.00	1.50
269 Bernie Williams ER	5.00	1.50
270 Tony Gwynn ER	10.00	3.00
S1 K.Griffey Jr. PE Sample	2.00	.60

1998 UD3 Die Cuts

The 1998 UD3 Die Cuts set consists of 270 cards and is a parallel to the 1998 Upper Deck UD3 base set. The cards were printed (and serial numbered) in the following quantities: numbers 1-90/2000 of each, numbers 91-180/1000 of each and numbers 181-270/100 of each. The cards were randomly inserted in packs.

Nm-Mt Ex-Mt

*DC'S 1-30: .5X TO 1.2X BASIC 1-30.
*DC'S 31-60: 2.5X TO 6X BASIC 31-60
*DC'S 61-90: 1.25X TO 3X BASIC 61-90
*DC'S 91-120: 1X TO 2.5X BASIC 91-120
*DC'S 121-150: 2.5X TO 6X BASIC 121-150
*DC'S 151-180: 5X TO 12X BASIC 151-180
*DC'S 181-210: 6X TO 15X BASIC 181-210
*DC RC'S 181-210: 4X TO 10X BASIC 181-210
*DC'S 211-240: 2X TO 5X BASIC 211-240
*DC'S 241-270: 1.25X TO 3X BASIC 241-270

1998 UD3 Power Corps Blowups

The 1998 UD3 Power Corps Blowups are exact parallels to ten selected basic issue UD3 Power Corps subset cards, except of course for their larger 5 inch x 7 inch dimensions. These ten cards were distributed exclusively in specially marked UD3 retail mini-boxes. Each box carried an SRP of $29.99, containing a handful of UD3 retail packs and one Power Corps Blowup.

	Nm-Mt	Ex-Mt
COMPLETE SET (10)	80.00	24.00
35 Nomar Garciaparra	10.00	3.00
38 Sammy Sosa	8.00	2.40
40 Mike Piazza	12.00	3.60
45 Frank Thomas	5.00	1.50
48 Alex Rodriguez	10.00	3.00
50 Mark McGwire	15.00	4.50
55 Barry Bonds	8.00	2.40
58 Chipper Jones	8.00	2.40
59 Juan Gonzalez	5.00	1.50
60 Ken Griffey Jr.	8.00	2.40

1995-97 UDA Commemorative Cards

Upper Deck Authenticated, in addition to its line of certified autograph products, has produced a series of double-size (3 1/2 by 5 inch) unsigned cards commemorating various events, players and teams. These are often referred to as "C-Cards." These cards typically are serially numbered out of limited editions of 10,000, 5,000 or less, and encased in clear plastic holders. This limited edition number is noted at the end of the card description. Most of these cards are unnumbered. No complete set price is given since most of these cards are one-offs.

	Nm-Mt	Ex-Mt
CR1 Cal Ripken 1995 SP Champ. 2131/2131	25.00	7.50
NH1 Ken Griffey Jr. National Hero/5000 1996	15.00	4.50
NH2 Cal Ripken National Hero/5000 1996	15.00	4.50
NNO Tony Gwynn 8 batting titles/2500 1997	25.00	7.50
NNO Ken Griffey Jr. AS Game/2500 1996	25.00	7.50
NNO Hideo Nomo 1995 ROY/5000 1996	15.00	4.50
NNO Ken Griffey Jr. Gold Glove/5000 1997	15.00	4.50
NNO Jackie Robinson debut/5000 1997	15.00	4.50
NNO Florida Marlins Champs/5000 Moises Alou Bobby Bonilla Kevin Brown Alex Fernandez Charles Johnson Gary Sheffield 1997	15.00	4.50

1998 UDA Mark McGwire Die-Cuts

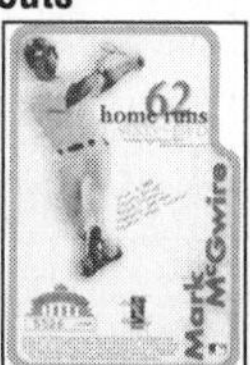

These two cards were sold on the Upper Deck Website. This set features two die-cut oversized Mark McGwire cards encapsulated in "PKK" snap-tite holders. One card features his 62nd homerun, while the other pictures his 70th homerun of the season.

	Nm-Mt	Ex-Mt
COMPLETE SET (2)	20.00	6.00
COMMON CARD (1-2)	10.00	3.00

2000 UDA 22kt Gold Ken Griffey Jr.

This 22kt Gold card was issued on the Upper Deck website in 2000. The card is a replica of the 1989 Upper Deck Griffey rookie card produced in 22kt gold.

	Nm-Mt	Ex-Mt
1 Ken Griffey Jr.	30.00	9.00

2002 UD Authentics

This 200 card was set was released in March, 2002. These cards were issued in five card packs which were packed 18 to a box and 12 boxes to a case with an SRP of $6.99 per pack. Cards numbered 171 through 200 feature 30 Rookie Cards but were printed in the same quantity as the other cards in this set.

	Nm-Mt	Ex-Mt
COMPLETE SET (200)	60.00	18.00
COMMON CARD (1-170)	.50	.15
COMMON CARD (171-200)	1.25	.35
1 Brad Fullmer	.50	.15
2 Garret Anderson	.50	.15
3 Darin Erstad	.50	.15
4 Jarrod Washburn	.50	.15
5 Troy Glaus	.75	.23
6 Barry Zito	.75	.23
7 David Justice	.50	.15
8 Eric Chavez	.50	.15
9 Tim Hudson	.50	.15
10 Miguel Tejada	.50	.15
11 Jermaine Dye	.50	.15
12 Mark Mulder	.50	.15
13 Carlos Delgado	.50	.15
14 Jose Cruz Jr.	.50	.15
15 Mo Vaughn UER Card is incorrectly numbered as 145	.50	.15
16 Shannon Stewart	.50	.15
17 Raul Mondesi	.50	.15
18 Tanyon Sturtze	.50	.15
19 Toby Hall	.50	.15
20 Greg Vaughn	.50	.15
21 Aubrey Huff	.50	.15
22 Ben Grieve	.50	.15
23 Brent Abernathy	.50	.15
24 Jim Thome	1.25	.35
25 C.C. Sabathia	.50	.15
26 Matt Lawton	.50	.15
27 Omar Vizquel	.50	.15
28 Ellis Burks	.50	.15
29 Russ Branyan	.50	.15
30 Bartolo Colon	.50	.15
31 Ichiro Suzuki	2.00	.60
32 John Olerud	.50	.15
33 Freddy Garcia	.50	.15
34 Mike Cameron	.50	.15
35 Jeff Cirillo	.50	.15
36 Kazuhiro Sasaki	.50	.15
37 Edgar Martinez	.75	.23
38 Bret Boone	.50	.15
39 Jeff Conine	.50	.15
40 Melvin Mora	.50	.15
41 Jason Johnson	.50	.15
42 Chris Richard	.50	.15
43 Tony Batista	.50	.15
44 Ivan Rodriguez	1.25	.35
45 Gabe Kapler	.50	.15
46 Rafael Palmeiro	.75	.23
47 Alex Rodriguez	2.00	.60
48 Juan Gonzalez	1.25	.35
49 Carl Everett	.50	.15
50 Nomar Garciaparra	2.00	.60
51 Trot Nixon	.75	.23
52 Manny Ramirez	.50	.15
53 Pedro Martinez	1.25	.35
54 Johnny Damon	.50	.15
55 Shea Hillenbrand	.50	.15
56 Mike Sweeney	.50	.15
57 Mark Quinn	.50	.15
58 Joe Randa	.50	.15
59 Carlos Beltran	.50	.15
60 Chuck Knoblauch	.50	.15
61 Robert Fick	.50	.15
62 Jeff Weaver	.50	.15
63 Bobby Higginson	.50	.15
64 Dean Palmer	.50	.15
65 Dmitri Young	.50	.15
66 Corey Koskie	.50	.15
67 Doug Mientkiewicz	.50	.15
68 Joe Mays	.50	.15
69 Torii Hunter	.50	.15
70 Cristian Guzman	.50	.15
71 Jacque Jones	.50	.15
72 Magglio Ordonez	.50	.15
73 Paul Konerko	.50	.15
74 Carlos Lee	.50	.15
75 Mark Buehrle	.50	.15
76 Jose Canseco	1.25	.35
77 Frank Thomas	1.25	.35
78 Roger Clemens	2.50	.75
79 Derek Jeter	3.00	.90
80 Jason Giambi Yankees	1.25	.35
81 Rondell White	.50	.15
82 Bernie Williams	.75	.23
83 Jorge Posada	.75	.23
84 Mike Mussina	1.25	.35
85 Alfonso Soriano	.75	.23
86 Wade Miller	.50	.15
87 Jeff Bagwell	.75	.23
88 Craig Biggio	.75	.23
89 Roy Oswalt	.50	.15
90 Lance Berkman	.50	.15
91 Daryle Ward	.50	.15
92 Chipper Jones	1.25	.35
93 Greg Maddux	2.00	.60
94 Marcus Giles	.50	.15
95 Gary Sheffield	.50	.15
96 Tom Glavine	.75	.23
97 Andruw Jones	.50	.15
98 Rafael Furcal	.50	.15
99 Richie Sexson	.50	.15
100 Ben Sheets	.50	.15
101 Jose Hernandez	.50	.15
102 Geoff Jenkins	.50	.15
103 Jeffrey Hammonds	.50	.15
104 Edgar Renteria	.50	.15
105 Matt Morris	.50	.15
106 Tino Martinez	.75	.23
107 Jim Edmonds	.50	.15
108 Albert Pujols	2.50	.75
109 J.D. Drew	.50	.15
110 Fernando Vina	.50	.15
111 Darryl Kile	.50	.15
112 Sammy Sosa	2.00	.60
113 Fred McGriff	.75	.23
114 Kerry Wood	1.25	.35
115 Moises Alou	.50	.15
116 Jon Lieber	.50	.15
117 Mark Grace	.75	.23
118 Randy Johnson	1.25	.35
119 Curt Schilling	.75	.23
120 Luis Gonzalez	.50	.15
121 Steve Finley	.50	.15
122 Matt Williams	.50	.15
123 Shawn Green	.50	.15
124 Kevin Brown	.50	.15
125 Adrian Beltre	.50	.15
126 Paul LoDuca	.50	.15
127 Hideo Nomo	1.25	.35
128 Brian Jordan	.50	.15
129 Vladimir Guerrero	1.25	.35

130 Javier Vazquez .50 .15
131 Jose Vidro .50 .15
132 Orlando Cabrera .50 .15
133 Jeff Kent .50 .15
134 Rich Aurilia .50 .15
135 Russ Ortiz .50 .15
136 Barry Bonds 3.00 .90
137 Preston Wilson .50 .15
138 Ryan Dempster .50 .15
139 Cliff Floyd .50 .15
140 Josh Beckett .75 .23
141 Mike Lowell .50 .15
142 Mike Piazza 2.00 .60
143 Roberto Alomar 1.25 .35
144 Al Leiter .50 .15
145 Edgardo Alfonzo .50 .15
146 Roger Cedeno .50 .15
147 Jeromy Burnitz .50 .15
148 Phil Nevin .50 .15
149 Mark Kotsay .50 .15
150 Ryan Klesko .50 .15
151 Trevor Hoffman .50 .15
152 Bobby Abreu .50 .15
153 Scott Rolen .75 .23
154 Jimmy Rollins .50 .15
155 Robert Person .50 .15
156 Pat Burrell .50 .15
157 Randy Wolf .50 .15
158 Brian Giles .50 .15
159 Aramis Ramirez .50 .15
160 Kris Benson .50 .15
161 Jason Kendall .50 .15
162 Ken Griffey Jr. 2.00 .60
163 Sean Casey .50 .15
164 Adam Dunn .50 .15
165 Barry Larkin 1.25 .35
166 Todd Helton .75 .23
167 Mike Hampton .50 .15
168 Larry Walker .75 .23
169 Juan Pierre .50 .15
170 Juan Uribe .50 .15
171 So Taguchi SR RC 2.00 .60
172 Brendan Donnelly SR RC 1.25 .35
173 Chris Baker SR RC 1.25 .35
174 John Ennis SR RC 1.25 .35
175 Francis Beltran SR RC 1.25 .35
176 Danny Wright SR 1.25 .35
177 Brandon Backe SR RC 1.25 .35
178 Mark Corey SR RC 1.25 .35
179 Kazuhisa Ishii SR RC 2.50 .75
180 Ron Calloway SR RC 1.25 .35
181 Kevin Frederick SR RC 1.25 .35
182 Jaime Cerda SR RC 1.25 .35
183 Doug Devore SR RC 1.25 .35
184 Brandon Puffer SR RC 1.25 .35
185 Andy Pratt SR RC 1.25 .35
186 Adrian Burnside SR RC 1.25 .35
187 Josh Hancock SR RC 1.25 .35
188 Jorge Nunez SR RC 1.25 .35
189 Tyler Yates SR RC 2.00 .60
190 Kyle Kane SR RC 1.25 .35
191 Jose Valverde SR RC 2.00 .60
192 Matt Thornton SR RC 1.25 .35
193 Ben Howard SR RC 1.25 .35
194 Reed Johnson SR RC 2.00 .60
195 Rene Reyes SR RC 1.25 .35
196 Jeremy Ward SR RC 1.25 .35
197 Steve Bechler SR RC 1.25 .35
198 Cam Esslinger SR RC 1.25 .35
199 Michael Crudale SR RC 1.25 .35
200 Todd Donovan SR RC 1.25 .35

2002 UD Authentics Reverse Negatives

Issued at stated odds of one in nine packs, this is a parallel to the 2002 UD Authentics set. These cards honor the reverse negatives which helped Upper Deck get some hobby publicity in 1989 (Dale Murphy, et. al). Another way a collector can differentiate these cards from the regular UD Authentic cards is by the airbrushing of all the team logos on these cards.

Nm-Mt Ex-Mt
*REV.NEG 1-170: 2.5X TO 6X BASIC..
*REV.NEG 171-200: 1X TO 2.5X BASIC

2002 UD Authentics 1989 Flashbacks

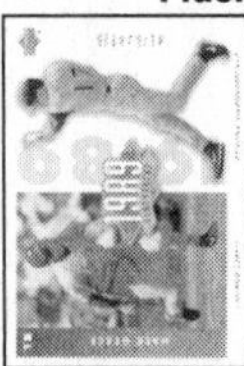
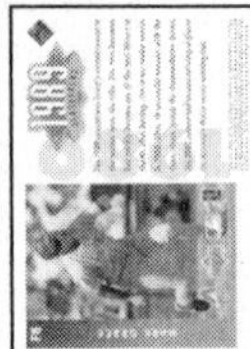

Randomly inserted in packs, these 12 cards feature players who were in the majors in 1989. These cards were issued to a stated print run of 4225 sets.

Nm-Mt Ex-Mt
COMPLETE SET (12) 50.00 15.00
F1 Ken Griffey Jr. 6.00 1.80
F2 Gary Sheffield 3.00 .90
F3 Randy Johnson 4.00 1.20
F4 Roger Clemens 8.00 2.40
F5 Greg Maddux 6.00 1.80
F6 Mark Grace 3.00 .90
F7 Barry Bonds 10.00 3.00
F8 Roberto Alomar 4.00 1.20
F9 Sammy Sosa 6.00 1.80
F10 Rafael Palmeiro 3.00 .90
F11 Edgar Martinez 3.00 .90
F12 Jose Canseco 4.00 1.20

2002 UD Authentics Heroes of Baseball

Randomly inserted in packs, these 30 cards feature three players who have been associated with Upper Deck over the years and also all played in Seattle during their career. Ken

Griffey Jr., Alex Rodriguez and Ichiro Suzuki all have 10 cards dedicated to their career in this set. Each of these 30 cards are printed to a stated print run of 1989 serial numbered cards.

Nm-Mt Ex-Mt
COMP.GRIFFEY SET (10) 60.00 18.00
COMMON GRIFFEY (G1-G10) 8.00 2.40
COMP.ICHIRO SET (10) 60.00 18.00
COMMON ICHIRO (I1-I10) 8.00 2.40
COMP.A.ROD SET (10) 60.00 18.00
COMMON A.ROD (R1-R10) 8.00 2.40

2002 UD Authentics Heroes of Baseball Autographs

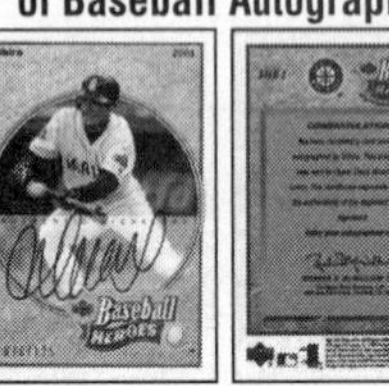
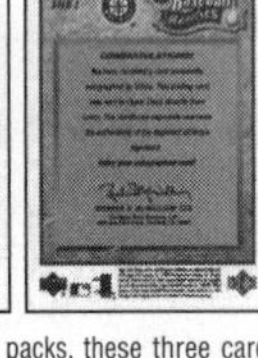

Randomly inserted in packs, these three cards feature autographs from the "Heroes of Baseball" autograph set. These cards are signed to a different amount and we have put the stated print run next to the player's name in our checklist.

Nm-Mt Ex-Mt
SHB-G K.Griffey Jr. Reds/185 . 150.00 45.00
SHB-I Ichiro Suzuki/125 400.00 120.00
SHB-R Alex Rodriguez 120.00 36.00
Rangers/185

2002 UD Authentics Reverse Negative Jerseys

Inserted at stated odds of one in 16, these 29 cards feature not only classic images from a past Upper Deck release but also a game-worn jersey swatch of the featured player.

Nm-Mt Ex-Mt
R-AJ Andruw Jones 10.00 3.00
R-AR Alex Rodriguez 15.00 4.50
R-BW Bernie Williams 15.00 4.50
R-BZ Barry Zito 15.00 4.50
R-CD Carlos Delgado 10.00 3.00
R-CJ Chipper Jones 15.00 4.50
R-DE Darin Erstad 10.00 3.00
R-EC Eric Chavez 10.00 3.00
R-FT Frank Thomas 15.00 4.50
R-GM Greg Maddux 15.00 4.50
R-IR Ivan Rodriguez 15.00 4.50
R-JB Jeff Bagwell 15.00 4.50
R-JD J.D. Drew 10.00 3.00
R-JE Jim Edmonds 10.00 3.00
R-JG Jason Giambi 15.00 4.50
R-KB Kevin Brown 10.00 3.00
R-KG Ken Griffey Jr. 15.00 4.50
R-LG Luis Gonzalez 10.00 3.00
R-MP Mike Piazza 15.00 4.50
R-MR Manny Ramirez 10.00 3.00
R-MS Mike Sweeney 10.00 3.00
R-RC Roger Clemens SP 40.00 12.00
R-RF Rafael Furcal 10.00 3.00
R-RJ Randy Johnson 15.00 4.50
R-SR Scott Rolen SP/25
R-SS Sammy Sosa SP 25.00 7.50
R-TG Tom Glavine 15.00 4.50
R-TH Todd Helton 15.00 4.50
R-TM Tino Martinez SP/25

2002 UD Authentics Retro Star Rookie Jerseys

Inserted at stated odds of one in 16, these 28 cards feature not only a design from a classic Upper Deck Rookie Card but also a a game-worn jersey swatch.

Nm-Mt Ex-Mt
SR-AP Albert Pujols 25.00 7.50
SR-AR Alex Rodriguez 25.00 7.50
SR-BG Brian Giles 10.00 3.00
SR-CB Craig Biggio 15.00 4.50
SR-CJ Chipper Jones 15.00 4.50
SR-DJ David Justice 10.00 3.00
SR-GK Gabe Kapler SP 10.00 3.00
SR-GS Gary Sheffield 10.00 3.00
SR-HN Hideo Nomo 20.00 6.00
SR-I Ichiro Suzuki 40.00 12.00
SR-IR Ivan Rodriguez 15.00 4.50
SR-JG Juan Gonzalez 15.00 4.50
SR-JO John Olerud 10.00 3.00
SR-JT Jim Thome 15.00 4.50
SR-KG Ken Griffey Jr. 25.00 7.50
SR-KL Kenny Lofton 10.00 3.00
SR-KS Kazuhiro Sasaki 10.00 3.00
SR-LG Luis Gonzalez 10.00 3.00
SR-LW Larry Walker 15.00 4.50
SR-MO Magglio Ordonez 10.00 3.00
SR-MR Manny Ramirez SP 10.00 3.00
SR-PB Pat Burrell 10.00 3.00
SR-PM Pedro Martinez 15.00 4.50
SR-RJ Randy Johnson 15.00 4.50
SR-RK Ryan Klesko 10.00 3.00
SR-RP Robert Person 10.00 3.00
SR-SG Shawn Green 10.00 3.00
SR-SS Sammy Sosa SP 25.00 7.50

2002 UD Authentics Retro Star Rookie Jerseys Autographs

Randomly inserted into packs, these three cards feature not only the Retro Star Rookie Jersey swatch but also an authentic signature of the featured player. These cards were issued to a stated print run of 40 serial numbered sets.

Nm-Mt Ex-Mt
SSR-AR Alex Rodriguez 200.00 60.00
SSR-JT Jim Thome
SSR-KG Ken Griffey Jr.

2002 UD Authentics Stars of 89 Jerseys

Inserted into packs at stated odds of one in 16, these 28 cards feature players who were in the majors in 1989 along with a game-worn jersey swatch of that player.

Nm-Mt Ex-Mt
SL-AG Andres Galarraga 10.00 3.00
SL-AL Al Leiter 10.00 3.00
SL-BL Barry Larkin SP 15.00 4.50
SL-CS Curt Schilling 15.00 4.50
SL-DC David Cone 10.00 3.00
SL-DJ David Justice 10.00 3.00
SL-EB Ellis Burks 10.00 3.00
SL-EM Edgar Martinez 15.00 4.50
SL-FM Fred McGriff 15.00 4.50
SL-GM Greg Maddux 15.00 4.50
SL-GS Gary Sheffield 10.00 3.00
SL-JC Jose Canseco 15.00 4.50
SL-JG Juan Gonzalez 15.00 4.50
SL-JO John Olerud 10.00 3.00
SL-KB Kevin Brown 10.00 3.00
SL-KG Ken Griffey Jr. 20.00 6.00
SL-LW Larry Walker 15.00 4.50
SL-MG Mark Grace 15.00 4.50
SL-MW Matt Williams 10.00 3.00
SL-PO Paul O'Neill 15.00 4.50
SL-RA Roberto Alomar 15.00 4.50
SL-RC Roger Clemens 25.00 7.50
SL-RH Rickey Henderson 15.00 4.50
SL-RJ Randy Johnson 15.00 4.50
SL-RP Rafael Palmeiro 15.00 4.50
SL-RV Robin Ventura 10.00 3.00
SL-SS Sammy Sosa 20.00 6.00
SL-TG Tom Glavine 15.00 4.50

2003 UD Authentics

This 140 card set was issued in two separate series. The primary UD Authentics product - containing the first 130 cards within the basic set - was released in August, 2003. These cards were issued in four card packs carrying a $12.50 SRP. Each box contained 10 packs and each case contained six boxes. Cards 1-100 featured a mix of active veterans and retired legends while cards 101 through 130 featured rookie cards. Those final 30 "low series" cards, of which were randomly inserted into packs, were issued to a stated print run of 999 serial numbered sets. Cards 131-140 are each serial numbered to a scant 150 copies per and were randomly seeded into 2003 UD Finite Bonus Packs. Each sealed box of UD Finite contained one 3-card Bonus Pack.

MINT NRMT
COMP.SET w/o SP's (100) 40.00 18.00
COMMON ACTIVE (1-100) .40 .18
COMMON RETIRED (1-100) .50 .23
COMMON CARD (101-130) 5.00 2.20
101-130 RANDOM INSERTS IN PACKS
101-130 PRINT RUN 999 SERIAL #'d SETS
COMMON CARD (131-140) 8.00 3.60
131-140 RANDOM IN FINITE BONUS PACKS
131-140 PRINT RUN 150 SERIAL #'d SETS
1 Pee Wee Reese .75 .35
2 Richie Ashburn .75 .35
3 Derek Jeter 2.50 1.10
4 Alex Rodriguez 1.50 .70
5 Jose Vidro .40 .18
6 Miguel Tejada .40 .18
7 Nomar Garciaparra 1.50 .70
8 Pat Burrell .40 .18
9 Albert Pujols 2.00 .90
10 Jeff Bagwell .60 .25
11 Stan Musial 2.00 .90
12 Mickey Mantle 5.00 2.20
13 J.D. Drew .40 .18
14 Ivan Rodriguez 1.00 .45
15 Joe Morgan .50 .23
16 Ted Williams 3.00 1.35
17 Travis Hafner .40 .18
18 Chipper Jones 1.00 .45
19 Hideo Nomo 1.00 .45
20 Gary Sheffield .40 .18
21 Jacque Jones .40 .18
22 Alfonso Soriano .60 .25
23 Roberto Alomar 1.00 .45
24 Jeff Kent .40 .18
25 Omar Vizquel .40 .18
26 Ernie Banks 1.25 .55
27 Shawn Green .40 .18
28 Tim Hudson .40 .18
29 Jim Edmonds .40 .18
30 Brandon Larson .40 .18
31 Doug Mientkiewicz .40 .18
32 Darin Erstad .40 .18
33 Bobby Hill .40 .18
34 Todd Helton .60 .25
35 Kazuhisa Ishii .40 .18
36 Lance Berkman .40 .18
37 Eric Hinske .40 .18
38 Jason Kendall .40 .18
39 Bob Feller .75 .35
40 Luis Gonzalez .40 .18
41 Sammy Sosa 1.50 .70
42 Mike Piazza 1.50 .70
43 Roger Clemens 2.00 .90
44 Jose Cruz Jr. .40 .18
45 Mark Prior 2.00 .90
46 Mark Teixeira .60 .25
47 Phil Nevin .40 .18
48 Lyle Overbay .40 .18
49 Manny Ramirez .40 .18
50 Brian Giles .40 .18
51 Preston Wilson .40 .18
52 Jermaine Dye .40 .18
53 Troy Glaus .60 .25
54 Frank Thomas 1.00 .45
55 Jim Thome 1.00 .45
56 Barry Bonds 2.50 1.10
57 Carlos Delgado .40 .18
58 Jason Giambi 1.00 .45
59 Joe Mays .40 .18
60 Andruw Jones .40 .18
61 Billy Williams .50 .23
62 Vladimir Guerrero 1.00 .45
63 Scott Rolen .60 .25
64 Juan Marichal .50 .23
65 Austin Kearns .40 .18
66 Kerry Wood 1.00 .45
67 Bret Boone .40 .18
68 Shea Hillenbrand .40 .18
69 Mike Sweeney .40 .18
70 Rocco Baldelli 1.50 .70
71 Ken Griffey Jr. 1.50 .70
72 Cliff Floyd .40 .18
73 Greg Maddux 1.50 .70
74 Mike Hampton .40 .18
75 Larry Walker .60 .25
76 Nolan Ryan 3.00 1.35
77 Rollie Fingers .50 .23
78 Mike Mussina 1.00 .45
79 Matt Morris .40 .18
80 Robin Roberts .50 .23
81 Barry Zito .60 .25
82 Curt Schilling .60 .25
83 Ken Harvey .40 .18
84 Troy Percival .40 .18
85 Tom Seaver .75 .35
86 Mariano Rivera .60 .25
87 Raul Mondesi .40 .18
88 Adam Dunn .40 .18
89 Roy Oswalt .40 .18
90 Pedro Martinez 1.00 .45
91 Andy Pettitte .60 .25
92 Tom Glavine .60 .25
93 Torii Hunter .40 .18
94 Joe Thurston .40 .18
95 Runelvys Hernandez .40 .18
96 Randy Johnson 1.00 .45
97 Bernie Williams .60 .25
98 Ichiro Suzuki 1.50 .70
99 C.C. Sabathia .40 .18
100 Bobby Abreu .40 .18
101 Jose Contreras RH RC 8.00 3.60
102 Hideki Matsui RH RC 20.00 9.00
103 Chris Capuano RH RC 5.00 2.20
104 Willie Eyre RH RC 5.00 2.20
105 Lew Ford RH RC 8.00 3.60
106 Shane Bazzell RH RC 5.00 2.20
107 Guillermo Quiroz RH RC 8.00 3.60
108 Fern. Cabrera RH RC 5.00 2.20
109 Francisco Cruceta RH RC 5.00 2.20
110 Jhonny Peralta RH RC 5.00 2.20
111 Bobby Madritsch RH RC 5.00 2.20
112 Diego Markwell RH RC 5.00 2.20
113 Matt Bruback RH RC 5.00 2.20
114 Matt Kata RH RC 8.00 3.60
115 Rob Hammock RH RC 8.00 3.60
116 Brandon Webb RH RC 10.00 4.50
117 Jon Leicester RH RC 5.00 2.20
118 Josh Willingham RH RC 8.00 3.60
119 Prentice Redman RH RC 5.00 2.20
120 Jeff Duncan RH RC 8.00 3.60
121 Craig Brazell RH RC 8.00 3.60
122 Jeremy Griffiths RH RC 8.00 3.60
123 Phil Seibel RH RC 5.00 2.20
124 Luis Ayala RH RC 5.00 2.20
125 Miguel Ojeda RH RC 5.00 2.20
126 Jeremy Wedel RH RC 5.00 2.20
127 Josh Hall RH RC 8.00 3.60
128 Oscar Villarreal RH RC 5.00 2.20
129 Clint Barmes RH RC 8.00 3.60
130 Nook Logan RH RC 5.00 2.20
131 Dan Haren RH RC 10.00 4.50
132 Delmon Young RH RC 50.00 22.00
133 Dontrelle Willis RH 8.00 3.60
134 Edwin Jackson RH RC 20.00 9.00
135 Jeremy Bonderman RH RC 10.00 4.50
136 Khalil Greene RH 10.00 4.50
137 Rich Harden RH 10.00 4.50
138 Rickie Weeks RH RC 40.00 18.00
139 Rosman Garcia RH RC 8.00 3.60
140 Ryan Wagner RH RC 12.00 5.50

2003 UD Authentics Rookie Hype Gold

Randomly inserted into packs, these cards parallel the final 30 cards of the regular UD Authentics set. These cards were issued to a stated print run of 50 serial numbered sets.

MINT NRMT
*RH GOLD: 1X TO 2.5X BASIC
RANDOM INSERTS IN PACKS
STATED PRINT RUN 50 SERIAL #'d SETS

2003 UD Authentics Autograph Frames

Inserted at a stated rate of one per box, these oversized frames featured an 8" by 10" photo of the featured player along with some design and authentic autograph. Since these were issued in varying quantities we have provided the print run next to the player's name in our checklist. Please note that if one of these frames was issued to a stated print run of 25 or fewer, no pricing is provided due to market scarcity.

MINT NRMT
RANDOM INSERTS IN PACKS
PRINT RUNS B/WN 1-350 COPIES PER
AK1 Austin Kearns 28/175 40.00 18.00
AK2 Austin Kearns 28/200 40.00 18.00
AK3 Austin Kearns 28/325 40.00 18.00
AK4 Austin Kearns Mascot/300. 40.00 18.00
AK5 Austin Kearns TL Jsy/28 80.00 36.00
BG1 Bob Gibson 45/200 80.00 36.00
BG2 Bob Gibson Cap/50 150.00 70.00
BG3 Bob Gibson TL Jsy/45 150.00 70.00
CF1 Carlton Fisk 27/250 60.00 27.00
CF2 Carlton Fisk B/70 100.00 45.00
CF3 Carlton Fisk Socks/125 80.00 36.00
CF4 Carlton Fisk TL Jsy/27 200.00 90.00
CJ1 Chipper Jones 10/350 80.00 36.00
CJ2 Chipper Jones A/200 80.00 36.00
CJ3 Chipper Jones MVP/100 100.00 45.00
CJ4 Chipper Jones TL Jsy/10
CR1 Cal Ripken 8/125 200.00 90.00
CR2 Cal Ripken Mascot/50 250.00 110.00
CR3 Cal Ripken TL Jsy/8
DH1 Drew Henson 57/100 60.00 27.00
DH2 Drew Henson 57/250 50.00 22.00
DH3 Drew Henson 57/350 50.00 22.00
DH4 Drew Henson NY/300 50.00 22.00
DS1 Duke Snider 4/150 80.00 36.00
DS2 Duke Snider 55 WS/50 150.00 70.00
DS3 Duke Snider B Jsy/4
GC1 Gary Carter 8/225 60.00 27.00
GC2 Gary Carter 86 WS/75 100.00 45.00
GC3 Gary Carter TL Jsy/8
HB1 Hank Blalock 9/175 50.00 22.00
HB2 Hank Blalock 9/200 50.00 22.00
HB3 Hank Blalock 9/325 50.00 22.00
HB4 Hank Blalock Flag/300 50.00 22.00
HB5 Hank Blalock TL Jsy/12
HM1 Hideki Matsui 75/175 400.00 180.00
HM2 Hideki Matsui NY/75 400.00 180.00
HM3 Hideki Matsui TL Jsy/55 . 500.00 220.00
IS1 Ichiro Suzuki 51/75 400.00 180.00
IS2 Ichiro Suzuki S/75 400.00 180.00
IS3 Ichiro Suzuki TL Jsy/51 400.00 180.00
JC1 Jose Contreras 52/350 60.00 27.00
JC2 Jose Contreras NY/120 60.00 27.00
JG1 J.Giambi A's Cap/75 80.00 36.00
JG2 J.Giambi A's Mascot/150 60.00 27.00
JG3 J.Giambi Yanks 25/100 100.00 45.00
JG4 J.Giambi Yanks 25/200 80.00 36.00
JG5 J.Giambi Yanks 25/300 80.00 36.00
JG6 J.Giambi Yanks NY/350 80.00 36.00
JG7 J.Giambi Yanks TL Jsy/25
KG1 K.Griffey M's MVP/75 200.00 90.00
KG2 K.Griffey Reds 30/325 150.00 70.00
KG3 K.Griffey Reds Mascot/200 150.00 70.00
KG4 K.Griffey Reds TL Jsy/30. 250.00 110.00
LB1 Lance Berkman 17/150 40.00 18.00
LB2 Lance Berkman Cap/50 60.00 27.00
LB3 Lance Berkman TL Jsy/17
MM1 Mickey Mantle 7/25
MM2 Mickey Mantle 56 WS Pants/7
MP1 Mark Prior 22/25
MP2 Mark Prior 22/175 120.00 55.00
MP3 Mark Prior 22/250 120.00 55.00
MP4 Mark Prior C/300 120.00 55.00
MP5 Mark Prior Mascot/100 150.00 70.00
MP6 Mark Prior TL Jsy/22
MT1 Mark Teixeira 23/175 50.00 22.00
MT2 Mark Teixeira 23/200 50.00 22.00
MT3 Mark Teixeira 23/250 50.00 22.00
MT4 Mark Teixeira Flag/150 50.00 22.00
MT5 Mark Teixeira TL Jsy/23

NG1 N.Garciaparra 5/250 150.00 70.00
NG2 N.Garciaparra B/150 150.00 70.00
NG3 N.Garciaparra Socks/75 200.00 90.00
NG4 N.Garciaparra TL Jsy/5
NR1 Nolan Ryan Angels A/100 200.00 90.00
NR2 Nolan Ryan Mets TL/50 250.00 110.00
NR3 Nolan Ryan Rgr 34/150 150.00 70.00
NR4 Nolan Ryan Rgr TL Jsy/34 300.00 135.00
OS1 Ozzie Smith 1/150 100.00 45.00
OS2 Ozzie Smith Cap/50 150.00 70.00
OS3 Ozzie Smith TL Jsy/1
PB1 Pat Burrell 5/330 40.00 18.00
PB2 Pat Burrell Comm/150 40.00 18.00
PB3 Pat Burrell P/240 40.00 18.00
PB4 Pat Burrell TL Jsy/5
PR1 Phil Rizzuto 10/350 60.00 27.00
PR2 Phil Rizzuto 51 WS/100 100.00 45.00
PR3 Phil Rizzuto NY/200 80.00 36.00
PR4 Phil Rizzuto TL Jsy/10
SR1 Scott Rolen 27/300 60.00 27.00
SR2 Scott Rolen STL/100 80.00 36.00
SR3 Scott Rolen TL Jsy/27 150.00 70.00
TGL1 Tom Glavine 47/275 60.00 27.00
TGL2 Tom Glavine Mascot/150 60.00 27.00
TGL3 Tom Glavine TL Jsy/47
TG1 Troy Glaus 25/350 50.00 22.00
TG2 Troy Glaus 02 WS/100 80.00 36.00
TG3 Troy Glaus A/200 50.00 22.00
TG4 Troy Glaus TL Jsy/25
TS1 Tom Seaver 41/100 100.00 45.00
TS2 Tom Seaver Mascot/50 150.00 70.00
TS3 Tom Seaver NY/50 150.00 70.00
TS4 Tom Seaver TL Jsy/41 150.00 70.00
TW1 Ted Williams 9/25
TW2 Ted Williams TL Pants/9
VG1 Vladimir Guerrero 27/150 60.00 27.00
VG2 Vladimir Guerrero TL Jsy/27 150.00 70.00

2003 UD Authentics Star Quality Memorabilia

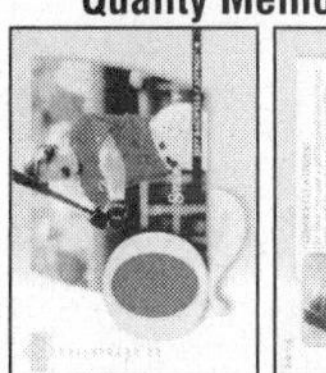

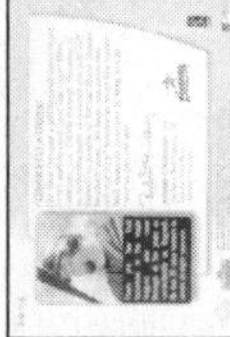

MINT NRMT
PRINT RUNS B/WN 130-350 COPIES PER
ALL COPIES ARE #'d TO 350 UNLESS NOTED
*GOLD: .75X TO 2X BASIC
GOLD PRINT RUNS B/WN 10-50 COPIES PER
NO GOLD PRICING ON QTY OF 25 OR LESS
RANDOM INSERTS IN PACKS
AD Adam Dunn Jsy 8.00 3.60
AK Austin Kearns Jsy 8.00 3.60
AP Albert Pujols Jsy 25.00 11.00
AS Alfonso Soriano Jsy 10.00 4.50
BW Bernie Williams Jsy 10.00 4.50
CD Carlos Delgado Jsy 8.00 3.60
CJ Chipper Jones Jsy 10.00 4.50
CR Cal Ripken Jsy/250 50.00 22.00
CS Casey Stengel Pants 20.00 9.00
GS Gary Sheffield Jsy 8.00 3.60
HM Hideki Matsui Jsy/250 80.00 36.00
HN Hideo Nomo Jsy 15.00 6.75
JB Jeff Bagwell Jsy 10.00 4.50
JD J.D. Drew Jsy 8.00 3.60
JG Jason Giambi Jsy 10.00 4.50
JK Jeff Kent Jsy 8.00 3.60
JO Josh Beckett Jsy 10.00 4.50
JT Jim Thome Jsy 10.00 4.50
KG Ken Griffey Jr. Jsy/250 15.00 6.75
KW Kerry Wood Jsy 10.00 4.50
LB Lance Berkman Jsy 8.00 3.60
MM Mickey Mantle Pants/250 100.00 45.00
MP Mark Prior Jsy 20.00 9.00
MU Mike Mussina Jsy 10.00 4.50
NR Nolan Ryan Jsy/130 50.00 22.00
PM Paul Molitor Pants/250 15.00 6.75
RA Roberto Alomar Jsy 10.00 4.50
RC Roger Clemens White Jsy 15.00 6.75
RC1 Roger Clemens Blue Jsy 15.00 6.75
RO Roy Oswalt Jsy 8.00 3.60
RP Rafael Palmeiro Jsy 10.00 4.50
SG Shawn Green Jsy 8.00 3.60
SS Sammy Sosa Jsy/250 15.00 6.75
TB Eric Hinske Jsy 8.00 3.60
TG Tom Glavine Jsy/250 10.00 4.50
TH Todd Helton PT Jsy 10.00 4.50
TR Troy Glaus Jsy 10.00 4.50
TS Tom Seaver Pants 15.00 6.75
TW Ted Williams Pants/250 80.00 36.00
VG Vladimir Guerrero PT Jsy 10.00 4.50

2003 UD Authentics Threads of Time

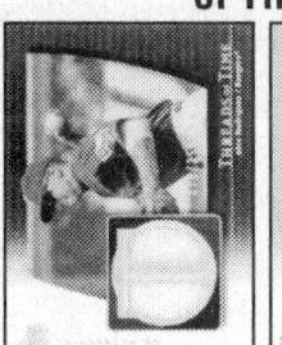

MINT NRMT
PRINT RUNS B/WN 250-350 COPIES PER
ALL COPIES ARE #'d TO 350 UNLESS NOTED
*GOLD ACTIVE: .75X TO 2X BASIC
*GOLD RETIRED: 1.25X TO 3X BASIC
GOLD PRINT RUNS B/WN 10-50 COPIES PER
NO GOLD PRICING ON QTY OF 25 OR LESS
RANDOM INSERTS IN PACKS
APE Andy Pettitte Jsy 10.00 4.50
APU Albert Pujols Jsy 25.00 11.00
AR Alex Rodriguez Jsy 15.00 6.75
CJ Chipper Jones Jsy 10.00 4.50
CR Cal Ripken Jsy 50.00 22.00

DD Don Drysdale Pants 15.00 6.75
DE Dennis Eckersley Jsy 10.00 4.50
DM Don Mattingly Jsy 40.00 18.00
DW Dave Winfield Jsy/250 10.00 4.50
FR Frank Robinson Jsy 15.00 6.75
FT Frank Thomas Jsy 10.00 4.50
GC Gary Carter Jsy 10.00 4.50
GM Greg Maddux Jsy 15.00 6.75
HK Harmon Killebrew Jsy 15.00 6.75
HM Hideo Nomo Jsy 15.00 6.75
HW Honus Wagner Pants 100.00 45.00
IR Ivan Rodriguez Jsy 10.00 4.50
IS Ichiro Suzuki Jsy/250 50.00 22.00
JB Johnny Bench Pants 15.00 6.75
JGI Jason Giambi Jsy/250 10.00 4.50
JGO Juan Gonzalez Jsy 10.00 4.50
JT Jim Thome Jsy 10.00 4.50
KG Ken Griffey Jr. Jsy/250 15.00 6.75
LG Lou Gehrig Jsy/250 200.00 90.00
MM Mickey Mantle Pants/250 120.00 55.00
MP Mike Piazza Jsy 15.00 6.75
MW Maury Wills Jsy 10.00 4.50
NR Nolan Ryan Pants 40.00 18.00
OS Ozzie Smith Jsy 25.00 11.00
PM Pedro Martinez Jsy 10.00 4.50
RC Roger Clemens Jsy 15.00 6.75
RF Rollie Fingers Jsy 10.00 4.50
RJ Randy Johnson Jsy 10.00 4.50
RM Roger Maris Pants 50.00 22.00
RS Ryne Sandberg Jsy 25.00 11.00
SS Sammy Sosa Jsy/250 15.00 6.75
TC Ty Cobb Pants 100.00 45.00
TM Tom Seaver Pants 15.00 6.75
TW Ted Williams Pants/250 80.00 36.00
VG Vladimir Guerrero PT Jsy 10.00 4.50

1999 UD Choice Preview

This 55-card standard size set was issued through retail channels. The cards were issued in five card packs with a suggested retail pack of 79 cents per and featured a selection of players in the regular UD Choice set. One important difference between these cards and the regular UD Choice cards is the word "Preview" in large foil letters on the top of the card. The set is skip-numbered to accommodate the feature of doing the leading players of the set.

Nm-Mt Ex-Mt
COMPLETE SET (55) 15.00 4.50
46 Tim Salmon .20 .06
48 Chuck Finley .20 .06
50 Matt Williams .30 .09
52 Travis Lee .20 .06
54 Andres Galarraga .40 .12
56 Greg Maddux 1.25 .35
58 Cal Ripken Jr. 2.00 .60
60 Rafael Palmeiro .40 .12
62 Nomar Garciaparra 1.00 .30
64 Pedro Martinez .50 .15
66 Kerry Wood .40 .12
67 Sammy Sosa 1.00 .30
70 Albert Belle .20 .06
72 Frank Thomas .50 .15
74 Pete Harnisch .10 .03
76 Manny Ramirez .50 .15
78 Travis Fryman .20 .06
80 Kenny Lofton .30 .09
82 Larry Walker .20 .06
84 Gabe Alvarez .10 .03
86 Damion Easley .10 .03
88 Mark Kotsay .10 .03
90 Jeff Bagwell .50 .15
93 Craig Biggio .30 .09
94 Larry Sutton .10 .03
96 Johnny Damon .30 .09
98 Gary Sheffield .50 .15
100 Mark Grudzielanek .10 .03
102 Jeff Cirillo .10 .03
104 Mark Loretta .10 .03
106 David Ortiz .30 .09
108 Brad Fullmer .20 .06
110 Vladimir Guerrero .50 .15
112 Brian McRae .10 .03
114 Rey Ordonez .10 .03
115 Derek Jeter 2.00 .60
118 Paul O'Neill .40 .12
120 A.J. Hinch .10 .03
122 Miguel Tejada .50 .15
124 Scott Rolen .40 .12
126 Bob Abreu .40 .12
128 Jason Kendall .20 .06
130 Mark McGwire 1.50 .45
132 Eli Marrero .10 .03
136 Kevin Brown .30 .09
137 Tony Gwynn 1.00 .30
138 Bill Mueller .10 .03
140 Barry Bonds 1.00 .30
142 Ken Griffey Jr. 1.00 .30
143 Alex Rodriguez 1.00 .30
146 Rolando Arrojo .10 .03
148 Quinton McCracken .10 .03
150 Will Clark .40 .12
152 Juan Gonzalez .50 .15
154 Carlos Delgado .40 .12

1999 UD Choice

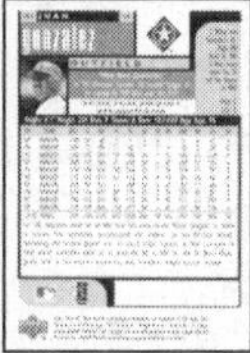

This 155-card set features color action player photos in white borders. The backs carry player information. The set contains the following subsets: Rookie Class (1-27) and Cover Glory (28-45). Approximately 350 Eddie Murray A Piece of History 500 Club bat cards were randomly seeded into packs. Pricing for this card can be referenced under 1999 Upper Deck A Piece of History 500 Club.

Nm-Mt Ex-Mt
COMPLETE SET (155) 20.00 6.00
1 Gabe Kapler .20 .06
2 Jin Ho Cho .20 .06
3 Matt Anderson .20 .06
4 Ricky Ledee .20 .06
5 Bruce Chen .20 .06
6 Alex Gonzalez .20 .06
7 Ryan Minor .20 .06
8 Michael Barrett .20 .06
9 Carlos Beltran .20 .06
10 Ramon E.Martinez RC .20 .06
11 Dermal Brown .20 .06
12 Robert Fick .20 .06
13 Preston Wilson .20 .06
14 Orlando Hernandez .20 .06
15 Troy Glaus .30 .09
16 Calvin Pickering .20 .06
17 Corey Koskie .20 .06
18 Fernando Seguignol .20 .06
19 Carlos Guillen .20 .06
20 Kevin Witt .20 .06
21 Mike Kinkade .20 .06
22 Eric Chavez .20 .06
23 Mike Lowell .20 .06
24 Adrian Beltre .20 .06
25 George Lombard .20 .06
26 Jeremy Giambi .20 .06
27 J.D. Drew .20 .06
28 Mark McGwire CG .60 .18
29 Kerry Wood CG .30 .09
30 David Wells CG .20 .06
31 Juan Gonzalez CG .30 .09
32 Randy Johnson CG .30 .09
33 Derek Jeter CG .60 .18
34 Tony Gwynn CG .30 .09
35 Greg Maddux CG .50 .15
36 Cal Ripken CG .75 .23
37 Ken Griffey Jr. CG .50 .15
38 Bartolo Colon CG .20 .06
39 Troy Glaus CG .20 .06
40 Ben Grieve CG .20 .06
41 Roger Clemens CG .50 .15
42 Chipper Jones CG .30 .09
43 Scott Rolen CG .30 .09
44 Nomar Garciaparra CG .50 .15
45 Sammy Sosa CG .50 .15
46 Tim Salmon .30 .09
47 Darin Erstad .20 .06
48 Chuck Finley .20 .06
49 Garret Anderson .20 .06
50 Matt Williams .20 .06
51 Jay Bell .20 .06
52 Travis Lee .20 .06
53 Andruw Jones .20 .06
54 Andres Galarraga .20 .06
55 Chipper Jones .50 .15
56 Greg Maddux .75 .23
57 Javy Lopez .20 .06
58 Cal Ripken 1.50 .45
59 Brady Anderson .20 .06
60 Rafael Palmeiro .30 .09
61 B.J. Surhoff .20 .06
62 Nomar Garciaparra .75 .23
63 Troy O'Leary .20 .06
64 Pedro Martinez .50 .15
65 Jason Varitek .20 .06
66 Kerry Wood .50 .15
67 Sammy Sosa .75 .23
68 Mark Grace .30 .09
69 Mickey Morandini .20 .06
70 Albert Belle .20 .06
71 Mike Caruso .20 .06
72 Frank Thomas .50 .15
73 Sean Casey .20 .06
74 Pete Harnisch .20 .06
75 Dmitri Young .20 .06
76 Manny Ramirez .20 .06
77 Omar Vizquel .20 .06
78 Travis Fryman .20 .06
79 Jim Thome .50 .15
80 Kenny Lofton .20 .06
81 Todd Helton .30 .09
82 Larry Walker .30 .09
83 Vinny Castilla .20 .06
84 Gabe Alvarez .20 .06
85 Tony Clark .20 .06
86 Damion Easley .20 .06
87 Livan Hernandez .20 .06
88 Mark Kotsay .20 .06
89 Cliff Floyd .20 .06
90 Jeff Bagwell .20 .06
91 Moises Alou .20 .06
92 Randy Johnson .50 .15
93 Craig Biggio .30 .09
94 Larry Sutton .20 .06
95 Dean Palmer .20 .06
96 Johnny Damon .20 .06
97 Charles Johnson .20 .06
98 Gary Sheffield .20 .06
99 Raul Mondesi .20 .06
100 Mark Grudzielanek .20 .06
101 Jeromy Burnitz .20 .06
102 Jeff Cirillo .20 .06
103 Jose Valentin .20 .06
104 Mark Loretta .20 .06
105 Todd Walker .20 .06
106 David Ortiz .20 .06
107 Brad Radke .20 .06
108 Brad Fullmer .20 .06
109 Rondell White .20 .06
110 Vladimir Guerrero .50 .15
111 Mike Piazza .75 .23
112 Brian McRae .20 .06
113 John Olerud .20 .06
114 Rey Ordonez .20 .06
115 Derek Jeter 1.25 .35
116 Bernie Williams .30 .09
117 David Wells .20 .06
118 Paul O'Neill .30 .09
119 Tino Martinez .30 .09
120 A.J. Hinch .20 .06
121 Jason Giambi .50 .15
122 Miguel Tejada .20 .06
123 Ben Grieve .20 .06
124 Scott Rolen .30 .09
125 Desi Relaford .20 .06
126 Bob Abreu .20 .06
127 Jose Guillen .20 .06
128 Jason Kendall .20 .06
129 Aramis Ramirez .20 .06
130 Mark McGwire 1.25 .35
131 Ray Lankford .20 .06
132 Eli Marrero .20 .06
133 Wally Joyner .20 .06
134 Greg Vaughn .20 .06
135 Trevor Hoffman .20 .06
136 Kevin Brown .30 .09
137 Tony Gwynn .60 .18
138 Bill Mueller .20 .06
139 Ellis Burks .20 .06
140 Barry Bonds 1.25 .35
141 Robb Nen .20 .06
142 Ken Griffey Jr. .75 .23
143 Alex Rodriguez .75 .23
144 Jay Buhner .20 .06
145 Edgar Martinez .30 .09
146 Rolando Arrojo .20 .06
147 Robert Smith .20 .06
148 Quinton McCracken .20 .06
149 Ivan Rodriguez .50 .15
150 Will Clark .50 .15
151 Mark McLemore .20 .06
152 Juan Gonzalez .50 .15
153 Jose Cruz Jr. .20 .06
154 Carlos Delgado .20 .06
155 Roger Clemens 1.00 .30

1999 UD Choice Prime Choice Reserve

Randomly inserted in hobby only packs, this 155-card set is a parallel version of the base set. Only 100 sets were produced and serially numbered.

Nm-Mt Ex-Mt
*STARS: 20X TO 40X BASIC CARDS

1999 UD Choice Blow Up

This 10-card set features action color photos of top players printed on jumbo-sized cards. The backs carry player information.

Nm-Mt Ex-Mt
COMPLETE SET (10) 20.00 6.00
1 Ken Griffey Jr. 2.00 .60
2 Sammy Sosa 2.00 .60
3 Mark McGwire 3.00 .90
4 Cal Ripken 4.00 1.20
5 Roger Clemens 2.00 .60
6 Derek Jeter 3.00 .90
7 Kerry Wood .50 .15
8 Alex Rodriguez 2.00 .60
9 Nomar Garciaparra 2.00 .60
10 Greg Maddux 2.50 .75

1999 UD Choice Blow Up Cover Glory

This 10-card set features action color photos of star players printed on jumbo-sized cards. The backs carry player information.

Nm-Mt Ex-Mt
COMPLETE SET (10) 20.00 6.00
1 Mark McGwire 3.00 .90
2 Kerry Wood .75 .23
3 Juan Gonzalez 1.00 .30
4 Derek Jeter 3.00 .90
5 Tony Gwynn 2.00 .60
6 Cal Ripken 4.00 1.20
7 Ken Griffey Jr. 3.00 .90
8 Roger Clemens 2.00 .60
9 Nomar Garciaparra 2.00 .60
10 Sammy Sosa 2.00 .60

1999 UD Choice Homerun Heroes

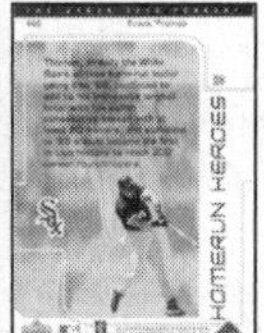

These cards were randomly inserted into speciual UD Choice cans released through special retail outlets.

Nm-Mt Ex-Mt
COMPLETE SET 10.00 3.00
H1 Ken Griffey Jr. 1.50 .45
H2 Mark McGwire 2.00 .60
H3 Sammy Sosa 1.50 .45
H4 Troy Glaus 1.00 .30
H5 Mike Piazza 2.00 .60
H6 Chipper Jones 1.50 .45
H7 Vladimir Guerrero 1.00 .30
H8 Frank Thomas 1.25 .35
H9 Juan Gonzalez 1.00 .30
H10 Alex Rodriguez 1.50 .45

1999 UD Choice Mini Bobbing Head

Randomly inserted one in every five packs, this 30-card set features head photos and a body figure of the some of the game's top players. If assembled, they represented mini Bobbing Heads.

Nm-Mt Ex-Mt
COMPLETE SET (30) 25.00 7.50
B1 Randy Johnson 1.25 .35
B2 Troy Glaus .75 .23
B3 Chipper Jones 1.25 .35
B4 Cal Ripken 4.00 1.20
B5 Nomar Garciaparra 2.00 .60
B6 Pedro Martinez 1.25 .35
B7 Kerry Wood 1.25 .35
B8 Sammy Sosa 2.00 .60
B9 Frank Thomas 1.25 .35
B10 Paul Konerko .50 .15
B11 Omar Vizquel .50 .15
B12 Kenny Lofton .50 .15
B13 Gabe Kapler .50 .15
B14 Adrian Beltre .50 .15
B15 Orlando Hernandez .50 .15
B16 Derek Jeter 3.00 .90
B17 Mike Piazza 2.00 .60
B18 Tino Martinez .75 .23
B19 Ben Grieve .50 .15
B20 Rickey Henderson 1.25 .35
B21 Scott Rolen .75 .23
B22 Aramis Ramirez .50 .15
B23 Greg Vaughn .50 .15
B24 Tony Gwynn 1.50 .45
B25 Barry Bonds 3.00 .90
B26 Alex Rodriguez 2.00 .60
B27 Ken Griffey Jr. 2.00 .60
B28 Mark McGwire 3.00 .90
B29 J.D. Drew .50 .15
B30 Juan Gonzalez 1.25 .35

1999 UD Choice Rookie Class

Inserted in 1999 Upper Deck Opening Day packs, these 10 cards feature players who were considered to be the leading prospects going into the 1999 season.

Nm-Mt Ex-Mt
COMPLETE SET 8.00 2.40
R1 J.D. Drew 1.00 .30
R2 Gabe Kapler .50 .15
R3 Eric Chavez 2.00 .60
R4 Troy Glaus 2.00 .60
R5 Ryan Minor .25 .07
R6 Corey Koskie 1.00 .30
R7 Jeremy Giambi .25 .07
R8 Carlos Beltran 1.25 .35
R9 Carlos Guillen .25 .07
R10 Mike Kinkade .25 .07

1999 UD Choice StarQuest

Inserted one in every pack, this 30-card set features color action photos of top players in a striped blue foil border. The backs carry player information.

Nm-Mt Ex-Mt
COMP.BLUE SET (30) 20.00 6.00
*GREEN: 1X TO 2.5X BASIC BLUE STARQUEST
GREEN STATED ODDS 1:8
*RED: 2.5X TO 6X BASIC BLUE STARQUEST
RED STATED ODDS 1:23
*GOLD: 30X TO 80X BASIC BLUE STARQUEST
GOLD RANDOM INSERTS IN PACKS
1 Ken Griffey Jr. 1.25 .35
2 Sammy Sosa 1.25 .35
3 Alex Rodriguez 1.25 .35
4 Derek Jeter 2.00 .60
5 Troy Glaus .50 .15
6 Mike Piazza 1.25 .35
7 Barry Bonds 2.00 .60
8 Tony Gwynn 1.00 .30
9 Juan Gonzalez .75 .23
10 Chipper Jones .75 .23
11 Greg Maddux 1.25 .35
12 Randy Johnson .75 .23
13 Roger Clemens 1.50 .45
14 Ben Grieve .30 .09
15 Nomar Garciaparra 1.25 .35
16 Travis Lee .30 .09
17 Frank Thomas .75 .23
18 Vladimir Guerrero .75 .23
19 Scott Rolen .50 .15
20 Ivan Rodriguez .75 .23
21 Cal Ripken 2.50 .75
22 Mark McGwire 2.00 .60
23 Jeff Bagwell .50 .15
24 Tony Clark .30 .09
25 Kerry Wood .75 .23
26 Kenny Lofton .30 .09
27 Adrian Beltre .30 .09
28 Larry Walker .50 .15
29 Curt Schilling .30 .09
30 Jim Thome .75 .23

1999 UD Choice Superstars

This insert set was randomly inserted into special UD Choice cans distributed through special retail outlets

Nm-Mt Ex-Mt
COMPLETE SET 10.00 3.00
S1 Ken Griffey Jr 1.50 .45
S2 Mark McGwire 2.00 .60
S3 Sammy Sosa 1.50 .45
S4 Cal Ripken Jr. 3.00 .90
S5 Nomar Garciaparra 1.50 .45

	Nm-Mt	Ex-Mt
S6 Alex Rodriguez	1.50	.45
S7 Kerry Wood	1.00	.30
S8 Juan Gonzalez	1.00	.30
S9 Derek Jeter	3.00	.90
S10 Greg Maddux	2.00	.60

1999 UD Choice Yard Work

Randomly inserted in packs at the rate of one in 13, this 30-card set features action color photos of 1998's most explosive power hitters.

	Nm-Mt	Ex-Mt
COMPLETE SET (30)	60.00	18.00
Y1 Andres Galarraga	1.00	.30
Y2 Chipper Jones	2.50	.75
Y3 Rafael Palmeiro	1.50	.45
Y4 Nomar Garciaparra	4.00	1.20
Y5 Sammy Sosa	4.00	1.20
Y6 Frank Thomas	2.50	.75
Y7 J.D. Drew	1.00	.30
Y8 Albert Belle	1.00	.30
Y9 Jim Thome	2.50	.75
Y10 Manny Ramirez	1.00	.30
Y11 Larry Walker	1.50	.45
Y12 Vinny Castilla	1.00	.30
Y13 Tony Clark	1.00	.30
Y14 Jeff Bagwell	1.50	.45
Y15 Moises Alou	1.00	.30
Y16 Dean Palmer	1.00	.30
Y17 Gary Sheffield	1.00	.30
Y18 Vladimir Guerrero	2.50	.75
Y19 Mike Piazza	4.00	1.20
Y20 Tino Martinez	1.50	.45
Y21 Ben Grieve	1.00	.30
Y22 Greg Vaughn	1.00	.30
Y23 Ken Caminiti	1.00	.30
Y24 Barry Bonds	6.00	1.80
Y25 Ken Griffey Jr.	4.00	1.20
Y26 Alex Rodriguez	4.00	1.20
Y27 Mark McGwire	6.00	1.80
Y28 Juan Gonzalez	2.50	.75
Y29 Jose Canseco	2.50	.75
Y30 Jose Cruz Jr.	1.00	.30

2004 UD Diamond All-Star

This 120 card set was released in March, 2004. The set was issued solely through Upper Deck's "retail" outlets. The set was issued in six card packs with an $3 SRP which came 24 packs to a box and 20 boxes to a case. Cards numbered 1-90 feature active veterans which cards numbered 91 through 120 feature rookies. The Rookie Cards were issued at a stated rate of one in six.

	Nm-Mt	Ex-Mt
COMP.SET w/o SP's (90)	25.00	7.50
COMMON CARD (1-90)	.30	.09
COMMON CARD (91-120)	3.00	.90
1 Garret Anderson	.30	.09
2 Darin Erstad	.30	.09
3 Troy Glaus	.50	.15
4 Curt Schilling	.50	.15
5 Brandon Webb	.30	.09
6 Randy Johnson	.75	.23
7 Andruw Jones	.30	.09
8 Chipper Jones	.75	.23
9 Gary Sheffield	.30	.09
10 Jay Gibbons	.30	.09
11 Miguel Tejada	.30	.09
12 Tony Batista	.30	.09
13 Nomar Garciaparra	1.25	.35
14 Manny Ramirez	.30	.09
15 Pedro Martinez	.75	.23
16 Mark Prior	1.50	.45
17 Kerry Wood	.75	.23
18 Sammy Sosa	1.25	.35
19 Bartolo Colon	.30	.09
20 Magglio Ordonez	.30	.09
21 Frank Thomas	.75	.23
22 Adam Dunn	.30	.09
23 Austin Kearns	.30	.09
24 Ken Griffey Jr.	1.25	.35
25 Brandon Phillips	.30	.09
26 Milton Bradley	.30	.09
27 Jody Gerut	.30	.09
28 Todd Helton	.50	.15
29 Larry Walker	.50	.15
30 Preston Wilson	.30	.09
31 Jeremy Bonderman	.30	.09
32 Carlos Pena	.30	.09
33 Dmitri Young	.30	.09
34 Dontrelle Willis	.30	.09
35 Miguel Cabrera	.75	.23
36 Mike Lowell	.30	.09
37 Jeff Bagwell	.50	.15
38 Roy Oswalt	.30	.09
39 Lance Berkman	.30	.09
40 Carlos Beltran	.30	.09
41 Mike Sweeney	.30	.09
42 Rondell White	.30	.09
43 Hideo Nomo	.75	.23
44 Kevin Brown	.30	.09
45 Shawn Green	.30	.09
46 Ben Sheets	.30	.09
47 Geoff Jenkins	.30	.09
48 Richie Sexson	.30	.09
49 Jacque Jones	.30	.09
50 Johan Santana	.30	.09
51 Torii Hunter	.30	.09
52 Javier Vazquez	.30	.09
53 Jose Vidro	.30	.09
54 Vladimir Guerrero	.75	.23
55 Cliff Floyd	.30	.09
56 Mike Piazza	1.25	.35
57 Jose Reyes	.50	.15
58 Derek Jeter	2.00	.60
59 Jason Giambi	.75	.23
60 Alfonso Soriano	.50	.15
61 Eric Chavez	.30	.09
62 Barry Zito	.50	.15
63 Tim Hudson	.30	.09
64 Bobby Abreu	.30	.09
65 Jim Thome	.75	.23
66 Kevin Millwood	.30	.09
67 Roger Clemens	1.50	.45
68 Jason Kendall	.30	.09
69 Reggie Sanders	.30	.09
70 Phil Nevin	.30	.09
71 Ryan Klesko	.30	.09
72 Brian Giles	.30	.09
73 A.J. Pierzynski	.30	.09
74 Jason Schmidt	.30	.09
75 Sidney Ponson	.30	.09
76 Edgar Martinez	.50	.15
77 Ichiro Suzuki	1.25	.35
78 Bret Boone	.30	.09
79 Albert Pujols	1.50	.45
80 Scott Rolen	.50	.15
81 Jim Edmonds	.30	.09
82 Aubrey Huff	.30	.09
83 Delmon Young	.75	.23
84 Rocco Baldelli	.75	.23
85 Alex Rodriguez	1.25	.35
86 Mark Teixeira	.30	.09
87 Rafael Palmeiro	.50	.15
88 Carlos Delgado	.30	.09
89 Vernon Wells	.30	.09
90 Roy Halladay	.30	.09
91 Brandon Medders FC RC	3.00	.90
92 Colby Miller FC RC	3.00	.90
93 Dave Crouthers FC RC	3.00	.90
94 Dennis Sarfate FC RC	4.00	1.20
95 Donald Kelly FC RC	3.00	.90
96 Alec Zumwalt FC RC	3.00	.90
97 Frank Brooks FC RC	3.00	.90
98 Greg Dobbs FC RC	3.00	.90
99 Ian Snell FC RC	4.00	1.20
100 Jake Woods FC RC	3.00	.90
101 Jamie Brown FC RC	3.00	.90
102 Jason Frasor FC RC	3.00	.90
103 Jerome Gamble FC RC	3.00	.90
104 Jesse Harper FC RC	3.00	.90
105 Josh Labandeira FC RC	3.00	.90
106 Justin Hampson FC RC	3.00	.90
107 Justin Huisman FC RC	3.00	.90
108 Justin Leone FC RC	3.00	.90
109 Chris Aguila FC RC	3.00	.90
110 Lincoln Holdzkom FC RC	3.00	.90
111 Mike Bumatay FC RC	3.00	.90
112 Mike Gosling FC RC	3.00	.90
113 Mike Johnston FC RC	3.00	.90
114 Mike Rouse FC RC	3.00	.90
115 Nick Regilio FC RC	3.00	.90
116 Ryan Meaux FC RC	3.00	.90
117 Scott Dohmann FC RC	3.00	.90
118 Sean Henn FC RC	4.00	1.20
119 Tim Bausher FC RC	3.00	.90
120 Tim Bittner FC RC	3.00	.90

2004 UD Diamond All-Star Gold Honors

	Nm-Mt	Ex-Mt
*GOLD 1-90: 6X TO 15X BASIC		
*GOLD 91-120: 1X TO 2.5X BASIC		
RANDOM INSERTS IN PACKS		
STATED PRINT RUN 50 SERIAL #'d SETS		

2004 UD Diamond All-Star Silver Honors

	Nm-Mt	Ex-Mt
*SILVER 1-90: 2X TO 5X BASIC		
*SILVER 91-120: .6X TO 1.5X BASIC		
1-90 STATED ODDS 1:6		
91-120 STATED ODDS 1:48		

2004 UD Diamond All-Star Class of 2004 Autographs

	Nm-Mt	Ex-Mt
STATED ODDS 1:5800		
PRINT RUNS B/WN 50-100 COPIES PER		
BZ Barry Zito/100	40.00	12.00
DW Dontrelle Willis/100	25.00	7.50
HM Hideki Matsui/50		
JR Jose Reyes/100	25.00	7.50
KG Ken Griffey Jr./100	150.00	45.00
MC Miguel Cabrera/50	50.00	15.00
MP Mark Prior/100	100.00	30.00
RH Rich Harden/100	25.00	7.50
VG Vladimir Guerrero/100	40.00	12.00

2004 UD Diamond All-Star Dean's List Jersey

	Nm-Mt	Ex-Mt
STATED ODDS 1:72		
AP Albert Pujols	15.00	4.50
AR Alex Rodriguez	10.00	3.00
AS Alfonso Soriano	10.00	3.00
BA Jeff Bagwell	10.00	3.00
CS Curt Schilling	10.00	3.00
DW Dontrelle Willis	8.00	2.40
GL Troy Glaus	10.00	3.00
GM Greg Maddux	10.00	3.00
HB Hank Blalock	8.00	2.40
HM Hideki Matsui	40.00	12.00
HN Hideo Nomo	10.00	3.00
IS Ichiro Suzuki	25.00	7.50
JG Jason Giambi	10.00	3.00
JT Jim Thome	10.00	3.00
KG Ken Griffey Jr.	15.00	4.50
LG Luis Gonzalez	8.00	2.40
MP Mark Prior	15.00	4.50
PI Mike Piazza	10.00	3.00
SG Shawn Green	8.00	2.40
SS Sammy Sosa	10.00	3.00
VG Vladimir Guerrero	10.00	3.00

2004 UD Diamond All-Star Future Gems Jersey

	Nm-Mt	Ex-Mt
STATED ODDS 1:72		
AE Adam Eaton	8.00	2.40
AH Aaron Heilman	8.00	2.40
BA Josh Bard	8.00	2.40
BO Jeremy Bonderman	8.00	2.40
BS Ben Sheets	8.00	2.40
DS David Sanders	8.00	2.40
EM Eric Milton	8.00	2.40
GU Jeremy Guthrie	8.00	2.40
IS Kazuhisa Ishii	8.00	2.40
JB Josh Beckett	10.00	3.00
JJ Jason Jennings	8.00	2.40
JL Jon Leicester	8.00	2.40
JR Jose Reyes	10.00	3.00
KA Matt Kata	8.00	2.40
LF Lew Ford	8.00	2.40
MC Mike Cameron	8.00	2.40
MK Mark Kotsay	8.00	2.40
MT Mark Teixeira	8.00	2.40
PS Phil Seibel	8.00	2.40
RH Roy Halladay	8.00	2.40
RR Rick Roberts	8.00	2.40
SB Sean Burroughs	8.00	2.40
TH Travis Hafner	8.00	2.40
TW Todd Wellemeyer	8.00	2.40
WE Willie Eyre	8.00	2.40
WI Josh Willingham	8.00	2.40

2004 UD Diamond All-Star Premium Stars

	Nm-Mt	Ex-Mt
STATED ODDS 1:4 MASS BLASTER		
AP Albert Pujols		
AR Alex Rodriguez		
AS Alfonso Soriano		
CD Carlos Delgado		
DJ Derek Jeter		
GS Gary Sheffield		
HM Hideki Matsui		
IS Ichiro Suzuki		
JG Jason Giambi		
KG Ken Griffey Jr.		
MP Mike Piazza		
NG Nomar Garciaparra		
SG Shawn Green		
SS Sammy Sosa		
VG Vladimir Guerrero		

2004 UD Diamond All-Star Promo

	Nm-Mt	Ex-Mt
ONE PER PACK		
AD Adam Dunn	1.00	.30
AJ Andruw Jones	1.00	.30
AK Austin Kearns	1.00	.30
BA Bobby Abreu	1.00	.30
BC Bartolo Colon	1.00	.30
BE Josh Beckett	1.25	.35
BO Bret Boone	1.00	.30
BZ Barry Zito	1.25	.35
CB Carlos Beltran	1.00	.30
CJ Chipper Jones	2.00	.60
CS Curt Schilling	1.25	.35
DJ Derek Jeter	5.00	1.50
DW Dontrelle Willis	1.00	.30
EC Eric Chavez	1.00	.30
ER Edgar Renteria	1.00	.30
FT Frank Thomas	2.00	.60
GA Garret Anderson	1.00	.30
GS Gary Sheffield	1.00	.30
HB Hank Blalock	1.00	.30
HM Hideki Matsui	3.00	.90
HU Tim Hudson	1.00	.30
IR Ivan Rodriguez	2.00	.60
JB Jeff Bagwell	1.25	.35
JD Johnny Damon	1.00	.30
JE Jim Edmonds	1.00	.30
JG Jason Giambi	2.00	.60
JJ Jacque Jones	1.00	.30
JK Jeff Kent	1.00	.30
JL Javy Lopez	1.00	.30
JP Jorge Posada	1.25	.35
JS Jason Schmidt	1.00	.30
JT Jim Thome	2.00	.60
JV Jason Varitek	1.00	.30
KG Ken Griffey Jr.	3.00	.90
KW Kerry Wood	2.00	.60
MG Marcus Giles	1.00	.30
ML Mike Lowell	1.00	.30
MM Mark Mulder	1.00	.30
MO Magglio Ordonez	1.00	.30
MP Mark Prior	4.00	1.20
MR Manny Ramirez	1.00	.30
MS Mike Sweeney	1.00	.30
MT Mark Teixeira	1.00	.30
MU Mike Mussina	2.00	.60
OC Orlando Cabrera	1.00	.30
PI Mike Piazza	3.00	.90
PM Pedro Martinez	2.00	.60
PW Preston Wilson	1.00	.30
RF Rafael Furcal	1.00	.30
RH Roy Halladay	1.00	.30
RJ Randy Johnson	2.00	.60
RP Rafael Palmeiro	1.25	.35
RS Richie Sexson	1.00	.30
SG Shawn Green	1.00	.30
SR Scott Rolen	1.25	.35
TE Miguel Tejada	1.00	.30
TG Troy Glaus	1.25	.35
TH Torii Hunter	1.00	.30
VI Jose Vidro	1.00	.30
VW Vernon Wells	1.00	.30

2004 UD Diamond All-Star Promo e-Card

	Nm-Mt	Ex-Mt
STATED ODDS 1:12		
AP Albert Pujols	5.00	1.50
AR Alex Rodriguez	4.00	1.20
AS Alfonso Soriano	1.50	.45
CD Carlos Delgado	1.50	.45
IS Ichiro Suzuki	4.00	1.20
NG Nomar Garciaparra	4.00	1.20
SS Sammy Sosa	4.00	1.20
TH Todd Helton	1.50	.45
VG Vladimir Guerrero	2.50	.75

1999 UD Ionix

This 90-card set (produced by Upper Deck) was distributed in four-card packs with a suggested retail price of $4.99. The set features color action photos of top MLB players printed on super-thick, double-laminated, metalized cards. The set contains a 30-card short-printed subset, Techno (61-90), of which cards were randomly inserted in packs at the rate of one in four. A game-used bat from Hall of Fame slugger Frank Robinson was cut up and incorporated into 370 special 500 Home Run Bat Cards. Robinson signed 20 of these cards. Pack odds for these cards was not officially released, but suffice to say, they're few and far between. Pricing for these bat cards can be referenced under 1999 Upper Deck A Piece of History 500 Club. In addition, a Ken Griffey Jr. sample card was distributed to dealers and hobby media several weeks prior to the product's release. The card can be readily identified by the bold "SAMPLE" text running diagonally across the back.

	Nm-Mt	Ex-Mt
COMPLETE SET (90)	120.00	36.00
COMP.SET w/o SP's (60)	20.00	6.00
COMMON CARD (1-60)	.40	.12
COMMON TECH (61-90)	2.00	.60
1 Troy Glaus	.60	.18
2 Darin Erstad	.40	.12
3 Travis Lee	.40	.12
4 Matt Williams	.40	.12
5 Chipper Jones	1.00	.30
6 Greg Maddux	1.50	.45
7 Andruw Jones	.40	.12
8 Andres Galarraga	.40	.12
9 Tom Glavine	.60	.18
10 Cal Ripken	3.00	.90
11 Ryan Minor	.40	.12
12 Nomar Garciaparra	1.50	.45
13 Mo Vaughn	.40	.12
14 Pedro Martinez	1.00	.30
15 Sammy Sosa	1.50	.45
16 Kerry Wood	1.00	.30
17 Albert Belle	.40	.12
18 Frank Thomas	1.00	.30
19 Sean Casey	.40	.12
20 Kenny Lofton	.40	.12
21 Manny Ramirez	.40	.12
22 Jim Thome	1.00	.30
23 Bartolo Colon	.40	.12
24 Jaret Wright	.40	.12
25 Larry Walker	.60	.18
26 Tony Clark	.40	.12
27 Gabe Kapler	.40	.12
28 Edgar Renteria	.40	.12
29 Randy Johnson	1.00	.30
30 Craig Biggio	.60	.18
31 Jeff Bagwell	.60	.18
32 Moises Alou	.40	.12
33 Johnny Damon	.40	.12
34 Adrian Beltre	.40	.12
35 Jeromy Burnitz	.40	.12
36 Todd Walker	.40	.12
37 Corey Koskie	.40	.12
38 Vladimir Guerrero	1.00	.30
39 Mike Piazza	1.50	.45
40 Hideo Nomo	1.00	.30
41 Derek Jeter	2.50	.75
42 Tino Martinez	.60	.18
43 Orlando Hernandez	.40	.12
44 Ben Grieve	.40	.12
45 Rickey Henderson	1.00	.30
46 Scott Rolen	.60	.18
47 Curt Schilling	.60	.18
48 Aramis Ramirez	.40	.12
49 Tony Gwynn	1.25	.35
50 Kevin Brown	.40	.12
51 Barry Bonds	2.50	.75
52 Ken Griffey Jr.	1.50	.45
53 Alex Rodriguez	1.50	.45
54 Mark McGwire	2.50	.75
55 J.D. Drew	.40	.12
56 Rolando Arrojo	.40	.12
57 Ivan Rodriguez	1.00	.30
58 Juan Gonzalez	1.00	.30
59 Roger Clemens	2.00	.60
60 Jose Cruz Jr.	.40	.12
61 Travis Lee TECH	2.00	.60
62 Andres Galarraga TECH	2.00	.60
63 Andruw Jones TECH	2.00	.60
64 Chipper Jones TECH	4.00	1.20
65 Greg Maddux TECH	6.00	1.80
66 Cal Ripken TECH	12.00	3.60
67 N.Garciaparra TECH	6.00	1.80
68 Mo Vaughn TECH	2.00	.60
69 Sammy Sosa TECH	6.00	1.80
70 Frank Thomas TECH	4.00	1.20
71 Kerry Wood TECH	4.00	1.20
72 Kenny Lofton TECH	2.00	.60
73 Manny Ramirez TECH	2.00	.60
74 Larry Walker TECH	2.50	.75
75 Jeff Bagwell TECH	2.50	.75
76 Randy Johnson TECH	4.00	1.20
77 Paul Molitor TECH	2.50	.75
78 Derek Jeter TECH	10.00	3.00
79 Tino Martinez TECH	2.50	.75
80 Mike Piazza TECH	6.00	1.80
81 Ben Grieve TECH	2.00	.60
82 Scott Rolen TECH	2.50	.75
83 Mark McGwire TECH	10.00	3.00
84 Tony Gwynn TECH	5.00	1.50
85 Barry Bonds TECH	10.00	3.00
86 Ken Griffey Jr. TECH	6.00	1.80
87 Alex Rodriguez TECH	6.00	1.80
88 Juan Gonzalez TECH	4.00	1.20
89 Roger Clemens TECH	8.00	2.40
90 J.D. Drew TECH	2.00	.60
S100 K.Griffey Jr. Sample	2.00	.60

1999 UD Ionix Reciprocal

This 90-card set is a parallel version of the base set and swaps the photos from the backs of the regular cards and places them on the fronts. Only 750 of cards 1-60 were produced and sequentially numbered. Only 100 of the 30-card Techno subset (61-90) were produced and sequentially numbered.

	Nm-Mt	Ex-Mt
*RECIP.1-60: 4X TO 10X BASIC 1-60		
*TECH RECIP: 3X TO 8X BASIC TECH		

1999 UD Ionix Cyber

Randomly inserted in packs at the rate of one in 53, this 25-card set features color action photos of some of the current most collectible superstars, hot rookies and crowd-pleasing favorites.

	Nm-Mt	Ex-Mt
COMPLETE SET (25)	500.00	150.00
C1 Ken Griffey Jr.	25.00	7.50
C2 Cal Ripken	50.00	15.00
C3 Frank Thomas	15.00	4.50
C4 Greg Maddux	25.00	7.50
C5 Mike Piazza	25.00	7.50
C6 Alex Rodriguez	25.00	7.50
C7 Chipper Jones	15.00	4.50
C8 Derek Jeter	40.00	12.00
C9 Mark McGwire	40.00	12.00
C10 Juan Gonzalez	15.00	4.50
C11 Kerry Wood	15.00	4.50
C12 Tony Gwynn	20.00	6.00
C13 Scott Rolen	10.00	3.00
C14 Nomar Garciaparra	25.00	7.50
C15 Roger Clemens	30.00	9.00
C16 Sammy Sosa	25.00	7.50
C17 Travis Lee	6.00	1.80
C18 Ben Grieve	6.00	1.80
C19 Jeff Bagwell	10.00	3.00
C20 Ivan Rodriguez	15.00	4.50
C21 Barry Bonds	40.00	12.00
C22 J.D. Drew	6.00	1.80

C23 Kenny Lofton	6.00	1.80
C24 Andruw Jones	6.00	1.80
C25 Vladimir Guerrero	15.00	4.50

1999 UD Ionix HoloGrFX

Randomly inserted in packs at the rate of one in 1500, this 10-card set features color action photos of the current best players in the game.

	Nm-Mt	Ex-Mt
COMPLETE SET (10)	600.00	180.00
HG1 Ken Griffey Jr.	50.00	15.00
HG2 Cal Ripken	100.00	30.00
HG3 Frank Thomas	30.00	9.00
HG4 Greg Maddux	50.00	15.00
HG5 Mike Piazza	50.00	15.00
HG6 Alex Rodriguez	50.00	15.00
HG7 Chipper Jones	30.00	9.00
HG8 Derek Jeter	80.00	24.00
HG9 Mark McGwire	80.00	24.00
HG10 Juan Gonzalez	30.00	9.00

1999 UD Ionix Hyper

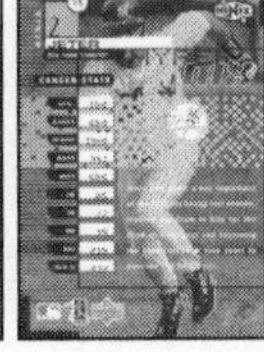

Randomly inserted in packs at the rate of one in nine, this 20-card set features color action photos of some of the current great MLB performers.

	Nm-Mt	Ex-Mt
COMPLETE SET (20)	150.00	45.00
H1 Ken Griffey Jr.	8.00	2.40
H2 Cal Ripken	15.00	4.50
H3 Frank Thomas	5.00	1.50
H4 Greg Maddux	8.00	2.40
H5 Mike Piazza	8.00	2.40
H6 Alex Rodriguez	8.00	2.40
H7 Chipper Jones	5.00	1.50
H8 Derek Jeter	12.00	3.60
H9 Mark McGwire	12.00	3.60
H10 Juan Gonzalez	5.00	1.50
H11 Kerry Wood	5.00	1.50
H12 Tony Gwynn	6.00	1.80
H13 Scott Rolen	3.00	.90
H14 Nomar Garciaparra	8.00	2.40
H15 Roger Clemens	10.00	3.00
H16 Sammy Sosa	8.00	2.40
H17 Travis Lee	2.00	.60
H18 Ben Grieve	2.00	.60
H19 Jeff Bagwell	3.00	.90
H20 J.D. Drew	2.00	.60

1999 UD Ionix Nitro

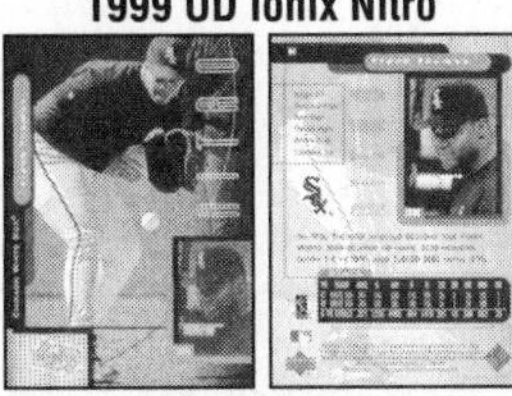

Randomly inserted in packs at the rate of one in 18, this 10-card set features color action photos of the ten most collectible players in the game printed on rainbow foil IONIX cards.

	Nm-Mt	Ex-Mt
COMPLETE SET (10)	80.00	24.00
N1 Ken Griffey Jr.	8.00	2.40
N2 Cal Ripken	15.00	4.50
N3 Frank Thomas	5.00	1.50
N4 Greg Maddux	8.00	2.40
N5 Mike Piazza	8.00	2.40
N6 Alex Rodriguez	8.00	2.40
N7 Chipper Jones	5.00	1.50
N8 Derek Jeter	12.00	3.60
N9 Mark McGwire	12.00	3.60
N10 J.D. Drew	2.00	.60

1999 UD Ionix Warp Zone

Randomly inserted in packs at the rate of one in 216, this 15-card set features color action player photos with a special holographic foil enhancement.

	Nm-Mt	Ex-Mt
COMPLETE SET (15)	400.00	120.00
WZ1 Ken Griffey Jr.	25.00	7.50
WZ2 Cal Ripken	50.00	15.00
WZ3 Frank Thomas	15.00	4.50
WZ4 Greg Maddux	25.00	7.50
WZ5 Mike Piazza	25.00	7.50
WZ6 Alex Rodriguez	25.00	7.50
WZ7 Chipper Jones	15.00	4.50
WZ8 Derek Jeter	40.00	12.00
WZ9 Mark McGwire	40.00	12.00
WZ10 Juan Gonzalez	15.00	4.50
WZ11 Kerry Wood	15.00	4.50
WZ12 Tony Gwynn	20.00	6.00
WZ13 Scott Rolen	10.00	3.00
WZ14 Nomar Garciaparra	25.00	7.50
WZ15 J.D. Drew	10.00	3.00

2000 UD Ionix

The 90 card standard-size set (produced by Upper Deck) was issued in four card packs issued in 24 count boxes and 12 box cases. The packs had an SRP of $3.99 per pack and were issued early in 2000. The final 30 cards in the set feature stars of the future and were inserted at a rate on every four packs. Also, a selection of A Piece of History 3000 Club Roberto Clemente memorabilia cards were randomly seeded into packs. 350 bat cards, four hand-numbered, autograph cut cards and five hand-numbered, combination bat chip and autograph cut cards were produced. Pricing for these memorabilia cards can be referenced under 2000 Upper Deck A Piece of History 3000 Club.

	Nm-Mt	Ex-Mt
COMPLETE SET (90)	80.00	24.00
COMP.SET w/o SP's (60)	25.00	7.50
COMMON CARD (1-60)	.40	.12
COMMON FUT. (61-90)	2.00	.60
1 Mo Vaughn	.40	.12
2 Troy Glaus	.60	.18
3 Jeff Bagwell	.60	.18
4 Craig Biggio	.60	.18
5 Jose Lima	.40	.12
6 Jason Giambi	1.00	.30
7 Tim Hudson	.60	.18
8 Shawn Green	.40	.12
9 Carlos Delgado	.40	.12
10 Chipper Jones	1.00	.30
11 Andruw Jones	.40	.12
12 Greg Maddux	1.50	.45
13 Jeromy Burnitz	.40	.12
14 Mark McGwire	2.50	.75
15 J.D. Drew	.40	.12
16 Sammy Sosa	1.50	.45
17 Jose Canseco	1.00	.30
18 Fred McGriff	.60	.18
19 Randy Johnson	1.00	.30
20 Matt Williams	.40	.12
21 Kevin Brown	.60	.18
22 Gary Sheffield	.40	.12
23 Vladimir Guerrero	1.00	.30
24 Barry Bonds	2.50	.75
25 Jim Thome	1.00	.30
26 Manny Ramirez	.40	.12
27 Roberto Alomar	1.00	.30
28 Kenny Lofton	.40	.12
29 Ken Griffey Jr.	1.50	.45
30 Alex Rodriguez	1.50	.45
31 Alex Gonzalez	.40	.12
32 Preston Wilson	.40	.12
33 Mike Piazza	1.50	.45
34 Robin Ventura	.60	.18
35 Cal Ripken	3.00	.90
36 Albert Belle	.40	.12
37 Tony Gwynn	1.25	.35
38 Scott Rolen	.60	.18
39 Curt Schilling	.60	.18
40 Brian Giles	.40	.12
41 Juan Gonzalez	1.00	.30
42 Ivan Rodriguez	1.00	.30
43 Rafael Palmeiro	.60	.18
44 Pedro Martinez	1.00	.30
45 Nomar Garciaparra	1.50	.45
46 Sean Casey	.40	.12
47 Aaron Boone	.40	.12
48 Barry Larkin	1.00	.30
49 Larry Walker	.60	.18
50 Vinny Castilla	.40	.12
51 Carlos Beltran	.40	.12
52 Gabe Kapler	.40	.12
53 Dean Palmer	.40	.12
54 Eric Milton	.40	.12
55 Corey Koskie	.40	.12
56 Frank Thomas	1.00	.30
57 Magglio Ordonez	.40	.12
58 Roger Clemens	2.00	.60
59 Bernie Williams	.60	.18
60 Derek Jeter	2.50	.75
61 Josh Beckett FUT	5.00	1.50
62 Eric Munson FUT	2.00	.60
63 Rick Ankiel FUT	2.00	.60
64 Matt Riley FUT	2.00	.60
65 Rob Ramsay FUT	2.00	.60
66 Vernon Wells FUT	2.00	.60
67 Eric Gagne FUT	4.00	1.20
68 Robert Fick FUT	2.00	.60
69 Mark Quinn FUT	2.00	.60
70 Kip Wells FUT	2.00	.60
71 Peter Bergeron FUT	2.00	.60
72 Ed Yarnall FUT	2.00	.60
73 Jorge Toca FUT	2.00	.60
74 Alfonso Soriano FUT	4.00	1.20
75 Calvin Murray FUT	2.00	.60
76 Ramon Ortiz FUT	2.00	.60
77 Chad Meyers FUT	2.00	.60
78 Jason LaRue FUT	2.00	.60
79 Pat Burrell FUT	2.50	.75
80 Chad Hermansen FUT	2.00	.60
81 Lance Berkman FUT	2.00	.60
82 Erubiel Durazo FUT	2.00	.60
83 Juan Pena FUT	2.00	.60
84 Adam Kennedy FUT	2.00	.60
85 Ben Petrick FUT	2.00	.60
86 Kevin Barker FUT	2.00	.60
87 Bruce Chen FUT	2.00	.60
88 Jerry Hairston Jr. FUT	2.00	.60
89 A.J. Burnett FUT	2.00	.60
90 Gary Matthews Jr. FUT	2.00	.60

2000 UD Ionix Reciprocal

This 90 card set is a parallel to the regular UD Ionix set. They were issued one every four packs for the lower numbers (R1-R60) and one every 11 packs for the future cards (R61-R90).

Nm-Mt Ex-Mt

*STARS 1-60: 1.5X TO 4X BASIC 1-60
*FUTURE 61-90: .6X TO 1.5X BASIC 61-90

2000 UD Ionix Atomic

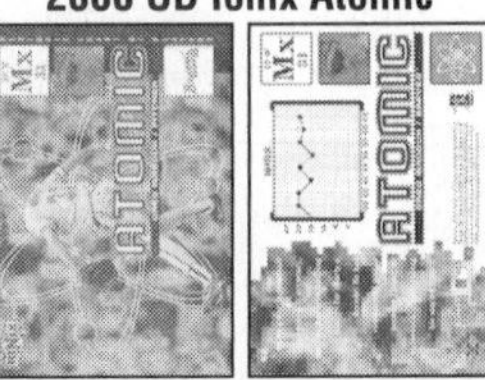

Issued one every eight packs, this set features 15 of the most popular and collectible hitters and pitchers currently active.

	Nm-Mt	Ex-Mt
COMPLETE SET (15)	60.00	18.00
A1 Pedro Martinez	3.00	.90
A2 Mark McGwire	10.00	3.00
A3 Ken Griffey Jr.	8.00	2.40
A4 Jeff Bagwell	3.00	.90
A5 Greg Maddux	6.00	1.80
A6 Derek Jeter	10.00	3.00
A7 Cal Ripken	10.00	3.00
A8 Manny Ramirez	3.00	.90
A9 Randy Johnson	3.00	.90
A10 Nomar Garciaparra	8.00	2.40
A11 Tony Gwynn	5.00	1.50
A12 Bernie Williams	2.50	.75
A13 Mike Piazza	6.00	1.80
A14 Roger Clemens	6.00	1.80
A15 Alex Rodriguez	8.00	2.40

2000 UD Ionix Awesome Powers

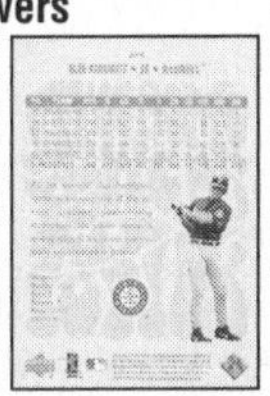

These cards, with a design based on 1960's psychedelic art, highlights some of the most prolific power hitters of the current crop of sluggers. These cards were inserted one every 23 packs.

	Nm-Mt	Ex-Mt
COMPLETE SET (15)	120.00	36.00
AP1 Ken Griffey Jr.	6.00	1.80
AP2 Mike Piazza	6.00	1.80
AP3 Carlos Delgado	1.50	.45
AP4 Mark McGwire	10.00	3.00
AP5 Chipper Jones	4.00	1.20
AP6 Scott Rolen	2.50	.75
AP7 Cal Ripken	12.00	3.60
AP8 Alex Rodriguez	6.00	1.80
AP9 Larry Walker	2.50	.75
AP10 Sammy Sosa	6.00	1.80
AP11 Barry Bonds	10.00	3.00
AP12 Nomar Garciaparra	6.00	1.80
AP13 Jose Canseco	4.00	1.20
AP14 Manny Ramirez	1.50	.45
AP15 Jeff Bagwell	2.50	.75

2000 UD Ionix BIOrhythm

Issued one every 11 packs, this 15-card set features many of the leading players of the game.

	Nm-Mt	Ex-Mt
COMPLETE SET (15)	80.00	24.00
B1 Randy Johnson	3.00	.90
B2 Derek Jeter	8.00	2.40
B3 Sammy Sosa	5.00	1.50
B4 Jose Lima	1.25	.35
B5 Chipper Jones	3.00	.90
B6 Barry Bonds	8.00	2.40
B7 Ken Griffey Jr.	5.00	1.50
B8 Nomar Garciaparra	5.00	1.50
B9 Frank Thomas	3.00	.90
B10 Pedro Martinez	3.00	.90
B11 Larry Walker	2.00	.60
B12 Greg Maddux	5.00	1.50
B13 Alex Rodriguez	5.00	1.50
B14 Mark McGwire	8.00	2.40
B15 Cal Ripken	10.00	3.00

2000 UD Ionix Pyrotechnics

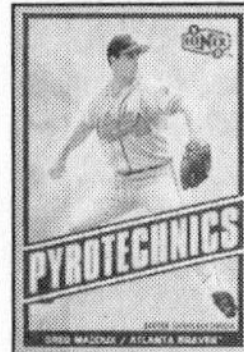

Inserted one every 72 packs, these 15 cards feature baseball's most popular players.

	Nm-Mt	Ex-Mt
COMPLETE SET (15)	350.00	105.00
P1 Roger Clemens	12.00	3.60
P2 Chipper Jones	6.00	1.80
P3 Alex Rodriguez	10.00	3.00
P4 Jeff Bagwell	4.00	1.20
P5 Mark McGwire	15.00	4.50
P6 Pedro Martinez	6.00	1.80
P7 Manny Ramirez	2.50	.75
P8 Cal Ripken	20.00	6.00
P9 Mike Piazza	10.00	3.00
P10 Derek Jeter	15.00	4.50
P11 Ken Griffey Jr.	10.00	3.00
P12 Frank Thomas	6.00	1.80
P13 Sammy Sosa	10.00	3.00
P14 Nomar Garciaparra	10.00	3.00
P15 Greg Maddux	10.00	3.00

2000 UD Ionix Shockwave

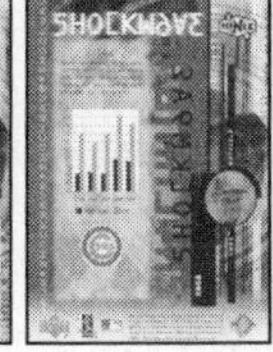

Using a rainbow foil Ionix technology, these 15 cards featuring the most powerful sluggers were inserted into packs at a rate of one every four packs.

	Nm-Mt	Ex-Mt
COMPLETE SET (15)	20.00	6.00
S1 Mark McGwire	3.00	.90
S2 Sammy Sosa	2.00	.60
S3 Manny Ramirez	.50	.15
S4 Ken Griffey Jr.	2.00	.60
S5 Vladimir Guerrero	1.25	.35
S6 Barry Bonds	3.00	.90
S7 Albert Belle	.50	.15
S8 Ivan Rodriguez	1.25	.35
S9 Chipper Jones	1.25	.35
S10 Mo Vaughn	.50	.15
S11 Jose Canseco	1.25	.35
S12 Jeff Bagwell	.75	.23
S13 Matt Williams	.50	.15
S14 Alex Rodriguez	2.00	.60
S15 Carlos Delgado	.50	.15

2000 UD Ionix UD Authentics

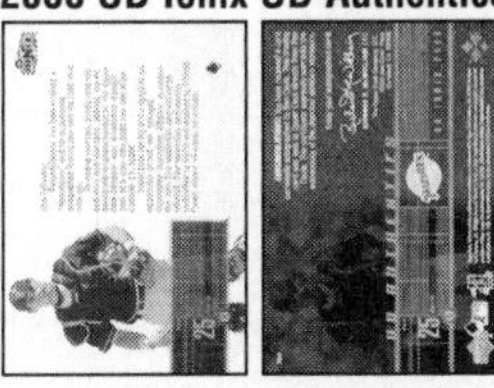

Randomly inserted into packs at an overall rate of one in 144, these 13 cards feature signed cards of various major leaguers. Please note that the Ben Davis, Derek Jeter and Manny Ramirez cards were exchange cards with a deadline date of September 20th, 2000.

	Nm-Mt	Ex-Mt
AB Adrian Beltre	15.00	4.50
BD Ben Davis	10.00	3.00
DJ Derek Jeter	150.00	45.00
JC Jose Canseco	40.00	12.00
JR Ken Griffey Jr.	150.00	45.00
MR Manny Ramirez	25.00	7.50
PB Pat Burrell	25.00	7.50
RM Ruben Mateo	10.00	3.00
SC Sean Casey	15.00	4.50
SG Shawn Green	15.00	4.50
SR Scott Rolen	25.00	7.50
VG Vladimir Guerrero	40.00	12.00
CBE Carlos Beltran	15.00	4.50

2000 UD Ionix Warp Zone

The toughest of the UD Ionix inserts, these 15 cards featured on holographic Ionix technology were inserted at a rate of one every 288 packs.

	Nm-Mt	Ex-Mt
COMPLETE SET (15)	600.00	180.00
WZ1 Cal Ripken	40.00	12.00
WZ2 Barry Bonds	30.00	9.00
WZ3 Ken Griffey Jr.	20.00	6.00
WZ4 Nomar Garciaparra	20.00	6.00
WZ5 Chipper Jones	12.00	3.60
WZ6 Ivan Rodriguez	12.00	3.60
WZ7 Greg Maddux	20.00	6.00
WZ8 Derek Jeter	30.00	9.00
WZ9 Mike Piazza	20.00	6.00
WZ10 Sammy Sosa	20.00	6.00
WZ11 Roger Clemens	25.00	7.50
WZ12 Alex Rodriguez	20.00	6.00
WZ13 Vladimir Guerrero	12.00	3.60
WZ14 Pedro Martinez	12.00	3.60
WZ15 Mark McGwire	30.00	9.00

2003 UD Patch Collection

This 161 card set was released in July, 2003. The set was issued in five card packs which came 20 packs to a box and 12 boxes to a case. Cards numbered 1 through 120 feature veterans. However, many of those cards were issued in shorter supply and we have notated that information with an SP next to the player's name in our checklist. The SP's were issued at a stated rate of one in four. Cards numbered 121 through 135 feature an All-Star subset and those cards were issued at a stated rate of one in 40. Cards numbered 136 through 150 featured HOFers and those cards were also issued at a stated rate of one in 40. Cards number 151 through 161 feature rookies and those cards were issued at a stated rate of one in 20. An Ichiro Suzuki sample card was produced to preview this set and that card can be located at the end of our checklist.

	Nm-Mt	Ex-Mt
COMP.SET w/o SP's (90)	25.00	7.50
COMMON CARD (1-120)	.50	.15
COMMON RC	.50	.15
COMMON SP (1-120)	5.00	1.50
COMMON CARD (121-135)	8.00	2.40
COMMON CARD (136-150)	8.00	2.40
COMMON CARD (151-161)	4.00	1.20
1 Darin Erstad	.50	.15
2 Troy Glaus	.75	.23
3 Robby Hammock RC	1.25	.35
4 Luis Gonzalez	.50	.15
5 Randy Johnson SP	8.00	2.40
6 Curt Schilling SP	8.00	2.40
7 Oscar Villarreal RC	.75	.23
8 Gary Sheffield	.50	.15
9 Mike Hampton SP	5.00	1.50
10 Greg Maddux SP	8.00	2.40
11 Chipper Jones	1.25	.35
12 Tony Batista	.50	.15
13 Rodrigo Lopez	.50	.15
14 Jay Gibbons	.50	.15
15 Shea Hillenbrand	.50	.15
16 Johnny Damon	.50	.15
17 Derek Lowe SP	5.00	1.50
18 Nomar Garciaparra	2.00	.60
19 Pedro Martinez SP	8.00	2.40
20 Manny Ramirez	.50	.15
21 Mark Prior SP	10.00	3.00
22 Kerry Wood SP	8.00	2.40
23 Corey Patterson	.50	.15
24 Sammy Sosa	2.00	.60
25 Troy O'Leary	.50	.15
26 Frank Thomas	1.25	.35
27 Magglio Ordonez	.50	.15
28 Bartolo Colon SP	5.00	1.50
29 Austin Kearns	.50	.15
30 Aaron Boone	.50	.15
31 Ken Griffey Jr.	2.00	.60
32 Adam Dunn	.50	.15
33 C.C. Sabathia	.50	.15
34 Karim Garcia	.50	.15
35 Larry Walker	.75	.23
36 Preston Wilson	.50	.15
37 Jason Jennings SP	5.00	1.50
38 Todd Helton	.75	.23
39 Carlos Pena	.50	.15
40 Eric Munson	.50	.15
41 Ivan Rodriguez	1.25	.35
42 Josh Beckett SP	8.00	2.40
43 A.J. Burnett SP	5.00	1.50
44 Roy Oswalt SP	5.00	1.50
45 Craig Biggio	.75	.23
46 Jeff Bagwell	.75	.23
47 Lance Berkman	.50	.15
48 Jeff Kent	.50	.15
49 Carlos Beltran	.50	.15
50 Mike Sweeney	.50	.15
51 Hideo Nomo SP	8.00	2.40
52 Adrian Beltre	.50	.15
53 Shawn Green	.50	.15
54 Kazuhisa Ishii SP	5.00	1.50
55 Ben Sheets SP	5.00	1.50
56 Richie Sexson	.50	.15
57 Torii Hunter	.50	.15
58 Doug Mientkiewicz	.50	.15
59 Eric Milton SP	5.00	1.50
60 Corey Koskie	.50	.15
61 Joe Mays SP	5.00	1.50
62 Jose Vidro	.50	.15
63 Vladimir Guerrero	1.25	.35
64 Luis Ayala RC	.75	.23
65 Cliff Floyd	.50	.15
66 Tom Glavine SP	8.00	2.40
67 Mike Piazza	2.00	.60
68 Roberto Alomar	1.25	.35
69 Al Leiter SP	5.00	1.50
70 Mike Mussina SP	8.00	2.40
71 Mariano Rivera SP	8.00	2.40
72 Drew Henson	.50	.15
73 Roger Clemens SP	10.00	3.00
74 Jason Giambi	1.25	.35
75 Bernie Williams	.75	.23
76 Alfonso Soriano	.75	.23
77 Derek Jeter	3.00	.90
78 Miguel Tejada	.50	.15

79 Jermaine Dye .50 .15
80 Tim Hudson SP 5.00 1.50
81 Barry Zito SP 8.00 2.40
82 Mark Mulder SP 5.00 1.50
83 Pat Burrell .50 .15
84 Jim Thome 1.25 .35
85 Bobby Abreu .50 .15
86 Kevin Millwood SP 5.00 1.50
87 Jason Kendall .50 .15
88 Brian Giles .50 .15
89 Phil Nevin .50 .15
90 Sean Burroughs .50 .15
91 Oliver Perez SP 5.00 1.50
92 Jose Cruz Jr. .50 .15
93 Rich Aurilia .50 .15
94 Edgardo Alfonzo .50 .15
95 Barry Bonds 3.00 .90
96 J.T. Snow .50 .15
97 Mike Cameron .50 .15
98 John Olerud .50 .15
99 Bret Boone .50 .15
100 Ichiro Suzuki 2.00 .60
101 J.D. Drew .50 .15
102 Jim Edmonds .50 .15
103 Scott Rolen .75 .23
104 Matt Morris SP 5.00 1.50
105 Tino Martinez .75 .23
106 Albert Pujols 2.50 .75
107 Rocco Baldelli 2.00 .60
108 Carl Crawford .50 .15
109 Mark Teixeira .75 .23
110 Rafael Palmeiro .75 .23
111 Hank Blalock .75 .23
112 Alex Rodriguez 2.00 .60
113 Kevin Mench .50 .15
114 Juan Gonzalez 1.25 .35
115 Shannon Stewart .50 .15
116 Vernon Wells .50 .15
117 Josh Phelps .50 .15
118 Eric Hinske SP 5.00 1.50
119 Orlando Hudson .50 .15
120 Carlos Delgado .50 .15
121 Alex Rodriguez AS 15.00 4.50
122 Nomar Garciaparra AS 12.00 3.60
123 Miguel Tejada AS 8.00 2.40
124 Jim Thome AS 10.00 3.00
125 Alfonso Soriano AS 10.00 3.00
126 Vladimir Guerrero AS 10.00 3.00
127 Derek Jeter AS 20.00 6.00
128 Mike Piazza AS 15.00 4.50
129 Ichiro Suzuki AS 15.00 4.50
130 Pedro Martinez AS 10.00 3.00
131 Luis Gonzalez AS 8.00 2.40
132 Adam Dunn AS 8.00 2.40
133 Shawn Green AS 8.00 2.40
134 Barry Zito AS 10.00 3.00
135 Torii Hunter AS UER 8.00 2.40
Name misspelled as Torri
136 Ted Williams HOF 30.00 9.00
137 Mickey Mantle HOF 40.00 12.00
138 Ernie Banks HOF 10.00 3.00
139 Yogi Berra HOF 10.00 3.00
140 Rollie Fingers HOF 8.00 2.40
141 Catfish Hunter HOF 10.00 3.00
142 Juan Marichal HOF 8.00 2.40
143 Eddie Mathews HOF 10.00 3.00
144 Willie McCovey HOF 8.00 2.40
145 Joe Morgan HOF 8.00 2.40
146 Stan Musial HOF 20.00 6.00
147 Pee Wee Reese HOF 10.00 3.00
148 Phil Rizzuto HOF 10.00 3.00
149 Nolan Ryan HOF 20.00 6.00
150 Tom Seaver HOF 10.00 3.00
151 Hideki Matsui RI RC 15.00 4.50
152 Jose Contreras RI RC 8.00 2.40
153 Lew Ford RI RC 5.00 1.50
154 Jeremy Griffiths RI RC 5.00 1.50
155 Guillermo Quiroz RI RC 8.00 2.40
156 Ryan Cameron RI RC 4.00 1.20
157 Jon Leicester RI RC 4.00 1.20
158 Josh Willingham RI RC 6.00 1.80
159 Shane Bazell RI RC UER 4.00 1.20
Name misspelled on front
160 Willie Eyre RI RC 4.00 1.20
161 Prentice Redman RI RC 4.00 1.20
IS Ichiro Suzuki SAMPLE 3.00 .90

2003 UD Patch Collection All-Star Game Patches

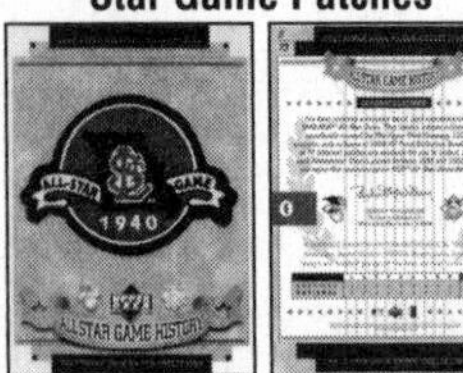

Nm-Mt Ex-Mt
COMMON CARD (1-27) 15.00 4.50
COMMON CARD (28-73) 10.00 3.00
TWO PER SEALED BOX-TOPPER PACK
1 Chicago White Sox 1933 15.00 4.50
2 New York Giants 1934 15.00 4.50
3 Cleveland Indians 1935 15.00 4.50
4 Boston Braves 1936 15.00 4.50
5 Washington Senators 1937 15.00 4.50
6 Cincinnati Reds 1938 15.00 4.50
7 New York Yankees 1939 25.00 7.50
8 St. Louis Cardinals 1940 15.00 4.50
9 Detroit Tigers 1941 15.00 4.50
10 New York Giants 1942 15.00 4.50
11 Philadelphia A's 1943 15.00 4.50
12 Pittsburgh Pirates 1944 15.00 4.50
13 Boston Red Sox 1946 15.00 4.50
14 Chicago Cubs 1947 20.00 6.00
15 St. Louis Browns 1948 20.00 6.00
16 Brooklyn Dodgers 1949 20.00 6.00
17 Chicago White Sox 1950 15.00 4.50
18 Detroit Tigers 1951 15.00 4.50
19 Philadelphia Phillies 1952 20.00 6.00
20 Cincinnati Reds 1953 15.00 4.50
21 Cleveland Indians 1954 15.00 4.50
22 Milwaukee Braves 1955 15.00 4.50
23 Washington Senators 1956 15.00 4.50
24 St. Louis Cardinals 1957 20.00 6.00
25 Baltimore Orioles 1958 15.00 4.50
26 Pittsburgh Pirates 1959 15.00 4.50
27 Los Angeles Dodgers 1959 15.00 4.50
28 Kansas City A's 1960 10.00 3.00
29 New York Yankees 1960 25.00 7.50
30 San Francisco Giants 1961 10.00 3.00
31 Boston Red Sox 1961 15.00 4.50
32 Washington Senators 1962 10.00 3.00
33 Chicago Cubs 1962 10.00 3.00
34 Cleveland Indians 1963 10.00 3.00
35 New York Mets 1964 15.00 4.50
36 Minnesota Twins 1965 10.00 3.00
37 St. Louis Cardinals 1966 15.00 4.50
38 Anaheim Angels 1967 10.00 3.00
39 Houston Astros 1968 10.00 3.00
40 Washington Senators 1969 UER 10.00 3.00
Card erroneously lists the Baltimore Orioles as the home franchise for this game
41 Cincinnati Reds 1970 10.00 3.00
42 Detroit Tigers 1971 15.00 4.50
43 Atlanta Braves 1972 10.00 3.00
44 Kansas City Royals 1973 10.00 3.00
45 Pittsburgh Pirates 1974 10.00 3.00
46 Milwaukee Brewers 1975 10.00 3.00
47 Philadelphia Phillies 1976 10.00 3.00
48 New York Yankees 1977 25.00 7.50
49 San Diego Padres 1978 10.00 3.00
50 Seattle Mariners 1979 10.00 3.00
51 Los Angeles Dodgers 1980 10.00 3.00
52 Cleveland Indians 1981 10.00 3.00
53 Montreal Expos 1982 10.00 3.00
54 Chicago White Sox 1983 10.00 3.00
55 San Francisco Giants 1984 10.00 3.00
56 Minnesota Twins 1985 10.00 3.00
57 Houston Astros 1986 10.00 3.00
58 Oakland A's 1987 10.00 3.00
59 Cincinnati Reds 1988 10.00 3.00
60 Anaheim Angels 1989 10.00 3.00
61 Chicago Cubs 1990 10.00 3.00
62 Toronto Blue Jays 1991 10.00 3.00
63 San Diego Padres 1992 10.00 3.00
64 Baltimore Orioles 1993 10.00 3.00
65 Pittsburgh Pirates 1994 10.00 3.00
66 Texas Rangers 1995 10.00 3.00
67 Philadelphia Phillies 1996 10.00 3.00
68 Cleveland Indians 1997 10.00 3.00
69 Colorado Rockies 1998 10.00 3.00
70 Boston Red Sox 1999 15.00 4.50
71 Atlanta Braves 2000 10.00 3.00
72 Seattle Mariners 2001 10.00 3.00
73 Milwaukee Brewers 2002 10.00 3.00

2003 UD Patch Collection MVP's

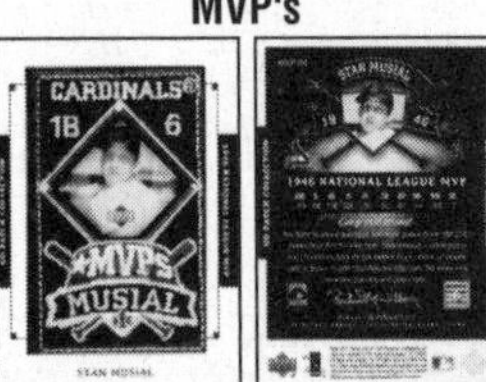

Nm-Mt Ex-Mt
STATED ODDS 1:20
MVP1 Derek Jeter 00 WS 15.00 4.50
MVP2 Randy Johnson 01 WS 8.00 2.40
MVP3 Curt Schilling 01 WS 8.00 2.40
MVP4 Troy Glaus 02 WS 8.00 2.40
MVP5 Ted Williams 46 MVP 20.00 6.00
MVP6 Ted Williams 49 MVP 20.00 6.00
MVP7 Mickey Mantle 56 MVP 25.00 7.50
MVP8 Mickey Mantle 57 MVP 25.00 7.50
MVP9 Phil Rizzuto 50 MVP 8.00 2.40
MVP10 Roger Clemens 86 MVP 10.00 3.00
MVP11 Ken Griffey Jr. 97 MVP 10.00 3.00
MVP12 Jason Giambi 00 MVP 8.00 2.40
MVP13 Ichiro Suzuki 01 MVP 10.00 3.00
MVP14 Roger Clemens AS MVP 10.00 3.00
MVP15 Yogi Berra 54 MVP 8.00 2.40
MVP16 Sammy Sosa 98 MVP 10.00 3.00
MVP17 Derek Jeter 00 AS MVP 15.00 4.50
MVP18 Mike Piazza 96 AS MVP 10.00 3.00
MVP19 Barry Bonds 02 MVP 15.00 4.50
MVP20 Stan Musial 46 MVP 15.00 4.50
MVP21 Joe Morgan 75 MVP 5.00 1.50

2003 UD Patch Collection Signature Patches

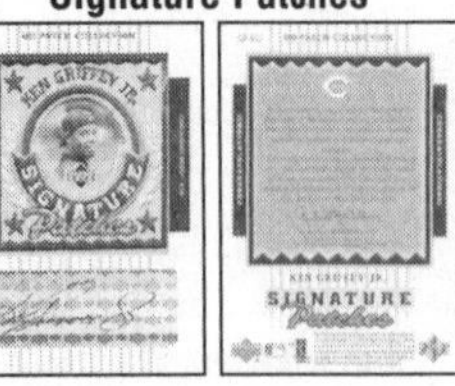

Inserted at a stated rate of one in 320, these 19 cards feature authentic autographs from the featured player. Please note that a few players signed fewer copies and we have noted that information with an SP next to the player's name in our checklist. In addition, Freddy Garcia did not return his cards in time for pack-out and those cards could be exchanged until June 19, 2006.

Nm-Mt Ex-Mt
AD Adam Dunn 60.00 18.00
BZ Barry Zito 60.00 18.00
CS Curt Schilling 60.00 18.00
DH Drew Henson 60.00 18.00
EH Eric Hinske 40.00 12.00
FG Freddy Garcia EXCH 40.00 12.00
GS Gary Sheffield 60.00 18.00
HM Hideki Matsui SP
IS Ichiro Suzuki SP
JB Jeff Bagwell 100.00 30.00
JG Jason Giambi SP
KG Ken Griffey Jr. 150.00 45.00
LB Lance Berkman 50.00 15.00
LG Luis Gonzalez 50.00 15.00
MT Miguel Tejada 50.00 15.00
RC Roger Clemens SP 200.00 60.00
SR Scott Rolen 60.00 18.00
SS Sammy Sosa SP 250.00 75.00
TP Troy Percival 40.00 12.00

2002 UD Piece of History

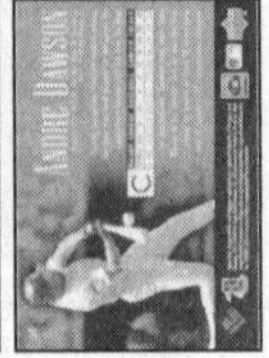

This 132 card set was released in April, 2002. The cards were issued in five card packs with an SRP of $2.99 per pack which were packed 24 to a box and 14 boxes to a case. Cards number 1-90 feature a mix of the best current player as well as various greats of the past. Within this group of cards, 10 cards belong to players who were short printed and we have notated those cards with SP in our checklist. In addition, cards numbered 91-132 featured leading prospects. These cards were issued in two different formats (portrait and action) and each of those cards are printed to a stated serial numbering of 625 cards.

Nm-Mt Ex-Mt
COMP.SET w/SP'S (90) 150.00 45.00
COMP.SET w/o SP'S (80) 20.00 6.00
COMMON CARD (1-90) .30 .09
COMMON CARD (91A-132P) 8.00 2.40
1 Troy Glaus .50 .15
2 Darin Erstad .30 .09
3 Reggie Jackson .50 .15
4 Miguel Tejada .30 .09
5 Tim Hudson .30 .09
6 Catfish Hunter .50 .15
7 Joe Carter .30 .09
8 Carlos Delgado .30 .09
9 Greg Vaughn .30 .09
10 Early Wynn .30 .09
11 Omar Vizquel .30 .09
12 Jim Thome .75 .23
13 Ichiro Suzuki 1.25 .35
14 Edgar Martinez .50 .15
15 Freddy Garcia .30 .09
16 Cal Ripken SP 25.00 7.50
17 Jeff Conine .30 .09
18 Juan Gonzalez .75 .23
19 Nolan Ryan SP 20.00 6.00
20 Alex Rodriguez SP 15.00 4.50
21 Rafael Palmeiro .50 .15
22 Ivan Rodriguez .75 .23
23 Carlton Fisk .50 .15
24 Wade Boggs .50 .15
25 Pedro Martinez .75 .23
26 Nomar Garciaparra 1.25 .35
27 Manny Ramirez .30 .09
28 Mike Sweeney UER .30 .09
Spelled Sweeny on front
29 Bobby Higginson .30 .09
30 Kirby Puckett .75 .23
31 Doug Mientkiewicz .30 .09
32 Corey Koskie .30 .09
33 Joe Mays .30 .09
34 Frank Thomas .75 .23
35 Magglio Ordonez .30 .09
36 Jason Giambi SP 15.00 4.50
37 Derek Jeter SP 20.00 6.00
38 Mickey Mantle SP 30.00 9.00
39 Joe DiMaggio 1.50 .45
40 Roger Maris 1.25 .35
41 Roger Clemens 1.50 .45
42 Bernie Williams .50 .15
43 Jeff Bagwell .50 .15
44 Lance Berkman .30 .09
45 Eddie Mathews .75 .23
46 Andruw Jones .30 .09
47 Phil Niekro .30 .09
48 Gary Sheffield .30 .09
49 Chipper Jones .75 .23
50 Greg Maddux 1.25 .35
51 Robin Yount 1.25 .35
52 Richie Sexson .30 .09
53 Jim Edmonds .30 .09
54 J.D. Drew .30 .09
55 Albert Pujols 1.50 .45
56 Andre Dawson .30 .09
57 Billy Williams .30 .09
58 Ernie Banks .75 .23
59 Sammy Sosa SP 15.00 4.50
60 Randy Johnson .75 .23
61 Curt Schilling .50 .15
62 Luis Gonzalez .30 .09
63 Kirk Gibson .30 .09
64 Steve Garvey .30 .09
65 Sandy Koufax SP 20.00 6.00
66 Shawn Green .30 .09
67 Hideo Nomo .75 .23
68 Kevin Brown .30 .09
69 Vladimir Guerrero .75 .23
70 Tim Raines .30 .09
71 Gaylord Perry .30 .09
72 Mel Ott .50 .15
73 Willie McCovey .30 .09
74 Barry Bonds SP 20.00 6.00
75 Jeff Kent .30 .09
76 Cliff Floyd .30 .09
77 Dwight Gooden .50 .15
78 Tom Seaver .50 .15
79 Mike Piazza 1.25 .35
80 Roberto Alomar .75 .23
81 Dave Winfield .30 .09
82 Tony Gwynn 1.00 .30
83 Scott Rolen .50 .15
84 Bill Mazeroski .30 .09
85 Willie Stargell .50 .15
86 Brian Giles .30 .09
87 Ken Griffey Jr. SP 15.00 4.50
88 Sean Casey .30 .09
89 Todd Helton .50 .15
90 Larry Walker .50 .15
91A Brendan Donnelly 21CP RC 8.00 2.40
91P Brendan Donnelly 21CP RC 8.00 2.40
92A Tom Shearn 21CP RC 8.00 2.40
92P Tom Shearn 21CP RC 8.00 2.40
93A Brandon Puffer 21CP RC 8.00 2.40
93P Brandon Puffer 21CP RC 8.00 2.40
94A Corey Thurman 21CP RC 8.00 2.40
94P Corey Thurman 21CP RC 8.00 2.40
95A Reed Johnson 21CP RC 8.00 2.40
95P Reed Johnson 21CP RC 8.00 2.40
96A Gustavo Chacin 21CP 8.00 2.40
96P Gustavo Chacin 21CP RC 8.00 2.40
97A Chris Baker 21CP RC 8.00 2.40
97P Chris Baker 21CP RC 8.00 2.40
98A John Ennis 21CP RC 8.00 2.40
98P John Ennis 21CP RC 8.00 2.40
99A So Taguchi 21CP RC 8.00 2.40
99P So Taguchi 21CP RC 8.00 2.40
100A Michael Crudale 21CP RC 8.00 2.40
100P Michael Crudale 21CP RC 8.00 2.40
101A Francis Beltran 21CP RC 8.00 2.40
101P Francis Beltran 21CP RC 8.00 2.40
102A Jose Valverde 21CP RC 8.00 2.40
102P Jose Valverde 21CP RC 8.00 2.40
103A Doug Devore 21CP RC 8.00 2.40
103P Doug Devore 21CP RC 8.00 2.40
104A Jeremy Ward 21CP RC 8.00 2.40
104P Jeremy Ward 21CP RC 8.00 2.40
105A P.J. Bevis 21CP RC 8.00 2.40
105P P.J. Bevis 21CP RC 8.00 2.40
106A Steve Kent 21CP RC 8.00 2.40
106P Steve Kent 21CP RC 8.00 2.40
107A Brandon Backe 21CP RC 8.00 2.40
107P Brandon Backe 21CP RC 8.00 2.40
108A Jorge Nunez 21CP RC 8.00 2.40
108P Jorge Nunez 21CP RC 8.00 2.40
109A Kazuhisa Ishii 21CP RC 15.00 4.50
109P Kazuhisa Ishii 21CP RC 15.00 4.50
110A Ron Calloway 21CP RC 8.00 2.40
110P Ron Calloway 21CP RC 8.00 2.40
111A Val Pascucci 21CP 8.00 2.40
111P Val Pascucci 21CP 8.00 2.40
112A J.J. Putz 21CP RC 8.00 2.40
112P J.J. Putz 21CP RC 8.00 2.40
113A Matt Thornton 21CP RC 8.00 2.40
113P Matt Thornton 21CP RC 8.00 2.40
114A Allan Simpson 21CP RC 8.00 2.40
114P Allan Simpson 21CP RC 8.00 2.40
115A Jaime Cerda 21CP RC 8.00 2.40
115P Jaime Cerda 21CP RC 8.00 2.40
116A Mark Corey 21CP RC 8.00 2.40
116P Mark Corey 21CP RC 8.00 2.40
117A Tyler Yates 21CP RC 12.00 3.60
117P Tyler Yates 21CP RC 12.00 3.60
118A Steve Bechler 21CP RC 8.00 2.40
118P Steve Bechler 21CP RC 8.00 2.40
119A Ben Howard 21CP RC 8.00 2.40
119P Ben Howard 21CP RC 8.00 2.40
120A Cliff Bartosh 21CP RC 8.00 2.40
120P Cliff Bartosh 21CP RC 8.00 2.40
121A Todd Donovan 21CP RC 8.00 2.40
121P Todd Donovan 21CP RC 8.00 2.40
122A Eric Junge 21CP RC 8.00 2.40
122P Eric Junge 21CP RC 8.00 2.40
123A Adrian Burnside 21CP RC 8.00 2.40
123P Adrian Burnside 21CP RC 8.00 2.40
124A Andy Pratt 21CP RC 8.00 2.40
124P Andy Pratt 21CP RC 8.00 2.40
125A Josh Hancock 21CP RC 8.00 2.40
125P Josh Hancock 21CP RC 8.00 2.40
126A Rene Reyes 21CP RC 8.00 2.40
126P Rene Reyes 21CP RC 8.00 2.40
127A Cam Esslinger 21CP RC 8.00 2.40
127P Cam Esslinger 21CP RC 8.00 2.40
128A Colin Young 21CP RC 8.00 2.40
128P Colin Young 21CP RC 8.00 2.40
129A Kevin Frederick 21CP RC 8.00 2.40
129P Kevin Frederick 21CP RC 8.00 2.40
130A Kyle Kane 21CP RC 8.00 2.40
130P Kyle Kane 21CP RC 8.00 2.40
131A Mitch Wylie 21CP RC 8.00 2.40
131P Mitch Wylie 21CP RC 8.00 2.40
132A Danny Wright 21CP 8.00 2.40
132P Danny Wright 21CP 8.00 2.40

2002 UD Piece of History 21st Century Phenoms 950

Randomly inserted into retail packs, these forty-two cards parallel the prospect section of the Piece of History set. These cards have a stated print run of 950 serial numbered sets and were only issued in portrait version in retail.

Nm-Mt Ex-Mt
*21ST CP 950: .25X TO .6X BASIC CARDS

2002 UD Piece of History 300 Game Winners

Inserted at stated odds one in 50 packs, these six cards feature pitchers who were able to achieve 300 victories in their career.

Nm-Mt Ex-Mt
COMPLETE SET (6) 30.00 9.00
GW1 Nolan Ryan 12.00 3.60
GW2 Tom Seaver 3.00 .90
GW3 Cy Young 5.00 1.50
GW4 Gaylord Perry 3.00 .90
GW5 Early Wynn 3.00 .90
GW6 Phil Niekro 3.00 .90

2002 UD Piece of History 300 Game Winners Jersey

Inserted at stated odds of one in 576 packs, these four cards feature not only 300 game winners but also a game-worn jersey swatch from that pitcher. Nolan Ryan and Tom Seaver were printed in shorter quantity and we have notated those cards as SP in our checklist.

Nm-Mt Ex-Mt
W-GP Gaylord Perry Pants 25.00 7.50
W-NR Nolan Ryan SP 50.00 15.00
W-PN Phil Niekro 25.00 7.50
W-TS Tom Seaver SP 25.00 7.50

2002 UD Piece of History 500 Home Run Club

Inserted at stated odds of one in nine, these nine cards feature members of the 500 home run club.

Nm-Mt Ex-Mt
COMPLETE SET (9) 60.00 18.00
HR1 Harmon Killebrew 8.00 2.40
HR2 Jimmie Foxx 8.00 2.40
HR3 Reggie Jackson 5.00 1.50
HR4 Mickey Mantle 20.00 6.00
HR5 Ernie Banks 8.00 2.40
HR6 Eddie Mathews 8.00 2.40
HR7 Mark McGwire 15.00 4.50
HR8 Willie McCovey 5.00 1.50
HR9 Mel Ott 8.00 2.40

2002 UD Piece of History 500 Home Run Club Jersey

Inserted at stated odds of one in 336, these eight cards feature not only a member of the 500 home run club but also a piece of a game-worn uniform. Ernie Banks and Mickey Mantle were issued in smaller quantities than the other players and we have notated that information with SP's next to their names in our checklist.

Nm-Mt Ex-Mt
EB Ernie Banks SP 50.00 15.00
EM Eddie Mathews 50.00 15.00
HA Hank Aaron 60.00 18.00
JF Jimmie Foxx 50.00 15.00
MO Mel Ott 50.00 15.00
RJ Reggie Jackson 40.00 12.00
WM Willie McCovey 40.00 12.00
MMA M.Mantle Pants SP/50 250.00 75.00

2002 UD Piece of History 500 Home Run Club Jersey Signatures

Randomly inserted into packs, this two card set features signatures of the players featured in this set. These cards have a stated print run of 10 serial numbered sets. There is no pricing on these cards due to market scarcity.

Nm-Mt Ex-Mt
SHR-EB Ernie Banks
SHR-RJ Reggie Jackson

2002 UD Piece of History Batting Champs

Inserted at stated odds of one in 30, these 10 cards feature players who won batting championships during their career.

	Nm-Mt	Ex-Mt
COMPLETE SET (10)	50.00	15.00
B1 Tony Gwynn	6.00	1.80
B2 Frank Thomas	5.00	1.50
B3 Billy Williams	2.00	.60
B4 Edgar Martinez	3.00	.90
B5 Bernie Williams	3.00	.90
B6 Mickey Mantle	15.00	4.50
B7 Larry Walker	3.00	.90
B8 Gary Sheffield	2.00	.60
B9 Wade Boggs	3.00	.90
B10 Alex Rodriguez	8.00	2.40

2002 UD Piece of History Batting Champs Jersey

Inserted at stated odds of one in 96, these 13 cards feature not only a card of a batting champion but also a game-worn uniform swatch of the featured player. A few players were issued in smaller quantities and we have notated this information with an SP next to the player's name in our checklist.

	Nm-Mt	Ex-Mt
AG Andres Galarraga	15.00	4.50
AR Alex Rodriguez	15.00	4.50
BEW Bernie Williams	15.00	4.50
EM Edgar Martinez	15.00	4.50
FT Frank Thomas	15.00	4.50
GS Gary Sheffield SP	15.00	4.50
JO John Olerud	15.00	4.50
LW Larry Walker SP	15.00	4.50
MM M.Mantle Pants SP/50	250.00	75.00
PO Paul O'Neill	15.00	4.50
TG Tony Gwynn	15.00	4.50
TR Tim Raines	15.00	4.50
WB Wade Boggs	15.00	4.50

2002 UD Piece of History Batting Champs Jersey Signatures

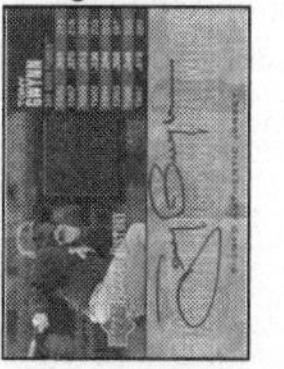

Randomly inserted in packs, these five cards feature not only the batting champs card but also a game-worn jersey piece and an authentic signature. These cards were issued to a stated print run of 24 cards. There is no pricing on these cards due to market scarcity.

	Nm-Mt	Ex-Mt
AR Alex Rodriguez		
FT Frank Thomas		
JO John Olerud		
PO Paul O'Neill		
TG Tony Gwynn		

2002 UD Piece of History ERA Leaders

Inserted at stated odds of one in 30, these 10 cards feature pitchers who won an ERA title during their career.

	Nm-Mt	Ex-Mt
COMPLETE SET	50.00	15.00
E1 Greg Maddux	8.00	2.40
E2 Pedro Martinez	5.00	1.50
E3 Freddy Garcia	2.00	.60
E4 Randy Johnson	5.00	1.50
E5 Tom Seaver	3.00	.90
E6 Early Wynn	2.00	.60
E7 Dwight Gooden	3.00	.90
E8 Kevin Brown	2.00	.60
E9 Roger Clemens	10.00	3.00
E10 Nolan Ryan	12.00	3.60

2002 UD Piece of History ERA Leaders Jersey

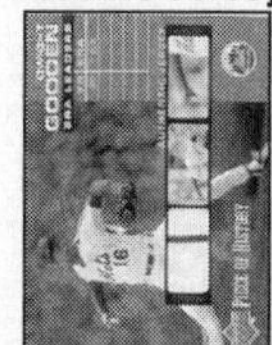

Inserted at stated odds of one in 96, these 12 cards feature not only pitchers who won an ERA title but also includes a game-worn jersey swatch of that player. A few of the cards in this set were issued in smaller quantities and we have notated that with an SP in our checklist.

	Nm-Mt	Ex-Mt
EL-CH Catfish Hunter SP	15.00	4.50
EL-DG Dwight Gooden	15.00	4.50
EL-FG Freddy Garcia	10.00	3.00
EL-GM Greg Maddux	15.00	4.50
EL-KB Kevin Brown	10.00	3.00
EL-NR Nolan Ryan SP	50.00	15.00
EL-PM Pedro Martinez	15.00	4.50
EL-PN Phil Niekro	10.00	3.00
EL-RC Roger Clemens	25.00	7.50
EL-RJ Randy Johnson	15.00	4.50
EL-SK Sandy Koufax SP	100.00	30.00
EL-TS Tom Seaver	15.00	4.50

2002 UD Piece of History ERA Leaders Jersey Signatures

Randomly inserted in packs, these three cards feature not only pitchers who won an ERA title but also includes a game-worn jersey swatch and an authentic signature of that player. These cards were issued to a stated print run of 24 serial numbered sets. Sandy Koufax did not return his cards in time for inclusion in packs and those cards could be redeemed until April 5, 2005. There is no pricing on these cards due to market scarcity.

	Nm-Mt	Ex-Mt
SEL-FG Freddy Garcia		
SEL-RC Roger Clemens		
SEL-SK Sandy Koufax EXCH		

2002 UD Piece of History Hitting for the Cycle

Inserted at stated odds of one in 15, these 20 cards feature players who hit for the cycle during their career.

	Nm-Mt	Ex-Mt
COMPLETE SET (20)	80.00	24.00
H1 Alex Rodriguez	8.00	2.40
H2 Andre Dawson	2.00	.60
H3 Cal Ripken	15.00	4.50
H4 Carlton Fisk	3.00	.90
H5 Dante Bichette	2.00	.60
H6 Dave Winfield	2.00	.60
H7 Eric Chavez	2.00	.60
H8 Robin Yount	8.00	2.40
H9 Jason Kendall	2.00	.60
H10 Jay Buhner	2.00	.60
H11 Jeff Kent	2.00	.60
H12 Joe DiMaggio	8.00	2.40
H13 John Olerud	2.00	.60
H14 Kirby Puckett	5.00	1.50
H15 Luis Gonzalez	2.00	.60
H16 Mark Grace	3.00	.90
H17 Mickey Mantle	15.00	4.50
H18 Miguel Tejada	2.00	.60
H19 Rondell White	2.00	.60
H20 Todd Helton	3.00	.90

2002 UD Piece of History Hitting for the Cycle Bats

Inserted at stated odds of one in 576, these 10 cards feature not only hitters who hit for the cycle in a game but also includes a game-used bat piece of that player. A few of the cards in this set were issued in smaller quantities and we have notated that with an SP in our checklist.

	Nm-Mt	Ex-Mt
HC-AD Andre Dawson	25.00	7.50
HC-AR Alex Rodriguez	40.00	12.00
HC-CF Carlton Fisk	30.00	9.00
HC-CR Cal Ripken SP	120.00	36.00
HC-DB Dante Bichette	25.00	7.50
HC-DW Dave Winfield	25.00	7.50
HC-EC Eric Chavez	25.00	7.50
HC-JB Jay Buhner	25.00	7.50
HC-LG Luis Gonzalez	25.00	7.50
HC-MM Mickey Mantle SP/50	250.00	75.00

2002 UD Piece of History Hitting for the Cycle Bats Signatures

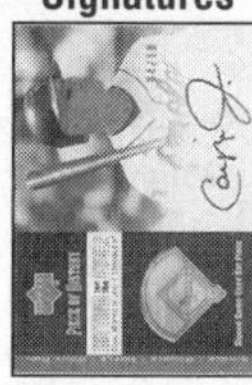

Randomly inserted in packs, these three cards feature not only hitters who hit for the cycle in a game but also includes a game-used bat piece and an authentic signature of that player. These cards were issued to a stated print run of 10 serial numbered sets. There is no pricing on these cards due to market scarcity.

	Nm-Mt	Ex-Mt
SHC-AR Alex Rodriguez		
SHC-CR Cal Ripken		
SHC-LG Luis Gonzalez		

2002 UD Piece of History MVP Club

Inserted at stated odds of one in 22, these 14 cards feature players who won an MVP award during their career.

	Nm-Mt	Ex-Mt
COMPLETE SET (14)	80.00	24.00
M1 Jason Giambi	5.00	1.50
M2 Sammy Sosa	8.00	2.40
M3 Cal Ripken	15.00	4.50
M4 Robin Yount	8.00	2.40
M5 Ken Griffey Jr.	8.00	2.40
M6 Kirk Gibson	2.00	.60
M7 Mickey Mantle	15.00	4.50
M8 Barry Bonds	12.00	3.60
M9 Frank Thomas	5.00	1.50
M10 Reggie Jackson	3.00	.90
M11 Jeff Bagwell	3.00	.90
M12 Roger Clemens	10.00	3.00
M13 Steve Garvey	2.00	.60
M14 Chipper Jones	5.00	1.50

2002 UD Piece of History MVP Club Jersey

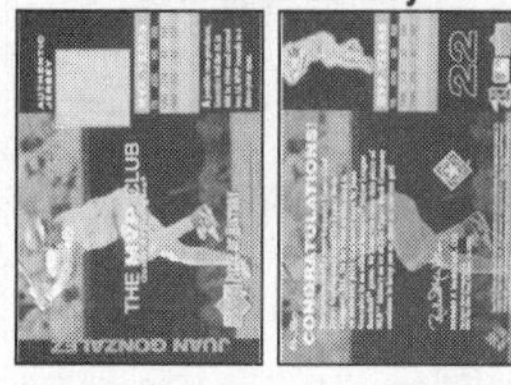

Inserted at stated odds of one in 96, these 18 cards feature not only players who won MVP awards but also includes a game-worn jersey swatch of that player. A few of the cards in this set were issued in smaller quantities and we have notated that with an SP in our checklist.

	Nm-Mt	Ex-Mt
M-BL Barry Larkin SP	40.00	12.00
M-CJ Chipper Jones	20.00	6.00
M-CR Cal Ripken	50.00	15.00
M-FT Frank Thomas	20.00	6.00
M-IR Ivan Rodriguez	20.00	6.00
M-JB Jeff Bagwell	15.00	4.50
M-JGI Jason Giambi	20.00	6.00
M-JGO Juan Gonzalez	20.00	6.00
M-JK Jeff Kent	15.00	4.50
M-KGI Kirk Gibson	15.00	4.50
M-KGR Ken Griffey Jr.	25.00	7.50
M-MM Mickey Mantle Pants SP/50	250.00	75.00
M-RC Roger Clemens	25.00	7.50
M-RJ Reggie Jackson	15.00	4.50
M-RM Roger Maris Pants SP/50		
M-RY Robin Yount Pants SP	40.00	12.00
M-SG Steve Garvey	15.00	4.50
M-SS Sammy Sosa	25.00	7.50

2002 UD Piece of History MVP Club Jersey Signatures

Randomly inserted in packs, these three cards feature not only players who won an MVP award during their career but also includes a game-worn jersey swatch and an authentic signature of that player. These cards were issued to a stated print run of 10 serial numbered sets. There is no pricing on these cards due to market scarcity.

	Nm-Mt	Ex-Mt
SM-CR Cal Ripken		
SM-KG Ken Griffey Jr.		
SM-SS Sammy Sosa		

2002 UD Piece of History Tape Measure Heroes

Inserted into packs at stated odds of one in 10, these 30 cards feature players who either hit many homers or a very crucial homer in baseball history.

	Nm-Mt	Ex-Mt
COMPLETE SET (30)	150.00	45.00
TM1 Joe Carter	2.00	.60
TM2 Cal Ripken	15.00	4.50
TM3 Mike Piazza	8.00	2.40
TM4 Shawn Green	2.00	.60
TM5 Mark McGwire	12.00	3.60
TM6 Reggie Jackson	3.00	.90
TM7 Mickey Mantle	15.00	4.50
TM8 Manny Ramirez	2.00	.60
TM9 Mo Vaughn	2.00	.60
TM10 Jeff Bagwell	3.00	.90
TM11 Sammy Sosa	8.00	2.40
TM12 Tony Gwynn	6.00	1.80
TM13 Bill Mazeroski	3.00	.90
TM14 Jose Canseco	5.00	1.50
TM15 Brian Giles	2.00	.60
TM16 Kirk Gibson	2.00	.60
TM17 Kirby Puckett	5.00	1.50
TM18 Wade Boggs	3.00	.90
TM19 Albert Pujols	10.00	3.00
TM20 David Justice	2.00	.60
TM21 Steve Garvey	2.00	.60
TM22 Luis Gonzalez	2.00	.60
TM23 Derek Jeter	12.00	3.60
TM24 Robin Yount	8.00	2.40
TM25 Barry Bonds	12.00	3.60
TM26 Alex Rodriguez	8.00	2.40
TM27 Willie Stargell	3.00	.90
TM28 Carlton Fisk	3.00	.90
TM29 Carlos Delgado	2.00	.60
TM30 Ken Griffey Jr.	8.00	2.40

2002 UD Piece of History Tape Measure Heroes Jersey

Inserted at stated odds of one in 96, these 23 cards feature not only players who hit many important homers but also includes a game-worn jersey swatch of that player. A few of the cards in this set were issued in smaller quantities and we have notated that with an SP in our checklist.

	Nm-Mt	Ex-Mt
AR Alex Rodriguez	20.00	6.00
BG Brian Giles	15.00	4.50
BM Bill Mazeroski	15.00	4.50
CD Carlos Delgado	15.00	4.50
CF Carlton Fisk	15.00	4.50
CR Cal Ripken	50.00	15.00
JB Jeff Bagwell	15.00	4.50
JCA Jose Canseco	20.00	6.00
JOC Joe Carter	15.00	4.50
KGI Kirk Gibson	15.00	4.50
KGR Ken Griffey Jr. SP/90		
MMA Mickey Mantle Pants SP/50	250.00	75.00
MP Mike Piazza	15.00	4.50
MR Manny Ramirez	15.00	4.50
RJ Reggie Jackson SP/23		
RM Roger Maris Pants SP/50		
RY Robin Yount Pants SP		
SGA Steve Garvey	15.00	4.50
SGR Shawn Green	15.00	4.50
SS Sammy Sosa	25.00	7.50
TG Tony Gwynn SP		
WB Wade Boggs	15.00	4.50
WS Willie Stargell	15.00	4.50

2001 UD Reserve

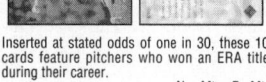

The 2001 UD Reserve product was released in late July, 2001 and featured a 210-card base set. The base set was broken into tiers as follows: Base Veterans (1-180), and Prospects (181-210) that are serial numbered to 2500 sets. Each pack contained 5 cards, and carried a suggested retail price of $2.49.

	Nm-Mt	Ex-Mt
COMP.SET w/o SP's (180)	25.00	7.50
COMMON CARD (1-180)	.30	.09
COMMON (181-210)	5.00	1.50
1 Darin Erstad	.30	.09
2 Tim Salmon	.50	.15
3 Bengie Molina	.30	.09
4 Troy Glaus	.50	.15
5 Glenallen Hill	.30	.09
6 Garret Anderson	.30	.09
7 Jason Giambi	.75	.23
8 Johnny Damon	.30	.09
9 Eric Chavez	.30	.09
10 Tim Hudson	.30	.09
11 Miguel Tejada	.30	.09
12 Barry Zito	.75	.23
13 Jose Ortiz	.30	.09
14 Tony Batista	.30	.09
15 Carlos Delgado	.30	.09
16 Shannon Stewart	.30	.09
17 Raul Mondesi	.30	.09
18 Ben Grieve	.30	.09
19 Aubrey Huff	.30	.09
20 Greg Vaughn	.30	.09
21 Fred McGriff	.50	.15
22 Gerald Williams	.30	.09
23 Bartolo Colon	.30	.09
24 Roberto Alomar	.75	.23
25 Jim Thome	.75	.23
26 Omar Vizquel	.30	.09
27 Juan Gonzalez	.75	.23
28 Ellis Burks	.30	.09
29 Edgar Martinez	.50	.15
30 Aaron Sele	.30	.09
31 Jay Buhner	.30	.09
32 Mike Cameron	.30	.09
33 Kazuhiro Sasaki	.30	.09
34 John Olerud	.30	.09
35 Cal Ripken	2.50	.75
36 Brady Anderson	.30	.09
37 Pat Hentgen	.30	.09
38 Chris Richard	.30	.09
39 Jerry Hairston Jr.	.30	.09
40 Mike Bordick	.30	.09
41 Ivan Rodriguez	.75	.23
42 Rick Helling	.30	.09
43 Rafael Palmeiro	.50	.15
44 Alex Rodriguez	1.25	.35
45 Andres Galarraga	.30	.09
46 Rusty Greer	.30	.09
47 Ruben Mateo	.30	.09
48 Ken Caminiti	.30	.09
49 Nomar Garciaparra	1.25	.35
50 Pedro Martinez	.75	.23
51 Manny Ramirez	.30	.09
52 Carl Everett	.30	.09
53 Dante Bichette	.30	.09
54 Hideo Nomo	.75	.23
55 Mike Sweeney	.30	.09
56 Carlos Beltran	.30	.09
57 Jeff Suppan	.30	.09
58 Jermaine Dye	.30	.09
59 Mark Quinn	.30	.09
60 Joe Randa	.30	.09
61 Bobby Higginson	.30	.09
62 Tony Clark	.30	.09
63 Brian Moehler	.30	.09
64 Dean Palmer	.30	.09
65 Brandon Inge	.30	.09
66 Damion Easley	.30	.09
67 Brad Radke	.30	.09
68 Corey Koskie	.30	.09
69 Cristian Guzman	.30	.09
70 Eric Milton	.30	.09
71 Jacque Jones	.30	.09
72 Matt Lawton	.30	.09
73 Frank Thomas	.75	.23
74 David Wells	.30	.09
75 Magglio Ordonez	.30	.09
76 Paul Konerko	.30	.09
77 Sandy Alomar Jr.	.30	.09
78 Ray Durham	.30	.09
79 Roger Clemens	1.50	.45
80 Bernie Williams	.50	.15
81 Derek Jeter	2.00	.60
82 David Justice	.30	.09
83 Paul O'Neill	.50	.15
84 Mike Mussina	.75	.23
85 Jorge Posada	.50	.15
86 Jeff Bagwell	.50	.15
87 Richard Hidalgo	.30	.09
88 Craig Biggio	.50	.15
89 Scott Elarton	.30	.09
90 Moises Alou	.30	.09
91 Greg Maddux	1.25	.35
92 Rafael Furcal	.30	.09
93 Andruw Jones	.30	.09
94 Tom Glavine	.50	.15
95 Chipper Jones	.75	.23
96 Javy Lopez	.30	.09
97 Richie Sexson	.30	.09
98 Jeromy Burnitz	.30	.09
99 Jeff D'Amico	.30	.09
100 Jeffrey Hammonds	.30	.09
101 Geoff Jenkins	.30	.09
102 Ben Sheets	.30	.09
103 Mark McGwire	2.00	.60
104 Rick Ankiel	.30	.09
105 Darryl Kile	.30	.09
106 Edgar Renteria	.30	.09
107 Jim Edmonds	.30	.09
108 J.D. Drew	.30	.09
109 Sammy Sosa	1.25	.35
110 Corey Patterson	.30	.09
111 Kerry Wood	.75	.23
112 Todd Hundley	.30	.09
113 Rondell White	.30	.09
114 Matt Stairs	.30	.09
115 Randy Johnson	.75	.23
116 Mark Grace	.50	.15
117 Steve Finley	.30	.09
118 Luis Gonzalez	.30	.09
119 Matt Williams	.30	.09
120 Curt Schilling	.50	.15
121 Gary Sheffield	.30	.09
122 Kevin Brown	.30	.09
123 Shawn Green	.30	.09
124 Eric Karros	.30	.09
125 Chan Ho Park	.30	.09
126 Adrian Beltre	.30	.09

127 Vladimir Guerrero .75 .23
128 Fernando Tatis .30 .09
129 Lee Stevens .30 .09
130 Jose Vidro .30 .09
131 Peter Bergeron .30 .09
132 Michael Barrett .30 .09
133 Jeff Kent .30 .09
134 Russ Ortiz .30 .09
135 Barry Bonds 2.00 .60
136 J.T. Snow .30 .09
137 Livan Hernandez .30 .09
138 Rich Aurilia .30 .09
139 Preston Wilson .30 .09
140 Mike Lowell .30 .09
141 Ryan Dempster .30 .09
142 Charles Johnson .30 .09
143 Matt Clement .30 .09
144 Luis Castillo .30 .09
145 Mike Piazza UER 1.25 .35
Card lists him as a Dodger
146 Al Leiter .30 .09
147 Robin Ventura .30 .09
148 Jay Payton .30 .09
149 Todd Zeile .30 .09
150 Edgardo Alfonzo .30 .09
151 Tony Gwynn 1.00 .30
152 Ryan Klesko .30 .09
153 Phil Nevin .30 .09
154 Mark Kotsay .30 .09
155 Trevor Hoffman .30 .09
156 Damian Jackson .30 .09
157 Scott Rolen .50 .15
158 Mike Lieberthal .30 .09
159 Bruce Chen .30 .09
160 Bobby Abreu .30 .09
161 Pat Burrell .30 .09
162 Travis Lee .30 .09
163 Jason Kendall .30 .09
164 Derek Bell .30 .09
165 Kris Benson .30 .09
166 Kevin Young .30 .09
167 Brian Giles .30 .09
168 Pat Meares .30 .09
169 Sean Casey .30 .09
170 Pokey Reese .30 .09
171 Pete Harnisch .30 .09
172 Barry Larkin .75 .23
173 Ken Griffey Jr. 1.25 .35
174 Dmitri Young .30 .09
175 Mike Hampton .30 .09
176 Todd Helton .50 .15
177 Jeff Cirillo .30 .09
178 Denny Neagle .30 .09
179 Larry Walker .50 .15
180 Todd Hollandsworth .30 .09
181 Ichiro Suzuki SP RC 25.00 7.50
182 Wilson Betemit SP RC 5.00 1.50
183 A. Hernandez SP RC 5.00 1.50
184 Travis Hafner SP RC 10.00 3.00
185 Sean Douglass SP RC 5.00 1.50
186 Juan Diaz SP RC 5.00 1.50
187 H. Ramirez SP RC 8.00 2.40
188 M. Ensberg SP RC 8.00 2.40
189 B. Duckworth SP RC 5.00 1.50
190 Jack Wilson SP RC 5.00 1.50
191 Erick Almonte SP RC 5.00 1.50
192 R. Rodriguez SP RC 5.00 1.50
193 E. Guzman SP RC 5.00 1.50
194 Juan Uribe SP RC 5.00 1.50
195 Ryan Freel SP RC 5.00 1.50
196 C. Parker SP RC 5.00 1.50
197 J. Melian SP RC 5.00 1.50
198 Jose Mieses SP RC 5.00 1.50
199 Andres Torres SP RC 5.00 1.50
200 Jason Smith SP RC 5.00 1.50
201 J. Estrada SP RC 5.00 1.50
202 Cesar Crespo SP RC 5.00 1.50
203 C. Valderrama SP RC 5.00 1.50
204 Albert Pujols SP RC 40.00 12.00
205 Wilkin Ruan SP RC 5.00 1.50
206 Josh Fogg SP RC 5.00 1.50
207 Bert Snow SP RC 5.00 1.50
208 B. Lawrence SP RC 5.00 1.50
209 Esix Snead SP RC 5.00 1.50
210 T. Shinjo SP RC 8.00 2.40

2001 UD Reserve Ball-Base Duos

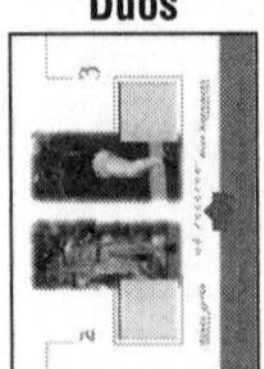

Randomly inserted into packs at one in 240, this 15-card insert set features swatches of both game-used baseball and base. Each of these cards feature two superstar caliber players on the card front. Card backs carry a "B" prefix followed by the players' initials.

Nm-Mt Ex-Mt
B-BH Barry Bonds 40.00 12.00
Todd Helton
B-CR Roger Clemens 30.00 9.00
Alex Rodriguez
B-GD Vladimir Guerrero 20.00 6.00
Carlos Delgado
B-GJ Ken Griffey Jr. 40.00 12.00
Derek Jeter
B-GR Nomar Garciaparra 30.00 9.00
Alex Rodriguez
B-GS Ken Griffey Jr. 25.00 7.50
Sammy Sosa
B-JN Chipper Jones 25.00 7.50
Nomar Garciaparra
B-JP Derek Jeter 40.00 12.00
Mike Piazza
B-JR Derek Jeter 40.00 12.00
Alex Rodriguez
B-MG Mark McGwire 50.00 15.00
Ken Griffey Jr.
B-MJ Mark McGwire 50.00 15.00
Derek Jeter
B-MP Mark McGwire 50.00 15.00
Mike Piazza
B-NJ Nomar Garciaparra 40.00 12.00
Derek Jeter
B-RM Alex Rodriguez 50.00 15.00
Mark McGwire
B-ST Sammy Sosa 25.00 7.50
Frank Thomas

2001 UD Reserve Ball-Base Quads

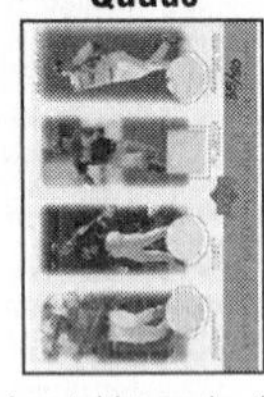

Randomly inserted into packs, this five card insert set features swatches of both game-used baseball and base. Each of these cards feature four superstar caliber players on the card front. Card backs carry a "B" prefix followed by the players' initials. Please note that there were only 50 serial numbered sets produced.

Nm-Mt Ex-Mt
GBJE Ken Griffey Jr. 100.00 30.00
Barry Bonds
Andruw Jones
Jim Edmonds
GPJG Vladimir Guerrero 80.00 24.00
Mike Piazza
Chipper Jones
Nomar Garciaparra
PMJR Mike Piazza 200.00 60.00
Mark McGwire
Derek Jeter
Alex Rodriguez
SGRM Alex Rodriguez 150.00 45.00
Ken Griffey Jr.
Sammy Sosa
Mark McGwire
THMJ Frank Thomas 120.00 36.00
Todd Helton
Mark McGwire
Derek Jeter

2001 UD Reserve Ball-Base Trios

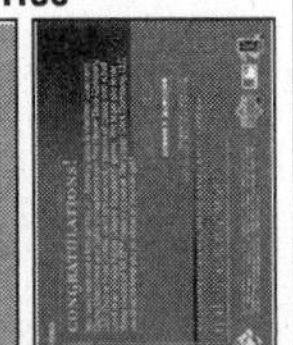

Randomly inserted into packs at one in 480, this 10-card insert set features swatches of both game-used baseball and base. Each of these cards feature three superstar caliber players on the card front. Card backs carry a "B" prefix followed by the players' initials.

Nm-Mt Ex-Mt
BSH Barry Bonds 50.00 15.00
Gary Sheffield
Todd Helton
CMJ Roger Clemens 60.00 18.00
Pedro Martinez
Derek Jeter
GPJ Vladimir Guerrero 40.00 12.00
Mike Piazza
Chipper Jones
GSG Ken Griffey Jr. 40.00 12.00
Sammy Sosa
Vladimir Guerrero
JGS Derek Jeter 60.00 18.00
Ken Griffey Jr.
Sammy Sosa
JRG Derek Jeter 60.00 18.00
Alex Rodriguez
Nomar Garciaparra
MJR Mark McGwire 100.00 30.00
Derek Jeter
Alex Rodriguez
PRS Mike Piazza 60.00 18.00
Alex Rodriguez
Sammy Sosa
SGM Sammy Sosa 100.00 30.00
Ken Griffey Jr.
Mark McGwire
THM Frank Thomas 100.00 30.00
Todd Helton
Mark McGwire

2001 UD Reserve Big Game

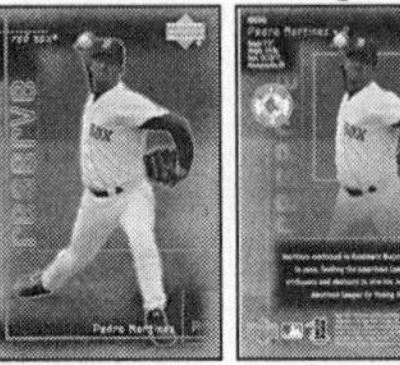

Randomly inserted into packs at one in 24, this 10-card insert set features players that usually come up big in clutch situations. Card backs carry a "BG" prefix.

Nm-Mt Ex-Mt
COMPLETE SET (10) 50.00 15.00
BG1 Alex Rodriguez 5.00 1.50
BG2 Ken Griffey Jr. 5.00 1.50
BG3 Mark McGwire 8.00 2.40
BG4 Derek Jeter 8.00 2.40
BG5 Sammy Sosa 5.00 1.50
BG6 Pedro Martinez 3.00 .90
BG7 Jason Giambi 3.00 .90
BG8 Todd Helton 2.00 .60
BG9 Carlos Delgado 2.00 .60
BG10 Mike Piazza 5.00 1.50

2001 UD Reserve Game Jersey Duos

Randomly inserted into packs at one in 240, this 15-card insert set features swatches of game-used jerseys. Each of these cards feature two superstar caliber players on the card front. Card backs carry a "J" prefix followed by the players' initials.

Nm-Mt Ex-Mt
J-BK Barry Bonds 50.00 15.00
Jeff Kent
J-DG Carlos Delgado 25.00 7.50
Jason Giambi
J-GE Troy Glaus 25.00 7.50
Darin Erstad
J-GK Jason Giambi 25.00 7.50
Jeff Kent
J-GW Brian Giles 25.00 7.50
Bernie Williams
J-HE Todd Helton 25.00 7.50
Darin Erstad
J-HG Tim Hudson 25.00 7.50
Jason Giambi
J-JG Chipper Jones 25.00 7.50
Troy Glaus
J-JJ Andruw Jones 25.00 7.50
Chipper Jones
J-JW Randy Johnson 25.00 7.50
David Wells
J-RB Alex Rodriguez 40.00 12.00
Tony Batista
J-SB Gary Sheffield 50.00 15.00
Barry Bonds
J-SG Sammy Sosa 40.00 12.00
Troy Glaus
J-WE Bernie Williams 25.00 7.50
Jim Edmonds
J-WO David Wells 25.00 7.50
Magglio Ordonez

2001 UD Reserve Game Jersey Quads

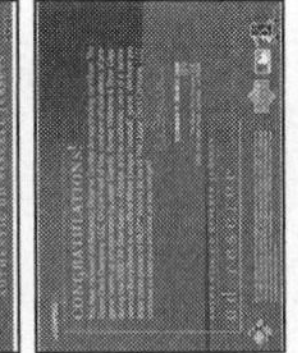

Randomly inserted into packs at one in 480, this five card insert set features swatches of game-used jerseys. Each of these cards feature four superstar caliber players on the card front. Card backs carry a "J" prefix followed by the players' initials.

Nm-Mt Ex-Mt
RGS Carlos Delgado 80.00 24.00
Alex Rodriguez
Troy Glaus
Sammy Sosa
WBG Jason Giambi 80.00 24.00
Bernie Williams
Barry Bonds
Brian Giles
HKEJ Todd Helton 50.00 15.00
Jeff Kent
Jim Edmonds
Chipper Jones
JRSB Andruw Jones 100.00 30.00
Alex Rodriguez
Sammy Sosa
Barry Bonds
SOEB Gary Sheffield 40.00 12.00
Magglio Ordonez
Darin Erstad
Tony Batista

2001 UD Reserve Game Jersey Trios

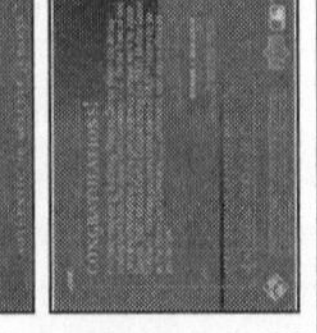

Randomly inserted into packs at one in 480, this 10-card insert set features swatches of game-used jerseys. Each of these cards feature three superstar caliber players on the card front. Card backs carry a "J" prefix followed by the players' initials.

Nm-Mt Ex-Mt
J-BSH Barry Bonds 60.00 18.00
Gary Sheffield
Todd Helton
J-BWD Tony Batista 40.00 12.00
Bernie Williams
Carlos Delgado
J-EKE Darin Erstad 40.00 12.00
Jeff Kent
Jim Edmonds
J-GGR Jason Giambi 50.00 15.00
Troy Glaus
Alex Rodriguez
J-GHD Jason Giambi 40.00 12.00
Todd Helton
Carlos Delgado
J-HJW Tim Hudson 40.00 12.00
Randy Johnson
David Wells
J-RSS Alex Rodriguez 60.00 18.00
Sammy Sosa
Gary Sheffield
J-SOD Sammy Sosa 50.00 15.00
Magglio Ordonez
Carlos Delgado
J-WEJ Bernie Williams 40.00 12.00
Jim Edmonds
Andruw Jones
J-WSH David Wells 50.00 15.00
Sammy Sosa
Todd Helton

2001 UD Reserve New Order

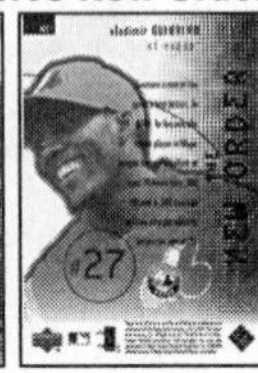

Randomly inserted into packs at one in 24, this 10-card insert set features players that are part of the "new generation" of baseball. Card backs carry a "NO" prefix.

Nm-Mt Ex-Mt
COMPLETE SET (10) 50.00 15.00
NO1 Vladimir Guerrero 3.00 .90
NO2 Andruw Jones 1.25 .35
NO3 Corey Patterson 1.25 .35
NO4 Derek Jeter 8.00 2.40
NO5 Alex Rodriguez 5.00 1.50
NO6 Pat Burrell 1.25 .35
NO7 Ichiro Suzuki 20.00 6.00
NO8 Barry Zito 3.00 .90
NO9 Rafael Furcal 1.25 .35
NO10 Troy Glaus 2.00 .60

2001 UD Reserve Royalty

Randomly inserted into packs at one in 24, this 10-card insert set features players that are among baseball's most elite. Card backs carry a "R" prefix.

Nm-Mt Ex-Mt
COMPLETE SET (10) 50.00 15.00
R1 Ken Griffey Jr. 5.00 1.50
R2 Derek Jeter 8.00 2.40
R3 Alex Rodriguez 5.00 1.50
R4 Sammy Sosa 5.00 1.50
R5 Mark McGwire 8.00 2.40
R6 Mike Piazza 5.00 1.50
R7 Vladimir Guerrero 3.00 .90
R8 Chipper Jones 3.00 .90
R9 Frank Thomas 3.00 .90
R10 Nomar Garciaparra 5.00 1.50

1988 Uecker Blue Shield

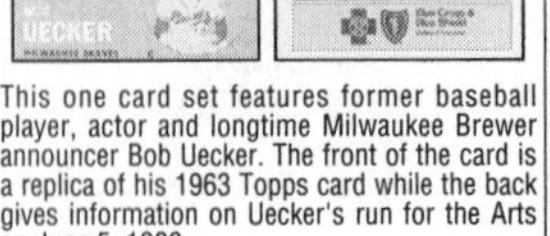

This one card set features former baseball player, actor and longtime Milwaukee Brewer announcer Bob Uecker. The front of the card is a replica of his 1963 Topps card while the back gives information on Uecker's run for the Arts on June 5, 1988.

Nm-Mt Ex-Mt
1 Bob Uecker 5.00 2.00

1985 Ultimate Baseball Card

This 15-card set by the Decathlon Corporation measures approximately 4" by 5 5/8". The fronts display color artwork of great players by Gerry Dvorak. The white backs carry the card name, player's name and career information.

Nm-Mt Ex-Mt
COMPLETE SET (15) 35.00 14.00
1 Ty Cobb 8.00 3.20
2 Honus Wagner 2.50 1.00
3 Babe Ruth 10.00 4.00
4 Lou Gehrig 8.00 3.20
5 Frank Baker 1.50 .60
6 Casey Stengel 2.00 .80
7 Moses Walker 1.00 .40
8 Cy Young 2.50 1.00
9 Joe DiMaggio 8.00 3.20
10 John McGraw 2.00 .80
11 Josh Gibson 5.00 2.00
12 Johnny Mize 1.50 .60
13 Walter Johnson 2.50 1.00
14 Walter Alston 1.00 .40
15 Enos Slaughter 1.50 .60

2001 Ultimate Collection

This product was released in mid-January 2002, and featured a 120-card base set that was broken up into tiers as follows: 90 Base Veterans, 10 Prospects numbered to 1000, 10 Prospects numbered to 750, and 10 Prospects numbered to 250. Exchange cards were seeded into packs for signed cards of Mark Prior and Mark Teixiera.

Nm-Mt Ex-Mt
COMMON CARD (1-90) 4.00 1.20
COMMON CARD (91-100) 10.00 3.00
COMMON CARD (101-110) 10.00 3.00
COMMON CARD (111-120) 25.00 7.50
1 Troy Glaus 4.00 1.20
2 Darin Erstad 4.00 1.20
3 Jason Giambi 6.00 1.80
4 Barry Zito 6.00 1.80
5 Tim Hudson 4.00 1.20
6 Miguel Tejada 4.00 1.20
7 Carlos Delgado 4.00 1.20
8 Shannon Stewart 4.00 1.20
9 Greg Vaughn 4.00 1.20
10 Toby Hall 4.00 1.20
11 Roberto Alomar 6.00 1.80
12 Juan Gonzalez 6.00 1.80
13 Jim Thome 6.00 1.80
14 Edgar Martinez 4.00 1.20
15 Freddy Garcia 4.00 1.20
16 Bret Boone 4.00 1.20
17 Kazuhiro Sasaki 4.00 1.20
18 Cal Ripken 20.00 6.00
19 Tim Raines Jr. 4.00 1.20
20 Alex Rodriguez 10.00 3.00
21 Ivan Rodriguez 6.00 1.80
22 Rafael Palmeiro 4.00 1.20
23 Pedro Martinez 6.00 1.80
24 Nomar Garciaparra 10.00 3.00
25 Manny Ramirez 4.00 1.20
26 Hideo Nomo 6.00 1.80
27 Mike Sweeney 4.00 1.20
28 Carlos Beltran 4.00 1.20
29 Tony Clark 4.00 1.20
30 Dean Palmer 4.00 1.20
31 Doug Mientkiewicz 4.00 1.20
32 Cristian Guzman 4.00 1.20
33 Corey Koskie 4.00 1.20
34 Frank Thomas 6.00 1.80
35 Magglio Ordonez 4.00 1.20
36 Jose Canseco 6.00 1.80
37 Roger Clemens 12.00 3.60
38 Derek Jeter 15.00 4.50
39 Bernie Williams 4.00 1.20
40 Mike Mussina 6.00 1.80
41 Tino Martinez 4.00 1.20
42 Jeff Bagwell 4.00 1.20
43 Lance Berkman 4.00 1.20
44 Roy Oswalt 4.00 1.20
45 Chipper Jones 6.00 1.80
46 Greg Maddux 10.00 3.00
47 Andruw Jones 4.00 1.20
48 Tom Glavine 4.00 1.20
49 Richie Sexson 4.00 1.20
50 Jeromy Burnitz 4.00 1.20
51 Ben Sheets 4.00 1.20
52 Mark McGwire 15.00 4.50
53 Matt Morris 4.00 1.20
54 Jim Edmonds 4.00 1.20
55 J.D. Drew 4.00 1.20
56 Sammy Sosa 10.00 3.00
57 Fred McGriff 4.00 1.20
58 Kerry Wood 6.00 1.80
59 Randy Johnson 6.00 1.80
60 Luis Gonzalez 4.00 1.20
61 Curt Schilling 4.00 1.20
62 Shawn Green 4.00 1.20
63 Kevin Brown 4.00 1.20
64 Gary Sheffield 4.00 1.20
65 Vladimir Guerrero 6.00 1.80
66 Barry Bonds 15.00 4.50
67 Jeff Kent 4.00 1.20
68 Rich Aurilia 4.00 1.20
69 Cliff Floyd 4.00 1.20
70 Charles Johnson 4.00 1.20
71 Josh Beckett 4.00 1.20
72 Mike Piazza 10.00 3.00
73 Edgardo Alfonzo 4.00 1.20
74 Robin Ventura 4.00 1.20
75 Tony Gwynn 8.00 2.40
76 Ryan Klesko 4.00 1.20
77 Phil Nevin 4.00 1.20
78 Scott Rolen 4.00 1.20
79 Bobby Abreu 4.00 1.20
80 Jimmy Rollins 4.00 1.20
81 Brian Giles 4.00 1.20
82 Jason Kendall 4.00 1.20

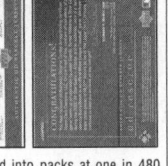

Card	Nm-Mt	Ex-Mt
83 Aramis Ramirez	4.00	1.20
84 Ken Griffey Jr.	10.00	3.00
85 Adam Dunn	4.00	1.20
86 Sean Casey	4.00	1.20
87 Barry Larkin	6.00	1.80
88 Larry Walker	4.00	1.20
89 Mike Hampton	4.00	1.20
90 Todd Helton	4.00	1.20
91 Ken Harvey T1	10.00	3.00
92 Bill Ortega T1 RC	10.00	3.00
93 Juan Diaz T1 RC	10.00	3.00
94 Greg Miller T1 RC	10.00	3.00
95 Brandon Berger T1 RC	10.00	3.00
96 Brandon Lyon T1 RC	10.00	3.00
97 Jay Gibbons T1 RC	20.00	6.00
98 Rob Mackowiak T1 RC	10.00	3.00
99 Erick Almonte T1 RC	10.00	3.00
100 J.Middlebrook T1 RC	10.00	3.00
101 Johnny Estrada T2 RC	12.00	3.60
102 Juan Uribe T2 RC	10.00	3.00
103 Travis Hafner T2 RC	25.00	7.50
104 M.Ensberg T2 RC	25.00	7.50
105 Mike Rivera T2 RC	10.00	3.00
106 Josh Towers T2 RC	10.00	3.00
107 A.Hernandez T2 RC	10.00	3.00
108 Rafael Soriano T2 RC	25.00	7.50
109 Jackson Melian T2 RC	10.00	3.00
110 Wilkin Ruan T2 RC	10.00	3.00
111 Albert Pujols T3 RC	200.00	60.00
112 T.Shinjo T3 RC	40.00	12.00
113 B.Duckworth T3 RC	25.00	7.50
114 Juan Cruz T3 RC	25.00	7.50
115 D.Brazelton T3 RC	25.00	7.50
116 Mark Prior T3 AU RC	600.00	180.00
117 Mark Teixeira T3 AU RC	300.00	90.00
118 Wilson Betemit T3 RC	25.00	7.50
119 Bud Smith T3 RC	25.00	7.50
120 I.Suzuki T3 AU RC	800.00	240.00

2001 Ultimate Collection Game Jersey

These cards feature swatches of actual game-used jerseys from various major league stars. Game Jersey cards (including Copper, Silver and Gold parallel versions) were cumulatively issued into packs at 1:2. Each card is serial-numbered to 150.

COPPER RANDOM INSERTS IN PACKS
COPPER PRINT RUN 24 SERIAL #'d SETS
NO COPPER PRICING DUE TO SCARCITY
GOLD RANDOM INSERTS IN PACKS..
GOLD PRINT RUN 15 SERIAL #'d SETS
NO GOLD PRICING DUE TO SCARCITY
SILVER RANDOM INSERTS IN PACKS
SILVER PRINT RUN 20 SERIAL #'d SETS
NO SILVER PRICING DUE TO SCARCITY

Card	Nm-Mt	Ex-Mt
U-AJ Andruw Jones	15.00	4.50
U-AP Albert Pujols	80.00	24.00
U-AR Alex Rodriguez	50.00	15.00
U-BB Barry Bonds	50.00	15.00
U-BW Bernie Williams	25.00	7.50
U-CD Carlos Delgado	15.00	4.50
U-CJ Chipper Jones	25.00	7.50
U-CR Cal Ripken	80.00	24.00
U-DE Darin Erstad	15.00	4.50
U-FT Frank Thomas	25.00	7.50
U-GM Greg Maddux	40.00	12.00
U-GS Gary Sheffield	15.00	4.50
U-IR Ivan Rodriguez	25.00	7.50
U-JAG Jason Giambi	25.00	7.50
U-JB Jeff Bagwell	25.00	7.50
U-JC Jose Canseco	25.00	7.50
U-JG Juan Gonzalez	25.00	7.50
U-KG Ken Griffey Jr.	50.00	15.00
U-LG Luis Gonzalez	15.00	4.50
U-LW Larry Walker	25.00	7.50
U-MO Magglio Ordonez	15.00	4.50
U-MP Mike Piazza	40.00	12.00
U-RA Roberto Alomar	25.00	7.50
U-RC Roger Clemens	60.00	18.00
U-RJ Randy Johnson	25.00	7.50
U-SG Shawn Green	15.00	4.50
U-SR Scott Rolen	25.00	7.50
U-SS Sammy Sosa	50.00	15.00
U-TG Tony Gwynn	25.00	7.50
U-TH Todd Helton	25.00	7.50

2001 Ultimate Collection Ichiro Ball

This five-card insert set features game-used ball cards from the 2001 Rookie of the Year, Ichiro Suzuki. There is a Base, Copper, Silver, Gold and Autographed version. Card backs carry a "BB" prefix. Print runs are listed in our checklist. The signed Ichiro Ball card was available via an exchange card seeded into packs. The redemption date for the exchange card was February, 25th, 2004.

Card	Nm-Mt	Ex-Mt
BI Ichiro Suzuki AU/25		
IA Ichiro Suzuki SP	80.00	24.00
IG Ichiro Suzuki Gold/25		
IH I.Suzuki Copper/150	120.00	36.00
IS I.Suzuki Silver/50	150.00	45.00

2001 Ultimate Collection Ichiro Base

This five-card insert set features game-used base cards from the 2001 Rookie of the Year, Ichiro Suzuki. There is a Base, Copper, Silver, Gold and Autographed version. Card backs carry a "U" preifx. Print runs are listed in our checklist. The autograph card was seeded into packs in the form of an exchange card of which carried a redemption deadline of 02/25/04.

Card	Nm-Mt	Ex-Mt
SUI Ichiro Suzuki AU/25		
UIA Ichiro Suzuki	40.00	12.00
UIC Ichiro Suzuki Copper/150	100.00	30.00
UIG Ichiro Suzuki Gold/25		
UIS Ichiro Suzuki Silver/50	120.00	36.00

2001 Ultimate Collection Ichiro Bat

This five-card insert set features game-used bat cards from the 2001 Rookie of the Year, Ichiro Suzuki. There is a Base, Copper, Silver, Gold and Autographed version. Card backs carry a "B" prefix.. Print runs are listed in our checklist. The autographed card was seeded into packs in the form of an exchange card of which carried a redemption deadline of 02/25/04.

Card	Nm-Mt	Ex-Mt
BIA I.Suzuki Away SP	80.00	24.00
BIC I.Suzuki Home SP	100.00	30.00
BIG I.Suzuki Gold/200	120.00	36.00
BIS I.Suzuki Silver/250	100.00	30.00
SBI Ichiro Suzuki AU/50	800.00	240.00

2001 Ultimate Collection Ichiro Batting Glove

This two-card insert set features game-used batting glove cards from the 2001 Rookie of the Year, Ichiro Suzuki. There are two versions available, Base and Gold. Cards carry a "BG" prefix. Print runs are listed in our checklist.

Card	Nm-Mt	Ex-Mt
BGI Ichiro Suzuki/75	200.00	60.00
BGIG Ichiro Suzuki Gold/25		

2001 Ultimate Collection Ichiro Fielders Glove

Randomly inserted into Ultimate Collection packs, these two cards feature swatches of Ichiro Suzuki gloves. The cards are printed to different amounts and we have listed those cards in our checklist.

Card	Nm-Mt	Ex-Mt
FGI Ichiro Suzuki/75	250.00	75.00
FGIG Ichiro Suzuki Gold/25		

2001 Ultimate Collection Ichiro Jersey

This five-card insert set features game-used jersey cards from the 2001 Rookie of the Year, Ichiro Suzuki. There is a Base, Copper, Silver, Gold and Autographed version. Card backs carry a "J" prefix. Print runs listed in our checklist. The autographed card was seeded into packs in the form of an exchange card of which carried a redemption deadline of 02/25/04.

Card	Nm-Mt	Ex-Mt
JIA Ichiro Suzuki Away	50.00	15.00
JIG I.Suzuki Gold/200	120.00	36.00
JIH I.Suzuki Home SP	80.00	24.00
JIS I.Suzuki Silver/250	100.00	30.00
SJI Ichiro Suzuki AU/50	800.00	240.00

2001 Ultimate Collection Magic Numbers Game Jersey

These cards feature swatches of actual game-used jerseys from various major league stars. They were issued into packs at 1:2. Card backs carry a "MN" prefix.

GAME JERSEY CUMULATIVE ODDS 1:2
STATED PRINT RUN 150 SERIAL #'d SETS
*RED: .75X TO 2X BASIC MAGIC NUMBERS
RED RANDOM INSERTS IN PACKS.....
RED PRINT RUN 30 SERIAL #'d SETS
COPPER RANDOM INSERTS IN PACKS
COPPER PRINT RUN 24 SERIAL #'d SETS
NO COPPER PRICING DUE TO SCARCITY
SILVER RANDOM INSERTS IN PACKS
SILVER PRINT RUN 20 SERIAL #'d SETS
NO SILVER PRICING DUE TO SCARCITY
GOLD RANDOM INSERTS IN PACKS..
GOLD PRINT RUN 15 SERIAL #'d SETS
NO GOLD PRICING DUE TO SCARCITY

Card	Nm-Mt	Ex-Mt
MN-G Tony Gwynn	25.00	7.50
MNAJ Andruw Jones	15.00	4.50
MNAP Albert Pujols	80.00	24.00
MNAR Alex Rodriguez	50.00	15.00
MNBB Barry Bonds	50.00	15.00
MNBW Bernie Williams	25.00	7.50
MNCD Carlos Delgado	15.00	4.50
MNCJ Chipper Jones	25.00	7.50
MNCR Cal Ripken	80.00	24.00
MNDE Darin Erstad	15.00	4.50
MNFT Frank Thomas	25.00	7.50
MNGM Greg Maddux	40.00	12.00
MNGS Gary Sheffield	15.00	4.50
MNIR Ivan Rodriguez	25.00	7.50
MNJAG Jason Giambi	25.00	7.50
MNJB Jeff Bagwell	25.00	7.50
MNJC Jose Canseco	25.00	7.50
MNJG Juan Gonzalez	25.00	7.50
MNKG Ken Griffey Jr.	50.00	15.00
MNLG Luis Gonzalez	15.00	4.50
MNLW Larry Walker	25.00	7.50
MNMO Magglio Ordonez	15.00	4.50
MNMP Mike Piazza	40.00	12.00
MNRA Roberto Alomar	25.00	7.50
MNRC Roger Clemens	60.00	18.00
MNRJ Randy Johnson	25.00	7.50
MNSG Shawn Green	15.00	4.50
MNSR Scott Rolen	25.00	7.50
MNSS Sammy Sosa	50.00	15.00
MNTH Todd Helton	25.00	7.50

2001 Ultimate Collection Signatures

These cards feature authentic autographs from various major league stars. They were issued into packs at 1:4. Card backs carry the player's initials as numbering. Please note that there were only 150 sets produced. The following players cards were seeded into packs as exchange cards with a redemption deadline of 02/25/04: Cal Ripken, Edgar Martinez, Ken Griffey Jr. and Tom Glavine.

Card	Nm-Mt	Ex-Mt
AR Alex Rodriguez	100.00	30.00
BAB Barry Bonds	200.00	60.00
CD Carlos Delgado	25.00	7.50
CF Carlton Fisk	40.00	12.00
CR Cal Ripken	150.00	45.00
DS Duke Snider	40.00	12.00
EB Ernie Banks	50.00	15.00
EM Edgar Martinez	50.00	15.00
FT Frank Thomas	50.00	15.00
GS Gary Sheffield	40.00	12.00
IR Ivan Rodriguez	50.00	15.00
JAG Jason Giambi	50.00	15.00
JT Jim Thome	50.00	15.00
KG Ken Griffey Jr.	150.00	45.00
KP Kirby Puckett	50.00	15.00
LG Luis Gonzalez	25.00	7.50
RA Roberto Alomar	50.00	15.00
RC Roger Clemens	150.00	45.00
RK Ryan Klesko	25.00	7.50
RY Robin Yount	60.00	18.00
SK Sandy Koufax	300.00	90.00
SS Sammy Sosa	200.00	60.00
TG Tony Gwynn	80.00	24.00
TGL Tom Glavine	50.00	15.00
TP Tony Perez	25.00	7.50
TS Tom Seaver	40.00	12.00

2001 Ultimate Collection Signatures Copper

This 27-card insert is a complete parallel of the 2001 Upper Deck Ultimate Collection Signatures insert set. Each card features a copper-foiled variation, and is individually serial numbered to 70. The following players cards were seeded into packs as exchange cards with a redemption deadline of 02/25/04: Cal Ripken, Edgar Martinez, Ken Griffey Jr. and Tom Glavine.

Nm-Mt Ex-Mt

*COPPER: .75X TO 1.5X BASIC SIGS .
SIGNATURES CUMULATIVE ODDS 1:4

2001 Ultimate Collection Signatures Gold

This 27-card insert is a complete parallel of the 2001 Upper Deck Ultimate Collection Signatures insert set. Each card features a gold-foiled variation, and is individually serial numbered to 15. The following players cards were seeded into packs as exchange cards with a redemption deadline of 02/25/04: Cal Ripken, Edgar Martinez, Ken Griffey Jr. and Tom Glavine.

Nm-Mt Ex-Mt

SIGNATURES CUMULATIVE ODDS 1:4

2001 Ultimate Collection Signatures Silver

This 26-card insert is a complete parallel of the 2001 Upper Deck Ultimate Collection Signatures insert set. Each card features a silver-foiled variation, and is individually serial numbered to 24. The following players cards were seeded into packs as exchange cards with a redemption deadline of 02/25/04: Cal Ripken, Edgar Martinez, Ken Griffey Jr. and Tom Glavine.

Nm-Mt Ex-Mt

SIGNATURES CUMULATIVE ODDS 1:4

2002 Ultimate Collection

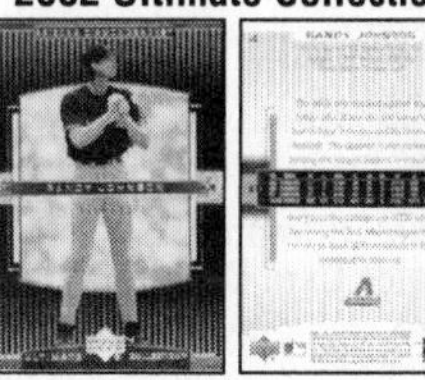

This 120 card set was released in late December, 2002. These cards were issued in five card packs which came four packs to a box and four boxes to a case with an SRP of approximately $100 per pack. Card numbered 61 through 120 featured Rookie Cards with cards numbered 110 through 120 being autographed by the player. The cards between 61 and 110 were issued to a stated print run of 500 serial numbered sets while cards numbered 111 through 113 were issued to a stated print run of 300 serial numbered sets and cards numbered 114 through 120 were issued to a stated print run of 550 serial numbered sets. One hundred Mark McGwire Priority Signing exchange cards were randomly seeded in to packs (at a believed odds of 1:1000 packs). The bearer of the card was allowed to send in one item of his or her choice to Upper Deck for McGwire to sign.

Card	Nm-Mt	Ex-Mt
COMMON CARD (1-60)	4.00	1.20
COMMON CARD (61-110)	10.00	3.00
61-110 PRINT RUN 550 SERIAL #'d SETS		
COMMON CARD (111-113)	25.00	7.50
COMMON CARD (114-120)	15.00	4.50
1 Troy Glaus	4.00	1.20
2 Luis Gonzalez	4.00	1.20
3 Curt Schilling	4.00	1.20
4 Randy Johnson	6.00	1.80
5 Andruw Jones	4.00	1.20
6 Greg Maddux	10.00	3.00
7 Chipper Jones	6.00	1.80
8 Gary Sheffield	4.00	1.20
9 Cal Ripken	20.00	6.00
10 Manny Ramirez	4.00	1.20
11 Pedro Martinez	6.00	1.80
12 Nomar Garciaparra	10.00	3.00
13 Sammy Sosa	10.00	3.00
14 Kerry Wood	6.00	1.80
15 Mark Prior	12.00	3.60
16 Magglio Ordonez	4.00	1.20
17 Frank Thomas	6.00	1.80
18 Adam Dunn	4.00	1.20
19 Ken Griffey Jr.	10.00	3.00
20 Jim Thome	6.00	1.80
21 Larry Walker	4.00	1.20
22 Todd Helton	4.00	1.20
23 Nolan Ryan	15.00	4.50
24 Jeff Bagwell	4.00	1.20
25 Roy Oswalt	4.00	1.20
26 Lance Berkman	4.00	1.20
27 Mike Sweeney	4.00	1.20
28 Shawn Green	4.00	1.20
29 Hideo Nomo	6.00	1.80
30 Torii Hunter	4.00	1.20
31 Vladimir Guerrero	6.00	1.80
32 Tom Seaver	4.00	1.20
33 Mike Piazza	10.00	3.00
34 Roberto Alomar	6.00	1.80
35 Derek Jeter	15.00	4.50
36 Alfonso Soriano	4.00	1.20
37 Jason Giambi	6.00	1.80
38 Roger Clemens	12.00	3.60
39 Mike Mussina	6.00	1.80
40 Bernie Williams	4.00	1.20
41 Joe DiMaggio	12.00	3.60
42 Mickey Mantle	25.00	7.50
43 Miguel Tejada	4.00	1.20
44 Eric Chavez	4.00	1.20
45 Barry Zito	4.00	1.20
46 Pat Burrell	4.00	1.20
47 Jason Kendall	4.00	1.20
48 Brian Giles	4.00	1.20
49 Barry Bonds	15.00	4.50
50 Ichiro Suzuki	10.00	3.00
51 Stan Musial	10.00	3.00
52 J.D. Drew	4.00	1.20
53 Scott Rolen	4.00	1.20
54 Albert Pujols	12.00	3.60
55 Mark McGwire	15.00	4.50
56 Alex Rodriguez	10.00	3.00
57 Ivan Rodriguez	6.00	1.80
58 Juan Gonzalez	6.00	1.80
59 Rafael Palmeiro	4.00	1.20
60 Carlos Delgado	4.00	1.20
61 Jose Valverde UR RC	15.00	4.50
62 Doug Devore UR RC	10.00	3.00
63 John Ennis UR RC	10.00	3.00
64 Joey Dawley UR RC	10.00	3.00
65 Trey Hodges UR RC	10.00	3.00
66 Mike Mahoney UR	10.00	3.00
67 Aaron Cook UR RC	10.00	3.00
68 Rene Reyes UR RC	10.00	3.00
69 Mark Corey UR RC	10.00	3.00
70 Hansel Izquierdo UR RC	10.00	3.00
71 Brandon Puffer UR RC	10.00	3.00
72 Jeriome Robertson UR RC	10.00	3.00
73 Jose Diaz UR RC	10.00	3.00
74 David Ross UR RC	10.00	3.00
75 Jayson Durocher UR RC	10.00	3.00
76 Eric Good UR RC	10.00	3.00
77 Satoru Komiyama UR RC	10.00	3.00
78 Tyler Yates UR RC	15.00	4.50
79 Eric Junge UR RC	10.00	3.00
80 Anderson Machado UR RC	10.00	3.00
81 Adrian Burnside UR RC	10.00	3.00
82 Ben Howard UR RC	10.00	3.00
83 Clay Condrey UR RC	10.00	3.00
84 Nelson Castro UR RC	10.00	3.00
85 So Taguchi UR RC	15.00	4.50
86 Mike Crudale UR RC	10.00	3.00
87 Scotty Layfield UR RC	10.00	3.00
88 Steve Bechler UR RC	10.00	3.00
89 Travis Driskill UR RC	10.00	3.00
90 Howie Clark UR RC	10.00	3.00
91 Josh Hancock UR RC	10.00	3.00
92 Jorge De La Rosa UR RC	10.00	3.00
93 Anastacio Martinez UR RC	10.00	3.00
94 Brian Tallet UR RC	15.00	4.50
95 Carl Sadler UR RC	10.00	3.00
96 Cliff Lee UR RC	15.00	4.50
97 Josh Bard UR RC	10.00	3.00
98 Wes Obermueller UR RC	10.00	3.00
99 Juan Brito UR RC	10.00	3.00
100 Aaron Guiel UR RC	10.00	3.00
101 Jeremy Hill UR RC	10.00	3.00
102 Kevin Frederick UR RC	10.00	3.00
103 Nate Field UR RC	10.00	3.00
104 Julio Mateo UR RC	10.00	3.00
105 Chris Snelling UR RC	15.00	4.50
106 Felix Escalona UR RC	10.00	3.00
107 Reynaldo Garcia UR RC	10.00	3.00
108 Mike Smith UR RC	10.00	3.00
109 Ken Huckaby UR RC	10.00	3.00
110 Kevin Cash UR RC	10.00	3.00
111 Kazuhisa Ishii UR AU RC	50.00	15.00
112 Fr. Sanchez UR AU RC	25.00	7.50
113 J.Simontacchi UR AU RC	25.00	7.50
114 Jorge Padilla UR AU RC	15.00	4.50
115 Kirk Saarloos UR AU RC	15.00	4.50
116 Ro. Rosario UR AU RC	15.00	4.50
117 Oliver Perez UR AU RC	25.00	7.50
118 Mi. Asencio UR AU RC	15.00	4.50
119 Fr. German UR AU RC	15.00	4.50
120 Jaime Cerda UR AU RC	15.00	4.50
MM M.McGwire AU EXCH/100	600.00	180.00

2002 Ultimate Collection Double Barrel Action

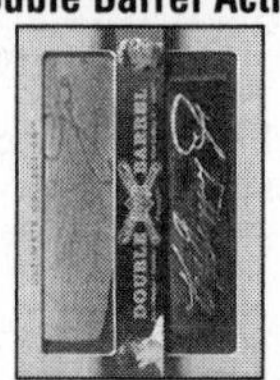

Randomly inserted into packs, these 18 cards feature two bat "barrell" cards of the featured player. As each of these cards have a stated print run of nine or fewer cards, we have not priced these cards due to market scarcity.

Card	Nm-Mt	Ex-Mt
BR Jeff Bagwell / Manny Ramirez/1		
DG Joe DiMaggio / Ken Griffey Jr./5		
DJ Carlos Delgado / Jason Giambi/2		
GH Shawn Green / Todd Helton/2		
GI Ken Griffey Jr. / Ichiro Suzuki/3		
GJ Luis Gonzalez / Randy Johnson/1		
GP Juan Gonzalez / Rafael Palmeiro/3		
IM Ichiro Suzuki / Edgar Martinez/1		
JJ Chipper Jones / Andruw Jones/2		
JM Chipper Jones / Greg Maddux/1		
RI Alex Rodriguez / Ivan Rodriguez/5		
RM Alex Rodriguez / Miguel Tejada/2		
RR Alex Rodriguez		

Cal Ripken/9
RS Manny Ramirez....................................
Sammy Sosa/1
SC Sammy Sosa....................................
Fred McGriff/3
SM Sammy Sosa....................................
Mark McGwire/1
TD Jim Thome....................................
Carlos Delgado/3
TO Frank Thomas....................................
Magglio Ordonez/4

2002 Ultimate Collection Game Jersey Tier 1

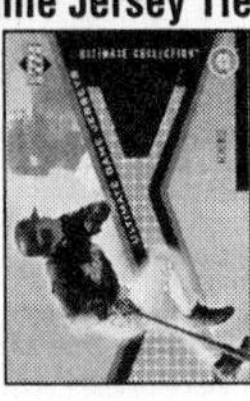

Randomly inserted into packs, these 21 cards were issued to a stated print run of 99 serial numbered sets. These cards can be differentiated from the other game jersey as they have a "JB" numbering prefix as well as featuring batting images and the swatches are on the right side.

	Nm-Mt	Ex-Mt
AD Adam Dunn	15.00	4.50
AJ Andruw Jones	15.00	4.50
AR Alex Rodriguez	40.00	12.00
AS Alfonso Soriano	25.00	7.50
CJ Chipper Jones	25.00	7.50
CR Cal Ripken	60.00	18.00
IR Ivan Rodriguez	25.00	7.50
IS Ichiro Suzuki	80.00	24.00
JD Joe DiMaggio	120.00	36.00
JG Jason Giambi	25.00	7.50
KG Ken Griffey Jr.	40.00	12.00
KI Kazuhisa Ishii	25.00	7.50
MC Mark McGwire	80.00	24.00
MM Mickey Mantle	150.00	45.00
MP Mike Piazza	40.00	12.00
MR Manny Ramirez	15.00	4.50
PM Pedro Martinez	25.00	7.50
PR Mark Prior	40.00	12.00
RC Roger Clemens	40.00	12.00
RJ Randy Johnson	25.00	7.50
SS Sammy Sosa	40.00	12.00

2002 Ultimate Collection Game Jersey Tier 1 Gold

Randomly inserted into packs, this is a parallel to the Tier 1 set. These cards have a stated print run of 50 serial numbered sets.

Nm-Mt Ex-Mt
*TIER 1 GOLD: .75X TO 1.5X TIER 1 JSY

2002 Ultimate Collection Game Jersey Tier 2

Randomly inserted into packs, these 21 cards were issued to a stated print run of 99 serial numbered sets. These cards can be differentiated from the other game jersey as they have a "JF" numbering prefix as well as featuring fielding images and the swatches are on the left side.

Nm-Mt Ex-Mt
*TIER 2: .4X TO 1X TIER 1 JSY ....

2002 Ultimate Collection Game Jersey Tier 2 Gold

Randomly inserted into packs, this is a parallel to the Tier 1 set. These cards have a stated print run of 30 serial numbered sets.

Nm-Mt Ex-Mt
*TIER 2 GOLD: .75X TO 2X TIER JSY .

2002 Ultimate Collection Game Jersey Tier 3

Randomly inserted into packs, these 21 cards were issued to a stated print run of 199 serial numbered sets. These cards can be differentiated from the other game jersey as they have a "JP" numbering prefix as well as featuring profile images and the swatches are on the right side.

Nm-Mt Ex-Mt
*TIER 3: .3X TO .8X TIER JSY ....

2002 Ultimate Collection Game Jersey Tier 4

Randomly inserted into packs, these 21 cards were issued to a stated print run of 199 serial numbered sets. These cards can be differentiated from the other game jersey as they have a "JR" numbering prefix as well as featuring running images and the swatches are on the left side.

Nm-Mt Ex-Mt
*TIER 4: .3X TO .8X TIER 1 JSY ....

2002 Ultimate Collection Patch Card

Randomly inserted into packs, these 10 cards featue game-used patch swatched of the feature player. Each of these cards were issued to a stated print run of 100 serial numbered sets.

	Nm-Mt	Ex-Mt
*3-COLOR PATCH: 1X TO 1.5X HI COLUMN		
CJ Chipper Jones	50.00	15.00
IR Ivan Rodriguez	50.00	15.00
IS Ichiro Suzuki	200.00	60.00
KI Kazuhisa Ishii	60.00	18.00
LG Luis Gonzalez	40.00	12.00

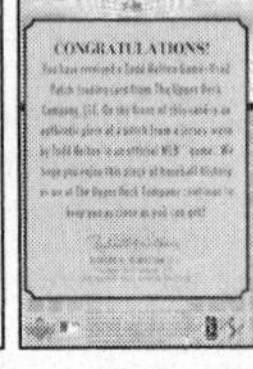

MM Mark McGwire	150.00	45.00
MP Mark Prior	60.00	18.00
SG Shawn Green	40.00	12.00
SS Sammy Sosa	80.00	24.00
TH Todd Helton	50.00	15.00

2002 Ultimate Collection Patch Card Double

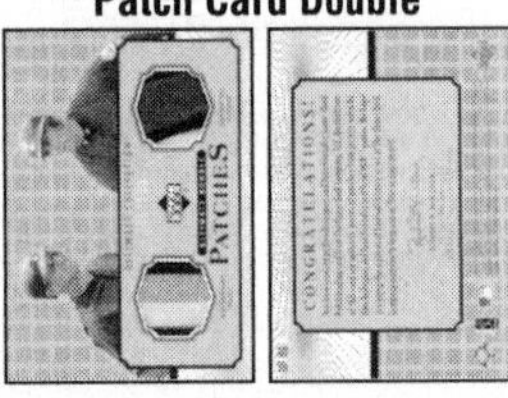

Randomly inserted into packs, these nine cards feature two game-used patch swatches of the featured players and were printed to a stated print run of 100 serial numbered sets.

	Nm-Mt	Ex-Mt
DE J.D. Drew / Jim Edmonds	80.00	24.00
GC Jason Giambi / Roger Clemens	120.00	36.00
IG Ichiro Suzuki / Ken Griffey Jr.	150.00	45.00
JS Randy Johnson / Curt Schilling	80.00	24.00
MG Greg Maddux / Tom Glavine	100.00	30.00
MS Mark McGwire / Sammy Sosa	150.00	45.00
PA Mike Piazza / Roberto Alomar	100.00	30.00
RG Alex Rodriguez / Juan Gonzalez	120.00	36.00
RM Manny Ramirez / Pedro Martinez	80.00	24.00

2002 Ultimate Collection Patch Card Double Gold

Randomly inserted into packs, these cards parallel the Patch Card Double insert set are were issued to a stated print run of 50 serial numbered sets. Please note that a card featuring Mickey Mantle and Joe DiMaggio was issued to a stated print run of 13 serial numbered sets and is not priced due to market scarcity.

Nm-Mt Ex-Mt
*GOLD: .75X TO 1.5X BASIC PATCH ..
MD Mickey Mantle ....
Joe DiMaggio/13

2002 Ultimate Collection Signatures Tier 1

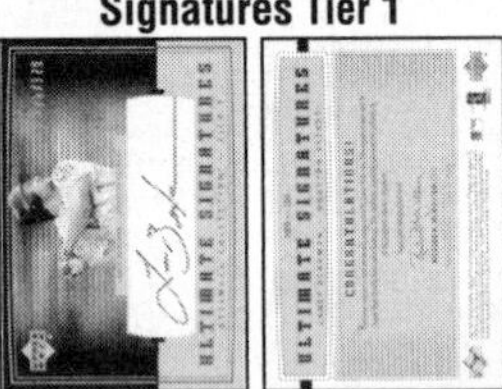

Randomly inserted into packs, these 19 cards feature signatures of some of the leading players in baseball. As the cards are signed to a differing amount of signatures, we have notated that information next to their name in our checklist.

	Nm-Mt	Ex-Mt
AD1 Adam Dunn/125	50.00	15.00
AR1 Alex Rodriguez/329	120.00	36.00
BG1 Brian Giles/220	20.00	6.00
BZ1 Barry Zito/199	50.00	15.00
CD1 Carlos Delgado/95	30.00	9.00
CR1 Cal Ripken/75	200.00	60.00
GS1 Gary Sheffield/95	30.00	9.00
JD1 J.D. Drew/220	20.00	6.00
JG1 Jason Giambi/295	50.00	15.00
JK1 Jason Kendall/220	20.00	6.00
JT1 Jim Thome/90	60.00	18.00
KG1 Ken Griffey Jr./195	150.00	45.00
LB1 Lance Berkman/179	20.00	6.00
LG1 Luis Gonzalez/199	20.00	6.00
MP1 Mark Prior/160	100.00	30.00
PB1 Pat Burrell/95	30.00	9.00
RA1 Roberto Alomar/155	50.00	15.00
RC1 Roger Clemens/320	100.00	30.00
SR1 Scott Rolen/160	30.00	9.00

2002 Ultimate Collection Signatures Tier 2

Randomly inserted into packs, these 16 cards feature signatures of some of the leading players in baseball. As the cards are signed to a differing amount of signatures, we have notated that information next to their name in our checklist.

	Nm-Mt	Ex-Mt
AJ2 Andruw Jones/51	80.00	24.00
AR2 Alex Rodriguez/75	150.00	45.00
BZ2 Barry Zito/70	60.00	18.00

DS2 Duke Snider/51	80.00	24.00
FT2 Frank Thomas/51	100.00	30.00
JB2 Jeff Bagwell/51	100.00	30.00
JG2 Jason Giambi/50	80.00	24.00
KG2 Ken Griffey Jr./30		
KP2 Kirby Puckett/75	80.00	24.00
KW2 Kerry Wood/51	100.00	30.00
LB2 Lance Berkman/85	30.00	9.00
LG2 Luis Gonzalez/70	30.00	9.00
MP2 Mark Prior/60	150.00	45.00
SR2 Scott Rolen/60	80.00	24.00
TG2 Tony Gwynn/51	120.00	36.00
TH2 Todd Helton/51	80.00	24.00

2002 Ultimate Collection Signatures Tier 2 Gold

Randomly inserted into packs, these cards partially parallel the Tier 2 Signatures and were printed to a stated print run of 10 serial numbered sets. Due to market scarcity, no pricing is provided for these cards.

Nm-Mt Ex-Mt
AR2 Alex Rodriguez ....
JG2 Jason Giambi ....
KG2 Ken Griffey Jr. ....
KP2 Kirby Puckett ....

2002 Ultimate Collection Signed Excellence

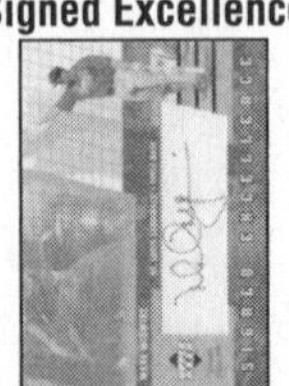

Randomly inserted into packs, these 20 cards feature signed cards of Upper Deck Spokespeople. Most of the cards were issued to a stated print run of 100 or fewer cards. Mark McGwire added a 583 HR notation to some of his signatures.

	Nm-Mt	Ex-Mt
*MCGWIRE 583 HR: 1X TO 1.5X HI COLUMN		
I1 Ichiro Suzuki/56	400.00	120.00
I2 Ichiro Suzuki/51	400.00	120.00
I3 Ichiro Suzuki/23		
I4 Ichiro Suzuki/12		
I5 Ichiro Suzuki Batting	300.00	90.00
I6 Ichiro Suzuki Throwing	300.00	90.00
MM1 Mark McGwire/70	400.00	120.00
MM2 Mark McGwire/65	400.00	120.00
MM3 Mark McGwire A's/49	400.00	120.00
MM4 Mark McGwire/25		
MM5 Mark McGwire Standing	300.00	90.00
MM6 Mark McGwire Waving	300.00	90.00
MM7 Mark McGwire A's Fldg.	300.00	90.00
SS1 Sammy Sosa/66	200.00	60.00
SS2 Sammy Sosa/64	200.00	60.00
SS3 Sammy Sosa/54	200.00	60.00
SS4 Sammy Sosa/21		
SS5 Sammy Sosa Running	150.00	45.00
SS6 Sammy Sosa Holding Bat	150.00	45.00
SS7 Sammy Sosa Throwing	150.00	45.00

2002 Ultimate Collection Signed Excellence Gold

Randomly inserted into packs, these cards partially parallel the Signed Excellence insert set and were printed to a stated print run of 1 serial numbered sets. Due to market scarcity, no pricing is provided for these cards.

Nm-Mt Ex-Mt
I4 Ichiro Suzuki ....
MM4 Mark McGwire....................................
SS4 Sammy Sosa ....

2003 Ultimate Collection

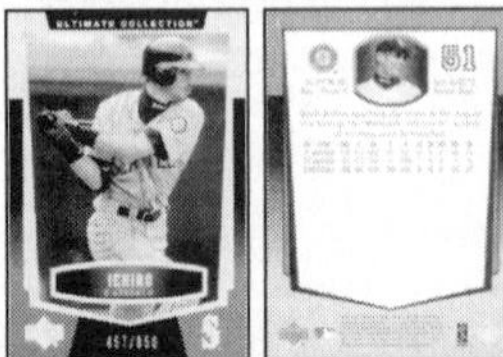

This 180 card set was released in very early January, 2004. The set was issued in four card packs with an $100 SRP which came four packs to a box and four boxes to a case. Cards numbered 1-84 feature veterans and were issued to a stated print run of 850 serial numbered sets. Cards 85-117 are Tier 1 Rookie Cards and were issued to a stated print run of 625 serial numbered sets. Cards numbered 118 through 140 are Tier 2 Rookie Cards and were issued to a stated print run of 399 serial numbered sets. Cards numbered 141 through 158 are Tier 3 Rookie Cards and were issued to a stated print run of 250 serial numbered sets. Cards numbered 159 through 168 are Tier 4 Rookie Cards and were issued to a stated print run of 100 serial numbered sets. Cards numbered 169 through 180 were each signed and inserted into packs at slightly different odds.

	MINT	NRMT
COMMON CARD (1-84)	3.00	1.35
1-84 STATED ODDS TWO PER PACK..		
COMMON CARD (85-117)	5.00	2.20
COMMON CARD (118-140)	5.00	2.20
118-140 PRINT RUN 399 SERIAL #'d SETS		
COMMON CARD (141-158)	6.00	2.70
COMMON CARD (159-168)	10.00	4.50
159-168 PRINT RUN 100 SERIAL #'d SETS		
85-168 STATED ODDS ONE PER PACK		
COMMON CARD (169-174)	40.00	18.00
169-174 AND ULT.SIG.OVERALL ODDS 1:4		
COMMON CARD (175-180)	15.00	6.75
175-180 AND BUYBACK OVERALL ODDS 1:8		
169-180 PRINT RUN 250 SERIAL #'d SETS		
MATSUI PART LIVE/ PART EXCH		
EXCHANGE DEADLINE 12/17/06........		
1 Ichiro Suzuki	8.00	3.60
2 Ken Griffey Jr.	8.00	3.60
3 Sammy Sosa	8.00	3.60
4 Jason Giambi	5.00	2.20
5 Mike Piazza	8.00	3.60
6 Derek Jeter	12.00	5.50
7 Randy Johnson	5.00	2.20
8 Barry Bonds	12.00	5.50
9 Carlos Delgado	3.00	1.35
10 Mark Prior	10.00	4.50
11 Vladimir Guerrero	5.00	2.20
12 Alfonso Soriano	5.00	2.20
13 Jim Thome	5.00	2.20
14 Pedro Martinez	5.00	2.20
15 Nomar Garciaparra	8.00	3.60
16 Chipper Jones	5.00	2.20
17 Rocco Baldelli	8.00	3.60
18 Dontrelle Willis	5.00	2.20
19 Garret Anderson	3.00	1.35
20 Jeff Bagwell	5.00	2.20
21 Jim Edmonds	3.00	1.35
22 Rickey Henderson	5.00	2.20
23 Torii Hunter	3.00	1.35
24 Tom Glavine	5.00	2.20
25 Hideo Nomo	5.00	2.20
26 Luis Gonzalez	3.00	1.35
27 Alex Rodriguez	8.00	3.60
28 Albert Pujols	10.00	4.50
29 Manny Ramirez	3.00	1.35
30 Rafael Palmeiro	5.00	2.20
31 Bernie Williams	5.00	2.20
32 Curt Schilling	5.00	2.20
33 Roger Clemens	10.00	4.50
34 Andruw Jones	3.00	1.35
35 J.D. Drew	3.00	1.35
36 Kerry Wood	5.00	2.20
37 Scott Rolen	5.00	2.20
38 Darin Erstad	3.00	1.35
39 Joe DiMaggio	8.00	3.60
40 Magglio Ordonez	3.00	1.35
41 Todd Helton	5.00	2.20
42 Barry Zito	5.00	2.20
43 Mickey Mantle	15.00	6.75
44 Miguel Tejada	3.00	1.35
45 Troy Glaus	5.00	2.20
46 Kazuhisa Ishii	3.00	1.35
47 Adam Dunn	3.00	1.35
48 Ted Williams	10.00	4.50
49 Mike Mussina	5.00	2.20
50 Ivan Rodriguez	5.00	2.20
51 Jacque Jones	3.00	1.35
52 Stan Musial	8.00	3.60
53 Mariano Rivera	5.00	2.20
54 Larry Walker	5.00	2.20
55 Aaron Boone	3.00	1.35
56 Hank Blalock	5.00	2.20
57 Rich Harden	5.00	2.20
58 Lance Berkman	3.00	1.35
59 Eric Chavez	3.00	1.35
60 Carlos Beltran	3.00	1.35
61 Roy Oswalt	3.00	1.35
62 Moises Alou	3.00	1.35
63 Nolan Ryan	10.00	4.50
64 Jeff Kent	3.00	1.35
65 Roberto Alomar	5.00	2.20
66 Runelvys Hernandez	3.00	1.35
67 Roy Halladay	3.00	1.35
68 Tim Hudson	3.00	1.35
69 Tom Seaver	5.00	2.20
70 Edgardo Alfonzo	3.00	1.35
71 Andy Pettitte	5.00	2.20
72 Preston Wilson	3.00	1.35
73 Frank Thomas	5.00	2.20
74 Jerome Williams	3.00	1.35
75 Shawn Green	3.00	1.35
76 David Wells	3.00	1.35
77 John Smoltz	5.00	2.20
78 Jorge Posada	5.00	2.20
79 Marlon Byrd	3.00	1.35
80 Austin Kearns	3.00	1.35
81 Bret Boone	3.00	1.35
82 Rafael Furcal	3.00	1.35
83 Jay Gibbons	3.00	1.35
84 Shane Reynolds	3.00	1.35
85 Nate Bland UR T1 RC	5.00	2.20
86 Willie Eyre UR T1 RC	5.00	2.20
87 Jeremy Guthrie UR T1	5.00	2.20
88 Jeremy Wedel UR T1 RC	5.00	2.20
89 Jhonny Peralta UR T1 RC	5.00	2.20
90 Luis Ayala UR T1 RC	5.00	2.20
91 Michael Hessman UR T1 RC	5.00	2.20
92 Michael Nakamura UR T1 RC	5.00	2.20
93 Nook Logan UR T1 RC	5.00	2.20
94 Rett Johnson UR T1 RC	8.00	3.60
95 Josh Hall UR T1 RC	8.00	3.60
96 Julio Manon UR T1 RC	5.00	2.20
97 Heath Bell UR T1 RC	5.00	2.20
98 Ian Ferguson UR T1 RC	5.00	2.20
99 Jason Gilfillan UR T1 RC	5.00	2.20
100 Jason Roach UR T1 RC	5.00	2.20
101 Jason Shiell UR T1 RC	5.00	2.20
102 Termel Sledge UR T1 RC	8.00	3.60
103 Phil Seibel UR T1 RC	5.00	2.20
104 Jeff Duncan UR T1 RC	8.00	3.60
105 Mike Neu UR T1 RC	5.00	2.20
106 Colin Porter UR T1 RC	5.00	2.20
107 David Matranga UR T1 RC	5.00	2.20
108 Aaron Looper UR T1 RC	5.00	2.20
109 Jeremy Bonderman UR T1 RC	8.00	3.60
110 Miguel Ojeda UR T1 RC	5.00	2.20
111 Chad Cordero UR T1 RC	5.00	2.20
112 Shane Bazzell UR T1 RC	5.00	2.20
113 Tim Olson UR T1 RC	8.00	3.60
114 Michel Hernandez UR T1 RC	5.00	2.20
115 Chien-Ming Wang UR T1 RC	15.00	6.75
116 Josh Stewart UR T1 RC	5.00	2.20
117 Clint Barmes UR T1 RC	8.00	3.60
118 Craig Brazell UR T2 RC	8.00	3.60
119 Josh Willingham UR T2 RC	10.00	4.50
120 Brent Hoard UR T2 RC	5.00	2.20
121 Francisco Rosario UR T2 RC	5.00	2.20
122 Rick Roberts UR T2 RC	5.00	2.20
123 Geoff Geary UR T2 RC	5.00	2.20
124 Edgar Gonzalez UR T2 RC	5.00	2.20
125 Kevin Correia UR T2 RC	5.00	2.20
126 Ryan Cameron UR T2 RC	5.00	2.20
127 Beau Kemp UR T2 RC	5.00	2.20
128 Tommy Phelps UR T2	5.00	2.20
129 Mark Malaska UR T2 RC	5.00	2.20
130 Kevin Ohme UR T2 RC	5.00	2.20
131 Humberto Quintero UR T2 RC	5.00	2.20
132 Aquilino Lopez UR T2 RC	5.00	2.20
133 Andrew Brown UR T2 RC	5.00	2.20
134 Wilfredo Ledezma UR T2 RC	5.00	2.20
135 Luis De Los Santos UR T2	5.00	2.20
136 Garrett Atkins UR T2	5.00	2.20
137 Fernando Cabrera UR T2 RC	5.00	2.20
138 D.J. Carrasco UR T2 RC	5.00	2.20
139 Alfredo Gonzalez UR T2 RC	5.00	2.20
140 Alex Prieto UR T2 RC	5.00	2.20
141 Matt Kata UR T3 RC	10.00	4.50
142 Chris Capuano UR T3 RC	6.00	2.70
143 Bobby Madritsch UR T3 RC	6.00	2.70
144 Greg Jones UR T3 RC	6.00	2.70
145 Pete Zoccolillo UR T3 RC	6.00	2.70
146 Chad Gaudin UR T3 RC	6.00	2.70
147 Rosman Garcia UR T3 RC	6.00	2.70
148 Gerald Laird UR T3	6.00	2.70
149 Danny Garcia UR T3 RC	6.00	2.70
150 Stephen Randolph UR T3 RC	6.00	2.70
151 Pete LaForest UR T3 RC	10.00	4.50
152 Brian Sweeney UR T3 RC	6.00	2.70
153 Aaron Miles UR T3 RC	10.00	4.50
154 Jorge DePaula UR T3 UER	6.00	2.70
Real name is Julio DePaula		
155 Graham Koonce UR T3 RC	25.00	11.00
156 Tom Gregorio UR T3 RC	6.00	2.70
157 Javier Lopez UR T3 RC	6.00	2.70
158 Oscar Villarreal UR T3 RC	6.00	2.70
159 Prentice Redman UR T4 RC	10.00	4.50
160 Francisco Cruceta UR T4 RC	10.00	4.50
161 Guillermo Quiroz UR T4 RC	20.00	9.00
162 Jeremy Griffiths UR T4 RC	15.00	6.75
163 Lew Ford UR T4 RC	15.00	6.75
164 Rob Hammock UR T4 RC	15.00	6.75
165 Todd Wellemeyer UR T4 RC	15.00	6.75
166 Ryan Wagner UR T4 RC	20.00	9.00
167 Edwin Jackson UR T4 RC	40.00	18.00
168 Dan Haren UR T4 RC	15.00	6.75
169 Hideki Matsui AU RC	300.00	135.00
170 Jose Contreras AU RC	50.00	22.00
171 Delmon Young AU RC	225.00	100.00
172 Rickie Weeks AU RC	200.00	90.00
173 Brandon Webb AU RC	50.00	22.00
174 Bo Hart AU RC	40.00	18.00
175 Rocco Baldelli YS AU	50.00	22.00
176 Jose Reyes YS AU	40.00	18.00
177 Dontrelle Willis YS AU	40.00	18.00
178 Bobby Hill YS AU	15.00	6.75
179 Jae Weong Seo YS AU	25.00	11.00
180 Jesse Foppert YS AU	25.00	11.00

2003 Ultimate Collection Gold

Nm-Mt Ex-Mt
*GOLD ACTIVE 1-84: 1.25X TO 3X BASIC
*GOLD RETIRED 1-84: 1.5X TO 4X BASIC
1-84 PRINT RUN 50 SERIAL #'d SETS
*GOLD 84-117: 1X TO 2.5X BASIC ....
84-117 PRINT RUN 50 SERIAL #'d SETS
*GOLD 118-140: 1X TO 2.5X BASIC ....
118-140 PRINT RUN 35 SERIAL #'d SETS
*GOLD 141-158: 1X TO 2.5X BASIC ...
141-158 PRINT RUN 25 SERIAL #'d SETS
159-168 PRINT RUN 10 SERIAL #'d SETS
159-168 NO PRICING DUE TO SCARCITY
169-174 AU PRINT RUN 25 SERIAL #'d SETS
169-174 AU NO PRICING DUE TO SCARCITY
175-180 AU PRINT RUN 25 SERIAL #'d SETS
175-180 AU NO PRICING DUE TO SCARCITY
RANDOM INSERTS IN PACKS ....

2003 Ultimate Collection Buybacks

These 231 cards, which were randomly inserted into packs, feature mainly 2003 cards (with a smattering of earlier year cards) from varying Upper Deck products which UD bought back and had the player signed. Please note that for cards with print runs of 15 or fewer copies pricing is not provided due to scarity of market evidence.

Nm-Mt Ex-Mt
BUYBACKS & YS 175-180 OVERALL ODDS 1:8

1 Rocco Baldelli 03 UDA Blue/10
2 Rocco Baldelli 03 UDA Red/10
3 Hank Blalock 02-3 SUP/10
4 Hank Blalock 02-3 SUP/35 ..... 40.00 12.00
5 Hank Blalock 03 40M/25 .... 50.00 15.00
6 Hank Blalock 03 GF/25 .... 50.00 15.00
7 Hank Blalock 03 MVP/10
8 Hank Blalock 03 Patch/25 ...... 50.00 15.00
9 Hank Blalock 03 SPA/20 .... 50.00 15.00
10 Hank Blalock 03 SPA/25 .... 50.00 15.00
11 Hank Blalock 03 UD/10
12 Hank Blalock 03 VIN/25 .... 50.00 15.00
13 Carlos Delgado 03 40M/10
14 Carlos Delgado 03 40M Flag/2
15 Carlos Delgado 03 GF/2
16 Carlos Delgado 03 MVP/3
17 Carlos Delgado 03 Patch/2
18 Carlos Delgado 03 PB/5
19 Carlos Delgado 03 PB Red/3
20 Carlos Delgado 03 SPA/11
21 Carlos Delgado 03 UD/1
22 Carlos Delgado 03 UD LS Jsy/4
23 Carlos Delgado 03 UDA/5
24 Carlos Delgado 03 VIN/2
25 Adam Dunn 03 40M Rain/1
26 Adam Dunn 03 40M Rain AS/5
27 Adam Dunn 03 GF/1
28 Adam Dunn 03 MVP/5
29 Adam Dunn 03 Patch/7
30 Adam Dunn 03 PB/9
31 Adam Dunn 03 PB Red/1
32 Adam Dunn 03 UD/7
33 Adam Dunn 03 UDA/5
34 Adam Dunn 03 VIN/1
35 Adam Dunn 03 VIN 3D/7
36 Nomar Garciaparra 03 40M/2
37 Nomar Garciaparra 03 40M Flag/1
38 Nomar Garciaparra 03 GF/3
39 Nomar Garciaparra 03 MVP/1
40 Nomar Garciaparra 03 PB/7
41 Nomar Garciaparra 03 PB Red/2
42 Nomar Garciaparra 03 SPA/1
43 Nomar Garciaparra 03 UD/3
44 Nomar Garciaparra 03 UD MP/2
45 Nomar Garciaparra 03 UDA/2
46 Nomar Garciaparra 03 VIN/1
47 Tom Glavine 03 40M/1
48 Tom Glavine 03 40M Flag/3
49 Tom Glavine 03 GF/3
50 Tom Glavine 03 GF w/Vlad/2
51 Tom Glavine 03 MVP/1
52 Tom Glavine 03 PB/5
53 Tom Glavine 03 PB Red/3
54 Tom Glavine 03 SPA/7
55 Tom Glavine 03 UD/8
56 Tom Glavine 03 UD/5
57 Tom Glavine 03 UDA/5
58 Tom Glavine 03 VIN/7
59 Luis Gonzalez 03 40M/10
60 Luis Gonzalez 03 40M AS/15
61 Luis Gonzalez 03 40M HR/25 50.00 15.00
62 Luis Gonzalez 03 40M T40/15
63 Luis Gonzalez 03 40M Flag/5
64 Luis Gonzalez 03 GF/15
65 Luis Gonzalez 03 MVP/3
66 Luis Gonzalez 03 Patch/17 ... 50.00 15.00
67 Luis Gonzalez 03 PB/15
68 Luis Gonzalez 03 SPA/25 ...... 50.00 15.00
69 Luis Gonzalez 03 SWS/15
70 Luis Gonzalez 03 UDA/15
71 Luis Gonzalez 03 VIN/25 ...... 50.00 15.00
72 K.Griffey Jr. 02-3 SUP/75... 175.00 52.50
73 K.Griffey 02-3 SUP Spok/50 200.00 60.00
74 K.Griffey Jr. 03 40M/50...... 200.00 60.00
75 K.Griffey 03 40M HR824/50 200.00 60.00
76 K.Griffey 03 40M HR825/50 200.00 60.00
77 K.Griffey 03 40M HR829/50 200.00 60.00
78 K.Griffey Jr. 03 40M T40/50 200.00 60.00
79 K.Griffey Jr. 03 GF/50......... 200.00 60.00
80 K.Griffey Jr. 03 GF GF/3
81 K.Griffey Jr. 03 GF w/Oswalt/9
82 K.Griffey Jr. 03 HON/50....... 200.00 60.00
83 K.Griffey Jr. 03 HON SP/30 250.00 75.00
84 K.Griffey Jr. 03 Patch/75..... 175.00 52.50
85 K.Griffey Jr. 03 PB/75 .... 175.00 52.50
86 K.Griffey Jr. 03 SPA/50...... 200.00 60.00
87 K.Griffey Jr. 03 SPA/75....... 175.00 52.50
88 K.Griffey Jr. 03 SPx/75....... 175.00 52.50
89 K.Griffey Jr. 03 SWS/75...... 175.00 52.50
90 K.Griffey Jr. 03 UD MP2/3
91 K.Griffey Jr. 03 UD MP4/3
92 K.Griffey Jr. 03 UD MP7/3
93 K.Griffey Jr. 03 UD MP26/3
94 K.Griffey Jr. 03 UDA/75...... 175.00 52.50
95 K.Griffey Jr. 03 VIN/50....... 200.00 60.00
96 Torii Hunter 03 40M/18......... 50.00 15.00
97 Torii Hunter 03 40M Flag/7
98 Torii Hunter 03 MVP/1
99 Torii Hunter 03 Patch/25....... 50.00 15.00
100 Torii Hunter 03 PB/50 .... 40.00 12.00
101 Torii Hunter 03 PB Red/5
102 Torii Hunter 03 SPA/4
103 Torii Hunter 03 UD/10
104 Torii Hunter 03 UDA/5
105 Torii Hunter 03 VIN/25....... 50.00 15.00
106 Randy Johnson 03 40M/7
107 Randy Johnson 03 40M Flag/5
108 Randy Johnson 03 GF/10
109 Randy Johnson 03 MVP/1
110 Randy Johnson 03 PB/10
111 Randy Johnson 03 PB Red/5
112 Randy Johnson 03 SPA/1
113 Randy Johnson 03 UD/3
114 Randy Johnson 03 UDA/5
115 Randy Johnson 03 VIN/3
116 Austin Kearns 02-3 SUP/10
117 Austin Kearns 03 40M/8
118 Austin Kearns 03 40M/33.... 40.00 12.00
119 Austin Kearns 03 40M Flag/10
120 Austin Kearns 03 GF/10
121 Austin Kearns 03 MVP/3
122 Austin Kearns 03 Patch/10
123 Austin Kearns 03 SPA/9
124 Austin Kearns 03 UDA/5
125 Austin Kearns 03 VIN/10
126 Matsui 03 40M NR/20...... 400.00 120.00
127 Matsui 03 40M FlagNR/20 400.00 120.00
128 Matsui 03 GFw/Pedro/18.. 400.00 120.00
129 Hideki Matsui 03 MVP/12
130 Hideki Matsui 03 PB/17.... 400.00 120.00
131 Hideki Matsui 03 PB Red/6
132 Hideki Matsui 03 UD/25 .... 400.00 120.00
133 Hideki Matsui 03 UD LS Jsy/4
134 Hideki Matsui 03 UD MP/3
135 Hideki Matsui 03 VIN/25 .. 400.00 120.00
136 Stan Musial 99 CL/15
137 Stan Musial 99 HIT/25
138 Stan Musial 00 LG/5
139 Stan Musial 01 HF/10
140 Stan Musial 01 LG/10
141 Stan Musial 01 SPLC/15
142 Stan Musial 02 SPLC/1
143 Stan Musial 02 SPLC/30 .... 80.00 24.00
144 Stan Musial 02 WSH/25
145 Stan Musial 03 PB/50........ 80.00 24.00
146 Stan Musial 03 PB Red/15
147 Stan Musial 03 SWSC/37 ... 80.00 24.00
148 Stan Musial 03 UD MP/3
149 Stan Musial 03 UDA/9
150 Stan Musial 03 VIN/50 .... 80.00 24.00
151 Mark Prior 03 40M/1
152 Mark Prior 03 40M Flag/5
153 Mark Prior 03 GF/5
154 Mark Prior 03 GF w/Berkman/7
155 Mark Prior 03 MVP/1
156 Mark Prior 03 Patch/3
157 Mark Prior 03 PB/10
158 Mark Prior 03 PB Red/1
159 Mark Prior 03 UD/7
160 Mark Prior 03 UDA/5
161 Mark Prior 03 VIN/5
162 Scott Rolen 03 40M/5
163 Scott Rolen 03 40M AS/7
164 Scott Rolen 03 40M Flag/1
165 Scott Rolen 03 GF/4
166 Scott Rolen 03 MVP/1
167 Scott Rolen 03 Patch/1
168 Scott Rolen 03 PB/5
169 Scott Rolen 03 PB Red/5
170 Scott Rolen 03 SPA/6
171 Scott Rolen 03 UD/5
172 Scott Rolen 03 UDA/5
173 Scott Rolen 03 VIN/4
174 Curt Schilling 02 SPA/1
175 Curt Schilling 03 40M/1
176 Curt Schilling 03 40M AS/1
177 Curt Schilling 03 GF/2
178 Curt Schilling 03 MVP/1
179 Curt Schilling 03 Patch/1
180 Curt Schilling 03 PB/6
181 Curt Schilling 03 PB Red/1
182 Curt Schilling 03 SPA/6
183 Curt Schilling 03 SWS/1
184 Curt Schilling 03 UDA/1
185 Curt Schilling 03 VIN/3
186 Sammy Sosa 02-3 SUP/25 200.00 60.00
187 Sammy Sosa 03 40M/13
188 Sammy Sosa 03 40M AS/1
189 Sammy Sosa 03 GF/10
190 Sammy Sosa 03 GF GF/10
191 S.Sosa 03 GF w/Mac/17
192 Sammy Sosa 03 MVP/7
193 Sammy Sosa 03 Patch/10
194 Sammy Sosa 03 PB/25 .... 200.00 60.00
195 Sammy Sosa 03 SPA/25 .. 200.00 60.00
196 Sammy Sosa 03 UD/7
197 Sammy Sosa 03 UD LS Jsy/5
198 Sammy Sosa 03 UD MP/3
199 Sammy Sosa 03 UDA/17.. 200.00 60.00
200 Sammy Sosa 03 UDA Blue/10
201 Sammy Sosa 03 UDA Red/10
202 Sammy Sosa 03 VIN/25 ... 200.00 60.00
203 Mark Teixeira 03 40M/50 ... 40.00 12.00
204 Mark Teixeira 03 40M Rain/15
205 Mark Teixeira 03 Patch/50.. 40.00 12.00
206 Mark Teixeira 03 SPA RA/25 50.00 15.00
207 Mark Teixeira 03 SWS/23... 50.00 15.00
208 Mark Teixeira 03 UD/25...... 50.00 15.00
209 Mark Teixeira 03 UDA/15
210 Mark Teixeira 03 VIN/25...... 50.00 15.00
211 Kerry Wood 03 40M Flag/13
212 Kerry Wood 03 GF/7
213 Kerry Wood 03 GF w/Pujols/3
214 Kerry Wood 03 MVP/3
215 Kerry Wood 03 PB/10
216 Kerry Wood 03 PB Red/13
217 Kerry Wood 03 SPA/10
218 Kerry Wood 03 UD/7
219 Kerry Wood 03 UDA/5
220 Kerry Wood 03 VIN/4
221 Barry Zito 03 40M/2
222 Barry Zito 03 40M Flag/2
223 Barry Zito 03 GF/7
224 Barry Zito 03 MVP/2
225 Barry Zito 03 Patch/2
226 Barry Zito 03 PB/1
227 Barry Zito 03 PB Red/2
228 Barry Zito 03 SPA/7
229 Barry Zito 03 SPx/10
230 Barry Zito 03 UD/10
231 Barry Zito 03 UDA/5

2003 Ultimate Collection Double Barrel

Nm-Mt Ex-Mt
RANDOM INSERTS IN PACKS
PRINT RUNS B/WN 1-3 COPIES PER..
NO PRICING DUE TO SCARCITY
AB Roberto Alomar
Craig Biggio/3
AC Edgardo Alfonzo
Jose Cruz Jr./2
AE Garrett Anderson
Darin Erstad/3
AJ Bobby Abreu
Chipper Jones/1
BC Bret Boone
Mike Cameron/1
BH Rocco Baldelli
Torii Hunter/1
BK Sean Burroughs
Mark Kotsay/1
BL Kevin Brown
Paul Lo Duca/1
BR Pat Burrell
Jimmy Rollins/1
BS Carlos Beltran
Mike Sweeney/2
DP Carlos Delgado
Albert Pujols/1
DR Johnny Damon
Manny Ramirez/1
DT Adam Dunn
Jim Thome/1
EM Jim Edmonds
Stan Musial/2
FS Rafael Furcal
Gary Sheffield/3
GK Brian Giles
Jason Kendall/2
GM Ken Griffey Jr.
Fred McGriff/2
GS Tom Glavine
Tom Seaver/2
HL Mike Hampton
Javy Lopez/1
HP Rickey Henderson
Juan Pierre/1
HV Shea Hillenbrand
Jose Vidro/1
JB Jeff Bagwell
Barry Larkin/1
KN Ryan Klesko
Phil Nevin/1
KT Paul Konerko
Frank Thomas/1
LO Carlos Lee
Magglio Ordonez/1
LP Mike Lieberthal
Mike Piazza/2
LR Luis Gonzalez
Raul Mondesi/1
LV Al Leiter
Mo Vaughn/1
MN Hideki Matsui
Hideo Nomo/1
MO Edgar Martinez
John Olerud/1
MR Tino Martinez
Scott Rolen/1
PP Corey Patterson
Jay Payton/3
PR Jorge Posada
Mariano Rivera/1
TP Todd Helton
Preston Wilson/1

2003 Ultimate Collection Dual Jersey

Nm-Mt Ex-Mt
STATED PRINT RUN 50 SERIAL #'d SETS
*GOLD: .75X TO 1.5X BASIC
GOLD PRINT RUN 25 SERIAL #'d SETS
OVERALL GU ODDS 3:4
ALL ARE DUAL JSY UNLESS NOTED..
AH Alfonso Soriano Jsy........... 80.00 24.00
Hideki Matsui Jsy
AI Albert Pujols Jsy 60.00 18.00
Ichiro Suzuki Jsy
BK Jeff Bagwell Jsy 25.00 7.50
Jeff Kent Jsy
CA Chipper Jones Jsy 25.00 7.50
Andruw Jones Jsy
CJ Carlos Delgado Jsy............. 25.00 7.50
Jason Giambi Jsy
DE J.D. Drew Jsy...................... 15.00 4.50
Jim Edmonds Jsy
DG Carlos Delgado Jsy............. 25.00 7.50
Vladimir Guerrero Jsy
DM Joe DiMaggio Pants......... 275.00 80.00
Mickey Mantle Jsy/Pants
DP Carlos Delgado Jsy............. 25.00 7.50
Rafael Palmeiro Jsy
DW Joe DiMaggio Jsy/Pants... 175.00 52.50
Ted Williams Jsy
GB Shawn Green Jsy................ 15.00 4.50
Kevin Brown Jsy
GD Ken Griffey Jr. Jsy 40.00 12.00
Adam Dunn Jsy
GE Troy Glaus Jsy................... 25.00 7.50
Darin Erstad Jsy
GP Ken Griffey Jr. Jsy 40.00 12.00
Rafael Palmeiro Jsy
GR Nomar Garciaparra Jsy....... 40.00 12.00
Alex Rodriguez Jsy
GS Vladimir Guerrero Jsy.......... 25.00 7.50
Sammy Sosa Jsy
HJ Torii Hunter Jsy 15.00 4.50
Jacque Jones Jsy
HZ Roy Halladay Jsy 25.00 7.50
Barry Zito Jsy
IG Ichiro Suzuki Jsy 60.00 18.00
Ken Griffey Jr. Jsy
IN Ichiro Suzuki Jsy 80.00 24.00
Hideo Nomo Jsy
IS Ichiro Suzuki Jsy................. 60.00 18.00
Sammy Sosa Jsy
JF Andruw Jones Jsy 15.00 4.50
Rafael Furcal Jsy
JM Jorge Posada Jsy............... 40.00 12.00
Mike Piazza Jsy
MC Greg Maddux Jsy............... 40.00 12.00
Roger Clemens Jsy
MW Mickey Mantle Jsy/Pants . 250.00 75.00
Ted Williams Jsy
NI Hideo Nomo Jsy 40.00 12.00
Kazuhusa Ishii Jsy
NM Hideo Nomo Jsy 80.00 24.00
Hideki Matsui Jsy
PC Pedro Martinez Jsy............ 40.00 12.00
Roger Clemens Jsy
PM Andy Pettitte Jsy 25.00 7.50
Mike Mussina Jsy
PS Mark Prior Jsy 50.00 15.00
Sammy Sosa Jsy
RM Manny Ramirez Jsy 25.00 7.50
Pedro Martinez Jsy
RP Alex Rodriguez Jsy 25.00 7.50
Rafael Palmeiro Jsy
SA Scott Rolen Jsy.................. 50.00 15.00
Albert Pujols Jsy
SB Alfonso Soriano Jsy........... 25.00 7.50
Bernie Williams Jsy
SJ Curt Schilling Jsy 25.00 7.50
Randy Johnson Jsy
SM John Smoltz Jsy 40.00 12.00
Greg Maddux Jsy
TB Mark Teixeira Jsy 25.00 7.50
Hank Blalock Jsy
TH Jim Thome Jsy 25.00 7.50
Todd Helton Jsy
TR Miguel Tejada Jsy.............. 25.00 7.50
Alex Rodriguez Jsy
WL Dontrelle Willis Jsy 25.00 7.50
Mike Lowell Jsy
YW Delmon Young Pants......... 60.00 18.00
Rickie Weeks Jsy

2003 Ultimate Collection Dual Patch

Nm-Mt Ex-Mt
OVERALL GU ODDS 3:4
PRINT RUNS B/WN 14-99 COPIES PER
NO PRICING ON QTY OF 14 OR LESS.
AI Albert Pujols 150.00 45.00
Ichiro Suzuki/99
AM Andy Pettitte 50.00 15.00
Mike Mussina/99
BK Jeff Bagwell 50.00 15.00
Jeff Kent/99
CA Chipper Jones 50.00 15.00
Andruw Jones/99
CV Carlos Delgado 50.00 15.00
Vladimir Guerrero/99
DE J.D. Drew 40.00 12.00
Jim Edmonds/99
DG Carlos Delgado................... 50.00 15.00
Jason Giambi/99
DP Carlos Delgado
Rafael Palmeiro/14
GB Shawn Green 40.00 12.00
Kevin Brown/99
GD Ken Griffey Jr. 60.00 18.00
Adam Dunn/99
GE Troy Glaus 50.00 15.00
Darin Erstad/99
GP Ken Griffey Jr.
Rafael Palmeiro/14
GR Nomar Garciaparra 100.00 30.00
Alex Rodriguez/99
GS Vladimir Guerrero 50.00 15.00
Sammy Sosa/99
HJ Torii Hunter 40.00 12.00
Jacque Jones/83
HZ Roy Halladay...................... 50.00 15.00
Barry Zito/99
IG Ichiro Suzuki..................... 120.00 36.00
Ken Griffey Jr./99
IN Ichiro Suzuki 200.00 60.00
Hideo Nomo/99
IS Ichiro Suzuki...................... 120.00 36.00
Sammy Sosa/99
JF Andruw Jones..................... 40.00 12.00
Rafael Furcal/99
JG John Smoltz....................... 60.00 18.00
Greg Maddux/99
MC Greg Maddux 80.00 24.00
Roger Clemens/75
NI Hideo Nomo...................... 100.00 30.00
Kazuhisa Ishii/63
PM Jorge Posada 60.00 18.00
Mike Piazza/73
PS Mark Prior........................... 80.00 24.00
Sammy Sosa/99
RM Manny Ramirez 50.00 15.00
Pedro Martinez/99
SA Scott Rolen 100.00 30.00
Albert Pujols/99
SB Alfonso Soriano 80.00 24.00
Bernie Williams/21
SJ Curt Schilling...................... 50.00 15.00
Randy Johnson/99
SM Alfonso Soriano 120.00 36.00
Hideki Matsui/99
TB Mark Teixeira 50.00 15.00
Hank Blalock/99
TH Jim Thome.......................... 50.00 15.00
Todd Helton/99
TR Miguel Tejada 60.00 18.00
Alex Rodriguez/99
WL Dontrelle Willis.................. 50.00 15.00
Mike Lowell/85
YW Delmon Young................. 120.00 36.00
Rickie Weeks/28

2003 Ultimate Collection Dual Patch Gold

Nm-Mt Ex-Mt
*GOLD: .6X TO 1.2X BASIC PATCH p/r 63-99
*GOLD: .5X TO 1X BASIC PATCH p/r 21-28
OVERALL GU ODDS 3:4
STATED PRINT RUN 35 SERIAL #'d SETS
DIMAGGIO/WILLIAMS PRINT RUN 1 #'d CARD
SORIANO/MATSUI PRINT RUN 15 #'d CARDS
NO PRICING ON QTY OF 15 OR LESS.
DP Carlos Delgado 60.00 18.00
Rafael Palmeiro
DW Joe DiMaggio
Ted Williams/1
GP Ken Griffey Jr..................... 80.00 24.00
Rafael Palmeiro
NM Hideo Nomo...................... 300.00 90.00
Hideki Matsui
PR Pedro Martinez 80.00 24.00
Roger Clemens
RP Alex Rodriguez 80.00 24.00
Rafael Palmeiro

2003 Ultimate Collection Signatures

Nm-Mt Ex-Mt
ULT.SIG. & AU RC OVERALL ODDS 1:4
PRINT RUNS B/WN 30-350 COPIES PER
GRIFFEY/MATSUI PART LIVE/ PART EXCH.
EXCHANGE DEADLINE 12/17/06
AP1 Albert Pujols w/Glove/40 . 200.00 60.00
AP2 Albert Pujols w/Bat/35 ..... 200.00 60.00
AR1 Alex Rodriguez/75 EXCH . 150.00 45.00
AR2 Alex Rodriguez/60 EXCH . 150.00 45.00
BG1 Bob Gibson Arm Up/299.... 30.00 9.00
BG2 Bob Gibson Stance/199..... 30.00 9.00
CD1 Carlos Delgado Hitting/150 30.00 9.00
CR1 Cal Ripken w/Helmet/85 .. 175.00 52.50
CR2 Cal Ripken Fielding/85...... 175.00 52.50
CY1 Carl Yastrzemski w/Bat/199 80.00 24.00
DY1 Delmon Young Run/300.... 60.00 18.00
DY2 Delmon Young w/Bat/300.. 60.00 18.00
EG1 Eric Gagne Arm Down/350 50.00 15.00
GC1 Gary Carter Hitting/199...... 30.00 9.00
GM1 Greg Maddux New Uni/250 80.00 24.00
GM2 G.Maddux Retro Uni/140 100.00 30.00
HM1 H.Matsui w/Glove/250 ..... 250.00 75.00
HM2 H.Matsui Throwing/240 .. 250.00 75.00
IS1 Ichiro Suzuki w/Shades/199 300.00 90.00
IS2 Ichiro Suzuki Running/99 . 300.00 90.00
JG1 Jason Giambi Torso/35..... 80.00 24.00
JG2 J.Giambi Open Swing/35.... 80.00 24.00
KG1 Ken Griffey Jr. Hitting/350 120.00 36.00
KG2 Ken Griffey Jr. w/Bat/350. 120.00 36.00
KW1 K.Wood Black Glv/170....... 50.00 15.00
KW2 K.Wood Brown Glv/85 ...... 60.00 18.00
MP1 Mark Prior w/Glove/299.. 100.00 30.00
MP2 Mark Prior Arm Up/225 .. 100.00 30.00
NG1 N.Garciaparra/125 EXCH . 120.00 36.00
NG2 N.Garciaparra Hitting/180 120.00 36.00
NR1 Nolan Ryan Blue Uni/85 .. 150.00 45.00
NR2 Nolan Ryan White Uni/75 150.00 45.00
OS1 Ozzie Smith Hitting/199..... 60.00 18.00
RC1 R.Clemens Glove Out/70.. 150.00 45.00
RC2 R.Clemens Arm Up/30.... 175.00 52.50
RJ1 R.Johnson Stripe Uni/75.. 100.00 30.00
RJ2 R.Johnson Black Uni/50... 120.00 36.00
RS1 R.Sandberg Blue Uni/240 .. 60.00 18.00
RS2 R.Sandberg Stripe Uni/200 60.00 18.00
RW1 R.Weeks White Uni/300..... 50.00 15.00
RW2 R.Weeks Red Uni/300 .... 50.00 15.00
TS1 Tom Seaver Arms Up/75..... 50.00 15.00
TS2 Tom Seaver Arm Down/60. 50.00 15.00
VG1 V.Guerrero Smiling/75...... 60.00 18.00
VG2 V.Guerrero Hitting/50 .... 80.00 24.00

2003 Ultimate Collection Signatures Gold

Nm-Mt Ex-Mt
ULT.SIG. & AU RC OVERALL ODDS 1:4
STATED PRINT RUN 25 SERIAL #'d SETS
AP Albert Pujols w/Glove......... 200.00 60.00
AR Alex Rodriguez EXCH.......... 250.00 75.00
BG Bob Gibson Arm Up............. 60.00 18.00
CD Carlos Delgado Hitting......... 60.00 18.00
CR Cal Ripken w/Helmet 300.00 90.00
CY Carl Yastrzemski w/Bat 150.00 45.00
DY Delmon Young Run 200.00 60.00
EG Eric Gagne Arm Down........ 100.00 30.00
GC Gary Carter Hitting............. 60.00 18.00
GM Greg Maddux New Uni....... 250.00 75.00
HM H.Matsui w/Glove 500.00 150.00
IS Ichiro Suzuki w/Shades....... 500.00 150.00
JG Jason Giambi Torso........... 100.00 30.00
KG Ken Griffey Jr. Hitting 250.00 75.00
KW K.Wood Black Glv.............. 100.00 30.00
MP Mark Prior w/Glove............ 200.00 60.00
NG N.Garciaparra EXCH.......... 200.00 60.00
NR Nolan Ryan Blue Uni.......... 200.00 60.00
OS Ozzie Smith Hitting............ 150.00 45.00

RC R.Clemens Glove Out.......... 250.00 75.00
RJ R.Johnson Stripe Uni.......... 150.00 45.00
RS R.Sandberg Blue Uni 150.00 45.00
RW R.Weeks White Uni............ 200.00 60.00
TS Tom Seaver Arms Up............ 60.00 18.00
VG V.Guerrero Smiling............. 100.00 30.00

2003 Ultimate Collection Game Jersey Tier 1

Nm-Mt Ex-Mt
STATED PRINT RUN 99 SERIAL #'d SETS
COPPER PRINT RUN 10 SERIAL #'d SETS
NO COPPER PRICING DUE TO SCARCITY
*GOLD p/r 75: .4X TO 1X BASIC ....
*GOLD MATSUI p/r 55: .6X TO 1.5X BASIC
*GOLD p/r 51: .6X TO 1.5X BASIC ......
*GOLD p/r 44-48: .75X TO 2X BASIC..
*GOLD p/r 25-35: 1X TO 2.5X BASIC..
*GOLD p/r 17-24: 1.25X TO 3X BASIC
GOLD PRINT RUNS B/WN 1-75 COPIES PER
NO GOLD PRICING ON QTY OF 15 OR LESS
OVERALL GU ODDS 3:4.......................
AD0 Adam Dunn Red Jsy.......... 10.00 3.00
AJ Andruw Jones w/Bat............ 10.00 3.00
AP Albert Pujols Running.......... 25.00 7.50
AR Alex Rodriguez Throw 20.00 6.00
AS Alfonso Soriano No Glv........ 15.00 4.50
BW Bernie Williams White Jsy .. 15.00 4.50
BZ Barry Zito Green Jsy 15.00 4.50
CD Carlos Delgado Blue Jsy 10.00 3.00
CJ Chipper Jones No Bat........... 15.00 4.50
CS Curt Schilling Arm Up.......... 15.00 4.50
DW Dontrelle Willis Black Jsy ... 15.00 4.50
DY Delmon Young Throw.......... 25.00 7.50
FT Frank Thomas Black Jsy....... 15.00 4.50
GM Greg Maddux White Jsy...... 20.00 6.00
GS Gary Sheffield Throw........... 10.00 3.00
HM Hideki Matsui Ball Toss 80.00 24.00
HN Hideo Nomo Gray Jsy.......... 25.00 7.50
IS Ichiro Suzuki Gray Jsy 60.00 18.00
JE Jim Edmonds White Jsy....... 10.00 3.00
JG Jason Giambi No Bat............ 15.00 4.50
JR Jose Reyes Throw................ 15.00 4.50
JT Jim Thome Red Jsy.............. 15.00 4.50
KG Ken Griffey Jr. Gray Jsy....... 25.00 7.50
KI Kazuhisa Ishii Arms Up.......... 10.00 3.00
KW Kerry Wood Pitching........... 15.00 4.50
MI Mike Piazza Mask On 20.00 6.00
MM Mike Mussina Blue Jsy 15.00 4.50
MP Mark Prior Pitching............. 25.00 7.50
MR Manny Ramirez Red Jsy 10.00 3.00
MT Miguel Tejada White Jsy 10.00 3.00
PB Pat Burrell Running 10.00 3.00
RB Rocco Baldelli Batting.......... 20.00 6.00
RC Roger Clemens White Jsy.... 25.00 7.50
RF Rafael Furcal Fielding........... 10.00 3.00
RJ Randy Johnson White Jsy.... 15.00 4.50
RW Rickie Weeks Bat Up 25.00 7.50
SG Shawn Green White Jsy....... 10.00 3.00
SS Sammy Sosa Running 25.00 7.50
TG Tom Glavine Black Jsy......... 15.00 4.50
TH Torii Hunter Running 10.00 3.00
TR Troy Glaus Dirty Jsy 15.00 4.50
VG Vladimir Guerrero w/Bat...... 15.00 4.50

2003 Ultimate Collection Game Jersey Tier 2

Nm-Mt Ex-Mt
STATED PRINT RUN 75 SERIAL #'d SETS
COPPER PRINT RUN 10 SERIAL #'d SETS
NO COPPER PRICING DUE TO SCARCITY
*GOLD p/r 75: .4X TO 1X BASIC ....
*GOLD MATSUI p/r 55: .6X TO 1.5X BASIC
*GOLD p/r 51: .6X TO 1.5X BASIC ......
*GOLD p/r 44-48: .75X TO 2X BASIC..
*GOLD p/r 25-35: 1X TO 2.5X BASIC..
*GOLD p/r 17-24: 1.25X TO 3X BASIC
GOLD PRINT RUNS B/WN 1-75 COPIES PER
NO GOLD PRICING ON QTY OF 15 OR LESS
OVERALL GU ODDS 3:4.......................
AD2 Adam Dunn Swing............. 10.00 3.00
AJ2 Andruw Jones w/Glv 10.00 3.00
AP2 Albert Pujols Batting.......... 25.00 7.50
AR2 Alex Rodriguez Running 20.00 6.00
AS2 Alfonso Soriano w/Glv 15.00 4.50
BW2 Bernie Williams Gray Jsy .. 15.00 4.50
BZ2 Barry Zito Gray Jsy 15.00 4.50
CD2 Carlos Delgado Gray Jsy.... 10.00 3.00
CJ2 Chipper Jones w/Bat 15.00 4.50
CS2 Curt Schilling Arm Down ... 15.00 4.50
DW Dontrelle Willis Gray Jsy 15.00 4.50
DY2 Delmon Young w/Ball 25.00 7.50
FT2 Frank Thomas White Jsy 15.00 4.50
GM2 Greg Maddux Blue Jsy...... 20.00 6.00
GS2 Gary Sheffield Batting........ 10.00 3.00
HM2 Hideki Matsui w/Bat.......... 80.00 24.00
HN2 Hideo Nomo Blue Jsy........ 25.00 7.50
IS2 Ichiro Suzuki w/Bat............ 60.00 18.00
JE2 Jim Edmonds Gray Jsy....... 10.00 3.00
JG2 Jason Giambi w/Bat 15.00 4.50
JR2 Jose Reyes Walking........... 15.00 4.50
JT2 Jim Thome White Jsy......... 15.00 4.50
KG2 Ken Griffey Jr. Red Jsy...... 25.00 7.50
KI2 Kazuhisa Ishii Arms Down .. 10.00 3.00
KW2 Kerry Wood Standing 15.00 4.50
MI2 Mike Piazza w/Bat 20.00 6.00
MM2 Mike Mussina Gray Jsy.... 15.00 4.50
MP2 Mark Prior Hitting 25.00 7.50
MR2 Manny Ramirez Gray Jsy.. 10.00 3.00
MT2 Miguel Tejada Green Jsy ... 10.00 3.00
PB2 Pat Burrell Swinging.......... 10.00 3.00
RB2 Rocco Baldelli Running 20.00 6.00
RC2 Roger Clemens Blue Jsy.... 25.00 7.50
RF2 Rafael Furcal Running........ 10.00 3.00
RJ2 Randy Johnson Black Jsy .. 15.00 4.50
RW2 Rickie Weeks Bat Forward 25.00 7.50

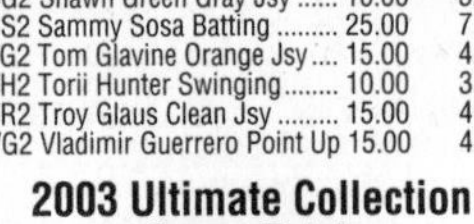

SG2 Shawn Green Gray Jsy 10.00 3.00
SS2 Sammy Sosa Batting 25.00 7.50
TG2 Tom Glavine Orange Jsy.... 15.00 4.50
TH2 Torii Hunter Swinging........ 10.00 3.00
TR2 Troy Glaus Clean Jsy 15.00 4.50
VG2 Vladimir Guerrero Point Up 15.00 4.50

2003 Ultimate Collection Game Patch

Nm-Mt Ex-Mt
STATED PRINT RUN 99 SERIAL #'d SETS
SORIANO PRINT RUN 42 SERIAL #'d CARDS
*COPPER: .6X TO 1.2X BASIC p/r 99..
*COPPER: .6X TO 1.2X BASIC p/r 42..
COPPER PRINT RUN 35 SERIAL #'d SETS
*GOLD: .75X TO 1.5X BASIC p/r 99....
*GOLD: .75X TO 1.5X BASIC p/r 42....
GOLD PRINT RUN 25 SERIAL #'d SETS
OVERALL GU ODDS 3:4.......................
AD Adam Dunn 25.00 7.50
AJ Andruw Jones 25.00 7.50
AP Albert Pujols 60.00 18.00
AR Alex Rodriguez 50.00 15.00
AS Alfonso Soriano/42.............. 40.00 12.00
BW Bernie Williams................... 40.00 12.00
BZ Barry Zito 40.00 12.00
CD Carlos Delgado 25.00 7.50
CJ Chipper Jones 40.00 12.00
CS Curt Schilling 40.00 12.00
DW Dontrelle Willis 40.00 12.00
DY Delmon Young..................... 50.00 15.00
FT Frank Thomas....................... 40.00 12.00
GM Greg Maddux 50.00 15.00
HM Hideki Matsui.................... 120.00 36.00
HN Hideo Nomo 80.00 24.00
IS Ichiro Suzuki...................... 150.00 45.00
JE Jim Edmonds 25.00 7.50
JG Jason Giambi 40.00 12.00
JR Jose Reyes........................... 40.00 12.00
JT Jim Thome 40.00 12.00
KG Ken Griffey Jr...................... 60.00 18.00
KI Kazuhisa Ishii........................ 25.00 7.50
KW Kerry Wood 40.00 12.00
MI Mike Piazza 50.00 15.00
MM Mike Mussina..................... 40.00 12.00
MP Mark Prior........................... 60.00 18.00
MR Manny Ramirez................... 25.00 7.50
MT Miguel Tejada...................... 25.00 7.50
PB Pat Burrell............................ 25.00 7.50
RB Rocco Baldelli....................... 40.00 12.00
RC Roger Clemens..................... 60.00 18.00
RF Rafael Furcal 25.00 7.50
RH Roy Halladay 25.00 7.50
RJ Randy Johnson..................... 40.00 12.00
RW Rickie Weeks 50.00 15.00
SG Shawn Green 25.00 7.50
SS Sammy Sosa 50.00 15.00
TG Tom Glavine......................... 40.00 12.00
TH Torii Hunter......................... 25.00 7.50
TR Troy Glaus 40.00 12.00
VG Vladimir Guerrero 40.00 12.00

1991 Ultra

This 400-card standard-size set marked Fleer's first entry into the premium card market. The cards were distributed exclusively in foil-wrapped packs. Fleer claimed in their original press release that there would only be 15 percent the amount of Ultra issued as there was of the regular 1991 Fleer issue. The cards feature full color action photography on the fronts and three full-color photos on the backs. Fleer also issued the sets in their now traditional alphabetical order as well as the teams in alphabetical order. Subsets include Major League Prospects (373-390), Elite Performance (391-396), and Checklists (397-400). Rookie Cards include Eric Karros and Denny Neagle.

Nm-Mt Ex-Mt
COMPLETE SET (400)............... 20.00 6.00
1 Steve Avery .... .10 .03
2 Jeff Blauser .... .10 .03
3 Francisco Cabrera .... .10 .03
4 Ron Gant.................................... .20 .06
5 Tom Glavine .... .30 .09
6 Tommy Gregg .... .10 .03
7 Dave Justice............................... .20 .06
8 Oddibe McDowell .... .10 .03
9 Greg Olson .... .10 .03
10 Terry Pendleton....................... .20 .06
11 Lonnie Smith........................... .10 .03
12 John Smoltz .... .30 .09
13 Jeff Treadway .... .10 .03
14 Glenn Davis............................. .10 .03
15 Mike Devereaux....................... .10 .03
16 Leo Gomez .... .10 .03
17 Chris Hoiles............................. .10 .03
18 Dave Johnson .... .10 .03
19 Ben McDonald......................... .10 .03
20 Randy Milligan .... .10 .03
21 Gregg Olson .... .10 .03
22 Joe Orsulak .... .10 .03
23 Bill Ripken .... .10 .03
24 Cal Ripken .... 1.50 .45
25 David Segui.............................. .10 .03
26 Craig Worthington.................... .10 .03
27 Wade Boggs............................. .30 .09
28 Tom Bolton .... .10 .03
29 Tom Brunansky .... .10 .03
30 Ellis Burks .... .20 .06
31 Roger Clemens...................... 1.00 .30
32 Mike Greenwell........................ .10 .03
33 Greg A. Harris .... .10 .03
34 Daryl Irvine.............................. .10 .03
35 Mike Marshall UER.................. .10 .03
(1990 in stats is shown as 990)
36 Tim Naehring........................... .10 .03
37 Tony Pena .... .10 .03
38 Phil Plantier RC .... .15 .04
39 Carlos Quintana....................... .10 .03
40 Jeff Reardon............................ .20 .06
41 Jody Reed .... .10 .03
42 Luis Rivera .... .10 .03
43 Jim Abbott .... .30 .09
44 Chuck Finley............................ .20 .06
45 Bryan Harvey........................... .10 .03
46 Donnie Hill............................... .10 .03
47 Jack Howell .... .10 .03
48 Wally Joyner .... .20 .06
49 Mark Langston......................... .10 .03
50 Kirk McCaskill .... .10 .03
51 Lance Parrish........................... .20 .06
52 Dick Schofield .... .10 .03
53 Lee Stevens............................. .10 .03
54 Dave Winfield .... .20 .06
55 George Bell.............................. .10 .03
56 Damon Berryhill .... .10 .03
57 Mike Bielecki .... .10 .03
58 Andre Dawson.......................... .20 .06
59 Shawon Dunston...................... .10 .03
60 Joe Girardi UER....................... .10 .03
(Bats right, LH hitter shown is Doug Dascenzo)
61 Mark Grace.............................. .30 .09
62 Mike Harkey .... .10 .03
63 Les Lancaster.......................... .10 .03
64 Greg Maddux........................... .75 .23
65 Derrick May............................. .10 .03
66 Ryne Sandberg........................ .75 .23
67 Luis Salazar............................. .10 .03
68 Dwight Smith .... .10 .03
69 Hector Villanueva .... .10 .03
70 Jerome Walton......................... .10 .03
71 Mitch Williams .... .10 .03
72 Carlton Fisk .... .30 .09
73 Scott Fletcher .... .10 .03
74 Ozzie Guillen........................... .10 .03
75 Greg Hibbard........................... .10 .03
76 Lance Johnson......................... .10 .03
77 Steve Lyons............................. .10 .03
78 Jack McDowell .... .10 .03
79 Dan Pasqua............................. .10 .03
80 Melido Perez .... .10 .03
81 Tim Raines .... .20 .06
82 Sammy Sosa......................... 1.00 .30
83 Cory Snyder .... .10 .03
84 Bobby Thigpen .... .10 .03
85 Frank Thomas .... .50 .15
(Card says he is an outfielder)
86 Robin Ventura .... .20 .06
87 Todd Benzinger .... .10 .03
88 Glenn Braggs........................... .10 .03
89 Tom Browning UER.................. .10 .03
(Front photo actually Norm Charlton)
90 Norm Charlton......................... .10 .03
91 Eric Davis .... .20 .06
92 Rob Dibble .... .20 .06
93 Bill Doran .... .10 .03
94 Mariano Duncan UER.............. .10 .03
(Right back photo is Billy Hatcher)
95 Billy Hatcher............................ .10 .03
96 Barry Larkin............................. .50 .15
97 Randy Myers .... .10 .03
98 Hal Morris .... .10 .03
99 Joe Oliver .... .10 .03
100 Paul O'Neill............................ .30 .09
101 Jeff Reed .... .10 .03
(See also 104)
102 Jose Rijo .... .10 .03
103 Chris Sabo............................. .10 .03
(See also 106)
104 Beau Allred UER .... .10 .03
(Card number is 101)
105 Sandy Alomar Jr..................... .10 .03
106 Carlos Baerga UER .... .10 .03
(Card number is 103)
107 Albert Belle............................ .20 .06
108 Jerry Browne.......................... .10 .03
109 Tom Candiotti......................... .10 .03
110 Alex Cole .... .10 .03
111 John Farrell .... .10 .03
(See also 114)
112 Felix Fermin........................... .10 .03
113 Brook Jacoby .... .10 .03
114 Chris James UER .... .10 .03
(Card number is 111)
115 Doug Jones............................ .10 .03
116 Steve Olin.............................. .10 .03
(See also 119)
117 Greg Swindell......................... .10 .03
118 Turner Ward RC .... .15 .04
119 Mitch Webster UER................ .10 .03
(Card number is 116)
120 Dave Bergman........................ .10 .03
121 Cecil Fielder........................... .20 .06
122 Travis Fryman .... .20 .06
123 Mike Henneman .... .10 .03
124 Lloyd Moseby......................... .10 .03
125 Dan Petry .... .10 .03
126 Tony Phillips .... .10 .03
127 Mark Salas .... .10 .03
128 Frank Tanana......................... .10 .03
129 Alan Trammell........................ .30 .09
130 Lou Whitaker.......................... .20 .06
131 Eric Anthony........................... .10 .03
132 Craig Biggio............................ .30 .09
133 Ken Caminiti.......................... .20 .06
134 Casey Candaele .... .10 .03
135 Andujar Cedeno...................... .10 .03
136 Mark Davidson .... .10 .03
137 Jim Deshaies.......................... .10 .03
138 Mark Portugal .... .10 .03
139 Rafael Ramirez .... .10 .03
140 Mike Scott.............................. .10 .03
141 Eric Yelding............................ .10 .03
142 Gerald Young .... .10 .03
143 Kevin Appier.......................... .20 .06
144 George Brett....................... 1.25 .35
145 Jeff Conine RC .... .75 .23
146 Jim Eisenreich........................ .10 .03
147 Tom Gordon........................... .10 .03
148 Mark Gubicza .... .10 .03
149 Bo Jackson............................. .50 .15
150 Brent Mayne.......................... .10 .03
151 Mike Macfarlane.................... .10 .03
152 Brian McRae RC .... .40 .12
153 Jeff Montgomery.................... .10 .03
154 Bret Saberhagen.................... .20 .06
155 Kevin Seitzer .... .10 .03
156 Terry Shumpert...................... .10 .03
157 Kurt Stillwell........................... .10 .03
158 Danny Tartabull .... .10 .03
159 Tim Belcher .... .10 .03
160 Kal Daniels .... .10 .03
161 Alfredo Griffin........................ .10 .03
162 Lenny Harris........................... .10 .03
163 Jay Howell.............................. .10 .03
164 Ramon Martinez..................... .10 .03
165 Mike Morgan .... .10 .03
166 Eddie Murray.......................... .50 .15
167 Jose Offerman........................ .10 .03
168 Juan Samuel .... .10 .03
169 Mike Scioscia .... .10 .03
170 Mike Sharperson.................... .10 .03
171 Darryl Strawberry................... .30 .09
172 Greg Brock .... .10 .03
173 Chuck Crim .... .10 .03
174 Jim Gantner............................ .10 .03
175 Ted Higuera............................ .10 .03
176 Mark Knudson........................ .10 .03
177 Tim McIntosh......................... .10 .03
178 Paul Molitor........................... .30 .09
179 Dan Plesac .... .10 .03
180 Gary Sheffield........................ .20 .06
181 Bill Spiers............................... .10 .03
182 B.J. Surhoff .... .20 .06
183 Greg Vaughn .... .20 .06
184 Robin Yount........................... .75 .23
185 Rick Aguilera.......................... .20 .06
186 Greg Gagne .... .10 .03
187 Dan Gladden.......................... .10 .03
188 Brian Harper........................... .10 .03
189 Kent Hrbek .... .20 .06
190 Gene Larkin............................ .10 .03
191 Shane Mack............................ .10 .03
192 Pedro Munoz RC .... .15 .04
193 Al Newman............................. .10 .03
194 Junior Ortiz .... .10 .03
195 Kirby Puckett......................... .50 .15
196 Kevin Tapani.......................... .10 .03
197 Dennis Boyd.......................... .10 .03
198 Tim Burke.............................. .10 .03
199 Ivan Calderon .... .10 .03
200 Delino DeShields .... .20 .06
201 Mike Fitzgerald .... .10 .03
202 Steve Frey .... .10 .03
203 Andres Galarraga.................. .20 .06
204 Marquis Grissom................... .10 .03
205 Dave Martinez .... .10 .03
206 Dennis Martinez .... .20 .06
207 Junior Noboa......................... .10 .03
208 Spike Owen .... .10 .03
209 Scott Ruskin.......................... .10 .03
210 Tim Wallach .... .10 .03
211 Daryl Boston .... .10 .03
212 Vince Coleman .... .10 .03
213 David Cone............................ .20 .06
214 Ron Darling........................... .10 .03
215 Kevin Elster .... .10 .03
216 Sid Fernandez........................ .10 .03
217 John Franco .... .20 .06
218 Dwight Gooden .... .30 .09
219 Tom Herr................................ .10 .03
220 Todd Hundley........................ .10 .03
221 Gregg Jefferies...................... .10 .03
222 Howard Johnson................... .10 .03
223 Dave Magadan....................... .10 .03
224 Kevin McReynolds................. .10 .03
225 Keith Miller............................ .10 .03
226 Mackey Sasser .... .10 .03
227 Frank Viola .... .20 .06
228 Jesse Barfield........................ .10 .03
229 Greg Cadaret .... .10 .03
230 Alvaro Espinoza.................... .10 .03
231 Bob Geren .... .10 .03
232 Lee Guetterman..................... .10 .03
233 Mel Hall................................. .10 .03
234 Andy Hawkins UER................ .10 .03
(Back center photo is not him)
235 Roberto Kelly......................... .10 .03
236 Tim Leary .... .10 .03
237 Jim Leyritz............................. .10 .03
238 Kevin Maas............................ .10 .03
239 Don Mattingly..................... 1.25 .35
240 Hensley Meulens................... .10 .03
241 Eric Plunk.............................. .10 .03
242 Steve Sax .... .10 .03
243 Todd Burns .... .10 .03
244 Jose Canseco........................ .50 .15
245 Dennis Eckersley................... .20 .06
246 Mike Gallego .... .10 .03
247 Dave Henderson.................... .10 .03
248 Rickey Henderson .... .50 .15
249 Rick Honeycutt...................... .10 .03
250 Carney Lansford.................... .20 .06
251 Mark McGwire.................... 1.25 .35
252 Mike Moore .... .10 .03
253 Terry Steinbach..................... .10 .03
254 Dave Stewart......................... .20 .06
255 Walt Weiss .... .10 .03
256 Bob Welch............................. .10 .03
257 Curt Young............................ .10 .03
258 Wes Chamberlain RC .... .40 .12
259 Pat Combs .... .10 .03
260 Darren Daulton...................... .20 .06
261 Jose DeJesus .... .10 .03
262 Len Dykstra........................... .20 .06
263 Charlie Hayes .... .10 .03
264 Von Hayes............................. .10 .03
265 Ken Howell .... .10 .03
266 John Kruk............................... .20 .06
267 Roger McDowell..................... .10 .03
268 Mickey Morandini................... .10 .03
269 Terry Mulholland .... .10 .03
270 Dale Murphy........................... .50 .15
271 Randy Ready .... .10 .03
272 Dickie Thon .... .10 .03
273 Stan Belinda .... .10 .03
274 Jay Bell................................... .20 .06
275 Barry Bonds .... 1.25 .35
276 Bobby Bonilla .... .20 .06
277 Doug Drabek .... .10 .03
278 Carlos Garcia RC .... .15 .04
279 Neal Heaton........................... .10 .03
280 Jeff King................................. .10 .03
281 Bill Landrum........................... .10 .03
282 Mike LaValliere...................... .10 .03
283 Jose Lind................................ .10 .03
284 Orlando Merced RC............... .15 .04
285 Gary Redus .... .10 .03
286 Don Slaught .... .10 .03
287 Andy Van Slyke .... .20 .06
288 Jose DeLeon .... .10 .03
289 Pedro Guerrero .... .20 .06
290 Ray Lankford.......................... .10 .03
291 Joe Magrane .... .10 .03
292 Jose Oquendo .... .10 .03
293 Tom Pagnozzi......................... .10 .03
294 Bryn Smith .... .10 .03
295 Lee Smith............................... .20 .06
296 Ozzie Smith UER .... .75 .23
(Born 12-26, 54, should have hyphen)
297 Milt Thompson........................ .10 .03
298 Craig Wilson........................... .10 .03
299 Todd Zeile .... .10 .03
300 Shawn Abner.......................... .10 .03
301 Andy Benes .... .10 .03
302 Paul Faries............................. .10 .03
303 Tony Gwynn .... .60 .18
304 Greg W. Harris .... .10 .03
305 Thomas Howard..................... .10 .03
306 Bruce Hurst............................ .10 .03
307 Craig Lefferts......................... .10 .03
308 Fred McGriff .... .30 .09
309 Dennis Rasmussen .... .10 .03
310 Bip Roberts .... .10 .03
311 Benito Santiago..................... .20 .06
312 Garry Templeton .... .10 .03
313 Ed Whitson............................ .10 .03
314 Dave Anderson...................... .10 .03
315 Kevin Bass............................. .10 .03
316 Jeff Brantley .... .10 .03
317 John Burkett.......................... .10 .03
318 Will Clark............................... .50 .15
319 Steve Decker .... .10 .03
320 Scott Garrelts .... .10 .03
321 Terry Kennedy....................... .10 .03
322 Mark Leonard......................... .10 .03
323 Darren Lewis......................... .10 .03
324 Greg Litton............................ .10 .03
325 Willie McGee .... .20 .06
326 Kevin Mitchell........................ .10 .03
327 Don Robinson .... .10 .03
328 Andres Santana..................... .10 .03
329 Robby Thompson................... .10 .03
330 Jose Uribe............................. .10 .03
331 Matt Williams .... .20 .06
332 Scott Bradley......................... .10 .03
333 Henry Cotto........................... .10 .03
334 Alvin Davis .... .10 .03
335 Ken Griffey Sr........................ .20 .06
336 Ken Griffey Jr. .... 1.00 .30
337 Erik Hanson........................... .10 .03
338 Brian Holman .... .10 .03
339 Randy Johnson .... .60 .18
340 Edgar Martinez UER .... .30 .09
(Listed as playing SS)
341 Tino Martinez .... .30 .09
342 Pete O'Brien .... .10 .03
343 Harold Reynolds.................... .20 .06
344 Dave Valle .... .10 .03
345 Omar Vizquel......................... .20 .06
346 Brad Arnsberg....................... .10 .03
347 Kevin Brown.......................... .20 .06
348 Julio Franco........................... .20 .06
349 Jeff Huson............................. .10 .03
350 Rafael Palmeiro .... .30 .09
351 Geno Petralli......................... .10 .03
352 Gary Pettis............................. .10 .03
353 Kenny Rogers........................ .20 .06
354 Jeff Russell .... .10 .03
355 Nolan Ryan........................ 2.00 .60
356 Ruben Sierra .... .10 .03
357 Bobby Witt .... .10 .03
358 Roberto Alomar..................... .50 .15
359 Pat Borders .... .10 .03
360 Joe Carter UER...................... .20 .06
(Reverse negative on back photo)
361 Kelly Gruber .... .10 .03
362 Tom Henke............................ .10 .03
363 Glenallen Hill .... .10 .03
364 Jimmy Key .... .20 .06
365 Manny Lee............................ .10 .03
366 Rance Mulliniks..................... .10 .03
367 John Olerud UER................... .20 .06
(Throwing left on card; back has throws right; he does throw lefty)
368 Dave Stieb .... .10 .03
369 Duane Ward .... .10 .03
370 David Wells .... .20 .06
371 Mark Whiten.......................... .10 .03
372 Mookie Wilson .... .20 .06
373 Willie Banks MLP .... .10 .03
374 Steve Carter MLP .... .10 .03
375 S.Chiamparino MLP .... .10 .03
376 Steve Chitren MLP .... .10 .03
377 Darrin Fletcher MLP .... .10 .03
378 Rich Garces MLP RC............. .15 .04
379 Reggie Jefferson MLP............ .10 .03
380 Eric Karros MLP RC .... .75 .23
381 Pat Kelly MLP RC .... .15 .04
382 C.Knoblauch MLP .... .20 .06
383 D.Neagle MLP RC.................. .40 .12
384 Dan Opperman MLP.............. .10 .03
385 John Ramos MLP.................. .10 .03
386 H.Rodriguez MLP RC .... .40 .12
387 Mo Vaughn MLP .... .20 .06
388 G.Williams MLP RC............... .40 .12

389 Mike York MLP .10 .03
390 Eddie Zosky MLP .10 .03
391 Barry Bonds EP .60 .18
392 Cecil Fielder EP .10 .03
393 Rickey Henderson EP .30 .09
394 Dave Justice EP .10 .03
395 Nolan Ryan EP 1.00 .30
396 Bobby Thigpen EP .10 .03
397 Gregg Jefferies CL .10 .03
398 Von Hayes CL .10 .03
399 Terry Kennedy CL .10 .03
400 Nolan Ryan CL .50 .15

1991 Ultra Gold

This ten-card standard-size set presents Fleer's 1991 Ultra Team. These cards were randomly inserted into Ultra packs. The set is sequenced in alphabetical order.

	Nm-Mt	Ex-Mt
COMPLETE SET (10)	10.00	3.00
1 Barry Bonds	2.50	.75
2 Will Clark	1.00	.30
3 Doug Drabek	.20	.06
4 Ken Griffey Jr.	2.00	.60
5 Rickey Henderson	1.00	.30
6 Bo Jackson	1.00	.30
7 Ramon Martinez	.20	.06
8 Kirby Puckett UER (Boggs won 1988 batting title, so Puckett didn't win consecutive titles)	1.00	.30
9 Chris Sabo	.20	.06
10 Ryne Sandberg UER (Johnson and Hornsby didn't hit 40 homers in 1990, Fielder did hit 51 in '90)	1.50	.45

1991 Ultra Update

The 120-card set was distributed exclusively in factory set form along with 20 team logo stickers through hobby dealers. The set includes the year's hottest rookies and important veteran players traded after the original Ultra series was produced. Card design is identical to regular issue 1991 cards except for the U-prefixed numbering on back. Cards are ordered alphabetically within and according to teams for each league. Rookie Cards in this set include Jeff Bagwell, Mike Mussina, and Ivan Rodriguez.

	Nm-Mt	Ex-Mt
COMP.FACT.SET (120)	40.00	12.00
1 Dwight Evans	.50	.15
2 Chito Martinez	.25	.07
3 Bob Melvin	.25	.07
4 Mike Mussina RC	5.00	1.50
5 Jack Clark	.50	.15
6 Dana Kiecker	.25	.07
7 Steve Lyons	.25	.07
8 Gary Gaetti	.50	.15
9 Dave Gallagher	.25	.07
10 Dave Parker	.50	.15
11 Luis Polonia	.25	.07
12 Luis Sojo	.25	.07
13 Wilson Alvarez	.25	.07
14 Alex Fernandez	.25	.07
15 Craig Grebeck	.25	.07
16 Ron Karkovice	.25	.07
17 Warren Newson	.25	.07
18 Scott Radinsky	.25	.07
19 Glenallen Hill	.25	.07
20 Charles Nagy	.25	.07
21 Mark Whiten	.25	.07
22 Milt Cuyler	.25	.07
23 Paul Gibson	.25	.07
24 Mickey Tettleton	.25	.07
25 Todd Benzinger	.25	.07
26 Storm Davis	.25	.07
27 Kirk Gibson	.50	.15
28 Bill Pecota	.25	.07
29 Gary Thurman	.25	.07
30 Darryl Hamilton	.25	.07
31 Jaime Navarro	.25	.07
32 Willie Randolph	.50	.15
33 Bill Wegman	.25	.07
34 Randy Bush	.25	.07
35 Chili Davis	.50	.15
36 Scott Erickson	.25	.07
37 Chuck Knoblauch	.50	.15
38 Scott Leius	.25	.07
39 Jack Morris	.50	.15
40 John Habyan	.25	.07
41 Pat Kelly	.25	.07
42 Matt Nokes	.25	.07
43 Scott Sanderson	.25	.07
44 Bernie Williams	3.00	.90
45 Harold Baines	.50	.15
46 Brook Jacoby	.25	.07
47 Earnest Riles	.25	.07
48 Willie Wilson	.25	.07
49 Jay Buhner	.50	.15
50 Rich DeLucia	.25	.07
51 Mike Jackson	.25	.07
52 Bill Krueger	.25	.07
53 Bill Swift	.25	.07
54 Brian Downing	.25	.07
55 Juan Gonzalez	5.00	1.50
56 Dean Palmer	.50	.15
57 Kevin Reimer	.25	.07
58 Ivan Rodriguez RC	10.00	3.00
59 Tom Candiotti	.25	.07
60 Juan Guzman RC	.50	.15
61 Bob MacDonald	.25	.07
62 Greg Myers	.25	.07
63 Ed Sprague	.25	.07
64 Devon White	.25	.07
65 Rafael Belliard	.25	.07
66 Juan Berenguer	.25	.07
67 Brian R. Hunter RC	.50	.15
68 Kent Mercker	.25	.07
69 Otis Nixon	.25	.07
70 Danny Jackson	.25	.07
71 Chuck McElroy	.25	.07
72 Gary Scott	.25	.07
73 Heathcliff Slocumb RC	.25	.07
74 Chico Walker	.25	.07
75 Rick Wilkins RC	.25	.07
76 Chris Hammond	.25	.07
77 Luis Quinones	.25	.07
78 Herm Winningham	.25	.07
79 Jeff Bagwell RC	8.00	2.40
80 Jim Corsi	.25	.07
81 Steve Finley	.50	.15
82 Luis Gonzalez RC	4.00	1.20
83 Pete Harnisch	.25	.07
84 Darryl Kile	.50	.15
85 Brett Butler	.50	.15
86 Gary Carter	.75	.23
87 Tim Crews	.25	.07
88 Orel Hershiser	.50	.15
89 Bob Ojeda	.25	.07
90 Bret Barberie RC**	.25	.07
91 Barry Jones	.25	.07
92 Gilberto Reyes	.25	.07
93 Larry Walker	1.25	.35
94 Hubie Brooks	.25	.07
95 Tim Burke	.25	.07
96 Rick Cerone	.25	.07
97 Jeff Innis	.25	.07
98 Wally Backman	.25	.07
99 Tommy Greene	.25	.07
100 Ricky Jordan	.25	.07
101 Mitch Williams	.25	.07
102 John Smiley	.25	.07
103 Randy Tomlin RC	.25	.07
104 Gary Varsho	.25	.07
105 Cris Carpenter	.25	.07
106 Ken Hill	.25	.07
107 Felix Jose	.25	.07
108 Omar Olivares RC	.25	.07
109 Gerald Perry	.25	.07
110 Jerald Clark	.25	.07
111 Tony Fernandez	.25	.07
112 Darrin Jackson	.25	.07
113 Mike Maddux	.25	.07
114 Tim Teufel	.25	.07
115 Bud Black	.25	.07
116 Kelly Downs	.25	.07
117 Mike Felder	.25	.07
118 Willie McGee	.50	.15
119 Trevor Wilson	.25	.07
120 Checklist 1-120	.25	.07

1992 Ultra

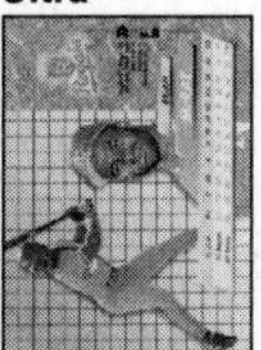

Consisting of 600 standard-size cards, the 1992 Ultra set was issued in two series of 300 cards each. Cards were distributed exclusively in foil packs. The cards are numbered on the back and ordered below alphabetically within and according to teams for each league with AL preceding NL. Some cards have been found without the word Fleer on the front.

	Nm-Mt	Ex-Mt
COMPLETE SET (600)	30.00	9.00
COMP. SERIES 1 (300)	20.00	6.00
COMP. SERIES 2 (300)	10.00	3.00
1 Glenn Davis	.10	.03
2 Mike Devereaux	.10	.03
3 Dwight Evans	.20	.06
4 Leo Gomez	.10	.03
5 Chris Hoiles	.10	.03
6 Sam Horn	.10	.03
7 Chito Martinez	.10	.03
8 Randy Milligan	.10	.03
9 Mike Mussina	.50	.15
10 Billy Ripken	.10	.03
11 Cal Ripken	1.50	.45
12 Tom Brunansky	.10	.03
13 Ellis Burks	.20	.06
14 Jack Clark	.20	.06
15 Roger Clemens	1.00	.30
16 Mike Greenwell	.10	.03
17 Joe Hesketh	.10	.03
18 Tony Pena	.10	.03
19 Carlos Quintana	.10	.03
20 Jeff Reardon	.20	.06
21 Jody Reed	.10	.03
22 Luis Rivera	.10	.03
23 Mo Vaughn	.20	.06
24 Gary DiSarcina	.10	.03
25 Chuck Finley	.20	.06
26 Gary Gaetti	.20	.06
27 Bryan Harvey	.10	.03
28 Lance Parrish	.20	.06
29 Luis Polonia	.10	.03
30 Dick Schofield	.10	.03
31 Luis Sojo	.10	.03
32 Wilson Alvarez	.10	.03
33 Carlton Fisk	.30	.09
34 Craig Grebeck	.10	.03
35 Ozzie Guillen	.10	.03
36 Greg Hibbard	.10	.03
37 Charlie Hough	.20	.06
38 Lance Johnson	.10	.03
39 Ron Karkovice	.10	.03
40 Jack McDowell	.10	.03
41 Donn Pall	.10	.03
42 Melido Perez	.10	.03
43 Tim Raines	.20	.06
44 Frank Thomas	.50	.15
45 Sandy Alomar Jr.	.10	.03
46 Carlos Baerga	.10	.03
47 Albert Belle	.20	.06
48 Jerry Browne UER (Reversed negative on card back)	.10	.03
49 Felix Fermin	.10	.03
50 Reggie Jefferson UER (Born 1968, not 1966)	.10	.03
51 Mark Lewis	.10	.03
52 Carlos Martinez	.10	.03
53 Steve Olin	.10	.03
54 Jim Thome	.50	.15
55 Mark Whiten	.10	.03
56 Dave Bergman	.10	.03
57 Milt Cuyler	.10	.03
58 Rob Deer	.10	.03
59 Cecil Fielder	.20	.06
60 Travis Fryman	.20	.06
61 Scott Livingstone	.10	.03
62 Tony Phillips	.10	.03
63 Mickey Tettleton	.10	.03
64 Alan Trammell	.30	.09
65 Lou Whitaker	.20	.06
66 Kevin Appier	.20	.06
67 Mike Boddicker	.10	.03
68 George Brett	1.25	.35
69 Jim Eisenreich	.10	.03
70 Mark Gubicza	.10	.03
71 David Howard	.10	.03
72 Joel Johnson	.10	.03
73 Mike Macfarlane	.10	.03
74 Brent Mayne	.10	.03
75 Brian McRae	.10	.03
76 Jeff Montgomery	.10	.03
77 Danny Tartabull	.10	.03
78 Don August	.10	.03
79 Dante Bichette	.20	.06
80 Ted Higuera	.10	.03
81 Paul Molitor	.30	.09
82 Jaime Navarro	.10	.03
83 Gary Sheffield	.20	.06
84 Bill Spiers	.10	.03
85 B.J. Surhoff	.20	.06
86 Greg Vaughn	.20	.06
87 Robin Yount	.75	.23
88 Rick Aguilera	.20	.06
89 Chili Davis	.20	.06
90 Scott Erickson	.10	.03
91 Brian Harper	.10	.03
92 Kent Hrbek	.20	.06
93 Chuck Knoblauch	.20	.06
94 Scott Leius	.10	.03
95 Shane Mack	.10	.03
96 Mike Pagliarulo	.10	.03
97 Kirby Puckett	.50	.15
98 Kevin Tapani	.10	.03
99 Jesse Barfield	.10	.03
100 Alvaro Espinoza	.10	.03
101 Mel Hall	.10	.03
102 Pat Kelly	.10	.03
103 Roberto Kelly	.10	.03
104 Kevin Maas	.10	.03
105 Don Mattingly	1.25	.35
106 Hensley Meulens	.10	.03
107 Matt Nokes	.10	.03
108 Steve Sax	.10	.03
109 Harold Baines	.20	.06
110 Jose Canseco	.50	.15
111 Ron Darling	.10	.03
112 Mike Gallego	.10	.03
113 Dave Henderson	.10	.03
114 Rickey Henderson	.50	.15
115 Mark McGwire	1.25	.35
116 Terry Steinbach	.10	.03
117 Dave Stewart	.20	.06
118 Todd Van Poppel	.10	.03
119 Bob Welch	.10	.03
120 Greg Briley	.10	.03
121 Jay Buhner	.20	.06
122 Rick DeLucia	.10	.03
123 Ken Griffey Jr.	.75	.23
124 Erik Hanson	.10	.03
125 Randy Johnson	.50	.15
126 Edgar Martinez	.30	.09
127 Tino Martinez	.30	.09
128 Pete O'Brien	.10	.03
129 Harold Reynolds	.20	.06
130 Dave Valle	.10	.03
131 Julio Franco	.20	.06
132 Juan Gonzalez	.50	.15
133 Jeff Huson (Shows Jose Canseco sliding into second)	.20	.06
134 Mike Jeffcoat	.10	.03
135 Terry Mathews	.10	.03
136 Rafael Palmeiro	.30	.09
137 Dean Palmer	.20	.06
138 Geno Petralli	.10	.03
139 Ivan Rodriguez	.50	.15
140 Jeff Russell	.10	.03
141 Nolan Ryan	2.00	.60
142 Ruben Sierra	.10	.03
143 Roberto Alomar	.50	.15
144 Pat Borders	.10	.03
145 Joe Carter	.20	.06
146 Kelly Gruber	.10	.03
147 Jimmy Key	.20	.06
148 Manny Lee	.10	.03
149 Rance Mulliniks	.10	.03
150 Greg Myers	.10	.03
151 John Olerud	.20	.06
152 Dave Stieb	.10	.03
153 Todd Stottlemyre	.10	.03
154 Duane Ward	.10	.03
155 Devon White	.10	.03
156 Eddie Zosky	.10	.03
157 Steve Avery	.10	.03
158 Rafael Belliard	.10	.03
159 Jeff Blauser	.10	.03
160 Sid Bream	.10	.03
161 Ron Gant	.20	.06
162 Tom Glavine	.30	.09
163 Brian Hunter	.10	.03
164 Dave Justice	.20	.06
165 Mark Lemke	.10	.03
166 Greg Olson	.10	.03
167 Terry Pendleton	.20	.06
168 Lonnie Smith	.10	.03
169 John Smoltz	.30	.09
170 Mike Stanton	.10	.03
171 Jeff Treadway	.10	.03
172 Paul Assenmacher	.10	.03
173 George Bell	.10	.03
174 Shawon Dunston	.10	.03
175 Mark Grace	.30	.09
176 Danny Jackson	.10	.03
177 Les Lancaster	.10	.03
178 Greg Maddux	.75	.23
179 Luis Salazar	.10	.03
180 Rey Sanchez RC	.20	.06
181 Ryne Sandberg	.75	.23
182 Jose Vizcaino	.10	.03
183 Chico Walker	.10	.03
184 Jerome Walton	.10	.03
185 Glenn Braggs	.10	.03
186 Tom Browning	.10	.03
187 Rob Dibble	.20	.06
188 Bill Doran	.10	.03
189 Chris Hammond	.10	.03
190 Billy Hatcher	.10	.03
191 Barry Larkin	.50	.15
192 Hal Morris	.10	.03
193 Joe Oliver	.10	.03
194 Paul O'Neill	.30	.09
195 Jeff Reed	.10	.03
196 Jose Rijo	.10	.03
197 Chris Sabo	.10	.03
198 Jeff Bagwell	.50	.15
199 Craig Biggio	.30	.09
200 Ken Caminiti	.20	.06
201 Andujar Cedeno	.10	.03
202 Steve Finley	.20	.06
203 Luis Gonzalez	.30	.09
204 Pete Harnisch	.10	.03
205 Xavier Hernandez	.10	.03
206 Darryl Kile	.20	.06
207 Al Osuna	.10	.03
208 Curt Schilling	.30	.09
209 Brett Butler	.20	.06
210 Kal Daniels	.10	.03
211 Lenny Harris	.10	.03
212 Stan Javier	.10	.03
213 Ramon Martinez	.10	.03
214 Roger McDowell	.10	.03
215 Jose Offerman	.10	.03
216 Juan Samuel	.10	.03
217 Mike Scioscia	.10	.03
218 Mike Sharperson	.10	.03
219 Darryl Strawberry	.30	.09
220 Delino DeShields	.10	.03
221 Tom Foley	.10	.03
222 Steve Frey	.10	.03
223 Dennis Martinez	.20	.06
224 Spike Owen	.10	.03
225 Gilberto Reyes	.10	.03
226 Tim Wallach	.10	.03
227 Daryl Boston	.10	.03
228 Tim Burke	.10	.03
229 Vince Coleman	.10	.03
230 David Cone	.20	.06
231 Kevin Elster	.10	.03
232 Dwight Gooden	.30	.09
233 Todd Hundley	.10	.03
234 Jeff Innis	.10	.03
235 Howard Johnson	.10	.03
236 Dave Magadan	.10	.03
237 Mackey Sasser	.10	.03
238 Anthony Young	.10	.03
239 Wes Chamberlain	.10	.03
240 Darren Daulton	.20	.06
241 Len Dykstra	.20	.06
242 Tommy Greene	.10	.03
243 Charlie Hayes	.10	.03
244 Dave Hollins	.10	.03
245 Ricky Jordan	.10	.03
246 John Kruk	.20	.06
247 Mickey Morandini	.10	.03
248 Terry Mulholland	.10	.03
249 Dale Murphy	.50	.15
250 Jay Bell	.20	.06
251 Barry Bonds	1.25	.35
252 Steve Buechele	.10	.03
253 Doug Drabek	.10	.03
254 Mike LaValliere	.10	.03
255 Jose Lind	.10	.03
256 Lloyd McClendon	.10	.03
257 Orlando Merced	.10	.03
258 Don Slaught	.10	.03
259 John Smiley	.10	.03
260 Zane Smith	.10	.03
261 Randy Tomlin	.10	.03
262 Andy Van Slyke	.20	.06
263 Pedro Guerrero	.20	.06
264 Felix Jose	.10	.03
265 Ray Lankford	.10	.03
266 Omar Olivares	.10	.03
267 Jose Oquendo	.10	.03
268 Tom Pagnozzi	.10	.03
269 Bryn Smith	.10	.03
270 Lee Smith UER (1991 record listed as 61-61)	.20	.06
271 Ozzie Smith UER (Comma before year of birth on card back)	.75	.23
272 Milt Thompson	.10	.03
273 Todd Zeile	.10	.03
274 Andy Benes	.10	.03
275 Jerald Clark	.10	.03
276 Tony Fernandez	.10	.03
277 Tony Gwynn	.60	.18
278 Greg W. Harris	.10	.03
279 Thomas Howard	.10	.03
280 Bruce Hurst	.10	.03
281 Mike Maddux	.10	.03
282 Fred McGriff	.30	.09
283 Benito Santiago	.20	.06
284 Kevin Bass	.10	.03
285 Jeff Brantley	.10	.03
286 John Burkett	.10	.03
287 Will Clark	.50	.15
288 Royce Clayton	.10	.03
289 Steve Decker	.10	.03
290 Kelly Downs	.10	.03
291 Mike Felder	.10	.03
292 Darren Lewis	.10	.03
293 Kirt Manwaring	.10	.03
294 Willie McGee	.20	.06
295 Robby Thompson	.10	.03
296 Matt Williams	.20	.06
297 Trevor Wilson	.10	.03
298 Checklist 1-100	.10	.03
299 Checklist 101-200	.10	.03
300 Checklist 201-300	.10	.03
301 Brady Anderson	.20	.06
302 Todd Frohwirth	.10	.03
303 Ben McDonald	.10	.03
304 Mark McLemore	.10	.03
305 Jose Mesa	.10	.03
306 Bob Milacki	.10	.03
307 Gregg Olson	.10	.03
308 David Segui	.10	.03
309 Rick Sutcliffe	.20	.06
310 Jeff Tackett	.10	.03
311 Wade Boggs	.30	.09
312 Scott Cooper	.10	.03
313 John Flaherty	.10	.03
314 Wayne Housie	.10	.03
315 Peter Hoy	.10	.03
316 John Marzano	.10	.03
317 Tim Naehring	.10	.03
318 Phil Plantier	.10	.03
319 Frank Viola	.20	.06
320 Matt Young	.10	.03
321 Jim Abbott	.30	.09
322 Hubie Brooks	.10	.03
323 Chad Curtis RC	.20	.06
324 Alvin Davis	.10	.03
325 Junior Felix	.10	.03
326 Von Hayes	.10	.03
327 Mark Langston	.10	.03
328 Scott Lewis	.10	.03
329 Don Robinson	.10	.03
330 Bobby Rose	.10	.03
331 Lee Stevens	.10	.03
332 George Bell	.10	.03
333 Esteban Beltre	.10	.03
334 Joey Cora	.10	.03
335 Alex Fernandez	.10	.03
336 Roberto Hernandez	.10	.03
337 Mike Huff	.10	.03
338 Kirk McCaskill	.10	.03
339 Dan Pasqua	.10	.03
340 Scott Radinsky	.10	.03
341 Steve Sax	.10	.03
342 Bobby Thigpen	.10	.03
343 Robin Ventura	.20	.06
344 Jack Armstrong	.10	.03
345 Alex Cole	.10	.03
346 Dennis Cook	.10	.03
347 Glenallen Hill	.10	.03
348 Thomas Howard	.10	.03
349 Brook Jacoby	.10	.03
350 Kenny Lofton	.50	.15
351 Charles Nagy	.10	.03
352 Rod Nichols	.10	.03
353 Junior Ortiz	.10	.03
354 Dave Otto	.10	.03
355 Tony Perezchica	.10	.03
356 Scott Scudder	.10	.03
357 Paul Sorrento	.10	.03
358 Skeeter Barnes	.10	.03
359 Mark Carreon	.10	.03
360 John Doherty RC	.10	.03
361 Dan Gladden	.10	.03
362 Bill Gullickson	.10	.03
363 Shawn Hare RC	.10	.03
364 Mike Henneman	.10	.03
365 Chad Kreuter	.10	.03
366 Mark Leiter	.10	.03
367 Mike Munoz	.10	.03
368 Kevin Ritz	.10	.03
369 Mark Davis	.10	.03
370 Tom Gordon	.10	.03
371 Chris Gwynn	.10	.03
372 Gregg Jefferies	.10	.03
373 Wally Joyner	.20	.06
374 Kevin McReynolds	.10	.03
375 Keith Miller	.10	.03
376 Rico Rossy	.10	.03
377 Curtis Wilkerson	.10	.03
378 Ricky Bones	.10	.03
379 Chris Bosio	.10	.03
380 Cal Eldred	.10	.03
381 Scott Fletcher	.10	.03
382 Jim Gantner	.10	.03
383 Darryl Hamilton	.10	.03
384 Doug Henry RC	.10	.03
385 Pat Listach RC	.20	.06
386 Tim McIntosh	.10	.03
387 Edwin Nunez	.10	.03
388 Dan Plesac	.10	.03
389 Kevin Seitzer	.10	.03
390 Franklin Stubbs	.10	.03
391 William Suero	.10	.03
392 Bill Wegman	.10	.03
393 Willie Banks	.10	.03
394 Jarvis Brown	.10	.03
395 Greg Gagne	.10	.03
396 Mark Guthrie	.10	.03
397 Bill Krueger	.10	.03
398 Pat Mahomes RC	.10	.03
399 Pedro Munoz	.10	.03
400 John Smiley	.10	.03
401 Gary Wayne	.10	.03
402 Lenny Webster	.10	.03
403 Carl Willis	.10	.03
404 Greg Cadaret	.10	.03
405 Steve Farr	.10	.03
406 Mike Gallego	.10	.03
407 Charlie Hayes	.10	.03
408 Steve Howe	.10	.03
409 Dion James	.10	.03
410 Jeff Johnson	.10	.03
411 Tim Leary	.10	.03
412 Jim Leyritz	.10	.03
413 Melido Perez	.10	.03
414 Scott Sanderson	.10	.03

415 Andy Stankiewicz .10 .03
416 Mike Stanley .10 .03
417 Danny Tartabull .10 .03
418 Lance Blankenship .10 .03
419 Mike Bordick .10 .03
420 Scott Brosius RC .75 .23
421 Dennis Eckersley .20 .06
422 Scott Hemond .10 .03
423 Carney Lansford .20 .06
424 Henry Mercedes .10 .03
425 Mike Moore .10 .03
426 Gene Nelson .10 .03
427 Randy Ready .10 .03
428 Bruce Walton .10 .03
429 Willie Wilson .10 .03
430 Rich Amaral .10 .03
431 Dave Cochrane .10 .03
432 Henry Cotto .10 .03
433 Calvin Jones .10 .03
434 Kevin Mitchell .10 .03
435 Clay Parker .10 .03
436 Omar Vizquel .20 .06
437 Floyd Bannister .10 .03
438 Kevin Brown .20 .06
439 John Cangelosi .10 .03
440 Brian Downing .10 .03
441 Monty Fariss .10 .03
442 Jose Guzman .10 .03
443 Donald Harris .10 .03
444 Kevin Reimer .10 .03
445 Kenny Rogers .20 .06
446 Wayne Rosenthal .10 .03
447 Dickie Thon .10 .03
448 Derek Bell .20 .06
449 Juan Guzman .10 .03
450 Tom Henke .10 .03
451 Candy Maldonado .10 .03
452 Jack Morris .20 .06
453 David Wells .20 .06
454 Dave Winfield .20 .06
455 Juan Berenguer .10 .03
456 Damon Berryhill .10 .03
457 Mike Bielecki .10 .03
458 Marvin Freeman .10 .03
459 Charlie Leibrandt .10 .03
460 Kent Mercker .10 .03
461 Otis Nixon .10 .03
462 Alejandro Pena .10 .03
463 Ben Rivera .10 .03
464 Deion Sanders .30 .09
465 Mark Wohlers .10 .03
466 Shawn Boskie .10 .03
467 Frank Castillo .10 .03
468 Andre Dawson .20 .06
469 Joe Girardi .10 .03
470 Chuck McElroy .10 .03
471 Mike Morgan .10 .03
472 Ken Patterson .10 .03
473 Bob Scanlan .10 .03
474 Gary Scott .10 .03
475 Dave Smith .10 .03
476 Sammy Sosa .75 .23
477 Hector Villanueva .10 .03
478 Scott Bankhead .10 .03
479 Tim Belcher .10 .03
480 Freddie Benavides .10 .03
481 Jacob Brumfield .10 .03
482 Norm Charlton .10 .03
483 Dwayne Henry .10 .03
484 Dave Martinez .10 .03
485 Bip Roberts .10 .03
486 Reggie Sanders .20 .06
487 Greg Swindell .10 .03
488 Ryan Bowen .10 .03
489 Casey Candaele .10 .03
490 Juan Guerrero UER .10 .03
(photo on front is Andujar Cedeno)
491 Pete Incaviglia .10 .03
492 Jeff Juden .10 .03
493 Rob Murphy .10 .03
494 Mark Portugal .10 .03
495 Rafael Ramirez .10 .03
496 Scott Servais .10 .03
497 Ed Taubensee RC .20 .06
498 Brian Williams RC .20 .06
499 Todd Benzinger .10 .03
500 John Candelaria .10 .03
501 Tom Candiotti .10 .03
502 Tim Crews .10 .03
503 Eric Davis .20 .06
504 Jim Gott .10 .03
505 Dave Hansen .10 .03
506 Carlos Hernandez .10 .03
507 Orel Hershiser .20 .06
508 Eric Karros .20 .06
509 Bob Ojeda .10 .03
510 Steve Wilson .10 .03
511 Moises Alou .20 .06
512 Bret Barberie .10 .03
513 Ivan Calderon .10 .03
514 Gary Carter .30 .09
515 Archi Cianfrocco RC .10 .03
516 Jeff Fassero .10 .03
517 Darrin Fletcher .10 .03
518 Marquis Grissom .10 .03
519 Chris Haney .10 .03
520 Ken Hill .10 .03
521 Chris Nabholz .10 .03
522 Bill Sampen .10 .03
523 John Vander Wal .10 .03
524 Dave Wainhouse .10 .03
525 Larry Walker .30 .09
526 John Wetteland .20 .06
527 Bobby Bonilla .20 .06
528 Sid Fernandez .10 .03
529 John Franco .20 .06
530 Dave Gallagher .10 .03
531 Paul Gibson .10 .03
532 Eddie Murray .50 .15
533 Junior Noboa .10 .03
534 Charlie O'Brien .10 .03
535 Bill Pecota .10 .03
536 Willie Randolph .20 .06
537 Bret Saberhagen .20 .06
538 Dick Schofield .10 .03
539 Pete Schourek .10 .03
540 Ruben Amaro .10 .03
541 Andy Ashby .10 .03
542 Kim Batiste .10 .03
543 Cliff Brantley .10 .03
544 Mariano Duncan .10 .03
545 Jeff Grotewold .10 .03
546 Barry Jones .10 .03
547 Julio Peguero .10 .03
548 Curt Schilling .30 .09
549 Mitch Williams .10 .03
550 Stan Belinda .10 .03
551 Scott Bullett RC .10 .03
552 Cecil Espy .10 .03
553 Jeff King .10 .03
554 Roger Mason .10 .03
555 Paul Miller .10 .03
556 Denny Neagle .20 .06
557 Vicente Palacios .10 .03
558 Bob Patterson .10 .03
559 Tom Prince .10 .03
560 Gary Redus .10 .03
561 Gary Varsho .10 .03
562 Juan Agosto .10 .03
563 Cris Carpenter .10 .03
564 Mark Clark RC .20 .06
565 Jose DeLeon .10 .03
566 Rich Gedman .10 .03
567 Bernard Gilkey .10 .03
568 Rex Hudler .20 .06
569 Tim Jones .10 .03
570 Donovan Osborne .10 .03
571 Mike Perez .10 .03
572 Gerald Perry .10 .03
573 Bob Tewksbury .10 .03
574 Todd Worrell .10 .03
575 Dave Eiland .10 .03
576 Jeremy Hernandez RC .10 .03
577 Craig Lefferts .10 .03
578 Jose Melendez .10 .03
579 Randy Myers .10 .03
580 Gary Pettis .10 .03
581 Rich Rodriguez .10 .03
582 Gary Sheffield .20 .06
583 Craig Shipley .10 .03
584 Kurt Stillwell .10 .03
585 Tim Teufel .10 .03
586 Rod Beck RC .50 .15
587 Dave Burba .10 .03
588 Craig Colbert .10 .03
589 Bryan Hickerson RC .10 .03
590 Mike Jackson .10 .03
591 Mark Leonard .10 .03
592 Jim McNamara .10 .03
593 John Patterson RC .10 .03
594 Dave Righetti .20 .06
595 Cory Snyder .10 .03
596 Bill Swift .10 .03
597 Ted Wood .10 .03
598 Checklist 301-400 .10 .03
599 Checklist 401-500 .10 .03
600 Checklist 501-600 .10 .03

1992 Ultra All-Rookies

Cards from this ten-card standard-size set highlighting a selection of top rookies were randomly inserted in 1992 Ultra II foil packs.

	Nm-Mt	Ex-Mt
COMPLETE SET (10)	6.00	1.80
1 Eric Karros	1.00	.30
2 Andy Stankiewicz	.50	.15
3 Gary DiSarcina	.50	.15
4 Archi Cianfrocco	.50	.15
5 Jim McNamara	.50	.15
6 Chad Curtis	1.00	.30
7 Kenny Lofton	2.50	.75
8 Reggie Sanders	1.00	.30
9 Pat Mahomes	.50	.15
10 Donovan Osborne	.50	.15

1992 Ultra All-Stars

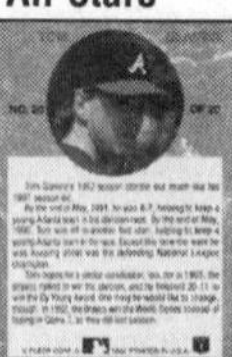

Featuring many of the 1992 season's stars, cards from this 20-card standard-size set were randomly inserted in 1992 Ultra II foil packs.

	Nm-Mt	Ex-Mt
COMPLETE SET (20)	25.00	7.50
1 Mark McGwire	4.00	1.20
2 Roberto Alomar	1.50	.45
3 Cal Ripken Jr.	5.00	1.50
4 Wade Boggs	1.00	.30
5 Mickey Tettleton	.30	.09
6 Ken Griffey Jr.	2.50	.75
7 Roberto Kelly	.30	.09
8 Kirby Puckett	1.50	.45
9 Frank Thomas	1.50	.45
10 Jack McDowell	.30	.09
11 Will Clark	1.50	.45
12 Ryne Sandberg	2.50	.75
13 Barry Larkin	1.50	.45
14 Gary Sheffield	.60	.18
15 Tom Pagnozzi	.30	.09
16 Barry Bonds	4.00	1.20
17 Deion Sanders	1.00	.30
18 Darryl Strawberry	1.00	.30
19 David Cone	.60	.18
20 Tom Glavine	1.00	.30

1992 Ultra Award Winners

This 25-card standard-size set features 18 Gold Glove winners, both Cy Young Award winners, both Rookies of the Year, both league MVP's, and the World Series MVP. The cards were randomly inserted in 1992 Fleer Ultra I packs.

	Nm-Mt	Ex-Mt
COMPLETE SET (25)	40.00	12.00
1 Jack Morris	1.00	.30
2 Chuck Knoblauch	1.00	.30
3 Jeff Bagwell	2.50	.75
4 Terry Pendleton	1.00	.30
5 Cal Ripken	8.00	2.40
6 Roger Clemens	5.00	1.50
7 Tom Glavine	1.50	.45
8 Tom Pagnozzi	.50	.15
9 Ozzie Smith	4.00	1.20
10 Andy Van Slyke	1.00	.30
11 Barry Bonds	6.00	1.80
12 Tony Gwynn	3.00	.90
13 Matt Williams	1.00	.30
14 Will Clark	2.50	.75
15 Robin Ventura	1.00	.30
16 Mark Langston	.50	.15
17 Tony Pena	.50	.15
18 Devon White	.50	.15
19 Don Mattingly	6.00	1.80
20 Roberto Alomar	2.50	.75
21A Cal Ripken ERR (Reversed negative on card back)	8.00	2.40
21B Cal Ripken COR	8.00	2.40
22 Ken Griffey Jr.	4.00	1.20
23 Kirby Puckett	2.50	.75
24 Greg Maddux	4.00	1.20
25 Ryne Sandberg	4.00	1.20

1992 Ultra Gwynn

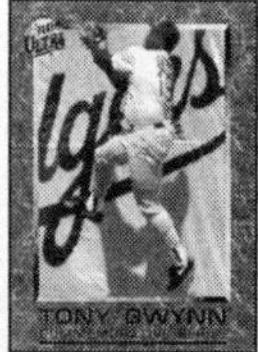

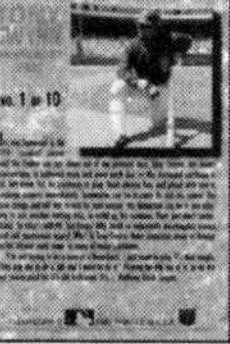

Tony Gwynn served as a spokesperson for Ultra during 1992 and was the exclusive subject of this 12-card standard-size set. The first ten cards of this set were randomly inserted in 1992 Ultra one packs. More than 2,000 of these cards were personally autographed by Gwynn. These cards are numbered on the back as " X of 10." An additional special two-card subset was available through a mail-in offer for ten 1992 Ultra baseball wrappers plus 1.00 for shipping and handling. This offer was good through October 31st and, according to Fleer, over 100,000 sets were produced. The standard-size cards display action shots of Gwynn framed by green marbled borders. The player's name and the words "Commemorative Series" appear in gold-foil lettering in the bottom border. On a green marbled background, the backs features a color head shot and either a player profile (Special No. 1 on the card back) or Gwynn's comments about other players or the game itself (Special No. 2 on the card back).

	Nm-Mt	Ex-Mt
COMPLETE SET (10)	10.00	3.00
COMMON GWYNN (1-10)	1.00	.30
COMMON MAIL(S1-S2)	1.00	.30
AU Tony Gwynn AU (Autographed with certified signature)	80.00	24.00

1993 Ultra

The 1993 Ultra baseball set was issued in two series and totaled 650 standard-size cards. The cards are numbered on the back, grouped alphabetically within teams, with NL teams preceding AL. The first series closes with checklist cards (298-300). The second series features 83 Ultra Rookies, 51 Rockies and Marlins, traded veteran players, and other major league veterans not included in the first series. The Rookie cards show a gold foil stamped Rookie "flag" as part of the card design. The key Rookie Card in this set is Jim Edmonds.

	Nm-Mt	Ex-Mt
COMPLETE SET (650)	30.00	9.00
COMP. SERIES 1 (300)	15.00	4.50
COMP. SERIES 2 (350)	15.00	4.50
1 Steve Avery	.15	.04
2 Rafael Belliard	.15	.04
3 Damon Berryhill	.15	.04
4 Sid Bream	.15	.04
5 Ron Gant	.30	.09
6 Tom Glavine	.50	.15
7 Ryan Klesko	.30	.09
8 Mark Lemke	.15	.04
9 Javier Lopez	.50	.15
10 Greg Olson	.15	.04
11 Terry Pendleton	.30	.09
12 Deion Sanders	.50	.15
13 Mike Stanton	.15	.04
14 Paul Assenmacher	.15	.04
15 Steve Buechele	.15	.04
16 Frank Castillo	.15	.04
17 Shawon Dunston	.15	.04
18 Mark Grace	.50	.15
19 Derrick May	.15	.04
20 Chuck McElroy	.15	.04
21 Mike Morgan	.15	.04
22 Bob Scanlan	.15	.04
23 Dwight Smith	.15	.04
24 Sammy Sosa	1.25	.35
25 Rick Wilkins	.15	.04
26 Tim Belcher	.15	.04
27 Jeff Branson	.15	.04
28 Bill Doran	.15	.04
29 Chris Hammond	.15	.04
30 Barry Larkin	.75	.23
31 Hal Morris	.15	.04
32 Joe Oliver	.15	.04
33 Jose Rijo	.15	.04
34 Bip Roberts	.15	.04
35 Chris Sabo	.15	.04
36 Reggie Sanders	.30	.09
37 Craig Biggio	.50	.15
38 Ken Caminiti	.30	.09
39 Steve Finley	.30	.09
40 Luis Gonzalez	.30	.09
41 Juan Guerrero	.15	.04
42 Pete Harnisch	.15	.04
43 Xavier Hernandez	.15	.04
44 Doug Jones	.15	.04
45 Al Osuna	.15	.04
46 Eddie Taubensee	.15	.04
47 Scooter Tucker	.15	.04
48 Brian Williams	.15	.04
49 Pedro Astacio	.15	.04
50 Rafael Bournigal	.15	.04
51 Brett Butler	.30	.09
52 Tom Candiotti	.15	.04
53 Eric Davis	.30	.09
54 Lenny Harris	.15	.04
55 Orel Hershiser	.30	.09
56 Eric Karros	.30	.09
57 Pedro Martinez	1.50	.45
58 Roger McDowell	.15	.04
59 Jose Offerman	.15	.04
60 Mike Piazza	2.00	.60
61 Moises Alou	.30	.09
62 Kent Bottenfield	.15	.04
63 Archi Cianfrocco	.15	.04
64 Greg Colbrunn	.15	.04
65 Wil Cordero	.15	.04
66 Delino DeShields	.15	.04
67 Darrin Fletcher	.15	.04
68 Ken Hill	.15	.04
69 Chris Nabholz	.15	.04
70 Mel Rojas	.15	.04
71 Larry Walker	.50	.15
72 Sid Fernandez	.15	.04
73 John Franco	.30	.09
74 Dave Gallagher	.15	.04
75 Todd Hundley	.15	.04
76 Howard Johnson	.15	.04
77 Jeff Kent	.75	.23
78 Eddie Murray	.75	.23
79 Bret Saberhagen	.30	.09
80 Chico Walker	.15	.04
81 Anthony Young	.15	.04
82 Kyle Abbott	.15	.04
83 Ruben Amaro	.15	.04
84 Juan Bell	.15	.04
85 Wes Chamberlain	.15	.04
86 Darren Daulton	.30	.09
87 Mariano Duncan	.15	.04
88 Dave Hollins	.15	.04
89 Ricky Jordan	.15	.04
90 John Kruk	.30	.09
91 Mickey Morandini	.15	.04
92 Terry Mulholland	.15	.04
93 Ben Rivera	.15	.04
94 Mike Williams	.15	.04
95 Stan Belinda	.15	.04
96 Jay Bell	.30	.09
97 Jeff King	.15	.04
98 Mike LaValliere	.15	.04
99 Lloyd McClendon	.15	.04
100 Orlando Merced	.15	.04
101 Zane Smith	.15	.04
102 Randy Tomlin	.15	.04
103 Andy Van Slyke	.30	.09
104 Tim Wakefield	.30	.09
105 John Wehner	.15	.04
106 Bernard Gilkey	.15	.04
107 Brian Jordan	.30	.09
108 Ray Lankford	.15	.04
109 Donovan Osborne	.15	.04
110 Tom Pagnozzi	.15	.04
111 Mike Perez	.15	.04
112 Lee Smith	.30	.09
113 Ozzie Smith	1.25	.35
114 Bob Tewksbury	.15	.04
115 Todd Zeile	.15	.04
116 Andy Benes	.15	.04
117 Greg W. Harris	.15	.04
118 Darrin Jackson	.15	.04
119 Fred McGriff	.50	.15
120 Rich Rodriguez	.15	.04
121 Frank Seminara	.15	.04
122 Gary Sheffield	.30	.09
123 Craig Shipley	.15	.04
124 Kurt Stillwell	.15	.04
125 Dan Walters	.15	.04
126 Rod Beck	.15	.04
127 Mike Benjamin	.15	.04
128 Jeff Brantley	.15	.04
129 John Burkett	.15	.04
130 Will Clark	.75	.23
131 Royce Clayton	.15	.04
132 Steve Hosey	.15	.04
133 Mike Jackson	.15	.04
134 Darren Lewis	.15	.04
135 Kirt Manwaring	.15	.04
136 Bill Swift	.15	.04
137 Robby Thompson	.15	.04
138 Brady Anderson	.30	.09
139 Glenn Davis	.15	.04
140 Leo Gomez	.15	.04
141 Chito Martinez	.15	.04
142 Ben McDonald	.15	.04
143 Alan Mills	.15	.04
144 Mike Mussina	.75	.23
145 Gregg Olson	.15	.04
146 David Segui	.15	.04
147 Jeff Tackett	.15	.04
148 Jack Clark	.30	.09
149 Scott Cooper	.15	.04
150 Danny Darwin	.15	.04
151 John Dopson	.15	.04
152 Mike Greenwell	.15	.04
153 Tim Naehring	.15	.04
154 Tony Pena	.15	.04
155 Paul Quantrill	.15	.04
156 Mo Vaughn	.30	.09
157 Frank Viola	.30	.09
158 Bob Zupcic	.15	.04
159 Chad Curtis	.15	.04
160 Gary DiSarcina	.15	.04
161 Damion Easley	.15	.04
162 Chuck Finley	.30	.09
163 Tim Fortugno	.15	.04
164 Rene Gonzales	.15	.04
165 Joe Grahe	.15	.04
166 Mark Langston	.15	.04
167 John Orton	.15	.04
168 Luis Polonia	.15	.04
169 Julio Valera	.15	.04
170 Wilson Alvarez	.15	.04
171 George Bell	.15	.04
172 Joey Cora	.15	.04
173 Alex Fernandez	.15	.04
174 Lance Johnson	.15	.04
175 Ron Karkovice	.15	.04
176 Jack McDowell	.15	.04
177 Scott Radinsky	.15	.04
178 Tim Raines	.30	.09
179 Steve Sax	.15	.04
180 Bobby Thigpen	.15	.04
181 Frank Thomas	.75	.23
182 Sandy Alomar Jr.	.15	.04
183 Carlos Baerga	.15	.04
184 Felix Fermin	.15	.04
185 Thomas Howard	.15	.04
186 Mark Lewis	.15	.04
187 Derek Lilliquist	.15	.04
188 Carlos Martinez	.15	.04
189 Charles Nagy	.15	.04
190 Scott Scudder	.15	.04
191 Paul Sorrento	.15	.04
192 Jim Thome	.75	.23
193 Mark Whiten	.15	.04
194 Milt Cuyler UER (Reversed negative on card front)	.15	.04
195 Rob Deer	.15	.04
196 John Doherty	.15	.04
197 Travis Fryman	.30	.09
198 Dan Gladden	.15	.04
199 Mike Henneman	.15	.04
200 John Kiely	.15	.04
201 Chad Kreuter	.15	.04
202 Scott Livingstone	.15	.04
203 Tony Phillips	.15	.04
204 Alan Trammell	.50	.15
205 Mike Boddicker	.15	.04
206 George Brett	2.00	.60
207 Tom Gordon	.15	.04
208 Mark Gubicza	.15	.04
209 Gregg Jefferies	.15	.04
210 Wally Joyner	.30	.09
211 Kevin Koslofski	.15	.04
212 Brent Mayne	.15	.04
213 Brian McRae	.15	.04
214 Kevin McReynolds	.15	.04
215 Rusty Meacham	.15	.04
216 Steve Shifflett	.15	.04
217 Jim Austin	.15	.04
218 Cal Eldred	.15	.04
219 Darryl Hamilton	.15	.04
220 Doug Henry	.15	.04
221 John Jaha	.15	.04
222 Dave Nilsson	.15	.04
223 Jesse Orosco	.15	.04
224 B.J. Surhoff	.30	.09
225 Greg Vaughn	.30	.09
226 Bill Wegman	.15	.04
227 Robin Yount UER (Born in Illinois, not in Virginia)	1.25	.35
228 Rick Aguilera	.15	.04
229 J.T. Bruett	.15	.04
230 Scott Erickson	.15	.04
231 Kent Hrbek	.30	.09
232 Terry Jorgensen	.15	.04
233 Scott Leius	.15	.04
234 Pat Mahomes	.15	.04
235 Pedro Munoz	.15	.04
236 Kirby Puckett	.75	.23
237 Kevin Tapani	.15	.04
238 Lenny Webster	.15	.04
239 Carl Willis	.15	.04
240 Mike Gallego	.15	.04
241 John Habyan	.15	.04
242 Pat Kelly	.15	.04
243 Kevin Maas	.15	.04
244 Don Mattingly	2.00	.60
245 Hensley Meulens	.15	.04
246 Sam Militello	.15	.04
247 Matt Nokes	.15	.04
248 Melido Perez	.15	.04
249 Andy Stankiewicz	.15	.04
250 Randy Velarde	.15	.04
251 Bob Wickman	.15	.04
252 Bernie Williams	.50	.15
253 Lance Blankenship	.15	.04
254 Mike Bordick	.15	.04
255 Jerry Browne	.15	.04
256 Ron Darling	.15	.04
257 Dennis Eckersley	.30	.09
258 Rickey Henderson	.75	.23
259 Vince Horsman	.15	.04
260 Troy Neel	.15	.04
261 Jeff Parrett	.15	.04
262 Terry Steinbach	.15	.04
263 Bob Welch	.15	.04
264 Bobby Witt	.15	.04
265 Rich Amaral	.15	.04

266 Bret Boone .50 .15
267 Jay Buhner .30 .09
268 Dave Fleming .15 .04
269 Randy Johnson .75 .23
270 Edgar Martinez .50 .15
271 Mike Schooler .15 .04
272 Russ Swan .15 .04
273 Dave Valle .15 .04
274 Omar Vizquel .30 .09
275 Kerry Woodson .15 .04
276 Kevin Brown .30 .09
277 Julio Franco .30 .09
278 Jeff Frye .15 .04
279 Juan Gonzalez .75 .23
280 Jeff Huson .15 .04
281 Rafael Palmeiro .50 .15
282 Dean Palmer .30 .09
283 Roger Pavlik .15 .04
284 Ivan Rodriguez .75 .23
285 Kenny Rogers .30 .09
286 Derek Bell .15 .04
287 Pat Borders .15 .04
288 Joe Carter .30 .09
289 Bob MacDonald .15 .04
290 Jack Morris .30 .09
291 John Olerud .30 .09
292 Ed Sprague .15 .04
293 Todd Stottlemyre .15 .04
294 Mike Timlin .15 .04
295 Duane Ward .15 .04
296 David Wells .30 .09
297 Devon White .15 .04
298 Ray Lankford CL .15 .04
299 Bobby Witt CL .15 .04
300 Mike Piazza CL .75 .23
301 Steve Bedrosian .15 .04
302 Jeff Blauser .15 .04
303 Francisco Cabrera .15 .04
304 Marvin Freeman .15 .04
305 Brian Hunter .15 .04
306 David Justice .30 .09
307 Greg Maddux 1.25 .35
308 Greg McMichael RC .15 .04
309 Kent Mercker .15 .04
310 Otis Nixon .15 .04
311 Pete Smith .15 .04
312 John Smoltz .50 .15
313 Jose Guzman .15 .04
314 Mike Harkey .15 .04
315 Greg Hibbard .15 .04
316 Candy Maldonado .15 .04
317 Randy Myers .15 .04
318 Dan Plesac .15 .04
319 Rey Sanchez .15 .04
320 Ryne Sandberg 1.25 .35
321 Tommy Shields .15 .04
322 Jose Vizcaino .15 .04
323 Matt Walbeck RC .15 .04
324 Willie Wilson .15 .04
325 Tom Browning .15 .04
326 Tim Costo .15 .04
327 Rob Dibble .30 .09
328 Steve Foster .15 .04
329 Roberto Kelly .15 .04
330 Randy Milligan .15 .04
331 Kevin Mitchell .15 .04
332 Tim Pugh RC .15 .04
333 Jeff Reardon .30 .09
334 John Roper .15 .04
335 Juan Samuel .15 .04
336 John Smiley .15 .04
337 Dan Wilson .30 .09
338 Scott Aldred .15 .04
339 Andy Ashby .15 .04
340 Freddie Benavides .15 .04
341 Dante Bichette .30 .09
342 Willie Blair .15 .04
343 Daryl Boston .15 .04
344 Vinny Castilla .30 .09
345 Jerald Clark .15 .04
346 Alex Cole .15 .04
347 Andres Galarraga .30 .09
348 Joe Girardi .15 .04
349 Ryan Hawblitzel .15 .04
350 Charlie Hayes .15 .04
351 Butch Henry .15 .04
352 Darren Holmes .15 .04
353 Dale Murphy .75 .23
354 David Nied .15 .04
355 Jeff Parrett .15 .04
356 Steve Reed RC .15 .04
357 Bruce Ruffin .15 .04
358 Danny Sheaffer RC .15 .04
359 Bryn Smith .15 .04
360 Jim Tatum RC .15 .04
361 Eric Young .15 .04
362 Gerald Young .15 .04
363 Luis Aquino .15 .04
364 Alex Arias .15 .04
365 Jack Armstrong .15 .04
366 Bret Barberie .15 .04
367 Ryan Bowen .15 .04
368 Greg Briley .15 .04
369 Cris Carpenter .15 .04
370 Chuck Carr .15 .04
371 Jeff Conine .30 .09
372 Steve Decker .15 .04
373 Orestes Destrade .15 .04
374 Monty Fariss .15 .04
375 Junior Felix .15 .04
376 Chris Hammond .15 .04
377 Bryan Harvey .15 .04
378 Trevor Hoffman .30 .09
379 Charlie Hough .30 .09
380 Joe Klink .15 .04
381 Richie Lewis RC .15 .04
382 Dave Magadan .15 .04
383 Bob McClure .15 .04
384 Scott Pose RC .15 .04
385 Rich Renteria .15 .04
386 Benito Santiago .30 .09
387 Walt Weiss .15 .04
388 Nigel Wilson .15 .04
389 Eric Anthony .15 .04
390 Jeff Bagwell .50 .15
391 Andujar Cedeno .15 .04
392 Doug Drabek .15 .04
393 Darryl Kile .30 .09
394 Mark Portugal .15 .04
395 Karl Rhodes .15 .04
396 Scott Servais .15 .04
397 Greg Swindell .15 .04
398 Tom Goodwin .15 .04
399 Kevin Gross .15 .04
400 Carlos Hernandez .15 .04
401 Ramon Martinez .15 .04
402 Raul Mondesi .30 .09
403 Jody Reed .15 .04
404 Mike Sharperson .15 .04
405 Cory Snyder .15 .04
406 Darryl Strawberry .50 .15
407 Rick Trlicek .15 .04
408 Tim Wallach .15 .04
409 Todd Worrell .15 .04
410 Tavo Alvarez .15 .04
411 Sean Berry .15 .04
412 Frank Bolick .15 .04
413 Cliff Floyd .50 .15
414 Mike Gardiner .15 .04
415 Marquis Grissom .15 .04
416 Tim Laker RC .15 .04
417 Mike Lansing RC .30 .09
418 Dennis Martinez .30 .09
419 John Vander Wal .15 .04
420 John Wetteland .30 .09
421 Rondell White .30 .09
422 Bobby Bonilla .15 .04
423 Jeromy Burnitz .30 .09
424 Vince Coleman .15 .04
425 Mike Draper .15 .04
426 Tony Fernandez .15 .04
427 Dwight Gooden .50 .15
428 Jeff Innis .15 .04
429 Bobby Jones .30 .09
430 Mike Maddux .15 .04
431 Charlie O'Brien .15 .04
432 Joe Orsulak .15 .04
433 Pete Schourek .15 .04
434 Frank Tanana .15 .04
435 Ryan Thompson .15 .04
436 Kim Batiste .15 .04
437 Mark Davis .15 .04
438 Jose DeLeon .15 .04
439 Len Dykstra .30 .09
440 Jim Eisenreich .15 .04
441 Tommy Greene .15 .04
442 Pete Incaviglia .15 .04
443 Danny Jackson .15 .04
444 Todd Pratt RC .30 .09
445 Curt Schilling .50 .15
446 Milt Thompson .15 .04
447 David West .15 .04
448 Mitch Williams .15 .04
449 Steve Cooke .15 .04
450 Carlos Garcia .15 .04
451 Al Martin .15 .04
452 Blas Minor .15 .04
453 Dennis Moeller .15 .04
454 Denny Neagle .30 .09
455 Don Slaught .15 .04
456 Lonnie Smith .15 .04
457 Paul Wagner .15 .04
458 Bob Walk .15 .04
459 Kevin Young .30 .09
460 Rene Arocha RC .30 .09
461 Brian Barber .15 .04
462 Rheal Cormier .15 .04
463 Gregg Jefferies .15 .04
464 Joe Magrane .15 .04
465 Omar Olivares .15 .04
466 Geronimo Pena .15 .04
467 Allen Watson .15 .04
468 Mark Whiten .15 .04
469 Derek Bell .15 .04
470 Phil Clark .15 .04
471 Pat Gomez RC .15 .04
472 Tony Gwynn 1.00 .30
473 Jeremy Hernandez .15 .04
474 Bruce Hurst .15 .04
475 Phil Plantier .15 .04
476 Scott Sanders RC .15 .04
477 Tim Scott .15 .04
478 Darrell Sherman RC .15 .04
479 Guillermo Velasquez .15 .04
480 Tim Worrell RC .15 .04
481 Todd Benzinger .15 .04
482 Bud Black .15 .04
483 Barry Bonds 2.00 .60
484 Dave Burba .15 .04
485 Bryan Hickerson .15 .04
486 Dave Martinez .15 .04
487 Willie McGee .30 .09
488 Jeff Reed .15 .04
489 Kevin Rogers .15 .04
490 Matt Williams .30 .09
491 Trevor Wilson .15 .04
492 Harold Baines .30 .09
493 Mike Devereaux .15 .04
494 Todd Frohwirth .15 .04
495 Chris Hoiles .15 .04
496 Luis Mercedes .15 .04
497 Sherman Obando RC .15 .04
498 Brad Pennington .15 .04
499 Harold Reynolds .30 .09
500 Arthur Rhodes .15 .04
501 Cal Ripken 2.50 .75
502 Rick Sutcliffe .30 .09
503 Fernando Valenzuela .30 .09
504 Mark Williamson .15 .04
505 Scott Bankhead .15 .04
506 Greg Blosser .15 .04
507 Ivan Calderon .15 .04
508 Roger Clemens 1.50 .45
509 Andre Dawson .30 .09
510 Scott Fletcher .15 .04
511 Greg A. Harris .15 .04
512 Billy Hatcher .15 .04
513 Bob Melvin .15 .04
514 Carlos Quintana .15 .04
515 Luis Rivera .15 .04
516 Jeff Russell .15 .04
517 Ken Ryan RC .15 .04
518 Chili Davis .30 .09
519 Jim Edmonds RC 2.50 .75
520 Gary Gaetti .30 .09
521 Torey Lovullo .15 .04
522 Troy Percival .50 .15
523 Tim Salmon .50 .15
524 Scott Sanderson .15 .04
525 J.T. Snow RC .75 .23
526 Jerome Walton .15 .04
527 Jason Bere .15 .04
528 Rod Bolton .15 .04
529 Ellis Burks .30 .09
530 Carlton Fisk .50 .15
531 Craig Grebeck .15 .04
532 Ozzie Guillen .15 .04
533 Roberto Hernandez .15 .04
534 Bo Jackson .75 .23
535 Kirk McCaskill .15 .04
536 Dave Stieb .15 .04
537 Robin Ventura .30 .09
538 Albert Belle .30 .09
539 Mike Bielecki .15 .04
540 Glenallen Hill .15 .04
541 Reggie Jefferson .15 .04
542 Kenny Lofton .30 .09
543 Jeff Mutis .15 .04
544 Junior Ortiz .15 .04
545 Manny Ramirez .75 .23
546 Jeff Treadway .15 .04
547 Kevin Wickander .15 .04
548 Cecil Fielder .30 .09
549 Kirk Gibson .30 .09
550 Greg Gohr .15 .04
551 David Haas .15 .04
552 Bill Krueger .15 .04
553 Mike Moore .30 .09
554 Mickey Tettleton .15 .04
555 Lou Whitaker .30 .09
556 Kevin Appier .30 .09
557 Billy Brewer .15 .04
558 David Cone .30 .09
559 Greg Gagne .15 .04
560 Mark Gardner .15 .04
561 Phil Hiatt .15 .04
562 Felix Jose .15 .04
563 Jose Lind .15 .04
564 Mike Macfarlane .15 .04
565 Keith Miller .15 .04
566 Jeff Montgomery .15 .04
567 Hipolito Pichardo .15 .04
568 Ricky Bones .15 .04
569 Tom Brunansky .15 .04
570 Joe Kmak .15 .04
571 Pat Listach .15 .04
572 Graeme Lloyd RC .30 .09
573 Carlos Maldonado .15 .04
574 Josias Manzanillo .15 .04
575 Matt Mieske .15 .04
576 Kevin Reimer .15 .04
577 Bill Spiers .15 .04
578 Dickie Thon .15 .04
579 Willie Banks .15 .04
580 Jim Deshaies .15 .04
581 Mark Guthrie .15 .04
582 Brian Harper .15 .04
583 Chuck Knoblauch .30 .09
584 Gene Larkin .15 .04
585 Shane Mack .15 .04
586 David McCarty .15 .04
587 Mike Pagliarulo .15 .04
588 Mike Trombley .15 .04
589 Dave Winfield .30 .09
590 Jim Abbott .50 .15
591 Wade Boggs .50 .15
592 Russ Davis RC .30 .09
593 Steve Farr .15 .04
594 Steve Howe .15 .04
595 Mike Humphreys .15 .04
596 Jimmy Key .30 .09
597 Jim Leyritz .15 .04
598 Bobby Munoz .15 .04
599 Paul O'Neill .50 .15
600 Spike Owen .15 .04
601 Mike Stanley .15 .04
602 Danny Tartabull .15 .04
603 Scott Brosius .30 .09
604 Storm Davis .15 .04
605 Eric Fox .15 .04
606 Rich Gossage .30 .09
607 Scott Hemond .15 .04
608 Dave Henderson .15 .04
609 Mark McGwire 2.00 .60
610 Mike Mohler RC .15 .04
611 Edwin Nunez .15 .04
612 Kevin Seitzer .15 .04
613 Ruben Sierra .15 .04
614 Chris Bosio .15 .04
615 Norm Charlton .15 .04
616 Jim Converse RC .15 .04
617 John Cummings RC .15 .04
618 Mike Felder .15 .04
619 Ken Griffey Jr. 1.25 .35
620 Mike Hampton .30 .09
621 Erik Hanson .15 .04
622 Bill Haselman .15 .04
623 Tino Martinez .50 .15
624 Lee Tinsley .15 .04
625 Fernando Vina RC 1.50 .45
626 David Wainhouse .15 .04
627 Jose Canseco .75 .23
628 Benji Gil .15 .04
629 Tom Henke .30 .09
630 David Hulse RC .15 .04
631 Manuel Lee .15 .04
632 Craig Lefferts .15 .04
633 Robb Nen .30 .09
634 Gary Redus .15 .04
635 Bill Ripken .15 .04
636 Nolan Ryan 3.00 .90
637 Dan Smith .15 .04
638 Matt Whiteside RC .15 .04
639 Roberto Alomar .75 .23
640 Juan Guzman .15 .04
641 Pat Hentgen .15 .04
642 Darrin Jackson .15 .04
643 Randy Knorr .15 .04
644 Domingo Martinez RC .15 .04
645 Paul Molitor .50 .15
646 Dick Schofield .15 .04
647 Dave Stewart .30 .09
648 Rey Sanchez CL .15 .04
649 Jeremy Hernandez CL .15 .04
650 Junior Ortiz CL .15 .04

1993 Ultra All-Rookies

Inserted into series II packs at a rate of one in 18, this ten-card standard-size set features

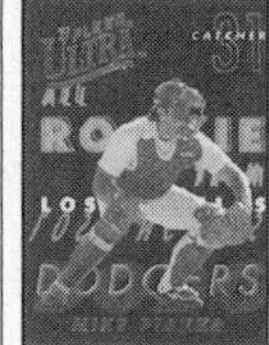

cutout color player action shots that are superposed upon a black background, which carries the player's uniform number, position, team name, and the set's title in multicolored lettering. The set is sequenced in alphabetical order. The key cards in this set are Mike Piazza and Tim Salmon.

Nm-Mt Ex-Mt
COMPLETE SET (10) 15.00 4.50
1 Rene Arocha 1.25 .35
2 Jeff Conine 1.25 .35
3 Phil Hiatt .60 .18
4 Mike Lansing 1.25 .35
5 Al Martin .60 .18
6 David Nied .60 .18
7 Mike Piazza 8.00 2.40
8 Tim Salmon 2.00 .60
9 J.T. Snow 3.00 .90
10 Kevin Young 1.25 .35

1993 Ultra All-Stars

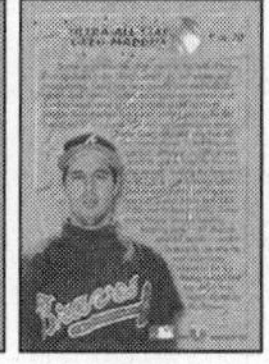

Inserted into series II packs at a rate of one in nine, this 20-card standard-size set features National League (1-10) and American League (11-20) All-Stars.

Nm-Mt Ex-Mt
COMPLETE SET (20) 40.00 12.00
1 Darren Daulton 1.25 .35
2 Will Clark 3.00 .90
3 Ryne Sandberg 5.00 1.50
4 Barry Larkin 3.00 .90
5 Gary Sheffield 1.25 .35
6 Barry Bonds 8.00 2.40
7 Ray Lankford .60 .18
8 Larry Walker 2.00 .60
9 Greg Maddux 5.00 1.50
10 Lee Smith 1.25 .35
11 Ivan Rodriguez 3.00 .90
12 Mark McGwire 8.00 2.40
13 Carlos Baerga .60 .18
14 Cal Ripken 10.00 3.00
15 Edgar Martinez 2.00 .60
16 Juan Gonzalez 3.00 .90
17 Ken Griffey Jr. 5.00 1.50
18 Kirby Puckett 3.00 .90
19 Frank Thomas 3.00 .90
20 Mike Mussina 3.00 .90

1993 Ultra Award Winners

Randomly inserted in first series packs, this 25-card standard-size insert set of 1993 Ultra Award Winners honors the Top Glove for the National (1-9) and American (10-18) Leagues and other major award winners (19-25).

Nm-Mt Ex-Mt
COMPLETE SET (25) 40.00 12.00
1 Greg Maddux 5.00 1.50
2 Tom Pagnozzi .60 .18
3 Mark Grace 2.00 .60
4 Jose Lind .60 .18
5 Terry Pendleton 1.25 .35
6 Ozzie Smith 5.00 1.50
7 Barry Bonds 8.00 2.40
8 Andy Van Slyke 1.25 .35
9 Larry Walker 2.00 .60
10 Mark Langston .60 .18
11 Ivan Rodriguez 3.00 .90
12 Don Mattingly 8.00 2.40
13 Roberto Alomar 3.00 .90
14 Robin Ventura 1.25 .35
15 Cal Ripken 10.00 3.00
16 Ken Griffey 5.00 1.50
17 Kirby Puckett 3.00 .90
18 Devon White .60 .18
19 Pat Listach .60 .18
20 Eric Karros 1.25 .35
21 Pat Borders .60 .18
22 Greg Maddux 5.00 1.50
23 Dennis Eckersley 1.25 .35
24 Barry Bonds 8.00 2.40
25 Gary Sheffield 1.25 .35

1993 Ultra Eckersley

Randomly inserted in first series foil packs, this 10-card (cards 11 and 12 were mail-aways) standard-size set salutes one of baseball's greatest relief pitchers, Dennis Eckersley. Two additional cards (11 and 12) were available through a mail-in offer for ten 1993 Fleer Ultra baseball wrappers plus 1.00 for postage and

handling. The expiration for this offer was September 30, 1993. Eckersley personally autographed more than 2,000 of these cards. The cards feature silver foil stamping on both sides.

Nm-Mt Ex-Mt
COMPLETE SET (10) 4.00 1.20
COMMON CARD (1-10) .50 .15
COMMON MAIL (11-12) 1.00 .30
P1 Dennis Eckersley 4.00 1.20
Paul Mullan Promo
AU Dennis Eckersley AU 50.00 15.00
(Certified autograph)

1993 Ultra Home Run Kings

Randomly inserted into all 1993 Ultra packs, this ten-card standard-size set features the best long ball hitters in baseball.

Nm-Mt Ex-Mt
COMPLETE SET (10) 20.00 6.00
1 Juan Gonzalez 4.00 1.20
2 Mark McGwire 10.00 3.00
3 Cecil Fielder 1.50 .45
4 Fred McGriff 2.50 .75
5 Albert Belle 1.50 .45
6 Barry Bonds 10.00 3.00
7 Joe Carter 1.50 .45
8 Gary Sheffield 1.50 .45
9 Darren Daulton 1.50 .45
10 Dave Hollins .75 .23

1993 Ultra Performers

This ten-card standard-size set could only be ordered directly from Fleer by sending in 9.95, five Fleer/Ultra baseball wrappers, and an order blank found in hobby and sports periodicals.

Nm-Mt Ex-Mt
COMPLETE SET (10) 20.00 6.00
1 Barry Bonds 5.00 1.50
2 Juan Gonzalez 2.00 .60
3 Ken Griffey Jr. 3.00 .90
4 Eric Karros .75 .23
5 Pat Listach .40 .12
6 Greg Maddux 3.00 .90
7 David Nied .40 .12
8 Gary Sheffield .75 .23
9 J.T. Snow 2.00 .60
10 Frank Thomas 2.00 .60

1993 Ultra Strikeout Kings

Inserted into series II packs at a rate of one in 37, this five-card standard-size set showcases outstanding pitchers from both leagues.

Nm-Mt Ex-Mt
COMPLETE SET (5) 25.00 7.50
1 Roger Clemens 10.00 3.00
2 Juan Guzman 1.00 .30
3 Randy Johnson 5.00 1.50
4 Nolan Ryan 20.00 6.00
5 John Smoltz 3.00 .90

1994 Ultra

The 1994 Ultra baseball set consists of 600 standard-size cards that were issued in two series of 300. Each pack contains at least one insert card, while "Hot Packs" have nothing but insert cards in them. The cards are numbered on the back, grouped alphabetically within teams, and checklisted below alphabetically according to teams for each league with AL preceding NL. Rookie Cards include Ray Durham and Chan Ho Park.

Nm-Mt Ex-Mt
COMPLETE SET (600) 30.00 9.00
COMP. SERIES 1 (300) 15.00 4.50
COMP. SERIES 2 (300) 15.00 4.50
1 Jeffrey Hammonds .15 .04
2 Chris Hoiles .15 .04
3 Ben McDonald .15 .04
4 Mark McLemore .15 .04
5 Alan Mills .15 .04
6 Jamie Moyer .30 .09
7 Brad Pennington .15 .04
8 Jim Poole .15 .04
9 Cal Ripken Jr. 2.50 .75
10 Jack Voigt .15 .04
11 Roger Clemens 1.50 .45
12 Danny Darwin .15 .04
13 Andre Dawson .30 .09
14 Scott Fletcher .15 .04
15 Greg A. Harris .15 .04
16 Billy Hatcher .15 .04
17 Jeff Russell .15 .04
18 Aaron Sele .15 .04
19 Mo Vaughn .30 .09
20 Mike Butcher .15 .04
21 Rod Correia .15 .04
22 Steve Frey .15 .04
23 Phil Leftwich RC .15 .04
24 Torey Lovullo .15 .04
25 Ken Patterson .15 .04
26 Eduardo Perez UER .15 .04
(listed as a Twin instead of Angel)
27 Tim Salmon .50 .15
28 J.T. Snow .30 .09
29 Chris Turner .15 .04
30 Wilson Alvarez .15 .04
31 Jason Bere .15 .04
32 Joey Cora .15 .04
33 Alex Fernandez .15 .04
34 Roberto Hernandez .15 .04
35 Lance Johnson .15 .04
36 Ron Karkovice .15 .04
37 Kirk McCaskill .15 .04
38 Jeff Schwarz .15 .04
39 Frank Thomas .75 .23
40 Sandy Alomar Jr. .15 .04
41 Albert Belle .30 .09
42 Felix Fermin .15 .04
43 Wayne Kirby .15 .04
44 Tom Kramer .15 .04
45 Kenny Lofton .30 .09
46 Jose Mesa .15 .04
47 Eric Plunk .15 .04
48 Paul Sorrento .15 .04
49 Jim Thome .75 .23
50 Bill Wertz .15 .04
51 John Doherty .15 .04
52 Cecil Fielder .30 .09
53 Travis Fryman .30 .09
54 Chris Gomez .15 .04
55 Mike Henneman .15 .04
56 Chad Kreuter .15 .04
57 Bob MacDonald .15 .04
58 Mike Moore .15 .04
59 Tony Phillips .15 .04
60 Lou Whitaker .30 .09
61 Kevin Appier .30 .09
62 Greg Gagne .15 .04
63 Chris Gwynn .15 .04
64 Bob Hamelin .15 .04
65 Chris Haney .15 .04
66 Phil Hiatt .15 .04
67 Felix Jose .15 .04
68 Jose Lind .15 .04
69 Mike Macfarlane .15 .04
70 Jeff Montgomery .15 .04
71 Hipolito Pichardo .15 .04
72 Juan Bell .15 .04
73 Cal Eldred .15 .04
74 Darryl Hamilton .15 .04
75 Doug Henry .15 .04
76 Mike Ignasiak .15 .04
77 John Jaha .15 .04
78 Graeme Lloyd .15 .04
79 Angel Miranda .15 .04
80 Dave Nilsson .15 .04
81 Troy O'Leary .15 .04
82 Kevin Reimer .15 .04
83 Willie Banks .15 .04
84 Larry Casian .15 .04
85 Scott Erickson .15 .04
86 Eddie Guardado .30 .09
87 Kent Hrbek .30 .09
88 Terry Jorgensen .15 .04
89 Chuck Knoblauch .30 .09
90 Pat Meares .15 .04
91 Mike Trombley .15 .04
92 Dave Winfield .30 .09
93 Wade Boggs .50 .15
94 Scott Kamieniecki .15 .04
95 Pat Kelly .15 .04
96 Jimmy Key .30 .09
97 Jim Leyritz .15 .04
98 Bobby Munoz .15 .04
99 Paul O'Neill .50 .15
100 Melido Perez .15 .04
101 Mike Stanley .15 .04
102 Danny Tartabull .15 .04
103 Bernie Williams .50 .15
104 Kurt Abbott RC .30 .09
105 Mike Bordick .15 .04
106 Ron Darling .15 .04
107 Brent Gates .15 .04
108 Miguel Jimenez .15 .04
109 Steve Karsay .15 .04
110 Scott Lydy .15 .04
111 Mark McGwire 2.00 .60
112 Troy Neel .15 .04
113 Craig Paquette .15 .04
114 Bob Welch .15 .04
115 Bobby Witt .15 .04
116 Rich Amaral .15 .04
117 Mike Blowers .15 .04
118 Jay Buhner .30 .09
119 Dave Fleming .15 .04
120 Ken Griffey Jr. 1.25 .35
121 Tino Martinez .50 .15
122 Marc Newfield .15 .04
123 Ted Power .15 .04
124 Mackey Sasser .15 .04
125 Omar Vizquel .30 .09
126 Kevin Brown .30 .09
127 Juan Gonzalez .75 .23
128 Tom Henke .15 .04
129 David Hulse .15 .04
130 Dean Palmer .30 .09
131 Roger Pavlik .15 .04
132 Ivan Rodriguez .75 .23
133 Kenny Rogers .30 .09
134 Doug Strange .15 .04
135 Pat Borders .15 .04
136 Joe Carter .30 .09
137 Darnell Coles .15 .04
138 Pat Hentgen .15 .04
139 Al Leiter .30 .09
140 Paul Molitor .50 .15
141 John Olerud .30 .09
142 Ed Sprague .15 .04
143 Dave Stewart .30 .09
144 Mike Timlin .15 .04
145 Duane Ward .15 .04
146 Devon White .15 .04
147 Steve Avery .15 .04
148 Steve Bedrosian .15 .04
149 Damon Berryhill .15 .04
150 Jeff Blauser .15 .04
151 Tom Glavine .50 .15
152 Chipper Jones .75 .23
153 Mark Lemke .15 .04
154 Fred McGriff .50 .15
155 Greg McMichael .15 .04
156 Deion Sanders .50 .15
157 John Smoltz .50 .15
158 Mark Wohlers .15 .04
159 Jose Bautista .15 .04
160 Steve Buechele .15 .04
161 Mike Harkey .15 .04
162 Greg Hibbard .15 .04
163 Chuck McElroy .15 .04
164 Mike Morgan .15 .04
165 Kevin Roberson .15 .04
166 Ryne Sandberg 1.25 .35
167 Jose Vizcaino .15 .04
168 Rick Wilkins .15 .04
169 Willie Wilson .15 .04
170 Willie Greene .15 .04
171 Roberto Kelly .15 .04
172 Larry Luebbers RC .15 .04
173 Kevin Mitchell .15 .04
174 Joe Oliver .15 .04
175 John Roper .15 .04
176 Johnny Ruffin .15 .04
177 Reggie Sanders .30 .09
178 John Smiley .15 .04
179 Jerry Spradlin RC .15 .04
180 Freddie Benavides .15 .04
181 Dante Bichette .30 .09
182 Willie Blair .15 .04
183 Kent Bottenfield .15 .04
184 Jerald Clark .15 .04
185 Joe Girardi .15 .04
186 Roberto Mejia .15 .04
187 Steve Reed .15 .04
188 Armando Reynoso .15 .04
189 Bruce Ruffin .15 .04
190 Eric Young .30 .09
191 Luis Aquino .15 .04
192 Bret Barberie .15 .04
193 Ryan Bowen .15 .04
194 Chuck Carr .15 .04
195 Orestes Destrade .15 .04
196 Richie Lewis .15 .04
197 Dave Magadan .15 .04
198 Bob Natal .15 .04
199 Gary Sheffield .30 .09
200 Matt Turner .15 .04
201 Darrell Whitmore .15 .04
202 Eric Anthony .15 .04
203 Jeff Bagwell .50 .15
204 Andujar Cedeno .15 .04
205 Luis Gonzalez .30 .09
206 Xavier Hernandez .15 .04
207 Doug Jones .15 .04
208 Darryl Kile .30 .09
209 Scott Servais .15 .04
210 Greg Swindell .15 .04
211 Brian Williams .15 .04
212 Pedro Astacio .15 .04
213 Brett Butler .30 .09
214 Omar Daal .15 .04
215 Jim Gott .15 .04
216 Raul Mondesi .30 .09
217 Jose Offerman .15 .04
218 Mike Piazza 1.50 .45
219 Cory Snyder .15 .04
220 Tim Wallach .15 .04
221 Todd Worrell .15 .04
222 Moises Alou .30 .09
223 Sean Berry .15 .04
224 Wil Cordero .15 .04
225 Jeff Fassero .15 .04
226 Darrin Fletcher .15 .04
227 Cliff Floyd .30 .09
228 Marquis Grissom .30 .09
229 Ken Hill .15 .04
230 Mike Lansing .15 .04
231 Kirk Rueter .30 .09
232 John Wetteland .30 .09
233 Rondell White .30 .09
234 Tim Bogar .15 .04
235 Jeromy Burnitz .30 .09
236 Dwight Gooden .50 .15
237 Todd Hundley .15 .04
238 Jeff Kent .30 .09
239 Josias Manzanillo .15 .04
240 Joe Orsulak .15 .04
241 Ryan Thompson .15 .04
242 Kim Batiste .15 .04
243 Darren Daulton .30 .09
244 Tommy Greene .15 .04
245 Dave Hollins .15 .04
246 Pete Incaviglia .15 .04
247 Danny Jackson .15 .04
248 Ricky Jordan .15 .04
249 John Kruk .30 .09
250 Mickey Morandini .15 .04
251 Terry Mulholland .15 .04
252 Ben Rivera .15 .04
253 Kevin Stocker .15 .04
254 Jay Bell .30 .09
255 Steve Cooke .15 .04
256 Jeff King .15 .04
257 Al Martin .15 .04
258 Danny Miceli .15 .04
259 Blas Minor .15 .04
260 Don Slaught .15 .04
261 Paul Wagner .15 .04
262 Tim Wakefield .30 .09
263 Kevin Young .15 .04
264 Rene Arocha .15 .04
265 Richard Batchelor RC .15 .04
266 Gregg Jefferies .15 .04
267 Brian Jordan .30 .09
268 Jose Oquendo .15 .04
269 Donovan Osborne .15 .04
270 Erik Pappas .15 .04
271 Mike Perez .15 .04
272 Bob Tewksbury .15 .04
273 Mark Whiten .15 .04
274 Todd Zeile .15 .04
275 Andy Ashby .15 .04
276 Brad Ausmus .15 .04
277 Phil Clark .15 .04
278 Jeff Gardner .15 .04
279 Ricky Gutierrez .15 .04
280 Tony Gwynn 1.00 .30
281 Tim Mauser .15 .04
282 Scott Sanders .15 .04
283 Frank Seminara .15 .04
284 Wally Whitehurst .15 .04
285 Rod Beck .15 .04
286 Barry Bonds 2.00 .60
287 Dave Burba .15 .04
288 Mark Carreon .15 .04
289 Royce Clayton .15 .04
290 Mike Jackson .15 .04
291 Darren Lewis .15 .04
292 Kirt Manwaring .15 .04
293 Dave Martinez .15 .04
294 Billy Swift .15 .04
295 Salomon Torres .15 .04
296 Matt Williams .30 .09
297 Checklist 1-75 .15 .04
298 Checklist 76-150 .15 .04
299 Checklist 151-225 .15 .04
300 Checklist 226-300 .15 .04
301 Brady Anderson .30 .09
302 Harold Baines .30 .09
303 Damon Buford .15 .04
304 Mike Devereaux .15 .04
305 Sid Fernandez .15 .04
306 Rick Krivda RC .15 .04
307 Mike Mussina .75 .23
308 Rafael Palmeiro .50 .15
309 Arthur Rhodes .15 .04
310 Chris Sabo .15 .04
311 Lee Smith .30 .09
312 Gregg Zaun RC .15 .04
313 Scott Cooper .15 .04
314 Mike Greenwell .15 .04
315 Tim Naehring .15 .04
316 Otis Nixon .15 .04
317 Paul Quantrill .15 .04
318 John Valentin .15 .04
319 Dave Valle .15 .04
320 Frank Viola .30 .09
321 Brian Anderson RC .30 .09
322 Garret Anderson .75 .23
323 Chad Curtis .15 .04
324 Chili Davis .30 .09
325 Gary DiSarcina .15 .04
326 Damion Easley .15 .04
327 Jim Edmonds .50 .15
328 Chuck Finley .30 .09
329 Joe Grahe .15 .04
330 Bo Jackson .75 .23
331 Mark Langston .15 .04
332 Harold Reynolds .30 .09
333 James Baldwin .15 .04
334 Ray Durham RC 1.00 .30
335 Julio Franco .30 .09
336 Craig Grebeck .15 .04
337 Ozzie Guillen .15 .04
338 Joe Hall RC .15 .04
339 Darrin Jackson .15 .04
340 Jack McDowell .15 .04
341 Tim Raines .30 .09
342 Robin Ventura .30 .09
343 Carlos Baerga .15 .04
344 Derek Lilliquist .15 .04
345 Dennis Martinez .30 .09
346 Jack Morris .30 .09
347 Eddie Murray .75 .23
348 Chris Nabholz .15 .04
349 Charles Nagy .15 .04
350 Chad Ogea .15 .04
351 Manny Ramirez .50 .15
352 Omar Vizquel .30 .09
353 Tim Belcher .15 .04
354 Eric Davis .30 .09
355 Kirk Gibson .30 .09
356 Rick Greene .15 .04
357 Mickey Tettleton .15 .04
358 Alan Trammell .50 .15
359 David Wells .30 .09
360 Stan Belinda .15 .04
361 Vince Coleman .15 .04
362 David Cone .30 .09
363 Gary Gaetti .30 .09
364 Tom Gordon .15 .04
365 Dave Henderson .15 .04
366 Wally Joyner .30 .09
367 Brent Mayne .15 .04
368 Brian McRae .15 .04
369 Michael Tucker .30 .09
370 Ricky Bones .15 .04
371 Brian Harper .15 .04
372 Tyrone Hill .15 .04
373 Mark Kiefer .15 .04
374 Pat Listach .15 .04
375 Mike Matheny RC .30 .09
376 Jose Mercedes RC .15 .04
377 Jody Reed .15 .04
378 Kevin Seitzer .15 .04
379 B.J. Surhoff .30 .09
380 Greg Vaughn .30 .09
381 Turner Ward .15 .04
382 Wes Weger RC .15 .04
383 Bill Wegman .15 .04
384 Rick Aguilera .15 .04
385 Rich Becker .15 .04
386 Alex Cole .15 .04
387 Steve Dunn .15 .04
388 Keith Garagozzo RC .15 .04
389 LaTroy Hawkins RC .30 .09
390 Shane Mack .15 .04
391 David McCarty .15 .04
392 Pedro Munoz .15 .04
393 Derek Parks .15 .04
394 Kirby Puckett .75 .23
395 Kevin Tapani .15 .04
396 Matt Walbeck .15 .04
397 Jim Abbott .50 .15
398 Mike Gallego .15 .04
399 Xavier Hernandez .15 .04
400 Don Mattingly 2.00 .60
401 Terry Mulholland .15 .04
402 Matt Nokes .15 .04
403 Luis Polonia .15 .04
404 Bob Wickman .15 .04
405 Mark Acre RC .15 .04
406 Fausto Cruz RC .15 .04
407 Dennis Eckersley .30 .09
408 Rickey Henderson .75 .23
409 Stan Javier .15 .04
410 Carlos Reyes RC .15 .04
411 Ruben Sierra .15 .04
412 Terry Steinbach .15 .04
413 Bill Taylor RC .30 .09
414 Todd Van Poppel .15 .04
415 Eric Anthony .15 .04
416 Bobby Ayala .15 .04
417 Chris Bosio .15 .04
418 Tim Davis .15 .04
419 Randy Johnson .75 .23
420 Kevin King RC .15 .04
421 Anthony Manahan RC .15 .04
422 Edgar Martinez .50 .15
423 Keith Mitchell .15 .04
424 Roger Salkeld .15 .04
425 Mac Suzuki RC .30 .09
426 Dan Wilson .15 .04
427 Duff Brumley RC .15 .04
428 Jose Canseco .75 .23
429 Will Clark .75 .23
430 Steve Dreyer RC .15 .04
431 Rick Helling .15 .04
432 Chris James .15 .04
433 Matt Whiteside .15 .04
434 Roberto Alomar .75 .23
435 Scott Brow .15 .04
436 Domingo Cedeno .15 .04
437 Carlos Delgado .50 .15
438 Juan Guzman .15 .04
439 Paul Spoljaric .15 .04
440 Todd Stottlemyre .15 .04
441 Woody Williams .15 .04
442 David Justice .30 .09
443 Mike Kelly .15 .04
444 Ryan Klesko .30 .09
445 Javier Lopez .30 .09
446 Greg Maddux 1.25 .35
447 Kent Mercker .15 .04
448 Charlie O'Brien .15 .04
449 Terry Pendleton .30 .09
450 Mike Stanton .15 .04
451 Tony Tarasco .15 .04
452 Terrell Wade RC .15 .04
453 Willie Banks .15 .04
454 Shawon Dunston .15 .04
455 Mark Grace .50 .15
456 Jose Guzman .15 .04
457 Jose Hernandez .15 .04
458 Glenallen Hill .15 .04
459 Blaise Ilsley RC .15 .04
460 Brooks Kieschnick RC .15 .04
461 Derrick May .15 .04
462 Randy Myers .15 .04
463 Karl Rhodes .15 .04
464 Sammy Sosa 1.00 .30
465 Steve Trachsel .15 .04
466 Anthony Young .15 .04
467 Eddie Zambrano RC .15 .04
468 Bret Boone .30 .09
469 Tom Browning .15 .04
470 Hector Carrasco .15 .04
471 Rob Dibble .30 .09
472 Erik Hanson .15 .04
473 Thomas Howard .15 .04
474 Barry Larkin .75 .23
475 Hal Morris .15 .04
476 Jose Rijo .15 .04
477 John Burke .15 .04
478 Ellis Burks .30 .09
479 Marvin Freeman .15 .04
480 Andres Galarraga .30 .09
481 Greg W. Harris .15 .04
482 Charlie Hayes .15 .04
483 Darren Holmes .15 .04
484 Howard Johnson .15 .04
485 Marcus Moore .15 .04
486 David Nied .15 .04
487 Mark Thompson .15 .04
488 Walt Weiss .15 .04
489 Kurt Abbott .30 .09
490 Matias Carrillo RC .15 .04
491 Jeff Conine .30 .09
492 Chris Hammond .15 .04
493 Bryan Harvey .15 .04
494 Charlie Hough .30 .09
495 Yorkis Perez .15 .04
496 Pat Rapp .15 .04
497 Benito Santiago .30 .09
498 David Weathers .15 .04
499 Craig Biggio .50 .15
500 Ken Caminiti .30 .09
501 Doug Drabek .15 .04
502 Tony Eusebio .15 .04
503 Steve Finley .30 .09
504 Pete Harnisch .15 .04
505 Brian L. Hunter .15 .04
506 Domingo Jean .15 .04
507 Todd Jones .15 .04
508 Orlando Miller .15 .04
509 James Mouton .15 .04
510 Roberto Petagine .15 .04
511 Shane Reynolds .15 .04
512 Mitch Williams .15 .04
513 Billy Ashley .15 .04
514 Tom Candiotti .15 .04
515 Delino DeShields .15 .04
516 Kevin Gross .15 .04
517 Orel Hershiser .30 .09
518 Eric Karros .30 .09
519 Ramon Martinez .15 .04
520 Chan Ho Park RC .75 .23
521 Henry Rodriguez .15 .04
522 Joey Eischen .15 .04
523 Rod Henderson .15 .04
524 Pedro Martinez .75 .23
525 Mel Rojas .15 .04
526 Larry Walker .50 .15
527 Gabe White .15 .04
528 Bobby Bonilla .30 .09
529 Jonathan Hurst .15 .04
530 Bobby Jones .15 .04
531 Kevin McReynolds .15 .04
532 Bill Pulsipher .30 .09
533 Bret Saberhagen .30 .09
534 David Segui .15 .04
535 Pete Smith .15 .04
536 Kelly Stinnett RC .30 .09
537 Dave Telgheder .15 .04
538 Quilvio Veras .15 .04
539 Jose Vizcaino .15 .04
540 Pete Walker RC .15 .04
541 Ricky Bottalico RC .30 .09
542 Wes Chamberlain .15 .04
543 Mariano Duncan .15 .04
544 Lenny Dykstra .30 .09
545 Jim Eisenreich .15 .04
546 Phil Geisler RC .15 .04
547 Wayne Gomes RC .15 .04
548 Doug Jones .15 .04
549 Jeff Juden .15 .04
550 Mike Lieberthal .30 .09
551 Tony Longmire .15 .04
552 Tom Marsh .15 .04
553 Bobby Munoz .15 .04
554 Curt Schilling .50 .15
555 Carlos Garcia .15 .04
556 Ravelo Manzanillo RC .15 .04
557 Orlando Merced .15 .04
558 Will Pennyfeather .15 .04
559 Zane Smith .15 .04
560 Andy Van Slyke .30 .09
561 Rick White .15 .04
562 Luis Alicea .15 .04
563 Brian Barber .15 .04
564 Clint Davis RC .15 .04
565 Bernard Gilkey .15 .04
566 Ray Lankford .15 .04
567 Tom Pagnozzi .15 .04
568 Ozzie Smith 1.25 .35
569 Rick Sutcliffe .30 .09
570 Allen Watson .15 .04
571 Dmitri Young .30 .09
572 Derek Bell .15 .04
573 Andy Benes .15 .04
574 Archi Cianfrocco .15 .04
575 Joey Hamilton .15 .04
576 Gene Harris .15 .04
577 Trevor Hoffman .30 .09
578 Tim Hyers RC .15 .04
579 Brian Johnson RC .15 .04
580 Keith Lockhart RC .30 .09
581 Pedro A. Martinez RC .15 .04
582 Ray McDavid .15 .04
583 Phil Plantier .15 .04
584 Bip Roberts .15 .04
585 Dave Staton .15 .04
586 Todd Benzinger .15 .04
587 John Burkett .15 .04
588 Bryan Hickerson .15 .04
589 Willie McGee .30 .09
590 John Patterson .15 .04
591 Mark Portugal .15 .04
592 Kevin Rogers .15 .04
593 Joe Rosselli .15 .04
594 Steve Soderstrom RC .15 .04
595 Robby Thompson .15 .04
596 125th Anniversary .15 .04
597 Jaime Navarro CL .15 .04
598 Andy Van Slyke CL .15 .04
599 Checklist .15 .04
600 Bryan Harvey CL .15 .04
P243 D.Daulton Promo 2.00 .60
P249 John Kruk Promo 2.00 .60

1994 Ultra All-Rookies

This 10-card standard-size set features top rookies of 1994 and were randomly inserted in second series jumbo and foil packs at a rate of one in 10.

Nm-Mt Ex-Mt
COMPLETE SET (10) 8.00 2.40
*JUMBOS: .75X TO 2X BASIC CARDS
ONE JUMBO SET PER 2ND SERIES HOBBY CASE
1 Kurt Abbott 1.00 .30
2 Carlos Delgado 1.00 .30
3 Cliff Floyd 1.00 .30
4 Jeffrey Hammonds .50 .15
5 Ryan Klesko 1.00 .30
6 Javier Lopez 1.00 .30
7 Raul Mondesi 1.00 .30
8 James Mouton .50 .15
9 Chan Ho Park 2.00 .60
10 Dave Staton .50 .15

1994 Ultra All-Stars

Randomly inserted in second series foil and jumbo packs at a rate of one in three, this 20-

card standard-size set contains top major league stars.

	Nm-Mt	Ex-Mt
COMPLETE SET (20)	15.00	4.50
1 Chris Hoiles	.25	.07
2 Frank Thomas	1.25	.35
3 Roberto Alomar	1.25	.35
4 Cal Ripken Jr.	4.00	1.20
5 Robin Ventura	.50	.15
6 Albert Belle	.50	.15
7 Juan Gonzalez	1.25	.35
8 Ken Griffey Jr.	2.00	.60
9 John Olerud	.50	.15
10 Jack McDowell	.25	.07
11 Mike Piazza	2.50	.75
12 Fred McGriff	.75	.23
13 Ryne Sandberg	2.00	.60
14 Jay Bell	.50	.15
15 Matt Williams	.50	.15
16 Barry Bonds	3.00	.90
17 Lenny Dykstra	.50	.15
18 David Justice	.50	.15
19 Tom Glavine	.75	.23
20 Greg Maddux	2.00	.60

1994 Ultra Award Winners

Randomly inserted in all first series packs at a rate of one in three, this 25-card standard-size set features three MVP's, two Rookies of the Year, and 18 Top Glove defensive standouts. The set is divided into American League Top Gloves (1-9), National League Top Gloves (10-18), and Award Winners (19-25).

	Nm-Mt	Ex-Mt
COMPLETE SET (25)	15.00	4.50
1 Ivan Rodriguez	1.25	.35
2 Don Mattingly	3.00	.90
3 Roberto Alomar	1.25	.35
4 Robin Ventura	.50	.15
5 Omar Vizquel	.50	.15
6 Ken Griffey Jr.	2.00	.60
7 Kenny Lofton	.50	.15
8 Devon White	.25	.07
9 Mark Langston	.25	.07
10 Kirt Manwaring	.25	.07
11 Mark Grace	.75	.23
12 Robby Thompson	.25	.07
13 Matt Williams	.50	.15
14 Jay Bell	.50	.15
15 Barry Bonds	3.00	.90
16 Marquis Grissom	.25	.07
17 Larry Walker	.75	.23
18 Greg Maddux	2.00	.60
19 Frank Thomas	1.25	.35
20 Barry Bonds	3.00	.90
21 Paul Molitor	.75	.23
22 Jack McDowell	.25	.07
23 Greg Maddux	2.00	.60
24 Tim Salmon	.75	.23
25 Mike Piazza	2.50	.75

1994 Ultra Career Achievement

Randomly inserted in all second series packs at a rate of one in 21, this five card standard-size set highlights veteran stars and milestones they have reached during their brilliant careers.

	Nm-Mt	Ex-Mt
COMPLETE SET (5)	10.00	3.00
1 Joe Carter	1.00	.30
2 Paul Molitor	1.50	.45
3 Cal Ripken Jr.	8.00	2.40
4 Ryne Sandberg	4.00	1.20
5 Dave Winfield	1.00	.30

1994 Ultra Firemen

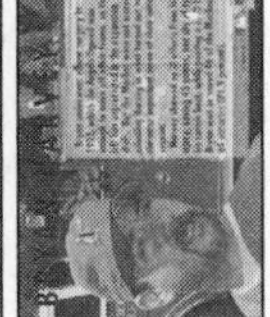

Randomly inserted in all first series packs at a rate of one in 11, this ten-card standard-size set features ten of baseball's top relief pitchers. The set is arranged according to American League (1-5) and National League (6-10) players.

	Nm-Mt	Ex-Mt
COMPLETE SET (10)	5.00	1.50
1 Jeff Montgomery	.50	.15
2 Duane Ward	.50	.15
3 Tom Henke	.50	.15
4 Roberto Hernandez	.50	.15
5 Dennis Eckersley	1.00	.30
6 Randy Myers	.50	.15
7 Rod Beck	.50	.15
8 Bryan Harvey	.50	.15
9 John Wetteland	1.00	.30
10 Mitch Williams	.50	.15

1994 Ultra Hitting Machines

Randomly inserted in all second series packs at a rate of one in five, this 10-card horizontally designed standard-size set features top hitters from 1993.

	Nm-Mt	Ex-Mt
COMPLETE SET (10)	10.00	3.00
1 Roberto Alomar	1.25	.35
2 Carlos Baerga	.25	.07
3 Barry Bonds	3.00	.90
4 Andres Galarraga	.50	.15
5 Juan Gonzalez	1.25	.35
6 Tony Gwynn	1.50	.45
7 Paul Molitor	.75	.23
8 John Olerud	.50	.15
9 Mike Piazza	2.50	.75
10 Frank Thomas	1.25	.35

1994 Ultra Home Run Kings

Randomly inserted exclusively in first series foil packs at a rate of one in 36, these 12 standard-size cards highlight home run hitters by an etched metalized look. Cards 1-6 feature American League Home Run Kings while cards 7-12 present National League Home Run Kings.

	Nm-Mt	Ex-Mt
COMPLETE SET (12)	60.00	18.00
1 Juan Gonzalez	6.00	1.80
2 Ken Griffey Jr.	10.00	3.00
3 Frank Thomas	6.00	1.80
4 Albert Belle	2.50	.75
5 Rafael Palmeiro	4.00	1.20
6 Joe Carter	2.50	.75
7 Barry Bonds	15.00	4.50
8 David Justice	2.50	.75
9 Matt Williams	2.50	.75
10 Fred McGriff	4.00	1.20
11 Ron Gant	1.25	.35
12 Mike Piazza	12.00	3.60

1994 Ultra League Leaders

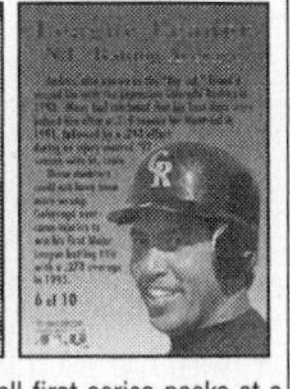

Randomly inserted in all first series packs at a rate of one in 11, this ten-card standard-size set features ten of 1993's leading players. The set is arranged according to American League (1-5) and National League (6-10) players.

	Nm-Mt	Ex-Mt
COMPLETE SET (10)	5.00	1.50
1 John Olerud	.75	.23
2 Rafael Palmeiro	1.25	.35
3 Kenny Lofton	.75	.23
4 Jack McDowell	.40	.12
5 Randy Johnson	2.00	.60
6 Andres Galarraga	.75	.23
7 Lenny Dykstra	.75	.23
8 Chuck Carr	.40	.12
9 Tom Glavine	1.25	.35
10 Jose Rijo	.40	.12

1994 Ultra On-Base Leaders

Randomly inserted in second series jumbo packs at a rate of one in 36, this 12-card standard-size set features those that were among the Major League leaders in on-base percentage.

	Nm-Mt	Ex-Mt
COMPLETE SET (12)	100.00	30.00
1 Roberto Alomar	12.00	3.60
2 Barry Bonds	30.00	9.00
3 Lenny Dykstra	5.00	1.50
4 Andres Galarraga	5.00	1.50
5 Mark Grace	8.00	2.40
6 Ken Griffey Jr.	20.00	6.00
7 Gregg Jefferies	2.50	.75
8 Orlando Merced	2.50	.75
9 Paul Molitor	8.00	2.40
10 John Olerud	5.00	1.50
11 Tony Phillips	2.50	.75
12 Frank Thomas	12.00	3.60

1994 Ultra Phillies Finest

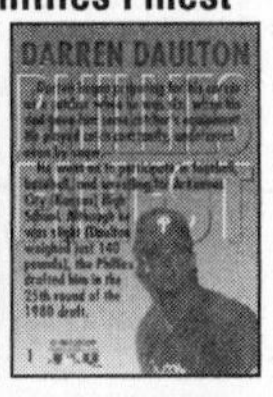

As the "Highlight Series" insert set, this 20-card standard-size set features Darren Daulton and John Kruk of the 1993 National League champion Philadelphia Phillies. The cards were inserted at a rate of one in six first series and one in 10 second series packs. Ten cards spotlight each player's career. Daulton and Kruk each signed more than 1,000 of their cards for random insertion. Moreover, the collector could receive four more cards (two of each player) through a mail-in offer by sending in ten 1994 series I wrappers plus 1.50 for postage and handling. The expiration for this redemption was September 30, 1994.

	Nm-Mt	Ex-Mt
COMPLETE SET (20)	10.00	3.00
COMPLETE SERIES 1 (10)	5.00	1.50
COMPLETE SERIES 2 (10)	5.00	1.50
COMMON (1-5/11-15)	.50	.15
COMMON (6-10/16-20)	.50	.15
COMMON MAIL-IN (M1-M4)	1.00	.30
AU1 Darren Daulton Certified Autograph	60.00	18.00
AU2 John Kruk Certified Autograph	60.00	18.00

1994 Ultra RBI Kings

Randomly inserted in first series jumbo packs at a rate of one in 36, this 12-card standard-size set features RBI leaders. These horizontal, metallized cards have a color player photo on front that superimposes a player image.The backs have a write-up and a small color player photo. Cards 1-6 feature American League RBI Kings while cards 7-12 present National League RBI Kings.

	Nm-Mt	Ex-Mt
COMPLETE SET (12)	60.00	18.00
1 Albert Belle	3.00	.90
2 Frank Thomas	8.00	2.40
3 Joe Carter	3.00	.90
4 Juan Gonzalez	8.00	2.40
5 Cecil Fielder	3.00	.90
6 Carlos Baerga	1.50	.45
7 Barry Bonds	20.00	6.00
8 David Justice	3.00	.90
9 Ron Gant	1.50	.45
10 Mike Piazza	15.00	4.50
11 Matt Williams	3.00	.90
12 Darren Daulton	3.00	.90

1994 Ultra Rising Stars

Randomly inserted in second series foil packs and jumbo packs at a rate of one in 36, this 12-card set spotlights top young major league stars.

	Nm-Mt	Ex-Mt
COMPLETE SET (12)	60.00	18.00
1 Carlos Baerga	2.00	.60
2 Jeff Bagwell	6.00	1.80
3 Albert Belle	4.00	1.20
4 Cliff Floyd	4.00	1.20
5 Travis Fryman	4.00	1.20
6 Marquis Grissom	2.00	.60
7 Kenny Lofton	4.00	1.20
8 John Olerud	4.00	1.20
9 Mike Piazza	20.00	6.00
10 Kirk Rueter	4.00	1.20
11 Tim Salmon	6.00	1.80
12 Aaron Sele	2.00	.60

1994 Ultra Second Year Standouts

Randomly inserted in all first series packs at a rate of one in 11, this 10-card standard-size set included 10 1993 outstanding rookies who are destined to become future stars. The set is arranged in alphabetical order according to American League (1-5) and National League (6-10) players.

	Nm-Mt	Ex-Mt
COMPLETE SET (10)	10.00	3.00
1 Jason Bere	.60	.18
2 Brent Gates	.60	.18
3 Jeffrey Hammonds	.60	.18
4 Tim Salmon	2.00	.60
5 Aaron Sele	.60	.18
6 Chuck Carr	.60	.18
7 Jeff Conine	1.25	.35
8 Greg McMichael	.60	.18
9 Mike Piazza	6.00	1.80
10 Kevin Stocker	.60	.18

1994 Ultra Strikeout Kings

Randomly inserted in all second series packs at a rate of one in seven, this five-card standard-size set features top strikeout artists.

	Nm-Mt	Ex-Mt
COMPLETE SET (5)	4.00	1.20
1 Randy Johnson	1.25	.35
2 Mark Langston	.25	.07
3 Greg Maddux	2.00	.60
4 Jose Rijo	.25	.07
5 John Smoltz	.75	.23

1995 Ultra

This 450-card standard-size set was issued in two series. The first series contained 250 cards while the second series consisted of 200 cards. They were issued in 12-card packs (either hobby or retail) with a suggested retail price of $1.99. Also, 15-card pre-priced packs with a suggested retail of $2.69. Each pack contained two inserts: one is a Gold Medallion parallel while the other is from one of Ultra's many insert sets. "Hot Packs" contained nothing but insert cards. The full-bleed fronts feature the player's photo with the team name and player's name at the bottom. The "95 Fleer Ultra" logo is in the upper right corner. The backs have a two-photo design; one of which is a full-size duotone shot with the other being a full-color action shot. In each series the cards were grouped alphabetically within teams and checklisted alphabetically according to teams for each league with AL preceding NL.

	Nm-Mt	Ex-Mt
COMPLETE SET (450)	30.00	9.00
COMP. SERIES 1 (250)	18.00	5.50
COMP.SERIES 2 (200)	12.00	3.60
1 Brady Anderson	.30	.09
2 Sid Fernandez	.15	.04
3 Jeffrey Hammonds	.15	.04
4 Chris Hoiles	.15	.04
5 Ben McDonald	.15	.04
6 Mike Mussina	.75	.23
7 Rafael Palmeiro	.50	.15
8 Jack Voigt	.15	.04
9 Wes Chamberlain	.15	.04
10 Roger Clemens	1.50	.45
11 Chris Howard	.15	.04
12 Tim Naehring	.15	.04
13 Otis Nixon	.15	.04
14 Rich Rowland	.15	.04
15 Ken Ryan	.15	.04
16 John Valentin	.15	.04
17 Mo Vaughn	.30	.09
18 Brian Anderson	.15	.04
19 Chili Davis	.30	.09
20 Damion Easley	.15	.04
21 Jim Edmonds	.30	.09
22 Mark Langston	.15	.04
23 Tim Salmon	.50	.15
24 J.T. Snow	.30	.09
25 Chris Turner	.15	.04
26 Wilson Alvarez	.15	.04
27 Joey Cora	.15	.04
28 Alex Fernandez	.15	.04
29 Roberto Hernandez	.15	.04
30 Lance Johnson	.15	.04
31 Ron Karkovice	.15	.04
32 Kirk McCaskill	.15	.04
33 Tim Raines	.30	.09
34 Frank Thomas	.75	.23
35 Sandy Alomar Jr.	.15	.04
36 Albert Belle	.30	.09
37 Mark Clark	.15	.04
38 Kenny Lofton	.30	.09
39 Eddie Murray	.75	.23
40 Eric Plunk	.15	.04
41 Manny Ramirez	.30	.09
42 Jim Thome	.75	.23
43 Omar Vizquel	.30	.09
44 Danny Bautista	.15	.04
45 Junior Felix	.15	.04
46 Cecil Fielder	.30	.09
47 Chris Gomez	.15	.04
48 Chad Kreuter	.15	.04
49 Mike Moore	.15	.04
50 Tony Phillips	.15	.04
51 Alan Trammell	.50	.15
52 David Wells	.30	.09
53 Kevin Appier	.30	.09
54 Billy Brewer	.15	.04
55 David Cone	.30	.09
56 Greg Gagne	.15	.04
57 Bob Hamelin	.15	.04
58 Jose Lind	.15	.04
59 Brent Mayne	.15	.04
60 Brian McRae	.15	.04
61 Terry Shumpert	.15	.04
62 Ricky Bones	.15	.04
63 Mike Fetters	.15	.04
64 Darryl Hamilton	.15	.04
65 John Jaha	.15	.04
66 Graeme Lloyd	.15	.04
67 Matt Mieske	.15	.04
68 Kevin Seitzer	.15	.04
69 Jose Valentin	.15	.04
70 Turner Ward	.15	.04
71 Rick Aguilera	.15	.04
72 Rich Becker	.15	.04
73 Alex Cole	.15	.04
74 Scott Leius	.15	.04
75 Pat Meares	.15	.04
76 Kirby Puckett	.75	.23
77 Dave Stevens	.15	.04
78 Kevin Tapani	.15	.04
79 Matt Walbeck	.15	.04
80 Wade Boggs	.50	.15
81 Scott Kamieniecki	.15	.04
82 Pat Kelly	.15	.04
83 Jimmy Key	.30	.09
84 Paul O'Neill	.50	.15
85 Luis Polonia	.15	.04
86 Mike Stanley	.15	.04
87 Danny Tartabull	.15	.04
88 Bob Wickman	.15	.04
89 Mark Acre	.15	.04
90 Geronimo Berroa	.15	.04
91 Mike Bordick	.15	.04
92 Ron Darling	.15	.04
93 Stan Javier	.15	.04
94 Mark McGwire	2.00	.60
95 Troy Neel	.15	.04
96 Ruben Sierra	.15	.04
97 Terry Steinbach	.15	.04
98 Eric Anthony	.15	.04
99 Chris Bosio	.15	.04
100 Dave Fleming	.15	.04
101 Ken Griffey Jr.	1.25	.35
102 Reggie Jefferson	.15	.04
103 Randy Johnson	.75	.23
104 Edgar Martinez	.50	.15
105 Bill Risley	.15	.04
106 Dan Wilson	.15	.04
107 Cris Carpenter	.15	.04
108 Will Clark	.75	.23
109 Juan Gonzalez	.75	.23
110 Rusty Greer	.30	.09
111 David Hulse	.15	.04
112 Roger Pavlik	.15	.04
113 Ivan Rodriguez	.75	.23
114 Doug Strange	.15	.04
115 Matt Whiteside	.15	.04
116 Roberto Alomar	.75	.23
117 Brad Cornett	.15	.04
118 Carlos Delgado	.30	.09
119 Alex Gonzalez	.15	.04
120 Darren Hall	.15	.04
121 Pat Hentgen	.15	.04
122 Paul Molitor	.50	.15
123 Ed Sprague	.15	.04
124 Devon White	.30	.09
125 Tom Glavine	.50	.15
126 David Justice	.30	.09
127 Roberto Kelly	.15	.04
128 Mark Lemke	.15	.04
129 Greg Maddux	1.25	.35
130 Greg McMichael	.15	.04
131 Kent Mercker	.15	.04
132 Charlie O'Brien	.15	.04
133 John Smoltz	.50	.15
134 Willie Banks	.15	.04
135 Steve Buechele	.15	.04
136 Kevin Foster	.15	.04
137 Glenallen Hill	.15	.04
138 Rey Sanchez	.15	.04
139 Sammy Sosa	1.25	.35
140 Steve Trachsel	.15	.04
141 Rick Wilkins	.15	.04
142 Jeff Brantley	.15	.04
143 Hector Carrasco	.15	.04
144 Kevin Jarvis	.15	.04
145 Barry Larkin	.75	.23
146 Chuck McElroy	.15	.04
147 Jose Rijo	.15	.04
148 Johnny Ruffin	.15	.04
149 Deion Sanders	.50	.15
150 Eddie Taubensee	.15	.04
151 Dante Bichette	.30	.09
152 Ellis Burks	.30	.09
153 Joe Girardi	.15	.04
154 Charlie Hayes	.15	.04
155 Mike Kingery	.15	.04
156 Steve Reed	.15	.04
157 Kevin Ritz	.15	.04
158 Bruce Ruffin	.15	.04
159 Eric Young	.15	.04
160 Kurt Abbott	.15	.04
161 Chuck Carr	.15	.04

162 Chris Hammond .15 .04
163 Bryan Harvey .15 .04
164 Terry Mathews .15 .04
165 Yorkis Perez .15 .04
166 Pat Rapp .15 .04
167 Gary Sheffield .30 .09
168 Dave Weathers .15 .04
169 Jeff Bagwell .50 .15
170 Ken Caminiti .30 .09
171 Doug Drabek .15 .04
172 Steve Finley .30 .09
173 John Hudek .15 .04
174 Todd Jones .15 .04
175 James Mouton .15 .04
176 Shane Reynolds .15 .04
177 Scott Servais .15 .04
178 Tom Candiotti .15 .04
179 Omar Daal .15 .04
180 Darren Dreifort .15 .04
181 Eric Karros .30 .09
182 Ramon J.Martinez .15 .04
183 Raul Mondesi .30 .09
184 Henry Rodriguez .15 .04
185 Todd Worrell .15 .04
186 Moises Alou .30 .09
187 Sean Berry .15 .04
188 Wil Cordero .15 .04
189 Jeff Fassero .15 .04
190 Darrin Fletcher .15 .04
191 Butch Henry .15 .04
192 Ken Hill .15 .04
193 Mel Rojas .15 .04
194 John Wetteland .30 .09
195 Bobby Bonilla .30 .09
196 Rico Brogna .15 .04
197 Bobby Jones .15 .04
198 Jeff Kent .30 .09
199 Josias Manzanillo .15 .04
200 Kelly Stinnett .15 .04
201 Ryan Thompson .15 .04
202 Jose Vizcaino .15 .04
203 Lenny Dykstra .30 .09
204 Jim Eisenreich .15 .04
205 Dave Hollins .15 .04
206 Mike Lieberthal .30 .09
207 Mickey Morandini .15 .04
208 Bobby Munoz .15 .04
209 Curt Schilling .50 .15
210 Heathcliff Slocumb .15 .04
211 David West .15 .04
212 Dave Clark .15 .04
213 Steve Cooke .15 .04
214 Midre Cummings .15 .04
215 Carlos Garcia .15 .04
216 Jeff King .15 .04
217 Jon Lieber .15 .04
218 Orlando Merced .15 .04
219 Don Slaught .15 .04
220 Rick White .15 .04
221 Rene Arocha .15 .04
222 Bernard Gilkey .15 .04
223 Brian Jordan .30 .09
224 Tom Pagnozzi .15 .04
225 Vicente Palacios .15 .04
226 Geronimo Pena .15 .04
227 Ozzie Smith 1.25 .35
228 Allen Watson .15 .04
229 Mark Whiten .15 .04
230 Brad Ausmus .15 .04
231 Derek Bell .15 .04
232 Andy Benes .15 .04
233 Tony Gwynn 1.00 .30
234 Joey Hamilton .15 .04
235 Luis Lopez .15 .04
236 Pedro A.Martinez .15 .04
237 Scott Sanders .15 .04
238 Eddie Williams .15 .04
239 Rod Beck .15 .04
240 Dave Burba .15 .04
241 Darren Lewis .15 .04
242 Kirt Manwaring .15 .04
243 Mark Portugal .15 .04
244 Darryl Strawberry .50 .15
245 Robby Thompson .15 .04
246 Wm.VanLandingham .15 .04
247 Matt Williams .30 .09
248 Checklist .15 .04
249 Checklist .15 .04
250 Checklist .15 .04
251 Harold Baines .30 .09
252 Bret Barberie .15 .04
253 Armando Benitez .30 .09
254 Mike Devereaux .15 .04
255 Leo Gomez .15 .04
256 Jamie Moyer .30 .09
257 Arthur Rhodes .15 .04
258 Cal Ripken 2.50 .75
259 Luis Alicea .15 .04
260 Jose Canseco .75 .23
261 Scott Cooper .15 .04
262 Andre Dawson .30 .09
263 Mike Greenwell .15 .04
264 Aaron Sele .15 .04
265 Garret Anderson .30 .09
266 Chad Curtis .15 .04
267 Gary DiSarcina .15 .04
268 Chuck Finley .30 .09
269 Rex Hudler .15 .04
270 Andrew Lorraine .15 .04
271 Spike Owen .15 .04
272 Lee Smith .30 .09
273 Jason Bere .15 .04
274 Ozzie Guillen .15 .04
275 Norberto Martin .15 .04
276 Scott Ruffcorn .15 .04
277 Robin Ventura .30 .09
278 Carlos Baerga .15 .04
279 Jason Grimsley .15 .04
280 Dennis Martinez .30 .09
281 Charles Nagy .15 .04
282 Paul Sorrento .15 .04
283 Dave Winfield .30 .09
284 John Doherty .15 .04
285 Travis Fryman .30 .09
286 Kirk Gibson .30 .09
287 Lou Whitaker .30 .09
288 Gary Gaetti .30 .09
289 Tom Gordon .15 .04
290 Mark Gubicza .15 .04
291 Wally Joyner .30 .09
292 Mike Macfarlane .15 .04
293 Jeff Montgomery .15 .04
294 Jeff Cirillo .15 .04
295 Cal Eldred .15 .04
296 Pat Listach .15 .04
297 Jose Mercedes .15 .04
298 Dave Nilsson .15 .04
299 Duane Singleton .15 .04
300 Greg Vaughn .30 .09
301 Scott Erickson .15 .04
302 Denny Hocking .15 .04
303 Chuck Knoblauch .30 .09
304 Pat Mahomes .15 .04
305 Pedro Munoz .15 .04
306 Erik Schullstrom .15 .04
307 Jim Abbott .50 .15
308 Tony Fernandez .15 .04
309 Sterling Hitchcock .15 .04
310 Jim Leyritz .15 .04
311 Don Mattingly 2.00 .60
312 Jack McDowell .15 .04
313 Melido Perez .15 .04
314 Bernie Williams .50 .15
315 Scott Brosius .30 .09
316 Dennis Eckersley .30 .09
317 Brent Gates .15 .04
318 Rickey Henderson .75 .23
319 Steve Karsay .15 .04
320 Steve Ontiveros .15 .04
321 Bill Taylor .15 .04
322 Todd Van Poppel .15 .04
323 Bob Welch .15 .04
324 Bobby Ayala .15 .04
325 Mike Blowers .15 .04
326 Jay Buhner .30 .09
327 Felix Fermin .15 .04
328 Tino Martinez .50 .15
329 Marc Newfield .15 .04
330 Greg Pirkl .15 .04
331 Alex Rodriguez 2.00 .60
332 Kevin Brown .30 .09
333 John Burkett .15 .04
334 Jeff Frye .15 .04
335 Kevin Gross .15 .04
336 Dean Palmer .30 .09
337 Joe Carter .30 .09
338 Shawn Green .30 .09
339 Juan Guzman .15 .04
340 Mike Huff .15 .04
341 Al Leiter .30 .09
342 John Olerud .30 .09
343 Dave Stewart .30 .09
344 Todd Stottlemyre .15 .04
345 Steve Avery .15 .04
346 Jeff Blauser .15 .04
347 Chipper Jones .75 .23
348 Mike Kelly .15 .04
349 Ryan Klesko .30 .09
350 Javier Lopez .30 .09
351 Fred McGriff .50 .15
352 Jose Oliva .15 .04
353 Terry Pendleton .30 .09
354 Mike Stanton .15 .04
355 Tony Tarasco .15 .04
356 Mark Wohlers .15 .04
357 Jim Bullinger .15 .04
358 Shawon Dunston .15 .04
359 Mark Grace .50 .15
360 Derrick May .15 .04
361 Randy Myers .15 .04
362 Karl Rhodes .15 .04
363 Bret Boone .30 .09
364 Brian Dorsett .15 .04
365 Ron Gant .30 .09
366 Brian R.Hunter .15 .04
367 Hal Morris .15 .04
368 Jack Morris .30 .09
369 John Roper .15 .04
370 Reggie Sanders .30 .09
371 Pete Schourek .15 .04
372 John Smiley .15 .04
373 Marvin Freeman .15 .04
374 Andres Galarraga .30 .09
375 Mike Munoz .15 .04
376 David Nied .15 .04
377 Walt Weiss .15 .04
378 Greg Colbrunn .15 .04
379 Jeff Conine .30 .09
380 Charles Johnson .30 .09
381 Kurt Miller .15 .04
382 Robb Nen .30 .09
383 Benito Santiago .30 .09
384 Craig Biggio .50 .15
385 Tony Eusebio .15 .04
386 Luis Gonzalez .30 .09
387 Brian L.Hunter .30 .09
388 Darryl Kile .30 .09
389 Orlando Miller .15 .04
390 Phil Plantier .15 .04
391 Greg Swindell .15 .04
392 Billy Ashley .15 .04
393 Pedro Astacio .15 .04
394 Brett Butler .30 .09
395 Delino DeShields .15 .04
396 Orel Hershiser .30 .09
397 Garey Ingram .15 .04
398 Chan Ho Park .30 .09
399 Mike Piazza 1.25 .35
400 Ismael Valdes .15 .04
401 Tim Wallach .15 .04
402 Cliff Floyd .30 .09
403 Marquis Grissom .15 .04
404 Mike Lansing .15 .04
405 Pedro Martinez .75 .23
406 Kirk Rueter .15 .04
407 Tim Scott .15 .04
408 Jeff Shaw .15 .04
409 Larry Walker .50 .15
410 Rondell White .30 .09
411 John Franco .30 .09
412 Todd Hundley .15 .04
413 Jason Jacome .15 .04
414 Joe Orsulak .15 .04
415 Bret Saberhagen .30 .09
416 David Segui .15 .04
417 Darren Daulton .30 .09
418 Mariano Duncan .15 .04
419 Tommy Greene .15 .04
420 Gregg Jefferies .15 .04
421 John Kruk .30 .09
422 Kevin Stocker .15 .04
423 Jay Bell .30 .09
424 Al Martin .15 .04
425 Denny Neagle .30 .09
426 Zane Smith .15 .04
427 Andy Van Slyke .30 .09
428 Paul Wagner .15 .04
429 Tom Henke .15 .04
430 Danny Jackson .15 .04
431 Ray Lankford .15 .04
432 John Mabry .15 .04
433 Bob Tewksbury .15 .04
434 Todd Zeile .15 .04
435 Andy Ashby .15 .04
436 Andujar Cedeno .15 .04
437 Donnie Elliott .15 .04
438 Bryce Florie .15 .04
439 Trevor Hoffman .30 .09
440 Melvin Nieves .15 .04
441 Bip Roberts .15 .04
442 Barry Bonds 2.00 .60
443 Royce Clayton .15 .04
444 Mike Jackson .15 .04
445 John Patterson .15 .04
446 J.R. Phillips .15 .04
447 Bill Swift .15 .04
448 Checklist .15 .04
449 Checklist .15 .04
450 Checklist .15 .04

1995 Ultra Gold Medallion

This 450-card parallels the regular Ultra issue. These cards were issued one per pack and are differentiated from the regular cards by the Ultra logo being replaced by the "Ultra Gold Medallion Edition logo."

Nm-Mt Ex-Mt
COMPLETE SET (450) 110.00 33.00
COMP. SERIES 1 (250) 60.00 18.00
COMP. SERIES 2 (200) 50.00 15.00
*STARS: 1.25X TO 3X BASIC CARDS.

1995 Ultra All-Rookies

This 10-card standard-size set features rookies who emerged with an impact in 1994. These cards were inserted one in every five second series packs. The cards are numbered in the lower left as "X" of 10 and are sequenced in alphabetical order.

Nm-Mt Ex-Mt
COMPLETE SET (10) 5.00 1.50
*GOLD MEDAL: .75X TO 2X BASIC AR
GM SER.2 STATED ODDS 1:50
1 Cliff Floyd .75 .23
2 Chris Gomez .40 .12
3 Rusty Greer .75 .23
4 Bob Hamelin .40 .12
5 Joey Hamilton .40 .12
6 John Hudek .40 .12
7 Ryan Klesko .75 .23
8 Raul Mondesi .75 .23
9 Manny Ramirez .75 .23
10 Steve Trachsel .40 .12

1995 Ultra All-Stars

This 20-card standard-size set feature players who are considered to be the top players in the game. Cards were inserted one in every four second series packs. The fronts feature two photos. The cards are numbered in the bottom left as "X" of 20 and are sequenced in alphabetical order.

Nm-Mt Ex-Mt
COMPLETE SET (20) 15.00 4.50
*GOLD MEDAL: .75X TO 2X BASIC ALL-STARS
GM SER.2 STATED ODDS 1:40
1 Moises Alou .50 .15
2 Albert Belle .50 .15
3 Craig Biggio .75 .23
4 Wade Boggs .75 .23
5 Barry Bonds 3.00 .90
6 David Cone .50 .15
7 Ken Griffey Jr. 2.00 .60
8 Tony Gwynn 1.50 .45
9 Chuck Knoblauch .50 .15
10 Barry Larkin 1.25 .35
11 Kenny Lofton .50 .15
12 Greg Maddux 2.00 .60
13 Fred McGriff .75 .23
14 Paul O'Neill .75 .23
15 Mike Piazza 2.00 .60
16 Kirby Puckett 1.25 .35
17 Cal Ripken 4.00 1.20
18 Ivan Rodriguez 1.25 .35
19 Frank Thomas 1.25 .35
20 Matt Williams .50 .15

1995 Ultra Award Winners

Featuring players who won major awards in 1994, this 25-card standard-size set was inserted one in every four first series packs. The cards are numbered as "X" of 25.

Nm-Mt Ex-Mt
COMPLETE SET (25) 20.00 6.00
*GOLD MEDAL: .75X TO 2X BASIC BASIC AW

GM SER.1 STATED ODDS 1:40
1 Ivan Rodriguez 1.25 .35
2 Don Mattingly 3.00 .90
3 Roberto Alomar 1.25 .35
4 Wade Boggs .75 .23
5 Omar Vizquel .50 .15
6 Ken Griffey Jr. 2.00 .60
7 Kenny Lofton .50 .15
8 Devon White .50 .15
9 Mark Langston .25 .07
10 Tom Pagnozzi .25 .07
11 Jeff Bagwell .75 .23
12 Craig Biggio .75 .23
13 Matt Williams .50 .15
14 Barry Larkin 1.25 .35
15 Barry Bonds 3.00 .90
16 Marquis Grissom .25 .07
17 Darren Lewis .25 .07
18 Greg Maddux 2.00 .60
19 Frank Thomas 1.25 .35
20 Jeff Bagwell .75 .23
21 David Cone .50 .15
22 Greg Maddux 2.00 .60
23 Bob Hamelin .25 .07
24 Raul Mondesi .50 .15
25 Moises Alou .50 .15

1995 Ultra Gold Medallion Rookies

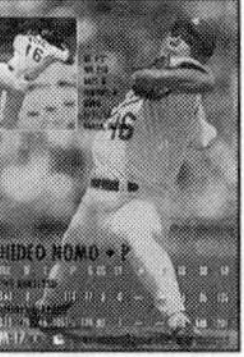

This 20-card standard-size set was available through a mail-in wrapper offer that expired 9/30/95. These players featured were all rookies in 1995 and were not included in the regular Ultra set. The design is essentially the same as the corresponding basic cards save for the medallion in the upper left-hand corner. The cards are numbered with an "M" prefix. The set is sequenced in alphabetical order.

Nm-Mt Ex-Mt
COMPLETE SET (20) 8.00 2.40
M1 Manny Alexander .25 .07
M2 Edgardo Alfonzo .50 .15
M3 Jason Bates .25 .07
M4 Andres Berumen .25 .07
M5 Darren Bragg .25 .07
M6 Jamie Brewington .25 .07
M7 Jason Christiansen .25 .07
M8 Brad Clontz .25 .07
M9 Marty Cordova .25 .07
M10 Johnny Damon .75 .23
M11 Vaughn Eshelman .25 .07
M12 Chad Fonville .25 .07
M13 Curtis Goodwin .25 .07
M14 Tyler Green .25 .07
M15 Bobby Higginson 1.25 .35
M16 Jason Isringhausen .50 .15
M17 Hideo Nomo 2.50 .75
M18 Jon Nunnally .25 .07
M19 Carlos Perez .50 .15
M20 Julian Tavarez .25 .07

1995 Ultra Golden Prospects

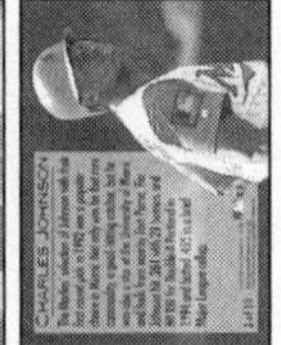

Inserted one every eight first series hobby packs, this 10-card standard-size set features potential impact players. The cards are numbered as "X" of 10 and are sequenced alphabetically.

Nm-Mt Ex-Mt
COMPLETE SET (10) 10.00 3.00
*GOLD MEDAL: .75X TO 2X BASIC PROSPECTS
GM SER.1 STATED ODDS 1:80
1 James Baldwin .50 .15
2 Alan Benes .50 .15
3 Armando Benitez 1.00 .30
4 Ray Durham 1.00 .30
5 LaTroy Hawkins .50 .15
6 Brian L.Hunter .50 .15
7 Derek Jeter 4.00 1.20
8 Charles Johnson 1.00 .30
9 Alex Rodriguez 4.00 1.20
10 Michael Tucker .50 .15

1995 Ultra Hitting Machines

This 10-card standard-size set features some of baseball's leading batters. Inserted one in every eight second-series retail packs, these horizontal cards have the player's photo against a background of the words "Hitting Machine." The cards are numbered as "X" of 10 in the

upper right and are sequenced in alphabetical order.

Nm-Mt Ex-Mt
COMPLETE SET (10) 12.00 3.60
*GOLD MEDAL: .75X TO 2X BASIC HIT.MACH.
GM SER.2 STATED ODDS 1:80 RETAIL
1 Jeff Bagwell .75 .23
2 Albert Belle .50 .15
3 Dante Bichette .50 .15
4 Barry Bonds 3.00 .90
5 Jose Canseco 1.25 .35
6 Ken Griffey Jr. 2.00 .60
7 Tony Gwynn 1.50 .45
8 Fred McGriff .75 .23
9 Mike Piazza 2.00 .60
10 Frank Thomas 1.25 .35

1995 Ultra Home Run Kings

This 10-card standard-size set featured the five leading home run hitters in each league. These cards were issued one every eight first series retail packs. The cards are numbered as "X" of 10 and are sequenced by league according to 1994's home rum standings. A Barry Bonds sample card was issued to dealers to prior to the release of 1995 Ultra.

Nm-Mt Ex-Mt
COMPLETE SET (10) 30.00 9.00
*GOLD MEDAL: .75X TO 2X BASIC HR KINGS
GM SER.1 STATED ODDS 1:80 RETAIL
1 Ken Griffey Jr. 5.00 1.50
2 Frank Thomas 3.00 .90
3 Albert Belle 1.25 .35
4 Jose Canseco 3.00 .90
5 Cecil Fielder 1.25 .35
6 Matt Williams 1.25 .35
7 Jeff Bagwell 2.00 .60
8 Barry Bonds 8.00 2.40
9 Fred McGriff 2.00 .60
10 Andres Galarraga 1.25 .35
S8 Barry Bonds Sample 2.00 .60

1995 Ultra League Leaders

This 10-card standard-size set was inserted one every three first series packs.

Nm-Mt Ex-Mt
COMPLETE SET (10) 6.00 1.80
*GOLD MEDAL: .75X TO 2X BASIC LL
GM SER.1 STATED ODDS 1:30
1 Paul O'Neill .75 .23
2 Kenny Lofton .50 .15
3 Jimmy Key .50 .15
4 Randy Johnson 1.25 .35
5 Lee Smith .50 .15
6 Tony Gwynn 1.50 .45
7 Craig Biggio .75 .23
8 Greg Maddux 2.00 .60
9 Andy Benes .25 .07
10 John Franco .50 .15

1995 Ultra On-Base Leaders

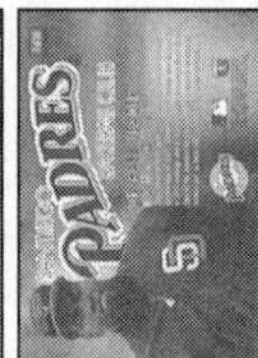

This 10-card standard-size set features ten players who are constantly reaching base safely. These cards were inserted one in every eight pre-priced second series jumbo packs. The cards are numbered in the upper right corner as "X" of 10 and are sequenced in alphabetical order.

Nm-Mt Ex-Mt
COMPLETE SET (10) 40.00 12.00
*GOLD MEDAL: .75X TO 2X BASIC OBL
GM SER.2 STATED ODDS 1:80 JUMBO
1 Jeff Bagwell 3.00 .90
2 Albert Belle 2.00 .60
3 Craig Biggio 3.00 .90
4 Wade Boggs 3.00 .90
5 Barry Bonds 12.00 3.60
6 Will Clark 5.00 1.50

7 Tony Gwynn 6.00 1.80
8 David Justice 2.00 .60
9 Paul O'Neill 3.00 .90
10 Frank Thomas 5.00 1.50

1995 Ultra Power Plus

This six-card standard-size set was inserted one in every 37 first series packs. The six players portrayed are not only sluggers, but also excel at another part of the game. Unlike the 1995 Ultra cards and the other insert sets, these cards are 100 percent foil. The cards are numbered on the bottom right as "X" of 6 and are sequenced in alphabetical order by league.

Nm-Mt Ex-Mt
COMPLETE SET (6) 25.00 7.50
*GOLD MEDAL: .75X TO 2X BASIC PLUS
GM SER.1 STATED ODDS 1:370
1 Albert Belle 1.50 .45
2 Ken Griffey Jr. 6.00 1.80
3 Frank Thomas 4.00 1.20
4 Jeff Bagwell 2.50 .75
5 Barry Bonds 10.00 3.00
6 Matt Williams 1.50 .45

1995 Ultra RBI Kings

This 10-card standard-size set was inserted into series one jumbo packs at a rate of one every 11. The cards are numbered in the upper left as "X" of 10 and are sequenced in order by league.

Nm-Mt Ex-Mt
COMPLETE SET (10) 30.00 9.00
*GOLD MEDAL: .75X TO 2X BASIC RBI KINGS
GM SER.1 STATED ODDS 1:110 JUMBO
1 Kirby Puckett 5.00 1.50
2 Joe Carter 2.00 .60
3 Albert Belle 2.00 .60
4 Frank Thomas 5.00 1.50
5 Julio Franco 1.00 .30
6 Jeff Bagwell 3.00 .90
7 Matt Williams 2.00 .60
8 Dante Bichette 2.00 .60
9 Fred McGriff 3.00 .90
10 Mike Piazza 8.00 2.40

1995 Ultra Rising Stars

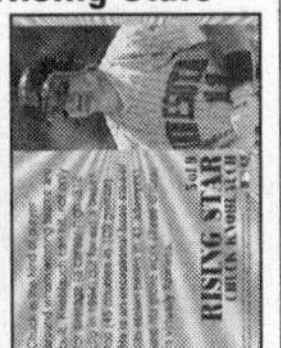

This nine-card standard-size set was inserted one every 37 second series packs. The cards are numbered "X" of 9 and are sequenced in alphabetical order.

Nm-Mt Ex-Mt
COMPLETE SET (9) 40.00 12.00
*GOLD MEDAL: .75X TO 2X BASIC RISING
GM SER.2 STATED ODDS 1:370
1 Moises Alou 3.00 .90
2 Jeff Bagwell 5.00 1.50
3 Albert Belle 3.00 .90
4 Juan Gonzalez 8.00 2.40
5 Chuck Knoblauch 3.00 .90
6 Kenny Lofton 3.00 .90
7 Raul Mondesi 3.00 .90
8 Mike Piazza 12.00 3.60
9 Frank Thomas 8.00 2.40

1995 Ultra Second Year Standouts

This 15-card standard-size set was inserted into first series packs at a rate of not greater than one in six packs. The players in this set were all rookies in 1994 whom big things were expected from in 1995. The cards are numbered in the lower right as "X" of 15 and are sequenced in alphabetical order.

Nm-Mt Ex-Mt
COMPLETE SET (15) 8.00 2.40
*GOLD MEDAL: .75X TO 2X BASIC 2YS
GM SER.1 STATED ODDS 1:60
1 Cliff Floyd 1.25 .35
2 Chris Gomez .60 .18
3 Rusty Greer 1.25 .35
4 Darren Hall .60 .18
5 Bob Hamelin .60 .18
6 Joey Hamilton .60 .18
7 Jeffrey Hammonds .60 .18
8 John Hudek .60 .18
9 Ryan Klesko 1.25 .35
10 Raul Mondesi 1.25 .35
11 Manny Ramirez 1.25 .35
12 Bill Risley .60 .18
13 Steve Trachsel .60 .18
14 W.VanLandingham .60 .18
15 Rondell White 1.25 .35

1995 Ultra Strikeout Kings

This six-card standard-size set was inserted one every five second series packs. The cards are numbered as "X" of 6 and are sequenced in alphabetical order.

Nm-Mt Ex-Mt
COMPLETE SET (6) 5.00 1.50
*GOLD MEDAL: .75X TO 2X BASIC K KINGS
GM SER.2 STATED ODDS 1:50
1 Andy Benes .25 .07
2 Roger Clemens 2.50 .75
3 Randy Johnson 1.25 .35
4 Greg Maddux 2.00 .60
5 Pedro Martinez 1.25 .35
6 Jose Rijo .25 .07

1996 Ultra Promos

This six card standard-size set previews the 1996 Ultra series. The Griffey card represents the basic set and has the same front and back as its regular issue counterpart. The Bonds and Ripken cards are from insert series and carry advertisements on their backs. The Gwynn and Lofton cards hail from the Season Crowns insert. Each card has the disclaimer "PROMOTIONAL SAMPLE" stamped diagonally across it.

Nm-Mt Ex-Mt
COMPLETE SET (6) 8.00 2.40
SC2 Tony Gwynn 1.50 .45
Season Crown
SC4 Kenny Lofton .75 .23
Season Crown
NNO Roberto Alomar .75 .23
Prime Leather
NNO Ken Griffey Jr. 2.00 .60
NNO Cal Ripken 3.00 .90
Prime Leather
NNO Barry Bonds 1.50 .45
HR King

1996 Ultra

The 1996 Ultra set, produced by Fleer, contains 600 standard-size cards. The cards were distributed in packs that included two inserts. One insert is a Gold Medallion parallel while the other insert comes from one of the many Ultra insert sets. The cards are thicker than their 1995 counterparts and the fronts feature the player in an action shot in full-bleed color. The cards are sequenced in alphabetical order within league and team order.

Nm-Mt Ex-Mt
COMPLETE SET (600) 50.00 15.00
COMP.SERIES 1 (300) 25.00 7.50
COMP.SERIES 2 (300) 25.00 7.50
1 Manny Alexander .30 .09
2 Brady Anderson .30 .09
3 Bobby Bonilla .30 .09
4 Scott Erickson .30 .09
5 Curtis Goodwin .30 .09
6 Chris Hoiles .30 .09
7 Doug Jones .30 .09
8 Jeff Manto .30 .09
9 Mike Mussina .75 .23
10 Rafael Palmeiro .50 .15
11 Cal Ripken 2.50 .75
12 Rick Aguilera .30 .09
13 Luis Alicea .30 .09
14 Stan Belinda .30 .09
15 Jose Canseco .75 .23
16 Roger Clemens 1.50 .45
17 Mike Greenwell .30 .09
18 Mike Macfarlane .30 .09
19 Tim Naehring .30 .09
20 Troy O'Leary .30 .09
21 John Valentin .30 .09
22 Mo Vaughn .30 .09
23 Tim Wakefield .30 .09
24 Brian Anderson .30 .09
25 Garret Anderson .30 .09
26 Chili Davis .30 .09
27 Gary DiSarcina .30 .09
28 Jim Edmonds .30 .09
29 Jorge Fabregas .30 .09
30 Chuck Finley .30 .09
31 Mark Langston .30 .09
32 Troy Percival .30 .09
33 Tim Salmon .50 .15
34 Lee Smith .30 .09
35 Wilson Alvarez .30 .09
36 Ray Durham .30 .09
37 Alex Fernandez .30 .09
38 Ozzie Guillen .30 .09
39 Roberto Hernandez .30 .09
40 Lance Johnson .30 .09
41 Ron Karkovice .30 .09
42 Lyle Mouton .30 .09
43 Tim Raines .30 .09
44 Frank Thomas .75 .23
45 Carlos Baerga .30 .09
46 Albert Belle .30 .09
47 Orel Hershiser .30 .09
48 Kenny Lofton .30 .09
49 Dennis Martinez .30 .09
50 Jose Mesa .30 .09
51 Eddie Murray .75 .23
52 Chad Ogea .30 .09
53 Manny Ramirez .30 .09
54 Jim Thome .75 .23
55 Omar Vizquel .30 .09
56 Dave Winfield .30 .09
57 Chad Curtis .30 .09
58 Cecil Fielder .30 .09
59 John Flaherty .30 .09
60 Travis Fryman .30 .09
61 Chris Gomez .30 .09
62 Bob Higginson .30 .09
63 Felipe Lira .30 .09
64 Brian Maxcy .30 .09
65 Alan Trammell .50 .15
66 Lou Whitaker .30 .09
67 Kevin Appier .30 .09
68 Gary Gaetti .30 .09
69 Tom Goodwin .30 .09
70 Tom Gordon .30 .09
71 Jason Jacome .30 .09
72 Wally Joyner .30 .09
73 Brent Mayne .30 .09
74 Jeff Montgomery .30 .09
75 Jon Nunnally .30 .09
76 Joe Vitiello .30 .09
77 Ricky Bones .30 .09
78 Jeff Cirillo .30 .09
79 Mike Fetters .30 .09
80 Darryl Hamilton .30 .09
81 David Hulse .30 .09
82 Dave Nilsson .30 .09
83 Kevin Seitzer .30 .09
84 Steve Sparks .30 .09
85 B.J. Surhoff .30 .09
86 Jose Valentin .30 .09
87 Greg Vaughn .30 .09
88 Marty Cordova .30 .09
89 Chuck Knoblauch .30 .09
90 Pat Meares .30 .09
91 Pedro Munoz .30 .09
92 Kirby Puckett .75 .23
93 Brad Radke .30 .09
94 Scott Stahoviak .30 .09
95 Dave Stevens .30 .09
96 Mike Trombley .30 .09
97 Matt Walbeck .30 .09
98 Wade Boggs .50 .15
99 Russ Davis .30 .09
100 Jim Leyritz .30 .09
101 Don Mattingly 2.00 .60
102 Jack McDowell .30 .09
103 Paul O'Neill .50 .15
104 Andy Pettitte .50 .15
105 Mariano Rivera .50 .15
106 Ruben Sierra .30 .09
107 Darryl Strawberry .50 .15
108 John Wetteland .30 .09
109 Bernie Williams .50 .15
110 Geronimo Berroa .30 .09
111 Scott Brosius .30 .09
112 Dennis Eckersley .30 .09
113 Brent Gates .30 .09
114 Rickey Henderson .75 .23
115 Mark McGwire 2.00 .60
116 Ariel Prieto .30 .09
117 Terry Steinbach .30 .09
118 Todd Stottlemyre .30 .09
119 Todd Van Poppel .30 .09
120 Steve Wojciechowski .30 .09
121 Rich Amaral .30 .09
122 Bobby Ayala .30 .09
123 Mike Blowers .30 .09
124 Chris Bosio .30 .09
125 Joey Cora .30 .09
126 Ken Griffey Jr. 1.25 .35
127 Randy Johnson .75 .23
128 Edgar Martinez .50 .15
129 Tino Martinez .50 .15
130 Alex Rodriguez 1.50 .45
131 Dan Wilson .30 .09
132 Will Clark .75 .23
133 Jeff Frye .30 .09
134 Benji Gil .30 .09
135 Juan Gonzalez .75 .23
136 Rusty Greer .30 .09
137 Mark McLemore .30 .09
138 Roger Pavlik .30 .09
139 Ivan Rodriguez .75 .23
140 Kenny Rogers .30 .09
141 Mickey Tettleton .30 .09
142 Roberto Alomar .75 .23
143 Joe Carter .30 .09
144 Tony Castillo .30 .09
145 Alex Gonzalez .30 .09
146 Shawn Green .30 .09
147 Pat Hentgen .30 .09
148 Sandy Martinez .30 .09
149 Paul Molitor .50 .15
150 John Olerud .30 .09
151 Ed Sprague .30 .09
152 Jeff Blauser .30 .09
153 Brad Clontz .30 .09
154 Tom Glavine .50 .15
155 Marquis Grissom .30 .09
156 Chipper Jones .75 .23
157 David Justice .30 .09
158 Ryan Klesko .30 .09
159 Javier Lopez .30 .09
160 Greg Maddux 1.25 .35
161 John Smoltz .50 .15
162 Mark Wohlers .30 .09
163 Jim Bullinger .30 .09
164 Frank Castillo .30 .09
165 Shawon Dunston .30 .09
166 Kevin Foster .30 .09
167 Luis Gonzalez .30 .09
168 Mark Grace .50 .15
169 Rey Sanchez .30 .09
170 Scott Servais .30 .09
171 Sammy Sosa 1.25 .35
172 Ozzie Timmons .30 .09
173 Steve Trachsel .30 .09
174 Bret Boone .30 .09
175 Jeff Branson .30 .09
176 Jeff Brantley .30 .09
177 Dave Burba .30 .09
178 Ron Gant .30 .09
179 Barry Larkin .75 .23
180 Darren Lewis .30 .09
181 Mark Portugal .30 .09
182 Reggie Sanders .30 .09
183 Pete Schourek .30 .09
184 John Smiley .30 .09
185 Jason Bates .30 .09
186 Dante Bichette .30 .09
187 Ellis Burks .30 .09
188 Vinny Castilla .30 .09
189 Andres Galarraga .30 .09
190 Darren Holmes .30 .09
191 Armando Reynoso .30 .09
192 Kevin Ritz .30 .09
193 Bill Swift .30 .09
194 Larry Walker .50 .15
195 Kurt Abbott .30 .09
196 John Burkett .30 .09
197 Greg Colbrunn .30 .09
198 Jeff Conine .30 .09
199 Andre Dawson .30 .09
200 Chris Hammond .30 .09
201 Charles Johnson .30 .09
202 Robb Nen .30 .09
203 Terry Pendleton .30 .09
204 Quilvio Veras .30 .09
205 Jeff Bagwell .50 .15
206 Derek Bell .30 .09
207 Doug Drabek .30 .09
208 Tony Eusebio .30 .09
209 Mike Hampton .30 .09
210 Brian L. Hunter .30 .09
211 Todd Jones .30 .09
212 Orlando Miller .30 .09
213 James Mouton .30 .09
214 Shane Reynolds .30 .09
215 Dave Veres .30 .09
216 Billy Ashley .30 .09
217 Brett Butler .30 .09
218 Chad Fonville .30 .09
219 Todd Hollandsworth .30 .09
220 Eric Karros .30 .09
221 Ramon Martinez .30 .09
222 Raul Mondesi .30 .09
223 Hideo Nomo .75 .23
224 Mike Piazza 1.25 .35
225 Kevin Tapani .30 .09
226 Ismael Valdes .30 .09
227 Todd Worrell .30 .09
228 Moises Alou .30 .09
229 Wil Cordero .30 .09
230 Jeff Fassero .30 .09
231 Darrin Fletcher .30 .09
232 Mike Lansing .30 .09
233 Pedro Martinez .75 .23
234 Carlos Perez .30 .09
235 Mel Rojas .30 .09
236 David Segui .30 .09
237 Tony Tarasco .30 .09
238 Rondell White .30 .09
239 Edgardo Alfonzo .30 .09
240 Rico Brogna .30 .09
241 Carl Everett .30 .09
242 Todd Hundley .30 .09
243 Butch Huskey .30 .09
244 Jason Isringhausen .30 .09
245 Bobby Jones .30 .09
246 Jeff Kent .30 .09
247 Bill Pulsipher .30 .09
248 Jose Vizcaino .30 .09
249 Ricky Bottalico .30 .09
250 Darren Daulton .30 .09
251 Jim Eisenreich .30 .09
252 Tyler Green .30 .09
253 Charlie Hayes .30 .09
254 Gregg Jefferies .30 .09
255 Tony Longmire .30 .09
256 Michael Mimbs .30 .09
257 Mickey Morandini .30 .09
258 Paul Quantrill .30 .09
259 Heathcliff Slocumb .30 .09
260 Jay Bell .30 .09
261 Jacob Brumfield .30 .09
262 A.Encarnacion RC .30 .09
263 John Ericks .30 .09
264 Mark Johnson .30 .09
265 Esteban Loaiza .30 .09
266 Al Martin .30 .09
267 Orlando Merced .30 .09
268 Dan Miceli .30 .09
269 Denny Neagle .30 .09
270 Brian Barber .30 .09
271 Scott Cooper .30 .09
272 Tripp Cromer .30 .09
273 Bernard Gilkey .30 .09
274 Tom Henke .30 .09
275 Brian Jordan .30 .09
276 John Mabry .30 .09
277 Tom Pagnozzi .30 .09
278 Mark Petkovsek .30 .09
279 Ozzie Smith 1.25 .35
280 Andy Ashby .30 .09
281 Brad Ausmus .30 .09
282 Ken Caminiti .30 .09
283 Glenn Dishman .30 .09
284 Tony Gwynn 1.00 .30
285 Joey Hamilton .30 .09
286 Trevor Hoffman .30 .09
287 Phil Plantier .30 .09
288 Jody Reed .30 .09
289 Eddie Williams .30 .09
290 Barry Bonds 2.00 .60
291 Jamie Brewington RC .30 .09
292 Mark Carreon .30 .09
293 Royce Clayton .30 .09
294 Glenallen Hill .30 .09
295 Mark Leiter .30 .09
296 Kirt Manwaring .30 .09
297 J.R. Phillips .30 .09
298 Deion Sanders .50 .15
299 Wm. VanLandingham .30 .09
300 Matt Williams .30 .09
301 Roberto Alomar .75 .23
302 Armando Benitez .30 .09
303 Mike Devereaux .30 .09
304 Jeffrey Hammonds .30 .09
305 Jimmy Haynes .30 .09
306 Scott McClain .30 .09
307 Kent Mercker .30 .09
308 Randy Myers .30 .09
309 B.J. Surhoff .30 .09
310 Tony Tarasco .30 .09
311 David Wells .30 .09
312 Wil Cordero .30 .09
313 Alex Delgado .30 .09
314 Tom Gordon .30 .09
315 Dwayne Hosey .30 .09
316 Jose Malave .30 .09
317 Kevin Mitchell .30 .09
318 Jamie Moyer .30 .09
319 Aaron Sele .30 .09
320 Heathcliff Slocumb .30 .09
321 Mike Stanley .30 .09
322 Jeff Suppan .30 .09
323 Jim Abbott .50 .15
324 George Arias .30 .09
325 Todd Greene .30 .09
326 Bryan Harvey .30 .09
327 J.T. Snow .30 .09
328 Randy Velarde .30 .09
329 Tim Wallach .30 .09
330 Harold Baines .30 .09
331 Jason Bere .30 .09
332 Darren Lewis .30 .09
333 Norberto Martin .30 .09
334 Tony Phillips .30 .09
335 Bill Simas .30 .09
336 Chris Snopek .30 .09
337 Kevin Tapani .30 .09
338 Danny Tartabull .30 .09
339 Robin Ventura .30 .09
340 Sandy Alomar Jr. .30 .09
341 Julio Franco .30 .09
342 Jack McDowell .30 .09
343 Charles Nagy .30 .09
344 Julian Tavarez .30 .09
345 Kimera Bartee .30 .09
346 Greg Keagle .30 .09
347 Mark Lewis .30 .09
348 Jose Lima .30 .09
349 Melvin Nieves .30 .09
350 Mark Parent .30 .09
351 Eddie Williams .30 .09
352 Johnny Damon .30 .09
353 Sal Fasano .30 .09
354 Mark Gubicza .30 .09
355 Bob Hamelin .30 .09
356 Chris Haney .30 .09
357 Keith Lockhart .30 .09
358 Mike Macfarlane .30 .09
359 Jose Offerman .30 .09
360 Bip Roberts .30 .09
361 Michael Tucker .30 .09
362 Chuck Carr .30 .09
363 Bobby Hughes .30 .09
364 John Jaha .30 .09
365 Mark Loretta .30 .09
366 Mike Matheny .30 .09
367 Ben McDonald .30 .09
368 Matt Mieske .30 .09
369 Angel Miranda .30 .09
370 Fernando Vina .30 .09
371 Rick Aguilera .30 .09
372 Rich Becker .30 .09
373 LaTroy Hawkins .30 .09
374 Dave Hollins .30 .09
375 Roberto Kelly .30 .09
376 Matt Lawton RC .40 .12
377 Paul Molitor .50 .15
378 Dan Naulty .30 .09
379 Rich Robertson .30 .09
380 Frank Rodriguez .30 .09
381 David Cone .30 .09
382 Mariano Duncan .30 .09
383 Andy Fox .30 .09
384 Joe Girardi .30 .09
385 Dwight Gooden .50 .15
386 Derek Jeter 2.00 .60
387 Pat Kelly .30 .09
388 Jimmy Key .30 .09
389 Matt Luke .30 .09
390 Tino Martinez .50 .15
391 Jeff Nelson .30 .09
392 Melido Perez .30 .09
393 Tim Raines .30 .09
394 Ruben Rivera .30 .09
395 Kenny Rogers .30 .09
396 Tony Batista RC 1.50 .45
397 Allen Battle .30 .09
398 Mike Bordick .30 .09
399 Steve Cox .30 .09
400 Jason Giambi .75 .23
401 Doug Johns .30 .09
402 Pedro Munoz .30 .09
403 Phil Plantier .30 .09
404 Scott Spiezio .30 .09
405 George Williams .30 .09
406 Ernie Young .30 .09
407 Darren Bragg .30 .09
408 Jay Buhner .30 .09
409 Norm Charlton .30 .09
410 Russ Davis .30 .09
411 Sterling Hitchcock .30 .09
412 Edwin Hurtado .30 .09
413 Raul Ibanez RC 1.25 .35
414 Mike Jackson .30 .09
415 Luis Sojo .30 .09
416 Paul Sorrento .30 .09
417 Bob Wolcott .30 .09
418 Damon Buford .30 .09
419 Kevin Gross .30 .09
420 Darryl Hamilton UER .30 .09

421 Mike Henneman .30 .09
422 Ken Hill .30 .09
423 Dean Palmer .30 .09
424 Bobby Witt .30 .09
425 Tilson Brito RC .30 .09
426 Giovanni Carrara RC .30 .09
427 Domingo Cedeno .30 .09
428 Felipe Crespo .30 .09
429 Carlos Delgado .30 .09
430 Juan Guzman .30 .09
431 Erik Hanson .30 .09
432 Marty Janzen .30 .09
433 Otis Nixon .30 .09
434 Robert Perez .30 .09
435 Paul Quantrill .30 .09
436 Bill Risley .30 .09
437 Steve Avery .30 .09
438 Jermaine Dye .30 .09
439 Mark Lemke .30 .09
440 Marty Malloy RC .30 .09
441 Fred McGriff .50 .15
442 Greg McMichael .30 .09
443 Wonderful Monds RC .30 .09
444 Eddie Perez .30 .09
445 Jason Schmidt .30 .09
446 Terrell Wade .30 .09
447 Terry Adams .30 .09
448 Scott Bullett .30 .09
449 Robin Jennings .30 .09
450 Doug Jones .30 .09
451 Brooks Kieschnick .30 .09
452 Dave Magadan .30 .09
453 Jason Maxwell RC .30 .09
454 Brian McRae .30 .09
455 Rodney Myers RC .30 .09
456 Jaime Navarro .30 .09
457 Ryne Sandberg 1.25 .35
458 Vince Coleman .30 .09
459 Eric Davis .30 .09
460 Steve Gibralter .30 .09
461 Thomas Howard .30 .09
462 Mike Kelly .30 .09
463 Hal Morris .30 .09
464 Eric Owens .30 .09
465 Jose Rijo .30 .09
466 Chris Sabo .30 .09
467 Eddie Taubensee .30 .09
468 Trenidad Hubbard .30 .09
469 Curt Leskanic .30 .09
470 Quinton McCracken .30 .09
471 Jayhawk Owens .30 .09
472 Steve Reed .30 .09
473 Bryan Rekar .30 .09
474 Bruce Ruffin .30 .09
475 Bret Saberhagen .30 .09
476 Walt Weiss .30 .09
477 Eric Young .30 .09
478 Kevin Brown .30 .09
479 Al Leiter .30 .09
480 Pat Rapp .30 .09
481 Gary Sheffield .30 .09
482 Devon White .30 .09
483 Bob Abreu .30 .09
484 Sean Berry .30 .09
485 Craig Biggio .50 .15
486 Jim Dougherty .30 .09
487 Richard Hidalgo .30 .09
488 Darryl Kile .30 .09
489 Derrick May .30 .09
490 Greg Swindell .30 .09
491 Rick Wilkins .30 .09
492 Mike Blowers .30 .09
493 Tom Candiotti .30 .09
494 Roger Cedeno .30 .09
495 Delino DeShields .30 .09
496 Greg Gagne .30 .09
497 Karim Garcia .30 .09
498 Wilton Guerrero RC .40 .12
499 Chan Ho Park .30 .09
500 Israel Alcantara .30 .09
501 Shane Andrews .30 .09
502 Yamil Benitez .30 .09
503 Cliff Floyd .30 .09
504 Mark Grudzielanek .30 .09
505 Ryan McGuire .30 .09
506 Sherman Obando .30 .09
507 Jose Paniagua .30 .09
508 Henry Rodriguez .30 .09
509 Kirk Rueter .30 .09
510 Juan Acevedo .30 .09
511 John Franco .30 .09
512 Bernard Gilkey .30 .09
513 Lance Johnson .30 .09
514 Rey Ordonez .30 .09
515 Robert Person .30 .09
516 Paul Wilson .30 .09
517 Toby Borland .30 .09
518 David Doster RC .30 .09
519 Lenny Dykstra .30 .09
520 Sid Fernandez .30 .09
521 Mike Grace RC .30 .09
522 Rich Hunter .30 .09
523 Benito Santiago .30 .09
524 Gene Schall .30 .09
525 Curt Schilling .50 .15
526 Kevin Sefcik RC .30 .09
527 Lee Tinsley .30 .09
528 David West .30 .09
529 Mark Whiten .30 .09
530 Todd Zeile .30 .09
531 Carlos Garcia .30 .09
532 Charlie Hayes .30 .09
533 Jason Kendall .30 .09
534 Jeff King .30 .09
535 Mike Kingery .30 .09
536 Nelson Liriano .30 .09
537 Dan Plesac .30 .09
538 Paul Wagner .30 .09
539 Luis Alicea .30 .09
540 David Bell .30 .09
541 Alan Benes .30 .09
542 Andy Benes .30 .09
543 Mike Busby RC .30 .09
544 Royce Clayton .30 .09
545 Dennis Eckersley .30 .09
546 Gary Gaetti .30 .09
547 Ron Gant .30 .09
548 Aaron Holbert .30 .09
549 Ray Lankford .30 .09
550 T.J. Mathews .30 .09
551 Willie McGee .30 .09
552 Miguel Mejia .30 .09
553 Todd Stottlemyre .30 .09
554 Sean Bergman .30 .09
555 Willie Blair .30 .09
556 Andujar Cedeno .30 .09
557 Steve Finley .30 .09
558 Rickey Henderson .75 .23
559 Wally Joyner .30 .09
560 Scott Livingstone .30 .09
561 Marc Newfield .30 .09
562 Bob Tewksbury .30 .09
563 Fernando Valenzuela .30 .09
564 Rod Beck .30 .09
565 Doug Creek .30 .09
566 Shawon Dunston .30 .09
567 O.Fernandez RC .30 .09
568 Stan Javier .30 .09
569 Marcus Jensen .30 .09
570 Steve Scarsone .30 .09
571 Robby Thompson .30 .09
572 Allen Watson .30 .09
573 Roberto Alomar STA .30 .09
574 Jeff Bagwell STA .30 .09
575 Albert Belle STA .30 .09
576 Wade Boggs STA .30 .09
577 Barry Bonds STA .75 .23
578 Juan Gonzalez STA .50 .15
579 Ken Griffey Jr. STA .75 .23
580 Tony Gwynn STA .50 .15
581 Randy Johnson STA .50 .15
582 Chipper Jones STA .50 .15
583 Barry Larkin STA .30 .09
584 Kenny Lofton STA .30 .09
585 Greg Maddux STA .75 .23
586 Raul Mondesi STA .30 .09
587 Mike Piazza STA .75 .23
588 Cal Ripken STA 1.25 .35
589 Tim Salmon STA .30 .09
590 Frank Thomas STA .50 .15
591 Mo Vaughn STA .30 .09
592 Matt Williams STA .30 .09
593 Marty Cordova RAW .30 .09
594 Jim Edmonds RAW .30 .09
595 Cliff Floyd RAW .30 .09
596 Chipper Jones RAW .50 .15
597 Ryan Klesko RAW .30 .09
598 Raul Mondesi RAW .30 .09
599 Manny Ramirez RAW .30 .09
600 Ruben Rivera RAW .30 .09
DD1 C. Ripken DD 50.00 15.00
Issued through dealers
Serial numbered to 2131
DD2 Cal Ripken DD 25.00 7.50
Issued through a wrapper redemption

1996 Ultra Gold Medallion

The 1996 Ultra Gold Medallion is a parallel to the regular Ultra issue. The cards were inserted one per pack in both first and second series. The card consists of a full gold foil paper with a full-color player cut out on top. Backs are identical to the regular cards.

Nm-Mt Ex-Mt
COMPLETE SET (600) 200.00 60.00
COMP.SERIES 1 (300) 100.00 30.00
COMP.SERIES 2 (300) 100.00 30.00
*STARS: 1.25X TO 3X BASIC CARDS .
*ROOKIES: 1.25X TO 3X BASIC CARDS

1996 Ultra Call to the Hall

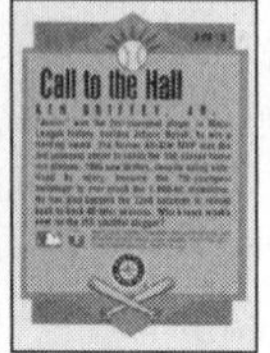

Randomly inserted in second series packs at a rate of one in 24, this ten-card set features original illustrations of possible future Hall of Famers. The backs state why the player is a possible HOF.

Nm-Mt Ex-Mt
COMPLETE SET (10) 60.00 18.00
*GOLD MEDAL: .75X TO 2X BASIC CALL
GM SER.2 STATED ODDS 1:240
1 Barry Bonds 12.00 3.60
2 Ken Griffey Jr. 8.00 2.40
3 Tony Gwynn 6.00 1.80
4 Rickey Henderson 5.00 1.50
5 Greg Maddux 8.00 2.40
6 Eddie Murray 5.00 1.50
7 Cal Ripken 15.00 4.50
8 Ryne Sandberg 8.00 2.40
9 Ozzie Smith 8.00 2.40
10 Frank Thomas 5.00 1.50

1996 Ultra Checklists

Randomly inserted in packs at a rate of one every four packs, this set of 20 standard-size cards features superstars of the game. Fronts are full-bleed color action photos of players with "Checklist" written in gold foil across the card. The horizontal backs are numbered and show the different card sets that are included in the Ultra line. The cards are sequenced in alphabetical order. A gold medallion parallel version of each card was issued.

Nm-Mt Ex-Mt
COMPLETE SERIES 1 (10) 10.00 3.00
COMPLETE SERIES 2 (10) 8.00 2.40
*GOLD MEDAL: .75X TO 2X BASIC CL
GM STATED ODDS 1:40
A1 Jeff Bagwell .60 .18
A2 Barry Bonds 2.50 .75
A3 Juan Gonzalez 1.00 .30
A4 Ken Griffey Jr. 1.50 .45
A5 Chipper Jones 1.00 .30
A6 Mike Piazza 1.50 .45
A7 Manny Ramirez .40 .12
A8 Cal Ripken 3.00 .90
A9 Frank Thomas 1.00 .30
A10 Matt Williams .40 .12
B1 Albert Belle .40 .12
B2 Cecil Fielder .40 .12
B3 Ken Griffey Jr. 1.50 .45
B4 Tony Gwynn 1.25 .35
B5 Derek Jeter 2.50 .75
B6 Jason Kendall .40 .12
B7 Ryan Klesko .40 .12
B8 Greg Maddux 1.50 .45
B9 Cal Ripken 3.00 .90
B10 Frank Thomas 1.00 .30

1996 Ultra Diamond Producers

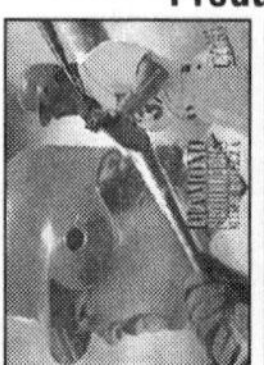

This 12-card standard-size set highlights the achievements of Major League stars. The cards were randomly inserted at a rate of one in 20. The cards are sequenced in alphabetical order and there are also gold medallion versions of these cards.

Nm-Mt Ex-Mt
COMPLETE SET (12) 60.00 18.00
*GOLD MEDAL: .75X TO 2X BASIC DIAMOND
GM SER.1 STATED ODDS 1:200
1 Albert Belle 1.50 .45
2 Barry Bonds 10.00 3.00
3 Ken Griffey Jr. 6.00 1.80
4 Tony Gwynn 5.00 1.50
5 Greg Maddux 6.00 1.80
6 Hideo Nomo 4.00 1.20
7 Mike Piazza 6.00 1.80
8 Kirby Puckett 4.00 1.20
9 Cal Ripken 12.00 3.60
10 Frank Thomas 4.00 1.20
11 Mo Vaughn 1.50 .45
12 Matt Williams 1.50 .45

1996 Ultra Fresh Foundations

Randomly inserted one every three packs, this 10-card standard-size set highlights the play of hot young players. The cards are sequenced in alphabetical order and there are also gold medallion versions of these cards.

Nm-Mt Ex-Mt
COMPLETE SET (10) 3.00 .90
*GOLD MEDAL: .75X TO 2X BASIC FRESH
GM SER.1 STATED ODDS 1:30
1 Garret Anderson .30 .09
2 Marty Cordova .30 .09
3 Jim Edmonds .30 .09
4 Brian L.Hunter .30 .09
5 Chipper Jones .75 .23
6 Ryan Klesko .30 .09
7 Raul Mondesi .30 .09
8 Hideo Nomo .75 .23
9 Manny Ramirez .30 .09
10 Rondell White .30 .09

1996 Ultra Golden Prospects

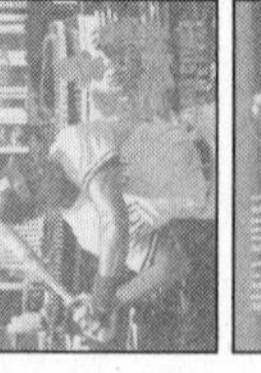

Randomly inserted at a rate of one in five hobby packs, this 10-card standard-size set features players who are likely to make it as major leaguers. The cards are sequenced in alphabetical order and there are also gold medallion versions of these cards.

Nm-Mt Ex-Mt
COMPLETE SET (10) 5.00 1.50
*GOLD MEDAL: .75X TO 2X BASIC GOLDEN
GM SER.1 STATED ODDS 1:50 HOBBY
1 Yamil Benitez .60 .18
2 Alberto Castillo .60 .18
3 Roger Cedeno .60 .18
4 Johnny Damon .60 .18
5 Micah Franklin .60 .18
6 Jason Giambi 1.50 .45
7 Jose Herrera .60 .18
8 Derek Jeter 4.00 1.20
9 Kevin Jordan .60 .18
10 Ruben Rivera .60 .18

1996 Ultra Golden Prospects Hobby

Randomly inserted in hobby packs only at a rate of one in 72, this 15-card set is printed on crystal card stock and showcases players awaiting their Major League debut. The backs carry some information about their accomplishments in the Minor Leagues. A first year card of Tony Batista is featured within this set.

Nm-Mt Ex-Mt
COMPLETE SET (15) 100.00 30.00
*GOLD MED: .75X TO 2X BASIC GOLD.HOB
GM SER.2 STATED ODDS 1:720 HOBBY
1 Bob Abreu 4.00 1.20
2 Israel Alcantara 4.00 1.20
3 Tony Batista 10.00 3.00
4 Mike Cameron 12.00 3.60
5 Steve Cox 4.00 1.20
6 Jermaine Dye 4.00 1.20
7 Wilton Guerrero 4.00 1.20
8 Richard Hidalgo 4.00 1.20
9 Raul Ibanez 10.00 3.00
10 Marty Janzen 4.00 1.20
11 Robin Jennings 4.00 1.20
12 Jason Maxwell 4.00 1.20
13 Scott McClain 4.00 1.20
14 Wonderful Monds 4.00 1.20
15 Chris Singleton 4.00 1.20

1996 Ultra Hitting Machines

Randomly inserted in second series packs at a rate of one in 288, this 10-card set features players who hit the ball hard and often.

Nm-Mt Ex-Mt
COMPLETE SET (10) 100.00 30.00
*GOLD MEDAL: .75X TO 2X BASIC HIT.MACH.
GM SER.2 STATED ODDS 1:2880
1 Albert Belle 6.00 1.80
2 Barry Bonds 40.00 12.00
3 Juan Gonzalez 15.00 4.50
4 Ken Griffey Jr. 25.00 7.50
5 Edgar Martinez 10.00 3.00
6 Rafael Palmeiro 10.00 3.00
7 Mike Piazza 25.00 7.50
8 Tim Salmon 10.00 3.00
9 Frank Thomas 15.00 4.50
10 Matt Williams 6.00 1.80

1996 Ultra Home Run Kings

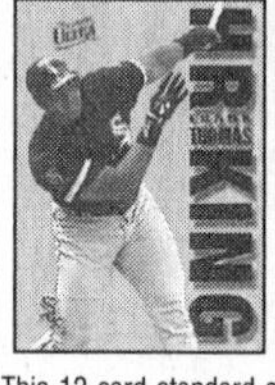

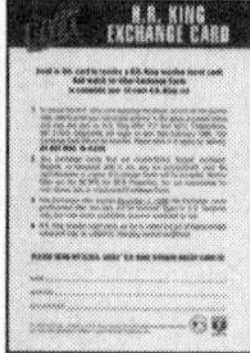

This 12-card standard-size set features leading power hitters. These cards were randomly inserted at a rate of one in 75 packs. The card fronts are thin wood with a color cut out of the player and HR KING printed diagonally in copper foil down the left side. The Fleer company was not happy with the final look of the card because of the transfer of the copper foil. Therefore all cards were made redemption cards. Backs of the cards have information about how to redeem the cards for replacement. The exchange offer expired on December 1, 1996. The cards are sequenced in alphabetical order.

Nm-Mt Ex-Mt
COMPLETE SET (12) 50.00 15.00
*GOLD MEDAL: 4X TO 10X BASIC HR KINGS
GM SER.1 STATED ODDS 1:750
*REDEMPTION: .6X TO 1.5X BASIC HR KINGS
ONE RDMP.CARD VIA MAIL PER HR CARD
1 Albert Belle 2.00 .60
2 Dante Bichette 2.00 .60
3 Barry Bonds 12.00 3.60
4 Jose Canseco 5.00 1.50
5 Juan Gonzalez 5.00 1.50
6 Ken Griffey Jr. 8.00 2.40
7 Mark McGwire 12.00 3.60
8 Manny Ramirez 2.00 .60
9 Tim Salmon 3.00 .90
10 Frank Thomas 5.00 1.50
11 Mo Vaughn 2.00 .60
12 Matt Williams 2.00 .60

1996 Ultra Home Run Kings Redemption Gold Medallion

These cards are parallel to the regular Home Run Kings Redemption cards. They are differentiated from the regular Home Run Kings Redemption cards by the Gold Medallion logo on the front of the cards.

Nm-Mt Ex-Mt
*GM REDEMPTION CARDS: 4X TO 10X BASIC HOME RUN KINGS

1996 Ultra On-Base Leaders

Randomly inserted in second series packs at a rate of one in four, this 10-card set features players with consistently high on-base percentage.

Nm-Mt Ex-Mt
COMPLETE SET (10) 5.00 1.50
*GOLD MEDAL: .75X TO 2X BASIC OBL
GM SER.2 STATED ODDS 1:40
1 Wade Boggs .60 .18
2 Barry Bonds 2.50 .75
3 Tony Gwynn 1.25 .35
4 Rickey Henderson 1.00 .30
5 Chuck Knoblauch .40 .12
6 Edgar Martinez .60 .18
7 Mike Piazza 1.50 .45
8 Tim Salmon .60 .18
9 Frank Thomas 1.00 .30
10 Jim Thome 1.00 .30

1996 Ultra Power Plus

Randomly inserted at a rate of one in ten packs, this 12-card standard-size set features top all-around players. The cards are sequenced in alphabetical order and gold medallion versions of these cards were also issued.

Nm-Mt Ex-Mt
COMPLETE SET (12) 25.00 7.50
*GOLD MEDAL: .75X TO 2X BASIC PLUS
GM SER.1 STATED ODDS 1:100
1 Jeff Bagwell 1.50 .45
2 Barry Bonds 6.00 1.80
3 Ken Griffey Jr. 4.00 1.20
4 Raul Mondesi 1.00 .30
5 Rafael Palmeiro 1.50 .45
6 Mike Piazza 4.00 1.20
7 Manny Ramirez 1.00 .30
8 Tim Salmon 1.50 .45
9 Reggie Sanders 1.00 .30
10 Frank Thomas 2.50 .75
11 Larry Walker 1.50 .45
12 Matt Williams 1.00 .30

1996 Ultra Prime Leather

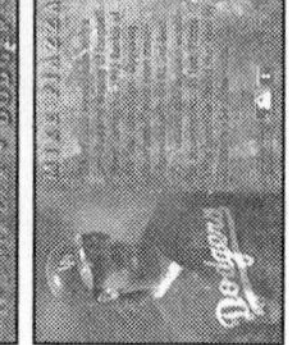

Eighteen outstanding defensive players are featured in this standard-size set which is inserted approximately one in every eight packs. The cards are sequenced in alphabetical order and gold medallion versions of these cards were also issued.

Nm-Mt Ex-Mt
COMPLETE SET (18) 25.00 7.50
*GOLD MEDAL: .75X TO 2X BASIC LEATHER
GM SER.1 STATED ODDS 1:80
1 Ivan Rodriguez 2.50 .75
2 Will Clark 2.50 .75
3 Roberto Alomar 2.50 .75
4 Cal Ripken 8.00 2.40
5 Wade Boggs 1.50 .45
6 Ken Griffey Jr. 4.00 1.20
7 Kenny Lofton 1.00 .30
8 Kirby Puckett 2.50 .75
9 Tim Salmon 1.50 .45
10 Mike Piazza 4.00 1.20
11 Mark Grace 1.50 .45
12 Craig Biggio 1.50 .45
13 Barry Larkin 2.50 .75
14 Matt Williams 1.00 .30
15 Barry Bonds 6.00 1.80
16 Tony Gwynn 3.00 .90
17 Brian McRae 1.00 .30
18 Raul Mondesi 1.00 .30
S4 Cal Ripken Jr Promo 8.00 2.40

1996 Ultra Rawhide

Randomly inserted in second series packs at a rate of one in eight, this 10-card set features leading defensive players.

Nm-Mt Ex-Mt
COMPLETE SET (10) 15.00 4.50
*GOLD MEDAL: .75X TO 2X BASIC RAWHIDE
GM SER.2 STATED ODDS 1:80
1 Roberto Alomar 1.50 .45
2 Barry Bonds 4.00 1.20

3 Mark Grace 1.00 .30
4 Ken Griffey Jr. 2.50 .75
5 Kenny Lofton .60 .18
6 Greg Maddux 2.50 .75
7 Raul Mondesi .60 .18
8 Mike Piazza 2.50 .75
9 Cal Ripken 5.00 1.50
10 Matt Williams .60 .18

1996 Ultra RBI Kings

This 10-card standard-size set was randomly inserted at a rate of one in five retail packs. The cards are sequenced in alphabetical order and gold medallion versions of these cards were also issued.

Nm-Mt Ex-Mt
COMPLETE SET (10) 30.00 9.00
*GOLD MEDAL: .75X TO 2X BASIC RBI KINGS
GM SER.1 STATED ODDS 1:50 RETAIL
1 Derek Bell 2.00 .60
2 Albert Belle 2.00 .60
3 Dante Bichette 2.00 .60
4 Barry Bonds 12.00 3.60
5 Jim Edmonds 2.00 .60
6 Manny Ramirez 2.00 .60
7 Reggie Sanders 2.00 .60
8 Sammy Sosa 8.00 2.40
9 Frank Thomas 5.00 1.50
10 Mo Vaughn 2.00 .60

1996 Ultra Respect

Randomly inserted in second series packs at a rate of one in 18, this 10-card set features players who are well regarded by their peers for both on and off field activies.

Nm-Mt Ex-Mt
COMPLETE SET (10) 50.00 15.00
*GOLD MEDAL: .75X TO 2X BASIC RESPECT
GM SER.2 STATED ODDS 1:180
1 Joe Carter 1.50 .45
2 Ken Griffey Jr. 6.00 1.80
3 Tony Gwynn 5.00 1.50
4 Greg Maddux 6.00 1.80
5 Eddie Murray 4.00 1.20
6 Kirby Puckett 4.00 1.20
7 Cal Ripken 12.00 3.60
8 Ryne Sandberg 6.00 1.80
9 Frank Thomas 4.00 1.20
10 Mo Vaughn 1.50 .45

1996 Ultra Rising Stars

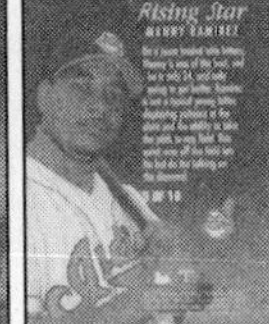

Randomly inserted in second series packs at a rate of one in four, this 10-card set features leading players of tomorrow.

Nm-Mt Ex-Mt
COMPLETE SET (10) 4.00 1.20
*GOLD MEDAL: .75X TO 2X BASIC RISING
GM SER.2 STATED ODDS 1:40
1 Garret Anderson .30 .09
2 Marty Cordova .30 .09
3 Jim Edmonds .30 .09
4 Cliff Floyd .30 .09
5 Brian L.Hunter .30 .09
6 Chipper Jones .75 .23
7 Ryan Klesko .30 .09
8 Hideo Nomo .75 .23
9 Manny Ramirez .30 .09
10 Rondell White .30 .09

1996 Ultra Season Crowns

This set features ten award winners and stat leaders. The cards were randomly inserted at a rate of one in ten. The clear acetate cards feature a full-color player cutout against a background of colored foliage and laurels.

Nm-Mt Ex-Mt
COMPLETE SET (10) 30.00 9.00

*GOLD MEDAL: .75X TO 2X BASIC CROWNS
GM SER.1 STATED ODDS 1:100
1 Barry Bonds 6.00 1.80
2 Tony Gwynn 3.00 .90
3 Randy Johnson 2.50 .75
4 Kenny Lofton 1.00 .30
5 Greg Maddux 4.00 1.20
6 Edgar Martinez 1.50 .45
7 Hideo Nomo 2.50 .75
8 Cal Ripken 8.00 2.40
9 Frank Thomas 2.50 .75
10 Tim Wakefield 1.00 .30

1996 Ultra Thunderclap

Randomly inserted one in 72 retail packs, these cards feature the leading power hitters.

Nm-Mt Ex-Mt
COMPLETE SET (20) 100.00 30.00
*GOLD MEDAL: .75X TO 2X BASIC THUNDER
GM SER.2 STATED ODDS 1:720 RETAIL
1 Albert Belle 5.00 1.50
2 Barry Bonds 30.00 9.00
3 Bobby Bonilla 5.00 1.50
4 Jose Canseco 12.00 3.60
5 Joe Carter 5.00 1.50
6 Will Clark 12.00 3.60
7 Andre Dawson 5.00 1.50
8 Cecil Fielder 5.00 1.50
9 Andres Galarraga 5.00 1.50
10 Juan Gonzalez 12.00 3.60
11 Ken Griffey Jr. 20.00 6.00
12 Fred McGriff 8.00 2.40
13 Mark McGwire 30.00 9.00
14 Eddie Murray 12.00 3.60
15 Rafael Palmeiro 8.00 2.40
16 Kirby Puckett 12.00 3.60
17 Cal Ripken 40.00 12.00
18 Ryne Sandberg 25.00 7.50
19 Frank Thomas 12.00 3.60
20 Matt Williams 5.00 1.50

1997 Ultra

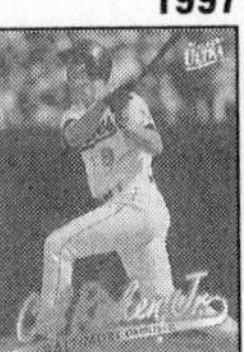

The 1997 Ultra was issued in two series totalling 553 cards. The first series consisted of 300 cards with the second containing 253. The 10-card packs had a suggested retail price of 2.49 each. Each pack had two insert cards, with one insert being a gold medallion parallel and the other insert being from one of serveral other insert sets. The fronts features borderless color action player photos with career statistics on the backs. As in most Fleer produced sets, the cards are arranged in alphabetical order by league, player and team. Second series retail packs contained only cards 301-450 while second series hobby packs contained all cards from 301-553. Rookie Cards include Jose Cruz Jr., Brian Giles and Fernando Tatis.

Nm-Mt Ex-Mt
COMPLETE SET (553) 60.00 18.00
COMP.SERIES 1 (300) 30.00 9.00
COMP.SERIES 2 (253) 30.00 9.00
COMMON CARD (1-553) .30 .09
COMMON RC .40 .12
1 Roberto Alomar .75 .23
2 Brady Anderson .30 .09
3 Rocky Coppinger .30 .09
4 Jeffrey Hammonds .30 .09
5 Chris Hoiles .30 .09
6 Eddie Murray .75 .23
7 Mike Mussina .75 .23
8 Jimmy Myers .30 .09
9 Randy Myers .30 .09
10 Arthur Rhodes .30 .09
11 Cal Ripken 2.50 .75
12 Jose Canseco .75 .23
13 Roger Clemens 1.50 .45
14 Tom Gordon .30 .09
15 Jose Malave .30 .09
16 Tim Naehring .30 .09
17 Troy O'Leary .30 .09
18 Bill Selby .30 .09
19 Heathcliff Slocumb .30 .09
20 Mike Stanley .30 .09
21 Mo Vaughn .30 .09
22 Garret Anderson .30 .09
23 George Arias .30 .09
24 Chili Davis .30 .09
25 Jim Edmonds .30 .09
26 Darin Erstad .30 .09
27 Chuck Finley .30 .09
28 Todd Greene .30 .09
29 Troy Percival .30 .09
30 Tim Salmon .50 .15
31 Jeff Schmidt .30 .09
32 Randy Velarde .30 .09
33 Shad Williams .30 .09
34 Wilson Alvarez .30 .09
35 Harold Baines .30 .09
36 James Baldwin .30 .09
37 Mike Cameron .30 .09
38 Ray Durham .30 .09
39 Ozzie Guillen .30 .09
40 Roberto Hernandez .30 .09
41 Darren Lewis .30 .09
42 Jose Munoz .30 .09
43 Tony Phillips .30 .09
44 Frank Thomas .75 .23
45 Sandy Alomar Jr. .30 .09
46 Albert Belle .30 .09
47 Mark Carreon .30 .09
48 Julio Franco .30 .09
49 Orel Hershiser .30 .09
50 Kenny Lofton .30 .09
51 Jack McDowell .30 .09
52 Jose Mesa .30 .09
53 Charles Nagy .30 .09
54 Manny Ramirez .30 .09
55 Julian Tavarez .30 .09
56 Omar Vizquel .30 .09
57 Raul Casanova .30 .09
58 Tony Clark .30 .09
59 Travis Fryman .30 .09
60 Bob Higginson .30 .09
61 Melvin Nieves .30 .09
62 Curtis Pride .30 .09
63 Justin Thompson .30 .09
64 Alan Trammell .50 .15
65 Kevin Appier .30 .09
66 Johnny Damon .30 .09
67 Keith Lockhart .30 .09
68 Jeff Montgomery .30 .09
69 Jose Offerman .30 .09
70 Bip Roberts .30 .09
71 Jose Rosado .30 .09
72 Chris Stynes .30 .09
73 Mike Sweeney .30 .09
74 Jeff Cirillo .30 .09
75 Jeff D'Amico .30 .09
76 John Jaha .30 .09
77 Scott Karl .30 .09
78 Mike Matheny .30 .09
79 Ben McDonald .30 .09
80 Matt Mieske .30 .09
81 Marc Newfield .30 .09
82 Dave Nilsson .30 .09
83 Jose Valentin .30 .09
84 Fernando Vina .30 .09
85 Rick Aguilera .30 .09
86 Marty Cordova .30 .09
87 Chuck Knoblauch .30 .09
88 Matt Lawton .30 .09
89 Pat Meares .30 .09
90 Paul Molitor .50 .15
91 Greg Myers .30 .09
92 Dan Naulty .30 .09
93 Kirby Puckett .75 .23
94 Frank Rodriguez .30 .09
95 Wade Boggs .50 .15
96 Cecil Fielder .30 .09
97 Joe Girardi .30 .09
98 Dwight Gooden .50 .15
99 Derek Jeter 2.00 .60
100 Tino Martinez .50 .15
101 Ramiro Mendoza RC .30 .09
102 Andy Pettitte .50 .15
103 Mariano Rivera .50 .15
104 Ruben Rivera .30 .09
105 Kenny Rogers .30 .09
106 Darryl Strawberry .50 .15
107 Bernie Williams .50 .15
108 Tony Batista .30 .09
109 Geronimo Berroa .30 .09
110 Bobby Chouinard .30 .09
111 Brent Gates .30 .09
112 Jason Giambi .75 .23
113 Damon Mashore .30 .09
114 Mark McGwire 2.00 .60
115 Scott Spiezio .30 .09
116 John Wasdin .30 .09
117 Steve Wojciechowski .30 .09
118 Ernie Young .30 .09
119 Norm Charlton .30 .09
120 Joey Cora .30 .09
121 Ken Griffey Jr. 1.25 .35
122 Sterling Hitchcock .30 .09
123 Raul Ibanez .30 .09
124 Randy Johnson .75 .23
125 Edgar Martinez .50 .15
126 Alex Rodriguez 1.25 .35
127 Matt Wagner .30 .09
128 Bob Wells .30 .09
129 Dan Wilson .30 .09
130 Will Clark .75 .23
131 Kevin Elster .30 .09
132 Juan Gonzalez .75 .23
133 Rusty Greer .30 .09
134 Darryl Hamilton .30 .09
135 Mike Henneman .30 .09
136 Ken Hill .30 .09
137 Mark McLemore .30 .09
138 Dean Palmer .30 .09
139 Roger Pavlik .30 .09
140 Ivan Rodriguez .75 .23
141 Joe Carter .30 .09
142 Carlos Delgado .30 .09
143 Alex Gonzalez .30 .09
144 Juan Guzman .30 .09
145 Pat Hentgen .30 .09
146 Marty Janzen .30 .09
147 Otis Nixon .30 .09
148 Charlie O'Brien .30 .09
149 John Olerud .30 .09
150 Robert Perez .30 .09
151 Jermaine Dye .30 .09
152 Tom Glavine .50 .15
153 Andruw Jones .30 .09
154 Chipper Jones .75 .23
155 Ryan Klesko .30 .09
156 Javier Lopez .30 .09
157 Greg Maddux 1.25 .35
158 Fred McGriff .50 .15
159 Wonderful Monds .30 .09
160 John Smoltz .50 .15
161 Terrell Wade .30 .09
162 Mark Wohlers .30 .09
163 Brant Brown .30 .09
164 Mark Grace .50 .15
165 Tyler Houston .30 .09
166 Robin Jennings .30 .09
167 Jason Maxwell .30 .09
168 Ryne Sandberg 1.25 .35
169 Sammy Sosa 1.25 .35
170 Amaury Telemaco .30 .09
171 Steve Trachsel .30 .09
172 Pedro Valdes RC .30 .09
173 Tim Belk .30 .09
174 Bret Boone .30 .09
175 Jeff Brantley .30 .09
176 Eric Davis .30 .09
177 Barry Larkin .75 .23
178 Chad Mottola .30 .09
179 Mark Portugal .30 .09
180 Reggie Sanders .30 .09
181 John Smiley .30 .09
182 Eddie Taubensee .30 .09
183 Dante Bichette .30 .09
184 Ellis Burks .30 .09
185 Andres Galarraga .30 .09
186 Curt Leskanic .30 .09
187 Quinton McCracken .30 .09
188 Jeff Reed .30 .09
189 Kevin Ritz .30 .09
190 Walt Weiss .30 .09
191 Jamey Wright .30 .09
192 Eric Young .30 .09
193 Kevin Brown .30 .09
194 Luis Castillo .30 .09
195 Jeff Conine .30 .09
196 Andre Dawson .30 .09
197 Charles Johnson .30 .09
198 Al Leiter .30 .09
199 Ralph Milliard .30 .09
200 Robb Nen .30 .09
201 Edgar Renteria .30 .09
202 Gary Sheffield .30 .09
203 Bob Abreu .30 .09
204 Jeff Bagwell .50 .15
205 Derek Bell .30 .09
206 Sean Berry .30 .09
207 Richard Hidalgo .30 .09
208 Todd Jones .30 .09
209 Darryl Kile .30 .09
210 Orlando Miller .30 .09
211 Shane Reynolds .30 .09
212 Billy Wagner .30 .09
213 Donne Wall .30 .09
214 Roger Cedeno .30 .09
215 Greg Gagne .30 .09
216 Karim Garcia .30 .09
217 Wilton Guerrero .30 .09
218 Todd Hollandsworth .30 .09
219 Ramon Martinez .30 .09
220 Raul Mondesi .30 .09
221 Hideo Nomo .75 .23
222 Chan Ho Park .30 .09
223 Mike Piazza 1.25 .35
224 Ismael Valdes .30 .09
225 Moises Alou .30 .09
226 Derek Aucoin .30 .09
227 Yamil Benitez .30 .09
228 Jeff Fassero .30 .09
229 Darrin Fletcher .30 .09
230 Mark Grudzielanek .30 .09
231 Barry Manuel .30 .09
232 Pedro Martinez .75 .23
233 Henry Rodriguez .30 .09
234 Ugueth Urbina .30 .09
235 Rondell White .30 .09
236 Carlos Baerga .30 .09
237 John Franco .30 .09
238 Bernard Gilkey .30 .09
239 Todd Hundley .30 .09
240 Butch Huskey .30 .09
241 Jason Isringhausen .30 .09
242 Lance Johnson .30 .09
243 Bobby Jones .30 .09
244 Alex Ochoa .30 .09
245 Rey Ordonez .30 .09
246 Paul Wilson .30 .09
247 Ron Blazier .30 .09
248 David Doster .30 .09
249 Jim Eisenreich .30 .09
250 Mike Grace .30 .09
251 Mike Lieberthal .30 .09
252 Wendell Magee .30 .09
253 Mickey Morandini .30 .09
254 Ricky Otero .30 .09
255 Scott Rolen .50 .15
256 Curt Schilling .50 .15
257 Todd Zeile .30 .09
258 Jermaine Allensworth .30 .09
259 Trey Beamon .30 .09
260 Carlos Garcia .30 .09
261 Mark Johnson .30 .09
262 Jason Kendall .30 .09
263 Jeff King .30 .09
264 Al Martin .30 .09
265 Denny Neagle .30 .09
266 Matt Ruebel .30 .09
267 Marc Wilkins .30 .09
268 Alan Benes .30 .09
269 Dennis Eckersley .30 .09
270 Ron Gant .30 .09
271 Aaron Holbert .30 .09
272 Brian Jordan .30 .09
273 Ray Lankford .30 .09
274 John Mabry .30 .09
275 T.J. Mathews .30 .09
276 Ozzie Smith 1.25 .35
277 Todd Stottlemyre .30 .09
278 Mark Sweeney .30 .09
279 Andy Ashby .30 .09
280 Steve Finley .30 .09
281 John Flaherty .30 .09
282 Chris Gomez .30 .09
283 Tony Gwynn 1.00 .30
284 Joey Hamilton .30 .09
285 Rickey Henderson .75 .23
286 Trevor Hoffman .30 .09
287 Jason Thompson .30 .09
288 Fernando Valenzuela .30 .09
289 Greg Vaughn .30 .09
290 Barry Bonds 2.00 .60
291 Jay Canizaro .30 .09
292 Jacob Cruz .30 .09
293 Shawon Dunston .30 .09
294 Shawn Estes .30 .09
295 Mark Gardner .30 .09
296 Marcus Jensen .30 .09
297 Bill Mueller RC 2.00 .60
298 Chris Singleton .30 .09
299 Allen Watson .30 .09
300 Matt Williams .30 .09
301 Rod Beck .30 .09
302 Jay Bell .30 .09
303 Shawon Dunston .30 .09
304 Reggie Jefferson .30 .09
305 Darren Oliver .30 .09
306 Benito Santiago .30 .09
307 Gerald Williams .30 .09
308 Damon Buford .30 .09
309 Jeromy Burnitz .30 .09
310 Sterling Hitchcock .30 .09
311 Dave Hollins .30 .09
312 Mel Rojas .30 .09
313 Robin Ventura .30 .09
314 David Wells .30 .09
315 Cal Eldred .30 .09
316 Gary Gaetti .30 .09
317 John Hudek .30 .09
318 Brian Johnson .30 .09
319 Denny Neagle .30 .09
320 Larry Walker .50 .15
321 Russ Davis .30 .09
322 Delino DeShields .30 .09
323 Charlie Hayes .30 .09
324 Jermaine Dye .30 .09
325 John Ericks .30 .09
326 Jeff Fassero .30 .09
327 Nomar Garciaparra 1.25 .35
328 Willie Greene .30 .09
329 Greg McMichael .30 .09
330 Damion Easley .30 .09
331 Ricky Bones .30 .09
332 John Burkett .30 .09
333 Royce Clayton .30 .09
334 Greg Colbrunn .30 .09
335 Tony Eusebio .30 .09
336 Gregg Jefferies .30 .09
337 Wally Joyner .30 .09
338 Jim Leyritz .30 .09
339 Paul O'Neill .50 .15
340 Bruce Ruffin .30 .09
341 Michael Tucker .30 .09
342 Andy Benes .30 .09
343 Craig Biggio .50 .15
344 Rex Hudler .30 .09
345 Brad Radke .30 .09
346 Deion Sanders .50 .15
347 Moises Alou .30 .09
348 Brad Ausmus .30 .09
349 Armando Benitez .30 .09
350 Mark Gubicza .30 .09
351 Terry Steinbach .30 .09
352 Mark Whiten .30 .09
353 Ricky Bottalico .30 .09
354 Brian Giles RC 1.50 .45
355 Eric Karros .30 .09
356 Jimmy Key .30 .09
357 Carlos Perez .30 .09
358 Alex Fernandez .30 .09
359 J.T. Snow .30 .09
360 Bobby Bonilla .30 .09
361 Scott Brosius .30 .09
362 Greg Swindell .30 .09
363 Jose Vizcaino .30 .09
364 Matt Williams .30 .09
365 Darren Daulton .30 .09
366 Shane Andrews .30 .09
367 Jim Eisenreich .30 .09
368 Ariel Prieto .30 .09
369 Bob Tewksbury .30 .09
370 Mike Bordick .30 .09
371 Rheal Cormier .30 .09
372 Cliff Floyd .30 .09
373 David Justice .30 .09
374 John Wetteland .30 .09
375 Mike Blowers .30 .09
376 Jose Canseco .75 .23
377 Roger Clemens 1.50 .45
378 Kevin Mitchell .30 .09
379 Todd Zeile .30 .09
380 Jim Thome .75 .23
381 Turk Wendell .30 .09
382 Rico Brogna .30 .09
383 Eric Davis .30 .09
384 Mike Lansing .30 .09
385 Devon White .30 .09
386 Marquis Grissom .30 .09
387 Todd Worrell .30 .09
388 Jeff Kent .30 .09
389 Mickey Tettleton .30 .09
390 Steve Avery .30 .09
391 David Cone .30 .09
392 Scott Cooper .30 .09
393 Lee Stevens .30 .09
394 Kevin Elster .30 .09
395 Tom Goodwin .30 .09
396 Shawn Green .30 .09
397 Pete Harnisch .30 .09
398 Eddie Murray .75 .23
399 Joe Randa .30 .09
400 Scott Sanders .30 .09
401 John Valentin .30 .09
402 Todd Jones .30 .09
403 Terry Adams .30 .09
404 Brian Hunter .30 .09
405 Pat Listach .30 .09
406 Kenny Lofton .30 .09
407 Hal Morris .30 .09
408 Ed Sprague .30 .09
409 Rich Becker .30 .09
410 Edgardo Alfonzo .30 .09
411 Albert Belle .30 .09
412 Jeff King .30 .09
413 Kirt Manwaring .30 .09
414 Jason Schmidt .30 .09
415 Allen Watson .30 .09
416 Lee Tinsley .30 .09
417 Brett Butler .30 .09

418 Carlos Garcia	.30	.09
419 Mark Lemke	.30	.09
420 Jaime Navarro	.30	.09
421 David Segui	.30	.09
422 Ruben Sierra	.30	.09
423 B.J. Surhoff	.30	.09
424 Julian Tavarez	.30	.09
425 Billy Taylor	.30	.09
426 Ken Caminiti	.30	.09
427 Chuck Carr	.30	.09
428 Benji Gil	.30	.09
429 Terry Mulholland	.30	.09
430 Mike Stanton	.30	.09
431 Wil Cordero	.30	.09
432 Chili Davis	.30	.09
433 Mariano Duncan	.30	.09
434 Orlando Merced	.30	.09
435 Kent Mercker	.30	.09
436 John Olerud	.30	.09
437 Quilvio Veras	.30	.09
438 Mike Fetters	.30	.09
439 Glenallen Hill	.30	.09
440 Bill Swift	.30	.09
441 Tim Wakefield	.30	.09
442 Pedro Astacio	.30	.09
443 Vinny Castilla	.30	.09
444 Doug Drabek	.30	.09
445 Alan Embree	.30	.09
446 Lee Smith	.30	.09
447 Darryl Hamilton	.30	.09
448 Brian McRae	.30	.09
449 Mike Timlin	.30	.09
450 Bob Wickman	.30	.09
451 Jason Dickson	.30	.09
452 Chad Curtis	.30	.09
453 Mark Leiter	.30	.09
454 Damon Berryhill	.30	.09
455 Kevin Orie	.30	.09
456 Dave Burba	.30	.09
457 Chris Holt	.30	.09
458 Ricky Ledee RC	.40	.12
459 Mike Devereaux	.30	.09
460 Pokey Reese	.30	.09
461 Tim Raines	.30	.09
462 Ryan Jones	.30	.09
463 Shane Mack	.30	.09
464 Darren Dreifort	.30	.09
465 Mark Parent	.30	.09
466 Mark Portugal	.30	.09
467 Dante Powell	.30	.09
468 Craig Grebeck	.30	.09
469 Ron Villone	.30	.09
470 Dmitri Young	.30	.09
471 Shannon Stewart	.30	.09
472 Rick Helling	.30	.09
473 Bill Haselman	.30	.09
474 Albie Lopez	.30	.09
475 Glendon Rusch	.30	.09
476 Derrick May	.30	.09
477 Chad Ogea	.30	.09
478 Kirk Rueter	.30	.09
479 Chris Hammond	.30	.09
480 Russ Johnson	.30	.09
481 James Mouton	.30	.09
482 Mike Macfarlane	.30	.09
483 Scott Ruffcorn	.30	.09
484 Jeff Frye	.30	.09
485 Richie Sexson	.30	.09
486 Emil Brown RC	.40	.12
487 Desi Wilson	.30	.09
488 Brent Gates	.30	.09
489 Tony Graffanino	.30	.09
490 Dan Miceli	.30	.09
491 Orlando Cabrera RC	.40	.12
492 Tony Womack RC	.40	.12
493 Jerome Walton	.30	.09
494 Mark Thompson	.30	.09
495 Jose Guillen	.30	.09
496 Willie Blair	.30	.09
497 T.J. Staton RC	.40	.12
498 Scott Kamieniecki	.30	.09
499 Vince Coleman	.30	.09
500 Jeff Abbott	.30	.09
501 Chris Widger	.30	.09
502 Kevin Tapani	.30	.09
503 Carlos Castillo RC	.40	.12
504 Luis Gonzalez	.30	.09
505 Tim Belcher	.30	.09
506 Armando Reynoso	.30	.09
507 Jamie Moyer	.30	.09
508 Randall Simon RC	.60	.18
509 Vladimir Guerrero	.75	.23
510 Wady Almonte RC	.40	.12
511 Dustin Hermanson	.30	.09
512 Deivi Cruz RC	.40	.12
513 Luis Alicea	.30	.09
514 Felix Heredia RC	.40	.12
515 Don Slaught	.30	.09
516 S.Hasegawa RC	1.00	.30
517 Matt Walbeck	.30	.09
518 David Arias-Ortiz RC	3.00	.90
519 Brady Raggio RC	.40	.12
520 Rudy Pemberton	.30	.09
521 Wayne Kirby	.30	.09
522 Calvin Maduro	.30	.09
523 Mark Lewis	.30	.09
524 Mike Jackson	.30	.09
525 Sid Fernandez	.30	.09
526 Mike Bielecki	.30	.09
527 Bubba Trammell RC	.40	.12
528 Brent Brede RC	.40	.12
529 Matt Morris	.30	.09
530 Joe Borowski RC	.40	.12
531 Orlando Miller	.30	.09
532 Jim Bullinger	.30	.09
533 Robert Person	.30	.09
534 Doug Glanville	.30	.09
535 Terry Pendleton	.30	.09
536 Jorge Posada	.50	.15
537 Marc Sagmoen RC	.40	.12
538 Fernando Tatis RC	.40	.12
539 Aaron Sele	.30	.09
540 Brian Banks	.30	.09
541 Derrek Lee	.30	.09
542 John Wasdin	.30	.09
543 Justin Towle RC	.40	.12
544 Pat Cline	.30	.09
545 Dave Magadan	.30	.09
546 Jeff Blauser	.30	.09
547 Phil Nevin	.30	.09
548 Todd Walker	.30	.09
549 Eli Marrero	.30	.09
550 Bartolo Colon	.30	.09
551 Jose Cruz Jr. RC	1.50	.45
552 Todd Dunwoody	.30	.09
553 Hideki Irabu RC	.40	.12
P11 Cal Ripken Promo Three Card Strip	2.00	.60

1997 Ultra Gold Medallion

This 553-card set is a gold-holofoil-stamped parallel version of the regular Ultra set and was inserted one per pack of both series one and series two cards. Unlike previous Gold Medallion sets, the 1997 edition features different photos than the corresponding regular cards.

	Nm-Mt	Ex-Mt
COMPLETE SET (553)	270.00	80.00
COMP. SERIES 1 (300)	150.00	45.00
COMP. SERIES 2 (253)	120.00	36.00
*STARS: 1.25X TO 3X BASIC CARDS		
*ROOKIES: .75X TO 2X BASIC CARDS		

1997 Ultra Platinum Medallion

This 553-card set is a parallel to the regular Ultra and was inserted one per 100 packs of both series 1 and series 2 cards. Sparkling platinum lettering on front differentiates these cards from their far more common regular issue brethren. No set price is provided due to scarcity. As with the 1997 Gold Medallion set, the Platinum Medallion set features different photos than the corresponding regular cards.

	Nm-Mt	Ex-Mt
*STARS 1-450: 12.5X TO 30X BASIC CARDS		
*STARS 451-553: 10X TO 25X BASIC CARDS		
*ROOKIES 1-450: 8X TO 20X BASIC CARDS		
*ROOKIES: 451-553: 5X TO 12X BASIC		

1997 Ultra Autographstix Emeralds

This six-card hobby exclusive Series two insert set consists of individually numbered Redemption cards for autographed bats from the players checklisted below. Only 25 of each card was produced. The deadline to exchange cards was July 1st, 1998. The bat a collector received for these cards was not easily identifiable as a special bat. Prices listed refer to the exchange cards.

	Nm-Mt	Ex-Mt
1 Alex Ochoa		
2 Todd Walker		
3 Scott Rolen		
4 Darin Erstad		
5 Alex Rodriguez		
6 Todd Hollandsworth		

1997 Ultra Baseball Rules

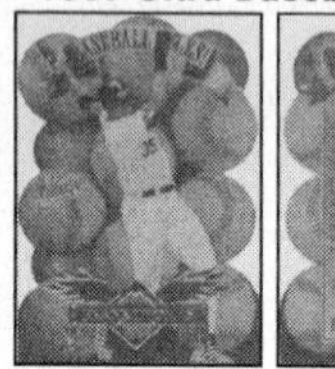

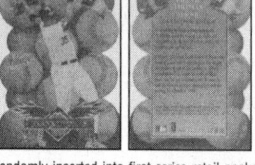

Randomly inserted into first series retail packs of 1997 Ultra at a rate of 1:36, cards from this 10-card set feature a selection of baseball's top performers from the 1996 season. The die cut cards feature a player photo surrounded by a group of baseballs. The back explains some of the rules involved in making various awards.

	Nm-Mt	Ex-Mt
COMPLETE SET (10)	120.00	36.00
1 Barry Bonds	15.00	4.50
2 Ken Griffey Jr.	10.00	3.00
3 Derek Jeter	15.00	4.50
4 Chipper Jones	6.00	1.80
5 Greg Maddux	10.00	3.00
6 Mark McGwire	15.00	4.50
7 Troy Percival	2.50	.75
8 Mike Piazza	10.00	3.00
9 Cal Ripken	20.00	6.00
10 Frank Thomas	6.00	1.80

1997 Ultra Checklists

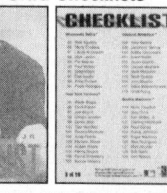

Randomly inserted in all first and second series packs at a rate of one in four, this 20-card set features borderless player photos on the front along with the word "Checklist", the player's name as well as the "ultra" logo at the bottom. The backs are checklists. The checklists for Series 1 are listed below with an "A" prefix and for Series 2 with a "B" prefix.

	Nm-Mt	Ex-Mt
COMPLETE SERIES 1 (10)	8.00	2.40
COMPLETE SERIES 2 (10)	12.00	3.60
A1 Dante Bichette	.30	.09
A2 Barry Bonds	2.00	.60
A3 Ken Griffey Jr.	1.25	.35
A4 Greg Maddux	1.25	.35
A5 Mark McGwire	2.00	.60
A6 Mike Piazza	1.25	.35
A7 Cal Ripken	2.50	.75
A8 John Smoltz	.50	.15
A9 Sammy Sosa	1.25	.35
A10 Frank Thomas	.75	.23
B1 Andruw Jones	.30	.09
B2 Ken Griffey Jr.	1.25	.35
B3 Frank Thomas	.75	.23
B4 Alex Rodriguez	1.25	.35
B5 Cal Ripken	2.50	.75
B6 Mike Piazza	1.25	.35
B7 Greg Maddux	1.25	.35
B8 Chipper Jones	.75	.23
B9 Derek Jeter	2.00	.60
B10 Juan Gonzalez	.75	.23

1997 Ultra Diamond Producers

Randomly inserted in all first series packs at a rate of one in 288, this 12-card set features "flannel" material mounted on card stock and attempt to look and feel like actual uniforms.

	Nm-Mt	Ex-Mt
COMPLETE SET (12)	250.00	75.00
1 Jeff Bagwell	10.00	3.00
2 Barry Bonds	40.00	12.00
3 Ken Griffey Jr.	25.00	7.50
4 Chipper Jones	15.00	4.50
5 Kenny Lofton	6.00	1.80
6 Greg Maddux	25.00	7.50
7 Mark McGwire	40.00	12.00
8 Mike Piazza	25.00	7.50
9 Cal Ripken	50.00	15.00
10 Alex Rodriguez	25.00	7.50
11 Frank Thomas	15.00	4.50
12 Matt Williams	6.00	1.80

1997 Ultra Double Trouble

Randomly inserted in series one packs at a rate of one in four, this 20-card set features two players from each team. The horizontal cards feature players photos with their names in silver foil on the bottom and the words "double trouble" on the top. The backs feature information on what the players contributed to their team in 1996

	Nm-Mt	Ex-Mt
COMPLETE SET (20)	10.00	3.00
1 Roberto Alomar Cal Ripken	2.50	.75
2 Mo Vaughn Jose Canseco	.30	.09
3 Jim Edmonds Tim Salmon	.30	.09
4 Harold Baines Frank Thomas	.75	.23
5 Albert Belle Kenny Lofton	.30	.09
6 Marty Cordova Chuck Knoblauch	.30	.09
7 Derek Jeter Andy Pettitte	2.00	.60
8 Jason Giambi Mark McGwire	2.00	.60
9 Ken Griffey Jr. Alex Rodriguez	1.25	.35
10 Juan Gonzalez Will Clark	.75	.23
11 Greg Maddux Chipper Jones	1.25	.35
12 Mark Grace Sammy Sosa	1.25	.35
13 Dante Bichette Andres Galarraga	.30	.09
14 Jeff Bagwell Derek Bell	.50	.15
15 Hideo Nomo Mike Piazza	1.25	.35
16 Henry Rodriguez Moises Alou	.30	.09
17 Rey Ordonez Alex Ochoa	.30	.09
18 Ray Lankford Ron Gant	.30	.09
19 Tony Gwynn Rickey Henderson	1.00	.30
20 Barry Bonds Matt Williams	2.00	.60

1997 Ultra Fame Game

Randomly inserted in series two hobby packs only at a rate of one in eight, this 18-card set features color photos of players who have displayed Hall of Fame potential on an elegant card design.

	Nm-Mt	Ex-Mt
COMPLETE SET (18)	60.00	18.00
1 Ken Griffey Jr.	5.00	1.50
2 Frank Thomas	3.00	.90
3 Alex Rodriguez	5.00	1.50
4 Cal Ripken	10.00	3.00
5 Mike Piazza	5.00	1.50
6 Greg Maddux	5.00	1.50
7 Derek Jeter	8.00	2.40
8 Jeff Bagwell	2.00	.60
9 Juan Gonzalez	3.00	.90
10 Albert Belle	1.25	.35
11 Tony Gwynn	4.00	1.20
12 Mark McGwire	8.00	2.40
13 Andy Pettitte	2.00	.60
14 Kenny Lofton	1.25	.35
15 Roberto Alomar	3.00	.90
16 Ryne Sandberg	5.00	1.50
17 Barry Bonds	8.00	2.40
18 Eddie Murray	3.00	.90

1997 Ultra Fielder's Choice

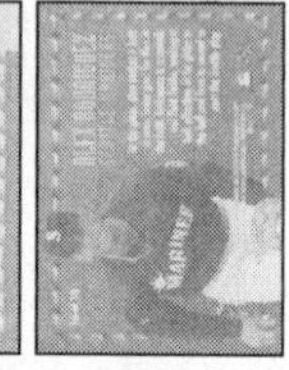

Randomly inserted in series one packs at a rate of one in 144, this 18-card set uses leather and gold foil to honor leading defensive players. The horizontal cards also include a player photo on the front as well as the big bold words "97 Fleer Ultra", "Fielder's Choice" and the player's name. The horizontal backs have another player photo as well as information about their defensive prowess.

	Nm-Mt	Ex-Mt
COMPLETE SET (18)	200.00	60.00
1 Roberto Alomar	12.00	3.60
2 Jeff Bagwell	8.00	2.40
3 Wade Boggs	8.00	2.40
4 Barry Bonds	30.00	9.00
5 Mark Grace	8.00	2.40
6 Ken Griffey Jr.	20.00	6.00
7 Marquis Grissom	5.00	1.50
8 Charles Johnson	5.00	1.50
9 Chuck Knoblauch	5.00	1.50
10 Barry Larkin	12.00	3.60
11 Kenny Lofton	5.00	1.50
12 Greg Maddux	20.00	6.00
13 Raul Mondesi	5.00	1.50
14 Rey Ordonez	5.00	1.50
15 Cal Ripken	40.00	12.00
16 Alex Rodriguez	20.00	6.00
17 Ivan Rodriguez	12.00	3.60
18 Matt Williams	5.00	1.50

1997 Ultra Golden Prospects

Randomly inserted in series two hobby packs only at a rate of one in four, this 10-card set features color action player images on a gold baseball background with commentary on what makes these players so promising..

	Nm-Mt	Ex-Mt
COMPLETE SET (10)	5.00	1.50
1 Andruw Jones	.30	.09
2 Vladimir Guerrero	.75	.23
3 Todd Walker	.30	.09
4 Karim Garcia	.30	.09
5 Kevin Orie	.30	.09
6 Brian Giles	1.50	.45
7 Jason Dickson	.30	.09
8 Jose Guillen	.30	.09
9 Ruben Rivera	.30	.09
10 Derrek Lee	.30	.09

1997 Ultra Hitting Machines

Randomly inserted in series two hobby packs only at a rate of one in 36, this 18-card set features color action player images of the MLB's most productive hitters in "machine-style" die-cut settings.

	Nm-Mt	Ex-Mt
COMPLETE SET (18)	120.00	36.00
1 Andruw Jones	2.50	.75
2 Ken Griffey Jr.	10.00	3.00
3 Frank Thomas	6.00	1.80
4 Alex Rodriguez	10.00	3.00
5 Cal Ripken	20.00	6.00
6 Mike Piazza	10.00	3.00
7 Derek Jeter	15.00	4.50
8 Albert Belle	2.50	.75
9 Tony Gwynn	8.00	2.40
10 Jeff Bagwell	4.00	1.20
11 Mark McGwire	15.00	4.50
12 Kenny Lofton	2.50	.75
13 Manny Ramirez	2.50	.75
14 Roberto Alomar	6.00	1.80
15 Ryne Sandberg	10.00	3.00
16 Eddie Murray	6.00	1.80
17 Sammy Sosa	10.00	3.00
18 Ken Caminiti	2.50	.75

1997 Ultra Home Run Kings

Randomly inserted in series one hobby packs only at a rate of one in 36, this 12-card set features ultra crystal cards with transparent refractive holo-foil technology. The players pictured are all leading power hitters.

	Nm-Mt	Ex-Mt
COMPLETE SET (12)	80.00	24.00
1 Albert Belle	2.50	.75
2 Barry Bonds	15.00	4.50
3 Juan Gonzalez	6.00	1.80
4 Ken Griffey Jr.	10.00	3.00
5 Todd Hundley	2.50	.75
6 Ryan Klesko	2.50	.75
7 Mark McGwire	15.00	4.50
8 Mike Piazza	10.00	3.00
9 Sammy Sosa	10.00	3.00
10 Frank Thomas	6.00	1.80
11 Mo Vaughn	2.50	.75
12 Matt Williams	2.50	.75

1997 Ultra Irabu Commemorative

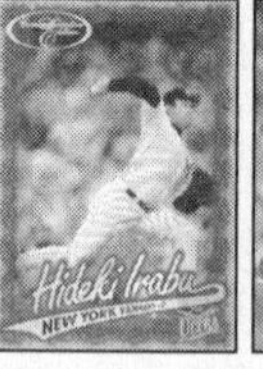

These seven Irabu cards were distributed exclusively in 1997 Ultra series two International hobby boxes. Three of the seven cards are over-sized 5 x 7 issues, placed in each box as a chiptopper (within the sealed box, but laying on top of the packs). These three cards are serial numbered "of 2750" in silver foil on back. Due to poor sales overseas a number of these boxes made their way back to America but are still considered quite tricky to find.

	Nm-Mt	Ex-Mt
COMPLETE SET (7)	15.00	4.50
COMMON 5 x 7 (C1-C3)	2.00	.60
COMMON CARD (C4-C7)	3.00	.90

1997 Ultra Leather Shop

Randomly inserted in series two hobby packs only at a rate of one in six, this 12-card set features color player images of some of the best fielders in the game highlighted by simulated leather backgrounds.

	Nm-Mt	Ex-Mt
COMPLETE SET (12)	15.00	4.50
1 Ken Griffey Jr.	1.50	.45
2 Alex Rodriguez	1.50	.45
3 Cal Ripken	3.00	.90
4 Derek Jeter	2.50	.75
5 Juan Gonzalez	1.00	.30
6 Tony Gwynn	1.25	.35
7 Jeff Bagwell	.60	.18
8 Roberto Alomar	1.00	.30
9 Ryne Sandberg	1.50	.45
10 Ken Caminiti	.40	.12
11 Kenny Lofton	.40	.12
12 John Smoltz	.60	.18

1997 Ultra Power Plus

Randomly inserted in series one packs at a rate of one in 24 and Series two hobby packs at the rate of one in eight, this 12-card set utilizes silver rainbow holo-foil and features players who not only hit with power but also excel at other parts of the game. The cards in the Series one insert set have an "A" prefix

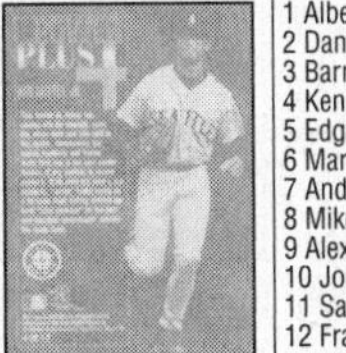

while the cards in the Series two insert set carry a "B" prefix in the checklist below.

	Nm-Mt	Ex-Mt
COMPLETE SERIES 1 (12)	80.00	24.00
COMPLETE SERIES 2 (12)	30.00	9.00
A1 Jeff Bagwell	2.50	.75
A2 Barry Bonds	10.00	3.00
A3 Juan Gonzalez	4.00	1.20
A4 Ken Griffey Jr.	6.00	1.80
A5 Chipper Jones	4.00	1.20
A6 Mark McGwire	10.00	3.00
A7 Mike Piazza	6.00	1.80
A8 Cal Ripken	12.00	3.60
A9 Alex Rodriguez	6.00	1.80
A10 Sammy Sosa	6.00	1.80
A11 Frank Thomas	4.00	1.20
A12 Matt Williams	1.50	.45
B1 Ken Griffey Jr.	2.50	.75
B2 Frank Thomas	1.50	.45
B3 Alex Rodriguez	2.50	.75
B4 Cal Ripken	5.00	1.50
B5 Mike Piazza	2.50	.75
B6 Chipper Jones	1.50	.45
B7 Albert Belle	.60	.18
B8 Juan Gonzalez	1.50	.45
B9 Jeff Bagwell	1.00	.30
B10 Mark McGwire	4.00	1.20
B11 Mo Vaughn	.60	.18
B12 Barry Bonds	4.00	1.20

1997 Ultra RBI Kings

Randomly inserted in series one packs at a rate of one in 18, this 10-card set features 100 percent etched-foil cards. The cards feature players who drive in many runs. The horizontal backs contain player information and another player photo.

	Nm-Mt	Ex-Mt
COMPLETE SET (10)	30.00	9.00
1 Jeff Bagwell	2.50	.75
2 Albert Belle	1.50	.45
3 Dante Bichette	1.50	.45
4 Barry Bonds	10.00	3.00
5 Jay Buhner	1.50	.45
6 Juan Gonzalez	4.00	1.20
7 Ken Griffey Jr.	6.00	1.80
8 Sammy Sosa	6.00	1.80
9 Frank Thomas	4.00	1.20
10 Mo Vaughn	1.50	.45

1997 Ultra Rookie Reflections

Randomly inserted in series one packs at a rate of one in four, this 10-card set uses a silver foil design to feature young players. The horizontal backs contain player information as well as another player photo.

	Nm-Mt	Ex-Mt
COMPLETE SET (10)	4.00	1.20
1 James Baldwin	.40	.12
2 Jermaine Dye	.40	.12
3 Darin Erstad	.40	.12
4 Todd Hollandsworth	.40	.12
5 Derek Jeter	2.50	.75
6 Jason Kendall	.40	.12
7 Alex Ochoa	.40	.12
8 Rey Ordonez	.40	.12
9 Edgar Renteria	.40	.12
10 Scott Rolen	.60	.18

1997 Ultra Season Crowns

Randomly inserted in series one packs at a rate of one in eight, this 12-card set features color photos of baseball's top stars with etched foil backgrounds.

	Nm-Mt	Ex-Mt
COMPLETE SET (12)	10.00	3.00
1 Albert Belle	.40	.12
2 Dante Bichette	.40	.12
3 Barry Bonds	2.50	.75
4 Kenny Lofton	.40	.12
5 Edgar Martinez	.60	.18
6 Mark McGwire	2.50	.75
7 Andy Pettitte	.60	.18
8 Mike Piazza	1.50	.45
9 Alex Rodriguez	1.50	.45
10 John Smoltz	.60	.18
11 Sammy Sosa	1.50	.45
12 Frank Thomas	1.00	.30

1997 Ultra Starring Role

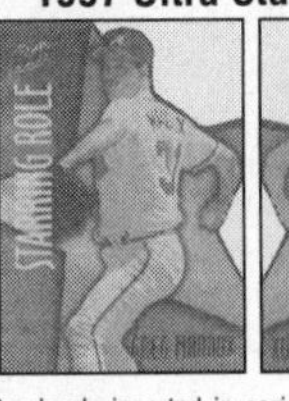
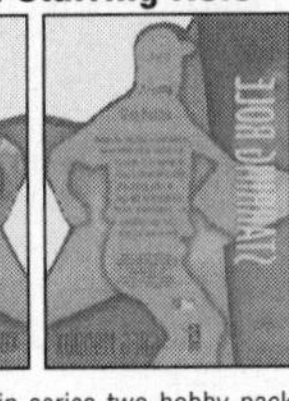

Randomly inserted in series two hobby packs only at a rate of one in 288, this 12-card set featues color photos of tried-and-true clutch performers on die-cut plastic cards with foil stamping.

	Nm-Mt	Ex-Mt
COMPLETE SET (12)	250.00	75.00
1 Andruw Jones	6.00	1.80
2 Ken Griffey Jr.	25.00	7.50
3 Frank Thomas	15.00	4.50
4 Alex Rodriguez	25.00	7.50
5 Cal Ripken	50.00	15.00
6 Mike Piazza	25.00	7.50
7 Greg Maddux	25.00	7.50
8 Chipper Jones	15.00	4.50
9 Derek Jeter	40.00	12.00
10 Juan Gonzalez	15.00	4.50
11 Albert Belle	6.00	1.80
12 Tony Gwynn	20.00	6.00

1997 Ultra Thunderclap

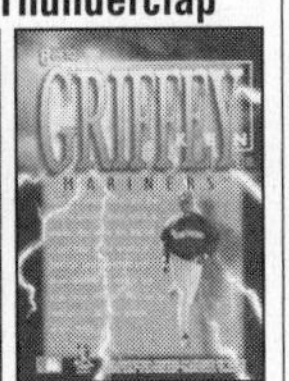

Randomly inserted in series two hobby packs only at a rate of one in 18, this 10-card set features color images of superstars who are feared by opponents for their ability to totally dominate a game on a background displaying lightning from a thunderstorm.

	Nm-Mt	Ex-Mt
COMPLETE SET (10)	60.00	18.00
1 Barry Bonds	10.00	3.00
2 Mo Vaughn	1.50	.45
3 Mark McGwire	10.00	3.00
4 Jeff Bagwell	2.50	.75
5 Juan Gonzalez	4.00	1.20
6 Alex Rodriguez	6.00	1.80
7 Chipper Jones	4.00	1.20
8 Ken Griffey Jr.	6.00	1.80
9 Mike Piazza	6.00	1.80
10 Frank Thomas	4.00	1.20

1997 Ultra Top 30

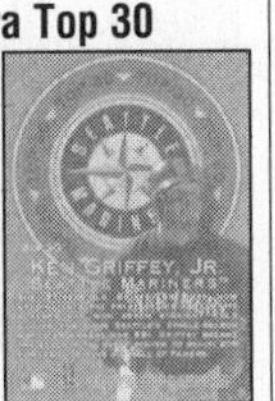

Randomly inserted one in every Ultra series two retail packs only, this 30-card set features color action player images of top stars with a "Top 30" circle in the team-colored background. The backs carry another player image with his team logo the backsground circle.

	Nm-Mt	Ex-Mt
COMPLETE SET (30)	40.00	12.00
*GOLD MED: 2.5X TO 6X BASIC TOP 30		
G.MED SER.2 STATED ODDS 1:18 RETAIL		
1 Andruw Jones	.50	.15
2 Ken Griffey	2.00	.60
3 Frank Thomas	1.25	.35
4 Alex Rodriguez	2.00	.60
5 Cal Ripken	4.00	1.20
6 Mike Piazza	2.00	.60
7 Greg Maddux	2.00	.60
8 Chipper Jones	1.25	.35
9 Derek Jeter	3.00	.90
10 Juan Gonzalez	1.25	.35
11 Albert Belle	.50	.15
12 Tony Gwynn	1.50	.45
13 Jeff Bagwell	.75	.23
14 Mark McGwire	3.00	.90
15 Andy Pettitte	.75	.23
16 Mo Vaughn	.50	.15
17 Kenny Lofton	.50	.15
18 Manny Ramirez	.50	.15
19 Roberto Alomar	1.25	.35
20 Ryne Sandberg	2.00	.60
21 Hideo Nomo	1.25	.35
22 Barry Bonds	3.00	.90
23 Eddie Murray	1.25	.35
24 Ken Caminiti	.50	.15
25 John Smoltz	.75	.23
26 Pat Hentgen	.50	.15
27 Todd Hollandsworth	.50	.15
28 Matt Williams	.50	.15
29 Bernie Williams	.75	.23
30 Brady Anderson	.50	.15

1998 Ultra

The complete 1998 Ultra set features 501 cards and was distributed in 10-card first and second series packs with a suggested retail price of $2.59. The fronts carry UV coated color action player photos printed on 20 pt. card stock. The backs display another player photo with player information and career statistics. The set contains the following subsets: Season's Crown (211-220) seeded 1:12 packs, Prospects (221-245) seeded 1:4 packs, Checklists (246-250), and Checklists (473-475) seeded 1:4 packs and Pizzazz (476-500) seeded 1:4 packs. Rookie Cards include Kevin Millwood and Maggio Ordonez. Though not confirmed by the manufacturer, it's believed that several cards within the Prospects subset are in shorter supply than others - most notably number 238 Ricky Ledee and number 243 Jorge Velandia. Also, seeded one in every pack, was one of 50 Million Dollar Moment cards which pictured some of the greatest moments in baseball histroy and gave the collector a chance to win a million dollars. As a special last minute promotion, Fleer/SkyBox got Alex Rodriguez to autograph 750 of his 1998 Fleer Promo cards. Each card is serial-numbered by hand on the card front. The signed cards were randomly seeded into Ultra Series two hobby packs.

	Nm-Mt	Ex-Mt
COMPLETE SET (501)	160.00	47.50
COMP.SERIES 1 (250)	100.00	30.00
COMP.SERIES 2 (251)	60.00	18.00
COMP.SER.1 w/o SP's (210)	15.00	4.50
COMP.SER.2 w/o SP's (226)	15.00	4.50
COMMON (1-220/246-250)	.30	.09
COMMON (251-475/501)	.30	.09
COMMON SC (211-220)	2.00	.60
COMMON (221-245)	3.00	.90
COMMON PZ (476-500)	1.00	.30
1 Ken Griffey Jr.	1.25	.35
2 Matt Morris	.30	.09
3 Roger Clemens	1.50	.45
4 Matt Williams	.30	.09
5 Roberto Hernandez	.30	.09
6 Rondell White	.30	.09
7 Tim Salmon	.50	.15
8 Brad Radke	.30	.09
9 Brett Butler	.30	.09
10 Carl Everett	.30	.09
11 Chili Davis	.30	.09
12 Chuck Finley	.30	.09
13 Darryl Kile	.30	.09
14 Deivi Cruz	.30	.09
15 Gary Gaetti	.30	.09
16 Matt Stairs	.30	.09
17 Pat Meares	.30	.09
18 Will Cunnane	.30	.09
19 Steve Woodard	.30	.09
20 Andy Ashby	.30	.09
21 Bobby Higginson	.30	.09
22 Brian Jordan	.30	.09
23 Craig Biggio	.50	.15
24 Jim Edmonds	.30	.09
25 Ryan McGuire	.30	.09
26 Scott Hatteberg	.30	.09
27 Willie Greene	.30	.09
28 Albert Belle	.30	.09
29 Ellis Burks	.30	.09
30 Hideo Nomo	.75	.23
31 Jeff Bagwell	.50	.15
32 Kevin Brown	.50	.15
33 Nomar Garciaparra	1.25	.35
34 Pedro Martinez	.75	.23
35 Raul Mondesi	.30	.09
36 Ricky Bottalico	.30	.09
37 Shawn Estes	.30	.09
38 Otis Nixon	.30	.09
39 Terry Steinbach	.30	.09
40 Tom Glavine	.50	.15
41 Todd Dunwoody	.30	.09
42 Deion Sanders	.50	.15
43 Gary Sheffield	.30	.09
44 Mike Lansing	.30	.09
45 Mike Lieberthal	.30	.09
46 Paul Sorrento	.30	.09
47 Paul O'Neill	.50	.15
48 Tom Goodwin	.30	.09
49 Andruw Jones	.30	.09
50 Barry Bonds	2.00	.60
51 Bernie Williams	.50	.15
52 Jeremi Gonzalez	.30	.09
53 Mike Piazza	1.25	.35
54 Russ Davis	.30	.09
55 Vinny Castilla	.30	.09
56 Rod Beck	.30	.09
57 Andres Galarraga	.30	.09
58 Ben McDonald	.30	.09
59 Billy Wagner	.30	.09
60 Charles Johnson	.30	.09
61 Fred McGriff	.50	.15
62 Dean Palmer	.30	.09
63 Frank Thomas	.75	.23
64 Ismael Valdes	.30	.09
65 Mark Bellhorn	.30	.09
66 Jeff King	.30	.09
67 John Wetteland	.30	.09
68 Mark Grace	.50	.15
69 Mark Kotsay	.50	.15
70 Scott Rolen	.50	.15
71 Todd Hundley	.30	.09
72 Todd Worrell	.30	.09
73 Wilson Alvarez	.30	.09
74 Bobby Jones	.30	.09
75 Jose Canseco	.75	.23
76 Kevin Appier	.30	.09
77 Neifi Perez	.30	.09
78 Paul Molitor	.50	.15
79 Quilvio Veras	.30	.09
80 Randy Johnson	.75	.23
81 Glendon Rusch	.30	.09
82 Curt Schilling	.50	.15
83 Alex Rodriguez	1.25	.35
84 Rey Ordonez	.30	.09
85 Jeff Juden	.30	.09
86 Mike Cameron	.30	.09
87 Ryan Klesko	.30	.09
88 Trevor Hoffman	.30	.09
89 Chuck Knoblauch	.30	.09
90 Larry Walker	.50	.15
91 Mark McLemore	.30	.09
92 B.J. Surhoff	.30	.09
93 Darren Daulton	.30	.09
94 Ray Durham	.30	.09
95 Sammy Sosa	1.25	.35
96 Eric Young	.30	.09
97 Gerald Williams	.30	.09
98 Javy Lopez	.30	.09
99 John Smiley	.30	.09
100 Juan Gonzalez	.75	.23
101 Shawn Green	.30	.09
102 Charles Nagy	.30	.09
103 David Justice	.30	.09
104 Joey Hamilton	.30	.09
105 Pat Hentgen	.30	.09
106 Raul Casanova	.30	.09
107 Tony Phillips	.30	.09
108 Tony Gwynn	1.00	.30
109 Will Clark	.75	.23
110 Jason Giambi	.75	.23
111 Jay Bell	.30	.09
112 Johnny Damon	.30	.09
113 Alan Benes	.30	.09
114 Jeff Suppan	.30	.09
115 Kevin Polcovich	.30	.09
116 Shigetoshi Hasegawa	.30	.09
117 Steve Finley	.30	.09
118 Tony Clark	.30	.09
119 David Cone	.30	.09
120 Jose Guillen	.30	.09
121 Kevin Millwood RC	1.25	.35
122 Greg Maddux	1.25	.35
123 Dave Nilsson	.30	.09
124 Hideki Irabu	.30	.09
125 Jason Kendall	.30	.09
126 Jim Thome	.75	.23
127 Delino DeShields	.30	.09
128 Edgar Renteria	.30	.09
129 Edgardo Alfonzo	.30	.09
130 J.T. Snow	.30	.09
131 Jeff Abbott	.30	.09
132 Jeffrey Hammonds	.30	.09
133 Todd Greene	.30	.09
134 Vladimir Guerrero	.75	.23
135 Jay Buhner	.30	.09
136 Jeff Cirillo	.30	.09
137 Jeromy Burnitz	.30	.09
138 Mickey Morandini	.30	.09
139 Tino Martinez	.50	.15
140 Jeff Shaw	.30	.09
141 Rafael Palmeiro	.50	.15
142 Bobby Bonilla	.30	.09
143 Cal Ripken	2.50	.75
144 Chad Fox RC	.30	.09
145 Dante Bichette	.30	.09
146 Dennis Eckersley	.30	.09
147 Mariano Rivera	.50	.15
148 Mo Vaughn	.30	.09
149 Reggie Sanders	.30	.09
150 Derek Jeter	2.00	.60
151 Rusty Greer	.30	.09
152 Brady Anderson	.30	.09
153 Brett Tomko	.30	.09
154 Jaime Navarro	.30	.09
155 Kevin Orie	.30	.09
156 Roberto Alomar	.75	.23
157 Edgar Martinez	.50	.15
158 John Olerud	.30	.09
159 John Smoltz	.50	.15
160 Ryne Sandberg	1.25	.35
161 Billy Taylor	.30	.09
162 Chris Holt	.30	.09
163 Damion Easley	.30	.09
164 Darin Erstad	.30	.09
165 Joe Carter	.30	.09
166 Kelvim Escobar	.30	.09
167 Ken Caminiti	.30	.09
168 Pokey Reese	.30	.09
169 Ray Lankford	.30	.09
170 Livan Hernandez	.30	.09
171 Steve Kline	.30	.09
172 Tom Gordon	.30	.09
173 Travis Fryman	.30	.09
174 Al Martin	.30	.09
175 Andy Pettitte	.50	.15
176 Jeff Kent	.30	.09
177 Jimmy Key	.30	.09
178 Mark Grudzielanek	.30	.09
179 Tony Saunders	.30	.09
180 Barry Larkin	.75	.23
181 Bubba Trammell	.30	.09
182 Carlos Delgado	.30	.09
183 Carlos Baerga	.30	.09
184 Derek Bell	.30	.09
185 Henry Rodriguez	.30	.09
186 Jason Dickson	.30	.09
187 Ron Gant	.30	.09
188 Tony Womack	.30	.09
189 Justin Thompson	.30	.09
190 Fernando Tatis	.30	.09
191 Mark Wohlers	.30	.09
192 Takashi Kashiwada	.30	.09
193 Garret Anderson	.30	.09
194 Jose Cruz Jr.	.30	.09
195 Ricardo Rincon	.30	.09
196 Tim Naehring	.30	.09
197 Moises Alou	.30	.09
198 Eric Karros	.30	.09
199 John Jaha	.30	.09
200 Marty Cordova	.30	.09
201 Ken Hill	.30	.09
202 Chipper Jones	.75	.23
203 Kenny Lofton	.30	.09
204 Mike Mussina	.75	.23
205 Manny Ramirez	.30	.09
206 Todd Hollandsworth	.30	.09
207 Cecil Fielder	.30	.09
208 Mark McGwire	2.00	.60
209 Jim Leyritz	.30	.09
210 Ivan Rodriguez	.75	.23
211 Jeff Bagwell SC	2.00	.60
212 Barry Bonds SC	8.00	2.40
213 Roger Clemens SC	6.00	1.80
214 N.Garciaparra SC	5.00	1.50
215 Ken Griffey Jr. SC	5.00	1.50
216 Tony Gwynn SC	4.00	1.20
217 Randy Johnson SC	3.00	.90
218 Mark McGwire SC	8.00	2.40
219 Scott Rolen SC	2.00	.60
220 Frank Thomas SC	3.00	.90
221 Matt Perisho PROS	3.00	.90
222 Wes Helms PROS	3.00	.90
223 D.Dellucci PROS RC	3.00	.90
224 Todd Helton PROS	3.00	.90
225 Brian Rose PROS	3.00	.90
226 Aaron Boone PROS	3.00	.90
227 Keith Foulke PROS	3.00	.90
228 Homer Bush PROS	3.00	.90
229 S.Stewart PROS	3.00	.90
230 R.Hidalgo PROS	3.00	.90
231 Russ Johnson PROS	3.00	.90
232 H.Blanco PROS RC	3.00	.90
233 Paul Konerko PROS	3.00	.90
234 A.Williamson PROS	3.00	.90
235 S.Bowers PROS RC	3.00	.90
236 Jose Vidro PROS	3.00	.90
237 Derek Wallace PROS	3.00	.90
238 Ricky Ledee PROS SP	5.00	1.50
239 Ben Grieve PROS	3.00	.90
240 Lou Collier PROS	3.00	.90
241 Derrek Lee PROS	3.00	.90
242 Ruben Rivera PROS	3.00	.90
243 J.Velandia PROS SP	5.00	1.50
244 Andrew Vessel PROS	3.00	.90
245 Chris Carpenter PROS	3.00	.90
246 Ken Griffey Jr. CL	.75	.23
247 Alex Rodriguez CL	.75	.23
248 Diamond Ink CL	.30	.09
249 Frank Thomas CL	.50	.15
250 Cal Ripken CL	1.25	.35
251 Carlos Perez	.30	.09
252 Larry Sutton	.30	.09
253 Gary Sheffield	.30	.09
254 Wally Joyner	.30	.09
255 Todd Stottlemyre	.30	.09
256 Nerio Rodriguez	.30	.09
257 Charles Johnson	.30	.09
258 Pedro Astacio	.30	.09
259 Cal Eldred	.30	.09
260 Chili Davis	.30	.09
261 Freddy Garcia	.30	.09
262 Bobby Witt	.30	.09
263 Michael Coleman	.30	.09
264 Mike Caruso	.30	.09
265 Mike Lansing	.30	.09
266 Dennis Reyes	.30	.09
267 F.P. Santangelo	.30	.09
268 Darryl Hamilton	.30	.09
269 Mike Fetters	.30	.09
270 Charlie Hayes	.30	.09
271 Royce Clayton	.30	.09
272 Doug Drabek	.30	.09
273 James Baldwin	.30	.09
274 Brian Hunter	.30	.09
275 Chan Ho Park	.30	.09
276 John Franco	.30	.09
277 David Wells	.30	.09
278 Eli Marrero	.30	.09
279 Kerry Wood	.75	.23
280 Donnie Sadler	.30	.09
281 Scott Winchester RC	.30	.09
282 Hal Morris	.30	.09
283 Brad Fullmer	.30	.09
284 Bernard Gilkey	.30	.09
285 Ramiro Mendoza	.30	.09
286 Kevin Brown	.50	.15
287 David Segui	.30	.09
288 Willie McGee	.30	.09
289 Darren Oliver	.30	.09
290 Antonio Alfonseca	.30	.09
291 Eric Davis	.30	.09
292 Mickey Morandini	.30	.09
293 Frank Catalanotto RC	.50	.15
294 Derrek Lee	.30	.09
295 Todd Zeile	.30	.09
296 Chuck Knoblauch	.30	.09
297 Wilson Delgado	.30	.09
298 Bobby Bonilla	.30	.09
299 Orel Hershiser	.30	.09
300 Ozzie Guillen	.30	.09
301 Aaron Sele	.30	.09
302 Joe Carter	.30	.09
303 Darryl Kile	.30	.09
304 Shane Reynolds	.30	.09
305 Todd Dunn	.30	.09
306 Bob Abreu	.30	.09
307 Doug Strange	.30	.09
308 Jose Canseco	.75	.23
309 Lance Johnson	.30	.09
310 Harold Baines	.30	.09
311 Todd Pratt	.30	.09
312 Greg Colbrunn	.30	.09
313 Masato Yoshii RC	.50	.15
314 Felix Heredia	.30	.09
315 Dennis Martinez	.30	.09
316 Geronimo Berroa	.30	.09
317 Darren Lewis	.30	.09
318 Bill Ripken	.30	.09
319 Enrique Wilson	.30	.09
320 Alex Ochoa	.30	.09
321 Doug Glanville	.30	.09
322 Mike Stanley	.30	.09
323 Gerald Williams	.30	.09
324 Pedro Martinez	.75	.23
325 Jaret Wright	.30	.09
326 Terry Pendleton	.30	.09
327 LaTroy Hawkins	.30	.09
328 Emil Brown	.30	.09
329 Walt Weiss	.30	.09
330 Omar Vizquel	.30	.09
331 Carl Everett	.30	.09

332 Fernando Vina .30 .09
333 Mike Blowers .30 .09
334 Dwight Gooden .30 .09
335 Mark Lewis .30 .09
336 Jim Leyritz .30 .09
337 Kenny Lofton .30 .09
338 John Halama RC .30 .09
339 Jose Valentin .30 .09
340 Desi Relaford .30 .09
341 Dante Powell .30 .09
342 Ed Sprague .30 .09
343 Reggie Jefferson .30 .09
344 Mike Hampton .30 .09
345 Marquis Grissom .30 .09
346 Heathcliff Slocumb .30 .09
347 Francisco Cordova .30 .09
348 Ken Cloude .30 .09
349 Benito Santiago .30 .09
350 Denny Neagle .30 .09
351 Sean Casey .30 .09
352 Robb Nen .30 .09
353 Orlando Merced .30 .09
354 Adrian Brown .30 .09
355 Gregg Jefferies .30 .09
356 Otis Nixon .30 .09
357 Michael Tucker .30 .09
358 Eric Milton .30 .09
359 Travis Fryman .30 .09
360 Gary DiSarcina .30 .09
361 Mario Valdez .30 .09
362 Craig Counsell .30 .09
363 Jose Offerman .30 .09
364 Tony Fernandez .30 .09
365 Jason McDonald .30 .09
366 Sterling Hitchcock .30 .09
367 Donovan Osborne .30 .09
368 Troy Percival .30 .09
369 Henry Rodriguez .30 .09
370 Dmitri Young .30 .09
371 Jay Powell .30 .09
372 Jeff Conine .30 .09
373 Orlando Cabrera .30 .09
374 Butch Huskey .30 .09
375 Mike Lowell RC 1.50 .45
376 Kevin Young .30 .09
377 Jamie Moyer .30 .09
378 Jeff D'Amico .30 .09
379 Scott Erickson .30 .09
380 Magglio Ordonez RC 2.50 .75
381 Melvin Nieves .30 .09
382 Ramon Martinez .30 .09
383 A.J. Hinch .30 .09
384 Jeff Brantley .30 .09
385 Kevin Elster .30 .09
386 Allen Watson .30 .09
387 Moises Alou .30 .09
388 Jeff Blauser .30 .09
389 Pete Harnisch .30 .09
390 Shane Andrews .30 .09
391 Rico Brogna .30 .09
392 Stan Javier .30 .09
393 David Howard .30 .09
394 Darryl Strawberry .50 .15
395 Kent Mercker .30 .09
396 Juan Encarnacion .30 .09
397 Sandy Alomar Jr. .30 .09
398 Al Leiter .30 .09
399 Tony Graffanino .30 .09
400 Terry Adams .30 .09
401 Bruce Aven .30 .09
402 Derrick Gibson .30 .09
403 Jose Cabrera RC .30 .09
404 Rich Becker .30 .09
405 David Ortiz .30 .09
406 Brian McRae .30 .09
407 Bobby Estalella .30 .09
408 Bill Mueller .30 .09
409 Dennis Eckersley .30 .09
410 Sandy Martinez .30 .09
411 Jose Vizcaino .30 .09
412 Jermaine Allensworth .30 .09
413 Miguel Tejada .50 .15
414 Turner Ward .30 .09
415 Glenallen Hill .30 .09
416 Lee Stevens .30 .09
417 Cecil Fielder .30 .09
418 Ruben Sierra .30 .09
419 Jon Nunnally .30 .09
420 Rod Myers .30 .09
421 Dustin Hermanson .30 .09
422 James Mouton .30 .09
423 Dan Wilson .30 .09
424 Roberto Kelly .30 .09
425 Antonio Osuna .30 .09
426 Jacob Cruz .30 .09
427 Brent Mayne .30 .09
428 Matt Karchner .30 .09
429 Damian Jackson .30 .09
430 Roger Cedeno .30 .09
431 Rickey Henderson .75 .23
432 Joe Randa .30 .09
433 Greg Vaughn .30 .09
434 Andres Galarraga .30 .09
435 Rod Beck .30 .09
436 Curtis Goodwin .30 .09
437 Brad Ausmus .30 .09
438 Bob Hamelin .30 .09
439 Todd Walker .30 .09
440 Scott Brosius .30 .09
441 Len Dykstra .30 .09
442 Abraham Nunez .30 .09
443 Brian Johnson .30 .09
444 Randy Myers .30 .09
445 Bret Boone .30 .09
446 Oscar Henriquez .30 .09
447 Mike Sweeney .30 .09
448 Kenny Rogers .30 .09
449 Mark Langston .30 .09
450 Luis Gonzalez .30 .09
451 John Burkett .30 .09
452 Bip Roberts .30 .09
453 Travis Lee .30 .09
454 Felix Rodriguez .30 .09
455 Andy Benes .30 .09
456 Willie Blair .30 .09
457 Brian Anderson .30 .09
458 Jay Bell .30 .09
459 Matt Williams .30 .09
460 Devon White .30 .09
461 Karim Garcia .30 .09
462 Jorge Fabregas .30 .09
463 Wilson Alvarez .30 .09
464 Roberto Hernandez .30 .09
465 Tony Saunders .30 .09
466 Rolando Arrojo RC .30 .09
467 Wade Boggs .75 .23
468 Fred McGriff .50 .15
469 Paul Sorrento .30 .09
470 Kevin Stocker .30 .09
471 Bubba Trammell .30 .09
472 Quinton McCracken .30 .09
473 Ken Griffey Jr. CL .75 .23
474 Cal Ripken CL 1.25 .35
475 Frank Thomas CL .50 .15
476 Ken Griffey Jr. PZ 4.00 1.20
477 Cal Ripken PZ 8.00 2.40
478 Frank Thomas PZ 2.50 .75
479 Alex Rodriguez PZ 4.00 1.20
480 Nomar Garciaparra PZ 4.00 1.20
481 Derek Jeter PZ 6.00 1.80
482 Andruw Jones PZ 1.00 .30
483 Chipper Jones PZ 2.50 .75
484 Greg Maddux PZ 4.00 1.20
485 Mike Piazza PZ 4.00 1.20
486 Juan Gonzalez PZ 2.50 .75
487 Jose Cruz Jr. PZ 1.00 .30
488 Jaret Wright PZ 1.00 .30
489 Hideo Nomo PZ 2.50 .75
490 Scott Rolen PZ 1.50 .45
491 Tony Gwynn PZ 3.00 .90
492 Roger Clemens PZ 5.00 1.50
493 Darin Erstad PZ 1.00 .30
494 Mark McGwire PZ 6.00 1.80
495 Jeff Bagwell PZ 1.50 .45
496 Mo Vaughn PZ 1.00 .30
497 Albert Belle PZ 1.00 .30
498 Kenny Lofton PZ 1.00 .30
499 Ben Grieve PZ 1.00 .30
500 Barry Bonds PZ 6.00 1.80
501 Mike Piazza 1.25 .35
S100 A.Rodriguez AU/750 80.00 24.00

1998 Ultra Gold Medallion

Randomly inserted one in every first and second series hobby pack, this 501-card set is parallel to the base set and features a gold metallic foil background.

Nm-Mt Ex-Mt
COMPLETE SET (501) 300.00 90.00
COMP.SERIES 1 (250) 150.00 45.00
COMP.SERIES 2 (251) 150.00 45.00
*STARS: 1.25X TO 3X BASIC CARDS .
*ROOKIES: .75X TO 2X BASIC CARDS
*SEASON CROWNS: .3X TO .8X BASIC SC
*PROSPECTS: .25X TO .6X BASIC PROS.
*CHECKLISTS: 1.25X TO 3X BASIC CL'S
*PIZZAZZ: .4X TO 1.X BASIC PIZZAZZ

1998 Ultra Platinum Medallion

Randomly inserted in first and second series hobby packs, this 498-card set is parallel to the base set. Only 100 first series sets and 98 second series sets were produced and each card is serially numbered in gold foil on back. Ten Platinum exchange cards good for a complete series one set were inserted into first series hobby packs. Another ten Platinum exchange cards good for a complete series two set were inserted in second series hobby packs. The three basic-issue checklist cards (473,474 and 475) were never printed in platinum form.

Nm-Mt Ex-Mt
*STARS: 10X TO 25X BASIC CARDS..
*ROOKIES: 10X TO 25X BASIC CARDS
*SEASON CROWNS: 1.5X TO 4X BASIC SC
*PROSPECTS: 2.5X TO 6X BASIC PROSP.
*CHECKLISTS: 12.5X TO 30X BASIC CL'S
*PIZZAZZ: 2X TO 5X BASIC PIZZAZZ..

1998 Ultra Artistic Talents

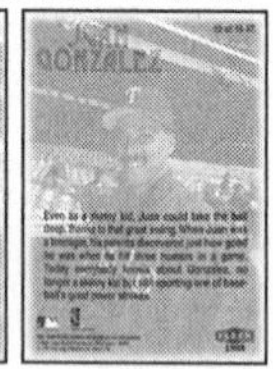

Randomly inserted in Series one packs at the rate of one in eight, this 18-card set features color pictures of top players on art enhanced cards.

Nm-Mt Ex-Mt
COMPLETE SET (18) 50.00 15.00
1 Ken Griffey Jr. 4.00 1.20
2 Andruw Jones 1.00 .30
3 Alex Rodriguez 4.00 1.20
4 Frank Thomas 2.50 .75
5 Cal Ripken 8.00 2.40
6 Derek Jeter 6.00 1.80
7 Chipper Jones 2.50 .75
8 Greg Maddux 4.00 1.20
9 Mike Piazza 4.00 1.20
10 Albert Belle 1.00 .30
11 Darin Erstad 1.00 .30
12 Juan Gonzalez 2.50 .75
13 Jeff Bagwell 1.50 .45
14 Tony Gwynn 3.00 .90
15 Mark McGwire 6.00 1.80
16 Scott Rolen 1.50 .45
17 Barry Bonds 6.00 1.80
18 Kenny Lofton 1.00 .30

1998 Ultra Back to the Future

Randomly inserted in Series one packs at the rate of one in six, this 15-card set features color photos of top Rookies. The backs carry player information.

Nm-Mt Ex-Mt
COMPLETE SET (15) 12.00 3.60
1 Andruw Jones .50 .15
2 Alex Rodriguez 2.00 .60

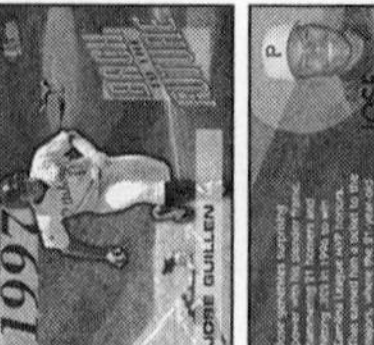

3 Derek Jeter 3.00 .90
4 Darin Erstad .50 .15
5 Mike Cameron .50 .15
6 Scott Rolen .75 .23
7 Nomar Garciaparra 2.00 .60
8 Hideki Irabu .50 .15
9 Jose Cruz Jr. .50 .15
10 Vladimir Guerrero 1.25 .35
11 Mark Kotsay .50 .15
12 Tony Womack .50 .15
13 Jason Dickson .50 .15
14 Jose Guillen .50 .15
15 Tony Clark .50 .15

1998 Ultra Big Shots

Randomly inserted in Series one packs at the rate of one in four, this 15-card set features color photos of players who hit the longest home runs in the 1997 season.

Nm-Mt Ex-Mt
COMPLETE SET (15) 10.00 3.00
1 Ken Griffey Jr. 1.50 .45
2 Frank Thomas 1.00 .30
3 Chipper Jones 1.00 .30
4 Albert Belle .40 .12
5 Juan Gonzalez 1.00 .30
6 Jeff Bagwell .60 .18
7 Mark McGwire 2.50 .75
8 Barry Bonds 2.50 .75
9 Manny Ramirez .40 .12
10 Mo Vaughn .40 .12
11 Matt Williams .40 .12
12 Jim Thome 1.00 .30
13 Tino Martinez .60 .18
14 Mike Piazza 1.50 .45
15 Tony Clark .40 .12

1998 Ultra Diamond Immortals

Randomly inserted in packs at a rate of one in 288, this 15-card insert set highlights color action photos of future Hall of Famers on die-cut cards with full silver holofoil backgrounds.

Nm-Mt Ex-Mt
COMPLETE SET (15) 400.00 120.00
1 Ken Griffey Jr. 40.00 12.00
2 Frank Thomas 25.00 7.50
3 Alex Rodriguez 40.00 12.00
4 Cal Ripken 80.00 24.00
5 Mike Piazza 40.00 12.00
6 Mark McGwire 60.00 18.00
7 Greg Maddux 40.00 12.00
8 Andruw Jones 10.00 3.00
9 Chipper Jones 25.00 7.50
10 Derek Jeter 60.00 18.00
11 Tony Gwynn 30.00 9.00
12 Juan Gonzalez 25.00 7.50
13 Jose Cruz Jr. 10.00 3.00
14 Roger Clemens 50.00 15.00
15 Barry Bonds 60.00 18.00

1998 Ultra Diamond Producers

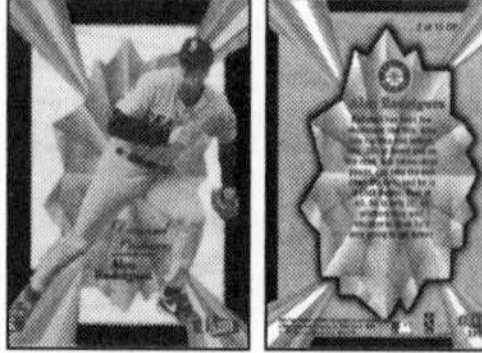

Randomly inserted in Series one packs at the rate of one in 288, this 15-card set features color photos of Major League Baseball's top players.

Nm-Mt Ex-Mt
COMPLETE SET (15) 400.00 120.00
1 Ken Griffey Jr. 30.00 9.00
2 Andruw Jones 8.00 2.40
3 Alex Rodriguez 30.00 9.00
4 Frank Thomas 20.00 6.00
5 Cal Ripken 60.00 18.00
6 Derek Jeter 50.00 15.00
7 Chipper Jones 20.00 6.00
8 Greg Maddux 30.00 9.00
9 Mike Piazza 30.00 9.00
10 Juan Gonzalez 20.00 6.00
11 Jeff Bagwell 12.00 3.60
12 Tony Gwynn 25.00 7.50
13 Mark McGwire 50.00 15.00
14 Barry Bonds 50.00 15.00
15 Jose Cruz Jr. 8.00 2.40

1998 Ultra Double Trouble

Randomly inserted in Series one packs at the rate of one in four, this 20-card set features color photos of two star players per card.

Nm-Mt Ex-Mt
COMPLETE SET (20) 12.00 3.60
1 Ken Griffey Jr. 1.50 .45
Alex Rodriguez
2 Vladimir Guerrero .60 .18
Pedro Martinez
3 Andruw Jones .30 .09
Kenny Lofton
4 Chipper Jones 1.00 .30
Greg Maddux
5 Derek Jeter 1.50 .45
Tino Martinez
6 Frank Thomas .60 .18
Albert Belle
7 Cal Ripken 2.50 .75
Roberto Alomar
8 Mike Piazza 1.25 .35
Hideo Nomo
9 Darin Erstad .25 .07
Jason Dickson
10 Juan Gonzalez .60 .18
Ivan Rodriguez
11 Jeff Bagwell .40 .12
Darryl Kile
UER front Kyle
12 Tony Gwynn 1.25 .35
Steve Finley
13 Mark McGwire 2.00 .60
Ray Lankford
14 Barry Bonds 1.00 .30
Jeff Kent
15 Andy Pettitte .40 .12
Bernie Williams
16 Mo Vaughn 1.25 .35
Nomar Garciaparra
17 Matt Williams .60 .18
Jim Thome
18 Hideki Irabu .30 .09
Mariano Rivera
19 Roger Clemens 2.00 .60
Jose Cruz Jr.
20 Manny Ramirez .30 .09
David Justice

1998 Ultra Fall Classics

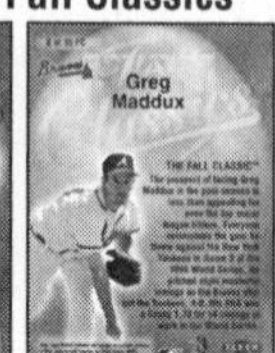

Randomly inserted in Series one packs at the rate of one in 18, this 15-card set features color photos of the top potential postseason heroes. The backs carry player information.

Nm-Mt Ex-Mt
COMPLETE SET (15) 100.00 30.00
1 Ken Griffey Jr. 8.00 2.40
2 Andruw Jones 2.00 .60
3 Alex Rodriguez 8.00 2.40
4 Frank Thomas 5.00 1.50
5 Cal Ripken 15.00 4.50
6 Derek Jeter 12.00 3.60
7 Chipper Jones 5.00 1.50
8 Greg Maddux 8.00 2.40
9 Mike Piazza 8.00 2.40
10 Albert Belle 2.00 .60
11 Juan Gonzalez 5.00 1.50
12 Jeff Bagwell 3.00 .90
13 Tony Gwynn 6.00 1.80
14 Mark McGwire 12.00 3.60
15 Barry Bonds 12.00 3.60

1998 Ultra Kid Gloves

Radomly inserted in Series one packs at the rate of one in eight, this 12-card set features color photos of top young defensive players. The backs carry player information.

Nm-Mt Ex-Mt
COMPLETE SET (12) 15.00 4.50
1 Andruw Jones .60 .18
2 Alex Rodriguez 2.50 .75
3 Derek Jeter 4.00 1.20
4 Chipper Jones 1.50 .45
5 Darin Erstad .60 .18
6 Todd Walker .60 .18
7 Scott Rolen 1.00 .30
8 Nomar Garciaparra 2.50 .75
9 Jose Cruz Jr. .60 .18
10 Charles Johnson .60 .18
11 Rey Ordonez .60 .18
12 Vladimir Guerrero 1.50 .45

1998 Ultra Millennium Men

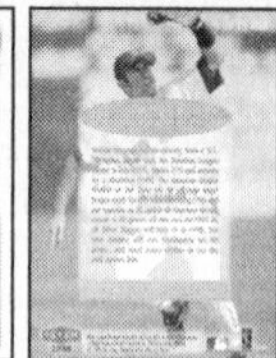

Randomly inserted in hobby only packs at a rate of one in 35, this 15-card insert set features a player action photo on an irridescent silver foil underlay that opens to reveal a second photo with a personal profile. For an added touch, a foil stamp embossed in the center gives the feel of a wax seal.

Nm-Mt Ex-Mt
COMPLETE SET (15) 120.00 36.00
1 Jose Cruz Jr. 2.50 .75
2 Ken Griffey Jr. 10.00 3.00
3 Cal Ripken 20.00 6.00
4 Derek Jeter 15.00 4.50
5 Andruw Jones 2.50 .75
6 Alex Rodriguez 10.00 3.00
7 Chipper Jones 6.00 1.80
8 Scott Rolen 4.00 1.20
9 Nomar Garciaparra 10.00 3.00
10 Frank Thomas 6.00 1.80
11 Mike Piazza 10.00 3.00
12 Greg Maddux 10.00 3.00
13 Juan Gonzalez 6.00 1.80
14 Ben Grieve 25.00 7.50
15 Jaret Wright 2.50 .75

1998 Ultra Notables

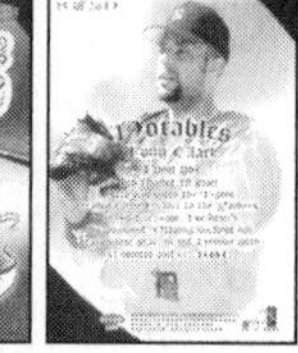

Randomly inserted in packs at a rate of one in four, this 20-card insert set features a color action player photo on a borderless UV coated front with a design of the American Eagle in the background.

Nm-Mt Ex-Mt
COMPLETE SET (20) 25.00 7.50
1 Frank Thomas 1.25 .35
2 Ken Griffey Jr. 2.00 .60
3 Edgar Renteria .50 .15
4 Albert Belle .50 .15
5 Juan Gonzalez 1.25 .35
6 Jeff Bagwell .75 .23
7 Mark McGwire 3.00 .90
8 Barry Bonds 3.00 .90
9 Scott Rolen .75 .23
10 Mo Vaughn .50 .15
11 Andruw Jones .50 .15
12 Chipper Jones 1.25 .35
13 Tino Martinez .75 .23
14 Mike Piazza 2.00 .60
15 Tony Clark .50 .15
16 Jose Cruz Jr. .50 .15
17 Nomar Garciaparra 2.00 .60
18 Cal Ripken 4.00 1.20
19 Alex Rodriguez 2.00 .60
20 Derek Jeter 3.00 .90

1998 Ultra Power Plus

Randomly inserted in Series one packs at the rate of one in 36, this 10-card set features color action photos of top young and veteran players. The backs carry player information.

Nm-Mt Ex-Mt
COMPLETE SET (10) 60.00 18.00
1 Ken Griffey Jr. 12.00 3.60
2 Andruw Jones 3.00 .90
3 Alex Rodriguez 12.00 3.60
4 Frank Thomas 8.00 2.40
5 Mike Piazza 12.00 3.60
6 Albert Belle 3.00 .90
7 Juan Gonzalez 8.00 2.40
8 Jeff Bagwell 5.00 1.50
9 Barry Bonds 20.00 6.00
10 Jose Cruz Jr. 3.00 .90

1998 Ultra Prime Leather

mly inserted in Series one packs at the rate of one in 144, this 18-card set features color photos of young and veteran players considered to be good glove men. The backs carry player information.

Nm-Mt Ex-Mt
1 Ken Griffey Jr. 25.00 7.50
2 Andruw Jones 6.00 1.80

3 Alex Rodriguez 25.00 7.50
4 Frank Thomas 15.00 4.50
5 Cal Ripken 50.00 15.00
6 Derek Jeter 40.00 12.00
7 Chipper Jones 15.00 4.50
8 Greg Maddux 25.00 7.50
9 Mike Piazza 25.00 7.50
10 Albert Belle 6.00 1.80
11 Darin Erstad 6.00 1.80
12 Juan Gonzalez 15.00 4.50
13 Jeff Bagwell 10.00 3.00
14 Tony Gwynn 20.00 6.00
15 Roberto Alomar 15.00 4.50
16 Barry Bonds 40.00 12.00
17 Kenny Lofton 6.00 1.80
18 Jose Cruz Jr. 6.00 1.80

1998 Ultra Rocket to Stardom

Randomly inserted in packs at a rate of one in 20, this 15-card insert set showcases rookies on a sculpted embossed and die-cut card designed to resemble a cloud of smoke.

Nm-Mt Ex-Mt
COMPLETE SET (15) 30.00 9.00
1 Ben Grieve 2.00 .60
2 Magglio Ordonez 8.00 2.40
3 Travis Lee 2.00 .60
4 Mike Caruso 2.00 .60
5 Brian Rose 2.00 .60
6 Brad Fullmer 2.00 .60
7 Michael Coleman 2.00 .60
8 Juan Encarnacion 2.00 .60
9 Karim Garcia 2.00 .60
10 Todd Helton 3.00 .90
11 Richard Hidalgo 2.00 .60
12 Paul Konerko 2.00 .60
13 Rod Myers 2.00 .60
14 Jaret Wright 2.00 .60
15 Miguel Tejada 3.00 .90

1998 Ultra Ticket Studs

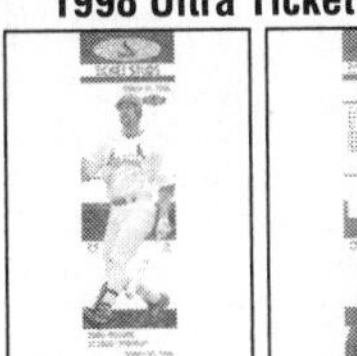

Randomly inserted in packs at a rate of one in 144, this 15-card insert set features color action player photos on sculpture embossed ticket-like designed cards. The cards open up to give details on what makes fans so crazy about their favorite players.

Nm-Mt Ex-Mt
COMPLETE SET (15) 250.00 75.00
1 Travis Lee 6.00 1.80
2 Tony Gwynn 20.00 6.00
3 Scott Rolen 10.00 3.00
4 Nomar Garciaparra 25.00 7.50
5 Mike Piazza 25.00 7.50
6 Mark McGwire 40.00 12.00
7 Ken Griffey Jr. 25.00 7.50
8 Juan Gonzalez 15.00 4.50
9 Jose Cruz Jr. 6.00 1.80
10 Frank Thomas 15.00 4.50
11 Derek Jeter 40.00 12.00
12 Chipper Jones 15.00 4.50
13 Cal Ripken 50.00 15.00
14 Andruw Jones 6.00 1.80
15 Alex Rodriguez 25.00 7.50

1998 Ultra Top 30

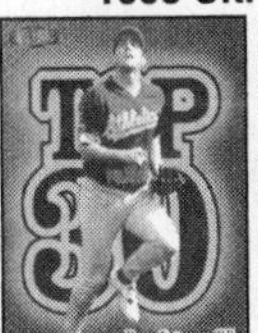

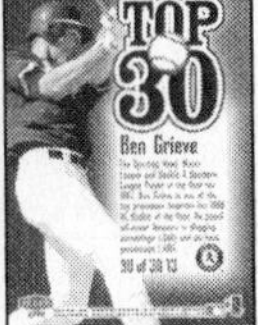

These cards which feature 30 of the leading baseball players were issued one per retail series two pack.

Nm-Mt Ex-Mt
COMPLETE SET (30) 25.00 7.50
1 Barry Bonds 2.50 .75
2 Ivan Rodriguez 1.00 .30
3 Kenny Lofton .40 .12
4 Albert Belle .40 .12
5 Mo Vaughn .40 .12
6 Jeff Bagwell .60 .18
7 Mark McGwire 2.50 .75
8 Darin Erstad .40 .12
9 Roger Clemens 2.00 .60
10 Tony Gwynn 1.25 .35
11 Scott Rolen .60 .18
12 Hideo Nomo 1.00 .30
13 Juan Gonzalez 1.00 .30
14 Mike Piazza 1.50 .45
15 Greg Maddux 1.50 .45
16 Chipper Jones 1.00 .30
17 Andruw Jones .40 .12
18 Derek Jeter 2.50 .75
19 Nomar Garciaparra 1.50 .45
20 Alex Rodriguez 1.50 .45
21 Frank Thomas 1.00 .30
22 Cal Ripken 3.00 .90
23 Ken Griffey Jr. 1.50 .45
24 Jose Cruz Jr. .40 .12
25 Jaret Wright .40 .12
26 Travis Lee .40 .12
27 Wade Boggs 1.00 .30
28 Chuck Knoblauch .40 .12
29 Joe Carter .40 .12
30 Ben Grieve .40 .12

1998 Ultra Win Now

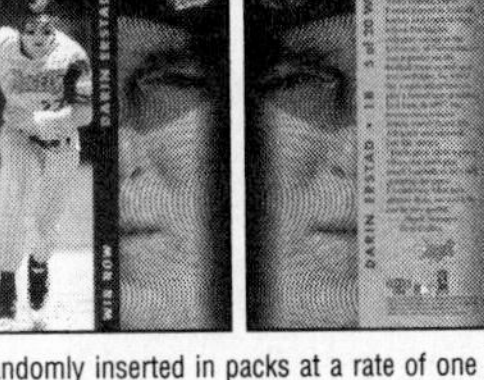

Randomly inserted in packs at a rate of one in 72, this 20-card insert set features color action photos on plastic cards. A transparent section of the front allows you to see the player image in reverse from the back.

Nm-Mt Ex-Mt
COMPLETE SET (20) 250.00 75.00
1 Alex Rodriguez 20.00 6.00
2 Andruw Jones 5.00 1.50
3 Cal Ripken 40.00 12.00
4 Chipper Jones 12.00 3.60
5 Darin Erstad 5.00 1.50
6 Derek Jeter 30.00 9.00
7 Frank Thomas 12.00 3.60
8 Greg Maddux 20.00 6.00
9 Hideo Nomo 12.00 3.60
10 Jeff Bagwell 8.00 2.40
11 Jose Cruz Jr. 5.00 1.50
12 Juan Gonzalez 12.00 3.60
13 Ken Griffey Jr. 20.00 6.00
14 Mark McGwire 30.00 9.00
15 Mike Piazza 20.00 6.00
16 Mo Vaughn 5.00 1.50
17 Nomar Garciaparra 20.00 6.00
18 Roger Clemens 25.00 7.50
19 Scott Rolen 8.00 2.40
20 Tony Gwynn 15.00 4.50

1999 Ultra Promo Sheet

This six card uncut sheet was distributed in dealer wholesale order forms and hobby media releases in late October, several weeks prior to the release of 1999 Ultra 1 baseball. The sheet is made up of six player cards, each of which parallel the player's regular issue Ultra card, except of course, for bold diagonal text stating "PROMOTIONAL SAMPLE" on the front and back of the cards.

Nm-Mt Ex-Mt
NNO 99 Ultra 1 Sheet 5.00 1.50
Nomar Garciaparra
Andruw Jones
Kenny Lofton
Mark McGwire
Alex Rodriguez
Kerry Wood

1999 Ultra

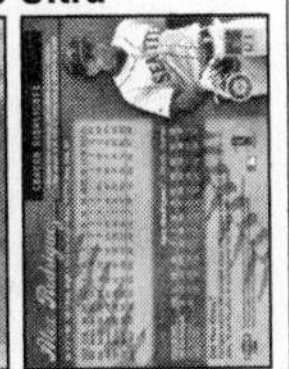

This 250-card single-series set was distributed in 10-card packs with a suggested retail price of $2.69 and features color player photos on the fronts with stats by year in 15 categories and career highlights on the backs for 210 veterans. The set contains the following subsets: Prospects (25 rookie cards seeded 1:4 packs), Season Crowns (10 1998 statistical leaders seeded 1:8) and five checklist cards.

Nm-Mt Ex-Mt
COMPLETE SET (250) 80.00 24.00
COMP.SET w/o SP's (215) 25.00 7.50
COMMON CARD (1-215) .30 .09
COMMON SC (216-225) .75 .23
COMMON (226-250) 2.00 .60
1 Greg Maddux 1.25 .35
2 Greg Vaughn .30 .09
3 John Wetteland .30 .09
4 Tino Martinez .50 .15
5 Todd Walker .30 .09
6 Troy O'Leary .30 .09
7 Barry Larkin .75 .23
8 Mike Lansing .30 .09
9 Delino DeShields .30 .09
10 Brett Tomko .30 .09
11 Carlos Perez .30 .09
12 Mark Langston .30 .09
13 Jamie Moyer .30 .09
14 Jose Guillen .30 .09
15 Bartolo Colon .30 .09
16 Brady Anderson .30 .09
17 Walt Weiss .30 .09
18 Shane Reynolds .30 .09
19 David Segui .30 .09
20 Vladimir Guerrero .75 .23
21 Freddy Garcia .30 .09
22 Carl Everett .30 .09
23 Jose Cruz Jr. .30 .09
24 David Ortiz .30 .09
25 Andruw Jones .30 .09
26 Darren Lewis .30 .09
27 Ray Lankford .30 .09
28 Wally Joyner .30 .09
29 Charles Johnson .30 .09
30 Derek Jeter 2.00 .60
31 Sean Casey .30 .09
32 Bobby Bonilla .30 .09
33 Todd Zeile .30 .09
34 Todd Helton .50 .15
35 David Wells .30 .09
36 Darin Erstad .30 .09
37 Ivan Rodriguez .75 .23
38 Antonio Osuna .30 .09
39 Mickey Morandini .30 .09
40 Rusty Greer .30 .09
41 Rod Beck .30 .09
42 Larry Sutton .30 .09
43 Edgar Renteria .30 .09
44 Otis Nixon .30 .09
45 Eli Marrero .30 .09
46 Reggie Jefferson .30 .09
47 Trevor Hoffman .30 .09
48 Andres Galarraga .30 .09
49 Scott Brosius .30 .09
50 Vinny Castilla .30 .09
51 Bret Boone .30 .09
52 Masato Yoshii .30 .09
53 Matt Williams .30 .09
54 Robin Ventura .30 .09
55 Jay Powell .30 .09
56 Dean Palmer .30 .09
57 Eric Milton .30 .09
58 Willie McGee .30 .09
59 Tony Gwynn 1.00 .30
60 Tom Gordon .30 .09
61 Dante Bichette .30 .09
62 Jaret Wright .30 .09
63 Devon White .30 .09
64 Frank Thomas .75 .23
65 Mike Piazza 1.25 .35
66 Jose Offerman .30 .09
67 Pat Meares .30 .09
68 Brian Meadows .30 .09
69 Nomar Garciaparra 1.25 .35
70 Mark McGwire 2.00 .60
71 Tony Graffanino .30 .09
72 Ken Griffey Jr. 1.25 .35
73 Ken Caminiti .30 .09
74 Todd Jones .30 .09
75 A.J. Hinch .30 .09
76 Marquis Grissom .30 .09
77 Jay Buhner .30 .09
78 Albert Belle .30 .09
79 Brian Anderson .30 .09
80 Quinton McCracken .30 .09
81 Omar Vizquel .30 .09
82 Todd Stottlemyre .30 .09
83 Cal Ripken 2.50 .75
84 Magglio Ordonez .30 .09
85 John Olerud .30 .09
86 Hal Morris .30 .09
87 Derrek Lee .30 .09
88 Doug Glanville .30 .09
89 Marty Cordova .30 .09
90 Kevin Brown .30 .09
91 Kevin Young .30 .09
92 Rico Brogna .30 .09
93 Wilson Alvarez .30 .09
94 Bob Wickman .30 .09
95 Jim Thome .75 .23
96 Mike Mussina .75 .23
97 Al Leiter .30 .09
98 Travis Lee .30 .09
99 Jeff King .30 .09
100 Kerry Wood .75 .23
101 Cliff Floyd .30 .09
102 Jose Valentin .30 .09
103 Manny Ramirez .30 .09
104 Butch Huskey .30 .09
105 Scott Erickson .30 .09
106 Ray Durham .30 .09
107 Johnny Damon .30 .09
108 Craig Counsell .30 .09
109 Rolando Arrojo .30 .09
110 Bob Abreu .30 .09
111 Tony Womack .30 .09
112 Mike Stanley .30 .09
113 Kenny Lofton .30 .09
114 Eric Davis .30 .09
115 Jeff Conine .30 .09
116 Carlos Baerga .30 .09
117 Rondell White .30 .09
118 Billy Wagner .30 .09
119 Ed Sprague .30 .09
120 Jason Schmidt .30 .09
121 Edgar Martinez .50 .15
122 Travis Fryman .30 .09
123 Armando Benitez .30 .09
124 Matt Stairs .30 .09
125 Roberto Hernandez .30 .09
126 Jay Bell .30 .09
127 Justin Thompson .30 .09
128 John Jaha .30 .09
129 Mike Caruso .30 .09
130 Miguel Tejada .30 .09
131 Geoff Jenkins .30 .09
132 Wade Boggs .50 .15
133 Andy Benes .30 .09
134 Aaron Sele .30 .09
135 Bret Saberhagen .30 .09
136 Mariano Rivera .50 .15
137 Neifi Perez .30 .09
138 Paul Konerko .30 .09
139 Barry Bonds 2.00 .60
140 Garret Anderson .30 .09
141 Bernie Williams .50 .15
142 Gary Sheffield .30 .09
143 Rafael Palmeiro .50 .15
144 Orel Hershiser .30 .09
145 Craig Biggio .50 .15
146 Dmitri Young .30 .09
147 Damion Easley .30 .09
148 Henry Rodriguez .30 .09
149 Brad Radke .30 .09
150 Pedro Martinez .75 .23
151 Mike Lieberthal .30 .09
152 Jim Leyritz .30 .09
153 Chuck Knoblauch .30 .09
154 Darryl Kile .30 .09
155 Brian Jordan .30 .09
156 Chipper Jones .75 .23
157 Pete Harnisch .30 .09
158 Moises Alou .30 .09
159 Ismael Valdes .30 .09
160 Stan Javier .30 .09
161 Mark Grace .50 .15
162 Jason Giambi .75 .23
163 Chuck Finley .30 .09
164 Juan Encarnacion .30 .09
165 Chan Ho Park .30 .09
166 Randy Johnson .75 .23
167 J.T. Snow .30 .09
168 Tim Salmon .50 .15
169 Brian L.Hunter .30 .09
170 Rickey Henderson .75 .23
171 Cal Eldred .30 .09
172 Curt Schilling .50 .15
173 Alex Rodriguez 1.25 .35
174 Dustin Hermanson .30 .09
175 Mike Hampton .30 .09
176 Shawn Green .30 .09
177 Roberto Alomar .75 .23
178 Sandy Alomar Jr. .30 .09
179 Larry Walker .50 .15
180 Mo Vaughn .30 .09
181 Raul Mondesi .30 .09
182 Hideki Irabu .30 .09
183 Jim Edmonds .30 .09
184 Shawn Estes .30 .09
185 Tony Clark .30 .09
186 Dan Wilson .30 .09
187 Michael Tucker .30 .09
188 Jeff Shaw .30 .09
189 Mark Grudzielanek .30 .09
190 Roger Clemens 1.50 .45
191 Juan Gonzalez .75 .23
192 Sammy Sosa 1.25 .35
193 Troy Percival .30 .09
194 Robb Nen .30 .09
195 Bill Mueller .30 .09
196 Ben Grieve .30 .09
197 Luis Gonzalez .30 .09
198 Will Clark .75 .23
199 Jeff Cirillo .30 .09
200 Scott Rolen .50 .15
201 Reggie Sanders .30 .09
202 Fred McGriff .50 .15
203 Denny Neagle .30 .09
204 Brad Fullmer .30 .09
205 Royce Clayton .30 .09
206 Jose Canseco .75 .23
207 Jeff Bagwell .50 .15
208 Hideo Nomo .75 .23
209 Karim Garcia .30 .09
210 Kenny Rogers .30 .09
211 Kerry Wood CL .50 .15
212 Alex Rodriguez CL .75 .23
213 Cal Ripken CL 1.25 .35
214 Frank Thomas CL .50 .15
215 Ken Griffey Jr. CL .75 .23
216 Alex Rodriguez SC 3.00 .90
217 Greg Maddux SC 3.00 .90
218 Juan Gonzalez SC 2.00 .60
219 Ken Griffey Jr. SC 3.00 .90
220 Kerry Wood SC 2.00 .60
221 Mark McGwire SC 5.00 1.50
222 Mike Piazza SC 3.00 .90
223 Rickey Henderson SC 2.00 .60
224 Sammy Sosa SC 3.00 .90
225 Travis Lee SC .75 .23
226 Gabe Alvarez PROS 2.00 .60
227 Matt Anderson PROS 2.00 .60
228 Adrian Beltre PROS 2.00 .60
229 O.Cabrera PROS 2.00 .60
230 Orl. Hernandez PROS 2.00 .60
231 A.Ramirez PROS 2.00 .60
232 Troy Glaus PROS 3.00 .90
233 Gabe Kapler PROS 2.00 .60
234 Jeremy Giambi PROS 2.00 .60
235 Derrick Gibson PROS 2.00 .60
236 Carlton Loewer PROS 2.00 .60
237 Mike Frank PROS 2.00 .60
238 Carlos Guillen PROS 2.00 .60
239 Alex Gonzalez PROS 2.00 .60
240 Enrique Wilson PROS 2.00 .60
241 J.D. Drew PROS 2.00 .60
242 Bruce Chen PROS 2.00 .60
243 Ryan Minor PROS 2.00 .60
244 Preston Wilson PROS 2.00 .60
245 Josh Booty PROS 2.00 .60
246 Luis Ordaz PROS 2.00 .60
247 G.Lombard PROS 2.00 .60
248 Matt Clement PROS 2.00 .60
249 Eric Chavez PROS 2.00 .60
250 Corey Koskie PROS 2.00 .60

1999 Ultra Gold Medallion

Randomly inserted one in every hobby only pack for regular cards, one in 40 for Prospects, and one in 80 for Season Crowns, this 250-card set is a gold parallel version of the base set.

Nm-Mt Ex-Mt
*STARS: 1.25X TO 3X BASIC CARDS .
*SC STARS: 2X TO 5X BASIC SC........
*PROSPECTS: 1X TO 2.5X BASIC PROSPECTS

1999 Ultra Platinum Medallion

Randomly inserted in hobby packs only, this 250-card set is a parallel version of the base set. Only 99 of the 210 veteran cards were produced and numbered. Only 65 of the Prospects (cards numbered from 226 through 250) subset was produced and serially numbered. Only 50 of the Season Crowns (cards numbered from 216 through 225) subset was produced and serially numbered.

Nm-Mt Ex-Mt
*STARS: 15X TO 40X BASIC CARDS ..
*SC STARS: 12.5X TO 30X BASIC SC.
*PROSPECTS: 2.5X TO 6X BASE PROSPECTS

1999 Ultra The Book On

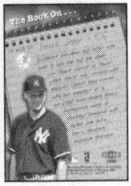

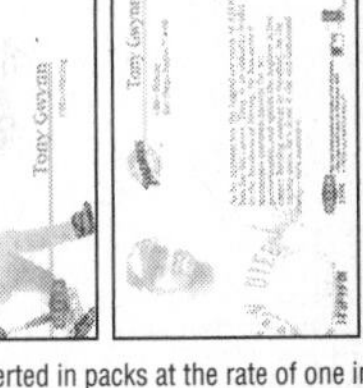

Randomly inserted in packs at the rate of one in six, this 20-card set features action color photos of top players with a detailed analysis of why they are so good printed on the backs.

Nm-Mt Ex-Mt
COMPLETE SET (20) 50.00 15.00
1 Kerry Wood 2.00 .60
2 Ken Griffey Jr. 3.00 .90
3 Frank Thomas 2.00 .60
4 Albert Belle .75 .23
5 Juan Gonzalez 2.00 .60
6 Jeff Bagwell 1.25 .35
7 Mark McGwire 5.00 1.50
8 Barry Bonds 5.00 1.50
9 Andruw Jones .75 .23
10 Mo Vaughn .75 .23
11 Scott Rolen 1.25 .35
12 Travis Lee .75 .23
13 Tony Gwynn 2.50 .75
14 Greg Maddux 3.00 .90
15 Mike Piazza 3.00 .90
16 Chipper Jones 2.00 .60
17 Nomar Garciaparra 3.00 .90
18 Cal Ripken 6.00 1.80
19 Derek Jeter 5.00 1.50
20 Alex Rodriguez 3.00 .90

1999 Ultra Damage Inc.

Randomly inserted in packs at the rate of one in 72, this 15-card set features color images of top players printed on a business card design.

Nm-Mt Ex-Mt
COMPLETE SET (15) 200.00 60.00
1 Alex Rodriguez 15.00 4.50
2 Greg Maddux 15.00 4.50
3 Cal Ripken 30.00 9.00
4 Chipper Jones 10.00 3.00
5 Derek Jeter 25.00 7.50
6 Frank Thomas 10.00 3.00
7 Juan Gonzalez 10.00 3.00
8 Ken Griffey Jr. 15.00 4.50
9 Kerry Wood 10.00 3.00
10 Mark McGwire 25.00 7.50
11 Mike Piazza 15.00 4.50
12 Nomar Garciaparra 15.00 4.50
13 Scott Rolen 6.00 1.80
14 Tony Gwynn 12.00 3.60
15 Travis Lee 4.00 1.20

1999 Ultra Diamond Producers

Randomly inserted in packs at the rate of one in 288, this 10-card set features action color player photos printed on full foil plastic die-cut cards with custom embossing.

Nm-Mt Ex-Mt
COMPLETE SET (10) 300.00 90.00
1 Ken Griffey Jr. 20.00 6.00
2 Frank Thomas 12.00 3.60
3 Alex Rodriguez 20.00 6.00
4 Cal Ripken 40.00 12.00
5 Mike Piazza 20.00 6.00
6 Mark McGwire 30.00 9.00
7 Greg Maddux 20.00 6.00
8 Kerry Wood 12.00 3.60
9 Chipper Jones 12.00 3.60
10 Derek Jeter 30.00 9.00

1999 Ultra RBI Kings

Randomly inserted one in every retail pack only, this 30-card set features action color photos of top run producing players.

	Nm-Mt	Ex-Mt
COMPLETE SET (30)	30.00	9.00
1 Rafael Palmeiro	.60	.18
2 Mo Vaughn	.40	.12
3 Ivan Rodriguez	1.00	.30
4 Barry Bonds	2.50	.75
5 Albert Belle	.40	.12
6 Jeff Bagwell	.60	.18
7 Mark McGwire	2.50	.75
8 Darin Erstad	.40	.12
9 Manny Ramirez	.40	.12
10 Chipper Jones	1.00	.30
11 Jim Thome	1.00	.30
12 Scott Rolen	.60	.18
13 Tony Gwynn	1.25	.35
14 Juan Gonzalez	1.00	.30
15 Mike Piazza	1.50	.45
16 Sammy Sosa	1.50	.45
17 Andruw Jones	.40	.12
18 Derek Jeter	2.50	.75
19 Nomar Garciaparra	1.50	.45
20 Alex Rodriguez	1.50	.45
21 Frank Thomas	1.00	.30
22 Cal Ripken	3.00	.90
23 Ken Griffey Jr.	1.50	.45
24 Travis Lee	.40	.12
25 Paul O'Neill	.40	.12
26 Greg Vaughn	.40	.12
27 Andres Galarraga	.40	.12
28 Tino Martinez	.60	.18
29 Jose Canseco	1.00	.30
30 Ben Grieve	.40	.12

1999 Ultra Thunderclap

Randomly inserted in packs at the rate of one in 36, this 15-card set features color player photos printed on embossed cards with silver pattern holofoil.

	Nm-Mt	Ex-Mt
COMPLETE SET (15)	100.00	30.00
1 Alex Rodriguez	8.00	2.40
2 Andruw Jones	2.00	.60
3 Cal Ripken	15.00	4.50
4 Chipper Jones	5.00	1.50
5 Darin Erstad	2.00	.60
6 Derek Jeter	12.00	3.60
7 Frank Thomas	5.00	1.50
8 Jeff Bagwell	3.00	.90
9 Juan Gonzalez	5.00	1.50
10 Ken Griffey Jr.	8.00	2.40
11 Mark McGwire	12.00	3.60
12 Mike Piazza	8.00	2.40
13 Travis Lee	2.00	.60
14 Nomar Garciaparra	8.00	2.40
15 Scott Rolen	3.00	.90

1999 Ultra World Premiere

Randomly inserted in packs at the rate of one in 18, this 15-card set features action color photos of top 1998 rookies printed on sculpture embossed silver holofoil cards.

	Nm-Mt	Ex-Mt
COMPLETE SET (15)	20.00	6.00
1 Gabe Alvarez	1.25	.35
2 Kerry Wood	5.00	1.50
3 Orlando Hernandez	1.25	.35
4 Mike Caruso	2.00	.60
5 Matt Anderson	1.25	.35
6 Randall Simon	2.00	.60
7 Adrian Beltre	1.25	.35
8 Scott Elarton	2.00	.60
9 Karim Garcia	2.00	.60
10 Mike Frank	1.25	.35
11 Richard Hidalgo	2.00	.60
12 Paul Konerko	2.00	.60
13 Travis Lee	2.00	.60
14 J.D. Drew	1.50	.45
15 Miguel Tejada	2.00	.60

2000 Ultra

This 300 card set was issued late in 1999. The cards were distributed in 10 card packs with an SRP of $2.69. The product was issued in either 8, 12 or 30 box cases. The prospect subset were numbered from 251 through 300 and were printed in shorter quantity than the regular cards and inserted one every four packs. Two separate Alex Rodriguez Promo cards were distributed to dealers and hobby media several weeks prior to the product's release. The first card features identical glossy card front stock as the basic Ultra 2000 product and has the words "PROMOTIONAL SAMPLE" running diagonally across the back of the card. The second, more scarce, card features a lenticular ribbed plastic card front (creating a primitive 3-D effect). Both promos share the same photo of Rodriguez as is used on the basic issue A-Rod 2000 Ultra card.

	Nm-Mt	Ex-Mt
COMPLETE SET (300)	100.00	30.00
COMP.SET w/o SP's (250)	25.00	7.50
COMMON CARD (1-250)	.30	.09
COMMON (251-300)	4.00	1.20
1 Alex Rodriguez	1.25	.35
2 Shawn Green	.30	.09
3 Magglio Ordonez	.30	.09
4 Tony Gwynn	1.00	.30
5 Joe McEwing	.30	.09
6 Jose Rosado	.30	.09
7 Sammy Sosa	1.25	.35
8 Gary Sheffield	.30	.09
9 Mickey Morandini	.30	.09
10 Mo Vaughn	.30	.09
11 Todd Hollandsworth	.30	.09
12 Tom Gordon	.30	.09
13 Charles Johnson	.30	.09
14 Derek Bell	.30	.09
15 Kevin Young	.30	.09
16 Jay Buhner	.30	.09
17 J.T. Snow	.30	.09
18 Jay Bell	.30	.09
19 John Rocker	.30	.09
20 Ivan Rodriguez	.75	.23
21 Pokey Reese	.30	.09
22 Paul O'Neill	.50	.15
23 Ronnie Belliard	.30	.09
24 Ryan Rupe	.30	.09
25 Travis Fryman	.30	.09
26 Trot Nixon	.50	.15
27 Wally Joyner	.30	.09
28 Andy Pettitte	.50	.15
29 Dan Wilson	.30	.09
30 Orlando Hernandez	.30	.09
31 Dmitri Young	.30	.09
32 Edgar Renteria	.30	.09
33 Eric Karros	.30	.09
34 Fernando Seguignol	.30	.09
35 Jason Kendall	.30	.09
36 Jeff Shaw	.30	.09
37 Matt Lawton	.30	.09
38 Robin Ventura	.50	.15
39 Scott Williamson	.30	.09
40 Ben Grieve	.30	.09
41 Billy Wagner	.30	.09
42 Javy Lopez	.30	.09
43 Joe Randa	.30	.09
44 Neifi Perez	.30	.09
45 David Justice	.30	.09
46 Ray Durham	.30	.09
47 Dustin Hermanson	.30	.09
48 Andres Galarraga	.30	.09
49 Brad Fullmer	.30	.09
50 Nomar Garciaparra	1.25	.35
51 David Cone	.30	.09
52 David Nilsson	.30	.09
53 David Wells	.30	.09
54 Miguel Tejada	.30	.09
55 Ismael Valdes	.30	.09
56 Jose Lima	.30	.09
57 Juan Encarnacion	.30	.09
58 Fred McGriff	.50	.15
59 Kenny Rogers	.30	.09
60 Vladimir Guerrero	.75	.23
61 Benito Santiago	.30	.09
62 Chris Singleton	.30	.09
63 Carlos Lee	.30	.09
64 Sean Casey	.30	.09
65 Tom Goodwin	.30	.09
66 Todd Hundley	.30	.09
67 Ellis Burks	.30	.09
68 Tim Hudson	.50	.15
69 Matt Stairs	.30	.09
70 Chipper Jones UER Dodgers logo on the back	.75	.23
71 Craig Biggio	.50	.15
72 Brian Rose	.30	.09
73 Carlos Delgado	.30	.09
74 Eddie Taubensee	.30	.09
75 John Smoltz	.50	.15
76 Ken Caminiti	.30	.09
77 Rafael Palmeiro	.50	.15
78 Sidney Ponson	.30	.09
79 Todd Helton	.50	.15
80 Juan Gonzalez	.75	.23
81 Bruce Aven	.30	.09
82 Desi Relaford	.30	.09
83 Johnny Damon	.30	.09
84 Albert Belle	.30	.09
85 Mark McGwire	2.00	.60
86 Rico Brogna	.30	.09
87 Tom Glavine	.50	.15
88 Harold Baines	.30	.09
89 Chad Allen	.30	.09
90 Barry Bonds	2.00	.60
91 Mark Grace	.50	.15
92 Paul Byrd	.30	.09
93 Roberto Alomar	.75	.23
94 Roberto Hernandez	.30	.09
95 Steve Finley	.30	.09
96 Bret Boone	.30	.09
97 Charles Nagy	.30	.09
98 Eric Chavez	.30	.09
99 Jamie Moyer	.30	.09
100 Ken Griffey Jr.	1.25	.35
101 J.D. Drew	.30	.09
102 Todd Stottlemyre	.30	.09
103 Tony Fernandez	.30	.09
104 Jeromy Burnitz	.30	.09
105 Jeremy Giambi	.30	.09
106 Livan Hernandez	.30	.09
107 Marlon Anderson	.30	.09
108 Troy Glaus	.50	.15
109 Troy O'Leary	.30	.09
110 Scott Rolen	.50	.15
111 Bernard Gilkey	.30	.09
112 Brady Anderson	.30	.09
113 Chuck Knoblauch	.30	.09
114 Jeff Weaver	.30	.09
115 B.J. Surhoff	.30	.09
116 Alex Gonzalez	.30	.09
117 Vinny Castilla	.30	.09
118 Tim Salmon	.50	.15
119 Brian Jordan	.30	.09
120 Corey Koskie	.30	.09
121 Dean Palmer	.30	.09
122 Gabe Kapler	.30	.09
123 Jim Edmonds	.30	.09
124 John Jaha	.30	.09
125 Mark Grudzielanek	.30	.09
126 Mike Bordick	.30	.09
127 Mike Lieberthal	.30	.09
128 Pete Harnisch	.30	.09
129 Russ Ortiz	.30	.09
130 Kevin Brown	.50	.15
131 Troy Percival	.30	.09
132 Alex Gonzalez	.30	.09
133 Bartolo Colon	.30	.09
134 John Valentin	.30	.09
135 Jose Hernandez	.30	.09
136 Marquis Grissom	.30	.09
137 Wade Boggs	.50	.15
138 Dante Bichette	.30	.09
139 Bobby Higginson	.30	.09
140 Frank Thomas	.75	.23
141 Geoff Jenkins	.30	.09
142 Jason Giambi	.75	.23
143 Jeff Cirillo	.30	.09
144 Sandy Alomar Jr	.30	.09
145 Luis Gonzalez	.30	.09
146 Preston Wilson	.30	.09
147 Carlos Beltran	.30	.09
148 Greg Vaughn	.30	.09
149 Carlos Febles	.30	.09
150 Jose Canseco	.75	.23
151 Kris Benson	.30	.09
152 Chuck Finley	.30	.09
153 Michael Barrett	.30	.09
154 Rey Ordonez	.30	.09
155 Adrian Beltre	.30	.09
156 Andruw Jones	.30	.09
157 Barry Larkin	.75	.23
158 Brian Giles	.30	.09
159 Carl Everett	.30	.09
160 Manny Ramirez	.30	.09
161 Darryl Kile	.30	.09
162 Edgar Martinez	.50	.15
163 Jeff Kent	.30	.09
164 Matt Williams	.30	.09
165 Mike Piazza	1.25	.35
166 Pedro Martinez	.75	.23
167 Ray Lankford	.30	.09
168 Roger Cedeno	.30	.09
169 Ron Coomer	.30	.09
170 Cal Ripken	2.50	.75
171 Jose Offerman	.30	.09
172 Kenny Lofton	.30	.09
173 Kent Bottenfield	.30	.09
174 Kevin Millwood	.30	.09
175 Omar Daal	.30	.09
176 Orlando Cabrera	.30	.09
177 Pat Hentgen	.30	.09
178 Tino Martinez	.50	.15
179 Tony Clark	.30	.09
180 Roger Clemens	1.50	.45
181 Brad Radke	.30	.09
182 Darin Erstad	.30	.09
183 Jose Jimenez	.30	.09
184 Jim Thome	.75	.23
185 John Wetteland	.30	.09
186 Justin Thompson	.30	.09
187 John Halama	.30	.09
188 Lee Stevens	.30	.09
189 Miguel Cairo	.30	.09
190 Mike Mussina	.75	.23
191 Raul Mondesi	.30	.09
192 Armando Rios	.30	.09
193 Trevor Hoffman	.30	.09
194 Tony Batista	.30	.09
195 Will Clark	.75	.23
196 Brad Ausmus	.30	.09
197 Chili Davis	.30	.09
198 Cliff Floyd	.30	.09
199 Curt Schilling	.50	.15
200 Derek Jeter	2.00	.60
201 Henry Rodriguez	.30	.09
202 Jose Cruz Jr.	.30	.09
203 Omar Vizquel	.30	.09
204 Randy Johnson	.75	.23
205 Reggie Sanders	.30	.09
206 Al Leiter	.30	.09
207 Damion Easley	.30	.09
208 David Bell	.30	.09
209 Fernando Tatis	.30	.09
210 Kerry Wood	.75	.23
211 Kevin Appier	.30	.09
212 Mariano Rivera	.50	.15
213 Mike Caruso	.30	.09
214 Moises Alou	.30	.09
215 Randy Winn	.30	.09
216 Roy Halladay	.30	.09
217 Shannon Stewart	.30	.09
218 Todd Walker	.30	.09
219 Jim Parque	.30	.09
220 Travis Lee	.30	.09
221 Andy Ashby	.30	.09
222 Ed Sprague	.30	.09
223 Larry Walker	.50	.15
224 Rick Helling	.30	.09
225 Rusty Greer	.30	.09
226 Todd Zeile	.30	.09
227 Freddy Garcia	.30	.09
228 Hideo Nomo	.75	.23
229 Marty Cordova	.30	.09
230 Greg Maddux	1.25	.35
231 Rondell White	.30	.09
232 Paul Konerko	.30	.09
233 Warren Morris	.30	.09
234 Bernie Williams	.50	.15
235 Bob Abreu	.30	.09
236 John Olerud	.30	.09
237 Doug Glanville	.30	.09
238 Eric Young	.30	.09
239 Robb Nen	.30	.09
240 Jeff Bagwell	.50	.15
241 Sterling Hitchcock	.30	.09
242 Todd Greene	.30	.09
243 Bill Mueller	.30	.09
244 Rickey Henderson	.75	.23
245 Chan Ho Park	.30	.09
246 Jason Schmidt	.30	.09
247 Jeff Zimmerman	.30	.09
248 Jermaine Dye	.30	.09
249 Randall Simon	.30	.09
250 Richie Sexson	.30	.09
251 Micah Bowie PROS	4.00	1.20
252 Joe Nathan PROS	4.00	1.20
253 C.Woodward PROS	4.00	1.20
254 Lance Berkman PROS	4.00	1.20
255 Ruben Mateo PROS	4.00	1.20
256 R.Branyan PROS	4.00	1.20
257 Randy Wolf PROS	4.00	1.20
258 A.J. Burnett PROS	4.00	1.20
259 Mark Quinn PROS	4.00	1.20
260 Buddy Carlyle PROS	4.00	1.20
261 Ben Davis PROS	4.00	1.20
262 Yamid Haad PROS	4.00	1.20
263 Mike Colangelo PROS	4.00	1.20
264 Rick Ankiel PROS	4.00	1.20
265 Jacque Jones PROS	4.00	1.20
266 Kelly Dransfeldt PROS	4.00	1.20
267 Matt Riley PROS	4.00	1.20
268 Adam Kennedy PROS	4.00	1.20
269 Octavio Dotel PROS	4.00	1.20
270 F.Cordero PROS	4.00	1.20
271 Wilton Veras PROS	4.00	1.20
272 C.Pickering PROS	4.00	1.20
273 Alex Sanchez PROS	4.00	1.20
274 Tony Armas Jr. PROS	4.00	1.20
275 Pat Burrell PROS	5.00	1.50
276 Chad Meyers PROS	4.00	1.20
277 Ben Petrick PROS	4.00	1.20
278 R.Hernandez PROS	4.00	1.20
279 Ed Yarnall PROS	4.00	1.20
280 Erubiel Durazo PROS	4.00	1.20
281 Vernon Wells PROS	4.00	1.20
282 G.Matthews Jr. PROS	4.00	1.20
283 Kip Wells PROS	4.00	1.20
284 Peter Bergeron PROS	4.00	1.20
285 Travis Dawkins PROS	4.00	1.20
286 Jorge Toca PROS	4.00	1.20
287 Cole Liniak PROS	4.00	1.20
288 C.Hermansen PROS	4.00	1.20
289 Eric Gagne PROS	5.00	1.50
290 C.Hutchinson PROS	4.00	1.20
291 Eric Munson PROS	4.00	1.20
292 Wiki Gonzalez PROS	4.00	1.20
293 A.Soriano PROS	5.00	1.50
294 T.Durrington PROS	4.00	1.20
295 Ben Molina PROS	4.00	1.20
296 Aaron Myette PROS	4.00	1.20
297 Wily Pena PROS	4.00	1.20
298 Kevin Barker PROS	4.00	1.20
299 Geoff Blum PROS	4.00	1.20
300 Josh Beckett PROS	6.00	1.80
P1 Alex Rodriguez Promo	1.50	.45
P2 A.Rodriguez Promo 3-D	5.00	1.50

2000 Ultra Gold Medallion

This set is a parallel to the regular Ultra set. The regular cards from 1 through 250 were issued one per hobby pack and the prospect cards were issued one every 24 hobby packs. These cards have special die-cutting and have gold coating and gold foil stamping.

Nm-Mt Ex-Mt

*STARS 1-250: 1.25X TO 3X BASIC CARDS
*PROSPECTS: .75X TO 2X BASIC CARDS

2000 Ultra Platinum Medallion

Randomly inserted into hobby packs, these cards parallel the regular Ultra set. These cards are serial numbered to 50 for the veterans and 25 for the prospects (251-300). These die cut cards have silver coating and silver foil. Pricing is unavaiable due to scarcity on cards 251-300.

Nm-Mt Ex-Mt

*STARS 1-250: 15X TO 40X BASIC CARDS
*PROSPECTS: 4X TO 10X BASIC CARDS
251-300 NO PRICING DUE TO SCARCITY

2000 Ultra Crunch Time

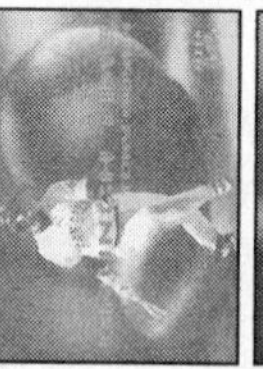

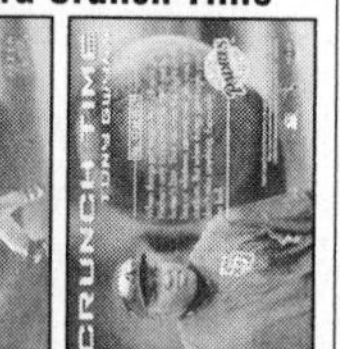

Inserted one every 72 packs, these 15 cards feature players who are among those players known for their clutch performances. The horizontal cards are printed on suede stock and then are gold foil stamped.

	Nm-Mt	Ex-Mt
COMPLETE SET (15)	200.00	60.00
1 Nomar Garciaparra	12.00	3.60
2 Ken Griffey Jr.	12.00	3.60
3 Mark McGwire	20.00	6.00
4 Alex Rodriguez	12.00	3.60
5 Derek Jeter	20.00	6.00
6 Sammy Sosa	12.00	3.60
7 Mike Piazza	12.00	3.60
8 Cal Ripken	25.00	7.50
9 Frank Thomas	8.00	2.40
10 Juan Gonzalez	8.00	2.40
11 J.D. Drew	3.00	.90
12 Greg Maddux	12.00	3.60
13 Tony Gwynn	10.00	3.00
14 Vladimir Guerrero	8.00	2.40
15 Ben Grieve	3.00	.90

2000 Ultra Diamond Mine

Inserted one every six packs, these 15 cards feature some of the brightest stars of the baseball diamond. The cards are printed on silver metallic ink and have silver foil stamping.

	Nm-Mt	Ex-Mt
COMPLETE SET (15)	30.00	9.00
1 Greg Maddux	2.00	.60
2 Mark McGwire	3.00	.90
3 Ken Griffey Jr.	2.00	.60
4 Cal Ripken	4.00	1.20
5 Nomar Garciaparra	2.00	.60
6 Mike Piazza	2.00	.60
7 Alex Rodriguez	2.00	.60
8 Frank Thomas	1.25	.35
9 Juan Gonzalez	1.25	.35
10 Derek Jeter	3.00	.90
11 Tony Gwynn	1.50	.45
12 Chipper Jones	1.25	.35
13 Sammy Sosa	2.00	.60
14 Roger Clemens	2.50	.75
15 Vladimir Guerrero	1.25	.35

2000 Ultra Feel the Game

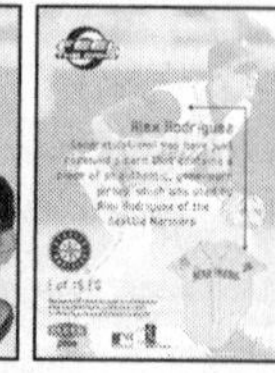

Inserted at a rate of one in 168, these cards feature pieces of game used memorabilia of some of today's stars. There is a player photo to go with the swatch of clothing used. It is widely believed that the Frank Thomas is the toughest card to find in the set.

	Nm-Mt	Ex-Mt
1 Alex Rodriguez Jsy	25.00	7.50
2 Chipper Jones Jsy	15.00	4.50
3 Rob Alomar Btg Glv SP	50.00	15.00
4 Greg Maddux Jsy	15.00	4.50
5 Pedro Martinez Jsy	15.00	4.50
6 Cal Ripken Jsy	50.00	15.00
7 Robin Ventura Jsy	10.00	3.00
8 J.D. Drew Jsy	10.00	3.00
9 Randy Johnson Jsy	15.00	4.50
10 Scott Rolen Jsy	15.00	4.50
11 Kevin Millwood Jsy	10.00	3.00
12 Frank Thomas Btg Glv SP	80.00	24.00
13 Tony Gwynn Btg Glv SP	60.00	18.00
14 Curt Schilling Jsy	15.00	4.50
15 Edgar Martinez Btg Glv	15.00	4.50

2000 Ultra Fresh Ink

Randomly inserted into packs, these cards feature signed cards of either young players or veteran stars. One card in this set is a combo signature card of the three players used in the Club 3000 series. After each player name in our checklist is a number indicating how many cards they signed for this promotion.

	Nm-Mt	Ex-Mt
1 Bob Abreu/200	25.00	7.50
2 Chad Allen/975	10.00	3.00
3 Marlon Anderson/975	10.00	3.00
4 Rick Ankiel/500	10.00	3.00
5 Glen Barker/975	10.00	3.00
6 Michael Barrett/975	10.00	3.00
7 Carlos Beltran/975	15.00	4.50
8 Adrian Beltre/900	15.00	4.50
9 Peter Bergeron/1000	10.00	3.00
10 Wade Boggs/250	60.00	18.00
11 Barry Bonds/250	200.00	60.00
12 Pat Burrell/600	25.00	7.50
13 Roger Cedeno/500	15.00	4.50
14 Eric Chavez/800	15.00	4.50
15 Bruce Chen/600	10.00	3.00
16 Johnny Damon/750	15.00	4.50
17 Ben Davis/1000	10.00	3.00
18 Carlos Delgado/275	25.00	7.50
19 Einar Diaz/975	10.00	3.00
20 Octavio Dotel/950	10.00	3.00
21 J.D. Drew/600	15.00	4.50
22 Scott Elarton/1000	10.00	3.00
23 Freddy Garcia/500	15.00	4.50
24 Jeremy Giambi/975	10.00	3.00
25 Troy Glaus/500	25.00	7.50
26 Shawn Green/350	25.00	7.50
27 Tony Gwynn/250	60.00	18.00
28 Richard Hidalgo/500	15.00	4.50
29 Bobby Higginson/975	10.00	3.00
30 Tim Hudson/975	25.00	7.50
31 Norm Hutchins/1000	10.00	3.00
32 Derek Jeter/95	250.00	75.00
33 Randy Johnson/240	80.00	24.00
34 Gabe Kapler/725	10.00	3.00
35 Jason Kendall/375	25.00	7.50
36 Paul Konerko/500	15.00	4.50
37 Matt Lawton/1000	10.00	3.00
38 Carlos Lee/900	15.00	4.50
39 Jose Macias/1000	10.00	3.00
40 Greg Maddux/225	120.00	36.00
41 Kevin Millwood/500	15.00	4.50
42 Warren Morris/1000	10.00	3.00
43 Eric Munson/900	15.00	4.50
44 Heath Murray/925	10.00	3.00
45 Joe Nathan/1000	10.00	3.00
46 Magglio Ordonez/335	25.00	7.50
47 Angel Pena/1000	10.00	3.00

Card	Nm-Mt	Ex-Mt
48 Cal Ripken/350	150.00	45.00
49 Alex Rodriguez/350	120.00	36.00
50 Scott Rolen/250	40.00	12.00
51 Ryan Rupe/1000	10.00	3.00
52 Curt Schilling/375	40.00	12.00
53 Randall Simon/1000	10.00	3.00
54 Alfonso Soriano/975	40.00	12.00
55 Shannon Stewart/275	25.00	7.50
56 Miguel Tejada/1000	15.00	4.50
57 Frank Thomas/150	100.00	30.00
58 Jeff Weaver/1000	15.00	4.50
59 Randy Wolf/1000	15.00	4.50
60 Ed Yarnall/1000	10.00	3.00
61 Kevin Young/1000	10.00	3.00
62 Wade Boggs	500.00	150.00
Tony Gwynn		
Nolan Ryan 100		

2000 Ultra Swing Kings

Inserted one every 24 packs, these 10 cards feature some of the leading power hitters in baseball. These cards are made of contemporary plastice with glittering silver foil highlights.

Card	Nm-Mt	Ex-Mt
COMPLETE SET (10)	50.00	15.00
1 Cal Ripken	8.00	2.40
2 Nomar Garciaparra	4.00	1.20
3 Frank Thomas	2.50	.75
4 Tony Gwynn	3.00	.90
5 Ken Griffey Jr.	4.00	1.20
6 Chipper Jones	2.50	.75
7 Mark McGwire	6.00	1.80
8 Sammy Sosa	4.00	1.20
9 Derek Jeter	6.00	1.80
10 Alex Rodriguez	4.00	1.20

2000 Ultra Talented

Randomly inserted into hobby packs, these 10 cards feature multi-talented players. These cards feature metallic ink on holofoil background with gold fil stamped accents.

Card	Nm-Mt	Ex-Mt
COMPLETE SET (10)	600.00	180.00
1 Sammy Sosa	50.00	15.00
2 Derek Jeter	80.00	24.00
3 Alex Rodriguez	50.00	15.00
4 Mike Piazza	50.00	15.00
5 Ken Griffey Jr.	50.00	15.00
6 Nomar Garciaparra	50.00	15.00
7 Mark McGwire	80.00	24.00
8 Cal Ripken	100.00	30.00
9 Frank Thomas	30.00	9.00
10 J.D. Drew	12.00	3.60

2000 Ultra World Premiere

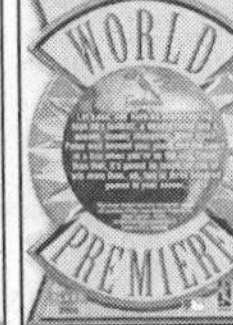

Inserted one every 12 packs, these 10 cards feature 12 of the leading prospects in baseball. The die cut cards are printed with etched foil.

Card	Nm-Mt	Ex-Mt
COMPLETE SET (10)	12.00	3.60
1 Ruben Mateo	1.00	.30
2 Lance Berkman	1.25	.35
3 Octavio Dotel	1.00	.30
4 Ben Davis	1.00	.30
5 Warren Morris	1.00	.30
6 Carlos Beltran	1.25	.35
7 Rick Ankiel	1.00	.30
8 Adam Kennedy	1.00	.30
9 Tim Hudson	2.00	.60
10 Jorge Toca	1.00	.30

2001 Ultra

The 2001 Ultra product was released in December, 2000 and features a 275-card base set. The base set is broken into tiers as follows: 250 Base Veterans, and 25 Prospects (1:4). Each pack contained 10-cards, and carried a suggested retail price of $2.99.

Card	Nm-Mt	Ex-Mt
COMPLETE SET (275)	120.00	36.00
COMP.SET w/o SP's (250)	25.00	7.50
COMMON CARD (1-250)	.30	.09
COMMON (251-275)	3.00	.90
COMMON (276-280)	5.00	1.50
1 Pedro Martinez	.75	.23
2 Derek Jeter	2.00	.60
3 Cal Ripken	2.50	.75
4 Alex Rodriguez	1.25	.35
5 Vladimir Guerrero	.75	.23
6 Troy Glaus	.50	.15
7 Sammy Sosa	1.25	.35
8 Mike Piazza	1.25	.35
9 Tony Gwynn	1.00	.30
10 Tim Hudson	.30	.09
11 John Flaherty	.30	.09
12 Jeff Cirillo	.30	.09
13 Ellis Burks	.30	.09
14 Carlos Lee	.30	.09
15 Carlos Beltran	.30	.09
16 Ruben Rivera	.30	.09
17 Richard Hidalgo	.30	.09
18 Omar Vizquel	.30	.09
19 Michael Barrett	.30	.09
20 Jose Canseco	.75	.23
21 Jason Giambi	.75	.23
22 Greg Maddux	1.25	.35
23 Charles Johnson	.30	.09
24 Sandy Alomar Jr.	.30	.09
25 Rick Ankiel	.30	.09
26 Richie Sexson	.30	.09
27 Matt Williams	.30	.09
28 Joe Girardi	.30	.09
29 Jason Kendall	.30	.09
30 Brad Fullmer	.30	.09
31 Alex Gonzalez	.30	.09
32 Rick Helling	.30	.09
33 Mike Mussina	.75	.23
34 Joe Randa	.30	.09
35 J.T. Snow	.30	.09
36 Edgardo Alfonzo	.30	.09
37 Dante Bichette	.30	.09
38 Brad Ausmus	.30	.09
39 Bobby Abreu	.30	.09
40 Warren Morris	.30	.09
41 Tony Womack	.30	.09
42 Russell Branyan	.30	.09
43 Mike Lowell	.30	.09
44 Mark Grace	.50	.15
45 Jeromy Burnitz	.30	.09
46 J.D. Drew	.30	.09
47 David Justice	.30	.09
48 Alex Gonzalez	.30	.09
49 Tino Martinez	.50	.15
50 Raul Mondesi	.30	.09
51 Rafael Furcal	.30	.09
52 Marquis Grissom	.30	.09
53 Kevin Young	.30	.09
54 Jon Lieber	.30	.09
55 Henry Rodriguez	.30	.09
56 Dave Burba	.30	.09
57 Shannon Stewart	.30	.09
58 Preston Wilson	.30	.09
59 Paul O'Neill	.50	.15
60 Jimmy Haynes	.30	.09
61 Darryl Kile	.30	.09
62 Bret Boone	.30	.09
63 Bartolo Colon	.30	.09
64 Andres Galarraga	.30	.09
65 Trot Nixon	.50	.15
66 Steve Finley	.30	.09
67 Shawn Green	.30	.09
68 Robert Person	.30	.09
69 Kenny Rogers	.30	.09
70 Bobby Higginson	.30	.09
71 Barry Larkin	.75	.23
72 Al Martin	.30	.09
73 Tom Glavine	.50	.15
74 Rondell White	.30	.09
75 Ray Lankford	.30	.09
76 Moises Alou	.30	.09
77 Matt Clement	.30	.09
78 Geoff Jenkins	.30	.09
79 David Wells	.30	.09
80 Chuck Finley	.30	.09
81 Andy Pettitte	.50	.15
82 Travis Fryman	.30	.09
83 Ron Coomer	.30	.09
84 Mark McGwire	2.00	.60
85 Kerry Wood	.75	.23
86 Jorge Posada	.50	.15
87 Jeff Bagwell	.50	.15
88 Andruw Jones	.30	.09
89 Ryan Klesko	.30	.09
90 Mariano Rivera	.50	.15
91 Lance Berkman	.30	.09
92 Kenny Lofton	.30	.09
93 Jacque Jones	.30	.09
94 Eric Young	.30	.09
95 Edgar Renteria	.30	.09
96 Chipper Jones	.75	.23
97 Todd Helton	.50	.15
98 Shawn Estes	.30	.09
99 Mark Mulder	.30	.09
100 Lee Stevens	.30	.09
101 Jermaine Dye	.30	.09
102 Greg Vaughn	.30	.09
103 Chris Singleton	.30	.09
104 Brady Anderson	.30	.09
105 Terrence Long	.30	.09
106 Quilvio Veras	.30	.09
107 Magglio Ordonez	.30	.09
108 Johnny Damon	.30	.09
109 Jeffrey Hammonds	.30	.09
110 Fred McGriff	.50	.15
111 Carl Pavano	.30	.09
112 Bobby Estalella	.30	.09
113 Todd Hundley	.30	.09
114 Scott Rolen	.50	.15
115 Robin Ventura	.30	.09
116 Pokey Reese	.30	.09
117 Luis Gonzalez	.30	.09
118 Jose Offerman	.30	.09
119 Edgar Martinez	.50	.15
120 Dean Palmer	.30	.09
121 David Segui	.30	.09
122 Troy O'Leary	.30	.09
123 Tony Batista	.30	.09
124 Todd Zeile	.30	.09
125 Randy Johnson	.75	.23
126 Luis Castillo	.30	.09
127 Kris Benson	.30	.09
128 John Olerud	.30	.09
129 Eric Karros	.30	.09
130 Eddie Taubensee	.30	.09
131 Neifi Perez	.30	.09
132 Matt Stairs	.30	.09
133 Luis Alicea	.30	.09
134 Jeff Kent	.30	.09
135 Javier Vazquez	.30	.09
136 Garret Anderson	.30	.09
137 Frank Thomas	.75	.23
138 Carlos Febles	.30	.09
139 Albert Belle	.30	.09
140 Tony Clark	.30	.09
141 Pat Burrell	.30	.09
142 Mike Sweeney	.30	.09
143 Jay Buhner	.30	.09
144 Gabe Kapler	.30	.09
145 Derek Bell	.30	.09
146 B.J. Surhoff	.30	.09
147 Adam Kennedy	.30	.09
148 Aaron Boone	.30	.09
149 Todd Stottlemyre	.30	.09
150 Roberto Alomar	.75	.23
151 Orlando Hernandez	.30	.09
152 Jason Varitek	.30	.09
153 Gary Sheffield	.30	.09
154 Cliff Floyd	.30	.09
155 Chad Hermansen	.30	.09
156 Carlos Delgado	.30	.09
157 Aaron Sele	.30	.09
158 Sean Casey	.30	.09
159 Ruben Mateo	.30	.09
160 Mike Bordick	.30	.09
161 Mike Cameron	.30	.09
162 Doug Glanville	.30	.09
163 Damion Easley	.30	.09
164 Carl Everett	.30	.09
165 Bengie Molina	.30	.09
166 Adrian Beltre	.30	.09
167 Tom Goodwin	.30	.09
168 Rickey Henderson	.75	.23
169 Mo Vaughn	.30	.09
170 Mike Lieberthal	.30	.09
171 Ken Griffey Jr.	1.25	.35
172 Juan Gonzalez	.75	.23
173 Ivan Rodriguez	.75	.23
174 Al Leiter	.30	.09
175 Vinny Castilla	.30	.09
176 Peter Bergeron	.30	.09
177 Pedro Astacio	.30	.09
178 Paul Konerko	.30	.09
179 Mitch Meluskey	.30	.09
180 Kevin Millwood	.30	.09
181 Ben Grieve	.30	.09
182 Barry Bonds	2.00	.60
183 Rusty Greer	.30	.09
184 Miguel Tejada	.30	.09
185 Mark Quinn	.30	.09
186 Larry Walker	.50	.15
187 Jose Valentin	.30	.09
188 Jose Vidro	.30	.09
189 Delino DeShields	.30	.09
190 Darin Erstad	.30	.09
191 Bill Mueller	.30	.09
192 Ray Durham	.30	.09
193 Ken Caminiti	.30	.09
194 Jim Thome	.75	.23
195 Javy Lopez	.30	.09
196 Fernando Vina	.30	.09
197 Eric Chavez	.30	.09
198 Eric Owens	.30	.09
199 Brad Radke	.30	.09
200 Travis Lee	.30	.09
201 Tim Salmon	.50	.15
202 Rafael Palmeiro	.50	.15
203 Nomar Garciaparra	1.25	.35
204 Mike Hampton	.30	.09
205 Kevin Brown	.30	.09
206 Juan Encarnacion	.30	.09
207 Danny Graves	.30	.09
208 Carlos Guillen	.30	.09
209 Phil Nevin	.30	.09
210 Matt Lawton	.30	.09
211 Manny Ramirez	.50	.15
212 James Baldwin	.30	.09
213 Fernando Tatis	.30	.09
214 Craig Biggio	.50	.15
215 Brian Jordan	.30	.09
216 Bernie Williams	.50	.15
217 Ryan Dempster	.30	.09
218 Roger Clemens	1.50	.45
219 Jose Cruz Jr.	.30	.09
220 John Valentin	.30	.09
221 Dmitri Young	.30	.09
222 Curt Schilling	.50	.15
223 Jim Edmonds	.30	.09
224 Chan Ho Park	.30	.09
225 Brian Giles	.30	.09
226 Jimmy Anderson	.30	.09
Tike Redman		
227 Adam Piatt	.30	.09
Jose Ortiz		
228 Kenny Kelly	.30	.09
Aubrey Huff		
229 Randy Choate	.30	.09
Craig Dingman		
230 Eric Cammack	.30	.09
Grant Roberts		
231 Yovanny Lara	.30	.09
Andy Tracy		
232 Wayne Franklin	.30	.09
Scott Linebrink		
233 Cameron Cairncross	.30	.09
Chan Perry		
234 J.C. Romero	.30	.09
Matt LeCroy		
235 Geraldo Guzman	.30	.09
Jason Conti		
236 Morgan Burkhart	.30	.09
Paxton Crawford		
237 Pasqual Coco	.30	.09
Leo Estrella		
238 John Parrish	.30	.09
Fernando Lunar		
239 Keith McDonald	.30	.09
Justin Brunette		
240 Carlos Casimiro	.30	.09
Ivanon Coffie		
241 Daniel Garibay	.30	.09
Ruben Quevedo		
242 Sang-Hoon Lee	.30	.09
Tomo Ohka		
243 Hector Ortiz	.30	.09
Jeff D'Amico		
244 Jeff Sparks	.30	.09
Travis Harper		
245 Jason Boyd	.30	.09
David Coggin		
246 Mark Buehrle	.30	.09
Lorenzo Barcelo		
247 Adam Melhuse	.30	.09
Ben Petrick		
248 Kane Davis	.30	.09
Paul Rigdon		
249 Mike Darr	.30	.09
Kory DeHaan		
250 Vicente Padilla	3.00	.90
Mark Brownson		
251 Barry Zito PROS	5.00	1.50
252 Tim Drew PROS	3.00	.90
253 Luis Matos PROS	4.00	1.20
254 Alex Cabrera PROS	3.00	.90
255 Jon Garland PROS	3.00	.90
256 Milton Bradley PROS	4.00	1.20
257 Juan Pierre PROS	4.00	1.20
258 Ismael Villegas PROS	3.00	.90
259 Eric Munson PROS	3.00	.90
260 T.De la Rosa PROS	3.00	.90
261 Chris Richard PROS	3.00	.90
262 Jason Tyner PROS	3.00	.90
263 B.J. Waszgis PROS	3.00	.90
264 Jason Marquis PROS	3.00	.90
265 Dusty Allen PROS	3.00	.90
266 C.Patterson PROS	4.00	1.20
267 Eric Byrnes PROS	3.00	.90
268 Xavier Nady PROS	4.00	1.20
269 G.Lombard PROS	3.00	.90
270 Timo Perez PROS	3.00	.90
271 G.Matthews Jr. PROS	3.00	.90
272 Chad Durbin PROS	3.00	.90
273 Tony Armas Jr. PROS	3.00	.90
274 F.Cordero PROS	3.00	.90
275 A.Soriano PROS	4.00	1.20
276 Junior Spivey RC	8.00	2.40
Juan Uribe RC		
277 Albert Pujols RC	40.00	12.00
Bud Smith RC		
278 Ichiro Suzuki RC	25.00	7.50
Tsuyoshi Shinjo RC		
279 Drew Henson RC	8.00	2.40
Jackson Melian RC		
280 Matt White RC	5.00	1.50
Adrian Hernandez RC		

2001 Ultra Gold Medallion

Inserted into packs at a rate of one per pack (251-275 were inserted at 1:24), this 275-card set is a complete parallel of the Ultra base set. Please note that these cards were produced with gold coating and gold foil stamping.

Nm-Mt Ex-Mt

*STARS 1-225: 1.25X TO 3X BASIC CARDS
*PROSPECTS 226-250: 1.25X TO 3X BASIC
*PROSPECTS 251-275: .75X TO 2X BASIC

2001 Ultra Platinum Medallion

Randomly inserted into packs, this 275-card set is a complete parallel of the Ultra base set. Cards 1-250 were individually serial numbered to 50, and cards 251-275 were individually serial numbered to 25. Please note that these cards were produced with a silver coating and silver foil stamping.

Nm-Mt Ex-Mt

*STARS 1-225: 20X TO 50X BASIC CARDS
*PROSPECTS 251-275: 4X TO 10X BASIC

2001 Ultra Decade of Dominance

Randomly inserted into packs at one in eight, this 15-card insert set features players that dominated Major League Baseball in the 1990's. Card backs carry a "DD" prefix.

Card	Nm-Mt	Ex-Mt
COMPLETE SET (15)	30.00	9.00
PLATINUM RANDOM INSERTS IN PACKS		
PLATINUM PRINT RUN 10 SERIAL #'d SETS		
PLATINUM NO PRICING DUE TO SCARCITY		
DD1 Barry Bonds	4.00	1.20
DD2 Mark McGwire	4.00	1.20
DD3 Sammy Sosa	2.50	.75
DD4 Ken Griffey Jr.	2.50	.75
DD5 Cal Ripken	5.00	1.50
DD6 Tony Gwynn	2.00	.60
DD7 Albert Belle	.75	.23
DD8 Frank Thomas	1.50	.45
DD9 Randy Johnson	1.50	.45
DD10 Juan Gonzalez	1.50	.45
DD11 Greg Maddux	2.50	.75
DD12 Craig Biggio	1.00	.30
DD13 Edgar Martinez	1.00	.30
DD14 Roger Clemens	3.00	.90
DD15 Andres Galarraga	.75	.23

2001 Ultra Fall Classics

Inserted into packs at one in 20, this 37-card insert set features some of the most legendary

players of all time. Card backs carry a "FC" prefix.

Card	Nm-Mt	Ex-Mt
FC1 Jackie Robinson	8.00	2.40
FC2 Enos Slaughter	3.00	.90
FC3 Mariano Rivera	3.00	.90
FC4 Hank Bauer	3.00	.90
FC5 Cal Ripken	15.00	4.50
FC6 Babe Ruth	15.00	4.50
FC7 Thurman Munson	8.00	2.40
FC8 Tom Glavine	3.00	.90
FC9 Fred Lynn	3.00	.90
FC10 Johnny Bench	5.00	1.50
FC11 Tony Lazzeri	3.00	.90
FC12 Al Kaline	5.00	1.50
FC13 Reggie Jackson	3.00	.90
FC14 Derek Jeter	12.00	3.60
FC15 Willie Stargell	3.00	.90
FC16 Roy Campanella	5.00	1.50
FC17 Phil Rizzuto	5.00	1.50
FC18 Roberto Clemente	15.00	4.50
FC19 Carlton Fisk	3.00	.90
FC20 Duke Snider	3.00	.90
FC21 Ted Williams	15.00	4.50
FC22 Bill Skowron	3.00	.90
FC23 Bucky Dent	3.00	.90
FC24 Mike Schmidt	10.00	3.00
FC25 Lou Brock	3.00	.90
FC26 Whitey Ford	3.00	.90
FC27 Brooks Robinson	5.00	1.50
FC28 Roberto Alomar	5.00	1.50
FC29 Yogi Berra	5.00	1.50
FC30 Joe Carter	3.00	.90
FC31 Bill Mazeroski	3.00	.90
FC32 Bob Gibson	3.00	.90
FC33 Hank Greenberg	6.00	1.80
FC34 Andrew Jones	3.00	.90
FC35 Bernie Williams	3.00	.90
FC36 Don Larsen	3.00	.90
FC37 Billy Martin	5.00	1.50

2001 Ultra Fall Classics Memorabilia

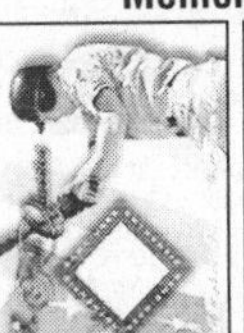

Randomly inserted into packs, this 26-card insert features game-used memorabilia from players like Derek Jeter, Al Kaline, and Cal Ripken. Please note that the cards a checklisted below in alphabetical order for convience.

Card	Nm-Mt	Ex-Mt
1 Hank Bauer Bat	15.00	4.50
2 Johnny Bench Jsy	25.00	7.50
3 Lou Brock Jsy	25.00	7.50
4 Roy Campanella Bat	60.00	18.00
5 Roberto Clemente Bat	120.00	36.00
6 Bucky Dent Bat	15.00	4.50
7 Carlton Fisk Jsy	25.00	7.50
8 Tom Glavine Jsy	25.00	7.50
9 Reggie Jackson Jsy	25.00	7.50
10 Derek Jeter Jsy	40.00	12.00
11 Al Kaline Jsy	25.00	7.50
12 Tony Lazzeri Bat	15.00	4.50
13 Fred Lynn Bat	15.00	4.50
14 Thurman Munson Bat	40.00	12.00
15 Cal Ripken Jsy	40.00	12.00
16 Mariano Rivera Jsy	25.00	7.50
17 Phil Rizzuto Bat	25.00	7.50
18 Brooks Robinson Bat	25.00	7.50
19 Jackie Robinson Pants	80.00	24.00
20 Babe Ruth Bat	200.00	60.00
21 Mike Schmidt Jsy	30.00	9.00
22 Bill Skowron Bat	15.00	4.50
23 Enos Slaughter Bat	15.00	4.50
24 Duke Snider Bat	25.00	7.50
25 Willie Stargell Bat	25.00	7.50
26 Ted Williams Bat	120.00	36.00

2001 Ultra Fall Classics Memorabilia Autograph

Randomly inserted into packs, this nine-card insert features game-used memorabilia and autographs of legendary players. Due to market scarcity, not all cards are priced. All are listed for checklisting purposes. Please note that the Al Kaline jersey/autograph card contained an error, Kaline actually wore jersey number 6. However, Fleer produced seven of these cards. Reggie Jackson's card was distributed as an exchange card in packs. The exchange deadline was January 2nd, 2002.

Nm-Mt Ex-Mt
1 Lou Brock Jsy AU/20
2 Carlton Fisk Jsy AU/27
3 Reggie Jackson 120.00 36.00
Bat-Jsy/44
4 Derek Jeter Jsy AU/2
5 Al Kaline Jsy AU/7 UER
Kaline wore Jersey number 6
6 Cal Ripken Jsy AU/8
7 Mike Schmidt Jsy AU/20
8 Enos Slaughter Jsy AU/9
9 Willie Stargell Jsy AU/8

2001 Ultra Greatest Hits

Randomly inserted into packs at one in 12, this 10-card insert set features players that dominante the Major Leagues. Card backs carry a "GH" prefix.

Nm-Mt Ex-Mt
COMPLETE SET (10) 25.00 7.50
PLATINUM RANDOM INSERTS IN PACKS
PLATINUM PRINT RUN 10 SERIAL #'d SETS
PLATINUM NO PRICING DUE TO SCARCITY
GH1 Mark McGwire 4.00 1.20
GH2 Alex Rodriguez 2.50 .75
GH3 Ken Griffey Jr. 2.50 .75
GH4 Ivan Rodriguez 1.50 .45
GH5 Cal Ripken 5.00 1.50
GH6 Todd Helton 1.00 .30
GH7 Derek Jeter 4.00 1.20
GH8 Pedro Martinez 1.50 .45
GH9 Tony Gwynn 2.00 .60
GH10 Jim Edmonds 1.00 .30

2001 Ultra Power Plus

Randomly inserted into packs at one in 24, this 10-card insert set features players that are among the league leaders in homeruns every year. Card backs carry a "PP" prefix.

Nm-Mt Ex-Mt
COMPLETE SET (10) 40.00 12.00
PLATINUM RANDOM INSERTS IN PACKS
PLATINUM PRINT RUN 10 SERIAL #'d SETS
PLATINUM NO PRICING DUE TO SCARCITY
PP1 Vladimir Guerrero 2.50 .75
PP2 Mark McGwire 6.00 1.80
PP3 Mike Piazza 4.00 1.20
PP4 Derek Jeter 6.00 1.80
PP5 Chipper Jones 2.50 .75
PP6 Carlos Delgado 1.50 .45
PP7 Sammy Sosa 4.00 1.20
PP8 Ken Griffey Jr. 4.00 1.20
PP9 Nomar Garciaparra 4.00 1.20
PP10 Alex Rodriguez 4.00 1.20

2001 Ultra Tomorrow's Legends

Randomly inserted into packs at one in 4, this 15-card insert set features players that will most likely make the Hall of Fame when their careers are through. Card backs carry a "TL" prefix.

Nm-Mt Ex-Mt
COMPLETE SET (15) 15.00 4.50
PLATINUM RANDOM INSERTS IN PACKS
PLATINUM PRINT RUN 10 SERIAL #'d SETS
PLATINUM NO PRICING DUE TO SCARCITY
TL1 Rick Ankiel .50 .15
TL2 J.D. Drew .50 .15
TL3 Carlos Delgado .50 .15
TL4 Todd Helton .75 .23
TL5 Andruw Jones .50 .15
TL6 Troy Glaus .75 .23
TL7 Jermaine Dye .50 .15
TL8 Vladimir Guerrero 1.25 .35
TL9 Brian Giles .50 .15
TL10 Scott Rolen .75 .23
TL11 Darin Erstad .50 .15
TL12 Derek Jeter 3.00 .90
TL13 Alex Rodriguez 2.00 .60
TL14 Pat Burrell .50 .15
TL15 Nomar Garciaparra 2.00 .60

2002 Ultra

This 285 card set was issued in November, 2001. The following subsets were issued for this set: All-Stars (cards numbered 201-220), Teammates (a veteran and prospect from each team, numbered 221-250), and Prospects (cards numbered 251-285). All three of these subsets were issued at a rate of one in four packs.

Nm-Mt Ex-Mt
COMPLETE SET (285) 200.00 60.00
COMP.SET w/o SP's (200) 25.00 7.50
COMMON CARD (1-200) .30 .09
COMMON (201-220) 1.00 .30
COMMON (221-250) 1.00 .30
COMMON (251-285) 3.00 .90
1 Jeff Bagwell .50 .15
2 Derek Jeter 2.00 .60
3 Alex Rodriguez 1.25 .35
4 Eric Chavez .30 .09
5 Tsuyoshi Shinjo .30 .09
6 Chris Stynes .30 .09
7 Ivan Rodriguez .75 .23
8 Cal Ripken 2.50 .75
9 Freddy Garcia .30 .09
10 Chipper Jones .75 .23
11 Hideo Nomo .75 .23
12 Rafael Furcal .30 .09
13 Preston Wilson .30 .09
14 Jimmy Rollins .30 .09
15 Cristian Guzman .30 .09
16 Garret Anderson .30 .09
17 Todd Helton .50 .15
18 Moises Alou .30 .09
19 Tony Gwynn 1.00 .30
20 Jorge Posada .50 .15
21 Sean Casey .30 .09
22 Kazuhiro Sasaki .30 .09
23 Ray Lankford .30 .09
24 Manny Ramirez .30 .09
25 Barry Bonds 2.00 .60
26 Fred McGriff .50 .15
27 Vladimir Guerrero .75 .23
28 Jermaine Dye .30 .09
29 Adrian Beltre .30 .09
30 Ken Griffey Jr. 1.25 .35
31 Ramon Hernandez .30 .09
32 Kerry Wood .75 .23
33 Greg Maddux 1.25 .35
34 Rondell White .30 .09
35 Mike Mussina .75 .23
36 Jim Edmonds .30 .09
37 Scott Rolen .50 .15
38 Mike Lowell .30 .09
39 Al Leiter .30 .09
40 Tony Clark .30 .09
41 Joe Mays .30 .09
42 Mo Vaughn .30 .09
43 Geoff Jenkins .30 .09
44 Curt Schilling .50 .15
45 Pedro Martinez .75 .23
46 Andy Pettitte .50 .15
47 Tim Salmon .50 .15
48 Carl Everett .30 .09
49 Lance Berkman .30 .09
50 Troy Glaus .50 .15
51 Ichiro Suzuki 1.25 .35
52 Alfonso Soriano .50 .15
53 Tomo Ohka .30 .09
54 Dean Palmer .30 .09
55 Kevin Brown .30 .09
56 Albert Pujols 1.50 .45
57 Homer Bush .30 .09
58 Tim Hudson .30 .09
59 Frank Thomas .75 .23
60 Joe Randa .30 .09
61 Chan Ho Park .30 .09
62 Bobby Higginson .30 .09
63 Bartolo Colon .30 .09
64 Aramis Ramirez .30 .09
65 Jeff Cirillo .30 .09
66 Roberto Alomar .75 .23
67 Mark Kotsay .30 .09
68 Mike Cameron .30 .09
69 Mike Hampton .30 .09
70 Trot Nixon .50 .15
71 Juan Gonzalez .75 .23
72 Damian Rolls .30 .09
73 Brad Fullmer .30 .09
74 David Ortiz .30 .09
75 Brandon Inge .30 .09
76 Orlando Hernandez .30 .09
77 Matt Stairs .30 .09
78 Jay Gibbons .30 .09
79 Greg Vaughn .30 .09
80 Brady Anderson .30 .09
81 Jim Thome .75 .23
82 Ben Sheets .30 .09
83 Rafael Palmeiro .50 .15
84 Edgar Renteria .30 .09
85 Doug Mientkiewicz .30 .09
86 Raul Mondesi .30 .09
87 Shane Reynolds .30 .09
88 Steve Finley .30 .09
89 Jose Cruz Jr. .30 .09
90 Edgardo Alfonzo .30 .09
91 Jose Valentin .30 .09
92 Mark McGwire 2.00 .60
93 Mark Grace .50 .15
94 Mike Lieberthal .30 .09
95 Barry Larkin .75 .23
96 Chuck Knoblauch .30 .09
97 Deivi Cruz .30 .09
98 Jeromy Burnitz .30 .09
99 Shannon Stewart .30 .09
100 David Wells .30 .09
101 Brook Fordyce .30 .09
102 Rusty Greer .30 .09
103 Andruw Jones .30 .09
104 Jason Kendall .30 .09
105 Nomar Garciaparra 1.25 .35
106 Shawn Green .30 .09
107 Craig Biggio .50 .15
108 Masato Yoshii .30 .09
109 Ben Petrick .30 .09
110 Gary Sheffield .30 .09
111 Travis Lee .30 .09
112 Matt Williams .30 .09
113 Billy Wagner .30 .09
114 Robin Ventura .30 .09
115 Jerry Hairston .30 .09
116 Paul LoDuca .30 .09
117 Darin Erstad .30 .09
118 Ruben Sierra .30 .09
119 Ricky Gutierrez .30 .09
120 Bret Boone .30 .09
121 John Rocker .30 .09
122 Roger Clemens 1.50 .45
123 Eric Karros .30 .09
124 J.D. Drew .30 .09
125 Carlos Delgado .30 .09
126 Jeffrey Hammonds .30 .09
127 Jeff Kent .30 .09
128 David Justice .30 .09
129 Cliff Floyd .30 .09
130 Omar Vizquel .30 .09
131 Matt Morris .30 .09
132 Rich Aurilia .30 .09
133 Larry Walker .50 .15
134 Miguel Tejada .30 .09
135 Eric Young .30 .09
136 Aaron Sele .30 .09
137 Eric Milton .30 .09
138 Travis Fryman .30 .09
139 Magglio Ordonez .30 .09
140 Sammy Sosa 1.25 .35
141 Pokey Reese .30 .09
142 Adam Eaton .30 .09
143 Adam Kennedy .30 .09
144 Mike Piazza 1.25 .35
145 Larry Barnes .30 .09
146 Darryl Kile .30 .09
147 Tom Glavine .50 .15
148 Ryan Klesko .30 .09
149 Jose Vidro .30 .09
150 Joe Kennedy .30 .09
151 Bernie Williams .50 .15
152 C.C. Sabathia .30 .09
153 Alex Ochoa .30 .09
154 A.J. Pierzynski .30 .09
155 Johnny Damon .30 .09
156 Omar Daal .30 .09
157 A.J. Burnett .30 .09
158 Eric Munson .30 .09
159 Fernando Vina .30 .09
160 Chris Singleton .30 .09
161 Juan Pierre .30 .09
162 John Olerud .30 .09
163 Randy Johnson .75 .23
164 Paul Konerko .30 .09
165 Tino Martinez .50 .15
166 Richard Hidalgo .30 .09
167 Luis Gonzalez .30 .09
168 Ben Grieve .30 .09
169 Matt Lawton .30 .09
170 Gabe Kapler .30 .09
171 Mariano Rivera .50 .15
172 Kenny Lofton .30 .09
173 Brian Jordan .30 .09
174 Brian Giles .30 .09
175 Mark Quinn .30 .09
176 Neifi Perez .30 .09
177 Ellis Burks .30 .09
178 Bobby Abreu .30 .09
179 Jeff Weaver .30 .09
180 Andres Galarraga .30 .09
181 Javy Lopez .30 .09
182 Todd Walker .30 .09
183 Fernando Tatis .30 .09
184 Charles Johnson .30 .09
185 Pat Burrell .30 .09
186 Jay Bell .30 .09
187 Aaron Boone .30 .09
188 Jason Giambi .75 .23
189 Jay Payton .30 .09
190 Carlos Lee .30 .09
191 Phil Nevin .30 .09
192 Mike Sweeney .30 .09
193 J.T. Snow .30 .09
194 Dmitri Young .30 .09
195 Richie Sexson .30 .09
196 Derrek Lee .30 .09
197 Corey Koskie .30 .09
198 Edgar Martinez .50 .15
199 Wade Miller .30 .09
200 Tony Batista .30 .09
201 John Olerud AS 1.00 .30
202 Bret Boone AS 1.00 .30
203 Cal Ripken AS 5.00 1.50
204 Alex Rodriguez AS 2.50 .75
205 Ichiro Suzuki AS 2.50 .75
206 Manny Ramirez AS .30 .09
207 Juan Gonzalez AS 1.50 .45
208 Ivan Rodriguez AS 1.50 .45
209 Roger Clemens AS 3.00 .90
210 Edgar Martinez AS 1.00 .30
211 Todd Helton AS 1.00 .30
212 Jeff Kent AS 1.00 .30
213 Chipper Jones AS 1.50 .45
214 Rich Aurilia AS 1.00 .30
215 Barry Bonds AS 4.00 1.20
216 Sammy Sosa AS 2.50 .75
217 Luis Gonzalez AS 1.00 .30
218 Mike Piazza AS 2.50 .75
219 Randy Johnson AS 1.50 .45
220 Larry Walker AS 1.00 .30
221 Todd Helton 1.00 .30
Juan Uribe
222 Pat Burrell 1.00 .30
Eric Valent
223 Edgar Martinez 2.50 .75
Ichiro Suzuki
224 Ben Grieve 1.00 .30
Jason Tyner
225 Mark Quinn 1.00 .30
Dee Brown
226 Cal Ripken 5.00 1.50
Brian Roberts
227 Cliff Floyd 1.00 .30
Abraham Nunez
228 Jeff Bagwell 1.00 .30
Adam Everett
229 Mark McGwire 4.00 1.20
Albert Pujols
230 Doug Mientkiewicz 1.00 .30
Luis Rivas
231 Juan Gonzalez 1.50 .45
Danny Peoples
232 Kevin Brown 1.00 .30
Luke Prokopec
233 Richie Sexson 1.00 .30
Ben Sheets
234 Jason Giambi 1.50 .45
Jason Hart
235 Barry Bonds 4.00 1.20
Carlos Valderrama
236 Tony Gwynn 2.00 .60
Cesar Crespo
237 Ken Griffey Jr. 2.50 .75
Adam Dunn
238 Frank Thomas .75 .23
Joe Crede
239 Derek Jeter 4.00 1.20
Drew Henson
240 Chipper Jones 1.50 .45
Wilson Betemit
241 Luis Gonzalez 1.00 .30
Junior Spivey
242 Bobby Higginson 1.00 .30
Andres Torres
243 Carlos Delgado 1.00 .30
Vernon Wells
244 Sammy Sosa 2.50 .75
Corey Patterson
245 Nomar Garciaparra 2.50 .75
Shea Hillenbrand
246 Alex Rodriguez 2.50 .75
Jason Romano
247 Troy Glaus 1.00 .30
David Eckstein
248 Mike Piazza 2.50 .75
Alex Escobar
249 Brian Giles 1.00 .30
Jack Wilson
250 Vladimir Guerrero 1.50 .45
Scott Hodges
251 Bud Smith PROS 3.00 .90
252 Juan Diaz PROS 3.00 .90
253 Wilkin Ruan PROS 3.00 .90
254 C. Spurling PROS RC 3.00 .90
255 Toby Hall PROS 3.00 .90
256 Jason Jennings PROS 3.00 .90
257 George Perez PROS 3.00 .90
258 D. Jimenez PROS 3.00 .90
259 Jose Acevedo PROS 3.00 .90
260 Josue Perez PROS 3.00 .90
261 Brian Rogers PROS 3.00 .90
262 C. Maldonado PROS RC 3.00 .90
263 Travis Phelps PROS 3.00 .90
264 R. Mackowiak PROS 3.00 .90
265 Ryan Drese PROS 3.00 .90
266 Carlos Garcia PROS 3.00 .90
267 Alexis Gomez PROS 3.00 .90
268 Jeremy Affeldt PROS 3.00 .90
269 S. Podsednik PROS 8.00 2.40
270 Adam Johnson PROS 3.00 .90
271 Pedro Santana PROS 3.00 .90
272 Les Walrond PROS 3.00 .90
273 Jackson Melian PROS 3.00 .90
274 C. Hernandez PROS 3.00 .90
275 M. Nussbeck PROS RC 3.00 .90
276 Cory Aldridge PROS 3.00 .90
277 Troy Mattes PROS 3.00 .90
278 B. Abernathy PROS 3.00 .90
279 J.J. Davis PROS 3.00 .90
280 B. Duckworth PROS 3.00 .90
281 Kyle Lohse PROS 3.00 .90
282 Justin Kaye PROS 3.00 .90
283 Cody Ransom PROS 3.00 .90
284 Dave Williams PROS 3.00 .90
285 Luis Lopez PROS 3.00 .90

2002 Ultra Gold Medallion

Issued at packs at different rates, this is a parallel to the Ultra set. Cards numbered 1-200 were issued at a rate of one per pack, cards numbered 201-250 were issued at a rate of one in 24 packs and cards numbered 251-285 were randomly inserted in packs. Cards numbered 251-285 were issued to 100 serial numbered sets.

Nm-Mt Ex-Mt
COMP.SET w/o SP's (200) 150.00 45.00
*GOLD 1-200: 1.25X TO 3X BASIC
*GOLD 201-220: .75X TO 2X BASIC
*GOLD 221-250: 1X TO 2.5X BASIC
*GOLD 251-285: 3X TO 8X BASIC

2002 Ultra Fall Classic

Issued at a rate of one in 20 hobby packs, these 36 cards feature players who participated in the World Series.

Nm-Mt Ex-Mt
COMPLETE SET (36) 200.00 60.00
1 Ty Cobb 10.00 3.00
2 Lou Gehrig 10.00 3.00
3 Babe Ruth 20.00 6.00
4 Stan Musial 10.00 3.00
5 Ted Williams 15.00 4.50
6 Dizzy Dean 8.00 2.40
7 Mickey Cochrane 5.00 1.50
8 Jimmie Foxx 8.00 2.40
9 Mel Ott 8.00 2.40
10 Rogers Hornsby 8.00 2.40
12 Clete Boyer 5.00 1.50
13 George Brett 15.00 4.50
14 Bob Gibson 8.00 2.40
15 Carlton Fisk 8.00 2.40
16 Johnny Bench 8.00 2.40
18 Willie McCovey 5.00 1.50
19 Paul Molitor 8.00 2.40
20 Jim Palmer 5.00 1.50
21 Frank Robinson 8.00 2.40
22 Derek Jeter 12.00 3.60
23 Earl Weaver 5.00 1.50
24 Lefty Grove 5.00 1.50
25 Tony Perez 5.00 1.50
26 Reggie Jackson 8.00 2.40
27 Sparky Anderson 5.00 1.50
28 Casey Stengel 5.00 1.50
29 Roy Campanella 8.00 2.40
31 Don Drysdale 8.00 2.40
32 Joe Morgan 5.00 1.50
33 Eddie Murray 8.00 2.40
34 Nolan Ryan 15.00 4.50
35 Tom Seaver 8.00 2.40
36 Bill Mazeroski 5.00 1.50
37 Jackie Robinson 10.00 3.00
38 Kirk Gibson 5.00 1.50
39 Robin Yount 10.00 3.00

2002 Ultra Fall Classic Autographs

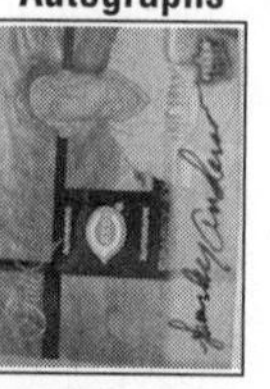

This partial parallel to the Fall Classic set features authentic autographs from the featured players. Almost all of the players except for Sparky Anderson and Earl Weaver were exchange cards. A few players were produced in lower quantities and those have been notated with SP's in our checklist.

Nm-Mt Ex-Mt
1 Sparky Anderson 15.00 4.50
2 Johnny Bench SP 50.00 15.00
3 George Brett SP 100.00 30.00
4 Carlton Fisk 25.00 7.50
5 Bob Gibson 25.00 7.50
6 Kirk Gibson 25.00 7.50
7 Reggie Jackson SP 50.00 15.00
8 Derek Jeter SP
9 Bill Mazeroski 25.00 7.50
10 Willie McCovey SP 40.00 12.00
11 Joe Morgan 15.00 4.50
12 Eddie Murray SP 50.00 15.00
13 Stan Musial SP
14 Jim Palmer 15.00 4.50
15 Tony Perez 15.00 4.50
16 Frank Robinson 25.00 7.50
17 Nolan Ryan SP 250.00 75.00
18 Tom Seaver SP 40.00 12.00
19 Earl Weaver 15.00 4.50
20 Robin Yount SP 60.00 18.00

2002 Ultra Fall Classic Memorabilia

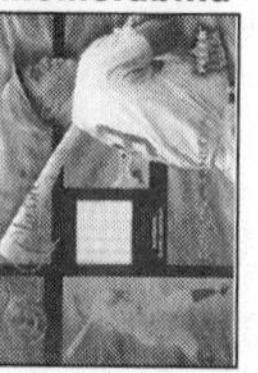

Inserted at a rate of one in 113, these 37 cards feature memorabilia from players who participated in World Series. A few cards were printed in lesser quantities and those have been notated with print runs as provided by Fleer.

Nm-Mt Ex-Mt
1 Sparky Anderson Pants 10.00 3.00
2 Johnny Bench Pants 15.00 4.50
3 Johnny Bench Jsy 15.00 4.50
4 George Brett White Jsy 25.00 7.50
5 George Brett Bat 25.00 7.50
6 George Brett Blue Jsy/65
7 Roy Campanella Bat/21
8 Carlton Fisk Jsy 15.00 4.50
9 Carlton Fisk Bat/42 50.00 15.00
10 Jimmie Foxx Bat 50.00 15.00
11 Bob Gibson Jsy 15.00 4.50
12 Kirk Gibson Bat 10.00 3.00
13 Reggie Jackson Bat 15.00 4.50
14 Reggie Jackson Bat
15 Reggie Jackson Jsy/73
16 Derek Jeter Pants 40.00 12.00
17 Willie McCovey Jsy 10.00 3.00
18 Paul Molitor Bat 15.00 4.50
19 Paul Molitor Jsy
20 Joe Morgan Bat 10.00 3.00
21 Joe Morgan Jsy
22 Eddie Murray Bat 15.00 4.50
23 Eddie Murray Jsy/91 50.00 15.00
24 Jim Palmer White Jsy 10.00 3.00
25 J.Palmer Gray Jsy/85 40.00 12.00
26 Tony Perez Bat 10.00 3.00
27 Frank Robinson Bat/40 40.00 12.00
28 Jackie Robinson Pants 80.00 24.00
29 Babe Ruth Bat/44 200.00 60.00
30 Nolan Ryan Pants 50.00 15.00
31 Tom Seaver Jsy 15.00 4.50
32 Earl Weaver Jsy 10.00 3.00
33 Ted Williams Jsy 100.00 30.00
34 Ted Williams Bat/30
35 Robin Yount Gray Jsy
36 Robin Yount White Jsy/30
37 Robin Yount Bat 15.00 4.50

2002 Ultra Glove Works

Inserted at a rate of one in 20, these 15 cards feature some of the leading fielders in the game.

Nm-Mt Ex-Mt
COMPLETE SET (15) 50.00 15.00
1 Andruw Jones 3.00 .90

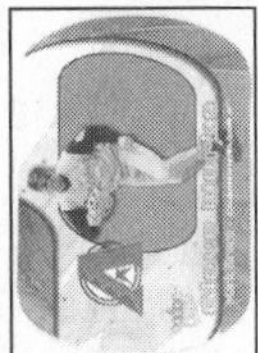

2 Derek Jeter 8.00 2.40
3 Cal Ripken 10.00 3.00
4 Larry Walker 3.00 .90
5 Chipper Jones 4.00 1.20
6 Barry Bonds 8.00 2.40
7 Scott Rolen 3.00 .90
8 Jim Edmonds 3.00 .90
9 Robin Ventura 3.00 .90
10 Darin Erstad 3.00 .90
11 Barry Larkin 4.00 1.20
12 Raul Mondesi 3.00 .90
13 Mark Grace 3.00 .90
14 Bernie Williams 3.00 .90
15 Ivan Rodriguez 4.00 1.20

2002 Ultra Glove Works Memorabilia

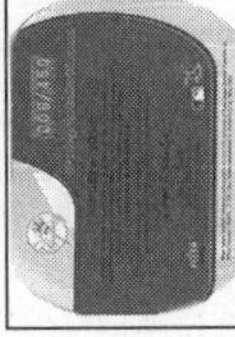

This 11-card insert set features game-used fielding mitts and batting gloves incorporated into the actual card. Each card is serial numbered to 450 copies - except for Barry Larkin (375 cards), Andruw Jones (100 cards) and Chipper Jones (100 cards). The first 75 serial numbered copies of the Cal Ripken, Barry Bonds and Ivan Rodriguez cards feature batting glove patches and cards serial numbered 76-450 for these players feature fielding mitt patches. The short-printed Andruw and Chipper Jones cards feature batting glove patches.

Nm-Mt Ex-Mt
PLATINUM RANDOM INSERTS IN PACKS
PLATINUM PRINT RUN 25 SERIAL #'d SETS
PLATINUM NO PRICING DUE TO SCARCITY
1 Derek Jeter 40.00 12.00
2 Andruw Jones SP/100
3 Cal Ripken 60.00 18.00
5 Chipper Jones SP/100
6 Barry Bonds 40.00 12.00
8 Robin Ventura 15.00 4.50
9 Barry Larkin SP/375 20.00 6.00
10 Raul Mondesi 15.00 4.50
11 Ivan Rodriguez 20.00 6.00

2002 Ultra Hitting Machines

Inserted at a rate of one in 20 retail packs, these 25 cards feature some of baseball's leading hitters.

Nm-Mt Ex-Mt
COMPLETE SET (25) 120.00 36.00
1 Frank Thomas 5.00 1.50
2 Derek Jeter 12.00 3.60
3 Vladimir Guerrero 5.00 1.50
4 Jim Edmonds 2.50 .75
5 Mike Piazza 8.00 2.40
6 Ivan Rodriguez 5.00 1.50
7 Chipper Jones 5.00 1.50
8 Tony Gwynn 6.00 1.80
9 Manny Ramirez 2.50 .75
10 Andruw Jones 2.50 .75
11 Carlos Delgado 2.50 .75
12 Bernie Williams 3.00 .90
13 Larry Walker 3.00 .90
14 Juan Gonzalez 5.00 1.50
15 Ichiro Suzuki 8.00 2.40
16 Albert Pujols 10.00 3.00
17 Barry Bonds 12.00 3.60
18 Cal Ripken 15.00 4.50
19 Edgar Martinez 3.00 .90
20 Luis Gonzalez 2.50 .75
21 Moises Alou 2.50 .75
22 Roberto Alomar 5.00 1.50
23 Todd Helton 3.00 .90
24 Rafael Palmeiro 3.00 .90
25 Bobby Abreu 2.50 .75

2002 Ultra Hitting Machines Game Bat

Issued at a rate of one in 81 packs, these cards feature not only some of the leading hitters but also a slice of a game-used bat.

Nm-Mt Ex-Mt
PLATINUM RANDOM INSERTS IN PACKS
PLATINUM PRINT RUN 25 SERIAL #'d SETS
PLATINUM: NO PRICING DUE TO SCARCITY
1 Bobby Abreu 10.00 3.00
2 Roberto Alomar 15.00 4.50
3 Moises Alou 10.00 3.00
4 Barry Bonds 30.00 9.00

5 Carlos Delgado 10.00 3.00
6 Jim Edmonds 10.00 3.00
7 Juan Gonzalez 15.00 4.50
8 Luis Gonzalez 10.00 3.00
9 Tony Gwynn 15.00 4.50
10 Todd Helton 15.00 4.50
11 Derek Jeter 30.00 9.00
12 Andruw Jones 10.00 3.00
13 Chipper Jones 15.00 4.50
14 Edgar Martinez 15.00 4.50
15 Rafael Palmeiro 15.00 4.50
16 Mike Piazza 15.00 4.50
17 Albert Pujols 40.00 12.00
18 Manny Ramirez 10.00 3.00
19 Cal Ripken 50.00 15.00
20 Ivan Rodriguez 15.00 4.50
21 Frank Thomas 15.00 4.50
22 Larry Walker 15.00 4.50
23 Bernie Williams 15.00 4.50

2002 Ultra On the Road Game Jersey

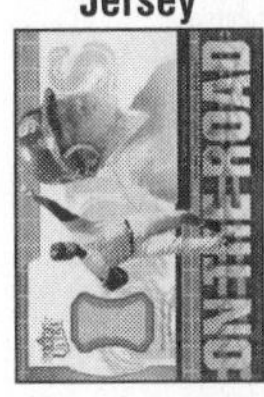

Inserted at a rate of one in 93, these 14 cards feature swatches of away uniforms used by the featured players.

Nm-Mt Ex-Mt
PLATINUM RANDOM INSERTS IN PACKS
PLATINUM PRINT RUN 25 SERIAL #'d SETS
PLATINUM: NO PRICING DUE TO SCARCITY
1 Derek Jeter 40.00 12.00
2 Ivan Rodriguez 20.00 6.00
3 Carlos Delgado 15.00 4.50
4 Larry Walker 20.00 6.00
5 Roberto Alomar 20.00 6.00
6 Tony Gwynn 20.00 6.00
7 Greg Maddux 20.00 6.00
8 Barry Bonds 40.00 12.00
9 Todd Helton 20.00 6.00
10 Kazuhiro Sasaki 15.00 4.50
11 Jeff Bagwell 20.00 6.00
12 Omar Vizquel 15.00 4.50
13 Chan Ho Park 15.00 4.50
14 Tom Glavine 20.00 6.00

2002 Ultra Rising Stars

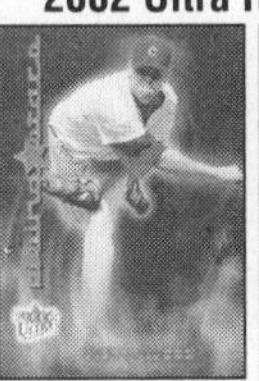

Issued at a rate of one in 12 packs, these 15 cards feature some of the leading young players in baseball.

Nm-Mt Ex-Mt
COMPLETE SET (15) 30.00 9.00
1 Ichiro Suzuki 4.00 1.20
2 Derek Jeter 6.00 1.80
3 Albert Pujols 5.00 1.50
4 Jimmy Rollins 2.00 .60
5 Adam Dunn 2.00 .60
6 Sean Casey 2.00 .60
7 Kerry Wood 2.50 .75
8 Tsuyoshi Shinjo 2.00 .60
9 Shea Hillenbrand 2.00 .60
10 Pat Burrell 2.00 .60
11 Ben Sheets 2.00 .60
12 Alfonso Soriano 2.00 .60
13 J.D. Drew 2.00 .60
14 Kazuhiro Sasaki 2.00 .60
15 Corey Patterson 2.00 .60

2002 Ultra Rising Stars Game Hat

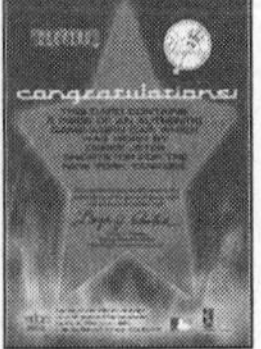

Randomly inserted in packs, these six cards feature not only some of the best young players in baseball but also a sliver of a cap they wore while playing.

Nm-Mt Ex-Mt
PLATINUM RANDOM IN HOBBY PACKS
PLATINUM PRINT RUN 25 SERIAL #'d SETS
PLATINUM NO PRICING DUE TO SCARCITY
1 Derek Jeter 80.00 24.00
2 Albert Pujols 50.00 15.00
3 Tsuyoshi Shinjo 40.00 12.00
4 Alfonso Soriano 40.00 12.00
5 J.D. Drew 40.00 12.00
6 Kazuhiro Sasaki 40.00 12.00

2003 Ultra

This 265-card set was issued in two separate series. The primary Ultra product - containing the first 250 cards from the basic set - was released in November, 2002. It was issued in 10 card packs which were packed 24 packs to a box and 16 boxes to a case. Cards numbered 1 through 200 featured veterans while cards numbered 201 through 220 featured All-Stars, cards numbered 221 through 240 featured rookies of 2002 and cards numbered 241 through 250 featured rookies of 2003. Cards numbered 201 through 220 were inserted at a stated rate of one in four while cards numbered 221 through 250 were inserted at a stated rate of one in two. Cards 251-265 were randomly seeded within Fleer Rookies and Greats packs of which was distributed in December, 2003. Each of these 15 update cards features a top prospect and is serial numbered to 1,500 copies.

Nm-Mt Ex-Mt
COMP.LO SET (250) 100.00 30.00
COMP.LO SET w/o SP's (200) 25.00 7.50
COMMON CARD (201-220) 1.50 .45
COMMON CARD (221-250) 2.00 .60
COMMON CARD (251-265) 3.00 .90
1 Barry Bonds 2.00 .60
2 Derek Jeter 2.00 .60
3 Ichiro Suzuki 1.25 .35
4 Mike Lowell .30 .09
5 Hideo Nomo .75 .23
6 Javier Vazquez .30 .09
7 Jeremy Giambi .30 .09
8 Jamie Moyer .30 .09
9 Rafael Palmeiro .50 .15
10 Magglio Ordonez .30 .09
11 Trot Nixon .50 .15
12 Luis Castillo .30 .09
13 Paul Byrd .30 .09
14 Adam Kennedy .30 .09
15 Trevor Hoffman .30 .09
16 Matt Morris .30 .09
17 Nomar Garciaparra 1.25 .35
18 Matt Lawton .30 .09
19 Carlos Beltran .30 .09
20 Jason Giambi .75 .23
21 Brian Giles .30 .09
22 Jim Edmonds .30 .09
23 Garret Anderson .30 .09
24 Tony Batista .30 .09
25 Aaron Boone .30 .09
26 Mike Hampton .30 .09
27 Billy Wagner .30 .09
28 Kazuhisa Ishii .30 .09
29 Al Leiter .30 .09
30 Pat Burrell .30 .09
31 Jeff Kent .30 .09
32 Randy Johnson .75 .23
33 Ray Durham .30 .09
34 Josh Beckett .50 .15
35 Cristian Guzman .30 .09
36 Roger Clemens 1.50 .45
37 Freddy Garcia .30 .09
38 Roy Halladay .30 .09
39 David Eckstein .30 .09
40 Jerry Hairston .30 .09
41 Barry Larkin .75 .23
42 Larry Walker .50 .15
43 Craig Biggio .50 .15
44 Edgardo Alfonzo .30 .09
45 Marlon Byrd .30 .09
46 J.T. Snow .30 .09
47 Juan Gonzalez .75 .23
48 Ramon Ortiz .30 .09
49 Jay Gibbons .30 .09
50 Adam Dunn .30 .09
51 Juan Pierre .30 .09
52 Jeff Bagwell .50 .15
53 Kevin Brown .30 .09
54 Pedro Astacio .30 .09
55 Mike Lieberthal .30 .09
56 Johnny Damon .30 .09
57 Tim Salmon .50 .15
58 Mike Bordick .30 .09
59 Ken Griffey Jr. 1.25 .35
60 Jason Jennings .30 .09
61 Lance Berkman .30 .09
62 Jeromy Burnitz .30 .09
63 Jimmy Rollins .30 .09
64 Tsuyoshi Shinjo .30 .09
65 Alex Rodriguez 1.25 .35
66 Greg Maddux 1.25 .35
67 Mark Prior 1.50 .45
68 Mike Maroth .30 .09
69 Geoff Jenkins .30 .09
70 Tony Armas Jr. .30 .09
71 Jermaine Dye .30 .09
72 Albert Pujols 1.50 .45
73 Shannon Stewart .30 .09
74 Troy Glaus .50 .15
75 Brook Fordyce .30 .09
76 Juan Encarnacion .30 .09
77 Todd Hollandsworth .30 .09
78 Roy Oswalt .30 .09
79 Paul Lo Duca .30 .09
80 Mike Piazza 1.25 .35
81 Bobby Abreu .30 .09
82 Sean Burroughs .30 .09
83 Randy Winn .30 .09
84 Curt Schilling .50 .15
85 Chris Singleton .30 .09
86 Sean Casey .30 .09
87 Todd Zeile .30 .09
88 Richard Hidalgo .30 .09
89 Roberto Alomar .75 .23
90 Tim Hudson .30 .09
91 Ryan Klesko .30 .09
92 Greg Vaughn .30 .09
93 Tony Womack .30 .09
94 Fred McGriff .50 .15
95 Tom Glavine .50 .15
96 Todd Walker .30 .09
97 Travis Fryman .30 .09
98 Shane Reynolds .30 .09
99 Shawn Green .30 .09
100 Mo Vaughn .30 .09
101 Adam Piatt .30 .09
102 Deivi Cruz .30 .09
103 Steve Cox .30 .09
104 Luis Gonzalez .30 .09
105 Russell Branyan .30 .09
106 Daryle Ward .30 .09
107 Mariano Rivera .50 .15
108 Phil Nevin .30 .09
109 Ben Grieve .30 .09
110 Moises Alou .30 .09
111 Omar Vizquel .30 .09
112 Joe Randa .30 .09
113 Jorge Posada .50 .15
114 Mark Kotsay .30 .09
115 Ryan Rupe .30 .09
116 Javy Lopez .30 .09
117 Corey Patterson .30 .09
118 Bobby Higginson .30 .09
119 Jose Vidro .30 .09
120 Barry Zito .50 .15
121 Scott Rolen .50 .15
122 Gary Sheffield .30 .09
123 Kerry Wood .75 .23
124 Brandon Inge .30 .09
125 Jose Hernandez .30 .09
126 Michael Barrett .30 .09
127 Miguel Tejada .30 .09
128 Edgar Renteria .30 .09
129 Junior Spivey .30 .09
130 Jose Valentin .30 .09
131 Derrek Lee .30 .09
132 A.J. Pierzynski .30 .09
133 Mike Mussina .75 .23
134 Bret Boone .30 .09
135 Chan Ho Park .30 .09
136 Steve Finley .30 .09
137 Mark Buehrle .30 .09
138 A.J. Burnett .30 .09
139 Ben Sheets .30 .09
140 David Ortiz .30 .09
141 Nick Johnson .30 .09
142 Randall Simon .30 .09
143 Carlos Delgado .30 .09
144 Darin Erstad .30 .09
145 Shea Hillenbrand .30 .09
146 Todd Helton .50 .15
147 Preston Wilson .30 .09
148 Eric Gagne .50 .15
149 Vladimir Guerrero .75 .23
150 Brandon Duckworth .30 .09
151 Rich Aurilia .30 .09
152 Ivan Rodriguez .75 .23
153 Andruw Jones .30 .09
154 Carlos Lee .30 .09
155 Robert Fick .30 .09
156 Jacque Jones .30 .09
157 Bernie Williams .50 .15
158 John Olerud .30 .09
159 Eric Hinske .30 .09
160 Matt Clement .30 .09
161 Dmitri Young .30 .09
162 Torii Hunter .30 .09
163 Carlos Pena .30 .09
164 Mike Cameron .30 .09
165 Raul Mondesi .30 .09
166 Pedro Martinez .75 .23
167 Bob Wickman .30 .09
168 Mike Sweeney .30 .09
169 David Wells .30 .09
170 Jason Kendall .30 .09
171 Tino Martinez .50 .15
172 Matt Williams .50 .15
173 Frank Thomas .75 .23
174 Cliff Floyd .30 .09
175 Corey Koskie .30 .09
176 Orlando Hernandez .30 .09
177 Edgar Martinez .50 .15
178 Richie Sexson .30 .09
179 Manny Ramirez .30 .09
180 Jim Thome .75 .23
181 Andy Pettitte .50 .15
182 Aramis Ramirez .30 .09
183 J.D. Drew .30 .09
184 Brian Jordan .30 .09
185 Sammy Sosa 1.25 .35
186 Jeff Weaver .30 .09
187 Jeffrey Hammonds .30 .09
188 Eric Milton .30 .09
189 Eric Chavez .30 .09
190 Kazuhiro Sasaki .30 .09
191 Jose Cruz Jr. .30 .09
192 Derek Lowe .30 .09
193 C.C. Sabathia .30 .09
194 Adrian Beltre .30 .09
195 Alfonso Soriano .50 .15
196 Jack Wilson .30 .09
197 Fernando Vina .30 .09
198 Chipper Jones .75 .23
199 Paul Konerko .30 .09
200 Rusty Greer .30 .09
201 Jason Giambi AS 1.50 .45
202 Alfonso Soriano AS 1.50 .45
203 Shea Hillenbrand AS 1.50 .45
204 Alex Rodriguez AS 2.50 .75
205 Jorge Posada AS 1.50 .45
206 Ichiro Suzuki AS 2.50 .75
207 Manny Ramirez AS 1.50 .45
208 Torii Hunter AS 1.50 .45
209 Todd Helton AS 1.50 .45
210 Jose Vidro AS 1.50 .45
211 Scott Rolen AS 1.50 .45
212 Jimmy Rollins AS 1.50 .45
213 Mike Piazza AS 2.50 .75
214 Barry Bonds AS 4.00 1.20
215 Sammy Sosa AS 2.50 .75
216 Vladimir Guerrero AS 1.50 .45
217 Lance Berkman AS 1.50 .45
218 Derek Jeter AS 4.00 1.20
219 Nomar Garciaparra AS 2.50 .75
220 Luis Gonzalez AS 1.50 .45
221 Kazuhisa Ishii 02R 2.00 .60
222 Satoru Komiyama 02R 2.00 .60
223 So Taguchi 02R 2.00 .60
224 Jorge Padilla 02R 2.00 .60
225 Ben Howard 02R 2.00 .60
226 Jason Simontacchi 02R 2.00 .60
227 Barry Wesson 02R 2.00 .60
228 Howie Clark 02R 2.00 .60
229 Aaron Guiel 02R 2.00 .60
230 Oliver Perez 02R 2.00 .60
231 David Ross 02R 2.00 .60
232 Julius Matos 02R 2.00 .60
233 Chris Snelling 02R 2.00 .60
234 Rodrigo Lopez 02R 2.00 .60
235 Will Nieves 02R 2.00 .60
236 Joe Borchard 02R 2.00 .60
237 Aaron Cook 02R 2.00 .60
238 Anderson Machado 02R 2.00 .60
239 Corey Thurman 02R 2.00 .60
240 Tyler Yates 02R 2.00 .60
241 Coco Crisp 03R 2.00 .60
242 Andy Van Hekken 03R 2.00 .60
243 Jim Rushford 03R 2.00 .60
244 Jeriome Robertson 03R 2.00 .60
245 Shane Nance 03R 2.00 .60
246 Kevin Cash 03R 2.00 .60
247 Kirk Saarloos 03R 2.00 .60
248 Josh Bard 03R 2.00 .60
249 Dave Pember 03R RC 2.00 .60
250 Freddy Sanchez 03R 2.00 .60
251 Chien-Ming Wang PROS RC 4.00 1.20
252 Rickie Weeks PROS RC 10.00 3.00
253 Brandon Webb PROS RC 5.00 1.50
254 Hideki Matsui PROS RC 10.00 3.00
255 Michael Hessman PROS RC 3.00 .90
256 Ryan Wagner PROS RC 4.00 1.20
257 Matt Kata PROS RC 4.00 1.20
258 Edwin Jackson PROS RC 6.00 1.80
259 Jose Contreras PROS RC 4.00 1.20
260 Delmon Young PROS RC 10.00 3.00
261 Bo Hart PROS RC 4.00 1.20
262 Jeff Duncan PROS RC 4.00 1.20
263 Robby Hammock PROS RC 4.00 1.20
264 Jeremy Bonderman PROS RC 4.00 1.20
265 Clint Barmes PROS RC 4.00 1.20

2003 Ultra Gold Medallion

This 250 card set is a parallel to the 2003 Ultra set. The first 200 cards were inserted at a stated rate of one per pack while cards numbered 221 through 250 were issued at a stated rate of one per 24 packs.

Nm-Mt Ex-Mt
*GOLD MED 1-200: 1.25X TO 3X BASIC
*GOLD MED 201-220: 1X TO 2.5X BASIC
*GOLD MED 221-250: 1X TO 2.5X BASIC

2003 Ultra Back 2 Back

Randomly inserted into packs, these 17 cards feature some of the leading players in baseball. Each of these cards were printed to a stated print run of 1000 serial numbered sets.

Nm-Mt Ex-Mt
1 Derek Jeter 15.00 4.50
2 Barry Bonds 15.00 4.50
3 Mike Piazza 10.00 3.00
4 Alex Rodriguez 10.00 3.00
5 Todd Helton 6.00 1.80
6 Edgar Martinez 6.00 1.80
7 Chipper Jones 6.00 1.80
8 Shawn Green 6.00 1.80
9 Chan Ho Park 6.00 1.80
10 Preston Wilson 6.00 1.80
11 Manny Ramirez 6.00 1.80
12 Aramis Ramirez 6.00 1.80
13 Pedro Martinez 6.00 1.80
14 Ivan Rodriguez 6.00 1.80
15 Ichiro Suzuki 10.00 3.00
16 Sammy Sosa 10.00 3.00
17 Jason Giambi 6.00 1.80

2003 Ultra Back 2 Back Memorabilia

Randomly inserted into packs, this is a parallel of the Ultra Back 2 Back insert set. Each of these cards feature a game-used memorabilia piece of the featured player and is issued to a stated print run of 500 serial numbered sets.

Nm-Mt Ex-Mt
*GOLD: 1.25X TO 3X BASIC B2B MEMORABILIA
GOLD PRINT RUN 50 SERIAL #'d SETS
1 Derek Jeter Jsy 25.00 7.50
2 Barry Bonds Bat 25.00 7.50
3 Mike Piazza Jsy 15.00 4.50
4 Alex Rodriguez Jsy 20.00 6.00
5 Todd Helton Jsy 15.00 4.50

6 Edgar Martinez Jsy 15.00 4.50
7 Chipper Jones Jsy 15.00 4.50
8 Shawn Green Jsy 10.00 3.00
9 Chan Ho Park Bat 10.00 3.00
10 Preston Wilson Jsy 10.00 3.00
11 Manny Ramirez Jsy 10.00 3.00
12 Aramis Ramirez Pants 10.00 3.00
13 Pedro Martinez Jsy 15.00 4.50
14 Ivan Rodriguez Jsy 15.00 4.50
15 Ichiro Suzuki Base 20.00 6.00
16 Sammy Sosa Base 15.00 4.50
17 Jason Giambi Base 15.00 4.50

2003 Ultra Double Up

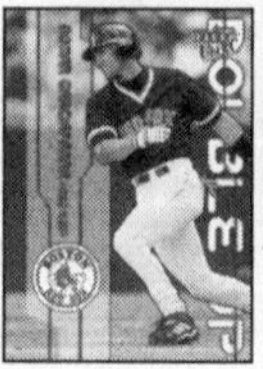

Inserted into packs at a stated rate of one in eight, each of these 16 cards feature two players with something in common. Among the common threads are teammates, nationality and position played.

Nm-Mt Ex-Mt
COMPLETE SET (16) 40.00 12.00
1 Derek Jeter 6.00 1.80
Mike Piazza
2 Alex Rodriguez 4.00 1.20
Rafael Palmeiro
3 Chipper Jones 2.50 .75
Andruw Jones
4 Derek Jeter 6.00 1.80
Alex Rodriguez
5 Nomar Garciaparra 6.00 1.80
Derek Jeter
6 Barry Bonds 6.00 1.80
Jason Giambi
7 Ichiro Suzuki 4.00 1.20
Hideo Nomo
8 Randy Johnson 2.50 .75
Curt Schilling
9 Pedro Martinez 4.00 1.20
Nomar Garciaparra
10 Roger Clemens 5.00 1.50
Kevin Brown
11 Nomar Garciaparra 4.00 1.20
Manny Ramirez
12 Kazuhiro Sasaki 2.50 .75
Hideo Nomo
13 Mike Piazza 4.00 1.20
Ivan Rodriguez
14 Ichiro Suzuki 4.00 1.20
Ken Griffey Jr.
15 Barry Bonds 6.00 1.80
Sammy Sosa
16 Alfonso Soriano 2.50 .75
Roberto Alomar

2003 Ultra Double Up Memorabilia

Randomly inserted into packs, this is a parallel to the Double Up insert set. Each of these cards feature a piece of memorabilia from each of the players featured.

Nm-Mt Ex-Mt
1 Derek Jeter Jsy 60.00 18.00
Mike Piazza Jsy
2 Alex Rodriguez Jsy 40.00 12.00
Rafael Palmeiro Jsy
3 Chipper Jones Bat 25.00 7.50
Andruw Jones Jsy
4 Derek Jeter Jsy 60.00 18.00
Alex Rodriguez Jsy
5 Nomar Garciaparra Jsy 60.00 18.00
Derek Jeter Jsy
6 Barry Bonds Bat 40.00 12.00
Jason Giambi Base
7 Ichiro Suzuki Base 120.00 36.00
Hideo Nomo Jsy
8 Randy Johnson Jsy 25.00 7.50
Curt Schilling Jsy
9 Pedro Martinez Jsy 40.00 12.00
Nomar Garciaparra Jsy
10 Roger Clemens Jsy 40.00 12.00
Kevin Brown Jsy
11 Nomar Garciaparra Jsy 40.00 12.00
Manny Ramirez Jsy
12 Kazuhiro Sasaki Jsy 60.00 18.00
Hideo Nomo Jsy
13 Mike Piazza Jsy 40.00 12.00
Ivan Rodriguez Jsy
14 Ichiro Suzuki Base 80.00 24.00
Ken Griffey Jr. Base
15 Barry Bonds Bat 60.00 18.00
Sammy Sosa Base
16 Alfonso Soriano Pants 25.00 7.50
Roberto Alomar Jsy

2003 Ultra Moonshots

Inserted into packs at a stated rate of one in 12, these 20 cards feature some of the leading power hitters in baseball.

Nm-Mt Ex-Mt
1 Mike Piazza 4.00 1.20
2 Alex Rodriguez 4.00 1.20
3 Manny Ramirez 2.00 .60
4 Ivan Rodriguez 2.50 .75

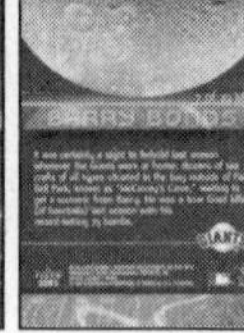

5 Luis Gonzalez 2.00 .60
6 Shawn Green 2.00 .60
7 Barry Bonds 6.00 1.80
8 Jason Giambi 2.50 .75
9 Nomar Garciaparra 4.00 1.20
10 Edgar Martinez 2.00 .60
11 Mo Vaughn 2.00 .60
12 Chipper Jones 2.50 .75
13 Todd Helton 2.00 .60
14 Raul Mondesi 2.00 .60
15 Preston Wilson 2.00 .60
16 Rafael Palmeiro 2.00 .60
17 Jim Edmonds 2.00 .60
18 Bernie Williams 2.00 .60
19 Vladimir Guerrero 2.50 .75
20 Alfonso Soriano 2.00 .60

2003 Ultra Moonshots Memorabilia

Inserted into packs at a stated rate of one in 20, this set parallels the Moonshot insert set except a game-used memorabilia piece is used on each of these cards.

Nm-Mt Ex-Mt
1 Mike Piazza Jsy 15.00 4.50
2 Alex Rodriguez Jsy 15.00 4.50
3 Manny Ramirez Jsy 8.00 2.40
4 Ivan Rodriguez Jsy 10.00 3.00
5 Luis Gonzalez Jsy 8.00 2.40
6 Shawn Green Jsy 8.00 2.40
7 Barry Bonds Jsy 15.00 4.50
8 Jason Giambi Base 10.00 3.00
9 Nomar Garciaparra Jsy 15.00 4.50
10 Edgar Martinez Jsy 10.00 3.00
11 Mo Vaughn Jsy 8.00 2.40
12 Chipper Jones Jsy 10.00 3.00
13 Todd Helton Jsy 10.00 3.00
14 Raul Mondesi Jsy 8.00 2.40
15 Preston Wilson Jsy 8.00 2.40
16 Rafael Palmeiro Jsy 10.00 3.00
17 Jim Edmonds Jsy 8.00 2.40
18 Bernie Williams Jsy 10.00 3.00
19 Vladimir Guerrero Base 10.00 3.00
20 Alfonso Soriano Pants 10.00 3.00

2003 Ultra Photo Effex

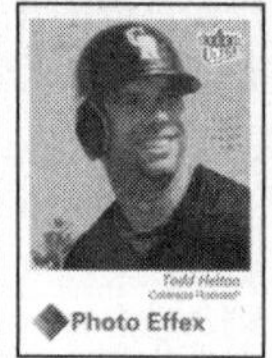

Inserted into packs at a stated rate of one in 12, these 20 cards feature intriguing photos of some of the leading players in the game.

Nm-Mt Ex-Mt
GOLD RANDOM INSERTS IN PACKS
GOLD PRINT RUN 25 SERIAL #'d SETS
GOLD NO PRICING DUE TO SCARCITY
1 Derek Jeter 6.00 1.80
2 Barry Bonds 6.00 1.80
3 Sammy Sosa 4.00 1.20
4 Troy Glaus 2.00 .60
5 Albert Pujols 5.00 1.50
6 Alex Rodriguez 4.00 1.20
7 Ichiro Suzuki 4.00 1.20
8 Greg Maddux 4.00 1.20
9 Nomar Garciaparra 4.00 1.20
10 Jeff Bagwell 2.00 .60
11 Chipper Jones 2.50 .75
12 Mike Piazza 4.00 1.20
13 Randy Johnson 2.50 .75
14 Vladimir Guerrero 2.50 .75
15 Alfonso Soriano 2.00 .60
16 Lance Berkman 2.00 .60
17 Todd Helton 2.00 .60
18 Mike Lowell 2.00 .60
19 Carlos Delgado 2.00 .60
20 Jason Giambi 2.50 .75

2003 Ultra When It Was A Game

Inserted into packs at a stated rate of one in 20, these 40 cards basically feature retired stars from baseball's past. Other than Derek Jeter and Barry Bonds, all the players in this set were retired at the time of issue.

Nm-Mt Ex-Mt
1 Derek Jeter 12.00 3.60
2 Barry Bonds 12.00 3.60
3 Luis Aparicio 5.00 1.50
4 Richie Ashburn 8.00 2.40
5 Ernie Banks 8.00 2.40
6 Enos Slaughter 5.00 1.50
7 Yogi Berra 8.00 2.40
8 Lou Boudreau 5.00 1.50
9 Lou Brock 8.00 2.40
10 Jim Bunning 5.00 1.50
11 Rod Carew 8.00 2.40
12 Orlando Cepeda 5.00 1.50
13 Larry Doby 5.00 1.50
14 Bobby Doerr 5.00 1.50
15 Bob Feller 8.00 2.40
16 Brooks Robinson 8.00 2.40
17 Rollie Fingers 5.00 1.50
18 Whitey Ford 8.00 2.40
19 Bob Gibson 8.00 2.40
20 Catfish Hunter 8.00 2.40
21 Nolan Ryan 15.00 4.50
22 Reggie Jackson 8.00 2.40
23 Fergie Jenkins 5.00 1.50
24 Al Kaline 8.00 2.40
25 Mike Schmidt 15.00 4.50
26 Harmon Killebrew 8.00 2.40
27 Ralph Kiner 5.00 1.50
28 Willie Stargell 8.00 2.40
29 Billy Williams 5.00 1.50
30 Tom Seaver 8.00 2.40
31 Juan Marichal 5.00 1.50
32 Eddie Mathews 8.00 2.40
33 Willie McCovey 5.00 1.50
34 Joe Morgan 5.00 1.50
35 Stan Musial 10.00 3.00
36 Robin Roberts 5.00 1.50
37 Robin Yount 10.00 3.00
38 Jim Palmer 5.00 1.50
39 Phil Rizzuto 8.00 2.40
40 Pee Wee Reese 8.00 2.40

2003 Ultra When It Was A Game Used

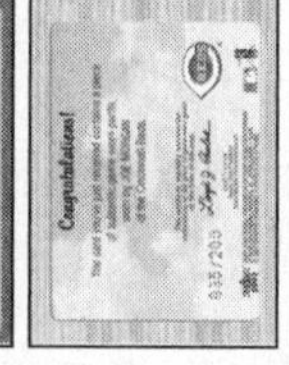

Randomly inserted into packs, these 12 cards form a partial parallel to the When it was a Game Insert set. Since several different print runs were used, we have notated that print run information next to the player's name in our checklist.

Nm-Mt Ex-Mt
1 Yogi Berra Pants/100 50.00 15.00
2 Barry Bonds Bat/200 40.00 12.00
3 Larry Doby Bat/150 20.00 6.00
4 Catfish Hunter Jsy/200 20.00 6.00
5 Reggie Jackson Bat/300 20.00 6.00
6 Derek Jeter Jsy/200 40.00 12.00
7 Juan Marichal Jsy/300 15.00 4.50
8 Eddie Mathews Bat/300 25.00 7.50
9 Willie McCovey Jsy/150 20.00 6.00
10 Joe Morgan Pants/200 15.00 4.50
11 Jim Palmer Pants/300 15.00 4.50
12 Tom Seaver Pants/100 25.00 7.50

2004 Ultra

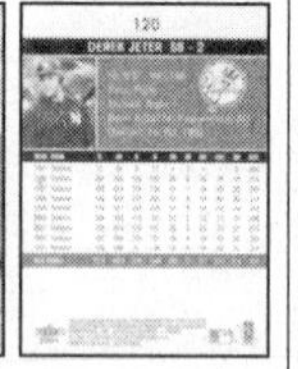

This 220-card set was released in November, 2003. This set was issued in eight-card packs with an $2.99 SRP which came 24 packs to a box and 16 boxes to a case. Please note that cards 201-220 feature leading prospects and were randomly inserted into packs.

MINT NRMT
COMPLETE SET (220) 60.00 27.00
COMP.SET w/o SP's (200) 25.00 11.00
COMMON CARD (1-200) .30 .14
COMMON CARD (201-220) 2.00 .90
1 Magglio Ordonez .30 .14
2 Bobby Abreu .30 .14
3 Eric Munson .30 .14
4 Eric Byrnes .30 .14
5 Bartolo Colon .30 .14
6 Juan Encarnacion .30 .14
7 Jody Gerut .30 .14
8 Eddie Guardado .30 .14
9 Shea Hillenbrand .30 .14
10 Andruw Jones .30 .14
11 Carlos Lee .30 .14
12 Pedro Martinez .75 .35
13 Barry Larkin .75 .35
14 Angel Berroa .30 .14
15 Edgar Martinez .50 .23
16 Sidney Ponson .30 .14
17 Mariano Rivera .50 .23
18 Richie Sexson .30 .14
19 Frank Thomas .75 .35
20 Jerome Williams .30 .14
21 Barry Zito .50 .23
22 Roberto Alomar .75 .35
23 Rocky Biddle .30 .14
24 Orlando Cabrera .30 .14
25 Placido Polanco .30 .14
26 Morgan Ensberg .30 .14
27 Jason Giambi .75 .35
28 Jim Thome .75 .35
29 Vladimir Guerrero .75 .35
30 Tim Hudson .30 .14
31 Jacque Jones .30 .14
32 Derrek Lee .30 .14
33 Rafael Palmeiro .50 .23
34 Mike Mussina .75 .35
35 Corey Patterson .30 .14
36 Mike Cameron .30 .14
37 Ivan Rodriguez .75 .35
38 Ben Sheets .30 .14
39 Woody Williams .30 .14
40 Ichiro Suzuki 1.25 .55
41 Moises Alou .30 .14
42 Craig Biggio .50 .23
43 Jorge Posada .50 .23
44 Craig Monroe .30 .14
45 Darin Erstad .30 .14
46 Jay Gibbons .30 .14
47 Aaron Guiel .30 .14
48 Travis Lee .30 .14
49 Jorge Julio .30 .14
50 Torii Hunter .30 .14
51 Luis Matos .30 .14
52 Brett Myers .30 .14
53 Sean Casey .30 .14
54 Mark Prior 1.50 .70
55 Alex Rodriguez 1.25 .55
56 Gary Sheffield .30 .14
57 Jason Varitek .30 .14
58 Dontrelle Willis .30 .14
59 Garret Anderson .30 .14
60 Casey Blake .30 .14
61 Jay Payton .30 .14
62 Carl Crawford .30 .14
63 Carl Everett .30 .14
64 Marcus Giles .30 .14
65 Jose Guillen .30 .14
66 Eric Karros .30 .14
67 Mike Lieberthal .30 .14
68 Hideki Matsui 1.25 .55
69 Xavier Nady .30 .14
70 Hank Blalock .30 .14
71 Albert Pujols 1.50 .70
72 Jose Cruz Jr. .30 .14
73 Randall Simon .30 .14
74 Javier Vazquez .30 .14
75 Preston Wilson .30 .14
76 Danys Baez .30 .14
77 Alex Cintron .30 .14
78 Jake Peavy .30 .14
79 Scott Rolen .50 .23
80 Robert Fick .30 .14
81 Brian Giles .30 .14
82 Roy Halladay .30 .14
83 Kazuhisa Ishii .30 .14
84 Austin Kearns .30 .14
85 Paul Lo Duca .30 .14
86 Darrell May .30 .14
87 Phil Nevin .30 .14
88 Carlos Pena .30 .14
89 Manny Ramirez .30 .14
90 C.C. Sabathia .30 .14
91 John Smoltz .50 .23
92 Jose Vidro .30 .14
93 Randy Wolf .30 .14
94 Jeff Bagwell .50 .23
95 Barry Bonds 2.00 .90
96 Frank Catalanotto .30 .14
97 Zach Day .30 .14
98 David Ortiz .30 .14
99 Troy Glaus .50 .23
100 Bo Hart .30 .14
101 Geoff Jenkins .30 .14
102 Jason Kendall .30 .14
103 Esteban Loaiza .30 .14
104 Doug Mientkiewicz .30 .14
105 Trot Nixon .50 .23
106 Troy Percival .30 .14
107 Aramis Ramirez .30 .14
108 Alex Sanchez .30 .14
109 Alfonso Soriano .50 .23
110 Omar Vizquel .30 .14
111 Kerry Wood .75 .35
112 Rocco Baldelli .75 .35
113 Bret Boone .30 .14
114 Shawn Chacon .30 .14
115 Carlos Delgado .30 .14
116 Shawn Green .30 .14
117 Tim Worrell .30 .14
118 Tom Glavine .50 .23
119 Shigetoshi Hasegawa .30 .14
120 Derek Jeter 2.00 .90
121 Jeff Kent .30 .14
122 Braden Looper .30 .14
123 Kevin Millwood .30 .14
124 Hideo Nomo .75 .35
125 Jason Phillips .30 .14
126 Tim Redding .30 .14
127 Reggie Sanders .30 .14
128 Sammy Sosa 1.25 .55
129 Billy Wagner .30 .14
130 Miguel Batista .30 .14
131 Milton Bradley .30 .14
132 Eric Chavez .30 .14
133 J.D. Drew .30 .14
134 Keith Foulke .30 .14
135 Luis Gonzalez .30 .14
136 LaTroy Hawkins .30 .14
137 Randy Johnson .75 .35
138 Byung-Hyun Kim .30 .14
139 Javy Lopez .30 .14
140 Melvin Mora .30 .14
141 Aubrey Huff .30 .14
142 Mike Piazza 1.25 .55
143 Mark Redman .30 .14
144 Kazuhiro Sasaki .30 .14
145 Shannon Stewart .30 .14
146 Larry Walker .50 .23
147 Dmitri Young .30 .14
148 Josh Beckett .50 .23
149 Jae Weong Seo .30 .14
150 Hee Seop Choi .30 .14
151 Adam Dunn .30 .14
152 Rafael Furcal .30 .14
153 Juan Gonzalez .75 .35
154 Todd Helton .50 .23
155 Carlos Zambrano .30 .14
156 Ryan Klesko .30 .14
157 Mike Lowell .30 .14
158 Jamie Moyer .30 .14
159 Russ Ortiz .30 .14
160 Juan Pierre .30 .14
161 Edgar Renteria .30 .14
162 Curt Schilling .50 .23
163 Mike Sweeney .30 .14
164 Brandon Webb .30 .14
165 Michael Young .30 .14
166 Carlos Beltran .30 .14
167 Sean Burroughs .30 .14
168 Luis Castillo .30 .14
169 David Eckstein .30 .14
170 Eric Gagne .50 .23
171 Chipper Jones .75 .35
172 Livan Hernandez .30 .14
173 Nick Johnson .30 .14
174 Corey Koskie .30 .14
175 Jason Schmidt .30 .14
176 Bill Mueller .30 .14
177 Steve Finley .30 .14
178 A.J. Pierzynski .30 .14
179 Rene Reyes .30 .14
180 Jason Johnson .30 .14
181 Mark Teixeira .30 .14
182 Kip Wells .30 .14
183 Mike MacDougal .30 .14
184 Lance Berkman .30 .14
185 Victor Zambrano .30 .14
186 Roger Clemens 1.50 .70
187 Jim Edmonds .30 .14
188 Nomar Garciaparra 1.25 .55
189 Ken Griffey Jr. 1.25 .55
190 Richard Hidalgo .30 .14
191 Cliff Floyd .30 .14
192 Greg Maddux 1.25 .55
193 Mark Mulder .30 .14
194 Roy Oswalt .30 .14
195 Marlon Byrd .30 .14
196 Jose Reyes .50 .23
197 Kevin Brown .30 .14
198 Miguel Tejada .30 .14
199 Vernon Wells .30 .14
200 Joel Pineiro .30 .14
201 Rickie Weeks AR 4.00 1.80
202 Chad Gaudin AR 2.00 .90
203 Ryan Wagner AR 2.00 .90
204 Chris Bootcheck AR 2.00 .90
205 Koyie Hill AR 2.00 .90
206 Jeff Duncan AR 2.00 .90
207 Rich Harden AR 2.00 .90
208 Edwin Jackson AR 3.00 1.35
209 Robby Hammock AR 2.00 .90
210 Khalil Greene AR 2.00 .90
211 Chien-Ming Wang AR 2.00 .90
212 Prentice Redman AR 2.00 .90
213 Todd Wellemeyer AR 2.00 .90
214 Clint Barmes AR 2.00 .90
215 Matt Kata AR 2.00 .90
216 Jon Leicester AR 2.00 .90
217 Jeremy Guthrie AR 2.00 .90
218 Chin-Hui Tsao AR 2.00 .90
219 Dan Haren AR 2.00 .90
220 Delmon Young AR 3.00 1.35

2004 Ultra Gold Medallion

MINT NRMT
*GOLD 1-200: 1.25X TO 3X BASIC
1-200 STATED ODDS 1:1
*GOLD 201-220: 1X TO 2.5X BASIC
201-220 STATED ODDS 1:8

2004 Ultra Platinum Medallion

MINT NRMT
*PLATINUM 1-200: 8X TO 20X BASIC
STATED ODDS 1:36
STATED PRINT RUN 66 SERIAL #'d SETS

2004 Ultra Season Crowns Autograph

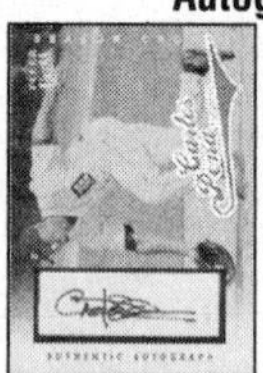
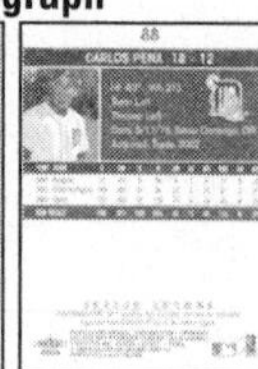

Rickie Weeks did not return his autographs in time for pack-out, thus those cards were issued as exchange cards. There is no expiration date for those redemptions.

MINT NRMT
STATED PRINT RUN 150 SERIAL #'d SETS
GOLD PRINT RUN 25 SERIAL #'d SETS
NO GOLD PRICING DUE TO SCARCITY
OVERALL AUTO PARALLEL ODDS 1:192
EXCHANGE DEADLINE INDEFINITE
35 Corey Patterson 25.00 11.00
58 Dontrelle Willis 40.00 18.00
70 Hank Blalock 40.00 18.00
79 Scott Rolen 40.00 18.00
84 Austin Kearns 25.00 11.00
88 Carlos Pena 15.00 6.75
100 Bo Hart 25.00 11.00
112 Rocco Baldelli 50.00 22.00
141 Aubrey Huff 25.00 11.00
151 Mike Lowell 25.00 11.00
164 Brandon Webb 25.00 11.00
171 Chipper Jones 80.00 36.00
196 Jose Reyes 40.00 18.00
198 Miguel Tejada 25.00 11.00
201 Rickie Weeks EXCH 60.00 27.00

2004 Ultra Season Crowns Game Used

MINT NRMT
STATED PRINT RUN 399 SERIAL #'d SETS
*GOLD: .75X TO 2X BASIC

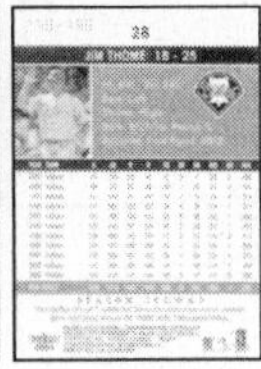

	MINT	NRMT
GOLD PRINT RUN 99 SERIAL #'d SETS		
PLATINUM PRINT RUN 25 SERIAL #'d SETS		
OVERALL GU PARALLEL ODDS 1:24..		
10 Andruw Jones Bat	8.00	3.60
12 Pedro Martinez Jsy	10.00	4.50
14 Angel Berroa Jsy	8.00	3.60
19 Frank Thomas Jsy	10.00	4.50
22 Roberto Alomar Bat	10.00	4.50
27 Jason Giambi Jsy	10.00	4.50
28 Jim Thome Jsy	10.00	4.50
29 Vladimir Guerrero Jsy	10.00	4.50
30 Tim Hudson Jsy	8.00	3.60
40 Ichiro Suzuki Base	25.00	11.00
50 Torii Hunter Bat	8.00	3.60
53 Sean Casey Bat	8.00	3.60
55 Alex Rodriguez Jsy	15.00	6.75
56 Gary Sheffield Bat	8.00	3.60
58 Dontrelle Willis Jsy	8.00	3.60
68 Hideki Matsui Base	25.00	11.00
70 Hank Blalock Bat	8.00	3.60
71 Albert Pujols Jsy	20.00	9.00
79 Scott Rolen Bat	10.00	4.50
84 Austin Kearns Bat	8.00	3.60
88 Carlos Pena Bat	8.00	3.60
89 Manny Ramirez Jsy	8.00	3.60
94 Jeff Bagwell Pants	10.00	4.50
95 Barry Bonds Base	20.00	9.00
99 Troy Glaus Jsy	10.00	4.50
102 Jason Kendall Jsy	8.00	3.60
109 Alfonso Soriano Bat	10.00	4.50
110 Omar Vizquel Jsy	8.00	3.60
112 Rocco Baldelli Jsy	10.00	4.50
115 Carlos Delgado Jsy	8.00	3.60
116 Shawn Green Jsy	8.00	3.60
118 Tom Glavine Bat	10.00	4.50
120 Derek Jeter Jsy	25.00	11.00
124 Hideo Nomo Jsy	10.00	4.50
128 Sammy Sosa Jsy	15.00	6.75
137 Randy Johnson Jsy	10.00	4.50
142 Mike Piazza Bat	15.00	6.75
144 Kazuhiro Sasaki Jsy	8.00	3.60
146 Larry Walker Jsy	10.00	4.50
151 Adam Dunn Bat	8.00	3.60
154 Todd Helton Jsy	10.00	4.50
164 Brandon Webb Jsy	8.00	3.60
166 Carlos Beltran Jsy	8.00	3.60
167 Sean Burroughs Jsy	8.00	3.60
171 Chipper Jones Jsy	10.00	4.50
184 Lance Berkman Bat	8.00	3.60
186 Roger Clemens Jsy	15.00	6.75
192 Greg Maddux Jsy	15.00	6.75
193 Mark Mulder Jsy	8.00	3.60
196 Jose Reyes Jsy	10.00	4.50

2004 Ultra Diamond Producers

	MINT	NRMT
STATED ODDS 1:144		
1 Greg Maddux	20.00	9.00
2 Dontrelle Willis	20.00	9.00
3 Jim Thome	20.00	9.00
4 Alfonso Soriano	20.00	9.00
5 Alex Rodriguez	20.00	9.00
6 Sammy Sosa	20.00	9.00
7 Nomar Garciaparra	20.00	9.00
8 Derek Jeter	30.00	13.50
9 Adam Dunn	20.00	9.00
10 Mark Prior	25.00	11.00

2004 Ultra Diamond Producers Game Used

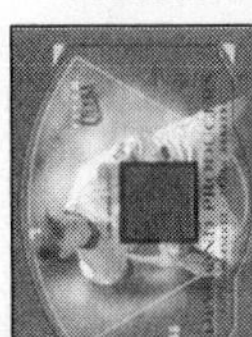
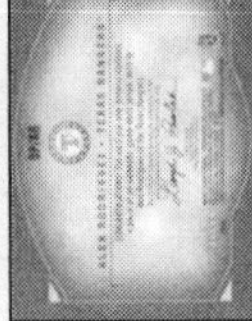

	MINT	NRMT
OVERALL GU INSERT ODDS 1:12		
STATED PRINT RUN 1000 SERIAL #'d SETS		
1 Greg Maddux Jsy	10.00	4.50
2 Dontrelle Willis Jsy	8.00	3.60
3 Jim Thome Jsy	10.00	4.50
4 Alfonso Soriano Bat	10.00	4.50
5 Alex Rodriguez Jsy	15.00	6.75
6 Sammy Sosa Jsy	15.00	6.75
7 Nomar Garciaparra Jsy	15.00	6.75
8 Derek Jeter Jsy	25.00	11.00
9 Adam Dunn Bat	8.00	3.60
10 Mark Prior Jsy	20.00	9.00

2004 Ultra Diamond Producers Game Used UltraSwatch

	MINT	NRMT
OVERALL GU INSERT ODDS 1:12		
PRINT RUNS B/WN 2-44 COPIES PER		
NO PRICING DUE TO SCARCITY		
1 Greg Maddux Jsy/31		
2 Dontrelle Willis Jsy/35		
3 Jim Thome Jsy/25		
4 Alfonso Soriano Bat/12		
5 Alex Rodriguez Jsy/3		
6 Sammy Sosa Jsy/21		
7 Nomar Garciaparra Jsy/5		
8 Derek Jeter Jsy/2		
9 Adam Dunn Bat/44		
10 Mark Prior Jsy/22		

2004 Ultra HR Kings

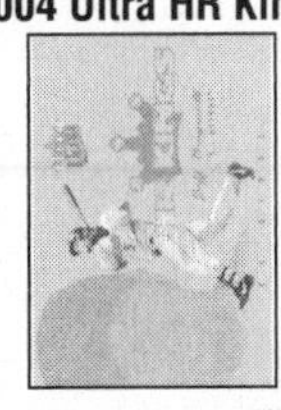

	MINT	NRMT
OVERALL HR/K/RBI KING ODDS 1:12		
*GOLD: 2X TO 5X BASIC		
GOLD OVERALL HR/K/RBI KING ODDS 1:350		
GOLD PRINT RUN 50 SERIAL #'d SETS		
1 Barry Bonds	6.00	2.70
2 Albert Pujols	5.00	2.20
3 Jason Giambi	2.50	1.10
4 Jeff Bagwell	2.50	1.10
5 Ken Griffey Jr.	4.00	1.80
6 Alex Rodriguez	4.00	1.80
7 Sammy Sosa	4.00	1.80
8 Alfonso Soriano	2.50	1.10
9 Chipper Jones	2.50	1.10
10 Mike Piazza	4.00	1.80

2004 Ultra K Kings

	MINT	NRMT
OVERALL HR/K/RBI KING ODDS 1:12		
*GOLD: 2X TO 5X BASIC		
OVERALL GOLD HR/K/RBI KING ODDS 1:350		
GOLD PRINT RUN 50 SERIAL #'d SETS		
1 Randy Johnson	2.50	1.10
2 Pedro Martinez	2.50	1.10
3 Curt Schilling	2.50	1.10
4 Roger Clemens	5.00	2.20
5 Mike Mussina	2.50	1.10
6 Roy Halladay	2.50	1.10
7 Kerry Wood	2.50	1.10
8 Dontrelle Willis	2.50	1.10
9 Greg Maddux	4.00	1.80
10 Mark Prior	5.00	2.20

2004 Ultra Kings Triple Swatch

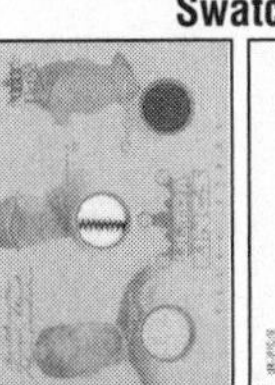
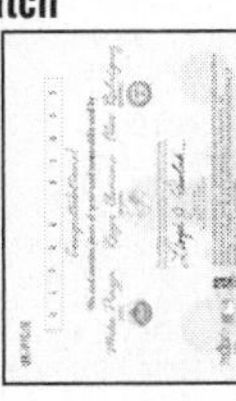

	MINT	NRMT
OVERALL GU INSERT ODDS 1:12		
STATED PRINT RUN 33 SERIAL #'d SETS		
NO PRICING DUE TO SCARCITY		
1 Mike Piazza Bat Roger Clemens Jsy Alex Rodriguez Jsy		
2 Albert Pujols Jsy Mark Prior Jsy Todd Helton Jsy		
3 Alfonso Soriano Bat Dontrelle Willis Jsy Albert Pujols Jsy		
4 Pedro Martinez Jsy Sammy Sosa Jsy Albert Pujols Jsy		
5 Greg Maddux Jsy Chipper Jones Jsy Vladimir Guerrero Jsy		
6 Randy Johnson Jsy Albert Pujols Jsy Todd Helton Jsy		
7 Dontrelle Willis Jsy Chipper Jones Jsy Albert Pujols Jsy		
8 Kerry Wood Jsy Sammy Sosa Jsy Nomar Garciaparra Jsy		
9 Dontrelle Willis Jsy Jeff Bagwell Pants Jim Thome Jsy		
10 Greg Maddux Jsy Jason Giambi Jsy Manny Ramirez Jsy		

2004 Ultra Performers

	MINT	NRMT
COMPLETE SET (15)	25.00	11.00
STATED ODDS 1:6		
1 Ichiro Suzuki	3.00	1.35
2 Albert Pujols	4.00	1.80
3 Barry Bonds	5.00	2.20
4 Hideki Matsui	3.00	1.35
5 Randy Johnson	2.00	.90
6 Jason Giambi	2.00	.90
7 Pedro Martinez	2.00	.90
8 Hank Blalock	2.00	.90
9 Chipper Jones	2.00	.90
10 Mike Piazza	3.00	1.35
11 Derek Jeter	5.00	2.20
12 Vladimir Guerrero	2.00	.90
13 Barry Zito	2.00	.90
14 Rocco Baldelli	2.00	.90
15 Hideo Nomo	2.00	.90

2004 Ultra Performers Game Used

	MINT	NRMT
OVERALL GU INSERT ODDS 1:12		
STATED PRINT RUN 500 SERIAL #'d SETS		
1 Albert Pujols Jsy	20.00	9.00
2 Barry Bonds Base	20.00	9.00
3 Randy Johnson Jsy	10.00	4.50
4 Jason Giambi Jsy	10.00	4.50
5 Pedro Martinez Jsy	10.00	4.50
6 Hank Blalock Bat	8.00	3.60
7 Chipper Jones Jsy	10.00	4.50
8 Mike Piazza Bat	10.00	4.50
9 Derek Jeter Jsy	25.00	11.00
10 Vladimir Guerrero Jsy	10.00	4.50
11 Rocco Baldelli Jsy	10.00	4.50
12 Hideo Nomo Jsy	10.00	4.50

2004 Ultra Performers Game Used UltraSwatch

	MINT	NRMT
OVERALL GU INSERT ODDS 1:12		
PRINT RUNS B/WN 2-51 COPIES PER		
NO PRICING DUE TO SCARCITY		
1 Albert Pujols Jsy/5		
2 Barry Bonds Base/25		
3 Randy Johnson Jsy/51		
4 Jason Giambi Jsy/25		
5 Pedro Martinez Jsy/45		
6 Hank Blalock Bat/9		
7 Chipper Jones Jsy/10		
8 Mike Piazza Bat/31		
9 Derek Jeter Jsy/2		
10 Vladimir Guerrero Jsy/27		
11 Rocco Baldelli Jsy/5		
12 Hideo Nomo Jsy/10		

2004 Ultra RBI Kings

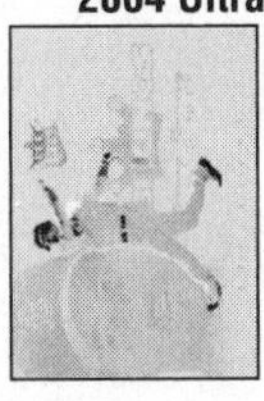

	MINT	NRMT
OVERALL HR/K/RBI KING ODDS 1:12		
*GOLD: 2X TO 5X BASIC		
OVERALL GOLD HR/K/RBI KING ODDS 1:350		
GOLD PRINT RUN 50 SERIAL #'d SETS		
1 Hideki Matsui	4.00	1.80
2 Albert Pujols	5.00	2.20
3 Todd Helton	2.50	1.10
4 Jim Thome	2.50	1.10
5 Carlos Delgado	2.50	1.10
6 Alex Rodriguez	4.00	1.80
7 Barry Bonds	6.00	2.70
8 Manny Ramirez	2.50	1.10
9 Vladimir Guerrero	2.50	1.10
10 Nomar Garciaparra	4.00	1.80

1925 Universal Toy and Novelty W-504

Issued in uncut sheet form, by Universal Toy and Novelty, this "Strip card" series appears to have been issued early in the 1925 season. Presently, examples of individual players representing four teams are accounted for. Three of the checklists appear to be complete (Brooklyn, Giants, Yankees - as listed below). The cards are numbered on the fronts, although the number is sometimes cut off when being separated from the sheet. The backs are blank. Like all "Strip cards" these were cut down by hand, after they were

marketed. As such, size variances may very well exist. Approximate size is 1 3/8" x 2 1/4".

	Ex-Mt	VG
COMPLETE SET (58)	1500.00	750.00
101 Eddie Brown	20.00	10.00
102 Hank DeBerry	20.00	10.00
103 Bill Doak	20.00	10.00
104 Rube Ehrhardt	20.00	10.00
105 Jake Fournier	25.00	12.50
106 Tommy Griffith	20.00	10.00
107 Burleigh Grimes	40.00	20.00
108 Charlie Hargreaves	20.00	10.00
109 Andy High	20.00	10.00
110 Jimmy Johnston	20.00	10.00
111 John Mitchell	20.00	10.00
112 Tiny Osborne	20.00	10.00
113 Milt Stock	20.00	10.00
114 Zack Taylor	20.00	10.00
115 Dazzy Vance	40.00	20.00
116 Zach Wheat	40.00	20.00
117 Bennie Bengough	20.00	10.00
118 Joe Dugan	20.00	10.00
119 Waite Hoyt	40.00	20.00
120 Sam Jones	25.00	12.50
121 Bob Meusel	30.00	15.00
122 Wally Pipp	20.00	10.00
123 Babe Ruth	150.00	75.00
124 Wally Schang	20.00	10.00
125 Bob Shawkey	25.00	12.50
126 Everett Scott	20.00	10.00
127 Urban Shocker	20.00	10.00
128 Aaron Ward	20.00	10.00
129 Whitey Witt	20.00	10.00
130 Carl Mays	20.00	10.00
131 Miller Huggins MG	40.00	20.00
132 Ben. Paschal	20.00	10.00
133 Virgil Barnes	20.00	10.00
134 Jack Bentley	20.00	10.00
135 Frank Frisch	40.00	20.00
136 Hank Gowdy	20.00	10.00
137 Heinie Groh	25.00	12.50
138 Travis Jackson	40.00	20.00
139 George Kelly	40.00	20.00
140 Emil Meusel	20.00	10.00
141 Hugh McQuillan	20.00	10.00
142 Arthur Nehf	20.00	10.00
143 Rosy Ryan	20.00	10.00
144 Pancho Snyder	20.00	10.00
145 Hack Wilson	40.00	20.00
146 Ross Youngs	40.00	20.00
147 Hugh Jennings CO	40.00	20.00
148 John McGraw MG	50.00	25.00
149 Joe Judge	25.00	12.50
151 Roger Peckinpaugh	25.00	12.50
152 Ossie Bluege	20.00	10.00
153 Mike McNally	20.00	10.00
154 Sam Rice	40.00	20.00
159 Pinky Hargrave	20.00	10.00
162 Muddy Ruel	20.00	10.00
164 George Mogridge	20.00	10.00
NNO Brooklyn Dodgers Team Photo	40.00	20.00
NNO New York Yankees Team Photo	40.00	20.00
NNO New York Giants Team Photo	40.00	20.00

1933 Uncle Jack

These blank-backed cards, which measure approximately 1 7/8" by 2 7/8" feauture the leading players in baseball at this time. The fronts feature a blue duotone photo with the players name on the bottom. Since the cards are unnumbered, they are sequenced in alphabetical order.

	Ex-Mt	VG
COMPLETE SET (30)	3600.00	1800.00
1 Earl Averill	120.00	60.00
2 James Bottomley	120.00	60.00
3 Ed Brandt	60.00	30.00
4 Ben Chapman	60.00	30.00
5 Gordon Cochrane	120.00	60.00
6 Joe Cronin	120.00	60.00
7 Kiki Cuyler	120.00	60.00
8 George Earnshaw	60.00	30.00
9 Wes Ferrell	100.00	50.00
10 Jimmie Foxx	200.00	100.00
11 Frank Frisch	120.00	60.00
12 Burleigh Grimes	120.00	60.00
13 Lefty Grove	200.00	100.00
14 Wild Bill Hallahan	80.00	40.00
15 Gabby Hartnett	120.00	60.00
16 Babe Herman	100.00	50.00
17 Rogers Hornsby	300.00	150.00
18 Charles Klein	120.00	60.00
19 Tony Lazzeri	120.00	60.00
20 Fred Lindstrom	120.00	60.00
21 Ted Lyons	120.00	60.00
22 Pepper Martin	100.00	50.00
23 Herb Pennock	120.00	60.00
24 Babe Ruth	500.00	250.00
25 Al Simmons	120.00	60.00
26 Bill Terry	120.00	60.00
27 Dazzy Vance	120.00	60.00
28 Lloyd Waner	120.00	60.00
29 Paul Waner	120.00	60.00
30 Hack Wilson	120.00	60.00

1976 UPI Superstars

It is believed that this known as the 1976 UPI set. The biographies on the cards do not really help either, as the time frame mentioned on these cards range anywhere from the 1960's until 1972. These cards measure 2 1/4" by 3" and have color photos as well as brief biographies. The backs are blank. Hobbyists who have seen these cards believe that they could have been cut from record album covers. We have sequenced this set in alphabetical order.

	NM	Ex
COMPLETE SET (12)	150.00	60.00
1 Ken Boyer	4.00	1.60
2 Don Drysdale	12.00	4.80
3 Whitey Ford	15.00	6.00
4 Jim Gentile	2.00	.80
5 Al Kaline	12.00	4.80
6 Sandy Koufax	20.00	8.00
7 Mickey Mantle	40.00	16.00
8 Roger Maris	15.00	6.00
9 Willie Mays	30.00	12.00
10 Bill Mazeroski	8.00	3.20
11 Frank Robinson	15.00	6.00
12 Pete Ward	2.00	.80

1988 Upper Deck Promos

The first two cards were test issues given away as samples during the summer of 1988 in anticipation of Upper Deck obtaining licenses from Major League Baseball and the Major League Baseball Players Association. Not many were produced (probably less than 25,000 of each) but few were thrown away as they were distributed basically only to those who would hold on to them. There are three versions based on where the hologram is located. Type A, the most common variety, has a hologram on the bottom that extends as far as the photo. On Type B, the hologram is on the bottom but extends to the edge of the card. Type C, by far the scarcest, has the hologram at the top. Joyner and Buice were supposedly interested in investing in Upper Deck (conflict of interest prohibited them) and apparently were helpful in getting Upper Deck the necessary licenses. Cards were passed out freely to every dealer at the National Sports Collectors Convention in Atlantic City, New Jersey in August 1988.

	Nm-Mt	Ex-Mt
A1 DeWayne Buice	10.00	4.00
A700 Wally Joyner	50.00	20.00
B1 DeWayne Buice	20.00	8.00
B700 Wally Joyner	100.00	40.00
C1 DeWayne Buice	50.00	20.00
C700 Wally Joyner	250.00	100.00

1989 Upper Deck

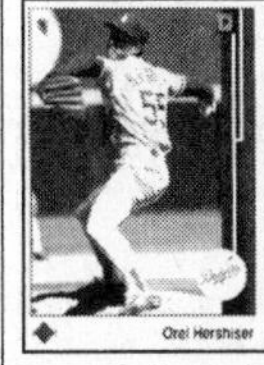

This attractive 800-card standard-size set was introduced in 1989 as the premier issue by the then-fledgling Upper Deck company. Unlike other 1989 releases, this set was issued in two separate series - a low series numbered 1-700 and a high series numbered 701-800. Cards were primarily issued in fin-wrapped low and high series foil packs, complete 800-card factory sets and 100-card high series factory sets. High series packs contained a mixture of both low and high series cards. Collectors should also note that many dealers consider that Upper Deck's "planned" production of 1,000,000 of each player was increased (perhaps even doubled) later in the year due to the explosion in popularity of the product. The cards feature slick paper stock, full color on both the front and the back and carry a hologram on the reverse to protect against counterfeiting. Subsets include Rookie Stars (1-26) and Collector's Choice art cards (668-693). The more significant variations involving changed photos or changed type are listed below. According to the company, the Murphy and Sheridan cards were corrected very early, after only two percent of the cards had been produced. Similarly, the Sheffield was corrected after 15 percent had been printed; Varsho, Gallego, and Schroeder were corrected after 20 percent; and Holton, Manrique, and Winningham were corrected 30 percent of the way through. Rookie Cards in the set include Jim Abbott, Sandy Alomar Jr., Dante Bichette, Craig Biggio, Steve Finley, Ken Griffey Jr., Randy Johnson, Gary Sheffield, John Smoltz and Todd Zeile. Cards with missing or duplicate holograms appear to be relatively common and are generally considered to be flawed copies that sell for substantial discounts.

Card	Nm-Mt	Ex-Mt
COMPLETE SET (800)	80.00	32.00
COMP.FACT.SET (800)	100.00	40.00
COMP.HI FACT.SET (100)	10.00	4.00
1 Ken Griffey Jr. RC	60.00	24.00
2 Luis Medina RC	.25	.10
3 Tony Chance RC	.25	.10
4 Dave Otto	.25	.10
5 S.Alomar Jr. RC UER	1.00	.40
Born 6/16/66, should be 6/18/66		
6 Rolando Roomes RC	.25	.10
7 Dave West RC	.25	.10
8 Cris Carpenter RC	.25	.10
9 Gregg Jefferies	.40	.16
10 Doug Dascenzo RC	.25	.10
11 Ron Jones RC	.25	.10
12 Luis DeLosSantos RC	.25	.10
13 Gary Sheffield COR RC	6.00	2.40
13A G.Sheffield ERR RC	6.00	2.40
SS upside down on card front		
14 Mike Harkey RC	.25	.10
15 Lance Blankenship RC	.25	.10
16 William Brennan RC	.25	.10
17 John Smoltz RC	4.00	1.60
18 Ramon Martinez RC	1.00	.40
19 Mark Lemke RC	.50	.20
20 Juan Bell RC	.25	.10
21 Rey Palacios RC	.25	.10
22 Felix Jose RC	.25	.10
23 Van Snider RC	.25	.10
24 Dante Bichette RC	1.00	.40
25 Randy Johnson RC	15.00	6.00
26 Carlos Quintana RC	.25	.10
27 Star Rookie CL	.25	.10
28 Mike Schooler	.25	.10
29 Randy St.Claire	.25	.10
30 Jerald Clark RC	.25	.10
31 Kevin Gross	.25	.10
32 Dan Firova	.25	.10
33 Jeff Calhoun	.25	.10
34 Tommy Hinzo	.25	.10
35 Ricky Jordan RC	.50	.20
36 Larry Parrish	.25	.10
37 Bret Saberhagen UER	.40	.16
Hit total 931, should be 1031		
38 Mike Smithson	.25	.10
39 Dave Dravecky	.40	.16
40 Ed Romero	.25	.10
41 Jeff Musselman	.25	.10
42 Ed Hearn	.25	.10
43 Rance Mulliniks	.25	.10
44 Jim Eisenreich	.25	.10
45 Sil Campusano	.25	.10
46 Mike Krukow	.25	.10
47 Paul Gibson	.25	.10
48 Mike LaCoss	.25	.10
49 Larry Herndon	.25	.10
50 Scott Garrelts	.25	.10
51 Dwayne Henry	.25	.10
52 Jim Acker	.25	.10
53 Steve Sax	.25	.10
54 Pete O'Brien	.25	.10
55 Paul Runge	.25	.10
56 Rick Rhoden	.25	.10
57 John Dopson	.25	.10
58 Casey Candaele UER	.25	.10
(No stats for Astros for '88 season)		
59 Dave Righetti	.25	.10
60 Joe Hesketh	.25	.10
61 Frank DiPino	.25	.10
62 Tim Laudner	.25	.10
63 Jamie Moyer	.40	.16
64 Fred Toliver	.25	.10
65 Mitch Webster	.25	.10
66 John Tudor	.25	.10
67 John Cangelosi	.25	.10
68 Mike Devereaux	.25	.10
69 Brian Fisher	.25	.10
70 Mike Marshall	.25	.10
71 Zane Smith	.25	.10
72A Brian Holton ERR	1.00	.40
(Photo actually Shawn Hillegas)		
72B Brian Holton COR	.40	.16
73 Jose Guzman	.25	.10
74 Rick Mahler	.25	.10
75 John Shelby	.25	.10
76 Jim Deshaies	.25	.10
77 Bobby Meacham	.25	.10
78 Bryn Smith	.25	.10
79 Joaquin Andujar	.25	.10
80 Richard Dotson	.25	.10
81 Charlie Lea	.25	.10
82 Calvin Schiraldi	.25	.10
83 Les Straker	.25	.10
84 Les Lancaster	.25	.10
85 Allan Anderson	.25	.10
86 Junior Ortiz	.25	.10
87 Jesse Orosco	.25	.10
88 Felix Fermin	.25	.10
89 Dave Anderson	.25	.10
90 Rafael Belliard UER	.25	.10
(Born '61, not '51)		
91 Franklin Stubbs	.25	.10
92 Cecil Espy	.25	.10
93 Albert Hall	.25	.10
94 Tim Leary	.25	.10
95 Mitch Williams	.25	.10
96 Tracy Jones	.25	.10
97 Danny Darwin	.25	.10
98 Gary Ward	.25	.10
99 Neal Heaton	.25	.10
100 Jim Pankovits	.25	.10
101 Bill Doran	.25	.10
102 Tim Wallach	.25	.10
103 Joe Magrane	.25	.10
104 Ozzie Virgil	.25	.10
105 Alvin Davis	.25	.10
106 Tom Brookens	.25	.10
107 Shawon Dunston	.25	.10
108 Tracy Woodson	.25	.10
109 Nelson Liriano	.25	.10
110 Devon White UER	.40	.16
(Doubles total 46, should be 56)		
111 Steve Balboni	.25	.10
112 Buddy Bell	.40	.16
113 German Jimenez	.25	.10
114 Ken Dayley	.25	.10
115 Andres Galarraga	.40	.16
116 Mike Scioscia	.25	.10
117 Gary Pettis	.25	.10
118 Ernie Whitt	.25	.10
119 Bob Boone	.40	.16
120 Ryne Sandberg	1.50	.60
121 Bruce Benedict	.25	.10
122 Hubie Brooks	.25	.10
123 Mike Moore	.25	.10
124 Wallace Johnson	.25	.10
125 Bob Horner	.25	.10
126 Chili Davis	.40	.16
127 Manny Trillo	.25	.10
128 Chet Lemon	.25	.10
129 John Cerutti	.25	.10
130 Orel Hershiser	.40	.16
131 Terry Pendleton	.25	.10
132 Jeff Blauser	.40	.16
133 Mike Fitzgerald	.25	.10
134 Henry Cotto	.25	.10
135 Gerald Young	.25	.10
136 Luis Salazar	.25	.10
137 Alejandro Pena	.25	.10
138 Jack Howell	.25	.10
139 Tony Fernandez	.25	.10
140 Mark Grace	1.00	.40
141 Ken Caminiti	.40	.16
142 Mike Jackson	.25	.10
143 Larry McWilliams	.25	.10
144 Andres Thomas	.25	.10
145 Nolan Ryan 3X	4.00	1.60
146 Mike Davis	.25	.10
147 DeWayne Buice	.25	.10
148 Jody Davis	.25	.10
149 Jesse Barfield	.25	.10
150 Matt Nokes	.25	.10
151 Jerry Reuss	.25	.10
152 Rick Cerone	.25	.10
153 Storm Davis	.25	.10
154 Marvell Wynne	.25	.10
155 Will Clark	1.00	.40
156 Luis Aguayo	.25	.10
157 Willie Upshaw	.25	.10
158 Randy Bush	.25	.10
159 Ron Darling	.25	.10
160 Kal Daniels	.25	.10
161 Spike Owen	.25	.10
162 Luis Polonia	.25	.10
163 Kevin Mitchell UER	.40	.16
('88/total HR's 18/52, should be 19/53)		
164 Dave Gallagher	.25	.10
165 Benito Santiago	.40	.16
166 Greg Gagne	.25	.10
167 Ken Phelps	.25	.10
168 Sid Fernandez	.25	.10
169 Bo Diaz	.25	.10
170 Cory Snyder	.25	.10
171 Eric Show	.25	.10
172 Robby Thompson	.25	.10
173 Marty Barrett	.25	.10
174 Dave Henderson	.25	.10
175 Ozzie Guillen	.25	.10
176 Barry Lyons	.25	.10
177 Kelvin Torve	.25	.10
178 Don Slaught	.25	.10
179 Steve Lombardozzi	.25	.10
180 Chris Sabo RC	1.00	.40
181 Jose Uribe	.25	.10
182 Shane Mack	.25	.10
183 Ron Karkovice	.25	.10
184 Todd Benzinger	.25	.10
185 Dave Stewart	.40	.16
186 Julio Franco	.25	.10
187 Ron Robinson	.25	.10
188 Wally Backman	.25	.10
189 Randy Velarde	.25	.10
190 Joe Carter	.60	.24
191 Bob Welch	.25	.10
192 Kelly Paris	.25	.10
193 Chris Brown	.25	.10
194 Rick Reuschel	.25	.10
195 Roger Clemens	2.00	.80
196 Dave Concepcion	.40	.16
197 Al Newman	.25	.10
198 Brook Jacoby	.25	.10
199 Mookie Wilson	.40	.16
200 Don Mattingly	2.50	1.00
201 Dick Schofield	.25	.10
202 Mark Gubicza	.25	.10
203 Gary Gaetti	.40	.16
204 Dan Pasqua	.25	.10
205 Andre Dawson	.40	.16
206 Chris Speier	.25	.10
207 Kent Tekulve	.25	.10
208 Rod Scurry	.25	.10
209 Scott Bailes	.25	.10
210 R.Henderson UER	1.00	.40
Throws Right		
211 Harold Baines	.40	.16
212 Tony Armas	.25	.10
213 Kent Hrbek	.40	.16
214 Darrin Jackson	.25	.10
215 George Brett	2.50	1.00
216 Rafael Santana	.25	.10
217 Andy Allanson	.25	.10
218 Brett Butler	.40	.16
219 Steve Jeltz	.25	.10
220 Jay Buhner	.40	.16
221 Bo Jackson	1.00	.40
222 Angel Salazar	.25	.10
223 Kirk McCaskill	.25	.10
224 Steve Lyons	.25	.10
225 Bert Blyleven	.40	.16
226 Scott Bradley	.25	.10
227 Bob Melvin	.25	.10
228 Ron Kittle	.25	.10
229 Phil Bradley	.25	.10
230 Tommy John	.40	.16
231 Greg Walker	.25	.10
232 Juan Berenguer	.25	.10
233 Pat Tabler	.25	.10
234 Terry Clark	.25	.10
235 Rafael Palmeiro	.60	.24
236 Paul Zuvella	.25	.10
237 Willie Randolph	.40	.16
238 Bruce Fields	.25	.10
239 Mike Aldrete	.25	.10
240 Lance Parrish	.25	.10
241 Greg Maddux	2.50	1.00
242 John Moses	.25	.10
243 Melido Perez	.25	.10
244 Willie Wilson	.25	.10
245 Mark McLemore	.25	.10
246 Von Hayes	.25	.10
247 Matt Williams	1.00	.40
248 John Candelaria UER	.25	.10
Listed as Yankee for part of '87, should be Mets		
249 Harold Reynolds	.40	.16
250 Greg Swindell	.25	.10
251 Juan Agosto	.25	.10
252 Mike Felder	.25	.10
253 Vince Coleman	.25	.10
254 Larry Sheets	.25	.10
255 George Bell	.25	.10
256 Terry Steinbach	.40	.16
257 Jack Armstrong RC	.50	.20
258 Dickie Thon	.25	.10
259 Ray Knight	.25	.10
260 Darryl Strawberry	.60	.24
261 Doug Sisk	.25	.10
262 Alex Trevino	.25	.10
263 Jeffrey Leonard	.25	.10
264 Tom Henke	.25	.10
265 Ozzie Smith	1.50	.60
266 Dave Bergman	.25	.10
267 Tony Phillips	.25	.10
268 Mark Davis	.25	.10
269 Kevin Elster	.25	.10
270 Barry Larkin	1.00	.40
271 Manny Lee	.25	.10
272 Tom Brunansky	.25	.10
273 Craig Biggio RC	3.00	1.20
274 Jim Gantner	.25	.10
275 Eddie Murray	1.00	.40
276 Jeff Reed	.25	.10
277 Tim Teufel	.25	.10
278 Rick Honeycutt	.25	.10
279 Guillermo Hernandez	.25	.10
280 John Kruk	.40	.16
281 Luis Alicea RC	.50	.20
282 Jim Clancy	.25	.10
283 Billy Ripken	.25	.10
284 Craig Reynolds	.25	.10
285 Robin Yount	1.50	.60
286 Jimmy Jones	.25	.10
287 Ron Oester	.25	.10
288 Terry Leach	.25	.10
289 Dennis Eckersley	.40	.16
290 Alan Trammell	.60	.24
291 Jimmy Key	.40	.16
292 Chris Bosio	.25	.10
293 Jose DeLeon	.25	.10
294 Jim Traber	.25	.10
295 Mike Scott	.25	.10
296 Roger McDowell	.25	.10
297 Garry Templeton	.25	.10
298 Doyle Alexander	.25	.10
299 Nick Esasky	.25	.10
300 Mark McGwire UER	5.00	2.00
(Doubles total 52, should be 51)		
301 Darryl Hamilton RC	.50	.20
302 Dave Smith	.25	.10
303 Rick Sutcliffe	.40	.16
304 Dave Stapleton	.25	.10
305 Alan Ashby	.25	.10
306 Pedro Guerrero	.25	.10
307 Ron Guidry	.40	.16
308 Steve Farr	.25	.10
309 Curt Ford	.25	.10
310 Claudell Washington	.25	.10
311 Tom Prince	.25	.10
312 Chad Kreuter RC	.50	.20
313 Ken Oberkfell	.25	.10
314 Jerry Browne	.25	.10
315 R.J. Reynolds	.25	.10
316 Scott Bankhead	.25	.10
317 Milt Thompson	.25	.10
318 Mario Diaz	.25	.10
319 Bruce Ruffin	.25	.10
320 Dave Valle	.25	.10
321A Gary Varsho ERR	2.00	.80
(Back photo actually Mike Bielecki bunting)		
321B Gary Varsho COR	.25	.10
(In road uniform)		
322 Paul Mirabella	.25	.10
323 Chuck Jackson	.25	.10
324 Drew Hall	.25	.10
325 Don August	.25	.10
326 Israel Sanchez	.25	.10
327 Denny Walling	.25	.10
328 Joel Skinner	.25	.10
329 Danny Tartabull	.25	.10
330 Tony Pena	.25	.10
331 Jim Sundberg	.25	.10
332 Jeff D. Robinson	.25	.10
333 Oddibe McDowell	.25	.10
334 Jose Lind	.25	.10
335 Paul Kilgus	.25	.10
336 Juan Samuel	.25	.10
337 Mike Campbell	.25	.10
338 Mike Maddux	.25	.10
339 Darnell Coles	.25	.10
340 Bob Dernier	.25	.10
341 Rafael Ramirez	.25	.10
342 Scott Sanderson	.25	.10
343 B.J. Surhoff	.40	.16
344 Billy Hatcher	.25	.10
345 Pat Perry	.25	.10
346 Jack Clark	.25	.10
347 Gary Thurman	.25	.10
348 Tim Jones	.25	.10
349 Dave Winfield	.40	.16
350 Frank White	.40	.16
351 Dave Collins	.25	.10
352 Jack Morris	.40	.16
353 Eric Plunk	.25	.10
354 Leon Durham	.25	.10
355 Ivan DeJesus	.25	.10
356 Brian Holman RC	.25	.10
357A Dale Murphy ERR	30.00	12.00
(Front has reverse negative)		
357B Dale Murphy COR	.60	.24
358 Mark Portugal	.25	.10
359 Andy McGaffigan	.25	.10
360 Tom Glavine	1.00	.40
361 Keith Moreland	.25	.10
362 Todd Stottlemyre	.60	.24
363 Dave Leiper	.25	.10
364 Cecil Fielder	.40	.16
365 Carmelo Martinez	.25	.10
366 Dwight Evans	.40	.16
367 Kevin McReynolds	.25	.10
368 Rich Gedman	.25	.10
369 Len Dykstra	.40	.16
370 Jody Reed	.25	.10
371 Jose Canseco UER	1.00	.40
(Strikeout total 391, should be 491)		
372 Rob Murphy	.25	.10
373 Mike Henneman	.25	.10
374 Walt Weiss	.25	.10
375 Rob Dibble RC	1.50	.60
376 Kirby Puckett	1.00	.40
(Mark McGwire in background)		
377 Dennis Martinez	.40	.16
378 Ron Gant	.40	.16
379 Brian Harper	.25	.10
380 Nelson Santovenia	.25	.10
381 Lloyd Moseby	.25	.10
382 Lance McCullers	.25	.10
383 Dave Stieb	.25	.10
384 Tony Gwynn	1.25	.50
385 Mike Flanagan	.25	.10
386 Bob Ojeda	.25	.10
387 Bruce Hurst	.25	.10
388 Dave Magadan	.25	.10
389 Wade Boggs	.60	.24
390 Gary Carter	.60	.24
391 Frank Tanana	.25	.10
392 Curt Young	.25	.10
393 Jeff Treadway	.25	.10
394 Darrell Evans	.40	.16
395 Glenn Hubbard	.25	.10
396 Chuck Cary	.25	.10
397 Frank Viola	.25	.10
398 Jeff Parrett	.25	.10
399 Terry Blocker	.25	.10
400 Dan Gladden	.25	.10
401 Louie Meadows	.25	.10
402 Tim Raines	.40	.16
403 Joey Meyer	.25	.10
404 Larry Andersen	.25	.10
405 Rex Hudler	.25	.10
406 Mike Schmidt	2.00	.80
407 John Franco	.40	.16
408 Brady Anderson RC	1.50	.60
409 Don Carman	.25	.10
410 Eric Davis	.40	.16
411 Bob Stanley	.25	.10
412 Pete Smith	.25	.10
413 Jim Rice	.40	.16
414 Bruce Sutter	.25	.10
415 Oil Can Boyd	.25	.10
416 Ruben Sierra	.25	.10
417 Mike LaValliere	.25	.10
418 Steve Buechele	.25	.10
419 Gary Redus	.25	.10
420 Scott Fletcher	.25	.10
421 Dale Sveum	.25	.10
422 Bob Knepper	.25	.10
423 Luis Rivera	.25	.10
424 Ted Higuera	.25	.10
425 Kevin Bass	.25	.10
426 Ken Gerhart	.25	.10
427 Shane Rawley	.25	.10
428 Paul O'Neill	.60	.24
429 Joe Orsulak	.25	.10
430 Jackie Gutierrez	.25	.10
431 Gerald Perry	.25	.10
432 Mike Greenwell	.25	.10
433 Jerry Royster	.25	.10
434 Ellis Burks	.60	.24
435 Ed Olwine	.25	.10
436 Dave Rucker	.25	.10
437 Charlie Hough	.40	.16
438 Bob Walk	.25	.10
439 Bob Brower	.25	.10
440 Barry Bonds	5.00	2.00
441 Tom Foley	.25	.10
442 Rob Deer	.25	.10
443 Glenn Davis	.25	.10
444 Dave Martinez	.25	.10
445 Bill Wegman	.25	.10
446 Lloyd McClendon	.25	.10
447 Dave Schmidt	.25	.10
448 Darren Daulton	.40	.16
449 Frank Williams	.25	.10
450 Don Aase	.25	.10
451 Lou Whitaker	.40	.16
452 Rich Gossage	.40	.16
453 Ed Whitson	.25	.10
454 Jim Walewander	.25	.10
455 Damon Berryhill	.25	.10
456 Tim Burke	.25	.10
457 Barry Jones	.25	.10
458 Joel Youngblood	.25	.10
459 Floyd Youmans	.25	.10
460 Mark Salas	.25	.10
461 Jeff Russell	.25	.10
462 Darrell Miller	.25	.10
463 Jeff Kunkel	.25	.10
464 Sherman Corbett	.25	.10
465 Curtis Wilkerson	.25	.10
466 Bud Black	.25	.10
467 Cal Ripken	3.00	1.20
468 John Farrell	.25	.10
469 Terry Kennedy	.25	.10
470 Tom Candiotti	.25	.10
471 Roberto Alomar	1.25	.50
472 Jeff M. Robinson	.25	.10
473 Vance Law	.25	.10
474 Randy Ready UER	.25	.10
(Strikeout total 136, should be 115)		
475 Walt Terrell	.25	.10
476 Kelly Downs	.25	.10
477 Johnny Paredes	.25	.10
478 Shawn Hillegas	.25	.10
479 Bob Brenly	.25	.10
480 Otis Nixon	.25	.10
481 Johnny Ray	.25	.10
482 Geno Petralli	.25	.10
483 Stu Cliburn	.25	.10
484 Pete Incaviglia	.25	.10
485 Brian Downing	.25	.10
486 Jeff Stone	.25	.10
487 Carmen Castillo	.25	.10
488 Tom Niedenfuer	.25	.10
489 Jay Bell	.60	.24
490 Rick Schu	.25	.10
491 Jeff Pico	.25	.10
492 Mark Parent	.25	.10
493 Eric King	.25	.10
494 Al Nipper	.25	.10
495 Andy Hawkins	.25	.10
496 Daryl Boston	.25	.10
497 Ernie Riles	.25	.10
498 Pascual Perez	.25	.10
499 Bill Long UER	.25	.10
(Games started total 70, should be 44)		
500 Kurt Manwaring	.25	.10
501 Chuck Crim	.25	.10
502 Candy Maldonado	.25	.10
503 Dennis Lamp	.25	.10
504 Glenn Braggs	.25	.10
505 Joe Price	.25	.10
506 Ken Williams	.25	.10
507 Bill Pecota	.25	.10
508 Rey Quinones	.25	.10
509 Jeff Bittiger	.25	.10
510 Kevin Seitzer	.25	.10
511 Steve Bedrosian	.25	.10
512 Todd Worrell	.40	.16
513 Chris James	.25	.10
514 Jose Oquendo	.25	.10
515 David Palmer	.25	.10
516 John Smiley	.25	.10
517 Dave Clark	.25	.10
518 Mike Dunne	.25	.10
519 Ron Washington	.25	.10
520 Bob Kipper	.25	.10
521 Lee Smith	.40	.16
522 Juan Castillo	.25	.10
523 Don Robinson	.25	.10
524 Kevin Romine	.25	.10
525 Paul Molitor	.60	.24
526 Mark Langston	.25	.10
527 Donnie Hill	.25	.10
528 Larry Owen	.25	.10
529 Jerry Reed	.25	.10
530 Jack McDowell	.40	.16
531 Greg Mathews	.25	.10
532 John Russell	.25	.10
533 Dan Quisenberry	.25	.10
534 Greg Gross	.25	.10
535 Danny Cox	.25	.10
536 Terry Francona	.40	.16
537 Andy Van Slyke	.40	.16
538 Mel Hall	.25	.10
539 Jim Gott	.25	.10
540 Doug Jones	.25	.10
541 Craig Lefferts	.25	.10
542 Mike Boddicker	.25	.10
543 Greg Brock	.25	.10
544 Atlee Hammaker	.25	.10
545 Tom Bolton	.25	.10
546 Mike Macfarlane RC	.50	.20
547 Rich Renteria	.25	.10
548 John Davis	.25	.10
549 Floyd Bannister	.25	.10
550 Mickey Brantley	.25	.10
551 Duane Ward	.25	.10
552 Dan Petry	.25	.10
553 Mickey Tettleton UER	.25	.10
(Walks total 175, should be 136)		
554 Rick Leach	.25	.10
555 Mike Witt	.25	.10
556 Sid Bream	.25	.10
557 Bobby Witt	.25	.10
558 Tommy Herr	.25	.10
559 Randy Milligan	.25	.10
560 Jose Cecena	.25	.10
561 Mackey Sasser	.25	.10
562 Carney Lansford	.40	.16
563 Rick Aguilera	.40	.16
564 Ron Hassey	.25	.10
565 Dwight Gooden	.60	.24
566 Paul Assenmacher	.25	.10
567 Neil Allen	.25	.10
568 Jim Morrison	.25	.10
569 Mike Pagliarulo	.25	.10
570 Ted Simmons	.40	.16
571 Mark Thurmond	.25	.10
572 Fred McGriff	1.00	.40
573 Wally Joyner	.40	.16
574 Jose Bautista RC	.25	.10
575 Kelly Gruber	.25	.10
576 Cecilio Guante	.25	.10
577 Mark Davidson	.25	.10
578 Bobby Bonilla UER	.40	.16
(Total steals 2 in '87, should be 3)		
579 Mike Stanley	.25	.10
580 Gene Larkin	.25	.10
581 Stan Javier	.25	.10
582 Howard Johnson	.25	.10
583A Mike Gallego ERR	1.00	.40
(Front reversed negative)		
583B Mike Gallego COR	1.00	.40
584 David Cone	.40	.16
585 Doug Jennings	.25	.10
586 Charles Hudson	.25	.10
587 Dion James	.25	.10
588 Al Leiter	1.00	.40
589 Charlie Puleo	.25	.10
590 Roberto Kelly	.40	.16
591 Thad Bosley	.25	.10
592 Pete Stanicek	.25	.10
593 Pat Borders RC	.50	.20
594 Bryan Harvey RC	.50	.20
595 Jeff Ballard	.25	.10
596 Jeff Reardon	.40	.16
597 Doug Drabek	.25	.10
598 Edwin Correa	.25	.10
599 Keith Atherton	.25	.10
600 Dave LaPoint	.25	.10
601 Don Baylor	.40	.16
602 Tom Pagnozzi	.25	.10
603 Tim Flannery	.25	.10
604 Gene Walter	.25	.10
605 Dave Parker	.40	.16
606 Mike Diaz	.25	.10

607 Chris Gwynn .25 .10
608 Odell Jones .25 .10
609 Carlton Fisk .60 .24
610 Jay Howell .25 .10
611 Tim Crews .25 .10
612 Keith Hernandez .60 .24
613 Willie Fraser .25 .10
614 Jim Eppard .25 .10
615 Jeff Hamilton .25 .10
616 Kurt Stillwell .25 .10
617 Tom Browning .25 .10
618 Jeff Montgomery .40 .16
619 Jose Rijo .25 .10
620 Jamie Quirk .25 .10
621 Willie McGee .40 .16
622 Mark Grant UER .25 .10
(Glove on wrong hand)
623 Bill Swift .25 .10
624 Orlando Mercado .25 .10
625 John Costello .25 .10
626 Jose Gonzalez .25 .10
627A Bill Schroeder ERR .60 .24
(Back photo actually Ronn Reynolds buckling shin guards)
627B Bill Schroeder COR .60 .24
628A Fred Manrique ERR .60 .24
(Back photo actually Ozzie Guillen throwing)
628B Fred Manrique COR .25 .10
(Swinging bat on back)
629 Ricky Horton .25 .10
630 Dan Plesac .25 .10
631 Alfredo Griffin .25 .10
632 Chuck Finley .40 .16
633 Kirk Gibson .40 .16
634 Randy Myers .40 .16
635 Greg Minton .25 .10
636A Herm Winningham 1.00 .40
ERR (W1nningham on back)
636B H.Winningham COR .25 .10
637 Charlie Leibrandt .25 .10
638 Tim Birtsas .25 .10
639 Bill Buckner .40 .16
640 Danny Jackson .25 .10
641 Greg Booker .25 .10
642 Jim Presley .25 .10
643 Gene Nelson .25 .10
644 Rod Booker .25 .10
645 Dennis Rasmussen .25 .10
646 Juan Nieves .25 .10
647 Bobby Thigpen .25 .10
648 Tim Belcher .25 .10
649 Mike Young .25 .10
650 Ivan Calderon .25 .10
651 Oswald Peraza .25 .10
652A Pat Sheridan ERR 15.00 6.00
(No position on front)
652B Pat Sheridan COR .25 .10
653 Mike Morgan .25 .10
654 Mike Heath .25 .10
655 Jay Tibbs .25 .10
656 Fernando Valenzuela .40 .16
657 Lee Mazzilli .25 .10
658 Frank Viola AL CY .25 .10
659A J.Canseco AL MVP .40 .16
Eagle logo in black
659B J.Canseco AL MVP .40 .16
Eagle logo in blue
660 Walt Weiss AL ROY .25 .10
661 Orel Hershiser NL CY .40 .16
662 Kirk Gibson NL MVP .40 .16
663 Chris Sabo NL ROY .25 .10
664 Dennis Eckersley .40 .16
ALCS MVP
665 Orel Hershiser .40 .16
NLCS MVP
666 Kirk Gibson WS 1.00 .40
667 O.Hershiser WS MVP .40 .16
668 Wally Joyner TC .25 .10
669 Nolan Ryan TC 1.25 .50
670 Jose Canseco TC .40 .16
671 Fred McGriff TC .40 .16
672 Dale Murphy TC .60 .24
673 Paul Molitor TC .40 .16
674 Ozzie Smith TC 1.00 .40
675 Ryne Sandberg TC 1.00 .40
676 Kirk Gibson TC .25 .10
677 Andres Galarraga TC .25 .10
678 Will Clark TC .40 .16
679 Cory Snyder TC .25 .10
680 Alvin Davis TC .25 .10
681 Darryl Strawberry TC .40 .16
682 Cal Ripken TC 1.00 .40
683 Tony Gwynn TC .60 .24
684 Mike Schmidt TC 1.00 .40
685 A.Van Slyke TC UER .25 .10
96 Junior Ortiz
686 Ruben Sierra TC .25 .10
687 Wade Boggs TC .40 .16
688 Eric Davis TC .25 .10
689 George Brett TC 1.00 .40
690 Alan Trammell TC .25 .10
691 Frank Viola TC .25 .10
692 Harold Baines TC .25 .10
693 Don Mattingly TC 1.00 .40
694 Checklist 1-100 .25 .10
695 Checklist 101-200 .25 .10
696 Checklist 201-300 .25 .10
697 Checklist 301-400 .25 .10
698 CL 401-500 UER .25 .10
467 Cal Ripkin Jr.
699 CL 501-600 UER .25 .10
543 Greg Booker
700 Checklist 601-700 .25 .10
701 Checklist 701-800 .25 .10
702 Jesse Barfield .25 .10
703 Walt Terrell .25 .10
704 Dickie Thon .25 .10
705 Al Leiter 1.00 .40
706 Dave LaPoint .25 .10
707 Charlie Hayes RC .50 .20
708 Andy Hawkins .25 .10
709 Mickey Hatcher .25 .10
710 Lance McCullers .25 .10
711 Ron Kittle .25 .10
712 Bert Blyleven .40 .16
713 Rick Dempsey .25 .10
714 Ken Williams .25 .10
715 Steve Rosenberg .25 .10
716 Joe Skalski .25 .10
717 Spike Owen .25 .10
718 Todd Burns .25 .10
719 Kevin Gross .25 .10
720 Tommy Herr .25 .10
721 Rob Ducey .25 .10
722 Gary Green .25 .10
723 Gregg Olson RC .50 .20
724 Greg W. Harris RC .25 .10
725 Craig Worthington .25 .10
726 Tom Howard RC .25 .10
727 Dale Mohorcic .25 .10
728 Rich Yett .25 .10
729 Mel Hall .25 .10
730 Floyd Youmans .25 .10
731 Lonnie Smith .25 .10
732 Wally Backman .25 .10
733 Trevor Wilson RC .25 .10
734 Jose Alvarez RC .25 .10
735 Bob Milacki .25 .10
736 Tom Gordon RC .50 .20
737 Wally Whitehurst RC .25 .10
738 Mike Aldrete .25 .10
739 Keith Miller .25 .10
740 Randy Milligan .25 .10
741 Jeff Parrett .25 .10
742 Steve Finley RC 1.50 .60
743 Junior Felix RC .25 .10
744 Pete Harnisch RC .50 .20
745 Bill Spiers RC .50 .20
746 Hensley Meulens RC .25 .10
747 Juan Bell RC .25 .10
748 Steve Sax .25 .10
749 Phil Bradley .25 .10
750 Rey Quinones .25 .10
751 Tommy Gregg .25 .10
752 Kevin Brown 1.00 .40
753 Derek Lilliquist RC .25 .10
754 Todd Zeile RC 1.00 .40
755 Jim Abbott RC 1.50 .60
Triple exposure
756 Ozzie Canseco .25 .10
757 Nick Esasky .25 .10
758 Mike Moore .25 .10
759 Rob Murphy .25 .10
760 Rick Mahler .25 .10
761 Fred Lynn .25 .10
762 Kevin Blankenship .25 .10
763 Eddie Murray 1.00 .40
764 Steve Searcy .25 .10
765 Jerome Walton RC .50 .20
766 Erik Hanson RC .50 .20
767 Bob Boone .40 .16
768 Edgar Martinez 1.00 .40
769 Jose DeJesus .25 .10
770 Greg Briley .25 .10
771 Steve Peters .25 .10
772 Rafael Palmeiro .60 .24
773 Jack Clark .25 .10
774 Nolan Ryan 4.00 1.60
(Throwing football)
775 Lance Parrish .25 .10
776 Joe Girardi RC 1.00 .40
777 Willie Randolph .40 .16
778 Mitch Williams .25 .10
779 Dennis Cook RC .50 .20
780 Dwight Smith RC .50 .20
781 Lenny Harris RC .50 .20
782 Torey Lovullo RC .25 .10
783 Norm Charlton RC .50 .20
784 Chris Brown .25 .10
785 Todd Benzinger .25 .10
786 Shane Rawley .25 .10
787 Omar Vizquel RC 2.00 .80
788 LaVel Freeman .25 .10
789 Jeffrey Leonard .25 .10
790 Eddie Williams .25 .10
791 Jamie Moyer .40 .16
792 Bruce Hurst UER .25 .10
(Workd Series)
793 Julio Franco .25 .10
794 Claudell Washington .25 .10
795 Jody Davis .25 .10
796 Oddibe McDowell .25 .10
797 Paul Kilgus .25 .10
798 Tracy Jones .25 .10
799 Steve Wilson .25 .10
800 Pete O'Brien .25 .10

1989 Upper Deck Sheets

These blank-backed, 8 1/2" by 11" sheets feature pictures of Upper Deck baseball cards and were distributed at conventions in Chicago and Washington, D.C. The sheets carried a production run number but not the total number produced. The sheets are listed below in chronological order.

	Nm-Mt	Ex-Mt
COMPLETE SET (3)	35.00	14.00
1 10th National Sports Collectors Convention Chicago, Illinois June 29-July 2, 1989 Kevin Mitchell Mickey Tettleton Dwight Gooden Harold Baines Mark Grace Jim Abbott Wade Boggs Will Clark	10.00	4.00
2 National Candy Wholesalers Expo Washington, D.C. July 27-29, 1989 Ken Griffey Jr. Mark McGwire Junior Felix Cal Ripken Barry Larkin Todd Zeile Tim Raines Todd Benzinger	20.00	8.00
3 Sun-Times Card Show Chicago, Illinois Dec. 16-17, 1989 Ken Griffey Jr. Gary Gaetti Don Mattingly Andre Dawson Kevin Seitzer Tom Browning Andres Galarraga Kevin Mitchell	10.00	4.00

1990 Upper Deck

The 1990 Upper Deck set contains 800 standard-size cards issued in two series, low numbers (1-700) and high numbers (701-800). Cards were distributed in fin-wrapped low and high series foil packs, complete 800-card factory sets and 100-card high series factory sets. High series foil packs contained a mixture of low and high series cards. The front and back borders are white, and both sides feature full-color photos. The horizontally oriented backs have recent stats and anti-counterfeiting holograms. Team checklist cards are mixed in with the first 100 cards of the set. Rookie Cards in the set include Juan Gonzalez, David Justice, Ray Lankford, Dean Palmer, Sammy Sosa and Larry Walker. The high series contains a Nolan Ryan variation; all cards produced before August 12th only discuss Ryan's sixth no-hitter while the later-issue cards include a stripe honoring Ryan's 300th victory. Card 702 (Rookie Threats) was originally scheduled to be Mike Witt. A few Witt cards with 702 on back and checklist cards showing Witt as 702 escaped into early packs; they are characterized by a black rectangle covering much of the card's back.

Nm-Mt Ex-Mt
COMPLETE SET (800) 25.00 7.50
COMP.FACT.SET (800) 25.00 7.50
COMPLETE LO SET (700) 25.00 7.50
COMPLETE HI SET (100) 5.00 1.50
COMP.HI FACT.SET (100) 4.00 1.20
1 Star Rookie Checklist .10 .03
2 Randy Nosek .10 .03
3 Tom Drees UER .10 .03
(11th line, hulred, should be hurled
4 Curt Young .10 .03
5 Devon White TC .10 .03
6 Luis Salazar .10 .03
7 Von Hayes TC .10 .03
8 Jose Bautista .10 .03
9 Marquis Grissom RC .25 .07
10 Orel Hershiser TC .10 .03
11 Rick Aguilera .20 .06
12 Benito Santiago TC .10 .03
13 Deion Sanders .50 .15
14 Marvell Wynne .10 .03
15 Dave West .10 .03
16 Bobby Bonilla TC .10 .03
17 Sammy Sosa RC 8.00 2.40
18 Steve Sax TC .10 .03
19 Jack Howell .10 .03
20 Mike Schmidt Special 1.00 .30
UER (Suprising, should be surprising)
21 Robin Ventura UER .50 .15
(Samta Maria)
22 Brian Meyer .10 .03
23 Blaine Beatty .10 .03
24 Ken Griffey Jr. TC .60 .18
25 Greg Vaughn UER .20 .06
(Association misspelled as assiocation)
26 Xavier Hernandez RC .10 .03
27 Jason Grimsley RC .10 .03
28 Eric Anthony RC UER .10 .03
(Ashville, should be Asheville)
29 Tim Raines TC UER .10 .03
(Wallach listed before Walker)
30 David Wells .20 .06
31 Hal Morris .10 .03
32 Bo Jackson TC .20 .06
33 Kelly Mann .10 .03
34 Nolan Ryan Special 1.00 .30
35 Scott Service UER .10 .03
(Born Cincinatti on 7/27/67, should be Cincinnati 2/27)
36 Mark McGwire TC .60 .18
37 Tino Martinez .50 .15
38 Chili Davis .20 .06
39 Scott Sanderson .10 .03
40 Kevin Mitchell TC .10 .03
41 Lou Whitaker TC .10 .03
42 Scott Coolbaugh UER .10 .03
(Definately) RC
43 Jose Cano UER .10 .03
(Born 9/7/62, should be 3/7/62)
44 Jose Vizcaino RC .25 .07
45 Bob Hamelin RC .25 .07
46 Jose Offerman RC UER .25 .07
(Posesses)
47 Kevin Blankenship .10 .03
48 Kirby Puckett TC .30 .09
49 Tommy Greene RC UER .10 .03
(Livest, should be liveliest)
50 Will Clark Special .20 .06
UER (Perenial, should be perennial)
51 Rob Nelson .10 .03
52 C.Hammond RC UER .10 .03
Chatanooga
53 Joe Carter TC .10 .03
54A B.McDonald RC ERR 2.00 .60
No Rookie designation on card front
54B B.McDonald COR RC .25 .07
55 Andy Benes UER .20 .06
(Whichita)
56 John Olerud RC .75 .23
57 Roger Clemens TC .50 .15
58 Tony Armas .10 .03
59 George Canale .10 .03
60A Mickey Tettleton TC 2.00 .60
ERR (683 Jamie Weston)
60B Mickey Tettleton TC .10 .03
COR (683 Mickey Weston)
61 Mike Stanton RC .25 .07
62 Dwight Gooden TC .20 .06
63 Kent Mercker RC UER .25 .07
(Albuguerque)
64 Francisco Cabrera .10 .03
65 Steve Avery UER .10 .03
(Born NJ, should be MI, Merker should be Mercker
66 Jose Canseco .50 .15
67 Matt Merullo .10 .03
68 Vince Coleman TC UER .10 .03
(Guererro)
69 Ron Karkovice .10 .03
70 Kevin Maas RC .25 .07
71 Dennis Cook UER .10 .03
(Shown with righty glove on card back)
72 Juan Gonzalez RC UER 2.50 .75
(135 games for Tulsa in '89, should be 133)
73 Andre Dawson TC .10 .03
74 Dean Palmer RC UER .25 .07
(Permanent misspelled as perminant)
75 Bo Jackson Special .20 .06
UER (Monsterous, should be monstrous)
76 Rob Richie .10 .03
77 Bobby Rose UER .10 .03
(Pickin, should be pick in)
78 Brian DuBois UER .10 .03
(Commiting)
79 Ozzie Guillen TC .10 .03
80 Gene Nelson .10 .03
81 Bob McClure .10 .03
82 Julio Franco TC .10 .03
83 Greg Minton .10 .03
84 John Smoltz TC UER .30 .09
(Oddibe not Odibbe)
85 Willie Fraser .10 .03
86 Neal Heaton .10 .03
87 Kevin Tapani RC UER .25 .07
(24th line has excpet, should be except)
88 Mike Scott TC .10 .03
89A Jim Gott ERR 2.00 .60
(Photo actually Rick Reed)
89B Jim Gott COR .10 .03
90 Lance Johnson .10 .03
91 Robin Yount TC UER .50 .15
(Checklist on back has 178 Rob Deer and 176 Mike Felder)
92 Jeff Parrett .10 .03
93 Julio Machado UER .10 .03
(Valenzuelan, should be Venezuelan)
94 Ron Jones .10 .03
95 George Bell TC .10 .03
96 Jerry Reuss .10 .03
97 Brian Fisher .10 .03
98 Kevin Ritz UER .10 .03
(Amercian)
99 Barry Larkin TC .20 .06
100 Checklist 1-100 .10 .03
101 Gerald Perry .10 .03
102 Kevin Appier .50 .15
103 Julio Franco .10 .03
104 Craig Biggio .30 .09
105 Bo Jackson UER .50 .15
('89 BA wrong, should be .256)
106 Junior Felix .10 .03
107 Mike Harkey .10 .03
108 Fred McGriff .50 .15
109 Rick Sutcliffe .20 .06
110 Pete O'Brien .10 .03
111 Kelly Gruber .10 .03
112 Dwight Evans .20 .06
113 Pat Borders .10 .03
114 Dwight Gooden .30 .09
115 Kevin Batiste .10 .03
116 Eric Davis .20 .06
117 Kevin Mitchell UER .10 .03
(Career HR total 99, should be 100)
118 Ron Oester .10 .03
119 Brett Butler .20 .06
120 Danny Jackson .10 .03
121 Tommy Gregg .10 .03
122 Ken Caminiti .20 .06
123 Kevin Brown .20 .06
124 George Brett UER 1.25 .35
(133 runs, should be 1300)
125 Mike Scott .10 .03
126 Cory Snyder .10 .03
127 George Bell .10 .03
128 Mark Grace .30 .09
129 Devon White .10 .03
130 Tony Fernandez .10 .03
131 Don Aase .10 .03
132 Rance Mulliniks .10 .03
133 Marty Barrett .10 .03
134 Nelson Liriano .10 .03
135 Mark Carreon .10 .03
136 Candy Maldonado .10 .03
137 Tim Birtsas .10 .03
138 Tom Brookens .10 .03
139 John Franco .20 .06
140 Mike LaCoss .10 .03
141 Jeff Treadway .10 .03
142 Pat Tabler .10 .03
143 Darrell Evans .20 .06
144 Rafael Ramirez .10 .03
145 O.McDowell UER .10 .03
Misspelled Odibbe
146 Brian Downing .10 .03
147 Curt Wilkerson .10 .03
148 Ernie Whitt .10 .03
149 Bill Schroeder .10 .03
150 Domingo Ramos UER .10 .03
(Says throws right, but shows him throwing lefty)
151 Rick Honeycutt .10 .03
152 Don Slaught .10 .03
153 Mitch Webster .10 .03
154 Tony Phillips .10 .03
155 Paul Kilgus .10 .03
156 Ken Griffey Jr. UER 1.50 .45
(Simultaniously)
157 Gary Sheffield .50 .15
158 Wally Backman .10 .03
159 B.J. Surhoff .20 .06
160 Louie Meadows .10 .03
161 Paul O'Neill .30 .09
162 Jeff McKnight .10 .03
163 Alvaro Espinoza .10 .03
164 Scott Scudder .10 .03
165 Jeff Reed .10 .03
166 Gregg Jefferies .20 .06
167 Barry Larkin .50 .15
168 Gary Carter .30 .09
169 Robby Thompson .10 .03
170 Rolando Roomes .10 .03
171 Mark McGwire UER 1.25 .35
(Total games 427 and hits 479, should be 467 and 427)
172 Steve Sax .10 .03
173 Mark Williamson .10 .03
174 Mitch Williams .10 .03
175 Brian Holton .10 .03
176 Rob Deer .10 .03
177 Tim Raines .20 .06
178 Mike Felder .10 .03
179 Harold Reynolds .20 .06
180 Terry Francona .20 .06
181 Chris Sabo .10 .03
182 Darryl Strawberry .30 .09
183 Willie Randolph .20 .06
184 Bill Ripken .10 .03
185 Mackey Sasser .10 .03
186 Todd Benzinger .10 .03
187 Kevin Elster UER .10 .03
(16 homers in 1989, should be 10)
188 Jose Uribe .10 .03
189 Tom Browning .10 .03
190 Keith Miller .10 .03
191 Don Mattingly 1.25 .35
192 Dave Parker .20 .06
193 Roberto Kelly UER .10 .03
(96 RBI, should be 62)
194 Phil Bradley .10 .03
195 Ron Hassey .10 .03
196 Gerald Young .10 .03
197 Hubie Brooks .10 .03
198 Bill Doran .10 .03
199 Al Newman .10 .03
200 Checklist 101-200 .10 .03
201 Terry Puhl .10 .03
202 Frank DiPino .10 .03
203 Jim Clancy .10 .03
204 Bob Ojeda .10 .03
205 Alex Trevino .10 .03
206 Dave Henderson .10 .03
207 Henry Cotto .10 .03
208 Rafael Belliard UER .10 .03
(Born 1961, not 1951)
209 Stan Javier .10 .03
210 Jerry Reed .10 .03
211 Doug Dascenzo .10 .03
212 Andres Thomas .10 .03
213 Greg Maddux .75 .23
214 Mike Schooler .10 .03
215 Lonnie Smith .10 .03
216 Jose Rijo .10 .03
217 Greg Gagne .10 .03
218 Jim Gantner .10 .03
219 Allan Anderson .10 .03
220 Rick Mahler .10 .03
221 Jim Deshaies .10 .03
222 Keith Hernandez .30 .09
223 Vince Coleman .10 .03
224 David Cone .20 .06
225 Ozzie Smith .75 .23
226 Matt Nokes .10 .03
227 Barry Bonds 1.25 .35
228 Felix Jose .10 .03
229 Dennis Powell .10 .03
230 Mike Gallego .10 .03
231 Shawon Dunston UER .10 .03
('89 stats are Andre Dawson's)
232 Ron Gant .20 .06
233 Omar Vizquel .50 .15
234 Derek Lilliquist .10 .03
235 Erik Hanson .10 .03
236 Kirby Puckett UER .50 .15
(824 games, should be 924)
237 Bill Spiers .10 .03
238 Dan Gladden .10 .03
239 Bryan Clutterbuck .10 .03
240 John Moses .10 .03
241 Ron Darling .10 .03
242 Joe Magrane .10 .03
243 Dave Magadan .10 .03
244 Pedro Guerrero UER .10 .03
(Misspelled Guererro)
245 Glenn Davis .10 .03
246 Terry Steinbach .10 .03

247 Fred Lynn .10 .03
248 Gary Redus .10 .03
249 Ken Williams .10 .03
250 Sid Bream .10 .03
251 Bob Welch UER .10 .03
(2587 career strike-
outs, should be 1587)
252 Bill Buckner .10 .03
253 Carney Lansford .20 .06
254 Paul Molitor .30 .09
255 Jose DeJesus .10 .03
256 Orel Hershiser .20 .06
257 Tom Brunansky .10 .03
258 Mike Davis .10 .03
259 Jeff Ballard .10 .03
260 Scott Terry .10 .03
261 Sid Fernandez .10 .03
262 Mike Marshall .10 .03
263 Howard Johnson UER .10 .03
(192 SO, should be 592)
264 Kirk Gibson UER .20 .06
(659 runs, should
be 669)
265 Kevin McReynolds .10 .03
266 Cal Ripken 1.50 .45
267 Ozzie Guillen UER .10 .03
(Career triples 27,
should be 29)
268 Jim Traber .10 .03
269 Bobby Thigpen UER .10 .03
(31 saves in 1989,
should be 34)
270 Joe Orsulak .10 .03
271 Bob Boone .20 .06
272 Dave Stewart UER .20 .06
(Totals wrong due to
omission of '86 stats)
273 Tim Wallach .10 .03
274 Luis Aquino UER .10 .03
(Says throws lefty,
but shows him
throwing righty)
275 Mike Moore .10 .03
276 Tony Pena .10 .03
277 Eddie Murray UER .50 .15
(Several typos in
career total stats)
278 Milt Thompson .10 .03
279 Alejandro Pena .10 .03
280 Ken Dayley .10 .03
281 Carmelo Castillo .10 .03
282 Tom Henke .10 .03
283 Mickey Hatcher .10 .03
284 Roy Smith .10 .03
285 Manny Lee .10 .03
286 Dan Pasqua .10 .03
287 Larry Sheets .10 .03
288 Garry Templeton .10 .03
289 Eddie Williams .10 .03
290 Brady Anderson UER .20 .06
(Home: Silver Springs,
not Siver Springs)
291 Spike Owen .10 .03
292 Storm Davis .10 .03
293 Chris Bosio .10 .03
294 Jim Eisenreich .10 .03
295 Don August .10 .03
296 Jeff Hamilton .10 .03
297 Mickey Tettleton .10 .03
298 Mike Scioscia .10 .03
299 Kevin Hickey .10 .03
300 Checklist 201-300 .10 .03
301 Shawn Abner .10 .03
302 Kevin Bass .10 .03
303 Bip Roberts .10 .03
304 Joe Girardi .30 .09
305 Danny Darwin .10 .03
306 Mike Heath .10 .03
307 Mike Macfarlane .10 .03
308 Ed Whitson .10 .03
309 Tracy Jones .10 .03
310 Scott Fletcher .10 .03
311 Darnell Coles .10 .03
312 Mike Brumley .10 .03
313 Bill Swift .10 .03
314 Charlie Hough .20 .06
315 Jim Presley .10 .03
316 Luis Polonia .10 .03
317 Mike Morgan .10 .03
318 Lee Guetterman .10 .03
319 Jose Oquendo .10 .03
320 Wayne Tolleson .10 .03
321 Jody Reed .10 .03
322 Damon Berryhill .10 .03
323 Roger Clemens 1.00 .30
324 Ryne Sandberg .75 .23
325 Benito Santiago UER .20 .06
(Misspelled Santago
on card back)
326 Bret Saberhagen UER .20 .06
(1140 hits, should be
1240; 56 CG, should
be 52)
327 Lou Whitaker .20 .06
328 Dave Gallagher .10 .03
329 Mike Pagliarulo .10 .03
330 Doyle Alexander .10 .03
331 Jeffrey Leonard .10 .03
332 Torey Lovullo .10 .03
333 Pete Incaviglia .10 .03
334 Rickey Henderson .50 .15
335 Rafael Palmeiro .30 .09
336 Ken Hill .20 .06
337 Dave Winfield UER .20 .06
(1418 RBI, should
be 1438)
338 Alfredo Griffin .10 .03
339 Andy Hawkins .10 .03
340 Ted Power .10 .03
341 Steve Wilson .10 .03
342 Jack Clark UER .20 .06
(916 BB, should be
1006; 1142 SO,
should be 1130)
343 Ellis Burks .30 .09
344 Tony Gwynn UER .60 .18
(Doubles stats on
card back are wrong)
345 Jerome Walton UER .10 .03
(Total At Bats 476,
should be 475)
346 Roberto Alomar UER .50 .15
(61 doubles, should
be 51)
347 Carlos Martinez UER .10 .03
(Born 8/11/64, should
be 8/11/65)
348 Chet Lemon .10 .03
349 Willie Wilson .10 .03
350 Greg Walker .10 .03
351 Tom Bolton .10 .03
352 German Gonzalez .10 .03
353 Harold Baines .20 .06
354 Mike Greenwell .10 .03
355 Ruben Sierra .10 .03
356 Andres Galarraga .20 .06
357 Andre Dawson .20 .06
358 Jeff Brantley .10 .03
359 Mike Bielecki .10 .03
360 Ken Oberkfell .10 .03
361 Kurt Stillwell .10 .03
362 Brian Holman .10 .03
363 Kevin Seitzer UER .10 .03
(Career triples total
does not add up)
364 Alvin Davis .10 .03
365 Tom Gordon .20 .06
366 Bobby Bonilla UER .20 .06
(Two steals in 1987,
should be 3)
367 Carlton Fisk .30 .09
368 Steve Carter UER .10 .03
(Charlotesville)
369 Joel Skinner .10 .03
370 John Cangelosi .10 .03
371 Cecil Espy .10 .03
372 Gary Wayne .10 .03
373 Jim Rice .20 .06
374 Mike Dyer RC .10 .03
375 Joe Carter .20 .06
376 Dwight Smith .10 .03
377 John Wetteland .50 .15
378 Earnie Riles .10 .03
379 Otis Nixon .10 .03
380 Vance Law .10 .03
381 Dave Bergman .10 .03
382 Frank White .20 .06
383 Scott Bradley .10 .03
384 Israel Sanchez UER .10 .03
(Totals don't in-
clude '89 stats)
385 Gary Pettis .10 .03
386 Donn Pall .10 .03
387 John Smiley .10 .03
388 Tom Candiotti .10 .03
389 Junior Ortiz .10 .03
390 Steve Lyons .10 .03
391 Brian Harper .10 .03
392 Fred Manrique .10 .03
393 Lee Smith .20 .06
394 Jeff Kunkel .10 .03
395 Claudell Washington .10 .03
396 John Tudor .10 .03
397 Terry Kennedy UER .10 .03
(Career totals all
wrong)
398 Lloyd McClendon .10 .03
399 Craig Lefferts .10 .03
400 Checklist 301-400 .10 .03
401 Keith Moreland .10 .03
402 Rich Gedman .10 .03
403 Jeff D. Robinson .10 .03
404 Randy Ready .10 .03
405 Rick Cerone .10 .03
406 Jeff Blauser .10 .03
407 Larry Andersen .10 .03
408 Joe Boever .10 .03
409 Felix Fermin .10 .03
410 Glenn Wilson .10 .03
411 Rex Hudler .10 .03
412 Mark Grant .10 .03
413 Dennis Martinez .20 .06
414 Darrin Jackson .10 .03
415 Mike Aldrete .10 .03
416 Roger McDowell .10 .03
417 Jeff Reardon .20 .06
418 Darren Daulton .20 .06
419 Tim Laudner .10 .03
420 Don Carman .10 .03
421 Lloyd Moseby .10 .03
422 Doug Drabek .10 .03
423 Lenny Harris UER .10 .03
(Walks 2 in '89,
should be 20)
424 Jose Lind .10 .03
425 Dave Johnson (P) .10 .03
426 Jerry Browne .10 .03
427 Eric Yelding .10 .03
428 Brad Komminsk .10 .03
429 Jody Davis .10 .03
430 Mariano Duncan .10 .03
431 Mark Davis .10 .03
432 Nelson Santovenia .10 .03
433 Bruce Hurst .10 .03
434 Jeff Huson RC .10 .03
435 Chris James .10 .03
436 Mark Guthrie .10 .03
437 Charlie Hayes .10 .03
438 Shane Rawley .10 .03
439 Dickie Thon .10 .03
440 Juan Berenguer .10 .03
441 Kevin Romine .10 .03
442 Bill Landrum .10 .03
443 Todd Frohwirth .10 .03
444 Craig Worthington .10 .03
445 Fernando Valenzuela .20 .06
446 Joey Belle .50 .15
447 Ed Whited UER .10 .03
(Ashville, should
be Asheville)
448 Dave Smith .10 .03
449 Dave Clark .10 .03
450 Juan Agosto .10 .03
451 Dave Valle .10 .03
452 Kent Hrbek .20 .06
453 Von Hayes .10 .03
454 Gary Gaetti .20 .06
455 Greg Briley .10 .03
456 Glenn Braggs .10 .03
457 Kirt Manwaring .10 .03
458 Mel Hall .10 .03
459 Brook Jacoby .10 .03
460 Pat Sheridan .10 .03
461 Rob Murphy .10 .03
462 Jimmy Key .20 .06
463 Nick Esasky .10 .03
464 Rob Ducey .10 .03
465 Carlos Quintana UER .10 .03
(Internatinoal)
466 Larry Walker RC 1.50 .45
467 Todd Worrell .10 .03
468 Kevin Gross .10 .03
469 Terry Pendleton .20 .06
470 Dave Martinez .10 .03
471 Gene Larkin .10 .03
472 Len Dykstra UER .20 .06
('89 and total runs
understated by 10)
473 Barry Lyons .10 .03
474 Terry Mulholland .10 .03
475 Chip Hale .10 .03
476 Jesse Barfield .10 .03
477 Dan Plesac .10 .03
478A Scott Garrelts ERR 2.00 .60
(Photo actually
Bill Bathe)
478B Scott Garrelts COR .10 .03
479 Dave Righetti .10 .03
480 Gus Polidor UER .10 .03
Wearing 14 on front,
but 10 on back
481 Mookie Wilson .20 .06
482 Luis Rivera .10 .03
483 Mike Flanagan .10 .03
484 Dennis Boyd .10 .03
485 John Cerutti .10 .03
486 John Costello .10 .03
487 Pascual Perez .10 .03
488 Tommy Herr .10 .03
489 Tom Foley .10 .03
490 Curt Ford .10 .03
491 Steve Lake .10 .03
492 Tim Teufel .10 .03
493 Randy Bush .10 .03
494 Mike Jackson .10 .03
495 Steve Jeltz .10 .03
496 Paul Gibson .10 .03
497 Steve Balboni .10 .03
498 Bud Black .10 .03
499 Dale Sveum .10 .03
500 Checklist 401-500 .10 .03
501 Tim Jones .10 .03
502 Mark Portugal .10 .03
503 Ivan Calderon .10 .03
504 Rick Rhoden .10 .03
505 Willie McGee .20 .06
506 Kirk McCaskill .10 .03
507 Dave LaPoint .10 .03
508 Jay Howell .10 .03
509 Johnny Ray .10 .03
510 Dave Anderson .10 .03
511 Chuck Crim .10 .03
512 Joe Hesketh .10 .03
513 Dennis Eckersley .20 .06
514 Greg Brock .10 .03
515 Tim Burke .10 .03
516 Frank Tanana .10 .03
517 Jay Bell .20 .06
518 Guillermo Hernandez .10 .03
519 Randy Kramer UER .10 .03
(Codiroli misspelled
as Codoroli)
520 Charles Hudson .10 .03
521 Jim Corsi .10 .03
Word "originally" is
misspelled on back
522 Steve Rosenberg .10 .03
523 Cris Carpenter .10 .03
524 Matt Winters .10 .03
525 Melido Perez .10 .03
526 Chris Gwynn UER .10 .03
(Albeguergue)
527 Bert Blyleven UER .20 .06
(Games career total is
wrong, should be 644)
528 Chuck Cary .10 .03
529 Daryl Boston .10 .03
530 Dale Mohorcic .10 .03
531 Geronimo Berroa .10 .03
532 Edgar Martinez .30 .09
533 Dale Murphy .50 .15
534 Jay Buhner .20 .06
535 John Smoltz UER .50 .15
(HEA Stadium)
536 Andy Van Slyke .20 .06
537 Mike Henneman .10 .03
538 Miguel Garcia .10 .03
539 Frank Williams .10 .03
540 R.J. Reynolds .10 .03
541 Shawn Hillegas .10 .03
542 Walt Weiss .10 .03
543 Greg Hibbard RC .10 .03
544 Nolan Ryan 2.00 .60
545 Todd Zeile .20 .06
546 Hensley Meulens .10 .03
547 Tim Belcher .10 .03
548 Mike Witt .10 .03
549 Greg Cadaret UER .10 .03
(Aquiring, should
be Acquiring)
550 Franklin Stubbs .10 .03
551 Tony Castillo .10 .03
552 Jeff M. Robinson .10 .03
553 Steve Olin RC .25 .07
554 Alan Trammell .30 .09
555 Wade Boggs 4X .30 .09
(Bo Jackson
in background)
556 Will Clark .50 .15
557 Jeff King .10 .03
558 Mike Fitzgerald .10 .03
559 Ken Howell .10 .03
560 Bob Kipper .10 .03
561 Scott Bankhead .10 .03
562A Jeff Innis ERR 2.00 .60
(Photo actually
David West)
562B Jeff Innis COR .10 .03
563 Randy Johnson .75 .23
564 Wally Whitehurst .10 .03
565 Gene Harris .10 .03
566 Norm Charlton .10 .03
567 Robin Yount UER .75 .23
(7602 career hits,
should be 2606)
568 Joe Oliver UER .10 .03
(Fl.orida)
569 Mark Parent .10 .03
570 John Farrell UER .10 .03
(Loss total added wrong)
571 Tom Glavine .30 .09
572 Rod Nichols .10 .03
573 Jack Morris .20 .06
574 Greg Swindell .10 .03
575 Steve Searcy .10 .03
576 Ricky Jordan .10 .03
577 Matt Williams .20 .06
578 Mike LaValliere .10 .03
579 Bryn Smith .10 .03
580 Bruce Ruffin .10 .03
581 Randy Myers .20 .06
582 Rick Wrona .10 .03
583 Juan Samuel .10 .03
584 Les Lancaster .10 .03
585 Jeff Musselman .10 .03
586 Rob Dibble .20 .06
587 Eric Show .10 .03
588 Jesse Orosco .10 .03
589 Herm Winningham .10 .03
590 Andy Allanson .10 .03
591 Dion James .10 .03
592 Carmelo Martinez .10 .03
593 Luis Quinones .10 .03
594 Dennis Rasmussen .10 .03
595 Rich Yett .10 .03
596 Bob Walk .10 .03
597A A.McGaffigan ERR 2.00 .60
Photo actually
Rich Thompson
597B A.McGaffigan COR .10 .03
598 Billy Hatcher .10 .03
599 Bob Knepper .10 .03
600 CL 501-600 UER .10 .03
599 Bob Kneppers
601 Joey Cora .20 .06
602 Steve Finley .20 .06
603 Kal Daniels UER .10 .03
(12 hits in '87, should
be 123; 335 runs,
should be 235)
604 Gregg Olson .20 .06
605 Dave Stieb .20 .06
606 Kenny Rogers .20 .06
(Shown catching
football)
607 Zane Smith .10 .03
608 Bob Geren UER .10 .03
(Origionally)
609 Chad Kreuter .10 .03
610 Mike Smithson .10 .03
611 Jeff Wetherby .10 .03
612 Gary Mielke .10 .03
613 Pete Smith .10 .03
614 Jack Daugherty UER .10 .03
(Born 7/30/60, should
be 7/3/60)
615 Lance McCullers .10 .03
616 Don Robinson .10 .03
617 Jose Guzman .10 .03
618 Steve Bedrosian .10 .03
619 Jamie Moyer .20 .06
620 Atlee Hammaker .10 .03
621 Rick Luecken UER .10 .03
(Innings pitched wrong)
622 Greg W. Harris .10 .03
623 Pete Harnisch .10 .03
624 Jerald Clark .10 .03
625 Jack McDowell UER .10 .03
(Career totals for Games
and GS don't include
1987 season)
626 Frank Viola .10 .03
627 Teddy Higuera .10 .03
628 Marty Pevey .10 .03
629 Bill Wegman .10 .03
630 Eric Plunk .10 .03
631 Drew Hall .10 .03
632 Doug Jones .10 .03
633 Geno Petralli UER .10 .03
(Sacremento)
634 Jose Alvarez .10 .03
635 Bob Milacki .10 .03
636 Bobby Witt .10 .03
637 Trevor Wilson .10 .03
638 Jeff Russell UER .10 .03
(Shutout stats wrong)
639 Mike Krukow .10 .03
640 Rick Leach .10 .03
641 Dave Schmidt .10 .03
642 Terry Leach .10 .03
643 Calvin Schiraldi .10 .03
644 Bob Melvin .10 .03
645 Jim Abbott .30 .09
646 Jaime Navarro .10 .03
647 Mark Langston UER .10 .03
(Several errors in
stats totals)
648 Juan Nieves .10 .03
649 Damaso Garcia .10 .03
650 Charlie O'Brien .10 .03
651 Eric King .10 .03
652 Mike Boddicker .10 .03
653 Duane Ward .10 .03
654 Bob Stanley .10 .03
655 Sandy Alomar Jr. .20 .06
656 Danny Tartabull UER .10 .03
(395 BB, should be 295)
657 Randy McCament .10 .03
658 Charlie Leibrandt .10 .03
659 Dan Quisenberry .10 .03
660 Paul Assenmacher .10 .03
661 Walt Terrell .10 .03
662 Tim Leary .10 .03
663 Randy Milligan .10 .03
664 Bo Diaz .10 .03
665 Mark Lemke UER .10 .03
(Richmond misspelled
as Richomond)
666 Jose Gonzalez .10 .03
667 Chuck Finley UER .20 .06
(Born 11/16/62, should
be 11/26/62)
668 John Kruk .20 .06
669 Dick Schofield .10 .03
670 Tim Crews .10 .03
671 John Dopson .10 .03
672 John Orton RC .10 .03
673 Eric Hetzel .10 .03
674 Lance Parrish .10 .03
675 Ramon Martinez .10 .03
676 Mark Gubicza .10 .03
677 Greg Litton .10 .03
678 Greg Mathews .10 .03
679 Dave Dravecky .20 .06
680 Steve Farr .10 .03
681 Mike Devereaux .10 .03
682 Ken Griffey Sr. .20 .06
683A Mickey Weston ERR 2.00 .60
(Listed as Jamie
on card)
683B Mickey Weston COR .10 .03
(Technically still an
error as birthdate is
listed as 3/26/81)
684 Jack Armstrong .10 .03
685 Steve Buechele .10 .03
686 Bryan Harvey .10 .03
687 Lance Blankenship .10 .03
688 Dante Bichette .50 .15
689 Todd Burns .10 .03
690 Dan Petry .10 .03
691 Kent Anderson .10 .03
692 Todd Stottlemyre .20 .06
693 Wally Joyner UER .20 .06
(Several stats errors)
694 Mike Rochford .10 .03
695 Floyd Bannister .10 .03
696 Rick Reuschel .10 .03
697 Jose DeLeon .10 .03
698 Jeff Montgomery .20 .06
699 Kelly Downs .10 .03
700A Checklist 601-700 2.00 .60
(683 Jamie Weston)
700B Checklist 601-700 .10 .03
(683 Mickey Weston)
701 Jim Gott .10 .03
702 Delino DeShields .50 .15
Marquis Grissom
Larry Walker
702A Mike Witt 10.00 3.00
Black rectangle covers much of back
703 Alejandro Pena .10 .03
704 Willie Randolph .20 .06
705 Tim Leary .10 .03
706 Chuck McElroy RC .10 .03
707 Gerald Perry .10 .03
708 Tom Brunansky .10 .03
709 John Franco .20 .06
710 Mark Davis .10 .03
711 David Justice RC .75 .23
712 Storm Davis .10 .03
713 Scott Ruskin .10 .03
714 Glenn Braggs .10 .03
715 Kevin Bearse .10 .03
716 Jose Nunez .10 .03
717 Tim Layana .10 .03
718 Greg Myers .10 .03
719 Pete O'Brien .10 .03
720 John Candelaria .10 .03
721 Craig Grebeck RC .10 .03
722 Shawn Boskie RC .10 .03
723 Jim Leyritz RC .25 .07
724 Bill Sampen .10 .03
725 Scott Radinsky RC .10 .03
726 Todd Hundley RC .25 .07
727 Scott Hemond RC .10 .03
728 Lenny Webster RC .10 .03
729 Jeff Reardon .20 .06
730 Mitch Webster .10 .03
731 Brian Bohanon RC .10 .03
732 Rick Parker .10 .03
733 Terry Shumpert .10 .03
734A Nolan Ryan 3.00 .90
6th No-Hitter
(No stripe on front)
734B Nolan Ryan 1.00 .30
6th No-Hitter
(stripe added on card
front for 300th win)
735 John Burkett .10 .03
736 Derrick May RC .10 .03
737 Carlos Baerga RC .25 .07
738 Greg Smith .10 .03
739 Scott Sanderson .10 .03
740 Joe Kraemer .10 .03
741 Hector Villanueva RC .10 .03
742 Mike Fetters RC .25 .07
743 Mark Gardner RC .10 .03
744 Matt Nokes .10 .03
745 Dave Winfield .20 .06
746 Delino DeShields RC .25 .07
747 Dann Howitt .10 .03
748 Tony Pena .10 .03
749 Oil Can Boyd .10 .03
750 Mike Benjamin .10 .03
751 Alex Cole RC .10 .03
752 Eric Gunderson .10 .03
753 Howard Farmer .10 .03
754 Joe Carter .20 .06
755 Ray Lankford RC .25 .07
756 Sandy Alomar Jr. .20 .06
757 Alex Sanchez .10 .03
758 Nick Esasky .10 .03
759 Stan Belinda RC .10 .03
760 Jim Presley .10 .03
761 Gary DiSarcina RC .25 .07
762 Wayne Edwards .10 .03
763 Pat Combs .10 .03
764 Mickey Pina .10 .03
765 Wilson Alvarez RC .25 .07
766 Dave Parker .20 .06
767 Mike Blowers RC .10 .03
768 Tony Phillips .10 .03
769 Pascual Perez .10 .03
770 Gary Pettis .10 .03
771 Fred Lynn .10 .03
772 Mel Rojas RC .10 .03
773 David Segui RC .25 .07
774 Gary Carter .30 .09
775 Rafael Valdez .10 .03
776 Glenallen Hill .10 .03
777 Keith Hernandez .30 .09
778 Billy Hatcher .10 .03
779 Marty Clary .10 .03
780 Candy Maldonado .10 .03

781 Mike Marshall .10 .03
782 Billy Joe Robidoux .10 .03
783 Mark Langston .10 .03
784 Paul Sorrento RC .25 .07
785 Dave Hollins RC .25 .07
786 Cecil Fielder .20 .06
787 Matt Young .10 .03
788 Jeff Huson .10 .03
789 Lloyd Moseby .10 .03
790 Ron Kittle .10 .03
791 Hubie Brooks .10 .03
792 Craig Lefferts .10 .03
793 Kevin Bass .10 .03
794 Bryn Smith .10 .03
795 Juan Samuel .10 .03
796 Sam Horn .10 .03
797 Randy Myers .20 .06
798 Chris James .10 .03
799 Bill Gullickson .10 .03
800 Checklist 701-800 .10 .03

1990 Upper Deck Jackson Heroes

This ten-card standard-size set was issued as an insert in 1990 Upper Deck High Number packs as part of the Upper Deck promotional giveaway of 2,500 officially signed and personally numbered Reggie Jackson cards. Signed cards ending with 00 have the words "Mr. October" added to the autograph. These cards cover Jackson's major league career. The complete set price refers only to the unautographed card set of ten. One-card packs of over-sized (3 1/2" by 5") versions of these cards were later inserted into retail blister repacks containing one foil pack each of 1993 Upper Deck Series I and II. These cards were later inserted into various forms of repackaging. The larger cards are also distinguishable by the Upper Deck Fifth Anniversary logo and "1993 Hall of Fame Inductee" logo on the front of the card. These over-sized cards were a limited edition of 10,000 numbered cards and have no extra value than the basic cards.

Nm-Mt Ex-Mt
COMPLETE SET (10) 15.00 4.50
COMMON REGGIE (1-9) 1.50 .45
NNO Reggie Jackson 3.00 .90
Header Card
AU1 Reggie Jackson AU 120.00 36.00
(Signed and Numbered
out of 2500)

1990 Upper Deck Sheets

These blank-backed, 8 1/2" by 11" sheets feature pictures of Upper Deck baseball cards and were distributed at various specific events and times around the country. The sheets carried a production run number but not necessarily a total number produced. There were four regionally-issued sheets bound inside Street and Smith's 1990 Baseball Annual magazines to celebrate its 50th anniversary. The top five 1990 Upper Deck cards featured on all four sheets were the same: Carlton Fisk, Tim Raines, Jose Canseco and Will Clark. The Street and Smith sheets are listed below by their regions and regional players. The sheets are listed below in chronological order.

Nm-Mt Ex-Mt
COMPLETE SET (5) 40.00 12.00
1 11th Annual National 8.00 2.40
Sports Collectors Convention
Arlington, Texas
July 5-8, 1990
(26,000)
Pat Combs
Bill Doran
Ruben Sierra
Mark McGwire
Howard Johnson
Nolan Ryan
Bugs Bunny
Daffy Duck
(Comic Ball)
2 San Francisco 8.00 2.40
Conv. Center Show
Aug. 31-Sept. 3, 1990
(45,000 est.)
Marquis Grissom
Delino DeShields
Larry Walker
Matt Williams
Kevin Maas
Nolan Ryan
Bob Welch
Cecil Fielder
Reggie Jackson
3 Street/Smith: West 15.00 4.50
Ken Griffey Jr.
Roberto Alomar
Bert Blyleven
4 Street/Smith: East 8.00 2.40
Gregg Olson
Wade Boggs
Gregg Jefferies
5 Street/Smith: Midwest 8.00 2.40
Tom Gordon
Pedro Guerrero
Ryne Sandberg

1991 Upper Deck

This set marked the third year Upper Deck issued a 800-card standard-size set in two separate series of 700 and 100 cards respectively. Cards were distributed in low and high series foil packs and factory sets. The 100-card extended or high-number series was issued by Upper Deck several months after the release of their first series. For the first time in Upper Deck's three-year history, they did not issue a factory Extended set. The basic cards are made on the typical Upper Deck slick, white card stock and features full-color photos on both the front and the back. Subsets include Star Rookies (1-26), Team Cards (28-34, 43-49, 77-82, 95-99) and Top Prospects (50-76). Several other special achievement cards are seeded throughout the set. The team checklist (TC) cards in the set feature an attractive Vernon Wells drawing of a featured player for that particular team. Rookie Cards in this set include Jeff Bagwell, Luis Gonzalez, Chipper Jones, Eric Karros, and Mike Mussina. A special Michael Jordan card (numbered SP1) was randomly included in packs on a somewhat limited basis. The Hank Aaron hologram card was randomly inserted in the 1991 Upper Deck high number foil packs. Neither card is included in the price of the regular issue set though both are listed at the end of our checklist.

Nm-Mt Ex-Mt
COMPLETE SET (800) 15.00 4.50
COMP.FACT.SET (800) 20.00 6.00
COMPLETE LO SET (700) 15.00 4.50
COMPLETE HI SET (100) 5.00 1.50
1 Star Rookie Checklist .05 .02
2 Phil Plantier RC .10 .03
3 D.J. Dozier .05 .02
4 Dave Hansen .05 .02
5 Maurice Vaughn .10 .03
6 Leo Gomez .05 .02
7 Scott Aldred .05 .02
8 Scott Chiamparino .05 .02
9 Lance Dickson RC .10 .03
10 Sean Berry RC .10 .03
11 Bernie Williams .25 .07
12 Brian Barnes UER .10 .03
(Photo either not him
or in wrong jersey)
13 Narciso Elvira .05 .02
14 Mike Gardiner .05 .02
15 Greg Colbrunn RC .25 .07
16 Bernard Gilkey .05 .02
17 Mark Lewis .05 .02
18 Mickey Morandini .05 .02
19 Charles Nagy .05 .02
20 Geronimo Pena .05 .02
21 Henry Rodriguez RC .25 .07
22 Scott Cooper .05 .02
23 Andujar Cedeno UER .05 .02
(Shown batting left,
back says right)
24 Eric Karros RC .50 .15
25 Steve Decker UER .05 .02
Lewis-Clark State
College, not Lewis
and Clark
26 Kevin Belcher .05 .02
27 Jeff Conine RC .50 .15
28 Dave Stewart TC .05 .02
29 Carlton Fisk TC .10 .03
30 Rafael Palmeiro TC .10 .03
31 Chuck Finley TC .05 .02
32 Harold Reynolds TC .05 .02
33 Bret Saberhagen TC .05 .02
34 Gary Gaetti TC .05 .02
35 Scott Leius .05 .02
36 Neal Heaton .05 .02
37 Terry Lee .05 .02
38 Gary Redus .05 .02
39 Barry Jones .05 .02
40 Chuck Knoblauch .10 .03
41 Larry Andersen .05 .02
42 Darryl Hamilton .05 .02
43 Mike Greenwell TC .05 .02
44 Kelly Gruber TC .05 .02
45 Jack Morris TC .05 .02
46 Sandy Alomar Jr. TC .05 .02
47 Gregg Olson TC .05 .02
48 Dave Parker TC .05 .02
49 Roberto Kelly TC .05 .02
50 Top Prospect Checklist .05 .02
51 Kyle Abbott .05 .02
52 Jeff Juden .05 .02
53 T.Van Poppel UER RC .25 .07
Born Arlington and
attended John Martin HS,
should say Hinsdale and
James Martin HS
54 Steve Karsay RC .25 .07
55 Chipper Jones RC 4.00 1.20
56 Chris Johnson RC UER .10 .03
(Called Tim on back)
57 John Ericks .05 .02
58 Gary Scott .05 .02
59 Kiki Jones .05 .02
60 Wil Cordero RC .10 .03
61 Royce Clayton .05 .02
62 Tim Costo RC .10 .03
63 Roger Salkeld .05 .02
64 Brook Fordyce RC .25 .07
65 Mike Mussina RC 1.50 .45
66 Dave Staton RC .10 .03
67 Mike Lieberthal RC .40 .12
68 Kurt Miller RC .05 .02
69 Dan Peltier RC .10 .03
70 Greg Blosser .05 .02
71 Reggie Sanders RC .40 .12
72 Brent Mayne .05 .02
73 Rico Brogna .05 .02
74 Willie Banks .05 .02
75 Len Brutcher .05 .02
76 Pat Kelly RC .10 .03
77 Chris Sabo TC .05 .02
78 Ramon Martinez TC .05 .02
79 Matt Williams TC .05 .02
80 Roberto Alomar TC .10 .03
81 Glenn Davis TC .05 .02
82 Ron Gant TC .05 .02
83 Cecil Fielder FEAT .05 .02
84 Orlando Merced RC .10 .03
85 Domingo Ramos .05 .02
86 Tom Bolton .05 .02
87 Andres Santana .05 .02
88 John Dopson .05 .02
89 Kenny Williams .05 .02
90 Marty Barrett .05 .02
91 Tom Pagnozzi .05 .02
92 Carmelo Martinez .05 .02
93 Bobby Thigpen SAVE .05 .02
94 Barry Bonds TC .30 .09
95 Gregg Jefferies TC .05 .02
96 Tim Wallach TC .05 .02
97 Len Dykstra TC .05 .02
98 Pedro Guerrero TC .05 .02
99 Mark Grace TC .10 .03
100 Checklist 1-100 .05 .02
101 Kevin Elster .05 .02
102 Tom Brookens .05 .02
103 Mackey Sasser .05 .02
104 Felix Fermin .05 .02
105 Kevin McReynolds .05 .02
106 Dave Stieb .05 .02
107 Jeffrey Leonard .05 .02
108 Dave Henderson .05 .02
109 Sid Bream .05 .02
110 Henry Cotto .05 .02
111 Shawon Dunston .05 .02
112 Mariano Duncan .05 .02
113 Joe Girardi .05 .02
114 Billy Hatcher .05 .02
115 Greg Maddux .40 .12
116 Jerry Browne .05 .02
117 Juan Samuel .05 .02
118 Steve Olin .05 .02
119 Alfredo Griffin .05 .02
120 Mitch Webster .05 .02
121 Joel Skinner .05 .02
122 Frank Viola .10 .03
123 Cory Snyder .05 .02
124 Howard Johnson .05 .02
125 Carlos Baerga .05 .02
126 Tony Fernandez .05 .02
127 Dave Stewart .10 .03
128 Jay Buhner .10 .03
129 Mike LaValliere .05 .02
130 Scott Bradley .05 .02
131 Tony Phillips .05 .02
132 Ryne Sandberg .40 .12
133 Paul O'Neill .15 .04
134 Mark Grace .15 .04
135 Chris Sabo .05 .02
136 Ramon Martinez .05 .02
137 Brook Jacoby .05 .02
138 Candy Maldonado .05 .02
139 Mike Scioscia .05 .02
140 Chris James .05 .02
141 Craig Worthington .05 .02
142 Manny Lee .05 .02
143 Tim Raines .10 .03
144 Sandy Alomar Jr. .05 .02
145 John Olerud .10 .03
146 Ozzie Canseco .10 .03
(With Jose)
147 Pat Borders .05 .02
148 Harold Reynolds .10 .03
149 Tom Henke .05 .02
150 R.J. Reynolds .05 .02
151 Mike Gallego .05 .02
152 Bobby Bonilla .10 .03
153 Terry Steinbach .05 .02
154 Barry Bonds .60 .18
155 Jose Canseco .25 .07
156 Gregg Jefferies .05 .02
157 Matt Williams .10 .03
158 Craig Biggio .15 .04
159 Daryl Boston .05 .02
160 Ricky Jordan .05 .02
161 Stan Belinda .05 .02
162 Ozzie Smith .40 .12
163 Tom Brunansky .05 .02
164 Todd Zeile .05 .02
165 Mike Greenwell .05 .02
166 Kal Daniels .05 .02
167 Kent Hrbek .10 .03
168 Franklin Stubbs .05 .02
169 Dick Schofield .05 .02
170 Junior Ortiz .05 .02
171 Hector Villanueva .05 .02
172 Dennis Eckersley .10 .03
173 Mitch Williams .05 .02
174 Mark McGwire .60 .18
175 F.Valenzuela 3X .10 .03
176 Gary Carter .15 .04
177 Dave Magadan .05 .02
178 Robby Thompson .05 .02
179 Bob Ojeda .05 .02
180 Ken Caminiti .10 .03
181 Don Slaught .05 .02
182 Luis Rivera .05 .02
183 Jay Bell .10 .03
184 Jody Reed .05 .02
185 Wally Backman .05 .02
186 Dave Martinez .05 .02
187 Luis Polonia .05 .02
188 Shane Mack .05 .02
189 Spike Owen .05 .02
190 Scott Bailes .05 .02
191 John Russell .05 .02
192 Walt Weiss .05 .02
193 Jose Oquendo .05 .02
194 Carney Lansford .10 .03
195 Jeff Huson .05 .02
196 Keith Miller .05 .02
197 Eric Yelding .05 .02
198 Ron Darling .05 .02
199 John Kruk .10 .03
200 Checklist 101-200 .05 .02
201 John Shelby .05 .02
202 Bob Geren .05 .02
203 Lance McCullers .05 .02
204 Alvaro Espinoza .05 .02
205 Mark Salas .05 .02
206 Mike Pagliarulo .05 .02
207 Jose Uribe .05 .02
208 Jim Deshaies .05 .02
209 Ron Karkovice .05 .02
210 Rafael Ramirez .05 .02
211 Donnie Hill .05 .02
212 Brian Harper .05 .02
213 Jack Howell .05 .02
214 Wes Gardner .05 .02
215 Tim Burke .05 .02
216 Doug Jones .05 .02
217 Hubie Brooks .05 .02
218 Tom Candiotti .05 .02
219 Gerald Perry .05 .02
220 Jose DeLeon .05 .02
221 Wally Whitehurst .05 .02
222 Alan Mills .05 .02
223 Alan Trammell .15 .04
224 Dwight Gooden .15 .04
225 Travis Fryman .10 .03
226 Joe Carter .10 .03
227 Julio Franco .10 .03
228 Craig Lefferts .05 .02
229 Gary Pettis .05 .02
230 Dennis Rasmussen .05 .02
231A Brian Downing ERR .05 .02
(No position on front)
231B Brian Downing COR .25 .07
(DH on front)
232 Carlos Quintana .05 .02
233 Gary Gaetti .10 .03
234 Mark Langston .05 .02
235 Tim Wallach .05 .02
236 Greg Swindell .05 .02
237 Eddie Murray .25 .07
238 Jeff Manto .05 .02
239 Lenny Harris .05 .02
240 Jesse Orosco .05 .02
241 Scott Lusader .05 .02
242 Sid Fernandez .05 .02
243 Jim Leyritz .05 .02
244 Cecil Fielder .10 .03
245 Darryl Strawberry .15 .04
246 Frank Thomas UER .25 .07
(Comiskey Park
misspelled Comisky)
247 Kevin Mitchell .05 .02
248 Lance Johnson .05 .02
249 Rick Reuschel .05 .02
250 Mark Portugal .05 .02
251 Derek Lilliquist .05 .02
252 Brian Holman .05 .02
253 Rafael Valdez UER .05 .02
(Born 4/17/68,
should be 12/17/67)
254 B.J. Surhoff .10 .03
255 Tony Gwynn .30 .09
256 Andy Van Slyke .10 .03
257 Todd Stottlemyre .05 .02
258 Jose Lind .05 .02
259 Greg Myers .05 .02
260 Jeff Ballard .05 .02
261 Bobby Thigpen .05 .02
262 Jimmy Kremers .05 .02
263 Robin Ventura .10 .03
264 John Smoltz .15 .04
265 Sammy Sosa .50 .15
266 Gary Sheffield .10 .03
267 Len Dykstra .10 .03
268 Bill Spiers .05 .02
269 Charlie Hayes .05 .02
270 Brett Butler .10 .03
271 Bip Roberts .05 .02
272 Rob Deer .05 .02
273 Fred Lynn .05 .02
274 Dave Parker .10 .03
275 Andy Benes .10 .03
276 Glenallen Hill .05 .02
277 Steve Howard .05 .02
278 Doug Drabek .05 .02
279 Joe Oliver .05 .02
280 Todd Benzinger .05 .02
281 Eric King .05 .02
282 Jim Presley .05 .02
283 Ken Patterson .05 .02
284 Jack Daugherty .05 .02
285 Ivan Calderon .05 .02
286 Edgar Diaz .05 .02
287 Kevin Bass .05 .02
288 Don Carman .05 .02
289 Greg Brock .05 .02
290 John Franco .10 .03
291 Joey Cora .05 .02
292 Bill Wegman .05 .02
293 Eric Show .05 .02
294 Scott Bankhead .05 .02
295 Garry Templeton .05 .02
296 Mickey Tettleton .05 .02
297 Luis Sojo .05 .02
298 Jose Rijo .05 .02
299 Dave Johnson .05 .02
300 Checklist 201-300 .05 .02
301 Mark Grant .05 .02
302 Pete Harnisch .05 .02
303 Greg Olson .05 .02
304 Anthony Telford .05 .02
305 Lonnie Smith .05 .02
306 Chris Hoiles .05 .02
307 Bryn Smith .05 .02
308 Mike Devereaux .05 .02
309A Milt Thompson ERR .25 .07
(Under yr information
has print dot)
309B Milt Thompson COR .05 .02
(Under yr information
says 86)
310 Bob Melvin .05 .02
311 Luis Salazar .05 .02
312 Ed Whitson .05 .02
313 Charlie Hough .10 .03
314 Dave Clark .05 .02
315 Eric Gunderson .05 .02
316 Dan Petry .05 .02
317 Dante Bichette UER .10 .03
(Assists misspelled
as assissts)
318 Mike Heath .05 .02
319 Damon Berryhill .05 .02
320 Walt Terrell .05 .02
321 Scott Fletcher .05 .02
322 Dan Plesac .05 .02
323 Jack McDowell .05 .02
324 Paul Molitor .15 .04
325 Ozzie Guillen .05 .02
326 Gregg Olson .05 .02
327 Pedro Guerrero .10 .03
328 Bob Milacki .05 .02
329 John Tudor UER .05 .02
('90 Cardinals,
should be '90 Dodgers)
330 Steve Finley UER .10 .03
(Born 3/12/65,
should be 5/12)
331 Jack Clark .10 .03
332 Jerome Walton .05 .02
333 Andy Hawkins .05 .02
334 Derrick May .05 .02
335 Roberto Alomar .25 .07
336 Jack Morris .10 .03
337 Dave Winfield .10 .03
338 Steve Searcy .05 .02
339 Chili Davis .10 .03
340 Larry Sheets .05 .02
341 Ted Higuera .05 .02
342 David Segui .05 .02
343 Greg Cadaret .05 .02
344 Robin Yount .40 .12
345 Nolan Ryan 1.00 .30
346 Ray Lankford .05 .02
347 Cal Ripken .75 .23
348 Lee Smith .10 .03
349 Brady Anderson .10 .03
350 Frank DiPino .05 .02
351 Hal Morris .05 .02
352 Deion Sanders .15 .04
353 Barry Larkin .25 .07
354 Don Mattingly .60 .18
355 Eric Davis .10 .03
356 Jose Offerman .05 .02
357 Mel Rojas .05 .02
358 Rudy Seanez .05 .02
359 Oil Can Boyd .05 .02
360 Nelson Liriano .05 .02
361 Ron Gant .10 .03
362 Howard Farmer .05 .02
363 David Justice .10 .03
364 Delino DeShields .10 .03
365 Steve Avery .05 .02
366 David Cone .10 .03
367 Lou Whitaker .10 .03
368 Von Hayes .05 .02
369 Frank Tanana .05 .02
370 Tim Teufel .05 .02
371 Randy Myers .05 .02
372 Roberto Kelly .05 .02
373 Jack Armstrong .05 .02
374 Kelly Gruber .05 .02
375 Kevin Maas .05 .02
376 Randy Johnson .30 .09
377 David West .05 .02
378 Brent Knackert .05 .02
379 Rick Honeycutt .05 .02
380 Kevin Gross .05 .02
381 Tom Foley .05 .02
382 Jeff Blauser .05 .02
383 Scott Ruskin .05 .02
384 Andres Thomas .05 .02
385 Dennis Martinez .10 .03
386 Mike Henneman .05 .02
387 Felix Jose .05 .02
388 Alejandro Pena .05 .02
389 Chet Lemon .05 .02
390 Craig Wilson .05 .02
391 Chuck Crim .05 .02
392 Mel Hall .05 .02
393 Mark Knudson .05 .02
394 Norm Charlton .05 .02
395 Mike Felder .05 .02
396 Tim Layana .05 .02
397 Steve Frey .05 .02
398 Bill Doran .05 .02
399 Dion James .05 .02
400 Checklist 301-400 .05 .02
401 Ron Hassey .05 .02
402 Don Robinson .05 .02
403 Gene Nelson .05 .02
404 Terry Kennedy .05 .02
405 Todd Burns .05 .02
406 Roger McDowell .05 .02
407 Bob Kipper .05 .02
408 Darren Daulton .10 .03
409 Chuck Cary .05 .02
410 Bruce Ruffin .05 .02
411 Juan Berenguer .05 .02
412 Gary Ward .05 .02
413 Al Newman .05 .02
414 Danny Jackson .05 .02
415 Greg Gagne .05 .02
416 Tom Herr .05 .02
417 Jeff Parrett .05 .02
418 Jeff Reardon .10 .03
419 Mark Lemke .05 .02
420 Charlie O'Brien .05 .02
421 Willie Randolph .10 .03
422 Steve Bedrosian .05 .02
423 Mike Moore .05 .02
424 Jeff Brantley .05 .02
425 Bob Welch .05 .02
426 Terry Mulholland .05 .02
427 Willie Blair .05 .02
428 Darrin Fletcher .05 .02
429 Mike Witt .05 .02
430 Joe Boever .05 .02
431 Tom Gordon .05 .02

432 Pedro Munoz RC .10 .03
433 Kevin Seitzer .05 .02
434 Kevin Tapani .05 .02
435 Bret Saberhagen .10 .03
436 Ellis Burks .10 .03
437 Chuck Finley .10 .03
438 Mike Boddicker .05 .02
439 Francisco Cabrera .05 .02
440 Todd Hundley .05 .02
441 Kelly Downs .05 .02
442 Dann Howitt .05 .02
443 Scott Garrelts .05 .02
444 Rickey Henderson 3X .25 .07
445 Will Clark .25 .07
446 Ben McDonald .05 .02
447 Dale Murphy .25 .07
448 Dave Righetti .10 .03
449 Dickie Thon .05 .02
450 Ted Power .05 .02
451 Scott Coolbaugh .05 .02
452 Dwight Smith .05 .02
453 Pete Incaviglia .05 .02
454 Andre Dawson .10 .03
455 Ruben Sierra .05 .02
456 Andres Galarraga .10 .03
457 Alvin Davis .05 .02
458 Tony Castillo .05 .02
459 Pete O'Brien .05 .02
460 Charlie Leibrandt .05 .02
461 Vince Coleman .05 .02
462 Steve Sax .05 .02
463 Omar Olivares RC .10 .03
464 Oscar Azocar .05 .02
465 Joe Magrane .05 .02
466 Karl Rhodes .05 .02
467 Benito Santiago .10 .03
468 Joe Klink .05 .02
469 Sil Campusano .05 .02
470 Mark Parent .05 .02
471 Shawn Boskie UER .05 .02
(Depleted misspelled
as depleated)
472 Kevin Brown .10 .03
473 Rick Sutcliffe .10 .03
474 Rafael Palmeiro .15 .04
475 Mike Harkey .05 .02
476 Jaime Navarro .05 .02
477 Marquis Grissom UER .05 .02
(DeShields misspelled
as DeSheilds)
478 Marty Clary .05 .02
479 Greg Briley .05 .02
480 Tom Glavine .15 .04
481 Lee Guetterman .05 .02
482 Rex Hudler .05 .02
483 Dave LaPoint .05 .02
484 Terry Pendleton .10 .03
485 Jesse Barfield .05 .02
486 Jose DeJesus .05 .02
487 Paul Abbott RC .25 .07
488 Ken Howell .05 .02
489 Greg W. Harris .05 .02
490 Roy Smith .05 .02
491 Paul Assenmacher .05 .02
492 Geno Petralli .05 .02
493 Steve Wilson .05 .02
494 Kevin Reimer .05 .02
495 Bill Long .05 .02
496 Mike Jackson .05 .02
497 Oddibe McDowell .05 .02
498 Bill Swift .05 .02
499 Jeff Treadway .05 .02
500 Checklist 401-500 .05 .02
501 Gene Larkin .05 .02
502 Bob Boone .10 .03
503 Allan Anderson .05 .02
504 Luis Aquino .05 .02
505 Mark Guthrie .05 .02
506 Joe Orsulak .05 .02
507 Dana Kiecker .05 .02
508 Dave Gallagher .05 .02
509 Greg A. Harris .05 .02
510 Mark Williamson .05 .02
511 Casey Candaele .05 .02
512 Mookie Wilson .10 .03
513 Dave Smith .05 .02
514 Chuck Carr .05 .02
515 Glenn Wilson .05 .02
516 Mike Fitzgerald .05 .02
517 Devon White .05 .02
518 Dave Hollins .05 .02
519 Mark Eichhorn .05 .02
520 Otis Nixon .05 .02
521 Terry Shumpert .05 .02
522 Scott Erickson .05 .02
523 Danny Tartabull .05 .02
524 Orel Hershiser .10 .03
525 George Brett .60 .18
526 Greg Vaughn .10 .03
527 Tim Naehring .05 .02
528 Curt Schilling .15 .04
529 Chris Bosio .05 .02
530 Sam Horn .05 .02
531 Mike Scott .05 .02
532 George Bell .05 .02
533 Eric Anthony .05 .02
534 Julio Valera .05 .02
535 Glenn Davis .05 .02
536 Larry Walker UER .25 .07
(Should have comma
after Expos in text)
537 Pat Combs .05 .02
538 Chris Nabholz .05 .02
539 Kirk McCaskill .05 .02
540 Randy Ready .05 .02
541 Mark Gubicza .05 .02
542 Rick Aguilera .10 .03
543 Brian McRae RC .25 .07
544 Kirby Puckett .25 .07
545 Bo Jackson .25 .07
546 Wade Boggs .15 .04
547 Tim McIntosh .05 .02
548 Randy Milligan .05 .02
549 Dwight Evans .10 .03
550 Billy Ripken .05 .02
551 Erik Hanson .05 .02
552 Lance Parrish .10 .03
553 Tino Martinez .15 .04
554 Jim Abbott .15 .04
555 Ken Griffey Jr. UER .50 .15
(Second most votes for
1991 All-Star Game)
556 Milt Cuyler .05 .02
557 Mark Leonard .05 .02
558 Jay Howell .05 .02
559 Lloyd Moseby .05 .02
560 Chris Gwynn .05 .02
561 Mark Whiten .05 .02
562 Harold Baines .10 .03
563 Junior Felix .05 .02
564 Darren Lewis .05 .02
565 Fred McGriff .15 .04
566 Kevin Appier .10 .03
567 Luis Gonzalez RC 1.25 .35
568 Frank White .10 .03
569 Juan Agosto .05 .02
570 Mike Macfarlane .05 .02
571 Bert Blyleven .10 .03
572 Ken Griffey Sr. .25 .07
Ken Griffey Jr.
573 Lee Stevens .05 .02
574 Edgar Martinez .15 .04
575 Wally Joyner .10 .03
576 Tim Belcher .05 .02
577 John Burkett .05 .02
578 Mike Morgan .05 .02
579 Paul Gibson .05 .02
580 Jose Vizcaino .05 .02
581 Duane Ward .05 .02
582 Scott Sanderson .05 .02
583 David Wells .10 .03
584 Willie McGee .10 .03
585 John Cerutti .05 .02
586 Danny Darwin .05 .02
587 Kurt Stillwell .05 .02
588 Rich Gedman .05 .02
589 Mark Davis .05 .02
590 Bill Gullickson .05 .02
591 Matt Young .05 .02
592 Bryan Harvey .05 .02
593 Omar Vizquel .10 .03
594 Scott Lewis RC .10 .03
595 Dave Valle .05 .02
596 Tim Crews .05 .02
597 Mike Bielecki .05 .02
598 Mike Sharperson .05 .02
599 Dave Bergman .05 .02
600 Checklist 501-600 .05 .02
601 Steve Lyons .05 .02
602 Bruce Hurst .05 .02
603 Donn Pall .05 .02
604 Jim Vatcher .05 .02
605 Dan Pasqua .05 .02
606 Kenny Rogers .10 .03
607 Jeff Schulz .05 .02
608 Brad Arnsberg .05 .02
609 Willie Wilson .05 .02
610 Jamie Moyer .10 .03
611 Ron Oester .05 .02
612 Dennis Cook .05 .02
613 Rick Mahler .05 .02
614 Bill Landrum .05 .02
615 Scott Scudder .05 .02
616 Tom Edens .05 .02
617 1917 Revisited .10 .03
(White Sox vintage uniforms)
618 Jim Gantner .05 .02
619 Darrel Akerfelds .05 .02
620 Ron Robinson .05 .02
621 Scott Radinsky .05 .02
622 Pete Smith .05 .02
623 Melido Perez .05 .02
624 Jerald Clark .05 .02
625 Carlos Martinez .05 .02
626 Wes Chamberlain RC .25 .07
627 Bobby Witt .05 .02
628 Ken Dayley .05 .02
629 John Barfield .05 .02
630 Bob Tewksbury .05 .02
631 Glenn Braggs .05 .02
632 Jim Neidlinger .05 .02
633 Tom Browning .05 .02
634 Kirk Gibson .10 .03
635 Rob Dibble .10 .03
636 Rickey Henderson SB .25 .07
Lou Brock
May 1, 1991 on front
636A R.Henderson SB .25 .07
Lou Brock
no date on card
637 Jeff Montgomery .05 .02
638 Mike Schooler .05 .02
639 Storm Davis .05 .02
640 Rich Rodriguez .05 .02
641 Phil Bradley .05 .02
642 Kent Mercker .05 .02
643 Carlton Fisk .15 .04
644 Mike Bell .05 .02
645 Alex Fernandez .05 .02
646 Juan Gonzalez .25 .07
647 Ken Hill .05 .02
648 Jeff Russell .05 .02
649 Chuck Malone .05 .02
650 Steve Buechele .05 .02
651 Mike Benjamin .05 .02
652 Tony Pena .05 .02
653 Trevor Wilson .05 .02
654 Alex Cole .05 .02
655 Roger Clemens .50 .15
656 Mark McGwire BASH .30 .09
657 Joe Grahe RC .10 .03
658 Jim Eisenreich .05 .02
659 Dan Gladden .05 .02
660 Steve Farr .05 .02
661 Bill Sampen .05 .02
662 Dave Rohde .05 .02
663 Mark Gardner .05 .02
664 Mike Simms .05 .02
665 Moises Alou .10 .03
666 Mickey Hatcher .05 .02
667 Jimmy Key .10 .03
668 John Wetteland .10 .03
669 John Smiley .05 .02
670 Jim Acker .05 .02
671 Pascual Perez .05 .02
672 Reggie Harris UER .05 .02
(Opportunity misspelled
as oppurtinity)
673 Matt Nokes .05 .02
674 Rafael Novoa .05 .02
675 Hensley Meulens .05 .02
676 Jeff M. Robinson .05 .02
677 Ground Breaking .10 .03
(New Comiskey Park;
Carlton Fisk and
Robin Ventura)
678 Johnny Ray .05 .02
679 Greg Hibbard .05 .02
680 Paul Sorrento .05 .02
681 Mike Marshall .05 .02
682 Jim Clancy .05 .02
683 Rob Murphy .05 .02
684 Dave Schmidt .05 .02
685 Jeff Gray .05 .02
686 Mike Hartley .05 .02
687 Jeff King .05 .02
688 Stan Javier .05 .02
689 Bob Walk .05 .02
690 Jim Gott .05 .02
691 Mike LaCoss .05 .02
692 John Farrell .05 .02
693 Tim Leary .05 .02
694 Mike Walker .05 .02
695 Eric Plunk .05 .02
696 Mike Fetters .05 .02
697 Wayne Edwards .05 .02
698 Tim Drummond .05 .02
699 Willie Fraser .05 .02
700 Checklist 601-700 .05 .02
701 Mike Heath .05 .02
702 Luis Gonzalez 1.00 .30
Karl Rhodes
Jeff Bagwell
703 Jose Mesa .05 .02
704 Dave Smith .05 .02
705 Danny Darwin .05 .02
706 Rafael Belliard .05 .02
707 Rob Murphy .05 .02
708 Terry Pendleton .10 .03
709 Mike Pagliarulo .05 .02
710 Sid Bream .05 .02
711 Junior Felix .05 .02
712 Dante Bichette .10 .03
713 Kevin Gross .05 .02
714 Luis Sojo .05 .02
715 Bob Ojeda .05 .02
716 Julio Machado .05 .02
717 Steve Farr .05 .02
718 Franklin Stubbs .05 .02
719 Mike Boddicker .05 .02
720 Willie Randolph .10 .03
721 Willie McGee .10 .03
722 Chili Davis .10 .03
723 Danny Jackson .05 .02
724 Cory Snyder .05 .02
725 Andre Dawson .25 .07
George Bell
Ryne Sandberg
726 Rob Deer .05 .02
727 Rich DeLucia .05 .02
728 Mike Perez RC .10 .03
729 Mickey Tettleton .05 .02
730 Mike Blowers .05 .02
731 Gary Gaetti .10 .03
732 Brett Butler .10 .03
733 Dave Parker .10 .03
734 Eddie Zosky .05 .02
735 Jack Clark .10 .03
736 Jack Morris .10 .03
737 Kirk Gibson .10 .03
738 Steve Bedrosian .05 .02
739 Candy Maldonado .05 .02
740 Matt Young .05 .02
741 Rich Garces RC .10 .03
742 George Bell .05 .02
743 Deion Sanders .15 .04
744 Bo Jackson .25 .07
745 Luis Mercedes RC .10 .03
746 Reggie Jefferson UER .05 .02
(Throwing left on card;
back has throws right)
747 Pete Incaviglia .05 .02
748 Chris Hammond .05 .02
749 Mike Stanton .05 .02
750 Scott Sanderson .05 .02
751 Paul Faries .05 .02
752 Al Osuna RC .05 .02
753 Steve Chitren .05 .02
754 Tony Fernandez .05 .02
755 Jeff Bagwell RC UER 1.50 .45
(Strikeout and walk
totals reversed)
756 K.Dressendorfer RC .10 .03
757 Glenn Davis .05 .02
758 Gary Carter .15 .04
759 Zane Smith .05 .02
760 Vance Law .05 .02
761 Denis Boucher RC .10 .03
762 Turner Ward RC .10 .03
763 Roberto Alomar .25 .07
764 Albert Belle .10 .03
765 Joe Carter .10 .03
766 Pete Schourek RC .10 .03
767 H.Slocumb RC .10 .03
768 Vince Coleman .05 .02
769 Mitch Williams .05 .02
770 Brian Downing .05 .02
771 Dana Allison .05 .02
772 Pete Harnisch .05 .02
773 Tim Raines .10 .03
774 Darryl Kile .10 .03
775 Fred McGriff .15 .04
776 Dwight Evans .10 .03
777 Joe Slusarski .05 .02
778 Dave Righetti .10 .03
779 Jeff Hamilton .05 .02
780 Ernest Riles .05 .02
781 Ken Dayley .05 .02
782 Eric King .05 .02
783 Devon White .05 .02
784 Beau Allred .05 .02
785 Mike Timlin RC .25 .07
786 Ivan Calderon .05 .02
787 Hubie Brooks .05 .02
788 Juan Agosto .05 .02
789 Barry Jones .05 .02
790 Wally Backman .05 .02
791 Jim Presley .05 .02
792 Charlie Hough .10 .03
793 Larry Andersen .05 .02
794 Steve Finley .10 .03
795 Shawn Abner .05 .02
796 Jeff M. Robinson .05 .02
797 Joe Bitker .05 .02
798 Eric Show .05 .02
799 Bud Black .05 .02
800 Checklist 701-800 .05 .02
HH1 H.Aaron Hologram 1.50 .45
SP1 Michael Jordan SP 8.00 2.40
(Shown batting in
White Sox uniform)
SP2 Rickey Henderson 2.00 .60
Nolan Ryan
May 1, 1991 Records

1991 Upper Deck Aaron Heroes

These standard-size cards were issued in honor of Hall of Famer Hank Aaron and inserted in Upper Deck high number wax packs. Aaron autographed 2,500 of card number 27, which featured his portrait by noted sports artist Vernon Wells. The cards are numbered on the back in continuation of the Baseball Heroes set.

	Nm-Mt	Ex-Mt
COMPLETE SET (10)	5.00	1.50
COMMON AARON (19-27)	.50	.15
NNO Title/Header card SP	1.00	.30
AU3 Hank Aaron AU (Signed and Numbered out of 2500)	150.00	45.00

1991 Upper Deck Heroes of Baseball

These standard-size cards were randomly inserted in Upper Deck Baseball Heroes wax packs. The fourth card features a color portrait of the three players by noted sports artist Vernon Wells. Each of the features heroes also signed 3,000 of each card for inclusion in this product.

	Nm-Mt	Ex-Mt
COMPLETE SET (4)	25.00	7.50
H1 Harmon Killebrew	8.00	2.40
H2 Gaylord Perry	5.00	1.50
H3 Ferguson Jenkins	5.00	1.50
H4 Harmon Killebrew ART (Ferguson Jenkins, Gaylord Perry)	8.00	2.40
AU1 Harmon Killebrew AU 3000	40.00	12.00
AU2 Gaylord Perry AU 3000	25.00	7.50
AU3 Fergie Jenkins AU 3000	25.00	7.50

1991 Upper Deck Ryan Heroes

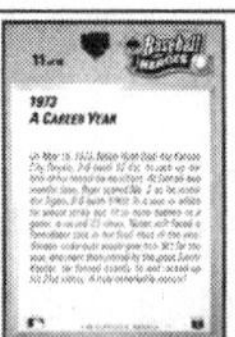

This nine-card standard-size set was included in first series 1991 Upper Deck packs. The set which honors Nolan Ryan and is numbered as a continuation of the Baseball Heroes set which began with Reggie Jackson in 1990. This set honors Ryan's long career and his place in Baseball History. Card number 18 features the artwork of Vernon Wells while the other cards are photos. The complete set price below does not include the signed Ryan card of which only 2500 were made. Signed cards ending with 00 have the expression "Strikeout King" added. These Ryan cards were apparently issued on 100-card sheets with the following configuration: ten each of the nine Ryan Baseball Heroes cards, five Michael Jordan cards and five Baseball Heroes header cards. The Baseball Heroes header card is a standard size card which explains the continuation of the Baseball Heroes series on the back while the front just says Baseball Heroes.

	Nm-Mt	Ex-Mt
COMPLETE SET (10)	5.00	1.50
COMMON RYAN (10-18)	.50	.15
NNO Baseball Heroes SP (Header card)	1.00	.30
AU2 Nolan Ryan AU (Signed and Numbered out of 2500)	200.00	60.00

1991 Upper Deck Silver Sluggers

The Upper Deck Silver Slugger set features nine players from each league, representing the nine batting positions on the team. The cards were issued one per 1991 Upper Deck jumbo pack. The cards measure the standard size. The cards are numbered on the back with an "SS" prefix.

	Nm-Mt	Ex-Mt
COMPLETE SET (18)	15.00	4.50
SS1 Julio Franco	.75	.23
SS2 Alan Trammell	1.25	.35
SS3 Rickey Henderson	2.00	.60
SS4 Jose Canseco	2.00	.60
SS5 Barry Bonds	5.00	1.50
SS6 Eddie Murray	2.00	.60
SS7 Kelly Gruber	.40	.12
SS8 Ryne Sandberg	3.00	.90
SS9 Darryl Strawberry	1.25	.35
SS10 Ellis Burks	.75	.23
SS11 Lance Parrish	.75	.23
SS12 Cecil Fielder	.75	.23
SS13 Matt Williams	.75	.23
SS14 Dave Parker	.75	.23
SS15 Bobby Bonilla	.75	.23
SS16 Don Robinson	.40	.12
SS17 Benito Santiago	.75	.23
SS18 Barry Larkin	2.00	.60

1991 Upper Deck Final Edition

The 1991 Upper Deck Final Edition boxed set contains 100 standard-size cards and showcases players who made major contributions during their team's late-season pennant drive. In addition to the late season traded and impact rookie cards (22-78), the set includes two special subsets: Diamond Skills cards (1-21), depicting the best Minor League prospects, and All-Star cards (80-99). Six assorted team logo hologram cards were issued with each set. The cards are numbered on the back with an F suffix. Among the outstanding Rookie Cards in this set are Ryan Klesko, Kenny Lofton, Pedro Martinez, Ivan Rodriguez, Jim Thome, Rondell White, and Dmitri Young.

	Nm-Mt	Ex-Mt
COMP.FACT.SET (100)	10.00	3.00
1F Ryan Klesko CL (Reggie Sanders)	.10	.03
2F Pedro Martinez RC	8.00	2.40
3F Lance Dickson	.05	.02
4F Royce Clayton	.05	.02
5F Scott Bryant	.05	.02
6F Dan Wilson RC	.25	.07
7F Dmitri Young RC	.50	.15
8F Ryan Klesko RC	.50	.15
9F Tom Goodwin	.05	.02
10F Rondell White RC	.40	.12
11F Reggie Sanders	.25	.07
12F Todd Van Poppel	.05	.02
13F Arthur Rhodes RC	.25	.07
14F Eddie Zosky	.05	.02
15F Gerald Williams RC	.25	.07
16F Robert Eenhoorn RC	.10	.03
17F Jim Thome RC	2.00	.60
18F Marc Newfield RC	.10	.03
19F Kerwin Moore RC	.10	.03
20F Jeff McNeely RC	.10	.03
21F Frankie Rodriguez RC	.10	.03
22F Andy Mota	.05	.02
23F Chris Haney RC	.10	.03
24F Kenny Lofton RC	.50	.15
25F Dave Nilsson RC	.25	.07
26F Derek Bell	.10	.03
27F Frank Castillo RC	.25	.07
28F Candy Maldonado	.05	.02
29F Chuck McElroy	.05	.02
30F Chito Martinez	.05	.02
31F Steve Howe	.05	.02
32F Freddie Benavides	.05	.02
33F Scott Kamieniecki RC	.10	.03
34F Denny Neagle RC	.25	.07
35F Mike Humphreys RC	.10	.03
36F Mike Remlinger	.05	.02
37F Scott Coolbaugh	.05	.02
38F Darren Lewis	.05	.02
39F Thomas Howard	.05	.02
40F John Candelaria	.05	.02
41F Todd Benzinger	.05	.02
42F Wilson Alvarez	.05	.02
43F Patrick Lennon RC	.10	.03
44F Rusty Meacham RC	.10	.03
45F Ryan Bowen RC	.10	.03
46F Rick Wilkins RC	.10	.03
47F Ed Sprague	.05	.02
48F Bob Scanlan	.05	.02
49F Tom Candiotti	.05	.02
50F Dennis Martinez (Perfecto)	.10	.03
51F Oil Can Boyd	.05	.02
52F Glenallen Hill	.05	.02

53F Scott Livingstone RC .10 .03
54F Brian R. Hunter RC .25 .07
55F Ivan Rodriguez RC 1.50 .45
56F Kevin Mitchell RC .10 .03
57F Roger McDowell .05 .02
58F Otis Nixon .05 .02
59F Juan Bell .05 .02
60F Bill Krueger .05 .02
61F Chris Donnels .05 .02
62F Tommy Greene .05 .02
63F Doug Simons .05 .02
64F Andy Ashby RC .25 .07
65F Anthony Young RC .10 .03
66F Kevin Morton .05 .02
67F Bret Barberie RC** .10 .03
68F Scott Servais RC .25 .07
69F Ron Darling .05 .02
70F Tim Burke .05 .02
71F Vicente Palacios .05 .02
72F Gerald Alexander .05 .02
73F Reggie Jefferson .05 .02
74F Dean Palmer .10 .03
75F Mark Whiten .05 .02
76F Randy Tomlin RC .10 .03
77F Mark Wohlers RC .25 .07
78F Brook Jacoby .05 .02
79F Ken Griffey Jr. CL .40 .12
Ryne Sandberg
80F Jack Morris AS .05 .02
81F Sandy Alomar Jr. AS .05 .02
82F Cecil Fielder AS .05 .02
83F Roberto Alomar AS .10 .03
84F Wade Boggs AS .10 .03
85F Cal Ripken AS .40 .12
86F Rickey Henderson AS .15 .04
87F Ken Griffey Jr. AS .25 .07
88F Dave Henderson AS .05 .02
89F Danny Tartabull AS .05 .02
90F Tom Glavine AS .10 .03
91F Benito Santiago AS .05 .02
92F Will Clark AS .10 .03
93F Ryne Sandberg AS .25 .07
94F Chris Sabo AS .05 .02
95F Ozzie Smith AS .25 .07
96F Ivan Calderon AS .05 .02
97F Tony Gwynn AS .15 .04
98F Andre Dawson AS .05 .02
99F Bobby Bonilla AS .05 .02
100F Checklist 1-100 .05 .02

1991 Upper Deck Comic Ball Promos

These promo cards measure the standard size and are horizontally oriented. The fronts feature color photos of the players with Looney Tunes characters superimposed on the pictures. An orange banner on the top of each picture has the Looney Tunes and Upper Deck logos. The backs of all four cards form a composite cartoon in which Tweety is standing on the pitcher's mound as Sylvester drags it from the field. The cards are unnumbered and checklisted below by the date of distribution at the 1991 National Sports Collectors Convention in Anaheim.

Nm-Mt Ex-Mt
COMPLETE SET (4) 12.00 3.60
1 The National 7/4/91 5.00 1.50
Nolan Ryan with Daffy
Duck and Bugs Bunny
2 The National 7/5/91 2.50 .75
Reggie Jackson and
the Tasmanian Devil
3 The National 7/6/91 5.00 1.50
Nolan Ryan and
Speedy Gonzales
4 The National 7/7/91 2.50 .75
Reggie Jackson
Elmer Fudd
Sylvester

1991 Upper Deck Heroes of Baseball 5x7

This unnumbered sheet measures 5" by 7" and was distributed to herald the 1991 Heroes of Baseball sheets, listing on its back the dates and sites of the old-timers games where they were to be distributed. The front features artist renderings of the players listed below.

Nm-Mt Ex-Mt
1 Date sheet 5x7 20.00 6.00
Reggie Jackson
Lou Brock
Harmon Killebrew
Boog Powell
Gaylord Perry
Ferguson Jenkins

1991 Upper Deck Sheets

These 23 commemorative sheets were issued in 1991 to fans attending old-timers games preceding major league games. The sheets measure 8 1/2" by 11" and feature artist renderings of players from the teams recreated for the old-timers game. The front carries the individual production number out of the total number produced, but otherwise the sheets are unnumbered and so listed below in chronological order. The cover sheet was produced in two different versions, one numbered to 10,000, the other to 20,000. After the original 10,000 were produced, another 10,000 were needed for promotions.

Nm-Mt Ex-Mt
COMPLETE SET (23) 150.00 45.00
1 Cover sheet 5.00 1.50
Reggie Jackson
(20,000)
Dates and sites of
Old-Timers Games
2 Philadelphia Scholars 15.00 4.50
Fund Sports Show
Oct. 17, 1991 (21,500)
Mike Schmidt
Charles Barkley
Rick Tocchet
Reggie White
3 Tribute to Baltimore 10.00 3.00
Orioles Heroes
April 21, 1991 (17,000)
Memorial Stadium
Frank Robinson
Earl Weaver
Brooks Robinson
Robin Roberts
Boog Powell
4 Tribute to Joe 10.00 3.00
DiMaggio and Ted
Williams in celebration
of their Summer of '41
May 11, 1991 (17,000)
Fenway Park
Ken Keltner
Dom DiMaggio
Johnny Pesky
Bobby Doerr
Mickey Owen
5 Heroes of the '70s 10.00 3.00
May 18, 1991 (22,000)
Cleveland Municipal Stadium
Ray Fosse
Reggie Jackson
Gaylord Perry
Boog Powell
Mark Fidrych
6 Atlanta Braves Heroes 10.00 3.00
National League Heroes
June 8, 1991 (22,000)
Fulton County Stadium
Rico Carty
Chris Chambliss
Jeff Burroughs
Darrell Evans
Lou Brock
7 Oakland A's 10.00 3.00
June 9, 1991 (22,000)
Oakland Coliseum
Jim(Catfish) Hunter
8 World Series Heroes 6.00 1.80
June 15, 1991 (47,000)
Shea Stadium
Ron Swoboda
Yogi Berra MG
Ray Knight
Donn Clendenon
Tug McGraw
9 Cincinnati Reds Heroes 15.00 4.50
vs. World Series Heroes
June 22, 1991 (22,000)
Riverfront Stadium
Leo Cardenas
Ed Bailey
Joe Nuxhall
John Edwards
Tony Perez
10 1981 American League 6.00 1.80
Divisional Playoff Heroes
June 29, 1991 (27,000)
County Stadium
Ben Oglivie
Charlie Moore
Cecil Cooper
Rollie Fingers
Gorman Thomas
11 A Tribute to All-Star 5.00 1.50
Heroes
Toronto
July 8, 1991 (95,000)
SkyDome
Reggie Jackson
Ferguson Jenkins
Brooks Robinson
Lou Brock
Bob Gibson
12 Tribute to Home 6.00 1.80
Run Heroes
July 14, 1991 (44,000)
Anaheim Stadium
George Foster
Bobby Grich
Bobby Bonds
Reggie Jackson
Billy Williams
13 Pittsburgh Pirates 10.00 3.00
July 20, 1991 (18,000)
Three Rivers Stadium
Steve Blass
Bruce Kison
Willie Stargell
Al Oliver
Richie Hebner
14 Battle of Missouri 10.00 3.00
July 21, 1991 (17,000)
Busch Stadium
Mike Shannon
Al Hrabosky
Bob Gibson
Red Schoendeinst
Lou Brock
15 David vs. Goliath 10.00 3.00
July 27, 1991 (17,000)
Astrodome
Lou Brock
Eddie Mathews
Cesar Cedeno
Gaylord Perry
Billy Williams
16 45th Annual Old-Timer's 6.00 1.80
Day Classic
July 27, 1991 (47,000)
Yankee Stadium
Joe Pepitone
Bobby Murcer
Catfish Hunter
Ron Guidry
Bobby Richardson
17 1971 Phillies vs. 6.00 1.80
Upper Deck Heroes
Aug. 10, 1991 (42,000)
Veterans Stadium
Larry Bowa
Willie Montanez
Don Money
Jim Bunning
18 Tribute to Hall 10.00 3.00
of Famers
Aug. 10, 1991 (17,000)
Arlington Stadium
Ferguson Jenkins
Gaylord Perry
19 All-Star Joes vs. 8.00 2.40
All-Star Bobs
Aug. 16, 1991 (27,000)
Jack Murphy Stadium
Bobby Bonds
Bobby Doerr
Bob Gibson
Joe Pepitone
Joe Rudi
20 Giants Reunion with 6.00 1.80
Newest Hall of Famer
Aug. 18, 1991 (42,000)
Candlestick Park
Gaylord Perry
21 American League vs. 10.00 3.00
National League
Aug. 24, 1991 (22,000)
Wrigley Field
Ron Santo
Don Kessinger
Billy Williams
Dave Kingman
Ferguson Jenkins
22 Tribute to 1971 Heroes 8.00 2.40
Aug. 25, 1991 (32,000)
Tiger Stadium
Bill Freehan
Mickey Lolich
Al Kaline
Willie Horton
23 10th Anniversary of 6.00 1.80
Expos' Divisional Championship
Sept. 1, 1991 (22,000)
Olympic Stadium
Larry Parrish
Chris Speier
Jerry White
Steve Rogers
Charlie Lea

1992 Upper Deck

The 1992 Upper Deck set contains 800 standard-size cards issued in two separate series of 700 and 100 cards respectively. The cards were distributed in low and high series foil packs in addition to factory sets. Factory sets feature a unique gold-foil hologram on the card backs (in contrast to the silver hologram on foil pack cards). Special subsets included in the set are Star Rookies (1-27), Team Checklists (29-40/86-99), with player portraits by Vernon Wells Sr.; Top Prospects (52-77); Bloodlines (79-85), Diamond Skills (640-650/711-721) and Diamond Debuts (771-780). Rookie Cards in the set include Shawn Green, Brian Jordan and Manny Ramirez. A special card picturing Tom Selleck and Frank Thomas, commemorating the forgettable movie "Mr. Baseball", was randomly inserted into high series packs. A standard-size Ted Williams hologram card was randomly inserted into low series packs. By mailing in 15 low series foil wrappers, a completed order form, and a handling fee, the collector could receive an 8 1/2" by 11" numbered, black and white lithograph picturing Ted Williams in his batting swing.

Nm-Mt Ex-Mt
COMPLETE SET (800) 25.00 7.50
COMPLETE LO SET (700) 20.00 6.00
COMPLETE HI SET (100) 5.00 1.50
1 Ryan Klesko CL .25 .07
Jim Thome
2 Royce Clayton SR .05 .02
3 Brian Jordan SR RC .50 .15
4 Dave Fleming SR .05 .02
5 Jim Thome SR .25 .07
6 Jeff Juden SR .05 .02
7 Roberto Hernandez SR .05 .02
8 Kyle Abbott SR .05 .02
9 Chris George SR .05 .02
10 Rob Maurer SR .05 .02
11 Donald Harris SR .05 .02
12 Ted Wood SR .05 .02
13 Patrick Lennon SR .05 .02
14 Willie Banks SR .05 .02
15 Roger Salkeld SR UER .05 .02
(Bill was his grand-
father, not his father)
16 Wil Cordero SR .05 .02
17 Arthur Rhodes SR .05 .02
18 Pedro Martinez SR 1.00 .30
19 Andy Ashby SR .05 .02
20 Tom Goodwin SR .05 .02
21 Braulio Castillo SR .05 .02
22 Todd Van Poppel SR .05 .02
23 Brian Williams SR RC .05 .02
24 Ryan Klesko SR .10 .03
25 Kenny Lofton SR .25 .07
26 Derek Bell SR .10 .03
27 Reggie Sanders SR .10 .03
28 Dave Winfield's 400th .05 .02
29 David Justice TC .05 .02
30 Rob Dibble TC .05 .02
31 Craig Biggio TC .10 .03
32 Eddie Murray TC .15 .04
33 Fred McGriff TC .10 .03
34 Willie McGee TC .05 .02
35 Shawon Dunston TC .05 .02
36 Delino DeShields TC .05 .02
37 Howard Johnson TC .05 .02
38 John Kruk TC .05 .02
39 Doug Drabek TC .05 .02
40 Todd Zeile TC .05 .02
41 Steve Avery .05 .02
Playoff Perfection
42 Jeremy Hernandez RC .05 .02
43 Doug Henry RC .10 .03
44 Chris Donnels .05 .02
45 Mo Sanford .05 .02
46 Scott Kamieniecki .05 .02
47 Mark Lemke .05 .02
48 Steve Farr .05 .02
49 Francisco Oliveras .05 .02
50 Ced Landrum .05 .02
51 Rondell White CL .10 .03
Mark Newfield
52 Eduardo Perez TP RC .25 .07
53 Tom Nevers TP .05 .02
54 David Zancanaro TP .05 .02
55 Shawn Green TP RC 1.50 .45
56 Mark Wohlers TP .05 .02
57 Dave Nilsson TP .05 .02
58 Dmitri Young TP .10 .03
59 Ryan Hawblitzel TP RC .10 .03
60 Raul Mondesi TP .25 .07
61 Rondell White TP .10 .03
62 Steve Hosey TP .05 .02
63 Manny Ramirez TP RC 1.50 .45
64 Marc Newfield TP .05 .02
65 Jeromy Burnitz TP .10 .03
66 Mark Smith TP RC .10 .03
67 Joey Hamilton TP RC .25 .07
68 Tyler Green TP RC .10 .03
69 Jon Farrell TP RC .10 .03
70 Kurt Miller TP .05 .02
71 Jeff Plympton TP .05 .02
72 Dan Wilson TP .05 .02
73 Joe Vitiello TP RC .10 .03
74 Rico Brogna TP .05 .02
75 David McCarty TP RC .25 .07
76 Bob Wickman TP .05 .02
77 Carlos Rodriguez TP .05 .02
78 Jim Abbott .10 .03
Stay In School
79 Ramon Martinez .25 .07
Pedro Martinez
80 Kevin Mitchell .05 .02
Keith Mitchell
81 Sandy Alomar Jr. .10 .03
Roberto Alomar
82 Cal Ripken .50 .15
Billy Ripken
83 Tony Gwynn .15 .04
Chris Gwynn
84 Dwight Gooden .10 .03
Gary Sheffield
85 Ken Griffey Sr. .25 .07
Ken Griffey Jr.
Craig Griffey
86 Jim Abbott TC .10 .03
87 Frank Thomas TC .15 .04
88 Danny Tartabull TC .05 .02
89 Scott Erickson TC .05 .02
90 Rickey Henderson TC .15 .04
91 Edgar Martinez TC .10 .03
92 Nolan Ryan TC .50 .15
93 Ben McDonald TC .05 .02
94 Ellis Burks TC .05 .02
95 Greg Swindell TC .05 .02
96 Cecil Fielder TC .05 .02
97 Greg Vaughn TC .05 .02
98 Kevin Maas TC .05 .02
99 Dave Stieb TC .05 .02
100 Checklist 1-100 .05 .02
101 Joe Oliver .05 .02
102 Hector Villanueva .05 .02
103 Ed Whitson .05 .02
104 Danny Jackson .05 .02
105 Chris Hammond .05 .02
106 Ricky Jordan .05 .02
107 Kevin Bass .05 .02
108 Darrin Fletcher .05 .02
109 Junior Ortiz .05 .02
110 Tom Bolton .05 .02
111 Jeff King .05 .02
112 Dave Magadan .05 .02
113 Mike LaValliere .05 .02
114 Hubie Brooks .05 .02
115 Jay Bell .10 .03
116 David Wells .10 .03
117 Jim Leyritz .05 .02
118 Manuel Lee .05 .02
119 Alvaro Espinoza .05 .02
120 B.J. Surhoff .10 .03
121 Hal Morris .05 .02
122 Shawon Dawson .05 .02
123 Chris Sabo .05 .02
124 Andre Dawson .10 .03
125 Eric Davis .10 .03
126 Chili Davis .10 .03
127 Dale Murphy .25 .07
128 Kirk McCaskill .05 .02
129 Terry Mulholland .05 .02
130 Rick Aguilera .10 .03
131 Vince Coleman .05 .02
132 Andy Van Slyke .10 .03
133 Gregg Jefferies .05 .02
134 Barry Bonds .60 .18
135 Dwight Gooden .15 .04
136 Dave Stieb .05 .02
137 Albert Belle .10 .03
138 Teddy Higuera .05 .02
139 Jesse Barfield .05 .02
140 Pat Borders .05 .02
141 Bip Roberts .05 .02
142 Rob Dibble .10 .03
143 Mark Grace .15 .04
144 Barry Larkin .25 .07
145 Ryne Sandberg .40 .12
146 Scott Erickson .05 .02
147 Luis Polonia .05 .02
148 John Burkett .05 .02
149 Luis Sojo .05 .02
150 Dickie Thon .05 .02
151 Walt Weiss .05 .02
152 Mike Scioscia .05 .02
153 Mark McGwire .60 .18
154 Matt Williams .10 .03
155 Rickey Henderson .25 .07
156 Sandy Alomar Jr. .05 .02
157 Brian McRae .05 .02
158 Harold Baines .10 .03
159 Kevin Appier .10 .03
160 Felix Fermin .05 .02
161 Leo Gomez .05 .02
162 Craig Biggio .15 .04
163 Ben McDonald .05 .02
164 Randy Johnson .25 .07
165 Cal Ripken .75 .23
166 Frank Thomas .25 .07
167 Delino DeShields .05 .02
168 Greg Gagne .05 .02
169 Ron Karkovice .05 .02
170 Charlie Leibrandt .05 .02
171 Dave Righetti .10 .03
172 Dave Henderson .05 .02
173 Steve Decker .05 .02
174 Darryl Strawberry .15 .04
175 Will Clark .25 .07
176 Ruben Sierra .05 .02
177 Ozzie Smith .40 .12
178 Charles Nagy .05 .02
179 Gary Pettis .05 .02
180 Kirk Gibson .10 .03
181 Randy Milligan .05 .02
182 Dave Valle .05 .02
183 Chris Hoiles .05 .02
184 Tony Phillips .05 .02
185 Brady Anderson .10 .03
186 Scott Fletcher .05 .02
187 Gene Larkin .05 .02
188 Lance Johnson .05 .02
189 Greg Olson .05 .02
190 Melido Perez .05 .02
191 Lenny Harris .05 .02
192 Terry Kennedy .05 .02
193 Mike Gallego .05 .02
194 Willie McGee .10 .03
195 Juan Samuel .05 .02
196 Jeff Huson .10 .03
(Shows Jose Canseco
sliding into second)
197 Alex Cole .05 .02
198 Ron Robinson .05 .02
199 Joel Skinner .05 .02
200 Checklist 101-200 .05 .02
201 Kevin Reimer .05 .02
202 Stan Belinda .05 .02
203 Pat Tabler .05 .02
204 Jose Guzman .05 .02
205 Jose Lind .05 .02
206 Spike Owen .05 .02
207 Joe Orsulak .05 .02
208 Charlie Hayes .05 .02
209 Mike Devereaux .05 .02
210 Mike Fitzgerald .05 .02
211 Willie Randolph .10 .03
212 Rod Nichols .05 .02
213 Mike Boddicker .05 .02
214 Bill Spiers .05 .02
215 Steve Olin .05 .02
216 David Howard .05 .02
217 Gary Varsho .05 .02
218 Mike Harkey .05 .02
219 Luis Aquino .05 .02
220 Chuck McElroy .05 .02
221 Doug Drabek .05 .02
222 Dave Winfield .10 .03
223 Rafael Palmeiro .15 .04
224 Joe Carter .10 .03
225 Bobby Bonilla .10 .03
226 Ivan Calderon .05 .02
227 Gregg Olson .05 .02
228 Tim Wallach .05 .02
229 Terry Pendleton .10 .03
230 Gilberto Reyes .05 .02
231 Carlos Baerga .05 .02
232 Greg Vaughn .10 .03
233 Bret Saberhagen .10 .03
234 Gary Sheffield .10 .03
235 Mark Lewis .05 .02
236 George Bell .05 .02
237 Danny Tartabull .05 .02
238 Willie Wilson .05 .02
239 Doug Dascenzo .05 .02
240 Bill Pecota .05 .02
241 Julio Franco .10 .03
242 Ed Sprague .10 .03
243 Juan Gonzalez .25 .07
244 Chuck Finley .10 .03
245 Ivan Rodriguez .25 .07
246 Len Dykstra .10 .03
247 Deion Sanders .15 .04
248 Dwight Evans .10 .03
249 Larry Walker .15 .04
250 Billy Ripken .05 .02
251 Mickey Tettleton .05 .02
252 Tony Pena .05 .02
253 Benito Santiago .10 .03
254 Kirby Puckett .25 .07
255 Cecil Fielder .10 .03
256 Howard Johnson .05 .02
257 Andujar Cedeno .05 .02
258 Jose Rijo .05 .02
259 Al Osuna .05 .02
260 Todd Hundley .05 .02
261 Orel Hershiser .10 .03
262 Ray Lankford .10 .03
263 Robin Ventura .10 .03
264 Felix Jose .05 .02
265 Eddie Murray .25 .07
266 Kevin Mitchell .05 .02
267 Gary Carter .15 .04
268 Mike Benjamin .05 .02
269 Dick Schofield .05 .02
270 Jose Uribe .05 .02
271 Pete Incaviglia .05 .02
272 Tony Fernandez .05 .02
273 Alan Trammell .15 .04
274 Tony Gwynn .30 .09
275 Mike Greenwell .05 .02
276 Jeff Bagwell .25 .07
277 Frank Viola .10 .03
278 Randy Myers .05 .02
279 Ken Caminiti .10 .03
280 Bill Doran .05 .02
281 Dan Pasqua .05 .02
282 Alfredo Griffin .05 .02
283 Jose Oquendo .05 .02
284 Kal Daniels .05 .02
285 Bobby Thigpen .05 .02
286 Robby Thompson .05 .02
287 Mark Eichhorn .05 .02

288 Mike Felder .05 .02
289 Dave Gallagher .05 .02
290 Dave Anderson .05 .02
291 Mel Hall .05 .02
292 Jerald Clark .05 .02
293 Al Newman .05 .02
294 Rob Deer .05 .02
295 Matt Nokes .05 .02
296 Jack Armstrong .05 .02
297 Jim Deshaies .05 .02
298 Jeff Innis .05 .02
299 Jeff Reed .05 .02
300 Checklist 201-300 .05 .02
301 Lonnie Smith .05 .02
302 Jimmy Key .10 .03
303 Junior Felix .05 .02
304 Mike Heath .05 .02
305 Mark Langston .05 .02
306 Greg W. Harris .05 .02
307 Brett Butler .10 .03
308 Luis Rivera .05 .02
309 Bruce Ruffin .05 .02
310 Paul Faries .05 .02
311 Terry Leach .05 .02
312 Scott Brosius RC .40 .12
313 Scott Leius .05 .02
314 Harold Reynolds .10 .03
315 Jack Morris .10 .03
316 David Segui .05 .02
317 Bill Gullickson .05 .02
318 Todd Frohwirth .05 .02
319 Mark Leiter .05 .02
320 Jeff M. Robinson .05 .02
321 Gary Gaetti .10 .03
322 John Smoltz .15 .04
323 Andy Benes .05 .02
324 Kelly Gruber .05 .02
325 Jim Abbott .15 .04
326 John Kruk .10 .03
327 Kevin Seitzer .05 .02
328 Darrin Jackson .05 .02
329 Kurt Stillwell .05 .02
330 Mike Maddux .05 .02
331 Dennis Eckersley .10 .03
332 Dan Gladden .05 .02
333 Jose Canseco .25 .07
334 Kent Hrbek .10 .03
335 Ken Griffey Sr. .10 .03
336 Greg Swindell .05 .02
337 Trevor Wilson .05 .02
338 Sam Horn .05 .02
339 Mike Henneman .05 .02
340 Jerry Browne .05 .02
341 Glenn Braggs .05 .02
342 Tom Glavine .15 .04
343 Wally Joyner .10 .03
344 Fred McGriff .15 .04
345 Ron Gant .10 .03
346 Ramon Martinez .05 .02
347 Wes Chamberlain .05 .02
348 Terry Shumpert .05 .02
349 Tim Teufel .05 .02
350 Wally Backman .05 .02
351 Joe Girardi .05 .02
352 Devon White .05 .02
353 Greg Maddux .40 .12
354 Ryan Bowen .05 .02
355 Roberto Alomar .25 .07
356 Don Mattingly .60 .18
357 Pedro Guerrero .10 .03
358 Steve Sax .05 .02
359 Joey Cora .05 .02
360 Jim Gantner .05 .02
361 Brian Barnes .05 .02
362 Kevin McReynolds .05 .02
363 Bret Barberie .05 .02
364 David Cone .10 .03
365 Dennis Martinez .10 .03
366 Brian Hunter .05 .02
367 Edgar Martinez .15 .04
368 Steve Finley .10 .03
369 Greg Briley .05 .02
370 Jeff Blauser .05 .02
371 Todd Stottlemyre .05 .02
372 Luis Gonzalez .15 .04
373 Rick Wilkins .05 .02
374 Darryl Kile .10 .03
375 John Olerud .10 .03
376 Lee Smith .10 .03
377 Kevin Maas .05 .02
378 Dante Bichette .10 .03
379 Tom Pagnozzi .05 .02
380 Mike Flanagan .05 .02
381 Charlie O'Brien .05 .02
382 Dave Martinez .05 .02
383 Keith Miller .05 .02
384 Scott Ruskin .05 .02
385 Kevin Elster .05 .02
386 Alvin Davis .05 .02
387 Casey Candaele .05 .02
388 Pete O'Brien .05 .02
389 Jeff Treadway .05 .02
390 Scott Bradley .05 .02
391 Mookie Wilson .10 .03
392 Jimmy Jones .05 .02
393 Candy Maldonado .05 .02
394 Eric Yelding .05 .02
395 Tom Henke .05 .02
396 Franklin Stubbs .05 .02
397 Milt Thompson .05 .02
398 Mark Carreon .05 .02
399 Randy Velarde .05 .02
400 Checklist 301-400 .05 .02
401 Omar Vizquel .10 .03
402 Joe Boever .05 .02
403 Bill Krueger .05 .02
404 Jody Reed .05 .02
405 Mike Schooler .05 .02
406 Jason Grimsley .05 .02
407 Greg Myers .05 .02
408 Randy Ready .05 .02
409 Mike Timlin .05 .02
410 Mitch Williams .05 .02
411 Garry Templeton .05 .02
412 Greg Cadaret .05 .02
413 Donnie Hill .05 .02
414 Wally Whitehurst .05 .02
415 Scott Sanderson .05 .02
416 Thomas Howard .05 .02
417 Neal Heaton .05 .02
418 Charlie Hough .10 .03
419 Jack Howell .05 .02
420 Greg Hibbard .05 .02
421 Carlos Quintana .05 .02
422 Kim Batiste .05 .02
423 Paul Molitor .15 .04
424 Ken Griffey Jr. .40 .12
425 Phil Plantier .05 .02
426 Denny Neagle .10 .03
427 Von Hayes .05 .02
428 Shane Mack .05 .02
429 Darren Daulton .10 .03
430 Dwayne Henry .05 .02
431 Lance Parrish .10 .03
432 Mike Humphreys .05 .02
433 Tim Burke .05 .02
434 Bryan Harvey .05 .02
435 Pat Kelly .05 .02
436 Ozzie Guillen .05 .02
437 Bruce Hurst .05 .02
438 Sammy Sosa .40 .12
439 Dennis Rasmussen .05 .02
440 Ken Patterson .05 .02
441 Jay Buhner .10 .03
442 Pat Combs .05 .02
443 Wade Boggs .15 .04
444 George Brett .60 .18
445 Mo Vaughn .10 .03
446 Chuck Knoblauch .10 .03
447 Tom Candiotti .05 .02
448 Mark Portugal .05 .02
449 Mickey Morandini .05 .02
450 Duane Ward .05 .02
451 Otis Nixon .05 .02
452 Bob Welch .05 .02
453 Rusty Meacham .05 .02
454 Keith Mitchell .05 .02
455 Marquis Grissom .05 .02
456 Robin Yount .40 .12
457 Harvey Pulliam .05 .02
458 Jose DeLeon .05 .02
459 Mark Gubicza .05 .02
460 Darryl Hamilton .05 .02
461 Tom Browning .05 .02
462 Monty Fariss .05 .02
463 Jerome Walton .05 .02
464 Paul O'Neill .15 .04
465 Dean Palmer .10 .03
466 Travis Fryman .10 .03
467 John Smiley .05 .02
468 Lloyd Moseby .05 .02
469 John Wehner .05 .02
470 Skeeter Barnes .05 .02
471 Steve Chitren .05 .02
472 Kent Mercker .05 .02
473 Terry Steinbach .05 .02
474 Andres Galarraga .10 .03
475 Steve Avery .05 .02
476 Tom Gordon .05 .02
477 Cal Eldred .05 .02
478 Omar Olivares .05 .02
479 Julio Machado .05 .02
480 Bob Milacki .05 .02
481 Les Lancaster .05 .02
482 John Candelaria .05 .02
483 Brian Downing .05 .02
484 Roger McDowell .05 .02
485 Scott Scudder .05 .02
486 Zane Smith .05 .02
487 John Cerutti .05 .02
488 Steve Buechele .05 .02
489 Paul Gibson .05 .02
490 Curtis Wilkerson .05 .02
491 Marvin Freeman .05 .02
492 Tom Foley .05 .02
493 Juan Berenguer .05 .02
494 Ernest Riles .05 .02
495 Sid Bream .05 .02
496 Chuck Crim .05 .02
497 Mike Macfarlane .05 .02
498 Dale Sveum .05 .02
499 Storm Davis .05 .02
500 Checklist 401-500 .05 .02
501 Jeff Reardon .10 .03
502 Shawn Abner .05 .02
503 Tony Fossas .05 .02
504 Cory Snyder .05 .02
505 Matt Young .05 .02
506 Allan Anderson .05 .02
507 Mark Lee .05 .02
508 Gene Nelson .05 .02
509 Mike Pagliarulo .05 .02
510 Rafael Belliard .05 .02
511 Jay Howell .05 .02
512 Bob Tewksbury .05 .02
513 Mike Morgan .05 .02
514 John Franco .10 .03
515 Kevin Gross .05 .02
516 Lou Whitaker .10 .03
517 Orlando Merced .05 .02
518 Todd Benzinger .05 .02
519 Gary Redus .05 .02
520 Walt Terrell .05 .02
521 Jack Clark .10 .03
522 Dave Parker .10 .03
523 Tim Naehring .05 .02
524 Mark Whiten .05 .02
525 Ellis Burks .10 .03
526 Frank Castillo .05 .02
527 Brian Harper .05 .02
528 Brook Jacoby .05 .02
529 Rick Sutcliffe .10 .03
530 Joe Klink .05 .02
531 Terry Bross .05 .02
532 Jose Offerman .05 .02
533 Todd Zeile .05 .02
534 Eric Karros .10 .03
535 Anthony Young .05 .02
536 Milt Cuyler .05 .02
537 Randy Tomlin .05 .02
538 Scott Livingstone .05 .02
539 Jim Eisenreich .05 .02
540 Don Slaught .05 .02
541 Scott Cooper .05 .02
542 Joe Grahe .05 .02
543 Tom Brunansky .05 .02
544 Eddie Zosky .05 .02
545 Roger Clemens .50 .15
546 David Justice .10 .03
547 Dave Stewart .10 .03
548 David West .05 .02
549 Dave Smith .05 .02
550 Dan Plesac .05 .02
551 Alex Fernandez .05 .02
552 Bernard Gilkey .05 .02
553 Jack McDowell .05 .02
554 Tino Martinez .15 .04
555 Bo Jackson .25 .07
556 Bernie Williams .15 .04
557 Mark Gardner .05 .02
558 Glenallen Hill .05 .02
559 Oil Can Boyd .05 .02
560 Chris James .05 .02
561 Scott Servais .05 .02
562 Rey Sanchez RC .25 .07
563 Paul McClellan .05 .02
564 Andy Mota .05 .02
565 Darren Lewis .05 .02
566 Jose Melendez .05 .02
567 Tommy Greene .05 .02
568 Rich Rodriguez .05 .02
569 Heathcliff Slocumb .05 .02
570 Joe Hesketh .05 .02
571 Carlton Fisk .15 .04
572 Erik Hanson .05 .02
573 Wilson Alvarez .05 .02
574 Rheal Cormier .05 .02
575 Tim Raines .10 .03
576 Bobby Witt .05 .02
577 Roberto Kelly .05 .02
578 Kevin Brown .10 .03
579 Chris Nabholz .05 .02
580 Jesse Orosco .05 .02
581 Jeff Brantley .05 .02
582 Rafael Ramirez .05 .02
583 Kelly Downs .05 .02
584 Mike Simms .05 .02
585 Mike Remlinger .05 .02
586 Dave Hollins .05 .02
587 Larry Andersen .05 .02
588 Mike Gardiner .05 .02
589 Craig Lefferts .05 .02
590 Paul Assenmacher .05 .02
591 Bryn Smith .05 .02
592 Donn Pall .05 .02
593 Mike Jackson .05 .02
594 Scott Radinsky .05 .02
595 Brian Holman .05 .02
596 Geronimo Pena .05 .02
597 Mike Jeffcoat .05 .02
598 Carlos Martinez .05 .02
599 Geno Petralli .05 .02
600 Checklist 501-600 .05 .02
601 Jerry Don Gleaton .05 .02
602 Adam Peterson .05 .02
603 Craig Grebeck .05 .02
604 Mark Guthrie .05 .02
605 Frank Tanana .05 .02
606 Hensley Meulens .05 .02
607 Mark Davis .05 .02
608 Eric Plunk .05 .02
609 Mark Williamson .05 .02
610 Lee Guetterman .05 .02
611 Bobby Rose .05 .02
612 Bill Wegman .05 .02
613 Mike Hartley .05 .02
614 Chris Beasley .05 .02
615 Chris Bosio .05 .02
616 Henry Cotto .05 .02
617 Chico Walker .05 .02
618 Russ Swan .05 .02
619 Bob Walk .05 .02
620 Bill Swift .05 .02
621 Warren Newson .05 .02
622 Steve Bedrosian .05 .02
623 Ricky Bones .05 .02
624 Kevin Tapani .05 .02
625 Juan Guzman .05 .02
626 Jeff Johnson .05 .02
627 Jeff Montgomery .05 .02
628 Ken Hill .05 .02
629 Gary Thurman .05 .02
630 Steve Howe .05 .02
631 Jose DeJesus .05 .02
632 Kirk Dressendorfer .05 .02
633 Jaime Navarro .05 .02
634 Lee Stevens .05 .02
635 Pete Harnisch .05 .02
636 Bill Landrum .05 .02
637 Rich DeLucia .05 .02
638 Luis Salazar .05 .02
639 Rob Murphy .05 .02
640 Jose Canseco CL .15 .04
Rickey Henderson
641 Roger Clemens DS .25 .07
642 Jim Abbott DS .10 .03
643 Travis Fryman DS .05 .02
644 Jesse Barfield DS .05 .02
645 Cal Ripken DS .40 .12
646 Wade Boggs DS .10 .03
647 Cecil Fielder DS .05 .02
648 Rickey Henderson DS .15 .04
649 Jose Canseco DS .10 .03
650 Ken Griffey Jr. DS .25 .07
651 Kenny Rogers .10 .03
652 Luis Mercedes .05 .02
653 Mike Stanton .05 .02
654 Glenn Davis .05 .02
655 Nolan Ryan 1.00 .30
656 Reggie Jefferson .05 .02
657 Javier Ortiz .05 .02
658 Greg A. Harris .05 .02
659 Mariano Duncan .05 .02
660 Jeff Shaw .05 .02
661 Mike Moore .05 .02
662 Chris Haney .05 .02
663 Joe Slusarski .05 .02
664 Wayne Housie .05 .02
665 Carlos Garcia .05 .02
666 Bob Ojeda .05 .02
667 Bryan Hickerson RC .10 .03
668 Tim Belcher .05 .02
669 Ron Darling .05 .02
670 Rex Hudler .05 .02
671 Sid Fernandez .05 .02
672 Chito Martinez .05 .02
673 Pete Schourek .05 .02
674 Armando Reynoso RC .25 .07
675 Mike Mussina .25 .07
676 Kevin Morton .05 .02
677 Norm Charlton .05 .02
678 Danny Darwin .05 .02
679 Eric King .05 .02
680 Ted Power .05 .02
681 Barry Jones .05 .02
682 Carney Lansford .10 .03
683 Mel Rojas .05 .02
684 Rick Honeycutt .05 .02
685 Jeff Fassero .05 .02
686 Cris Carpenter .05 .02
687 Tim Crews .05 .02
688 Scott Terry .05 .02
689 Chris Gwynn .05 .02
690 Gerald Perry .05 .02
691 John Barfield .05 .02
692 Bob Melvin .05 .02
693 Juan Agosto .05 .02
694 Alejandro Pena .05 .02
695 Jeff Russell .05 .02
696 Carmelo Martinez .05 .02
697 Bud Black .05 .02
698 Dave Otto .05 .02
699 Billy Hatcher .05 .02
700 Checklist 601-700 .05 .02
701 Clemente Nunez RC .05 .02
702 Mark Clark .05 .02
Donovan Osborne
Brian Jordan
703 Mike Morgan .05 .02
704 Keith Miller .05 .02
705 Kurt Stillwell .05 .02
706 Damon Berryhill .05 .02
707 Von Hayes .05 .02
708 Rick Sutcliffe .10 .03
709 Hubie Brooks .05 .02
710 Ryan Turner RC .10 .03
711 Barry Bonds CL .30 .09
Andy Van Slyke
712 Jose Rijo DS .05 .02
713 Tom Glavine DS .10 .03
714 Shawon Dunston DS .05 .02
715 Andy Van Slyke DS .05 .02
716 Ozzie Smith DS .25 .07
717 Tony Gwynn DS .15 .04
718 Will Clark DS .10 .03
719 Marquis Grissom DS .05 .02
720 Howard Johnson DS .05 .02
721 Barry Bonds DS .30 .09
722 Kirk McCaskill .05 .02
723 Sammy Sosa .75 .23
724 George Bell .05 .02
725 Gregg Jefferies .05 .02
726 Gary DiSarcina .05 .02
727 Mike Bordick .05 .02
728 Eddie Murray 400 HR .15 .04
729 Rene Gonzales .05 .02
730 Mike Bielecki .05 .02
731 Calvin Jones .05 .02
732 Jack Morris .10 .03
733 Frank Viola .10 .03
734 Dave Winfield .10 .03
735 Kevin Mitchell .05 .02
736 Bill Swift .05 .02
737 Dan Gladden .05 .02
738 Mike Jackson .05 .02
739 Mark Carreon .05 .02
740 Kirt Manwaring .05 .02
741 Randy Myers .05 .02
742 Kevin McReynolds .05 .02
743 Steve Sax .05 .02
744 Wally Joyner .10 .03
745 Gary Sheffield .10 .03
746 Danny Tartabull .05 .02
747 Julio Valera .05 .02
748 Denny Neagle .10 .03
749 Lance Blankenship .05 .02
750 Mike Gallego .05 .02
751 Bret Saberhagen .10 .03
752 Ruben Amaro .05 .02
753 Eddie Murray .25 .07
754 Kyle Abbott .05 .02
755 Bobby Bonilla .10 .03
756 Eric Davis .10 .03
757 Eddie Taubensee RC .25 .07
758 Andres Galarraga .10 .03
759 Pete Incaviglia .05 .02
760 Tom Candiotti .05 .02
761 Tim Belcher .05 .02
762 Ricky Bones .05 .02
763 Bip Roberts .05 .02
764 Pedro Munoz .05 .02
765 Greg Swindell .05 .02
766 Kenny Lofton .25 .07
767 Gary Carter .15 .04
768 Charlie Hayes .05 .02
769 Dickie Thon .05 .02
770 D. Osborne DD CL .05 .02
771 Bret Boone DD .25 .07
772 A. Cianfrocco DD RC .10 .03
773 Mark Clark DD RC .10 .03
774 Chad Curtis DD RC .25 .07
775 Pat Listach DD RC .25 .07
776 Pat Mahomes DD RC .25 .07
777 Donovan Osborne DD .05 .02
778 John Patterson DD RC .10 .03
779 Andy Stankiewicz DD .05 .02
780 Turk Wendell DD RC .25 .07
781 Bill Krueger .05 .02
782 Rickey Henderson 1000 .15 .04
783 Kevin Seitzer .05 .02
784 Dave Martinez .05 .02
785 John Smiley .05 .02
786 Matt Stairs RC .25 .07
787 Scott Scudder .05 .02
788 John Wetteland .10 .03
789 Jack Armstrong .05 .02
790 Ken Hill .05 .02
791 Dick Schofield .05 .02
792 Mariano Duncan .05 .02
793 Bill Pecota .05 .02
794 Mike Kelly RC .10 .03
795 Willie Randolph .10 .03
796 Butch Henry .05 .02
797 Carlos Hernandez .05 .02
798 Doug Jones .05 .02
799 Melido Perez .05 .02
800 Checklist 701-800 .05 .02
HH2 T.Williams Hologram 2.00 .60
Top left corner says
91 Upper Deck 92
SP3 Deion Sanders FB/BB 1.00 .30
SP4 Tom Selleck 1.00 .30
Frank Thomas SP
(Mr. Baseball)

1992 Upper Deck Gold Hologram

All cards issued in 1992 Upper Deck factory sets have a gold hologram on the back.

	Nm-Mt	Ex-Mt
COMP.FACT.SET (800)	25.00	7.50
*STARS: .4X TO 1X BASIC CARDS		
*ROOKIES: .4X TO 1X BASIC		

1992 Upper Deck Bench/Morgan Heroes

This standard size 10-card set was randomly inserted in 1992 Upper Deck high number packs. Both Bench and Morgan autographed 2,500 of card number 45, which displays a portrait by sports artist Vernon Wells. The fronts feature color photos of Bench (37-39), Morgan (40-42), or both (43-44) at various stages of their baseball careers.

	Nm-Mt	Ex-Mt
COMPLETE SET (10)	15.00	4.50
COMMON CARD (37-45)	1.50	.45
NNO Baseball Heroes SP (Header card)	2.50	.75
AU5 Johnny Bench and Joe Morgan AU (Signed and Numbered of 2500)	100.00	30.00

1992 Upper Deck College POY Holograms

This three-card standard-size set was randomly inserted in 1992 Upper Deck high series foil packs. This set features College Player of the Year winners for 1989 through 1991. The cards are numbered on the back with the prefix "CP".

	Nm-Mt	Ex-Mt
COMPLETE SET (3)	2.00	.60
CP1 David McCarty	1.00	.30
CP2 Mike Kelly	1.00	.30
CP3 Ben McDonald	1.00	.30

1992 Upper Deck Heroes of Baseball

Continuing a popular insert set introduced the previous year, Upper Deck produced four new commemorative cards, including three player cards and one portrait card by sports artist Vernon Wells. These cards were randomly inserted in 1992 Upper Deck baseball low number foil packs. Three thousand of each card were personally numbered and autographed by each player.

	Nm-Mt	Ex-Mt
H5 Vida Blue	2.00	.60
H6 Lou Brock	2.00	.60
H7 Rollie Fingers	2.00	.60
H8 Vida Blue ART Lou Brock Rollie Fingers	2.00	.60
AU5 Vida Blue AU/3000	15.00	4.50
AU6 Lou Brock AU/3000	25.00	7.50
AU7 R.Fingers AU/3000	15.00	4.50

1992 Upper Deck Heroes Highlights

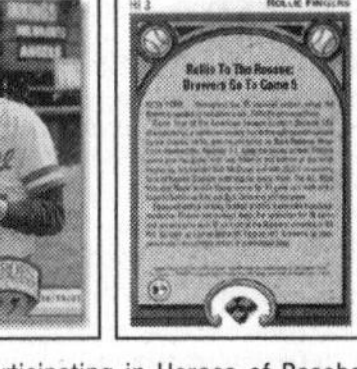

To dealers participating in Heroes of Baseball Collectors shows, Upper Deck made available this ten-card insert standard-size set, which commemorates one of the greatest moments in the careers of ten of baseball's all-time players. The cards were primarily randomly inserted in high number packs sold at these shows. However at the first Heroes show in Anaheim, the cards were inserted into low number packs. The fronts feature color player photos with a shadowed strip for a three-dimensional effect. The player's name and the date of the great moment in the hero's career appear with a "Heroes Highlights" logo in a bottom border of varying shades of brown and blue-green. The backs have white borders and display a blue-green and brown bordered monument design accented with baseballs. The major portion of the design is parchment-textured and contains text highlighting a special moment in the player's career. The cards are numbered on the back with an "HI" prefix. The card numbering follows alphabetical order by player's name.

	Nm-Mt	Ex-Mt
COMPLETE SET (10)	15.00	4.50
HI1 Bobby Bonds	.50	.15
HI2 Lou Brock	3.00	.90
HI3 Rollie Fingers	2.00	.60
HI4 Bob Gibson	3.00	.90
HI5 Reggie Jackson	4.00	1.20
HI6 Gaylord Perry	2.00	.60
HI7 Robin Roberts	2.00	.60
HI8 Brooks Robinson	4.00	1.20
HI9 Billy Williams	2.00	.60
HI10 Ted Williams	6.00	1.80

1992 Upper Deck Home Run Heroes

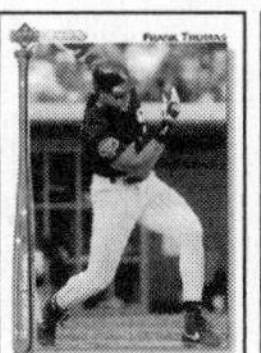

This 26-card standard-size set was inserted one per pack into 1992 Upper Deck low series jumbo packs. The set spotlights the 1991 home run leaders from each of the 26 Major League teams.

	Nm-Mt	Ex-Mt
COMPLETE SET (26)	12.00	3.60
HR1 Jose Canseco	.75	.23
HR2 Cecil Fielder	.30	.09
HR3 Howard Johnson	.15	.04
HR4 Cal Ripken	2.50	.75
HR5 Matt Williams	.30	.09
HR6 Joe Carter	.30	.09
HR7 Ron Gant	.30	.09
HR8 Frank Thomas	.75	.23
HR9 Andre Dawson	.30	.09
HR10 Fred McGriff	.50	.15
HR11 Danny Tartabull	.15	.04
HR12 Chili Davis	.30	.09
HR13 Albert Belle	.30	.09
HR14 Jack Clark	.30	.09
HR15 Paul O'Neill	.50	.15
HR16 Darryl Strawberry	.50	.15
HR17 Dave Winfield	.30	.09
HR18 Jay Buhner	.30	.09
HR19 Juan Gonzalez	.75	.23
HR20 Greg Vaughn	.30	.09
HR21 Barry Bonds	2.00	.60
HR22 Matt Nokes	.15	.04
HR23 John Kruk	.30	.09
HR24 Ivan Calderon	.15	.04
HR25 Jeff Bagwell	.75	.23
HR26 Todd Zeile	.15	.04

1992 Upper Deck Scouting Report

Inserted one per high series jumbo pack, cards from this 25-card standard-size set feature outstanding prospects in baseball. Please note these cards are highly condition sensitive and are priced below in NmMt condition. Mint copies trade for premiums.

	Nm-Mt	Ex-Mt
COMPLETE SET (25)	20.00	6.00
SR1 Andy Ashby	1.00	.30
SR2 Willie Banks	1.00	.30
SR3 Kim Batiste	1.00	.30
SR4 Derek Bell	1.00	.30
SR5 Archi Cianfrocco	1.00	.30
SR6 Royce Clayton	1.00	.30
SR7 Gary DiSarcina	1.00	.30
SR8 Dave Fleming	1.00	.30
SR9 Butch Henry	1.00	.30
SR10 Todd Hundley	1.00	.30
SR11 Brian Jordan	2.00	.60
SR12 Eric Karros	1.00	.30
SR13 Pat Listach	1.00	.30
SR14 Scott Livingstone	1.00	.30
SR15 Kenny Lofton	1.00	.30
SR16 Pat Mahomes	1.00	.30
SR17 Denny Neagle	1.00	.30
SR18 Dave Nilsson	1.00	.30
SR19 Donovan Osborne	1.00	.30
SR20 Reggie Sanders	1.00	.30
SR21 Andy Stankiewicz	1.00	.30
SR22 Jim Thome	2.00	.60
SR23 Julio Valera	1.00	.30
SR24 Mark Wohlers	1.00	.30
SR25 Anthony Young	1.00	.30

1992 Upper Deck Williams Best

This 20-card standard-size set contains Ted Williams' choices of best current and future hitters in the game. The cards were randomly inserted in Upper Deck high number foil packs. These cards are condition sensitive and priced below in NmMt condition. True mint condition copies do sell for more than these listed prices.

	Nm-Mt	Ex-Mt
COMPLETE SET (20)	20.00	6.00
T1 Wade Boggs	.75	.23
T2 Barry Bonds	3.00	.90
T3 Jose Canseco	1.25	.35
T4 Will Clark	1.25	.35
T5 Cecil Fielder	.50	.15
T6 Tony Gwynn	1.50	.45
T7 Rickey Henderson	1.25	.35
T8 Fred McGriff	.75	.23
T9 Kirby Puckett	1.25	.35
T10 Ruben Sierra	.25	.07
T11 Roberto Alomar	1.25	.35
T12 Jeff Bagwell	1.25	.35
T13 Albert Belle	.50	.15
T14 Juan Gonzalez	1.25	.35
T15 Ken Griffey Jr.	2.00	.60
T16 Chris Hoiles	.25	.07
T17 David Justice	.50	.15
T18 Phil Plantier	.25	.07
T19 Frank Thomas	1.25	.35
T20 Robin Ventura	.50	.15

1992 Upper Deck Williams Heroes

This standard-size ten-card set was randomly inserted in 1992 Upper Deck low number foil packs. Williams autographed 2,500 of card 36, which displays his portrait by sports artist Vernon Wells. The cards are numbered on the back in continuation of the Upper Deck heroes series.

	Nm-Mt	Ex-Mt
COMPLETE SET (10)	6.00	1.80
COMMON (28-36)	.50	.15
NNO Baseball Heroes SP (Header card)	2.00	.60
AU4 Ted Williams (Signed and Numbered of 2500)	500.00	150.00

1992 Upper Deck Williams Wax Boxes

These eight oversized blank-backed "cards," measuring approximately 5 1/4" by 7 1/4", were featured on the bottom panels of 1992 Upper Deck low series wax boxes. They are identical in design to the Williams Heroes insert cards, displaying color player photos in an oval frame. These boxes are unnumbered. We have checklisted them below according to the numbering of the Heroes cards.

	Nm-Mt	Ex-Mt
COMMON CARD (28-35)	.50	.15

1992 Upper Deck FanFest

As a title sponsor of the 1992 All-Star FanFest in San Diego, Upper Deck produced this 54-card standard size set to commemorate past, present, and future All-Stars Heroes of Major League Baseball. Sixty sets were packaged in a case, and each case had at least one gold foil set. Cards 1-10 feature ten Future Heroes that are, in Upper Deck's opinion, sure bets to make an upcoming team; cards 11-44 present active All-Star alumni; and cards 45-54 salute All-Star Heroes of the past with ten fan favorites.

	Nm-Mt	Ex-Mt
COMP.FACT SET (54)	10.00	3.00
*GOLD: 10X VALUE		
1 Steve Avery	.10	.03
2 Ivan Rodriguez	.75	.23
3 Jeff Bagwell	.75	.23
4 Delino DeShields	.20	.06
5 Royce Clayton	.10	.03
6 Robin Ventura	.50	.15
7 Phil Plantier	.10	.03
8 Ray Lankford	.20	.06
9 Juan Gonzalez	.75	.23
10 Frank Thomas	1.00	.30
11 Roberto Alomar	.50	.15
12 Sandy Alomar Jr.	.20	.06
13 Wade Boggs	.75	.23
14 Barry Bonds	1.50	.45
15 Bobby Bonilla	.10	.03
16 George Brett	1.50	.45
17 Jose Canseco	.60	.18
18 Will Clark	.50	.15
19 Roger Clemens	1.50	.45
20 Eric Davis	.20	.06
21 Rob Dibble	.10	.03
22 Cecil Fielder	.20	.06
23 Dwight Gooden	.20	.06
24 Ken Griffey Jr.	2.00	.60
25 Tony Gwynn	1.50	.45
26 Bryan Harvey	.10	.03
27 Rickey Henderson	1.00	.30
28 Howard Johnson	.10	.03
29 Wally Joyner	.20	.06
30 Barry Larkin	.50	.15
31 Don Mattingly	1.50	.45
32 Mark McGwire	2.50	.75
33 Dale Murphy	.50	.15
34 Rafael Palmeiro	.50	.15
35 Kirby Puckett	.75	.23
36 Cal Ripken	3.00	.90
37 Nolan Ryan	3.00	.90
38 Chris Sabo	.10	.03
39 Ryne Sandberg	1.50	.45
40 Benito Santiago	.20	.06
41 Ruben Sierra	.20	.06
42 Ozzie Smith	1.50	.45
43 Darryl Strawberry	.20	.06
44 Robin Yount	.75	.23
45 Rollie Fingers	.20	.06
46 Reggie Jackson	.50	.15
47 Billy Williams	.20	.06
48 Lou Brock	.50	.15
49 Gaylord Perry	.20	.06
50 Ted Williams	3.00	.90
51 Brooks Robinson	.50	.15
52 Bob Gibson	.50	.15
53 Bobby Bonds	.20	.06
54 Robin Roberts	.20	.06

1992 Upper Deck Heroes of Baseball 5x7

This sheet measures approximately 5" by 7" and was distributed to herald the 1992 Heroes of Baseball sheets. Superimposed upon a black-and-white photo of Ted Williams, the back carries the dates and sites of the old-timers games at which the sheets were to be distributed. The front carries a story about the Baseball Assistance Team, (BAT) an organization that offers help to members of the baseball family who may have fallen on hard times. A total of 5,000 were produced.

	Nm-Mt	Ex-Mt
1 Ted Williams	50.00	15.00

1992 Upper Deck Sheets

The 35 commemorative sheets listed below in chronological order were issued by Upper Deck in 1992. The Upper Deck Heroes of Baseball made stops in all 26 MLB ballparks, as well as Mile High Stadium in Denver. They sponsored old-timer baseball games and donated $10,000 to the Baseball Assistance Team, a group dedicated to helping members of the baseball family that have fallen upon hard times. At each game a limited edition commemorative sheet was distributed. Four other commemorative sheets were produced in honor of other events. When the Orioles moved to Oriole Park at Camden Yards on April 6, Upper Deck distributed 17,000 individually numbered sheets free to fans. These sheets feature four artistic views of the new stadium. The first 1992 sheet listed below was issued at the Yankee Fan Festival held at the Jacob Javits Convention Center in New York Jan. 31-Feb. 2. Sheets 17 and 18 were issued at the All-Star Game in San Diego. Sheets 31 and 32 were inserted into retail repacks of eight 1992 Upper Deck foil packs. Displaying different player cards, sheets 33-34 are two different versions of the same sheet and list dates and locations of collectors shows. All the sheets measure 8 1/2" by 11" and most feature artist renderings of players from the teams recreated for the old-timers games. The front carries the individual production number out of the total number produced, but otherwise the sheets are unnumbered.

	Nm-Mt	Ex-Mt
COMPLETE SET (35)	250.00	75.00
1 Yankee Fan Festival Jan. 31-Feb. 2, 1992 12,500 Pictures regular-issue 1992 Upper Deck cards Don Mattingly Mel Hall Pat Kelly Matt Nokes Alvaro Espinoza Bernie Williams	15.00	4.50
2 Opening of Oriole Park at Camden Yards April 6, 1992 (17,000) Features four artist renderings of the Park	30.00	9.00
3 Toronto Blue Jays April 25, 1992 52,000) SkyDome Bob Bailor John Mayberry Rick Bosetti Balor Moore Garth Iorg	5.00	1.50
4 '72 Upper Deck Heroes vs. Atlanta Braves Heroes May 1, 1992 (22,000) Fulton County Coliseum Bruce Benedict Darrell Evans Glenn Hubbard Dave Johnson Reggie Jackson	8.00	2.40
5 Rangers Heroes vs. White Sox Heroes May 3, 1992 (22,000) Comiskey Park Bill Melton Dick Allen Wilbur Wood Carlos May Chuck Tanner MG	6.00	1.80
6 Silver Anniversary of the Impossible Dream May 16, 1992 (38,000) Fenway Park Jim Lonborg George Scott Carl Yastrzemski Tony Conigliaro Dick Williams MG	6.00	1.80
7 Nickname Heroes at the 'Stick May 17, 1992 (37,000) Candlestick Park Orlando Cepeda Jim Davenport Juan Marichal Dave Kingman John Montefusco	6.00	1.80
8 American League Heroes vs. National League Heroes May 30, 1992 (17,000) Astrodome Tony Oliva Joe Niekro Jose Cruz Mark Fidrych Jim Wynn	8.00	2.40
9 Harvey's Wallbangers May 30, 1992 (32,000) County Stadium Ben Oglivie Harvey Kuenn Cecil Cooper Gorman Thomas	6.00	1.80
10 30 Years of Mets Baseball June 13, 1992 (47,000) Shea Stadium Cleon Jones Bud Harrelson Rusty Staub Jerry Koosman Ed Kranepool	5.00	1.50
11 Cardinals' 100th Anniversary June 14, 1992 (22,000) Busch Stadium Red Schoendeinst Bob Gibson Enos Slaughter Lou Brock	10.00	3.00
12 N.L. Heroes vs. American League Heroes June 20. 1992 (47.000) Arlington Stadium former Texas Rangers Jim Sundberg Toby Harrah Jim Kern Al Oliver Jim Spencer	5.00	1.50
13 Record Setters June 21, 1992 (52,000) Anaheim Stadium Nolan Ryan Jim Abbott Jimmie Reese CO	15.00	4.50
14 Cubs Heroes vs. Reds Heroes June 28, 1992 (27,000) Riverfront Stadium George Foster Gary Nolan Pedro Borbon Cesar Cedeno Bernie Carbo	8.00	2.40
15 The Record-Setting Infield July 5, 1992 (62,000) Dodger Stadium Bill Russell Davey Lopes Steve Garvey Ron Cey	6.00	1.80
16 46th Annual Old-Timers Day Classic July 11, 1992 (50,000) Yankee Stadium Phil Rizzuto Bobby Brown Allie Reynolds Hank Bauer Tom Henrich	6.00	1.80
17 Heroes of Baseball All-Star Game July 13, 1992 (67,000) Jack Murphy Stadium Reggie Jackson Rollie Fingers Steve Garvey Brooks Robinson Bob Feller	8.00	2.40
18 All-Star Fanfest July 13, 1992 (12,000) Jack Murphy Stadium Larry Doby Steve Garvey Rollie Fingers This card measures 5 1/2" by 8 1/2".	15.00	4.50
19 All-Star Game Heroes July 18, 1992 (27,000) Three Rivers Stadium Kent Tekulve Frank Thomas Elroy Face Bob Veale Chuck Tanner	8.00	2.40
20 Royals HOF Inductees July 18-19, 1992 (42,000) Royal Stadium Fred Patek Joe Burke GM Larry Gura	5.00	1.50
21 More Than 100 Years of Baseball in Montreal July 26, 1992 (22,000) Olympic Stadium Claude Raymond Duke Snider Jean-Pierre Roy ANN Rusty Staub Steve Rogers	8.00	2.40
22 Seattle Mariners Heroes of Baseball July 26, 1992 Kingdome	6.00	1.80
23 A Tribute to Rocky Colavito Aug. 1, 1992 (22,000) Municipal Stadium	8.00	2.40
24 '70s A's vs. '76 Phillies Aug. 8, 1992 (44,000) Veterans Stadium Tug McGraw Steve Carlton Greg Luzinski Larry Bowa Dick Allen	8.00	2.40
25 Rollie Fingers Hall of Fame Day Aug. 9, 1992 (32,000) County Stadium	6.00	1.80
26 200 Club Aug. 9, 1992 (50,000) Camden Yards Luis Aparicio J.R. Richard Brooks Robinson Milt Pappas Bill Buckner	8.00	2.40
27 25th Anniversary of the Oakland Athletics Aug. 15, 1992 (22,000) Oakland-Alameda County Stadium Jim(Catfish) Hunter Reggie Jackson Rollie Fingers Vida Blue Bert Campaneris	10.00	3.00
28 Chicago Cubs August 16, 1982 Ron Santo Ernie Banks Randy Hundley Billy Williams Don Kessinger	5.00	1.50
29 Minnesota Twins World Series Heroes Aug. 23, 1992 (22,000) Metrodome Maury Wills Bob Gibson Zoilo Versalles Jim(Mudcat) Grant Tony Oliva	8.00	2.40
30 1972 Division Winners Detroit Tigers Aug. 30, 1992 (32,000) Bert Campaneris Aurelio Rodriguez Sparky Anderson MG Al Oliver	8.00	2.40
31 Upper Deck Authenticated Salutes The Legends Past, Present and Future Nov. 13-15, 1992 (18,000) Midwest Sports Collectors Show List of Tri-Star Sports, Inc. shows	5.00	1.50
32 50 Year Anniversary of the 1942 Triple Crown Season by Ted Williams (Numbered, but without total production number) Ted Williams	10.00	3.00
33 Upper Deck Honors Lou Brock Vida Blue Rollie Fingers 50,000	8.00	2.40
34 Upper Deck Heroes of Baseball Shows Rollie Fingers Reggie Jackson Gaylord Perry Brooks Robinson Ted Williams 76,400)	5.00	1.50
35 Upper Deck Heroes of Baseball Shows Bobby Bonds Lou Brock Bob Gibson Robin Roberts Billy Williams 76,400	5.00	1.50

1992 Upper Deck Team MVP Holograms

The 54 hologram cards in this standard size set feature the top offensive player and pitcher

from each Major League team plus two checklist cards. Only 216,000 number sets were produced, and each set was packaged in a custom-designed box with protective sleeve and included a numbered certificate. To display the set, Upper Deck also made available a custom album through a mail-in offer for 10.00. Cards 1-2 feature the AL and NL MVPs (with checklists) while cards 3-54 are arranged in alphabetical order.

Nm-Mt Ex-Mt
COMP. FACT SET (54) 15.00 4.50
1 Cal Ripken MVP CL 1.50 .45
2 Terry Pendleton MVP CL .10 .03
3 Jim Abbott .20 .06
4 Roberto Alomar .50 .15
5 Kevin Appier .20 .06
6 Steve Avery .10 .03
7 Jeff Bagwell .75 .23
8 Albert Belle .20 .06
9 Andy Benes .10 .03
10 Wade Boggs .75 .23
11 Barry Bonds 1.50 .45
12 George Brett 1.50 .45
13 Ivan Calderon .10 .03
14 Jose Canseco .75 .23
15 Will Clark .50 .15
16 Roger Clemens 1.50 .45
17 David Cone .30 .09
18 Doug Drabek .10 .03
19 Dennis Eckersley .60 .18
20 Scott Erickson .10 .03
21 Cecil Fielder .20 .06
22 Ken Griffey Jr. 2.00 .60
23 Bill Gullickson .10 .03
24 Juan Guzman .10 .03
25 Pete Harnisch .10 .03
26 Howard Johnson .10 .03
27 Randy Johnson .75 .23
28 John Kruk .20 .06
29 Barry Larkin .50 .15
30 Greg Maddux 1.50 .45
31 Dennis Martinez .20 .06
32 Ramon Martinez .10 .03
33 Don Mattingly 1.50 .45
34 Jack McDowell .10 .03
35 Fred McGriff .30 .09
36 Paul Molitor .60 .18
37 Charles Nagy .10 .03
38 Gregg Olson .20 .06
39 Terry Pendleton .10 .03
40 Luis Polonia .10 .03
41 Kirby Puckett .60 .18
42 Dave Righetti .10 .03
43 Jose Rijo .10 .03
44 Cal Ripken 3.00 .90
45 Nolan Ryan 3.00 .90
46 Ryne Sandberg 1.50 .45
47 Scott Sanderson .10 .03
48 Ruben Sierra .20 .06
49 Lee Smith .20 .06
50 Ozzie Smith 1.50 .45
51 Darryl Strawberry .20 .06
52 Frank Thomas .75 .23
53 Bill Wegman .10 .03
54 Mitch Williams .10 .03

1993 Upper Deck

The 1993 Upper Deck set consists of two series of 420 standard-size cards. Special subsets featured include Star Rookies (1-29), Community Heroes (30-40), and American League Teammates (41-55), Top Prospects (421-449), Inside the Numbers (450-470), Team Stars (471-485), Award Winners (486-499), and Diamond Debuts (500-510). Derek Jeter is the only notable Rookie Card in this set. A special card (SP5) was randomly inserted in first series packs to commemorate the 3,000th hit of George Brett and Robin Yount. A special card (SP6) commemorating Nolan Ryan's last season was randomly inserted into second series packs. Both SP cards were inserted at a rate of one every 72 packs

Nm-Mt Ex-Mt
COMPLETE SET (840) 40.00 12.00
COMP.FACT.SET (840) 50.00 15.00
COMP. SERIES 1 (420) 15.00 4.50
COMP. SERIES 2 (420) 25.00 7.50
1 Tim Salmon CL .20 .06
2 Mike Piazza SR 1.25 .35
3 Rene Arocha SR RC .20 .06
4 Willie Greene SR .10 .03
5 Manny Alexander .10 .03
6 Dan Wilson .20 .06
7 Dan Smith .10 .03
8 Kevin Rogers .10 .03
9 Kurt Miller SR .10 .03
10 Joe Vitko .10 .03
11 Tim Costo .10 .03
12 Alan Embree SR .10 .03
13 Jim Tatum SR RC .10 .03
14 Cris Colon .10 .03
15 Steve Hosey .10 .03
16 S. Hitchcock SR RC .20 .06
17 Dave Milicki .10 .03
18 Jessie Hollins .10 .03
19 Bobby Jones SR .20 .06
20 Kurt Miller .10 .03
21 Melvin Nieves SR .10 .03
22 Billy Ashley SR .10 .03
23 J.T. Snow SR RC .50 .15
24 Chipper Jones SR .50 .15
25 Tim Salmon SR .30 .09
26 Tim Pugh SR RC .10 .03
27 David Nied SR .10 .03
28 Mike Trombley .10 .03
29 Javier Lopez SR .30 .09
30 Jim Abbott CH CL .20 .06
31 Jim Abbott CH .10 .03
32 Dale Murphy CH .30 .09
33 Tony Pena CH .10 .03
34 Kirby Puckett CH .30 .09
35 Harold Reynolds CH .10 .03
36 Cal Ripken CH .75 .23
37 Nolan Ryan CH 1.00 .30
38 Ryne Sandberg CH .50 .15
39 Dave Stewart CH .10 .03
40 Dave Winfield CH .10 .03
41 Joe Carter CL .50 .15
Mark McGwire
42 Joe Carter .20 .06
Roberto Alomar
43 Paul Molitor .50 .15
Pat Listach
Robin Yount
44 Cal Ripken .50 .15
Brady Anderson
45 Albert Belle .30 .09
Sandy Alomar Jr.
Jim Thome
Carlos Baerga
Kenny Lofton
46 Cecil Fielder .10 .03
Mickey Tettleton
47 Roberto Kelly .60 .18
Don Mattingly
48 Frank Viola .50 .15
Roger Clemens
49 Ruben Sierra .50 .15
Mark McGwire
50 Kent Hrbek .30 .09
Kirby Puckett
51 Robin Ventura .30 .09
Frank Thomas
52 Juan Gonzalez .50 .15
Jose Canseco
Ivan Rodriguez
Rafael Palmeiro
53 Mark Langston .20 .06
Jim Abbott
Chuck Finley
54 Wally Joyner .50 .15
Gregg Jefferies
George Brett
55 Kevin Mitchell .50 .15
Ken Griffey Jr.
Jay Buhner
56 George Brett 1.25 .35
57 Scott Cooper .10 .03
58 Mike Maddux .10 .03
59 Rusty Meacham .10 .03
60 Wil Cordero .10 .03
61 Tim Teufel .10 .03
62 Jeff Montgomery .10 .03
63 Scott Livingstone .10 .03
64 Doug Dascenzo .10 .03
65 Bret Boone .30 .09
66 Tim Wakefield .20 .06
67 Curt Schilling .30 .09
68 Frank Tanana .10 .03
69 Len Dykstra .20 .06
70 Derek Lilliquist .10 .03
71 Anthony Young .10 .03
72 Hipolito Pichardo .10 .03
73 Rod Beck .10 .03
74 Kent Hrbek .20 .06
75 Tom Glavine .30 .09
76 Kevin Brown .20 .06
77 Chuck Finley .20 .06
78 Bob Walk .10 .03
79 Rheal Cormier UER .10 .03
(Born in New Brunswick, not British Columbia)
80 Rick Sutcliffe .20 .06
81 Harold Baines .20 .06
82 Lee Smith .20 .06
83 Geno Petralli .10 .03
84 Jose Oquendo .10 .03
85 Mark Gubicza .10 .03
86 Mickey Tettleton .10 .03
87 Bobby Witt .10 .03
88 Mark Lewis .10 .03
89 Kevin Appier .20 .06
90 Mike Stanton .10 .03
91 Rafael Belliard .10 .03
92 Kenny Rogers .20 .06
93 Randy Velarde .10 .03
94 Luis Sojo .10 .03
95 Mark Leiter .10 .03
96 Jody Reed .10 .03
97 Pete Harnisch .10 .03
98 Tom Candiotti .10 .03
99 Mark Portugal .10 .03
100 Dave Valle .10 .03
101 Shawon Dunston .10 .03
102 B.J. Surhoff .20 .06
103 Jay Bell .20 .06
104 Sid Bream .10 .03
105 Frank Thomas CL .30 .09
106 Mike Morgan .10 .03
107 Bill Doran .10 .03
108 Lance Blankenship .10 .03
109 Mark Lemke .10 .03
110 Brian Harper .10 .03
111 Brady Anderson .20 .06
112 Bip Roberts .10 .03
113 Mitch Williams .10 .03
114 Craig Biggio .30 .09
115 Eddie Murray .50 .15
116 Matt Nokes .10 .03
117 Lance Parrish .20 .06
118 Bill Swift .10 .03
119 Jeff Innis .10 .03
120 Mike LaValliere .10 .03
121 Hal Morris .10 .03
122 Walt Weiss .10 .03
123 Ivan Rodriguez .50 .15
124 Andy Van Slyke .20 .06
125 Roberto Alomar .50 .15
126 Robby Thompson .10 .03
127 Sammy Sosa .75 .23
128 Mark Langston .10 .03
129 Jerry Browne .10 .03
130 Chuck McElroy .10 .03
131 Frank Viola .20 .06
132 Leo Gomez .10 .03
133 Ramon Martinez .10 .03
134 Don Mattingly 1.25 .35
135 Roger Clemens 1.00 .30
136 Rickey Henderson .50 .15
137 Darren Daulton .20 .06
138 Ken Hill .10 .03
139 Ozzie Guillen .10 .03
140 Jerald Clark .10 .03
141 Dave Fleming .10 .03
142 Delino DeShields .10 .03
143 Matt Williams .20 .06
144 Larry Walker .30 .09
145 Ruben Sierra .10 .03
146 Ozzie Smith .75 .23
147 Chris Sabo .10 .03
148 Carlos Hernandez .10 .03
149 Pat Borders .10 .03
150 Orlando Merced .10 .03
151 Royce Clayton .10 .03
152 Kurt Stillwell .10 .03
153 Dave Hollins .10 .03
154 Mike Greenwell .10 .03
155 Nolan Ryan 2.00 .60
156 Felix Jose .10 .03
157 Junior Felix .10 .03
158 Derek Bell .10 .03
159 Steve Buechele .10 .03
160 John Burkett .10 .03
161 Pat Howell .10 .03
162 Milt Cuyler .10 .03
163 Terry Pendleton .20 .06
164 Jack Morris .20 .06
165 Tony Gwynn .60 .18
166 Deion Sanders .30 .09
167 Mike Devereaux .10 .03
168 Ron Darling .10 .03
169 Orel Hershiser .20 .06
170 Mike Jackson .10 .03
171 Doug Jones .10 .03
172 Dan Walters .10 .03
173 Darren Lewis .10 .03
174 Carlos Baerga .10 .03
175 Ryne Sandberg .75 .23
176 Gregg Jefferies .10 .03
177 John Jaha .10 .03
178 Luis Polonia .10 .03
179 Kirt Manwaring .10 .03
180 Mike Magnante .10 .03
181 Billy Ripken .10 .03
182 Mike Moore .10 .03
183 Eric Anthony .10 .03
184 Lenny Harris .10 .03
185 Tony Pena .10 .03
186 Mike Felder .10 .03
187 Greg Olson .10 .03
188 Rene Gonzales .10 .03
189 Mike Bordick .10 .03
190 Mel Rojas .10 .03
191 Todd Frohwirth .10 .03
192 Darryl Hamilton .10 .03
193 Mike Fetters .10 .03
194 Omar Olivares .10 .03
195 Tony Phillips .10 .03
196 Paul Sorrento .10 .03
197 Trevor Wilson .10 .03
198 Kevin Gross .10 .03
199 Ron Karkovice .10 .03
200 Brook Jacoby .10 .03
201 Mariano Duncan .10 .03
202 Dennis Cook .10 .03
203 Daryl Boston .10 .03
204 Mike Perez .10 .03
205 Manuel Lee .10 .03
206 Steve Olin .10 .03
207 Charlie Hough .20 .06
208 Scott Scudder .10 .03
209 Charlie O'Brien .10 .03
210 Barry Bonds CL .60 .18
211 Jose Vizcaino .10 .03
212 Scott Leius .10 .03
213 Kevin Mitchell .10 .03
214 Brian Barnes .10 .03
215 Pat Kelly .10 .03
216 Chris Hammond .10 .03
217 Rob Deer .10 .03
218 Cory Snyder .10 .03
219 Gary Carter .30 .09
220 Danny Darwin .10 .03
221 Tom Gordon .10 .03
222 Gary Sheffield .20 .06
223 Joe Carter .20 .06
224 Jay Buhner .20 .06
225 Jose Offerman .10 .03
226 Jose Rijo .10 .03
227 Mark Whiten .10 .03
228 Randy Milligan .10 .03
229 Bud Black .10 .03
230 Gary DiSarcina .10 .03
231 Steve Finley .20 .06
232 Dennis Martinez .20 .06
233 Mike Mussina .50 .15
234 Joe Oliver .10 .03
235 Chad Curtis .10 .03
236 Shane Mack .10 .03
237 Jaime Navarro .10 .03
238 Brian McRae .10 .03
239 Chili Davis .20 .06
240 Jeff King .10 .03
241 Dean Palmer .20 .06
242 Danny Tartabull .10 .03
243 Charles Nagy .10 .03
244 Ray Lankford .10 .03
245 Barry Larkin .50 .15
246 Steve Avery .10 .03
247 John Kruk .20 .06
248 Derrick May .10 .03
249 Stan Javier .10 .03
250 Roger McDowell .10 .03
251 Dan Gladden .10 .03
252 Wally Joyner .20 .06
253 Pat Listach .10 .03
254 Chuck Knoblauch .20 .06
255 Sandy Alomar Jr. .10 .03
256 Jeff Bagwell .30 .09
257 Andy Stankiewicz .10 .03
258 Darrin Jackson .10 .03
259 Brett Butler .20 .06
260 Joe Orsulak .10 .03
261 Andy Benes .10 .03
262 Kenny Lofton .20 .06
263 Robin Ventura .20 .06
264 Ron Gant .20 .06
265 Ellis Burks .20 .06
266 Juan Guzman .10 .03
267 Wes Chamberlain .10 .03
268 John Smiley .10 .03
269 Franklin Stubbs .10 .03
270 Tom Browning .10 .03
271 Dennis Eckersley .20 .06
272 Carlton Fisk .30 .09
273 Lou Whitaker .20 .06
274 Phil Plantier .10 .03
275 Bobby Bonilla .20 .06
276 Ben McDonald .10 .03
277 Bob Zupcic .10 .03
278 Terry Steinbach .10 .03
279 Terry Mulholland .10 .03
280 Lance Johnson .10 .03
281 Willie McGee .20 .06
282 Bret Saberhagen .20 .06
283 Randy Myers .10 .03
284 Randy Tomlin .10 .03
285 Mickey Morandini .10 .03
286 Brian Williams .10 .03
287 Tino Martinez .30 .09
288 Jose Melendez .10 .03
289 Jeff Huson .10 .03
290 Joe Grahe .10 .03
291 Mel Hall .10 .03
292 Otis Nixon .10 .03
293 Todd Hundley .10 .03
294 Casey Candaele .10 .03
295 Kevin Seitzer .10 .03
296 Eddie Taubensee .10 .03
297 Moises Alou .20 .06
298 Scott Radinsky .10 .03
299 Thomas Howard .10 .03
300 Kyle Abbott .10 .03
301 Omar Vizquel .20 .06
302 Keith Miller .10 .03
303 Rick Aguilera .10 .03
304 Bruce Hurst .10 .03
305 Ken Caminiti .20 .06
306 Mike Pagliarulo .10 .03
307 Frank Seminara .10 .03
308 Andre Dawson .20 .06
309 Jose Lind .10 .03
310 Joe Boever .10 .03
311 Jeff Parrett .10 .03
312 Alan Mills .10 .03
313 Kevin Tapani .10 .03
314 Darryl Kile .20 .06
315 Will Clark CL .20 .06
316 Mike Sharperson .10 .03
317 John Orton .10 .03
318 Bob Tewksbury .10 .03
319 Xavier Hernandez .10 .03
320 Paul Assenmacher .10 .03
321 John Franco .20 .06
322 Mike Timlin .10 .03
323 Jose Guzman .10 .03
324 Pedro Martinez 1.00 .30
325 Bill Spiers .10 .03
326 Melido Perez .10 .03
327 Mike Macfarlane .10 .03
328 Ricky Bones .10 .03
329 Scott Bankhead .10 .03
330 Rich Rodriguez .10 .03
331 Geronimo Pena .10 .03
332 Bernie Williams .30 .09
333 Paul Molitor .30 .09
334 Carlos Garcia .10 .03
335 David Cone .20 .06
336 Randy Johnson .50 .15
337 Pat Mahomes .10 .03
338 Erik Hanson .10 .03
339 Duane Ward .10 .03
340 Al Martin .10 .03
341 Pedro Munoz .10 .03
342 Greg Colbrunn .10 .03
343 Julio Valera .10 .03
344 John Olerud .20 .06
345 George Bell .10 .03
346 Devon White .10 .03
347 Donovan Osborne .10 .03
348 Mark Gardner .10 .03
349 Zane Smith .10 .03
350 Wilson Alvarez .10 .03
351 Kevin Koslofski .10 .03
352 Roberto Hernandez .10 .03
353 Glenn Davis .10 .03
354 Reggie Sanders .20 .06
355 Ken Griffey Jr. .75 .23
356 Marquis Grissom .10 .03
357 Jack McDowell .10 .03
358 Jimmy Key .20 .06
359 Stan Belinda .10 .03
360 Gerald Williams .10 .03
361 Sid Fernandez .10 .03
362 Alex Fernandez .10 .03
363 John Smoltz .30 .09
364 Travis Fryman .20 .06
365 Jose Canseco .50 .15
366 David Justice .20 .06
367 Pedro Astacio .10 .03
368 Tim Belcher .10 .03
369 Steve Sax .10 .03
370 Gary Gaetti .20 .06
371 Jeff Frye .10 .03
372 Bob Wickman .10 .03
373 Ryan Thompson .10 .03
374 David Hulse RC .10 .03
375 Cal Eldred .10 .03
376 Ryan Klesko .20 .06
377 Damion Easley .10 .03
378 John Kiely .10 .03
379 Jim Bullinger .10 .03
380 Brian Bohanon .10 .03
381 Rod Brewer .10 .03
382 Fernando Ramsey RC .10 .03
383 Sam Militello .10 .03
384 Arthur Rhodes .10 .03
385 Eric Karros .20 .06
386 Rico Brogna .10 .03
387 John Valentin .10 .03
388 Kerry Woodson .10 .03
389 Ben Rivera .10 .03
390 Matt Whiteside RC .10 .03
391 Henry Rodriguez .10 .03
392 John Wetteland .20 .06
393 Kent Mercker .10 .03
394 Bernard Gilkey .10 .03
395 Doug Henry .10 .03
396 Mo Vaughn .20 .06
397 Scott Erickson .10 .03
398 Bill Gullickson .10 .03
399 Mark Guthrie .10 .03
400 Dave Martinez .10 .03
401 Jeff Kent .50 .15
402 Chris Hoiles .10 .03
403 Mike Henneman .10 .03
404 Chris Nabholz .10 .03
405 Tom Pagnozzi .10 .03
406 Kelly Gruber .10 .03
407 Bob Welch .10 .03
408 Frank Castillo .10 .03
409 John Dopson .10 .03
410 Steve Farr .10 .03
411 Henry Cotto .10 .03
412 Bob Patterson .10 .03
413 Todd Stottlemyre .10 .03
414 Greg A. Harris .10 .03
415 Denny Neagle .20 .06
416 Bill Wegman .10 .03
417 Willie Wilson .10 .03
418 Terry Leach .10 .03
419 Willie Randolph .20 .06
420 Mark McGwire CL .30 .09
421 Calvin Murray CL .10 .03
422 Pete Janicki TP RC .10 .03
423 Todd Jones TP .10 .03
424 Mike Neill TP .10 .03
425 Carlos Delgado TP .50 .15
426 Jose Oliva TP .10 .03
427 Tyrone Hill TP .10 .03
428 Dmitri Young TP .20 .06
429 Derek Wallace TP RC .10 .03
430 Michael Moore TP RC .10 .03
431 Cliff Floyd TP .30 .09
432 Calvin Murray TP .10 .03
433 Manny Ramirez TP .50 .15
434 Marc Newfield TP .10 .03
435 Charles Johnson TP .20 .06
436 Butch Huskey TP .10 .03
437 Brad Pennington TP .10 .03
438 Ray McDavid TP RC .10 .03
439 Chad McConnell TP .10 .03
440 M.Cummings TP RC .10 .03
441 Benji Gil TP .10 .03
442 Frankie Rodriguez TP .10 .03
443 Chad Mottola TP RC .10 .03
444 John Burke TP RC .10 .03
445 Michael Tucker TP .10 .03
446 Rick Greene TP .10 .03
447 Rich Becker TP .10 .03
448 Mike Robertson TP .10 .03
449 Derek Jeter TP RC 15.00 4.50
450 Ivan Rodriguez CL .30 .09
David McCarty
451 Jim Abbott IN .20 .06
452 Jeff Bagwell IN .20 .06
453 Jason Bere IN .10 .03
454 Delino DeShields IN .10 .03
455 Travis Fryman IN .10 .03
456 Alex Gonzalez IN .10 .03
457 Phil Hiatt IN .10 .03
458 Dave Hollins IN .10 .03
459 Chipper Jones IN .30 .09
460 David Justice IN .10 .03
461 Ray Lankford IN .10 .03
462 David McCarty IN .10 .03
463 Mike Mussina IN .30 .09
464 Jose Offerman IN .10 .03
465 Dean Palmer IN .10 .03
466 Geronimo Pena IN .10 .03
467 Eduardo Perez IN .10 .03
468 Ivan Rodriguez IN .30 .09
469 Reggie Sanders IN .10 .03
470 Bernie Williams IN .20 .06
471 Barry Bonds CL .50 .15
Matt Williams
Will Clark
472 Greg Maddux .50 .15
Steve Avery
John Smoltz
Tom Glavine
473 Jose Rijo .10 .03
Rob Dibble
Roberto Kelly
Reggie Sanders
Barry Larkin
474 Gary Sheffield .20 .06
Phil Plantier
Tony Gwynn
Fred McGriff
475 Doug Drabek .20 .06
Craig Biggio
Jeff Bagwell
476 Will Clark .50 .15
Barry Bonds
Matt Williams
477 Eric Davis .20 .06
Darryl Strawberry
478 Dante Bichette .20 .06
David Nied
Andres Galarraga
479 Dave Magadan .10 .03
Orestes Destrade
Bret Barberie
Jeff Conine
480 Tim Wakefield .20 .06
Andy Van Slyke
Jay Bell
481 Marquis Grissom .10 .03
Delino DeShields
Dennis Martinez
Larry Walker
482 Geronimo Pena .50 .15
Ray Lankford
Ozzie Smith
Bernard Gilkey

483 Randy Myers .50 .15
Ryne Sandberg
Mark Grace
484 Eddie Murray .30 .09
Howard Johnson
Bobby Bonilla
485 John Kruk .10 .03
Dave Hollins
Darren Daulton
Len Dykstra
486 Barry Bonds AW .60 .18
487 Dennis Eckersley AW .20 .06
488 Greg Maddux AW .50 .15
489 Dennis Eckersley AW .20 .06
490 Eric Karros AW .10 .03
491 Pat Listach AW .10 .03
492 Gary Sheffield AW .10 .03
493 Mark McGwire AW .60 .18
494 Gary Sheffield AW .10 .03
495 Edgar Martinez AW .20 .06
496 Fred McGriff AW .20 .06
497 Juan Gonzalez AW .30 .09
498 Darren Daulton AW .10 .03
499 Cecil Fielder AW .10 .03
500 Brent Gates CL .10 .03
501 Tavo Alvarez DD .10 .03
502 Rod Bolton .10 .03
503 J.Cummings DD RC .10 .03
504 Brent Gates DD .10 .03
505 Tyler Green .10 .03
506 Jose Martinez DD RC .10 .03
507 Troy Percival .30 .09
508 Kevin Stocker DD .10 .03
509 Matt Walbeck DD RC .10 .03
510 Rondell White DD .20 .06
511 Billy Ripken .10 .03
512 Mike Moore .10 .03
513 Jose Lind .10 .03
514 Chito Martinez .10 .03
515 Jose Guzman .10 .03
516 Kim Batiste .10 .03
517 Jeff Tackett .10 .03
518 Charlie Hough .20 .06
519 Marvin Freeman .10 .03
520 Carlos Martinez .10 .03
521 Eric Young .10 .03
522 Pete Incaviglia .10 .03
523 Scott Fletcher .10 .03
524 Orestes Destrade .10 .03
525 Ken Griffey Jr. CL .50 .15
526 Ellis Burks .20 .06
527 Juan Samuel .10 .03
528 Dave Magadan .10 .03
529 Jeff Parrett .10 .03
530 Bill Krueger .10 .03
531 Frank Bolick .10 .03
532 Alan Trammell .30 .09
533 Walt Weiss .10 .03
534 David Cone .20 .06
535 Greg Maddux .75 .23
536 Kevin Young .20 .06
537 Dave Hansen .10 .03
538 Alex Cole .10 .03
539 Greg Hibbard .10 .03
540 Gene Larkin .10 .03
541 Jeff Reardon .20 .06
542 Felix Jose .10 .03
543 Jimmy Key .20 .06
544 Reggie Jefferson .10 .03
545 Gregg Jefferies .10 .03
546 Dave Stewart .20 .06
547 Tim Wallach .10 .03
548 Spike Owen .10 .03
549 Tommy Greene .10 .03
550 Fernando Valenzuela .20 .06
551 Rich Amaral .10 .03
552 Bret Barberie .10 .03
553 Edgar Martinez .30 .09
554 Jim Abbott .30 .09
555 Frank Thomas .50 .15
556 Wade Boggs .30 .09
557 Tom Henke .10 .03
558 Milt Thompson .10 .03
559 Lloyd McClendon .10 .03
560 Vinny Castilla .20 .06
561 Ricky Jordan .10 .03
562 Andujar Cedeno .10 .03
563 Greg Vaughn .20 .06
564 Cecil Fielder .20 .06
565 Kirby Puckett .50 .15
566 Mark McGwire 1.25 .35
567 Barry Bonds 1.25 .35
568 Jody Reed .10 .03
569 Todd Zeile .10 .03
570 Mark Carreon .10 .03
571 Joe Girardi .10 .03
572 Luis Gonzalez .20 .06
573 Mark Grace .30 .09
574 Rafael Palmeiro .30 .09
575 Darryl Strawberry .30 .09
576 Will Clark .50 .15
577 Fred McGriff .30 .09
578 Kevin Reimer .10 .03
579 Dave Righetti .20 .06
580 Juan Bell .10 .03
581 Jeff Brantley .10 .03
582 Brian Hunter .10 .03
583 Tim Naehring .10 .03
584 Glenallen Hill .10 .03
585 Cal Ripken 1.50 .45
586 Albert Belle .20 .06
587 Robin Yount .75 .23
588 Chris Bosio .10 .03
589 Pete Smith .10 .03
590 Chuck Carr .10 .03
591 Jeff Blauser .10 .03
592 Kevin McReynolds .10 .03
593 Andres Galarraga .20 .06
594 Kevin Maas .10 .03
595 Eric Davis .20 .06
596 Brian Jordan .20 .06
597 Tim Raines .20 .06
598 Rick Wilkins .10 .03
599 Steve Cooke .10 .03
600 Mike Gallego .10 .03
601 Mike Munoz .10 .03
602 Luis Rivera .10 .03
603 Junior Ortiz .10 .03
604 Brent Mayne .10 .03
605 Luis Alicea .10 .03
606 Damon Berryhill .10 .03
607 Dave Henderson .10 .03
608 Kirk McCaskill .10 .03
609 Jeff Fassero .10 .03
610 Mike Harkey .10 .03
611 Francisco Cabrera .10 .03
612 Rey Sanchez .10 .03
613 Scott Servais .10 .03
614 Darrin Fletcher .10 .03
615 Felix Fermin .10 .03
616 Kevin Seitzer .10 .03
617 Bob Scanlan .10 .03
618 Billy Hatcher .10 .03
619 John Vander Wal .10 .03
620 Joe Hesketh .10 .03
621 Hector Villanueva .10 .03
622 Randy Milligan .10 .03
623 Tony Tarasco RC .10 .03
624 Russ Swan .10 .03
625 Willie Wilson .10 .03
626 Frank Tanana .10 .03
627 Pete O'Brien .10 .03
628 Lenny Webster .10 .03
629 Mark Clark .10 .03
630 Roger Clemens CL .50 .15
631 Alex Arias .10 .03
632 Chris Gwynn .10 .03
633 Tom Bolton .10 .03
634 Greg Briley .10 .03
635 Kent Bottenfield .10 .03
636 Kelly Downs .10 .03
637 Manuel Lee .10 .03
638 Al Leiter .20 .06
639 Jeff Gardner .10 .03
640 Mike Gardiner .10 .03
641 Mark Gardner .10 .03
642 Jeff Branson .10 .03
643 Paul Wagner .10 .03
644 Sean Berry .10 .03
645 Phil Hiatt .10 .03
646 Kevin Mitchell .10 .03
647 Charlie Hayes .10 .03
648 Jim Deshaies .10 .03
649 Dan Pasqua .10 .03
650 Mike Maddux .10 .03
651 Domingo Martinez RC .10 .03
652 Greg McMichael RC .10 .03
653 Eric Wedge RC .10 .03
654 Mark Whiten .10 .03
655 Roberto Kelly .10 .03
656 Julio Franco .20 .06
657 Gene Harris .10 .03
658 Pete Schourek .10 .03
659 Mike Bielecki .10 .03
660 Ricky Gutierrez .10 .03
661 Chris Hammond .10 .03
662 Tim Scott .10 .03
663 Norm Charlton .10 .03
664 Doug Drabek .10 .03
665 Dwight Gooden .30 .09
666 Jim Gott .10 .03
667 Randy Myers .10 .03
668 Darren Holmes .10 .03
669 Tim Spehr .10 .03
670 Bruce Ruffin .10 .03
671 Bobby Thigpen .10 .03
672 Tony Fernandez .10 .03
673 Darrin Jackson .10 .03
674 Gregg Olson .10 .03
675 Rob Dibble .20 .06
676 Howard Johnson .10 .03
677 Mike Lansing RC .20 .06
678 Charlie Leibrandt .10 .03
679 Kevin Bass .10 .03
680 Hubie Brooks .10 .03
681 Scott Brosius .20 .06
682 Randy Knorr .10 .03
683 Dante Bichette .20 .06
684 Bryan Harvey .10 .03
685 Greg Gohr .10 .03
686 Willie Banks .10 .03
687 Robb Nen .20 .06
688 Mike Scioscia .10 .03
689 John Farrell .10 .03
690 John Candelaria .10 .03
691 Damon Buford .10 .03
692 Todd Worrell .10 .03
693 Pat Hentgen .10 .03
694 John Smiley .10 .03
695 Greg Swindell .10 .03
696 Derek Bell .10 .03
697 Terry Jorgensen .10 .03
698 Jimmy Jones .10 .03
699 David Wells .20 .06
700 Dave Martinez .10 .03
701 Steve Bedrosian .10 .03
702 Jeff Russell .10 .03
703 Joe Magrane .10 .03
704 Matt Mieske .10 .03
705 Paul Molitor .30 .09
706 Dale Murphy .50 .15
707 Steve Howe .10 .03
708 Greg Gagne .10 .03
709 Dave Eiland .10 .03
710 David West .10 .03
711 Luis Aquino .10 .03
712 Joe Orsulak .10 .03
713 Eric Plunk .10 .03
714 Mike Felder .10 .03
715 Joe Klink .10 .03
716 Lonnie Smith .10 .03
717 Monty Fariss .10 .03
718 Craig Lefferts .10 .03
719 John Habyan .10 .03
720 Willie Blair .10 .03
721 Darnell Coles .10 .03
722 Mark Williamson .10 .03
723 Bryn Smith .10 .03
724 Greg W. Harris .10 .03
725 Graeme Lloyd RC .20 .06
726 Cris Carpenter .10 .03
727 Chico Walker .10 .03
728 Tracy Woodson .10 .03
729 Jose Uribe .10 .03
730 Stan Javier .10 .03
731 Jay Howell .10 .03
732 Freddie Benavides .10 .03
733 Jeff Reboulet .10 .03
734 Scott Sanderson .10 .03
735 Ryne Sandberg CL .50 .15
736 Archi Cianfrocco .10 .03
737 Daryl Boston .10 .03
738 Craig Grebeck .10 .03
739 Doug Dascenzo .10 .03
740 Gerald Young .10 .03
741 Candy Maldonado .10 .03
742 Joey Cora .10 .03
743 Don Slaught .10 .03
744 Steve Decker .10 .03
745 Blas Minor .10 .03
746 Storm Davis .10 .03
747 Carlos Quintana .10 .03
748 Vince Coleman .10 .03
749 Todd Burns .10 .03
750 Steve Frey .10 .03
751 Ivan Calderon .10 .03
752 Steve Reed RC .10 .03
753 Danny Jackson .10 .03
754 Jeff Conine .20 .06
755 Juan Gonzalez .50 .15
756 Mike Kelly .10 .03
757 John Doherty .10 .03
758 Jack Armstrong .10 .03
759 John Wehner .10 .03
760 Scott Bankhead .10 .03
761 Jim Tatum .10 .03
762 Scott Pose RC .10 .03
763 Andy Ashby .10 .03
764 Ed Sprague .10 .03
765 Harold Baines .20 .06
766 Kirk Gibson .20 .06
767 Troy Neel .10 .03
768 Dick Schofield .10 .03
769 Dickie Thon .10 .03
770 Butch Henry .10 .03
771 Junior Felix .10 .03
772 Ken Ryan RC .10 .03
773 Trevor Hoffman .20 .06
774 Phil Plantier .10 .03
775 Bo Jackson .50 .15
776 Benito Santiago .20 .06
777 Andre Dawson .20 .06
778 Bryan Hickerson .10 .03
779 Dennis Moeller .10 .03
780 Ryan Bowen .10 .03
781 Eric Fox .10 .03
782 Joe Kmak .10 .03
783 Mike Hampton .20 .06
784 Darrell Sherman RC .10 .03
785 J.T. Snow .50 .15
786 Dave Winfield .20 .06
787 Jim Austin .10 .03
788 Craig Shipley .10 .03
789 Greg Myers .10 .03
790 Todd Benzinger .10 .03
791 Cory Snyder .10 .03
792 David Segui .10 .03
793 Armando Reynoso .10 .03
794 Chili Davis .20 .06
795 Dave Nilsson .10 .03
796 Paul O'Neill .30 .09
797 Jerald Clark .10 .03
798 Jose Mesa .10 .03
799 Brain Holman .10 .03
800 Jim Eisenreich .10 .03
801 Mark McLemore .10 .03
802 Luis Sojo .10 .03
803 Harold Reynolds .20 .06
804 Dan Plesac .10 .03
805 Dave Stieb .10 .03
806 Tom Brunansky .10 .03
807 Kelly Gruber .10 .03
808 Bob Ojeda .10 .03
809 Dave Burba .10 .03
810 Joe Boever .10 .03
811 Jeremy Hernandez .10 .03
812 Tim Salmon TC .20 .06
813 Jeff Bagwell TC .20 .06
814 Dennis Eckersley TC .20 .06
815 Roberto Alomar TC .20 .06
816 Steve Avery TC .10 .03
817 Pat Listach TC .10 .03
818 Gregg Jefferies TC .10 .03
819 Sammy Sosa TC .50 .15
820 Darryl Strawberry TC .20 .06
821 Dennis Martinez TC .10 .03
822 Robby Thompson TC .10 .03
823 Albert Belle TC .20 .06
824 Randy Johnson TC .30 .09
825 Nigel Wilson TC .10 .03
826 Bobby Bonilla TC .10 .03
827 Glenn Davis TC .10 .03
828 Gary Sheffield TC .10 .03
829 Darren Daulton TC .10 .03
830 Jay Bell TC .10 .03
831 Juan Gonzalez TC .30 .09
832 Andre Dawson TC .10 .03
833 Hal Morris TC .10 .03
834 David Nied TC .10 .03
835 Felix Jose TC .10 .03
836 Travis Fryman TC .50 .15
837 Shane Mack TC .10 .03
838 Robin Ventura TC .10 .03
839 Danny Tartabull TC .10 .03
840 Roberto Alomar CL .20 .06
SP5 George Brett 1.00 .30
Robin Yount
SP6 Nolan Ryan 2.00 .60

1993 Upper Deck Gold Hologram

These gold parallel cards were made available exclusively in factory set form. One set in every 15 ct. case of factory sets featured cards with gold foil holograms on the card backs, rather than the traditional silver foil holograms. The factory boxes for the basic sets and the much scarcer Gold Hologram sets are identical, thus all Gold Hologram sets offered for sale are for opened factory sets. Please refer to the multipliers provided below for values on single cards.

	Nm-Mt	Ex-Mt
COMP.FACT.SET (840)	150.00	45.00
*STARS: 3X TO 8X BASIC CARDS		
*ROOKIES: 3X TO 8X BASIC CARDS		

1993 Upper Deck Clutch Performers

These 20 standard-size cards were inserted one every nine series II retail foil packs, as well as inserted one per series II retail jumbo packs. The cards are numbered on the back with an "R" prefix and appear in alphabetical order. These 20 cards represent Reggie Jackson's selection of players who have come through under pressure. Please note these cards are condition sensitive and trade for premium values if found in Mint.

	Nm-Mt	Ex-Mt
COMPLETE SET (20)	20.00	6.00
R1 Roberto Alomar	1.25	.35
R2 Wade Boggs	.75	.23
R3 Barry Bonds	3.00	.90
R4 Jose Canseco	1.25	.35
R5 Joe Carter	.50	.15
R6 Will Clark	1.25	.35
R7 Roger Clemens	2.50	.75
R8 Dennis Eckersley	.50	.15
R9 Cecil Fielder	.50	.15
R10 Juan Gonzalez	1.25	.35
R11 Ken Griffey Jr.	2.00	.60
R12 Rickey Henderson	1.25	.35
R13 Barry Larkin	1.25	.35
R14 Don Mattingly	3.00	.90
R15 Fred McGriff	.75	.23
R16 Terry Pendleton	.50	.15
R17 Kirby Puckett	1.25	.35
R18 Ryne Sandberg	2.00	.60
R19 John Smoltz	.75	.23
R20 Frank Thomas	1.25	.35

1993 Upper Deck Fifth Anniversary

This 15-card standard-size set celebrates Upper Deck's five years in the sports card business.The cards are essentially reprinted versions of some of Upper Deck's most popular cards in the last five years. These cards were inserted one every nine second series hobby packs. The black-bordered fronts feature player photos that previously appeared on an Upper Deck card. The cards are numbered on the back with an "A" prefix. These cards are condition sensitive and trade for premium values in Mint.

	Nm-Mt	Ex-Mt
COMPLETE SET (15)	15.00	4.50
A1 Ken Griffey Jr.	2.00	.60
A2 Gary Sheffield	.50	.15
A3 Roberto Alomar	1.25	.35
A4 Jim Abbott	.75	.23
A5 Nolan Ryan	5.00	1.50
A6 Juan Gonzalez	1.25	.35
A7 David Justice	.50	.15
A8 Carlos Baerga	.25	.07
A9 Reggie Jackson	.50	.15
A10 Eric Karros	.50	.15
A11 Chipper Jones	1.25	.35
A12 Ivan Rodriguez	1.25	.35
A13 Pat Listach	.25	.07
A14 Frank Thomas	1.25	.35
A15 Tim Salmon	.75	.23

1993 Upper Deck Future Heroes

Inserted in second series foil packs at a rate of one every nine pack; this set continues the Heroes insert set begun in the 1990 Upper Deck high-number set, this ten-card standard-size set features eight different "Future Heroes" along with a checklist and header card.

	Nm-Mt	Ex-Mt
COMPLETE SET (10)	12.00	3.60
55 Roberto Alomar	1.25	.35
56 Barry Bonds	3.00	.90
57 Roger Clemens	2.50	.75
58 Juan Gonzalez	1.25	.35
59 Ken Griffey Jr.	2.00	.60
60 Mark McGwire	3.00	.90
61 Kirby Puckett	1.25	.35
62 Frank Thomas	1.25	.35
63 Checklist	.50	.15
NNO Header Card SP	.25	.07

1993 Upper Deck Home Run Heroes

This 28-card standard-size set features the home run leader from each Major League team. Each 1993 first series 27-card jumbo pack contained one of these cards. The cards are numbered on the back with an "HR" prefix and the set is arranged in descending order according to the number of home runs.

	Nm-Mt	Ex-Mt
COMPLETE SET (28)	15.00	4.50
HR1 Juan Gonzalez	1.25	.35
HR2 Mark McGwire	3.00	.90
HR3 Cecil Fielder	.50	.15
HR4 Fred McGriff	.75	.23
HR5 Albert Belle	.50	.15
HR6 Barry Bonds	3.00	.90
HR7 Joe Carter	.50	.15
HR8 Darren Daulton	.50	.15
HR9 Ken Griffey Jr.	2.00	.60
HR10 Dave Hollins	.25	.07
HR11 Ryne Sandberg	2.00	.60
HR12 George Bell	.25	.07
HR13 Danny Tartabull	.25	.07
HR14 Mike Devereaux	.25	.07
HR15 Greg Vaughn	.50	.15
HR16 Larry Walker	.75	.23
HR17 David Justice	.50	.15
HR18 Terry Pendleton	.50	.15
HR19 Eric Karros	.50	.15
HR20 Ray Lankford	.25	.07
HR21 Matt Williams	.50	.15
HR22 Eric Anthony	.25	.07
HR23 Bobby Bonilla	.50	.15
HR24 Kirby Puckett	1.25	.35
HR25 Mike Macfarlane	.25	.07
HR26 Tom Brunansky	.25	.07
HR27 Paul O'Neill	.75	.23
HR28 Gary Gaetti	.50	.15

1993 Upper Deck Iooss Collection

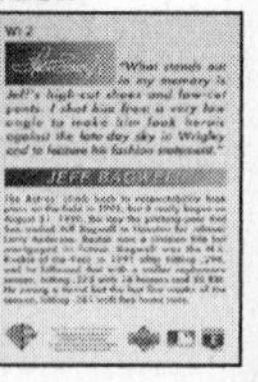

This 27-card standard-size set spotlights the work of famous sports photographer Walter Iooss Jr. by presenting 26 of the game's current greats in a candid photo set. The cards were inserted in series I retail foil packs at a rate of one every nine packs. They were also in retail jumbo packs at a rate of one in five packs. The cards are numbered on the back with a "WI" prefix. Please note these cards are condition sensitive and trade for premium values in Mint.

	Nm-Mt	Ex-Mt
COMPLETE SET (27)	30.00	9.00
WI1 Tim Salmon	1.00	.30
WI2 Jeff Bagwell	1.00	.30
WI3 Mark McGwire	4.00	1.20
WI4 Roberto Alomar	1.50	.45
WI5 Steve Avery	.30	.09
WI6 Paul Molitor	1.00	.30
WI7 Ozzie Smith	2.50	.75
WI8 Mark Grace	1.00	.30
WI9 Eric Karros	.60	.18
WI10 Delino DeShields	.30	.09
WI11 Will Clark	1.50	.45
WI12 Albert Belle	.60	.18
WI13 Ken Griffey Jr.	2.50	.75
WI14 Howard Johnson	.30	.09
WI15 Cal Ripken Jr.	5.00	1.50
WI16 Fred McGriff	1.00	.30
WI17 Darren Daulton	.60	.18
WI18 Andy Van Slyke	.60	.18
WI19 Nolan Ryan	6.00	1.80
WI20 Wade Boggs	1.00	.30
WI21 Barry Larkin	1.50	.45
WI22 George Brett	4.00	1.20
WI23 Cecil Fielder	.60	.18
WI24 Kirby Puckett	1.50	.45
WI25 Frank Thomas	1.50	.45
WI26 Don Mattingly	4.00	1.20
NNO Title Card	.30	.09
Iooss Header		

1993 Upper Deck Mays Heroes

This standard-size ten-card set was randomly inserted in 1993 Upper Deck first series foil packs. The fronts feature color photos of Mays at various stages of his career that are partially contained within a black bordered circle. The cards are numbered in continuation of Upper Deck's Heroes series.

	Nm-Mt	Ex-Mt
COMPLETE SET (10)	3.00	.90
COMMON (46-54/HDR)	.50	.15

1993 Upper Deck On Deck

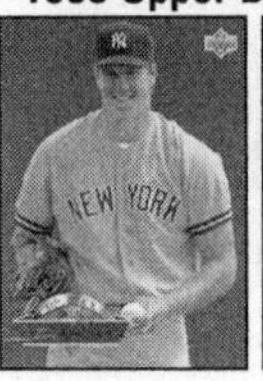
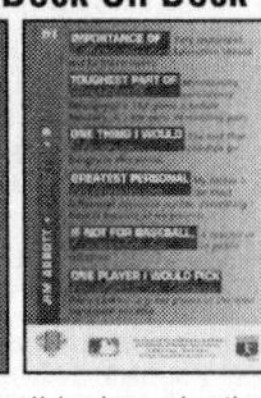

Inserted one per series II jumbo packs, these 25 standard-size cards profile baseball's top players. The cards are numbered on the back with a "D" prefix in alphabetical order by name.

	Nm-Mt	Ex-Mt
COMPLETE SET (25)	20.00	6.00
D1 Jim Abbott	.75	.23
D2 Roberto Alomar	1.25	.35
D3 Carlos Baerga	.25	.07
D4 Albert Belle	.50	.15
D5 Wade Boggs	.75	.23
D6 George Brett	3.00	.90
D7 Jose Canseco	1.25	.35
D8 Will Clark	1.25	.35
D9 Roger Clemens	2.50	.75
D10 Dennis Eckersley	.50	.15
D11 Cecil Fielder	.50	.15
D12 Juan Gonzalez	1.25	.35
D13 Ken Griffey Jr.	2.00	.60
D14 Tony Gwynn	1.50	.45
D15 Bo Jackson	1.25	.35
D16 Chipper Jones	1.25	.35
D17 Eric Karros	.50	.15
D18 Mark McGwire	3.00	.90
D19 Kirby Puckett	1.25	.35
D20 Nolan Ryan	5.00	1.50
D21 Tim Salmon	.75	.23
D22 Ryne Sandberg	2.00	.60
D23 Darryl Strawberry	.75	.23
D24 Frank Thomas	1.25	.35
D25 Andy Van Slyke	.50	.15

1993 Upper Deck Season Highlights

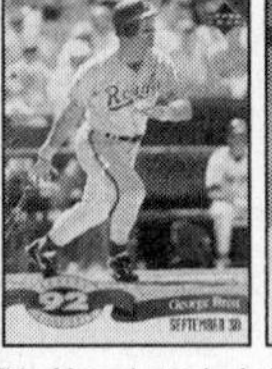
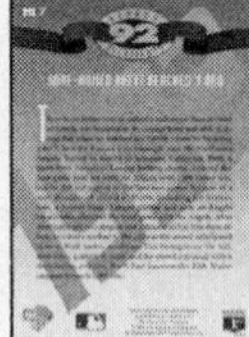

This 20-card standard-size insert set captures great moments of the 1992 Major League Baseball season. The cards were exclusively distributed in specially marked cases that were available only at Upper Deck Heroes of Baseball Card Shows and through the purchase of a specified quantity of second series cases. In these packs, the cards were inserted at a rate of one every nine. The cards are numbered on the back with an "HI" prefix in alphabetical order by player's name.

	Nm-Mt	Ex-Mt
COMPLETE SET (20)	120.00	36.00
HI1 Roberto Alomar	8.00	2.40
HI2 Steve Avery	1.50	.45
HI3 Harold Baines	3.00	.90
HI4 Damon Berryhill	1.50	.45
HI5 Barry Bonds	20.00	6.00
HI6 Bret Boone	5.00	1.50
HI7 George Brett	20.00	6.00
HI8 Francisco Cabrera	1.50	.45
HI9 Ken Griffey Jr.	12.00	3.60
HI10 Rickey Henderson	8.00	2.40
HI11 Kenny Lofton	3.00	.90
HI12 Mickey Morandini	1.50	.45
HI13 Eddie Murray	8.00	2.40
HI14 David Nied	1.50	.45
HI15 Jeff Reardon	3.00	.90
HI16 Bip Roberts	1.50	.45
HI17 Nolan Ryan	30.00	9.00
HI18 Ed Sprague	1.50	.45
HI19 Dave Winfield	3.00	.90
HI20 Robin Yount	12.00	3.60

1993 Upper Deck Then And Now

This 18-card, standard-size hologram set highlights veteran stars in their rookie year and today, reflecting on how they and the game have changed. Cards 1-9 were randomly inserted in series I foil packs; cards 10-18 were randomly inserted in series II foil packs. In either series, the cards were inserted one every 27 packs. The nine lithogram cards in the second series feature one card each of Hall of Famers Reggie Jackson, Mickey Mantle, and Willie Mays, as well as six active players. The cards are numbered on the back with a "TN" prefix and arranged alphabetically within subgroup according to player's last name.

	Nm-Mt	Ex-Mt
COMPLETE SET (18)	40.00	12.00
COMPLETE SERIES 1 (9)	15.00	4.50
COMPLETE SERIES 2 (9)	25.00	7.50
TN1 Wade Boggs	1.25	.35
TN2 George Brett	5.00	1.50
TN3 Rickey Henderson	2.00	.60
TN4 Cal Ripken	6.00	1.80
TN5 Nolan Ryan	8.00	2.40
TN6 Ryne Sandberg	3.00	.90
TN7 Ozzie Smith	3.00	.90
TN8 Darryl Strawberry	1.25	.35
TN9 Dave Winfield	.75	.23
TN10 Dennis Eckersley	.75	.23
TN11 Tony Gwynn	2.50	.75
TN12 Howard Johnson	.40	.12
TN13 Don Mattingly	5.00	1.50
TN14 Eddie Murray	2.00	.60
TN15 Robin Yount	3.00	.90
TN16 Reggie Jackson	2.50	.75
TN17 Mickey Mantle	12.00	3.60
TN18 Willie Mays	6.00	1.80

1993 Upper Deck Triple Crown

This ten-card, standard-size insert set highlights ten players who were selected by Upper Deck as having the best shot at winning Major League Baseball's Triple Crown. The cards were randomly inserted in series I hobby foil packs at a rate of one in 15. The cards are numbered on the back with a "TC" prefix and arranged alphabetically by player's last name.

	Nm-Mt	Ex-Mt
COMPLETE SET (10)	12.00	3.60
TC1 Barry Bonds	3.00	.90
TC2 Jose Canseco	1.25	.35
TC3 Will Clark	1.25	.35
TC4 Ken Griffey Jr.	2.00	.60
TC5 Fred McGriff	.75	.23
TC6 Kirby Puckett	1.25	.35
TC7 Cal Ripken Jr.	4.00	1.20
TC8 Gary Sheffield	.50	.15
TC9 Frank Thomas	1.25	.35
TC10 Larry Walker	.75	.23

1993 Upper Deck All-Time Heroes Preview

This four-card boxed preview set was distributed to herald the release of the 165-card main set. The cards are patterned after the T-202 Hassan Triple Folders cards, which first appeared in 1912. The cards measure approximately 2 1/4" by 5 1/4" and feature two side panels and a larger middle panel. The fronts feature two-player color drawings by Todd Reigle in their middle panels. The side panels feature photos of the two players. The white backs include player biographies and career highlights printed in red lettering. The cards are numbered on the back with an "HOB" prefix.

	Nm-Mt	Ex-Mt
COMPLETE SET (4)	5.00	1.50
1 Ted Williams Mickey Mantle	1.50	.45
2 Reggie Jackson Mickey Mantle	1.50	.45
3 Ted Williams Reggie Jackson	1.50	.45
4 Reggie Jackson Mickey Mantle Ted Williams	1.50	.45

1993 Upper Deck All-Time Heroes

This 165-card set of All-Time Heroes of Baseball is patterned after the T-202 Hassan Triple Folders cards, which first appeared in 1912. The cards measure approximately 2 1/4" by 5 1/4" and feature two side panels and a larger middle panel. The set consists of 130 regular cards and the Classic Combinations subset (131-165). The fronts feature candid or action photos of the featured player on the center panel, along with a portrait on one of the side panels and the B.A.T. (Baseball Assistance Team) logo on the other. The backs include player biographies and career highlights, as well as an explanation of the B.A.T. cause. The Classic Combinations subset have center panels that feature either artwork by Todd Reigle or a photograph of multiple greats. The side panels feature photos of two players. The backs include player biographies on the side panels, with the center panel detailing the association between the players. The foil packs contained 12 cards per pack. Each card is holographically enhanced. Reggie Jackson and Mickey Mantle were the spokespersons for this set and they are featured prominently on the front of the box. The grand prize for the set's mail-in contest was an actual, original set of T202 Hassan Triplefolders, which Upper Deck had purchased in the open hobby market expressly for the promotion.

	Nm-Mt	Ex-Mt
COMPLETE SET (165)	25.00	7.50
1 Hank Aaron	2.00	.60
2 Tommie Agee	.10	.03
3 Bob Allison	.10	.03
4 Matty Alou	.10	.03
5 Sal Bando	.10	.03
6 Hank Bauer	.10	.03
7 Don Baylor	.15	.04
8 Glenn Beckert	.10	.03
9 Yogi Berra	1.00	.30
10 Buddy Biancalana	.10	.03
11 Jack Billingham	.10	.03
12 Joe Black	.15	.04
13 Paul Blair	.10	.03
14 Steve Blass	.10	.03
15 Ray Boone	.10	.03
16 Lou Boudreau	.20	.06
17 Ken Brett	.10	.03
18 Nellie Briles	.10	.03
19 Bobby Brown	.15	.04
20 Bill Buckner	.15	.04
21 Don Buford	.10	.03
22 Al Bumbry	.10	.03
23 Lew Burdette	.15	.04
24 Jeff Burroughs	.10	.03
25 Johnny Callison	.10	.03
26 Bert Campaneris	.10	.03
27 Rico Carty	.10	.03
28 Dave Cash	.10	.03
29 Cesar Cedeno	.15	.04
30 Frank Chance	.20	.06
31 Joe Charboneau	.15	.04
32 Ty Cobb	2.00	.60
33 Jerry Coleman	.10	.03
34 Cecil Cooper	.10	.03
35 Frankie Crosetti	.10	.03
36 Alvin Dark	.10	.03
37 Tommy Davis	.10	.03
38 Dizzy Dean	.50	.15
39 Doug DeCinces	.10	.03
40 Bucky Dent	.10	.03
41 Larry Dierker	.10	.03
42 Larry Doby	.40	.12
43 Moe Drabowsky	.10	.03
44 Dave Dravecky	.10	.03
45 Del Ennis	.10	.03
46 Carl Erskine	.15	.04
47 Johnny Evers	.20	.06
48 Roy Face	.10	.03
49 Rick Ferrell	.20	.06
50 Mark Fidrych	.15	.04
51 Curt Flood	.15	.04
52 Whitey Ford	.75	.23
53 George Foster	.15	.04
54 Jimmie Foxx	.50	.15
55 Jim Fregosi	.10	.03
56 Phil Garner	.10	.03
57 Ralph Garr	.10	.03
58 Lou Gehrig	2.50	.75
59 Bobby Grich	.15	.04
60 Jerry Grote	.10	.03
61 Harvey Haddix	.10	.03
62 Toby Harrah	.10	.03
63 Bud Harrelson	.15	.04
64 Jim Hegan	.10	.03
65 Gil Hodges	.25	.07
66 Ken Holtzman	.10	.03
67 Bob Horner	.10	.03
68 Rogers Hornsby	.50	.15
69 Carl Hubbell	.20	.06
70 Ron Hunt	.10	.03
71 Monte Irvin	.20	.06
72 Reggie Jackson	.75	.23
73 Larry Jansen	.10	.03
74 Ferguson Jenkins	.20	.06
75 Tommy John	.15	.04
76 Cliff Johnson	.10	.03
77 Davey Johnson	.15	.04
78 Walter Johnson	.50	.15
79 George Kell	.20	.06
80 Don Kessinger	.10	.03
81 Vern Law	.10	.03
82 Dennis Leonard	.10	.03
83 Johnny Logan	.10	.03
84 Mickey Lolich	.15	.04
85 Jim Lonborg	.10	.03
86 Bill Madlock	.10	.03
87 Mickey Mantle	5.00	1.50
88 Billy Martin	.20	.06
89 Christy Mathewson	.50	.15
90 Lee May	.10	.03
91 Willie Mays	2.00	.60
92 Bill Mazeroski	.25	.07
93 Gil McDougald	.15	.04
94 Sam McDowell	.10	.03
95 Minnie Minoso	.15	.04
96 Johnny Mize	.20	.06
97 Rick Monday	.10	.03
98 Wally Moon	.10	.03
99 Manny Mota	.10	.03
100 Bobby Murcer	.10	.03
101 Ron Necciai	.10	.03
102 Al Oliver	.15	.04
103 Mel Ott	.20	.06
104 Mel Parnell	.10	.03
105 Jimmy Piersall	.15	.04
106 Johnny Podres	.15	.04
107 Bobby Richardson	.15	.04
108 Robin Roberts	.20	.06
109 Al Rosen	.15	.04
110 Babe Ruth	5.00	1.50
111 Joe Sambito	.10	.03
112 Manny Sanguillen	.10	.03
113 Ron Santo	.15	.04
114 Bill Skowron	.10	.03
115 Enos Slaughter	.20	.06
116 Warren Spahn	.20	.06
117 Tris Speaker	.20	.06
118 Frank Thomas	.10	.03
119 Bobby Thomson	.15	.04
120 Andre Thornton	.10	.03
121 Marv Throneberry	.10	.03
122 Luis Tiant	.15	.04
123 Joe Tinker	.20	.06
124 Honus Wagner	.50	.15
125 Bill White	.15	.04
126 Ted Williams	4.00	1.20
127 Earl Wilson	.10	.03
128 Joe Wood	.15	.04
129 Cy Young	.20	.06
130 Richie Zisk	.10	.03
131 Babe Ruth Lou Gehrig	2.00	.60
132 Ted Williams Rogers Hornsby	1.00	.30
133 Lou Gehrig Babe Ruth	2.00	.60
134 Babe Ruth Mickey Mantle	2.00	.60
135 Mickey Mantle Reggie Jackson	1.25	.35
136 Mel Ott Carl Hubbell	.15	.04
137 Mickey Mantle Willie Mays	1.50	.45
138 Cy Young Walter Johnson	.20	.06
139 Honus Wagner Rogers Hornsby	.20	.06
140 Mickey Mantle Whitey Ford	1.25	.35
141 Mickey Mantle Billy Martin	1.25	.35
142 Cy Young Walter Johnson	.20	.06
143 Christy Mathewson Walter Johnson	.20	.06
144 Warren Spahn Christy Mathewson	.20	.06
145 Honus Wagner Ty Cobb	1.00	.30
146 Babe Ruth Ty Cobb	2.00	.60
147 Joe Tinker Johnny Evers	.20	.06
148 Johnny Evers Frank Chance	.20	.06
149 Hank Aaron Babe Ruth	2.00	.60
150 Willie Mays Hank Aaron	1.25	.35
151 Babe Ruth Willie Mays	2.00	.60
152 Babe Ruth Whitey Ford	1.25	.35
153 Larry Doby Minnie Minoso	.10	.03
154 Joe Black Monte Irvin	.15	.04
155 Joe Wood Christy Mathewson	.15	.04
156 Christy Mathewson Cy Young	.20	.06
157 Cy Young Joe Wood	.15	.04
158 Cy Young Whitey Ford	.15	.04
159 Cy Young Ferguson Jenkins	.15	.04
160 Ty Cobb Rogers Hornsby	1.00	.30
161 Tris Speaker Ted Williams	1.00	.30
162 Rogers Hornsby Ted Williams	1.00	.30
163 Willie Mays Monte Irvin	.75	.23
164 Willie Mays Bobby Thomson	.75	.23
165 Reggie Jackson Mickey Mantle	1.50	.45

1993 Upper Deck All-Time Heroes T202 Reprints

Inserted in 1993 Upper Deck All-Time Heroes of Baseball foil packs at a stated rate of one in five, this ten-card set of reprints feature players from the 1912 Hassan "Triplefolders. The Hassan cigarette ads were replaced by the Upper Deck hologram and their designation of "T202" comes from their assignment in the American Card Catalog. The reprints are unnumbered and appear alphabetically

	Nm-Mt	Ex-Mt
COMPLETE SET (10)	15.00	4.50
1 Art Devlin Christy Mathewson	1.00	.30
2 Hugh Jennings Ty Cobb	2.50	.75
3 John Kling Cy Young	1.00	.30
4 Jack Knight Walter Johnson	1.00	.30
5 John McGraw Hugh Jennings	1.50	.45
6 George Moriarty Ty Cobb	2.00	.60
7 Charles O'Leary Ty Cobb	2.00	.60
8 Charles O'Leary Ty Cobb	2.00	.60
9 Joe Tinker Frank Chance	2.50	.75
10 Joe Wood Tris Speaker	1.00	.30

1993 Upper Deck Clark Reggie Jackson

Issued to promote the reintroduction of the Reggie bar by the Clark Candy Co., these three standard-size cards highlight Jackson's career and feature on their fronts white-bordered color photos of Jackson as an Athletic and as a Yankee, with all team logos airbrushed out. The cards are numbered on the back with a "C" prefix. One card was inserted in each Reggie bar and Jackson autographed 200 cards that were randomly inserted into the candy bar packages.

	Nm-Mt	Ex-Mt
COMPLETE SET (3)	5.00	1.50
COMMON CARD (C1-C3)	2.00	.60
RJ Reggie Jackson AU Autograph card		

1993 Upper Deck Diamond Gallery

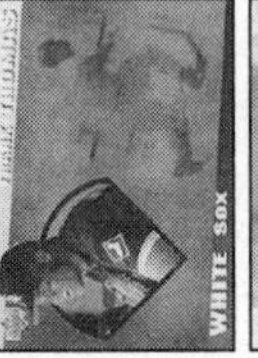

This 38-card standard-size boxed set features two player action photos on its horizontal fronts. One is a hologram, the other is a color action shot of the player, which is displayed on the left side projecting from a baseball diamond design. In the hologram, the player's uniform number appears behind him. Two subsets are present in this set; cards 29-31 are Gallery Heroes subset, and cards 32-36 are Diamonds in the Rough. Also included in the set are the checklist bearing the production number out of 123,600 sets produced, and a mail-away card for the Diamond Gallery card album.

	Nm-Mt	Ex-Mt
COMP. FACT SET (38)	15.00	4.50
1 Tim Salmon	.50	.15
2 Jeff Bagwell	.75	.23
3 Mark McGwire	2.50	.75
4 Roberto Alomar	.50	.15
5 Terry Pendleton	.10	.03
6 Robin Yount	.50	.15
7 Ray Lankford	.20	.06
8 Ryne Sandberg	1.50	.45
9 Darryl Strawberry	.20	.06
10 Marquis Grissom	.20	.06
11 Barry Bonds	1.50	.45
12 Carlos Baerga	.20	.06
13 Ken Griffey Jr.	2.00	.60
14 Benito Santiago	.20	.06
15 Dwight Gooden	.20	.06
16 Cal Ripken	3.00	.90
17 Tony Gwynn	1.50	.45
18 Dave Hollins	.10	.03
19 Andy Van Slyke	.10	.03
20 Juan Gonzalez	.75	.23
21 Roger Clemens	1.50	.45
22 Barry Larkin	.50	.15
23 David Nied	.10	.03
24 George Brett	1.50	.45
25 Travis Fryman	.20	.06
26 Kirby Puckett	.75	.23
27 Frank Thomas	.75	.23
28 Don Mattingly	1.50	.45
29 Rickey Henderson	1.00	.30
30 Nolan Ryan	3.00	.90
31 Ozzie Smith	1.50	.45
32 Wil Cordero	.10	.03
33 Phil Hiatt	.10	.03
34 Mike Piazza	3.00	.90
35 J.T. Snow	.50	.15
36 Kevin Young	.10	.03
NNO Checklist Card	.10	.03
NNO Album Offer Card	.10	.03

1993 Upper Deck Folder

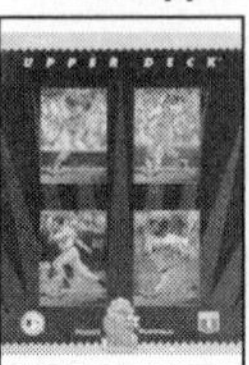

This folder features four 1993 Upper Deck Triple Crown Contenders insert cards on the front. The back of the folder features the back of the cards involved. Inside the folder is room to place some of a collectors favorite cards.

	Nm-Mt	Ex-Mt
1 Ken Griffey Jr. Will Clark Cal Ripken Jr Kirby Puckett	2.00	.60

1993 Upper Deck Jackson Heroes Jumbo

This jumbo set (3 1/2" by 5") utilizes the same design as the 1990 standard-size high series inserts. It is currently uncertain whether the unnumbered header card was reproduced in jumbo form. The jumbos were issued in 1993 as a retail blister pack insert in a pack which included one pack of each 1993 Upper Deck series. These cards also include a 5th Anniversary Upper Deck logo and "1993 Hall of Fame inductee" on the front. Ten thousand of each card were issued.

	Nm-Mt	Ex-Mt
COMPLETE SET (9)	25.00	7.50
COMMON REGGIE (1-9)	3.00	.90

1993 Upper Deck Sheets

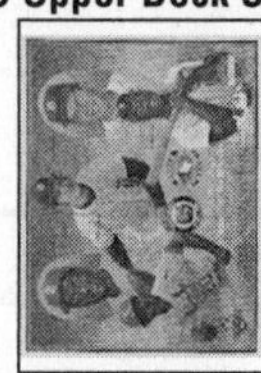

The 31 commemorative sheets listed below in chronological order were issued by Upper Deck in 1993. The Upper Deck Heroes of Baseball made stops in MLB ballparks and sponsored old-timer baseball games preceding major league games. At each game a limited edition commemorative sheet was distributed. Commemorative sheets were produced in honor of other events. Days prior to the All-Star Game, sheets 16 and 17 were issued to fans who were at Camden Yards to watch the All-Star Workout. Sheet 19 was issued at the National in Chicago. Sheet 21 commemorates the World Children's Baseball Fair. And sheet 29 was handed out at by Upper Deck to collectors at various shows during the year. All the sheets measure 8 1/2" by 11" and most feature artist renderings of players from the teams recreated for the old-timers games. The front of each sheet carries the individual production number out of the total number produced, but otherwise the sheets are unnumbered.

	Nm-Mt	Ex-Mt
COMPLETE SET (31)	175.00	52.50
1 Blue Jays Heroes vs. Upper Deck Heroes April 25, 1993 (53,600) SkyDome Bob Bailor Reggie Jackson Ferguson Jenkins Alan Ashby	6.00	1.80
2 Atlanta Braves Heroes Upper Deck Award Winners May 14, 1993 (44,100) Fulton County Coliseum Jeff Burroughs George Kell Gary Matthews Earl Williams Ralph Garr	6.00	1.80
3 Upper Deck Heroes of Baseball vs. St. Louis Cardinals May 15, 1993 (51,600) Busch Stadium Art Shamsky Reggie Jackson Dick Williams Earl Weaver MG Ken Holtzman Bob Feller	6.00	1.80
4 '69 Royals vs. '69 Twins May 22, 1993 (42,600) Royal Stadium Bob Oliver Ellie Rodriguez Moe Drabowsky Dick Drago Joe Keough	6.00	1.80
5 Ewing M. Kauffman Induction into Royals Hall of Fame May 23, 1993 (42,600) Royal Stadium Ewing M. Kauffman	5.00	1.50
6 Upper Deck Heroes vs. Red Sox Heroes May 29, 1993 (36,600) Fenway Park Minnie Minoso Ernie Banks Earl Wilson Carl Yastrzemski	8.00	2.40
7 Heroes of the '60s June 6, 1993 (31,600) Candlestick Park Jim Ray Hart Jim Davenport Tom Haller Juan Marichal Orlando Cepeda	6.00	1.80
8 125 Years of Cincinnati Baseball June 6, 1993 (51,600) Riverfront Stadium Tommy Helms Bobby Tolan Brooks Lawrence Gordy Coleman	4.00	1.20
9 Nickname Heroes Milwaukee County Stad. June 12, 1993 (31,600) County Stadium Bill Madlock Mark Fidrych Jerry Augustine John Montefusco Cecil Cooper	6.00	1.80
10 20th Anniversary of the 1973 World Series June 12, 1993 (46,600) Shea Stadium Felix Millan Dick Williams MG Vida Blue Jerry Grote Wayne Garrett	6.00	1.80
11 Colorado Rockies Inaugural Season June 19, 1993 (21,600) Mile High Stadium Roger Freed Johnny Blanchard Graig Nettles J.R. Richard	10.00	3.00
12 '83 Phillies vs. '83 Heroes June 19, 1993 (56,600) Veterans Stadium Mike Schmidt Gary Matthews John Denny Joe Morgan Al Holland	8.00	2.40
13 25 Years of Padres Baseball June 25, 1993 (41,600) Jack Murphy Stadium Randy Jones Dick Williams MG Graig Nettles Steve Garvey Nate Colbert	6.00	1.80
14 White Sox 1983 Winning Ugly vs. 1983 Baltimore Orioles July 4, 1993 (21,600) Comiskey Park Dick Tidrow Floyd Bannister Tom Paciorek Richard Dotson Julio Cruz	6.00	1.80
15 All-Time Home Run Hitters July 4, 1993 (21,600) Metrodome Dick Allen George Foster Harmon Killebrew Tony Oliva Willie Horton	8.00	2.40
16 1993 Upper Deck All-Star FanFest Autograph Sheet July 8-13, 1993 unnumbered	2.00	.60
17 A Celebration of Early Black Baseball July 10, 1993 (50,000) Camden Yards Roy Campanella Bill Wright Andy Porter Leon Day Henry Kimbro Luis Villodas Buck Leonard Verdell Mathis Buck O'Neil Ray Dandridge Piper Davis Ted Radcliffe	8.00	2.40
18 Upper Deck Heroes of Baseball All-Star Game July 12, 1993 (unnumbered) Camden Yards Reggie Jackson Brooks Robinson Frank Robinson Jim Palmer Al Kaline	6.00	1.80
19 The 1993 National Chicago Upper Deck 5 Year Anniversary July 20-25, 1993 unnumbered Tim Salmon Gary Sheffield Nolan Ryan Juan Gonzalez Dave Justice Ivan Rodriguez Ken Griffey Jr. Frank Thomas Ken Griffey Jr.	4.00	1.20
20 1978 Yankees 22nd World Championship July 24, 1993 (51,600) Yankee Stadium Thurman Munson Mike Torrez Reggie Jackson Steve Garvey Dennis Leonard	6.00	1.80
21 Astros All-Star Heroes Game July 24, 1993 Ferguson Jenkins Juan Marichal Billy Williams Jim Wynn	2.00	.60
22 World Children's Baseball Fair July 31, 1993 (61,000) Jack Murphy Stadium Randy Jones Sachio Kinugasa George Foster Orlando Cepeda Minnie Minoso Bill Madlock Sadaharu Oh	8.00	2.40
23 Reggie Jackson Hall of Fame Induction Aug. 1, 1993 (51,600) Anaheim Stadium	6.00	1.80
24 Seattle Mariners Salutes Heroes of the 70's August 15, 1993 26,600 Bill Madlock Mark Fidrych Ron Cey George Foster Wilbur Wood	2.00	.60
25 A Tribute to Billy Ball Billy Martin Aug. 15, 1993 (46,600) Oakland-Alameda County Stadium	6.00	1.80
26 25th Anniversary of the 1968 World Series August 22, 1993 (31,600) Tiger Stadium Curt Flood Lou Brock Mickey Lolich Jim Northrup Willie Horton	10.00	3.00
27 The Expos' 25th Anniversary August 28, 1993 (41,600) Olympic Stadium Warren Cromartie Rusty Staub Gene Mauch MG Steve Rogers Gary Carter	6.00	1.80
28 Florida Marlins Inaugural Season September 25, 1993 (47,600) Tony Perez Minnie Minoso Luis Tiant Orlando Cepeda Cookie Rojas	8.00	2.40
29 Upper Deck Company Salutes the Heroes of Arlington Stadium October 2, 1993 (46,600) Arlington Stadium	4.00	1.20
30 Tribute to Cleveland Stadium October 2, 1993 (76,600) Cleveland Stadium Andre Thornton Mel Harder Bob Feller Lou Boudreau	4.00	1.20
31 Upper Deck Heroes of Baseball Autograph Sheet No date (21,600)	2.00	.60

1994 Upper Deck

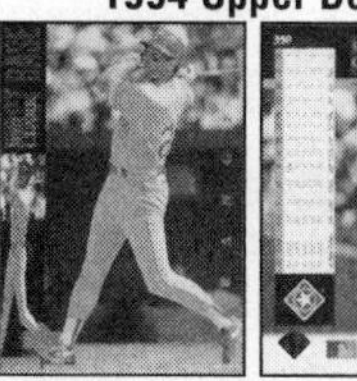

The 1994 Upper Deck set was issued in two series of 280 and 270 standard-size cards for a total of 550. There are number of topical subsets including Star Rookies (1-30), Fantasy Team (31-40), The Future is Now (41-55), Home Field Advantage (267-294), Upper Deck Classic Alumni (295-299), Diamond Debuts (511-522) and Top Prospects (523-550). Three autograph cards were randomly inserted into first series retail packs. They are Ken Griffey Jr. (KG), Mickey Mantle (MM) and a combo card with Griffey and Mantle (GM). An Alex Rodriguez (298A) autograph card was randomly inserted into second series retail packs. Rookie Cards include Michael Jordan (as an baseball player), Chan Ho Park, Alex Rodriguez and Billy Wagner. Many cards have been found with a significant variation on the back. The player's name, the horizontal bar containing the biographical information and the vertical bar containing the stats header are normally printed in copper-gold color. On the variation cards, these areas are printed in silver. It is not known exactly how many of the 550 cards have silver versions, nor has any premium been established for them. Also, all of the American League Home Field Advantage subset cards (numbers 281-294) are minor uncorrected errors because the Upper Deck logos on the front are missing the year "1994".

	Nm-Mt	Ex-Mt
COMPLETE SET (550)	50.00	15.00
COMP. SERIES 1 (280)	30.00	9.00
COMP. SERIES 2 (270)	20.00	6.00
1 Brian Anderson RC	.40	.12
2 Shane Andrews	.15	.04
3 James Baldwin	.15	.04
4 Rich Becker	.15	.04
5 Greg Blosser	.15	.04
6 Ricky Bottalico RC	.40	.12
7 Midre Cummings	.15	.04
8 Carlos Delgado	.50	.15
9 Steve Dreyer RC	.15	.04
10 Joey Eischen	.15	.04
11 Carl Everett	.30	.09
12 Cliff Floyd UER (text indicates he throws left; should be right)	.30	.09
13 Alex Gonzalez	.15	.04
14 Jeff Granger	.15	.04
15 Shawn Green	.75	.23
16 Brian L. Hunter	.15	.04
17 Butch Huskey	.15	.04
18 Mark Hutton	.15	.04
19 Michael Jordan RC	10.00	3.00
20 Steve Karsay	.15	.04
21 Jeff McNeely	.15	.04
22 Marc Newfield	.15	.04
23 Manny Ramirez	.50	.15
24 Alex Rodriguez RC	20.00	6.00
25 Scott Ruffcorn UER (photo on back is Robert Ellis)	.15	.04
26 Paul Spoljaric UER (Expos logo on back)	.15	.04
27 Salomon Torres	.15	.04
28 Steve Trachsel	.15	.04
29 Chris Turner	.15	.04
30 Gabe White	.15	.04
31 Randy Johnson FT	.50	.15
32 John Wetteland FT	.15	.04
33 Mike Piazza FT	.75	.23
34 Rafael Palmeiro FT	.30	.09
35 Roberto Alomar FT	.30	.09
36 Matt Williams FT	.15	.04
37 Travis Fryman FT	.15	.04
38 Barry Bonds FT	1.00	.30
39 Marquis Grissom FT	.15	.04
40 Albert Belle FT	.30	.09
41 Steve Avery FUT	.15	.04
42 Jason Bere FUT	.15	.04
43 Alex Fernandez FUT	.15	.04
44 Mike Mussina FUT	.50	.15
45 Aaron Sele FUT	.15	.04
46 Rod Beck FUT	.15	.04
47 Mike Piazza FUT	.75	.23
48 John Olerud FUT	.15	.04
49 Carlos Baerga FUT	.15	.04
50 Gary Sheffield FUT	.15	.04
51 Travis Fryman FUT	.15	.04
52 Juan Gonzalez FUT	.50	.15
53 Ken Griffey Jr. FUT	.75	.23
54 Tim Salmon FUT	.30	.09
55 Frank Thomas FUT	.50	.15
56 Tony Phillips	.15	.04
57 Julio Franco	.30	.09
58 Kevin Mitchell	.15	.04
59 Raul Mondesi	.30	.09
60 Rickey Henderson	.75	.23
61 Jay Buhner	.30	.09
62 Bill Swift	.15	.04
63 Brady Anderson	.30	.09
64 Ryan Klesko	.30	.09
65 Darren Daulton	.30	.09
66 Damion Easley	.15	.04
67 Mark McGwire	2.00	.60
68 John Roper	.15	.04
69 Dave Telgheder	.15	.04
70 David Nied	.15	.04
71 Mo Vaughn	.30	.09
72 Tyler Green	.15	.04
73 Dave Magadan	.15	.04
74 Chili Davis	.30	.09
75 Archi Cianfrocco	.15	.04
76 Joe Girardi	.15	.04
77 Chris Hoiles	.15	.04
78 Ryan Bowen	.15	.04
79 Greg Gagne	.15	.04
80 Aaron Sele	.15	.04
81 Dave Winfield	.30	.09
82 Chad Curtis	.15	.04
83 Andy Van Slyke	.30	.09
84 Kevin Stocker	.15	.04
85 Deion Sanders	.50	.15
86 Bernie Williams	.50	.15
87 John Smoltz	.50	.15
88 Ruben Santana	.15	.04
89 Dave Stewart	.30	.09
90 Don Mattingly	2.00	.60
91 Joe Carter	.30	.09
92 Ryne Sandberg	1.25	.35
93 Chris Gomez	.15	.04
94 Tino Martinez	.50	.15
95 Terry Pendleton	.30	.09
96 Andre Dawson	.30	.09
97 Wil Cordero	.15	.04
98 Kent Hrbek	.30	.09
99 John Olerud	.30	.09
100 Kirt Manwaring	.15	.04
101 Tim Bogar	.15	.04
102 Mike Mussina	.75	.23
103 Nigel Wilson	.15	.04
104 Ricky Gutierrez	.15	.04
105 Roberto Mejia	.15	.04
106 Tom Pagnozzi	.15	.04
107 Mike Macfarlane	.15	.04
108 Jose Bautista	.15	.04
109 Luis Ortiz	.15	.04
110 Brent Gates	.15	.04
111 Tim Salmon	.50	.15
112 Wade Boggs	.50	.15
113 Tripp Cromer	.15	.04
114 Denny Hocking	.15	.04
115 Carlos Baerga	.15	.04
116 J.R. Phillips	.15	.04
117 Bo Jackson	.75	.23
118 Lance Johnson	.15	.04
119 Bobby Jones	.15	.04
120 Bobby Witt	.15	.04
121 Ron Karkovice	.15	.04
122 Jose Vizcaino	.15	.04
123 Danny Darwin	.15	.04
124 Eduardo Perez	.15	.04
125 Brian Looney RC	.15	.04
126 Pat Hentgen	.15	.04
127 Frank Viola	.30	.09
128 Darren Holmes	.15	.04
129 Wally Whitehurst	.15	.04
130 Matt Walbeck	.15	.04
131 Albert Belle	.30	.09
132 Steve Cooke	.15	.04
133 Kevin Appier	.30	.09
134 Joe Oliver	.15	.04
135 Benji Gil	.15	.04
136 Steve Buechele	.15	.04
137 Devon White	.15	.04
138 S.Hitchcock UER two losses for career; should be four	.15	.04
139 Phil Leftwich RC	.15	.04
140 Jose Canseco	.75	.23
141 Rick Aguilera	.15	.04
142 Rod Beck	.15	.04
143 Jose Rijo	.15	.04
144 Tom Glavine	.50	.15
145 Phil Plantier	.15	.04
146 Jason Bere	.15	.04
147 Jamie Moyer	.30	.09
148 Wes Chamberlain	.15	.04
149 Glenallen Hill	.15	.04
150 Mark Whiten	.15	.04
151 Bret Barberie	.15	.04
152 Chuck Knoblauch	.30	.09
153 Trevor Hoffman	.30	.09
154 Rick Wilkins	.15	.04
155 Juan Gonzalez	.75	.23
156 Ozzie Guillen	.15	.04
157 Jim Eisenreich	.15	.04
158 Pedro Astacio	.15	.04
159 Joe Magrane	.15	.04
160 Ryan Thompson	.15	.04
161 Jose Lind	.15	.04
162 Jeff Conine	.30	.09
163 Todd Benzinger	.15	.04
164 Roger Salkeld	.15	.04
165 Gary DiSarcina	.15	.04
166 Kevin Gross	.15	.04
167 Charlie Hayes	.15	.04
168 Tim Costo	.15	.04
169 Wally Joyner	.30	.09
170 Johnny Ruffin	.15	.04
171 Kirk Rueter	.30	.09
172 Lenny Dykstra	.30	.09
173 Ken Hill	.15	.04
174 Mike Bordick	.15	.04
175 Billy Hall	.15	.04
176 Rob Butler	.15	.04
177 Jay Bell	.30	.09
178 Jeff Kent	.30	.09
179 David Wells	.30	.09
180 Dean Palmer	.30	.09
181 Mariano Duncan	.15	.04
182 Orlando Merced	.15	.04
183 Brett Butler	.30	.09
184 Milt Thompson	.15	.04
185 Chipper Jones	.75	.23
186 Paul O'Neill	.50	.15
187 Mike Greenwell	.15	.04
188 Harold Baines	.30	.09
189 Todd Stottlemyre	.15	.04
190 Jeromy Burnitz	.30	.09
191 Rene Arocha	.15	.04
192 Jeff Fassero	.15	.04
193 Robby Thompson	.15	.04
194 Greg W. Harris	.15	.04
195 Todd Van Poppel	.15	.04
196 Jose Guzman	.15	.04
197 Shane Mack	.15	.04
198 Carlos Garcia	.15	.04
199 Kevin Roberson	.15	.04
200 David McCarty	.15	.04
201 Alan Trammell	.50	.15
202 Chuck Carr	.15	.04
203 Tommy Greene	.15	.04
204 Wilson Alvarez	.15	.04
205 Dwight Gooden	.50	.15
206 Tony Tarasco	.15	.04
207 Darren Lewis	.15	.04
208 Eric Karros	.30	.09
209 Chris Hammond	.15	.04
210 Jeffrey Hammonds	.15	.04
211 Rich Amaral	.15	.04
212 Danny Tartabull	.15	.04
213 Jeff Russell	.15	.04
214 Dave Staton	.15	.04
215 Kenny Lofton	.30	.09
216 Manuel Lee	.15	.04
217 Brian Koelling	.15	.04
218 Scott Lydy	.15	.04
219 Tony Gwynn	1.00	.30
220 Cecil Fielder	.30	.09
221 Royce Clayton	.15	.04
222 Reggie Sanders	.30	.09
223 Brian Jordan	.30	.09
224 Ken Griffey Jr.	1.25	.35
225 Fred McGriff	.50	.15
226 Felix Jose	.15	.04
227 Brad Pennington	.15	.04
228 Chris Bosio	.15	.04
229 Mike Stanley	.15	.04
230 Willie Greene	.15	.04
231 Alex Fernandez	.15	.04
232 Brad Ausmus	.15	.04
233 Darrell Whitmore	.15	.04
234 Marcus Moore	.15	.04
235 Allen Watson	.15	.04
236 Jose Offerman	.15	.04
237 Rondell White	.30	.09
238 Jeff King	.15	.04
239 Luis Alicea	.15	.04
240 Dan Wilson	.15	.04
241 Ed Sprague	.15	.04
242 Todd Hundley	.15	.04
243 Al Martin	.15	.04
244 Mike Lansing	.15	.04
245 Ivan Rodriguez	.75	.23
246 Dave Fleming	.15	.04
247 John Doherty	.15	.04
248 Mark McLemore	.15	.04
249 Bob Hamelin	.15	.04
250 Curtis Pride RC	.40	.12
251 Zane Smith	.15	.04
252 Eric Young	.15	.04
253 Brian McRae	.15	.04
254 Tim Raines	.30	.09
255 Javier Lopez	.30	.09
256 Melvin Nieves	.15	.04
257 Randy Myers	.15	.04
258 Willie McGee	.30	.09
259 Jimmy Key UER (birthdate missing on back)	.30	.09
260 Tom Candiotti	.15	.04
261 Eric Davis	.30	.09
262 Craig Paquette	.15	.04
263 Robin Ventura	.30	.09
264 Pat Kelly	.15	.04
265 Gregg Jefferies	.15	.04
266 Cory Snyder	.15	.04
267 David Justice HFA	.15	.04
268 Sammy Sosa HFA	.75	.23
269 Barry Larkin HFA	.30	.09
270 Andres Galarraga HFA	.15	.04
271 Gary Sheffield HFA	.15	.04
272 Jeff Bagwell HFA	.30	.09

1994 Upper Deck

273 Mike Piazza HFA .75 .23
274 Larry Walker HFA .15 .04
275 Bobby Bonilla HFA .15 .04
276 John Kruk HFA .15 .04
277 Jay Bell HFA .15 .04
278 Ozzie Smith HFA .75 .23
279 Tony Gwynn HFA .50 .15
280 Barry Bonds HFA 1.00 .30
281 Cal Ripken Jr. HFA 1.25 .35
282 Mo Vaughn HFA .15 .04
283 Tim Salmon HFA .30 .09
284 Frank Thomas HFA .50 .15
285 Albert Belle HFA .30 .09
286 Cecil Fielder HFA .15 .04
287 Wally Joyner HFA .15 .04
288 Greg Vaughn HFA .15 .04
289 Kirby Puckett HFA .50 .15
290 Don Mattingly HFA 1.00 .30
291 Terry Steinbach HFA .15 .04
292 Ken Griffey Jr. HFA .75 .23
293 Juan Gonzalez HFA .50 .15
294 Paul Molitor HFA .30 .09
295 Tavo Alvarez UDC .15 .04
296 Matt Brunson UDC .15 .04
297 Shawn Green UDC .30 .09
298 Alex Rodriguez UDC 6.00 1.80
299 S.Stewart UDC .75 .23
300 Frank Thomas .75 .23
301 Mickey Tettleton .15 .04
302 Pedro Munoz .15 .04
303 Jose Valentin .15 .04
304 Orestes Destrade .15 .04
305 Pat Listach .15 .04
306 Scott Brosius .30 .09
307 Kurt Miller .15 .04
308 Rob Dibble .30 .09
309 Mike Blowers .15 .04
310 Jim Abbott .50 .15
311 Mike Jackson .15 .04
312 Craig Biggio .50 .15
313 Kurt Abbott RC .40 .12
314 Chuck Finley .30 .09
315 Andres Galarraga .30 .09
316 Mike Moore .15 .04
317 Doug Strange .15 .04
318 Pedro Martinez .75 .23
319 Kevin McReynolds .15 .04
320 Greg Maddux 1.25 .35
321 Mike Henneman .15 .04
322 Scott Leius .15 .04
323 John Franco .30 .09
324 Jeff Blauser .15 .04
325 Kirby Puckett .75 .23
326 Darryl Hamilton .15 .04
327 John Smiley .15 .04
328 Derrick May .15 .04
329 Jose Vizcaino .15 .04
330 Randy Johnson .75 .23
331 Jack Morris .30 .09
332 Graeme Lloyd .15 .04
333 Dave Valle .15 .04
334 Greg Myers .15 .04
335 John Wetteland .30 .09
336 Jim Gott .15 .04
337 Tim Naehring .15 .04
338 Mike Kelly .15 .04
339 Jeff Montgomery .15 .04
340 Rafael Palmeiro .50 .15
341 Eddie Murray .75 .23
342 Xavier Hernandez .15 .04
343 Bobby Munoz .15 .04
344 Bobby Bonilla .30 .09
345 Travis Fryman .30 .09
346 Steve Finley .30 .09
347 Chris Sabo .15 .04
348 Armando Reynoso .15 .04
349 Ramon Martinez .15 .04
350 Will Clark .75 .23
351 Moises Alou .30 .09
352 Jim Thome .75 .23
353 Bob Tewksbury .15 .04
354 Andujar Cedeno .15 .04
355 Orel Hershiser .30 .09
356 Mike Devereaux .15 .04
357 Mike Perez .15 .04
358 Dennis Martinez .30 .09
359 Dave Nilsson .15 .04
360 Ozzie Smith 1.25 .35
361 Eric Anthony .15 .04
362 Scott Sanders .15 .04
363 Paul Sorrento .15 .04
364 Tim Belcher .15 .04
365 Dennis Eckersley .30 .09
366 Mel Rojas .15 .04
367 Tom Henke .15 .04
368 Randy Tomlin .15 .04
369 B.J. Surhoff .30 .09
370 Larry Walker .50 .15
371 Joey Cora .15 .04
372 Mike Harkey .15 .04
373 John Valentin .15 .04
374 Doug Jones .15 .04
375 David Justice .30 .09
376 Vince Coleman .15 .04
377 David Hulse .15 .04
378 Kevin Seitzer .15 .04
379 Pete Harnisch .15 .04
380 Ruben Sierra .15 .04
381 Mark Lewis .15 .04
382 Bip Roberts .15 .04
383 Paul Wagner .15 .04
384 Stan Javier .15 .04
385 Barry Larkin .75 .23
386 Mark Portugal .15 .04
387 Roberto Kelly .15 .04
388 Andy Benes .15 .04
389 Felix Fermin .15 .04
390 Marquis Grissom .15 .04
391 Troy Neel .15 .04
392 Chad Kreuter .15 .04
393 Gregg Olson .15 .04
394 Charles Nagy .15 .04
395 Jack McDowell .15 .04
396 Luis Gonzalez .30 .09
397 Benito Santiago .30 .09
398 Chris James .15 .04
399 Terry Mulholland .15 .04
400 Barry Bonds 2.00 .60
401 Joe Grahe .15 .04
402 Duane Ward .15 .04
403 John Burkett .15 .04
404 Scott Servais .15 .04
405 Bryan Harvey .15 .04
406 Bernard Gilkey .15 .04
407 Greg McMichael .15 .04
408 Tim Wallach .15 .04
409 Ken Caminiti .30 .09
410 John Kruk .30 .09
411 Darrin Jackson .15 .04
412 Mike Gallego .15 .04
413 David Cone .30 .09
414 Lou Whitaker .30 .09
415 Sandy Alomar Jr. .15 .04
416 Bill Wegman .15 .04
417 Pat Borders .15 .04
418 Roger Pavlik .15 .04
419 Pete Smith .15 .04
420 Steve Avery .15 .04
421 David Segui .15 .04
422 Rheal Cormier .15 .04
423 Harold Reynolds .30 .09
424 Edgar Martinez .50 .15
425 Cal Ripken Jr. 2.50 .75
426 Jaime Navarro .15 .04
427 Sean Berry .15 .04
428 Bret Saberhagen .30 .09
429 Bob Welch .15 .04
430 Juan Guzman .15 .04
431 Cal Eldred .15 .04
432 Dave Hollins .15 .04
433 Sid Fernandez .15 .04
434 Willie Banks .15 .04
435 Darryl Kile .30 .09
436 Henry Rodriguez .15 .04
437 Tony Fernandez .15 .04
438 Walt Weiss .15 .04
439 Kevin Tapani .15 .04
440 Mark Grace .50 .15
441 Brian Harper .15 .04
442 Kent Mercker .15 .04
443 Anthony Young .15 .04
444 Todd Zeile .15 .04
445 Greg Vaughn .30 .09
446 Ray Lankford .15 .04
447 Dave Weathers .15 .04
448 Bret Boone .30 .09
449 Charlie Hough .30 .09
450 Roger Clemens 1.50 .45
451 Mike Morgan .15 .04
452 Doug Drabek .15 .04
453 Danny Jackson .15 .04
454 Dante Bichette .30 .09
455 Roberto Alomar .75 .23
456 Ben McDonald .15 .04
457 Kenny Rogers .30 .09
458 Bill Gullickson .15 .04
459 Darrin Fletcher .15 .04
460 Curt Schilling .50 .15
461 Billy Hatcher .15 .04
462 Howard Johnson .15 .04
463 Mickey Morandini .15 .04
464 Frank Castillo .15 .04
465 Delino DeShields .15 .04
466 Gary Gaetti .30 .09
467 Steve Farr .15 .04
468 Roberto Hernandez .15 .04
469 Jack Armstrong .15 .04
470 Paul Molitor .50 .15
471 Melido Perez .15 .04
472 Greg Hibbard .15 .04
473 Jody Reed .15 .04
474 Tom Gordon .15 .04
475 Gary Sheffield .30 .09
476 John Jaha .15 .04
477 Shawon Dunston .15 .04
478 Reggie Jefferson .15 .04
479 Don Slaught .15 .04
480 Jeff Bagwell .50 .15
481 Tim Pugh .15 .04
482 Kevin Young .15 .04
483 Ellis Burks .30 .09
484 Greg Swindell .15 .04
485 Mark Langston .15 .04
486 Omar Vizquel .30 .09
487 Kevin Brown .30 .09
488 Terry Steinbach .15 .04
489 Mark Lemke .15 .04
490 Matt Williams .30 .09
491 Pete Incaviglia .15 .04
492 Karl Rhodes .15 .04
493 Shawn Green .75 .23
494 Hal Morris .15 .04
495 Derek Bell .15 .04
496 Luis Polonia .15 .04
497 Otis Nixon .15 .04
498 Ron Darling .15 .04
499 Mitch Williams .15 .04
500 Mike Piazza 1.50 .45
501 Pat Meares .15 .04
502 Scott Cooper .15 .04
503 Scott Erickson .15 .04
504 Jeff Juden .15 .04
505 Lee Smith .30 .09
506 Bobby Ayala .15 .04
507 Dave Henderson .15 .04
508 Erik Hanson .15 .04
509 Bob Wickman .15 .04
510 Sammy Sosa 1.25 .35
511 Hector Carrasco .15 .04
512 Tim Davis .15 .04
513 Joey Hamilton .15 .04
514 Robert Eenhoorn .15 .04
515 Jorge Fabregas .15 .04
516 Tim Hyers RC .15 .04
517 John Hudek RC .15 .04
518 James Mouton .15 .04
519 Herbert Perry RC .40 .12
520 Chan Ho Park RC 1.00 .30
521 W.Va Landingham RC .15 .04
522 Paul Shuey .15 .04
523 Ryan Hancock RC .15 .04
524 Billy Wagner RC 1.00 .30
525 Jason Giambi .75 .23
526 Jose Silva RC .15 .04
527 Terrell Wade RC .15 .04
528 Todd Dunn .15 .04
529 Alan Benes RC .40 .12
530 B.Kieschnick RC .40 .12
531 T.Hollandsworth .15 .04
532 Brad Fullmer RC 1.00 .30
533 S.Soderstrom RC .15 .04
534 Daron Kirkreit .15 .04
535 Arquimedez Pozo RC .15 .04
536 Charles Johnson .30 .09
537 Preston Wilson .50 .15
538 Alex Ochoa .15 .04
539 Derrek Lee RC 1.25 .35
540 Wayne Gomes RC .15 .04
541 J.Allensworth RC .15 .04
542 Mike Bell RC .15 .04
543 Trot Nixon RC 1.00 .30
544 Pokey Reese .15 .04
545 Neifi Perez RC .40 .12
546 Johnny Damon .75 .23
547 Matt Brunson RC .15 .04
548 L.Hawkins RC .40 .12
549 Eddie Pearson RC .15 .04
550 Derek Jeter 2.50 .75
A298 Alex Rodriguez AU 375.00 110.00
P224 K.Griffey Jr. Promo 2.00 .60
GM1 Ken Griffey Jr. AU 1000.00 300.00
Mickey Mantle AU/1000
KG1 K.Griffey Jr. AU/1000 200.00 60.00
MM1 M.Mantle AU/1000 500.00 150.00

1994 Upper Deck Electric Diamond

This 550-card set is a parallel issue to the basic 1994 Upper Deck cards. The cards were issued one per foil pack and two per mini jumbo. The only differences between these and the basic cards is the "Electric Diamond" in silver foil toward the bottom and the player's name is also in silver foil.

Nm-Mt Ex-Mt
COMPLETE SET (550) 100.00 30.00
COMP.SERIES 1 (280) 60.00 18.00
COMP.SERIES 2 (270) 40.00 12.00
*STARS: .75X TO 2X BASIC CARDS ...
*ROOKIES: .6X TO 1.5X BASIC CARDS

1994 Upper Deck Diamond Collection

This 30-card standard-size set was inserted regionally in first series hobby packs at a rate of one in 18. The three regions are Central (C1-C10), East (E1-E10) and West (W1-W10). While each card has the same horizontal format, the color scheme differs by region. The Central cards have a blue background, the East green and the West a deep shade of red. Color player photos are superimposed over the backgrounds. Each card has, "The Upper Deck Diamond Collection" as part of the background. The backs have a small photo and career highlights.

Nm-Mt Ex-Mt
COMPLETE SET (30) 180.00 55.00
COMPLETE CENTRAL (10) 80.00 24.00
COMPLETE EAST (10) 40.00 12.00
COMPLETE WEST (10) 60.00 18.00
C1 Jeff Bagwell 4.00 1.20
C2 Michael Jordan 25.00 7.50
C3 Barry Larkin 6.00 1.80
C4 Kirby Puckett 6.00 1.80
C5 Manny Ramirez 4.00 1.20
C6 Ryne Sandberg 10.00 3.00
C7 Ozzie Smith 10.00 3.00
C8 Frank Thomas 6.00 1.80
C9 Andy Van Slyke 2.50 .75
C10 Robin Yount 6.00 1.80
E1 Roberto Alomar 6.00 1.80
E2 Roger Clemens 12.00 3.60
E3 Lenny Dykstra 2.50 .75
E4 Cecil Fielder 2.50 .75
E5 Cliff Floyd 2.50 .75
E6 Dwight Gooden 4.00 1.20
E7 David Justice 2.50 .75
E8 Don Mattingly 15.00 4.50
E9 Cal Ripken Jr. 20.00 6.00
E10 Gary Sheffield 2.50 .75
W1 Barry Bonds 15.00 4.50
W2 Andres Galarraga 2.50 .75
W3 Juan Gonzalez 6.00 1.80
W4 Ken Griffey Jr. 10.00 3.00
W5 Tony Gwynn 8.00 2.40
W6 Rickey Henderson 6.00 1.80
W7 Bo Jackson 6.00 1.80
W8 Mark McGwire 15.00 4.50
W9 Mike Piazza 12.00 3.60
W10 Tim Salmon 4.00 1.20

1994 Upper Deck Mantle Heroes

Randomly inserted in second series packs at a rate of one in 35, this 10-card standard-size set looks at various moments from The Mick's career. Metallic fronts feature a vintage photo with the card title at the bottom. The backs contain career highlights with a small scrapbook like photo. The numbering (64-72) is a continuation from previous Heroes sets.

Nm-Mt Ex-Mt
COMPLETE SET (10) 80.00 24.00
COMMON (64-72/HDR) 10.00 3.00

1994 Upper Deck Mantle's Long Shots

Randomly inserted in first series retail packs at a rate of one in 18, this 21-card silver foil standard-size set features top longball hitters as selected by Mickey Mantle. The cards are numbered on the back with a "MM" prefix and sequenced in alphabetical order. Two trade cards, were also random inserts and were redeemable (expiration: December 31, 1994) for either the basic silver foil set version (Silver Trade card) or the Electric Diamond version (blue Trade card).

Nm-Mt Ex-Mt
COMPLETE SET (21) 40.00 12.00
*ED: .5X TO 1.2X BASIC MANTLE LS .
ONE ED SET VIA MAIL PER BLUE TRADE CARD
MANTLE TRADES: RANDOM IN SER.1 HOB
MM1 Jeff Bagwell 1.50 .45
MM2 Albert Belle 1.00 .30
MM3 Barry Bonds 6.00 1.80
MM4 Jose Canseco 2.50 .75
MM5 Joe Carter 1.00 .30
MM6 Carlos Delgado 1.50 .45
MM7 Cecil Fielder 1.00 .30
MM8 Cliff Floyd 1.00 .30
MM9 Juan Gonzalez 2.50 .75
MM10 Ken Griffey Jr. 4.00 1.20
MM11 David Justice 1.00 .30
MM12 Fred McGriff 1.50 .45
MM13 Mark McGwire 6.00 1.80
MM14 Dean Palmer 1.00 .30
MM15 Mike Piazza 5.00 1.50
MM16 Manny Ramirez 1.50 .45
MM17 Tim Salmon 1.50 .45
MM18 Frank Thomas 2.50 .75
MM19 Mo Vaughn 1.00 .30
MM20 Matt Williams 1.00 .30
MM21 Mickey Mantle 15.00 4.50
NNO Mickey Mantle 6.00 1.80
Silver Trade
NNO Mickey Mantle 15.00 4.50
Blue ED Trade

1994 Upper Deck Next Generation

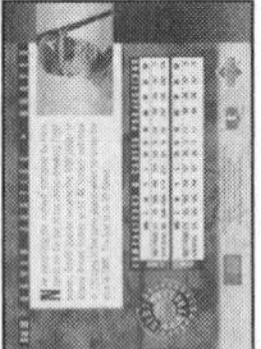

Randomly inserted in second series retail packs at a rate of one in 20, this 18-card standard-size set spotlights young established stars and promising prospects. The set is sequenced in alphabetical order. A Next Generation Electric Diamond Trade Card and a Next Generation Trade Card were seeded randomly in second series hobby packs. Each card could be redeemed for that set. Expiration date for redemption was October 31, 1994.

Nm-Mt Ex-Mt
COMPLETE SET (18) 120.00 36.00
1 Roberto Alomar 5.00 1.50
2 Carlos Delgado 3.00 .90
3 Cliff Floyd 2.00 .60
4 Alex Gonzalez 1.00 .30
5 Juan Gonzalez 5.00 1.50
6 Ken Griffey Jr. 8.00 2.40
7 Jeffrey Hammonds 1.00 .30
8 Michael Jordan 20.00 6.00
9 David Justice 2.00 .60
10 Ryan Klesko 2.00 .60
11 Javier Lopez 2.00 .60
12 Raul Mondesi 2.00 .60
13 Mike Piazza 10.00 3.00
14 Kirby Puckett 5.00 1.50
15 Manny Ramirez 3.00 .90
16 Alex Rodriguez 40.00 12.00
17 Tim Salmon 3.00 .90
18 Gary Sheffield 2.00 .60
NNO Exp. NG Trade Card 1.00 .30

1994 Upper Deck Next Generation Electric Diamond

This 18 card set parallels the regular Next Generation insert set. The cards are differentiated by an "Electric Diamond" logo on the bottom. These cards were sent if a collector received a ED trade card in a pack.

Nm-Mt Ex-Mt
*ELEC.DIAM: .5X TO 1.2X BASIC NEXT.GEN.
8 Michael Jordan 25.00 7.50
16 Alex Rodriguez 60.00 18.00

1994 Upper Deck All-Star Jumbos

This 48-card boxed set captures the photography of Walter Iooss Jr. Iooss shot 42 of the 49 cards in the set. The set included an order form for an album. The cards are oversized, measuring 3 1/2" by 5 1/4". The full-bleed color player photos are edged on one side by a green stripe carrying the player's name. A special green foil All-Star logo appears in one of the lower corners. One set per 40-box case uses gold foil in place of green. The horizontal back has a thick black stripe carrying a small color photo and Iooss' comments on the left, with a career summary and another closeup photo on the remainder of the back. The set closes with six cards commemorating historic events during the 125-year history of baseball (43-48). Some dealers believe that gold production was limited to 1,200 sets.

Nm-Mt Ex-Mt
COMP.FACT SET (48) 15.00 4.50
1 Ken Griffey Jr. 1.50 .45
2 Ruben Sierra .10 .03
Todd Van Poppel
3 Bryan Harvey .40 .12
Gary Sheffield
4 Gregg Jefferies .20 .06
Brian Jordan
5 Ryne Sandberg .75 .23
6 Matt Williams .30 .09
John Burkett
7 Darren Daulton .20 .06
John Kruk
8 Don Mattingly 1.00 .30
Wade Boggs
9 Pat Listach .10 .03
Greg Vaughn
10 Tim Salmon .40 .12
Eduardo Perez
11 Fred McGriff .30 .09
Tom Glavine
12 Mo Vaughn .20 .06
Andre Dawson
13 Brian McRae .10 .03
Kevin Appier
14 Kirby Puckett 1.00 .30
Kent Hrbek
15 Cal Ripken 2.00 .60
16 Roberto Alomar .40 .12
Paul Molitor
17 Tony Gwynn 1.00 .30
Phil Plantier
18 Greg Maddux 1.25 .35
Steve Avery
19 Mike Mussina .40 .12
Chris Hoiles
20 Randy Johnson .40 .12
21 Roger Clemens 1.00 .30
Aaron Sele
22 Will Clark .40 .12
Dean Palmer
23 Cecil Fielder .20 .06
Travis Fryman
24 John Olerud .20 .06
Joe Carter
25 Juan Gonzalez .40 .12
26 Jose Rijo .30 .09
Barry Larkin
27 Andy Van Slyke .20 .06
Jeff King
28 Larry Walker .20 .06
Marquis Grissom
29 Kenny Lofton .20 .06
Albert Belle
30 Mark Grace 1.25 .35
Sammy Sosa
31 Mike Piazza 1.50 .45
32 Ramon Martinez .50 .15
Pedro Martinez
Orel Hershiser
33 David Justice .40 .12
Terry Pendleton
34 Ivan Rodriguez .50 .15
Jose Canseco
35 Barry Bonds 1.00 .30
36 Jeff Bagwell .75 .23
Craig Biggio
37 Jay Bell .10 .03
Orlando Merced
38 Jeff Kent .20 .06
Dwight Gooden
39 Andres Galarraga .40 .12
Charlie Hayes
40 Frank Thomas .75 .23
41 Bobby Bonilla .10 .03
42 Jack McDowell .10 .03
Tim Raines
43 1869 Red Stockings .10 .03
44 Ty Cobb 25th Ann. .75 .23
45 Babe Ruth 50th Ann. 2.00 .60
46 M.Mantle 75th Ann. 2.00 .60
47 Hank Aaron 100th Ann. .75 .23
48 K.Griffey Jr. 125th Ann. 1.25 .35
P48 Ken Griffey Jr. Promo 5.00 1.50

1994 Upper Deck All-Time Heroes

This set consists of 225 standard-size cards. According to Upper Deck, production was limited to 4,015 numbered cases. Special subsets featured are Off The Wire (1-18), All-Time Heroes (101-125), Diamond Legends (151-177), and Heroes of Baseball (208-224). Mickey Mantle and three other superstars (Reggie Jackson, Tom Seaver, and George Brett) each autographed 1,000 cards that were randomly inserted into packs. (Nolan Ryan had been expected to sign cards for this product but did not. Instead, Brett signed an additional 1,000 cards). According to Upper Deck, a signed card would be found in one of every 385 packs. A Reggie Jackson Promo card was distributed to dealers and hobby media to preview the set.

	Nm-Mt	Ex-Mt
COMPLETE SET (225)	15.00	4.50
1 Ted Williams OW	.60	.18
2 J. Vander Meer OW	.10	.03
3 Lou Brock OW	.30	.09
4 Lou Gehrig OW	.50	.15
5 Hank Aaron OW	.50	.15
6 Tommie Agee OW	.10	.03
7 Mickey Mantle OW	1.00	.30
8 Bill Mazeroski OW	.20	.06
9 Reggie Jackson OW	.30	.09
10 Willie Mays Mickey Mantle	1.00	.30
11 Roy Campanella OW	.20	.06
12 Harvey Haddix OW	.10	.03
13 Jimmy Piersall OW	.10	.03
14 Enos Slaughter OW	.10	.03
15 Nolan Ryan OW	.75	.23
16 Bobby Thomson OW	.10	.03
17 Willie Mays OW	.50	.15
18 Bucky Dent OW	.10	.03
19 Joe Garagiola	.20	.06
20 George Brett	1.25	.35
21 Cecil Cooper	.20	.06
22 Ray Boone	.10	.03
23 King Kelly	.20	.06
24 Willie Mays	1.00	.30
25 Napoleon Lajoie	.30	.09
26 Gil McDougald	.20	.06
27 Nelson Briles	.10	.03
28 Bucky Dent	.20	.06
29 Manny Sanguillen	.10	.03
30 Ty Cobb	.75	.23
31 Jim Grant	.10	.03
32 Del Ennis	.10	.03
33 Ron Hunt	.10	.03
34 Nolan Ryan	1.50	.45
35 Christy Mathewson	.30	.09
36 Robin Roberts	.20	.06
37 Frank Crosetti	.10	.03
38 Johnny Vander Meer	.10	.03
39 Virgil Trucks	.10	.03
40 Lou Gehrig	1.00	.30
41 Luke Appling	.20	.06
42 Rico Petrocelli	.10	.03
43 Harry Walker	.10	.03
44 Reggie Jackson	.30	.09
45 Mel Ott	.30	.09
46 Phil Cavarretta	.20	.06
47 Larry Doby	.20	.06
48 Johnny Mize	.20	.06
49 Ralph Kiner	.30	.09
50 Ted Williams	1.25	.35
51 Bobby Thomson	.20	.06
52 Joe Black	.20	.06
53 Monte Irvin	.20	.06
54 Bill Virdon	.20	.06
55 Honus Wagner	.50	.15
56 Herb Score	.20	.06
57 Jerry Coleman	.10	.03
58 Jimmie Foxx	.30	.09
59 Roy Face	.10	.03
60 Babe Ruth	1.50	.45
61 Jimmy Piersall	.20	.06
62 Ed Charles	.10	.03
63 Johnny Podres	.20	.06
64 Charlie Neal	.10	.03
65 Bill White	.20	.06
66 Bill Skowron	.30	.09
67 Al Rosen	.20	.06
68 Eddie Lopat	.10	.03
69 Bud Harrelson	.20	.06
70 Steve Carlton	.20	.06
71 Vida Blue	.10	.03
72 Don Newcombe	.20	.06
73 Al Bumbry	.10	.03
74 Bill Madlock	.20	.06
75 Hank Aaron CL	.30	.09
76 Bill Mazeroski	.30	.09
77 Ron Cey	.20	.06
78 Tommy John	.20	.06
79 Lou Brock	.30	.09
80 Walter Johnson	.50	.15
81 Harvey Haddix	.20	.06
82 Al Oliver	.20	.06
83 Johnny Logan	.20	.06
84 Dave Dravecky	.20	.06
85 Tony Oliva	.20	.06
86 Dave Kingman	.20	.06
87 Luis Tiant	.20	.06
88 Sal Bando	.20	.06
89 Cesar Cedeno	.20	.06
90 Warren Spahn	.30	.09
91 Mickey Lolich	.10	.03
92 Lew Burdette	.20	.06
93 Hank Bauer	.20	.06
94 Marv Throneberry	.10	.03
95 Willie Stargell	.30	.09
96 George Kell	.30	.09
97 Ferguson Jenkins	.20	.06
98 Al Kaline	.50	.15
99 Billy Martin	.30	.09
100 Mickey Mantle	2.00	.60
101 1869 Red Stockings ATH	.10	.03
102 King Kelly ATH	.10	.03
103 Nap Lajoie ATH	.20	.06
104 C. Mathewson ATH	.20	.06
105 Cy Young ATH	.20	.06
106 Ty Cobb ATH	.50	.15
107 Reggie Jackson CL	.20	.06
108 Rogers Hornsby ATH	.20	.06
109 Walter Johnson ATH	.20	.06
110 Babe Ruth ATH	.75	.23
111 Hack Wilson ATH	.20	.06
112 Lou Gehrig ATH	.50	.15
113 Ted Williams ATH	.60	.18
114 Yogi Berra ATH	.30	.09
115 Bobby Thomson ATH	.10	.03
116 Mickey Mantle ATH	1.00	.30
117 Willie Mays ATH	.50	.15
118 Bill Mazeroski ATH	.20	.06
119 Bob Gibson ATH	.20	.06
120 Nolan Ryan Tom Seaver Tommie Agee	.50	.15
121 Hank Aaron ATH	.50	.15
122 Reggie Jackson ATH	.30	.09
123 George Brett ATH	.60	.18
124 Steve Carlton ATH	.10	.03
125 Nolan Ryan ATH	.75	.23
126 Frank Thomas	.20	.06
127 Sam McDowell	.20	.06
128 Jim Lonborg	.10	.03
129 Bert Campaneris	.10	.03
130 Bob Gibson	.30	.09
131 Bobby Richardson	.20	.06
132 Bobby Grich	.20	.06
133 Billy Pierce	.20	.06
134 Enos Slaughter	.20	.06
135 Honus Wagner CL	.20	.06
136 Orlando Cepeda	.20	.06
137 Rennie Stennett	.10	.03
138 Gene Alley	.10	.03
139 Manny Mota	.10	.03
140 Rogers Hornsby	.30	.09
141 Joe Charboneau	.10	.03
142 Rick Ferrell	.20	.06
143 Toby Harrah	.10	.03
144 Hank Aaron	1.00	.30
145 Yogi Berra	.50	.15
146 Whitey Ford	.30	.09
147 Roy Campanella	.50	.15
148 Graig Nettles	.20	.06
149 Bobby Brown	.10	.03
150 Willie Mays CL	.30	.09
151 Cy Young LGD	.20	.06
152 Walter Johnson LGD	.20	.06
153 C. Mathewson LGD	.20	.06
154 Warren Spahn LGD	.30	.09
155 Steve Carlton LGD	.10	.03
156 Bob Gibson LGD	.20	.06
157 Whitey Ford LGD	.20	.06
158 Yogi Berra LGD	.30	.09
159 Roy Campanella LGD	.20	.06
160 Lou Gehrig LGD	.50	.15
161 Johnny Mize LGD	.10	.03
162 Rogers Hornsby LGD	.20	.06
163 Honus Wagner LGD	.20	.06
164 Hank Aaron LGD	.50	.15
165 Babe Ruth LGD	.75	.23
166 Willie Mays LGD	.50	.15
167 Reggie Jackson LGD	.30	.09
168 Mickey Mantle LGD	1.00	.30
169 Jimmie Foxx LGD	.20	.06
170 Ted Williams LGD	.60	.18
171 Mel Ott LGD	.20	.06
172 Willie Stargell LGD	.20	.06
173 Al Kaline LGD	.20	.06
174 Ty Cobb LGD	.50	.15
175 Nap Lajoie LGD	.20	.06
176 Lou Brock LGD	.30	.09
177 Tom Seaver LGD	.30	.09
178 Mark Fidrych	.20	.06
179 Don Baylor	.20	.06
180 Tom Seaver	.30	.09
181 Jerry Grote	.20	.06
182 George Foster	.10	.03
183 Buddy Bell	.20	.06
184 Ralph Garr	.20	.06
185 Steve Garvey	.20	.06
186 Joe Torre	.20	.06
187 Carl Erskine	.30	.09
188 Tommy Davis	.10	.03
189 Bill Buckner	.20	.06
190 Hack Wilson	.30	.09
191 Steve Blass	.10	.03
192 Ken Brett	.10	.03
193 Lee May	.10	.03
194 Bob Horner	.20	.06
195 Boog Powell	.20	.06
196 Darrell Evans	.20	.06
197 Paul Blair	.10	.03
198 Johnny Callison	.20	.06
199 Jimmie Reese	.10	.03
200 Cy Young	.50	.15
201 Ron Santo	.20	.06
202 Rico Carty	.10	.03
203 Ron Necciai	.10	.03
204 Lou Boudreau	.20	.06
205 Minnie Minoso	.20	.06
206 Eddie Yost	.10	.03
207 Tommie Agee	.10	.03
208 Dave Kingman HB	.10	.03
209 Tony Oliva HB	.20	.06
210 Reggie Jackson HB	.30	.09
211 Paul Blair HB	.10	.03
212 Ferguson Jenkins HB	.10	.03
213 Steve Garvey HB	.20	.06
214 Bert Campaneris HB	.10	.03
215 Orlando Cepeda HB	.20	.06
216 Bill Madlock HB	.10	.03
217 Rennie Stennett HB	.10	.03
218 Frank Thomas HB	.10	.03
219 Bob Gibson HB	.20	.06
220 Lou Brock HB	.30	.09
221 Rico Carty HB	.10	.03
222 Mickey Mantle HB	1.00	.30
223 Robin Roberts HB	.20	.06
224 Manny Sanguillen HB	.10	.03
225 Mickey Mantle CL	.50	.15
P44 R.Jackson Promo	3.00	.90

1994 Upper Deck All-Time Heroes 125th

This 225-card standard-size set is identical to the regular issue 1994 Upper Deck All-Time Heroes of Baseball series, except that each card has on its front "Major League Baseball" and "125th Anniversary" stamped in bronze foil along the right edge. Every pack contained one 125th Anniversary gold card.

	Nm-Mt	Ex-Mt
COMPLETE SET (225)	50.00	15.00
*STARS: 1.5X TO 4X BASIC CARDS...		

1994 Upper Deck All-Time Heroes 1954 Archives

Measuring the standard-size, these three chase cards were randomly inserted in the foil packs at a ratio of one card per 30 ten-card foil packs. Cards numbered 1 and 250 of Ted Williams, which are similar in design to the two that were originally issued by Topps in 1954, were not included in that company's 1954 Archives edition due to the terms of his contract with Upper Deck. Like Williams, Mickey Mantle had an exclusive agreement with Upper Deck that precluded his appearance in the 1954 Topps

Archives set. Mantle didn't even appear in the original 1954 Topps set due to his then exclusive contract with Bowman. This "card that never was" is similar to the original 1954 set design.

	Nm-Mt	Ex-Mt
1 Ted Williams	50.00	15.00
250 Ted Williams	50.00	15.00
259 Mickey Mantle	100.00	30.00

1994 Upper Deck All-Time Heroes Autographs

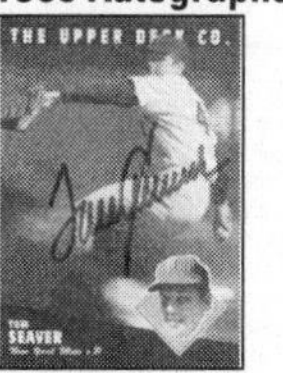

These four autograph cards were inserted one every 385 packs into the All-Time Heroes packs. Three players signed 1,000 cards while George Brett signed 2,000 cards since Nolan Ryan did not sign the 1,000 cards he had been expected to sign for this product. Each card came with a certification of authenticity on the back and could be registered with Upper Deck upon receipt.

	Nm-Mt	Ex-Mt
1 George Brett	60.00	18.00
2 Reggie Jackson	30.00	9.00
3 Mickey Mantle	500.00	150.00
4 Tom Seaver	30.00	9.00

1994 Upper Deck All-Time Heroes Next In Line

Capturing up and coming Minor League stars, this 20-card standard-size set was randomly inserted at a ratio of one in every 39 packs. Production was limited to 2,500 of each card. The fronts have a metallic finish with a color player cutout on the left, silhouetted by a blue-foil line. A black border on the right features the words "Next In Line," a color player headshot, and the player's name. The backs carry another color player photo, player information, and 1993 statistics. The cards are numbered on the back as "X of 20".

	Nm-Mt	Ex-Mt
COMPLETE SET (20)	50.00	15.00
1 Mike Bell	2.00	.60
2 Alan Benes	2.00	.60
3 D.J. Boston	2.00	.60
4 Johnny Damon	3.00	.90
5 Brad Fullmer	5.00	1.50
6 LaTroy Hawkins	2.00	.60
7 Derek Jeter	25.00	7.50
8 Daron Kirkreit	2.00	.60
9 Trot Nixon	5.00	1.50
10 Alex Ochoa	2.00	.60
11 Kirk Presley	2.00	.60
12 Jose Silva	2.00	.60
13 Terrell Wade	2.00	.60
14 Billy Wagner	3.00	.90
15 Glenn Williams	2.00	.60
16 Preston Wilson	5.00	1.50
17 Wayne Gomes	2.00	.60
18 Ben Grieve	3.00	.90
19 Dustin Hermanson	3.00	.90
20 Paul Wilson	2.00	.60

1994 Upper Deck: The American Epic

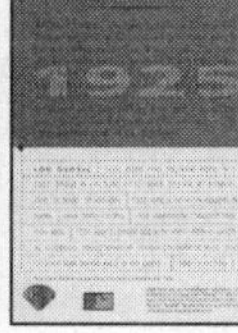

This 80-card boxed standard-size set recounts the story behind the PBS documentary "Baseball: The American Epic," produced by Ken Burns and sponsored by GM. The suggested retail price for the set, including the storage container, was 19.95. It was available from leading retail stores, the QVC television network, direct mail solicitation, and the Upper Deck Authenticated catalog. Like the documentary, the set is divided into "nine innings" and arranged chronologically as follows: 1st Inning (the 19th century [1-10], 2nd Inning (the 1900s [11-20], 3rd Inning (the 1910s [21-29], 4th Inning (the 1920s [30-39], 5th Inning (the 1930s [40-49], 6th Inning (the 1940s [50-56], 7th Inning (the 1950s [57-64], 8th Inning (the 1960s [65-71], and 9th Inning (1970-present [72-80]. Three insert cards were included with the set. A Michael Jordan card was available for direct mail customers, a Babe Ruth card for retail customers and a Mickey Mantle card for QVC customers. These cards are horizontal, full-bleed cards with black and white player photos. The backs are black and white with player information. The set price applies to either of the three versions and includes either of the three inserts. Recently, some autographs of Mickey Mantle from this set have surfaced on one of the home shopping channels. Since no information on how these cards were issued, or whether they were actually inserted into packs is available we are not pricing or listing this card at this point. Any further information on this card is appreciated.

	Nm-Mt	Ex-Mt
COMP.FACT SET (81)	15.00	4.50
1 Our Game	.05	.02
2 Alexander Cartwright	.10	.03
3 Henry Chadwick	.05	.02
4 The Fair Sex	.05	.02
5 Harry Wright	.05	.02
6 Albert Goodwill Spalding	.10	.03
7 Cap Anson	.15	.04
8 Moses Fleet. Walker	.10	.03
9 King Kelly	.10	.03
10 John Mont. Ward	.10	.03
11 Ty Cobb	1.25	.35
12 John McGraw	.15	.04
13 Rube Waddell	.10	.03
14 Christy Mathewson	.20	.06
15 Walter Johnson	.50	.15
16 Alta Weiss	.05	.02
17 Fred Merkle	.05	.02
18 Take Me Out To The Ballgame	.05	.02
19 John Henry(Pop) Lloyd	.10	.03
20 Honus Wagner	.75	.23
21 Woodrow Wilson	.15	.04
22 Nap Lajoie	.10	.03
23 Addie Joss	.10	.03
24 Joe Wood	.15	.04
25 Royal Rooters	.05	.02
26 Ebbets Field	.05	.02
27 Johnny Evers	.10	.03
28 World War I	.05	.02
29 Joe Jackson	1.00	.30
30 Babe Ruth	3.00	.90
31 George(Rube) Foster	.05	.02
32 Ray Chapman	.05	.02
33 Kenesaw M. Landis	.10	.03
34 Yankee Stadium	.05	.02
35 Rogers Hornsby	.20	.06
36 Warren G. Harding	.05	.02
37 Lou Gehrig	2.00	.60
38 Grover C. Alexander	.10	.03
39 House of David	.05	.02
40 Satchel Paige	.75	.23
41 Lefty Grove	.10	.03
42 Jimmie Foxx	.15	.04
43 Connie Mack	.15	.04
44 Josh Gibson	.20	.06
45 Dizzy Dean	.10	.03
46 Carl Hubbell	.10	.03
47 Franklin D. Roosevelt	.15	.04
48 Bob Feller	.10	.03
49 Cool Papa Bell	.10	.03
50 Jackie Robinson	2.00	.60
51 Ted Williams	2.00	.60
52 Sym-phony Band	.05	.02
53 Annabel Lee	.05	.02
54 Hank Greenberg	.10	.03
55 Branch Rickey	.10	.03
56 Harry S. Truman	.20	.06
57 Casey Stengel	.20	.06
58 Bobby Thomson	.10	.03
59 Dwight D. Eisenhower	.15	.04
60 Mario Cuomo	.10	.03
61 Buck O'Neil	.10	.03
62 Yogi Berra	.50	.15
63 Mickey Mantle	3.00	.90
64 Don Larsen	.10	.03
65 John F. Kennedy	1.50	.45
66 Bill Mazeroski	.10	.03
67 Roger Maris	.20	.06
68 Frank Robinson	.10	.03
69 Bob Gibson	.10	.03
70 Tom Seaver UER Wrong Birthdate of March 17th	.50	.15
71 Curt Flood	.05	.02
72 Roberto Clemente	2.00	.60
73 Luis Tiant	.05	.02
74 Marvin Miller	.05	.02
75 Reggie Jackson	.50	.15
76 Willie(Pops) Stargell	.10	.03
77 Pete Rose	.50	.15
78 Bill Clinton	1.00	.30
79 Nolan Ryan	2.50	.75
80 George Brett	.20	.06
BC1 Mickey Mantle Home shopping insert	5.00	1.50
BC2 Michael Jordan Direct mail insert	5.00	1.50
BC3 Babe Ruth Retail insert	5.00	1.50

1994 Upper Deck: The American Epic GM

This nine-card set recounts part of the story behind the PBS documentary "Baseball: The American Epic," produced by Ken Burns and sponsored by GM. A GM Merchandise and Memorabilia Catalog was based on the American Epic series and available at GM dealers. The catalog included an offer for this nine-card set for 1.00. The GM logo appears in the lower right corner.

	Nm-Mt	Ex-Mt
COMPLETE SET (9)	4.00	1.20
1 Hank Aaron	.50	.15
2 Roberto Clemente	.75	.23
3 Ty Cobb	.50	.15
4 Hank Greenberg	.10	.03
5 Mickey Mantle	1.25	.35
6 Satchel Paige	.25	.07
7 Jackie Robinson	.75	.23
8 Babe Ruth	1.25	.35
9 Ted Williams	.75	.23

1994 Upper Deck: The American Epic Little Debbies

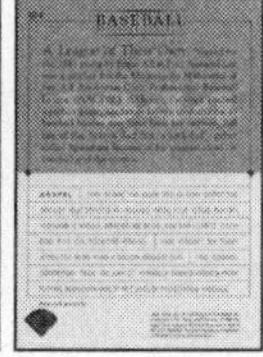

This 15-card set recounts part of the story behind the PBS documentary "Baseball: The American Epic," produced by Ken Burns. The cards could be ordered through an on-pack offer on Little Debbies cakes for 3.99. The Little Debbies logo appears on the bottom of the checklist card.

	Nm-Mt	Ex-Mt
COMPLETE SET (15)	5.00	1.50
LD1 Our Game CL	.10	.03
LD2 Alexander Cartwright	.10	.03
LD3 King Kelly	.10	.03
LD4 John McGraw	.20	.06
LD5 Christy Mathewson	.20	.06
LD6 Walter Johnson	.30	.09
LD7 Ted Williams	1.50	.45
LD8 Annabel Lee	.10	.03
LD9 Jackie Robinson	1.00	.30
LD10 Bobby Thomson	.20	.06
LD11 Buck O'Neil	.20	.06
LD12 Mickey Mantle	1.50	.45
LD13 Bob Gibson	.30	.09
LD14 Curt Flood	.10	.03
LD15 Reggie Jackson	.40	.12

1994 Upper Deck Mantle Phone Cards

Upper Deck in conjunction with Global Telecommunication Solutions produced this set of 10 phone cards to honor Mickey Mantle, the greatest switch-hitter in baseball history. The set was issued in two five-card sets: series one in early October, and series two later that year. Each five-card set retailed for $59.95. Chronicling his career from 1951 until his 1974 Hall of Fame Induction, the set is a replica of the "Baseball Heroes" insert cards featured in the 1994 Upper Deck baseball series 2. Just 5,000 sets of series 1 were produced, with each card including a bonus one-minute Mantle highlight replay moment. As an added bonus, 500 1869 Cincinnati Red Stockings phone cards were randomly inserted in series two sets, while Upper Deck distributed its allotment to the first 450 orders received from hobby dealers. Only 2,000 Red Stocking cards were produced. The phone cards are unnumbered and checklisted below in chronological order.

	Nm-Mt	Ex-Mt
COMPLETE SET (11)	60.00	18.00
COMMON CARD (1-10)	8.00	2.40
NNO0 1869 Cincinnati Red Stockings	10.00	3.00

1994 Upper Deck Sheets

These ten 8 1/2" by 11" sheets were produced by Upper Deck. They were issued to commemorate various special events sponsored by Upper Deck. We have listed the production quantities when known.

	Nm-Mt	Ex-Mt
COMPLETE SET (10)	35.00	10.50
1 Heroes of Baseball Day The Ballpark in Arlington April 3, 1994	2.00	.60
2 1964 Season Tribute	8.00	2.40

June 4, 1994 (50,000)
Lou Brock
Dick Groat
Bobby Richardson
Bob Gibson
3 Milwaukee Brewers 2.00 .60
Silver Anniversary
June 25, 1994 (30,000)
Robin Yount
Hank Aaron
Rollie Fingers
4 Hollywood Softball Game 6.00 1.80
June 26
5 Heroes of Baseball 6.00 1.80
All-Star Game
July 11, 1994 (60,000)
Bill Mazeroski
Reggie Jackson
Chuck Tanner
Steve Garvey
Willie Stargell
6 25th Anniversary of the 8.00 2.40
1969 Season and the
Miracle Mets
July 17
7 All-Time Homerun Kings 8.00 2.40
July 23
8 Baseball 125th Anniversary 2.00 .60
August 6, 1994 (40,000)
Jim Lonborg
Ted Williams
Reggie Jackson
Bobby Thomson
Bill Mazeroski
9 All Star Fanfest 2.00 .60
Autograph Sheet
Drawing of
baseball field
10 Upper Deck Authenticated 2.00 .60
Triple Crown Winners
2,500 produced
Ted Williams
Frank Robinson
Mickey Mantle
Carl Yastrzemski
11 UDA Ted Williams Career
Commemorative 2.00 .60

1994 Upper Deck Top Ten Promo

This one-card Ken Griffey promo was issued to promote the never issued 1994 Upper Deck Top Ten set. The set which was supposed to honor the best players in baseball was never issued by Upper Deck due to the baseball strike in 1994.

	Nm-Mt	Ex-Mt
P6 Ken Griffey Jr.	5.00	1.50

1995 Upper Deck

The 1995 Upper Deck baseball set was issued in two series of 225 cards for a total of 450. The cards were distributed in 12-card packs (36 per box) with a suggested retail price of $1.99. Subsets include Top Prospect (1-15, 251-265), 90's Midpoint (101-110), Star Rookie (211-240), and Diamond Debuts (241-250). Rookie Cards in this set include Hideo Nomo. Five randomly inserted Trade Cards were each redeemable for nine updated cards of new rookies or players who changed teams, comprising a 45-card Trade Redemption set. The Trade cards expired Feb 1, 1996. Autographed jumbo cards (Roger Clemens for series one, Alex Rodriguez for either series) were available through a wrapper redemption offer.

	Nm-Mt	Ex-Mt
COMP.MASTER SET (495)	110.00	33.00
COMPLETE SET (450)	50.00	15.00
COMP. SERIES 1 (225)	25.00	7.50
COMP. SERIES 2 (225)	25.00	7.50
COMMON CARD (1-450)	.15	.04
COMP.TRADE SET (45)	60.00	18.00
COMMON (451T-495T)	1.00	.30
1 Ruben Rivera	.15	.04
2 Bill Pulsipher	.15	.04
3 Ben Grieve	.30	.09
4 Curtis Goodwin	.15	.04
5 Damon Hollins	.15	.04
6 Todd Greene	.15	.04
7 Glenn Williams	.15	.04
8 Bret Wagner	.15	.04
9 Karim Garcia RC	.30	.09
10 Nomar Garciaparra	2.50	.75
11 Raul Casanova RC	.15	.04
12 Matt Smith	.15	.04
13 Paul Wilson	.15	.04
14 Jason Isringhausen	.30	.09
15 Reid Ryan	.30	.09
16 Lee Smith	.30	.09
17 Chili Davis	.30	.09
18 Brian Anderson	.15	.04
19 Gary DiSarcina	.15	.04
20 Bo Jackson	.75	.23
21 Chuck Finley	.30	.09
22 Darryl Kile	.30	.09
23 Shane Reynolds	.15	.04
24 Tony Eusebio	.15	.04
25 Craig Biggio	.50	.15
26 Doug Drabek	.15	.04
27 Brian L. Hunter	.15	.04
28 James Mouton	.15	.04
29 Geronimo Berroa	.15	.04
30 Rickey Henderson	.75	.23
31 Steve Karsay	.15	.04
32 Steve Ontiveros	.15	.04
33 Ernie Young	.15	.04
34 Dennis Eckersley	.30	.09
35 Mark McGwire	2.00	.60
36 Dave Stewart	.30	.09
37 Pat Hentgen	.15	.04
38 Carlos Delgado	.30	.09
39 Joe Carter	.30	.09
40 Roberto Alomar	.75	.23
41 John Olerud	.30	.09
42 Devon White	.30	.09
43 Roberto Kelly	.15	.04
44 Jeff Blauser	.15	.04
45 Fred McGriff	.50	.15
46 Tom Glavine	.50	.15
47 Mike Kelly	.15	.04
48 Javier Lopez	.30	.09
49 Greg Maddux	1.25	.35
50 Matt Mieske	.15	.04
51 Troy O'Leary	.15	.04
52 Jeff Cirillo	.15	.04
53 Cal Eldred	.15	.04
54 Pat Listach	.15	.04
55 Jose Valentin	.15	.04
56 John Mabry	.15	.04
57 Bob Tewksbury	.15	.04
58 Brian Jordan	.30	.09
59 Gregg Jefferies	.15	.04
60 Ozzie Smith	1.25	.35
61 Geronimo Pena	.15	.04
62 Mark Whiten	.15	.04
63 Rey Sanchez	.15	.04
64 Willie Banks	.15	.04
65 Mark Grace	.50	.15
66 Randy Myers	.15	.04
67 Steve Trachsel	.15	.04
68 Derrick May	.15	.04
69 Brett Butler	.30	.09
70 Eric Karros	.30	.09
71 Tim Wallach	.15	.04
72 Delino DeShields	.15	.04
73 Darren Dreifort	.15	.04
74 Orel Hershiser	.30	.09
75 Billy Ashley	.15	.04
76 Sean Berry	.15	.04
77 Ken Hill	.15	.04
78 John Wetteland	.30	.09
79 Moises Alou	.30	.09
80 Cliff Floyd	.30	.09
81 Marquis Grissom	.15	.04
82 Larry Walker	.50	.15
83 Rondell White	.30	.09
84 W.VanLandingham	.15	.04
85 Matt Williams	.30	.09
86 Rod Beck	.15	.04
87 Darren Lewis	.15	.04
88 Robby Thompson	.15	.04
89 Darryl Strawberry	.50	.15
90 Kenny Lofton	.30	.09
91 Charles Nagy	.15	.04
92 Sandy Alomar Jr.	.15	.04
93 Mark Clark	.15	.04
94 Dennis Martinez	.30	.09
95 Dave Winfield	.30	.09
96 Jim Thome	.75	.23
97 Manny Ramirez	.30	.09
98 Goose Gossage	.30	.09
99 Tino Martinez	.50	.15
100 Ken Griffey Jr.	1.25	.35
101 Greg Maddux ANA	.75	.23
102 Randy Johnson ANA	.50	.15
103 Barry Bonds ANA	1.00	.30
104 Juan Gonzalez ANA	.50	.15
105 Frank Thomas ANA	.50	.15
106 Matt Williams ANA	.15	.04
107 Paul Molitor ANA	.30	.09
108 Fred McGriff ANA	.30	.09
109 Carlos Baerga ANA	.15	.04
110 Ken Griffey Jr. ANA	.75	.23
111 Reggie Jefferson	.15	.04
112 Randy Johnson	.75	.23
113 Marc Newfield	.15	.04
114 Robb Nen	.30	.09
115 Jeff Conine	.30	.09
116 Kurt Abbott	.15	.04
117 Charlie Hough	.30	.09
118 Dave Weathers	.15	.04
119 Juan Castillo	.15	.04
120 Bret Saberhagen	.30	.09
121 Rico Brogna	.15	.04
122 John Franco	.30	.09
123 Todd Hundley	.15	.04
124 Jason Jacome	.15	.04
125 Bobby Jones	.15	.04
126 Bret Barberie	.15	.04
127 Ben McDonald	.15	.04
128 Harold Baines	.30	.09
129 Jeffrey Hammonds	.15	.04
130 Mike Mussina	.75	.23
131 Chris Hoiles	.15	.04
132 Brady Anderson	.30	.09
133 Eddie Williams	.15	.04
134 Andy Benes	.15	.04
135 Tony Gwynn	1.00	.30
136 Bip Roberts	.15	.04
137 Joey Hamilton	.15	.04
138 Luis Lopez	.15	.04
139 Ray McDavid	.15	.04
140 Lenny Dykstra	.30	.09
141 Mariano Duncan	.15	.04
142 Fernando Valenzuela	.30	.09
143 Bobby Munoz	.15	.04
144 Kevin Stocker	.15	.04
145 John Kruk	.30	.09
146 Jon Lieber	.15	.04
147 Zane Smith	.15	.04
148 Steve Cooke	.15	.04
149 Andy Van Slyke	.30	.09
150 Jay Bell	.30	.09
151 Carlos Garcia	.15	.04
152 John Dettmer	.15	.04
153 Darren Oliver	.15	.04
154 Dean Palmer	.30	.09
155 Otis Nixon	.15	.04
156 Rusty Greer	.30	.09
157 Rick Helling	.15	.04
158 Jose Canseco	.75	.23
159 Roger Clemens	1.50	.45
160 Andre Dawson	.30	.09
161 Mo Vaughn	.30	.09
162 Aaron Sele	.15	.04
163 John Valentin	.15	.04
164 Brian R. Hunter	.15	.04
165 Bret Boone	.30	.09
166 Hector Carrasco	.15	.04
167 Pete Schourek	.15	.04
168 Willie Greene	.15	.04
169 Kevin Mitchell	.15	.04
170 Deion Sanders	.50	.15
171 John Roper	.15	.04
172 Charlie Hayes	.15	.04
173 David Nied	.15	.04
174 Ellis Burks	.30	.09
175 Dante Bichette	.30	.09
176 Marvin Freeman	.15	.04
177 Eric Young	.15	.04
178 David Cone	.30	.09
179 Greg Gagne	.15	.04
180 Bob Hamelin	.15	.04
181 Wally Joyner	.30	.09
182 Jeff Montgomery	.15	.04
183 Jose Lind	.15	.04
184 Chris Gomez	.15	.04
185 Travis Fryman	.30	.09
186 Kirk Gibson	.30	.09
187 Mike Moore	.15	.04
188 Lou Whitaker	.30	.09
189 Sean Bergman	.15	.04
190 Shane Mack	.15	.04
191 Rick Aguilera	.15	.04
192 Denny Hocking	.15	.04
193 Chuck Knoblauch	.30	.09
194 Kevin Tapani	.15	.04
195 Kent Hrbek	.30	.09
196 Ozzie Guillen	.15	.04
197 Wilson Alvarez	.15	.04
198 Tim Raines	.30	.09
199 Scott Ruffcorn	.15	.04
200 Michael Jordan	2.50	.75
201 Robin Ventura	.30	.09
202 Jason Bere	.15	.04
203 Darrin Jackson	.15	.04
204 Russ Davis	.15	.04
205 Jimmy Key	.30	.09
206 Jack McDowell	.15	.04
207 Jim Abbott	.50	.15
208 Paul O'Neill	.50	.15
209 Bernie Williams	.50	.15
210 Don Mattingly	2.00	.60
211 Orlando Miller	.15	.04
212 Alex Gonzalez	.15	.04
213 Terrell Wade	.15	.04
214 Jose Oliva	.15	.04
215 Alex Rodriguez	2.00	.60
216 Garret Anderson	.30	.09
217 Alan Benes	.15	.04
218 Armando Benitez	.30	.09
219 Dustin Hermanson	.15	.04
220 Charles Johnson	.30	.09
221 Julian Tavarez	.15	.04
222 Jason Giambi	.75	.23
223 LaTroy Hawkins	.15	.04
224 Todd Hollandsworth	.15	.04
225 Derek Jeter	2.00	.60
226 Hideo Nomo RC	2.00	.60
227 Tony Clark	.15	.04
228 Roger Cedeno	.15	.04
229 Scott Stahoviak	.15	.04
230 Michael Tucker	.15	.04
231 Joe Rosselli	.15	.04
232 Antonio Osuna	.15	.04
233 Bobby Higginson RC	.75	.23
234 Mark Grudzielanek RC	.50	.15
235 Ray Durham	.30	.09
236 Frank Rodriguez	.15	.04
237 Quilvio Veras	.15	.04
238 Darren Bragg	.15	.04
239 Ugueth Urbina	.15	.04
240 Jason Bates	.15	.04
241 David Bell	.15	.04
242 Ron Villone	.15	.04
243 Joe Randa	.30	.09
244 Carlos Perez RC	.30	.09
245 Brad Clontz	.15	.04
246 Steve Rodriguez	.15	.04
247 Joe Vitiello	.15	.04
248 Ozzie Timmons	.15	.04
249 Rudy Pemberton	.15	.04
250 Marty Cordova	.15	.04
251 Tony Graffanino	.15	.04
252 Mark Johnson RC	.30	.09
253 Tomas Perez RC	.15	.04
254 Jimmy Hurst	.15	.04
255 Edgardo Alfonzo	.30	.09
256 Jose Malave	.15	.04
257 Brad Radke RC	1.25	.35
258 Jon Nunnally	.15	.04
259 Dilson Torres RC	.15	.04
260 Esteban Loaiza	.30	.09
261 Freddy Adrian Garcia RC	.15	.04
262 Don Wengert	.15	.04
263 Robert Person RC	.30	.09
264 Tim Unroe RC	.15	.04
265 Juan Acevedo RC	.15	.04
266 Eduardo Perez	.15	.04
267 Tony Phillips	.15	.04
268 Jim Edmonds	.30	.09
269 Jorge Fabregas	.15	.04
270 Tim Salmon	.50	.15
271 Mark Langston	.15	.04
272 J.T. Snow	.30	.09
273 Phil Plantier	.15	.04
274 Derek Bell	.15	.04
275 Jeff Bagwell	.50	.15
276 Luis Gonzalez	.30	.09
277 John Hudek	.15	.04
278 Todd Stottlemyre	.15	.04
279 Mark Acre	.15	.04
280 Ruben Sierra	.15	.04
281 Mike Bordick	.15	.04
282 Ron Darling	.15	.04
283 Brent Gates	.15	.04
284 Todd Van Poppel	.15	.04
285 Paul Molitor	.50	.15
286 Ed Sprague	.15	.04
287 Juan Guzman	.15	.04
288 David Cone	.30	.09
289 Shawn Green	.30	.09
290 Marquis Grissom	.15	.04
291 Kent Mercker	.15	.04
292 Steve Avery	.15	.04
293 Chipper Jones	.75	.23
294 John Smoltz	.50	.15
295 David Justice	.30	.09
296 Ryan Klesko	.30	.09
297 Joe Oliver	.15	.04
298 Ricky Bones	.15	.04
299 John Jaha	.15	.04
300 Greg Vaughn	.30	.09
301 Dave Nilsson	.15	.04
302 Kevin Seitzer	.15	.04
303 Bernard Gilkey	.15	.04
304 Allen Battle	.15	.04
305 Ray Lankford	.15	.04
306 Tom Pagnozzi	.15	.04
307 Allen Watson	.15	.04
308 Danny Jackson	.15	.04
309 Ken Hill	.15	.04
310 Todd Zeile	.15	.04
311 Kevin Roberson	.15	.04
312 Steve Buechele	.15	.04
313 Rick Wilkins	.15	.04
314 Kevin Foster	.15	.04
315 Sammy Sosa	1.25	.35
316 Howard Johnson	.15	.04
317 Greg Hansell	.15	.04
318 Pedro Astacio	.15	.04
319 Rafael Bournigal	.15	.04
320 Mike Piazza	1.25	.35
321 Ramon Martinez	.15	.04
322 Raul Mondesi	.30	.09
323 Ismael Valdes	.15	.04
324 Wil Cordero	.15	.04
325 Tony Tarasco	.15	.04
326 Roberto Kelly	.15	.04
327 Jeff Fassero	.15	.04
328 Mike Lansing	.15	.04
329 Pedro Martinez	.75	.23
330 Kirk Rueter	.15	.04
331 Glenallen Hill	.15	.04
332 Kirt Manwaring	.15	.04
333 Royce Clayton	.15	.04
334 J.R. Phillips	.15	.04
335 Barry Bonds	2.00	.60
336 Mark Portugal	.15	.04
337 Terry Mulholland	.15	.04
338 Omar Vizquel	.30	.09
339 Carlos Baerga	.15	.04
340 Albert Belle	.30	.09
341 Eddie Murray	.75	.23
342 Wayne Kirby	.15	.04
343 Chad Ogea	.15	.04
344 Tim Davis	.15	.04
345 Jay Buhner	.30	.09
346 Bobby Ayala	.15	.04
347 Mike Blowers	.15	.04
348 Dave Fleming	.15	.04
349 Edgar Martinez	.50	.15
350 Andre Dawson	.30	.09
351 Darrell Whitmore	.15	.04
352 Chuck Carr	.15	.04
353 John Burkett	.15	.04
354 Chris Hammond	.15	.04
355 Gary Sheffield	.30	.09
356 Pat Rapp	.15	.04
357 Greg Colbrunn	.15	.04
358 David Segui	.15	.04
359 Jeff Kent	.30	.09
360 Bobby Bonilla	.30	.09
361 Pete Harnisch	.15	.04
362 Ryan Thompson	.15	.04
363 Jose Vizcaino	.15	.04
364 Brett Butler	.30	.09
365 Cal Ripken Jr.	2.50	.75
366 Rafael Palmeiro	.50	.15
367 Leo Gomez	.15	.04
368 Andy Van Slyke	.30	.09
369 Arthur Rhodes	.15	.04
370 Ken Caminiti	.30	.09
371 Steve Finley	.30	.09
372 Melvin Nieves	.15	.04
373 Andujar Cedeno	.15	.04
374 Trevor Hoffman	.30	.09
375 Fernando Valenzuela	.30	.09
376 Ricky Bottalico	.15	.04
377 Dave Hollins	.15	.04
378 Charlie Hayes	.15	.04
379 Tommy Greene	.15	.04
380 Darren Daulton	.30	.09
381 Curt Schilling	.50	.15
382 Midre Cummings	.15	.04
383 Al Martin	.15	.04
384 Jeff King	.15	.04
385 Orlando Merced	.15	.04
386 Denny Neagle	.30	.09
387 Don Slaught	.15	.04
388 Dave Clark	.15	.04
389 Kevin Gross	.15	.04
390 Will Clark	.75	.23
391 Ivan Rodriguez	.75	.23
392 Benji Gil	.15	.04
393 Jeff Frye	.15	.04
394 Kenny Rogers	.30	.09
395 Juan Gonzalez	.75	.23
396 Mike Macfarlane	.15	.04
397 Lee Tinsley	.15	.04
398 Tim Naehring	.15	.04
399 Tim Vanegmond	.15	.04
400 Mike Greenwell	.15	.04
401 Ken Ryan	.15	.04
402 John Smiley	.15	.04
403 Tim Pugh	.15	.04
404 Reggie Sanders	.30	.09
405 Barry Larkin	.75	.23
406 Hal Morris	.15	.04
407 Jose Rijo	.15	.04
408 Lance Painter	.15	.04
409 Joe Girardi	.15	.04
410 Andres Galarraga	.30	.09
411 Mike Kingery	.15	.04
412 Roberto Mejia	.15	.04
413 Walt Weiss	.15	.04
414 Bill Swift	.15	.04
415 Larry Walker	.50	.15
416 Billy Brewer	.15	.04
417 Pat Borders	.15	.04
418 Tom Gordon	.15	.04
419 Kevin Appier	.30	.09
420 Gary Gaetti	.30	.09
421 Greg Gohr	.15	.04
422 Felipe Lira	.15	.04
423 John Doherty	.15	.04
424 Chad Curtis	.15	.04
425 Cecil Fielder	.30	.09
426 Alan Trammell	.50	.15
427 David McCarty	.15	.04
428 Scott Erickson	.15	.04
429 Pat Mahomes	.15	.04
430 Kirby Puckett	.75	.23
431 Dave Stevens	.15	.04
432 Pedro Munoz	.15	.04
433 Chris Sabo	.15	.04
434 Alex Fernandez	.15	.04
435 Frank Thomas	.75	.23
436 Roberto Hernandez	.15	.04
437 Lance Johnson	.15	.04
438 Jim Abbott	.50	.15
439 John Wetteland	.30	.09
440 Melido Perez	.15	.04
441 Tony Fernandez	.15	.04
442 Pat Kelly	.15	.04
443 Mike Stanley	.15	.04
444 Danny Tartabull	.15	.04
445 Wade Boggs	.50	.15
446 Robin Yount	1.25	.35
447 Ryne Sandberg	1.25	.35
448 Nolan Ryan	3.00	.90
449 George Brett	2.00	.60
450 Mike Schmidt	1.25	.35
451 Jim Abbott TRADE	2.00	.60
452 D.Tartabull TRADE	1.00	.30
453 Ariel Prieto TRADE	1.00	.30
454 Scott Cooper TRADE	1.00	.30
455 Tom Henke TRADE	1.00	.30
456 Todd Zeile TRADE	1.00	.30
457 Brian McRae TRADE	1.00	.30
458 Luis Gonzalez TRADE	1.50	.45
459 Jaime Navarro TRADE	1.00	.30
460 Todd Worrell TRADE	1.00	.30
461 Roberto Kelly TRADE	1.00	.30
462 Chad Fonville TRADE	1.00	.30
463 S.Andrews TRADE	1.00	.30
464 David Segui TRADE	1.00	.30
465 Deion Sanders TRADE	2.00	.60
466 Orel Hershiser TRADE	1.50	.45
467 Ken Hill TRADE	1.00	.30
468 Andy Benes TRADE	1.00	.30
469 T.Pendleton TRADE	1.50	.45
470 Bobby Bonilla TRADE	1.50	.45
471 Scott Erickson TRADE	1.00	.30
472 Kevin Brown TRADE	1.50	.45
473 G.Dishman TRADE	1.00	.30
474 Phil Plantier TRADE	1.00	.30
475 G.Jefferies TRADE	1.00	.30
476 Tyler Green TRADE	1.00	.30
477 H. Slocumb TRADE	1.00	.30
478 Mark Whiten TRADE	1.00	.30
479 M.Tettleton TRADE	1.00	.30
480 Tim Wakefield TRADE	1.50	.45
481 V. Eshelman TRADE	1.00	.30
482 Rick Aguilera TRADE	1.00	.30
483 Erik Hanson TRADE	1.00	.30
484 Willie McGee TRADE	1.50	.45
485 Troy O'Leary TRADE	1.00	.30
486 B.Santiago TRADE	1.50	.45
487 Darren Lewis TRADE	1.00	.30
488 Dave Burba TRADE	1.00	.30
489 Ron Gant TRADE	1.50	.45
490 B.Saberhagen TRADE	1.50	.45
491 Vinny Castilla TRADE	1.50	.45
492 F.Rodriguez TRADE	1.00	.30
493 Andy Pettitte TRADE	2.00	.60
494 Ruben Sierra TRADE	1.00	.30
495 David Cone TRADE	1.50	.45
J159 R. Clemens Jumbo AU	50.00	15.00
J215 A. Rodriguez Jumbo AU	120.00	36.00
P100 K.Griffey Jr. Promo	2.00	.60

1995 Upper Deck Electric Diamond

This 450-card parallel set was inserted one per retail pack or two per mini-jumbo pack. These cards are distinguished from their regular issue counterparts in that they are printed on a heavier cardstock and use a special foil treatment.

	Nm-Mt	Ex-Mt
COMPLETE SET (450)	100.00	30.00
COMP. SERIES 1 (225)	50.00	15.00
COMP. SERIES 2 (225)	60.00	18.00

*STARS: 1.25X to 3X BASIC CARDS ..
*ROOKIES: 1X TO 2.5X BASIC CARDS

1995 Upper Deck Autographs

Trade cards to redeem these autographed issues were randomly seeded into second series packs. The actual signed cards share the same front design as the basic issue 1995 Upper Deck cards. The cards were issued along with a card signed in fascimile by Brain Burr of Upper Deck along with instructions on how to register these cards.

	Nm-Mt	Ex-Mt
AC1 Reggie Jackson	40.00	12.00
AC2 Willie Mays	100.00	30.00
AC3 Frank Robinson	40.00	12.00
AC4 Roger Clemens	100.00	30.00
AC5 Raul Mondesi	25.00	7.50

1995 Upper Deck Checklists

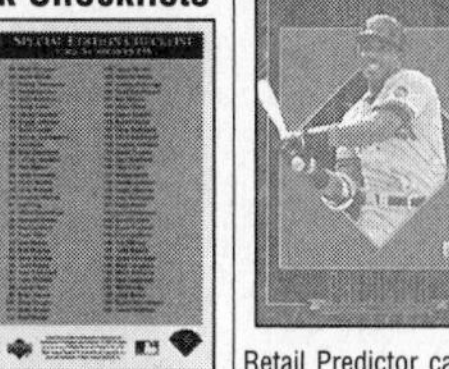

Each of these 10 cards features a star player(s) on the front and a checklist on the back. The cards were randomly inserted in hobby and retail packs at a rate of one in 17. The horizontal fronts feature a player photo along with a sentence about the 1994 highlight. The cards are numbered as "X" of 5 in the upper left.

	Nm-Mt	Ex-Mt
COMPLETE SET (5)	12.00	3.60
COMPLETE SERIES 1 (5)	4.00	1.20
COMPLETE SERIES 2 (5)	8.00	2.40
1A Montreal Expos	.30	.09
2A Fred McGriff	1.00	.30
3A John Valentin	.30	.09
4A Kenny Rogers	.60	.18
5A Greg Maddux	2.50	.75
1B Cecil Fielder	.60	.18
2B Tony Gwynn	2.00	.60
3B Greg Maddux	2.50	.75
4B Randy Johnson	1.50	.45
5B Mike Schmidt	2.50	.75

1995 Upper Deck Predictor Award Winners

Cards from this set were inserted in hobby packs at a rate of approximately one in 30. This 40-card standard-size set features nine players and a Long Shot in each league for each of two categories -- MVP and Rookie of the Year. If the player pictured on the card won his category, the card was redeemable for a special foil version of all 20 Hobby Predictor cards. Winning cards are marked with a "W" in the checklist below. Both MVP winners for the season (Barry Larkin in the NL and Mo Vaughn in the AL) were not featured on their own Predictor cards and thus the Longshot card became the winner. Fronts are full-color player action photos. Backs include the rules of the contest. These cards were redeemable until December 31, 1995.

	Nm-Mt	Ex-Mt
COMPLETE SERIES 1 (20)	40.00	12.00
COMPLETE SERIES 2 (20)	40.00	12.00
*AW EXCH: .4X TO 1X BASIC PRED.AW		
ONE EXCH.SET VIA MAIL PER PRED.WINNER		
H1 Albert Belle MVP	1.25	.35
H2 Juan Gonzalez MVP	3.00	.90
H3 Ken Griffey Jr. MVP	5.00	1.50
H4 Kirby Puckett MVP	3.00	.90
H5 Frank Thomas MVP	3.00	.90
H6 Jeff Bagwell MVP	2.00	.60
H7 Barry Bonds MVP	8.00	2.40
H8 Mike Piazza MVP	5.00	1.50
H9 Matt Williams MVP	1.25	.35
H10 MVP Wild Card W	.60	.18
Mo Vaughn, Barry Larkin		
H11 A.Benitez ROY	1.25	.35
H12 Alex Gonzalez ROY	.60	.18
H13 Shawn Green ROY	1.25	.35
H14 Derek Jeter ROY	8.00	2.40
H15 Alex Rodriguez ROY	8.00	2.40
H16 Alan Benes ROY	.60	.18
H17 Brian L.Hunter ROY	.60	.18
H18 Charles Johnson ROY	1.25	.35
H19 Jose Oliva ROY	.60	.18
H20 ROY Wild Card	.60	.18
H21 Cal Ripken MVP	10.00	3.00
H22 Don Mattingly MVP	8.00	2.40
H23 Roberto Alomar MVP	3.00	.90
H24 Kenny Lofton MVP	1.25	.35
H25 Will Clark MVP	3.00	.90
H26 Mark McGwire MVP	8.00	2.40
H27 Greg Maddux MVP	5.00	1.50
H28 Fred McGriff MVP	2.00	.60
H29 A.Galarraga MVP	1.25	.35
H30 Jose Canseco MVP	3.00	.90
H31 Ray Durham ROY	1.25	.35
H32 M.Grudzielanek ROY	2.00	.60
H33 Scott Ruffcorn ROY	.60	.18
H34 Michael Tucker ROY	.60	.18
H35 Garret Anderson ROY	1.25	.35
H36 Darren Bragg ROY	.60	.18
H37 Quilvio Veras ROY	.60	.18
H38 Hideo Nomo ROY W	8.00	2.40
H39 Chipper Jones ROY	3.00	.90
H40 M.Cordova ROY W	.60	.18

1995 Upper Deck Predictor League Leaders

Cards from this 60-card standard size set were seeded exclusively in first and second series retail packs at a rate of 1:30 and ANCO packs at 1:17. Cards 1-30 were distributed in series one packs and cards 31-60 in series two packs. The set includes nine players and a Long Shot in each league for each of three categories -- Batting Average Leader, Home Run Leader and Runs Batted In Leader. If the player pictured on the card won his category, the card was redeemable for a special foil version of 30

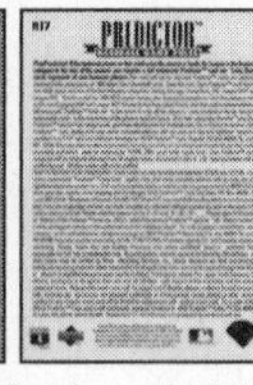

Retail Predictor cards (based upon the first or second series that it was associated with). These cards were redeemable until December 31, 1995. Card fronts are full-color action photos of the player emerging from a marble diamond. Backs list the rules of the game. Winning cards are designated with a W in our listings and are in noticeably shorter supply than other cards from this set as the bulk of them were mailed in to Upper Deck (and destroyed) in exchange for the parallel card prizes.

	Nm-Mt	Ex-Mt
COMPLETE SERIES 1 (30)	60.00	18.00
COMPLETE SERIES 2 (30)	40.00	12.00
*EXCH: .5X TO 1.2X BASIC PREDICTOR LL		
ONE EXCH.SET VIA MAIL PER PRED.WINNER		
R1 Albert Belle HR W	1.25	.35
R2 Jose Canseco HR	3.00	.90
R3 Juan Gonzalez HR	3.00	.90
R4 Ken Griffey Jr. HR	5.00	1.50
R5 Frank Thomas HR	3.00	.90
R6 Jeff Bagwell HR	2.00	.60
R7 Barry Bonds HR	8.00	2.40
R8 Fred McGriff HR	2.00	.60
R9 Matt Williams HR	1.25	.35
R10 HR Wild Card W	.60	.18
Dante Bichette		
R11 Albert Belle RBI W	1.25	.35
R12 Joe Carter RBI	1.25	.35
R13 Cecil Fielder RBI	1.25	.35
R14 Kirby Puckett RBI	3.00	.90
R15 Frank Thomas RBI	3.00	.90
R16 Jeff Bagwell RBI	2.00	.60
R17 Barry Bonds RBI	8.00	2.40
R18 Mike Piazza RBI	5.00	1.50
R19 Matt Williams RBI	1.25	.35
R20 RBI Wild Card W	.60	.18
Mo Vaughn		
R21 Wade Boggs BAT	2.00	.60
R22 Kenny Lofton BAT	1.25	.35
R23 Paul Molitor BAT	2.00	.60
R24 Paul O'Neill BAT	2.00	.60
R25 Frank Thomas BAT	3.00	.90
R26 Jeff Bagwell BAT	2.00	.60
R27 Tony Gwynn BAT W	4.00	1.20
R28 Gregg Jefferies BAT	.60	.18
R29 Hal Morris BAT	.60	.18
R30 Batting WC W	.60	.18
Edgar Martinez		
R31 Joe Carter HR	1.25	.35
R32 Cecil Fielder HR	1.25	.35
R33 Rafael Palmeiro HR	2.00	.60
R34 Larry Walker HR	2.00	.60
R35 Manny Ramirez HR	1.25	.35
R36 Tim Salmon HR	2.00	.60
R37 Mike Piazza HR	5.00	1.50
R38 Andres Galarraga HR	1.25	.35
R39 David Justice HR	1.25	.35
R40 Gary Sheffield HR	1.25	.35
R41 Juan Gonzalez RBI	3.00	.90
R42 Jose Canseco RBI	3.00	.90
R43 Will Clark RBI	3.00	.90
R44 Rafael Palmeiro RBI	2.00	.60
R45 Ken Griffey Jr. RBI	5.00	1.50
R46 Ruben Sierra RBI	.60	.18
R47 Larry Walker RBI	2.00	.60
R48 Fred McGriff RBI	2.00	.60
R49 Dante Bichette RBI W	1.25	.35
R50 Darren Daulton RBI	1.25	.35
R51 Will Clark BAT	3.00	.90
R52 Ken Griffey Jr. BAT	5.00	1.50
R53 Don Mattingly BAT	8.00	2.40
R54 John Olerud BAT	1.25	.35
R55 Kirby Puckett BAT	3.00	.90
R56 Raul Mondesi BAT	1.25	.35
R57 Moises Alou BAT	1.25	.35
R58 Bret Boone BAT	1.25	.35
R59 Albert Belle BAT	1.25	.35
R60 Mike Piazza BAT	5.00	1.50

1995 Upper Deck Ruth Heroes

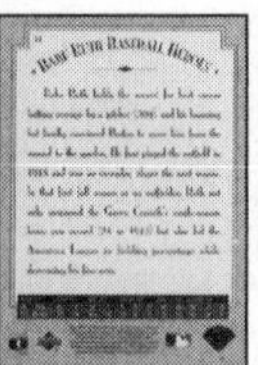

Randomly inserted in second series hobby and retail packs at a rate of 1:34, this set of 10 standard-size cards celebrates the achievements of one of baseball's all-time greats. The set was issued on the Centennial of Ruth's birth. The numbering (73-81) is a continuation from previous Heroes sets.

	Nm-Mt	Ex-Mt
COMPLETE SET (10)	100.00	30.00
COMMON (73-81/HDR)	15.00	4.50

1995 Upper Deck Special Edition

Inserted at a rate of one per pack, this 270 standard-size card set features full color action shots of players on a silver foil background. The back highlights the player's previous performance, including 1994 and career

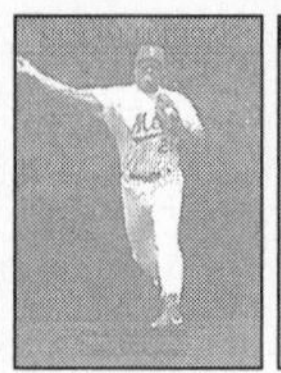

statistics. Another player photo is also featured on the back.

	Nm-Mt	Ex-Mt
COMPLETE SET (270)	100.00	30.00
COMP. SERIES 1 (135)	50.00	15.00
COMP. SERIES 2 (135)	50.00	15.00
*SE GOLD: 2.5X TO 6X BASIC SE		
*SE GOLD RC's: 2.5X TO 6X BASIC SE		
SE GOLD ODDS 1:35 HOBBY		
1 Cliff Floyd	.75	.23
2 Wil Cordero	.40	.12
3 Pedro Martinez	2.00	.60
4 Larry Walker	1.25	.35
5 Derek Jeter	5.00	1.50
6 Mike Stanley	.40	.12
7 Melido Perez	.40	.12
8 Jim Leyritz	.40	.12
9 Danny Tartabull	.40	.12
10 Wade Boggs	1.25	.35
11 Ryan Klesko	.75	.23
12 Steve Avery	.40	.12
13 Damon Hollins	.40	.12
14 Chipper Jones	2.00	.60
15 David Justice	.75	.23
16 Glenn Williams	.40	.12
17 Jose Oliva	.40	.12
18 Terrell Wade	.40	.12
19 Alex Fernandez	.40	.12
20 Frank Thomas	2.00	.60
21 Ozzie Guillen	.40	.12
22 Roberto Hernandez	.40	.12
23 Albie Lopez	.40	.12
24 Eddie Murray	2.00	.60
25 Albert Belle	.75	.23
26 Omar Vizquel	.75	.23
27 Carlos Baerga	.40	.12
28 Jose Rijo	.40	.12
29 Hal Morris	.40	.12
30 Reggie Sanders	.75	.23
31 Jack Morris	.75	.23
32 Raul Mondesi	.75	.23
33 Karim Garcia	.75	.23
34 Todd Hollandsworth	.40	.12
35 Mike Piazza	3.00	.90
36 Chan Ho Park	.75	.23
37 Ramon Martinez	.40	.12
38 Kenny Rogers	.40	.12
39 Will Clark	2.00	.60
40 Juan Gonzalez	2.00	.60
41 Ivan Rodriguez	2.00	.60
42 Orlando Miller	.40	.12
43 John Hudek	.40	.12
44 Luis Gonzalez	.75	.23
45 Jeff Bagwell	1.25	.35
46 Cal Ripken	6.00	1.80
47 Mike Oquist	.40	.12
48 Armando Benitez	.75	.23
49 Ben McDonald	.40	.12
50 Rafael Palmeiro	1.25	.35
51 Curtis Goodwin	.40	.12
52 Vince Coleman	.40	.12
53 Tom Gordon	.40	.12
54 Mike Macfarlane	.40	.12
55 Brian McRae	.40	.12
56 Matt Smith	.40	.12
57 David Segui	.40	.12
58 Paul Wilson	.40	.12
59 Bill Pulsipher	.40	.12
60 Bobby Bonilla	.75	.23
61 Jeff Kent	.75	.23
62 Ryan Thompson	.40	.12
63 Jason Isringhausen	.75	.23
64 Ed Sprague	.40	.12
65 Paul Molitor	1.25	.35
66 Juan Guzman	.40	.12
67 Alex Gonzalez	.40	.12
68 Shawn Green	.75	.23
69 Mark Portugal	.40	.12
70 Barry Bonds	5.00	1.50
71 Robby Thompson	.40	.12
72 Royce Clayton	.40	.12
73 Ricky Bottalico	.40	.12
74 Doug Jones	.40	.12
75 Darren Daulton	.75	.23
76 Gregg Jefferies	.40	.12
77 Scott Cooper	.40	.12
78 Nomar Garciaparra	6.00	1.80
79 Ken Ryan	.40	.12
80 Mike Greenwell	.40	.12
81 LaTroy Hawkins	.40	.12
82 Rich Becker	.40	.12
83 Scott Erickson	.40	.12
84 Pedro Munoz	.40	.12
85 Kirby Puckett	2.00	.60
86 Orlando Merced	.40	.12
87 Jeff King	.40	.12
88 Midre Cummings	.40	.12
89 Bernard Gilkey	.40	.12
90 Ray Lankford	.40	.12
91 Todd Zeile	.40	.12
92 Alan Benes	.40	.12
93 Bret Wagner	.40	.12
94 Rene Arocha	.40	.12
95 Cecil Fielder	.75	.23
96 Alan Trammell	1.25	.35
97 Tony Phillips	.40	.12
98 Junior Felix	.40	.12
99 Brian Harper	.40	.12
100 Greg Vaughn	.75	.23
101 Ricky Bones	.40	.12
102 Walt Weiss	.40	.12
103 Lance Painter	.40	.12
104 Roberto Mejia	.40	.12
105 Andres Galarraga	.75	.23
106 Todd Van Poppel	.40	.12
107 Ben Grieve	.75	.23
108 Brent Gates	.40	.12
109 Jason Giambi	2.00	.60
110 Ruben Sierra	.40	.12
111 Terry Steinbach	.40	.12
112 Chris Hammond	.40	.12
113 Charles Johnson	.75	.23
114 Jesus Tavarez	.40	.12
115 Gary Sheffield	.75	.23
116 Chuck Carr	.40	.12
117 Bobby Ayala	.40	.12
118 Randy Johnson	2.00	.60
119 Edgar Martinez	1.25	.35
120 Alex Rodriguez	5.00	1.50
121 Kevin Foster	.40	.12
122 Kevin Roberson	.40	.12
123 Sammy Sosa	3.00	.90
124 Steve Trachsel	.40	.12
125 Eduardo Perez	.40	.12
126 Tim Salmon	1.25	.35
127 Todd Greene	.40	.12
128 Jorge Fabregas	.40	.12
129 Mark Langston	.40	.12
130 Mitch Williams	.40	.12
131 Raul Casanova	.40	.12
132 Mel Nieves	.40	.12
133 Andy Benes	.40	.12
134 Dustin Hermanson	.40	.12
135 Trevor Hoffman	.75	.23
136 Mark Grudzielanek	1.25	.35
137 Ugueth Urbina	.40	.12
138 Moises Alou	.75	.23
139 Roberto Kelly	.40	.12
140 Rondell White	.75	.23
141 Paul O'Neill	1.25	.35
142 Jimmy Key	.75	.23
143 Jack McDowell	.40	.12
144 Ruben Rivera	.40	.12
145 Don Mattingly	5.00	1.50
146 John Wetteland	.75	.23
147 Tom Glavine	1.25	.35
148 Marquis Grissom	.40	.12
149 Javier Lopez	.75	.23
150 Fred McGriff	1.25	.35
151 Greg Maddux	3.00	.90
152 Chris Sabo	.40	.12
153 Ray Durham	.75	.23
154 Robin Ventura	.75	.23
155 Jim Abbott	1.25	.35
156 Jimmy Hurst	.40	.12
157 Tim Raines	.75	.23
158 Dennis Martinez	.75	.23
159 Kenny Lofton	.75	.23
160 Dave Winfield	.75	.23
161 Manny Ramirez	.75	.23
162 Jim Thome	2.00	.60
163 Barry Larkin	2.00	.60
164 Bret Boone	.75	.23
165 Deion Sanders	1.25	.35
166 Ron Gant	.75	.23
167 Benito Santiago	.75	.23
168 Hideo Nomo	5.00	1.50
169 Billy Ashley	.40	.12
170 Roger Cedeno	.40	.12
171 Ismael Valdes	.40	.12
172 Eric Karros	.75	.23
173 Rusty Greer	.75	.23
174 Rick Helling	.40	.12
175 Nolan Ryan	8.00	2.40
176 Dean Palmer	.75	.23
177 Phil Plantier	.40	.12
178 Darryl Kile	.75	.23
179 Derek Bell	.40	.12
180 Doug Drabek	.40	.12
181 Craig Biggio	1.25	.35
182 Kevin Brown	.75	.23
183 Harold Baines	.75	.23
184 Jeffrey Hammonds	.40	.12
185 Chris Hoiles	.40	.12
186 Mike Mussina	2.00	.60
187 Bob Hamelin	.40	.12
188 Jeff Montgomery	.40	.12
189 Michael Tucker	.40	.12
190 George Brett	5.00	1.50
191 Edgardo Alfonzo	.75	.23
192 Brett Butler	.75	.23
193 Bobby Jones	.40	.12
194 Todd Hundley	.40	.12
195 Bret Saberhagen	.75	.23
196 Pat Hentgen	.40	.12
197 Roberto Alomar	2.00	.60
198 David Cone	.75	.23
199 Carlos Delgado	.75	.23
200 Joe Carter	.75	.23
201 Wm. VanLandingham	.40	.12
202 Rod Beck	.40	.12
203 J.R. Phillips	.40	.12
204 Darren Lewis	.40	.12
205 Matt Williams	.75	.23
206 Lenny Dykstra	.75	.23
207 Dave Hollins	.40	.12
208 Mike Schmidt	3.00	.90
209 Charlie Hayes	.40	.12
210 Mo Vaughn	.75	.23
211 Jose Malave	.40	.12
212 Roger Clemens	4.00	1.20
213 Jose Canseco	2.00	.60
214 Mark Whiten	.40	.12
215 Marty Cordova	.40	.12
216 Rick Aguilera	.40	.12
217 Kevin Tapani	.40	.12
218 Chuck Knoblauch	.75	.23
219 Al Martin	.40	.12
220 Jay Bell	.75	.23
221 Carlos Garcia	.40	.12
222 Freddy Adrian Garcia	.40	.12
223 Jon Lieber	.40	.12
224 Danny Jackson	.40	.12
225 Ozzie Smith	3.00	.90
226 Brian Jordan	.75	.23
227 Ken Hill	.40	.12
228 Scott Cooper	.40	.12
229 Chad Curtis	.40	.12
230 Lou Whitaker	.75	.23
231 Kirk Gibson	.75	.23
232 Travis Fryman	.75	.23
233 Jose Valentin	.40	.12
234 Dave Nilsson	.40	.12
235 Cal Eldred	.40	.12
236 Matt Mieske	.40	.12
237 Bill Swift	.40	.12
238 Marvin Freeman	.40	.12
239 Jason Bates	.40	.12
240 Larry Walker	1.25	.35
241 Dave Nied	.40	.12
242 Dante Bichette	.75	.23
243 Dennis Eckersley	.75	.23
244 Todd Stottlemyre	.40	.12
245 Rickey Henderson	2.00	.60
246 Geronimo Berroa	.40	.12
247 Mark McGwire	5.00	1.50
248 Quilvio Veras	.40	.12
249 Terry Pendleton	.75	.23
250 Andre Dawson	.75	.23
251 Jeff Conine	.75	.23
252 Kurt Abbott	.40	.12
253 Jay Buhner	.75	.23
254 Darren Bragg	.40	.12
255 Ken Griffey Jr.	3.00	.90
256 Tino Martinez	1.25	.35
257 Mark Grace	1.25	.35
258 Ryne Sandberg	3.00	.90
259 Randy Myers	.40	.12
260 Howard Johnson	.40	.12
261 Lee Smith	.75	.23
262 J.T. Snow	.75	.23
263 Chili Davis	.75	.23
264 Chuck Finley	.75	.23
265 Eddie Williams	.40	.12
266 Joey Hamilton	.40	.12
267 Ken Caminiti	.75	.23
268 Andujar Cedeno	.40	.12
269 Steve Finley	.75	.23
270 Tony Gwynn	2.50	.75

1995 Upper Deck Steal of a Deal

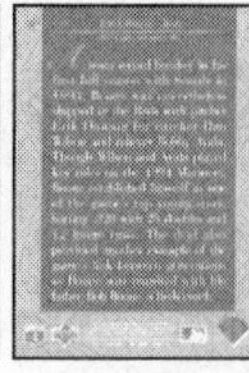

This set was inserted in hobby and retail packs at a rate of approximately one in 34. This 15-card standard-size set focuses on players who were acquired through, according to Upper Deck, "astute trades" or low round draft picks. The cards are numbered in the upper left with an "SD" prefix.

	Nm-Mt	Ex-Mt
COMPLETE SET (15)	80.00	24.00
SD1 Mike Piazza	12.00	3.60
SD2 Fred McGriff	5.00	1.50
SD3 Kenny Lofton	3.00	.90
SD4 Jose Oliva	1.50	.45
SD5 Jeff Bagwell	5.00	1.50
SD6 Roberto Alomar	8.00	2.40
Joe Carter		
SD7 Steve Karsay	1.50	.45
SD8 Ozzie Smith	12.00	3.60
SD9 Dennis Eckersley	3.00	.90
SD10 Jose Canseco	8.00	2.40
SD11 Carlos Baerga	1.50	.45
SD12 Cecil Fielder	3.00	.90
SD13 Don Mattingly	20.00	6.00
SD14 Bret Boone	3.00	.90
SD15 Michael Jordan	25.00	7.50

1995 Upper Deck Trade Exchange

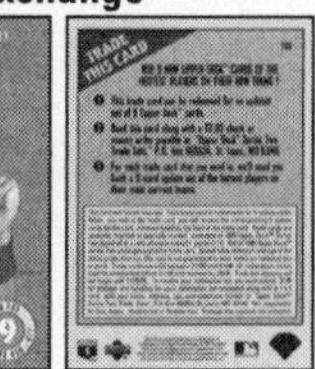

These five cards were randomly inserted into second series Upper Deck packs. A collector could send in these cards and receive nine cards from the trade set for the base 1995 Upper Deck set (numbers 451-495). These cards were redeemable until February 1, 1996.

	Nm-Mt	Ex-Mt
COMPLETE SET (5)	5.00	1.50
TC1 Orel Hershiser	1.50	.45
TC2 Terry Pendleton	1.00	.30
TC3 Benito Santiago	1.50	.45
TC4 Kevin Brown	2.00	.60
TC5 Gregg Jefferies	1.00	.30

1995 Upper Deck/GTS Phone Cards

Upper Deck joined with GTS (Global Telecommunication Solutions Inc.) to produce a series of MLB player phone cards. Each card contained 15 minutes of long distance phone time and was priced at $12.00. Card numbers 1-5 were released March 1, April 15, and May 15, for a total of fifteen cards. Moreover, other cards were to be released later in the year. The cards are unnumbered and checklisted below in alphabetical order in two sections--the first five that were released (MLB1-MLB5) and then the other ten cards (MLB6-MLB15).

	Nm-Mt	Ex-Mt
COMPLETE SET (15)	120.00	36.00
MLB1 Tony Gwynn	12.00	3.60
MLB2 Fred McGriff	3.00	.90
MLB3 Frank Thomas	6.00	1.80
MLB4 Ken Griffey Jr.	15.00	4.50
MLB5 Cecil Fielder	2.00	.60
MLB6 Roberto Alomar	5.00	1.50
MLB7 Jeff Bagwell	6.00	1.80
MLB8 Barry Bonds	12.00	3.60
MLB9 Roger Clemens	12.00	3.60
MLB10 David Justice	5.00	1.50
MLB11 Don Mattingly	12.00	3.60
MLB12 Kirby Puckett	6.00	1.80
MLB13 Cal Ripken	25.00	7.50
MLB14 Gary Sheffield	6.00	1.80
MLB15 Ozzie Smith	10.00	3.00

1995 Upper Deck Mantle Metallic Impressions

This eight-card set features vintage photos of career highlights of Mickey Mantle printed on metal cards. The backs carry information about the various stages of his career with a small stamp-like photo. The set was distributed in a collector's edition metal box containing a Certificate of Authenticity.

	Nm-Mt	Ex-Mt
COMPLETE SET (8)	20.00	6.00
COMMON CARD (1-8)	3.00	.90

1995 Upper Deck Sonic Heroes of Baseball

These standard-size cards were given out in three-card cello packs to customers who purchased a combo meal at participating Sonic Restaurants. The fronts feature black-and-white player photos with white borders. The words "Exclusive Edition" are printed in a blue bar at the top, with the player's name in a red bar directly below. The team name and the player's position appear on the bottom. The backs carry stats, career highlights, and sponsor and producer logos.

	Nm-Mt	Ex-Mt
COMPLETE SET (20)	6.00	1.80
1 Whitey Ford	.30	.09
2 Cy Young	.40	.12
3 Babe Ruth	1.50	.45
4 Lou Gehrig	.75	.23
5 Mike Schmidt	.40	.12
6 Nolan Ryan	1.50	.45
7 Robin Yount	.40	.12
8 Gary Carter	.20	.06
9 Tom Seaver	.30	.09
10 Reggie Jackson	.30	.09
11 Bob Gibson	.20	.06
12 Gil Hodges	.30	.09
13 Monte Irvin	.10	.03
14 Minnie Minoso	.10	.03
15 Willie Stargell	.20	.06
16 Al Kaline	.20	.06
17 Joe Jackson	.50	.15
18 Walter Johnson	.40	.12
19 Ty Cobb	.50	.15
20 Satchel Paige	.30	.09

1995 Upper Deck Sports Drink Jackson

Upper Deck and Energy Foods have joined together to produce the Upper Deck Authentic Sports Drink. The drink was available in four flavors (lemon lime, madarin orange, fruit cooler and tropical berry), and each package included one of three Reggie Jackson Heroes cards. Six-bottle packages retail for $2.00. The cards are similar to those that were included with Reggie Candy Bars in 1993, and come with and without a gold facsimile autograph. The cards are numbered on the back "X of 3."

	Nm-Mt	Ex-Mt
COMPLETE SET (3)	5.00	1.50
COMMON CARD (1-3)	2.00	.60

1996 Upper Deck

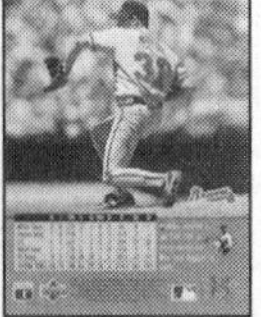

The 1996 Upper Deck set was issued in two series of 240 cards, and a 30 card update set, for a total of 510 cards. The cards were distributed in 10-card packs with a suggested retail price of $1.99, and 28 packs were contained in each box. Upper Deck issued 15,000 factory sets (containing all 510 cards) at season's end. In addition to being included in factory sets, the 30-card Update sets (U481-U510) were also available via mail through a wrapper exchange program. The attractive fronts of each basic card feature a full-bleed photo above a bronze foil bar that includes the player's name, team and position in a white oval. Subsets include Young at Heart (100-117), Beat the Odds (145-153), Postseason Checklist (218-222), Best of a Generation (370-387), Strange But True (415-423) and Managerial Salute Checklists (476-480). The only Rookie Card of note is Livan Hernandez.

	Nm-Mt	Ex-Mt
COMPLETE SET (480)	50.00	15.00
COMP.FACT.SET (510)	100.00	30.00
COMP. SERIES 1 (240)	25.00	7.50
COMP. SERIES 2 (240)	25.00	7.50
COMMON CARD (1-480)	.30	.09
COMP.UPDATE SET (30)	20.00	6.00
COMMON (481U-510U)	.50	.15
1 Cal Ripken 2131	4.00	1.20
2 Eddie Murray 3000 Hits	.50	.15
3 Mark Wohlers	.30	.09
4 David Justice	.30	.09
5 Chipper Jones	.75	.23
6 Javier Lopez	.30	.09
7 Mark Lemke	.30	.09
8 Marquis Grissom	.30	.09
9 Tom Glavine	.50	.15
10 Greg Maddux	1.25	.35
11 Manny Alexander	.30	.09
12 Curtis Goodwin	.30	.09
13 Scott Erickson	.30	.09
14 Chris Hoiles	.30	.09
15 Rafael Palmeiro	.50	.15
16 Rick Krivda	.30	.09
17 Jeff Manto	.30	.09
18 Mo Vaughn	.30	.09
19 Tim Wakefield	.30	.09
20 Roger Clemens	1.50	.45
21 Tim Naehring	.30	.09
22 Troy O'Leary	.30	.09
23 Mike Greenwell	.30	.09
24 Stan Belinda	.30	.09
25 John Valentin	.30	.09
26 J.T. Snow	.30	.09
27 Gary DiSarcina	.30	.09
28 Mark Langston	.30	.09
29 Brian Anderson	.30	.09
30 Jim Edmonds	.30	.09
31 Garret Anderson	.30	.09
32 Orlando Palmeiro	.30	.09
33 Brian McRae	.30	.09
34 Kevin Foster	.30	.09
35 Sammy Sosa	1.25	.35
36 Todd Zeile	.30	.09
37 Jim Bullinger	.30	.09
38 Luis Gonzalez	.30	.09
39 Lyle Mouton	.30	.09
40 Ray Durham	.30	.09
41 Ozzie Guillen	.30	.09
42 Alex Fernandez	.30	.09
43 Brian Keyser	.30	.09
44 Robin Ventura	.30	.09
45 Reggie Sanders	.30	.09
46 Pete Schourek	.30	.09
47 John Smiley	.30	.09
48 Jeff Brantley	.30	.09
49 Thomas Howard	.30	.09
50 Bret Boone	.30	.09
51 Kevin Jarvis	.30	.09
52 Jeff Branson	.30	.09
53 Carlos Baerga	.30	.09
54 Jim Thome	.75	.23
55 Manny Ramirez	.30	.09
56 Omar Vizquel	.30	.09
57 Jose Mesa	.30	.09
58 Julian Tavarez UER	.30	.09
59 Orel Hershiser	.30	.09
60 Larry Walker	.50	.15
61 Bret Saberhagen	.30	.09
62 Vinny Castilla	.30	.09
63 Eric Young	.30	.09
64 Bryan Rekar	.30	.09
65 Andres Galarraga	.30	.09
66 Steve Reed	.30	.09
67 Chad Curtis	.30	.09
68 Bobby Higginson	.30	.09
69 Phil Nevin	.30	.09
70 Cecil Fielder	.30	.09
71 Felipe Lira	.30	.09
72 Chris Gomez	.30	.09
73 Charles Johnson	.30	.09
74 Quilvio Veras	.30	.09
75 Jeff Conine	.30	.09
76 John Burkett	.30	.09
77 Greg Colbrunn	.30	.09
78 Terry Pendleton	.30	.09
79 Shane Reynolds	.30	.09
80 Jeff Bagwell	.50	.15
81 Orlando Miller	.30	.09
82 Mike Hampton	.30	.09
83 James Mouton	.30	.09
84 Brian L. Hunter	.30	.09
85 Derek Bell	.30	.09
86 Kevin Appier	.30	.09
87 Joe Vitiello	.30	.09
88 Wally Joyner	.30	.09
89 Michael Tucker	.30	.09
90 Johnny Damon	.30	.40
91 Jon Nunnally	.30	.09
92 Jason Jacome	.30	.09
93 Chad Fonville	.30	.09
94 Chan Ho Park	.30	.09
95 Hideo Nomo	.75	.23
96 Ismael Valdes	.30	.09
97 Greg Gagne	.30	.09
98 Arizona Diamondbacks	.75	.23
Tampa Bay Devil Rays		
99 Raul Mondesi	.30	.09
100 Dave Winfield YH	.30	.09
101 Dennis Eckersley YH	.30	.09
102 Andre Dawson YH	.30	.09
103 Dennis Martinez YH	.30	.09
104 Lance Parrish YH	.30	.09
105 Eddie Murray YH	.50	.15
106 Alan Trammell YH	.30	.09
107 Lou Whitaker YH	.30	.09
108 Ozzie Smith YH	.75	.23
109 Paul Molitor YH	.30	.09
110 Rickey Henderson YH	.50	.15
111 Tim Raines YH	.30	.09
112 Harold Baines YH	.30	.09
113 Lee Smith YH	.30	.09
114 F.Valenzuela YH	.30	.09
115 Cal Ripken YH	1.25	.35
116 Tony Gwynn YH	.50	.15
117 Wade Boggs	.50	.15
118 Todd Hollandsworth	.30	.09
119 Dave Nilsson	.30	.09
120 Jose Valentin	.30	.09
121 Steve Sparks	.30	.09
122 Chuck Carr	.30	.09
123 John Jaha	.30	.09
124 Scott Karl	.30	.09
125 Chuck Knoblauch	.30	.09
126 Brad Radke	.30	.09
127 Pat Meares	.30	.09
128 Ron Coomer	.30	.09
129 Pedro Munoz	.30	.09
130 Kirby Puckett	.75	.23
131 David Segui	.30	.09
132 Mark Grudzielanek	.30	.09
133 Mike Lansing	.30	.09
134 Sean Berry	.30	.09
135 Rondell White	.30	.09
136 Pedro Martinez	.75	.23
137 Carl Everett	.30	.09
138 Dave Mlicki	.30	.09
139 Bill Pulsipher	.30	.09
140 Jason Isringhausen	.30	.09
141 Rico Brogna	.30	.09
142 Edgardo Alfonzo	.30	.09
143 Jeff Kent	.30	.09
144 Andy Pettitte	.50	.15
145 Mike Piazza BO	.75	.23
146 Cliff Floyd BO	.30	.09
147 J.Isringhausen BO	.30	.09
148 Tim Wakefield BO	.30	.09
149 Chipper Jones BO	.50	.15
150 Hideo Nomo BO	.50	.15
151 Mark McGwire BO	1.00	.30
152 Ron Gant BO	.30	.09
153 Gary Gaetti BO	.30	.09
154 Don Mattingly	2.00	.60
155 Paul O'Neill	.50	.15
156 Derek Jeter	2.00	.60
157 Joe Girardi	.30	.09
158 Ruben Sierra	.30	.09
159 Jorge Posada	.50	.15
160 Geronimo Berroa	.30	.09
161 Steve Ontiveros	.30	.09
162 George Williams	.30	.09
163 Doug Johns	.30	.09
164 Ariel Prieto	.30	.09
165 Scott Brosius	.30	.09
166 Mike Bordick	.30	.09
167 Tyler Green	.30	.09
168 Mickey Morandini	.30	.09
169 Darren Daulton	.30	.09
170 Gregg Jefferies	.30	.09
171 Jim Eisenreich	.30	.09
172 Heathcliff Slocumb	.30	.09
173 Kevin Stocker	.30	.09
174 Esteban Loaiza	.30	.09
175 Jeff King	.30	.09
176 Mark Johnson	.30	.09
177 Denny Neagle	.30	.09
178 Orlando Merced	.30	.09
179 Carlos Garcia	.30	.09
180 Brian Jordan	.30	.09
181 Mike Morgan	.30	.09
182 Mark Petkovsek	.30	.09
183 Bernard Gilkey	.30	.09
184 John Mabry	.30	.09
185 Tom Henke	.30	.09
186 Glenn Dishman	.30	.09
187 Andy Ashby	.30	.09
188 Bip Roberts	.30	.09
189 Melvin Nieves	.30	.09
190 Ken Caminiti	.30	.09
191 Brad Ausmus	.30	.09
192 Deion Sanders	.50	.15
193 Jamie Brewington RC	.30	.09
194 Glenallen Hill	.30	.09
195 Barry Bonds	2.00	.60
196 Wm. Van Landingham	.30	.09
197 Mark Carreon	.30	.09
198 Royce Clayton	.30	.09
199 Joey Cora	.30	.09
200 Ken Griffey Jr.	1.25	.35
201 Jay Buhner	.30	.09
202 Alex Rodriguez	1.50	.45
203 Norm Charlton	.30	.09
204 Andy Benes	.30	.09
205 Edgar Martinez	.50	.15
206 Juan Gonzalez	.75	.23
207 Will Clark	.75	.23
208 Kevin Gross	.30	.09
209 Roger Pavlik	.30	.09
210 Ivan Rodriguez	.75	.23
211 Rusty Greer	.30	.09
212 Angel Martinez	.30	.09
213 Tomas Perez	.30	.09
214 Alex Gonzalez	.30	.09
215 Joe Carter	.30	.09
216 Shawn Green	.30	.09
217 Edwin Hurtado	.30	.09
218 Edgar Martinez	.30	.09
Tony Pena CL		
219 Chipper Jones	.50	.15
Barry Larkin CL		
220 Orel Hershiser CL	.30	.09
221 Mike Devereaux CL	.30	.09
222 Tom Glavine CL	.30	.09
223 Karim Garcia	.30	.09
224 Arquimedez Pozo	.30	.09
225 Billy Wagner	.30	.09
226 John Wasdin	.30	.09
227 Jeff Suppan	.30	.09
228 Steve Gibralter	.30	.09
229 Jimmy Haynes	.30	.09
230 Ruben Rivera	.30	.09
231 Chris Snopek	.30	.09
232 Alex Ochoa	.30	.09
233 Shannon Stewart	.30	.09
234 Quinton McCracken	.30	.09
235 Trey Beamon	.30	.09
236 Billy McMillon	.30	.09
237 Steve Cox	.30	.09
238 George Arias	.30	.09
239 Yamil Benitez	.30	.09
240 Todd Greene	.30	.09
241 Jason Kendall	.30	.09
242 Brooks Kieschnick	.30	.09
243 O. Fernandez RC	.30	.09
244 Livan Hernandez RC	.60	.18
245 Rey Ordonez	.30	.09
246 Mike Grace RC	.30	.09
247 Jay Canizaro	.30	.09
248 Bob Wolcott	.30	.09
249 Jermaine Dye	.30	.09
250 Jason Schmidt	.30	.09
251 Mike Sweeney RC	2.00	.60
252 Marcus Jensen	.30	.09
253 Mendy Lopez	.30	.09
254 Wilton Guerrero RC	.40	.12
255 Paul Wilson	.30	.09
256 Edgar Renteria	.30	.09
257 Richard Hidalgo	.30	.09
258 Bob Abreu	.30	.09
259 Robert Smith RC	.30	.09
260 Sal Fasano	.30	.09
261 Enrique Wilson	.30	.09
262 Rich Hunter RC	.30	.09
263 Sergio Nunez	.30	.09
264 Dan Serafini	.30	.09
265 David Doster	.30	.09
266 Ryan McGuire	.30	.09
267 Scott Spiezio	.30	.09
268 Rafael Orellano	.30	.09
269 Steve Avery	.30	.09
270 Fred McGriff	.50	.15
271 John Smoltz	.50	.15
272 Ryan Klesko	.30	.09
273 Jeff Blauser	.30	.09
274 Brad Clontz	.30	.09
275 Roberto Alomar	.75	.23
276 B.J. Surhoff	.30	.09
277 Jeffrey Hammonds	.30	.09
278 Brady Anderson	.30	.09
279 Bobby Bonilla	.30	.09
280 Cal Ripken	2.50	.75
281 Mike Mussina	.75	.23
282 Wil Cordero	.30	.09
283 Mike Stanley	.30	.09
284 Aaron Sele	.30	.09
285 Jose Canseco	.75	.23
286 Tom Gordon	.30	.09
287 Heathcliff Slocumb	.30	.09
288 Lee Smith	.30	.09
289 Troy Percival	.30	.09
290 Tim Salmon	.50	.15
291 Chuck Finley	.30	.09
292 Jim Abbott	.50	.15
293 Chili Davis	.30	.09
294 Steve Trachsel	.30	.09
295 Mark Grace	.50	.15
296 Rey Sanchez	.30	.09
297 Scott Servais	.30	.09
298 Jaime Navarro	.30	.09
299 Frank Castillo	.30	.09
300 Frank Thomas	.75	.23
301 Jason Bere	.30	.09
302 Danny Tartabull	.30	.09
303 Darren Lewis	.30	.09
304 Roberto Hernandez	.30	.09
305 Tony Phillips	.30	.09
306 Wilson Alvarez	.30	.09
307 Jose Rijo	.30	.09
308 Hal Morris	.30	.09
309 Mark Portugal	.30	.09
310 Barry Larkin	.75	.23
311 Dave Burba	.30	.09
312 Eddie Taubensee	.30	.09
313 Sandy Alomar Jr.	.30	.09
314 Dennis Martinez	.30	.09
315 Albert Belle	.30	.09
316 Eddie Murray	.75	.23
317 Charles Nagy	.30	.09
318 Chad Ogea	.30	.09
319 Kenny Lofton	.30	.09
320 Dante Bichette	.30	.09
321 Armando Reynoso	.30	.09
322 Walt Weiss	.30	.09
323 Ellis Burks	.30	.09
324 Kevin Ritz	.30	.09
325 Bill Swift	.30	.09
326 Jason Bates	.30	.09
327 Tony Clark	.30	.09
328 Travis Fryman	.30	.09
329 Mark Parent	.30	.09
330 Alan Trammell	.50	.15
331 C.J. Nitkowski	.30	.09
332 Jose Lima	.30	.09
333 Phil Plantier	.30	.09
334 Kurt Abbott	.30	.09
335 Andre Dawson	.30	.09
336 Chris Hammond	.30	.09
337 Robb Nen	.30	.09
338 Pat Rapp	.30	.09
339 Al Leiter	.30	.09
340 Gary Sheffield UER	.30	.09
(HR total says 17		
341 Todd Jones	.30	.09
342 Doug Drabek	.30	.09
343 Greg Swindell	.30	.09
344 Tony Eusebio	.30	.09
345 Craig Biggio	.50	.15
346 Darryl Kile	.30	.09
347 Mike Macfarlane	.30	.09
348 Jeff Montgomery	.30	.09
349 Chris Haney	.30	.09
350 Bip Roberts	.30	.09
351 Tom Goodwin	.30	.09
352 Mark Gubicza	.30	.09
353 Joe Randa	.30	.09
354 Ramon Martinez	.30	.09
355 Eric Karros	.30	.09
356 Delino DeShields	.30	.09
357 Brett Butler	.30	.09
358 Todd Worrell	.30	.09
359 Mike Blowers	.30	.09
360 Mike Piazza	1.25	.35
361 Ben McDonald	.30	.09
362 Ricky Bones	.30	.09
363 Greg Vaughn	.30	.09
364 Matt Mieske	.30	.09
365 Kevin Seitzer	.30	.09
366 Jeff Cirillo	.30	.09
367 LaTroy Hawkins	.30	.09
368 Frank Rodriguez	.30	.09
369 Rick Aguilera	.30	.09
370 Roberto Alomar BG	.30	.09
371 Albert Belle BG	.30	.09
372 Wade Boggs BG	.30	.09
373 Barry Bonds BG	.75	.23
374 Roger Clemens BG	.75	.23
375 Dennis Eckersley BG	.30	.09
376 Ken Griffey Jr. BG	.75	.23
377 Tony Gwynn BG	.50	.15
378 Rickey Henderson BG	.50	.15
379 Greg Maddux BG	.75	.23
380 Fred McGriff BG	.30	.09
381 Paul Molitor BG	.30	.09
382 Eddie Murray BG	.50	.15
383 Mike Piazza BG	.75	.23
384 Kirby Puckett BG	.50	.15
385 Cal Ripken BG	1.25	.35
386 Ozzie Smith BG	.75	.23
387 Frank Thomas BG	.50	.15
388 Matt Walbeck	.30	.09
389 Dave Stevens	.30	.09
390 Marty Cordova	.30	.09
391 Darrin Fletcher	.30	.09
392 Cliff Floyd	.30	.09
393 Mel Rojas	.30	.09
394 Shane Andrews	.30	.09
395 Moises Alou	.30	.09
396 Carlos Perez	.30	.09
397 Jeff Fassero	.30	.09
398 Bobby Jones	.30	.09
399 Todd Hundley	.30	.09
400 John Franco	.30	.09
401 Jose Vizcaino	.30	.09
402 Bernard Gilkey	.30	.09
403 Pete Harnisch	.30	.09
404 Pat Kelly	.30	.09
405 David Cone	.30	.09
406 Bernie Williams	.50	.15
407 John Wetteland	.30	.09
408 Scott Kamieniecki	.30	.09
409 Tim Raines	.30	.09
410 Wade Boggs	.50	.15
411 Terry Steinbach	.30	.09
412 Jason Giambi	.75	.23
413 Todd Van Poppel	.30	.09
414 Pedro Munoz	.30	.09
415 Eddie Murray SBT	.50	.15
416 Dennis Eckersley SBT	.30	.09
417 Bip Roberts SBT	.30	.09
418 Glenallen Hill SBT	.30	.09
419 John Hudek SBT	.30	.09
420 Derek Bell SBT	.30	.09
421 Larry Walker SBT	.30	.09
422 Greg Maddux SBT	.75	.23
423 Ken Caminiti SBT	.30	.09
424 Brent Gates	.30	.09
425 Mark McGwire	2.00	.60
426 Mark Whiten	.30	.09
427 Sid Fernandez	.30	.09
428 Ricky Bottalico	.30	.09
429 Mike Mimbs	.30	.09
430 Lenny Dykstra	.30	.09
431 Todd Zeile	.30	.09
432 Benito Santiago	.30	.09
433 Danny Miceli	.30	.09
434 Al Martin	.30	.09
435 Jay Bell	.30	.09
436 Charlie Hayes	.30	.09
437 Mike Kingery	.30	.09
438 Paul Wagner	.30	.09
439 Tom Pagnozzi	.30	.09
440 Ozzie Smith	1.25	.35
441 Ray Lankford	.30	.09
442 Dennis Eckersley	.30	.09
443 Ron Gant	.30	.09
444 Alan Benes	.30	.09
445 Rickey Henderson	.75	.23
446 Jody Reed	.30	.09
447 Trevor Hoffman	.30	.09
448 Andujar Cedeno	.30	.09
449 Steve Finley	.30	.09
450 Tony Gwynn	1.00	.30
451 Joey Hamilton	.30	.09
452 Mark Leiter	.30	.09
453 Rod Beck	.30	.09
454 Kirt Manwaring	.30	.09
455 Matt Williams	.30	.09
456 Robby Thompson	.30	.09
457 Shawon Dunston	.30	.09
458 Russ Davis	.30	.09
459 Paul Sorrento	.30	.09
460 Randy Johnson	.75	.23
461 Chris Bosio	.30	.09
462 Luis Sojo	.30	.09
463 Sterling Hitchcock	.30	.09
464 Benji Gil	.30	.09
465 Mickey Tettleton	.30	.09
466 Mark McLemore	.30	.09
467 Darryl Hamilton	.30	.09
468 Ken Hill	.30	.09
469 Dean Palmer	.30	.09
470 Carlos Delgado	.30	.09
471 Ed Sprague	.30	.09
472 Otis Nixon	.30	.09
473 Pat Hentgen	.30	.09
474 Juan Guzman	.30	.09
475 John Olerud	.30	.09
476 Buck Showalter CL	.30	.09
477 Bobby Cox CL	.30	.09
478 Tommy Lasorda CL	.30	.09
479 Buck Showalter CL	.30	.09
480 Sparky Anderson CL	.30	.09
481U Randy Myers	.50	.15
482U Kent Mercker	.50	.15
483U David Wells	.75	.23
484U Kevin Mitchell	.50	.15
485U Randy Velarde	.50	.15
486U Ryne Sandberg	4.00	1.20
487U Doug Jones	.50	.15
488U Terry Adams	.50	.15
489U Kevin Tapani	.50	.15
490U Harold Baines	.75	.23
491U Eric Davis	.75	.23
492U Julio Franco	.75	.23
493U Jack McDowell	.50	.15
494U Devon White	.75	.23

495U Kevin Brown .75 .23
496U Rick Wilkins .50 .15
497U Sean Berry .50 .15
498U Keith Lockhart .50 .15
499U Mark Loretta .50 .15
500U Paul Molitor 1.25 .35
501U Roberto Kelly .50 .15
502U Lance Johnson .50 .15
503U Tino Martinez 1.25 .35
504U Kenny Rogers .75 .23
505U Todd Stottlemyre .50 .15
506U Gary Gaetti .75 .23
507U Royce Clayton .50 .15
508U Andy Benes .50 .15
509U Wally Joyner .75 .23
510U Erik Hanson .50 .15
P100 Ken Griffey Jr Promo 3.00 .90

1996 Upper Deck Blue Chip Prospects

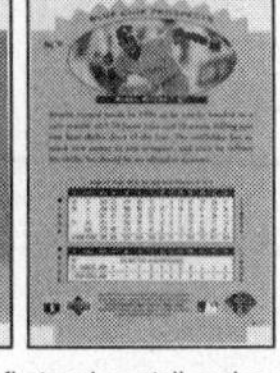

Randomly inserted in first series retail packs at a rate of one in 72, this 20-card set, diecut on the top and bottom, features some of the best young stars in the majors against a bluish background.

	Nm-Mt	Ex-Mt
COMPLETE SET (20)	100.00	30.00
BC1 Hideo Nomo	10.00	3.00
BC2 Johnny Damon	4.00	1.20
BC3 Jason Isringhausen	4.00	1.20
BC4 Bill Pulsipher	4.00	1.20
BC5 Marty Cordova	4.00	1.20
BC6 Michael Tucker	4.00	1.20
BC7 John Wasdin	4.00	1.20
BC8 Karim Garcia	4.00	1.20
BC9 Ruben Rivera	4.00	1.20
BC10 Chipper Jones	10.00	3.00
BC11 Billy Wagner	4.00	1.20
BC12 Brooks Kieschnick	4.00	1.20
BC13 Alan Benes	4.00	1.20
BC14 Roger Cedeno	4.00	1.20
BC15 Alex Rodriguez	20.00	6.00
BC16 Jason Schmidt	4.00	1.20
BC17 Derek Jeter	25.00	7.50
BC18 Brian L.Hunter	4.00	1.20
BC19 Garret Anderson	4.00	1.20
BC20 Manny Ramirez	4.00	1.20

1996 Upper Deck Diamond Destiny

Issued one per Wal Mart pack, these 40 cards feature leading players of baseball. The cards have two photos on the front with the player's name listed on the bottom. The backs have another photo along with biographical information.

	Nm-Mt	Ex-Mt
COMPLETE SET (40)	80.00	24.00
*GOLD: 5X TO 12 X BASIC DESTINY		
GOLD: ONE IN 143 UD TECH RETAIL PACKS		
*SILVER: 1.5X TO 4X BASIC DESTINY		
SILVER: ONE IN 35 UD TECH RETAIL PACKS		
DD1 Chipper Jones	2.50	.75
DD2 Fred McGriff	1.50	.45
DD3 John Smoltz	1.50	.45
DD4 Ryan Klesko	1.00	.30
DD5 Greg Maddux	4.00	1.20
DD6 Cal Ripken	8.00	2.40
DD7 Roberto Alomar	2.50	.75
DD8 Eddie Murray	2.50	.75
DD9 Brady Anderson	1.00	.30
DD10 Mo Vaughn	1.00	.30
DD11 Roger Clemens	5.00	1.50
DD12 Darin Erstad	2.50	.75
DD13 Sammy Sosa	4.00	1.20
DD14 Frank Thomas	2.50	.75
DD15 Barry Larkin	2.50	.75
DD16 Albert Belle	1.00	.30
DD17 Manny Ramirez	1.00	.30
DD18 Kenny Lofton	1.00	.30
DD19 Dante Bichette	1.00	.30
DD20 Gary Sheffield	1.00	.30
DD21 Jeff Bagwell	1.50	.45
DD22 Hideo Nomo	2.50	.75
DD23 Mike Piazza	4.00	1.20
DD24 Kirby Puckett	2.50	.75
DD25 Paul Molitor	4.00	1.20
DD26 Chuck Knoblauch	1.00	.30
DD27 Wade Boggs	1.50	.45
DD28 Derek Jeter	6.00	1.80
DD29 Rey Ordonez	1.00	.30
DD30 Mark McGwire	6.00	1.80
DD31 Ozzie Smith	4.00	1.20
DD32 Tony Gwynn	3.00	.90
DD33 Barry Bonds	6.00	1.80
DD34 Matt Williams	1.00	.30
DD35 Ken Griffey Jr.	4.00	1.20
DD36 Jay Buhner	1.00	.30
DD37 Randy Johnson	2.50	.75
DD38 Alex Rodriguez	5.00	1.50
DD39 Juan Gonzalez	2.50	.75
DD40 Joe Carter	1.00	.30

1996 Upper Deck Future Stock Prospects

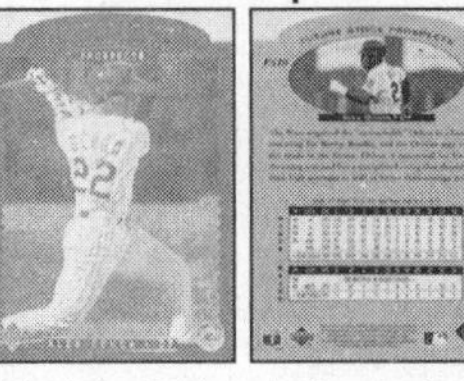

Randomly inserted in packs at a rate of one in 6, this 20-card set highlights the top prospects who made their major league debuts in 1995. The cards are diecut at the top and feature a purple border surrounding the player's picture.

	Nm-Mt	Ex-Mt
COMPLETE SET (20)	8.00	2.40
FS1 George Arias	1.00	.30
FS2 Brian Barber	1.00	.30
FS3 Trey Beamon	1.00	.30
FS4 Yamil Benitez	1.00	.30
FS5 Jamie Brewington	1.00	.30
FS6 Tony Clark	1.00	.30
FS7 Steve Cox	1.00	.30
FS8 Carlos Delgado	1.00	.30
FS9 Chad Fonville	1.00	.30
FS10 Alex Ochoa	1.00	.30
FS11 Curtis Goodwin	1.00	.30
FS12 Todd Greene	1.00	.30
FS13 Jimmy Haynes	1.00	.30
FS14 Quinton McCracken	1.00	.30
FS15 Billy McMillon	1.00	.30
FS16 Chan Ho Park	1.00	.30
FS17 Arquimedez Pozo	1.00	.30
FS18 Chris Snopek	1.00	.30
FS19 Shannon Stewart	1.00	.30
FS20 Jeff Suppan	1.00	.30

1996 Upper Deck Gameface

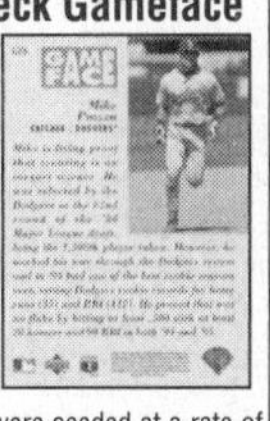

These Gameface cards were seeded at a rate of one per Upper Deck and Collector's Choice Wal Mart retail pack. The Upper Deck packs contained eight cards and the Collector's Choice packs contained sixteen cards. Both packs carried a suggested retail price of $1.50. The card fronts feature the player's photo surrounded by a "cloudy" white border along with a Gameface logo at the bottom.

	Nm-Mt	Ex-Mt
COMPLETE SET (10)	12.00	3.60
GF1 Ken Griffey Jr.	1.25	.35
GF2 Frank Thomas	.75	.23
GF3 Barry Bonds	2.00	.60
GF4 Albert Belle	.30	.09
GF5 Cal Ripken	2.50	.75
GF6 Mike Piazza	1.25	.35
GF7 Chipper Jones	.75	.23
GF8 Matt Williams	.30	.09
GF9 Hideo Nomo	.75	.23
GF10 Greg Maddux	1.25	.35

1996 Upper Deck Hot Commodities

Cards from this 20 card set double die-cut set were randomly inserted into series two Upper Deck packs at a rate of one in 37. The set features some of baseball's most popular players.

	Nm-Mt	Ex-Mt
COMPLETE SET (20)	150.00	45.00
HC1 Ken Griffey Jr.	12.00	3.60
HC2 Hideo Nomo	8.00	2.40
HC3 Roberto Alomar	8.00	2.40
HC4 Paul Wilson	3.00	.90
HC5 Albert Belle	3.00	.90
HC6 Manny Ramirez	3.00	.90
HC7 Kirby Puckett	8.00	2.40
HC8 Johnny Damon	3.00	.90
HC9 Randy Johnson	8.00	2.40
HC10 Greg Maddux	12.00	3.60
HC11 Chipper Jones	8.00	2.40
HC12 Barry Bonds	20.00	6.00
HC13 Mo Vaughn	3.00	.90
HC14 Mike Piazza	12.00	3.60
HC15 Cal Ripken	25.00	7.50
HC16 Tim Salmon	5.00	1.50
HC17 Sammy Sosa	12.00	3.60
HC18 Kenny Lofton	3.00	.90
HC19 Tony Gwynn	10.00	3.00
HC20 Frank Thomas	8.00	2.40

1996 Upper Deck V.J. Lovero Showcase

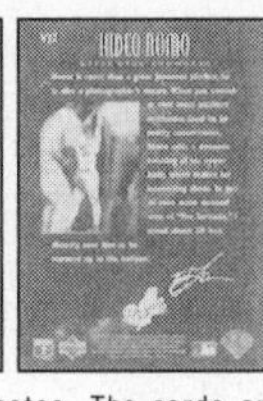

Upper Deck utilized photos from the files of V.J. Lovero to produce this set. The cards feature the photos along with a story of how Lovero took the photos. The cards are numbered with a "VJ" prefix. These cards were inserted at a rate of one every six packs.

	Nm-Mt	Ex-Mt
COMPLETE SET (19)	25.00	7.50
VJ1 Jim Abbott	1.25	.35
VJ2 Hideo Nomo	2.00	.60
VJ3 Derek Jeter	5.00	1.50
VJ4 Barry Bonds	5.00	1.50
VJ5 Greg Maddux	3.00	.90
VJ6 Mark McGwire	5.00	1.50
VJ7 Jose Canseco	2.00	.60
VJ8 Ken Caminiti	.75	.23
VJ9 Raul Mondesi	.75	.23
VJ10 Ken Griffey Jr.	3.00	.90
VJ11 Jay Buhner	.75	.23
VJ12 Randy Johnson	2.00	.60
VJ13 Roger Clemens	4.00	1.20
VJ14 Brady Anderson	.75	.23
VJ15 Frank Thomas	2.00	.60
VJ16 Garret Anderson Jim Edmonds Tim Salmon	.75	.23
VJ17 Mike Piazza	3.00	.90
VJ18 Dante Bichette	.75	.23
VJ19 Tony Gwynn	2.50	.75

1996 Upper Deck Nomo Highlights

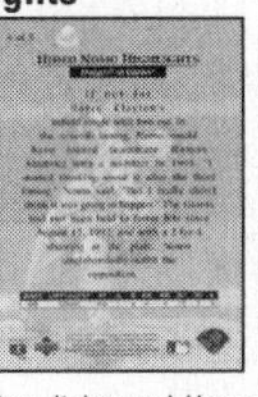

Los Angeles Dodgers star pitcher and Upper Deck spokesperson Hideo Nomo was featured in this special five card set. The cards were randomly seeded into second series packs at a rate of one in 24 and feature game action as well as descriptions of some of Nomo's key 1995 games.

	Nm-Mt	Ex-Mt
COMPLETE SET (5)	20.00	6.00
COMMON CARD (1-5)	5.00	1.50

1996 Upper Deck Power Driven

Randomly inserted in first series packs at a rate of one in 36, this 20-card set consists of embossed rainbow foil inserts of baseball's top power hitters.

	Nm-Mt	Ex-Mt
COMPLETE SET (20)	120.00	36.00
PD1 Albert Belle	3.00	.90
PD2 Barry Bonds	20.00	6.00
PD3 Jay Buhner	3.00	.90
PD4 Jose Canseco	8.00	2.40
PD5 Cecil Fielder	3.00	.90
PD6 Juan Gonzalez	8.00	2.40
PD7 Ken Griffey Jr.	12.00	3.60
PD8 Eric Karros	3.00	.90
PD9 Fred McGriff	5.00	1.50
PD10 Mark McGwire	20.00	6.00
PD11 Rafael Palmeiro	5.00	1.50
PD12 Mike Piazza	12.00	3.60
PD13 Manny Ramirez	3.00	.90
PD14 Tim Salmon	5.00	1.50
PD15 Reggie Sanders	3.00	.90
PD16 Sammy Sosa	12.00	3.60
PD17 Frank Thomas	8.00	2.40
PD18 Mo Vaughn	3.00	.90
PD19 Larry Walker	5.00	1.50
PD20 Matt Williams	3.00	.35

1996 Upper Deck Predictor Hobby

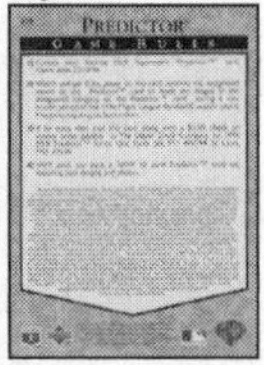

Randomly inserted in both series hobby packs at a rate of one in 12, this 60-card predictor set offered six different 10-card parallel exchange sets for prizes as featured players competed for monthly milestones and awards. The fronts feature a cutout player photo against a pinstriped background surrounded by a gray marble border. Card backs feature game rules and guidelines. Winner cards are signified with a W in our listings and are in noticeably shorter supply since they had to be mailed in to Upper Deck (where they were destroyed) to claim your exchange cards. The deadline to mail in winning cards was November 18th, 1996.

	Nm-Mt	Ex-Mt
COMPLETE SERIES 1 (30)	30.00	9.00
COMPLETE SERIES 2 (30)	30.00	9.00
*EXCHANGE: .4X TO 1X BASIC PREDICTOR		
ONE EXCH.SET VIA MAIL PER PRED.WINNER		
H1 Albert Belle	.60	.18
H2 Kenny Lofton	.60	.18
H3 Rafael Palmeiro	1.00	.30
H4 Ken Griffey Jr.	2.50	.75
H5 Tim Salmon	1.00	.30
H6 Cal Ripken	5.00	1.50
H7 Mark McGwire W	4.00	1.20
H8 Frank Thomas W	1.50	.45
H9 Mo Vaughn W	.60	.18
H10 Player of Month LS W	.60	.18
H11 Roger Clemens	3.00	.90
H12 David Cone	.60	.18
H13 Jose Mesa	.60	.18
H14 Randy Johnson	1.50	.45
H15 Chuck Finley	.60	.18
H16 Mike Mussina	1.50	.45
H17 Kevin Appier	.60	.18
H18 Kenny Rogers	1.50	.45
H19 Lee Smith	.60	.18
H20 Pitcher of Month LS W	.60	.18
H21 George Arias	.60	.18
H22 Jose Herrera	.60	.18
H23 Tony Clark	.60	.18
H24 Todd Greene	.60	.18
H25 Derek Jeter W	4.00	1.20
H26 Arquimedez Pozo	.60	.18
H27 Matt Lawton	.60	.18
H28 Shannon Stewart	.60	.18
H29 Chris Snopek	.60	.18
H30 Most Rookie Hits LS	.60	.18
H31 Jeff Bagwell W	1.00	.30
H32 Dante Bichette	.60	.18
H33 Barry Bonds W	4.00	1.20
H34 Tony Gwynn	2.00	.60
H35 Chipper Jones	1.50	.45
H36 Eric Karros	.60	.18
H37 Barry Larkin	1.50	.45
H38 Mike Piazza	2.50	.75
H39 Matt Williams	.60	.18
H40 Long Shot Card	.60	.18
H41 Osvaldo Fernandez	.60	.18
H42 Tom Glavine	1.00	.30
H43 Jason Isringhausen	.60	.18
H44 Greg Maddux	2.50	.75
H45 Pedro Martinez	1.50	.45
H46 Hideo Nomo	1.50	.45
H47 Pete Schourek	.60	.18
H48 Paul Wilson	.60	.18
H49 Mark Wohlers	.60	.18
H50 Long Shot Card	.60	.18
H51 Bob Abreu	.60	.18
H52 Trey Beamon	.60	.18
H53 Yamil Benitez	.60	.18
H54 Roger Cedeno	.60	.18
H55 Todd Hollandsworth	.60	.18
H56 Marvin Benard	.60	.18
H57 Jason Kendall	.60	.18
H58 Brooks Kieschnick	.60	.18
H59 Rey Ordonez W	.60	.18
H60 Long Shot Card	.60	.18

1996 Upper Deck Predictor Retail

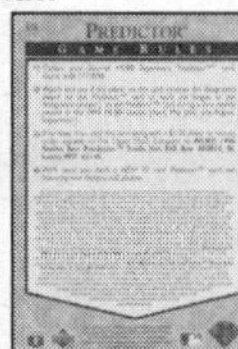

Randomly inserted in both series retail packs at a rate of one in 12, this 60-card Predictor set offered six different 10-card parallel exchange sets as featured players competed for "monthly milestones and awards." The fronts feature a "cutout" player photo against a pinstriped background surrounded by a gray marble border. Card backs feature game rules and guidelines. Winner cards are signified with a W in our listings and are in noticeably shorter supply since they had to be mailed in to Upper Deck (where they were destroyed) to claim your exchange cards. The expiration date to send in cards was November 18th, 1996.

	Nm-Mt	Ex-Mt
COMPLETE SERIES 1 (30)	40.00	12.00
COMPLETE SERIES 2 (30)	40.00	12.00
*EXCHANGE: .4X TO 1X BASIC PREDICTOR		
ONE EXCH.SET VIA MAIL PER PRED.WINNER		
R1 Albert Belle W	.60	.18
R2 Jay Buhner W	.60	.18
R3 Juan Gonzalez	1.50	.45
R4 Ken Griffey Jr.	2.50	.75
R5 Mark McGwire W	4.00	1.20
R6 Rafael Palmeiro	1.00	.30
R7 Tim Salmon	1.00	.30
R8 Frank Thomas	1.50	.45
R9 Mo Vaughn W	.60	.18
R10 Monthly HR Ldr LS W	.60	.18
R11 Albert Belle W	.60	.18
R12 Jay Buhner	.60	.18
R13 Jim Edmonds	.60	.18
R14 Cecil Fielder	.60	.18
R15 Ken Griffey Jr.	2.50	.75
R16 Edgar Martinez	1.00	.30
R17 Manny Ramirez	.60	.18
R18 Frank Thomas	1.50	.45
R19 Mo Vaughn W	.60	.18
R20 Monthly RBI Ldr LS W	.60	.18
R21 Roberto Alomar W	1.50	.45
R22 Carlos Baerga	.60	.18
R23 Wade Boggs	1.00	.30
R24 Ken Griffey Jr.	2.50	.75
R25 Chuck Knoblauch	.60	.18
R26 Kenny Lofton	.60	.18
R27 Edgar Martinez	1.00	.30
R28 Tim Salmon	1.00	.30
R29 Frank Thomas	1.50	.45
R30 Monthly Hits Ldr Longshot W	.60	.18
R31 Dante Bichette	.60	.18
R32 Barry Bonds W	4.00	1.20
R33 Ron Gant	.60	.18
R34 Chipper Jones	1.50	.45
R35 Fred McGriff	1.00	.30
R36 Mike Piazza	2.50	.75
R37 Sammy Sosa	2.50	.75
R38 Larry Walker	1.00	.30
R39 Matt Williams	.60	.18
R40 Long Shot Card	.60	.18
R41 Jeff Bagwell W	1.00	.30
R42 Dante Bichette	.60	.18
R43 Barry Bonds W	4.00	1.20
R44 Jeff Conine	.60	.18
R45 Andres Galarraga	.60	.18
R46 Mike Piazza	2.50	.75
R47 Reggie Sanders	.60	.18
R48 Sammy Sosa	2.50	.75
R49 Matt Williams	.60	.18
R50 Long Shot Card	.60	.18
R51 Jeff Bagwell	1.00	.30
R52 Derek Bell	.60	.18
R53 Dante Bichette	.60	.18
R54 Craig Biggio	1.00	.30
R55 Barry Bonds	4.00	1.20
R56 Bret Boone	.60	.18
R57 Tony Gwynn	2.00	.60
R58 Barry Larkin	1.50	.45
R59 Mike Piazza W	2.50	.75
R60 Long Shot Card	.60	.18

1996 Upper Deck Ripken Collection

This 23 card set was issued across all the various Upper Deck brands. The cards were issued to commemorate Cal Ripken's career, which had been capped the previous season by the breaking of the consecutive game streak long held by Lou Gehrig. The cards were inserted at the following ratios: Cards 1-4 were in Collector Choice first series packs at a rate of one in 12. Cards 5-8 were inserted into Upper Deck series one packs at a rate of one in 24. Cards 9-12 were placed into second series Collector Choice packs at a rate of one in 12. Cards 13-17 were in second series Upper Deck packs at a rate of one in 24. And Cards 18-22 were in SP Packs at a rate of one in 45. The header card (number 23) was also inserted into only Collector Choice packs.

	Nm-Mt	Ex-Mt
COMMON COLC (1-4/9-12)	3.00	.90
COMMON UD (5-8/13-17)	6.00	1.80
COMMON SP (18-22)	15.00	4.50
NNO C.Ripken Header COLC	3.00	.90

1996 Upper Deck Ripken Collection Jumbos

With a suggested retail price of $19.95, cards from this 22-card boxed set measures approximately 3 1/2" by 5" and features color borderless photos of Cal Ripken Jr. with a gold foil facsimile autograph. The cards parallel the standard Ripken Collection inserted into various 1996 Upper Deck Baseball products. The backs carry information about the player.

	Nm-Mt	Ex-Mt
COMP.FACT SET	20.00	6.00
COMMON CARD	1.00	.30
1 Cal Ripken COLC after playing in 2131 consecutive games	2.00	.60
22 Cal Ripken SP Eddie Murray 1981	1.00	.30

1996 Upper Deck Run Producers

This 20 card set was randomly inserted into series two packs at a rate of one every 71 packs. The cards are thermographically printed, which gives the card a rubber surface texture. The cards are double die-cut and are foil stamped. These cards are highly condition sensitive, often found with noticable chipping on the edges.

	Nm-Mt	Ex-Mt
COMPLETE SET (20)	150.00	45.00
RP1 Albert Belle	4.00	1.20
RP2 Dante Bichette	4.00	1.20
RP3 Barry Bonds	25.00	7.50
RP4 Jay Buhner	4.00	1.20

RP5 Jose Canseco 10.00 3.00
RP6 Juan Gonzalez 10.00 3.00
RP7 Ken Griffey Jr. 15.00 4.50
RP8 Tony Gwynn 12.00 3.60
RP9 Kenny Lofton 4.00 1.20
RP10 Edgar Martinez 6.00 1.80
RP11 Fred McGriff 6.00 1.80
RP12 Mark McGwire 25.00 7.50
RP13 Rafael Palmeiro 6.00 1.80
RP14 Mike Piazza 15.00 4.50
RP15 Manny Ramirez 4.00 1.20
RP16 Tim Salmon 6.00 1.80
RP17 Sammy Sosa 15.00 4.50
RP18 Frank Thomas 10.00 3.00
RP19 Mo Vaughn 4.00 1.20
RP20 Matt Williams 4.00 1.20

1996 Upper Deck All-Stars Jumbos

This 18-card set measures approximately 3 1/2" by 5" with a suggested retail price of $19.95 a set. The fronts feature borderless color player photos and are foil stamped with the official 1996 Major League Baseball All-Star game logo. The backs carry another player photo with player information and statistics. The cards are checklisted below in alphabetical order.

Nm-Mt Ex-Mt
1 Roberto Alomar .75 .23
2 Sandy Alomar Jr. .40 .12
3 Jeff Bagwell 1.00 .30
4 Albert Belle .40 .12
5 Dante Bichette .40 .12
6 Craig Biggio .60 .18
7 Wade Boggs 1.00 .30
8 Barry Bonds 2.00 .60
9 Ken Griffey Jr. 2.50 .75
10 Tony Gwynn 2.00 .60
11 Barry Larkin .75 .23
12 Kenny Lofton .60 .18
13 Charles Nagy .20 .06
14 Mike Piazza 3.00 .90
15 Cal Ripken Jr. 4.00 1.20
16 John Smoltz .40 .12
17 Frank Thomas 1.00 .30
18 Matt Williams .60 .18

1996 Upper Deck Meet the Stars Griffey Redemption

This one-card set features a postcard-size action photo of Ken Griffey Jr. with a "Magic Moment" from a 1995 Post-Season game printed on one side of the three-sided black-and-aqua border. The back is blank.

Nm-Mt Ex-Mt
1 Ken Griffey Jr 3.00 .90
1995 Post-Season

1996 Upper Deck Nomo Collection Jumbos

This 16-card set measures approximately 3 1/2" by 5" and features color action photos of Hideo Nomo with a small black-and-white head photo in the upper left. The backs carry a smaller black-and-white version of the front photo with a continuing story highlighting Nomo's major league career.

Nm-Mt Ex-Mt
COMPLETE SET (16) 15.00 4.50
COMMON CARD (1-16) 1.00 .30

1996 Upper Deck Nomo ROY Japanese

Produced by Upper Deck, this 3 1/2" by 5" card commemorates Hideo Nomo being named the Rookie-of-the-Year of the National League for 1995. The front features a color action player photo while the back displays a blue-tinted player portrait with player information in Japanese.

Nm-Mt Ex-Mt
1 Hideo Nomo 5.00 1.50

1996 Upper Deck Sheet

This one 8 1/2" by 11" sheet was issued so fans at Fan Fest could have an item for players to sign at the show. The sheet has very little on the front so more signatures can be signed and the back is blank.

Nm-Mt Ex-Mt
1 All-Star Fanfest 2.00 .60
Autograph Sheet

1997 Upper Deck

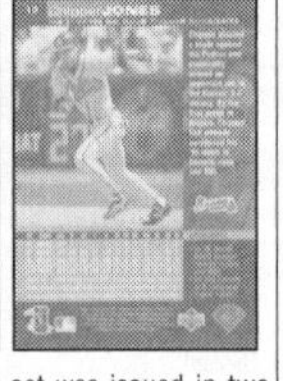

The 1997 Upper Deck set was issued in two series (series one 1-240, series two 271-520). The 12-card packs retailed for $2.49 each. Many cards have dates on the front to identify when, and when possible, what significant event is pictured. The backs include a player photo, stats and a brief blurb to go with vital statistics. Subsets include Jackie Robinson Tribute (1-9), Strike Force (64-72), Defensive Gems (136-153), Global Impact (181-207), Season Highlight Checklists (214-222/316-324), Star Rookies (223-240/271-288), Capture the Flag (370-387), Griffey's Hot List (415-424) and Diamond Debuts (470-483). It's critical to note that the Griffey's Hot List subset cards (in an unannounced move by the manufacturer) were shortprinted (about 1:7 packs) in relation to other cards in the series two set. The comparatively low print run on these cards created a dramatic surge in demand amongst set collectors and the cards soared in value on the secondary market. A 30-card first series Update set (numbered 241-270) was available to collectors that mailed in 10 series one wrappers along with $3 for postage and handling. The Series One Update set is composed primarily of 1996 post-season highlights. An additional 30-card series two Trade set (numbered 521-550) was also released around the end of the season. It too was available to collectors that mailed in ten series two wrappers along with $3 for postage and handling. The Series Two Trade set is composed primarily of traded players pictured in their new uniforms and a selection of rookies and prospects highlighted by the inclusion of Jose Cruz Jr. and Hideki Irabu.

Nm-Mt Ex-Mt
COMP.MASTER SET (550) 200.00 60.00
COMPLETE SET (490) 100.00 30.00
COMP. SERIES 1 (240) 40.00 12.00
COMP. SERIES 2 (250) 60.00 18.00
COMP.SER.2 w/o GHL (240) 25.00 7.50
COMMON (1-240/271-520) .30 .09
COMP.UPDATE SET (30) 80.00 24.00
COMMON (241-270) 1.00 .30
COMMON GHL (415-424) 1.50 .45
COMP.TRADE SET (30) 20.00 6.00
COMMON (521-550) .50 .15
1 Jackie Robinson .50 .15
The Beginnings
2 Jackie Robinson .50 .15
Breaking the Barrier
3 Jackie Robinson .50 .15
The MVP Season, 1949
4 Jackie Robinson .50 .15
1951 season
5 Jackie Robinson .50 .15
1952 and 1953 seasons
6 Jackie Robinson .50 .15
1954 season
7 Jackie Robinson .50 .15
1955 season
8 Jackie Robinson .50 .15
1956 season
9 Jackie Robinson HOF .50 .15
10 Chipper Jones .75 .23
11 Marquis Grissom .30 .09
12 Jermaine Dye .30 .09
13 Mark Lemke .30 .09
14 Terrell Wade .30 .09
15 Fred McGriff .50 .15
16 Tom Glavine .50 .15
17 Mark Wohlers .30 .09
18 Randy Myers .30 .09
19 Roberto Alomar .75 .23
20 Cal Ripken 2.50 .75
21 Rafael Palmeiro .50 .15
22 Mike Mussina .75 .23
23 Brady Anderson .30 .09
24 Jose Canseco .75 .23
25 Mo Vaughn .30 .09
26 Roger Clemens 1.50 .45
27 Tim Naehring .30 .09
28 Jeff Suppan .30 .09
29 Troy Percival .30 .09
30 Sammy Sosa 1.25 .35
31 Amaury Telemaco .30 .09
32 Rey Sanchez .30 .09
33 Scott Servais .30 .09
34 Steve Trachsel .30 .09
35 Mark Grace .50 .15
36 Wilson Alvarez .30 .09
37 Harold Baines .30 .09
38 Tony Phillips .30 .09
39 James Baldwin .30 .09
40 Frank Thomas UER .75 .23
Bio information is Ken Griffey Jr.'s
41 Lyle Mouton .30 .09
42 Chris Snopek .30 .09
43 Hal Morris .30 .09
44 Eric Davis .30 .09
45 Barry Larkin .75 .23
46 Reggie Sanders .30 .09
47 Pete Schourek .30 .09
48 Lee Smith .30 .09
49 Charles Nagy .30 .09
50 Albert Belle .30 .09
51 Julio Franco .30 .09
52 Kenny Lofton .30 .09
53 Orel Hershiser .30 .09
54 Omar Vizquel .30 .09
55 Eric Young .30 .09
56 Curtis Leskanic .30 .09
57 Quinton McCracken .30 .09
58 Kevin Ritz .30 .09
59 Walt Weiss .30 .09
60 Dante Bichette .30 .09
61 Mark Lewis .30 .09
62 Tony Clark .30 .09
63 Travis Fryman .30 .09
64 John Smoltz SF .30 .09
65 Greg Maddux SF .75 .23
66 Tom Glavine SF .30 .09
67 Mike Mussina SF .50 .15
68 Andy Pettitte SF .30 .09
69 Mariano Rivera SF .30 .09
70 Hideo Nomo SF .30 .09
71 Kevin Brown SF .30 .09
72 Randy Johnson SF .50 .15
73 Felipe Lira .30 .09
74 Kimera Bartee .30 .09
75 Alan Trammell .50 .15
76 Kevin Brown .30 .09
77 Edgar Renteria .30 .09
78 Al Leiter .30 .09
79 Charles Johnson .30 .09
80 Andre Dawson .30 .09
81 Billy Wagner .30 .09
82 Donne Wall .30 .09
83 Jeff Bagwell .50 .15
84 Keith Lockhart .30 .09
85 Jeff Montgomery .30 .09
86 Tom Goodwin .30 .09
87 Tim Belcher .30 .09
88 Mike Macfarlane .30 .09
89 Joe Randa .30 .09
90 Brett Butler .30 .09
91 Todd Worrell .30 .09
92 Todd Hollandsworth .30 .09
93 Ismael Valdes .30 .09
94 Hideo Nomo .75 .23
95 Mike Piazza 1.25 .35
96 Jeff Cirillo .30 .09
97 Ricky Bones .30 .09
98 Fernando Vina .30 .09
99 Ben McDonald .30 .09
100 John Jaha .30 .09
101 Mark Loretta .30 .09
102 Paul Molitor .50 .15
103 Rick Aguilera .30 .09
104 Marty Cordova .30 .09
105 Kirby Puckett .75 .23
106 Dan Naulty .30 .09
107 Frank Rodriguez .30 .09
108 Shane Andrews .30 .09
109 Henry Rodriguez .30 .09
110 Mark Grudzielanek .30 .09
111 Pedro Martinez .75 .23
112 Ugueth Urbina .30 .09
113 David Segui .30 .09
114 Rey Ordonez .30 .09
115 Bernard Gilkey .30 .09
116 Butch Huskey .30 .09
117 Paul Wilson .30 .09
118 Alex Ochoa .30 .09
119 John Franco .30 .09
120 Dwight Gooden .50 .15
121 Ruben Rivera .50 .15
122 Andy Pettitte .50 .15
123 Tino Martinez .50 .15
124 Bernie Williams .50 .15
125 Wade Boggs .50 .15
126 Paul O'Neill .50 .15
127 Scott Brosius .30 .09
128 Ernie Young .30 .09
129 Doug Johns .30 .09
130 Geronimo Berroa .30 .09
131 Jason Giambi .75 .23
132 John Wasdin .30 .09
133 Jim Eisenreich .30 .09
134 Ricky Otero .30 .09
135 Ricky Bottalico .30 .09
136 Mark Langston DG .30 .09
137 Greg Maddux DG .75 .23
138 Ivan Rodriguez DG .50 .15
139 Charles Johnson DG .30 .09
140 J.T. Snow DG .30 .09
141 Mark Grace DG .30 .09
142 Roberto Alomar DG .30 .09
143 Craig Biggio DG .30 .09
144 Ken Caminiti DG .30 .09
145 Matt Williams DG .30 .09
146 Omar Vizquel DG .30 .09
147 Cal Ripken DG 1.25 .35
148 Ozzie Smith DG .75 .23
149 Rey Ordonez DG .30 .09
150 Ken Griffey Jr. DG .75 .23
151 Devon White DG .30 .09
152 Barry Bonds DG .75 .23
153 Kenny Lofton DG .30 .09
154 Mickey Morandini .30 .09
155 Gregg Jefferies .30 .09
156 Curt Schilling .50 .15
157 Jason Kendall .30 .09
158 Francisco Cordova .30 .09
159 Dennis Eckersley .30 .09
160 Ron Gant .30 .09
161 Ozzie Smith 1.25 .35
162 Brian Jordan .30 .09
163 John Mabry .30 .09
164 Andy Ashby .30 .09
165 Steve Finley .30 .09
166 Fernando Valenzuela .30 .09
167 Archi Cianfrocco .30 .09
168 Wally Joyner .30 .09
169 Greg Vaughn .30 .09
170 Barry Bonds 2.00 .60
171 W.VanLandingham .30 .09
172 Marvin Benard .30 .09
173 Rich Aurilia .30 .09
174 Jay Canizaro .30 .09
175 Ken Griffey Jr. 1.25 .35
176 Bob Wells .30 .09
177 Jay Buhner .30 .09
178 Sterling Hitchcock .30 .09
179 Edgar Martinez .50 .15
180 Rusty Greer .30 .09
181 Dave Nilsson GI .30 .09
182 Larry Walker GI .30 .09
183 Edgar Renteria GI .30 .09
184 Rey Ordonez GI .30 .09
185 Rafael Palmeiro GI .30 .09
186 Osvaldo Fernandez GI .30 .09
187 Raul Mondesi GI .30 .09
188 Manny Ramirez GI .30 .09
189 Sammy Sosa GI UER .75 .23
The flag pictured is wrong
190 Robert Eenhoorn GI .30 .09
191 Devon White GI .30 .09
192 Hideo Nomo GI .30 .09
193 Mac Suzuki GI .30 .09
194 Chan Ho Park GI .30 .09
195 F.Valenzuela GI .30 .09
196 Andruw Jones GI .30 .09
197 Vinny Castilla GI .30 .09
198 Dennis Martinez GI .30 .09
199 Ruben Rivera GI .30 .09
200 Juan Gonzalez GI .50 .15
201 Roberto Alomar GI .30 .09
202 Edgar Martinez GI .30 .09
203 Ivan Rodriguez GI .50 .15
204 Carlos Delgado GI .30 .09
205 Andres Galarraga GI .30 .09
206 Ozzie Guillen GI .30 .09
207 Midre Cummings GI .30 .09
208 Roger Pavlik .30 .09
209 Darren Oliver .30 .09
210 Dean Palmer .30 .09
211 Ivan Rodriguez .75 .23
212 Otis Nixon .30 .09
213 Pat Hentgen .30 .09
214 Ozzie Smith .50 .15
Andre Dawson
Kirby Pucket HL CL
215 Barry Bonds .50 .15
Gary Sheffield
Brady Anderson HL CL
216 Ken Caminiti SH CL .30 .09
217 John Smoltz SH CL .30 .09
218 Eric Young SH CL .30 .09
219 Juan Gonzalez SH CL .50 .15
220 Eddie Murray SH CL .50 .15
221 T. Lasorda SH CL .30 .09
222 Paul Molitor SH CL .30 .09
223 Luis Castillo .30 .09
224 Justin Thompson .30 .09
225 Rocky Coppinger .30 .09
226 Jermaine Allensworth .30 .09
227 Jeff D'Amico .30 .09
228 Jamey Wright .30 .09
229 Scott Rolen .50 .15
230 Darin Erstad .30 .09
231 Marty Janzen .30 .09
232 Jacob Cruz .30 .09
233 Raul Ibanez .30 .09
234 Nomar Garciaparra 1.25 .35
235 Todd Walker .30 .09
236 Brian Giles RC 1.25 .35
237 Matt Beech .30 .09
238 Mike Cameron .30 .09
239 Jose Paniagua .30 .09
240 Andruw Jones .30 .09
241 Brant Brown UPD 1.00 .30
242 Robin Jennings UPD 1.00 .30
243 Willie Adams UPD 1.00 .30
244 Ken Caminiti UPD 1.50 .45
245 Brian Jordan UPD 1.50 .45
246 Chipper Jones UPD 4.00 1.20
247 Juan Gonzalez UPD 4.00 1.20
248 Bernie Williams UPD 2.50 .75
249 Roberto Alomar UPD 4.00 1.20
250 Bernie Williams UPD 2.50 .75
251 David Wells UPD 1.50 .45
252 Cecil Fielder UPD 1.50 .45
253 D.Strawberry UPD 2.50 .75
254 Andy Pettitte UPD 2.50 .75
255 Javier Lopez UPD 1.50 .45
256 Gary Gaetti UPD 1.50 .45
257 Ron Gant UPD 1.50 .45
258 Brian Jordan UPD 1.50 .45
259 John Smoltz UPD 2.50 .75
260 Greg Maddux UPD 8.00 2.40
261 Tom Glavine UPD 2.50 .75
262 Andruw Jones UPD 1.50 .45
263 Greg Maddux UPD 8.00 2.40
264 David Cone UPD 1.50 .45
265 Jim Leyritz UPD 1.00 .30
266 Andy Pettitte UPD 2.50 .75
267 John Wetteland UPD 1.50 .45
268 Dario Veras UPD 1.00 .30
269 Neifi Perez UPD 1.00 .30
270 Bill Mueller UPD 10.00 3.00
271 Vladimir Guerrero .75 .23
272 Dmitri Young .30 .09
273 Nerio Rodriguez RC .30 .09
274 Kevin Orie .30 .09
275 Felipe Crespo .30 .09
276 Danny Graves .30 .09
277 Rod Myers .30 .09
278 Felix Heredia RC .30 .09
279 Ralph Milliard .30 .09
280 Greg Norton .30 .09
281 Derek Wallace .30 .09
282 Trot Nixon .50 .15
283 Bobby Chouinard .30 .09
284 Jay Witasick .30 .09
285 Travis Miller .30 .09
286 Brian Bevil RC .30 .09
287 Bobby Estalella .30 .09
288 Steve Soderstrom .30 .09
289 Mark Langston .30 .09
290 Tim Salmon .50 .15
291 Jim Edmonds .30 .09
292 Garret Anderson .30 .09
293 George Arias .30 .09
294 Gary DiSarcina .30 .09
295 Chuck Finley .30 .09
296 Todd Greene .30 .09
297 Randy Velarde .30 .09
298 David Justice .30 .09
299 Ryan Klesko .30 .09
300 John Smoltz .50 .15
301 Javier Lopez .30 .09
302 Greg Maddux 1.25 .35
303 Denny Neagle .30 .09
304 B.J. Surhoff .30 .09
305 Chris Hoiles .30 .09
306 Eric Davis .30 .09
307 Scott Erickson .30 .09
308 Mike Bordick .30 .09
309 John Valentin .30 .09
310 Heathcliff Slocumb .30 .09
311 Tom Gordon .30 .09
312 Mike Stanley .30 .09
313 Reggie Jefferson .30 .09
314 Darren Bragg .30 .09
315 Troy O'Leary .30 .09
316 John Mabry SH CL .30 .09
317 Mark Whiten SH CL .30 .09
318 Edgar Martinez SH CL .30 .09
319 Alex Rodriguez SH CL .75 .23
320 Mark McGwire SH CL 1.00 .30
321 Hideo Nomo SH CL .30 .09
322 Todd Hundley SH CL .30 .09
323 Barry Bonds SH CL .75 .23
324 Andruw Jones SH CL .30 .09
325 Ryne Sandberg 1.25 .35
326 Brian McRae .30 .09
327 Frank Castillo .30 .09
328 Shawon Dunston .30 .09
329 Ray Durham .30 .09
330 Robin Ventura .30 .09
331 Ozzie Guillen .30 .09
332 Roberto Hernandez .30 .09
333 Albert Belle .30 .09
334 Dave Martinez .30 .09
335 Willie Greene .30 .09
336 Jeff Brantley .30 .09
337 Kevin Jarvis .30 .09
338 John Smiley .30 .09
339 Eddie Taubensee .30 .09
340 Bret Boone .30 .09
341 Kevin Seitzer .30 .09
342 Jack McDowell .30 .09
343 Sandy Alomar Jr. .30 .09
344 Chad Curtis .30 .09
345 Manny Ramirez .30 .09
346 Chad Ogea .30 .09
347 Jim Thome .75 .23
348 Mark Thompson .30 .09
349 Ellis Burks .30 .09
350 Andres Galarraga .30 .09
351 Vinny Castilla .30 .09
352 Kirt Manwaring .30 .09
353 Larry Walker .50 .15
354 Omar Olivares .30 .09
355 Bobby Higginson .30 .09
356 Melvin Nieves .30 .09
357 Brian Johnson .30 .09
358 Devon White .30 .09
359 Jeff Conine .30 .09
360 Gary Sheffield .30 .09
361 Robb Nen .30 .09
362 Mike Hampton .30 .09
363 Bob Abreu .30 .09
364 Luis Gonzalez .30 .09
365 Derek Bell .30 .09
366 Sean Berry .30 .09
367 Craig Biggio .50 .15
368 Darryl Kile .30 .09
369 Shane Reynolds .30 .09
370 Jeff Bagwell CF .30 .09
371 Ron Gant CF .30 .09
372 Andy Benes CF .30 .09
373 Gary Gaetti CF .30 .09
374 Ramon Martinez CF .30 .09
375 Raul Mondesi CF .30 .09
376 Steve Finley CF .30 .09
377 Ken Caminiti CF .30 .09
378 Tony Gwynn CF .50 .15
379 Dario Veras RC .30 .09
380 Andy Pettitte CF .30 .09
381 Ruben Rivera CF .30 .09
382 David Cone CF .30 .09
383 Roberto Alomar CF .30 .09
384 Edgar Martinez CF .30 .09
385 Ken Griffey Jr. CF .75 .23
386 Mark McGwire CF 1.00 .30
387 Rusty Greer CF .30 .09
388 Jose Rosado .30 .09
389 Kevin Appier .30 .09
390 Johnny Damon .30 .09
391 Jose Offerman .30 .09
392 Michael Tucker .30 .09
393 Craig Paquette .30 .09
394 Bip Roberts .30 .09
395 Ramon Martinez .30 .09
396 Greg Gagne .30 .09
397 Chan Ho Park .30 .09
398 Karim Garcia .30 .09
399 Wilton Guerrero .30 .09
400 Eric Karros .30 .09
401 Raul Mondesi .30 .09
402 Matt Mieske .30 .09
403 Mike Fetters .30 .09
404 Dave Nilsson .30 .09
405 Jose Valentin .30 .09
406 Scott Karl .30 .09
407 Marc Newfield .30 .09
408 Cal Eldred .30 .09
409 Rich Becker .30 .09
410 Terry Steinbach .30 .09
411 Chuck Knoblauch .30 .09
412 Pat Meares .30 .09
413 Brad Radke .30 .09
414 Kirby Puckett UER .75 .23
Card numbered 415
415 A.Jones GHL SP 1.50 .45
416 C.Jones GHL SP 2.50 .75
417 Mo Vaughn GHL SP 1.50 .45
418 F.Thomas GHL SP 2.50 .75
419 Albert Belle GHL SP 1.50 .45
420 M.McGwire GHL SP 8.00 2.40
421 Derek Jeter GHL SP 8.00 2.40
422 A.Rodriguez GHL SP 5.00 1.50
423 J.Gonzalez GHL SP 2.50 .75
424 K.Griffey Jr. GHL SP 5.00 1.50
425 Rondell White .30 .09
426 Darrin Fletcher .30 .09
427 Cliff Floyd .30 .09
428 Mike Lansing .30 .09

429 F.P. Santangelo .30 .09
430 Todd Hundley .30 .09
431 Mark Clark .30 .09
432 Pete Harnisch .30 .09
433 Jason Isringhausen .30 .09
434 Bobby Jones .30 .09
435 Lance Johnson .30 .09
436 Carlos Baerga .30 .09
437 Mariano Duncan .30 .09
438 David Cone .30 .09
439 Mariano Rivera .50 .15
440 Derek Jeter 2.00 .60
441 Joe Girardi .30 .09
442 Charlie Hayes .30 .09
443 Tim Raines .30 .09
444 Darryl Strawberry .50 .15
445 Cecil Fielder .30 .09
446 Ariel Prieto .30 .09
447 Tony Batista .30 .09
448 Brent Gates .30 .09
449 Scott Spiezio .30 .09
450 Mark McGwire 2.00 .60
451 Don Wengert .30 .09
452 Mike Lieberthal .30 .09
453 Lenny Dykstra .30 .09
454 Rex Hudler .30 .09
455 Darren Daulton .30 .09
456 Kevin Stocker .30 .09
457 Trey Beamon .30 .09
458 Midre Cummings .30 .09
459 Mark Johnson .30 .09
460 Al Martin .30 .09
461 Kevin Elster .30 .09
462 Jon Lieber .30 .09
463 Jason Schmidt .30 .09
464 Paul Wagner .30 .09
465 Andy Benes .30 .09
466 Alan Benes .30 .09
467 Royce Clayton .30 .09
468 Gary Gaetti .30 .09
469 Curt Lyons RC .30 .09
470 Eugene Kingsale DD .30 .09
471 Damian Jackson DD .30 .09
472 Wendell Magee DD .30 .09
473 Kevin L. Brown DD .30 .09
474 Raul Casanova DD .30 .09
475 R.Mendoza DD RC .30 .09
476 Todd Dunn DD .30 .09
477 Chad Mottola DD .30 .09
478 Andy Larkin DD .30 .09
479 Jaime Bluma DD .30 .09
480 Mac Suzuki DD .30 .09
481 Brian Banks DD .30 .09
482 Desi Wilson DD .30 .09
483 Einar Diaz DD .30 .09
484 Tom Pagnozzi .30 .09
485 Ray Lankford .30 .09
486 Todd Stottlemyre .30 .09
487 Donovan Osborne .30 .09
488 Trevor Hoffman .30 .09
489 Chris Gomez .30 .09
490 Ken Caminiti .30 .09
491 John Flaherty .30 .09
492 Tony Gwynn 1.00 .30
493 Joey Hamilton .30 .09
494 Rickey Henderson .75 .23
495 Glenallen Hill .30 .09
496 Rod Beck .30 .09
497 Osvaldo Fernandez .30 .09
498 Rick Wilkins .30 .09
499 Joey Cora .30 .09
500 Alex Rodriguez 1.25 .35
501 Randy Johnson .75 .23
502 Paul Sorrento .30 .09
503 Dan Wilson .30 .09
504 Jamie Moyer .30 .09
505 Will Clark .75 .23
506 Mickey Tettleton .30 .09
507 John Burkett .30 .09
508 Ken Hill .30 .09
509 Mark McLemore .30 .09
510 Juan Gonzalez .75 .23
511 Bobby Witt .30 .09
512 Carlos Delgado .30 .09
513 Alex Gonzalez .30 .09
514 Shawn Green .30 .09
515 Joe Carter .30 .09
516 Juan Guzman .30 .09
517 Charlie O'Brien .30 .09
518 Ed Sprague .30 .09
519 Mike Timlin .30 .09
520 Roger Clemens 1.50 .45
521 Eddie Murray TRADE 2.00 .60
522 Jason Dickson TRADE .50 .15
523 Jim Leyritz TRADE .50 .15
524 M.Tucker TRADE .50 .15
525 Kenny Lofton TRADE .75 .23
526 Jimmy Key TRADE .75 .23
527 Mel Rojas TRADE .50 .15
528 Deion Sanders TRADE 1.25 .35
529 Bartolo Colon TRADE .75 .23
530 Matt Williams TRADE .75 .23
531 M.Grissom TRADE .50 .15
532 David Justice TRADE .75 .23
533 B.Trammell TRADE .75 .23
534 Moises Alou TRADE .75 .23
535 Bobby Bonilla TRADE .75 .23
536 A.Fernandez TRADE .50 .15
537 Jay Bell TRADE .75 .23
538 Chili Davis TRADE .75 .23
539 Jeff King TRADE .50 .15
540 Todd Zeile TRADE .50 .15
541 John Olerud TRADE .75 .23
542 Jose Guillen TRADE .75 .23
543 Derrek Lee TRADE .75 .23
544 Dante Powell TRADE .50 .15
545 J.T. Snow TRADE .75 .23
546 Jeff Kent TRADE .75 .23
547 Jose Cruz Jr. TRADE 3.00 .90
548 J.Wetteland TRADE .75 .23
549 O.Merced TRADE .50 .15
550 Hideki Irabu TRADE .75 .23

1997 Upper Deck Amazing Greats

Randomly inserted in all first series packs at a rate of one in 69, this 20-card set features a horizontal design along with two player photos

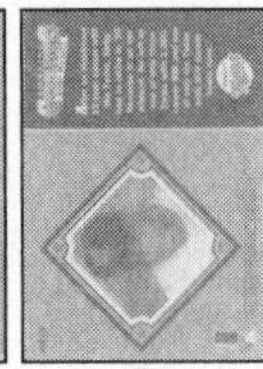

on the front. The cards feature translucent player images against a real wood grain stock.

Nm-Mt Ex-Mt
COMPLETE SET (20) 300.00 90.00
AG1 Ken Griffey Jr. 20.00 6.00
AG2 Roberto Alomar 12.00 3.60
AG3 Alex Rodriguez 20.00 6.00
AG4 Paul Molitor 8.00 2.40
AG5 Chipper Jones 12.00 3.60
AG6 Tony Gwynn 15.00 4.50
AG7 Kenny Lofton 5.00 1.50
AG8 Albert Belle 5.00 1.50
AG9 Matt Williams 5.00 1.50
AG10 Frank Thomas 12.00 3.60
AG11 Greg Maddux 20.00 6.00
AG12 Sammy Sosa 20.00 6.00
AG13 Kirby Puckett 12.00 3.60
AG14 Jeff Bagwell 8.00 2.40
AG15 Cal Ripken 40.00 12.00
AG16 Manny Ramirez 5.00 1.50
AG17 Barry Bonds 30.00 9.00
AG18 Mo Vaughn 5.00 1.50
AG19 Eddie Murray 12.00 3.60
AG20 Mike Piazza 20.00 6.00

1997 Upper Deck Blue Chip Prospects

This rare 20-card set, randomly inserted into series two packs, features color photos of high expectation prospects who are likely to have a big impact on Major League Baseball. Only 500 of this crash numbered, limited edition set was produced.

Nm-Mt Ex-Mt
BC1 Andruw Jones 10.00 3.00
BC2 Derek Jeter 60.00 18.00
BC3 Scott Rolen 15.00 4.50
BC4 Manny Ramirez 10.00 3.00
BC5 Todd Walker 10.00 3.00
BC6 Rocky Coppinger 10.00 3.00
BC7 Nomar Garciaparra 40.00 12.00
BC8 Darin Erstad 10.00 3.00
BC9 Jermaine Dye 10.00 3.00
BC10 Vladimir Guerrero 25.00 7.50
BC11 Edgar Renteria 10.00 3.00
BC12 Bob Abreu 10.00 3.00
BC13 Karim Garcia 10.00 3.00
BC14 Jeff D'Amico 10.00 3.00
BC15 Chipper Jones 25.00 7.50
BC16 Todd Hollandsworth 10.00 3.00
BC17 Andy Pettitte 15.00 4.50
BC18 Ruben Rivera 10.00 3.00
BC19 Jason Kendall 10.00 3.00
BC20 Alex Rodriguez 40.00 12.00

1997 Upper Deck Game Jersey

Randomly inserted in all first series packs at a rate of one in 800, this three-card set feaures swatches of real game-worn jerseys cut up and placed on the cards. These cards represent the first memorabilia insert cards to hit the baseball card market and thus carry a significant impact in the development of the hobby in the late 1990's.

Nm-Mt Ex-Mt
GJ1 Ken Griffey Jr. 120.00 36.00
GJ2 Tony Gwynn 50.00 15.00
GJ3 Rey Ordonez 25.00 7.50

1997 Upper Deck Hot Commodities

Randomly inserted in series two packs at a rate of one in 13, this 20-card set features color player images on a flame background in a black border. The backs carry a player head photo, statistics, and a commentary by ESPN sportscarster Dan Patrick.

Nm-Mt Ex-Mt
COMPLETE SET (20) 60.00 18.00
HC1 Alex Rodriguez 4.00 1.20
HC2 Andruw Jones 1.00 .30
HC3 Derek Jeter 6.00 1.80
HC4 Frank Thomas 2.50 .75
HC5 Ken Griffey Jr. 4.00 1.20
HC6 Chipper Jones 2.50 .75
HC7 Juan Gonzalez 2.50 .75
HC8 Cal Ripken 8.00 2.40
HC9 John Smoltz 1.50 .45
HC10 Mark McGwire 6.00 1.80
HC11 Barry Bonds 6.00 1.80
HC12 Albert Belle 1.00 .30
HC13 Mike Piazza 4.00 1.20
HC14 Manny Ramirez 1.00 .30
HC15 Mo Vaughn 1.00 .30
HC16 Tony Gwynn 3.00 .90
HC17 Vladimir Guerrero 2.50 .75
HC18 Hideo Nomo 2.50 .75
HC19 Greg Maddux 4.00 1.20
HC20 Kirby Puckett 2.50 .75

1997 Upper Deck Long Distance Connection

Randomly inserted in series two packs at a rate of one in 35, this 20-card set features color player images of some of the League's top power hitters on backgrounds utilizing Light/FX technology. The backs carry the pictured player's statistics.

Nm-Mt Ex-Mt
COMPLETE SET (20) 150.00 45.00
LD1 Mark McGwire 15.00 4.50
LD2 Brady Anderson 2.50 .75
LD3 Ken Griffey Jr. 10.00 3.00
LD4 Albert Belle 2.50 .75
LD5 Juan Gonzalez 6.00 1.80
LD6 Andres Galarraga 2.50 .75
LD7 Jay Buhner 2.50 .75
LD8 Mo Vaughn 2.50 .75
LD9 Barry Bonds 15.00 4.50
LD10 Gary Sheffield 2.50 .75
LD11 Todd Hundley 2.50 .75
LD12 Frank Thomas 6.00 1.80
LD13 Sammy Sosa 10.00 3.00
LD14 Rafael Palmeiro 4.00 1.20
LD15 Alex Rodriguez 10.00 3.00
LD16 Mike Piazza 10.00 3.00
LD17 Ken Caminiti 2.50 .75
LD18 Chipper Jones 6.00 1.80
LD19 Manny Ramirez 2.50 .75
LD20 Andruw Jones 2.50 .75

1997 Upper Deck Memorable Moments

Cards from these sets were distributed exclusively in six-card retail Collector's Choice series one and two packs. Each pack contained one of ten different Memorable Moments inserts. Each set features a selection of top stars captured in highlights of season's gone by. Each card features wave-like die cut top and bottom borders wth gold foil.

Nm-Mt Ex-Mt
COMPLETE SERIES 1 (10) 12.00 3.60
COMPLETE SERIES 2 (10) 12.00 3.60
A1 Andruw Jones .30 .09
A2 Chipper Jones .75 .23
A3 Cal Ripken 2.50 .75
A4 Frank Thomas .75 .23
A5 Manny Ramirez .30 .09
A6 Mike Piazza 1.25 .35
A7 Mark McGwire 2.00 .60
A8 Barry Bonds 2.00 .60
A9 Ken Griffey Jr. 1.25 .35
A10 Alex Rodriguez 1.25 .35
B1 Ken Griffey Jr. 1.25 .35
B2 Albert Belle .30 .09
B3 Derek Jeter 2.00 .60
B4 Greg Maddux 1.25 .35
B5 Tony Gwynn 1.00 .30
B6 Ryne Sandberg 1.25 .35
B7 Juan Gonzalez .75 .23
B8 Roger Clemens 1.50 .45
B9 Jose Cruz Jr. 1.25 .35
B10 Mo Vaughn .30 .09

1997 Upper Deck Power Package

Randomly inserted in all first series packs at a rate of one in 24, this 20-card set feaures some of the best longball hitters. The die cut cards feature some of baseball's leading power hitters.

Nm-Mt Ex-Mt
COMPLETE SET (20) 80.00 24.00
*JUMBO VERSIONS: HALF VALUE

JUMBOS: ONE PER RETAIL JUMBO PACK
PP1 Ken Griffey Jr. 8.00 2.40
PP2 Joe Carter 2.00 .60
PP3 Rafael Palmeiro 3.00 .90
PP4 Jay Buhner 2.00 .60
PP5 Sammy Sosa 8.00 2.40
PP6 Fred McGriff 3.00 .90
PP7 Jeff Bagwell 3.00 .90
PP8 Albert Belle 2.00 .60
PP9 Matt Williams 2.00 .60
PP10 Mark McGwire 12.00 3.60
PP11 Gary Sheffield 2.00 .60
PP12 Tim Salmon 3.00 .90
PP13 Ryan Klesko 2.00 .60
PP14 Manny Ramirez 2.00 .60
PP15 Mike Piazza 8.00 2.40
PP16 Barry Bonds 12.00 3.60
PP17 Mo Vaughn 2.00 .60
PP18 Jose Canseco 5.00 1.50
PP19 Juan Gonzalez 5.00 1.50
PP20 Frank Thomas 5.00 1.50

1997 Upper Deck Predictor

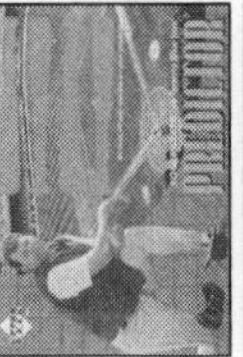

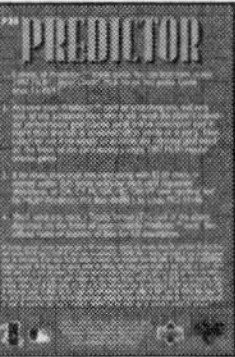

Randomly inserted in series two packs at a rate of one in five, this 30-card set featues a color player photo alongside a series of bats. The collector could activate the card by scratching off one of the bats to predict the performance of the pictured player during a single game. If the player matches or exceeds the predicted performance, the card could be mailed in with $2 to receive a Totally Virtual high-tech cel-card of the player pictured on the front. The backs carry the rules of the game. The deadline to redeem these cards was November 22nd, 1997. Winners and Losers are specified in our checklist with a "W" or a "L" after the player's name.

Nm-Mt Ex-Mt
COMPLETE SET (30) 30.00 9.00
*SCRATCH LOSER: .25X TO .6X UNSCRATCH
*EXCH.WIN: 1X TO 2.5X BASIC PREDICTOR
SER.2 STATED ODDS 1:5
1 Andruw Jones L .40 .12
2 Chipper Jones L 1.00 .30
3 Greg Maddux W 1.50 .45
Complete Game Shutout
4 Fred McGriff W .60 .18
4 Hits/2HR/3B
5 John Smoltz W .60 .18
Complete Game Shutout
6 Brady Anderson W .40 .12
Leadoff HR
7 Cal Ripken W 3.00 .90
Grand Slam
8 Mo Vaughn W .40 .12
3HR/6RBI
9 Sammy Sosa L 1.50 .45
10 Albert Belle W .40 .12
Grand Slam/9th HR
11 Frank Thomas L 1.00 .30
12 Kenny Lofton W .40 .12
5 Hits
13 Jim Thome L 1.00 .30
14 Dante Bichette W .40 .12
6RBI's
15 Andres Galarraga L .40 .12
16 Gary Sheffield L .40 .12
17 Hideo Nomo W 1.00 .30
Base Hit
18 Mike Piazza W 1.50 .45
Steal/9th HR
19 Derek Jeter W 2.50 .75
2HR
20 Bernie Williams L .60 .18
21 Mark McGwire W 2.50 .75
Grand Slam/4HR
22 Ken Caminiti W .40 .12
5RBI's
23 Tony Gwynn W 1.25 .35
2 2B/3RBI
24 Barry Bonds W 2.50 .75
5RBI's
25 Jay Buhner W .40 .12
5RBI's
26 Ken Griffey Jr. W 1.50 .45
3HR's
27 Alex Rodriguez W 1.50 .45
Cycle
28 Juan Gonzalez W 1.00 .30
5RBI's/4 Hits
29 Dean Palmer W .40 .12
2HR's/5RBI's
30 Roger Clemens W 2.00 .60
Complete Game Shutout

1997 Upper Deck Rock Solid Foundation

Randomly inserted in all first series packs at a rate of one in seven, this 20-card set features players 25 and under who have made an impact in the majors. The fronts feature a player photo against a "silver" type background.

The backs give player information as well as another player photo and are numbered with a "RS" prefix.

Nm-Mt Ex-Mt
COMPLETE SET (20) 40.00 12.00
RS1 Alex Rodriguez 6.00 1.80
RS2 Rey Ordonez 1.50 .45
RS3 Derek Jeter 10.00 3.00
RS4 Darin Erstad 1.50 .45
RS5 Chipper Jones 4.00 1.20
RS6 Johnny Damon 1.50 .45
RS7 Ryan Klesko 1.50 .45
RS8 Charles Johnson 1.50 .45
RS9 Andy Pettitte 2.50 .75
RS10 Manny Ramirez 1.50 .45
RS11 Ivan Rodriguez 4.00 1.20
RS12 Jason Kendall 1.50 .45
RS13 Rondell White 1.50 .45
RS14 Alex Ochoa 1.50 .45
RS15 Javier Lopez 1.50 .45
RS16 Pedro Martinez 4.00 1.20
RS17 Carlos Delgado 1.50 .45
RS18 Paul Wilson 1.50 .45
RS19 Alan Benes 1.50 .45
RS20 Raul Mondesi 1.50 .45

1997 Upper Deck Run Producers

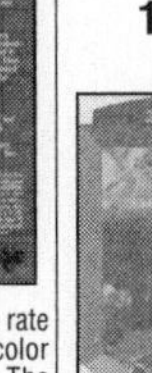

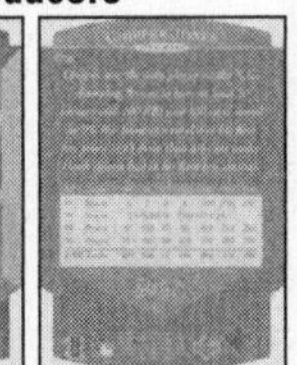

Randomly inserted in series two packs at a rate of one in 69, this 24-card set features color player images on die-cut cards that actually look and feel like home plate. The backs carry player information and career statistics.

Nm-Mt Ex-Mt
COMPLETE SET (24) 150.00 45.00
RP1 Ken Griffey Jr. 15.00 4.50
RP2 Barry Bonds 25.00 7.50
RP3 Albert Belle 4.00 1.20
RP4 Mark McGwire 25.00 7.50
RP5 Frank Thomas 10.00 3.00
RP6 Juan Gonzalez 10.00 3.00
RP7 Brady Anderson 4.00 1.20
RP8 Andres Galarraga 4.00 1.20
RP9 Rafael Palmeiro 6.00 1.80
RP10 Alex Rodriguez 15.00 4.50
RP11 Jay Buhner 4.00 1.20
RP12 Gary Sheffield 4.00 1.20
RP13 Sammy Sosa 15.00 4.50
RP14 Dante Bichette 4.00 1.20
RP15 Mike Piazza 15.00 4.50
RP16 Manny Ramirez 4.00 1.20
RP17 Kenny Lofton 4.00 1.20
RP18 Mo Vaughn 4.00 1.20
RP19 Tim Salmon 6.00 1.80
RP20 Chipper Jones 10.00 3.00
RP21 Jim Thome 10.00 3.00
RP22 Ken Caminiti 4.00 1.20
RP23 Jeff Bagwell 6.00 1.80
RP24 Paul Molitor 6.00 1.80

1997 Upper Deck Star Attractions

These 20 cards were issued one per pack in special Upper Deck Memorabilia Madness packs. The Memorabilia Madness packs included various redemptions for signed 8 by 10 photos with the grand prize being a grouping of Ken Griffey Jr. signed jersey, baseball and 8 by 10 photo. The die cut cards feature the words "Star Attraction" on the top with the player and team identification on the sides. The backs have a photo and a brief blurb on the player. Cards numbered 1-10 were inserted in Upper Deck packs while cards numbered 11-20 were in Collectors Choice packs.

Nm-Mt Ex-Mt
COMPLETE SET (20) 25.00 7.50
*GOLD: 2X TO 5X BASE STAR ATT.
GOLD INSERTS IN UD/CC MADNESS RETAIL
1 Ken Griffey Jr. 1.50 .45
2 Barry Bonds 2.50 .75
3 Jeff Bagwell .60 .18
4 Nomar Garciaparra 1.50 .45
5 Tony Gwynn 1.25 .35
6 Roger Clemens 2.00 .60
7 Chipper Jones 1.00 .30
8 Tino Martinez .60 .18
9 Albert Belle .40 .12
10 Kenny Lofton .40 .12

11 Alex Rodriguez 1.50 .45
12 Mark McGwire 2.50 .75
13 Cal Ripken 3.00 .90
14 Larry Walker .60 .18
15 Mike Piazza 1.50 .45
16 Frank Thomas 1.00 .30
17 Juan Gonzalez 1.00 .30
18 Greg Maddux 1.50 .45
19 Jose Cruz Jr. 1.00 .30
20 Mo Vaughn .40 .12

1997 Upper Deck Ticket To Stardom

Randomly inserted in all first series packs at a rate of one in 34, this 20-card set is designed in the form of a ticket and are designed to be matched. The horizontal fronts feature two player photos as well as using "light f/x technology and embossed player images.

Nm-Mt Ex-Mt
TS1 Chipper Jones 6.00 1.80
TS2 Jermaine Dye 2.50 .75
TS3 Rey Ordonez 2.50 .75
TS4 Alex Ochoa 2.50 .75
TS5 Derek Jeter 15.00 4.50
TS6 Ruben Rivera 2.50 .75
TS7 Billy Wagner 2.50 .75
TS8 Jason Kendall 2.50 .75
TS9 Darin Erstad 2.50 .75
TS10 Alex Rodriguez 10.00 3.00
TS11 Bob Abreu 2.50 .75
TS12 Richard Hidalgo 6.00 1.80
TS13 Karim Garcia 2.50 .75
TS14 Andruw Jones 2.50 .75
TS15 Carlos Delgado 2.50 .75
TS16 Rocky Coppinger 2.50 .75
TS17 Jeff D'Amico 2.50 .75
TS18 Johnny Damon 2.50 .75
TS19 John Wasdin 2.50 .75
TS20 Manny Ramirez 2.50 .75

1997 Upper Deck Ticket To Stardom Combos

These ten dual-player cards parallel a selection of cards from the Ticket to Stardom cards randomly seeded in basic 1997 UD packs. These "Combo" cards, however, measure twice as long as a standard size card (2 1/2" tall by 6 1/2 inches wide) and are essentially the mutated offspring of two standard size cards fused together side by side. Interestingly, these Combo cards were distributed one per Collector's Choice retail "Ticket to Stardom" box. Each of these boxes contained three packs of Collector's Choice series one packs plus the Ticket to Stardom Combo card (of which was clearly displayed through a viewing window on thje box front - thus one could select the exact Combo card they wanted).

Nm-Mt Ex-Mt
COMPLETE SET (10) 25.00 7.50
TS1 Chipper Jones 3.00 .90
Andruw Jones
TS2 Rey Ordonez 2.00 .60
Kevin Orie
TS3 Derek Jeter 5.00 1.50
Nomar Garciaparra
TS4 Billy Wagner 2.00 .60
Jason Kendall
TS5 Darin Erstad 4.00 1.20
Alex Rodriguez
TS6 Bob Abreu 2.00 .60
Jose Guillen
TS7 Wilton Guerrero 2.50 .75
Vladimir Guerrero
TS8 Carlos Delgado 2.50 .75
Rocky Coppinger
TS9 Jason Dickson 2.00 .60
Johnny Damon
TS10 Bartolo Colon 2.50 .75
Manny Ramirez

1997 Upper Deck 1996 Award Winner Jumbos

This 23-card set measures approximately 3 1/2" by 5" and features borderless color player photos with gold and silver foil highlights of both American and National League award winners. The backs carry another player photo and statistics with a sentence about winning his award. The set was issued through retail outlets and television promotions with a suggested retail set price of $19.95.

Nm-Mt Ex-Mt
COMP.FACT SET (23) 10.00 3.00
1 Alex Rodriguez 3.00 .90
2 Tony Gwynn 2.50 .75
3 Mark McGwire 5.00 1.50
4 Andres Galarraga 1.00 .30
5 Albert Belle .75 .23
6 Andres Galarraga 1.00 .30
7 Kenny Lofton .75 .23
8 Eric Young .50 .15
9 Andy Pettitte .75 .23
10 John Smoltz .50 .15
11 Roger Clemens 2.50 .75
12 John Smoltz .50 .15
13 Juan Guzman .25 .07
14 Kevin Brown .75 .23
15 John Wetteland .50 .15
16 Jeff Brantley .25 .07
17 Todd Worrell .25 .07
18 Derek Jeter 5.00 1.50
19 Todd Hollandsworth .25 .07
20 Juan Gonzalez 1.25 .35
21 Ken Caminiti .50 .15
22 Pat Hentgen .50 .15
23 John Smoltz .50 .15

1997 Upper Deck Chris Berman Rock 'N Roll Hall of Fame

This one-card set features a borderless color picture of Chris Berman performing and was given away at the Rock 'N Roll Hall of Fame as part of the party Chris Berman hosted for ESPN. The back displays a small head shot of Berman along with a list of players and nicknames under the heading, "Baseball Nickname Hall of Fame."

Nm-Mt Ex-Mt
1 Chris Berman 1.00 .30

1997 Upper Deck Home Team Heroes

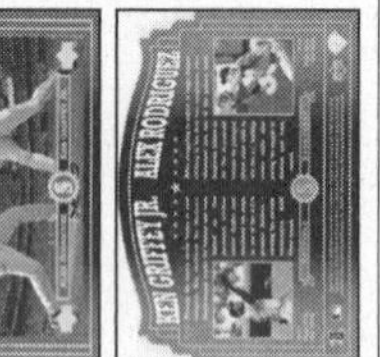

This 12-card set measures approximately 5" by 3 1/2" and features two color action embossed images of top players from the same team printed on a die-cut card with silver foil enhancements. The backs carry two small color action player photos with player information in paragraph form.

Nm-Mt Ex-Mt
COMPLETE SET (12) 10.00 3.00
HT1 Alex Rodriguez 4.00 1.20
Ken Griffey Jr.
HT2 Bernie Williams 2.00 .60
Derek Jeter
HT3 Bernard Gilkey .50 .15
Todd Hundley
HT4 Hideo Nomo .75 .23
Mike Piazza
HT5 Andruw Jones 2.50 .75
Chipper Jones
HT6 John Smoltz 2.50 .75
Greg Maddux
HT7 Mike Mussina 3.00 .90
Cal Ripken Jr.
HT8 Andres Galarraga .75 .23
Dante Bichette
HT9 Juan Gonzalez 2.00 .60
Ivan Rodriguez
HT10 Albert Belle 2.00 .60
Frank Thomas
HT11 Kenny Lofton .75 .23
Manny Ramirez
HT12 Ken Caminiti 2.00 .60
Tony Gwynn

1997 Upper Deck Ken Griffey Jr. Highlight Reels

This five-card hi-tech Diamond Vision set features actual MLB video footage of Ken Griffey Jr.'s most unbelievable plays. Each card was distributed in clamshell packaging for a suggested retail price of $9.99. The cards measure approximately 3.5" by 5" with each card containing over 20 frames of actual video footage of the player.

Nm-Mt Ex-Mt
COMMON CARD (1-5) 10.00 3.00

1997 Upper Deck Sister Assumpta Trivia

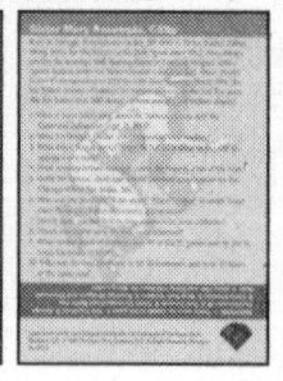

This one-card set was introduced at the National in Cleveland, Ohio, on August 7, 1997, and is a tribute to Indians fan, Sister Mary Assumpta, who began baking chocolate chip cookies for the players in 1986. The front features the nun's picture holding a bat and a cookie. The back displays ten trivia questions with the answers printed upside down in a blue bar at the bottom.

Nm-Mt Ex-Mt
1 Sister Mary Assumpta .50 .15

1998 Upper Deck

The 1998 Upper Deck set was issued in three series consisting of a 270-card first series, a 270-card second series and a 211-card third series. Each series was distributed in 12-card packs which carried a suggested retail price of $2.49. Card fronts feature game dated photographs of some of the season's most memorable moments. The following subsets are contained within the set: History in the Making (1-8/361-369), Griffey's Hot List (9-18), Define the Game (136-153), Season Highlights (244-252/532-540/748-750), Star Rookies (253-288/541-600), Postseason Headliners (415-432), Upper Echelon (451-459) and Eminent Prestige (601-630). The Eminent Prestige subset cards were slightly shortprinted (approximately 1:4 packs) and Upper Deck offered a free service to collectors trying to finish their Series three sets whereby Eminent Prestige cards were mailed to collectors who sent in proof of purchase of one-and-a-half boxes or more. The print run for Mike Piazza card number 681 was split exactly in half creating two shortprints: card number 681 (picturing Piazza as a New York Met) and card number 681A (picturing Piazza as a Florida Marlin). Both cards are exactly two times tougher to pull from packs than other regular issue Series three cards. The series three set is considered complete with both versions at 251 total cards. Notable Rookie Cards include Gabe Kapler and Magglio Ordonez.

Nm-Mt Ex-Mt
COMPLETE SET (751) 200.00 60.00
COMP.SERIES 1 (270) 40.00 12.00
COMP.SERIES 2 (270) 40.00 12.00
COMP.SERIES 3 (211) 120.00 36.00
COMMON (1-600/631-750) .30 .09
COMMON EP (601-630) 2.00 .60
1 Tino Martinez HIST .30 .09
2 Jimmy Key HIST .30 .09
3 Jay Buhner HIST .30 .09
4 Mark Gardner HIST .30 .09
5 Greg Maddux HIST .75 .23
6 Pedro Martinez HIST .50 .15
7 Hideo Nomo HIST .50 .15
8 Sammy Sosa HIST .75 .23
9 Mark McGwire GHL 1.00 .30
10 Ken Griffey Jr. GHL .75 .23
11 Larry Walker GHL .30 .09
12 Tino Martinez GHL .30 .09
13 Mike Piazza GHL .75 .23
14 Jose Cruz Jr. GHL .30 .09
15 Tony Gwynn GHL .50 .15
16 Greg Maddux GHL .75 .23
17 Roger Clemens GHL .75 .23
18 Alex Rodriguez GHL .75 .23
19 Shigetoshi Hasegawa .30 .09
20 Eddie Murray .75 .23
21 Jason Dickson .30 .09
22 Darin Erstad .30 .09
23 Chuck Finley .30 .09
24 Dave Hollins .30 .09
25 Garret Anderson .30 .09
26 Michael Tucker .30 .09
27 Kenny Lofton .30 .09
28 Javier Lopez .30 .09
29 Fred McGriff .50 .15
30 Greg Maddux 1.25 .35
31 Jeff Blauser .30 .09
32 John Smoltz .50 .15
33 Mark Wohlers .30 .09
34 Scott Erickson .30 .09
35 Jimmy Key .30 .09
36 Harold Baines .30 .09
37 Randy Myers .30 .09
38 B.J. Surhoff .30 .09
39 Eric Davis .30 .09
40 Rafael Palmeiro .50 .15
41 Jeffrey Hammonds .30 .09
42 Mo Vaughn .30 .09
43 Tom Gordon .30 .09
44 Tim Naehring .30 .09
45 Darren Bragg .30 .09
46 Aaron Sele .30 .09
47 Troy O'Leary .30 .09
48 John Valentin .30 .09
49 Doug Glanville .30 .09
50 Ryne Sandberg 1.25 .35
51 Steve Trachsel .30 .09
52 Mark Grace .50 .15
53 Kevin Foster .30 .09
54 Kevin Tapani .30 .09
55 Kevin Orie .30 .09
56 Lyle Mouton .30 .09
57 Ray Durham .30 .09
58 Jaime Navarro .30 .09
59 Mike Cameron .30 .09
60 Albert Belle .30 .09
61 Doug Drabek .30 .09
62 Chris Snopek .30 .09
63 Eddie Taubensee .30 .09
64 Terry Pendleton .30 .09
65 Barry Larkin .75 .23
66 Willie Greene .30 .09
67 Deion Sanders .50 .15
68 Pokey Reese .30 .09
69 Jeff Shaw .30 .09
70 Jim Thome .75 .23
71 Orel Hershiser .30 .09
72 Omar Vizquel .30 .09
73 Brian Giles .30 .09
74 David Justice .30 .09
75 Bartolo Colon .30 .09
76 Sandy Alomar Jr. .30 .09
77 Neifi Perez .30 .09
78 Dante Bichette .30 .09
79 Vinny Castilla .30 .09
80 Eric Young .30 .09
81 Quinton McCracken .30 .09
82 Jamey Wright .30 .09
83 John Thomson .30 .09
84 Damion Easley .30 .09
85 Justin Thompson .30 .09
86 Willie Blair .30 .09
87 Raul Casanova .30 .09
88 Bobby Higginson .30 .09
89 Bubba Trammell .30 .09
90 Tony Clark .30 .09
91 Livan Hernandez .30 .09
92 Charles Johnson .30 .09
93 Edgar Renteria .30 .09
94 Alex Fernandez .30 .09
95 Gary Sheffield .30 .09
96 Moises Alou .30 .09
97 Tony Saunders .30 .09
98 Robb Nen .30 .09
99 Darryl Kile .30 .09
100 Craig Biggio .50 .15
101 Chris Holt .30 .09
102 Bob Abreu .30 .09
103 Luis Gonzalez .30 .09
104 Billy Wagner .30 .09
105 Brad Ausmus .30 .09
106 Chili Davis .30 .09
107 Tim Belcher .30 .09
108 Dean Palmer .30 .09
109 Jeff King .30 .09
110 Jose Rosado .30 .09
111 Mike Macfarlane .30 .09
112 Jay Bell .30 .09
113 Todd Worrell .30 .09
114 Chan Ho Park .30 .09
115 Raul Mondesi .30 .09
116 Brett Butler .30 .09
117 Greg Gagne .30 .09
118 Hideo Nomo .75 .23
119 Todd Zeile .30 .09
120 Eric Karros .30 .09
121 Cal Eldred .30 .09
122 Jeff D'Amico .30 .09
123 Antone Williamson .30 .09
124 Doug Jones .30 .09
125 Dave Nilsson .30 .09
126 Gerald Williams .30 .09
127 Fernando Vina .30 .09
128 Ron Coomer .30 .09
129 Matt Lawton .30 .09
130 Paul Molitor .50 .15
131 Todd Walker .30 .09
132 Rick Aguilera .30 .09
133 Brad Radke .30 .09
134 Bob Tewksbury .30 .09
135 Vladimir Guerrero .75 .23
136 Tony Gwynn DG .50 .15
137 Roger Clemens DG .75 .23
138 Dennis Eckersley DG .30 .09
139 Brady Anderson DG .30 .09
140 Ken Griffey Jr. DG .75 .23
141 Derek Jeter DG 1.00 .30
142 Ken Caminiti DG .30 .09
143 Frank Thomas DG .50 .15
144 Barry Bonds DG .75 .23
145 Cal Ripken DG 1.25 .35
146 Alex Rodriguez DG .75 .23
147 Greg Maddux DG .75 .23
148 Kenny Lofton DG .30 .09
149 Mike Piazza DG .75 .23
150 Mark McGwire DG 1.00 .30
151 Andruw Jones DG .50 .15
152 Rusty Greer DG .30 .09
153 F.P. Santangelo DG .30 .09
154 Mike Lansing .30 .09
155 Lee Smith .30 .09
156 Carlos Perez .30 .09
157 Pedro Martinez .75 .23
158 Ryan McGuire .30 .09
159 F.P. Santangelo .30 .09
160 Rondell White .50 .15
161 T.Kashiwada RC .40 .12
162 Butch Huskey .30 .09
163 Edgardo Alfonzo .30 .09
164 John Franco .30 .09
165 Todd Hundley .30 .09
166 Rey Ordonez .30 .09
167 Armando Reynoso .30 .09
168 John Olerud .30 .09
169 Bernie Williams .50 .15
170 Andy Pettitte .50 .15
171 Wade Boggs .50 .15
172 Paul O'Neill .50 .15
173 Cecil Fielder .30 .09
174 Charlie Hayes .30 .09
175 David Cone .30 .09
176 Hideki Irabu .30 .09
177 Mark Bellhorn .30 .09
178 Steve Karsay .30 .09
179 Damon Mashore .30 .09
180 Jason McDonald .30 .09
181 Scott Spiezio .30 .09
182 Ariel Prieto .30 .09
183 Jason Giambi .75 .23
184 Wendell Magee .30 .09
185 Rico Brogna .30 .09
186 Garrett Stephenson .30 .09
187 Wayne Gomes .30 .09
188 Ricky Bottalico .30 .09
189 Mickey Morandini .30 .09
190 Mike Lieberthal .30 .09
191 Kevin Polcovich .30 .09
192 Francisco Cordova .30 .09
193 Kevin Young .30 .09
194 Jon Lieber .30 .09
195 Kevin Elster .30 .09
196 Tony Womack .30 .09
197 Lou Collier .30 .09
198 Mike Difelice RC .40 .12
199 Gary Gaetti .30 .09
200 Dennis Eckersley .30 .09
201 Alan Benes .30 .09
202 Willie McGee .30 .09
203 Ron Gant .30 .09
204 Fernando Valenzuela .30 .09
205 Mark McGwire 2.00 .60
206 Archi Cianfrocco .30 .09
207 Andy Ashby .30 .09
208 Steve Finley .30 .09
209 Quilvio Veras .30 .09
210 Ken Caminiti .30 .09
211 Rickey Henderson .75 .23
212 Joey Hamilton .30 .09
213 Derrek Lee .30 .09
214 Bill Mueller .30 .09
215 Shawn Estes .30 .09
216 J.T. Snow .30 .09
217 Mark Gardner .30 .09
218 Terry Mulholland .30 .09
219 Dante Powell .30 .09
220 Jeff Kent .30 .09
221 Jamie Moyer .30 .09
222 Joey Cora .30 .09
223 Jeff Fassero .30 .09
224 Dennis Martinez .30 .09
225 Ken Griffey Jr. 1.25 .35
226 Edgar Martinez .50 .15
227 Russ Davis .30 .09
228 Dan Wilson .30 .09
229 Will Clark .75 .23
230 Ivan Rodriguez .75 .23
231 Benji Gil .30 .09
232 Lee Stevens .30 .09
233 Mickey Tettleton .30 .09
234 Julio Santana .30 .09
235 Rusty Greer .30 .09
236 Bobby Witt .30 .09
237 Ed Sprague .30 .09
238 Pat Hentgen .30 .09
239 Kelvim Escobar .30 .09
240 Joe Carter .30 .09
241 Carlos Delgado .30 .09
242 Shannon Stewart .30 .09
243 Benito Santiago .30 .09
244 Tino Martinez SH .30 .09
245 Ken Griffey Jr. SH .75 .23
246 Kevin Brown SH .30 .09
247 Ryne Sandberg SH .50 .15
248 Mo Vaughn SH .30 .09
249 Darryl Hamilton SH .30 .09
250 Randy Johnson SH .50 .15
251 Steve Finley SH .30 .09
252 Bobby Higginson SH .30 .09
253 Brett Tomko .30 .09
254 Mark Kotsay .30 .09
255 Jose Guillen .30 .09
256 Eli Marrero .30 .09
257 Dennis Reyes .30 .09
258 Richie Sexson .30 .09
259 Pat Cline .30 .09
260 Todd Helton .50 .15
261 Juan Melo .30 .09
262 Matt Morris .30 .09
263 Jeremi Gonzalez .30 .09
264 Jeff Abbott .30 .09
265 Aaron Boone .30 .09
266 Todd Dunwoody .30 .09
267 Jaret Wright .50 .15
268 Derrick Gibson .30 .09
269 Mario Valdez .30 .09
270 Fernando Tatis .30 .09
271 Craig Counsell .30 .09
272 Brad Rigby .30 .09
273 Danny Clyburn .30 .09
274 Brian Rose .30 .09
275 Miguel Tejada .50 .15
276 Jason Varitek .30 .09
277 Dave Dellucci RC .40 .12
278 Michael Coleman .30 .09
279 Adam Riggs .30 .09
280 Ben Grieve .30 .09
281 Brad Fullmer .30 .09
282 Ken Cloude .30 .09
283 Tom Evans .30 .09
284 Kevin Millwood RC 1.50 .45
285 Paul Konerko .30 .09
286 Juan Encarnacion .30 .09
287 Chris Carpenter .30 .09
288 Tom Fordham .30 .09
289 Gary DiSarcina .30 .09
290 Tim Salmon .50 .15
291 Troy Percival .30 .09
292 Todd Greene .30 .09
293 Ken Hill .30 .09
294 Dennis Springer .30 .09
295 Jim Edmonds .30 .09
296 Allen Watson .30 .09
297 Brian Anderson .30 .09
298 Keith Lockhart .30 .09
299 Tom Glavine .50 .15
300 Chipper Jones .75 .23
301 Randall Simon .30 .09
302 Mark Lemke .30 .09
303 Ryan Klesko .30 .09
304 Denny Neagle .30 .09
305 Andruw Jones .30 .09
306 Mike Mussina .75 .23

307 Brady Anderson .30 .09
308 Chris Hoiles .30 .09
309 Mike Bordick .30 .09
310 Cal Ripken 2.50 .75
311 Geronimo Berroa .30 .09
312 Armando Benitez .30 .09
313 Roberto Alomar .75 .23
314 Tim Wakefield .30 .09
315 Reggie Jefferson .30 .09
316 Jeff Frye .30 .09
317 Scott Hatteberg .30 .09
318 Steve Avery .30 .09
319 Robinson Checo .30 .09
320 Nomar Garciaparra 1.25 .35
321 Lance Johnson .30 .09
322 Tyler Houston .30 .09
323 Mark Clark .30 .09
324 Terry Adams .30 .09
325 Sammy Sosa 1.25 .35
326 Scott Servais .30 .09
327 Manny Alexander .30 .09
328 Norberto Martin .30 .09
329 Scott Eyre .30 .09
330 Frank Thomas .75 .23
331 Robin Ventura .30 .09
332 Matt Karchner .30 .09
333 Keith Foulke .30 .09
334 James Baldwin .30 .09
335 Chris Stynes .30 .09
336 Bret Boone .30 .09
337 Jon Nunnally .30 .09
338 Dave Burba .30 .09
339 Eduardo Perez .30 .09
340 Reggie Sanders .30 .09
341 Mike Remlinger .30 .09
342 Pat Watkins .30 .09
343 Chad Ogea .30 .09
344 John Smiley .30 .09
345 Kenny Lofton .30 .09
346 Jose Mesa .30 .09
347 Charles Nagy .30 .09
348 Enrique Wilson .30 .09
349 Bruce Aven .30 .09
350 Manny Ramirez .30 .09
351 Jerry DiPoto .30 .09
352 Ellis Burks .30 .09
353 Kirt Manwaring .30 .09
354 Vinny Castilla .30 .09
355 Larry Walker .50 .15
356 Kevin Ritz .30 .09
357 Pedro Astacio .30 .09
358 Scott Sanders .30 .09
359 Deivi Cruz .30 .09
360 Brian L. Hunter .30 .09
361 Pedro Martinez HM .50 .15
362 Tom Glavine HM .30 .09
363 Willie McGee HM .30 .09
364 J.T. Snow HM .30 .09
365 Rusty Greer HM .30 .09
366 Mike Grace HM .30 .09
367 Tony Clark HM .30 .09
368 Ben Grieve HM .30 .09
369 Gary Sheffield HM .30 .09
370 Joe Oliver .30 .09
371 Todd Jones .30 .09
372 Frank Catalanotto RC .60 .18
373 Brian Moehler .30 .09
374 Cliff Floyd .30 .09
375 Bobby Bonilla .30 .09
376 Al Leiter .30 .09
377 Josh Booty .30 .09
378 Darren Daulton .30 .09
379 Jay Powell .30 .09
380 Felix Heredia .30 .09
381 Jim Eisenreich .30 .09
382 Richard Hidalgo .30 .09
383 Mike Hampton .30 .09
384 Shane Reynolds .30 .09
385 Jeff Bagwell .50 .15
386 Derek Bell .30 .09
387 Ricky Gutierrez .30 .09
388 Bill Spiers .30 .09
389 Jose Offerman .30 .09
390 Johnny Damon .30 .09
391 Jermaine Dye .30 .09
392 Jeff Montgomery .30 .09
393 Glendon Rusch .30 .09
394 Mike Sweeney .30 .09
395 Kevin Appier .30 .09
396 Joe Vitiello .30 .09
397 Ramon Martinez .30 .09
398 Darren Dreifort .30 .09
399 Wilton Guerrero .30 .09
400 Mike Piazza 1.25 .35
401 Eddie Murray .75 .23
402 Ismael Valdes .30 .09
403 Todd Hollandsworth .30 .09
404 Mark Loretta .30 .09
405 Jeromy Burnitz .30 .09
406 Jeff Cirillo .30 .09
407 Scott Karl .30 .09
408 Mike Matheny .30 .09
409 Jose Valentin .30 .09
410 John Jaha .30 .09
411 Terry Steinbach .30 .09
412 Torii Hunter .30 .09
413 Pat Meares .30 .09
414 Marty Cordova .30 .09
415 Jaret Wright PH .30 .09
416 Mike Mussina PH .50 .15
417 John Smoltz PH .30 .09
418 Devon White PH .30 .09
419 Denny Neagle PH .30 .09
420 Livan Hernandez PH .30 .09
421 Kevin Brown PH .30 .09
422 Marquis Grissom PH .30 .09
423 Mike Mussina PH .50 .15
424 Eric Davis PH .30 .09
425 Tony Fernandez PH .30 .09
426 Moises Alou PH .30 .09
427 Sandy Alomar Jr. PH .30 .09
428 Gary Sheffield PH .30 .09
429 Jaret Wright PH .30 .09
430 Livan Hernandez PH .30 .09
431 Chad Ogea PH .30 .09
432 Edgar Renteria PH .30 .09
433 LaTroy Hawkins .30 .09
434 Rich Robertson .30 .09
435 Chuck Knoblauch .30 .09
436 Jose Vidro .30 .09
437 Dustin Hermanson .30 .09
438 Jim Bullinger .30 .09
439 Orlando Cabrera .30 .09
440 Vladimir Guerrero .75 .23
441 Ugueth Urbina .30 .09
442 Brian McRae .30 .09
443 Matt Franco .30 .09
444 Bobby Jones .30 .09
445 Bernard Gilkey .30 .09
446 Dave Mlicki .30 .09
447 Brian Bohanon .30 .09
448 Mel Rojas .30 .09
449 Tim Raines .30 .09
450 Derek Jeter 2.00 .60
451 Roger Clemens UE .75 .23
452 N.Garciaparra UE .75 .23
453 Mike Piazza UE .75 .23
454 Mark McGwire UE 1.00 .30
455 Ken Griffey Jr. UE .75 .23
456 Larry Walker UE .30 .09
457 Alex Rodriguez UE .75 .23
458 Tony Gwynn UE .50 .15
459 Frank Thomas UE .50 .15
460 Tino Martinez .50 .15
461 Chad Curtis .30 .09
462 Ramiro Mendoza .30 .09
463 Joe Girardi .30 .09
464 David Wells .30 .09
465 Mariano Rivera .50 .15
466 Willie Adams .30 .09
467 George Williams .30 .09
468 Dave Telgheder .30 .09
469 Dave Magadan .30 .09
470 Matt Stairs .30 .09
471 Bill Taylor .30 .09
472 Jimmy Haynes .30 .09
473 Gregg Jefferies .30 .09
474 Midre Cummings .30 .09
475 Curt Schilling .50 .15
476 Mike Grace .30 .09
477 Mark Leiter .30 .09
478 Matt Beech .30 .09
479 Scott Rolen .50 .15
480 Jason Kendall .30 .09
481 Esteban Loaiza .30 .09
482 Jermaine Allensworth .30 .09
483 Mark Smith .30 .09
484 Jason Schmidt .30 .09
485 Jose Guillen .30 .09
486 Al Martin .30 .09
487 Delino DeShields .30 .09
488 Todd Stottlemyre .30 .09
489 Brian Jordan .30 .09
490 Ray Lankford .30 .09
491 Matt Morris .30 .09
492 Royce Clayton .30 .09
493 John Mabry .30 .09
494 Wally Joyner .30 .09
495 Trevor Hoffman .30 .09
496 Chris Gomez .30 .09
497 Sterling Hitchcock .30 .09
498 Pete Smith .30 .09
499 Greg Vaughn .30 .09
500 Tony Gwynn 1.00 .30
501 Will Cunnane .30 .09
502 Darryl Hamilton .30 .09
503 Brian Johnson .30 .09
504 Kirk Rueter .30 .09
505 Barry Bonds 2.00 .60
506 Osvaldo Fernandez .30 .09
507 Stan Javier .30 .09
508 Julian Tavarez .30 .09
509 Rich Aurilia .30 .09
510 Alex Rodriguez 1.25 .35
511 David Segui .30 .09
512 Rich Amaral .30 .09
513 Raul Ibanez .30 .09
514 Jay Buhner .30 .09
515 Randy Johnson .75 .23
516 Heathcliff Slocumb .30 .09
517 Tony Saunders .30 .09
518 Kevin Elster .30 .09
519 John Burkett .30 .09
520 Juan Gonzalez .75 .23
521 John Wetteland .30 .09
522 Domingo Cedeno .30 .09
523 Darren Oliver .30 .09
524 Roger Pavlik .30 .09
525 Jose Cruz Jr. .30 .09
526 Woody Williams .30 .09
527 Alex Gonzalez .30 .09
528 Robert Person .30 .09
529 Juan Guzman .30 .09
530 Roger Clemens 1.50 .45
531 Shawn Green .30 .09
532 Francisco Cordova SH .30 .09
Ricardo Rincon
Mark Smith
533 N.Garciaparra SH .75 .23
534 Roger Clemens SH .75 .23
535 Mark McGwire SH 1.00 .30
536 Larry Walker SH .30 .09
537 Mike Piazza SH .75 .23
538 Curt Schilling SH .30 .09
539 Tony Gwynn SH .50 .15
540 Ken Griffey Jr. SH .75 .23
541 Carl Pavano .30 .09
542 Shane Monahan .30 .09
543 Gabe Kapler RC .60 .18
544 Eric Milton .30 .09
545 Gary Matthews Jr. RC .40 .12
546 Mike Kinkade RC .30 .09
547 Ryan Christenson RC .30 .09
548 Corey Koskie RC 1.25 .35
549 Norm Hutchins .30 .09
550 Russell Branyan .30 .09
551 Masato Yoshii RC .60 .18
552 Jesus Sanchez RC .30 .09
553 Anthony Sanders .30 .09
554 Edwin Diaz .30 .09
555 Gabe Alvarez .30 .09
556 Carlos Lee RC 1.25 .35
557 Mike Darr .30 .09
558 Kerry Wood .75 .23
559 Carlos Guillen .30 .09
560 Sean Casey .30 .09
561 Manny Aybar RC .30 .09
562 Octavio Dotel .30 .09
563 Jarrod Washburn .30 .09
564 Mark L. Johnson .30 .09
565 Ramon Hernandez .30 .09
566 Rich Butler RC .30 .09
567 Mike Caruso .30 .09
568 Cliff Politte .30 .09
569 Scott Elarton .30 .09
570 Magglio Ordonez RC 3.00 .90
571 Adam Butler RC .30 .09
572 Marlon Anderson .30 .09
573 Julio Ramirez RC .30 .09
574 Darron Ingram RC .30 .09
575 Bruce Chen .30 .09
576 Steve Woodard .30 .09
577 Hiram Bocachica .30 .09
578 Kevin Witt .30 .09
579 Javier Vazquez .30 .09
580 Alex Gonzalez .30 .09
581 Brian Powell .30 .09
582 Wes Helms .30 .09
583 Ron Wright .30 .09
584 Rafael Medina .30 .09
585 Daryle Ward .30 .09
586 Geoff Jenkins .30 .09
587 Preston Wilson .30 .09
588 Jim Chamblee RC .30 .09
589 Mike Lowell RC 2.00 .60
590 A.J. Hinch .30 .09
591 Francisco Cordero RC .30 .09
592 Rolando Arrojo RC .40 .12
593 Braden Looper .30 .09
594 Sidney Ponson .30 .09
595 Matt Clement .30 .09
596 Carlton Loewer .30 .09
597 Brian Meadows .30 .09
598 Danny Klassen .30 .09
599 Larry Sutton .30 .09
600 Travis Lee .30 .09
601 Randy Johnson EP 2.50 .75
602 Greg Maddux EP 4.00 1.20
603 Roger Clemens EP 5.00 1.50
604 Jaret Wright EP 2.00 .60
605 Mike Piazza EP 4.00 1.20
606 Tino Martinez EP 2.00 .60
607 Frank Thomas EP 2.50 .75
608 Mo Vaughn EP 2.00 .60
609 Todd Helton EP 2.00 .60
610 Mark McGwire EP 6.00 1.80
611 Jeff Bagwell EP 2.00 .60
612 Travis Lee EP 2.00 .60
613 Scott Rolen EP 2.00 .60
614 Cal Ripken EP 8.00 2.40
615 Chipper Jones EP 2.50 .75
616 Nomar Garciaparra EP 4.00 1.20
617 Alex Rodriguez EP 4.00 1.20
618 Derek Jeter EP 6.00 1.80
619 Tony Gwynn EP 3.00 .90
620 Ken Griffey Jr. EP 4.00 1.20
621 Kenny Lofton EP 2.00 .60
622 Juan Gonzalez EP 2.50 .75
623 Jose Cruz Jr. EP 2.00 .60
624 Larry Walker EP 2.00 .60
625 Barry Bonds EP 6.00 1.80
626 Ben Grieve EP 2.00 .60
627 Andruw Jones EP 2.00 .60
628 Vladimir Guerrero EP 2.50 .75
629 Paul Konerko EP 2.00 .60
630 Paul Molitor EP 2.00 .60
631 Cecil Fielder .30 .09
632 Jack McDowell .30 .09
633 Mike James .30 .09
634 Brian Anderson .30 .09
635 Jay Bell .30 .09
636 Devon White .30 .09
637 Andy Stankiewicz .30 .09
638 Tony Batista .30 .09
639 Omar Daal .30 .09
640 Matt Williams .30 .09
641 Brent Brede .30 .09
642 Jorge Fabregas .30 .09
643 Karim Garcia .30 .09
644 Felix Rodriguez .30 .09
645 Andy Benes .30 .09
646 Willie Blair .30 .09
647 Jeff Suppan .30 .09
648 Yamil Benitez .30 .09
649 Walt Weiss .30 .09
650 Andres Galarraga .30 .09
651 Doug Drabek .30 .09
652 Ozzie Guillen .30 .09
653 Joe Carter .30 .09
654 Dennis Eckersley .30 .09
655 Pedro Martinez .75 .23
656 Jim Leyritz .30 .09
657 Henry Rodriguez .30 .09
658 Rod Beck .30 .09
659 Mickey Morandini .30 .09
660 Jeff Blauser .30 .09
661 Ruben Sierra .30 .09
662 Mike Sirotka .30 .09
663 Pete Harnisch .30 .09
664 Damian Jackson .30 .09
665 Dmitri Young .30 .09
666 Steve Cooke .30 .09
667 Geronimo Berroa .30 .09
668 Shawon Dunston .30 .09
669 Mike Jackson .30 .09
670 Travis Fryman .30 .09
671 Dwight Gooden .30 .09
672 Paul Assenmacher .30 .09
673 Eric Plunk .30 .09
674 Mike Lansing .30 .09
675 Darryl Kile .30 .09
676 Luis Gonzalez .30 .09
677 Frank Castillo .30 .09
678 Joe Randa .30 .09
679 Bip Roberts .30 .09
680 Derrek Lee .30 .09
681 Mike Piazza SP 3.00 .90
New York Mets
681A Mike Piazza SP 3.00 .90
Florida Marlins
682 Sean Berry .30 .09
683 Ramon Garcia .30 .09
684 Carl Everett .30 .09
685 Moises Alou .30 .09
686 Hal Morris .30 .09
687 Jeff Conine .30 .09
688 Gary Sheffield .30 .09
689 Jose Vizcaino .30 .09
690 Charles Johnson .30 .09
691 Bobby Bonilla .30 .09
692 Marquis Grissom .30 .09
693 Alex Ochoa .30 .09
694 Mike Morgan .30 .09
695 Orlando Merced .30 .09
696 David Ortiz .30 .09
697 Brent Gates .30 .09
698 Otis Nixon .30 .09
699 Trey Moore .30 .09
700 Derrick May .30 .09
701 Rich Becker .30 .09
702 Al Leiter .30 .09
703 Chili Davis .30 .09
704 Scott Brosius .30 .09
705 Chuck Knoblauch .30 .09
706 Kenny Rogers .30 .09
707 Mike Blowers .30 .09
708 Mike Fetters .30 .09
709 Tom Candiotti .30 .09
710 Rickey Henderson .75 .23
711 Bob Abreu .30 .09
712 Mark Lewis .30 .09
713 Doug Glanville .30 .09
714 Desi Relaford .30 .09
715 Kent Mercker .30 .09
716 Kevin Brown .50 .15
717 James Mouton .30 .09
718 Mark Langston .30 .09
719 Greg Myers .30 .09
720 Orel Hershiser .30 .09
721 Charlie Hayes .30 .09
722 Robb Nen .30 .09
723 Glenallen Hill .30 .09
724 Tony Saunders .30 .09
725 Wade Boggs .50 .15
726 Kevin Stocker .30 .09
727 Wilson Alvarez .30 .09
728 Albie Lopez .30 .09
729 Dave Martinez .30 .09
730 Fred McGriff .50 .15
731 Quinton McCracken .30 .09
732 Bryan Rekar .30 .09
733 Paul Sorrento .30 .09
734 Roberto Hernandez .30 .09
735 Bubba Trammell .30 .09
736 Miguel Cairo .30 .09
737 John Flaherty .30 .09
738 Terrell Wade .30 .09
739 Roberto Kelly .30 .09
740 Mark McLemore .30 .09
741 Danny Patterson .30 .09
742 Aaron Sele .30 .09
743 Tony Fernandez .30 .09
744 Randy Myers .30 .09
745 Jose Canseco .75 .23
746 Darrin Fletcher .30 .09
747 Mike Stanley .30 .09
748 M.Grissom SH CL .30 .09
749 Fred McGriff SH CL .30 .09
750 Travis Lee SH CL .30 .09

1998 Upper Deck 5 x 7 Blow Ups

These jumbo parallel cards capture a selection of players taken from each of the three basic series of the 1998 Upper Deck set. Besides the obvious difference in size, these 5" by 7" cards also lack the silver foil coating on front that the standard 2 1/2" by 3 1/2" cards have. The first fifteen cards checklisted below (skip-numbered between 30 and 230) comprise the first series 5 x 7 Blow Up set. These first series jumbo cards were available only via redemption from Upper Deck. Collector's had to send in ten first series wrappers plus $3 to the UD redemption center. The next ten cards checklisted below (skip-numbered between 310 and 530) comprise the second series 5 x 7 Blow Up set. These second series jumbo cards were available only in specially marked mass market retail series 2 boxes (carrying an $11.99 SRP). Each box contained five basic series 2 retail packs and one 5 x 7 Blow Up. The third series 5 x 7 Blow Ups (numbered between 605 and 620 in the listings below) are comprised of selected stars from the Eminent Prestige subset within the basic issue Series 3 set.

Nm-Mt Ex-Mt
27 Kenny Lofton 1.00 .30
30 Greg Maddux 3.00 .90
40 Rafael Palmeiro 1.25 .35
50 Ryne Sandberg 3.00 .90
60 Albert Belle .75 .23
65 Barry Larkin 1.25 .35
68 Deion Sanders .75 .23
95 Gary Sheffield 1.50 .45
130 Paul Molitor 1.50 .45
135 Vladimir Guerrero 1.50 .45
176 Hideki Irabu .50 .15
205 Mark McGwire 5.00 1.50
211 Rickey Henderson 2.00 .60
225 Ken Griffey Jr. 4.00 1.20
230 Ivan Rodriguez 1.50 .45
310 Cal Ripken 6.00 1.80
320 Nomar Garciaparra 3.00 .90
330 Frank Thomas 2.00 .60
355 Larry Walker .75 .23
385 Jeff Bagwell 1.50 .45
400 Mike Piazza 4.00 1.20
450 Derek Jeter 6.00 1.80
500 Tony Gwynn 3.00 .90
510 Alex Rodriguez 4.00 1.20
530 Roger Clemens 3.00 .90
605 Mike Piazza EP 4.00 1.20
607 Frank Thomas EP 2.00 .60
610 Mark McGwire EP 5.00 1.50
611 Jeff Bagwell EP 1.50 .45
612 Travis Lee EP .75 .23
614 Cal Ripken EP 6.00 1.80
616 Nomar Garciaparra EP 3.00 .90
617 Alex Rodriguez EP 4.00 1.20
619 Tony Gwynn EP 3.00 .90
620 Ken Griffey Jr. EP 4.00 1.20

1998 Upper Deck 10th Anniversary Preview

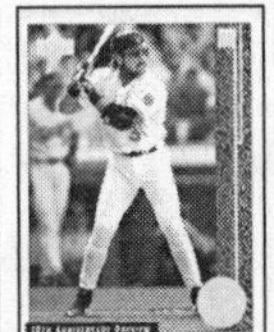

Randomly inserted in Series one packs at the rate of one in five, this 60-card set features color player photos in a design similar to the inaugural 1989 Upper Deck series. The backs carry a photo of that player's previous Upper Deck card. A 10th Anniversary Ballot Card was inserted one in four packs which allowed the collector to vote for the players they wanted to see in the 1999 Upper Deck tenth anniversary series.

Nm-Mt Ex-Mt
COMPLETE SET (60) 120.00 36.00
*RETAIL: .4X TO .1X BASIC 10TH ANN
RETAIL DISTRIBUTED AS FACTORY SET
1 Greg Maddux 5.00 1.50
2 Mike Mussina 3.00 .90
3 Roger Clemens 6.00 1.80
4 Hideo Nomo 3.00 .90
5 David Cone 1.25 .35
6 Tom Glavine 2.00 .60
7 Andy Pettitte 2.00 .60
8 Jimmy Key 1.25 .35
9 Randy Johnson 3.00 .90
10 Dennis Eckersley 1.25 .35
11 Lee Smith 1.25 .35
12 John Franco 1.25 .35
13 Randy Myers 1.25 .35
14 Mike Piazza 5.00 1.50
15 Ivan Rodriguez 3.00 .90
16 Todd Hundley 1.25 .35
17 Sandy Alomar Jr. 1.25 .35
18 Frank Thomas 3.00 .90
19 Rafael Palmeiro 2.00 .60
20 Mark McGwire 8.00 2.40
21 Mo Vaughn 1.25 .35
22 Fred McGriff 2.00 .60
23 Andres Galarraga 1.25 .35
24 Mark Grace 2.00 .60
25 Jeff Bagwell 2.00 .60
26 Roberto Alomar 3.00 .90
27 Chuck Knoblauch 1.25 .35
28 Ryne Sandberg 5.00 1.50
29 Eric Young 1.25 .35
30 Craig Biggio 2.00 .60
31 Carlos Baerga 1.25 .35
32 Robin Ventura 1.25 .35
33 Matt Williams 1.25 .35
34 Wade Boggs 2.00 .60
35 Dean Palmer 1.25 .35
36 Chipper Jones 3.00 .90
37 Vinny Castilla 1.25 .35
38 Ken Caminiti 1.25 .35
39 Omar Vizquel 1.25 .35
40 Cal Ripken 10.00 3.00
41 Derek Jeter 8.00 2.40
42 Alex Rodriguez 5.00 1.50
43 Barry Larkin 3.00 .90
44 Mark Grudzielanek 1.25 .35
45 Albert Belle 1.25 .35
46 Manny Ramirez 1.25 .35
47 Jose Canseco 3.00 .90
48 Ken Griffey Jr. 5.00 1.50
49 Juan Gonzalez 3.00 .90
50 Kenny Lofton 1.25 .35
51 Sammy Sosa 5.00 1.50
52 Larry Walker 2.00 .60
53 Gary Sheffield 1.25 .35
54 Rickey Henderson 3.00 .90
55 Tony Gwynn 4.00 1.20
56 Barry Bonds 8.00 2.40
57 Paul Molitor 2.00 .60
58 Edgar Martinez 2.00 .60
59 Chili Davis 1.25 .35
60 Eddie Murray 3.00 .90

1998 Upper Deck 10th Anniversary Preview Retail

This 60 card set is a parallel to the 10th Anniversary Preview set inserted into 1998 Upper Deck Series 1. This set was only available as part of a retail package which also included 200 better 1997 Collectors Choice cards. The difference between these cards and the pack inserts are the gold foil printed on the card along with the words "Preview Edition" printed on the side. The box which contained all these cards had a SRP of $19.99.

Nm-Mt Ex-Mt
COMPLETE SET (60) 20.00 6.00
*:STARS: .4X TO 1X BASIC CARDS ....

1998 Upper Deck A Piece of the Action 1

Randomly inserted in first series packs at the rate of one in 2,500, cards from this set feature color photos of top players with pieces of actual game worn jerseys and/or game used bats embedded in the cards.

Nm-Mt Ex-Mt
1 Jay Buhner Bat 25.00 7.50
2 Tony Gwynn Bat 40.00 12.00
3 Tony Gwynn Jersey 40.00 12.00
4 Todd Hollandsworth Bat 20.00 6.00
5 T.Hollandsworth Jersey 20.00 6.00
6 Greg Maddux Jersey 60.00 18.00

	Nm-Mt	Ex-Mt
7 Alex Rodriguez Bat	50.00	15.00
8 Alex Rodriguez Jersey	50.00	15.00
9 Gary Sheffield Bat	25.00	7.50
10 Gary Sheffield Jersey	25.00	7.50

1998 Upper Deck A Piece of the Action 2

Randomly seeded into second series packs at a rate of 1:2500, each of these four different cards features pieces of both game-used bats and jerseys incorporated into the design of the card. According to information provided on the media release, only 225 of each card was produced. The cards are numbered by the player's initials.

	Nm-Mt	Ex-Mt
AJ Andruw Jones	50.00	15.00
GS Gary Sheffield	50.00	15.00
JB Jay Buhner	50.00	15.00
RA Roberto Alomar	80.00	24.00

1998 Upper Deck A Piece of the Action 3

Randomly seeded into third series packs, each of these cards featured a jersey swatch embedded on the card. The portion of the bat which was in series two is now just a design element. Ken Griffey, Jr. signed 24 of these cards and they were inserted into the packs as well.

	Nm-Mt	Ex-Mt
BG Ben Grieve/200	25.00	7.50
JC Jose Cruz Jr./200	25.00	7.50
KG Ken Griffey Jr./300	120.00	36.00
TL Travis Lee/200	25.00	7.50
KGS Ken Griffey Jr. AU/24		

1998 Upper Deck All-Star Credentials

Randomly inserted in packs at a rate of one in nine, this 30-card insert set features players who have the best chance of appearing in future All-Star games.

	Nm-Mt	Ex-Mt
COMPLETE SET (30)	100.00	30.00
AS1 Ken Griffey Jr.	5.00	1.50
AS2 Travis Lee	1.25	.35
AS3 Ben Grieve	1.25	.35
AS4 Jose Cruz Jr.	1.25	.35
AS5 Andruw Jones	1.25	.35
AS6 Craig Biggio	2.00	.60
AS7 Hideo Nomo	3.00	.90
AS8 Cal Ripken	10.00	3.00
AS9 Jaret Wright	1.25	.35
AS10 Mark McGwire	8.00	2.40
AS11 Derek Jeter	8.00	2.40
AS12 Scott Rolen	2.00	.60
AS13 Jeff Bagwell	2.00	.60
AS14 Manny Ramirez	1.25	.35
AS15 Alex Rodriguez	5.00	1.50
AS16 Chipper Jones	3.00	.90
AS17 Larry Walker	2.00	.60
AS18 Barry Bonds	8.00	2.40
AS19 Tony Gwynn	4.00	1.20
AS20 Mike Piazza	5.00	1.50
AS21 Roger Clemens	6.00	1.80
AS22 Greg Maddux	5.00	1.50
AS23 Jim Thome	3.00	.90
AS24 Tino Martinez	2.00	.60
AS25 Nomar Garciaparra	5.00	1.50
AS26 Juan Gonzalez	3.00	.90
AS27 Kenny Lofton	1.25	.35
AS28 Randy Johnson	3.00	.90
AS29 Todd Helton	2.00	.60
AS30 Frank Thomas	3.00	.90

1998 Upper Deck Amazing Greats

Randomly inserted in Series one packs, this 30-card set features color photos of amazing players printed on a hi-tech plastic card. Only 2000 of this set were produced and are sequentially numbered.

	Nm-Mt	Ex-Mt
COMPLETE SET (30)	400.00	120.00
*DIE CUTS: 1X TO 2.5X BASIC AMAZING		
DIE CUT PRINT RUN 250 SERIAL #'d SETS		
RANDOM INSERTS IN SER.1 PACKS..		

	Nm-Mt	Ex-Mt
AG1 Ken Griffey Jr.	12.00	3.60
AG2 Derek Jeter	20.00	6.00
AG3 Alex Rodriguez	12.00	3.60
AG4 Paul Molitor	5.00	1.50
AG5 Jeff Bagwell	5.00	1.50
AG6 Larry Walker	5.00	1.50
AG7 Kenny Lofton	3.00	.90
AG8 Cal Ripken	25.00	7.50
AG9 Juan Gonzalez	8.00	2.40
AG10 Chipper Jones	8.00	2.40
AG11 Greg Maddux	12.00	3.60
AG12 Roberto Alomar	8.00	2.40
AG13 Mike Piazza	12.00	3.60
AG14 Andres Galarraga	3.00	.90
AG15 Barry Bonds	20.00	6.00
AG16 Andy Pettitte	5.00	1.50
AG17 Nomar Garciaparra	12.00	3.60
AG18 Tino Martinez	5.00	1.50
AG19 Tony Gwynn	10.00	3.00
AG20 Frank Thomas	8.00	2.40
AG21 Roger Clemens	15.00	4.50
AG22 Sammy Sosa	12.00	3.60
AG23 Jose Cruz Jr.	3.00	.90
AG24 Manny Ramirez	3.00	.90
AG25 Mark McGwire	20.00	6.00
AG26 Randy Johnson	8.00	2.40
AG27 Mo Vaughn	3.00	.90
AG28 Gary Sheffield	3.00	.90
AG29 Andruw Jones	3.00	.90
AG30 Albert Belle	3.00	.90

1998 Upper Deck Blue Chip Prospects

Randomly inserted in Series two packs, this 30-card set features color photos of some of the league's most impressive prospects printed on die-cut acetate cards. Only 2,000 of each card were produced.

	Nm-Mt	Ex-Mt
COMPLETE SET (30)	250.00	75.00
BC1 Nomar Garciaparra	25.00	7.50
BC2 Scott Rolen	10.00	3.00
BC3 Jason Dickson	4.00	1.20
BC4 Darin Erstad	6.00	1.80
BC5 Brad Fullmer	4.00	1.20
BC6 Jaret Wright	4.00	1.20
BC7 Justin Thompson	4.00	1.20
BC8 Matt Morris	6.00	1.80
BC9 Fernando Tatis	4.00	1.20
BC10 Alex Rodriguez	25.00	7.50
BC11 Todd Helton	10.00	3.00
BC12 Andy Pettitte	10.00	3.00
BC13 Jose Cruz Jr.	6.00	1.80
BC14 Mark Kotsay	4.00	1.20
BC15 Derek Jeter	40.00	12.00
BC16 Paul Konerko	6.00	1.80
BC17 Todd Dunwoody	4.00	1.20
BC18 Vladimir Guerrero	15.00	4.50
BC19 Miguel Tejada	10.00	3.00
BC20 Chipper Jones	15.00	4.50
BC21 Kevin Orie	4.00	1.20
BC22 Juan Encarnacion	4.00	1.20
BC23 Brian Rose	4.00	1.20
BC24 Livan Hernandez	4.00	1.20
BC25 Andruw Jones	6.00	1.80
BC26 Brian Giles	6.00	1.80
BC27 Brett Tomko	4.00	1.20
BC28 Jose Guillen	4.00	1.20
BC29 Aaron Boone	6.00	1.80
BC30 Ben Grieve	4.00	1.20

1998 Upper Deck Clearly Dominant

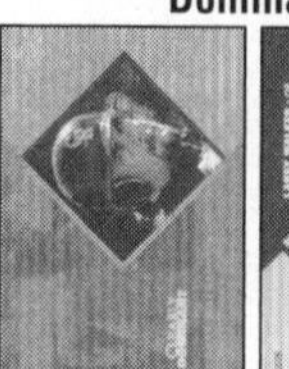
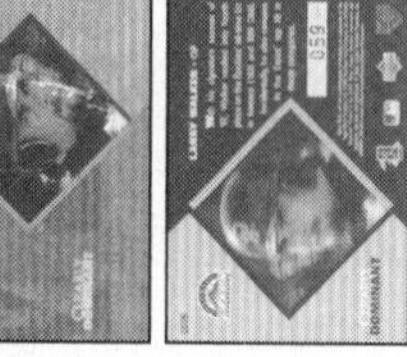

Randomly inserted in Series two packs, this 30-card set features color head photos of top players with a black-and-white action shot in the background printed on Light F/X plastic stock. Only 250 sequentially numbered sets were produced.

	Nm-Mt	Ex-Mt
COMPLETE SET (30)	800.00	240.00
CD1 Mark McGwire	40.00	12.00
CD2 Derek Jeter	40.00	12.00
CD3 Alex Rodriguez	25.00	7.50
CD4 Paul Molitor	10.00	3.00
CD5 Jeff Bagwell	10.00	3.00
CD6 Ivan Rodriguez	15.00	4.50
CD7 Kenny Lofton	6.00	1.80
CD8 Cal Ripken	50.00	15.00
CD9 Albert Belle	6.00	1.80
CD10 Chipper Jones	15.00	4.50
CD11 Gary Sheffield	6.00	1.80
CD12 Roberto Alomar	15.00	4.50
CD13 Mo Vaughn	6.00	1.80
CD14 Andres Galarraga	6.00	1.80
CD15 Nomar Garciaparra	25.00	7.50
CD16 Randy Johnson	15.00	4.50
CD17 Mike Mussina	15.00	4.50
CD18 Greg Maddux	25.00	7.50
CD19 Tony Gwynn	20.00	6.00
CD20 Frank Thomas	15.00	4.50
CD21 Roger Clemens	30.00	9.00
CD22 Dennis Eckersley	6.00	1.80
CD23 Juan Gonzalez	15.00	4.50
CD24 Tino Martinez	10.00	3.00
CD25 Andruw Jones	6.00	1.80
CD26 Larry Walker	10.00	3.00
CD27 Ken Caminiti	6.00	1.80
CD28 Mike Piazza	25.00	7.50
CD29 Barry Bonds	40.00	12.00
CD30 Ken Griffey Jr.	25.00	7.50

1998 Upper Deck Destination Stardom

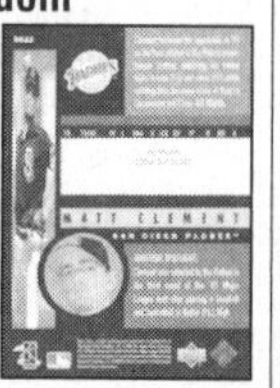

Randomly inserted in packs at a rate of one in five, this 60-card insert set features color action photos of today's star potential placed in a diamond-cut center with four colored corners. The cards are foil enhanced and die-cut.

	Nm-Mt	Ex-Mt
COMPLETE SET (60)	100.00	30.00
DS1 Travis Lee	1.00	.30
DS2 Nomar Garciaparra	6.00	1.80
DS3 Alex Gonzalez	1.00	.30
DS4 Richard Hidalgo	1.50	.45
DS5 Jaret Wright	1.00	.30
DS6 Mike Kinkade	4.00	1.20
DS7 Matt Morris	1.50	.45
DS8 Gary Matthews Jr.	4.00	1.20
DS9 Brett Tomko	1.00	.30
DS10 Todd Helton	2.50	.75
DS11 Scott Elarton	1.00	.30
DS12 Scott Rolen	2.50	.75
DS13 Jose Cruz Jr.	1.50	.45
DS14 Jarrod Washburn	1.50	.45
DS15 Sean Casey	1.50	.45
DS16 Magglio Ordonez	8.00	2.40
DS17 Gabe Alvarez	1.00	.30
DS18 Todd Dunwoody	1.00	.30
DS19 Kevin Witt	1.00	.30
DS20 Ben Grieve	1.00	.30
DS21 Daryle Ward	1.00	.30
DS22 Matt Clement	1.50	.45
DS23 Carlton Loewer	1.00	.30
DS24 Javier Vazquez	1.50	.45
DS25 Paul Konerko	1.50	.45
DS26 Preston Wilson	1.50	.45
DS27 Wes Helms	1.00	.30
DS28 Derek Jeter	10.00	3.00
DS29 Corey Koskie	4.00	1.20
DS30 Russell Branyan	1.00	.30
DS31 Vladimir Guerrero	4.00	1.20
DS32 Ryan Christenson	1.50	.45
DS33 Carlos Lee	4.00	1.20
DS34 Dave Dellucci	1.50	.45
DS35 Bruce Chen	1.00	.30
DS36 Ricky Ledee	1.00	.30
DS37 Ron Wright	1.00	.30
DS38 Derrek Lee	1.50	.45
DS39 Miguel Tejada	2.50	.75
DS40 Brad Fullmer	1.00	.30
DS41 Rich Butler	1.00	.30
DS42 Chris Carpenter	1.00	.30
DS43 Alex Rodriguez	6.00	1.80
DS44 Darron Ingram	1.50	.45
DS45 Kerry Wood	4.00	1.20
DS46 Jason Varitek	1.50	.45
DS47 Ramon Hernandez	1.00	.30
DS48 Aaron Boone	1.50	.45
DS49 Juan Encarnacion	1.00	.30
DS50 A.J. Hinch	1.00	.30
DS51 Mike Lowell	6.00	1.80
DS52 Fernando Tatis	1.00	.30
DS53 Jose Guillen	1.00	.30
DS54 Mike Caruso	1.00	.30
DS55 Carl Pavano	1.00	.30
DS56 Chris Clemons	1.00	.30
DS57 Mark L. Johnson	1.00	.30
DS58 Ken Cloude	1.00	.30
DS59 Rolando Arrojo	4.00	1.20
DS60 Mark Kotsay	1.00	.30

1998 Upper Deck Griffey Home Run Chronicles

Randomly inserted in first and second series packs at the rate of one in nine, this 56-card set features color photos of Ken Griffey Jr.'s 56 home runs of the 1997 season. The fronts of the Series one inserts have photos and a brief headline of each homer. The backs all have the same photo and more details about each homer. The cards are notated on the back with what date each homer was hit. Series two inserts feature game-dated photos from the actual games in which the homers were hit.

	Nm-Mt	Ex-Mt
COMPLETE SET (56)	100.00	30.00
COMMON GRIFFEY (1-56)	2.00	.60
COMMON GRIFFEY (1-7)	2.00	.60
COMMON PIAZZA (8-14)	2.50	.75
COMMON THOMAS (15-21)	.75	.23
COMMON MCGWIRE (22-28)	3.00	.90
COMMON RIPKEN (29-35)	4.00	1.20
COMMON GONZALEZ (36-42)	1.25	.35
COMMON GWYNN (43-49)	2.00	.60
COMMON BONDS (50-55)	3.00	.90
COMMON MADDUX (56-60)	2.50	.75

1998 Upper Deck National Pride

Randomly inserted in Series one packs at the rate of one in 23, this 42-card set features color photos of some of the league's great players from countries other than the United States printed on die-cut ranbow foil cards. The backs carry player information.

	Nm-Mt	Ex-Mt
NP1 Dave Nilsson	5.00	1.50
NP2 Larry Walker	8.00	2.40
NP3 Edgar Renteria	5.00	1.50
NP4 Jose Canseco	12.00	3.60
NP5 Rey Ordonez	5.00	1.50
NP6 Rafael Palmeiro	8.00	2.40
NP7 Livan Hernandez	5.00	1.50
NP8 Andruw Jones	5.00	1.50
NP9 Manny Ramirez	5.00	1.50
NP10 Sammy Sosa	20.00	6.00
NP11 Raul Mondesi	5.00	1.50
NP12 Moises Alou	5.00	1.50
NP13 Pedro Martinez	12.00	3.60
NP14 Vladimir Guerrero	12.00	3.60
NP15 Chili Davis	5.00	1.50
NP16 Hideo Nomo	12.00	3.60
NP17 Hideki Irabu	5.00	1.50
NP18 S.Hasegawa	5.00	1.50
NP19 Takashi Kashiwada	6.00	1.80
NP20 Chan Ho Park	5.00	1.50
NP21 Fernando Valenzuela	5.00	1.50
NP22 Vinny Castilla	5.00	1.50
NP23 Armando Reynoso	5.00	1.50
NP24 Karim Garcia	5.00	1.50
NP25 Marvin Benard	5.00	1.50
NP26 Mariano Rivera	8.00	2.40
NP27 Juan Gonzalez	12.00	3.60
NP28 Roberto Alomar	12.00	3.60
NP29 Ivan Rodriguez	12.00	3.60
NP30 Carlos Delgado	5.00	1.50
NP31 Bernie Williams	8.00	2.40
NP32 Edgar Martinez	8.00	2.40
NP33 Frank Thomas	12.00	3.60
NP34 Barry Bonds	30.00	9.00
NP35 Mike Piazza	20.00	6.00
NP36 Chipper Jones	12.00	3.60
NP37 Cal Ripken	40.00	12.00
NP38 Alex Rodriguez	20.00	6.00
NP39 Ken Griffey Jr.	20.00	6.00
NP40 Andres Galarraga	5.00	1.50
NP41 Omar Vizquel	5.00	1.50
NP42 Ozzie Guillen	5.00	1.50

1998 Upper Deck Power Deck Audio Griffey

In an effort to premier their new Power Deck Audio technology, Upper Deck created three special Ken Griffey Jr. cards (blue, green and silver backgrounds), each of which contained the same five minute interview with the Mariner's superstar. These cards were randomly seeded exclusively into test packs comprising only 10 percent of the total first series 1998 Upper Deck print run. The seeding ratios are as follows: blue 1:8, green 1:100 and silver 1:2400. Each test issue box contained a clear CD disc for which the card could be placed upon for playing on any common CD player. To play the card, the center hole had to be punched out. Prices below are for Mint unpunched cards. Punched out cards trade at twenty-five percent of the listed values.

	Nm-Mt	Ex-Mt
1 Ken Griffey Jr. Blue	2.00	.60
2 Ken Griffey Jr. Green	12.00	3.60
3 Ken Griffey Jr. Silver	40.00	12.00

1998 Upper Deck Prime Nine

Randomly inserted in Series two packs at the rate of one in five, this 60-card set features color photos of the current most popular players printed on premium silver card stock.

	Nm-Mt	Ex-Mt
COMPLETE SET (60)	100.00	30.00

1998 Upper Deck Retrospectives

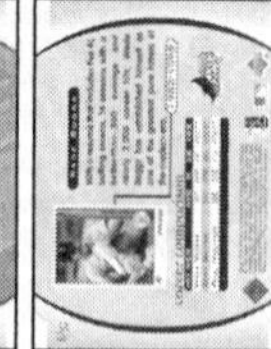

Randomly inserted in series three packs at a rate of one in 24, this 30-card insert set takes a look back at the unforgettable careers of some of baseball's most valuable contributors. The fronts feature a color action photo from each player's rookie season.

	Nm-Mt	Ex-Mt
1 Dennis Eckersley	3.00	.90
2 Rickey Henderson	8.00	2.40
3 Harold Baines	3.00	.90
4 Cal Ripken	25.00	7.50
5 Tony Gwynn	10.00	3.00
6 Wade Boggs	5.00	1.50
7 Orel Hershiser	3.00	.90
8 Joe Carter	3.00	.90
9 Roger Clemens	15.00	4.50
10 Barry Bonds	20.00	6.00
11 Mark McGwire	20.00	6.00
12 Greg Maddux	12.00	3.60
13 Fred McGriff	5.00	1.50
14 Rafael Palmeiro	5.00	1.50
15 Craig Biggio	5.00	1.50
16 Brady Anderson	3.00	.90
17 Randy Johnson	8.00	2.40
18 Gary Sheffield	3.00	.90
19 Albert Belle	3.00	.90
20 Ken Griffey Jr.	12.00	3.60
21 Juan Gonzalez	8.00	2.40
22 Larry Walker	5.00	1.50
23 Tino Martinez	5.00	1.50
24 Frank Thomas	8.00	2.40
25 Jeff Bagwell	5.00	1.50
26 Kenny Lofton	3.00	.90
27 Mo Vaughn	3.00	.90
28 Mike Piazza	12.00	3.60
29 Alex Rodriguez	12.00	3.60
30 Chipper Jones	8.00	2.40

1998 Upper Deck Rookie Edition Preview

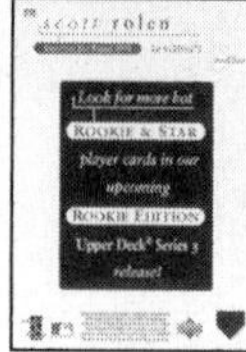

Randomly inserted in Upper Deck Series two packs at an approximate rate of one in six, this 10-card set features color photos of players who were top rookies. The backs carry player information.

	Nm-Mt	Ex-Mt
COMPLETE SET (10)	6.00	1.80
1 Nomar Garciaparra	2.00	.60
2 Scott Rolen	.75	.23
3 Mark Kotsay	.50	.15
4 Todd Helton	.75	.23
5 Paul Konerko	.50	.15
6 Juan Encarnacion	.50	.15
7 Brad Fullmer	.50	.15
8 Miguel Tejada	.75	.23
9 Richard Hidalgo	.50	.15
10 Ben Grieve	.50	.15

1998 Upper Deck Tape Measure Titans

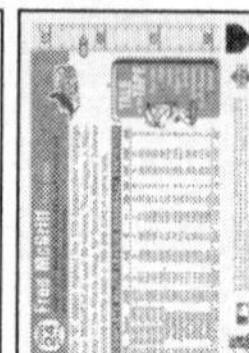

Randomly inserted in Series two packs at the rate of one in 23, this 30-card set features color photos of the league's most productive long-ball hitters printed on unique retro cards.

	Nm-Mt	Ex-Mt
COMPLETE SET (30)	150.00	45.00
*GOLD: .4X TO 1X BASIC TITAN		
GOLD: RANDOM IN RETAIL PACKS		
GOLD PRINT RUN 2667 SERIAL #'d SETS		
1 Mark McGwire	20.00	6.00
2 Andres Galarraga	3.00	.90
3 Jeff Bagwell	5.00	1.50
4 Larry Walker	5.00	1.50
5 Frank Thomas	8.00	2.40
6 Rafael Palmeiro	5.00	1.50
7 Nomar Garciaparra	12.00	3.60
8 Mo Vaughn	3.00	.90

9 Albert Belle 3.00 .90
10 Ken Griffey Jr. 12.00 3.60
11 Manny Ramirez 3.00 .90
12 Jim Thome 8.00 2.40
13 Tony Clark 3.00 .90
14 Juan Gonzalez 8.00 2.40
15 Mike Piazza 12.00 3.60
16 Jose Canseco 8.00 2.40
17 Jay Buhner 3.00 .90
18 Alex Rodriguez 12.00 3.60
19 Jose Cruz Jr. 3.00 .90
20 Tino Martinez 5.00 1.50
21 Carlos Delgado 3.00 .90
22 Andruw Jones 3.00 .90
23 Chipper Jones 8.00 2.40
24 Fred McGriff 5.00 1.50
25 Matt Williams 3.00 .90
26 Sammy Sosa 12.00 3.60
27 Vinny Castilla 3.00 .90
28 Tim Salmon 5.00 1.50
29 Ken Caminiti 3.00 .90
30 Barry Bonds 20.00 6.00

1998 Upper Deck Unparalleled

Randomly inserted in series three hobby packs only at a rate of one in 72, this 20-card insert set features color action photos on a high-tech designed card.

	Nm-Mt	Ex-Mt
COMPLETE SET (20)	250.00	75.00
1 Ken Griffey Jr.	15.00	4.50
2 Travis Lee	4.00	1.20
3 Ben Grieve	4.00	1.20
4 Jose Cruz Jr.	4.00	1.20
5 Nomar Garciaparra	15.00	4.50
6 Hideo Nomo	10.00	3.00
7 Kenny Lofton	4.00	1.20
8 Cal Ripken	30.00	9.00
9 Roger Clemens	20.00	6.00
10 Mike Piazza	15.00	4.50
11 Jeff Bagwell	6.00	1.80
12 Chipper Jones	10.00	3.00
13 Greg Maddux	15.00	4.50
14 Randy Johnson	10.00	3.00
15 Alex Rodriguez	15.00	4.50
16 Barry Bonds	25.00	7.50
17 Frank Thomas	10.00	3.00
18 Juan Gonzalez	10.00	3.00
19 Tony Gwynn	12.00	3.60
20 Mark McGwire	25.00	7.50

1998 Upper Deck Griffey Most Memorable Home Runs

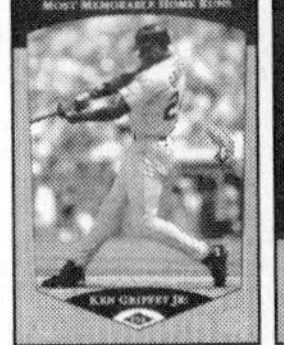

This 10-card set features color action photos of Ken Griffey Jr. hitting the most memorable home runs of his career printed on cards measuring approximately 3 1/2" by 5" with gold foil highlights. The backs carry another photo of the home run along with the date and why the home run was important in his career. Limited Edition Ken Griffey Jr. Autograph cards were randomly inserted in the set boxes. Also inserted was a special redemption card to be redeemed for an exclusive Ken Griffey Jr. 300th HR Commemorative Card or a special oversized card of equal or geater value.

	Nm-Mt	Ex-Mt
COMMON CARD (1-10)	1.25	.35

1998 Upper Deck Griffey Most Memorable Home Runs Autographed

Randomly inserted into the boxes Griffey Most Memorable Home Runs were these autographed cards. Ken Griffey Jr. signed 10 each of the cards in the set and the cards are all serial numbered on the front "x"/10. These cards were real difficult to pull and are rarely seen within the hobby so no pricing is currently provided for them.

	Nm-Mt	Ex-Mt
1 Ken Griffey Jr. 4/10/89		
2 Ken Griffey Jr. 9/14/90		
3 Ken Griffey Jr. 7/14/92		
4 Ken Griffey Jr. 7/28/93		
5 Ken Griffey Jr. 6/30/94		
6 Ken Griffey Jr. 8/24/95		
7 Ken Griffey Jr. 10/8/95		
8 Ken Griffey Jr. 4/25/97		
9 Ken Griffey Jr. 9/7/97		
10 Ken Griffey Jr. 9/27/97		

1998 Upper Deck Mark McGwire's Chase for 62

This 31-card set features color action photos of memorable moments in the 1998 season for Mark McGwire in his chase for 62 home runs. One oversized 3 1/2" by 5" commemorative card was included showing Big Mac's historical 61st and 62nd home runs. The set was distributed by the Home Shopping Network in a red box. The hobby box is yellow. The set carries a suggested retail price of $19.99. The oversize card is slightly different in each version (Home Shopping, Hobby and Retail) issued. However, there is no difference in the values of this card.

	Nm-Mt	Ex-Mt
COMP.FACT SET (31)	15.00	4.50
COMMON CARD (1-30)	.50	.15
4 Mark McGwire Ken Griffey Jr.	1.00	.30
NNO Mark McGwire 61st and 62nd homers	3.00	.90

1998 Upper Deck McGwire Jumbo

This one-card set measuring 3 1/2" by 5" commemorates Mark McGwire's 62nd Home Run. The front features two action player photos with a reproduction of a ticket stub from the game in the center with a red border. The card was originally offered on the Home Shopping Network and then sold to Hobby dealers. Only 16,200 of this card were produced and sequentially numbered.

	Nm-Mt	Ex-Mt
1 Mark McGwire	20.00	6.00

1998 Upper Deck Richie Ashburn

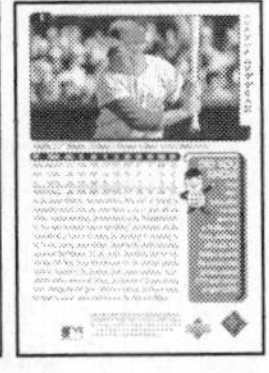

This one-card set was distributed as a wrapper redemption at SportsFest 98 held in Philadelphia. The front features a color action photo of Richie Ashburn with a white border. The back carries the top part of the photo with career statistics and player information.

	Nm-Mt	Ex-Mt
1 Richie Ashburn	2.00	.60

1999 Upper Deck

This 525-card set was distributed in two separate series. Series one packs contained cards 1-255 and series two contained 266-535. Cards 256-265 were never created. Subsets are as follows: Star Rookies (1-18, 266-292), Foreign Focus (229-246), Season Highlights Checklists (247-255, 527-535), and Arms Race '99 (518-526). The product was distributed in 10-card packs with a suggested retail price of $2.99. Though not confirmed by Upper Deck, it's widely believed by dealers that these subset cards were slightly short-printed in comparison to other cards in the set. Notable Rookie Cards include Pat Burrell. 100 signed 1989 Upper Deck Ken Griffey Jr. RC's were randomly seeded into series one packs. These signed cards are real 89 RC's and they contain an additional diamond shaped hologram on back signifying that UD has verified Griffey's signature. Approximately 350 Babe Ruth A Piece of History cards were randomly seeded into all series one packs at a rate of one in 15,000. 50 Babe Ruth A Piece of History 500 Club bat cards were randomly seeded into second series packs. Pricing for these bat cards can be referenced under 1999 Upper Deck A Piece of History 500 Club.

	Nm-Mt	Ex-Mt
COMPLETE SET (525)	100.00	30.00
COMP. SERIES 1 (255)	60.00	18.00
COMP. SERIES 2 (270)	40.00	12.00
COMMON (19-255/293-535)	.30	.09
COMMON SER.1 SR (1-18)	.50	.15
COMMON (266-292)	.50	.15
1 Troy Glaus SR	.75	.23
2 Adrian Beltre SR	.50	.15
3 Matt Anderson SR	.50	.15
4 Eric Chavez SR	.50	.15
5 Jin Ho Cho SR	.50	.15
6 Robert Smith SR	.50	.15
7 George Lombard SR	.50	.15
8 Mike Kinkade SR	.50	.15
9 Seth Greisinger SR	.50	.15
10 J.D. Drew SR	.50	.15
11 Aramis Ramirez SR	.50	.15
12 Carlos Guillen SR	.50	.15
13 Justin Baughman SR	.50	.15
14 Jim Parque SR	.50	.15
15 Ryan Jackson SR	.50	.15
16 Ramon E.Martinez SR RC	.50	.15
17 Orlando Hernandez SR	.50	.15
18 Jeremy Giambi SR	.50	.15
19 Gary DiSarcina	.30	.09
20 Darin Erstad	.30	.09
21 Troy Glaus	.50	.15
22 Chuck Finley	.30	.09
23 Dave Hollins	.30	.09
24 Troy Percival	.30	.09
25 Tim Salmon	.50	.15
26 Brian Anderson	.30	.09
27 Jay Bell	.30	.09
28 Andy Benes	.30	.09
29 Brent Brede	.30	.09
30 David Dellucci	.30	.09
31 Karim Garcia	.30	.09
32 Travis Lee	.30	.09
33 Andres Galarraga	.30	.09
34 Ryan Klesko	.30	.09
35 Keith Lockhart	.30	.09
36 Kevin Millwood	.30	.09
37 Denny Neagle	.30	.09
38 John Smoltz	.50	.15
39 Michael Tucker	.30	.09
40 Walt Weiss	.30	.09
41 Dennis Martinez	.30	.09
42 Javy Lopez	.30	.09
43 Brady Anderson	.30	.09
44 Harold Baines	.30	.09
45 Mike Bordick	.30	.09
46 Roberto Alomar	.75	.23
47 Scott Erickson	.30	.09
48 Mike Mussina	.75	.23
49 Cal Ripken	2.50	.75
50 Darren Bragg	.30	.09
51 Dennis Eckersley	.30	.09
52 Nomar Garciaparra	1.25	.35
53 Scott Hatteberg	.30	.09
54 Troy O'Leary	.30	.09
55 Bret Saberhagen	.30	.09
56 John Valentin	.30	.09
57 Rod Beck	.30	.09
58 Jeff Blauser	.30	.09
59 Brant Brown	.30	.09
60 Mark Clark	.30	.09
61 Mark Grace	.50	.15
62 Kevin Tapani	.30	.09
63 Henry Rodriguez	.30	.09
64 Mike Cameron	.30	.09
65 Mike Caruso	.30	.09
66 Ray Durham	.30	.09
67 Jaime Navarro	.30	.09
68 Magglio Ordonez	.30	.09
69 Mike Sirotka	.30	.09
70 Sean Casey	.30	.09
71 Barry Larkin	.75	.23
72 Jon Nunnally	.30	.09
73 Paul Konerko	.30	.09
74 Chris Stynes	.30	.09
75 Brett Tomko	.30	.09
76 Dmitri Young	.30	.09
77 Sandy Alomar Jr.	.30	.09
78 Bartolo Colon	.30	.09
79 Travis Fryman	.30	.09
80 Brian Giles	.30	.09
81 David Justice	.30	.09
82 Omar Vizquel	.30	.09
83 Jaret Wright	.30	.09
84 Jim Thome	.75	.23
85 Charles Nagy	.30	.09
86 Pedro Astacio	.30	.09
87 Todd Helton	.50	.15
88 Darryl Kile	.30	.09
89 Mike Lansing	.30	.09
90 Neifi Perez	.30	.09
91 John Thomson	.30	.09
92 Larry Walker	.50	.15
93 Tony Clark	.30	.09
94 Deivi Cruz	.30	.09
95 Damion Easley	.30	.09
96 Brian L.Hunter	.30	.09
97 Todd Jones	.30	.09
98 Brian Moehler	.30	.09
99 Gabe Alvarez	.30	.09
100 Craig Counsell	.30	.09
101 Cliff Floyd	.30	.09
102 Livan Hernandez	.30	.09
103 Andy Larkin	.30	.09
104 Derrek Lee	.30	.09
105 Brian Meadows	.30	.09
106 Moises Alou	.30	.09
107 Sean Berry	.30	.09
108 Craig Biggio	.50	.15
109 Ricky Gutierrez	.30	.09
110 Mike Hampton	.30	.09
111 Jose Lima	.30	.09
112 Billy Wagner	.30	.09
113 Hal Morris	.30	.09
114 Johnny Damon	.30	.09
115 Jeff King	.30	.09
116 Jeff Montgomery	.30	.09
117 Glendon Rusch	.30	.09
118 Larry Sutton	.30	.09
119 Bobby Bonilla	.30	.09
120 Jim Eisenreich	.30	.09
121 Eric Karros	.30	.09
122 Matt Luke	.30	.09
123 Ramon Martinez	.30	.09
124 Gary Sheffield	.30	.09
125 Eric Young	.30	.09
126 Charles Johnson	.30	.09
127 Jeff Cirillo	.30	.09
128 Marquis Grissom	.30	.09
129 Jeromy Burnitz	.30	.09
130 Bob Wickman	.30	.09
131 Scott Karl	.30	.09
132 Mark Loretta	.30	.09
133 Fernando Vina	.30	.09
134 Matt Lawton	.30	.09
135 Pat Meares	.30	.09
136 Eric Milton	.30	.09
137 Paul Molitor	.50	.15
138 David Ortiz	.30	.09
139 Todd Walker	.30	.09
140 Shane Andrews	.30	.09
141 Brad Fullmer	.30	.09
142 Vladimir Guerrero	.75	.23
143 Dustin Hermanson	.30	.09
144 Ryan McGuire	.30	.09
145 Ugueth Urbina	.30	.09
146 John Franco	.30	.09
147 Butch Huskey	.30	.09
148 Bobby Jones	.30	.09
149 John Olerud	.30	.09
150 Rey Ordonez	.30	.09
151 Mike Piazza	1.25	.35
152 Hideo Nomo	.75	.23
153 Masato Yoshii	.30	.09
154 Derek Jeter	2.00	.60
155 Chuck Knoblauch	.30	.09
156 Paul O'Neill	.50	.15
157 Andy Pettitte	.50	.15
158 Mariano Rivera	.50	.15
159 Darryl Strawberry	.50	.15
160 David Wells	.30	.09
161 Jorge Posada	.50	.15
162 Ramiro Mendoza	.30	.09
163 Miguel Tejada	.30	.09
164 Ryan Christenson	.30	.09
165 Rickey Henderson	.75	.23
166 A.J. Hinch	.30	.09
167 Ben Grieve	.30	.09
168 Kenny Rogers	.30	.09
169 Matt Stairs	.30	.09
170 Bob Abreu	.30	.09
171 Rico Brogna	.30	.09
172 Doug Glanville	.30	.09
173 Mike Grace	.30	.09
174 Desi Relaford	.30	.09
175 Scott Rolen	.50	.15
176 Jose Guillen	.30	.09
177 Francisco Cordova	.30	.09
178 Al Martin	.30	.09
179 Jason Schmidt	.30	.09
180 Turner Ward	.30	.09
181 Kevin Young	.30	.09
182 Mark McGwire	2.00	.60
183 Delino DeShields	.30	.09
184 Eli Marrero	.30	.09
185 Tom Lampkin	.30	.09
186 Ray Lankford	.30	.09
187 Willie McGee	.30	.09
188 Matt Morris UER Career strikeout totals are wrong	.30	.09
189 Andy Ashby	.30	.09
190 Kevin Brown	.50	.15
191 Ken Caminiti	.30	.09
192 Trevor Hoffman	.30	.09
193 Wally Joyner	.30	.09
194 Greg Vaughn	.30	.09
195 Danny Darwin	.30	.09
196 Shawn Estes	.30	.09
197 Orel Hershiser	.30	.09
198 Jeff Kent	.30	.09
199 Bill Mueller	.30	.09
200 Robb Nen	.30	.09
201 J.T. Snow	.30	.09
202 Ken Cloude	.30	.09
203 Russ Davis	.30	.09
204 Jeff Fassero	.30	.09
205 Ken Griffey Jr.	1.25	.35
206 Shane Monahan	.30	.09
207 David Segui	.30	.09
208 Dan Wilson	.30	.09
209 Wilson Alvarez	.30	.09
210 Wade Boggs	.50	.15
211 Miguel Cairo	.30	.09
212 Bubba Trammell	.30	.09
213 Quinton McCracken	.30	.09
214 Paul Sorrento	.30	.09
215 Kevin Stocker	.30	.09
216 Will Clark	.75	.23
217 Rusty Greer	.30	.09
218 Rick Helling	.30	.09
219 Mark McLemore	.30	.09
220 Ivan Rodriguez	.75	.23
221 John Wetteland	.30	.09
222 Jose Canseco	.75	.23
223 Roger Clemens	1.50	.45
224 Carlos Delgado	.30	.09
225 Darrin Fletcher	.30	.09
226 Alex Gonzalez	.30	.09
227 Jose Cruz Jr.	.30	.09
228 Shannon Stewart	.30	.09
229 Rolando Arrojo FF	.30	.09
230 Livan Hernandez FF	.30	.09
231 Orlando Hernandez FF	.30	.09
232 Raul Mondesi FF	.30	.09
233 Moises Alou FF	.30	.09
234 Pedro Martinez FF	.75	.23
235 Sammy Sosa FF	1.25	.35
236 Vladimir Guerrero FF	.75	.23
237 Bartolo Colon FF	.30	.09
238 Miguel Tejada FF	.30	.09
239 Ismael Valdes FF	.30	.09
240 Mariano Rivera FF	.50	.15
241 Jose Cruz Jr. FF	.30	.09
242 Juan Gonzalez FF	.75	.23
243 Ivan Rodriguez FF	.75	.23
244 Sandy Alomar Jr. FF	.30	.09
245 Roberto Alomar FF	.75	.23
246 Magglio Ordonez FF	.30	.09
247 Kerry Wood SH CL	.50	.15
248 Mark McGwire SH CL	2.00	.60
249 David Wells SH CL	.30	.09
250 Rolando Arrojo SH CL	.30	.09
251 Ken Griffey Jr. SH CL	1.25	.35
252 T.Hoffman SH CL	.30	.09
253 Travis Lee SH CL	.30	.09
254 R.Alomar SH CL	.50	.15
255 Sammy Sosa SH CL	1.25	.35
266 Pat Burrell SR RC	3.00	.90
267 S.Hillenbrand SR RC	1.50	.45
268 Robert Fick SR	.50	.15
269 Roy Halladay SR	.50	.15
270 Ruben Mateo SR	.50	.15
271 Bruce Chen SR	.50	.15
272 Angel Pena SR	.50	.15
273 Michael Barrett SR	.50	.15
274 Kevin Witt SR	.50	.15
275 Damon Minor SR	.50	.15
276 Ryan Minor SR	.50	.15
277 A.J. Pierzynski SR	.50	.15
278 A.J. Burnett SR RC	1.00	.30
279 Dermal Brown SR	.50	.15
280 Joe Lawrence SR	.50	.15
281 Derrick Gibson SR	.50	.15
282 Carlos Febles SR	.50	.15
283 Chris Haas SR	.50	.15
284 Cesar King SR	.50	.15
285 Calvin Pickering SR	.50	.15
286 Mitch Meluskey SR	.50	.15
287 Carlos Beltran SR	.50	.15
288 Ron Belliard SR	.50	.15
289 Jerry Hairston Jr. SR	.50	.15
290 F.Seguignol SR	.50	.15
291 Kris Benson SR	.50	.15
292 C.Hutchinson SR RC	.50	.15
293 Jarrod Washburn	.30	.09
294 Jason Dickson	.30	.09
295 Mo Vaughn	.30	.09
296 Garret Anderson	.30	.09
297 Jim Edmonds	.30	.09
298 Ken Hill	.30	.09
299 Shigetoshi Hasegawa	.30	.09
300 Todd Stottlemyre	.30	.09
301 Randy Johnson	.75	.23
302 Omar Daal	.30	.09
303 Steve Finley	.30	.09
304 Matt Williams	.30	.09
305 Danny Klassen	.30	.09
306 Tony Batista	.30	.09
307 Brian Jordan	.30	.09
308 Greg Maddux	1.25	.35
309 Chipper Jones	.75	.23
310 Bret Boone	.30	.09
311 Ozzie Guillen	.30	.09
312 John Rocker	.30	.09
313 Tom Glavine	.50	.15
314 Andruw Jones	.30	.09
315 Albert Belle	.30	.09
316 Charles Johnson	.30	.09
317 Will Clark	.75	.23
318 B.J. Surhoff	.30	.09
319 Delino DeShields	.30	.09
320 Heathcliff Slocumb	.30	.09
321 Sidney Ponson	.30	.09
322 Juan Guzman	.30	.09
323 Reggie Jefferson	.30	.09
324 Mark Portugal	.30	.09
325 Tim Wakefield	.30	.09
326 Jason Varitek	.30	.09
327 Jose Offerman	.30	.09
328 Pedro Martinez	.75	.23
329 Trot Nixon	.50	.15
330 Kerry Wood	.75	.23
331 Sammy Sosa	1.25	.35
332 Glenallen Hill	.30	.09
333 Gary Gaetti	.30	.09
334 Mickey Morandini	.30	.09
335 Benito Santiago	.30	.09
336 Jeff Blauser	.30	.09
337 Frank Thomas	.75	.23
338 Paul Konerko	.30	.09
339 Jaime Navarro	.30	.09
340 Carlos Lee	.30	.09
341 Brian Simmons	.30	.09
342 Mark Johnson	.30	.09
343 Jeff Abbott	.30	.09
344 Steve Avery	.30	.09
345 Mike Cameron	.30	.09
346 Michael Tucker	.30	.09
347 Greg Vaughn	.30	.09
348 Hal Morris	.30	.09
349 Pete Harnisch	.30	.09
350 Denny Neagle	.30	.09
351 Manny Ramirez	.30	.09
352 Roberto Alomar	.75	.23
353 Dwight Gooden	.50	.15
354 Kenny Lofton	.30	.09
355 Mike Jackson	.30	.09
356 Charles Nagy	.30	.09
357 Enrique Wilson	.30	.09
358 Russ Branyan	.30	.09
359 Richie Sexson	.30	.09
360 Vinny Castilla	.30	.09
361 Dante Bichette	.30	.09
362 Kirt Manwaring	.30	.09
363 Darryl Hamilton	.30	.09
364 Jamey Wright	.30	.09
365 Curtis Leskanic	.30	.09
366 Jeff Reed	.30	.09
367 Bobby Higginson	.30	.09
368 Justin Thompson	.30	.09
369 Brad Ausmus	.30	.09
370 Dean Palmer	.30	.09
371 Gabe Kapler	.30	.09
372 Juan Encarnacion	.30	.09
373 Karim Garcia	.30	.09
374 Alex Gonzalez	.30	.09
375 Braden Looper	.30	.09
376 Preston Wilson	.30	.09

377 Todd Dunwoody	.30	.09
378 Alex Fernandez	.30	.09
379 Mark Kotsay	.30	.09
380 Matt Mantei	.30	.09
381 Ken Caminiti	.30	.09
382 Scott Elarton	.30	.09
383 Jeff Bagwell	.50	.15
384 Derek Bell	.30	.09
385 Ricky Gutierrez	.30	.09
386 Richard Hidalgo	.30	.09
387 Shane Reynolds	.30	.09
388 Carl Everett	.30	.09
389 Scott Service	.30	.09
390 Jeff Suppan	.30	.09
391 Joe Randa	.30	.09
392 Kevin Appier	.30	.09
393 Shane Halter	.30	.09
394 Chad Kreuter	.30	.09
395 Mike Sweeney	.30	.09
396 Kevin Brown	.50	.15
397 Devon White	.30	.09
398 Todd Hollandsworth	.30	.09
399 Todd Hundley	.30	.09
400 Chan Ho Park	.30	.09
401 Mark Grudzielanek	.30	.09
402 Raul Mondesi	.30	.09
403 Ismael Valdes	.30	.09
404 Rafael Roque RC	.30	.09
405 Sean Berry	.30	.09
406 Kevin Barker	.30	.09
407 Dave Nilsson	.30	.09
408 Geoff Jenkins	.30	.09
409 Jim Abbott	.50	.15
410 Bobby Hughes	.30	.09
411 Corey Koskie	.30	.09
412 Rick Aguilera	.30	.09
413 LaTroy Hawkins	.30	.09
414 Ron Coomer	.30	.09
415 Denny Hocking	.30	.09
416 Marty Cordova	.30	.09
417 Terry Steinbach	.30	.09
418 Rondell White	.30	.09
419 Wilton Guerrero	.30	.09
420 Shane Andrews	.30	.09
421 Orlando Cabrera	.30	.09
422 Carl Pavano	.30	.09
423 Javier Vazquez	.30	.09
424 Chris Widger	.30	.09
425 Robin Ventura	.30	.09
426 Rickey Henderson	.75	.23
427 Al Leiter	.30	.09
428 Bobby Jones	.30	.09
429 Brian McRae	.30	.09
430 Roger Cedeno	.30	.09
431 Bobby Bonilla	.30	.09
432 Edgardo Alfonzo	.30	.09
433 Bernie Williams	.50	.15
434 Ricky Ledee	.30	.09
435 Chili Davis	.30	.09
436 Tino Martinez	.50	.15
437 Scott Brosius	.30	.09
438 David Cone	.30	.09
439 Joe Girardi	.30	.09
440 Roger Clemens	1.50	.45
441 Chad Curtis	.30	.09
442 Hideki Irabu	.30	.09
443 Jason Giambi	.75	.23
444 Scott Spiezio	.30	.09
445 Tony Phillips	.30	.09
446 Ramon Hernandez	.30	.09
447 Mike Macfarlane	.30	.09
448 Tom Candiotti	.30	.09
449 Billy Taylor	.30	.09
450 Bobby Estalella	.30	.09
451 Curt Schilling	.50	.15
452 Carlton Loewer	.30	.09
453 Marlon Anderson	.30	.09
454 Kevin Jordan	.30	.09
455 Ron Gant	.30	.09
456 Chad Ogea	.30	.09
457 Abraham Nunez	.30	.09
458 Jason Kendall	.30	.09
459 Pat Meares	.30	.09
460 Brant Brown	.30	.09
461 Brian Giles	.30	.09
462 Chad Hermansen	.30	.09
463 Freddy Adrian Garcia	.30	.09
464 Edgar Renteria	.30	.09
465 Fernando Tatis	.30	.09
466 Eric Davis	.30	.09
467 Darren Bragg	.30	.09
468 Donovan Osborne	.30	.09
469 Manny Aybar	.30	.09
470 Jose Jimenez	.30	.09
471 Kent Mercker	.30	.09
472 Reggie Sanders	.30	.09
473 Ruben Rivera	.30	.09
474 Tony Gwynn	1.00	.30
475 Jim Leyritz	.30	.09
476 Chris Gomez	.30	.09
477 Matt Clement	.30	.09
478 Carlos Hernandez	.30	.09
479 Sterling Hitchcock	.30	.09
480 Ellis Burks	.30	.09
481 Barry Bonds	2.00	.60
482 Marvin Benard	.30	.09
483 Kirk Rueter	.30	.09
484 F.P. Santangelo	.30	.09
485 Stan Javier	.30	.09
486 Jeff Kent	.30	.09
487 Alex Rodriguez	1.25	.35
488 Tom Lampkin	.30	.09
489 Jose Mesa	.30	.09
490 Jay Buhner	.30	.09
491 Edgar Martinez	.50	.15
492 Butch Huskey	.30	.09
493 John Mabry	.30	.09
494 Jamie Moyer	.30	.09
495 Roberto Hernandez	.30	.09
496 Tony Saunders	.30	.09
497 Fred McGriff	.50	.15
498 Dave Martinez	.30	.09
499 Jose Canseco	.75	.23
500 Rolando Arrojo	.30	.09
501 Esteban Yan	.30	.09
502 Juan Gonzalez	.75	.23
503 Rafael Palmeiro	.50	.15
504 Aaron Sele	.30	.09
505 Royce Clayton	.30	.09
506 Todd Zeile	.30	.09
507 Tom Goodwin	.30	.09
508 Lee Stevens	.30	.09
509 Esteban Loaiza	.30	.09
510 Joey Hamilton	.30	.09
511 Homer Bush	.30	.09
512 Willie Greene	.30	.09
513 Shawn Green	.30	.09
514 David Wells	.30	.09
515 Kelvim Escobar	.30	.09
516 Tony Fernandez	.30	.09
517 Pat Hentgen	.30	.09
518 Mark McGwire AR	1.00	.30
519 Ken Griffey Jr. AR	.75	.23
520 Sammy Sosa AR	.75	.23
521 Juan Gonzalez AR	.50	.15
522 J.D. Drew AR	.30	.09
523 Chipper Jones AR	.50	.15
524 Alex Rodriguez AR	.75	.23
525 Mike Piazza AR	.75	.23
526 N.Garciaparra AR	.75	.23
527 Mark McGwire SH CL	1.00	.30
528 Sammy Sosa SH CL	.75	.23
529 Scott Brosius SH CL	.30	.09
530 Cal Ripken SH CL	1.25	.35
531 Barry Bonds SH CL	.75	.23
532 Roger Clemens SH CL	.75	.23
533 Ken Griffey Jr. SH CL	.75	.23
534 Alex Rodriguez SH CL	.75	.23
535 Curt Schilling SH CL	.30	.09
NNO Ken Griffey Jr. 1989 AU/100	1000.00	300.00

1999 Upper Deck Exclusives Level 1

This 525-card set is a hobby only parallel version of the base set. Each card is sequentially numbered to 100 on back. In addition, Bronze foil fronts make them easy to differentiate from their silver foiled basic issue brethren. As is the case with the basic set, cards 256-265 were never printed due to a numbering error at the manufacturer.

Nm-Mt Ex-Mt

*STARS: 10X TO 25X BASIC CARDS ..
*SER.1 STAR ROOK: 4X TO 10X BASIC SR
*SER.2 STAR ROOK: 6X TO 15X BASIC SR

1999 Upper Deck 10th Anniversary Sweepstakes

These exchange cards were randomly seeded into first series hobby and retail packs. The lucky recipients were entitled to exchange their card to receive one of six different prizes (detailed in the listings below). Cards were seeded at an approximate rate of 1:1600 packs. Specific print runs for each prize are detailed below. It was later determined that due to an insertion error, three cards for the batting lesson, rather than the original one, was put into packs. The winners of the batting lesson never got a batting lesson with Griffey although they did get to meet Griffey during a UDA signing session.

	Nm-Mt	Ex-Mt
1 Ken Griffey Jr Batting Lesson 3		
2 1989 UD Factory Set 100	2.00	.60
3 Ken Griffey Jr. Autographed Photo/100	2.00	.60
4 1999 UD Baseball Box 250	2.00	.60
5 10th Ann. Cap/500	2.00	.60
6 Ken Griffey Jr. Commemorative Card/2400	2.00	.60

1999 Upper Deck 10th Anniversary Team

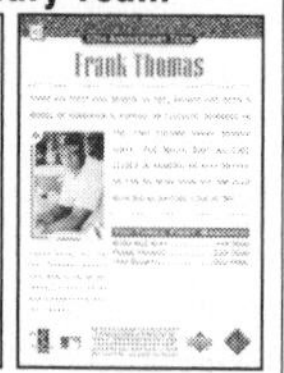

Randomly inserted in first series packs at the rate of one in four, this 30-card set features color photos of collectors' favorite players selected for this special All-Star team.

	Nm-Mt	Ex-Mt
COMPLETE SET (30)	50.00	15.00

*DOUBLES: 1.25X TO 3X BASIC 10TH ANN.
DOUBLES RANDOM INSERTS IN SER.1 PACKS
DOUBLES PRINT RUN 4000 SERIAL #'d SETS
*TRIPLES: 8X TO 20X BASIC 10TH ANN
TRIPLES RANDOM INSERTS IN SER.1 PACKS
TRIPLES PRINT RUN 100 SERIAL #'d SETS
HR'S RANDOM INSERTS IN SER.1 PACKS
HOME RUN PRINT RUN 1 SERIAL #'d SET
HR'S NOT PRICED DUE TO SCARCITY

X1 Mike Piazza	2.50	.75
X2 Mark McGwire	4.00	1.20
X3 Roberto Alomar	1.50	.45
X4 Chipper Jones	1.50	.45
X5 Cal Ripken	5.00	1.50
X6 Ken Griffey Jr.	2.50	.75
X7 Barry Bonds	4.00	1.20
X8 Tony Gwynn	2.00	.60
X9 Nolan Ryan	6.00	1.80
X10 Randy Johnson	1.50	.45
X11 Dennis Eckersley	.60	.18
X12 Ivan Rodriguez	1.50	.45
X13 Frank Thomas	1.50	.45
X14 Craig Biggio	1.00	.30
X15 Wade Boggs	1.00	.30
X16 Alex Rodriguez	2.50	.75
X17 Albert Belle	.60	.18
X18 Juan Gonzalez	1.50	.45
X19 Rickey Henderson	1.50	.45
X20 Greg Maddux	2.50	.75
X21 Tom Glavine	1.00	.30
X22 Randy Myers	.60	.18
X23 Sandy Alomar Jr.	.60	.18
X24 Jeff Bagwell	1.00	.30
X25 Derek Jeter	4.00	1.20
X26 Matt Williams	.60	.18
X27 Kenny Lofton	.60	.18
X28 Sammy Sosa	2.50	.75
X29 Larry Walker	1.00	.30
X30 Roger Clemens	3.00	.90

1999 Upper Deck A Piece of History

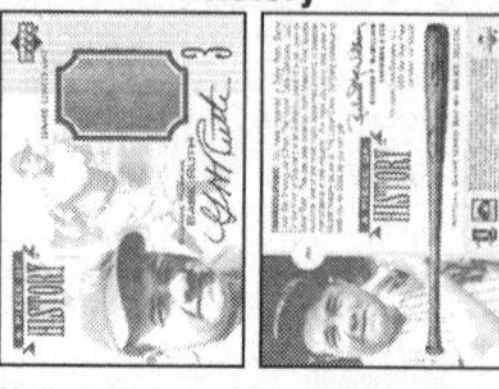

This limited edition set features photos of Babe Ruth along with a bat chip from an actual game-used Louisville Slugger swung by him during the late 20's. Approximately 350 cards were made and seeded into packs at a rate of 1:15,000. Another insert card incorporates both a "cut" signature of Ruth along with a piece of his game-used bat. Only three of these cards were produced.

	Nm-Mt	Ex-Mt
PHLC Babe Ruth AU/3		
PH Babe Ruth	800.00	240.00

1999 Upper Deck A Piece of History 500 Club

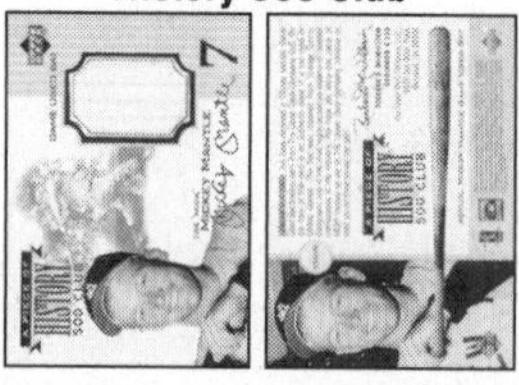

During the 1999 season, Upper Deck inserted into various products these cards which are cut up bats from all except one of the members of the 500 homer club. Mark McGwire asked that one of his bats not be included in this set, thus there was no Mark McGwire card in this grouping (until 2003 when McGwire signed a deal with Upper Deck). With the exception of Babe Ruth, approximately 350 of each card was produced. Only 50 Babe Ruth's were made. The cards were released in the following products: 1999 SP Authentic: Ernie Banks; 1999 SP Signature: Mel Ott; 1999 SPx: Willie Mays, 1999 UD Choice: Eddie Murray; 1999 UD Ionix: Frank Robinson; 1999 Upper Deck 2: Babe Ruth; 1999 Upper Deck Century Legends: Jimmie Foxx; 1999 Upper Deck Challengers for 70: Harmon Killebrew; 1999 Upper Deck HoloGrFx: Eddie Mathews and Willie McCovey; 1999 Upper Deck MVP: Mike Schmidt; 1999 Upper Deck Ovation: Mickey Mantle: 1999 Upper Deck Retro: Ted Williams; 2000 Black Diamond: Reggie Jackson; 2000 Upper Deck 1: Hank Aaron.

	Nm-Mt	Ex-Mt
BR Babe Ruth/50		
EB Ernie Banks	150.00	45.00
EM Eddie Mathews	150.00	45.00
EM Eddie Murray	150.00	45.00
FR Frank Robinson	120.00	36.00
HA Hank Aaron	250.00	75.00
HK Harmon Killebrew	150.00	45.00
JF Jimmie Foxx	200.00	60.00
MM Mickey Mantle	600.00	180.00
MO Mel Ott	150.00	45.00
MS Mike Schmidt	200.00	60.00
RJ Reggie Jackson	120.00	36.00
TW Ted Williams	250.00	75.00
WM Willie Mays	250.00	75.00
WM Willie McCovey	120.00	36.00
XX Instant Winner Card		

1999 Upper Deck A Piece of History 500 Club Autographs

As part of the Upper Deck A Piece of History 500 Club Autograph promotion, Upper Deck had most of the living members of the 500 homer club sign a number of cards which matched their uniform number. On some of the players, the cards are not priced due to scarcity. Each card is serial numbered on the front.

	Nm-Mt	Ex-Mt
EBAU Ernie Banks/14		
EMAU Eddie Mathews/41	1000.00	300.00
FRAU Frank Robinson/20		
HAAU Hank Aaron/44	1200.00	350.00
HKAU Harmon Killebrew/3		
MSAU Mike Schmidt/20		
RJAU Reggie Jackson/44	600.00	180.00
TWAU Ted Williams/9		
WMAU Willie Mays/24		
WMAU Willie McCovey/44	800.00	240.00

1999 Upper Deck Crowning Glory

Randomly inserted in first series packs at the rate of one in 23, this three-card set features color photos of players who reached major milestones during the '98 MLB season and printed on double sided cards.

	Nm-Mt	Ex-Mt
COMPLETE SET (3)	60.00	18.00

*DOUBLES: .6X TO 1.5X BASIC CROWN
DOUBLES RANDOM INSERTS IN SER.1 PACKS

DOUBLES PRINT RUN 1000 SERIAL #'d SETS
*TRIPLES: 4X TO 10X BASIC CROWN
TRIPLES RANDOM INSERTS IN SER.1 PACKS
TRIPLES PRINT RUN 25 SERIAL #'d SETS
HR'S RANDOM INSERTS IN SER.1 PACKS
HOME RUNS PRINT RUN 1 SERIAL #'d SET
HOME RUNS NOT PRICED DUE TO SCARCITY

CG1 Roger Clemens Kerry Wood	15.00	4.50
CG2 Mark McGwire Barry Bonds	20.00	6.00
CG3 Ken Griffey Jr. Mark McGwire	15.00	4.50

1999 Upper Deck Forte

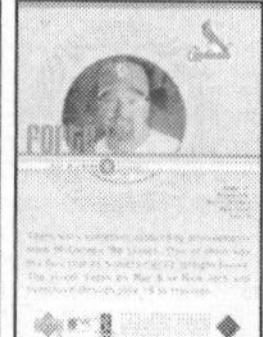

Randomly inserted in series two packs at the rate of one in 23, this 30-card set features color photos of the most collectible superstars captured on super premium cards with extensive rainbow foil coverage. Three limited parallel sets were also produced and randomly inserted into Series two packs. Forte Doubles was serially numbered to 2000; Forte Triples, to 100; and Forte Quadruples, to 10.

	Nm-Mt	Ex-Mt
COMPLETE SET (30)	200.00	60.00

*DOUBLES: .6X TO 1.5X BASIC FORTE
DOUBLES RANDOM INSERTS IN SER.2 PACKS
DOUBLES PRINT RUN 2000 SERIAL #'d SETS
*TRIPLES: 2X TO 5X BASIC FORTE ....
TRIPLES RANDOM INSERTS IN SER.2 PACKS
TRIPLES PRINT RUN 100 SERIAL #'d SETS
QUADS RANDOM INSERTS IN SER.2 PACKS
QUADRUPLES NOT PRICED DUE TO SCARCITY

F1 Darin Erstad	2.50	.75
F2 Troy Glaus	4.00	1.20
F3 Mo Vaughn	2.50	.75
F4 Greg Maddux	10.00	3.00
F5 Andres Galarraga	2.50	.75
F6 Chipper Jones	6.00	1.80
F7 Cal Ripken	20.00	6.00
F8 Albert Belle	2.50	.75
F9 Nomar Garciaparra	10.00	3.00
F10 Sammy Sosa	10.00	3.00
F11 Kerry Wood	6.00	1.80
F12 Frank Thomas	6.00	1.80
F13 Jim Thome	6.00	1.80
F14 Jeff Bagwell	4.00	1.20
F15 Vladimir Guerrero	6.00	1.80
F16 Mike Piazza	10.00	3.00
F17 Derek Jeter	15.00	4.50
F18 Ben Grieve	2.50	.75
F19 Eric Chavez	1.25	.35
F20 Scott Rolen	4.00	1.20
F21 Mark McGwire	15.00	4.50
F22 J.D. Drew	1.25	.35
F23 Tony Gwynn	8.00	2.40
F24 Barry Bonds	15.00	4.50
F25 Alex Rodriguez	10.00	3.00
F26 Ken Griffey Jr.	10.00	3.00
F27 Ivan Rodriguez	6.00	1.80
F28 Juan Gonzalez	6.00	1.80
F29 Roger Clemens	12.00	3.60
F30 Andruw Jones	2.50	.75

1999 Upper Deck Game Jersey

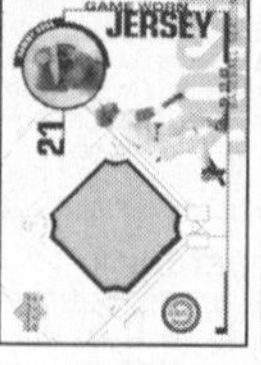
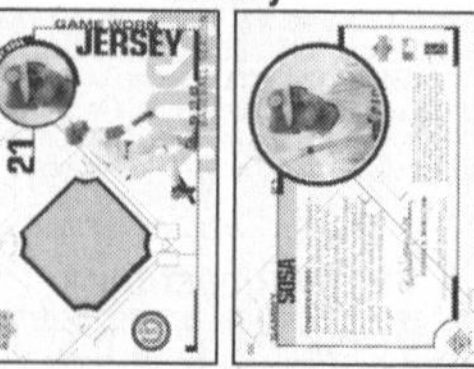

This set consists of 23 cards inserted in first and second series packs. Hobby packs contained Game Jersey hobby cards (signified in the listings with an H after the player's name) at a rate of 1:288. Hobby and retail packs contained much scarcer Game Jersey hobby/retail cards (signified with an H/R after the player's name in the listings below) at a rate of 1:2500. Each card features a piece of an actual game worn jersey. Five additional cards were signed by the athlete and serial numbered by hand to the player's respective jersey number. These rare signed Game Jersey cards are priced below but not considered part of the complete set.

	Nm-Mt	Ex-Mt
AB Adrian Beltre H1	25.00	7.50
AR Alex Rodriguez HR1	50.00	15.00
BF Brad Fullmer H2	15.00	4.50
BG Ben Grieve H1	15.00	4.50
BT Bubba Trammell H2	15.00	4.50
CJ Charles Johnson HR1	25.00	7.50
CJ Chipper Jones H2	40.00	12.00
DE Darin Erstad H1	25.00	7.50
EC Eric Chavez H2	25.00	7.50
FT Frank Thomas HR2	40.00	12.00
GM Greg Maddux HR2	50.00	15.00
IR Ivan Rodriguez H1	40.00	12.00
JD J.D. Drew H2	25.00	7.50
JG Juan Gonzalez HR1	40.00	12.00
JR K.Griffey Jr. HR2	50.00	15.00
KG K.Griffey Jr. H1	50.00	15.00
KW Kerry Wood HR1	40.00	12.00
MP Mike Piazza HR1	50.00	15.00
MR Manny Ramirez H2	25.00	7.50
NRA Nolan Ryan Astros H2	80.00	24.00
NRB Nolan Ryan Rangers HR2	80.00	24.00
SS Sammy Sosa H2	50.00	15.00
TH Todd Helton H2	40.00	12.00
TGW Tony Gwynn H2	40.00	12.00
TL Travis Lee H1	15.00	4.50
JDS J.Drew AU/8 H2		
JRS Ken Griffey Jr. AU/24 HR2		
KGAU Ken Griffey Jr. AU/24 H1		
KWAU Kerry Wood AU/34 HR1	250.00	75.00
NRAS Nolan Ryan Astros AU/34, H2	800.00	240.00

1999 Upper Deck Ken Griffey Jr. Box Blasters

These ten 5" by 7" cards were inserted one per Upper Deck special retail boxes. The cards feature oversize reprints of the regular issue Ken Griffey Jr. Upper Deck cards during both his 10 year career and the 10 seasons Upper Deck has made cards for. We have numbered the cards 1-10 based on the year of the card's original issue.

	Nm-Mt	Ex-Mt
COMPLETE SET (1-10)	50.00	15.00
COMMON CARD (1-10)	5.00	1.50

1999 Upper Deck Ken Griffey Jr. Box Blasters Autographs

Randomly seeded into one in every 64 special retail boxes, each of these attractive cards was signed by Ken Griffey Jr. The cards are oversized 5" by 7" replicas of each of Griffey's basic issue Upper Deck cards from 1989-1999. The backs of the cards provide a certificate of authenticity from UD Chairman and CEO Richard McWilliam.

	Nm-Mt	Ex-Mt
COMMON CARD	100.00	30.00
KG1989 Ken Griffey Jr. AU 89	200.00	60.00

1999 Upper Deck Immaculate Perception

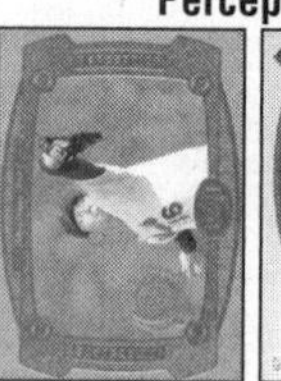

Randomly inserted in Series one packs at the rate of one in 23, this 27-card set features top player photos printed on unique, foil-enhanced cards.

	Nm-Mt	Ex-Mt
COMPLETE SET (27)	250.00	75.00

*DOUBLES: .75X TO 2X BASIC IMM.PERC.
DOUBLES RANDOM INSERTS IN SER.1 PACKS
DOUBLES PRINT RUN 1000 SERIAL #'d SETS
*TRIPLES: 5X TO 12X BASIC IMM.PERC.
TRIPLES RANDOM INSERTS IN SER.1 PACKS
TRIPLES PRINT RUN 25 SERIAL #'d SETS
HR'S RANDOM INSERTS IN SER.1 PACKS
HOME RUNS PRINT RUN 1 SERIAL #'d SET
HOME RUNS NOT PRICED DUE TO SCARCITY

I1 Jeff Bagwell	5.00	1.50
I2 Craig Biggio	5.00	1.50
I3 Barry Bonds	20.00	6.00
I4 Roger Clemens	15.00	4.50
I5 Jose Cruz Jr.	3.00	.90
I6 Nomar Garciaparra	12.00	3.60
I7 Tony Clark	3.00	.90
I8 Ben Grieve	3.00	.90
I9 Ken Griffey Jr.	12.00	3.60
I10 Tony Gwynn	10.00	3.00
I11 Randy Johnson	8.00	2.40
I12 Chipper Jones	8.00	2.40
I13 Travis Lee	3.00	.90
I14 Kenny Lofton	3.00	.90
I15 Greg Maddux	12.00	3.60

I16 Mark McGwire 20.00 6.00
I17 Hideo Nomo 8.00 2.40
I18 Mike Piazza 12.00 3.60
I19 Manny Ramirez 3.00 .90
I20 Cal Ripken 25.00 7.50
I21 Alex Rodriguez 12.00 3.60
I22 Scott Rolen 5.00 1.50
I23 Frank Thomas 8.00 2.40
I24 Kerry Wood 8.00 2.40
I25 Larry Walker 5.00 1.50
I26 Vinny Castilla 3.00 .90
I27 Derek Jeter 20.00 6.00

1999 Upper Deck Textbook Excellence

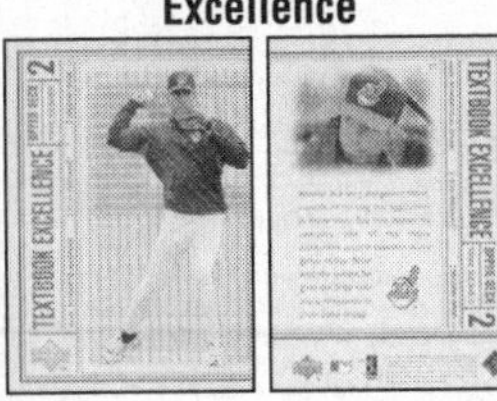

Inserted one every 23 second series packs, these cards offer information on the skills of some of the game's most fundamentally sound performers.

Nm-Mt Ex-Mt
COMPLETE SET (30) 50.00 15.00
*DOUBLES: 1.5X TO 4X BASIC TEXTBOOK
DOUBLES RANDOM INSERTS IN SER.2 PACKS
DOUBLES PRINT RUN 2000 SERIAL #'d SETS
*TRIPLES: 6X TO 15X BASIC TEXTBOOK
TRIPLES RANDOM INSERTS IN SER.2 PACKS
TRIPLES PRINT RUN 100 SERIAL #'d SETS
QUADS RANDOM INSERTS IN SER.2 PACKS
QUADRUPLES PRINT RUN 10 SERIAL #'d SETS
QUADRUPLES NOT PRICED DUE TO SCARCITY
T1 Mo Vaughn .75 .23
T2 Greg Maddux 3.00 .90
T3 Chipper Jones 2.00 .60
T4 Andruw Jones .75 .23
T5 Cal Ripken 6.00 1.80
T6 Albert Belle .75 .23
T7 Roberto Alomar 2.00 .60
T8 Nomar Garciaparra 3.00 .90
T9 Kerry Wood 2.00 .60
T10 Sammy Sosa 3.00 .90
T11 Greg Vaughn .75 .23
T12 Jeff Bagwell 1.25 .35
T13 Kevin Brown 1.25 .35
T14 Vladimir Guerrero 2.00 .60
T15 Mike Piazza 3.00 .90
T16 Bernie Williams 1.25 .35
T17 Derek Jeter 5.00 1.50
T18 Ben Grieve .75 .23
T19 Eric Chavez .40 .12
T20 Scott Rolen 1.25 .35
T21 Mark McGwire 5.00 1.50
T22 David Wells .75 .23
T23 J.D. Drew .40 .12
T24 Tony Gwynn 2.50 .75
T25 Barry Bonds 5.00 1.50
T26 Alex Rodriguez 3.00 .90
T27 Ken Griffey Jr. 3.00 .90
T28 Juan Gonzalez 2.00 .60
T29 Ivan Rodriguez 2.00 .60
T30 Roger Clemens 4.00 1.20

1999 Upper Deck View to a Thrill

These cards, inserted one every seven second series packs feature special die-cuts and embossing and takes a new look at 30 of the best overall athletes in baseball.

Nm-Mt Ex-Mt
COMPLETE SET (30) 100.00 30.00
*DOUBLES: 1X TO 2.5X BASIC VIEW .
DOUBLES RANDOM INSERTS IN SER.2 PACKS
DOUBLES PRINT RUN 2000 SERIAL #'d SETS
*TRIPLES: 4X TO 10X BASIC VIEW ....
TRIPLES RANDOM INSERTS IN SER.2 PACKS
TRIPLES PRINT RUN 100 SERIAL #'d SETS
QUADS RANDOM INSERTS IN SER.2 PACKS
QUADRUPLES PRINT RUN 10 SERIAL #'d SETS
QUADRUPLES NOT PRICED DUE TO SCARCITY
V1 Mo Vaughn 1.25 .35
V2 Darin Erstad 1.25 .35
V3 Travis Lee 1.25 .35
V4 Chipper Jones 3.00 .90
V5 Greg Maddux 5.00 1.50
V6 Gabe Kapler 1.25 .35
V7 Cal Ripken 10.00 3.00
V8 Nomar Garciaparra 5.00 1.50
V9 Kerry Wood 3.00 .90
V10 Frank Thomas 3.00 .90
V11 Manny Ramirez 1.25 .35
V12 Larry Walker 2.00 .60
V13 Tony Clark 1.25 .35
V14 Jeff Bagwell 2.00 .60
V15 Craig Biggio 2.00 .60
V16 Vladimir Guerrero 3.00 .90
V17 Mike Piazza 5.00 1.50
V18 Bernie Williams 2.00 .60
V19 Derek Jeter 8.00 2.40
V20 Ben Grieve 1.25 .35
V21 Eric Chavez .60 .18
V22 Scott Rolen 2.00 .60
V23 Mark McGwire 8.00 2.40
V24 Tony Gwynn 4.00 1.20
V25 Barry Bonds 8.00 2.40
V26 Ken Griffey Jr. 5.00 1.50
V27 Alex Rodriguez 5.00 1.50
V28 J.D. Drew .60 .18
V29 Juan Gonzalez 3.00 .90
V30 Roger Clemens 6.00 1.80

1999 Upper Deck Wonder Years

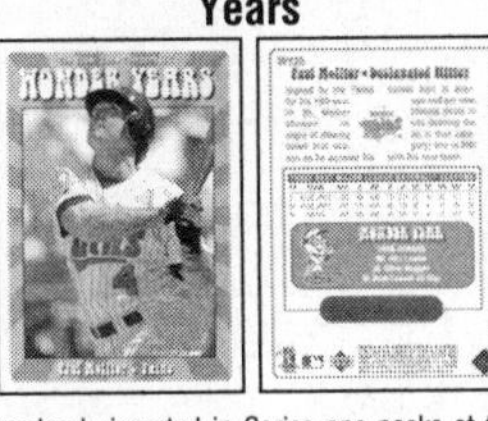

Randomly inserted in Series one packs at the rate of one in seven, this 30-card set features color photos of top stars.

Nm-Mt Ex-Mt
COMPLETE SET (30) 80.00 24.00
*DOUBLES: 1X TO 2.5X BASIC WONDER
DOUBLES RANDOM INSERTS IN SER.1 PACKS
DOUBLES PRINT RUN 2000 SERIAL #'d SETS
*TRIPLES: 8X TO 20X BASIC WONDER
TRIPLES RANDOM INSERTS IN SER.1 PACKS
TRIPLES PRINT RUN 50 SERIAL #'d SETS
HR'S RANDOM INSERTS IN SER.1 PACKS
HOME RUNS PRINT RUN 1 SERIAL #'d SET
HOME RUNS NOT PRICED DUE TO SCARCITY
W1 Kerry Wood 3.00 .90
W2 Travis Lee 1.25 .35
W3 Jeff Bagwell 2.00 .60
W4 Barry Bonds 8.00 2.40
W5 Roger Clemens 6.00 1.80
W6 Jose Cruz Jr. 1.25 .35
W7 Andres Galarraga 1.25 .35
W8 Nomar Garciaparra 5.00 1.50
W9 Juan Gonzalez 3.00 .90
W10 Ken Griffey Jr. 5.00 1.50
W11 Tony Gwynn 4.00 1.20
W12 Derek Jeter 8.00 2.40
W13 Randy Johnson 3.00 .90
W14 Andruw Jones 1.25 .35
W15 Chipper Jones 3.00 .90
W16 Kenny Lofton 1.25 .35
W17 Greg Maddux 5.00 1.50
W18 Tino Martinez 2.00 .60
W19 Mark McGwire 8.00 2.40
W20 Paul Molitor 2.00 .60
W21 Mike Piazza 5.00 1.50
W22 Manny Ramirez 1.25 .35
W23 Cal Ripken 10.00 3.00
W24 Alex Rodriguez 5.00 1.50
W25 Sammy Sosa 5.00 1.50
W26 Frank Thomas 3.00 .90
W27 Mo Vaughn 1.25 .35
W28 Larry Walker 2.00 .60
W29 Scott Rolen 2.00 .60
W30 Ben Grieve 1.25 .35

1999 Upper Deck Employment Promo

This card was used as a promotional tool by Upper Deck to thank anyone who applied for a job there. The card features Upper Deck corporate spokesperson Ken Griffey Jr.

Nm-Mt Ex-Mt
NNO Ken Griffey Jr. 2.00 .60

1999 Upper Deck Ken Griffey Jr Santa

This one card was issued to Upper Deck employees as well as some of their direct dealers. The card features a photo of Griffey on the front along a swatch of the "Santa" hat he wore for the shoot. The back has a congratulatory message from Upper Deck.

Nm-Mt Ex-Mt
1 Ken Griffey Jr. 50.00 15.00

1999 Upper Deck Mark McGwire Tribute

This 30 card standard-size set was released by Upper Deck in 1999 to commemorate Mark McGwire's 70 home run season in 1998. The set was issued in a lunch box and each card features a highlight from the 1998 season. There is an action shot on the front of the card along with a little inset portrait photo. The back gives big play to the date along with a description of what happenned on that day.

Nm-Mt Ex-Mt
COMP. FACT SET 15.00 4.50
COMMON CARD .75 .23

1999 Upper Deck McGwire 500 Home Run Set

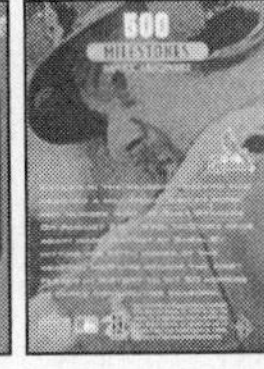

This 30 card box set honors Mark McGwire hitting his 500th homer during the 1999 season. The cards were issued in a special box which also commemorated the feat.

Nm-Mt Ex-Mt
COMP. FACT SET (30) 20.00 6.00
COMMON CARD (1-30) .75 .23

2000 Upper Deck

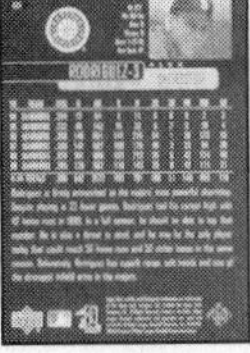

Upper Deck Series one was released in December, 1999 and offered 270 standard-size cards. The first series was distributed in 10 card packs with a SRP of $2.99 per pack. The second series was released in July, 2000 and offered 270 standard-size cards. The cards were issued in 24 pack boxes. Cards numbered 1-28 and 271-297 are Star Rookie subsets while cards numbered 262-270 and 532-540 feature 1999 season highlights and have checklists on back. Cards 523-531 feature the All-UD Team subset - a collection of top stars as selected by Upper Deck. Notable Rookie Cards include Kazuhiro Sasaki. Also, 350 1999 A Piece of History 500 Club Hank Aaron bat cards were randomly seeded into first series packs. In addition, Aaron signed and numbered 44 copies. Pricing for these bat cards can be referenced under 1999 Upper Deck A Piece of History 500 Club. Also, a selection of A Piece of History 3000 Club Hank Aaron memorabilia cards were randomly seeded into second series packs. 350 bat cards, 350 jersey cards, 100 hand-numbered, combination bat-jersey cards and forty-four hand-numbered, autographed, combination bat-jersey cards were produced. Pricing for these memorabilia cards can be referenced under 2000 Upper Deck A Piece of History 3000 Club.

Nm-Mt Ex-Mt
COMPLETE SET (540) 100.00 30.00
COMP. SERIES 1 (270) 50.00 15.00
COMP. SERIES 2 (270) 50.00 15.00
COMMON (28-270/298-540) .30 .09
COMMON (1-28/271-297) .50 .15
1 Rick Ankiel SR .50 .15
2 Vernon Wells SR .75 .23
3 Ryan Anderson SR .50 .15
4 Ed Yarnall SR .50 .15
5 Brian McNichol SR .50 .15
6 Ben Petrick SR .50 .15
7 Kip Wells SR .50 .15
8 Eric Munson SR .50 .15
9 Matt Riley SR .50 .15
10 Peter Bergeron SR .50 .15
11 Eric Gagne SR 2.00 .60
12 Ramon Ortiz SR .50 .15
13 Josh Beckett SR 4.00 1.20
14 Alfonso Soriano SR 2.00 .60
15 Jorge Toca SR .50 .15
16 Buddy Carlyle SR .50 .15
17 Chad Hermansen SR .50 .15
18 Matt Perisho SR .50 .15
19 Tomokazu Ohka SR RC .75 .23
20 Jacque Jones SR .75 .23
21 Josh Paul SR .50 .15
22 Dermal Brown SR .50 .15
23 Adam Kennedy SR .50 .15
24 Chad Harville SR .50 .15
25 Calvin Murray SR .50 .15
26 Chad Meyers SR .50 .15
27 Brian Cooper SR .50 .15
28 Troy Glaus .50 .15
29 Ben Molina .30 .09
30 Troy Percival .50 .15
31 Ken Hill .30 .09
32 Chuck Finley .50 .15
33 Todd Greene .30 .09
34 Tim Salmon .50 .15
35 Gary DiSarcina .30 .09
36 Luis Gonzalez .30 .09
37 Tony Womack .30 .09
38 Omar Daal .30 .09
39 Randy Johnson .75 .23
40 Erubiel Durazo .30 .09
41 Jay Bell .30 .09
42 Steve Finley .30 .09
43 Travis Lee .30 .09
44 Greg Maddux 1.25 .35
45 Bret Boone .30 .09
46 Brian Jordan .30 .09
47 Kevin Millwood .30 .09
48 Odalis Perez .30 .09
49 Javy Lopez .30 .09
50 John Smoltz .50 .15
51 Bruce Chen .30 .09
52 Albert Belle .30 .09
53 Jerry Hairston Jr. .30 .09
54 Will Clark .75 .23
55 Sidney Ponson .30 .09
56 Charles Johnson .30 .09
57 Cal Ripken 2.50 .75
58 Ryan Minor .30 .09
59 Mike Mussina .75 .23
60 Tom Gordon .30 .09
61 Jose Offerman .30 .09
62 Trot Nixon .50 .15
63 Pedro Martinez .75 .23
64 John Valentin .30 .09
65 Jason Varitek .30 .09
66 Juan Pena .30 .09
67 Troy O'Leary .30 .09
68 Sammy Sosa 1.25 .35
69 Henry Rodriguez .30 .09
70 Kyle Farnsworth .30 .09
71 Glenallen Hill .30 .09
72 Lance Johnson .30 .09
73 Mickey Morandini .30 .09
74 Jon Lieber .30 .09
75 Kevin Tapani .30 .09
76 Carlos Lee .30 .09
77 Ray Durham .30 .09
78 Jim Parque .30 .09
79 Bob Howry .30 .09
80 Magglio Ordonez .30 .09
81 Paul Konerko .30 .09
82 Mike Caruso .30 .09
83 Chris Singleton .30 .09
84 Sean Casey .30 .09
85 Barry Larkin .75 .23
86 Pokey Reese .30 .09
87 Eddie Taubensee .30 .09
88 Scott Williamson .30 .09
89 Jason LaRue .30 .09
90 Aaron Boone .30 .09
91 Jeffrey Hammonds .30 .09
92 Omar Vizquel .30 .09
93 Manny Ramirez .30 .09
94 Kenny Lofton .30 .09
95 Jaret Wright .30 .09
96 Einar Diaz .30 .09
97 Charles Nagy .30 .09
98 David Justice .30 .09
99 Richie Sexson .30 .09
100 Steve Karsay .30 .09
101 Todd Helton .50 .15
102 Dante Bichette .30 .09
103 Larry Walker .50 .15
104 Pedro Astacio .30 .09
105 Neifi Perez .30 .09
106 Brian Bohanon .30 .09
107 Edgard Clemente .30 .09
108 Dave Veres .30 .09
109 Gabe Kapler .30 .09
110 Juan Encarnacion .30 .09
111 Jeff Weaver .30 .09
112 Damion Easley .30 .09
113 Justin Thompson .30 .09
114 Brad Ausmus .30 .09
115 Frank Catalanotto .30 .09
116 Todd Jones .30 .09
117 Preston Wilson .30 .09
118 Cliff Floyd .30 .09
119 Mike Lowell .30 .09
120 Antonio Alfonseca .30 .09
121 Alex Gonzalez .30 .09
122 Braden Looper .30 .09
123 Bruce Aven .30 .09
124 Richard Hidalgo .30 .09
125 Mitch Meluskey .30 .09
126 Jeff Bagwell .50 .15
127 Jose Lima .30 .09
128 Derek Bell .30 .09
129 Billy Wagner .30 .09
130 Shane Reynolds .30 .09
131 Moises Alou .30 .09
132 Carlos Beltran .30 .09
133 Carlos Febles .30 .09
134 Jermaine Dye .30 .09
135 Jeremy Giambi .30 .09
136 Joe Randa .30 .09
137 Jose Rosado .30 .09
138 Chad Kreuter .30 .09
139 Jose Vizcaino .30 .09
140 Adrian Beltre .30 .09
141 Kevin Brown .50 .15
142 Ismael Valdes .30 .09
143 Angel Pena .30 .09
144 Chan Ho Park .30 .09
145 Mark Grudzielanek .30 .09
146 Jeff Shaw .30 .09
147 Geoff Jenkins .30 .09
148 Jeromy Burnitz .30 .09
149 Hideo Nomo .75 .23
150 Ron Belliard .30 .09
151 Sean Berry .30 .09
152 Mark Loretta .30 .09
153 Steve Woodard .30 .09
154 Joe Mays .30 .09
155 Eric Milton .30 .09
156 Corey Koskie .30 .09
157 Ron Coomer .30 .09
158 Brad Radke .30 .09
159 Terry Steinbach .30 .09
160 Cristian Guzman .30 .09
161 Vladimir Guerrero .75 .23
162 Wilton Guerrero .30 .09
163 Michael Barrett .30 .09
164 Chris Widger .30 .09
165 Fernando Seguignol .30 .09
166 Ugueth Urbina .30 .09
167 Dustin Hermanson .30 .09
168 Kenny Rogers .30 .09
169 Edgardo Alfonzo .30 .09
170 Orel Hershiser .30 .09
171 Robin Ventura .30 .09
172 Octavio Dotel .30 .09
173 Rickey Henderson .75 .23
174 Roger Cedeno .30 .09
175 John Olerud .30 .09
176 Derek Jeter 2.00 .60
177 Tino Martinez .50 .15
178 Orlando Hernandez .30 .09
179 Chuck Knoblauch .30 .09
180 Bernie Williams .50 .15
181 Chili Davis .30 .09
182 David Cone .30 .09
183 Ricky Ledee .30 .09
184 Paul O'Neill .50 .15
185 Jason Giambi .75 .23
186 Eric Chavez .30 .09
187 Matt Stairs .30 .09
188 Miguel Tejada .30 .09
189 Olmedo Saenz .30 .09
190 Tim Hudson .50 .15
191 John Jaha .30 .09
192 Randy Velarde .30 .09
193 Rico Brogna .30 .09
194 Mike Lieberthal .30 .09
195 Marlon Anderson .30 .09
196 Bob Abreu .30 .09
197 Ron Gant .30 .09
198 Randy Wolf .30 .09
199 Desi Relaford .30 .09
200 Doug Glanville .30 .09
201 Warren Morris .30 .09
202 Kris Benson .30 .09
203 Kevin Young .30 .09
204 Brian Giles .30 .09
205 Jason Schmidt .30 .09
206 Ed Sprague .30 .09
207 Francisco Cordova .30 .09
208 Mark McGwire 2.00 .60
209 Jose Jimenez .30 .09
210 Fernando Tatis .30 .09
211 Kent Bottenfield .30 .09
212 Eli Marrero .30 .09
213 Edgar Renteria .30 .09
214 Joe McEwing .30 .09
215 J.D. Drew .30 .09
216 Tony Gwynn 1.00 .30
217 Gary Matthews Jr. .30 .09
218 Eric Owens .30 .09
219 Damian Jackson .30 .09
220 Reggie Sanders .30 .09
221 Trevor Hoffman .30 .09
222 Ben Davis .30 .09
223 Shawn Estes .30 .09
224 F.P. Santangelo .30 .09
225 Livan Hernandez .30 .09
226 Ellis Burks .30 .09
227 J.T. Snow .30 .09
228 Jeff Kent .30 .09
229 Robb Nen .30 .09
230 Marvin Benard .30 .09
231 Ken Griffey Jr. 1.25 .35
232 John Halama .30 .09
233 Gil Meche .30 .09
234 David Bell .30 .09
235 Brian Hunter .30 .09
236 Jay Buhner .30 .09
237 Edgar Martinez .50 .15
238 Jose Mesa .30 .09
239 Wilson Alvarez .30 .09
240 Wade Boggs .50 .15
241 Fred McGriff .50 .15
242 Jose Canseco .75 .23
243 Kevin Stocker .30 .09
244 Roberto Hernandez .30 .09
245 Bubba Trammell .30 .09
246 John Flaherty .30 .09
247 Ivan Rodriguez .75 .23
248 Rusty Greer .30 .09
249 Rafael Palmeiro .50 .15
250 Jeff Zimmerman .30 .09
251 Royce Clayton .30 .09
252 Todd Zeile .30 .09
253 John Wetteland .30 .09
254 Ruben Mateo .30 .09
255 Kelvim Escobar .30 .09
256 David Wells .30 .09
257 Shawn Green .30 .09
258 Homer Bush .30 .09
259 Shannon Stewart .30 .09
260 Carlos Delgado .30 .09
261 Roy Halladay .30 .09
262 Fernando Tatis SH CL .30 .09
263 Jose Jimenez SH CL .30 .09
264 Tony Gwynn SH CL .50 .15
265 Wade Boggs SH CL .30 .09
266 Cal Ripken SH CL 1.25 .35
267 David Cone SH CL .30 .09
268 Mark McGwire SH CL 1.25 .35
269 Pedro Martinez SH CL .50 .15
270 N. Garciaparra SH CL .75 .23
271 Nick Johnson SR .75 .23
272 Mark Quinn SR .50 .15
273 Roosevelt Brown SR .50 .15
274 Terrence Long SR .75 .23
275 Jason Marquis SR .50 .15
276 K.Sasaki SR RC 2.00 .60
277 Aaron Myette SR .75 .23
278 Danys Baez SR RC 1.25 .35
279 Travis Dawkins SR .50 .15
280 Mark Mulder SR 1.25 .35
281 Chris Haas SR .50 .15
282 Milton Bradley SR .75 .23
283 Brad Penny SR .50 .15
284 Rafael Furcal SR .75 .23
285 Luis Matos SR RC 2.00 .60
286 Victor Santos SR RC .75 .23
287 R.Washington SR RC .75 .23
288 Rob Bell SR .50 .15
289 Joe Crede SR .75 .23
290 Pablo Ozuna SR .50 .15
291 W.Serrano SR RC .75 .23
292 S-H. Lee SR RC .50 .15
293 C.Wakeland SR RC .50 .15
294 Luis Rivera SR RC .50 .15
295 Mike Lamb SR RC .75 .23
296 Wily Mo Pena SR .50 .15
297 Mike Meyers SR RC .75 .23
298 Mo Vaughn .30 .09
299 Darin Erstad .30 .09
300 Garret Anderson .30 .09
301 Tim Belcher .30 .09
302 Scott Spiezio .30 .09
303 Kent Bottenfield .30 .09
304 Orlando Palmeiro .30 .09
305 Jason Dickson .30 .09
306 Matt Williams .30 .09
307 Brian Anderson .30 .09
308 Hanley Frias .30 .09
309 Todd Stottlemyre .30 .09
310 Matt Mantei .30 .09
311 David Dellucci .30 .09
312 Armando Reynoso .30 .09
313 Bernard Gilkey .30 .09

314 Chipper Jones .75 .23
315 Tom Glavine .50 .15
316 Quilvio Veras .30 .09
317 Andruw Jones .30 .09
318 Bobby Bonilla .30 .09
319 Reggie Sanders .30 .09
320 Andres Galarraga .30 .09
321 George Lombard .30 .09
322 John Rocker .30 .09
323 Wally Joyner .30 .09
324 B.J. Surhoff .30 .09
325 Scott Erickson .30 .09
326 Delino DeShields .30 .09
327 Jeff Conine .30 .09
328 Mike Timlin .30 .09
329 Brady Anderson .30 .09
330 Mike Bordick .30 .09
331 Harold Baines .30 .09
332 Nomar Garciaparra 1.25 .35
333 Bret Saberhagen .30 .09
334 Ramon Martinez .30 .09
335 Donnie Sadler .30 .09
336 Wilton Veras .30 .09
337 Mike Stanley .30 .09
338 Brian Rose .30 .09
339 Carl Everett .30 .09
340 Tim Wakefield .30 .09
341 Mark Grace .50 .15
342 Kerry Wood .75 .23
343 Eric Young .30 .09
344 Jose Nieves .30 .09
345 Ismael Valdes .30 .09
346 Joe Girardi .30 .09
347 Damon Buford .30 .09
348 Ricky Gutierrez .30 .09
349 Frank Thomas .75 .23
350 Brian Simmons .30 .09
351 James Baldwin .30 .09
352 Brook Fordyce .30 .09
353 Jose Valentin .30 .09
354 Mike Sirotka .30 .09
355 Greg Norton .30 .09
356 Dante Bichette .30 .09
357 Deion Sanders .50 .15
358 Ken Griffey Jr. 1.25 .35
359 Denny Neagle .30 .09
360 Dmitri Young .30 .09
361 Pete Harnisch .30 .09
362 Michael Tucker .30 .09
363 Roberto Alomar .75 .23
364 Dave Roberts .30 .09
365 Jim Thome .75 .23
366 Bartolo Colon .30 .09
367 Travis Fryman .30 .09
368 Chuck Finley .30 .09
369 Russell Branyan .30 .09
370 Alex Ramirez .30 .09
371 Jeff Cirillo .30 .09
372 Jeffrey Hammonds .30 .09
373 Scott Karl .30 .09
374 Brent Mayne .30 .09
375 Tom Goodwin .30 .09
376 Jose Jimenez .30 .09
377 Rolando Arrojo .30 .09
378 Terry Shumpert .30 .09
379 Juan Gonzalez .75 .23
380 Bobby Higginson .30 .09
381 Tony Clark .30 .09
382 Dave Mlicki .30 .09
383 Deivi Cruz .30 .09
384 Brian Moehler .30 .09
385 Dean Palmer .30 .09
386 Luis Castillo .30 .09
387 Mike Redmond .30 .09
388 Alex Fernandez .30 .09
389 Brant Brown .30 .09
390 Dave Berg .30 .09
391 A.J. Burnett .30 .09
392 Mark Kotsay .30 .09
393 Craig Biggio .50 .15
394 Daryle Ward .30 .09
395 Lance Berkman .30 .09
396 Roger Cedeno .30 .09
397 Scott Elarton .30 .09
398 Octavio Dotel .30 .09
399 Ken Caminiti .30 .09
400 Johnny Damon .30 .09
401 Mike Sweeney .30 .09
402 Jeff Suppan .30 .09
403 Rey Sanchez .30 .09
404 Blake Stein .30 .09
405 Ricky Bottalico .30 .09
406 Jay Witasick .30 .09
407 Shawn Green .30 .09
408 Orel Hershiser .30 .09
409 Gary Sheffield .30 .09
410 Todd Hollandsworth .30 .09
411 Terry Adams .30 .09
412 Todd Hundley .30 .09
413 Eric Karros .30 .09
414 F.P. Santangelo .30 .09
415 Alex Cora .30 .09
416 Marquis Grissom .30 .09
417 Henry Blanco .30 .09
418 Jose Hernandez .30 .09
419 Kyle Peterson .30 .09
420 John Snyder RC .30 .09
421 Bob Wickman .30 .09
422 Jamey Wright .30 .09
423 Chad Allen .30 .09
424 Todd Walker .30 .09
425 J.C. Romero RC .30 .09
426 Butch Huskey .30 .09
427 Jacque Jones .30 .09
428 Matt Lawton .30 .09
429 Rondell White .30 .09
430 Jose Vidro .30 .09
431 Hideki Irabu .30 .09
432 Javier Vazquez .30 .09
433 Lee Stevens .30 .09
434 Mike Thurman .30 .09
435 Geoff Blum .30 .09
436 Mike Hampton .30 .09
437 Mike Piazza 1.25 .35
438 Al Leiter .30 .09
439 Derek Bell .30 .09
440 Armando Benitez .30 .09
441 Rey Ordonez .30 .09
442 Todd Zeile .30 .09
443 Roger Clemens 1.50 .45
444 Ramiro Mendoza .30 .09
445 Andy Pettitte .50 .15
446 Scott Brosius .30 .09
447 Mariano Rivera .50 .15
448 Jim Leyritz .30 .09
449 Jorge Posada .50 .15
450 Omar Olivares .30 .09
451 Ben Grieve .30 .09
452 A.J. Hinch .30 .09
453 Gil Heredia .30 .09
454 Kevin Appier .30 .09
455 Ryan Christenson .30 .09
456 Ramon Hernandez .30 .09
457 Scott Rolen .50 .15
458 Alex Arias .30 .09
459 Andy Ashby .30 .09
460 K.Jordan UER 474 .30 .09
461 Robert Person .30 .09
462 Paul Byrd .30 .09
463 Curt Schilling .50 .15
464 Mike Jackson .30 .09
465 Jason Kendall .30 .09
466 Pat Meares .30 .09
467 Bruce Aven .30 .09
468 Todd Ritchie .30 .09
469 Wil Cordero .30 .09
470 Aramis Ramirez .30 .09
471 Andy Benes .30 .09
472 Ray Lankford .30 .09
473 Fernando Vina .30 .09
474 Jim Edmonds .30 .09
475 Craig Paquette .30 .09
476 Pat Hentgen .30 .09
477 Darryl Kile .30 .09
478 Sterling Hitchcock .30 .09
479 Ruben Rivera .30 .09
480 Ryan Klesko .30 .09
481 Phil Nevin .30 .09
482 Woody Williams .30 .09
483 Carlos Hernandez .30 .09
484 Brian Meadows .30 .09
485 Bret Boone .30 .09
486 Barry Bonds 2.00 .60
487 Russ Ortiz .30 .09
488 Bobby Estalella .30 .09
489 Rich Aurilia .30 .09
490 Bill Mueller .30 .09
491 Joe Nathan .30 .09
492 Russ Davis .30 .09
493 John Olerud .30 .09
494 Alex Rodriguez 1.25 .35
495 Freddy Garcia .30 .09
496 Carlos Guillen .30 .09
497 Aaron Sele .30 .09
498 Brett Tomko .30 .09
499 Jamie Moyer .30 .09
500 Mike Cameron .30 .09
501 Vinny Castilla .30 .09
502 Gerald Williams .30 .09
503 Mike DiFelice .30 .09
504 Ryan Rupe .30 .09
505 Greg Vaughn .30 .09
506 Miguel Cairo .30 .09
507 Juan Guzman .30 .09
508 Jose Guillen .30 .09
509 Gabe Kapler .30 .09
510 Rick Helling .30 .09
511 David Segui .30 .09
512 Doug Davis .30 .09
513 Justin Thompson .30 .09
514 Chad Curtis .30 .09
515 Tony Batista .30 .09
516 Billy Koch .30 .09
517 Raul Mondesi .30 .09
518 Joey Hamilton .30 .09
519 Darrin Fletcher .30 .09
520 Brad Fullmer .30 .09
521 Jose Cruz Jr. .30 .09
522 Kevin Witt .30 .09
523 Mark McGwire AUT 1.00 .30
524 Roberto Alomar AUT .30 .09
525 Chipper Jones AUT .50 .15
526 Derek Jeter AUT 1.00 .30
527 Ken Griffey Jr. AUT .75 .23
528 Sammy Sosa AUT .75 .23
529 Manny Ramirez AUT .30 .09
530 Ivan Rodriguez AUT .50 .15
531 Pedro Martinez AUT .50 .15
532 Mariano Rivera CL .50 .15
533 Sammy Sosa CL .75 .23
534 Cal Ripken CL 1.25 .35
535 Vladimir Guerrero CL .50 .15
536 Tony Gwynn CL .50 .15
537 Mark McGwire CL 1.00 .30
538 Bernie Williams CL .30 .09
539 Pedro Martinez CL .50 .15
540 Ken Griffey Jr. CL .75 .23

2000 Upper Deck Exclusives Silver

This set parallels the regular Upper Deck set and cards were randomly seeded into packs. The cards feature coral and red borders and utilize silver foil stamping on front (instead of blue borders and bronze foil in the base set). In addition, each Exclusive Silver parallel is machine serial numbered to 100 on front.

Nm-Mt Ex-Mt
*STARS: 8X TO 20X BASIC CARDS
*SR NON-RC'S: 2.5X TO 6X BASIC SR
*SR RC'S: 4X TO 10X BASIC SR

2000 Upper Deck 2K Plus

Inserted one every 23 first series packs, these 12 cards feature some players who are expected to be stars in the beginning of the 21st century.

Nm-Mt Ex-Mt
COMPLETE SET (12) 60.00 18.00
*DIE CUTS: 2.5X TO 6X BASIC 2K PLUS
DIE CUTS RANDOM INSERTS IN SER.1 HOBBY
DIE CUTS PRINT RUN 100 SERIAL #'d SETS
GOLD DIE CUTS RANDOM IN SER.1 HOBBY
GOLD DIE CUT PRINT RUN 1 SERIAL #'d SET
GOLD DC NOT PRICED DUE TO SCARCITY
2K1 Ken Griffey Jr. 6.00 1.80
2K2 J.D. Drew 1.50 .45
2K3 Derek Jeter 10.00 3.00
2K4 Nomar Garciaparra 6.00 1.80
2K5 Pat Burrell 10.00 3.00
2K6 Ruben Mateo 1.50 .45
2K7 Carlos Beltran 1.50 .45
2K8 Vladimir Guerrero 4.00 1.20
2K9 Scott Rolen 2.50 .75
2K10 Chipper Jones 4.00 1.20
2K11 Alex Rodriguez 6.00 1.80
2K12 Maggio Ordonez 1.50 .45

2000 Upper Deck A Piece of History 3000 Club

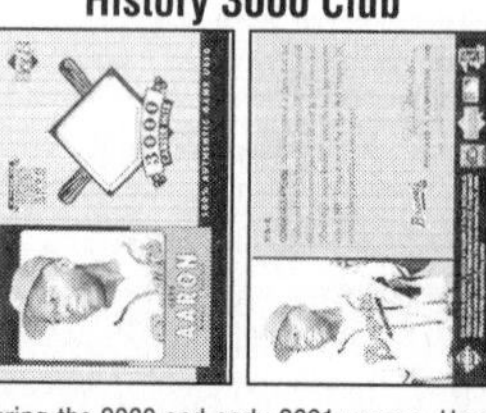

During the 2000 and early 2001 season, Upper Deck inserted a selection of memorabilia cards celebrating members of the 3000 hit club. Approximately 350 of each bat or jersey card was produced. In addition, a wide array of scarce, hand-numbered, autographed cards and combination memorabilia cards were made available. Complete print run information for these cards is provided in our checklist. The cards were released in the following products: 2000 SP Authentic: Tris Speaker and Paul Waner; 2000 SPx: Ty Cobb; 2000 UD Ionix: Roberto Clemente; 2000 Upper Deck 2: Hank Aaron; 2000 Upper Deck Gold Reserve: Al Kaline; 2000 Upper Deck Hitter's Club: Wade Boggs and Tony Gwynn; 2000 Upper Deck HoloGrFx: George Brett and Robin Yount; 2000 Upper Deck Legends: Paul Molitor and Carl Yastrzemski; 2000 Upper Deck MVP: Stan Musial; 2000 Upper Deck Ovation: Willie Mays; 2000 Upper Deck Pros and Prospects: Lou Brock and Rod Carew; 2000 Upper Deck Yankees Legends: Dave Winfield; 2001 Upper Deck: Eddie Murray and Cal Ripken. Exchange cards were seeded into packs for the following cards: Al Kaline Bat AU, Eddie Murray Bat AU, Cal Ripken Bat and Cal Ripken Bat-Jsy. The deadline to exchange the Kaline card was April 10th, 2001 and the Murray/Ripken cards was August 22nd, 2001.

Nm-Mt Ex-Mt
AK-B Al Kaline Bat/400 40.00 12.00
AK-BS Al Kaline Bat AU/6 EXCH
BG-B Wade Boggs 150.00 45.00
Uncommon Gwynn Bat/99
BY-B George Brett 200.00 60.00
Robin Yount
Bat/99
BY-BS George Brett
Robin Yount
Bat AU/10
BY-J George Brett 200.00 60.00
Robin Yount
Jersey/99
BY-JS George Brett
Robin Yount
Jersey AU/10
CR-B Cal Ripken 60.00 18.00
Bat/350 EXCH
CR-J Cal Ripken 60.00 18.00
Jersey/350
CR-JB Cal Ripken 200.00 60.00
Bat-Jsy/100
CR-JBS Cal Ripken
Bat-Jsy AU/8
CY-B Carl Yaz 40.00 12.00
Bat/350
CY-J Carl Yaz 50.00 15.00
Jersey/350
CY-JB Carl Yaz 120.00 36.00
Bat-Jsy/100
CY-JBS Carl Yaz
Bat-Jsy AU/8
DW-B Dave Winf. 15.00 4.50
Bat/350
DW-J Dave Winf. 15.00 4.50
Jersey/350
DW-JB Dave Winf. 40.00 12.00
Bat-Jsy/100
DW-JBS Dave Winfield
Bat-Jsy AU/31
EM-B Eddie Murray 40.00 12.00
Bat/350
EM-J Eddie Murray 40.00 12.00
Jersey/350
EM-JB Eddie Murray 100.00 30.00
Bat-Jsy/100
EM-JBS Eddie Murray
Bat-Jsy AU/33 EXCH
GB-B George Brett 40.00 12.00
Bat/350
GB-J George Brett 40.00 12.00
Jersey/350
HA-B Hank Aaron 60.00 18.00
Bat/350
HA-BS Hank Aaron 1000.00 300.00
Bat-Jsy AU/44
HA-J Hank Aaron 80.00 24.00
Jersey/350
HA-JB Hank Aaron 200.00 60.00
Bat-Jsy/100
LB-B Lou Brock 25.00 7.50
Bat/350
LB-J Lou Brock 25.00 7.50
Jsy/350
LB-JB Lou Brock 60.00 18.00
Bat-Jsy/100
LB-JBS Lou Brock
Bat-Jsy AU/20
PM-B Paul Molitor 25.00 7.50
Bat/350
PW-B Paul Waner 50.00 15.00
Bat/350
PW-BC Paul Waner
Bat-Cut AU/5
RCA-B Rod Carew 25.00 7.50
Bat/350
RCA-J Rod Carew 25.00 7.50
Jsy/350
RCA-BJ Rod Carew 60.00 18.00
Bat-Jsy/100
RCA-JS Rod Carew
Bat-Jsy AU/30
RCL-B Roberto Clemente 120.00 36.00
Bat/350
RCL-C Roberto Clemente
Cut AU/4
RCL-BC Roberto Clemente
Bat-Cut AU/5
RY-B Robin Yount 25.00 7.50
Bat/350
RY-J Robin Yount 25.00 7.50
Jersey/350
SM-B Stan Musial 50.00 15.00
Bat/350
SM-J Stan Musial 60.00 18.00
Jersey/350
SM-JB Stan Musial 150.00 45.00
Bat-Jsy/100
SM-JBS Stan Musial
Bat-Jsy AU/6
TC-B Ty Cobb 150.00 45.00
Bat/350
TC-BC Ty Cobb
Bat-Cut AU/1
TC-C Ty Cobb
Cut AU/3
TG-B Tony Gwynn 40.00 12.00
Bat/350
TG-BC Tony Gwynn 150.00 45.00
Bat-Cap/50
TG-BS Tony Gwynn
Bat AU/19
TS-B Tris Speaker 100.00 30.00
Bat/350
TS-BC Tris Speaker
Bat-Cut AU/5
WB-B Wade Boggs 25.00 7.50
Bat/350
WB-BC Wade Boggs 100.00 30.00
Bat-Cap/50
WB-BS Wade Boggs
Bat AU/12
WM-B Willie Mays 60.00 18.00
Bat/300
WM-J Willie Mays 80.00 24.00
Jersey/350
WM-JB Willie Mays 250.00 75.00
Bat-Jsy/50
WM-JBS Willie Mays
Bat-Jsy AU/24

2000 Upper Deck Cooperstown Calling

Randomly inserted into Upper Deck Series two packs at one in 23, this 15-card insert features players that will be going to Cooperstown after they retire from baseball. Card backs carry a "CC" prefix.

Nm-Mt Ex-Mt
COMPLETE SET (15) 100.00 30.00
CC1 Roger Clemens 8.00 2.40
CC2 Cal Ripken 12.00 3.60
CC3 Ken Griffey Jr. 6.00 1.80
CC4 Mike Piazza 6.00 1.80
CC5 Tony Gwynn 5.00 1.50
CC6 Sammy Sosa 6.00 1.80
CC7 Jose Canseco 4.00 1.20
CC8 Larry Walker 2.50 .75
CC9 Barry Bonds 10.00 3.00
CC10 Greg Maddux 6.00 1.80
CC11 Derek Jeter 10.00 3.00
CC12 Mark McGwire 10.00 3.00
CC13 Randy Johnson 4.00 1.20
CC14 Frank Thomas 4.00 1.20
CC15 Jeff Bagwell 2.50 .75

2000 Upper Deck e-Card

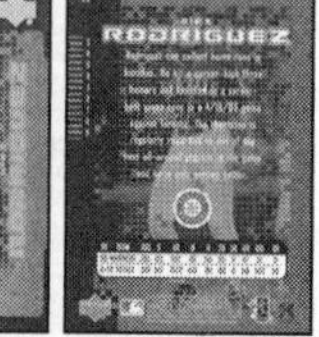

Inserted as a two-pack box-topper in Upper Deck Series two, this six-card insert features cards that can be viewed over the Upper Deck website. Cards feature a serial number that is to be typed in a the Upper Deck website to reveal that card. Card backs carry an "E" prefix.

Nm-Mt Ex-Mt
COMPLETE SET (6) 8.00 2.40
E1 Ken Griffey Jr. 1.50 .45
E2 Alex Rodriguez 1.50 .45
E3 Cal Ripken Jr. 3.00 .90
E4 Jeff Bagwell .60 .18
E5 Barry Bonds 2.50 .75
E6 Manny Ramirez .40 .12

2000 Upper Deck eVolve Autograph

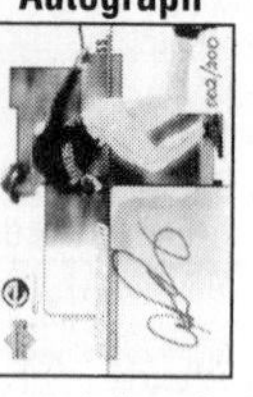

Lucky participants in Upper Deck's E-Card program received special upgraded E-Cards available by checking the UD website (www.upperdeck.com) and entering their basic E-Card serial code (printed on the front of each basic E-Card). When viewed on the Upper Deck website, if an autographed card of the depicted player appeared, the bearer of the base card could then exchange their basic E-Card and receive the signed upgrade via mail. Only 200 serial numbered E-Card Autograph sets were produced. Signed E-Cards all have an ES prefix on the card numbers.

Nm-Mt Ex-Mt
ES-1 Ken Griffey Jr. 120.00 36.00
ES-2 Alex Rodriguez 120.00 36.00
ES-3 Cal Ripken 150.00 45.00
ES-4 Jeff Bagwell 80.00 24.00
ES-5 Barry Bonds 200.00 60.00
ES-6 Manny Ramirez 50.00 15.00

2000 Upper Deck eVolve Game Jersey

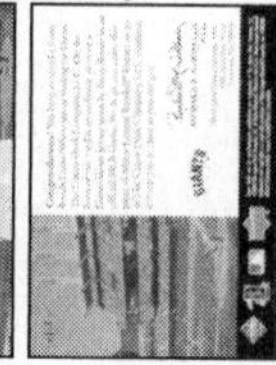

Lucky participants in Upper Deck's E-Card program received special upgraded E-Cards available by checking the UD website (www.upperdeck.com) and entering their basic E-Card serial code (printed on the front of each basic E-Card). When viewed on the Upper Deck website, if a jersey card of the depicted player appeared, the bearer of the base card could then exchange their basic E-Card and receive the Game Jersey upgrade via mail. The cards closely parallel basic 2000 Game Jerseys that were distributed in first and second series packs except for the gold foil "e-volve" logo on front. Only 300 serial numbered E-Card Jersey sets were produced with each card being serial -numbered by hand in blue ink sharpie at the bottom right front corner. Unsigned E-Card Game Jerseys all have an EJ prefix on the card numbers.

Nm-Mt Ex-Mt
EJ-1 Ken Griffey Jr. 40.00 12.00
EJ-2 Alex Rodriguez 40.00 12.00
EJ-3 Cal Ripken 60.00 18.00
EJ-4 Jeff Bagwell 25.00 7.50
EJ-5 Barry Bonds 50.00 15.00
EJ-6 Manny Ramirez 15.00 4.50

2000 Upper Deck eVolve Game Jersey Autograph

Lucky participants in Upper Deck's E-Card program received special upgraded E-Cards available by checking the UD website (www.upperdeck.com) and entering their basic E-Card serial code (printed on the front of each basic E-Card). When viewed on the Upper Deck website, if an autographed card of the depicted player appeared, the bearer of the base card could then exchange their basic E-Card and receive the signed jersey upgrade via mail. A mere 50 serial numbered sets were produced. Signed jersey E-Cards all have an ESJ prefix on the card numbers.

Nm-Mt Ex-Mt
ESJ-1 Ken Griffey Jr. 200.00 60.00
ESJ-2 Alex Rodriguez 200.00 60.00
ESJ-3 Cal Ripken 250.00 75.00
ESJ-4 Jeff Bagwell 120.00 36.00
ESJ-5 Barry Bonds 400.00 120.00
ESJ-6 Manny Ramirez 80.00 24.00

2000 Upper Deck Faces of the Game

Inserted one every 11 first series packs, these 20 cards feature leading players captured by exceptional photography.

Nm-Mt Ex-Mt
COMPLETE SET (20) 80.00 24.00
*DIE CUTS: 3X TO 8X BASIC FACES...

DIE CUTS RANDOM INSERTS IN SER.1 HOBBY
DIE CUTS PRINT RUN 100 SERIAL #'d SETS
GOLD DIE CUTS RANDOM IN SER.1 HOBBY
GOLD DIE CUT PRINT RUN 1 SERIAL #'d SET
GOLD DC NOT PRICED DUE TO SCARCITY

Card	Nm-Mt	Ex-Mt
F1 Ken Griffey Jr.	5.00	1.50
F2 Mark McGwire	8.00	2.40
F3 Sammy Sosa	5.00	1.50
F4 Alex Rodriguez	5.00	1.50
F5 Manny Ramirez	1.25	.35
F6 Derek Jeter	8.00	2.40
F7 Jeff Bagwell	2.00	.60
F8 Roger Clemens	6.00	1.80
F9 Scott Rolen	2.00	.60
F10 Tony Gwynn	4.00	1.20
F11 Nomar Garciaparra	5.00	1.50
F12 Randy Johnson	3.00	.90
F13 Greg Maddux	5.00	1.50
F14 Mike Piazza	5.00	1.50
F15 Frank Thomas	3.00	.90
F16 Cal Ripken	10.00	3.00
F17 Ivan Rodriguez	3.00	.90
F18 Mo Vaughn	1.25	.35
F19 Chipper Jones	3.00	.90
F20 Sean Casey	1.25	.35

2000 Upper Deck Five-Tool Talents

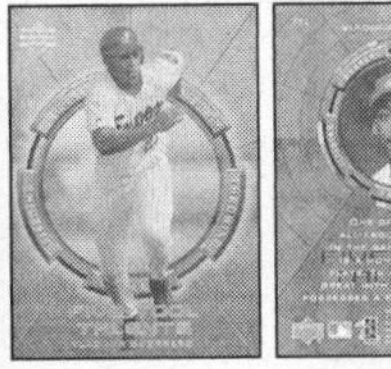

Randomly inserted into packs at one in 11, this 15-card insert features players that possess all of the tools needed to succeed in the Major Leagues. Card backs carry a "FT" prefix.

Card	Nm-Mt	Ex-Mt
COMPLETE SET (15)	30.00	9.00
FT1 Vladimir Guerrero	2.00	.60
FT2 Barry Bonds	5.00	1.50
FT3 Jason Kendall	.75	.23
FT4 Derek Jeter	5.00	1.50
FT5 Ken Griffey Jr.	3.00	.90
FT6 Andruw Jones	.75	.23
FT7 Bernie Williams	1.25	.35
FT8 Jose Canseco	2.00	.60
FT9 Scott Rolen	1.25	.35
FT10 Shawn Green	.75	.23
FT11 Nomar Garciaparra	3.00	.90
FT12 Jeff Bagwell	1.25	.35
FT13 Larry Walker	1.25	.35
FT14 Chipper Jones	2.00	.60
FT15 Alex Rodriguez	3.00	.90

2000 Upper Deck Game Ball

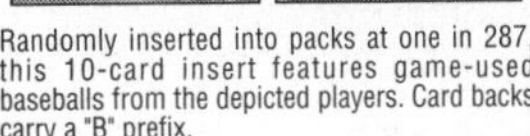

Randomly inserted into packs at one in 287, this 10-card insert features game-used baseballs from the depicted players. Card backs carry a "B" prefix.

Card	Nm-Mt	Ex-Mt
B-AJ Andruw Jones	10.00	3.00
B-AR Alex Rodriguez	15.00	4.50
B-BW Bernie Williams	10.00	3.00
B-DJ Derek Jeter	25.00	7.50
B-JB Jeff Bagwell	10.00	3.00
B-KG Ken Griffey Jr.	15.00	4.50
B-MM Mark McGwire	40.00	12.00
B-RC Roger Clemens	15.00	4.50
B-TG Tony Gwynn	15.00	4.50
B-VG Vladimir Guerrero	10.00	3.00

2000 Upper Deck Game Jersey

These cards feature swatches of jerseys of various major league stars. The cards with an "H" after the player names are available only in hobby packs at a rate of one every 288 first series and 1:287 second series. The cards which have an "HR" after the player names are available in either hobby or retail packs at a rate of one every 2500 packs.

Card	Nm-Mt	Ex-Mt
AJ Andruw Jones HR2	15.00	4.50
AR Alex Rodriguez H1	50.00	15.00
AR Alex Rodriguez HR2	50.00	15.00
BG Ben Grieve HR2	15.00	4.50
CJ Chipper Jones HR1	40.00	12.00
CR Cal Ripken HR1	60.00	18.00
CY Tom Glavine H1	25.00	7.50
DC David Cone HR2	15.00	4.50
DJ Derek Jeter H1	60.00	18.00
EC Eric Chavez HR2	15.00	4.50
EM Edgar Martinez HR2	25.00	7.50
FT Frank Thomas H1	40.00	12.00
FT Frank Thomas HR2	40.00	12.00
GK Gabe Kapler HR1	15.00	4.50
GM Greg Maddux HR1	50.00	15.00
GM Greg Maddux HR2	50.00	15.00
GV Greg Vaughn HR1	15.00	4.50
JB Jeff Bagwell H1	25.00	7.50
JC Jose Canseco HR1	40.00	12.00
JR Ken Griffey Jr. H1	50.00	15.00
KG K.Griffey Jr. Reds HR2	50.00	15.00
KM Kevin Millwood HR2	15.00	4.50
MH Mike Hampton HR2	15.00	4.50
MP Mike Piazza H1	50.00	15.00
MR Manny Ramirez HR1	15.00	4.50
MV Mo Vaughn HR2	15.00	4.50
MW Matt Williams HR2	15.00	4.50
PM Pedro Martinez H1	40.00	12.00
RJ Randy Johnson HR2	40.00	12.00
RV Robin Ventura HR2	15.00	4.50
SA Sandy Alomar Jr. HR2	15.00	4.50
TG Tony Gwynn HR2	40.00	12.00
TH Todd Helton HR1	25.00	7.50
TH Todd Helton HR2	25.00	7.50
VG Vladimir Guerrero HR1	40.00	12.00
TGL Tom Glavine HR2	25.00	7.50
TRG Troy Glaus H1	25.00	7.50
TRG Troy Glaus HR2	25.00	7.50

2000 Upper Deck Game Jersey Autograph

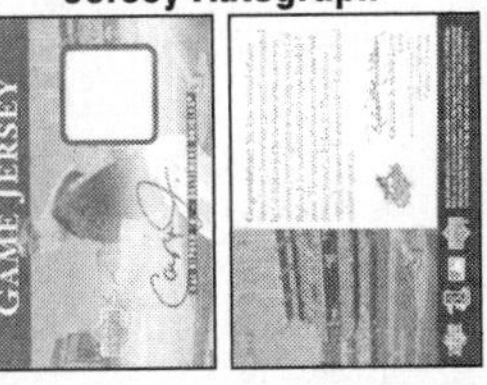

Randomly inserted into Upper Deck Series two hobby packs, this insert set features autographed game-used jersey cards from some of the hottest players in major league baseball. Card backs carry an "H" prefix. A few autographs were not available in packs and had to be exchanged for signed cards. These cards had to be returned to Upper Deck by March 6th, 2001.

Card	Nm-Mt	Ex-Mt
HAR A.Rodriguez EXCH	150.00	45.00
HBB Barry Bonds	250.00	75.00
HCR Cal Ripken	150.00	45.00
HDJ Derek Jeter	200.00	60.00
HIR I.Rodriguez AU H2	80.00	24.00
HJB Jeff Bagwell	80.00	24.00
HJC Jose Canseco	50.00	15.00
HJK Jason Kendall	40.00	12.00
HKG K.Griffey Jr. Reds EXCH	200.00	60.00
HMR M.Ramirez EXCH	50.00	15.00
HPO Paul O'Neill	50.00	15.00
HSR Scott Rolen	50.00	15.00
HVG Vladimir Guerrero	80.00	24.00

2000 Upper Deck Game Jersey Autograph Numbered

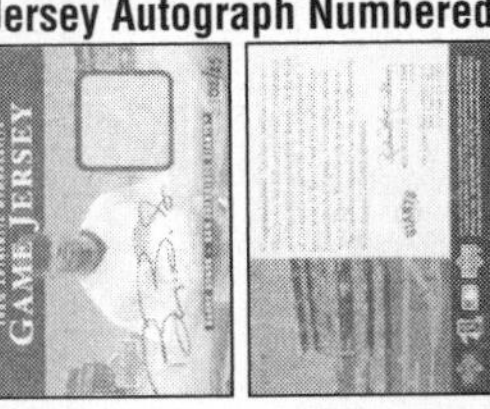

Randomly inserted into Upper Deck hobby packs, this insert set features autographed game-used jersey cards of the hottest players in baseball. Please note that these cards are hand-numbered on front in blue ink sharpie pen to the depicted players jersey number. Due to scarcity, some of these cards are not priced. A few cards were available via exchange: Series one exchange cards had to be redeemed by July 15th, 2000 while series two exchange cards were to be redeemed by March 6th, 2001. Cards tagged with an H1 or H2 suffix in the description were distributed exclusively in first and second series hobby packs. Cards tagged with an HR1 or HR2 suffix were distributed in both hobby and retail packs. The "hobby-only" cards carry an "HN" prefix for the numbering on the back of each card (i.e. Scott Rolen is HN-SR). In addition, each of these cards features features a congratulations from UD President Richard McWilliams with the reference to the card being "crash numbered". These two differences make these scarce numbered inserts easy to legitimize against possible fakes whereby unscrupulous parties may have numbered the cards themselves on front (not very tough to do given the cards were hand-numbered by UD). Unfortunately, the hobby-retail cards do not carry these key differences in design. It's believed that these Numbered inserts feature a gold hologram on back (lower left corner) rather than the silver hologram featured on the more common non-Numbered Game Jersey Autograph cards. Nonetheless, buyers are encouraged to exercise extreme caution for fakes when purchasing the hobby-retail versions of these cards.

Card	Nm-Mt	Ex-Mt
AJ Andruw Jones/25 H2		
AR Alex Rodriguez/3 HR1		
BB Barry Bonds/25 H2		
BG Ben Grieve /14 HR2		
CR Cal Ripken/8 H2		
DJ Derek Jeter/2 HR1		
EM Edgar Martinez /11 HR2		
FT Frank Thomas/35 HR2	200.00	60.00
GM Greg Maddux/31 HR2	300.00	90.00
IR Ivan Rodriguez/7 H2		
JB Jeff Bagwell/5 H2		
JC Jose Canseco/33 H2	250.00	75.00
JK Jason Kendall/18 H2		
JR K.Griffey Jr./24 H1 EX		
KG K.Griffey Jr. Reds/30 H2	400.00	120.00
MH Mike Hampton/10 HR2		
MR Manny Ramirez/24 H1		
MR M.Ramirez/24 H2 EX		
MV Mo Vaughn/42 HR2	80.00	24.00
MW Matt Williams/9 HR2		
PO Paul O'Neill/21 H2		
RJ R.Johnson/51 HR2	200.00	60.00
SR Scott Rolen/17 H2		
TG Tony Gwynn/19 HR2		
VG V.Guerrero/27 H2	300.00	90.00
TGI Tom Glavine/47 HR2	150.00	45.00
TRG Troy Glaus/14 HR2		

2000 Upper Deck Game Jersey Patch

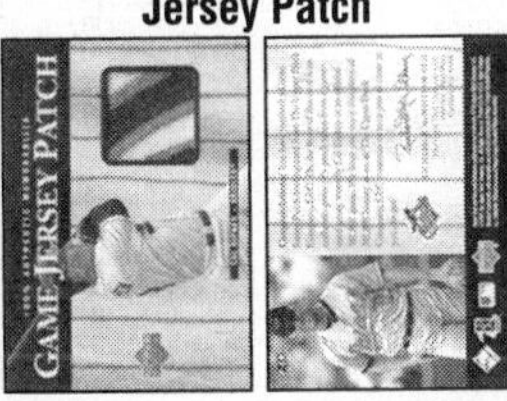

Randomly inserted into series one packs at one in 10,000 and series two packs at a rate of 1:7500, these cards feature game-worn uniform patches.

Card	Nm-Mt	Ex-Mt
P-AJ Andruw Jones 2	100.00	30.00
P-AR Alex Rodriguez 1	250.00	75.00
P-AR Alex Rodriguez 2	250.00	75.00
P-BB Barry Bonds 2	300.00	90.00
P-BG Ben Grieve 2	80.00	24.00
P-CJ Chipper Jones 1	150.00	45.00
P-CR Cal Ripken 1	300.00	90.00
P-CR Cal Ripken 2	300.00	90.00
P-CY Tom Glavine 1	120.00	36.00
P-DC David Cone	100.00	30.00
P-DJ Derek Jeter 1	300.00	90.00
P-DJ Derek Jeter 2	300.00	90.00
P-EC Eric Chavez 1	100.00	30.00
P-FT Frank Thomas 1	150.00	45.00
P-GK Gabe Kapler 1	80.00	24.00
P-GM Greg Maddux 1	200.00	60.00
P-GM Greg Maddux 2	200.00	60.00
P-GV Greg Vaughn 1	100.00	30.00
P-IR Ivan Rodriguez 2	150.00	45.00
P-JB Jeff Bagwell 1	120.00	36.00
P-JC Jose Canseco 1	150.00	45.00
P-JR Ken Griffey Jr. 1	250.00	75.00
P-KG K.Griffey Jr. Reds 2	250.00	75.00
P-MP Mike Piazza 1	200.00	60.00
P-MR Manny Ramirez 1	100.00	30.00
P-MR Manny Ramirez 2	100.00	30.00
P-MV Mo Vaughn 2	100.00	30.00
P-MW Matt Williams 2	100.00	30.00
P-PM Pedro Martinez 1	150.00	45.00
P-RJ Randy Johnson 2	150.00	45.00
P-SR Scott Rolen 2	120.00	36.00
P-TG Tony Gwynn 2	200.00	60.00
P-TH Todd Helton 1	120.00	36.00
P-TRG Troy Glaus 1	120.00	36.00
P-TRG Troy Glaus 2	120.00	36.00
P-VG Vladimir Guerrero 1	150.00	45.00
P-VG Vladimir Guerrero 2	150.00	45.00

2000 Upper Deck Hit Brigade

Inserted into first series packs at a rate of one in eight, these 15 cards feature some of the best hitters. These cards are printed in etched foil.

Card	Nm-Mt	Ex-Mt
COMPLETE SET (15)	30.00	9.00

*DIE CUTS: 6X TO 15X BASIC HIT BRIGADE
DIE CUTS RANDOM INSERTS IN SER.1 PACKS
DIE CUTS PRINT RUN 100 SERIAL #'d SETS
GOLD DIE CUTS RANDOM IN SER.1 PACKS
GOLD DIE CUT PRINT RUN 1 SERIAL #'d SET
GOLD DC NOT PRICED DUE TO SCARCITY

Card	Nm-Mt	Ex-Mt
H1 Ken Griffey Jr.	2.50	.75
H2 Tony Gwynn	2.00	.60
H3 Alex Rodriguez	2.50	.75
H4 Derek Jeter	4.00	1.20
H5 Mike Piazza	2.50	.75
H6 Sammy Sosa	2.50	.75
H7 Juan Gonzalez	1.50	.45
H8 Scott Rolen	1.00	.30
H9 Nomar Garciaparra	2.50	.75
H10 Barry Bonds	4.00	1.20
H11 Craig Biggio	1.00	.30
H12 Chipper Jones	1.50	.45
H13 Frank Thomas	1.50	.45
H14 Larry Walker	1.00	.30
H15 Mark McGwire	4.00	1.20

2000 Upper Deck Hot Properties

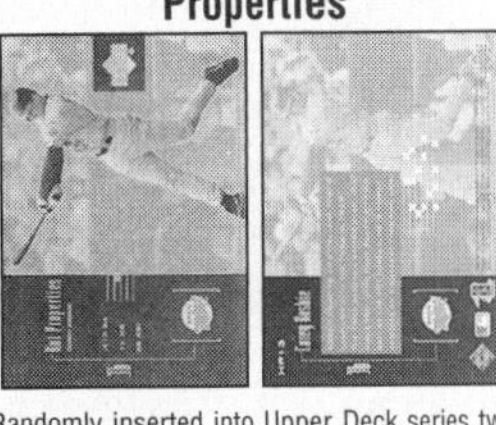

Randomly inserted into Upper Deck series two packs at one in 11, this 15-card insert features the major league's top prospects. Card backs carry a "HP" prefix.

Card	Nm-Mt	Ex-Mt
COMPLETE SET (15)	12.00	3.60
HP1 Carlos Beltran	.75	.23
HP2 Rick Ankiel	.75	.23
HP3 Sean Casey	.75	.23
HP4 Preston Wilson	.75	.23
HP5 Vernon Wells	1.25	.35
HP6 Pat Burrell	1.00	.30
HP7 Eric Chavez	.75	.23
HP8 J.D. Drew	.75	.23
HP9 Alfonso Soriano	3.00	.90
HP10 Gabe Kapler	.75	.23
HP11 Rafael Furcal	1.25	.35
HP12 Ruben Mateo	.75	.23
HP13 Corey Koskie	.50	.15
HP14 Kip Wells	.75	.23
HP15 Ramon Ortiz	.75	.23

2000 Upper Deck Legendary Cuts

Randomly inserted into Upper Deck series two packs, this eight-card insert features cut-signatures from some of the all-time great players of the 20th Century. Please note that only one set was produced of this insert.

Card	Nm-Mt	Ex-Mt
1 Cap Anson		
2 Roberto Clemente		
3 Ty Cobb		
4 Eddie Collins		
5 Nap Lajoie		
6 Tris Speaker		
7 Honus Wagner		
8 Paul Waner		

2000 Upper Deck Pennant Driven

Randomly inserted into packs at one in four, this 10-card insert features players that are driven to win the pennant. Card backs carry a "PD" prefix.

Card	Nm-Mt	Ex-Mt
COMPLETE SET (10)	10.00	3.00
PD1 Derek Jeter	2.00	.60
PD2 Roberto Alomar	.75	.23
PD3 Chipper Jones	.75	.23
PD4 Jeff Bagwell	.50	.15
PD5 Roger Clemens	1.50	.45
PD6 Nomar Garciaparra	1.25	.35
PD7 Manny Ramirez	.30	.09
PD8 Mike Piazza	1.25	.35
PD9 Ivan Rodriguez	.75	.23
PD10 Randy Johnson	.75	.23

2000 Upper Deck People's Choice

Randomly inserted into second series packs at one in 23, this 15-card set features players that people have voted as their favorites to watch. Card backs carry a "PC" prefix.

Card	Nm-Mt	Ex-Mt
COMPLETE SET (15)	100.00	30.00
PC1 Mark McGwire	10.00	3.00
PC2 Nomar Garciaparra	6.00	1.80
PC3 Derek Jeter	10.00	3.00
PC4 Shawn Green	1.50	.45
PC5 Manny Ramirez	1.50	.45
PC6 Pedro Martinez	4.00	1.20
PC7 Ivan Rodriguez	4.00	1.20
PC8 Alex Rodriguez	6.00	1.80
PC9 Juan Gonzalez	4.00	1.20
PC10 Ken Griffey Jr.	6.00	1.80
PC11 Sammy Sosa	6.00	1.80
PC12 Jeff Bagwell	2.50	.75
PC13 Chipper Jones	4.00	1.20
PC14 Cal Ripken	12.00	3.60
PC15 Mike Piazza	6.00	1.80

2000 Upper Deck Power MARK

Inserted one every 23 first series packs, these 10 cards all feature Mark McGwire.

Card	Nm-Mt	Ex-Mt
COMPLETE SET (10)	50.00	15.00
COMMON (MC1-MC10)	6.00	1.80

*DIE CUTS: 3X TO 8X BASIC POWER MARK
DIE CUTS RANDOM INSERTS IN SER.1 HOBBY
DIE CUTS PRINT RUN 100 SERIAL #'d SETS
GOLD DIE CUTS RANDOM IN SER.1 HOBBY
GOLD DIE CUT PRINT RUN 1 SERIAL #'d SET
GOLD DC NOT PRICED DUE TO SCARCITY

2000 Upper Deck Power Rally

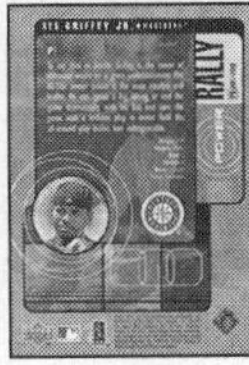

Inserted one every 11 first series packs, these 15 cards feature baseball's leading power hitters.

Card	Nm-Mt	Ex-Mt
COMPLETE SET (15)	40.00	12.00

*DIE CUTS: 5X TO 12X BASIC POWER RALLY
DIE CUTS RANDOM INSERTS IN SER.1 PACKS
DIE CUTS PRINT RUN 100 SERIAL #'d SETS
GOLD DIE CUTS RANDOM IN SER.1 PACKS
GOLD DIE CUT PRINT RUN 1 SERIAL #'d SET
GOLD DC NOT PRICED DUE TO SCARCITY

Card	Nm-Mt	Ex-Mt
P1 Ken Griffey Jr.	3.00	.90
P2 Mark McGwire	5.00	1.50
P3 Sammy Sosa	3.00	.90
P4 Jose Canseco	2.00	.60
P5 Juan Gonzalez	2.00	.60
P6 Bernie Williams	1.25	.35
P7 Jeff Bagwell	1.25	.35
P8 Chipper Jones	2.00	.60
P9 Vladimir Guerrero	2.00	.60
P10 Mo Vaughn	.75	.23
P11 Derek Jeter	5.00	1.50
P12 Mike Piazza	3.00	.90
P13 Barry Bonds	5.00	1.50
P14 Alex Rodriguez	3.00	.90
P15 Nomar Garciaparra	3.00	.90

2000 Upper Deck PowerDeck Inserts

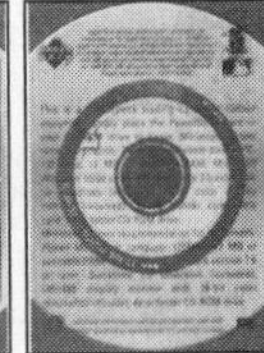

These CD's were inserted into packs at two different rates. PD1 through PD 8 were inserted at a rate of one every 23 packs while PD9 through PD 11 were inserted at a rate of one every 287 packs. Due to problems at the manufacturer, the Alex Rodriguez CD was not inserted into the first series packs so a collector could acquire one of those by sending in a UPC code on the bottom of the 2000 Upper Deck first series boxes. Also, some of the 1999 Upper Deck PowerDeck CD's were mistakenly inserted into this product. Those CD's are priced under the 1999 Upper Deck PowerDeck listings. Finally, Ken Griffey Jr., Reggie Jackson and Mark McGwire have all been confirmed as short prints by representatives at Upper Deck.

Card	Nm-Mt	Ex-Mt
COMPLETE SET (11)	120.00	36.00
PD1 Ken Griffey Jr.	6.00	1.80
PD2 Cal Ripken	12.00	3.60
PD3 Mark McGwire	10.00	3.00
PD4 Tony Gwynn	5.00	1.50
PD5 Roger Clemens	8.00	2.40
PD6 Alex Rodriguez EXCH	8.00	2.40
PD7 Sammy Sosa	6.00	1.80
PD8 Derek Jeter	10.00	3.00
PD9 Ken Griffey Jr. SP	15.00	4.50
PD10 Mark McGwire SP	25.00	7.50
PD11 Reggie Jackson SP	15.00	4.50

2000 Upper Deck Prime Performers

Randomly inserted into series two packs at one in eight, this 10-card insert features players that are prime performers. Card backs carry a "PP" prefix.

Card	Nm-Mt	Ex-Mt
COMPLETE SET (10)	12.00	3.60
PP1 Manny Ramirez	.40	.12
PP2 Pedro Martinez	1.00	.30
PP3 Carlos Delgado	.40	.12
PP4 Ken Griffey Jr.	1.50	.45
PP5 Derek Jeter	2.50	.75

PP6 Chipper Jones	1.00	.30
PP7 Sean Casey	.40	.12
PP8 Shawn Green	.40	.12
PP9 Sammy Sosa	1.50	.45
PP10 Alex Rodriguez	1.50	.45

2000 Upper Deck Statitude

Inserted one every four packs, these 30 cards feature some of the most statistically dominant players in baseball.

	Nm-Mt	Ex-Mt
COMPLETE SET (30)	40.00	12.00
*DIE CUTS: 6X TO 15X BASIC STATITUDE		
DIE CUTS RANDOM INSERTS IN SER.1 RETAIL		
DIE CUTS PRINT RUN 100 SERIAL #'d SETS		
GOLD DIE CUTS RANDOM IN SER.1 RETAIL		
GOLD DIE CUT PRINT RUN 1 SERIAL #'d SET		
GOLD DC NOT PRICED DUE TO SCARCITY		
S1 Mo Vaughn	.60	.18
S2 Matt Williams	.60	.18
S3 Travis Lee	.60	.18
S4 Chipper Jones	1.50	.45
S5 Greg Maddux	2.50	.75
S6 Gabe Kapler	.60	.18
S7 Cal Ripken	5.00	1.50
S8 Nomar Garciaparra	2.50	.75
S9 Sammy Sosa	2.50	.75
S10 Frank Thomas	1.50	.45
S11 Manny Ramirez	.60	.18
S12 Larry Walker	1.00	.30
S13 Ivan Rodriguez	1.50	.45
S14 Jeff Bagwell	1.00	.30
S15 Craig Biggio	1.00	.30
S16 Vladimir Guerrero	1.50	.45
S17 Mike Piazza	2.50	.75
S18 Bernie Williams	1.00	.30
S19 Derek Jeter	4.00	1.20
S20 Jose Canseco	1.50	.45
S21 Eric Chavez	.60	.18
S22 Scott Rolen	1.00	.30
S23 Mark McGwire	4.00	1.20
S24 Tony Gwynn	2.00	.60
S25 Barry Bonds	4.00	1.20
S26 Ken Griffey Jr.	2.50	.75
S27 Alex Rodriguez	2.50	.75
S28 J.D. Drew	.60	.18
S29 Juan Gonzalez	1.50	.45
S30 Roger Clemens	3.00	.90

2000 Upper Deck Subway Series

This 30-card box set was released shortly after the 2000 World Series, in mid-November. The set features 13 New York Yankee players, 13 New York Met players and four Subway Series Flashback cards. Each set also incuded one 3x5 Commemorative 2000 World Series Championship card. Each set carried a suggested retail price of $19.99.

	Nm-Mt	Ex-Mt
COMP. FACT SET (30)	15.00	4.50
NY1 Derek Jeter	3.00	.90
NY2 Bernie Williams	.60	.18
NY3 Roger Clemens	1.50	.45
NY4 Paul O'Neill	.60	.18
NY5 Tino Martinez	.20	.06
NY6 Jorge Posada	.40	.12
NY7 David Justice	.60	.18
NY8 Andy Pettitte	.20	.06
NY9 Orlando Hernandez	.20	.06
NY10 Mariano Rivera	.40	.12
NY11 Scott Brosius	.20	.06
NY12 Dwight Gooden	.20	.06
NY13 Jose Canseco	.75	.23
NY14 Mike Hampton	.20	.06
NY15 Al Leiter	.20	.06
NY16 Armando Benitez	.20	.06
NY17 Bobby Jones	.10	.03
NY18 Mike Piazza	2.00	.60
NY19 Todd Zeile	.20	.06
NY20 Edgardo Alfonzo	.60	.18
NY21 Mike Bordick	.10	.03
NY22 Robin Ventura	.40	.12
NY23 Jay Payton	.20	.06
NY24 Timo Perez	.20	.06
NY25 John Franco	.20	.06
NY26 Turk Wendell	.10	.03
NY27 Mickey Mantle	3.00	.90
NY28 Don Larsen	.20	.06
NY29 Jackie Robinson	1.50	.45
NY30 Pee Wee Reese	1.00	.30
NNO N.Y. Yankees 3x5	.60	.18

2001 Upper Deck

The 2001 Upper Deck Series one product was released in November, 2000 and featured a 270-card base set. Series two (entitled Mid-Summer Classic) was released in June, 2001 and featured a 180-card base set. The complete set is broken into subsets as follows: Star Rookies (1-45/271-300), basic cards (46-261/301-444), and Season Highlight checklists (262-270/445-450). Each pack contained 10-cards and carried a suggested retail price of $1.99. Key Rookie Cards in the set include Albert Pujols and Ichiro Suzuki. Also, a selection of A Piece of History 3000 Club Eddie Murray and Cal Ripken memorabilia cards were randomly seeded into series one packs. 350 bat cards, 350 jersey cards and 100 hand-numbered, combination bat-jersey cards were produced for each player. In addition, thirty-three autographed, hand-numbered, combination bat-jersey Eddie Murray cards and eight autographed, hand-numbered, combination bat-jersey Cal Ripken cards were produced. The Ripken Bat, Ripken Bat-Jsy Combo and Murray Bat-Jsy Combo Autograph were all exchange cards. The deadline to send in the exchange cards was August 22nd, 2001. Pricing for these memorabilia cards can be referenced under 2000 Upper Deck A Piece of History 3000 Club.

	Nm-Mt	Ex-Mt
COMPLETE SET (450)	100.00	30.00
COMP. SERIES 1 (270)	40.00	12.00
COMP. SERIES 2 (180)	60.00	18.00
COMMON (46-270/300-450)	.30	.09
COMMON SR (1-45)	.50	.15
1 Jeff DaVanon SR	.50	.15
2 Aubrey Huff SR	.50	.15
3 Pasqual Coco SR	.50	.15
4 Barry Zito SR	1.00	.30
5 Augie Ojeda SR	.50	.15
6 Chris Richard SR	.50	.15
7 Josh Phelps SR	.50	.15
8 Kevin Nicholson SR	.50	.15
9 Juan Guzman SR	.50	.15
10 Brandon Kolb SR	.50	.15
11 Johan Santana SR	.60	.18
12 Josh Kalinowski SR	.50	.15
13 Tike Redman SR	.50	.15
14 Ivanon Coffie SR	.50	.15
15 Chad Durbin SR	.50	.15
16 Derrick Turnbow SR	.50	.15
17 Scott Downs SR	.50	.15
18 Jason Grilli SR	.50	.15
19 Mark Buehrle SR	.50	.15
20 Paxton Crawford SR	.50	.15
21 Bronson Arroyo SR	.50	.15
22 Tomas De la Rosa SR	.50	.15
23 Paul Rigdon SR	.50	.15
24 Rob Ramsay SR	.50	.15
25 Damian Rolls SR	.50	.15
26 Jason Conti SR	.50	.15
27 John Parrish SR	.50	.15
28 Geraldo Guzman SR	.50	.15
29 Tony Mota SR	.50	.15
30 Luis Rivas SR	.50	.15
31 Brian Tollberg SR	.50	.15
32 Adam Bernero SR	.50	.15
33 Michael Cuddyer SR	.50	.15
34 Josue Espada SR	.50	.15
35 Joe Lawrence SR	.50	.15
36 Chad Moeller SR	.50	.15
37 Nick Bierbrodt SR	.50	.15
38 DeWayne Wise SR	.50	.15
39 Javier Cardona SR	.50	.15
40 Hiram Bocachica SR	.50	.15
41 G.Chiaramonte SR	.50	.15
42 Alex Cabrera SR	.50	.15
43 Jimmy Rollins SR	.50	.15
44 Pat Flury SR RC	.50	.15
45 Leo Estrella SR	.50	.15
46 Darin Erstad	.30	.09
47 Seth Etherton	.30	.09
48 Troy Glaus	.50	.15
49 Brian Cooper	.30	.09
50 Tim Salmon	.50	.15
51 Adam Kennedy	.30	.09
52 Bengie Molina	.30	.09
53 Jason Giambi	.75	.23
54 Miguel Tejada	.30	.09
55 Tim Hudson	.30	.09
56 Eric Chavez	.30	.09
57 Terrence Long	.30	.09
58 Jason Isringhausen	.30	.09
59 Ramon Hernandez	.30	.09
60 Raul Mondesi	.30	.09
61 David Wells	.30	.09
62 Shannon Stewart	.30	.09
63 Tony Batista	.30	.09
64 Brad Fullmer	.30	.09
65 Chris Carpenter	.30	.09
66 Homer Bush	.30	.09
67 Gerald Williams	.30	.09
68 Miguel Cairo	.30	.09
69 Ryan Rupe	.30	.09
70 Greg Vaughn	.30	.09
71 John Flaherty	.30	.09
72 Dan Wheeler	.30	.09
73 Fred McGriff	.50	.15
74 Roberto Alomar	.75	.23
75 Bartolo Colon	.30	.09
76 Kenny Lofton	.30	.09
77 David Segui	.30	.09
78 Omar Vizquel	.30	.09
79 Russ Branyan	.30	.09
80 Chuck Finley	.30	.09
81 Manny Ramirez UER	.30	.09
Back photo is of David Segui		
82 Alex Rodriguez	1.25	.35
83 John Halama	.30	.09
84 Mike Cameron	.30	.09
85 David Bell	.30	.09
86 Jay Buhner	.30	.09
87 Aaron Sele	.30	.09
88 Rickey Henderson	.75	.23
89 Brook Fordyce	.30	.09
90 Cal Ripken	2.50	.75
91 Mike Mussina	.75	.23
92 Delino DeShields	.30	.09
93 Melvin Mora	.30	.09
94 Sidney Ponson	.30	.09
95 Brady Anderson	.30	.09
96 Ivan Rodriguez	.75	.23
97 Ricky Ledee	.30	.09
98 Rick Helling	.30	.09
99 Ruben Mateo	.30	.09
100 Luis Alicea	.30	.09
101 John Wetteland	.30	.09
102 Mike Lamb	.30	.09
103 Carl Everett	.30	.09
104 Troy O'Leary	.30	.09
105 Wilton Veras	.30	.09
106 Pedro Martinez	.75	.23
107 Rolando Arrojo	.30	.09
108 Scott Hatteberg	.30	.09
109 Jason Varitek	.30	.09
110 Jose Offerman	.30	.09
111 Carlos Beltran	.30	.09
112 Johnny Damon	.30	.09
113 Mark Quinn	.30	.09
114 Rey Sanchez	.30	.09
115 Mac Suzuki	.30	.09
116 Jermaine Dye	.30	.09
117 Chris Fussell	.30	.09
118 Jeff Weaver	.30	.09
119 Dean Palmer	.30	.09
120 Robert Fick	.30	.09
121 Brian Moehler	.30	.09
122 Damion Easley	.30	.09
123 Juan Encarnacion	.30	.09
124 Tony Clark	.30	.09
125 Cristian Guzman	.30	.09
126 Matt LeCroy	.30	.09
127 Eric Milton	.30	.09
128 Jay Canizaro	.30	.09
129 David Ortiz	.30	.09
130 Brad Radke	.30	.09
131 Jacque Jones	.30	.09
132 Magglio Ordonez	.30	.09
133 Carlos Lee	.30	.09
134 Mike Sirotka	.30	.09
135 Ray Durham	.30	.09
136 Paul Konerko	.30	.09
137 Charles Johnson	.30	.09
138 James Baldwin	.30	.09
139 Jeff Abbott	.30	.09
140 Roger Clemens	1.50	.45
141 Derek Jeter	2.00	.60
142 David Justice	.30	.09
143 Ramiro Mendoza	.30	.09
144 Chuck Knoblauch	.30	.09
145 Orlando Hernandez	.30	.09
146 Alfonso Soriano	.50	.15
147 Jeff Bagwell	.50	.15
148 Julio Lugo	.30	.09
149 Mitch Meluskey	.30	.09
150 Jose Lima	.30	.09
151 Richard Hidalgo	.30	.09
152 Moises Alou	.30	.09
153 Scott Elarton	.30	.09
154 Andruw Jones	.30	.09
155 Quilvio Veras	.30	.09
156 Greg Maddux	1.25	.35
157 Brian Jordan	.30	.09
158 Andres Galarraga	.30	.09
159 Kevin Millwood	.30	.09
160 Rafael Furcal	.30	.09
161 Jeromy Burnitz	.30	.09
162 Jimmy Haynes	.30	.09
163 Mark Loretta	.30	.09
164 Ron Belliard	.30	.09
165 Richie Sexson	.30	.09
166 Kevin Barker	.30	.09
167 Jeff D'Amico	.30	.09
168 Rick Ankiel	.30	.09
169 Mark McGwire	2.00	.60
170 J.D. Drew	.30	.09
171 Eli Marrero	.30	.09
172 Darryl Kile	.30	.09
173 Edgar Renteria	.30	.09
174 Will Clark	.75	.23
175 Eric Young	.30	.09
176 Mark Grace	.50	.15
177 Jon Lieber	.30	.09
178 Damon Buford	.30	.09
179 Kerry Wood	.75	.23
180 Rondell White	.30	.09
181 Joe Girardi	.30	.09
182 Curt Schilling	.50	.15
183 Randy Johnson	.75	.23
184 Steve Finley	.30	.09
185 Kelly Stinnett	.30	.09
186 Jay Bell	.30	.09
187 Matt Mantei	.30	.09
188 Luis Gonzalez	.30	.09
189 Shawn Green	.30	.09
190 Todd Hundley	.30	.09
191 Chan Ho Park	.30	.09
192 Adrian Beltre	.30	.09
193 Mark Grudzielanek	.30	.09
194 Gary Sheffield	.30	.09
195 Tom Goodwin	.30	.09
196 Lee Stevens	.30	.09
197 Javier Vazquez	.30	.09
198 Milton Bradley	.30	.09
199 Vladimir Guerrero	.75	.23
200 Carl Pavano	.30	.09
201 Orlando Cabrera	.30	.09
202 Tony Armas Jr.	.30	.09
203 Jeff Kent	.30	.09
204 Calvin Murray	.30	.09
205 Ellis Burks	.30	.09
206 Barry Bonds	2.00	.60
207 Russ Ortiz	.30	.09
208 Marvin Benard	.30	.09
209 Joe Nathan	.30	.09
210 Preston Wilson	.30	.09
211 Cliff Floyd	.30	.09
212 Mike Lowell	.30	.09
213 Ryan Dempster	.30	.09
214 Brad Penny	.30	.09
215 Mike Redmond	.30	.09
216 Luis Castillo	.30	.09
217 Derek Bell	.30	.09
218 Mike Hampton	.30	.09
219 Todd Zeile	.30	.09
220 Robin Ventura	.30	.09
221 Mike Piazza	1.25	.35
222 Al Leiter	.30	.09
223 Edgardo Alfonzo	.30	.09
224 Mike Bordick	.30	.09
225 Phil Nevin	.30	.09
226 Ryan Klesko	.30	.09
227 Adam Eaton	.30	.09
228 Eric Owens	.30	.09
229 Tony Gwynn	1.00	.30
230 Matt Clement	.30	.09
231 Wiki Gonzalez	.30	.09
232 Robert Person	.30	.09
233 Doug Glanville	.30	.09
234 Scott Rolen	.50	.15
235 Mike Lieberthal	.30	.09
236 Randy Wolf	.30	.09
237 Bob Abreu	.30	.09
238 Pat Burrell	.30	.09
239 Bruce Chen	.30	.09
240 Kevin Young	.30	.09
241 Todd Ritchie	.30	.09
242 Adrian Brown	.30	.09
243 Chad Hermansen	.30	.09
244 Warren Morris	.30	.09
245 Kris Benson	.30	.09
246 Jason Kendall	.30	.09
247 Pokey Reese	.30	.09
248 Rob Bell	.30	.09
249 Ken Griffey Jr.	1.25	.35
250 Sean Casey	.30	.09
251 Aaron Boone	.30	.09
252 Pete Harnisch	.30	.09
253 Barry Larkin	.75	.23
254 Dmitri Young	.30	.09
255 Todd Hollandsworth	.30	.09
256 Pedro Astacio	.30	.09
257 Todd Helton	.50	.15
258 Terry Shumpert	.30	.09
259 Neifi Perez	.30	.09
260 Jeffrey Hammonds	.30	.09
261 Ben Petrick	.30	.09
262 Mark McGwire SH	1.00	.30
263 Derek Jeter SH	1.00	.30
264 Sammy Sosa SH	.75	.23
265 Cal Ripken SH	1.25	.35
266 Pedro Martinez SH	.50	.15
267 Barry Bonds SH	.75	.23
268 Fred McGriff SH	.30	.09
269 Randy Johnson SH	.50	.15
270 Darin Erstad SH	.30	.09
271 Ichiro Suzuki SR RC	15.00	4.50
272 W. Betemit SR RC	.50	.15
273 Corey Patterson SR	.50	.15
274 Sean Douglass SR RC	.50	.15
275 Mike Penney SR RC	.50	.15
276 Nate Teut SR RC	.50	.15
277 R. Rodriguez SR RC	.50	.15
278 B. Duckworth SR RC	.50	.15
279 Rafael Soriano SR RC	1.50	.45
280 Juan Diaz SR RC	.50	.15
281 H. Ramirez SR RC	1.00	.30
282 T. Shinjo SR RC	1.25	.35
283 Keith Ginter SR	.50	.15
284 Esix Snead SR RC	.50	.15
285 Erick Almonte SR RC	.50	.15
286 Travis Hafner SR RC	1.50	.45
287 Jason Smith SR RC	.50	.15
288 J. Melian SR RC	.50	.15
289 Tyler Walker SR RC	.50	.15
290 Jason Standridge SR	.50	.15
291 Juan Uribe SR RC	.50	.15
292 A. Hernandez SR RC	.50	.15
293 J. Michaels SR RC	.50	.15
294 Jason Hart SR	.50	.15
295 Albert Pujols SR RC	40.00	12.00
296 M. Ensberg SR RC	1.25	.35
297 Brandon Inge SR	.50	.15
298 Jesus Colome SR	.50	.15
299 K. Kessel SR RC UER	.50	.15
L Missing from MLB experience		
300 Timo Perez SR	.50	.15
301 Mo Vaughn	.30	.09
302 Ismael Valdes	.30	.09
303 Glenallen Hill	.30	.09
304 Garret Anderson	.30	.09
305 Johnny Damon	.30	.09
306 Jose Ortiz	.30	.09
307 Mark Mulder	.30	.09
308 Adam Piatt	.30	.09
309 Gil Heredia	.30	.09
310 Mike Sirotka	.30	.09
311 Carlos Delgado	.30	.09
312 Alex Gonzalez	.30	.09
313 Jose Cruz Jr.	.30	.09
314 Darrin Fletcher	.30	.09
315 Ben Grieve	.30	.09
316 Vinny Castilla	.30	.09
317 Wilson Alvarez	.30	.09
318 Brent Abernathy	.30	.09
319 Ellis Burks	.30	.09
320 Jim Thome	.75	.23
321 Juan Gonzalez	.75	.23
322 Ed Taubensee	.30	.09
323 Travis Fryman	.30	.09
324 John Olerud	.30	.09
325 Edgar Martinez	.50	.15
326 Freddy Garcia	.30	.09
327 Bret Boone	.50	.15
328 Kazuhiro Sasaki	.30	.09
329 Albert Belle	.30	.09
330 Mike Bordick	.30	.09
331 David Segui	.30	.09
332 Pat Hentgen	.30	.09
333 Alex Rodriguez	1.25	.35
334 Andres Galarraga	.30	.09
335 Gabe Kapler	.30	.09
336 Ken Caminiti	.30	.09
337 Rafael Palmeiro	.50	.15
338 Manny Ramirez	.30	.09
339 David Cone	.30	.09
340 Nomar Garciaparra	1.25	.35
341 Trot Nixon	.50	.15
342 Derek Lowe	.30	.09
343 Roberto Hernandez	.30	.09
344 Mike Sweeney	.30	.09
345 Carlos Febles	.30	.09
346 Jeff Suppan	.30	.09
347 Roger Cedeno	.30	.09
348 Bobby Higginson	.30	.09
349 Deivi Cruz	.30	.09
350 Mitch Meluskey	.30	.09
351 Matt Lawton	.30	.09
352 Mark Redman	.30	.09
353 Jay Canizaro	.30	.09
354 Corey Koskie	.30	.09
355 Matt Kinney	.30	.09
356 Frank Thomas	.75	.23
357 Sandy Alomar Jr.	.30	.09
358 David Wells	.30	.09
359 Jim Parque	.30	.09
360 Chris Singleton	.30	.09
361 Tino Martinez	.50	.15
362 Paul O'Neill	.50	.15
363 Mike Mussina	.75	.23
364 Bernie Williams	.50	.15
365 Andy Pettite	.50	.15
366 Mariano Rivera	.50	.15
367 Brad Ausmus	.30	.09
368 Craig Biggio	.50	.15
369 Lance Berkman	.30	.09
370 Shane Reynolds	.30	.09
371 Chipper Jones	.75	.23
372 Tom Glavine	.50	.15
373 B.J. Surhoff	.30	.09
374 John Smoltz	.50	.15
375 Rico Brogna	.30	.09
376 Geoff Jenkins	.30	.09
377 Jose Hernandez	.30	.09
378 Tyler Houston	.30	.09
379 Henry Blanco	.30	.09
380 Jeffrey Hammonds	.30	.09
381 Jim Edmonds	.30	.09
382 Fernando Vina	.30	.09
383 Andy Benes	.30	.09
384 Ray Lankford	.30	.09
385 Dustin Hermanson	.30	.09
386 Todd Hundley	.30	.09
387 Sammy Sosa	1.25	.35
388 Tom Gordon	.30	.09
389 Bill Mueller	.30	.09
390 Ron Coomer	.30	.09
391 Matt Stairs	.30	.09
392 Mark Grace	.50	.15
393 Matt Williams	.30	.09
394 Todd Stottlemyre	.30	.09
395 Tony Womack	.30	.09
396 Erubiel Durazo	.30	.09
397 Reggie Sanders	.30	.09
398 Andy Ashby	.30	.09
399 Eric Karros	.30	.09
400 Kevin Brown	.30	.09
401 Darren Dreifort	.30	.09
402 Fernando Tatis	.30	.09
403 Jose Vidro	.30	.09
404 Peter Bergeron	.30	.09
405 Geoff Blum	.30	.09
406 J.T. Snow	.30	.09
407 Livan Hernandez	.30	.09
408 Robb Nen	.30	.09
409 Bobby Estalella	.30	.09
410 Rich Aurilia	.30	.09
411 Eric Davis	.30	.09
412 Charles Johnson	.30	.09
413 Alex Gonzalez	.30	.09
414 A.J. Burnett	.30	.09
415 Antonio Alfonseca	.30	.09
416 Derek Lee	.30	.09
417 Jay Payton	.30	.09
418 Kevin Appier	.30	.09
419 Steve Trachsel	.30	.09
420 Rey Ordonez	.30	.09
421 Darryl Hamilton	.30	.09
422 Ben Davis	.30	.09
423 Damian Jackson	.30	.09
424 Mark Kotsay	.30	.09
425 Trevor Hoffman	.30	.09
426 Travis Lee	.30	.09
427 Omar Daal	.30	.09
428 Paul Byrd	.30	.09
429 Reggie Taylor	.30	.09
430 Brian Giles	.30	.09
431 Derek Bell	.30	.09
432 Francisco Cordova	.30	.09
433 Pat Meares	.30	.09
434 Scott Williamson	.30	.09
435 Jason LaRue	.30	.09
436 Michael Tucker	.30	.09
437 Wilton Guerrero	.30	.09
438 Mike Hampton	.30	.09
439 Ron Gant	.30	.09
440 Jeff Cirillo	.30	.09
441 Denny Neagle	.30	.09
442 Larry Walker	.50	.15
443 Juan Pierre	.30	.09
444 Todd Walker	.30	.09
445 Jason Giambi SH CL	.50	.15
446 Jeff Kent SH CL	.30	.09
447 Mariano Rivera SH CL	.30	.09
448 Edgar Martinez SH CL	.30	.09
449 Troy Glaus SH CL	.30	.09
450 Alex Rodriguez SH CL	.75	.23

2001 Upper Deck Exclusives Gold

Randomly inserted into series one packs, this 270-card set is a complete parallel of the 2001 Upper Deck series one base set. Please note that these cards were produced with gold lettering on the front and are individually serial numbered to 25. The words "Gold UD Exclusives" also run down the left side of each card front.

	Nm-Mt	Ex-Mt
*STARS: 40X TO 80X BASIC CARDS		
*SR STARS: 20X TO 40X BASIC SR		
*SR ROOKIES: 20X TO 40X BASIC SR		

2001 Upper Deck Exclusives Silver

Randomly inserted into series one packs, this 270-card set is a complete parallel of the 2001 Upper Deck series one base set. Please note that these cards were produced with silver lettering on the front and are individually serial numbered to 100. The words "UD Exclusives" also run down the left side of each card front.

	Nm-Mt	Ex-Mt
STARS: 12.5X TO 30X BASIC CARDS .		
*SR YNG.STARS: 6X TO 15X BASIC...		
*SR RC's: 6X TO 15X BASIC SR		

2001 Upper Deck 1971 All-Star Game Salute

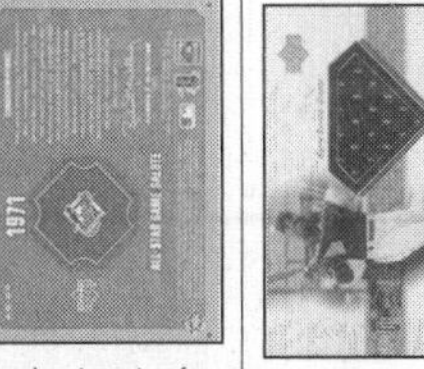

Inserted in second series packs at a rate of one in 288, these 12 memorabilia cards feature players who participated in the 1971 All-Star Game which was highlighted by Reggie Jackson's home run off the light tower at Tiger Stadium.

	Nm-Mt	Ex-Mt
AS-BR B. Robinson Bat	20.00	6.00
AS-FR Frank Robinson Jsy	15.00	4.50
AS-HA Hank Aaron Bat	40.00	12.00
AS-HA Hank Aaron Jsy	50.00	15.00
AS-JB Johnny Bench Bat	20.00	6.00
AS-JB Johnny Bench Jsy	20.00	6.00
AS-LA Luis Aparicio Jsy	15.00	4.50
AS-LB Lou Brock Bat	20.00	6.00
AS-RC R. Clemente Jsy	120.00	36.00
AS-RJ Reggie Jackson Jsy	20.00	6.00
AS-TM T. Munson Jsy	40.00	12.00
AS-TS Tom Seaver Jsy	20.00	6.00

2001 Upper Deck All-Star Heroes

Randomly inserted in second series packs, these 14 cards feature a mix of past and present players who have starred in All-Star Games. Since each player was issued to a different amount, we have notated that information in our checklist.

	Nm-Mt	Ex-Mt
ASH-AR Alex Rodriguez Bat/1998	15.00	4.50
ASH-BR Babe Ruth Bat/1933	150.00	45.00
ASH-CR Cal Ripken Bat/1991	40.00	12.00
ASH-DJ Derek Jeter Base/2000	25.00	7.50
ASH-JD Joe DiMaggio Jsy/36		
ASH-KG Ken Griffey Jr. Bat/1992	20.00	6.00
ASH-MM Mickey Mantle Jsy/54	350.00	105.00
ASH-MP Mike Piazza Base/1996	15.00	4.50
ASH-RC Roger Clemens Jsy/1986	20.00	6.00
ASH-RJ Randy Johnson Jsy/1993	15.00	4.50
ASH-SS Sammy Sosa Jsy/2000	20.00	6.00
ASH-TG Tony Gwynn Jsy/1994	15.00	4.50
ASH-TP Tony Perez Bat 1967	10.00	3.00
ASH-ROC R.Clemente Bat/1961	100.00	30.00

2001 Upper Deck Big League Beat

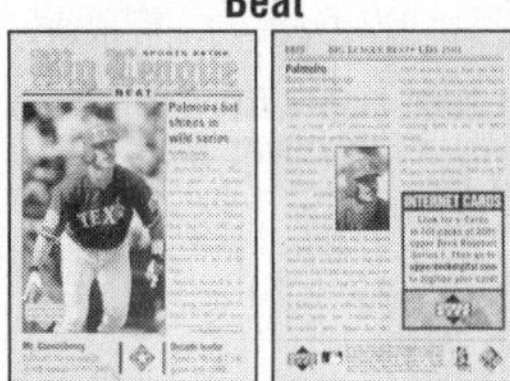

Randomly inserted into packs at one in three, this 20-card insert features some of the most prolific players in the Major Leagues. Card backs carry a "BB" prefix.

	Nm-Mt	Ex-Mt
COMPLETE SET (20)	20.00	6.00
BB1 Barry Bonds	2.00	.60
BB2 Nomar Garciaparra	1.25	.35
BB3 Mark McGwire	2.00	.60
BB4 Roger Clemens	1.50	.45
BB5 Chipper Jones	.75	.23
BB6 Jeff Bagwell	.50	.15
BB7 Sammy Sosa	1.25	.35
BB8 Cal Ripken	2.50	.75
BB9 Randy Johnson	.75	.23
BB10 Carlos Delgado	.50	.15
BB11 Manny Ramirez	.50	.15
BB12 Derek Jeter	2.00	.60
BB13 Tony Gwynn	1.00	.30
BB14 Pedro Martinez	.75	.23
BB15 Jose Canseco	.75	.23
BB16 Frank Thomas	.75	.23
BB17 Alex Rodriguez	1.25	.35
BB18 Bernie Williams	.50	.15
BB19 Greg Maddux	1.25	.35
BB20 Rafael Palmeiro	.50	.15

2001 Upper Deck Big League Challenge Game Jerseys

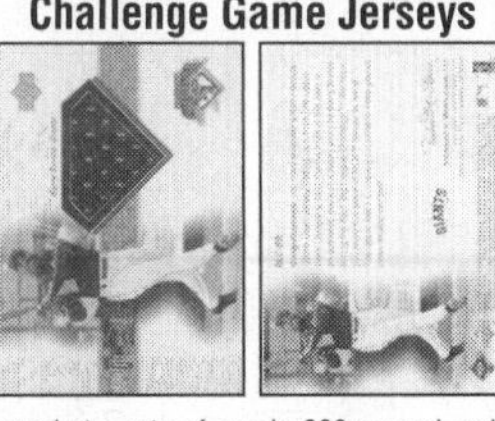

Issued at a rate of one in 288 second series packs, these 11 cards feature jersey pieces from participants in the 2001 Big League Challenge home run hitting contest.

	Nm-Mt	Ex-Mt
BLC-BB Barry Bonds	40.00	12.00
BLC-FT Frank Thomas	20.00	6.00
BLC-GS Gary Sheffield	15.00	4.50
BLC-JC Jose Canseco	20.00	6.00
BLC-JE Jim Edmonds	15.00	4.50
BLC-MP Mike Piazza	25.00	7.50
BLC-RH Richard Hidalgo	15.00	4.50
BLC-RP Rafael Palmeiro	20.00	6.00
BLC-SF Steve Finley	15.00	4.50
BLC-TG Troy Glaus	20.00	6.00
BLC-TH Todd Helton	20.00	6.00

2001 Upper Deck e-Card

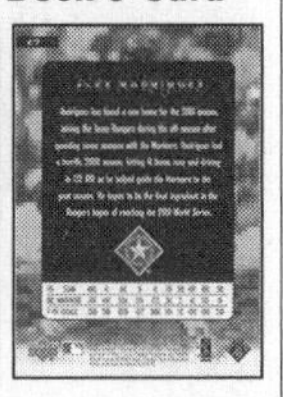

Inserted as a two-pack box-topper, this six-card insert features cards that can be viewed over the Upper Deck website. Cards feature a serial number that is to be typed in a the Upper Deck website to reveal that card. Card backs carry an "E" prefix.

	Nm-Mt	Ex-Mt
COMPLETE SET (12)	15.00	4.50
COMPLETE SERIES 1 (6)	6.00	1.80
COMPLETE SERIES 2 (6)	10.00	3.00
E1 Andruw Jones	1.00	.30
E2 Alex Rodriguez	1.50	.45
E3 Frank Thomas	1.00	.30
E4 Todd Helton	1.00	.30
E5 Troy Glaus	1.00	.30
E6 Barry Bonds	2.50	.75
E7 Alex Rodriguez	1.50	.45
E8 Ken Griffey Jr.	1.50	.45
E9 Sammy Sosa	1.50	.45
E10 Gary Sheffield	1.00	.30
E11 Barry Bonds	2.50	.75
E12 Andruw Jones	1.00	.30

2001 Upper Deck eVolve Autograph

Lucky participants in Upper Deck's E-Card program received special upgraded E-Cards available by checking the UD website (www.upperdeck.com) and entering their basic E-Card serial code (printed on the front of each basic E-Card). When viewed on the Upper Deck website, if an autographed card of the depicted player appeared, the bearer of the base card could then exchange their basic E-Card and receive the signed upgrade via mail. Only 200 serial numbered E-Card Autograph sets were produced. Signed E-Cards all have an ES prefix on the card numbers.

	Nm-Mt	Ex-Mt
ES-AJ Andruw Jones S1		
ES-AJ Andruw Jones S2		
ES-AR Alex Rodriguez S1		
ES-AR Alex Rodriguez S2		
ES-BB Barry Bonds S1		
ES-BB Barry Bonds S2		
ES-FT Frank Thomas S1		
ES-GS Gary Sheffield S2		
ES-KG Ken Griffey Jr. S2		
ES-SS Sammy Sosa S2		
ES-TG Troy Glaus S1		
ES-TH Todd Helton S1		

2001 Upper Deck eVolve Game Jersey

Lucky participants in Upper Deck's E-Card program received special upgraded E-Cards available by checking the UD website (www.upperdeck.com) and entering their basic E-Card serial code (printed on the front of each basic E-Card). When viewed on the Upper Deck website, if a jersey card of the depicted player appeared, the bearer of the base card could then exchange their basic E-Card and receive the Game Jersey upgrade via mail. The cards closely parallel basic 2000 Game Jerseys that were distributed in first and second series packs except for the gold foil "e-volve" logo on front. Only 300 serial numbered E-Card Jersey sets were produced with each card being serial -numbered by hand in blue ink sharpie at the bottom right front corner. Unsigned E-Card Game Jerseys all have an EJ prefix on the card numbers.

	Nm-Mt	Ex-Mt
EJ-AJ Andruw Jones S1		
EJ-AJ Andruw Jones S2		
EJ-AR Alex Rodriguez S1		
EJ-AR Alex Rodriguez S2		
EJ-BB Barry Bonds S1		
EJ-BB Barry Bonds S2		
EJ-FT Frank Thomas S1		
EJ-GS Gary Sheffield S2		
EJ-KG Ken Griffey Jr. S2		
EJ-SS Sammy Sosa S2		
EJ-TG Troy Glaus S1		
EJ-TH Todd Helton S1		

2001 Upper Deck eVolve Game Jersey Autograph

Lucky participants in Upper Deck's E-Card program received special upgraded E-Cards available by checking the UD website (www.upperdeck.com) and entering their basic E-Card serial code (printed on the front of each basic E-Card). When viewed on the Upper Deck website, if an autographed card of the depicted player appeared, the bearer of the base card could then exchange their basic E-Card and receive the signed jersey upgrade via mail. A mere 50 serial numbered sets were produced. Signed jersey E-Cards all have an ESJ prefix on the card numbers.

	Nm-Mt	Ex-Mt
ESJ-AJ Andruw Jones S1		
ESJ-AJ Andruw Jones S2		
ESJ-AR Alex Rodriguez S1		
ESJ-AR Alex Rodriguez S2		
ESJ-BB Barry Bonds S1		
ESJ-BB Barry Bonds S2		
ESJ-FT Frank Thomas S1		
ESJ-GS Gary Sheffield S2		
ESJ-KG Ken Griffey Jr. S2		
ESJ-SS Sammy Sosa S2		
ESJ-TG Troy Glaus S1		
ESJ-TH Todd Helton S1		

2001 Upper Deck Franchise

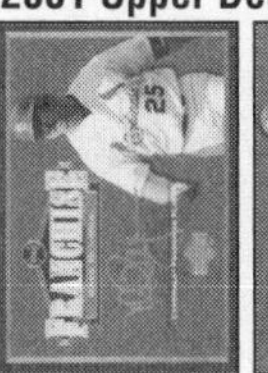

Inserted at a rate of one in 36 second series packs, these 10 cards feature players who are considered the money players for their franchise.

	Nm-Mt	Ex-Mt
COMPLETE SET (10)	60.00	18.00
F1 Frank Thomas	4.00	1.20
F2 Mark McGwire	10.00	3.00
F3 Ken Griffey Jr.	6.00	1.80
F4 Manny Ramirez	4.00	1.20
F5 Alex Rodriguez	6.00	1.80
F6 Greg Maddux	6.00	1.80
F7 Sammy Sosa	6.00	1.80
F8 Derek Jeter	10.00	3.00
F9 Mike Piazza	6.00	1.80
F10 Vladimir Guerrero	4.00	1.20

2001 Upper Deck Game Ball 1

Randomly inserted into packs, this 18-card insert features game-used baseballs from the depicted players. Card backs carry a "B" prefix.

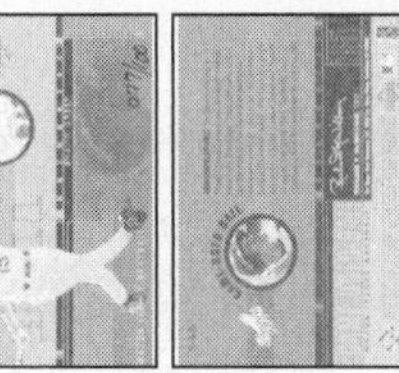

Please note that only 100 serial numbered sets were produced.

	Nm-Mt	Ex-Mt
B-AJ Andruw Jones	25.00	7.50
B-AR A.Rodriguez Mariners	60.00	18.00
B-BB Barry Bonds	80.00	24.00
B-DJ Derek Jeter	80.00	24.00
B-IR Ivan Rodriguez	40.00	12.00
B-JG Jeff Bagwell	40.00	12.00
B-JG Jason Giambi	40.00	12.00
B-KG Ken Griffey Jr.	50.00	15.00
B-MM Mark McGwire	100.00	30.00
B-MP Mike Piazza	60.00	18.00
B-RA Rick Ankiel	25.00	7.50
B-RJ Randy Johnson	40.00	12.00
B-SG Shawn Green	25.00	7.50
B-SS Sammy Sosa	50.00	15.00
B-TH Todd Helton	40.00	12.00
B-TOG Tony Gwynn	40.00	12.00
B-TRG Troy Glaus	40.00	12.00
B-VG Vladimir Guerrero	40.00	12.00

2001 Upper Deck Game Ball 2

Inserted into second series packs at a rate of one in 288 , this 18-card insert features game-used baseballs from the depicted players. Card backs carry a "B" prefix. The Nomar Garciaparra card was short printed and has been notated as such in our checklist.

	Nm-Mt	Ex-Mt
B-AJ Andruw Jones	10.00	3.00
B-AR A.Rodriguez Rangers	25.00	7.50
B-BB Barry Bonds	40.00	12.00
B-BW Bernie Williams	15.00	4.50
B-CJ Chipper Jones	15.00	4.50
B-CR Cal Ripken	40.00	12.00
B-DJ Derek Jeter	40.00	12.00
B-GS Gary Sheffield	10.00	3.00
B-JB Jeff Bagwell	15.00	4.50
B-JK Jeff Kent	10.00	3.00
B-KG Ken Griffey Jr.	25.00	7.50
B-MM Mark McGwire	50.00	15.00
B-MP Mike Piazza	25.00	7.50
B-MR Mariano Rivera	15.00	4.50
B-NG N.Garciaparra SP	40.00	12.00
B-RC Roger Clemens	25.00	7.50
B-SS Sammy Sosa	25.00	7.50
B-VG Vladimir Guerrero	15.00	4.50

2001 Upper Deck Game Ball Gold Autograph

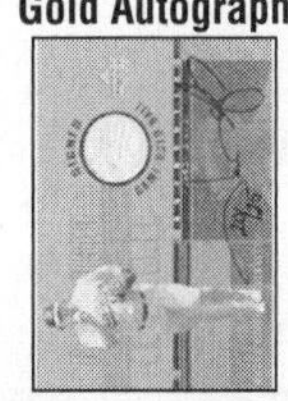

Randomly inserted into packs, this nine-card insert set features autographs and game-used baseball swatches from the depicted players below. Card backs carry a "SB" prefix. Please note that only 25 serial numbered sets were produced. The following cards packed out as exchange cards with a redmption deadline of August 7th, 2001: Alex Rodriguez, Jeff Bagwell, Ken Griffey Jr. and Rick Ankiel.

	Nm-Mt	Ex-Mt
SB-AR Alex Rodriguez		
SB-BB Barry Bonds		
SB-JB Jeff Bagwell		
SB-JG Jason Giambi		
SB-KG Ken Griffey Jr.		
SB-RA Rick Ankiel		
SB-RJ Randy Johnson		
SB-SG Shawn Green		
SB-TH Todd Helton		

2001 Upper Deck Game Jersey

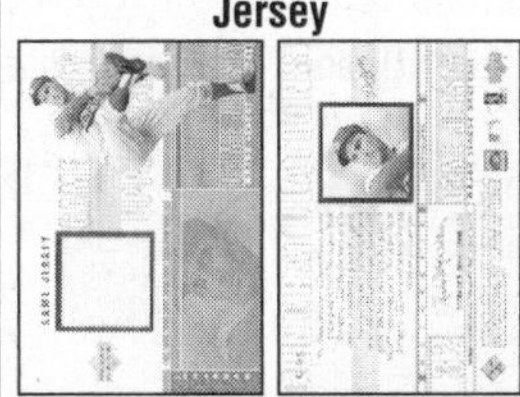

These cards feature swatches of jerseys of various major league stars. These cards were available in either series one hobby or retail packs at a rate of one every 288 packs. Card backs carry a "C" prefix.

	Nm-Mt	Ex-Mt
C-AJ A.Jones HR1	15.00	4.50
C-AR Alex Rodriguez	50.00	15.00
C-BW B.Williams HR1	25.00	7.50
C-CR Cal Ripken	80.00	24.00
C-DJ Derek Jeter	60.00	18.00
C-FT Fernando Tatis	15.00	4.50
C-IR Ivan Rodriguez	25.00	7.50
C-KG Ken Griffey Jr.	50.00	15.00
C-MR M.Ramirez HR1	15.00	4.50
C-MW Matt Williams	15.00	4.50
C-NRA Nolan Ryan Astros HR1	80.00	24.00
C-NRR Nolan Ryan Rangers HR1	80.00	24.00
C-PO Paul O'Neill	25.00	7.50
C-RV Robin Ventura	15.00	4.50
C-SK Sandy Koufax	150.00	45.00
C-TG Tony Gwynn	30.00	9.00
C-TH Todd Helton	25.00	7.50
C-TIH Tim Hudson	15.00	4.50

2001 Upper Deck Game Jersey Autograph 1

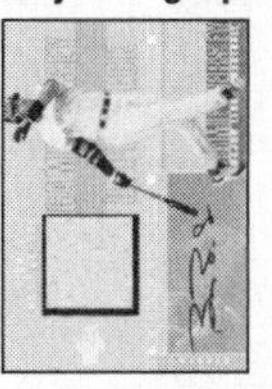

These cards feature both autographs and swatches of jerseys from various major league stars. The cards which have an "H1" after the player names are available in series one hobby packs at a rate of one in every 288 packs. Card backs carry a "H" prefix. The following cards were distributed in packs as exchange cards: Alex Rodriguez, Jeff Bagwell, Ken Griffey Jr., Mike Hampton and Rick Ankiel. The deadline to exchange these cards was August 7th, 2001.

	Nm-Mt	Ex-Mt
H-AR A.Rodriguez H1	150.00	45.00
H-BB Barry Bonds	250.00	75.00
H-FT Frank Thomas	80.00	24.00
H-GM Greg Maddux	150.00	45.00
H-JB J.Bagwell H1	80.00	24.00
H-JC Jose Canseco	80.00	24.00
H-JD J.D. Drew	40.00	12.00
H-JG Jason Giambi	80.00	24.00
H-JL Javy Lopez	40.00	12.00
H-KG K.Griffey Jr. H1	150.00	45.00
H-MH M.Hampton H1	40.00	12.00
H-NRA Nolan Ryan Angels	200.00	60.00
H-NRM Nolan Ryan Mets	200.00	60.00
H-RA R.Ankiel H1	30.00	9.00
H-RJ Randy Johnson	120.00	36.00
H-RP Rafael Palmeiro	80.00	24.00
H-SC Sean Casey	40.00	12.00
H-SG Shawn Green	40.00	12.00

2001 Upper Deck Game Jersey Autograph 2

These cards feature both autographs and swatches of jerseys from various major league stars. The cards which have an "H2" after the player names are available in series one hobby packs at a rate of one in every 288 packs. Card backs carry a "H" prefix. Please note a few of the players were issued in lesser quantites and we have notated those as SP's. The following players packed out as exchange cards: Alex Rodriguez and Ken Griffey Jr. The deadline for exchange is June 26th, 2006.

	Nm-Mt	Ex-Mt
AJ Andruw Jones	50.00	15.00
AR Alex Rodriguez EXCH	150.00	45.00
BB Barry Bonds	250.00	75.00
CJ Chipper Jones	80.00	24.00
CR Cal Ripken SP	250.00	75.00
GS Gary Sheffield	50.00	15.00
IR Ivan Rodriguez SP	100.00	30.00
JB Johnny Bench	80.00	24.00
JC Jose Canseco	80.00	24.00
KG Ken Griffey Jr. EXCH	150.00	45.00
NR Nolan Ryan	200.00	60.00
RC Roger Clemens	150.00	45.00
SS Sammy Sosa SP	250.00	75.00
TG Troy Glaus	50.00	15.00

2001 Upper Deck Game Jersey Autograph Numbered

These cards feature both autographs and swatches of jerseys from various major league stars. The cards which have an "H" after the player names were only available in series one hobby packs, while the cards with a "C" can be found in either series one hobby or retail packs. Hobby cards feature gold backgrounds and say "Signed Game Jersey" on front. Hobby/Retail cards feature white backgrounds and simply say "Game Jersey" on front. These cards are individually serial numbered to the depicted player's jersey number. The following players packed out as exchange cards: Alex Rodriguez, Ken Griffey Jr., Jeff Bagwell, Mike Hampton and Rick Ankiel. The exchange deadline was August 7th, 2001.

	Nm-Mt	Ex-Mt
C-AJ Andruw Jones/25		
C-AR Alex Rodriguez/3		
C-FT Fernando Tatis/23		
C-IR Ivan Rodriguez/7		
C-JL Javy Lopez/8		
C-KG Ken Griffey Jr./30	400.00	120.00
HR1		
C-MW Matt Williams/9		
C-NRA Nolan Ryan	400.00	120.00
Astros/34 HR1		
C-NRR Nolan Ryan	400.00	120.00
Rangers 34 HR1		
C-PO Paul O'Neill/21		
C-RV Robin Ventura/4		
C-SK Sandy Koufax	1000.00	300.00
32 HR1		
C-TG Tony Gwynn/19		
C-TH Todd Helton/17		
C-TIH Tim Hudson/15		
H-AR Alex Rodriguez/3		
H-BB Barry Bonds/25		
H-FT Frank Thomas/35	150.00	45.00
H-GM Greg Maddux/31	300.00	90.00
H-JB Jeff Bagwell/5		
H-JC Jose Canseco/33	150.00	45.00
H-JD J.D. Drew/7		
H-JG Jason Giambi/16		
H-KG Ken Griffey Jr.	400.00	120.00
30 H1		
H-MH Mike Hampton/32	60.00	18.00
H-NRA Nolan Ryan	400.00	120.00
30/Angels H1		
H-NRM Nolan Ryan	500.00	150.00
30/Mets H1		
H-RA Rick Ankiel	40.00	12.00
66 H1		
H-RJ Randy Johnson	150.00	45.00
51 H1		
H-RP Rafael Palmeiro		
25 H1		
H-SC Sean Casey/21		
H-SG Shawn Green/15		

2001 Upper Deck Game Jersey Combo

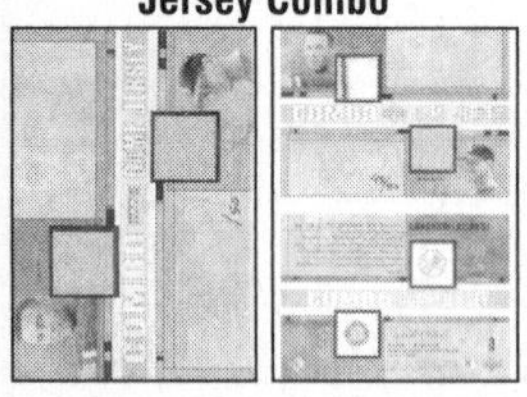

Randomly inserted into series one packs, these 13 cards feature dual player game-worn uniform patches. Card backs carry both players initials as numbering. Please note that there were only 50 serial numbered sets produced.

	Nm-Mt	Ex-Mt
AJKG Andruw Jones	80.00	24.00
Ken Griffey Jr.		
BBJC Barry Bonds	120.00	36.00
Jose Canseco		
BBKG Barry Bonds	120.00	36.00
Ken Griffey Jr.		
DJAR Derek Jeter	150.00	45.00
Alex Rodriguez		
FTJB Frank Thomas	50.00	15.00
Jeff Bagwell		
IRRP Ivan Rodriguez	50.00	15.00
Rafael Palmeiro		
JDRA J.D. Drew	40.00	12.00
Rick Ankiel		
MMKG Mickey Mantle		
Ken Griffey Jr.		
NRAR Nolan Rya	150.00	45.00
Astros-Rangers		
NRMA Nolan Ryan	150.00	45.00
Mets-Angels		
RATH Rick Ankiel	40.00	12.00
Tim Hudson		
RJGM Randy Johnson	80.00	24.00
Greg Maddux		
TGCR Tony Gwynn	150.00	45.00
Cal Ripken		
VGMR Vladimir Guerrero	50.00	15.00
Manny Ramirez		

2001 Upper Deck Game Jersey Combo Autograph

Randomly inserted into series one hobby packs, these seven cards feature autographed dual player game-worn uniform patches. Card backs carry both players initials as numbering with a "S" prefix. Please note that there were only 10 serial numbered sets produced. Cards SAJ-KG and SJD-RA both packed out as exchange cards with a redemption deadline of 8/07/01. Due to market scarcity, no pricing is provided.

	Nm-Mt	Ex-Mt
SAJ-KG Andruw Jones		
Ken Griffey Jr. EXCH		
SBB-JC Barry Bonds		
Jose Canseco		
SBB-KG Barry Bonds		
Ken Griffey Jr.		
SDJ-AR Derek Jeter		
Alex Rodriguez		
SJD-RA J.D. Drew		
Rick Ankiel		
SNR-AR Nolan Ryan Astros-Rangers		
SNR-MA Nolan Ryan Mets-Angels		

2001 Upper Deck Game Jersey Patch

Randomly inserted into series one packs at one in 7500 and series 2 packs at 1:5000, these cards feature game-worn uniform patches. Card backs carry a "P" prefix.

	Nm-Mt	Ex-Mt
P-AR Alex Rodriguez S1	150.00	45.00
P-AR Alex Rodriguez S2	150.00	45.00
P-BB Barry Bonds S1	150.00	45.00
P-BB Barry Bonds S2	150.00	45.00
P-CJ Chipper Jones S2	120.00	36.00
P-CR Cal Ripken S1	150.00	45.00
P-CR Cal Ripken S2	150.00	45.00
P-DJ Derek Jeter S1	150.00	45.00
P-FT Frank Thomas S1	120.00	36.00
P-IR Ivan Rodriguez S1	120.00	36.00
P-IR Ivan Rodriguez S2	120.00	36.00
P-JB Johnny Bench S2	120.00	36.00
P-JB Jeff Bagwell S1	120.00	36.00
P-JC Jose Canseco S1	120.00	36.00
P-JG Jason Giambi S1	120.00	36.00
P-KG Ken Griffey Jr. S1	150.00	45.00
P-KG Ken Griffey Jr. S2	150.00	45.00
P-NRA Nolan Ryan Astros	200.00	60.00
P-NRR N.Ryan Rangers S1	200.00	60.00
P-NRR N.Ryan Rangers S2	200.00	60.00
P-RA Rick Ankiel S1	80.00	24.00
P-RP Rafael Palmeiro S1	120.00	36.00
P-SS Sammy Sosa S2	150.00	45.00
P-TG Tony Gwynn S1	120.00	36.00

2001 Upper Deck Game Jersey Patch Autograph Numbered

Randomly inserted into series one hobby packs, these cards feature both autographs and game-worn uniform patches. Card backs carry a "SP" prefix. Please note that these cards are hand-numbered to the depicted players jersey number. All of these cards packed out as exchange cards with a redemption deadline of 8/07/01.

	Nm-Mt	Ex-Mt
SP-AR Alex Rodriguez/3		
SP-KG K.Griffey Jr./30	800.00	240.00
SP-RA Rick Ankiel/66	80.00	24.00

2001 Upper Deck Home Run Derby Heroes

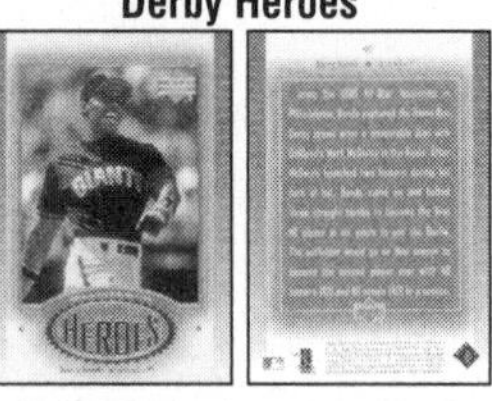

Inserted in second series packs at a rate of one in 36, these 10 cards features a look back at some of the most explosive performances from past Home Run Derby competitions.

	Nm-Mt	Ex-Mt
COMPLETE SET (10)	50.00	15.00
HD1 Mark McGwire 99	10.00	3.00
HD2 Sammy Sosa 00	6.00	1.80
HD3 Frank Thomas 96	4.00	1.20
HD4 Cal Ripken 91	12.00	3.60
HD5 Tino Martinez 97	2.50	.75
HD6 Ken Griffey Jr. 99	6.00	1.80
HD7 Barry Bonds 96	10.00	3.00
HD8 Albert Belle 95	2.00	.60
HD9 Mark McGwire 92	10.00	3.00
HD10 Juan Gonzalez 93	4.00	1.20

2001 Upper Deck Home Run Explosion

Randomly inserted into series one packs at one in 12, this 15-card insert features players that are among the league leaders in homeruns every year. Card backs carry a "HR" prefix.

	Nm-Mt	Ex-Mt
COMPLETE SET (15)	40.00	12.00
HR1 Mark McGwire	5.00	1.50
HR2 Chipper Jones	2.00	.60
HR3 Jeff Bagwell	1.25	.35
HR4 Carlos Delgado	1.00	.30
HR5 Barry Bonds	5.00	1.50
HR6 Troy Glaus	1.25	.35
HR7 Sammy Sosa	3.00	.90
HR8 Alex Rodriguez	3.00	.90
HR9 Mike Piazza	3.00	.90
HR10 Vladimir Guerrero	2.00	.60
HR11 Ken Griffey Jr.	3.00	.90
HR12 Frank Thomas	2.00	.60
HR13 Ivan Rodriguez	2.00	.60
HR14 Jason Giambi	2.00	.60
HR15 Carl Everett	1.00	.30

2001 Upper Deck Midseason Superstar Summit

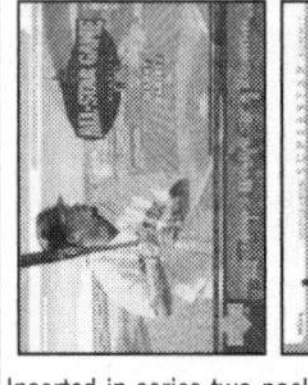

Inserted in series two packs at a rate of one in 24, these 15 cards feature some of the most dominant players of the 2000 season.

	Nm-Mt	Ex-Mt
COMPLETE SET (15)	60.00	18.00
MS1 Derek Jeter	10.00	3.00
MS2 Sammy Sosa	6.00	1.80
MS3 Jeff Bagwell	2.50	.75
MS4 Tony Gwynn	5.00	1.50
MS5 Alex Rodriguez	6.00	1.80
MS6 Greg Maddux	6.00	1.80
MS7 Jason Giambi	4.00	1.20
MS8 Mark McGwire	10.00	3.00
MS9 Barry Bonds	10.00	3.00
MS10 Ken Griffey Jr.	6.00	1.80
MS11 Carlos Delgado	2.00	.60
MS12 Troy Glaus	2.50	.75
MS13 Todd Helton	2.50	.75
MS14 Manny Ramirez	2.00	.60
MS15 Jeff Kent	2.00	.60

2001 Upper Deck Midsummer Classic Moments

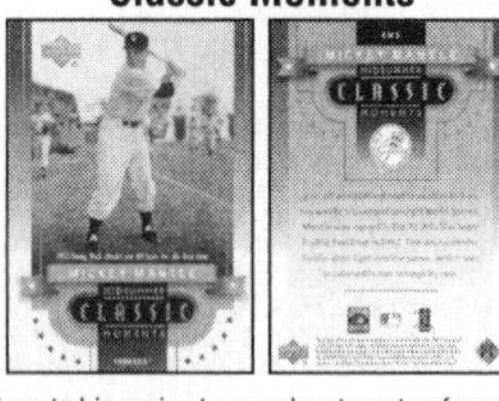

Inserted in series two packs at a rate of one in 12, these 20 cards feature some of the most memorable moments from All Star Game history.

	Nm-Mt	Ex-Mt
COMPLETE SET (20)	40.00	12.00
CM1 Joe DiMaggio 36	3.00	.90
CM2 Joe DiMaggio 51	3.00	.90
CM3 Mickey Mantle 52	6.00	1.80
CM4 Mickey Mantle 68	6.00	1.80
CM5 Roger Clemens 86	4.00	1.20
CM6 Mark McGwire 87	5.00	1.50
CM7 Cal Ripken 91	6.00	1.80
CM8 Ken Griffey Jr. 92	3.00	.90
CM9 Randy Johnson 93	2.00	.60
CM10 Tony Gwynn 94	2.50	.75
CM11 Fred McGriff 94	1.25	.35
CM12 Hideo Nomo 95	2.00	.60
CM13 Jeff Conine 95	1.00	.30
CM14 Mike Piazza 96	3.00	.90
CM15 Sandy Alomar Jr.	1.00	.30
CM16 Alex Rodriguez 98	2.50	.75
CM17 Roberto Alomar 98	2.00	.60
CM18 Pedro Martinez 99	2.00	.60
CM19 Andres Galarraga	1.00	.30
CM20 Derek Jeter 00	4.00	1.20

2001 Upper Deck People's Choice

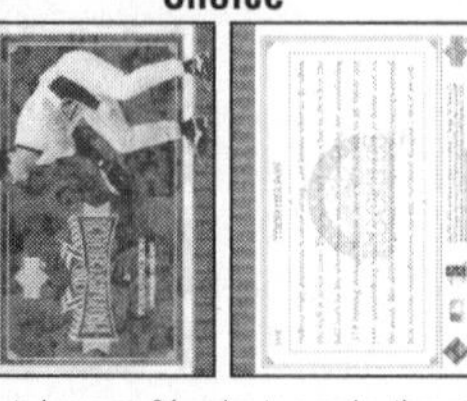

Inserted one per 24 series two packs, these 15 cards feature the players who fans want to see the most.

	Nm-Mt	Ex-Mt
COMPLETE SET (15)	80.00	24.00
PC1 Alex Rodriguez	6.00	1.80
PC2 Ken Griffey Jr.	6.00	1.80
PC3 Mark McGwire	10.00	3.00
PC4 Todd Helton	2.50	.75
PC5 Manny Ramirez	2.50	.75
PC6 Mike Piazza	6.00	1.80
PC7 Vladimir Guerrero	4.00	1.20
PC8 Randy Johnson	4.00	1.20
PC9 Cal Ripken	12.00	3.60
PC10 Andruw Jones	2.50	.75
PC11 Sammy Sosa	6.00	1.80
PC12 Derek Jeter	10.00	3.00
PC13 Pedro Martinez	4.00	1.20
PC14 Frank Thomas	4.00	1.20
PC15 Nomar Garciaparra	6.00	1.80

2001 Upper Deck Rookie Roundup

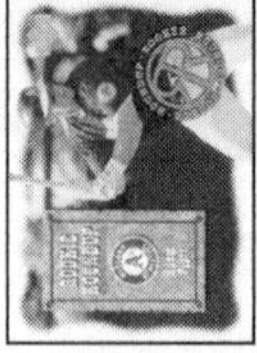

Randomly inserted into series one packs at one in six, this 10-card insert features some of the younger players in Major League baseball. Card backs carry a "RR" prefix.

	Nm-Mt	Ex-Mt
COMPLETE SET (10)	5.00	1.50
RR1 Rick Ankiel	.50	.15
RR2 Adam Kennedy	.50	.15
RR3 Mike Lamb	.50	.15
RR4 Adam Eaton	.50	.15
RR5 Rafael Furcal	.75	.23
RR6 Pat Burrell	.75	.23
RR7 Adam Piatt	.50	.15
RR8 Eric Munson	.50	.15
RR9 Brad Penny	.50	.15
RR10 Mark Mulder	.75	.23

2001 Upper Deck Subway Series Game Jerseys

While the set name seemed to indicate that these cards were from jerseys worn during the 2000 World series, they were actually swatches from regular-season game jerseys.

	Nm-Mt	Ex-Mt
SS-AL Al Leiter	10.00	3.00
SS-AP Andy Pettitte	25.00	7.50
SS-BW Bernie Williams	25.00	7.50
SS-EA Edgardo Alfonzo	10.00	3.00
SS-JF John Franco	10.00	3.00
SS-JP Jay Payton	8.00	2.40
SS-OH Orlando Hernandez	20.00	6.00
SS-PO Paul O'Neill	25.00	7.50
SS-RC Roger Clemens	40.00	12.00
SS-TP Timo Perez	8.00	2.40

2001 Upper Deck Superstar Summit

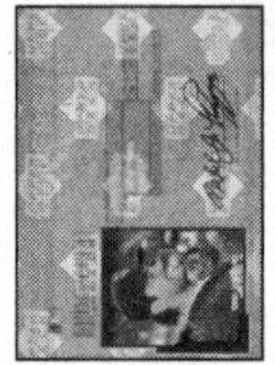

Randomly inserted into packs at one in 12, this 15-card insert features the Major League's top superstar caliber players. Card backs carry a "SS" prefix.

	Nm-Mt	Ex-Mt
COMPLETE SET (15)	50.00	15.00
SS1 Derek Jeter	5.00	1.50
SS2 Randy Johnson	2.00	.60
SS3 Barry Bonds	5.00	1.50
SS4 Frank Thomas	2.00	.60
SS5 Cal Ripken	6.00	1.80
SS6 Pedro Martinez	2.00	.60
SS7 Ivan Rodriguez	2.00	.60
SS8 Mike Piazza	3.00	.90
SS9 Mark McGwire	5.00	1.50
SS10 Manny Ramirez	2.00	.60
SS11 Ken Griffey Jr.	3.00	.90
SS12 Sammy Sosa	3.00	.90
SS13 Alex Rodriguez	3.00	.90
SS14 Chipper Jones	2.00	.60
SS15 Nomar Garciaparra	3.00	.90

2001 Upper Deck UD's Most Wanted

Randomly inserted into packs at one in 14, this 15-card insert features players that are in high demand on the collectibles market. Card backs carry a "MW" prefix.

	Nm-Mt	Ex-Mt
COMPLETE SET (15)	60.00	18.00
MW1 Mark McGwire	6.00	1.80
MW2 Cal Ripken	8.00	2.40
MW3 Ivan Rodriguez	2.50	.75
MW4 Pedro Martinez	2.50	.75
MW5 Sammy Sosa	4.00	1.20
MW6 Tony Gwynn	3.00	.90
MW7 Vladimir Guerrero	2.50	.75
MW8 Derek Jeter	6.00	1.80
MW9 Mike Piazza	4.00	1.20
MW10 Chipper Jones	2.50	.75
MW11 Alex Rodriguez	4.00	1.20
MW12 Barry Bonds	6.00	1.80
MW13 Jeff Bagwell	2.50	.75
MW14 Frank Thomas	2.50	.75
MW15 Nomar Garciaparra	4.00	1.20

2001 Upper Deck Pinstripe Exclusives DiMaggio

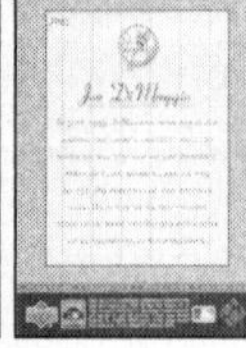

This 56-card set features a wide selection of cards focusing on Yankees legend Joe DiMaggio. The cards were distributed in special three-card foil wrapped packs, exclusively seeded into 2001 SP Game Bat Milestone, SP Game-Used, SPx, Upper Deck Decade 1970's, Upper Deck Gold Glove, Upper Deck Legends, Upper Deck Ovation and Upper Deck Sweet Spot hobby boxes at a rate of one pack per sealed box.

	Nm-Mt	Ex-Mt
COMPLETE SET (56)	60.00	18.00
COMMON (JD1-JD56)	1.50	.45

2001 Upper Deck Pinstripe Exclusives DiMaggio Memorabilia

Randomly seeded into special three-card Pinstripe Exclusives DiMaggio foil packs (of which were distributed exclusively in 2001 SP Game Bat Milestone, SP Game-Used, SPx, Upper Deck Decade 1970's, Upper Deck Gold Glove, Upper Deck Legends, Upper Deck Ovation and Upper Deck Sweet Spot Sweet Spot hobby boxes) were a selection of scarce game-used memorabilia and autograph cut cards featuring Joe DiMaggio. Each card is serial-numbered and features either a game-used bat chip, jersey swatch or autograph cut.

	Nm-Mt	Ex-Mt
COMMON BAT (B1-B9)	100.00	30.00
COMMON JERSEY (J1-J9)	120.00	36.00
COMMON BAT CUT (BC1-BC7)		
COMMON CUT (C1-C8)		
SUFFIX 1 CARDS DIST.IN SWEET SPOT		
SUFFIX 2 CARDS DIST.IN OVATION		
SUFFIX 3 CARDS DIST.IN SPX		
SUFFIX 4 CARDS DIST.IN SP GAME USED		
SUFFIX 5 CARDS DIST.IN LEGENDS		
SUFFIX 6 CARDS DIST. IN DECADE 1970		
SUFFIX 7 CARDS DIST.IN SP BAT MILE		
SUFFIX 8 CARDS DIST.IN UD GOLD GLOVE		
BAT 1-9 PRINT RUN 100 SERIAL #'d SETS		
BAT-CUT 1-7 PRINT RUN 5 SERIAL #'d SETS		
COMBO 1-6 PRINT RUN 50 SERIAL #'D SETS		
CUT 1-8 PRINT RUN 5 SERIAL #'d SETS		
JERSEY 1-8 PRINT RUN 100 SERIAL #'d SETS		
CJ1 Joe DiMaggio Jsy	600.00	180.00
Lou Gehrig Pants/50		
CJ2 Joe DiMaggio Jsy	400.00	120.00
Mickey Mantle Jsy/50		
CJ3 Joe DiMaggio Jsy	200.00	60.00
Ken Griffey Jr. Jsy/50		
CJ4 Joe DiMaggio Jsy	250.00	75.00
Dom DiMaggio Jsy/50		
CJ5 Joe DiMaggio Jsy	400.00	120.00
Mickey Mantle Jsy/50		
CJ6 Joe DiMaggio Jsy	400.00	120.00
Mickey Mantle Jsy/50		

2001 Upper Deck Pinstripe Exclusives Mantle

This 56-card set features a wide selection of cards focusing on Yankees legend Mickey Mantle. The cards were distributed in special three-card foil wrapped packs, seeded into 2001 Upper Deck Series 2, Upper Deck Hall of Famers, Upper Deck MVP and Upper Deck

Vintage hobby boxes at a rate of one pack per 24 ct. box.

	Nm-Mt	Ex-Mt
COMPLETE SET (56)	100.00	30.00
COMMON (MM1-MM56)	2.50	.75

2001 Upper Deck Pinstripe Exclusives Mantle Memorabilia

Randomly seeded into special three-card Pinstripe Exclusives Mantle foil packs (of which were distributed in hobby boxes of 2001 SP Authentic, 2001 SP Game Bat Milestone, 2001 Upper Deck series 2, 2001 Upper Deck Hall of Famers, 2001 Upper Deck Legends of New York, 2001 Upper Deck MVP and 2001 Upper Deck Vintage) were a selection of scarce game-used memorabilia and autograph cut cards featuring Mickey Mantle. Each card is serial-numbered and features either a game-used bat chip, jersey swatch or autograph cut.

	Nm-Mt	Ex-Mt
COMMON BAT (B1-B4)	150.00	45.00
COMMON JERSEY (J1-J7)	200.00	60.00
COMMON BAT CUT (BC1-BC4)		
COMMON CUT (C1-C4)		

SUFFIX 1 CARDS DIST.IN UD VINTAGE
SUFFIX 2 CARDS DIST.IN UD HOF'ers
SUFFIX 3 CARDS DIST.IN UD MVP
SUFFIX 4 CARDS DIST.IN SP AUTH
SUFFIX 5 CARDS DIST.IN SP AUTH...
SUFFIX 6 CARDS DIST. IN SP GAME BAT MILE
SUFFIX 7 CARDS DIST. IN UD LEG OF NY
BAT 1-9 PRINT RUN 100 SERIAL #'d SETS
BAT-CUT 1-4 PRINT RUN 7 SERIAL #'d SETS
COMBO 1-6 PRINT RUN 50 SERIAL #'d SETS
CUT 1-4 PRINT RUN 7 SERIAL #'D SETS
JERSEY 1-7 PRINT RUN 100 SERIAL #'d SETS

	Nm-Mt	Ex-Mt
CJ1 Mickey Mantle / Roger Maris Jsy/50	400.00	120.00
CJ2 Mickey Mantle / Joe DiMag Jsy/50	400.00	120.00
CJ3 Mickey Mantle / Ken Griffey Jsy/50	250.00	75.00
CJ4 Mickey Mantle / Roger Maris Jsy/50	400.00	120.00
CJ5 Mickey Mantle / Joe DiMaggio Jsy/50	400.00	120.00
CJ6 Mickey Mantle / Joe DiMaggio Jsy/50	400.00	120.00
CJ7 Mickey Mantle / Joe DiMaggio Jsy 50	400.00	120.00

2001 Upper Deck Gwynn

This five-card standard-size set was issued by Upper Deck to honor Tony Gwynn during his final days as an active player. These cards feature shots of Tony Gwynn along with a blurb on the back and career stats. Each card also has a "Thanks Tony" logo on the bottom left corner.

	Nm-Mt	Ex-Mt
COMPLETE SET	25.00	7.50
COMMON CARD	5.00	1.50

2001 Upper Deck Collectibles Ichiro Tribute to 51

This set was issued by Upper Deck to commemorate both the sensational rookie season of Ichiro Suzuki and the signing of Suzuki to an Upper Deck spokesman contract. Cards numbered I1 through I20 are regular cards while I21 through I25 are milestone cards. The set was issued in a box which contained these 25 cards as well as as a special bonus jumbo commemorative card. The set originally retailed for $19.95.

	Nm-Mt	Ex-Mt
COMPLETE FACT. SET (26)	20.00	6.00
COMMON ICHIRO (I1-I25)	.75	.23
XX Ichiro Suzuki / 3 1/2" by 5" commemorative card	2.00	.60

2001 Upper Deck DiMaggio Kit Young Game Bat

These cards were passed out to paid attendees of the 2001 Kit Young Hawaii Trade Conference on the day of Tuesday, February 27th (during day one of the popular Meet the Industry session). The basic card features a piece of bat in the shape of the classic NY logo that was used by Joe DiMaggio in an official Major League Baseball game. Each card was presented in a special silver foil Kit Young Hawaii wrapper. Please note that each pack also contained a special card explaining Upper Deck's 2001 Pinstripe Exclusive Promotion. Five lucky attendees got one of the rare autograph cut variation cards. Please note that each basic card is serial numbered to 450 in gold foil on the back.

	Nm-Mt	Ex-Mt
KY-JD1 Joe DiMaggio Bat/450	125.00	38.00
KY-JD3 Joe DiMaggio Bat AU/5		

2001 Upper Deck Subway Series Heroes

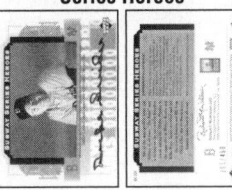

These four cards were distributed exclusively to paid attendees of the 2001 Kit Young Trade Show in Hawaii that took place in late February of that year. Each card was handed out on a different day of the week long trade show. The cards measure the standard 2 1/2" by 3 1/2" dimensions and feature a vintage era black and white image on a horizontal card front. Each player signed his cards in blue sharpie on front. Only 450 sets were produced and each card is serial numbered to that figure in gold foil on back.

	Nm-Mt	Ex-Mt
COMPLETE SET (4)	100.00	30.00
KY-SS1 Don Larsen	15.00	4.50
KY-SS2 Whitey Ford	40.00	12.00
KY-SS3 Johnny Podres	10.00	3.00
KY-SS4 Duke Snider	40.00	12.00

2002 Upper Deck

The 500 card first series set was issued in November, 2001. The 245-card second series set was issued in May, 2002. The cards were issued in eight card packs with 24 packs to a box. Subsets include Star Rookies (cards numbered 1-50, 501-545), World Stage (cards numbered 461-480), Griffey Gallery (481-490) and Checklists (491-500, 736-745) and Year of the Record (726-735). Star Rookies were inserted at a rate of one per pack into second series packs, making them 1.75X times tougher to pull than veteran second series cards.

	Nm-Mt	Ex-Mt
COMPLETE SET (745)	160.00	47.50
COMPLETE SERIES 1 (500)	110.00	33.00
COMPLETE SERIES 2 (245)	50.00	15.00
COMMON (51-500/546-745)	.30	.09
COMMON SR (1-50/501-545)	1.00	.30
1 Mark Prior SR	5.00	1.50
2 Mark Teixeira SR	1.50	.45
3 Brian Roberts SR	1.00	.30
4 Jason Romano SR	1.00	.30
5 Dennis Stark SR	1.00	.30
6 Oscar Salazar SR	1.00	.30
7 John Patterson SR	1.00	.30
8 Shane Loux SR	1.00	.30
9 Marcus Giles SR	1.00	.30
10 Juan Cruz SR	1.00	.30
11 Jorge Julio SR	1.00	.30
12 Adam Dunn SR	1.00	.30
13 Delvin James SR	1.00	.30
14 Jeremy Affeldt SR	1.00	.30
15 Tim Raines Jr. SR	1.00	.30
16 Luke Hudson SR	1.00	.30
17 Todd Sears SR	1.00	.30
18 George Perez SR	1.00	.30
19 Wilmy Caceres SR	1.00	.30
20 Abraham Nunez SR	1.00	.30
21 Mike Amrhein SR RC	1.00	.30
22 Carlos Hernandez SR	1.00	.30
23 Scott Hodges SR	1.00	.30
24 Brandon Knight SR	1.00	.30
25 Geoff Goetz SR	1.00	.30
26 Carlos Garcia SR	1.00	.30
27 Luis Pineda SR	1.00	.30
28 Chris Gissell SR	1.00	.30
29 Jae Weong Seo SR	1.00	.30
30 Paul Phillips SR	1.00	.30
31 Cory Aldridge SR	1.00	.30
32 Aaron Cook SR RC	1.00	.30
33 Rendy Espina SR RC	1.00	.30
34 Jason Phillips SR	1.00	.30
35 Carlos Silva SR	1.00	.30
36 Ryan Mills SR	1.00	.30
37 Pedro Santana SR	1.00	.30
38 John Grabow SR	1.00	.30
39 Cody Ransom SR	1.00	.30
40 Orlando Woodards SR	1.00	.30
41 Bud Smith SR	1.00	.30
42 Junior Guerrero SR	1.00	.30
43 David Brous SR	1.00	.30
44 Steve Green SR	1.00	.30
45 Brian Rogers SR	1.00	.30
46 Juan Figueroa SR RC	1.00	.30
47 Nick Punto SR	1.00	.30
48 Junior Herndon SR	1.00	.30
49 Justin Kaye SR	1.00	.30
50 Jason Karnuth SR	1.00	.30
51 Troy Glaus	.50	.15
52 Bengie Molina	.30	.09
53 Ramon Ortiz	.30	.09
54 Aaron Kennedy	.30	.09
55 Jarrod Washburn	.30	.09
56 Troy Percival	.30	.09
57 David Eckstein	.30	.09
58 Ben Weber	.30	.09
59 Larry Barnes	.30	.09
60 Ismael Valdes	.30	.09
61 Benji Gil	.30	.09
62 Scott Schoeneweis	.30	.09
63 Pat Rapp	.30	.09
64 Jason Giambi	.75	.23
65 Mark Mulder	.30	.09
66 Ron Gant	.30	.09
67 Johnny Damon	.30	.09
68 Adam Piatt	.30	.09
69 Jermaine Dye	.30	.09
70 Jason Hart	.30	.09
71 Eric Chavez	.30	.09
72 Jim Mecir	.30	.09
73 Barry Zito	.50	.15
74 Jason Isringhausen	.30	.09
75 Jeremy Giambi	.30	.09
76 Olmedo Saenz	.30	.09
77 Terrence Long	.30	.09
78 Ramon Hernandez	.30	.09
79 Chris Carpenter	.30	.09
80 Raul Mondesi	.30	.09
81 Carlos Delgado	.30	.09
82 Billy Koch	.30	.09
83 Vernon Wells	.30	.09
84 Darrin Fletcher	.30	.09
85 Homer Bush	.30	.09
86 Pasqual Coco	.30	.09
87 Shannon Stewart	.30	.09
88 Chris Woodward	.30	.09
89 Joe Lawrence	.30	.09
90 Esteban Loaiza	.30	.09
91 Cesar Izturis	.30	.09
92 Kelvim Escobar	.30	.09
93 Greg Vaughn	.30	.09
94 Brent Abernathy	.30	.09
95 Tanyon Sturtze	.30	.09
96 Steve Cox	.30	.09
97 Aubrey Huff	.30	.09
98 Jesus Colome	.30	.09
99 Ben Grieve	.30	.09
100 Esteban Yan	.30	.09
101 Joe Kennedy	.30	.09
102 Felix Martinez	.30	.09
103 Nick Bierbrodt	.30	.09
104 Damian Rolls	.30	.09
105 Russ Johnson	.30	.09
106 Toby Hall	.30	.09
107 Roberto Alomar	.75	.23
108 Bartolo Colon	.30	.09
109 John Rocker	.30	.09
110 Juan Gonzalez	.75	.23
111 Einar Diaz	.30	.09
112 Chuck Finley	.30	.09
113 Kenny Lofton	.30	.09
114 Danys Baez	.30	.09
115 Travis Fryman	.30	.09
116 C.C. Sabathia	.30	.09
117 Paul Shuey	.30	.09
118 Marty Cordova	.30	.09
119 Ellis Burks	.30	.09
120 Bob Wickman	.30	.09
121 Edgar Martinez	.50	.15
122 Freddy Garcia	.30	.09
123 Ichiro Suzuki	1.25	.35
124 John Olerud	.30	.09
125 Gil Meche	.30	.09
126 Dan Wilson	.30	.09
127 Aaron Sele	.30	.09
128 Kazuhiro Sasaki	.30	.09
129 Mark McLemore	.30	.09
130 Carlos Guillen	.30	.09
131 Al Martin	.30	.09
132 David Bell	.30	.09
133 Jay Buhner	.30	.09
134 Stan Javier	.30	.09
135 Tony Batista	.30	.09
136 Jason Johnson	.30	.09
137 Brook Fordyce	.30	.09
138 Mike Kinkade	.30	.09
139 Willis Roberts	.30	.09
140 David Segui	.30	.09
141 Josh Towers	.30	.09
142 Jeff Conine	.30	.09
143 Chris Richard	.30	.09
144 Pat Hentgen	.30	.09
145 Melvin Mora	.30	.09
146 Jerry Hairston Jr.	.30	.09
147 Calvin Maduro	.30	.09
148 Brady Anderson	.30	.09
149 Alex Rodriguez	1.25	.35
150 Kenny Rogers	.30	.09
151 Chad Curtis	.30	.09
152 Ricky Ledee	.30	.09
153 Rafael Palmeiro	.50	.15
154 Rob Bell	.30	.09
155 Rick Helling	.30	.09
156 Doug Davis	.30	.09
157 Mike Lamb	.30	.09
158 Gabe Kapler	.30	.09
159 Jeff Zimmerman	.30	.09
160 Bill Haselman	.30	.09
161 Tim Crabtree	.30	.09
162 Carlos Pena	.30	.09
163 Nomar Garciaparra	1.25	.35
164 Shea Hillenbrand	.30	.09
165 Hideo Nomo	.75	.23
166 Manny Ramirez	.30	.09
167 Jose Offerman	.30	.09
168 Scott Hatteberg	.30	.09
169 Trot Nixon	.50	.15
170 Darren Lewis	.30	.09
171 Derek Lowe	.30	.09
172 Troy O'Leary	.30	.09
173 Tim Wakefield	.30	.09
174 Chris Stynes	.30	.09
175 John Valentin	.30	.09
176 David Cone	.30	.09
177 Neifi Perez	.30	.09
178 Brent Mayne	.30	.09
179 Dan Reichert	.30	.09
180 A.J. Hinch	.30	.09
181 Chris George	.30	.09
182 Mike Sweeney	.30	.09
183 Jeff Suppan	.30	.09
184 Roberto Hernandez	.30	.09
185 Joe Randa	.30	.09
186 Paul Byrd	.30	.09
187 Luis Ordaz	.30	.09
188 Kris Wilson	.30	.09
189 Dee Brown	.30	.09
190 Tony Clark	.30	.09
191 Matt Anderson	.30	.09
192 Robert Fick	.30	.09
193 Juan Encarnacion	.30	.09
194 Dean Palmer	.30	.09
195 Victor Santos	.30	.09
196 Damion Easley	.30	.09
197 Jose Lima	.30	.09
198 Deivi Cruz	.30	.09
199 Roger Cedeno	.30	.09
200 Jose Macias	.30	.09
201 Jeff Weaver	.30	.09
202 Brandon Inge	.30	.09
203 Brian Moehler	.30	.09
204 Brad Radke	.30	.09
205 Doug Mientkiewicz	.30	.09
206 Cristian Guzman	.30	.09
207 Corey Koskie	.30	.09
208 LaTroy Hawkins	.30	.09
209 J.C. Romero	.30	.09
210 Chad Allen	.30	.09
211 Torii Hunter	.30	.09
212 Travis Miller	.30	.09
213 Joe Mays	.30	.09
214 Todd Jones	.30	.09
215 David Ortiz	.30	.09
216 Brian Buchanan	.30	.09
217 A.J. Pierzynski	.30	.09
218 Carlos Lee	.30	.09
219 Gary Glover	.30	.09
220 Jose Valentin	.30	.09
221 Aaron Rowand	.30	.09
222 Sandy Alomar Jr.	.30	.09
223 Herbert Perry	.30	.09
224 Jon Garland	.30	.09
225 Mark Buehrle	.30	.09
226 Chris Singleton	.30	.09
227 Kip Wells	.30	.09
228 Ray Durham	.30	.09
229 Joe Crede	.30	.09
230 Keith Foulke	.30	.09
231 Royce Clayton	.30	.09
232 Andy Pettitte	.50	.15
233 Derek Jeter	2.00	.60
234 Jorge Posada	.50	.15
235 Roger Clemens	1.50	.45
236 Paul O'Neill	.50	.15
237 Nick Johnson	.30	.09
238 Gerald Williams	.30	.09
239 Mariano Rivera	.50	.15
240 Alfonso Soriano	.50	.15
241 Ramiro Mendoza	.30	.09
242 Mike Mussina	.75	.23
243 Luis Sojo	.30	.09
244 Scott Brosius	.30	.09
245 David Justice	.30	.09
246 Wade Miller	.30	.09
247 Brad Ausmus	.30	.09
248 Jeff Bagwell	.50	.15
249 Daryle Ward	.30	.09
250 Shane Reynolds	.30	.09
251 Chris Truby	.30	.09
252 Billy Wagner	.30	.09
253 Craig Biggio	.50	.15
254 Moises Alou	.30	.09
255 Vinny Castilla	.30	.09
256 Tim Redding	.30	.09
257 Roy Oswalt	.30	.09
258 Julio Lugo	.30	.09
259 Chipper Jones	.75	.23
260 Greg Maddux	1.25	.35
261 Ken Caminiti	.30	.09
262 Kevin Millwood	.30	.09
263 Keith Lockhart	.30	.09
264 Rey Sanchez	.30	.09
265 Jason Marquis	.30	.09
266 Brian Jordan	.30	.09
267 Steve Karsay	.30	.09
268 Wes Helms	.30	.09
269 B.J. Surhoff	.30	.09
270 Wilson Betemit	.30	.09
271 John Smoltz	.50	.15
272 Rafael Furcal	.30	.09
273 Jeromy Burnitz	.30	.09
274 Jimmy Haynes	.30	.09
275 Mark Loretta	.30	.09
276 Jose Hernandez	.30	.09
277 Paul Rigdon	.30	.09
278 Alex Sanchez	.30	.09
279 Chad Fox	.30	.09
280 Devon White	.30	.09
281 Tyler Houston	.30	.09
282 Ronnie Belliard	.30	.09
283 Luis Lopez	.30	.09
284 Ben Sheets	.30	.09
285 Curtis Leskanic	.30	.09
286 Henry Blanco	.30	.09
287 Mark McGwire	2.00	.60
288 Edgar Renteria	.30	.09
289 Matt Morris	.30	.09
290 Gene Stechschulte	.30	.09
291 Dustin Hermanson	.30	.09
292 Eli Marrero	.30	.09
293 Albert Pujols	1.50	.45
294 Luis Saturria	.30	.09
295 Bobby Bonilla	.30	.09
296 Garrett Stephenson	.30	.09
297 Jim Edmonds	.30	.09
298 Rick Ankiel	.30	.09
299 Placido Polanco	.30	.09
300 Dave Veres	.30	.09
301 Sammy Sosa	1.25	.35
302 Eric Young	.30	.09
303 Kerry Wood	.75	.23
304 Jon Lieber	.30	.09
305 Joe Girardi	.30	.09
306 Fred McGriff	.50	.15
307 Jeff Fassero	.30	.09
308 Julio Zuleta	.30	.09
309 Kevin Tapani	.30	.09
310 Rondell White	.30	.09
311 Julian Tavarez	.30	.09
312 Tom Gordon	.30	.09
313 Corey Patterson	.30	.09
314 Bill Mueller	.30	.09
315 Randy Johnson	.75	.23
316 Chad Moeller	.30	.09
317 Tony Womack	.30	.09
318 Erubiel Durazo	.30	.09
319 Luis Gonzalez	.30	.09
320 Brian Anderson	.30	.09
321 Reggie Sanders	.30	.09
322 Greg Colbrunn	.30	.09
323 Robert Ellis	.30	.09
324 Jack Cust	.30	.09
325 Bret Prinz	.30	.09
326 Steve Finley	.30	.09
327 Byung-Hyun Kim	.30	.09
328 Albie Lopez	.30	.09
329 Gary Sheffield	.30	.09
330 Mark Grudzielanek	.30	.09
331 Paul LoDuca	.30	.09
332 Tom Goodwin	.30	.09
333 Andy Ashby	.30	.09
334 Hiram Bocachica	.30	.09
335 Dave Hansen	.30	.09
336 Kevin Brown	.30	.09
337 Marquis Grissom	.30	.09
338 Terry Adams	.30	.09
339 Chan Ho Park	.30	.09
340 Adrian Beltre	.30	.09
341 Luke Prokopec	.30	.09
342 Jeff Shaw	.30	.09
343 Vladimir Guerrero	.75	.23
344 Orlando Cabrera	.30	.09
345 Tony Armas Jr.	.30	.09
346 Michael Barrett	.30	.09
347 Geoff Blum	.30	.09
348 Ryan Minor	.30	.09
349 Peter Bergeron	.30	.09
350 Graeme Lloyd	.30	.09
351 Jose Vidro	.30	.09
352 Javier Vazquez	.30	.09
353 Matt Blank	.30	.09
354 Masato Yoshii	.30	.09
355 Carl Pavano	.30	.09
356 Barry Bonds	2.00	.60
357 Shawon Dunston	.30	.09
358 Livan Hernandez	.30	.09
359 Felix Rodriguez	.30	.09
360 Pedro Feliz	.30	.09
361 Calvin Murray	.30	.09
362 Robb Nen	.30	.09
363 Marvin Benard	.30	.09
364 Russ Ortiz	.30	.09
365 Jason Schmidt	.30	.09
366 Rich Aurilia	.30	.09
367 John Vander Wal	.30	.09
368 Benito Santiago	.30	.09
369 Ryan Dempster	.30	.09
370 Charles Johnson	.30	.09
371 Alex Gonzalez	.30	.09
372 Luis Castillo	.30	.09
373 Mike Lowell	.30	.09
374 Antonio Alfonseca	.30	.09
375 A.J. Burnett	.30	.09
376 Brad Penny	.30	.09
377 Jason Grilli	.30	.09
378 Derrek Lee	.30	.09
379 Matt Clement	.30	.09
380 Eric Owens	.30	.09
381 Vladimir Nunez	.30	.09
382 Cliff Floyd	.30	.09
383 Mike Piazza	1.25	.35
384 Lenny Harris	.30	.09
385 Glendon Rusch	.30	.09
386 Todd Zeile	.30	.09
387 Al Leiter	.30	.09
388 Armando Benitez	.30	.09
389 Alex Escobar	.30	.09
390 Kevin Appier	.30	.09
391 Matt Lawton	.30	.09
392 Bruce Chen	.30	.09
393 John Franco	.30	.09
394 Tsuyoshi Shinjo	.30	.09
395 Rey Ordonez	.30	.09
396 Joe McEwing	.30	.09
397 Ryan Klesko	.30	.09
398 Brian Lawrence	.30	.09
399 Kevin Walker	.30	.09
400 Phil Nevin	.30	.09
401 Bubba Trammell	.30	.09
402 Wiki Gonzalez	.30	.09
403 D'Angelo Jimenez	.30	.09
404 Rickey Henderson	.75	.23
405 Mike Darr	.30	.09
406 Trevor Hoffman	.30	.09
407 Damian Jackson	.30	.09
408 Santiago Perez	.30	.09
409 Cesar Crespo	.30	.09
410 Robert Person	.30	.09
411 Travis Lee	.30	.09
412 Scott Rolen	.50	.15
413 Turk Wendell	.30	.09
414 Randy Wolf	.30	.09
415 Kevin Jordan	.30	.09
416 Jose Mesa	.30	.09
417 Mike Lieberthal	.30	.09
418 Bobby Abreu	.30	.09
419 Tomas Perez	.30	.09
420 Doug Glanville	.30	.09
421 Reggie Taylor	.30	.09
422 Jimmy Rollins	.30	.09
423 Brian Giles	.30	.09
424 Rob Mackowiak	.30	.09
425 Bronson Arroyo	.30	.09
426 Kevin Young	.30	.09
427 Jack Wilson	.30	.09
428 Adrian Brown	.30	.09
429 Chad Hermansen	.30	.09
430 Jimmy Anderson	.30	.09
431 Aramis Ramirez	.30	.09
432 Todd Ritchie	.30	.09
433 Pat Meares	.30	.09
434 Warren Morris	.30	.09
435 Derek Bell	.30	.09
436 Ken Griffey Jr.	1.25	.35
437 Elmer Dessens	.30	.09
438 Ruben Rivera	.30	.09
439 Jason LaRue	.30	.09
440 Sean Casey	.30	.09
441 Pete Harnisch	.30	.09
442 Danny Graves	.30	.09
443 Aaron Boone	.30	.09
444 Dmitri Young	.30	.09
445 Brandon Larson	.30	.09

446 Pokey Reese .30 .09
447 Todd Walker .30 .09
448 Juan Castro .30 .09
449 Todd Helton .50 .15
450 Ben Petrick .30 .09
451 Juan Pierre .30 .09
452 Jeff Cirillo .30 .09
453 Juan Uribe .30 .09
454 Brian Bohanon .30 .09
455 Terry Shumpert .30 .09
456 Mike Hampton .30 .09
457 Shawn Chacon .30 .09
458 Adam Melhuse .30 .09
459 Greg Norton .30 .09
460 Gabe White .30 .09
461 Ichiro Suzuki WS .75 .23
462 Carlos Delgado WS .30 .09
463 Manny Ramirez WS .30 .09
464 Miguel Tejada WS .30 .09
465 Tsuyoshi Shinjo WS .30 .09
466 Bernie Williams WS .30 .09
467 Juan Gonzalez WS .50 .15
468 Andruw Jones WS .30 .09
469 Ivan Rodriguez WS .50 .15
470 Larry Walker WS .50 .15
471 Hideo Nomo WS .30 .09
472 Albert Pujols WS .75 .23
473 Pedro Martinez WS .50 .15
474 Vladimir Guerrero WS .50 .15
475 Tony Batista WS .30 .09
476 Kazuhiro Sasaki WS .30 .09
477 Richard Hidalgo WS .30 .09
478 Carlos Lee WS .30 .09
479 Roberto Alomar WS .30 .09
480 Rafael Palmeiro WS .30 .09
481 Ken Griffey Jr. GG .75 .23
482 Ken Griffey Jr. GG .75 .23
483 Ken Griffey Jr. GG .75 .23
484 Ken Griffey Jr. GG .75 .23
485 Ken Griffey Jr. GG .75 .23
486 Ken Griffey Jr. GG .75 .23
487 Ken Griffey Jr. GG .75 .23
488 Ken Griffey Jr. GG .75 .23
489 Ken Griffey Jr. GG .75 .23
490 Ken Griffey Jr. GG .75 .23
491 Barry Bonds CL .75 .23
492 Hideo Nomo CL .30 .09
493 Ichiro Suzuki CL .75 .23
494 Cal Ripken CL 1.25 .35
495 Tony Gwynn CL .50 .15
496 Randy Johnson CL .50 .15
497 A.J. Burnett CL .30 .09
498 Rickey Henderson CL .50 .15
499 Albert Pujols CL .75 .23
500 Luis Gonzalez CL .30 .09
501 Brandon Puffer SR RC 1.00 .30
502 Rodrigo Rosario SR RC 1.00 .30
503 Tom Shearn SR RC 1.00 .30
504 Reed Johnson SR RC 1.00 .30
505 Chris Baker SR RC 1.00 .30
506 John Ennis SR RC 1.00 .30
507 Luis Martinez SR RC 1.00 .30
508 So Taguchi SR RC 1.00 .30
509 Scotty Layfield SR RC 1.00 .30
510 Francis Beltran SR RC 1.00 .30
511 Brandon Backe SR RC 1.00 .30
512 Doug Devore SR RC 1.00 .30
513 Jeremy Ward SR RC 1.00 .30
514 Jose Valverde SR RC 1.00 .30
515 P.J. Bevis SR RC 1.00 .30
516 Victor Alvarez SR RC 1.00 .30
517 Kazuhisa Ishii SR RC 2.50 .75
518 Jorge Nunez SR RC 1.00 .30
519 Eric Good SR RC 1.00 .30
520 Ron Calloway SR RC 1.00 .30
521 Val Pascucci SR 1.00 .30
522 Nelson Castro SR RC 1.00 .30
523 Deivis Santos SR 1.00 .30
524 Luis Ugueto SR RC 1.00 .30
525 Matt Thornton SR RC 1.00 .30
526 Hansel Izquierdo SR RC 1.00 .30
527 Tyler Yates SR RC 1.50 .45
528 Mark Corey SR RC 1.00 .30
529 Jaime Cerda SR RC 1.00 .30
530 Satoru Komiyama SR RC 1.00 .30
531 Steve Bechler SR RC 1.00 .30
532 Ben Howard SR RC 1.00 .30
533 An. Machado SR RC 1.00 .30
534 Jorge Padilla SR RC 1.00 .30
535 Eric Junge SR RC 1.00 .30
536 Adrian Burnside SR RC 1.00 .30
537 Mike Gonzalez SR RC 1.00 .30
538 Josh Hancock SR RC 1.00 .30
539 Colin Young SR RC 1.00 .30
540 Rene Reyes SR RC 1.00 .30
541 Cam Esslinger SR RC 1.00 .30
542 Tim Kalita SR RC 1.00 .30
543 Kevin Frederick SR RC 1.00 .30
544 Kyle Kane SR RC 1.00 .30
545 Edwin Almonte SR RC 1.00 .30
546 Aaron Sele .30 .09
547 Garret Anderson .30 .09
548 Darin Erstad .30 .09
549 Brad Fullmer .30 .09
550 Kevin Appier .30 .09
551 Tim Salmon .50 .15
552 David Justice .30 .09
553 Billy Koch .30 .09
554 Scott Hatteberg .30 .09
555 Tim Hudson .30 .09
556 Miguel Tejada .30 .09
557 Carlos Pena .30 .09
558 Mike Sirotka .30 .09
559 Jose Cruz Jr. .30 .09
560 Josh Phelps .30 .09
561 Brandon Lyon .30 .09
562 Luke Prokopec .30 .09
563 Felipe Lopez .30 .09
564 Jason Standridge .30 .09
565 Chris Gomez .30 .09
566 John Flaherty .30 .09
567 Jason Tyner .30 .09
568 Bobby Smith .30 .09
569 Wilson Alvarez .30 .09
570 Matt Lawton .30 .09
571 Omar Vizquel .30 .09
572 Jim Thome .75 .23
573 Brady Anderson .30 .09
574 Alex Escobar .30 .09
575 Russell Branyan .30 .09
576 Bret Boone .30 .09
577 Ben Davis .30 .09
578 Mike Cameron .30 .09
579 Jamie Moyer .30 .09
580 Ruben Sierra .30 .09
581 Jeff Cirillo .30 .09
582 Marty Cordova .30 .09
583 Mike Bordick .30 .09
584 Brian Roberts .30 .09
585 Luis Matos .30 .09
586 Geronimo Gil .30 .09
587 Jay Gibbons .30 .09
588 Carl Everett .30 .09
589 Ivan Rodriguez .75 .23
590 Chan Ho Park .30 .09
591 Juan Gonzalez .75 .23
592 Hank Blalock .75 .23
593 Todd Van Poppel .30 .09
594 Pedro Martinez .75 .23
595 Jason Varitek .30 .09
596 Tony Clark .30 .09
597 Johnny Damon .30 .09
598 Dustin Hermanson .30 .09
599 John Burkett .30 .09
600 Carlos Beltran .30 .09
601 Mark Quinn .30 .09
602 Chuck Knoblauch .30 .09
603 Michael Tucker .30 .09
604 Carlos Febles .30 .09
605 Jose Rosado .30 .09
606 Dmitri Young .30 .09
607 Bobby Higginson .30 .09
608 Craig Paquette .30 .09
609 Mitch Meluskey .30 .09
610 Wendell Magee .30 .09
611 Mike Rivera .30 .09
612 Jacque Jones .30 .09
613 Luis Rivas .30 .09
614 Eric Milton .30 .09
615 Eddie Guardado .30 .09
616 Matt LeCroy .30 .09
617 Mike Jackson .30 .09
618 Magglio Ordonez .30 .09
619 Frank Thomas .75 .23
620 Rocky Biddle .30 .09
621 Paul Konerko .30 .09
622 Todd Ritchie .30 .09
623 Jon Rauch .30 .09
624 John Vander Wal .30 .09
625 Rondell White .30 .09
626 Jason Giambi .75 .23
627 Robin Ventura .30 .09
628 David Wells .30 .09
629 Bernie Williams .50 .15
630 Lance Berkman .30 .09
631 Richard Hidalgo .30 .09
632 Greg Zaun .30 .09
633 Jose Vizcaino .30 .09
634 Octavio Dotel .30 .09
635 Morgan Ensberg .30 .09
636 Andruw Jones .30 .09
637 Tom Glavine .50 .15
638 Gary Sheffield .30 .09
639 Vinny Castilla .30 .09
640 Javy Lopez .30 .09
641 Albie Lopez .30 .09
642 Geoff Jenkins .30 .09
643 Jeffrey Hammonds .30 .09
644 Alex Ochoa .30 .09
645 Richie Sexson .30 .09
646 Eric Young .30 .09
647 Glendon Rusch .30 .09
648 Tino Martinez .50 .15
649 Fernando Vina .30 .09
650 J.D. Drew .30 .09
651 Woody Williams .30 .09
652 Darryl Kile .30 .09
653 Jason Isringhausen .30 .09
654 Moises Alou .30 .09
655 Alex Gonzalez .30 .09
656 Delino DeShields .30 .09
657 Todd Hundley .30 .09
658 Chris Stynes .30 .09
659 Jason Bere .30 .09
660 Curt Schilling .50 .15
661 Craig Counsell .30 .09
662 Mark Grace .50 .15
663 Matt Williams .30 .09
664 Jay Bell .30 .09
665 Rick Helling .30 .09
666 Shawn Green .30 .09
667 Eric Karros .30 .09
668 Hideo Nomo .75 .23
669 Omar Daal .30 .09
670 Brian Jordan .30 .09
671 Cesar Izturis .30 .09
672 Fernando Tatis .30 .09
673 Lee Stevens .30 .09
674 Tomo Ohka .30 .09
675 Brian Schneider .30 .09
676 Brad Wilkerson .30 .09
677 Bruce Chen .30 .09
678 Tsuyoshi Shinjo .30 .09
679 Jeff Kent .30 .09
680 Kirk Rueter .30 .09
681 J.T. Snow .30 .09
682 David Bell .30 .09
683 Reggie Sanders .30 .09
684 Preston Wilson .30 .09
685 Vic Darensbourg .30 .09
686 Josh Beckett .50 .15
687 Pablo Ozuna .30 .09
688 Mike Redmond .30 .09
689 Scott Strickland .30 .09
690 Mo Vaughn .30 .09
691 Roberto Alomar .75 .23
692 Edgardo Alfonzo .30 .09
693 Shawn Estes .30 .09
694 Roger Cedeno .30 .09
695 Jeromy Burnitz .30 .09
696 Ray Lankford .30 .09
697 Mark Kotsay .30 .09
698 Kevin Jarvis .30 .09
699 Bobby Jones .30 .09
700 Sean Burroughs .30 .09
701 Ramon Vazquez .30 .09
702 Pat Burrell .30 .09
703 Marlon Byrd .75 .23
704 Brandon Duckworth .30 .09
705 Marlon Anderson .30 .09
706 Vicente Padilla .30 .09
707 Kip Wells .30 .09
708 Jason Kendall .30 .09
709 Pokey Reese .30 .09
710 Pat Meares .30 .09
711 Kris Benson .30 .09
712 Armando Rios .30 .09
713 Mike Williams .30 .09
714 Barry Larkin .75 .23
715 Adam Dunn .30 .09
716 Juan Encarnacion .30 .09
717 Scott Williamson .30 .09
718 Wilton Guerrero .30 .09
719 Chris Reitsma .30 .09
720 Larry Walker .50 .15
721 Denny Neagle .30 .09
722 Todd Zeile .30 .09
723 Jose Ortiz .30 .09
724 Jason Jennings .30 .09
725 Tony Eusebio .30 .09
726 Ichiro Suzuki YR .75 .23
727 Barry Bonds YR .75 .23
728 Randy Johnson YR .50 .15
729 Albert Pujols YR .75 .23
730 Roger Clemens YR .75 .23
731 Sammy Sosa YR .75 .23
732 Alex Rodriguez YR .75 .23
733 Chipper Jones YR .50 .15
734 Rickey Henderson YR .50 .15
735 Ichiro Suzuki YR .75 .23
736 Luis Gonzalez SH CL .30 .09
737 Derek Jeter SH CL 1.00 .30
738 Ichiro Suzuki SH CL .75 .23
739 Barry Bonds SH CL .75 .23
740 Curt Schilling SH CL .30 .09
741 Shawn Green SH CL .30 .09
742 Jason Giambi SH CL .50 .15
743 Roberto Alomar SH CL .50 .15
744 Larry Walker SH CL .30 .09
745 Mark McGwire SH CL 1.00 .30

2002 Upper Deck 2001 Greatest Hits

Issued into first series packs at a rate of one in 14, these 10 cards feature some of the leading hitters during the 2001 season.

	Nm-Mt	Ex-Mt
COMPLETE SET (10)	40.00	12.00
GH1 Barry Bonds	6.00	1.80
GH2 Ichiro Suzuki	4.00	1.20
GH3 Albert Pujols	5.00	1.50
GH4 Mike Piazza	4.00	1.20
GH5 Alex Rodriguez	4.00	1.20
GH6 Mark McGwire	6.00	1.80
GH7 Manny Ramirez	2.50	.75
GH8 Ken Griffey Jr.	4.00	1.20
GH9 Sammy Sosa	4.00	1.20
GH10 Derek Jeter	6.00	1.80

2002 Upper Deck A Piece of History 500 Club

Randomly inserted in 2002 Upper Deck second series packs, this card features a bat slice from Mark McGwire and continues the Upper Deck A Piece of History set begun in 1999. This card was printed to a stated print run of 350 serial numbered sets.

	Nm-Mt	Ex-Mt
MMC Mark McGwire	400.00	120.00

2002 Upper Deck A Piece of History 500 Club Autograph

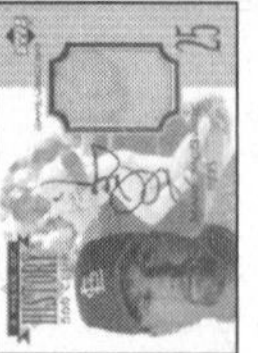

Randomly inserted in 2002 Upper Deck second series packs, this card features a bat slice from Mark McGwire and an authentic autograph and continues the Upper Deck A Piece of History set begun in 1999. This card was printed to a stated print run of 25 serial numbered sets.

	Nm-Mt	Ex-Mt
S-MMC Mark McGwire/25		

2002 Upper Deck AL Centennial Memorabilia

Inserted into first series packs at a rate of one in 144, these 10 cards feature memorabilia from some of the leading players in American League history. The bat jersey cards were produced in smaller quantites than the jersey cards and we have notated those cards with SP's in our checklist.

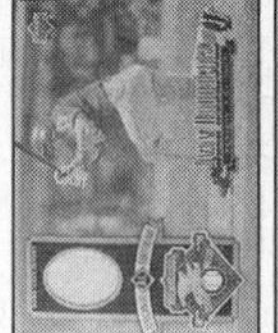

	Nm-Mt	Ex-Mt
ALB-BR Babe Ruth Bat SP	150.00	45.00
ALB-JD Joe DiMaggio Bat SP	120.00	36.00
ALB-MM M. Mantle Bat SP	150.00	45.00
ALJ-AR A. Rodriguez Jsy	20.00	6.00
ALJ-CR Cal Ripken Jsy	40.00	12.00
ALJ-FT Frank Thomas Jsy	15.00	4.50
ALJ-IR Ivan Rodriguez Jsy	15.00	4.50
ALJ-NR Nolan Ryan Jsy	40.00	12.00
ALJ-PM P. Martinez Jsy	15.00	4.50
ALJ-RA R. Alomar Jsy	15.00	4.50

2002 Upper Deck AL Centennial Memorabilia Autograph

Randomly inserted into first series packs, these four cards featured autographs of players whose memorabilia is featured in the Centennial Memorabilia set. These cards are serial numbered to 25. Due to market scarcity, no pricing is provided.

	Nm-Mt	Ex-Mt
SAL-CR Cal Ripken Jsy		
SAL-IR Ivan Rodriguez Jsy		
SAL-NR Nolan Ryan Jsy		
SAL-PM Pedro Martinez Jsy		

2002 Upper Deck All-Star Home Run Derby Game Jersey

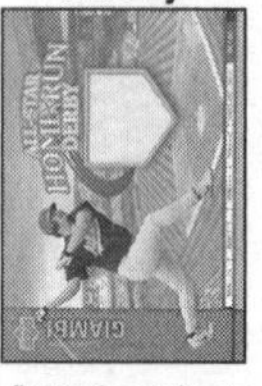

Inserted into first series packs at a rate of one in 288, these seven cards feature jersey swatches from these players who participated in the Home Run Derby. A couple of the jerseys were from regular use and we have notated that information in our checklist.

	Nm-Mt	Ex-Mt
GOLD RANDOM INSERTS IN PACKS		
GOLD PRINT RUN 25 SERIAL #'d SETS		
NO GOLD PRICING DUE TO SCARCITY		
AS-AR Alex Rodriguez	25.00	7.50
AS-BRB Bret Boone	15.00	4.50
AS-JG1 Jason Giambi	20.00	6.00
AS-JG2 Jason Giambi A's	20.00	6.00
AS-SS1 Sammy Sosa	30.00	9.00
AS-SS2 S. Sosa Cubs	30.00	9.00
AS-TH Todd Helton	15.00	4.50

2002 Upper Deck All-Star Salute Game Jersey

Inserted into first series packs at a rate of one in 288, these nine cards feature game jersey swatches of some of the most exciting All-Star performers.

	Nm-Mt	Ex-Mt
GOLD RANDOM INSERTS IN PACKS		
GOLD PRINT RUN 25 SERIAL #'d SETS		
NO GOLD PRICING DUE TO SCARCITY		
SJAR1 A.Rodriguez Mariners	25.00	7.50
SJAR2 A.Rodriguez Rangers	25.00	7.50
SJDE Dennis Eckersley	15.00	4.50
SJDS Don Sutton	15.00	4.50
SJIS Ichiro Suzuki	50.00	15.00
SJKG Ken Griffey Jr.	30.00	9.00
SJLB Lou Boudreau	15.00	4.50
SJNF Nellie Fox	15.00	4.50
SJSA Sparky Anderson	15.00	4.50

2002 Upper Deck Authentic McGwire

Randomly inserted in second series packs, these two cards feature authentic memorabilia from Mark McGwire's career. These cards have a stated print run of 70 serial numbered sets.

	Nm-Mt	Ex-Mt
AM-B Mark McGwire Bat	150.00	45.00
AM-J Mark McGwire Jsy	150.00	45.00

2002 Upper Deck Big Fly Zone

Issued into first series packs at a rate of one in 14, these 10 cards feature some of the leading power hitters in the game.

	Nm-Mt	Ex-Mt
COMPLETE SET (10)	30.00	9.00
Z1 Mark McGwire	6.00	1.80
Z2 Ken Griffey Jr.	4.00	1.20
Z3 Manny Ramirez	1.50	.45
Z4 Sammy Sosa	4.00	1.20
Z5 Todd Helton	1.50	.45
Z6 Barry Bonds	6.00	1.80
Z7 Luis Gonzalez	1.50	.45
Z8 Alex Rodriguez	4.00	1.20
Z9 Carlos Delgado	1.50	.45
Z10 Chipper Jones	2.50	.75

2002 Upper Deck Breakout Performers

Issued into first series packs at a rate of one in 14, these 10 cards feature players who had breakout seasons in 2001.

	Nm-Mt	Ex-Mt
COMPLETE SET (10)	25.00	7.50
BP1 Ichiro Suzuki	4.00	1.20
BP2 Albert Pujols	5.00	1.50
BP3 Doug Mientkiewicz	1.50	.45
BP4 Lance Berkman	1.50	.45
BP5 Tsuyoshi Shinjo	1.50	.45
BP6 Ben Sheets	1.50	.45
BP7 Jimmy Rollins	1.50	.45
BP8 J.D. Drew	1.50	.45
BP9 Bret Boone	1.50	.45
BP10 Alfonso Soriano	1.50	.45

2002 Upper Deck Championship Caliber

Inserted into first series packs at a rate of one in 23, these six cards feature players who have all earned World Series rings.

	Nm-Mt	Ex-Mt
COMPLETE SET (6)	20.00	6.00
CC1 Derek Jeter	6.00	1.80
CC2 Roberto Alomar	2.50	.75
CC3 Chipper Jones	2.50	.75
CC4 Gary Sheffield	1.50	.45
CC5 Roger Clemens	5.00	1.50
CC6 Greg Maddux	4.00	1.20

2002 Upper Deck Championship Caliber Swatch

Inserted in second series packs at a stated rate of one in 288, these 14 cards feature not only players who have been on World Champions but also a game-worn swatch. A few players were issued in shorter supply and we have notated that information in our checklist.

	Nm-Mt	Ex-Mt
AP Andy Pettitte	15.00	4.50
BL Barry Larkin	15.00	4.50
BW Bernie Williams	15.00	4.50
CF Cliff Floyd	10.00	3.00
CHJ Charles Johnson	10.00	3.00
CJO Chipper Jones SP		
CS Curt Schilling	15.00	4.50
GM Greg Maddux SP		
JO John Olerud	10.00	3.00
JP Jorge Posada	15.00	4.50
KB Kevin Brown SP	15.00	4.50

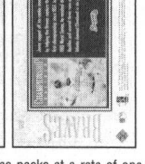

	Nm-Mt	Ex-Mt
RA Roberto Alomar SP		
RJ Randy Johnson	15.00	4.50
TM Tino Martinez	15.00	4.50

2002 Upper Deck Chasing History

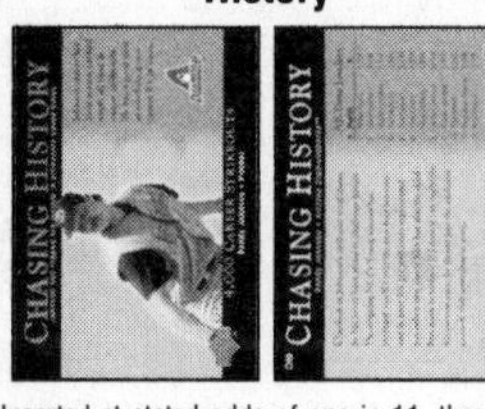

Inserted at stated odds of one in 11, these 15 cards feature players who are moving up in the record books.

	Nm-Mt	Ex-Mt
COMPLETE SET (15)	40.00	12.00
CH1 Sammy Sosa	5.00	1.50
CH2 Ken Griffey Jr.	5.00	1.50
CH3 Roger Clemens	6.00	1.80
CH4 Barry Bonds	8.00	2.40
CH5 Rafael Palmeiro	2.00	.60
CH6 Andres Galarraga	2.00	.60
CH7 Juan Gonzalez	3.00	.90
CH8 Roberto Alomar	3.00	.90
CH9 Randy Johnson	3.00	.90
CH10 Jeff Bagwell	2.00	.60
CH11 Fred McGriff	2.00	.60
CH12 Matt Williams	2.00	.60
CH13 Greg Maddux	5.00	1.50
CH14 Robb Nen	2.00	.60
CH15 Kenny Lofton	2.00	.60

2002 Upper Deck Combo Memorabilia

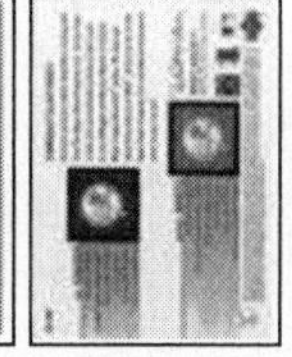

Issued into first series packs at a rate of one in 288, these seven cards feature two pieces of game-used memorabilia from players who have something in common.

	Nm-Mt	Ex-Mt
GOLD RANDOM INSERTS IN PACKS ..		
GOLD PRINT RUN 25 SERIAL #'d SETS		
NO GOLD PRICING DUE TO SCARCITY		
B-DM Joe DiMaggio / Mickey Mantle Bat	200.00	60.00
B-RG Alex Rodriguez / Ken Griffey Jr. Bat	40.00	12.00
J-BS Barry Bonds / Sammy Sosa Jsy	50.00	15.00
J-HK S. Hasegawa / Byung-Hyun Kim Jsy	15.00	4.50
J-RC Nolan Ryan / Roger Clemens Jsy	60.00	18.00
J-RM Nolan Ryan / Pedro Martinez Jsy	50.00	15.00
J-RS Alex Rodriguez / Sammy Sosa Jsy	40.00	12.00

2002 Upper Deck Double Game Worn Gems

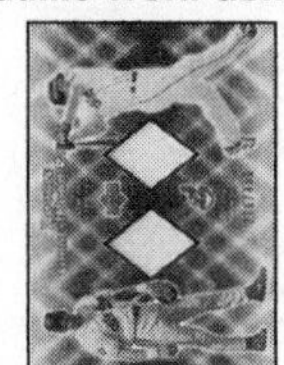

Randomly inserted in second series retail packs, these 12 cards feature two teammates along with pieces of game used memorabilia. These cards have a stated print run of 450 serial numbered sets.

	Nm-Mt	Ex-Mt
DG-AP Roberto Alomar / Mike Piazza	25.00	7.50
DG-DF Carlos Delgado / Shannon Stewart	15.00	4.50
DG-DH Jermaine Dye / Tim Hudson	15.00	4.50
DG-GS Luis Gonzalez / Curt Schilling	15.00	4.50
DG-KG Jason Kendall / Brian Giles	15.00	4.50
DG-MI Edgar Martinez / Ichiro Suzuki SP/150		
DG-MM Kevin Millwood / Greg Maddux	25.00	7.50
DG-NK Phil Nevin / Ryan Klesko	15.00	4.50
DG-PL Robert Person / Mike Lieberthal	15.00	4.50
DG-PN Chan Ho Park / Hideo Nomo	50.00	15.00
DG-TO Frank Thomas / Magglio Ordonez	20.00	6.00
DG-VB Omar Vizquel / Russell Branyan	15.00	4.50

2002 Upper Deck First Timers Game Jersey

Inserted into first series hobby packs at a rate of one in 288 hobby packs, these nine cards feature players who have never been featured on a Upper Deck game jersey card before.

	Nm-Mt	Ex-Mt
FT-AP Albert Pujols	50.00	15.00
FT-CP Corey Patterson	10.00	3.00
FT-EM Eric Milton	10.00	3.00
FT-FG Freddy Garcia	10.00	3.00
FT-JM Joe Mays	10.00	3.00
FT-ML Matt Lawton	10.00	3.00
FT-OD Omar Daal	10.00	3.00
FT-RB Russell Branyan	10.00	3.00
FT-SS Shannon Stewart	10.00	3.00

2002 Upper Deck First Timers Game Jersey Autograph

This parallel to the First Timers Game Jersey set features the players signing 25 copies of these cards. These cards were distributed exclusively in first series hobby packs. Freddy Garcia did not return his cards in time for packout and thus was available only in exchange format with a redemption deadline of 11/19/04. Due to market scarcity, no pricing is provided.

	Nm-Mt	Ex-Mt
SFT-AP Albert Pujols		
SFT-CP Corey Patterson		
SFT-FG Freddy Garcia EXCH		
SFT-JM Joe Mays		
SFT-SS Shannon Stewart		

2002 Upper Deck Game Base

Inserted into first series packs at a rate of one in 288, these 22 cards feature authentic pieces of bases used in official Major League games.

	Nm-Mt	Ex-Mt
B-AJ Andruw Jones	10.00	3.00
B-AR Alex Rodriguez	20.00	6.00
B-BB Barry Bonds	30.00	9.00
B-CD Carlos Delgado	10.00	3.00
B-CJ Chipper Jones	15.00	4.50
B-CR Cal Ripken	40.00	12.00
B-DJ Derek Jeter	30.00	9.00
B-IR Ivan Rodriguez	15.00	4.50
B-IS Ichiro Suzuki	50.00	15.00
B-JG Jason Giambi	15.00	4.50
B-JG Juan Gonzalez	15.00	4.50
B-KG Ken Griffey Jr.	20.00	6.00
B-KS Kazuhiro Sasaki	10.00	3.00
B-LG Luis Gonzalez	10.00	3.00
B-MM Mark McGwire	50.00	15.00
B-MP Mike Piazza	15.00	4.50
B-RC Roger Clemens	25.00	7.50
B-SG Shawn Green	10.00	3.00
B-SS Sammy Sosa	20.00	6.00
B-TG Troy Glaus	15.00	4.50
CB-MJ Mark McGwire / Derek Jeter	60.00	18.00
CB-RG Alex Rodriguez / Ken Griffey Jr.	40.00	12.00

2002 Upper Deck Game Base Autograph

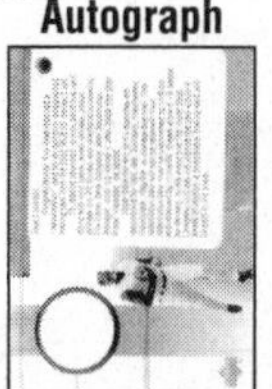

Randomly inserted into first series packs, Ken Griffey Jr. signed 25 cards for inclusion in this set. However, Griffey did not return his cards in time for inclusion in the packs and therefore these cards could be redeemed until November 5, 2004. Due to market scarcity, no pricing is provided.

	Nm-Mt	Ex-Mt
SB-KG Ken Griffey Jr. EXCH		

2002 Upper Deck Game Jersey

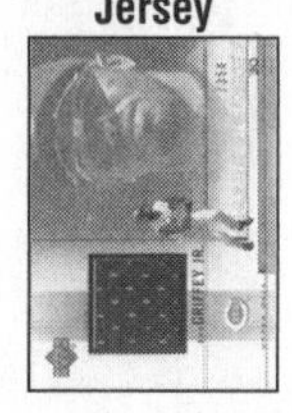

Randomly inserted in packs, these 11 cards feature some of today's star players along with a game-worn swatch of the featured player.

	Nm-Mt	Ex-Mt
AB Adrian Beltre	10.00	3.00
CS Curt Schilling	15.00	4.50
FT Frank Thomas	15.00	4.50
JC Jeff Cirillo Pants	10.00	3.00
KG Ken Griffey Jr.	25.00	7.50
MP Mike Piazza Pants	15.00	4.50
PW Preston Wilson	10.00	3.00
SR Scott Rolen	15.00	4.50
SS Sammy Sosa	25.00	7.50
TB Tony Batista	10.00	3.00
TH Tim Hudson	10.00	3.00

2002 Upper Deck Game Jersey Autograph

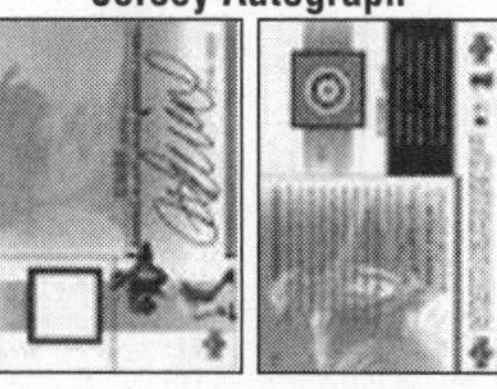

Randomly inserted into first series hobby packs, these 12 cards feature not only a game jersey swatch but also an authentic autograph of the player featured. These cards are serial numbered to 200. A few players did not return their signed cards in time for release in the packs and those cards have an exchange deadline of November 19, 2004.

	Nm-Mt	Ex-Mt
J-AJ Andruw Jones EXCH	40.00	12.00
J-AP Albert Pujols EXCH	150.00	45.00
J-BB Barry Bonds	250.00	75.00
J-CD Carlos Delgado	25.00	7.50
J-CR Cal Ripken	200.00	60.00
J-GS Gary Sheffield	40.00	12.00
J-IS Ichiro Suzuki UER / Word Close repeated in ninth line of text	300.00	90.00
J-JGI Jason Giambi	60.00	18.00
J-KG Ken Griffey Jr. EXCH	150.00	45.00
J-NR Nolan Ryan	150.00	45.00
J-PW Preston Wilson	25.00	7.50
J-RF Rafael Furcal	25.00	7.50

2002 Upper Deck Game Jersey Patch

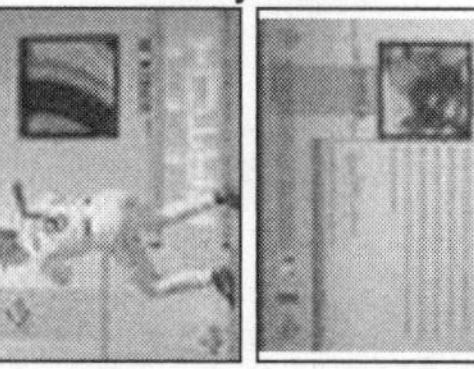

Inserted at a rate of one in 2,500 first series packs, these cards feature a jersey patch from the star players featured.

	Nm-Mt	Ex-Mt
PL-AR Alex Rodriguez L	120.00	36.00
PL-BB Barry Bonds L	150.00	45.00
PL-CR Cal Ripken L	150.00	45.00
PL-JG Jason Giambi L	100.00	30.00
PL-KG Ken Griffey Jr. L	120.00	36.00
PL-PM Pedro Martinez L	100.00	30.00
PL-SS Sammy Sosa L	100.00	30.00
PN-AR Alex Rodriguez N	120.00	36.00
PN-BB Barry Bonds N	150.00	45.00
PN-CR Cal Ripken N	150.00	45.00
PN-JG Jason Giambi N	100.00	30.00
PN-KG Ken Griffey Jr. N	120.00	36.00
PN-PM Pedro Martinez N	100.00	30.00
PN-SS Sammy Sosa N	100.00	30.00
PS-AR Alex Rodriguez S	120.00	36.00
PS-BB Barry Bonds S	150.00	45.00
PS-CR Cal Ripken S	150.00	45.00
PS-JG Jason Giambi S	100.00	30.00
PS-KG Ken Griffey Jr. S	120.00	36.00
PS-PM Pedro Martinez S	100.00	30.00
PS-SS Sammy Sosa S	100.00	30.00

2002 Upper Deck Game Jersey Patch Autograph

Randomly inserted into first series packs, these six cards feature not only a game jersey patch swatch but also an authentic autograph of the player featured. These cards are serial numbered to 25. Ken Griffey Jr. did not return his cards in time for pack out and those cards were issued as exchange cards. Due to market scarcity, no pricing is provided.

	Nm-Mt	Ex-Mt
SPNBB Barry Bonds N		
SPNCR Cal Ripken N		
SPNKG Ken Griffey Jr. N EXCH		

	Nm-Mt	Ex-Mt
SPNSS Sammy Sosa N		
SPSBB Barry Bonds S		
SPSCR Cal Ripken S		

2002 Upper Deck Game Worn Gems

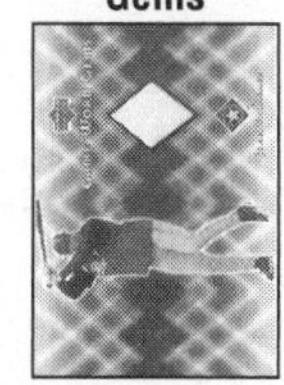

Inserted in second series retail packs at a stated rate of one in 48 retail packs, these 31 cards feature leading stars along a game-used memorabilia piece. A few cards were issued in shorter supply and those cards are notated in our checklist with an SP. Cards notated with an SP are not priced due to market scarcity.

	Nm-Mt	Ex-Mt
G-AS Aaron Sele	10.00	3.00
G-CD Carlos Delgado	10.00	3.00
G-CJ Chipper Jones	15.00	4.50
G-CR Cal Ripken	50.00	15.00
G-CS Curt Schilling	15.00	4.50
G-DE Darin Erstad SP		
G-EC Eric Chavez	10.00	3.00
G-EM Edgar Martinez	15.00	4.50
G-EM Eric Milton	10.00	3.00
G-FG Freddy Garcia SP		
G-FT Frank Thomas	15.00	4.50
G-GM Greg Maddux	15.00	4.50
G-GS Gary Sheffield SP		
G-HN Hideo Nomo SP		
G-IR Ivan Rodriguez	15.00	4.50
G-JG Juan Gonzalez	15.00	4.50
G-JK Jason Kendall	10.00	3.00
G-JM Joe Mays	10.00	3.00
G-JO John Olerud SP		
G-LG Luis Gonzalez SP		
G-MH Mike Hampton SP		
G-OV Omar Vizquel SP		
G-PM Pedro Martinez SP		
G-PN Phil Nevin	10.00	3.00
G-RA Roberto Alomar	15.00	4.50
G-RK Ryan Klesko SP		
G-RP Robert Person	10.00	3.00
G-RY Robin Yount	15.00	4.50
G-SR Scott Rolen	15.00	4.50
G-TG Tom Glavine	15.00	4.50
G-TM Tino Martinez	15.00	4.50

2002 Upper Deck Global Swatch Game Jersey

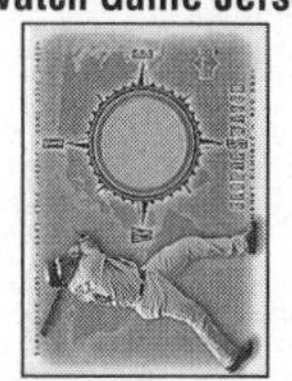

Issued at a rate of one in 144 first series packs, these 10 cards feature swatches of game jerseys worn by players who were born outside the continental United States.

	Nm-Mt	Ex-Mt
GSBK Byung-Hyun Kim	10.00	3.00
GSCD Carlos Delgado	10.00	3.00
GSCP Chan Ho Park	10.00	3.00
GSHN Hideo Nomo	40.00	12.00
GSIS Ichiro Suzuki	60.00	18.00
GSKS Kazuhiro Sasaki	10.00	3.00
GSMR Manny Ramirez	10.00	3.00
GSMY Masato Yoshii	10.00	3.00
GSSH S. Hasegawa	10.00	3.00
GSTS Tsuyoshi Shinjo	10.00	3.00

2002 Upper Deck Global Swatch Game Jersey Autograph

Randomly inserted into first series packs, these five cards feature not only a game-jersey swatch but also authentic autographs from the players. These cards are serial numbered to 25. Due to market scarcity, no pricing is provided.

	Nm-Mt	Ex-Mt
SGSBK Byung-Hyun Kim		
SGSCD Carlos Delgado		
SGSCP Chan Ho Park		
SGSHN Hideo Nomo		
SGSTS Tsuyoshi Shinjo		

2002 Upper Deck McGwire Combo Jersey

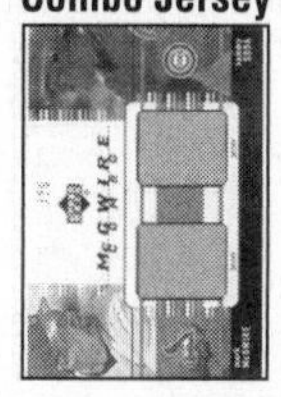

Randomly inserted in second series packs, these three cards feature swatches of both Mark McGwire and a player with which he says something in common. These cards were printed to a stated print run of 25 serial numbered sets and no pricing is available due to market scarcity.

	Nm-Mt	Ex-Mt
MMJG Mark McGwire / Jason Giambi		
MMKG Mark McGwire / Ken Griffey Jr.		
MMSS Mark McGwire / Sammy Sosa		

2002 Upper Deck Peoples Choice Game Jersey

Inserted in second series hobby packs at a stated rate of one in 24, these 39 cards feature some of the most popular player in baseball along with a game-worn memorablila swatch. A few cards were issued in lesser quantity and we have notated those cards with an SP in our checklist.

	Nm-Mt	Ex-Mt
PJ-AG Andres Galarraga SP	15.00	4.50
PJ-AP Andy Pettitte	15.00	4.50
PJ-AR Alex Rodriguez	15.00	4.50
PJ-BG Brian Giles	10.00	3.00
PJ-BW Bernie Williams	15.00	4.50
PJ-CD Carlos Delgado	10.00	3.00
PJ-CJ Charles Johnson	10.00	3.00
PJ-CS Curt Schilling	15.00	4.50
PJ-DL Derek Lowe	10.00	3.00
PJ-DW David Wells	10.00	3.00
PJ-EB Ellis Burks SP	15.00	4.50
PJ-FT Frank Thomas	15.00	4.50
PJ-GM Greg Maddux	15.00	4.50
PJ-HI Hideki Irabu	10.00	3.00
PJ-JG Juan Gonzalez	15.00	4.50
PJ-JN Jeff Nelson	10.00	3.00
PJ-JS J.T. Snow	10.00	3.00
PJ-JBA Jeff Bagwell	15.00	4.50
PJ-JBU Jeromy Burnitz	10.00	3.00
PJ-KG Ken Griffey Jr.	20.00	6.00
PJ-MP Mike Piazza	15.00	4.50
PJ-MS Mike Stanton	10.00	3.00
PJ-MW Matt Williams SP	15.00	4.50
PJ-MRA Manny Ramirez	10.00	3.00
PJ-MRI Mariano Rivera	15.00	4.50
PJ-OD Omar Daal	10.00	3.00
PJ-OV Omar Vizquel	10.00	3.00
PJ-RF Rafael Furcal	10.00	3.00
PJ-RO Rey Ordonez	10.00	3.00
PJ-RP Rafael Palmeiro SP	25.00	7.50
PJ-RP Robert Person SP	15.00	4.50
PJ-RV Robin Ventura	10.00	3.00
PJ-SH Sterling Hitchcock	10.00	3.00
PJ-SS Sammy Sosa	20.00	6.00
PJ-TG Tony Gwynn	15.00	4.50
PJ-TM Tino Martinez	15.00	4.50
PJ-TR Tim Raines Sr.	10.00	3.00
PJ-TS Tim Salmon	15.00	4.50
PJ-TSh Tsuyoshi Shinjo	10.00	3.00

2002 Upper Deck Return of the Ace

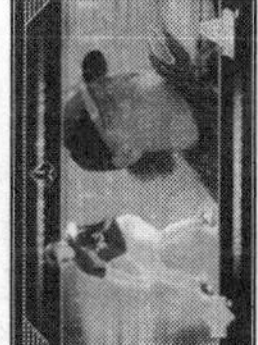

Inserted into second series packs at a stated rate of one in 11 packs, these 15 cards feature some of today's leading pitchers.

	Nm-Mt	Ex-Mt
COMPLETE SET (15)	30.00	9.00
RA1 Randy Johnson	3.00	.90
RA2 Greg Maddux	5.00	1.50
RA3 Pedro Martinez	3.00	.90
RA4 Freddy Garcia	2.00	.60
RA5 Matt Morris	2.00	.60
RA6 Mark Mulder	2.00	.60
RA7 Wade Miller	2.00	.60
RA8 Kevin Brown	2.00	.60
RA9 Roger Clemens	6.00	1.80
RA10 Jon Lieber	2.00	.60
RA11 C.C. Sabathia	2.00	.60
RA12 Tim Hudson	2.00	.60

RA13 Curt Schilling 2.00 .60
RA14 Al Leiter 2.00 .60
RA15 Mike Mussina 3.00 .90

2002 Upper Deck Sons of Summer Game Jersey

Inserted at a stated rate of one in 288 second series packs, these eight cards feature some of the best players in the game along with a game jersey swatch. According to Upper Deck, the Pedro Martinez card was issued in shorter supply.

	Nm-Mt	Ex-Mt
SS-AR Alex Rodriguez	20.00	6.00
SS-GM Greg Maddux	20.00	6.00
SS-JB Jeff Bagwell	20.00	6.00
SS-JG Juan Gonzalez	20.00	6.00
SS-MP Mike Piazza	20.00	6.00
SS-PM Pedro Martinez SP	25.00	7.50
SS-RA Roberto Alomar	20.00	6.00
SS-RC Roger Clemens	30.00	9.00

2002 Upper Deck Superstar Summit I

Inserted into first series packs at a rate of one in 23, these six cards feature the most popular players in the game.

	Nm-Mt	Ex-Mt
COMPLETE SET (6)	25.00	7.50
SS1 Sammy Sosa	4.00	1.20
SS2 Alex Rodriguez	4.00	1.20
SS3 Mark McGwire	6.00	1.80
SS4 Barry Bonds	6.00	1.80
SS5 Mike Piazza	4.00	1.20
SS6 Ken Griffey Jr.	4.00	1.20

2002 Upper Deck Superstar Summit II

Inserted into second series packs at a rate of one in 11, these fifteen cards feature the most popular players in the game.

	Nm-Mt	Ex-Mt
COMPLETE SET (15)	60.00	18.00
SS1 Alex Rodriguez	5.00	1.50
SS2 Jason Giambi	3.00	.90
SS3 Vladimir Guerrero	3.00	.90
SS4 Randy Johnson	3.00	.90
SS5 Chipper Jones	3.00	.90
SS6 Ichiro Suzuki	5.00	1.50
SS7 Sammy Sosa	5.00	1.50
SS8 Greg Maddux	5.00	1.50
SS9 Ken Griffey Jr.	5.00	1.50
SS10 Todd Helton	3.00	.90
SS11 Barry Bonds	8.00	2.40
SS12 Derek Jeter	8.00	2.40
SS13 Mike Piazza	5.00	1.50
SS14 Ivan Rodriguez	3.00	.90
SS15 Frank Thomas	3.00	.90

2002 Upper Deck UD Plus Hobby

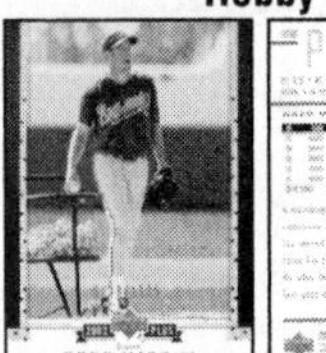

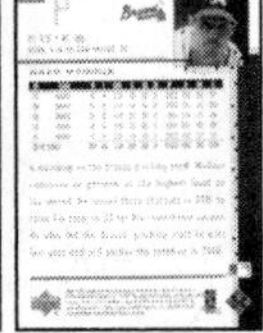

Issued as a two-card box topper in second series Upper Deck packs, these 100 cards could be exchanged for Joe DiMaggio or Mickey Mantle jersey cards if a collector finished the entire set. These cards were numbered to a stated print run of 1125 serial numbered sets. Hobby cards feature silver foil accents on front (unlike the Retail UD Plus cards - of which feature bronze fronts and backs). These cards could be exchanged until May 16, 2003.

	Nm-Mt	Ex-Mt
UD1 Darin Erstad	5.00	1.50
UD2 Troy Glaus	5.00	1.50
UD3 Tim Hudson	5.00	1.50
UD4 Jermaine Dye	5.00	1.50
UD5 Barry Zito	5.00	1.50
UD6 Carlos Delgado	5.00	1.50
UD7 Shannon Stewart	5.00	1.50
UD8 Greg Vaughn	5.00	1.50
UD9 Jim Thome	6.00	1.80
UD10 C.C. Sabathia	5.00	1.50
UD11 Ichiro Suzuki	10.00	3.00
UD12 Edgar Martinez	5.00	1.50
UD13 Bret Boone	5.00	1.50
UD14 Freddy Garcia	5.00	1.50
UD15 Matt Thornton	5.00	1.50
UD16 Jeff Conine	5.00	1.50
UD17 Steve Bechler	5.00	1.50
UD18 Rafael Palmeiro	5.00	1.50
UD19 Juan Gonzalez	6.00	1.80
UD20 Alex Rodriguez	10.00	3.00
UD21 Ivan Rodriguez	6.00	1.80
UD22 Carl Everett	5.00	1.50
UD23 Manny Ramirez	5.00	1.50
UD24 Nomar Garciaparra	10.00	3.00
UD25 Pedro Martinez	6.00	1.80
UD26 Mike Sweeney	5.00	1.50
UD27 Chuck Knoblauch	5.00	1.50
UD28 Dmitri Young	5.00	1.50
UD29 Bobby Higginson	5.00	1.50
UD30 Dean Palmer	5.00	1.50
UD31 Doug Mientkiewicz	5.00	1.50
UD32 Corey Koskie	5.00	1.50
UD33 Brad Radke	5.00	1.50
UD34 Cristian Guzman	5.00	1.50
UD35 Frank Thomas	6.00	1.80
UD36 Magglio Ordonez	5.00	1.50
UD37 Carlos Lee	5.00	1.50
UD38 Roger Clemens	12.00	3.60
UD39 Bernie Williams	5.00	1.50
UD40 Derek Jeter	15.00	4.50
UD41 Jason Giambi	6.00	1.80
UD42 Mike Mussina	6.00	1.80
UD43 Jeff Bagwell	5.00	1.50
UD44 Lance Berkman	5.00	1.50
UD45 Wade Miller	5.00	1.50
UD46 Greg Maddux	10.00	3.00
UD47 Chipper Jones	6.00	1.80
UD48 Andruw Jones	5.00	1.50
UD49 Gary Sheffield	5.00	1.50
UD50 Richie Sexson	5.00	1.50
UD51 Albert Pujols	12.00	3.60
UD52 J.D. Drew	5.00	1.50
UD53 Matt Morris	5.00	1.50
UD54 Jim Edmonds	5.00	1.50
UD55 So Taguchi	5.00	1.50
UD56 Sammy Sosa	10.00	3.00
UD57 Fred McGriff	5.00	1.50
UD58 Kerry Wood	6.00	1.80
UD59 Moises Alou	5.00	1.50
UD60 Randy Johnson	6.00	1.80
UD61 Luis Gonzalez	5.00	1.50
UD62 Mark Grace	5.00	1.50
UD63 Curt Schilling	5.00	1.50
UD64 Matt Williams	5.00	1.50
UD65 Kevin Brown	5.00	1.50
UD66 Brian Jordan	5.00	1.50
UD67 Shawn Green	5.00	1.50
UD68 Hideo Nomo	12.00	3.60
UD69 Kazuhisa Ishii	10.00	3.00
UD70 Vladimir Guerrero	6.00	1.80
UD71 Jose Vidro	5.00	1.50
UD72 Eric Good	5.00	1.50
UD73 Barry Bonds	15.00	4.50
UD74 Jeff Kent	5.00	1.50
UD75 Rich Aurilia	5.00	1.50
UD76 Deivis Santos	5.00	1.50
UD77 Preston Wilson	5.00	1.50
UD78 Cliff Floyd	5.00	1.50
UD79 Josh Beckett	5.00	1.50
UD80 Hansel Izquierdo	5.00	1.50
UD81 Mike Piazza	10.00	3.00
UD82 Roberto Alomar	6.00	1.80
UD83 Mo Vaughn	5.00	1.50
UD84 Jeromy Burnitz	5.00	1.50
UD85 Phil Nevin	5.00	1.50
UD86 Ryan Klesko	5.00	1.50
UD87 Bobby Abreu	5.00	1.50
UD88 Scott Rolen	5.00	1.50
UD89 Jimmy Rollins	5.00	1.50
UD90 Jason Kendall	5.00	1.50
UD91 Brian Giles	5.00	1.50
UD92 Aramis Ramirez	5.00	1.50
UD93 Ken Griffey Jr.	10.00	3.00
UD94 Sean Casey	5.00	1.50
UD95 Barry Larkin	6.00	1.80
UD96 Adam Dunn	5.00	1.50
UD97 Todd Helton	5.00	1.50
UD98 Larry Walker	5.00	1.50
UD99 Mike Hampton	5.00	1.50
UD100 Rene Reyes	5.00	1.50

2002 Upper Deck UD Plus Memorabilia Moments Game Uniform

These cards were available only through a mail exchange. Collectors who finished the UD Plus set earliest had an opportunity to receive cards with game-used jersey swatches of either Mickey Mantle or Joe DiMaggio. These cards were issued to a stated print run of 25 serial numbred sets. Due to market scarcity, no pricing will be provided for these cards.

	Nm-Mt	Ex-Mt
COMMON DIMAGGIO (1-5)	150.00	45.00
COMMON MANTLE (1-5)	300.00	90.00

AVAILABLE VIA MAIL EXCHANGE
STATED PRINT RUN 25 SERIAL #'d SETS

2002 Upper Deck World Series Heroes Memorabilia

Issued into first series packs at a rate of one in 288 hobby packs, these eight cards feature memorabilia from players who had star moments in the World Series.

	Nm-Mt	Ex-Mt
B-DJ Derek Jeter Base SP	40.00	12.00
B-ES E.Slaughter Bat	15.00	4.50
B-JD Joe DiMaggio Bat SP		
B-KP Kirby Puckett Bat	25.00	7.50
B-MM M.Mantle Bat	120.00	36.00
S-BM B.Mazeroski Jsy	20.00	6.00
S-CF Carlton Fisk Jsy	20.00	6.00
S-DL Don Larsen Jsy	20.00	6.00
S-JC Joe Carter Jsy	15.00	4.50

2002 Upper Deck World Series Heroes Memorabilia Autograph

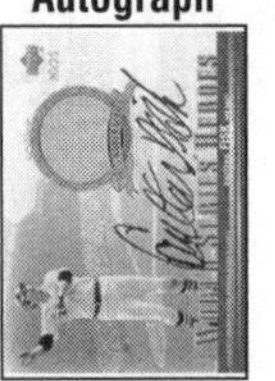

Randomly inserted in first series hobby packs, these four cards feature not only a piece of memorabilia from a World Series hero but also were signed by the featured player. A stated print run of twenty-five serial numbered cards were produced. Due to market scarcity, no pricing is provided for these cards.

	Nm-Mt	Ex-Mt
S-BM Bill Mazeroski Jsy		
S-CF Carlton Fisk Jsy		
S-DL Don Larsen Jsy		
S-JC Joe Carter Jsy		

2002 Upper Deck Yankee Dynasty Memorabilia

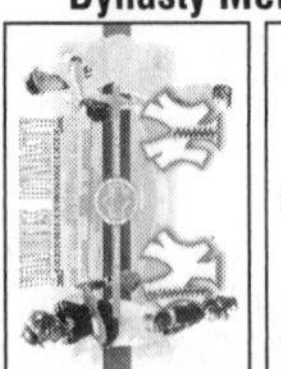

Issued into first series packs at a rate of one in 144, these 13 cards feature two pieces of game-worn memorabilia from various members of the Yankees Dynasty.

	Nm-Mt	Ex-Mt
YBCJ Roger Clemens Derek Jeter Bat SP	150.00	45.00
YBJW Derek Jeter Bernie Williams Bat	100.00	30.00
YJBJ Scott Brosius David Justice Jsy	25.00	7.50
YJBT Wade Boggs Joe Torre Jsy	25.00	7.50
YJCP Roger Clemens Jorge Posada Jsy	50.00	15.00
YJDM Joe DiMaggio Mickey Mantle Jsy	300.00	90.00
YJGC Joe Girardi David Cone Jsy	25.00	7.50
YJKR Chuck Knoblauch Tim Raines J	25.00	7.50
YJOM Paul O'Neill Tino Martinez Jsy	25.00	7.50
YJPR Andy Pettitte Mariano Rivera Jsy	25.00	7.50
YJRK Willie Randolph Chuck Knoblauch Jsy	25.00	7.50
YJWG David Wells Dwight Gooden Jsy	25.00	7.50
YJWO Bernie Williams Paul O'Neill Jsy	25.00	7.50

2002 Upper Deck Ichiro Mini Playmaker

This five card standard-size set features Japanese sensation Ichiro Suzuki. The fronts have the "Mini Play-maker" logo on the upper left and this set was issued by Upper Deck Collectibles. The fronts have the 51 Ichiro on the bottom, while the backs have some information about Ichiro's sensational 2001 rookie season.

	Nm-Mt	Ex-Mt
COMPLETE SET	20.00	6.00
COMMON CARD	4.00	1.20

2002 Upper Deck Mark McGwire Employee

This one card set features Upper Deck spokesperson Mark McGwire. The front has two photos of McGwire along with a game-

worn jersey swatch while the back has some words thanking the UD employees for their hard work. This card was issued to a stated print run of 350 serial numbered sets and was distributed as a bonus to Upper Deck employees.

	Nm-Mt	Ex-Mt
UDC-MM Mark McGwire	150.00	45.00

2002 Upper Deck Mark McGwire Holiday

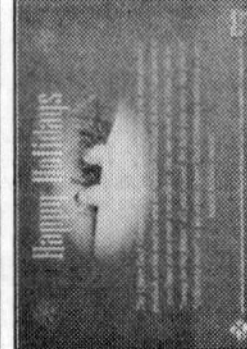

This one-card set, which measures 3" by 5" features a photo of Mark McGwire on the front hitting a snowball, while the back gives Upper Deck's message that everyone should enjoy a happy holiday season.

	MINT	NRMT
1 Mark McGwire	5.00	2.20

2003 Upper Deck

The 270 card first series was released in November, 2002. The 270 card second series was released in June, 2003. The final 60 cards were released as part of an special boxed insert in the 2004 Upper Deck Series one product. The first tw series cards were issued in eight card packs which came 24 packs to a box and 12 boxes to a case with an SRP of $3 per pack. Cards numbered from 1 through 30 featured leading rookie prospects while cards numbered from 261 through 270 featured checklist cards honoring the leading events of the 2002 season. In the second series the following subsets were issued: Cards numbered 501 through 530 feature Star Rookies while cards numbered 531 through 540 feature Season Highlight fronts and checklist backs. Due to an error in printing, card 19 was originally intended to feature Marcos Scutaro but the card was erroneously numbered as card 96. Thus, the set features two card 96's (Scutaro and Nomar Garciaparra) and no card number 19.

	Nm-Mt	Ex-Mt
COMPLETE SERIES 1 (270)	50.00	15.00
COMPLETE SERIES 2 (270)	50.00	15.00
COMP.UPDATE SET (60)	20.00	6.00
COMMON (31-500/531-600)	.30	.09
COMMON (1-30/501-530)	1.00	.30
COMMON RC (541-600)	.50	.15

SR 1-30/501-530 ARE NOT SHORT PRINTS
CARD 19 DOES NOT EXIST
SCUTARO/NOMAR ARE BOTH CARD 96
541-600 ISSUED IN 04 UD1 HOBBY BOXES
UPDATE SET EXCH 1:240 '04 UD1 RETAIL
UPDATE SET EXCH.DEADLINE 11/10/06

	Nm-Mt	Ex-Mt
1 John Lackey SR	1.00	.30
2 Alex Cintron SR	1.00	.30
3 Jose Leon SR	1.00	.30
4 Bobby Hill SR	1.00	.30
5 Brandon Larson SR	1.00	.30
6 Raul Gonzalez SR	1.00	.30
7 Ben Broussard SR	1.00	.30
8 Earl Snyder SR	1.00	.30
9 Ramon Santiago SR	1.00	.30
10 Jason Lane SR	1.00	.30
11 Keith Ginter SR	1.00	.30
12 Kirk Saarloos SR	1.00	.30
13 Juan Brito SR	1.00	.30
14 Runelvys Hernandez SR	1.00	.30
15 Shawn Sedlacek SR	1.00	.30
16 Jayson Durocher SR	1.00	.30
17 Kevin Frederick SR	1.00	.30
18 Zach Day SR	1.00	.30
19 Marcos Scutaro SR UER Card number 96 on back	1.00	.30
20 Marcus Thames SR	1.00	.30
21 Esteban German SR	1.00	.30
22 Brett Myers SR	1.00	.30
23 Oliver Perez SR	1.00	.30
24 Dennis Tankersley SR	1.00	.30
25 Julius Matos SR	1.00	.30
26 Jake Peavy SR	1.00	.30
27 Eric Cyr SR	1.00	.30
28 Mike Crudale SR	1.00	.30
29 Josh Pearce SR	1.00	.30
30 Carl Crawford SR	1.00	.30
31 Tim Salmon	.50	.15
32 Troy Glaus	.50	.15
33 Adam Kennedy	.30	.09
34 David Eckstein	.30	.09
35 Ben Molina	.30	.09
36 Jarrod Washburn	.30	.09
37 Ramon Ortiz	.30	.09
38 Eric Chavez	.30	.09
39 Miguel Tejada	.30	.09
40 Adam Piatt	.30	.09
41 Jermaine Dye	.30	.09
42 Olmedo Saenz	.30	.09
43 Tim Hudson	.30	.09
44 Barry Zito	.50	.15
45 Billy Koch	.30	.09
46 Shannon Stewart	.30	.09
47 Kelvim Escobar	.30	.09
48 Jose Cruz Jr.	.30	.09
49 Vernon Wells	.30	.09
50 Roy Halladay	.30	.09
51 Esteban Loaiza	.30	.09
52 Eric Hinske	.30	.09
53 Steve Cox	.30	.09
54 Brent Abernathy	.30	.09
55 Ben Grieve	.30	.09
56 Aubrey Huff	.30	.09
57 Jared Sandberg	.30	.09
58 Paul Wilson	.30	.09
59 Tanyon Sturtze	.30	.09
60 Jim Thome	.75	.23
61 Omar Vizquel	.30	.09
62 C.C. Sabathia	.30	.09
63 Chris Magruder	.30	.09
64 Ricky Gutierrez	.30	.09
65 Einar Diaz	.30	.09
66 Danys Baez	.30	.09
67 Ichiro Suzuki	1.25	.35
68 Ruben Sierra	.30	.09
69 Carlos Guillen	.30	.09
70 Mark McLemore	.30	.09
71 Dan Wilson	.30	.09
72 Jamie Moyer	.30	.09
73 Joel Pineiro	.30	.09
74 Edgar Martinez	.50	.15
75 Tony Batista	.30	.09
76 Jay Gibbons	.30	.09
77 Chris Singleton	.30	.09
78 Melvin Mora	.30	.09
79 Geronimo Gil	.30	.09
80 Rodrigo Lopez	.30	.09
81 Jorge Julio	.30	.09
82 Rafael Palmeiro	.50	.15
83 Juan Gonzalez	.75	.23
84 Mike Young	.30	.09
85 Hideki Irabu	.30	.09
86 Chan Ho Park	.30	.09
87 Kevin Mench	.30	.09
88 Doug Davis	.30	.09
89 Pedro Martinez	.75	.23
90 Shea Hillenbrand	.30	.09
91 Derek Lowe	.30	.09
92 Jason Varitek	.30	.09
93 Tony Clark	.30	.09
94 John Burkett	.30	.09
95 Frank Castillo	.30	.09
96 Nomar Garciaparra	1.25	.35
97 Rickey Henderson	.75	.23
98 Mike Sweeney	.30	.09
99 Carlos Febles	.30	.09
100 Mark Quinn	.30	.09
101 Raul Ibanez	.30	.09
102 A.J. Hinch	.30	.09
103 Paul Byrd	.30	.09
104 Chuck Knoblauch	.30	.09
105 Dmitri Young	.30	.09
106 Randall Simon	.30	.09
107 Brandon Inge	.30	.09
108 Damion Easley	.30	.09
109 Carlos Pena	.30	.09
110 George Lombard	.30	.09
111 Juan Acevedo	.30	.09
112 Torii Hunter	.30	.09
113 Doug Mientkiewicz	.30	.09
114 David Ortiz	.30	.09
115 Eric Milton	.30	.09
116 Eddie Guardado	.30	.09
117 Cristian Guzman	.30	.09
118 Corey Koskie	.30	.09
119 Magglio Ordonez	.30	.09
120 Mark Buehrle	.30	.09
121 Todd Ritchie	.30	.09
122 Jose Valentin	.30	.09
123 Paul Konerko	.30	.09
124 Carlos Lee	.30	.09
125 Jon Garland	.30	.09
126 Jason Giambi	.75	.23
127 Derek Jeter	2.00	.60
128 Roger Clemens	1.50	.45
129 Raul Mondesi	.30	.09
130 Jorge Posada	.50	.15
131 Rondell White	.30	.09
132 Robin Ventura	.30	.09
133 Mike Mussina	.75	.23
134 Jeff Bagwell	.50	.15
135 Craig Biggio	.50	.15
136 Morgan Ensberg	.30	.09
137 Richard Hidalgo	.30	.09
138 Brad Ausmus	.30	.09
139 Roy Oswalt	.30	.09
140 Carlos Hernandez	.30	.09
141 Shane Reynolds	.30	.09
142 Gary Sheffield	.30	.09
143 Andruw Jones	.30	.09
144 Tom Glavine	.50	.15
145 Rafael Furcal	.30	.09
146 Javy Lopez	.30	.09
147 Vinny Castilla	.30	.09
148 Marcus Giles	.30	.09
149 Kevin Millwood	.30	.09
150 Jason Marquis	.30	.09
151 Ruben Quevedo	.30	.09
152 Ben Sheets	.30	.09
153 Geoff Jenkins	.30	.09
154 Jose Hernandez	.30	.09
155 Glendon Rusch	.30	.09
156 Jeffrey Hammonds	.30	.09
157 Alex Sanchez	.30	.09
158 Jim Edmonds	.30	.09
159 Tino Martinez	.50	.15
160 Albert Pujols	1.50	.45
161 Eli Marrero	.30	.09
162 Woody Williams	.30	.09
163 Fernando Vina	.30	.09
164 Jason Isringhausen	.30	.09
165 Jason Simontacchi	.30	.09
166 Kerry Robinson	.30	.09
167 Sammy Sosa	1.25	.35

168 Juan Cruz .30 .09
169 Fred McGriff .50 .15
170 Antonio Alfonseca .30 .09
171 Jon Lieber .30 .09
172 Mark Prior 1.50 .45
173 Moises Alou .30 .09
174 Matt Clement .30 .09
175 Mark Bellhorn .30 .09
176 Randy Johnson .75 .23
177 Luis Gonzalez .30 .09
178 Tony Womack .30 .09
179 Mark Grace .50 .15
180 Junior Spivey .30 .09
181 Byung Hyun Kim .30 .09
182 Danny Bautista .30 .09
183 Brian Anderson .30 .09
184 Shawn Green .30 .09
185 Brian Jordan .30 .09
186 Eric Karros .30 .09
187 Andy Ashby .30 .09
188 Cesar Izturis .30 .09
189 Dave Roberts .30 .09
190 Eric Gagne .50 .15
191 Kazuhisa Ishii .30 .09
192 Adrian Beltre .30 .09
193 Vladimir Guerrero .75 .23
194 Tony Armas Jr. .30 .09
195 Bartolo Colon .30 .09
196 Troy O'Leary .30 .09
197 Tomo Ohka .30 .09
198 Brad Wilkerson .30 .09
199 Orlando Cabrera .30 .09
200 Barry Bonds 2.00 .60
201 David Bell .30 .09
202 Tsuyoshi Shinjo .30 .09
203 Benito Santiago .30 .09
204 Livan Hernandez .30 .09
205 Jason Schmidt .30 .09
206 Kirk Rueter .30 .09
207 Ramon E. Martinez .30 .09
208 Mike Lowell .30 .09
209 Luis Castillo .30 .09
210 Derrek Lee .30 .09
211 Andy Fox .30 .09
212 Eric Owens .30 .09
213 Charles Johnson .30 .09
214 Brad Penny .30 .09
215 A.J. Burnett .30 .09
216 Edgardo Alfonzo .30 .09
217 Roberto Alomar .75 .23
218 Rey Ordonez .30 .09
219 Al Leiter .30 .09
220 Roger Cedeno .30 .09
221 Timo Perez .30 .09
222 Jeromy Burnitz .30 .09
223 Pedro Astacio .30 .09
224 Joe McEwing .30 .09
225 Ryan Klesko .30 .09
226 Ramon Vazquez .30 .09
227 Mark Kotsay .30 .09
228 Bubba Trammell .30 .09
229 Wiki Gonzalez .30 .09
230 Trevor Hoffman .30 .09
231 Ron Gant .30 .09
232 Bob Abreu .30 .09
233 Marlon Anderson .30 .09
234 Jeremy Giambi .30 .09
235 Jimmy Rollins .30 .09
236 Mike Lieberthal .30 .09
237 Vicente Padilla .30 .09
238 Randy Wolf .30 .09
239 Pokey Reese .30 .09
240 Brian Giles .30 .09
241 Jack Wilson .30 .09
242 Mike Williams .30 .09
243 Kip Wells .30 .09
244 Rob Mackowiak .30 .09
245 Craig Wilson .30 .09
246 Adam Dunn .30 .09
247 Sean Casey .30 .09
248 Todd Walker .30 .09
249 Corky Miller .30 .09
250 Ryan Dempster .30 .09
251 Reggie Taylor .30 .09
252 Aaron Boone .30 .09
253 Larry Walker .50 .15
254 Jose Ortiz .30 .09
255 Todd Zeile .30 .09
256 Bobby Estalella .30 .09
257 Juan Pierre .30 .09
258 Terry Shumpert .30 .09
259 Mike Hampton .30 .09
260 Denny Stark .30 .09
261 Shawn Green SH CL .30 .09
262 Derek Lowe SH CL .30 .09
263 Barry Bonds SH CL .75 .23
264 Mike Cameron SH CL .30 .09
265 Luis Castillo SH CL .30 .09
266 Vladimir Guerrero SH CL .50 .15
267 Jason Giambi SH CL .50 .15
268 Eric Gagne SH CL .30 .09
269 Magglio Ordonez SH CL .30 .09
270 Jim Thome SH CL .50 .15
271 Garret Anderson .30 .09
272 Troy Percival .30 .09
273 Brad Fullmer .30 .09
274 Scott Spiezio .30 .09
275 Darin Erstad .30 .09
276 Francisco Rodriguez .30 .09
277 Kevin Appier .30 .09
278 Shawn Wooten .30 .09
279 Eric Owens .30 .09
280 Scott Hatteberg .30 .09
281 Terrence Long .30 .09
282 Mark Mulder .30 .09
283 Ramon Hernandez .30 .09
284 Ted Lilly .30 .09
285 Erubiel Durazo .30 .09
286 Mark Ellis .30 .09
287 Carlos Delgado .30 .09
288 Orlando Hudson .30 .09
289 Chris Woodward .30 .09
290 Mark Hendrickson .30 .09
291 Josh Phelps .30 .09
292 Ken Huckaby .30 .09
293 Justin Miller .30 .09
294 Travis Lee .30 .09
295 Jorge Sosa .30 .09
296 Joe Kennedy .30 .09
297 Carl Crawford .30 .09
298 Toby Hall .30 .09
299 Rey Ordonez .30 .09
300 Brandon Phillips .30 .09
301 Matt Lawton .30 .09
302 Ellis Burks .30 .09
303 Bill Selby .30 .09
304 Travis Hafner .30 .09
305 Milton Bradley .30 .09
306 Karim Garcia .30 .09
307 Cliff Lee .30 .09
308 Jeff Cirillo .30 .09
309 John Olerud .30 .09
310 Kazuhiro Sasaki .30 .09
311 Freddy Garcia .30 .09
312 Bret Boone .30 .09
313 Mike Cameron .30 .09
314 Ben Davis .30 .09
315 Randy Winn .30 .09
316 Gary Matthews Jr. .30 .09
317 Jeff Conine .30 .09
318 Sidney Ponson .30 .09
319 Jerry Hairston .30 .09
320 David Segui .30 .09
321 Scott Erickson .30 .09
322 Marty Cordova .30 .09
323 Hank Blalock .50 .15
324 Herbert Perry .30 .09
325 Alex Rodriguez 1.25 .35
326 Carl Everett .30 .09
327 Einar Diaz .30 .09
328 Ugueth Urbina .30 .09
329 Mark Teixeira .50 .15
330 Manny Ramirez .30 .09
331 Johnny Damon .30 .09
332 Trot Nixon .50 .15
333 Tim Wakefield .30 .09
334 Casey Fossum .30 .09
335 Todd Walker .30 .09
336 Jeremy Giambi .30 .09
337 Bill Mueller .30 .09
338 Ramiro Mendoza .30 .09
339 Carlos Beltran .30 .09
340 Jason Grimsley .30 .09
341 Brent Mayne .30 .09
342 Angel Berroa .30 .09
343 Albie Lopez .30 .09
344 Michael Tucker .30 .09
345 Bobby Higginson .30 .09
346 Shane Halter .30 .09
347 Jeremy Bonderman RC 1.00 .30
348 Eric Munson .30 .09
349 Andy Van Hekken .30 .09
350 Matt Anderson .30 .09
351 Jacque Jones .30 .09
352 A.J. Pierzynski .30 .09
353 Joe Mays .30 .09
354 Brad Radke .30 .09
355 Dustan Mohr .30 .09
356 Bobby Kielty .30 .09
357 Michael Cuddyer .30 .09
358 Luis Rivas .30 .09
359 Frank Thomas .75 .23
360 Joe Borchard .30 .09
361 D'Angelo Jimenez .30 .09
362 Bartolo Colon .30 .09
363 Joe Crede .30 .09
364 Miguel Olivo .30 .09
365 Billy Koch .30 .09
366 Bernie Williams .50 .15
367 Nick Johnson .30 .09
368 Andy Pettitte .50 .15
369 Mariano Rivera .50 .15
370 Alfonso Soriano .50 .15
371 David Wells .30 .09
372 Drew Henson .30 .09
373 Juan Rivera .30 .09
374 Steve Karsay .30 .09
375 Jeff Kent .30 .09
376 Lance Berkman .30 .09
377 Octavio Dotel .30 .09
378 Julio Lugo .30 .09
379 Jason Lane .30 .09
380 Wade Miller .30 .09
381 Billy Wagner .30 .09
382 Brad Ausmus .30 .09
383 Mike Hampton .30 .09
384 Chipper Jones .75 .23
385 John Smoltz .50 .15
386 Greg Maddux 1.25 .35
387 Javy Lopez .30 .09
388 Robert Fick .30 .09
389 Mark DeRosa .30 .09
390 Russ Ortiz .30 .09
391 Julio Franco .30 .09
392 Richie Sexson .30 .09
393 Eric Young .30 .09
394 Robert Machado .30 .09
395 Mike DeJean .30 .09
396 Todd Ritchie .30 .09
397 Royce Clayton .30 .09
398 Nick Neugebauer .30 .09
399 J.D. Drew .30 .09
400 Edgar Renteria .30 .09
401 Scott Rolen .50 .15
402 Matt Morris .30 .09
403 Garrett Stephenson .30 .09
404 Eduardo Perez .30 .09
405 Mike Matheny .30 .09
406 Miguel Cairo .30 .09
407 Brett Tomko .30 .09
408 Bobby Hill .30 .09
409 Troy O'Leary .30 .09
410 Corey Patterson .30 .09
411 Kerry Wood .75 .23
412 Eric Karros .30 .09
413 Hee Seop Choi .30 .09
414 Alex Gonzalez .30 .09
415 Matt Clement .30 .09
416 Mark Grudzielanek .30 .09
417 Curt Schilling .50 .15
418 Steve Finley .30 .09
419 Craig Counsell .30 .09
420 Matt Williams .30 .09
421 Quinton McCracken .30 .09
422 Chad Moeller .30 .09
423 Lyle Overbay .30 .09
424 Miguel Batista .30 .09
425 Paul Lo Duca .30 .09
426 Kevin Brown .30 .09
427 Hideo Nomo .75 .23
428 Fred McGriff .50 .15
429 Joe Thurston .30 .09
430 Odalis Perez .30 .09
431 Darren Dreifort .30 .09
432 Todd Hundley .30 .09
433 Dave Roberts .30 .09
434 Jose Vidro .30 .09
435 Javier Vazquez .30 .09
436 Michael Barrett .30 .09
437 Fernando Tatis .30 .09
438 Peter Bergeron .30 .09
439 Endy Chavez .30 .09
440 Orlando Hernandez .30 .09
441 Marvin Benard .30 .09
442 Rich Aurilia .30 .09
443 Pedro Feliz .30 .09
444 Robb Nen .30 .09
445 Ray Durham .30 .09
446 Marquis Grissom .30 .09
447 Damian Moss .30 .09
448 Edgardo Alfonzo .30 .09
449 Juan Pierre .30 .09
450 Braden Looper .30 .09
451 Alex Gonzalez .30 .09
452 Justin Wayne .30 .09
453 Josh Beckett .50 .15
454 Juan Encarnacion .30 .09
455 Ivan Rodriguez .75 .23
456 Todd Hollandsworth .30 .09
457 Cliff Floyd .30 .09
458 Rey Sanchez .30 .09
459 Mike Piazza 1.25 .35
460 Mo Vaughn .30 .09
461 Armando Benitez .30 .09
462 Tsuyoshi Shinjo .30 .09
463 Tom Glavine .50 .15
464 David Cone .30 .09
465 Phil Nevin .30 .09
466 Sean Burroughs .30 .09
467 Jake Peavy .30 .09
468 Brian Lawrence .30 .09
469 Mark Loretta .30 .09
470 Dennis Tankersley .30 .09
471 Jesse Orosco .30 .09
472 Jim Thome .75 .23
473 Kevin Millwood .30 .09
474 David Bell .30 .09
475 Pat Burrell .30 .09
476 Brandon Duckworth .30 .09
477 Jose Mesa .30 .09
478 Marlon Byrd .30 .09
479 Reggie Sanders .30 .09
480 Jason Kendall .30 .09
481 Aramis Ramirez .30 .09
482 Kris Benson .30 .09
483 Matt Stairs .30 .09
484 Kevin Young .30 .09
485 Kenny Lofton .30 .09
486 Austin Kearns .30 .09
487 Barry Larkin .75 .23
488 Jason LaRue .30 .09
489 Ken Griffey Jr. 1.25 .35
490 Danny Graves .30 .09
491 Russell Branyan .30 .09
492 Reggie Taylor .30 .09
493 Jimmy Haynes .30 .09
494 Charles Johnson .30 .09
495 Todd Helton .50 .15
496 Juan Uribe .30 .09
497 Preston Wilson .30 .09
498 Chris Stynes .30 .09
499 Jason Jennings .30 .09
500 Jay Payton .30 .09
501 Hideki Matsui SR RC 8.00 2.40
502 Jose Contreras SR RC 3.00 .90
503 Brandon Webb SR RC 4.00 1.20
504 Robby Hammock SR RC 1.50 .45
505 Matt Kata SR RC 1.50 .45
506 Tim Olson SR RC 1.50 .45
507 Michael Hessman SR RC 1.00 .30
508 Jon Leicester SR RC 1.00 .30
509 Todd Wellemeyer SR RC 1.50 .45
510 David Sanders SR RC 1.00 .30
511 Josh Stewart SR RC 1.00 .30
512 Luis Ayala SR RC 1.00 .30
513 Clint Barmes SR RC 1.50 .45
514 Josh Willingham SR RC 2.50 .75
515 Al. Machado SR RC 1.00 .30
516 Felix Sanchez SR RC 1.00 .30
517 Willie Eyre SR RC 1.00 .30
518 Brent Hoard SR RC 1.00 .30
519 Lew Ford SR RC 1.50 .45
520 Terrmel Sledge SR RC 1.50 .45
521 Jeremy Griffiths SR RC 1.50 .45
522 Phil Seibel SR RC 1.00 .30
523 Craig Brazell SR RC 1.50 .45
524 Prentice Redman SR RC 1.00 .30
525 Jeff Duncan SR RC 1.50 .45
526 Shane Bazzell SR RC 1.00 .30
527 Bernie Castro SR RC 1.00 .30
528 Rett Johnson SR RC 1.50 .45
529 Bobby Madritsch SR RC 1.00 .30
530 Rocco Baldelli SR 2.50 .75
531 Alex Rodriguez SH CL .75 .23
532 Eric Chavez SH CL .30 .09
533 Miguel Tejada SH CL .30 .09
534 Ichiro Suzuki SH CL .75 .23
535 Sammy Sosa SH CL .75 .23
536 Barry Zito SH CL .30 .09
537 Darin Erstad SH CL .30 .09
538 Alfonso Soriano SH CL .30 .09
539 Troy Glaus SH CL .30 .09
540 N.Garciaparra SH CL .75 .23
541 Bo Hart RC 1.50 .45
542 Dan Haren RC 1.00 .30
543 Ryan Wagner RC 1.25 .35
544 Rich Harden .50 .15
545 Dontrelle Willis .75 .23
546 Jerome Williams .30 .09
547 Bobby Crosby .50 .15
548 Greg Jones RC .50 .15
549 Todd Linden .30 .09
550 Byung-Hyun Kim .30 .09
551 Rickie Weeks RC 5.00 1.50
552 Jason Roach RC .50 .15
553 Oscar Villarreal RC .50 .15
554 Justin Duchscherer .30 .09
555 Chris Capuano RC .50 .15
556 Josh Hall RC .50 .15
557 Luis Matos .30 .09
558 Miguel Ojeda RC .50 .15
559 Kevin Ohme RC .50 .15
560 Julio Manon RC .50 .15
561 Kevin Correia RC .50 .15
562 Delmon Young RC 8.00 2.40
563 Aaron Boone .30 .09
564 Aaron Looper RC .50 .15
565 Mike Neu RC .50 .15
566 Aquilino Lopez RC .50 .15
567 Jhonny Peralta RC .50 .15
568 Duaner Sanchez .30 .09
569 Stephen Randolph RC .50 .15
570 Nate Bland RC .50 .15
571 Chin-Hui Tsao .30 .09
572 Michel Hernandez RC .50 .15
573 Rocco Baldelli 1.25 .35
574 Robb Quinlan .30 .09
575 Aaron Heilman .30 .09
576 Jae Weong Seo .30 .09
577 Joe Borowski .30 .09
578 Chris Bootcheck .30 .09
579 Michael Ryan RC .50 .15
580 Mark Malaska RC .50 .15
581 Jose Guillen .30 .09
582 Josh Towers .30 .09
583 Tom Gregorio RC .50 .15
584 Edwin Jackson RC 2.50 .75
585 Jason Anderson .30 .09
586 Jose Reyes .50 .15
587 Miguel Cabrera 1.25 .35
588 Nate Bump .30 .09
589 Jeromy Burnitz .30 .09
590 David Ross .30 .09
591 Chase Utley .30 .09
592 Brandon Webb 2.00 .60
593 Masao Kida .30 .09
594 Jimmy Journell .30 .09
595 Eric Young .30 .09
596 Tony Womack .30 .09
597 Amaury Telemaco .30 .09
598 Rickey Henderson .75 .23
599 Esteban Loaiza .30 .09
600 Sidney Ponson .30 .09
NNO Update Set Exchange Card

2003 Upper Deck Gold

MINT NRMT
COMP.FACT.SET (60) 40.00 18.00
*GOLD: 2X TO 5X BASIC
*GOLD: 1.25X TO 3X BASIC RC'S
ONE GOLD SET PER 12 CT HOBBY CASE

2003 Upper Deck A Piece of History 500 Club

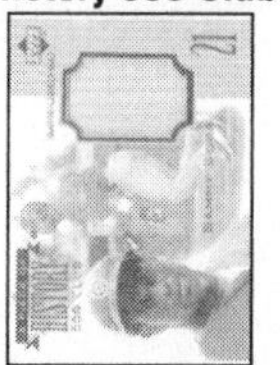

This card, which continues the Upper Deck A Piece of History 500 club set which began in 1999, was randomly inserted into second series packs. These cards were issued to a stated print run of 350 cards.

Nm-Mt Ex-Mt
SS Sammy Sosa 250.00 75.00

2003 Upper Deck A Piece of History 500 Club Autograph

Randomly inserted into packs, this is a parallel to the Piece of History insert card of Sammy Sosa. Sosa signed 21 copies of this card but did not return them in time for pack-out. Please note that the exchange date for these cards are June 9th, 2006 and since only 21 cards were created there is no pricing due to market scarcity.

Nm-Mt Ex-Mt
RANDOM INSERT IN SERIES 2 PACKS
STATED PRINT RUN 21 SERIAL #'d CARDS
NO PRICING DUE TO SCARCITY
EXCHANGE DEADLINE 06/09/06
SSAU Sammy Sosa AU/21 EXCH

2003 Upper Deck AL All-Star Swatches

Inserted into first series retail packs at a stated rate of one in 144, these 13 cards feature game-used uniform swatches of players who had made the AL All-Star game during their career.

Nm-Mt Ex-Mt
AP Andy Pettitte 15.00 4.50
AS Aaron Sele 10.00 3.00
CE Carl Everett 10.00 3.00
CF Chuck Finley 10.00 3.00
JG Juan Gonzalez 15.00 4.50
JM Joe Mays 10.00 3.00
JP Jorge Posada 15.00 4.50
MC Mike Cameron 10.00 3.00
MO Magglio Ordonez 10.00 3.00
MR Mariano Rivera 15.00 4.50
MS Mike Sweeney 10.00 3.00
RD Ray Durham 10.00 3.00
TF Travis Fryman 10.00 3.00

2003 Upper Deck Big League Breakdowns

Inserted into series one packs at a stated rate of one in eight, these 15 cards feature some of the leading hitters in the game.

Nm-Mt Ex-Mt
COMPLETE SET (15) 40.00 12.00
BL1 Troy Glaus 2.00 .60
BL2 Miguel Tejada 2.00 .60
BL3 Chipper Jones 2.50 .75
BL4 Torii Hunter 2.00 .60
BL5 Nomar Garciaparra 4.00 1.20
BL6 Sammy Sosa 4.00 1.20
BL7 Todd Helton 2.00 .60
BL8 Lance Berkman 2.00 .60
BL9 Shawn Green 2.00 .60
BL10 Vladimir Guerrero 2.50 .75
BL11 Jason Giambi 2.50 .75
BL12 Derek Jeter 6.00 1.80
BL13 Barry Bonds 6.00 1.80
BL14 Ichiro Suzuki 4.00 1.20
BL15 Alex Rodriguez 4.00 1.20

2003 Upper Deck Chase for 755

Inserted into first series packs at a stated rate of one in eight, these 15 cards feature players who are considered to have some chance of surpassing Hank Aaron's career home run total.

Nm-Mt Ex-Mt
COMPLETE SET (15) 30.00 9.00
C1 Troy Glaus 2.00 .60
C2 Andruw Jones 2.00 .60
C3 Manny Ramirez 2.00 .60
C4 Sammy Sosa 4.00 1.20
C5 Ken Griffey Jr. 4.00 1.20
C6 Adam Dunn 2.00 .60
C7 Todd Helton 2.00 .60
C8 Lance Berkman 2.00 .60
C9 Jeff Bagwell 2.00 .60
C10 Shawn Green 2.00 .60
C11 Vladimir Guerrero 2.50 .75
C12 Barry Bonds 6.00 1.80
C13 Alex Rodriguez 4.00 1.20
C14 Juan Gonzalez 2.50 .75
C15 Carlos Delgado 2.00 .60

2003 Upper Deck Game Swatches

Inserted into first series packs at a stated rate of one in 72, these 25 cards feature game-used memorabilia swatches. A few cards were printed to a lesser quantity and we have notated those cards in our checklist.

Nm-Mt Ex-Mt
HJ-AR Alex Rodriguez 15.00 4.50
HJ-BW Bernie Williams 10.00 3.00
HJ-CC C.C. Sabathia 8.00 2.40
HJ-CD Carlos Delgado SP 15.00 4.50
HJ-CP Carlos Pena 8.00 2.40
HJ-CS Curt Schilling SP/100 20.00 6.00
HJ-GM Greg Maddux 10.00 3.00
HJ-MM Mike Mussina 10.00 3.00
HJ-MO Magglio Ordonez 8.00 2.40
HJ-MP Mike Piazza SP 25.00 7.50
HJ-SB Sean Burroughs SP 15.00 4.50
HJ-SS Sammy Sosa 15.00 4.50
RJ-AD Adam Dunn 8.00 2.40
RJ-DE Darin Erstad 8.00 2.40
RJ-EM Edgar Martinez 10.00 3.00
RJ-FT Frank Thomas 10.00 3.00
RJ-IR Ivan Rodriguez 10.00 3.00
RJ-JD J.D. Drew 8.00 2.40
RJ-JE Jim Edmonds 8.00 2.40
RJ-JG Jason Giambi 10.00 3.00

RJ-JK Jeff Kent 8.00 2.40
RJ-KG Ken Griffey Jr. 15.00 4.50
RJ-RC Roger Clemens 20.00 6.00
RJ-RJ Randy Johnson 10.00 3.00
RJ-TH Tim Hudson 8.00 2.40

2003 Upper Deck Leading Swatches

Nm-Mt Ex-Mt
SERIES 2 STATED ODDS 1:24 HOB/1:48 RET
SP INFO PROVIDED BY UPPER DECK
SP'S ARE NOT SERIAL-NUMBERED
*GOLD: .75X TO 2X BASIC SWATCHES
*GOLD: .6X TO 1.5X BASIC SP SWATCHES
*GOLD MATSUI HR: .75X TO 1.5X BASIC HR
*GOLD MATSUI RBI: .6X TO 1.2X BASIC RBI
GOLD RANDOM INSERTS IN SER.2 PACKS
GOLD PRINT RUN 100 SERIAL #'d SETS
AB Adrian Beltre GM 8.00 2.40
AD Adam Dunn RUN 8.00 2.40
AD1 Adam Dunn BB SP 10.00 3.00
AJ Andruw Jones HR 8.00 2.40
AJ1 Andruw Jones AB SP 10.00 3.00
AP Andy Pettitte WIN SP 15.00 4.50
AR Alex Rodriguez HR 15.00 4.50
AR1 Alex Rodriguez RBI 15.00 4.50
AS Alfonso Soriano SB 10.00 3.00
AS1 Alfonso Soriano RUN 10.00 3.00
AS2 Aaron Sele WIN 8.00 2.40
BA Bobby Abreu 2B 8.00 2.40
BG Brian Giles HR 8.00 2.40
BG1 Brian Giles OBP 8.00 2.40
BW Bernie Williams 333 AVG 10.00 3.00
BW1 Bernie Williams 339 AVG 10.00 3.00
BZ Barry Zito WIN 10.00 3.00
CD Carlos Delgado RBI 8.00 2.40
CJ Chipper Jones AVG-RBI 10.00 3.00
CP Corey Patterson HR 8.00 2.40
CS Curt Schilling WIN 10.00 3.00
EC Eric Chavez HR 8.00 2.40
GA Garret Anderson RBI 8.00 2.40
GM Greg Maddux 2.62 ERA 10.00 3.00
GM1 Greg Maddux 1.56 ERA SP 15.00 4.50
GO Juan Gonzalez RBI 10.00 3.00
HM Hideki Matsui HR 100.00 30.00
HM1 Hideki Matsui RBI SP 120.00 36.00
HN Hideo Nomo WIN 15.00 4.50
IR Ivan Rodriguez AVG 10.00 3.00
IS Ichiro Suzuki HIT 30.00 9.00
IS1 Ichiro Suzuki SB SP 40.00 12.00
JB Jeff Bagwell RBI 10.00 3.00
JB1 Jeff Bagwell SLG SP 15.00 4.50
JD J.D. Drew RBI 8.00 2.40
JE Jim Edmonds RUN 8.00 2.40
JG Jason Giambi HR 10.00 3.00
JG1 Jason Giambi SLG 10.00 3.00
JL Javy Lopez NLCS 8.00 2.40
JP Jay Payton 3B 8.00 2.40
JS J.T. Snow GLV 8.00 2.40
JT Jim Thome HR 10.00 3.00
JT1 Jim Thome SLG 10.00 3.00
KE Jason Kendall RUN 8.00 2.40
KG Ken Griffey Jr. 40 HR 15.00 4.50
KG1 Ken Griffey Jr. 56 HR SP 20.00 6.00
KI Kazuhisa Ishii K 8.00 2.40
KS Kazuhiro Sasaki SV 8.00 2.40
KW Kerry Wood K 10.00 3.00
LB Lance Berkman HR 8.00 2.40
LG Luis Gonzalez RUN 8.00 2.40
LW Larry Walker AVG 10.00 3.00
MP Mike Piazza HR 15.00 4.50
MP1 Mike Piazza SLG 15.00 4.50
MR Manny Ramirez AVG 8.00 2.40
MSL Mike Sweeney AVG 8.00 2.40
MSW Mike Stanton Pants GM 8.00 2.40
MT Miguel Tejada RBI 8.00 2.40
MT1 Miguel Tejada GM SP 10.00 3.00
OV Omar Vizquel SAC 8.00 2.40
PB Pat Burrell HR 8.00 2.40
PB1 Pat Burrell RBI 8.00 2.40
PM Pedro Martinez K 10.00 3.00
RC Roger Clemens K 15.00 4.50
RC1 Roger Clemens ERA 15.00 4.50
RJ Randy Johnson K 10.00 3.00
RJ1 Randy Johnson ERA 10.00 3.00
RO Roy Oswalt WIN 8.00 2.40
RO1 Roy Oswalt PCT SP 10.00 3.00
RP Rafael Palmeiro RBI 10.00 3.00
RP1 Rafael Palmeiro 2B 10.00 3.00
SG Shawn Green HR 8.00 2.40
SG1 Shawn Green TB 8.00 2.40
SR Scott Rolen HR 10.00 3.00
SS Sammy Sosa 49 HR 15.00 4.50
SS1 Sammy Sosa 50 HR SP/170 20.00 6.00
TB Tony Batista HR 8.00 2.40
TG Troy Glaus HR 10.00 3.00
THE Todd Helton RBI 10.00 3.00
THU Tim Hudson IP 8.00 2.40
THU1 Tim Hudson GM SP 10.00 3.00
TP Troy Percival SV 8.00 2.40
VG Vladimir Guerrero HIT 10.00 3.00

2003 Upper Deck Lineup Time Jerseys

Inserted into first series hobby packs at a stated rate of one in 96, these 10 cards feature game-used uniform swatches from some of the leading players in the game. A couple of cards were printed to a smaller quantity and we have notated those cards with an SP in our checklist.

Nm-Mt Ex-Mt
BW Bernie Williams 10.00 3.00
CD Carlos Delgado 8.00 2.40
GM Greg Maddux 10.00 3.00
IS Ichiro Suzuki 40.00 12.00
JD J.D. Drew 8.00 2.40
JT Jim Thome 10.00 3.00
RC Roger Clemens SP 25.00 7.50
RJ Randy Johnson SP 20.00 6.00
SG Shawn Green 8.00 2.40
TH Todd Helton 10.00 3.00

2003 Upper Deck Magical Performances

Nm-Mt Ex-Mt
*GOLD: 1X TO 2.5X BASIC MAGIC
GOLD RANDOM INSERTS IN SER.2 PACKS
GOLD PRINT RUN 50 SERIAL #'d SETS
DUPE STARS EQUALLY VALUED
MP1 Hideki Matsui 40.00 12.00
MP2 Ken Griffey Jr. 20.00 6.00
MP3 Ichiro Suzuki 20.00 6.00
MP4 Ken Griffey Jr. 20.00 6.00
MP5 Hideo Nomo 15.00 4.50
MP6 Mickey Mantle 50.00 15.00
MP7 Ken Griffey Jr. 20.00 6.00
MP8 Barry Bonds 25.00 7.50
MP9 Mickey Mantle 50.00 15.00
MP10 Tom Seaver 15.00 4.50
MP11 Mike Piazza 20.00 6.00
MP12 Roger Clemens 20.00 6.00
MP13 Nolan Ryan 40.00 12.00
MP14 Nomar Garciaparra 20.00 6.00
MP15 Ernie Banks 15.00 4.50
MP16 Stan Musial 25.00 7.50
MP17 Mickey Mantle 50.00 15.00
MP18 Nolan Ryan 40.00 12.00
MP19 Nolan Ryan 40.00 12.00
MP20 Mickey Mantle 50.00 15.00
MP21 Ichiro Suzuki 20.00 6.00
MP22 Nolan Ryan 40.00 12.00
MP23 Tom Seaver 15.00 4.50
MP24 Ken Griffey Jr. 20.00 6.00
MP25 Hideo Nomo 15.00 4.50
MP26 Ken Griffey Jr. 20.00 6.00
MP27 Mark McGwire 25.00 7.50
MP28 Barry Bonds 25.00 7.50
MP29 Alex Rodriguez 20.00 6.00
MP30 Nolan Ryan 40.00 12.00
MP31 Mark McGwire 25.00 7.50
MP32 Nolan Ryan 40.00 12.00
MP33 Sammy Sosa 20.00 6.00
MP34 Ichiro Suzuki 20.00 6.00
MP35 Barry Bonds 25.00 7.50
MP36 Derek Jeter 25.00 7.50
MP37 Roger Clemens 20.00 6.00
MP38 Jason Giambi 15.00 4.50
MP39 Mickey Mantle 50.00 15.00
MP40 Ted Williams 40.00 12.00
MP41 Ted Williams 40.00 12.00
MP42 Ted Williams 40.00 12.00

2003 Upper Deck Mark of Greatness Autograph Jerseys

Randomly inserted into first series packs, these three cards feature authentically signed Mark McGwire cards. There are three different versions of this card, which were all signed to a different print run, and we have notated that information in our checklist.

Nm-Mt Ex-Mt
MOG Mark McGwire/400 400.00 120.00
MOGG Mark McGwire Gold/25
MOGS Mark McGwire Silver/70 500.00 150.00

2003 Upper Deck Masters with the Leather

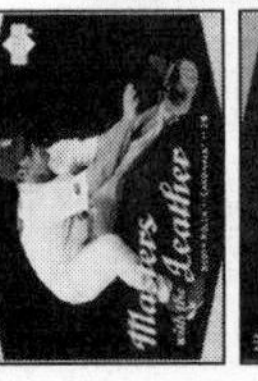

Nm-Mt Ex-Mt
COMPLETE SET (12) 25.00 7.50
L1 Darin Erstad 2.00 .60
L2 Andruw Jones 2.00 .60
L3 Greg Maddux 4.00 1.20
L4 Nomar Garciaparra 4.00 1.20
L5 Torii Hunter 2.00 .60
L6 Roberto Alomar 2.50 .75
L7 Derek Jeter 6.00 1.80
L8 Eric Chavez 2.00 .60
L9 Ichiro Suzuki 4.00 1.20
L10 Jim Edmonds 2.00 .60
L11 Scott Rolen 2.00 .60
L12 Alex Rodriguez 4.00 1.20

2003 Upper Deck Mid-Summer Stars Swatches

Inserted into first series packs at a stated rate of one in 72, these 23 cards feature a mix of players who shine all during the season. A few cards do not feature jersey swatches and we have notated that information in our checklist. In addition, a few cards were issued to a smaller quantity and we have notated those cards with an SP in our checklist.

Nm-Mt Ex-Mt
AJ Andruw Jones 8.00 2.40
AR Alex Rodriguez 15.00 4.50
BZ Barry Zito 10.00 3.00
CD Carlos Delgado 8.00 2.40
CS Curt Schilling 10.00 3.00
DE Darin Erstad 8.00 2.40
DW David Wells 8.00 2.40
EM Edgar Martinez 10.00 3.00
FG Freddy Garcia 8.00 2.40
FT Frank Thomas 10.00 3.00
HN Hideo Nomo 20.00 6.00
IS Ichiro Suzuki Turtleneck SP 50.00 15.00
JE Jim Edmonds SP * 10.00 3.00
JG Juan Gonzalez Pants 10.00 3.00
KS Kazuhiro Sasaki 8.00 2.40
MP Mike Piazza 15.00 4.50
MR Manny Ramirez 8.00 2.40
RC Roger Clemens 15.00 4.50
RJ Randy Johnson Shirt 10.00 3.00
RV Robin Ventura 10.00 3.00
SG Shawn Green SP 10.00 3.00
SS Sammy Sosa 15.00 4.50
TG Tom Glavine 10.00 3.00

2003 Upper Deck NL All-Star Swatches

Inserted into first series hobby packs at a stated rate of one in 72, these 12 cards feature game-used memorabilia swatch of players who had participated in the All-Star game for the National League.

Nm-Mt Ex-Mt
AL Al Leiter 8.00 2.40
CF Cliff Floyd 8.00 2.40
CS Curt Schilling 10.00 3.00
FM Fred McGriff 10.00 3.00
JV Jose Vidro 8.00 2.40
MH Mike Hampton 8.00 2.40
MM Matt Morris 8.00 2.40
RK Ryan Klesko 8.00 2.40
SC Sean Casey 8.00 2.40
TG Tom Glavine 10.00 3.00
TG Tony Gwynn 15.00 4.50
TH Trevor Hoffman 8.00 2.40

2003 Upper Deck National Pride Memorabilia

Nm-Mt Ex-Mt
SERIES 2 ODDS 1:24 HOBBY/1:48 RETAIL
SP PRINT RUNS PROVIDED BY UPPER DECK
SP'S ARE NOT SERIAL-NUMBERED
ALL FEATURE PANTS UNLESS NOTED
AA Abe Alvarez 8.00 2.40
AH Aaron Hill 8.00 2.40
AJ A.J. Hinch Jsy 8.00 2.40
AK A.Kearns Right Jsy 8.00 2.40
AK1 A.Kearns Left Jsy SP/250 15.00 4.50
BH Bobby Hill Field Jsy 8.00 2.40
BH1 Bobby Hill Run Jsy SP/100 20.00 6.00
BS Brad Sullivan Wind Up 8.00 2.40
BS1 Brad Sullivan Throw SP/250 15.00 4.50
BZ Bob Zimmermann 5.00 1.50
CC Chad Cordero 5.00 1.50
CJ Conor Jackson 8.00 2.40
CQ Carlos Quentin 8.00 2.40
CS Clint Sammons 5.00 1.50
DP Dustin Pedroia 5.00 1.50
EM Eric Milton White Jsy 8.00 2.40
EM1 Eric Milton Blue Jsy SP/50 20.00 6.00
EP Eric Patterson 8.00 2.40
GJ Grant Johnson 5.00 1.50
HS Huston Street 8.00 2.40
JJ0 J.Jones White Jsy 8.00 2.40
JJ1 J.Jones Blue Jsy SP/250 15.00 4.50
JJE Jason Jennings Jsy 8.00 2.40
KB Kyle Bakker 5.00 1.50
KSA K.Saarloos Red Jsy 8.00 2.40
KSL Kyle Sleeth 10.00 3.00
KSA1 K.Saarloos Grey Jsy SP/250 15.00 4.50
LP Landon Powell 5.00 1.50
MA Michael Aubrey 10.00 3.00
MJ Mark Jurich 5.00 1.50
MP Mark Prior Pinstripes Jsy 20.00 6.00
MP1 Mark Prior Grey Jsy SP/100
PH Philip Humber 8.00 2.40
RF Robert Fick Jsy 8.00 2.40
RO R.Oswalt Behind Jsy 8.00 2.40
RO1 R.Oswalt Beside Jsy SP/100 20.00 6.00
RW R.Weeks Glove-Chest 15.00 4.50
RW1 R.Weeks Glove-Head SP/250
SB Sean Burroughs 8.00 2.40
SC Shane Costa 8.00 2.40
SF Sam Fuld 5.00 1.50
WL Wes Littleton 8.00 2.40

2003 Upper Deck Piece of the Action Game Ball

Nm-Mt Ex-Mt
SERIES 2 ODDS 1:288 HOBBY/1:576 RETAIL
PRINT RUNS B/WN 10-175 COPIES PER
PRINT RUNS PROVIDED BY UPPER DECK
CARDS ARE NOT SERIAL-NUMBERED
NO PRICING ON QTY OF 25 OR LESS.
AB Adrian Beltre/100 10.00 3.00
ARA Aramis Ramirez/100 10.00 3.00
ARO Alex Rodriguez/100 25.00 7.50
BA Bobby Abreu/125 10.00 3.00
BB Barry Bonds/125 40.00 12.00
BG Brian Giles/100 10.00 3.00
BW Bernie Williams/125 15.00 4.50
CJ Chipper Jones/62 25.00 7.50
CS Curt Schilling/100 15.00 4.50
DE Darin Erstad/125 10.00 3.00
DJ Derek Jeter/65 60.00 18.00
EM Edgar Martinez/125 15.00 4.50
FG Freddy Garcia/100 10.00 3.00
FT Frank Thomas/150 15.00 4.50
GA Garret Anderson/150 10.00 3.00
GS Gary Sheffield/100 10.00 3.00
HN Hideo Nomo/100 40.00 12.00
IR Ivan Rodriguez/10
IS Ichiro Suzuki/25
JG Juan Gonzalez/100 15.00 4.50
JK Jason Kendall/100 10.00 3.00
JT Jim Thome/125 15.00 4.50
JV Jose Vidro/100 10.00 3.00
KB Kevin Brown/100 10.00 3.00
KE Jeff Kent/150 10.00 3.00
KS Kazuhiro Sasaki/100 10.00 3.00
LG Luis Gonzalez/100 10.00 3.00
LW Larry Walker/150 15.00 4.50
MP Mike Piazza/150 25.00 7.50
PB Pat Burrell/150 10.00 3.00
PM Pedro Martinez/150 15.00 4.50
PN Phil Nevin/75 15.00 4.50
RJ Randy Johnson/100 15.00 4.50
RK Ryan Klesko/75 15.00 4.50
RP Rafael Palmeiro/150 15.00 4.50
RS Richie Sexson/160 10.00 3.00
SG Shawn Green/175 10.00 3.00
SS Sammy Sosa/85 40.00 12.00
TG Troy Glaus/150 15.00 4.50
THE Todd Helton/100 15.00 4.50
THO Trevor Hoffman/150 10.00 3.00
VG Vladimir Guerrero/50 25.00 7.50

2003 Upper Deck Piece of the Action Game Ball Gold

Nm-Mt Ex-Mt
*GOLD: 1X TO 2.5X GAME BALL p/r 150-175
*GOLD: 1X TO 2.5X GAME BALL p/r 100-125
*GOLD: .6X TO 1.5X GAME BALL p/r 50-85
RANDOM INSERTS IN SERIES 2 PACKS
STATED PRINT RUN 50 SERIAL #'d SETS
IR Ivan Rodriguez 40.00 12.00
IS Ichiro Suzuki

2003 Upper Deck Signed Game Jerseys

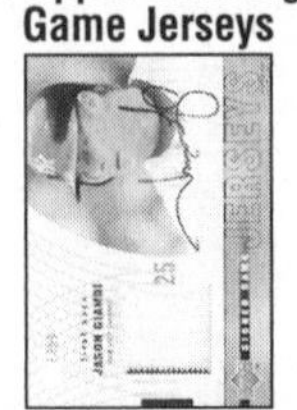

Randomly inserted into first series packs, these seven cards feature not only game-used memorabilia swatches but also an authentic autograph of the player. We have notated the print run for each card next to the player's name. In addition, Ken Griffey Jr. did not sign cards in time for inclusion into packs and those cards could be redeemed until February 11, 2006.

Nm-Mt Ex-Mt
RANDOM INSERTS IN SERIES 1 PACKS
PRINT RUNS B/WN 150-350 COPIES PER
EXCHANGE DEADLINE 02/11/06
AR Alex Rodriguez/350 150.00 45.00
CR Cal Ripken/350 150.00 45.00
JG Jason Giambi/350 100.00 30.00
KG Ken Griffey Jr./350 EXCH 150.00 45.00
MM Mark McGwire/150 400.00 120.00
RC Roger Clemens/350 150.00 45.00
SS Sammy Sosa/150 200.00 60.00

2003 Upper Deck Signed Game Jerseys Gold

Randomly inserted into first series packs, this is a partial parallel to the Signed Game Jersey insert set. These three cards were issued to a stated print run of 25 serial numbered sets and no pricing is provided due to market scarcity. Please note that Ken Griffey Jr. did not return his cards in time for inclusion in packs and those cards could be redeemed until February 11, 2006.

Nm-Mt Ex-Mt
KG Ken Griffey Jr. EXCH
MM Mark McGwire
SS Sammy Sosa

2003 Upper Deck Signed Game Jerseys Silver

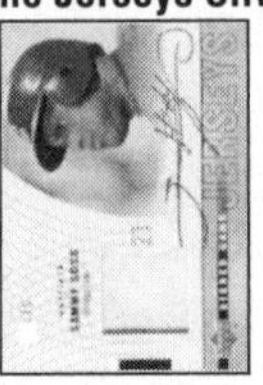

Randomly inserted into first series packs, this is a partial parallel to the Signed Game Jersey insert set. These five cards were issued to a stated print run of 75 serial numbered sets. Please note that Ken Griffey Jr. did not return his cards in time for inclusion in packs and those cards could be redeemed until February 11, 2006.

Nm-Mt Ex-Mt
AR Alex Rodriguez
JG Jason Giambi
KG Ken Griffey Jr. EXCH
MM Mark McGwire
SS Sammy Sosa

2003 Upper Deck Slammin Sammy Autograph Jerseys

Randomly inserted into first series packs, these three cards feature authentically signed Sammy Sosa cards. Each of these cards also have a game-worn uniform swatch on them. There are three different versions of this card, which were all signed to a different print run, and we have notated that information in our checklist.

Nm-Mt Ex-Mt
RANDOM INSERTS IN SERIES 1 PACKS
PRINT RUNS B/WN 25-384 COPIES PER
NO PRICING ON QTY OF 25 OR LESS.
SST Sammy Sosa/384 250.00 75.00
SSTG Sammy Sosa Gold/25
SSTS Sammy Sosa Silver/66 300.00 90.00

2003 Upper Deck Star-Spangled Swatches

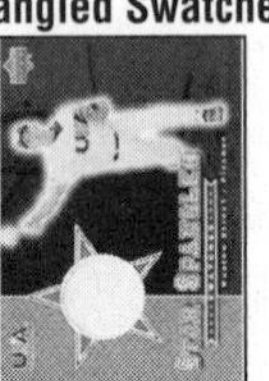

Inserted into first series packs at a stated rate of one in 72, these 16 cards feature game-worn uniform swatches of players who were on the USA National Team.

Nm-Mt Ex-Mt
AH Aaron Hill H 8.00 2.40
BS Brad Sullivan H 8.00 2.40
CC Chad Cordero H 5.00 1.50
CJ Conor Jackson Pants R 8.00 2.40
CQ Carlos Quentin H 8.00 2.40
DP Dustin Pedroia R 5.00 1.50
EP Eric Patterson H 8.00 2.40
GJ Grant Johnson H 5.00 1.50

Card	Nm-Mt	Ex-Mt
HS Huston Street R	8.00	2.40
KB Kyle Bakker R	5.00	1.50
KS Kyle Sleeth R	10.00	3.00
LP Landon Powell R	5.00	1.50
MA Michael Aubrey H	10.00	3.00
PH Philip Humber R	8.00	2.40
RW Rickie Weeks H	15.00	4.50
SC Shane Costa R	8.00	2.40

2003 Upper Deck Superior Sluggers

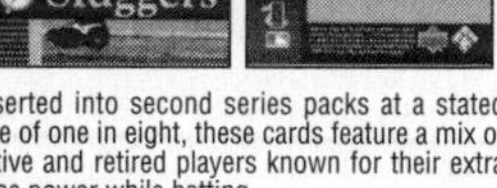

Inserted into second series packs at a stated rate of one in eight, these cards feature a mix of active and retired players known for their extra base power while batting.

	Nm-Mt	Ex-Mt
COMPLETE SET (18)	40.00	12.00
S1 Troy Glaus	2.00	.60
S2 Chipper Jones	2.50	.75
S3 Manny Ramirez	2.00	.60
S4 Ken Griffey Jr.	4.00	1.20
S5 Jim Thome	2.50	.75
S6 Todd Helton	2.00	.60
S7 Lance Berkman	2.00	.60
S8 Derek Jeter	6.00	1.80
S9 Vladimir Guerrero	2.50	.75
S10 Mike Piazza	4.00	1.20
S11 Hideki Matsui	8.00	2.40
S12 Barry Bonds	6.00	1.80
S13 Mickey Mantle	10.00	3.00
S14 Alex Rodriguez	4.00	1.20
S15 Ted Williams	8.00	2.40
S16 Carlos Delgado	2.00	.60
S17 Frank Thomas	2.50	.75
S18 Adam Dunn	2.00	.60

2003 Upper Deck Superstar Scrapbooks

Randomly inserted into series one packs, these seven cards feature game-worn jersey swatches of some of baseball's major superstars. Each of these cards was issued to a stated print run of 24 serial numbered sets and there is no pricing due to market scarcity.

	Nm-Mt	Ex-Mt
AR Alex Rodriguez		
IS Ichiro Suzuki		
JG Jason Giambi		
KG Ken Griffey Jr.		
MP Mike Piazza		
RC Roger Clemens		
SS Sammy Sosa		

2003 Upper Deck Superstar Scrapbooks Gold

Randomly inserted into series one packs, these seven cards are a parallel ot the Superstar Scrapbook set. Each of these cards feature game-worn jersey swatches of some of baseball's major superstars. Each of these cards was issued to a stated print run of one serial numbered set and there is no pricing due to market scarcity.

	Nm-Mt	Ex-Mt
IS Ichiro Suzuki		
KG Ken Griffey Jr.		
SS Sammy Sosa		

2003 Upper Deck Superstar Scrapbooks Silver

Randomly inserted into series one packs, these seven cards are a parallel ot the Superstar Scrapbook set. Each of these cards feature game-worn jersey swatches of some of baseball's major superstars. Each of these cards was issued to a stated print run of six serial numbered set and there is no pricing due to market scarcity.

	Nm-Mt	Ex-Mt
AR Alex Rodriguez		
IS Ichiro Suzuki		
JG Jason Giambi		
KG Ken Griffey Jr.		
SS Sammy Sosa		

2003 Upper Deck Triple Game Jersey

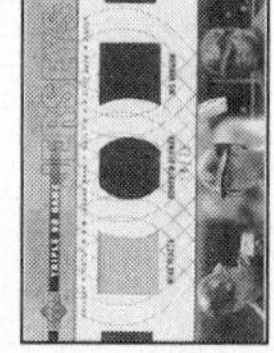

Randomly inserted into first series packs, these nine cards feature three game-worn uniform swatches of teammates. These cards were issued to a stated print run of anywhere from 25 to 150 serial numbered sets depending on which group the card belongs to. Please note the cards from group C are not priced due to market scarcity.

	Nm-Mt	Ex-Mt
GROUP A 150 SERIAL #'d SETS		
GROUP B 75 SERIAL #'d SETS		
GROUP C 25 SERIAL #'d SETS		
ARZ Randy Johnson / Curt Schilling / Luis Gonzalez A	50.00	15.00
ATL Chipper Jones / Greg Maddux / Gary Sheffield B	80.00	24.00
CHC Sammy Sosa / Moises Alou / Kerry Wood B	60.00	18.00
CIN Ken Griffey Jr. / Sean Casey / Adam Dunn A	40.00	12.00
HOU Jeff Bagwell / Lance Berkman / Craig Biggio A	50.00	15.00
NYM Mike Piazza Pants / Roberto Alomar / Mo Vaughn B	50.00	15.00
NYY Roger Clemens / Jason Giambi / Bernie Williams C		
SEA Ichiro Suzuki / Freddy Garcia / Bret Boone B	120.00	36.00
TEX Rafael Palmeiro / Alex Rodriguez / Juan Gonzalez A	50.00	15.00

2003 Upper Deck Triple Game Jersey Gold

Randomly inserted in packs, this is a parallel to the Triple Game Jersey insert set. Depending on the group, each card is printed to a stated print run of between 10 and 50 serial numbered sets. Those cards in group B and C are not priced due to market scarcity.

	Nm-Mt	Ex-Mt
GROUP A 50 SERIAL #'d SETS		
GROUP B 25 SERIAL #'d SETS		
GROUP C 10 SERIAL #'d SETS		

2003 Upper Deck UD Bonus

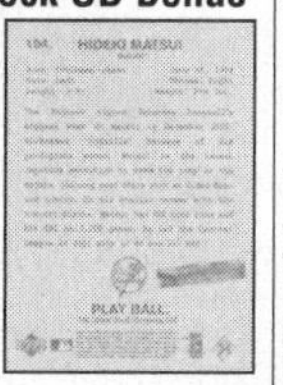

Inserted into second series packs at a stated rate of one in 288, these are copies of various recent year Upper Deck cards which were repurchased for insertion in 2003 Upper Deck 2nd series. Please note that these cards were all stamped with a "UD Bonus" logo. Each of these cards were issued to differening print runs and we have notated the print runs next to the player's name in our checklist.

	Nm-Mt	Ex-Mt
1 Jeff Bagwell 01 GG Glv/6		
2 Josh Beckett 01 TP AU/55	50.00	15.00
3 Carlos Beltran 00 SPA AU/118	25.00	7.50
4 Barry Bonds 01 UD Ball/34		
5 Barry Bonds 01 GG Glv/5		
6 Barry Bonds 01 P/P Jsy/117	40.00	12.00
7 Lou Brock 00 LGD AU/198	40.00	12.00
8 Gary Carter 00 LGD AU/63	40.00	12.00
9 Sean Casey 00 SPA AU/11		
10 Roger Clemens 00 HFX Base/12		
11 Roger Clemens 00 LGD Jsy/12		
12 Roger Clemens 01 P/P Jsy/117	40.00	12.00
13 A.Dawson 00 LGD AU/140	25.00	7.50
14 J.D. Drew 00 SPA AU/55	25.00	7.50
15 Rollie Fingers 00 LGD AU/116	25.00	7.50
16 Rafael Furcal 00 SPA AU/87	25.00	7.50
17 Rafael Furcal 00 SPA AU/39		
18 Jason Giambi 00 SPA AU/106		
19 Jason Giambi 01 UD Ball/35		
20 Jason Giambi 01 P/P Jsy/97	20.00	6.00
21 Troy Glaus 00 SPA AU/110	40.00	12.00
22 Shawn Green 01 UD Ball/10		
23 Ken Griffey Jr. 01 UD Ball/28		
24 Ken Griffey Jr. 01 GG Glv/2		
25 Vladimir Guerrero 00 SPA AU/8		
26 Vladimir Guerrero 00 LGD AU/26		
27 Vladimir Guerrero 00 OV Bat/16		
28 Brandon Inge 01 TP AU/113	15.00	4.50
29 Derek Jeter 01 UD Ball/17		
30 Randy Johnson 01 UD Ball/37		
31 Andruw Jones 01 UD Ball/38		
32 Chipper Jones 00 HFX AU/5		
33 Chipper Jones 00 OV Bat/19		
34 Harmon Killebrew 00 LGD AU/31		
35 Roger Maris 00 YL Jsy/11		
36 Eddie Mathews 00 LGD Jsy/12		
37 Hideki Matsui 03 PB AU/31		
38 Hideki Matsui 03 PB Red AU/20		
39 Don Mattingly 00 YL Jsy/26		
40 Don Mattingly 01 LGD NY Bat/20		
41 Joe Mays 00 SPA AU/30		
42 Mark McGwire 01 UD Ball/19		
43 D.Mientkiewicz 00 BD Jsy/57	15.00	4.50
44 Dale Murphy 00 LGD AU/91	80.00	24.00
45 Stan Musial 00 LGD AU/5		
46 Jim Palmer 00 LGD AU/121	25.00	7.50
47 P.Reese 01 HOF Jsy/46	25.00	7.50
48 Phil Rizzuto 00 YL Jsy/19		
49 Ivan Rodriguez 00 SPA AU/27		
50 Ivan Rodriguez 01 GG Glv/4		
51 Nolan Ryan 01 HOF Bat/37		
52 Nolan Ryan 01 HOF Jsy/76		
53 C.C. Sabathia 01 TP AU/64	25.00	7.50
54 Tim Salmon 01 GG Glv/12		
55 Tom Seaver 00 LGD Jsy/18		
56 Ben Sheets 01 TP AU/60	25.00	7.50
57 Ozzie Smith 00 LGD Jsy/14		
58 Alf Soriano 00 SPA AU/80	50.00	15.00
59 Sammy Sosa 01 P/P Jsy/77	30.00	9.00
60 Larry Walker 01 GG Glv/10		
61 Bernie Williams 01 GG Glv/10		
62 Maury Wills 00 LGD Jsy/22		
63 Dave Winfield 00 YL Bat/53	15.00	4.50
64 Bernie Williams / Ichiro Suzuki 01 P/P Bat/87	80.00	24.00
65 Sammy Sosa / Luis Gonzalez 01 P/P Bat/61	25.00	7.50

2003 Upper Deck UD Patch Logos

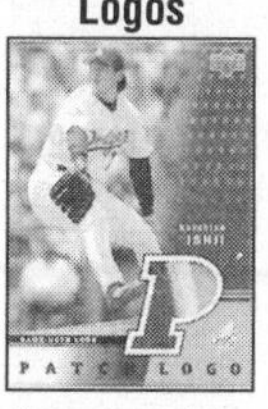

Inserted into first series packs at a stated rate of one in 7500, these eight cards feature game-used patch pieces. Each card has a print run between 41 and 54 and we have notated that print run information next to the player's name in our checklist.

	Nm-Mt	Ex-Mt
BW Bernie Williams/42		
CJ Chipper Jones/52	120.00	36.00
FT Frank Thomas/52	120.00	36.00
GM Greg Maddux/50		
JB Jeff Bagwell/41		
KI Kazuhisa Ishii/54	120.00	36.00
RJ Randy Johnson/50		
TH Todd Helton/41		

2003 Upper Deck UD Patch Logos Exclusives

Inserted into first series packs at a stated rate of one in 7500, these ten cards feature game-used patch pieces. Each card has a print run between nine and 61 and we have notated that print run information next to the player's name in our checklist. The cards with a print run of 25 or fewer are not priced due to market scarcity.

	Nm-Mt	Ex-Mt
AR Alex Rodriguez/34		
IS Ichiro Suzuki/46		
JD Joe DiMaggio/9		
JG Jason Giambi/34		
KG Ken Griffey Jr./50		
MG Mark McGwire/43		
MM Mickey Mantle/10		
MP Mike Piazza/61	200.00	60.00
RC Roger Clemens/34		
SS Sammy Sosa/60	120.00	36.00

2003 Upper Deck UD Patch Numbers

Inserted into first series packs at a stated rate of one in 7500, these six cards feature game-used patch number pieces. Each card has a print run between 27 and 90 and we have notated that print run information next to the player's name in our checklist.

	Nm-Mt	Ex-Mt
BW Bernie Williams/66	80.00	24.00
CJ Chipper Jones/44		
FT Frank Thomas/91	80.00	24.00
KI Kazuhisa Ishii/63	80.00	24.00
RJ Randy Johnson/90	100.00	30.00
TH Todd Helton/27		

2003 Upper Deck UD Patch Numbers Exclusives

Inserted into first series packs at a stated rate of one in 7500, these six cards feature game-used patch number pieces. Each card has a print run between 56 and 100 and we have notated that print run information next to the player's name in our checklist.

	Nm-Mt	Ex-Mt
AR Alex Rodriguez/56	120.00	36.00
JG Jason Giambi/68	80.00	24.00
KG Ken Griffey Jr./97	120.00	36.00
MG Mark McGwire/60	250.00	75.00
SS Sammy Sosa/100	100.00	30.00

2003 Upper Deck UD Patch Stripes

Inserted into first series packs at a stated rate of one in 7500, these seven cards feature game-used patch striped pieces. Each card has a print run between 43 and 73 and we have notated that print run information next to the player's name in our checklist.

	Nm-Mt	Ex-Mt
BW Bernie Williams/58	80.00	24.00
CJ Chipper Jones/58	80.00	24.00
FT Frank Thomas/58	80.00	24.00

	Nm-Mt	Ex-Mt
JB Jeff Bagwell/73	80.00	24.00
KI Kazuhisa Ishii/58	80.00	24.00
RJ Randy Johnson/58	120.00	36.00
TH Todd Helton/43		

2003 Upper Deck UD Patch Stripes Exclusives

Inserted into first series packs at a stated rate of one in 7500, these seven cards feature game-used patch striped pieces. Each card has a print run between 63 and 66 and we have notated that print run information next to the player's name in our checklist.

	Nm-Mt	Ex-Mt
AR Alex Rodriguez/63	120.00	36.00
IS Ichiro Suzuki/63	300.00	90.00
JG Jason Giambi/66	80.00	24.00
KG Ken Griffey Jr./63	150.00	45.00
MG Mark McGwire/63	250.00	75.00
SS Sammy Sosa/63	120.00	36.00

2003 Upper Deck UD Super Patch Logos

	Nm-Mt	Ex-Mt
AJ Andruw Jones/92		
AR Alex Rodriguez/45		
AS Alfonso Soriano/15		
GM Greg Maddux/95		
HM Hideki Matsui/8		
IS Ichiro Suzuki/20		
KG Ken Griffey Jr./22		
MP Mike Piazza/30		
MR Manny Ramirez/22		
SS Sammy Sosa/21		

2003 Upper Deck UD Super Patch Numbers

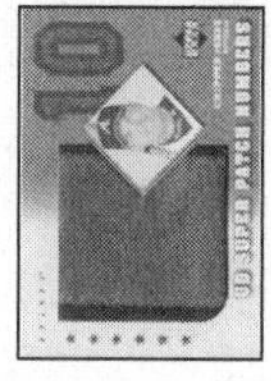

	Nm-Mt	Ex-Mt
AP Albert Pujols/8		
AR Alex Rodriguez/13		
CJ Chipper Jones/11		
CS Curt Schilling/18		
IR Ivan Rodriguez/10		
IS Ichiro Suzuki/14		
JB Jeff Bagwell/8		
JG Jason Giambi/40		
RC Roger Clemens/12		

2003 Upper Deck UD Super Patch Stripes

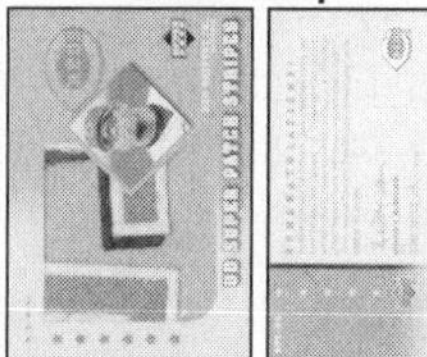

	Nm-Mt	Ex-Mt
AD Adam Dunn/70		
AS Alfonso Soriano/16		
JG Jason Giambi/50		
KG Ken Griffey Jr./12		
LB Lance Berkman/30		
MP Mike Piazza/10		
RJ Randy Johnson/73		
SS Sammy Sosa/70		
TH Todd Helton/50		
VG Vladimir Guerrero/75		

2003 Upper Deck UD Superstar Slam Jerseys

Inserted into first series hobby packs at a stated rate of one in 48, these 10 cards feature game-used jersey pieces of the featured players.

	Nm-Mt	Ex-Mt
AR Alex Rodriguez	15.00	4.50
CJ Chipper Jones	10.00	3.00
FT Frank Thomas	10.00	3.00
JB Jeff Bagwell	10.00	3.00

	Nm-Mt	Ex-Mt
JG Jason Giambi	10.00	3.00
KG Ken Griffey Jr.	15.00	4.50
LG Luis Gonzalez	8.00	2.40
MP Mike Piazza	15.00	4.50
SS Sammy Sosa	15.00	4.50
JGO Juan Gonzalez	10.00	3.00

2003 Upper Deck Gary Carter Hawaii Autograph

This one card set was distibuted at the Hawaii Trade Show conference. This card features an authentic autograph of recently inducted Hall of Famer Gary Carter.

	Nm-Mt	Ex-Mt
GC Gary Carter	25.00	7.50

2003 Upper Deck Star Rookie Hawaii

This card was produced to commemorate the Yankees signing of Japanese slugger Hideki Matsui. The card was distributed in February, 2003 to select attendees of the Kit Young Hawaii Trade Conference. It's estimated that only about 300 copies were produced. The card carries an HM number on back.

	Nm-Mt	Ex-Mt
HM Hideki Matsui	80.00	24.00

2004 Upper Deck

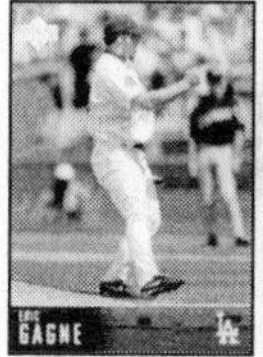

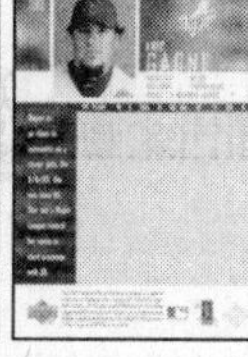

The 270-card first series was released in November, 2003. The cards were issued in eight-card hobby packs with an $3 SRP which came 24 packs to a box and 12 boxes to a case. These cards were also issued in nine-card retail packs also with a $3 SRP which came 24 packs to a box and 12 boxes to a case. Please note that insert cards were much more prevalent in the hobby packs. The following subsets were included in the first series: Super Rookies (1-30); Season Highlights Checklists (261-270). In addition, please note that the Super Rookie cards were not short printed.

	MINT	NRMT
COMPLETE SERIES 1 (270)	50.00	22.00
COMMON CARD (31-270)	.30	.14
COMMON CARD (1-30)	1.00	.45
1 Dontrelle Willis SR	1.00	.45
2 Edgar Gonzalez SR	1.00	.45
3 Jose Reyes SR	1.50	.70
4 Jae Weong Seo SR	1.00	.45
5 Miguel Cabrera SR	1.50	.70
6 Jesse Foppert SR	1.00	.45
7 Mike Neu SR	1.00	.45
8 Michael Nakamura SR	1.00	.45
9 Luis Ayala SR	1.00	.45
10 Jared Sandberg SR	1.00	.45
11 Jhonny Peralta SR	1.00	.45
12 Wil Ledezma SR	1.00	.45
13 Jason Roach SR	1.00	.45
14 Kirk Saarloos SR	1.00	.45
15 Cliff Lee SR	1.00	.45
16 Bobby Hill SR	1.00	.45
17 Lyle Overbay SR	1.00	.45
18 Josh Hall SR	1.00	.45
19 Joe Thurston SR	1.00	.45
20 Matt Kata SR	1.00	.45
21 Jeremy Bonderman SR	1.00	.45
22 Julio Manon SR	1.00	.45
23 Rodrigo Rosario SR	1.00	.45
24 Robby Hammock SR	1.00	.45
25 David Sanders SR	1.00	.45
26 Miguel Ojeda SR	1.00	.45
27 Mark Teixeira SR	1.00	.45
28 Franklyn German SR	1.00	.45
29 Ken Harvey SR	1.00	.45
30 Xavier Nady SR	1.00	.45

31 Tim Salmon .50 .23
32 Troy Glaus .50 .23
33 Adam Kennedy .30 .14
34 David Eckstein .30 .14
35 Ben Molina .30 .14
36 Jarrod Washburn .30 .14
37 Ramon Ortiz .30 .14
38 Eric Chavez .30 .14
39 Miguel Tejada .30 .14
40 Chris Singleton .30 .14
41 Jermaine Dye .30 .14
42 John Halama .30 .14
43 Tim Hudson .30 .14
44 Barry Zito .50 .23
45 Ted Lilly .30 .14
46 Bobby Kielty .30 .14
47 Kelvim Escobar .30 .14
48 Josh Phelps .30 .14
49 Vernon Wells .30 .14
50 Roy Halladay .30 .14
51 Orlando Hudson .30 .14
52 Eric Hinske .30 .14
53 Brandon Backe .30 .14
54 Dewon Brazelton .30 .14
55 Ben Grieve .30 .14
56 Aubrey Huff .30 .14
57 Toby Hall .30 .14
58 Rocco Baldelli .75 .35
59 Al Martin .30 .14
60 Brandon Phillips .30 .14
61 Omar Vizquel .30 .14
62 C.C. Sabathia .30 .14
63 Milton Bradley .30 .14
64 Ricky Gutierrez .30 .14
65 Matt Lawton .30 .14
66 Danys Baez .30 .14
67 Ichiro Suzuki 1.25 .55
68 Randy Winn .30 .14
69 Carlos Guillen .30 .14
70 Mark McLemore .30 .14
71 Dan Wilson .30 .14
72 Jamie Moyer .30 .14
73 Joel Pineiro .30 .14
74 Edgar Martinez .50 .23
75 Tony Batista .30 .14
76 Jay Gibbons .30 .14
77 Jeff Conine .30 .14
78 Melvin Mora .30 .14
79 Geronimo Gil .30 .14
80 Rodrigo Lopez .30 .14
81 Jorge Julio .30 .14
82 Rafael Palmeiro .50 .23
83 Juan Gonzalez .75 .35
84 Mike Young .30 .14
85 Alex Rodriguez 1.25 .55
86 Einar Diaz .30 .14
87 Kevin Mench .30 .14
88 Hank Blalock .30 .14
89 Pedro Martinez .75 .35
90 Byung-Hyun Kim .30 .14
91 Derek Lowe .30 .14
92 Jason Varitek .30 .14
93 Manny Ramirez .30 .14
94 John Burkett .30 .14
95 Todd Walker .30 .14
96 Nomar Garciaparra 1.25 .55
97 Trot Nixon .50 .23
98 Mike Sweeney .30 .14
99 Carlos Febles .30 .14
100 Mike MacDougal .30 .14
101 Raul Ibanez .30 .14
102 Jason Grimsley .30 .14
103 Chris George .30 .14
104 Brent Mayne .30 .14
105 Dmitri Young .30 .14
106 Eric Munson .30 .14
107 A.J. Hinch .30 .14
108 Andres Torres .30 .14
109 Bobby Higginson .30 .14
110 Shane Halter .30 .14
111 Matt Walbeck .30 .14
112 Torii Hunter .30 .14
113 Doug Mientkiewicz .30 .14
114 Lew Ford .30 .14
115 Eric Milton .30 .14
116 Eddie Guardado .30 .14
117 Cristian Guzman .30 .14
118 Corey Koskie .30 .14
119 Magglio Ordonez .30 .14
120 Mark Buehrle .30 .14
121 Billy Koch .30 .14
122 Jose Valentin .30 .14
123 Paul Konerko .30 .14
124 Carlos Lee .30 .14
125 Jon Garland .30 .14
126 Jason Giambi .75 .35
127 Derek Jeter 2.00 .90
128 Roger Clemens 1.50 .70
129 Andy Pettitte .50 .23
130 Jorge Posada .50 .23
131 David Wells .30 .14
132 Hideki Matsui 1.25 .55
133 Mike Mussina .75 .35
134 Jeff Bagwell .50 .23
135 Craig Biggio .50 .23
136 Morgan Ensberg .30 .14
137 Richard Hidalgo .30 .14
138 Brad Ausmus .30 .14
139 Roy Oswalt .30 .14
140 Billy Wagner .30 .14
141 Octavio Dotel .30 .14
142 Gary Sheffield .50 .23
143 Andruw Jones .30 .14
144 John Smoltz .50 .23
145 Rafael Furcal .30 .14
146 Javy Lopez .30 .14
147 Shane Reynolds .30 .14
148 Horacio Ramirez .30 .14
149 Mike Hampton .30 .14
150 Jung Bong .30 .14
151 Ruben Quevedo .30 .14
152 Ben Sheets .30 .14
153 Geoff Jenkins .30 .14
154 Royce Clayton .30 .14
155 Glendon Rusch .30 .14
156 John Vander Wal .30 .14
157 Scott Podsednik .75 .35
158 Jim Edmonds .30 .14
159 Tino Martinez .50 .23
160 Albert Pujols 1.50 .70
161 Matt Morris .30 .14
162 Woody Williams .30 .14
163 Edgar Renteria .30 .14
164 Jason Isringhausen .30 .14
165 Jason Simontacchi .30 .14
166 Kerry Robinson .30 .14
167 Sammy Sosa 1.25 .55
168 Joe Borowski .30 .14
169 Tony Womack .30 .14
170 Antonio Alfonseca .30 .14
171 Corey Patterson .30 .14
172 Mark Prior 1.50 .70
173 Moises Alou .30 .14
174 Matt Clement .30 .14
175 Randall Simon .30 .14
176 Randy Johnson .75 .35
177 Luis Gonzalez .30 .14
178 Craig Counsell .30 .14
179 Miguel Batista .30 .14
180 Steve Finley .30 .14
181 Brandon Webb .30 .14
182 Danny Bautista .30 .14
183 Oscar Villarreal .30 .14
184 Shawn Green .30 .14
185 Brian Jordan .30 .14
186 Fred McGriff .50 .23
187 Andy Ashby .30 .14
188 Rickey Henderson .75 .35
189 Dave Roberts .30 .14
190 Eric Gagne .50 .23
191 Kazuhisa Ishii .30 .14
192 Adrian Beltre .30 .14
193 Vladimir Guerrero .75 .35
194 Livan Hernandez .30 .14
195 Ron Calloway .30 .14
196 Sun Woo Kim .30 .14
197 Wil Cordero .30 .14
198 Brad Wilkerson .30 .14
199 Orlando Cabrera .30 .14
200 Barry Bonds 2.00 .90
201 Ray Durham .30 .14
202 Andres Galarraga .30 .14
203 Benito Santiago .30 .14
204 Jose Cruz Jr. .30 .14
205 Jason Schmidt .30 .14
206 Kirk Rueter .30 .14
207 Felix Rodriguez .30 .14
208 Mike Lowell .30 .14
209 Luis Castillo .30 .14
210 Derrek Lee .30 .14
211 Andy Fox .30 .14
212 Tommy Phelps .30 .14
213 Todd Hollandsworth .30 .14
214 Brad Penny .30 .14
215 Juan Pierre .30 .14
216 Mike Piazza 1.25 .55
217 Jae Weong Seo .30 .14
218 Ty Wigginton .30 .14
219 Al Leiter .30 .14
220 Roger Cedeno .30 .14
221 Timo Perez .30 .14
222 Aaron Heilman .30 .14
223 Pedro Astacio .30 .14
224 Joe McEwing .30 .14
225 Ryan Klesko .30 .14
226 Brian Giles .30 .14
227 Mark Kotsay .30 .14
228 Brian Lawrence .30 .14
229 Rod Beck .30 .14
230 Trevor Hoffman .30 .14
231 Sean Burroughs .30 .14
232 Bob Abreu .30 .14
233 Jim Thome .75 .35
234 David Bell .30 .14
235 Jimmy Rollins .30 .14
236 Mike Lieberthal .30 .14
237 Vicente Padilla .30 .14
238 Randy Wolf .30 .14
239 Reggie Sanders .30 .14
240 Jason Kendall .30 .14
241 Jack Wilson .30 .14
242 Jose Hernandez .30 .14
243 Kip Wells .30 .14
244 Carlos Rivera .30 .14
245 Craig Wilson .30 .14
246 Adam Dunn .30 .14
247 Sean Casey .30 .14
248 Danny Graves .30 .14
249 Ryan Dempster .30 .14
250 Barry Larkin .75 .35
251 Reggie Taylor .30 .14
252 Wily Mo Pena .30 .14
253 Larry Walker .50 .23
254 Mark Sweeney .30 .14
255 Preston Wilson .30 .14
256 Jason Jennings .30 .14
257 Charles Johnson .30 .14
258 Jay Payton .30 .14
259 Chris Stynes .30 .14
260 Juan Uribe .30 .14
261 Hideki Matsui SH CL .75 .35
262 Barry Bonds SH CL 1.00 .45
263 Dontrelle Willis SH CL .30 .14
264 Kevin Millwood SH CL .30 .14
265 Billy Wagner SH CL .30 .14
266 Rocco Baldelli SH CL .50 .23
267 Roger Clemens SH CL .75 .35
268 Rafael Palmeiro SH CL .30 .14
269 Miguel Cabrera SH CL .75 .35
270 Jose Contreras SH CL .30 .14

2004 Upper Deck A Piece of History 500 Club

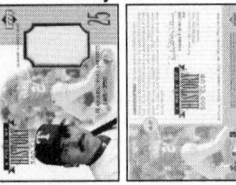

MINT NRMT
SERIES 1 STATED ODDS 1:8700
STATED PRINT RUN 350 SERIAL #'D CARDS
504HR Rafael Palmeiro 250.00 110.00

2004 Upper Deck A Piece of History 500 Club Autograph

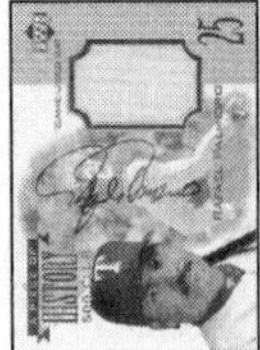

MINT NRMT
RANDOM INSERT IN SERIES 1 PACKS
STATED PRINT RUN 25 SERIAL #'d CARDS
NO PRICING DUE TO SCARCITY
RPAUO Rafael Palmeiro AU/25

2004 Upper Deck Authentic Stars Game Jersey

MINT NRMT
SERIES 1 ODDS 1:48 HOBBY, 1:96 RETAIL
*GOLD: .75X TO 2X BASIC AS JSY
GOLD RANDOM INSERTS IN SERIES 1 PACKS
GOLD PRINT RUN 100 SERIAL #'d SETS
AJ Andruw Jones 8.00 3.60
AP Albert Pujols 15.00 6.75
AR Alex Rodriguez 10.00 4.50
AS Alfonso Soriano 10.00 4.50
BA Bob Abreu 8.00 3.60
BW Bernie Williams 10.00 4.50
BZ Barry Zito 10.00 4.50
CD Carlos Delgado 8.00 3.60
CJ Chipper Jones 10.00 4.50
CS Curt Schilling 10.00 4.50
DE Darin Erstad 8.00 3.60
EC Eric Chavez 8.00 3.60
FT Frank Thomas 10.00 4.50
GM Greg Maddux 10.00 4.50
HB Hank Blalock 8.00 3.60
HM Hideki Matsui 40.00 18.00
IR Ivan Rodriguez 10.00 4.50
IS Ichiro Suzuki 25.00 11.00
JB Jeff Bagwell 10.00 4.50
JD J.D. Drew 8.00 3.60
JG Jason Giambi 10.00 4.50
JH Josh Beckett 10.00 4.50
JK Jeff Kent 8.00 3.60
KG Ken Griffey Jr. 15.00 6.75
LW Larry Walker 10.00 4.50
MI Mike Piazza 10.00 4.50
MP Mark Prior 15.00 6.75
MT Mark Teixeira 8.00 3.60
PM Pedro Martinez 10.00 4.50
PN Phil Nevin 8.00 3.60
RB Rocco Baldelli 10.00 4.50
RC Roger Clemens 15.00 6.75
RJ Randy Johnson 10.00 4.50
RO Roberto Alomar 10.00 4.50
SG Shawn Green 8.00 3.60
SS Sammy Sosa 15.00 6.75
TG Troy Glaus 10.00 4.50
TH Todd Helton 10.00 4.50
TL Tom Glavine 10.00 4.50
TM Tino Martinez 10.00 4.50
TO Torii Hunter 8.00 3.60
VG Vladimir Guerrero 10.00 4.50

2004 Upper Deck First Pitch Inserts

MINT NRMT
SERIES 1 STATED ODDS 1:72
CARD SP9 DOES NOT EXIST
SP7 LeBron James 25.00 11.00
SP8 Gordie Howe 15.00 6.75
SP9 Does Not Exist
SP10 Ernie Banks 15.00 6.75
SP11 General Tommy Franks 10.00 4.50
SP12 Ben Affleck 15.00 6.75
SP13 Halle Berry UER 15.00 6.75
Last name misspelled Barry
SP14 George H.W. Bush 10.00 4.50
SP15 George W. Bush 15.00 6.75

2004 Upper Deck Going Deep Game Bat

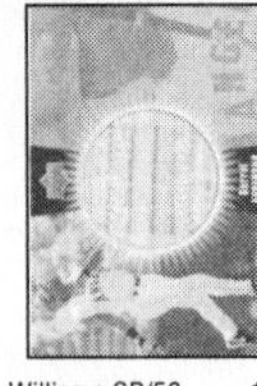

MINT NRMT
SERIES 1 ODDS 1:288 HOB, 1:576 RET
SP PRINT RUNS B/WN 12-123 COPIES PER
SP PRINT RUNS PROVIDED BY UPPER DECK
NO PRICING ON QTY OF 41 OR LESS.
GOLD RANDOM INSERTS IN PACKS
GOLD PRINT RUN 50 SERIAL #'d SETS
NO GOLD PRICING DUE TO SCARCITY
AJ Andruw Jones SP/12
AP Albert Pujols 25.00 11.00
AS Alfonso Soriano SP/53 15.00 6.75
BA Bob Abreu SP/110 10.00 4.50
BW Bernie Williams SP/56 15.00 6.75
CB Craig Biggio SP/89 15.00 6.75
CJ Chipper Jones SP/69 15.00 6.75
CP Corey Patterson SP/41
CS Curt Schilling SP/57 15.00 6.75
DE Darin Erstad 10.00 4.50
DM Doug Mientkiewicz SP/123 10.00 4.50
GA Garret Anderson 10.00 4.50
HM Hideki Matsui SP/70 40.00 18.00
HN Hideo Nomo 15.00 6.75
JB Jeff Bagwell SP/92 15.00 6.75
JE Jim Edmonds SP 10.00 4.50
JL Javy Lopez SP/77 10.00 4.50
JPA Jorge Posada 15.00 6.75
JPO Jay Payton SP/100 10.00 4.50
JT Jim Thome 15.00 6.75
KG Ken Griffey Jr. SP 40.00 18.00
KW Kerry Wood SP/108 15.00 6.75
MO Magglio Ordonez 10.00 4.50
MP Mike Piazza 15.00 6.75
MT Miguel Tejada SP/23
OV Omar Vizquel SP/115 10.00 4.50
RA Rich Aurilia SP/102 10.00 4.50
RB Rocco Baldelli SP 15.00 6.75
RF Rafael Furcal SP 10.00 4.50
RH Rickey Henderson SP/77 15.00 6.75
RO Roberto Alomar 15.00 6.75
SC Sandy Alomar Jr. SP/95 10.00 4.50
SG Shawn Green SP/100 10.00 4.50
SR Scott Rolen SP/77 15.00 6.75
TG Troy Glaus SP/113 15.00 6.75
TH Torii Hunter SP/115 10.00 4.50

2004 Upper Deck Headliners Game Jersey

MINT NRMT
SERIES 1 ODDS 1:48 HOBBY, 1:96 RETAIL
SP PRINT RUNS B/WN 97-153 COPIES PER
SP PRINT RUNS PROVIDED BY UPPER DECK
*GOLD: .75X TO 2X BASIC
GOLD RANDOM INSERTS IN SERIES 1 PACKS
GOLD PRINT RUN 100 SERIAL #'d SETS
AD Adam Dunn 8.00 3.60
BK Byung-Hyun Kim AS 8.00 3.60
BS Benito Santiago AS 8.00 3.60
CS Curt Schilling 10.00 4.50
GM Greg Maddux 10.00 4.50
HM Hideki Matsui 40.00 18.00
IS Ichiro Suzuki SP/153 40.00 18.00
JB Josh Beckett 10.00 4.50
JD Joe DiMaggio SP/153 100.00 45.00
JE Jim Edmonds 8.00 3.60
JH Jose Hernandez AS 8.00 3.60
JR Jimmy Rollins AS 8.00 3.60
JS Junior Spivey AS 8.00 3.60
JT Jim Thome 10.00 4.50
JV Jose Vidro AS 8.00 3.60
KG Ken Griffey Jr. 15.00 6.75
LB Lance Berkman 8.00 3.60
LC Luis Castillo AS 8.00 3.60
LG Luis Gonzalez 8.00 3.60
MA Mariano Rivera 10.00 4.50
MB Mark Buehrle AS 8.00 3.60
ML Mike Lowell AS 8.00 3.60
MM Mickey Mantle SP/97
MO Magglio Ordonez 8.00 3.60
MR Manny Ramirez 8.00 3.60
MS Matt Morris AS 8.00 3.60
MT Miguel Tejada 8.00 3.60
MU Mike Mussina 10.00 4.50
MY Mike Sweeney AS 8.00 3.60
PK Paul Konerko AS 8.00 3.60
PM Pedro Martinez 10.00 4.50
RF Robert Fick AS 8.00 3.60
RH Roy Halladay AS 8.00 3.60
RK Ryan Klesko 8.00 3.60
RO Roy Oswalt 8.00 3.60
SG Shawn Green 8.00 3.60
TB Tony Batista AS 8.00 3.60
TG Tom Glavine 10.00 4.50
TH Trevor Hoffman AS 8.00 3.60
TW Ted Williams SP/153 100.00 45.00
VG Vladimir Guerrero SP/153 15.00 6.75

2004 Upper Deck Magical Performances

MINT NRMT
SERIES 1 STATED ODDS 1:96 HOBBY
GOLD RANDOM INSERTS IN SER.1 HOBBY
GOLD STATED ODDS 1:1300 RETAIL
GOLD PRINT RUN 50 SERIAL #'d SETS
NO GOLD PRICING DUE TO SCARCITY
1 Mickey Mantle USC HR 50.00 22.00
2 Mickey Mantle 56 Triple Crown 50.00 22.00
3 Joe DiMaggio 56th Game 30.00 13.50
4 Joe DiMaggio Slides Home 30.00 13.50
5 Derek Jeter The Flip 30.00 13.50
6 Derek Jeter 00 AS/MVP 30.00 13.50
7 R.Clemens 300 Win/4000 K 25.00 11.00
8 Roger Clemens 20-1 25.00 11.00
9 Alfonso Soriano Walkoff 20.00 9.00
10 Andy Pettitte 96 20.00 9.00
11 Hideki Matsui Grand Slam 25.00 11.00
12 Mike Mussina 1-Hitter 20.00 9.00
13 Jorge Posada ALDS HR 20.00 9.00
14 Jason Giambi Grand Slam 20.00 9.00
15 David Wells Perfect 15.00 6.75
16 Mariano Rivera 99 WS MVP 20.00 9.00
17 Yogi Berra 12 K's 20.00 9.00
18 Phil Rizzuto 50 MVP 20.00 9.00
19 Whitey Ford 61 CY 20.00 9.00
20 Jose Contreras 1st Win 15.00 6.75
21 Catfish Hunter Free Agent 20.00 9.00
22 Mickey Mantle Cycle 50.00 22.00
23 M.Mantle HR's Both Sides 50.00 22.00
24 Joe DiMaggio 3-Time MVP 30.00 13.50
25 Joe DiMaggio Cycle 30.00 13.50
26 Derek Jeter 7 Seasons 30.00 13.50
27 Derek Jeter Mr. November 30.00 13.50
28 Roger Clemens 1-Hitter 25.00 11.00
29 Roger Clemens 01 CY 25.00 11.00
30 Alfonso Soriano HR Record 20.00 9.00
31 Andy Pettitte ALCS 20.00 9.00
32 Hideki Matsui 4 Hits 25.00 11.00
33 Mike Mussina 1st Postseason 20.00 9.00
34 Jorge Posada 40 Doubles 20.00 9.00
35 Jason Giambi 200th HR 20.00 9.00
36 David Wells 3-Hitter 15.00 6.75
37 Mariano Rivera Saves 3 20.00 9.00
38 Yogi Berra 3-Time MVP 20.00 9.00
39 Phil Rizzuto Broadcasting 20.00 9.00
40 Whitey Ford 10 WS Wins 20.00 9.00
41 Jose Contreras 2 Hits 15.00 6.75
42 Catfish Hunter 200th Win 20.00 9.00

2004 Upper Deck Matsui Chronicles

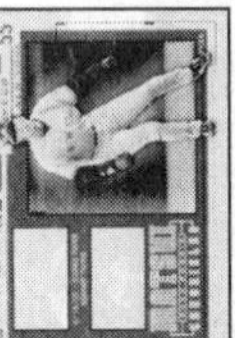

MINT NRMT
COMPLETE SET (60) 60.00 27.00
COMMON CARD (HM1-HM60) 2.00 .90
ONE PER SERIES 1 RETAIL PACK

2004 Upper Deck National Pride

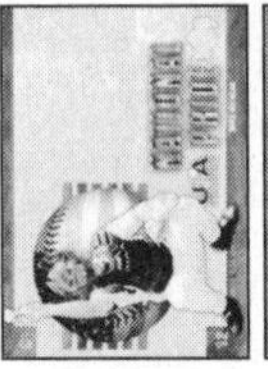
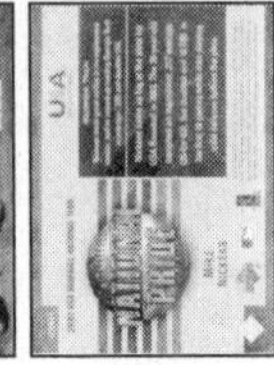

MINT NRMT
SERIES 1 STATED ODDS 1:6
1 Justin Orenduff 2.00 .90
2 Micah Owings 2.00 .90
3 Steven Register 2.00 .90
4 Huston Street 2.00 .90
5 Justin Verlander 2.00 .90
6 Jered Weaver 5.00 2.20
7 Matt Campbell 2.00 .90
8 Stephen Head 2.00 .90
9 Mark Romanczuk 2.00 .90
10 Jeff Clement 4.00 1.80
11 Mike Nickeas 2.00 .90
12 Tyler Greene 2.00 .90
13 Paul Janish 2.00 .90
14 Jeff Larish 3.00 1.35
15 Eric Patterson 2.00 .90
16 Dustin Pedroia 2.00 .90
17 Michael Griffin 2.00 .90
18 Brent Lillibridge 2.00 .90
19 Danny Putnam 2.00 .90
20 Seth Smith 2.00 .90

2004 Upper Deck National Pride Jersey Cards

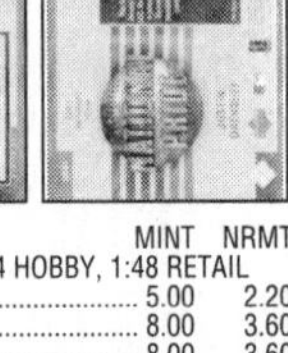

MINT NRMT
SERIES 1 ODDS 1:24 HOBBY, 1:48 RETAIL
1 Justin Orenduff 5.00 2.20
2 Micah Owings 8.00 3.60
3 Steven Register 8.00 3.60
4 Huston Street 5.00 2.20
5 Justin Verlander 8.00 3.60
6 Jered Weaver 10.00 4.50
7 Matt Campbell 5.00 2.20
8 Stephen Head 5.00 2.20

9 Mark Romanczuk 5.00 2.20
10 Jeff Clement 10.00 4.50
11 Mike Nickeas 5.00 2.20
12 Tyler Greene 5.00 2.20
13 Paul Janish 5.00 2.20
14 Jeff Larish 8.00 3.60
15 Eric Patterson 8.00 3.60
16 Dustin Pedroia 5.00 2.20
17 Michael Griffin 5.00 2.20
18 Brent Lillibridge 5.00 2.20
19 Danny Putnam 8.00 3.60
20 Seth Smith 8.00 3.60
21 Justin Orenduff SP 8.00 3.60
22 Micah Owings SP 10.00 4.50
23 Steven Register SP 10.00 4.50
24 Huston Street SP 8.00 3.60
25 Justin Verlander SP 10.00 4.50
26 Jered Weaver SP 15.00 6.75
27 Matt Campbell SP 8.00 3.60
28 Stephen Head SP 8.00 3.60
29 Mark Romanczuk SP 8.00 3.60
30 Jeff Clement SP 15.00 6.75
31 Mike Nickeas SP 8.00 3.60
32 Tyler Greene SP 8.00 3.60
33 Paul Janish SP 8.00 3.60
34 Jeff Larish SP 10.00 4.50
35 Eric Patterson SP 10.00 4.50
36 Dustin Pedroia SP 8.00 3.60
37 Michael Griffin SP 8.00 3.60
38 Brent Lillibridge SP 8.00 3.60
39 Danny Putnam SP 10.00 4.50
40 Seth Smith SP 10.00 4.50
41 Delmon Young SP 15.00 6.75
42 Rickie Weeks SP 15.00 6.75

2004 Upper Deck Signature Stars Black Ink

Please note that Roger Clemens did not return his cards in time for pack-out and those cards could be redeemed until November 10, 2006.

MINT NRMT
SER.1 ODDS 1:288 H,1:24 UPD BOX, 1:1800 R
PRINT RUNS B/WN 18-479 COPIES PER
NO PRICING ON QTY OF 25 OR LESS.
EXCHANGE DEADLINE 11/10/06
AG Andres Galarraga/248 15.00 6.75
AH Aaron Heilman/49 25.00 11.00
BG Bob Gibson/19
BK Billy Koch/429 10.00 4.50
CR Cal Ripken/69 200.00 90.00
DR Dave Roberts/278 10.00 4.50
HM Hideki Matsui/25
IS Ichiro Suzuki/19
JRA Joe Randa/271 10.00 4.50
KIO Kazuhisa Ishii/58 25.00 11.00
MO Magglio Ordonez/377 15.00 6.75
MU Mike Mussina/68 60.00 27.00
NG Nomar Garciaparra/69 150.00 70.00
NR Nolan Ryan/69 150.00 70.00
RA Rich Aurilia/479 10.00 4.50
RC Roger Clemens/19 EXCH
RH Rich Harden/163 15.00 6.75
RP Rafael Palmeiro/18
TH Torii Hunter/374 15.00 6.75
VG Vladimir Guerrero/68 60.00 27.00

2004 Upper Deck Signature Stars Blue Ink

MINT NRMT
SER.1 ODDS 1:288 H,1:24 UPD BOX, 1:1800 R
STATED PRINT RUN 25 SERIAL #'d SETS
MATSUI PRINT RUN 324 SERIAL #'d CARDS
NO PRICING ON QTY OF 25 OR LESS.
EXCHANGE DEADLINE 11/10/06
HM Hideki Matsui/324 250.00 110.00

2004 Upper Deck Signature Stars Red Ink

MINT NRMT
SER.1 ODDS 1:288 H,1:24 UPD BOX, 1:1800 R
STATED PRINT RUN 10 SERIAL #'d SETS
NO PRICING DUE TO SCARCITY
EXCHANGE DEADLINE 11/10/06

2004 Upper Deck Signature Stars Gold

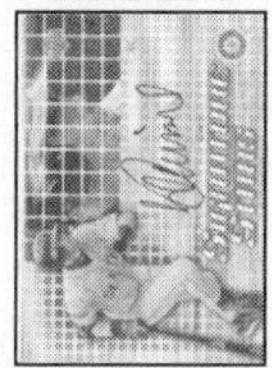

MINT NRMT
SER.1 ODDS 1:288 H, 1:24 MINI, 1:1800 R
STATED PRINT RUN 99 SERIAL #'d SETS
ALL EXCEPT MATSUI FEATURE BLUE INK
NO PRICING DUE TO SCARCITY
EXCHANGE DEADLINE 11/10/06

2004 Upper Deck Super Patch Logos

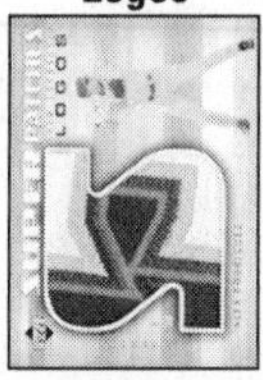

MINT NRMT
OVERALL PATCH SERIES 1 ODDS 1:7500
PRINT RUNS B/WN 8-25 COPIES PER
PRINT RUNS PROVIDED BY UPPER DECK
NO PRICING DUE TO SCARCITY
AD Adam Dunn/8
AJ Andruw Jones/25
AP Albert Pujols/20
AR Alex Rodriguez/20
AS Alfonso Soriano/10
CJ Chipper Jones/25
CS Curt Schilling/20
GM Greg Maddux/25
HM Hideki Matsui /10
IS Ichiro Suzuki/20

2004 Upper Deck Super Patch Numbers

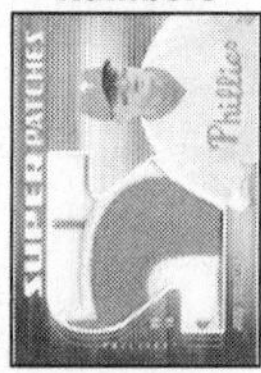

MINT NRMT
OVERALL PATCH SERIES 1 ODDS 1:7500
PRINT RUNS B/WN 10-25 COPIES PER
PRINT RUNS PROVIDED BY UPPER DECK
NO PRICING DUE TO SCARCITY
IR Ivan Rodriguez/14
JB Jeff Bagwell/16
JG Jason Giambi/10
JK Jeff Kent/20
JT Jim Thome/25
KG Ken Griffey Jr./15
LB Lance Berkman/10
MP Mark Prior/20
MR Manny Ramirez/18
SS Sammy Sosa/15

2004 Upper Deck Super Patch Stripes

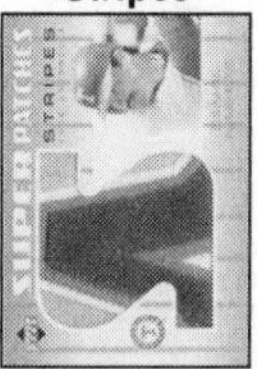

MINT NRMT
OVERALL PATCH SERIES 1 ODDS 1:7500
PRINT RUNS B/WN 25-40 COPIES PER
PRINT RUNS PROVIDED BY UPPER DECK
NO PRICING DUE TO SCARCITY
MP Mike Piazza/30
PM Pedro Martinez/25
RB Rocco Baldelli/30
RC Roger Clemens/30
RJ Randy Johnson/30
RP Rafael Palmeiro/40
SS Sammy Sosa/30
TH Todd Helton/30
TH Torii Hunter/30
VG Vladimir Guerrero/40

2004 Upper Deck Twenty-Five Salute

MINT NRMT
COMPLETE SET (10) 20.00 9.00
SERIES 1 STATED ODDS 1:12
1 Barry Bonds 6.00 2.70
2 Troy Glaus 2.00 .90
3 Andruw Jones 2.00 .90
4 Jay Gibbons 2.00 .90
5 Jeremy Giambi 2.00 .90
6 Jason Giambi 2.50 1.10

7 Jim Thome 2.50 1.10
8 Rafael Palmeiro 2.00 .90
9 Carlos Delgado 2.00 .90
10 Dmitri Young 2.00 .90

2002 Upper Deck 40-Man

This overwhelming 1182 card set was released in July, 2002. The set was issued in 10-card packs with an $3 SRP that were issued 24 packs to a box and 14 boxes to a case. These cards, feature just about every player on the 40 man rosters of the major league teams except for those players who had served as replacement players during the 1994-95 strike.

Nm-Mt Ex-Mt
COMPLETE SET (1182) 200.00 60.00
1 Darin Erstad .40 .12
2 Kevin Appier .40 .12
3 Scott Schoeneweis .40 .12
4 Ben Molina .40 .12
5 Troy Glaus .60 .18
6 Adam Kennedy .40 .12
7 Aaron Sele .40 .12
8 Garret Anderson .40 .12
9 Ramon Ortiz .40 .12
10 Dennis Cook .40 .12
11 Scott Spiezio .40 .12
12 Orlando Palmeiro .40 .12
13 Troy Percival .40 .12
14 David Eckstein .40 .12
15 Jarrod Washburn .40 .12
16 Nathan Haynes .40 .12
17 Benji Gil .40 .12
18 Alfredo Amezaga .40 .12
19 Ben Weber .40 .12
20 Al Levine .40 .12
21 Brad Fullmer .40 .12
22 Elpidio Guzman .40 .12
23 Tim Salmon .60 .18
24 Jose Nieves .40 .12
25 Shawn Wooten .40 .12
26 Lou Pote .40 .12
27 Mickey Callaway .40 .12
28 Steve Green .40 .12
29 John Lackey .40 .12
30 Mark Lukasiewicz .40 .12
31 Jorge Fabregas .40 .12
32 Jeff DaVanon .40 .12
33 Elvin Nina .40 .12
34 Donne Wall .40 .12
35 Eric Chavez .40 .12
36 Jermaine Dye .40 .12
37 Scott Hatteberg .40 .12
38 Mark Mulder .40 .12
39 Ramon Hernandez .40 .12
40 Jim Mecir .40 .12
41 Barry Zito .60 .18
42 Greg Myers .40 .12
43 David Justice .40 .12
44 Mike Magnante .40 .12
45 Terrence Long .40 .12
46 Tim Hudson .40 .12
47 Olmedo Saenz .40 .12
48 Billy Koch .40 .12
49 Carlos Pena .40 .12
50 Mike Venafro .40 .12
51 Mark Ellis .40 .12
52 Randy Velarde .40 .12
53 Jeremy Giambi .40 .12
54 Mike Colangelo .40 .12
55 Mike Holtz .40 .12
56 Chad Bradford .40 .12
57 Miguel Tejada .40 .12
58 Mike Fyhrie .40 .12
59 Erik Hiljus .40 .12
60 Juan Pena .40 .12
61 Mario Valdez .40 .12
62 Franklyn German RC .60 .18
63 Carlos Delgado .40 .12
64 Orlando Hudson .40 .12
65 Chris Carpenter .40 .12
66 Kelvim Escobar .40 .12
67 Felipe Lopez .40 .12
68 Brandon Lyon .40 .12
69 Jose Cruz Jr. .40 .12
70 Luke Prokopec .40 .12
71 Darrin Fletcher .40 .12
72 Bob File .40 .12
73 Felix Heredia .40 .12
74 Mike Sirotka .40 .12
75 Shannon Stewart .40 .12
76 Joe Lawrence .40 .12
77 Chris Woodward .40 .12
78 Dan Plesac .40 .12
79 Pedro Borbon .40 .12
80 Roy Halladay .40 .12
81 Raul Mondesi .40 .12
82 Steve Parris .40 .12
83 Homer Bush .40 .12
84 Esteban Loaiza .40 .12
85 Vernon Wells .40 .12
86 Justin Miller .40 .12
87 Scott Eyre .40 .12
88 Dave Berg .40 .12
89 Gustavo Chacin RC .60 .18
90 Joe Orloski RC .60 .18
91 Corey Thurman RC .60 .18
92 Tom Wilson RC .60 .18
93 Eric Hinske .40 .12
94 Chris Baker RC .60 .18
95 Reed Johnson RC 1.00 .30
96 Greg Vaughn .40 .12
97 Toby Hall .40 .12
98 Brent Abernathy .40 .12
99 Bobby Smith .40 .12
100 Tanyon Sturtze .40 .12
101 Chris Gomez .40 .12
102 Joe Kennedy .40 .12
103 Ben Grieve .40 .12
104 Aubrey Huff .40 .12
105 Jesus Colome .40 .12
106 Felix Escalona RC .60 .18
107 Paul Wilson .40 .12
108 Ryan Rupe .40 .12
109 Jason Tyner .40 .12
110 Esteban Yan .40 .12
111 Russ Johnson .40 .12
112 Randy Winn .40 .12
113 Wilson Alvarez .40 .12
114 Wilmy Caceres .40 .12
115 Steve Cox .40 .12
116 Dewon Brazelton .40 .12
117 Doug Creek .40 .12
118 Jason Conti .40 .12
119 John Flaherty .40 .12
120 Delvin James .40 .12
121 Steve Kent .40 .12
122 Kevin McGlinchy .40 .12
123 Travis Phelps .40 .12
124 Bobby Seay .40 .12
125 Travis Harper .40 .12
126 Victor Zambrano .40 .12
127 Jace Brewer .40 .12
128 Jason Smith .40 .12
129 Ramon Soler .40 .12
130 Brandon Backe RC .60 .18
131 Jorge Sosa RC .60 .18
132 Jim Thome 1.00 .30
133 Brady Anderson .40 .12
134 C.C. Sabathia .40 .12
135 Einar Diaz .40 .12
136 Ricky Gutierrez .40 .12
137 Danys Baez .40 .12
138 Bob Wickman .40 .12
139 Milton Bradley .40 .12
140 Bartolo Colon .40 .12
141 Jolbert Cabrera .40 .12
142 Eddie Taubensee .40 .12
143 Ellis Burks .40 .12
144 Omar Vizquel .40 .12
145 Eddie Perez .40 .12
146 Jaret Wright .40 .12
147 Chuck Finley .40 .12
148 Paul Shuey .40 .12
149 Travis Fryman .40 .12
150 Wil Cordero .40 .12
151 Ricardo Rincon .40 .12
152 Victor Martinez .40 .12
153 Charles Nagy .40 .12
154 Alex Escobar .40 .12
155 Russell Branyan .40 .12
156 Matt Lawton .40 .12
157 Ryan Drese .40 .12
158 Jerrod Riggan .40 .12
159 David Riske .40 .12
160 Jake Westbrook .40 .12
161 Mark Wohlers .40 .12
162 John McDonald .40 .12
163 Ichiro Suzuki 1.50 .45
164 Freddy Garcia .40 .12
165 Edgar Martinez .60 .18
166 Ben Davis .40 .12
167 Shigetoshi Hasegawa .40 .12
168 Carlos Guillen .40 .12
169 Ruben Sierra .40 .12
170 Joel Pineiro .40 .12
171 Norm Charlton .40 .12
172 Bret Boone .40 .12
173 Jamie Moyer .40 .12
174 Jeff Nelson .40 .12
175 Kazuhiro Sasaki .40 .12
176 Jeff Cirillo .40 .12
177 Mark McLemore .40 .12
178 Paul Abbott .40 .12
179 Mike Cameron .40 .12
180 Dan Wilson .40 .12
181 John Olerud .40 .12
182 Arthur Rhodes .40 .12
183 Desi Relaford .40 .12
184 John Halama .40 .12
185 Antonio Perez .40 .12
186 Ryan Anderson .40 .12
187 James Baldwin .40 .12
188 Ryan Franklin .40 .12
189 Justin Kaye .40 .12
190 J.J. Putz RC .60 .18
191 Allan Simpson RC .40 .12
192 Matt Thornton RC .60 .18
193 Luis Ugueto RC .60 .18
194 Chris Richard .40 .12
195 Sidney Ponson .40 .12
196 Brook Fordyce .40 .12
197 Luis Matos .40 .12
198 Josh Towers .40 .12
199 David Segui .40 .12
200 Chris Brock RC .40 .12
201 Tony Batista .40 .12
202 Erik Bedard .40 .12
203 Marty Cordova .40 .12
204 Jerry Hairston Jr. .40 .12
205 Jason Johnson .40 .12
206 Buddy Groom .40 .12
207 Mike Bordick .40 .12
208 Melvin Mora .40 .12
209 Calvin Maduro .40 .12
210 Jeff Conine .40 .12
211 Luis Rivera .40 .12
212 Jay Gibbons .40 .12
213 B.J. Ryan .40 .12
214 Sean Douglass .40 .12
215 Rodrigo Lopez .40 .12
216 Rick Bauer .40 .12
217 Scott Erickson .40 .12
218 Jorge Julio .40 .12
219 Willis Roberts .40 .12
220 John Stephens .40 .12
221 Geronimo Gil .40 .12
222 Chris Singleton .40 .12
223 Mike Paradis .40 .12
224 John Parrish .40 .12
225 Steve Bechler RC .60 .18
226 Mike Moriarty RC .40 .12
227 Luis Garcia RC .60 .18
228 Alex Rodriguez 1.50 .45
229 Mark Teixeira 1.50 .45
230 Chan Ho Park .40 .12
231 Todd Van Poppel .40 .12
232 Mike Young .40 .12
233 Kenny Rogers .40 .12
234 Rusty Greer .40 .12
235 Rafael Palmeiro .60 .18
236 Francisco Cordero .40 .12
237 John Rocker .40 .12
238 Dave Burba .40 .12
239 Travis Hafner .40 .12
240 Kevin Mench .40 .12
241 Carl Everett .40 .12
242 Ivan Rodriguez 1.00 .30
243 Jeff Zimmerman .40 .12
244 Juan Gonzalez 1.00 .30
245 Herbert Perry .40 .12
246 Rob Bell .40 .12
247 Doug Davis .40 .12
248 Frank Catalanotto .40 .12
249 Jay Powell .40 .12
250 Gabe Kapler .40 .12
251 Joaquin Benoit .40 .12
252 Jovanny Cedeno .40 .12
253 Hideki Irabu .40 .12
254 Dan Miceli .40 .12
255 Danny Kolb .40 .12
256 Colby Lewis .40 .12
257 Rich Rodriguez .40 .12
258 Ismael Valdes .40 .12
259 Bill Haselman .40 .12
260 Jason Hart .40 .12
261 Rudy Seanez .40 .12
262 Travis Hughes RC .60 .18
263 Hank Blalock 1.50 .45
264 Steve Woodard .40 .12
265 Nomar Garciaparra 1.50 .45
266 Pedro Martinez 1.00 .30
267 Frank Castillo .40 .12
268 Johnny Damon .40 .12
269 Doug Mirabelli .40 .12
270 Derek Lowe .40 .12
271 Shea Hillenbrand .40 .12
272 Paxton Crawford .40 .12
273 Tony Clark .40 .12
274 Dustin Hermanson .40 .12
275 Trot Nixon .60 .18
276 John Burkett .40 .12
277 Rich Garces .40 .12
278 Josh Hancock RC .60 .18
279 Michael Coleman .40 .12
280 Darren Oliver .40 .12
281 Jason Varitek .40 .12
282 Jose Offerman .40 .12
283 Tim Wakefield .40 .12
284 Rolando Arrojo .40 .12
285 Rickey Henderson 1.00 .30
286 Ugueth Urbina .40 .12
287 Casey Fossum .40 .12
288 Manny Ramirez .40 .12
289 Sun-Woo Kim .40 .12
290 Juan Diaz .40 .12
291 Willie Banks .40 .12
292 Jorge De La Rosa RC .60 .18
293 Juan Pena .40 .12
294 Jeff Wallace .40 .12
295 Calvin Pickering .40 .12
296 Anastacio Martinez RC .60 .18
297 Carlos Baerga .40 .12
298 Rey Sanchez .40 .12
299 Mike Sweeney .40 .12
300 Jeff Suppan .40 .12
301 Brent Mayne .40 .12
302 Chad Durbin .40 .12
303 Dan Reichert .40 .12
304 Raul Ibanez .40 .12
305 Joe Randa .40 .12
306 Chris George .40 .12
307 Michael Tucker .40 .12
308 Paul Byrd .40 .12
309 Kris Wilson .40 .12
310 Luis Alicea .40 .12
311 Neifi Perez .40 .12
312 Brian Shouse .40 .12
313 Chuck Knoblauch .40 .12
314 Dave McCarty .40 .12
315 Blake Stein .40 .12
316 Alexis Gomez .40 .12
317 Mark Quinn .40 .12
318 A.J. Hinch .40 .12
319 Carlos Febles .40 .12
320 Roberto Hernandez .40 .12
321 Brandon Berger .40 .12
322 Jeff Austin RC .60 .18
323 Cory Bailey .40 .12
324 Tony Cogan .40 .12
325 Nate Field RC .60 .18
326 Jason Grimsley .40 .12
327 Darrell May RC .40 .12
328 Donnie Sadler .40 .12
329 Carlos Beltran .40 .12
330 Miguel Asencio RC .60 .18
331 Jeff Weaver .40 .12
332 Bobby Higginson .40 .12
333 Mike Rivera .40 .12
334 Matt Anderson .40 .12
335 Craig Paquette .40 .12
336 Jose Lima .40 .12
337 Juan Acevedo .40 .12
338 Danny Patterson .40 .12
339 Andres Torres .40 .12
340 Dean Palmer .40 .12
341 Randall Simon .40 .12
342 Craig Monroe .40 .12
343 Damion Easley .40 .12
344 Robert Fick .40 .12
345 Steve Sparks .40 .12
346 Dmitri Young .40 .12
347 Nate Cornejo .40 .12
348 Matt Miller .40 .12

349 Wendell Magee .40 .12
350 Shane Halter .40 .12
351 Brian Moehler .40 .12
352 Mitch Meluskey .40 .12
353 Jose Macias .40 .12
354 Mark Redman .40 .12
355 Jeff Farnsworth .40 .12
356 Kris Keller .40 .12
357 Adam Pettyjohn .40 .12
358 Fernando Rodney .40 .12
359 Andy Van Hekken .40 .12
360 Damian Jackson .40 .12
361 Jose Paniagua .40 .12
362 Jacob Cruz .40 .12
363 Doug Mientkiewicz .40 .12
364 Torii Hunter .40 .12
365 Brad Radke .40 .12
366 Denny Hocking .40 .12
367 Mike Jackson .40 .12
368 Eddie Guardado .40 .12
369 Jacque Jones .40 .12
370 Joe Mays .40 .12
371 Matt Kinney .40 .12
372 Kyle Lohse .40 .12
373 David Ortiz .40 .12
374 Luis Rivas .40 .12
375 Jay Canizaro .40 .12
376 Dustan Mohr .40 .12
377 LaTroy Hawkins .40 .12
378 Warren Morris .40 .12
379 A.J. Pierzynski .40 .12
380 Eric Milton .40 .12
381 Bob Wells .40 .12
382 Cristian Guzman .40 .12
383 Brian Buchanan .40 .12
384 Bobby Kielty .40 .12
385 Corey Koskie .40 .12
386 J.C. Romero .40 .12
387 Jack Cressend .40 .12
388 Mike Duvall .40 .12
389 Tony Fiore .40 .12
390 Tom Prince .40 .12
391 Todd Sears .40 .12
392 Kevin Frederick RC .60 .18
393 Frank Thomas 1.00 .30
394 Mark Buehrle .40 .12
395 Jon Garland .40 .12
396 Jeff Liefer .40 .12
397 Magglio Ordonez .40 .12
398 Rocky Biddle .40 .12
399 Lorenzo Barcelo .40 .12
400 Ray Durham .40 .12
401 Bob Howry .40 .12
402 Aaron Rowand .40 .12
403 Keith Foulke .40 .12
404 Paul Konerko .40 .12
405 Sandy Alomar Jr. .40 .12
406 Mark Johnson .40 .12
407 Carlos Lee .40 .12
408 Jose Valentin .40 .12
409 Jon Rauch .40 .12
410 Royce Clayton .40 .12
411 Kenny Lofton .40 .12
412 Tony Graffanino .40 .12
413 Todd Ritchie .40 .12
414 Antonio Osuna .40 .12
415 Gary Glover .40 .12
416 Mike Porzio .40 .12
417 Danny Wright .40 .12
418 Kelly Wunsch .40 .12
419 Miguel Olivo .40 .12
420 Edwin Almonte RC .60 .18
421 Kyle Kane RC .40 .12
422 Mitch Wylie RC .60 .18
423 Derek Jeter 2.50 .75
424 Jason Giambi 1.00 .30
425 Roger Clemens 2.00 .60
426 Enrique Wilson .40 .12
427 David Wells .40 .12
428 Mike Mussina 1.00 .30
429 Bernie Williams .60 .18
430 Mike Stanton .40 .12
431 Sterling Hitchcock .40 .12
432 Alex Graman .40 .12
433 Robin Ventura .40 .12
434 Mariano Rivera .60 .18
435 Jay Tessmer .40 .12
436 Andy Pettitte .60 .18
437 John Vander Wal .40 .12
438 Adrian Hernandez .40 .12
439 Alberto Castillo .40 .12
440 Steve Karsay .40 .12
441 Alfonso Soriano .60 .18
442 Rondell White .40 .12
443 Nick Johnson .40 .12
444 Jorge Posada .60 .18
445 Ramiro Mendoza .40 .12
446 Gerald Williams .40 .12
447 Orlando Hernandez .40 .12
448 Randy Choate .40 .12
449 Randy Keisler .40 .12
450 Ted Lilly .40 .12
451 Christian Parker .40 .12
452 Ron Coomer .40 .12
453 Marcus Thames .40 .12
454 Drew Henson .60 .18
455 Jeff Bagwell .60 .18
456 Wade Miller .40 .12
457 Lance Berkman .40 .12
458 Julio Lugo .40 .12
459 Roy Oswalt .40 .12
460 Nelson Cruz .40 .12
461 Morgan Ensberg .40 .12
462 Geoff Blum .40 .12
463 Ryan Jamison .40 .12
464 Billy Wagner .40 .12
465 Dave Mlicki .40 .12
466 Brad Ausmus .40 .12
467 Jose Vizcaino .40 .12
468 Craig Biggio .60 .18
469 Shane Reynolds .40 .12
470 Greg Zaun .40 .12
471 Octavio Dotel .40 .12
472 Carlos Hernandez .40 .12
473 Richard Hidalgo .40 .12
474 Daryle Ward .40 .12
475 Orlando Merced .40 .12
476 John Buck .40 .12
477 Adam Everett .40 .12
478 Doug Brocail .40 .12
479 Brad Lidge .40 .12
480 Scott Linebrink .40 .12
481 T.J. Mathews .40 .12
482 Greg Miller .40 .12
483 Hipolito Pichardo .40 .12
484 Brandon Puffer RC .60 .18
485 Ricky Stone RC .40 .12
486 Jason Lane .40 .12
487 Brian L. Hunter .40 .12
488 Rodrigo Rosario RC .60 .18
489 Tom Shearn RC .60 .18
490 Gary Sheffield .40 .12
491 Tom Glavine .60 .18
492 Mike Remlinger .40 .12
493 Henry Blanco .40 .12
494 Vinny Castilla .40 .12
495 Chris Hammond .40 .12
496 Kevin Millwood .40 .12
497 Darren Holmes .40 .12
498 Cory Aldridge .40 .12
499 Tim Spooneybarger .40 .12
500 Rafael Furcal .40 .12
501 Albie Lopez .40 .12
502 Javy Lopez .40 .12
503 Greg Maddux 1.50 .45
504 Andruw Jones .40 .12
505 Steve Torrealba .40 .12
506 George Lombard .40 .12
507 B.J. Surhoff .40 .12
508 Marcus Giles .40 .12
509 Derrick Lewis .40 .12
510 Wes Helms .40 .12
511 John Smoltz .60 .18
512 Chipper Jones 1.00 .30
513 Jason Marquis .40 .12
514 Mark DeRosa .40 .12
515 Jung Bong .40 .12
516 Kevin Gryboski RC .40 .12
517 Damian Moss .40 .12
518 Horacio Ramirez .40 .12
519 Scott Sobkowiak .40 .12
520 Billy Sylvester .40 .12
521 Nick Green .40 .12
522 Travis Wilson UER .40 .12
Mistakenly numbered as 617
523 Ryan Langerhans .40 .12
524 John Ennis RC .60 .18
525 John Foster RC .60 .18
526 Keith Lockhart .40 .12
527 Julio Franco .40 .12
528 Richie Sexson .40 .12
529 Jeffrey Hammonds .40 .12
530 Ben Sheets .40 .12
531 Mike DeJean .40 .12
532 Mark Loretta .40 .12
533 Alex Ochoa .40 .12
534 Jamey Wright .40 .12
535 Jose Hernandez .40 .12
536 Glendon Rusch .40 .12
537 Geoff Jenkins .40 .12
538 Luis Lopez .40 .12
539 Curtis Leskanic .40 .12
540 Chad Fox .40 .12
541 Tyler Houston .40 .12
542 Nick Neugebauer .40 .12
543 Matt Stairs .40 .12
544 Paul Rigdon .40 .12
545 Bill Hall .40 .12
546 Luis Vizcaino .40 .12
547 Lenny Harris .40 .12
548 Alex Sanchez .40 .12
549 Raul Casanova .40 .12
550 Eric Young .40 .12
551 Jeff Deardorff .40 .12
552 Nelson Figueroa .40 .12
553 Ron Belliard .40 .12
554 Mike Buddie .40 .12
555 Jose Cabrera .40 .12
556 J.M. Gold .40 .12
557 Ray King .40 .12
558 Jose Mieses .40 .12
559 Takahito Nomura RC .60 .18
560 Ruben Quevedo .40 .12
561 Jackson Melian .40 .12
562 Cristian Guerrero .40 .12
563 Paul Bako .40 .12
564 Luis Martinez RC .60 .18
565 Brian Mallette RC .40 .12
566 Matt Morris .60 .18
567 Tino Martinez .60 .18
568 Fernando Vina .40 .12
569 Gene Stechschulte .40 .12
570 Andy Benes .40 .12
571 Placido Polanco .40 .12
572 Luis Garcia .40 .12
573 Jim Edmonds .40 .12
574 Bud Smith .40 .12
575 Mike Matheny .40 .12
576 Garrett Stephenson .40 .12
577 Miguel Cairo .40 .12
578 Darryl Kile .40 .12
579 Mike Timlin .40 .12
580 Rick Ankiel .40 .12
581 Jason Isringhausen .40 .12
582 Albert Pujols UER 2.00 .60
He is credited with a 13 yr career on the back
583 Eli Marrero .40 .12
584 Steve Kline .40 .12
585 J.D. Drew .40 .12
586 Mike DiFelice .40 .12
587 Dave Veres .40 .12
588 Kerry Robinson .40 .12
589 Edgar Renteria .40 .12
590 Woody Williams .40 .12
591 Chance Caple .40 .12
592 Mike Crudale RC .60 .18
593 Luther Hackman .40 .12
594 Josh Pearce .40 .12
595 Kevin Joseph .40 .12
596 Jim Journell .40 .12
597 Jeremy Lambert RC .60 .18
598 Mike Matthews .40 .12
599 Les Walrond .40 .12
600 Keith McDonald .40 .12
601 William Ortega .40 .12
602 Scotty Layfield RC .60 .18
603 So Taguchi RC 1.00 .30
604 Eduardo Perez .40 .12
605 Sammy Sosa 1.50 .45
606 Kerry Wood 1.00 .30
607 Kyle Farnsworth .40 .12
608 Alex Gonzalez .40 .12
609 Tom Gordon .40 .12
610 Carlos Zambrano .40 .12
611 Roosevelt Brown .40 .12
612 Bill Mueller .40 .12
613 Mark Prior 3.00 .90
614 Darren Lewis .40 .12
615 Joe Girardi .40 .12
616 Fred McGriff .60 .18
617 Jon Lieber .40 .12
618 Robert Machado .40 .12
619 Corey Patterson .40 .12
620 Joe Borowski .40 .12
621 Todd Hundley .40 .12
622 Jason Bere .40 .12
623 Moises Alou .40 .12
624 Jeff Fassero .40 .12
625 Jesus Sanchez .40 .12
626 Chris Stynes .40 .12
627 Delino Deshields .40 .12
628 Augie Ojeda .40 .12
629 Juan Cruz .40 .12
630 Ben Christensen .40 .12
631 Mike Meyers .40 .12
632 Will Ohman .40 .12
633 Steve Smyth .40 .12
634 Mark Bellhorn .40 .12
635 Nate Frese .40 .12
636 David Kelton .40 .12
637 Francis Beltran RC .60 .18
638 Antonio Alfonseca .40 .12
639 Donovan Osborne .40 .12
640 Shawn Sonnier .40 .12
641 Matt Clement .40 .12
642 Luis Gonzalez .40 .12
643 Brian Anderson .40 .12
644 Randy Johnson 1.00 .30
645 Mark Grace .60 .18
646 Danny Bautista .40 .12
647 Junior Spivey .40 .12
648 Jay Bell .40 .12
649 Miguel Batista .40 .12
650 Tony Womack .40 .12
651 Byung-Hyun Kim .40 .12
652 Steve Finley .40 .12
653 Rick Helling .40 .12
654 Curt Schilling .60 .18
655 Erubiel Durazo .40 .12
656 Chris Donnels .40 .12
657 Greg Colbrunn .40 .12
658 Mike Morgan .40 .12
659 Jose Guillen .40 .12
660 Matt Williams .40 .12
661 Craig Counsell .40 .12
662 Greg Swindell .40 .12
663 Rod Barajas .40 .12
664 David Dellucci .40 .12
665 Todd Stottlemyre .40 .12
666 P.J. Bevis RC .60 .18
667 Mike Koplove .40 .12
668 Mike Myers .40 .12
669 John Patterson .40 .12
670 Bret Prinz .40 .12
671 Jeremy Ward RC .60 .18
672 Danny Klassen .40 .12
673 Luis Terrero .40 .12
674 Jose Valverde RC 1.00 .30
675 Doug Devore RC .60 .18
676 Quinton McCracken .40 .12
677 Paul LoDuca .40 .12
678 Mark Grudzielanek .40 .12
679 Kevin Brown .40 .12
680 Paul Quantrill .40 .12
681 Shawn Green .40 .12
682 Hideo Nomo 1.00 .30
683 Eric Gagne .60 .18
684 Giovanni Carrara .40 .12
685 Marquis Grissom .40 .12
686 Hiram Bocachica .40 .12
687 Guillermo Mota .40 .12
688 Alex Cora .40 .12
689 Odalis Perez .40 .12
690 Brian Jordan .40 .12
691 Andy Ashby .40 .12
692 Eric Karros .40 .12
693 Chad Kreuter .40 .12
694 Dave Roberts .40 .12
695 Omar Daal .40 .12
696 Dave Hansen .40 .12
697 Adrian Beltre .40 .12
698 Terry Mulholland .40 .12
699 Cesar Izturis .40 .12
700 Steve Colyer .40 .12
701 Carlos Garcia .40 .12
702 Ricardo Rodriguez .40 .12
703 Darren Dreifort .60 .18
704 Jeff Reboulet .40 .12
705 Victor Alvarez RC .60 .18
706 Kazuhisa Ishii RC 2.50 .75
707 Jose Vidro .40 .12
708 Henry Mateo .40 .12
709 Tony Armas Jr. .40 .12
710 Carl Pavano .40 .12
711 Peter Bergeron .40 .12
712 Bruce Chen .40 .12
713 Orlando Cabrera .40 .12
714 Britt Reames .40 .12
715 Masato Yoshii .40 .12
716 Fernando Tatis .40 .12
717 Graeme Lloyd .40 .12
718 Scott Stewart .40 .12
719 Lou Collier .40 .12
720 Michael Barrett .40 .12
721 Vladimir Guerrero 1.00 .30
722 Troy Mattes .40 .12
723 Brian Schneider .40 .12
724 Lee Stevens .40 .12
725 Javier Vazquez .40 .12
726 Brad Wilkerson .40 .12
727 Zach Day .40 .12
728 Ed Vosberg .40 .12
729 Tomo Ohka .40 .12
730 Mike Mordecai .40 .12
731 Donnie Bridges .40 .12
732 Ron Chiavacci .40 .12
733 T.J. Tucker .40 .12
734 Scott Hodges .40 .12
735 Valentino Pascucci .40 .12
736 Andres Galarraga .40 .12
737 Scott Downs .40 .12
738 Eric Good RC .60 .18
739 Ron Calloway RC .60 .18
740 Jorge Nunez RC .60 .18
741 Henry Rodriguez .40 .12
742 Jeff Kent .40 .12
743 Russ Ortiz .40 .12
744 Felix Rodriguez .40 .12
745 Benito Santiago .40 .12
746 Tsuyoshi Shinjo .40 .12
747 Tim Worrell .40 .12
748 Marvin Benard .40 .12
749 Kurt Ainsworth .40 .12
750 Edwards Guzman .40 .12
751 J.T. Snow .40 .12
752 Jason Christiansen .40 .12
753 Robb Nen .40 .12
754 Barry Bonds 2.50 .75
755 Shawon Dunston .40 .12
756 Chad Zerbe .40 .12
757 Ramon E. Martinez .40 .12
758 Calvin Murray .40 .12
759 Pedro Feliz .40 .12
760 Jason Schmidt .40 .12
761 Damon Minor .40 .12
762 Reggie Sanders .40 .12
763 Rich Aurilia .40 .12
764 Kirk Rueter .40 .12
765 David Bell .40 .12
766 Yorvit Torrealba .40 .12
767 Livan Hernandez .40 .12
768 Felix Diaz .40 .12
769 Aaron Fultz .40 .12
770 Ryan Jensen .40 .12
771 Arturo McDowell .40 .12
772 Carlos Valderrama .40 .12
773 Nelson Castro RC .60 .18
774 Jay Witasick .40 .12
775 Deivis Santos .40 .12
776 Josh Beckett .60 .18
777 Charles Johnson .40 .12
778 Derrek Lee .40 .12
779 A.J. Burnett .40 .12
780 Vic Darensbourg .40 .12
781 Cliff Floyd .40 .12
782 Jose Cueto .40 .12
783 Nate Teut .40 .12
784 Alex Gonzalez .40 .12
785 Brad Penny .40 .12
786 Kevin Olsen .40 .12
787 Mike Lowell .40 .12
788 Mike Redmond .40 .12
789 Braden Looper .40 .12
790 Eric Owens .40 .12
791 Andy Fox .40 .12
792 Vladimir Nunez .40 .12
793 Luis Castillo .40 .12
794 Ryan Dempster .40 .12
795 Armando Almanza .40 .12
796 Preston Wilson .40 .12
797 Pablo Ozuna .40 .12
798 Gary Knotts .40 .12
799 Ramon Castro .40 .12
800 Benito Baez .40 .12
801 Michael Tejera .40 .12
802 Claudio Vargas .40 .12
803 Chip Ambres .40 .12
804 Hansel Izquierdo RC .60 .18
805 Tim Raines Sr. .40 .12
806 Marty Malloy .40 .12
807 Julian Tavarez .40 .12
808 Roberto Alomar 1.00 .30
809 Al Leiter .40 .12
810 Jeromy Burnitz .40 .12
811 John Franco .40 .12
812 Edgardo Alfonzo .40 .12
813 Mike Piazza 1.50 .45
814 Shawn Estes .40 .12
815 Joe McEwing .40 .12
816 David Weathers .40 .12
817 Pedro Astacio .40 .12
818 Timo Perez .40 .12
819 Grant Roberts .40 .12
820 Rey Ordonez .40 .12
821 Steve Trachsel .40 .12
822 Roger Cedeno .40 .12
823 Mark Johnson .40 .12
824 Armando Benitez .40 .12
825 Vance Wilson .40 .12
826 Jay Payton .40 .12
827 Mo Vaughn .40 .12
828 Scott Strickland .40 .12
829 Mark Guthrie .40 .12
830 Jeff D'Amico .40 .12
831 Mark Corey RC .60 .18
832 Kane Davis .40 .12
833 Jae Weong Seo .40 .12
834 Pat Strange .40 .12
835 Adam Walker RC .60 .18
836 Tyler Walker RC .60 .18
837 Gary Matthews Jr. .40 .12
838 Jaime Cerda RC .60 .18
839 Satoru Komiyama RC .60 .18
840 Tyler Yates RC 1.50 .45
841 John Valentin .40 .12
842 Ryan Klesko .40 .12
843 Wiki Gonzalez .40 .12
844 Trevor Hoffman .40 .12
845 Sean Burroughs .60 .18
846 Alan Embree .40 .12
847 Dennis Tankersley .40 .12
848 D'Angelo Jimenez .40 .12
849 Kevin Jarvis .40 .12
850 Mark Kotsay .40 .12
851 Phil Nevin .40 .12
852 Jeremy Fikac .40 .12
853 Brett Tomko .40 .12
854 Brian Lawrence .40 .12
855 Steve Reed .40 .12
856 Bubba Trammell .40 .12
857 Tom Davey .40 .12
858 Ramon Vazquez .40 .12
859 Tom Lampkin .40 .12
860 Bobby Jones .40 .12
861 Ray Lankford .40 .12
862 Mark Sweeney .40 .12
863 Adam Eaton .40 .12
864 Trenidad Hubbard .40 .12
865 Jason Boyd .40 .12
866 Javier Cardona .40 .12
867 Cliff Bartosh RC .60 .18
868 Mike Bynum .40 .12
869 Eric Cyr .40 .12
870 Jose Nunez .40 .12
871 Ron Gant .40 .12
872 Deivi Cruz .40 .12
873 Ben Howard RC .60 .18
874 Todd Donovan RC .60 .18
875 Andy Shibilo RC .60 .18
876 Scott Rolen .60 .18
877 Jose Mesa .40 .12
878 Rheal Cormier .40 .12
879 Travis Lee .40 .12
880 Mike Lieberthal .40 .12
881 Brandon Duckworth .40 .12
882 David Coggin .40 .12
883 Bob Abreu .40 .12
884 Turk Wendell .40 .12
885 Marlon Byrd .60 .18
886 Jason Michaels .40 .12
887 Robert Person .40 .12
888 Tomas Perez .40 .12
889 Jimmy Rollins .40 .12
890 Vicente Padilla .40 .12
891 Pat Burrell .40 .12
892 Dave Hollins .40 .12
893 Randy Wolf .40 .12
894 Jose Santiago .40 .12
895 Doug Glanville .40 .12
896 Cliff Politte .40 .12
897 Marlon Anderson .40 .12
898 Ricky Bottalico .40 .12
899 Terry Adams .40 .12
900 Brad Baisley .40 .12
901 Hector Mercado .40 .12
902 Elio Serrano RC .60 .18
903 Todd Pratt .40 .12
904 Pete Zamora RC .60 .18
905 Nick Punto .40 .12
906 Ricky Ledee .40 .12
907 Eric Junge RC .60 .18
908 Anderson Machado RC .60 .18
909 Jorge Padilla RC .60 .18
910 John Mabry .40 .12
911 Brian Giles .40 .12
912 Jason Kendall .40 .12
913 Jack Wilson .40 .12
914 Kris Benson .40 .12
915 Aramis Ramirez .40 .12
916 Mike Fetters .40 .12
917 Adrian Brown .40 .12
918 Pokey Reese .40 .12
919 Dave Williams .40 .12
920 Mike Benjamin .40 .12
921 Kip Wells .40 .12
922 Mike Williams .40 .12
923 Pat Meares .40 .12
924 Ron Villone .40 .12
925 Armando Rios .40 .12
926 Jimmy Anderson .40 .12
927 Rob Mackowiak .40 .12
928 Kevin Young .40 .12
929 Brian Boehringer .40 .12
930 Joe Beimel .40 .12
931 Chad Hermansen .40 .12
932 Scott Sauerbeck .40 .12
933 Josh Fogg .40 .12
934 Mike Gonzalez RC .60 .18
935 Mike Lincoln .40 .12
936 Sean Lowe .40 .12
937 Matt Guerrier .40 .12
938 Ryan Vogelsong .40 .12
939 J.R. House .40 .12
940 Craig Wilson .40 .12
941 Tony Alvarez .40 .12
942 J.J. Davis .40 .12
943 Abraham Nunez .40 .12
944 Adrian Burnside RC .60 .18
945 Ken Griffey Jr. 1.50 .45
946 Jimmy Haynes .40 .12
947 Juan Castro .40 .12
948 Jose Rijo .40 .12
949 Corky Miller .40 .12
950 Elmer Dessens .40 .12
951 Aaron Boone .40 .12
952 Juan Encarnacion .40 .12
953 Chris Reitsma .40 .12
954 Wilton Guerrero .40 .12
955 Danny Graves .40 .12
956 Jim Brower .40 .12
957 Barry Larkin 1.00 .30
958 Todd Walker .40 .12
959 Gabe White .40 .12
960 Adam Dunn .40 .12
961 Jason LaRue .40 .12
962 Reggie Taylor .40 .12
963 Sean Casey .40 .12
964 Scott Williamson .40 .12
965 Austin Kearns .60 .18
966 Kelly Stinnett .40 .12
967 Jose Acevedo .40 .12
968 Gookie Dawkins .40 .12
969 Brady Clark .40 .12
970 Scott Sullivan .40 .12
971 Ricardo Aramboles .40 .12
972 Lance Davis .40 .12
973 Seth Etherton .40 .12
974 Luke Hudson .40 .12
975 Joey Hamilton .40 .12
976 Luis Pineda .40 .12
977 John Riedling .40 .12
978 Jose Silva .40 .12
979 Dane Sardinha .40 .12
980 Ben Broussard .40 .12
981 David Espinosa .40 .12
982 Ruben Mateo .40 .12
983 Larry Walker .60 .18
984 Juan Uribe .40 .12
985 Mike Hampton .40 .12
986 Aaron Cook RC .60 .18
987 Jose Ortiz .40 .12
988 Todd Jones .40 .12
989 Todd Helton .60 .18
990 Shawn Chacon .40 .12
991 Jason Jennings .40 .12
992 Todd Zeile .40 .12
993 Ben Petrick .40 .12
994 Denny Neagle .40 .12
995 Jose Jimenez .40 .12
996 Juan Pierre .40 .12
997 Todd Hollandsworth .40 .12
998 Kent Mercker .40 .12
999 Greg Norton .40 .12
1000 Terry Shumpert .40 .12

735 Kelly Stinnett .40 .18
736 Ruben Mateo .40 .18
737 Wily Mo Pena .40 .18
738 Larry Walker .60 .25
739 Juan Uribe .40 .18
740 Denny Neagle .40 .18
741 Darren Oliver .40 .18
742 Charles Johnson .40 .18
743 Todd Jones .40 .18
744 Todd Helton .60 .25
745 Shawn Chacon .40 .18
746 Jason Jennings .40 .18
747 Preston Wilson .40 .18
748 Chris Richard .40 .18
749 Chris Stynes .40 .18
750 Jose Jimenez .40 .18
751 Gabe Kapler .40 .18
752 Jay Payton .40 .18
753 Aaron Cook .40 .18
754 Greg Norton .40 .18
755 Scott Elarton .40 .18
756 Brian Fuentes .40 .18
757 Jose Hernandez .40 .18
758 Nelson Cruz .40 .18
759 Justin Speier .40 .18
760 Javier A. Lopez RC .60 .25
761 Garret Anderson AS .40 .18
762 Tony Batista AS .40 .18
763 Mark Buehrle AS .40 .18
764 Johnny Damon AS .40 .18
765 Freddy Garcia AS .40 .18
766 Nomar Garciaparra AS 1.00 .45
767 Jason Giambi AS .60 .25
768 Roy Halladay AS .40 .18
769 Shea Hillenbrand AS .40 .18
770 Torii Hunter AS .40 .18
771 Derek Jeter AS 1.25 .55
772 Paul Konerko AS .40 .18
773 Derek Lowe AS .40 .18
774 Pedro Martinez AS .60 .25
775 A.J. Pierzynski AS .40 .18
776 Jorge Posada AS .40 .18
777 Manny Ramirez AS .40 .18
778 Mariano Rivera AS .40 .18
779 Alex Rodriguez AS 1.00 .45
780 Kazuhiro Sasaki AS .40 .18
781 Alfonso Soriano AS .40 .18
782 Ichiro Suzuki AS 1.00 .45
783 Mike Sweeney AS .40 .18
784 Miguel Tejada AS .40 .18
785 Ugueth Urbina AS .40 .18
786 Robin Ventura AS .40 .18
787 Omar Vizquel AS .40 .18
788 Randy Winn AS .40 .18
789 Barry Zito AS .40 .18
790 Lance Berkman AS .40 .18
791 Barry Bonds AS 1.25 .55
792 Adam Dunn AS .40 .18
793 Tom Glavine AS .40 .18
794 Luis Gonzalez AS .40 .18
795 Shawn Green AS .40 .18
796 Vladimir Guerrero AS .60 .25
797 Todd Helton AS .40 .18
798 Trevor Hoffman AS .40 .18
799 Randy Johnson AS .60 .25
800 Andruw Jones AS .40 .18
801 Byung-Hyun Kim AS .40 .18
802 Mike Lowell AS .40 .18
803 Eric Gagne AS .40 .18
804 Matt Morris AS .40 .18
805 Robb Nen AS .40 .18
806 Vicente Padilla AS .40 .18
807 Odalis Perez AS .40 .18
808 Mike Piazza AS 1.00 .45
809 Mike Remlinger AS .40 .18
810 Scott Rolen AS .40 .18
811 Jimmy Rollins AS .40 .18
812 Benito Santiago AS .40 .18
813 Curt Schilling AS .40 .18
814 Richie Sexson AS .40 .18
815 John Smoltz AS .40 .18
816 Sammy Sosa AS 1.00 .45
817 Junior Spivey AS .40 .18
818 Jose Vidro AS .40 .18
819 Mike Williams AS .40 .18
820 Luis Castillo AS .40 .18
821 Jason Giambi HR Derby .60 .25
822 Luis Gonzalez HR Derby .40 .18
823 Sammy Sosa HR Derby 1.00 .45
824 Ken Griffey Jr. HR Derby 1.00 .45
825 Ken Griffey Jr. HR Derby 1.00 .45
826 Tino Martinez HR Derby .40 .18
827 Barry Bonds HR Derby 1.25 .55
828 Frank Thomas HR Derby .60 .25
829 Ken Griffey Jr. HR Derby 1.00 .45
830 Barry Bonds 02 WS 1.25 .55
831 Tim Salmon 02 WS .40 .18
832 Troy Glaus 02 WS .40 .18
833 Robb Nen 02 WS .40 .18
834 Jeff Kent 02 WS .40 .18
835 Scott Spiezio 02 WS .40 .18
836 Darin Erstad 02 WS .40 .18
837 Randy Johnson T40 .60 .25
838 Chipper Jones T40 .60 .25
839 Greg Maddux T40 1.00 .45
840 Nomar Garciaparra T40 1.00 .45
841 Manny Ramirez T40 .40 .18
842 Pedro Martinez T40 .60 .25
843 Sammy Sosa T40 1.00 .45
844 Ken Griffey Jr. T40 1.00 .45
845 Jim Thome T40 .60 .25
846 Vladimir Guerrero T40 .60 .25
847 Mike Piazza T40 1.00 .45
848 Derek Jeter T40 1.25 .55
849 Jason Giambi T40 .60 .25
850 Roger Clemens T40 1.00 .45
851 Alfonso Soriano T40 .40 .18
852 Hideki Matsui T40 4.00 1.80
853 Barry Bonds T40 1.25 .55
854 Ichiro Suzuki T40 1.00 .45
855 Albert Pujols T40 1.00 .45
856 Alex Rodriguez T40 1.00 .45
857 Darin Erstad T40 .40 .18
858 Troy Glaus T40 .40 .18
859 Curt Schilling T40 .40 .18
860 Luis Gonzalez T40 .40 .18
861 Tom Glavine T40 .40 .18
862 Andruw Jones T40 .40 .18
863 Gary Sheffield T40 .40 .18
864 Frank Thomas T40 .60 .25
865 Mark Prior T40 1.00 .45
866 Ivan Rodriguez T40 .60 .25
867 Jeff Bagwell T40 .40 .18
868 Lance Berkman T40 .40 .18
869 Shawn Green T40 .40 .18
870 Hideo Nomo T40 .60 .25
871 Torii Hunter T40 .40 .18
872 Bernie Williams T40 .40 .18
873 Barry Zito T40 .40 .18
874 Pat Burrell T40 .40 .18
875 Carlos Delgado T40 .40 .18
876 Miguel Tejada T40 .40 .18
877 Hideki Matsui NR RC 8.00 3.60
878 Jose Contreras NR RC 3.00 1.35
879 Jason Anderson NR .40 .18
880 Jason Shiell NR RC .60 .25
881 Kevin Tolar NR RC .60 .25
882 Michel Hernandez NR RC .60 .25
883 Arnie Munoz NR RC .60 .25
884 David Sanders NR RC .60 .25
885 Willie Eyre NR RC .60 .25
886 Brent Hoard NR RC .60 .25
887 Lew Ford NR RC 1.00 .45
888 Beau Kemp NR RC .60 .25
889 Jon Pridie NR RC .60 .25
890 Mike Ryan NR RC 1.00 .45
891 Richard Fischer NR RC .60 .25
892 Luis Ayala NR RC .60 .25
893 Mike Neu NR RC .60 .25
894 Joe Valentine NR RC .60 .25
895 Nate Bland NR RC .60 .25
896 Shane Bazzell NR RC .60 .25
897 Aquilino Lopez NR RC .60 .25
898 D.Markwell NR RC .60 .25
899 Francisco Rosario NR RC .60 .25
900 Guillermo Quiroz NR RC 2.50 1.10
901 Luis De Los Santos NR .40 .18
902 Fern.Cabrera NR RC .60 .25
903 Francisco Cruceta NR RC .60 .25
904 Jhonny Peralta NR RC .60 .25
905 Rett Johnson NR RC 1.00 .45
906 Aaron Looper NR RC .60 .25
907 Bobby Madritsch NR RC .60 .25
908 Luis Matos NR .40 .18
909 Jose Castillo NR .40 .18
910 Chris Waters NR RC .60 .25
911 Jeremy Guthrie NR .40 .18
912 Pedro Liriano NR .40 .18
913 Joe Borowski NR .40 .18
914 Felix Sanchez NR RC .60 .25
915 Jon Leicester NR RC .60 .25
916 Todd Wellemeyer NR RC 1.00 .45
917 Matt Bruback NR RC .40 .18
918 Chris Capuano NR RC .60 .25
919 Oscar Villarreal NR RC .60 .25
920 Matt Kata NR RC 1.50 .70
921 Robby Hammock NR RC 1.00 .45
922 Gerald Laird NR .40 .18
923 Brandon Webb NR RC 4.00 1.80
924 Tommy Whiteman NR .40 .18
925 Andrew Brown NR RC .60 .25
926 Alfredo Gonzalez NR RC .60 .25
927 Carlos Rivera NR .40 .18
928 Rick Roberts NR RC .60 .25
929 Termel Sledge NR RC 1.00 .45
930 Josh Willingham NR RC 2.50 1.10
931 Prentice Redman NR RC .60 .25
932 Jeff Duncan NR RC 1.00 .45
933 Craig Brazell NR RC 1.00 .45
934 Jeremy Griffiths NR RC 1.00 .45
935 Phil Seibel NR RC .60 .25
936 Heath Bell NR RC .60 .25
937 Bernie Castro NR RC .60 .25
938 Mike Nicolas NR RC .60 .25
939 Cory Stewart NR RC .60 .25
940 Shane Victorino NR RC .60 .25
941 Brandon Villafuerte NR .40 .18
942 Jeremy Wedel NR RC .60 .25
943 Tommy Phelps NR .40 .18
944 Josh Hall NR RC 1.00 .45
945 Ryan Cameron NR RC .60 .25
946 Garrett Atkins NR .40 .18
947 Clint Barmes NR RC 1.00 .45
948 Mike Hessman NR RC .60 .25
949 Brian Stokes NR RC .60 .25
950 Rocco Baldelli NR 1.50 .70
951 Hector Luna NR RC .60 .25
952 Jaime Cerda NR .40 .18
953 D.J. Carrasco NR RC .60 .25
954 Ian Ferguson NR RC .60 .25
955 Tim Olson NR RC 1.00 .45
956 Al. Machado NR RC .60 .25
957 Jorge Cordova NR RC .60 .25
958 Wilfredo Ledezma NR RC .60 .25
959 Nate Robertson NR RC 1.00 .45
960 Nook Logan NR RC .60 .25
961 Troy Glaus TC .40 .18
962 Jay Gibbons TC .40 .18
963 Nomar Garciaparra TC .40 .18
964 Paul Konerko TC .40 .18
965 Ellis Burks TC .40 .18
966 Bobby Higginson TC .40 .18
967 Mike Sweeney TC .40 .18
968 Torii Hunter .40 .18
Doug Mientkiewicz TC
969 Jorge Posada TC .40 .18
970 Miguel Tejada TC .40 .18
971 Ichiro Suzuki TC .40 .18
972 Toby Hall TC .40 .18
973 Alex Rodriguez .40 .18
Juan Gonzalez TC
974 Shannon Stewart TC .40 .18
975 Luis Gonzalez .40 .18
Mark Grace TC
976 Andruw Jones TC .40 .18
977 Antonio Alfonseca TC .40 .18
978 Aaron Boone TC .40 .18
979 Todd Helton TC .40 .18
980 Ivan Rodriguez TC .40 .18
981 Craig Biggio TC .40 .18
982 Shawn Green TC .40 .18
983 Richie Sexson TC .40 .18
984 Vladimir Guerrero TC .40 .18
985 Roberto Alomar TC .40 .18
986 Jim Thome TC .40 .18
987 Humberto Cota TC .40 .18
988 Ryan Klesko TC .40 .18
989 Barry Bonds .40 .18
Benito Santiago TC
990 Albert Pujols .40 .18
J.D. Drew TC
P1 Ken Griffey Jr. Sample 1.00 .45

2003 Upper Deck 40-Man Rainbow

MINT NRMT
*RAINBOW: 10X TO 25X BASIC
*RAINBOW RC'S: 4X TO 10X BASIC
*RAINBOW NR: 10X TO 25X BASIC
*RAINBOW NR RC'S: 4X TO 10X BASIC
RANDOM INSERTS IN PACKS
STATED PRINT RUN 40 SERIAL #'d SETS

2003 Upper Deck 40-Man Red White and Blue

MINT NRMT
*RWB: 1.5X TO 4X BASIC
*RWB NR: 1.5X TO 4X BASIC
1-752 STATED ODDS 1:6
877-960 STATED ODDS 1:36

2003 Upper Deck 40-Man Endorsements Signatures

Inserted in packs at a stated rate of one in 500, these 33 cards feature authentic autographs from the player. Many of these cards were signed to print runs of 50 or fewer and we have put the stated print run next to the player's name in our checklist. Please note that if a card was signed to a print run of 25 or fewer copies there is no pricing due to market scarcity.

MINT NRMT
AGO Alex Graman/50
AV Andy Van Hekken/50
BC Brad Cresse/35
BD Ben Diggins 15.00 6.75
BH Ben Howard/25
BP Brandon Phillips/25
BR Brandon Claussen/35
CM Corwin Malone/50
CS C.C. Sabathia/10
DBO Dewon Brazelton/50
DH Drew Henson/25
DK David Kelton/50
HI Hansel Izquierdo/50
JA Jay Gibbons/24
JB John Buck/25
JD Johnny Damon/23
JG Jason Giambi/10
JJ Jimmy Journell/30
JL Jon Lieber 15.00 6.75
JU Justin Wayne/25
JW Jerome Williams/50
JYO Jayson Werth/50
KG Ken Griffey Jr./33
KGS Ken Griffey Sr. 15.00 6.75
KL Kenny Lofton/25
MA Mark Buehrle/23
MB Milton Bradley/50
MT Matt Thornton/50
MX Mark Teixeira/25
RA Rick Ankiel 25.00 11.00
SR Scott Rolen/10
TG Tony Gwynn/20
TO Tomo Ohka 40.00 18.00

2002 Upper Deck Ballpark Idols

This 245 card set was issued in five card packs with an SRP of $3 per pack. In addition, in the bigger box; there was also a "bobber" inserted into each box. Card numbered 201 through 245 feature mostly Rookie Cards and were issued to a stated print run of 1750 serial numbered sets.

Nm-Mt Ex-Mt
COMP.SET w/o SP's (200) 40.00 12.00
COMMON CARD (1-200) .30 .09
COMMON CARD (201-245) 5.00 1.50
1 Troy Glaus .50 .15
2 Kevin Appier .30 .09
3 Darin Erstad .30 .09
4 Garret Anderson .30 .09
5 Brad Fullmer .30 .09
6 Tim Salmon .50 .15
7 Eric Chavez .30 .09
8 Tim Hudson .30 .09
9 David Justice .30 .09
10 Barry Zito .50 .15
11 Miguel Tejada .30 .09
12 Mark Mulder .30 .09
13 Jermaine Dye .30 .09
14 Carlos Delgado .30 .09
15 Jose Cruz Jr. .30 .09
16 Brandon Lyon .30 .09
17 Shannon Stewart .30 .09
18 Eric Hinske .30 .09
19 Chris Carpenter .30 .09
20 Greg Vaughn .30 .09
21 Tanyon Sturtze .30 .09
22 Jason Tyner .30 .09
23 Toby Hall .30 .09
24 Ben Grieve .30 .09
25 Jim Thome .75 .23
26 Omar Vizquel .30 .09
27 Ricky Gutierrez .30 .09
28 C.C. Sabathia .30 .09
29 Ellis Burks .30 .09
30 Matt Lawton .30 .09
31 Milton Bradley .30 .09
32 Edgar Martinez .50 .15
33 Ichiro Suzuki 1.25 .35
34 Bret Boone .30 .09
35 Freddy Garcia .30 .09
36 Mike Cameron .30 .09
37 John Olerud .30 .09
38 Kazuhiro Sasaki .30 .09
39 Jeff Cirillo .30 .09
40 Jeff Conine .30 .09
41 Marty Cordova .30 .09
42 Tony Batista .30 .09
43 Jerry Hairston Jr. .30 .09
44 Jason Johnson .30 .09
45 David Segui .30 .09
46 Alex Rodriguez 1.25 .35
47 Rafael Palmeiro .50 .15
48 Carl Everett .30 .09
49 Chan Ho Park .30 .09
50 Ivan Rodriguez .75 .23
51 Juan Gonzalez .75 .23
52 Hank Blalock .75 .23
53 Manny Ramirez .30 .09
54 Pedro Martinez .75 .23
55 Tony Clark .30 .09
56 Nomar Garciaparra 1.25 .35
57 Johnny Damon .30 .09
58 Trot Nixon .50 .15
59 Rickey Henderson .75 .23
60 Mike Sweeney .30 .09
61 Neifi Perez .30 .09
62 Joe Randa .30 .09
63 Carlos Beltran .30 .09
64 Chuck Knoblauch .30 .09
65 Michael Tucker .30 .09
66 Dean Palmer .30 .09
67 Bobby Higginson .30 .09
68 Dmitri Young .30 .09
69 Randall Simon .30 .09
70 Mitch Meluskey .30 .09
71 Damion Easley .30 .09
72 Joe Mays .30 .09
73 Doug Mientkiewicz .30 .09
74 Corey Koskie .30 .09
75 Brad Radke .30 .09
76 Cristian Guzman .30 .09
77 Torii Hunter .30 .09
78 Eric Milton .30 .09
79 Frank Thomas .75 .23
80 Paul Konerko .30 .09
81 Mark Buehrle .30 .09
82 Magglio Ordonez .30 .09
83 Carlos Lee .30 .09
84 Joe Crede .30 .09
85 Derek Jeter 2.00 .60
86 Bernie Williams .50 .15
87 Mike Mussina .75 .23
88 Jorge Posada .50 .15
89 Roger Clemens 1.50 .45
90 Jason Giambi .75 .23
91 Alfonso Soriano .50 .15
92 Rondell White .30 .09
93 Jeff Bagwell .50 .15
94 Lance Berkman .30 .09
95 Roy Oswalt .30 .09
96 Richard Hidalgo .30 .09
97 Wade Miller .30 .09
98 Craig Biggio .50 .15
99 Greg Maddux 1.25 .35
100 Chipper Jones .75 .23
101 Gary Sheffield .30 .09
102 Rafael Furcal .30 .09
103 Andruw Jones .30 .09
104 Vinny Castilla .30 .09
105 Marcus Giles .30 .09
106 Tom Glavine .50 .15
107 Richie Sexson .30 .09
108 Geoff Jenkins .30 .09
109 Glendon Rusch .30 .09
110 Eric Young .30 .09
111 Ben Sheets .30 .09
112 Alex Sanchez .30 .09
113 Albert Pujols 1.50 .45
114 J.D. Drew .30 .09
115 Matt Morris .30 .09
116 Jim Edmonds .30 .09
117 Tino Martinez .50 .15
118 Scott Rolen .50 .15
119 Edgar Renteria .30 .09
120 Sammy Sosa 1.25 .35
121 Kerry Wood .75 .23
122 Moises Alou .30 .09
123 Jon Lieber .30 .09
124 Fred McGriff .50 .15
125 Juan Cruz .30 .09
126 Alex Gonzalez .30 .09
127 Corey Patterson .30 .09
128 Randy Johnson .75 .23
129 Luis Gonzalez .30 .09
130 Steve Finley .30 .09
131 Matt Williams .30 .09
132 Curt Schilling .50 .15
133 Mark Grace .50 .15
134 Craig Counsell .30 .09
135 Shawn Green .30 .09
136 Kevin Brown .30 .09
137 Hideo Nomo .75 .23
138 Paul Lo Duca .30 .09
139 Brian Jordan .30 .09
140 Eric Karros .30 .09
141 Adrian Beltre .30 .09
142 Vladimir Guerrero .75 .23
143 Fernando Tatis .30 .09
144 Javier Vazquez .30 .09
145 Orlando Cabrera .30 .09
146 Tony Armas Jr. .30 .09
147 Jose Vidro .30 .09
148 Barry Bonds 2.00 .60
149 Rich Aurilia .30 .09
150 Tsuyoshi Shinjo .30 .09
151 Jeff Kent .30 .09
152 Russ Ortiz .30 .09
153 Jason Schmidt .30 .09
154 Reggie Sanders .30 .09
155 Preston Wilson .30 .09
156 Luis Castillo .30 .09
157 Charles Johnson .30 .09
158 Josh Beckett .50 .15
159 Derrek Lee .30 .09
160 Mike Lowell .30 .09
161 Mike Piazza 1.25 .35
162 Roberto Alomar .75 .23
163 Al Leiter .30 .09
164 Mo Vaughn .30 .09
165 Jeromy Burnitz .30 .09
166 Edgardo Alfonzo .30 .09
167 Roger Cedeno .30 .09
168 Ryan Klesko .30 .09
169 Brian Lawrence .30 .09
170 Sean Burroughs .30 .09
171 Phil Nevin .30 .09
172 Ramon Vazquez .30 .09
173 Mark Kotsay .30 .09
174 Marlon Anderson .30 .09
175 Mike Lieberthal .30 .09
176 Bobby Abreu .30 .09
177 Pat Burrell .30 .09
178 Robert Person .30 .09
179 Brandon Duckworth .30 .09
180 Jimmy Rollins .30 .09
181 Brian Giles .30 .09
182 Pokey Reese .30 .09
183 Kris Benson .30 .09
184 Aramis Ramirez .30 .09
185 Jason Kendall .30 .09
186 Kip Wells .30 .09
187 Ken Griffey Jr. 1.25 .35
188 Adam Dunn .30 .09
189 Barry Larkin .75 .23
190 Sean Casey .30 .09
191 Austin Kearns .30 .09
192 Aaron Boone .30 .09
193 Todd Helton .50 .15
194 Juan Pierre .30 .09
195 Mike Hampton .30 .09
196 Jose Ortiz .30 .09
197 Larry Walker .50 .15
198 Juan Uribe .30 .09
199 Ichiro Suzuki CL .75 .23
200 Jason Giambi CL .50 .15
201 Franklyn German ROO RC 5.00 1.50
202 Rodrigo Rosario ROO RC 5.00 1.50
203 Brandon Puffer ROO RC 5.00 1.50
204 Kirk Saarloos ROO RC 5.00 1.50
205 Chris Baker ROO RC 5.00 1.50
206 John Ennis ROO RC 5.00 1.50
207 Luis Martinez ROO RC 5.00 1.50
208 So Taguchi ROO RC 8.00 2.40
209 Mike Crudale ROO RC 5.00 1.50
210 Francis Beltran ROO RC 5.00 1.50
211 Brandon Backe ROO RC 5.00 1.50
212 Felix Escalona ROO RC 5.00 1.50
213 Jose Valverde ROO RC 8.00 2.40
214 Doug Devore ROO RC 5.00 1.50
215 Kazuhisa Ishii ROO RC 10.00 3.00
216 Victor Alvarez ROO RC 5.00 1.50
217 Ron Calloway ROO RC 5.00 1.50
218 Eric Good ROO RC 5.00 1.50
219 Jorge Nunez ROO RC 5.00 1.50
220 Deivis Santos ROO 5.00 1.50
221 Nelson Castro ROO RC 5.00 1.50
222 Matt Thornton ROO RC 5.00 1.50
223 Jason Simontacchi ROO RC 5.00 1.50
224 Hansel Izquierdo ROO RC 5.00 1.50
225 Tyler Yates ROO RC 8.00 2.40
226 Jaime Cerda ROO RC 5.00 1.50
227 Satoru Komiyama ROO RC 5.00 1.50
228 Steve Bechler ROO RC 5.00 1.50
229 Ben Howard ROO RC 5.00 1.50
230 Todd Donovan ROO RC 5.00 1.50
231 Jorge Padilla ROO RC 5.00 1.50
232 Eric Junge ROO RC 5.00 1.50
233 Anderson Machado ROO RC 5.00 1.50
234 Adrian Burnside ROO RC 5.00 1.50
235 Mike Gonzalez ROO RC 5.00 1.50
236 Josh Hancock ROO RC 5.00 1.50
237 Anastacio Martinez ROO RC 5.00 1.50
238 Chris Booker ROO RC 5.00 1.50
239 Rene Reyes ROO RC 5.00 1.50
240 Cam Esslinger ROO RC 5.00 1.50
241 Oliver Perez ROO RC 8.00 2.40
242 Tim Kalita ROO RC 5.00 1.50
243 Kevin Frederick ROO RC 5.00 1.50
244 Mitch Wylie ROO RC 5.00 1.50
245 Edwin Almonte ROO RC 5.00 1.50

2002 Upper Deck Ballpark Idols Bronze

Randomly inserted into packs, this is a parallel to the Ballpark Idols set. These cards were issued to a stated print run of 100 serial numbered sets.

Nm-Mt Ex-Mt
*BRONZE 1-200: 8X TO 20X BASIC CARDS
COMMON CARD (201-245) 6.00 1.80
204 Kirk Saarloos ROO 6.00 1.80
215 Kazuhisa Ishii ROO 25.00 7.50
223 Jason Simontacchi ROO 6.00 1.80
241 Oliver Perez ROO 10.00 3.00

2002 Upper Deck Ballpark Idols Bobbers

Inserted one per sealed box, this 58 bobber set features both an home and an away version of each bobble piece. The bobbers with the players in their home uniform were printed to a smaller quantity and we have noted that information with an SP in our checklist.

Nm-Mt Ex-Mt
1 Roberto Alomar Away 15.00 4.50
2 Roberto Alomar Home SP
3 Jeff Bagwell 15.00 4.50
4 Josh Beckett Away 15.00 4.50
5 Josh Beckett Home SP
6 Barry Bonds Away 40.00 12.00
7 Barry Bonds Home SP
8 Sean Burroughs Away 10.00 3.00
9 Sean Burroughs Home SP
10 R.Clemens Red Sox SP
11 R.Clemens Yanks Away 30.00 9.00

12 R.Clemens Yanks Home SP		
13 Joe DiMaggio Away/555	40.00	12.00
14 Joe DiMaggio Home/361		
15 Nomar Garciaparra Away	25.00	7.50
16 Nomar Garciaparra Home SP		
17 Jason Giambi Away	15.00	4.50
18 Jason Giambi Home SP		
19 Luis Gonzalez Away	10.00	3.00
20 Luis Gonzalez Home SP		
21 Ken Griffey M's SP		
22 Ken Griffey Reds Away	25.00	7.50
23 Ken Griffey Reds Home SP		
24 Vladimir Guerrero	15.00	4.50
25 Kazuhisa Ishii Away	15.00	4.50
26 Kazuhisa Ishii Home SP		
27 Derek Jeter Away SP		
28 Derek Jeter Home SP		
29 Randy Johnson D'Backs	15.00	4.50
30 Randy Johnson Expos	15.00	4.50
31 Chipper Jones	15.00	4.50
32 Greg Maddux	25.00	7.50
33 Mickey Mantle Away/777	50.00	15.00
34 Mickey Mantle Home/536	60.00	18.00
35 Mark McGwire A's SP		
36 M.McGwire Cards Away	40.00	12.00
37 M.McGwire Cards Home SP		
38 Mike Piazza Dodgers SP		
39 Mike Piazza Mets	25.00	7.50
40 Mark Prior Away	25.00	7.50
41 Mark Prior Home SP		
42 Albert Pujols Away	30.00	9.00
43 Albert Pujols Home SP		
44 Alex Rodriguez Away	25.00	7.50
45 Alex Rodriguez Home SP		
46 Ivan Rodriguez Away	15.00	4.50
47 Ivan Rodriguez Home SP		
48 Curt Schilling D'Backs	15.00	4.50
49 Curt Schilling O's SP		
50 S.Sosa Cubs Away	25.00	7.50
51 S.Sosa Cubs Home SP		
52 Sammy Sosa Rgr SP		
53 Ichiro Suzuki Away SP		
54 Ichiro Suzuki Home SP		
55 Frank Thomas Away	15.00	4.50
56 Frank Thomas Home SP		
57 Jim Thome Away	15.00	4.50
58 Jim Thome Home SP		

2002 Upper Deck Ballpark Idols Bobbers Autographs

Randomly inserted into boxes, these 21 bobbers feature the player's signature on the bobber.

	Nm-Mt	Ex-Mt
1 Roberto Alomar Mets		
2 Josh Beckett		
3 Sean Burroughs		
4 Roger Clemens Red Sox		
5 Roger Clemens Yanks		
6 Frank Thomas		
7 Jason Giambi		
8 Luis Gonzalez		
9 Ken Griffey Jr. M's		
10 Ken Griffey Jr. Reds		
11 Mark McGwire A's		
12 Mark McGwire Away		
13 Mark McGwire Home		
14 Mark Prior		
15 Alex Rodriguez		
16 Ivan Rodriguez		
17 Sammy Sosa Cubs		
18 Sammy Sosa Rangers		
19 Ichiro Suzuki Away		
20 Ichiro Suzuki Home		
21 Jim Thome		

2002 Upper Deck Ballpark Idols Bobbers Gold

Randomly inserted into Ballpark Idol boxes, this is a partial parallel to the Bobbers inserts. Only Joe DiMaggio and Mickey Mantle are featured in this set and they are each issued to stated print runs which have importance to their careers.

	Nm-Mt	Ex-Mt
1 Joe DiMaggio Away/56		
2 Joe DiMaggio Home/41		
3 Mickey Mantle Away/77		
4 Mickey Mantle Home/61		

2002 Upper Deck Ballpark Idols Field Garb Jerseys

Inserted at a stated rate of one in 72, these 13 cards feature game-worn jersey swatches of some of the biggest stars in baseball.

	Nm-Mt	Ex-Mt
AR Alex Rodriguez	15.00	4.50
BG Brian Giles	10.00	3.00
BZ Barry Zito	15.00	4.50
IR Ivan Rodriguez	15.00	4.50
JK Jeff Kent	10.00	3.00
JO John Olerud	10.00	3.00
LW Larry Walker	15.00	4.50
MR Manny Ramirez	10.00	3.00
MS Mike Sweeney	10.00	3.00
RJ Randy Johnson	15.00	4.50
RV Robin Ventura	10.00	3.00
TB Tony Batista	10.00	3.00
TM Tino Martinez	15.00	4.50

2002 Upper Deck Ballpark Idols Figure-Heads

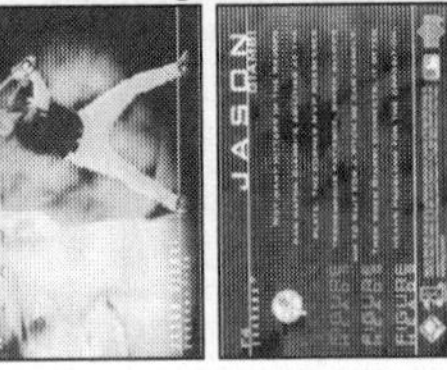

Issued at a a stated rate of one in 12, this 10 card set features baseball's leading superstars.

	Nm-Mt	Ex-Mt
COMPLETE SET (10)	30.00	9.00
F1 Ichiro Suzuki	4.00	1.20
F2 Sammy Sosa	4.00	1.20
F3 Alex Rodriguez	4.00	1.20
F4 Jason Giambi	3.00	.90
F5 Barry Bonds	6.00	1.80
F6 Chipper Jones	3.00	.90
F7 Mike Piazza	4.00	1.20
F8 Derek Jeter	6.00	1.80
F9 Nomar Garciaparra	4.00	1.20
F10 Ken Griffey Jr.	4.00	1.20

2002 Upper Deck Ballpark Idols Player's Club Jerseys

Inserted at a stated rate of one in 72, these 13 cards feature game-used jersey cards of some of baseball's most elite performers. A couple of these cards were issued in shorter quantity and we have notated that information with an SP next to the player's name in our checklist.

	Nm-Mt	Ex-Mt
AJ Andruw Jones	10.00	3.00
CS Curt Schilling	10.00	3.00
DE Darin Erstad	10.00	3.00
HN Hideo Nomo	30.00	9.00
IS Ichiro Suzuki SP	50.00	15.00
JK Jason Kendall	10.00	3.00
JT Jim Thome	15.00	4.50
KB Kevin Brown	10.00	3.00
MM Mark McGwire SP	100.00	30.00
MO Magglio Ordonez	10.00	3.00
PN Phil Nevin	10.00	3.00
RF Rafael Furcal	10.00	3.00
TH Tim Hudson	10.00	3.00

2002 Upper Deck Ballpark Idols Playmakers

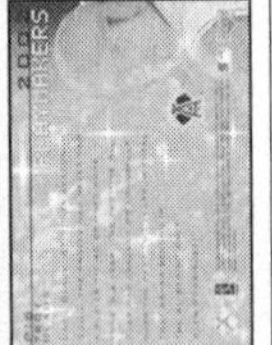

Inserted at a stated rate of one in six, this 20 card set features players who are always making important plays for their team.

	Nm-Mt	Ex-Mt
COMPLETE SET (20)	40.00	12.00
P1 Ken Griffey Jr.	3.00	.90
P2 Alex Rodriguez	3.00	.90
P3 Sammy Sosa	3.00	.90
P4 Derek Jeter	5.00	1.50
P5 Mike Piazza	3.00	.90
P6 Jason Giambi	2.00	.60
P7 Barry Bonds	5.00	1.50
P8 Frank Thomas	2.00	.60
P9 Randy Johnson	2.00	.60
P10 Chipper Jones	2.00	.60
P11 Jeff Bagwell	1.50	.45
P12 Vladimir Guerrero	2.00	.60
P13 Albert Pujols	4.00	1.20
P14 Nomar Garciaparra	3.00	.90
P15 Ichiro Suzuki	3.00	.90
P16 Troy Glaus	1.50	.45
P17 Ivan Rodriguez	2.00	.60
P18 Carlos Delgado	1.50	.45
P19 Greg Maddux	3.00	.90
P20 Todd Helton	1.50	.45

2002 Upper Deck Ballpark Idols Uniform Sluggers Jerseys

Inserted at a stated rate of one in 72, these 12 cards feature game-worn jersey swatches from the heaviest hitters in baseball. A few cards were issued in shorter quantity and those cards we have notated with an SP in our checklist.

	Nm-Mt	Ex-Mt
AR Alex Rodriguez	15.00	4.50
BW Bernie Williams	10.00	3.00
CJ Chipper Jones	15.00	4.50

JB Jeff Bagwell	10.00	3.00
KG Ken Griffey Jr. SP	40.00	12.00
MM Mickey Mantle SP	200.00	60.00
MP Mike Piazza	12.00	3.60
SG Shawn Green	10.00	3.00
SS Sammy Sosa SP/95		
TH Todd Helton	10.00	3.00
JGI Jason Giambi	15.00	4.50
JGO Juan Gonzalez	15.00	4.50

2002 Upper Deck Collectors Club

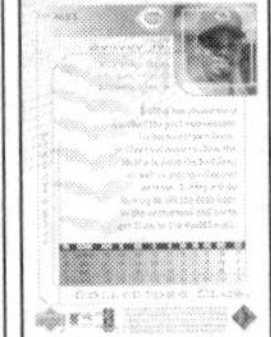

These cards were distributed in May, 2002 via mail exclusively to members of Upper Deck's Collectors Club program as part of their Starter Kit. Each member received a 20-card complete set plus a memorabilia cards wrapped in clear plastic cello, an Upper Deck baseball cap and a club membership card. Members received a quarterly newsletter with features on upcoming products and sample cards. In addition, if members attended a card show in which Upper Deck had a corporate presence, they could show their membership card to a UD staffer and receive complimentary items.

	Nm-Mt	Ex-Mt
COMP.FACT.SET (21)	30.00	9.00
COMPLETE SET (20)	20.00	6.00
MLB1 Alex Rodriguez	1.50	.45
MLB2 Barry Bonds	1.50	.45
MLB3 Ken Griffey Jr.	2.00	.60
MLB4 Sammy Sosa	1.50	.45
MLB5 Jason Giambi	1.25	.35
MLB6 Ichiro Suzuki	3.00	.90
MLB7 Chipper Jones	1.50	.45
MLB8 Derek Jeter	3.00	.90
MLB9 Nomar Garciaparra	1.25	.35
MLB10 Greg Maddux	1.50	.45
MLB11 Mike Piazza	1.50	.45
MLB12 Frank Thomas	1.00	.30
MLB13 Albert Pujols	1.50	.45
MLB14 Randy Johnson	1.25	.35
MLB15 Pedro Martinez	1.00	.30
MLB16 Todd Helton	1.00	.30
MLB17 Vladimir Guerrero	1.00	.30
MLB18 Jeff Bagwell	1.00	.30
MLB19 Roger Clemens	1.50	.45
MLB20 Shawn Green	.75	.23

2002 Upper Deck Collectors Club Game Jersey

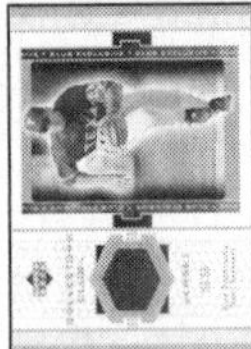

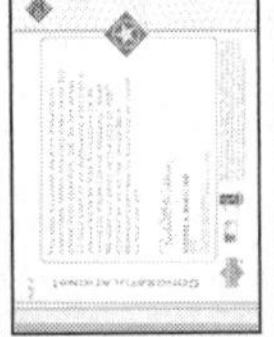

This card was inserted one per each Upper Deck Collectors Club set which all collectors who signed up for the Collectors Club received.

	Nm-Mt	Ex-Mt
AR-J Alex Rodriguez Jsy	10.00	3.00

2000 Upper Deck Brooklyn Dodgers Master Collection

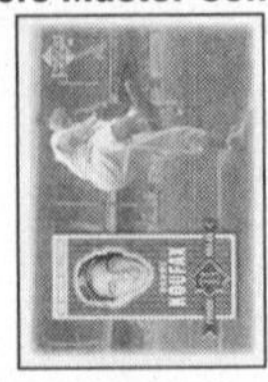

The 2000 Upper Deck Brooklyn Dodgers Master Collection was released in November, 2000 and included a 15-card base set, an 11-card Legends of Flatbush insert set, and one mystery pack card. Please note that only 250 Master Collections exist.

	Nm-Mt	Ex-Mt
COMPLETE SET (15)	300.00	90.00
BD1 Jackie Robinson	40.00	12.00
BD2 Duke Snider	25.00	7.50
BD3 Pee Wee Reese	40.00	12.00
BD4 Gil Hodges	40.00	12.00
BD5 Carl Furillo	15.00	4.50
BD6 Don Newcombe	15.00	4.50
BD7 Sandy Koufax	100.00	30.00
BD8 Roy Campanella	40.00	12.00
BD9 Jim Gilliam	15.00	4.50
BD10 Don Drysdale	40.00	12.00
BD11 Sandy Amoros	15.00	4.50
BD12 Joe Black	15.00	4.50
BD13 Carl Erskine	15.00	4.50
BD14 Johnny Podres	15.00	4.50
BD15 Zack Wheat	25.00	7.50
NNO Mini Bat Mail Out/750	5.00	1.50

2000 Upper Deck Brooklyn Dodgers Master Collection Legends of Flatbush

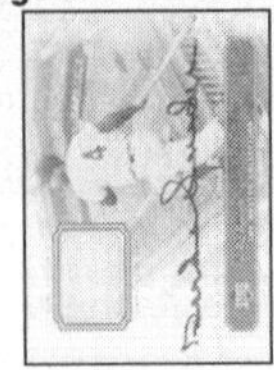

This insert set was issued in the 2000 Brooklyn Dodgers Master Collection. The set features game-used memorabilia cards from Dodger greats like Sandy Koufax and Duke Snider. Please note that Don Newcombe, Duke Snider, and Sandy Koufax autographed all of their cards.

	Nm-Mt	Ex-Mt
LOF1 Gil Hodges Bat	60.00	18.00
LOF2 Jackie Robinson Bat	100.00	30.00
LOF3 Pee Wee Reese Bat	50.00	15.00
LOF4 Jim Gilliam Bat	40.00	12.00
LOF5 Roy Campanella Bat	60.00	18.00
LOF6 Zach Wheat Bat	60.00	18.00
LOF7 Carl Furillo Bat	40.00	12.00
LOF8 D.Newcombe Bat AU	60.00	18.00
LOF9 Duke Snider Bat AU	100.00	30.00
LOF10 Don Drysdale Jsy	60.00	18.00
LOF11 S.Koufax Jsy AU	800.00	240.00

2000 Upper Deck Brooklyn Dodgers Master Collection Mystery Pack Inserts

Inserted into Brooklyn Dodgers Master Collection's at one per set, this 10-card insert features game-used memorablia and autographs of many Dodger greats. Please note that these cards came in a special mystery package that was inserted into every Brooklyn Dodgers Master Collection.

	Nm-Mt	Ex-Mt
DN-CF Don Newcombe / Carl Furillo Bat/35		
DS-DN Duke Snider AU / Don Newcombe AU		
GH-BC1-3 Gil Hodges Bat-Cut AU/3		
JR-BC1-5 Jackie Robinson Bat-Cut AU/5		
JR-DS Jackie Robinson / Duke Snider Bat/35		
JR-GH Jackie Robinson / Gil Hodges		
JR-PW Jackie Robinson / Pee Wee Reese Bat		
JR-RC Jackie Robinson / Roy Campanella Bat		
PW-BC1-8 Pee Wee Reese Bat-Cut AU/8		
SK-DD Sandy Koufax Jsy / Don Drysdale Jsy/35		

1999 Upper Deck Century Legends

This set was released in June, 1999 and was distributed in five card packs with an SRP of $4.99 per pack. The packs came 24 to a box. The first 47 card of the set feature an assortment of players honored from the Sporting News of 100 Greatest Players. The next 50 cards feature Upper Deck's choices of the best active players. The final cards are utilized for the following subsets: 21 CP (Cards numbered 101 through 120) and Memorablue Shots (Cards numbered 122 through 135.) Cards 11, 25, 26 and 126 do not exist. Due to contractual problems, Upper Deck had to pull the player's originally intended to be featured on these cards. Thus, though the set is numbered 1-135, it is complete at only 131 cards. A game-used bat from legendary slugger Jimmie Foxx was cut into approximately 350 pieces, incorporated into special A Piece of History 500 Club cards and randomly seeded into packs. Pricing for these scarce Foxx bat cards can be referenced under 1999 Upper Deck A Piece of History 500 Club. A Babe Ruth sample card was distributed to dealers and media several weeks prior to the product's national release. The card parallels Ruth's regular issue card except for the word "SAMPLE" running in red text diagonally across the card back.

	Nm-Mt	Ex-Mt
COMPLETE SET (131)	50.00	15.00
1 Babe Ruth	2.50	.75
2 Willie Mays	1.50	.45
3 Ty Cobb	1.25	.35
4 Walter Johnson	.75	.23
5 Hank Aaron	1.50	.45
6 Lou Gehrig	1.50	.45
7 Christy Mathewson	.75	.23
8 Ted Williams	2.00	.60
9 Rogers Hornsby	.75	.23
10 Stan Musial	1.25	.35
12 Grover Alexander	.75	.23
13 Honus Wagner	.75	.23
14 Cy Young	.75	.23
15 Jimmie Foxx	.75	.23
16 Johnny Bench	.75	.23
17 Mickey Mantle	3.00	.90
18 Josh Gibson	.75	.23
19 Satchel Paige	.75	.23
20 Roberto Clemente	1.50	.45
21 Warren Spahn	.50	.15
22 Frank Robinson	.50	.15
23 Lefty Grove	.75	.23
24 Eddie Collins	.50	.15
27 Tris Speaker	.75	.23
28 Mike Schmidt	1.50	.45
29 Napoleon Lajoie	.75	.23
30 Steve Carlton	.40	.12
31 Bob Gibson	.50	.15
32 Tom Seaver	.50	.15
33 George Sisler	.40	.12
34 Barry Bonds	2.00	.60
35 Joe Jackson NNO UER	1.00	.30
36 Bob Feller	.50	.15
37 Hank Greenberg	.75	.23
38 Ernie Banks	.75	.23
39 Greg Maddux	1.25	.35
40 Yogi Berra	.75	.23
41 Nolan Ryan	2.00	.60
42 Mel Ott	.75	.23
43 Al Simmons	.40	.12
44 Jackie Robinson	1.00	.30
45 Carl Hubbell	.50	.15
46 Charley Gehringer	.40	.12
47 Buck Leonard	.40	.12
48 Reggie Jackson	.50	.15
49 Tony Gwynn	1.00	.30
50 Roy Campanella	.75	.23
51 Ken Griffey Jr.	1.25	.35
52 Barry Bonds	2.00	.60
53 Roger Clemens	1.50	.45
54 Tony Gwynn	1.00	.30
55 Cal Ripken	2.50	.75
56 Greg Maddux	1.25	.35
57 Frank Thomas	.75	.23
58 Mark McGwire	2.00	.60
59 Mike Piazza	1.25	.35
60 Wade Boggs	.50	.15
61 Alex Rodriguez	1.25	.35
62 Juan Gonzalez	.75	.23
63 Mo Vaughn	.40	.12
64 Albert Belle	.40	.12
65 Sammy Sosa	1.25	.35
66 Nomar Garciaparra	1.25	.35
67 Derek Jeter	2.00	.60
68 Kevin Brown	.50	.15
69 Jose Canseco	.75	.23
70 Randy Johnson	.75	.23
71 Tom Glavine	.50	.15
72 Barry Larkin	.75	.23
73 Curt Schilling	.50	.15
74 Moises Alou	.40	.12
75 Fred McGriff	.50	.15
76 Pedro Martinez	.75	.23
77 Andres Galarraga	.40	.12
78 Will Clark	.75	.23
79 Larry Walker	.50	.15
80 Ivan Rodriguez	.75	.23
81 Chipper Jones	.75	.23
82 Jeff Bagwell	.50	.15
83 Craig Biggio	.50	.15
84 Kerry Wood	.75	.23
85 Roberto Alomar	.75	.23
86 Vinny Castilla	.40	.12
87 Kenny Lofton	.40	.12
88 Rafael Palmeiro	.50	.15
89 Manny Ramirez	.40	.12
90 David Wells	.40	.12
91 Mark Grace	.50	.15
92 Bernie Williams	.50	.15
93 David Cone	.40	.12
94 John Olerud	.40	.12
95 John Smoltz	.50	.15
96 Tino Martinez	.50	.15
97 Raul Mondesi	.40	.12
98 Gary Sheffield	.40	.12
99 Orel Hershiser	.40	.12
100 Rickey Henderson	.75	.23
101 J.D. Drew 21CP	.40	.12
102 Troy Glaus 21CP	.50	.15
103 N.Garciaparra 21CP	1.25	.35
104 Scott Rolen 21CP	.50	.15
105 Ryan Minor 21CP	.30	.09
106 Travis Lee 21CP	.30	.09
107 Roy Halladay 21CP	.40	.12
108 Carlos Beltran 21CP	.40	.12
109 Alex Rodriguez 21CP	1.25	.35
110 Eric Chavez 21CP	.40	.12
111 V.Guerrero 21CP	.75	.23
112 Ben Grieve 21CP	.30	.09
113 Kerry Wood 21CP	.75	.23
114 Alex Gonzalez 21CP	.30	.09
115 Darin Erstad 21CP	.40	.12
116 Derek Jeter 21CP	2.00	.60
117 Jaret Wright 21CP	.30	.09
118 Jose Cruz Jr. 21CP	.40	.12
119 Chipper Jones 21CP	.75	.23
120 Gabe Kapler 21CP	.30	.09
121 Satchel Paige MEM	.75	.23
122 Willie Mays MEM	1.50	.45
123 R.Clemente MEM	1.50	.45
124 Lou Gehrig MEM	1.50	.45
125 Mark McGwire MEM	2.00	.60
127 Bob Gibson MEM	.50	.15
128 J.VanderMeer MEM	.30	.09
129 Walter Johnson MEM	.75	.23
130 Ty Cobb MEM	1.25	.35

131 Don Larsen MEM .40 .12
132 Jackie Robinson MEM 1.00 .30
133 Tom Seaver MEM .40 .12
134 Johnny Bench MEM .50 .15
135 Frank Robinson MEM .50 .15
S1 Babe Ruth Sample 2.00 .60

1999 Upper Deck Century Legends Century Collection

Randomly inserted into hobby packs only, this 131-card set is a die-cut parallel version of the base set and is sequentially numbered to 100. Cards 11, 25, 26, and 126 do not exist.

Nm-Mt Ex-Mt
*ACTIVE STARS: 8X TO 20X BASIC
*POST-WAR STARS: 12.5X TO 30X BASIC
*PRE-WAR STARS: 6X TO 15X BASIC
*21ST CENT: 8X TO 20X BASIC

1999 Upper Deck Century Legends All-Century Team

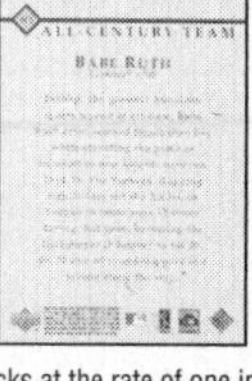

Randomly inserted in packs at the rate of one in 23, this 10-card set features photos of Upper Deck's All-Time All-Star Team.

	Nm-Mt	Ex-Mt
COMPLETE SET (10)	60.00	18.00
AC1 Babe Ruth	12.00	3.60
AC2 Ty Cobb	6.00	1.80
AC3 Willie Mays	8.00	2.40
AC4 Lou Gehrig	8.00	2.40
AC5 Jackie Robinson	5.00	1.50
AC6 Mike Schmidt	8.00	2.40
AC7 Ernie Banks	4.00	1.20
AC8 Johnny Bench	4.00	1.20
AC9 Cy Young	4.00	1.20
AC10 Lineup Sheet	1.50	.45

1999 Upper Deck Century Legends Artifacts

Randomly inserted in packs, this nine-card set features redemption cards for memorabilia from some of the top players of the century. Only one of each card was produced. No pricing is available due to the scarcity of these cards.

Nm-Mt Ex-Mt
1900 Ty Cobb Framed Cut
1910 Babe Ruth Framed Cut
1920 Rogers Hornsby Framed Cut
1930 Satchel Paige Framed Cut
1950 Hank Aaron
Willie Mays
Mickey Mantle AU Balls
1960 Ernie Banks
Bob Gibson
Johnny Bench AU Balls
1970 Tom Seaver
Mike Schmidt
Steve Carlton AU Balls
1980 Nolan Ryan
Ken Griffey Jr. AU Balls
1990 Ken Griffey Jr. AU Jersey

1999 Upper Deck Century Legends Epic Milestones

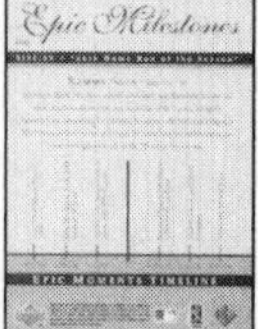

Randomly inserted into packs at the rate of one in 12, this nine-card set features color photos of players with the most impressive milestones in MLB history. Card EM1 does not exist.

	Nm-Mt	Ex-Mt
COMPLETE SET (9)	40.00	12.00
EM2 Jackie Robinson	3.00	.90
EM3 Nolan Ryan	6.00	1.80
EM4 Mark McGwire	6.00	1.80
EM5 Roger Clemens	5.00	1.50
EM6 Sammy Sosa	4.00	1.20
EM7 Cal Ripken	8.00	2.40
EM8 Rickey Henderson	2.50	.75
EM9 Hank Aaron	5.00	1.50
EM10 Barry Bonds	6.00	1.80

1999 Upper Deck Century Legends Epic Signatures

Randomly inserted into packs at the rate of one in 24, this 30-card set features autographed photos of retired stars and current players. Stickered exchange cards for Johnny Bench, Yogi Berra, Carlton Fisk and Willie McCovey were seeded into packs. The deadline to exchange those cards was December 31, 1999.

	Nm-Mt	Ex-Mt
AR Alex Rodriguez	150.00	45.00
BB Barry Bonds	200.00	60.00
BD Bucky Dent	15.00	4.50
BF Bob Feller	25.00	7.50
BG Bob Gibson	25.00	7.50
BM Bill Mazeroski	25.00	7.50
BT Bobby Thomson	15.00	4.50
CF Carlton Fisk	25.00	7.50
CFX Carlton Fisk EXCH	6.00	1.80
DL Don Larsen	15.00	4.50
EB Ernie Banks	40.00	12.00
EMA Eddie Mathews	50.00	15.00
FR Frank Robinson	25.00	7.50
FT Frank Thomas	80.00	24.00
GM Greg Maddux	100.00	30.00
HK Harmon Killebrew	40.00	12.00
JB Johnny Bench	40.00	12.00
JBX Johnny Bench EXCH	6.00	1.80
JG Juan Gonzalez	40.00	12.00
JR Ken Griffey Jr.	120.00	36.00
MS Mike Schmidt	50.00	15.00
NR Nolan Ryan	150.00	45.00
RJ Reggie Jackson	60.00	18.00
SC Steve Carlton	25.00	7.50
SM Stan Musial	60.00	18.00
SR Ken Griffey Sr.	15.00	4.50
TG Tony Gwynn	50.00	15.00
TS Tom Seaver	25.00	7.50
VG Vladimir Guerrero	40.00	12.00
WMC Willie McCovey	25.00	7.50
WMCX W.McCovey EXCH	4.00	1.20
WS Warren Spahn	40.00	12.00
YB Yogi Berra	40.00	12.00
YBX Yogi Berra EXCH	5.00	1.50

1999 Upper Deck Century Legends Epic Signatures Century

Randomly inserted in packs, this 32-card set features autographed color photos of past and present players with gold-foil stamping. Each card is hand-numbered to 100.

	Nm-Mt	Ex-Mt
AR Alex Rodriguez	250.00	75.00
BB Barry Bonds	300.00	90.00
BD Bucky Dent	25.00	7.50
BF Bob Feller	50.00	15.00
BG Bob Gibson	50.00	15.00
BM Bill Mazeroski	50.00	15.00
BT Bobby Thomson	25.00	7.50
CF Carlton Fisk	50.00	15.00
CFX Carlton Fisk EXCH	12.00	3.60
DL Don Larsen	25.00	7.50
EB Ernie Banks	80.00	24.00
EMA Eddie Mathews	80.00	24.00
FR Frank Robinson	50.00	15.00
FT Frank Thomas	120.00	36.00
GM Greg Maddux	150.00	45.00
HK Harmon Killebrew	80.00	24.00
JB Johnny Bench	80.00	24.00
JBX Johnny Bench EXCH	15.00	4.50
JG Juan Gonzalez	80.00	24.00
JR Ken Griffey Jr.	200.00	60.00
MS Mike Schmidt	120.00	36.00
NR Nolan Ryan	250.00	75.00
RJ Reggie Jackson	80.00	24.00
SC Steve Carlton	50.00	15.00
SM Stan Musial	100.00	30.00
SR Ken Griffey Sr.	25.00	7.50
TG Tony Gwynn	100.00	30.00
TS Tom Seaver	50.00	15.00
TW Ted Williams	1000.00	300.00
VG Vladimir Guerrero	80.00	24.00
WM Willie Mays	300.00	90.00
WMC Willie McCovey	50.00	15.00
WMCX W.McCovey EXCH	6.00	1.80
WS Warren Spahn	80.00	24.00
YB Yogi Berra	80.00	24.00
YBX Yogi Berra EXCH	15.00	4.50

1999 Upper Deck Century Legends Jerseys of the Century

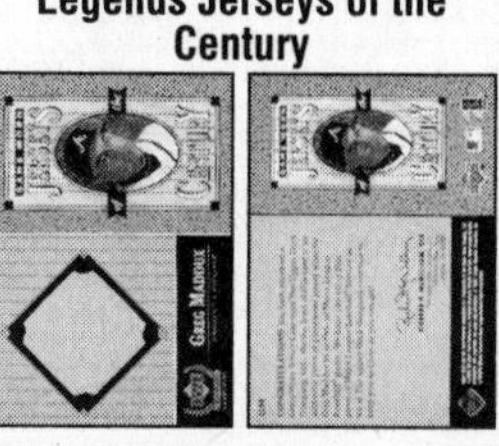

Randomly inserted in packs at the rate of one in 418, this nine-card set features color photos of top current and retired players with pieces of their actual game-worn jerseys embedded in the cards.

	Nm-Mt	Ex-Mt
DW Dave Winfield	15.00	4.50
EM Eddie Murray	25.00	7.50
GB George Brett	40.00	12.00
GM Greg Maddux	25.00	7.50
MS Mike Schmidt	40.00	12.00
NR Nolan Ryan	100.00	30.00
OZ Ozzie Smith	25.00	7.50
RC Roger Clemens	40.00	12.00
TG Tony Gwynn	30.00	9.00

1999 Upper Deck Century Legends Legendary Cuts

Randomly inserted into packs, this nine-card set features actual signature cuts from some of baseball's greatest players. Only one of each of these cards was produced.

Nm-Mt Ex-Mt
BR Babe Ruth
CY Cy Young
LG Lefty Grove
MO Mel Ott
RC Roy Campanella
SP Satchel Paige
TY Ty Cobb
WJ Walter Johnson
XX Jimmie Foxx

1999 Upper Deck Century Legends Memorable Shots

Randomly inserted into packs at the rate of one in 12, this 10-card set features photos of the most memorable home runs launched during this century.

	Nm-Mt	Ex-Mt
COMPLETE SET (10)	30.00	9.00
HR1 Babe Ruth	10.00	3.00
HR2 Bobby Thomson	1.00	.30
HR3 Kirk Gibson	1.00	.30
HR4 Carlton Fisk	1.00	.30
HR5 Bill Mazeroski	1.00	.30
HR6 Bucky Dent	1.00	.30
HR7 Mark McGwire	5.00	1.50
HR8 Mickey Mantle	10.00	3.00
HR9 Joe Carter	1.00	.30
HR10 Mark McGwire	5.00	1.50

1999 Upper Deck Century Legends MVPs

Randomly inserted in packs, this 100-card set features color action photos of Upper Deck's 1999 MVP players printed with rainbow-foil. Only one of each card was produced. Pricing for stars is unavailable due to scarcity. A checklist has been provided for cataloging purposes.

Nm-Mt Ex-Mt
C1 Mo Vaughn
C2 Troy Glaus
C3 Darin Erstad
C4 Randy Johnson
C5 Travis Lee
C6 Chipper Jones
C7 Greg Maddux
C8 Tom Glavine
C9 John Smoltz
C10 Cal Ripken
C11 Charles Johnson
C12 Albert Belle
C13 Nomar Garciaparra
C14 Pedro Martinez
C15 Kerry Wood
C16 Sammy Sosa
C17 Mark Grace
C18 Frank Thomas
C19 Paul Konerko
C20 Ray Durham
C21 Denny Neagle
C22 Sean Casey
C23 Barry Larkin
C24 Roberto Alomar
C25 Kenny Lofton
C26 Travis Fryman
C27 Jim Thome
C28 Manny Ramirez
C29 Vinny Castilla
C30 Todd Helton
C31 Dante Bichette
C32 Larry Walker
C33 Gabe Kapler
C34 Dean Palmer
C35 Tony Clark
C36 Juan Encarnacion
C37 Alex Gonzalez
C38 Preston Wilson
C39 Derrek Lee
C40 Ken Caminiti
C41 Jeff Bagwell
C42 Moises Alou
C43 Craig Biggio
C44 Carlos Beltran
C45 Jeremy Giambi
C46 Johnny Damon
C47 Kevin Brown
C48 Chan Ho Park
C49 Raul Mondesi
C50 Gary Sheffield
C51 Sean Berry
C52 Jeromy Burnitz
C53 Brad Radke
C54 Eric Milton
C55 Todd Walker
C56 Vladimir Guerrero
C57 Rondell White
C58 Mike Piazza
C59 Rickey Henderson
C60 Rey Ordonez
C61 Derek Jeter
C62 Bernie Williams
C63 Paul O'Neill
C64 Scott Brosius
C65 Tino Martinez
C66 Roger Clemens
C67 Orlando Hernandez
C68 Ben Grieve
C69 Eric Chavez
C70 Jason Giambi
C71 Curt Schilling
C72 Scott Rolen
C73 Pat Burrell
C74 Jason Kendall
C75 Aramis Ramirez
C76 Mark McGwire
C77 J.D. Drew
C78 Edgar Renteria
C79 Tony Gwynn
C80 Sterling Hitchcock
C81 Ruben Rivera
C82 Trevor Hoffman
C83 Barry Bonds
C84 Ellis Burks
C85 Robb Nen
C86 Ken Griffey Jr.
C87 Alex Rodriguez
C88 Carlos Guillen
C89 Edgar Martinez
C90 Jose Canseco
C91 Rolando Arrojo
C92 Wade Boggs
C93 Fred McGriff
C94 Juan Gonzalez
C95 Ivan Rodriguez
C96 Rafael Palmeiro
C97 David Wells
C98 Roy Halladay
C99 Carlos Delgado
C100 Jose Cruz Jr.

1999 Upper Deck Challengers for 70

This 90 card set was distributed in five card packs. The set is broken up into 45 regular player cards with the following themes: Power Corps, Rookie Power and Power Elite. The other 45 cards of the set are dedicated to 45 Home Run Highlight subset cards. A game-used bat from legendary slugger Harmon Killebrew was cut up and incorporated into approximately 350 A Piece of History 500 Club bat cards. In addition, Killebrew signed and numbered three copies (in concert with his jersey number). Pricing for these scarce bat cards can be referenced under 1999 Upper Deck A Piece of History 500 Club.

	Nm-Mt	Ex-Mt
COMPLETE SET (90)	40.00	12.00
1 Mark McGwire	2.00	.60
2 Sammy Sosa	1.25	.35
3 Ken Griffey Jr.	1.25	.35
4 Alex Rodriguez	1.25	.35
5 Albert Belle	.30	.09
6 Mo Vaughn	.30	.09
7 Mike Piazza	1.25	.35
8 Frank Thomas	.75	.23
9 Juan Gonzalez	.75	.23
10 Barry Bonds	2.00	.60
11 Rafael Palmeiro	.50	.15
12 Jose Canseco	.75	.23
13 Nomar Garciaparra	1.25	.35
14 Carlos Delgado	.30	.09
15 Brian Jordan	.30	.09
16 Vladimir Guerrero	.75	.23
17 Vinny Castilla	.30	.09
18 Chipper Jones	.75	.23
19 Jeff Bagwell	.50	.15
20 Moises Alou	.30	.09
21 Tony Clark	.30	.09
22 Jim Thome	.75	.23
23 Tino Martinez	.50	.15
24 Greg Vaughn	.30	.09
25 Javy Lopez	.30	.09
26 Jeromy Burnitz	.30	.09
27 Cal Ripken	2.50	.75
28 Manny Ramirez	.30	.09
29 Darin Erstad	.30	.09
30 Ken Caminiti	.30	.09
31 Edgar Martinez	.50	.15
32 Ivan Rodriguez	.75	.23
33 Larry Walker	.50	.15
34 Todd Helton	.50	.15
35 Andruw Jones	.30	.09
36 Ray Lankford	.30	.09
37 Travis Lee	.30	.09
38 Raul Mondesi	.30	.09
39 Scott Rolen	.50	.15
40 Ben Grieve	.30	.09
41 J.D. Drew	.30	.09
42 Troy Glaus	.50	.15
43 Eric Chavez	.30	.09
44 Gabe Kapler	.30	.09
45 Michael Barrett	.30	.09
46 Mark McGwire HRH	1.00	.30
47 Jose Canseco HRH	.50	.15
48 Greg Vaughn HRH	.30	.09
49 Albert Belle HRH	.30	.09
50 Mark McGwire HRH	1.00	.30
51 Vinny Castilla HRH	.30	.09
52 Vladimir Guerrero HRH	.50	.15
53 Andres Galarraga HRH	.30	.09
54 Rafael Palmeiro HRH	.30	.09
55 Juan Gonzalez HRH	.50	.15
56 Ken Griffey Jr. HRH	.75	.23
57 Barry Bonds HRH	.75	.23
58 Mo Vaughn HRH	.30	.09
59 N.Garciaparra HRH	.75	.23
60 Tino Martinez HRH	.30	.09
61 Mark McGwire HRH	1.00	.30
62 Mark McGwire HRH	1.00	.30
63 Mark McGwire HRH	1.00	.30
64 Mark McGwire HRH	1.00	.30
65 Mark McGwire HRH	1.00	.30
66 Sammy Sosa HRH	.75	.23
67 Mark McGwire HRH	1.00	.30
68 Mark McGwire HRH	1.00	.30
69 Mark McGwire HRH	1.00	.30
70 Mark McGwire HRH	1.00	.30
71 Mark McGwire HRH	1.00	.30
72 Scott Brosius HRH	.30	.09
73 Tony Gwynn HRH	.50	.15
74 Chipper Jones HRH	.50	.15
75 Jeff Bagwell HRH	.30	.09
76 Moises Alou HRH	.30	.09
77 Manny Ramirez HRH	.30	.09
78 Carlos Delgado HRH	.30	.09
79 Kerry Wood HRH	.50	.15
80 Ken Griffey Jr. HRH	.75	.23
81 Cal Ripken HRH	1.25	.35
82 Alex Rodriguez HRH	.75	.23
83 Barry Bonds HRH	.75	.23
84 Ken Griffey Jr. HRH	.75	.23
85 Travis Lee HRH	.30	.09
86 George Lombard HRH	.30	.09
87 Michael Barrett HRH	.30	.09
88 Jeremy Giambi HRH	.30	.09
89 Troy Glaus HRH	.30	.09
90 J.D. Drew HRH	.30	.09

1999 Upper Deck Challengers for 70 Challengers Edition

Randomly inserted in packs, this 90-card set is parallel to the base set. Only 600 serial-numbered sets were produced.

Nm-Mt Ex-Mt
*STARS: 5X TO 12X BASIC CARDS

1999 Upper Deck Challengers for 70 Challengers Inserts

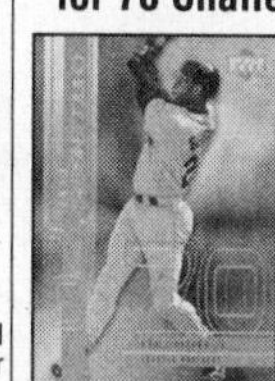
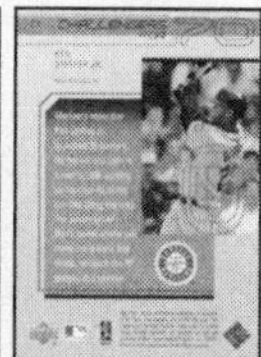

Inserted one per pack, this 30-card set features color photos of players trying for McGwire's single season Home Run record.

	Nm-Mt	Ex-Mt
COMPLETE SET (30)	25.00	7.50
*PARALLEL: 20X TO 50X BASIC CHALL.INS.		
PARALLEL: RANDOM INSERTS IN PACKS		
PARALLEL PRINT RUN 70 SERIAL #'d SETS		
C1 Mark McGwire	2.00	.60
C2 Sammy Sosa	1.25	.35
C3 Ken Griffey Jr.	1.25	.35
C4 Alex Rodriguez	1.25	.35
C5 Albert Belle	.30	.09
C6 Mo Vaughn	.30	.09
C7 Mike Piazza	1.25	.35
C8 Frank Thomas	.75	.23
C9 Juan Gonzalez	.75	.23
C10 Barry Bonds	2.00	.60
C11 Rafael Palmeiro	.50	.15
C12 Nomar Garciaparra	1.25	.35
C13 Vladimir Guerrero	.75	.23
C14 Vinny Castilla	.30	.09
C15 Chipper Jones	.75	.23
C16 Jeff Bagwell	.50	.15
C17 Moises Alou	.30	.09
C18 Tony Clark	.30	.09
C19 Jim Thome	.75	.23
C20 Tino Martinez	.50	.15
C21 Greg Vaughn	.30	.09
C22 Manny Ramirez	.30	.09
C23 Darin Erstad	.30	.09
C24 Ken Caminiti	.30	.09
C25 Ivan Rodriguez	.75	.23
C26 Andruw Jones	.30	.09
C27 Travis Lee	.30	.09
C28 Scott Rolen	.50	.15
C29 Ben Grieve	.30	.09
C30 J.D. Drew	.30	.09

1999 Upper Deck Challengers for 70 Longball Legends

Randomly inserted in packs at the rate of one in 39, this 30-card set features color photos of top hitters in the game printed on Light F/X cards.

Nm-Mt Ex-Mt
COMPLETE SET (30) 250.00 75.00
L1 Ken Griffey Jr. 12.00 3.60
L2 Mark McGwire 20.00 6.00
L3 Sammy Sosa 12.00 3.60
L4 Cal Ripken 25.00 7.50
L5 Barry Bonds 20.00 6.00
L6 Larry Walker 5.00 1.50
L7 Fred McGriff 5.00 1.50
L8 Alex Rodriguez 12.00 3.60
L9 Frank Thomas 8.00 2.40
L10 Juan Gonzalez 8.00 2.40
L11 Jeff Bagwell 5.00 1.50
L12 Mo Vaughn 3.00 .90
L13 Albert Belle 3.00 .90
L14 Mike Piazza 12.00 3.60
L15 Vladimir Guerrero 8.00 2.40
L16 Chipper Jones 8.00 2.40
L17 Ken Caminiti 3.00 .90
L18 Rafael Palmeiro 5.00 1.50
L19 Nomar Garciaparra 12.00 3.60
L20 Jim Thome 8.00 2.40
L21 Edgar Martinez 5.00 1.50
L22 Ivan Rodriguez 8.00 2.40
L23 Andres Galarraga 3.00 .90
L24 Scott Rolen 5.00 1.50
L25 Darin Erstad 3.00 .90
L26 Moises Alou 3.00 .90
L27 J.D. Drew 3.00 .90
L28 Andruw Jones 3.00 .90
L29 Manny Ramirez 3.00 .90
L30 Tino Martinez 5.00 1.50

1999 Upper Deck Challengers for 70 Mark on History

Randomly inserted in packs at the rate of one in five, this 25-card set features photos of Mark McGwire's most memorable Home Runs during the celebrated chase for history. A limited parallel set was also produced and sequentially numbered to 70.

Nm-Mt Ex-Mt
COMPLETE SET (25) 100.00 30.00
COMMON (M1-M25) 4.00 1.20
COMMON PAR. (M1-M25) 80.00 24.00
*PARALLEL HR 70: 6X TO 15X BASIC MARK
PARALLEL: RANDOM INSERTS IN PACKS
PARALLEL PRINT RUN 70 SERIAL #'d SETS

1999 Upper Deck Challengers for 70 Swinging for the Fences

Randomly inserted in packs at the rate of one in 19, this 15-card set features color photos of top Home Run hitters printed on futuristic-styled cards.

Nm-Mt Ex-Mt
COMPLETE SET (15) 60.00 18.00
S1 Ken Griffey Jr. 6.00 1.80
S2 Mark McGwire 10.00 3.00
S3 Sammy Sosa 6.00 1.80
S4 Alex Rodriguez 6.00 1.80
S5 Nomar Garciaparra 6.00 1.80
S6 J.D. Drew 1.50 .45
S7 Vladimir Guerrero 4.00 1.20
S8 Ben Grieve 1.50 .45
S9 Chipper Jones 4.00 1.20
S10 Gabe Kapler 1.50 .45
S11 Travis Lee 1.50 .45
S12 Todd Helton 2.50 .75
S13 Juan Gonzalez 4.00 1.20
S14 Mike Piazza 6.00 1.80
S15 Mo Vaughn 1.50 .45

1999 Upper Deck Challengers for 70 Swinging for the Fences Autograph

Randomly inserted in packs, this six-card set features autographed versions of some of the regular Swinging for the Fences insert cards. Only 2700 total cards were signed but not all players signed in equal quantities. Please note, a redemption card was seeded into packs for Alex Rodriguez.

Nm-Mt Ex-Mt
AR Alex Rodriguez 120.00 36.00
GK Gabe Kapler 15.00 4.50
JR Ken Griffey Jr. 150.00 45.00
TH Todd Helton 25.00 7.50
TL Travis Lee 15.00 4.50
VG Vladimir Guerrero 40.00 12.00

2003 Upper Deck Classic Portraits

This 232 card set was released in October, 2003. The set was issued in five card packs with an $5 SRP and the packs were 18 to a box with 12 boxes to a case. Each unopened box also included a special "bust." Cards numbered 1 through 100 feature veteran players. Cards numbered 101 through 190 feature 2003 rookies. Cards numbered 101 through 145 were issued at stated odds of one in four while cards numbered 146 through 190 were issued to a stated print run of 2003 serial numbered sets and were issued at a stated rate of three per box. Cards numbered 191 through 232 was a subset called Baseball Royalty and these cards were issued at a stated rate of two per box and were issued to a stated print run of 1200 serial numbered sets.

MINT NRMT
COMP.SET w/o SP's (100) 25.00 11.00
COMMON CARD (1-100) .40 .18
COMMON CARD (101-145) 3.00 1.35
COMMON RC (101-145) 3.00 1.35
COMMON CARD (146-190) 5.00 2.20
COMMON RC (146-190) 5.00 2.20
COMMON ACTIVE (191-232) 8.00 3.60
COMMON RETIRED (191-232) 8.00 3.60
191-232 STATED ODDS 2 PER BOX
191-232 PRINT RUN 1200 SERIAL #'d SETS
1 Ken Griffey Jr. 1.50 .70
2 Randy Johnson 1.00 .45
3 Rafael Furcal .40 .18
4 Omar Vizquel .40 .18
5 Shawn Green .40 .18
6 Roy Oswalt .40 .18
7 Hideo Nomo 1.00 .45
8 Jason Giambi 1.00 .45
9 Barry Bonds 2.50 1.10
10 Mike Piazza 1.50 .70
11 Ichiro Suzuki 1.50 .70
12 Carlos Delgado .40 .18
13 Preston Wilson .40 .18
14 Lance Berkman .40 .18
15 Magglio Ordonez .40 .18
16 Kerry Wood 1.00 .45
17 Ivan Rodriguez 1.00 .45
18 Chipper Jones 1.00 .45
19 Adam Dunn .40 .18
20 C.C. Sabathia .40 .18
21 Mike MacDougal .40 .18
22 Torii Hunter .40 .18
23 Jim Thome 1.00 .45
24 Hank Blalock .60 .25
25 Johnny Damon .40 .18
26 Troy Glaus .60 .25
27 Manny Ramirez .40 .18
28 Mark Prior 2.00 .90
29 Brent Mayne .40 .18
30 Derek Jeter 2.50 1.10
31 Tim Hudson .40 .18
32 Mike Cameron .40 .18
33 Mark Teixeira .60 .25
34 Shannon Stewart .40 .18
35 Tim Salmon .60 .25
36 Luis Gonzalez .40 .18
37 Jason Johnson .40 .18
38 Shea Hillenbrand .40 .18
39 Bartolo Colon .40 .18
40 Austin Kearns .40 .18
41 Vladimir Guerrero 1.00 .45
42 Tom Glavine .60 .25
43 Andres Galarraga .40 .18
44 Kazuhiro Sasaki .40 .18
45 Juan Gonzalez 1.00 .45
46 Vernon Wells .40 .18
47 Jeff Bagwell .60 .25
48 Mike Sweeney .40 .18
49 Carlos Beltran .40 .18
50 Dave Roberts .40 .18
51 Todd Helton .60 .25
52 Carlos Pena .40 .18
53 Darin Erstad .40 .18
54 Gary Sheffield .40 .18
55 Lyle Overbay .40 .18
56 Sammy Sosa 1.50 .70
57 Mike Mussina 1.00 .45
58 Matt Morris .40 .18
59 Roberto Alomar 1.00 .45
60 Larry Walker .60 .25
61 Jacque Jones .40 .18
62 Josh Beckett .60 .25
63 Richie Sexson .40 .18
64 Derek Lowe .40 .18
65 Pedro Martinez 1.00 .45
66 Moises Alou .40 .18
67 Craig Biggio .60 .25
68 Curt Schilling .60 .25
69 Jesse Foppert .40 .18
70 Nomar Garciaparra 1.50 .70
71 Barry Zito .60 .25
72 Alfonso Soriano .60 .25
73 Miguel Tejada .40 .18
74 Rafael Palmeiro .60 .25
75 Albert Pujols 2.00 .90
76 Mariano Rivera .60 .25
77 Bobby Abreu .40 .18
78 Alex Rodriguez 1.50 .70
79 Andruw Jones .40 .18
80 Frank Thomas 1.00 .45
81 Greg Maddux 1.50 .70
82 Jim Edmonds .40 .18
83 Bernie Williams .60 .25
84 Roger Clemens 2.00 .90
85 Eric Chavez .40 .18
86 Scott Rolen .60 .25
87 Jorge Posada .60 .25
88 Bret Boone .40 .18
89 Ben Sheets .40 .18
90 John Olerud .40 .18
91 J.D. Drew .40 .18
92 Aaron Boone .40 .18
93 Corey Koskie .40 .18
94 Sean Casey .40 .18
95 Jose Cruz Jr. .40 .18
96 Pat Burrell .40 .18
97 Jose Guillen .40 .18
98 Mark Mulder .40 .18
99 Garret Anderson .40 .18
100 Kazuhisa Ishii .40 .18
101 David Matranga SP RC 3.00 1.35
102 Colin Porter SP RC 3.00 1.35
103 Jason Gilfillan SP RC 3.00 1.35
104 Carlos Mendez SP RC 3.00 1.35
105 Jason Shiell SP RC 3.00 1.35
106 Kevin Tolar SP RC 3.00 1.35
107 Termel Sledge SP RC 4.00 1.80
108 Craig Brazell SP RC 4.00 1.80
109 Bernie Castro SP RC 3.00 1.35
110 Tim Olson SP RC 4.00 1.80
111 Kevin Ohme SP RC 3.00 1.35
112 Pedro Liriano SP 3.00 1.35
113 Joe Borowski SP 3.00 1.35
114 Edgar Gonzalez SP RC 3.00 1.35
115 Joe Thurston SP 3.00 1.35
116 Bobby Hill SP 3.00 1.35
117 Michel Hernandez SP RC 3.00 1.35
118 Arnie Munoz SP RC 3.00 1.35
119 David Sanders SP RC 3.00 1.35
120 Willie Eyre SP RC 3.00 1.35
121 Brent Hoard SP RC 3.00 1.35
122 Lew Ford SP RC 4.00 1.80
123 Beau Kemp SP RC 3.00 1.35
124 Jon Pridie SP RC 3.00 1.35
125 Mike Ryan SP RC 4.00 1.80
126 Richard Fischer SP RC 3.00 1.35
127 Luis Ayala SP RC 3.00 1.35
128 Mike Neu SP RC 3.00 1.35
129 Joe Valentine SP RC 3.00 1.35
130 Nate Bland SP RC 3.00 1.35
131 Shane Bazzell SP RC 3.00 1.35
132 Jason Roach SP RC 3.00 1.35
133 D.Markwell SP RC 3.00 1.35
134 Francisco Rosario SP RC 3.00 1.35
135 Guillermo Quiroz SP RC 6.00 2.70
136 Jerome Williams SP 3.00 1.35
137 Fernando Cabrera SP RC 3.00 1.35
138 Francisco Cruceta SP RC 3.00 1.35
139 Jhonny Peralta SP RC 3.00 1.35
140 Rett Johnson SP RC 4.00 1.80
141 Aaron Looper SP RC 3.00 1.35
142 Bobby Madritsch SP RC 3.00 1.35
143 Dan Haren SP RC 4.00 1.80
144 Jose Castillo SP 3.00 1.35
145 Chris Waters SP RC 3.00 1.35
146 Hideki Matsui MP RC 15.00 6.75
147 Jose Contreras MP RC 6.00 2.70
148 Felix Sanchez MP RC 5.00 2.20
149 Jon Leicester MP RC 5.00 2.20
150 Todd Wellemeyer MP RC 5.00 2.20
151 Matt Bruback MP RC 5.00 2.20
152 Chris Capuano MP RC 5.00 2.20
153 Oscar Villarreal MP RC 5.00 2.20
154 Matt Kata MP RC 5.00 2.20
155 Robby Hammock MP RC 5.00 2.20
156 Gerald Laird MP 5.00 2.20
157 Brandon Webb MP RC 8.00 3.60
158 Tommy Whiteman MP 5.00 2.20
159 Andrew Brown MP RC 5.00 2.20
160 Alfredo Gonzalez MP RC 5.00 2.20
161 Carlos Rivera MP 5.00 2.20
162 Rick Roberts MP RC 5.00 2.20
163 Dontrelle Willis MP 8.00 3.60
164 Josh Willingham MP RC 6.00 2.70
165 Prentice Redman MP RC 5.00 2.20
166 Jeff Duncan MP RC 5.00 2.20
167 Jose Reyes MP 8.00 3.60
168 Jeremy Griffiths MP RC 5.00 2.20
169 Phil Seibel MP RC 5.00 2.20
170 Heath Bell MP RC 5.00 2.20
171 Anthony Ferrari MP RC 5.00 2.20
172 Mike Nicolas MP RC 5.00 2.20
173 Cory Stewart MP RC 5.00 2.20
174 Miguel Ojeda MP RC 5.00 2.20
175 Rickie Weeks MP RC UER 10.00 4.50
Card back statistics is that of a pitcher
176 Delmon Young MP RC 15.00 6.75
177 Tommy Phelps MP 5.00 2.20
178 Josh Hall MP RC 5.00 2.20
179 Ryan Cameron MP RC 5.00 2.20
180 Garrett Atkins MP 5.00 2.20
181 Clint Barmes MP RC 5.00 2.20
182 Mike Hessman MP RC 5.00 2.20
183 Chin-Hui Tsao MP 5.00 2.20
184 Rocco Baldelli MP 8.00 3.60
185 Bo Hart MP RC 6.00 2.70
186 Wilfredo Ledezma MP RC 5.00 2.20
187 Miguel Cabrera MP 8.00 3.60
188 Ian Ferguson MP RC 5.00 2.20
189 Mi.Nakamura MP RC 5.00 2.20
190 Al.Machado MP RC 5.00 2.20
191 Mickey Mantle BBR 20.00 9.00
192 Ted Williams BBR 15.00 6.75
193 Mark Prior BBR 10.00 4.50
194 Stan Musial BBR 8.00 3.60
195 Phil Rizzuto BBR 8.00 3.60
196 Nolan Ryan BBR 12.00 5.50
197 Tom Seaver BBR 8.00 3.60
198 Robin Yount BBR 8.00 3.60
199 Yogi Berra BBR 8.00 3.60
200 Ernie Banks BBR 8.00 3.60
201 Willie McCovey BBR 8.00 3.60
202 Ralph Kiner BBR 8.00 3.60
203 Ken Griffey Jr. BBR 8.00 3.60
204 Sammy Sosa BBR 8.00 3.60
205 Derek Jeter BBR 12.00 5.50
206 Nomar Garciaparra BBR 8.00 3.60
207 Alex Rodriguez BBR 8.00 3.60
208 Ichiro Suzuki BBR 8.00 3.60
209 Mike Piazza BBR 8.00 3.60
210 Jackie Robinson BBR 10.00 4.50
211 Roberto Clemente BBR 15.00 6.75
212 Babe Ruth BBR 15.00 6.75
213 Duke Snider BBR 8.00 3.60
214 Greg Maddux BBR 8.00 3.60
215 Juan Marichal BBR 8.00 3.60
216 Joe Morgan BBR 8.00 3.60
217 Rollie Fingers BBR 8.00 3.60
218 Warren Spahn BBR 8.00 3.60
219 Pee Wee Reese BBR 8.00 3.60
220 Troy Glaus BBR 8.00 3.60
221 Jason Giambi BBR 8.00 3.60
222 Roger Clemens BBR 10.00 4.50
223 Pedro Martinez BBR 8.00 3.60
224 Chipper Jones BBR 8.00 3.60
225 Randy Johnson BBR 8.00 3.60
226 Jim Thome BBR 8.00 3.60
227 Barry Bonds BBR 12.00 5.50
228 Hideo Nomo BBR 8.00 3.60
229 Whitey Ford BBR 8.00 3.60
230 Bob Gibson BBR 8.00 3.60
231 Alfonso Soriano BBR 8.00 3.60
232 Richie Ashburn BBR 8.00 3.60

2003 Upper Deck Classic Portraits Gold

Please note that this parallel set does not include the Baseball Royalty subset.

MINT NRMT
RANDOM INSERTS IN PACKS
STATED PRINT RUN 25 SERIAL #'d SETS
NO PRICING DUE TO SCARCITY

2003 Upper Deck Classic Portraits Busts Bronze

MINT NRMT
STATED ODDS 1:2 BOXES
SP PRINT RUNS PROVIDED BY UD
SP'S ARE NOT SERIAL-NUMBERED
A IS AWAY UNIFORM, H IS HOME UNIFORM
AWAY ='s CITY NAME ACROSS BUST
HOME ='s TEAM NAME/LOGO ACROSS BUST
BG-H Bob Gibson H 30.00 13.50
BRS-H Babe Ruth Sox H/300 50.00 22.00
BRY-A Babe Ruth Yanks A 60.00 27.00
BRY-H Babe Ruth Yanks H 60.00 27.00
DS-A Duke Snider A 30.00 13.50
DS-H Duke Snider H 30.00 13.50
HM-H Hideki Matsui H 40.00 18.00
IS-H Ichiro Suzuki H/300 40.00 18.00
JG-H Jason Giambi H 30.00 13.50
KG-H Ken Griffey Jr. H/300 40.00 18.00
MM-A Mickey Mantle A 80.00 36.00
MM-H Mickey Mantle H 80.00 36.00
NG-H Nomar Garciaparra H 40.00 18.00
NRA-H Nolan Ryan Astros H/300 50.00 22.00
NRM-A Nolan Ryan Mets A 50.00 22.00
NRM-H Nolan Ryan Mets H 50.00 22.00
RC-H Roberto Clemente H 80.00 36.00
SM-H Stan Musial H 40.00 18.00
SS-H Sammy Sosa H/300 40.00 18.00
TSM-A Tom Seaver Mets A 30.00 13.50
TSM-H Tom Seaver Mets H 30.00 13.50
TSR-A Tom Seaver Reds A/300 30.00 13.50
TSR-H Tom Seaver Reds H 30.00 13.50
TW-A Ted Williams A 60.00 27.00
TW-H Ted Williams H 60.00 27.00
YB-A Yogi Berra A 30.00 13.50
YB-H Yogi Berra H 30.00 13.50

2003 Upper Deck Classic Portraits Busts Marble

MINT NRMT
STATED ODDS 1:4 BOXES
PRINT RUNS B/WN 100-250 COPIES PER
PRINT RUNS PROVIDED BY UPPER DECK
BUSTS ARE NOT SERIAL-NUMBERED
BG-H Bob Gibson H/250 40.00 18.00
BRS-H Babe Ruth Sox H/250 60.00 27.00
BRY-A Babe Ruth Yanks A/125 100.00 45.00
BRY-H Babe Ruth Yanks H/250 80.00 36.00
DS-A Duke Snider A/100 50.00 22.00
DS-H Duke Snider H/250 40.00 18.00
HM-H Hideki Matsui H/250 50.00 22.00
IS-H Ichiro Suzuki H/250 50.00 22.00
JG-H Jason Giambi H/250 40.00 18.00
KG-H Ken Griffey Jr. H/250 50.00 22.00
MM-A Mickey Mantle A/125 120.00 55.00
MM-H Mickey Mantle H/250 100.00 45.00
NG-H Nomar Garciaparra H/250 50.00 22.00
NRA-H Nolan Ryan Astros H/250 60.00 27.00
NRM-A Nolan Ryan Mets A/125 80.00 36.00
NRM-H Nolan Ryan Mets H/250 60.00 27.00
RC-H Roberto Clemente H/250 100.00 45.00
SM-H Stan Musial H/250 50.00 22.00
SS-H Sammy Sosa H/250 50.00 22.00
TSM-A Tom Seaver Mets A/125 50.00 22.00
TSM-H Tom Seaver Mets H/250 40.00 18.00
TSR-A Tom Seaver Reds A/125 50.00 22.00
TSR-H Tom Seaver Reds H/250 40.00 18.00
TW-A Ted Williams A/125 100.00 45.00
TW-H Ted Williams H/250 80.00 36.00
YB-A Yogi Berra A/125 50.00 22.00
YB-H Yogi Berra H/250 40.00 18.00

2003 Upper Deck Classic Portraits Busts Pewter

MINT NRMT
STATED ODDS 1:6 BOXES
PRINT RUNS B/WN 75-100 COPIES PER
PRINT RUNS PROVIDED BY UPPER DECK
BUSTS ARE NOT SERIAL-NUMBERED
BG-H Bob Gibson H/100 50.00 22.00
BRS-H Babe Ruth Sox H/100 100.00 45.00
BRY-A Babe Ruth Yanks A/75 120.00 55.00
BRY-H Babe Ruth Yanks H/100 120.00 55.00
DS-A Duke Snider A/75 50.00 22.00
DS-H Duke Snider H/100 50.00 22.00
HM-H Hideki Matsui H/100 80.00 36.00
IS-H Ichiro Suzuki H/100 80.00 36.00
JG-H Jason Giambi H/100 50.00 22.00
KG-H Ken Griffey Jr. H/100 80.00 36.00
MM-A Mickey Mantle A/75 200.00 90.00
MM-H Mickey Mantle H/100 200.00 90.00
NG-H Nomar Garciaparra H/100 80.00 36.00
NRA-H Nolan Ryan Astros H/100 100.00 45.00
NRM-A Nolan Ryan Mets A/75 100.00 45.00
NRM-H Nolan Ryan Mets H/100 100.00 45.00
RC-H Roberto Clemente H/100 150.00 70.00
SM-H Stan Musial H/100 80.00 36.00
SS-H Sammy Sosa H/100 80.00 36.00
TSM-A Tom Seaver Mets A/75 50.00 22.00
TSM-H Tom Seaver Mets H/100 50.00 22.00
TSR-A Tom Seaver Reds A/100 50.00 22.00
TSR-H Tom Seaver Reds H/75 50.00 22.00
TW-A Ted Williams A/75 120.00 55.00
TW-H Ted Williams H/100 100.00 45.00
YB-A Yogi Berra A/75 50.00 22.00
YB-H Yogi Berra H/100 50.00 22.00

2003 Upper Deck Classic Portraits Busts Pewter Wood

MINT NRMT
RANDOM INSERTS IN BOXES
PRINT RUNS B/WN 10-11 COPIES PER
PRINT RUNS PROVIDED BY UPPER DECK
BUSTS ARE NOT SERIAL-NUMBERED
BG-H Bob Gibson H/11
BRS-H Babe Ruth Sox H/11
BRY-H Babe Ruth Yanks H/11
DS-H Duke Snider H/11
HM-H Hideki Matsui H/11
IS-H Ichiro Suzuki H/11
JG-H Jason Giambi H/11
KG-H Ken Griffey Jr. H/11
MM-H Mickey Mantle H/11
NG-H Nomar Garciaparra H/11
NRA-H Nolan Ryan Astros H/11
NRM-H Nolan Ryan Mets H/11
RC-H Roberto Clemente H/11
SM-H Stan Musial H/11
SS-H Sammy Sosa H/11
TSM-H Tom Seaver Mets H/11
TSR-H Tom Seaver Reds H/11
TW-H Ted Williams H/10
YB-H Yogi Berra H/11

2003 Upper Deck Classic Portraits Busts Autograph Bronze

MINT NRMT
OVERALL AUTO ODDS 1:12 BOXES
SP PRINT RUNS B/WN 1-106 COPIES PER
SP PRINT RUNS PROVIDED BY UPPER DECK
SP'S ARE NOT SERIAL-NUMBERED
NO PRICING ON QTY OF 14 OR LESS.
A IS AWAY UNIFORM, H IS HOME UNIFORM
AWAY ='s CITY NAME ACROSS BUST
HOME ='s TEAM NAME/LOGO ACROSS BUST
BG-H Bob Gibson H 80.00 36.00
BRY-H Babe Ruth Yanks H/1
DS-A Duke Snider A/5
DS-H Duke Snider H 120.00 55.00
HM-H Hideki Matsui H 200.00 90.00
IS-H Ichiro Suzuki H/62 300.00 135.00
KG-H Ken Griffey Jr. H 120.00 55.00
MM-A Mickey Mantle A/1
MM-H Mickey Mantle H/2
NG-H Nomar Garciaparra H/106 200.00 90.00
NRA-H Nolan Ryan Astros H/14
NRM-A Nolan Ryan Mets A/1
NRM-H Nolan Ryan Mets H/14
RC-H Roberto Clemente H/1
SM-H Stan Musial H/62 200.00 90.00
TSM-A Tom Seaver Mets A/1
TSM-H Tom Seaver Mets H/14
TSR-A Tom Seaver Reds A/1
TSR-H Tom Seaver Reds H/14
TW-A Ted Williams A/1
TW-H Ted Williams H/4
YB-A Yogi Berra A/5
YB-H Yogi Berra H 120.00 55.00

2003 Upper Deck Classic Portraits Busts Autograph Marble

MINT NRMT
OVERALL AUTO ODDS 1:12 BOXES
PRINT RUNS B/WN 1-26 COPIES PER
PRINT RUNS PROVIDED BY UPPER DECK

BUSTS ARE NOT SERIAL-NUMBERED
NO PRICING DUE TO SCARCITY.........
A IS AWAY UNIFORM, H IS HOME UNIFORM
AWAY ='s CITY NAME ACROSS BUST
HOME ='s TEAM NAME/LOGO ACROSS BUST
BG-H Bob Gibson H/25 ....
BRY-H Babe Ruth Yanks H/1..............
DS-A Duke Snider A/1.....................
DS-H Duke Snider H/25....................
HM-H Hideki Matsui H/25 ....
IS-H Ichiro Suzuki H/25...................
KG-H Ken Griffey Jr. H/24 ....
MM-A Mickey Mantle A/1 ....
MM-H Mickey Mantle H/1 ....
NG-H Nomar Garciaparra H/26............
NRA-H Nolan Ryan Astros H/23...........
NRM-H Nolan Ryan Mets H/23.............
RC-H Roberto Clemente H/1 ....
SM-H Stan Musial H/25.....................
TSM-H Tom Seaver Mets H/25..............
TSR-H Tom Seaver Reds H/25 ....
TW-A Ted Williams A/1 ....
TW-H Ted Williams H/1......................
YB-A Yogi Berra A/1.........................
YB-H Yogi Berra H/25 ....

2003 Upper Deck Classic Portraits Busts Autograph Pewter

MINT NRMT
OVERALL AUTO ODDS 1:12 BOXES....
PRINT RUNS B/WN 1-17 COPIES PER
PRINT RUNS PROVIDED BY UPPER DECK
BUSTS ARE NOT SERIAL-NUMBERED
NO PRICING DUE TO SCARCITY.........
A IS AWAY UNIFORM, H IS HOME UNIFORM
AWAY ='s CITY NAME ACROSS BUST
HOME ='s TEAM NAME/LOGO ACROSS BUST
BG-H Bob Gibson H/10 ....
BRY-H Babe Ruth Yanks H/1...............
DS-A Duke Snider A/1.......................
DS-H Duke Snider H/10......................
HM-H Hideki Matsui H/17 ....
IS-H Ichiro Suzuki H/13.....................
KG-H Ken Griffey Jr. H/15 ....
MM-A Mickey Mantle A/1 ....
MM-H Mickey Mantle H/1 ....
NG-H Nomar Garciaparra H/17............
NRA-H Nolan Ryan Astros H/10...........
NRM-H Nolan Ryan Mets H/10.............
RC-H Roberto Clemente H/1 ....
SM-H Stan Musial H/13......................
TSM-H Tom Seaver Mets H/10..............
TSR-H Tom Seaver Reds H/10..............
TW-A Ted Williams A/1 ....
TW-H Ted Williams H/1.......................
YB-A Yogi Berra A/1..........................
YB-H Yogi Berra H/10 ....

2003 Upper Deck Classic Portraits Busts Autograph Pewter Wood

MINT NRMT
OVERALL AUTO ODDS 1:12 BOXES....
PRINT RUNS B/WN 1-3 COPIES PER..
PRINT RUNS PROVIDED BY UPPER DECK
BUSTS ARE NOT SERIAL-NUMBERED
NO PRICING DUE TO SCARCITY.........
A IS AWAY UNIFORM...........................
AWAY ='s CITY NAME ACROSS BUST
KG-A Ken Griffey Jr. A/3.....................
NG-A Nomar Garciaparra A/1...............
NRM-A Nolan Ryan Mets H/2...............
YB-A Yogi Berra A/2............................

2003 Upper Deck Classic Portraits Signs of Success

MINT NRMT
PRINT RUNS B/WN 9-299 COPIES PER
NO PRICING ON QTY OF 22 OR LESS.
GOLD PRINT RUN 25 SERIAL #'d SETS
NO GOLD PRICING DUE TO SCARCITY
RANDOM INSERTS IN PACKS ....
AG Alex Graman/215................. 10.00 4.50
AH Andy Van Hekken/299 .... 10.00 4.50
BC Brad Cresse/121 .... 10.00 4.50
BD Ben Diggins/299................. 10.00 4.50

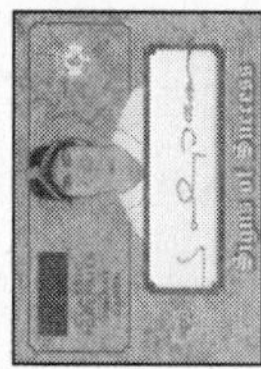

BH Ben Howard/299.................. 10.00 4.50
BP Brandon Phillips/131 .... 10.00 4.50
BR Brandon Claussen/121 .... 15.00 6.75
CC C.C. Sabathia/106 .... 15.00 6.75
CM Corwin Malone/103.............. 10.00 4.50
DB Dewon Brazelton/299 .... 10.00 4.50
DH Drew Henson/246................ 25.00 11.00
DK David Kelton/102................ 10.00 4.50
HI Hansel Izquierdo/299............ 10.00 4.50
JB John Buck/98 .... 10.00 4.50
JD Johnny Damon/297.............. 15.00 6.75
JE Jerome Williams/103............ 15.00 6.75
JI Jay Gibbons/22 ....
JJ Jimmy Journell/98................ 10.00 4.50
JU Justin Wayne/299 .... 10.00 4.50
JW Jayson Werth/299............... 10.00 4.50
KG Ken Griffey Jr./299 .... 120.00 55.00
KL Kenny Lofton/296 .... 15.00 6.75
MB Mark Buehrle/220 .... 15.00 6.75
MI Milton Bradley/220.............. 15.00 6.75
MT Mark Teixeira/280 .... 25.00 11.00
SR0 Scott Rolen/9.....................
TG Tony Gwynn/49................ 100.00 45.00
TH Matt Thornton/298.............. 10.00 4.50

2003 Upper Deck Classic Portraits Stitches

MINT NRMT
STATED PRINT RUN 299 SERIAL #'d SETS
GOLD PRINT RUN 25 SERIAL #'d SETS
NO GOLD PRICING DUE TO SCARCITY
RANDOM INSERTS IN PACKS ....
AD Adam Dunn 8.00 3.60
AJ Andruw Jones 8.00 3.60
AL Albert Pujols 20.00 9.00
AP Andy Pettitte 10.00 4.50
AR Alex Rodriguez 15.00 6.75
AS Alfonso Soriano 10.00 4.50
CJ Chipper Jones 10.00 4.50
CP Corey Patterson 8.00 3.60
CS Curt Schilling 10.00 4.50
DW Dontrelle Willis 10.00 4.50
GM Greg Maddux..................... 10.00 4.50
GS Gary Sheffield 8.00 3.60
HB Hank Blalock...................... 10.00 4.50
HC Hee Seop Choi 8.00 3.60
HM Hideki Matsui.................... 50.00 22.00
HN Hideo Nomo 15.00 6.75
IR Ivan Rodriguez.................... 10.00 4.50
IS Ichiro Suzuki...................... 25.00 11.00
JB Jeff Bagwell 10.00 4.50
JD J.D. Drew 8.00 3.60
JE Jim Edmonds 8.00 3.60
JG Jason Giambi 10.00 4.50
JK Jeff Kent............................ 8.00 3.60
JT Jim Thome 10.00 4.50
KG Ken Griffey Jr.................... 15.00 6.75
KW Kerry Wood 10.00 4.50
MI Mike Piazza 10.00 4.50
ML Mike Lowell........................ 8.00 3.60
MM Matt Morris 8.00 3.60
MO Maggio Ordonez 8.00 3.60
MP Mark Prior......................... 20.00 9.00
PM Pedro Martinez.................. 10.00 4.50
RB Rocco Baldelli.................... 15.00 6.75
RC Roger Clemens 15.00 6.75
RF Rafael Furcal 8.00 3.60
RJ Randy Johnson 10.00 4.50
RO Roy Oswalt.......................... 8.00 3.60
SG Shawn Green 8.00 3.60
SS Sammy Sosa 15.00 6.75
TG Troy Glaus 10.00 4.50
TH Torii Hunter......................... 8.00 3.60
VG Vladimir Guerrero 10.00 4.50

2003 Upper Deck Classic Portraits Stitches Patch

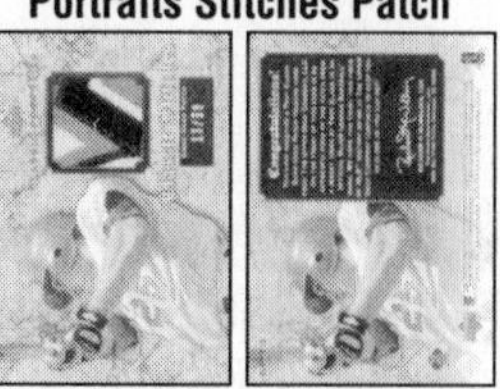

MINT NRMT
STATED PRINT RUN 99 SERIAL #'d SETS
PATCH GOLD PRINT 10 SERIAL #'d SETS
NO PATCH GOLD PRICING DUE TO SCARCITY
RANDOM INSERTS IN PACKS ....
AD Adam Dunn 25.00 11.00
AJ Andruw Jones 25.00 11.00
AL Albert Pujols 50.00 22.00
AP Andy Pettitte 30.00 13.50
AR Alex Rodriguez 60.00 27.00
AS Alfonso Soriano 30.00 13.50
CJ Chipper Jones 30.00 13.50
CP Corey Patterson 25.00 11.00
CS Curt Schilling 30.00 13.50
DW Dontrelle Willis 30.00 13.50
GM Greg Maddux..................... 40.00 18.00
GS Gary Sheffield 25.00 11.00
HB Hank Blalock...................... 30.00 13.50
HC Hee Seop Choi 25.00 11.00
HM Hideki Matsui.................. 150.00 70.00
HN Hideo Nomo 80.00 36.00
IR Ivan Rodriguez.................... 30.00 13.50
IS Ichiro Suzuki.................... 150.00 70.00
JB Jeff Bagwell 30.00 13.50
JD J.D. Drew 25.00 11.00
JE Jim Edmonds 25.00 11.00
JG Jason Giambi 30.00 13.50
JK Jeff Kent 25.00 11.00
JT Jim Thome 30.00 13.50
KG Ken Griffey Jr.................... 80.00 36.00
KW Kerry Wood 30.00 13.50
MI Mike Piazza 50.00 22.00
ML Mike Lowell....................... 25.00 11.00
MM Matt Morris 25.00 11.00
MO Magglio Ordonez 25.00 11.00
MP Mark Prior......................... 50.00 22.00
PM Pedro Martinez.................. 30.00 13.50
RB Rocco Baldelli.................... 40.00 18.00
RC Roger Clemens 50.00 22.00
RF Rafael Furcal 25.00 11.00
RJ Randy Johnson 30.00 13.50
RO Roy Oswalt........................ 25.00 11.00
SG Shawn Green 25.00 11.00
SS Sammy Sosa 40.00 18.00
TG Troy Glaus 30.00 13.50
TH Torii Hunter....................... 25.00 11.00
VG Vladimir Guerrero 30.00 13.50

2001 Upper Deck Decade 1970's

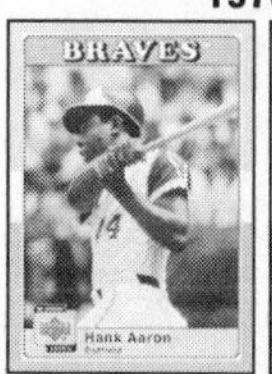

This 180 card set was issued in five card packs with an SRP of $2.99 per pack. Some topical subsets included: Rookie Flashback (91-110), Decade Dateline (111-140), Award Winners (141-170) and World Series Highlights (171-180).

Nm-Mt Ex-Mt
COMPLETE SET (180).............. 40.00 12.00
1 Nolan Ryan............................ 4.00 1.20
2 Don Baylor .... .60 .18
3 Bobby Grich .... .60 .18
4 Reggie Jackson...................... 1.00 .30
5 Catfish Hunter .... 1.00 .30
6 Gene Tenace............................ .60 .18
7 Rollie Fingers .... .60 .18
8 Sal Bando................................ .60 .18
9 Bert Campaneris...................... .60 .18
10 John Mayberry .... .40 .12
11 Rico Carty .... .40 .12
12 Gaylord Perry .... .60 .18
13 Andre Thornton .... .40 .12
14 Buddy Bell .... .60 .18
15 Dennis Eckersley.................... .60 .18
16 Ruppert Jones......................... .40 .12
17 Brooks Robinson.................. 1.50 .45
18 Tommy Davis .... .40 .12
19 Eddie Murray........................ 1.50 .45
20 Boog Powell .... 1.00 .30
21 Al Oliver................................ .60 .18
22 Jeff Burroughs .... .40 .12
23 Mike Hargrove .... .60 .18
24 Dwight Evans .... .60 .18
25 Fred Lynn .... .60 .18
26 Rico Petrocelli .... .40 .12
27 Carlton Fisk .... 1.00 .30
28 Luis Aparicio .... .60 .18
29 Amos Otis .... .40 .12
30 Hal McRae............................. .60 .18
31 Jason Thompson.................... .40 .12
32 Al Kaline .... 1.50 .45
33 Jim Perry............................... .60 .18
34 Bert Blyleven .... .60 .18
35 Harmon Killebrew................. 1.50 .45
36 Wilbur Wood.......................... .60 .18
37 Jim Kaat................................ .60 .18
38 Ron Guidry .... .60 .18
39 Thurman Munson................. 2.00 .60
40 Graig Nettles .... .60 .18
41 Bobby Murcer .... .60 .18
42 Chris Chambliss .... .60 .18
43 Roy White .... .40 .12
44 J.R. Richard .... .60 .18
45 Jose Cruz .... .60 .18
46 Hank Aaron .... 3.00 .90
47 Phil Niekro............................. .60 .18
48 Bob Horner............................ .40 .12
49 Darrell Evans .... .60 .18
50 Gorman Thomas .... .60 .18
51 Don Money............................ .40 .12
52 Robin Yount .... 2.50 .75
53 Joe Torre............................... .60 .18
54 Tim McCarver......................... .60 .18
55 Lou Brock............................ 1.00 .30
56 Keith Hernandez .... 1.00 .30
57 Bill Madlock........................... .60 .18
58 Ron Santo .... 1.00 .30
59 Billy Williams......................... .60 .18
60 Ferguson Jenkins .... .60 .18
61 Steve Garvey .... .60 .18
62 Bill Russell UER .... .60 .18
Trivia question has several wrong answers
63 Maury Wills .... .60 .18
64 Ron Cey................................. .60 .18
65 Manny Mota .... .40 .12
66 Ron Fairly .... .40 .12
67 Steve Rogers......................... .40 .12
68 Gary Carter......................... 1.00 .30
69 Andre Dawson........................ .60 .18
70 Bobby Bonds.......................... .60 .18
71 Jack Clark............................. .60 .18
72 Willie McCovey...................... .60 .18
73 Tom Seaver......................... 1.00 .30
74 Bud Harrelson .... .60 .18
75 Dave Kingman........................ .60 .18
76 Jerry Koosman....................... .60 .18
77 Jon Matlack .... .40 .12
78 Randy Jones .... .40 .12
79 Ozzie Smith .... 2.50 .75
80 Garry Maddox .... .40 .12
81 Mike Schmidt...................... 3.00 .90
82 Greg Luzinski .... .60 .18
83 Tug McGraw.......................... .60 .18
84 Willie Stargell .... 1.00 .30
85 Dave Parker........................... .60 .18
86 Roberto Clemente 4.00 1.20
87 Johnny Bench .... 1.50 .45
88 Joe Morgan .... .60 .18
89 George Foster......................... .60 .18
90 Ken Griffey Sr. .... .60 .18
91 Carlton Fisk RF .... 1.00 .30
92 Andre Dawson RF................... .60 .18
93 Fred Lynn RF .... .60 .18
94 Eddie Murray RF.................. 1.50 .45
95 Bob Horner RF .... .40 .12
96 Jon Matlack RF....................... .40 .12
97 Mike Hargrove RF................... .60 .18
98 Robin Yount RF.................... 2.50 .75
99 Mike Schmidt RF.................. 1.50 .45
100 Gary Carter RF...................... .60 .18
101 Ozzie Smith RF................... 1.50 .45
102 Paul Molitor RF .... 1.00 .30
103 Dennis Eckersley RF.............. .60 .18
104 Dale Murphy RF.................. 1.50 .45
105 Bert Blyleven RF .... .60 .18
106 Thurman Munson RF .... 2.00 .60
107 Dave Parker RF...................... .60 .18
108 Jack Clark RF .... .60 .18
109 Keith Hernandez RF............ 1.00 .30
110 Ron Cey RF .... .60 .18
111 Billy Williams DD................... .40 .12
112 Tom Seaver DD .... .60 .18
113 Reggie Jackson DD................ .60 .18
114 Bobby Bonds DD .... .40 .12
115 Willie Stargell DD .... .60 .18
116 Harmon Killebrew DD.......... 1.50 .45
117 Roberto Clemente DD.......... 2.00 .60
118 Wilbur Wood DD .... .40 .12
119 Billy Williams DD.................. .40 .12
120 Nolan Ryan DD.................... 2.00 .60
121 Ron Blomberg DD .... .40 .12
122 Hank Aaron DD.................... 1.50 .45
123 Lou Brock DD........................ .60 .18
124 Al Kaline DD UER .... 1.00 .30
Kaline got his 3,000 hit in 1974, not 1964
125 Brooks Robinson DD........... 1.00 .30
126 Bill Madlock DD..................... .40 .12
127 Rennie Stennett DD................ .40 .12
128 Carlton Fisk DD .... .60 .18
129 Chris Chambliss DD .... .40 .12
130 Ruppert Jones DD.................. .40 .12
131 Ron Fairly DD........................ .40 .12
132 George Foster DD.................. .40 .12
133 Reggie Jackson DD................ .60 .18
134 Ron Guidry DD .... .40 .12
135 Gaylord Perry DD .... .40 .12
136 Bucky Dent DD .... .40 .12
137 Dave Kingman DD .... .40 .12
138 Lou Brock DD........................ .60 .18
139 Thurman Munson DD........... 1.00 .30
140 Willie Stargell DD .... .60 .18
141 Johnny Bench AW............... 1.00 .30
142 Boog Powell AW .... .60 .18
143 Jim Perry AW......................... .40 .12
144 Joe Torre AW .... .40 .12
145 Chris Chambliss AW.............. .40 .12
146 Ferguson Jenkins AW .... .40 .12
147 Carlton Fisk AW .... .60 .18
148 Gaylord Perry AW.................. .60 .18
149 Johnny Bench AW............... 1.00 .30
150 Reggie Jackson AW .... .60 .18
151 Tom Seaver AW .... .60 .18
152 Thurman Munson AW .... 1.00 .30
153 Steve Garvey AW................... .40 .12
154 Catfish Hunter AW .... .60 .18
155 Mike Hargrove AW .... .40 .12
156 Joe Morgan AW .... .40 .12
157 Fred Lynn AW........................ .40 .12
158 Tom Seaver AW .... .60 .18
159 Thurman Munson AW .... 1.00 .30
160 Randy Jones AW.................... .40 .12
161 Joe Morgan AW .... .40 .12
162 George Foster AW .... .40 .12
163 Eddie Murray AW .... 1.00 .30
164 Andre Dawson AW................. .40 .12
165 Gaylord Perry AW.................. .40 .12
166 Ron Guidry AW .... .40 .12
167 Dave Parker AW .... .40 .12
168 Don Baylor AW...................... .40 .12
169 Bruce Sutter AW.................... .40 .12
170 Willie Stargell AW.................. .60 .18
171 Brooks Robinson WS.......... 1.00 .30
172 Roberto Clemente WS......... 2.00 .60
173 Gene Tenace WS .... .40 .12
174 Reggie Jackson WS .... .60 .18
175 Rollie Fingers WS .... .40 .12
176 Carlton Fisk WS .... .60 .18
177 Johnny Bench WS .... 1.00 .30
178 Reggie Jackson WS .... .60 .18
179 Bucky Dent WS .... .40 .12
180 Willie Stargell WS.................. .60 .18

2001 Upper Deck Decade 1970's Arms Race

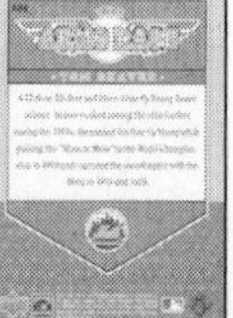

Issued at a rate of one in 14, these 10 cards pay homage to the great pitchers of yesteryear.

Nm-Mt Ex-Mt
COMPLETE SET (10)................. 25.00 7.50
AR1 Nolan Ryan......................... 8.00 2.40
AR2 Ferguson Jenkins .... 1.25 .35
AR3 Jim Hunter.......................... 2.00 .60
AR4 Tom Seaver .... 2.00 .60
AR5 Randy Jones .... 1.25 .35
AR6 J.R. Richard......................... 1.25 .35
AR7 Rollie Fingers...................... 1.25 .35
AR8 Gaylord Perry .... 1.25 .35
AR9 Ron Guidry .... 1.25 .35
AR10 Phil Niekro......................... 1.25 .35

2001 Upper Deck Decade 1970's Bellbottomed Bashers

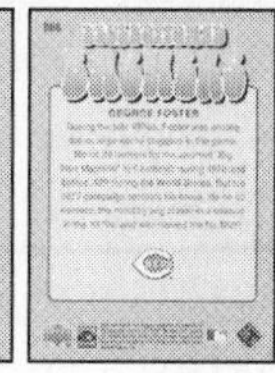

Issued at a rate of one in 14, these 10 cards feature some of the 1970's most powerful sluggers.

Nm-Mt Ex-Mt
COMPLETE SET (10)................. 25.00 7.50
BB1 Reggie Jackson................... 2.00 .60
BB2 Gorman Thomas.................. 1.25 .35
BB3 Willie McCovey .... 1.25 .35
BB4 Willie Stargell.................... 2.00 .60
BB5 Mike Schmidt..................... 6.00 1.80
BB6 George Foster .... 1.25 .35
BB7 Johnny Bench .... 3.00 .90
BB8 Dave Kingman..................... 1.25 .35
BB9 Graig Nettles...................... 1.25 .35
BB10 Steve Garvey..................... 1.25 .35

2001 Upper Deck Decade 1970's Disco Era Dandies

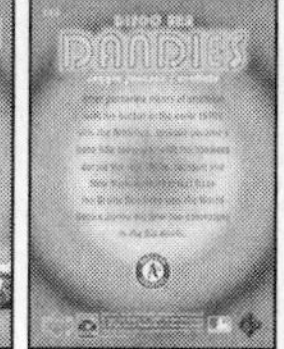

Issued at a rate of one in 23, these six cards feature some of the best players of the "disco" era.

Nm-Mt Ex-Mt
COMPLETE SET (6).................. 20.00 6.00
DE1 Mike Schmidt..................... 6.00 1.80
DE2 Johnny Bench.................... 3.00 .90
DE3 Lou Brock .... 2.00 .60
DE4 Reggie Jackson.................. 2.00 .60
DE5 Willie Stargell..................... 2.00 .60
DE6 Tom Seaver......................... 2.00 .60

2001 Upper Deck Decade 1970's Dynasties

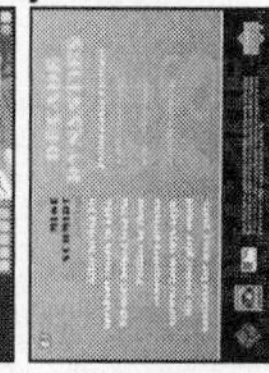

Issued at a rate of one in 14, these 10 cards feature stars from 10 of baseball's best teams during the 1970's.

Nm-Mt Ex-Mt
COMPLETE SET (10)................ 25.00 7.50
D1 Boog Powell......................... 1.25 .35
D2 Johnny Bench...................... 3.00 .90
D3 Willie Stargell....................... 2.00 .60
D4 Jim Hunter........................... 2.00 .60
D5 Steve Garvey........................ 1.25 .35
D6 Carlton Fisk.......................... 2.00 .60
D7 Mike Schmidt........................ 6.00 1.80
D8 Hal McRae .... 1.25 .35
D9 Tom Seaver........................... 2.00 .60
D10 Reggie Jackson.................... 2.00 .60

2001 Upper Deck Decade 1970's Game Bat

Issued at a rate of one in 24 hobby and one in 48 retail, these 48 cards featuure game-used pat pieces from various stars of the 1970's. A few players were printed in lesser quantities and we have notated them in our checklist with an SP along with print run information supplied by Upper Deck.

	Nm-Mt	Ex-Mt
B-AD Andre Dawson	10.00	3.00
B-AO Al Oliver	10.00	3.00
B-BB Bobby Bonds	10.00	3.00
B-BG Bobby Grich	10.00	3.00
B-BH B.Harrelson SP/290	10.00	3.00
B-BIM Bill Madlock	10.00	3.00
B-BOM Bobby Murcer	25.00	7.50
B-BP Boog Powell	15.00	4.50
B-BR Bill Russell	10.00	3.00
B-CF Carlton Fisk	15.00	4.50
B-DAE Darrell Evans	10.00	3.00
B-DB Don Baylor	10.00	3.00
B-DC Dave Concepcion	10.00	3.00
B-DP Dave Parker	10.00	3.00
B-DW Dave Winfield	10.00	3.00
B-DWE Dwight Evans	10.00	3.00
B-EM Eddie Murray	15.00	4.50
B-FL Fred Lynn	10.00	3.00
B-GC Gary Carter	15.00	4.50
B-GF George Foster	10.00	3.00
B-GL Greg Luzinski	10.00	3.00
B-GM Garry Maddox	10.00	3.00
B-GN Graig Nettles SP/219		
B-HA Hank Aaron	50.00	15.00
B-HM Hal McRae	10.00	3.00
B-JAC Jack Clark	10.00	3.00
B-JM Joe Morgan	10.00	3.00
B-JOC Jose Cruz	10.00	3.00
B-KG Ken Griffey Sr.	10.00	3.00
B-KH K.Hernandez SP/243	25.00	7.50
B-MM Manny Mota	10.00	3.00
B-MW Maury Wills	10.00	3.00
B-NR Nolan Ryan	80.00	24.00
B-OS Ozzie Smith	15.00	4.50
B-RAJ Randy Jones	10.00	3.00
B-RC R.Clemente SP/243	100.00	30.00
B-REJ Reggie Jackson	15.00	4.50
B-RH Ron Hunt	10.00	3.00
B-RM Rick Monday	10.00	3.00
B-RS Ron Santo	15.00	4.50
B-RW Roy White	10.00	3.00
B-SG Steve Garvey	10.00	3.00
B-TD Tommy Davis	10.00	3.00
B-TIM Tim McCarver	10.00	3.00
B-TOS T.Seaver SP/121	40.00	12.00
B-TUM Tug McGraw SP/97		
B-WM Willie Montanez	10.00	3.00
B-WR Willie Randolph	10.00	3.00

2001 Upper Deck Decade 1970's Game Bat Combos

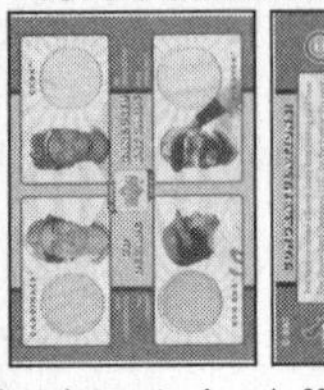

Issued at a rate of one in 336, these 19 cards feature game-used bat pieces from four different players. A handful of cards were announced as short-prints by Upper Deck with specific print runs revealed. That information is detailed in our checklist.

	Nm-Mt	Ex-Mt
LA Steve Garvey Ron Cey Bill Russell Rick Monday	25.00	7.50
RD George Foster Joe Morgan Ron Cey Bill Russell	25.00	7.50
RY Chris Chambliss Reggie Jackson Roy White Hal McRae	80.00	24.00
WS72 Reggie Jackson Bert Campaneris Dave Concepcion Johnny Bench SP/97	80.00	24.00
WS73 Reggie Jackson Bert Campaneris Tom Seaver Bud Harrelson	40.00	12.00
WS74 Reggie Jackson Bert Campaneris Steve Garvey Ron Cey	40.00	12.00
WS75 Carlton Fisk Fred Lynn George Foster Joe Morgan	40.00	12.00
WS76 Chris Chambliss Graig Nettles Johnny Bench Ken Griffey Sr.	80.00	24.00
WS77 Reggie Jackson Graig Nettles Steve Garvey Ron Cey	40.00	12.00
WS78 Graig Nettles Chris Chambliss Bill Russell Ron Cey	60.00	18.00
BAT Keith Hernandez Bill Madlock Fred Lynn Dave Parker	40.00	12.00
CIN Johnny Bench George Foster Ken Griffey Sr. Joe Morgan	50.00	15.00
GGA Carlton Fisk Graig Nettles Bobby Grich Fred Lynn	40.00	12.00
GGN Johnny Bench Roberto Clemente Dave Concepcion Garry Maddox	100.00	30.00
NYM Tom Seaver Ron Hunt Tug McGraw Bud Harrelson	40.00	12.00
NYY Reggie Jackson Graig Nettles Chris Chambliss Roy White	50.00	15.00
ROY Andre Dawson Fred Lynn Carlton Fisk Eddie Murray	50.00	15.00
ASMV Bill Madlock Joe Morgan Steve Garvey Dave Parker	25.00	7.50
MVPN Johnny Bench Steve Garvey Willie Stargell George Foster	50.00	15.00

2001 Upper Deck Decade 1970's Game Jersey

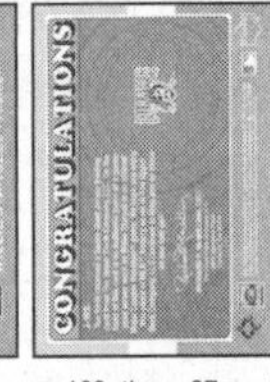

Issued at a rate of one on 168, these 27 cards feature swatches of their game-used uniforms. A few players were issued in shorter supply; we have notated them with an SP in our checklist along with print run information supplied by Upper Deck.

	Nm-Mt	Ex-Mt
J-BH Burt Hooton	10.00	3.00
J-BM Bobby Murcer	25.00	7.50
J-BM Bill Madlock	10.00	3.00
J-CF Carlton Fisk	15.00	4.50
J-CH Catfish Hunter	15.00	4.50
J-HA Hank Aaron	50.00	15.00
J-JB Johnny Bench	15.00	4.50
J-JKA Jim Kaat	10.00	3.00
J-JKO Jerry Koosman	10.00	3.00
J-JM Jon Matlack	10.00	3.00
J-JP Jim Perry	10.00	3.00
J-KG Ken Griffey Sr. SP/15		
J-LA Luis Aparicio	10.00	3.00
J-LP Lou Piniella	10.00	3.00
J-MW Maury Wills	10.00	3.00
J-NR Nolan Ryan SP/50	120.00	36.00
J-RC Roberto Clemente	100.00	30.00
J-RF Rollie Fingers	10.00	3.00
J-RG Ron Guidry	10.00	3.00
J-RJ Reggie Jackson		
J-RP Rico Petrocelli SP/15		
J-SB Sal Bando SP/15		
J-TM Tug McGraw	10.00	3.00
J-TS Tom Seaver	15.00	4.50
J-WD Willie Davis	10.00	3.00
J-WR Willie Randolph	10.00	3.00
J-WS Willie Stargell	15.00	4.50

2001 Upper Deck Decade 1970's Game Jersey Autograph

Issued at a rate of one in 168 hobby and one in 480 retail, these 18 cards have not only a game-used jersey piece but also an authentic autograph of the featured player. Some of the cards were released in lesser quantites and we have notated that information in our checklist with an SP along with print run information provided by Upper Deck.

	Nm-Mt	Ex-Mt
SJ-BH Burt Hooton	25.00	7.50
SJ-BM Bobby Murcer	80.00	24.00
SJ-BM Bill Madlock	25.00	7.50
SJ-CF Carlton Fisk SP/243	40.00	12.00
SJ-HA Hank Aaron SP/97	200.00	60.00
SJ-JB Johnny Bench	100.00	30.00
SJ-JKA Jim Kaat	25.00	7.50
SJ-JKO Jerry Koosman		
SJ-KG Ken Griffey Sr.	25.00	7.50
SJ-LA Luis Aparicio	25.00	7.50
SJ-MW Maury Wills	25.00	7.50
SJ-NR Nolan Ryan SP/291	150.00	45.00
SJ-RF Rollie Fingers	25.00	7.50
SJ-RG Ron Guidry	25.00	7.50
SJ-RJ R.Jackson SP/291	100.00	30.00
SJ-RP Rico Petrocelli	25.00	7.50
SJ-SB Sal Bando	25.00	7.50
SJ-TM Tug McGraw	50.00	15.00

2001 Upper Deck Decade 1970's Game Jersey Patch

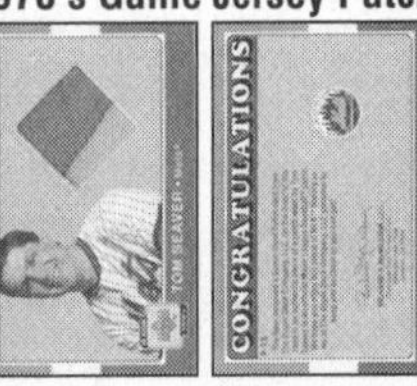

Issued at a rate of one in 7,500, these 26 cards features pieces of game-used uniform patches. Due to scarcity, no pricing is provided for these cards.

	Nm-Mt	Ex-Mt
P-BH Burt Hooton		
P-BM Bill Madlock		
P-BM Bobby Murcer		
P-CH Jim Hunter		
P-HA Hank Aaron		
P-JB Johnny Bench		
P-JKA Jim Kaat		
P-JKO Jerry Koosman		
P-JM Jon Matlack		
P-JP Jim Perry		
P-KG Ken Griffey Sr.		
P-LA Luis Aparicio		
P-LP Lou Piniella		
P-MW Maury Wills		
P-NR Nolan Ryan		
P-RC Roberto Clemente		
P-RF Rollie Fingers		
P-RG Ron Guidry		
P-RJ Reggie Jackson		
P-RP Rico Petrocelli		
P-SB Sal Bando		
P-TM Tug McGraw		
P-TS Tom Seaver		
P-WD Willie Davis		
P-WR Willie Randolph		
P-WS Willie Stargell		

2001 Upper Deck Decade 1970's Super Powers

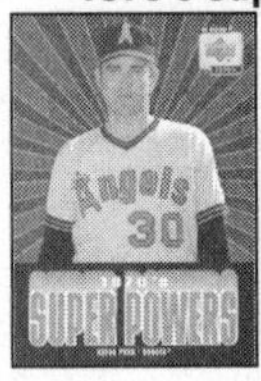

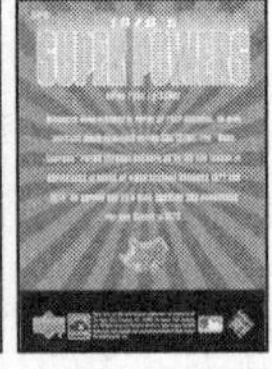

Inserted at a rate of one in 23, these six cards feature the players who carried the most clout during the 1970's.

	Nm-Mt	Ex-Mt
COMPLETE SET (6)	20.00	6.00
SP1 Reggie Jackson	2.00	.60
SP2 Joe Morgan	2.00	.60
SP3 Willie Stargell	2.00	.60
SP4 Willie McCovey	2.00	.60
SP5 Mike Schmidt	6.00	1.80
SP6 Nolan Ryan	8.00	2.40

2002 Upper Deck Diamond Connection

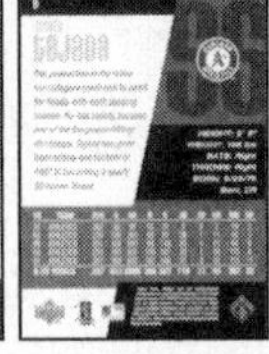

This 630-card standard-size set was released in two separate series. The basic Diamond Connection product was issued in August, 2002 and contained cards 1-570. It was issued in five card packs with an SRP of $7 per pack. The first 90 cards featured veteran players while cards 90 through 200 featured rookies and prospects. These cards were issued to a stated print run of 1500 serial numbered sets. The rest of the cards featured memorabilia pieces and were printed to various stated print runs. We have notated that information as to each cards print run. The original packaging of this product left each box short one jersey or bat card. Upper Deck would remedy that situation by later issuing redemption packs through their network of wholesale distributors who then sent the packs to their dealers. It's believed that most (if not all) of cards 536-570 were distributed in these redemption packs. Cards 571-630 were distributed in mid-December, 2002 within packs of 2002 Upper Deck Rookie Update. Cards 571-600 featured veterans on new teams and were commonly distributed in all packs. Cards 601-630 featured prospects and were serial #'d to 1,999. Though stated odds for cards 601-630 were never released by the manufacturer, we believe the cards seeded at an approximate rate of 1:7.

	Nm-Mt	Ex-Mt
COMP.LOW w/o SP's (90)	25.00	7.50
COMP.UPDATE w/o SP's (30)	10.00	3.00
COMMON CARD (1-90)	.40	.12
COMMON CARD (91-200)	5.00	1.50
DC JSY 201-270/537-547 PRINT 775 #'d SETS		
BLH JSY 271-320/548-550 PRINT 200 #'d SETS		
HM JSY 321-353/551-552 PRINT 150 #'d SETS		
FC JSY 354-368/553 PRINT 100 #'d SETS		
DC BAT 369-438/554-564 PRINT 775 #'d SETS		
BLH BAT 439-488/565-567 PRINT 200 #'d SETS		
HM BAT 489-521/568-569 PRINT 150 #'d SETS		
FC BAT 522-536/570 PRINT 100 #'d SETS		
COMMON CARD (571-600)	.60	.18
COMMON CARD (601-630)	5.00	1.50
1 Troy Glaus	.60	.18
2 Darin Erstad	.40	.12
3 Barry Zito	.60	.18
4 Eric Chavez	.40	.12
5 Tim Hudson	.40	.12
6 Miguel Tejada	.40	.12
7 Carlos Delgado	.40	.12
8 Shannon Stewart	.40	.12
9 Greg Vaughn	.40	.12
10 Jim Thome	1.00	.30
11 C.C. Sabathia	.40	.12
12 Ichiro Suzuki	1.50	.45
13 Edgar Martinez	.60	.18
14 Bret Boone	.40	.12
15 Freddy Garcia	.40	.12
16 Jeff Conine	.40	.12
17 Alex Rodriguez	1.50	.45
18 Rafael Palmeiro	.60	.18
19 Ivan Rodriguez	1.00	.30
20 Juan Gonzalez	1.00	.30
21 Pedro Martinez	1.00	.30
22 Nomar Garciaparra	1.50	.45
23 Manny Ramirez	.40	.12
24 Carlos Beltran	.40	.12
25 Mike Sweeney	.40	.12
26 Dmitri Young	.40	.12
27 Bobby Higginson	.40	.12
28 Corey Koskie	.40	.12
29 Cristian Guzman	.40	.12
30 Doug Mientkiewicz	.40	.12
31 Torii Hunter	.40	.12
32 Frank Thomas	1.00	.30
33 Mark Buehrle	.40	.12
34 Carlos Lee	.40	.12
35 Magglio Ordonez	.40	.12
36 Roger Clemens	2.00	.60
37 Bernie Williams	.60	.18
38 Jason Giambi	1.00	.30
39 Derek Jeter	2.50	.75
40 Mike Mussina	1.00	.30
41 Jeff Bagwell	.60	.18
42 Richard Hidalgo	.40	.12
43 Lance Berkman	.40	.12
44 Roy Oswalt	.40	.12
45 Chipper Jones	1.00	.30
46 Gary Sheffield	.40	.12
47 Andruw Jones	.40	.12
48 Greg Maddux	1.50	.45
49 Geoff Jenkins	.40	.12
50 Ben Sheets	.40	.12
51 Richie Sexson	.40	.12
52 Albert Pujols	2.00	.60
53 Matt Morris	.40	.12
54 J.D. Drew	.40	.12
55 Tino Martinez	.40	.12
56 Sammy Sosa	1.50	.45
57 Kerry Wood	1.00	.30
58 Moises Alou	.40	.12
59 Fred McGriff	.60	.18
60 Randy Johnson	1.00	.30
61 Luis Gonzalez	.40	.12
62 Curt Schilling	.60	.18
63 Kevin Brown	.40	.12
64 Shawn Green	.40	.12
65 Paul LoDuca	.40	.12
66 Vladimir Guerrero	1.00	.30
67 Jose Vidro	.40	.12
68 Barry Bonds	2.50	.75
69 Jeff Kent	.40	.12
70 Rich Aurilia	.40	.12
71 Preston Wilson	.40	.12
72 Josh Beckett	.60	.18
73 Cliff Floyd	.40	.12
74 Mike Piazza	1.50	.45
75 Mo Vaughn	.40	.12
76 Roberto Alomar	1.00	.30
77 Jeromy Burnitz	.40	.12
78 Phil Nevin	.40	.12
79 Sean Burroughs	.40	.12
80 Scott Rolen	.60	.18
81 Bob Abreu	.40	.12
82 Pat Burrell	.40	.12
83 Brian Giles	.40	.12
84 Jason Kendall	.40	.12
85 Ken Griffey Jr.	1.50	.45
86 Adam Dunn	.40	.12
87 Aaron Boone	.40	.12
88 Larry Walker	.60	.18
89 Todd Helton	.60	.18
90 Mike Hampton	.40	.12
91 Brandon Puffer DC RC	5.00	1.50
92 Rodrigo Rosario DC RC	5.00	1.50
93 Tom Shearn DC RC	5.00	1.50
94 Morgan Ensberg DC	5.00	1.50
95 Jason Lane DC	5.00	1.50
96 Franklyn German DC RC	5.00	1.50
97 Carlos Pena DC	5.00	1.50
98 Joe Orloski DC RC	5.00	1.50
99 Reed Johnson DC RC	8.00	2.40
100 Chris Baker DC RC	5.00	1.50
101 Corey Thurman DC RC	5.00	1.50
102 Gustavo Chacin DC RC	5.00	1.50
103 Eric Hinske DC	5.00	1.50
104 John Foster DC RC	5.00	1.50
105 John Ennis DC RC	5.00	1.50
106 Kevin Gryboski DC RC	5.00	1.50
107 Jung Bong DC	5.00	1.50
108 Travis Wilson DC	5.00	1.50
109 Luis Martinez DC RC	5.00	1.50
110 Brian Mallette DC RC	5.00	1.50
111 Takahito Nomura DC RC	5.00	1.50
112 Bill Hall DC	5.00	1.50
113 Jeff Deardorff DC	5.00	1.50
114 Cristian Guerrero DC	5.00	1.50
115 Scotty Layfield DC RC	5.00	1.50
116 Mike Crudale DC RC	5.00	1.50
117 So Taguchi DC RC	8.00	2.40
118 Jeremy Lambert DC RC	5.00	1.50
119 Jim Journell DC	5.00	1.50
120 Francis Beltran DC RC	5.00	1.50
121 Mark Prior DC	15.00	4.50
122 Ben Christensen DC	5.00	1.50
123 Jorge Sosa DC RC	5.00	1.50
124 Brandon Backe DC RC	5.00	1.50
125 Steve Kent DC RC	5.00	1.50
126 Felix Escalona DC RC	5.00	1.50
127 P.J. Bevis DC RC	5.00	1.50
128 Jose Valverde DC RC	8.00	2.40
129 Doug Devore DC RC	5.00	1.50
130 Jeremy Ward DC RC	5.00	1.50
131 Mike Koplove DC	5.00	1.50
132 Luis Terrero DC	5.00	1.50
133 John Patterson DC	5.00	1.50
134 Victor Alvarez DC RC	5.00	1.50
135 Kirk Saarloos DC RC	5.00	1.50
136 Kazuhisa Ishii DC RC	10.00	3.00
137 Steve Colyer DC	5.00	1.50
138 Cesar Izturis DC	5.00	1.50
139 Ron Calloway DC RC	5.00	1.50
140 Eric Good DC RC	5.00	1.50
141 Jorge Nunez DC RC	5.00	1.50
142 Ron Chiavacci DC	5.00	1.50
143 Donnie Bridges DC	5.00	1.50
144 Nelson Castro DC RC	5.00	1.50
145 Deivis Santos DC	5.00	1.50
146 Kurt Ainsworth DC	5.00	1.50
147 Arturo McDowell DC	5.00	1.50
148 Allan Simpson DC RC	5.00	1.50
149 Matt Thornton DC RC	5.00	1.50
150 Luis Ugueto DC RC	5.00	1.50
151 J.J. Putz DC RC	5.00	1.50
152 Hansel Izquierdo DC RC	5.00	1.50
153 Oliver Perez DC RC	8.00	2.40
154 Jaime Cerda DC RC	5.00	1.50
155 Mark Corey DC RC	5.00	1.50
156 Tyler Yates DC RC	8.00	2.40
157 Satoru Komiyama DC RC	5.00	1.50
158 Adam Walker DC RC	5.00	1.50
159 Steve Bechler DC RC	5.00	1.50
160 Erik Bedard DC	5.00	1.50
161 Todd Donovan DC RC	5.00	1.50
162 Clifford Bartosh DC RC	5.00	1.50
163 Ben Howard DC RC	5.00	1.50
164 Andy Shibilo DC RC	5.00	1.50
165 Dennis Tankersley DC	5.00	1.50
166 Mike Bynum DC	5.00	1.50
167 And. Machado DC RC	5.00	1.50
168 Pete Zamora DC RC	5.00	1.50
169 Eric Junge DC RC	5.00	1.50
170 Elio Serrano DC RC	5.00	1.50
171 Jorge Padilla DC RC	5.00	1.50
172 Marlon Byrd DC	5.00	1.50
173 Adrian Burnside DC RC	5.00	1.50
174 Mike Gonzalez DC RC	5.00	1.50
175 J.R. House DC	5.00	1.50
176 Hank Blalock DC	8.00	2.40
177 Travis Hughes DC RC	5.00	1.50
178 Mark Teixeira DC	8.00	2.40
179 Josh Hancock DC RC	5.00	1.50
180 An. Martinez DC RC	5.00	1.50
181 Jorge de la Rosa DC RC	5.00	1.50
182 Ben Broussard DC	5.00	1.50
183 Austin Kearns DC	5.00	1.50
184 Corky Miller DC	5.00	1.50
185 Colin Young DC RC	5.00	1.50
186 Cam Esslinger DC RC	5.00	1.50
187 Rene Reyes DC RC	5.00	1.50
188 Aaron Cook DC RC	5.00	1.50
189 Alexis Gomez DC	5.00	1.50
190 Nate Field DC RC	5.00	1.50
191 Miguel Asencio DC RC	5.00	1.50
192 Brandon Berger DC	5.00	1.50
193 Fernando Rodney DC	5.00	1.50
194 Andy Van Hekken DC	5.00	1.50
195 Kevin Frederick DC RC	5.00	1.50
196 Todd Sears DC	5.00	1.50
197 Edwin Almonte DC RC	5.00	1.50
198 Kyle Kane DC RC	5.00	1.50
199 Mitch Wylie DC RC	5.00	1.50
200 Mike Porzio DC	5.00	1.50
201 Darin Erstad DC Jsy	10.00	3.00
202 Tim Salmon DC Jsy	15.00	4.50
203 Jeff Bagwell DC Jsy	15.00	4.50
204 Lance Berkman DC Jsy	10.00	3.00
205 Eric Chavez DC Jsy	10.00	3.00
206 Tim Hudson DC Jsy	10.00	3.00
207 Carlos Delgado DC Jsy	10.00	3.00
208 Chipper Jones DC Jsy	15.00	4.50
209 Gary Sheffield DC Jsy	10.00	3.00
210 Greg Maddux DC Jsy	15.00	4.50
211 Tom Glavine DC Jsy	15.00	4.50
212 Mike Mussina DC Jsy	15.00	4.50
213 J.D. Drew DC Jsy	10.00	3.00
214 Rick Ankiel DC Jsy	10.00	3.00
215 Sammy Sosa DC Jsy	20.00	6.00
216 Mike Lieberthal DC Jsy	10.00	3.00
217 Fred McGriff DC Jsy	15.00	4.50
218 David Wells DC Jsy	10.00	3.00
219 Curt Schilling DC Jsy	15.00	4.50
220 Luis Gonzalez DC Jsy	10.00	3.00
221 Mark Grace DC Jsy	15.00	4.50
222 Kevin Brown DC Jsy	10.00	3.00
223 Hideo Nomo DC Jsy	25.00	7.50
224 Jose Vidro DC Jsy	10.00	3.00
225 Jeff Kent DC Jsy	10.00	3.00
226 Rich Aurilia DC Jsy	10.00	3.00
227 Kenny Lofton DC Jsy	10.00	3.00
228 C.C. Sabathia DC Jsy	10.00	3.00
229 Edgar Martinez DC Jsy	15.00	4.50
230 Freddy Garcia DC Jsy	10.00	3.00
231 Cliff Floyd DC Jsy	10.00	3.00
232 Preston Wilson DC Jsy	10.00	3.00
233 Mike Piazza DC Jsy	15.00	4.50
234 Roberto Alomar DC Jsy	15.00	4.50
235 Trevor Hoffman DC Jsy	10.00	3.00
236 Ryan Klesko DC Jsy	10.00	3.00
237 Sean Burroughs DC Jsy	10.00	3.00
238 Scott Rolen DC Jsy	15.00	4.50
239 Pat Burrell DC Jsy	10.00	3.00
240 Edgardo Alfonzo DC Jsy	10.00	3.00
241 Brian Giles DC Jsy	10.00	3.00
242 Jason Kendall DC Jsy	10.00	3.00
243 Alex Rodriguez DC Jsy	20.00	6.00
244 Juan Gonzalez DC Jsy	15.00	4.50
245 Ivan Rodriguez DC Jsy	15.00	4.50
246 Rafael Palmeiro DC Jsy	15.00	4.50
247 Ken Griffey Jr. DC Jsy	20.00	6.00
248 Adam Dunn DC Jsy	10.00	3.00
249 Barry Larkin DC Jsy	15.00	4.50
250 Manny Ramirez DC Jsy	10.00	3.00
251 Pedro Martinez DC Jsy	15.00	4.50
252 Todd Helton DC Jsy	15.00	4.50
253 Larry Walker DC Jsy	15.00	4.50
254 Randy Johnson DC Jsy	15.00	4.50
255 Mike Sweeney DC Jsy	10.00	3.00
256 Carlos Beltran DC Jsy	10.00	3.00
257 D.Young DC Jsy SP/380	10.00	3.00
258 Joe Mays DC Jsy	10.00	3.00
259 D.Mientkiewicz DC Jsy	10.00	3.00
260 Corey Koskie DC Jsy	10.00	3.00
261 Magglio Ordonez DC Jsy	10.00	3.00
262 Frank Thomas DC Jsy	15.00	4.50
263 Ray Durham DC Jsy	10.00	3.00
264 Jason Giambi DC Jsy	15.00	4.50
265 Bernie Williams DC Jsy	15.00	4.50
266 Roger Clemens DC Jsy	25.00	7.50
267 Mariano Rivera DC Jsy	15.00	4.50
268 Robin Ventura DC Jsy	10.00	3.00
269 Andy Pettitte DC Jsy	15.00	4.50
270 Jorge Posada DC Jsy	15.00	4.50
271 Mike Piazza BLH Jsy	20.00	6.00
272 Alex Rodriguez BLH Jsy	25.00	7.50
273 Ken Griffey Jr. BLH Jsy	25.00	7.50

274 Jason Giambi BLH Jsy....... 20.00 6.00
275 Frank Thomas BLH Jsy....... 20.00 6.00
276 Greg Maddux BLH Jsy....... 20.00 6.00
277 Sammy Sosa BLH Jsy....... 25.00 7.50
278 Roger Clemens BLH Jsy.... 30.00 9.00
279 Jeff Bagwell BLH Jsy....... 20.00 6.00
280 Todd Helton BLH Jsy....... 20.00 6.00
281 Ichiro Suzuki BLH Jsy....... 50.00 15.00
282 Randy Johnson BLH Jsy.... 20.00 6.00
283 Jim Thome BLH Jsy....... 20.00 6.00
284 Ivan Rodriguez BLH Jsy..... 20.00 6.00
285 Darin Erstad BLH Jsy....... 15.00 4.50
286 Eric Chavez BLH Jsy....... 15.00 4.50
287 Barry Zito BLH Jsy....... 20.00 6.00
288 Carlos Delgado BLH Jsy..... 15.00 4.50
289 Omar Vizquel BLH Jsy....... 15.00 4.50
290 Edgar Martinez BLH Jsy..... 20.00 6.00
291 Manny Ramirez BLH Jsy..... 15.00 4.50
292 Mike Sweeney BLH Jsy....... 15.00 4.50
293 Tom Glavine BLH Jsy....... 20.00 6.00
294 Joe Mays BLH Jsy....... 10.00 3.00
295 Eric Milton BLH Jsy....... 10.00 3.00
296 Mag. Ordonez BLH Jsy....... 15.00 4.50
297 Bernie Williams BLH Jsy..... 20.00 6.00
298 Trevor Hoffman BLH Jsy..... 15.00 4.50
299 Andruw Jones BLH Jsy....... 15.00 4.50
300 Aubrey Huff BLH Jsy....... 15.00 4.50
301 Jim Edmonds BLH Jsy....... 15.00 4.50
302 Kerry Wood BLH Jsy....... 20.00 6.00
303 Luis Gonzalez BLH Jsy....... 15.00 4.50
304 Shawn Green BLH Jsy....... 15.00 4.50
305 Jose Vidro BLH Jsy....... 15.00 4.50
306 Jeff Kent BLH Jsy....... 15.00 4.50
307 Edgardo Alfonzo BLH Jsy.... 15.00 4.50
308 Preston Wilson BLH Jsy..... 15.00 4.50
309 Roberto Alomar BLH Jsy..... 20.00 6.00
310 Jeromy Burnitz BLH Jsy..... 15.00 4.50
311 Phil Nevin BLH Jsy....... 15.00 4.50
312 Ryan Klesko BLH Jsy....... 15.00 4.50
313 Bob Abreu BLH Jsy....... 15.00 4.50
314 Scott Rolen BLH Jsy....... 20.00 6.00
315 Kazuhiro Sasaki BLH Jsy.... 15.00 4.50
316 Jason Kendall BLH Jsy....... 15.00 4.50
317 Sean Casey BLH Jsy....... 15.00 4.50
318 Larry Walker BLH Jsy....... 20.00 6.00
319 Mike Hampton BLH Jsy....... 15.00 4.50
320 Juan Gonzalez BLH Jsy....... 20.00 6.00
321 Darin Erstad HM Jsy....... 15.00 4.50
322 Tim Hudson HM Jsy....... 15.00 4.50
323 Carlos Delgado HM Jsy....... 15.00 4.50
324 Greg Vaughn HM Jsy....... 15.00 4.50
325 Jim Thome HM Jsy....... 20.00 6.00
326 Ichiro Suzuki HM Jsy....... 50.00 15.00
327 Rafael Palmeiro HM Jsy..... 20.00 6.00
328 Alex Rodriguez HM Jsy....... 25.00 7.50
329 Juan Gonzalez HM Jsy....... 20.00 6.00
330 Manny Ramirez HM Jsy....... 15.00 4.50
331 Carlos Beltran HM Jsy....... 15.00 4.50
332 Eric Milton HM Jsy....... 15.00 4.50
333 Frank Thomas HM Jsy....... 20.00 6.00
334 Roger Clemens HM Jsy....... 30.00 9.00
335 Jason Giambi HM Jsy....... 20.00 6.00
336 Lance Berkman HM Jsy....... 15.00 4.50
337 Greg Maddux HM Jsy....... 20.00 6.00
338 Chipper Jones HM Jsy....... 20.00 6.00
339 Sean Casey HM Jsy....... 15.00 4.50
340 Jim Edmonds HM Jsy....... 15.00 4.50
341 Kerry Wood HM Jsy....... 20.00 6.00
342 Sammy Sosa HM Jsy....... 25.00 7.50
343 Luis Gonzalez HM Jsy....... 15.00 4.50
344 Shawn Green HM Jsy....... 15.00 4.50
345 Jeff Kent HM Jsy....... 15.00 4.50
346 Preston Wilson HM Jsy....... 15.00 4.50
347 Roberto Alomar HM Jsy....... 20.00 6.00
348 Phil Nevin HM Jsy....... 15.00 4.50
349 Scott Rolen HM Jsy....... 20.00 6.00
350 Mike Sweeney HM Jsy....... 15.00 4.50
351 Ken Griffey Jr. HM Jsy....... 25.00 7.50
352 Todd Helton HM Jsy....... 20.00 6.00
353 Larry Walker HM Jsy....... 20.00 6.00
354 Alex Rodriguez FC Jsy....... 30.00 9.00
355 Pedro Martinez FC Jsy....... 25.00 7.50
356 Frank Thomas FC Jsy....... 25.00 7.50
357 Jason Giambi FC Jsy....... 25.00 7.50
358 Bernie Williams FC Jsy....... 25.00 7.50
359 Jeff Bagwell FC Jsy....... 25.00 7.50
360 Chipper Jones FC Jsy....... 25.00 7.50
361 Sammy Sosa FC Jsy....... 30.00 9.00
362 Randy Johnson FC Jsy....... 25.00 7.50
363 Shawn Green FC Jsy....... 20.00 6.00
364 Mike Piazza FC Jsy....... 25.00 7.50
365 Ichiro Suzuki FC Jsy....... 60.00 18.00
366 Ken Griffey Jr. FC Jsy....... 30.00 9.00
367 Larry Walker FC Jsy....... 25.00 7.50
368 Jim Edmonds FC Jsy....... 20.00 6.00
369 Darin Erstad DC Bat....... 10.00 3.00
370 Tim Salmon DC Bat....... 15.00 4.50
371 Mark Kotsay DC Bat....... 10.00 3.00
372 Craig Biggio DC Bat....... 15.00 4.50
373 Eric Chavez DC Bat....... 10.00 3.00
374 David Justice DC Bat....... 10.00 3.00
375 Carlos Delgado DC Bat....... 10.00 3.00
376 Chipper Jones DC Bat....... 15.00 4.50
377 Gary Sheffield DC Bat....... 10.00 3.00
378 Greg Maddux DC Bat....... 15.00 4.50
379 Eric Karros DC Bat....... 10.00 3.00
380 Fred McGriff DC Bat....... 15.00 4.50
381 J.D. Drew DC Bat....... 10.00 3.00
382 Rick Ankiel DC Bat....... 10.00 3.00
383 Sammy Sosa DC Bat....... 20.00 6.00
384 Moises Alou DC Bat....... 10.00 3.00
385 Ben Grieve DC Bat....... 10.00 3.00
386 Greg Vaughn DC Bat....... 10.00 3.00
387 Jay Payton DC Bat....... 10.00 3.00
388 Luis Gonzalez DC Bat....... 10.00 3.00
389 Ray Durham DC Bat....... 10.00 3.00
390 Shawn Green DC Bat....... 10.00 3.00
391 Hideo Nomo DC Bat....... 25.00 7.50
392 Jose Vidro DC Bat....... 10.00 3.00
393 Jeff Kent DC Bat....... 10.00 3.00
394 Adrian Beltre DC Bat....... 10.00 3.00
395 Jim Thome DC Bat....... 15.00 4.50
396 Bob Abreu DC Bat....... 10.00 3.00
397 Edgar Martinez DC Bat....... 15.00 4.50
398 Carl Everett DC Bat....... 10.00 3.00
399 Luis Castillo DC Bat....... 10.00 3.00
400 Preston Wilson DC Bat....... 10.00 3.00
401 Jermaine Dye DC Bat....... 10.00 3.00
402 Roberto Alomar DC Bat....... 15.00 4.50
403 Todd Hundley DC Bat....... 10.00 3.00
404 Ryan Klesko DC Bat....... 10.00 3.00
405 Phil Nevin DC Bat....... 10.00 3.00
406 Scott Rolen DC Bat....... 15.00 4.50
407 Rafael Furcal DC Bat....... 10.00 3.00
408 Miguel Tejada DC Bat....... 10.00 3.00
409 Brian Giles DC Bat....... 10.00 3.00
410 Jason Kendall DC Bat....... 10.00 3.00
411 Alex Rodriguez DC Bat....... 20.00 6.00
412 Juan Gonzalez DC Bat....... 15.00 4.50
413 Ivan Rodriguez DC Bat....... 15.00 4.50
414 Rafael Palmeiro DC Bat....... 15.00 4.50
415 Ken Griffey Jr. DC Bat....... 20.00 6.00
416 Edgardo Alfonzo DC Bat....... 10.00 3.00
417 Barry Larkin DC Bat....... 15.00 4.50
418 Manny Ramirez DC Bat....... 10.00 3.00
419 Pedro Martinez DC Bat....... 15.00 4.50
420 Todd Helton DC Bat....... 15.00 4.50
421 Larry Walker DC Bat....... 15.00 4.50
422 Garret Anderson DC Bat....... 10.00 3.00
423 Mike Sweeney DC Bat....... 10.00 3.00
424 Carlos Beltran DC Bat....... 10.00 3.00
425 Javier Lopez DC Bat....... 10.00 3.00
426 J.T. Snow DC Bat....... 10.00 3.00
427 D.Mientkiewicz DC Bat....... 10.00 3.00
428 John Olerud DC Bat....... 10.00 3.00
429 Magglio Ordonez DC Bat....... 10.00 3.00
430 Frank Thomas DC Bat....... 15.00 4.50
431 Kenny Lofton DC Bat....... 10.00 3.00
432 Al Leiter DC Bat....... 10.00 3.00
433 Bernie Williams DC Bat....... 15.00 4.50
434 Roger Clemens DC Bat....... 25.00 7.50
435 Tom Glavine DC Bat....... 15.00 4.50
436 Robin Ventura DC Bat....... 10.00 3.00
437 Chan Ho Park DC Bat....... 10.00 3.00
438 Jorge Posada DC Bat....... 15.00 4.50
439 Charles Johnson BLH Bat....... 15.00 4.50
440 Alex Rodriguez BLH Bat....... 25.00 7.50
441 Ken Griffey Jr. BLH Bat....... 25.00 7.50
442 Mark Kotsay BLH Bat....... 10.00 3.00
443 Frank Thomas BLH Bat....... 20.00 6.00
444 Greg Maddux BLH Bat....... 20.00 6.00
445 Sammy Sosa BLH Bat....... 25.00 7.50
446 Tom Glavine BLH Bat....... 20.00 6.00
447 Chipper Jones BLH Bat....... 20.00 6.00
448 Todd Helton BLH Bat....... 20.00 6.00
449 Jeff Cirillo BLH Bat....... 10.00 3.00
450 Steve Finley BLH Bat....... 15.00 4.50
451 Jim Thome BLH Bat....... 20.00 6.00
452 Ivan Rodriguez BLH Bat....... 20.00 6.00
453 Darin Erstad BLH Bat....... 15.00 4.50
454 Eric Chavez BLH Bat....... 15.00 4.50
455 Miguel Tejada BLH Bat....... 15.00 4.50
456 Carlos Delgado BLH Bat....... 15.00 4.50
457 Omar Vizquel BLH Bat....... 15.00 4.50
458 Edgar Martinez BLH Bat....... 20.00 6.00
459 Johnny Damon BLH Bat....... 15.00 4.50
460 Russell Branyan BLH Bat....... 10.00 3.00
461 Kenny Lofton BLH Bat....... 15.00 4.50
462 Jermaine Dye BLH Bat....... 15.00 4.50
463 Ellis Burks BLH Bat....... 15.00 4.50
464 Mag. Ordonez BLH Bat....... 15.00 4.50
465 Bernie Williams BLH Bat....... 20.00 6.00
466 Tim Salmon BLH Bat....... 20.00 6.00
467 Andruw Jones BLH Bat....... 20.00 6.00
468 J.Hammonds BLH Bat....... 10.00 3.00
469 Jim Edmonds BLH Bat....... 15.00 4.50
470 Kerry Wood BLH Bat....... 20.00 6.00
471 Luis Gonzalez BLH Bat....... 15.00 4.50
472 Shawn Green BLH Bat....... 15.00 4.50
473 Jose Vidro BLH Bat....... 15.00 4.50
474 Jeff Kent BLH Bat SP/189 .. 15.00 4.50
475 Javier Lopez BLH Bat....... 15.00 4.50
476 Preston Wilson BLH Bat....... 15.00 4.50
477 Roberto Alomar BLH Bat....... 20.00 6.00
478 Robin Ventura BLH Bat....... 15.00 4.50
479 Phil Nevin BLH Bat....... 15.00 4.50
480 Ryan Klesko BLH Bat....... 15.00 4.50
481 Bob Abreu BLH Bat....... 15.00 4.50
482 Scott Rolen BLH Bat....... 20.00 6.00
483 Brian Giles BLH Bat....... 15.00 4.50
484 Jason Kendall BLH Bat....... 15.00 4.50
485 Tsuyoshi Shinjo BLH Bat....... 15.00 4.50
486 Larry Walker BLH Bat....... 20.00 6.00
487 Mike Lieberthal BLH Bat....... 15.00 4.50
488 Juan Gonzalez BLH Bat....... 20.00 6.00
489 Darin Erstad HM Bat....... 15.00 4.50
490 Tom Glavine HM Bat....... 20.00 6.00
491 Carlos Delgado HM Bat....... 15.00 4.50
492 Greg Vaughn HM Bat....... 15.00 4.50
493 Jim Thome HM Bat....... 20.00 6.00
494 Mark Grace HM Bat....... 20.00 6.00
495 Rafael Palmeiro HM Bat....... 20.00 6.00
496 Alex Rodriguez HM Bat....... 25.00 7.50
497 Juan Gonzalez HM Bat....... 20.00 6.00
498 Miguel Tejada HM Bat....... 15.00 4.50
499 Carlos Beltran HM Bat....... 15.00 4.50
500 Andruw Jones HM Bat....... 15.00 4.50
501 Frank Thomas HM Bat....... 20.00 6.00
502 Andres Galarraga HM Bat....... 15.00 4.50
503 Gary Sheffield HM Bat....... 15.00 4.50
504 Craig Biggio HM Bat....... 20.00 6.00
505 Greg Maddux HM Bat....... 20.00 6.00
506 Chipper Jones HM Bat....... 20.00 6.00
507 Pat Burrell HM Bat....... 15.00 4.50
508 Jim Edmonds HM Bat....... 15.00 4.50
509 Kerry Wood HM Bat....... 20.00 6.00
510 Sammy Sosa HM Bat....... 25.00 7.50
511 Luis Gonzalez HM Bat....... 15.00 4.50
512 Shawn Green HM Bat....... 15.00 4.50
513 Edgardo Alfonzo HM Bat....... 15.00 4.50
514 Preston Wilson HM Bat....... 15.00 4.50
515 Roberto Alomar HM Bat....... 20.00 6.00
516 Phil Nevin HM Bat....... 15.00 4.50
517 Scott Rolen HM Bat....... 20.00 6.00
518 Brian Giles HM Bat....... 15.00 4.50
519 Jorge Posada HM Bat....... 20.00 6.00
520 Todd Helton HM Bat....... 20.00 6.00
521 Larry Walker HM Bat....... 20.00 6.00
522 Alex Rodriguez FC Bat....... 30.00 9.00
523 Pedro Martinez FC Bat....... 25.00 7.50
524 Frank Thomas FC Bat....... 25.00 7.50
525 Jason Giambi FC Bat....... 25.00 7.50
526 Bernie Williams FC Bat....... 25.00 7.50
527 J.D. Drew FC Bat....... 20.00 6.00
528 Chipper Jones FC Bat....... 25.00 7.50
529 Sammy Sosa FC Bat....... 30.00 9.00
530 Randy Johnson FC Bat....... 25.00 7.50
531 Shawn Green FC Bat....... 20.00 6.00
532 Kevin Brown FC Bat....... 20.00 6.00
533 Brian Giles FC Bat....... 20.00 6.00
534 Ken Griffey Jr. FC Bat....... 30.00 9.00
535 Larry Walker FC Bat....... 25.00 7.50
536 Jim Edmonds FC Bat....... 20.00 6.00
537 Barry Zito DC Jsy....... 15.00 4.50
538 Bobby Abreu DC Jsy....... 10.00 3.00
539 Eric Karros DC Jsy....... 10.00 3.00
540 Sean Casey DC Jsy....... 10.00 3.00
541 Phil Nevin DC Jsy....... 10.00 3.00
542 Andruw Jones DC Jsy....... 10.00 3.00
543 Jim Thome DC Jsy....... 15.00 4.50
544 Jim Edmonds DC Jsy....... 10.00 3.00
545 Ichiro Suzuki DC Jsy....... 40.00 12.00
546 Kerry Wood DC Jsy....... 15.00 4.50
547 Eric Milton DC Jsy....... 10.00 3.00
548 Pat Burrell BLH Jsy....... 15.00 4.50
549 Adam Dunn BLH Jsy....... 15.00 4.50
550 Lance Berkman BLH Jsy....... 15.00 4.50
551 Lance Berkman HM Jsy....... 15.00 4.50
552 Barry Zito HM Jsy....... 20.00 6.00
553 Roger Clemens FC Jsy....... 25.00 7.50
554 Andres Galarraga DC Bat....... 10.00 3.00
555 Johnny Damon DC Bat....... 10.00 3.00
556 Jose Cruz Jr. DC Bat....... 10.00 3.00
557 Charles Johnson DC Bat....... 10.00 3.00
558 Matt Williams DC Bat....... 10.00 3.00
559 Andruw Jones DC Bat....... 10.00 3.00
560 Tsuyoshi Shinjo DC Bat....... 10.00 3.00
561 Jim Thome DC Bat....... 15.00 4.50
562 Omar Vizquel DC Bat....... 10.00 3.00
563 Frank Thomas DC Bat....... 15.00 4.50
564 Corey Patterson DC Bat....... 10.00 3.00
565 Fred McGriff BLH Bat....... 20.00 6.00
566 Manny Ramirez BLH Bat....... 15.00 4.50
567 Gary Sheffield BLH Bat....... 15.00 4.50
568 Manny Ramirez HM Bat....... 15.00 4.50
569 Mike Sweeney HM Bat....... 15.00 4.50
570 Todd Helton FC Bat....... 25.00 7.50
571 Erubiel Durazo....... .60 .18
572 Geronimo Gil....... .60 .18
573 Shea Hillenbrand....... .60 .18
574 Cliff Floyd....... .60 .18
575 Corey Patterson....... .60 .18
576 Joe Borchard....... .60 .18
577 Austin Kearns....... .60 .18
578 Ryan Dempster....... .60 .18
579 Brandon Larson....... .60 .18
580 Luis Castillo....... .60 .18
581 Juan Encarnacion....... .60 .18
582 Chin-Feng Chen....... .60 .18
583 Hideo Nomo....... 1.50 .45
584 Bartolo Colon....... .60 .18
585 Raul Mondesi....... .60 .18
586 Eric Munson....... .60 .18
587 Alfonso Soriano....... 1.00 .30
588 Ted Lilly....... .60 .18
589 Ray Durham....... .60 .18
590 Brett Myers....... .60 .18
591 Brandon Phillips....... .60 .18
592 Kenny Lofton....... .60 .18
593 Scott Rolen....... 1.00 .30
594 Jim Edmonds....... .60 .18
595 Carl Crawford....... .60 .18
596 Hank Blalock....... 1.50 .45
597 Kevin Mench....... .60 .18
598 Josh Phelps....... .60 .18
599 Orlando Hudson....... .60 .18
600 Eric Hinske....... .60 .18
601 Mike Mahoney DC....... 5.00 1.50
602 Jason Davis DC RC....... 10.00 3.00
603 Trey Hodges DC RC....... 5.00 1.50
604 Josh Bard DC RC....... 5.00 1.50
605 Jer. Robertson DC RC....... 5.00 1.50
606 Jose Diaz DC RC....... 5.00 1.50
607 Jorge Nunez DC RC....... 5.00 1.50
608 Danny Mota DC RC....... 5.00 1.50
609 David Ross DC RC....... 5.00 1.50
610 Jayson Durocher DC RC....... 5.00 1.50
611 Freddy Sanchez DC RC....... 5.00 1.50
612 Julius Matos DC RC....... 5.00 1.50
613 Wil Nieves DC RC....... 5.00 1.50
614 Ben Kozlowski DC RC....... 5.00 1.50
615 J.Simontacchi DC RC....... 5.00 1.50
616 Mike Coolbaugh DC RC....... 5.00 1.50
617 Travis Driskill DC RC....... 5.00 1.50
618 Howie Clark DC RC....... 5.00 1.50
619 Earl Snyder DC RC....... 5.00 1.50
620 Carl Sadler DC RC....... 5.00 1.50
621 Jason Beverlin DC RC....... 5.00 1.50
622 Terry Pearson DC RC....... 5.00 1.50
623 Eric Eckenstahler DC RC....... 5.00 1.50
624 Shawn Sedlacek DC RC....... 5.00 1.50
625 Aaron Guiel DC RC....... 5.00 1.50
626 Ryan Bukvich DC RC....... 5.00 1.50
627 Julio Mateo DC RC....... 5.00 1.50
628 Chris Snelling DC RC....... 8.00 2.40
629 Lance Carter DC RC....... 5.00 1.50
630 Scott Wiggins DC RC....... 5.00 1.50

2002 Upper Deck Diamond Connection Bat Around Quads

This 30 card set was issued one per special "redemption" packs Upper Deck had to issued due to the problems with seeding the regular issued Diamond Connection boxes. Each card features four players

Nm-Mt Ex-Mt
GOLD: RANDOM IN REDEMPTION PACKS
GOLD PRINT RUN 50 SERIAL #'d SETS
NO GOLD PRICING DUE TO SCARCITY
ABBV Roberto Alomar....... 25.00 7.50
Bret Boone
Craig Biggio
Jose Vidro
ALAE Moises Alou....... 15.00 4.50
Kenny Lofton
Garret Anderson
Carl Everett
DGVC Carlos Delgado....... 15.00 4.50
Andres Galarraga
Jose Vidro
Jose Cruz Jr.
DMGS Joe DiMaggio....... 100.00 30.00
Mark McGwire
Ken Griffey Jr.
Sammy Sosa
DRME J.D. Drew....... 25.00 7.50
Scott Rolen
Tino Martinez
Jim Edmonds
FVRT Rafael Furcal....... 25.00 7.50
Omar Vizquel
Alex Rodriguez
Miguel Tejada
GRPR Juan Gonzalez....... 25.00 7.50
Ivan Rodriguez
Rafael Palmeiro
Alex Rodriguez
GSGB Shawn Green....... 40.00 12.00
Sammy Sosa
Ken Griffey Jr.
Pat Burrell
GSMJ Ken Griffey Jr....... 40.00 12.00
Sammy Sosa
Greg Maddux
Randy Johnson
GSWG Shawn Green....... 25.00 7.50
Sammy Sosa
Larry Walker
Luis Gonzalez
HGSR Todd Helton....... 40.00 12.00
Ken Griffey Jr.
Sammy Sosa
Alex Rodriguez
INSH Kazuhisa Ishii....... 25.00 7.50
Hideo Nomo
Tsuyoshi Shinjo
Shigetoshi Hasegawa
JMEG David Justice....... 25.00 7.50
Edgar Martinez
Darin Erstad
Juan Gonzalez
JWGF Randy Johnson....... 25.00 7.50
Matt Williams
Luis Gonzalez
Steve Finley
KRLJ Jason Kendall....... 25.00 7.50
Ivan Rodriguez
Mike Lieberthal
Charles Johnson
MGMC Pedro Martinez....... 40.00 12.00
Tom Glavine
Greg Maddux
Roger Clemens
MGSG Mark McGwire....... 60.00 18.00
Ken Griffey Jr.
Sammy Sosa
Jason Giambi
OSGA Magglio Ordonez....... 25.00 7.50
Tim Salmon
Shawn Green
Bobby Abreu
PBBD Corey Patterson....... 15.00 4.50
Adrian Beltre
Russell Branyan
Adam Dunn
PTMO Rafael Palmeiro....... 25.00 7.50
Frank Thomas
Doug Mientkiewicz
John Olerud
SAKS Gary Sheffield....... 40.00 12.00
Bobby Abreu
Ryan Klesko
Sammy Sosa
SGPM Sammy Sosa....... 40.00 12.00
Ken Griffey Jr.
Rafael Palmeiro
Fred McGriff
SJJM Gary Sheffield....... 40.00 12.00
Andruw Jones
Chipper Jones
Greg Maddux
SMTT Mike Sweeney....... 25.00 7.50
Edgar Martinez
Jim Thome
Frank Thomas
TGTD Jim Thome....... 25.00 7.50
Juan Gonzalez
Frank Thomas
Carlos Delgado
TROJ Jim Thome....... 25.00 7.50
Alex Rodriguez
Magglio Ordonez
David Justice
VRBA Robin Ventura....... 25.00 7.50
Scott Rolen
Adrian Beltre
Edgardo Alfonzo
WGGH Preston Wilson....... 25.00 7.50
Brian Giles
Shawn Green
Todd Helton
WGPV Bernie Williams....... 40.00 12.00
Jason Giambi
Jorge Posada
Robin Ventura
WLAV Bernie Williams....... 25.00 7.50
Al Leiter
Roberto Alomar
Robin Ventura

2002 Upper Deck Diamond Connection Great Connections

Randomly inserted in packs, these six cards feature two players as well as memorabilia pieces for each player. Each card was issued to a stated print run of 50 serial numbered sets.

Nm-Mt Ex-Mt
GR Jason Giambi....... 400.00 120.00
Babe Ruth
IG Ichiro Suzuki....... 250.00 75.00
Ken Griffey Jr.
MD Mickey Mantle....... 400.00 120.00
Joe DiMaggio
MR Mark McGwire....... 500.00 150.00
Babe Ruth
MS Mark McGwire....... 250.00 75.00
Sammy Sosa
RR Alex Rodriguez....... 200.00 60.00
Nolan Ryan

2002 Upper Deck Diamond Connection Memorable Signatures Bat

Randomly inserted into packs, these 12 cards feature not only a game-used bat piece of the featured player but also an authentic signature. These cards are all printed to different stated print runs and we have notated that information next to the card in our checklist.

Nm-Mt Ex-Mt
NO PRICING ON QTY OF 20 OR LESS.
AR Alex Rodriguez/145....... 150.00 45.00
BR Babe Ruth/3.......
CR Cal Ripken/145....... 150.00 45.00
IS Ichiro Suzuki/99....... 300.00 90.00
JD Joe DiMaggio/20.......
JG Jason Giambi/49....... 100.00 30.00
JM Joe Morgan/99....... 60.00 18.00
KG Ken Griffey Jr./49....... 200.00 60.00
KP Kirby Puckett/145....... 100.00 30.00
MMC Mark McGwire/49....... 400.00 120.00
NR Nolan Ryan/99....... 150.00 45.00
SS Sammy Sosa/99....... 200.00 60.00

2002 Upper Deck Diamond Connection Memorable Signatures Jersey

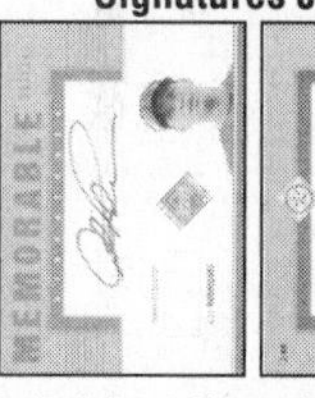

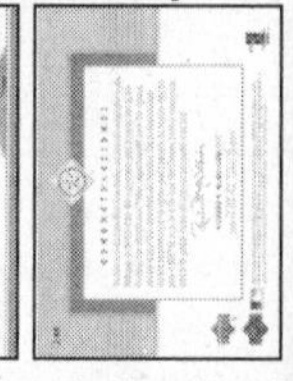

Randomly inserted into packs, these 14 cards feature not only a game-used jersey piece of the featured player but also an authentic signature. These cards are all printed to different stated print runs and we have notated that information next to the card in our checklist.

Nm-Mt Ex-Mt
NO PRICING ON QTY OF 20 OR LESS.
AR Alex Rodriguez/145....... 150.00 45.00
BR Babe Ruth/3.......
CR Cal Ripken/145....... 150.00 45.00
EB Ernie Banks/150....... 100.00 30.00
IS Ichiro Suzuki/99....... 300.00 90.00
JD Joe DiMaggio Pants/20.......
JG Jason Giambi/49.......
JM Joe Morgan/99....... 60.00 18.00
KG Ken Griffey Jr./49....... 200.00 60.00
MMA Mickey Mantle/1.......
MMC Mark McGwire/49....... 400.00 120.00
NR Nolan Ryan/99....... 150.00 45.00
SK Sandy Koufax/150....... 350.00 105.00
SS Sammy Sosa/99....... 200.00 60.00

2002 Upper Deck Diamond Connection Memorable Signatures Jerseys Gold

Randomly inserted into packs, this card featured not only a jersey swatch of Sandy Koufax but also an authentic autograph. This card was issued to a stated print run of 150 serial numbered copies.

Nm-Mt Ex-Mt
JSKO Sandy Koufax/150....... 350.00 105.00

1999 Upper Deck Encore

The 1999 Upper Deck Encore set was issued in one series for a total of 180 cards and was distributed in six-card packs with a suggested retail price of $3.99. The set features 90 of the best cards from the 1999 Upper Deck set

printed on rainbow-foil cards with three short-printed subsets: Star Rookies (91-135) with an insertion rate of 1:4, Homer Odyssey (136-165) inserted 1:6 packs, and Strokes of Genius (166-180) inserted 1:8 packs. Rookie Cards include Pat Burrell and Eric Munson.

	Nm-Mt	Ex-Mt
COMPLETE SET (180)	200.00	60.00
COMP.SET w/o SP's (90)	20.00	6.00
COMMON CARD (1-90)	.40	.12
COMMON SR (91-135)	1.00	.30
COMMON HO (136-165)	.75	.23
COMMON SG (166-180)	1.00	.30
1 Darin Erstad	.40	.12
2 Mo Vaughn	.40	.12
3 Travis Lee	.40	.12
4 Randy Johnson	1.00	.30
5 Matt Williams	.40	.12
6 John Smoltz	.60	.18
7 Greg Maddux	1.50	.45
8 Chipper Jones	1.00	.30
9 Tom Glavine	.60	.18
10 Andruw Jones	.40	.12
11 Cal Ripken	3.00	.90
12 Mike Mussina	1.00	.30
13 Albert Belle	.40	.12
14 Nomar Garciaparra	1.50	.45
15 Jose Offerman	.40	.12
16 Pedro Martinez	1.00	.30
17 Trot Nixon	.60	.18
18 Kerry Wood	1.00	.30
19 Sammy Sosa	1.50	.45
20 Frank Thomas	1.00	.30
21 Paul Konerko	.40	.12
22 Sean Casey	.40	.12
23 Barry Larkin	1.00	.30
24 Greg Vaughn	.40	.12
25 Travis Fryman	.40	.12
26 Jaret Wright	.40	.12
27 Jim Thome	1.00	.30
28 Manny Ramirez	.40	.12
29 Roberto Alomar	1.00	.30
30 Kenny Lofton	.40	.12
31 Todd Helton	.60	.18
32 Larry Walker	.60	.18
33 Vinny Castilla	.40	.12
34 Dante Bichette	.40	.12
35 Tony Clark	.40	.12
36 Dean Palmer	.40	.12
37 Gabe Kapler	.40	.12
38 Juan Encarnacion	.40	.12
39 Alex Gonzalez	.40	.12
40 Preston Wilson	.40	.12
41 Mark Kotsay	.40	.12
42 Moises Alou	.40	.12
43 Craig Biggio	.60	.18
44 Ken Caminiti	.40	.12
45 Jeff Bagwell	.60	.18
46 Johnny Damon	.40	.12
47 Gary Sheffield	.40	.12
48 Kevin Brown	.60	.18
49 Raul Mondesi	.40	.12
50 Jeff Cirillo	.40	.12
51 Jeromy Burnitz	.40	.12
52 Todd Walker	.40	.12
53 Corey Koskie	.40	.12
54 Brad Fullmer	.40	.12
55 Vladimir Guerrero	1.00	.30
56 Mike Piazza	1.50	.45
57 Robin Ventura	.40	.12
58 Rickey Henderson	1.00	.30
59 Derek Jeter	2.50	.75
60 Paul O'Neill	.60	.18
61 Bernie Williams	.60	.18
62 Tino Martinez	.60	.18
63 Roger Clemens	2.00	.60
64 Ben Grieve	.40	.12
65 Jason Giambi	1.00	.30
66 Bob Abreu	.40	.12
67 Scott Rolen	.60	.18
68 Curt Schilling	.60	.18
69 Marlon Anderson	.40	.12
70 Kevin Young	.40	.12
71 Jason Kendall	.40	.12
72 Brian Giles	.40	.12
73 Mark McGwire	2.50	.75
74 Fernando Tatis	.40	.12
75 Eric Davis	.40	.12
76 Trevor Hoffman	.40	.12
77 Tony Gwynn	1.25	.35
78 Matt Clement	.40	.12
79 Robb Nen	.40	.12
80 Barry Bonds	2.50	.75
81 Ken Griffey Jr.	1.50	.45
82 Alex Rodriguez	1.50	.45
83 Wade Boggs	.60	.18
84 Fred McGriff	.60	.18
85 Jose Canseco	1.00	.30
86 Ivan Rodriguez	1.00	.30
87 Juan Gonzalez	1.00	.30
88 Rafael Palmeiro	.60	.18
89 Carlos Delgado	.40	.12
90 David Wells	.40	.12
91 Troy Glaus SR	1.50	.45
92 Adrian Beltre SR	1.00	.30
93 Matt Anderson SR	1.00	.30
94 Eric Chavez SR	1.00	.30
95 Jeff Weaver SR RC	1.50	.45
96 Warren Morris SR	1.00	.30
97 George Lombard SR	1.00	.30
98 Mike Kinkade SR	1.00	.30
99 Kyle Farnsworth SR RC	2.50	.75
100 J.D. Drew SR	1.00	.30
101 Joe McEwing SR RC	1.00	.30
102 Carlos Guillen SR	1.00	.30
103 K.Dransfeldt SR RC	1.00	.30
104 Eric Munson SR RC	3.00	.90
105 Armando Rios SR	1.00	.30
106 Ramon E.Martinez SR RC	1.00	.30
107 O.Hernandez SR	1.00	.30
108 Jeremy Giambi SR	1.00	.30
109 Pat Burrell SR RC	10.00	3.00
110 S.Hillenbrand SR RC	5.00	1.50
111 Billy Koch SR	1.00	.30
112 Roy Halladay SR	1.00	.30
113 Ruben Mateo SR	1.00	.30
114 Bruce Chen SR	1.00	.30
115 Angel Pena SR	1.00	.30
116 Michael Barrett SR	1.00	.30
117 Kevin Witt SR	1.00	.30
118 Damon Minor SR	1.00	.30
119 Ryan Minor SR	1.00	.30
120 A.J. Pierzynski SR	1.00	.30
121 A.J. Burnett SR RC	2.50	.75
122 Cristian Guzman SR	1.00	.30
123 Joe Lawrence SR	1.00	.30
124 Derrick Gibson SR	1.00	.30
125 Carlos Febles SR	1.00	.30
126 Chris Haas SR	1.00	.30
127 Cesar King SR	1.00	.30
128 Calvin Pickering SR	1.00	.30
129 Mitch Meluskey SR	1.00	.30
130 Carlos Beltran SR	1.00	.30
131 Ron Belliard SR	1.00	.30
132 Jerry Hairston Jr. SR	1.00	.30
133 F.Seguignol SR	1.00	.30
134 Kris Benson SR	1.00	.30
135 C.Hutchinson SR RC	1.00	.30
136 Ken Griffey Jr. HO	3.00	.90
137 Mark McGwire HO	5.00	1.50
138 Sammy Sosa HO	3.00	.90
139 Albert Belle HO	.75	.23
140 Mo Vaughn HO	.75	.23
141 Alex Rodriguez HO	3.00	.90
142 Manny Ramirez HO	.75	.23
143 J.D. Drew HO	.75	.23
144 Juan Gonzalez HO	2.00	.60
145 Vladimir Guerrero HO	2.00	.60
146 Fernando Tatis HO	.75	.23
147 Mike Piazza HO	3.00	.90
148 Barry Bonds HO	5.00	1.50
149 Ivan Rodriguez HO	2.00	.60
150 Jeff Bagwell HO	1.25	.35
151 Raul Mondesi HO	.75	.23
152 N.Garciaparra HO	3.00	.90
153 Jose Canseco HO	2.00	.60
154 Greg Vaughn HO	.75	.23
155 Scott Rolen HO	1.25	.35
156 Vinny Castilla HO	.75	.23
157 Troy Glaus HO	1.25	.35
158 Craig Biggio HO	1.25	.35
159 Tino Martinez HO	1.25	.35
160 Jim Thome HO	2.00	.60
161 Frank Thomas HO	2.00	.60
162 Tony Clark HO	.75	.23
163 Ben Grieve HO	.75	.23
164 Matt Williams HO	.75	.23
165 Derek Jeter HO	5.00	1.50
166 Ken Griffey Jr. SG	2.50	.75
167 Tony Gwynn SG	2.00	.60
168 Mike Piazza SG	2.50	.75
169 Mark McGwire SG	4.00	1.20
170 Sammy Sosa SG	2.50	.75
171 Juan Gonzalez SG	1.50	.45
172 Mo Vaughn SG	1.00	.30
173 Derek Jeter SG	4.00	1.20
174 Bernie Williams SG	1.00	.30
175 Ivan Rodriguez SG	1.50	.45
176 Barry Bonds SG	4.00	1.20
177 Scott Rolen SG	1.00	.30
178 Larry Walker SG	1.00	.30
179 Chipper Jones SG	1.50	.45
180 Alex Rodriguez SG	2.50	.75

1999 Upper Deck Encore FX Gold

This 180-card set is a parallel version of the base set and is sequentially numbered to 125. These cards feature gold foil fronts instead of silver foil for the more common base set.

Nm-Mt Ex-Mt
*STARS 1-90: 6X TO 15X BASIC 1-90
*SR RC'S 91-135: 1.5X TO 4X BASIC SR RC
*HOMER ODYSSEY: 1.5X TO 4X BASIC HO
*STROKES OF GENIUS: 2X TO 5X BASIC SG

1999 Upper Deck Encore 2K Countdown

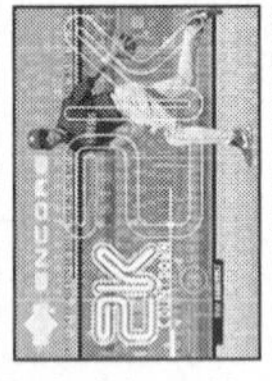

Randomly inserted in packs at the rate of one in 11, this 10-card set features color photos of top players who will be stars in the next century.

	Nm-Mt	Ex-Mt
COMPLETE SET (10)	25.00	7.50
2K1 Ken Griffey Jr.	2.50	.75
2K2 Derek Jeter	4.00	1.20
2K3 Mike Piazza	2.50	.75
2K4 J.D. Drew	1.00	.30
2K5 Vladimir Guerrero	1.50	.45
2K6 Chipper Jones	1.50	.45
2K7 Alex Rodriguez	2.50	.75
2K8 Nomar Garciaparra	2.50	.75
2K9 Mark McGwire	4.00	1.20
2K10 Sammy Sosa	2.50	.75

1999 Upper Deck Encore Batting Practice Caps

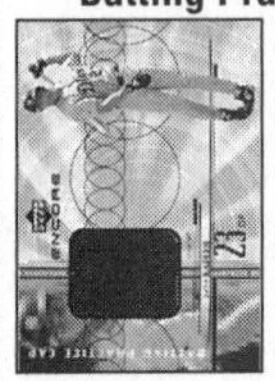
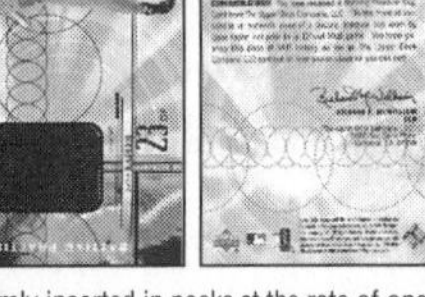

Randomly inserted in packs at the rate of one in 750, this 15-card set features color player photos with actual swatch pieces of the highlighted player's batting practice cap embedded in the card.

	Nm-Mt	Ex-Mt
C-BB Barry Bonds	60.00	18.00
C-BH Frank Thomas	25.00	7.50
C-CB Carlos Beltran	15.00	4.50
C-DP Dean Palmer	15.00	4.50
C-EC Eric Chavez	15.00	4.50
C-GK Gabe Kapler	10.00	3.00
C-GV Greg Vaughn	15.00	4.50
C-JD J.D. Drew	15.00	4.50
C-JK Jason Kendall	15.00	4.50
C-TC Tony Clark	10.00	3.00
C-TG Tony Gwynn	30.00	9.00
C-TH Todd Helton	25.00	7.50
C-TW Todd Walker	15.00	4.50
C-VC Vinny Castilla	15.00	4.50
C-VG Vladimir Guerrero	25.00	7.50

1999 Upper Deck Encore Driving Forces

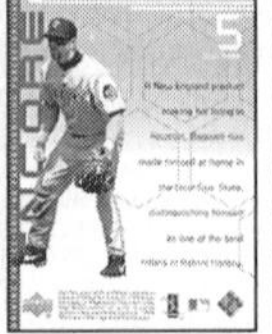

Randomly inserted in packs at the rate of one in 23, this 15-card set features color photos of some of the top players printed on super-thick, rainbow foil cards.

	Nm-Mt	Ex-Mt
COMPLETE SET (15)	80.00	24.00
FX GOLD RANDOM INSERTS IN PACKS		
FX GOLD PRINT RUN 10 SERIAL #'d SETS		
FX GOLD NOT PRICED DUE TO SCARCITY		
D1 Ken Griffey Jr.	6.00	1.80
D2 Mark McGwire	10.00	3.00
D3 Sammy Sosa	6.00	1.80
D4 Albert Belle	1.50	.45
D5 Alex Rodriguez	6.00	1.80
D6 Mo Vaughn	1.50	.45
D7 Juan Gonzalez	4.00	1.20
D8 Jeff Bagwell	2.50	.75
D9 Mike Piazza	6.00	1.80
D10 Frank Thomas	4.00	1.20
D11 Barry Bonds	10.00	3.00
D12 Vladimir Guerrero	4.00	1.20
D13 Chipper Jones	4.00	1.20
D14 Tony Gwynn	5.00	1.50
D15 J.D. Drew	2.50	.75

1999 Upper Deck Encore McGwired

Randomly inserted in packs at the rate of one in 23, this 10-card set features color photos of Mark McGwire.

	Nm-Mt	Ex-Mt
COMPLETE SET (10)	80.00	24.00
*FX GOLD: 1X TO 2.5X BASIC MCGWIRED		
FX GOLD RANDOM INSERTS IN PACKS		
FX GOLD PRINT RUN 500 SERIAL #'d SETS		
MC1 Mark McGwire Carl Pavano	10.00	3.00
MC2 Mark McGwire Mike Morgan	8.00	2.40
MC3 Mark McGwire Steve Trachsel	8.00	2.40
MC4 Mark McGwire Ramon Martinez	8.00	2.40
MC5 Mark McGwire Willie Blair	8.00	2.40
MC6 Mark McGwire Scott Elarton	8.00	2.40
MC7 Mark McGwire Jim Parque	8.00	2.40
MC8 Mark McGwire Livan Hernandez	8.00	2.40
MC9 Mark McGwire Rafael Roque	8.00	2.40
MC10 Mark McGwire Jaret Wright	8.00	2.40

1999 Upper Deck Encore Pure Excitement

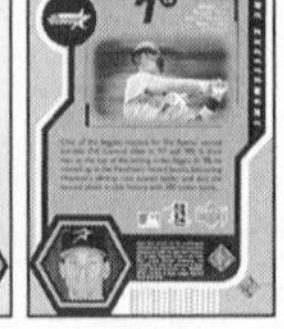

Randomly inserted at the rate of one in seven, this 30-card set features color photos of some of the most exciting players printed on Light F/X cards.

	Nm-Mt	Ex-Mt
COMPLETE SET (30)	80.00	24.00
P1 Mo Vaughn	1.00	.30
P2 Darin Erstad	1.00	.30
P3 Travis Lee	1.00	.30
P4 Chipper Jones	2.50	.75
P5 Greg Maddux	4.00	1.20
P6 Gabe Kapler	1.00	.30
P7 Cal Ripken	8.00	2.40
P8 Nomar Garciaparra	4.00	1.20
P9 Kerry Wood	2.50	.75
P10 Frank Thomas	2.50	.75
P11 Manny Ramirez	1.00	.30
P12 Larry Walker	1.50	.45
P13 Tony Clark	1.00	.30
P14 Jeff Bagwell	1.50	.45
P15 Craig Biggio	1.50	.45
P16 Vladimir Guerrero	2.50	.75
P17 Mike Piazza	4.00	1.20
P18 Bernie Williams	1.50	.45
P19 Derek Jeter	6.00	1.80
P20 Ben Grieve	1.00	.30
P21 Eric Chavez	1.00	.30
P22 Scott Rolen	1.50	.45
P23 Mark McGwire	6.00	1.80
P24 Tony Gwynn	3.00	.90
P25 Barry Bonds	6.00	1.80
P26 Ken Griffey Jr.	4.00	1.20
P27 Alex Rodriguez	4.00	1.20
P28 J.D. Drew	1.50	.45
P29 Juan Gonzalez	2.50	.75
P30 Roger Clemens	5.00	1.50

1999 Upper Deck Encore Rookie Encore

Randomly inserted in packs at the rate of one in 23, this 10-card set features color photos of top rookies of the 1999 season.

	Nm-Mt	Ex-Mt
COMPLETE SET (10)	15.00	4.50
*FX GOLD: 1.25X TO 3X BASIC ROOK.ENCORE		
FX GOLD RANDOM INSERTS IN PACKS		
FX GOLD PRINT RUN 500 SERIAL #'d SETS		
R1 J.D. Drew	.60	.18
R2 Eric Chavez	.60	.18
R3 Gabe Kapler	1.50	.45
R4 Bruce Chen	.60	.18
R5 Carlos Beltran	.60	.18
R6 Troy Glaus	1.00	.30
R7 Roy Halladay	.60	.18
R8 Adrian Beltre	.60	.18
R9 Michael Barrett	.60	.18
R10 Pat Burrell	5.00	1.50

1999 Upper Deck Encore UD Authentics

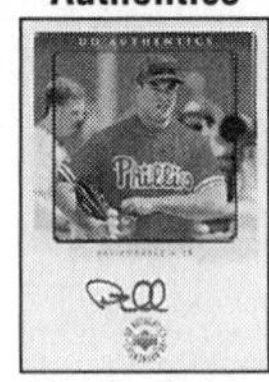

Randomly inserted in packs at the rate of one in 288, this six-card set features autographed color photos of top players.

	Nm-Mt	Ex-Mt
JD J.D. Drew	15.00	4.50
JR Ken Griffey Jr.	150.00	45.00
MB Michael Barrett	10.00	3.00
NG Nomar Garciaparra	150.00	45.00
PB Pat Burrell	25.00	7.50
TG Troy Glaus	25.00	7.50

1999 Upper Deck Encore Upper Realm

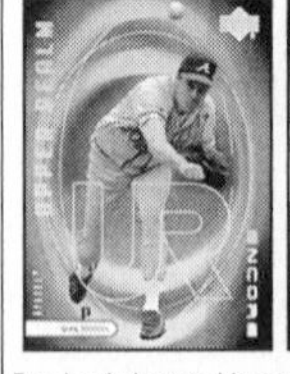

Randomly inserted in packs at the rate of one in 11, this 15-card set features color photos of the best players of the season.

	Nm-Mt	Ex-Mt
COMPLETE SET (15)	50.00	15.00
U1 Ken Griffey Jr.	3.00	.90
U2 Mark McGwire	5.00	1.50
U3 Sammy Sosa	3.00	.90
U4 Tony Gwynn	2.50	.75
U5 Alex Rodriguez	3.00	.90
U6 Juan Gonzalez	2.00	.60
U7 J.D. Drew	1.50	.45
U8 Roger Clemens	4.00	1.20
U9 Greg Maddux	3.00	.90
U10 Randy Johnson	2.00	.60
U11 Mo Vaughn	.75	.23
U12 Derek Jeter	5.00	1.50
U13 Vladimir Guerrero	2.00	.60
U14 Cal Ripken	6.00	1.80
U15 Nomar Garciaparra	3.00	.90

2001 Upper Deck Evolution

The 2001 Upper Deck Evolution product released in October, 2001 and featured a 120-card base set. Each pack contained 5 cards, and carried a suggested retail price of $2.99 per pack. The set was broken into two tiers, Base Cards (1-90) and Prospects (91-120).

The Prospects cards were serial numbered to 2250.

	Nm-Mt	Ex-Mt
COMP.SET w/o SP's (90)	20.00	6.00
COMMON CARD (1-90)	.30	.09
COMMON CARD (91-120)	5.00	1.50
1 Darin Erstad	.30	.09
2 Troy Glaus	.50	.15
3 Jason Giambi	.75	.23
4 Tim Hudson	.30	.09
5 Jermaine Dye	.30	.09
6 Barry Zito	.75	.23
7 Carlos Delgado	.30	.09
8 Shannon Stewart	.30	.09
9 Jose Cruz Jr.	.30	.09
10 Greg Vaughn	.30	.09
11 Juan Gonzalez	.75	.23
12 Roberto Alomar	.75	.23
13 Omar Vizquel	.30	.09
14 Jim Thome	.75	.23
15 Edgar Martinez	.50	.15
16 John Olerud	.30	.09
17 Kazuhiro Sasaki	.30	.09
18 Cal Ripken	2.50	.75
19 Alex Rodriguez	1.25	.35
20 Ivan Rodriguez	.75	.23
21 Rafael Palmeiro	.50	.15
22 Pedro Martinez	.75	.23
23 Nomar Garciaparra	1.25	.35
24 Manny Ramirez	.30	.09
25 Carl Everett	.30	.09
26 Mark Quinn	.30	.09
27 Mike Sweeney	.30	.09
28 Neifi Perez	.30	.09
29 Tony Clark	.30	.09
30 Eric Milton	.30	.09
31 Doug Mientkiewicz	.30	.09
32 Corey Koskie	.30	.09
33 Frank Thomas	.75	.23
34 David Wells	.30	.09
35 Magglio Ordonez	.30	.09
36 Derek Jeter	2.00	.60
37 Mike Mussina	.75	.23
38 Bernie Williams	.50	.15
39 Roger Clemens	1.50	.45
40 David Justice	.30	.09
41 Jeff Bagwell	.50	.15
42 Richard Hidalgo	.30	.09
43 Wade Miller	.30	.09
44 Chipper Jones	.75	.23
45 Greg Maddux	1.25	.35
46 Andruw Jones	.30	.09
47 Rafael Furcal	.30	.09
48 Geoff Jenkins	.30	.09
49 Jeromy Burnitz	.30	.09
50 Ben Sheets	.30	.09
51 Richie Sexson	.30	.09
52 Mark McGwire	2.00	.60
53 Jim Edmonds	.30	.09
54 Darryl Kile	.30	.09
55 J.D. Drew	.30	.09
56 Sammy Sosa	1.25	.35
57 Kerry Wood	.75	.23
58 Randy Johnson	.75	.23
59 Luis Gonzalez	.30	.09
60 Matt Williams	.30	.09
61 Kevin Brown	.30	.09
62 Gary Sheffield	.30	.09
63 Shawn Green	.30	.09
64 Chan Ho Park	.30	.09
65 Vladimir Guerrero	.75	.23
66 Jose Vidro	.30	.09
67 Fernando Tatis	.30	.09
68 Barry Bonds	2.00	.60
69 Jeff Kent	.30	.09
70 Russ Ortiz	.30	.09
71 Preston Wilson	.30	.09
72 Ryan Dempster	.30	.09
73 Charles Johnson	.30	.09
74 Mike Piazza	1.25	.35
75 Edgardo Alfonzo	.30	.09
76 Robin Ventura	.30	.09
77 Jay Payton	.30	.09
78 Tony Gwynn	1.00	.30
79 Phil Nevin	.30	.09
80 Pat Burrell	.30	.09
81 Scott Rolen	.50	.15
82 Bob Abreu	.30	.09
83 Brian Giles	.30	.09
84 Jason Kendall	.30	.09
85 Ken Griffey Jr.	1.25	.35
86 Barry Larkin	.75	.23
87 Sean Casey	.30	.09
88 Todd Helton	.50	.15
89 Larry Walker	.50	.15
90 Mike Hampton	.30	.09
91 Ichiro Suzuki PROS RC	25.00	7.50
92 Albert Pujols PROS RC	30.00	9.00
93 W.Betemit PROS RC	5.00	1.50
94 Jay Gibbons PROS RC	8.00	2.40
95 Juan Uribe PROS RC	5.00	1.50
96 M. Ensberg PROS RC	8.00	2.40
97 C. Parker PROS RC	5.00	1.50
98 T. Shinjo PROS RC	8.00	2.40
99 Jack Wilson PROS RC	5.00	1.50
100 D. Mendez PROS RC	5.00	1.50
101 Ryan Freel PROS RC	5.00	1.50
102 Juan Diaz PROS RC	5.00	1.50
103 H. Ramirez PROS RC	8.00	2.40
104 R. Rodriguez PROS RC	5.00	1.50
105 E. Almonte PROS RC	5.00	1.50
106 J. Towers PROS RC	5.00	1.50
107 A.Hernandez PROS RC	5.00	1.50
108 B.Duckworth PROS RC	5.00	1.50
109 T. Hafner PROS RC	10.00	3.00
110 M. Vargas PROS RC	5.00	1.50
111 Kris Keller PROS RC	5.00	1.50
112 B. Lawrence PROS RC	5.00	1.50

113 Esix Snead PROS RC 5.00 1.50
114 Wilkin Ruan PROS RC 5.00 1.50
115 J. Mieses PROS RC 5.00 1.50
116 J. Estrada PROS RC 5.00 1.50
117 E. Guzman PROS RC 5.00 1.50
118 S. Douglass PROS RC 5.00 1.50
119 B. Sylvester PROS RC 5.00 1.50
120 Bret Prinz PROS RC 5.00 1.50

2001 Upper Deck Evolution e-Card Classics

Randomly inserted at one in , this six-card insert features cards that can be viewed over the Upper Deck website. Cards feature a serial number that is to be typed in a the Upper Deck website to reveal that card. Card backs carry an "E" prefix.

	Nm-Mt	Ex-Mt
COMPLETE SET (15)	40.00	12.00
EC1 Ken Griffey Jr. 89	5.00	1.50
EC2 Gary Sheffield 89	1.00	.30
EC3 Randy Johnson 89	2.50	.75
EC4 Sammy Sosa 90	4.00	1.20
EC5 Carlos Delgado 93	1.00	.30
EC6 Ichiro Suzuki 01	15.00	4.50
EC7 Andruw Jones 97	1.00	.30
EC8 Chipper Jones 91	2.50	.75
EC9 Kazuhiro Sasaki 00	1.00	.30
EC10 Shawn Green 92	1.00	.30
EC11 Alex Rodriguez 94	4.00	1.20
EC12 Brian Giles 97	1.00	.30
EC13 J.D. Drew 99	1.00	.30
EC14 Pat Burrell 99	1.00	.30
EC15 Ivan Rodriguez 91	2.50	.75

2001 Upper Deck Evolution e-Card Game Bat

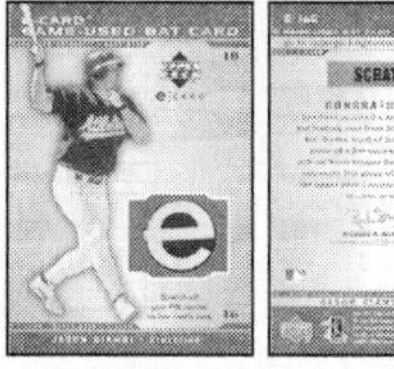

Randomly inserted into packs at one in 120, these 10-card set features a piece of game-used bat. The card backs have a scratch off box that reveals a number that can be entered at Upper Deck's website. Winning bat cards evolve in bat-jersey autograph cards. Card backs carry a "B" prefix.

	Nm-Mt	Ex-Mt
B-AJ Andruw Jones	10.00	3.00
B-AR Alex Rodriguez	25.00	7.50
B-CD Carlos Delgado	10.00	3.00
B-GS Gary Sheffield	10.00	3.00
B-JaG Jason Giambi	20.00	6.00
B-JD J.D. Drew	10.00	3.00
B-JK Jason Kendall	10.00	3.00
B-KG Ken Griffey Jr.	20.00	6.00
B-PB Pat Burrell	10.00	3.00
B-RB Russell Branyan	10.00	3.00

2001 Upper Deck Evolution e-Card Game Bat-Jersey Autograph

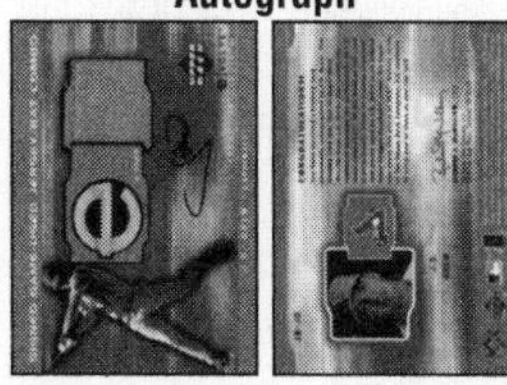

Issued at a rate of one in 480 Evolved upgrades, these cards have not only a game-used piece but also an autograph of the featured player.

Nm-Mt Ex-Mt
STATED ODDS 1:480 EVOLVE UPGRADES
STATED PRINT RUN 5 SERIAL #'d SETS

2001 Upper Deck Evolution Game Jersey

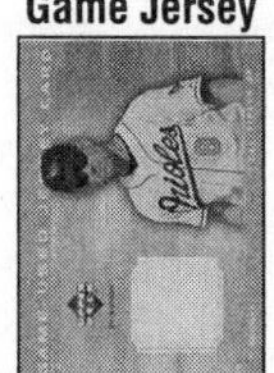

Randomly inserted into packs at one in 120, this 15-card set features game-used jersey cards of the players. Cards are numbered using the players intials with a "J" prefix.

	Nm-Mt	Ex-Mt
J-JaG Jason Giambi	15.00	4.50
J-AJ Andruw Jones	10.00	3.00
J-AR Alex Rodriguez	25.00	7.50
J-BG Brian Giles	10.00	3.00
J-CJ Chipper Jones	15.00	4.50
J-CR Cal Ripken	40.00	12.00
J-GS Gary Sheffield	10.00	3.00
J-JD J.D. Drew	10.00	3.00
J-JK Jason Kendall	10.00	3.00
J-KG Ken Griffey Jr.	20.00	6.00
J-PB Pat Burrell	10.00	3.00
J-RB Russell Branyan	10.00	3.00
J-SG Shawn Green	10.00	3.00
J-SS Sammy Sosa	20.00	6.00
J-TG Troy Glaus	15.00	4.50

2001 Upper Deck Evolution Ichiro Suzuki All-Star Game

Randomly inserted into packs, this card was originally intended to be distributed at the All-Star Game Fanfest in Seattle. The card comes in three versions, bronze, silver and gold. The silver and gold versions are serial numbered. Approximately 10 percent of the gold cards have been discovered without the serial numbering. We are continuing to evaluate more about that specific card and see if it is more than just a printing flaw.

	Nm-Mt	Ex-Mt
51B Ichiro Suzuki Bronze	10.00	3.00
51G Ichiro Suzuki Gold/51	150.00	45.00
51S Ichiro Suzuki Silver/2001	25.00	7.50

2003 Upper Deck Finite

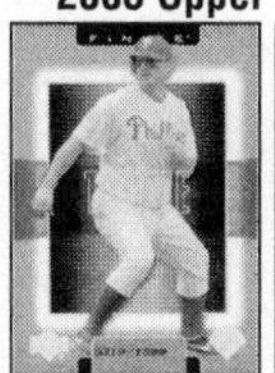
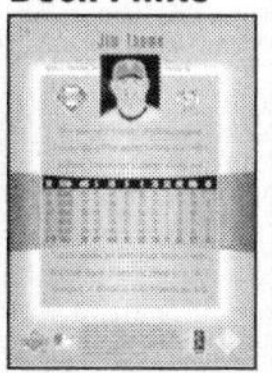

This 380-card set was released in December, 2003. This set was issued in three-card packs with an $9.99 SRP which came 11 packs to a box and 12 boxes to a case. This set is split into many different subsets: Cards numbered 1-100 feature veterans and those cards were issued to a stated print run of 1999 serial numbered sets. Cards numbered 101-150 are a Major Factors subset and they cards were issued to a stated print run of 1599 serial numbered sets. Cards numbered 151 through 180 were Prominent Powers subset and they were issued to a stated print run of 499 serial numbered sets. Cards numbered 181 through 200 were the First Class cards and they were issued to a stated print run of 199 serial numbered sets. Cards numbered 201 through 380 featured Rookies and those cards were issued in varying tiers. Cards numbered 201-300 were issued to a stated print run of 1299 serial numbered sets. Cards numbered 301-330 were issued to a stated print run of 599 serial numbered sets. Cards numbered 331 through 360 were issued to a stated print run of 299 serial numbered sets and cards numbered 361-380 were issued to a stated print run of 150 serial numbered sets. In addition, update cards for the following Upper Deck products: SP Authentic, SPX, Upper Deck Game Face and UD Authentics) were randomly inserted into these packs.

	MINT	NRMT
COMMON CARD (1-100)	2.00	.90
COMMON CARD (101-150)	2.50	1.10
COMMON CARD (151-180)	4.00	1.80
COMMON CARD (181-200)	5.00	2.20
1-200 STATED ODDS TWO PER PACK		
COMMON CARD (201-300)	3.00	1.35
COMMON CARD (301-330)	5.00	2.20
301-330 PRINT RUN 599 SERIAL #'d SETS		
COMMON CARD (331-360)	8.00	3.60
331-360 PRINT RUN 299 SERIAL #'d SETS		
COMMON CARD (361-380)	10.00	4.50
361-380 PRINT RUN 150 SERIAL #'d SETS		
201-380/STARS 'N STRIPES ODDS 1:1		
1 Darin Erstad	2.00	.90
2 Garret Anderson	2.00	.90
3 Tim Salmon	2.50	1.10
4 Troy Glaus	2.50	1.10
5 Luis Gonzalez	2.00	.90
6 Randy Johnson	2.50	1.10
7 Curt Schilling	2.50	1.10
8 Andruw Jones	2.00	.90
9 Gary Sheffield	2.00	.90
10 Rafael Furcal	2.00	.90
11 Greg Maddux	4.00	1.80
12 Chipper Jones	2.50	1.10
13 Tony Batista	2.00	.90
14 Jay Gibbons	2.00	.90
15 Johnny Damon	2.00	.90
16 Derek Lowe	2.00	.90
17 Nomar Garciaparra	4.00	1.80
18 Pedro Martinez	2.50	1.10
19 Manny Ramirez	2.00	.90
20 Mark Prior	5.00	2.20
21 Kerry Wood	2.50	1.10
22 Corey Patterson	2.00	.90
23 Sammy Sosa	4.00	1.80
24 Moises Alou	2.00	.90
25 Magglio Ordonez	2.00	.90
26 Frank Thomas	2.50	1.10
27 Paul Konerko	2.00	.90
28 Bartolo Colon	2.00	.90
29 Adam Dunn	2.00	.90
30 Austin Kearns	2.00	.90
31 Aaron Boone	2.00	.90
32 Ken Griffey Jr.	4.00	1.80
33 Omar Vizquel	2.00	.90
34 C.C. Sabathia	2.00	.90
35 Brandon Phillips	2.00	.90
36 Larry Walker	2.50	1.10
37 Preston Wilson	2.00	.90
38 Todd Helton	2.50	1.10
39 Eric Munson	2.00	.90
40 Ivan Rodriguez	2.50	1.10
41 Josh Beckett	2.50	1.10
42 Roy Oswalt	2.00	.90
43 Craig Biggio	2.50	1.10
44 Jeff Bagwell	2.50	1.10
45 Dontrelle Willis	2.50	1.10
46 Carlos Beltran	2.00	.90
47 Brent Mayne	2.00	.90
48 Hideo Nomo	2.50	1.10
49 Rickey Henderson	2.50	1.10
50 Adrian Beltre	2.00	.90
51 Miguel Cabrera	4.00	1.80
52 Kazuhisa Ishii	2.00	.90
53 Richie Sexson	2.00	.90
54 Torii Hunter	2.00	.90
55 Jacque Jones	2.00	.90
56 A.J. Pierzynski	2.00	.90
57 Jose Vidro	2.00	.90
58 Vladimir Guerrero	2.50	1.10
59 Tom Glavine	2.50	1.10
60 Jose Reyes	2.50	1.10
61 Mike Piazza	4.00	1.80
62 Jorge Posada	2.50	1.10
63 Mike Mussina	2.50	1.10
64 Robin Ventura	2.00	.90
65 Mariano Rivera	2.50	1.10
66 Roger Clemens	5.00	2.20
67 Jason Giambi	2.50	1.10
68 Bernie Williams	2.50	1.10
69 Alfonso Soriano	2.50	1.10
70 Derek Jeter	6.00	2.70
71 Miguel Tejada	2.00	.90
72 Eric Chavez	2.00	.90
73 Tim Hudson	2.00	.90
74 Barry Zito	2.50	1.10
75 Pat Burrell	2.00	.90
76 Jim Thome	2.50	1.10
77 Bobby Abreu	2.00	.90
78 Brian Giles	2.00	.90
79 Reggie Sanders	2.00	.90
80 Ryan Klesko	2.00	.90
81 Edgardo Alfonzo	2.00	.90
82 Rich Aurilia	2.00	.90
83 Barry Bonds	6.00	2.70
84 Mike Cameron	2.00	.90
85 Kazuhiro Sasaki	2.00	.90
86 Bret Boone	2.00	.90
87 Ichiro Suzuki	4.00	1.80
88 J.D. Drew	2.00	.90
89 Jim Edmonds	2.00	.90
90 Scott Rolen	2.50	1.10
91 Matt Morris	2.00	.90
92 Tino Martinez	2.50	1.10
93 Albert Pujols	5.00	2.20
94 Rocco Baldelli	4.00	1.80
95 Hank Blalock	2.50	1.10
96 Alex Rodriguez	4.00	1.80
97 Rafael Palmeiro	2.50	1.10
98 Eric Hinske	2.00	.90
99 Orlando Hudson	2.00	.90
100 Carlos Delgado	2.00	.90
101 Albert Pujols MF	6.00	2.70
102 Alex Rodriguez MF	5.00	2.20
103 Alfonso Soriano MF	3.00	1.35
104 Andruw Jones MF	2.50	1.10
105 Barry Zito MF	3.00	1.35
106 Bernie Williams MF	3.00	1.35
107 Carlos Delgado MF	3.00	1.35
108 Chipper Jones MF	3.00	1.35
109 Curt Schilling MF	3.00	1.35
110 Doug Mientkiewicz MF	2.50	1.10
111 Frank Thomas MF	3.00	1.35
112 Garret Anderson MF	2.50	1.10
113 Gary Sheffield MF	2.50	1.10
114 Greg Maddux MF	5.00	2.20
115 Hank Blalock MF	3.00	1.35
116 Hideki Matsui MF	6.00	2.70
117 Hideo Nomo MF	3.00	1.35
118 Ichiro Suzuki MF	5.00	2.20
119 Ivan Rodriguez MF	3.00	1.35
120 Jason Giambi MF	3.00	1.35
121 Jeff Bagwell MF	2.50	1.10
122 Jeff Kent MF	2.50	1.10
123 Jerome Williams MF	2.50	1.10
124 Jeromy Burnitz MF	2.50	1.10
125 Jim Thome MF	3.00	1.35
126 Jose Cruz Jr. MF	2.50	1.10
127 Ken Griffey Jr. MF	5.00	2.20
128 Kerry Wood MF	3.00	1.35
129 Lance Berkman MF	2.50	1.10
130 Luis Gonzalez MF	2.50	1.10
131 Manny Ramirez MF	2.50	1.10
132 Mark Prior MF	6.00	2.70
133 Miguel Cabrera MF	5.00	2.20
134 Miguel Tejada MF	2.50	1.10
135 Mike Piazza MF	5.00	2.20
136 Pat Burrell MF	2.50	1.10
137 Pedro Martinez MF	3.00	1.35
138 Rafael Furcal MF	3.00	1.35
139 Randy Johnson MF	3.00	1.35
140 Rich Harden MF	3.00	1.35
141 Rickey Henderson MF	3.00	1.35
142 Roberto Alomar MF	3.00	1.35
143 Roger Clemens MF	6.00	2.70
144 Sammy Sosa MF	5.00	2.20
145 Shawn Green MF	2.50	1.10
146 Todd Helton MF	3.00	1.35
147 Tom Glavine MF	3.00	1.35
148 Torii Hunter MF	2.50	1.10
149 Troy Glaus MF	3.00	1.35
150 Vladimir Guerrero MF	3.00	1.35
151 Adam Dunn PP	4.00	1.80
152 Albert Pujols PP	10.00	4.50
153 Alex Rodriguez PP	8.00	3.60
154 Alfonso Soriano PP	5.00	2.20
155 Andruw Jones PP	4.00	1.80
156 Barry Bonds PP	12.00	5.50
157 Carlos Delgado PP	4.00	1.80
158 Chipper Jones PP	5.00	2.20
159 Derek Jeter PP	12.00	5.50
160 Gary Sheffield PP	4.00	1.80
161 Hank Blalock PP	5.00	2.20
162 Hideki Matsui PP	10.00	4.50
163 Ichiro Suzuki PP	8.00	3.60
164 J.D. Drew PP	4.00	1.80
165 Jason Giambi PP	5.00	2.20
166 Jeff Bagwell PP	5.00	2.20
167 Jeff Kent PP	4.00	1.80
168 Jim Edmonds PP	4.00	1.80
169 Jim Thome PP	5.00	2.20
170 Ken Griffey Jr. PP	8.00	3.60
171 Luis Gonzalez PP	4.00	1.80
172 Magglio Ordonez PP	4.00	1.80
173 Manny Ramirez PP	4.00	1.80
174 Mike Lowell PP	4.00	1.80
175 Mike Piazza PP	8.00	3.60
176 Nomar Garciaparra PP	8.00	3.60
177 Rafael Palmeiro PP	5.00	2.20
178 Shawn Green PP	4.00	1.80
179 Troy Glaus PP	5.00	2.20
180 Vladimir Guerrero PP	5.00	2.20
181 Albert Pujols FC	12.00	5.50
182 Alex Rodriguez FC	10.00	4.50
183 Alfonso Soriano FC	6.00	2.70
184 Bernie Williams FC	6.00	2.70
185 Chipper Jones FC	6.00	2.70
186 Derek Jeter FC	15.00	6.75
187 Hideki Matsui FC	12.00	5.50
188 Ichiro Suzuki FC	10.00	4.50
189 Jim Thome FC	6.00	2.70
190 Joe DiMaggio FC	10.00	4.50
191 Ken Griffey Jr. FC	10.00	4.50
192 Mickey Mantle FC	20.00	9.00
193 Mike Piazza FC	10.00	4.50
194 Pedro Martinez FC	6.00	2.70
195 Randy Johnson FC	6.00	2.70
196 Roger Clemens FC	12.00	5.50
197 Sammy Sosa FC	10.00	4.50
198 Ted Williams FC	12.00	5.50
199 Troy Glaus FC	6.00	2.70
200 Vladimir Guerrero FC	6.00	2.70
201 Aaron Looper T1 RC	3.00	1.35
202 Alejandro Machado T1 RC	3.00	1.35
203 Alfredo Gonzalez T1 RC	3.00	1.35
204 Andrew Brown T1 RC	3.00	1.35
205 Anthony Ferrari T1 RC	3.00	1.35
206 Aquilino Lopez T1 RC	3.00	1.35
207 Beau Kemp T1 RC	3.00	1.35
208 Bernie Castro T1 RC	3.00	1.35
209 Bobby Madritsch T1 RC	3.00	1.35
210 Brandon Villafuerte T1	3.00	1.35
211 Brent Hoard T1 RC	3.00	1.35
212 Brian Stokes T1 RC	3.00	1.35
213 Carlos Mendez T1 RC	3.00	1.35
214 Chris Capuano T1 RC	3.00	1.35
215 Chris Waters T1 RC	3.00	1.35
216 Clint Barmes T1 RC	5.00	2.20
217 Colin Porter T1 RC	3.00	1.35
218 Cory Stewart T1 RC	3.00	1.35
219 Craig Brazell T1 RC	5.00	2.20
220 D.J. Carrasco T1 RC	3.00	1.35
221 Daniel Cabrera T1 RC	3.00	1.35
222 David Matranga T1 RC	3.00	1.35
223 David Sanders T1 RC	3.00	1.35
224 Diegomar Markwell T1 RC	3.00	1.35
225 Edgar Gonzalez T1 RC	3.00	1.35
226 Felix Sanchez T1 RC	3.00	1.35
227 Fernando Cabrera T1 RC	3.00	1.35
228 Francisco Cruceta T1 RC	3.00	1.35
229 Francisco Rosario T1 RC	3.00	1.35
230 Garrett Atkins T1	3.00	1.35
231 Gerald Laird T1	3.00	1.35
232 Guillermo Quiroz T1 RC	5.00	2.20
233 Heath Bell T1 RC	3.00	1.35
234 Delmon Young T1 RC	15.00	6.75
235 Jason Shiell T1 RC	3.00	1.35
236 Jeremy Bonderman T1 RC	5.00	2.20
237 Jeremy Griffiths T1 RC	5.00	2.20
238 Jeremy Guthrie T1	3.00	1.35
239 Jeremy Wedel T1 RC	3.00	1.35
240 Carlos Rivera T1	3.00	1.35
241 Joe Valentine T1 RC	3.00	1.35
242 Jon Leicester T1 RC	3.00	1.35
243 Jon Pridie T1 RC	3.00	1.35
244 Jorge Cordova T1 RC	3.00	1.35
245 Jose Castillo T1	3.00	1.35
246 Josh Hall T1 RC	5.00	2.20
247 Josh Stewart T1 RC	3.00	1.35
248 Josh Willingham T1 RC	6.00	2.70
249 Julio Manon T1 RC	3.00	1.35
250 Kevin Correia T1 RC	3.00	1.35
251 Kevin Ohme T1 RC	3.00	1.35
252 Kevin Tolar T1 RC	3.00	1.35
253 Luis De Los Santos T1	3.00	1.35
254 Jermaine Clark T1	3.00	1.35
255 Mark Malaska T1 RC	3.00	1.35
256 Juan Dominguez T1	3.00	1.35
257 Michael Hessman T1 RC	3.00	1.35
258 Michael Nakamura T1 RC	3.00	1.35
259 Miguel Ojeda T1 RC	3.00	1.35
260 Mike Gallo T1 RC	3.00	1.35
261 Edwin Jackson T1 RC	8.00	3.60
262 Mike Ryan T1 RC	5.00	2.20
263 Nate Bland T1 RC	3.00	1.35
264 Nate Robertson T1 RC	5.00	2.20
265 Nook Logan T1 RC	3.00	1.35
266 Phil Seibel T1 RC	3.00	1.35
267 Prentice Redman T1 RC	3.00	1.35
268 Rafael Betancourt T1 RC	5.00	2.20
269 Rett Johnson T1 RC	5.00	2.20
270 Richard Fischer T1 RC	3.00	1.35
271 Rick Roberts T1 RC	3.00	1.35
272 Roger Deago T1 RC	3.00	1.35
273 Ryan Cameron T1 RC	3.00	1.35
274 Shane Bazzell T1 RC	3.00	1.35
275 Erasmo Ramirez T1	3.00	1.35
276 Terrmel Sledge T1 RC	5.00	2.20
277 Tim Olson T1 RC	5.00	2.20
278 Tommy Phelps T1	3.00	1.35
279 Tommy Whiteman T1	3.00	1.35
280 Willie Eyre T1 RC	3.00	1.35
281 Alex Prieto T1 RC	3.00	1.35
282 Michel Hernandez T1 RC	3.00	1.35
283 Greg Jones T1 RC	3.00	1.35
284 Victor Martinez T1	3.00	1.35
285 Tom Gregorio T1 RC	3.00	1.35
286 Marcus Thames T1	3.00	1.35
287 Jorge DePaula T1	3.00	1.35
288 Aaron Miles T1 RC	5.00	2.20
289 Reynaldo Garcia T1	3.00	1.35
290 Brian Sweeney T1 RC	3.00	1.35
291 Pete LaForest T1 RC	5.00	2.20
292 Pete Zoccolillo T1 RC	3.00	1.35
293 Danny Garcia T1 RC	3.00	1.35
294 Jonny Gomes T1	3.00	1.35
295 Rosman Garcia T1 RC	3.00	1.35
296 Mike Edwards T1	3.00	1.35
297 Marlon Byrd T1	3.00	1.35
298 Khalil Greene T1	5.00	2.20
299 Jose Valverde T1	3.00	1.35
300 Drew Henson T1	3.00	1.35
301 Chris Bootcheck T2	5.00	2.20
302 Matt Belisle T2	5.00	2.20
303 Kevin Gregg T2	5.00	2.20
304 Bobby Jenks T2	5.00	2.20
305 Jason Young T2	5.00	2.20
306 Laynce Nix T2	5.00	2.20
307 Robb Quinlan T2	5.00	2.20
308 Chase Utley T2	5.00	2.20
309 Humberto Quintero T2 RC	5.00	2.20
310 Tim Raines Jr. T2	5.00	2.20
311 Stephen Smitherman T2	5.00	2.20
312 Jason Anderson T2	5.00	2.20
313 Joe Dawley T2	5.00	2.20
314 Chad Cordero T2 RC	5.00	2.20
315 Victor Alvarez T2	5.00	2.20
316 Jimmy Gobble T2	5.00	2.20
317 Jared Fernandez T2	5.00	2.20
318 Eric Bruntlett T2	5.00	2.20
319 Neal Cotts T2	5.00	2.20
320 Ryan Madson T2	5.00	2.20
321 Rocco Baldelli T2	8.00	3.60
322 Graham Koonce T2 RC	15.00	6.75
323 Bobby Crosby T2	8.00	3.60
324 Mike Wood T2	5.00	2.20
325 Jesse Garcia T2	5.00	2.20
326 Noah Lowry T2	5.00	2.20
327 Edwin Almonte T2	5.00	2.20
328 Justin Morneau T2	5.00	2.20
329 Steve Colyer T2	5.00	2.20
330 Vinnie Chulk T2	5.00	2.20
331 Brian Schmack T3 RC	8.00	3.60
332 Stephen Randolph T3 RC	8.00	3.60
333 Pedro Feliciano T3 RC	15.00	6.75
334 Koyie Hill T3	8.00	3.60
335 Geoff Geary T3 RC	8.00	3.60
336 Jon Switzer T3	8.00	3.60
337 Xavier Nady T3	8.00	3.60
338 Rich Harden T3	10.00	4.50
339 Dontrelle Willis T3	10.00	4.50
340 Angel Berroa T3	8.00	3.60
341 Jerome Williams T3	8.00	3.60
342 Brandon Claussen T3	8.00	3.60
343 Kurt Ainsworth T3	8.00	3.60
344 Horacio Ramirez T3	8.00	3.60
345 Hee Seop Choi T3	8.00	3.60
346 Billy Traber T3	8.00	3.60
347 Brandon Phillips T3	8.00	3.60
348 Jody Gerut T3	8.00	3.60
349 Mark Teixeira T3	10.00	4.50
350 Javier Lopez T3 RC	8.00	3.60
351 Miguel Cabrera T3	8.00	3.60
352 Brad Lidge T3	8.00	3.60
353 Mike MacDougal T3	8.00	3.60
354 Ken Harvey T3	8.00	3.60
355 Chien-Ming Wang T3 RC	10.00	4.50
356 Aaron Heilman T3	8.00	3.60
357 Jason Phillips T3	8.00	3.60
358 Jason Bay T3	8.00	3.60
359 Arnie Munoz T3 RC	8.00	3.60
360 Ian Ferguson T3 RC	8.00	3.60
361 Ryan Wagner T4 RC	15.00	6.75
362 Rickie Weeks T4 RC	50.00	22.00
363 Chad Gaudin T4 RC	10.00	4.50
364 Jason Gilfillan T4 RC	10.00	4.50
365 Jason Roach T4 RC	10.00	4.50
366 Jhonny Peralta T4 RC	10.00	4.50
367 Mike Neu T4 RC	10.00	4.50
368 Jose Contreras T4 RC	20.00	9.00
369 Wilfredo Ledezma T4 RC	10.00	4.50
370 Lew Ford T4 RC	15.00	6.75
371 Luis Ayala T4 RC	10.00	4.50
372 Bo Hart T4 RC	20.00	9.00
373 Brandon Webb T4 RC	25.00	11.00
374 Dan Haren T4 RC	15.00	6.75
375 Hideki Matsui T4 RC	50.00	22.00
376 Jeff Duncan T4 RC	15.00	6.75
377 Matt Kata T4 RC	15.00	6.75
378 Oscar Villarreal T4 RC	10.00	4.50
379 Rob Hammock T4 RC	15.00	6.75
380 Todd Wellemeyer T4 RC	15.00	6.75

2003 Upper Deck Finite Gold

MINT NRMT
*GOLD 1-100: .75X TO 2X BASIC
*GOLD 101-150: .6X TO 1.5X BASIC
*GOLD 151-180: .4X TO 1X BASIC
1-180 PRINT RUN 199 SERIAL #'d SETS
*GOLD 181-200 ACTIVE: .6X TO 1.5X BASIC
*GOLD 181-200 RETIRED: 1X TO 2.5X BASIC
181-200 PRINT RUN 99 SERIAL #'d SETS
RANDOM INSERTS IN PACKS

2003 Upper Deck Finite Elements Game Jersey

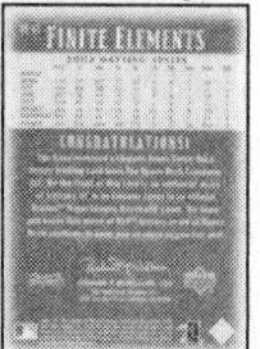

	MINT	NRMT
OVERALL GU ODDS 1:3		
SP INFO PROVIDED BY UPPER DECK		
AD Adam Dunn	8.00	3.60

AL Albert Pujols 15.00 6.75
AP Andy Pettitte 10.00 4.50
AR Alex Rodriguez 10.00 4.50
AS Alfonso Soriano 10.00 4.50
CJ Chipper Jones 10.00 4.50
CP Corey Patterson 8.00 3.60
DW Dontrelle Willis 10.00 4.50
DY Delmon Young SP/100 25.00 11.00
GM Greg Maddux 10.00 4.50
HB Hank Blalock 10.00 4.50
HC Hee Seop Choi 8.00 3.60
HM Hideki Matsui 30.00 13.50
IS Ichiro Suzuki 25.00 11.00
JB Jeff Bagwell 10.00 4.50
JD J.D. Drew 8.00 3.60
JE Jim Edmonds 8.00 3.60
JK Jeff Kent 8.00 3.60
JT Jim Thome 10.00 4.50
KG Ken Griffey Jr. SP 25.00 11.00
KW Kerry Wood 10.00 4.50
MI Mike Piazza 10.00 4.50
ML Mike Lowell 8.00 3.60
MM Matt Morris 8.00 3.60
MP Mark Prior 15.00 6.75
RB Rocco Baldelli 10.00 4.50
RO Roy Oswalt 8.00 3.60
RW Rickie Weeks SP/100 20.00 9.00
SG Shawn Green 8.00 3.60
TH Torii Hunter 8.00 3.60

2003 Upper Deck Finite Elements Game Patch

MINT NRMT
RANDOM INSERTS IN PACKS
STATED PRINT RUN 25 SERIAL #'d SETS
NO PRICING DUE TO SCARCITY

2003 Upper Deck Finite Elements Game Patch Gold

Nm-Mt Ex-Mt
RANDOM INSERTS IN PACKS
STATED PRINT RUN 10 SERIAL #'d SETS
NO PRICING DUE TO SCARCITY

2003 Upper Deck Finite First Class Game Jersey

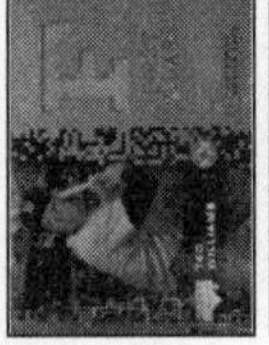

MINT NRMT
OVERALL GU ODDS 1:3
SP INFO PROVIDED BY UPPER DECK
AP Albert Pujols 15.00 6.75
AR Alex Rodriguez 10.00 4.50
AS Alfonso Soriano 10.00 4.50
BW Bernie Williams 10.00 4.50
CJ Chipper Jones 10.00 4.50
HM Hideki Matsui 30.00 13.50
IS Ichiro Suzuki 25.00 11.00
JD Joe DiMaggio Pants SP/200 80.00 36.00
JT Jim Thome 10.00 4.50
KG Ken Griffey Jr. 15.00 6.75
LG Luis Gonzalez 8.00 3.60
MM Mickey Mantle Pants SP/100 120.00 55.00
MP Mike Piazza 10.00 4.50
PM Pedro Martinez 10.00 4.50
RC Roger Clemens 15.00 6.75
RJ Randy Johnson 10.00 4.50
SS Sammy Sosa 15.00 6.75
TG Troy Glaus 10.00 4.50
TW Ted Williams Pants SP/100 80.00 36.00
VG Vladimir Guerrero 10.00 4.50

2003 Upper Deck Finite Signatures

MINT NRMT
STATED ODDS 1:120
PRINT RUNS B/WN 25-355 COPIES PER
NO PRICING ON QTY OF 25 OR LESS.
BH Bo Hart/150 40.00 18.00
BW Brandon Webb/150 40.00 18.00
CS C.C. Sabathia/50 25.00 11.00
DS David Sanders/150 10.00 4.50
DW Dontrelle Willis/50 50.00 22.00
DY Delmon Young/50 120.00 55.00
EA Erick Almonte/355 10.00 4.50
HM Hideki Matsui/99 350.00 160.00
IS Ichiro Suzuki/25
JR Jose Reyes/100 40.00 18.00
JW Jerome Williams/150 15.00 6.75
MC Miguel Cabrera/100 60.00 27.00
MP Mark Prior/75 100.00 45.00
MT Mark Teixeira/200 25.00 11.00
NG Nomar Garciaparra/50 200.00 90.00
PS Phil Seibel/200 10.00 4.50
RC Roger Clemens/50 175.00 80.00
RK Rob Hammock/200 15.00 6.75
RN Rich Harden/150 25.00 11.00
RW Rickie Weeks/25
SR Scott Rolen/100 40.00 18.00
SZ Shane Bazzell/250 10.00 4.50
WE Willie Eyre/200 10.00 4.50

2003 Upper Deck Finite Stars and Stripes

MINT NRMT
STRIPES/FINITE RC OVERALL ODDS 1:1
STATED PRINT RUN 299 SERIAL #'d SETS
1 Justin Orenduff 10.00 4.50
2 Micah Owings 10.00 4.50
3 Steven Register 10.00 4.50
4 Huston Street 10.00 4.50
5 Justin Verlander 12.00 5.50
6 Jered Weaver 25.00 11.00
7 Matt Campbell 8.00 3.60
8 Stephen Head 10.00 4.50
9 Mark Romanczuk 8.00 3.60
10 Jeff Clement 20.00 9.00
11 Mike Nickeas 8.00 3.60
12 Tyler Greene 10.00 4.50
13 Paul Janish 8.00 3.60
14 Jeff Larish 12.00 5.50
15 Eric Patterson 10.00 4.50
16 Dustin Pedroia 8.00 3.60
17 Michael Griffin 8.00 3.60
18 Brent Lillibridge 8.00 3.60
19 Danny Putnam 10.00 4.50
20 Seth Smith 10.00 4.50

2003 Upper Deck Finite Stars and Stripes Game Jersey

MINT NRMT
OVERALL GU ODDS 1:3
J1 Justin Orenduff 8.00 3.60
J2 Micah Owings 8.00 3.60
J3 Steven Register 8.00 3.60
J4 Huston Street 8.00 3.60
J5 Justin Verlander 10.00 4.50
J6 Jered Weaver 15.00 6.75
J7 Matt Campbell 5.00 2.20
J8 Stephen Head 8.00 3.60
J9 Mark Romanczuk 5.00 2.20
J10 Jeff Clement 15.00 6.75
J11 Mike Nickeas 5.00 2.20
J12 Tyler Greene 8.00 3.60
J13 Paul Janish 5.00 2.20
J14 Jeff Larish 10.00 4.50
J15 Eric Patterson 8.00 3.60
J16 Dustin Pedroia 5.00 2.20
J17 Michael Griffin 5.00 2.20
J18 Brent Lillibridge 5.00 2.20
J19 Danny Putnam 8.00 3.60
J20 Seth Smith 8.00 3.60

2003 Upper Deck First Pitch

This 300-card set was released in April, 2003. These cards were issued in five card packs with an 99 cent SRP which came 36 packs to a box and 20 boxes to a case. This set parallels the 2003 Upper Deck first series however, there is a rookie and prospect subset added (271-283) and a traded/free agent subset (284-300). Those cards (271-300) were issued at a stated rate of one in four.

Nm-Mt Ex-Mt
COMP.SET w/o SP's (270) 50.00 15.00
*FIRST PITCH 1-270: .4X TO 1X BASIC UD
COMMON CARD (271-283) 3.00 .90
COMMON CARD (284-300) 3.00 .90
271 Hideki Matsui SP RC 15.00 4.50
272 Jose Contreras SP RC 6.00 1.80
273 Robert Madritsch SP RC 3.00 .90
274 Shane Bazzell SP RC 3.00 .90
275 Felix Sanchez SP RC 3.00 .90
276 Todd Wellemeyer SP RC 4.00 1.20
277 Lew Ford SP RC 4.00 1.20
278 Jeremy Griffiths SP RC 4.00 1.20
279 Oscar Villarreal SP RC 3.00 .90
280 Brandon Webb SP RC 8.00 2.40
281 Delvis Lantigua SP RC 3.00 .90
282 Josh Willingham SP RC 5.00 1.50
283 Mike Nicolas SP RC 3.00 .90
284 Mike Hampton SP
285 Jim Thome SP 4.00 1.20
286 Bartolo Colon SP
287 Orlando Hernandez SP
288 Jeremy Giambi SP 3.00 .90
289 Jeff Kent SP
290 Tom Glavine SP 3.00 .90
291 Cliff Floyd SP
292 Tsuyoshi Shinjo SP
293 Jose Cruz Jr. SP
294 Edgardo Alfonzo SP
295 Andres Galarraga SP
296 Troy O'Leary SP 3.00 .90
297 Eric Karros SP
298 Ivan Rodriguez SP 4.00 1.20
299 Fred McGriff SP 3.00 .90
300 Preston Wilson SP

2003 Upper Deck First Pitch Signature Stars

Randomly inserted into packs, these six cards feature authentic player signatures. We have noted the stated print run for each player next to their name in our checklist. Please note that Ken Griffey Jr did not return his card in time for inclusion in packs and collectors could redeem exchange cards for his autograph until April 11, 2006.

Nm-Mt Ex-Mt
IS Ichiro Suzuki/50
JG Jason Giambi/100
KG Ken Griffey Jr./100 EXCH
KGS Ken Griffey Sr./800
NM Nomar Garciaparra/100
SS Sammy Sosa/50

2004 Upper Deck First Pitch

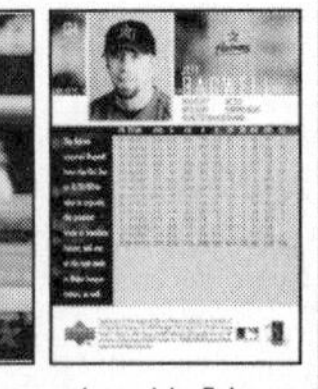

This 300 card set was released in February, 2004. The set was issued in five-card packs which came 36 packs to a box and 20 boxes to a case. The first 270 cards are issued in the same quantity while the final 30 cards which featture leading prospects of 2004 were issued at a stated rate of one in four.

Nm-Mt Ex-Mt
COMP.SET w/o SP'S (270) 50.00 15.00
*FIRST PITCH 1-270: .4X TO 1X BASIC UD
COMMON CARD (271-300) 3.00 .90
271-300 STATED ODDS 1:4
271 Rickie Weeks SP 4.00 1.20
272 Delmon Young SP 4.00 1.20
273 Chien-Ming Wang SP 3.00 .90
274 Rich Harden SP 3.00 .90
275 Edwin Jackson SP 4.00 1.20
276 Dan Haren SP 3.00 .90
277 Todd Wellemeyer SP 3.00 .90
278 Prentice Redman SP 3.00 .90
279 Ryan Wagner SP 3.00 .90
280 Aaron Looper SP 3.00 .90
281 Rick Roberts SP 3.00 .90
282 Josh Willingham SP 3.00 .90
283 Dave Crouthers SP RC 3.00 .90
284 Chris Capuano SP 3.00 .90
285 Mike Gosling SP RC 3.00 .90
286 Brian Sweeney SP 3.00 .90
287 Donald Kelly SP RC 3.00 .90
288 Ryan Meaux SP RC 3.00 .90
289 Colin Porter SP 3.00 .90
290 Jerome Gamble SP RC 3.00 .90
291 Colby Miller SP RC 3.00 .90
292 Ian Ferguson SP 3.00 .90
293 Tim Bittner SP RC 3.00 .90
294 Jason Frasor SP RC 3.00 .90
295 Brandon Medders SP RC 3.00 .90
296 Mike Johnston SP RC 3.00 .90
297 Tim Bausher SP RC 3.00 .90
298 Justin Leone SP RC 3.00 .90
299 Sean Henn SP RC 4.00 1.20
300 Michel Hernandez SP 3.00 .90

2004 Upper Deck First Pitch First and Foremost Jumbos

Nm-Mt Ex-Mt
BW Brandon Webb 5.00 1.50
DH Dan Haren 5.00 1.50
DW Dontrelle Willis 5.00 1.50
EB Ernie Banks 8.00 2.40
GH George H.W. Bush 10.00 3.00
GW George W. Bush 15.00 4.50
HR Horacio Ramirez 5.00 1.50
JC Jose Contreras 5.00 1.50
JW Jerome Williams 5.00 1.50
LT Luis Tiant 5.00 1.50
MS Mike Schmidt 10.00 3.00
RH Rich Harden 5.00 1.50
RW Ryan Wagner 5.00 1.50
WF Whitey Ford 8.00 2.40

2003 Upper Deck Game Face Promos

Inserted one per newstand copy of Tuff Stuff magazine, these cards parallel the Non-SP 1-120 cards. Each of these cards have a UD Promo notation promiently on the front.

Nm-Mt Ex-Mt
*PROMOS: 1.25X TO 3X BASIC CARDS

2003 Upper Deck Game Face

This 217 card set was issued in two separate series. The primary Game Face product was released in May, 2003. The "low series" set containing cards 1-192 was issued in four card packs with a $4 SRP which were packed 24 packs to a box and six boxes to a case. The first 120 cards featured veterans. But even within that group, there were cards that were shortprinted. The short-print cards from number 1-120 were issued at a stated rate of one in four packs. Cards numbered 121 through 150 feature leading prospects and rookies and were issued at a stated rate of one in eight. Cards numbered 151 through 171 feature cards with a game face subset and those cards were issued at a stated rate of one in 16. Cards numbered 172 through 192 were issued at a stated rate of one in eight and featured two players in a "faceoff" on each card. Cards 193-217 featured additional prospects, were serial numbered to 299 copies per and randomly seeded into Bonus Packs of 2003 Upper Deck Finite baseball of which was distributed in December, 2003. A Ken Griffey Jr sample card was issued to dealers and media before this product was released and we have added that card at the end of our checklist.

Nm-Mt Ex-Mt
COMP.SET w/o SP's (90) 25.00 7.50
COMMON CARD (1-120) .50 .15
COMMON SP (1-120) 4.00 1.20
COMMON CARD (121-150) 4.00 1.20
COMMON CARD (151-171) 8.00 2.40
COMMON CARD (172-192) 8.00 2.40
COMMON CARD (193-217) 8.00 2.40
193-217 RANDOM IN FINITE BONUS PACKS
193-217 PRINT RUN 299 SERIAL #'d SETS
1 Darin Erstad .50 .15
2 Garret Anderson .50 .15
3 Tim Salmon .75 .23
4 Jarrod Washburn .50 .15
5 Troy Glaus SP 5.00 1.50
6 Luis Gonzalez .50 .15
7 Junior Spivey .50 .15
8 Randy Johnson SP 5.00 1.50
9 Curt Schilling SP 5.00 1.50
10 Andruw Jones .50 .15
11 Gary Sheffield .50 .15
12 Rafael Furcal .50 .15
13 Greg Maddux SP 8.00 2.40
14 Chipper Jones SP 5.00 1.50
15 Tony Batista .50 .15
16 Rodrigo Lopez .50 .15
17 Jay Gibbons .50 .15
18 Shea Hillenbrand .50 .15
19 Johnny Damon .50 .15
20 Derek Lowe .50 .15
21 Nomar Garciaparra 2.00 .60
22 Pedro Martinez SP 5.00 1.50
23 Manny Ramirez SP 4.00 1.20
24 Mark Prior 2.50 .75
25 Kerry Wood 1.25 .35
26 Corey Patterson .50 .15
27 Sammy Sosa SP 8.00 2.40
28 Magglio Ordonez .50 .15
29 Frank Thomas 1.25 .35
30 Paul Konerko .50 .15
31 Adam Dunn .50 .15
32 Austin Kearns .50 .15
33 Aaron Boone .50 .15
34 Ken Griffey Jr. SP 8.00 2.40
35 Omar Vizquel .50 .15
36 C.C. Sabathia .50 .15
37 Karim Garcia SP 4.00 1.20
38 Larry Walker .75 .23
39 Preston Wilson .50 .15
40 Jay Payton .50 .15
41 Todd Helton SP 5.00 1.50
42 Carlos Pena .50 .15
43 Eric Munson .50 .15
44 Mike Lowell .50 .15
45 Josh Beckett .75 .23
46 A.J. Burnett .50 .15
47 Roy Oswalt .50 .15
48 Craig Biggio .75 .23
49 Jeff Bagwell SP 5.00 1.50
50 Lance Berkman SP 4.00 1.20
51 Mike Sweeney .50 .15
52 Carlos Beltran .50 .15
53 Hideo Nomo 1.25 .35
54 Odalis Perez .50 .15
55 Adrian Beltre .50 .15
56 Shawn Green SP 4.00 1.20
57 Kazuhisa Ishii SP 4.00 1.20
58 Ben Sheets .50 .15
59 Richie Sexson .50 .15
60 Torii Hunter .50 .15
61 Jacque Jones .50 .15
62 Eric Milton .50 .15
63 Corey Koskie .50 .15
64 A.J. Pierzynski .50 .15
65 Jose Vidro .50 .15
66 Bartolo Colon .50 .15
67 Vladimir Guerrero SP 5.00 1.50
68 Tom Glavine .75 .23
69 Mike Piazza SP 8.00 2.40
70 Roberto Alomar SP 5.00 1.50
71 Jorge Posada .75 .23
72 Mike Mussina 1.25 .35
73 Robin Ventura .50 .15
74 Raul Mondesi .50 .15
75 Roger Clemens SP UER 10.00 3.00
Card mistakenly numbered as 79
76 Jason Giambi SP 5.00 1.50
77 Bernie Williams SP 5.00 1.50
78 Alfonso Soriano SP 5.00 1.50
79 Derek Jeter SP 12.00 3.60
80 Miguel Tejada .50 .15
81 Eric Chavez .50 .15
82 Tim Hudson .50 .15
83 Barry Zito .75 .23
84 Mark Mulder .50 .15
85 Pat Burrell .50 .15
86 Jim Thome 1.25 .35
87 Bobby Abreu .50 .15
88 Brian Giles .50 .15
89 Jason Kendall .50 .15
90 Aramis Ramirez .50 .15
91 Ryan Klesko .50 .15
92 Phil Nevin .50 .15
93 Sean Burroughs .50 .15
94 J.T. Snow .50 .15
95 Rich Aurilia .50 .15
96 Benito Santiago .50 .15
97 Barry Bonds SP 12.00 3.60
98 Edgar Martinez .75 .23
99 John Olerud .50 .15
100 Bret Boone .50 .15
101 Ichiro Suzuki SP 8.00 2.40
102 J.D. Drew .50 .15
103 Jim Edmonds .50 .15
104 Scott Rolen .75 .23
105 Matt Morris .50 .15
106 Tino Martinez .75 .23
107 Albert Pujols SP 10.00 3.00
108 Aubrey Huff .50 .15
109 Carl Crawford .50 .15
110 Rafael Palmeiro .75 .23
111 Hank Blalock .75 .23
112 Alex Rodriguez SP 8.00 2.40
113 Kevin Mench SP 4.00 1.20
114 Juan Gonzalez SP 5.00 1.50
115 Shannon Stewart .50 .15
116 Vernon Wells .50 .15
117 Josh Phelps .50 .15
118 Eric Hinske .50 .15
119 Orlando Hudson .50 .15
120 Carlos Delgado SP 4.00 1.20
121 David Sanders FF RC 4.00 1.20
122 Rob Hammock FF RC 5.00 1.50
123 Rett Johnson FF RC 5.00 1.50
124 Mike Nicolas FF RC 4.00 1.20
125 Terrmel Sledge FF RC 5.00 1.50
126 Ryan Cameron FF RC 4.00 1.20
127 Prentice Redman FF RC 4.00 1.20
128 Clint Barmes FF RC 5.00 1.50
129 Brent Hoard FF RC 4.00 1.20
130 Willie Eyre FF RC 4.00 1.20
131 Phil Seibel FF RC 4.00 1.20
132 Chris Capuano FF RC 4.00 1.20
133 Bobby Madritsch FF RC 4.00 1.20
134 Shane Bazzell FF RC 4.00 1.20
135 Jeremy Griffiths FF RC 5.00 1.50
136 Jon Leicester FF RC 4.00 1.20
137 Brandon Webb FF RC 10.00 3.00
138 Todd Wellemeyer FF RC 5.00 1.50
139 Jose Contreras FF RC 8.00 2.40
140 Felix Sanchez FF RC 4.00 1.20
141 Arnie Munoz FF RC 4.00 1.20
142 Delvis Lantigua FF RC 4.00 1.20
143 Francisco Cruceta FF RC 4.00 1.20
144 Josh Willingham FF RC 6.00 1.80
145 Oscar Villarreal FF RC 4.00 1.20
146 Ian Ferguson FF RC 4.00 1.20
147 Pedro Liriano FF 4.00 1.20
148 Lew Ford FF RC 5.00 1.50
149 Jeff Duncan FF RC 5.00 1.50
150 Rich Fischer FF RC 4.00 1.20
151 Troy Glaus GF 8.00 2.40
152 Randy Johnson GF 10.00 3.00
153 Hideki Matsui GF RC 20.00 6.00
154 Chipper Jones GF 10.00 3.00
155 Nomar Garciaparra GF 15.00 4.50
156 Pedro Martinez GF 10.00 3.00
157 Ted Williams GF 25.00 7.50
158 Sammy Sosa GF 15.00 4.50
159 Ken Griffey Jr. GF 15.00 4.50
160 Vladimir Guerrero GF 10.00 3.00
161 Mike Piazza GF 12.00 3.60
162 Mickey Mantle GF 40.00 12.00
163 Alfonso Soriano GF 8.00 2.40
164 Derek Jeter GF 20.00 6.00
165 Roger Clemens GF 15.00 4.50
166 Jason Giambi GF 10.00 3.00
167 Barry Bonds GF 20.00 6.00
168 Ichiro Suzuki GF 12.00 3.60
169 Albert Pujols GF 15.00 4.50
170 Mark McGwire GF 20.00 6.00
171 Alex Rodriguez GF 12.00 3.60
172 Roy Oswalt 15.00 4.50
Ken Griffey Jr.
173 Barry Zito 8.00 2.40
Troy Glaus
174 Tim Hudson 15.00 4.50
Ichiro Suzuki
175 Mark Mulder 15.00 4.50
Alex Rodriguez
176 Tom Glavine 10.00 3.00
Vladimir Guerrero
177 Greg Maddux 15.00 4.50
Mike Piazza
178 Mark McGwire 30.00 9.00
Sammy Sosa
179 Mark Prior 15.00 4.50
Lance Berkman
180 Kerry Wood 15.00 4.50
Albert Pujols
181 Randy Johnson 10.00 3.00
Jeff Bagwell
182 Curt Schilling 20.00 6.00
Derek Jeter
183 Hideo Nomo 20.00 6.00
Barry Bonds
184 Kazuhisa Ishii 8.00 2.40
Todd Helton
185 Freddy Garcia 8.00 2.40
Eric Chavez

186 Al Leiter 10.00 3.00
Chipper Jones
187 Ted Williams 25.00 7.50
Nomar Garciaparra
188 Pedro Martinez 15.00 4.50
Hideki Matsui
189 Derek Lowe 8.00 2.40
Bernie Williams
190 Roger Clemens 20.00 6.00
Mike Piazza
191 Mike Mussina 10.00 3.00
Manny Ramirez
192 Mickey Mantle 30.00 9.00
Jason Giambi
193 Aaron Looper FF RC 8.00 2.40
194 Alex Prieto FF RC 8.00 2.40
195 Bo Hart FF RC 10.00 3.00
196 Chad Gaudin FF RC 8.00 2.40
197 Colin Porter FF RC 8.00 2.40
198 D.J. Carrasco FF RC 8.00 2.40
199 Dan Haren FF RC 10.00 3.00
200 Delmon Young FF RC 30.00 9.00
201 Dontrelle Willis FF 10.00 3.00
202 Jon Switzer FF 8.00 2.40
203 Edwin Jackson FF RC 15.00 4.50
204 Fernando Cabrera FF RC 8.00 2.40
205 Garrett Atkins FF 8.00 2.40
206 Jeremy Bonderman FF RC 10.00 3.00
207 Kevin Ohme FF RC 8.00 2.40
208 Khalil Greene FF 10.00 3.00
209 Luis Ayala FF RC 8.00 2.40
210 Matt Kata FF RC 10.00 3.00
211 Noah Lowry FF 8.00 2.40
212 Rich Harden FF 10.00 3.00
213 Rickie Weeks FF RC 25.00 7.50
214 Rosman Garcia FF RC 8.00 2.40
215 Ryan Wagner FF RC 10.00 3.00
216 Tom Gregorio FF RC 8.00 2.40
217 Wilfredo Ledezma FF RC 8.00 2.40
NNO Ken Griffey Jr. Sample 5.00 1.50

2003 Upper Deck Game Face Autographs

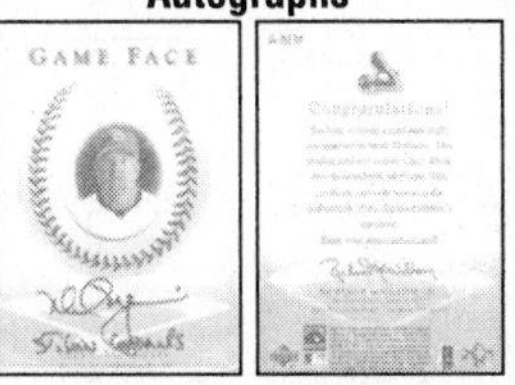

Issued at a stated rate of one in 576, these 11 cards featured authentic autographs on players from the game face set. A few players were issued in smaller quantities and we have notated that information with an SP in our data base. Andruw Jones, Ken Griffey Jr. and Hideki Matsui did not return their cards in time for inclusion in this product. Thus, exchange cards with a redemption deadline of May 12, 2006 were seeded into packs.

Nm-Mt Ex-Mt
AJ Andruw Jones SP EXCH
BZ Barry Zito 60.00 18.00
HM H.Matsui English SP/55 EX 500.00 150.00
IS Ichiro Suzuki SP 400.00 120.00
JG Jason Giambi 100.00 30.00
KG Ken Griffey Jr. EXCH 200.00 60.00
LB Lance Berkman SP
MM Mark McGwire SP 400.00 120.00
MP Mark Prior SP 200.00 60.00
SS Sammy Sosa 200.00 60.00
TH Todd Helton SP

2003 Upper Deck Game Face Gear

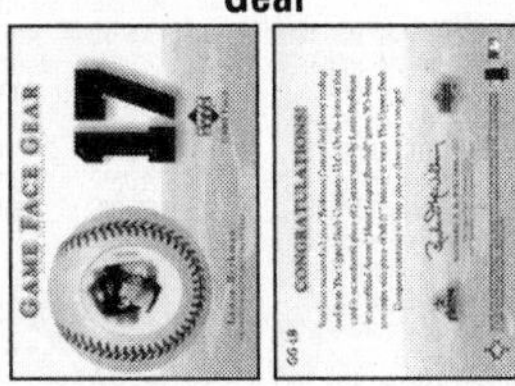

Inserted at a stated rate of one in eight, this 71 card set features game-used memorabilia from the featured player. A few cards were issued in smaller quantities and we have notated that information with the SP notation next to the player's name in our checklist. In addition, a few players were issued using both their home and away uniforms.

Nm-Mt Ex-Mt
AB Aaron Boone SP 15.00 4.50
AD Adam Dunn 10.00 3.00
AJ Andruw Jones 10.00 3.00
AK Austin Kearns 10.00 3.00
AR Alex Rodriguez Home 20.00 6.00
AR2 Alex Rodriguez Away 20.00 6.00
AS Alfonso Soriano 15.00 4.50
BA Bobby Abreu 10.00 3.00
BG Brian Giles 10.00 3.00
BW Bernie Williams 15.00 4.50
BZ Barry Zito Home 15.00 4.50
BZ2 Barry Zito Away 15.00 4.50
CB Carlos Beltran 10.00 3.00
CD Carlos Delgado 10.00 3.00
CJ Chipper Jones 15.00 4.50
CS Curt Schilling 15.00 4.50
DE Darin Erstad Home 10.00 3.00
DE2 Darin Erstad Away 10.00 3.00
DR J.D. Drew Home 10.00 3.00
DR2 J.D. Drew Away 10.00 3.00
EA Edgardo Alfonzo 10.00 3.00
EC Eric Chavez 10.00 3.00
EM Edgar Martinez 15.00 4.50
FT Frank Thomas 15.00 4.50
GM Greg Maddux Home 15.00 4.50
GM2 Greg Maddux Away 15.00 4.50
HN Hideo Nomo 25.00 7.50
HU Torii Hunter 10.00 3.00
IR Ivan Rodriguez 15.00 4.50
IS Ichiro Suzuki SP 60.00 18.00
JB Jeff Bagwell 15.00 4.50
JE Jim Edmonds 10.00 3.00
JG Jason Giambi 15.00 4.50
JG Juan Gonzalez 15.00 4.50
JJ Jacque Jones 10.00 3.00
JK Jason Kendall 10.00 3.00
JK Jeff Kent 10.00 3.00
JP Jorge Posada 15.00 4.50
JT Jim Thome 15.00 4.50
JV Jose Vidro 10.00 3.00
KG Ken Griffey Jr. SP 30.00 9.00
KI Kazuhisa Ishii 10.00 3.00
KW Kerry Wood 15.00 4.50
LB Lance Berkman 10.00 3.00
LG Luis Gonzalez Home 10.00 3.00
LG2 Luis Gonzalez Away 10.00 3.00
LW Larry Walker 15.00 4.50
ML Mike Lowell 10.00 3.00
MM Mike Mussina 15.00 4.50
MO Magglio Ordonez 10.00 3.00
MPI Mike Piazza 20.00 6.00
MPR Mark Prior 25.00 7.50
MR Manny Ramirez 10.00 3.00
MS Mike Sweeney 10.00 3.00
MT Miguel Tejada 10.00 3.00
OV Omar Vizquel 10.00 3.00
PB Pat Burrell 10.00 3.00
PM Pedro Martinez 15.00 4.50
PW Preston Wilson 10.00 3.00
RC Roger Clemens 20.00 6.00
RJ Randy Johnson 15.00 4.50
RK Ryan Klesko 10.00 3.00
RO Roy Oswalt 10.00 3.00
RP Rafael Palmeiro 15.00 4.50
RS Richie Sexson 10.00 3.00
SG Shawn Green 10.00 3.00
SR Scott Rolen 15.00 4.50
SS Sammy Sosa 20.00 6.00
TG Tom Glavine 15.00 4.50
TH Todd Helton SP 15.00 4.50
TI Tim Hudson 10.00 3.00

2003 Upper Deck Game Face Patch

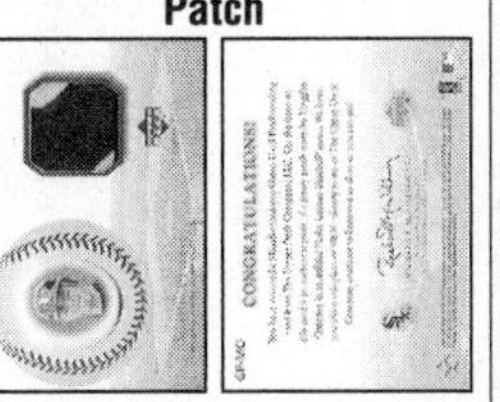

Randomly inserted in packs, these 70-cards feature game-used patch pieces of the featured players. Each of these cards were issued to a stated print run of 100 serial numbered sets.

Nm-Mt Ex-Mt
AB Aaron Boone 25.00 7.50
AD Adam Dunn 25.00 7.50
AJ Andruw Jones 25.00 7.50
AK Austin Kearns 25.00 7.50
AR Alex Rodriguez Home 100.00 30.00
AR2 Alex Rodriguez Away 100.00 30.00
AS Alfonso Soriano 40.00 12.00
BA Bobby Abreu 25.00 7.50
BW Bernie Williams 40.00 12.00
BZ Barry Zito Home 40.00 12.00
BZ2 Barry Zito Away 40.00 12.00
CB Carlos Beltran 25.00 7.50
CD Carlos Delgado 25.00 7.50
CJ Chipper Jones 60.00 18.00
CS Curt Schilling 40.00 12.00
DE Darin Erstad Home 25.00 7.50
DE2 Darin Erstad Away 25.00 7.50
DR J.D. Drew Home 25.00 7.50
DR2 J.D. Drew Away 25.00 7.50
EA Edgardo Alfonzo 25.00 7.50
EC Eric Chavez 25.00 7.50
EM Edgar Martinez 40.00 12.00
FT Frank Thomas 60.00 18.00
GM Greg Maddux Home 100.00 30.00
GM2 Greg Maddux Away 100.00 30.00
HN Hideo Nomo 200.00 60.00
HU Torii Hunter 25.00 7.50
IR Ivan Rodriguez 60.00 18.00
IS Ichiro Suzuki 300.00 90.00
JB Jeff Bagwell 40.00 12.00
JE Jim Edmonds 25.00 7.50
JG Jason Giambi 60.00 18.00
JG Juan Gonzalez 60.00 18.00
JJ Jacque Jones 25.00 7.50
JK Jason Kendall 25.00 7.50
JK Jeff Kent 25.00 7.50
JP Jorge Posada 40.00 12.00
JT Jim Thome 60.00 18.00
JV Jose Vidro 25.00 7.50
KG Ken Griffey Jr. 100.00 30.00
KI Kazuhisa Ishii 25.00 7.50
KW Kerry Wood 60.00 18.00
LB Lance Berkman 25.00 7.50
LG Luis Gonzalez Home 25.00 7.50
LG2 Luis Gonzalez Away 25.00 7.50
LW Larry Walker 40.00 12.00
ML Mike Lowell 25.00 7.50
MMO Mike Mussina SP/81 60.00 18.00
MO Magglio Ordonez 25.00 7.50
MP Mark Prior 100.00 30.00
MP Mike Piazza 100.00 30.00
MR Manny Ramirez 25.00 7.50
MS Mike Sweeney 25.00 7.50
MT Miguel Tejada 25.00 7.50
OV Omar Vizquel 25.00 7.50
PB Pat Burrell 25.00 7.50
PM Pedro Martinez 60.00 18.00
PW Preston Wilson 25.00 7.50
RC Roger Clemens 100.00 30.00
RJ Randy Johnson 60.00 18.00
RK Ryan Klesko 25.00 7.50
RO Roy Oswalt 25.00 7.50
RP Rafael Palmeiro 40.00 12.00
RS Richie Sexson 25.00 7.50
SG Shawn Green 25.00 7.50
SR Scott Rolen 40.00 12.00
SS Sammy Sosa 100.00 30.00
TG Tom Glavine 40.00 12.00
TH Todd Helton 40.00 12.00
TI Tim Hudson 25.00 7.50

2001 Upper Deck Gold Glove

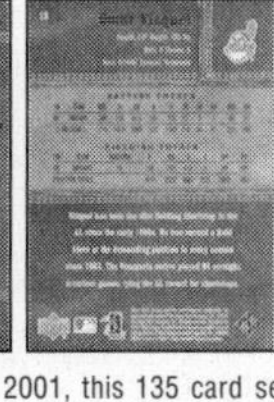

Issued in November 2001, this 135 card set featured many of the best defensive players in the majors. Cards numbered 91-135 were short printed and featured all Rookie Cards. Cards numbered 91-129 were serial numbered to 1000 and cards numbered 130-135 were serial numbered to 500.

Nm-Mt Ex-Mt
COMP.SET w/o SP'S (90) 25.00 7.50
COMMON CARD (1-90) .60 .18
COMMON CARD (91-129) 8.00 2.40
COMMON (130-135) 15.00 4.50
1 Troy Glaus 1.00 .30
2 Darin Erstad .60 .18
3 Jason Giambi 1.50 .45
4 Tim Hudson .60 .18
5 Jermaine Dye .60 .18
6 Raul Mondesi .60 .18
7 Carlos Delgado .60 .18
8 Shannon Stewart .60 .18
9 Greg Vaughn .60 .18
10 Aubrey Huff .60 .18
11 Juan Gonzalez 1.50 .45
12 Roberto Alomar 1.50 .45
13 Omar Vizquel .60 .18
14 Jim Thome 1.50 .45
15 John Olerud .60 .18
16 Edgar Martinez 1.00 .30
17 Kazuhiro Sasaki .60 .18
18 Aaron Sele .60 .18
19 Cal Ripken 5.00 1.50
20 Chris Richard .60 .18
21 Ivan Rodriguez 1.50 .45
22 Rafael Palmeiro 1.00 .30
23 Alex Rodriguez 2.50 .75
24 Pedro Martinez 1.50 .45
25 Nomar Garciaparra 2.50 .75
26 Manny Ramirez .60 .18
27 Neifi Perez .60 .18
28 Mike Sweeney .60 .18
29 Bobby Higginson .60 .18
30 Dean Palmer .60 .18
31 Tony Clark .60 .18
32 Doug Mientkiewicz .60 .18
33 Brad Radke .60 .18
34 Joe Mays .60 .18
35 Frank Thomas 1.50 .45
36 Magglio Ordonez .60 .18
37 Carlos Lee .60 .18
38 Bernie Williams 1.00 .30
39 Mike Mussina 1.50 .45
40 Derek Jeter 4.00 1.20
41 Roger Clemens 3.00 .90
42 Craig Biggio 1.00 .30
43 Jeff Bagwell 1.00 .30
44 Lance Berkman .60 .18
45 Andruw Jones .60 .18
46 Greg Maddux 2.50 .75
47 Chipper Jones 1.50 .45
48 Geoff Jenkins .60 .18
49 Ben Sheets .60 .18
50 Jeromy Burnitz .60 .18
51 Jim Edmonds .60 .18
52 Mark McGwire 4.00 1.20
53 Mike Matheny .60 .18
54 J.D. Drew .60 .18
55 Sammy Sosa 2.50 .75
56 Kerry Wood 1.50 .45
57 Fred McGriff 1.00 .30
58 Randy Johnson 1.50 .45
59 Steve Finley .60 .18
60 Mark Grace 1.00 .30
61 Matt Williams .60 .18
62 Luis Gonzalez .60 .18
63 Shawn Green .60 .18
64 Kevin Brown .60 .18
65 Gary Sheffield .60 .18
66 Vladimir Guerrero 1.50 .45
67 Tony Armas Jr. .60 .18
68 Barry Bonds 4.00 1.20
69 J.T. Snow .60 .18
70 Jeff Kent .60 .18
71 Charles Johnson .60 .18
72 Preston Wilson .60 .18
73 Cliff Floyd .60 .18
74 Robin Ventura .60 .18
75 Mike Piazza 2.50 .75
76 Edgardo Alfonzo .60 .18
77 Tony Gwynn 2.00 .60
78 Ryan Klesko .60 .18
79 Scott Rolen 1.00 .30
80 Mike Lieberthal .60 .18
81 Pat Burrell .60 .18
82 Jason Kendall .60 .18
83 Brian Giles .60 .18
84 Ken Griffey Jr. 2.50 .75
85 Barry Larkin 1.50 .45
86 Pokey Reese .60 .18
87 Larry Walker 1.00 .30
88 Mike Hampton .60 .18
89 Juan Pierre .60 .18
90 Todd Helton 1.00 .30
91 Mike Penney GD RC 8.00 2.40
92 Wilkin Ruan GD RC 8.00 2.40
93 Greg Miller GD RC 8.00 2.40
94 Johnny Estrada GD RC 8.00 2.40
95 Tsuyoshi Shinjo GD RC 12.00 3.60
96 Josh Towers GD RC 8.00 2.40
97 H. Ramirez GD RC 10.00 3.00
98 Ryan Freel GD RC 8.00 2.40
99 M. Ensberg GD RC 12.00 3.60
100 A. Hernandez GD RC 8.00 2.40
101 Juan Uribe GD RC 8.00 2.40
102 Jose Mieses GD RC 8.00 2.40
103 Jack Wilson GD RC 8.00 2.40
104 Cesar Crespo GD RC 8.00 2.40
105 Bud Smith GD RC 8.00 2.40
106 Erick Almonte GD RC 8.00 2.40
107 E. Guzman GD RC 8.00 2.40
108 B. Duckworth GD RC 8.00 2.40
109 Juan Diaz GD RC 8.00 2.40
110 Kris Keller GD RC 8.00 2.40
111 J. Michaels GD RC 8.00 2.40
112 Bret Prinz GD RC 8.00 2.40
113 Henry Mateo GD RC 8.00 2.40
114 R. Rodriguez GD RC 8.00 2.40
115 Travis Hafner GD RC 12.00 3.60
116 Nate Teut GD RC 8.00 2.40
117 Alexis Gomez GD RC 8.00 2.40
118 Billy Sylvester GD RC 8.00 2.40
119 A. Pettyjohn GD RC 8.00 2.40
120 Josh Fogg GD RC 8.00 2.40
121 Juan Cruz GD RC 8.00 2.40
122 C. Valderrama GD RC 8.00 2.40
123 Jay Gibbons GD RC 12.00 3.60
124 D. Mendez GD RC 8.00 2.40
125 Bill Ortega GD RC 8.00 2.40
126 Sean Douglass GD RC 8.00 2.40
127 C. Parker GD RC 8.00 2.40
128 Grant Balfour GD RC 8.00 2.40
129 Joe Kennedy GD RC 8.00 2.40
130 Albert Pujols GD RC 50.00 15.00
131 W. Betemit GD RC 15.00 4.50
132 Mark Teixeira GD RC 30.00 9.00
133 Mark Prior GD RC 50.00 15.00
134 D. Brazelton GD RC 15.00 4.50
135 Ichiro Suzuki GD RC 40.00 12.00

2001 Upper Deck Gold Glove Finite

This parallel to the basic Gold Glove set was randomly inserted in packs. The veterans are valued as a multiple of the basic cards while the rookies are serial numbered to 25.

Nm-Mt Ex-Mt
*STARS 1-90: 15X TO 40X BASIC CARDS

2001 Upper Deck Gold Glove Limited

Randomly inserted in packs, this is a parallel to the basic Gold Glove set. These cards are serial numbered to 100 and are valued as a multiple of the basic cards.

Nm-Mt Ex-Mt
*STARS 1-90: 5X TO 12X BASIC CARDS
*DEBUT 91-129: .6X TO 1.5X BASIC
*DEBUT 130-135: .6X TO 1.5X BASIC

2001 Upper Deck Gold Glove Game Jersey

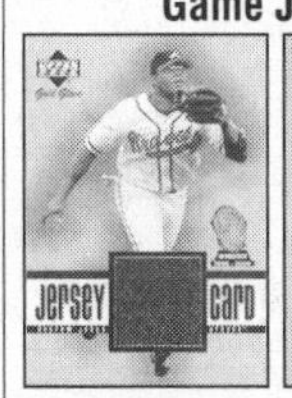

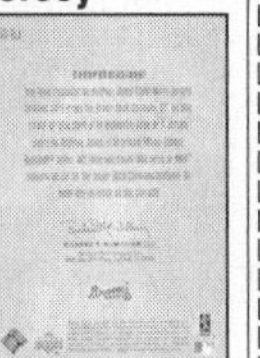

Issued at a rate of one in 20, these 27 cards feature game-used jerseys of defensive stars of the past and present. A few cards were issued in lesser quantities. Those cards are notated in our checklist with an SP along with specific print information provided by Upper Deck.

Nm-Mt Ex-Mt
STATED ODDS 1:20
SP PRINT RUNS PROVIDED BY UPPER DECK
SP'S ARE NOT SERIAL NUMBERED
GOLD RANDOM INSERTS IN PACKS
GOLD PRINT RUN 25 SERIAL #'d SETS
GOLD NO PRICING DUE TO SCARCITY
GG-AJ Andruw Jones 10.00 3.00
GG-BB Barry Bonds 30.00 9.00
GG-BR B.Richardson SP/274 25.00 7.50
GG-BW Bernie Williams 15.00 4.50
GG-CC Cesar Cedeno 10.00 3.00
GG-CF Carlton Fisk 15.00 4.50
GG-CR Cal Ripken 40.00 12.00
GG-DE Darin Erstad 10.00 3.00
GG-DM Don Mattingly 40.00 12.00
GG-GC Gary Carter 15.00 4.50
GG-GM Greg Maddux 15.00 4.50
GG-IR Ivan Rodriguez 15.00 4.50
GG-IS Ichiro Suzuki 80.00 24.00
GG-JB Jeff Bagwell 15.00 4.50
GG-JK Jim Kaat 10.00 3.00
GG-KG Ken Griffey Jr. 20.00 6.00
GG-LA Luis Aparicio 10.00 3.00
GG-MG Mark Grace 15.00 4.50
GG-MMA M. Mantle SP/264 200.00 60.00
GG-MMU Mike Mussina 15.00 4.50
GG-OS Ozzie Smith 15.00 4.50
GG-OV Omar Vizquel 10.00 3.00
GG-RG Ron Guidry 10.00 3.00
GG-RM R. Maris SP/265 80.00 24.00
GG-RP Rafael Palmeiro 15.00 4.50
GG-SG Shawn Green 10.00 3.00
GG-TM T. Munson SP/204 80.00 24.00

2001 Upper Deck Gold Glove Leather Bound

Inserted at a rate of one in 60, these 60 cards showcase the fielding talents of some of the best fielders in the game. It was originally reported by the manufacturer that a handful of cards were short-printed to a quantity of 100 copies each. Upon further investigation in 2003, Beckett price guide staff worked with representatives at Upper Deck to get final print run quantities on all cards. It was ultimately verified by the manufacturer, though they lack serial-numbering every card in the set was produced to a quantity of 100 copies each.

Nm-Mt Ex-Mt
GOLD RANDOM INSERTS IN PACKS
GOLD PRINT RUN 25 SERIAL #'d SETS
NO GOLD PRICING DUE TO SCARCITY
LB-AF Alex Fernandez
LB-AG Alex Gonzalez 15.00 4.50
LB-AR Alex Rodriguez 40.00 12.00
LB-AS Aaron Sele 15.00 4.50
LB-BB Barry Bonds 60.00 18.00
LB-BG Ben Grieve 15.00 4.50
LB-CB Craig Biggio 25.00 7.50
LB-CF Cliff Floyd 15.00 4.50
LB-CJ Chipper Jones 25.00 7.50
LB-CL Carlos Lee 15.00 4.50
LB-CP Chan Ho Park 15.00 4.50
LB-DE Dock Ellis 15.00 4.50
LB-DW Dave Winfield 15.00 4.50
LB-EM Edgar Martinez 25.00 7.50
LB-FR Frank Robinson
LB-FT Frank Thomas
LB-GA Garret Anderson
LB-GC Gary Carter 25.00 7.50
LB-GL Greg Luzinski 15.00 4.50
LB-GS Gary Sheffield 15.00 4.50
LB-HI Hideki Irabu 15.00 4.50
LB-HK Harvey Kuenn 15.00 4.50
LB-I Ichiro Suzuki 250.00 75.00
LB-IR Ivan Rodriguez 25.00 7.50
LB-JD Johnny Damon 15.00 4.50
LB-JE Jim Edmonds 15.00 4.50
LB-JI Jason Isringhausen
LB-JL Javy Lopez 15.00 4.50
LB-JM Jose Mesa
LB-JO John Olerud 15.00 4.50
LB-JBL Johnny Blanchard 15.00 4.50
LB-JBU Jay Buhner
LB-JKA Jim Kaat 15.00 4.50
LB-JKE Jason Kendall 15.00 4.50
LB-KC Ken Caminiti 15.00 4.50
LB-KG Ken Griffey Jr. 40.00 12.00
LB-KL Kenny Lofton 15.00 4.50
LB-LD Leon Day
LB-LG Lefty Grove 120.00 36.00
LB-MG Marquis Grissom 15.00 4.50
LB-MP Mike Piazza 40.00 12.00
LB-MR Manny Ramirez 15.00 4.50
LB-MY Masato Yoshii
LB-NF Nellie Fox 25.00 7.50
LB-OD Octavio Dotel 15.00 4.50
LB-OH Orlando Hernandez 15.00 4.50
LB-OS Ozzie Smith 50.00 15.00
LB-OV Omar Vizquel 15.00 4.50
LB-PM Pedro Martinez 25.00 7.50
LB-PO Paul O'Neill 25.00 7.50
LB-RF Rafael Furcal 15.00 4.50
LB-RJ Reggie Jackson 25.00 7.50
LB-RK Ryan Klesko 15.00 4.50
LB-RP Rafael Palmeiro 25.00 7.50
LB-RCA Roy Campanella 100.00 30.00
LB-RCE Roger Cedeno
LB-SS Sammy Sosa 40.00 12.00
LB-TS Tim Salmon 25.00 7.50
LB-THE Todd Helton 25.00 7.50
LB-THO T. Hollandsworth 15.00 4.50

2001 Upper Deck Gold Glove Leather Bound Autograph

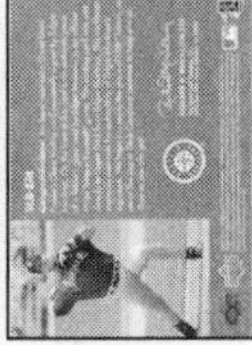

Issued at a rate of one in 240, these 31 cards feature not only information about the defensive star but also are signed by the player on the card. In 2003, more than two years after the product's intiial release, the Beckett price guide staff managed to obtain specific print runs for short prints within this set (of which are detailed in our checklist) and finally settled lingering questions about the possible existence of cards featuring Aaron Sele, Barry Bonds, Chipper Jones, Gary Sheffield, Jim Edmonds, Mike Piazza, Pedro Martinez, Rafael Palmeiro, Sammy Sosa and Todd Helton. None of these cards had been seen in the secondary market but all were originally detailed on press release materials. In 2003, however, UD officially verified that none of the cards were created.

Nm-Mt Ex-Mt
STATED ODDS 1:240
SP PRINT RUNS PROVIDED BY UPPER DECK
SP'S ARE NOT SERIAL-NUMBERED
SLB-I Ichiro Suzuki SP/50
SLB-AR Alex Rodriguez SP/29
SLB-CF Cliff Floyd 25.00 7.50
SLB-DW Dave Winfield 60.00 18.00
SLB-EM Edgar Martinez 80.00 24.00
SLB-FR Frank Robinson 60.00 18.00
SLB-FT Frank Thomas 80.00 24.00
SLB-GL Greg Luzinski 25.00 7.50
SLB-IR Ivan Rodriguez 80.00 24.00
SLB-JD Johnny Damon 25.00 7.50

SLB-JK Jim Kaat 25.00 7.50
SLB-JK Jason Kendall 25.00 7.50
SLB-JL Javy Lopez 25.00 7.50
SLB-JO John Olerud 25.00 7.50
SLB-KG Ken Griffey Jr. SP/49
SLB-KL Kenny Lofton 25.00 7.50
SLB-OS Ozzie Smith 100.00 30.00
SLB-PO Paul O'Neill 60.00 18.00
SLB-RF Rafael Furcal 25.00 7.50
SLB-RJ Reggie Jackson SP/68
SLB-RK Ryan Klesko 25.00 7.50

2001 Upper Deck Gold Glove Official Issue Game Ball

Inserted at a rate of one in 20, these 57 cards feature two players along with pieces of game-used memorabilia. A few cards were printed in lesser quantities and those have been noted as SP's in our checklist. We have also provided print run information provided by Upper Deck for these cards.

Nm-Mt Ex-Mt
OI-AG Roberto Alomar 15.00 4.50
Juan Gonzalez
OI-BA Pat Burrell 10.00 3.00
Bobby Abreu
OI-BB Jeff Bagwell 15.00 4.50
Lance Berkman
OI-BH Lance Berkman 10.00 3.00
Richard Hidalgo
OI-BK Barry Bonds 30.00 9.00
Jeff Kent
OI-BS Jeromy Burnitz 10.00 3.00
Richie Sexson
OI-CJ Roger Clemens
Derek Jeter SP/17
OI-DM Carlos Delgado 10.00 3.00
Raul Mondesi
OI-DP J.D.Drew 50.00 15.00
Albert Pujols
OI-EA Darin Erstad 10.00 3.00
Garrett Anderson
OI-FJ Cliff Floyd 10.00 3.00
Charles Johnson
OI-GB Shawn Green 10.00 3.00
Adrian Beltre
OI-GC Ken Griffey Jr. 20.00 6.00
Sean Casey
OI-GE Troy Glaus 15.00 4.50
Darin Erstad
OI-GG Luis Gonzalez 15.00 4.50
Mark Grace
OI-GJ Cristian Guzman 15.00 4.50
Jacque Jones SP/194
OI-GK Tony Gwynn 20.00 6.00
Ryan Klesko
OI-GR Brian Giles 10.00 3.00
Aramis Ramirez
OI-GT Jason Giambi 15.00 4.50
Miguel Tejada
OI-GV Vladimir Guerrero 15.00 4.50
Jose Vidro
OI-HC Bobby Higginson 15.00 4.50
Tony Clark SP/160
OI-HH Mike Hampton 15.00 4.50
Todd Helton
OI-HW Todd Helton 15.00 4.50
Larry Walker
OI-IO Ichiro Suzuki 50.00 15.00
John Olerud
OI-JB Geoff Jenkins 10.00 3.00
Jeromy Burnitz
OI-JF Andruw Jones 10.00 3.00
Rafael Furcal
OI-JG Randy Johnson 15.00 4.50
Luis Gonzalez
OI-JJ Chipper Jones 15.00 4.50
Andruw Jones
OI-JW Deter Jeter
Bernie Williams SP/17
OI-KA Jeff Kent 10.00 3.00
Rich Aurilia
OI-KG Jason Kendall 10.00 3.00
Brian Giles
OI-LG Barry Larkin 20.00 6.00
Ken Griffey Jr.
OI-MG Doug Mientkiewicz 15.00 4.50
Cristian Guzman SP/194
OI-MJ Greg Maddux 20.00 6.00
Chipper Jones
OI-MO Edgar Martinez 25.00 7.50
John Olerud SP/160
OI-MP Mark McGwire 100.00 30.00
Albert Pujols
OI-NK Phil Nevin 10.00 3.00
Ryan Klesko
OI-PE Albert Pujols 50.00 15.00
Jim Edmonds
OI-PR Rafael Palmeiro 25.00 7.50
Alex Rodriguez
OI-PS Mike Piazza 20.00 6.00
Tsuyoshi Shinjo
OI-RB Cal Ripken 40.00 12.00
Tony Batista
OI-RE Manny Ramirez 10.00 3.00
Carl Everett
OI-RP Ivan Rodriguez 15.00 4.50
Rafael Palmeiro
OI-RR Alex Rodriguez 25.00 7.50
Ivan Rodriguez
OI-RBU Scott Rolen 15.00 4.50
Pat Burrell
OI-SB Mike Sweeney 10.00 3.00
Carlos Beltran
OI-SG Gary Sheffield 10.00 3.00
Shawn Green
OI-SV Tsuyoshi Shinjo 15.00 4.50
Robin Ventura
OI-SW Sammy Sosa 20.00 6.00
Rondell White
OI-TC Miguel Tejada 10.00 3.00
Eric Chavez
OI-TO Frank Thomas 25.00 7.50
Magglio Ordonez SP/160
OI-VM Greg Vaughn 25.00 7.50
Fred McGriff SP/170
OI-VP Robin Ventura 20.00 6.00
Mike Piazza
OI-WF Preston Wilson 10.00 3.00
Cliff Floyd
OI-WP Larry Walker 15.00 4.50
Juan Pierre
OI-WS Kerry Wood 20.00 6.00
Sammy Sosa
OI-WPO Bernie Williams
Jorge Posada SP/17

2001 Upper Deck Gold Glove Slugger's Choice

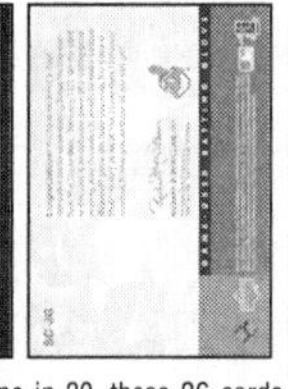

Issued at a rate of one in 20, these 26 cards feature authentic pieces of game-used batting gloves of baseball's top hitters. A few cards were short printed compared to the other cards. We have notated these cards with an SP and print run information provided by Upper Deck in our checklist.

Nm-Mt Ex-Mt
GOLD RANDOM INSERTS IN PACKS
GOLD PRINT RUN 25 SERIAL #'d SETS
NO GOLD PRICING DUE TO SCARCITY
SC-AG Andres Galarraga 10.00 3.00
SC-ARM A.Rodriguez Mariners 20.00 6.00
SC-ARR A.Rodriguez Rangers 20.00 6.00
SC-BA Bobby Abreu 10.00 3.00
SC-BA Brady Anderson 10.00 3.00
SC-BB Barry Bonds 30.00 9.00
SC-CJ Chipper Jones 15.00 4.50
SC-EM Edgar Martinez 15.00 4.50
SC-FT F.Tatis SP/147 10.00 3.00
SC-GS G.Sheffield SP/201 10.00 3.00
SC-HR H.Rodriguez SP/185 10.00 3.00
SC-IR Ivan Rodriguez 15.00 4.50
SC-JC J.Cruz Jr. SP/191 10.00 3.00
SC-JG Juan Gonzalez 15.00 4.50
SC-JI Jason Isringhausen 10.00 3.00
SC-KGM K.Griffey Jr. Mariners 20.00 6.00
SC-KGR K.Griffey Jr. Reds 20.00 6.00
SC-MC Marty Cordova 10.00 3.00
SC-MR Manny Ramirez 10.00 3.00
SC-MT Miguel Tejada 10.00 3.00
SC-NP Neifi Perez 10.00 3.00
SC-PO Paul O'Neill 15.00 4.50
SC-RF Rafael Furcal 10.00 3.00
SC-RP Rafael Palmeiro 15.00 4.50
SC-SS Sammy Sosa 20.00 6.00
SC-TB Tony Batista 10.00 3.00

2000 Upper Deck Gold Reserve

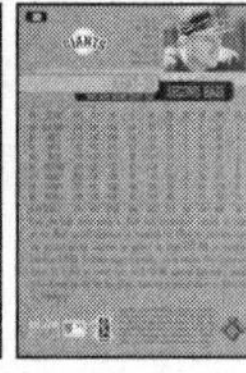

The 2000 Upper Deck Gold Reserve product was released in early August, 2000 as a retail only product. The 300-card set features 267-player cards, 30 short-printed Fantastic Find subset cards (each individually serial numbered to 2500), and three checklist cards. Each pack contained 10 cards and carried a suggested retail price of $2.99. Notable Rookie Cards include Kazuhiro Sasaki. Also, a selection of A Piece of History 3000 Club Al Kaline memorabilia cards were randomly seeded into packs. 350 bat cards and six hand-numbered, combination bat chip and autograph cut cards were produced. Exchange cards were seeded into packs for the bat chip-autograph cut combination card. The deadline to send these cards into Upper Deck was April 10th, 2001. Pricing for these memorabilia cards can be referenced under 2000 Upper Deck A Piece of History 3000 Club.

Nm-Mt Ex-Mt
COMPLETE SET (300) 350.00 105.00
COMP.SET w/o SP's (270) 50.00 15.00
COMMON (1-267/298-300) .30 .09
COMMON (268-297) 5.00 1.50
1 Mo Vaughn .30 .09
2 Darin Erstad .30 .09
3 Garret Anderson .30 .09
4 Troy Glaus .50 .15
5 Troy Percival .30 .09
6 Kent Bottenfield .30 .09
7 Orlando Palmeiro .30 .09
8 Tim Salmon .50 .15
9 Jason Giambi .75 .23
10 Eric Chavez .30 .09
11 Matt Stairs .30 .09
12 Miguel Tejada .30 .09
13 Tim Hudson .50 .15
14 John Jaha .30 .09
15 Ben Grieve .30 .09
16 Kevin Appier .30 .09
17 David Wells .30 .09
18 Jose Cruz Jr. .30 .09
19 Homer Bush .30 .09
20 Shannon Stewart .30 .09
21 Carlos Delgado .30 .09
22 Roy Halladay .30 .09
23 Tony Batista .30 .09
24 Raul Mondesi .30 .09
25 Fred McGriff .50 .15
26 Jose Canseco .75 .23
27 R.Hernandez UER .30 .09
Card erroneously numbered 73
28 Vinny Castilla .30 .09
29 Gerald Williams .30 .09
30 Ryan Rupe .30 .09
31 Greg Vaughn .30 .09
32 Miguel Cairo .30 .09
33 Roberto Alomar .75 .23
34 Jim Thome .75 .23
35 Bartolo Colon .30 .09
36 Omar Vizquel .30 .09
37 Manny Ramirez .30 .09
38 Chuck Finley .30 .09
39 Travis Fryman .30 .09
40 Kenny Lofton .30 .09
41 Richie Sexson .30 .09
42 Charles Nagy .30 .09
43 John Halama .30 .09
44 David Bell .30 .09
45 Jay Buhner .30 .09
46 Edgar Martinez .50 .15
47 Alex Rodriguez 1.25 .35
48 Freddy Garcia .30 .09
49 Aaron Sele .30 .09
50 Jamie Moyer .30 .09
51 Mike Cameron .30 .09
52 Albert Belle .30 .09
53 Jerry Hairston Jr. .30 .09
54 Sidney Ponson .30 .09
55 Cal Ripken 2.50 .75
56 Mike Mussina .75 .23
57 B.J. Surhoff .30 .09
58 Brady Anderson .30 .09
59 Mike Bordick .30 .09
60 Ivan Rodriguez .75 .23
61 Rusty Greer .30 .09
62 Rafael Palmeiro .50 .15
63 John Wetteland .30 .09
64 Ruben Mateo .30 .09
65 Gabe Kapler .30 .09
66 David Segui .30 .09
67 Justin Thompson .30 .09
68 Rick Helling .30 .09
69 Jose Offerman .30 .09
70 Trot Nixon .50 .15
71 Pedro Martinez .75 .23
72 Jason Varitek .30 .09
73 Troy O'Leary .30 .09
74 Nomar Garciaparra 1.25 .35
75 Carl Everett .30 .09
76 Wilton Veras .30 .09
77 Tim Wakefield .30 .09
78 Ramon Martinez .30 .09
79 Johnny Damon .30 .09
80 Mike Sweeney .30 .09
81 Rey Sanchez .30 .09
82 Carlos Beltran .30 .09
83 Carlos Febles .30 .09
84 Jermaine Dye .30 .09
85 Joe Randa .30 .09
86 Jose Rosado .30 .09
87 Jeff Suppan .30 .09
88 Juan Encarnacion .30 .09
89 Damion Easley .30 .09
90 Brad Ausmus .30 .09
91 Todd Jones .30 .09
92 Juan Gonzalez .75 .23
93 Bobby Higginson .30 .09
94 Tony Clark .30 .09
95 Brian Moehler .30 .09
96 Dean Palmer .30 .09
97 Joe Mays .30 .09
98 Eric Milton .30 .09
99 Corey Koskie .30 .09
100 Ron Coomer .30 .09
101 Brad Radke .30 .09
102 Todd Walker .30 .09
103 Butch Huskey .30 .09
104 Jacque Jones .30 .09
105 Frank Thomas .75 .23
106 Mike Sirotka .30 .09
107 Carlos Lee .30 .09
108 Ray Durham .30 .09
109 Bob Howry .30 .09
110 Magglio Ordonez .30 .09
111 Paul Konerko .30 .09
112 Chris Singleton .30 .09
113 James Baldwin .30 .09
114 Derek Jeter 2.00 .60
115 Tino Martinez .50 .15
116 Orlando Hernandez .30 .09
117 Chuck Knoblauch .30 .09
118 Bernie Williams .50 .15
119 David Cone .30 .09
120 Paul O'Neill .50 .15
121 Roger Clemens 1.50 .45
122 Mariano Rivera .50 .15
123 Ricky Ledee .30 .09
124 Richard Hidalgo .30 .09
125 Jeff Bagwell .50 .15
126 Jose Lima .30 .09
127 Billy Wagner .30 .09
128 Shane Reynolds .30 .09
129 Moises Alou .30 .09
130 Craig Biggio .50 .15
131 Roger Cedeno .30 .09
132 Octavio Dotel .30 .09
133 Greg Maddux 1.25 .35
134 Brian Jordan .30 .09
135 Kevin Millwood .30 .09
136 Javy Lopez .30 .09
137 Bruce Chen .30 .09
138 Chipper Jones .75 .23
139 Tom Glavine .50 .15
140 Andruw Jones .30 .09
141 Andres Galarraga .30 .09
142 Reggie Sanders .30 .09
143 Geoff Jenkins .30 .09
144 Jeromy Burnitz .30 .09
145 Ron Belliard .30 .09
146 Mark Loretta .30 .09
147 Steve Woodard .30 .09
148 Marquis Grissom .30 .09
149 Bob Wickman .30 .09
150 Mark McGwire 2.00 .60
151 Fernando Tatis .30 .09
152 Edgar Renteria .30 .09
153 J.D. Drew .30 .09
154 Ray Lankford .30 .09
155 Fernando Vina .30 .09
156 Pat Hentgen .30 .09
157 Jim Edmonds .30 .09
158 Mark Grace .50 .15
159 Kerry Wood .75 .23
160 Eric Young .30 .09
161 Ismael Valdes .30 .09
162 Sammy Sosa 1.25 .35
163 Henry Rodriguez .30 .09
164 Kyle Farnsworth .30 .09
165 Glenallen Hill .30 .09
166 Jon Lieber .30 .09
167 Luis Gonzalez .30 .09
168 Tony Womack .30 .09
169 Omar Daal .30 .09
170 Randy Johnson .75 .23
171 Erubiel Durazo .30 .09
172 Jay Bell .30 .09
173 Steve Finley .30 .09
174 Travis Lee .30 .09
175 Matt Williams .30 .09
176 Matt Mantei .30 .09
177 Adrian Beltre .30 .09
178 Kevin Brown .50 .15
179 Chan Ho Park .30 .09
180 Mark Grudzielanek .30 .09
181 Jeff Shaw .30 .09
182 Shawn Green .30 .09
183 Gary Sheffield .30 .09
184 Todd Hundley .30 .09
185 Eric Karros .30 .09
186 Kevin Elster .30 .09
187 Vladimir Guerrero .75 .23
188 Michael Barrett .30 .09
189 Chris Widger .30 .09
190 Ugueth Urbina .30 .09
191 Dustin Hermanson .30 .09
192 Rondell White .30 .09
193 Jose Vidro .30 .09
194 Hideki Irabu .30 .09
195 Lee Stevens .30 .09
196 Livan Hernandez .30 .09
197 Ellis Burks .30 .09
198 J.T. Snow .30 .09
199 Jeff Kent .30 .09
200 Robb Nen .30 .09
201 Marvin Benard .30 .09
202 Barry Bonds 2.00 .60
203 Russ Ortiz .30 .09
204 Rich Aurilia .30 .09
205 Joe Nathan .30 .09
206 Preston Wilson .30 .09
207 Cliff Floyd .30 .09
208 Mike Lowell .30 .09
209 Ryan Dempster .30 .09
210 Luis Castillo .30 .09
211 Alex Fernandez .30 .09
212 Mark Kotsay .30 .09
213 Brant Brown .30 .09
214 Edgardo Alfonzo .30 .09
215 Robin Ventura .30 .09
216 Rickey Henderson .75 .23
217 Mike Hampton .30 .09
218 Mike Piazza 1.25 .35
219 Al Leiter .30 .09
220 Derek Bell .30 .09
221 Armando Benitez .30 .09
222 Rey Ordonez .30 .09
223 Todd Zeile .30 .09
224 Tony Gwynn 1.00 .30
225 Eric Owens .30 .09
226 Damian Jackson .30 .09
227 Trevor Hoffman .30 .09
228 Ben Davis .30 .09
229 Sterling Hitchcock .30 .09
230 Ruben Rivera .30 .09
231 Ryan Klesko .30 .09
232 Phil Nevin .30 .09
233 Mike Lieberthal .30 .09
234 Bob Abreu .30 .09
235 Doug Glanville .30 .09
236 Rico Brogna .30 .09
237 Scott Rolen .50 .15
238 Andy Ashby .30 .09
239 Robert Person .30 .09
240 Curt Schilling .50 .15
241 Mike Jackson .30 .09
242 Warren Morris .30 .09
243 Kris Benson .30 .09
244 Kevin Young .30 .09
245 Brian Giles .30 .09
246 Jason Schmidt .30 .09
247 Jason Kendall .30 .09
248 Todd Ritchie .30 .09
249 Wil Cordero .30 .09
250 Aramis Ramirez .30 .09
251 Sean Casey .30 .09
252 Barry Larkin .75 .23
253 Pokey Reese .30 .09
254 Scott Williamson .30 .09
255 Aaron Boone .30 .09
256 Dante Bichette .30 .09
257 Ken Griffey Jr. 1.25 .35
258 Denny Neagle .30 .09
259 Dmitri Young .30 .09
260 Todd Helton .50 .15
261 Larry Walker .50 .15
262 Pedro Astacio .30 .09
263 Neifi Perez .30 .09
264 Jeff Cirillo .30 .09
265 Jeffrey Hammonds .30 .09
266 Tom Goodwin .30 .09
267 Rolando Arrojo .30 .09
268 Rick Ankiel FF 5.00 1.50
269 Pat Burrell FF 8.00 2.40
270 Eric Munson FF 5.00 1.50
271 Rafael Furcal FF 5.00 1.50
272 Brad Penny FF 5.00 1.50
273 Adam Kennedy FF 5.00 1.50
274 Mike Lamb FF RC 5.00 1.50
275 Matt Riley FF 5.00 1.50
276 Eric Gagne FF 8.00 2.40
277 K.Sasaki FF RC 10.00 3.00
278 Julio Lugo FF 5.00 1.50
279 Kip Wells FF 5.00 1.50
280 Danys Baez FF RC 8.00 2.40
281 Josh Beckett FF 10.00 3.00
282 Alfonso Soriano FF 8.00 2.40
283 Vernon Wells FF 5.00 1.50
284 Nick Johnson FF 5.00 1.50
285 Ramon Ortiz FF 5.00 1.50
286 Peter Bergeron FF 5.00 1.50
287 W.Serrano FF RC 5.00 1.50
288 Josh Paul FF 5.00 1.50
289 Mark Quinn FF 5.00 1.50
290 Jason Marquis FF 5.00 1.50
291 Rob Bell FF 5.00 1.50
292 Pablo Ozuna FF 5.00 1.50
293 Milton Bradley FF 5.00 1.50
294 Roosevelt Brown FF 5.00 1.50
295 Terrence Long FF 5.00 1.50
296 Chad Durbin FF RC 5.00 1.50
297 Matt LeCroy FF 5.00 1.50
298 Ken Griffey Jr. CL .75 .23
299 Mark McGwire CL 1.00 .30
300 Derek Jeter CL 1.00 .30

2000 Upper Deck Gold Reserve 24-Karat Gems

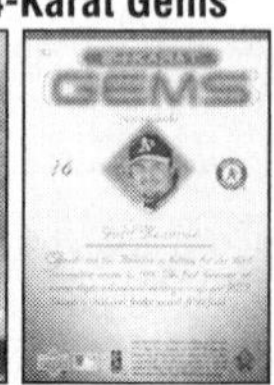

Randomly inserted into packs at one in seven, this 15-card insert features players that are as good as gold. Card backs carry a "K" prefix.

Nm-Mt Ex-Mt
COMPLETE SET (15) 25.00 7.50
K1 Pedro Martinez 1.50 .45
K2 Scott Rolen 1.00 .30
K3 Jason Giambi 1.50 .45
K4 Jeromy Burnitz .60 .18
K5 Rafael Palmeiro 1.00 .30
K6 Rick Ankiel 10.00 3.00
K7 Carlos Beltran .60 .18
K8 Derek Jeter 4.00 1.20
K9 Jason Kendall .60 .18
K10 Chipper Jones 1.50 .45
K11 Carlos Delgado .60 .18
K12 Alex Rodriguez 2.50 .75
K13 Randy Johnson 1.50 .45
K14 Tony Gwynn 2.00 .60
K15 Shawn Green .60 .18

2000 Upper Deck Gold Reserve Game Ball

Randomly inserted into packs at one in 480, this 20-card insert features swatches of actual Game-Used baseball's. The cards are numbered using the player's initials with a "B" prefix.

Nm-Mt Ex-Mt
B-AJ Andruw Jones 15.00 4.50
B-BB Barry Bonds 80.00 24.00
B-BW Bernie Williams 25.00 7.50
B-CJ Chipper Jones 25.00 7.50
B-DJ Derek Jeter 80.00 24.00
B-GM Greg Maddux 40.00 12.00
B-GS Gary Sheffield 15.00 4.50
B-IR Ivan Rodriguez
B-JB Jeff Bagwell
B-KG Ken Griffey Jr. 40.00 12.00
B-MM Mark McGwire 80.00 24.00
B-MP Mike Piazza 40.00 12.00
B-MR Manny Ramirez 15.00 4.50
B-NG Nomar Garciaparra 40.00 12.00
B-RC Roger Clemens 50.00 15.00
B-SC Sean Casey 15.00 4.50
B-SG Shawn Green 15.00 4.50
B-SR Scott Rolen 25.00 7.50
B-SS Sammy Sosa 40.00 12.00
B-TG Tony Gwynn 40.00 12.00

2000 Upper Deck Gold Reserve Setting the Standard

Randomly inserted into packs at one in 11, this 15-card insert features players that set the standard of play in the Major Leagues. Card backs carry a "S" prefix.

Nm-Mt Ex-Mt
COMPLETE SET (15) 40.00 12.00
S1 Tony Gwynn 2.50 .75
S2 Manny Ramirez .75 .23
S3 Derek Jeter 5.00 1.50
S4 Cal Ripken 6.00 1.80
S5 Mo Vaughn .75 .23

S6 Jose Canseco 2.00 .60
S7 Barry Bonds 5.00 1.50
S8 Nomar Garciaparra 3.00 .90
S9 Juan Gonzalez 2.00 .60
S10 Mark McGwire 5.00 1.50
S11 Alex Rodriguez 3.00 .90
S12 Jeff Bagwell 1.25 .35
S13 Ken Griffey Jr. 3.00 .90
S14 Frank Thomas 2.00 .60
S15 Sammy Sosa 3.00 .90

2000 Upper Deck Gold Reserve Solid Gold Gallery

Randomly inserted into packs at one in 13, this 12-card insert features superstar caliber players. Card backs carry a "G" prefix.

	Nm-Mt	Ex-Mt
COMPLETE SET (12)	40.00	12.00
G1 Ken Griffey Jr.	3.00	.90
G2 Alex Rodriguez	3.00	.90
G3 Mike Piazza	3.00	.90
G4 Sammy Sosa	3.00	.90
G5 Derek Jeter	5.00	1.50
G6 Jeff Bagwell	1.25	.35
G7 Mark McGwire	5.00	1.50
G8 Cal Ripken	6.00	1.80
G9 Pedro Martinez	2.00	.60
G10 Chipper Jones	2.00	.60
G11 Ivan Rodriguez	2.00	.60
G12 Vladimir Guerrero	2.00	.60

2000 Upper Deck Gold Reserve UD Authentics

Randomly inserted into packs at one in 480, this 10-card insert features autographed cards of players like Cal Ripken, Ken Griffey Jr, and Chipper Jones. Please note that Ken Griffey Jr., Manny Ramirez, and Shawn Green packed out as exchange cards. These exchange cards must be sent to Upper Deck by 04/10/01.

	Nm-Mt	Ex-Mt
AR Alex Rodriguez	120.00	36.00
CB Carlos Beltran	25.00	7.50
CJ Chipper Jones	50.00	15.00
CR Cal Ripken	150.00	45.00
IR Ivan Rodriguez		
JC Jose Canseco	50.00	15.00
KG Ken Griffey Jr.		
MR Manny Ramirez	40.00	12.00
SG Shawn Green	25.00	7.50
TG Tony Gwynn	80.00	24.00

2000 Upper Deck Gold Reserve UD Authentics Gold

Randomly inserted into packs, this 10-card insert is a complete parallel of the UD Authentics insert. Each card in this set is individually serial numbered to 25. Please note that Ken Griffey Jr., Manny Ramirez, and Shawn Green packed out as exchange cards. These exchange cards must be sent to Upper Deck by 04/10/01.

Nm-Mt Ex-Mt

RANDOM INSERTS IN PACKS
STATED PRINT RUN 25 SERIAL #'d SETS
NO PRICING DUE TO SCARCITY

2001 Upper Deck Hall of Famers

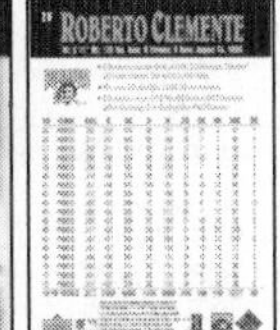

The 2001 Upper Deck Hall of Famers product was released in early April, 2001 and features a 90-card base set that is broken into tiers as follows: Base Veterans (1-50), Origins of the Game (51-60), National Pastime (61-80), and finally Hall of Records (81-90). Each pack contained 5 cards and carried a suggested retail price of $3.99.

	Nm-Mt	Ex-Mt
COMPLETE SET (90)	20.00	6.00
1 Reggie Jackson	.40	.12
2 Hank Aaron	1.25	.35
3 Eddie Mathews	.60	.18
4 Warren Spahn	.40	.12
5 Robin Yount	1.00	.30
6 Lou Brock	.40	.12
7 Dizzy Dean	.60	.18
8 Bob Gibson	.40	.12
9 Stan Musial	1.00	.30
10 Enos Slaughter	.25	.07
11 Rogers Hornsby	.60	.18
12 Ernie Banks	.60	.18
13 Fergie Jenkins	.25	.07
14 Roy Campanella	.60	.18
15 Pee Wee Reese	.60	.18
16 Jackie Robinson	1.00	.30
17 Juan Marichal	.25	.07
18 Christy Mathewson	.60	.18
19 Willie Mays	1.25	.35
20 Hoyt Wilhelm	.25	.07
21 Buck Leonard	.25	.07
22 Bob Feller	.40	.12
23 Cy Young	.60	.18
24 Satchel Paige	.60	.18
25 Tom Seaver	.40	.12
26 Brooks Robinson	.60	.18
27 Mike Schmidt	1.25	.35
28 Roberto Clemente	1.50	.45
29 Ralph Kiner	.25	.07
30 Willie Stargell	.40	.12
31 Honus Wagner	.75	.23
32 Josh Gibson	.60	.18
33 Nolan Ryan	1.50	.45
34 Carlton Fisk	.40	.12
35 Jimmie Foxx	.60	.18
36 Johnny Bench	.60	.18
37 Joe Morgan	.25	.07
38 George Brett	1.50	.45
39 Walter Johnson	.60	.18
40 Cool Papa Bell	.25	.07
41 Ty Cobb	1.00	.30
42 Al Kaline	.60	.18
43 Harmon Killebrew	.60	.18
44 Luis Aparicio	.25	.07
45 Yogi Berra	.60	.18
46 Joe DiMaggio	1.25	.35
47 Whitey Ford	.40	.12
48 Lou Gehrig	1.25	.35
49 Mickey Mantle	2.50	.75
50 Babe Ruth	2.00	.60
51 Josh Gibson OG	.40	.12
52 Honus Wagner OG	.60	.18
53 Hoyt Wilhelm OG	.25	.07
54 Cy Young OG	.40	.12
55 Walter Johnson OG	.40	.12
56 Satchel Paige OG	.40	.12
57 Rogers Hornsby OG	.40	.12
58 Christy Mathewson OG	.40	.12
59 Tris Speaker OG	.40	.12
60 Nap Lajoie OG	.60	.18
61 Mickey Mantle NP	1.25	.35
62 Jackie Robinson NP	.40	.12
63 Nolan Ryan NP	1.00	.30
64 Josh Gibson NP	.40	.12
65 Yogi Berra NP	.40	.12
66 Brooks Robinson NP	.40	.12
67 Stan Musial NP	.60	.18
68 Mike Schmidt NP	.60	.18
69 Joe DiMaggio NP	.60	.18
70 Ernie Banks NP	.40	.12
71 Willie Stargell NP	.25	.07
72 Johnny Bench NP	.40	.12
73 Willie Mays NP	.60	.18
74 Satchel Paige NP	.40	.12
75 Bob Gibson NP	.25	.07
76 Harmon Killebrew NP	.60	.18
77 Al Kaline NP	.40	.12
78 Carlton Fisk NP	.25	.07
79 Tom Seaver NP	.25	.07
80 Reggie Jackson NP	.25	.07
81 Bob Gibson HR	.25	.07
82 Nolan Ryan HR	1.00	.30
83 Walter Johnson HR	.40	.12
84 Stan Musial HR	.60	.18
85 Josh Gibson HR	.40	.12
86 Cy Young HR	.40	.12
87 Joe DiMaggio HR	.60	.18
88 Hoyt Wilhelm HR	.25	.07
89 Lou Brock HR	.25	.07
90 Mickey Mantle HR	1.25	.35

2001 Upper Deck Hall of Famers 20th Century Showcase

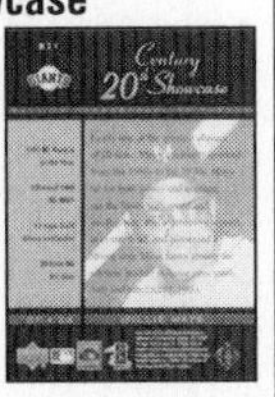

Randomly inserted into packs at one in eight, this 11-card insert set features some of the Major League's top players throughout the 20th Century. Card backs carry an "S" prefix.

	Nm-Mt	Ex-Mt
COMPLETE SET (11)	30.00	9.00
S1 Cy Young	2.00	.60
S2 Joe DiMaggio	4.00	1.20
S3 Harmon Killebrew	2.00	.60
S4 Stan Musial	3.00	.90
S5 Mickey Mantle	8.00	2.40
S6 Satchel Paige	2.00	.60
S7 Nolan Ryan	5.00	1.50
S8 Bob Gibson	1.50	.45
S9 Ernie Banks	2.00	.60
S10 Mike Schmidt	4.00	1.20
S11 Willie Mays	4.00	1.20

2001 Upper Deck Hall of Famers Class of '36

Randomly inserted into packs at one in 17, this 5-card insert features players that were inducted into the Major League Hall of Fame in 1936. Card backs carry a "C" prefix.

	Nm-Mt	Ex-Mt
COMPLETE SET (5)	15.00	4.50
C1 Ty Cobb	3.00	.90
C2 Babe Ruth	6.00	1.80
C3 Christy Mathewson	2.00	.60

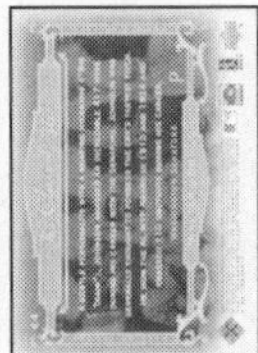

	Nm-Mt	Ex-Mt
C4 Walter Johnson	2.00	.60
C5 Honus Wagner	2.50	.75

2001 Upper Deck Hall of Famers Cut Signatures

Randomly inserted into packs, this five-card insert set features cut-signatures from deceased Major League Ballplayers. Card backs carry a "C" prefix followed by the player's initials. A total of only eleven cards were produced for this set.

Nm-Mt Ex-Mt

LC1 Honus Wagner
Ty Cobb
Babe Ruth
Christy Mathewson
Walter Johnson/1
C-BR Babe Ruth/2
C-CM Christy Mathewson/1
C-HW Honus Wagner/1
C-TC Ty Cobb/2
C-WJ Walter Johnson/5

2001 Upper Deck Hall of Famers Endless Summer

Randomly inserted into packs at one in eight, this 11-card insert set features classic players that had amazing careers in Major League Baseball. Card backs carry an "ES" prefix.

	Nm-Mt	Ex-Mt
COMPLETE SET (11)	30.00	9.00
ES1 Mickey Mantle	8.00	2.40
ES2 Yogi Berra	2.00	.60
ES3 Mike Schmidt	4.00	1.20
ES4 Jackie Robinson	2.50	.75
ES5 Johnny Bench	2.00	.60
ES6 Tom Seaver	2.00	.60
ES7 Ernie Banks	2.00	.60
ES8 Harmon Killebrew	2.00	.60
ES9 Joe DiMaggio	4.00	1.20
ES10 Willie Mays	4.00	1.20
ES11 Brooks Robinson	2.00	.60

2001 Upper Deck Hall of Famers Gallery

Randomly inserted into packs at one in six, this 15-card insert set features Major League Ballplayers that have been inducted into the Hall of Fame. Card backs carry a "G" prefix.

	Nm-Mt	Ex-Mt
COMPLETE SET (15)	40.00	12.00
G1 Reggie Jackson	1.25	.35
G2 Tom Seaver	1.25	.35
G3 Bob Gibson	1.25	.35
G4 Jackie Robinson	2.50	.75
G5 Joe DiMaggio	4.00	1.20
G6 Ernie Banks	2.00	.60
G7 Mickey Mantle	8.00	2.40
G8 Willie Mays	4.00	1.20
G9 Cy Young	2.00	.60
G10 Nolan Ryan	5.00	1.50
G11 Johnny Bench	2.00	.60
G12 Yogi Berra	2.00	.60
G13 Satchel Paige	2.00	.60
G14 George Brett	5.00	1.50
G15 Stan Musial	3.00	.90

2001 Upper Deck Hall of Famers Game Bat

Randomly inserted into packs at one in 24 (about one a box), this 40-card insert features slivers of actual game-used bats. Card backs carry a "B" prefix followed by the players initials. Though they lack any actual form of serial-numbering, Upper Deck announced

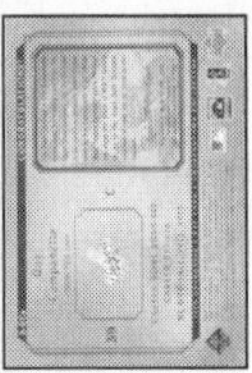

specific print runs for several short prints within this set. That information is detailed within our checklist. In addition, based upon extensive market research by our analysts, several cards are tagged with an asterisk within our checklist to indicate a perceived larger supply.

	Nm-Mt	Ex-Mt
B-BR Babe Ruth	175.00	52.50
B-BRO Brooks Robinson	15.00	4.50
B-BW Billy Williams	10.00	3.00
B-CF Carlton Fisk *	15.00	4.50
B-DD Don Drysdale	15.00	4.50
B-DS Duke Snider	15.00	4.50
B-EB Ernie Banks	15.00	4.50
B-ES Enos Slaughter	10.00	3.00
B-EW Early Wynn	15.00	4.50
B-FR Frank Robinson	15.00	4.50
B-GB George Brett *	25.00	7.50
B-GK George Kell	15.00	4.50
B-HA Hank Aaron *	40.00	12.00
B-HG Hank Greenberg	50.00	15.00
B-JB Johnny Bench *	15.00	4.50
B-JBO Jim Bottomley	15.00	4.50
B-JD Joe DiMaggio	100.00	30.00
B-JF Jimmie Foxx	60.00	18.00
B-JM Johnny Mize	15.00	4.50
B-JMO Joe Morgan *	10.00	3.00
B-JP Jim Palmer SP/372	50.00	15.00
B-JR J.Robinson SP/371	150.00	45.00
B-LA Luis Aparicio	10.00	3.00
B-MM Mickey Mantle	150.00	45.00
B-MO Mel Ott	60.00	18.00
B-NF Nellie Fox	15.00	4.50
B-NR Nolan Ryan	40.00	12.00
B-OC Orlando Cepeda	10.00	3.00
B-RC R.Clemente SP/409	120.00	36.00
B-RCA Roy Campanella	40.00	12.00
B-RF Rollie Fingers	10.00	3.00
B-RH Rogers Hornsby	100.00	30.00
B-RJ Reggie Jackson *	15.00	4.50
B-RK Ralph Kiner	15.00	4.50
B-RS Red Schoendienst	15.00	4.50
B-RY Robin Yount *	15.00	4.50
B-TP Tony Perez	10.00	3.00
B-WM Willie Mays *	40.00	12.00
B-WS Willie Stargell	15.00	4.50
B-YB Yogi Berra	15.00	4.50

2001 Upper Deck Hall of Famers Game Jersey

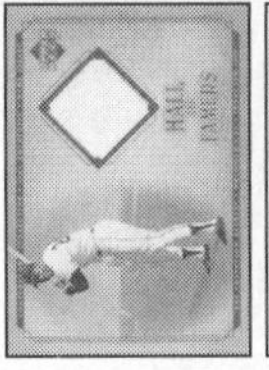
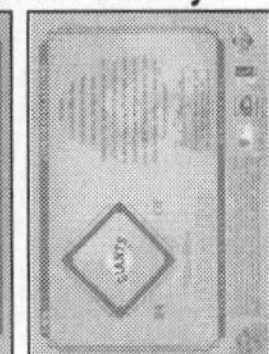

Randomly inserted into packs at one in 168, this 18-card insert features swatches of actual game-used jerseys. Card backs carry a "J" prefix followed by the players initials. Though they lack actual serial-numbering, Upper Deck announced specific print runs for several short-prints within this set. That information is detailed within our checklist. In addition, based upon extensive market research by our analysts, several cards are tagged with an asterisk within our checklist to indicate a perceived larger supply.

	Nm-Mt	Ex-Mt
J-BR Brooks Robinson	25.00	7.50
J-DD Don Drysdale SP/49		
J-DS Duke Snider SP/267	80.00	24.00
J-DSU Don Sutton	15.00	4.50
J-FR Frank Robinson	25.00	7.50
J-JD Joe DiMaggio	120.00	36.00
J-JM Joe Morgan	15.00	4.50
J-LA Luis Aparicio	15.00	4.50
J-LG L.Gehrig Pants SP/194	300.00	90.00
J-MM M.Mantle SP/216	300.00	90.00
J-NR Nolan Ryan *	40.00	12.00
J-OC Orlando Cepeda	15.00	4.50
J-PW Pee Wee Reese	25.00	7.50
J-RC Roberto Clemente	120.00	36.00
J-TP Tony Perez	15.00	4.50
J-TS Tom Seaver	25.00	7.50
J-WM Willie Mays	100.00	30.00
J-WS Willie Stargell	25.00	7.50

2001 Upper Deck Hall of Famers Game Jersey Autograph

Randomly inserted into packs at one in 504, this 14-card insert features swatches of actual game-used jerseys, as well as, an authentic autograph from the depicted player. Card backs carry a "SJ" prefix followed by the players initials. Willie Stargell was supposed to sign cards for this set but he passed away on April 9th, 2001 . . . before any of the exchange cards were produced.

	Nm-Mt	Ex-Mt
SJ-BR Brooks Robinson	100.00	30.00
SJ-DS Duke Snider	80.00	24.00
SJ-DSU Don Sutton	50.00	15.00
SJ-EB Ernie Banks	100.00	30.00
SJ-FR Frank Robinson	80.00	24.00
SJ-GB George Brett	150.00	45.00
SJ-JM Joe Morgan	50.00	15.00
SJ-LA Luis Aparicio	50.00	15.00
SJ-NR Nolan Ryan	150.00	45.00
SJ-OC Orlando Cepeda	50.00	15.00
SJ-RJ Reggie Jackson	100.00	30.00
SJ-TP Tony Perez	50.00	15.00
SJ-TS Tom Seaver	80.00	24.00
SJ-WS Willie Stargell EXCH	5.00	1.50

2000 Upper Deck Hitter's Club

This product was distributed in late February, 2000 exclusively in retail outlets. Five card packs carried an SRP of $2.99. The attractive 90-card set, featuring a selection of the best current and retired hitters in baseball, contains the following subsets: Why3K (51-72) and Hitting the Show (73-89). Ken Griffey Jr is featured on the checklist (card 90) to close out the set. Also, a selection of A Piece of History 3000 Club Wade Boggs and Tony Gwynn memorabilia cards were randomly seeded into packs. 350 bat cards and fifty hand-numbered, combination bat chip-baseball cap cards for each player were produced. In addition, ninety-nine hand-numbered cards featuring bat chips from both Boggs and Gwynn were produced. Also, twelve hand-numbered, autographed Wade Boggs bat cards and nineteen hand-numbered, autographed Tony Gwynn bat cards were produced. Pricing for these memorabilia cards can be referenced under 2000 Upper Deck A Piece of History 3000 Club.

	Nm-Mt	Ex-Mt
COMPLETE SET (90)	25.00	7.50
1 Mo Vaughn	.30	.09
2 Troy Glaus	.50	.15
3 Jeff Bagwell	.50	.15
4 Craig Biggio	.50	.15
5 Jason Giambi	.75	.23
6 Eric Chavez	.30	.09
7 Carlos Delgado	.30	.09
8 Chipper Jones	.75	.23
9 Andruw Jones	.30	.09
10 Andres Galarraga	.30	.09
11 Jeromy Burnitz	.30	.09
12 Mark McGwire	2.00	.60
13 Mark Grace	.50	.15
14 Sammy Sosa	1.25	.35
15 Jose Canseco	.75	.23
16 Vinny Castilla	.30	.09
17 Matt Williams	.30	.09
18 Gary Sheffield	.30	.09
19 Shawn Green	.30	.09
20 Vladimir Guerrero	.75	.23
21 Barry Bonds	2.00	.60
22 Manny Ramirez	.30	.09
23 Roberto Alomar	.75	.23
24 Jim Thome	.75	.23
25 Ken Griffey Jr.	1.25	.35
26 Alex Rodriguez	1.25	.35
27 Edgar Martinez	.50	.15
28 Preston Wilson	.30	.09
29 Mike Piazza	1.25	.35
30 Robin Ventura	.50	.15
31 Albert Belle	.30	.09
32 Cal Ripken	2.50	.75
33 Tony Gwynn	1.00	.30
34 Scott Rolen	.50	.15
35 Bob Abreu	.30	.09
36 Brian Giles	.30	.09
37 Ivan Rodriguez	.75	.23
38 Rafael Palmeiro	.50	.15
39 Nomar Garciaparra	1.25	.35
40 Sean Casey	.30	.09
41 Larry Walker	.50	.15
42 Todd Helton	.50	.15
43 Carlos Beltran	.30	.09
44 Dean Palmer	.30	.09
45 Juan Gonzalez	.75	.23
46 Corey Koskie	.30	.09
47 Frank Thomas	.75	.23
48 Magglio Ordonez	.30	.09
49 Derek Jeter	2.00	.60
50 Bernie Williams	.50	.15
51 Paul Waner W3K	.75	.23
52 Honus Wagner W3K	.75	.23
53 Tris Speaker W3K	.75	.23
54 Nap Lajoie W3K	.75	.23
55 Eddie Collins W3K	.75	.23
56 Roberto Clemente W3K	1.50	.45
57 Ty Cobb W3K	1.50	.45
58 Cap Anson W3K	.75	.23
59 Robin Yount W3K	1.25	.35
60 Carl Yastrzemski W3K	1.00	.30
61 Dave Winfield W3K	.30	.09
62 Stan Musial W3K	1.00	.30
63 Eddie Murray W3K	.75	.23
64 Paul Molitor W3K	.50	.15
65 Willie Mays W3K	1.50	.45
66 Al Kaline W3K	.75	.23
67 Tony Gwynn W3K	1.00	.30
68 Rod Carew W3K	.50	.15

69 Lou Brock W3K .50 .15
70 George Brett W3K 2.00 .60
71 Wade Boggs W3K .50 .15
72 Hank Aaron W3K 1.50 .45
73 Jorge Toca HS .30 .09
74 J.D. Drew HS .30 .09
75 Pat Burrell HS .50 .15
76 Vernon Wells HS .30 .09
77 Julio Ramirez HS .30 .09
78 Gabe Kapler HS .30 .09
79 Erubiel Durazo HS .30 .09
80 Lance Berkman HS .30 .09
81 Peter Bergeron HS .30 .09
82 Alfonso Soriano HS .75 .23
83 Jacque Jones HS .30 .09
84 Ben Petrick HS .30 .09
85 Jerry Hairston Jr. HS .30 .09
86 Kevin Witt HS .30 .09
87 Dermal Brown HS .30 .09
88 Chad Hermansen HS .30 .09
89 Ruben Mateo HS .30 .09
90 Ken Griffey Jr. CL .75 .23

2000 Upper Deck Hitter's Club Accolades

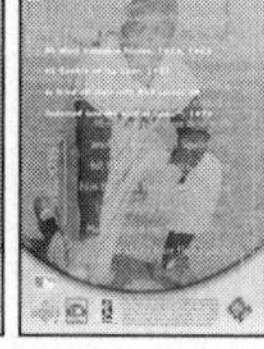

Randomly inserted in packs at one in eleven, this 10-card insert set features past and present stars of the game. Card backs carry an "A" prefix.

	Nm-Mt	Ex-Mt
COMPLETE SET (10)	40.00	12.00
A1 Robin Yount	4.00	1.20
A2 Tony Gwynn	3.00	.90
A3 Sammy Sosa	4.00	1.20
A4 Mike Piazza	4.00	1.20
A5 Cal Ripken	8.00	2.40
A6 Mark McGwire	6.00	1.80
A7 Barry Bonds	6.00	1.80
A8 Wade Boggs	1.50	.45
A9 Ken Griffey Jr.	4.00	1.20
A10 Willie Mays	5.00	1.50

2000 Upper Deck Hitter's Club Autographs

Randomly inserted in packs, this 15-card insert set features autographed cards of some of the greatest players to ever play the game. Card backs are numbered with the player's initials. The Hank Aaron card was originally issued as an exchange.

	Nm-Mt	Ex-Mt
AL Al Kaline	40.00	12.00
CAL Cal Ripken SP		
DW Dave Winfield	25.00	7.50
EM Eddie Murray	60.00	18.00
GB George Brett	120.00	36.00
HA Hank Aaron SP	250.00	75.00
LOU Lou Brock	25.00	7.50
MAN Stan Musial	80.00	24.00
PM Paul Molitor	25.00	7.50
ROD Rod Carew	25.00	7.50
RY Robin Yount	50.00	15.00
TG Tony Gwynn	50.00	15.00
WB Wade Boggs	25.00	7.50
WM Willie Mays	200.00	60.00
YAZ Carl Yastrzemski	80.00	24.00

2000 Upper Deck Hitter's Club Epic Performances

Randomly inserted in packs at one in three, this 10-card set features players that have produced epic performances over their careers. Card backs carry an "EP" prefix. Please note that card number EP2 does not exist, and was replaced with card number EP11.

	Nm-Mt	Ex-Mt
COMPLETE SET (10)	15.00	4.50
EP1 Mark McGwire	2.50	.75
EP2 Does Not Exist		
EP3 Sammy Sosa	1.50	.45
EP4 Ken Griffey Jr.	1.50	.45
EP5 Carl Yastrzemski	1.25	.35
EP6 Tony Gwynn	1.25	.35
EP7 Nomar Garciaparra	1.50	.45
EP8 Cal Ripken	3.00	.90
EP9 George Brett	2.50	.75
EP10 Hank Aaron	2.00	.60
EP11 Wade Boggs	.60	.18

2000 Upper Deck Hitter's Club Eternals

Randomly inserted in packs at a rate of one in 23, this 10-card insert set features players that are the heart and soul of their teams. Card backs carry an "E" prefix.

	Nm-Mt	Ex-Mt
COMPLETE SET (10)	80.00	24.00
E1 Cal Ripken	12.00	3.60
E2 Mark McGwire	10.00	3.00
E3 Ken Griffey Jr.	6.00	1.80
E4 Nomar Garciaparra	6.00	1.80
E5 Tony Gwynn	5.00	1.50
E6 Derek Jeter	10.00	3.00
E7 Jose Canseco	4.00	1.20
E8 Mike Piazza	6.00	1.80
E9 Alex Rodriguez	6.00	1.80
E10 Barry Bonds	10.00	3.00

2000 Upper Deck Hitter's Club Generations of Excellence

Randomly inserted in packs at a rate of one in six, this 10-card insert set features ten dual player cards that compare past stars with present stars. Card backs carry a "GE" prefix.

	Nm-Mt	Ex-Mt
COMPLETE SET (10)	30.00	9.00
GE1 Cal Ripken / Eddie Murray	5.00	1.50
GE2 Vladimir Guerrero / Roberto Clemente	1.50	.45
GE3 George Brett / Robin Yount	1.50	.45
GE4 Barry Bonds / Willie Mays	4.00	1.20
GE5 Chipper Jones / Hank Aaron	1.50	.45
GE6 Mark McGwire / Sammy Sosa	4.00	1.20
GE7 Tony Gwynn / Wade Boggs	2.00	.60
GE8 Rickey Henderson / Lou Brock	1.50	.45
GE9 Derek Jeter / Nomar Garciaparra	4.00	1.20
GE10 Alex Rodriguez / Ken Griffey Jr.	2.50	.75

2000 Upper Deck Hitter's Club Inserts

Randomly inserted in packs at a rate of one in 95, this 10-card insert set features past and present stars. Card backs carry a "HC" prefix.

	Nm-Mt	Ex-Mt
COMPLETE SET (10)	200.00	60.00
HC1 Rod Carew	10.00	3.00
HC2 Alex Rodriguez	25.00	7.50
HC3 Willie Mays	30.00	9.00
HC4 George Brett	40.00	12.00
HC5 Tony Gwynn	20.00	6.00
HC6 Stan Musial	20.00	6.00
HC7 Frank Thomas	15.00	4.50
HC8 Wade Boggs	10.00	3.00
HC9 Larry Walker	10.00	3.00
HC10 Nomar Garciaparra	25.00	7.50

2000 Upper Deck Hitter's Club On Target

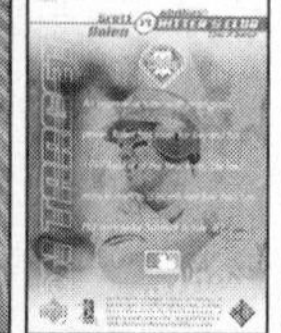

Randomly inserted in packs at a rate of one in 23, this 10-card insert set features ten players that are "on target" for success. Card backs carry an "OT" prefix.

	Nm-Mt	Ex-Mt
COMPLETE SET (10)	50.00	15.00
OT1 Nomar Garciaparra	6.00	1.80
OT2 Sean Casey	1.50	.45
OT3 Alex Rodriguez	6.00	1.80
OT4 Troy Glaus	2.50	.75
OT5 Ivan Rodriguez	4.00	1.20
OT6 Chipper Jones	4.00	1.20
OT7 Manny Ramirez	1.50	.45
OT8 Derek Jeter	10.00	3.00
OT9 Vladimir Guerrero	4.00	1.20
OT10 Scott Rolen	2.50	.75

1999 Upper Deck HoloGrFX

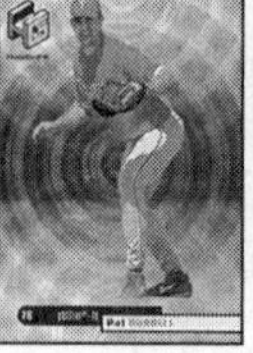
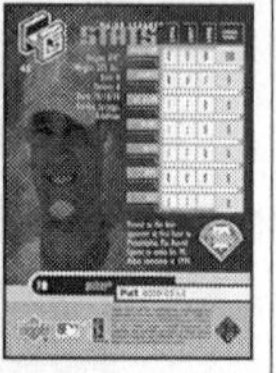

Issued only through Retail outlets, this 60 card set was distributed in the summer of 1999. There were 36 packs in a box with three cards per pack at a SRP of $1.99 per pack. All the cards in this set featured a hi-tech holographic treatment. Notable Rookie Cards include Pat Burrell. Two separate A Piece of History 500 Club bat cards featuring legendary sluggers Eddie Mathews and Willie McCovey were randomly seeded into HoloGrFX packs. Approximately 350 of each card were made. In addition, 41 signed Mathews cards and 44 signed McCovey cards were also included in packs. Both players signed to their jersey numbers. Pricing for these APH 500 Club cards can be found under 1999 Upper Deck A Piece of History 500 Club. A Ken Griffey Jr. HoloGrFX sample card was distributed to dealers and hobby media several weeks prior to the product's national release. The card is similar to the basic HoloGrFX Griffey except for it's numbering (the basic Griffey is number 53, the sample is number 60) and the white text "SAMPLE" running diagonally across the card back.

	Nm-Mt	Ex-Mt
COMPLETE SET (60)	25.00	7.50
1 Mo Vaughn	.40	.12
2 Troy Glaus	.60	.18
3 Tim Salmon	.60	.18
4 Randy Johnson	1.00	.30
5 Travis Lee	.40	.12
6 Chipper Jones	1.00	.30
7 Greg Maddux	1.50	.45
8 Andruw Jones	.40	.12
9 Tom Glavine	.60	.18
10 Cal Ripken	3.00	.90
11 Albert Belle	.40	.12
12 Nomar Garciaparra	1.50	.45
13 Pedro Martinez	1.00	.30
14 Sammy Sosa	1.50	.45
15 Frank Thomas	1.00	.30
16 Greg Vaughn	.40	.12
17 Kenny Lofton	.40	.12
18 Jim Thome	1.00	.30
19 Manny Ramirez	.40	.12
20 Todd Helton	.60	.18
21 Larry Walker	.60	.18
22 Tony Clark	.40	.12
23 Juan Encarnacion	.40	.12
24 Mark Kotsay	.40	.12
25 Jeff Bagwell	.60	.18
26 Craig Biggio	.60	.18
27 Ken Caminiti	.40	.12
28 Carlos Beltran	.40	.12
29 Jeremy Giambi	.40	.12
30 Raul Mondesi	.40	.12
31 Kevin Brown	.60	.18
32 Jeromy Burnitz	.40	.12
33 Corey Koskie	.40	.12
34 Todd Walker	.40	.12
35 Vladimir Guerrero	1.00	.30
36 Mike Piazza	1.50	.45
37 Robin Ventura	.40	.12
38 Derek Jeter	2.50	.75
39 Roger Clemens	2.00	.60
40 Bernie Williams	.60	.18
41 Orlando Hernandez	.40	.12
42 Ben Grieve	.40	.12
43 Eric Chavez	.40	.12
44 Scott Rolen	.60	.18
45 Pat Burrell RC	3.00	.90
46 Warren Morris	.40	.12
47 Jason Kendall	.40	.12
48 Mark McGwire	2.50	.75
49 J.D. Drew	.40	.12
50 Tony Gwynn	1.25	.35
51 Trevor Hoffman	.40	.12
52 Barry Bonds	2.50	.75
53 Ken Griffey Jr.	1.50	.45
54 Alex Rodriguez	1.50	.45
55 Jose Canseco	1.00	.30
56 Juan Gonzalez	1.00	.30
57 Ivan Rodriguez	1.00	.30
58 Rafael Palmeiro	.60	.18
59 David Wells	.40	.12
60 Carlos Delgado	.40	.12
S60 K.Griffey Jr. Sample	2.00	.60

1999 Upper Deck HoloGrFX AuSOME

Randomly inserted in packs at the rate of one in eight, this 60-card set is parallel to the regular set and is distinguished by the gold ink used on this set.

	Nm-Mt	Ex-Mt
COMPLETE SET (60)	150.00	45.00
*STARS: 2.5X TO 6X BASIC CARDS		
*ROOKIES: 1.25X TO 3X BASIC CARDS		

1999 Upper Deck HoloGrFX Future Fame

Randomly inserted in packs at the rate of one in 32, this six-card set features color photos of players destined for Hall-of-Fame greatness.

	Nm-Mt	Ex-Mt
COMPLETE SET (6)	50.00	15.00
*GOLD: 2X TO 5X BASIC FUTURE FAME		
GOLD STATED ODDS 1:432		
F1 Tony Gwynn	5.00	1.50
F2 Cal Ripken	12.00	3.60
F3 Mark McGwire	10.00	3.00
F4 Ken Griffey Jr.	6.00	1.80
F5 Greg Maddux	6.00	1.80
F6 Roger Clemens	8.00	2.40

1999 Upper Deck HoloGrFX Launchers

Randomly inserted in packs at the rate of one in four, this 15-card set features color photos of the top home run sluggers printed on holographic patterned foil cards.

	Nm-Mt	Ex-Mt
COMPLETE SET (15)	30.00	9.00
*GOLD: 2.5X TO 6X BASIC LAUNCHERS		
GOLD STATED ODDS 1:105		
L1 Mark McGwire	4.00	1.20
L2 Ken Griffey Jr.	2.50	.75
L3 Sammy Sosa	2.50	.75
L4 J.D. Drew	.60	.18
L5 Mo Vaughn	.60	.18
L6 Juan Gonzalez	1.50	.45
L7 Mike Piazza	2.50	.75
L8 Alex Rodriguez	2.50	.75
L9 Chipper Jones	1.50	.45
L10 Nomar Garciaparra	2.50	.75
L11 Vladimir Guerrero	1.50	.45
L12 Albert Belle	.60	.18
L13 Barry Bonds	4.00	1.20
L14 Frank Thomas	1.50	.45
L15 Jeff Bagwell	1.00	.30

1999 Upper Deck HoloGrFX StarView

Randomly inserted in packs at the rate of one in 16, this nine-card set features color photos of some of the most elite performers in the game today.

	Nm-Mt	Ex-Mt
COMPLETE SET (9)	40.00	12.00
*GOLD: 2X TO 5X BASIC STARVIEW		
GOLD STATED ODDS 1:210		
S1 Mark McGwire	6.00	1.80
S2 Ken Griffey Jr.	4.00	1.20
S3 Sammy Sosa	4.00	1.20
S4 Nomar Garciaparra	4.00	1.20
S5 Roger Clemens	5.00	1.50
S6 Greg Maddux	4.00	1.20
S7 Mike Piazza	4.00	1.20
S8 Alex Rodriguez	4.00	1.20
S9 Chipper Jones	2.50	.75

1999 Upper Deck HoloGrFX UD Authentics

Randomly inserted in packs at the rate of one in 431, this 12-card set features autographed color photos of some of the current top players in baseball.

	Nm-Mt	Ex-Mt
AG Alex Gonzalez	10.00	3.00
BC Bruce Chen	10.00	3.00
CB Carlos Beltran	15.00	4.50
CJ Chipper Jones	80.00	24.00
CK Corey Koskie	15.00	4.50
GK Gabe Kapler	10.00	3.00
GL George Lombard	10.00	3.00
JD J.D. Drew	15.00	4.50
JR Ken Griffey Jr.	150.00	45.00
MK Mike Kinkade	10.00	3.00
RM Ryan Minor	10.00	3.00
SM Shane Monahan	10.00	3.00

2000 Upper Deck HoloGrFX

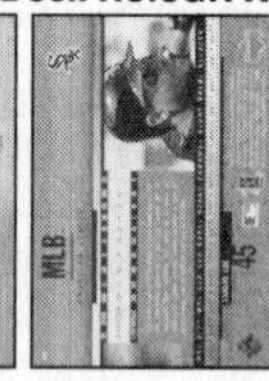

The 2000 Upper Deck HoloGrFX product was released in April, 2000 as a 90-card set. The set features some of the hottest players in major league baseball. Each pack contained three cards and carried a suggested retail price of 1.99. Also, a selection of A Piece of History 3000 Club George Brett and Robin Yount memorabilia cards were randomly seeded into packs. 350 bat cards and 350 jersey cards were produced for each player. In addition, ninety-nine hand-numbered Brett/Yount combination bat cards and ninety-nine hand-numbered Brett/Yount combination jersey cards were produced. Also, ten hand-numbered, autographed Brett/Yount combination bat and ten hand-numbered, autographed Brett/Yount combination jersey cards were produced. Pricing for these memorabilia cards can be referenced under 2000 Upper Deck A Piece of History 3000 Club.

	Nm-Mt	Ex-Mt
COMPLETE SET (90)	25.00	7.50
1 Mo Vaughn	.40	.12
2 Troy Glaus	.60	.18
3 Daryle Ward	.40	.12
4 Jeff Bagwell	.60	.18
5 Craig Biggio	.60	.18
6 Jose Lima	.40	.12
7 Jason Giambi	1.00	.30
8 Eric Chavez	.40	.12
9 Tim Hudson	.60	.18
10 Raul Mondesi	.40	.12
11 Carlos Delgado	.40	.12
12 David Wells	.40	.12
13 Chipper Jones	1.00	.30
14 Greg Maddux	1.50	.45
15 Andruw Jones	.40	.12
16 Brian Jordan	.40	.12
17 Jeromy Burnitz	.40	.12
18 Ron Belliard	.40	.12
19 Mark McGwire	2.50	.75
20 Fernando Tatis	.40	.12
21 J.D. Drew	.40	.12
22 Sammy Sosa	1.50	.45
23 Mark Grace	.60	.18
24 Greg Vaughn	.40	.12
25 Jose Canseco	1.00	.30
26 Vinny Castilla	.40	.12
27 Fred McGriff	.60	.18
28 Matt Williams	.40	.12
29 Randy Johnson	1.00	.30
30 Erubiel Durazo	.40	.12
31 Shawn Green	.40	.12
32 Gary Sheffield	.40	.12
33 Kevin Brown	.60	.18
34 Vladimir Guerrero	1.00	.30
35 Michael Barrett	.40	.12
36 Russ Ortiz	.40	.12
37 Barry Bonds	2.50	.75
38 Jeff Kent	.40	.12
39 Kenny Lofton	.40	.12
40 Manny Ramirez	.40	.12
41 Roberto Alomar	1.00	.30
42 Richie Sexson	.40	.12
43 Edgar Martinez	.60	.18
44 Alex Rodriguez	1.50	.45
45 Freddy Garcia	.40	.12
46 Preston Wilson	.40	.12
47 Alex Gonzalez	.40	.12
48 Mike Hampton	.40	.12
49 Mike Piazza	1.50	.45
50 Robin Ventura	.60	.18
51 Edgardo Alfonzo	.40	.12
52 Albert Belle	.40	.12
53 Cal Ripken	3.00	.90
54 B.J. Surhoff	.40	.12
55 Tony Gwynn	1.25	.35
56 Trevor Hoffman	.40	.12
57 Mike Lieberthal	.40	.12
58 Scott Rolen	.60	.18
59 Bob Abreu	.40	.12
60 Curt Schilling	.60	.18
61 Jason Kendall	.40	.12
62 Brian Giles	.40	.12
63 Kris Benson	.40	.12
64 Rafael Palmeiro	.60	.18
65 Ivan Rodriguez	1.00	.30
66 Gabe Kapler	.40	.12
67 Nomar Garciaparra	1.50	.45
68 Pedro Martinez	1.00	.30
69 Troy O'Leary	.40	.12
70 Barry Larkin	1.00	.30
71 Dante Bichette	.40	.12
72 Sean Casey	.40	.12
73 Ken Griffey Jr.	1.50	.45
74 Jeff Cirillo	.40	.12
75 Todd Helton	.60	.18
76 Larry Walker	.60	.18
77 Carlos Beltran	.40	.12
78 Jermaine Dye	.40	.12
79 Juan Gonzalez	1.00	.30
80 Juan Encarnacion	.40	.12
81 Dean Palmer	.40	.12
82 Corey Koskie	.40	.12
83 Eric Milton	.40	.12
84 Frank Thomas	1.00	.30
85 Magglio Ordonez	.40	.12
86 Carlos Lee	.40	.12
87 Derek Jeter	2.50	.75

	Nm-Mt	Ex-Mt
88 Tino Martinez	.60	.18
89 Bernie Williams	.60	.18
90 Roger Clemens	2.00	.60

2000 Upper Deck HoloGrFX A Piece of the Series

Randomly inserted in packs, this 11-card insert set features swatches of the bases used in the 1999 World series. Card backs carry a "PS" prefix. Card number 10 was pulled from production.

	Nm-Mt	Ex-Mt
PS1 Derek Jeter	50.00	15.00
PS2 Chipper Jones	25.00	7.50
PS3 Roger Clemens	40.00	12.00
PS4 Greg Maddux	25.00	7.50
PS5 Bernie Williams	25.00	7.50
PS6 Andruw Jones	15.00	4.50
PS7 Tino Martinez	25.00	7.50
PS8 Brian Jordan	15.00	4.50
PS9 Mariano Rivera	25.00	7.50
PS11 Paul O'Neill	25.00	7.50
PS12 Tom Glavine	25.00	7.50

2000 Upper Deck HoloGrFX A Piece of the Series Autographs

Randomly inserted in packs, this nine-card autographed insert set features swatches of the bases used in the 1999 World series. Card backs carry a "PS" prefix. Each card is hand numbered to 25. Card numbers 5, 9, and 10 were pulled from production. Unannounced signed variations (each serial numbered to the players jersey) were created as follows: Tom Glavine (of 47), Brian Jordan (of 33), Tino Martinez (of24) and Paul O'Neill (of 21).

	Nm-Mt	Ex-Mt
PSA1 Derek Jeter		
PSA2 Chipper Jones		
PSA3 Roger Clemens		
PSA4 Greg Maddux		
PSA6 Andruw Jones		
PSA7 Tino Martinez		
PSA7 Tino Martinez 24		
PSA8 Brian Jordan		
PSA8 Brian Jordan 33	60.00	18.00
PSA11 Paul O'Neill		
PSA11A Paul O'Neill 21		
PSA12 Tom Glavine		
PSA12A Tom Glavine 47	150.00	45.00

2000 Upper Deck HoloGrFX Bomb Squad

Randomly inserted into packs at one in 34, this six-card insert set features the greatest power hitters in major league baseball. Card backs carry a "BS" prefix.

	Nm-Mt	Ex-Mt
COMPLETE SET (6)	40.00	12.00
BS1 Ken Griffey Jr.	6.00	1.80
BS2 Mark McGwire	10.00	3.00
BS3 Chipper Jones	4.00	1.20
BS4 Alex Rodriguez	6.00	1.80
BS5 Sammy Sosa	6.00	1.80
BS6 Barry Bonds	10.00	3.00

2000 Upper Deck HoloGrFX Future Fame

Randomly inserted into packs at one in 34, this insert set features six players that are sure bets to make the Hall of Fame. Card backs carry a "FF" prefix.

	Nm-Mt	Ex-Mt
COMPLETE SET (6)	50.00	15.00
FF1 Cal Ripken	12.00	3.60
FF2 Mark McGwire	10.00	3.00
FF3 Greg Maddux	6.00	1.80
FF4 Tony Gwynn	5.00	1.50
FF5 Ken Griffey Jr.	6.00	1.80
FF6 Roger Clemens	8.00	2.40

2000 Upper Deck HoloGrFX Longball Legacy

Randomly inserted into packs at one in six, this 15-card insert set features the greatest homerun hitters in major league baseball. Card backs carry a "LL" prefix.

	Nm-Mt	Ex-Mt
COMPLETE SET (15)	30.00	9.00
LL1 Mike Piazza	3.00	.90
LL2 Ivan Rodriguez	2.00	.60
LL3 Jeff Bagwell	1.25	.35
LL4 Alex Rodriguez	3.00	.90
LL5 Jose Canseco	2.00	.60
LL6 Mark McGwire	5.00	1.50
LL7 Scott Rolen	1.25	.35
LL8 Carlos Delgado	.75	.23
LL9 Mo Vaughn	.75	.23
LL10 Manny Ramirez	.75	.23
LL11 Matt Williams	.75	.23
LL12 Sammy Sosa	3.00	.90
LL13 Ken Griffey Jr.	3.00	.90
LL14 Nomar Garciaparra	3.00	.90
LL15 Larry Walker	1.25	.35

2000 Upper Deck HoloGrFX Stars of the System

Randomly inserted into packs at one in eight, this 10-card insert set features some of the hottest young talent to enter major league baseball. Card backs carry a "SS" prefix.

	Nm-Mt	Ex-Mt
COMPLETE SET (10)	12.00	3.60
SS1 Rick Ankiel	1.00	.30
SS2 Alfonso Soriano	2.00	.60
SS3 Vernon Wells	1.00	.30
SS4 Ben Petrick	1.00	.30
SS5 Francisco Cordero	1.00	.30
SS6 Matt Riley	1.00	.30
SS7 A.J. Burnett	1.00	.30
SS8 Pat Burrell	1.25	.35
SS9 Ed Yarnall	1.00	.30
SS10 Dermal Brown	1.00	.30

2000 Upper Deck HoloGrFX StarView

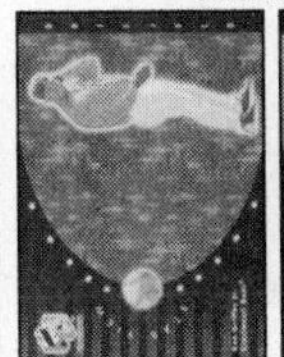

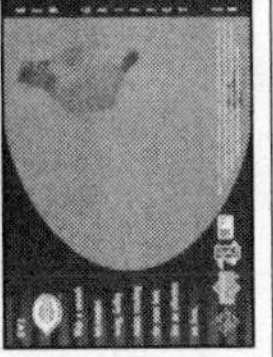

Randomly inserted into packs at one in 11, this eight-card insert set features the most popular players in MLB. Card backs carry a "SV" prefix.

	Nm-Mt	Ex-Mt
COMPLETE SET (8)	30.00	9.00
SV1 Ken Griffey Jr.	3.00	.90
SV2 Nomar Garciaparra	3.00	.90
SV3 Chipper Jones	2.00	.60
SV4 Mark McGwire	5.00	1.50
SV5 Sammy Sosa	3.00	.90
SV6 Derek Jeter	5.00	1.50
SV7 Mike Piazza	3.00	.90
SV8 Alex Rodriguez	3.00	.90

2002 Upper Deck Honor Roll

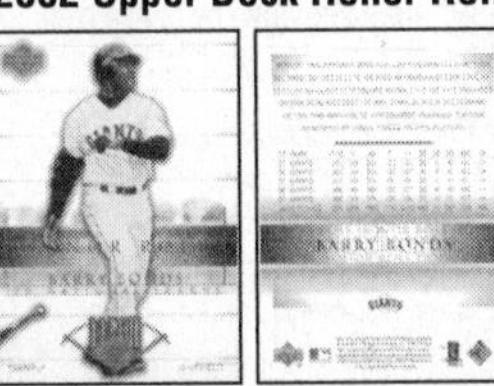

This 190-card retail-only set was distributed in two separate series. The first 100 cards (excluding cards 19-27) feature Upper Deck's dream team. Cards 19-27 feature nine prospects. These first 1000 cards were issued in the standard Honor Roll packs of which hit retail shelves in late April 2002. The standard-size card fronts highlight one player for each position and then dedicates each of the nine players in the set with unique color action shots. These cards were issued in five card packs which were packed 24 to a box and 20 boxes to a case with an SRP of $2.99 per pack. Cards 101-190 were distributed in mid-December 2002 within packs of Upper Deck Rookie Debut. Subset cards 101-130 feature Dream Moments and 131-190 feature a selection of prospects and rookies. All 90 cards were seeded at an equal rate of approximately one or two per Rookie Debut pack.

	Nm-Mt	Ex-Mt
COMP.LOW SET (100)	25.00	7.50
COMP.UPDATE SET (90)	25.00	7.50
COMMON CARD (101-130)	.30	.09
1 Randy Johnson NLD9	.50	.15
2 Mike Piazza NLD9	.75	.23
3 Albert Pujols NLD9	1.00	.30
4 Roberto Alomar NLD9	.50	.15
5 Chipper Jones NLD9	.50	.15
6 Rich Aurilia NLD9	.20	.06
7 Barry Bonds NLD9	1.25	.35
8 Ken Griffey Jr. NLD9	.75	.23
9 Sammy Sosa NLD9	.75	.23
10 Roger Clemens ALD9	1.00	.30
11 Ivan Rodriguez ALD9	.50	.15
12 Jason Giambi ALD9	.30	.09
13 Bret Boone ALD9	.20	.06
14 Troy Glaus ALD9	.30	.09
15 Alex Rodriguez ALD9	.75	.23
16 Manny Ramirez ALD9	.20	.06
17 Bernie Williams ALD9	.30	.09
18 Ichiro Suzuki ALD9	.75	.23
19 Matt Thornton PD9 RC	.50	.15
20 Chris Baker PD9 RC	.50	.15
21 Tyler Yates PD9 RC	1.00	.30
22 Jorge Nunez PD9 RC	.50	.15
23 Rene Reyes PD9 RC	.50	.15
24 Ben Howard PD9 RC	.50	.15
25 Ron Calloway PD9 RC	.50	.15
26 Dan Wright PD9	.50	.15
27 Reed Johnson PD9 RC	.60	.18
28 Randy Johnson	.50	.15
29 Randy Johnson	.50	.15
30 Randy Johnson	.50	.15
31 Randy Johnson	.50	.15
32 Mike Piazza	.75	.23
33 Mike Piazza	.75	.23
34 Mike Piazza	.75	.23
35 Mike Piazza	.75	.23
36 Albert Pujols	1.00	.30
37 Albert Pujols	1.00	.30
38 Albert Pujols	1.00	.30
39 Albert Pujols	1.00	.30
40 Roberto Alomar	.50	.15
41 Roberto Alomar	.50	.15
42 Roberto Alomar	.50	.15
43 Roberto Alomar	.50	.15
44 Chipper Jones	.50	.15
45 Chipper Jones	.50	.15
46 Chipper Jones	.50	.15
47 Chipper Jones	.50	.15
48 Rich Aurilia	.20	.06
49 Rich Aurilia	.20	.06
50 Rich Aurilia	.20	.06
51 Rich Aurilia	.20	.06
52 Barry Bonds	1.25	.35
53 Barry Bonds	1.25	.35
54 Barry Bonds	1.25	.35
55 Barry Bonds	1.25	.35
56 Ken Griffey Jr.	.75	.23
57 Ken Griffey Jr.	.75	.23
58 Ken Griffey Jr.	.75	.23
59 Ken Griffey Jr.	.75	.23
60 Sammy Sosa	.75	.23
61 Sammy Sosa	.75	.23
62 Sammy Sosa	.75	.23
63 Sammy Sosa	.75	.23
64 Roger Clemens	1.00	.30
65 Roger Clemens	1.00	.30
66 Roger Clemens	1.00	.30
67 Roger Clemens	1.00	.30
68 Ivan Rodriguez	.50	.15
69 Ivan Rodriguez	.50	.15
70 Ivan Rodriguez	.50	.15
71 Ivan Rodriguez	.50	.15
72 Jason Giambi	.50	.15
73 Jason Giambi	.50	.15
74 Jason Giambi	.50	.15
75 Jason Giambi	.50	.15
76 Bret Boone	.20	.06
77 Bret Boone	.20	.06
78 Bret Boone	.20	.06
79 Bret Boone	.20	.06
80 Troy Glaus	.30	.09
81 Troy Glaus	.30	.09
82 Troy Glaus	.30	.09
83 Troy Glaus	.30	.09
84 Alex Rodriguez	.75	.23
85 Alex Rodriguez	.75	.23
86 Alex Rodriguez	.75	.23
87 Alex Rodriguez	.75	.23
88 Manny Ramirez	.20	.06
89 Manny Ramirez	.20	.06
90 Manny Ramirez	.20	.06
91 Manny Ramirez	.20	.06
92 Bernie Williams	.30	.09
93 Bernie Williams	.30	.09
94 Bernie Williams	.30	.09
95 Bernie Williams	.30	.09
96 Ichiro Suzuki	.75	.23
97 Ichiro Suzuki	.75	.23
98 Ichiro Suzuki	.75	.23
99 Ichiro Suzuki	.75	.23
100 Checklist	.20	.06
101 Curt Schilling DM	.50	.15
102 Geronimo Gil DM	.30	.09
103 Cliff Floyd DM	.30	.09
104 Derek Lowe DM	.30	.09
105 Hee Seop Choi DM	.50	.15
106 Mark Prior DM	2.00	.60
107 Joe Borchard DM	.30	.09
108 Austin Kearns DM	.30	.09
109 Adam Dunn DM	.30	.09
110 Brandon Phillips DM	.30	.09
111 Carlos Pena DM	.30	.09
112 Andy Van Hekken DM	.30	.09
113 Juan Encarnacion DM	.30	.09
114 Lance Berkman DM	.30	.09
115 Torii Hunter DM	.30	.09
116 Bartolo Colon DM	.30	.09
117 Raul Mondesi DM	.30	.09
118 Alfonso Soriano DM	.50	.15
119 Miguel Tejada DM	.30	.09
120 Ray Durham DM	.30	.09
121 Eric Chavez DM	.30	.09
122 Brett Myers DM	.30	.09
123 Marlon Byrd DM	.30	.09
124 Sean Burroughs DM	.30	.09
125 Kenny Lofton DM	.30	.09
126 Scott Rolen DM	.50	.15
127 Carl Crawford DM	.30	.09
128 Josh Phelps DM	.30	.09
129 Eric Hinske DM	.30	.09
130 Orlando Hudson DM	.30	.09
131 Barry Wesson UDP RC	.50	.15
132 Jose Valverde UDP RC	.60	.18
133 Kevin Gryboski UDP RC	.50	.15
134 Trey Hodges UDP RC	.50	.15
135 Howie Clark UDP RC	.50	.15
136 Josh Hancock UDP RC	.50	.15
137 Freddy Sanchez UDP RC	.50	.15
138 Francis Beltran UDP RC	.50	.15
139 Mike Mahoney UDP	.50	.15
140 Brian Tallet UDP RC	.60	.18
141 Jason Davis UDP RC	1.00	.30
142 Carl Sadler UDP RC	.50	.15
143 Jason Beverlin UDP RC	.50	.15
144 Josh Bard UDP RC	.50	.15
145 Aaron Cook UDP RC	.50	.15
146 Eric Eckenstahler UDP RC	.50	.15
147 Tim Kalita UDP RC	.50	.15
148 Franklyn German UDP RC	.50	.15
149 Hansel Izquierdo UDP RC	.50	.15
150 Brandon Puffer UDP RC	.50	.15
151 Rodrigo Rosario UDP RC	.50	.15
152 Kirk Saarloos UDP RC	.50	.15
153 Jeriome Robertson UDP RC	.50	.15
154 Jeremy Hill UDP RC	.50	.15
155 Wes Obermueller UDP RC	.50	.15
156 Aaron Guiel UDP RC	.50	.15
157 Kazuhisa Ishii UDP RC	2.00	.60
158 David Ross UDP RC	.50	.15
159 Jayson Durocher UDP RC	.50	.15
160 Luis Martinez UDP RC	.50	.15
161 Shane Nance UDP RC	.50	.15
162 Eric Good UDP RC	.50	.15
163 Jamey Carroll UDP RC	.50	.15
164 Jaime Cerda UDP RC	.50	.15
165 Satoru Komiyama UDP RC	.50	.15
166 Adam Walker UDP RC	.50	.15
167 Nate Field UDP RC	.50	.15
168 Cody McKay UDP RC	.50	.15
169 Jose Flores UDP RC	.50	.15
170 Eric Junge UDP RC	.50	.15
171 Jorge Padilla UDP RC	.50	.15
172 Oliver Perez UDP RC	.60	.18
173 Julius Matos UDP RC	.50	.15
174 Wil Nieves UDP RC	.50	.15
175 Clay Condrey UDP RC	.50	.15
176 Mike Crudale UDP RC	.50	.15
177 Jason Simontacchi UDP RC	.50	.15
178 So Taguchi UDP RC	.60	.18
179 Jose Rodriguez UDP RC	.50	.15
180 Jorge Sosa UDP RC	.50	.15
181 Felix Escalona UDP RC	.50	.15
182 Lance Carter UDP RC	.50	.15
183 Travis Hughes UDP RC	.50	.15
184 Reynaldo Garcia UDP RC	.50	.15
185 Mike Smith UDP RC	.50	.15
186 Corey Thurman UDP RC	.50	.15
187 Ken Huckaby UDP RC	.50	.15
188 Reed Johnson UDP	.50	.15
189 Kevin Cash UDP RC	.50	.15
190 Scott Wiggins UDP RC	.50	.15

2002 Upper Deck Honor Roll Gold

This 190-card set is a parallel to the base set. Cards 1-100 were randomly seeded in Honor Roll packs and 101-190 in Upper Deck Rookie Debut packs. Only 25-serial numbered sets were produced for cards 1-100 and fifty serial-numbered sets for cards 101-190. The rare gold foil set features Upper Deck's Dream Team and along with a wide selection of prospects. The standard-size card fronts highlight one player for each position and then dedicates each of the nine players in the set with unique color action shots. The cards can be readily distinguished by the gold foil accents and serial-numbering on front.

	Nm-Mt	Ex-Mt
*GOLD 1-18/28-100: 25X TO 60X BASIC		
*GOLD 101-130: 12.5X TO 30X BASIC		
*GOLD 131-190: 8X TO 20X BASIC		

2002 Upper Deck Honor Roll Silver

This 100-card set is a parallel to the base set. Cards were randomly seeded in packs. 100 serial-numbered sets were produced. The set features Upper Deck's dream team. The standard-size card fronts highlight one player for each position and then dedicates each of the nine players in the set with unique color action shots.

	Nm-Mt	Ex-Mt
*SILVER 1-18/28-100: 8X TO 20X BASIC		
*SILVER RC's 19-27: 6X TO 15X BASIC		

2002 Upper Deck Honor Roll Batting Gloves

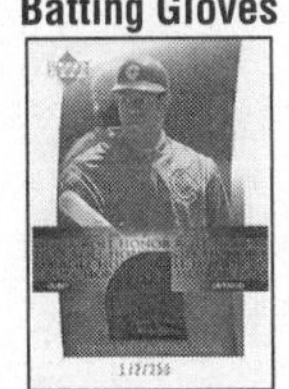

This eight-card limited edition insert set showcases authentic game-used batting gloves on standard-size card fronts. Cards were randomly seeded into packs we have notated the stated print run next to the player's name in our checklist.

	Nm-Mt	Ex-Mt
G-I Ichiro Suzuki/46		
G-AR Alex Rodriguez/250	30.00	9.00
G-BB Bret Boone/89		
G-IR1 I.Rodriguez Batting/250	25.00	7.50
G-IR2 Ivan Rodriguez w/cap/250	25.00	7.50
G-JG Jason Giambi/210	25.00	7.50
G-KG Ken Griffey Jr./250	40.00	12.00
G-SS Sammy Sosa/250	40.00	12.00

2002 Upper Deck Honor Roll Game Bats

This 30-card insert set is standard-size and features authentic game-used bats on the card fronts. Cards were randomly seeded into packs and 99 serial-numbered sets were produced.

	Nm-Mt	Ex-Mt
B-I1 Ichiro Suzuki Running	60.00	18.00
B-I2 I.Suzuki Batting Profile	60.00	18.00
B-I3 Ichiro Suzuki w/Cap	60.00	18.00
B-AR1 A.Rodriguez Btg Helmet	40.00	12.00
B-AR2 Alex Rodriguez Hand on Head	40.00	12.00
B-AR3 Alex Rodriguez Shades on Cap	40.00	12.00
B-AR4 Alex Rodriguez Wearing Shades	40.00	12.00
B-BB1 Bret Boone Looking Left	15.00	4.50
B-BB2 Bret Boone w/Cap Batting	15.00	4.50
B-BB3 B.Boone Looking Right	15.00	4.50
B-CJ1 Chipper Jones Batting	25.00	7.50
B-CJ2 C.Jones Looking Up	25.00	7.50
B-CJ3 Chipper Jones Running	25.00	7.50
B-IR1 I.Rodriguez Looking Up	25.00	7.50
B-IR2 I.Rodriguez Holding Bat	25.00	7.50
B-IR3 Ivan Rodriguez Fielding	25.00	7.50
B-IR4 I.Rodriguez Red Helmet	25.00	7.50
B-JG1 Jason Giambi Fielding	25.00	7.50
B-JG2 Jason Giambi Running	25.00	7.50
B-JG3 J.Giambi Studio Portrait	25.00	7.50
B-KG1 Ken Griffey Jr. Batting	50.00	15.00
B-KG2 Ken Griffey Jr. Walking	50.00	15.00
B-KG3 K.Griffey Jr. Looking Up	50.00	15.00
B-RC1 R.Clemens Look Right	60.00	18.00
B-RC2 Roger Clemens Arm in Motion	60.00	18.00
B-RC3 R.Clemens Ball in Glove	60.00	18.00
B-SS1 S.Sosa Looking Right	40.00	12.00
B-SS2 Sammy Sosa Btg Action	40.00	12.00
B-SS3 S.Sosa Btg Close Up	40.00	12.00
B-SS4 Sammy Sosa w/Cap	40.00	12.00

2002 Upper Deck Honor Roll Game Jersey

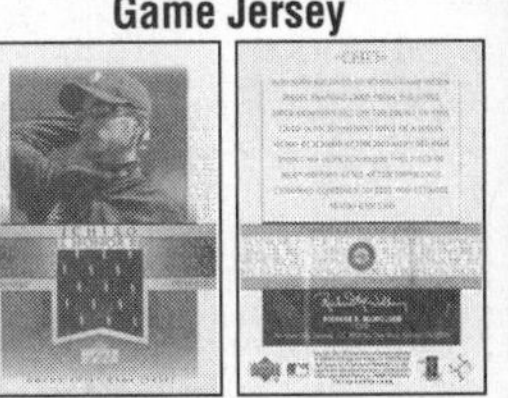

Inserted into packs at stated odds of one in 90, these 30 cards feature jersey swatched worn by the featured players. A few players were printed in smaller quantities and we have notated that information in our checklist.

	Nm-Mt	Ex-Mt
J-I1 Ichiro Suzuki Throw SP	60.00	18.00
J-I2 Ichiro Suzuki Cap SP	60.00	18.00
J-I3 Ichiro Suzuki Helmet SP	60.00	18.00
J-AR1 Alex Rodriguez Helmet	15.00	4.50
J-AR2 Alex Rodriguez Glasses	15.00	4.50
J-AR3 Alex Rodriguez Cap	15.00	4.50
J-AR4 Alex Rodriguez No Hat	15.00	4.50
J-BB1 Bret Boone Face Left SP/69		
J-BB2 Bret Boone White Jsy SP/69		
J-BB3 Bret Boone Gray Jsy SP/69		
J-CJ1 Chipper Jones Helmet	15.00	4.50
J-CJ2 Chipper Jones Face Right	15.00	4.50
J-CJ3 Chipper Jones Earflap	15.00	4.50
J-IR1 Ivan Rodriguez Hat	15.00	4.50
J-IR2 Ivan Rodriguez Helmet	15.00	4.50
J-IR3 Ivan Rodriguez Glove	15.00	4.50
J-IR4 Ivan Rodriguez Number	15.00	4.50
J-JG1 Jason Giambi Bat	15.00	4.50
J-JG2 Jason Giambi Helmet	15.00	4.50
J-JG3 Jason Giambi Cap	15.00	4.50
J-KG1 Ken Griffey Jr. No Hat	20.00	6.00
J-KG2 Ken Griffey Jr. Helmet	20.00	6.00
J-KG3 Ken Griffey Jr. Cap	20.00	6.00
J-RC1 Roger Clemens White	25.00	7.50
J-RC2 R.Clemens Face Right	25.00	7.50
J-RC3 Roger Clemens Gray	25.00	7.50
J-SS1 Sammy Sosa Glove SP	30.00	9.00
J-SS2 Sammy Sosa Cap SP	30.00	9.00
J-SS3 Sammy Sosa No Hat SP	30.00	9.00
J-SS4 Sammy Sosa Helmet SP	30.00	9.00

2002 Upper Deck Honor Roll Star Swatches Game Jersey

This 30-card insert set offers standard-size cards. The fronts feature jersey swatches cut into the shape of stars. Cards were seeded into packs at a rate of 1:90. A few cards were issued in smaller quantities and we have notated that information in our checklist.

Nm-Mt Ex-Mt
SP PRINT RUNS PROVIDED BY UPPER DECK
SP'S ARE NOT SERIAL-NUMBERED...
SS-AR1 Alex Rodriguez Batting. 15.00 4.50
SS-AR2 Alex Rodriguez Fielding 15.00 4.50
SS-AR3 Alex Rodriguez Throwing 15.00 4.50
SS-AR4 Alex Rodriguez Fist...... 15.00 4.50
SS-BB1 Bret Boone Batting SP/45.....
SS-BB2 Bret Boone Running SP/45.....
SS-BB3 Bret Boone Throwing SP/45...
SS-CJ1 C.Jones Batting Left..... 15.00 4.50
SS-CJ2 C.Jones Batting Right... 15.00 4.50
SS-CJ3 Chipper Jones Fielding . 15.00 4.50
SS-IR1 Ivan Rodriguez Throwing 15.00 4.50
SS-IR2 Ivan Rodriguez Running 15.00 4.50
SS-IR3 Ivan Rodriguez Cap....... 15.00 4.50
SS-IR4 Ivan Rodriguez Batting.. 15.00 4.50
SS-I1 I.Suzuki White Jsy SP 60.00 18.00
SS-I2 Ichiro Suzuki Helmet SP.. 60.00 18.00
SS-I3 Ichiro Suzuki Gray Jsy SP 60.00 18.00
SS-JG1 Jason Giambi Cap 15.00 4.50
SS-JG2 Jason Giambi Bat......... 15.00 4.50
SS-JG3 Jason Giambi Helmet ... 15.00 4.50
SS-KG1 Ken Griffey Jr. Bat SP .. 30.00 9.00
SS-KG2 Ken Griffey Jr............... 30.00 9.00
Red Helmet SP
SS-KG3 Ken Griffey Jr............... 30.00 9.00
Black Helmet SP
SS-RC1 Roger Clemens Windup SP/29
SS-RC2 Roger Clemens Follow Through SP/29
SS-RC3 Roger Clemens Release SP/29
SS-SS1 Sammy Sosa White Jsy 25.00 7.50
SS-SS2 Sammy Sosa Batting.... 25.00 7.50
SS-SS3 Sammy Sosa Fielding... 25.00 7.50
SS-SS4 Sammy Sosa Blue Jsy.. 25.00 7.50

2002 Upper Deck Honor Roll Stitch of Nine Game Jersey

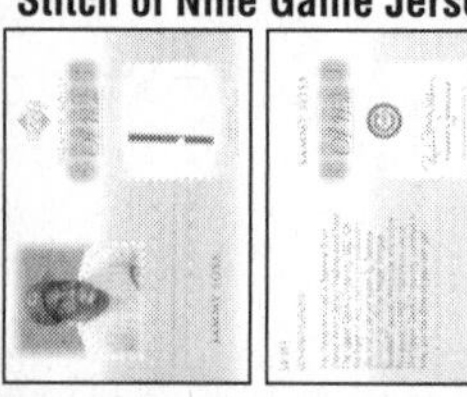

This 30-card insert set features standard-size cards with unique jersey die-cut fronts. Cards were seeded into packs at a rate of 1:90. A few playes were produced in smaller quantities and we have provided that information next to the player's name in our checklist.

Nm-Mt Ex-Mt
S9-I1 Ichiro Hat SP/85 .... 60.00 18.00
S9-I2 I.Suzuki Glasses SP/85.... 60.00 18.00
S9-I3 I.Suzuki Helmet SP/85..... 60.00 18.00
S9-AR1 Alex Rodriguez............ 15.00 4.50
Left Profile
S9-AR2 Alex Rodriguez Hat........ 15.00 4.50
S9-AR3 Alex Rodriguez No Hat . 15.00 4.50
S9-AR4 A.Rodriguez Right Profile 15.00 4.50
S9-BB1 Bret Boone Left SP/45.........
S9-BB2 Bret Boone Straight SP/45 .....
S9-BB3 Bret Boone SP/45..................
S9-CJ1 Chipper Jones Cap........ 15.00 4.50
S9-CJ2 Chipper Jones Helmet... 15.00 4.50
S9-CJ3 C.Jones Cap Right 15.00 4.50
S9-IR1 Ivan Rodriguez Helmet.. 15.00 4.50
S9-IR2 Ivan Rodriguez Hat........ 15.00 4.50
S9-IR3 Ivan Rodriguez No Hat .. 15.00 4.50
S9-IR4 Ivan Rodriguez............. 15.00 4.50
Helmet Left
S9-JG1 J.Giambi Helmet SP...... 15.00 4.50
S9-JG2 Jason Giambi Hat SP.... 15.00 4.50
S9-JG3 J.Giambi Hat Left SP ... 15.00 4.50
S9-KG1 Ken Griffey Jr. White.... 20.00 6.00
S9-KG2 Ken Griffey Jr. Red....... 20.00 6.00
S9-KG3 Ken Griffey Jr. Helmet.. 20.00 6.00
S9-RC1 Roger Clemens 25.00 7.50
Follow Through
S9-RC2 R.Clemens Throwing.... 25.00 7.50
S9-RC3 Roger Clemens 25.00 7.50
Chin on Shoulder
S9-SS1 Sammy Sosa Bat......... 25.00 7.50
S9-SS2 Sammy Sosa Helmet.... 25.00 7.50
S9-SS3 S.Sosa Facing Left...... 25.00 7.50
S9-SS4 S.Sosa Facing Right..... 25.00 7.50

2002 Upper Deck Honor Roll Time Capsule Game Jersey

This 30-card insert set is standard-size and features authentic game-used jersey swatches worn by the nine members of Upper Deck's Honor Roll. The card fronts highlight memorable moments from the career of each superstar through color photos. Cards were randomly seeded into packs at a rate of 1:90. A few players were produced in smaller quantities and we have notated that information in our checklist.

Nm-Mt Ex-Mt
TC-AR1 Alex Rodriguez 9-29-96 15.00 4.50
TC-AR2 Alex Rodriguez 9-27-98 15.00 4.50
TC-AR3 Alex Rodriguez............ 15.00 4.50
12-11-00
TC-AR4 Alex Rodriguez 10-4-01 15.00 4.50
TC-BB1 Bret Boone 9-28-97 SP/69.....
TC-BB2 Bret Boone 9-27-98 SP/69.....
TC-BB3 Bret Boone 10-7-01 SP/69.....
TC-CJ1 Chipper Jones 10-3-99. 15.00 4.50
TC-CJ2 Chipper Jones 11-1-00. 15.00 4.50
TC-CJ3 Chipper Jones 10-7-01. 15.00 4.50
TC-IR1 I.Rodriguez 10-4-92 SP 15.00 4.50
TC-IR2 I.Rodriguez 10-3-99 SP 15.00 4.50
TC-IR3 I.Rodriguez 10-1-00 SP 15.00 4.50
TC-IR4 I.Rodriguez 4-24-01 SP 15.00 4.50
TC-I1 Ichiro Suzuki 4-2-01........ 50.00 15.00
TC-I2 Ichiro Suzuki 7-10-01...... 50.00 15.00
TC-I3 Ichiro Suzuki 11-12-01.... 50.00 15.00
TC-JG1 Jason Giambi 10-27-98 SP/52
TC-JG2 Jason Giambi 10-1-00 SP/52 .
TC-JG3 Jason Giambi 10-7-01SP/52 ..
TC-KG1 Ken Griffey Jr. 9-14-90 SP/5..
TC-KG2 Ken Griffey Jr. 9-28-97 SP/5..
TC-KG3 Ken Griffey Jr. 4-10-00 SP/5..
TC-RC1 Roger Clemens 4-29-86 25.00 7.50
TC-RC2 Roger Clemens 9-27-98 25.00 7.50
TC-RC3 Roger Clemens 9-19-01 25.00 7.50
TC-SS1 Sammy Sosa 10-3-93 .. 25.00 7.50
TC-SS2 Sammy Sosa 9-27-98 .. 25.00 7.50
TC-SS3 Sammy Sosa 10-1-00 .. 25.00 7.50
TC-SS4 Sammy Sosa 10-2-01 .. 25.00 7.50

2003 Upper Deck Honor Roll

This 161 card set was released in August, 2003. These cards were issued in five card packs with an $3 SRP which came 24 packs to a box and 20 boxes to a case. Cards numbered 1 through 130 featured veterans with each player having 2 versions. The even cards 2 through 60 were issued at a stated rate of one in six. Cards numbered 131 through 161 featured rookies. Card number 131 featured a game-used jersey swatch of Hideki Matsui and that card was issued to a stated print run of 1000 serial numbered sets. Cards numbered 132-161 were issued to a stated print run of 2500 serial numbered sets.

MINT NRMT
COMP.SET w/o SP's (100)........ 25.00 11.00
COMMON CARD (1-130).............. .30 .14
COMMON EVEN (2-60) .... 2.00 .90
COMMON CARD (132-161)........... 4.00 1.80
1 Derek Jeter.............................. 2.00 .90
2 Derek Jeter SP 8.00 3.60
3 Alex Rodriguez .... 1.25 .55
4 Alex Rodriguez SP.................... 5.00 2.20
5 Roger Clemens......................... 1.50 .70
6 Roger Clemens SP 6.00 2.70
7 Mike Piazza .... 1.25 .55
8 Mike Piazza SP 5.00 2.20
9 Jeff Bagwell .... .50 .23
10 Jeff Bagwell SP .... 2.00 .90
11 Vladimir Guerrero.................... .75 .35
12 Vladimir Guerrero SP 3.00 1.35
13 Ken Griffey Jr. .... 1.25 .55
14 Ken Griffey Jr. SP 5.00 2.20
15 Greg Maddux.......................... 1.25 .55
16 Greg Maddux SP 5.00 2.20
17 Chipper Jones .... .75 .35
18 Chipper Jones SP................... 3.00 1.35
19 Randy Johnson .... .75 .35
20 Randy Johnson SP................. 3.00 1.35
21 Miguel Tejada......................... .30 .14
22 Miguel Tejada SP .... 2.00 .90
23 Nomar Garciaparra................ 1.25 .55
24 Nomar Garciaparra SP 5.00 2.20
25 Ichiro Suzuki .... 1.25 .55
26 Ichiro Suzuki SP.................... 5.00 2.20
27 Sammy Sosa.......................... 1.25 .55
28 Sammy Sosa SP 5.00 2.20
29 Albert Pujols.......................... 1.50 .70
30 Albert Pujols SP 6.00 2.70
31 Alfonso Soriano..................... .50 .23
32 Alfonso Soriano SP .... 2.00 .90
33 Barry Bonds .... 2.00 .90
34 Barry Bonds SP...................... 8.00 3.60
35 Jeff Kent................................ .30 .14
36 Jeff Kent SP .... 2.00 .90
37 Jim Thome .... .75 .35
38 Jim Thome SP........................ 3.00 1.35
39 Pedro Martinez....................... .75 .35
40 Pedro Martinez SP 3.00 1.35
41 Todd Helton........................... .50 .23
42 Todd Helton SP .... 2.00 .90
43 Troy Glaus............................. .50 .23
44 Troy Glaus SP .... 2.00 .90
45 Mark Prior............................. 1.50 .70
46 Mark Prior SP........................ 6.00 2.70
47 Tom Glavine .... .50 .23
48 Tom Glavine SP..................... 2.00 .90
49 Pat Burrell .... .30 .14
50 Pat Burrell SP........................ 2.00 .90
51 Barry Zito .... .50 .23
52 Barry Zito SP .... 2.00 .90
53 Bernie Williams .... .50 .23
54 Bernie Williams SP................ 2.00 .90
55 Curt Schilling........................ .50 .23
56 Curt Schilling SP .... 2.00 .90
57 Darin Erstad .... .30 .14
58 Darin Erstad SP.................... 2.00 .90
59 Carlos Delgado...................... .30 .14
60 Carlos Delgado SP .... 2.00 .90
61 Gary Sheffield....................... .30 .14
62 Gary Sheffield....................... .30 .14
63 Frank Thomas .... .75 .35
64 Frank Thomas .... .75 .35
65 Lance Berkman .... .30 .14
66 Lance Berkman .... .30 .14
67 Shawn Green......................... .30 .14
68 Shawn Green......................... .30 .14
69 Hideo Nomo .... .75 .35
70 Hideo Nomo .... .75 .35
71 Torii Hunter........................... .30 .14
72 Torii Hunter........................... .30 .14
73 Roberto Alomar...................... .75 .35
74 Roberto Alomar...................... .75 .35
75 Andruw Jones......................... .30 .14
76 Andruw Jones......................... .30 .14
77 Scott Rolen .... .50 .23
78 Scott Rolen .... .50 .23
79 Eric Chavez............................ .30 .14
80 Eric Chavez............................ .30 .14
81 Rafael Palmeiro .... .50 .23
82 Rafael Palmeiro .... .50 .23
83 Bobby Abreu .... .30 .14
84 Bobby Abreu .... .30 .14
85 Craig Biggio........................... .50 .23
86 Craig Biggio........................... .50 .23
87 Rafael Furcal .... .30 .14
88 Rafael Furcal .... .30 .14
89 Jose Vidro.............................. .30 .14
90 Jose Vidro.............................. .30 .14
91 Luis Gonzalez .... .30 .14
92 Luis Gonzalez .... .30 .14
93 Roy Oswalt............................. .30 .14
94 Roy Oswalt............................. .30 .14
95 Cliff Floyd.............................. .30 .14
96 Cliff Floyd.............................. .30 .14
97 Larry Walker........................... .50 .23
98 Larry Walker........................... .50 .23
99 Jim Edmonds .... .30 .14
100 Jim Edmonds .... .30 .14
101 Adam Dunn .... .30 .14
102 Adam Dunn .... .30 .14
103 J.D. Drew .... .30 .14
104 J.D. Drew .... .30 .14
105 Josh Beckett......................... .50 .23
106 Josh Beckett......................... .50 .23
107 Brian Giles........................... .30 .14
108 Brian Giles........................... .30 .14
109 Magglio Ordonez.................. .30 .14
110 Magglio Ordonez.................. .30 .14
111 Edgardo Alfonzo................... .30 .14
112 Edgardo Alfonzo................... .30 .14
113 Bartolo Colon .... .30 .14
114 Bartolo Colon .... .30 .14
115 Roy Halladay .... .30 .14
116 Roy Halladay .... .30 .14
117 Joe Thurston......................... .30 .14
118 Joe Thurston......................... .30 .14
119 Brandon Phillips................... .30 .14
120 Brandon Phillips................... .30 .14
121 Kazuhisa Ishii....................... .30 .14
122 Kazuhisa Ishii....................... .30 .14
123 Mike Mussina........................ .75 .35
124 Mike Mussina........................ .75 .35
125 Tim Hudson .... .30 .14
126 Tim Hudson .... .30 .14
127 Mariano Rivera .... .50 .23
128 Mariano Rivera .... .50 .23
129 Travis Hafner........................ .30 .14
130 Travis Hafner........................ .30 .14
131 Hideki Matsui DL Jsy 30.00 13.50
132 Jose Contreras FC RC 8.00 3.60
133 Jason Anderson FC 4.00 1.80
134 Willie Eyre FC RC................ 4.00 1.80
135 Shane Bazzell FC RC........... 4.00 1.80
136 Guillermo Quiroz FC RC....... 6.00 2.70
137 Francisco Cruceta FC RC..... 4.00 1.80
138 Jhonny Peralta FC RC.......... 4.00 1.80
139 Aaron Looper FC RC 4.00 1.80
140 Bobby Madritsch FC RC 4.00 1.80
141 Michael Hessman FC RC...... 4.00 1.80
142 Todd Wellemeyer FC RC....... 5.00 2.20
143 Matt Bruback FC RC 4.00 1.80
144 Chris Capuano FC RC 4.00 1.80
145 Oscar Villarreal FC RC 4.00 1.80
146 Prentice Redman FC RC....... 4.00 1.80
147 Jeff Duncan FC RC 5.00 2.20
148 Phil Seibel FC RC................ 4.00 1.80
149 Arnaldo Munoz FC RC......... 4.00 1.80
150 David Sanders FC RC 4.00 1.80
151 Rick Roberts FC RC............. 4.00 1.80
152 Terrmel Sledge FC RC.......... 5.00 2.20
153 Franklin Perez FC RC........... 4.00 1.80
154 Jeremy Wedel FC RC............ 4.00 1.80
155 Ian Ferguson FC RC.............. 4.00 1.80
156 Josh Hall FC RC.................... 5.00 2.20
157 Rocco Baldelli FC 10.00 4.50
158 Al. Machado FC RC............... 4.00 1.80
159 Jorge Cordova FC RC 4.00 1.80
160 Wilfredo Ledezma FC RC...... 4.00 1.80
161 Luis Ayala FC RC 4.00 1.80

2003 Upper Deck Honor Roll Gold

MINT NRMT
RANDOM INSERTS IN PACKS ....
STATED PRINT RUN 25 SERIAL #'d SETS
NO PRICING DUE TO SCARCITY........
CARD 131 DOES NOT EXIST..............

2003 Upper Deck Honor Roll Silver

MINT NRMT
*SILVER 1-130: 5X TO 12X BASIC .....
*SILVER 2-60 EVEN: 1.25X TO 3X BASIC
*SILVER 132-161: .5X TO 1.2X BASIC
RANDOM INSERTS IN PACKS ....
STATED PRINT RUN 150 SERIAL #'d SETS
CARD 131 DOES NOT EXIST...............

2003 Upper Deck Honor Roll Dean's List Jerseys

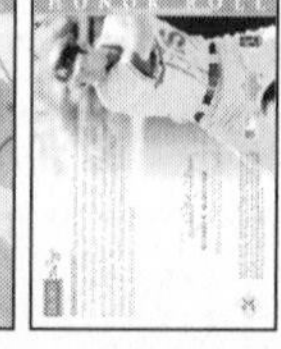

Issued at a stated rate of one in 24, almost each player had two different jersey cards issued. These cards could be differentiated by the jersey swatch being in the player's initials.

MINT NRMT
STATED ODDS 1:24 ....
AP Albert Pujols A................ 20.00 9.00
AP1 Albert Pujols P.............. 20.00 9.00
AR Alex Rodriguez A 15.00 6.75
AR1 Alex Rodriguez R........... 15.00 6.75
CJ Chipper Jones C.............. 10.00 4.50
CJ1 Chipper Jones J 10.00 4.50
HM Hideki Matsui H Pants 40.00 18.00
HM1 Hideki Matsui M Pants..... 40.00 18.00
HN Hideo Nomo H.................. 15.00 6.75
HN1 Hideo Nomo N................ 15.00 6.75
IS Ichiro Suzuki I 30.00 13.50
IS1 Ichiro Suzuki S............... 30.00 13.50
JG Jason Giambi J 10.00 4.50
JG1 Jason Giambi G.............. 10.00 4.50
KG Ken Griffey Jr. K 15.00 6.75
KG1 Ken Griffey Jr. G 15.00 6.75
MA Mark Prior M.................... 20.00 9.00
MA1 Mark Prior P 20.00 9.00
MP Mike Piazza M.................. 15.00 6.75
MP1 Mike Piazza P................. 15.00 6.75
NG Shawn Green S................. 8.00 3.60
NG1 Shawn Green G 8.00 3.60
RC Roger Clemens R.............. 15.00 6.75
RC1 Roger Clemens C............ 15.00 6.75
SS Sammy Sosa S 15.00 6.75
TG Troy Glaus T 10.00 4.50
TG1 Troy Glaus G................... 10.00 4.50
VG Vladimir Guerrero V.......... 10.00 4.50
VG1 Vladimir Guerrero G........ 10.00 4.50

2003 Upper Deck Honor Roll Grade A Batting Gloves

MINT NRMT
STATED ODDS 1:960 ....
PRINT RUNS B/WN 25-70 COPIES PER
PRINT RUNS PROVIDED BY UPPER DECK
CARDS ARE NOT SERIAL-NUMBERED
NO PRICING DUE TO SCARCITY.........
AR Alex Rodriguez/67
AR1 Alex Rodriguez/25
CD Carlos Delgado/65
FT Frank Thomas/70
IR Ivan Rodriguez/70
IR1 Ivan Rodriguez/25
JG Juan Gonzalez/65
KG Ken Griffey Jr./65
KG1 Ken Griffey Jr./25
MR Manny Ramirez/69
MT Miguel Tejada/70
MT1 Miguel Tejada/25
RA Roberto Alomar/65
RF Rafael Furcal/45
RM Raul Mondesi/65
RP Rafael Palmeiro/67
RP1 Rafael Palmeiro/25
SS Sammy Sosa/65
SS1 Sammy Sosa/25
TG Troy Glaus/60
TG1 Troy Glaus/25

2003 Upper Deck Honor Roll Leather of Distinction

MINT NRMT
STATED ODDS 1:960 ....
PRINT RUNS B/WN 9-70 COPIES PER
PRINT RUNS PROVIDED BY UPPER DECK
CARDS ARE NOT SERIAL-NUMBERED
NO PRICING DUE TO SCARCITY.........
AR Alex Rodriguez/70
AR1 Alex Rodriguez/25
CJ Chipper Jones/70
FT Frank Thomas/70
GS Gary Sheffield/70
IR Ivan Rodriguez/69
IS Ichiro Suzuki/9
JG Jason Giambi/65
KG Ken Griffey Jr./70
KG1 Ken Griffey Jr./25
MP Mike Piazza/50
MP1 Mike Piazza/25
MR Manny Ramirez/70
OV Omar Vizquel/65
PM Pedro Martinez/70
PM1 Pedro Martinez/25
RP Rafael Palmeiro/70
SS Sammy Sosa/70
SS1 Sammy Sosa/25
TS Tim Salmon/70

2000 Upper Deck Legends

The 2000 Upper Deck Legends product was released in late August, 2000 and featured a 135-card base set that was broken into tiers as follows: (90) Base Veterans (1-90), (15) Y2K Subset cards (91-105) (1:9), and (30) 20th Century Legends Subset cards (106-135) (1:5). Each pack contained five cards and carried a suggested retail price of $4.99. Also, a selection of A Piece of History 3000 Club Paul Molitor and Carl Yastrzemski memorabilia cards were randomly seeded into packs. 350 bat cards for each player were produced. Also for Carl Yatsrzemski only, 350 jersey cards, 100 hand-numbered bat-jersey combination cards and eight autographed, hand-numbered, combination bat-jersey cards were produced. Pricing for these memorabilia cards can be referenced under 2000 Upper Deck A Piece of History 3000 Club.

Nm-Mt Ex-Mt
COMPLETE SET (135)............. 80.00 24.00
COMP.SET w/o SP'S (90) 20.00 6.00
COMMON CARD (1-90)................. .30 .09
COMMON CARD (91-105)........... 2.00 .60
COMMON (106-135).................... 2.00 .60
1 Darin Erstad .... .30 .09
2 Troy Glaus................................ .50 .15
3 Mo Vaughn................................ .30 .09
4 Craig Biggio.............................. .50 .15
5 Jeff Bagwell .... .50 .15
6 Reggie Jackson......................... .50 .15
7 Tim Hudson............................... .50 .15
8 Jason Giambi .... .75 .23
9 Hank Aaron .... 1.50 .45
10 Greg Maddux....................... 1.25 .35
11 Chipper Jones .... .75 .23
12 Andres Galarraga.................... .30 .09
13 Robin Yount .... 1.25 .35
14 Jeromy Burnitz........................ .30 .09
15 Paul Molitor............................ .50 .15
16 David Wells .... .30 .09
17 Carlos Delgado....................... .30 .09
18 Ernie Banks .... .75 .23
19 Sammy Sosa........................ 1.25 .35
20 Kerry Wood .... .75 .23
21 Stan Musial .... 1.25 .35
22 Bob Gibson .... .50 .15
23 Mark McGwire...................... 2.00 .60
24 Fernando Tatis........................ .30 .09
25 Randy Johnson .... .75 .23
26 Matt Williams .... .30 .09
27 Jackie Robinson.................... 1.00 .30
28 Sandy Koufax .... 2.00 .60
29 Shawn Green.......................... .30 .09
30 Kevin Brown .... .50 .15
31 Gary Sheffield......................... .30 .09
32 Greg Vaughn .... .30 .09
33 Jose Canseco......................... .75 .23
34 Gary Carter............................. .50 .15
35 Vladimir Guerrero................... .75 .23
36 Willie Mays.......................... 1.50 .45
37 Barry Bonds .... 2.00 .60
38 Jeff Kent.................................. .30 .09
39 Bob Feller .... .50 .15
40 Roberto Alomar .... .75 .23
41 Jim Thome .... .75 .23
42 Manny Ramirez .... .30 .09
43 Alex Rodriguez .... 1.25 .35
44 Preston Wilson .... .30 .09
45 Tom Seaver .... .50 .15
46 Robin Ventura .... .30 .09
47 Mike Piazza .... 1.25 .35
48 Mike Hampton......................... .30 .09
49 Brooks Robinson.................... .75 .23
50 Frank Robinson .... .50 .15
51 Cal Ripken .... 2.50 .75
52 Albert Belle............................. .30 .09
53 Eddie Murray .... .75 .23
54 Tony Gwynn......................... 1.00 .30
55 Roberto Clemente .... 1.50 .45
56 Willie Stargell .... .50 .15
57 Brian Giles.............................. .30 .09
58 Jason Kendall......................... .30 .09
59 Mike Schmidt....................... 1.50 .45
60 Bob Abreu .... .30 .09
61 Scott Rolen .... .50 .15
62 Curt Schilling......................... .50 .15
63 Johnny Bench .... .75 .23
64 Sean Casey............................. .30 .09
65 Barry Larkin............................ .75 .23
66 Ken Griffey Jr. .... 1.25 .35
67 George Brett....................... 2.00 .60
68 Carlos Beltran .... .30 .09
69 Nolan Ryan.......................... 2.50 .75
70 Ivan Rodriguez .... .75 .23
71 Rafael Palmeiro .... .50 .15
72 Larry Walker........................... .50 .15
73 Todd Helton............................ .50 .15
74 Jeff Cirillo .... .30 .09
75 Carl Everett .... .30 .09
76 Nomar Garciaparra............... 1.25 .35
77 Pedro Martinez....................... .75 .23
78 Harmon Killebrew................... .75 .23
79 Corey Koskie .... .30 .09
80 Ty Cobb .... 1.25 .35
81 Dean Palmer........................... .30 .09
82 Juan Gonzalez .... .75 .23
83 Carlton Fisk............................ .50 .15
84 Frank Thomas .... .75 .23
85 Magglio Ordonez .... .30 .09
86 Lou Gehrig .... 1.50 .45
87 Babe Ruth .... 2.50 .75
88 Derek Jeter.......................... 2.00 .60
89 Roger Clemens.................... 1.50 .45
90 Bernie Williams .... .50 .15
91 Rick Ankiel Y2K.................. 2.00 .60
92 Kip Wells Y2K .... 2.00 .60
93 Pat Burrell Y2K.................... 2.00 .60
94 Mark Quinn Y2K................... 2.00 .60
95 Ruben Mateo Y2K .... 2.00 .60
96 Adam Kennedy Y2K............. 2.00 .60
97 Brad Penny Y2K................... 2.00 .60
98 K.Sasaki Y2K RC 4.00 1.20
99 Peter Bergeron Y2K.............. 2.00 .60
100 Rafael Furcal Y2K.............. 2.00 .60
101 Eric Munson Y2K .... 2.00 .60

102 Nick Johnson Y2K 2.00 .60
103 Rob Bell Y2K 2.00 .60
104 Vernon Wells Y2K 2.00 .60
105 Ben Petrick Y2K 2.00 .60
106 Babe Ruth 20C 8.00 2.40
107 Mark McGwire 20C 5.00 1.50
108 Nolan Ryan 20C 6.00 1.80
109 Hank Aaron 20C 4.00 1.20
110 Barry Bonds 20C 5.00 1.50
111 N.Garciaparra 20C 3.00 .90
112 Roger Clemens 20C 4.00 1.20
113 Johnny Bench 20C 2.00 .60
114 Alex Rodriguez 20C 3.00 .90
115 Cal Ripken 20C 6.00 1.80
116 Willie Mays 20C 4.00 1.20
117 Mike Piazza 20C 3.00 .90
118 Reggie Jackson 20C 2.00 .60
119 Tony Gwynn 20C 2.50 .75
120 Cy Young 20C 2.00 .60
121 George Brett 20C 4.00 1.20
122 Greg Maddux 20C 3.00 .90
123 Yogi Berra 20C 2.00 .60
124 Sammy Sosa 20C 3.00 .90
125 Randy Johnson 20C 2.00 .60
126 Bob Gibson 20C 2.00 .60
127 Lou Gehrig 20C 5.00 1.50
128 Ken Griffey Jr. 20C 3.00 .90
129 Derek Jeter 20C 5.00 1.50
130 Mike Schmidt 20C 4.00 1.20
131 Pedro Martinez 20C 2.00 .60
132 Jackie Robinson 20C 2.50 .75
133 Jose Canseco 20C 2.00 .60
134 Ty Cobb 20C 3.00 .90
135 Stan Musial 20C 3.00 .90

2000 Upper Deck Legends Commemorative Collection

Randomly inserted into packs, this 135-card insert is a complete parallel of the Upper Deck Legends base set. Each card in this set is individually serial numbered to 100.

Nm-Mt Ex-Mt
*ACTIVE STARS 1-90: 8X TO 20X BASIC
*POST-WAR STARS 1-90: 10X TO 25X BASIC
*PRE-WAR STARS 1-90: 6X TO 15X BASIC
*Y2K: 2X TO 5X BASIC Y2K
*ACTIVE 20C: 3X TO 8X BASIC 20C
*POST-WAR 20C: 5X TO 12X BASIC 20C
*PRE-WAR 20C: 2.5X TO 6X BASIC 20C

2000 Upper Deck Legends Defining Moments

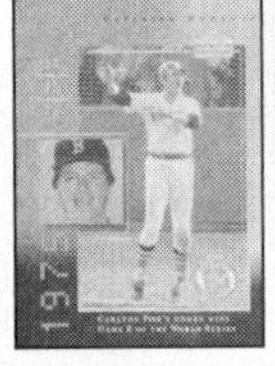

Randomly inserted into packs at one in 12, this 10-card insert focuses on some of Major League baseball's most defining moments Card backs carry a "DM" prefix.

Nm-Mt Ex-Mt
COMPLETE SET (10) 50.00 15.00
DM1 Reggie Jackson 1.50 .45
DM2 Hank Aaron 5.00 1.50
DM3 Babe Ruth 8.00 2.40
DM4 Cal Ripken 8.00 2.40
DM5 Carlton Fisk 1.50 .45
DM6 Ken Griffey Jr. 4.00 1.20
DM7 Nolan Ryan 8.00 2.40
DM8 Roger Clemens 5.00 1.50
DM9 Willie Mays 5.00 1.50
DM10 Mark McGwire 6.00 1.80

2000 Upper Deck Legends Eternal Glory

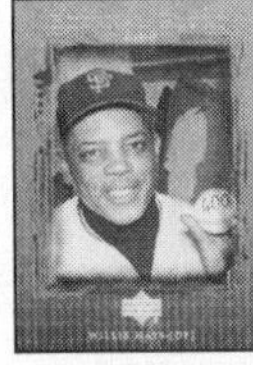

Randomly inserted into packs at one in 24, this six-card insert features players whose greatness will live on in the minds of many. Please note that card number 3 does not exist. Card backs carry an "EG" prefix.

Nm-Mt Ex-Mt
COMPLETE SET (6) 40.00 12.00
EG1 Nolan Ryan 10.00 3.00
EG2 Ken Griffey Jr. 5.00 1.50
EG3 Does Not Exist
EG4 Sammy Sosa 5.00 1.50
EG5 Derek Jeter 8.00 2.40
EG6 Willie Mays 6.00 1.80
EG7 Roger Clemens 6.00 1.80

2000 Upper Deck Legends Legendary Game Jerseys

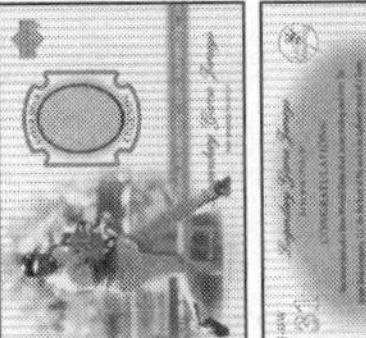

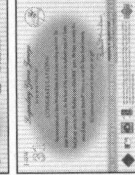

Randomly inserted into packs at one in 48, this 50-card insert set features game-used jersey cards of past and present Major League stars. Cards are numbered using the player's initials with a "J" prefix.

Nm-Mt Ex-Mt
J-AR Alex Rodriguez 25.00 7.50
J-BAB Barry Bonds 40.00 12.00
J-BG Bob Gibson Pants 15.00 4.50
J-BM Bill Mazeroski 10.00 3.00
J-BOB Bobby Bonds 10.00 3.00
J-BR Brooks Robinson 15.00 4.50
J-CJ Chipper Jones 15.00 4.50
J-CR Cal Ripken 40.00 12.00
J-DC Dave Concepcion 10.00 3.00
J-DD Don Drysdale 15.00 4.50
J-DJ Derek Jeter 40.00 12.00
J-DM Dale Murphy 15.00 4.50
J-DW Dave Winfield 10.00 3.00
J-EM Eddie Mathews 15.00 4.50
J-EW Earl Weaver 10.00 3.00
J-FR Frank Robinson 15.00 4.50
J-FT Frank Thomas 15.00 4.50
J-GB George Brett 25.00 7.50
J-GM Greg Maddux 25.00 7.50
J-GP Gaylord Perry 10.00 3.00
J-HA Hank Aaron 60.00 18.00
J-JB Jeff Bagwell 15.00 4.50
J-JB Johnny Bench 15.00 4.50
J-JC Jose Canseco 15.00 4.50
J-JP Jim Palmer 10.00 3.00
J-JT Joe Torre 15.00 4.50
J-KG Ken Griffey Jr. 25.00 7.50
J-LB Lou Brock 15.00 4.50
J-LG Lou Gehrig Pants 300.00 90.00
J-MM Mickey Mantle 150.00 45.00
J-MR Manny Ramirez 10.00 3.00
J-MS Mike Schmidt 25.00 7.50
J-MW Matt Williams 10.00 3.00
J-MW Maury Wills 10.00 3.00
J-NR Nolan Ryan 40.00 12.00
J-OS Ozzie Smith 15.00 4.50
J-RAJ Randy Johnson 15.00 4.50
J-RC Roger Clemens 25.00 7.50
J-RF Rollie Fingers 10.00 3.00
J-RJ Reggie Jackson 15.00 4.50
J-RM Roger Maris Pants 80.00 24.00
J-SK Sandy Koufax SP/95 300.00 90.00
J-SM Stan Musial SP/28
J-TG Tony Gwynn 15.00 4.50
J-TM Thurman Munson 50.00 15.00
J-TS Tom Seaver 15.00 4.50
J-WB Wade Boggs 15.00 4.50
J-WM Willie Mays SP/29
J-WMC Willie McCovey 10.00 3.00
J-WS Willie Stargell 15.00 4.50
S-JSK Sandy Koufax AU/32

2000 Upper Deck Legends Legendary Signatures

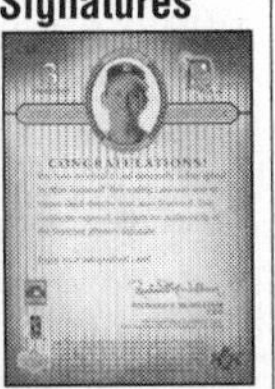

Randomly inserted into packs at one in 24, this 39-card insert features autographed cards of past and present superstars. Card backs are numbered using the player's initials and an "S" prefix. Though print run numbers were not initially released, Upper Deck did confirm to Beckett Publications that Hank Aaron, Derek Jeter and Manny Ramirez signed less cards than other players in the set. Specific quantities for each of these players is detailed in the checklist below. Finally, Dave Concepcion, Frank Thomas, Ken Griffey Jr., Manny Ramirez, Mo Vaughn, Ozzie Smith and Willie Stargell cards were inserted in packs as stickered exchange cards. The deadline for this exchange was April 22nd, 2001. In addition to the exchange cards, real autographed cards did make their into packs for the following players: Willie Stargell, Ozzie Smith and Dave Concepcion.

Nm-Mt Ex-Mt
S-AD Andre Dawson 15.00 4.50
S-AR Alex Rodriguez 120.00 36.00
S-AT Alan Trammell 25.00 7.50
S-BB Bobby Bonds 25.00 7.50
S-CJ Chipper Jones 40.00 12.00
S-CR Cal Ripken 150.00 45.00
S-DC D.Concepcion EXCH* 15.00 4.50
S-DJ Derek Jeter SP/61 600.00 180.00
S-DM Dale Murphy 40.00 12.00
S-FL Fred Lynn 15.00 4.50
S-FT Frank Thomas 50.00 15.00
S-GB George Brett 80.00 24.00
S-GC Gary Carter 25.00 7.50
S-HA Hank Aaron SP/94 300.00 90.00
S-HK Harmon Killebrew 40.00 12.00
S-IR Ivan Rodriguez 40.00 12.00
S-JB Johnny Bench 40.00 12.00
S-JC Jose Canseco 40.00 12.00
S-JP Jim Palmer 15.00 4.50
S-KG Ken Griffey Jr. 120.00 36.00
S-LB Lou Brock 25.00 7.50
S-MP Mike Piazza 250.00 75.00
S-MR Manny Ramirez SP/141 60.00 18.00
S-MS Mike Schmidt 60.00 18.00
S-MV Mo Vaughn 15.00 4.50
S-MW Matt Williams 15.00 4.50
S-NR Nolan Ryan 120.00 36.00
S-OS Ozzie Smith 50.00 15.00
S-PN Phil Niekro 15.00 4.50
S-RC Roger Clemens 100.00 30.00
S-RF Rollie Fingers 15.00 4.50
S-RJ Reggie Jackson 40.00 12.00
S-SC Sean Casey 15.00 4.50
S-SM Stan Musial 80.00 24.00
S-TG Tony Gwynn 50.00 15.00
S-TS Tom Seaver 25.00 7.50
S-VG Vladimir Guerrero 40.00 12.00
S-WS Willie Stargell 50.00 15.00
EXCH*
SRAJ Randy Johnson 80.00 24.00

2000 Upper Deck Legends Legendary Signatures Gold

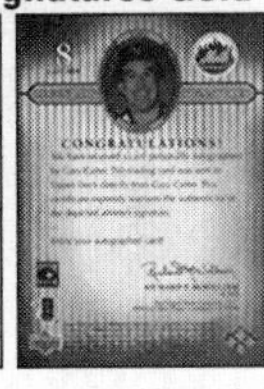

Randomly inserted into packs, this set is a parallel of the Legendary Signatures insert. Each card features gold colored fronts (instead of silver for the basic cards) and is individually serial numbered to 50 in front in blue ink sharpie. Each card is numbered on the back using the player's initials and an "S" prefix. Also, Dave Concepcion, Frank Thomas, Ken Griffey Jr., Manny Ramirez, Mo Vaughn, Ozzie Smith and Willie Stargell cards were inserted in packs as stickered exchange cards. The deadline for this exchange was April 22nd, 2001. In addition to the exchange cards, real autographed cards did make their into packs for the following players: Willie Stargell, Ozzie Smith and Dave Concepcion. Please note, that Derek Jeter did not sign any Gold cards. The Yankees star shortstop signed only 61 cards for this entire product - all of which were basic Legendary Signatures.

Nm-Mt Ex-Mt
S-AD Andre Dawson 40.00 12.00
S-AR Alex Rodriguez 200.00 60.00
S-AT Alan Trammell 50.00 15.00
S-BB Bobby Bonds 50.00 15.00
S-CJ Chipper Jones 80.00 24.00
S-CR Cal Ripken 250.00 75.00
S-DC D.Concepcion EXCH* 40.00 12.00
S-DM Dale Murphy 80.00 24.00
S-FL Fred Lynn 40.00 12.00
S-FT Frank Thomas 50.00 15.00
S-GB George Brett 200.00 60.00
S-GC Gary Carter 50.00 15.00
S-HA Hank Aaron 250.00 75.00
S-HK Harmon Killebrew 80.00 24.00
S-IR Ivan Rodriguez 80.00 24.00
S-JB Johnny Bench 80.00 24.00
S-JC Jose Canseco 80.00 24.00
S-JP Jim Palmer 40.00 12.00
S-KG Ken Griffey Jr. 200.00 60.00
S-LB Lou Brock 50.00 15.00
S-MP Mike Piazza 300.00 90.00
S-MR M.Ramirez EXCH 40.00 12.00
S-MS Mike Schmidt 150.00 45.00
S-MV Mo Vaughn 40.00 12.00
S-MW Matt Williams 40.00 12.00
S-NR Nolan Ryan 200.00 60.00
S-OS Ozzie Smith 100.00 30.00
S-PN Phil Niekro 40.00 12.00
S-RC Roger Clemens 200.00 60.00
S-RF Rollie Fingers 40.00 12.00
S-RJ Reggie Jackson 80.00 24.00
S-SC Sean Casey 40.00 12.00
S-SM Stan Musial 100.00 30.00
S-TG Tony Gwynn 100.00 30.00
S-TS Tom Seaver 50.00 15.00
S-VG Vladimir Guerrero 80.00 24.00
S-WS W.Stargell EXCH* 80.00 24.00
SRAJ Randy Johnson 150.00 45.00

2000 Upper Deck Legends Millennium Team

Randomly inserted into packs at one in four, this nine-card insert features the most famous players of the 20th Century. Please note that card number 6 does not exist. Card backs carry a "UD" prefix.

Nm-Mt Ex-Mt
COMPLETE SET (9) 10.00 3.00
UD1 Mark McGwire 2.00 .60
UD2 Jackie Robinson 1.00 .30
UD3 Mike Schmidt 1.50 .45
UD4 Cal Ripken 2.50 .75
UD5 Babe Ruth 2.50 .75
UD6 Does Not Exist
UD7 Willie Mays 1.50 .45
UD8 Johnny Bench .75 .23
UD9 Nolan Ryan 2.50 .75
UD10 Ken Griffey Jr. 1.25 .35

2000 Upper Deck Legends Ones for the Ages

Randomly inserted into packs at one in 24, this seven-card insert features Major League Baseball's most legendary players. Card backs carry an "O" prefix.

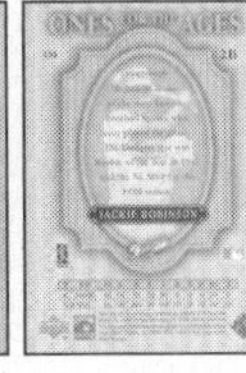

Nm-Mt Ex-Mt
COMPLETE SET (7) 25.00 7.50
O1 Ty Cobb 5.00 1.50
O2 Cal Ripken 10.00 3.00
O3 Babe Ruth 10.00 3.00
O4 Jackie Robinson 4.00 1.20
O5 Mark McGwire 8.00 2.40
O6 Alex Rodriguez 5.00 1.50
O7 Mike Piazza 5.00 1.50

2000 Upper Deck Legends Reflections in Time

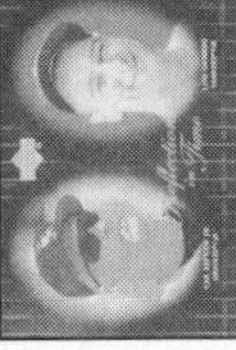

Randomly inserted into packs at one in 12, this 10-card insert features dual-player cards of players that have had very similar major league careers. Card backs carry a "R" prefix.

Nm-Mt Ex-Mt
COMPLETE SET (10) 40.00 12.00
R1 Ken Griffey Jr. 4.00 1.20
Hank Aaron
R2 Sammy Sosa 4.00 1.20
Roberto Clemente
R3 Roger Clemens 5.00 1.50
Nolan Ryan
R4 Ivan Rodriguez 2.50 .75
Johnny Bench
R5 Alex Rodriguez 4.00 1.20
Ernie Banks
R6 Tony Gwynn 4.00 1.20
Stan Musial
R7 Barry Bonds 5.00 1.50
Willie Mays
R8 Cal Ripken 5.00 1.50
Lou Gehrig
R9 Chipper Jones 5.00 1.50
Mike Schmidt
R10 Mark McGwire 8.00 2.40
Babe Ruth

2001 Upper Deck Legends

This 90 card set was released in July, 2001. The cards were issued in five card packs with an SRP of $4.99 per pack and these packs were issued 24 to a box. The set has a mixture of past and present superstars.

Nm-Mt Ex-Mt
COMPLETE SET (90) 20.00 6.00
1 Darin Erstad .30 .09
2 Troy Glaus .50 .15
3 Nolan Ryan 2.00 .60
4 Reggie Jackson .50 .15
5 Catfish Hunter .50 .15
6 Jason Giambi .75 .23
7 Tim Hudson .30 .09
8 Miguel Tejada .30 .09
9 Carlos Delgado .30 .09
10 Shannon Stewart .30 .09
11 Greg Vaughn .30 .09
12 Larry Doby .30 .09
13 Jim Thome .75 .23
14 Juan Gonzalez .75 .23
15 Roberto Alomar .75 .23
16 Edgar Martinez .50 .15
17 John Olerud .30 .09
18 Eddie Murray .75 .23
19 Cal Ripken 2.50 .75
20 Alex Rodriguez 1.25 .35
21 Ivan Rodriguez .75 .23
22 Rafael Palmeiro .50 .15
23 Jimmie Foxx .75 .23
24 Cy Young .75 .23
25 Manny Ramirez .30 .09
26 Pedro Martinez .75 .23
27 Nomar Garciaparra 1.25 .35
28 George Brett 2.00 .60
29 Mike Sweeney .30 .09
30 Jermaine Dye .30 .09
31 Ty Cobb 1.25 .35
32 Dean Palmer .30 .09
33 Harmon Killebrew .75 .23
34 Matt Lawton .30 .09
35 Luis Aparicio .30 .09
36 Frank Thomas .75 .23
37 Magglio Ordonez .30 .09
38 David Wells .30 .09
39 Mickey Mantle 3.00 .90
40 Joe DiMaggio 1.50 .45
41 Roger Maris 1.25 .35
42 Babe Ruth 2.50 .75
43 Derek Jeter 2.00 .60
44 Roger Clemens 1.50 .45
45 Bernie Williams .50 .15
46 Jeff Bagwell .50 .15
47 Richard Hidalgo .30 .09
48 Warren Spahn .50 .15
49 Greg Maddux 1.25 .35
50 Chipper Jones .75 .23
51 Andruw Jones .30 .09
52 Robin Yount 1.25 .35
53 Jeromy Burnitz .30 .09
54 Jeffrey Hammonds .30 .09
55 Ozzie Smith 1.25 .35
56 Stan Musial 1.25 .35
57 Mark McGwire 2.00 .60
58 Jim Edmonds .30 .09
59 Sammy Sosa 1.25 .35
60 Ernie Banks .75 .23
61 Kerry Wood .75 .23
62 Randy Johnson .75 .23
63 Luis Gonzalez .30 .09
64 Don Drysdale .75 .23
65 Jackie Robinson 1.00 .30
66 Gary Sheffield .30 .09
67 Kevin Brown .30 .09
68 Vladimir Guerrero .75 .23
69 Willie Mays 1.50 .45
70 Mel Ott .75 .23
71 Jeff Kent .30 .09
72 Barry Bonds 2.00 .60
73 Preston Wilson .30 .09
74 Ryan Dempster .30 .09
75 Tom Seaver .50 .15
76 Mike Piazza 1.25 .35
77 Robin Ventura .30 .09
78 Dave Winfield .30 .09
79 Tony Gwynn 1.00 .30
80 Bob Abreu .30 .09
81 Scott Rolen .50 .15
82 Mike Schmidt 1.50 .45
83 Roberto Clemente 2.00 .60
84 Brian Giles .30 .09
85 Ken Griffey Jr. 1.25 .35
86 Frank Robinson .50 .15
87 Johnny Bench .75 .23
88 Todd Helton .50 .15
89 Larry Walker .50 .15
90 Mike Hampton .30 .09

2001 Upper Deck Legends Fiorentino Collection

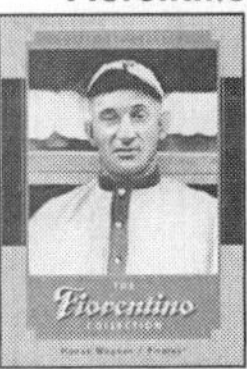
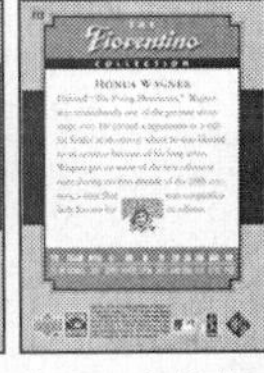

Inserted in packs at a rate of one in 12, these 14 cards feature the original artwork of James Fiorentino. The cards have a "F" prefix.

Nm-Mt Ex-Mt
COMPLETE SET (14) 40.00 12.00
F1 Babe Ruth 8.00 2.40
F2 Satchel Paige 2.50 .75
F3 Joe DiMaggio 5.00 1.50
F4 Willie Mays 5.00 1.50
F5 Ty Cobb 4.00 1.20
F6 Nolan Ryan 8.00 2.40
F7 Lou Gehrig 5.00 1.50
F8 Jackie Robinson 3.00 .90
F9 Hank Aaron 5.00 1.50
F10 Roberto Clemente 5.00 1.50
F11 Stan Musial 3.00 .90
F12 Johnny Bench 2.50 .75
F13 Honus Wagner 2.50 .75
F14 Reggie Jackson 2.50 .75

2001 Upper Deck Legends Legendary Cuts

Randomly inserted in packs, these six cards feature cut signatures from the five original members of the Hall of Fame. Due to scarcity, no pricing is provided.

Nm-Mt Ex-Mt
C-1 Ty Cobb
Babe Ruth
Christy Mathewson
Walter Johnson
Honus Wagner/1
C-BR Babe Ruth/3
C-CM Christy Mathewson/1
C-HW Honus Wagner/2
C-TC Ty Cobb/1
C-WJ Walter Johnson/3

2001 Upper Deck Legends Legendary Game Jersey

Issued at a rate of one in 24, these 33 cards feature authentic game jersey pieces from past and current players. A few players are perceived to be produced in larger quantities, we have notated those players with asterisks in our checklist. In addition, a few players were

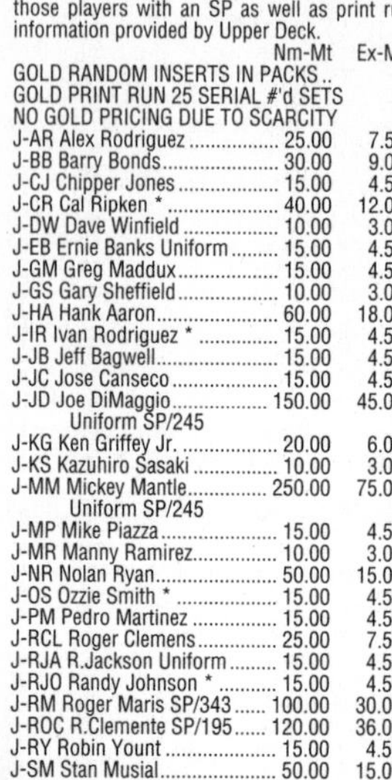

printed in shorter supply. We have notated those players with an SP as well as print run information provided by Upper Deck.

Nm-Mt Ex-Mt
GOLD RANDOM INSERTS IN PACKS..
GOLD PRINT RUN 25 SERIAL #'d SETS
NO GOLD PRICING DUE TO SCARCITY
J-AR Alex Rodriguez 25.00 7.50
J-BB Barry Bonds 30.00 9.00
J-CJ Chipper Jones 15.00 4.50
J-CR Cal Ripken * 40.00 12.00
J-DW Dave Winfield 10.00 3.00
J-EB Ernie Banks Uniform 15.00 4.50
J-GM Greg Maddux 15.00 4.50
J-GS Gary Sheffield 10.00 3.00
J-HA Hank Aaron 60.00 18.00
J-IR Ivan Rodriguez * 15.00 4.50
J-JB Jeff Bagwell 15.00 4.50
J-JC Jose Canseco 15.00 4.50
J-JD Joe DiMaggio 150.00 45.00
Uniform SP/245
J-KG Ken Griffey Jr. 20.00 6.00
J-KS Kazuhiro Sasaki 10.00 3.00
J-MM Mickey Mantle 250.00 75.00
Uniform SP/245
J-MP Mike Piazza 15.00 4.50
J-MR Manny Ramirez 10.00 3.00
J-NR Nolan Ryan 50.00 15.00
J-OS Ozzie Smith * 15.00 4.50
J-PM Pedro Martinez 15.00 4.50
J-RCL Roger Clemens 25.00 7.50
J-RJA R.Jackson Uniform 15.00 4.50
J-RJO Randy Johnson * 15.00 4.50
J-RM Roger Maris SP/343 100.00 30.00
J-ROC R.Clemente SP/195 120.00 36.00
J-RY Robin Yount 15.00 4.50
J-SM Stan Musial 50.00 15.00
Uniform SP/490
J-SS Sammy Sosa 20.00 6.00
J-TG T.Gwynn Uniform * 15.00 4.50
J-TS Tom Seaver 15.00 4.50
J-WM Willie Mays 50.00 15.00
J-YB Yogi Berra Uniform 15.00 4.50

2001 Upper Deck Legends Legendary Game Jersey Autographs

Issued at a rate of one in 288, these cards feature not only a game jersey piece but an authentic autograph of the player pictured. Ken Griffey Jr. did not return his cards in time for packout; those cards could be redeemed until July 9, 2004. In addition, a few cards were produced in lesser quantites. Those cards are notated in our checklist with an SP and print run information provided by Upper Deck.

Nm-Mt Ex-Mt
SJ-AR Alex Rodriguez 150.00 45.00
SJ-EB Ernie Banks 80.00 24.00
SJ-KG K.Griffey Jr. EXCH 150.00 45.00
SJ-NR Nolan Ryan 150.00 45.00
SJ-OS Ozzie Smith 80.00 24.00
SJ-RC R.Clemens SP/211 150.00 45.00
SJ-RJ R.Jackson SP/224 100.00 30.00
SJ-SM S.Musial SP/266 120.00 36.00
SJ-SS Sammy Sosa SP/91 300.00 90.00
SJ-TS Tom Seaver 60.00 18.00

2001 Upper Deck Legends Legendary Game Jersey Autographs Gold

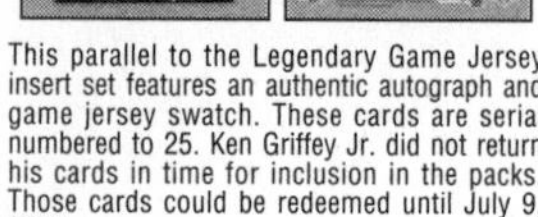

This parallel to the Legendary Game Jersey insert set features an authentic autograph and game jersey swatch. These cards are serial numbered to 25. Ken Griffey Jr. did not return his cards in time for inclusion in the packs. Those cards could be redeemed until July 9, 2004.

Nm-Mt Ex-Mt
GSJ-AR Alex Rodriguez
GSJ-EB Ernie Banks
GSJ-KG K.Griffey Jr. EXCH
GSJ-NR Nolan Ryan
GSJ-OS Ozzie Smith
GSJ-RC Roger Clemens
GSJ-RJ Reggie Jackson
GSJ-SM Stan Musial
GSJ-SS Sammy Sosa
GSJ-TS Tom Seaver

2001 Upper Deck Legends Legendary Lumber

Inserted in packs at a rate of one in 24, these 32 cards feature authentic game bat pieces from past and current players. A few cards are available in larger supply and we have notated those with asterisks in our checklist. In addition, certain cards were short printed. We have notated those with an SP as well as print run information provided by Upper Deck.

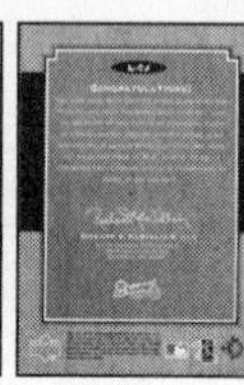

Nm-Mt Ex-Mt
GOLD RANDOM INSERTS IN PACKS..
GOLD PRINT RUN 25 SERIAL #'d SETS
NO GOLD PRICING DUE TO SCARCITY
L-AJ Andruw Jones 10.00 3.00
L-AP Albert Pujols 60.00 18.00
L-AR Alex Rodriguez 20.00 6.00
L-BB Barry Bonds * 25.00 7.50
L-CJ Chipper Jones 15.00 4.50
L-CR Cal Ripken 50.00 15.00
L-EB Ernie Banks SP/80 60.00 18.00
L-EM Eddie Murray 15.00 4.50
L-FR Frank Robinson 15.00 4.50
L-GS Gary Sheffield * 10.00 3.00
L-HA Hank Aaron 40.00 12.00
L-IR Ivan Rodriguez * 15.00 4.50
L-JB Johnny Bench 15.00 4.50
L-JC Jose Canseco 15.00 4.50
L-JD Joe DiMaggio 100.00 30.00
L-JF Jimmie Foxx SP/351 60.00 18.00
L-KG Ken Griffey Jr. 20.00 6.00
L-LA Luis Aparicio 10.00 3.00
L-MM Mickey Mantle 200.00 60.00
L-MO Mel Ott SP/355 50.00 15.00
L-MP Mike Piazza 15.00 4.50
L-MR Manny Ramirez 10.00 3.00
L-OS Ozzie Smith 15.00 4.50
L-RCA R.Campanella SP/335 60.00 18.00
L-RCL Roger Clemens 25.00 7.50
L-RJ Reggie Jackson 15.00 4.50
L-RJ Randy Johnson 15.00 4.50
L-RM Roger Maris 50.00 15.00
L-ROC R.Clemente SP/170 120.00 36.00
L-SS Sammy Sosa * 20.00 6.00
L-TG Tony Gwynn 15.00 4.50
L-WM Willie Mays * 40.00 12.00

2001 Upper Deck Legends Legendary Lumber Autographs

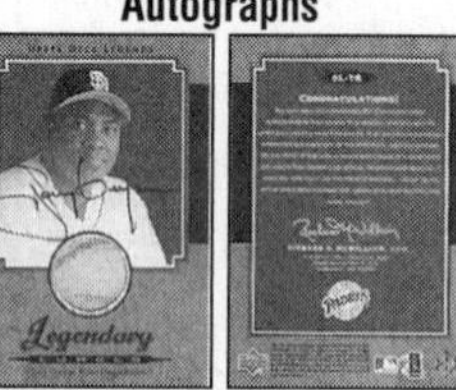

This partial parallel to the Legendary Lumber insert set features authentic autographs from the player on the card. Ken Griffey Jr. did not return his cards in time for inclusion in packs. These cards were redeemable until July 9, 2004. In addition, a few cards were signed in lesser quantites. We have notated those cards with an SP and print run information provided by Upper Deck.

Nm-Mt Ex-Mt
SL-AR Alex Rodriguez 150.00 45.00
SL-EB Ernie Banks 80.00 24.00
SL-EM Eddie Murray 60.00 18.00
SL-KG K.Griffey Jr. EXCH 150.00 45.00
SL-LA Luis Aparicio 50.00 15.00
SL-RC R.Clemens SP/227 120.00 36.00
SL-RJ R.Jackson SP/211 80.00 24.00
SL-SS S.Sosa SP/66 250.00 75.00
SL-TG Tony Gwynn 80.00 24.00

2001 Upper Deck Legends Legendary Lumber Autographs Gold

This partial parallel to the Legendary Lumber insert set features authentic autographs from the player on the card. Ken Griffey Jr. did not return his cards in time for inclusion in packs. These cards are serial numbered to 25. Due to scarcity, no pricing is provided.

Nm-Mt Ex-Mt
GSL-AR Alex Rodriguez
GSL-EB Ernie Banks
GSL-EM Eddie Murray
GSL-KG Ken Griffey Jr. EXCH
GSL-LA Luis Aparicio
GSL-RC Roger Clemens
GSL-RJ Reggie Jackson
GSL-SS Sammy Sosa
GSL-TG Tony Gwynn

2001 Upper Deck Legends Reflections in Time

Issued at a rate of one in 18, these 10 cards feature an past and present player from the same team.

Nm-Mt Ex-Mt
COMPLETE SET (10) 30.00 9.00
R1 Bernie Williams 10.00 3.00

Mickey Mantle
R2 Pedro Martinez 2.50 .75
Cy Young
R3 Barry Bonds 8.00 2.40
Willie Mays
R4 Scott Rolen 5.00 1.50
Mike Schmidt
R5 Mark McGwire 6.00 1.80
Stan Musial
R6 Ken Griffey Jr. 4.00 1.20
Frank Robinson
R7 Sammy Sosa 4.00 1.20
Andre Dawson
R8 Kevin Brown 2.50 .75
Don Drysdale
R9 Jason Giambi 2.50 .75
Reggie Jackson
R10 Tim Hudson 1.50 .45
Jim "Catfish" Hunter

2001 Upper Deck Legends of NY

This product was released in late December, 2001. The 200-card base set features baseball greats like Babe Ruth and Mickey Mantle. Each pack contained five cards and carried a suggested retail price of $2.99

Nm-Mt Ex-Mt
COMPLETE SET (200) 50.00 15.00
1 Billy Herman .50 .15
2 Carl Erskine .50 .15
3 Burleigh Grimes .50 .15
4 Don Newcombe .50 .15
5 Gil Hodges 1.25 .35
6 Pee Wee Reese 1.25 .35
7 Jackie Robinson 1.50 .45
8 Duke Snider .75 .23
9 Jim Gilliam .50 .15
10 Roy Campanella 1.25 .35
11 Carl Furillo .50 .15
12 Casey Stengel .75 .23
13 Casey Stengel DB .50 .15
14 Billy Herman DB .40 .12
15 Jackie Robinson DB .75 .23
16 Jackie Robinson DB .75 .23
17 Gil Hodges DB 1.25 .35
18 Carl Furillo DB .40 .12
19 Roy Campanella DB .75 .23
20 Don Newcombe DB .40 .12
21 Duke Snider DB .50 .15
22 Casey Stengel BNS .50 .15
23 Burleigh Grimes BNS .40 .12
24 Pee Wee Reese BNS .75 .23
25 Jackie Robinson BNS .75 .23
26 Jackie Robinson BNS .75 .23
27 Carl Erskine BNS .40 .12
28 Roy Campanella BNS .75 .23
29 Duke Snider BNS .75 .23
30 Rube Marquard .50 .15
31 Ross Youngs .50 .15
32 Bobby Thomson .50 .15
33 Christy Mathewson 1.25 .35
34 Carl Hubbell 1.25 .35
35 Hoyt Wilhelm .50 .15
36 Johnny Mize .50 .15
37 John McGraw .75 .23
38 Monte Irvin .50 .15
39 Travis Jackson .50 .15
40 Mel Ott 1.25 .35
41 Dusty Rhodes .40 .12
42 Leo Durocher .50 .15
43 John McGraw BG .50 .15
44 Christy Mathewson BG .75 .23
45 The Polo Grounds BG .40 .12
46 Travis Jackson BG .40 .12
47 Mel Ott BG .75 .23
48 Johnny Mize BG .40 .12
49 Leo Durocher BG .40 .12
50 Bobby Thomson BG .40 .12
51 Monte Irvin BG .40 .12
52 Bobby Thomson BG .40 .12
53 Christy Mathewson BNS .75 .23
54 Christy Mathewson BNS .75 .23
55 Christy Mathewson BNS .75 .23
56 John McGraw BNS .50 .15
57 John McGraw BNS .50 .15
58 John McGraw BNS .50 .15
59 Travis Jackson BNS .40 .12
60 Mel Ott BNS .75 .23
61 Mel Ott BNS .75 .23
62 Carl Hubbell BNS .50 .15
63 Bobby Thomson BNS .40 .12
64 Monte Irvin BNS .40 .12
65 Al Weis .40 .12
66 Donn Clendenon .40 .12
67 Ed Kranepool .50 .15
68 Gary Carter .75 .23
69 Tommie Agee .40 .12
70 Jon Matlack .40 .12
71 Ken Boswell .40 .12
72 Len Dykstra .50 .15
73 Nolan Ryan 3.00 .90
74 Ray Sadecki .40 .12
75 Ron Darling .50 .15
76 Ron Swoboda .50 .15
77 Dwight Gooden .75 .23
78 Tom Seaver .75 .23
79 Wayne Garrett .40 .12
80 Casey Stengel MM .50 .15
81 Tom Seaver MM .50 .15
82 Tommie Agee MM .40 .12
83 Tom Seaver MM .50 .15
84 Yogi Berra MM .75 .23
85 Yogi Berra MM .75 .23
86 Tom Seaver MM .50 .15
87 Dwight Gooden MM .50 .15
88 Gary Carter MM .50 .15
89 Ron Darling MM .40 .12
90 Tommie Agee BNS .40 .12
91 Tom Seaver BNS .50 .15
92 Gary Carter BNS .50 .15
93 Len Dykstra BNS .40 .12
94 Babe Ruth 4.00 1.20
95 Bill Dickey .75 .23
96 Rich Gossage .50 .15
97 Casey Stengel UER .75 .23
Card has a Dodger logo on the back
98 Catfish Hunter .75 .23
99 Charlie Keller .40 .12
100 Chris Chambliss .50 .15
101 Don Larsen .50 .15
102 Dave Winfield .50 .15
103 Don Mattingly 3.00 .90
104 Elston Howard .75 .23
105 Frankie Crosetti .50 .15
106 Hank Bauer .50 .15
107 Joe DiMaggio 2.50 .75
108 Graig Nettles .50 .15
109 Lefty Gomez .75 .23
110 Phil Rizzuto 1.25 .35
111 Lou Gehrig 2.50 .75
112 Lou Piniella .50 .15
113 Mickey Mantle 5.00 1.50
114 Red Rolfe .50 .15
115 Reggie Jackson .75 .23
116 Roger Maris 2.00 .60
117 Roy White .40 .12
118 Thurman Munson 1.50 .45
119 Tom Tresh .50 .15
120 Tommy Henrich .50 .15
121 Waite Hoyt .50 .15
122 Willie Randolph .50 .15
123 Whitey Ford .75 .23
124 Yogi Berra 1.25 .35
125 Babe Ruth BT 2.00 .60
126 Babe Ruth BT 2.00 .60
127 Lou Gehrig BT 1.25 .35
128 Babe Ruth BT 2.00 .60
129 Joe DiMaggio BT 1.25 .35
130 Joe DiMaggio BT 1.25 .35
131 Mickey Mantle BT 2.50 .75
132 Roger Maris BT 1.25 .35
133 Mickey Mantle BT 2.50 .75
134 Reggie Jackson BT .50 .15
135 Babe Ruth BNS 2.00 .60
136 Babe Ruth BNS 2.00 .60
137 Babe Ruth BNS 2.00 .60
138 Lefty Gomez BNS .50 .15
139 Lou Gehrig BNS 1.25 .35
140 Lou Gehrig BNS 1.25 .35
141 Joe DiMaggio BNS 1.25 .35
142 Joe DiMaggio BNS 1.25 .35
143 Casey Stengel BNS .50 .15
144 Mickey Mantle BNS 2.50 .75
145 Yogi Berra BNS .75 .23
146 Mickey Mantle BNS 2.50 .75
147 Elston Howard BNS .50 .15
148 Whitey Ford BNS .50 .15
149 Reggie Jackson BNS .50 .15
150 Reggie Jackson BNS .50 .15
151 John McGraw 2.00 .60
Babe Ruth
152 Babe Ruth 2.00 .60
John McGraw
153 Lou Gehrig 1.25 .35
Mel Ott
154 Joe DiMaggio 1.25 .35
Mel Ott
155 Joe DiMaggio 1.25 .35
Billy Herman
156 Joe DiMaggio 1.25 .35
Jackie Robinson
157 Mickey Mantle 2.50 .75
Bobby Thomson
158 Yogi Berra .75 .23
Pee Wee Reese
159 Roy Campanella 2.50 .75
Mickey Mantle
160 Don Larsen .50 .15
Duke Snider
161 Christy Mathewson TT .75 .23
162 Christy Mathewson TT .75 .23
163 Rube Marquard TT .40 .12
164 Christy Mathewson TT .75 .23
165 John McGraw TT .50 .15
166 Burleigh Grimes TT .40 .12
167 Babe Ruth TT 2.00 .60
168 Burleigh Grimes TT .40 .12
169 Babe Ruth TT 2.00 .60
170 John McGraw TT .50 .15
171 Lou Gehrig TT 1.25 .35
172 Babe Ruth TT 2.00 .60
173 Babe Ruth TT 2.00 .60
174 Carl Hubbell TT .50 .15
175 Joe DiMaggio TT 1.25 .35
176 Lou Gehrig TT 1.25 .35
177 Leo Durocher TT .40 .12
178 Mel Ott TT .75 .23
179 Joe DiMaggio TT 1.25 .35
180 Jackie Robinson TT .75 .23
181 Babe Ruth TT 2.00 .60
182 Bobby Thomson TT .40 .12
183 Joe DiMaggio TT 1.25 .35
184 Mickey Mantle TT 2.50 .75
185 Monte Irvin TT .40 .12
186 Roy Campanella TT .75 .23
187 Duke Snider TT .75 .23
188 Dusty Rhodes TT .40 .12
189 Yogi Berra TT .75 .23
190 Mickey Mantle TT 2.50 .75
191 Mickey Mantle TT 2.50 .75
192 Casey Stengel TT .50 .15
193 Tom Seaver TT .50 .15
194 Mickey Mantle TT UER 2.50 .75
Text has Mantle retiring in 1939
195 Tommie Agee TT .40 .12
196 Tom Seaver TT .50 .15
197 Chris Chambliss TT .40 .12
198 Reggie Jackson TT .50 .15
199 Reggie Jackson TT .50 .15
200 Gary Carter TT .50 .15

2001 Upper Deck Legends of NY Combo Autographs

Randomly inserted into packs, this nine-card insert set features dual-autographs from Hall of Famers like Nolan Ryan and Tom Seaver. Each card is individually serial numbered to 25. Due to market scarcity, no pricing is provided.

Nm-Mt Ex-Mt
SCN Chris Chambliss
Graig Nettles
SGJ Ron Guidry
Tommy John
SLB Don Larsen
Yogi Berra
SNP Don Newcombe
Johnny Podres
SRD Willie Randolph
Bucky Dent
SRS Nolan Ryan
Tom Seaver
SRW Mickey Rivers
Roy White
SWJ Dave Winfield
Reggie Jackson
SWM Dave Winfield
Don Mattingly

2001 Upper Deck Legends of NY Cut Signatures

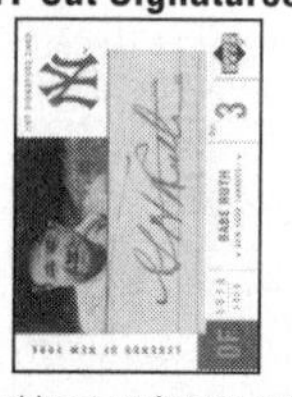

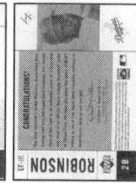

This five-card insert set features authentic cut signatures from deceased greats like Babe Ruth and Jackie Robinson. There were a total of 49 cut cards issued in this set. Specific print runs are listed in our checklist.

Nm-Mt Ex-Mt
LC-BR Babe Ruth/5
LC-GH Gil Hodges/1
LC-JD Joe DiMaggio/38
LC-JR Jackie Robinson/3
LC-MO Mel Ott/2

2001 Upper Deck Legends of NY Game Base

This two card set features game-used base cards of Jackie Robinson and Tom Seaver. Each card is individually serial numbered to 100.

Nm-Mt Ex-Mt
GOLD RANDOM INSERTS IN PACKS..
GOLD PRINT RUN 25 SERIAL #'d SETS
NO GOLD PRICING DUE TO SCARCITY
SILVER RANDOM INSERTS IN PACKS
SILVER PRINT RUN 50 SERIAL #'d SETS
SILVER NO PRICING DUE TO SCARCITY
EF-JR Jackie Robinson
SS-TS Tom Seaver

2001 Upper Deck Legends of NY Game Bat

This 33-card insert set features authentic game-used bat chips. Collectors received either on bat or jersey card per box. A few cards were produced in lesser quantites, those print runs are provided in our checklist.

Nm-Mt Ex-Mt
LDB-BH Billy Herman 10.00 3.00
LDB-DN Don Newcombe SP/67
LDB-JG Jim Gilliam 10.00 3.00
LGB-BT Bobby Thomson 10.00 3.00

Card	Nm-Mt	Ex-Mt
LMB-AW Al Weis	10.00	3.00
LMB-DC Donn Clendenon SP/60		
LMB-EK Ed Kranepool	10.00	3.00
LMB-GC Gary Carter	15.00	4.50
LMB-JM J.C. Martin	10.00	3.00
LMB-KB Ken Boswell	10.00	3.00
LMB-LD Len Dykstra	10.00	3.00
LMB-NR Nolan Ryan	40.00	12.00
LMB-RS Ron Swoboda	10.00	3.00
LMB-TS Tom Seaver	15.00	4.50
LMB-WG Wayne Garrett	10.00	3.00
LYB-BD Bill Dickey	15.00	4.50
LYB-BR Babe Ruth SP/107		
LYB-CC Chris Chambliss SP/130		
LYB-CK Charlie Keller	10.00	3.00
LYB-DM Don Mattingly	40.00	12.00
LYB-DW Dave Winfield UER Playing career has the wrong years	10.00	3.00
LYB-EH Elston Howard	15.00	4.50
LYB-HB Hank Bauer	10.00	3.00
LYB-JD Joe DiMaggio SP/43		
LYB-LP Lou Piniella	10.00	3.00
LYB-MM Mickey Mantle SP/134		
LYB-MR Mickey Rivers	10.00	3.00
LYB-RJ Reggie Jackson	15.00	4.50
LYB-RM Roger Maris SP/60	120.00	36.00
LYB-TH Tommy Henrich	10.00	3.00
LYB-TM Thurman Munson	30.00	9.00
LYB-TT Tom Tresh	10.00	3.00
LYB-YB Yogi Berra	15.00	4.50

2001 Upper Deck Legends of NY Game Bat Autograph

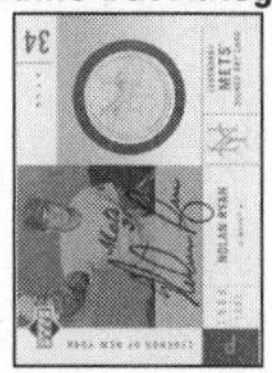

This insert set is a partial parallel to the 2001 Upper Deck Legends of NY Game Bat insert. Each of these cards were signed, and issued into packs at 1:336. A few cards were printed in lesser quantities, those print runs are provided in our checklist.

Card	Nm-Mt	Ex-Mt
SDB-DN Don Newcombe	40.00	12.00
SMB-DC Donn Clendenon	30.00	9.00
SMB-GC Gary Carter	50.00	15.00
SMB-NR N.Ryan SP/129	200.00	60.00
SMB-RS Ron Swoboda		
SMB-TS Tom Seaver SP/89		
SYB-CC Chris Chambliss	40.00	12.00
SYB-DM Don Mattingly	100.00	30.00
SYB-DW Dave Winfield SP/167		
SYB-MR Mickey Rivers	40.00	12.00
SYB-RJ Reggie Jackson SP/123		
SYB-RW Roy White	30.00	9.00
SYB-YB Yogi Berra	80.00	24.00

2001 Upper Deck Legends of NY Game Jersey

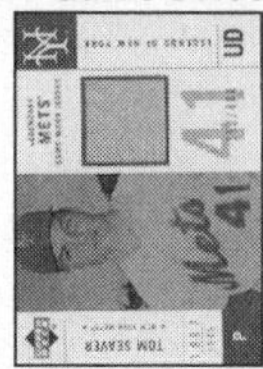

This 36-card insert set features authentic game-used jersey swatches. Collectors received either on bat or jersey card per box. A few cards were printed in small quantities, those print runs are provided in our checklist.

Card	Nm-Mt	Ex-Mt
BT Bob Turley	10.00	3.00
CD Chuck Dressen	10.00	3.00
CE Carl Erskine	10.00	3.00
CH Catfish Hunter	15.00	4.50
CM Christy Mathewson SP/63	500.00	150.00
CS Casey Stengel	15.00	4.50
DM Duke Maas	10.00	3.00
DW Dave Winfield	10.00	3.00
EH Elston Howard	15.00	4.50
FC Frank Crosetti	10.00	3.00
GN Graig Nettles	10.00	3.00
HB Hank Behrman	10.00	3.00
HB Hank Bauer	10.00	3.00
JD Joe DiMaggio SP/63		
JM Jon Matlack	10.00	3.00
JP Joe Pepitone	10.00	3.00
JR J.Robinson Pants SP/126	150.00	45.00
JT Joe Torre	15.00	4.50
LM Lindy McDaniel	10.00	3.00
MM Mickey Mantle SP/63		
PN Phil Niekro	10.00	3.00
RD Ron Darling	10.00	3.00
RM Roger Maris SP/63		
RR Red Rolfe	10.00	3.00
RS Ray Sadecki	10.00	3.00
SJ Spider Jorgensen	10.00	3.00
TH Tommy Henrich	10.00	3.00
TM Thurman Munson	40.00	12.00
TS Tom Seaver	15.00	4.50
WR Willie Randolph	10.00	3.00

2001 Upper Deck Legends of NY Game Jersey Autograph

This 22-card insert set is a partial parallel to the 2001 Upper Deck Legends of NY Game Jersey insert set. Each of these cards were signed, and issued into packs at 1:336. A few cards were printed in lesser quantity and those cards are notated in our checklist as SP's along with

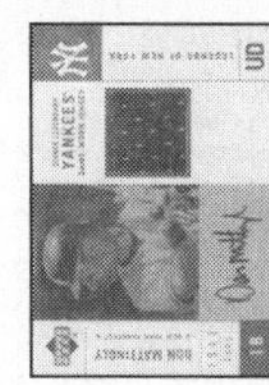

print run information provided by Upper Deck.

Card	Nm-Mt	Ex-Mt
SDJ-CE Carl Erskine	50.00	15.00
SDJ-JG Jim Gilliam SP/49		
SDJ-JP J. Podres SP/193	60.00	18.00
SMJ-CS Craig Swan	50.00	15.00
SMJ-GF G.Foster SP/196	50.00	15.00
SMJ-NR Nolan Ryan SP/47		
SMJ-TS Tom Seaver SP/60		
SYJ-BD Bucky Dent	50.00	15.00
SYJ-DL Don Larsen	60.00	18.00
SYJ-DM Don Mattingly SP/72	150.00	45.00
SYJ-DR Dave Righetti	50.00	15.00
SYJ-GN Graig Nettles	50.00	15.00
SYJ-HL H.Lopez SP/195	50.00	15.00
SYJ-JP Joe Pepitone	50.00	15.00
SYJ-PN P.Niekro SP/195	60.00	18.00
SYJ-RG Ron Guidry	60.00	18.00
SYJ-RG R.Gossage SP/145	50.00	15.00
SYJ-RJ Reggie Jackson SP/47		
SYJ-SL Sparky Lyle	50.00	15.00
SYJ-TJ Tommy John	50.00	15.00
SYJ-WR Willie Randolph	50.00	15.00
SYJ-YB Yogi Berra SP/73		

2001 Upper Deck Legends of NY Game Jersey Gold

This 24-card insert is a partial parallel set to the 2001 Upper Deck Legends of NY Game Jersey set, and features game-used jersey cards on a gold-foil based card. Print runs, of which vary between 125 and 500 numbered copies, are listed for each card in our checklist.

Card	Nm-Mt	Ex-Mt
LDJ-CD C.Dressen/400	12.00	3.60
LDJ-CE Carl Erskine/400	12.00	3.60
LDJ-HB H.Behrman/500	12.00	3.60
LDJ-SJ S.Jorgensen/500	12.00	3.60
LMJ-JM Jon Matlack/400	12.00	3.60
LMJ-JT Joe Torre/250	25.00	7.50
LMJ-RD Ron Darling/400	12.00	3.60
LMJ-RS Ray Sadecki/400	12.00	3.60
LMJ-TS Tom Seaver/400	20.00	6.00
LYJ-BT Bob Turley/400	12.00	3.60
LYJ-CH C.Hunter/500	20.00	6.00
LYJ-DM Duke Maas/400	12.00	3.60
LYJ-DW D.Winfield/250	15.00	4.50
LYJ-EH E.Howard/400	20.00	6.00
LYJ-FC Frank Crosetti/400	12.00	3.60
LYJ-GN Graig Nettles/250	15.00	4.50
LYJ-HB Hank Bauer/400	12.00	3.60
LYJ-JP Joe Pepitone/250	15.00	4.50
LYJ-LM L.McDaniel/400	12.00	3.60
LYJ-PN Phil Niekro/125	20.00	6.00
LYJ-RR Red Rolfe/400	12.00	3.60
LYJ-TH T.Henrich/400	12.00	3.60
LYJ-TM T.Munson/400	50.00	15.00
LYJ-WR W.Randolph/125	20.00	6.00

2001 Upper Deck Legends of NY Stadium Seat

This two card set features stadium seat cards of Jackie Robinson and Mickey Mantle. Each card is individually serial numbered to 100.

Card	Nm-Mt	Ex-Mt
GOLD RANDOM INSERTS IN PACKS..		
GOLD PRINT RUN 25 SERIAL #'d SETS		
GOLD NO PRICING DUE TO SCARCITY		
SILVER RANDOM INSERTS IN PACKS		
SILVER PRINT RUN 50 SERIAL #'d SETS		
SILVER NO PRICING DUE TO SCARCITY		
EFS-JR Jackie Robinson	40.00	12.00
YS-MM Mickey Mantle	120.00	36.00

2001 Upper Deck Legends of NY Tri-Combo Autographs

Randomly inserted into packs, this seven-card insert set features tri-combo autographs from greats like Ryan/Seaver/Swoboda. Each card is individually serial numbered to 25. Each card carries a "S" prefix. Due to market scarcity, no pricing is provided.

Card	Nm-Mt	Ex-Mt
S-CND Chris Chambliss Graig Nettles Bucky Dent		
S-GJG Ron Guidry Tommy John Goose Gossage		
S-LBP Don Larsen Yogi Berra Joe Pepitone		
S-LRG Sparky Lyle Dave Righetti Goose Gossage		
S-NPE Don Newcombe Johnny Podres Carl Erskine		
S-RSS Nolan Ryan Tom Seaver Ron Swoboda		
S-WMN Dave Winfield Don Mattingly Graig Nettles		

2001 Upper Deck Legends of NY United We Stand

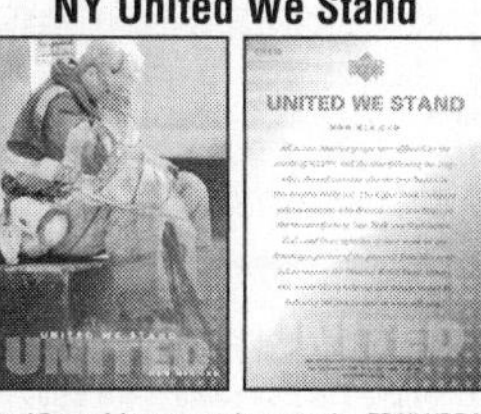

This 15-card insert set honors the FDNY/PDNY for their relief work in the Sept. 11, 2001 terrorist attacks in New York. Card backs carry a "USA" prefix. This insert was issued at a rate of 1:12 packs.

Card	Nm-Mt	Ex-Mt
COMPLETE SET (15)	60.00	18.00
COMMON CARD (1-15)	5.00	1.50

1999 Upper Deck MVP Preview

This skip numbered set was issued to preview what the 1999 Upper Deck MVP set would look like. Printed in the same style as the regular MVP cards, exactly one half of the 220 cards printed in the regular set were available in this set. This set was issued in five card packs available in retail stores for less than a dollar.

Card	Nm-Mt	Ex-Mt
COMPLETE SET (110)	25.00	7.50
3 Jack McDowell	.10	.03
4 Troy Glaus	.50	.15
5 Darin Erstad	.50	.15
6 Tim Salmon	.20	.06
10 Travis Lee	.20	.06
11 Matt Williams	.30	.09
13 Jay Bell	.10	.03
15 Chipper Jones	1.00	.30
16 Andruw Jones	.50	.15
17 Greg Maddux	1.25	.35
18 Tom Glavine	.40	.12
19 Javy Lopez	.20	.06
22 John Smoltz	.20	.06
23 Cal Ripken	2.00	.60
26 Brady Anderson	.20	.06
27 Mike Mussina	.40	.12
31 Nomar Garciaparra	1.00	.30
32 Pedro Martinez	.50	.15
34 Troy O'Leary	.10	.03
37 John Valentin	.10	.03
38 Kerry Wood	.30	.09
39 Sammy Sosa	1.00	.30
40 Mark Grace	.40	.12
41 Henry Rodriguez	.10	.03
42 Rod Beck	.20	.06
44 Kevin Tapani	.10	.03
45 Frank Thomas	.60	.18
47 Magglio Ordonez	.50	.15
49 Ray Durham	.20	.06
50 Jim Parque	.10	.03
53 Pete Harnisch	.10	.03
55 Sean Casey	.20	.06
57 Barry Larkin	.40	.12
58 Pokey Reese	.10	.03
59 Sandy Alomar Jr.	.20	.06
61 Bartolo Colon	.40	.12
62 Kenny Lofton	.30	.09
63 Omar Vizquel	.20	.06
64 Travis Fryman	.20	.06
65 Jim Thome	.30	.09
66 Manny Ramirez	.50	.15
67 Jaret Wright	.10	.03
68 Darryl Kile	.10	.03
69 Kirt Manwaring	.10	.03
70 Vinny Castilla	.10	.03
72 Dante Bichette	.20	.06
73 Larry Walker	.20	.06
77 Matt Anderson	.10	.03
79 Damion Easley	.10	.03
80 Tony Clark	.10	.03
81 Juan Encarnacion	.20	.06
82 Livan Hernandez	.10	.03
83 Alex Gonzalez	.10	.03
85 Derrek Lee	.10	.03
86 Mark Kotsay	.10	.03
87 Todd Dunwoody	.10	.03
88 Cliff Floyd	.20	.06
90 Jeff Bagwell	.50	.15
91 Moises Alou	.20	.06
92 Craig Biggio	.30	.09
93 Billy Wagner	.20	.06
95 Derek Bell	.10	.03
97 Jeff King	.10	.03
98 Carlos Beltran	.30	.09
100 Larry Sutton	.10	.03
101 Johnny Damon	.20	.06
104 Chan Ho Park	.10	.03
105 Raul Mondesi	.20	.06
106 Eric Karros	.20	.06
109 Gary Sheffield	.50	.15
112 Marquis Grissom	.20	.06
114 Jeff Cirillo	.10	.03
115 Geoff Jenkins	.20	.06
116 Jeromy Burnitz	.20	.06
117 Brad Radke	.20	.06
118 Eric Milton	.10	.03
120 Todd Walker	.10	.03
121 David Ortiz	.30	.09
123 Vladimir Guerrero	.75	.23
124 Rondell White	.20	.06
125 Brad Fullmer	.20	.06
127 Dustin Hermanson	.10	.03
130 Mike Piazza	1.25	.35
132 Rey Ordonez	.10	.03
133 John Olerud	.20	.06
135 Hideo Nomo	.40	.12
137 Al Leiter	.20	.06
138 Brian McRae	.10	.03
139 Derek Jeter	2.00	.60
140 Bernie Williams	.40	.12
141 Paul O'Neill	.40	.12
142 Scott Brosius	.10	.03
143 Tino Martinez	.20	.06
145 Orlando Hernandez	.10	.03
148 A.J. Hinch	.10	.03
149 Ben Grieve	.20	.06
151 Miguel Tejada	.50	.15
152 Matt Stairs	.10	.03
154 Jason Giambi	.50	.15
155 Curt Schilling	.50	.15
156 Scott Rolen	.40	.12
158 Doug Glanville	.10	.03
159 Bobby Abreu	.40	.12
160 Rico Brogna	.10	.03
169 Mark McGwire	1.50	.45
176 Tony Gwynn	1.00	.30
183 Barry Bonds	1.00	.30
190 Ken Griffey Jr.	1.25	.35
191 Alex Rodriguez	1.25	.35
204 Juan Gonzalez	.50	.15

1999 Upper Deck MVP

This 220 card set was distributed in 10 cards packs with an SRP of $1.59 per pack. Cards numbered from 218 through 220 are checklist subsets. Approximately 350 Mike Schmidt A Piece of History 500 Home Run Game-Used bat cards were distributed in this product. In addition, 20 hand serial numbered versions of this card personally signed by Schmidt himself were also randomly seeded into packs. Pricing for these bat cards can be referenced under 1999 Upper Deck A Piece of History 500 Club. A Ken Griffey Jr. Sample card was distributed to dealers and hobby media several weeks prior to the product's national release. Unlike most Upper Deck promotional cards, this card does not have the word "SAMPLE" pasted across the back of the card. The card, however, is numbered "S3". It's believed that cards S1 and S2 were Upper Deck MVP football and basketball promo cards.

Card	Nm-Mt	Ex-Mt
COMPLETE SET (220)	25.00	7.50
1 Mo Vaughn	.20	.06
2 Tim Belcher	.20	.06
3 Jack McDowell	.20	.06
4 Troy Glaus	.30	.09
5 Darin Erstad	.20	.06
6 Tim Salmon	.30	.09
7 Jim Edmonds	.20	.06
8 Randy Johnson	.50	.15
9 Steve Finley	.20	.06
10 Travis Lee	.20	.06
11 Matt Williams	.20	.06
12 Todd Stottlemyre	.20	.06
13 Jay Bell	.20	.06
14 David Dellucci	.20	.06
15 Chipper Jones	.50	.15
16 Andruw Jones	.20	.06
17 Greg Maddux	.75	.23
18 Tom Glavine	.30	.09
19 Javy Lopez	.20	.06
20 Brian Jordan	.20	.06
21 George Lombard	.20	.06
22 John Smoltz	.30	.09
23 Cal Ripken	1.50	.45
24 Charles Johnson	.20	.06
25 Albert Belle	.20	.06
26 Brady Anderson	.20	.06
27 Mike Mussina	.50	.15
28 Calvin Pickering	.20	.06
29 Ryan Minor	.20	.06
30 Jerry Hairston Jr.	.20	.06
31 Nomar Garciaparra	.75	.23
32 Pedro Martinez	.50	.15
33 Jason Varitek	.20	.06
34 Troy O'Leary	.20	.06
35 Donnie Sadler	.20	.06
36 Mark Portugal	.20	.06
37 John Valentin	.20	.06
38 Kerry Wood	.50	.15
39 Sammy Sosa	.75	.23
40 Mark Grace	.30	.09
41 Henry Rodriguez	.20	.06
42 Rod Beck	.20	.06
43 Benito Santiago	.20	.06
44 Kevin Tapani	.20	.06
45 Frank Thomas	.50	.15
46 Mike Caruso	.20	.06
47 Magglio Ordonez	.20	.06
48 Paul Konerko	.20	.06
49 Ray Durham	.20	.06
50 Jim Parque	.20	.06
51 Carlos Lee	.20	.06
52 Denny Neagle	.20	.06
53 Pete Harnisch	.20	.06
54 Michael Tucker	.20	.06
55 Sean Casey	.20	.06
56 Eddie Taubensee	.20	.06
57 Barry Larkin	.50	.15
58 Pokey Reese	.20	.06
59 Sandy Alomar Jr.	.20	.06
60 Roberto Alomar	.50	.15
61 Bartolo Colon	.20	.06
62 Kenny Lofton	.20	.06
63 Omar Vizquel	.20	.06
64 Travis Fryman	.20	.06
65 Jim Thome	.50	.15
66 Manny Ramirez	.20	.06
67 Jaret Wright	.20	.06
68 Darryl Kile	.20	.06
69 Kirt Manwaring	.20	.06
70 Vinny Castilla	.20	.06
71 Todd Helton	.30	.09
72 Dante Bichette	.20	.06
73 Larry Walker	.30	.09
74 Derrick Gibson	.20	.06
75 Gabe Kapler	.20	.06
76 Dean Palmer	.20	.06
77 Matt Anderson	.20	.06
78 Bobby Higginson	.20	.06
79 Damion Easley	.20	.06
80 Tony Clark	.20	.06
81 Juan Encarnacion	.20	.06
82 Livan Hernandez	.20	.06
83 Alex Gonzalez	.20	.06
84 Preston Wilson	.20	.06
85 Derrek Lee	.20	.06
86 Mark Kotsay	.20	.06
87 Todd Dunwoody	.20	.06
88 Cliff Floyd	.20	.06
89 Ken Caminiti	.20	.06
90 Jeff Bagwell	.30	.09
91 Moises Alou	.20	.06
92 Craig Biggio	.30	.09
93 Billy Wagner	.20	.06
94 Richard Hidalgo	.20	.06
95 Derek Bell	.20	.06
96 Hipolito Pichardo	.20	.06
97 Jeff King	.20	.06
98 Carlos Beltran	.20	.06
99 Jeremy Giambi	.20	.06
100 Larry Sutton	.20	.06
101 Johnny Damon	.20	.06
102 Dee Brown	.20	.06
103 Kevin Brown	.30	.09
104 Chan Ho Park	.20	.06
105 Raul Mondesi	.20	.06
106 Eric Karros	.20	.06
107 Adrian Beltre	.20	.06
108 Devon White	.20	.06
109 Gary Sheffield	.20	.06
110 Sean Berry	.20	.06
111 Alex Ochoa	.20	.06
112 Marquis Grissom	.20	.06
113 Fernando Vina	.20	.06
114 Jeff Cirillo	.20	.06
115 Geoff Jenkins	.20	.06
116 Jeromy Burnitz	.20	.06
117 Brad Radke	.20	.06
118 Eric Milton	.20	.06
119 A.J. Pierzynski	.20	.06
120 Todd Walker	.20	.06
121 David Ortiz	.20	.06
122 Corey Koskie	.20	.06
123 Vladimir Guerrero	.50	.15
124 Rondell White	.20	.06
125 Brad Fullmer	.20	.06
126 Ugueth Urbina	.20	.06
127 Dustin Hermanson	.20	.06
128 Michael Barrett	.20	.06
129 Fernando Seguignol	.20	.06
130 Mike Piazza	.75	.23
131 Rickey Henderson	.50	.15
132 Rey Ordonez	.20	.06
133 John Olerud	.20	.06
134 Robin Ventura	.20	.06
135 Hideo Nomo	.50	.15
136 Mike Kinkade	.20	.06
137 Al Leiter	.20	.06
138 Brian McRae	.20	.06
139 Derek Jeter	1.25	.35
140 Bernie Williams	.30	.09
141 Paul O'Neill	.30	.09
142 Scott Brosius	.20	.06
143 Tino Martinez	.30	.09
144 Roger Clemens	1.00	.30
145 Orlando Hernandez	.20	.06
146 Mariano Rivera	.30	.09
147 Ricky Ledee	.20	.06
148 A.J. Hinch	.20	.06
149 Ben Grieve	.20	.06
150 Eric Chavez	.20	.06
151 Miguel Tejada	.20	.06
152 Matt Stairs	.20	.06
153 Ryan Christenson	.20	.06
154 Jason Giambi	.50	.15
155 Curt Schilling	.30	.09
156 Scott Rolen	.30	.09
157 Pat Burrell RC	1.50	.45
158 Doug Glanville	.20	.06
159 Bobby Abreu	.20	.06
160 Rico Brogna	.20	.06
161 Ron Gant	.20	.06
162 Jason Kendall	.20	.06
163 Aramis Ramirez	.20	.06
164 Jose Guillen	.20	.06
165 Emil Brown	.20	.06
166 Pat Meares	.20	.06
167 Kevin Young	.20	.06
168 Brian Giles	.20	.06
169 Mark McGwire	1.25	.35
170 J.D. Drew	.20	.06
171 Edgar Renteria	.20	.06
172 Fernando Tatis	.20	.06
173 Matt Morris	.20	.06
174 Eli Marrero	.20	.06
175 Ray Lankford	.20	.06
176 Tony Gwynn	.60	.18
177 Sterling Hitchcock	.20	.06
178 Ruben Rivera	.20	.06
179 Wally Joyner	.20	.06
180 Trevor Hoffman	.20	.06
181 Jim Leyritz	.20	.06
182 Carlos Hernandez	.20	.06
183 Barry Bonds UER Uniform number 24 on front, 25 on back	1.25	.35
184 Ellis Burks	.20	.06
185 F.P. Santangelo	.20	.06
186 J.T. Snow	.20	.06
187 Ramon E.Martinez RC	.20	.06
188 Jeff Kent	.20	.06
189 Robb Nen	.20	.06

190 Ken Griffey Jr. .75 .23
191 Alex Rodriguez .75 .23
192 Shane Monahan .20 .06
193 Carlos Guillen .20 .06
194 Edgar Martinez .30 .09
195 David Segui .20 .06
196 Jose Mesa .20 .06
197 Jose Canseco .50 .15
198 Rolando Arrojo .20 .06
199 Wade Boggs .30 .09
200 Fred McGriff .30 .09
201 Quinton McCracken .20 .06
202 Bobby Smith .20 .06
203 Bubba Trammell .20 .06
204 Juan Gonzalez .50 .15
205 Ivan Rodriguez .50 .15
206 Rafael Palmeiro .30 .09
207 Royce Clayton .20 .06
208 Rick Helling .20 .06
209 Todd Zeile .20 .06
210 Rusty Greer .20 .06
211 David Wells .20 .06
212 Roy Halladay .20 .06
213 Carlos Delgado .20 .06
214 Darrin Fletcher .20 .06
215 Shawn Green .20 .06
216 Kevin Witt .20 .06
217 Jose Cruz Jr. .20 .06
218 Ken Griffey Jr. CL .50 .15
219 Sammy Sosa CL .50 .15
220 Mark McGwire CL .60 .18
S3 Ken Griffey Jr. Sample 1.00 .30

1999 Upper Deck MVP Gold Script

Randomly inserted into hobby packs, these parallel cards of the regular Upper Deck MVP set are serial numbered to 100 and have a gold foil fascimile signature on the front of the card.

Nm-Mt Ex-Mt
*STARS: 12.5X TO 30X BASIC CARDS
*ROOKIES: 12.5X TO 30X BASIC CARDS

1999 Upper Deck MVP Silver Script

These parallels were seeded at a rate of one in every two packs. Unlike basic MVP cards, each Silver Script parallel features the player's facsimile autograph in silver foil on the front of the card. A Ken Griffey Jr. sample card was distributed to dealers and hobby media several weeks prior to the product's national release. The card is numbered "S3" on back.

Nm-Mt Ex-Mt
COMPLETE SET (220) 150.00 45.00
*STARS: 1.5X TO 4X BASIC CARDS ...
*ROOKIES: 1.5X TO 4X BASIC CARDS
S3 Ken Griffey Jr. Sample 4.00 1.20

1999 Upper Deck MVP Super Script

This parallel set of the Upper Deck MVP set is serial numbered to 25. The fascimile signatures on these cards are printed in a special holo-foil format.

Nm-Mt Ex-Mt
*STARS: 30X TO 80X BASIC CARDS ..

1999 Upper Deck MVP Dynamics

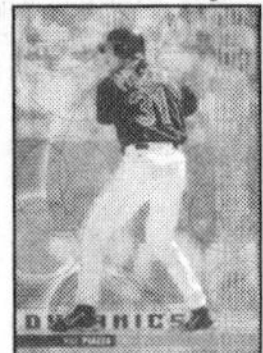
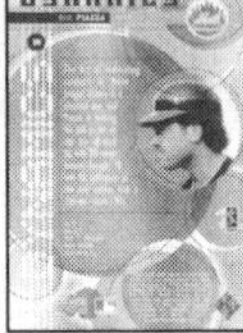

Inserted one every 28 packs, these cards feature the most collectible stars in basebll. The front of the card has a player photo, the word "Dynamics" in black ink on the bottom and lots of fancy graphics.

Nm-Mt Ex-Mt
COMPLETE SET (15) 100.00 30.00
D1 Ken Griffey Jr. 6.00 1.80
D2 Alex Rodriguez 6.00 1.80
D3 Nomar Garciaparra 6.00 1.80
D4 Mike Piazza 6.00 1.80
D5 Mark McGwire 10.00 3.00
D6 Sammy Sosa 6.00 1.80
D7 Chipper Jones 4.00 1.20
D8 Mo Vaughn 1.50 .45
D9 Tony Gwynn 5.00 1.50
D10 Vladimir Guerrero 4.00 1.20
D11 Derek Jeter 10.00 3.00
D12 Jeff Bagwell 2.50 .75
D13 Cal Ripken 12.00 3.60
D14 Juan Gonzalez 4.00 1.20
D15 J.D. Drew 1.50 .45

1999 Upper Deck MVP Game Used Souvenirs

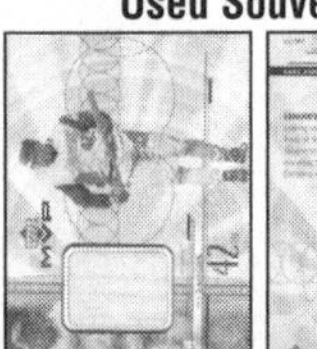

These 11 cards were randomly inserted into packs at a rate of one in 144. Each card features a chip of actual game-used bat from the player featured.

Nm-Mt Ex-Mt
GUBB Barry Bonds 40.00 12.00
GUCJ Chipper Jones 20.00 6.00
GUCR Cal Ripken 50.00 15.00
GUJB Jeff Bagwell 15.00 4.50
GUJD J.D. Drew 10.00 3.00
GUKG Ken Griffey Jr. 25.00 7.50
GUMP Mike Piazza 30.00 9.00
GUMV Mo Vaughn 10.00 3.00
GUSR Scott Rolen 15.00 4.50
GAKG K. Griffey Jr. AU/24
GACJ Chipper Jones AU/10

1999 Upper Deck MVP Power Surge

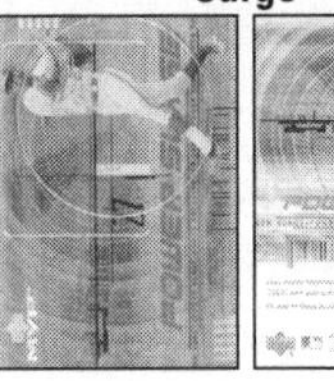

These cards were inserted one every nine packs. The horizontal cards feature some of the leading sluggers in baseball and are printed on rainbow foil.

Nm-Mt Ex-Mt
COMPLETE SET (15) 25.00 7.50
P1 Mark McGwire 3.00 .90
P2 Sammy Sosa 2.00 .60
P3 Ken Griffey Jr. 2.00 .60
P4 Alex Rodriguez 2.00 .60
P5 Juan Gonzalez 1.25 .35
P6 Nomar Garciaparra 2.00 .60
P7 Vladimir Guerrero 1.25 .35
P8 Chipper Jones 1.25 .35
P9 Albert Belle .50 .15
P10 Frank Thomas 1.25 .35
P11 Mike Piazza 2.00 .60
P12 Jeff Bagwell .75 .23
P13 Manny Ramirez .50 .15
P14 Mo Vaughn .50 .15
P15 Barry Bonds 3.00 .90

1999 Upper Deck MVP ProSign

Inserted as a rate of one every 216 retail packs, these cards feature autographs from various baseball players. It's believed that the veteran stars in this set are in much shorter supply than the various young prospects.Some of these star cards have rarely been seen in the secondary market and no pricing is yet available for those cards.

Nm-Mt Ex-Mt
AG Alex Gonzalez 10.00 3.00
AN Abraham Nunez 10.00 3.00
BC Bruce Chen 10.00 3.00
BF Brad Fullmer 10.00 3.00
BG Ben Grieve 10.00 3.00
CB Carlos Beltran 15.00 4.50
CG Chris Gomez 10.00 3.00
CJ Chipper Jones SP 100.00 30.00
CK Corey Koskie 15.00 4.50
CP Calvin Pickering 10.00 3.00
DG Derrick Gibson 10.00 3.00
EC Eric Chavez 15.00 4.50
GK Gabe Kapler 10.00 3.00
GL George Lombard 10.00 3.00
IR Ivan Rodriguez SP 100.00 30.00
JG Jeremy Giambi 10.00 3.00
JP Jim Parque 10.00 3.00
JR Ken Griffey Jr. SP 150.00 45.00
KW Kevin Witt 10.00 3.00
MA Matt Anderson 10.00 3.00
ML Mike Lincoln 10.00 3.00
NG Nomar Garciaparra SP 150.00 45.00
RB Russ Branyan 10.00 3.00
RH Richard Hidalgo 15.00 4.50
RL Ricky Ledee 10.00 3.00
RM Ryan Minor 10.00 3.00
RR Ruben Rivera 10.00 3.00
SH Shea Hillenbrand 15.00 4.50
SK Scott Karl 10.00 3.00
SM Shane Monahan 10.00 3.00
JRA Jason Rakers 10.00 3.00
MLO Mike Lowell 15.00 4.50

1999 Upper Deck MVP Scout's Choice

Inserted one every nine packs, these cards feature the best young stars and rookies captured on Light F/X packs.

Nm-Mt Ex-Mt
COMPLETE SET (15) 12.00 3.60
SC1 J.D. Drew .60 .18
SC2 Ben Grieve .60 .18
SC3 Troy Glaus 1.00 .30
SC4 Gabe Kapler .60 .18
SC5 Carlos Beltran .60 .18
SC6 Aramis Ramirez .60 .18
SC7 Pat Burrell 2.00 .60
SC8 Kerry Wood 1.50 .45
SC9 Ryan Minor .60 .18
SC10 Todd Helton 1.00 .30
SC11 Eric Chavez .60 .18
SC12 Russ Branyan .60 .18
SC13 Travis Lee .60 .18
SC14 Ruben Mateo .60 .18
SC15 Roy Halladay .60 .18

1999 Upper Deck MVP Super Tools

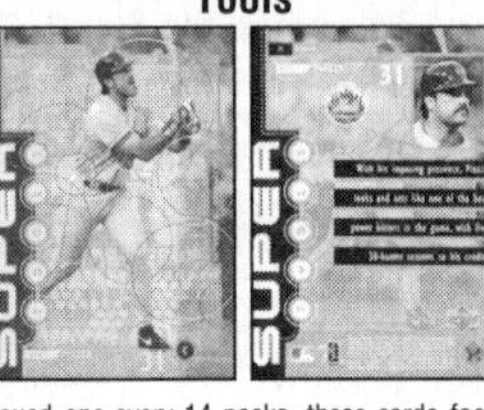

Issued one every 14 packs, these cards focus on big leaguers who posess various tools of greatness.

Nm-Mt Ex-Mt
COMPLETE SET (15) 50.00 15.00
T1 Ken Griffey Jr. 4.00 1.20
T2 Alex Rodriguez 4.00 1.20
T3 Sammy Sosa 4.00 1.20
T4 Derek Jeter 6.00 1.80
T5 Vladimir Guerrero 2.50 .75
T6 Ben Grieve 1.00 .30
T7 Mike Piazza 4.00 1.20
T8 Kenny Lofton 1.00 .30
T9 Barry Bonds 6.00 1.80
T10 Darin Erstad 1.00 .30
T11 Nomar Garciaparra 4.00 1.20
T12 Cal Ripken 8.00 2.40
T13 J.D. Drew 1.00 .30
T14 Larry Walker 1.50 .45
T15 Chipper Jones 2.50 .75

1999 Upper Deck MVP Swing Time

Issued one every six packs, these cards focus on players who have swings considered to be among the sweetest in the game.

Nm-Mt Ex-Mt
COMPLETE SET (12) 20.00 6.00
S1 Ken Griffey Jr. 1.50 .45
S2 Mark McGwire 2.50 .75
S3 Sammy Sosa 1.50 .45
S4 Tony Gwynn 1.25 .35
S5 Alex Rodriguez 1.50 .45
S6 Nomar Garciaparra 1.50 .45
S7 Barry Bonds 2.50 .75
S8 Frank Thomas 1.00 .30
S9 Chipper Jones 1.00 .30
S10 Ivan Rodriguez 1.00 .30
S11 Mike Piazza 1.50 .45
S12 Derek Jeter 2.50 .75

1999 Upper Deck MVP FanFest

This 30 card standard-size set was issued by Upper Deck during the annual FanFest celebration. The cards were issued in three-card packs with 15,000 packs produced and distributed during the show. The cards have a silver All-Star Game logo on the lower right corner of the card and they are all numbered with an "AS" prefix. Ten of the cards were printed in smaller quantities then the other 20 cards, those cards are notated with an SP in the listings below

Nm-Mt Ex-Mt
COMPLETE SET 60.00 18.00
COMMON (AS1-AS30) .30 .09
COMMON SP 2.00 .60
AS1 Mo Vaughn SP 2.00 .60
AS2 Randy Johnson .75 .23
AS3 Chipper Jones 1.50 .45
AS4 Greg Maddux SP 6.00 1.80
AS5 Cal Ripken 3.00 .90
AS6 Albert Belle .30 .09
AS7 N.Garciaparra SP 6.00 1.80
AS8 Pedro Martinez .75 .23
AS9 Sammy Sosa 1.50 .45
AS10 Frank Thomas .75 .23
AS11 Sean Casey .30 .09
AS12 Roberto Alomar .60 .18
AS13 Manny Ramirez .75 .23
AS14 Larry Walker .30 .09
AS15 Jeff Bagwell SP 3.00 .90
AS16 Craig Biggio .60 .18
AS17 Raul Mondesi .30 .09
AS18 Vladimir Guerrero .75 .23
AS19 Mike Piazza SP 8.00 2.40
AS20 Derek Jeter SP 12.00 3.60
AS21 Roger Clemens SP 6.00 1.80
AS22 Scott Rolen .60 .18
AS23 Mark McGwire SP 10.00 3.00
AS24 Tony Gwynn 1.50 .45
AS25 Barry Bonds 1.50 .45
AS26 Ken Griffey Jr SP 8.00 2.40
AS27 Alex Rodriguez 1.50 .45
AS28 Jose Canseco .75 .23
AS29 Juan Gonzalez .75 .23
AS30 Ivan Rodriguez .75 .23

2000 Upper Deck MVP

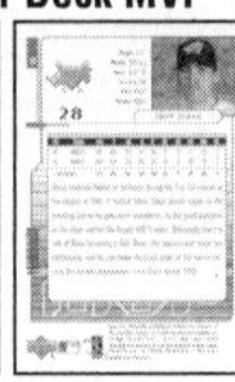

The 2000 Upper Deck MVP product was released in June, 2000 as a 220-card set. Each pack contained 10 cards and carried a suggested retail price of $1.59. Please note that cards 218-220 are player/checklist cards. Also, a selection of A Piece of History 3000 Club Stan Musial memorabilia cards were randomly seeded into packs. 350 bat cards, 350 jersey cards, 100 hand-numbered combination bat-jersey cards and six autographed, hand-numbered, combination bat-jersey cards were produced. Pricing for these memorabilia cards can be referenced under 2000 Upper Deck A Piece of History 3000 Club.

Nm-Mt Ex-Mt
COMPLETE SET (220) 15.00 4.50
1 Garret Anderson .20 .06
2 Mo Vaughn .20 .06
3 Tim Salmon .30 .09
4 Ramon Ortiz .20 .06
5 Darin Erstad .20 .06
6 Troy Glaus .30 .09
7 Troy Percival .20 .06
8 Jeff Bagwell .30 .09
9 Ken Caminiti .20 .06
10 Daryle Ward .20 .06
11 Craig Biggio .30 .09
12 Jose Lima .20 .06
13 Moises Alou .20 .06
14 Octavio Dotel .20 .06
15 Ben Grieve .20 .06
16 Jason Giambi .50 .15
17 Tim Hudson .30 .09
18 Eric Chavez .20 .06
19 Matt Stairs .20 .06
20 Miguel Tejada .20 .06
21 John Jaha .20 .06
22 Chipper Jones .50 .15
23 Kevin Millwood .20 .06
24 Brian Jordan .20 .06
25 Andruw Jones .20 .06
26 Andres Galarraga .20 .06
27 Greg Maddux .75 .23
28 Reggie Sanders .20 .06
29 Javy Lopez .20 .06
30 Jeromy Burnitz .20 .06
31 Kevin Barker .20 .06
32 Jose Hernandez .20 .06
33 Ron Belliard .20 .06
34 Henry Blanco .20 .06
35 Marquis Grissom .20 .06
36 Geoff Jenkins .20 .06
37 Carlos Delgado .20 .06
38 Raul Mondesi .20 .06
39 Roy Halladay .20 .06
40 Tony Batista .20 .06
41 David Wells .20 .06
42 Shannon Stewart .20 .06
43 Vernon Wells .20 .06
44 Sammy Sosa .75 .23
45 Ismael Valdes .20 .06
46 Joe Girardi .20 .06
47 Mark Grace .30 .09
48 Henry Rodriguez .20 .06
49 Kerry Wood .50 .15
50 Eric Young .20 .06
51 Mark McGwire 1.25 .35
52 Darryl Kile .20 .06
53 Fernando Vina .20 .06
54 Ray Lankford .20 .06
55 J.D. Drew .20 .06
56 Fernando Tatis .20 .06
57 Rick Ankiel .20 .06
58 Matt Williams .20 .06
59 Erubiel Durazo .20 .06
60 Tony Womack .20 .06
61 Jay Bell .20 .06
62 Randy Johnson .50 .15
63 Steve Finley .20 .06
64 Matt Mantei .20 .06
65 Luis Gonzalez .20 .06
66 Gary Sheffield .20 .06
67 Eric Gagne .50 .15
68 Adrian Beltre .20 .06
69 Mark Grudzielanek .20 .06
70 Kevin Brown .20 .06
71 Chan Ho Park .20 .06
72 Shawn Green .20 .06
73 Vinny Castilla .20 .06
74 Fred McGriff .30 .09
75 Wilson Alvarez .20 .06
76 Greg Vaughn .20 .06
77 Gerald Williams .20 .06
78 Ryan Rupe .20 .06
79 Jose Canseco .50 .15
80 Vladimir Guerrero .50 .15
81 Dustin Hermanson .20 .06
82 Michael Barrett .20 .06
83 Rondell White .20 .06
84 Tony Armas Jr. .20 .06
85 Wilton Guerrero .20 .06
86 Jose Vidro .20 .06
87 Barry Bonds 1.25 .35
88 Russ Ortiz .20 .06
89 Ellis Burks .20 .06
90 Jeff Kent .20 .06
91 Russ Davis .20 .06
92 J.T. Snow .20 .06
93 Roberto Alomar .50 .15
94 Manny Ramirez .20 .06
95 Chuck Finley .20 .06
96 Kenny Lofton .20 .06
97 Jim Thome .50 .15
98 Bartolo Colon .20 .06
99 Omar Vizquel .20 .06
100 Richie Sexson .20 .06
101 Mike Cameron .20 .06
102 Brett Tomko .20 .06
103 Edgar Martinez .30 .09
104 Alex Rodriguez .75 .23
105 John Olerud .20 .06
106 Freddy Garcia .20 .06
107 Kazuhiro Sasaki RC 1.00 .30
108 Preston Wilson .20 .06
109 Luis Castillo .20 .06
110 A.J. Burnett .20 .06
111 Mike Lowell .20 .06
112 Cliff Floyd .20 .06
113 Brad Penny .20 .06
114 Alex Gonzalez .20 .06
115 Mike Piazza .75 .23
116 Derek Bell .20 .06
117 Edgardo Alfonzo .20 .06
118 Rickey Henderson .50 .15
119 Todd Zeile .20 .06
120 Mike Hampton .20 .06
121 Al Leiter .20 .06
122 Robin Ventura .20 .06
123 Cal Ripken 1.50 .45
124 Mike Mussina .50 .15
125 B.J. Surhoff .20 .06
126 Jerry Hairston Jr. .20 .06
127 Brady Anderson .20 .06
128 Albert Belle .20 .06
129 Sidney Ponson .20 .06
130 Tony Gwynn .60 .18
131 Ryan Klesko .20 .06
132 Sterling Hitchcock .20 .06
133 Eric Owens .20 .06
134 Trevor Hoffman .20 .06
135 Al Martin .20 .06
136 Bret Boone .20 .06
137 Brian Giles .20 .06
138 Chad Hermansen .20 .06
139 Kevin Young .20 .06
140 Kris Benson .20 .06
141 Warren Morris .20 .06
142 Jason Kendall .20 .06
143 Wil Cordero .20 .06
144 Scott Rolen .30 .09
145 Curt Schilling .30 .09
146 Doug Glanville .20 .06
147 Mike Lieberthal .20 .06
148 Mike Jackson .20 .06
149 Rico Brogna .20 .06
150 Andy Ashby .20 .06
151 Bob Abreu .20 .06
152 Sean Casey .20 .06
153 Pete Harnisch .20 .06
154 Dante Bichette .20 .06
155 Pokey Reese .20 .06
156 Aaron Boone .20 .06
157 Ken Griffey Jr. .75 .23
158 Barry Larkin .50 .15
159 Scott Williamson .20 .06
160 Carlos Beltran .20 .06
161 Jermaine Dye .20 .06
162 Jose Rosado .20 .06
163 Joe Randa .20 .06
164 Johnny Damon .20 .06
165 Mike Sweeney .20 .06
166 Mark Quinn .20 .06
167 Ivan Rodriguez .50 .15
168 Rusty Greer .20 .06
169 Ruben Mateo .20 .06
170 Doug Davis .20 .06
171 Gabe Kapler .20 .06
172 Justin Thompson .20 .06
173 Rafael Palmeiro .30 .09
174 Larry Walker .30 .09
175 Neifi Perez .20 .06
176 Rolando Arrojo .20 .06
177 Jeffrey Hammonds .20 .06
178 Todd Helton .30 .09
179 Pedro Astacio .20 .06
180 Jeff Cirillo .20 .06
181 Pedro Martinez .50 .15
182 Carl Everett .20 .06
183 Troy O'Leary .20 .06
184 Nomar Garciaparra .75 .23
185 Jose Offerman .20 .06
186 Bret Saberhagen .20 .06
187 Trot Nixon .30 .09
188 Jason Varitek .20 .06
189 Todd Walker .20 .06
190 Eric Milton .20 .06
191 Chad Allen .20 .06
192 Jacque Jones .20 .06
193 Brad Radke .20 .06
194 Corey Koskie .20 .06
195 Joe Mays .20 .06
196 Juan Gonzalez .50 .15
197 Jeff Weaver .20 .06
198 Juan Encarnacion .20 .06
199 Deivi Cruz .20 .06
200 Damion Easley .20 .06
201 Tony Clark .20 .06
202 Dean Palmer .20 .06
203 Frank Thomas .50 .15
204 Carlos Lee .20 .06
205 Mike Sirotka .20 .06
206 Kip Wells .20 .06
207 Magglio Ordonez .20 .06
208 Paul Konerko .20 .06
209 Chris Singleton .20 .06
210 Derek Jeter 1.25 .35
211 Tino Martinez .30 .09
212 Mariano Rivera .30 .09
213 Roger Clemens 1.00 .30
214 Nick Johnson .20 .06

215 Paul O'Neill .30 .09
216 Bernie Williams .30 .09
217 David Cone .20 .06
218 Ken Griffey Jr. CL .50 .15
219 Sammy Sosa CL .50 .15
220 Mark McGwire CL .60 .18

2000 Upper Deck MVP Gold Script

Randomly inserted into packs, this 220-card insert is a complete parallel of the Upper Deck MVP base set. Each card in the set is individually serial numbered to 50. Please note that each card features a gold foiled facsimile autograph on the front of the card.

Nm-Mt Ex-Mt
*STARS: 25X TO 60X BASIC CARDS ..
*ROOKIES: 20X TO 50X BASIC CARDS

2000 Upper Deck MVP Silver Script

Randomly inserted into packs at one in two, this 220-card insert is a complete parallel of the Upper Deck MVP base set. Please note that each card features a silver foiled facsimile autograph on the front of the card.

Nm-Mt Ex-Mt
COMPLETE SET (220) 150.00 45.00
*STARS: 1.25X TO 3X BASIC CARDS .
*ROOKIES: 1.25X TO 3X BASIC CARDS

2000 Upper Deck MVP All Star Game

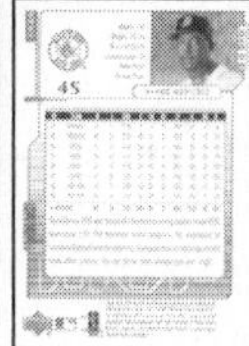

This 30-card insert set was released in three-card packs at the All-Star Fan Fest in Atlanta in July, 2000.

Nm-Mt Ex-Mt
COMPLETE SET (30) 40.00 12.00
AS1 Mo Vaughn .40 .12
AS2 Jeff Bagwell 1.00 .30
AS3 Jason Giambi 1.00 .30
AS4 Chipper Jones 1.50 .45
AS5 Greg Maddux 2.00 .60
AS6 Tony Batista .25 .07
AS7 Sammy Sosa 2.00 .60
AS8 Mark McGwire 3.00 .90
AS9 Randy Johnson 1.00 .30
AS10 Shawn Green .75 .23
AS11 Greg Vaughn .40 .12
AS12 Vladimir Guerrero 1.00 .30
AS13 Barry Bonds 2.00 .60
AS14 Manny Ramirez 1.00 .30
AS15 Alex Rodriguez 2.00 .60
AS16 Preston Wilson .40 .12
AS17 Mike Piazza 2.50 .75
AS18 Cal Ripken Jr. 4.00 1.20
AS19 Tony Gwynn 2.00 .60
AS20 Scott Rolen .75 .23
AS21 Ken Griffey Jr. 2.50 .75
AS22 Carlos Beltran .60 .18
AS23 Ivan Rodriguez 1.00 .30
AS24 Larry Walker .40 .12
AS25 Nomar Garciaparra 2.00 .60
AS26 Pedro Martinez 1.00 .30
AS27 Juan Gonzalez 1.00 .30
AS28 Frank Thomas 1.50 .45
AS29 Derek Jeter 4.00 1.20
AS30 Bernie Williams .75 .23

2000 Upper Deck MVP Draw Your Own Card

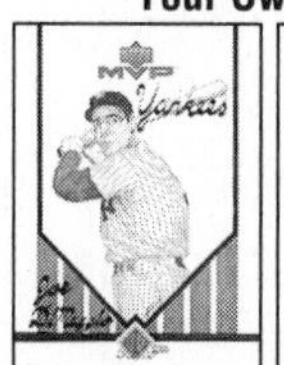
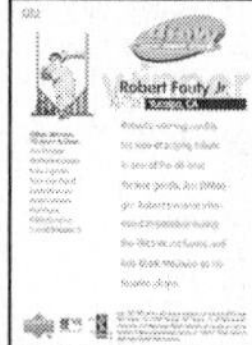

Randomly inserted into packs at one in six, this 31-card insert features player drawings from the 2000 Draw Your Own Card winners. Card backs carry a "DT" prefix.

Nm-Mt Ex-Mt
COMPLETE SET (31) 50.00 15.00
DT1 Frank Thomas 1.00 .30
DT2 Joe DiMaggio 2.00 .60
DT3 Barry Bonds 2.50 .75
DT4 Mark McGwire 2.50 .75
DT5 Ken Griffey Jr. 1.50 .45
DT6 Mark McGwire 2.50 .75
DT7 Mike Stanley .40 .12
DT8 Nomar Garciaparra 1.50 .45
DT9 Mickey Mantle 4.00 1.20
DT10 Randy Johnson 1.00 .30
DT11 Nolan Ryan 2.50 .75
DT12 Chipper Jones 1.00 .30
DT13 Ken Griffey Jr. 1.50 .45
DT14 Troy Glaus .60 .18
DT15 Manny Ramirez .40 .12
DT16 Mark McGwire 2.50 .75
DT17 Ivan Rodriguez 1.00 .30
DT18 Mike Piazza 1.50 .45
DT19 Sammy Sosa 1.50 .45
DT20 Ken Griffey Jr. 1.50 .45
DT21 Jeff Bagwell .60 .18
DT22 Ken Griffey Jr. 1.50 .45
DT23 Kerry Wood 1.00 .30
DT24 Mark McGwire 2.50 .75
DT25 Greg Maddux 1.50 .45
DT26 Sandy Alomar Jr. .40 .12
DT27 Albert Belle .40 .12
DT28 Sammy Sosa 1.50 .45
DT29 Alexandra Brunet .40 .12
DT30 Mark McGwire 2.50 .75
DT31 Nomar Garciaparra 1.50 .45

2000 Upper Deck MVP Drawing Power

Randomly inserted into packs at one in 28, this seven-card insert features players that bring fans to the ballpark. Card backs carry a "DP" prefix.

Nm-Mt Ex-Mt
COMPLETE SET (7) 30.00 9.00
DP1 Mark McGwire 6.00 1.80
DP2 Ken Griffey Jr. 4.00 1.20
DP3 Mike Piazza 4.00 1.20
DP4 Chipper Jones 2.50 .75
DP5 Nomar Garciaparra 4.00 1.20
DP6 Sammy Sosa 4.00 1.20
DP7 Jose Canseco 2.50 .75

2000 Upper Deck MVP Game Used Souvenirs

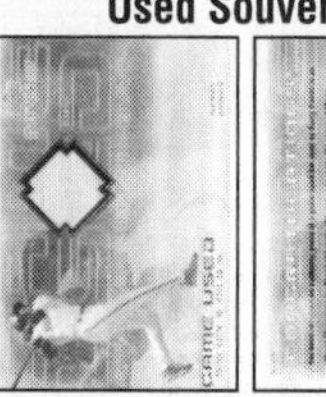
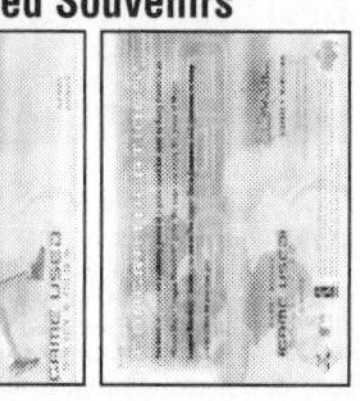

Randomly inserted into packs at one in 130, this 30-card insert features game-used bat and game used glove cards from players such as Chipper Jones and Ken Griffey Jr.

Nm-Mt Ex-Mt
AB-G Albert Belle Glove 20.00 6.00
AF-G Alex Fernandez Glove 15.00 4.50
AG-G Alex Gonzalez Glove 15.00 4.50
AR-B Alex Rodriguez Bat 15.00 4.50
AR-G Alex Rodriguez Glove 50.00 15.00
BB-B Barry Bonds Bat 25.00 7.50
BB-G Barry Bonds Glove 80.00 24.00
BG-G Ben Grieve Glove 15.00 4.50
BW-G Bernie Williams Glove 30.00 9.00
CR-G Cal Ripken Glove 80.00 24.00
IR-B Ivan Rodriguez Bat 15.00 4.50
IR-G Ivan Rodriguez Glove 30.00 9.00
JB-G Jeff Bagwell Glove 30.00 9.00
JC-B Jose Canseco Bat 15.00 4.50
KG-B Ken Griffey Jr. Bat 20.00 6.00
KG-G Ken Griffey Jr. Glove 50.00 15.00
KL-G Kenny Lofton Glove 20.00 6.00
LW-G Larry Walker Glove 30.00 9.00
MR-B Manny Ramirez Bat 15.00 4.50
NR-G Nolan Ryan Glove 80.00 24.00
PO-G Paul O'Neill Glove 30.00 9.00
RA-G Roberto Alomar Glove 30.00 9.00
RM-G Raul Mondesi Glove 20.00 6.00
RP-G Rafael Palmeiro Glove 50.00 15.00
TG-B Tony Gwynn Bat 20.00 6.00
TG-G Tony Gwynn Glove 40.00 12.00
TS-G Tim Salmon Glove 30.00 9.00
WC-G Will Clark Glove 30.00 9.00

2000 Upper Deck MVP Game Used Souvenirs Signed

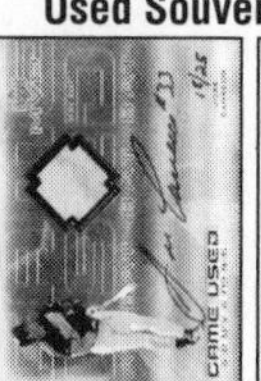
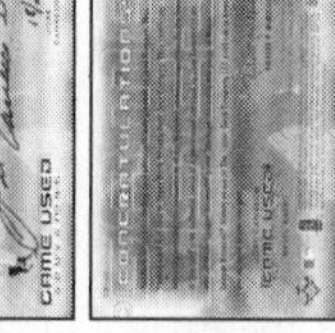

Randomly inserted into packs, this autographed insert features game-used bat and game-used glove cards from players such as Chipper Jones and Ken Griffey Jr. Each card was individually serial numbered to 25 on front. Stickered exchange cards were placed into packs for Ken Griffey Jr. The exchange deadline for these stickered redemption cards was February 2nd, 2001. Due to market scarcity, no pricing is provided for these cards.

Nm-Mt Ex-Mt
ABSG Albert Belle Glove
BBSB Barry Bonds Bat
BBSG Barry Bonds Glove
CJSB Chipper Jones Bat
JCSB Jose Canseco Bat
KGSB Ken Griffey Jr. Bat
KGSG Ken Griffey Jr. Glove EX
KLSG Kenny Lofton Glove
NRSG Nolan Ryan Glove
RASG Roberto Alomar Glove
RPSG Rafael Palmeiro Glove
TGSB Tony Gwynn Bat
TGSG Tony Gwynn Glove

2000 Upper Deck MVP Prolifics

Randomly inserted into packs at one in 28, this 7-card insert features some of the most prolific players in major league baseball. Card backs carry a "P" prefix.

Nm-Mt Ex-Mt
COMPLETE SET (7) 25.00 7.50
P1 Manny Ramirez 1.00 .30
P2 Vladimir Guerrero 2.50 .75
P3 Derek Jeter 6.00 1.80
P4 Pedro Martinez 2.50 .75
P5 Shawn Green 1.00 .30
P6 Alex Rodriguez 4.00 1.20
P7 Cal Ripken 8.00 2.40

2000 Upper Deck MVP ProSign

Randomly inserted into retail packs only at one in 143, this 18-card insert features autographs of players such as Mike Sweeney, Rick Ankiel, and Tim Hudson. Card backs are numbered using the players initials.

Nm-Mt Ex-Mt
BP Ben Petrick 10.00 3.00
BT Bubba Trammell 10.00 3.00
DD Doug Davis 10.00 3.00
EY Ed Yarnall 10.00 3.00
JM Jim Morris 25.00 7.50
JV Jose Vidro 15.00 4.50
JZ Jeff Zimmerman 10.00 3.00
KW Kevin Witt 10.00 3.00
MB Michael Barrett 10.00 3.00
MM Mike Meyers 15.00 4.50
MQ Mark Quinn 10.00 3.00
MS Mike Sweeney 15.00 4.50
PW Preston Wilson 15.00 4.50
RA Rick Ankiel 10.00 3.00
SW Scott Williamson 10.00 3.00
TH Tim Hudson 25.00 7.50
TN Trot Nixon 25.00 7.50
WM Warren Morris 10.00 3.00

2000 Upper Deck MVP Pure Grit

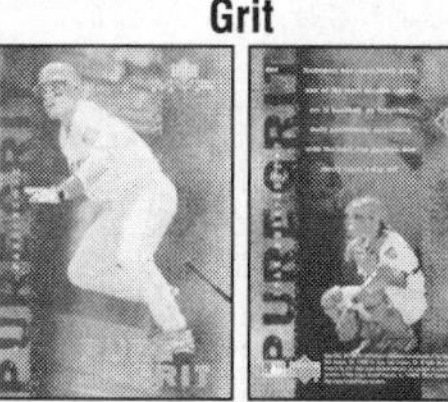

Randomly inserted into packs at one in six, this 10-card insert features players that constantly give their best day in, day out. Card backs carry a "G" prefix.

Nm-Mt Ex-Mt
COMPLETE SET (10) 15.00 4.50
G1 Derek Jeter 3.00 .90
G2 Kevin Brown .50 .15
G3 Craig Biggio .75 .23
G4 Ivan Rodriguez 1.25 .35
G5 Scott Rolen .75 .23
G6 Carlos Beltran .50 .15
G7 Ken Griffey Jr. 2.00 .60
G8 Cal Ripken 4.00 1.20
G9 Nomar Garciaparra 2.00 .60
G10 Randy Johnson 1.25 .35

2000 Upper Deck MVP Scout's Choice

Randomly inserted into packs at one in 14, this 10-card insert features players that major league scouts believe will be future stars in the major leagues. Card backs carry a "SC" prefix.

Nm-Mt Ex-Mt
COMPLETE SET (10) 10.00 3.00
SC1 Rick Ankiel 1.00 .30
SC2 Vernon Wells 1.00 .30
SC3 Pat Burrell 1.00 .30
SC4 Travis Dawkins 1.00 .30
SC5 Eric Munson 1.00 .30
SC6 Nick Johnson 1.00 .30
SC7 Dermal Brown 1.00 .30
SC8 Alfonso Soriano 1.50 .45
SC9 Ben Petrick 1.00 .30
SC10 Adam Everett 1.00 .30

2000 Upper Deck MVP Second Season Standouts

Randomly inserted into packs at one in six, this 10-card insert features players that had outstanding sophomore years in the major leagues. Card backs carry a "SS" prefix.

Nm-Mt Ex-Mt
COMPLETE SET (10) 10.00 3.00
SS1 Pedro Martinez 1.25 .35
SS2 Mariano Rivera .75 .23
SS3 Orlando Hernandez .50 .15
SS4 Ken Caminiti .50 .15
SS5 Bernie Williams .75 .23
SS6 Jim Thome 1.25 .35
SS7 Nomar Garciaparra 2.00 .60
SS8 Edgardo Alfonzo .50 .15
SS9 Derek Jeter 3.00 .90
SS10 Kevin Millwood .50 .15

2001 Upper Deck MVP

This 330-card set was released in May, 2001. These cards were issued in eight card packs with an SRP of $1.99. These packs were issued 24 packs to a box.

Nm-Mt Ex-Mt
COMPLETE SET (330) 50.00 15.00
1 Mo Vaughn .20 .06
2 Troy Percival .20 .06
3 Adam Kennedy .20 .06
4 Darin Erstad .20 .06
5 Tim Salmon .30 .09
6 Bengie Molina .20 .06
7 Troy Glaus .30 .09
8 Garret Anderson .20 .06
9 Ismael Valdes .20 .06
10 Glenallen Hill .20 .06
11 Tim Hudson .20 .06
12 Eric Chavez .20 .06
13 Johnny Damon .20 .06
14 Barry Zito .50 .15
15 Jason Giambi .50 .15
16 Terrence Long .20 .06
17 Jason Hart .20 .06
18 Jose Ortiz .20 .06
19 Miguel Tejada .20 .06
20 Jason Isringhausen .20 .06
21 Adam Piatt .20 .06
22 Jeremy Giambi .20 .06
23 Tony Batista .20 .06
24 Darrin Fletcher .20 .06
25 Mike Sirotka .20 .06
26 Carlos Delgado .20 .06
27 Billy Koch .20 .06
28 Shannon Stewart .20 .06
29 Raul Mondesi .20 .06
30 Brad Fullmer .20 .06
31 Jose Cruz Jr. .20 .06
32 Kelvim Escobar .20 .06
33 Greg Vaughn .20 .06
34 Aubrey Huff .20 .06
35 Albie Lopez .20 .06
36 Gerald Williams .20 .06
37 Ben Grieve .20 .06
38 John Flaherty .20 .06
39 Fred McGriff .30 .09
40 Ryan Rupe .20 .06
41 Travis Harper .20 .06
42 Steve Cox .20 .06
43 Roberto Alomar .50 .15
44 Jim Thome .50 .15
45 Russell Branyan .20 .06
46 Bartolo Colon .20 .06
47 Omar Vizquel .20 .06
48 Travis Fryman .20 .06
49 Kenny Lofton .20 .06
50 Chuck Finley .20 .06
51 Ellis Burks .20 .06
52 Eddie Taubensee .20 .06
53 Juan Gonzalez .50 .15
54 Edgar Martinez .30 .09
55 Aaron Sele .20 .06
56 John Olerud .20 .06
57 Jay Buhner .20 .06
58 Mike Cameron .20 .06
59 John Halama .20 .06
60 Ichiro Suzuki RC 10.00 3.00
61 David Bell .20 .06
62 Freddy Garcia .20 .06
63 Carlos Guillen .20 .06
64 Bret Boone .20 .06
65 Al Martin .20 .06
66 Cal Ripken 1.50 .45
67 Delino DeShields .20 .06
68 Chris Richard .20 .06
69 Sean Douglass RC .50 .15
70 Melvin Mora .20 .06
71 Luis Matos .20 .06
72 Sidney Ponson .20 .06
73 Mike Bordick .20 .06
74 Brady Anderson .20 .06
75 David Segui .20 .06
76 Jeff Conine .20 .06
77 Alex Rodriguez .75 .23
78 Gabe Kapler .20 .06
79 Ivan Rodriguez .50 .15
80 Rick Helling .20 .06
81 Kenny Rogers .20 .06
82 Andres Galarraga .20 .06
83 Rusty Greer .20 .06
84 Justin Thompson .20 .06
85 Ken Caminiti .20 .06
86 Rafael Palmeiro .30 .09
87 Ruben Mateo .20 .06
88 Travis Hafner RC 1.25 .35
89 Manny Ramirez .20 .06
90 Pedro Martinez .50 .15
91 Carl Everett .20 .06
92 Dante Bichette .20 .06
93 Derek Lowe .20 .06
94 Jason Varitek .20 .06
95 Nomar Garciaparra .75 .23
96 David Cone .20 .06
97 Tomokazu Ohka .20 .06
98 Troy O'Leary .20 .06
99 Trot Nixon .30 .09
100 Jermaine Dye .20 .06
101 Joe Randa .20 .06
102 Jeff Suppan .20 .06
103 Roberto Hernandez .20 .06
104 Mike Sweeney .20 .06
105 Mac Suzuki .20 .06
106 Carlos Febles .20 .06
107 Jose Rosado .20 .06
108 Mark Quinn .20 .06
109 Carlos Beltran .20 .06
110 Dean Palmer .20 .06
111 Mitch Meluskey .20 .06
112 Bobby Higginson .20 .06
113 Brandon Inge .20 .06
114 Tony Clark .20 .06
115 Brian Moehler .20 .06
116 Juan Encarnacion .20 .06
117 Damion Easley .20 .06
118 Roger Cedeno .20 .06
119 Jeff Weaver .20 .06
120 Matt Lawton .20 .06
121 Jay Canizaro .20 .06
122 Eric Milton .20 .06
123 Corey Koskie .20 .06
124 Mark Redman .20 .06
125 Jacque Jones .20 .06
126 Brad Radke .20 .06
127 Cristian Guzman .20 .06
128 Joe Mays .20 .06
129 Denny Hocking .20 .06
130 Frank Thomas .50 .15
131 David Wells .20 .06
132 Ray Durham .20 .06
133 Paul Konerko .20 .06
134 Joe Crede .20 .06
135 Jim Parque .20 .06
136 Carlos Lee .20 .06
137 Magglio Ordonez .20 .06
138 Sandy Alomar Jr. .20 .06
139 Chris Singleton .20 .06
140 Jose Valentin .20 .06
141 Roger Clemens 1.00 .30
142 Derek Jeter 1.25 .35
143 Orlando Hernandez .20 .06
144 Tino Martinez .30 .09
145 Bernie Williams .30 .09
146 Jorge Posada .30 .09
147 Mariano Rivera .30 .09
148 David Justice .20 .06
149 Paul O'Neill .30 .09
150 Mike Mussina .50 .15
151 Christian Parker RC .50 .15
152 Andy Pettitte .30 .09
153 Alfonso Soriano .30 .09
154 Jeff Bagwell .30 .09
155 Morgan Ensberg RC 1.00 .30
156 Daryle Ward .20 .06
157 Craig Biggio .30 .09
158 Richard Hidalgo .20 .06
159 Shane Reynolds .20 .06
160 Scott Elarton .20 .06
161 Julio Lugo .20 .06
162 Moises Alou .20 .06
163 Lance Berkman .20 .06
164 Chipper Jones .50 .15
165 Greg Maddux .75 .23
166 Javy Lopez .20 .06
167 Andruw Jones .20 .06
168 Rafael Furcal .20 .06
169 Brian Jordan .20 .06
170 Wes Helms .20 .06
171 Tom Glavine .30 .09
172 B.J. Surhoff .20 .06
173 John Smoltz .30 .09
174 Quilvio Veras .20 .06
175 Rico Brogna .20 .06
176 Jeromy Burnitz .20 .06
177 Jeff D'Amico .20 .06
178 Geoff Jenkins .20 .06
179 Henry Blanco .20 .06
180 Mark Loretta .20 .06
181 Richie Sexson .20 .06
182 Jimmy Haynes .20 .06
183 Jeffrey Hammonds .20 .06
184 Ron Belliard .20 .06
185 Tyler Houston .20 .06
186 Mark McGwire 1.25 .35
187 Rick Ankiel .20 .06
188 Darryl Kile .20 .06
189 Jim Edmonds .20 .06
190 Mike Matheny .20 .06
191 Edgar Renteria .20 .06
192 Ray Lankford .20 .06
193 Garrett Stephenson .20 .06
194 J.D. Drew .20 .06

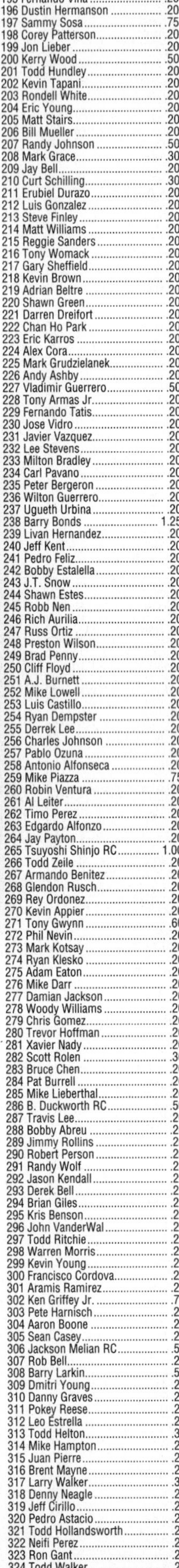

195 Fernando Vina .20 .06
196 Dustin Hermanson .20 .06
197 Sammy Sosa .75 .23
198 Corey Patterson .20 .06
199 Jon Lieber .20 .06
200 Kerry Wood .50 .15
201 Todd Hundley .20 .06
202 Kevin Tapani .20 .06
203 Rondell White .20 .06
204 Eric Young .20 .06
205 Matt Stairs .20 .06
206 Bill Mueller .20 .06
207 Randy Johnson .50 .15
208 Mark Grace .30 .09
209 Jay Bell .20 .06
210 Curt Schilling .30 .09
211 Erubiel Durazo .20 .06
212 Luis Gonzalez .20 .06
213 Steve Finley .20 .06
214 Matt Williams .20 .06
215 Reggie Sanders .20 .06
216 Tony Womack .20 .06
217 Gary Sheffield .20 .06
218 Kevin Brown .20 .06
219 Adrian Beltre .20 .06
220 Shawn Green .20 .06
221 Darren Dreifort .20 .06
222 Chan Ho Park .20 .06
223 Eric Karros .20 .06
224 Alex Cora .20 .06
225 Mark Grudzielanek .20 .06
226 Andy Ashby .20 .06
227 Vladimir Guerrero .50 .15
228 Tony Armas Jr. .20 .06
229 Fernando Tatis .20 .06
230 Jose Vidro .20 .06
231 Javier Vazquez .20 .06
232 Lee Stevens .20 .06
233 Milton Bradley .20 .06
234 Carl Pavano .20 .06
235 Peter Bergeron .20 .06
236 Wilton Guerrero .20 .06
237 Ugueth Urbina .20 .06
238 Barry Bonds 1.25 .35
239 Livan Hernandez .20 .06
240 Jeff Kent .20 .06
241 Pedro Feliz .20 .06
242 Bobby Estalella .20 .06
243 J.T. Snow .20 .06
244 Shawn Estes .20 .06
245 Robb Nen .20 .06
246 Rich Aurilia .20 .06
247 Russ Ortiz .20 .06
248 Preston Wilson .20 .06
249 Brad Penny .20 .06
250 Cliff Floyd .20 .06
251 A.J. Burnett .20 .06
252 Mike Lowell .20 .06
253 Luis Castillo .20 .06
254 Ryan Dempster .20 .06
255 Derrek Lee .20 .06
256 Charles Johnson .20 .06
257 Pablo Ozuna .20 .06
258 Antonio Alfonseca .20 .06
259 Mike Piazza .75 .23
260 Robin Ventura .20 .06
261 Al Leiter .20 .06
262 Timo Perez .20 .06
263 Edgardo Alfonzo .20 .06
264 Jay Payton .20 .06
265 Tsuyoshi Shinjo RC 1.00 .30
266 Todd Zeile .20 .06
267 Armando Benitez .20 .06
268 Glendon Rusch .20 .06
269 Rey Ordonez .20 .06
270 Kevin Appier .20 .06
271 Tony Gwynn .60 .18
272 Phil Nevin .20 .06
273 Mark Kotsay .20 .06
274 Ryan Klesko .20 .06
275 Adam Eaton .20 .06
276 Mike Darr .20 .06
277 Damian Jackson .20 .06
278 Woody Williams .20 .06
279 Chris Gomez .20 .06
280 Trevor Hoffman .20 .06
281 Xavier Nady .20 .06
282 Scott Rolen .30 .09
283 Bruce Chen .20 .06
284 Pat Burrell .20 .06
285 Mike Lieberthal .20 .06
286 B. Duckworth RC .50 .15
287 Travis Lee .20 .06
288 Bobby Abreu .20 .06
289 Jimmy Rollins .20 .06
290 Robert Person .20 .06
291 Randy Wolf .20 .06
292 Jason Kendall .20 .06
293 Derek Bell .20 .06
294 Brian Giles .20 .06
295 Kris Benson .20 .06
296 John VanderWal .20 .06
297 Todd Ritchie .20 .06
298 Warren Morris .20 .06
299 Kevin Young .20 .06
300 Francisco Cordova .20 .06
301 Aramis Ramirez .20 .06
302 Ken Griffey Jr. .75 .23
303 Pete Harnisch .20 .06
304 Aaron Boone .20 .06
305 Sean Casey .20 .06
306 Jackson Melian RC .50 .15
307 Rob Bell .20 .06
308 Barry Larkin .50 .15
309 Dmitri Young .20 .06
310 Danny Graves .20 .06
311 Pokey Reese .20 .06
312 Leo Estrella .20 .06
313 Todd Helton .30 .09
314 Mike Hampton .20 .06
315 Juan Pierre .20 .06
316 Brent Mayne .20 .06
317 Larry Walker .30 .09
318 Denny Neagle .20 .06
319 Jeff Cirillo .20 .06
320 Pedro Astacio .20 .06
321 Todd Hollandsworth .20 .06
322 Neifi Perez .20 .06
323 Ron Gant .20 .06
324 Todd Walker .20 .06
325 Alex Rodriguez CL .50 .15
326 Ken Griffey Jr. CL .50 .15
327 Mark McGwire CL .60 .18
328 Pedro Martinez CL .30 .09
329 Derek Jeter CL .60 .18
330 Mike Piazza CL .50 .15

2001 Upper Deck MVP Authentic Griffey

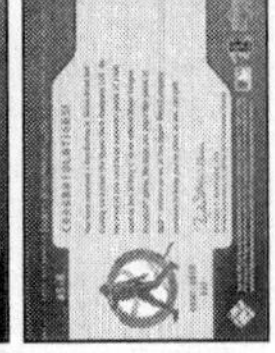

Inserted in packs at a rate of one in 288, these 12 cards feature memorabilia relating to the career of Ken Griffey Jr. A few cards were printed to a stated print run of 30 (Griffey's uniform number with the Reds), and we have notated those cards in our checklist. Griffey did not return his autographs in time for inclusion in the product and those cards could be redeemed until January 15th, 2002.

Nm-Mt Ex-Mt
B Ken Griffey Jr. Bat 25.00 7.50
C Ken Griffey Jr. Cap 50.00 15.00
J Ken Griffey Jr. Jsy 25.00 7.50
S K.Griffey Jr. AU EXCH* 120.00 36.00
U K.Griffey Jr. Uniform 25.00 7.50
GB Ken Griffey Jr. 150.00 45.00
Gold Bat/30
GC Ken Griffey Jr. 150.00 45.00
Gold Cap/30
GJ Ken Griffey Jr. 150.00 45.00
Gold Jsy/30
GS Ken Griffey Jr. 300.00 90.00
Gold AU/30 EXCH
CGR Ken Griffey Jr. 100.00 30.00
Alex Rodriguez
CGS Ken Griffey Jr. 100.00 30.00
Sammy Sosa
CGT Ken Griffey Jr. 60.00 18.00
Frank Thomas Jsy/100

2001 Upper Deck MVP Drawing Power

Inserted in packs at a rate of one in 12, these 10 cards feature the players who help to draw the most fans to ballparks.

Nm-Mt Ex-Mt
COMPLETE SET (10) 25.00 7.50
DP1 Mark McGwire 6.00 1.80
DP2 Vladimir Guerrero 2.50 .75
DP3 Manny Ramirez 2.50 .75
DP4 Frank Thomas 2.50 .75
DP5 Ken Griffey Jr. 4.00 1.20
DP6 Alex Rodriguez 4.00 1.20
DP7 Mike Piazza 4.00 1.20
DP8 Derek Jeter 6.00 1.80
DP9 Sammy Sosa 4.00 1.20
DP10 Todd Helton 2.50 .75

2001 Upper Deck MVP Game Souvenirs Bat Duos

Inserted one in 144, these 14 cards feature two pieces of game-used bats on the same card.

Nm-Mt Ex-Mt
B-3K Tony Gwynn 50.00 15.00
Cal Ripken
B-DV Carlos Delgado 15.00 4.50
Jose Vidro
B-GS Ken Griffey Jr. 40.00 12.00
Sammy Sosa
B-HR Jose Canseco 30.00 9.00
Ken Griffey Jr.
B-JF Chipper Jones 25.00 7.50
Rafael Furcal
B-JJ Andruw Jones 25.00 7.50
Chipper Jones
B-OW Paul O'Neill 25.00 7.50
Bernie Williams
B-RM Alex Rodriguez 30.00 9.00
Edgar Martinez
B-RP Ivan Rodriguez 25.00 7.50
Rafael Palmeiro
B-RR Alex Rodriguez 40.00 12.00
Ivan Rodriguez
B-TG Jim Thome 30.00 9.00
Ken Griffey Jr.
B-TO Frank Thomas 25.00 7.50
Magglio Ordonez
B-TS Frank Thomas 30.00 9.00
Sammy Sosa
B-WA Kerry Wood 25.00 7.50
Rick Ankiel

2001 Upper Deck MVP Game Souvenirs Bat Trios

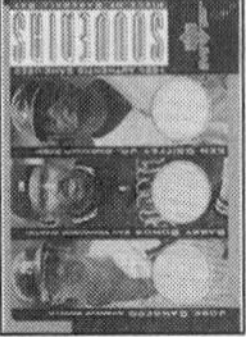

Randomly inserted in packs, these six cards feature three pieces of game-used bats. These cards are serial numbered to 25. Due to market scarcity, no pricing is provided.

Nm-Mt Ex-Mt
B-BGJ Barry Bonds
Ken Griffey Jr.
Andruw Jones
B-CBG Jose Canseco
Barry Bonds
Ken Griffey Jr.
B-JEG Andruw Jones
Jim Edmonds
Ken Griffey Jr.
B-JGC Chipper Jones
Troy Glaus
Eric Chavez
B-JWO David Justice
Bernie Williams
Paul O'Neill
B-SGR Sammy Sosa
Ken Griffey Jr.
Alex Rodriguez

2001 Upper Deck MVP Game Souvenirs Batting Glove

Inserted one per 96 hobby packs, these 18 cards feature a swatch of game-used batting glove of various major leaguers. A couple of players were issued in lesser quantities. We have notated those cards as SP's as well as print run information (as provided by Upper Deck) in our checklist.

Nm-Mt Ex-Mt
G-AR Alex Rodriguez 25.00 7.50
G-BB Barry Bonds 50.00 15.00
G-CJ Chipper Jones 15.00 4.50
G-CR Cal Ripken 60.00 18.00
G-EM Edgar Martinez 15.00 4.50
G-FM Fred McGriff 15.00 4.50
G-FT Frank Thomas 15.00 4.50
G-GM Greg Maddux SP/95 80.00 24.00
G-IR Ivan Rodriguez 15.00 4.50
G-JG Juan Gonzalez 15.00 4.50
G-JL Javy Lopez 10.00 3.00
G-KG Ken Griffey Jr. 25.00 7.50
G-MT Miguel Tejada 10.00 3.00
G-MV Mo Vaughn 10.00 3.00
G-RP Rafael Palmeiro 15.00 4.50
G-SS Sammy Sosa 25.00 7.50
G-TOG T.Gwynn SP/200 40.00 12.00
G-TRG Troy Glaus 15.00 4.50

2001 Upper Deck MVP Game Souvenirs Batting Glove Autograph

Randomly inserted in packs, these nine cards feature not only a swatch of a game-used batting glove but also an authentic autograph of the player. These cards have a stated print run of 25 sets. Troy Glaus did not return his cards in time for inclusion in the packs and these cards were only available as redemptions. Due to market scarcity, no pricing is provided.

Nm-Mt Ex-Mt
SG-AR Alex Rodriguez
SG-CJ Chipper Jones
SG-CR Cal Ripken
SG-FT Frank Thomas
SG-IR Ivan Rodriguez
SG-KG Ken Griffey Jr.
SG-SS Sammy Sosa
SG-TOG Tony Gwynn
SG-TRG Troy Glaus

2001 Upper Deck MVP Super Tools

Inserted one per six packs, these 20 cards feature players whose tools seem to be far above the other players.

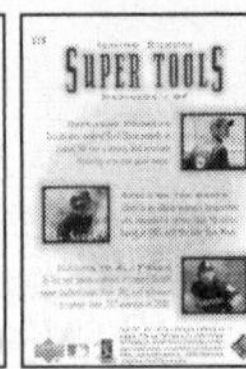

Nm-Mt Ex-Mt
COMPLETE SET (20) 40.00 12.00
ST1 Ken Griffey Jr. 4.00 1.20
ST2 Carlos Delgado 1.00 .30
ST3 Alex Rodriguez 4.00 1.20
ST4 Troy Glaus 1.50 .45
ST5 Jeff Bagwell 1.50 .45
ST6 Ichiro Suzuki 10.00 3.00
ST7 Derek Jeter 6.00 1.80
ST8 Jim Edmonds 1.00 .30
ST9 Vladimir Guerrero 2.50 .75
ST10 Jason Giambi 2.50 .75
ST11 Todd Helton 1.50 .45
ST12 Cal Ripken 8.00 2.40
ST13 Barry Bonds 6.00 1.80
ST14 N.Garciaparra UER 4.00 1.20
Spelled Garicaparra on the front
ST15 Randy Johnson 2.50 .75
ST16 Jermaine Dye 1.00 .30
ST17 Andruw Jones 1.00 .30
ST18 Ivan Rodriguez 2.50 .75
ST19 Sammy Sosa 4.00 1.20
ST20 Pedro Martinez 2.50 .75

2002 Upper Deck MVP

This 300 card set was issued in May, 2002. These cards were issued in eight card packs which came 24 packs to a box and 12 boxes to a case. Cards number 295-300 feature players on the front and checklisting information on the back. Card 301, featuring Kazuhisa Ishii, was added to the product at the last minute. According to representatives at Upper Deck, the card was seeded only into very late boxes of MVP.

Nm-Mt Ex-Mt
COMPLETE SET (301) 40.00 12.00
1 Darin Erstad .20 .06
2 Ramon Ortiz .20 .06
3 Garret Anderson .20 .06
4 Jarrod Washburn .20 .06
5 Troy Glaus .30 .09
6 Brendan Donnelly RC .50 .15
7 Troy Percival .20 .06
8 Tim Salmon .30 .09
9 Aaron Sele .20 .06
10 Brad Fullmer .20 .06
11 Scott Hatteberg .20 .06
12 Barry Zito .30 .09
13 Tim Hudson .20 .06
14 Miguel Tejada .20 .06
15 Jermaine Dye .20 .06
16 Mark Mulder .20 .06
17 Eric Chavez .20 .06
18 Terrence Long .20 .06
19 Carlos Pena .20 .06
20 David Justice .20 .06
21 Jeremy Giambi .20 .06
22 Shannon Stewart .20 .06
23 Raul Mondesi .20 .06
24 Chris Carpenter .20 .06
25 Carlos Delgado .20 .06
26 Mike Sirotka .20 .06
27 Reed Johnson RC .50 .15
28 Darrin Fletcher .20 .06
29 Jose Cruz Jr. .20 .06
30 Vernon Wells .20 .06
31 Tanyon Sturtze .20 .06
32 Toby Hall .20 .06
33 Brent Abernathy .20 .06
34 Ben Grieve .20 .06
35 Joe Kennedy .20 .06
36 Dewon Brazelton .20 .06
37 Aubrey Huff .20 .06
38 Steve Cox .20 .06
39 Greg Vaughn .20 .06
40 Brady Anderson .20 .06
41 Chuck Finley .20 .06
42 Jim Thome .50 .15
43 Russell Branyan .20 .06
44 C.C. Sabathia .20 .06
45 Matt Lawton .20 .06
46 Omar Vizquel .20 .06
47 Bartolo Colon .20 .06
48 Alex Escobar .20 .06
49 Ellis Burks .20 .06
50 Bret Boone .20 .06
51 John Olerud .20 .06
52 Jeff Cirillo .20 .06
53 Ichiro Suzuki .75 .23
54 Kazuhiro Sasaki .20 .06
55 Freddy Garcia .20 .06
56 Edgar Martinez .30 .09
57 Matt Thornton RC .50 .15
58 Mike Cameron .20 .06
59 Carlos Guillen .20 .06
60 Jeff Conine .20 .06
61 Tony Batista .20 .06
62 Jason Johnson .20 .06
63 Melvin Mora .20 .06
64 Brian Roberts .20 .06
65 Josh Towers .20 .06
66 Steve Bechler RC .50 .15
67 Jerry Hairston Jr. .20 .06
68 Chris Richard .20 .06
69 Alex Rodriguez .75 .23
70 Chan Ho Park .20 .06
71 Ivan Rodriguez .50 .15
72 Jeff Zimmerman .20 .06
73 Mark Teixeira .50 .15
74 Gabe Kapler .20 .06
75 Frank Catalanotto .20 .06
76 Rafael Palmeiro .30 .09
77 Doug Davis .20 .06
78 Carl Everett .20 .06
79 Pedro Martinez .50 .15
80 Nomar Garciaparra .75 .23
81 Tony Clark .20 .06
82 Trot Nixon .30 .09
83 Manny Ramirez .20 .06
84 Josh Hancock RC .50 .15
85 Johnny Damon .20 .06
86 Jose Offerman .20 .06
87 Rich Garces .20 .06
88 Shea Hillenbrand .20 .06
89 Carlos Beltran .20 .06
90 Mike Sweeney .20 .06
91 Jeff Suppan .20 .06
92 Joe Randa .20 .06
93 Chuck Knoblauch .20 .06
94 Mark Quinn .20 .06
95 Neifi Perez .20 .06
96 Carlos Febles .20 .06
97 Miguel Asencio RC .50 .15
98 Michael Tucker .20 .06
99 Dean Palmer .20 .06
100 Jose Lima .20 .06
101 Craig Paquette .20 .06
102 Dmitri Young .20 .06
103 Bobby Higginson .20 .06
104 Jeff Weaver .20 .06
105 Matt Anderson .20 .06
106 Damion Easley .20 .06
107 Eric Milton .20 .06
108 Doug Mientkiewicz .20 .06
109 Cristian Guzman .20 .06
110 Brad Radke .20 .06
111 Torii Hunter .20 .06
112 Corey Koskie .20 .06
113 Joe Mays .20 .06
114 Jacque Jones .20 .06
115 David Ortiz .20 .06
116 Kevin Frederick RC .50 .15
117 Maggio Ordonez .20 .06
118 Ray Durham .20 .06
119 Mark Buehrle .20 .06
120 Jon Garland .20 .06
121 Paul Konerko .20 .06
122 Todd Ritchie .20 .06
123 Frank Thomas .50 .15
124 Edwin Almonte RC .50 .15
125 Carlos Lee .20 .06
126 Kenny Lofton .20 .06
127 Roger Clemens 1.00 .30
128 Derek Jeter 1.25 .35
129 Jorge Posada .30 .09
130 Bernie Williams .30 .09
131 Mike Mussina .50 .15
132 Alfonso Soriano .30 .09
133 Robin Ventura .20 .06
134 John Vander Wal .20 .06
135 Jason Giambi Yankees .50 .15
136 Mariano Rivera .30 .09
137 Rondell White .20 .06
138 Jeff Bagwell .30 .09
139 Wade Miller .20 .06
140 Richard Hidalgo .20 .06
141 Julio Lugo .20 .06
142 Roy Oswalt .20 .06
143 Rodrigo Rosario RC .50 .15
144 Lance Berkman .20 .06
145 Craig Biggio .30 .09
146 Shane Reynolds .20 .06
147 John Smoltz .30 .09
148 Chipper Jones .50 .15
149 Gary Sheffield .20 .06
150 Rafael Furcal .20 .06
151 Greg Maddux .75 .23
152 Tom Glavine .30 .09
153 Andruw Jones .20 .06
154 John Ennis RC .50 .15
155 Vinny Castilla .20 .06
156 Marcus Giles .20 .06
157 Javy Lopez .20 .06
158 Richie Sexson .20 .06
159 Geoff Jenkins .20 .06
160 Jeffrey Hammonds .20 .06
161 Alex Ochoa .20 .06
162 Ben Sheets .20 .06
163 Jose Hernandez .20 .06
164 Eric Young .20 .06
165 Luis Martinez RC .50 .15
166 Albert Pujols 1.00 .30
167 Darryl Kile .20 .06
168 So Taguchi RC .50 .15
169 Jim Edmonds .20 .06
170 Fernando Vina .20 .06
171 Matt Morris .20 .06
172 J.D. Drew .20 .06
173 Bud Smith .20 .06
174 Edgar Renteria .20 .06
175 Placido Polanco .20 .06
176 Tino Martinez .30 .09
177 Sammy Sosa .75 .23
178 Moises Alou .20 .06
179 Kerry Wood .50 .15
180 Delino DeShields .20 .06
181 Alex Gonzalez .20 .06
182 Jon Lieber .20 .06
183 Fred McGriff .30 .09
184 Corey Patterson .20 .06
185 Mark Prior 1.00 .30
186 Tom Gordon .20 .06
187 Francis Beltran RC .50 .15
188 Randy Johnson .50 .15
189 Luis Gonzalez .20 .06
190 Matt Williams .20 .06
191 Mark Grace .30 .09
192 Curt Schilling .30 .09
193 Doug Devore RC .50 .15
194 Erubiel Durazo .20 .06
195 Steve Finley .20 .06
196 Craig Counsell .20 .06
197 Shawn Green .20 .06
198 Kevin Brown .20 .06
199 Paul LoDuca .20 .06
200 Brian Jordan .20 .06
201 Andy Ashby .20 .06
202 Darren Dreifort .20 .06
203 Adrian Beltre .20 .06

204 Victor Alvarez RC .50 .15
205 Eric Karros .20 .06
206 Hideo Nomo .50 .15
207 Vladimir Guerrero .50 .15
208 Javier Vazquez .20 .06
209 Michael Barrett .20 .06
210 Jose Vidro .20 .06
211 Brad Wilkerson .20 .06
212 Tony Armas Jr. .20 .06
213 Eric Good RC .50 .15
214 Orlando Cabrera .20 .06
215 Lee Stevens .20 .06
216 Jeff Kent .20 .06
217 Rich Aurilia .20 .06
218 Robb Nen .20 .06
219 Calvin Murray .20 .06
220 Russ Ortiz .20 .06
221 Deivis Santos .20 .06
222 Marvin Benard .20 .06
223 Jason Schmidt .20 .06
224 Reggie Sanders .20 .06
225 Barry Bonds 1.25 .35
226 Brad Penny .20 .06
227 Cliff Floyd .20 .06
228 Mike Lowell .20 .06
229 Derrek Lee .20 .06
230 Ryan Dempster .20 .06
231 Josh Beckett .30 .09
232 Hansel Izquierdo RC .50 .15
233 Preston Wilson .20 .06
234 A.J. Burnett .20 .06
235 Charles Johnson .20 .06
236 Mike Piazza .75 .23
237 Al Leiter .20 .06
238 Jay Payton .20 .06
239 Roger Cedeno .20 .06
240 Jeromy Burnitz .20 .06
241 Roberto Alomar .50 .15
242 Mo Vaughn .20 .06
243 Shawn Estes .20 .06
244 Armando Benitez .20 .06
245 Tyler Yates RC .75 .23
246 Phil Nevin .20 .06
247 D'Angelo Jimenez .20 .06
248 Ramon Vazquez .20 .06
249 Bubba Trammell .20 .06
250 Trevor Hoffman .20 .06
251 Ben Howard RC .50 .15
252 Mark Kotsay .20 .06
253 Ray Lankford .20 .06
254 Ryan Klesko .20 .06
255 Scott Rolen .30 .09
256 Robert Person .20 .06
257 Jimmy Rollins .20 .06
258 Pat Burrell .20 .06
259 Anderson Machado RC .50 .15
260 Randy Wolf .20 .06
261 Travis Lee .20 .06
262 Mike Lieberthal .20 .06
263 Doug Glanville .20 .06
264 Bobby Abreu .20 .06
265 Brian Giles .20 .06
266 Kris Benson .20 .06
267 Aramis Ramirez .20 .06
268 Kevin Young .20 .06
269 Jack Wilson .20 .06
270 Mike Williams .20 .06
271 Jimmy Anderson .20 .06
272 Jason Kendall .20 .06
273 Pokey Reese .20 .06
274 Rob Mackowiak .20 .06
275 Sean Casey .20 .06
276 Juan Encarnacion .20 .06
277 Austin Kearns .20 .06
278 Danny Graves .20 .06
279 Ken Griffey Jr. .75 .23
280 Barry Larkin .50 .15
281 Todd Walker .20 .06
282 Elmer Dessens .20 .06
283 Aaron Boone .20 .06
284 Adam Dunn .20 .06
285 Larry Walker .30 .09
286 Rene Reyes RC .50 .15
287 Juan Uribe .20 .06
288 Mike Hampton .20 .06
289 Todd Helton .30 .09
290 Juan Pierre .20 .06
291 Denny Neagle .20 .06
292 Jose Ortiz .20 .06
293 Todd Zeile .20 .06
294 Ben Petrick .20 .06
295 Ken Griffey Jr. CL .50 .15
296 Derek Jeter CL .60 .18
297 Sammy Sosa CL .50 .15
298 Ichiro Suzuki CL .50 .15
299 Barry Bonds CL .50 .15
300 Alex Rodriguez CL .50 .15
301 Kazuhisa Ishii RC 3.00 .90

2002 Upper Deck MVP Silver

Inserted randomly into hobby and retail packs, these cards parallel the regular MVP set and have a stated print run of 100 serial numbered sets.

Nm-Mt Ex-Mt
*SILVER STARS: 12.5X TO 30X BASIC CARDS
*SILVER ROOKIES: 6X TO 15X BASIC

2002 Upper Deck MVP Game Souvenirs Bat

Issued exclusively in hobby packs at stated odds of one in 144, these 27 cards feature bat chips from the featured players. A few players were issued to lesser quantities and we have notated that stated print run information in our checklist.

Nm-Mt Ex-Mt
B-AR Alex Rodriguez 25.00 7.50
B-BG Brian Giles 15.00 4.50
B-BW Bernie Williams 20.00 6.00
B-CD Carlos Delgado
B-DJ David Justice
B-DM Doug Mientkiewicz 15.00 4.50
B-EM Edgar Martinez 20.00 6.00
B-FT Frank Thomas SP/97
B-GM Greg Maddux
B-GS Gary Sheffield
B-GV Greg Vaughn 15.00 4.50
B-IR Ivan Rodriguez 20.00 6.00
B-JK Jeff Kent 15.00 4.50
B-JT Jim Thome 20.00 6.00
B-KG Ken Griffey Jr. 25.00 7.50
B-LG Luis Gonzalez 15.00 4.50
B-LW Larry Walker 20.00 6.00
B-MO Magglio Ordonez 15.00 4.50
B-MP Mike Piazza SP/97
B-MS Mike Sweeney
B-RA Roberto Alomar
B-RK Ryan Klesko 15.00 4.50
B-RP Rafael Palmeiro SP/97
B-SG Shawn Green 15.00 4.50
B-SR Scott Rolen
B-SS Sammy Sosa 25.00 7.50
B-TH Todd Helton

2002 Upper Deck MVP Game Souvenirs Bat Jersey Combos

Inserted exclusively in hobby packs at stated odds of one in 144, these 28 cards feature both a bat chip and a jersey swatch from the featured player. A few players were issued in smaller quantities and we have notated that information with the stated print run in our checklist.

Nm-Mt Ex-Mt
GOLD RANDOM INSERTS IN PACKS ..
GOLD PRINT RUN 25 SERIAL #'d SETS
NO GOLD PRICING DUE TO SCARCITY
C-AB Adrian Beltre 20.00 6.00
C-AR Alex Rodriguez 50.00 15.00
C-BG Brian Giles 20.00 6.00
C-BW Bernie Williams SP/97
C-CD Carlos Delgado w/Pants 20.00 6.00
C-CJ Chipper Jones 40.00 12.00
C-DE Darin Erstad 20.00 6.00
C-EA Edgardo Alfonzo 20.00 6.00
C-IR Ivan Rodriguez 40.00 12.00
C-JB Jeff Bagwell w/Pants
C-JG Jason Giambi 40.00 12.00
C-JK Jeff Kent 20.00 6.00
C-JT Jim Thome 40.00 12.00
C-KG Ken Griffey Jr. 50.00 15.00
C-LG Luis Gonzalez 20.00 6.00
C-MO Magglio Ordonez 20.00 6.00
C-MP Mike Piazza 50.00 15.00
C-OV Omar Vizquel w/Pants SP/97
C-PB Pat Burrell SP/97
C-RA Roberto Alomar w/Pants
C-RJ Randy Johnson 40.00 12.00
C-RP Rafael Palmeiro 25.00 7.50
C-RV Robin Ventura 20.00 6.00
C-SG Shawn Green 20.00 6.00
C-SR Scott Rolen 25.00 7.50
C-SS Sammy Sosa 50.00 15.00
C-TH Todd Helton 25.00 7.50
C-TZ Todd Zeile 20.00 6.00

2002 Upper Deck MVP Game Souvenirs Jersey

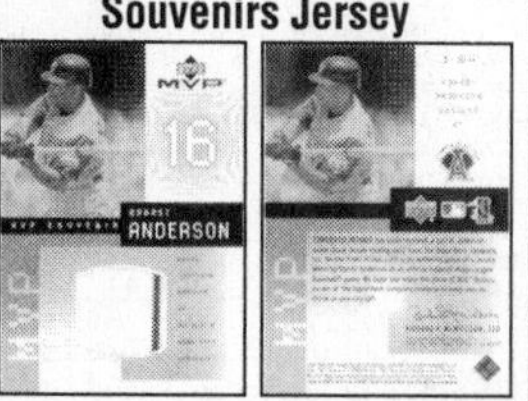

Inserted into hobby and retail packs at stated odds of one in 48, these 29 cards feature jersey swatches from the featured player. A few cards were printed in smaller quantity and we have notated those with an SP in our checklist. In addition, a few players appeared to be in larger supply and we have notated that information with an asterisk in our checklist.

Nm-Mt Ex-Mt
J-AB Adrian Beltre 10.00 3.00
J-AR Alex Rodriguez 15.00 4.50
J-CD Carlos Delgado Pants 10.00 3.00
J-DE Darin Erstad 10.00 3.00
J-EM Edgar Martinez 15.00 4.50
J-FT Frank Thomas 15.00 4.50
J-GA Garret Anderson 10.00 3.00
J-IR Ivan Rodriguez 15.00 4.50
J-JB Jeff Bagwell Pants 15.00 4.50
J-JB Jeromy Burnitz 10.00 3.00
J-JG Juan Gonzalez 15.00 4.50
J-JK Jeff Kent 10.00 3.00
J-JP Jay Payton SP 15.00 4.50
J-JT Jim Thome SP 25.00 7.50
J-KL Kenny Lofton 10.00 3.00
J-MK Mark Kotsay 10.00 3.00
J-MP Mike Piazza 15.00 4.50
J-OV Omar Vizquel Pants * 10.00 3.00
J-PK Paul Konerko SP 15.00 4.50
J-PW Preston Wilson 10.00 3.00
J-RA Roberto Alomar Pants 15.00 4.50
J-RC Roger Clemens 25.00 7.50
J-RF Rafael Furcal 10.00 3.00
J-RV Robin Ventura 10.00 3.00
J-SR Scott Rolen 15.00 4.50
J-THO Trevor Hoffman 10.00 3.00
J-THU Tim Hudson 10.00 3.00
J-TS Tim Salmon 15.00 4.50
J-TZ Todd Zeile 10.00 3.00

2002 Upper Deck MVP Ichiro A Season to Remember

Inserted in hobby and retail packs at stated odds of one in 12, these 10 cards feature highlights from Ichiro's rookie season.

Nm-Mt Ex-Mt
COMPLETE SET (10) 30.00 9.00
COMMON CARD (I1-I10) 3.00 .90

2002 Upper Deck MVP Ichiro A Season to Remember Memorabilia

Randomly inserted in hobby and retail packs, these cards feature memorabilia pieces from Ichiro's rookie season. These cards are serial numbered to 25 and no pricing is available due to market scarcity.

Nm-Mt Ex-Mt
I-B Ichiro Suzuki Bat
I-J Ichiro Suzuki Jsy

2003 Upper Deck MVP

This 220 card set was released in March, 2003. These cards were issued in eight card packs which came 24 packs to a box and 12 boxes to a case. Cards numbered 219 and 220 are checklists featuring Upper Deck spokespeople. Cards numbered 221 through 330 were issued in special factory "tin" sets.

Nm-Mt Ex-Mt
COMP.FACT.SET (330) 40.00 12.00
COMPLETE LO SET (220) 25.00 7.50
COMMON CARD (1-220) .20 .06
1 Troy Glaus .30 .09
2 Darin Erstad .20 .06
3 Jarrod Washburn .20 .06
4 Francisco Rodriguez .20 .06
5 Garret Anderson .20 .06
6 Tim Salmon .30 .09
7 Adam Kennedy .20 .06
8 Randy Johnson .50 .15
9 Luis Gonzalez .20 .06
10 Curt Schilling .30 .09
11 Junior Spivey .20 .06
12 Craig Counsell .20 .06
13 Mark Grace .30 .09
14 Steve Finley .20 .06
15 Javy Lopez .20 .06
16 Rafael Furcal .20 .06
17 John Smoltz .30 .09
18 Greg Maddux .75 .23
19 Chipper Jones .50 .15
20 Gary Sheffield .20 .06
21 Andruw Jones .20 .06
22 Tony Batista .20 .06
23 Geronimo Gil .20 .06
24 Jay Gibbons .20 .06
25 Rodrigo Lopez .20 .06
26 Chris Singleton .20 .06
27 Melvin Mora .20 .06
28 Jeff Conine .20 .06
29 Nomar Garciaparra .75 .23
30 Pedro Martinez .50 .15
31 Manny Ramirez .20 .06
32 Shea Hillenbrand .20 .06
33 Johnny Damon .20 .06
34 Jason Varitek .20 .06
35 Derek Lowe .20 .06
36 Trot Nixon .30 .09
37 Sammy Sosa .75 .23
38 Kerry Wood .50 .15
39 Mark Prior 1.00 .30
40 Moises Alou .20 .06
41 Corey Patterson .20 .06
42 Hee Seop Choi .20 .06
43 Mark Bellhorn .20 .06
44 Frank Thomas .50 .15
45 Mark Buehrle .20 .06
46 Magglio Ordonez .20 .06
47 Carlos Lee .20 .06
48 Paul Konerko .20 .06
49 Joe Borchard .20 .06
50 Joe Crede .20 .06
51 Ken Griffey Jr. .75 .23
52 Adam Dunn .20 .06
53 Austin Kearns .20 .06
54 Aaron Boone .20 .06
55 Sean Casey .20 .06
56 Danny Graves .20 .06
57 Russell Branyan .20 .06
58 Matt Lawton .20 .06
59 C.C. Sabathia .20 .06
60 Omar Vizquel .20 .06
61 Brandon Phillips .20 .06
62 Karim Garcia .20 .06
63 Ellis Burks .20 .06
64 Cliff Lee .20 .06
65 Todd Helton .30 .09
66 Larry Walker .30 .09
67 Jay Payton .20 .06
68 Brent Butler .20 .06
69 Juan Uribe .20 .06
70 Jason Jennings .20 .06
71 Denny Stark .20 .06
72 Dmitri Young .20 .06
73 Carlos Pena .20 .06
74 Andres Torres .20 .06
75 Andy Van Hekken .20 .06
76 George Lombard .20 .06
77 Eric Munson .20 .06
78 Bobby Higginson .20 .06
79 Luis Castillo .20 .06
80 A.J. Burnett .20 .06
81 Juan Encarnacion .20 .06
82 Ivan Rodriguez .50 .15
83 Mike Lowell .20 .06
84 Josh Beckett .30 .09
85 Brad Penny .20 .06
86 Craig Biggio .30 .09
87 Jeff Kent .20 .06
88 Morgan Ensberg .20 .06
89 Daryle Ward .20 .06
90 Jeff Bagwell .30 .09
91 Roy Oswalt .20 .06
92 Lance Berkman .20 .06
93 Mike Sweeney .20 .06
94 Carlos Beltran .20 .06
95 Raul Ibanez .20 .06
96 Carlos Febles .20 .06
97 Joe Randa .20 .06
98 Shawn Green .20 .06
99 Kevin Brown .20 .06
100 Paul Lo Duca .20 .06
101 Adrian Beltre .20 .06
102 Eric Gagne .30 .09
103 Kazuhisa Ishii .20 .06
104 Odalis Perez .20 .06
105 Brian Jordan .20 .06
106 Geoff Jenkins .20 .06
107 Richie Sexson .20 .06
108 Ben Sheets .20 .06
109 Alex Sanchez .20 .06
110 Eric Young .20 .06
111 Jose Hernandez .20 .06
112 Torii Hunter .20 .06
113 Eric Milton .20 .06
114 Corey Koskie .20 .06
115 Doug Mientkiewicz .20 .06
116 A.J. Pierzynski .20 .06
117 Jacque Jones .20 .06
118 Cristian Guzman .20 .06
119 Bartolo Colon .20 .06
120 Brad Wilkerson .20 .06
121 Michael Barrett .20 .06
122 Vladimir Guerrero .50 .15
123 Jose Vidro .20 .06
124 Javier Vazquez .20 .06
125 Endy Chavez .20 .06
126 Roberto Alomar .50 .15
127 Mike Piazza .75 .23
128 Jeromy Burnitz .20 .06
129 Mo Vaughn .20 .06
130 Tom Glavine .30 .09
131 Al Leiter .20 .06
132 Armando Benitez .20 .06
133 Timo Perez .20 .06
134 Roger Clemens 1.00 .30
135 Derek Jeter 1.25 .35
136 Jason Giambi .50 .15
137 Alfonso Soriano .30 .09
138 Bernie Williams .30 .09
139 Mike Mussina .50 .15
140 Jorge Posada .30 .09
141 Hideki Matsui RC 5.00 1.50
142 Robin Ventura .20 .06
143 David Wells .20 .06
144 Nick Johnson .20 .06
145 Tim Hudson .20 .06
146 Eric Chavez .20 .06
147 Barry Zito .30 .09
148 Miguel Tejada .20 .06
149 Jermaine Dye .20 .06
150 Mark Mulder .20 .06
151 Terrence Long .20 .06
152 Scott Hatteberg .20 .06
153 Marlon Byrd .20 .06
154 Jim Thome .50 .15
155 Marlon Anderson .20 .06
156 Vicente Padilla .20 .06
157 Bobby Abreu .20 .06
158 Jimmy Rollins .20 .06
159 Pat Burrell .20 .06
160 Brian Giles .20 .06
161 Aramis Ramirez .20 .06
162 Jason Kendall .20 .06
163 Josh Fogg .20 .06
164 Kip Wells .20 .06
165 Pokey Reese .20 .06
166 Kris Benson .20 .06
167 Ryan Klesko .20 .06
168 Brian Lawrence .20 .06
169 Mark Kotsay .20 .06
170 Jake Peavy .20 .06
171 Phil Nevin .20 .06
172 Sean Burroughs .20 .06
173 Trevor Hoffman .20 .06
174 Jason Schmidt .20 .06
175 Kirk Rueter .20 .06
176 Barry Bonds 1.25 .35
177 Pedro Feliz .20 .06
178 Rich Aurilia .20 .06
179 Benito Santiago .20 .06
180 J.T. Snow .20 .06
181 Robb Nen .20 .06
182 Ichiro Suzuki .75 .23
183 Edgar Martinez .30 .09
184 Bret Boone .20 .06
185 Freddy Garcia .20 .06
186 John Olerud .20 .06
187 Mike Cameron .20 .06
188 Joel Piniero .20 .06
189 Albert Pujols 1.00 .30
190 Matt Morris .20 .06
191 J.D. Drew .20 .06
192 Scott Rolen .30 .09
193 Tino Martinez .30 .09
194 Jim Edmonds .20 .06
195 Edgar Renteria .20 .06
196 Fernando Vina .20 .06
197 Jason Isringhausen .20 .06
198 Ben Grieve .20 .06
199 Carl Crawford .20 .06
200 Dewon Brazelton .20 .06
201 Aubrey Huff .20 .06
202 Jared Sandberg .20 .06
203 Steve Cox .20 .06
204 Carl Everett .20 .06
205 Kevin Mench .20 .06
206 Alex Rodriguez .75 .23
207 Rafael Palmeiro .30 .09
208 Michael Young .20 .06
209 Hank Blalock .30 .09
210 Juan Gonzalez .50 .15
211 Carlos Delgado .20 .06
212 Eric Hinske .20 .06
213 Josh Phelps .20 .06
214 Mark Hendrickson .20 .06
215 Roy Halladay .20 .06
216 Orlando Hudson .20 .06
217 Shannon Stewart .20 .06
218 Vernon Wells .20 .06
219 Ichiro Suzuki CL .50 .15
220 Jason Giambi CL .30 .09
221 Scott Spiezio .20 .06
222 Rich Fischer RC .40 .12
223 Bengie Molina .20 .06
224 David Eckstein .20 .06
225 Brandon Webb RC 2.00 .60
226 Oscar Villarreal RC .40 .12
227 Rob Hammock RC .50 .15
228 Matt Kata RC .75 .23
229 Lyle Overbay .20 .06
230 Chris Capuano RC .40 .12
231 Horacio Ramirez .20 .06
232 Shane Reynolds .20 .06
233 Russ Ortiz .20 .06
234 Mike Hampton .20 .06
235 Mike Hessman RC .40 .12
236 Byung-Hyun Kim .20 .06
237 Freddy Sanchez .20 .06
238 Jason Shiell RC .40 .12
239 Ryan Cameron RC .40 .12
240 Todd Wellemeyer RC .50 .15
241 Joe Borowski .20 .06
242 Alex Gonzalez .20 .06
243 Jon Leicester RC .40 .12
244 David Sanders RC .40 .12
245 Roberto Alomar .50 .15
246 Barry Larkin .50 .15
247 Jhonny Peralta RC .40 .12
248 Zach Sorensen .20 .06
249 Jason Davis .20 .06
250 Coco Crisp .20 .06
251 Greg Vaughn .20 .06
252 Preston Wilson .20 .06
253 Denny Neagle .20 .06
254 Clint Barmes RC .50 .15
255 Jeremy Bonderman RC 1.00 .30
256 Wilfredo Ledezma RC .40 .12
257 Dontrelle Willis .50 .15
258 Alex Gonzalez .20 .06
259 Tommy Phelps .20 .06
260 Kirk Saarloos .20 .06
261 Colin Porter RC .40 .12
262 Nate Bland RC .40 .12
263 Jason Gilfillan RC .40 .12
264 Mike MacDougal .20 .06
265 Ken Harvey .20 .06
266 Brent Mayne .20 .06
267 Miguel Cabrera .75 .23
268 Hideo Nomo .50 .15
269 Dave Roberts .20 .06
270 Fred McGriff .30 .09
271 Joe Thurston .20 .06
272 Royce Clayton .20 .06
273 Michael Nakamura RC .40 .12
274 Brad Radke .20 .06
275 Joe Mays .20 .06
276 Lew Ford RC .50 .15
277 Michael Cuddyer .20 .06
278 Luis Ayala RC .40 .12
279 Julio Manon RC .25 .07
280 Anthony Ferrari RC .40 .12
281 Livan Hernandez .20 .06
282 Jae Weong Seo .20 .06
283 Jose Reyes .30 .09
284 Tony Clark .20 .06
285 Ty Wigginton .20 .06
286 Cliff Floyd .20 .06
287 Jeremy Griffiths RC .50 .15
288 Jason Roach RC .40 .12
289 Jeff Duncan RC .50 .15
290 Phil Seibel RC .40 .12
291 Prentice Redman RC .40 .12
292 Jose Contreras RC 1.50 .45
293 Ruben Sierra .20 .06
294 Andy Pettitte .30 .09
295 Aaron Boone .20 .06
296 Mariano Rivera .30 .09
297 Michel Hernandez RC .40 .12
298 Mike Neu RC .40 .12
299 Erubiel Durazo .20 .06
300 Billy McMillon .20 .06
301 Rich Harden .30 .09
302 David Bell .20 .06
303 Kevin Millwood .20 .06
304 Mike Lieberthal .20 .06
305 Jeremy Wedel RC .40 .12
306 Kenny Lofton .20 .06
307 Reggie Sanders .20 .06
308 Randall Simon .20 .06
309 Xavier Nady .20 .06
310 Rod Beck .20 .06
311 Miguel Ojeda RC .40 .12
312 Mark Loretta .20 .06
313 Edgardo Alfonzo .20 .06
314 Andres Galarraga .20 .06
315 Jose Cruz Jr. .20 .06
316 Jesse Foppert .20 .06
317 Kurt Ainsworth .20 .06
318 Dan Wilson .20 .06
319 Ben Davis .20 .06

320 Rocco Baldelli .75 .23
321 Al Martin .20 .06
322 Runelvys Hernandez .20 .06
323 Dan Haren RC 1.00 .30
324 Bo Hart RC 1.50 .45
325 Einar Diaz .20 .06
326 Mike Lamb .20 .06
327 Aquilino Lopez RC .40 .12
328 Reed Johnson .20 .06
329 Diegomar Markwell RC .40 .12
330 Hideki Matsui CL 2.00 .60

2003 Upper Deck MVP Black

Randomly inserted in packs, this is a parallel to the Upper Deck MVP low number set. These cards were issued to a stated print run of 50 serial numbered sets.

Nm-Mt Ex-Mt
*BLACK: 15X TO 40X BASIC

2003 Upper Deck MVP Gold

Randomly inserted in packs, this is a parallel to the MVP low number set. These cards were issued to a stated print run of 125 serial numbered sets.

Nm-Mt Ex-Mt
*GOLD: 10X TO 25X BASIC
*GOLD RC'S: 2.5X TO 6X BASIC

2003 Upper Deck MVP Silver

These cards, which parallel the MVP low number set, were actually inserted at a stated rate of one in 12. This is different from the stated wrapper odds which said these cards were inserted at a rate of one in two.

Nm-Mt Ex-Mt
*SILVER: 3X TO 8X BASIC
*SILVER RC'S: .75X TO 2X BASIC

2003 Upper Deck MVP Base-to-Base

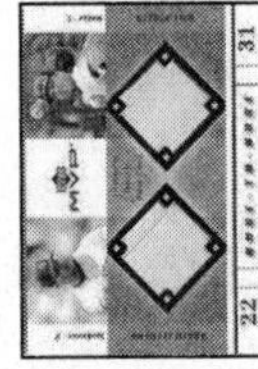

Issued at a stated rate of one in 488, these six cards feature two players as well as bases used in one of their games.

Nm-Mt Ex-Mt
CP Roger Clemens 25.00 7.50
Mike Piazza
IG Ichiro Suzuki 40.00 12.00
Ken Griffey Jr.
IJ Ichiro Suzuki 50.00 15.00
Derek Jeter
JW Derek Jeter 25.00 7.50
Bernie Williams
MB Mark McGwire 60.00 18.00
Barry Bonds
RJ Alex Rodriguez 40.00 12.00
Derek Jeter

2003 Upper Deck MVP Celebration

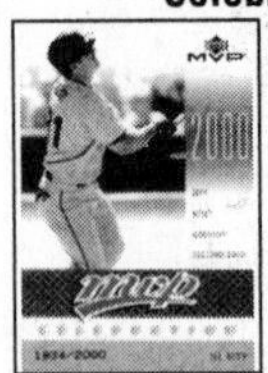

Randomly inserted into packs, these 90 cards honor various players leading achievements in baseball. Each of these cards were issued to a stated print run of between 1955 and 2002 cards and we have notated the print run information next to the player's name in our checklist.

Nm-Mt Ex-Mt
*GOLD: 1.25X TO 3X BASIC
GOLD PRINT RUN 75 SERIAL #'d SETS
1 Yogi Berra MVP/1955 4.00 1.20
2 Mickey Mantle MVP/1956 15.00 4.50
3 Mickey Mantle MVP/1957 15.00 4.50
4 Mickey Mantle MVP/1962 15.00 4.50
5 Roger Clemens MVP/1986 8.00 2.40
6 Rickey Henderson MVP/1990 4.00 1.20
7 Frank Thomas MVP/1993 4.00 1.20
8 Mo Vaughn MVP/1995 3.00 .90
9 Juan Gonzalez MVP/1996 4.00 1.20
10 Ken Griffey Jr. MVP/1997 6.00 1.80
11 Juan Gonzalez MVP/1998 4.00 1.20
12 Ivan Rodriguez MVP/1998 4.00 1.20
13 Jason Giambi MVP/2000 4.00 1.20
14 Ichiro Suzuki MVP/2001 6.00 1.80
15 Miguel Tejada MVP/2002 3.00 .90
16 Barry Bonds MVP/1990 10.00 3.00
17 Barry Bonds MVP/1992 10.00 3.00
18 Barry Bonds MVP/1993 10.00 3.00
19 Jeff Bagwell MVP/1994 3.00 .90
20 Barry Larkin MVP/1995 4.00 1.20
21 Larry Walker MVP/1997 3.00 .90
22 Sammy Sosa MVP/1998 6.00 1.80
23 Chipper Jones MVP/1999 4.00 1.20
24 Jeff Kent MVP/2000 3.00 .90
25 Barry Bonds MVP/2001 10.00 3.00
26 Barry Bonds MVP/2002 10.00 3.00
27 Ken Griffey Sr. AS/1980 3.00 .90
28 Roger Clemens AS/1986 8.00 2.40
29 Ken Griffey Jr. AS/1992 6.00 1.80
30 Fred McGriff AS/1994 3.00 .90
31 Jeff Conine AS/1995 3.00 .90
32 Mike Piazza AS/1996 6.00 1.80
33 Sandy Alomar Jr. AS/1997 3.00 .90
34 Roberto Alomar AS/1998 4.00 1.20
35 Pedro Martinez AS/1999 4.00 1.20
36 Derek Jeter AS/2000 10.00 3.00
37 Rickey Henderson ALCS/1989 4.00 1.20
38 Roberto Alomar ALCS/1992 4.00 1.20
39 Bernie Williams ALCS/1996 3.00 .90
40 Marquis Grissom ALCS/1997 3.00 .90
41 David Wells ALCS/1998 3.00 .90
42 Orlando Hernandez ALCS/1999 3.00 .90
43 David Justice ALCS/2000 3.00 .90
44 Andy Pettitte ALCS/2001 3.00 .90
45 Adam Kennedy ALCS/2002 3.00 .90
46 John Smoltz NLCS/1992 3.00 .90
47 Curt Schilling NLCS/1993 3.00 .90
48 Javy Lopez NLCS/1996 3.00 .90
49 Livan Hernandez NLCS/1997 3.00 .90
50 Sterling Hitchcock NLCS/1998 3.00 .90
51 Mike Hampton NLCS/2000 3.00 .90
52 Craig Counsell NLCS/2001 3.00 .90
53 Benito Santiago NLCS/2002 3.00 .90
54 Tom Glavine WS/1995 3.00 .90
55 Livan Hernandez WS/1997 3.00 .90
56 Mariano Rivera WS/1999 3.00 .90
57 Derek Jeter WS/2000 10.00 3.00
58 Randy Johnson WS/2001 4.00 1.20
59 Curt Schilling WS/2001 3.00 .90
60 Troy Glaus WS/2002 3.00 .90
61 Yogi Berra MM/1951 4.00 1.20
62 Yogi Berra MM/1955 4.00 1.20
63 Mickey Mantle MM/1956 15.00 4.50
64 Mickey Mantle MM/1957 15.00 4.50
65 Ken Griffey Sr. MM/1980 3.00 .90
66 Rickey Henderson MM/1989 4.00 1.20
67 Roberto Alomar MM/1992 4.00 1.20
68 Bernie Williams MM/1996 3.00 .90
69 Livan Hernandez MM/1997 3.00 .90
70 Sammy Sosa MM/1998 6.00 1.80
71 Sterling Hitchcock MM/1998 3.00 .90
72 David Wells MM/1998 3.00 .90
73 Mariano Rivera MM/1999 3.00 .90
74 Chipper Jones MM/1999 4.00 1.20
75 Ivan Rodriguez MM/1999 4.00 1.20
76 Derek Jeter MM/2000 10.00 3.00
77 Jason Giambi MM/2000 4.00 1.20
78 Jeff Kent MM/2000 3.00 .90
79 Mike Hampton MM/2000 3.00 .90
80 Randy Johnson MM/2001 4.00 1.20
81 Curt Schilling MM/2001 3.00 .90
82 Barry Bonds MM/2001 10.00 3.00
83 Ichiro Suzuki MM/2001 6.00 1.80
84 Ichiro Suzuki MM/2001 6.00 1.80
85 Adam Kennedy MM/2002 3.00 .90
86 Benito Santiago MM/2002 3.00 .90
87 Troy Glaus MM/2002 3.00 .90
88 Troy Glaus MM/2002 3.00 .90
89 Miguel Tejada MM/2002 3.00 .90
90 Barry Bonds MM/2002 10.00 3.00

2003 Upper Deck MVP Covering the Bases

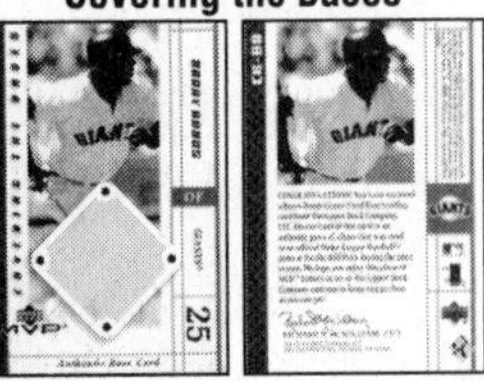

Issued at a stated rate of one in 125, these 15 cards feature game-used bases from the featured player's career.

Nm-Mt Ex-Mt
AR Alex Rodriguez 15.00 4.50
BB Barry Bonds 20.00 6.00
CD Carlos Delgado 8.00 2.40
DE Darin Erstad 8.00 2.40
DJ Derek Jeter 20.00 6.00
FT Frank Thomas 10.00 3.00
IR Ivan Rodriguez 10.00 3.00
IS Ichiro Suzuki 20.00 6.00
JD J.D. Drew 8.00 2.40
JT Jim Thome 10.00 3.00
LG Luis Gonzalez 8.00 2.40
MP Mike Piazza 15.00 4.50
MT Miguel Tejada 8.00 2.40
SG Shawn Green 8.00 2.40
TG Troy Glaus 10.00 3.00

2003 Upper Deck MVP Covering the Plate Game Bat

Issued at a stated rate of one in 160, these six cards feature game-used bat pieces from the featured player.

Nm-Mt Ex-Mt
FM Fred McGriff 15.00 4.50
JT Jim Thome 15.00 4.50
MG Mark McGwire 60.00 18.00
RA Roberto Alomar 15.00 4.50
RF Rafael Furcal 10.00 3.00
VG Vladimir Guerrero 15.00 4.50

2003 Upper Deck MVP Dual Aces Game Base

Issued at a stated rate of one in 488, these six cards feature bases used in games featuring two key pitchers.

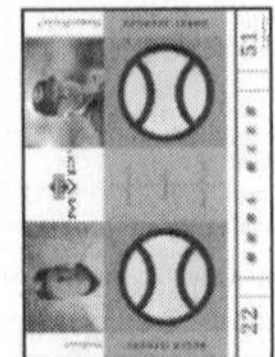

Nm-Mt Ex-Mt
BS Kevin Brown 10.00 3.00
Curt Schilling
CJ Roger Clemens 20.00 6.00
Randy Johnson
CL Roger Clemens 15.00 4.50
Al Leiter
ML Matt Morris 10.00 3.00
Al Leiter
SJ Curt Schilling 10.00 3.00
Randy Johnson
SP Curt Schilling 10.00 3.00
Andy Pettitte

2003 Upper Deck MVP Express Delivery

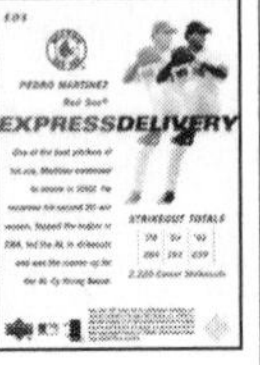

Inserted at a stated rate of one in 12, these 15 cards feature players who are among the leading pitchers in baseball.

Nm-Mt Ex-Mt
ED1 Randy Johnson 2.00 .60
ED2 Curt Schilling 1.50 .45
ED3 Pedro Martinez 2.00 .60
ED4 Kerry Wood 2.00 .60
ED5 Mark Prior 4.00 1.20
ED6 A.J. Burnett 1.50 .45
ED7 Josh Beckett 1.50 .45
ED8 Roy Oswalt 1.50 .45
ED9 Hideo Nomo 2.00 .60
ED10 Ben Sheets 1.50 .45
ED11 Bartolo Colon 1.50 .45
ED12 Roger Clemens 4.00 1.20
ED13 Mike Mussina 2.00 .60
ED14 Tim Hudson 1.50 .45
ED15 Matt Morris 1.50 .45

2003 Upper Deck MVP Pro Sign

Randomly inserted in packs, these 23 cards feature authentic autographs from the featured players. Each of these cards are printed to a stated print run of 25 serial numbered sets and no pricing is provided due to market scarcity.

Nm-Mt Ex-Mt
AD Adam Dunn
AK Austin Kearns
BG Brian Giles
BZ Barry Zito
CD Carlos Delgado
DH Drew Henson
DM Doug Mientkiewicz
FG Freddy Garcia
GI Jay Gibbons
HB Hank Blalock
IS Ichiro Suzuki
JD Johnny Damon
JG Jason Giambi
KG Ken Griffey Jr.
LB Lance Berkman
MM Mark McGwire
MP Mark Prior
MS Mike Sweeney
RS Richie Sexson
SB Sean Burroughs
SS Sammy Sosa
TG Tony Gwynn
TH Tim Hudson

2003 Upper Deck MVP Pro View

Issued as a two-card box topper pack, these 45 cards are a special hologram set.

Nm-Mt Ex-Mt
*GOLD: .75X TO 2X BASIC PRO VIEW
ONE 2-CARD PACK PER 6 SEALED BOXES
PV1 Troy Glaus 3.00 .90
PV2 Darin Erstad 3.00 .90
PV3 Randy Johnson 4.00 1.20
PV4 Curt Schilling 3.00 .90
PV5 Luis Gonzalez 3.00 .90
PV6 Chipper Jones 4.00 1.20
PV7 Andruw Jones 3.00 .90
PV8 Greg Maddux 6.00 1.80
PV9 Pedro Martinez 4.00 1.20
PV10 Manny Ramirez 3.00 .90
PV11 Sammy Sosa 6.00 1.80
PV12 Mark Prior 8.00 2.40
PV13 Magglio Ordonez 3.00 .90
PV14 Frank Thomas 4.00 1.20
PV15 Ken Griffey Jr. 6.00 1.80
PV16 Adam Dunn 3.00 .90
PV17 Jim Thome 4.00 1.20
PV18 Todd Helton 3.00 .90
PV19 Jeff Bagwell 3.00 .90
PV20 Lance Berkman 3.00 .90
PV21 Shawn Green 3.00 .90
PV22 Hideo Nomo 4.00 1.20
PV23 Vladimir Guerrero 4.00 1.20
PV24 Roberto Alomar 4.00 1.20
PV25 Mike Piazza 6.00 1.80
PV26 Jason Giambi 4.00 1.20
PV27 Roger Clemens 8.00 2.40
PV28 Alfonso Soriano 3.00 .90
PV29 Derek Jeter 10.00 3.00
PV30 Miguel Tejada 3.00 .90
PV31 Eric Chavez 3.00 .90
PV32 Barry Zito 3.00 .90
PV33 Pat Burrell 3.00 .90
PV34 Brian Giles 3.00 .90
PV35 Barry Bonds 10.00 3.00
PV36 Ichiro Suzuki 6.00 1.80
PV37 Albert Pujols 8.00 2.40
PV38 Scott Rolen 3.00 .90
PV39 J.D. Drew 3.00 .90
PV40 Mark McGwire 10.00 3.00
PV41 Alex Rodriguez 6.00 1.80
PV42 Rafael Palmeiro 3.00 .90
PV43 Juan Gonzalez 4.00 1.20
PV44 Eric Hinske 3.00 .90
PV45 Carlos Delgado 3.00 .90

2003 Upper Deck MVP SportsNut

Inserted at a stated rate of one in three, this 90 card insert set could be used as interactive game cards. The contest could be entered on either a season or a weekly basis.

Nm-Mt Ex-Mt
SN1 Troy Glaus 1.50 .45
SN2 Darin Erstad 1.00 .30
SN3 Luis Gonzalez 1.00 .30
SN4 Andruw Jones 1.00 .30
SN5 Chipper Jones 2.50 .75
SN6 Gary Sheffield 1.00 .30
SN7 Jay Gibbons 1.00 .30
SN8 Manny Ramirez 1.00 .30
SN9 Shea Hillenbrand 1.00 .30
SN10 Johnny Damon 1.00 .30
SN11 Nomar Garciaparra 4.00 1.20
SN12 Sammy Sosa 4.00 1.20
SN13 Magglio Ordonez 1.00 .30
SN14 Frank Thomas 2.50 .75
SN15 Ken Griffey Jr. 4.00 1.20
SN16 Adam Dunn 1.00 .30
SN17 Matt Lawton 1.00 .30
SN18 Larry Walker 1.50 .45
SN19 Todd Helton 1.50 .45
SN20 Carlos Pena 1.00 .30
SN21 Mike Lowell 1.00 .30
SN22 Jeff Bagwell 1.50 .45
SN23 Lance Berkman 1.00 .30
SN24 Mike Sweeney 1.00 .30
SN25 Carlos Beltran 1.00 .30
SN26 Shawn Green 1.00 .30
SN27 Richie Sexson 1.00 .30
SN28 Torii Hunter 1.00 .30
SN29 Jacque Jones 1.00 .30
SN30 Vladimir Guerrero 2.50 .75
SN31 Jose Vidro 1.00 .30
SN32 Roberto Alomar 2.50 .75
SN33 Mike Piazza 4.00 1.20
SN34 Alfonso Soriano 1.50 .45
SN35 Derek Jeter 6.00 1.80
SN36 Jason Giambi 2.50 .75
SN37 Bernie Williams 1.50 .45
SN38 Eric Chavez 1.00 .30
SN39 Miguel Tejada 1.00 .30
SN40 Jim Thome 2.50 .75
SN41 Pat Burrell 1.00 .30
SN42 Bobby Abreu 1.00 .30
SN43 Brian Giles 1.00 .30
SN44 Jason Kendall 1.00 .30
SN45 Ryan Klesko 1.00 .30
SN46 Phil Nevin 1.00 .30
SN47 Barry Bonds 6.00 1.80
SN48 Rich Aurilia 1.00 .30
SN49 Ichiro Suzuki 4.00 1.20
SN50 Bret Boone 1.00 .30
SN51 J.D. Drew 1.00 .30
SN52 Jim Edmonds 1.00 .30
SN53 Albert Pujols 5.00 1.50
SN54 Scott Rolen 1.50 .45
SN55 Ben Grieve 1.00 .30
SN56 Alex Rodriguez 4.00 1.20
SN57 Rafael Palmeiro 1.50 .45
SN58 Juan Gonzalez 2.50 .75
SN59 Carlos Delgado 1.00 .30
SN60 Josh Phelps 1.00 .30
SN61 Jarrod Washburn 1.00 .30
SN62 Randy Johnson 2.50 .75
SN63 Curt Schilling 1.50 .45
SN64 Greg Maddux 4.00 1.20
SN65 Mike Hampton 1.00 .30
SN66 Rodrigo Lopez 1.00 .30
SN67 Pedro Martinez 2.50 .75
SN68 Derek Lowe 1.00 .30
SN69 Mark Prior 5.00 1.50
SN70 Kerry Wood 2.50 .75
SN71 Mark Buehrle 1.00 .30
SN72 Roy Oswalt 1.00 .30
SN73 Wade Miller 1.00 .30
SN74 Odalis Perez 1.00 .30
SN75 Hideo Nomo 2.50 .75
SN76 Ben Sheets 1.00 .30
SN77 Eric Milton 1.00 .30
SN78 Bartolo Colon 1.00 .30
SN79 Tom Glavine 1.50 .45
SN80 Al Leiter 1.00 .30
SN81 Roger Clemens 5.00 1.50
SN82 Mike Mussina 2.50 .75
SN83 Tim Hudson 1.00 .30
SN84 Barry Zito 1.50 .45
SN85 Mark Mulder 1.00 .30
SN86 Vicente Padilla 1.00 .30
SN87 Jason Schmidt 1.00 .30
SN88 Freddy Garcia 1.00 .30
SN89 Matt Morris 1.00 .30
SN90 Roy Halladay 1.00 .30

2003 Upper Deck MVP Talk of the Town

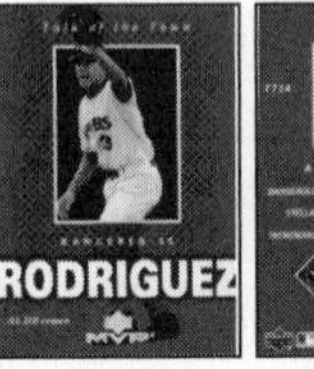

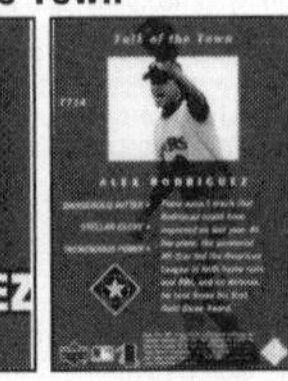

Inserted at a stated rate of one in 12, this 15 card set features some of the most talked about players in baseball.

Nm-Mt Ex-Mt
TT1 Hideki Matsui 6.00 1.80
TT2 Chipper Jones 2.00 .60
TT3 Manny Ramirez 1.50 .45
TT4 Sammy Sosa 3.00 .90
TT5 Ken Griffey Jr. 3.00 .90
TT6 Lance Berkman 1.50 .45
TT7 Shawn Green 1.50 .45
TT8 Vladimir Guerrero 2.00 .60
TT9 Mike Piazza 3.00 .90
TT10 Jason Giambi 2.00 .60
TT11 Alfonso Soriano 1.50 .45
TT12 Ichiro Suzuki 3.00 .90
TT13 Albert Pujols 4.00 1.20
TT14 Alex Rodriguez 3.00 .90
TT15 Eric Hinske 1.50 .45

2003 Upper Deck MVP Three Bagger Game Base

Inserted at a stated rate of one in 488, this six-card set features base pieces involving three players on each card.

Nm-Mt Ex-Mt
BMP Barry Bonds 100.00 30.00
Mark McGwire
Mike Piazza
GIB Ken Griffey Jr. 80.00 24.00
Ichiro Suzuki
Barry Bonds
GTD Troy Glaus 15.00 4.50
Frank Thomas
Carlos Delgado
IBJ Ichiro Suzuki 100.00 30.00
Barry Bonds
Derek Jeter
JWP Derek Jeter 40.00 12.00
Bernie Williams
Jorge Posada
SCB Curt Schilling 25.00 7.50
Roger Clemens
Kevin Brown

2003 Upper Deck MVP Total Bases

Randomly inserted into packs, this is an insert set featuring one base piece on each card. Each card was issued to a stated print run of 150 serial numbered sets.

Nm-Mt Ex-Mt
AR Alex Rodriguez 25.00 7.50
BB Barry Bonds 40.00 12.00
DJ Derek Jeter 40.00 12.00
IS Ichiro Suzuki 40.00 12.00
KG Ken Griffey Jr. 25.00 7.50
MM Mark McGwire 50.00 15.00
MP Mike Piazza 25.00 7.50
RC Roger Clemens 25.00 7.50
TG Troy Glaus 15.00 4.50

1999 Upper Deck Ovation

This 90-card set was distributed in five-card packs with a suggested retail price of $3.99. The cards feature action color player images printed on game-ball stock for the look and feel of an actual baseball. The set contains the following subsets: World Premiere (61-80) with an insertion rate of one in every 3.5 packs, and Superstar Spotlight (81-90) inserted at a rate of one in six packs. In addition, 350 Mickey Mantle A Piece of History 500 Home Run bat cards were randomly seeded into packs. Pricing for these scarce bat cards can be referenced under 1999 Upper Deck A Piece of History 500 Club. Finally, one special Mantle card was created by Upper Deck featuring both a chip of wood from a game used Mantle bat plus an authentic Mantle signature cut. Entitled "Legendary Cuts", only one of these cards was produced and it was randomly inserted into an Ovation pack.

	Nm-Mt	Ex-Mt
COMPLETE SET (90)	80.00	24.00
COMP.SET w/o SP's (60)	25.00	7.50
COMMON CARD (1-60)	.40	.12
COMMON WP (61-80)	2.00	.60
COMMON SS (81-90)	2.50	.75
1 Ken Griffey Jr.	1.50	.45
2 Rondell White	.40	.12
3 Tony Clark	.40	.12
4 Barry Bonds	2.50	.75
5 Larry Walker	.60	.18
6 Greg Vaughn	.40	.12
7 Mark Grace	.60	.18
8 John Olerud	.40	.12
9 Matt Williams	.40	.12
10 Craig Biggio	.60	.18
11 Quinton McCracken	.40	.12
12 Kerry Wood	1.00	.30
13 Derek Jeter	2.50	.75
14 Frank Thomas	1.00	.30
15 Tino Martinez	.60	.18
16 Albert Belle	.40	.12
17 Ben Grieve	.40	.12
18 Cal Ripken	3.00	.90
19 Johnny Damon	.40	.12
20 Jose Cruz Jr.	.40	.12
21 Barry Larkin	1.00	.30
22 Jason Giambi	1.00	.30
23 Sean Casey	.40	.12
24 Scott Rolen	.60	.18
25 Jim Thome	1.00	.30
26 Curt Schilling	.60	.18
27 Moises Alou	.40	.12
28 Alex Rodriguez	1.50	.45
29 Mark Kotsay	.40	.12
30 Darin Erstad	.40	.12
31 Mike Mussina	1.00	.30
32 Todd Walker	.40	.12
33 Nomar Garciaparra	1.50	.45
34 Vladimir Guerrero	1.00	.30
35 Jeff Bagwell	.60	.18
36 Mark McGwire	2.50	.75
37 Travis Lee	.40	.12
38 Dean Palmer	.40	.12
39 Fred McGriff	.60	.18
40 Sammy Sosa	1.50	.45
41 Mike Piazza	1.50	.45
42 Andres Galarraga	.40	.12
43 Pedro Martinez	1.00	.30
44 Juan Gonzalez	1.00	.30
45 Greg Maddux	1.50	.45
46 Jeromy Burnitz	.40	.12
47 Roger Clemens	2.00	.60
48 Vinny Castilla	.40	.12
49 Kevin Brown	.60	.18
50 Mo Vaughn	.40	.12
51 Raul Mondesi	.40	.12
52 Randy Johnson	1.00	.30
53 Ray Lankford	.40	.12
54 Jaret Wright	.40	.12
55 Tony Gwynn	1.25	.35
56 Chipper Jones	1.00	.30
57 Gary Sheffield	.40	.12
58 Ivan Rodriguez	1.00	.30
59 Kenny Lofton	.40	.12
60 Jason Kendall	.40	.12
61 J.D. Drew WP	2.00	.60
62 Gabe Kapler WP	2.00	.60
63 Adrian Beltre WP	2.00	.60
64 Carlos Beltran WP	2.00	.60
65 Eric Chavez WP	2.00	.60
66 Mike Lowell WP	2.00	.60
67 Troy Glaus WP	2.50	.75
68 George Lombard WP	2.00	.60
69 Alex Gonzalez WP	2.00	.60
70 Mike Kinkade WP	2.00	.60
71 Jeremy Giambi WP	2.00	.60
72 Bruce Chen WP	2.00	.60
73 Preston Wilson WP	2.00	.60
74 Kevin Witt WP	2.00	.60
75 Carlos Guillen WP	2.00	.60
76 Ryan Minor WP	2.00	.60
77 Corey Koskie WP	2.00	.60
78 Robert Fick WP	2.50	.75
79 Michael Barrett WP	2.00	.60
80 Calvin Pickering WP	2.00	.60
81 Ken Griffey Jr. SS	4.00	1.20
82 Mark McGwire SS	6.00	1.80
83 Cal Ripken SS	8.00	2.40
84 Derek Jeter SS	6.00	1.80
85 Chipper Jones SS	2.50	.75
86 Nomar Garciaparra SS	4.00	1.20
87 Sammy Sosa SS	4.00	1.20
88 Juan Gonzalez SS	2.50	.75
89 Mike Piazza SS	4.00	1.20
90 Alex Rodriguez SS	4.00	1.20
MICL M.Mantle Legendary Cut/1		

1999 Upper Deck Ovation Standing Ovation

Radomly inserted into packs, this 90-card set is a parallel version of the base set. Each card is sequentially numbered to 500.

Nm-Mt Ex-Mt

*STARS 1-60: 5X TO 12X BASIC 1-60
*WP CARDS 61-80: 1X TO 2.5X BASIC WP
*SS CARDS 81-90: 2X TO 5X BASIC SS

1999 Upper Deck Ovation A Piece of History

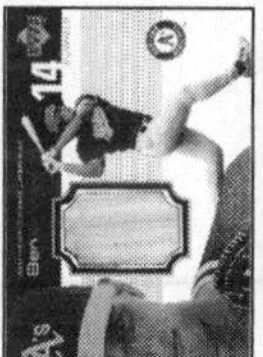

Randomly inserted in packs at the rate of one in 247, this set features pieces of actual game-used bats of some of MLB's biggest stars embedded in the cards. Only 25 Ben Grieve and Kerry Wood autographed cards were produced. The signed Grieve card contains a game-used bat chip. The signed Wood card contains a piece of a game-used baseball.

	Nm-Mt	Ex-Mt
AR Alex Rodriguez	40.00	12.00
BB Barry Bonds	50.00	15.00
BG Ben Grieve	10.00	3.00
BW Bernie Williams	25.00	7.50
CJ Chipper Jones	25.00	7.50
CR Cal Ripken	60.00	18.00
DJ Derek Jeter	50.00	15.00
JG Juan Gonzalez	25.00	7.50
MP Mike Piazza	40.00	12.00
NG Nomar Garciaparra	40.00	12.00
SS Sammy Sosa	40.00	12.00
TG Tony Gwynn	25.00	7.50
VG Vladimir Guerrero	25.00	7.50
KGJ Ken Griffey Jr.	40.00	12.00
BGAU B. Grieve Bat AU/25		
KWAU K.Wood Ball AU/25		

1999 Upper Deck Ovation Curtain Calls

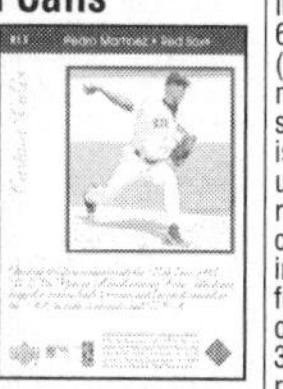

Randomly inserted in packs at the rate of one in eight, this 20-card set features color action photos of the pictured player's most memorable accomplishment during the 1998 season.

	Nm-Mt	Ex-Mt
COMPLETE SET (20)	80.00	24.00
R1 Mark McGwire	8.00	2.40
R2 Sammy Sosa	5.00	1.50
R3 Ken Griffey Jr.	5.00	1.50
R4 Alex Rodriguez	5.00	1.50
R5 Roger Clemens	6.00	1.80
R6 Cal Ripken	10.00	3.00
R7 Barry Bonds	8.00	2.40
R8 Kerry Wood	3.00	.90
R9 Nomar Garciaparra	5.00	1.50
R10 Derek Jeter	8.00	2.40
R11 Juan Gonzalez	3.00	.90
R12 Greg Maddux	5.00	1.50
R13 Pedro Martinez	3.00	.90
R14 David Wells	1.25	.35
R15 Moises Alou	1.25	.35
R16 Tony Gwynn	4.00	1.20
R17 Albert Belle	1.25	.35
R18 Mike Piazza	5.00	1.50
R19 Ivan Rodriguez	3.00	.90
R20 Randy Johnson	3.00	.90

1999 Upper Deck Ovation Major Production

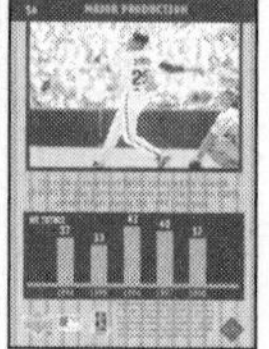

Randomly inserted in packs at the rate of one in 45, this 20-card set features color action photos of some of the game's most productive players printed using Thermography technology to simulate the look and feel of home plate.

	Nm-Mt	Ex-Mt
COMPLETE SET (20)	400.00	120.00
S1 Mike Piazza	20.00	6.00
S2 Mark McGwire	30.00	9.00
S3 Chipper Jones	12.00	3.60
S4 Cal Ripken	40.00	12.00
S5 Ken Griffey Jr.	20.00	6.00
S6 Barry Bonds	30.00	9.00
S7 Tony Gwynn	15.00	4.50
S8 Randy Johnson	12.00	3.60
S9 Ivan Rodriguez	12.00	3.60
S10 Frank Thomas	12.00	3.60
S11 Alex Rodriguez	20.00	6.00
S12 Albert Belle	5.00	1.50
S13 Juan Gonzalez	12.00	3.60
S14 Greg Maddux	20.00	6.00
S15 Jeff Bagwell	8.00	2.40
S16 Derek Jeter	30.00	9.00
S17 Matt Williams	5.00	1.50
S18 Kenny Lofton	5.00	1.50
S19 Sammy Sosa	20.00	6.00
S20 Roger Clemens	25.00	7.50

1999 Upper Deck Ovation ReMarkable Moments

This 15-card three-tiered insert set showcases Mark McGwire's dominant play during the 1998 home run race. Cards 1-5 feature bronze foil highlights with an insertion rate of 1:9. Cards 6-10 display silver foil highlights with an insertion rate of 1:25. Cards 11-15 are gold-foiled with a 1:99 insertion rate.

	Nm-Mt	Ex-Mt
COMMON CARD (1-5)	5.00	1.50
COMMON CARD (6-10)	10.00	3.00
COMMON CARD (11-15)	20.00	6.00

2000 Upper Deck Ovation

The 2000 Upper Deck Ovation set was released in March, 2000 as an 89-card set that featured 60 player cards, 19 World Premiere cards (1:3), and 10 Superstar cards (1:6). Card number 70 does exist, however, it is in very short supply. The featured player on that card is Ryan Anderson, who was not available for usage in the set as he was not on the 40 man roster at the time this set was printed. No copies of card number 70 are believed to exist in the Ovation parallel set. Each pack contained five cards and carried a suggested retail price of 3.99. Also, a selection of A Piece of History 3000 Club Willie Mays memorabilia cards were randomly seeded into packs. 300 bat cards, 350 jersey cards, 50 hand-numbered combination bat-jersey cards and twenty-four autographed, hand-numbered, combination bat-jersey cards were produced. Pricing for these memorabilia cards can be referenced under 2000 Upper Deck A Piece of History 3000 Club.

	Nm-Mt	Ex-Mt
COMPLETE SET (89)	80.00	24.00
COMP.SET w/o SP's (60)	20.00	6.00
COMMON CARD (1-60)	.40	.12
COMMON WP (61-80)	2.00	.60
COMMON SS (81-90)	3.00	.90
1 Mo Vaughn	.40	.12
2 Troy Glaus	.60	.18
3 Jeff Bagwell	.60	.18
4 Craig Biggio	.60	.18
5 Mike Hampton	.40	.12
6 Jason Giambi	1.00	.30
7 Tim Hudson	.60	.18
8 Chipper Jones	1.00	.30
9 Greg Maddux	1.50	.45
10 Kevin Millwood	.40	.12
11 Brian Jordan	.40	.12
12 Jeromy Burnitz	.40	.12
13 David Wells	.40	.12
14 Carlos Delgado	.40	.12
15 Sammy Sosa	1.50	.45
16 Mark McGwire	2.50	.75
17 Matt Williams	.40	.12
18 Randy Johnson	1.00	.30
19 Erubiel Durazo	.40	.12
20 Kevin Brown	.60	.18
21 Shawn Green	.40	.12
22 Gary Sheffield	.40	.12
23 Jose Canseco	1.00	.30
24 Vladimir Guerrero	1.00	.30
25 Barry Bonds	2.50	.75
26 Manny Ramirez	.40	.12
27 Roberto Alomar	1.00	.30
28 Richie Sexson	.40	.12
29 Jim Thome	1.00	.30
30 Alex Rodriguez	1.50	.45
31 Ken Griffey Jr.	1.50	.45
32 Preston Wilson	.40	.12
33 Mike Piazza	1.50	.45
34 Al Leiter	.40	.12
35 Robin Ventura	.60	.18
36 Cal Ripken	3.00	.90
37 Albert Belle	.40	.12
38 Tony Gwynn	1.25	.35
39 Brian Giles	.40	.12
40 Jason Kendall	.40	.12
41 Scott Rolen	.60	.18
42 Bob Abreu	.40	.12
43 Ken Griffey Jr. Reds	1.50	.45
44 Sean Casey	.40	.12
45 Carlos Beltran	.40	.12
46 Gabe Kapler	.40	.12
47 Ivan Rodriguez	1.00	.30
48 Rafael Palmeiro	.60	.18
49 Larry Walker	.60	.18
50 Nomar Garciaparra	1.50	.45
51 Pedro Martinez	1.00	.30
52 Eric Milton	.40	.12
53 Juan Gonzalez	1.00	.30
54 Tony Clark	.40	.12
55 Frank Thomas	1.00	.30
56 Magglio Ordonez	.40	.12
57 Roger Clemens	2.00	.60
58 Derek Jeter	2.50	.75
59 Bernie Williams	.60	.18
60 Orlando Hernandez	.40	.12
61 Rick Ankiel WP	2.00	.60
62 Josh Beckett WP	6.00	1.80
63 Vernon Wells WP	2.50	.75
64 Alfonso Soriano WP	5.00	1.50
65 Pat Burrell WP	3.00	.90
66 Eric Munson WP	2.00	.60
67 Chad Hutchinson WP	2.00	.60
68 Eric Gagne WP	5.00	1.50
69 Peter Bergeron WP	2.00	.60
70 Ryan Anderson WP SP	200.00	60.00
71 A.J. Burnett WP	2.00	.60
72 Jorge Toca WP	2.00	.60
73 Matt Riley WP	2.00	.60
74 Chad Hermansen WP	2.00	.60
75 Doug Davis WP	2.00	.60
76 Jim Morris WP	5.00	1.50
77 Ben Petrick WP	2.00	.60
78 Mark Quinn WP	2.00	.60
79 Ed Yarnall WP	2.00	.60
80 Ramon Ortiz WP	2.00	.60
81 Ken Griffey Jr. SS	5.00	1.50
82 Mark McGwire SS	8.00	2.40
83 Derek Jeter SS	8.00	2.40
84 Jeff Bagwell SS	3.00	.90
85 Nomar Garciaparra SS	5.00	1.50
86 Sammy Sosa SS	5.00	1.50
87 Mike Piazza SS	5.00	1.50
88 Alex Rodriguez SS	5.00	1.50
89 Cal Ripken SS	10.00	3.00
90 Pedro Martinez SS	3.00	.90

2000 Upper Deck Ovation Standing Ovation

Randomly inserted into packs, this 90-card set parallels the Upper Deck Ovation base set. Cards are serial numbered to 50.

Nm-Mt Ex-Mt

*STARS: 10X TO 25X BASIC CARDS ..
*WORLD PREM: 1.5X TO 4X BASIC WP
*SPOTLIGHT: 3X TO 8X BASIC SS .....

2000 Upper Deck Ovation A Piece of History

Randomly inserted into packs, this 16-card set features 12 player cards containing pieces of game-used bats. Production of 400 copies of each card was publicly announced by Upper Deck but the cards are not serial-numbered. Alex Rodriguez, Cal Ripken, Derek Jeter, and Ken Griffey Jr. have additional cards that contain both pieces of game-used bats and their autographs.

	Nm-Mt	Ex-Mt
AR Alex Rodriguez	40.00	12.00
CJ Chipper Jones	20.00	6.00
CR Cal Ripken	50.00	15.00
DJ Derek Jeter	50.00	15.00
IR Ivan Rodriguez	20.00	6.00
JC Jose Canseco	20.00	6.00
KG Ken Griffey Jr.	40.00	12.00
MR Manny Ramirez	15.00	4.50
PB Pat Burrell	15.00	4.50
SR Scott Rolen	15.00	4.50
TG Tony Gwynn	25.00	7.50
VG Vladimir Guerrero	20.00	6.00
ARA Alex Rodriguez AU/3		
CRA Cal Ripken AU/8		
DJA Derek Jeter AU/2		
KGA Ken Griffey Jr. AU/24		

2000 Upper Deck Ovation Center Stage Silver

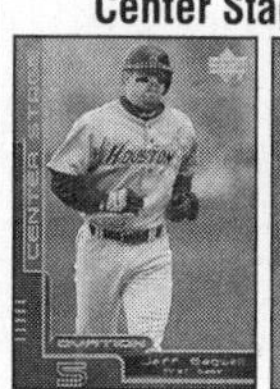

Randomly inserted in packs at one in nine, this insert set features ten players that are ready to take center stage on any given day. Card backs carry a "CS" prefix.

	Nm-Mt	Ex-Mt
COMPLETE SET (10)	60.00	18.00
*GOLD: .75X TO 2X CENTER SILVER .		
GOLD STATED ODDS 1:39		
*RAINBOW: 1.5X TO 4X CENTER SILVER		
RAINBOW STATED ODDS 1:99		
CS1 Jeff Bagwell	2.00	.60
CS2 Ken Griffey Jr.	5.00	1.50
CS3 Nomar Garciaparra	5.00	1.50
CS4 Mike Piazza	5.00	1.50
CS5 Mark McGwire	8.00	2.40
CS6 Alex Rodriguez	5.00	1.50
CS7 Cal Ripken	10.00	3.00
CS8 Derek Jeter	8.00	2.40
CS9 Chipper Jones	3.00	.90
CS10 Sammy Sosa	5.00	1.50

2000 Upper Deck Ovation Curtain Calls

Randomly inserted into packs at one in three, this insert features 20 major leaguers who deserve a standing ovation for their 1999 peformances. Card backs carry a "CC" prefix.

	Nm-Mt	Ex-Mt
COMPLETE SET (20)	40.00	12.00
CC1 David Cone	.75	.23
CC2 Mark McGwire	5.00	1.50
CC3 Sammy Sosa	3.00	.90
CC4 Eric Milton	.75	.23
CC5 Bernie Williams	1.25	.35
CC6 Tony Gwynn	2.50	.75
CC7 Nomar Garciaparra	3.00	.90
CC8 Manny Ramirez	.75	.23
CC9 Wade Boggs	2.00	.60
CC10 Randy Johnson	2.00	.60
CC11 Cal Ripken	6.00	1.80
CC12 Pedro Martinez	2.00	.60
CC13 Alex Rodriguez	3.00	.90
CC14 Fernando Tatis	.75	.23
CC15 Vladimir Guerrero	2.00	.60
CC16 Robin Ventura	1.25	.35
CC17 Larry Walker	1.25	.35
CC18 Carlos Beltran	.75	.23
CC19 Jose Canseco	2.00	.60
CC20 Ken Griffey Jr.	3.00	.90

2000 Upper Deck Ovation Diamond Futures

Randomly inserted in packs at one in six, this insert features 10 of the league's top players who are on the verge of greatness. Card backs carry a "DM" prefix.

	Nm-Mt	Ex-Mt
COMPLETE SET (10)	15.00	4.50
DM1 J.D. Drew	1.00	.30
DM2 Alfonso Soriano	2.00	.60
DM3 Preston Wilson	1.00	.30
DM4 Erubiel Durazo	1.00	.30
DM5 Rick Ankiel	1.00	.30
DM6 Octavio Dotel	1.00	.30
DM7 A.J. Burnett	1.00	.30
DM8 Carlos Beltran	1.00	.30
DM9 Vernon Wells	1.00	.30
DM10 Troy Glaus	1.25	.35

2000 Upper Deck Ovation Lead Performers

Randomly inserted in packs at one in 19, this insert set features 10 players that lead by example. Card backs carry a "LP" prefix.

	Nm-Mt	Ex-Mt
COMPLETE SET (10)	60.00	18.00
LP1 Mark McGwire	10.00	3.00
LP2 Derek Jeter	10.00	3.00
LP3 Vladimir Guerrero	4.00	1.20
LP4 Mike Piazza	6.00	1.80
LP5 Cal Ripken	12.00	3.60
LP6 Sammy Sosa	6.00	1.80
LP7 Jeff Bagwell	2.50	.75
LP8 Nomar Garciaparra	6.00	1.80
LP9 Chipper Jones	4.00	1.20
LP10 Ken Griffey Jr.	6.00	1.80

2000 Upper Deck Ovation Super Signatures

Randomly inserted into packs, this insert set features autographed cards of Ken Griffey Jr. and Mike Piazza. Each player has a silver, gold and rainbow version. Piazza did not return his cards in time for the product to ship, thus UD seeded exchange cards into their packs for all Piazza autographs. These exchange cards had a large, square white sticker with text explaining redemption guidelines placed on the card front. All Piazza exchange cards had to be mailed in prior to the December 9th, 2000 deadline.

	Nm-Mt	Ex-Mt
SSKGG Ken Griffey Jr. Gold/50	200.00	60.00
SSKGR Ken Griffey Jr. Rainbow/10		
SSKGS Ken Griffey Jr. Silver/100	150.00	45.00
SSMPG Mike Piazza Gold 50 EX	350.00	105.00
SSMPR Mike Piazza Rainbow/10 EX		
SSMPS Mike Piazza Silver/100 EX	300.00	90.00

2000 Upper Deck Ovation Superstar Theatre

Randomly inserted in packs at one in 19, this insert set features 20 players that have a flair for the dramatic. Card backs carry a "ST" prefix.

	Nm-Mt	Ex-Mt
COMPLETE SET (20)	120.00	36.00
ST1 Ivan Rodriguez	6.00	1.80
ST2 Brian Giles	2.50	.75
ST3 Bernie Williams	4.00	1.20
ST4 Greg Maddux	10.00	3.00
ST5 Frank Thomas	6.00	1.80
ST6 Sean Casey	2.50	.75
ST7 Mo Vaughn	2.50	.75
ST8 Carlos Delgado	2.50	.75
ST9 Tony Gwynn	8.00	2.40
ST10 Pedro Martinez	6.00	1.80
ST11 Scott Rolen	4.00	1.20
ST12 Mark McGwire	15.00	4.50
ST13 Manny Ramirez	2.50	.75
ST14 Rafael Palmeiro	4.00	1.20
ST15 Jose Canseco	6.00	1.80
ST16 Randy Johnson	6.00	1.80
ST17 Gary Sheffield	2.50	.75
ST18 Larry Walker	4.00	1.20
ST19 Barry Bonds	15.00	4.50
ST20 Roger Clemens	12.00	3.60

2001 Upper Deck Ovation

The 2001 Upper Deck Ovation product was released in early March 2001, and features a 90-card base set that was broken into tiers as follows: Base Veterans (1-60), and World Premiere Prospects (61-90) that were individually serial numbered to 2000. Each pack contained five cards and carried a suggested retail price of $2.99.

	Nm-Mt	Ex-Mt
COMP.SET w/o SP'S (60)	20.00	6.00
COMMON CARD (1-60)	.40	.12
COMMON WP (61-90)	5.00	1.50
1 Troy Glaus	.60	.18
2 Darin Erstad	.40	.12
3 Jason Giambi	1.00	.30
4 Tim Hudson	.40	.12
5 Eric Chavez	.40	.12
6 Carlos Delgado	.40	.12
7 David Wells	.40	.12
8 Greg Vaughn	.40	.12
9 Omar Vizquel Travis Fryman is pictured on card front UER	.40	.12
10 Jim Thome	1.00	.30
11 Roberto Alomar	1.00	.30
12 John Olerud	.40	.12
13 Edgar Martinez	.60	.18
14 Cal Ripken	3.00	.90
15 Alex Rodriguez	1.50	.45
16 Ivan Rodriguez	1.00	.30
17 Manny Ramirez	.40	.12
18 Nomar Garciaparra	1.50	.45
19 Pedro Martinez	1.00	.30
20 Jermaine Dye	.40	.12
21 Juan Gonzalez	1.00	.30
22 Matt Lawton	.40	.12
23 Frank Thomas	1.00	.30
24 Magglio Ordonez	.40	.12
25 Bernie Williams	.60	.18
26 Derek Jeter	2.50	.75
27 Roger Clemens	2.00	.60
28 Jeff Bagwell	.60	.18
29 Richard Hidalgo	.40	.12
30 Chipper Jones	1.00	.30
31 Greg Maddux	1.50	.45
32 Andruw Jones	.40	.12
33 Jeromy Burnitz	.40	.12
34 Mark McGwire	2.50	.75
35 Jim Edmonds	.40	.12
36 Sammy Sosa	1.50	.45
37 Kerry Wood	1.00	.30
38 Randy Johnson	1.00	.30
39 Steve Finley	.40	.12
40 Gary Sheffield	.40	.12
41 Kevin Brown	.40	.12
42 Shawn Green	.40	.12
43 Vladimir Guerrero	1.00	.30
44 Jose Vidro	.40	.12
45 Barry Bonds	2.50	.75
46 Jeff Kent	.40	.12
47 Preston Wilson	.40	.12
48 Luis Castillo	.40	.12
49 Mike Piazza	1.50	.45
50 Edgardo Alfonzo	.40	.12
51 Tony Gwynn	1.25	.35
52 Ryan Klesko	.40	.12
53 Scott Rolen	.60	.18
54 Bob Abreu	.40	.12
55 Jason Kendall	.40	.12
56 Brian Giles	.40	.12
57 Ken Griffey Jr.	1.50	.45
58 Barry Larkin	1.00	.30
59 Todd Helton	.60	.18
60 Mike Hampton	.40	.12
61 Corey Patterson WP	5.00	1.50
62 Timo Perez WP	5.00	1.50
63 Toby Hall WP	5.00	1.50
64 Brandon Inge WP	5.00	1.50
65 Joe Crede WP	5.00	1.50
66 Xavier Nady WP	5.00	1.50
67 A. Pettyjohn WP RC	5.00	1.50
68 Keith Ginter WP	5.00	1.50
69 Brian Cole WP	5.00	1.50
70 Tyler Walker WP RC	5.00	1.50
71 Juan Uribe WP RC	5.00	1.50
72 Alex Hernandez WP	5.00	1.50
73 Leo Estrella WP	5.00	1.50
74 Joey Nation WP	5.00	1.50
75 Aubrey Huff WP	5.00	1.50
76 Ichiro Suzuki WP RC	80.00	24.00
77 Jay Spurgeon WP	5.00	1.50
78 Sun Woo Kim WP	5.00	1.50
79 Pedro Feliz WP	5.00	1.50
80 Pablo Ozuna WP	5.00	1.50
81 Hiram Bocachica WP	5.00	1.50
82 Brad Wilkerson WP	5.00	1.50
83 Rocky Biddle WP	5.00	1.50
84 Aaron McNeal WP	5.00	1.50
85 Adam Bernero WP	5.00	1.50
86 Danys Baez WP	5.00	1.50
87 Dee Brown WP	5.00	1.50
88 Jimmy Rollins WP	5.00	1.50
89 Jason Hart WP	5.00	1.50
90 Ross Gload WP	5.00	1.50

2001 Upper Deck Ovation A Piece of History

Randomly inserted into packs at one in 40, this 40-card insert features slivers of actual game-used bats from Major League stars like Barry Bonds and Alex Rodriguez. Card backs carry the player's initials as numbering.

	Nm-Mt	Ex-Mt
COMMON RETIRED	15.00	4.50
AJ Andruw Jones	10.00	3.00
AR Alex Rodriguez	20.00	6.00
BB Barry Bonds	30.00	9.00
BR Brooks Robinson	25.00	7.50
BW Bernie Williams	15.00	4.50
CD Carlos Delgado	10.00	3.00
CF Carlton Fisk	25.00	7.50
CJ Chipper Jones	15.00	4.50
CR Cal Ripken	40.00	12.00
DC David Cone	10.00	3.00
DD Don Drysdale	15.00	4.50
DE Darin Erstad	10.00	3.00
EW Early Wynn	15.00	4.50
FT Frank Thomas	15.00	4.50
GM Greg Maddux	15.00	4.50
GS Gary Sheffield	10.00	3.00
IR Ivan Rodriguez	15.00	4.50
JB Johnny Bench	25.00	7.50
JC Jose Canseco	15.00	4.50
JD Joe DiMaggio	100.00	30.00
JE Jim Edmonds	10.00	3.00
JP Jim Palmer	15.00	4.50
KG Ken Griffey Jr.	20.00	6.00
KGS Ken Griffey Sr.	10.00	3.00
KKB Kevin Brown	10.00	3.00
MH Mike Hampton	10.00	3.00
MM Mickey Mantle	150.00	45.00
MW Matt Williams	10.00	3.00
NR Nolan Ryan SP	100.00	30.00
OS Ozzie Smith	25.00	7.50
RA Rick Ankiel	10.00	3.00
RC Roger Clemens	20.00	6.00
RF Rollie Fingers	15.00	4.50
RF Rafael Furcal	10.00	3.00
RJ Randy Johnson	15.00	4.50
SG Shawn Green	10.00	3.00
SS Sammy Sosa	20.00	6.00
TG Tom Glavine	15.00	4.50
TRG Troy Glaus	15.00	4.50
TS Tom Seaver	25.00	7.50

2001 Upper Deck Ovation A Piece of History Autographs

Randomly inserted into packs, this 7-card insert features slivers of actual game-used bats and authentic autographs from some of the Major League's top stars. Card backs carry a "S" prefix followed by the player's initials. Please note that the print runs are listed below.

	Nm-Mt	Ex-Mt
S-AR Alex Rodriguez/3		
S-BB Barry Bonds/25		
S-CD Carlos Delgado/25		
S-CJ Chipper Jones/10		
S-FT Frank Thomas/35		
S-IR Ivan Rodriguez/7		
S-KG Ken Griffey Jr./30	400.00	120.00

2001 Upper Deck Ovation A Piece of History Combos

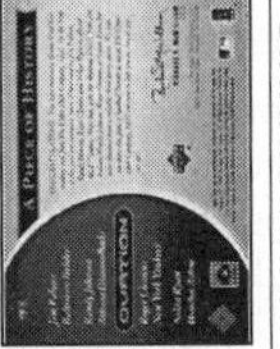

Randomly inserted into packs, this five-card insert set features a combination of slivers from actual game-used bats of historic Major League players. Card backs carry the player's initials as numbering. Please note that their were only 25 serial numbered sets produced. Due to market scarcity, no pricing is provided.

	Nm-Mt	Ex-Mt
GBTC Ken Griffey Jr. / Barry Bonds / Frank Thomas / Jose Canseco		
MDCW Mickey Mantle / Joe DiMaggio / Roger Clemens / Bernie Williams		
MGJC Greg Maddux / Tom Glavine / Randy Johnson / Roger Clemens		
PFBP Mike Piazza / Carlton Fisk / Johnny Bench / Ivan Rodriguez		
PJCR Jim Palmer / Randy Johnson / Roger Clemens / Nolan Ryan		

2001 Upper Deck Ovation Curtain Calls

Randomly inserted into packs at one in seven, this 10-card insert set features players that deserve a round of applause after the numbers they put up last year. Card backs carry a "CC" prefix.

	Nm-Mt	Ex-Mt
COMPLETE SET (10)	20.00	6.00
CC1 Sammy Sosa	3.00	.90
CC2 Darin Erstad	1.25	.35
CC3 Barry Bonds	5.00	1.50
CC4 Todd Helton	1.25	.35
CC5 Mike Piazza	3.00	.90
CC6 Ken Griffey Jr.	3.00	.90
CC7 Nomar Garciaparra	3.00	.90
CC8 Carlos Delgado	1.25	.35
CC9 Jason Giambi	2.00	.60
CC10 Alex Rodriguez	3.00	.90

2001 Upper Deck Ovation Lead Performers

Randomly inserted into packs at one in 12, this 11-card insert set features players that were among the league leaders in many of the offensive categories. Card backs carry a "LP" prefix.

	Nm-Mt	Ex-Mt
COMPLETE SET (11)	30.00	9.00
LP1 Mark McGwire	6.00	1.80
LP2 Derek Jeter	6.00	1.80
LP3 Alex Rodriguez	4.00	1.20
LP4 Frank Thomas	2.50	.75
LP5 Sammy Sosa	4.00	1.20
LP6 Mike Piazza	4.00	1.20
LP7 Vladimir Guerrero	2.50	.75
LP8 Pedro Martinez	2.50	.75
LP9 Carlos Delgado	1.50	.45
LP10 Ken Griffey Jr.	4.00	1.20
LP11 Jeff Bagwell	1.50	.45

2001 Upper Deck Ovation Superstar Theatre

Randomly inserted into packs at one in 12, this 11-card insert set features players that put on a "show" everytime they take the field. Card backs carry a "ST" prefix.

	Nm-Mt	Ex-Mt
COMPLETE SET (11)	30.00	9.00
ST1 Nomar Garciaparra	4.00	1.20
ST2 Ken Griffey Jr.	4.00	1.20
ST3 Frank Thomas	2.50	.75
ST4 Derek Jeter	6.00	1.80
ST5 Mike Piazza	4.00	1.20
ST6 Sammy Sosa	4.00	1.20
ST7 Barry Bonds	6.00	1.80
ST8 Alex Rodriguez	4.00	1.20
ST9 Todd Helton	2.50	.75
ST10 Mark McGwire	6.00	1.80
ST11 Jason Giambi	2.50	.75

2002 Upper Deck Ovation

This 180 card set was issued in two separate brands. The basic Ovation product, containing cards 1-120, was released in June, 2002. These cards were issued in five-card packs with a suggested retail price of $3 per pack of which were issued 24 to a box and 20 boxes to a case. These cards feature veteran stars from cards 1-60, rookie stars from 61-89 (of which have a stated print run of 2002 serial numbered copies) and then five cards each of the six Upper Deck spokesmen from 90-119. The first series set concludes with a card with a stated print run of 2002 serial numbered sets featuring the six Upper Deck spokemen. Cards 121-180 were distributed within retail-only packs of Upper Deck Rookie Debut in mid-December 2002. Cards 121-150 were seeded at an approximate rate of one per pack and feature traded players and young prospects. Cards 151-180 continue the World Premiere rookie subset with each card being serial-numbered to 2002 copies. Though the manufacturer did not release odds on these market research indicates an approximate seeding ratio of 1:8 packs.

	Nm-Mt	Ex-Mt
COMP.LOW w/o SP's (90)	25.00	7.50
COMP.UPDATE w/o SP's (30)	15.00	4.50
COMMON CARD (1-60)	.40	.12
COMMON (61-89/120/151-180)	8.00	2.40
COMMON CARD (90-119)	.50	.15
COMMON CARD (121-150)	.60	.18
1 Troy Glaus	.60	.18
2 David Justice	.40	.12
3 Tim Hudson	.40	.12
4 Jermaine Dye	.40	.12
5 Carlos Delgado	.40	.12
6 Greg Vaughn	.40	.12
7 Jim Thome	1.00	.30
8 C.C. Sabathia	.40	.12
9 Ichiro Suzuki	1.50	.45
10 Edgar Martinez	.60	.18
11 Chris Richard	.40	.12
12 Rafael Palmeiro	.60	.18
13 Alex Rodriguez	1.50	.45
14 Ivan Rodriguez	1.00	.30
15 Nomar Garciaparra	1.50	.45
16 Manny Ramirez	.40	.12
17 Pedro Martinez	1.00	.30
18 Mike Sweeney	.40	.12
19 Dmitri Young	.40	.12
20 Doug Mientkiewicz	.40	.12
21 Brad Radke	.40	.12
22 Cristian Guzman	.40	.12
23 Frank Thomas	1.00	.30
24 Magglio Ordonez	.40	.12
25 Bernie Williams	.60	.18
26 Derek Jeter	2.50	.75
27 Jason Giambi	1.00	.30
28 Roger Clemens	2.00	.60
29 Jeff Bagwell	.60	.18
30 Lance Berkman	.40	.12
31 Chipper Jones	1.00	.30
32 Gary Sheffield	.40	.12
33 Greg Maddux	1.50	.45
34 Richie Sexson	.40	.12
35 Albert Pujols	2.00	.60
36 Tino Martinez	.60	.18
37 J.D. Drew	.40	.12
38 Sammy Sosa	1.50	.45
39 Moises Alou	.40	.12
40 Randy Johnson	1.00	.30
41 Luis Gonzalez	.40	.12
42 Shawn Green	.40	.12
43 Kevin Brown	.40	.12
44 Vladimir Guerrero	1.00	.30
45 Barry Bonds	2.50	.75
46 Jeff Kent	.40	.12
47 Cliff Floyd	.40	.12
48 Josh Beckett	.60	.18
49 Mike Piazza	1.50	.45
50 Mo Vaughn	.40	.12
51 Jeromy Burnitz	.40	.12
52 Roberto Alomar	1.00	.30
53 Phil Nevin	.40	.12
54 Scott Rolen	.60	.18
55 Jimmy Rollins	.40	.12
56 Brian Giles	.40	.12
57 Ken Griffey Jr.	1.50	.45
58 Sean Casey	.40	.12
59 Larry Walker	.60	.18
60 Todd Helton	.60	.18
61 Rodrigo Rosario WP RC	8.00	2.40
62 Reed Johnson WP RC	10.00	3.00
63 John Ennis WP RC	8.00	2.40
64 Luis Martinez WP RC	8.00	2.40
65 So Taguchi WP RC	10.00	3.00
66 Brandon Backe WP RC	8.00	2.40
67 Doug Devore WP RC	8.00	2.40
68 Victor Alvarez WP RC	8.00	2.40
69 Kazuhisa Ishii WP RC	12.00	3.60
70 Eric Good WP RC	8.00	2.40
71 Deivis Santos WP	8.00	2.40
72 Matt Thornton WP RC	8.00	2.40
73 Hansel Izquierdo WP RC	8.00	2.40
74 Tyler Yates WP RC	10.00	3.00
75 Jaime Cerda WP RC	8.00	2.40
76 Satoru Komiyama WP RC	8.00	2.40
77 Steve Bechler WP RC	8.00	2.40
78 Ben Howard WP RC	8.00	2.40
79 Jorge Padilla WP RC	8.00	2.40
80 Eric Junge WP RC	8.00	2.40
81 And. Machado WP RC	8.00	2.40
82 Adrian Burnside WP RC	8.00	2.40
83 Josh Hancock WP RC	8.00	2.40
84 Anastacio Martinez WP RC	8.00	2.40
85 Rene Reyes WP RC	8.00	2.40
86 Nate Field WP RC	8.00	2.40
87 Tim Kalita WP RC	8.00	2.40
88 Kevin Frederick WP RC	8.00	2.40
89 Edwin Almonte WP RC	8.00	2.40
90 Ichiro Suzuki SS	.75	.23
91 Ichiro Suzuki SS	.75	.23
92 Ichiro Suzuki SS	.75	.23
93 Ichiro Suzuki SS	.75	.23
94 Ichiro Suzuki SS	.75	.23
95 Ken Griffey Jr. SS	.75	.23
96 Ken Griffey Jr. SS	.75	.23
97 Ken Griffey Jr. SS	.75	.23
98 Ken Griffey Jr. SS	.75	.23
99 Ken Griffey Jr. SS	.75	.23
100 Jason Giambi A's SS	.50	.15
101 Jason Giambi A's SS	.50	.15
102 Jason Giambi A's SS	.50	.15
103 J.Giambi Yankees SS	.50	.15
104 J.Giambi Yankees SS	.60	.18
105 Sammy Sosa SS	.75	.23
106 Sammy Sosa SS	.75	.23
107 Sammy Sosa SS	.75	.23
108 Sammy Sosa SS	.75	.23
109 Sammy Sosa SS	.75	.23
110 Alex Rodriguez SS	.75	.23
111 Alex Rodriguez SS	.75	.23
112 Alex Rodriguez SS	.75	.23
113 Alex Rodriguez SS	.75	.23
114 Alex Rodriguez SS	.75	.23
115 Mark McGwire SS	1.25	.35
116 Mark McGwire SS	1.25	.35
117 Mark McGwire SS	1.25	.35
118 Mark McGwire SS	1.25	.35
119 Mark McGwire SS	1.25	.35
120 Jason Giambi / Ken Griffey Jr. / Mark McGwire / Alex Rodriguez / Sammy Sosa / Ichiro Suzuki SP/2002	20.00	6.00
121 Curt Schilling	1.00	.30
122 Cliff Floyd	.60	.18
123 Derek Lowe	.60	.18
124 Hee Seop Choi	1.00	.30
125 Mark Prior	3.00	.90
126 Joe Borchard	.60	.18
127 Austin Kearns	.60	.18
128 Adam Dunn	.60	.18
129 Jay Payton	.60	.18
130 Carlos Pena	.60	.18
131 Andy Van Hekken	.60	.18
132 Andres Torres	.60	.18
133 Ben Diggins	.60	.18
134 Torii Hunter	.60	.18
135 Bartolo Colon	.60	.18
136 Raul Mondesi	.60	.18
137 Alfonso Soriano	1.00	.30
138 Miguel Tejada	.60	.18
139 Ray Durham	.60	.18
140 Eric Chavez	.60	.18
141 Marlon Byrd	.60	.18
142 Brett Myers	.60	.18
143 Sean Burroughs	.60	.18
144 Kenny Lofton	.60	.18
145 Scott Rolen	1.00	.30
146 Carl Crawford	.60	.18
147 Jayson Werth	.60	.18
148 Josh Phelps	.60	.18
149 Eric Hinske	.60	.18
150 Orlando Hudson	.60	.18
151 Jose Valverde WP RC	10.00	3.00
152 Trey Hodges WP RC	8.00	2.40
153 Joey Dawley WP RC	8.00	2.40
154 Travis Driskill WP RC	8.00	2.40
155 Howie Clark WP RC	8.00	2.40
156 J.De La Rosa WP RC	8.00	2.40
157 Freddy Sanchez WP RC	8.00	2.40
158 Earl Snyder WP RC	8.00	2.40
159 Cliff Lee WP RC	10.00	3.00
160 Josh Bard WP RC	8.00	2.40
161 Aaron Cook WP RC	8.00	2.40
162 Franklyn German WP RC	8.00	2.40
163 Brandon Puffer WP RC	8.00	2.40
164 Kirk Saarloos WP RC	8.00	2.40
165 Jer. Robertson WP RC	8.00	2.40
166 Miguel Asencio WP RC	8.00	2.40
167 Shawn Sedlacek WP RC	8.00	2.40
168 Jayson Durocher WP RC	8.00	2.40
169 Shane Nance WP RC	8.00	2.40
170 Jamey Carroll WP RC	8.00	2.40
171 Oliver Perez WP RC	10.00	3.00
172 Wil Nieves WP RC	8.00	2.40
173 Clay Condrey WP RC	8.00	2.40
174 Chris Snelling WP RC	10.00	3.00

175 Mike Crudale WP RC 8.00 2.40
176 J.Simontacchi WP RC 8.00 2.40
177 Felix Escalona WP RC 8.00 2.40
178 Lance Carter WP RC 8.00 2.40
179 Scott Wiggins WP RC 8.00 2.40
180 Kevin Cash WP RC 8.00 2.40

2002 Upper Deck Ovation Gold

Randomly inserted in packs, this is a complete parallel to the 2002 Upper Deck Ovation set. The cards between 1-60 are printed to an appropriate 2001 stat while the cards numbered from 61-120 are printed to a stated print run of 25 serial numbered sets. For those cards with specific print run information, we have published that information next to their name in our checklist. For all card with a print run of 25 or fewer, there is no pricing due to market scarcity.

	Nm-Mt	Ex-Mt
1 Troy Glaus/47	25.00	7.50
2 David Justice/41	15.00	4.50
3 Tim Hudson/20		
4 Jermaine Dye/33	20.00	6.00
5 Carlos Delgado/44	15.00	4.50
6 Greg Vaughn/50	15.00	4.50
7 Jim Thome/49	40.00	12.00
8 C.C. Sabathia/17		
9 Ichiro Suzuki/8		
10 Edgar Martinez/37	25.00	7.50
11 Chris Richard/15		
12 Rafael Palmeiro/47	25.00	7.50
13 Alex Rodriguez/52	50.00	15.00
14 Ivan Rodriguez/35	50.00	15.00
15 Nomar Garciaparra/35	80.00	24.00
16 Manny Ramirez/45	15.00	4.50
17 Pedro Martinez/23		
18 Mike Sweeney/29	20.00	6.00
19 Dmitri Young//21		
20 Doug Mientkiewicz/15		
21 Brad Radke/20		
22 Cristian Guzman/10		
23 Frank Thomas/43	40.00	12.00
24 Magglio Ordonez/32	20.00	6.00
25 Bernie Williams/30	30.00	9.00
26 Derek Jeter/24		
27 Jason Giambi/43	40.00	12.00
28 Roger Clemens/24		
29 Jeff Bagwell/47	25.00	7.50
30 Lance Berkman/34	20.00	6.00
31 Chipper Jones/45	40.00	12.00
32 Gary Sheffield/43	15.00	4.50
33 Greg Maddux/20		
34 Richie Sexson/45	15.00	4.50
35 Albert Pujols/37	80.00	24.00
36 Tino Martinez/44	25.00	7.50
37 J.D. Drew/27	20.00	6.00
38 Sammy Sosa/66	40.00	12.00
39 Moises Alou/38	15.00	4.50
40 Randy Johnson/21		
41 Luis Gonzalez/57	12.00	3.60
42 Shawn Green/49	15.00	4.50
43 Kevin Brown/21		
44 Vladimir Guerrero/44	40.00	12.00
45 Barry Bonds/73	60.00	18.00
46 Jeff Kent/33	20.00	6.00
47 Cliff Floyd/31	20.00	6.00
48 Josh Beckett/2		
49 Mike Piazza/40	60.00	18.00
50 Mo Vaughn/44	15.00	4.50
51 Jeromy Burnitz/38	15.00	4.50
52 Roberto Alomar/24		
53 Phil Nevin/41	15.00	4.50
54 Scott Rolen/31	30.00	9.00
55 Jimmy Rollins/14		
56 Brian Giles/39	15.00	4.50
57 Ken Griffey Jr./56	50.00	15.00
58 Sean Casey/25		
59 Larry Walker/49	25.00	7.50
60 Todd Helton/49	25.00	7.50

2002 Upper Deck Ovation Silver

Randomly inserted in packs, this is a complete parallel of the 2002 Upper Deck Ovation set. Cards numbered 1-60 and 90-119 were inserted at an overall approximate stated odds of one in four while cardds 61-89 and 120 were printed to a stated print run of 100 serial numbered sets.

Nm-Mt Ex-Mt
*SILVER 1-60: 1.25X TO 3X BASIC ....
*SILVER 61-89/120: .5X TO 1.2X BASIC
*SILVER 61-119: 2.5X TO 6X BASIC ..

2002 Upper Deck Ovation Authentic McGwire

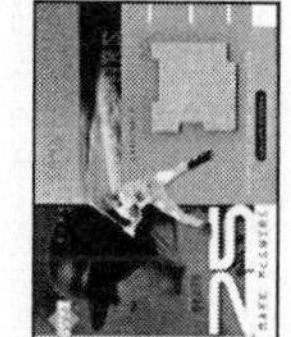

Randomly inserted into packs, these two cards feature authentic game-used memorabilia pieces from Mark McGwire's major league career. These two cards are each produced to a stated print run of 70 serial numbered sets.

	Nm-Mt	Ex-Mt
AMB Mark McGwire Bat	120.00	36.00
AMJ Mark McGwire Jsy	120.00	36.00

2002 Upper Deck Ovation Authentic McGwire Gold

Randomly inserted into packs, these two cards feature authentic game-used memorabilia pieces from Mark McGwire's major league career. These two cards are each produced to a stated print run of 50 serial numbered sets.

Nm-Mt Ex-Mt
AMBG Mark McGwire Bat
AMJG Mark McGwire Jsy

2002 Upper Deck Ovation Authentic McGwire Signatures

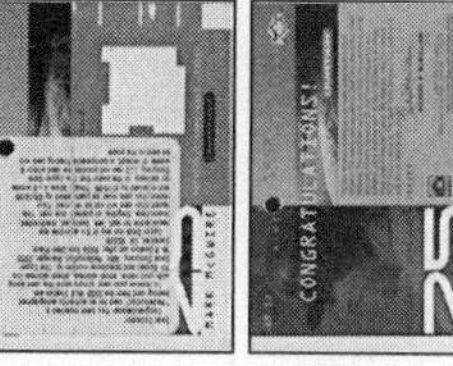

Randomly inserted into packs, these two cards feature authentic game-used memorabilia pieces from Mark McGwire's major league career as well as an authentic autograph. However, McGwire did not sign his cards in time for inclusion in this set so these cards were issued as exchange cards with an redemption deadline of July 3, 2005. These two cards are each produced to a stated print run of 25 serial numbered sets and no pricing is provided due to market scarcity.

Nm-Mt Ex-Mt
AMSB Mark McGwire Bat EXCH
AMSJ Mark McGwire Jsy EXCH

2002 Upper Deck Ovation Diamond Futures Jerseys

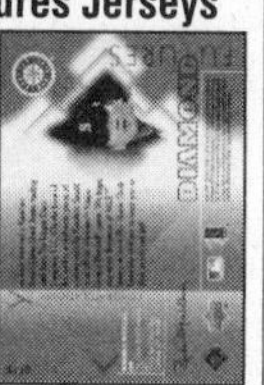

Inserted in packs at stated odds of one in 72, these 12 cards feature game-worn jersey swatches from 12 of baseball's future stars.

Nm-Mt Ex-Mt
GOLD RANDOM INSERTS IN PACKS ..
GOLD PRINT RUN 25 SERIAL #'d SETS
NO GOLD PRICING DUE TO SCARCITY

	Nm-Mt	Ex-Mt
DF-BZ Barry Zito	15.00	4.50
DF-FG Freddy Garcia	10.00	3.00
DF-IR Ivan Rodriguez	15.00	4.50
DF-JK Jason Kendall	10.00	3.00
DF-JP Jorge Posada	15.00	4.50
DF-JR Jimmy Rollins	10.00	3.00
DF-JV Jose Vidro	10.00	3.00
DF-KS Kazuhiro Sasaki	10.00	3.00
DF-LB Lance Berkman	10.00	3.00
DF-PB Pat Burrell	10.00	3.00
DF-RB Russell Branyan	10.00	3.00
DF-TH Tim Hudson	10.00	3.00

2002 Upper Deck Ovation Lead Performer Jerseys

Inserted in packs at stated odds of one in 72, these 12 cards feature game-worn swatches from some of the leading players in baseball. A couple of these cards were produced in shorter quantity and we have notated that information in our checklist next to their name.

Nm-Mt Ex-Mt
GOLD RANDOM INSERTS IN PACKS ..
GOLD PRINT RUN 25 SERIAL #'d SETS
NO GOLD PRICING DUE TO SCARCITY

	Nm-Mt	Ex-Mt
LP-AR Alex Rodriguez	15.00	4.50
LP-CD Carlos Delgado	10.00	3.00
LP-FT Frank Thomas	15.00	4.50
LP-IR Ivan Rodriguez	15.00	4.50
LP-IS Ichiro Suzuki Shirt	50.00	15.00
LP-JB Jeff Bagwell	15.00	4.50
LP-JG Jason Giambi	15.00	4.50
LP-JG Juan Gonzalez	15.00	4.50
LP-KG Ken Griffey Jr. SP	25.00	7.50
LP-LG Luis Gonzalez	10.00	3.00
LP-MP Mike Piazza	15.00	4.50
LP-SS Sammy Sosa SP	25.00	7.50

2002 Upper Deck Ovation Spokesman Spotlight Signatures

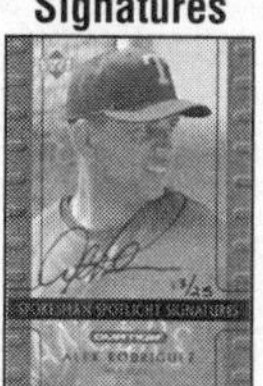

Randomly inserted into packs, these six cards feature authentic signatures of the six Upper Deck spokesman. Since each card is produced to a stated print run of 25 serial numbered sets, there is no pricing due to market scarcity.

Nm-Mt Ex-Mt
AR Alex Rodriguez
IS Ichiro Suzuki
JG Jason Giambi
KG Ken Griffey Jr.
MM Mark McGwire
SS Sammy Sosa

2002 Upper Deck Ovation Swatches

Inserted at stated odds of one in 72, these 12 cards feature game-used larger "swatches" from the players featured. The Roberto Alomar card was issued in smaller quantities and we have notated that information in our checklist.

Nm-Mt Ex-Mt
GOLD RANDOM INSERTS IN PACKS ..
GOLD PRINT RUN 25 SERIAL #'d SETS
NO GOLD PRICING DUE TO SCARCITY

	Nm-Mt	Ex-Mt
O-AR Alex Rodriguez	15.00	4.50
O-BW Bernie Williams	15.00	4.50
O-CD Carlos Delgado	10.00	3.00
O-CJ Chipper Jones	15.00	4.50
O-DE Darin Erstad	10.00	3.00
O-EB Ellis Burks	10.00	3.00
O-EC Eric Chavez	10.00	3.00
O-GM Greg Maddux	15.00	4.50
O-JB Jeromy Burnitz	10.00	3.00
O-MG Mark Grace	15.00	4.50
O-PM Pedro Martinez	15.00	4.50
O-RA Roberto Alomar SP		

2003 Upper Deck Play Ball Promos

These cards, which were issued to preview the 2003 Upper Deck Play Ball set were issued one per Tuff Stuff newstand copy. These cards can be differentiated from the regular cards as the words "UD Promo" are in large letters on the front.

Nm-Mt Ex-Mt
*PROMOS: 1.25X TO 3X BASIC CARDS

2003 Upper Deck Play Ball

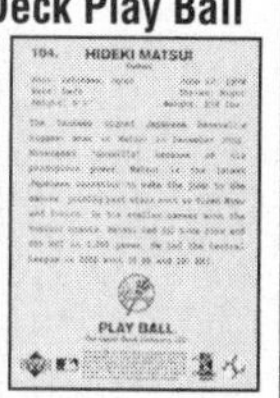

This 104 card set was released in February, 2004. The set was issued in five card packs with an $4 SRP. The packs were issued in 24 pack boxes which came 14 boxes to a case. The following subsets were included as part of the set: Summer of 1941 (74-88); Ted Williams Tribute (89-103). Cards numbered 74-103 were issued at stated rate of one in 24. In addition, one of the earliest cards of New York Yankee rookie Hideki Matsui was issued as card number 104. Shortly before the product debuted, an sample card of Mark McGwire was issued to preview what the set would look like.

	Nm-Mt	Ex-Mt
COMP.SET w/o SP's (74)	50.00	15.00
COMMON ACTIVE (1-73/104)	.40	.12
COMMON RETIRED (1-73/104)	.60	.18
COMMON CARD (74-88)	8.00	2.40
COMMON T.WILLIAMS (89-103)	15.00	4.50
1 Troy Glaus	.60	.18
2 Darin Erstad	.40	.12
3 Randy Johnson	1.00	.30
4 Luis Gonzalez	.40	.12
5 Curt Schilling	.60	.18
6 Tom Glavine	.60	.18
7 Chipper Jones	1.00	.30
8 Greg Maddux	1.50	.45
9 Andruw Jones	.40	.12
10 Pedro Martinez	1.00	.30
11 Manny Ramirez	.40	.12
12 Nomar Garciaparra	1.50	.45
13 Billy Williams	.60	.18
14 Sammy Sosa	1.50	.45
15 Kerry Wood	1.00	.30
16 Mark Prior	2.00	.60
17 Ernie Banks	1.50	.45
18 Frank Thomas	1.00	.30
19 Joe Morgan	.60	.18
20 Ken Griffey Jr.	1.50	.45
21 Adam Dunn	.40	.12
22 Jim Thome	1.00	.30
23 Todd Helton	.60	.18
24 Larry Walker	.60	.18
25 Lance Berkman	.40	.12
26 Roy Oswalt	.40	.12
27 Jeff Bagwell	.60	.18
28 Nolan Ryan	4.00	1.20
29 Mike Sweeney	.40	.12
30 Shawn Green	.40	.12
31 Hideo Nomo	1.00	.30
32 Kazuhisa Ishii	.40	.12
33 Richie Sexson	.40	.12
34 Robin Yount	2.50	.75
35 Harmon Killebrew	1.50	.45
36 Torii Hunter	.40	.12
37 Vladimir Guerrero	1.00	.30
38 Roberto Alomar	1.00	.30
39 Mike Piazza	1.50	.45
40 Tom Seaver	1.00	.30
41 Phil Rizzuto	1.00	.30
42 Yogi Berra	1.50	.45
43 Mike Mussina	1.00	.30
44 Roger Clemens	2.00	.60
45 Derek Jeter	2.50	.75
46 Jason Giambi	1.00	.30
47 Bernie Williams	.60	.18
48 Alfonso Soriano	.60	.18
49 Catfish Hunter	1.00	.30
50 Barry Zito	.60	.18
51 Eric Chavez	.40	.12
52 Tim Hudson	.40	.12
53 Rollie Fingers	.60	.18
54 Miguel Tejada	.40	.12
55 Pat Burrell	.40	.12
56 Brian Giles	.40	.12
57 Willie Stargell	1.00	.30
58 Phil Nevin	.40	.12
59 Orlando Cepeda	.60	.18
60 Barry Bonds	2.50	.75
61 Jeff Kent	.40	.12
62 Willie McCovey	.60	.18
63 Ichiro Suzuki	1.50	.45
64 Stan Musial	2.50	.75
65 Albert Pujols	2.00	.60
66 J.D. Drew	.40	.12
67 Scott Rolen	.60	.18
68 Mark McGwire	2.50	.75
69 Alex Rodriguez	1.50	.45
70 Juan Gonzalez	1.00	.30
71 Ivan Rodriguez	1.00	.30
72 Rafael Palmeiro	.60	.18
73 Carlos Delgado	.40	.12
74 Ted Williams S41	15.00	4.50
75 Hank Greenberg S41	10.00	3.00
76 Joe DiMaggio S41	15.00	4.50
77 Lefty Gomez S41	10.00	3.00
78 Tommy Henrich S41	8.00	2.40
79 Pee Wee Reese S41	10.00	3.00
80 Mel Ott S41	10.00	3.00
81 Carl Hubbell S41	10.00	3.00
82 Jimmie Foxx S41	10.00	3.00
83 Joe Cronin S41	8.00	2.40
84 Charlie Gehringer S41	8.00	2.40
85 Frank Hayes S41	8.00	2.40
86 Babe Dahlgren S41	8.00	2.40
87 Dolph Camilli S41	8.00	2.40
88 Johnny Vandermeer S41	8.00	2.40
89 Ted Williams TRIB	15.00	4.50
90 Ted Williams TRIB	15.00	4.50
91 Ted Williams TRIB	15.00	4.50
92 Ted Williams TRIB	15.00	4.50
93 Ted Williams TRIB	15.00	4.50
94 Ted Williams TRIB	15.00	4.50
95 Ted Williams TRIB	15.00	4.50
96 Ted Williams TRIB	15.00	4.50
97 Ted Williams TRIB	15.00	4.50
98 Ted Williams TRIB	15.00	4.50
99 Ted Williams TRIB	15.00	4.50
100 Ted Williams TRIB	15.00	4.50
101 Ted Williams TRIB	15.00	4.50
102 Ted Williams TRIB	15.00	4.50
103 Ted Williams TRIB	15.00	4.50
104 Hideki Matsui RC	8.00	2.40
MM1 Mark McGwire Sample	2.00	.60

2003 Upper Deck Play Ball 1941 Series

Issued at a stated rate of one in two, this is a partial parallel to the Play Ball set. These cards are issued to the size of the original 1941 Play Ball cards.

Nm-Mt Ex-Mt
*1941 ACTIVE: 1.25X TO 3X BASIC ....
*1941 RETIRED: 1.25X TO 3X BASIC .

2003 Upper Deck Play Ball Red Backs

Issued at a stated rate of one per pack for cards 1-73 and 104 and one in 96 for 74-103; this is a complete parallel to the Red Backs set. These cards can be identified as all the text on the card is in red ink.

Nm-Mt Ex-Mt
*RED BACK ACTIVE 1-73: .75X TO 2X BASIC
*RED BACK RETIRED 1-73: .75X TO 2X BASIC
*RED BACK 74-88: .6X TO 1.5X BASIC
*RED BACK 89-103: .6X TO 1.5X BASIC
*RED BACK 104: .75X TO 2X BASIC ...

2003 Upper Deck Play Ball 1941 Reprints

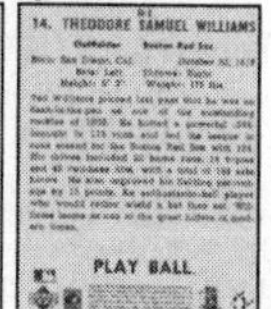

Issued at a stated rate of one in two, this 25 card insert set features cards reprinted from their 1941 originals.

	Nm-Mt	Ex-Mt
COMPLETE SET (25)	30.00	9.00
R1 Ted Williams	8.00	2.40
R2 Hank Greenberg	3.00	.90
R3 Joe DiMaggio	8.00	2.40
R4 Lefty Gomez	3.00	.90
R5 Tommy Henrich	2.00	.60
R6 Pee Wee Reese	3.00	.90
R7 Mel Ott	3.00	.90
R8 Carl Hubbell	3.00	.90
R9 Jimmie Foxx	3.00	.90
R10 Joe Cronin	2.00	.60
R11 Charley Gehringer	2.00	.60
R12 Frank Hayes	2.00	.60
R13 Babe Dahlgren	2.00	.60
R14 Dolph Camilli	2.00	.60
R15 Johnny Vandermeer	2.00	.60
R16 Bucky Walters	2.00	.60
R17 Red Ruffing	2.00	.60
R18 Charlie Keller	2.00	.60
R19 Indian Bob Johnson	2.00	.60
R20 Dutch Leonard	2.00	.60
R21 Barney McCosky	2.00	.60
R22 Soupy Campbell	2.00	.60
R23 Stormy Weatherly	2.00	.60
R24 Bobby Doerr	2.00	.60
R25 Bill Dickey	3.00	.90

2003 Upper Deck Play Ball Game Used Memorabilia Tier 1

Inserted at a stated rate of one in 82, these 21 cards feature game-used memorabilia of the featured players. Interestingly, the only retired player with a memorabilia piece in this set is Tommy Henrich.

Nm-Mt Ex-Mt
GOLD RANDOM INSERTS IN PACKS ..
GOLD PRINT RUN 25 SERIAL #'d SETS
NO GOLD PRICING DUE TO SCARCITY

	Nm-Mt	Ex-Mt
AD1 Adam Dunn Jsy	8.00	2.40
AS1 Alfonso Soriano Jsy	10.00	3.00
BW1 Bernie Williams Jsy	10.00	3.00
CD1 Carlos Delgado Jsy	8.00	2.40
CJ1 Chipper Jones Jsy	15.00	4.50
CS1 Curt Schilling Jsy	10.00	3.00
DR1 J.D. Drew Jsy	8.00	2.40
IR1 Ivan Rodriguez Jsy	15.00	4.50
IS1 Ichiro Suzuki Jsy	40.00	12.00
JG1 Jason Giambi Jsy	15.00	4.50
KG1 Ken Griffey Jr. Jsy	25.00	7.50
KI1 Kazuhisa Ishii Jsy	8.00	2.40
LG1 Luis Gonzalez Jsy	8.00	2.40
MM1 Mark McGwire Jsy	60.00	18.00
MP1 Mike Piazza Jsy	15.00	4.50
MS1 Mike Sweeney Jsy	8.00	2.40
PR1 Mark Prior Jsy	20.00	6.00
RC1 Roger Clemens Jsy	20.00	6.00
RP1 Rafael Palmeiro Jsy	10.00	3.00
SS1 Sammy Sosa Jsy	20.00	6.00
TH1 Tommy Henrich Pants	8.00	2.40

2003 Upper Deck Play Ball Game Used Memorabilia Tier 2

Randomly inserted in packs, these 21 cards feature game-used memorabilia of the featured players. These cards were issued to a stated print run of 150 serial numbered sets.

	Nm-Mt	Ex-Mt
AJ2 Andruw Jones Jsy	10.00	3.00
AR2 Alex Rodriguez Jsy	25.00	7.50
CJ2 Chipper Jones Jsy	20.00	6.00
CS2 Curt Schilling Jsy	15.00	4.50
DE2 Darin Erstad Jsy	10.00	3.00
GM2 Greg Maddux Jsy	15.00	4.50
IS2 Ichiro Suzuki Jsy	80.00	24.00
JB2 Jeff Bagwell Jsy	15.00	4.50
JD2 Joe DiMaggio Jsy	120.00	36.00
JG2 Jason Giambi Jsy	20.00	6.00
JT2 Jim Thome Jsy	20.00	6.00
KG2 Ken Griffey Jr. Jsy	25.00	7.50
KW2 Kerry Wood Jsy	20.00	6.00
LB2 Lance Berkman Jsy	10.00	3.00
MM2 Mark McGwire Jsy	80.00	24.00
MP2 Mike Piazza Jsy	15.00	4.50
MR2 Manny Ramirez Jsy	10.00	3.00
PM2 Pedro Martinez Jsy	20.00	6.00
RJ2 Randy Johnson Jsy	20.00	6.00
SG2 Shawn Green Jsy	10.00	3.00
SS2 Sammy Sosa Jsy	25.00	7.50

2003 Upper Deck Play Ball Game Used Memorabilia Tier 2 Signatures

Randomly isnerted in packs, these cards parallel the Game Used Memorabilia Tier 2 insert set. With the exception of the Alex Rodriguez card, these cards were issued to a stated print run of 50 serial numbered sets. The Alex Rodriguez card was issued to a stated print run of 285 sets. Please note that Mark McGwire signed all his cards with an "all century" notation.

	Nm-Mt	Ex-Mt
AJ2 Andruw Jones Jsy	100.00	30.00
AR2 Alex Rodriguez Jsy/285	150.00	45.00
CS2 Curt Schilling Jsy	100.00	30.00
DE2 Darin Erstad Jsy	100.00	30.00
IS2 Ichiro Suzuki Jsy	400.00	120.00
JB2 Jeff Bagwell Jsy	120.00	36.00
JG2 Jason Giambi Jsy	150.00	45.00
JT2 Jim Thome Jsy	120.00	36.00
KG2 Ken Griffey Jr. Jsy	250.00	75.00

KW2 Kerry Wood Jsy 120.00 36.00
LB2 Lance Berkman Jsy 100.00 30.00
MM2 Mark McGwire Jsy 400.00 120.00
SS2 Sammy Sosa Jsy 250.00 75.00

2003 Upper Deck Play Ball Yankee Clipper 1941 Streak

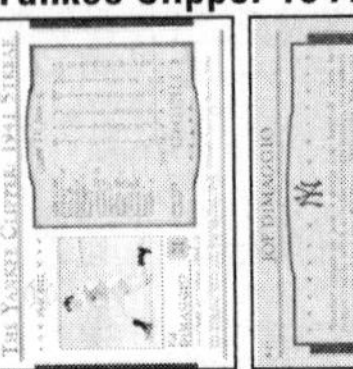
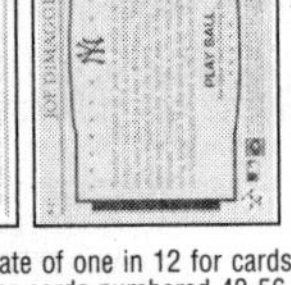

Inserted at a stated rate of one in 12 for cards 1-41 and one in 24 for cards numbered 42-56, this is a 56 card set honoring Joe DiMaggio's 56-game consecutive game hitting streak in 1941. Each card features a box score from the matching game during the streak.

	Nm-Mt	Ex-Mt
COMMON CARD (1-41)	10.00	3.00
COMMON CARD (42-56)	10.00	3.00

2003 Upper Deck Play Ball Hawaii

This 10-card set was distributed in complete form within a sealed cello packet to attendees of the February, 2003 Kit Young Hawaii Trade Show in Honolulu. The cards can be readily distinguished from basic 2003 Play Ball as follows: a) each card features a tropical background with palm trees, b) the card numbers on back each carry a "KY" prefix and most obviously c) the large "Hawaii Trade Conference" logo on the bottom right corner of each card front.

	Nm-Mt	Ex-Mt
COMPLETE SET (10)	200.00	60.00
KY1 Sammy Sosa	20.00	6.00
KY2 Ken Griffey Jr.	25.00	7.50
KY3 Jason Giambi	15.00	4.50
KY4 Ichiro Suzuki	30.00	9.00
KY5 Mark McGwire	25.00	7.50
KY6 Troy Glaus	15.00	4.50
KY7 Derek Jeter	40.00	12.00
KY8 Barry Bonds	25.00	7.50
KY9 Alex Rodriguez	25.00	7.50
KY10 Nomar Garciaparra	25.00	7.50

2003 Upper Deck Play Ball Hawaii Autographs

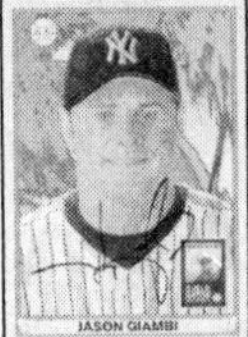
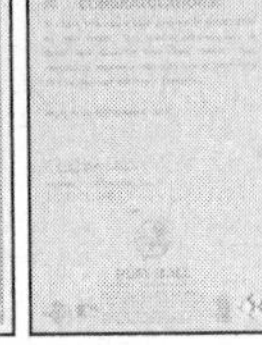

These four cards were distributed to select participants of the February, 2003 Kit Young Hawaii Trade Conference in Honolulu, HI. It's estimated as few as 50 copies of the McGwire and Sosa autographs were produced. The cards loosely parallel basic issue 2003 Play Ball except, of course, for the player's autograph of which appears in thin blue ink on front, the Hawaiian themed background of the card fronts and the certificate of authenticity nomenclature on the card back.

	Nm-Mt	Ex-Mt
IS Ichiro Suzuki		
JG Jason Giambi	30.00	9.00
MM Mark McGwire		
SS Sammy Sosa		

1999 Upper Deck PowerDeck

The Upper Deck Power Deck set featured both digital CD trading cards as well as more standard "paper" cards issued in three card packs. These packs which guaranteed having a digital card retailed for $4.99 per pack. Each digital card has game clips, sounds, photos and career highlights of the featured players. These cards can be played on almost any computer.

	Nm-Mt	Ex-Mt
COMPLETE SET (25)	50.00	15.00
1 Ken Griffey Jr.	3.00	.90
2 Mark McGwire	5.00	1.50
3 Cal Ripken	6.00	1.80
4 Sammy Sosa	3.00	.90
5 Derek Jeter	5.00	1.50
6 Mike Piazza	3.00	.90
7 Nomar Garciaparra	3.00	.90
8 Greg Maddux	3.00	.90
9 Tony Gwynn	2.50	.75
10 Roger Clemens	4.00	1.20
11 Scott Rolen	1.25	.35
12 Alex Rodriguez	3.00	.90
13 Manny Ramirez	1.00	.30
14 Chipper Jones	2.00	.60
15 Juan Gonzalez	2.00	.60
16 Ivan Rodriguez	2.00	.60
17 Frank Thomas	2.00	.60
18 Mo Vaughn	1.00	.30
19 Barry Bonds	5.00	1.50
20 Vladimir Guerrero	2.00	.60
21 Jose Canseco	2.00	.60
22 Jeff Bagwell	1.25	.35
23 Pedro Martinez	2.00	.60
24 Gabe Kapler	1.00	.30
25 J.D. Drew	1.00	.30

1999 Upper Deck PowerDeck Auxiliary

These "paper" cards are inserted two per pack. This set parallels the digital trading cards and feature more standard features like photos and statistics.

	Nm-Mt	Ex-Mt
COMPLETE SET (25)	20.00	6.00

*AUXILIARY: .1X TO .2X BASIC CD'S.

1999 Upper Deck PowerDeck Auxiliary Gold

This parallel of the PowerDeck Auxiliary set is printed in Gold and is limited to one card of each player. Due to the scarcity of these cards, no pricing is provided. The way to differentiate these cars is that they are printed in special gold deco foil versions.

	Nm-Mt	Ex-Mt
COMMON CARD (AUX1-AUX25)		

1999 Upper Deck PowerDeck A Season To Remember

This one per box chiptopper featured seven of the leading highlights of the 1999 season: Both Wade Boggs and Tony Gwynn reaching the 3000 hit club, Mark McGwire hitting his 500th homer, Ken Griffey's first homer at Safeco Field, Sammy Sosa on his way to more than 60 homers, David Cone's perfect game on Yogi Berra day at Yankee Stadium and Cal Ripken's march towards 3,000 hits. In addition, several thousand of these CD-Roms were given out at ball park promotions.

	Nm-Mt	Ex-Mt
1 Mark McGwire	8.00	2.40
Wade Boggs		
Tony Gwynn		
Ken Griffey Jr.		
Sammy Sosa		
David Cone		
Cal Ripken		

1999 Upper Deck PowerDeck Most Valuable Performances

These CD's which were inserted one every 287 packs featured players who had won MVP awards during their career.

	Nm-Mt	Ex-Mt
COMPLETE SET (7)	250.00	75.00

*AUXILIARY: .3X TO .8X BASIC MVP CD
AUXILIARY STATED ODDS 1:287
1 OF 1 AUXILIARY GOLD CARDS EXIST
1 OF 1 AUX.GOLD TOO SCARCE TO PRICE

	Nm-Mt	Ex-Mt
M1 Sammy Sosa	15.00	4.50
M2 Barry Bonds	25.00	7.50
M3 Cal Ripken	30.00	9.00
M4 Juan Gonzalez	10.00	3.00
M5 Ken Griffey Jr.	15.00	4.50
M6 Roger Clemens	20.00	6.00
M7 Mark McGwire	25.00	7.50

1999 Upper Deck PowerDeck Powerful Moments

These CD's, which was issued one every seven packs, feature game-action footabge pinpointing specific milestones in each of the players career. Among the highlights include Mark McGwire hitting his 70th homer in 1998 and Cal Ripken Jr. playing in his 2,131st game in 1995.

	Nm-Mt	Ex-Mt
COMPLETE SET (6)	50.00	15.00

*AUXILIARY: .3X TO .8X BASIC POW.MOM
AUXILIARY STATED ODDS 1:7
1 OF 1 AUXILIARY GOLD CARDS EXIST
1 OF 1 AUX.GOLD TOO SCARCE TO PRICE

	Nm-Mt	Ex-Mt
P1 Mark McGwire	5.00	1.50
P2 Sammy Sosa	3.00	.90
P3 Cal Ripken	6.00	1.80
P4 Ken Griffey Jr.	3.00	.90
P5 Derek Jeter	5.00	1.50
P6 Alex Rodriguez	3.00	.90

1999 Upper Deck PowerDeck Time Capsule

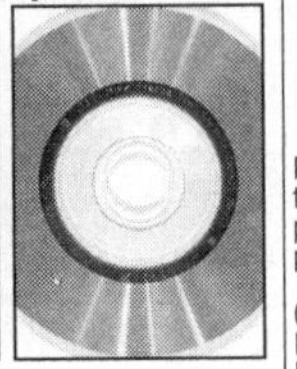

Five players who had won Rookie of the Year Awards as well as Ken Griffey Jr, who burst into the majors at the age of 19, are featured in this set. These CD's are inserted at a rate of one every 23 packs.

	Nm-Mt	Ex-Mt
COMPLETE SET (6)	60.00	18.00

*AUXILIARY: .3X TO .8X BASIC TIME CAP.
AUXILIARY STATED ODDS 1:23
1 OF 1 AUXILIARY GOLD CARDS EXIST
1 OF 1 AUX.GOLD TOO SCARCE TO PRICE

	Nm-Mt	Ex-Mt
R1 Ken Griffey Jr.	5.00	1.50
R2 Mike Piazza	5.00	1.50
R3 Mark McGwire	8.00	2.40
R4 Derek Jeter	8.00	2.40
R5 Jose Canseco	3.00	.90
R6 Nomar Garciaparra	5.00	1.50

2000 Upper Deck PowerDeck

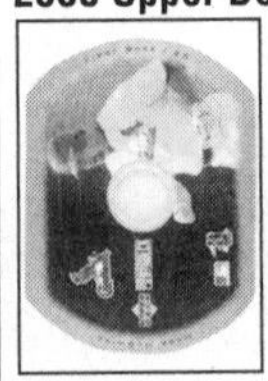

The 2000 Upper Deck PowerDeck product packed out in September, 2000 and featured a 12-card base set. Each pack contained one card, and carried a suggested retail price of $4.99.

	Nm-Mt	Ex-Mt
COMPLETE SET (12)	50.00	15.00
1 Sammy Sosa	4.00	1.20
2 Ken Griffey Jr.	4.00	1.20
3 Mark McGwire	6.00	1.80
4 Derek Jeter	6.00	1.80
5 Alex Rodriguez	4.00	1.20
6 Nomar Garciaparra	4.00	1.20
7 Mike Piazza	4.00	1.20
8 Cal Ripken	8.00	2.40
9 Ivan Rodriguez	2.50	.75
10 Chipper Jones	2.50	.75
11 Pedro Martinez	2.50	.75
12 Manny Ramirez	2.50	.75

2000 Upper Deck PowerDeck Magical Moments

Randomly inserted into hobby packs at one in 10, this two-card insert features a Ken Griffey Jr. 400th homerun card, and a Cal Ripken 3000th hit card. Card backs are numbered using the player's initials.

	Nm-Mt	Ex-Mt
COMPLETE SET (2)	15.00	4.50
CR Cal Ripken	10.00	3.00
KG Ken Griffey Jr.	5.00	1.50

2000 Upper Deck PowerDeck Magical Moments Autographs

Randomly inserted into hobby packs, this two-card set is a complete parallel of the Magical Moments insert. This parallel features autographed cards of Ken Griffey Jr. and Cal Ripken. Please note that each card is individually serial numbered to 50, and are numbered on the back using the player's initials.

	Nm-Mt	Ex-Mt
CR Cal Ripken	400.00	120.00
KG Ken Griffey Jr.	250.00	75.00

2000 Upper Deck PowerDeck Power Trio

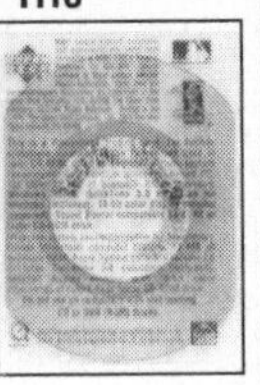

Randomly inserted into packs at one in seven, this three-card insert features three of the best players in baseball. Card backs carry a "PT" prefix.

	Nm-Mt	Ex-Mt
COMPLETE SET (3)	25.00	7.50
PT1 Derek Jeter	8.00	2.40
PT2 Ken Griffey Jr.	5.00	1.50
PT3 Mark McGwire	8.00	2.40

2000 Upper Deck Pros and Prospects

The 2000 Upper Deck Pros and Prospects product was initially released in early October as a 132-card basic set that was broken into tiers as follows: 90 Veterans (1-90), 30 Prospective Superstars (91-120) each serial numbered to 1350, and 12 Pro Fame cards (121-132) each serial numbered to 1000. Each pack contained five cards and carried a suggested retail price of $4.99. In late December, 2000, Upper Deck released their Rookie Update brand which carried a selection of new cards to extend the 2000 SP Authentic, SPx and UD Pros and Prospects brands. The new Pros and Prospects cards featured an extension of the Prospective Superstars subset (cards 133-162) with each card serial numbered to 1,600 and a selection of veterans (cards 163-192) composed of player's either initially not included in the basic set or traded to new teams. Notable Rookie Cards include Barry Zito (his first licensed MLB card), Xavier Nady, Jon Rauch and Ben Sheets. Also, a selection of A Piece of History 3000 Club Lou Brock and Rod Carew memorabilia cards were randomly seeded into packs. 350 bat cards, 350 jersey cards and 100 hand-numbered combination bat-jersey cards were produced for each player. In addition, twenty autographed, hand-numbered, combination bat-jersey Lou Brock cards and twenty nine autographed, hand-numbered, combination bat-jersey Rod Carew cards were produced. Pricing for these memorabilia cards can be referenced under 2000 Upper Deck A Piece of History 3000 Club.

	Nm-Mt	Ex-Mt
COMP.BASIC w/o SP's (90)	20.00	6.00
COMP.UPDATE w/o SP'S (30)	10.00	3.00
COMMON CARD (1-90)	.40	.12
COMMON PS (91-120)	5.00	1.50
COMMON PF (121-132)	6.00	1.80
COMMON PS (133-162)	8.00	2.40
COMMON (163-192)	.60	.18
1 Darin Erstad	.40	.12
2 Troy Glaus	.60	.18
3 Mo Vaughn	.40	.12
4 Jason Giambi	1.00	.30
5 Tim Hudson	.60	.18
6 Ben Grieve	.40	.12
7 Eric Chavez	.40	.12
8 Shannon Stewart	.40	.12
9 Raul Mondesi	.40	.12
10 Carlos Delgado	.40	.12
11 Jose Canseco	1.00	.30
12 Fred McGriff	.60	.18
13 Greg Vaughn	.40	.12
14 Manny Ramirez	.40	.12
15 Roberto Alomar	1.00	.30
16 Jim Thome	1.00	.30
17 Alex Rodriguez	1.50	.45
18 Freddy Garcia	.40	.12
19 John Olerud	.40	.12
20 Cal Ripken	3.00	.90
21 Albert Belle	.40	.12
22 Mike Mussina	1.00	.30
23 Ivan Rodriguez	1.00	.30
24 Rafael Palmeiro	.60	.18
25 Ruben Mateo	.40	.12
26 Gabe Kapler	.40	.12
27 Pedro Martinez	1.00	.30
28 Nomar Garciaparra	1.50	.45
29 Carl Everett	.40	.12
30 Carlos Beltran	.40	.12
31 Jermaine Dye	.40	.12
32 Johnny Damon UER	.40	.12
Picture on front is Joe Randa		
33 Juan Gonzalez	1.00	.30
34 Juan Encarnacion	.40	.12
35 Dean Palmer	.40	.12
36 Jacque Jones	.40	.12
37 Matt Lawton	.40	.12
38 Frank Thomas	1.00	.30
39 Paul Konerko	.40	.12
40 Magglio Ordonez	.40	.12
41 Derek Jeter	2.50	.75
42 Bernie Williams	.60	.18
43 Mariano Rivera	.60	.18
44 Roger Clemens	2.00	.60
45 Jeff Bagwell	.60	.18
46 Craig Biggio	.60	.18
47 Richard Hidalgo	.40	.12
48 Chipper Jones	1.00	.30
49 Andres Galarraga	.40	.12
50 Andruw Jones	.40	.12
51 Greg Maddux	1.50	.45
52 Jeromy Burnitz	.40	.12
53 Geoff Jenkins	.40	.12
54 Mark McGwire	2.50	.75
55 Jim Edmonds	.40	.12
56 Fernando Tatis	.40	.12
57 J.D. Drew	.40	.12
58 Sammy Sosa	1.50	.45
59 Kerry Wood	1.00	.30
60 Randy Johnson	1.00	.30
61 Matt Williams	.40	.12
62 Erubiel Durazo	.40	.12
63 Shawn Green	.40	.12
64 Kevin Brown	.40	.12
65 Gary Sheffield	.40	.12
66 Adrian Beltre	.40	.12
67 Vladimir Guerrero	1.00	.30
68 Jose Vidro	.40	.12
69 Barry Bonds	2.50	.75
70 Jeff Kent	.40	.12
71 Preston Wilson	.40	.12
72 Ryan Dempster	.40	.12
73 Mike Lowell	.40	.12
74 Mike Piazza	1.50	.45
75 Robin Ventura	.40	.12
76 Edgardo Alfonzo	.40	.12
77 Derek Bell	.40	.12
78 Tony Gwynn	1.25	.35
79 Matt Clement	.40	.12
80 Scott Rolen	.60	.18
81 Bobby Abreu	.40	.12
82 Curt Schilling	.60	.18
83 Brian Giles	.40	.12
84 Jason Kendall	.40	.12
85 Kris Benson	.40	.12
86 Ken Griffey Jr.	1.50	.45
87 Sean Casey	.40	.12
88 Pokey Reese	.40	.12
89 Larry Walker	.60	.18
90 Todd Helton	.60	.18
91 Rick Ankiel PS	5.00	1.50
92 Milton Bradley PS	5.00	1.50
93 Vernon Wells PS	5.00	1.50
94 Rafael Furcal PS	5.00	1.50
95 Kazuhiro Sasaki PS RC	10.00	3.00
96 Joe Torres PS RC	5.00	1.50
97 Adam Kennedy PS	5.00	1.50
98 Adam Piatt PS	5.00	1.50
99 Matt Wheatland PS RC	5.00	1.50
100 Alex Cabrera PS RC	5.00	1.50
101 Barry Zito PS RC	25.00	7.50
102 Mike Lamb PS RC	5.00	1.50
103 Scott Heard PS RC	5.00	1.50
104 Danys Baez PS RC	8.00	2.40
105 Matt Riley PS	5.00	1.50
106 Mark Mulder PS	8.00	2.40
107 W.Rodriguez PS RC	5.00	1.50
108 Luis Matos PS RC	10.00	3.00
109 Alfonso Soriano PS	8.00	2.40
110 Pat Burrell PS	8.00	2.40
111 Mike Tonis PS RC	8.00	2.40
112 Aaron McNeal PS RC	5.00	1.50
113 Dave Krynzel PS RC	5.00	1.50
114 Josh Beckett PS	10.00	3.00
115 Sean Burnett PS RC	10.00	3.00
116 Eric Munson PS	5.00	1.50
117 Scott Downs PS RC	5.00	1.50
118 Brian Tollberg PS RC	5.00	1.50
119 Nick Johnson PS	5.00	1.50
120 Leo Estrella PS RC	5.00	1.50
121 Ken Griffey Jr. PF	10.00	3.00
122 Frank Thomas PF	6.00	1.80
123 Cal Ripken PF	20.00	6.00
124 Ivan Rodriguez PF	6.00	1.80
125 Derek Jeter PF	15.00	4.50
126 Mark McGwire PF	15.00	4.50
127 Pedro Martinez PF	6.00	1.80
128 Chipper Jones PF	6.00	1.80
129 Sammy Sosa PF	10.00	3.00
130 Alex Rodriguez PF	10.00	3.00
131 Vladimir Guerrero PF	6.00	1.80
132 Jeff Bagwell PF	6.00	1.80
133 Dane Artman PS RC	8.00	2.40
134 Juan Pierre PS RC	10.00	3.00
135 Jace Brewer PS RC	8.00	2.40
136 Sun Woo Kim PS RC	8.00	2.40
137 Jon Rauch PS RC	8.00	2.40
138 Juan Guzman PS RC	8.00	2.40
139 Daylan Holt PS RC	8.00	2.40
140 R.Washington PS RC	8.00	2.40
141 Ben Diggins PS RC	8.00	2.40
142 Mike Meyers PS RC	8.00	2.40
143 C.Wakeland PS RC	8.00	2.40
144 Cory Vance PS RC	8.00	2.40
145 Keith Ginter PS RC	8.00	2.40
146 Koyie Hill PS RC	10.00	3.00
147 Julio Zuleta PS RC	5.00	1.50
148 G.Guzman PS RC	8.00	2.40
149 Jay Spurgeon PS RC	8.00	2.40
150 Ross Gload PS RC	8.00	2.40
151 Ben Sheets PS RC	10.00	3.00
152 J.Kalinowski PS RC	8.00	2.40
153 Kurt Ainsworth PS RC	10.00	3.00
154 P.Crawford PS RC	8.00	2.40
155 Xavier Nady PS RC	10.00	3.00
156 B.Wilkerson PS RC	10.00	3.00
157 Kris Wilson PS RC	8.00	2.40
158 Paul Rigdon PS RC	8.00	2.40
159 R.Kohlmeier PS RC	8.00	2.40
160 Dane Sardinha PS RC	8.00	2.40
161 Javier Cardona PS RC	8.00	2.40
162 Brad Cresse PS RC	8.00	2.40
163 Ron Gant	.60	.18
164 Mark Mulder	1.00	.30
165 David Wells	.60	.18
166 Jason Tyner	.60	.18
167 David Segui	.60	.18
168 Al Martin	.60	.18
169 Melvin Mora	.60	.18
170 Ricky Ledee	.60	.18
171 Rolando Arrojo	.60	.18
172 Mike Sweeney	.60	.18
173 Bobby Higginson	.60	.18
174 Eric Milton	.60	.18
175 Charles Johnson	.60	.18
176 David Justice	.60	.18

177 Moises Alou .60 .18
178 Andy Ashby .60 .18
179 Richie Sexson .60 .18
180 Will Clark 1.50 .45
181 Rondell White .60 .18
182 Curt Schilling 1.00 .30
183 Tom Goodwin .60 .18
184 Lee Stevens .60 .18
185 Ellis Burks .60 .18
186 Henry Rodriguez .60 .18
187 Mike Bordick .60 .18
188 Ryan Klesko .60 .18
189 Travis Lee .60 .18
190 Kevin Young .60 .18
191 Barry Larkin 1.50 .45
192 Jeff Cirillo .60 .18

2000 Upper Deck Pros and Prospects Best in the Bigs

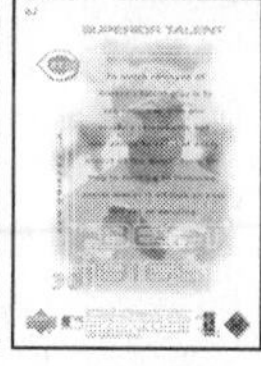

Randomly inserted into packs at one in 12, this 10-card insert features the best players in Major League Baseball. Card backs carry a "B" prefix.

Nm-Mt Ex-Mt
COMPLETE SET (10) 40.00 12.00
B1 Sammy Sosa 4.00 1.20
B2 Tony Gwynn 3.00 .90
B3 Pedro Martinez 2.50 .75
B4 Mark McGwire 6.00 1.80
B5 Chipper Jones 2.50 .75
B6 Derek Jeter 6.00 1.80
B7 Ken Griffey Jr. 4.00 1.20
B8 Cal Ripken 8.00 2.40
B9 Greg Maddux 4.00 1.20
B10 Ivan Rodriguez 2.50 .75

2000 Upper Deck Pros and Prospects Future Forces

Randomly inserted into packs at one in six, this 10-card insert features Major League prospects that hope to play a major role on their teams. Card backs carry a "F" prefix.

Nm-Mt Ex-Mt
COMPLETE SET (10) 10.00 3.00
F1 Pat Burrell 1.50 .45
F2 Brad Penny 1.00 .30
F3 Rick Ankiel 1.00 .30
F4 Adam Kennedy 1.00 .30
F5 Eric Munson 1.00 .30
F6 Rafael Furcal 1.00 .30
F7 Mark Mulder 1.50 .45
F8 Vernon Wells 1.00 .30
F9 Matt Riley 1.00 .30
F10 Nick Johnson 1.00 .30

2000 Upper Deck Pros and Prospects Game Jersey Autograph

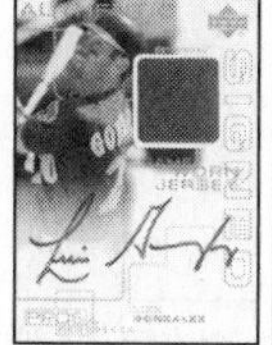

Randomly inserted into packs at an approximate rate of one in 96, this 21-card insert features autographs of many of the Major Leagues elite players. Card backs are numbered using the players initials. The following players packed out as stickered exchange cards: Cal Ripken, Ivan Rodriguez, Jose Canseco, Ken Griffey Jr., Mo Vaughn and Tom Glavine. Please note that Jose Canseco and Tom Glavine both only signed partial quantities of their cards, thus half packed out as proper autos and the other half packed out as exchange cards. Due to problems with the players, UD was not able to get the athletes to sign their remaining cards and were forced to redeem the exchange cards with signed Mo Vaughn cards instead. The deadline to redeem exchange cards was July 5th, 2001. Representatives at Upper Deck have confirmed that the Derek Jeter card was produced in shorter supply than other cards from this set. This set also contains the first-ever certified autograph of Luis Gonzalez.

Nm-Mt Ex-Mt
AR Alex Rodriguez 175.00 52.50
BB Barry Bonds 250.00 75.00
CJ Chipper Jones 80.00 24.00
CR Cal Ripken 175.00 52.50
DJ Derek Jeter SP 500.00 150.00
FT Frank Thomas 50.00 15.00
GS Gary Sheffield 50.00 15.00
IR Ivan Rodriguez 50.00 15.00
JC Jose Canseco EXCH NO AU 10.00 3.00
JC Jose Canseco 50.00 15.00
JD J.D. Drew 40.00 12.00
KG Ken Griffey Jr. 150.00 45.00
KL Kenny Lofton 40.00 12.00
LG Luis Gonzalez 40.00 12.00
MV Mo Vaughn 40.00 12.00
MW Matt Williams 40.00 12.00
PW Preston Wilson 40.00 12.00
RJ Randy Johnson 100.00 30.00
RV Robin Ventura 40.00 12.00
SR Scott Rolen 50.00 15.00
TGL Tom Glavine EXCH NO AU 10.00 3.00
TGL Tom Glavine 50.00 15.00
TGW Tony Gwynn 80.00 24.00

2000 Upper Deck Pros and Prospects Game Jersey Autograph Gold

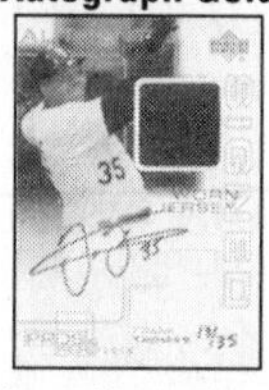

Randomly inserted into packs, this 21-card insert is a complete parallel of the 2000 Pros and Prospects Game Jerseys. Each card is serial numbered to the player's jersey number, and are numbered on the back using the player's initials. Please note that Upper Deck has announced the exchange cards of Jose Canseco and Tom Glavine will be redeemed with Mo Vaughn. Some cards are not priced due to market scarcity. The following cards packed out as exchnage cards with a redemption deadline of 07/05/01: Cal Ripken, Ivan Rodriguez, Ken Griffey Jr. and Mo Vaughn.

Nm-Mt Ex-Mt
AR Alex Rodriguez/3
BB Barry Bonds/25
CJ Chipper Jones/10
CR Cal Ripken/8
DJ Derek Jeter/2
FT Frank Thomas/35 150.00 45.00
GS Gary Sheffield/10
IR Ivan Rodriguez/7
JC Jose Canseco/33
JD J.D. Drew/7
KG Ken Griffey Jr. 400.00 120.00
30 EXCH
KL Kenny Lofton/7
LG Luis Gonzalez/20
MV Mo Vaughn/42 60.00 18.00
MW Matt Williams/9
PW Preston Wilson/44 60.00 18.00
RJ Randy Johnson/51 250.00 75.00
RV Robin Ventura/4
SR Scott Rolen/17
TGL Tom Glavine/47 120.00 36.00
TGW Tony Gwynn/19

2000 Upper Deck Pros and Prospects ProMotion

Randomly inserted into packs at one in six, this 10-card insert features baseball's greatest all-around players. Card backs carry a "P" prefix.

Nm-Mt Ex-Mt
COMPLETE SET (10) 25.00 7.50
P1 Derek Jeter 4.00 1.20
P2 Mike Piazza 2.50 .75
P3 Mark McGwire 4.00 1.20
P4 Ivan Rodriguez 1.50 .45
P5 Kerry Wood 1.50 .45
P6 Nomar Garciaparra 2.50 .75
P7 Sammy Sosa 2.50 .75
P8 Alex Rodriguez 2.50 .75
P9 Ken Griffey Jr. 2.50 .75
P10 Vladimir Guerrero 1.50 .45

2000 Upper Deck Pros and Prospects Rare Breed

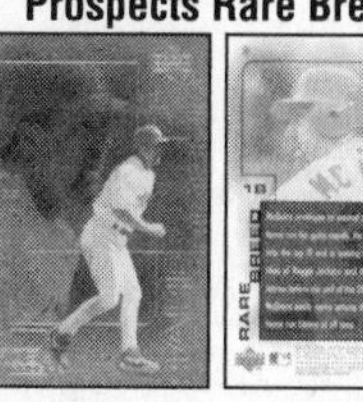

Randomly inserted into packs at one in 12, this 12-card insert features players that have rare talents. Card backs carry a "R" prefix.

Nm-Mt Ex-Mt
COMPLETE SET (12) 40.00 12.00
R1 Mark McGwire 6.00 1.80
R2 Frank Thomas 2.50 .75
R3 Mike Piazza 4.00 1.20
R4 Barry Bonds 6.00 1.80
R5 Manny Ramirez 1.00 .30
R6 Ken Griffey Jr. 4.00 1.20
R7 Nomar Garciaparra 4.00 1.20
R8 Randy Johnson 2.50 .75
R9 Vladimir Guerrero 2.50 .75
R10 Jeff Bagwell 1.50 .45
R11 Rick Ankiel 12.00 3.60
R12 Alex Rodriguez 4.00 1.20

2001 Upper Deck Pros and Prospects

This 135 card set was issued in five card packs. Cards numbered 91-141 were shorter printed than the other cards. Cards numbered 91-135 had a print run of 1,250 serial numbered sets while cards numbered 136-141 had a print run of 500 sets.

Nm-Mt Ex-Mt
COMP.SET w/o SP's (90) 20.00 6.00
COMMON CARD (1-90) .40 .12
COMMON CARD (91-135) 8.00 2.40
COMMON (136-141) 20.00 6.00
1 Troy Glaus .60 .18
2 Darin Erstad .40 .12
3 Tim Hudson .40 .12
4 Jason Giambi 1.00 .30
5 Jermaine Dye .40 .12
6 Barry Zito 1.00 .30
7 Carlos Delgado .40 .12
8 Shannon Stewart .40 .12
9 Raul Mondesi .40 .12
10 Greg Vaughn .40 .12
11 Ben Grieve .40 .12
12 Roberto Alomar 1.00 .30
13 Juan Gonzalez 1.00 .30
14 Jim Thome 1.00 .30
15 C.C. Sabathia .40 .12
16 Edgar Martinez .60 .18
17 Kazuhiro Sasaki .40 .12
18 Aaron Sele .40 .12
19 John Olerud .40 .12
20 Cal Ripken 3.00 .90
21 Rafael Palmeiro .60 .18
22 Ivan Rodriguez 1.00 .30
23 Alex Rodriguez 1.50 .45
24 Manny Ramirez .40 .12
25 Pedro Martinez 1.00 .30
26 Carl Everett .40 .12
27 Nomar Garciaparra 1.50 .45
28 Neifi Perez .40 .12
29 Mike Sweeney .40 .12
30 Bobby Higginson .40 .12
31 Tony Clark .40 .12
32 Doug Mientkiewicz .40 .12
33 Cristian Guzman .40 .12
34 Brad Radke .40 .12
35 Magglio Ordonez .40 .12
36 Carlos Lee .40 .12
37 Frank Thomas 1.00 .30
38 Roger Clemens 2.00 .60
39 Bernie Williams .60 .18
40 Derek Jeter 2.50 .75
41 Tino Martinez .60 .18
42 Wade Miller .40 .12
43 Jeff Bagwell .60 .18
44 Lance Berkman .40 .12
45 Richard Hidalgo .40 .12
46 Greg Maddux 1.50 .45
47 Andruw Jones .40 .12
48 Chipper Jones 1.00 .30
49 Rafael Furcal .40 .12
50 Jeromy Burnitz .40 .12
51 Geoff Jenkins .40 .12
52 Ben Sheets .40 .12
53 Mark McGwire 2.50 .75
54 Jim Edmonds .40 .12
55 J.D. Drew .40 .12
56 Fred McGriff .60 .18
57 Sammy Sosa 1.50 .45
58 Kerry Wood 1.00 .30
59 Randy Johnson 1.00 .30
60 Luis Gonzalez .40 .12
61 Curt Schilling .60 .18
62 Kevin Brown .40 .12
63 Shawn Green .40 .12
64 Gary Sheffield .40 .12
65 Vladimir Guerrero 1.00 .30
66 Jose Vidro .40 .12
67 Barry Bonds 2.50 .75
68 Jeff Kent .40 .12
69 Rich Aurilia .40 .12
70 Preston Wilson .40 .12
71 Charles Johnson .40 .12
72 Cliff Floyd .40 .12
73 Mike Piazza 1.50 .45
74 Al Leiter .40 .12
75 Matt Lawton .40 .12
76 Tony Gwynn 1.25 .35
77 Ryan Klesko .40 .12
78 Phil Nevin .40 .12
79 Scott Rolen .60 .18
80 Pat Burrell .40 .12
81 Jimmy Rollins .40 .12
82 Jason Kendall .40 .12
83 Brian Giles .40 .12
84 Aramis Ramirez .40 .12
85 Ken Griffey Jr. 1.50 .45
86 Barry Larkin 1.00 .30
87 Sean Casey .40 .12
88 Larry Walker .60 .18
89 Todd Helton .60 .18
90 Mike Hampton .40 .12
91 Juan Cruz PS RC 8.00 2.40
92 Brian Lawrence PS RC 8.00 2.40
93 Brandon Lyon PS RC 8.00 2.40
94 A.Hernandez PS RC 8.00 2.40
95 Jose Mieses PS RC 8.00 2.40
96 Juan Uribe PS RC 8.00 2.40
97 M.Ensberg PS RC 12.00 3.60
98 Wilson Betemit PS RC 8.00 2.40
99 Ryan Freel PS RC 8.00 2.40
100 Jack Wilson PS RC 8.00 2.40
101 Cesar Crespo PS RC 8.00 2.40
102 Bret Prinz PS RC 8.00 2.40
103 H.Ramirez PS RC 10.00 3.00
104 E. Guzman PS RC 8.00 2.40
105 Josh Towers PS RC 8.00 2.40
106 B. Duckworth PS RC 8.00 2.40
107 Esix Snead PS RC 8.00 2.40
108 Billy Sylvester PS RC 8.00 2.40
109 Alexis Gomez PS RC 8.00 2.40
110 J. Estrada PS RC 10.00 3.00
111 Joe Kennedy PS RC 8.00 2.40
112 Travis Hafner PS RC 10.00 3.00
113 Martin Vargas PS RC 8.00 2.40
114 Jay Gibbons PS RC 10.00 3.00
115 Andres Torres PS RC 8.00 2.40
116 Sean Douglass PS RC 8.00 2.40
117 Juan Diaz PS RC 8.00 2.40
118 Greg Miller PS RC 8.00 2.40
119 C. Valderrama PS RC 8.00 2.40
120 Bill Ortega PS RC 8.00 2.40
121 Josh Fogg PS RC 8.00 2.40
122 Wilken Ruan PS RC 8.00 2.40
123 Kris Keller PS RC 8.00 2.40
124 Erick Almonte PS RC 8.00 2.40
125 R. Rodriguez PS RC 8.00 2.40
126 Grant Balfour PS RC 8.00 2.40
127 Nick Maness PS RC 8.00 2.40
128 Jeremy Owens PS RC 8.00 2.40
129 Doug Nickle PS RC 8.00 2.40
130 Bert Snow PS RC 8.00 2.40
131 Jason Smith PS RC 8.00 2.40
132 Henry Mateo PS RC 8.00 2.40
133 Mike Penney PS RC 8.00 2.40
134 Bud Smith PS RC 8.00 2.40
135 Junior Spivey PS RC 10.00 3.00
136 Ichiro Suzuki JSY RC 100.00 30.00
137 Albert Pujols JSY RC 120.00 36.00
138 Mark Teixeira JSY RC 120.00 36.00
139 D. Brazelton JSY RC 20.00 6.00
140 Mark Prior JSY RC 120.00 36.00
141 T. Shinjo JSY RC 25.00 7.50

2001 Upper Deck Pros and Prospects Franchise Building Blocks

Issued at a rate of one in six, these 30 cards feature leading player as well as the leading prospect or rookie from each major league franchise.

Nm-Mt Ex-Mt
COMPLETE SET (30) 50.00 15.00
F1 Darin Erstad 1.00 .30
Elpidio Guzman
F2 Jason Giambi 1.50 .45
Jason Hart
F3 Carlos Delgado 1.00 .30
Vernon Wells
F4 Greg Vaughn 1.00 .30
Aubrey Huff
F5 Jim Thome 1.50 .45
C.C. Sabathia
F6 Edgar Martinez 5.00 1.50
Ichiro Suzuki
F7 Cal Ripken Jr. 5.00 1.50
Josh Towers
F8 Ivan Rodriguez 1.50 .45
Carlos Pena
F9 Nomar Garciaparra 2.50 .75
Dernell Stenson
F10 Mike Sweeney 1.00 .30
Dee Brown
F11 Bobby Higginson 1.00 .30
Brandon Inge
F12 Brad Radke 1.00 .30
Adam Johnson
F13 Frank Thomas 1.50 .45
Joe Crede
F14 Derek Jeter 4.00 1.20
Nick Johnson
F15 Jeff Bagwell 1.50 .45
Morgan Ensberg
F16 Chipper Jones 1.50 .45
Wilson Betemit
F17 Jeromy Burnitz 1.00 .30
Ben Sheets
F18 Mark McGwire 8.00 2.40
Albert Pujols
F19 Sammy Sosa 2.50 .75
Corey Patterson
F20 Luis Gonzalez 1.00 .30
Jack Cust
F21 Kevin Brown 1.00 .30
Luke Prokopec
F22 Vladimir Guerrero 1.50 .45
Wilkin Ruan
F23 Barry Bonds 4.00 1.20
Carlos Valderrama
F24 Preston Wilson 1.00 .30
Abraham Nunez
F25 Mike Piazza 2.50 .75
Alex Escobar
F26 Tony Gwynn 2.00 .60
Xavier Nady
F27 Scott Rolen 1.00 .30
Jimmy Rollins
F28 Jason Kendall 1.00 .30
Jack Wilson
F29 Ken Griffey Jr. 2.50 .75
Adam Dunn
F30 Todd Helton 1.00 .30
Juan Uribe

2001 Upper Deck Pros and Prospects Game Bat

Issued at a rate of one in 24, these 13 cards feature two bat pieces on each card.

Nm-Mt Ex-Mt
GOLD RANDOM INSERTS IN PACKS ..
GOLD PRINT RUN 25 SERIAL #'d SETS
NO GOLD PRICING DUE TO SCARCITY
PPBT Jeff Bagwell 15.00 4.50
Frank Thomas
PPGBO Ken Griffey Jr. 40.00 12.00
Barry Bonds
PPGBU Shawn Green 10.00 3.00
Jeromy Burnitz
PPJL Andruw Jones 10.00 3.00
Kenny Lofton
PPJP Chipper Jones 50.00 15.00
Albert Pujols
PPKA Jeff Kent 15.00 4.50
Roberto Alomar
PPMJ Greg Maddux 15.00 4.50
Randy Johnson
PPPT Rafael Palmeiro 15.00 4.50
Jim Thome
PPRF Alex Rodriguez 20.00 6.00
Rafael Furcal
PPRG Manny Ramirez 15.00 4.50
Juan Gonzalez
PPRP Ivan Rodriguez 15.00 4.50
Mike Piazza
PPSG Sammy Sosa 20.00 6.00
Luis Gonzalez
PPWI Bernie Williams 40.00 12.00
Ichiro Suzuki

2001 Upper Deck Pros and Prospects Ichiro World Tour

Issued one per 12 packs, these 15 cards feature Ichrio Suzuki and information about various ballparks he played in.

Nm-Mt Ex-Mt
COMPLETE SET (15) 100.00 30.00
COMMON CARD (WT1-WT15) 8.00 2.40

2001 Upper Deck Pros and Prospects Legends Game Bat

Issued one per 216 packs, these six cards feature two bat pieces from players whose careers are related to each other.

Nm-Mt Ex-Mt
GOLD RANDOM INSERTS IN PACKS ..
GOLD PRINT RUN 25 SERIAL #'d SETS
NO GOLD PRICING DUE TO SCARCITY
PL-BY Jeromy Burnitz 25.00 7.50
Robin Yount
PL-GM Ken Griffey Jr.
Joe Morgan
PL-RF Manny Ramirez 15.00 4.50
Carlton Fisk
PL-RG Cal Ripken Jr. 50.00 15.00
Tony Gwynn
PL-SB Sammy Sosa
Ernie Banks
PL-WJ Bernie Williams 25.00 7.50
Reggie Jackson

2001 Upper Deck Pros and Prospects Specialty Game Jersey

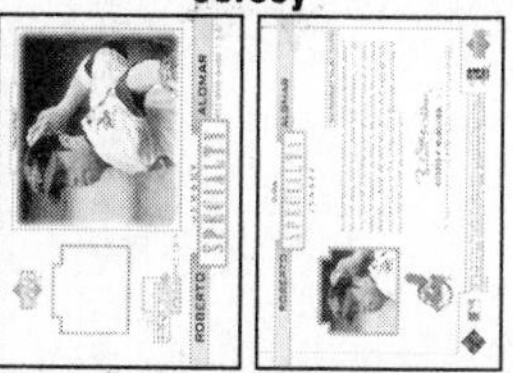

Inserted one per 24 packs, these cards feature a piece of a jersey worn by the featured player in a special event.

Nm-Mt Ex-Mt
GOLD RANDOM INSERTS IN PACKS ..

GOLD PRINT RUN 25 SERIAL #'d SETS
NO GOLD PRICING DUE TO SCARCITY
S-I Ichiro Suzuki 80.00 24.00
S-AR Alex Rodriguez 20.00 6.00
S-BB Barry Bonds 25.00 7.50
S-CR Cal Ripken 40.00 12.00
S-JE Jim Edmonds 8.00 2.40
S-JG Juan Gonzalez 10.00 3.00
S-JT Jim Thome 10.00 3.00
S-LW Larry Walker 10.00 3.00
S-RA Roberto Alomar 10.00 3.00
S-RJ Randy Johnson 10.00 3.00
S-SG Shawn Green 8.00 2.40
S-SR Scott Rolen 10.00 3.00
S-SS Sammy Sosa 20.00 6.00
S-TG Tony Gwynn 15.00 4.50

2001 Upper Deck Pros and Prospects Then and Now Game Jersey

Issued at a rate of one in 24, these 25 cards feature a retrospective look at the showcased player's career by including a jersey swatch from both his past team and his current team. Nolan Ryan is featured with three different swatches.

Nm-Mt Ex-Mt
GOLD RANDOM INSERTS IN PACKS ..
GOLD PRINT RUN 25 SERIAL #'d SETS
NO GOLD PRICING DUE TO SCARCITY
TN-AR Alex Rodriguez 25.00 7.50
TN-B Barry Bonds 40.00 12.00
TN-CS Curt Schilling 15.00 4.50
TN-FG Freddy Garcia 10.00 3.00
TN-GM Greg Maddux 15.00 4.50
TN-GS Gary Sheffield 10.00 3.00
TN-JE Jim Edmonds 10.00 3.00
TN-JG Jason Giambi 15.00 4.50
TN-JG Juan Gonzalez 15.00 4.50
TN-KB Kevin Brown 10.00 3.00
TN-KG Ken Griffey Jr. 20.00 6.00
TN-MP Mike Piazza 15.00 4.50
TN-MR Manny Ramirez 10.00 3.00
TN-NR Nolan Ryan 120.00 36.00
TN-PM Pedro Martinez 15.00 4.50
TN-PN Phil Nevin 10.00 3.00
TN-RA Rick Ankiel 10.00 3.00
TN-RC Roger Clemens 30.00 9.00
TN-RJ Randy Johnson 15.00 4.50
TN-RV Robin Ventura 10.00 3.00
TN-XN Xavier Nady 10.00 3.00

2001 Upper Deck Prospect Premieres

The 2001 Upper Deck Prospect Premieres was released in October 2001 and features a 102-card set. The first 90 cards are regular and the last 12 are autographed cards numbered to 1000 randomly inserted into packs. The packs contain four cards and have a SRP of $2.99 per pack. There were 18 packs per box.

Nm-Mt Ex-Mt
COMP.SET w/o SP's (90) 25.00 7.50
COMMON CARD (1-90) .40 .12
COMMON AUTO (91-102) 15.00 4.50
1 Jeff Mathis XRC 1.50 .45
2 Jake Woods XRC .40 .12
3 Dallas McPherson XRC 2.00 .60
4 Steven Shell XRC .40 .12
5 Ryan Budde XRC .40 .12
6 Kirk Saarloos XRC .40 .12
7 Ryan Stegall XRC .40 .12
8 Bobby Crosby XRC 3.00 .90
9 J.T. Stotts XRC .40 .12
10 Neal Cotts XRC 1.50 .45
11 J.Bonderman XRC 1.00 .30
12 Brandon League XRC .40 .12
13 Tyrell Godwin XRC .40 .12
14 Gabe Gross XRC .50 .15
15 Chris Neylan XRC .40 .12
16 Macay McBride XRC .40 .12
17 Josh Burrus XRC .40 .12
18 Adam Stern XRC .40 .12
19 Richard Lewis XRC .40 .12
20 Cole Barthel XRC .40 .12
21 Mike Jones XRC .50 .15
22 J.J. Hardy XRC 2.50 .75
23 Jon Steitz XRC .40 .12
24 Brad Nelson XRC 1.25 .35
25 Justin Pope XRC .40 .12
26 Dan Haren XRC UER 1.00 .30
Blurb incorrectly lists him as a lefty
27 Andy Sisco XRC 1.25 .35
28 Ryan Theriot XRC .40 .12
29 Ricky Nolasco XRC .40 .12
30 Jon Switzer XRC .40 .12
31 Justin Wechsler XRC .40 .12
32 Mike Gosling XRC .40 .12
33 Scott Hairston XRC 1.50 .45
34 Brian Pilkington XRC .75 .23
35 Kole Strayhorn XRC .40 .12
36 David Taylor XRC .40 .12
37 Donald Levinski XRC .40 .12
38 Mike Hinckley XRC .75 .23
39 Nick Long XRC .40 .12
40 Brad Hennessey XRC .40 .12
41 Noah Lowry XRC .40 .12
42 Josh Cram XRC .40 .12
43 Jesse Foppert XRC 1.50 .45
44 Julian Benavidez XRC .40 .12
45 Dan Denham XRC .40 .12
46 Travis Foley XRC .40 .12
47 Mike Conroy XRC .40 .12
48 Jake Dittler XRC .40 .12
49 Rene Rivera XRC .40 .12
50 John Cole XRC .40 .12
51 Lazaro Abreu XRC .40 .12
52 David Wright XRC 1.50 .45
53 Aaron Heilman XRC .75 .23
54 Len DiNardo XRC .40 .12
55 Alhaji Turay XRC .50 .15
56 Chris Smith XRC .40 .12
57 Rommie Lewis XRC .40 .12
58 Bryan Bass XRC .40 .12
59 David Crouthers XRC .40 .12
60 Josh Barfield XRC 2.50 .75
61 Jake Peavy XRC 1.25 .35
62 Ryan Howard XRC 1.00 .30
63 Gavin Floyd XRC 2.00 .60
64 Michael Floyd XRC .40 .12
65 Stefan Bailie XRC .40 .12
66 Jon DeVries XRC .40 .12
67 Steve Kelly XRC .40 .12
68 Alan Moye XRC .40 .12
69 Justin Gillman XRC .40 .12
70 Jayson Nix XRC .75 .23
71 John Draper XRC .40 .12
72 Kenny Baugh XRC .40 .12
73 Michael Woods XRC .40 .12
74 Preston Larrison XRC .50 .15
75 Matt Coenen XRC .40 .12
76 Scott Tyler XRC .50 .15
77 Jose Morales XRC .40 .12
78 Corwin Malone XRC .40 .12
79 Dennis Ulacia XRC .50 .15
80 Andy Gonzalez XRC .40 .12
81 Kris Honel XRC 1.50 .45
82 Wyatt Allen XRC .40 .12
83 Ryan Wing XRC .40 .12
84 Sean Henn XRC .50 .15
85 John-Ford Griffin XRC .50 .15
86 Bronson Sardinha XRC .50 .15
87 Jon Skaggs XRC .40 .12
88 Shelley Duncan XRC .40 .12
89 Jason Arnold XRC 1.00 .30
90 Aaron Rifkin XRC .50 .15
91 Colt Griffin AU XRC 25.00 7.50
92 J.D. Martin AU XRC 15.00 4.50
93 Justin Wayne AU XRC 25.00 7.50
94 J. VanBenschoten AU XRC 40.00 12.00
95 Chris Burke AU XRC 25.00 7.50
96 C. Kotchman AU XRC 60.00 18.00
97 M. Garciaparra AU XRC 25.00 7.50
98 Jake Gautreau AU XRC 15.00 4.50
99 J. Williams AU XRC 40.00 12.00
100 Toe Nash AU XRC 15.00 4.50
101 Joe Borchard AU XRC 40.00 12.00
102 Mark Prior AU XRC 200.00 60.00

2001 Upper Deck Prospect Premieres Heroes of Baseball Game Bat

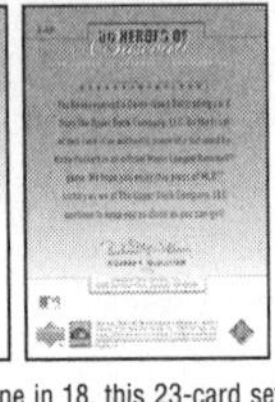

Inserted at a rate of one in 18, this 23-card set features bat pieces of retired players. The cards carry a 'B' prefix.

Nm-Mt Ex-Mt
B-AO Al Oliver 10.00 3.00
B-BB Bill Buckner 10.00 3.00
B-BM Bill Madlock 10.00 3.00
B-DB Don Baylor 10.00 3.00
B-DE Dwight Evans 10.00 3.00
B-DL Davey Lopes 10.00 3.00
B-DP Dave Parker 10.00 3.00
B-DW Dave Winfield 10.00 3.00
B-EM Eddie Murray 15.00 4.50
B-FL Fred Lynn 10.00 3.00
B-GC Gary Carter 15.00 4.50
B-GM Gary Matthews 10.00 3.00
B-JM Joe Morgan 10.00 3.00
B-KEG Ken Griffey Sr. 10.00 3.00
B-KIG Kirk Gibson 10.00 3.00
B-KP Kirby Puckett 15.00 4.50
B-MM Manny Mota 10.00 3.00
B-OS Ozzie Smith 15.00 4.50
B-RJ Reggie Jackson 15.00 4.50
B-SG Steve Garvey 10.00 3.00
B-TM Tim McCarver 10.00 3.00
B-TP Tony Perez 10.00 3.00
B-WB Wade Boggs 15.00 4.50

2001 Upper Deck Prospect Premieres Heroes of Baseball Game Jersey Duos

Inserted at a rate of one in 144, this seven card set featured dual game jerseys of both current and retired players. The cards carry a 'J' prefix.

Nm-Mt Ex-Mt
J-BH Bryan Bass 15.00 4.50
J.J. Hardy
J-DG Shelley Duncan 8.00 2.40
Tyrell Godwin
J-GS Steve Garvey 10.00 3.00
Reggie Smith
J-HB Aaron Heilman 10.00 3.00
Jeremy Bonderman
J-JJ Michael Jordan 100.00 30.00
Michael Jordan
J-SG Jon Switzer 8.00 2.40
Mike Gosling
J-WP Dave Winfield 25.00 7.50
Kirby Puckett

2001 Upper Deck Prospect Premieres Heroes of Baseball Game Jersey Duos Autograph

Randomly inserted into packs, this six card set featured dual game jerseys with autographs of both current and retired players. The cards were serial numbered to 25.The cards carry a 'SJ' prefix. Due to scarcity, no pricing is provided.

Nm-Mt Ex-Mt
SJBH Bryan Bass
J.J. Hardy
SJGS Steve Garvey
Reggie Smith
SJHB Aaron Heilman
Jeremy Bonderman
SJJJ Michael Jordan
Michael Jordan
SJMG Joe Morgan
Ken Griffey Sr
SJWP Dave Winfield
Kirby Puckett

2001 Upper Deck Prospect Premieres Heroes of Baseball Game Jersey Trios

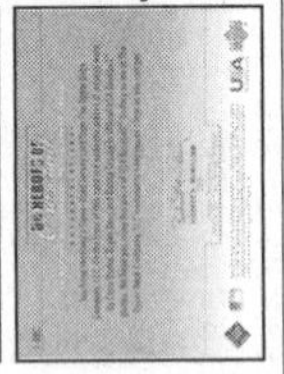

Inserted in packs at a rate of one in 144, these 9 cards feature three swatches of game-worn jerseys on a card. Representatives at Upper Deck have confirmed that the Maris-Mantle-DiMaggio card is in noticeably short supply.

Nm-Mt Ex-Mt
BBC Chris Burke 20.00 6.00
Bryan Bass
Bobby Crosby UER
CGS Bobby Crosby UER 20.00 6.00
Michael Garciaparra
Bronson Sardinha EXCH
GGH Jake Gautreau 10.00 3.00
Tyrell Godwin
Aaron Heilman EXCH
GKB Gabe Gross 15.00 4.50
Casey Kotchmann
Kenny Baugh EXCH
GMS Colt Griffin 8.00 2.40
J.D. Martin
Jon Switzer EXCH
JMD Michael Jordan 400.00 120.00
Mickey Mantle
Joe DiMaggio
JPW Michael Jordan 80.00 24.00
Kirby Puckett
Dave Winfield
MMD Roger Maris 400.00 120.00
Mickey Mantle
Joe DiMaggio SP
VPJ J.VanBenschoten 40.00 12.00
Mark Prior
Mike Jones EXCH

2001 Upper Deck Prospect Premieres Heroes of Baseball Game Jersey Trios Autograph

Randomly inserted in packs, these cards feature not only three swatches of game-worn jerseys but also autographs of the featured players. These cards are serial numbered to 25. Due to scarcity, no pricing is provided.

Nm-Mt Ex-Mt
SJ-BBC Chris Burke
Bryan Bass
Bobby Crosby UER
SJ-JPW Michael Jordan
Kirby Puckett
Dave Winfield
SJ-MGP Joe Morgan
Ken Griffey Sr.
Tony Perez

2001 Upper Deck Prospect Premieres MJ Grandslam Game Bat

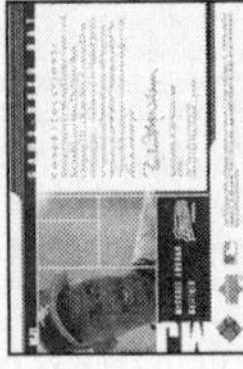

Randomly inserted in packs, these five cards feature bat cards from basketball legend turned baseball prospect. Card number "MJ5" was printed in lesser quantities and is notated in our checklist as an SP.

Nm-Mt Ex-Mt
COMMON CARD (MJ1-MJ4) 30.00 9.00
MJ5 Michael Jordan SP 60.00 18.00

2001 Upper Deck Prospect Premieres Tribute to 42

Issued at a rate of one in 750, these seven cards honor the memory of the integration trail blazer and all time great.

Nm-Mt Ex-Mt
B Jackie Robinson Bat 50.00 15.00
C Jackie Robinson Cut AU
J Jackie Robinson Pants 50.00 15.00
BC Jackie Robinson Bat-Cut AU
GB Jackie Robinson 100.00 30.00
Gold Bat/42
GJ J.Robinson Pants Gold/42 . 100.00 30.00
JC Jackie Robinson Pants-Cut AU

2002 Upper Deck Prospect Premieres

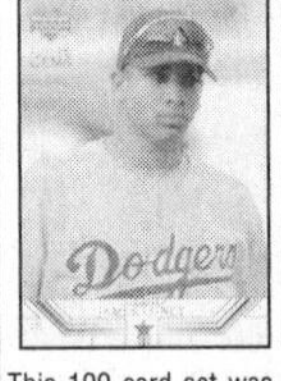

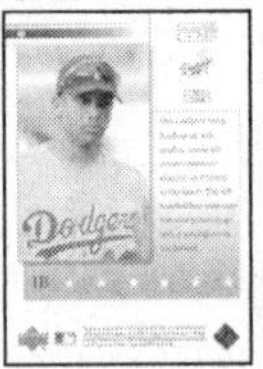

This 109 card set was released in November, 2002. It was issued in four count packs which came 24 packs to a box and 20 boxes to a case with an SRP of $3 per pack. Cards number 61 through 85 feature game-worn jersey pieces and were inserted at a stated rate of one in 18 packs. Cards numbered 86 through 97 feature player's autographs and were issued at a stated rate of one in 18 packs. Cards numbered 98 through 109 feature tribute cards to recently retired superstars Cal Ripken and Mark McGwire along with Yankee great Joe DiMaggio. Matt Pender's basic XRC erroneously packed out picturing Curtis Granderson. A corrected version of the card was made available to collectors a few months after the product went live via a mail exchange program directly from Upper Deck.

Nm-Mt Ex-Mt
COMP.SET w/o SP's (72) 25.00 7.50
COMMON CARD (1-60) .40 .12
COMMON CARD (61-85) 8.00 2.40
COMMON CARD (86-97) 10.00 3.00
COMMON RIPKEN (98-99) 2.00 .60
COMMON MCGWIRE (100-105) . 2.00 .60
COMMON DIMAGGIO (106-109). 1.50 .45
PENDER COR AVAIL.VIA MAIL EXCHANGE
1 Josh Rupe XRC .40 .12
2 Blair Johnson XRC .40 .12
3 Jason Pridie XRC 1.00 .30
4 Tim Gilhooly XRC .40 .12
5 Kennard Jones XRC .40 .12
6 Darrell Rasner XRC .40 .12
7 Adam Donachie XRC .40 .12
8 Josh Murray XRC .40 .12
9 Brian Dopirak XRC 1.25 .35
10 Jason Cooper XRC .40 .12
11 Zach Hammes XRC .50 .15
12 Jon Lester XRC .40 .12
13 Kevin Jepsen XRC .40 .12
14 Curtis Granderson XRC .75 .23
15 David Bush XRC 1.25 .35
16 Joel Guzman .40 .12
17A Matt Pender UER XRC .40 .12
Pictures Curtis Granderson
17B Matt Pender COR
18 Derick Grigsby XRC .40 .12
19 Jeremy Reed XRC 2.50 .75
20 Jonathan Broxton XRC .40 .12
21 Jesse Crain XRC .40 .12
22 Justin Jones XRC 1.25 .35
23 Brian Slocum XRC .40 .12
24 Brian McCann XRC .75 .23
25 Francisco Liriano XRC .50 .15
26 Fred Lewis XRC .40 .12
27 Steve Stanley XRC .40 .12
28 Chris Snyder XRC .40 .12
29 Dan Cevette XRC .40 .12
30 Kiel Fisher XRC .50 .15
31 Brandon Weeden XRC .40 .12
32 Pat Osborn XRC .40 .12
33 Taber Lee XRC .40 .12
34 Dan Ortmeier XRC .75 .23
35 Josh Johnson XRC .40 .12
36 Val Majewski XRC .75 .23
37 Larry Broadway XRC 1.25 .35
38 Joey Gomes XRC .40 .12
39 Eric Thomas XRC .40 .12
40 James Loney XRC 2.50 .75
41 Charlie Morton XRC .40 .12
42 Mark McLemore XRC .40 .12
43 Matt Craig XRC .40 .12
44 Ryan Rodriguez XRC .40 .12
45 Rich Hill XRC .40 .12
46 Bob Malek XRC .40 .12
47 Justin Maureau XRC .40 .12
48 Randy Braun XRC .40 .12
49 Brian Grant XRC .40 .12
50 Tyler Davidson XRC .40 .12
51 Travis Hanson XRC .50 .15
52 Kyle Boyer XRC .40 .12
53 James Holcomb XRC .40 .12
54 Ryan Williams XRC .40 .12
55 Ben Crockett XRC .40 .12
56 Adam Greenberg XRC .40 .12
57 John Baker XRC .40 .12
58 Matt Carson XRC .40 .12
59 Jonathan George XRC .40 .12
60 David Jensen XRC .40 .12
61 Nick Swisher JSY XRC 10.00 3.00
62 Br.Clevlen JSY XRC UER 10.00 3.00
Name mispelled as Cleven
63 Royce Ring JSY XRC 10.00 3.00
64 Mike Nixon JSY XRC 8.00 2.40
65 Ricky Barrett JSY XRC 8.00 2.40
66 Russ Adams JSY XRC 10.00 3.00
67 Joe Mauer JSY XRC 25.00 7.50
68 Jeff Francoeur JSY XRC 30.00 9.00
69 Joseph Blanton JSY XRC 15.00 4.50
70 Micah Schilling JSY XRC 8.00 2.40
71 John McCurdy JSY XRC 8.00 2.40
72 Sergio Santos JSY XRC 10.00 3.00
73 Josh Womack JSY XRC 8.00 2.40
74 Jared Doyle JSY XRC 8.00 2.40
75 Ben Fritz JSY XRC 8.00 2.40
76 Greg Miller JSY XRC 15.00 4.50
77 Luke Hagerty JSY XRC 8.00 2.40
78 Matt Whitney JSY XRC 10.00 3.00
79 Dan Meyer JSY XRC 10.00 3.00
80 Bill Murphy JSY XRC 8.00 2.40
81 Zach Segovia JSY XRC 10.00 3.00
82 St. Obenchain JSY XRC 8.00 2.40
83 Matt Clanton JSY XRC 8.00 2.40
84 Mark Teahen JSY XRC 8.00 2.40
85 Kyle Pawelczyk JSY XRC 8.00 2.40
86 Khalil Greene AU XRC 40.00 12.00
87 Joe Saunders AU XRC 10.00 3.00
88 Jeremy Hermida AU XRC 30.00 9.00
89 Drew Meyer AU XRC 10.00 3.00
90 Jeff Francis AU XRC 10.00 3.00
91 Scott Moore AU XRC 15.00 4.50
92 Prince Fielder AU XRC 80.00 24.00
93 Zack Greinke AU XRC 50.00 15.00
94 Chris Gruler AU XRC 10.00 3.00
95 Scott Kazmir AU XRC 80.00 24.00
96 B.J. Upton AU XRC 60.00 18.00
97 Clint Everts AU XRC 20.00 6.00
98 Cal Ripken TRIB 2.00 .60
99 Cal Ripken TRIB 2.00 .60
100 Mark McGwire TRIB 2.00 .60
101 Mark McGwire TRIB 2.00 .60
102 Mark McGwire TRIB 2.00 .60
103 Mark McGwire TRIB 2.00 .60
104 Mark McGwire TRIB 2.00 .60
105 Joe DiMaggio TRIB 1.50 .45
106 Joe DiMaggio TRIB 1.50 .45
107 Joe DiMaggio TRIB 1.50 .45
108 Joe DiMaggio TRIB 1.50 .45
109 Joe DiMaggio TRIB 1.50 .45

2002 Upper Deck Prospect Premieres Future Gems Quads

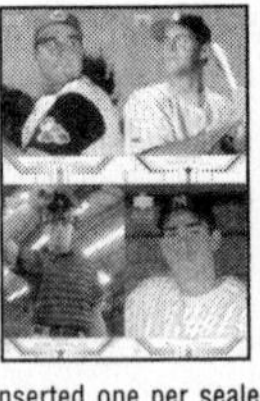

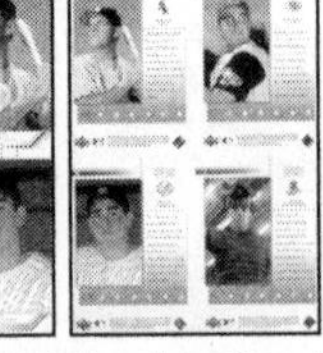

Inserted one per sealed box, these 33 cards feature four different cards in a panel and were issued to a stated print run of 600 serial numbered sets.

Nm-Mt Ex-Mt
1 David Bush 8.00 2.40
Matt Craig
Josh Johnson
Brian McCann
2 Jason Cooper 8.00 2.40
Jonathan George
Larry Broadway
Joel Guzman
3 Matt Craig 8.00 2.40
Josh Murray
Brian McCann
Jason Pridie
4 Jesse Crain 8.00 2.40
Brian Grant
Curtis Granderson
Joey Gomes
5 Tyler Davidson 8.00 2.40
Val Majewski
Justin Jones
Daniel Cevette
6 Joe DiMaggio 8.00 2.40
Jon Lester
Mark McGwire
Mark McLemore
7 Jonathan George 8.00 2.40
Jeremy Reed
Adam Donachie

Matt Carson
8 Jonathan George 8.00 2.40
Eric Thomas
Joel Guzman
Kiel Fisher
9 Tim Gilhooly 8.00 2.40
Brandon Weeden
Brian Slocum
Brian Dopirak
10 Brian Grant 8.00 2.40
Rich Hill
Joey Gomes
Joe DiMaggio
11 Derick Grigsby 8.00 2.40
Bob Malek
James Loney
Fred Lewis
12 Zach Hammes 8.00 2.40
James Holcomb
Cal Ripken
Kennard Jones
13 Rich Hill 8.00 2.40
Mark McGwire
Brian Grant
Matt Carson
14 James Holcomb 8.00 2.40
David Jensen
Kennard Jones
Ryan Williams
15 David Jensen 8.00 2.40
Francisco Liriano
Ryan Williams
Travis Hanson
16 Josh Johnson 8.00 2.40
Jesse Crain
Adam Greenberg
Curtis Granderson
17 Jon Lester 8.00 2.40
Jonathan George
Mark McLemore
Adam Donachie
18 Francisco Liriano 8.00 2.40
Mark McGwire
Travis Hanson
Taber Lee
19 Val Majewski 8.00 2.40
Charlie Morton
Daniel Cevette
Joey Gomes
20 Bob Malek 8.00 2.40
Zach Hammes
Fred Lewis
Cal Ripken
21 Justin Maureau 8.00 2.40
Joe DiMaggio
Chris Snyder
Mark McGwire
22 Mark McGwire 8.00 2.40
Bob Malek
Joe DiMaggio
Kyle Boyer
23 Charlie Morton 8.00 2.40
David Bush#Joey Gomes
Josh Johnson
24 Josh Murray 8.00 2.40
Mark McGwire
Jason Pridie
Joe DiMaggio
25 Matt Pender UER 8.00 2.40
Mark McGwire
Mark McLemore
Ryan Rodriguez
26 Jason Pridie 8.00 2.40
Josh Murray
Matt Craig
Brian McCann
27 Jeremy Reed 8.00 2.40
Josh Johnson
Matt Carson
Adam Greenberg
28 Cal Ripken 8.00 2.40
Jason Cooper
Matt Carson
Larry Broadway
29 Ryan Rodriguez 8.00 2.40
Eric Thomas
Pat Osborn
Randy Braun
30 Josh Rupe 8.00 2.40
Tyler Davidson
John Baker
Justin Jones
31 Eric Thomas 8.00 2.40
Derick Grigsby
Randy Braun
James Loney
32 Eric Thomas 8.00 2.40
Matt Pender UER
Kiel Fisher
Mark McLemore
33 Brandon Weeden 8.00 2.40
Rich Hill
Brian Dopirak
Brian Grant

2002 Upper Deck Prospect Premieres Heroes of Baseball

Inserted at stated odds of one per pack, these 90 cards feature 10 cards each of various baseball legends. Each player featured has nine regular cards and one header card.

	Nm-Mt	Ex-Mt
COMP.RIPKEN SET (10)	20.00	6.00
COMMON RIPKEN (CR1-HDR)	2.50	.75
COMP.DIMAGGIO SET (10)	10.00	3.00
COMMON DIMAGGIO (JD1-HDR)	1.25	.35
COMP.MORGAN SET (10)	5.00	1.50
COMMON MORGAN (JM1-HDR)	.75	.23
COMP.MCGWIRE SET (10)	20.00	6.00
COMMON MCGWIRE (MC1-HDR)	2.50	.75
COMP.MANTLE SET (10)	25.00	7.50
COMMON MANTLE (MM1-HDR)	3.00	.90
COMP.OZZIE SET (10)	15.00	4.50
COMMON OZZIE (OS1-HDR)	2.00	.60
COMP.GWYNN SET (10)	15.00	4.50
COMMON GWYNN (TG1-HDR)	2.00	.60
COMP.SEAVER SET (10)	10.00	3.00
COMMON SEAVER (TS1-HDR)	1.25	.35
COMP.STARGELL SET (10)	5.00	1.50
COMMON STARGELL (WS1-HDR)	.75	.23

2002 Upper Deck Prospect Premieres Heroes of Baseball 85 Quads

Randomly inserted as boxtoppers, these eight panels feature a mix of four cards of the players featured in the Heroes of Baseball insert set. Each of these cards are issued to a stated print run of 85 serial numbered sets.

Nm-Mt Ex-Mt
1 Joe DiMaggio 15.00 4.50
Tony Gwynn
Tony Gwynn
Joe DiMaggio
2 Joe DiMaggio 25.00 7.50
Tony Gwynn
Cal Ripken
Cal Ripken
3 Joe DiMaggio Hdr 25.00 7.50
Mickey Mantle
Willie Stargell Hdr
Mickey Mantle
4 Tony Gwynn 15.00 4.50
Tony Gwynn
Ozzie Smith
Willie Stargell
5 Tony Gwynn 15.00 4.50
Willie Stargell
Joe DiMaggio
Joe Morgan
6 Tony Gwynn 15.00 4.50
Willie Stargell
Cal Ripken
Ozzie Smith
7 Mickey Mantle 25.00 7.50
Mark McGwire
Joe Morgan
Tom Seaver
8 Mickey Mantle 25.00 7.50
Tom Seaver
Mickey Mantle
Tom Seaver
9 Mark McGwire 25.00 7.50
Joe Morgan
Mark McGwire
Joe Morgan
10 Mark McGwire Hdr 25.00 7.50
Cal Ripken
Tony Gwynn
Joe DiMaggio
11 Mark McGwire 15.00 4.50
Tom Seaver
Joe Morgan
Ozzie Smith
12 Joe Morgan 15.00 4.50
Tony Gwynn
Joe Morgan
Tony Gwynn
13 Joe Morgan 25.00 7.50
Joe DiMaggio
Mickey Mantle
Cal Ripken
14 Joe Morgan 15.00 4.50
Joe DiMaggio
Willie Stargell
Tony Gwynn
15 Ozzie Smith 15.00 4.50
Joe DiMaggio
Ozzie Smith
Willie Stargell
16 Ozzie Smith 15.00 4.50
Mark McGwire
Willie Stargell
Tony Gwynn
17 Ozzie Smith 15.00 4.50
Tom Seaver
Tom Seaver
Mark McGwire
18 Cal Ripken 25.00 7.50
Mickey Mantle
Joe DiMaggio
Joe Morgan
19 Cal Ripken 25.00 7.50
Mark McGwire
Cal Ripken
Mark McGwire
20 Tom Seaver 15.00 4.50
Joe DiMaggio
Tom Seaver
Joe DiMaggio
21 Tom Seaver 15.00 4.50
Joe Morgan
Ozzie Smith
Willie Stargell
22 Tom Seaver 25.00 7.50
Cal Ripken
Mark McGwire
Mickey Mantle
23 Willie Stargell 15.00 4.50
Ozzie Smith
Ozzie Smith
Willie Stargell
24 Willie Stargell 15.00 4.50
Ozzie Smith
Tom Seaver
Joe Morgan

2003 Upper Deck Prospect Premieres

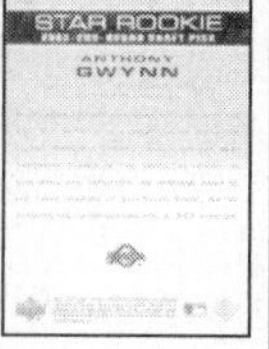

For the third consecutive year, Upper Deck produced a set consisting solely of players who had been taken during that season's amateur draft. This was a 90-card standard-size set which was released in December, 2003. This set was issued in four-card packs with an $2.99 SRP which came 16 packs to a box and 18 boxes to a case.

	MINT	NRMT
COMPLETE SET (90)	50.00	22.00
1 Bryan Opdyke XRC	.50	.23
2 Gabriel Sosa XRC	.50	.23
3 Tila Reynolds XRC	.50	.23
4 Aaron Hill XRC	1.50	.70
5 Aaron Marsden XRC	.75	.35
6 Abe Alvarez XRC	.75	.35
7 Adam Jones XRC	1.00	.45
8 Adam Miller XRC	1.00	.45
9 Andre Ethier XRC	.50	.23
10 Anthony Gwynn XRC	1.50	.70
11 Brad Snyder XRC	1.25	.55
12 Brad Sullivan XRC	1.00	.45
13 Brian Anderson XRC	1.50	.70
14 Brian Buscher XRC	.50	.23
15 Brian Snyder XRC	.75	.35
16 Carlos Quentin XRC	1.25	.55
17 Chad Billingsley XRC	1.00	.45
18 Fraser Dizard XRC	.75	.35
19 Chris Durbin XRC	.50	.23
20 Chris Ray XRC	.75	.35
21 Conor Jackson XRC	1.50	.70
22 Kory Casto XRC	.50	.23
23 Craig Whitaker XRC	1.00	.45
24 Daniel Moore XRC	.50	.23
25 Daric Barton XRC	1.50	.70
26 Darin Downs XRC	1.00	.45
27 David Murphy XRC	1.50	.70
28 Dustin Majewski XRC	.75	.35
29 Edgardo Baez XRC	1.00	.45
30 Jake Fox XRC	.75	.35
31 Jake Stevens XRC	.75	.35
32 Jamie D'Antona XRC	2.00	.90
33 James Houser XRC	1.00	.45
34 Jar. Saltalamacchia XRC	1.00	.45
35 Jason Hirsh XRC	.75	.35
36 Javi Herrera XRC	.75	.35
37 Jeff Allison XRC	2.00	.90
38 John Hudgins XRC	.50	.23
39 Jo Jo Reyes XRC	1.00	.45
40 Justin James XRC	.50	.23
41 Kurt Isenberg XRC	.50	.23
42 Kyle Boyer XRC	.75	.35
43 Lastings Milledge XRC	2.50	1.10
44 Luis Atilano XRC	.50	.23
45 Matt Murton XRC	1.00	.45
46 Matt Moses XRC	2.00	.90
47 Matt Harrison XRC	.75	.35
48 Michael Bourn XRC	.75	.35
49 Miguel Vega XRC	.50	.23
50 Mitch Maier XRC	1.00	.45
51 Omar Quintanilla XRC	1.00	.45
52 Ryan Sweeney XRC	3.00	1.35
53 Scott Baker XRC	.50	.23
54 Sean Rodriguez XRC	1.25	.55
55 Steve Lerud XRC	.50	.23
56 Thomas Pauly XRC	.50	.23
57 Tom Gorzelanny XRC	.75	.35
58 Tim Moss XRC	.75	.35
59 Robbie Wooley XRC	.75	.35
60 Trey Webb XRC	.50	.23
61 Wes Littleton XRC	1.00	.45
62 Beau Vaughan XRC	.75	.35
63 Willy Jo Ronda XRC	1.00	.45
64 Chris Lubanski XRC	1.50	.70
65 Ian Stewart XRC	4.00	1.80
66 John Danks XRC	1.25	.55
67 Kyle Sleeth XRC	2.00	.90
68 Michael Aubrey XRC	2.50	1.10
69 Kevin Kouzmanoff XRC	1.25	.55
70 Ryan Harvey XRC	2.50	1.10
71 Tim Stauffer XRC	1.00	.45
72 Tony Richie XRC	.50	.23
73 Brandon Wood XRC	1.25	.55
74 David Aardsma XRC	1.25	.55
75 David Shinskie XRC	.50	.23
76 Dennis Dove XRC	.75	.35
77 Eric Sultemeier XRC	.50	.23
78 Jay Sborz XRC	.75	.35
79 Jimmy Barthmaier XRC	.50	.23
80 Josh Whitesell XRC	.50	.23
81 Josh Anderson XRC	.75	.35
82 Kenny Lewis XRC	1.00	.45
83 Mateo Miramontes XRC	.50	.23
84 Nick Markakis XRC	1.25	.55
85 Paul Bacot XRC	.75	.35
86 Peter Stonard XRC	.50	.23
87 Reggie Willits XRC	.50	.23
88 Shane Costa XRC	.75	.35
89 Billy Sadler XRC	.50	.23
90 Delmon Young XRC	4.00	1.80

2003 Upper Deck Prospect Premieres Autographs

Please note that a few players who were anticipated to have cards in this set do not exist. Those card numbers are P18, P28, P47, P54, P59 and P69.

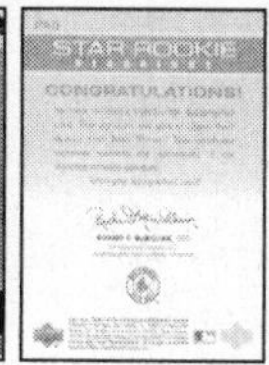

	MINT	NRMT
STATED ODDS 1:9		
P1 Bryan Opdyke	10.00	4.50
P2 Gabriel Sosa	10.00	4.50
P3 Tila Reynolds	10.00	4.50
P4 Aaron Hill	30.00	13.50
P5 Aaron Marsden	15.00	6.75
P6 Abe Alvarez	15.00	6.75
P7 Adam Jones	20.00	9.00
P8 Adam Miller	20.00	9.00
P9 Andre Ethier	10.00	4.50
P10 Anthony Gwynn	30.00	13.50
P11 Brad Snyder	20.00	9.00
P12 Brad Sullivan	15.00	6.75
P13 Brian Anderson	30.00	13.50
P14 Brian Buscher	10.00	4.50
P15 Brian Snyder	15.00	6.75
P16 Carlos Quentin	25.00	11.00
P17 Chad Billingsley	20.00	9.00
P19 Chris Durbin	10.00	4.50
P20 Chris Ray	15.00	6.75
P21 Conor Jackson	30.00	13.50
P22 Kory Casto	10.00	4.50
P23 Craig Whitaker	15.00	6.75
P24 Daniel Moore	10.00	4.50
P25 Daric Barton	25.00	11.00
P26 Darin Downs	20.00	9.00
P27 David Murphy	30.00	13.50
P29 Edgardo Baez	15.00	6.75
P30 Jake Fox	15.00	6.75
P31 Jake Stevens	15.00	6.75
P32 Jamie D'Antona	25.00	11.00
P33 James Houser	15.00	6.75
P34 Jarrod Saltalamacchia	20.00	9.00
P35 Jason Hirsh	15.00	6.75
P36 Javi Herrera	15.00	6.75
P37 Jeff Allison	40.00	18.00
P38 John Hudgins	10.00	4.50
P39 Jo Jo Reyes	15.00	6.75
P40 Justin James	10.00	4.50
P41 Kurt Isenberg	10.00	4.50
P42 Kyle Boyer	15.00	6.75
P43 Lastings Milledge	50.00	22.00
P44 Luis Atilano	10.00	4.50
P45 Matt Murton	15.00	6.75
P46 Matt Moses	40.00	18.00
P48 Michael Bourn	10.00	4.50
P49 Miguel Vega	10.00	4.50
P50 Mitch Maier	15.00	6.75
P51 Omar Quintanilla	15.00	6.75
P52 Ryan Sweeney	50.00	22.00
P53 Scott Baker	10.00	4.50
P55 Steve Lerud	15.00	6.75
P56 Thomas Pauly	10.00	4.50
P57 Tom Gorzelanny	15.00	6.75
P58 Tim Moss	15.00	6.75
P60 Trey Webb	10.00	4.50
P61 Wes Littleton	15.00	6.75
P62 Beau Vaughan	15.00	6.75
P63 Willy Jo Ronda	15.00	6.75
P64 Chris Lubanski	25.00	11.00
P65 Ian Stewart	70.00	32.00
P66 John Danks	25.00	11.00
P67 Kyle Sleeth	40.00	18.00
P68 Michael Aubrey	50.00	22.00
P70 Ryan Harvey	40.00	18.00
P71 Tim Stauffer	20.00	9.00

2003 Upper Deck Prospect Premieres Game Jersey

Please note that card number P90 does not exist.

	MINT	NRMT
STATED ODDS 1:18		
P72 Tony Richie	8.00	3.60
P73 Brandon Wood	15.00	6.75
P74 David Aardsma	20.00	9.00
P75 David Shinskie	8.00	3.60
P76 Dennis Dove	10.00	4.50
P77 Eric Sultimeier	8.00	3.60
P78 Jay Sborz	10.00	4.50
P79 Jimmy Barthmaier	8.00	3.60
P80 Josh Whitesell	8.00	3.60
P81 Josh Anderson	10.00	4.50
P82 Kenny Lewis	10.00	4.50
P83 Mateo Miramontes	8.00	3.60
P84 Nick Markakis	15.00	6.75
P85 Paul Bacot	10.00	4.50
P86 Peter Stonard	8.00	3.60
P87 Reggie Willits	8.00	3.60
P88 Shane Costa	10.00	4.50
P89 Billy Sadler	8.00	3.60
P91 Kyle Sleeth	10.00	4.50
P92 Ian Stewart	20.00	9.00
P93 Fraser Dizard	10.00	4.50
P94 Abe Alvarez	10.00	4.50
P95 Adam Jones	10.00	4.50
P96 Brian Anderson	15.00	6.75
P97 Chris Durbin	8.00	3.60
P98 Craig Whitaker	10.00	4.50
P99 Jake Fox	10.00	4.50
P100 Kurt Isenberg	8.00	3.60
P101 Luis Atilano	8.00	3.60
P102 Miguel Vega	8.00	3.60
P103 Mitch Maier	10.00	4.50
P104 Ryan Sweeney	15.00	6.75
P105 Scott Baker	8.00	3.60
P106 Sean Rodriguez	10.00	4.50
P108 Trey Webb	8.00	3.60
P109 Willy Jo Ronda	10.00	4.50
P110 John Danks	10.00	4.50
P111 Michael Aubrey	15.00	6.75
P112 Lastings Milledge	15.00	6.75
P113 Chris Lubanski	15.00	6.75

1998 Upper Deck Retro

The 1998 Upper Deck Retro set contains 129 standard size cards. The six-card packs retailed for $4.99 each. The set contains the subset: Futurama (101-130). The fronts feature current superstars as well as some retired legends surrounded by a four-sided white border and printed on super-thick, uncoated 24-pt stock card. The featured player's name lines the bottom border of the card. Card number 82 (originally slated to be Stan Musial) does not exist. Rookie Cards include Troy Glaus.

	Nm-Mt	Ex-Mt
COMPLETE SET (129)	40.00	12.00
1 Jim Edmonds	.40	.12
2 Darin Erstad	.40	.12
3 Tim Salmon	.60	.18
4 Jay Bell	.40	.12
5 Matt Williams	.40	.12
6 Andres Galarraga	.40	.12
7 Andruw Jones	.40	.12
8 Chipper Jones	1.00	.30
9 Greg Maddux	1.50	.45
10 Rafael Palmeiro	.60	.18
11 Cal Ripken	3.00	.90
12 Brooks Robinson	1.00	.30
13 Nomar Garciaparra	1.50	.45
14 Pedro Martinez	1.00	.30
15 Mo Vaughn	.40	.12
16 Ernie Banks	1.00	.30
17 Mark Grace	.60	.18
18 Gary Matthews Sr.	.40	.12
19 Sammy Sosa	1.50	.45
20 Albert Belle	.40	.12
21 Carlton Fisk	.60	.18
22 Frank Thomas	1.00	.30
23 Ken Griffey Sr.	.40	.12
24 Paul Konerko	.40	.12
25 Barry Larkin	1.00	.30
26 Sean Casey	.40	.12
27 Tony Perez	.40	.12
28 Bob Feller	.60	.18
29 Kenny Lofton	.40	.12
30 Manny Ramirez	.40	.12
31 Jim Thome	1.00	.30
32 Omar Vizquel	.40	.12
33 Dante Bichette	.40	.12
34 Larry Walker	.60	.18
35 Tony Clark	.40	.12
36 Damion Easley	.40	.12
37 Cliff Floyd	.40	.12
38 Livan Hernandez	.40	.12
39 Jeff Bagwell	.60	.18
40 Craig Biggio	.60	.18
41 Al Kaline	1.00	.30
42 Johnny Damon	.40	.12
43 Dean Palmer	.40	.12
44 Charles Johnson	.40	.12
45 Eric Karros	.40	.12
46 Gaylord Perry	.40	.12
47 Raul Mondesi	.40	.12
48 Gary Sheffield	.40	.12
49 Eddie Mathews	1.00	.30
50 Warren Spahn	.60	.18
51 Jeromy Burnitz	.40	.12
52 Jeff Cirillo	.40	.12
53 Marquis Grissom	.40	.12
54 Paul Molitor	.60	.18
55 Kirby Puckett	1.00	.30
56 Brad Radke	.40	.12
57 Todd Walker	.40	.12
58 Vladimir Guerrero	1.00	.30
59 Brad Fullmer	.40	.12
60 Rondell White	.40	.12
61 Bobby Jones	.40	.12
62 Hideo Nomo	1.00	.30
63 Mike Piazza	1.50	.45
64 Tom Seaver	.60	.18
65 Frank Thomas	.40	.12
66 Yogi Berra	1.00	.30
67 Derek Jeter	2.50	.75
68 Tino Martinez	.60	.18
69 Paul O'Neill	.60	.18
70 Andy Pettitte	.60	.18
71 Rollie Fingers	.40	.12
72 Rickey Henderson	1.00	.30
73 Matt Stairs	.40	.12
74 Scott Rolen	.60	.18
75 Curt Schilling	.60	.18
76 Jose Guillen	.40	.12
77 Jason Kendall	.40	.12
78 Lou Brock	.60	.18
79 Bob Gibson	.60	.18
80 Ray Lankford	.40	.12
81 Mark McGwire	2.50	.75
83 Kevin Brown	.60	.18
84 Ken Caminiti	.40	.12
85 Tony Gwynn	1.25	.35
86 Greg Vaughn	.40	.12
87 Barry Bonds	2.50	.75
88 Willie Stargell	.60	.18
89 Willie McCovey	.40	.12
90 Ken Griffey Jr.	1.50	.45
91 Randy Johnson	1.00	.30
92 Alex Rodriguez	1.50	.45

93 Quinton McCracken .40 .12
94 Fred McGriff .60 .18
95 Juan Gonzalez 1.00 .30
96 Ivan Rodriguez 1.00 .30
97 Nolan Ryan 2.50 .75
98 Jose Canseco 1.00 .30
99 Roger Clemens 2.00 .60
100 Jose Cruz Jr. .40 .12
101 J.Baughman FUT RC .40 .12
102 Dave Dellucci FUT RC .40 .12
103 Travis Lee FUT .40 .12
104 Troy Glaus FUT RC 3.00 .90
105 Kerry Wood FUT 1.00 .30
106 Mike Caruso FUT .40 .12
107 Jim Parque FUT RC .40 .12
108 Brett Tomko FUT .40 .12
109 Russell Branyan FUT .40 .12
110 Jaret Wright FUT .40 .12
111 Todd Helton FUT .60 .18
112 Gabe Alvarez FUT .40 .12
113 M.Anderson FUT RC .40 .12
114 Alex Gonzalez FUT .40 .12
115 Mark Kotsay FUT .40 .12
116 Derrek Lee FUT .40 .12
117 Richard Hidalgo FUT .40 .12
118 Adrian Beltre FUT .40 .12
119 Geoff Jenkins FUT .40 .12
120 Eric Milton FUT .40 .12
121 Brad Fullmer FUT .40 .12
122 V.Guerrero FUT 1.00 .30
123 Carl Pavano FUT .40 .12
124 O.Hernandez FUT RC 1.00 .30
125 Ben Grieve FUT .40 .12
126 A.J. Hinch FUT .40 .12
127 Matt Clement FUT .40 .12
128 G.Matthews Jr. FUT RC .40 .12
129 Aramis Ramirez FUT .40 .12
130 R.Arrojo FUT RC .40 .12

1998 Upper Deck Retro Big Boppers

Randomly inserted in packs, this 30-card set is an insert to the Upper Deck Retro base set. The set is serially numbered to 500. The fronts feature today's most powerful hitters on a nostalgic four-sided white bordered card. The featured player's name runs vertically along the left side border.

	Nm-Mt	Ex-Mt
COMPLETE SET (30)	400.00	120.00
BB1 Darin Erstad	4.00	1.20
BB2 Rafael Palmeiro	6.00	1.80
BB3 Cal Ripken	30.00	9.00
BB4 Nomar Garciaparra	15.00	4.50
BB5 Mo Vaughn	4.00	1.20
BB6 Frank Thomas	10.00	3.00
BB7 Albert Belle	4.00	1.20
BB8 Jim Thome	10.00	3.00
BB9 Manny Ramirez	4.00	1.20
BB10 Tony Clark	4.00	1.20
BB11 Tino Martinez	6.00	1.80
BB12 Ben Grieve	4.00	1.20
BB13 Ken Griffey Jr.	15.00	4.50
BB14 Alex Rodriguez	15.00	4.50
BB15 Jay Buhner	4.00	1.20
BB16 Juan Gonzalez	10.00	3.00
BB17 Jose Cruz Jr.	4.00	1.20
BB18 Jose Canseco	10.00	3.00
BB19 Travis Lee	4.00	1.20
BB20 Chipper Jones	10.00	3.00
BB21 Andres Galarraga	4.00	1.20
BB22 Andruw Jones	4.00	1.20
BB23 Sammy Sosa	15.00	4.50
BB24 Vinny Castilla	4.00	1.20
BB25 Larry Walker	6.00	1.80
BB26 Jeff Bagwell	6.00	1.80
BB27 Gary Sheffield	4.00	1.20
BB28 Mike Piazza	15.00	4.50
BB29 Mark McGwire	25.00	7.50
BB30 Barry Bonds	25.00	7.50

1998 Upper Deck Retro Groovy Kind of Glove

Randomly inserted in packs at a rate of one in seven, this 30-card set is an insert to the Upper Deck Retro base set. The fronts feature today's top defensive players surrounded by a four-sided white border and flourescent inks.

	Nm-Mt	Ex-Mt
COMPLETE SET (30)	120.00	36.00
G1 Roberto Alomar	5.00	1.50
G2 Cal Ripken	15.00	4.50
G3 Nomar Garciaparra	8.00	2.40
G4 Frank Thomas	5.00	1.50
G5 Robin Ventura	2.00	.60
G6 Omar Vizquel	2.00	.60
G7 Kenny Lofton	2.00	.60
G8 Ben Grieve	2.00	.60
G9 Alex Rodriguez	8.00	2.40
G10 Ken Griffey Jr.	8.00	2.40
G11 Ivan Rodriguez	5.00	1.50
G12 Travis Lee	2.00	.60
G13 Matt Williams	2.00	.60
G14 Greg Maddux	8.00	2.40
G15 Andres Galarraga	2.00	.60
G16 Andruw Jones	2.00	.60
G17 Kerry Wood	5.00	1.50
G18 Mark Grace	3.00	.90
G19 Craig Biggio	3.00	.90
G20 Charles Johnson	2.00	.60
G21 Raul Mondesi	2.00	.60
G22 Mike Piazza	8.00	2.40
G23 Rey Ordonez	2.00	.60
G24 Derek Jeter	12.00	3.60
G25 Scott Rolen	3.00	.90
G26 Mark McGwire	12.00	3.60
G27 Ken Caminiti	2.00	.60
G28 Tony Gwynn	6.00	1.80
G29 J.T. Snow	2.00	.60
G30 Barry Bonds	12.00	3.60

1998 Upper Deck Retro Legendary Cuts

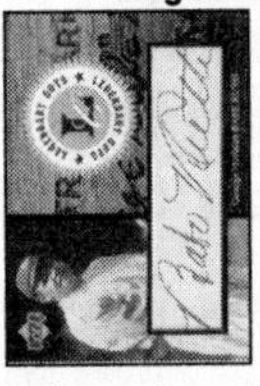

The three copies produced of this card were randomly inserted into 1998 Upper Deck Retro packs. Upper Deck acquired an autograph album including Babe Ruth signatures and carefully cut out the Ruth's to create these cards. Due to extreme scarcity these cards are not priced.

	Nm-Mt	Ex-Mt
LC Babe Ruth/3		

1998 Upper Deck Retro Lunchboxes

This set features six top Baseball stars pictured on collectible lunchboxes. The lunchboxes themselves doubled as packaging for the 24 packs of Retro trading cards inside and a collectible item in it's own right.

	Nm-Mt	Ex-Mt
COMPLETE SET (6)	40.00	12.00
1 Nomar Garciaparra	8.00	2.40
2 Ken Griffey Jr.	8.00	2.40
3 Chipper Jones	5.00	1.50
4 Travis Lee	2.00	.60
5 Mark McGwire	12.00	3.60
6 Cal Ripken	15.00	4.50

1998 Upper Deck Retro New Frontier

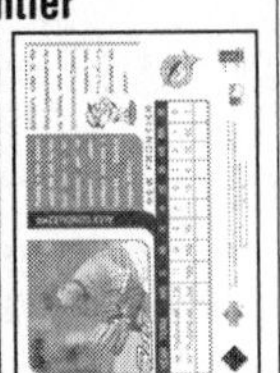

Randomly inserted in packs, this limited edition 30-card set features color player photos sequentially numbered to 1,000. A first year card of Troy Glaus is featured in this set.

	Nm-Mt	Ex-Mt
COMPLETE SET (30)	100.00	30.00
NF1 Justin Baughman	3.00	.90
NF2 David Dellucci	3.00	.90
NF3 Travis Lee	3.00	.90
NF4 Troy Glaus	15.00	4.50
NF5 Mike Caruso	3.00	.90
NF6 Jim Parque	3.00	.90
NF7 Kerry Wood	8.00	2.40
NF8 Brett Tomko	3.00	.90
NF9 Russell Branyan	3.00	.90
NF10 Jaret Wright	3.00	.90
NF11 Todd Helton	5.00	1.50
NF12 Gabe Alvarez	3.00	.90
NF13 Matt Anderson	3.00	.90
NF14 Alex Gonzalez	3.00	.90
NF15 Mark Kotsay	3.00	.90
NF16 Derrek Lee	3.00	.90
NF17 Richard Hidalgo	3.00	.90
NF18 Adrian Beltre	3.00	.90
NF19 Geoff Jenkins	3.00	.90
NF20 Eric Milton	3.00	.90
NF21 Brad Fullmer	3.00	.90
NF22 Vladimir Guerrero	8.00	2.40
NF23 Carl Pavano	3.00	.90
NF24 Orlando Hernandez	8.00	2.40
NF25 Ben Grieve	3.00	.90
NF26 A.J. Hinch	3.00	.90
NF27 Matt Clement	3.00	.90
NF28 Gary Matthews Jr.	3.00	.90
NF29 Aramis Ramirez	3.00	.90
NF30 Rolando Arrojo	3.00	.90

1998 Upper Deck Retro Quantum Leap

Randomly inserted in packs, this scarce 30-card die cut set features a selection of the leagues top players. Only 50 sets were printed and each card is serial numbered. The fronts

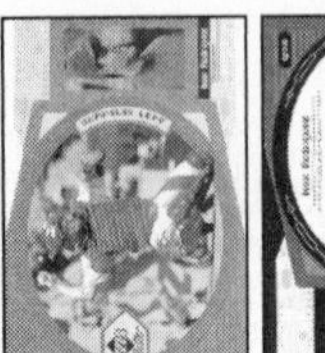

feature color action photos surrounded by a computer chip design background that highlights the technology of today.

	Nm-Mt	Ex-Mt
Q1 Darin Erstad	20.00	6.00
Q2 Cal Ripken	150.00	45.00
Q3 Nomar Garciaparra	80.00	24.00
Q4 Frank Thomas	50.00	15.00
Q5 Kenny Lofton	20.00	6.00
Q6 Ben Grieve	20.00	6.00
Q7 Ken Griffey Jr.	80.00	24.00
Q8 Alex Rodriguez	80.00	24.00
Q9 Juan Gonzalez	50.00	15.00
Q10 Jose Cruz Jr.	20.00	6.00
Q11 Roger Clemens	100.00	30.00
Q12 Travis Lee	20.00	6.00
Q13 Chipper Jones	50.00	15.00
Q14 Greg Maddux	80.00	24.00
Q15 Kerry Wood	50.00	15.00
Q16 Jeff Bagwell	30.00	9.00
Q17 Mike Piazza	80.00	24.00
Q18 Scott Rolen	30.00	9.00
Q19 Mark McGwire	120.00	36.00
Q20 Tony Gwynn	80.00	24.00
Q21 Larry Walker	30.00	9.00
Q22 Derek Jeter	120.00	36.00
Q23 Sammy Sosa	80.00	24.00
Q24 Barry Bonds	120.00	36.00
Q25 Mo Vaughn	20.00	6.00
Q26 Roberto Alomar	50.00	15.00
Q27 Todd Helton	30.00	9.00
Q28 Ivan Rodriguez	50.00	15.00
Q29 Vladimir Guerrero	50.00	15.00
Q30 Albert Belle	20.00	6.00

1998 Upper Deck Retro Sign of the Times

Randomly inserted in packs at a rate of one in 36, this 31-card set is an insert to the Upper Deck Retro base set. The fronts feature retro style autographs from retired baseball legends and some of today's players surrounded by a four-sided white border. The featured player's name lines the bottom border.

	Nm-Mt	Ex-Mt
AK Al Kaline/600	40.00	12.00
BF Bob Feller/600	40.00	12.00
BGI Bob Gibson/300	40.00	12.00
BGR Ben Grieve/300	10.00	3.00
BR Brooks Robinson/300	40.00	12.00
CF Carlton Fisk/600	40.00	12.00
EB Ernie Banks/300	40.00	12.00
EM Eddie Mathews/600	50.00	15.00
FT Frank Thomas/600	15.00	4.50
GMJ G.Matthews Jr./750	10.00	3.00
GMS G.Matthews Sr./600	15.00	4.50
GP Gaylord Perry/1000	15.00	4.50
JC Jose Cruz Jr./300	15.00	4.50
KGJ Ken Griffey Jr./100	200.00	60.00
KGS Ken Griffey Sr./600	15.00	4.50
KP Kirby Puckett/450	50.00	15.00
KW Kerry Wood/200	50.00	15.00
LB Lou Brock/300	40.00	12.00
NR Nolan Ryan/500	100.00	30.00
PK Paul Konerko/750	15.00	4.50
RB Russell Branyan/750	10.00	3.00
RF Rollie Fingers/600	15.00	4.50
SR Scott Rolen/300	40.00	12.00
TG Tony Gwynn/200	50.00	15.00
TLE Travis Lee/300	10.00	3.00
TP Tony Perez/600	25.00	7.50
TS Tom Seaver/300	40.00	12.00
WIS Willie Stargell/600	50.00	15.00
WM Willie McCovey/600	40.00	12.00
WS Warren Spahn/600	40.00	12.00
YB Yogi Berra/150	80.00	24.00

1998 Upper Deck Retro Time Capsule

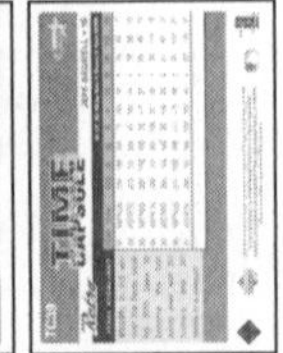

Randomly inserted in packs at the rate of one in two, this 50-card set features color photos of current stars who are destined to earn a place in baseball history.

	Nm-Mt	Ex-Mt
COMPLETE SET (50)	120.00	36.00
TC1 Mike Mussina	3.00	.90
TC2 Rafael Palmeiro	2.00	.60
TC3 Cal Ripken	10.00	3.00
TC4 Nomar Garciaparra	5.00	1.50
TC5 Pedro Martinez	3.00	.90
TC6 Mo Vaughn	1.25	.35
TC7 Albert Belle	1.25	.35
TC8 Frank Thomas	3.00	.90
TC9 David Justice	1.25	.35
TC10 Kenny Lofton	1.25	.35
TC11 Manny Ramirez	1.25	.35
TC12 Jim Thome	3.00	.90
TC13 Derek Jeter	8.00	2.40
TC14 Tino Martinez	2.00	.60
TC15 Ben Grieve	3.00	.90
TC16 Rickey Henderson	3.00	.90
TC17 Ken Griffey Jr.	5.00	1.50
TC18 Randy Johnson	3.00	.90
TC19 Alex Rodriguez	5.00	1.50
TC20 Wade Boggs	3.00	.90
TC21 Fred McGriff	2.00	.60
TC22 Juan Gonzalez	3.00	.90
TC23 Ivan Rodriguez	3.00	.90
TC24 Nolan Ryan	8.00	2.40
TC25 Jose Canseco	3.00	.90
TC26 Roger Clemens	6.00	1.80
TC27 Jose Cruz Jr.	1.25	.35
TC28 Travis Lee	1.25	.35
TC29 Matt Williams	1.25	.35
TC30 Andres Galarraga	1.25	.35
TC31 Andruw Jones	1.25	.35
TC32 Chipper Jones	3.00	.90
TC33 Greg Maddux	5.00	1.50
TC34 Kerry Wood	3.00	.90
TC35 Barry Larkin	3.00	.90
TC36 Dante Bichette	1.25	.35
TC37 Larry Walker	2.00	.60
TC38 Livan Hernandez	1.25	.35
TC39 Jeff Bagwell	2.00	.60
TC40 Craig Biggio	2.00	.60
TC41 Charles Johnson	1.25	.35
TC42 Gary Sheffield	1.25	.35
TC43 Marquis Grissom	1.25	.35
TC44 Mike Piazza	5.00	1.50
TC45 Scott Rolen	2.00	.60
TC46 Curt Schilling	2.00	.60
TC47 Mark McGwire	8.00	2.40
TC48 Ken Caminiti	1.25	.35
TC49 Tony Gwynn	4.00	1.20
TC50 Barry Bonds	8.00	2.40

1999 Upper Deck Retro

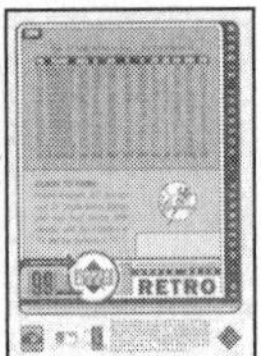

This 110 card set features a mix of active stars and retired superstars. Similar to the 1998 Upper Deck Retro set, these cards were issued in special "Luncboxes" which were designed to give the packaging a vintage. The lunchboxes had six cards per pack, 24 packs per box and 12 boxes per case at a SRP of $4.99 each. 350 Ted Williams A Piece of History 500 Club bat cards were randomly seeded into packs. In addition, Williams signed and numbered nine copies. Pricing for these bat cards can be referenced under 1999 Upper Deck A Piece of History 500 Club.

	Nm-Mt	Ex-Mt
COMPLETE SET (110)	25.00	7.50
1 Mo Vaughn	.30	.09
2 Troy Glaus	.50	.15
3 Tim Salmon	.50	.15
4 Randy Johnson	.75	.23
5 Travis Lee	.30	.09
6 Matt Williams	.30	.09
7 Greg Maddux	1.25	.35
8 Chipper Jones	.75	.23
9 Andruw Jones	.30	.09
10 Tom Glavine	.50	.15
11 Javy Lopez	.30	.09
12 Albert Belle	.30	.09
13 Cal Ripken	2.50	.75
14 Brady Anderson	.30	.09
15 Nomar Garciaparra	1.25	.35
16 Pedro Martinez	.75	.23
17 Sammy Sosa	1.25	.35
18 Mark Grace	.50	.15
19 Frank Thomas	.75	.23
20 Ray Durham	.30	.09
21 Sean Casey	.30	.09
22 Greg Vaughn	.30	.09
23 Barry Larkin	.75	.23
24 Manny Ramirez	.30	.09
25 Jim Thome	.75	.23
26 Jaret Wright	.30	.09
27 Kenny Lofton	.30	.09
28 Larry Walker	.50	.15
29 Todd Helton	.50	.15
30 Vinny Castilla	.30	.09
31 Tony Clark	.30	.09
32 Juan Encarnacion	.30	.09
33 Dean Palmer	.30	.09
34 Mark Kotsay	.30	.09
35 Alex Gonzalez	.30	.09
36 Shane Reynolds	.30	.09
37 Ken Caminiti	.30	.09
38 Jeff Bagwell	.50	.15
39 Craig Biggio	.50	.15
40 Carlos Febles	.30	.09
41 Carlos Beltran	.30	.09
42 Jeremy Giambi	.30	.09
43 Raul Mondesi	.30	.09
44 Adrian Beltre	.30	.09
45 Kevin Brown	.50	.15
46 Jeromy Burnitz	.30	.09
47 Jeff Cirillo	.30	.09
48 Corey Koskie	.30	.09
49 Todd Walker	.30	.09
50 Vladimir Guerrero	.75	.23
51 Michael Barrett	.30	.09
52 Mike Piazza	1.25	.35
53 Robin Ventura	.30	.09
54 Edgardo Alfonzo	.30	.09
55 Derek Jeter	2.00	.60
56 Roger Clemens	1.50	.45
57 Tino Martinez	.50	.15
58 Orlando Hernandez	.30	.09
59 Chuck Knoblauch	.30	.09
60 Bernie Williams	.50	.15
61 Eric Chavez	.30	.09
62 Ben Grieve	.30	.09
63 Jason Giambi	.75	.23
64 Scott Rolen	.50	.15
65 Curt Schilling	.50	.15
66 Bobby Abreu	.30	.09
67 Jason Kendall	.30	.09
68 Kevin Young	.30	.09
69 Mark McGwire	2.00	.60
70 J.D. Drew	.30	.09
71 Eric Davis	.30	.09
72 Tony Gwynn	1.00	.30
73 Trevor Hoffman	.30	.09
74 Barry Bonds	2.00	.60
75 Robb Nen	.30	.09
76 Ken Griffey Jr.	1.25	.35
77 Alex Rodriguez	1.25	.35
78 Jay Buhner	.30	.09
79 Carlos Guillen	.30	.09
80 Jose Canseco	.75	.23
81 Bobby Smith	.30	.09
82 Juan Gonzalez	.75	.23
83 Ivan Rodriguez	.75	.23
84 Rafael Palmeiro	.50	.15
85 Rick Helling	.30	.09
86 Jose Cruz Jr.	.30	.09
87 David Wells	.30	.09
88 Carlos Delgado	.30	.09
89 Nolan Ryan	3.00	.90
90 George Brett	2.00	.60
91 Robin Yount	1.25	.35
92 Paul Molitor	.50	.15
93 Dave Winfield	.30	.09
94 Steve Garvey	.30	.09
95 Ozzie Smith	1.25	.35
96 Ted Williams	2.50	.75
97 Don Mattingly	2.00	.60
98 Mickey Mantle	3.00	.90
99 Harmon Killebrew	.75	.23
100 Rollie Fingers	.30	.09
101 Kirk Gibson	.30	.09
102 Bucky Dent	.30	.09
103 Willie Mays	1.50	.45
104 Babe Ruth	2.50	.75
105 Gary Carter	.50	.15
106 Reggie Jackson	.50	.15
107 Frank Robinson	.50	.15
108 Ernie Banks	.75	.23
109 Eddie Murray	.75	.23
110 Mike Schmidt	1.50	.45

1999 Upper Deck Retro Gold

Randomly inserted into packs, these cards parallel the regular Retro set and are serial numbered to 250. These cards can be differentiated by the gold foil borders on them.

Nm-Mt Ex-Mt

*ACTIVE STARS 1-88: 6X TO 15X BASIC
*RETIRED STARS 89-110: 10X TO 25X BASIC

1999 Upper Deck Retro Distant Replay

These cards which were issued one every eight packs, featured the most memorable plays from 15 of the most memorable players active in baseball.

	Nm-Mt	Ex-Mt
COMPLETE SET (15)	60.00	18.00
*LEVEL 2: 2.5X TO 6X BASIC DIST.REPLAY		
LEVEL 2 RANDOM INSERTS IN PACKS		
LEVEL 2 PRINT RUN 100 SERIAL #'d SETS		
D1 Ken Griffey Jr.	4.00	1.20
D2 Mark McGwire	6.00	1.80
D3 Cal Ripken	8.00	2.40
D4 Greg Maddux	4.00	1.20
D5 Nomar Garciaparra	4.00	1.20
D6 Roger Clemens	5.00	1.50
D7 Alex Rodriguez	4.00	1.20
D8 Frank Thomas	2.50	.75
D9 Mike Piazza	4.00	1.20
D10 Chipper Jones	2.50	.75
D11 Juan Gonzalez	2.50	.75
D12 Tony Gwynn	3.00	.90
D13 Barry Bonds	6.00	1.80
D14 Ivan Rodriguez	2.50	.75
D15 Derek Jeter	6.00	1.80

1999 Upper Deck Retro Inkredible

Inserted one every 24 packs, these cards feature autographs from both active and retired players.The horizontal cards are designed so the primary focus on most of the card is actually the autograph. Eddie Murray and Sean Casey did not return their cards when this set was packed out so their autographs were available via redemption. The deadline for this redemption was April 15th, 2000.

Nm-Mt Ex-Mt
AP Angel Pena 10.00 3.00
BD Bucky Dent 15.00 4.50
BW Bernie Williams 80.00 24.00
CBE Carlos Beltran 15.00 4.50
CJ Chipper Jones 40.00 12.00
DE Darin Erstad 15.00 4.50
DM Don Mattingly 60.00 18.00
DW Dave Winfield 25.00 7.50
EM Eddie Murray SP 80.00 24.00
FL Fred Lynn 15.00 4.50
GB George Brett SP 120.00 36.00
GK Gabe Kapler 10.00 3.00
HK Harmon Killebrew 40.00 12.00
IR Ivan Rodriguez 40.00 12.00
JR Ken Griffey Jr. 150.00 45.00
KG Kirk Gibson 15.00 4.50
MR Manny Ramirez 15.00 4.50
NR Nolan Ryan 200.00 60.00
OZ Ozzie Smith 40.00 12.00
PB Pat Burrell 25.00 7.50
PM Paul Molitor 25.00 7.50
PO Paul O'Neill 25.00 7.50
RF Rollie Fingers 15.00 4.50
RG Rusty Greer 15.00 4.50
RY Robin Yount 40.00 12.00
SC Sean Casey 15.00 4.50
SG Steve Garvey 15.00 4.50
TC Tony Clark 10.00 3.00
TG Tony Gwynn 40.00 12.00

1999 Upper Deck Retro Inkredible Level 2

Randomly inserted into packs, these cards parallel the regular Inkredible inserts. The difference is that these cards are serial numbered to the featured player's jersey number. No pricing is available on some of these cards due to their scarcity.

Nm-Mt Ex-Mt
AP Angel Pena/36 25.00 7.50
BD Bucky Dent/20
BW Bernie Williams/51 100.00 30.00
CBE Carlos Beltran/36 40.00 12.00
CJ Chipper Jones/10
DE Darin Erstad/17
DM Don Mattingly/23
DW Dave Winfield/31 60.00 18.00
EM Eddie Murray/33 200.00 60.00
FL Fred Lynn/19
GB George Brett/5
GK Gabe Kapler/23
HK Harmon Killebrew/3
IR Ivan Rodriguez/7
JR Ken Griffey Jr./24
KG Kirk Gibson/23
MR Manny Ramirez/24
NR Nolan Ryan/34 500.00 150.00
OZ Ozzie Smith/1
PB Pat Burrell/76 120.00 36.00
PM Paul Molitor/4
PO Paul O'Neill/21
RF Rollie Fingers/34 40.00 12.00
RG Rusty Greer/29 40.00 12.00
RY Robin Yount/19
SC Sean Casey/21
SG Steve Garvey/6
TC Tony Clark/17
TG Tony Gwynn/19

1999 Upper Deck Retro Lunchboxes

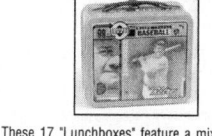

These 17 "Lunchboxes" feature a mix of active and retired players on them. In 1999, there were also some dual pairings of players on the boxes. The dual player boxes were issued one per 12 box case and are therefore in shorter supply than the regular player lunchboxes.

Nm-Mt Ex-Mt
1 Roger Clemens 12.00 3.60
2 Ken Griffey Jr. 25.00 7.50
3 Mickey Mantle 25.00 7.50
4 Mark McGwire 25.00 7.50
5 Mike Piazza 15.00 4.50
6 Alex Rodriguez 15.00 4.50
7 Babe Ruth 25.00 7.50
8 Sammy Sosa 12.00 3.60
9 Ted Williams 20.00 6.00
10 Ken Griffey Jr. 15.00 4.50
Mickey Mantle
11 Ken Griffey Jr. 15.00 4.50
Mark McGwire
12 K.Griffey Jr. 15.00 4.50
Babe Ruth
13 Ken Griffey Jr. 15.00 4.50
Ted Williams
14 Mickey Mantle 15.00 4.50
Babe Ruth
15 Mark McGwire 15.00 4.50
Mickey Mantle
16 Mark McGwire 15.00 4.50
Babe Ruth
17 Marlk McGwire 15.00 4.50
Ted Williams

1999 Upper Deck Retro Old School/New School

Sequentially numbered to 1000, these cards feature active players broken into "Old School" or veteran and "New School" or youngsters in two different designs.

Nm-Mt Ex-Mt
COMPLETE SET (30) 200.00 60.00
*LEVEL 2 STARS: 1.25X TO 3X BASIC SCHOOL
*LEVEL 2 ROOKIES: .75X TO 2X BASIC OLD/NEW SCHOOL
STATED PRINT RUN 50 SERIAL #'d SETS

RANDOM INSERTS IN PACKS
S1 Ken Griffey Jr. 10.00 3.00
S2 Alex Rodriguez 10.00 3.00
S3 Frank Thomas 6.00 1.80
S4 Cal Ripken 20.00 6.00
S5 Chipper Jones 6.00 1.80
S6 Craig Biggio 4.00 1.20
S7 Greg Maddux 10.00 3.00
S8 Jeff Bagwell 4.00 1.20
S9 Juan Gonzalez 6.00 1.80
S10 Mark McGwire 15.00 4.50
S11 Mike Piazza 10.00 3.00
S12 Mo Vaughn 2.50 .75
S13 Roger Clemens 12.00 3.60
S14 Sammy Sosa 10.00 3.00
S15 Tony Gwynn 8.00 2.40
S16 Gabe Kapler 2.50 .75
S17 J.D. Drew 2.50 .75
S18 Pat Burrell 10.00 3.00
S19 Roy Halladay 2.50 .75
S20 Jeff Weaver 2.00 .60
S21 Troy Glaus 4.00 1.20
S22 Vladimir Guerrero 6.00 1.80
S23 Michael Barrett 2.50 .75
S24 Carlos Beltran 2.50 .75
S25 Scott Rolen 4.00 1.20
S26 Nomar Garciaparra 10.00 3.00
S27 Warren Morris 2.50 .75
S28 Alex Gonzalez 2.50 .75
S29 Kyle Farnsworth 2.50 .75
S30 Derek Jeter 15.00 4.50

1999 Upper Deck Retro Throwback Attack

Using a design reminiscent of the 1959 Topps set, these cards were inserted one every five packs. The players featured are among the leading players in the game and this insert set is designed to show how cards of these players would have looked many years ago.

Nm-Mt Ex-Mt
COMPLETE SET (15) 40.00 12.00
*LEVEL 2: 1.25X TO 3X BASIC THROWBACK
LEVEL 2 RANDOM INSERTS IN PACKS
T1 Ken Griffey Jr. 3.00 .90
T2 Mark McGwire 5.00 1.50
T3 Sammy Sosa 3.00 .90
T4 Roger Clemens 4.00 1.20
T5 J.D. Drew .75 .23
T6 Alex Rodriguez 3.00 .90
T7 Greg Maddux 3.00 .90
T8 Mike Piazza 3.00 .90
T9 Juan Gonzalez 2.00 .60
T10 Mo Vaughn .75 .23
T11 Cal Ripken 6.00 1.80
T12 Frank Thomas 2.00 .60
T13 Nomar Garciaparra 3.00 .90
T14 Vladimir Guerrero 2.00 .60
T15 Tony Gwynn 2.50 .75

2002 Upper Deck Rookie Debut Climbing the Ladder

Randomly inserted in rookie debut packs, these cards were issued to a stated print run of 25 serial numbered sets. Due to market scarcity no pricing is provided for these cards.

Nm-Mt Ex-Mt
AR Alex Rodriguez
GM Greg Maddux
GO Juan Gonzalez
IS Ichiro Suzuki
JG Jason Giambi
JT Jim Thome
KG Ken Griffey Jr.
LW Larry Walker
MM Mark McGwire
RP Rafael Palmeiro
SG Shawn Green
SS Sammy Sosa

2002 Upper Deck Rookie Debut Elite Company

Randomly inserted into packs, these two cards feature the leading sluggers of 1998 and each of these cards was issued to a stated print run of 25 serial numbered sets. Due to market scarcity, no pricing is provided for these cards.

Nm-Mt Ex-Mt
MM Mark McGwire
SS Sammy Sosa

2002 Upper Deck Rookie Debut Making Their Marks

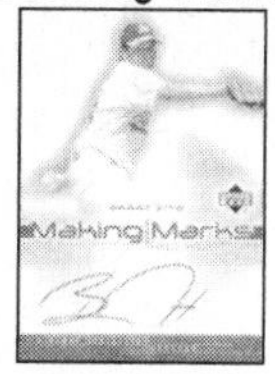

Randomly inserted into packs, these two cards feature some of the leading young players in baseball. Each of these cards was issued to a stated print run of 25 serial numbered sets. Due to market scarcity, no pricing is provided for these cards.

Nm-Mt Ex-Mt
BG Brian Giles
BZ Barry Zito
DM Doug Mientkiewicz
HB Hank Blalock
LB Lance Berkman
MB Mark Buehrle
MP Mark Prior
MS Mike Sweeney
RS Richie Sexson
SB Sean Burroughs
TO Tomo Ohka
TR Tim Redding

2002 Upper Deck Rookie Debut Solid Contact

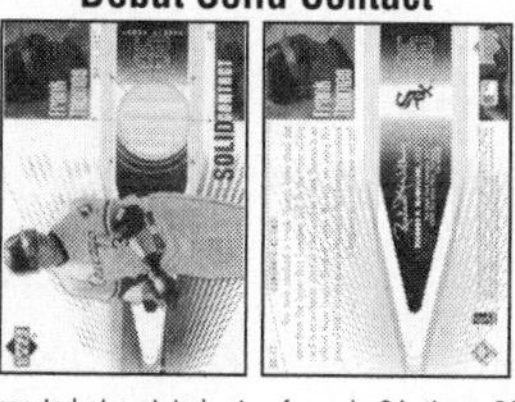

Inserted at a stated rate of one in 24, these 30 cards feature leading hitters in baseball.

Nm-Mt Ex-Mt
AR Alex Rodriguez 15.00 4.50
BA Bobby Abreu 10.00 3.00
BG Brian Giles 10.00 3.00
BL Barry Larkin 15.00 4.50
BW Bernie Williams 15.00 4.50
CD Carlos Delgado SP 15.00 4.50
CE Carl Everett 10.00 3.00
DM Doug Mientkiewicz 15.00 4.50
EA Edgardo Alfonzo 10.00 3.00
EM Edgar Martinez 15.00 4.50
FM Fred McGriff 15.00 4.50
FT Frank Thomas 15.00 4.50
GS Gary Sheffield 10.00 3.00
IR Ivan Rodriguez 15.00 4.50
JC Jose Cruz Jr. 10.00 3.00
JE Jim Edmonds 10.00 3.00
JG Jason Giambi SP/50 20.00 6.00
JK Jason Kendall 10.00 3.00
JO John Olerud 10.00 3.00
JP Jorge Posada 15.00 4.50
JT Jim Thome 15.00 4.50
KG Ken Griffey Jr. 20.00 6.00
MA Moises Alou 10.00 3.00
MO Magglio Ordonez 10.00 3.00
MW Matt Williams 10.00 3.00
OV Omar Vizquel 10.00 3.00
RA Roberto Alomar 15.00 4.50
SS Sammy Sosa 20.00 6.00
TA Fernando Tatis 10.00 3.00
TH Todd Helton 15.00 4.50

2001 Upper Deck Rookie Update

The 2001 Upper Deck Rookie Update product released in late December,2001 and features updates to three of Upper Deck's 2000 products. This product contains updated players and rookies from SP Authentic, SPx, and Sweet Spot. Each pack contained four-cards and carried a suggested retail price of $4.99. Please see 2001 SP Authentic, 2001 SPx and 2001Upper Deck Sweet Spot for checklists and prices.

Nm-Mt Ex-Mt
SEE SP AUTH, SPX AND SW.SPOT FOR PRICING

2001 Upper Deck Rookie Update Ichiro Rookie BuyBacks

As a last minute addition to their Rookie Update brand, Upper Deck added a total of 50 Ichiro Suzuki Rookie Cards into packs. The 50 cards are an assortion from SP Authentic, SPx, Sweet Spot and UD Reserve. Each of the SPx, SP Authentic and Sweet Spot cards have their original serial-numbering, as well as an additional hand numbering by Upper Deck coupled with a serial-numbered hologram on back and an accompanying 2 1/2" by 3" certificate of authenticity of which carries a matching hologram number. Unlike the other cards from this set, the UD Reserve cards were not repurchased from the secondary market and do not carry any type of serial-numbered hologram. Though the original UD Reserve Ichiro cards were serial numbered to 2,500 these BuyBacks, do not carry any factory serial-numbering at all. Collectors who pulled an unnumbered UD Reserve BuyBack Ichiro card were instructed to send it back to Upper Deck for a numbered version. Though the cards are serial numbered cumulatively to 50, representatives at Upper Deck did release actual quantities of each card used for this promotion. They are as follows: SP Authentic - 16, SPx - 3, Sweet Spot - 4 and UD Reserve - 27.

Nm-Mt Ex-Mt
1 Ichiro Suzuki SP Authentic/16
2 Ichiro Suzuki SPx/3
3 Ichiro Suzuki Sweet Spot/4
4 Ichiro Suzuki UD Reserve/27

2001 Upper Deck Rookie Update Ichiro Tribute

This 51-card set was distributed in special three-card Ichiro Tribute mini packs seeded exclusively into 2001 Upper Deck Rookie Update boxes at a rate of one pack per 24-ct box. The set commemorates Ichiro's amazing 2001 MLB campaign. The set is broken down as follows: Basic Cards (1-30), Five Tool Star (31-35), Salute to Ichiro (36-50) and Checklist Card (51).

Nm-Mt Ex-Mt
COMPLETE SET (51) 60.00 18.00
COMMON CARD (1-51) 2.00 .60
*GOLD: 5X TO 12X BASIC ICHIRO TRIB.
GOLD PRINT RUN 100 SERIAL #'d SETS
*PLATINUM: 12.5X TO 30X BASIC TRIB
PLATINUM PRINT RUN 25 SERIAL #'d SETS

2001 Upper Deck Rookie Update Ichiro Tribute Game Bat

Randomly inserted into 2001 Ichiro Tribute packs, this 20-card insert features game-used bat cards from the 2001 American Rookie of the Year, Ichiro Suzuki. Card backs carry a "B" prefix. Cards numbered 1 through 12 are serial numbered to 100, cards numbered 13 through 17 are serial numbered to 50, cards numbered 18 and 19 are serial numbered to 25 and card number 20 is serial numbered to 1.

Nm-Mt Ex-Mt
COMMON (B-I1-B-I12) 50.00 15.00
COMMON (B-I13-B-I17) 80.00 24.00
COMMON (B-I18-B-I19) 150.00 45.00

2001 Upper Deck Rookie Update Ichiro Tribute Game Pants

Randomly inserted into 2001 Ichiro Tribute packs, this 20-card insert features game-used pants cards from the 2001 American Rookie of the Year, Ichiro Suzuki. Card backs carry a "J" prefix. Cards numbered 1 through 12 are serial numbered to 100, cards numbered 13 through 17 are serial numbered to 50, cards numbered 18 and 19 are serial numbered to 25 and card number 20 is serial numbered to 1.

Nm-Mt Ex-Mt
COMMON (J-I1-J-I12) 50.00 15.00
COMMON (J-I13-J-I17) 80.00 24.00
COMMON (J-I18-J-I19) 150.00 45.00

2001 Upper Deck Rookie Update USA Touch of Gold Autographs

Randomly inserted into packs, this 24-card insert features authentic autographs from members of the 2000 U.S.A. Olympic Team. Each card is individually serial numbered to 500.

Nm-Mt Ex-Mt
AE Adam Everett 10.00 3.00
AS Anthony Sanders 10.00 3.00
BA Brent Abernathy 10.00 3.00
BW Brad Wilkerson 10.00 3.00
CG Chris George 10.00 3.00
DM Doug Mientkiewicz 15.00 4.50
EY Ernie Young 10.00 3.00
JC John Cotton 10.00 3.00
JR Jon Rauch 10.00 3.00
KU Kurt Ainsworth 10.00 3.00
MJ Marcus Jensen 10.00 3.00
MK Mike Kinkade 10.00 3.00
MN Mike Neill 10.00 3.00
PB Pat Borders 10.00 3.00
RF Ryan Franklin 10.00 3.00
RK Rick Krivda 10.00 3.00
RO Roy Oswalt 25.00 7.50
SB Sean Burroughs 15.00 4.50
SH Shane Heams 10.00 3.00
TD Gookie Dawkins 10.00 3.00
TW Todd Williams 10.00 3.00
TY Tim Young 10.00 3.00
BSE Bobby Seay 10.00 3.00
BSH Ben Sheets 15.00 4.50

2002 Upper Deck Rookie Update Star Tributes

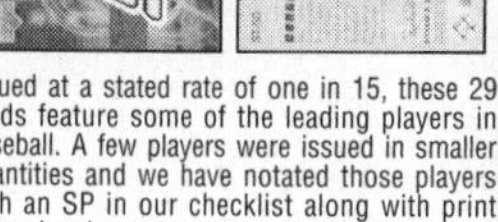

Issued at a stated rate of one in 15, these 29 cards feature some of the leading players in baseball. A few players were issued in smaller quantities and we have notated those players with an SP in our checklist along with print runs when known.

Nm-Mt Ex-Mt
AD Adam Dunn 8.00 2.40
AR Alex Rodriguez 15.00 4.50
AS Alfonso Soriano 10.00 3.00
CD Carlos Delgado 8.00 2.40
CJ Chipper Jones 10.00 3.00
CS Curt Schilling 10.00 3.00
FT Frank Thomas 10.00 3.00
IR Ivan Rodriguez 10.00 3.00
IS Ichiro Suzuki SP/19
JB Josh Beckett 10.00 3.00
JD Joe DiMaggio SP 100.00 30.00
JG Jason Giambi 10.00 3.00
KG Ken Griffey Jr. 15.00 4.50
KI Kazuhisa Ishii 15.00 4.50
KS Kazuhiro Sasaki 8.00 2.40
LB Lance Berkman 8.00 2.40
LG Luis Gonzalez SP 10.00 3.00
MM Mark McGwire SP 60.00 18.00
MPI Mike Piazza 12.00 3.60
MPR Mark Prior 15.00 4.50
MS Mike Sweeney 8.00 2.40
PM Pedro Martinez 10.00 3.00
RC Roger Clemens 15.00 4.50
RJ Randy Johnson 10.00 3.00
RP Rafael Palmeiro 10.00 3.00
SG Shawn Green 8.00 2.40
SS Sammy Sosa 15.00 4.50
TG Tom Glavine 10.00 3.00
TS Tsuyoshi Shinjo 8.00 2.40

2002 Upper Deck Rookie Update Star Tributes Signatures

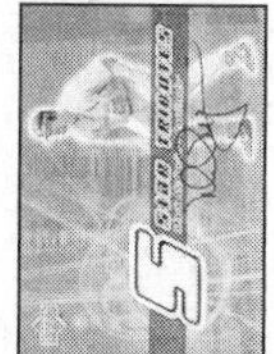

Randomly inserted into packs, this is a partial parallel to the Star Tributes insert set. These cards were signed by the player and were issued to a stated print run of 50 serial numbered sets.

Nm-Mt Ex-Mt
AR Alex Rodriguez
JG Jason Giambi
KG Ken Griffey Jr.
MM Mark McGwire

2002 Upper Deck Rookie Update Star Tributes Signatures Copper

This is a parallel to the Star Tribute Signature insert set. These sets have copper borders and

were issued to a stated print run of 25 serial numbered sets. Due to market scarcity, no pricing is provided.

Nm-Mt Ex-Mt

AR Alex Rodriguez
CR Cal Ripken
MM Mark McGwire
SS Sammy Sosa

2002 Upper Deck Rookie Update Star Tributes Signatures Gold

This is a parallel to the Star Tribute Signature insert set. These sets have gold borders and were issued to a stated print run of five serial numbered sets. Due to market scarcity, no pricing is provided.

Nm-Mt Ex-Mt

JG Jason Giambi
MM Mark McGwire

2002 Upper Deck Rookie Update Star Tributes Signatures Silver

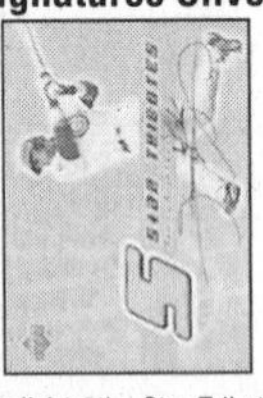

This is a parallel to the Star Tribute Signature insert set. These sets have silver borders and were issued to a stated print run of 25 serial numbered sets. Due to market scarcity, no pricing is provided.

Nm-Mt Ex-Mt

AR Alex Rodriguez
SS Sammy Sosa

2002 Upper Deck Rookie Update USA Future Watch Swatches

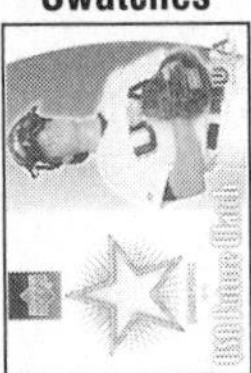

Inserted at a stated rate of one in 15, these 22 cards feature game-used jersey swatches of players from the 2002 USA National team.

	Nm-Mt	Ex-Mt
AA Abe Alvarez	10.00	3.00
AH Aaron Hill	10.00	3.00
BS Brad Sullivan	10.00	3.00
BZ Bob Zimmermann	8.00	2.40
CC Chad Cordero	8.00	2.40
CJ Conor Jackson	10.00	3.00
CQ Carlos Quentin	10.00	3.00
CS Clint Sammons	8.00	2.40
DP Dustin Pedroia	8.00	2.40
EP Eric Patterson	10.00	3.00
GJ Grant Johnson	8.00	2.40
HS Huston Street	10.00	3.00
KB Kyle Bakker	8.00	2.40
KS Kyle Sleeth	15.00	4.50
LP Landon Powell	8.00	2.40
MA Michael Aubrey	15.00	4.50
MJ Mark Jurich	8.00	2.40
PH Philip Humber	10.00	3.00
RW Rickie Weeks	20.00	6.00
SC Shane Costa	10.00	3.00
SF Sam Fuld	8.00	2.40
WL Wes Littleton	10.00	3.00

2002 Upper Deck Rookie Update USA Future Watch Swatches Copper

Randomly inserted into packs, this is a parallel to the Future Watch Swatch insert set. These cards were issued to a stated print run of 25 serial numbered sets and no pricing is available due to market scarcity.

Nm-Mt Ex-Mt

BS Brad Sullivan
CJ Conor Jackson
KS Kyle Sleeth
LP Landon Powell

2002 Upper Deck Rookie Update USA Future Watch Swatches Gold

Randomly inserted into packs, this is a parallel to the Future Watch Swatch insert set. These cards, which have gold borders, were issued to a stated print run of five serial numbered sets and no pricing is available due to market scarcity.

Nm-Mt Ex-Mt

AH Aaron Hill
EP Eric Patterson

2002 Upper Deck Rookie Update USA Future Watch Swatches Red

Randomly inserted into packs, this is a parallel to the Future Watch Swatch insert set. These cards, which have red borders, were issued to a stated print run of 50 serial numbered sets.

Nm-Mt Ex-Mt

CC Chad Cordero
GJ Grant Johnson
HS Huston Street
PH Philip Humber

2002 Upper Deck Rookie Update USA Future Watch Swatches Silver

Randomly inserted into packs, this is a parallel to the Future Watch Swatch insert set. These cards, which have silver borders, were issued to a stated print run of 25 serial numbered sets and no pricing is provided due to market scarcity.

Nm-Mt Ex-Mt

CQ Carlos Quentin
MA Michael Aubrey

1998 Upper Deck Special F/X

The 1998 Upper Deck Special F/X set was issued in one series totalling 150 cards. Distributed exclusively in retail outlets, six-card packs carried a $2.97 suggested retail price. The set contains a selection of the top 150 cards from the basic issue 1998 Upper Deck first series set including the topical subsets Griffey's Hot List (1-10) and Star Rookies (136-150). Each Special F/X card features a special foil treatment on the card fronts and is printed on sturdy 20 pt. stock.

	Nm-Mt	Ex-Mt
COMPLETE SET (150)	40.00	12.00
1 Ken Griffey Jr. GHL	2.00	.60
2 Mark McGwire GHL	3.00	.90
3 Alex Rodriguez GHL	2.00	.60
4 Larry Walker GHL	.75	.23
5 Tino Martinez GHL	.75	.23
6 Mike Piazza GHL	2.00	.60
7 Jose Cruz Jr. GHL	.50	.15
8 Greg Maddux GHL	2.00	.60
9 Tony Gwynn GHL	1.50	.45
10 Roger Clemens GHL	2.50	.75
11 Jason Dickson	.50	.15
12 Darin Erstad	.50	.15
13 Chuck Finley	.50	.15
14 Dave Hollins	.50	.15
15 Garret Anderson	.50	.15
16 Michael Tucker	.50	.15
17 Javier Lopez	.50	.15
18 John Smoltz	.75	.23
19 Mark Wohlers	.50	.15
20 Greg Maddux	2.00	.60
21 Scott Erickson	.50	.15
22 Jimmy Key	.50	.15
23 B.J. Surhoff	.50	.15
24 Eric Davis	.50	.15
25 Rafael Palmeiro	.75	.23
26 Tim Naehring	.50	.15
27 Darren Bragg	.50	.15
28 Troy O'Leary	.50	.15
29 John Valentin	.50	.15
30 Mo Vaughn	.50	.15
31 Mark Grace	.75	.23
32 Kevin Foster	.50	.15
33 Kevin Tapani	.50	.15
34 Kevin Orie	.50	.15
35 Albert Belle	.50	.15
36 Ray Durham	.50	.15
37 Jaime Navarro	.50	.15
38 Mike Cameron	.50	.15
39 Eddie Taubensee	.50	.15
40 Barry Larkin	1.25	.35
41 Willie Greene	.50	.15
42 Jeff Shaw	.50	.15
43 Omar Vizquel	.50	.15
44 Brian Giles	.50	.15
45 Jim Thome	1.25	.35
46 David Justice	.50	.15
47 Sandy Alomar Jr.	.50	.15
48 Neifi Perez	.50	.15
49 Dante Bichette	.50	.15
50 Vinny Castilla	.50	.15
51 John Thomson	.50	.15
52 Damion Easley	.50	.15
53 Justin Thompson	.50	.15
54 Bobby Higginson	.50	.15
55 Tony Clark	.50	.15
56 Charles Johnson	.50	.15
57 Edgar Renteria	.50	.15
58 Alex Fernandez	.50	.15
59 Gary Sheffield	.50	.15
60 Livan Hernandez	.50	.15
61 Craig Biggio	.75	.23
62 Chris Holt	.50	.15
63 Billy Wagner	.50	.15
64 Brad Ausmus	.50	.15
65 Dean Palmer	.50	.15
66 Tim Belcher	.50	.15
67 Jeff King	.50	.15
68 Jose Rosado	.50	.15
69 Chan Ho Park	.50	.15
70 Raul Mondesi	.50	.15
71 Hideo Nomo	1.25	.35
72 Todd Zeile	.50	.15
73 Eric Karros	.50	.15
74 Cal Eldred	.50	.15
75 Jeff D'Amico	.50	.15
76 Doug Jones	.50	.15
77 Dave Nilsson	.50	.15
78 Todd Walker	.50	.15
79 Rick Aguilera	.50	.15
80 Paul Molitor	.75	.23
81 Brad Radke	.50	.15
82 Vladimir Guerrero	1.25	.35
83 Carlos Perez	.50	.15
84 F.P. Santangelo	.50	.15
85 Rondell White	.50	.15
86 Butch Huskey	.50	.15
87 Edgardo Alfonzo	.50	.15
88 John Franco	.50	.15
89 John Olerud	.50	.15
90 Todd Hundley	.50	.15
91 Bernie Williams	.75	.23
92 Andy Pettitte	.75	.23
93 Paul O'Neill	.75	.23
94 David Cone	.50	.15
95 Jason Giambi	1.25	.35
96 Damon Mashore	.50	.15
97 Scott Spiezio	.50	.15
98 Ariel Prieto	.50	.15
99 Rico Brogna	.50	.15
100 Mike Lieberthal	.50	.15
101 Garrett Stephenson	.50	.15
102 Ricky Bottalico	.50	.15
103 Kevin Polcovich	.50	.15
104 Jon Lieber	.50	.15
105 Kevin Young	.50	.15
106 Tony Womack	.50	.15
107 Gary Gaetti	.50	.15
108 Alan Benes	.50	.15
109 Willie McGee	.50	.15
110 Mark McGwire	3.00	.90
111 Ron Gant	.50	.15
112 Andy Ashby	.50	.15
113 Steve Finley	.50	.15
114 Quilvio Veras	.50	.15
115 Ken Caminiti	.50	.15
116 Joey Hamilton	.50	.15
117 Bill Mueller	.50	.15
118 Mark Gardner	.50	.15
119 Shawn Estes	.50	.15
120 J.T. Snow	.50	.15
121 Dante Powell	.50	.15
122 Jeff Kent	.50	.15
123 Jamie Moyer	.50	.15
124 Joey Cora	.50	.15
125 Ken Griffey Jr.	2.00	.60
126 Jeff Fassero	.50	.15
127 Edgar Martinez	.75	.23
128 Will Clark	1.25	.35
129 Lee Stevens	.50	.15
130 Ivan Rodriguez	1.25	.35
131 Rusty Greer	.50	.15
132 Ed Sprague	.50	.15
133 Pat Hentgen	.50	.15
134 Shannon Stewart	.50	.15
135 Carlos Delgado	.50	.15
136 Brett Tomko	.50	.15
137 Jose Guillen	.50	.15
138 Eli Marrero	.50	.15
139 Dennis Reyes	.50	.15
140 Mark Kotsay	.50	.15
141 Richie Sexson	.50	.15
142 Todd Helton	.75	.23
143 Jeremi Gonzalez	.50	.15
144 Jeff Abbott	.50	.15
145 Matt Morris	.50	.15
146 Aaron Boone	.50	.15
147 Todd Dunwoody	.50	.15
148 Mario Valdez	.50	.15
149 Fernando Tatis	.50	.15
150 Jaret Wright	.50	.15

1998 Upper Deck Special F/X Power Zone

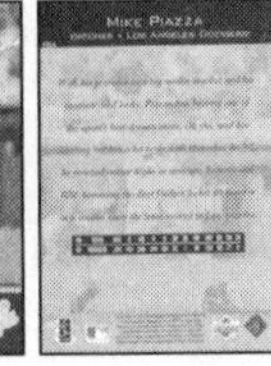

Randomly seeded into Special F/X packs at a rate of one in seven, cards from this 20-card set feature a selection of baseball's top stars printed on special silver Light F/X technology.

	Nm-Mt	Ex-Mt
COMPLETE SET (20)	50.00	15.00
PZ1 Jose Cruz Jr.	1.25	.35
PZ2 Frank Thomas	3.00	.90
PZ3 Juan Gonzalez	3.00	.90
PZ4 Mike Piazza	5.00	1.50
PZ5 Mark McGwire	8.00	2.40
PZ6 Barry Bonds	8.00	2.40
PZ7 Greg Maddux	5.00	1.50
PZ8 Alex Rodriguez	5.00	1.50
PZ9 Nomar Garciaparra	5.00	1.50
PZ10 Ken Griffey Jr.	5.00	1.50
PZ11 John Smoltz	2.00	.60
PZ12 Andruw Jones	1.25	.35
PZ13 Sandy Alomar Jr.	1.25	.35
PZ14 Roberto Alomar	3.00	.90
PZ15 Chipper Jones	3.00	.90
PZ16 Kenny Lofton	1.25	.35
PZ17 Larry Walker	2.00	.60
PZ18 Jeff Bagwell	2.00	.60
PZ19 Mo Vaughn	1.25	.35
PZ20 Tom Glavine	2.00	.60

1998 Upper Deck Special F/X Power Zone OctoberBest

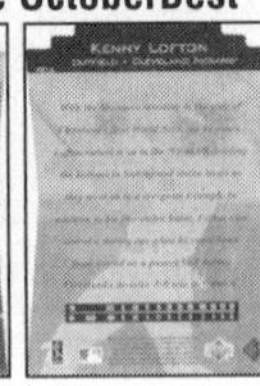

Randomly seeded into Special F/X packs at a rate of one in 34, cards from this 15-card set feature some of the league's top stars printed on silver die-cut Light F/X technology.

	Nm-Mt	Ex-Mt
COMPLETE SET (15)	120.00	36.00
PZ1 Frank Thomas	10.00	3.00
PZ2 Juan Gonzalez	10.00	3.00
PZ3 Mike Piazza	15.00	4.50
PZ4 Mark McGwire	25.00	7.50
PZ5 Jeff Bagwell	6.00	1.80
PZ6 Barry Bonds	25.00	7.50
PZ7 Ken Griffey Jr.	15.00	4.50
PZ8 John Smoltz	6.00	1.80
PZ9 Andruw Jones	4.00	1.20
PZ10 Greg Maddux	15.00	4.50
PZ11 Sandy Alomar Jr.	4.00	1.20
PZ12 Roberto Alomar	10.00	3.00
PZ13 Chipper Jones	10.00	3.00
PZ14 Kenny Lofton	4.00	1.20
PZ15 Tom Glavine	6.00	1.80

1998 Upper Deck Special F/X Power Zone Power Driven

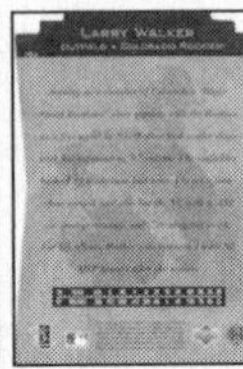

Randomly seeded into Special F/X packs at a rate of one in 69, cards from this 10-card set feature a selection of top stars printed on Light F/X gold-foil.

	Nm-Mt	Ex-Mt
COMPLETE SET (10)	120.00	36.00
PZ1 Frank Thomas	12.00	3.60
PZ2 Juan Gonzalez	12.00	3.60
PZ3 Mike Piazza	20.00	6.00
PZ4 Larry Walker	8.00	2.40
PZ5 Mark McGwire	30.00	9.00
PZ6 Jeff Bagwell	8.00	2.40
PZ7 Mo Vaughn	5.00	1.50
PZ8 Barry Bonds	30.00	9.00
PZ9 Tino Martinez	8.00	2.40
PZ10 Ken Griffey Jr.	20.00	6.00

1998 Upper Deck Special F/X Power Zone Superstar Xcitement

Randomly seeded in packs, cards from this 10-card set feature ten of the league's top stars printed on die-cut Light F/X gold-foil stock. In addition, only 250 sets were printed and each card is "crash-numbered" on back "of 250".

	Nm-Mt	Ex-Mt
COMPLETE SET (10)	250.00	75.00
PZ1 Jose Cruz Jr.	8.00	2.40
PZ2 Frank Thomas	20.00	6.00
PZ3 Juan Gonzalez	20.00	6.00
PZ4 Mike Piazza	30.00	9.00
PZ5 Mark McGwire	50.00	15.00
PZ6 Barry Bonds	50.00	15.00
PZ7 Greg Maddux	30.00	9.00
PZ8 Alex Rodriguez	30.00	9.00
PZ9 Nomar Garciaparra	30.00	9.00
PZ10 Ken Griffey Jr.	30.00	9.00

2003 Upper Deck Standing O

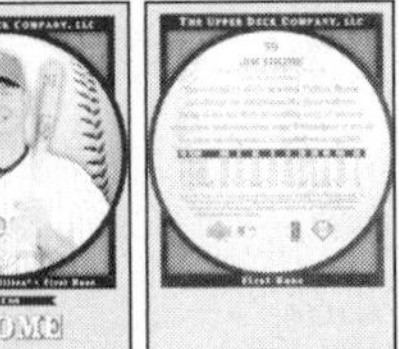

This 126 card set was released in May, 2003. The set was issued in 13 card packs with a $2 SRP which came 24 packs to a box and 20 boxes to a case. Cards numbered 1 through 84 featured veterans while cards 85 through 126 feature rookies and those cards were seeded into packs at a stated rate of one in four.

	Nm-Mt	Ex-Mt
COMP.SET w/o SP's (84)	15.00	4.50
COMMON CARD (1-84)	.30	.09
COMMON CARD (85-126)	2.00	.60
1 Darin Erstad	.30	.09
2 Troy Glaus	.50	.15
3 Tim Salmon	.50	.15
4 Luis Gonzalez	.30	.09
5 Randy Johnson	.75	.23
6 Curt Schilling	.50	.15
7 Andruw Jones	.30	.09
8 Greg Maddux	1.25	.35
9 Chipper Jones	.75	.23
10 Gary Sheffield	.30	.09
11 Rodrigo Lopez	.30	.09
12 Geronimo Gil	.30	.09
13 Nomar Garciaparra	1.25	.35
14 Pedro Martinez	.75	.23
15 Manny Ramirez	.30	.09
16 Mark Prior	1.50	.45
17 Kerry Wood	.75	.23
18 Sammy Sosa	1.25	.35
19 Magglio Ordonez	.30	.09
20 Frank Thomas	.75	.23
21 Adam Dunn	.30	.09
22 Ken Griffey Jr.	1.25	.35
23 Sean Casey	.30	.09
24 Omar Vizquel	.30	.09
25 C.C. Sabathia	.30	.09
26 Larry Walker	.50	.15
27 Todd Helton	.50	.15
28 Ivan Rodriguez	.75	.23
29 Josh Beckett	.50	.15
30 Roy Oswalt	.30	.09
31 Jeff Kent	.30	.09
32 Jeff Bagwell	.50	.15
33 Lance Berkman	.30	.09
34 Mike Sweeney	.30	.09
35 Carlos Beltran	.30	.09
36 Hideo Nomo	.75	.23
37 Shawn Green	.30	.09
38 Kazuhisa Ishii	.30	.09
39 Geoff Jenkins	.30	.09
40 Richie Sexson	.30	.09
41 Torii Hunter	.30	.09
42 Jacque Jones	.30	.09
43 Jose Vidro	.30	.09
44 Vladimir Guerrero	.75	.23
45 Cliff Floyd	.30	.09
46 Al Leiter	.30	.09
47 Mike Piazza	1.25	.35
48 Tom Glavine	.50	.15
49 Roberto Alomar	.75	.23
50 Roger Clemens	1.50	.45
51 Jason Giambi	.75	.23
52 Bernie Williams	.50	.15
53 Alfonso Soriano	.50	.15
54 Derek Jeter	2.00	.60
55 Miguel Tejada	.30	.09
56 Eric Chavez	.30	.09
57 Barry Zito	.50	.15
58 Pat Burrell	.30	.09
59 Jim Thome	.75	.23
60 Brian Giles	.30	.09
61 Jason Kendall	.30	.09
62 Ryan Klesko	.30	.09
63 Phil Nevin	.30	.09
64 Sean Burroughs	.30	.09
65 Jason Schmidt	.30	.09
66 Rich Aurilia	.30	.09
67 Barry Bonds	2.00	.60
68 Randy Winn	.30	.09
69 Freddy Garcia	.30	.09
70 Ichiro Suzuki	1.25	.35
71 J.D. Drew	.30	.09
72 Jim Edmonds	.30	.09
73 Scott Rolen	.50	.15
74 Matt Morris	.30	.09
75 Albert Pujols	1.50	.45
76 Tino Martinez	.50	.15
77 Rey Ordonez	.30	.09
78 Carl Crawford	.30	.09
79 Rafael Palmeiro	.50	.15
80 Kevin Mench	.30	.09
81 Alex Rodriguez	1.25	.35
82 Juan Gonzalez	.75	.23
83 Carlos Delgado	.30	.09
84 Eric Hinske	.30	.09
85 Rich Fischer WP RC	2.00	.60
86 Brandon Webb WP RC	6.00	1.80
87 Rob Hammock WP RC	3.00	.90
88 Matt Kata WP RC	3.00	.90
89 Tim Olson WP RC	3.00	.90
90 Oscar Villarreal WP RC	2.00	.60
91 Michael Hessman WP RC	2.00	.60
92 Daniel Cabrera WP RC	2.00	.60
93 Jon Leicester WP RC	2.00	.60
94 Todd Wellemeyer WP RC	3.00	.90
95 Felix Sanchez WP RC	2.00	.60
96 David Sanders WP RC	2.00	.60
97 Josh Stewart WP RC	2.00	.60
98 Arnie Munoz WP RC	2.00	.60
99 Ryan Cameron WP RC	2.00	.60
100 Clint Barmes WP RC	3.00	.90
101 Josh Willingham WP RC	4.00	1.20
103 Willie Eyre WP RC	2.00	.60
104 Brent Hoard WP RC	2.00	.60
105 Termel Sledge WP RC	3.00	.90
106 Phil Seibel WP RC	2.00	.60
107 Craig Brazell WP RC	3.00	.90
108 Jeff Duncan WP RC	3.00	.90
110 Bernie Castro WP RC	2.00	.60
111 Mike Nicolas WP RC	2.00	.60
112 Rett Johnson WP RC	3.00	.90
113 Bobby Madritsch WP RC	2.00	.60
114 Luis Ayala WP RC	2.00	.60
115 Hideki Matsui WP RC	12.00	3.60
116 Jose Contreras WP RC	5.00	1.50
117 Lew Ford WP RC	3.00	.90
118 Jeremy Griffiths WP RC	3.00	.90
119 Guillermo Quiroz WP RC	4.00	1.20
120 Al. Machado WP RC	2.00	.60
121 Fran. Cruceta WP RC	2.00	.60
122 Prentice Redman WP RC	2.00	.60
123 Shane Bazzell WP RC	2.00	.60
124 Jason Anderson WP	2.00	.60
125 Ian Ferguson WP RC	2.00	.60
126 Nook Logan WP RC	2.00	.60

2003 Upper Deck Standing O Die Cuts

Nm-Mt Ex-Mt

*DIE CUTS 1-84: 1.25X TO 3X BASIC
*DIE CUTS 85-126: .75X TO 2X BASIC

2003 Upper Deck Standing O Starring Role Game Jersey

Collectors who pulled an exchange card for a game-used jersey card from this set were not given any assurances as to what card they would receive from Upper Deck. Those random exchange cards had an expiration date of May 20, 2006.

	Nm-Mt	Ex-Mt
AR Alex Rodriguez		
GO Juan Gonzalez		
HN Hideo Nomo Dodgers		
HN2 Hideo Nomo Red Sox SP/66		
JG Jason Giambi SP		
KG Ken Griffey Jr. SP/35		
LG Luis Gonzalez		
MC Mark McGwire SP		
MCA Mike Cameron		
MM Mickey Mantle SP/100		
MP Mike Piazza		
MT Miguel Tejada		
RC Roger Clemens		
RJ Randy Johnson		
SG Shawn Green		
XX Random Player EXCH	25.00	7.50

1999 Upper Deck Ultimate Victory

The 1999 Upper Deck Ultimate Victory Product was issued late in 1999. The cards were distributed in five card packs with a SRP of $2.99 per pack and each box had 24 packs in it. The set, consisting of 180 cards has 120 cards printed in normal quantites and 60 short prints. The cards from 121 through 150 feature players in their rookie campaign and cards numbered 151 through 180 all feature Mark McGwire in a set entitled "McGwire's Magic". Cards 121-180 were all released at a rate of one in four. Rookie Cards of Rick Ankiel, Josh Beckett, Pat Burrell, Freddy Garcia, Eric Munson, and Alfonso Soriano are all included in this set.

	Nm-Mt	Ex-Mt
COMPLETE SET (180)	200.00	60.00
COMP.SET w/o SP's (120)	25.00	7.50
COMMON CARD (1-120)	.30	.09
COMMON SP (121-150)	2.00	.60
COMMON (151-180)	2.00	.60
1 Troy Glaus	.50	.15
2 Tim Salmon	.50	.15
3 Mo Vaughn	.30	.09
4 Garret Anderson	.30	.09
5 Darin Erstad	.30	.09
6 Randy Johnson	.75	.23
7 Matt Williams	.30	.09
8 Travis Lee	.30	.09
9 Jay Bell	.30	.09
10 Steve Finley	.30	.09
11 Luis Gonzalez	.30	.09
12 Greg Maddux	1.25	.35
13 Chipper Jones	.75	.23
14 Javy Lopez	.30	.09
15 Tom Glavine	.50	.15
16 John Smoltz	.50	.15
17 Cal Ripken	2.50	.75
18 Charles Johnson	.30	.09
19 Albert Belle	.30	.09
20 Mike Mussina	.75	.23
21 Pedro Martinez	.75	.23
22 Nomar Garciaparra	1.25	.35
23 Jose Offerman	.30	.09
24 Sammy Sosa	1.25	.35
25 Mark Grace	.50	.15
26 Kerry Wood	.75	.23
27 Frank Thomas	.75	.23
28 Ray Durham	.30	.09
29 Paul Konerko	.30	.09
30 Pete Harnisch	.30	.09
31 Greg Vaughn	.30	.09
32 Sean Casey	.30	.09
33 Manny Ramirez	.30	.09
34 Jim Thome	.75	.23
35 Sandy Alomar Jr.	.30	.09
36 Roberto Alomar	.75	.23
37 Travis Fryman	.30	.09
38 Kenny Lofton	.30	.09
39 Omar Vizquel	.30	.09
40 Larry Walker	.50	.15
41 Todd Helton	.50	.15
42 Vinny Castilla	.30	.09
43 Tony Clark	.30	.09
44 Juan Encarnacion	.30	.09
45 Dean Palmer	.30	.09
46 Damion Easley	.30	.09
47 Mark Kotsay	.30	.09
48 Cliff Floyd	.30	.09
49 Jeff Bagwell	.50	.15
50 Ken Caminiti	.30	.09
51 Craig Biggio	.50	.15
52 Moises Alou	.30	.09
53 Johnny Damon	.30	.09
54 Larry Sutton	.30	.09
55 Kevin Brown	.50	.15
56 Adrian Beltre	.30	.09
57 Raul Mondesi	.30	.09
58 Gary Sheffield	.30	.09
59 Jeromy Burnitz	.30	.09
60 Sean Berry	.30	.09
61 Jeff Cirillo	.30	.09
62 Brad Radke	.30	.09
63 Todd Walker	.30	.09
64 Matt Lawton	.30	.09
65 Vladimir Guerrero	.75	.23
66 Rondell White	.30	.09
67 Dustin Hermanson	.30	.09
68 Mike Piazza	1.25	.35
69 Rickey Henderson	.75	.23
70 Robin Ventura	.30	.09
71 John Olerud	.30	.09
72 Derek Jeter	2.00	.60
73 Roger Clemens	1.50	.45
74 Orlando Hernandez	.30	.09
75 Paul O'Neill	.50	.15
76 Bernie Williams	.50	.15
77 Chuck Knoblauch	.30	.09
78 Tino Martinez	.50	.15
79 Jason Giambi	.75	.23
80 Ben Grieve	.30	.09
81 Matt Stairs	.30	.09
82 Scott Rolen	.50	.15
83 Ron Gant	.30	.09
84 Bobby Abreu	.30	.09
85 Curt Schilling	.50	.15
86 Brian Giles	.30	.09
87 Jason Kendall	.30	.09
88 Kevin Young	.30	.09
89 Mark McGwire	2.00	.60
90 Fernando Tatis	.30	.09
91 Ray Lankford	.30	.09
92 Eric Davis	.30	.09
93 Tony Gwynn	1.00	.30
94 Reggie Sanders	.30	.09
95 Wally Joyner	.30	.09
96 Trevor Hoffman	.30	.09
97 Robb Nen	.30	.09
98 Barry Bonds	2.00	.60
99 Jeff Kent	.30	.09
100 J.T. Snow	.30	.09
101 Ellis Burks	.30	.09
102 Ken Griffey Jr.	1.25	.35
103 Alex Rodriguez	1.25	.35
104 Jay Buhner	.30	.09
105 Edgar Martinez	.50	.15
106 David Bell	.30	.09
107 Bobby Smith	.30	.09
108 Wade Boggs	.50	.15
109 Fred McGriff	.50	.15
110 Rolando Arrojo	.30	.09
111 Jose Canseco	.75	.23
112 Ivan Rodriguez	.75	.23
113 Juan Gonzalez	.75	.23
114 Rafael Palmeiro	.50	.15
115 Rusty Greer	.30	.09
116 Todd Zeile	.30	.09
117 Jose Cruz Jr.	.30	.09
118 Carlos Delgado	.30	.09
119 Shawn Green	.30	.09
120 David Wells	.30	.09
121 Eric Munson SP RC	10.00	3.00
122 Lance Berkman SP	3.00	.90
123 Ed Yarnall SP	2.00	.60
124 Jacque Jones SP	3.00	.90
125 K.Farnsworth SP RC	8.00	2.40
126 Ryan Rupe SP RC	3.00	.90
127 Jeff Weaver SP RC	5.00	1.50
128 Gabe Kapler SP	2.00	.60
129 Alex Gonzalez SP	2.00	.60
130 Randy Wolf SP	3.00	.90
131 Ben Davis SP	2.00	.60
132 Carlos Beltran SP	3.00	.90
133 Jim Morris SP RC	8.00	2.40
134 J.Zimmerman SP RC	3.00	.90
135 Bruce Aven SP	2.00	.60
136 A.Soriano SP RC	50.00	15.00
137 Tim Hudson SP RC	25.00	7.50
138 Josh Beckett SP RC	60.00	18.00
139 Michael Barrett SP	2.00	.60
140 Eric Chavez SP	3.00	.90
141 Pat Burrell SP RC	20.00	6.00
142 Kris Benson SP	2.00	.60
143 J.D. Drew SP	3.00	.90
144 Matt Clement SP	3.00	.90
145 Rick Ankiel SP RC	10.00	3.00
146 Vernon Wells SP	3.00	.90
147 Ruben Mateo SP UER Card is misnumbered	2.00	.60
148 Roy Halladay SP	3.00	.90
149 Joe McEwing SP RC	3.00	.90
150 Freddy Garcia SP RC	8.00	2.40
151 Mark McGwire MM	2.00	.60
152 Mark McGwire MM	2.00	.60
153 Mark McGwire MM	2.00	.60
154 Mark McGwire MM	2.00	.60
155 Mark McGwire MM	2.00	.60
156 Mark McGwire MM	2.00	.60
157 Mark McGwire MM	2.00	.60
158 Mark McGwire MM	2.00	.60
159 Mark McGwire MM	2.00	.60
160 Mark McGwire MM	2.00	.60
161 Mark McGwire MM	2.00	.60
162 Mark McGwire MM	2.00	.60
163 Mark McGwire MM	2.00	.60
164 Mark McGwire MM	2.00	.60
165 Mark McGwire MM	2.00	.60
166 Mark McGwire MM	2.00	.60
167 Mark McGwire MM	2.00	.60
168 Mark McGwire MM	2.00	.60
169 Mark McGwire MM	2.00	.60
170 Mark McGwire MM	2.00	.60
171 Mark McGwire MM	2.00	.60
172 Mark McGwire MM	2.00	.60
173 Mark McGwire MM	2.00	.60
174 Mark McGwire MM	2.00	.60
175 Mark McGwire MM	2.00	.60
176 Mark McGwire MM	2.00	.60
177 Mark McGwire MM	2.00	.60
178 Mark McGwire MM	2.00	.60
179 Mark McGwire MM	2.00	.60
180 Mark McGwire MM	2.00	.60

1999 Upper Deck Ultimate Victory Parallel

Inserted at a rate of one in 12, these card parallel the regular set. They can be differentiated from the regular cards with the addition of linear holographic foil on each card.

Nm-Mt Ex-Mt

*STARS 1-120: 2X TO 5X BASIC CARDS
*PROSPECT 121-150: .6X TO 1.5X BASIC
*PROSPECT RC'S 121-150: .6X TO 1.5X BASIC

1999 Upper Deck Ultimate Victory Parallel 100

Randomly inserted into packs, these cards parallel the regular Ultimate Victory set. They feature silver holographic foil in trippy circular patterns and are sequentially numbered to 100 on the front.

Nm-Mt Ex-Mt

*STARS 1-120: 5X TO 12X BASIC CARDS
*PROSPECT 121-150: 1.5X TO 4X BASIC
*PROSP.RC'S 121-150: 2X TO 4X BASIC
*MCGWIRE 151-180: 3X TO 8X BASIC

1999 Upper Deck Ultimate Victory Bleacher Reachers

Inserted one every 23 packs, these horizontal cards feature 11 players who are among baseball's leading sluggers.

	Nm-Mt	Ex-Mt
COMPLETE SET (11)	50.00	15.00
BR1 Ken Griffey Jr.	4.00	1.20
BR2 Mark McGwire	6.00	1.80
BR3 Sammy Sosa	4.00	1.20
BR4 Barry Bonds	6.00	1.80
BR5 Nomar Garciaparra	4.00	1.20
BR6 Juan Gonzalez	2.50	.75
BR7 Jose Canseco	2.50	.75
BR8 Manny Ramirez	1.00	.30
BR9 Mike Piazza	4.00	1.20
BR10 Jeff Bagwell	1.50	.45
BR11 Alex Rodriguez	4.00	1.20

1999 Upper Deck Ultimate Victory Fame-Used Memorabilia

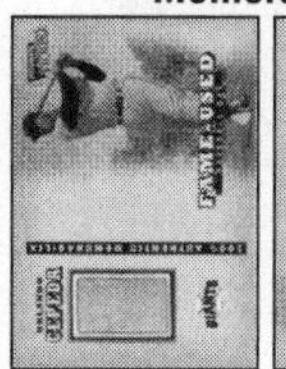

Randomly inserted into packs, these cards feature pieces of bats used by the four inductees into the Hall of Fame in 1999. Similar to the other bat cards Upper Deck has produced, approximately 350 of each card were made. There was also a special card made with bat pieces of all four of these players. Ninety-nine copies of that combo card were produced.

	Nm-Mt	Ex-Mt
GB George Brett	25.00	7.50
NR Nolan Ryan	40.00	12.00
OC Orlando Cepeda	10.00	3.00
RY Robin Yount	15.00	4.50
HOF Nolan Ryan George Brett Robin Yount Orlando Cepeda	150.00	45.00

1999 Upper Deck Ultimate Victory Frozen Ropes

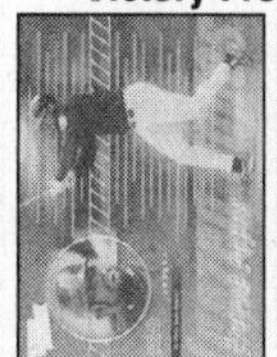

Inserted one every 23 packs, these 10 cards feature players who consistently are among the best in the majors.

	Nm-Mt	Ex-Mt
COMPLETE SET (10)	50.00	15.00
F1 Ken Griffey Jr.	4.00	1.20
F2 Mark McGwire	6.00	1.80
F3 Sammy Sosa	4.00	1.20
F4 Derek Jeter	6.00	1.80
F5 Tony Gwynn	3.00	.90
F6 Nomar Garciaparra	4.00	1.20
F7 Alex Rodriguez	4.00	1.20
F8 Mike Piazza	4.00	1.20
F9 Mo Vaughn	1.00	.30
F10 Craig Biggio	1.50	.45

2000 Upper Deck Ultimate Victory Lasting Impressions

Randomly inserted into packs at one in 11, this 10-card insert set features players that leave a lasting impression on those who watch them perform. Card backs carry a "L" prefix.

	Nm-Mt	Ex-Mt
COMPLETE SET (10)	30.00	9.00
L1 Barry Bonds	5.00	1.50
L2 Mike Piazza	3.00	.90
L3 Manny Ramirez	.75	.23
L4 Pedro Martinez	2.00	.60
L5 Mark McGwire	5.00	1.50
L6 Ken Griffey Jr.	3.00	.90
L7 Ivan Rodriguez	2.00	.60
L8 Jeff Bagwell	1.25	.35
L9 Randy Johnson	2.00	.60
L10 Alex Rodriguez	3.00	.90

2000 Upper Deck Ultimate Victory Starstruck

Randomly inserted into packs at one in 11, this 10-card insert set features players that have been starstruck. Card backs carry a "S" prefix.

	Nm-Mt	Ex-Mt
COMPLETE SET (10)	30.00	9.00
S1 Alex Rodriguez	3.00	.90
S2 Frank Thomas	2.00	.60
S3 Derek Jeter	5.00	1.50
S4 Mark McGwire	5.00	1.50
S5 Nomar Garciaparra	3.00	.90
S6 Chipper Jones	2.00	.60
S7 Cal Ripken	6.00	1.80
S8 Sammy Sosa	3.00	.90
S9 Vladimir Guerrero	2.00	.60
S10 Ken Griffey Jr.	3.00	.90

1999 Upper Deck Ultimate Victory STATure

Inserted one every six packs, these fifteen cards featured players who are among the statistical leaders.

	Nm-Mt	Ex-Mt
COMPLETE SET (15)	25.00	7.50
S1 Ken Griffey Jr.	1.25	.35
S2 Mark McGwire	2.00	.60
S3 Sammy Sosa	1.25	.35
S4 Nomar Garciaparra	1.25	.35
S5 Roger Clemens	1.50	.45
S6 Greg Maddux	1.25	.35
S7 Alex Rodriguez	1.25	.35
S8 Derek Jeter	2.00	.60
S9 Juan Gonzalez	.75	.23
S10 Manny Ramirez	.30	.09
S11 Mike Piazza	1.25	.35
S12 Tony Gwynn	1.00	.30
S13 Chipper Jones	.75	.23
S14 Pedro Martinez	.75	.23
S15 Frank Thomas	.75	.23

1999 Upper Deck Ultimate Victory Tribute 1999

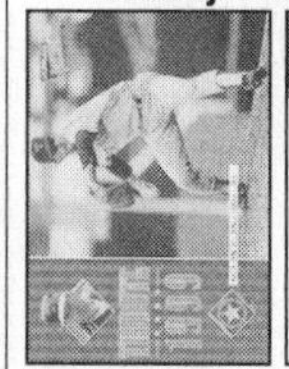
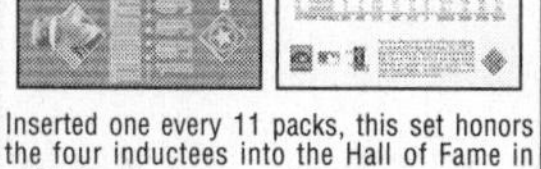

Inserted one every 11 packs, this set honors the four inductees into the Hall of Fame in 1999. Card backs carry a "T" prefix.

	Nm-Mt	Ex-Mt
COMPLETE SET (4)	15.00	4.50
T1 Nolan Ryan	6.00	1.80
T2 Robin Yount	4.00	1.20
T3 George Brett	6.00	1.80
T4 Orlando Cepeda	1.50	.45

1999 Upper Deck Ultimate Victory Ultimate Competitors

Inserted one every 23 packs, this 12 card set highlights the players who bring an winning attitude to the ballpark every day.

	Nm-Mt	Ex-Mt
COMPLETE SET (12)	60.00	18.00
U1 Ken Griffey Jr.	5.00	1.50
U2 Roger Clemens	6.00	1.80
U3 Scott Rolen	2.00	.60
U4 Greg Maddux	5.00	1.50
U5 Mark McGwire	8.00	2.40
U6 Derek Jeter	8.00	2.40
U7 Randy Johnson	3.00	.90
U8 Cal Ripken	10.00	3.00
U9 Craig Biggio	2.00	.60
U10 Kevin Brown	2.00	.60
U11 Chipper Jones	3.00	.90
U12 Vladimir Guerrero	3.00	.90

1999 Upper Deck Ultimate Victory Ultimate Hit Men

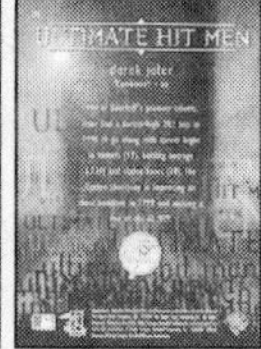

Inserted one every 23 packs, this eight card set features players who were among the leading contenders for the 1999 batting titles in their respective leagues.

	Nm-Mt	Ex-Mt
COMPLETE SET (8)	30.00	9.00
H1 Tony Gwynn	2.50	.75
H2 Cal Ripken	6.00	1.80
H3 Wade Boggs	1.25	.35
H4 Larry Walker	1.25	.35
H5 Alex Rodriguez	3.00	.90
H6 Derek Jeter	5.00	1.50
H7 Ivan Rodriguez	2.00	.60
H8 Ken Griffey Jr.	3.00	.90

2000 Upper Deck Ultimate Victory

The 2000 Upper Deck Ultimate Victory product was released in October, 2000. The set features 120 cards broken into tiers as follows: 90 veterans (1-90), 10 Rookies serial numbered to 3500, 10 Rookies serial numbered to 2500, and 10 Rookies serial numbered to 1000. Each pack contained five cards and carried a suggested retail price of $3.99.

	Nm-Mt	Ex-Mt
COMP.SET w/o SP's (90)	25.00	7.50
COMMON CARD (1-90)	.30	.09
1 Mo Vaughn	.30	.09
2 Darin Erstad	.30	.09
3 Troy Glaus	.50	.15
4 Adam Kennedy	.30	.09
5 Jason Giambi	.75	.23
6 Ben Grieve	.30	.09
7 Terrence Long	.30	.09
8 Tim Hudson	.50	.15
9 David Wells	.30	.09
10 Carlos Delgado	.30	.09
11 Shannon Stewart	.30	.09
12 Greg Vaughn	.30	.09
13 Gerald Williams	.30	.09
14 Manny Ramirez	.30	.09
15 Roberto Alomar	.75	.23
16 Jim Thome	.75	.23
17 Edgar Martinez	.50	.15
18 Alex Rodriguez	1.25	.35
19 Matt Riley	.30	.09
20 Cal Ripken	2.50	.75
21 Mike Mussina	.75	.23
22 Albert Belle	.30	.09
23 Ivan Rodriguez	.75	.23
24 Rafael Palmeiro	.50	.15
25 Nomar Garciaparra	1.25	.35
26 Pedro Martinez	.75	.23
27 Carl Everett	.30	.09
28 Tomokazu Ohka RC	.30	.09
29 Jermaine Dye	.30	.09
30 Johnny Damon	.30	.09
31 Dean Palmer	.30	.09
32 Juan Gonzalez	.75	.23
33 Eric Milton	.30	.09
34 Matt Lawton	.30	.09
35 Frank Thomas	.75	.23
36 Paul Konerko	.30	.09
37 Magglio Ordonez	.30	.09
38 Jon Garland	.30	.09
39 Derek Jeter	2.00	.60
40 Roger Clemens	1.50	.45
41 Bernie Williams	.50	.15
42 Nick Johnson	.30	.09
43 Julio Lugo	.30	.09
44 Jeff Bagwell	.50	.15
45 Richard Hidalgo	.30	.09
46 Chipper Jones	.75	.23
47 Greg Maddux	1.25	.35
48 Andruw Jones	.30	.09
49 Andres Galarraga	.30	.09
50 Rafael Furcal	.30	.09
51 Jeromy Burnitz	.30	.09
52 Geoff Jenkins	.30	.09
53 Mark McGwire	2.00	.60
54 Jim Edmonds	.30	.09
55 Rick Ankiel	.30	.09
56 Sammy Sosa	1.25	.35
57 Julio Zuleta RC	.30	.09
58 Kerry Wood	.75	.23

59 Randy Johnson .75 .23
60 Matt Williams .30 .09
61 Steve Finley .30 .09
62 Gary Sheffield .30 .09
63 Kevin Brown .30 .09
64 Shawn Green .30 .09
65 Milton Bradley .30 .09
66 Vladimir Guerrero .75 .23
67 Jose Vidro .30 .09
68 Barry Bonds 2.00 .60
69 Jeff Kent .30 .09
70 Preston Wilson .30 .09
71 Mike Lowell .30 .09
72 Mike Piazza 1.25 .35
73 Robin Ventura .30 .09
74 Edgardo Alfonzo .30 .09
75 Jay Payton .30 .09
76 Tony Gwynn 1.00 .30
77 Adam Eaton .30 .09
78 Phil Nevin .30 .09
79 Scott Rolen .50 .15
80 Bob Abreu .30 .09
81 Pat Burrell .50 .15
82 Brian Giles .30 .09
83 Jason Kendall .30 .09
84 Kris Benson .30 .09
85 Gookie Dawkins .30 .09
86 Ken Griffey Jr. 1.25 .35
87 Barry Larkin .75 .23
88 Larry Walker .50 .15
89 Todd Helton .50 .15
90 Ben Petrick .30 .09
91 Alex Cabrera/3500 RC 4.00 1.20
92 M.Wheatland/1000 RC 10.00 3.00
93 Joe Torres/1000 RC 10.00 3.00
94 Xavier Nady/1000 RC 25.00 7.50
95 Kenny Kelly/3500 RC 4.00 1.20
96 Matt Ginter/3500 RC 4.00 1.20
97 Ben Diggins/1000 RC 10.00 3.00
98 Danys Baez/3500 RC 6.00 1.80
99 Daylan Holt/2500 RC 5.00 1.50
100 K.Sasaki/3500 RC 8.00 2.40
101 D.Artman/2500 RC 5.00 1.50
102 Mike Tonis/1000 RC 15.00 4.50
103 Timo Perez/2500 RC 5.00 1.50
104 Barry Zito/2500 RC 30.00 9.00
105 Koyie Hill/2500 RC 8.00 2.40
106 B.Wilkerson/2500 RC 8.00 2.40
107 Juan Pierre/3500 RC 10.00 3.00
108 A.McNeal/3500 RC 4.00 1.20
109 J.Spurgeon/3500 RC 4.00 1.20
110 Sean Burnett/1000 RC 25.00 7.50
111 Luis Matos/3500 RC 10.00 3.00
112 Dave Krynzel/1000 RC 10.00 3.00
113 Scott Heard/1000 RC 10.00 3.00
114 Ben Sheets/2500 RC 8.00 2.40
115 D.Sardinha/1000 RC 10.00 3.00
116 D.Espinosa/1000 RC 10.00 3.00
117 Leo Estrella/3500 RC 4.00 1.20
118 K.Ainsworth/2500 RC 8.00 2.40
119 Jon Rauch/2500 RC 5.00 1.50
120 R.Franklin/2500 RC 5.00 1.50

2000 Upper Deck Ultimate Victory Parallel 250

Randomly inserted into packs, this 120-card insert is a complete parallel of the base set. They can be differentiated from the regular cards with the addition of silver foil on each card. Each card is serial numbered to 250.

Nm-Mt Ex-Mt
*STARS 1-90: 3X TO 8X BASIC 1-90..
*ROOKIES 1-90: 6X TO 15X BASIC 1-90
*TIER 1 91-120: .2X TO .5X BASIC RC 1000
*TIER 2 91-120: .4X TO 1X BASIC RC 2500
*TIER 3 91-120: .6X TO 1.5X BASIC RC 3500

2000 Upper Deck Ultimate Victory Parallel 100

Randomly inserted into packs, this 120-card insert is a complete parallel of the base set. They can be differentiated from the regular cards with the addition of red foil on each card. Each card is serial numbered to 100.

Nm-Mt Ex-Mt
*STARS 1-90: 8X TO 20X BASIC 1-90
*ROOKIES 1-90: 10X TO 25X BASIC 1-90
*TIER 1 91-120: &&.4X TO 1X BASIC RC 1000
*TIER 2 91-120: .75X TO 2X BASIC 2500
*TIER 3 91-120: 1X TO 2.5X BASIC 3500

2000 Upper Deck Ultimate Victory Parallel 25

Randomly inserted into packs, this 120-card insert is a complete parallel of the base set. They can be differentiated from the regular cards with the addition of gold foil on each card. Each card is serial numbered to 25.

Nm-Mt Ex-Mt
*STARS 1-90: 15X TO 40X BASIC 1-90

2000 Upper Deck Ultimate Victory Diamond Dignitaries

Randomly inserted into packs at one in 23, this 10-card insert set features players that are leaders on the playing field. Card backs carry a "D" prefix.

Nm-Mt Ex-Mt
COMPLETE SET (10) 60.00 18.00
D1 Ken Griffey Jr. 6.00 1.80
D2 Nomar Garciaparra 6.00 1.80
D3 Chipper Jones 4.00 1.20
D4 Ivan Rodriguez 4.00 1.20
D5 Mark McGwire 10.00 3.00
D6 Cal Ripken 12.00 3.60
D7 Vladimir Guerrero 4.00 1.20
D8 Alex Rodriguez 6.00 1.80
D9 Sammy Sosa 6.00 1.80
D10 Derek Jeter 10.00 3.00

2000 Upper Deck Ultimate Victory Hall of Fame Game Jersey

Randomly inserted into packs, this four-card insert set features jersey cards of players that were inducted into the Hall of Fame in 2000. Each card was serial numbered to 500, and the card backs carry the player's initials as numbering. Please note that the combo card of Fisk/Anderson/Perez was serial numbered to 100.

Nm-Mt Ex-Mt
CF Carlton Fisk 15.00 4.50
SA Sparky Anderson 15.00 4.50
TP Tony Perez 15.00 4.50
HOF Carlton Fisk 60.00 18.00
Sparky Anderson
Tony Perez/100

1999 Upper Deck Victory

This 470 standard-size set was issued in 12 card packs with 39 packs per box and 12 boxes per case. The SRP on these packs was only 99 cents and no insert cards were made for this product. The Subsets include 50 cards featuring 1999 rookies, 20 Rookie Flashback cards (451-470), 15 Power Trip cards, 10 History in the Making cards, 30 Team Checklist cards and 30 Mark McGwire Magic cards (421-450). Unless noted the subset cards are interspersed throughout the set. Also, through an internet-oriented contest, 10 autographed Ken Griffey Jr. jerseys were available through a contest which was entered through the Upper Deck website.

Nm-Mt Ex-Mt
COMPLETE SET (470) 75.00 22.00
COMMON CARD (1-470) .20 .06
COMMON (421-450) .75 .23
1 Anaheim Angels TC .20 .06
2 Mark Harriger RC .20 .06
3 Mo Vaughn PT .20 .06
4 Darin Erstad BP .20 .06
5 Troy Glaus .30 .09
6 Tim Salmon .30 .09
7 Mo Vaughn .20 .06
8 Darin Erstad .20 .06
9 Garret Anderson .20 .06
10 Todd Greene .20 .06
11 Troy Percival .20 .06
12 Chuck Finley .20 .06
13 Jason Dickson .20 .06
14 Jim Edmonds .20 .06
15 Ariz. Diamondbacks TC .20 .06
16 Randy Johnson .50 .15
17 Matt Williams .20 .06
18 Travis Lee .20 .06
19 Jay Bell .20 .06
20 Tony Womack .20 .06
21 Steve Finley .20 .06
22 Bernard Gilkey .20 .06
23 Tony Batista .20 .06
24 Todd Stottlemyre .20 .06
25 Omar Daal .20 .06
26 Atlanta Braves TC .20 .06
27 Bruce Chen .20 .06
28 George Lombard .20 .06
29 Chipper Jones PT .30 .09
30 Chipper Jones BP .30 .09
31 Greg Maddux .75 .23
32 Chipper Jones .50 .15
33 Javy Lopez .20 .06
34 Tom Glavine .30 .09
35 John Smoltz .30 .09
36 Andruw Jones .20 .06
37 Brian Jordan .20 .06
38 Walt Weiss .20 .06
39 Bret Boone .20 .06
40 Andres Galarraga .20 .06
41 Baltimore Orioles TC .20 .06
42 Ryan Minor .20 .06
43 Jerry Hairston Jr. .20 .06
44 Calvin Pickering .20 .06
45 Cal Ripken HM .75 .23
46 Cal Ripken 1.50 .45
47 Charles Johnson .20 .06
48 Albert Belle .20 .06
49 Delino DeShields .20 .06
50 Mike Mussina .50 .15
51 Scott Erickson .20 .06
52 Brady Anderson .20 .06
53 B.J. Surhoff .20 .06
54 Harold Baines .20 .06
55 Will Clark .50 .15
56 Boston Red Sox TC .20 .06
57 Shea Hillenbrand RC 1.25 .35
58 Trot Nixon .30 .09
59 Jin Ho Cho .20 .06
60 Nomar Garciaparra PT .50 .15
61 Nomar Garciaparra BP .50 .15
62 Pedro Martinez .50 .15
63 Nomar Garciaparra .75 .23
64 Jose Offerman .20 .06
65 Jason Varitek .20 .06
66 Darren Lewis .20 .06
67 Troy O'Leary .20 .06
68 Donnie Sadler .20 .06
69 John Valentin .20 .06
70 Tim Wakefield .20 .06
71 Bret Saberhagen .20 .06
72 Chicago Cubs TC .20 .06
73 Kyle Farnsworth RC .75 .23
74 Sammy Sosa PT .50 .15
75 Sammy Sosa BP .50 .15
76 Sammy Sosa HM .50 .15
77 Kerry Wood HM .30 .09
78 Sammy Sosa .75 .23
79 Mark Grace .30 .09
80 Kerry Wood .50 .15
81 Kevin Tapani .20 .06
82 Benito Santiago .20 .06
83 Gary Gaetti .20 .06
84 Mickey Morandini .20 .06
85 Glenallen Hill .20 .06
86 Henry Rodriguez .20 .06
87 Rod Beck .20 .06
88 Chicago White Sox TC .20 .06
89 Carlos Lee .20 .06
90 Mark Johnson .20 .06
91 Frank Thomas PT .30 .09
92 Frank Thomas .50 .15
93 Jim Parque .20 .06
94 Mike Sirotka .20 .06
95 Mike Caruso .20 .06
96 Ray Durham .20 .06
97 Magglio Ordonez .20 .06
98 Paul Konerko .20 .06
99 Bob Howry .20 .06
100 Brian Simmons .20 .06
101 Jaime Navarro .20 .06
102 Cincinnati Reds TC .20 .06
103 Denny Neagle .20 .06
104 Pete Harnisch .20 .06
105 Greg Vaughn .20 .06
106 Brett Tomko .20 .06
107 Mike Cameron .20 .06
108 Sean Casey .20 .06
109 Aaron Boone .20 .06
110 Michael Tucker .20 .06
111 Dmitri Young .20 .06
112 Barry Larkin .50 .15
113 Cleveland Indians TC .20 .06
114 Russ Branyan .20 .06
115 Jim Thome PT .30 .09
116 Manny Ramirez PT .20 .06
117 Manny Ramirez .20 .06
118 Jim Thome .50 .15
119 David Justice .20 .06
120 Sandy Alomar Jr. .20 .06
121 Roberto Alomar .50 .15
122 Jaret Wright .20 .06
123 Bartolo Colon .20 .06
124 Travis Fryman .20 .06
125 Kenny Lofton .20 .06
126 Omar Vizquel .20 .06
127 Colorado Rockies TC .20 .06
128 Derrick Gibson .20 .06
129 Larry Walker BP .30 .09
130 Larry Walker .30 .09
131 Dante Bichette .20 .06
132 Todd Helton .30 .09
133 Neifi Perez .20 .06
134 Vinny Castilla .20 .06
135 Darryl Kile .20 .06
136 Pedro Astacio .20 .06
137 Darryl Hamilton .20 .06
138 Mike Lansing .20 .06
139 Kirt Manwaring .20 .06
140 Detroit Tigers TC .20 .06
141 Jeff Weaver RC .50 .15
142 Gabe Kapler .20 .06
143 Tony Clark PT .20 .06
144 Tony Clark .20 .06
145 Juan Encarnacion .20 .06
146 Dean Palmer .20 .06
147 Damion Easley .20 .06
148 Bobby Higginson .20 .06
149 Karim Garcia .20 .06
150 Justin Thompson .20 .06
151 Matt Anderson .20 .06
152 Willie Blair .20 .06
153 Brian Hunter .20 .06
154 Florida Marlins TC .20 .06
155 Alex Gonzalez .20 .06
156 Mark Kotsay .20 .06
157 Livan Hernandez .20 .06
158 Cliff Floyd .20 .06
159 Todd Dunwoody .20 .06
160 Alex Fernandez .20 .06
161 Matt Mantei .20 .06
162 Derrek Lee .20 .06
163 Kevin Orie .20 .06
164 Craig Counsell .20 .06
165 Rafael Medina .20 .06
166 Houston Astros TC .20 .06
167 Daryle Ward .20 .06
168 Mitch Meluskey .20 .06
169 Jeff Bagwell PT .20 .06
170 Jeff Bagwell .30 .09
171 Ken Caminiti .20 .06
172 Craig Biggio .30 .09
173 Derek Bell .20 .06
174 Moises Alou .20 .06
175 Billy Wagner .20 .06
176 Shane Reynolds .20 .06
177 Carl Everett .20 .06
178 Scott Elarton .20 .06
179 Richard Hidalgo .20 .06
180 K.C Royals TC .20 .06
181 Carlos Beltran .20 .06
182 Carlos Febles .20 .06
183 Jeremy Giambi .20 .06
184 Johnny Damon .20 .06
185 Joe Randa .20 .06
186 Jeff King .20 .06
187 Hipolito Pichardo .20 .06
188 Kevin Appier .20 .06
189 Chad Kreuter .20 .06
190 Rey Sanchez .20 .06
191 Larry Sutton .20 .06
192 Jeff Montgomery .20 .06
193 Jermaine Dye .20 .06
194 L.A. Dodgers TC .20 .06
195 Adam Riggs .20 .06
196 Angel Pena .20 .06
197 Todd Hundley .20 .06
198 Kevin Brown .30 .09
199 Ismael Valdes .20 .06
200 Chan Ho Park .20 .06
201 Adrian Beltre .20 .06
202 Mark Grudzielanek .20 .06
203 Raul Mondesi .20 .06
204 Gary Sheffield .20 .06
205 Eric Karros .20 .06
206 Devon White .20 .06
207 Milw. Brewers TC .20 .06
208 Ron Belliard .20 .06
209 Rafael Roque RC .20 .06
210 Jeromy Burnitz .20 .06
211 Fernando Vina .20 .06
212 Scott Karl .20 .06
213 Jim Abbott .30 .09
214 Sean Berry .20 .06
215 Marquis Grissom .20 .06
216 Geoff Jenkins .20 .06
217 Jeff Cirillo .20 .06
218 Dave Nilsson .20 .06
219 Jose Valentin .20 .06
220 Minnesota Twins TC .20 .06
221 Corey Koskie .20 .06
222 Cristian Guzman .20 .06
223 A.J. Pierzynski .20 .06
224 David Ortiz .20 .06
225 Brad Radke .20 .06
226 Todd Walker .20 .06
227 Matt Lawton .20 .06
228 Rick Aguilera .20 .06
229 Eric Milton .20 .06
230 Marty Cordova .20 .06
231 Torii Hunter .20 .06
232 Ron Coomer .20 .06
233 LaTroy Hawkins .20 .06
234 Montreal Expos TC .20 .06
235 Fernando Seguignol .20 .06
236 Michael Barrett .20 .06
237 Vladimir Guerrero BP .30 .09
238 Vladimir Guerrero .50 .15
239 Brad Fullmer .20 .06
240 Rondell White .20 .06
241 Ugueth Urbina .20 .06
242 Dustin Hermanson .20 .06
243 Orlando Cabrera .20 .06
244 Wilton Guerrero .20 .06
245 Carl Pavano .20 .06
246 Javier Vazquez .20 .06
247 Chris Widger .20 .06
248 New York Mets TC .20 .06
249 Mike Kinkade .20 .06
250 Octavio Dotel .20 .06
251 Mike Piazza PT .50 .15
252 Mike Piazza .75 .23
253 Rickey Henderson .50 .15
254 Edgardo Alfonzo .20 .06
255 Robin Ventura .20 .06
256 Al Leiter .20 .06
257 Brian McRae .20 .06
258 Rey Ordonez .20 .06
259 Bobby Bonilla .20 .06
260 Orel Hershiser .20 .06
261 John Olerud .20 .06
262 New York Yankees TC .20 .06
263 Ricky Ledee .20 .06
264 Bernie Williams BP .20 .06
265 Derek Jeter BP .60 .18
266 Scott Brosius HM .20 .06
267 Derek Jeter 1.25 .35
268 Roger Clemens 1.00 .30
269 Orlando Hernandez .20 .06
270 Scott Brosius .20 .06
271 Paul O'Neill .30 .09
272 Bernie Williams .30 .09
273 Chuck Knoblauch .20 .06
274 Tino Martinez .30 .09
275 Mariano Rivera .30 .09
276 Jorge Posada .30 .09
277 Oakland Athletics TC .20 .06
278 Eric Chavez .20 .06
279 Ben Grieve HM .20 .06
280 Jason Giambi .50 .15
281 John Jaha .20 .06
282 Miguel Tejada .20 .06
283 Ben Grieve .20 .06
284 Matt Stairs .20 .06
285 Ryan Christenson .20 .06
286 A.J. Hinch .20 .06
287 Kenny Rogers .20 .06
288 Tom Candiotti .20 .06
289 Scott Spiezio .20 .06
290 Phi. Phillies TC .20 .06
291 Pat Burrell RC 2.50 .75
292 Marlon Anderson .20 .06
293 Scott Rolen BP .30 .09
294 Scott Rolen .30 .09
295 Doug Glanville .20 .06
296 Rico Brogna .20 .06
297 Ron Gant .20 .06
298 Bobby Abreu .20 .06
299 Desi Relaford .20 .06
300 Curt Schilling .30 .09
301 Chad Ogea .20 .06
302 Kevin Jordan .20 .06
303 Carlton Loewer .20 .06
304 Pittsburgh Pirates TC .20 .06
305 Kris Benson .20 .06
306 Brian Giles .20 .06
307 Jason Kendall .20 .06
308 Jose Guillen .20 .06
309 Pat Meares .20 .06
310 Brant Brown .20 .06
311 Kevin Young .20 .06
312 Ed Sprague .20 .06
313 Francisco Cordova .20 .06
314 Aramis Ramirez .20 .06
315 Freddy Adrian Garcia .20 .06
316 St. Louis Cardinals TC .20 .06
317 J.D. Drew .20 .06
318 Chad Hutchinson RC .30 .09
319 Mark McGwire PT .60 .18
320 J.D. Drew PT .20 .06
321 Mark McGwire BP .60 .18
322 Mark McGwire HM .60 .18
323 Mark McGwire 1.25 .35
324 Fernando Tatis .20 .06
325 Edgar Renteria .20 .06
326 Ray Lankford .20 .06
327 Willie McGee .20 .06
328 Ricky Bottalico .20 .06
329 Eli Marrero .20 .06
330 Matt Morris .20 .06
331 Eric Davis .20 .06
332 Darren Bragg .20 .06
333 San Diego Padres TC .20 .06
334 Matt Clement .20 .06
335 Ben Davis .20 .06
336 Gary Matthews Jr. .20 .06
337 Tony Gwynn BP .30 .09
338 Tony Gwynn HM .30 .09
339 Tony Gwynn .60 .18
340 Reggie Sanders .20 .06
341 Ruben Rivera .20 .06
342 Wally Joyner .20 .06
343 Sterling Hitchcock .20 .06
344 Carlos Hernandez .20 .06
345 Andy Ashby .20 .06
346 Trevor Hoffman .20 .06
347 Chris Gomez .20 .06
348 Jim Leyritz .20 .06
349 S.F. Giants TC .20 .06
350 Armando Rios .20 .06
351 Barry Bonds PT .50 .15
352 Barry Bonds BP .50 .15
353 Barry Bonds HM .50 .15
354 Robb Nen .20 .06
355 Bill Mueller .20 .06
356 Barry Bonds 1.25 .35
357 Jeff Kent .20 .06
358 J.T. Snow .20 .06
359 Ellis Burks .20 .06
360 F.P. Santangelo .20 .06
361 Marvin Benard .20 .06
362 Stan Javier .20 .06
363 Shawn Estes .20 .06
364 Seattle Mariners TC .20 .06
365 Carlos Guillen .20 .06
366 Ken Griffey Jr. PT .50 .15
367 Alex Rodriguez PT .50 .15
368 Ken Griffey Jr. BP .50 .15
369 Alex Rodriguez BP .50 .15
370 Ken Griffey Jr. HM .50 .15
371 Alex Rodriguez HM .50 .15
372 Ken Griffey Jr. .75 .23
373 Alex Rodriguez .75 .23
374 Jay Buhner .20 .06
375 Edgar Martinez .30 .09
376 Jeff Fassero .20 .06
377 David Bell .20 .06
378 David Segui .20 .06
379 Russ Davis .20 .06
380 Dan Wilson .20 .06
381 Jamie Moyer .20 .06
382 T.B. Devil Rays TC .20 .06
383 Roberto Hernandez .20 .06
384 Bobby Smith .20 .06
385 Wade Boggs .30 .09
386 Fred McGriff .30 .09
387 Rolando Arrojo .20 .06
388 Jose Canseco .50 .15
389 Wilson Alvarez .20 .06
390 Kevin Stocker .20 .06
391 Miguel Cairo .20 .06
392 Quinton McCracken .20 .06
393 Texas Rangers TC .20 .06
394 Ruben Mateo .20 .06
395 Cesar King .20 .06
396 Juan Gonzalez PT .30 .09
397 Juan Gonzalez BP .30 .09
398 Ivan Rodriguez .50 .15
399 Juan Gonzalez .50 .15
400 Rafael Palmeiro .30 .09
401 Rick Helling .20 .06
402 Aaron Sele .20 .06
403 John Wetteland .20 .06
404 Rusty Greer .20 .06
405 Todd Zeile .20 .06
406 Royce Clayton .20 .06
407 Tom Goodwin .20 .06
408 Toronto Blue Jays TC .20 .06
409 Kevin Witt .20 .06
410 Roy Halladay .20 .06
411 Jose Cruz Jr. .20 .06
412 Carlos Delgado .20 .06
413 Willie Greene .20 .06
414 Shawn Green .20 .06
415 Homer Bush .20 .06
416 Shannon Stewart .20 .06
417 David Wells .20 .06
418 Kelvim Escobar .20 .06
419 Joey Hamilton .20 .06
420 Alex Gonzalez .20 .06
421 Mark McGwire MM .75 .23
422 Mark McGwire MM .75 .23
423 Mark McGwire MM .75 .23
424 Mark McGwire MM .75 .23
425 Mark McGwire MM .75 .23
426 Mark McGwire MM .75 .23
427 Mark McGwire MM .75 .23
428 Mark McGwire MM .75 .23
429 Mark McGwire MM .75 .23
430 Mark McGwire MM .75 .23
431 Mark McGwire MM .75 .23
432 Mark McGwire MM .75 .23
433 Mark McGwire MM .75 .23
434 Mark McGwire MM .75 .23
435 Mark McGwire MM .75 .23
436 Mark McGwire MM .75 .23
437 Mark McGwire MM .75 .23
438 Mark McGwire MM .75 .23
439 Mark McGwire MM .75 .23
440 Mark McGwire MM .75 .23
441 Mark McGwire MM .75 .23
442 Mark McGwire MM .75 .23
443 Mark McGwire MM .75 .23
444 Mark McGwire MM .75 .23
445 Mark McGwire MM .75 .23
446 Mark McGwire MM .75 .23
447 Mark McGwire MM .75 .23
448 Mark McGwire MM .75 .23
449 Mark McGwire MM .75 .23
450 Mark McGwire MM .75 .23

451 Chipper Jones RF .30 .09
452 Cal Ripken RF .75 .23
453 Roger Clemens RF .50 .15
454 Wade Boggs RF .20 .06
455 Greg Maddux RF .50 .15
456 Frank Thomas RF .30 .09
457 Jeff Bagwell RF .20 .06
458 Mike Piazza RF .50 .15
459 Randy Johnson RF .30 .09
460 Mo Vaughn RF .20 .06
461 Mark McGwire RF .60 .18
462 Rickey Henderson RF .30 .09
463 Barry Bonds RF .50 .15
464 Tony Gwynn RF .30 .09
465 Ken Griffey Jr. RF .50 .15
466 Alex Rodriguez RF .50 .15
467 Sammy Sosa RF .50 .15
468 Juan Gonzalez RF .30 .09
469 Kevin Brown RF .20 .06
470 Fred McGriff RF .20 .06

2000 Upper Deck Victory

The Upper Deck Victory set was initially released in March, 2000 as a 440-card set that featured 300 player cards, 40 Rookie Subset cards, 20 Big Play Makers, 30 Team Checklists, and 50 Junior Circuit subset cards. Each pack contained 12 cards and carried a suggested retail price of ninety-nine cents. A 466-card factory set was released in December, 2000 containing an exclusive 26-card Team USA subset (cards 441-466) featuring the team that won the Olympic gold medal in Sydney, Australia in September, 2000. Finally, special packs were issued in April, 2000 for the season-opening Mets/Cubs series in Japan. These packs contained three regular issue Victory cards featuring either Cubs or Mets and two Japanese header cards. One of those cards featured a checklist of the 21 players in the packs and the other one provided set information. Notable rookies in the set include Jon Rauch and Ben Sheets.

	Nm-Mt	Ex-Mt
COMPLETE SET (440)	15.00	4.50
COMP.FACT.SET (466)	20.00	6.00
COMMON CARD (1-390)	.20	.06
COMMON (391-440)	.50	.15
COMMON USA (441-466)	.30	.09

1 Mo Vaughn .20 .06
2 Garret Anderson .20 .06
3 Tim Salmon .30 .09
4 Troy Percival .20 .06
5 Orlando Palmeiro .20 .06
6 Darin Erstad .20 .06
7 Ramon Ortiz .20 .06
8 Ben Molina .20 .06
9 Troy Glaus .30 .09
10 Jim Edmonds .20 .06
11 Mo Vaughn .20 .06
Troy Percival CL
12 Craig Biggio .30 .09
13 Roger Cedeno .20 .06
14 Shane Reynolds .20 .06
15 Jeff Bagwell .30 .09
16 Octavio Dotel .20 .06
17 Moises Alou .20 .06
18 Jose Lima .20 .06
19 Ken Caminiti .20 .06
20 Richard Hidalgo .20 .06
21 Billy Wagner .20 .06
22 Lance Berkman .20 .06
23 Jeff Bagwell .20 .06
Jose Lima CL
24 Jason Giambi .50 .15
25 Randy Velarde .20 .06
26 Miguel Tejada .20 .06
27 Matt Stairs .20 .06
28 A.J. Hinch .20 .06
29 Olmedo Saenz .20 .06
30 Ben Grieve .20 .06
31 Ryan Christenson .20 .06
32 Eric Chavez .20 .06
33 Tim Hudson .30 .09
34 John Jaha .20 .06
35 Jason Giambi .50 .15
Matt Stairs CL
36 Raul Mondesi .20 .06
37 Tony Batista .20 .06
38 David Wells .20 .06
39 Homer Bush .20 .06
40 Carlos Delgado .20 .06
41 Billy Koch .20 .06
42 Darrin Fletcher .20 .06
43 Tony Fernandez .20 .06
44 Shannon Stewart .20 .06
45 Roy Halladay .20 .06
46 Chris Carpenter .20 .06
47 Carlos Delgado .20 .06
David Wells CL
48 Chipper Jones .50 .15
49 Greg Maddux .75 .23
50 Andruw Jones .20 .06
51 Andres Galarraga .20 .06
52 Tom Glavine .30 .09
53 Brian Jordan .20 .06
54 John Smoltz .30 .09
55 John Rocker .20 .06
56 Javy Lopez .20 .06
57 Eddie Perez .20 .06
58 Kevin Millwood .20 .06
59 Chipper Jones .30 .09
Greg Maddux CL
60 Jeromy Burnitz .20 .06
61 Steve Woodard .20 .06
62 Ron Belliard .20 .06
63 Geoff Jenkins .20 .06
64 Bob Wickman .20 .06
65 Marquis Grissom .20 .06
66 Henry Blanco .20 .06
67 Mark Loretta .20 .06
68 Alex Ochoa .20 .06
69 Marquis Grissom .20 .06
Jeromy Burnitz CL
70 Mark McGwire 1.25 .35
71 Edgar Renteria .20 .06
72 Dave Veres .20 .06
73 Eli Marrero .20 .06
74 Fernando Tatis .20 .06
75 J.D. Drew .20 .06
76 Ray Lankford .20 .06
77 Darryl Kile .20 .06
78 Kent Bottenfield .20 .06
79 Joe McEwing .20 .06
80 Mark McGwire .60 .18
Ray Lankford CL
81 Sammy Sosa .75 .23
82 Jose Nieves .20 .06
83 Jon Lieber .20 .06
84 Henry Rodriguez .20 .06
85 Mark Grace .30 .09
86 Eric Young .20 .06
87 Kerry Wood .50 .15
88 Ismael Valdes .20 .06
89 Glenallen Hill .20 .06
90 Sammy Sosa .30 .09
Mark Grace CL
91 Greg Vaughn .20 .06
92 Fred McGriff .30 .09
93 Ryan Rupe .20 .06
94 Bubba Trammell .20 .06
95 Miguel Cairo .20 .06
96 Roberto Hernandez .20 .06
97 Jose Canseco .50 .15
98 Wilson Alvarez .20 .06
99 John Flaherty .20 .06
100 Vinny Castilla .20 .06
101 Jose Canseco .20 .06
Ramon Hernandez CL
102 Randy Johnson .50 .15
103 Matt Williams .20 .06
104 Matt Mantei .20 .06
105 Steve Finley .20 .06
106 Luis Gonzalez .20 .06
107 Travis Lee .20 .06
108 Omar Daal .20 .06
109 Jay Bell .20 .06
110 Erubiel Durazo .20 .06
111 Tony Womack .20 .06
112 Todd Stottlemyre .20 .06
113 Randy Johnson .20 .06
Matt Williams CL
114 Gary Sheffield .20 .06
115 Adrian Beltre .20 .06
116 Kevin Brown .30 .09
117 Todd Hundley .20 .06
118 Eric Karros .20 .06
119 Shawn Green .20 .06
120 Chan Ho Park .20 .06
121 Mark Grudzielanek .20 .06
122 Todd Hollandsworth .20 .06
123 Jeff Shaw .20 .06
124 Darren Dreifort .20 .06
125 Gary Sheffield .20 .06
Kevin Brown CL
126 Vladimir Guerrero .50 .15
127 Michael Barrett .20 .06
128 Dustin Hermanson .20 .06
129 Jose Vidro .20 .06
130 Chris Widger .20 .06
131 Mike Thurman .20 .06
132 Wilton Guerrero .20 .06
133 Brad Fullmer .20 .06
134 Rondell White .20 .06
135 Ugueth Urbina .20 .06
136 Vladimir Guerrero .20 .06
Rondell White CL
137 Barry Bonds 1.25 .35
138 Russ Ortiz .20 .06
139 J.T. Snow .20 .06
140 Joe Nathan .20 .06
141 Rich Aurilia .20 .06
142 Jeff Kent .20 .06
143 Armando Rios .20 .06
144 Ellis Burks .20 .06
145 Robb Nen .20 .06
146 Marvin Benard .20 .06
147 Barry Bonds .50 .15
Russ Ortiz CL
148 Manny Ramirez .20 .06
149 Bartolo Colon .20 .06
150 Kenny Lofton .20 .06
151 Sandy Alomar Jr. .20 .06
152 Travis Fryman .20 .06
153 Omar Vizquel .20 .06
154 Roberto Alomar .50 .15
155 Richie Sexson .20 .06
156 David Justice .20 .06
157 Jim Thome .50 .15
158 Manny Ramirez .20 .06
Roberto Alomar CL
159 Ken Griffey Jr. .75 .23
160 Edgar Martinez .30 .09
161 Freddy Garcia .20 .06
162 Alex Rodriguez .75 .23
163 John Halama .20 .06
164 Russ Davis .20 .06
165 David Bell .20 .06
166 Gil Meche .20 .06
167 Jamie Moyer .20 .06
168 John Olerud .20 .06
169 Ken Griffey Jr. .50 .15
Freddy Garcia CL
170 Preston Wilson .20 .06
171 Antonio Alfonseca .20 .06
172 A.J. Burnett .20 .06
173 Luis Castillo .20 .06
174 Mike Lowell .20 .06
175 Alex Fernandez .20 .06
176 Mike Redmond .20 .06
177 Alex Gonzalez .20 .06
178 Vladimir Nunez .20 .06
179 Mark Kotsay .20 .06
180 Preston Wilson .20 .06
Luis Castillo CL
181 Mike Piazza .75 .23
182 Darryl Hamilton .20 .06
183 Al Leiter .20 .06
184 Robin Ventura .30 .09
185 Rickey Henderson .50 .15
186 Rey Ordonez .20 .06
187 Edgardo Alfonzo .20 .06
188 Derek Bell .20 .06
189 Mike Hampton .20 .06
190 Armando Benitez .20 .06
191 Mike Piazza .30 .09
Rickey Henderson CL
192 Cal Ripken 1.50 .45
193 B.J. Surhoff .20 .06
194 Mike Mussina .50 .15
195 Albert Belle .20 .06
196 Jerry Hairston Jr. .20 .06
197 Will Clark .50 .15
198 Sidney Ponson .20 .06
199 Brady Anderson .20 .06
200 Scott Erickson .20 .06
201 Ryan Minor .20 .06
202 Cal Ripken .75 .23
Albert Belle CL
203 Tony Gwynn .60 .18
204 Bret Boone .20 .06
205 Ryan Klesko .20 .06
206 Ben Davis .20 .06
207 Matt Clement .20 .06
208 Eric Owens .20 .06
209 Trevor Hoffman .20 .06
210 Sterling Hitchcock .20 .06
211 Phil Nevin .20 .06
212 Tony Gwynn .30 .09
Trevor Hoffman CL
213 Scott Rolen .30 .09
214 Bob Abreu .20 .06
215 Curt Schilling .30 .09
216 Rico Brogna .20 .06
217 Robert Person .20 .06
218 Doug Glanville .20 .06
219 Mike Lieberthal .20 .06
220 Andy Ashby .20 .06
221 Randy Wolf .20 .06
222 Bob Abreu .20 .06
Curt Schilling CL
223 Brian Giles .20 .06
224 Jason Kendall .20 .06
225 Kris Benson .20 .06
226 Warren Morris .20 .06
227 Kevin Young .20 .06
228 Al Martin .20 .06
229 Wil Cordero .20 .06
230 Bruce Aven .20 .06
231 Todd Ritchie .20 .06
232 Jason Kendall .20 .06
Brian Giles CL
233 Ivan Rodriguez .50 .15
234 Rusty Greer .20 .06
235 Ruben Mateo .20 .06
236 Justin Thompson .20 .06
237 Rafael Palmeiro .30 .09
238 Chad Curtis .20 .06
239 Royce Clayton UER .20 .06
Mark McLemore pictured on back
240 Gabe Kapler .20 .06
241 Jeff Zimmerman .20 .06
242 John Wetteland .20 .06
243 Ivan Rodriguez .30 .09
Rafael Palmeiro CL
244 Nomar Garciaparra .75 .23
245 Pedro Martinez .50 .15
246 Jose Offerman .20 .06
247 Jason Varitek .20 .06
248 Troy O'Leary .20 .06
249 John Valentin .20 .06
250 Trot Nixon .30 .09
251 Carl Everett .20 .06
252 Wilton Veras .20 .06
253 Bret Saberhagen .20 .06
254 Nomar Garciaparra .50 .15
Pedro Martinez CL
255 Sean Casey .20 .06
256 Barry Larkin .50 .15
257 Pokey Reese .20 .06
258 Pete Harnisch .20 .06
259 Aaron Boone .20 .06
260 Dante Bichette .20 .06
261 Scott Williamson .20 .06
262 Steve Parris .20 .06
263 Dmitri Young .20 .06
264 Mike Cameron .20 .06
265 Sean Casey .20 .06
Scott Williamson CL
266 Larry Walker .30 .09
267 Rolando Arrojo .20 .06
268 Pedro Astacio .20 .06
269 Todd Helton .30 .09
270 Jeff Cirillo .20 .06
271 Neifi Perez .20 .06
272 Brian Bohanon .20 .06
273 Jeffrey Hammonds .20 .06
274 Tom Goodwin .20 .06
275 Larry Walker .20 .06
Todd Helton CL
276 Carlos Beltran .20 .06
277 Jermaine Dye .20 .06
278 Mike Sweeney .20 .06
279 Joe Randa .20 .06
280 Jose Rosado .20 .06
281 Carlos Febles .20 .06
282 Jeff Suppan .20 .06
283 Johnny Damon .20 .06
284 Jeremy Giambi .20 .06
285 Mike Sweeney .20 .06
Carlos Beltran CL
286 Tony Clark .20 .06
287 Damion Easley .20 .06
288 Jeff Weaver .20 .06
289 Dean Palmer .20 .06
290 Juan Gonzalez .50 .15
291 Juan Encarnacion .20 .06
292 Todd Jones .20 .06
293 Karim Garcia .20 .06
294 Deivi Cruz .20 .06
295 Dean Palmer .20 .06
Juan Encarnacion CL
296 Corey Koskie .20 .06
297 Brad Radke .20 .06
298 Doug Mientkiewicz .20 .06
299 Ron Coomer .20 .06
300 Joe Mays .20 .06
301 Eric Milton .20 .06
302 Jacque Jones .20 .06
303 Chad Allen .20 .06
304 Cristian Guzman .20 .06
305 Jason Ryan .20 .06
306 Todd Walker .20 .06
307 Corey Koskie .20 .06
Eric Milton CL
308 Frank Thomas .50 .15
309 Paul Konerko .20 .06
310 Mike Sirotka .20 .06
311 Jim Parque .20 .06
312 Magglio Ordonez .20 .06
313 Bob Howry .20 .06
314 Carlos Lee .20 .06
315 Ray Durham .20 .06
316 Chris Singleton .20 .06
317 Brook Fordyce .20 .06
318 Frank Thomas .30 .09
Magglio Ordonez CL
319 Derek Jeter 1.25 .35
320 Roger Clemens 1.00 .30
321 Paul O'Neill .30 .09
322 Bernie Williams .30 .09
323 Mariano Rivera .30 .09
324 Tino Martinez .30 .09
325 David Cone .20 .06
326 Chuck Knoblauch .20 .06
327 Darryl Strawberry .30 .09
328 Orlando Hernandez .20 .06
329 Ricky Ledee .20 .06
330 Derek Jeter .60 .18
Bernie Williams CL
331 Pat Burrell .30 .09
332 Alfonso Soriano .50 .15
333 Josh Beckett 1.50 .45
334 Matt Riley .20 .06
335 Brian Cooper .20 .06
336 Eric Munson .20 .06
337 Vernon Wells .20 .06
338 Juan Pena .20 .06
339 Mark DeRosa .20 .06
340 Kip Wells .20 .06
341 Roosevelt Brown .20 .06
342 Jason LaRue .20 .06
343 Ben Petrick .20 .06
344 Mark Quinn .20 .06
345 Julio Ramirez .20 .06
346 Rod Barajas .20 .06
347 Robert Fick .20 .06
348 David Newhan .20 .06
349 Eric Gagne .50 .15
350 Jorge Toca .20 .06
351 Mitch Meluskey .20 .06
352 Ed Yarnall .20 .06
353 Chad Hermansen .20 .06
354 Peter Bergeron .20 .06
355 Dermal Brown .20 .06
356 Adam Kennedy .20 .06
357 Kevin Barker .20 .06
358 Francisco Cordero .20 .06
359 Travis Dawkins .20 .06
360 Jeff Williams RC .20 .06
361 Chad Hutchinson .20 .06
362 D'Angelo Jimenez .20 .06
363 Derrick Gibson .20 .06
364 Calvin Murray .20 .06
365 Doug Davis .20 .06
366 Rob Ramsay .20 .06
367 Mark Redman .20 .06
368 Rick Ankiel .20 .06
369 Domingo Guzman RC .20 .06
370 Eugene Kingsale .20 .06
371 N.Garciaparra BPM .50 .15
372 Ken Griffey Jr. BPM .50 .15
373 Randy Johnson BPM .30 .09
374 Jeff Bagwell BPM .30 .09
375 Ivan Rodriguez BPM .30 .09
376 Derek Jeter BPM .60 .18
377 Carlos Beltran BPM .20 .06
378 V.Guerrero BPM .30 .09
379 Sammy Sosa BPM .50 .15
380 Barry Bonds BPM .50 .15
381 Pedro Martinez BPM .30 .09
382 Chipper Jones BPM .30 .09
383 Mo Vaughn BPM .20 .06
384 Mike Piazza BPM .50 .15
385 Alex Rodriguez BPM .50 .15
386 Manny Ramirez BPM .20 .06
387 Mark McGwire BPM .60 .18
388 Tony Gwynn BPM .30 .09
389 Sean Casey BPM .20 .06
390 Cal Ripken BPM .75 .23
391 Ken Griffey Jr. JC .50 .15
392 Ken Griffey Jr. JC .50 .15
393 Ken Griffey Jr. JC .50 .15
394 Ken Griffey Jr. JC .50 .15
395 Ken Griffey Jr. JC .50 .15
396 Ken Griffey Jr. JC .50 .15
397 Ken Griffey Jr. JC .50 .15
398 Ken Griffey Jr. JC .50 .15
399 Ken Griffey Jr. JC .50 .15
400 Ken Griffey Jr. JC .50 .15
401 Ken Griffey Jr. JC .50 .15
402 Ken Griffey Jr. JC .50 .15
403 Ken Griffey Jr. JC .50 .15
404 Ken Griffey Jr. JC .50 .15
405 Ken Griffey Jr. JC .50 .15
406 Ken Griffey Jr. JC .50 .15
407 Ken Griffey Jr. JC .50 .15
408 Ken Griffey Jr. JC .50 .15
409 Ken Griffey Jr. JC .50 .15
410 Ken Griffey Jr. JC .50 .15
411 Ken Griffey Jr. JC .50 .15
412 Ken Griffey Jr. JC .50 .15
413 Ken Griffey Jr. JC .50 .15
414 Ken Griffey Jr. JC .50 .15
415 Ken Griffey Jr. JC .50 .15
416 Ken Griffey Jr. JC .50 .15
417 Ken Griffey Jr. JC .50 .15
418 Ken Griffey Jr. JC .50 .15
419 Ken Griffey Jr. JC .50 .15
420 Ken Griffey Jr. JC .50 .15
421 Ken Griffey Jr. JC .50 .15
422 Ken Griffey Jr. JC .50 .15
423 Ken Griffey Jr. JC .50 .15
424 Ken Griffey Jr. JC .50 .15
425 Ken Griffey Jr. JC .50 .15
426 Ken Griffey Jr. JC .50 .15
427 Ken Griffey Jr. JC .50 .15
428 Ken Griffey Jr. JC .50 .15
429 Ken Griffey Jr. JC .50 .15
430 Ken Griffey Jr. JC .50 .15
431 Ken Griffey Jr. JC .50 .15
432 Ken Griffey Jr. JC .50 .15
433 Ken Griffey Jr. JC .50 .15
434 Ken Griffey Jr. JC .50 .15
435 Ken Griffey Jr. JC .50 .15
436 Ken Griffey Jr. JC .50 .15
437 Ken Griffey Jr. JC .50 .15
438 Ken Griffey Jr. JC .50 .15
439 Ken Griffey Jr. JC .50 .15
440 Ken Griffey Jr. JC .50 .15
441 T.Lasorda USA MG .30 .09
442 Sean Burroughs USA .30 .09
443 Rick Krivda USA .30 .09
444 Ben Sheets USA RC 1.50 .45
445 Pat Borders USA .30 .09
446 B.Abernathy USA RC .30 .09
447 Tim Young USA .30 .09
448 Adam Everett USA .30 .09
449 Anthony Sanders USA .30 .09
450 Ernie Young USA .30 .09
451 B.Wilkerson USA RC .60 .18
452 K.Ainsworth USA RC 1.00 .30
453 Ryan Franklin USA RC .30 .09
454 Todd Williams USA .30 .09
455 Jon Rauch USA RC .30 .09
456 Roy Oswalt USA RC 4.00 1.20
457 S.Heams USA RC .30 .09
458 Chris George USA .30 .09
459 Bobby Seay USA .30 .09
460 Mike Kinkade USA .30 .09
461 Marcus Jensen USA .30 .09
462 Travis Dawkins USA .30 .09
463 D.Mientkiewicz USA .30 .09
464 John Cotton USA RC .30 .09
465 Mike Neill USA .30 .09
466 Team Photo USA 1.00 .30
NNO Japanese Checklist .25 .07
NNO Jap. Product Info. .25 .07

2001 Upper Deck Victory

The 2001 Upper Deck Victory product was released in late February, 2001 and features a 660-card base set. The base set is broken into tiers as follows: 550 Veterans (1-550), (40) Prospects (551-590), (20) Big Play Makers (591-610), and (50) Victory Best cards (611-660). Each pack contains 13 cards and carries a suggested retail price of $1.99.

	Nm-Mt	Ex-Mt
COMPLETE SET (660)	60.00	18.00

1 Troy Glaus .30 .09
2 Scott Spiezio .20 .06
3 Gary DiSarcina .20 .06
4 Darin Erstad .20 .06
5 Tim Salmon .30 .09
6 Troy Percival .20 .06
7 Ramon Ortiz .20 .06
8 Orlando Palmeiro .20 .06
9 Tim Belcher .20 .06
10 Mo Vaughn .20 .06
11 Bengie Molina .20 .06
12 Benji Gil .20 .06
13 Scott Schoeneweis .20 .06
14 Garret Anderson .20 .06
15 Matt Wise .20 .06
16 Adam Kennedy .20 .06
17 Jarrod Washburn .20 .06
18 Darin Erstad .20 .06
Troy Percival CL
19 Jason Giambi .50 .15
20 Tim Hudson .20 .06
21 Ramon Hernandez .20 .06
22 Eric Chavez .20 .06
23 Gil Heredia .20 .06
24 Jason Isringhausen .20 .06
25 Jeremy Giambi .20 .06
26 Miguel Tejada .20 .06
27 Barry Zito .50 .15
28 Terrence Long .20 .06
29 Ryan Christenson .20 .06
30 Mark Mulder .20 .06
31 Olmedo Saenz .20 .06
32 Adam Piatt .20 .06
33 Ben Grieve .20 .06
34 Omar Olivares .20 .06
35 John Jaha .20 .06
36 Jason Giambi .20 .06
Tim Hudson CL
37 Carlos Delgado .20 .06
38 Esteban Loaiza .20 .06
39 Brad Fullmer .20 .06
40 David Wells .20 .06
41 Chris Woodward .20 .06
42 Billy Koch .20 .06
43 Shannon Stewart .20 .06
44 Chris Carpenter .20 .06
45 Steve Parris .20 .06
46 Darrin Fletcher .20 .06
47 Joey Hamilton .20 .06
48 Jose Cruz Jr. .20 .06
49 Vernon Wells .20 .06
50 Raul Mondesi .20 .06
51 Kelvim Escobar .20 .06
52 Tony Batista .20 .06
53 Alex Gonzalez .20 .06
54 Carlos Delgado .20 .06
David Wells CL
55 Greg Vaughn .20 .06
56 Albie Lopez .20 .06
57 Randy Winn .20 .06
58 Ryan Rupe .20 .06
59 Steve Cox .20 .06
60 Vinny Castilla .20 .06
61 Jose Guillen .20 .06

2001 Upper Deck Victory

62 Wilson Alvarez .20 .06
63 Bryan Rekar .20 .06
64 Gerald Williams .20 .06
65 Esteban Yan .20 .06
66 Felix Martinez .20 .06
67 Fred McGriff .30 .09
68 John Flaherty .20 .06
69 Jason Tyner .20 .06
70 Russ Johnson .20 .06
71 Roberto Hernandez .20 .06
72 Greg Vaughn .20 .06
Albie Lopez CL
73 Eddie Taubensee .20 .06
74 Bob Wickman .20 .06
75 Ellis Burks .20 .06
76 Kenny Lofton .20 .06
77 Einar Diaz .20 .06
78 Travis Fryman .20 .06
79 Omar Vizquel .20 .06
80 Jason Bere .20 .06
81 Bartolo Colon .20 .06
82 Jim Thome .50 .15
83 Roberto Alomar .50 .15
84 Chuck Finley .20 .06
85 Steve Woodard .20 .06
86 Russ Branyan .20 .06
87 Dave Burba .20 .06
88 Jaret Wright .20 .06
89 Jacob Cruz .20 .06
90 Steve Karsay .20 .06
91 Manny Ramirez .20 .06
Bartolo Colon CL
92 Raul Ibanez .20 .06
93 Freddy Garcia .20 .06
94 Edgar Martinez .30 .09
95 Jay Buhner .20 .06
96 Jamie Moyer .20 .06
97 John Olerud .20 .06
98 Aaron Sele .20 .06
99 Kazuhiro Sasaki .20 .06
100 Mike Cameron .20 .06
101 John Halama .20 .06
102 David Bell .20 .06
103 Gil Meche .20 .06
104 Carlos Guillen .20 .06
105 Mark McLemore .20 .06
106 Stan Javier .20 .06
107 Al Martin .20 .06
108 Dan Wilson .20 .06
109 Alex Rodriguez .50 .15
Kazuhiro Sasaki CL
110 Cal Ripken 1.50 .45
111 Delino DeShields .20 .06
112 Sidney Ponson .20 .06
113 Albert Belle .20 .06
114 Jose Mercedes .20 .06
115 Scott Erickson .20 .06
116 Jerry Hairston Jr. .20 .06
117 Brook Fordyce .20 .06
118 Luis Matos .20 .06
119 Eugene Kingsale .20 .06
120 Jeff Conine .20 .06
121 Chris Richard .20 .06
122 Fernando Lunar .20 .06
123 John Parrish .20 .06
124 Brady Anderson .20 .06
125 Ryan Kohlmeier .20 .06
126 Melvin Mora .20 .06
127 Albert Belle .20 .06
Jose Mercedes CL
128 Ivan Rodriguez .50 .15
129 Justin Thompson .20 .06
130 Kenny Rogers .20 .06
131 Rafael Palmeiro .30 .09
132 Rusty Greer .20 .06
133 Gabe Kapler .20 .06
134 John Wetteland .20 .06
135 Mike Lamb .20 .06
136 Doug Davis .20 .06
137 Ruben Mateo .20 .06
138 A. Rodriguez Rangers 1.50 .45
139 Chad Curtis .20 .06
140 Rick Helling .20 .06
141 Ryan Glynn .20 .06
142 Andres Galarraga .20 .06
143 Ricky Ledee .20 .06
144 Frank Catalanotto .20 .06
145 Rafael Palmeiro .20 .06
Rick Helling CL
146 Pedro Martinez .50 .15
147 Wilton Veras .20 .06
148 M. Ramirez Red Sox .20 .06
149 Rolando Arrojo .20 .06
150 Nomar Garciaparra .75 .23
151 Darren Lewis .20 .06
152 Troy O'Leary .20 .06
153 Tomokazu Ohka .20 .06
154 Carl Everett .20 .06
155 Jason Varitek .20 .06
156 Frank Castillo .20 .06
157 Pete Schourek .20 .06
158 Jose Offerman .20 .06
159 Derek Lowe .20 .06
160 John Valentin .20 .06
161 Dante Bichette .20 .06
162 Trot Nixon .30 .09
163 Nomar Garciaparra .50 .15
Pedro Martinez CL
164 Jermaine Dye .20 .06
165 Dave McCarty .20 .06
166 Jose Rosado .20 .06
167 Mike Sweeney .20 .06
168 Rey Sanchez .20 .06
169 Jeff Suppan .20 .06
170 Chad Durbin .20 .06
171 Carlos Beltran .20 .06
172 Brian Meadows .20 .06
173 Todd Dunwoody .20 .06
174 Johnny Damon .20 .06
175 Blake Stein .20 .06
176 Carlos Febles .20 .06
177 Joe Randa .20 .06
178 Mac Suzuki .20 .06
179 Mark Quinn .20 .06
180 Gregg Zaun .20 .06
181 Mike Sweeney .20 .06
Jeff Suppan
182 Juan Gonzalez .50 .15
183 Dean Palmer .20 .06
184 Wendell Magee .20 .06
185 Todd Jones .20 .06
186 Bobby Higginson .20 .06
187 Brian Moehler .20 .06
188 Juan Encarnacion .20 .06
189 Tony Clark .20 .06
190 Rich Becker .20 .06
191 Roger Cedeno .20 .06
192 Mitch Meluskey .20 .06
193 Shane Halter .20 .06
194 Jeff Weaver .20 .06
195 Deivi Cruz .20 .06
196 Damion Easley .20 .06
197 Robert Fick .20 .06
198 Matt Anderson .20 .06
199 Bobby Higginson .20 .06
Brian Moehler
200 Brad Radke .20 .06
201 Mark Redman .20 .06
202 Corey Koskie .20 .06
203 Matt Lawton .20 .06
204 Eric Milton .20 .06
205 Chad Moeller .20 .06
206 Jacque Jones .20 .06
207 Matt Kinney .20 .06
208 Jay Canizaro .20 .06
209 Torii Hunter .20 .06
210 Ron Coomer .20 .06
211 Chad Allen .20 .06
212 Denny Hocking .20 .06
213 Cristian Guzman .20 .06
214 LaTroy Hawkins .20 .06
215 Joe Mays .20 .06
216 David Ortiz .20 .06
217 Matt Lawton .20 .06
Eric Milton CL
218 Frank Thomas .50 .15
219 Jose Valentin .20 .06
220 Mike Sirotka .20 .06
221 Kip Wells .20 .06
222 Magglio Ordonez .20 .06
223 Herbert Perry .20 .06
224 James Baldwin .20 .06
225 Jon Garland .20 .06
226 Sandy Alomar Jr. .20 .06
227 Chris Singleton .20 .06
228 Keith Foulke .20 .06
229 Paul Konerko .20 .06
230 Jim Parque .20 .06
231 Greg Norton .20 .06
232 Carlos Lee .20 .06
233 Cal Eldred .20 .06
234 Ray Durham .20 .06
235 Jeff Abbott .20 .06
236 Frank Thomas .30 .09
Mike Sirotka CL
237 Derek Jeter 1.25 .35
238 Glenallen Hill .20 .06
239 Roger Clemens 1.00 .30
240 Bernie Williams .30 .09
241 David Justice .20 .06
242 Luis Sojo .20 .06
243 Orlando Hernandez .20 .06
244 Mike Mussina .50 .15
245 Jorge Posada .30 .09
246 Andy Pettitte .30 .09
247 Paul O'Neill .30 .09
248 Scott Brosius .20 .06
249 Alfonso Soriano .30 .09
250 Mariano Rivera .30 .09
251 Chuck Knoblauch .20 .06
252 Ramiro Mendoza .20 .06
253 Tino Martinez .30 .09
254 David Cone .20 .06
255 Derek Jeter .60 .18
Andy Pettite CL
256 Jeff Bagwell .30 .09
257 Lance Berkman .20 .06
258 Craig Biggio .30 .09
259 Scott Elarton .20 .06
260 Bill Spiers .20 .06
261 Moises Alou .20 .06
262 Billy Wagner .20 .06
263 Shane Reynolds .20 .06
264 Tony Eusebio .20 .06
265 Julio Lugo .20 .06
266 Jose Lima .20 .06
267 Octavio Dotel .20 .06
268 Brad Ausmus .20 .06
269 Daryle Ward .20 .06
270 Glen Barker .20 .06
271 Wade Miller .20 .06
272 Richard Hidalgo .20 .06
273 Chris Truby .20 .06
274 Jeff Bagwell .20 .06
Scott Elarton CL
275 Greg Maddux .75 .23
276 Chipper Jones .50 .15
277 Tom Glavine .30 .09
278 Brian Jordan .20 .06
279 Andruw Jones .20 .06
280 Kevin Millwood .20 .06
281 Rico Brogna .20 .06
282 George Lombard .20 .06
283 Reggie Sanders .20 .06
284 John Rocker .20 .06
285 Rafael Furcal .20 .06
286 John Smoltz .30 .09
287 Javy Lopez .50 .15
288 Walt Weiss .20 .06
289 Quilvio Veras .20 .06
290 Eddie Perez .20 .06
291 B.J. Surhoff .20 .06
292 Chipper Jones .30 .09
Tom Glavine CL
293 Jeromy Burnitz .20 .06
294 Charlie Hayes .20 .06
295 Jeff D'Amico .20 .06
296 Jose Hernandez .20 .06
297 Richie Sexson .20 .06
298 Tyler Houston .20 .06
299 Paul Rigdon .20 .06
300 Jamey Wright .20 .06
301 Mark Loretta .20 .06
302 Geoff Jenkins .20 .06
303 Luis Lopez .20 .06
304 John Snyder .20 .06
305 Henry Blanco .20 .06
306 Curtis Leskanic .20 .06
307 Ron Belliard .20 .06
308 Jimmy Haynes .20 .06
309 Marquis Grissom .20 .06
310 Geoff Jenkins .20 .06
Jeff D'Amico CL
311 Mark McGwire 1.25 .35
312 Rick Ankiel .20 .06
313 Dave Veres .20 .06
314 Carlos Hernandez .20 .06
315 Jim Edmonds .20 .06
316 Andy Benes .20 .06
317 Garrett Stephenson .20 .06
318 Ray Lankford .20 .06
319 Dustin Hermanson .20 .06
320 Steve Kline .20 .06
321 Mike Matheny .20 .06
322 Edgar Renteria .20 .06
323 J.D. Drew .20 .06
324 Craig Paquette .20 .06
325 Darryl Kile .20 .06
326 Fernando Vina .20 .06
327 Eric Davis .20 .06
328 Placido Polanco .20 .06
329 Jim Edmonds .20 .06
Darryl Kile CL
330 Sammy Sosa .75 .23
331 Rick Aguilera .20 .06
332 Willie Greene .20 .06
333 Kerry Wood .50 .15
334 Todd Hundley .20 .06
335 Rondell White .20 .06
336 Julio Zuleta .20 .06
337 Jon Lieber .20 .06
338 Joe Girardi .20 .06
339 Damon Buford .20 .06
340 Kevin Tapani .20 .06
341 Ricky Gutierrez .20 .06
342 Bill Mueller .20 .06
343 Ruben Quevedo .20 .06
344 Eric Young .20 .06
345 Gary Matthews Jr. .20 .06
346 Daniel Garibay .20 .06
347 Sammy Sosa .30 .09
Jon Lieber CL
348 Randy Johnson .50 .15
349 Matt Williams .20 .06
350 Kelly Stinnett .20 .06
351 Brian Anderson .20 .06
352 Steve Finley .20 .06
353 Curt Schilling .30 .09
354 Erubiel Durazo .20 .06
355 Todd Stottlemyre .20 .06
356 Mark Grace .30 .09
357 Luis Gonzalez .20 .06
358 Danny Bautista .20 .06
359 Matt Mantei .20 .06
360 Tony Womack .20 .06
361 Armando Reynoso .20 .06
362 Greg Colbrunn .20 .06
363 Jay Bell .20 .06
364 Byung-Hyun Kim .20 .06
365 Luis Gonzalez .30 .09
Randy Johnson CL
366 Gary Sheffield .20 .06
367 Eric Karros .20 .06
368 Jeff Shaw .20 .06
369 Jim Leyritz .20 .06
370 Kevin Brown .20 .06
371 Alex Cora .20 .06
372 Andy Ashby .20 .06
373 Eric Gagne .30 .09
374 Chan Ho Park .20 .06
375 Shawn Green .20 .06
376 Kevin Elster .20 .06
377 Mark Grudzielanek .20 .06
378 Darren Dreifort .20 .06
379 Dave Hansen .20 .06
380 Bruce Aven .20 .06
381 Adrian Beltre .20 .06
382 Tom Goodwin .20 .06
383 Gary Sheffield .20 .06
Chan Ho Park CL
384 Vladimir Guerrero .50 .15
385 Ugueth Urbina .20 .06
386 Michael Barrett .20 .06
387 Geoff Blum .20 .06
388 Fernando Tatis .20 .06
389 Carl Pavano .20 .06
390 Jose Vidro .20 .06
391 Orlando Cabrera .20 .06
392 Terry Jones .20 .06
393 Mike Thurman .20 .06
394 Lee Stevens .20 .06
395 Tony Armas Jr. .20 .06
396 Wilton Guerrero .20 .06
397 Peter Bergeron .20 .06
398 Milton Bradley .20 .06
399 Javier Vazquez .20 .06
400 Fernando Seguignol .20 .06
401 Vladimir Guerrero .30 .09
Dustin Hermanson CL
402 Barry Bonds 1.25 .35
403 Russ Ortiz .20 .06
404 Calvin Murray .20 .06
405 Armando Rios .20 .06
406 Livan Hernandez .20 .06
407 Jeff Kent .20 .06
408 Bobby Estalella .20 .06
409 Felipe Crespo .20 .06
410 Shawn Estes .20 .06
411 J.T. Snow .20 .06
412 Marvin Benard .20 .06
413 Joe Nathan .20 .06
414 Robb Nen .20 .06
415 Shawon Dunston .20 .06
416 Mark Gardner .20 .06
417 Kirk Rueter .20 .06
418 Rich Aurilia .20 .06
419 Doug Mirabelli .20 .06
420 Russ Davis .20 .06
421 Barry Bonds .60 .18
Livan Hernandez CL
422 Cliff Floyd .20 .06
423 Luis Castillo .20 .06
424 Antonio Alfonseca .20 .06
425 Preston Wilson .20 .06
426 Ryan Dempster .20 .06
427 Jesus Sanchez .20 .06
428 Derrek Lee .20 .06
429 Brad Penny .20 .06
430 Mark Kotsay .20 .06
431 Alex Fernandez .20 .06
432 Mike Lowell .20 .06
433 Chuck Smith .20 .06
434 Alex Gonzalez .20 .06
435 Dave Berg .20 .06
436 A.J. Burnett .20 .06
437 Charles Johnson .20 .06
438 Reid Cornelius .20 .06
439 Mike Redmond .20 .06
440 Preston Wilson .20 .06
Ryan Dempster CL
441 Mike Piazza .75 .23
442 Kevin Appier .20 .06
443 Jay Payton .20 .06
444 Steve Trachsel .20 .06
445 Al Leiter .20 .06
446 Joe McEwing .20 .06
447 Armando Benitez .20 .06
448 Edgardo Alfonzo .20 .06
449 Glendon Rusch .20 .06
450 Mike Bordick .20 .06
451 Lenny Harris .20 .06
452 Matt Franco .20 .06
453 Darryl Hamilton .20 .06
454 Bobby Jones .20 .06
455 Robin Ventura .20 .06
456 Todd Zeile .20 .06
457 John Franco .20 .06
458 Mike Piazza .50 .15
Al Leiter CL
459 Tony Gwynn .60 .18
460 John Mabry .20 .06
461 Trevor Hoffman .20 .06
462 Phil Nevin .20 .06
463 Ryan Klesko .20 .06
464 Wiki Gonzalez .20 .06
465 Matt Clement .20 .06
466 Alex Arias .20 .06
467 Woody Williams .20 .06
468 Ruben Rivera .20 .06
469 Sterling Hitchcock .20 .06
470 Ben Davis .20 .06
471 Bubba Trammell .20 .06
472 Jay Witasick .20 .06
473 Eric Owens .20 .06
474 Damian Jackson .20 .06
475 Adam Eaton .20 .06
476 Mike Darr .20 .06
477 Phil Nevin .20 .06
Trevor Hoffman CL
478 Scott Rolen .30 .09
479 Robert Person .20 .06
480 Mike Lieberthal .20 .06
481 Reggie Taylor .20 .06
482 Paul Byrd .20 .06
483 Bruce Chen .20 .06
484 Pat Burrell .20 .06
485 Kevin Jordan .20 .06
486 Bobby Abreu .20 .06
487 Randy Wolf .20 .06
488 Kevin Sefcik .20 .06
489 Brian Hunter .20 .06
490 Doug Glanville .20 .06
491 Kent Bottenfield .20 .06
492 Travis Lee .20 .06
493 Jeff Brantley .20 .06
494 Omar Daal .20 .06
495 Bobby Abreu .20 .06
Randy Wolf CL
496 Jason Kendall .20 .06
497 Adrian Brown .20 .06
498 Warren Morris .20 .06
499 Brian Giles .20 .06
500 Jimmy Anderson .20 .06
501 John VanderWal .20 .06
502 Mike Williams .20 .06
503 Aramis Ramirez .20 .06
504 Pat Meares .20 .06
505 Jason Schmidt .20 .06
506 Todd Ritchie .20 .06
507 Abraham Nunez .20 .06
508 Jose Silva .20 .06
509 Francisco Cordova .20 .06
510 Kevin Young .20 .06
511 Derek Bell .20 .06
512 Kris Benson .20 .06
513 Brian Giles .20 .06
Jose Silva CL
514 Ken Griffey Jr. .75 .23
515 Scott Williamson .20 .06
516 Dmitri Young .20 .06
517 Sean Casey .20 .06
518 Barry Larkin .50 .15
519 Juan Castro .20 .06
520 Danny Graves .20 .06
521 Aaron Boone .20 .06
522 Pokey Reese .20 .06
523 Elmer Dessens .20 .06
524 Michael Tucker .20 .06
525 Benito Santiago .20 .06
526 Pete Harnisch .20 .06
527 Alex Ochoa .20 .06
528 Gookie Dawkins .20 .06
529 Seth Etherton .20 .06
530 Rob Bell .20 .06
531 Ken Griffey Jr. .50 .15
Steve Parris CL
532 Todd Helton .30 .09
533 Jose Jimenez .20 .06
534 Todd Walker .20 .06
535 Ron Gant .20 .06
536 Neifi Perez .20 .06
537 Butch Huskey .20 .06
538 Pedro Astacio .20 .06
539 Juan Pierre .20 .06
540 Jeff Cirillo .20 .06
541 Ben Petrick .20 .06
542 Brian Bohanon .20 .06
543 Larry Walker .30 .09
544 Masato Yoshii .20 .06
545 Denny Neagle .20 .06
546 Brent Mayne .20 .06
547 Mike Hampton .20 .06
548 Todd Hollandsworth .20 .06
549 Brian Rose .20 .06
550 Todd Helton .20 .06
Pedro Astacio CL
551 Jason Hart .20 .06
552 Joe Crede .20 .06
553 Timo Perez .20 .06
554 Brady Clark .20 .06
555 Adam Pettyjohn RC .20 .06
556 Jason Grilli .20 .06
557 Paxton Crawford .20 .06
558 Jay Spurgeon .20 .06
559 Hector Ortiz .20 .06
560 Vernon Wells .20 .06
561 Aubrey Huff .20 .06
562 Xavier Nady .20 .06
563 Billy McMillon .20 .06
564 Ichiro Suzuki RC 5.00 1.50
565 Tomas De la Rosa .20 .06
566 Matt Ginter .20 .06
567 Sun Woo Kim .20 .06
568 Nick Johnson .20 .06
569 Pablo Ozuna .20 .06
570 Tike Redman .20 .06
571 Brian Cole .20 .06
572 Ross Gload .20 .06
573 Dee Brown .20 .06
574 Tony McKnight .20 .06
575 Allen Levrault .20 .06
576 Lesli Brea .20 .06
577 Adam Bernero .20 .06
578 Tom Davey .20 .06
579 Morgan Burkhart .20 .06
580 Britt Reames .20 .06
581 Dave Coggin .20 .06
582 Trey Moore .20 .06
583 Matt Kinney .20 .06
584 Pedro Feliz .20 .06
585 Brandon Inge .20 .06
586 Alex Hernandez .20 .06
587 Toby Hall .20 .06
588 Grant Roberts .20 .06
589 Brian Sikorski .20 .06
590 Aaron Myette .20 .06
591 Derek Jeter PM 1.25 .35
592 Ivan Rodriguez PM .30 .09
593 Alex Rodriguez PM .75 .23
594 Carlos Delgado PM .20 .06
595 Mark McGwire PM 1.25 .35
596 Troy Glaus PM .30 .09
597 Sammy Sosa PM .75 .23
598 Vladimir Guerrero PM .50 .15
599 Manny Ramirez PM .20 .06
600 Pedro Martinez PM .30 .09
601 Chipper Jones PM .30 .09
602 Jason Giambi PM .20 .06
603 Frank Thomas PM .30 .09
604 Ken Griffey Jr. PM .75 .23
605 Nomar Garciaparra PM .75 .23
606 Randy Johnson PM .30 .09
607 Mike Piazza PM .75 .23
608 Barry Bonds PM 1.25 .35
609 Todd Helton PM .20 .06
610 Jeff Bagwell PM .20 .06
611 Ken Griffey Jr. VB .75 .23
612 Carlos Delgado VB .20 .06
613 Jeff Bagwell VB .20 .06
614 Jason Giambi VB .20 .06
615 Cal Ripken VB 1.50 .45
616 Brian Giles VB .20 .06
617 Bernie Williams VB .20 .06
618 Greg Maddux VB .75 .23
619 Troy Glaus VB .30 .09
620 Greg Vaughn VB .20 .06
621 Sammy Sosa VB .75 .23
622 Pat Burrell VB .20 .06
623 Ivan Rodriguez VB .30 .09
624 Chipper Jones VB .30 .09
625 Barry Bonds VB 1.25 .35
626 Roger Clemens VB 1.00 .30
627 Jim Edmonds VB .20 .06
628 Nomar Garciaparra VB .75 .23
629 Frank Thomas VB .30 .09
630 Mike Piazza VB .75 .23
631 Randy Johnson VB .30 .09
632 Andruw Jones VB .20 .06
633 David Wells VB .20 .06
634 Manny Ramirez VB .20 .06
635 Preston Wilson VB .20 .06
636 Todd Helton VB .20 .06
637 Kerry Wood VB .30 .09
638 Albert Belle VB .20 .06
639 Juan Gonzalez VB .30 .09
640 Vladimir Guerrero VB .50 .15
641 Gary Sheffield VB .20 .06
642 Larry Walker VB .30 .09
643 Magglio Ordonez VB .20 .06
644 Jermaine Dye VB .20 .06
645 Scott Rolen VB .20 .06
646 Tony Gwynn VB .60 .18
647 Shawn Green VB .20 .06
648 Roberto Alomar VB .20 .06
649 Eric Milton VB .20 .06
650 Mark McGwire VB 1.25 .35
651 Tim Hudson VB .20 .06
652 Jose Canseco VB .20 .06
653 Tom Glavine VB .20 .06
654 Derek Jeter VB 1.25 .35
655 Alex Rodriguez VB .75 .23
656 Darin Erstad VB .20 .06
657 Jason Kendall VB .20 .06
658 Pedro Martinez VB .30 .09
659 Richie Sexson VB .20 .06
660 Rafael Palmeiro VB .20 .06

2002 Upper Deck Victory

This 660 card set was issued in two separate products. The basic Vistory brand, containing cards 1-550, was released in February 2002. These cards were issued in ten count packs which were issued 24 packs to a box and twelve boxes to a case. The following subsets were also included in this product: Cards numbered 491-530 feature rookie prospects and cards numbered 531-550 were Big Play Makers. Cards 551-660 were distributed within retail-only packs of Upper Deck Rookie Debut in mid-December 2002. The 110-card update set features traded veterans in their new uniforms and a wide array of prospects and rookies. The cards were issued at a rate of approximately two per pack.

	Nm-Mt	Ex-Mt
COMPLETE SET (660)	75.00	22.00
COMP.LOW SET (550)	50.00	15.00
COMP.UPDATE SET (110)	25.00	7.50
COMMON (1-490/531-550)	.20	.06
COMMON CARD (491-530)	.25	.07
COMMON CARD (551-605)	.40	.12
COMMON CARD (606-660)	.40	.12

1 Troy Glaus .30 .09
2 Tim Salmon .30 .09
3 Troy Percival .20 .06
4 Darin Erstad .20 .06
5 Adam Kennedy .20 .06
6 Scott Spiezio .20 .06
7 Ramon Ortiz .20 .06
8 Ismael Valdes .20 .06
9 Jarrod Washburn .20 .06
10 Garrett Anderson .20 .06
11 David Eckstein .20 .06
12 Mo Vaughn .20 .06
13 Benji Gil .20 .06
14 Bengie Molina .20 .06
15 Scott Schoeneweis .20 .06
16 Troy Glaus .30 .09
Ramon Ortiz
17 David Justice .20 .06
18 Jermaine Dye .20 .06
19 Eric Chavez .20 .06
20 Jeremy Giambi .20 .06
21 Terrence Long .20 .06
22 Miguel Tejada .20 .06
23 Johnny Damon .20 .06
24 Jason Hart .20 .06
25 Adam Piatt .20 .06
26 Billy Koch .20 .06
27 Ramon Hernandez .20 .06
28 Eric Byrnes .20 .06
29 Olmedo Saenz .20 .06
30 Barry Zito .30 .09
31 Tim Hudson .20 .06
32 Mark Mulder .20 .06
33 Jason Giambi .20 .06
Mark Mulder
34 Carlos Delgado .20 .06
35 Shannon Stewart .20 .06
36 Vernon Wells .20 .06
37 Homer Bush .20 .06
38 Brad Fullmer .20 .06
39 Jose Cruz Jr. .20 .06
40 Felipe Lopez .20 .06
41 Raul Mondesi .20 .06
42 Esteban Loaiza .20 .06
43 Darrin Fletcher .20 .06
44 Mike Sirotka .20 .06
45 Luke Prokopec .20 .06
46 Chris Carpenter .20 .06
47 Roy Halladay .20 .06
48 Kelvim Escobar .20 .06
49 Carlos Delgado .20 .06
Billy Koch
50 Nick Bierbrodt .20 .06
51 Greg Vaughn .20 .06
52 Ben Grieve .20 .06
53 Damian Rolls .20 .06
54 Russ Johnson .20 .06
55 Brent Abernathy .20 .06
56 Steve Cox .20 .06
57 Aubrey Huff .20 .06
58 Randy Winn .20 .06
59 Jason Tyner .20 .06
60 Tanyon Sturtze .20 .06
61 Joe Kennedy .20 .06
62 Jared Sandberg .20 .06
63 Esteban Yan .20 .06
64 Ryan Rupe .20 .06
65 Toby Hall .20 .06
66 Greg Vaughn .20 .06
Tanyon Sturtze
67 Matt Lawton .20 .06
68 Juan Gonzalez .50 .15
69 Jim Thome .50 .15
70 Einar Diaz .20 .06
71 Ellis Burks .20 .06
72 Kenny Lofton .20 .06
73 Omar Vizquel .20 .06
74 Russell Branyan .20 .06
75 Brady Anderson .20 .06
76 John Rocker .20 .06
77 Travis Fryman .20 .06
78 Wil Cordero .20 .06
79 Chuck Finley .20 .06
80 C.C. Sabathia .20 .06
81 Bartolo Colon .20 .06
82 Bob Wickman .20 .06
83 Roberto Alomar .20 .06
C.C. Sabathia
84 Ichiro Suzuki .75 .23
85 Edgar Martinez .30 .09
86 Aaron Sele .20 .06
87 Carlos Guillen .20 .06
88 Bret Boone .20 .06
89 John Olerud .20 .06
90 Jamie Moyer .20 .06
91 Ben Davis .20 .06
92 Dan Wilson .20 .06
93 Jeff Cirillo .20 .06
94 John Halama .20 .06
95 Freddy Garcia .20 .06
96 Kazuhiro Sasaki .20 .06
97 Mike Cameron .20 .06
98 Paul Abbott .20 .06
99 Mark McLemore .20 .06
100 Ichiro Suzuki .50 .15
Freddy Garcia
101 Jeff Conine .20 .06
102 David Segui .20 .06
103 Marty Cordova .20 .06
104 Tony Batista .20 .06
105 Chris Richard .20 .06
106 Willis Roberts .20 .06
107 Melvin Mora .20 .06
108 Mike Bordick .20 .06
109 Jay Gibbons .20 .06
110 Mike Kinkade .20 .06
111 Brian Roberts .20 .06
112 Jerry Hairston Jr. .20 .06
113 Jason Johnson .20 .06
114 Josh Towers .20 .06
115 Calvin Maduro .20 .06
116 Sidney Ponson .20 .06
117 Jeff Conine .20 .06
Jason Johnson
118 Alex Rodriguez .75 .23
119 Ivan Rodriguez .50 .15
120 Frank Catalanotto .20 .06
121 Mike Lamb .20 .06
122 Ruben Sierra .20 .06
123 Rusty Greer .20 .06
124 Rafael Palmeiro .30 .09
125 Gabe Kapler .20 .06
126 Aaron Myette .20 .06
127 Kenny Rogers .20 .06
128 Carl Everett .20 .06
129 Rick Helling .20 .06
130 Ricky Ledee .20 .06
131 Michael Young .20 .06
132 Doug Davis .20 .06
133 Jeff Zimmerman .20 .06
134 Alex Rodriguez .50 .15
Rick Helling
135 Manny Ramirez .20 .06
136 Nomar Garciaparra .75 .23
137 Jason Varitek .20 .06
138 Dante Bichette .20 .06
139 Tony Clark .20 .06
140 Scott Hatteberg .20 .06
141 Trot Nixon .30 .09
142 Hideo Nomo .50 .15
143 Dustin Hermanson .20 .06
144 Chris Stynes .20 .06
145 Jose Offerman .20 .06
146 Pedro Martinez .50 .15
147 Shea Hillenbrand .20 .06
148 Tim Wakefield .20 .06
149 Troy O'Leary .20 .06
150 Ugueth Urbina .20 .06
151 Manny Ramirez .20 .06
Hideo Nomo
152 Carlos Beltran .20 .06
153 Dee Brown .20 .06
154 Mike Sweeney .20 .06
155 Luis Alicea .20 .06
156 Raul Ibanez .20 .06
157 Mark Quinn .20 .06
158 Joe Randa .20 .06
159 Roberto Hernandez .20 .06
160 Neifi Perez .20 .06
161 Carlos Febles .20 .06
162 Jeff Suppan .20 .06
163 Dave McCarty .20 .06
164 Blake Stein .20 .06
165 Chad Durbin .20 .06
166 Paul Byrd .20 .06
167 Carlos Beltran .20 .06
Jeff Suppan
168 Craig Paquette .20 .06
169 Dean Palmer .20 .06
170 Shane Halter .20 .06
171 Bobby Higginson .20 .06
172 Robert Fick .20 .06
173 Jose Macias .20 .06
174 Deivi Cruz .20 .06
175 Damion Easley .20 .06
176 Brandon Inge .20 .06
177 Mark Redman .20 .06
178 Dmitri Young .20 .06
179 Steve Sparks .20 .06
180 Jeff Weaver .20 .06
181 Victor Santos .20 .06
182 Jose Lima .20 .06
183 Matt Anderson .20 .06
184 Roger Cedeno .20 .06
Steve Sparks
185 Doug Mientkiewicz .20 .06
186 Cristian Guzman .20 .06
187 Torii Hunter .20 .06
188 Matt LeCroy .20 .06
189 Corey Koskie .20 .06
190 Jacque Jones .20 .06
191 Luis Rivas .20 .06
192 David Ortiz .20 .06
193 A.J. Pierzynski .20 .06
194 Brian Buchanan .20 .06
195 Joe Mays .20 .06
196 Brad Radke .20 .06
197 Denny Hocking .20 .06
198 Eric Milton .20 .06
199 LaTroy Hawkins .20 .06
200 Doug Mientkiewicz .20 .06
Joe Mays
201 Magglio Ordonez .20 .06
202 Jose Valentin .20 .06
203 Chris Singleton .20 .06
204 Aaron Rowand .20 .06
205 Paul Konerko .20 .06
206 Carlos Lee .20 .06
207 Ray Durham .20 .06
208 Keith Foulke .20 .06
209 Todd Ritchie .20 .06
210 Royce Clayton .20 .06
211 Jose Canseco .50 .15
212 Frank Thomas .50 .15
213 David Wells .20 .06
214 Mark Buehrle .20 .06
215 Jon Garland .20 .06
216 Magglio Ordonez .20 .06
Mark Buehrle
217 Derek Jeter 1.25 .35
218 Bernie Williams .30 .09
219 Rondell White .20 .06
220 Jorge Posada .30 .09
221 Alfonso Soriano .30 .09
222 Ramiro Mendoza .20 .06
223 Jason Giambi Yankees 1.25 .35
224 John Vander Wal .20 .06
225 Steve Karsay .20 .06
226 Nick Johnson .20 .06
227 Mariano Rivera .30 .09
228 Orlando Hernandez .20 .06
229 Andy Pettitte .30 .09
230 Robin Ventura .20 .06
231 Roger Clemens 1.00 .30
232 Mike Mussina .50 .15
233 Derek Jeter .60 .18
Roger Clemens
234 Moises Alou .20 .06
235 Lance Berkman .20 .06
236 Craig Biggio .30 .09
237 Octavio Dotel .20 .06
238 Jeff Bagwell .30 .09
239 Richard Hidalgo .20 .06
240 Morgan Ensberg .20 .06
241 Julio Lugo .20 .06
242 Daryle Ward .20 .06
243 Roy Oswalt .20 .06
244 Billy Wagner .20 .06
245 Brad Ausmus .20 .06
246 Jose Vizcaino .20 .06
247 Wade Miller .20 .06
248 Shane Reynolds .20 .06
249 Jeff Bagwell .20 .06
Wade Miller
250 Chipper Jones .50 .15
251 Brian Jordan .20 .06
252 B.J. Surhoff .20 .06
253 Rafael Furcal .20 .06
254 Julio Franco .20 .06
255 Javy Lopez .20 .06
256 John Burkett .20 .06
257 Andruw Jones .20 .06
258 Marcus Giles .20 .06
259 Wes Helms .20 .06
260 Greg Maddux .75 .23
261 John Smoltz .30 .09
262 Tom Glavine .30 .09
263 Vinny Castilla .20 .06
264 Kevin Millwood .20 .06
265 Jason Marquis .20 .06
266 Chipper Jones .30 .09
Greg Maddux
267 Tyler Houston .20 .06
268 Mark Loretta .20 .06
269 Richie Sexson .20 .06
270 Jeromy Burnitz .20 .06
271 Jimmy Haynes .20 .06
272 Geoff Jenkins .20 .06
273 Ron Belliard .20 .06
274 Jose Hernandez .20 .06
275 Jeffrey Hammonds .20 .06
276 Curtis Leskanic .20 .06
277 Devon White .20 .06
278 Ben Sheets .20 .06
279 Henry Blanco .20 .06
280 Jamey Wright .20 .06
281 Allen Levrault .20 .06
282 Jeff D'Amico .20 .06
283 Richie Sexson .20 .06
Jimmy Haynes
284 Albert Pujols 1.00 .30
285 Jason Isringhausen .20 .06
286 J.D. Drew .20 .06
287 Placido Polanco .20 .06
288 Jim Edmonds .20 .06
289 Fernando Vina .20 .06
290 Edgar Renteria .20 .06
291 Mike Matheny .20 .06
292 Bud Smith .20 .06
293 Mike DiFelice .20 .06
294 Woody Williams .20 .06
295 Eli Marrero .20 .06
296 Matt Morris .20 .06
297 Darryl Kile .20 .06
298 Kerry Robinson .20 .06
299 Luis Saturria .20 .06
300 Albert Pujols .50 .15
Matt Morris
301 Sammy Sosa .75 .23
302 Michael Tucker .20 .06
303 Bill Mueller .20 .06
304 Ricky Gutierrez .20 .06
305 Fred McGriff .30 .09
306 Eric Young .20 .06
307 Corey Patterson .20 .06
308 Alex Gonzalez .20 .06
309 Ron Coomer .20 .06
310 Kerry Wood .50 .15
311 Delino DeShields .20 .06
312 Jon Lieber .20 .06
313 Tom Gordon .20 .06
314 Todd Hundley .20 .06
315 Jason Bere .20 .06
316 Kevin Tapani .20 .06
317 Sammy Sosa .30 .09
Jon Lieber
318 Steve Finley .20 .06
319 Luis Gonzalez .20 .06
320 Mark Grace .30 .09
321 Craig Counsell .20 .06
322 Matt Williams .20 .06
323 Tony Womack .20 .06
324 Junior Spivey .20 .06
325 David Dellucci .20 .06
326 Jay Bell .20 .06
327 Curt Schilling .30 .09
328 Randy Johnson .50 .15
329 Danny Bautista .20 .06
330 Miguel Batista .20 .06
331 Erubiel Durazo .20 .06
332 Brian Anderson .20 .06
333 Byung-Hyun Kim .20 .06
334 Luis Gonzalez .30 .09
Curt Schilling
335 Paul LoDuca .20 .06
336 Gary Sheffield .20 .06
337 Shawn Green .20 .06
338 Adrian Beltre .20 .06
339 Darren Dreifort .20 .06
340 Mark Grudzielanek .20 .06
341 Eric Karros .20 .06
342 Cesar Izturis .20 .06
343 Tom Goodwin .20 .06
344 Marquis Grissom .20 .06
345 Kevin Brown .20 .06
346 James Baldwin .20 .06
347 Terry Adams .20 .06
348 Alex Cora .20 .06
349 Andy Ashby .20 .06
350 Chan Ho Park .20 .06
351 Shawn Green .20 .06
Chan Ho Park
352 Jose Vidro .20 .06
353 Vladimir Guerrero .50 .15
354 Orlando Cabrera .20 .06
355 Fernando Tatis .20 .06
356 Michael Barrett .20 .06
357 Lee Stevens .20 .06
358 Geoff Blum .20 .06
359 Brad Wilkerson .20 .06
360 Peter Bergeron .20 .06
361 Javier Vazquez .20 .06
362 Tony Armas Jr. .20 .06
363 Tomo Ohka .20 .06
364 Scott Strickland .20 .06
365 Vladimir Guerrero .20 .06
Javier Vazquez
366 Barry Bonds 1.25 .35
367 Rich Aurilia .20 .06
368 Jeff Kent .20 .06
369 Andres Galarraga .20 .06
370 Desi Relaford .20 .06
371 Shawon Dunston .20 .06
372 Benito Santiago .20 .06
373 Tsuyoshi Shinjo .20 .06
374 Calvin Murray .20 .06
375 Marvin Benard .20 .06
376 J.T. Snow .20 .06
377 Livan Hernandez .20 .06
378 Russ Ortiz .20 .06
379 Robb Nen .20 .06
380 Jason Schmidt .20 .06
381 Barry Bonds .50 .15
Russ Ortiz
382 Cliff Floyd .20 .06
383 Antonio Alfonseca .20 .06
384 Mike Redmond .20 .06
385 Mike Lowell .20 .06
386 Derrek Lee .20 .06
387 Preston Wilson .20 .06
388 Luis Castillo .20 .06
389 Charles Johnson .20 .06
390 Eric Owens .20 .06
391 Alex Gonzalez .20 .06
392 Josh Beckett .30 .09
393 Brad Penny .20 .06
394 Ryan Dempster .20 .06
395 Matt Clement .20 .06
396 A.J. Burnett .20 .06
397 Cliff Floyd .20 .06
Ryan Dempster
398 Mike Piazza .75 .23
399 Joe McEwing .20 .06
400 Todd Zeile .20 .06
401 Jay Payton .20 .06
402 Roger Cedeno .20 .06
403 Rey Ordonez .20 .06
404 Edgardo Alfonzo .20 .06
405 Roberto Alomar .50 .15
406 Glendon Rusch .20 .06
407 Timo Perez .20 .06
408 Al Leiter .20 .06
409 Lenny Harris .20 .06
410 Shawn Estes .20 .06
411 Armando Benitez .20 .06
412 Kevin Appier .20 .06
413 Bruce Chen .20 .06
414 Mike Piazza .30 .09
Al Leiter
415 Phil Nevin .20 .06
416 Ryan Klesko .20 .06
417 Mark Kotsay .20 .06
418 Ray Lankford .20 .06
419 Mike Darr .20 .06
420 D'Angelo Jimenez .20 .06
421 Bubba Trammell .20 .06
422 Adam Eaton .20 .06
423 Ramon Vazquez .20 .06
424 Cesar Crespo .20 .06
425 Trevor Hoffman .20 .06
426 Kevin Jarvis .20 .06
427 Wiki Gonzalez .20 .06
428 Damian Jackson .20 .06
429 Brian Lawrence .20 .06
430 Phil Nevin .20 .06
Trevor Hoffman
431 Scott Rolen .30 .09
432 Marlon Anderson .20 .06
433 Bobby Abreu .20 .06
434 Jimmy Rollins .20 .06
435 Doug Glanville .20 .06
436 Travis Lee .20 .06
437 Brandon Duckworth .20 .06
438 Pat Burrell .20 .06
439 Kevin Jordan .20 .06
440 Robert Person .20 .06
441 Johnny Estrada .20 .06
442 Randy Wolf .20 .06
443 Jose Mesa .20 .06
444 Mike Lieberthal .20 .06
445 Bobby Abreu .20 .06
Robert Person
446 Brian Giles .20 .06
447 Jason Kendall .20 .06
448 Aramis Ramirez .20 .06
449 Rob Mackowiak .20 .06
450 Abraham Nunez .20 .06
451 Pat Meares .20 .06
452 Craig Wilson .20 .06
453 Jack Wilson .20 .06
454 Gary Matthews Jr. .20 .06
455 Kevin Young .20 .06
456 Derek Bell .20 .06
457 Kip Wells .20 .06
458 Jimmy Anderson .20 .06
459 Kris Benson .20 .06
460 Brian Giles .20 .06
Todd Ritchie
461 Sean Casey .20 .06
462 Wilton Guerrero .20 .06
463 Jason LaRue .20 .06
464 Juan Encarnacion .20 .06
465 Todd Walker .20 .06
466 Aaron Boone .20 .06
467 Pete Harnisch .20 .06
468 Ken Griffey Jr. .75 .23
469 Adam Dunn .20 .06
470 Barry Larkin .50 .15
471 Kelly Stinnett .20 .06
472 Pokey Reese .20 .06
473 Brady Clark .20 .06
474 Scott Williamson .20 .06
475 Danny Graves .20 .06
476 Ken Griffey Jr. .50 .15
Elmer Dessens
477 Larry Walker .30 .09
478 Todd Helton .30 .09
479 Juan Pierre .20 .06
480 Juan Uribe .20 .06
481 Mario Encarnacion .20 .06
482 Jose Ortiz .20 .06
483 Todd Hollandsworth .20 .06
484 Alex Ochoa .20 .06
485 Mike Hampton .20 .06
486 Terry Shumpert .20 .06
487 Denny Neagle .20 .06
488 Jose Jimenez .20 .06
489 Jason Jennings .20 .06
490 Todd Helton .20 .06
Mike Hampton
491 Tim Redding ROO .25 .07
492 Mark Teixeira ROO 1.00 .30
493 Alex Cintron ROO .40 .12
494 Tim Raines Jr. ROO .25 .07
495 Juan Cruz ROO .25 .07
496 Joe Crede ROO .25 .07
497 Steve Green ROO .25 .07
498 Mike Rivera ROO .25 .07
499 Mark Prior ROO 4.00 1.20
500 Ken Harvey ROO .25 .07
501 Tim Spooneybarger ROO .25 .07
502 Adam Everett ROO .25 .07
503 Jason Standridge ROO .25 .07
504 Nick Neugebauer ROO .25 .07
505 Adam Johnson ROO .25 .07
506 Sean Douglass ROO .25 .07
507 Brandon Berger ROO .25 .07
508 Alex Escobar ROO .25 .07
509 Doug Nickle ROO .25 .07
510 Jason Middlebrook ROO .25 .07
511 Dewon Brazelton ROO .25 .07
512 Yorvit Torrealba ROO .25 .07
513 Henry Mateo ROO .25 .07
514 Dennis Tankersley ROO .25 .07
515 Marlon Byrd ROO .40 .12
516 Andy Barkett ROO .25 .07
517 Orlando Hudson ROO .25 .07
518 Josh Fogg ROO .25 .07
519 Ryan Drese ROO .25 .07
520 Mike MacDougal ROO .25 .07
521 Luis Pineda ROO .25 .07
522 Jack Cust ROO .25 .07
523 Kurt Ainsworth ROO .25 .07
524 Bart Miadich ROO .25 .07
525 Dernell Stenson ROO .40 .12
526 Carlos Zambrano ROO .40 .12
527 Austin Kearns ROO .40 .12
528 Larry Barnes ROO .25 .07
529 Mike Cuddyer ROO .25 .07
530 Carlos Pena ROO .25 .07
531 Derek Jeter BPM .60 .18
532 Ken Griffey Jr. BPM .50 .15
533 Manny Ramirez BPM .20 .06
534 Luis Gonzalez BPM .20 .06
535 Sammy Sosa BPM .50 .15
536 Roger Clemens BPM .50 .15
537 Phil Nevin BPM .20 .06
538 Mike Piazza BPM .50 .15
539 Alex Rodriguez BPM .50 .15
540 Jason Giambi Yankees BPM .60 .18
541 Randy Johnson BPM .30 .09
542 Albert Pujols BPM .50 .15
543 Jeff Bagwell BPM .20 .06
544 Shawn Green BPM .20 .06
545 Carlos Delgado BPM .20 .06
546 Pedro Martinez BPM .30 .09
547 Todd Helton BPM .20 .06
548 Roberto Alomar BPM .20 .06
549 Barry Bonds BPM .50 .15
550 Ichiro Suzuki BPM .50 .15
551 John Lackey .40 .12
552 Francisco Rodriguez .20 .06
553 Cliff Floyd .40 .12
554 Derek Lowe .40 .12
555 Mark Bellhorn .40 .12
556 Matt Clement .40 .12
557 Hee Seop Choi .50 .15
558 Joe Borchard .40 .12
559 Ryan Dempster .40 .12
560 Russell Branyan .40 .12
561 Brandon Larson .40 .12
562 Coco Crisp .40 .12
563 Karim Garcia .40 .12
564 Brandon Phillips .40 .12
565 Jay Payton .40 .12
566 Gabe Kapler .40 .12
567 Carlos Pena .40 .12
568 George Lombard .40 .12
569 Andy Van Hekken .40 .12
570 Andres Torres .40 .12
571 Justin Wayne .40 .12
572 Juan Encarnacion .40 .12
573 Abraham Nunez .40 .12
574 Peter Munro .40 .12
575 Jason Lane .40 .12
576 Dave Roberts .40 .12
577 Eric Gagne .50 .15
578 Alex Sanchez .40 .12
579 Jim Rushford RC .40 .12
580 Ben Diggins .40 .12
581 Eddie Guardado .40 .12
582 Bartolo Colon .40 .12
583 Endy Chavez .40 .12
584 Raul Mondesi .40 .12
585 Jeff Weaver .40 .12
586 Marcus Thames .40 .12
587 Ted Lilly .40 .12
588 Ray Durham .40 .12
589 Jeremy Giambi .40 .12
590 Vicente Padilla .40 .12
591 Brett Myers .40 .12
592 Josh Fogg .40 .12
593 Tony Alvarez .40 .12
594 Jake Peavy .40 .12
595 Dennis Tankersley .40 .12
596 Sean Burroughs .40 .12
597 Kenny Lofton .40 .12
598 Scott Rolen .50 .15
599 Chuck Finley .40 .12
600 Carl Crawford .40 .12
601 Kevin Mench .40 .12
602 Juan Gonzalez .75 .23
603 Jayson Werth .40 .12
604 Eric Hinske .40 .12
605 Josh Phelps .40 .12
606 Jose Valverde ROO RC .50 .15
607 John Ennis ROO RC .40 .12
608 Trey Hodges ROO RC .40 .12
609 Kevin Gryboski ROO RC .40 .12

610 Travis Driskill ROO RC .... .40 .12
611 Howie Clark ROO RC .... .40 .12
612 Freddy Sanchez ROO RC .... .40 .12
613 Josh Hancock ROO RC .... .40 .12
614 Jorge De La Rosa ROO RC..... .40 .12
615 Mike Mahoney ROO .... .40 .12
616 Jason Davis ROO RC .... .75 .23
617 Josh Bard ROO RC .... .40 .12
618 Jason Beverlin ROO RC .... .40 .12
619 Carl Sadler ROO RC .... .40 .12
620 Earl Snyder ROO RC .... .40 .12
621 Aaron Cook ROO RC .... .40 .12
622 Eric Eckenstahler ROO RC ...... .40 .12
623 Franklyn German ROO RC ...... .40 .12
624 Kirk Saarloos ROO RC .... .40 .12
625 Rodrigo Rosario ROO RC .... .40 .12
626 Jeriome Robertson ROO RC... .40 .12
627 Brandon Puffer ROO RC .... .40 .12
628 Miguel Asencio ROO RC .... .40 .12
629 Aaron Guiel ROO RC .... .40 .12
630 Ryan Bukvich ROO RC .... .40 .12
631 Jeremy Hill ROO RC .... .40 .12
632 Kazuhisa Ishii ROO RC .... 1.50 .45
633 Jayson Durocher ROO RC ...... .40 .12
634 Shane Nance ROO RC .... .40 .12
635 Eric Good ROO RC .... .40 .12
636 Jamey Carroll ROO RC .... .40 .12
637 Jaime Cerda ROO RC .... .40 .12
638 Nate Field ROO RC .... .40 .12
639 Cody McKay ROO RC .... .40 .12
640 Jose Flores ROO RC .... .40 .12
641 Jorge Padilla ROO RC .... .40 .12
642 Anderson Machado ROO RC .. .40 .12
643 Eric Junge ROO RC .... .40 .12
644 Oliver Perez ROO RC .... .50 .15
645 Julius Matos ROO RC .... .40 .12
646 Ben Howard ROO RC .... .40 .12
647 Julio Mateo ROO RC .... .40 .12
648 Matt Thornton ROO RC .... .40 .12
649 Chris Snelling ROO RC .... 1.00 .30
650 Jason Simontacchi ROO RC... .40 .12
651 So Taguchi ROO RC .... .50 .15
652 Mike Crudale ROO RC .... .40 .12
653 Mike Coolbaugh ROO RC .... .40 .12
654 Felix Escalona ROO RC .... .40 .12
655 Jorge Sosa ROO RC .... .40 .12
656 Lance Carter ROO RC .... .40 .12
657 Reynaldo Garcia ROO RC .... .40 .12
658 Kevin Cash ROO RC .... .40 .12
659 Ken Huckaby ROO RC .... .40 .12
660 Scott Wiggins ROO RC .... .40 .12

2002 Upper Deck Victory Gold

This set parallels the regular 2002 Upper Deck Victory set and were issued at stated odds of one in two packs.

Nm-Mt Ex-Mt
COMMON CARD (1-550) .... 1.00 .30
*GOLD 1-490/531-550: 4X TO 10X BASIC
*GOLD 491-530: 3X TO 8X BASIC ......

2003 Upper Deck Victory

This 200 card set was issued in Feburary, 2003. This set was issued in six card packs with an $1 SRP. The packs were issued 36 to a box and 20 boxes to a case. Cards number 1 through 100 comprise the base set while cards numbered 101 through 200 were produced in smaller quantity. The following subsets were produced: Solid Hits (101-128) were issued at a stated rate of one in four; Clutch Players (129-148) and Laying it on the Line (149-168) were issued at a stated rate of one in five; True Gamers (169-178) and Run Producers (179-188) were issued at a stated rate of one in 10; Difference Makers (189-194) and Winning Formula (195-200) were issued at a stated rate of one in 20.

Nm-Mt Ex-Mt
COMPLETE SET (200) 80.00 24.00
COMP.SET w/o SP's (100) 25.00 7.50
COMMON CARD (101-200) .... .75 .23
101-128 STATED ODDS 1:4 ....
129-168 STATED ODDS 1:5 ....
169-188 STATED ODDS 1:10 ....
189-200 STATED ODDS 1:20 ....
1 Troy Glaus .... .50 .15
2 Garret Anderson .... .30 .09
3 Tim Salmon .... .50 .15
4 Darin Erstad .... .30 .09
5 Luis Gonzalez .... .30 .09
6 Curt Schilling .... .50 .15
7 Randy Johnson .... .75 .23
8 Junior Spivey .... .30 .09
9 Andruw Jones .... .30 .09
10 Greg Maddux .... 1.25 .35
11 Chipper Jones .... .75 .23
12 Gary Sheffield .... .30 .09
13 John Smoltz .... .50 .15
14 Geronimo Gil .... .30 .09
15 Tony Batista .... .30 .09
16 Trot Nixon .... .50 .15
17 Manny Ramirez .... .30 .09
18 Pedro Martinez .... .75 .23
19 Nomar Garciaparra .... 1.25 .35
20 Derek Lowe .... .30 .09
21 Shea Hillenbrand .... .30 .09
22 Sammy Sosa .... 1.25 .35
23 Kerry Wood .... .75 .23
24 Mark Prior .... 1.50 .45
25 Magglio Ordonez .... .30 .09
26 Frank Thomas .... .75 .23
27 Mark Buehrle .... .30 .09
28 Paul Konerko .... .30 .09
29 Adam Dunn .... .30 .09
30 Ken Griffey Jr. .... 1.25 .35
31 Austin Kearns .... .30 .09
32 Matt Lawton .... .30 .09
33 Larry Walker .... .50 .15
34 Todd Helton .... .50 .15
35 Jeff Bagwell .... .50 .15
36 Roy Oswalt .... .30 .09
37 Lance Berkman .... .30 .09
38 Mike Sweeney .... .30 .09
39 Carlos Beltran .... .30 .09
40 Kazuhisa Ishii .... .30 .09
41 Shawn Green .... .30 .09
42 Hideo Nomo .... .75 .23
43 Adrian Beltre .... .30 .09
44 Richie Sexson .... .30 .09
45 Ben Sheets .... .30 .09
46 Torii Hunter .... .30 .09
47 Jacque Jones .... .30 .09
48 Corey Koskie .... .30 .09
49 Vladimir Guerrero .... .75 .23
50 Jose Vidro .... .30 .09
51 Mo Vaughn .... .30 .09
52 Mike Piazza .... 1.25 .35
53 Roberto Alomar .... .75 .23
54 Derek Jeter .... 2.00 .60
55 Alfonso Soriano .... .50 .15
56 Jason Giambi .... .75 .23
57 Roger Clemens .... 1.50 .45
58 Mike Mussina .... .50 .15
59 Bernie Williams .... .50 .15
60 Jorge Posada .... .50 .15
61 Nick Johnson .... .30 .09
62 Hideki Matsui RC 5.00 1.50
63 Eric Chavez .... .30 .09
64 Barry Zito .... .50 .15
65 Miguel Tejada .... .30 .09
66 Tim Hudson .... .30 .09
67 Pat Burrell .... .30 .09
68 Bobby Abreu .... .30 .09
69 Jimmy Rollins .... .30 .09
70 Brett Myers .... .30 .09
71 Jim Thome .... .75 .23
72 Jason Kendall .... .30 .09
73 Brian Giles .... .30 .09
74 Aramis Ramirez .... .30 .09
75 Sean Burroughs .... .30 .09
76 Ryan Klesko .... .30 .09
77 Phil Nevin .... .30 .09
78 Barry Bonds .... 2.00 .60
79 J.T.Snow .... .30 .09
80 Rich Aurilia .... .30 .09
81 Ichiro Suzuki .... 1.25 .35
82 Edgar Martinez .... .50 .15
83 Freddy Garcia .... .30 .09
84 Jim Edmonds .... .30 .09
85 J.D. Drew .... .30 .09
86 Scott Rolen .... .50 .15
87 Albert Pujols .... 1.50 .45
88 Mark McGwire .... 2.00 .60
89 Matt Morris .... .30 .09
90 Ben Grieve .... .30 .09
91 Carl Crawford .... .30 .09
92 Alex Rodriguez .... 1.25 .35
93 Carl Everett .... .30 .09
94 Juan Gonzalez .... .75 .23
95 Rafael Palmeiro .... .50 .15
96 Hank Blalock .... .50 .15
97 Carlos Delgado .... .30 .09
98 Josh Phelps .... .30 .09
99 Eric Hinske .... .30 .09
100 Shannon Stewart .... .30 .09
101 Albert Pujols SH .... 3.00 .90
102 Alex Rodriguez SH .... 2.50 .75
103 Alfonso Soriano SH .... 1.00 .30
104 Barry Bonds SH 4.00 1.20
105 Bernie Williams SH .... 1.00 .30
106 Brian Giles SH .... .75 .23
107 Chipper Jones SH .... 1.50 .45
108 Darin Erstad SH .... .75 .23
109 Derek Jeter SH 4.00 1.20
110 Eric Chavez SH .... .75 .23
111 Miguel Tejada SH .... .75 .23
112 Ichiro Suzuki SH .... 2.50 .75
113 Rafael Palmeiro SH .... 1.00 .30
114 Jason Giambi SH .... .75 .23
115 Jeff Bagwell SH .... 1.00 .30
116 Jim Thome SH .... 1.50 .45
117 Ken Griffey Jr. SH .... 2.50 .75
118 Lance Berkman SH .... .75 .23
119 Luis Gonzalez SH .... .75 .23
120 Manny Ramirez SH .... .75 .23
121 Mike Piazza SH .... 2.50 .75
122 J.D. Drew SH .... .75 .23
123 Sammy Sosa SH .... 2.50 .75
124 Scott Rolen SH .... 1.00 .30
125 Shawn Green SH .... .75 .23
126 Todd Helton SH .... 1.00 .30
127 Troy Glaus SH .... 1.00 .30
128 Vladimir Guerrero SH .... 1.50 .45
129 Albert Pujols CP .... 3.00 .90
130 Brian Giles CP .... .75 .23
131 Carlos Delgado CP .... .75 .23
132 Curt Schilling CP .... 1.00 .30
133 Derek Jeter CP 4.00 1.20
134 Frank Thomas CP .... 1.50 .45
135 Greg Maddux CP .... 2.50 .75
136 Jeff Bagwell CP .... 1.00 .30
137 Jim Thome CP .... 1.50 .45
138 Jorge Posada CP .... 1.00 .30
139 Kazuhisa Ishii CP .... .75 .23
140 Larry Walker CP .... 1.00 .30
141 Luis Gonzalez CP .... .75 .23
142 Miguel Tejada CP .... .75 .23
143 Pat Burrell CP .... .75 .23
144 Pedro Martinez CP .... 1.50 .45
145 Rafael Palmeiro CP .... 1.00 .30
146 Roger Clemens CP .... 3.00 .90
147 Tim Hudson CP .... .75 .23
148 Troy Glaus CP .... 1.00 .30
149 Alfonso Soriano LL .... 1.00 .30
150 Andruw Jones LL .... .75 .23
151 Barry Zito LL .... 1.00 .30
152 Darin Erstad LL .... .75 .23
153 Eric Chavez LL .... .75 .23
154 Alex Rodriguez LL .... 2.50 .75
155 J.D. Drew LL .... .75 .23
156 Jason Giambi LL .... .75 .23
157 Jason Kendall LL .... .75 .23
158 Ken Griffey Jr. LL .... 2.50 .75
159 Lance Berkman LL .... .75 .23
160 Mike Mussina LL .... 1.50 .45
161 Mike Piazza LL .... 2.50 .75
162 Nomar Garciaparra LL .... 2.50 .75
163 Randy Johnson LL .... 1.50 .45
164 Roberto Alomar LL .... 1.50 .45
165 Scott Rolen LL .... 1.00 .30
166 Shawn Green LL .... .75 .23
167 Torii Hunter LL .... .75 .23
168 Vladimir Guerrero LL .... 1.50 .45
169 Alex Rodriguez TG .... 2.50 .75
170 Andruw Jones TG .... .75 .23
171 Bernie Williams TG .... 1.00 .30
172 Ichiro Suzuki TG .... 2.50 .75
173 Miguel Tejada TG .... .75 .23
174 Nomar Garciaparra TG .... 2.50 .75
175 Pedro Martinez TG .... 1.50 .45
176 Randy Johnson TG .... 1.50 .45
177 Todd Helton TG .... 1.00 .30
178 Vladimir Guerrero TG .... 1.50 .45
179 Barry Bonds RP 4.00 1.20
180 Carlos Delgado RP .... .75 .23
181 Chipper Jones RP .... 1.50 .45
182 Frank Thomas RP .... 1.50 .45
183 Lance Berkman RP .... .75 .23
184 Larry Walker RP .... 1.00 .30
185 Manny Ramirez RP .... .75 .23
186 Mike Piazza RP .... 2.50 .75
187 Sammy Sosa RP .... 2.50 .75
188 Shawn Green RP .... .75 .23
189 Chipper Jones DM .... 1.50 .45
190 Curt Schilling DM .... 1.00 .30
191 Derek Jeter DM 4.00 1.20
192 Ken Griffey Jr. DM .... 2.50 .75
193 Sammy Sosa DM .... 2.50 .75
194 Vladimir Guerrero DM .... 1.50 .45
195 Alex Rodriguez WF .... 2.50 .75
196 Barry Bonds WF 4.00 1.20
197 Greg Maddux WF .... 2.50 .75
198 Ichiro Suzuki WF .... 2.50 .75
199 Jason Giambi WF .... .75 .23
200 Mike Piazza WF .... 2.50 .75

2003 Upper Deck Victory Tier 1 Green

Issued at a stated rate of one per pack, this a parallel to the first 100 cards of the Victory set. These cards can be identified by their green borders.

Nm-Mt Ex-Mt
COMPLETE SET (100) 50.00 15.00
*GREEN: 1X TO 2.5X BASIC
*GREEN MATSUI: .6X TO 1.5X BASIC

2003 Upper Deck Victory Tier 2 Orange

Issued at a stated rate of one per eight packs, this a parallel to the first 100 cards of the Victory set. These cards can be identified by their orange borders.

Nm-Mt Ex-Mt
COMPLETE SET (100) 80.00 24.00
*ORANGE: 2X TO 5X BASIC ....
*ORANGE MATSUI: 1X TO 2.5X BASIC

2003 Upper Deck Victory Tier 3 Blue

Randomly inserted in packs, this a parallel to the first 100 cards of the basic Victory set. These cards can be identified by their blue borders. These cards were issued to a stated print run of 650 serial numbered sets.

Nm-Mt Ex-Mt
*BLUE: 4X TO 10X BASIC ....

2003 Upper Deck Victory Tier 4 Purple

Randomly inserted in packs, this a parallel to the first 100 cards of the basic Victory set. These cards can be identified by their purple borders. These cards were issued to a stated print run of 50 serial numbered sets.

Nm-Mt Ex-Mt
*PURPLE: 12.5X TO 30X BASIC ....

2003 Upper Deck Victory Tier 5 Red

Randomly inserted in packs, this a parallel to the first 100 cards of the basic Victory set. These cards can be identified by their red borders. These cards were issued to a stated print run of 25 serial numbered sets. No pricing is available on these cards due to market scarcity.

Nm-Mt Ex-Mt
NO PRICING DUE TO SCARCITY ....

2001 Upper Deck Vintage

The 2001 Upper Deck Vintage product released in late January,2001 and featured a 400-card base set. Each pack contained 10 cards, and carried a suggested retail price of $2.99 per pack. The set was broken into tiers as follows: Base Veterans (1-340), Prospects (341-370), Series Highlights (371-390) and League Leaders (391-400). A Sample card featuring Ken Griffey Jr. was distributed to dealers and hobby media several weeks prior to the product's release national release date. The card can be readily identified by the bold "SAMPLE" text running diagonally across the back.

Nm-Mt Ex-Mt
COMPLETE SET (400) 50.00 15.00
COMMON (1-340/371-400) .... .30 .09
COMMON (341-370) .... .50 .15
1 Darin Erstad .... .30 .09
2 Seth Etherton .... .30 .09
3 Troy Glaus .... .50 .15
4 Bengie Molina .... .30 .09
5 Mo Vaughn .... .30 .09
6 Tim Salmon .... .50 .15
7 Ramon Ortiz .... .30 .09
8 Adam Kennedy .... .30 .09
9 Garret Anderson .... .30 .09
10 Troy Percival .... .30 .09
11 Tim Salmon .... .30 .09
Bengie Molina
MoVaughn
Adam Kennedy
Troy Glaus
Kevin Stocker
Darin Erstad
Garret Anderson
Ron Gant CL
12 Jason Giambi .... .75 .23
13 Tim Hudson .... .30 .09
14 Adam Piatt .... .30 .09
15 Miguel Tejada .... .30 .09
16 Mark Mulder .... .30 .09
17 Eric Chavez .... .30 .09
18 Ramon Hernandez .... .30 .09
19 Terrence Long .... .30 .09
20 Jason Isringhausen .... .30 .09
21 Barry Zito .... .75 .23
22 Ben Grieve .... .30 .09
23 Olmedo Saenz .... .30 .09
Ramon Hernandez
Jason Giambi
Randy Velarde
Eric Chavez
Miguel Tejada
Ben Grieve
Terrence Long
Adam Piatt CL
24 David Wells .... .30 .09
25 Raul Mondesi .... .30 .09
26 Darrin Fletcher .... .30 .09
27 Shannon Stewart .... .30 .09
28 Kelvim Escobar .... .30 .09
29 Tony Batista .... .30 .09
30 Carlos Delgado .... .30 .09
31 Brad Fullmer .... .30 .09
32 Billy Koch .... .30 .09
33 Jose Cruz Jr. .... .30 .09
34 Brad Fullmer .... .30 .09
Darrin Fletcher
Carlos Delgado
Homer Bush
Tony Batista
Alex Gonzalez
Shannon Stewart
Jose Cruz Jr.
Raul Mondesi CL
35 Greg Vaughn .... .30 .09
36 Roberto Hernandez .... .30 .09
37 Vinny Castilla .... .30 .09
38 Gerald Williams .... .30 .09
39 Aubrey Huff .... .30 .09
40 Bryan Rekar .... .30 .09
41 Albie Lopez .... .30 .09
42 Fred McGriff .... .50 .15
43 Miguel Cairo .... .30 .09
44 Ryan Rupe .... .30 .09
45 Greg Vaughn .... .30 .09
John Flaherty
Fred McGriff
Miguel Cairo
Vinny Castilla
Felix Martinez
Gerald Williams
Jose Guillen
Steve Cox CL
46 Jim Thome .... .75 .23
47 Roberto Alomar .... .75 .23
48 Bartolo Colon .... .30 .09
49 Omar Vizquel .... .30 .09
50 Travis Fryman .... .30 .09
51 Manny Ramirez UER .... .30 .09
Picture is of David Segui
52 Dave Burba .... .30 .09
53 Chuck Finley .... .30 .09
54 Russ Branyan .... .30 .09
55 Kenny Lofton .... .30 .09
56 Russell Branyan .... .30 .09
Sandy Alomar Jr.
Jim Thome
Roberto Alomar
Travis Fryman
Omar Vizquel
Wil Cordero
Kenny Lofton
Manny Ramirez
Picture is off David Segui CL UER
57 Alex Rodriguez .... 1.25 .35
58 Jay Buhner .... .30 .09
59 Aaron Sele .... .30 .09
60 Kazuhiro Sasaki .... .30 .09
61 Edgar Martinez .... .50 .15
62 John Halama .... .30 .09
63 Mike Cameron .... .30 .09
64 Freddy Garcia .... .30 .09
65 John Olerud .... .30 .09
66 Jamie Moyer .... .30 .09
67 Gil Meche .... .30 .09
68 Edgar Martinez .... .30 .09
Joe Oliver
John Olerud
David Bell
Carlos Guillen
Alex Rodriguez
Jay Buhner
Mike Cameron
Al Martin CL
69 Cal Ripken .... 2.50 .75
70 Sidney Ponson .... .30 .09
71 Chris Richard .... .30 .09
72 Jose Mercedes .... .30 .09
73 Albert Belle .... .30 .09
74 Mike Mussina .... .75 .23
75 Brady Anderson .... .30 .09
76 Delino DeShields .... .30 .09
77 Melvin Mora .... .30 .09
78 Luis Matos .... .30 .09
79 Brook Fordyce .... .30 .09
80 Jeff Conine .... .30 .09
Brook Fordyce
Chris Richard
Delino DeShields
Cal Ripken
Melvin Mora
Luis Matos
Brady Anderson
Albert Belle CL
81 Rafael Palmeiro .... .50 .15
82 Rick Helling .... .30 .09
83 Ruben Mateo .... .30 .09
84 Rusty Greer .... .30 .09
85 Ivan Rodriguez .... .75 .23
86 Doug Davis .... .30 .09
87 Gabe Kapler .... .30 .09
88 Mike Lamb .... .30 .09
89 A.Rodriguez Rangers .... 3.00 .90
90 Kenny Rogers .... .30 .09
91 David Segui .... .50 .15
Ivan Rodriguez
Rafael Palmeiro
Frank Catalanotto
Mike Lamb
Royce Clayton
Ruben Mateo
Gabe Kapler
Rusty Greer CL
92 Nomar Garciaparra .... 1.25 .35
93 Trot Nixon .... .50 .15
94 Tomokazu Ohka .... .30 .09
95 Pedro Martinez .... .75 .23
96 Dante Bichette .... .30 .09
97 Jason Varitek .... .30 .09
98 Rolando Arrojo .... .30 .09
99 Carl Everett .... .30 .09
100 Derek Lowe .... .30 .09
101 Troy O'Leary .... .30 .09
102 Tim Wakefield .... .30 .09
103 Troy O'Leary .... .30 .09
Jason Varitek
Jose Offerman
Mike Lansing
Wilton Veras
Nomar Garciaparra
Carl Everett
Trot Nixon
Dante Bichette CL
104 Mike Sweeney .... .30 .09
105 Carlos Febles .... .30 .09
106 Joe Randa .... .30 .09
107 Jeff Suppan .... .30 .09
108 Mac Suzuki .... .30 .09
109 Jermaine Dye .... .30 .09
110 Carlos Beltran .... .30 .09
111 Mark Quinn .... .30 .09
112 Johnny Damon .... .30 .09
113 Mark Quinn .... .30 .09
Gregg Zaun
Mike Sweeney
Carlos Febles
Joe Randa
Rey Sanchez
Carlos Beltran
Johnny Damon
Jermaine Dye CL
114 Tony Clark .... .30 .09
115 Dean Palmer .... .30 .09
116 Brian Moehler .... .30 .09
117 Brad Ausmus .... .30 .09
118 Juan Gonzalez .... .75 .23
119 Juan Encarnacion .... .30 .09
120 Jeff Weaver .... .30 .09
121 Bobby Higginson .... .30 .09
122 Todd Jones .... .30 .09
123 Deivi Cruz .... .30 .09
124 Juan Gonzalez .... .30 .09
Brad Ausmus
Tony Clark
Damion Easley
Dean Palmer
Deivi Cruz
Bobby Higginson
Juan Encarnacion
Rich Becker CL
125 Corey Koskie .... .30 .09
126 Matt Lawton .... .30 .09
127 Mark Redman .... .30 .09
128 David Ortiz .... .30 .09
129 Jay Canizaro .... .30 .09
130 Eric Milton .... .30 .09
131 Jacque Jones .... .30 .09
132 J.C. Romero .... .30 .09
133 Ron Coomer .... .30 .09
134 Brad Radke .... .30 .09
135 David Ortiz .... .30 .09
Matt LeCroy
Ron Coomer
Jay Canizaro
Corey Koskie
Cristian Guzman
Jacque Jones
Matt Lawton
Torii Hunter CL
136 Carlos Lee .... .30 .09
137 Frank Thomas .... .75 .23
138 Mike Sirotka .... .30 .09
139 Charles Johnson .... .30 .09
140 James Baldwin .... .30 .09
141 Magglio Ordonez .... .30 .09
142 Jon Garland .... .30 .09
143 Paul Konerko .... .30 .09
144 Ray Durham .... .30 .09
145 Keith Foulke .... .30 .09
146 Chris Singleton .... .30 .09
147 Frank Thomas .... .50 .15
Charles Johnson
Paul Konerko
Ray Durham
Herbert Perry
Jose Valentin
Carlos Lee
Magglio Ordonez
Chris Singleton CL
148 Bernie Williams .... .50 .15
149 Orlando Hernandez .... .30 .09
150 David Justice .... .30 .09
151 Andy Pettitte .... .50 .15
152 Mariano Rivera .... .50 .15

153 Derek Jeter 2.00 .60
154 Jorge Posada .50 .15
155 Jose Canseco .75 .23
156 Glenallen Hill .30 .09
157 Paul O'Neill .50 .15
158 Denny Neagle .30 .09
159 Chuck Knoblauch .30 .09
160 Roger Clemens 1.50 .45
161 Glenallen Hill .75 .23
Jorge Posada
Tino Martinez
Chuck Knoblauch
Scott Brosius
Derek Jeter
Paul O'Neill
Bernie Williams
David Justice CL
162 Jeff Bagwell .50 .15
163 Moises Alou .30 .09
164 Lance Berkman .30 .09
165 Shane Reynolds .30 .09
166 Ken Caminiti .30 .09
167 Craig Biggio .50 .15
168 Jose Lima .30 .09
169 Octavio Dotel .30 .09
170 Richard Hidalgo .30 .09
171 Scott Elarton .30 .09
172 Scott Elarton .50 .15
Mitch Meluskey
Jeff Bagwell
Craig Biggio
Bill Spiers
Julio Lugo
Moises Alou
Richard Hidalgo
Lance Berkman CL
173 Rafael Furcal .30 .09
174 Greg Maddux 1.25 .35
175 Quilvio Veras .30 .09
176 Chipper Jones .75 .23
177 Andres Galarraga .30 .09
178 Brian Jordan .30 .09
179 Tom Glavine .50 .15
180 Kevin Millwood .30 .09
181 Javier Lopez .30 .09
182 B.J. Surhoff .30 .09
183 Andruw Jones .30 .09
184 Andy Ashby .30 .09
185 Tom Glavine .30 .09
Javy Lopez
Andres Galarraga
Quilvio Veras
Chipper Jones
Rafael Furcal
Reggie Sanders
Brian Jordan
Andruw Jones CL
186 Richie Sexson .30 .09
187 Jeff D'Amico .30 .09
188 Ron Belliard .30 .09
189 Jeromy Burnitz .30 .09
190 Jimmy Haynes .30 .09
191 Marquis Grissom .30 .09
192 Jose Hernandez .30 .09
193 Geoff Jenkins .30 .09
194 Jamey Wright .30 .09
195 Mark Loretta .30 .09
196 Jeff D'Amico .30 .09
Henry Blanco
Richie Sexson
Ron Belliard
Tyler Houston
Mark Loretta
Jeromy Burnitz
Marquis Grissom
Geoff Jenkins CL
197 Rick Ankiel .30 .09
198 Mark McGwire 2.00 .60
199 Fernando Vina .30 .09
200 Edgar Renteria .30 .09
201 Darryl Kile .30 .09
202 Jim Edmonds .30 .09
203 Ray Lankford .30 .09
204 Garrett Stephenson .30 .09
205 Fernando Tatis .30 .09
206 Will Clark .75 .23
207 J.D. Drew .30 .09
208 Darryl Kile .30 .09
Mike Matheny
Mark McGwire
Fernando Vina
Fernando Tatis
Edgar Renteria
Ray Lankford
Jim Edmonds
J.D. Drew CL
209 Mark Grace .50 .15
210 Eric Young .30 .09
211 Sammy Sosa 1.25 .35
212 Jon Lieber .30 .09
213 Joe Girardi .30 .09
214 Kevin Tapani .30 .09
215 Ricky Gutierrez .30 .09
216 Kerry Wood .75 .23
217 Rondell White .30 .09
218 Damon Buford .30 .09
219 Jon Lieber .30 .09
Joe Girardi
Mark Grace
Eric Young
Willie Greene
Ricky Gutierrez
Sammy Sosa
Damon Bufford
Rondell White CL
220 Luis Gonzalez .30 .09
221 Randy Johnson .75 .23
222 Jay Bell .30 .09
223 Erubiel Durazo .30 .09
224 Matt Williams .30 .09
225 Steve Finley .30 .09
226 Curt Schilling .50 .15
227 Todd Stottlemyre .30 .09
228 Tony Womack .30 .09
229 Brian Anderson .30 .09
230 Randy Johnson .30 .09
Kelly Stinnett
Greg Colbrunn
Jay Bell
Matt Williams
Tony Womack
Luis Gonzalez
Steve Finley
Danny Bautista CL
231 Gary Sheffield .30 .09
232 Adrian Beltre .30 .09
233 Todd Hundley .30 .09
234 Chan Ho Park .30 .09
235 Shawn Green .30 .09
236 Kevin Brown .30 .09
237 Tom Goodwin .30 .09
238 Mark Grudzielanek .30 .09
239 Ismael Valdes .30 .09
240 Eric Karros .30 .09
241 Kevin Brown .30 .09
Todd Hundley
Eric Karros
Mark Grudzielanek
Adrian Beltre
Alex Cora
Gary Sheffield
Shawn Green
Tom Goodwin CL
242 Jose Vidro .30 .09
243 Javier Vazquez .30 .09
244 Orlando Cabrera .30 .09
245 Peter Bergeron .30 .09
246 Vladimir Guerrero .75 .23
247 Dustin Hermanson .30 .09
248 Tony Armas Jr. .30 .09
249 Lee Stevens .30 .09
250 Milton Bradley .30 .09
251 Carl Pavano .30 .09
252 Dustin Hermanson .30 .09
Michael Barrett
Lee Stevens
Jose Vidro
Geoff Jenkins
Orlando Cabrera
Vladimir Guerrero
Peter Bergeron
Milton Bradley CL
253 Ellis Burks .30 .09
254 Robb Nen .30 .09
255 J.T. Snow .30 .09
256 Barry Bonds 2.00 .60
257 Shawn Estes .30 .09
258 Jeff Kent .30 .09
259 Kirk Rueter .30 .09
260 Bill Mueller .30 .09
261 Livan Hernandez .30 .09
262 Rich Aurilia .30 .09
263 Livan Hernadez .30 .09
Bobby Estalella
J.T. Snow
Jeff Kent
Bill Mueller
Rich Aurilia
Barry Bonds
Marvin Benard
Ellis Burks CL
264 Ryan Dempster .30 .09
265 Cliff Floyd .30 .09
266 Mike Lowell .30 .09
267 A.J. Burnett .30 .09
268 Preston Wilson .30 .09
269 Luis Castillo .30 .09
270 Henry Rodriguez .30 .09
271 Antonio Alfonseca .30 .09
272 Derrek Lee .30 .09
273 Mark Kotsay .30 .09
274 Brad Penny .30 .09
275 Ryan Dempster .30 .09
Mike Redmond
Derrek Lee
Luis Castillo
Mike Lowell
Alex Gonzalez
Cliff Floyd
Mark Kotsay
Preston Wilson CL
276 Mike Piazza 1.25 .35
277 Jay Payton .30 .09
278 Al Leiter .30 .09
279 Mike Bordick .30 .09
280 Armando Benitez .30 .09
281 Todd Zeile .30 .09
282 Mike Hampton .30 .09
283 Edgardo Alfonzo .30 .09
284 Derek Bell .30 .09
285 Robin Ventura .30 .09
286 Mike Hampton .30 .09
Mike Piazza
Todd Zeile
Edgardo Alfonzo
Robin Ventura
Mike Bordick
Derek Bell
Jay Payton
Timo Perez CL
287 Tony Gwynn 1.00 .30
288 Trevor Hoffman .30 .09
289 Ryan Klesko .30 .09
290 Phil Nevin .30 .09
291 Matt Clement .30 .09
292 Ben Davis .30 .09
293 Ruben Rivera .30 .09
294 Bret Boone .30 .09
295 Adam Eaton .30 .09
296 Eric Owens .30 .09
297 Matt Clement .30 .09
Ben Davis
Ryan Klesko
Bret Boone
Phil Nevin
Damian Jackson
Ruben Rivera
Eric Owens
Tony Gwynn CL
298 Bob Abreu .30 .09
299 Mike Lieberthal .30 .09
300 Robert Person .30 .09
301 Scott Rolen .50 .15
302 Randy Wolf .30 .09
303 Bruce Chen .30 .09
304 Travis Lee .30 .09
305 Kent Bottenfield .30 .09
306 Pat Burrell .30 .09
307 Doug Glanville .30 .09
308 Robert Person .30 .09
Mike Lieberthal
Pat Burrell
Kevin Jordan
Scott Rolen
Alex Arias
Bob Abreu
Doug Glanville
Travis Lee CL
309 Brian Giles .30 .09
310 Todd Ritchie .30 .09
311 Warren Morris .30 .09
312 John VanderWal .30 .09
313 Kris Benson .30 .09
314 Jason Kendall .30 .09
315 Kevin Young .30 .09
316 Francisco Cordova .30 .09
317 Jimmy Anderson .30 .09
318 Kris Benson .30 .09
Jason Kendall
Kevin Young
Warren Morris
Mike Benjamin
Pat Meares
John VanderWal
Brian Giles
Adrian Brown CL
319 Ken Griffey Jr. 1.25 .35
320 Pokey Reese .30 .09
321 Chris Stynes .30 .09
322 Barry Larkin .75 .23
323 Steve Parris .30 .09
324 Michael Tucker .30 .09
325 Dmitri Young .30 .09
326 Pete Harnisch .30 .09
327 Danny Graves .30 .09
328 Aaron Boone .30 .09
329 Sean Casey .30 .09
330 Steve Parris .30 .09
Ed Taubensee
Sean Casey
Pokey Reese
Aaron Boone
Barry Larkin
Ken Griffey Jr.
Dmitri Young
Michael Tucker CL
331 Todd Helton .50 .15
332 Pedro Astacio .30 .09
333 Larry Walker .50 .15
334 Ben Petrick .30 .09
335 Brian Bohanon .30 .09
336 Juan Pierre .30 .09
337 Jeffrey Hammonds .30 .09
338 Jeff Cirillo .30 .09
339 Todd Hollandsworth .30 .09
340 Pedro Astacio .30 .09
Brent Mayne
Todd Helton
Todd Walker
Jeff Cirillo
Neifi Perez
Larry Walker
Jeffrey Hammonds
Juan Pierre CL
341 Matt Wise .50 .15
Keith Luuola
Derrick Turnbow
342 Jason Hart .50 .15
Jose Ortiz
Mario Encarnacion
343 Vernon Wells .50 .15
Pasqual Coco
Josh Phelps
344 Travis Harper .50 .15
Kenny Kelley
Tbby Hall
345 Danys Baez .50 .15
Tim Drew
Martin Vargas
346 Ichiro Suzuki 15.00 4.50
Ryan Franklin
Ryan Christianson
347 Jay Spurgeon .50 .15
Lesli Brea
Carlos Casimiro
348 B.J. Waszgis .50 .15
Brian Sikorski
Joaquin Benoit
349 Sun-Woo Kim .50 .15
Paxton Crawford
Steve Lomasney
350 Kris Wilson .50 .15
Orber Moreno
Dee Brown
351 Mark Johnson .50 .15
Brandon Inge
Adam Bernero
352 Danny Ardoin .50 .15
Matt Kinney
Jason Ryan
353 Rocky Biddle .50 .15
Joe Crede
Josh Paul
354 Nick Johnson .50 .15
D'Angelo Jimenez
Wily Mo Pena
355 Tony McKnight .50 .15
Aaron McNeal
Keith Ginter
356 Mark DeRosa .30 .09
Jason Marquis
Wes Helms UER
Photos do not match the players ID'd
357 Allen Levrault .50 .15
Horacio Estrada
Santiago Perez
358 Luis Saturria .50 .15
Gene Stechschulte
Britt Reames
359 Joey Nation .50 .15
Corey Patterson
Cole Liniak
360 Alex Cabrera .50 .15
Geraldo Guzman
Nelson Figuero
361 Hiram Bocachica .50 .15
Mike Judd
Luke Prokopec
362 Tomas de la Rosa .50 .15
Yohanny Valera
Talmadge Nunnari
363 Ryan Vogelsong .50 .15
Juan Melo
Chad Zerbe
364 Jason Grilli .50 .15
Pablo Ozuna
Ramon Castro
365 Timo Perez .50 .15
Grant Roberts
Brian Cole
366 Tom Davey .50 .15
Xavier Nady
Dave Maurer
367 Jimmy Rollins .50 .15
Mark Brownson
Reggie Taylor
368 Alex Hernandez .50 .15
Adam Hyzdu
Tike Redman
369 Brady Clark .50 .15
John Riedling
Mike Bell
370 Giovanni Carrara .50 .15
Josh Kalinowski
Craig House
371 Jim Edmonds SH .30 .09
372 Edgar Martinez SH .30 .09
373 Rickey Henderson SH .75 .23
374 Barry Zito SH .75 .23
375 Tino Martinez SH .50 .15
376 J.T. Snow SH .30 .09
377 Bobby Jones SH .30 .09
378 Alex Rodriguez SH .75 .23
379 Mike Hampton SH .30 .09
380 Roger Clemens SH .75 .23
381 Jay Payton SH .30 .09
382 John Olerud SH .30 .09
383 David Justice SH .30 .09
384 Mike Hampton SH .30 .09
385 New York Yankees SH .75 .23
386 Jose Vizcaino SH .30 .09
387 Roger Clemens SH .75 .23
388 Todd Zeile SH .30 .09
389 Derek Jeter SH 1.00 .30
390 New York Yankees SH .75 .23
391 Nomar Garciaparra .75 .23
Darin Erstad
Manny Ramirez
Derek Jeter
Carlos Delgado LL
392 Todd Helton .50 .15
Luis Castillo
Jeffrey Hammonds
Vladimir Guerrero
Moises Alou LL
393 Troy Glaus .75 .23
Frank Thomas
Alex Rodriguez
Jason Giambi
David Justice LL
394 Sammy Sosa .50 .15
Jeff Bagwell
Barry Bonds
Vladimir Guerrero
Richard Hidalgo LL
395 Edgar Martinez .50 .15
Mike Sweeney
Frank Thomas
Carlos Delgado
Jason Giambi LL
396 Todd Helton .30 .09
Jeff Kent
Brian Giles
Sammy Sosa
Jeff Bagwell LL
397 Pedro Martinez .50 .15
Roger Clemens
Mike Mussina
Bartolo Colon
Mike Sirotka LL
398 Kevin Brown .30 .09
Randy Johnson
Jeff D'Amico
Greg Maddux
Mike Hampton LL
399 Tim Hudson .30 .09
David Wells
Aaron Sele
Andy Pettitte
Pedro Martinez LL
400 Tom Glavine .50 .15
Darryl Kile
Randy Johnson
Chan Ho Park
Greg Maddux LL
S30 K.Griffey Jr. Sample 1.25 .35

2001 Upper Deck Vintage All-Star Tributes

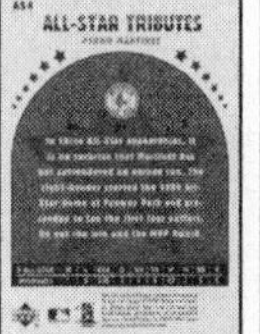

Randomly inserted into packs at one in 23, this 10-card insert features players that make the All-Star team on a consistent basis. Card backs carry an "AS" prefix.

	Nm-Mt	Ex-Mt
COMPLETE SET (10)	40.00	12.00
AS1 Derek Jeter	6.00	1.80
AS2 Mike Piazza	4.00	1.20
AS3 Carlos Delgado	1.50	.45
AS4 Pedro Martinez	2.50	.75
AS5 Vladimir Guerrero	2.50	.75
AS6 Mark McGwire	6.00	1.80
AS7 Alex Rodriguez	4.00	1.20
AS8 Barry Bonds	6.00	1.80
AS9 Chipper Jones	2.50	.75
AS10 Sammy Sosa	4.00	1.20

2001 Upper Deck Vintage Glory Days

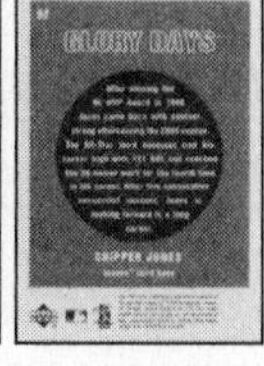

Randomly inserted into packs at one in 15, this 15-card insert features players that remind us of baseball's glory days of the past. Card backs carry a "G" prefix.

	Nm-Mt	Ex-Mt
COMPLETE SET (15)	40.00	12.00
G1 Jermaine Dye	1.50	.45
G2 Chipper Jones	2.50	.75
G3 Todd Helton	1.50	.45
G4 Magglio Ordonez	1.50	.45
G5 Tony Gwynn	3.00	.90
G6 Jim Edmonds	1.50	.45
G7 Rafael Palmeiro	1.50	.45
G8 Barry Bonds	6.00	1.80
G9 Carl Everett	1.50	.45
G10 Mike Piazza	4.00	1.20
G11 Brian Giles	1.50	.45
G12 Tony Batista	1.50	.45
G13 Jeff Bagwell	1.50	.45
G14 Ken Griffey Jr.	4.00	1.20
G15 Troy Glaus	1.50	.45

2001 Upper Deck Vintage Matinee Idols

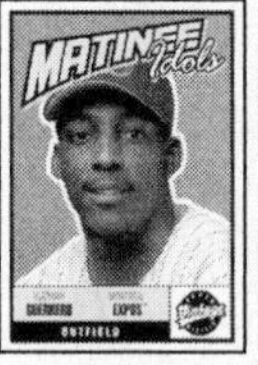
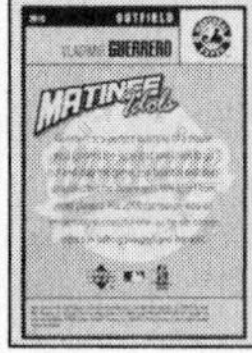

Randomly inserted into packs at one in four, this 20-card insert features players that are idolized by every young baseball player in America. Card backs carry a "M" prefix.

	Nm-Mt	Ex-Mt
COMPLETE SET (20)	25.00	7.50
M1 Ken Griffey Jr.	2.00	.60
M2 Derek Jeter	3.00	.90
M3 Barry Bonds	3.00	.90
M4 Chipper Jones	1.25	.35
M5 Mike Piazza	2.00	.60
M6 Todd Helton	.75	.23
M7 Randy Johnson	1.25	.35
M8 Alex Rodriguez	2.00	.60
M9 Sammy Sosa	2.00	.60
M10 Cal Ripken	4.00	1.20
M11 Nomar Garciaparra	2.00	.60
M12 Carlos Delgado	.75	.23
M13 Jason Giambi	1.25	.35
M14 Ivan Rodriguez	1.25	.35
M15 Vladimir Guerrero	1.25	.35
M16 Gary Sheffield	.75	.23
M17 Frank Thomas	1.25	.35
M18 Jeff Bagwell	.75	.23
M19 Pedro Martinez	1.25	.35
M20 Mark McGwire	3.00	.90

2001 Upper Deck Vintage Retro Rules

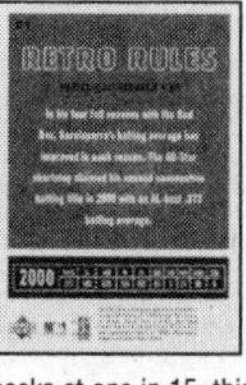

Randomly inserted into packs at one in 15, this 15-card insert features players whose performances remind us of baseball's good ol' days. Card backs carry a "R" prefix.

	Nm-Mt	Ex-Mt
COMPLETE SET (15)	40.00	12.00
R1 Nomar Garciaparra	4.00	1.20
R2 Frank Thomas	2.50	.75
R3 Jeff Bagwell	1.50	.45
R4 Sammy Sosa	4.00	1.20
R5 Derek Jeter	6.00	1.80
R6 David Wells	1.50	.45
R7 Vladimir Guerrero	2.50	.75
R8 Jim Thome	2.50	.75
R9 Mark McGwire	6.00	1.80
R10 Todd Helton	1.50	.45
R11 Tony Gwynn	3.00	.90
R12 Bernie Williams	1.50	.45
R13 Cal Ripken	8.00	2.40
R14 Brian Giles	1.50	.45
R15 Jason Giambi	2.50	.75

2001 Upper Deck Vintage Timeless Teams

Randomly inserted into packs at one in 72 (Bats) and one in 288 (Jerseys), this 39-card insert features swatches of game-used memorabilia from powerhouse clubs of the past. Card backs carry the team initials/player's initials as numbering.

	Nm-Mt	Ex-Mt
CI2JB Johnny Bench Bat	25.00	7.50

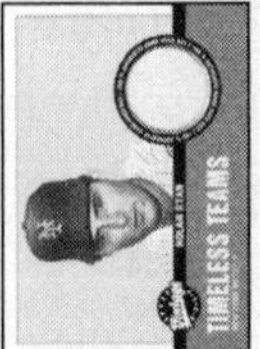
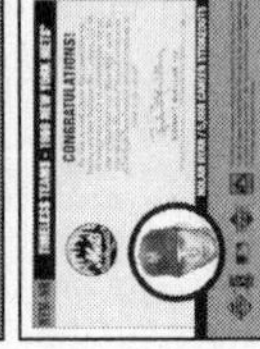

CI2JM Joe Morgan Bat 15.00 4.50
CI2KG Ken Griffey Sr. Bat 25.00 7.50
CI2TP Tony Perez Bat 15.00 4.50
BABP Boog Powell Bat 25.00 7.50
BABR B. Robinson Bat 25.00 7.50
BAFR Frank Robinson Bat 25.00 7.50
BAMB Mark Belanger Bat 15.00 4.50
BKDN Don Newcombe Bat 25.00 7.50
BKGH Gil Hodges Bat 25.00 7.50
BKJR Jackie Robinson Bat 100.00 30.00
BKRC Roy Campanella Bat 60.00 18.00
CIDC D. Concepcion Jsy 15.00 4.50
CIJM Joe Morgan Jsy 15.00 4.50
CIKG Ken Griffey Sr. Jsy 25.00 7.50
CITP Tony Perez Jsy 15.00 4.50
LABR Bill Russell Bat 15.00 4.50
LADB Dusty Baker Bat 15.00 4.50
LARC Ron Cey Bat 15.00 4.50
LASG Steve Garvey Bat 15.00 4.50
NYMEK Ed Kranepool Bat 15.00 4.50
NYMNR Nolan Ryan Bat 50.00 15.00
NYMRS Ron Swoboda Bat 15.00 4.50
NYMTA Tommie Agee Bat 15.00 4.50
NYYBD Bill Dickey Bat 25.00 7.50
NYYBR B. Richardson Jsy 15.00 4.50
NYYCK Charlie Keller Bat 15.00 4.50
NYYJD Joe DiMaggio Bat 120.00 36.00
NYYMM M. Mantle Jsy 200.00 60.00
NYYRM Roger Maris Jsy 60.00 18.00
NYYTH T. Henrich Bat 15.00 4.50
OAGT Gene Tenace Bat 15.00 4.50
OAJR Joe Rudi Bat 15.00 4.50
OARJ Reggie Jackson Bat 25.00 7.50
OASB Sal Bando Bat 15.00 4.50
PIAO Al Oliver Bat 15.00 4.50
PIMS M. Sanguillen Bat 15.00 4.50
PIRC R. Clemente Bat 120.00 36.00
PIWS Willie Stargell Bat 25.00 7.50

2001 Upper Deck Vintage Timeless Teams Combos

Randomly inserted into packs, this 11-card insert features swatches of game-used memorabilia from powerhouse clubs of the past. Please note that these cards feature dual players, and are individually serial numbered to 100. Card backs carry the team initials/year as numbering. Unlike the other cards in this set, only twenty-five serial-numbered copies of the "Fantasy Outfield" card featuring DiMaggio, Mantle and Griffey Jr. were created.

Nm-Mt Ex-Mt
LA81 Steve Garvey 80.00 24.00
Ron Cey
Dusty Baker
Bill Russell Bat
BAL70 Brooks Robinson 100.00 30.00
Frank Robinson
Mark Belanger
Boog Powell Bat
BKN55 Jackie Robinson 200.00 60.00
Roy Campanella
Gil Hodges
Don Newcombe Bat
CIN75B Johnny Bench 100.00 30.00
Tony Perez
Joe Morgan
Ken Griffey Sr. Bat
CIN75J Dave Concepcion 80.00 24.00
Tony Perez
Ken Griffey Sr. Jsy
NYM69 Nolan Ryan 150.00 45.00
Ron Swoboda
Ed Kranepool
Tommie Agee Bat
NYY41 Joe DiMaggio 250.00 75.00
Tommy Henrich
Bill Dickey
Charlie Keller Bat
NYY61 Mickey Mantle 300.00 90.00
Roger Maris
Bobby Richardson Jsy
OAK72 Reggie Jackson 100.00 30.00
Sal Bando
Gene Tenace
Joe Rudi Bat
PIT71 Roberto Clemente 200.00 60.00
Willie Stargell
Manny Sanguillen
Al Oliver Bat UER
Card back says it is a Bill Mazeroski piece
Manny Sanguillen replaced Mazeroski on card
FO-CJ Joe DiMaggio
Mickey Mantle
Ken Griffey Jr. Jsy/25

2002 Upper Deck Vintage

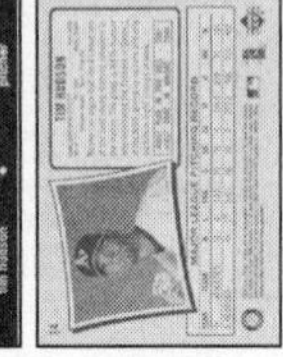

Released In January, 2002 this 300 card set features Upper Deck honoring the popular 1971 Topps design for this set. Subsets include Team Checklists, Vintage Rookies (both seeded throughout the set), League Leaders (271-280) and Postseason Scrapbook (281-300). Please note that card number 274 has a variation. A few cards issued very early in the printing cycle featured the players listed as AL Home Run Leaders and no names listed for the players. It is believed this card was corrected very early in the printing cycle.

Nm-Mt Ex-Mt
COMPLETE SET (300) 60.00 18.00
1 Darin Erstad .40 .12
2 Mo Vaughn .40 .12
3 Ramon Ortiz .40 .12
4 Garret Anderson .40 .12
5 Troy Glaus .50 .15
6 Troy Percival .40 .12
7 Tim Salmon .50 .15
8 Wilmy Caceres .40 .12
Elpidio Guzman
9 Ramon Ortiz TC .40 .12
10 Jason Giambi .75 .23
11 Mark Mulder .40 .12
12 Jermaine Dye .40 .12
13 Miguel Tejada .40 .12
14 Tim Hudson .40 .12
15 Eric Chavez .40 .12
16 Barry Zito .50 .15
17 Oscar Salazar .40 .12
Juan Pena
18 Miguel Tejada .40 .12
Jason Giambi TC
19 Carlos Delgado .40 .12
20 Raul Mondesi .40 .12
21 Chris Carpenter .40 .12
22 Jose Cruz Jr. .40 .12
23 Alex Gonzalez .40 .12
24 Brad Fullmer .40 .12
25 Shannon Stewart .40 .12
26 Brandon Lyon .40 .12
Vernon Wells
27 Carlos Delgado TC .40 .12
28 Greg Vaughn .40 .12
29 Toby Hall .40 .12
30 Ben Grieve .40 .12
31 Aubrey Huff .40 .12
32 Tanyon Sturtze .40 .12
33 Brent Abernathy .40 .12
34 Dewon Brazelton .40 .12
Delvin James
35 Greg Vaughn .40 .12
Fred McGriff TC
36 Roberto Alomar .75 .23
37 Juan Gonzalez .75 .23
38 Bartolo Colon .40 .12
39 C.C. Sabathia .40 .12
40 Jim Thome .75 .23
41 Omar Vizquel .40 .12
42 Russell Branyan .40 .12
43 Ryan Drese .40 .12
Roy Smith
44 C.C. Sabathia TC .40 .12
45 Edgar Martinez .50 .15
46 Bret Boone .40 .12
47 Freddy Garcia .40 .12
48 John Olerud .40 .12
49 Kazuhiro Sasaki .40 .12
50 Ichiro Suzuki 1.25 .35
51 Mike Cameron .40 .12
52 Rafael Soriano .40 .12
Dennis Stark
53 Jamie Moyer TC .40 .12
54 Tony Batista .40 .12
55 Jeff Conine .40 .12
56 Jason Johnson .40 .12
57 Jay Gibbons .40 .12
58 Chris Richard .40 .12
59 Josh Towers .40 .12
60 Jerry Hairston Jr. .40 .12
61 Sean Douglass .40 .12
Tim Raines Jr.
62 Cal Ripken TC 1.25 .35
63 Alex Rodriguez 1.25 .35
64 Ruben Sierra .40 .12
65 Ivan Rodriguez .75 .23
66 Gabe Kapler .40 .12
67 Rafael Palmeiro .50 .15
68 Frank Catalanotto .40 .12
69 Mark Teixeira 1.00 .30
Carlos Pena
70 Alex Rodriguez TC .75 .23
71 Nomar Garciaparra 1.25 .35
72 Pedro Martinez .75 .23
73 Trot Nixon .50 .15
74 Dante Bichette .40 .12
75 Manny Ramirez .40 .12
76 Carl Everett .40 .12
77 Hideo Nomo .75 .23
78 Dernell Stenson .40 .12
Juan Diaz
79 Manny Ramirez TC .40 .12
80 Mike Sweeney .40 .12
81 Carlos Febles .40 .12
82 Dee Brown .40 .12
83 Neifi Perez .40 .12
84 Mark Quinn .40 .12
85 Carlos Beltran .40 .12
86 Joe Randa .40 .12
87 Ken Harvey .40 .12
Mike MacDougal
88 Mike Sweeney TC .40 .12
89 Dean Palmer .40 .12
90 Jeff Weaver .40 .12
91 Jose Lima .40 .12
92 Tony Clark .40 .12
93 Damion Easley .40 .12
94 Bobby Higginson .40 .12
95 Robert Fick .40 .12
96 Pedro Santana .40 .12
Mike Rivera
97 Juan Encarnacion .40 .12
Roger Cedeno TC
98 Doug Mientkiewicz .40 .12
99 David Ortiz .40 .12
100 Joe Mays .40 .12
101 Corey Koskie .40 .12
102 Eric Milton .40 .12
103 Cristian Guzman .40 .12
104 Brad Radke .40 .12
105 Adam Johnson .40 .12
Juan Rincon
106 Corey Koskie TC .40 .12
107 Frank Thomas .75 .23
108 Carlos Lee .40 .12
109 Mark Buehrle .40 .12
110 Jose Canseco .75 .23
111 Magglio Ordonez .40 .12
112 Jon Garland .40 .12
113 Ray Durham .40 .12
114 Joe Crede .40 .12
Josh Fogg
115 Carlos Lee TC .40 .12
116 Derek Jeter 2.00 .60
117 Roger Clemens 1.50 .45
118 Alfonso Soriano .50 .15
119 Paul O'Neill .50 .15
120 Jorge Posada .50 .15
121 Bernie Williams .50 .15
122 Mariano Rivera .50 .15
123 Tino Martinez .50 .15
124 Mike Mussina .75 .23
125 Nick Johnson .40 .12
Erick Almonte
126 Jorge Posada .75 .23
David Justice
Scott Brosius TC
127 Jeff Bagwell .50 .15
128 Wade Miller .40 .12
129 Lance Berkman .40 .12
130 Moises Alou .40 .12
131 Craig Biggio .50 .15
132 Roy Oswalt .40 .12
133 Richard Hidalgo .40 .12
134 Morgan Ensberg .40 .12
Tim Redding
135 Lance Berkman .40 .12
Richard Hidalgo TC
136 Greg Maddux 1.25 .35
137 Chipper Jones .75 .23
138 Brian Jordan .40 .12
139 Marcus Giles .40 .12
140 Andruw Jones .40 .12
141 Tom Glavine .50 .15
142 Rafael Furcal .40 .12
143 Wilson Betemit .40 .12
Horacio Ramirez
144 Chipper Jones .50 .15
Brian Jordan TC
145 Jeromy Burnitz .40 .12
146 Ben Sheets .40 .12
147 Geoff Jenkins .40 .12
148 Devon White .40 .12
149 Jimmy Haynes .40 .12
150 Richie Sexson .40 .12
151 Jose Hernandez .40 .12
152 Jose Mieses .40 .12
Alex Sanchez
153 Richie Sexson TC .40 .12
154 Mark McGwire 2.00 .60
155 Albert Pujols 1.50 .45
156 Matt Morris .40 .12
157 J.D. Drew .40 .12
158 Jim Edmonds .40 .12
159 Bud Smith .40 .12
160 Darryl Kile .40 .12
161 Bill Ortega .40 .12
Luis Saturria
162 Albert Pujols 1.50 .45
Mark McGwire TC
163 Sammy Sosa 1.25 .35
164 Jon Lieber .40 .12
165 Eric Young .40 .12
166 Kerry Wood .75 .23
167 Fred McGriff .50 .15
168 Corey Patterson .40 .12
169 Rondell White .40 .12
170 Juan Cruz 2.50 .75
Mark Prior
171 Sammy Sosa TC .75 .23
172 Luis Gonzalez .40 .12
173 Randy Johnson .75 .23
174 Matt Williams .40 .12
175 Mark Grace .50 .15
176 Steve Finley .40 .12
177 Reggie Sanders .40 .12
178 Curt Schilling .50 .15
179 Alex Cintron .40 .12
Jack Cust
180 Arizona Diamondbacks TC .75 .23
181 Gary Sheffield .40 .12
182 Paul LoDuca .40 .12
183 Chan Ho Park .40 .12
184 Shawn Green .40 .12
185 Eric Karros .40 .12
186 Adrian Beltre .40 .12
187 Kevin Brown .40 .12
188 Ricardo Rodriguez .40 .12
Carlos Garcia
189 Shawn Green .40 .12
Gary Sheffield TC
190 Vladimir Guerrero .75 .23
191 Javier Vazquez .40 .12
192 Jose Vidro .40 .12
193 Fernando Tatis .40 .12
194 Orlando Cabrera .40 .12
195 Lee Stevens .40 .12
196 Tony Armas Jr. .40 .12
197 Donnie Bridges .40 .12
Henry Mateo
198 Vladimir Guerrero .50 .15
Jose Vidro TC
199 Barry Bonds 2.00 .60
200 Rich Aurilia .40 .12
201 Russ Ortiz .40 .12
202 Jeff Kent .40 .12
203 Jason Schmidt .40 .12
204 John Vander Wal .40 .12
205 Robb Nen .40 .12
206 Yorvit Torrealba .40 .12
Kurt Ainsworth
207 Barry Bonds TC .75 .23
208 Preston Wilson .40 .12
209 Brad Penny .40 .12
210 Cliff Floyd .40 .12
211 Luis Castillo .40 .12
212 Ryan Dempster .40 .12
213 Charles Johnson .40 .12
214 A.J. Burnett .40 .12
215 Abraham Nunez .60 .18
Josh Beckett
216 Cliff Floyd TC .40 .12
217 Mike Piazza 1.25 .35
218 Al Leiter .40 .12
219 Edgardo Alfonzo .40 .12
220 Tsuyoshi Shinjo .40 .12
221 Matt Lawton .40 .12
222 Robin Ventura .40 .12
223 Jay Payton .40 .12
224 Alex Escobar .40 .12
Jae Weong Seo
225 Mike Piazza .75 .23
Robin Ventura TC
226 Ryan Klesko .40 .12
227 D'Angelo Jimenez .40 .12
228 Trevor Hoffman .40 .12
229 Phil Nevin .40 .12
230 Mark Kotsay .40 .12
231 Brian Lawrence .40 .12
232 Bubba Trammell .40 .12
233 Jason Middlebrook .40 .12
Xavier Nady
234 Tony Gwynn TC .50 .15
235 Scott Rolen .50 .15
236 Jimmy Rollins .40 .12
237 Mike Lieberthal .40 .12
238 Bobby Abreu .40 .12
239 Brandon Duckworth .40 .12
240 Robert Person .40 .12
241 Pat Burrell .40 .12
242 Nick Punto .40 .12
Carlos Silva
243 Mike Lieberthal TC .40 .12
244 Brian Giles .40 .12
245 Jack Wilson .40 .12
246 Kris Benson .40 .12
247 Jason Kendall .40 .12
248 Aramis Ramirez .40 .12
249 Todd Ritchie .40 .12
250 Rob Mackowiak .40 .12
251 John Grabow .40 .12
Humberto Cota
252 Brian Giles TC .40 .12
253 Ken Griffey Jr. 1.25 .35
254 Barry Larkin .75 .23
255 Sean Casey .40 .12
256 Aaron Boone .40 .12
257 Dmitri Young .40 .12
258 Pokey Reese .40 .12
259 Adam Dunn .40 .12
260 David Espinosa .40 .12
Dane Sardinha
261 Ken Griffey TC .75 .23
262 Todd Helton .50 .15
263 Mike Hampton .40 .12
264 Juan Pierre .40 .12
265 Larry Walker .50 .15
266 Juan Uribe .40 .12
267 Jose Ortiz .40 .12
268 Jeff Cirillo .40 .12
269 Jason Jennings .40 .12
Luke Hudson
270 Larry Walker TC .40 .12
271 Ichiro Suzuki .75 .23
Jason Giambi
Roberto Alomar LL
272 Larry Walker .40 .12
Todd Helton
Moises Alou LL
273 Alex Rodriguez .50 .15
Jim Thome
Rafael Palmeiro LL
274 Barry Bonds 1.00 .30
Sammy Sosa
Luis Gonzalez LL
274A Barry Bonds 15.00 4.50
Sammy Sosa
Luis Gonzalez LL ERR
Card has AL Home Run Leaders
No player names on cards
275 Mark Mulder .50 .15
Roger Clemens
Jamie Moyer LL
276 Curt Schilling .50 .15
Matt Morris
Randy Johnson LL
277 Freddy Garcia .50 .15
Mike Mussina
Joe Mays LL
278 Randy Johnson .50 .15
Curt Schilling
John Burkett LL
279 Mariano Rivera .40 .12
Kazuhiro Sasaki
Keith Foulke LL
280 Robb Nen .50 .15
Armando Benitez
Trevor Hoffman LL
281 Jason Giambi PS .50 .15
282 Jorge Posada PS .40 .12
283 Jim Thome .50 .15
Juan Gonzalez PS
284 Edgar Martinez PS .40 .12
285 Andruw Jones PS .40 .12
286 Chipper Jones PS .50 .15
287 Matt Williams PS .40 .12
288 Curt Schilling PS .40 .12
289 Derek Jeter PS 1.00 .30
290 Mike Mussina PS .50 .15
291 Bret Boone PS .40 .12
292 Alfonso Soriano PS UER .40 .12
Alfonso is spelled incorrectly
293 Randy Johnson PS .50 .15
294 Tom Glavine PS .40 .12
295 Curt Schilling PS .40 .12
296 Randy Johnson PS .50 .15
297 Derek Jeter PS 1.00 .30
298 Tino Martinez PS .40 .12
299 Curt Schilling PS .40 .12
300 Luis Gonzalez PS .40 .12

2002 Upper Deck Vintage Aces Game Jersey

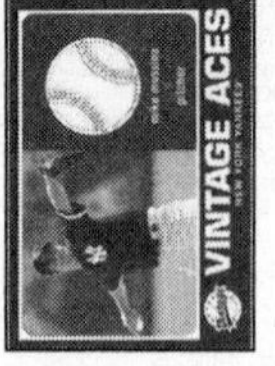

Inserted into packs at stated odds of one in 144 hobby and one in 210 retail, these 14 cards feature a mix of active and retired pitchers along with a game jersey swatch. Roger Clemens was produced in shorter quantity than the other players and we have notated that with an SP in our checklist.

Nm-Mt Ex-Mt
A-FJ Ferguson Jenkins 15.00 4.50
A-GM Greg Maddux 25.00 7.50
A-HN Hideo Nomo 40.00 12.00
A-JD John Denny 10.00 3.00
A-JM Juan Marichal 15.00 4.50
A-JS Johnny Sain 25.00 7.50
A-MMA Mike Marshall 15.00 4.50
A-MMU Mike Mussina 25.00 7.50
A-MT Mike Torrez 10.00 3.00
A-NR Nolan Ryan 120.00 36.00
A-PM Pedro Martinez 25.00 7.50
A-RC Roger Clemens SP
A-RJ Randy Johnson 25.00 7.50
A-TH Tim Hudson 15.00 4.50

2002 Upper Deck Vintage Day At The Park

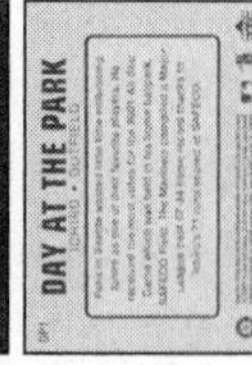

Inserted into packs at stated odds of one in 23, these six cards feature active players in a design dedicated to capturing the nostaglia of Baseball.

Nm-Mt Ex-Mt
COMPLETE SET (6) 20.00 6.00
DP1 Ichiro Suzuki 4.00 1.20
DP2 Derek Jeter 6.00 1.80
DP3 Alex Rodriguez 4.00 1.20
DP4 Mark McGwire 6.00 1.80
DP5 Barry Bonds 6.00 1.80
DP6 Sammy Sosa 4.00 1.20

2002 Upper Deck Vintage Night Gamers

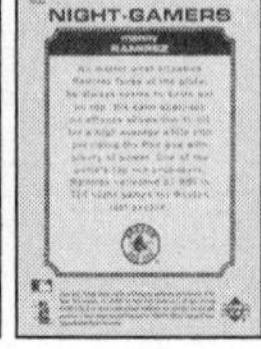

Inserted into packs at stated odds of one in 11, these 12 cards features a salute to primetime games with some of the leading players.

Nm-Mt Ex-Mt
COMPLETE SET (12) 15.00 4.50
NG1 Todd Helton 1.00 .30
NG2 Manny Ramirez 1.00 .30
NG3 Ivan Rodriguez 1.50 .45
NG4 Albert Pujols 3.00 .90
NG5 Greg Maddux 2.50 .75
NG6 Carlos Delgado 1.00 .30
NG7 Frank Thomas 1.50 .45
NG8 Derek Jeter 4.00 1.20
NG9 Troy Glaus 1.00 .30
NG10 Jeff Bagwell 1.00 .30
NG11 Juan Gonzalez 1.50 .45
NG12 Randy Johnson 1.50 .45

2002 Upper Deck Vintage Sandlot Stars

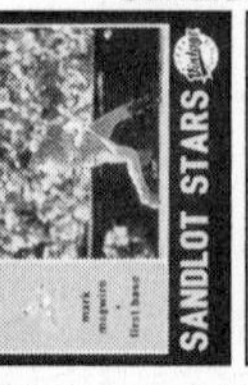

Inserted in packs at stated odds of one in 11, these 12 cards feature some of today's stars in a playful salute to the old days where many players were "discovered" while playing sandlot ball.

Nm-Mt Ex-Mt
COMPLETE SET (12) 20.00 6.00
SS1 Ken Griffey Jr. 2.50 .75
SS2 Derek Jeter 4.00 1.20
SS3 Ichiro Suzuki 2.50 .75
SS4 Nomar Garciaparra 2.50 .75
SS5 Sammy Sosa 2.50 .75
SS6 Chipper Jones 1.50 .45

SS7 Jason Giambi 1.50 .45
SS8 Alex Rodriguez 2.50 .75
SS9 Mark McGwire 4.00 1.20
SS10 Barry Bonds 4.00 1.20
SS11 Mike Piazza 2.50 .75
SS12 Vladimir Guerrero 1.50 .45

2002 Upper Deck Vintage Signature Combos

Randomly inserted in packs, these nine cards feature two signatures of various baseball stars on each card. These cards all have a stated print run of 100 copies.

Nm-Mt Ex-Mt
VS-AT Roberto Alomar
Jim Thome
VS-BB Yogi Berra
Johnny Bench
VS-BR Sal Bando
Joe Rudi
VS-EL Dwight Evans
Fred Lynn
VS-FB Carlton Fisk 120.00 36.00
Johnny Bench
VS-GR Ken Griffey Jr.
Alex Rodriguez
VS-JM Reggie Jackson
Willie McCovey
VS-JO Edgar Martinez
John Olerud
VS-SD Ryne Sandberg
Andre Dawson

2002 Upper Deck Vintage Special Collection Game Jersey

Issued in packs at stated odds of one in 144 hobby and one in 210 retail, these 15 cards feature past and present stars along with a memorabilia swatch. A few players were produced in smaller quantities and we have notated those players with an SP in our checklist. These cards honored players from the famed Oakland A's "Mustache Gang" which won three straight world series in the 1970's and various Cubs stars who were still looking for their first World Series appearance since 1945.

Nm-Mt Ex-Mt
S-AD Andre Dawson Pants 15.00 4.50
S-BC Bert Campaneris Jsy 15.00 4.50
S-BW Billy Williams Jsy 15.00 4.50
S-CH Catfish Hunter Jsy SP
S-FJ Fergie Jenkins Pants SP 15.00 4.50
S-JR Joe Rudi Jsy 15.00 4.50
S-MG Mark Grace Jsy 20.00 6.00
S-MH Mike Hegan Jsy 10.00 3.00
S-PL Paul Lindblad Jsy 10.00 3.00
S-RF Rollie Fingers Jsy 15.00 4.50
S-RJ Reggie Jackson Jsy SP 20.00 6.00
S-RS Ryne Sandberg Jsy 50.00 15.00
S-SAB Sal Bando Jsy 15.00 4.50
S-SS Sammy Sosa Jsy 30.00 9.00
S-STB Stan Bahnsen Jsy 10.00 3.00

2002 Upper Deck Vintage Timeless Teams Game Bat Quads

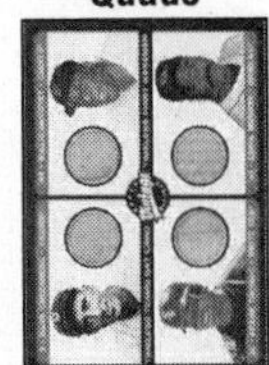

Issued in packs at stated odds of one in 288 hobby and one in 480 retail, these eight cards feature either teammates or position mates along with a bat chip from each of these players career.

Nm-Mt Ex-Mt
B Hank Greenberg 40.00 12.00
Willie McCovey
Frank Thomas
Eddie Murray
OF2 Ken Griffey Jr. 60.00 18.00
Barry Bonds
Rickey Henderson
Tony Gwynn
ATL Tom Glavine 50.00 15.00
Greg Maddux
Chipper Jones
Andruw Jones
CLE Juan Gonzalez 40.00 12.00
Jim Thome
Roberto Alomar
Kenny Lofton
NYY Mariano Rivera 50.00 15.00
Bernie Williams
Paul O'Neill
Jorge Posada
OAK Dave Parker 40.00 12.00
Jose Canseco
Rickey Henderson
Don Baylor
SEA Ichiro Suzuki 80.00 24.00
Edgar Martinez
John Olerud
Bret Boone
OFNY Mickey Mantle
Joe DiMaggio
Reggie Jackson
Babe Ruth SP

2002 Upper Deck Vintage Timeless Teams Game Jersey

Issued in packs at stated odds of one in 144 hobby and one in 210 retail, these 14 cards feature players from a great team of the past or present along with a jersey swatch. Some players were produced in shorter quantities and we have notated those players with an SP in our checklist.

Nm-Mt Ex-Mt
J-AJ Andruw Jones Jsy 15.00 4.50
J-CH Catfish Hunter Jsy 20.00 6.00
J-CJ Chipper Jones Jsy 20.00 6.00
J-DE Dwight Evans Jsy 20.00 6.00
J-EMA Edgar Martinez Jsy 20.00 6.00
J-EMU Eddie Murray Jsy 25.00 7.50
J-FL Fred Lynn Jsy 20.00 6.00
J-GM Greg Maddux Jsy SP
J-IS Ichiro Suzuki Pants SP
J-JB Johnny Bench Jsy 25.00 7.50
J-KS Kazuhiro Sasaki Jsy 15.00 4.50
J-RF Rollie Fingers Jsy 20.00 6.00
J-RJ Reggie Jackson Jsy 20.00 6.00
J-WM Willie McCovey Pants 20.00 6.00

2002 Upper Deck Vintage Timeless Teams Game Jersey Combos

Issued in hobby packs at stated odds one in 288, these four cards feature either teammates or players with something in common along with a jersey swatch of all three players featured. The card featuring the three Hall of Famers was produced in smaller quantites than the other cards and we have notated that with an SP in our checklist.

Nm-Mt Ex-Mt
ATL Greg Maddux 60.00 18.00
Chipper Jones
Andruw Jones
HOF Ty Cobb
Babe Ruth
Honus Wagner SP
NYY Roger Clemens 60.00 18.00
Mariano Rivera
Bernie Williams
OAK Rollie Fingers 50.00 15.00
Catfish Hunter
Reggie Jackson

2003 Upper Deck Vintage

This 280 card set, designed to resemble the 1965 Topps set, was released in January 2003. This set was issued in eight card packs which came 24 packs to a box and 12 boxes to a case. These packs had an SRP of $2. Cards numbered from 223 through 232 feature a pair of prospects from an organiztion. Cards numbered from 233 through 247 are titled Stellar Stat Men. Cards from 248 through 277 were produced in a style reminscent of the Kellogs 3-D cards of the 1970's. Those 3D cards were seeded at a rate of one in 48. In addition, there were other short print cards scattered throughout the set. Those cards which we have noted as either SP, TR1 SP or TR2 SP were inserted at a rate between one in 20 and one in 40. Please note, Eddie Mathews is listed below as card 37 (as was the manufacturer's original intent), but the card is mistakenly numbered as 376. Jason Jennings who was supposed to be card number 178 was mistakenly numbered as 28. In addition, cards number 281 through 341 were later issued at a stated rate of one per Upper Deck 40-man pack.

Nm-Mt Ex-Mt
COMP.SET w/o SP's (200) 50.00 15.00
COMP.UPDATE SET (60) 25.00 7.50
COMMON ACTIVE (1-280) .30 .09
COMMON RETIRED .60 .18
COMMON SP (1-220) 5.00 1.50
COMMON TR1 SP 5.00 1.50
COMMON TR2 SP 5.00 1.50
COMMON CARD (223-232) 2.00 .60
COMMON CARD (233-247) 2.00 .60
COMMON CARD (248-277) 10.00 3.00
COMMON CARD (281-341) .60 .18
COMMON RC (281-341) .60 .18
281-341 ONE PER 2003 UD 40-MAN PACK
1 Troy Glaus .50 .15
2 Darin Erstad .30 .09
3 Garret Anderson .30 .09
4 Jarrod Washburn .30 .09
5 Nolan Ryan 4.00 1.20
6 Tim Salmon .50 .15
7 Troy Percival .30 .09
8 Alex Ochoa TR1 SP 5.00 1.50
9 Daryle Ward .30 .09
10 Jeff Bagwell .50 .15
11 Roy Oswalt .30 .09
12 Lance Berkman .30 .09
13 Craig Biggio .50 .15
14 Richard Hidalgo .30 .09
15 Tim Hudson .30 .09
16 Eric Chavez .30 .09
17 Barry Zito .50 .15
18 Miguel Tejada .30 .09
19 Mark Mulder .30 .09
20 Rollie Fingers .60 .18
21 Catfish Hunter 1.00 .30
22 Jermaine Dye .30 .09
23 Ray Durham TR2 SP 5.00 1.50
24 Carlos Delgado .30 .09
25 Eric Hinske .30 .09
26 Josh Phelps .30 .09
27 Shannon Stewart .30 .09
28 Vernon Wells .30 .09
29 John Smoltz .50 .15
30 Greg Maddux 1.25 .35
31 Chipper Jones .75 .23
32 Gary Sheffield .30 .09
33 Andruw Jones .30 .09
34 Tom Glavine .50 .15
35 Rafael Furcal .30 .09
36 Phil Niekro .60 .18
37 Eddie Mathews UER 376 1.50 .45
38 Robin Yount 2.50 .75
39 Richie Sexson .30 .09
40 Ben Sheets .30 .09
41 Geoff Jenkins .30 .09
42 Alex Sanchez .30 .09
43 Jason Isringhausen .30 .09
44 Albert Pujols 1.50 .45
45 Matt Morris .30 .09
46 J.D. Drew .30 .09
47 Jim Edmonds .30 .09
48 Stan Musial 2.50 .75
49 Red Schoendienst .60 .18
50 Edgar Renteria .30 .09
51 Mark McGwire SP 12.00 3.60
52 Scott Rolen TR2 SP 8.00 2.40
53 Mark Bellhorn .30 .09
54 Kerry Wood .75 .23
55 Mark Prior 1.50 .45
56 Moises Alou .30 .09
57 Corey Patterson .30 .09
58 Ernie Banks 1.50 .45
59 Hee Seop Choi .30 .09
60 Billy Williams .60 .18
61 Sammy Sosa SP 10.00 3.00
62 Ben Grieve .30 .09
63 Jared Sandberg .30 .09
64 Carl Crawford .30 .09
65 Randy Johnson .75 .23
66 Luis Gonzalez .30 .09
67 Steve Finley .30 .09
68 Junior Spivey .30 .09
69 Erubiel Durazo .30 .09
70 Curt Schilling SP 8.00 2.40
71 Al Lopez .60 .18
72 Pee Wee Reese 1.00 .30
73 Eric Gagne .50 .15
74 Shawn Green .30 .09
75 Kevin Brown .30 .09
76 Paul Lo Duca .30 .09
77 Adrian Beltre .30 .09
78 Hideo Nomo .75 .23
79 Eric Karros .30 .09
80 Odalis Perez .30 .09
81 Kazuhisa Ishii SP 5.00 1.50
82 Tommy Lasorda .60 .18
83 Fernando Tatis .30 .09
84 Vladimir Guerrero .75 .23
85 Jose Vidro .30 .09
86 Javier Vazquez .30 .09
87 Brad Wilkerson .30 .09
88 Bartolo Colon TR1 SP 5.00 1.50
89 Monte Irvin .60 .18
90 Robb Nen .30 .09
91 Reggie Sanders .30 .09
92 Jeff Kent .30 .09
93 Rich Aurilia .30 .09
94 Orlando Cepeda .60 .18
95 Juan Marichal .60 .18
96 Willie McCovey .60 .18
97 David Bell .30 .09
98 Barry Bonds SP 12.00 3.60
99 Kenny Lofton TR2 SP 5.00 1.50
100 Jim Thome .75 .23
101 C.C. Sabathia .30 .09
102 Omar Vizquel .30 .09
103 Lou Boudreau .60 .18
104 Larry Doby .60 .18
105 Bob Lemon .60 .18
106 John Olerud .30 .09
107 Edgar Martinez .50 .15
108 Bret Boone .30 .09
109 Freddy Garcia .30 .09
110 Mike Cameron .30 .09
111 Kazuhiro Sasaki .30 .09
112 Ichiro Suzuki SP 10.00 3.00
113 Mike Lowell .30 .09
114 Josh Beckett .50 .15
115 A.J. Burnett .30 .09
116 Juan Pierre .30 .09
117 Derrek Lee .30 .09
118 Luis Castillo .30 .09
119 Juan Encarnacion TR1 SP 5.00 1.50
120 Roberto Alomar .75 .23
121 Edgardo Alfonzo .30 .09
122 Jeromy Burnitz .30 .09
123 Mo Vaughn .30 .09
124 Tom Seaver 1.00 .30
125 Al Leiter .30 .09
126 Mike Piazza SP 10.00 3.00
127 Tony Batista .30 .09
128 Geronimo Gil .30 .09
129 Chris Singleton .30 .09
130 Rodrigo Lopez .30 .09
131 Jay Gibbons .30 .09
132 Melvin Mora .30 .09
133 Earl Weaver .60 .18
134 Trevor Hoffman .30 .09
135 Phil Nevin .30 .09
136 Sean Burroughs .30 .09
137 Ryan Klesko .30 .09
138 Mark Kotsay .30 .09
139 Mike Lieberthal .30 .09
140 Bobby Abreu .30 .09
141 Jimmy Rollins .30 .09
142 Pat Burrell .30 .09
143 Vicente Padilla .30 .09
144 Richie Ashburn 1.00 .30
145 Jeremy Giambi TR1 SP 5.00 1.50
146 Josh Fogg .30 .09
147 Brian Giles .30 .09
148 Aramis Ramirez .30 .09
149 Jason Kendall .30 .09
150 Ralph Kiner .60 .18
151 Willie Stargell 1.00 .30
152 Kevin Mench .30 .09
153 Rafael Palmeiro .50 .15
154 Ivan Rodriguez .75 .23
155 Hank Blalock .50 .15
156 Juan Gonzalez .75 .23
157 Carl Everett .30 .09
158 Alex Rodriguez SP 10.00 3.00
159 Nomar Garciaparra 1.25 .35
160 Derek Lowe .30 .09
161 Manny Ramirez .30 .09
162 Shea Hillenbrand .30 .09
163 Bobby Doerr .60 .18
164 Johnny Damon .30 .09
165 Jason Varitek .30 .09
166 Pedro Martinez SP 8.00 2.40
167 Cliff Floyd TR2 SP 5.00 1.50
168 Ken Griffey Jr. 1.25 .35
169 Adam Dunn .30 .09
170 Austin Kearns .30 .09
171 Aaron Boone .30 .09
172 Joe Morgan .60 .18
173 Sean Casey .30 .09
174 Todd Walker .30 .09
175 Ryan Dempster TR1 SP 5.00 1.50
176 Shawn Estes TR1 SP 5.00 1.50
177 Gabe Kapler TR1 SP 5.00 1.50
178 Jason Jennings UER .30 .09
Card numbered as 28
179 Todd Helton .50 .15
180 Larry Walker .50 .15
181 Preston Wilson .30 .09
182 Jay Payton TR1 SP 5.00 1.50
183 Mike Sweeney .30 .09
184 Carlos Beltran .30 .09
185 Paul Byrd .30 .09
186 Raul Ibanez .30 .09
187 Rick Ferrell .60 .18
188 Early Wynn .60 .18
189 Dmitri Young .30 .09
190 Jim Bunning 1.00 .30
191 George Kell .60 .18
192 Hal Newhouser .60 .18
193 Bobby Higginson .30 .09
194 Carlos Pena TR1 SP 5.00 1.50
195 Sparky Anderson .60 .18
196 Torii Hunter .30 .09
197 Eric Milton .30 .09
198 Corey Koskie .30 .09
199 Jacque Jones .30 .09
200 Harmon Killebrew 1.50 .45
201 Doug Mientkiewicz .30 .09
202 Frank Thomas .75 .23
203 Mark Buehrle .30 .09
204 Magglio Ordonez .30 .09
205 Paul Konerko .30 .09
206 Joe Borchard .30 .09
207 Hoyt Wilhelm .60 .18
208 Carlos Lee .30 .09
209 Roger Clemens 1.50 .45
210 Nick Johnson .30 .09
211 Jason Giambi .75 .23
212 Alfonso Soriano .50 .15
213 Bernie Williams .50 .15
214 Robin Ventura .30 .09
215 Jorge Posada .50 .15
216 Mike Mussina .75 .23
217 Yogi Berra 1.50 .45
218 Phil Rizzuto 1.00 .30
219 Mariano Rivera .50 .15
220 Derek Jeter SP 12.00 3.60
221 Jeff Weaver TR1 SP 5.00 1.50
222 Raul Mondesi TR2 SP 5.00 1.50
223 Freddy Sanchez 2.00 .60
Josh Hancock
224 Joe Borchard 2.00 .60
Miguel Olivo
225 Brandon Phillips 2.00 .60
Josh Bard
226 Andy Van Hekken 2.00 .60
Andres Torres
227 Jason Lane 2.00 .60
Jeriome Robertson
228 Chin-Feng Chen 2.00 .60
Joe Thurston
229 Endy Chavez 2.00 .60
Jamey Carroll
230 Drew Henson 2.00 .60
Alex Graman
231 Dewon Brazelton 2.00 .60
Lance Carter
232 Jayson Werth 2.00 .60
Kevin Cash
233 Randy Johnson 3.00 .90
Curt Schilling
Barry Zito
234 Pedro Martinez 3.00 .90
Randy Johnson
Derek Lowe
235 Randy Johnson 3.00 .90
Curt Schilling
Pedro Martinez
236 John Smoltz 3.00 .90
Eric Gagne
Mike Williams
237 Randy Johnson 3.00 .90
Bartolo Colon
A.J. Burnett
238 Alfonso Soriano 4.00 1.20
Ichiro Suzuki
Vladimir Guerrero
239 Alex Rodriguez 4.00 1.20
Jim Thome
Sammy Sosa
240 Barry Bonds 4.00 1.20
Manny Ramirez
Mike Sweeney
241 Alfonso Soriano 4.00 1.20
Alex Rodriguez
Derek Jeter
242 Alex Rodriguez 4.00 1.20
Magglio Ordonez
Miguel Tejada
243 Luis Castillo 2.00 .60
Juan Pierre
Dave Roberts
244 Nomar Garciaparra 4.00 1.20
Garrett Anderson
Alfonso Soriano
245 Johnny Damon 2.00 .60
Jimmy Rollins
Kenny Lofton
246 Barry Bonds 4.00 1.20
Jim Thome
Manny Ramirez
247 Barry Bonds 4.00 1.20
Brian Giles
Manny Ramirez
248 Troy Glaus 3D 15.00 4.50
249 Luis Gonzalez 3D 10.00 3.00
250 Chipper Jones 3D 15.00 4.50
251 Nomar Garciaparra 3D 15.00 4.50
252 Manny Ramirez 3D 10.00 3.00
253 Sammy Sosa 3D 15.00 4.50
254 Frank Thomas 3D 15.00 4.50
255 Magglio Ordonez 3D 10.00 3.00
256 Adam Dunn 3D 10.00 3.00
257 Ken Griffey Jr. 3D 15.00 4.50
258 Jim Thome 3D 15.00 4.50
259 Todd Helton 3D 15.00 4.50
260 Larry Walker 3D 15.00 4.50
261 Lance Berkman 3D 10.00 3.00
262 Jeff Bagwell 3D 15.00 4.50
263 Mike Sweeney 3D 10.00 3.00
264 Shawn Green 3D 10.00 3.00
265 Vladimir Guerrero 3D 15.00 4.50
266 Mike Piazza 3D 15.00 4.50
267 Jason Giambi 3D 15.00 4.50
268 Pat Burrell 3D 10.00 3.00
269 Barry Bonds 3D 25.00 7.50
270 Mark McGwire 3D 25.00 7.50
271 Alex Rodriguez 3D 20.00 6.00
272 Carlos Delgado 3D 10.00 3.00
273 Richie Sexson 3D 10.00 3.00
274 Andruw Jones 3D 10.00 3.00
275 Derek Jeter 3D 25.00 7.50
276 Juan Gonzalez 3D 15.00 4.50
277 Albert Pujols 3D 20.00 6.00
278 Jason Giambi CL .50 .15
279 Sammy Sosa CL .75 .23
280 Ichiro Suzuki CL .75 .23
281 Tom Glavine 1.00 .30
282 Josh Stewart RC .60 .18
283 Aquilino Lopez RC .60 .18
284 Horacio Ramirez .60 .18
285 Brandon Phillips .60 .18
286 Kirk Saarloos .60 .18
287 Runelvys Hernandez .60 .18
288 Hideki Matsui RC 8.00 2.40
289 Jeremy Bonderman RC 2.00 .60
290 Russ Ortiz .60 .18
291 Ken Harvey .60 .18
292 Edgardo Alfonzo .60 .18
293 Oscar Villareal RC .60 .18
294 Marlon Byrd .60 .18
295 Josh Bard .60 .18
296 David Cone .60 .18
297 Mike Neu RC .60 .18
298 Cliff Floyd .60 .18
299 Travis Lee .60 .18
300 Jeff Kent .60 .18
301 Ron Calloway .60 .18
302 Bartolo Colon .60 .18
303 Jose Contreras RC 3.00 .90
304 Mark Teixeira 1.00 .30
305 Ivan Rodriguez 1.50 .45
306 Jim Thome 1.50 .45
307 Shane Reynolds .60 .18
308 Luis Ayala RC .60 .18
309 Lyle Overbay .60 .18
310 Travis Hafner .60 .18
311 Wilfredo Ledezma RC .60 .18
312 Rocco Baldelli 2.50 .75
313 Jason Anderson .60 .18
314 Kenny Lofton .60 .18
315 Brandon Larson .60 .18
316 Ty Wigginton .60 .18
317 Fred McGriff 1.00 .30
318 Antonio Osuna .60 .18
319 Corey Patterson .60 .18
320 Erubiel Durazo .60 .18
321 Mike MacDougal .60 .18
322 Sammy Sosa 2.50 .75
323 Mike Hampton .60 .18
324 Ramiro Mendoza .60 .18
325 Kevin Millwood .60 .18
326 Dave Roberts .60 .18
327 Todd Zeile .60 .18

328 Reggie Sanders	.60	.18
329 Billy Koch	.60	.18
330 Mike Stanton	.60	.18
331 Orlando Hernandez	.60	.18
332 Tony Clark	.60	.18
333 Chris Hammond	.60	.18
334 Michael Cuddyer	.30	.09
335 Sandy Alomar Jr.	.60	.18
336 Jose Cruz Jr.	.60	.18
337 Omar Daal	.60	.18
338 Robert Fick	.60	.18
339 Daryle Ward	.60	.18
340 David Bell	.60	.18
341 Checklist	.60	.18

2003 Upper Deck Vintage All Caps

Randomly inserted into packs, these 15 cards feature swatches of game-used caps. Each of these cards have a stated print run of 250 serial numbered sets.

	Nm-Mt	Ex-Mt
CP Chan Ho Park	15.00	4.50
DE Darin Erstad	15.00	4.50
GM Greg Maddux	40.00	12.00
JB Jeff Bagwell	20.00	6.00
JG Juan Gonzalez	20.00	6.00
KS Kazuhiro Sasaki	15.00	4.50
LB Lance Berkman	15.00	4.50
LG Luis Gonzalez	15.00	4.50
MP Mike Piazza	40.00	12.00
MV Mo Vaughn	15.00	4.50
RF Rafael Furcal	15.00	4.50
RP Rafael Palmeiro	20.00	6.00
RV Robin Ventura	15.00	4.50
TG Tony Gwynn	25.00	7.50
TH Tim Hudson	15.00	4.50

2003 Upper Deck Vintage Capping the Action

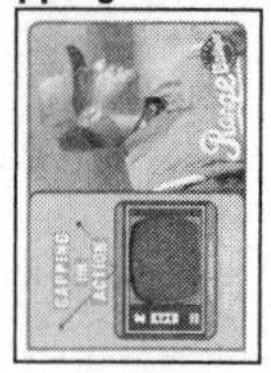

Randomly inserted into packs, these 15 cards feature pieces of game-worn caps embedded into the card. Each of these cards were issued to a stated print run of between 91 and 125 copies.

	Nm-Mt	Ex-Mt
AR Alex Rodriguez/101	40.00	12.00
AS Alfonso Soriano/109	25.00	7.50
CD Carlos Delgado/91	20.00	6.00
HM Hideo Nomo/117	60.00	18.00
IR Ivan Rodriguez/125	25.00	7.50
JG Juan Gonzalez/99	25.00	7.50
KG Ken Griffey Jr./102	40.00	12.00
MM Mike Mussina/109	50.00	15.00
PM Pedro Martinez/125	25.00	7.50
RA Roberto Alomar/101	25.00	7.50
RP Rafael Palmeiro/125	25.00	7.50
SG Shawn Green/125	20.00	6.00
SR Scott Rolen/109	25.00	7.50
SS Sammy Sosa/125	40.00	12.00
TH Todd Helton/99	25.00	7.50

2003 Upper Deck Vintage Cracking the Lumber

Randomly inserted into packs, these two cards feature authentic game-used bat chips of either Ichiro Suzuki or Jason Giambi. These cards were issued to a stated print run of 25 serial numbered sets. Due to marrket scarcity, no pricing is provided.

	Nm-Mt	Ex-Mt
GOLD PRINT RUN 5 SERIAL #'d SETS		
RANDOM INSERTS IN PACKS		
NO PRICING DUE TO SCARCITY		
IS Ichiro Suzuki		
JG Jason Giambi		

2003 Upper Deck Vintage Crowning Glory

Randomly inserted into packs, these 15 cards feature pieces of game-worn caps attached to the card front. These cards were issued to a stated print run of 25 serial numbered sets. Due to market scarcity, no pricing is provided for these cards.

	Nm-Mt	Ex-Mt
AJ Andruw Jones		
AR Alex Rodriguez		
CJ Chipper Jones		
GM Greg Maddux		
IR Ivan Rodriguez		
IS Ichiro Suzuki		
JG Jason Giambi		
KG Ken Griffey Jr.		
LG Luis Gonzalez		
MP Mike Piazza		
MR Manny Ramirez		
PM Pedro Martinez		
SC Sean Casey		
SG Shawn Green		
SS Sammy Sosa		

2003 Upper Deck Vintage Dropping the Hammer

Inserted into packs at a stated rate of one in 130, these cards feature game-used bat pieces.

	Nm-Mt	Ex-Mt
*GOLD: .75X TO 2X BASIC HAMMER		
GOLD RANDOM INSERTS IN PACKS		
GOLD PRINT RUN 100 SERIAL #'d SETS		
AJ Andruw Jones	10.00	3.00
AR Alex Rodriguez	20.00	6.00
BA Bobby Abreu	10.00	3.00
DJ David Justice	10.00	3.00
FM Fred McGriff	15.00	4.50
FT Frank Thomas	15.00	4.50
JG Jason Giambi	15.00	4.50
JT Jim Thome	15.00	4.50
KG Ken Griffey Jr.	20.00	6.00
KL Kenny Lofton	10.00	3.00
LB Lance Berkman	10.00	3.00
LW Larry Walker	15.00	4.50
MO Magglio Ordonez	10.00	3.00
MP Mike Piazza	25.00	7.50
MT Miguel Tejada	10.00	3.00
OV Omar Vizquel	10.00	3.00
PW Preston Wilson	10.00	3.00
RA Roberto Alomar	15.00	4.50
RF Rafael Furcal	10.00	3.00
RP Rafael Palmeiro	15.00	4.50
RV Robin Ventura	10.00	3.00
SG Shawn Green	10.00	3.00
SS Sammy Sosa	25.00	7.50
TA Fernando Tatis	10.00	3.00
TH Todd Helton	15.00	4.50

2003 Upper Deck Vintage Hitmen

Randomly inserted into packs, these four cards feature game-used bat pieces from Upper Deck spokespeople. Each of these cards were issued to a stated print run of 150 serial numbered sets.

	Nm-Mt	Ex-Mt
GOLD PRINT RUN 10 SERIAL #'d SETS		
NO GOLD PRICING DUE TO SCARCITY		
IS Ichiro Suzuki	80.00	24.00
JG Jason Giambi	25.00	7.50
KG Ken Griffey Jr.	40.00	12.00
MM Mark McGwire	80.00	24.00

2003 Upper Deck Vintage Hitmen Double Signed

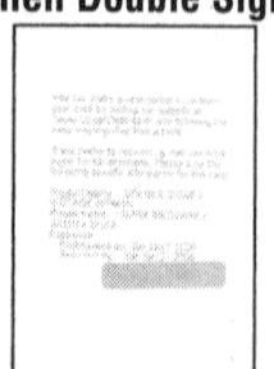

Randomly inserted into packs, this card features not only game-used bat chips but authentic signatures from the two leading homer hitters in the summer of 1998. This card was issued to a stated print run of 75 serial numbered sets.

	Nm-Mt	Ex-Mt
GOLD PRINT RUN 5 SERIAL #'d CARDS		
MS Mark McGwire Sammy Sosa	700.00	210.00

2003 Upper Deck Vintage Men with Hats

Inserted at a stated rate of one in 285, these 15 cards feature leading players with pieces of game-worn caps embedded in them.

	Nm-Mt	Ex-Mt
MH-AD Adam Dunn	15.00	4.50
MH-AJ Andruw Jones	15.00	4.50
MH-AR Alex Rodriguez	25.00	7.50
MH-BW Bernie Williams	20.00	6.00
MH-EC Eric Chavez	15.00	4.50
MH-FT Frank Thomas	20.00	6.00
MH-HU Tim Hudson	15.00	4.50
MH-JD Johnny Damon	15.00	4.50
MH-JG Jason Giambi	20.00	6.00
MH-JK Jason Kendall	15.00	4.50
MH-KL Kenny Lofton	15.00	4.50
MH-MT Miguel Tejada	15.00	4.50
MH-TH Todd Helton	20.00	6.00
MH-TW Todd Walker	15.00	4.50
MH-VC Vinny Castilla	15.00	4.50

2003 Upper Deck Vintage Slugfest

Randomly inserted into packs, this 10 card set feature pieces of game-used bat chips honoring some of the leading sluggers in baseball. These cards were issued to a stated print run of 200 serial numbered sets.

	Nm-Mt	Ex-Mt
*GOLD: .75X TO 2X BASIC SLUGFEST		
GOLD PRINT RUN 50 SERIAL #'d SETS		
S-AJ Andruw Jones	10.00	3.00
S-AR Alex Rodriguez	25.00	7.50
S-BW Bernie Williams	15.00	4.50
S-CD Carlos Delgado	10.00	3.00
S-FT Frank Thomas	15.00	4.50
S-JT Jim Thome	15.00	4.50
S-LW Larry Walker	15.00	4.50
S-MP Mike Piazza	30.00	9.00
S-RP Rafael Palmeiro	15.00	4.50
S-SG Shawn Green	10.00	3.00

2003 Upper Deck Vintage Timeless Teams Bat Quads

Randomly inserted into packs, this is a set featuring four bat pieces from teammates. These cards were issued to a stated print run of 175 serial numbered sets.

	Nm-Mt	Ex-Mt
BLAR Pat Burrell Mike Lieberthal Bobby Abreu Jimmy Rollins	25.00	7.50
CTDJ Eric Chavez Miguel Tejada Jermaine Dye David Justice	25.00	7.50
DEMR J.D. Drew Jim Edmonds Tino Martinez Scott Rolen	40.00	12.00
DGCL Adam Dunn Ken Griffey Jr. Sean Casey Barry Larkin	40.00	12.00
GNBL Shawn Green Hideo Nomo Adrian Beltre Paul Lo Duca	50.00	15.00
GPMS Jason Giambi Jorge Posada Raul Mondesi Alfonso Soriano	40.00	12.00
GWVS Jason Giambi Bernie Williams Robin Ventura Alfonso Soriano	40.00	12.00
HWPZ Todd Helton Larry Walker Juan Pierre Todd Zeile	40.00	12.00
IMBC Ichiro Suzuki Edgar Martinez Bret Boone Mike Cameron	100.00	30.00
JGSW Randy Johnson Luis Gonzalez Curt Schilling Matt Williams	40.00	12.00
JJSF Chipper Jones Andruw Jones Gary Sheffield Rafael Furcal	40.00	12.00
KNKB Ryan Klesko Phil Nevin Mark Kotsay Sean Burroughs	25.00	7.50
MGLJ Greg Maddux Tom Glavine Javy Lopez Chipper Jones	60.00	18.00
OTLK Magglio Ordonez Frank Thomas Carlos Lee Paul Konerko	40.00	12.00
PVAA Mike Piazza Mo Vaughn Roberto Alomar Edgardo Alfonzo	60.00	18.00
RGRP Alex Rodriguez Juan Gonzalez Ivan Rodriguez Rafael Palmeiro	50.00	15.00
RMHN Manny Ramirez Pedro Martinez Shea Hillenbrand Trot Nixon	40.00	12.00
SMAP Sammy Sosa Fred McGriff Moises Alou Corey Patterson	50.00	15.00

2003 Upper Deck Vintage UD Giants

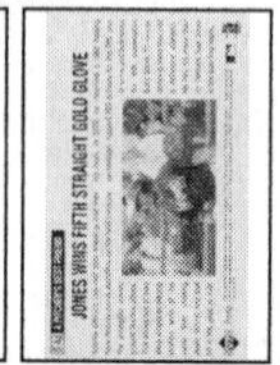

Inserted as a sealed box-topper, these 42 cards, which were designed in the style of the 1964 Topps Giant set, feature most of the leading players in baseball.

	Nm-Mt	Ex-Mt
AD Adam Dunn	3.00	.90
AJ Andruw Jones	3.00	.90
AP Albert Pujols	8.00	2.40
AR Alex Rodriguez	6.00	1.80
BB Barry Bonds	10.00	3.00
BG Brian Giles	3.00	.90
BW Bernie Williams	3.00	.90
CD Carlos Delgado	3.00	.90
CJ Chipper Jones	4.00	1.20
CS Curt Schilling	3.00	.90
FT Frank Thomas	4.00	1.20
GM Greg Maddux	6.00	1.80
GO Juan Gonzalez	4.00	1.20
HN Hideo Nomo	4.00	1.20
IR Ivan Rodriguez	4.00	1.20
IS Ichiro Suzuki	6.00	1.80
JB Jeff Bagwell	3.00	.90
JD J.D. Drew	3.00	.90
JG Jason Giambi	4.00	1.20
JT Jim Thome	4.00	1.20
KG Ken Griffey Jr.	6.00	1.80
KI Kazuhisa Ishii	3.00	.90
KW Kerry Wood	4.00	1.20
LB Lance Berkman	3.00	.90
LG Luis Gonzalez	3.00	.90
MM Mike Mussina	4.00	1.20
MO Magglio Ordonez	3.00	.90
MP Mike Piazza	6.00	1.80
MR Manny Ramirez	3.00	.90
NG Nomar Garciaparra	6.00	1.80
PB Pat Burrell	3.00	.90
PM Pedro Martinez	4.00	1.20
PR Mark Prior	8.00	2.40
RA Roberto Alomar	4.00	1.20
RC Roger Clemens	8.00	2.40
RJ Randy Johnson	4.00	1.20
RP Rafael Palmeiro	3.00	.90
SG Shawn Green	3.00	.90
SR Scott Rolen	3.00	.90
SS Sammy Sosa	6.00	1.80
TH Todd Helton	3.00	.90
VG Vladimir Guerrero	4.00	1.20

2004 Upper Deck Vintage

This 450-card standard set was released in January, 2004. The set was issued in eight card packs with an $2.99 SRP which came 24 packs to a box and 12 boxes to a case. Cards numbered from 1 through 300 were printed in heavier quantity than the rest of the set. In that group of 300 the final three cards feature checklists. Cards numbered 301 through 315 are Play Ball Preview Cards while cards numbered 316 through 325 are World Series Highlight Cards. Cards numbered 326 through 335 were players who were traded during the 2003 season. A few leading 2003 rookies were issued as Short Prints between cards 335 and 350. Those cards were issued in two different tiers which we have notated in our checklist. Similar to the 2003 set, many cards (351-440) were issued with lenticular technology and feature 90 of the majors leading sluggers. The set concludes with 10 cards made in the style of the 19th century Old Judge cards. Those cards were issued in "Old Judge Packs" which were issued as one per box "boxtoppers".

	Nm-Mt	Ex-Mt
COMP.SET w/o SP's (300)	60.00	18.00
COMMON CARD (1-300)	.30	.09
301-315 STATED ODDS 1:5		
COMMON CARD (316-325)	2.00	.60
316-325 STATED ODDS 1:7		
COMMON CARD (326-350)	4.00	1.20
326-350 STATED ODDS 1:5		
COMMON CARD (351-440)	10.00	3.00
351-440 STATED ODDS 1:12		
COMMON CARD (441-450)	4.00	1.20
1 Albert Pujols	1.50	.45
2 Carlos Delgado	.30	.09
3 Todd Helton	.50	.15
4 Nomar Garciaparra	1.25	.35
5 Vladimir Guerrero	.75	.23
6 Alfonso Soriano	.50	.15
7 Alex Rodriguez	1.25	.35
8 Jason Giambi	.75	.23
9 Derek Jeter	2.00	.60
10 Pedro Martinez	.75	.23
11 Ivan Rodriguez	.75	.23
12 Mark Prior	1.50	.45
13 Marquis Grissom	.30	.09
14 Barry Zito	.50	.15
15 Alex Cintron	.30	.09
16 Wade Miller	.30	.09
17 Eric Chavez	.30	.09
18 Matt Clement	.30	.09
19 Orlando Cabrera	.30	.09
20 Odalis Perez	.30	.09
21 Lance Berkman	.30	.09
22 Keith Foulke	.30	.09
23 Shawn Green	.30	.09
24 Byung-Hyun Kim	.30	.09
25 Geoff Jenkins	.30	.09
26 Torii Hunter	.30	.09
27 Richard Hidalgo	.30	.09
28 Edgar Martinez	.50	.15
29 Placido Polanco	.30	.09
30 Brad Lidge	.30	.09
31 Alex Escobar	.30	.09
32 Garret Anderson	.30	.09
33 Larry Walker	.50	.15
34 Ken Griffey Jr.	1.25	.35
35 Junior Spivey	.30	.09
36 Carlos Beltran	.30	.09
37 Bartolo Colon	.30	.09
38 Ichiro Suzuki	1.25	.35
39 Ramon Ortiz	.30	.09
40 Roy Oswalt	.30	.09
41 Mike Piazza	1.25	.35
42 Benito Santiago	.30	.09
43 Mike Mussina	.75	.23
44 Jeff Kent	.30	.09
45 Curt Schilling	.50	.15
46 Adam Dunn	.30	.09
47 Mike Sweeney	.30	.09
48 Chipper Jones	.75	.23
49 Frank Thomas	.75	.23
50 Kerry Wood	.75	.23
51 Rod Beck	.30	.09
52 Brian Giles	.30	.09
53 Hank Blalock	.30	.09
54 Andruw Jones	.30	.09
55 Dmitri Young	.30	.09
56 Juan Pierre	.30	.09
57 Jacque Jones	.30	.09
58 Phil Nevin	.30	.09
59 Rocco Baldelli	.75	.23
60 Greg Maddux	1.25	.35
61 Eric Gagne	.50	.15
62 Tim Hudson	.30	.09
63 Brian Lawrence	.30	.09
64 Sammy Sosa	1.25	.35
65 Corey Koskie	.30	.09
66 Bobby Abreu	.30	.09
67 Preston Wilson	.30	.09
68 Jay Gibbons	.30	.09
69 Dontrelle Willis	.30	.09
70 Richie Sexson	.30	.09
71 Kevin Millwood	.30	.09
72 Randy Johnson	.75	.23
73 Jack Cust	.30	.09
74 Randy Wolf	.30	.09
75 Johan Santana	.30	.09
76 Magglio Ordonez	.30	.09
77 Sean Casey	.30	.09
78 Billy Wagner	.30	.09
79 Javier Vazquez	.30	.09
80 Jorge Posada	.50	.15
81 Jason Schmidt	.30	.09
82 Bret Boone	.30	.09
83 Jeff Bagwell	.50	.15
84 Rickie Weeks	.75	.23
85 Troy Percival	.30	.09
86 Jose Vidro	.30	.09
87 Freddy Garcia	.30	.09
88 Manny Ramirez	.30	.09
89 John Smoltz	.50	.15
90 Moises Alou	.30	.09
91 Ugueth Urbina	.30	.09
92 Bobby Hill	.30	.09
93 Marcus Giles	.30	.09
94 Aramis Ramirez	.30	.09
95 Brad Wilkerson	.30	.09
96 Ray Durham	.30	.09
97 David Wells	.30	.09
98 Paul Lo Duca	.30	.09
99 Danny Graves	.30	.09
100 Jason Kendall	.30	.09
101 Carlos Lee	.30	.09
102 Rafael Furcal	.30	.09
103 Mike Lowell	.30	.09
104 Kevin Brown	.30	.09
105 Vicente Padilla	.30	.09
106 Miguel Tejada	.30	.09
107 Bernie Williams	.50	.15
108 Octavio Dotel	.30	.09
109 Steve Finley	.30	.09
110 Lyle Overbay	.30	.09
111 Delmon Young	.75	.23
112 Bo Hart	.30	.09
113 Jason Lane	.30	.09
114 Matt Roney	.30	.09
115 Brian Roberts	.30	.09
116 Tom Glavine	.50	.15

117 Rich Aurilia .30 .09
118 Adam Kennedy .30 .09
119 Hee Seop Choi .30 .09
120 Trot Nixon .50 .15
121 Gary Sheffield .30 .09
122 Jay Payton .30 .09
123 Brad Penny .30 .09
124 Garrett Atkins .30 .09
125 Aubrey Huff .30 .09
126 Juan Gonzalez .75 .23
127 Jason Jennings .30 .09
128 Luis Gonzalez .30 .09
129 Vinny Castilla .30 .09
130 Esteban Loaiza .30 .09
131 Erubiel Durazo .30 .09
132 Eric Hinske .30 .09
133 Scott Rolen .50 .15
134 Craig Biggio .50 .15
135 Tim Wakefield .30 .09
136 Darin Erstad .30 .09
137 Denny Stark .30 .09
138 Ben Sheets .30 .09
139 Hideo Nomo .75 .23
140 Derrek Lee .30 .09
141 Matt Mantei .30 .09
142 Reggie Sanders .30 .09
143 Jose Guillen .30 .09
144 Joe Mays .30 .09
145 Jimmy Rollins .30 .09
146 Juan Encarnacion .30 .09
147 Joe Crede .30 .09
148 Aaron Guiel .30 .09
149 Mark Mulder .30 .09
150 Travis Lee .30 .09
151 Josh Phelps .30 .09
152 Michael Young .30 .09
153 Paul Konerko .30 .09
154 John Lackey .30 .09
155 Damian Moss .30 .09
156 Javy Lopez .50 .15
157 Joe Borowski .30 .09
158 Jose Cruz Jr. .30 .09
159 Ramon Hernandez .30 .09
160 Raul Ibanez .30 .09
161 Adrian Beltre .30 .09
162 Bobby Higginson .30 .09
163 Jorge Julio .30 .09
164 Miguel Batista .30 .09
165 Luis Castillo .30 .09
166 Aaron Harang .30 .09
167 Ken Harvey .30 .09
168 Rocky Biddle .30 .09
169 Mariano Rivera .50 .15
170 Matt Morris .30 .09
171 Laynce Nix .30 .09
172 Mike Maroth .30 .09
173 Francisco Rodriguez .30 .09
174 Livan Hernandez .30 .09
175 Aaron Heilman .30 .09
176 Nick Johnson .30 .09
177 Woody Williams .30 .09
178 Joe Kennedy .30 .09
179 Jesse Foppert .30 .09
180 Ryan Franklin .30 .09
181 Endy Chavez .30 .09
182 Chin-Hui Tsao .30 .09
183 Todd Walker .30 .09
184 Edgardo Alfonzo .30 .09
185 Edgar Renteria .30 .09
186 Matt LeCroy .30 .09
187 Carl Everett .30 .09
188 Jeff Conine .30 .09
189 Jason Varitek .30 .09
190 Russ Ortiz .30 .09
191 Melvin Mora .30 .09
192 Mark Buehrle .30 .09
193 Bill Mueller .30 .09
194 Miguel Cabrera .75 .23
195 Carlos Zambrano .30 .09
196 Jose Valverde .30 .09
197 Danys Baez .30 .09
198 Mike MacDougal .30 .09
199 Zach Day .30 .09
200 Roy Halladay .30 .09
201 Jerome Williams .30 .09
202 Josh Fogg .30 .09
203 Mark Kotsay .30 .09
204 Pat Burrell .30 .09
205 A.J. Pierzynski .30 .09
206 Fred McGriff .50 .15
207 Brandon Larson .30 .09
208 Robb Quinlan .30 .09
209 David Ortiz .30 .09
210 A.J. Burnett .30 .09
211 John Vander Wal .30 .09
212 Jim Thome .75 .23
213 Matt Kata .30 .09
214 Kip Wells .30 .09
215 Scott Podsednik .75 .23
216 Rickey Henderson .75 .23
217 Travis Hafner .30 .09
218 Tony Batista .30 .09
219 Robert Fick .30 .09
220 Derek Lowe .30 .09
221 Ryan Klesko .30 .09
222 Joe Beimel .30 .09
223 Doug Mientkiewicz .30 .09
224 Angel Berroa .30 .09
225 Adam Eaton .30 .09
226 C.C. Sabathia .30 .09
227 Wilfredo Ledezma .30 .09
228 Jason Johnson .30 .09
229 Ryan Wagner .30 .09
230 Al Leiter .30 .09
231 Joel Pineiro .30 .09
232 Jason Isringhausen .30 .09
233 John Olerud .30 .09
234 Ron Calloway .30 .09
235 Jose Reyes .50 .15
236 J.D. Drew .30 .09
237 Jared Sandberg .30 .09
238 Gil Meche .30 .09
239 Jose Contreras .30 .09
240 Eric Milton .30 .09
241 Jason Phillips .30 .09
242 Luis Ayala .30 .09
243 Bobby Kielty .30 .09
244 Jose Lima .30 .09
245 Brooks Kieschnick .30 .09
246 Xavier Nady .30 .09
247 Danny Haren .30 .09
248 Victor Zambrano .30 .09
249 Kelvim Escobar .30 .09
250 Oliver Perez .30 .09
251 Jamie Moyer .30 .09
252 Orlando Hudson .30 .09
253 Danny Kolb .30 .09
254 Jake Peavy .30 .09
255 Kris Benson .30 .09
256 Roger Clemens 1.50 .45
257 Jim Edmonds .30 .09
258 Rafael Palmeiro .50 .15
259 Jae Weong Seo .30 .09
260 Chase Utley .30 .09
261 Rich Harden .30 .09
262 Mark Teixeira .30 .09
263 Johnny Damon .30 .09
264 Luis Matos .30 .09
265 Shigetoshi Hasegawa .30 .09
266 Alfredo Amezaga .30 .09
267 Tim Worrell .30 .09
268 Kazuhisa Ishii .30 .09
269 Miguel Ojeda .30 .09
270 Kazuhiro Sasaki .30 .09
271 Hideki Matsui 1.25 .35
272 Troy Glaus .50 .15
273 Michael Tucker .30 .09
274 Lew Ford .30 .09
275 Brian Jordan .30 .09
276 David Eckstein .30 .09
277 Robby Hammock .30 .09
278 Corey Patterson .30 .09
279 Wes Helms .30 .09
280 Jermaine Dye .30 .09
281 Cliff Floyd .30 .09
282 Dustan Mohr .30 .09
283 Kevin Mench .30 .09
284 Ellis Burks .30 .09
285 Jerry Hairston Jr. .30 .09
286 Tim Salmon .50 .15
287 Omar Vizquel .50 .15
288 Andy Pettitte .50 .15
289 Guillermo Mota .30 .09
290 Tino Martinez .50 .15
291 Lance Carter .30 .09
292 Francisco Cordero .30 .09
293 Robb Nen .30 .09
294 Mike Cameron .30 .09
295 Jhonny Peralta .30 .09
296 Braden Looper .30 .09
297 Jarrod Washburn .30 .09
298 Mark Prior CL .75 .23
299 Alfonso Soriano CL .30 .09
300 Rocco Baldelli CL .50 .15
301 Pedro Martinez PBP 2.50 .75
302 Mark Prior PBP 5.00 1.50
303 Barry Zito PBP 2.00 .60
304 Roger Clemens PBP 5.00 1.50
305 Randy Johnson PBP 2.50 .75
306 Roy Halladay PBP 2.00 .60
307 Hideo Nomo PBP 2.50 .75
308 Roy Oswalt PBP 2.00 .60
309 Kerry Wood PBP 2.50 .75
310 Dontrelle Willis PBP 2.00 .60
311 Mark Mulder PBP 2.00 .60
312 Brandon Webb PBP 2.00 .60
313 Mike Mussina PBP 2.50 .75
314 Curt Schilling PBP 2.00 .60
315 Tim Hudson PBP 2.00 .60
316 Dontrelle Willis WSH 2.00 .60
317 Juan Pierre WSH 2.00 .60
318 Hideki Matsui WSH 4.00 1.20
319 Andy Pettitte WSH 2.00 .60
320 Mike Mussina WSH 2.50 .75
321 Roger Clemens WSH 5.00 1.50
322 Alex Gonzalez WSH 2.00 .60
323 Brad Penny WSH 2.00 .60
324 Ivan Rodriguez WSH 2.50 .75
325 Josh Beckett WSH 2.00 .60
326 Aaron Boone TR 4.00 1.20
327 Jeff Suppan TR 4.00 1.20
328 Shea Hillenbrand TR 4.00 1.20
329 Jeromy Burnitz TR 4.00 1.20
330 Sidney Ponson TR 4.00 1.20
331 Rondell White TR 4.00 1.20
332 Shannon Stewart TR 4.00 1.20
333 Armando Benitez TR 4.00 1.20
334 Roberto Alomar TR 5.00 1.50
335 Raul Mondesi TR 4.00 1.20
336 Morgan Ensberg SP1 4.00 1.20
337 Milton Bradley SP1 4.00 1.20
338 Brandon Webb SP1 4.00 1.20
339 Marlon Byrd SP1 4.00 1.20
340 Carlos Pena SP1 4.00 1.20
341 Brandon Phillips SP1 4.00 1.20
342 Josh Beckett SP1 4.00 1.20
343 Eric Munson SP1 4.00 1.20
344 Brett Myers SP1 4.00 1.20
345 Aubrey Huff SP1 4.00 1.20
346 Jody Gerut SP2 4.00 1.20
347 Vernon Wells SP2 4.00 1.20
348 Jeff Duncan SP2 4.00 1.20
349 Sean Burroughs SP2 4.00 1.20
350 Jeremy Bonderman SP2 4.00 1.20
351 Hideki Matsui 3D 15.00 4.50
352 Jason Giambi 3D 15.00 4.50
353 Alfonso Soriano 3D 10.00 3.00
354 Derek Jeter 3D 25.00 7.50
355 Aaron Boone 3D 10.00 3.00
356 Jorge Posada 3D 10.00 3.00
357 Bernie Williams 3D 10.00 3.00
358 Manny Ramirez 3D 10.00 3.00
359 Nomar Garciaparra 3D 15.00 4.50
360 Johnny Damon 3D 10.00 3.00
361 Jason Varitek 3D 10.00 3.00
362 Carlos Delgado 3D 10.00 3.00
363 Vernon Wells 3D 10.00 3.00
364 Jay Gibbons 3D 10.00 3.00
365 Tony Batista 3D 10.00 3.00
366 Rocco Baldelli 3D 15.00 4.50
367 Aubrey Huff 3D 10.00 3.00
368 Carlos Beltran 3D 10.00 3.00
369 Mike Sweeney 3D 10.00 3.00
370 Maggio Ordonez 3D 10.00 3.00
371 Frank Thomas 3D 15.00 4.50
372 Carlos Lee 3D 10.00 3.00
373 Roberto Alomar 3D 15.00 4.50
374 Jacque Jones 3D 10.00 3.00
375 Torii Hunter 3D 10.00 3.00
376 Milton Bradley 3D 10.00 3.00
377 Travis Hafner 3D 10.00 3.00
378 Jody Gerut 3D 10.00 3.00
379 Dmitri Young 3D 10.00 3.00
380 Carlos Pena 3D 10.00 3.00
381 Ichiro Suzuki 3D 15.00 4.50
382 Bret Boone 3D 10.00 3.00
383 Edgar Martinez 3D 10.00 3.00
384 Eric Chavez 3D 10.00 3.00
385 Miguel Tejada 3D 10.00 3.00
386 Erubiel Durazo 3D 10.00 3.00
387 Jose Guillen 3D 10.00 3.00
388 Garret Anderson 3D 10.00 3.00
389 Troy Glaus 3D 10.00 3.00
390 Alex Rodriguez 3D 15.00 4.50
391 Rafael Palmeiro 3D 10.00 3.00
392 Hank Blalock 3D 10.00 3.00
393 Mark Teixeira 3D 10.00 3.00
394 Gary Sheffield 3D 10.00 3.00
395 Andruw Jones 3D 10.00 3.00
396 Chipper Jones 3D 15.00 4.50
397 Javy Lopez 3D 10.00 3.00
398 Marcus Giles 3D 10.00 3.00
399 Rafael Furcal 3D 10.00 3.00
400 Jim Thome 3D 15.00 4.50
401 Bobby Abreu 3D 10.00 3.00
402 Pat Burrell 3D 10.00 3.00
403 Mike Lowell 3D 10.00 3.00
404 Ivan Rodriguez 3D 15.00 4.50
405 Derrek Lee 3D 10.00 3.00
406 Miguel Cabrera 3D 15.00 4.50
407 Vladimir Guerrero 3D 15.00 4.50
408 Orlando Cabrera 3D 10.00 3.00
409 Jose Vidro 3D 10.00 3.00
410 Mike Piazza 3D 15.00 4.50
411 Cliff Floyd 3D 10.00 3.00
412 Albert Pujols 3D 20.00 6.00
413 Scott Rolen 3D 10.00 3.00
414 Jim Edmonds 3D 10.00 3.00
415 Edgar Renteria 3D 10.00 3.00
416 Lance Berkman 3D 10.00 3.00
417 Jeff Bagwell 3D 10.00 3.00
418 Jeff Kent 3D 10.00 3.00
419 Richard Hidalgo 3D 10.00 3.00
420 Morgan Ensberg 3D 10.00 3.00
421 Sammy Sosa 3D 15.00 4.50
422 Moises Alou 3D 10.00 3.00
423 Ken Griffey Jr. 3D 15.00 4.50
424 Adam Dunn 3D 10.00 3.00
425 Austin Kearns 3D 10.00 3.00
426 Richie Sexson 3D 10.00 3.00
427 Geoff Jenkins 3D 10.00 3.00
428 Brian Giles 3D 10.00 3.00
429 Reggie Sanders 3D 10.00 3.00
430 Rich Aurilia 3D 10.00 3.00
431 Jose Cruz Jr. 3D 10.00 3.00
432 Shawn Green 3D 10.00 3.00
433 Jeromy Burnitz 3D 10.00 3.00
434 Luis Gonzalez 3D 10.00 3.00
435 Todd Helton 3D 10.00 3.00
436 Preston Wilson 3D 10.00 3.00
437 Larry Walker 3D 10.00 3.00
438 Ryan Klesko 3D 10.00 3.00
439 Phil Nevin 3D 10.00 3.00
440 Sean Burroughs 3D 10.00 3.00
441 Sammy Sosa OJ 8.00 2.40
442 Albert Pujols OJ 10.00 3.00
443 Magglio Ordonez OJ 4.00 1.20
444 Vladimir Guerrero OJ 5.00 1.50
445 Todd Helton OJ 4.00 1.20
446 Jason Giambi OJ 5.00 1.50
447 Ichiro Suzuki OJ 8.00 2.40
448 Alex Rodriguez OJ 8.00 2.40
449 Carlos Delgado OJ 4.00 1.20
450 Manny Ramirez OJ 4.00 1.20

2004 Upper Deck Vintage Black and White

These cards, pictured in black and white, are a complete parallel of the first 350 cards in the Vintage set.

Nm-Mt Ex-Mt
*B/W 1-300: 3X TO 8X BASIC
1-300 STATED ODDS 1:6
*B/W 301-315: .6X TO 1.5X BASIC
301-315 STATED ODDS 1:24
*B/W 316-325: .6X TO 1.5X BASIC
316-325 STATED ODDS 1:24
*B/W 326-350: .4X TO 1X BASIC
326-350 STATED ODDS 1:20

2004 Upper Deck Vintage Black and White Color Variation

Issued at stated odds of one in 48, these skip-numbered cards are a variation to the black and white parallel cards.

Nm-Mt Ex-Mt
*B/W COLOR: 5X TO 12X BASIC

2004 Upper Deck Vintage Old Judge Subset Blue Back

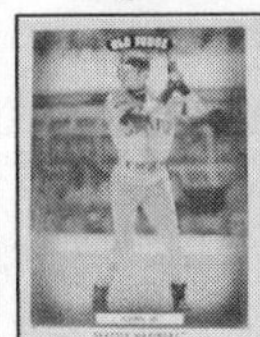
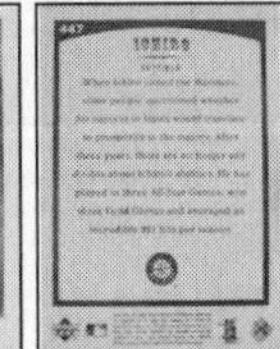

Nm-Mt Ex-Mt
*OJ BLUE BACK 441-450: .6X TO 1.5X BASIC
STATED ODD 1:4 OJ HOBBY PACKS
ONE 3-CARD OJ PACK PER HOBBY BOX

2004 Upper Deck Vintage Old Judge Subset Red Back

Nm-Mt Ex-Mt
*OJ RED BACK 441-450: 1X TO 2.5X BASIC OJ
STATED ODDS 1:12 OJ HOBBY PACKS
ONE 3-CARD OJ PACK PER HOBBY BOX

2004 Upper Deck Vintage Old Judge

Nm-Mt Ex-Mt
DISTRIBUTED IN OLD JUDGE HOBBY PACKS
ONE 3-CARD OJ PACK PER HOBBY BOX
*OJ BLUE BACK 11-30: .6X TO 1.5X BASIC
OJ BLUE BACK ODDS 1:4 OJ HOBBY PACKS
*OJ RED BACK 11-30: 1X TO 2.5X BASIC
OJ RED BACK ODDS 1:12 OJ HOBBY PACKS
11 Randy Johnson 5.00 1.50
12 Pedro Martinez 5.00 1.50
13 Mark Prior 10.00 3.00
14 Barry Zito 4.00 1.20
15 Roy Oswalt 4.00 1.20
16 Roy Halladay 4.00 1.20
17 Curt Schilling 4.00 1.20
18 Mike Mussina 5.00 1.50
19 Kevin Brown 4.00 1.20
20 Roger Clemens 10.00 3.00
21 Eric Gagne 4.00 1.20
22 Mariano Rivera 4.00 1.20
23 Mike Piazza 8.00 2.40
24 Jorge Posada 4.00 1.20
25 Jeff Kent 4.00 1.20
26 Alfonso Soriano 4.00 1.20
27 Scott Rolen 4.00 1.20
28 Eric Chavez 4.00 1.20
29 Edgar Renteria 4.00 1.20
30 Hideki Matsui 8.00 2.40

2004 Upper Deck Vintage Stellar Signatures

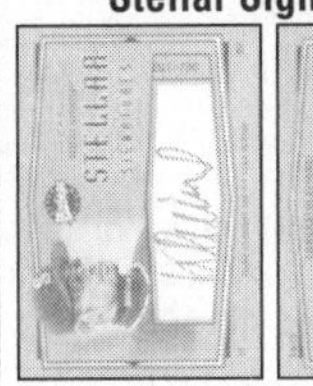
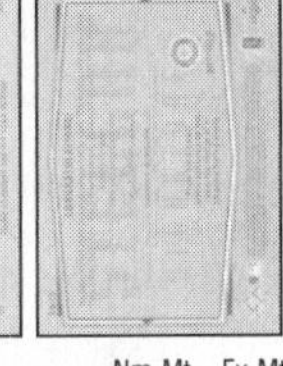

Nm-Mt Ex-Mt
STATED ODDS 1:600
STATED PRINT RUN 150 SERIAL #'d SETS
EXCHANGE DEADLINE 01/27/07
AR Alex Rodriguez EXCH 120.00 36.00
BZ Barry Zito 40.00 12.00
CY Carl Yastrzemski 60.00 18.00
HM Hideki Matsui 300.00 90.00
IS Ichiro Suzuki 300.00 90.00
MP Mike Piazza 200.00 60.00
TS Tom Seaver 40.00 12.00

2004 Upper Deck Vintage Stellar Stat Men Jerseys

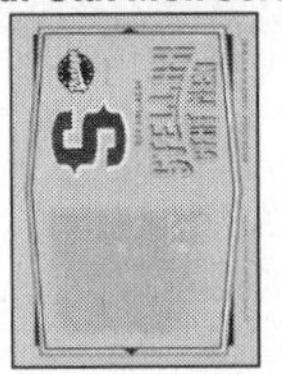

Nm-Mt Ex-Mt
STATED ODDS 1:24
SP PRINT RUNS PROVIDED BY UPPER DECK
SP'S ARE NOT SERIAL-NUMBERED
1 Jose Reyes 10.00 3.00
2 Bo Hart 8.00 2.40
3 Hideki Matsui Pants 25.00 7.50
4 Dontrelle Willis 8.00 2.40
5 Rocco Baldelli 10.00 3.00
6 Ichiro Suzuki 30.00 9.00
7 Mike Lowell 8.00 2.40
8 Derek Jeter 30.00 9.00
9 Ken Griffey Jr. 15.00 4.50
10 Sammy Sosa 15.00 4.50
11 Kerry Wood 10.00 3.00
12 Chipper Jones 10.00 3.00
13 Alfonso Soriano 10.00 3.00
14 Khalil Greene 8.00 2.40
15 Jim Thome 10.00 3.00
16 Rafael Furcal 8.00 2.40
17 Andrew Brown 8.00 2.40
18 Mark Prior 15.00 4.50
19 Barry Zito 10.00 3.00
20 Al Leiter 8.00 2.40
21 Carlos Delgado 8.00 2.40
22 Pedro Martinez 10.00 3.00
23 Alex Rodriguez 15.00 4.50
24 Lance Berkman 8.00 2.40
25 Jeff Bagwell 10.00 3.00
26 Bernie Williams 10.00 3.00
27 Hideo Nomo 15.00 4.50
28 Randy Johnson 10.00 3.00
29 Curt Schilling 10.00 3.00
30 Mike Piazza 15.00 4.50
31 Albert Pujols 15.00 4.50
32 Joe DiMaggio Pants SP/300
33 Ted Williams Pants SP/300 80.00 24.00
34 Mickey Mantle Pants SP/300 150.00 45.00
35 Mike Mussina 10.00 3.00
36 Rich Harden 8.00 2.40
37 Roy Oswalt 8.00 2.40
38 Torii Hunter 8.00 2.40
39 Jorge Posada 10.00 3.00
40 Troy Glaus 10.00 3.00
41 Manny Ramirez 8.00 2.40
42 Roy Halladay 8.00 2.40

2004 Upper Deck Vintage Timeless Teams Quad Bats

Nm-Mt Ex-Mt
STATED ODDS 1:400
STATED PRINT RUN 175 SERIAL #'d SETS
CARD NUMBER 3 DOES NOT EXIST
TT1 Alfonso Soriano 120.00 36.00
Derek Jeter
Hideki Matsui
Jason Giambi
TT2 Luis Gonzalez 40.00 12.00
Curt Schilling
Randy Johnson
Steve Finley
TT4 Manny Ramirez 50.00 15.00
Nomar Garciaparra
Trot Nixon
Johnny Damon
TT5 Alex Rodriguez 40.00 12.00
Rafael Palmeiro
Mark Teixeira
Hank Blalock
TT6 Magglio Ordonez 40.00 12.00
Frank Thomas
Roberto Alomar
Carl Everett
TT7 Jacque Jones 25.00 7.50
Torii Hunter
Doug Mientkiewicz
Shannon Stewart
TT8 Jim Edmonds 50.00 15.00
Scott Rolen
J.D. Drew
Albert Pujols
TT9 Ichiro Suzuki 80.00 24.00
John Olerud
Bret Boone
Mike Cameron
TT10 Jeff Kent 40.00 12.00
Jeff Bagwell
Craig Biggio
Lance Berkman
TT11 Troy Glaus 40.00 12.00
Darin Erstad
Garret Anderson
Tim Salmon
TT12 Bernie Williams 80.00 24.00
Jorge Posada
Hideki Matsui
Alfonso Soriano
TT13 Michael Tucker 25.00 7.50
Carlos Beltran
Mike Sweeney
Brent Mayne
TT14 Jim Thome 40.00 12.00
Marlon Byrd
Mike Lieberthal
Bobby Abreu
TT15 Miguel Cabrera 40.00 12.00
Ivan Rodriguez
Juan Encarnacion
Mike Lowell
TT16 Sammy Sosa 50.00 15.00
Corey Patterson
Moises Alou
Kerry Wood
TT17 Jose Cruz Jr. 25.00 7.50
Edgardo Alfonzo
Rich Aurilia
Andres Galarraga
TT18 Alfonso Soriano 120.00 36.00
Derek Jeter
Hideki Matsui
Bernie Williams

2002 Upper Deck World Series Heroes

This 180 card set was released in September, 2002. The five card packs were issued in 24 pack boxes which came 20 boxes to a case with an $3 SRP per pack. Cards numbered 1-90 featured a mix of active and retired players who had played in the World Series. Cards numbered 91 through 135 feature Rookie Cards while cards numbered 136 through 180 feature active players who had yet to participate in a World Series. Cards numbered 91 through 180 were all issued at a stated rate of one in 10.

	Nm-Mt	Ex-Mt
COMP.SET w/o SP's (90)	20.00	6.00
COMMON CARD (1-90)	.30	.09
COMMON CARD (91-135)	3.00	.90
COMMON CARD (136-180)	4.00	1.20
1 Catfish Hunter	.50	.15
2 Jimmie Foxx	.75	.23
3 Mark McGwire	2.00	.60
4 Rollie Fingers	.30	.09
5 Rickey Henderson	.75	.23
6 Joe Carter	.30	.09
7 John Olerud	.30	.09
8 Roberto Alomar	.75	.23
9 Pat Hentgen	.30	.09
10 Devon White	.30	.09
11 Eddie Mathews	.75	.23
12 Greg Maddux	1.25	.35
13 Chipper Jones	.75	.23
14 Tom Glavine	.50	.15
15 Andruw Jones	.30	.09
16 Dave Justice	.30	.09
17 Fred McGriff	.50	.15
18 Ryan Klesko	.30	.09
19 John Smoltz	.50	.15
20 Javy Lopez	.30	.09
21 Marquis Grissom	.30	.09
22 Robin Yount	1.25	.35
23 Ozzie Smith	1.25	.35
24 Frankie Frisch	.50	.15
25 Stan Musial	1.25	.35
26 Randy Johnson	.75	.23
27 Luis Gonzalez	.30	.09
28 Matt Williams	.30	.09
29 Steve Finley	.30	.09
30 Sandy Koufax	2.00	.60
31 Duke Snider	.50	.15
32 Kirk Gibson	.30	.09
33 Steve Garvey	.30	.09
34 Jackie Robinson	1.00	.30
35 Don Drysdale	.75	.23
36 Juan Marichal	.30	.09
37 Mel Ott	.75	.23
38 Orlando Cepeda	.30	.09
39 Jim Thome	.75	.23
40 Manny Ramirez	.30	.09
41 Omar Vizquel	.30	.09
42 Lou Boudreau	.30	.09
43 Gary Sheffield	.30	.09
44 Moises Alou	.30	.09
45 Livan Hernandez	.30	.09
46 Edgar Renteria	.30	.09
47 Al Leiter	.30	.09
48 Tom Seaver	.50	.15
49 Gary Carter	.50	.15
50 Mike Piazza	1.25	.35
51 Nolan Ryan	2.00	.60
52 Robin Ventura	.30	.09
53 Mike Hampton	.30	.09
54 Jesse Orosco	.30	.09
55 Cal Ripken	2.50	.75
56 Brooks Robinson	.75	.23
57 Tony Gwynn	1.00	.30
58 Kevin Brown	.30	.09
59 Curt Schilling	.50	.15
60 Cy Young	.75	.23
61 Honus Wagner	1.25	.35
62 Willie Stargell	.50	.15
63 Wade Boggs	.50	.15
64 Carlton Fisk	.50	.15
65 Ken Griffey Sr.	.30	.09
66 Joe Morgan	.30	.09
67 Johnny Bench	.75	.23
68 Barry Larkin	.75	.23
69 Jose Rijo	.30	.09
70 Ty Cobb	1.25	.35
71 Kirby Puckett	.75	.23
72 Chuck Knoblauch	.30	.09
73 Harmon Killebrew	.75	.23
74 Mickey Mantle	3.00	.90
75 Joe DiMaggio	1.50	.45
76 Don Larsen	.50	.15
77 Thurman Munson	1.00	.30
78 Roger Maris	1.25	.35
79 Phil Rizzuto	.50	.15
80 Babe Ruth	2.50	.75
81 Lou Gehrig	1.50	.45
82 Billy Martin	.50	.15
83 Derek Jeter	2.00	.60
84 Roger Clemens	1.50	.45
85 Tino Martinez	.50	.15
86 Bernie Williams	.50	.15
87 Mariano Rivera	.50	.15
88 Andy Pettitte	.50	.15
89 David Wells	.30	.09
90 Jorge Posada	.50	.15
91 Rodrigo Rosario PH RC	3.00	.90
92 Brandon Puffer PH RC	3.00	.90
93 Franklyn German PH RC	3.00	.90
94 Reed Johnson PH RC	5.00	1.50
95 Chris Baker PH RC	3.00	.90
96 John Ennis PH RC	3.00	.90
97 Luis Martinez PH RC	3.00	.90
98 Takaki Nomura PH RC	3.00	.90
99 So Taguchi PH RC	5.00	1.50
100 Michael Crudale PH RC	3.00	.90
101 Francis Beltran PH RC	3.00	.90
102 Steve Kent PH RC	3.00	.90
103 Jorge Sosa PH RC	3.00	.90
104 Felix Escalona PH RC	3.00	.90
105 Jose Valverde PH RC	5.00	1.50
106 Doug Devore PH RC	3.00	.90
107 Kazuhisa Ishii PH RC	6.00	1.80
108 Victor Alvarez PH RC	3.00	.90
109 Eric Good PH RC	3.00	.90
110 Jorge Nunez PH RC	3.00	.90
111 Ron Calloway PH RC	3.00	.90
112 Nelson Castro PH RC	3.00	.90
113 Matt Thornton PH RC	3.00	.90
114 Luis Ugueto PH RC	3.00	.90
115 Hansel Izquierdo PH RC	3.00	.90
116 Jaime Cerda PH RC	3.00	.90
117 Mark Corey PH RC	3.00	.90
118 Tyler Yates PH RC	5.00	1.50
119 Satoru Komiyama PH RC	3.00	.90
120 Steve Bechler PH RC	3.00	.90
121 Ben Howard PH RC	3.00	.90
122 Anderson Machado PH RC	3.00	.90
123 Jorge Padilla PH RC	3.00	.90
124 Eric Junge PH RC	3.00	.90
125 Adrian Burnside PH RC	3.00	.90
126 Mike Gonzalez PH RC	3.00	.90
127 Anastacio Martinez PH RC	3.00	.90
128 Josh Hancock PH RC	3.00	.90
129 Rene Reyes PH RC	3.00	.90
130 Aaron Cook PH RC	3.00	.90
131 Cam Esslinger PH RC	3.00	.90
132 Juan Brito PH RC	3.00	.90
133 Miguel Asencio PH RC	3.00	.90
134 Kevin Frederick PH RC	3.00	.90
135 Edwin Almonte PH RC	3.00	.90
136 Troy Glaus FWS	4.00	1.20
137 Darin Erstad FWS	4.00	1.20
138 Jeff Bagwell FWS	4.00	1.20
139 Lance Berkman FWS	4.00	1.20
140 Tim Hudson FWS	4.00	1.20
141 Eric Chavez FWS	4.00	1.20
142 Barry Zito FWS	4.00	1.20
143 Carlos Delgado FWS	4.00	1.20
144 Richie Sexson FWS	4.00	1.20
145 Albert Pujols FWS	12.00	3.60
146 Sammy Sosa FWS	10.00	3.00
147 Kerry Wood FWS	6.00	1.80
148 Greg Vaughn FWS	4.00	1.20
149 Shawn Green FWS	4.00	1.20
150 Vladimir Guerrero FWS	6.00	1.80
151 Barry Bonds FWS	15.00	4.50
152 C.C. Sabathia FWS	4.00	1.20
153 Ichiro Suzuki FWS	10.00	3.00
154 Freddy Garcia FWS	4.00	1.20
155 Edgar Martinez FWS	4.00	1.20
156 Josh Beckett FWS	4.00	1.20
157 Cliff Floyd FWS	4.00	1.20
158 Mo Vaughn FWS	4.00	1.20
159 Jeromy Burnitz FWS	4.00	1.20
160 Sean Burroughs FWS	4.00	1.20
161 Phil Nevin FWS	4.00	1.20
162 Scott Rolen FWS	4.00	1.20
163 Brian Giles FWS	4.00	1.20
164 Alex Rodriguez FWS	10.00	3.00
165 Ivan Rodriguez FWS	6.00	1.80
166 Juan Gonzalez FWS	6.00	1.80
167 Rafael Palmeiro FWS	4.00	1.20
168 Nomar Garciaparra FWS	10.00	3.00
169 Pedro Martinez FWS	6.00	1.80
170 Ken Griffey Jr. FWS	10.00	3.00
171 Adam Dunn FWS	4.00	1.20
172 Todd Helton FWS	4.00	1.20
173 Mike Sweeney FWS	4.00	1.20
174 Carlos Beltran FWS	4.00	1.20
175 Dmitri Young FWS	4.00	1.20
176 Doug Mientkiewicz FWS	4.00	1.20
177 Torii Hunter FWS	4.00	1.20
178 Frank Thomas FWS	6.00	1.80
179 Maggio Ordonez FWS	4.00	1.20
180 Jason Giambi FWS	6.00	1.80

2002 Upper Deck World Series Heroes Classic Match-Ups Memorabilia

Issued at a stated rate of one in 24, these cards feature two player along with a piece of memorabilia from the player listed first in our checklist. A few cards were produced in lesser quantity and we have notated the information next to their name in our checklist.

	Nm-Mt	Ex-Mt
MU Mike Piazza Jersey Roger Clemens	15.00	4.50
MUa Andy Pettitte Pants Mike Piazza	15.00	4.50
MUb Al Leiter Jersey Derek Jeter	10.00	3.00
MUc Robin Ventura Jersey Roger Clemens	10.00	3.00
MUd Edgardo Alfonzo Jersey Mariano Rivera	10.00	3.00
MUe John Franco Jersey Derek Jeter	10.00	3.00
MU1 Mariano Rivera Jersey Luis Gonzalez	15.00	4.50
MU1a Paul O'Neill Pants Curt Schilling	15.00	4.50
MU1b Bernie Williams Randy Johnson	10.00	3.00
MU1c David Justice Jersey Curt Schilling	10.00	3.00
MU1d Randy Johnson Jersey Bernie Williams	15.00	4.50
MU1e Curt Schilling Jersey Tino Martinez	15.00	4.50
MU1f Roger Clemens Jersey Luis Gonzalez	20.00	6.00
MU1g Paul O'Neill Pants Byung-Hyun Kim	15.00	4.50
MU1h Luis Gonzalez Jersey Mariano Rivera SP/97	15.00	4.50
MU3 Honus Wagner Pants Cy Young	150.00	45.00
MU9 Ty Cobb Pants Honus Wagner SP	200.00	60.00
MU30 Jimmie Foxx Pants Frankie Frisch	50.00	15.00
MU36 Joe DiMaggio Pants Mel Ott SP	120.00	36.00
MU49 Duke Snider Jersey Joe DiMaggio	25.00	7.50
MU53 Jackie Robinson Pants Billy Martin	50.00	15.00
MU55 Mickey Mantle Pants Jackie Robinson	150.00	45.00
MU56 Don Larsen Pants Duke Snider	25.00	7.50
MU56a Don Larsen Pants Jackie Robinson	25.00	7.50
MU57 Eddie Mathews Jersey Yogi Berra	25.00	7.50
MU58 Yogi Berra Jersey Eddie Mathews	25.00	7.50
MU62 Roger Maris Pants Juan Marichal	60.00	18.00
MU63 Sandy Koufax Jersey Mickey Mantle	100.00	30.00
MU66 Don Drysdale Jersey Brooks Robinson SP	50.00	15.00
MU69 Nolan Ryan Jersey Brooks Robinson	80.00	24.00
MU72 Joe Morgan Jersey Catfish Hunter	10.00	3.00
MU72a Rollie Fingers Jersey Johnny Bench	10.00	3.00
MU73 Tom Seaver Pants Catfish Hunter	15.00	4.50
MU74 Catfish Hunter Jersey Steve Garvey	15.00	4.50
MU74a Davey Lopes Jersey Catfish Hunter	10.00	3.00
MU76 Ken Griffey Sr. Jersey Thurman Munson	10.00	3.00
MU76a Thurman Munson Pants Johnny Bench	25.00	7.50
MU78 Thurman Munson Pants Steve Garvey	25.00	7.50
MU78a Bill Russell Jersey Thurman Munson	10.00	3.00
MU81 Steve Garvey Jersey Dave Winfield	10.00	3.00
MU82 Robin Yount Jersey Ozzie Smith	15.00	4.50
MU83 Cal Ripken Pants Joe Morgan	30.00	9.00
MU84 Jack Morris Jersey Tony Gwynn	10.00	3.00
MU86 Jesse Orosco Jersey Roger Clemens	10.00	3.00
MU87 Ozzie Smith Jersey Kirby Puckett	15.00	4.50
MU88 Mark McGwire Jersey Kirk Gibson SP	100.00	30.00
MU90 Barry Larkin Jersey Mark McGwire SP	20.00	6.00
MU91 Tom Glavine Jersey Kirby Puckett	15.00	4.50
MU93 Joe Carter Jersey Curt Schilling	10.00	3.00
MU95 Dennis Martinez Jersey David Justice	10.00	3.00
MU95a Kenny Lofton Jersey John Smoltz	15.00	4.50
MU96 Andruw Jones Jersey Andy Pettitte	10.00	3.00
MU96a Tim Raines Pants Tom Glavine	10.00	3.00
MU96b Kenny Rogers Jersey Chipper Jones	10.00	3.00
MU97 Jim Thome Jersey Kevin Brown	15.00	4.50
MU98 Tony Gwynn Pants Bernie Williams	15.00	4.50
MU98a Trevor Hoffman Jersey Bernie Williams SP	15.00	4.50
MU99 Jorge Posada Jersey Greg Maddux	15.00	4.50
MU99a Greg Maddux Jersey Derek Jeter	15.00	4.50
MU99b Paul O'Neill Pants John Smoltz	15.00	4.50
MU99c Chipper Jones Jersey Mariano Rivera	15.00	4.50

2002 Upper Deck World Series Heroes Patch Collection

Inserted one per jumbo pack, these 98 "oversized" cards feature patches from each of the previously played World Series. These cards were issued to a stated print run of 298 sets. Exchange cards for a randomly selected patch were seeded into retail packs at a rate of 1:24. The deadline for this redemption was May 17th, 2005.

	Nm-Mt	Ex-Mt
COMMON PATCH	20.00	6.00
WS3 1903 World Series	25.00	7.50
WS12 1912 World Series	25.00	7.50
WS18 1918 World Series	25.00	7.50
WS19 1919 World Series	30.00	9.00
WS27 1927 World Series	30.00	9.00
WS32 1932 World Series	25.00	7.50
WS34 1934 World Series	25.00	7.50
WS55 1955 World Series	40.00	12.00
WS56 1956 World Series	25.00	7.50
WS60 1960 World Series	25.00	7.50
WS61 1961 World Series	40.00	12.00
WS69 1969 World Series	40.00	12.00
WS75 1975 World Series	30.00	9.00
WS77 1977 World Series	25.00	7.50
WS88 1988 World Series	25.00	7.50
WS96 1996 World Series	25.00	7.50
WS2000 2000 World Series	25.00	7.50
NNO Random Patch EXCH	20.00	6.00

2002 Upper Deck World Series Heroes Patch Collection Signatures

Inserted at a stated rate of one in 24 jumbo packs, these 16 cards feature player's

signatures on a Patch Card.

	Nm-Mt	Ex-Mt
WS55 Duke Snider	120.00	36.00
WS56 Don Larsen	60.00	18.00
WS65 Sandy Koufax	250.00	75.00
WS69 Nolan Ryan	200.00	60.00
WS70 Brooks Robinson	80.00	24.00
WS73 Tom Seaver	60.00	18.00
WS74 Rollie Fingers	40.00	12.00
WS75 Carlton Fisk	120.00	36.00
WS76 Joe Morgan	40.00	12.00
WS81 Steve Garvey	60.00	18.00
WS82 Ozzie Smith	100.00	30.00
WS83 Cal Ripken	250.00	75.00
WS89 Mark McGwire	300.00	90.00
WS91 Kirby Puckett	80.00	24.00
WS93 Joe Carter	40.00	12.00
WS99 Roger Clemens	100.00	30.00

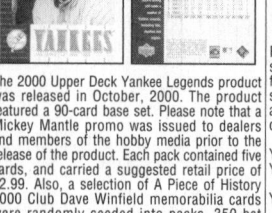

2003 Upper Deck Yankees 100th Anniversary

This 30-card set featuring many of the great New York Yankees of the past and present was issued in a special tin with an $19.99 SRP. The first 26 cards featured players from past World Champion teams while cards number 27 through 29 feature key moments from the 2003 season.

	MINT	NRMT
COMP.FACT SET (30)	20.00	9.00
DISTRIBUTED IN TIN FACTORY SET...		
1 Babe Ruth 23	3.00	1.35
2 Tony Lazzeri 27	.40	.18
3 Lou Gehrig 28	2.50	1.10
4 Lou Gehrig 32	2.50	1.10
5 Red Rolfe 36	.40	.18
6 Lou Gehrig 37	2.50	1.10
7 Bill Dickey 38	.60	.25
8 Joe DiMaggio 39	2.50	1.10
9 Charlie Keller 41	.40	.18
10 Frank Crosetti 43	.40	.18
11 Phil Rizzuto 47	.60	.25
12 Joe DiMaggio 49	2.50	1.10
13 Joe DiMaggio 50	2.50	1.10
14 Phil Rizzuto 51	.60	.25
15 Mickey Mantle 52	4.00	1.80
16 Yogi Berra 53	1.00	.45
17 Yogi Berra 56	1.00	.45
18 Mickey Mantle 58	4.00	1.80
19 Whitey Ford 61	.60	.25
20 Mickey Mantle 62	4.00	1.80
21 Thurman Munson 77	1.25	.55
22 Thurman Munson 78	1.25	.55
23 Bernie Williams 96	.60	.25
24 Jorge Posada 98	.60	.25
25 Mariano Rivera 99	.60	.25
26 Derek Jeter 00	2.50	1.10
27 Hideki Matsui RH 03 HR	5.00	2.20
28 Hideki Matsui RH 03 AS	5.00	2.20
29 Roger Clemens 300th Win	2.00	.90
30 Yankee Stadium CL	.40	.18

2000 Upper Deck Yankees Legends

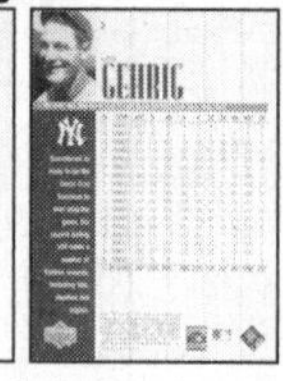

The 2000 Upper Deck Yankee Legends product was released in October, 2000. The product featured a 90-card base set. Please note that a Mickey Mantle promo was issued to dealers and members of the hobby media prior to the release of the product. Each pack contained five cards, and carried a suggested retail price of $2.99. Also, a selection of A Piece of History 3000 Club Dave Winfield memorabilia cards were randomly seeded into packs. 350 bat cards, 350 jersey cards, 100 hand-numbered combination bat-jersey cards and thrity-one autographed, hand-numbered, combination bat-jersey cards were produced. Pricing for these memorabilia cards can be referenced under 2000 Upper Deck A Piece of History 3000 Club.

	Nm-Mt	Ex-Mt
COMPLETE SET (90)	25.00	7.50
1 Babe Ruth	3.00	.90
2 Mickey Mantle	4.00	1.20
3 Lou Gehrig	2.00	.60
4 Joe DiMaggio	2.00	.60
5 Yogi Berra	1.00	.30
6 Don Mattingly	2.50	.75
7 Reggie Jackson	.60	.18
8 Dave Winfield	.40	.12
9 Bill Skowron	.40	.12
10 Willie Randolph	.40	.12
11 Phil Rizzuto	1.00	.30
12 Tony Kubek	.60	.18
13 Thurman Munson	1.50	.45
14 Roger Maris	1.50	.45
15 Billy Martin	1.00	.30
16 Elston Howard	.60	.18
17 Graig Nettles	.40	.12
18 Whitey Ford	.60	.18
19 Earle Combs	.40	.12
20 Tony Lazzeri	.40	.12
21 Bob Meusel	.40	.12
22 Joe Gordon	.40	.12
23 Jerry Coleman	.40	.12
24 Joe Torre	1.00	.30
25 Bucky Dent	.40	.12
26 Don Larsen	.60	.18
27 Bobby Richardson	.40	.12
28 Ron Guidry	.40	.12
29 Bobby Murcer	.40	.12
30 Tommy Henrich	.40	.12
31 Hank Bauer	.40	.12
32 Joe Pepitone	.40	.12
33 Clete Boyer	.40	.12
34 Chris Chambliss	.40	.12
35 Tommy John	.40	.12
36 Goose Gossage	.40	.12
37 Red Ruffing	.40	.12
38 Charlie Keller	.40	.12
39 Billy Gardner	.40	.12
40 Hector Lopez	.40	.12
41 Cliff Johnson	.40	.12
42 Oscar Gamble	.40	.12
43 Allie Reynolds	.40	.12
44 Mickey Rivers	.40	.12
45 Bill Dickey	.60	.18
46 Dave Righetti	.40	.12
47 Mel Stottlemyre	.40	.12
48 Waite Hoyt	.40	.12
49 Lefty Gomez	.60	.18
50 Wade Boggs	.60	.18
51 Billy Martin MN	.60	.18
52 Babe Ruth MN	1.50	.45
53 Lou Gehrig MN	1.00	.30
54 Joe DiMaggio MN	1.00	.30
55 Mickey Mantle MN	2.00	.60
56 Yogi Berra MN	.60	.18
57 Bill Dickey MN	.40	.12
58 Roger Maris MN	1.00	.30
59 Phil Rizzuto MN	.60	.18
60 Thurman Munson MN	1.00	.30
61 Whitey Ford MN	.40	.12
62 Don Mattingly MN	1.25	.35
63 Elston Howard MN	.40	.12
64 Casey Stengel MN	.60	.18
65 Reggie Jackson MN	.40	.12
66 Babe Ruth '23 TCY	1.50	.45
67 Lou Gehrig '27 TCY	1.00	.30
68 Tony Lazzeri '28 TCY	.40	.12
69 Babe Ruth '32 TCY	1.50	.45
70 Lou Gehrig '36 TCY	1.00	.30
71 Lefty Gomez '37 TCY	.60	.18
72 Bill Dickey '38 TCY	.40	.12
73 T.Henrich '39 TCY	.40	.12
74 Joe DiMaggio '41 TCY	1.00	.30
75 Spud Chandler '43 TCY	.40	.12
76 T.Henrich '47 TCY	.40	.12
77 Phil Rizzuto '49 TCY	.60	.18
78 Whitey Ford '50 TCY	.40	.12
79 Yogi Berra '51 TCY	.60	.18
80 Casey Stengel '52 TCY	.60	.18
81 Billy Martin '53 TCY	.60	.18
82 Don Larsen '56 TCY	.40	.12
83 Elston Howard '58 TCY	.60	.18
84 Roger Maris '61 TCY	1.00	.30
85 Mickey Mantle '62 TCY	2.00	.60
86 R.Jackson '77 TCY	.40	.12
87 Bucky Dent '78 TCY	.40	.12
88 Wade Boggs '96 TCY	.40	.12
89 Joe Torre '98 TCY	.60	.18
90 Joe Torre '99 TCY	.60	.18
NNO M.Mantle Promo	3.00	.90

2000 Upper Deck Yankees Legends DiMaggio Memorabilia

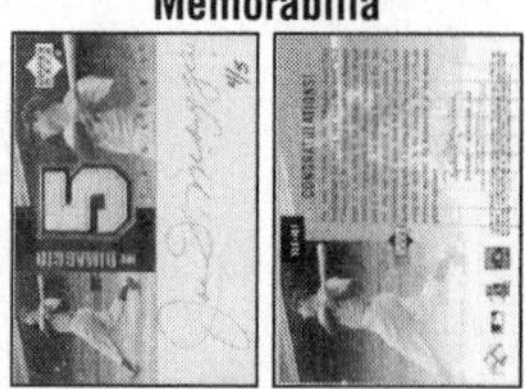

Randomly inserted into packs, this three-card set features game-used memorabilia cards from Yankee great Joe DiMaggio. Cards in the set include game-used bat, bat-cut signature, and a bat card numbered to 56. Card backs carry a "YLG" prefix.

	Nm-Mt	Ex-Mt
YLBJD Joe DiMaggio Bat	150.00	45.00
YLCJD1 Joe DiMaggio Bat-Cut AU/5		
YLGJD Joe DiMaggio Gold Bat/56	250.00	75.00

2000 Upper Deck Yankees Legends Golden Years

Randomly inserted into packs at one in 11, this 10-card insert set features players that played for the Yankees during their golden years. Card backs carry a "GY" prefix.

	Nm-Mt	Ex-Mt
COMPLETE SET (10)	25.00	7.50
GY1 Joe DiMaggio	5.00	1.50
GY2 Phil Rizzuto	2.50	.75
GY3 Yogi Berra	2.50	.75
GY4 Billy Martin	2.50	.75
GY5 Whitey Ford	1.50	.45
GY6 Roger Maris	4.00	1.20
GY7 Mickey Mantle	10.00	3.00
GY8 Elston Howard	1.50	.45
GY9 Tommy Henrich	1.00	.30
GY10 Joe Gordon	1.00	.30

2000 Upper Deck Yankees Legends Legendary Lumber

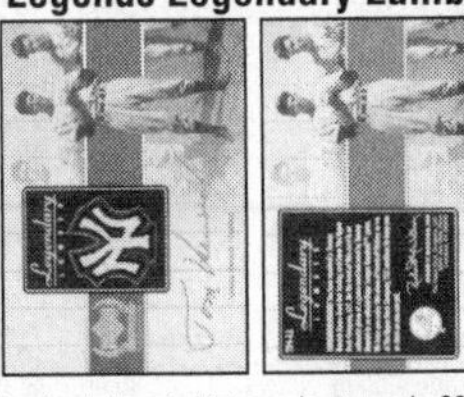

Randomly inserted into packs at one in 23, this 30-card insert set features game-used bat cards from Yankee greats. Card backs carry a "LL" suffix. Please note that the hologram on the back of these cards is silver and the Bat Chip features a wood "NY"..

	Nm-Mt	Ex-Mt
BD-LL Bucky Dent	10.00	3.00
BG-LL Billy Gardner	10.00	3.00
BM-LL Bobby Murcer	25.00	7.50
BR-LL Babe Ruth	200.00	60.00
CB-LL Clete Boyer	10.00	3.00
CC-LL Chris Chambliss	10.00	3.00
CJ-LL Cliff Johnson	10.00	3.00
CK-LL Charlie Keller	10.00	3.00
DM-LL Don Mattingly	40.00	12.00
DW-LL Dave Winfield	10.00	3.00
EH-LL Elston Howard	10.00	3.00
GN-LL Graig Nettles	10.00	3.00
HB-LL Hank Bauer	10.00	3.00
HL-LL Hector Lopez	10.00	3.00
JC-LL Joe Collins	10.00	3.00
JP-LL Joe Pepitone	10.00	3.00
MM-LL Mickey Mantle	200.00	60.00
MR-LL Mickey Rivers	10.00	3.00
MS-LL Moose Skowron	10.00	3.00
OG-LL Oscar Gamble	10.00	3.00
PB-LL Paul Blair	10.00	3.00
RH-LL Ralph Houk	10.00	3.00
RJ-LL Reggie Jackson	15.00	4.50
RM-LL Roger Maris	80.00	24.00
TH-LL Tommy Henrich	10.00	3.00
TJ-LL Tommy John	10.00	3.00
TK-LL Tony Kubek	15.00	4.50
TM-LL Thurman Munson	50.00	15.00
WR-LL Willie Randolph	10.00	3.00
YB-LL Yogi Berra	25.00	7.50

2000 Upper Deck Yankees Legends Legendary Lumber Signature Cut

Randomly inserted into packs, this six card insert features cut-signatures from some of the Yankee's greatest players of all time. Card backs carry a "LC" suffix.

	Nm-Mt	Ex-Mt
BM-LC Billy Martin/1		
BR-LC Babe Ruth/3		
MM-LC Mickey Mantle/7		
RM-LC Roger Maris/9		
TM-LC Thurman Munson/15		

2000 Upper Deck Yankees Legends Legendary Pinstripes

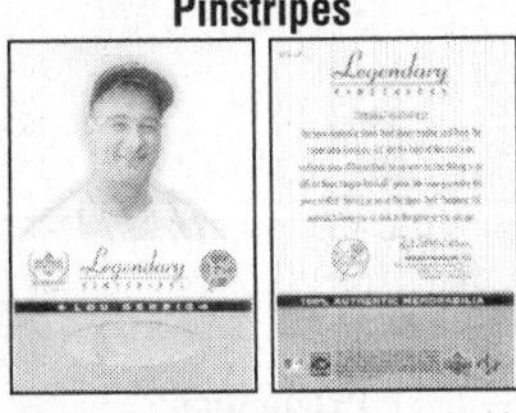

Randomly inserted into packs at one in 144, this 20-card insert set features game-used jersey cards from Yankee greats. Card backs carry a "LP" suffix.

	Nm-Mt	Ex-Mt
AR-LP Allie Reynolds	25.00	7.50
BD-LP Bucky Dent	15.00	4.50
BM-LP Billy Martin	40.00	12.00
BR-LP Bobby Richardson	15.00	4.50
DM-LP Don Mattingly	60.00	18.00
DW-LP Dave Winfield	15.00	4.50
EH-LP Elston Howard	25.00	7.50
GG-LP Goose Gossage	15.00	4.50
GM-LP Gil McDougald	15.00	4.50
HL-LP Hector Lopez	15.00	4.50
JP-LP Joe Pepitone	15.00	4.50
LG-LP Lou Gehrig Pants	300.00	90.00
MM-LP Mickey Mantle	250.00	75.00
PR-LP Phil Rizzuto	25.00	7.50
RG-LP Ron Guidry	15.00	4.50
RJ-LP Reggie Jackson	25.00	7.50
RM-LP Roger Maris	100.00	30.00
TH-LP Tommy Henrich	15.00	4.50
TM-LP Thurman Munson	80.00	24.00
WF-LP Whitey Ford	25.00	7.50

2000 Upper Deck Yankees Legends Legendary Pinstripes Autograph

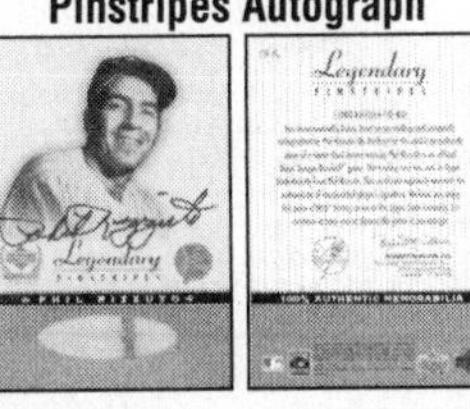

Randomly inserted into packs at one in 287, this 10-card insert set features autographed game-used jersey cards from Yankee greats. Card backs carry an "A" suffix. Please note that Ron Guidry packed out as exchange card with a deadline to redeem no later than July 18th, 2001.

	Nm-Mt	Ex-Mt
BD-A Bucky Dent	50.00	15.00
DM-A Don Mattingly	150.00	45.00
DW-A Dave Winfield	80.00	24.00
GG-A Goose Gossage	50.00	15.00
GM-A Gil McDougald	50.00	15.00
JP-A Joe Pepitone	40.00	12.00
PR-A Phil Rizzuto	80.00	24.00
RG-A Ron Guidry	50.00	15.00
TH-A Tommy Henrich	50.00	15.00
WF-A Whitey Ford	80.00	24.00

2000 Upper Deck Yankees Legends Monument Park

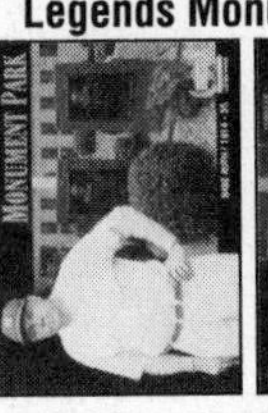

Randomly inserted into packs at one in 23, this six-card insert set features all-time Yankee greats. Card backs carry a "MP" suffix.

	Nm-Mt	Ex-Mt
COMPLETE SET (6)	25.00	7.50
MP1 Lou Gehrig	6.00	1.80
MP2 Babe Ruth	10.00	3.00
MP3 Mickey Mantle	12.00	3.60
MP4 Joe DiMaggio	6.00	1.80
MP5 Thurman Munson	5.00	1.50
MP6 Elston Howard	2.00	.60

2000 Upper Deck Yankees Legends Murderer's Row

Randomly inserted into packs at one in 11, this 10-card insert set features some of the most dominating New York Yankee players of all-time. Card backs carry a "MR" suffix.

	Nm-Mt	Ex-Mt
COMPLETE SET (10)	20.00	6.00
MR1 Tony Lazzeri	1.00	.30
MR2 Babe Ruth	8.00	2.40
MR3 Bob Meusel	1.00	.30
MR4 Lou Gehrig	5.00	1.50
MR5 Joe Dugan	1.00	.30
MR6 Bill Dickey	1.50	.45
MR7 Waite Hoyt	1.00	.30
MR8 Red Ruffing	1.00	.30
MR9 Earle Combs	1.00	.30
MR10 Lefty Gomez	1.50	.45

2000 Upper Deck Yankees Legends New Dynasty

Randomly inserted into packs at one in 11, this 10-card insert set features New York Yankee greats from the last twenty years. Card backs carry a "ND" suffix.

	Nm-Mt	Ex-Mt
COMPLETE SET (10)	15.00	4.50
ND1 Reggie Jackson	1.50	.45
ND2 Graig Nettles	1.00	.30
ND3 Don Mattingly	6.00	1.80
ND4 Goose Gossage	1.00	.30
ND5 Dave Winfield	1.00	.30
ND6 Chris Chambliss	1.00	.30
ND7 Thurman Munson	4.00	1.20
ND8 Willie Randolph	1.00	.30
ND9 Ron Guidry	1.00	.30
ND10 Bucky Dent	1.00	.30

2000 Upper Deck Yankees Legends Pride of the Pinstripes

Randomly inserted into packs at one in 23, this six-card insert set features legendary Yankee greats. Card backs carry a "PP" suffix.

	Nm-Mt	Ex-Mt
COMPLETE SET (6)	25.00	7.50
PP1 Babe Ruth	10.00	3.00
PP2 Mickey Mantle	12.00	3.60
PP3 Joe DiMaggio	6.00	1.80
PP4 Lou Gehrig	6.00	1.80
PP5 Reggie Jackson	2.00	.60
PP6 Yogi Berra	3.00	.90

2000 Upper Deck Yankees Master Collection

The 2000 Upper Deck Yankees Master Collection was released in early June, 2000. Each box set contains 37 cards. The box set includes a 25-card base set that is individually serial numbered to 500, an 11-card game-used bat set that includes players such a Mickey Mantle, and Babe Ruth, and a one card mystery pack that includes various memorabilia and autographed cards. Card backs carry a "NYY" prefix.

	Nm-Mt	Ex-Mt
COMPLETE SET (25)	500.00	150.00
NYY1 Babe Ruth 23	50.00	15.00
NYY2 Lou Gehrig 27	30.00	9.00
NYY3 Tony Lazzeri 28	10.00	3.00
NYY4 Babe Ruth 32	50.00	15.00
NYY5 Lou Gehrig 36	30.00	9.00
NYY6 Lefty Gomez 37	10.00	3.00
NYY7 Bill Dickey 38	10.00	3.00
NYY8 Bill Dickey 39	10.00	3.00
NYY9 Tommy Henrich 41	10.00	3.00
NYY10 Spud Chandler 43	10.00	3.00
NYY11 T.Henrich 47	10.00	3.00
NYY12 Phil Rizzuto 49	15.00	4.50
NYY13 Whitey Ford 50	10.00	3.00
NYY14 Yogi Berra 51	15.00	4.50
NYY15 Casey Stengel 52	10.00	3.00
NYY16 Billy Martin 53	10.00	3.00
NYY17 Don Larsen 56	10.00	3.00
NYY18 Elston Howard 58	10.00	3.00
NYY19 Roger Maris 61	25.00	7.50
NYY20 Mickey Mantle 62	60.00	18.00
NYY21 Reggie Jackson 77	10.00	3.00
NYY22 Bucky Dent 78	10.00	3.00
NYY23 Derek Jeter 96	30.00	9.00
NYY24 Derek Jeter 98	30.00	9.00
NYY25 Derek Jeter 99	30.00	9.00

2000 Upper Deck Yankees Master Collection All-Time Yankees Game Bats

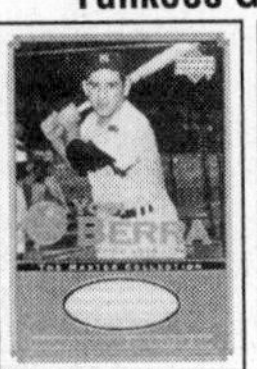

One complete 11-card set of All-Time Yankees Game Bats was inserted into each sealed Yankees Master Collection box. Only 500 sets were produced and each card carries serial-numbering. This 11-card game-used bat card set features some of the greatest New York Yankee players of all time. Card backs carry an "ATY" prefix. Please note that card number eleven of Lou Gehrig is a special commemorative card that does not included a piece of game-used bat.

	Nm-Mt	Ex-Mt
ATY1 Babe Ruth	150.00	45.00
ATY2 Mickey Mantle	150.00	45.00
ATY3 Reggie Jackson	25.00	7.50
ATY4 Don Mattingly	80.00	24.00
ATY5 Billy Martin	25.00	7.50
ATY6 Graig Nettles	15.00	4.50
ATY7 Derek Jeter	80.00	24.00
ATY8 Yogi Berra	25.00	7.50
ATY9 Thurman Munson	60.00	18.00
ATY10 Whitey Ford	25.00	7.50
ATY11 Lou Gehrig COMM	25.00	7.50

2000 Upper Deck Yankees Master Collection Mystery Pack Inserts

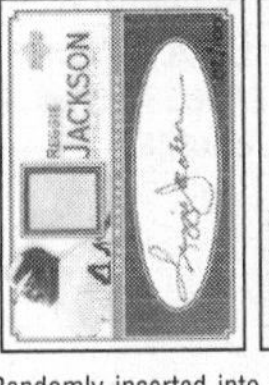

Randomly inserted into each Yankees Master Collection at one per box, this one card mystery pack includes various game-used memorabilia and autographed insert cards.

	Nm-Mt	Ex-Mt
BM1-2 Billy Martin Bat-Cut AU/2		
BR1-3 Babe Ruth Bat-Cut AU/3		
MM1-7 Mickey Mantle Bat-Cut AU/7		
BRC1-3 Babe Ruth Cut AU/3		
LGC1-3 Lou Gehrig Cut AU/3		
TMC1-2 Thurman Munson Cut AU/2		
DJ-B Derek Jeter Bat AU/100	500.00	150.00
DJ-J Derek Jeter Jsy AU/100	500.00	150.00
RJ-B Reggie Jackson Bat AU/100	150.00	45.00
WF-J Whitey Ford Bat AU/100	150.00	45.00
YB-B Yogi Berra Bat AU/80	150.00	45.00

2003 Upper Deck Yankees Signature

This 90 card set was released in April, 2003. These cards were issued in three card packs with an $30 SRP. These packs came 10 packs to a box and eight boxes to a case. In an interesting note this set is sequenced by the first name of the player.

	Nm-Mt	Ex-Mt
COMPLETE SET (90)	100.00	30.00
1 Al Downing	1.00	.30
2 Al Gettel	1.00	.30
3 Art Ditmar	1.00	.30
4 Babe Ruth	15.00	4.50
5 Bill Virdon MG	1.00	.30
6 Billy Martin	3.00	.90
7 Bob Cerv	1.00	.30
8 Bob Turley	1.00	.30
9 Bobby Cox	2.00	.60
10 Bobby Richardson	2.00	.60
11 Bobby Shantz	1.00	.30
12 Bucky Dent	2.00	.60
13 Bud Metheny XRC	1.00	.30
14 Casey Stengel	3.00	.90
15 Charlie Hayes	1.00	.30
16 Charlie Silvera	1.00	.30
17 Chris Chambliss	2.00	.60
18 Danny Cater	1.00	.30
19 Dave Kingman	2.00	.60
20 Dave Righetti	2.00	.60
21 Dave Winfield	2.00	.60
22 David Cone	2.00	.60
23 Dick Tidrow	1.00	.30
24 Doc Medich	1.00	.30
25 Dock Ellis	2.00	.60
26 Don Gullett	2.00	.60
27 Don Mattingly	15.00	4.50
28 Dwight Gooden	3.00	.90
29 Eddie Robinson	1.00	.30
30 Felipe Alou	2.00	.60
31 Fred Sanford	1.00	.30
32 Fred Stanley	1.00	.30
33 Gene Michael	1.00	.30
34 Hank Bauer	2.00	.60
35 Hector Lopez	1.00	.30
36 Horace Clarke	1.00	.30
37 Jake Gibbs	1.00	.30
38 Jerry Coleman	1.00	.30
39 Jerry Lumpe	1.00	.30
40 Jim Bouton	2.00	.60
41 Jim Kaat	2.00	.60
42 Jim Mason	1.00	.30
43 Jimmy Key	2.00	.60
44 Joe DiMaggio	10.00	3.00
45 Joe Torre	5.00	1.50
46 John Montefusco	2.00	.60
47 Johnny Blanchard	1.00	.30
48 Johnny Callison	2.00	.60
49 Lew Burdette	2.00	.60
50 Johnny Kucks	1.00	.30
51 Steve Balboni	1.00	.30
52 Ken Singleton ANC	2.00	.60
53 Lee Mazzilli	2.00	.60
54 Lou Gehrig	10.00	3.00
55 Lou Piniella	2.00	.60
56 Luis Tiant	2.00	.60
57 Marius Russo XRC	1.00	.30
58 Mel Stottlemyre	2.00	.60
59 Mickey Mantle	15.00	4.50
60 Mike Pagliarulo	1.00	.30
61 Mike Torrez	1.00	.30
62 Miller Huggins MG	1.00	.30
63 Norm Siebern	1.00	.30
64 Paul O'Neill	3.00	.90
65 Phil Niekro	2.00	.60
66 Phil Rizzuto	3.00	.90
67 Ralph Branca	2.00	.60
68 Ralph Houk	2.00	.60
69 Ralph Terry	2.00	.60
70 Randy Gumpert	1.00	.30
71 Roger Maris	10.00	3.00
72 Ron Blomberg	1.00	.30
73 Ron Guidry	2.00	.60
74 Ruben Amaro	1.00	.30
75 Ryne Duren	1.00	.30
76 Sam McDowell	2.00	.60
77 Sparky Lyle	2.00	.60
78 Thurman Munson	10.00	3.00
79 Tom Sturdivant	1.00	.30
80 Tom Tresh	2.00	.60
81 Tommy Byrne	1.00	.30
82 Tommy Henrich	2.00	.60
83 Tommy John	2.00	.60
84 Tony Kubek	3.00	.90
85 Tony Lazzeri	2.00	.60
86 Virgil Trucks	1.00	.30
87 Wade Boggs	3.00	.90
88 Whitey Ford	3.00	.90
89 Willie Randolph	2.00	.60
90 Yogi Berra	5.00	1.50

2003 Upper Deck Yankees Signature Monumental Cuts

Randomly inserted into packs, these 30 combined cards feature autographs of Yankee Legends who have passed on. We have notated the print run next to the player's name in our checklist.

	Nm-Mt	Ex-Mt
RANDOM INSERTS IN PACKS		
B/WN 1-9 COPIES OF EACH CARD		
NO PRICING DUE TO SCARCITY		
BM Billy Martin/9		
BR Babe Ruth/1		
CS Casey Stengel/3		
JD Joe DiMaggio/4		
LG Lou Gehrig/1		
MH Miller Huggins/2		
MM Mickey Mantle/1		
RM Roger Maris/6		
TL Tony Lazzeri/2		
TM Thurman Munson/1		

2003 Upper Deck Yankees Signature Pinstripe Excellence Autographs

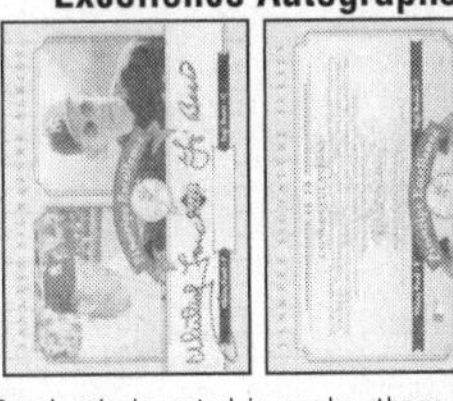

Randomly inserted in packs, these cards feature two autographs on each card. These cards were issued to a stated print run of 125 serial numbered sets.

	Nm-Mt	Ex-Mt
AA Felipe Alou / Ruben Amaro	60.00	18.00
BA Hank Bauer / Felipe Alou	60.00	18.00
BP Wade Boggs / Mike Pagliarulo	100.00	30.00
BR1 Hank Bauer / Phil Rizzuto	100.00	30.00
BR2 Tommy Byrne / Marius Russo	40.00	12.00
BT Jim Bouton / Ralph Terry	60.00	18.00
CK Chris Chambliss / Dave Kingman	100.00	30.00
DC Bucky Dent / Chris Chambliss	60.00	18.00
DR Bucky Dent / Willie Randolph	100.00	30.00
DS Ryne Duren / Tom Sturdivant	40.00	12.00
FB Whitey Ford / Yogi Berra	200.00	60.00
GB Jake Gibbs / Johnny Blanchard	40.00	12.00
GM Ron Guidry / John Montefusco	60.00	18.00
GR Ron Guidry / Willie Randolph	100.00	30.00
JK Tommy John / Jim Kaat	60.00	18.00
LG Sparky Lyle / Ron Guidry	100.00	30.00
LM Jerry Lumpe / Jim Mason	40.00	12.00
MC John Montefusco / Chris Chambliss	60.00	18.00
MK Gene Michael / Tony Kubek	100.00	30.00
ML Sam McDowell / Sparky Lyle	60.00	18.00
MR Don Mattingly / Dave Righetti	200.00	60.00
NT Phil Niekro	100.00	30.00

Luis Tiant
RB Bobby Richardson 100.00 30.00
Hank Bauer
RC Bobby Richardson 100.00 30.00
Jerry Coleman
SC Ken Singleton 60.00 18.00
Jerry Coleman
ST Tom Sturdivant 40.00 12.00
Bob Turley
TK Luis Tiant 60.00 18.00
Jim Kaat
TM Mike Torrez 60.00 18.00
Lee Mazzilli

2003 Upper Deck Yankees Signature Pride of New York Autographs

Inserted at a stated rate of one per pack, these 88 cards feature authentic autographs from either retired Yankee players or people associated with the franchise in some way. This set included the first certified autographed sports cards for figures such as Yankee GM Brian Cashman, actors John Goodman and Jason Alexander. Bud Metheny was supposed to sign cards for this product but he passed away before he could sign his cards. In addition a few players did not return their cards in time for inclusion in this product and we have notated that information with an EXCH in our checklist. Collectors could redeem those cards until March 27, 2006. David Cone signed some of his cards in time for inclusion and others were available as an exchange card. Upper Deck announced some shorter print runs and we have put that stated print run information next to the player's name in our checklist.

Nm-Mt Ex-Mt
EXCH * = PART LIVE/PART REDEMPTION
AD Al Downing 10.00 3.00
AG Al Gettel 10.00 3.00
BD Brian Doyle 10.00 3.00
BL Johnny Blanchard 10.00 3.00
BR Bobby Richardson 15.00 4.50
BS Bobby Shantz 10.00 3.00
BT Bob Turley 10.00 3.00
BV Bill Virdon MG 10.00 3.00
CA1 Johnny Callison 10.00 3.00
CA2 Brian Cashman/100 EX 400.00 120.00
CC Chris Chambliss 10.00 3.00
CE Bob Cerv 10.00 3.00
CH Charlie Hayes 10.00 3.00
CO David Cone EXCH * 25.00 7.50
CS Charlie Silvera 10.00 3.00
CX Bobby Cox 10.00 3.00
DC Danny Cater 10.00 3.00
DE Bucky Dent 10.00 3.00
DG Don Gullett 10.00 3.00
DI Art Ditmar 10.00 3.00
DK Dave Kingman 10.00 3.00
DM Doc Medich 10.00 3.00
DR Dave Righetti 10.00 3.00
DT Dick Tidrow 10.00 3.00
DW Dave Winfield/350 60.00 18.00
DZ Don Zimmer 40.00 12.00
EL Dock Ellis 10.00 3.00
ER Eddie Robinson 10.00 3.00
FA Felipe Alou 10.00 3.00
FS Fred Sanford 10.00 3.00
GM Gene Michael 10.00 3.00
GO Dwight Gooden EXCH 15.00 4.50
HB Hank Bauer 10.00 3.00
HC Horace Clarke 10.00 3.00
HL Hector Lopez 10.00 3.00
HR Hal Reniff 10.00 3.00
JA Jason Alexander/50 1000.00 300.00
JB Jim Bouton 10.00 3.00
JC Jerry Coleman 10.00 3.00
JG1 Jake Gibbs 10.00 3.00
JG2 John Goodman/100 EX 500.00 150.00
JK Jim Kaat 10.00 3.00
JL Jerry Lumpe 10.00 3.00
JM Jim Mason 10.00 3.00
JT Joe Torre 40.00 12.00
JW Jim Wynn 10.00 3.00
KE Jimmy Key 15.00 4.50
KS Ken Singleton ANC 10.00 3.00
KU Johnny Kucks 10.00 3.00
LB Lew Burdette 10.00 3.00
LM Lee Mazzilli 10.00 3.00
LP Lou Piniella/542 15.00 4.50
LT Luis Tiant 10.00 3.00
MA Don Mattingly 100.00 30.00
MO John Montefusco 10.00 3.00
MP Mike Pagliarulo 10.00 3.00
MR Marius Russo 10.00 3.00
MS Mel Stottlemyre 10.00 3.00
MT Mike Torrez 10.00 3.00
NS Norm Siebern 10.00 3.00
PN Phil Niekro 25.00 7.50
PO Paul O'Neill/500 25.00 7.50
PR Phil Rizzuto 50.00 15.00
RA Ruben Amaro 10.00 3.00
RB1 Ron Blomberg 10.00 3.00
RB2 Ralph Branca 10.00 3.00
RD Ryne Duren 10.00 3.00
RG1 Ron Guidry 25.00 7.50
RG2 Randy Gumpert 10.00 3.00
RH Ralph Houk 10.00 3.00
RT Ralph Terry 10.00 3.00
SB Steve Balboni 10.00 3.00
SL Sparky Lyle 10.00 3.00
SM Sam McDowell 10.00 3.00
ST Fred Stanley 10.00 3.00
TB Tommy Byrne 10.00 3.00
TC Tom Carroll 10.00 3.00
TH Tommy Henrich 40.00 12.00
TJ Tommy John 10.00 3.00
TK Tony Kubek 40.00 12.00
TS Tom Sturdivant 10.00 3.00
TT Tom Tresh 15.00 4.50
VT Virgil Trucks 10.00 3.00
WB Wade Boggs 50.00 15.00
WF Whitey Ford 50.00 15.00
WR Willie Randolph/283 15.00 4.50
YB Yogi Berra EXCH 60.00 18.00

2003 Upper Deck Yankees Signature Yankees Forever Autographs

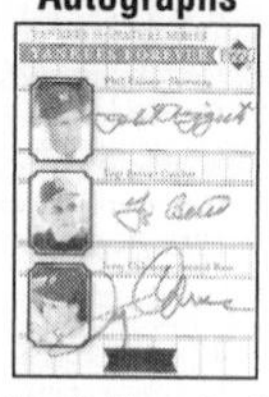

Randomly inserted in packs, these cards feature three Yankee players (usually with something in common) all signing the same card. These cards were issued to a stated print run of 50 serial numbered sets. A few cards were issued as exchange cards and those cards could be redeemed until March 27, 2006.

Nm-Mt Ex-Mt
RANDOM INSERTS IN PACKS
STATED PRINT RUN 50 SERIAL #'d SETS
EXCHANGE DEADLINE 03/27/06
ALB Felipe Alou 120.00 36.00
Hector Lopez
Hank Bauer
AOM Felipe Alou 150.00 45.00
Paul O'Neill
Lee Mazzilli
BSB Yogi Berra 150.00 45.00
Bobby Shantz
Hank Bauer
DFB Al Downing 200.00 60.00
Whitey Ford
Yogi Berra
DRC Bucky Dent 120.00 36.00
Willie Randolph
Chris Chambliss
EMG Dock Ellis 120.00 36.00
Doc Medich
Don Gullett
FKB Whitey Ford 150.00 45.00
Johnny Kucks
Jim Bouton
GCK Dwight Gooden 150.00 45.00
David Cone
Jimmy Key EXCH
GRJ Ron Guidry 150.00 45.00
Dave Righetti
Tommy John EXCH
HMC Ralph Houk 100.00 30.00
Gene Michael
Bobby Cox
HRB Tommy Henrich 150.00 45.00
Phil Rizzuto
Ralph Branca
JKL Tommy John 120.00 36.00
Jim Kaat
Sparky Lyle
KCC Dave Kingman 120.00 36.00
Chris Chambliss
Danny Cater
KGT Jim Kaat 120.00 36.00
Don Gullet
Mike Torrez
KJB Jim Kaat 120.00 36.00
Tommy John
Jim Bouton
MTT John Montefusco 100.00 30.00
Mike Torrez
Dick Tidrow EXCH
OBK Paul O'Neill 200.00 60.00
Wade Boggs
Jimmy Key
PTV Lou Piniella 150.00 45.00
Joe Torre
Bill Virdon
RBC Phil Rizzuto 150.00 45.00
Yogi Berra
Jerry Coleman
RKD Phil Rizzuto 150.00 45.00
Tony Kubek
Bucky Dent
RRC Bobby Richardson 150.00 45.00
Willie Randolph
Jerry Coleman
RSB Marius Russo 100.00 30.00
Tom Sturdivant
Tommy Byrne
SSB Fred Stanley 100.00 30.00
Charlie Silvera
Johnny Blanchard
STE Mel Stottlemyre 120.00 36.00
Luis Tiant
Dock Ellis
TCO Joe Torre 200.00 60.00
David Cone
Paul O'Neill EXCH
TLN Luis Tiant 120.00 36.00
Sparky Lyle
Phil Niekro
TMT Luis Tiant 120.00 36.00
Sam McDowell
Ralph Terry
WHM Dave Winfield 150.00 45.00
Tommy Henrich
Lee Mazzilli
WMG Dave Winfield 350.00 105.00
Don Mattingly
Ron Guidry EXCH
WPC Dave Winfield 150.00 45.00
Lou Piniella
Chris Chambliss EXCH

1989 USPS Legends Stamp Cards

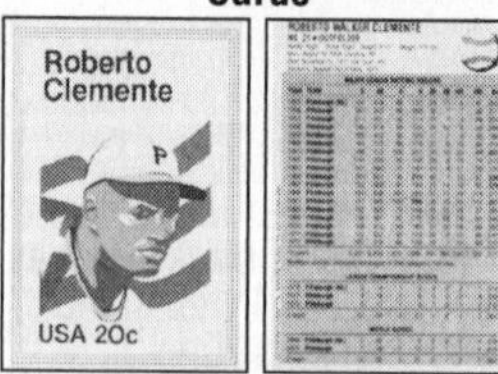

The 1989 USPS Legends Stamp Cards set includes four cards each measuring 2 1/2" by 3 9/16". On the fronts, the cards depict the four baseball-related stamp designs which featured actual players. The outer front borders are white; the inner front borders are orange and purple. The vertically oriented backs are beige and pink. These cards were sold by the U.S. Postal Service as a set (kit) for $7.95 along with the actual stamps, an attractive booklet, and other materials. The first printing of the set was sold out and so a second printing was made. The first printing cards did not have the USPS copyright logo. All the stamps in the set are drawings; for example, the Gehrig stamp was painted by noted sports artist, Bart Forbes. All of the stamps except Gehrig (25 cents) are 20-cent stamps.

Nm-Mt Ex-Mt
COMPLETE SET (4) 25.00 10.00
1 Roberto Clemente 6.00 2.40
Issued August 17, 1984
2 Lou Gehrig 6.00 2.40
Issued June 10, 1989
3 Jackie Robinson 6.00 2.40
Issued August 2, 1982
4 Babe Ruth 7.50 3.00
Issued July 6, 1983

2000 USPS Legends of Baseball Postcards

Issued as a companion piece to the Legends of Baseball stamps, these 20 oversize postcards were also issued by the USPS as part of the stamp collecting program. The SRP from the Post Office for this set was $5.95. Since the cards are unnumbered we have sequenced them in alphabetical order.

Nm-Mt Ex-Mt
COMPLETE SET (20) 6.00 1.80
1 Roberto Clemente 1.00 .30
2 Ty Cobb .75 .23
3 Mickey Cochrane .25 .07
4 Eddie Collins .25 .07
5 Dizzy Dean .25 .07
6 Jimmie Foxx .50 .15
7 Lou Gehrig 1.25 .35
8 Josh Gibson .75 .23
9 Lefty Grove .50 .15
10 Rogers Hornsby .50 .15
11 Walter Johnson .75 .23
12 Christy Mathewson .75 .23
13 Satchel Paige .50 .15
14 Jackie Robinson 1.00 .30
15 Babe Ruth 1.50 .45
16 George Sisler .25 .07
17 Tris Speaker .25 .07
18 Pie Traynor .25 .07
19 Honus Wagner .75 .23
20 Cy Young .50 .15

2000 USPS Legends of Baseball Stamps

This 20 stamp collection was released by the U.S. Postal service in Late July, 2000. The collection features an assortment of Hall of Fame baseball players.

Nm-Mt Ex-Mt
COMPLETE SET (20) 6.60 2.00
1 Roberto Clemente .33 .10
2 Ty Cobb .33 .10
3 Mickey Cochrane .33 .10
4 Eddie Collins .33 .10
5 Dizzy Dean .33 .10
6 Jimmie Foxx .33 .10
7 Lou Gehrig .33 .10
8 Josh Gibson .33 .10
9 Lefty Grove .33 .10
10 Rogers Hornsby .33 .10
11 Walter Johnson .33 .10
12 Christy Mathewson .33 .10
13 Satchel Paige .33 .10
14 Jackie Robinson .33 .10
15 Babe Ruth .33 .10
16 George Sisler .33 .10
17 Tris Speaker .33 .10
18 Pie Traynor .33 .10
19 Honus Wagner .33 .10
20 Cy Young .33 .10

1912 Vassar Sweaters

This oversized set measures approximately 4" by 6 1/2" and features black-and-white photos of players in sweaters with white borders. The only known players in the set are listed below in alphabetical order. Other cards may exist and any confirmed additions are welcomed.

Ex-Mt VG
COMPLETE SET 2500.00 1250.00
1 Ty Cobb 1000.00 500.00
2 Sam Crawford 300.00 150.00
3 Walter Johnson 600.00 300.00
4 Larry Lajoie 600.00 300.00
5 Smokey Joe Wood 250.00 125.00

1915 Victory T214

The cards in this 30-card set measure 1 1/2" by 2 5/8". The set is easily distinguished by the presence of the reference to Victory Tobacco on the card backs. The players in this unnumbered set have been alphabetized and numbered for reference in the checklist below. The set can be dated to 1915 with Chief Bender's appearence as a Baltimore Federal.

Ex-Mt VG
COMPLETE SET (31) 25000.00 12500.00
1 Chief Bender 1000.00 500.00
2 Roger Bresnahan 1000.00 500.00
3 Howie Camnitz 600.00 300.00
4 Ty Cobb 3000.00 1500.00
5 Birdie Cree 600.00 300.00
6 Ray Demmitt 600.00 300.00
7 Mickey Doolan 600.00 300.00
8 Tom Downey 600.00 300.00
9 Kid Elberfeld 800.00 400.00
10 Russ Ford 600.00 300.00
11 Art Fromme 600.00 300.00
12 Rube Geyer 600.00 300.00
13 Clark Griffith MG 1000.00 500.00
14 Bob Groom 600.00 300.00
15 Hugh Jennings MG 1200.00 600.00
16 Walter Johnson 1500.00 750.00
17 Ed Konetchy 600.00 300.00
18 Nap Lajoie 1200.00 600.00
19 Ed Lennox 600.00 300.00
20 Sherry Magee 800.00 400.00
21 Chief Meyers 800.00 400.00
22 George Mullin 800.00 400.00
23 Tom Needham 600.00 300.00
24 Rebel Oakes 600.00 300.00
25 Jack Quinn 600.00 300.00
26 Frank Schulte 800.00 400.00
28 Ed Sweeney 600.00 300.00
28 Joe Tinker 1000.00 500.00
29 Heinie Wagner 600.00 300.00
30 Zack Wheat 1000.00 500.00
31 Hooks Wiltse 600.00 300.00

1909 W.W. Smith Postcards

In 1909 W.W. Smith of Pittsburgh produced a set of Postcards for the 1909 World Series between the Pittsburgh Pirates and Detroit Tigers. One card is titled "World's Series Souvenir" titled two of a kind featuring the stars of each team, Ty Cobb of the Tigers and Honus Wagner of the Pirates featuring caracitures of the two stars. The other known card titled "The Mighty Honus" shows a caracature of Wagner. It is possible that a caracature of Cobb exists as well as some of the other prominent players from both teams but they have yet to be identified.

Ex-Mt VG
COMPLETE SET (2) 700.00 350.00
1 Ty Cobb 500.00 250.00
Honus Wagner
World Series Souvenir
2 Honus Wagner 250.00 125.00
The Mighty Honus

1922 W501

This 120-card set, referenced by the catalog designation W501, measures approximately 1 15/16" by 3 1/2". The cards have white borders which frame a posed black and white photo. The cards are blank backed and have the number in the upper right hand corner. The cards are thought to have been issued about 1922. All these pictures are the same as the ones in E-121. All photos are all identified by a G-4-22, which is the best guess to how the set is dated as 1922.

Ex-Mt VG
COMPLETE SET (120) 4000.00 2000.00
1 Ed Rommel 20.00 10.00
2 Urban Shocker 30.00 15.00
3 Frank Davis 20.00 10.00
4 George Sisler 100.00 50.00
5 Bobby Veach 20.00 10.00
6 Harry Heilmann 80.00 40.00
7 Ira Flagstead 20.00 10.00
8 Ty Cobb 300.00 150.00
9 Oscar Vitt 20.00 10.00
10 Muddy Ruel 20.00 10.00
11 Del Pratt 20.00 10.00
12 Joe Gharrity 20.00 10.00
13 Joe Judge 30.00 15.00
14 Sam Rice 50.00 25.00
15 Clyde Milan 30.00 15.00
16 Joe Sewell 50.00 25.00
17 Walter Johnson 200.00 100.00
18 Stuffy McInnis 30.00 15.00
19 Tris Speaker 120.00 60.00
20 Jim Bagby 20.00 10.00
21 Stan Coveleski 50.00 25.00
22 Bill Wambsganss 30.00 15.00
23 John Mails 20.00 10.00
24 Larry Gardner 20.00 10.00
25 Aaron Ward 20.00 10.00
26 Miller Huggins MG 50.00 25.00
27 Wally Schang 30.00 15.00
28 Thomas Rogers 20.00 10.00
29 Carl Mays 30.00 15.00
30 Everett Scott 20.00 10.00
31 Bob Shawkey 30.00 15.00
32 Waite Hoyt 80.00 40.00
33 Mike McNally 20.00 10.00
34 Joe Bush 20.00 10.00
35 Bob Meusel 40.00 20.00
36 Irish Meusel 20.00 10.00
37 Dickie Kerr 20.00 10.00
38 Eddie Collins 80.00 40.00
39 Kid Gleason MG 30.00 15.00
40 Johnny Mostil 20.00 10.00
41 Bibb Falk 20.00 10.00
42 Clarence Hodge 20.00 10.00
43 Ray Schalk 50.00 25.00
44 Amos Strunk 20.00 10.00
45 Edward Mulligan 20.00 10.00
46 Earl Sheely 20.00 10.00
47 Harry Hooper 80.00 40.00
48 Red Faber 50.00 25.00
49 Babe Ruth 500.00 250.00
50 Ivy Wingo 20.00 10.00
51 Greasy Neale 30.00 15.00
52 Jake Daubert 20.00 10.00
53 Edd Roush 80.00 40.00
54 Eppa Rixey 50.00 25.00
55 Speed Martin 20.00 10.00
56 Bill Killifer 20.00 10.00
57 Charlie Hollocher 20.00 10.00
58 Zeb Terry 20.00 10.00
59 Grover Alexander 100.00 50.00
60 Turner Barber 20.00 10.00
61 Johnny Rawlings 20.00 10.00
62 Frankie Frisch 120.00 60.00
63 Red Shea 20.00 10.00
64 Dave Bancroft 50.00 25.00
65 Red Causey 20.00 10.00
66 Pancho Snyder 20.00 10.00
67 Heinie Groh 30.00 15.00
68 Ross Youngs 50.00 25.00
69 Fred Toney 20.00 10.00
70 Art Nehf 20.00 10.00
71 Earl Smith 20.00 10.00
72 George Kelly 50.00 25.00
73 John McGraw MG 80.00 40.00
74 Phil Douglas 20.00 10.00
75 Rosy Ryan 20.00 10.00
76 Jesse Haines 50.00 25.00
77 Milt Stock 20.00 10.00
78 Bill Doak 20.00 10.00
79 Specs Toporcer 20.00 10.00
80 Wilbur Cooper 20.00 10.00
81 Possum Whitted 20.00 10.00
82 Charlie Grimm 30.00 15.00
83 Rabbit Maranville 50.00 25.00
84 Babe Adams 30.00 15.00
85 Carson Bigbee 20.00 10.00
86 Max Carey 80.00 40.00
87 Whitey Glazner 20.00 10.00
88 George Gibson 20.00 10.00
89 Billy Southworth 30.00 15.00
90 Hank Gowdy 20.00 10.00
91 Walter Holke 20.00 10.00
92 Joe Oeschger 20.00 10.00
93 Pete Kilduff 20.00 10.00
94 Chief Meyers 30.00 15.00
95 Otto Miller 20.00 10.00
96 Wilbert Robinson MG 50.00 25.00
97 Zack Wheat 50.00 25.00
98 Dutch Ruether 20.00 10.00
99 Tilly Walker 20.00 10.00
100 Cy Williams 30.00 15.00
101 Dave Danforth 20.00 10.00
102 Ed Rommell 20.00 10.00
103 John McGraw MG 80.00 40.00
104 Frank Frisch 80.00 40.00
105 Al DeVormer 20.00 10.00
106 Tommy Griffith 20.00 10.00
107 George Harper 20.00 10.00
108 Doc Lavan 20.00 10.00
109 Elmer Smith 20.00 10.00
110 Hooks Dauss 20.00 10.00
111 Alex Gaston 20.00 10.00
112 Jack Graney 20.00 10.00
113 Irish Meusel 20.00 10.00
114 Rogers Hornsby 120.00 60.00
115 Les Nunamaker 20.00 10.00
116 Steve O'Neill 30.00 15.00
117 Max Flack 20.00 10.00
118 Billy Southworth 20.00 10.00
119 Art Nehf 20.00 10.00
120 Chick Fewster 20.00 10.00

1928 W502

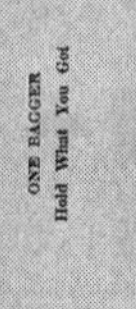

2003 Upper Deck Yankees Signature Pride of New York Autographs

This 60-card set, referenced by the catalog designation W502, measures approximately 1 5/16" by 2 1/2". The photo is a black and white action-posed photo, while the back reads "One Bagger. Hold what you've got." The cards are thought to have been issued about 1928.

	Ex-Mt	VG
COMPLETE SET (60)	1500.00	750.00
1 Burleigh Grimes	25.00	12.50
2 Walter Reuther	12.00	6.00
3 Joe Dugan	15.00	7.50
4 Red Faber	25.00	12.50
5 Gabby Hartnett	25.00	12.50
6 Babe Ruth	200.00	100.00
7 Bob Meusel	20.00	10.00
8 Herb Pennock	25.00	12.50
9 George Burns	12.00	6.00
10 Joe Sewell	25.00	12.50
11 George Uhle	12.00	6.00
12 Bob O'Farrell	12.00	6.00
13 Rogers Hornsby	50.00	25.00
14 Pie Traynor	25.00	12.50
15 Clarence Mitchell	12.00	6.00
16 Eppa Rixey	25.00	12.50
17 Carl Mays	12.00	6.00
18 Adolfo Luque	15.00	7.50
19 Dave Bancroft	25.00	12.50
20 George Kelly	25.00	12.50
21 Earle Combs	25.00	12.50
22 Harry Heilmann	25.00	12.50
23 Ray W. Schalk	25.00	12.50
24 Johnny Mostil	12.00	6.00
25 Hack Wilson	25.00	12.50
26 Lou Gehrig	120.00	60.00
27 Ty Cobb	120.00	60.00
28 Tris Speaker	50.00	25.00
29 Tony Lazzeri	25.00	12.50
30 Waite Hoyt	25.00	12.50
31 Sherwood Smith	12.00	6.00
32 Max Carey	25.00	12.50
33 Eugene Hargrave	12.00	6.00
34 Miguel J. Gonzalez	12.00	6.00
35 Joe Judge	15.00	7.50
36 E.C. (Sam) Rice	25.00	12.50
37 Earl Sheely	12.00	6.00
38 Sam Jones	12.00	6.00
39 Bob A. Falk	12.00	6.00
40 Willie Kamm	15.00	7.50
41 Stanley Harris	25.00	12.50
42 John J. McGraw MG	25.00	12.50
43 Artie Nehf	12.00	6.00
44 Grover Alexander	50.00	25.00
45 Paul Waner	25.00	12.50
46 William H. Terry	25.00	12.50
47 Glenn Wright	12.00	6.00
48 Earl Smith	12.00	6.00
49 Leon (Goose) Goslin	25.00	12.50
50 Frank Frisch	25.00	12.50
51 Joe Harris	12.00	6.00
52 Fred (Cy) Wiliams	15.00	7.50
53 Ed Roush	25.00	12.50
54 George Sisler	25.00	12.50
55 Ed Rommel	12.00	6.00
56 Roger Peckinpaugh	12.00	6.00
57 Stanley Coveleski	25.00	12.50
58 Lester Bell	12.00	6.00
59 Lloyd Waner	25.00	12.50
60 John P. McInnis	15.00	7.50

1923 W503

This 64-card set, referenced by the catalog designation W503, measures approximately 1 3/4" by 2 3/4". The cards have white borders which frame a black-and-white player portrait or action photo and the card number. The backs are blank, and there is no evidence of a manufacturer. The set is thought to have been issued in early 1923.

	Ex-Mt	VG
COMPLETE SET (64)	2500.00	1250.00
1 Joe Bush	40.00	20.00
2 Wally Schang	40.00	20.00
3 Dave Robertson	25.00	12.50
4 Wally Pipp	25.00	12.50
5 Bill Ryan	25.00	12.50
6 George Kelly	80.00	40.00
7 Frank Snyder	25.00	12.50
8 Jimmy O'Connell	25.00	12.50
9 Bill Cunningham	25.00	12.50
10 Norman McMillan	25.00	12.50
11 Waite Hoyt	80.00	40.00
12 Art Nehf	25.00	12.50
13 George Sisler	100.00	50.00
14 Al Devormer	25.00	12.50
15 Casey Stengel	120.00	60.00
16 Ken Williams	40.00	20.00
17 Joe Dugan	40.00	20.00
18 Irish Muesel	25.00	12.50
19 Bob Meusel	60.00	30.00
20 Carl Mays	25.00	12.50
21 Frank Frisch	80.00	40.00
22 Jess Barnes	25.00	12.50
23 Walter Johnson	150.00	75.00
24 Claude Jonnard	25.00	12.50
25 Dave Bancroft	80.00	40.00
26 Johnny Rawlings	25.00	12.50
27 Pep Young	25.00	12.50
28 Earl Smith	25.00	12.50
29 Willie Kamm	25.00	12.50
30 Art Fletcher	25.00	12.50
31 Kid Gleason MG	25.00	12.50
32 Babe Ruth	500.00	250.00
33 Guy Morton	25.00	12.50
34 Heinie Groh	25.00	12.50
35 Leon Cadore	25.00	12.50
36 Joe Tobin	25.00	12.50
37 Rube Marquard	80.00	40.00
38 Grover Alexander	120.00	60.00
39 George Burns	25.00	12.50
40 Joe Oeschger	25.00	12.50
41 Chick Shorten	25.00	12.50
42 Roger Hornsby UER	150.00	75.00
misspelled Rogers		
43 Adolfo Luque	40.00	20.00
44 Zack Wheat	80.00	40.00
45 Hub Pruett UER	25.00	12.50
misspelled Herb		
46 Rabbit Maranville	80.00	40.00
47 Jimmy Ring	25.00	12.50
48 Sherrod Smith	25.00	12.50
49 Lea Meadows UER	25.00	12.50
misspelled Lee		
50 Aaron Ward	25.00	12.50
51 Herb Pennock	80.00	40.00
52 Carlson Bigbee UER	25.00	12.50
misspelled Carson		
53 Max Carey	80.00	40.00
54 Charles Robertson	25.00	12.50
55 Urban Shocker	40.00	20.00
56 Dutch Ruether	25.00	12.50
57 Jake Daubert	40.00	20.00
58 Louis Guisto	25.00	12.50
59 Ivy Wingo	25.00	12.50
60 Bill Pertica	25.00	12.50
61 Luke Sewell	25.00	12.50
62 Hank Gowdy	25.00	12.50
63 Jack Scott	25.00	12.50
64 Stan Coveleskie UER	80.00	40.00
misspelled Coveleski		

1919 W514

This 120-card set measures approximately 1 7/16" by 2 1/2" and are numbered in the lower right The cards portray drawings of the athletes portrayed. The cards are thought to have been issued about 1919. Variations on team names are known to exist. This might suggest that these cards were actually issued over a period of years. Any further information on this fact would be appreciated.

	Ex-Mt	VG
COMPLETE SET (120)	1500.00	750.00
1 Ira Flagstead	10.00	5.00
2 Babe Ruth	200.00	100.00
3 Happy Felsch	20.00	10.00
4 Doc Lavan	10.00	5.00
5 Phil Douglas	10.00	5.00
6 Earl Neale	12.00	6.00
7 Leslie Nunamaker	10.00	5.00
8 Sam Jones	12.00	6.00
9 Claude Hendrix	10.00	5.00
10 Frank Schulte	10.00	5.00
11 Cactus Cravath	10.00	5.00
12 Pat Moran MG	10.00	5.00
13 Dick Rudolph	10.00	5.00
14 Arthur Fletcher	10.00	5.00
15 Joe Jackson	150.00	75.00
16 Bill Southworth	12.00	6.00
17 Ad Luque	12.00	6.00
18 Charlie Deal	10.00	5.00
19 Al Mamaux	10.00	5.00
20 Stuffy McInnis	12.00	6.00
21 Rabbit Maranville	20.00	10.00
22 Max Carey	20.00	10.00
23 Dick Kerr	12.00	6.00
24 George Burns	10.00	5.00
25 Eddie Collins	20.00	10.00
26 Steve O'Neil	10.00	5.00
27 Bill Fisher	10.00	5.00
28 Rube Bressler	10.00	5.00
29 Bob Shawkey	12.00	6.00
30 Donie Bush	10.00	5.00
31 Chick Gandil	20.00	10.00
32 Ollie Zeider	10.00	5.00
33 Vean Gregg	10.00	5.00
34 Miller Huggins MG	20.00	10.00
35 Lefty Williams	20.00	10.00
36 Tub Spencer	10.00	5.00
37 Lew McCarthy	10.00	5.00
38 Hod Eller	10.00	5.00
39 Joe Gedeon	10.00	5.00
40 Dave Bancroft	20.00	10.00
41 Clark Griffith MG	20.00	10.00
42 Wilbur Cooper	10.00	5.00
43 Ty Cobb	80.00	40.00
44 Roger Peckinpaugh	12.00	6.00
45 Nic Carter	10.00	5.00
46 Heinie Groh	10.00	5.00
47 Bob Roth	10.00	5.00
48 Frank Davis	10.00	5.00
49 Leslie Mann	10.00	5.00
50 Fielder Jones	10.00	5.00
51 Bill Doak	10.00	5.00
52 John J. McGraw MG	20.00	10.00
53 Charles Hollocher	10.00	5.00
54 Babe Adams	12.00	6.00
55 Dode Paskert	10.00	5.00
56 Rogers Hornsby	30.00	15.00
57 Max Rath	10.00	5.00
58 Jeff Pfeffer	10.00	5.00
59 Nick Cullop	10.00	5.00
60 Ray Schalk	20.00	10.00
61 Bill Jacobson	10.00	5.00
62 Nap Lajoie	20.00	10.00
63 George Gibson	10.00	5.00
64 Harry Hooper	20.00	10.00
65 Grover Alexander	20.00	10.00
66 Ping Bodie	10.00	5.00
67 Hank Gowdy	10.00	5.00
68 Jake Daubert	12.00	6.00
69 Red Faber	20.00	10.00
70 Ivan Olson	10.00	5.00
71 Pickles Dilhoefer	10.00	5.00
72 Christy Mathewson	30.00	15.00
73 Ira Wingo	10.00	5.00
74 Fred Merkle	12.00	6.00
75 Frank Baker	20.00	10.00
76 Bert Gallia	10.00	5.00
77 Milton Watson	10.00	5.00
78 Bert Shotten	10.00	5.00
79 Sam Rice	20.00	10.00
80 Dan Greiner	10.00	5.00
81 Larry Doyle	12.00	6.00
82 Eddie Cicotte	20.00	10.00
83 Hugo Bezdek	10.00	5.00
84 Wally Pipp	12.00	6.00
85 Eddie Roush	20.00	10.00
86 Slim Sallee	10.00	5.00
87 Bill Killifer	10.00	5.00
88 Bob Veach	10.00	5.00
89 Jim Burke	10.00	5.00
90 Everett Scott	10.00	5.00
91 Buck Weaver	20.00	10.00
92 George Whitted	10.00	5.00
93 Ed Konetchy	10.00	5.00
94 Walter Johnson	30.00	15.00
95 Sam Crawford	20.00	10.00
96 Fred Mitchell	10.00	5.00
97 Ira Thomas	10.00	5.00
98 Jimmy Ring	10.00	5.00
99 Wally Schang	10.00	5.00
100 Benny Kauff	10.00	5.00
101 George Sisler	20.00	10.00
102 Tris Speaker	20.00	10.00
103 Carl Mays	10.00	5.00
104 Buck Herzog	10.00	5.00
105 Swede Risberg	20.00	10.00
106 Hugh Jennings MG	20.00	10.00
107 Pep Young	10.00	5.00
108 Walter Reuther	10.00	5.00
109 Joe Gharrity	10.00	5.00
110 Zack Wheat	20.00	10.00
111 Jim Vaughn	10.00	5.00
112 Kid Gleason MG	15.00	7.50
113 Casey Stengel	30.00	15.00
114 Hal Chase	12.00	6.00
115 Oscar Stanage	10.00	5.00
116 Larry Shean	10.00	5.00
117 Steve Pendergast	10.00	5.00
118 Larry Kopf	10.00	5.00
119 Charles Whiteman	10.00	5.00
120 Jesse Barnes	10.00	5.00

1923 W515

This 60-card set, referenced by the catalog designation W515, measures approximately 1 5/16" by 2 3/16". The cards are blank backed and feature drawings on the front with the name of the player, his position, and his team on the bottom of the card.

	Ex-Mt	VG
COMPLETE SET (60)	1000.00	500.00
1 Bill Cunningham	8.00	4.00
2 Al Mamauz	8.00	4.00
3 Babe Ruth	150.00	75.00
4 Dave Bancroft	15.00	7.50
5 Ed Rommell	8.00	4.00
6 Babe Adams	10.00	5.00
7 Clarence Walker	8.00	4.00
8 Waite Hoyt	15.00	7.50
9 Bob Shawkey	10.00	5.00
10 Ty Cobb	80.00	40.00
11 George Sisler	25.00	12.50
12 Jack Bentley	8.00	4.00
13 Jim O'Connell	8.00	4.00
14 Frank Frisch	25.00	12.50
15 Frank Baker	15.00	7.50
16 Burleigh Grimes	15.00	7.50
17 Wally Schang	10.00	5.00
18 Harry Heilman	15.00	7.50
19 Aaron Ward	8.00	4.00
20 Carl Mays	8.00	4.00
21 Bob Meusel	12.00	6.00
Irish Meusel		
22 Arthur Nehf	8.00	4.00
23 Lee Meadows	8.00	4.00
24 Casey Stengel	40.00	20.00
25 Jack Scott	8.00	4.00
26 Kenneth Williams	10.00	5.00
27 Joe Bush	8.00	4.00
28 Tris Speaker	25.00	12.50
29 Ross Youngs	15.00	7.50
30 Joe Dugan	10.00	5.00
31 Jesse Barnes	10.00	5.00
Virgil Barnes		
32 George Kelly	15.00	7.50
33 Hugh McQuillen	8.00	4.00
34 Hugh Jennings MG	15.00	7.50
35 Tom Griffith	8.00	4.00
36 Miller Huggins MG	15.00	7.50
37 Whitey Witt	8.00	4.00
38 Walter Johnson	40.00	20.00
39 Wally Pipp	10.00	5.00
40 Dutch Reuther	8.00	4.00
41 Jim Johnston	8.00	4.00
42 Willie Kamm	10.00	5.00
43 Sam Jones	8.00	4.00
44 Frank Snyder	8.00	4.00
45 John McGraw MG	15.00	7.50
46 Everett Scott	8.00	4.00
47 Babe Ruth	150.00	75.00
48 Urban Shocker	10.00	5.00
49 Grover Alexander	25.00	12.50
50 Rabbit Maranville	15.00	7.50
51 Ray Schalk	15.00	7.50
52 Heinie Groh	10.00	5.00
53 Wilbert Robinson MG	15.00	7.50
54 George Burns	8.00	4.00
55 Rogers Hornsby	40.00	20.00
56 Zack Wheat	15.00	7.50
57 Eddie Roush	15.00	7.50
58 Eddie Collins	15.00	7.50
59 Charlie Hollocher	8.00	4.00
60 Red Faber	15.00	7.50

1920 W516-1

This 30-card set, referenced by the catalog designation W516, measures approximately 1 7/16" by 2 5/16". The cards have colorful photos with a blank back. The copyright is reversed on the front of the card. There is also the name of the player and position on the bottom of the card.

	Ex-Mt	VG
COMPLETE SET (30)	800.00	400.00
1 Babe Ruth	200.00	100.00
2 Heine Groh	15.00	7.50
3 Ping Bodie	12.00	6.00
4 Ray Shalk (sic)	25.00	12.50
5 Tris Speaker	50.00	25.00
6 Ty Cobb	100.00	50.00
7 Roger Hornsby (sic)	80.00	40.00
8 Walter Johnson	80.00	40.00
9 Grover Alexander	50.00	25.00
10 George Burns	12.00	6.00
11 Jimmy Ring	12.00	6.00
12 Jess Barnes	12.00	6.00
13 Larry Doyle	15.00	7.50
14 Arty Fletcher	12.00	6.00
15 Dick Rudolph	12.00	6.00
16 Benny Kauff	12.00	6.00
17 Art Nehf	12.00	6.00
18 Babe Adams	15.00	7.50
19 Will Cooper	12.00	6.00
20 R.Peckingpaugh (sic)	12.00	6.00
21 Eddie Cicotte	25.00	12.50
22 Hank Gowdy	12.00	6.00
23 Eddie Collins	25.00	12.50
24 Christy Mathewson	80.00	40.00
25 Clyde Milan	15.00	7.50
26 M. Kelley	12.00	6.00
27 Ed Hooper	12.00	6.00
28 Pep Young	25.00	12.50
29 Eddie Rousch (sic)	25.00	12.50
30 George Bancroft	12.00	6.00

1931 W517

The cards in this 54-card set measure approximately 3" by 4". This 1931 set of numbered, blank-backed cards was placed in the "W~ category in the original American Card Catalog because (1) its producer was unknown and (2) it was issued in strips of three. The photo is black and white but the entire obverse of each card is generally found tinted in tones of sepia, blue, green, yellow, rose, black or gray. The cards are numbered in a small circle on the front. A solid dark line at one end of a card entitled the purchaser to another piece of candy as a prize. There are two different cards of both Babe Ruth and Mickey Cochrane. There may be other variations in this set: such as cards without numbers (e.g., Paul Waner and Dazzy Vance) as well as Chalmer Cissell with both Chicago and Cleveland, Chick Hafey with both the Cardinals and Cincinnati, and George Kelly and Lefty O'Doul with Brooklyn.

	Ex-Mt	VG
COMPLETE SET (54)	7500.00	3800.00
1 Earle Combs	80.00	40.00
2 Pie Traynor	100.00	50.00
3 Eddie Roush	100.00	50.00
(Wearing Cincinnati uniform& but listed as a New York Giant)		
4 Babe Ruth	1500.00	750.00
(Throwing)		
5 Chalmer Cissell	40.00	20.00
6 Bill Sherdel	40.00	20.00
7 Bill Shore	40.00	20.00
8 George Earnshaw	40.00	20.00
9 Bucky Harris	80.00	40.00
10 Chuck Klein	100.00	50.00
11 George Kelly	80.00	40.00
12 Travis Jackson	80.00	40.00
13 Willie Kamm	40.00	20.00
14 Harry Heilmann	100.00	50.00
15 Grover Alexander	150.00	75.00
16 Frank Frisch	100.00	50.00
17 Jack Quinn	60.00	30.00
18 Cy Williams	60.00	30.00
19 Kiki Cuyler	80.00	40.00
20 Babe Ruth	2000.00	1000.00
(Portrait)		
21 Jimmy Foxx	250.00	125.00
22 Jimmy Dykes	60.00	30.00
23 Bill Terry	120.00	60.00
24 Freddy Lindstrom	80.00	40.00
25 Hugh Critz	40.00	20.00
26 Pete Donahue	40.00	20.00
27 Tony Lazzeri	100.00	50.00
28 Heinie Manush	80.00	40.00
29 Chick Hafey	80.00	40.00
30 Melvin Ott	200.00	100.00
31 Bing Miller	40.00	20.00
32 Mule Haas	40.00	20.00
33 Lefty O'Doul	60.00	30.00
34 Paul Waner	80.00	40.00
35 Lou Gehrig	1000.00	500.00
36 Dazzy Vance	80.00	40.00
37 Mickey Cochrane	100.00	50.00
(Catching pose)		
38 Rogers Hornsby	250.00	125.00
39 Lefty Grove	200.00	100.00
40 Al Simmons	100.00	50.00
41 Rube Walberg	40.00	20.00
42 Hack Wilson	100.00	50.00
43 Art Shires	40.00	20.00
44 Sammy Hale	40.00	20.00
45 Ted Lyons	80.00	40.00
46 Joe Sewell	80.00	40.00
47 Goose Goslin	80.00	40.00
48 Lou Fonseca	40.00	20.00
49 Bob Meusel	60.00	30.00
50 Lu Blue	40.00	20.00
51 Earl Averill	80.00	40.00
52 Eddie Collins	100.00	50.00
53 Joe Judge	40.00	20.00
54 Mickey Cochrane	100.00	50.00
(Portrait)		

1920 W520

These cards which measure 1 3/*" by 2 1/4" are numbered in the lower right hand corner. For some unexplicable reason, there are two Mike Gonzales cards in this set.

	Ex-Mt	VG
COMPLETE SET (20)	800.00	400.00
1 Dave Bancroft	40.00	20.00
2 Christy Mathewson	150.00	75.00
3 Larry Doyle	25.00	12.50
4 Jess Barnes	20.00	10.00
5 Art Fletcher	20.00	10.00
6 Wilbur Cooper	20.00	10.00
7 Mike Gonzalez	20.00	10.00
8 Zach Wheat	40.00	20.00
9 Tris Speaker	100.00	50.00
10 Benny Kauff	20.00	10.00
11 Zach Wheat	40.00	20.00
12 Phil Douglas	20.00	10.00
13 Babe Ruth	300.00	150.00
14 Stan Coveleski	40.00	20.00
Spelled Koveleski		
15 Goldie Rapp	20.00	10.00
16 Pol Perritt	20.00	10.00
17 Otto Miller	20.00	10.00
18 George Kelly	40.00	20.00
19 Mike Gonzalez	20.00	10.00
20 Les Nunamaker	20.00	10.00

1923 W551

This 10-card set features color drawings of players that measure approximately 1 3/8" by 3 1/4" and were printed in strips. The players name and team name are printed in the bottom margin. The backs are blank. The cards are unnumbered and checklisted below in alphabetical order.

	Ex-Mt	VG
COMPLETE SET (10)	600.00	300.00
1 Frank Baker	30.00	15.00
2 Dave Bancroft	20.00	10.00
3 Jess Barnes	10.00	5.00
4 Ty Cobb	150.00	75.00
5 Walter Johnson	120.00	60.00
6 Wally Pipp	10.00	5.00
7 Babe Ruth	200.00	100.00
8 George Sisler	50.00	25.00
9 Tris Speaker	80.00	40.00
10 Casey Stengel	80.00	40.00

1929 W553

These cards, which measure 1 3/4" by 2 3/4", are very obscure and feature star players from the late 1920's. These blank-backed cards are known to exist in either green, red or B&W. The photos are framed with ornate picture frame style borders. Varified cards are listed below and more may exsist so any additions to this checklist are appreciated.

	Ex-Mt	VG
COMPLETE SET	4000.00	2000.00
1 Lu Blue	100.00	50.00
2 Mickey Cochrane	250.00	125.00
3 Jimmy Foxx	300.00	150.00
4 Frank Frisch	250.00	125.00

5 Lou Gehrig 500.00 250.00
6 Goose Goslin 250.00 125.00
7 Burleigh Grimes 250.00 125.00
8 Lefty Grove 300.00 150.00
9 Rogers Hornsby 300.00 150.00
10 Rabbit Maranville 250.00 125.00
11 Bing Miller 150.00 75.00
12 Lefty O'Doul 150.00 75.00
13 Babe Ruth 800.00 400.00
14 Al Simmons 250.00 125.00
15 Pie Traynor 250.00 125.00

1930 W554

This set corresponds to the poses in R316 and R306. The cards measure 5" by 7" and are reasonably available within the Hobby.

	Ex-Mt	VG
COMPLETE SET (18)	300.00	150.00
1 Gordon S. (Mickey) Cochrane	75.00	38.00
2 Lewis A. Fonseca	25.00	12.50
3 Jimmy Foxx	100.00	50.00
4 Lou Gehrig	250.00	125.00
5 Burleigh Grimes	75.00	38.00
6 Robert M. Grove	100.00	50.00
7 Waite Hoyt	75.00	38.00
8 Joe Judge	50.00	25.00
9 Charles(Chuck)Klein	75.00	38.00
10 Douglas McWeeny	25.00	12.50
11 Frank O'Doul	50.00	25.00
12 Melvin Ott	75.00	38.00
13 Herbert Pennock	75.00	38.00
14 Eddie Rommel	50.00	25.00
15 Babe Ruth	400.00	200.00
16 Al Simmons	75.00	38.00
17 Lloyd Waner	75.00	38.00
18 Hack Wilson	75.00	38.00

1910 W555

This 66 card set measures 1 1/8" by 1 3/16" and have sepia pictures surrounded by a black border, which is framed by a white line. Little is known about how these cards were released and it is speculated thay they are part of the strip card family which explains why they have the "W" designation. Eight cards: Bates, Bescher, Byrne, Collins, Crawford, Devlin, Lake and Mowery are frequently found on want lists. The Eddie Cicotte card was the most recent discovery and is also assumed to be one of the tougher cards. The set is also considered to be related to the E93, E94, E97 and E98 sets.

	Ex-Mt	VG
COMPLETE SET (66)	5000.00	2500.00
1 Red Ames	40.00	20.00
2 Jimmy Austin	40.00	20.00
3 Johnny Bates	80.00	40.00
4 Chief Bender	100.00	50.00
5 Bob Bescher	80.00	40.00
6 Joe Birmingham	40.00	20.00
7 Bill Bradley	40.00	20.00
8 Kitty Bransfield	40.00	20.00
9 Mordecai Brown	100.00	50.00
10 Bobby Byrne	80.00	40.00
11 Frank Chance	100.00	50.00
12 Hal Chase	80.00	40.00
13 Eddie Cicotte	100.00	50.00
14 Fred Clarke	100.00	50.00
15 Ty Cobb	500.00	250.00
16 Eddie Collins dark uniform	300.00	150.00
17 Eddie Collins light uniform	300.00	150.00
18 Harry Covelskie	40.00	20.00
19 Sam Crawford	150.00	75.00
20 Harry Davis	40.00	20.00
21 Jim Delahanty	40.00	20.00
22 Art Devlin	80.00	40.00
23 Josh Devore	40.00	20.00
24 Bill Donovan	60.00	30.00
25 Red Dooin	40.00	20.00
26 Mickey Doolan	40.00	20.00
27 Bull Durham	40.00	20.00
28 Jimmy Dygert	40.00	20.00
29 Johnny Evers	100.00	50.00
30 Russ Ford	40.00	20.00
31 George Gibson	40.00	20.00
32 Clark Griffith	100.00	50.00
33 Topsy Hartsell	40.00	20.00
34 Bill Hinchman Sic, Heinchman	40.00	20.00
35 Charlie Hemphill	40.00	20.00
36 Hugh Jennings MG	100.00	50.00
37 Davy Jones	40.00	20.00
38 Addie Joss	100.00	50.00
39 Willie Keeler	100.00	50.00
40 Red Kleinow	40.00	20.00
41 Nap Lajoie	150.00	75.00
42 Joe Lake	40.00	20.00
43 Tommy Leach	40.00	20.00
44 Sherry Magee	60.00	30.00
45 Christy Mathewson	250.00	125.00
46 Ambrose McConnell	40.00	20.00
47 John McGraw MG	150.00	75.00
48 Chief Meyers	60.00	30.00
49 Earl Moore	40.00	20.00
50 Mike Mowrey	40.00	20.00
51 George Mullin	60.00	30.00
52 Red Murray	40.00	20.00
53 Simon Nicholls	40.00	20.00
54 Jim Pastorius	40.00	20.00
55 Deacon Phillipe	60.00	30.00
56 Eddie Plank	100.00	50.00
57 Fred Snodgrass	40.00	20.00
58 Harry Steinfeldt	60.00	30.00
59 Joe Tinker	100.00	50.00
60 Hippo Vaughn	40.00	20.00
61 Honus Wagner	250.00	125.00
62 Rube Waddell	100.00	50.00
63 Hooks Wiltse	40.00	20.00
64 Cy Young Cleveland Amer.	200.00	100.00
65 Cy Young Same pose as E93	200.00	100.00
66 Cy Young Same pose as E97-8	200.00	100.00

1922 W572

This 119-card set was issued in 1922 in ten-card strips along with strips of boxer cards. The cards measure approximately 1 5/16" by 2 1/2" and are blank backed. Most of the player photos on the fronts are black and white, although a few photos are sepia-toned. The pictures are the same ones used in the E120 set, but they have been cropped to fit on the smaller format. The player's signature and team appear at the bottom of the pictures, along with an IFS (International Feature Service) copyright notice. The cards are unnumbered and checklisted below in alphabetical order.

	Ex-Mt	VG
COMPLETE SET (119)	4000.00	2000.00
1 Eddie Ainsmith	15.00	7.50
2 Vic Aldridge	15.00	7.50
3 Grover C. Alexander	100.00	50.00
4 Dave Bancroft	30.00	15.00
5 Jesse Barnes	15.00	7.50
6 John Bassler	15.00	7.50
7 Lu Blue	15.00	7.50
8 Norm Boeckel	15.00	7.50
9 George Burns	15.00	7.50
10 Joe Bush	18.00	9.00
11 Leon Cadore	15.00	7.50
12 Virgil Cheevers	15.00	7.50
13 Ty Cobb	500.00	250.00
14 Eddie Collins	40.00	20.00
15 John Collins	15.00	7.50
16 Wilbur Cooper	15.00	7.50
17 Stanley Coveleski	30.00	15.00
18 Walton Cruise	15.00	7.50
19 Dave Danforth	15.00	7.50
20 Jake Daubert	18.00	9.00
21 Hank DeBerry	15.00	7.50
22 Lou DeVormer	15.00	7.50
23 Bill Doak	15.00	7.50
24 Pete Donohue	15.00	7.50
25 Pat Duncan	15.00	7.50
26 Jimmy Dykes	18.00	9.00
27 Urban Faber	30.00	15.00
28 Bibb Falk	15.00	7.50
29 Frank Frisch	50.00	25.00
30 Chick Galloway	15.00	7.50
31 Ed Gharrity	15.00	7.50
32 Charles Glazner	15.00	7.50
33 Hank Gowdy	18.00	9.00
34 Tom Griffith	15.00	7.50
35 Burleigh Grimes	30.00	15.00
36 Ray Grimes	15.00	7.50
37 Heinie Groh	18.00	9.00
38 Joe Harris	15.00	7.50
39 Bucky Harris	30.00	15.00
40 Joe Hauser	15.00	7.50
41 Harry Heilmann	30.00	15.00
42 Walter Henline	15.00	7.50
43 Charles Hollocher	15.00	7.50
44 Harry Hooper	30.00	15.00
45 Rogers Hornsby	120.00	60.00
46 Waite Hoyt	30.00	15.00
47 Wilbur Hubbell	15.00	7.50
48 William Jacobson	15.00	7.50
49 Charles Jamieson	15.00	7.50
50 Syl Johnson	15.00	7.50
51 Walter Johnson	200.00	100.00
52 Jimmy Johnston	15.00	7.50
53 Joe Judge	18.00	9.00
54 George Kelly	30.00	15.00
55 Lee King	15.00	7.50
56 Larry Kopf	15.00	7.50
57 George Leverette	15.00	7.50
58 Al Mamaux	15.00	7.50
59 Rabbit Maranville	30.00	15.00
60 Rube Marquard	30.00	15.00
61 Martin McManus	15.00	7.50
62 Lee Meadows	15.00	7.50
63 Mike Menosky	15.00	7.50
64 Bob Meusel	20.00	10.00
65 Emil Meusel	15.00	7.50
66 George Mogridge	15.00	7.50
67 John Morrison	15.00	7.50
68 Johnny Mostil	15.00	7.50
69 Roleine Naylor	15.00	7.50
70 Art Nehf	15.00	7.50
71 Joe Oeschger	15.00	7.50
72 Bob O'Farrell	15.00	7.50
73 Steve O'Neill	18.00	9.00
74 Frank Parkinson	15.00	7.50
75 Ralph Perkins	15.00	7.50
76 Herman Pillette	15.00	7.50
77 Babe Pinelli	18.00	9.00
78 Wallie Pipp	20.00	10.00
79 Ray Powell	15.00	7.50
80 Jack Quinn	15.00	7.50
81 Goldie Rapp	15.00	7.50
82 Walt Reuther	15.00	7.50
83 Sam Rice	30.00	15.00
84 Emory Rigney	15.00	7.50
85 Eppa Rixey	30.00	15.00
86 Ed Rommel	18.00	9.00
87 Eddie Roush	50.00	25.00
88 Babe Ruth	1000.00	500.00
89 Ray Schalk	30.00	15.00
90 Wally Schang	18.00	9.00
91 Walter Schmidt	15.00	7.50
92 Joe Schultz	15.00	7.50
93 Hank Severeid	15.00	7.50
94 Joe Sewell	30.00	15.00
95 Bob Shawkey	18.00	9.00
96 Earl Sheely	15.00	7.50
97 Will Sherdel	15.00	7.50
98 Urban Shocker	18.00	9.00
99 George Sisler	80.00	40.00
100 Earl Smith	15.00	7.50
101 Elmer Smith	15.00	7.50
102 Jack Smith	15.00	7.50
103 Bill Southworth	18.00	9.00
104 Tris Speaker	100.00	50.00
105 Jigger Statz	15.00	7.50
106 Milton Stock	15.00	7.50
107 Jim Tierney	15.00	7.50
108 Harold Traynor	30.00	15.00
109 George Uhle	15.00	7.50
110 Bob Veach	15.00	7.50
111 Clarence Walker	15.00	7.50
112 Curtis Walker	15.00	7.50
113 Bill Wambsganss	18.00	9.00
114 Aaron Ward	15.00	7.50
115 Zach Wheat	30.00	15.00
116 Fred Williams	15.00	7.50
117 Ken Williams	20.00	10.00
118 Ivy Wingo	15.00	7.50
119 Joe Wood	20.00	10.00
120 Tom Zachary	15.00	7.50

1922 W573

This set's design is similiar to the E120 American Caramel set. The backs are blank. These cards have been described as a "small strip card type of E120. Albums for these cards exist. They are made of black construction paper and the inside has pages for each team and specific places for each player.

	Ex-Mt	VG
COMPLETE SET (143)	2000.00	1000.00
1 Babe Adams	12.00	6.00
2 Eddie Ainsmith	10.00	5.00
3 Vic Aldridge	10.00	5.00
4 Grover C. Alexander	60.00	30.00
5 Frank Baker	20.00	10.00
6 Dave Bancroft	20.00	10.00
7 Turner Barber	10.00	5.00
8 Jesse Barnes	10.00	5.00
9 Johnny Bassler	10.00	5.00
10 Carson Bigbee	10.00	5.00
11 Lu Blue	10.00	5.00
12 Tony Boeckel	10.00	5.00
13 George H. Burns	10.00	5.00
14 George J. Burns	10.00	5.00
15 Marty Callaghan	10.00	5.00
16 Max Carey	20.00	10.00
17 Ike Caveney	10.00	5.00
18 Virgil Cheeves	10.00	5.00
19 Verne Clemons	10.00	5.00
20 Ty Cobb	150.00	75.00
21 Al Cole	10.00	5.00
22 Eddie Collins	20.00	10.00
23 Pat Collins	10.00	5.00
24 Wilbur Cooper	10.00	5.00
25 Dick Cox	10.00	5.00
26 Bill Cunningham	10.00	5.00
27 George Cutshaw	10.00	5.00
28 Dave Danforth	10.00	5.00
29 Hooks Dauss	10.00	5.00
30 Dixie Davis	10.00	5.00
31 Hank DeBerry	10.00	5.00
32 Al DeVormer	10.00	5.00
33 Bill Doak	10.00	5.00
34 Joe Dugan	12.00	6.00
35 Howard Ehmke	12.00	6.00
36 Frank Ellerbe	10.00	5.00
37 Red Faber	20.00	10.00
38 Bibb Falk	10.00	5.00
39 Max Flack	10.00	5.00
40 Ira Flagstead	10.00	5.00
41 Art Fletcher	10.00	5.00
42 Hod Ford	10.00	5.00
43 Jacques Fournier	10.00	5.00
44 Frank Frisch	40.00	20.00
45 Ollie Fuhrman	10.00	5.00
46 Chick Galloway	10.00	5.00
47 Wally Gerber	10.00	5.00
48 Patsy Gharrity	10.00	5.00
49 Whitey Glazner	10.00	5.00
50 Goose Goslin	20.00	10.00
51 Hank Gowdy	12.00	6.00
52 Jack Graney	10.00	5.00
53 Burleigh Grimes	20.00	10.00
54 Heinie Groh	12.00	6.00
55 Jesse Haines	20.00	10.00
56 Bubbles Hargrave	10.00	5.00
57 Joe Harris	10.00	5.00
58 Earl Hamilton	10.00	5.00
59 Cliff Heathcote	10.00	5.00
60 Harry Heilmann	20.00	10.00
61 Clarence Hodge	10.00	5.00
62 Charlie Hollocher	10.00	5.00
63 Harry Hooper	20.00	10.00
64 Rogers Hornsby	80.00	40.00
65 Waite Hoyt	20.00	10.00
66 Ernie Johnson	10.00	5.00
67 Syl Johnson	10.00	5.00
68 Walter Johnson	80.00	40.00
69 Paul Johnson	10.00	5.00
70 Sam Jones	12.00	6.00
71 Benjamin Karr	10.00	5.00
72 Doc Lavan	10.00	5.00
73 Dixie Levrette	10.00	5.00
74 Rabbit Maranville	20.00	10.00
75 Cliff Markle	10.00	5.00
76 Carl Mays	10.00	5.00
77 Harvey McClellan	10.00	5.00
78 Marty McManus	10.00	5.00
79 Lee Meadows	10.00	5.00
80 Mike Menosky	10.00	5.00
81 Irish Meusel	10.00	5.00
82 Clyde Milan	12.00	6.00
83 Bing Miller	10.00	5.00
84 Elmer Miller	10.00	5.00
85 Ralph Miller	10.00	5.00
86 Hack Miller	10.00	5.00
87 Clarence Mitchell	10.00	5.00
88 George Mogridge	10.00	5.00
89 John Morrison	10.00	5.00
90 Johnny Mostil	10.00	5.00
91 Elmer Myers	10.00	5.00
92 Roleine Naylor	10.00	5.00
93 Les Nunamaker	10.00	5.00
94 Bob O'Farrell	10.00	5.00
95 Steve O'Neill	12.00	6.00
96 Herb Pennock	20.00	10.00
97 Cy Perkins	10.00	5.00
98 Thomas Phillips	10.00	5.00
99 Val Picinich	10.00	5.00
100 Herman Pillette	10.00	5.00
101 Babe Pinelli	10.00	5.00
102 Wally Pipp	12.00	6.00
103 Clark Pittenger	10.00	5.00
104 Del Pratt	10.00	5.00
105 Goldie Rapp	10.00	5.00
106 Johnny Rawlings	10.00	5.00
107 Topper Rigney	10.00	5.00
108 Charlie Robertson	10.00	5.00
109 Ed Rommel	10.00	5.00
110 Muddy Ruel	10.00	5.00
111 Dutch Ruether	10.00	5.00
112 Babe Ruth	250.00	125.00
113 Ray Schalk	20.00	10.00
114 Wally Schang	12.00	6.00
115 Ray Schmandt	10.00	5.00
116 Walter Schmidt	10.00	5.00
117 Germany Schultz	10.00	5.00
118 Henry Severeid	10.00	5.00
119 Joe Sewell	20.00	10.00
120 Bob Shawkey	15.00	7.50
121 Earl Sheely	10.00	5.00
122 Ralph Shinners	10.00	5.00
123 Urban Shocker	10.00	5.00
124 George Sisler	40.00	20.00
125 Earl L. Smith	10.00	5.00
126 Earl S. Smith	10.00	5.00
127 Jack Smith	10.00	5.00
128 Allen Sothoron	10.00	5.00
129 Tris Speaker	60.00	30.00
130 Amos Strunk	10.00	5.00
131 Cotton Tierney	10.00	5.00
132 Jack Tobin	10.00	5.00
133 Specs Toporcer	10.00	5.00
134 George Uhle	10.00	5.00
135 Bobby Veach	10.00	5.00
136 John Watson	10.00	5.00
137 Zack Wheat	20.00	10.00
138 Ken Williams	12.00	6.00
139 Cy Williams	10.00	5.00
140 Charles Woodall	10.00	5.00
141 Russell Wrightstone	10.00	5.00
142 Ross Youngs	20.00	10.00
143 Tom Zachary	10.00	5.00

1922 W575

This 154-card set, referenced by the catalog designation W575, measures approximately 1 15/16" by 3 3/16". The cards have a black and white action posed photo are are blank backed. The players name and position are under the photo on the front. Cards that are part of the "autograph on shoulder" series are marked with an asterisk in the checklist below and are worth a little more.

	Ex-Mt	VG
COMPLETE SET (154)	2750.00	1400.00
1 Babe Adams	10.00	5.00
2 Grover C. Alexander (2)	50.00	25.00
3 Jim Bagby	10.00	5.00
4 Frank Baker	25.00	12.50
5 Dave Bancroft (2)	50.00	25.00
6 Jesse Barnes	10.00	5.00
7 Johnny Bassler	20.00	10.00
8 Joe Berry	10.00	5.00
9 Carson Bigbee	10.00	5.00
10 Ping Bodie	10.00	5.00
11 Eddie Brown	10.00	5.00
12 Jesse Burkett CO	25.00	12.50
13 George H. Burns	10.00	5.00
14 Donie Bush	20.00	10.00
15 Joe Bush	10.00	5.00
16 Max Carey (2)	25.00	12.50
17 Ty Cobb	150.00	75.00
18 Eddie Collins*	25.00	12.50
19 Rip Collins	10.00	5.00
20 Stan Coveleski*	25.00	12.50
21 Bill Cunningham	10.00	5.00
22 Jake Daubert	20.00	10.00
23 Hooks Dauss (2)	10.00	5.00
24 Dixie Davis	10.00	5.00
25 Charlie Deal (2)	10.00	5.00
26 Al Devormer	10.00	5.00
27 Bill Doak	10.00	5.00
28 Bill Donovan MG	10.00	5.00
29 Phil Douglas	10.00	5.00
30 Joe Dugan	20.00	10.00
31 Johnny Evers MG (2)	25.00	12.50
32 Red Faber	25.00	12.50
33 Bibb Falk	10.00	5.00
34 Alex Ferguson	10.00	5.00
35 Chick Fewster	10.00	5.00
36 Eddie Foster	10.00	5.00
37 Frank Frisch	50.00	25.00
38 Larry Gardner	10.00	5.00
39 Alex Gaston	10.00	5.00
40 Wally Gerber	20.00	10.00
41 Patsy Gharrity	10.00	5.00
42 Whitey Glazner	10.00	5.00
43 Kid Gleason MG	15.00	7.50
44 Mike Gonzales	10.00	5.00
45 Hank Gowdy	15.00	7.50
46 Jack Graney (2)	10.00	5.00
47 Tommy Griffith	10.00	5.00
48 Charlie Grimm	15.00	7.50
49 Heinie Groh New York NL	15.00	7.50
50 Henie Groh Cincinnati NL	15.00	7.50
51 Jesse Haines	25.00	12.50
52 Harry Harper	10.00	5.00
53 Chicken Hawks	10.00	5.00
54 Harry Heilmann	25.00	12.50
55 Fred Hoffman	10.00	5.00
56 Walter Holke (3)	10.00	5.00
57 Charlie Hollocher (2)	10.00	5.00
58 Harry Hooper	25.00	12.50
59 Rogers Hornsby	50.00	25.00
60 Waite Hoyt	25.00	12.50
61 Miller Huggins MG	25.00	12.50
62 Baby Doll Jacobson	10.00	5.00
63 Hugh Jennings CO	25.00	12.50
64 Walter Johnson (2)	100.00	50.00
65 Jimmy Johnston	10.00	5.00
66 Joe Judge	20.00	10.00
67 George Kelly (2)	25.00	12.50
68 Dickie Kerr	15.00	7.50
69 Pete Kilduff	10.00	5.00
70 Doc Lavan	10.00	5.00
71 Nemo Leibold	10.00	5.00
72 Duffy Lewis	15.00	7.50
73 Al Mamaux	10.00	5.00
74 Rabbit Maranville*	25.00	12.50
75 Rube Marquard	25.00	12.50
76 Carl Mays (2)	15.00	7.50
77 John McGraw MG	50.00	25.00
78 Stuffy McInnis	15.00	7.50
79 Mike McNally	10.00	5.00
80 Bob Meusel	20.00	10.00
81 Irish Meusel	10.00	5.00
82 Clyde Milan	15.00	7.50
83 Elmer Miller	10.00	5.00
84 Otto Miller	10.00	5.00
85 Johnny Mitchell	10.00	5.00
86 Guy Morton	20.00	10.00
87 Eddie Mulligan	10.00	5.00
88 Eddie Murphy	10.00	5.00
89 Hy Myers (3)	10.00	5.00
90 Greasy Neale	15.00	7.50
91 Art Nehf	20.00	10.00
92 Joe Oeschger	10.00	5.00
93 Charley O'Leary CO	10.00	5.00
94 Steve O'Neill	15.00	7.50
95 Roger Peckinpaugh (2)	15.00	7.50
96 Bill Piercy	10.00	5.00
97 Jeff Pfeffer Brook. NL	10.00	5.00
98 Jeff Pfeffer St. L. NL	10.00	5.00
99 Wally Pipp	15.00	7.50
100 Jack Quinn	10.00	5.00
101 Johnny Rawlings (2)	10.00	5.00
102 Sam Rice (2)	25.00	12.50
103 Jimmy Ring	20.00	10.00
104 Eppa Rixey	25.00	12.50
105 Charlie Robertson*	20.00	10.00
106 Wilbert Robinson MG	25.00	12.50
107 Tom Rogers	10.00	5.00
108 Ed Rommel#(sic.Rounnel	20.00	10.00
109 Braggo Roth	10.00	5.00
110 Edd Roush (2)	25.00	12.50
111 Muddy Ruel	10.00	5.00
112 Babe Ruth (2)	250.00	125.00
113 Rosy Ryan (2)	10.00	5.00
114 Slim Sallee (2)	10.00	5.00
115 Ray Schalk (2)	25.00	12.50
116 Wally Schang* (2)	20.00	10.00
117 Ferd Schupp (2)	10.00	5.00
118 Everett Scott Boston AL	20.00	4.00
119 Everett Scott New York AL	10.00	5.00
120 Hank Severeid *	20.00	10.00
121 Joe Sewell*	25.00	12.50
122 Bob Shawkey	20.00	10.00
123 Red Shea	10.00	5.00
124 Earl Sheely	10.00	5.00
125 Urban Shocker	15.00	7.50
126 George Sisler* (2)	50.00	25.00
127 Elmer Smith	10.00	5.00
128 Earl Smith	10.00	5.00
129 Pancho Snyder	10.00	5.00
130 Tris Speaker* (2)	50.00	25.00
131 Casey Stengel New York NL	50.00	25.00
132 Casey Stengel Phila. NL	50.00	25.00
133 Riggs Stephenson	20.00	10.00
134 Milt Stock	10.00	5.00
135 Amos Strunk (2)	10.00	5.00
136 Zeb Terry	50.00	25.00
137 Pinch Thomas	10.00	5.00
138 Fred Toney (2)	10.00	5.00
139 Specs Torporcer	10.00	5.00
140 Lefty Tyler	10.00	5.00
141 Hippo Vaughn (2)	15.00	7.50
142 Bobby Veach (3)	20.00	10.00
143 Ossie Vitt	20.00	10.00
144 Frank Walker	20.00	10.00
145 Curt Walker	20.00	10.00
146 Bill Wambsganss (2)	15.00	7.50
147 Zack Wheat	25.00	12.50
148 Possum Whitted	10.00	5.00
149 Williams Chicago AL *	20.00	10.00
150 Cy Williams	10.00	5.00

151 Ivy Wingo 10.00 5.00
152 Joe Wood 20.00 10.00
153 Ralph Young 50.00 25.00
154 Ross Youngs 25.00 12.50

1926-28 W590

Issued over a period of years, this set which measure approximately 1 3/8" by 2 1/2" features some of the leading players from the 1920's. The fronts have a photo on the front with the players name, position and team on the bottom. The backs are blank and as these cards are unnumbered we have sequenced them in alphabetical order.

Ex-Mt VG
COMPLETE SET 3500.00 1800.00
1 Grover Cleveland Alexander 150.00 75.00
2 Dave Bancroft 80.00 40.00
3 Jess Barnes 25.00 12.50
4 Ray Blades 25.00 12.50
5 Ozzie Bluege 25.00 12.50
6 George Burns 40.00 20.00
NY NL
7 George Burns 40.00 20.00
Phi NL
8 George Burns 40.00 20.00
Cleveland
9 Max Carey 80.00 40.00
10 Jimmy Caveney 25.00 12.50
11 Ty Cobb 250.00 125.00
12 Eddie Collins 150.00 75.00
13 George Dauss 25.00 12.50
14 Red Faber 80.00 40.00
15 Frankie Frisch 100.00 50.00
16 Lou Gehrig 300.00 150.00
17 Sam Gray 25.00 12.50
18 Hank Gowdy 25.00 12.50
19 Charley Grimm 40.00 20.00
20 Bucky Harris 80.00 40.00
21 Rogers Hornsby 200.00 100.00
St Louis
22 Rogers Hornsby 200.00 100.00
Boston
23 Travis Jackson 80.00 40.00
24 Walter Johnson 200.00 100.00
25 George Kelly 40.00 20.00
26 Fred Lindstrom 80.00 40.00
27 Rabbit Maranville 80.00 40.00
28 Bob Meusel 60.00 30.00
29 Jack Quinn 40.00 20.00
30 Eppa Rixey 40.00 20.00
31 Eddie Rommel 25.00 12.50
32 Babe Ruth 500.00 250.00
33 Heinie Sand 25.00 12.50
34 Earl Smith 25.00 12.50
35 Tris Speaker 150.00 75.00
36 Roy Spencer 25.00 12.50
37 Milt Stock 25.00 12.50
38 Phil Todt 25.00 12.50
Phi AL
39 Phil Todt 25.00 12.50
Bos AL
40 Dazzy Vance 80.00 40.00
41 Ken Williams 40.00 20.00
St Louis AL
42 Ken Williams 40.00 20.00
Bos AL
43 Zack Wheat 80.00 40.00
44 Ross Youngs 80.00 40.00

1963 Wagner Otto Milk Carton

This is the only baseball player featured in this set which honored promiment Western Pennsylvanians. The side panel of the milk carton inlcuded a drawing of Wagner as well as some brief biographical informaion as well as a biography.

MINT NRMT
1 Honus Wagner 80.00 36.00

1995 Wagner T-206 Reprint IMT

This one card reprint was issued as part of the promotion which celebrated the contest in which one very lucky collector could win a real T206 Wagner. This card resembles the original but has the information about who the producer is as well as who allowed the usage of Wagner's picture on the card.

Nm-Mt Ex-Mt
1 Honus Wagner 1.00 .30

1920 Walter Mails WG7

These cards were distributed as part of a baseball game produced in 1920. The cards each measure approximately 2 5/16" by 3 1/4" and have rounded corners. The card fronts show a black and white photo of the player, his name, position, his team, and the game outcome associated with that particular card. The card backs are all the same, each showing an ornate red and white design with "Walter Mails" inside a red circle in the middle all surrounded by a thin white outer border. Since the cards are unnumbered, they are listed below in alphabetical order.

Ex-Mt VG
COMPLETE SET 3500.00 1800.00
1 Buzz Arlett 50.00 25.00
2 Jim Bagby 50.00 25.00
3 Dave Bancroft 100.00 50.00
4 Johnny Bassler 50.00 25.00
Sic, Basseler
5 Jack Bentley 50.00 25.00
6 Rube Benton 50.00 25.00
7 George Burns 50.00 25.00
8 Joe Bush 50.00 25.00
9 Harold P. Chavez 50.00 25.00
10 Hugh Critz 50.00 25.00
11 Jake Daubert 80.00 40.00
12 Wheezer Dell 50.00 25.00
13 Joe Dugan 60.00 30.00
14 Pat Duncan 50.00 25.00
15 Howard Ehmke 50.00 25.00
16 Lew Fonseca 50.00 25.00
17 Ray French 50.00 25.00
18 Ed Gharity 50.00 25.00
Sic, Gharitty
19 Heinie Groh 60.00 30.00
20 George Grove 50.00 25.00
21 Bubbles Hargrave 50.00 25.00
22 Elmer Jacobs 50.00 25.00
23 Walter Johnson 500.00 250.00
24 Duke Kenworthy 50.00 25.00
25 Harry Krause 50.00 25.00
26 Ray Kremer 50.00 25.00
27 Walter Mails 50.00 25.00
28 Rabbit Maranville 100.00 50.00
29 Stuffy McInnis 60.00 30.00
30 Marty McManus 50.00 25.00
31 Bob Meusel 80.00 40.00
32 Hack Miller 50.00 25.00
33 Pat J. Moran 60.00 30.00
34 Guy Morton 50.00 25.00
35 Johnny Mostil 50.00 25.00
36 Red Murphy 50.00 25.00
37 Jimmy O'Connell 50.00 25.00
38 Joe Oeschger 50.00 25.00
39 Steve O'Neil 60.00 30.00
40 Roger Peckinpaugh 60.00 30.00
41 Babe Pinelli 50.00 25.00
42 Wally Pipp 80.00 40.00
43 Elmer Ponder 50.00 25.00
44 Sam Rice 100.00 50.00
45 Ed Rommell 50.00 25.00
46 Walter Schmidt 50.00 25.00
47 Joe Sewell 100.00 50.00
48 Pat Shea 50.00 25.00
49 Wilford Shupe 50.00 25.00
50 Paddy Siglin 50.00 25.00
51 George Sisler 150.00 75.00
52 Bill Skiff 50.00 25.00
53 Jack Smith 50.00 25.00
54 Suds Sutherland 50.00 25.00
55 Cotton Tierney 50.00 25.00
56 George Uhle 50.00 25.00

1910 Washington Times

This very rare and obscure issue was apparently a supplement for the Washington Times newspaper. The cards measure approximately 2 1/2" by 3 1/2" and feature black-and-white player photos with blank backs. The cards are unnumbered and checklisted below in alphabetical order. The Walter Johnson card is rumored as being in the set. The checklist is probably incomplete and any confirmed additions are welcomed.

Ex-Mt VG
COMPLETE SET 10000.00 5000.00
1 Ty Cobb 3000.00 1500.00
2 Eddie Collins 1000.00 500.00
3 Wid Conroy 250.00 125.00
4 Walter Johnson 1500.00 750.00
5 Nap Lajoie 1000.00 500.00
6 George McBride 250.00 125.00
7 Clyde Milan 300.00 150.00
8 Frank Oberlin 250.00 125.00
9 Jack O'Connor 250.00 125.00
10 Gabby Street 250.00 125.00
11 Lee Tannehill 250.00 125.00
12 Bob Unglaub 250.00 125.00
13 Dixie Walker 250.00 125.00
14 Ed Walsh 500.00 250.00
15 Joe Wood 400.00 200.00
16 Cy Young 1500.00 750.00

1987 Weis Market Discs

These discs are a parallel issue to the 1987 MSA Iced Tea Discs. They say Weis on the front and are valued the same as the MSA Discs.

Nm-Mt Ex-Mt
COMPLETE SET (20) 8.00 3.20
1 Darryl Strawberry .20 .08
2 Roger Clemens 1.50 .60
3 Ron Darling .10 .04
4 Keith Hernandez .20 .08
5 Tony Pena .20 .08
6 Don Mattingly 1.50 .60
7 Eric Davis .20 .08
8 Gary Carter .75 .30
9 Dave Winfield .75 .30
10 Wally Joyner .60 .24
11 Mike Schmidt .75 .30
12 Robby Thompson .10 .04
13 Wade Boggs .75 .30
14 Cal Ripken 3.00 1.20
15 Dale Murphy .40 .16
16 Tony Gwynn 1.50 .60
17 Jose Canseco .75 .30
18 Rickey Henderson 1.00 .40
19 Lance Parrish .10 .04
20 Dave Righetti .10 .04

1988 Weis Market Discs

For the second year, Weis Markets was one of the distributors of these MSA Baseball Superstar Discs. These discs are valued the same as the MSA Iced Tea Discs.

Nm-Mt Ex-Mt
COMPLETE SET (20) 10.00 4.00
1 Wade Boggs 1.00 .40
2 Ellis Burks 1.00 .40
3 Don Mattingly 2.00 .80
4 Mark McGwire 3.00 1.20
5 Matt Nokes .10 .04
6 Kirby Puckett 1.00 .40
7 Billy Ripken .10 .04
8 Kevin Seitzer .10 .04
9 Roger Clemens 2.00 .80
10 Will Clark .75 .30
11 Vince Coleman .10 .04
12 Eric Davis .25 .10
13 Dave Magadan .10 .04
14 Dale Murphy .50 .20
15 Benito Santiago .25 .10
16 Mike Schmidt 1.00 .40
17 Darryl Strawberry .25 .10
18 Steve Bedrosian .10 .04
19 Dwight Gooden .25 .10
20 Fernando Valenzuela .25 .10

1989 Weis Market Discs

For the third year, the MSA Iced Tea Discs were issued under the Weis Market name. They are valued the same as the regular MSA Iced Tea Discs.

Nm-Mt Ex-Mt
COMPLETE SET (20) 30.00 12.00
1 Don Mattingly 6.00 2.40
2 Dave Cone 1.00 .40
3 Mark McGwire 10.00 4.00
4 Will Clark 2.50 1.00
5 Darryl Strawberry 1.50 .60
6 Dwight Gooden 1.50 .60
7 Wade Boggs 4.00 1.60
8 Roger Clemens 6.00 2.40
9 Benito Santiago 1.50 .60
10 Orel Hershiser 1.50 .60
11 Eric Davis 1.50 .60
12 Kirby Puckett 3.00 1.20
13 Dave Winfield 3.00 1.20
14 Andre Dawson 2.50 1.00
15 Steve Bedrosian 1.00 .40
16 Cal Ripken 12.00 4.80
17 Andy Van Slyke 1.00 .40
18 Jose Canseco 3.00 1.20
19 Jose Oquendo 1.00 .40
20 Dale Murphy 2.00 .80

1977 Wendy's Discs

These discs were issued of popular baseball players through the popular hamburger chain. They, like all the other discs, feature the players photo on the front and a back publicizing where the disc was obtained. These are the most expensive of the 1977 discs.

NM Ex
COMPLETE SET (70) 600.00 240.00
1 Sal Bando 5.00 2.00
2 Buddy Bell 10.00 4.00
3 Johnny Bench 80.00 32.00
4 Lou Brock 60.00 24.00
5 Larry Bowa 10.00 4.00
6 Steve Braun 5.00 2.00
7 George Brett 120.00 47.50
8 Jeff Burroughs 5.00 2.00
9 Campy Campaneris 10.00 4.00
10 John Candelaria 5.00 2.00
11 Jose Cardenal 5.00 2.00
12 Rod Carew 60.00 24.00
13 Steve Carlton 60.00 24.00
14 Dave Cash 5.00 2.00
15 Cesar Cedeno 5.00 2.00
16 Ron Cey 10.00 4.00
17 Dave Concepcion 15.00 6.00
18 Dennis Eckersley 60.00 24.00
19 Mark Fidrych 60.00 24.00
20 Rollie Fingers 40.00 16.00
21 Carlton Fisk 60.00 24.00
22 George Foster 15.00 6.00
23 Wayne Garland 5.00 2.00
24 Ralph Garr 10.00 4.00
25 Steve Garvey 30.00 12.00
26 Cesar Geronimo 5.00 2.00
27 Bobby Grich 10.00 4.00
28 Ken Griffey 15.00 6.00
29 Don Gullett 5.00 2.00
30 Mike Hargrove 10.00 4.00
31 Al Hrabosky 5.00 2.00
32 Catfish Hunter 40.00 16.00
33 Reggie Jackson 80.00 32.00
34 Randy Jones 5.00 2.00
35 Dave Kingman 20.00 8.00
36 Jerry Koosman 10.00 4.00
37 Dave LaRoche 5.00 2.00
38 Greg Luzinski 15.00 6.00
39 Fred Lynn 10.00 4.00
40 Bill Madlock 10.00 4.00
41 Rick Manning 5.00 2.00
42 Jon Matlack 5.00 2.00
43 John Mayberry 5.00 2.00
44 Hal McRae 10.00 4.00
45 Andy Messersmith 5.00 2.00
46 Rick Monday 5.00 2.00
47 John Montefusco 5.00 2.00
48 Joe Morgan 40.00 16.00
49 Thurman Munson 30.00 12.00
50 Bobby Murcer 15.00 6.00
51 Bill North 5.00 2.00
52 Jim Palmer 40.00 16.00
53 Tony Perez 40.00 16.00
54 Jerry Reuss 5.00 2.00
55 Brooks Robinson 60.00 24.00
56 Pete Rose 80.00 32.00
57 Joe Rudi 5.00 2.00
58 Nolan Ryan 150.00 60.00
59 Manny Sanguillen 5.00 2.00
60 Mike Schmidt 80.00 32.00
61 Tom Seaver 80.00 32.00
62 Bill Singer 5.00 2.00
63 Willie Stargell 40.00 16.00
64 Rusty Staub 15.00 6.00
65 Luis Tiant 10.00 4.00
66 Bob Watson 10.00 4.00
67 Butch Wynegar 5.00 2.00
68 Carl Yastrzemski 60.00 24.00
69 Robin Yount 60.00 24.00
70 Richie Zisk 5.00 2.00

1888 WG1 Card Game

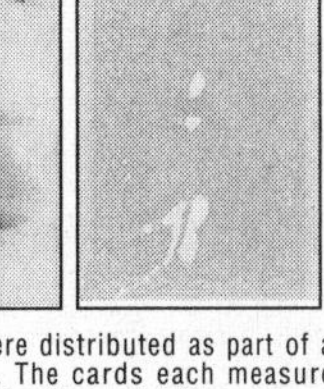

These cards were distributed as part of a baseball game. The cards each measure approximately 2 1/2" by 3 1/2" and have rounded corners. The card fronts show a color drawing of the player, his name, his position, and the game outcome associated with that particular card. The card backs are all the same, each showing a geometric graphic design in blue. Since the cards are unnumbered, they are listed below in alphabetical order within each of the eight teams. The box features a photo of King Kelly on the front along with the words, "Patented Feb. 28, 1888".

Ex-Mt VG
COMPLETE SET (72) 30000.00 15000.00
1 Tom Brown 400.00 200.00
2 John Clarkson 1000.00 500.00
3 Joe Hornung 400.00 200.00
4 Dick Johnston 400.00 200.00
5 King Kelly 1500.00 750.00
6 John Morrill 400.00 200.00
7 Billy Nash 400.00 200.00
8 Ezra Sutton 400.00 200.00
9 Sam Wise 400.00 200.00
10 Cap Anson 3000.00 1500.00
11 Tom Burns 400.00 200.00
12 Silver Flint 400.00 200.00
13 Bob Pettit 400.00 200.00
14 Fred Pfeffer 400.00 200.00
15 Jimmy Ryan 400.00 200.00
16 Marty Sullivan 800.00 400.00
17 George Van Haltren 400.00 200.00
18 Ned Williamson 500.00 250.00
19 Charlie Bennett 500.00 250.00
20 Dan Brouthers 1200.00 600.00
21 Charlie Getzein 400.00 200.00
22 Ned Hanlon 800.00 400.00
23 Hardy Richardson 400.00 200.00
24 Jack Rowe 400.00 200.00
25 Sam Thompson 800.00 400.00
26 Larry Twitchell 400.00 200.00
27 Deacon White 500.00 250.00
28 Charley Bassett 400.00 200.00
29 Henry Boyle 400.00 200.00
30 Jerry Denny 400.00 200.00
31 Dude Esterbrook 400.00 200.00
32 Jack Glasscock 800.00 400.00
33 Paul Hines 400.00 200.00
34 George Meyers 400.00 200.00
35 Emmett Seery 400.00 200.00
36 Jumbo Shoeneck 400.00 200.00
37 Roger Connor 800.00 400.00
38 Buck Ewing 1200.00 600.00
39 Elmer Foster 400.00 200.00
40 George Gore 400.00 200.00
41 Tim Keefe 800.00 400.00
42 Jim O'Rourke 800.00 400.00
43 Danny Richardson 400.00 200.00
44 Mike Tiernan 400.00 200.00
45 John Ward 1200.00 600.00
46 Ed Andrews 400.00 200.00
47 Charlie Bastian 400.00 200.00
48 Don Casey 400.00 200.00
49 Jack Clements 400.00 200.00
50 Sid Farrar 500.00 250.00
51 Jim Fogarty 400.00 200.00
52 Arthur Irwin 400.00 200.00
53 Joe Mulvey 400.00 200.00
54 George Wood 400.00 200.00
55 Fred Carroll 400.00 200.00
56 John Coleman 400.00 200.00
57 Abner Dalrymple 400.00 200.00
58 Fred Dunlap 400.00 200.00
59 Pud Galvin 800.00 400.00
60 Willie Kuehne 400.00 1600.00
61 Al Maul 400.00 200.00
62 Pop Smith 400.00 200.00
63 Billy Sunday 800.00 400.00
64 Jim Donelly 400.00 200.00
65 Dummy Hoy 800.00 400.00
66 John Irwin 400.00 200.00
67 Connie Mack 2000.00 1000.00
68 Al Myers 400.00 200.00
69 Billy O'Brien 400.00 200.00
70 George Shoch 400.00 200.00
71 Jim Whitney 400.00 200.00
72 Walt Wilmot 400.00 200.00

1935 Wheaties BB1

This set is referred to as "Fancy Frame with Script Signature". These cards (which made up the back of the Wheaties cereal box) measure 6" by 6 1/4" with the frame and about 5" by 5 1/2" if the frame is trimmed off. The player photo appears in blue on a blue-tinted field with a solid orange background behind the player. The player's facsimile autograph is displayed at the bottom of the card.

Ex-Mt VG
COMPLETE SET (27) 2000.00 1000.00
1 Jack Armstrong 40.00 20.00
(batting pose)
(fictional character)
2 Jack Armstrong 40.00 20.00
(throwing)
(your friend)
(fictional character)
3 Wally Berger 40.00 20.00
(batting follow through)
Sincerely Yours
4 Tommy Bridges 40.00 20.00
(pitching)
5A Mickey Cochrane 80.00 40.00
(squatting, wearing black hat and uniform with stripes)
5B Mickey Cochrane 250.00 125.00
(squatting, wearing white hat and uniform with no stripes)
6 James "Rip" Collins 40.00 20.00
(jumping)
7 Dizzy Dean 150.00 75.00
(pitching follow through)
8 Dizzy Dean and 100.00 50.00
Paul Dean
(squatting)
9 Paul Dean 50.00 25.00
(pitching)
10 William Delancey 40.00 20.00
(catching)
11 Jimmie Foxx 120.00 60.00
(facing camera knee up)
12 Frank Frisch 80.00 40.00
(stooping to field)
13 Lou Gehrig 500.00 250.00
(batting follow through)
14 Goose Goslin 80.00 40.00
(batting)
15 Lefty Grove 120.00 60.00
(holding trophy)
16 Carl Hubbell 80.00 40.00
(pitching)
17 Travis C. Jackson 50.00 25.00
(stooping to field)
18 Chuck Klein 80.00 40.00
(with four bats)
19 Gus Mancuso 40.00 20.00
(catching)
20A Pepper Martin 40.00 20.00
(batting)
20B Pepper Martin 40.00 20.00
(portrait)
Sincerely Yours
21 Joe Medwick 80.00 65.00
(batting follow through)
22 Mel Ott 120.00 60.00
(batting follow through)
23 Harold Schumacher 40.00 20.00
(pitching)
24 Al Simmons 80.00 40.00
(batting follow through)
Sincerely Yours
25 Jo Jo White 40.00 20.00
(batting follow through)

1936 Wheaties BB3

This set is referred to as "Fancy Frame with Printed Name and Data." These cards (which made up the back of the Wheaties cereal box) measure 6" by 6 1/4" with the frame and about 5" by 5 1/2" if the frame is trimmed off. This set is distinguished from BB1 (above) in that this set also shows the player's name and some fact about him. The player's facsimile autograph is displayed at the bottom of the card. In the checklist below, the first few words of the printed data found on the card is also provided.

Ex-Mt VG
COMPLETE SET (12) 850.00 425.00
1 Earl Averill 60.00 30.00
(batting)

Star Outfielder
2 Mickey Cochrane.......... 100.00 50.00
(catching)
Manager, World
Champion Detroit
3 Jimmie Foxx.......... 120.00 60.00
(batting)
All Around Star
4 Lou Gehrig.......... 400.00 200.00
(stooping to field)
Iron Man
5 Hank Greenberg.......... 100.00 50.00
(jumping)
Home Run Champion
6 Gabby Hartnett.......... 80.00 40.00
(squatting)
Catcher Voted
Most Valuable
7 Carl Hubbell.......... 80.00 40.00
(ready to throw)
Star Pitcher
8 Pepper Martin.......... 40.00 20.00
(jumping)
Heavy Hitter
9 Van L. Mungo.......... 40.00 20.00
(pitching)
Star Pitcher
10 Buck Newsom.......... 40.00 20.00
(pitching)
Star Pitcher
11 Arky Vaughan.......... 60.00 30.00
(batting)
Batting Champion
12 Jimmy Wilson.......... 40.00 20.00
(squatting)
Manager and
Star Catcher

1936 Wheaties BB4

This set is refered to as the "Thin Orange Border / Figures in Border." These unnumbered cards (which made up the back of the Wheaties cereal box) mwasure 6" by 8 1/2". The set is the first in this larger size. The figures in the border include drawings of men and women competing baseball, football, hockey, track, golf, tennis, skiing and swimming. A train and an airplane also appear. The rectangular photo of the player appears in a box above an endorsment for Wheaties. The player's name is in script below the endorsment, A printed name, team and other information is near the top in the solid orange background.

	Ex-Mt	VG
COMPLETE SET (12)	750.00	375.00
1 Curt Davis Philadelphia Phillies	40.00	20.00
2 Lou Gehrig New York Yankees	400.00	200.00
3 Charlie Gehringer Detroit Tigers	80.00	40.00
4 Lefty Grove Boston Red Sox	100.00	50.00
5 Rollie Hemsley St. Louis Browns	40.00	20.00
6 Billy Herman Chicago Cubs	60.00	30.00
7 Joe Medwick St. Louis Cardinals	80.00	40.00
8 Mel Ott New York Giants	100.00	50.00
9 Schoolboy Rowe Detroit Tigers	40.00	20.00
10 Arky Vaughan Detroit Tigers	60.00	30.00
11 Joe Vosmik Cleveland Indians	40.00	20.00
12 Lon Warneke Chicago Cubs	40.00	20.00

1936 Wheaties BB5

This set is referred to as "How to Play Winning Baseball." These cards, which made up the back of the Wheaties box. measure 6" X 8 1/2" These panels combine a photo of the player with a series of blue and white drawings illustrating playing instrustions. All of the players are shown in full length poses, except Earl Averill, who is pictured to the thighs. The players appear against a solid orange background. In addition to the numbers 1 thru 12, these panels are also found with a small number 28 combined with captial letters "A" thru "L." However, panels are know without these letter-number combinations. This set is sometimes refered to as the "28 Series."

	Ex-Mt	VG
COMPLETE SET (13)	650.00	325.00
1 Lefty Gomez (28E) Pitching, How to Throw the Fast Ball	60.00	30.00
2 Billy Herman	50.00	25.00
3 Luke Appling (28C) Shortstop, Putting 'Em Out at Second	50.00	25.00
4 Jimmie Foxx (28A) Tells How to Play First Base...	80.00	40.00
5 Joe Medwick (28K) Tells How to Play Outfield...	60.00	30.00
6 Charlie Gehringer(28G) Tells How to Play Second Base...	80.00	40.00
7A Mel Ott Bunting, Put 'Em Where They Count (large figure, tips in vertical sequence)	80.00	40.00
7B Mel Ott (28H) Bunting, Put 'Em Where They Count" (small figure, tips in two horiz. rows)	80.00	40.00
8 Odell Hale (28B) Third Base -- Fine Play at Hot Corner	40.00	20.00
9 Bill Dickey (28I) Catching Pointers Behind the Plate	80.00	40.00
10 Lefty Grove (28J) Tells You About Pitching...	80.00	40.00
11 Carl Hubbell	60.00	30.00
12 Earl Averill (28L) Batting -- Get Those Extra Bases	50.00	25.00

1937 Wheaties BB6

This set is refered to as "How to Star in Baseball." These numbered cards, which made up the back of the cereal box, measure 6" X 8 1/4". This series is very similar to BB5. Both are instructional series' and the text and drawings used to illuatrate the tips are similar and in some cases identical. Each panel is a full length photo, The players name, team and script signature also appears on the card.

	Ex-Mt	VG
COMPLETE SET (12)	800.00	400.00
1 Bill Dickey How to Catch	100.00	50.00
2 Red Ruffing Pitching the Fast Ball	60.00	30.00
3 Zeke Bonura First Base - Make More Outs	40.00	20.00
4 Charlie Gehringer Second Base as the Stars Play It	100.00	50.00
5 Arky Vaughan Shortstop, Play It Right	60.00	30.00
6 Carl Hubbell Pitching the Slow Ball	80.00	40.00
7 John Lewis Third Base, Field Those Hot Ones	40.00	20.00
8 Heinie Manush Fielding for Extra Outs	60.00	30.00
9 Lefty Grove Pitching the Outdrop Ball	100.00	50.00
10 Billy Herman How to Score (baserunning)	60.00	30.00
11 Joe DiMaggio Bat Like a Home Run King	400.00	200.00
12 Joe Medwick Batting for Extra Bases	60.00	30.00

1937 Wheaties BB7

This set is refered to as the "29 Series" These numbered cards which make up the back of the box measure 6" X 8 1/4". The players name, position, team and some information about him are printed near the top. His signature appears on the lower part of the panel near a printed endorsment for the cereal. This set contains several different card designs. One design shows the player outlined aganist an orange (nearly red) background. A two or three line endorsment is at the bottom. DiMaggio, Bonura and Bridges appear in this form. Another design shows a player against a solid white background , but the panel is rimmed by a red, white and blue border. Players shown in this fashion are Moore, Radcliff and Martin. A third style offers a panel with an orange border and a large orange circle behind the player. The rest of the background is white. Lombardi, Travis and Mungo appear in this design. The final style is a titled, orange background picture of the player with white and blue framing the photo. Trosky, Demaree and Vaughan show up in this design. The set also has three known Pacific Coast League players. One number, 29N, which could be a PCL player, is unknown.

	Ex-Mt	VG
COMPLETE SET (15)	900.00	450.00
29A Zeke Bonura (batting)	40.00	20.00
29B Cecil Travis (reaching left)	40.00	20.00
29C Frank Demaree (batting)	40.00	20.00
29D Joe Moore (batting)	40.00	20.00
29E Ernie Lombardi (crouch)	60.00	30.00
29F John L. "Pepper" Martin (reaching)	40.00	20.00
29G Harold Trosky (batting)	40.00	20.00
29H Ray Radcliff (batting)	40.00	20.00
29I Joe DiMaggio (batting)	400.00	200.00
29J Tommy Bridges (hands over head)	40.00	20.00
29K Van L. Mungo (pitching)	40.00	20.00
29L Arky Vaughan (batting)	60.00	30.00
29M Arnold Statz (PCL)	150.00	75.00
29N Uuknown		
29O Fred Muller (PCL)	150.00	75.00
29P Gene Lillard (PCL)	150.00	75.00

1937 Wheaties BB8

This set is refered to as the "Speckled Orange, White and Blue Series." These unnumbered cards which made up the back of the Wheaties box measure 6" X 8 1/2". The set contains several different card designs. One design (DiMaggio and Feller) shows the player surrounded by orange sprreckles on a white backgroung with a group of four blue and white drawings of players in action along the panel's right side. Another design shows the panel divided into four rectangles -- white at upper right and lower left and orange on the other two. -- with the players (Appling and Averill) leaping to catch the ball. Blue circles surrounded by orange and white speckles appear on the pictures of Hubbel and Grove. Medwick and Gehringer appear on white panels with a cloud of orange speckles behind them. The player's name in script style appears along with printed data about his 1936 season and a brief endorsement for the cereal.

	Ex-Mt	VG
COMPLETE SET (8)	750.00	375.00
1 Luke Appling (reaching)	50.00	25.00
2 Earl Averill (reaching)	50.00	25.00
3 Joe DiMaggio (batting)	400.00	200.00
4 Bob Feller (throwing)	120.00	60.00
5 Charlie Gehringer (batting)	100.00	50.00
6 Lefty Grove (throwing)	100.00	50.00
7 Carl Hubbell (throwing)	100.00	50.00
8 Joe Medwick (fielding)	50.00	25.00

1937 Wheaties BB9

This set is refered to as the "Color Series." These unnumbered cards measure 6" X 8 1/2" Photos of the players appear in circles. "V" shapes and rectangles, and stars among others. A player from every major League team is included. The player's name is in script with the team name below. The name , endorsment and player's 1936 highlights are printed near the bottom. John Moore and Harland Cliff have been reported on paper stock. Whether they were part of a store display is unknown.

	Ex-Mt	VG
COMPLETE SET (16)	1000.00	500.00
1 Zeke Bonura Chicago White Sox (fielding, crossed bats, glove, ball at upper left)	40.00	20.00
2 Tom Bridges Detroit Tigers (pitching, figure in large orange circle)	40.00	20.00
3 Harland Clift St. Louis Browns (batting, large baseball behind him)	40.00	20.00
4 Kiki Cuyler Cincinnati Reds (batting on green background)	60.00	30.00
5 Joe DiMaggio New York Yankees (leaping, green and white circle behind)	400.00	200.00
6 Bob Feller Cleveland Indians (pitching, blue circle on left knee)	120.00	60.00
7 Lefty Grove Boston Red Sox (pitching, red orange home plate)	100.00	50.00
8 Billy Herman Chicago Cubs (throwing, yellow star behind him)	60.00	30.00
9 Carl Hubbell New York Giants (pitching, orange, yellow V's behind)	80.00	40.00
10 Buck Jordan Boston Bees (batting, dark orange rectangle, blue sides)	40.00	20.00
11 Pepper Martin St. Louis Cardinals (reaching, orange rectangle)	50.00	25.00
12 John Moore Philadelphia Phillies (batting, blue background, stands on green)	40.00	20.00
13 Wally Moses Philadelphia A's (leaping, dark orange background, yellow and blue)	40.00	20.00
14 Van L. Mungo Brooklyn Dodgers (pitching, green background, orange and blue)	50.00	25.00
15 Cecil Travis Washington Senators (batting, orange lightning)	40.00	20.00
16 Arky Vaughan Pittsburgh Pirates (batting, blue diamond, green frame)	60.00	30.00

1937 Wheaties BB14

This set is referred to as the "Small Panels with Orange Background Series." These numbered (and unnumbered) cards, which made up the back of the Wheaties individual serving cereal box, measure about 2 5/8" by 3 7/8". These small panels have orange backgrounds and some, but not all, use poses that appear in some of the regular sized panels. Joe DiMaggio, for example, is the same pose as in the large Wheaties BB7 set and the Mel Ott is similar to the BB5 pose, but cropped a little differently. Some panels have been seen with and without the number 29 in combination with a letter, so apparently there were several printings. The player's name is in all capitals with his position and team in smaller caps. A printed block of data about him is on the main part of the card with a Wheaties endorsement in a white strip at the bottom.

	Ex-Mt	VG
COMPLETE SET (17)	1600.00	800.00
1 Zeke Bonura (29A) Led all A.L. First Basemen (BB7 pose)	60.00	30.00
2 Tommy Bridges (29J) Struck Out Most Batters, 173 ..." (not BB7 pose)	60.00	30.00
3 Dolph Camilli Most Put Outs, 1446 ..." (unnumbered)	80.00	40.00
4 Frank Demaree	60.00	30.00
5 Joe DiMaggio (29I) Outstanding Rookie, 1936 ..." (BB7 pose)	500.00	250.00
6 Billy Herman Lifetime .300 Hitter ... (unnumbered)	100.00	50.00
7 Carl Hubbell Won Most Games, 26 ... (unnumbered)	150.00	75.00
8 Ernie Lombardi	100.00	50.00
9 Pepper Martin	80.00	40.00
10 Joe Moore	60.00	30.00
11 Van L. Mungo	80.00	40.00
12 Mel Ott	150.00	75.00
13 Raymond Radcliff (29H) (most one-base hits) (BB7 pose)	60.00	30.00
14 Cecil Travis (29B) One of the Leading Bats in ... (BB7 pose)	60.00	30.00
15 Harold Trosky	60.00	30.00
16A Arky Vaughan (unnumbered)	120.00	60.00
16B Arky Vaughan (29L) Lifetime .300 Hitter who ..." (BB7 pose)	120.00	60.00

1938 Wheaties BB10

This set is refered to as the "Biggest Thrills in Baseball." These numbered cards which make up the back of the cereal box measure 6" X 8 1/2." A player from every Major League team is included. Each panel describes the player's greatest thrill playing the game. The thrill is announced in large banner headline type and described in a block of copy over the players script signature, His team name and position are printed below the name. All sixteen are known to exist on both paper stock as well as heavy cardboard.

	Ex-Mt	VG
COMPLETE SET (16)	1000.00	500.00
1 Bob Feller Cleveland Indians (Two Hits in One Inning for Feller)	120.00	60.00
2 Cecil Travis Washington Nationals (Clicks in First Big League Games)	40.00	20.00
3 Joe Medwick St. Louis Cardinals (Goes on Batting Spree Twice)	60.00	30.00
4 Gerald Walker Chicago White Sox (World Series Game& 1934& Gives ...)	40.00	20.00
5 Carl Hubbell New York Giants (Strikes Out Murderer's Row)	80.00	40.00
6 Bob Johnson Philadelphia A's (Setting New A.L. Record)	40.00	20.00
7 Beau Bell St. Louis Browns (Smacks First Major League Homer)	40.00	20.00
8 Ernie Lombardi Cincinnati Reds (Sold to Majors)	50.00	25.00
9 Lefty Grove Boston Red Sox (Fans Babe Ruth)	100.00	50.00
10 Lou Fette Boston Bees (Wins 20 Games)	40.00	20.00
11 Joe DiMaggio New York Yankees (Home Run King Gets Biggest Thrill ...)	400.00	200.00
12 Pinky Whitney Philadelphia Phillies (Hits Three in a Row)	40.00	20.00
13 Dizzy Dean Chicago Cubs (11-0 Victory Clinches World Series)	100.00	50.00
14 Charlie Gehringer Detroit Tigers (Homers Off Dizzy Dean)	80.00	40.00
15 Paul Waner Pittsburgh Pirates (Four Perfect Sixes)	60.00	30.00
16 Dolph Camilli Brooklyn Dodgers (First Hit a Homer)	50.00	25.00

1938 Wheaties BB11

This set is refered to as the "Dress Clothes or Civies Series." The cards are unnumbered and measure 6" 8 1/4" The panels feature the players and their friends in blue photos. The remainder of the panel uses the traditional orange, blue and white Wheaties colors.

	Ex-Mt	VG
COMPLETE SET (8)	300.00	150.00
1 Lou Fette (pouring milk over his Wheaties)	40.00	20.00
2 Jimmie Foxx (slices banana for his son's Wheaties)	80.00	40.00
3 Charlie Gehringer (and his young fan)	60.00	30.00
4 Lefty Grove (watches waitress pour Wheaties)	60.00	30.00
5 Hank Greenberg and Roxie Lawson	80.00	40.00

(eat breakfast)		
6 Ernie Lombardi and Lee Grissom (prepare to eat)	40.00	20.00
7 Joe Medwick (pours milk over cereal)	50.00	25.00
8 Lon Warneke (smiles in anticipation of Wheaties)	40.00	20.00

1938 Wheaties BB15

This set is referred to as the "Small Panels with Orange, Blue and White Background Series." These numbered (and unnumbered) cards, which made up the back of the Wheaties individual serving cereal box, measure about 2 5/8" by 3 7/8". These small panels have orange, blue and white backgrounds and some, but not all, use poses that appear in some of the regular, larger-sized panels. Greenberg and Lewis are featured with a horizontal (HOR) pose.

	Ex-Mt	VG
COMPLETE SET (11)	1000.00	500.00
1 Zeke Bonura (batted .345)	50.00	25.00
2 Joe DiMaggio (46 home runs)	400.00	200.00
3A Charlie Gehringer (leaping, MVP, American League)	100.00	50.00
3B Charlie Gehringer (batting, 1937 batting king)	100.00	50.00
4 Hank Greenberg HOR (second in home runs)	120.00	60.00
5 Lefty Grove (17-9 won-lost record)	120.00	60.00
6 Carl Hubbell (star pitcher, 1937 Giants)	100.00	50.00
7 John (Buddy) Lewis (batted .314) HOR	50.00	25.00
8 Heinie Manush (batted .332)	80.00	40.00
9 Joe Medwick	80.00	40.00
10 Arky Vaughan	80.00	40.00

1939 Wheaties BB12

This set is refered to as the "Personal Pointers Series." These numbered cards measure 6" X 8 1/4'. The panels feature an instructional format similar to both the BB5 and BB6 Wheaties sets. Drawings again illustrate the tips on batting and pitching. The colors are orange, blue and white and the players appear in photographs.

	Ex-Mt	VG
COMPLETE SET (9)	500.00	250.00
1 Ernie Lombardi How to Place Hits For Scores	60.00	30.00
2 Johnny Allen It's Windup That Counts	40.00	20.00
3 Lefty Gomez Delivery That Keeps 'Em Guessing	80.00	40.00
4 Bill Lee Follow Through For Stops	40.00	20.00
5 Jimmie Foxx Stance Helps Sluggers	100.00	50.00
6 Joe Medwick Power-Drive Grip	60.00	30.00
7 Hank Greenberg Smooth Swing	100.00	50.00
8 Mel Ott Study That Pitcher	80.00	40.00
9 Arky Vaughan Beat 'Em With Bunts	60.00	30.00

1939 Wheaties BB13

This set is referred to as the "100 Years of Baseball or Baseball Centennial Series." These numbered cards which make up the back of the Wheaties box measure 6" X 6 3/4". Each panel has a drawing that depicts various aspects and events in baseball in the traditional orange, blue and white Wheaties colors.

	Ex-Mt	VG
COMPLETE SET (8)	200.00	100.00
1 Design of First Diamond with Picture of Abner Doubleday - 1938	40.00	20.00
2 Lincoln Gets News of Nomination on Base-ball Field - 1860	40.00	20.00
3 Crowd Boos First Baseball Glove (pictures of gloves) - 1869	25.00	12.50
4 Curve Ball Just an Illusion Say Scientists - 1877	25.00	12.50
5 Fencer's Mask is Pattern for First Catcher's Cage - 1877	25.00	12.50
6 Baseball Gets "All Dressed Up" pictures of uniforms) - 1890	25.00	12.50
7 Modern Bludgeon Enters Game (pictures of bats) - 1895	25.00	12.50
8 Casey at the Bat (eight verses of the famous Mudville poem)	40.00	20.00

1964 Wheaties Stamps

In 1964 General Mills issued the Wheaties Major League All-Star Baseball Player Stamp Album. The album is orange, blue and white and measures approximately 8 3/8" by 11"; it contains 48 pages with places for one or two stamps per page. The individual stamps are in full color with a thick white border and measure approximately 2 9/16" by 2 3/4". The stamps are unnumbered so they listed below in alphabetical order.

	NM	Ex
COMPLETE SET (50)	140.00	55.00
1 Hank Aaron	15.00	6.00
2 Bob Allison	1.25	.50
3 Luis Aparicio	4.00	1.60
4 Ed Bailey	1.00	.40
5 Steve Barber	1.00	.40
6 Earl Battey	1.00	.40
7 Jim Bouton	1.25	.50
8 Ken Boyer	1.50	.60
9 Jim Bunning	4.00	1.60
10 Orlando Cepeda	4.00	1.60
11 Roberto Clemente	25.00	10.00
12 Ray Culp	1.00	.40
13 Tommy Davis	1.25	.50
14 John Edwards	1.00	.40
15 Whitey Ford	6.00	2.40
16 Nelson Fox	4.00	1.60
18 Jim Gilliam	1.50	.60
19 Jim Grant	1.00	.40
20 Dick Groat	1.25	.50
21 Elston Howard	1.50	.60
22 Larry Jackson	1.00	.40
23 Julian Javier	1.00	.40
24 Al Kaline	8.00	3.20
25 Harmon Killebrew	6.00	2.40
26 Don Leppert	1.00	.40
27 Frank Malzone	1.25	.50
28 Juan Marichal	5.00	2.00
29 Willie Mays	15.00	6.00
30 Ken McBride	1.00	.40
31 Willie McCovey	5.00	2.00
32 Jim O'Toole	1.00	.40
33 Albie Pearson	1.00	.40
34 Joe Pepitone	1.25	.50
35 Ron Perranoski	1.25	.50
36 Juan Pizarro	1.00	.40
37 Dick Radatz	1.00	.40
38 Bobby Richardson	2.00	.80
39 Brooks Robinson	8.00	3.20
40 Ron Santo	2.00	.80
41 Norm Siebern	1.00	.40
42 Duke Snider	8.00	3.20
43 Warren Spahn	8.00	3.20
44 Joe Torre	2.00	.80
45 Tom Tresh	1.25	.50
46 Zoilo Versalles	1.25	.50
47 Leon Wagner	1.00	.40
48 Bill White	1.25	.50
49 Hal Woodeshick	1.00	.40
50 Carl Yastrzemski	6.00	2.40

1907 White Sox George W. Hull

This 12 card set measures 3 1/2" by 5 1/2" and contains World Champion White Sox players only. Each postcard contains club president Charles Comiskey's picture in a circle on the lower left on the front; assorted White Sox players pictures in ovals on socks in a clothesline; and the subject player's picture on the right side of the card. The George W. Hall identification is also pictured on the front.

	Ex-Mt	VG
COMPLETE SET (12)	1600.00	800.00
1 Nick Altrock	120.00	60.00
2 George Davis	200.00	100.00
3 Jiggs Donohue	100.00	50.00
4 Pat Dougherty	100.00	50.00
5 Eddie Hahn	100.00	50.00
6 Frank Isbell	100.00	50.00
7 Fielder Jones	100.00	50.00
8 Ed McFarland	100.00	50.00
9 Frank Owens	100.00	50.00
10 Ray Patterson	100.00	50.00
11 George Rohe	100.00	50.00
12 Frank Smith	100.00	50.00
13 Billy Sullivan	100.00	50.00
14 Lee Tannehill	100.00	50.00
15 Ed Walsh	200.00	100.00
16 Doc White	100.00	50.00

1917 White Sox Team Issue

These cards which measure 1 3/4" by 2 3/4" were issued in a box labeled "Davis Printing Works". The fronts feature clear photos and glossy photographs. The cards are unnumbered and we have sequenced them in alphabetical order.

	Ex-Mt	VG
COMPLETE SET (25)	28000.00	14000.00
1 Charles Comiskey OWN	1200.00	600.00
2 Joe Benz	400.00	200.00
3 Eddie Cicotte	2000.00	1000.00
4 Eddie Collins	2000.00	1000.00
5 Shano Collins	400.00	200.00
6 Dave Danforth	400.00	200.00
7 Red Faber	1200.00	600.00
8 Happy Felsch	1200.00	600.00
9 Chick Gandil	1200.00	600.00
10 Kid Gleason CO	800.00	400.00
11 Joe Jackson	8000.00	4000.00
12 Joe Jenkins	400.00	200.00
13 Ted Jourdan	400.00	200.00
14 Nemo Leibold	400.00	200.00
15 Byrd Lynn	400.00	200.00
16 Fred McMullen	800.00	400.00
17 Eddie Murphy	400.00	200.00
18 Swede Risberg	800.00	400.00
19 Pants Rowland MG	400.00	200.00
20 Reb Russell	400.00	200.00
21 Ray Schalk	2000.00	1000.00
22 James Scott	400.00	200.00
23 Buck Weaver	2000.00	1000.00
24 Claude Williams	1200.00	600.00
25 Meldon Wolfgang	400.00	200.00

1930 White Sox Blue Ribbon Malt

In addition to the smaller photos which were cut out of the team panorama, Blue Ribbon Malt also issued larger sized photos of members of the 1930 Chicago White Sox. These photos measure approximately 5" by 7" and are attached to grey mounts in a similar fashion to the Cubs issue. This checklist is probably incomplete and any additions are welcome.

	MINT	NRMT
COMPLETE SET	60.00	27.00
1 Bill Cissell	10.00	4.50
2 Smead Jolley	12.00	5.50
3 Willie Kamm	12.00	5.50
4 Ted Lyons	25.00	11.00
5 Johnny Watwood	10.00	4.50

1930 White Sox Team Issue

These cards, which measure between 1 7/16 to 2 7/8" by 3 1/2" are actually photos cut out of a 1930 White Sox Team Panorama issued by Blue Ribbon Malt.

	Ex-Mt	VG
COMPLETE SET (27)	300.00	150.00
1 Chick Autry	10.00	5.00
2 Red Barnes	10.00	5.00
3 Moe Berg	25.00	12.50
4 Garland Braxton	10.00	5.00
5 Donie Bush MG	12.00	6.00
6 Pat Caraway	10.00	5.00
7 Bill Cissell	10.00	5.00
8 Bud Clancy	10.00	5.00
9 Clyde Crouse	10.00	5.00
10 Red Faber	25.00	12.50
11 Bob Fothergill	12.00	6.00
12 Dutch Henry	10.00	5.00
13 Smead Jolley	12.00	6.00
14 Willie Kamm	12.00	6.00
15 Mike Kelly	10.00	5.00
16 Johnny Kerr	10.00	5.00
17 Ted Lyons	25.00	12.50
18 Harold McKain	10.00	5.00
19 Jim Moore	10.00	5.00
20 Greg Mulleavy	10.00	5.00
21 Carl Reynolds	12.00	6.00
22 Blondy Ryan	10.00	5.00
23 Benny Tate	10.00	5.00
24 Tommy Thomas	10.00	5.00
25 Ed Walsh Jr.	12.00	6.00
26 Johnny Watwood	10.00	5.00
27 Bob Weiland	10.00	5.00

1939 White Sox Team Issue

These 23 photos measure approximately 5 1/4" by 6 3/4". They feature player photos and a fascimile autograph. The backs are blank and we have sequenced them in alphabetical order.

	Ex-Mt	VG
COMPLETE SET (23)	125.00	60.00
1 Pete Appleton	5.00	2.50
2 Luke Appling	15.00	7.50
3 Clint Brown	5.00	2.50
4 Bill Dietrich	5.00	2.50
5 Mule Haas	5.00	2.50
6 Jack Hayes	5.00	2.50
7 Bob Kennedy	5.00	2.50
8 Jack Knott	5.00	2.50
9 Mike Kreevich	5.00	2.50
10 Joe Kuhel	5.00	2.50
11 Thornton Lee	10.00	5.00
12 Ted Lyons	15.00	7.50
13 Eric McNair	5.00	2.50
14 John Rigney	5.00	2.50
15 Larry Rosenthal	5.00	2.50
16 Ken Silvestri	5.00	2.50
17 Eddie Smith	5.00	2.50
18 Moose Solters	5.00	2.50
19 Monty Stratton	10.00	5.00
20 Mike Tresh	5.00	2.50
21 Skeeter Webb	5.00	2.50
22 Ed Weiland	5.00	2.50
23 Taft Wright	5.00	2.50

1948 White Sox Team Issue

These 30 photos represent members of the 1948 Chicago White Sox. They measure approximately 6 1/2" by 9" are black and white and have blank backs. We have sequenced this set in alphabetical order.

	NM	Ex
COMPLETE SET (30)	150.00	75.00
1 Luke Appling	20.00	10.00
2 Floyd Baker	4.00	2.00
3 Fred Bradley	4.00	2.00
4 Earl Caldwell	4.00	.16
5 Red Faber CO	15.00	7.50
6 Bob Gillespie	4.00	2.00
7 Jim Goodwin	4.00	2.00
8 Orval Grove	4.00	2.00
9 Earl Harrist	4.00	2.00
10 Joe Haynes	4.00	2.00
11 Ralph Hodgin	4.00	2.00
12 Howie Judson	4.00	2.00
13 Bob Kennedy	5.00	2.50
14 Don Kolloway	4.00	2.00
15 Tony Lupien	4.00	2.00
16 Ted Lyons MG	15.00	7.50
17 Cass Michaels	4.00	2.00
18 Bing Miller CO	4.00	2.00
19 Buster Mills CO	4.00	2.00
20 Glen Moulder	4.00	2.00
21 Frank Papish	4.00	2.00
22 Ike Pearson	4.00	2.00
23 Dave Philley	4.00	2.00
24 Aaron Robinson	4.00	2.00
25 Mike Tresh	4.00	2.00
26 Jack Wallaesa	4.00	2.00
27 Ralph Weigel	4.00	2.00
28 Bill Wight	4.00	2.00
29 Taft Wright	4.00	2.00
30 Team Photo	25.00	12.50

1958 White Sox Jay Publishing

This 12-card set of the Chicago White Sox measures approximately 5" by 7" and features black-and-white player photos in a white border. These cards were packaged 12 to a packet. The backs are blank. The cards are unnumbered and checklisted below in alphabetical order.

	NM	Ex
COMPLETE SET (12)	50.00	25.00
1 Luis Aparicio	10.00	5.00
2 Dick Donovan	3.00	1.50
3 Nelson Fox	10.00	5.00
4 Tito Francona	3.00	1.50
5 Bill Goodman	3.00	1.50
6 Sherman Lollar	3.00	1.50
7 Ray Moore	3.00	1.50
8 Billy Pierce	5.00	2.50
9 Jim Rivera	3.00	1.50
10 Al Smith	3.00	1.50
11 Jim Wilson	3.00	1.50
12 Early Wynn	10.00	5.00

1959 White Sox Jay Publishing

This 12-card set of the Chicago White Sox measures approximately 5" by 7" and features black-and-white player photos in a white border. These cards were packaged 12 to a packet. The backs are blank. The cards are unnumbered and checklisted below in alphabetical order.

	NM	Ex
COMPLETE SET	60.00	30.00
1 Luis Aparicio	10.00	5.00
2 Johnny Callison	6.00	3.00
3 Dick Donovan	3.00	1.50
4 Nellie Fox	10.00	5.00
5 Billy Goodman	4.00	2.00
6 Jim Landis	3.00	1.50
7 Sherm Lollar	3.00	1.50
8 Al Lopez MG	6.00	3.00
9 Bubba Phillips	3.00	1.50
10 Billy Pierce	6.00	3.00
11 Al Smith	3.00	1.50
12 Early Wynn	10.00	5.00

1960 White Sox Jay Publishing

This 12-card set of the Chicago White Sox measures approximately 5" by 7" and features black-and-white player photos in a white border. These cards were packaged 12 to a packet. The backs are blank. The cards are unnumbered and checklisted below in alphabetical order.

	NM	Ex
COMPLETE SET (12)	40.00	16.00
1 Luis Aparicio	10.00	4.00
2 Nelson Fox	10.00	4.00
3 Gene Freese	2.00	.80
4 Ted Kluszewski	4.00	1.60
5 Jim Landis	2.00	.80
6 Sherman Lollar	2.00	.80
7 Al Lopez MG	4.00	1.60
8 Minnie Minoso	4.00	1.60
9 Bob Shaw	2.00	.80
10 Roy Sievers	2.50	1.00
11 Al Smith	2.00	.80
12 Early Wynn	10.00	4.00

1960 White Sox Ticket Stubs

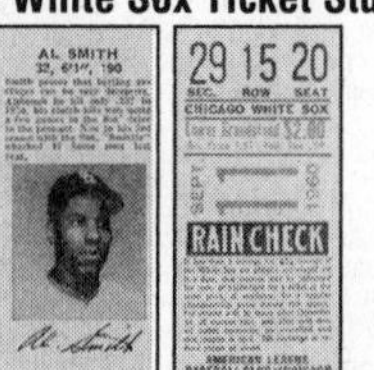

This set was the brainchild of famed owner Bill Veeck. Player's photos were put on a ticket stub so they could be collected. The players marked UNC below in the checklist are unconfirmed at this time and may not exist. These tickets come in mulitple colors. No extra value is attached for any color.

	NM	Ex
COMPLETE SET	100.00	40.00
1 Luis Aparicio	8.00	3.20
2 Earl Battey UNC	4.00	1.60
3 Frank Baumann	4.00	1.60
4 Dick Donovan	4.00	1.60
5 Nelson Fox	15.00	6.00
6 Gene Freese	4.00	1.60
7 Billy Goodman UNC	4.00	1.60
8 Ted Kluzewski	8.00	3.20
9 Jim Landis	4.00	1.60
10 Barry Latman	4.00	1.60
11 Sherman Lollar	4.00	1.60
12 Al Lopez MG	6.00	2.40
13 Turk Lown	4.00	1.60
14 Minnie Minoso	8.00	3.20
15 Billy Pierce	6.00	2.40
16 Jim Rivera	4.00	1.60
17 Bob Shaw	4.00	1.60
18 Roy Sievers	5.00	2.00
19 Al Smith	4.00	1.60
20 Gerry Staley	4.00	1.60
21 Earl Torgeson UNC	4.00	1.60
22 Early Wynn	8.00	3.20

1961 White Sox Rainbow Orchard Laundry Cleaners

This Pizzaro card is assumed to be part of a 20 card set. When unfolded the card measures 19 1/2" by 2 1/2" and has the player's photo on it as well as the 1961 White Sox home schedule. Since it is assumed this is part of a set any additions to this checklist is appreciated

	NM	Ex
9 Juan Pizzaro	50.00	20.00

1961 White Sox Ticket Stubs

For the second year, the White Sox placed player photos on ticket stubs to promote interest in their players.

	NM	Ex
COMPLETE SET	75.00	30.00
1 Luis Aparicio	6.00	2.40

	NM	Ex
2 Frank Baumann	3.00	1.20
3 Cam Carreon	3.00	1.20
4 Sam Esposito	3.00	1.20
5 Nelson Fox	10.00	4.00
6 Jim Landis	3.00	1.20
7 Sherm Lollar	3.00	1.20
8 Al Lopez MG	5.00	2.00
9 Cal McLish	3.00	1.20
10 J.C. Martin	3.00	1.20
11 Minnie Minoso	6.00	2.40
12 Billy Pierce	5.00	2.00
13 Juan Pizarro	3.00	1.20
14 Bob Roselli	3.00	1.20
15 Herb Score	5.00	2.00
16 Bob Shaw	3.00	1.20
17 Roy Sievers	4.00	1.60
18 Al Smith	3.00	1.20
19 Gerry Staley	3.00	1.20
20 Early Wynn	8.00	3.20

1962 White Sox Jay Publishing

This 12-card set of the Chicago White Sox measures approximately 5" by 7". The fronts feature black-and-white posed player photos with the player's and team name printed below in the white border. These cards were packaged 12 to a packet. The backs are blank. The cards are unnumbered and checklisted below in alphabetical order.

	NM	Ex
COMPLETE SET (12)	50.00	20.00
1 Luis Aparicio	10.00	4.00
2 Frank Baumann	2.50	1.00
3 Nellie Fox	10.00	4.00
4 Russ Kemmerer	2.50	1.00
5 Jim Landis	2.50	1.00
6 Sherm Lollar	2.50	1.00
7 Al Lopez MG	5.00	2.00
8 Joe Martin	2.50	1.00
9 Juan Pizzarro	2.50	1.00
10 Floyd Robinson	2.50	1.00
11 Al Smith	2.50	1.00
12 Early Wynn	10.00	4.00

1962 White Sox Ticket Stubs

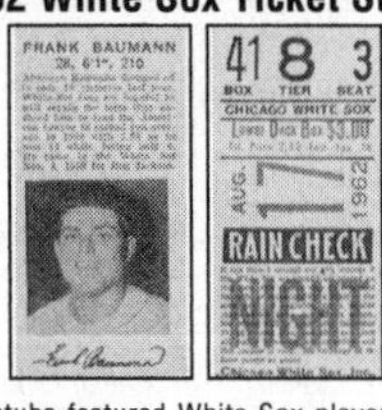

This stubs featured White Sox players. The stubs had the player photo imprinted so fans could have more keepsakes of their favorite players.

	NM	Ex
COMPLETE SET	100.00	40.00
1 Luis Aparicio	8.00	3.20
2 Frank Baumann	4.00	1.60
3 John Buzhardt	4.00	1.60
4 Camilo Carreon	4.00	1.60
5 Joe Cunningham	4.00	1.60
6 Bob Farley	4.00	1.60
7 Eddie Fisher	4.00	1.60
8 Nelson Fox	8.00	3.20
9 Jim Landis	4.00	1.60
10 Sherm Lollar	5.00	2.00
11 Al Lopez MG	6.00	2.40
12 Turk Lown	4.00	1.60
13 J.C. Martin	4.00	1.60
14 Cal McLish	4.00	1.60
15 Gary Peters	5.00	2.00
16 Juan Pizarro	4.00	1.60
17 Floyd Robinson	4.00	1.60
18 Bob Roselli	4.00	1.60
19 Herb Score	6.00	2.40
20 Al Smith	4.00	1.60
21 Charles Smith	4.00	1.60
22 Early Wynn	8.00	3.20

1963 White Sox Jay Publishing

This 12-card set of the Chicago White Sox measures approximately 5" by 7". The fronts feature black-and-white posed player photos with the player's and team name printed below in the white border. These cards were packaged 12 to a packet. The backs are blank. The cards are unnumbered and checklisted below in alphabetical order.

	NM	Ex
COMPLETE SET (12)	30.00	12.00
1 Frank Baumann	2.00	.80
2 Camilio Carreon	2.00	.80
3 Joe Cunningham	2.00	.80
4 Sam Esposito	2.00	.80
5 Nellie Fox	8.00	3.20
6 Ray Herbert	2.00	.80
7 Joel Horlen	2.50	1.00
8 Jim Landis	2.00	.80
9 Sherm Lollar	2.00	.80
10 Al Lopez MG	4.00	1.60
11 Juan Pizzaro	2.00	.80
12 Floyd Robinson	2.00	.80

1963 White Sox Ticket Stubs

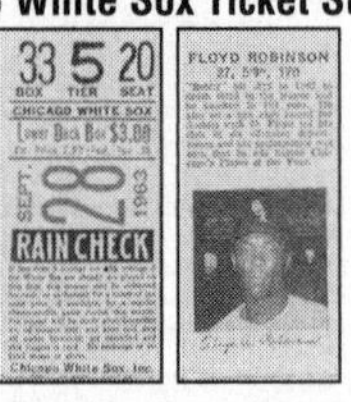

Again, the White Sox featured player photos on their ticket stubs. These photos were originally the idea of Hall of Famer Bill Vecck, but the promotion continued even after he had sold all his interest in the White Sox.

	NM	Ex
COMPLETE SET	80.00	32.00
1 Frank Baumann	3.00	1.20
2 John Buzhardt	3.00	1.20
3 Camilo Carreon	3.00	1.20
4 Joe Cunningham	3.00	1.20
5 Dave DeBusschere	5.00	2.00
6 Eddie Fisher	3.00	1.20
7 Nelson Fox	10.00	4.00
8 Ron Hansen	3.00	1.20
9 Ray Herbert	3.00	1.20
10 Mike Hershberger	3.00	1.20
11 Joel Horlen	4.00	1.60
12 Grover Jones	3.00	1.20
13 Mike Joyce	3.00	1.20
14 Frank Kreutzer	3.00	1.20
15 Jim Landis	3.00	1.20
16 Sherm Lollar	3.00	1.20
17 Al Lopez MG	6.00	2.40
18 J.C. Martin	3.00	1.20
19 Charlie Maxwell	3.00	1.20
20 Dave Nicholson	3.00	1.20
21 Juan Pizarro	3.00	1.20
22 Floyd Robinson	3.00	1.20
23 Charlie Smith	3.00	1.20
24 Pete Ward	3.00	1.20
25 Al Weis	3.00	1.20
26 Hoyt Wilhelm	10.00	4.00
27 Dom Zanni	3.00	1.20

1964 White Sox Iron-Ons

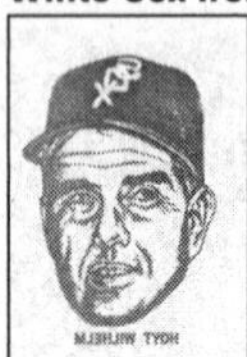

This 27-card set of the Chicago White Sox features head player drawings that could be ironed on various items and articles of clothing. The set was distributed in packages of three sheets with nine players to a sheet. One sheet displayed blue heads, another red, and another black. The cards are unnumbered and checklisted below in alphabetical order.

	NM	Ex
COMPLETE SET (27)	15.00	6.00
1 Fritz Ackley	.50	.20
2 Frank Bauman	.50	.20
3 Jim Brosnan	1.00	.40
4 Don Buford	.50	.20
5 John Buzhardt	.50	.20
6 Camilo Carreon	.50	.20
7 Joe Cunningham	.50	.20
8 Dave DeBusschere	2.00	.80
9 Ed Fisher	.50	.20
10 Jim Golden	.50	.20
11 Ron Hansen	.50	.20
12 Ray Herbert	.50	.20
13 Mike Hershberger	.50	.20
14 Joel Horlen	.50	.20
15 Mike Joyce	.50	.20
16 Jim Landis	.50	.20
17 J.C. Martin	.50	.20
18 Charlie Maxwell	.50	.20
19 Tom McCraw	.50	.20
20 Dave Nicholson	.50	.20
21 Gary Peters	.50	.20
22 Floyd Robinson	.50	.20
23 Gene Stephens	.50	.20
24 Pete Ward	.50	.20
25 Al Weis	.50	.20
26 Hoyt Wilhelm	3.00	1.20
27 Team Logo	.50	.20

1964 White Sox Jay Publishing

This 12-card set of the Chicago White Sox measures approximately 5" by 7". The fronts feature black-and-white posed player photos with the player's and team name printed below in the white border. These cards were packaged 12 to a packet. The backs are blank. The cards are unnumbered and checklisted below in alphabetical order.

	NM	Ex
COMPLETE SET (12)	25.00	10.00
1 Camilio Carreon	2.00	.80
2 Joe Cunningham	2.00	.80
3 Ron Hansen	2.00	.80
4 Ray Herbert	2.00	.80
5 Mike Hershberger	2.00	.80
6 Joel Horlen	2.00	.80
7 Jim Landis	2.00	.80
8 Al Lopez MG	4.00	1.60
9 Dave Nicholson	2.00	.80
10 Gary Peters	2.50	1.00
11 Juan Pizarro	2.50	1.00
12 Pete Ward	2.00	.80

1964 White Sox Ticket Stubs

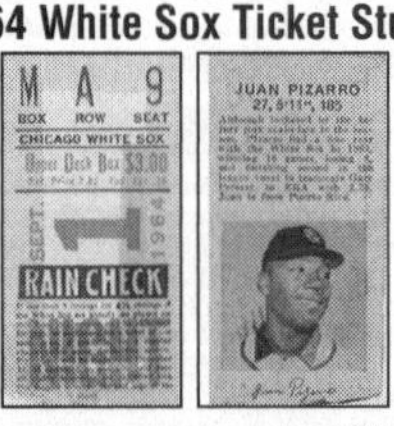

For the fifth consecutive year, White Sox players were featured on these collector strips. These stubs were issued so fans could have another way of collecting memorabilia of their favorite players.

	NM	Ex
COMPLETE SET	75.00	30.00
1 Fritz Ackley	3.00	1.20
2 Frank Baumann	3.00	1.20
3 Don Buford	3.00	1.20
4 John Buzhardt	3.00	1.20
5 Camilo Carreon	3.00	1.20
6 Joe Cunningham	3.00	1.20
7 Dave DeBusschere	5.00	2.00
8 Eddie Fisher	3.00	1.20
9 Jim Golden	3.00	1.20
10 Ron Hansen	3.00	1.20
11 Ray Herbert	3.00	1.20
12 Mike Hershberger	3.00	1.20
13 Joe Horlen	3.00	1.20
14 Jim Landis	3.00	1.20
15 Al Lopez MG	6.00	2.40
16 J.C. Martin	3.00	1.20
17 Dave Nicholson	3.00	1.20
18 Gary Peters	4.00	1.60
19 Juan Pizarro	3.00	1.20
20 Floyd Robinson	3.00	1.20
21 Gene Stephens	3.00	1.20
22 Pete Ward	4.00	1.60
23 Hoyt Wilhelm	8.00	3.20

1965 White Sox Jay Publishing

This 12-card set of the Chicago White Sox measures approximately 5" by 7". The fronts feature black-and-white posed player photos with the player's and team name printed below in the white border. These cards were packaged 12 to a packet. The backs are blank. The cards are unnumbered and checklisted below in alphabetical order.

	NM	Ex
COMPLETE SET (12)	30.00	12.00
1 Ron Hansen	2.00	.80
2 Al Lopez MG	4.00	1.60
3 J.C. Martin	2.00	.80
4 Tom McCraw	2.00	.80
5 Dave Nicholson	2.00	.80
6 Gary Peters	2.50	1.00
7 Juan Pizarro	2.00	.80
8 Floyd Robinson	2.00	.80
9 John Romano	2.00	.80
10 Bill Skowron	2.50	1.00
11 Pete Ward	2.00	.80
12 Hoyt Wilhelm	8.00	3.20

1966 White Sox Team Issue

This 12-card set of the Chicago White Sox measures 4 7/8" by 7" and features black-and-white player photos in a white border with blank backs. These cards were originally packaged 12 to a packet. The cards are unnumbered and checklisted below in alphabetical order.

	MINT	NRMT
COMPLETE SET (12)	25.00	11.00
1 Tommy Agee	2.50	1.10
2 John Buzhardt	2.00	.90
3 Don Buford	2.00	.90
4 Joel Horlen	2.00	.90
5 Tommy John	4.00	1.80
6 Bob Locker	2.00	.90
7 Gary Peters	2.00	.90
8 Juan Pizarro	2.00	.90
9 Floyd Robinson	2.00	.90
10 Johnny Romano	2.00	.90
11 Bill Skowron	3.00	1.35
12 Eddie Stanky MG	2.00	.90

1967 White Sox Team Issue

This 12-card set of the Chicago White Sox measures 4 7/8" by 7" and features black-and-white player photos in a white border with blank backs. These cards were originally packaged 12 to a packet. The cards are unnumbered and checklisted below in alphabetical order.

	NM	Ex
COMPLETE SET (12)	25.00	10.00
1 Jerry Adair	2.00	.80
2 Tom Agee	2.00	.80
3 Ken Berry	2.00	.80
4 Don Buford	2.00	.80
5 Ron Hansen	2.00	.80
6 Joe Horlen	2.00	.80
7 Tommy John	4.00	1.60
8 Duane Josephson	2.00	.80
9 Tom McCraw	2.00	.80
10 Gary Peters	2.00	.80
11 Ed Stanky MG	2.00	.80
12 Pete Ward	2.00	.80

1969 White Sox Team Issue Black and White

This 12-card set of the Chicago White Sox measures approximately 4 1/4" by 7". The fronts display black-and-white player portraits bordered in white. The player's name and team are printed in the top margin. The backs are blank. The cards are unnumbered and checklisted below in alphabetical order.

	NM	Ex
COMPLETE SET (12)	20.00	8.00
1 Sandy Alomar	2.00	.80
2 Luis Aparicio	4.00	1.60
3 Ken Berry	1.50	.60
4 Charles Bradford	1.50	.60
5 Joe Horlen	1.50	.60
6 Tommy John	2.50	1.00
7 Duane Josephson	1.50	.60
8 Al Lopez MG	3.00	1.20
9 Carlos May	1.50	.60
10 Bill Melton	1.50	.60
11 Gary Peters	2.00	.80
12 Pete Ward	1.50	.60

1969 White Sox Team Issue Color

Similar to the Jewel food store issues, these color photos measure approximately 5" by 7" and feature members of the 1969 Chicago White Sox. Since these are unnumbered, we have sequenced them in alphabetical order.

	NM	Ex
COMPLETE SET	30.00	12.00
1 Luis Aparicio	6.00	2.40
2 Ken Berry	2.00	.80
3 Buddy Bradford	2.00	.80
4 Kerby Farrell CO	2.00	.80
5 Don Gutteridge MG	2.00	.80
6 Ed Herrmann	2.00	.80
7 Gail Hopkins	2.00	.80
8 Joel Horlen	2.00	.80
9 Tommy John	4.00	1.60
10 Duane Josephson	2.00	.80
11 Carlos May	2.00	.80
12 Rich Morales	2.00	.80
13 Bill Melton	2.00	.80
14 Dan Osinski	2.00	.80
15 Gary Peters	2.50	1.00
16 Wilbur Wood	2.50	1.00

1970 White Sox Team Issue

This 12-card set of the Chicago White Sox measures approximately 4 1/4" by 7" and features black-and-white player photos in a white border. Packaged 12 to a packet with blank backs, the cards are unnumbered and checklisted below in alphabetical order.

	NM	Ex
COMPLETE SET (12)	25.00	10.00
1 Luis Aparicio	6.00	2.40
2 Ken Berry	2.00	.80
3 Charles Bradford	2.00	.80
4 Don Gutteridge MG	2.00	.80
5 Gail Hopkins	2.00	.80
6 Joe Horlen	2.00	.80
7 Tommy John	4.00	1.60
8 Duane Josephson	2.00	.80
9 Bobby Knoop	2.00	.80
10 Carlos May	2.00	.80
11 Bill Melton	2.00	.80
12 Walter Williams	2.00	.80

1972 White Sox

The 1972 Chicago White Sox are featured in this set of 12 approximately 7 1/2" by 9 3/8" glossy color player photos. The photos are bordered in white, and the player's name is given below the picture. The backs are blank and the photos are checklisted below in alphabetical order.

	NM	Ex
COMPLETE SET (12)	35.00	14.00
1 Dick Allen	5.00	2.00
2 Stan Bahnsen	3.00	1.20
3 Terry Forster	4.00	1.60
4 Ken Henderson	3.00	1.20
5 Ed Herrmann	3.00	1.20
6 Pat Kelly	3.00	1.20
7 Eddie Leon	3.00	1.20
8 Carlos May	3.00	1.20
9 Bill Melton	4.00	1.60
10 Jorge Orta	3.00	1.20
11 Steve Stone	4.00	1.60
12 Wilbur Wood	4.00	1.60

1972 White Sox Chi-Foursome

These drawings feature members of the Chicago White Sox. These drawings measure 11" by 14" and also have the player's fascimile signature. The backs are blank and we have sequenced this set in alphabetical order.

	NM	Ex
COMPLETE SET (7)	40.00	16.00
1 Mike Andrews	5.00	2.00
2 Ed Herrmann	5.00	2.00
3 Pat Kelly	5.00	2.00
4 Carlos May	6.00	2.40
5 Bill Melton	6.00	2.40
6 Chuck Tanner MG	6.00	2.40
7 Wilbur Wood	8.00	3.20

1972 White Sox Durochrome Stickers

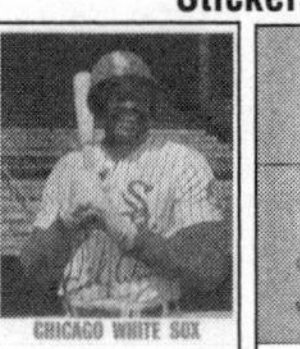

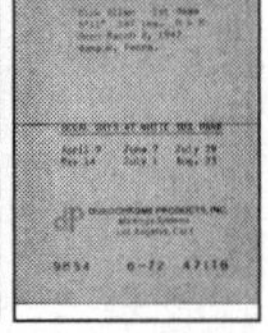

These stickers measure 3 1/2" by 4 1/2". They are unnumbered and we have sequenced them in alphabetical order.

	NM	Ex
COMPLETE SET (6)	12.00	4.80
1 Dick Allen	4.00	1.60
2 Ed Herrmann	1.50	.60
3 Bart Johnson	1.50	.60
4 Carlos May	1.50	.60
5 Bill Melton	2.00	.80
6 Wilbur Wood	3.00	1.20

1972 White Sox Team Issue

These cards measure 4 1/4" by 7" and were issued in groups of 12. The fronts feature a player photo against a white border along with the player's name and team on the bottom. The backs are blank. These cards were issued continually throughout the year so there is not an exact number divisible by 12.

	NM	Ex
COMPLETE SET	50.00	20.00
1 Dick Allen	6.00	2.40
2 Mike Andrews	3.00	1.20
3 Stan Bahnsen	4.00	1.60
4 Tom Bradley	3.00	1.20
5 Tom Egan	3.00	1.20
6 Terry Forster	4.00	1.60
7 Ed Herrmann	3.00	1.20
8 Jay Johnstone	4.00	1.60
9 Pat Kelly	3.00	1.20
10 Carlos May	3.00	1.20
10 Rick Reichardt	3.00	1.20

11 Bill Melton	4.00	1.60
12 Jorge Orta	3.00	1.20
13 Chuck Tanner MG	3.00	1.20
14 Walt Williams	3.00	1.20
15A Wilbur Wood UER	5.00	2.00
(Says Wilber on card)		
15B Wilbur Wood COR	5.00	2.00

1973 White Sox Jewel

These 6 1/2" by 9 1/2" blank-backed, white bordered, full-color photos were issued as a premium by Jewel Foods. The photos have a fascimile autograph and since they are unnumbered we have sequenced them in alphabetical order.

	NM	Ex
COMPLETE SET	20.00	8.00
1 Dick Allen	3.00	1.20
2 Mike Andrews	1.50	.60
3 Stan Bahnsen	1.50	.60
4 Eddie Fisher	1.50	.60
5 Terry Forster	1.50	.60
6 Ken Henderson	1.50	.60
7 Ed Herrmann	1.50	.60
8 Johnny Jeter	1.50	.60
9 Pat Kelly	1.50	.60
10 Eddie Leon	1.50	.60
11 Carlos May	1.50	.60
12 Bill Melton	1.50	.60
13 Tony Muser	1.50	.60
14 Jorge Orta	1.50	.60
15 Rick Reichardt	1.50	.60
16 Wilbur Wood	2.00	.80

1973 White Sox Team Issue

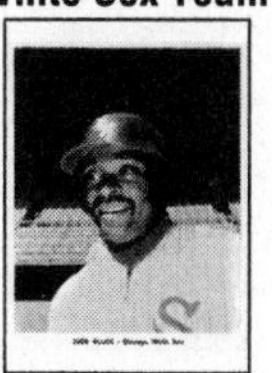

Measuring approximately 7" by 8 3/4" these blank-backed photos were issued to promote some of the leading players of the White Sox. The full-color photos are surrounded by white borders with the player's name and team on the bottom. Since these photos are unnumbered, we have sequenced them in alphabetical order.

	MINT	NRMT
COMPLETE SET	10.00	4.50
1 Dick Allen	3.00	1.35
2 Stan Bahnsen	1.50	.70
3 Pat Kelly	1.50	.70
4 Carlos May	1.50	.70
5 Bill Melton	1.50	.70
6 Wilbur Wood UER	2.00	.90
Spelled Wilber		

1975 White Sox 1919 TCMA

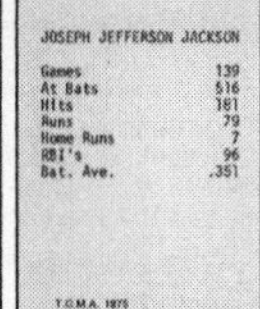

This 28-card set features the 1919 Chicago White Sox Team. The fronts display black-and-white player photos while the backs carry player statistics. The set includes one team picture jumbo card which measures approximately 3 1/2" by 4 3/4". The cards are unnumbered and checklisted below in alphabetical order.

	NM	Ex
COMPLETE SET (28)	25.00	10.00
1 Joe Benz	.50	.20
2 Eddie Cicotte	2.00	.80
3 Eddie Collins	3.00	1.20
4 Shano Collins	.50	.20
5 Dave Danforth	.50	.20
6 Red Faber	2.00	.80
7 Happy Felsch	1.50	.60
8 Charles "Chick" Gandil	1.50	.60
9 Kid Gleason MG	1.00	.40
10 Joe Jackson	5.00	2.00
11 Bill James	.50	.20
12 Dickie Kerr	1.00	.40
13 Nemo Leibold	.50	.20
14 Byrd Lynn	.50	.20
15 Erskine Mayer	.50	.20
16 Harvey McClellan	.50	.20
17 Fred McMullin	1.00	.40
18 Eddie Murphy	.50	.20
19 Pat Ragan	.50	.20
20 Swede Risberg	1.00	.40
21 Charlie Robertson	.50	.20
22 Red Russell	.50	.20
23 Ray Schalk	2.00	.80
24 Frank Shellenback	.50	.20
Grover Lowdermilk		
Joe Jenkins		
Dickie Kerr		
Ray Schalk		
25 Buck Weaver	2.00	.80
26 Roy Wilkinson	.50	.20
27 Lefty Williams	1.50	.60
28 Team Picture	1.00	.40

1976 White Sox TCMA All-Time Greats

All-Time
Chicago White Sox
Eddie Robinson 1B
Eddie Collins 2B
Willie Kamm 3B
Luke Appling SS
Ray Schalk C
Al Simmons LF
Johnny Mostil CF
Harry Hooper RF
Ted Lyons RHP
Billy Pierce LHP
Gerry Staley RP
Al Lopez Mgr

This 12-card set of the All-Time Chicago White Sox Team features black-and-white player photos bordered in white with the player's name and position printed in red in the bottom margin. The white backs carry the roster of the team. The cards are unnumbered and checklisted below in alphabetical order.

	NM	Ex
COMPLETE SET (12)	10.00	4.00
1 Luke Appling	1.00	.40
2 Eddie Collins	1.50	.60
3 Harry Hooper	1.00	.40
4 Willie Kamm	.50	.20
5 Al Lopez MG	.75	.30
6 Ted Lyons	1.00	.40
7 Johnny Mostil	.50	.20
8 Billy Pierce	.75	.30
9 Eddie Robinson	.50	.20
10 Ray Schalk	.75	.30
11 Al Simmons	1.50	.60
12 Gerry Staley	.50	.20

1977 White Sox Jewel Tea

This 16-card set of the Chicago White Sox measures approximately 5 7/8" by 9". The white-bordered fronts feature color player head photos with a facsimile autograph below. The backs are blank. The cards are unnumbered and checklisted below in alphabetical order.

	NM	Ex
COMPLETE SET (16)	15.00	6.00
1 Alan Bannister	1.00	.40
2 Francisco Barrios	1.00	.40
3 Jim Essian	1.00	.40
4 Oscar Gamble	1.50	.60
5 Ralph Garr	1.50	.60
6 Lamar Johnson	1.00	.40
7 Chris Knapp	1.00	.40
8 Ken Kravec	1.00	.40
9 Lerrin LaGrow	1.00	.40
10 Chet Lemon	1.50	.60
11 Jorge Orta	1.00	.40
12 Eric Soderholm	1.00	.40
13 Jim Spencer	1.00	.40
14 Steve Stone	1.50	.60
15 Wilbur Wood	1.00	.40
16 Richie Zisk	1.50	.60

1977 White Sox Tribune

These portraits were issued as inserts in the Chicago Tribune newspaper and were issued two at a time. One player pictured was a Chicago Cub and another was a Chicago White Sox. The photos are black and white and are posed head shots, the bottom of the photo features statistics up to that time. The photos are unnumbered so we have sequenced them in alphabetical order.

	NM	Ex
COMPLETE SET	25.00	10.00
1 Alan Bannister	1.00	.40
2 Francisco Barrios	1.00	.40
3 Kevin Bell	1.00	.40
4 Jack Brohamer	1.00	.40
5 Bruce Dal Canton	1.00	.40
6 Brian Downing	1.00	.40
7 Jim Essian	1.00	.40
8 Oscar Gamble	1.50	.60
9 Ralph Garr	1.00	.40
10 Dave Hamilton	1.00	.40
11 Bart Johnson	1.00	.40
12 Lamar Johnson	1.00	.40
13 Don Kirkwood	1.00	.40
14 Chris Knapp	1.00	.40
15 Ken Kravec	1.00	.40
16 Jack Kucek	1.00	.40
17 Lerrin LaGrow	1.00	.40
18 Chet Lemon	1.00	.40
19 Tim Nordbrook	1.00	.40
20 Wayne Nordhagen	1.00	.40
21 Jorge Orta	1.00	.40
22 Eric Soderholm	1.00	.40
23 Jim Spencer	1.00	.40
24 Royle Stillman	1.00	.40
25 Steve Stone	1.50	.60
26 Wilbur Wood	1.50	.60
27 Richie Zisk	1.00	.40

1980 White Sox Greats TCMA

This 12-card standard-size set features various all-time White Sox greats. The fronts display a player photo, while the backs carry information about the player.

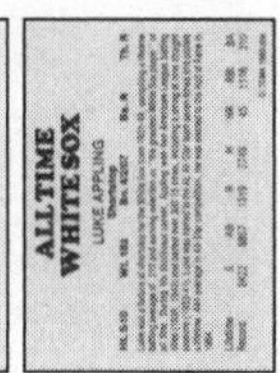

	NM	Ex
COMPLETE SET (12)	5.00	2.00
1 Ted Lyons	.75	.30
2 Eddie Collins	1.00	.40
3 Al Lopez MG	.50	.20
4 Luke Appling	1.00	.40
5 Billy Pierce	.50	.20
6 Willie Kamm	.25	.10
7 Johnny Mostil	.25	.10
8 Al Simmons	.75	.30
9 Ray Schalk	.75	.30
10 Gerry Staley	.25	.10
11 Harry Hooper	.75	.30
12 Eddie Robinson	.25	.10

1981 White Sox 1959 TCMA

This 45-card set features photos of the 1959 Chicago White Sox team in blue borders. The backs carry player information.

	Nm-Mt	Ex-Mt
COMPLETE SET (45)	15.00	6.00
1 Earl Torgeson	.25	.10
2 Nellie Fox	1.50	.60
3 Luis Aparicio	1.50	.60
4 Bubba Phillips	.25	.10
5 Jim McAnany	.25	.10
6 Jim Landis	.25	.10
7 Al Smith	.25	.10
8 Sherman Lollar	.50	.20
9 Billy Goodman	.25	.10
10 Jim Rivera	.25	.10
11 Sammy Esposito	.25	.10
12 Norm Cash	.75	.30
13 Johnny Romano	.25	.10
14 Johnny Callison	.50	.20
15 Harry Simpson	.25	.10
16 Ted Kluszewski	1.00	.40
17 Del Ennis	.50	.20
18 Earl Battey	.25	.10
19 Larry Doby	1.50	.60
20 Ron Jackson	.25	.10
21 Ray Boone	.25	.10
22 Lou Skizas	.25	.10
23 Joe Hicks	.25	.10
24 Don Mueller	.25	.10
25 J.C. Martin	.25	.10
26 Cam Carreon	.25	.10
27 Early Wynn	1.50	.60
28 Bob Shaw	.25	.10
29 Billy Pierce	.50	.20
30 Turk Lown	.25	.10
31 Dick Donovan	.25	.10
32 Gerry Staley	.25	.10
33 Barry Latman	.25	.10
34 Ray Moore	.25	.10
35 Rudy Arias	.25	.10
36 Joe Stanka	.25	.10
37 Ken McBride	.25	.10
38 Don Rudolph	.25	.10
39 Claude Raymond	.25	.10
40 Gary Peters	.25	.10
41 Al Lopez MG	.75	.30
42 Don Gutteridge CO	.25	.10
43 Ray Berres CO	.25	.10
44 Tony Cuccinello CO	.25	.10
45 John Cooney CO	.25	.10

1983 White Sox True Value

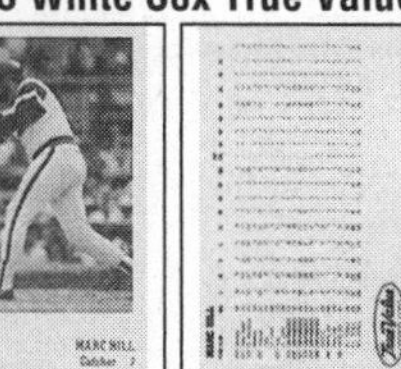

This 23-card set was sponsored by True Value Hardware Stores and features full-color (approximately 2 5/8" by 4 1/4") cards of the Chicago White Sox. Most of the set was intended for distribution two cards per game at selected White Sox Tuesday night home games. The cards are unnumbered except for uniform number given in the lower right corner of the obverse. The card backs contain statistical information in basic black and white. The cards of Harold Baines, Salome Barojas, and Marc Hill were not issued at the park; hence they are more difficult to obtain than the other 20 cards and are marked SP in the checklist below.

	Nm-Mt	Ex-Mt
COMPLETE SET (23)	35.00	14.00
COMMON SP	5.00	2.00
1 Scott Fletcher	.50	.20
3 Harold Baines SP	8.00	3.20
5 Vance Law	.50	.20
7 Marc Hill SP	5.00	2.00
10 Tony LaRussa MG	1.50	.60
11 Rudy Law	.50	.20
14 Tony Bernazard	.50	.20
17 Jerry Hairston	.50	.20
19 Greg Luzinski	1.00	.40
24 Floyd Bannister	.50	.20
25 Mike Squires	.50	.20
30 Salome Barojas SP	5.00	2.00
31 LaMarr Hoyt	.75	.30
34 Richard Dotson	.50	.20
36 Jerry Koosman	1.00	.40
40 Britt Burns	.50	.20
41 Dick Tidrow	.50	.20
42 Ron Kittle	1.50	.60
44 Tom Paciorek	.50	.20
45 Kevin Hickey	.50	.20
53 Dennis Lamp	.50	.20
67 Jim Kern	.50	.20
72 Carlton Fisk	8.00	3.20

1984 White Sox Jewel

These 16 blank backed cards feature members of the 1984 Chicago White Sox. The fronts have the players photo against a blue background with a fascimile autograph on the bottom and the MLBPA logo in the upper left. These cards are unnumbered so we have sequenced them in alphabetical order.

	Nm-Mt	Ex-Mt
COMPLETE SET (16)	15.00	6.00
1 Harold Baines	1.50	.60
2 Floyd Bannister	.50	.20
3 Julio Cruz	.50	.20
4 Rich Dotson	.50	.20
5 Jerry Dybzinski	.50	.20
6 Carlton Fisk	3.00	1.20
7 Scott Fletcher	.50	.20
8 Lamarr Hoyt	.75	.30
9 Rudy Law	.50	.20
10 Vance Law	.50	.20
11 Greg Luzinski	1.00	.40
12 Ron Kittle	.75	.30
13 Tom Paciorek	.50	.20
14 Tom Seaver	5.00	2.00
15 Mike Squires	.50	.20
16 Greg Walker	.50	.20

1984 White Sox True Value

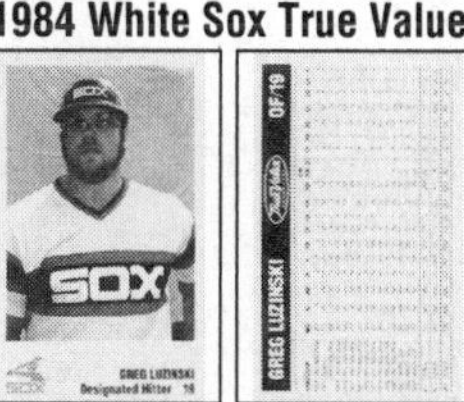

This 30-card set features full color (approximately 2 1/2" by 4") cards of the Chicago White Sox. Most of the set was distributed two cards per game at selected White Sox Tuesday home games. Faust and Minoso were not given out although their cards were available through direct (promotional) contact with them. Brennan and Hulett were not released directly since they were sent down to the minors. The cards are unnumbered except for uniform number given in the lower right corner of the obverse; they are arbitrarily listed below in alphabetical order. The card backs contain statistical information in basic black and white.

	Nm-Mt	Ex-Mt
COMPLETE SET (30)	25.00	10.00
COMMON SP	3.00	1.20
1 Juan Agosto	.50	.20
2 Luis Aparicio	3.00	1.20
3 Harold Baines	1.50	.60
4 Floyd Bannister	.50	.20
5 Salome Barojas	.50	.20
6 Tom Brennan SP	3.00	1.20
7 Britt Burns	.50	.20
8 Coaching Staff	.75	.30
(Blank back)		
9 Julio Cruz	.50	.20
10 Richard Dotson	.50	.20
11 Jerry Dybzinski	.50	.20
12 Nancy Faust ORG	1.50	.60
(Blank back)		
13 Carlton Fisk	6.00	2.40
14 Scott Fletcher	.50	.20
15 Jerry Hairston	.50	.20
16 Marc Hill	.50	.20
17 LaMarr Hoyt	.50	.20
18 Tim Hulett SP	3.00	1.20
19 Ron Kittle	.75	.30
20 Tony LaRussa MG	1.50	.60
21 Rudy Law	.50	.20
22 Vance Law	.50	.20
23 Greg Luzinski	1.00	.40
24 Minnie Minoso	3.00	1.20
25 Tom Paciorek	.50	.20
26 Ron Reed	.50	.20
27 Tom Seaver	6.00	2.40
28 Dave Stegman	.50	.20
29 Mike Squires	.50	.20
30 Greg Walker	.75	.30

1985 White Sox Coke

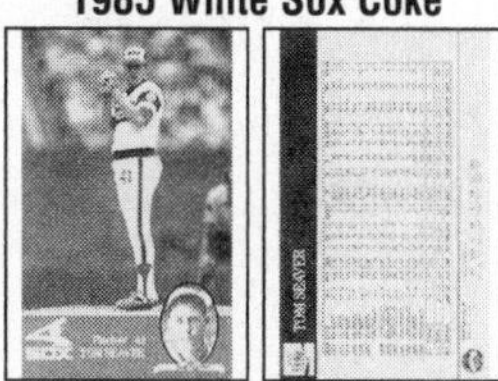

This 30-card set features present and past Chicago White Sox players and personnel. Cards measure approximately 2 5/8" by 4 1/8" and feature a red band at the bottom of the card. Within the red band are the White Sox logo, the player's name, position, uniform number, and a small oval portrait of an all-time White Sox Great at a similar position. The cards were available two at a time at Tuesday night White Sox home games or as a complete set through membership in the Coca-Cola White Sox Fan Club. The cards below are numbered by uniform number; the last three cards are unnumbered.

	Nm-Mt	Ex-Mt
COMPLETE SET (30)	12.00	4.80
0 Oscar Gamble	.25	.10
Zeke Bonura		
1 Scott Fletcher	1.00	.40
Luke Appling		
3 Harold Baines	.75	.30
Bill Melton		
5 Luis Salazar	.25	.10
Chico Carrasquel		
7 Marc Hill	.25	.10
Sherm Lollar		
8 Daryl Boston	.25	.10
Jim Landis		
10 Tony LaRussa MG	1.00	.40
Al Lopez MG		
12 Julio Cruz	1.00	.40
Nellie Fox		
13 Ozzie Guillen	2.50	1.00
Luis Aparicio		
17 Jerry Hairston	.25	.10
Smoky Burgess		
20 Joe DeSa	.25	.10
Carlos May		
22 Joel Skinner	.25	.10
J.C. Martin		
23 Rudy Law	.25	.10
Bill Skowron		
24 Floyd Bannister	.50	.20
Red Faber		
29 Greg Walker	.75	.30
Dick Allen		
30 Gene Nelson	1.00	.40
Early Wynn		
32 Tim Hulett	.25	.10
Pete Ward		
34 Richard Dotson	.50	.20
Ed Walsh		
37 Dan Spillner	.25	.10
Thornton Lee		
40 Britt Burns	.25	.10
Gary Peters		
41 Tom Seaver	2.50	1.00
Ted Lyons		
42 Ron Kittle	1.00	.40
Minnie Minoso		
43 Bob James	.25	.10
Hoyt Wilhelm		
44 Tom Paciorek	1.00	.40
Eddie Collins		
46 Tim Lollar	.50	.20
Billy Pierce		
50 Juan Agosto	.25	.10
Wilbur Wood		
72 Carlton Fisk	2.50	1.00
Ray Schalk		
NNO Comiskey Park	.25	.10
NNO Nancy Faust ORG	.25	.10
NNO Ribbie and Roobarb	.25	.10

1986 White Sox Coke

This colorful 30-card set features a borderless photo on top of a blue-on-white name, position, and uniform number. Card backs provide complete major and minor season-by-season career statistical information. Since the cards are unnumbered, they are numbered below according to uniform number. The cards measure approximately 2 5/8" by 4". The five unnumbered non-player cards are listed at the end of the checklist below.

	Nm-Mt	Ex-Mt
COMPLETE SET (30)	12.00	4.80
1 Wayne Tolleson	.25	.10
3 Harold Baines	1.00	.40
7 Marc Hill	.25	.10
8 Daryl Boston	.25	.10
12 Julio Cruz	.25	.10
13 Ozzie Guillen	1.50	.60
17 Jerry Hairston	.25	.10
19 Floyd Bannister	.25	.10
20 Reid Nichols	.25	.10
22 Joel Skinner	.25	.10
24 Dave Schmidt	.25	.10
26 Bobby Bonilla	3.00	1.20
29 Greg Walker	.25	.10
30 Gene Nelson	.25	.10
32 Tim Hulett	.25	.10
33 Neil Allen	.25	.10
34 Richard Dotson	.25	.10
40 Joe Cowley	.25	.10
41 Tom Seaver	3.00	1.20
42 Ron Kittle	.50	.20
43 Bob James	.25	.10
44 John Cangelosi	.25	.10
50 Juan Agosto	.25	.10
52 Joel Davis	.25	.10
72 Carlton Fisk	3.00	1.20
NNO Nancy Faust ORG	.25	.10
NNO Ken(Hawk) Harrelson GM	.50	.20
NNO Tony LaRussa MG	.75	.30
NNO Minnie Minoso CO	.75	.30
NNO Ribbie and Roobarb	.25	.10

1987 White Sox Coke

This colorful 30-card set features a card front with a blue-bordered photo and name, position,

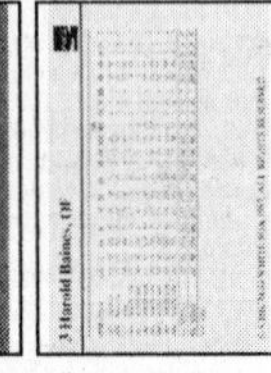

and uniform number. Card backs provide complete major and minor season-by-season career statistical information. Since the cards are unnumbered, they are numbered below in alphabetical order. The cards measure approximately 2 5/8" by 4". The card set, sponsored by Coca-Cola, is an exclusive for fan club members who join (for 10.00) in 1987.

	Nm-Mt	Ex-Mt
COMPLETE SET (30)	12.00	4.80
1 Neil Allen	.25	.10
2 Harold Baines	1.50	.60
3 Floyd Bannister	.25	.10
4 Daryl Boston	.25	.10
5 Ivan Calderon	.50	.20
6 Joel Davis	.25	.10
7 Jose DeLeon	.25	.10
8 Richard Dotson	.25	.10
9 Nancy Faust ORG	.25	.10
10 Carlton Fisk	3.00	1.20
11 Jim Fregosi MG	.25	.10
12 Ozzie Guillen	1.00	.40
13 Jerry Hairston	.25	.10
14 Ron Hassey	.25	.10
15 Donnie Hill	.25	.10
16 Tim Hulett	.25	.10
17 Bob James	.25	.10
18 Ron Karkovice	.50	.20
19 Steve Lyons	.50	.20
20 Fred Manrique	.25	.10
21 Joel McKeon	.25	.10
22 Minnie Minoso	1.00	.40
23 Russ Morman	.25	.10
24 Gary Redus	.25	.10
25 Ribbie and Roobarb	.25	.10
26 Jerry Royster	.25	.10
27 Ray Searage	.25	.10
28 Bobby Thigpen	.50	.20
29 Greg Walker	.25	.10
30 Jim Winn	.25	.10

1988 White Sox Coke

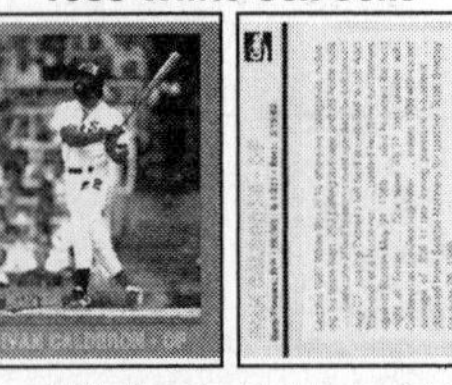

This colorful 30-card set features a card front with a red-bordered photo and name and position. Card backs provide a narrative without any statistical tables. Since the cards are unnumbered, they are numbered below in alphabetical order according to the subject's name or card's title. The cards measure approximately 2 5/8" by 3 1/2". The card set, sponsored by Coca-Cola, was for fan club members who join (for 10.00) in 1988. The cards were also given out at the May 22nd game at Comiskey Park. These cards do not even list the player's uniform number anywhere on the card. Card backs are printed in black and gray on thin white card stock.

	Nm-Mt	Ex-Mt
COMPLETE SET (30)	8.00	3.20
1 Harold Baines	1.00	.40
2 Daryl Boston	.25	.10
3 Ivan Calderon	.25	.10
4 Comiskey Park	.25	.10
5 John Davis	.25	.10
6 Nancy Faust ORG	.25	.10
7 Jim Fregosi MG	.25	.10
8 Carlton Fisk	2.00	.80
9 Ozzie Guillen	1.00	.40
10 Donnie Hill	.25	.10
11 Ricky Horton	.25	.10
12 Lance Johnson	2.00	.80
13 Dave LaPoint	.25	.10
14 Bill Long	.25	.10
15 Steve Lyons	.50	.20
16 Jack McDowell	2.50	1.00
17 Fred Manrique	.25	.10
18 Minnie Minoso CO	1.00	.40
19 Dan Pasqua	.25	.10
20 John Pawlowski	.25	.10
21 Melido Perez	.25	.10
22 Billy Pierce	.50	.20
23 Jerry Reuss	.50	.20
24 Gary Redus	.25	.10
25 Ribbie and Roobarb	.25	.10
26 Mark Salas	.25	.10
27 Jose Segura	.25	.10
28 Bobby Thigpen	.50	.20
29 Greg Walker	.25	.10
30 Kenny Williams	1.00	.40

1988 White Sox Kodak

This five-card, approximately 8" by 11 1/2" set was issued by Kodak including members of the 1988 Chicago White Sox. The cards are borderless and say "1988 Kodak Collectible Series" on top with the player's photo dominating the middle of the photo. Underneath the photo is a facsimile autograph and on the bottom left of the photo is an advertisment for Kodak and the bottom right of the card the White Sox logo is featured.

	Nm-Mt	Ex-Mt
COMPLETE SET (5)	8.00	3.20
1 Ozzie Guillen	2.50	1.00
2 Carlton Fisk	3.00	1.20
3 Rick Horton	1.50	.60
4 Ivan Calderon	1.50	.60
5 Harold Baines	3.00	1.20

1989 White Sox Coke

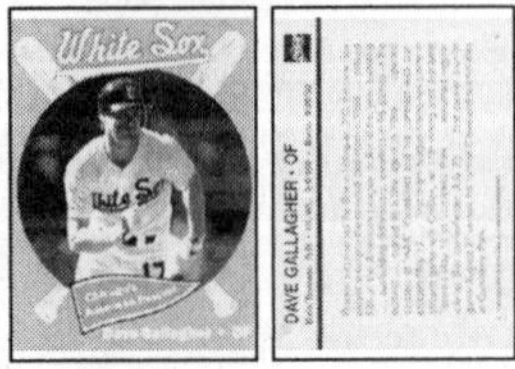

The 1989 Coke Chicago White Sox set contains 30 cards measuring approximately 2 5/8" by 3 1/2". The players in the set represent the White Sox opening day roster. The fronts are blue. The horizontally oriented backs are gray and white, and feature biographical information. The set was a promotional give-away August 10, 1989 at the Baseball Card Night game against the Oakland A's to the first 15,000 fans. The set includes a special "New Comiskey Park, 1991" card. The complete set was also available with (10.00) membership in the Chi-Sox Fan Club. The cards in the set are numbered on the backs in the lower right corner in very small print.

	Nm-Mt	Ex-Mt
COMPLETE SET (30)	8.00	3.20
1 New Comiskey Park 1991	.25	.10
2 Comiskey Park	.25	.10
3 Jeff Torborg MG	.25	.10
4 Coaching Staff	.25	.10
5 Harold Baines	.75	.30
6 Daryl Boston	.25	.10
7 Ivan Calderon	.50	.20
8 Carlton Fisk	1.50	.60
9 Dave Gallagher	.25	.10
10 Ozzie Guillen	1.00	.40
11 Shawn Hillegas	.25	.10
12 Barry Jones	.25	.10
13 Ron Karkovice	.25	.10
14 Eric King	.25	.10
15 Ron Kittle	.25	.10
16 Bill Long	.25	.10
17 Steve Lyons	.50	.20
18 Donn Pall	.25	.10
19 Dan Pasqua	.25	.10
20 Ken Patterson	.25	.10
21 Melido Perez	.25	.10
22 Jerry Reuss	.50	.20
23 Billy Joe Robidoux	.25	.10
24 Steve Rosenberg	.25	.10
25 Jeff Schaefer	.25	.10
26 Bobby Thigpen	.25	.10
27 Greg Walker	.25	.10
28 Eddie Williams	.25	.10
29 Nancy Faust ORG	.25	.10
30 Minnie Minoso	1.00	.40

1989 White Sox Kodak

For the second consecutive year Kodak in conjunction with the Chicago White Sox issued a set about the White Sox. The 1989 set was marked by a color photo of the active star dominating the upper right half of the card with the bottom half of the card depicting two other famous White Sox players at the same position that the current star played. This six-card, approximately 8" by 11 1/2", set was given away at various games at Comiskey Park.

	Nm-Mt	Ex-Mt
COMPLETE SET (6)	8.00	3.20
1 Greg Walker	1.50	.60
Dick Allen		
Ted Kluszewski		
2 Steve Lyons	2.00	.80
Eddie Collins		
Nellie Fox		
3 Carlton Fisk	3.00	1.20
Sherm Lollar		
Ray Schalk		
4 Harold Baines	1.50	.60
Minnie Minoso		
Jim Landis		
5 Bobby Thigpen	1.50	.60
Gerry Staley		
Hoyt Wilhelm		
6 Ozzie Guillen	3.00	1.20
Luke Appling		
Luis Aparicio		

1990 White Sox Coke

The 1990 Coca Cola White Sox set contains 30 cards. The set is a beautiful full-color set commemorating the 1990 White Sox who were

celebrating the eightieth and last season played in old Comiskey Park. This (approximately) 2 5/8" by 3 1/2" set has a Comiskey Park logo on the front with 1989 statistics and a brief biography on the back. The set is checklisted alphabetically. The set features early cards of Sammy Sosa and Frank Thomas.

	Nm-Mt	Ex-Mt
COMPLETE SET (30)	50.00	15.00
1 Ivan Calderon	.25	.07
2 Wayne Edwards	.25	.07
3 Carlton Fisk	2.00	.60
4 Scott Fletcher	.25	.07
5 Dave Gallagher	.25	.07
6 Craig Grebeck	.25	.07
7 Ozzie Guillen	1.00	.30
8 Greg Hibbard	.25	.07
9 Lance Johnson	1.00	.30
10 Barry Jones	.25	.07
11 Ron Karkovice	.25	.07
12 Eric King	.25	.07
13 Ron Kittle	.25	.07
14 Jerry Kutzler	.25	.07
15 Steve Lyons	.50	.15
16 Carlos Martinez	.25	.07
17 Jack McDowell	1.00	.30
18 Donn Pall	.25	.07
19 Dan Pasqua	.25	.07
20 Ken Patterson	.25	.07
21 Melido Perez	.25	.07
22 Scott Radinsky	.25	.07
23 Sammy Sosa	30.00	9.00
24 Bobby Thigpen	.50	.15
25 Frank Thomas	15.00	4.50
26 Jeff Torborg MG	.50	.15
27 Robin Ventura	3.00	.90
28 Jerry Kutzler	.75	.23
Wayne Edwards		
Craig Grebeck		
Scott Radinsky		
Robin Ventura		
29 Ozzie Guillen	.50	.15
Carlton Fisk		
30 Barry Foote CO	.25	.07
Sammy Ellis CO		
Walt Hriniak CO		
Terry Bevington CO		
Dave LaRoche CO		
Joe Nossek CO		
Ron Clark CO		

1990 White Sox Kodak

In 1990 Kodak again in conjunction with the Chicago White Sox issued a beautiful six-card set about some key members of the 1990 White Sox. This was slightly reduced in size (from the previous two years) to be approximately 7" by 11" and featured a full-color picture with an advertisement for Kodak on the lower left corner of the front of the card and the White Sox logo in the lower right hand corner. The cards were again borderless and blank-backed.

	Nm-Mt	Ex-Mt
COMPLETE SET (6)	10.00	3.00
1 Carlton Fisk	4.00	1.20
2 Melido Perez	1.25	.35
3 Ozzie Guillen	2.00	.60
4 Ron Kittle	1.25	.35
5 Scott Fletcher	1.25	.35
6 Comiskey Park	1.25	.35

1991 White Sox Kodak

This 28-card set was sponsored by Kodak and measures approximately 2 5/8" by 3 1/2". The cards are skip-numbered by uniform number and checklisted below accordingly, with the unnumbered cards listed at the end.

	Nm-Mt	Ex-Mt
COMPLETE SET (28)	30.00	9.00
1 Lance Johnson	.25	.07
5 Matt Merullo	.25	.07
7 Scott Fletcher	.25	.07
8 Bo Jackson	1.00	.30
10 Jeff Torborg MG	.25	.07
13 Ozzie Guillen	.75	.23
14 Craig Grebeck	.25	.07
20 Ron Karkovice	.25	.07
21 Joey Cora	.25	.07
22 Donn Pall	.25	.07
23 Robin Ventura	2.00	.60
25 Sammy Sosa	15.00	4.50
27 Greg Hibbard	.25	.07
28 Cory Snyder	.25	.07
29 Jack McDowell	.75	.23
30 Tim Raines	.50	.15
31 Scott Radinsky	.25	.07
32 Alex Fernandez	.25	.07
33 Melido Perez	.25	.07
34 Ken Patterson	.25	.07
35 Frank Thomas	8.00	2.40
37 Bobby Thigpen	.25	.07
44 Dan Pasqua	.25	.07
45 Wayne Edwards	.25	.07
49 Charlie Hough	.50	.15
50 Brian Drahman	.25	.07
72 Carlton Fisk	2.50	.75
NNO Jack McDowell	5.00	1.50
Robin Ventura		
Alex Fernandez		
Frank Thomas		
NNO Carlton Fisk	.75	.23
Ozzie Guillen		
NNO Walt Hriniak CO	.25	.07
Sammy Ellis CO		
Terry Bevington CO		
Barry Foote CO		
Joe Nossek CO		
John Stephenson CO		
Dave LaRoche CO		

1992 White Sox Kodak

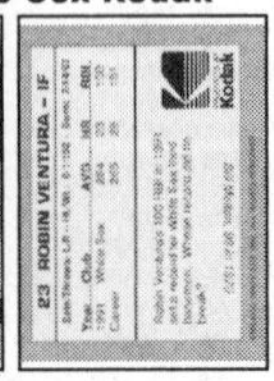

This 30-card set was sponsored by Kodak and measures slightly larger (2 5/8" by 3 1/2") than standard size. The set was distributed at a White Sox vs. Milwaukee four-game series at Comiskey Park. The cards are skip-numbered on the front by uniform number and checklisted below accordingly.

	Nm-Mt	Ex-Mt
COMPLETE SET (30)	15.00	4.50
0 Waldo the Wolf	.25	.07
1 Lance Johnson	.25	.07
5 Matt Merullo	.25	.07
7 Steve Sax	.25	.07
12 Mike Huff	.25	.07
13 Ozzie Guillen	.75	.23
14 Craig Grebeck	.25	.07
20 Ron Karkovice	.25	.07
21 George Bell	.50	.15
22 Donn Pall	.25	.07
23 Robin Ventura	2.00	.60
24 Warren Newson	.25	.07
25 Kirk McCaskill	.25	.07
27 Greg Hibbard	.25	.07
28 Joey Cora	.25	.07
29 Jack McDowell	.75	.23
30 Tim Raines	.50	.15
31 Scott Radinsky	.25	.07
32 Alex Fernandez	.25	.07
33 Gene Lamont MG	.25	.07
34 Terry Leach	.25	.07
35 Frank Thomas	6.00	1.80
37 Bobby Thigpen	.25	.07
39 Roberto Hernandez	2.50	.75
40 Wilson Alvarez	1.00	.30
44 Dan Pasqua	.25	.07
45 Shawn Abner	.25	.07
49 Charlie Hough	.50	.15
72 Carlton Fisk	3.00	.90
NNO Walt Hriniak CO	.25	.07
Doug Mansolino CO		
Dave Huppert CO		
Mike Squires CO		
Terry Bevington CO		
Gene Lamont MG		
Joe Nossek CO		
Jackie Brown CO		

1993 White Sox Kodak

This 30-card set measures approximately 2 5/8" by 3 1/2" and features color player action photos on the fronts. The cards are unnumbered and checklisted below in alphabetical order.

	Nm-Mt	Ex-Mt
COMPLETE SET (30)	12.00	3.60
1 Wilson Alvarez	.25	.07
2 George Bell	.50	.15
3 Jason Bere	.25	.07
4 Rod Bolton	.25	.07
5 Ellis Burks	1.00	.30
6 Chuck Cary	.25	.07
7 Joey Cora	.25	.07
8 Alex Fernandez	.25	.07
9 Craig Grebeck	.25	.07
10 Ozzie Guillen	.75	.23
11 Roberto Hernandez	.50	.15
12 Mike Huff	.25	.07
13 Bo Jackson	1.00	.30
14 Lance Johnson	.25	.07
15 Ron Karkovice	.25	.07
16 Gene Lamont MG	.25	.07
17 Mike LaValliere	.25	.07
18 Terry Leach	.25	.07
19 Kirk McCaskill	.25	.07
20 Jack McDowell	.50	.15
21 Donn Pall	.25	.07
22 Dan Pasqua	.25	.07
23 Scott Radinsky	.25	.07
24 Tim Raines	.75	.23
25 Steve Sax	.25	.07
26 Jeff Schwarz	.25	.07
27 Bobby Thigpen	.25	.07
28 Frank Thomas	4.00	1.20
29 Robin Ventura	1.50	.45
30 Jose Antigua CO	.25	.07
Terry Bevington CO		
Jackie Brown CO		
Walt Hriniak CO		
Gene Lamont MG		
Doug Mansolino CO		
Joe Nossek CO		
Dewey Robinson CO		

1993 White Sox Stadium Club

This 30-card standard-size set features the 1993 Chicago White Sox. The set was issued in hobby (plastic box) and retail (blister) form.

	Nm-Mt	Ex-Mt
COMP. FACT SET (30)	6.00	1.80
1 Frank Thomas	1.50	.45
2 Bo Jackson	.75	.23
3 Rod Bolton	.10	.03
4 Dave Stieb	.25	.07
5 Tim Raines	.25	.07
6 Joey Cora	.10	.03
7 Warren Newson	.10	.03
8 Roberto Hernandez	.25	.07
9 Brandon Wilson	.10	.03
10 Wilson Alvarez	.25	.07
11 Dan Pasqua	.10	.03
12 Ozzie Guillen	.50	.15
13 Robin Ventura	.75	.23
14 Craig Grebeck	.10	.03
15 Lance Johnson	.25	.07
16 Carlton Fisk	1.00	.30
17 Ron Karkovice	.10	.03
18 Jack McDowell	.25	.07
19 Scott Radinsky	.10	.03
20 Bobby Thigpen	.25	.07
21 Donn Pall	.10	.03
22 George Bell	.25	.07
23 Alex Fernandez	.10	.03
24 Mike Huff	.10	.03
25 Jason Bere	.25	.07
26 Johnny Ruffin	.10	.03
27 Ellis Burks	.75	.23
28 Kirk McCaskill	.10	.03
29 Terry Leach	.10	.03
30 Shawn Gilbert	.10	.03

1994 White Sox Kodak

These 30 cards measure 2 5/8" by 3 1/2" and feature borderless color player action shots on their fronts. The cards are unnumbered and checklisted below in alphabetical order.

	Nm-Mt	Ex-Mt
COMPLETE SET (30)	12.00	3.60
1 Wilson Alvarez	.50	.15
2 Paul Assenmacher	.25	.07
3 Jason Bere	.25	.07
4 Dennis Cook	.25	.07
5 Joey Cora	.25	.07
6 Jose DeLeon	.25	.07
7 Alex Fernandez	.25	.07
8 Julio Franco	.50	.15
9 Craig Grebeck	.25	.07
10 Ozzie Guillen	.75	.23
11 Joe Hall	.25	.07
12 Roberto Hernandez	.50	.15
13 Dann Howitt	.25	.07
14 Darrin Jackson	.25	.07
15 Dane Johnson	.25	.07
16 Lance Johnson	.25	.07
17 Ron Karkovice	.25	.07
18 Gene Lamont MG	.25	.07
19 Mike LaValliere	.25	.07
20 Norberto Martin	.25	.07
21 Kirk McCaskill	.25	.07
22 Jack McDowell	.75	.23
23 Warren Newson	.25	.07
24 Dan Pasqua	.25	.07
25 Tim Raines	.75	.23
26 Scott Sanderson	.50	.15
27 Frank Thomas	4.00	1.20
28 Robin Ventura	2.00	.60
29 Bob Zupcic	.25	.07
30 Doug Mansolino CO	.25	.07
Rick Peterson CO		
Roly de Armas CO		
Jackie Brown CO		
Gene Lamont MG		
Terry Bevington CO		
Joe Nossek CO		
Walt Hriniak CO		

1995 White Sox Kodak

Sponsored by Kodak, this 31-card set commemorates the 95th anniversary of the Chicago White Sox. The cards measure 2 5/8" by 3 1/2". The cards are unnumbered and checklisted below in alphabetical order.

	Nm-Mt	Ex-Mt
COMPLETE SET (31)	12.00	3.60
1 Jim Abbott	.50	.15
2 Wilson Alvarez	.50	.15
3 Jason Bere	.25	.07
4 Terry Bevington MG	.25	.07
5 Jose DeLeon	.25	.07
6 Mike Devereaux	.25	.07
7 Rob Dibble	.25	.07
8 Ray Durham	1.50	.45
9 Alex Fernandez	.25	.07
10 Tim Fortugno	.25	.07
11 Craig Grebeck	.25	.07
12 Ozzie Guillen	.75	.23
13 Roberto Hernandez	.75	.23
14 Lance Johnson	.25	.07
15 Ron Karkovice	.25	.07
16 Brian Keyser	.25	.07
17 John Kruk	.50	.15
18 Mike LaValliere	.25	.07
19 Norberto Martin	.25	.07
20 Dave Martinez	.25	.07
21 Kirk McCaskill	.25	.07
22 Warren Newson	.25	.07
24 Steve Odgers	.25	.07
Dir. of Conditioning		
25 Scott Radinsky	.25	.07
26 Tim Raines	.75	.23
27 Herm Schneider TR	.25	.07
Mark Anderson TR		
28 Frank Thomas	3.00	.90
29 Frank Thomas AS	1.50	.45
30 Robin Ventura	1.50	.45
31 Terry Bevington MG	.25	.07
Don Cooper CO		
Walt Hriniak CO		
Joe Nossek CO		
Doug Mansolino CO		
Ron Jackson CO		
Mark Salas CO		
Roly de Armas CO		

1996 White Sox Dannon

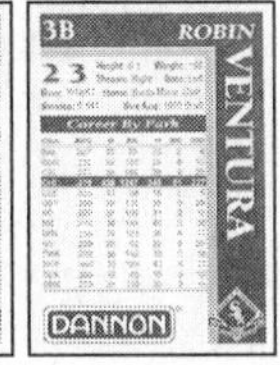

These 30 cards were issued in conjunction with Dannon Yogurt and were given away at a special night at Comiskey Park. The cards are unnumbered so we have sequenced them in alphabetical order.

	Nm-Mt	Ex-Mt
COMPLETE SET (30)	12.00	3.60
1 Wilson Alvarez	.50	.15
2 James Baldwin	.25	.07
3 Harold Baines	1.00	.30
4 Jason Bere	.25	.07
5 Terry Bevington MG	.25	.07
6 Ray Durham	1.00	.30
7 Alex Fernandez	.25	.07
8 Ozzie Guillen	.75	.23
9 Roberto Hernandez	.75	.23
10 Ron Karkovice	.25	.07
11 Brian Keyser	.25	.07
12 Matt Karchner	.25	.07
13 Chad Kreuter	.25	.07
14 Darren Lewis	.25	.07
15 Joe Magrane	.25	.07
16 Norberto Martin	.25	.07
17 Dave Martinez	.25	.07
18 Kirk McCaskill	.25	.07
19 Lyle Mouton	.25	.07
20 Jose Munoz	.25	.07
21 Tony Philips	.25	.07
22 Bill Simas	.25	.07
23 Chris Snopek	.25	.07
24 Kevin Tapani	.25	.07
25 Danny Tartabull	.50	.15
26 Frank Thomas	2.00	.60
27 Larry Thomas	.25	.07
28 Robin Ventura	1.50	.45
29 Frank Thomas	1.50	.45
Ray Durham		
Robin Ventura		
Ozzie Guillen		
30 Mark Salas CO	.25	.07
Bill Buckner CO		
Mike Pazik CO		
Roly de Armas CO		
Doug Mansolino CO		
Joe Nossek CO		
Terry Bevington CO		
Ron Jackson CO		

1996 White Sox Fleer

These 20 standard-size cards have the same design as the regular Fleer issue, except they are UV coated, they use silver foil and they are numbered "x of 20". The team set packs were

available at retail locations and hobby shops in 10-card packs for a suggested price of $1.99.

	Nm-Mt	Ex-Mt
COMPLETE SET (20)	3.00	.90
1 Wilson Alvarez	.20	.06
2 Harold Baines	.40	.12
3 Jason Bere	.10	.03
4 Ray Durham	.40	.12
5 Alex Fernandez	.10	.03
6 Ozzie Guillen	.20	.06
7 Roberto Hernandez	.20	.06
8 Matt Karchner	.10	.03
9 Ron Karkovice	.10	.03
10 Darren Lewis	.10	.03
11 Dave Martinez	.10	.03
12 Lyle Mouton	.10	.03
13 Tony Phillips	.10	.03
14 Chris Snopek	.10	.03
15 Kevin Tapani	.10	.03
16 Danny Tartabull	.10	.03
17 Frank Thomas	1.00	.30
18 Robin Ventura	.50	.15
19 Logo card	.10	.03
20 Checklist	.10	.03

1997 White Sox Coke Magnet

This four-card set distributed by Coca-Cola features action color player photos printed on die-cut magnets. The magnets are unnumbered and checklisted below in alphabetical order.

	Nm-Mt	Ex-Mt
COMPLETE SET (4)	8.00	2.40
1 Mike Cameron	4.00	1.20
2 Ray Durham	3.00	.90
3 Jorge Fabregas	2.00	.60
4 Lyle Mouton	2.00	.60

1997 White Sox Score

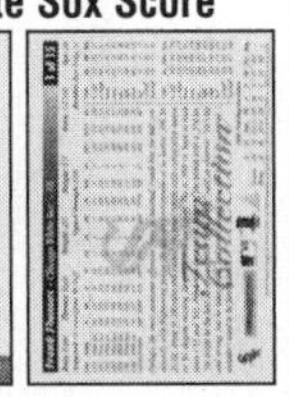

This 15-card set of the Chicago White Sox was issued in five-card packs with a suggested retail price of $1.30 each. The fronts feature color player photos with special team specific color foil stamping. The backs carry player information. Only 100 cases were made for each team. Platinum parallel cards were inserted at a rate of 1:6, Premier parallel cards at a rate of 1:31.

	Nm-Mt	Ex-Mt
COMPLETE SET (15)	5.00	1.50
*PLATINUM: 4X BASIC CARDS		
*PREMIER: 20X BASIC CARDS		
1 Frank Thomas	2.00	.60
2 James Baldwin	.25	.07
3 Danny Tartabull	.25	.07
4 Jeff Darwin	.25	.07
5 Harold Baines	1.00	.30
6 Roberto Hernandez	.40	.12
7 Ray Durham	1.00	.30
8 Robin Ventura	1.00	.30
9 Wilson Alvarez	.40	.12
10 Lyle Mouton	.25	.07
11 Alex Fernandez	.25	.07
12 Ron Karkovice	.25	.07
13 Kevin Tapani	.25	.07
14 Tony Phillips	.25	.07
15 Mike Cameron	.60	.18

1997 White Sox Team Issue

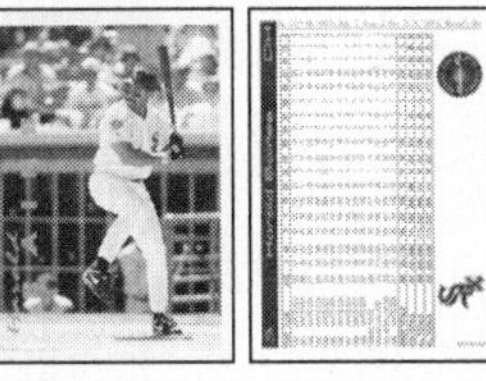

This 30-card set of the Chicago White Sox features color action player photos in white borders. The backs carry player information and career statistics.

	Nm-Mt	Ex-Mt
COMPLETE SET (30)	12.00	3.60
2 Nellie Fox	1.00	.30
3 Harold Baines	1.00	.30
5 Ray Durham	.75	.23
7 Norberto Martin	.25	.07
8 Albert Belle	.50	.15
10 Darren Lewis	.25	.07
12 Jorge Fabregas	.25	.07
13 Ozzie Guillen	.50	.15
14 Dave Martinez	.25	.07
15 Doug Drabek	.25	.07
18 Terry Bevington MG	.25	.07
20 Ron Karkovice	.25	.07
23 Robin Ventura	1.00	.30
24 Mike Cameron	1.00	.30
26 Chuck McElroy	.25	.07
27 Chris Snopek	.25	.07
28 Lyle Mouton	.25	.07
29 Tony Pena	.50	.15
35 Frank Thomas	3.00	.90
37 James Baldwin	.25	.07
38 Jaime Navarro	.25	.07
39 Roberto Hernandez	.75	.23
40 Wilson Alvarez	.50	.15
41 Bill Simas	.25	.07
43 Carlos Castillo	.25	.07
44 Danny Darwin	.25	.07
47 Matt Karchner	.25	.07
49 Tony Castillo	.25	.07
NNO White Sox Training Staff	.25	.07
NNO White Sox Coaches Trivia	.25	.07

1998 White Sox Lemon Chill

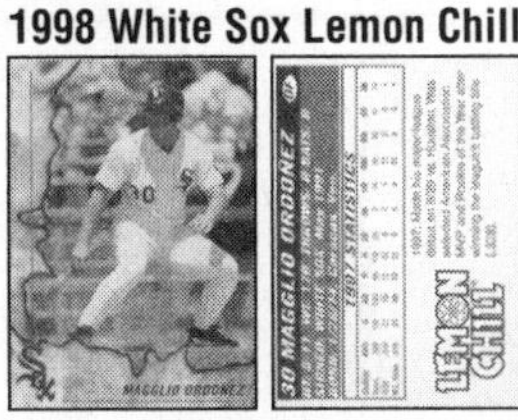

This 30-card standard-size set features members of the 1998 Chicago White Sox. The full bleed borders feature a player photos set up by a design on the left and the players name on the bottom. The horizontal backs have vital statistics, 1997 statistics and a blurb about the players 1997 season. Since the cards are unnumbered we have sequenced them in alphabetical order. Please note that Magglio Ordonez appears in his Rookie Card year.

	Nm-Mt	Ex-Mt
COMPLETE SET (30)	12.00	3.60
1 Jeff Abbott	.25	.07
2 James Baldwin	.25	.07
3 Albert Belle	.50	.15
4 Mike Cameron	.75	.23
5 Mike Caruso	.25	.07
6 Carlos Castillo	.25	.07
7 Wil Cordero	.25	.07
8 Ray Durham	1.00	.30
9 Scott Eyre	.25	.07
10 Keith Foulke	1.00	.30
11 Bob Howry	.25	.07
12 Matt Karchner	.25	.07
13 Chad Krueter	.25	.07
14 Jerry Manuel MG	.25	.07
15 Jaime Navarro	.25	.07
16 Greg Norton	.25	.07
17 Charlie O'Brien	.25	.07
18 Magglio Ordonez	4.00	1.20
19 Jim Parque	.25	.07
20 Bill Simas	.25	.07
21 Mike Sirotka	.25	.07
22 Chris Snopek	.25	.07
23 John Snyder	.25	.07
24 Frank Thomas	1.50	.45
25 Robin Ventura	1.00	.30
26 Bryan Ward	.25	.07
27 Nardi Contreras CO	.25	.07
Von Joshua CO		
28 Wallace Johnson CO	.25	.07
Bryan Little CO		
29 Joe Nossek CO	.25	.07
Art Kusnyer CO		
30 Mark Salas CO	.25	.07
Steve Odgers COND		
Herm Schneider TR		
Mark Anderson ATR		

1998 White Sox Score

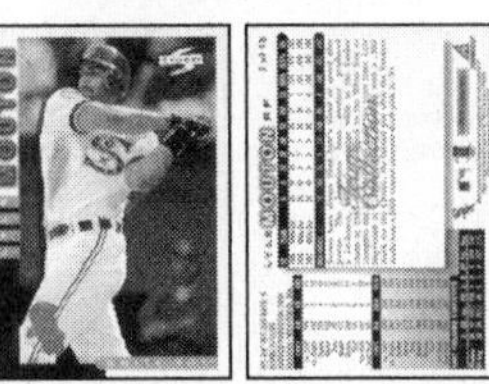

This 15-card set was issued in special retail packs and features color photos of the Chicago White Sox team. The backs carry player information. A special platinum parallel set was also issued and randomly inserted in packs.

	Nm-Mt	Ex-Mt
COMPLETE SET (15)	5.00	1.50
*PLATINUM: 5X BASIC CARDS		
1 Albert Belle	.50	.15
2 Chuck McElroy	.25	.07
3 Mike Cameron	.75	.23
4 Ozzie Guillen	.50	.15
5 Jaime Navarro	.25	.07
6 Chris Clemons	.25	.07
7 Lyle Mouton	.25	.07
8 Frank Thomas	1.25	.35
9 Doug Drabek	.25	.07
10 Robin Ventura	1.00	.30
11 Dave Martinez	.25	.07
12 Ray Durham	.75	.23
13 Chris Snopek	.25	.07
14 James Baldwin	.25	.07
15 Jorge Fabregas	.25	.07

1999 White Sox Sheldon

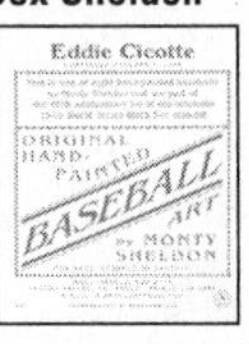

These eight small cards (approximately 2" by 2 3/8") feature special art baseballs drawn by Monty Sheldon and feature members of the 1919 White Sox on the 80th anniversary of the Black Sox Scandal. The fronts feature a photo of the ball while the backs promote the artwork of Sheldon. Since these cards are unnumbered, we have sequenced them in alphabetical order.

	Nm-Mt	Ex-Mt
COMPLETE SET (8)	15.00	4.50
1 Eddie Cicotte	2.50	.75
2 Happy Felsch	1.50	.45
3 Chick Gandil	2.00	.60
4 Joe Jackson	5.00	1.50
5 Fred McMullin	1.00	.30
6 Swede Risberg	1.00	.30
7 Buck Weaver	2.50	.75
8 Lefty Williams	1.50	.45

1992 Whitehall Prototypes

This five-card standard-size set features color close-up photos inside a tan inner border and a white outer border. By a process known as Photonix, old photographs from the National Baseball Library underwent extensive pixel value recomputation to restore contrast, resolution, and light balance. The cards are stamped "Prototype" across the text. The cards are unnumbered and checklisted below in alphabetical order.

	Nm-Mt	Ex-Mt
COMPLETE SET (5)	12.00	3.60
1 Ty Cobb	4.00	1.20
2 Lou Gehrig	4.00	1.20
3 Babe Ruth	6.00	1.80
4 Honus Wagner	3.00	.90
5 Cy Young	2.00	.60

1992 Whitehall Legends to Life

This five-card hologram set from the Whitehall Collection, which measures the standard size, features hologram images created from actual photographs on the card fronts. The cards are unnumbered and checklisted below in alphabetical order.

	Nm-Mt	Ex-Mt
COMPLETE SET (5)	12.00	3.60
1 Ty Cobb	4.00	1.20
2 Lou Gehrig	4.00	1.20
3 Babe Ruth	6.00	1.80
4 Honus Wagner	3.00	.90
5 Cy Young	2.00	.60

1978 Wiffle Ball Discs

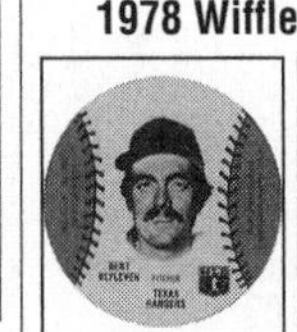

These discs were on the side of Wiffle Ball boxes. Even though the copyright date on the discs are 1976, the player selection implies that this set was issued early in 1978. For some reason, Thurman Munson discs seem to be available in significantly higher quantities and we have labeled Munson as a DP. These discs are unnumbered and we have sequenced this set in alphabetical order.

	NM	Ex
COMPLETE SET (79)	125.00	50.00
1 Sal Bando	.50	.20
2 Buddy Bell	1.00	.40
3 Johnny Bench	8.00	3.20
4 Vida Blue	.50	.20
5 Bert Blyleven	1.00	.40
6 Bobby Bonds	.50	.20
7 George Brett	30.00	12.00
8 Lou Brock	5.00	2.00
9 Bill Buckner	.50	.20
10 Ray Burris	.25	.10
11 Jeff Burroughs	.25	.10
12 Campy Campaneris	.50	.20
13 Rod Carew	5.00	2.00
14 Steve Carlton	5.00	2.00
15 Dave Cash	.25	.10
16 Cesar Cedeno	.50	.20
17 Ron Cey	1.00	.40
18 Chris Chambliss	.25	.10
19 Dave Concepcion	1.00	.40
20 Dennis Eckersley	5.00	2.00
21 Mark Fidrych	4.00	1.60
22 Rollie Fingers	5.00	2.00
23 Carlton Fisk	8.00	3.20
24 George Foster	.50	.20
25 Wayne Garland	.25	.10
26 Ralph Garr	.25	.10
27 Steve Garvey	4.00	1.60
28 Don Gullett	.25	.10
29 Larry Hisle	.25	.10
30 Al Hrabosky	.25	.10
31 Catfish Hunter	5.00	2.00
32 Reggie Jackson	10.00	4.00
33 Randy Jones	.25	.10
34 Dave Kingman	1.50	.60
35 Jerry Koosman	1.00	.40
36 Ed Kranepool	.25	.10
37 Ron LeFlore	.50	.20
38 Sixto Lezcano	.25	.10
39 Davey Lopes	.50	.20
40 Greg Luzinski	1.00	.40
41 Fred Lynn	.50	.20
42 Garry Maddox	.25	.10
43 Jon Matlack	.25	.10
44 Gary Matthews	.50	.20
45 Lee May	.50	.20
46 John Mayberry	.25	.10
47 Bake McBride	.25	.10
48 Tug McGraw	1.00	.40
49 Hal McRae	.50	.20
50 Andy Messersmith	.25	.10
51 Randy Moffitt	.25	.10
52 John Montefusco	.25	.10
53 Joe Morgan	5.00	2.00
54 Thurman Munson DP	1.50	.60
55 Graig Nettles	1.00	.40
56 Al Oliver	.50	.20
57 Jorge Orta	.25	.10
58 Jim Palmer	5.00	2.00
59 Dave Parker	1.50	.60
60 Tony Perez	4.00	1.60
61 Gaylord Perry	5.00	2.00
62 Jim Rice	1.50	.60
63 Steve Rogers	.25	.10
64 Pete Rose	10.00	4.00
65 Joe Rudi	.25	.10
66 Nolan Ryan	30.00	12.00
67 Manny Sanguillen	.25	.10
68 Mike Schmidt	10.00	4.00
69 Tom Seaver	10.00	4.00
70 Ted Simmons	1.00	.40
71 Reggie Smith	.50	.20
72 Willie Stargell	5.00	2.00
73 Rusty Staub	1.00	.40
74 Frank Tanana	.50	.20
75 Gene Tenace	.25	.10
76 Luis Tiant	1.00	.40
77 Manny Trillo	.25	.10
78 Bob Watson	.50	.20
79 Richie Zisk	.25	.10
80 Carl Yastrzemski	5.00	2.00

1963 Wilhelm Motel

This one card postcard set was issued on November 2, 1963 to commemorate the opening of a motel in Georgia that Wilhelm had a stake in. The front of the postcard shows a photo of Wilhelm warming up in front of the White Sox dugout while the back has an ad for the motel.

	NM	Ex
1 Hoyt Wilhelm	10.00	4.00

1923 Willards Chocolates V100

Issued in Canada by Willards Chocolates, these 180 blank-backed cards measure approximately 2" by 3 1/4". The catalog designation for this set is V100. The white-bordered fronts feature sepia-tone player photos. The player's facsimile autograph appears on the card face. The cards are unnumbered and checklisted below in alphabetical order.

	Ex-Mt	VG
COMPLETE SET (180)	10500.00	5200.00
1 Babe Adams	50.00	25.00
2 Grover C. Alexander	120.00	60.00
3 James Austin MG	40.00	20.00
4 Jim Bagby	40.00	20.00
5 Frank Baker	80.00	40.00
6 Dave Bancroft	80.00	40.00
7 Turner Barber	40.00	20.00
8 Jesse L. Barnes	40.00	20.00
9 John Bassler	40.00	20.00
10 Lu Blue	40.00	20.00
11 Norman Boekel	40.00	20.00
12 Frank Brazill	40.00	20.00
13 George H. Burns	40.00	20.00
14 George J. Burns	40.00	20.00
15 Leon Cadore	50.00	25.00
16 Max Carey	80.00	40.00
17 Harold G. Carlson	40.00	20.00
18 Lloyd Christenberry	40.00	20.00
19 Vernon J. Clemons	40.00	20.00
20 Ty Cobb	600.00	300.00
21 Bert Cole	40.00	20.00
22 John F. Collins	40.00	20.00
23 Stan Coveleski	80.00	40.00
24 Walton E. Cruise	40.00	20.00

25 George W. Cutshaw 40.00 20.00
26 Jake Daubert 50.00 25.00
27 George Dauss 40.00 20.00
28 Frank Davis 40.00 20.00
29 Charles A. Deal 40.00 20.00
30 William L. Doak 40.00 20.00
31 Wild Bill Donovan MG 40.00 20.00
32 Hugh Duffy MG 80.00 40.00
33 Joe Dugan 50.00 25.00
34 Louis B. Duncan 40.00 20.00
35 Jimmy Dykes 50.00 25.00
36 Howard Ehmke 50.00 25.00
37 Francis R. Ellerbe 40.00 20.00
38 Eric G. Erickson 40.00 20.00
39 Johnny Evers MG 80.00 40.00
40 Urban Faber 80.00 40.00
41 Bibb Falk 40.00 20.00
42 Max Flack 40.00 20.00
43 Lee Fohl MG 40.00 20.00
44 Jack Fournier 40.00 20.00
45 Frank Frisch 80.00 40.00
46 C.E. Galloway 40.00 20.00
47 Billy Gardner 40.00 20.00
48 Edward Gharrity 40.00 20.00
49 George Gibson 40.00 20.00
50 Kid Gleason MG 60.00 30.00
51 William Gleason 40.00 20.00
52 Hank Gowdy 50.00 25.00
53 I.M. Griffin 40.00 20.00
54 Thomas Griffith 40.00 20.00
55 Burleigh Grimes 80.00 40.00
56 Charlie Grimm 50.00 25.00
57 Jesse Haines 80.00 40.00
58 Bill Harris 40.00 20.00
59 Bucky Harris 80.00 40.00
60 Robert Hasty 40.00 20.00
61 Harry Heilmann 80.00 40.00
62 Walter Henline 40.00 20.00
63 Walter Holke 40.00 20.00
64 Charles Hollocher 40.00 20.00
65 Harry Hooper 80.00 40.00
66 Rogers Hornsby 200.00 100.00
67 Waite Hoyt 80.00 40.00
68 Miller Huggins MG 80.00 40.00
69 W.C. Jacobson 40.00 20.00
70 Charlie Jamieson 40.00 20.00
71 E. Johnson 40.00 20.00
72 Walter Johnson 300.00 150.00
73 James H. Johnston 40.00 20.00
74 Bob Jones 40.00 20.00
75 Sam Jones 50.00 25.00
76 Joe Judge 50.00 25.00
77 James W. Keenan 40.00 20.00
78 Geo. L. Kelly 80.00 40.00
79 Peter J. Kilduff 40.00 20.00
80 William Killefer 40.00 20.00
81 Lee King 40.00 20.00
82 Ray Kolp 40.00 20.00
83 John Lavan 40.00 20.00
84 Nemo Leibold 40.00 20.00
85 Connie Mack MG 120.00 60.00
86 Duster Mails 40.00 20.00
87 Walter Maranville 80.00 40.00
88 Richard W. Marquard 80.00 40.00
89 Carl W. Mays 50.00 25.00
90 Geo. F. McBride 40.00 20.00
91 Harvey McClellan 40.00 20.00
92 John J. McGraw MG 100.00 50.00
93 Austin B. McHenry 40.00 20.00
94 Snuffy McInnis 50.00 25.00
95 Douglas McWeeny 40.00 20.00
96 Mike Menosky 40.00 20.00
97 Emil F. Meusel 40.00 20.00
98 Bob Meusel 50.00 25.00
99 Henry W. Meyers 40.00 20.00
100 Clyde Milan MG 50.00 25.00
101 John K. Miljus 40.00 20.00
102 Edmund J. Miller 50.00 25.00
103 Elmer Miller 40.00 20.00
104 Otto L. Miller 40.00 20.00
105 Fred Mitchell MG 40.00 20.00
106 Geo. Mogridge 40.00 20.00
107 Patrick J. Moran MG 40.00 20.00
108 John D. Morrison 40.00 20.00
109 Johnny Mostil 40.00 20.00
110 Clarence F. Mueller 40.00 20.00
111 Greasy Neale 60.00 30.00
112 Joseph Oeschger 40.00 20.00
113 Robert J. O'Farrell 40.00 20.00
114 John Oldham 40.00 20.00
115 Ivy Olson 40.00 20.00
116 Geo. M. O'Neil 40.00 20.00
117 Steve O'Neill 50.00 25.00
118 Frank J. Parkinson 40.00 20.00
119 Dode Paskert 40.00 20.00
120 Roger Peckinpaugh 50.00 25.00
121 Herb Pennock 80.00 40.00
122 Ralph Perkins 40.00 20.00
123 Jeff Pfeffer 40.00 20.00
124 Wally Pipp 50.00 25.00
125 Charles Ponder 40.00 20.00
126 Raymond R. Powell 40.00 20.00
127 Del Pratt 40.00 20.00
128 Joseph Rapp 40.00 20.00
129 John H. Rawlings 40.00 20.00
130 Edgar Rice 80.00 40.00
131 Branch Rickey MG 100.00 50.00
132 James J. Ring 40.00 20.00
133 Eppa J. Rixey 80.00 40.00
134 Davis A. Robertson 40.00 20.00
135 Edwin Rommel 50.00 25.00
136 Edd J. Roush 80.00 40.00
137 Harold Ruel 40.00 20.00
138 Allen Russell 40.00 20.00
139 Babe Ruth 1000.00 500.00
140 Wilfred D. Ryan 40.00 20.00
141 Henry F. Sallee 40.00 20.00
142 Wally Schang 50.00 25.00
143 Raymond H. Schmandt 40.00 20.00
144 Everett Scott 50.00 25.00
145 Henry Severeid 40.00 20.00
146 Joseph W. Sewell 80.00 40.00
147 Howard S. Shanks 40.00 20.00
148 Earl Sheely 40.00 20.00
149 Ralph Shinners 40.00 20.00
150 Urban J. Shocker 50.00 25.00
151 George H. Sisler 100.00 50.00
152 Earl L. Smith 40.00 20.00
153 Earl S. Smith 40.00 20.00
154 George A. Smith 40.00 20.00
155 John Smith 40.00 20.00
156 Tris Speaker MG 120.00 60.00
157 Arnold Staatz 40.00 20.00
158 Riggs Stephenson 60.00 30.00
159 Milton J. Stock 40.00 20.00
160 John L. Sullivan 40.00 20.00
161 Herb Thormahlen 40.00 20.00
162 James A. Tierney 40.00 20.00
163 John Tobin 40.00 20.00
164 James L. Vaughn 40.00 20.00
165 Bobby Veach 40.00 20.00
166 Tilly Walker 40.00 20.00
167 Aaron Ward 40.00 20.00
168 Zack D. Wheat 80.00 40.00
169 George B. Whitted 40.00 20.00
170 Irvin K. Wilhelm 40.00 20.00
171 Roy H. Wilkinson 40.00 20.00
172 Fred C. Williams 50.00 25.00
173 Ken Williams 50.00 25.00
174 Samuel W. Wilson 40.00 20.00
175 Ivy B. Wingo 40.00 20.00
176 Whitey Witt 50.00 25.00
177 Joseph Wood 60.00 30.00
178 Clarence Yaryan 40.00 20.00
179 Ralph Young 40.00 20.00
180 Ross Youngs 80.00 40.00

1922 William Paterson V89

This 50-card set was inserted in packages of caramel candy. The cards measure approximately 2" by 3 1/4". the fronts feature sepia-toned player photos framed by white borders. The following information appears in the bottom border beneath the picture: card number, player's name, team name and imprint information (Wm. Paterson, Limited; Brantford, Canada). The backs are blank.

	Ex-Mt	VG
COMPLETE SET (50)	6000.00	3000.00
1 Ed Roush	100.00	50.00
2 Rube Marquard	100.00	50.00
3 Del Gainer	50.00	25.00
4 George Sisler	100.00	50.00
5 Joe Bush	60.00	30.00
6 Joe Oeschger	50.00	25.00
7 Willie Kamm	50.00	25.00
8 John Watson	50.00	25.00
9 Adolfo Luque	60.00	30.00
10 Miller Huggins MG	100.00	50.00
11 Wally Schang	60.00	30.00
12 Bob Shawkey	60.00	30.00
13 Tris Speaker MG	100.00	50.00
14 Hugh McQuillen	50.00	25.00
15 George Kelly	100.00	50.00
16 Ray Schalk	100.00	50.00
17 Sam Jones	60.00	30.00
18 Grover Alexander	200.00	100.00
19 Bob Meusel	80.00	40.00
20 Emil Meusel	50.00	25.00
21 Rogers Hornsby	250.00	125.00
22 Harry Heilmann	100.00	50.00
23 Heinie Groh	60.00	30.00
24 Frankie Frisch	100.00	50.00
25 Babe Ruth	1500.00	750.00
26 Jack Bentley	50.00	25.00
27 Everett Scott	50.00	25.00
28 Max Carey	100.00	50.00
29 Chick Fewster	50.00	25.00
30 Cy Williams	60.00	30.00
31 Burleigh Grimes	100.00	50.00
32 Waite Hoyt	100.00	50.00
33 Frank Snyder	50.00	25.00
34 Clyde Milan MG	50.00	25.00
35 Eddie Collins	100.00	50.00
36 Travis Jackson	100.00	50.00
37 Ken Williams	60.00	30.00
38 Dave Bancroft	100.00	50.00
39 Mike McNally	50.00	25.00
40 John McGraw MG	200.00	100.00
41 Art Nehf	60.00	30.00
42 Rabbit Maranville	100.00	50.00
43 Charlie Grimm	60.00	30.00
44 Joe Judge	60.00	30.00
45 Wally Pipp	60.00	30.00
46 Ty Cobb	800.00	400.00
47 Walter Johnson	300.00	150.00
48 Jake Daubert	50.00	25.00
49 Zach Wheat	100.00	50.00
50 Herb Pennock	100.00	50.00

1910 Williams Caramels E103

The cards in this 30-card set measure 1 1/2" by 2 3/4". E103 is distinctive for its black and white player portraits set onto a solid red background. Player names and teams are listed below each photo, with "Williams", the manufacturer's name, in the line below. Printed on thin cardboard, the blank back Williams set was released to the public about 1910. Since the cards are unnumbered, they are ordered below alphabetically

	Ex-Mt	VG
COMPLETE SET (30)	20000.00	
10000.00		
1 Chief Bender	600.00	300.00
2 Roger Bresnahan	600.00	300.00
3 Mordecai Brown	600.00	300.00
4 Frank Chance	600.00	300.00
5 Hal Chase	500.00	250.00
6 Ty Cobb	5000.00	2500.00
7 Eddie Collins	600.00	300.00
8 Sam Crawford	600.00	300.00
9 Harry Davis	300.00	150.00
10 Art Devlin	300.00	150.00
11 Bill Donovan	300.00	150.00
12 Red Dooin	300.00	150.00
13 Larry Doyle	400.00	200.00
14 John Ewing	300.00	150.00
15 George Gibson	300.00	150.00
16 Hugh Jennings	600.00	300.00
17 Davy Jones	300.00	150.00
18 Tim Jordan	300.00	150.00
19 Nap Lajoie	1200.00	600.00
20 Tommy Leach	300.00	150.00
21 Harry Lord	300.00	150.00
22 Christy Mathewson	2000.00	1000.00
23 Larry McLean	300.00	150.00
24 George McQuillan	300.00	150.00
25 Jim Pastorious	300.00	150.00
26 Nap Rucker	400.00	200.00
27 Fred Tenney	300.00	150.00
28 Ira Thomas	300.00	150.00
29 Honus Wagner	2500.00	1250.00
30 Joe Wood	500.00	250.00

1912 Gus Williams Lemon Drop

Measuring approximately 2 1/4" by 4" this card feature a photo of Gus Williams taken by Johnston and Co. The front has a photo of Wiliams in street clothes while the back has the words "Compliments of W.T. Crane's Lemon Drop Package". It is possible that other players were created for this set.

	MINT	NRMT
1 Gus Williams	50.00	22.00

1989 Ted Williams Museum Postcards

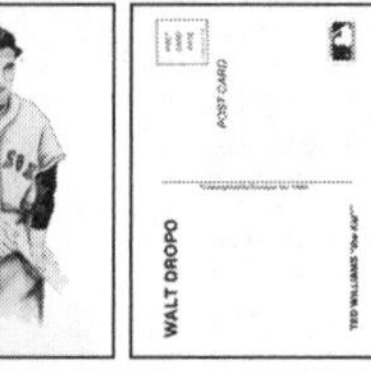

These postcards, which measure 3 1/2" by 5 1/2" feature a mix of then active and retired players as well as a mix of superstars and noted people in baseball. Each postcard has a drawing on the front while the horizontal postcard back gives the player's name and states that it was approved by Ted Williams with each drawing copyrighted by "Thumper Inc" in 1989. Since these are not numbered, we have sequenced them in alphabetical order.

	MINT	NRMT
COMPLETE SET	125.00	55.00
1 Vida Blue Posed shot	2.50	1.10
2 Vida Blue In Windup	2.50	1.10
3 Lou Boudreau	4.00	1.80
4 Lou Brock Running	4.00	1.80
5 Lou Brock Fielding	4.00	1.80
6 Happy Chandler	2.50	1.10
7 Steve Carlton	5.00	2.20
8 Lou Dials	2.50	1.10
9 Larry Doby	4.00	1.80
10 Bill Doran	2.50	1.10
11 Walt Dropo	2.50	1.10
12 Dwight Evans	3.00	1.35
13 Bob Feller	5.00	2.20
14 Rick Ferrell	2.50	1.10
15 Charlie Gehringer	4.00	1.80
16 Billy Herman	4.00	1.80
17 Catfish Hunter	4.00	1.80
18 Monte Irvin	4.00	1.80
19 Bo Jackson	5.00	2.20
20 Howard Johnson	2.50	1.10
21 Al Kaline	5.00	2.20
22 Ralph Kiner	5.00	2.20
23 Hal Lanier Posed Shot	2.50	1.10
24 Hal Lanier Throwing	2.50	1.10
25 Max Lanier	2.50	1.10
26 Bob Lemon	4.00	1.80
27 Bill Madlock	3.00	1.35
28 Willie McCovey	5.00	2.20
29 Johnny Mize	4.00	1.80
30 Don Newcombe	3.00	1.35
31 Johnny Pesky	3.00	1.35
32 Johnny Podres	3.00	1.35
33 Pee Wee Reese	5.00	2.20
34 Red Schoendienst	4.00	1.80
35 Enos Slaughter	4.00	1.80
36 Willie Stargell	4.00	1.80
37 Hoyt Wilhelm	4.00	1.80
38 Ted Williams	10.00	4.50

2001 Ted Williams Museum

The card is measured 2 1/2" x 3" and is designed in the style of the 1930's Sports King set. This card is serial numbered to 1941 (the year Williams hit .406) and features a drawing of Williams on the front as well as a blurb on the back.

	Nm-Mt	Ex-Mt
1 Ted Williams	10.00	3.00

1995 Ted Williams Tunnel

These twelve cards were issued to honor the opening of the "Ted Williams Tunnel" in Boston. The set was issued by Choice Marketing Inc. except for one of the card number 9's which was issued by Topps.

	Nm-Mt	Ex-Mt
COMPLETE SET (12)	50.00	15.00
COMMON CARD (1-12)	1.00	.30
9A Ted Williams Topps Header Card	50.00	15.00

1929 Hack Wilson All-Weather Tire

This one card blank-backed photo set, measuring approximately 7" by 9" features Cub slugger Hack Wilson as a promotion for All-Weather Tire Co. on July 2, 1929.

	Ex-Mt	VG
1 Hack Wilson	100.00	50.00

1931 Hack Wilson Blue Ribbon Malt

This photo was issued to promote both Blue Ribbon Malt as well as Hack Wilson. The front has a posed action shot of Wilson with the words "Compliments of Blue Ribbon Malt" on the bottom. There might be other players issued as part of this series (just like the previous year) so any additional information would be appreciated.

	MINT	NRMT
1 Hack Wilson	100.00	45.00

1954 Wilson

The cards in this 20-card set measure approximately 2 5/8" by 3 3/4". The 1954 "Wilson Wieners" set contains 20 full color, unnumbered cards. The obverse design of a package of hot dogs appearing to fly through the air is a distinctive feature of this set. Uncut sheets have been seen. Cards are numbered below alphabetically by player's name.

	NM	Ex
COMPLETE SET (20)	9000.00	4500.00
1 Roy Campanella	1000.00	500.00
2 Del Ennis	250.00	125.00
3 Carl Erskine	300.00	150.00
4 Ferris Fain	200.00	100.00
5 Bob Feller	800.00	400.00
6 Nellie Fox	400.00	200.00
7 Johnny Groth	200.00	100.00
8 Stan Hack MG	200.00	100.00
9 Gil Hodges	400.00	200.00
10 Ray Jablonski	200.00	100.00
11 Harvey Kuenn	250.00	125.00
12 Roy McMillan	200.00	100.00
13 Andy Pafko	200.00	100.00
14 Paul Richards MG	200.00	100.00
15 Hank Sauer	200.00	100.00
16 Red Schoendienst	400.00	200.00
17 Enos Slaughter	400.00	200.00
18 Vern Stephens	200.00	100.00
19 Sammy White	200.00	100.00
20 Ted Williams	4000.00	2000.00

1959-61 Wilson Sporting Goods

This seven-card set measures approximately 8" by 10" and features white-bordered black-and-white player photos with a facsimile autograph. The player's and sponsor's names are printed in the bottom margin. The backs are blank. The cards are unnumbered and checklisted below in alphabetical order.

	NRMT	VG-E
COMPLETE SET (8)	125.00	55.00
1 Luis Aparicio	25.00	11.00
2 Ernie Banks	25.00	11.00
3 Nellie Fox	25.00	11.00
4 Harmon Killebrew	25.00	11.00
5 Billy Pierce	15.00	6.75
6 Pete Runnels	10.00	4.50
7 Larry Sherry	10.00	4.50
8 Early Wynn	20.00	9.00

1961 Wilson Sporting Goods H828

This three-card set features black-and-white player images on a gray background with a black border and looks as if the cards were cut from boxes. A player facsimile autograph is printed at the bottom. The cards measure approximately 1 7/8" by 5 1/4" and the catalog number is H828. The cards are unnumbered and checklisted below in alphabetical order.

	NM	Ex
COMPLETE SET (3)	300.00	120.00
1 Don Hoak	100.00	40.00
2 Harvey Kuenn	100.00	40.00
3 Jim Piersall	100.00	40.00

1961 Wilson Sporting Goods H828-1

This six card set measures approximately 2 1/4" by 4" and features black and white blank backed photos containing a blue facsimile autograph and "Member - Advisory Staff Wilson Sporting Goods Co." across the bottom of the card. According to old hobby experts, this set may very well have more than six players. All additions to this checklist are appreciated. The catalog designation for this set is H828-1.

	NM	Ex
COMPLETE SET (6)	60.00	24.00
1 Dick Ellsworth	10.00	4.00
2 Don Hoak	10.00	4.00
3 Harvey Kuenn	10.00	4.00
4 Roy McMillan	10.00	4.00
5 Jim Piersall	15.00	6.00
6 Ron Santo	20.00	8.00

1990 Windwalker Discs

This nine-disc set features 1990 American League All-Stars. The discs measure approximately 3 13/16" in diameter. Inside a pale yellow outer border with red baseball stitching, the fronts have a color action player photo. A facsimile autograph is inscribed across the picture. The player's name and the words "1990 All-Star" appear below the picture. The reverse of each disc features a different player. The discs are unnumbered; they are listed below in alphabetical order according to the player on one of the sides.

	Nm-Mt	Ex-Mt
COMPLETE SET (9)	25.00	7.50
1 Sandy Alomar Jr. Dave Parker	1.50	.45
2 Wade Boggs Kirby Puckett	6.00	1.80
3 Roger Clemens Bob Welch	2.50	.75
4 Cecil Fielder Bret Saberhagen	1.50	.45
5 Chuck Finley Kelly Gruber	1.00	.30
6 Julio Franco George Bell	1.00	.30
7 Ken Griffey Jr. Steve Sax	8.00	2.40
8 Rickey Henderson Jose Canseco	5.00	1.50
9 Cal Ripken Jr. Ozzie Guillen	6.00	1.80

1993 Winfield Rainbow Foods

This ten-card standard-size set was sponsored by Rainbow Foods, with a portion of the sales proceeds donated to the Minnesota Twins Rookie League youth baseball program. The blue-bordered fronts contain color and sepia photos of Winfield beginning with his college years and following his career in the major leagues. Winfield's name in red script is displayed on a gold stripe under the picture. The Rainbow Foods logo appears in the lower right. The horizontal backs contain a close-up picture on the left and the appropriate statistics and career summary on the right side. Cards 9 and 10 have vertical backs. The cards are numbered on the back. The cards originally sold in five-card packs for 99 cents. Each pack contained four blue-bordered cards and one gold-bordered card. The gold-bordered set is otherwise identical to the blue-bordered set but due to its relative scarcity sells for two to three times the values listed below.

	Nm-Mt	Ex-Mt
COMPLETE SET (10)	6.00	1.80
COMMON CARD (1-10)	.75	.23

1990 Wonder Bread Stars

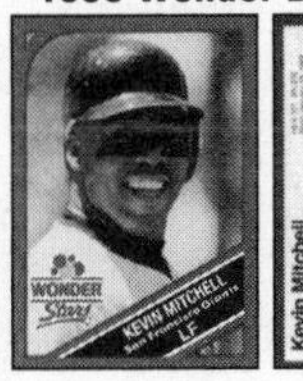
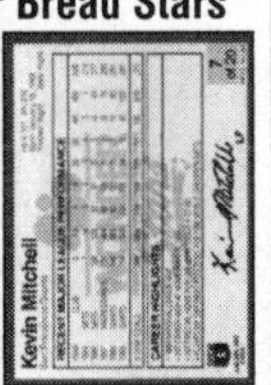

The 1990 Wonder Bread set was issued in 1990 by MSA (Michael Schechter Associates) in conjunction with Wonder Bread. One card was issued inside each specially marked package of Wonder Bread. Cards were available in grocery stores through June 15, 1990. The card was sealed in a pouch in the bread wrapper. This standard-size card set was issued without logos like many of the sets produced by MSA. Cards were printed on thin stock and hence were easily creased during bread handling making the set more difficult to put together one card at a time for condition-conscious collectors. Cards are numbered on the back in the lower right corner. Wonder Bread also offered sets in uncut sheet form to collectors mailing in with 3.00 and five proofs of purchase.

	Nm-Mt	Ex-Mt
COMPLETE SET (20)	30.00	9.00
1 Bo Jackson	1.50	.45
2 Roger Clemens	5.00	1.50
3 Jim Abbott	1.00	.30
4 Orel Hershiser	.75	.23
5 Ozzie Smith	3.00	.90
6 Don Mattingly	5.00	1.50
7 Kevin Mitchell	.50	.15
8 Jerome Walton	.50	.15
9 Kirby Puckett	2.00	.60
10 Darryl Strawberry	.75	.23
11 Robin Yount	2.50	.75
12 Tony Gwynn	5.00	1.50
13 Alan Trammell	1.00	.30
14 Jose Canseco	2.00	.60
15 Greg Swindell	.50	.15
16 Nolan Ryan	10.00	3.00
17 Howard Johnson	.50	.15
18 Ken Griffey Jr.	8.00	2.40
19 Will Clark	1.50	.45
20 Ryne Sandberg	2.50	.75

1985 Woolworth's

This 44-card standard-size set features color as well as black and white cards of All Time Record Holders. The cards are printed with blue ink on an orange and white back. The set was produced for Woolworth's by Topps and was packaged in a colorful box which contained a checklist of the cards in the set on the back panel. The numerical order of the cards coincides alphabetically with the player's name.

	Nm-Mt	Ex-Mt
COM. FACT SET (44)	6.00	2.40
1 Hank Aaron	.75	.30
2 Grover C. Alexander	.20	.08
3 Ernie Banks	.20	.08
4 Yogi Berra	.20	.08
5 Lou Brock	.15	.06
6 Steve Carlton	.20	.08
7 Jack Chesbro	.05	.02
8 Ty Cobb	.75	.30
9 Sam Crawford	.15	.06
10 Rollie Fingers	.15	.06
11 Whitey Ford	.20	.08
12 John Frederick	.05	.02
13 Frankie Frisch	.15	.06
14 Lou Gehrig	.75	.30
15 Jim Gentile	.05	.02
16 Dwight Gooden	.50	.20
17 Rickey Henderson	.40	.16
18 Rogers Hornsby	.20	.08
19 Frank Howard	.10	.04
20 Cliff Johnson	.05	.02
21 Walter Johnson	.20	.08
22 Hub Leonard	.05	.02
23 Mickey Mantle	1.00	.40
24 Roger Maris	.50	.20
25 Christy Mathewson	.20	.08
26 Willie Mays	.75	.30
27 Stan Musial	.50	.20
28 Dan Quisenberry	.05	.02
29 Frank Robinson	.20	.08
30 Pete Rose	.50	.20
31 Babe Ruth	1.00	.40
32 Nolan Ryan	1.00	.40
33 George Sisler	.20	.08
34 Tris Speaker	.20	.08
35 Ed Walsh	.15	.06
36 Lloyd Waner	.15	.06
37 Earl Webb	.05	.02
38 Ted Williams	.75	.30
39 Maury Wills	.10	.04
40 Hack Wilson	.15	.06
41 Owen Wilson	.05	.02
42 Willie Wilson	.05	.02
43 Rudy York	.05	.02
44 Cy Young	.20	.08

1986 Woolworth's

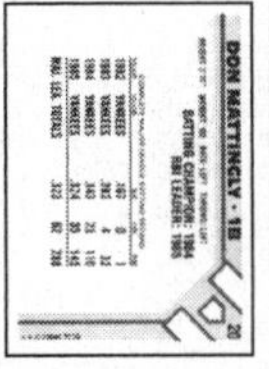

This boxed set of 33 standard-size cards was produced by Topps for Woolworth's variety stores. The set features players who hold or have held hitting, home run or RBI titles. The cards have a glossy finish. The card fronts are bordered in yellow with the subtitle "Topps Collectors' Series" across the top. The card backs are printed in green and blue ink on white card stock. The custom box gives the set checklist on the back.

	Nm-Mt	Ex-Mt
COMP. FACT SET (33)	6.00	2.40
1 Tony Armas	.05	.02
2 Don Baylor	.10	.04
3 Wade Boggs	.50	.20
4 George Brett	1.25	.50
5 Bill Buckner	.05	.02
6 Rod Carew	.40	.16
7 Gary Carter	.50	.20
8 Cecil Cooper	.10	.04
9 Darrell Evans	.05	.02
10 Dwight Evans	.10	.04
11 George Foster	.10	.04
12 Bob Grich	.05	.02
13 Tony Gwynn	1.00	.40
14 Keith Hernandez	.10	.04
15 Reggie Jackson	.50	.20
16 Dave Kingman	.05	.02
17 Carney Lansford	.05	.02
18 Fred Lynn	.10	.04
19 Bill Madlock	.05	.02
20 Don Mattingly	1.50	.60
21 Willie McGee	.10	.04
22 Hal McRae	.05	.02
23 Dale Murphy	.20	.08
24 Eddie Murray	.50	.20
25 Ben Oglivie	.05	.02
26 Al Oliver	.05	.02
27 Dave Parker	.10	.04
28 Jim Rice	.10	.04
29 Pete Rose	.75	.30
30 Mike Schmidt	.75	.30
31 Gorman Thomas	.05	.02
32 Willie Wilson	.05	.02
33 Dave Winfield	.50	.20

1987 Woolworth's

Topps produced this 33-card standard-size set for Woolworth's stores. The set is subtitled "Topps Collectors Series Baseball Highlights" and consists of high gloss card fronts with full-color photos. The cards show and describe highlights of the previous season. The card backs are printed in gold and purple and are numbered. The set was sold nationally in Woolworth's for a 1.99 suggested retail price.

	Nm-Mt	Ex-Mt
COMP. FACT SET (33)	5.00	2.00
1 Steve Carlton	.40	.16
2 Cecil Cooper	.10	.04
3 Rickey Henderson	.50	.20
4 Reggie Jackson	.40	.16
5 Jim Rice	.10	.04
6 Don Sutton	.40	.16
7 Roger Clemens	1.00	.40
8 Mike Schmidt	.50	.20
9 Jesse Barfield	.05	.02
10 Wade Boggs	.40	.16
11 Tim Raines	.10	.04
12 Jose Canseco	.40	.16
13 Todd Worrell	.10	.04
14 Dave Righetti	.05	.02
15 Don Mattingly	1.00	.40
16 Tony Gwynn	1.00	.40
17 Marty Barrett	.05	.02
18 Mike Scott	.05	.02
19 Bruce Hurst	.05	.02
20 Calvin Schiraldi	.05	.02
21 Dwight Evans	.10	.04
22 Dave Henderson	.05	.02
23 Len Dykstra	.15	.06
24 Bob Ojeda	.05	.02
25 Gary Carter	.40	.16
26 Ron Darling	.05	.02
27 Jim Rice	.10	.04
28 Bruce Hurst	.05	.02
29 Darryl Strawberry	.10	.04
30 Ray Knight	.05	.02
31 Keith Hernandez	.10	.04
32 Mets Celebration	.05	.02
33 Ray Knight	.05	.02

1988 Woolworth's

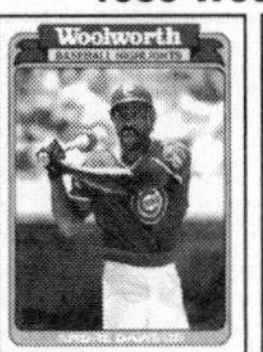
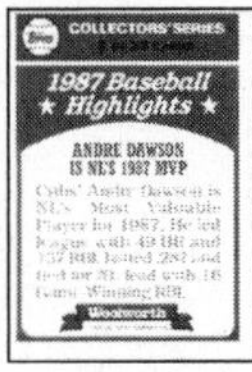

Topps produced this 33-card standard-size set for Woolworth's stores. The set is subtitled "Topps Collectors Series Baseball Highlights" and consists of high gloss card fronts with full-color photos. The cards show and describe highlights of the previous season. Cards 19-33 commemorate the World Series with highlights and key players of each game in the series. The card backs are printed in red and blue on white card stock and are numbered. The set was sold nationally in Woolworth's for a 1.99 suggested retail price.

	Nm-Mt	Ex-Mt
COMP. FACT SET (33)	5.00	2.00
1 Don Baylor	.10	.04
2 Vince Coleman	.05	.02
3 Darrell Evans	.10	.04
4 Don Mattingly	1.00	.40
5 Eddie Murray	.40	.16
6 Nolan Ryan	2.00	.80
7 Mike Schmidt	.50	.20
8 Andre Dawson	.20	.08
9 George Bell	.05	.02
10 Steve Bedrosian	.05	.02
11 Roger Clemens	1.00	.40
12 Tony Gwynn	1.00	.40
13 Wade Boggs	.40	.16
14 Benito Santiago	.10	.04
15 Mark McGwire UER (Referenced on card back as NL ROY, sic)	1.50	.60
16 Dave Righetti	.05	.02
17 Jeffrey Leonard	.05	.02
18 Gary Gaetti	.10	.04
19 Frank Viola WS1	.05	.02
20 Dan Gladden WS1	.05	.02
21 Bert Blyleven WS2	.10	.04
22 Gary Gaetti WS2	.10	.04
23 John Tudor WS3	.05	.02
24 Todd Worrell WS3	.10	.04
25 Tom Lawless WS4	.05	.02
26 Willie McGee WS4	.10	.04
27 Danny Cox WS5	.05	.02
28 Curt Ford WS5	.05	.02
29 Don Baylor WS6	.10	.04
30 Kent Hrbek WS6	.10	.04
31 Kirby Puckett WS7	.40	.16
32 Greg Gagne WS7	.05	.02
33 Frank Viola WS-MVP	.05	.02

1989 Woolworth's

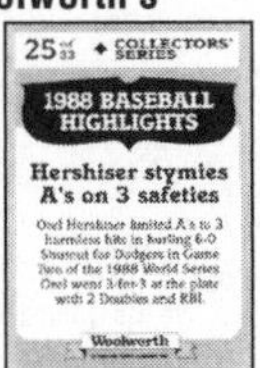

The 1989 Woolworth's Highlights set contains 33 standard-size glossy cards. The fronts have red and white borders. The vertically oriented backs are yellow and red, and describe highlights from the 1988 season including the World Series. The cards were distributed through Woolworth stores as a boxed set.

	Nm-Mt	Ex-Mt
COMP. FACT SET (33)	5.00	2.00
1 Jose Canseco MVP	.30	.12
2 Kirk Gibson MVP	.15	.06
3 Frank Viola CY	.05	.02
4 Orel Hershiser CY	.10	.04
5 Walt Weiss ROY	.05	.02
6 Chris Sabo ROY	.05	.02
7 George Bell	.05	.02
8 Wade Boggs	.40	.16
9 Tom Browning	.05	.02
10 Gary Carter	.40	.16
11 Andre Dawson	.20	.08
12 John Franco	.10	.04
13 Randy Johnson	2.00	.80
14 Doug Jones	.05	.02
15 Kevin McReynolds	.05	.02
16 Gene Nelson	.05	.02
17 Jeff Reardon	.10	.04
18 Pat Tabler	.05	.02
19 Tim Belcher	.05	.02
20 Dennis Eckersley	.40	.16
21 Orel Hershiser	.10	.04
22 Gregg Jefferies	.05	.02
23 Jose Canseco	.50	.20
24 Kirk Gibson	.10	.04
25 Orel Hershiser	.10	.04
26 Mike Marshall	.05	.02
27 Mark McGwire	1.50	.60
28 Rick Honeycutt	.05	.02
29 Tim Belcher	.05	.02
30 Jay Howell	.05	.02
31 Mickey Hatcher	.05	.02
32 Mike Davis	.05	.02
33 Orel Hershiser	.10	.04

1990 Woolworth's

The 1990 Woolworth set is a 33-card standard-size set highlighting some of the more important events of the 1989 season. This set is broken down between major award winners, career highlights, and post-season heroes. The first six cards of the set feature the award winners while the last 11 cards of the set feature post-season heroes.

	Nm-Mt	Ex-Mt
COMP. FACT SET (33)	6.00	1.80
1 Robin Yount MVP	.50	.15
2 Kevin Mitchell MVP	.05	.02
3 Bret Saberhagen CY	.10	.03
4 Mark Davis CY	.05	.02
5 Gregg Olson ROY	.05	.02
6 Jerome Walton ROY	.05	.02
7 Bert Blyleven	.10	.03
8 Wade Boggs	.50	.15
9 George Brett	1.00	.30
10 Vince Coleman	.05	.02
11 Andre Dawson	.20	.06
12 Dwight Evans	.10	.03
13 Carlton Fisk	.40	.12
14 Rickey Henderson	.50	.15
15 Dale Murphy	.20	.06
16 Eddie Murray	.40	.12
17 Jeff Reardon	.10	.03
18 Rick Reuschel	.05	.02
19 Cal Ripken	2.00	.60
20 Nolan Ryan	2.00	.60
21 Ryne Sandberg	.75	.23
22 Robin Yount	.50	.15
23 Rickey Henderson	.50	.15
24 Will Clark	.20	.06
25 Dave Stewart	.10	.03
26 Walt Weiss	.05	.02
27 Mike Moore	.05	.02
28 Terry Steinbach	.05	.02
29 Dave Henderson	.05	.02
30 Matt Williams	.20	.06
31 Rickey Henderson	.60	.18
32 Kevin Mitchell	.05	.02
33 Dave Stewart	.10	.03

1991 Woolworth's

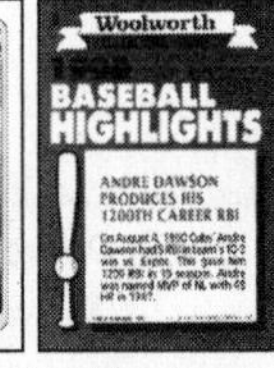

Topps produced this 33-card boxed standard-size set for Woolworth stores. The cards feature glossy color player photos on the fronts, with yellow borders on a white card face. The backs are printed in red, black, and white, and commemorate outstanding achievements of the players featured on the cards. The set can be subdivided as follows: MVPs (1-2), Cy Young winners (3-4), ROYs (5-6), '90 highlights in alphabetical order (7-22), playoff MVPs (23-24), and World Series action in chronological order (25-33).

	Nm-Mt	Ex-Mt
COMP. FACT SET (33)	5.00	1.50
1 Barry Bonds	1.00	.30
2 Rickey Henderson (Bat on shoulder)	.50	.15
3 Doug Drabek	.05	.02
4 Bob Welch	.05	.02
5 David Justice	.20	.06
6 Sandy Alomar Jr.	.10	.03
7 Bert Blyleven	.10	.03
8 George Brett	1.00	.30
9 Andre Dawson	.20	.06
10 Dwight Evans	.10	.03
11 Alex Fernandez	.05	.02
12 Carlton Fisk	.50	.15
13 Kevin Maas	.05	.02
14 Dale Murphy	.20	.06
15 Eddie Murray	.20	.06
16 Dave Parker	.10	.03
17 Jeff Reardon	.10	.03
18 Cal Ripken	2.00	.60
19 Nolan Ryan	2.00	.60
20 Ryne Sandberg	.75	.23
21 Bobby Thigpen	.05	.02
22 Robin Yount	.50	.15
23 Rob Dibble and Randy Myers	.05	.02
24 Dave Stewart	.10	.03
25 Eric Davis	.15	.04
26 Rickey Henderson (Running bases)	.50	.15
27 Billy Hatcher	.05	.02
28 Joe Oliver	.05	.02
29 Chris Sabo	.05	.02
30 Barry Larkin	.20	.06
31 Jose Rijo (Pitching Game 4)	.05	.02
32 Reds Celebrate (1990 World Champions)	.05	.02
33 Jose Rijo World Series MVP	.05	.02

1910 World Series Photo Pack

These 12 pictures, which measure 4 1/2" by 6" are blank-backed and may have been cut from a larger album which featured all these cards. Since these cards are unnumbered, we are listing them in alphabetical order.

	Ex-Mt	VG
COMPLETE SET	2000.00	1000.00
1 Harry Davis / Eddie Collins	300.00	150.00
2 Rube Oldring / Topsy Hartsell	100.00	50.00
3 Lew Richie / Harry McIntyre	100.00	50.00
4 Ginger Beaumont / Solly Hofman	100.00	50.00
5 King Cole / Jimmy Archer	100.00	50.00
6 Frank Chance / Johnny Evers	400.00	200.00
7 John Kane / Ed Reulbach	100.00	50.00
8 Joe Tinker / Harry Steinfeldt	250.00	125.00
9 Orvie Overall / Tom Needham	100.00	50.00
10 Mordecai Brown / Johnny Kling	300.00	150.00
11 Frank Schulte / Jimmy Sheckard	100.00	50.00
12 Jack Pfeister / Heinie Zimmerman	150.00	75.00

1936 World Wide Gum V355

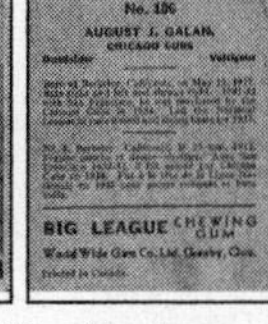
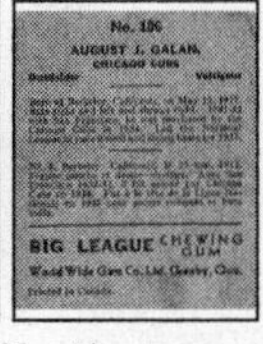

The cards in this 135-card set measure approximately 2 1/2" by 3". The 1936 Canadian Goudey set was issued by World Wide Gum Company and contains black and white cards. This issue is the most difficult to obtain of the Canadian Goudeys. The fronts feature player photos with white borders. The bilingual (French and English) backs carry player biography and career highlights. The World Wide Gum Company has its location listed as Granby, Quebec on these cards (as opposed to Montreal on earlier issues). The cards are numbered on both sides. The Phil Weintraub card (number 135) is very scarce and on many collectors wantlists.

	Ex-Mt	VG
COMPLETE SET (135)	20000.00	10000.00
1 Jimmy Dykes	100.00	50.00
2 Paul Waner	150.00	75.00
3 Cy Blanton	60.00	30.00
4 Sam Leslie	60.00	30.00
5 Johnny Vergez	60.00	30.00
6 Arky Vaughan	150.00	75.00
7 Bill Terry	150.00	75.00
8 Joe Moore	60.00	30.00
9 Gus Mancuso	60.00	30.00
10 Fred Marberry	60.00	30.00
11 George Selkirk	100.00	50.00
12 Spud Davis	60.00	30.00
13 Chuck Klein	150.00	75.00
14 Fred Fitzsimmons	100.00	50.00
15 Bill DeLancey	60.00	30.00
16 Billy Herman	150.00	75.00
17 George Davis	60.00	30.00
18 Rip Collins	60.00	30.00
19 Dizzy Dean	400.00	200.00
20 Roy Parmelee	60.00	30.00
21 Vic Sorrell	60.00	30.00
22 Harry Danning	60.00	30.00
23 Hal Schumacher	100.00	50.00
24 Cy Perkins	60.00	30.00
25 Leo Durocher	250.00	125.00
26 Glenn Myatt	60.00	30.00
27 Bob Seeds	60.00	30.00
28 Jimmy Ripple	60.00	30.00
29 Al Schacht	100.00	50.00
30 Pete Fox	60.00	30.00
31 Del Baker	60.00	30.00
32 Herman(Flea) Clifton	60.00	30.00
33 Tommy Bridges	100.00	50.00
34 Bill Dickey	250.00	125.00
35 Wally Berger	100.00	50.00
36 Slick Castleman	60.00	30.00
37 Dick Bartell	100.00	50.00
38 Red Rolfe	100.00	50.00
39 Waite Hoyt	150.00	75.00
40 Wes Ferrell	120.00	60.00
41 Hank Greenberg	250.00	125.00
42 Charlie Gehringer	150.00	75.00
43 Goose Goslin	150.00	75.00
44 Schoolboy Rowe	100.00	50.00
45 Mickey Cochrane MG	150.00	75.00
46 Joe Cronin	150.00	75.00
47 Jimmie Foxx	400.00	200.00
48 Jerry Walker	60.00	30.00
49 Charlie Gelbert	60.00	30.00
50 Ray Hayworth	60.00	30.00
51 Joe DiMaggio	4000.00	2000.00
52 Billy Rogell	60.00	30.00

53 John McCarthy 60.00 30.00
54 Phil Cavarretta 100.00 50.00
55 KiKi Cuyler 150.00 75.00
56 Lefty Gomez 150.00 75.00
57 Gabby Hartnett 150.00 75.00
58 John Marcum 60.00 30.00
59 Burgess Whitehead 60.00 30.00
60 Whitey Whitehill 60.00 30.00
61 Bucky Walters 100.00 50.00
62 Luke Sewell 100.00 50.00
63 Joe Kuhel 60.00 30.00
64 Lou Finney 60.00 30.00
65 Fred Lindstrom 150.00 75.00
66 Paul Derringer 100.00 50.00
67 Steve O'Neill MG 100.00 50.00
68 Mule Haas 60.00 30.00
69 Marv Owen 60.00 30.00
70 Bill Hallahan 60.00 30.00
71 Billy Urbanski 60.00 30.00
72 Dan Taylor 60.00 30.00
73 Heinie Manush 150.00 75.00
74 Jo Jo White 60.00 30.00
75 Joe Medwick 150.00 75.00
76 Joe Vosmik 60.00 30.00
77 Al Simmons 150.00 75.00
78 Shaug Shaughnessy 60.00 30.00
79 Harry Smythe 60.00 30.00
80 Bennie Tate 60.00 30.00
81 Billy Rheil 60.00 30.00
82 Lauri Myllykangas 60.00 30.00
83 Ben Sankey 60.00 30.00
84 Crip Polli 60.00 30.00
85 Jim Bottomley 150.00 75.00
86 Watson Clark 60.00 30.00
87 Ossie Bluege 100.00 50.00
88 Lefty Grove 250.00 125.00
89 Charlie Grimm MG 100.00 50.00
90 Ben Chapman 100.00 50.00
91 Frank Crosetti 120.00 60.00
Not him pictured on card
92 John Pomorski 60.00 30.00
93 Jess Haines 150.00 75.00
94 Chick Hafey 150.00 75.00
95 Tony Piet 60.00 30.00
96 Lou Gehrig 3000.00 1500.00
97 Billy Jurges 100.00 50.00
98 Smead Jolley 100.00 50.00
99 Jimmy Wilson 100.00 50.00
100 Lon Warneke 100.00 50.00
101 Vito Tamulis 60.00 30.00
102 Red Ruffing 150.00 75.00
103 Earl Grace 60.00 30.00
104 Rox Lawson 60.00 30.00
105 Stan Hack 100.00 50.00
106 Augie Galan 60.00 30.00
107 Frank Frisch MG 150.00 75.00
108 Bill McKechnie MG 150.00 75.00
109 Bill Lee 100.00 50.00
110 Connie Mack MG 150.00 75.00
111 Frank Reiber 60.00 30.00
112 Zeke Bonura 100.00 50.00
113 Luke Appling 150.00 75.00
114 Monte Pearson 60.00 30.00
115 Bob O'Farrell 100.00 50.00
116 Marvin Duke 60.00 30.00
117 Paul Florence 60.00 30.00
118 John Berley 60.00 30.00
119 Tom Oliver 60.00 30.00
120 Norman Kies 60.00 30.00
121 Hal King 60.00 30.00
122 Tom Abernathy 60.00 30.00
123 Phil Hensich 60.00 30.00
124 Ray Schalk 150.00 75.00
125 Paul Dunlap 60.00 30.00
126 Benny Bates 60.00 30.00
127 George Puccinelli 60.00 30.00
128 Stevie Stevenson 60.00 30.00
129 Rabbit Maranville MG 150.00 75.00
130 Bucky Harris MG 150.00 75.00
131 Al Lopez 150.00 75.00
132 Buddy Myer 100.00 50.00
133 Cliff Bolton 60.00 30.00
134 Estel Crabtree 60.00 30.00
135 Phil Weintraub 400.00 200.00

1939 World Wide Gum V351A

These 25 photos measure approximately 4" by 5 3/4" and feature on their fronts white-bordered sepia-toned posed player photos. The player's facsimile autograph appears across the picture. The backs carry tips printed in brown ink on how to play baseball. The photos are unnumbered and checklisted below in alphabetical order.

	Ex-Mt	VG
COMPLETE SET (25)	2000.00	1000.00
1 Morris Arnovich	30.00	15.00
2 Sam Bell	30.00	15.00
3 Zeke Bonura	40.00	20.00
4 Earl Caldwell	30.00	15.00
5 Flea Clifton	30.00	15.00
6 Frank Crosetti	50.00	25.00
7 Harry Danning	30.00	15.00
8 Dizzy Dean	150.00	75.00
9 Emile De Jonghe	30.00	15.00
10 Paul Derringer	30.00	15.00
11 Joe DiMaggio	600.00	300.00
12 Vince DiMaggio	60.00	30.00
13 Charles Gehringer	150.00	75.00
14 Gene Hasson	30.00	15.00
15 Tommy Henrich	60.00	30.00
16 Fred Hutchinson	50.00	25.00
17 Phil Marchildon	40.00	20.00
18 Mike Meola	30.00	15.00
19 Arnold Moser	30.00	15.00
20 Frank Pytlak	30.00	15.00
21 Frank Reiber	30.00	15.00
22 Lee Rogers	30.00	15.00
23 Cecil Travis	40.00	20.00
24 Hal Trosky	40.00	20.00
25 Ted Williams	600.00	300.00

1939 World Wide Gum Trimmed Premiums V351B

These 48 photos measure approximately 4" by 5 3/4" and feature on their fronts white-bordered sepia-toned posed player photos. The set is essentially a re-issue of the R303A set. The white borders at the top and bottom were trimmed (during the manufacturing process) to the same size as the Series A photos. The player's facsimile autograph appears across the photo. The backs carry tips printed in brown ink on how to play baseball. The photos are unnumbered and checklisted below in alphabetical order.

	Ex-Mt	VG
COMPLETE SET (48)	1600.00	800.00
1 Luke Appling	40.00	20.00
2 Earl Averill	40.00	20.00
3 Wally Berger	25.00	12.50
4 Darrell Blanton	20.00	10.00
5 Zeke Bonura	25.00	12.50
6 Mace Brown	20.00	10.00
7 George Case	25.00	12.50
8 Ben Chapman	20.00	10.00
9 Joe Cronin	40.00	20.00
10 Frank Crosetti	30.00	15.00
11 Paul Derringer	25.00	12.50
12 Bill Dickey	40.00	20.00
13 Joe DiMaggio	250.00	125.00
14 Bob Feller	80.00	40.00
15 Jimmy Foxx	60.00	30.00
16 Charlie Gehringer	40.00	20.00
17 Lefty Gomez	40.00	20.00
18 Ival Goodman	20.00	10.00
19 Joe Gordon	30.00	15.00
20 Hank Greenberg	40.00	20.00
21 Buddy Hassett	20.00	10.00
22 Jeff Heath	20.00	10.00
23 Tommy Henrich	30.00	15.00
24 Billy Herman	40.00	20.00
25 Frank Higgins	20.00	10.00
26 Fred Hutchinson	25.00	12.50
27 Bob Johnson	25.00	12.50
28 Ken Keltner	25.00	12.50
29 Mike Kreevich	20.00	10.00
30 Ernie Lombardi	40.00	20.00
31 Gus Mancuso	20.00	10.00
32 Eric McNair	20.00	10.00
33 Van Mungo	25.00	12.50
34 Buck Newsom	25.00	12.50
35 Mel Ott	40.00	20.00
36 Marvin Owen	20.00	10.00
37 Frankie Pytlak	20.00	10.00
38 Woody Rich	20.00	10.00
39 Charlie Root	25.00	12.50
40 Al Simmons	40.00	20.00
41 Jim Tabor	20.00	10.00
42 Cecil Travis	20.00	10.00
43 Hal Trosky	20.00	10.00
44 Arky Vaughan	40.00	20.00
45 Joe Vosmik	20.00	10.00
46 Lon Warneke	20.00	10.00
47 Ted Williams	250.00	125.00
48 Rudy York	25.00	12.50

1933 Worch Cigar

These 3 7/16" by 5 7/16" photos were issued by Worch Cigars. They feature both major and minor leaguers and according to documentation issued by Worch in 1933 the players issued were the players they figured to be in the most demand and had negatives on hand to make. Interesting to note that just as many minor leaguers as major leaguers were produced.

	Ex-Mt	VG
COMPLETE SET	3500.00	1800.00
1 Sparky Adams	10.00	5.00
2 Dale Alexander	10.00	5.00
3 Ivy Paul Andrews	10.00	5.00
4 Earl Averill	20.00	10.00
Name at left)		
5 Earl Averill	20.00	10.00
Name at right)		
6 Richard Bartell	12.00	6.00
7 Walter Berger	12.00	6.00
Bos NL		
8 Walter Berger	12.00	6.00
No team name		
9 Huck Betts	10.00	5.00
10 Max Bishop	10.00	5.00
11 Jim Bottomley	20.00	10.00
12 Tom Bridges	10.00	5.00
13 Clint Brown	10.00	5.00
14 Max Carey MG	20.00	10.00
15 Tex Carleton	10.00	5.00
16 Ben Chapman	10.00	5.00
Name not in box		
17 Ben Chapman	10.00	5.00
Name in box		
18 Chalmer Cissell	10.00	5.00
19 Mickey Cochrane	30.00	15.00
20 Mickey Cochrane	30.00	15.00
Name spelled Cochran		
21 Earle Combs	20.00	10.00
22 Rip Collins	10.00	5.00
23 Adam Comorosky	10.00	5.00
24 Estel Crabtree	10.00	5.00
25 Roger Cramer	12.00	6.00
26 Pat Crawford	10.00	5.00
27 Hugh Critz	10.00	5.00
28 Joe Cronin	30.00	15.00
29 Frank Crosetti	15.00	7.50
30 Alvin Crowder	10.00	5.00
31 Tony Cuccinello	10.00	5.00
32 Kiki Cuyler	20.00	10.00
33 Geo. Davis	10.00	5.00
34 Dizzy Dean	50.00	25.00
35 Bill Dickey	40.00	20.00
Name not in box		
36 Bill Dickey	40.00	20.00
Name in Box		
37 Leo Durocher	40.00	20.00
38 James Dykes	15.00	7.50
39 George Earnshaw	10.00	5.00
40 Woody English	12.00	6.00
41 Richard Ferrel	20.00	10.00
Name Spelled incorrectly		
42 Richard Ferrell	20.00	10.00
43 Wesley Ferrell	12.00	6.00
44 James Foxx	100.00	50.00
45 Fred Frankhouse	10.00	5.00
46 Frank Frisch	40.00	20.00
Large cropping)		
47 Frank Frisch	40.00	20.00
Small cropping)		
48 George Grantham	10.00	5.00
Name spelled Gantham		
49 Lou Gehrig	300.00	150.00
Box on Card		
50 Lou Gehrig	300.00	150.00
No Box on Card		
51 Charlie Gehringer	40.00	20.00
52 Geo. Gibson MG	10.00	5.00
53 Lefty Gomez	50.00	25.00
No Box		
54 Vernon Gomez	50.00	25.00
Box on Card		
55 Leon Goslin(Name spelled Gaslin 20.00		
10.00		
56 Leon Goslin	20.00	10.00
Name correctly spelled		
57 Charlie Grimm	15.00	7.50
58 Robert Grove	50.00	25.00
Name in box		
59 Robert Grove	50.00	25.00
Name not in box		
60 Chic Hafey	20.00	10.00
No Background on card		
61 Chic Hafey	20.00	10.00
Photo Background on Card		
62 Bill Hallahan	12.00	6.00
63 Mel Harder	12.00	6.00
64 Gabby Hartnett	20.00	10.00
65 Dutch Henry	10.00	5.00
66 Babe Herman	15.00	7.50
67 Bill Herman	20.00	10.00
68 Oral Hildebrand	10.00	5.00
Box on Card		
69 Oral Hildebrand	10.00	5.00
No Box on Card		
70 Rogers Hornsby	50.00	25.00
St Louis AL		
71 Rogers Hornsby	50.00	25.00
St Louis Cards NL		
72 Carl Hubbell	40.00	20.00
73 Travis Jackson	20.00	10.00
New York N.L.		
74 Travis Jackson	20.00	10.00
No team name		
75 Charles Klein	20.00	10.00
Philadelphia N.L., No Background		
76 Chuck Klein	20.00	10.00
Chicago NL, no background		
77 Chuck Klein	20.00	10.00
Philadelphia NL, background		
78 Joe Kuhel	10.00	5.00
79 Tony Lazzeri	20.00	10.00
New York A.L.		
80 Tony Lazzeri	20.00	10.00
N.Y. A.L.		
81 Ernie Lombardi	20.00	10.00
82 Al Lopez	20.00	10.00
83 Red Lucas	10.00	5.00
84 Henry Manush	20.00	10.00
85 Fred Marberry	10.00	5.00
86 Pepper Martin	12.00	6.00
Has Background		
87 Pepper Martin	12.00	6.00
No background		
88 Joe Medwick	20.00	10.00
89 Joe Moore	10.00	5.00
90 Van Mungo	12.00	6.00
91 Buddy Myer	10.00	5.00
92 Bob O'Farrell	10.00	5.00
93 Lefty O'Doul	15.00	7.50
New York N.L>		
94 Lefty O'Doul	15.00	7.50
No team name)		
95 Ernie Orsatti	10.00	5.00
standing)		
96 Ernie Orsatti	10.00	5.00
batting)		
97 Melvin Ott	20.00	10.00
98 Homer Peel	10.00	5.00
99 Red Ruffing	20.00	10.00
100 Jack Russell	10.00	5.00
101 Babe Ruth	500.00	250.00
Box on Card		
102 Babe Ruth	500.00	250.00
No Box on Card		
103 Blondy Ryan	10.00	5.00
104 Wilfred Ryan	10.00	5.00
105 Hal Schumacher	10.00	5.00
106 Luke Sewell	10.00	5.00
Name in a Box		
107 Luke Sewell	10.00	5.00
No Box Around Name		
108 Al Simmons	30.00	15.00
Name at left)		
109 Al Simmons	30.00	15.00
Name at right)		
110 Ray Spencer	10.00	5.00
111 Gus Suhr	10.00	5.00
112 Bill Terry	30.00	15.00
113 Pie Traynor	40.00	20.00
114 Dazzy Vance	20.00	10.00
115 Gerald Walker	10.00	5.00
116 Lloyd Waner	20.00	10.00
With background)		
117 Lloyd Waner	20.00	10.00
Without background)		
118 Paul Waner	25.00	12.50
With background)		
119 Paul Waner	25.00	12.50
Without background)		
120 Lon Warneke	10.00	5.00
Brown background)		
121 Lon Warneke	10.00	5.00
White background)		
122 Monte Weaver	10.00	5.00
123 Sam West	10.00	5.00
124 Burgess Whitehead	10.00	5.00
125 Hack Wilson	20.00	10.00
126 Jimmy Wilson	10.00	5.00

1992 Carol Wright Proofs

These "proofs" which measure 2" by 2" were issued to Carol Wright to promote their products. Each of these proofs were issued to a stated print run of 1500 sets. Since these cards are not numbered, we have listed this set in alphabetical order.

	MINT	NRMT
COMPLETE SET	12.00	5.50
1 Craig Biggio	.20	.09
2 Wade Boggs	.50	.23
3 Barry Bonds	1.25	.55
4 Bobby Bonilla	.15	.07
5 Jose Canseco	.40	.18
6 Will Clark	.25	.11
7 Joe Carter	.15	.07
8 Len Dykstra	.15	.07
9 Cecil Fielder	.15	.07
10 Ken Griffey Jr.	1.50	.70
11 Tony Gwynn	1.25	.55
12 Don Mattingly	1.25	.55
13 Kirby Puckett	.75	.35
14 Cal Ripken Jr.	2.50	1.10
15 Chris Sabo	.10	.05
16 Ryne Sandberg	1.25	.55
17 Ozzie Smith	1.25	.55
18 Darryl Strawberry	.15	.07
19 Frank Thomas	.75	.35
20 Robin Yount	.75	.35

1944 Yankees Stamps

This stamp set commemorates the New York Yankees and their World Series victory in 1943. The stamps were perforated together in a sheet with five rows of six stamps across. The stamps are ordered alphabetically on the stamp sheet left to right. Each stamp measures approximately 1 3/4" by 2 3/8" and is in full color. The player's name is printed in white on a red background at the bottom of each stamp. An album for the set was issued but it is more difficult to find than the stamps. The catalog designation for this set is ST101.

	Ex-Mt	VG
COMPLETE SET (30)	75.00	38.00
1 Ernie Bonham	2.00	1.00
2 Hank Borowy	2.00	1.00
3 Marvin Breuer	1.50	.75
4 Tommy Byrne	2.00	1.00
5 Spud Chandler	2.50	1.25
6 Earle Combs CO	5.00	2.50
7 Frank Crosetti	2.50	1.25
8 Bill Dickey	10.00	5.00
9 Atley Donald	1.50	.75
10 Nick Etten	1.50	.75
11 Art Fletcher CO	1.50	.75
12 Joe Gordon	2.50	1.25
13 Oscar Grimes	1.50	.75
14 Rollie Hemsley	1.50	.75
15 Bill Johnson	1.50	.75
16 Charlie Keller	2.50	1.25
17 John Lindell	2.00	1.00
18 Joe McCarthy MG	5.00	2.50
19 Bud Metheny	1.50	.75
20 Johnny Murphy	2.00	1.00
21 Pat O'Dougherty	1.50	.75
22 Marius Russo	1.50	.75
23 John Schulte	1.50	.75
24 Ken Sears	1.50	.75
25 Tuck Stainback	1.50	.75
26 George Stirnweiss	2.00	1.00
27 Jim Turner	2.00	1.00
28 Roy Weatherly	1.50	.75
29 Charley Wensloff	1.50	.75
30 Bill Zuber	1.50	.75
NNO Album	25.00	12.50

1947 Yankees Team Issue

This 25-card set of the New York Yankees measures approximately 6 1/2" by 9" and features black-and-white player portraits with white borders and facsimile autographs. The backs are blank. The cards are unnumbered and checklisted below in alphabetical order. This set was available from the Yankees at time of issue for 50 cents.

	Ex-Mt	VG
COMPLETE SET (25)	250.00	125.00
1 Yogi Berra	50.00	25.00
2 Bill Bevans	5.00	2.50
3 Bobby Brown	10.00	5.00
4 Spud Chandler	5.00	2.50
5 Gerry Coleman	5.00	2.50
6 John Corriden CO	5.00	2.50
7 Frank Crosetti	5.00	2.50
8 Joe DiMaggio	80.00	40.00
9 Chuck Dressen CO	8.00	4.00
10 Randy Gumpert	5.00	2.50
11 Bucky Harris MG	10.00	5.00
12 Tommy Henrich	8.00	4.00
13 Ralph Houk	6.00	3.00
14 Don Johnson	5.00	2.50
15 Bill Johnson	5.00	2.50
16 Charlie Keller	5.00	2.50
17 John Lindell	5.00	2.50
18 George McQuinn	5.00	2.50
19 Joe Page	5.00	2.50
20 Allie Reynolds	8.00	4.00
21 Phil Rizzuto	20.00	10.00
22 Aaron Robinson	5.00	2.50
23 Frank Shea	5.00	2.50
24 Ken Silvestri	5.00	2.50
25 George Stirnweiss	5.00	2.50

1948 Yankees Team Issue

These 26 photos measure approximately 6 1/2" by 9". They feature members of the 1948 New York Yankees. These black and white photos also feature a facsimile signature and are framed by white borders. The photos are unnumbered and we have sequenced them in alphabetical order.

	NM	Ex
COMPLETE SET (26)	275.00	140.00
1 Mel Allen ANN	10.00	5.00
2 Yogi Berra	40.00	20.00
3 Bobby Brown	6.00	3.00
4 Red Corriden CO	5.00	2.50
5 Frank Crosetti	8.00	4.00
6 Joe DiMaggio	80.00	40.00
7 Chuck Dressen CO	6.00	3.00
8 Karl Drews	5.00	2.50
9 Red Embree	5.00	2.50
10 Randy Gumpert	5.00	2.50
11 Bucky Harris MG	10.00	5.00
12 Tommy Henrich	8.00	4.00
13 Frank Hiller	5.00	2.50
14 Bill Johnson	5.00	2.50
15 Charlie Keller	6.00	3.00
16 Ed Lopat	8.00	4.00
17 John Lindell	5.00	2.50
18 Cliff Mapes	5.00	2.50
19 Gus Niarhos	5.00	2.50
20 George McQuinn	5.00	2.50
21 Joe Page	6.00	3.00
22 Vic Raschi	8.00	4.00
23 Allie Reynolds	8.00	4.00
24 Phil Rizzuto	30.00	15.00
25 Frank Shea	5.00	2.50
26 Snuffy Stirnweiss	6.00	3.00

1949 Yankees Team Issue

This 25-card set of the New York Yankees measures approximately 6 1/2" by 9" and features black-and-white player portraits with white borders. The backs are blank. The cards are unnumbered and checklisted below in alphabetical order.

	NM	Ex
COMPLETE SET (25)	300.00	150.00
1 Mel Allen ANN	10.00	5.00
2 Larry Berra	40.00	20.00
3 Bobby Brown	10.00	5.00
4 Tommy Byrne	5.00	2.50
5 Jerry Coleman	8.00	4.00
6 Frank Crosetti CO	8.00	4.00
7 Bill Dickey CO	20.00	10.00
8 Joe DiMaggio	80.00	40.00
9 Tom Henrich	8.00	4.00
10 Bill Johnson	5.00	2.50
11 Charlie Keller	5.00	2.50
12 John Lindell	5.00	2.50
13 Ed Lopat	8.00	4.00
14 Gus Niarhos	5.00	2.50
15 Joe Page	5.00	2.50
16 Bob Porterfield	5.00	2.50
17 Vic Raschi	8.00	4.00
18 Allie Reynolds	8.00	4.00
19 Phil Rizzuto	30.00	15.00
20 Fred Sanford	5.00	2.50
21 Frank Shea	5.00	2.50
22 Casey Stengel MG	25.00	12.50
23 George Stirnweiss	5.00	2.50
24 Jim Turner CO	5.00	2.50
25 Gene Woodling	6.00	3.00

1950 Yankees Team Issue

This 25-card set of the New York Yankees measures approximately 6 1/2" by 9" and features black-and-white player portraits with white borders. The backs are blank. The cards are unnumbered and checklisted below in alphabetical order.

	NM	Ex
COMPLETE SET (25)	300.00	150.00
1 Mel Allen ANN	10.00	5.00
2 Hank Bauer	10.00	5.00
3 Larry Berra	40.00	20.00
4 Bobby Brown	10.00	5.00
5 Tommy Byrne	5.00	2.50
6 Jerry Coleman	8.00	4.00
7 Frank Crosetti CO	8.00	4.00
8 Bill Dickey CO	20.00	10.00
9 Joe DiMaggio	80.00	40.00
10 Tom Henrich	8.00	4.00
11 Jack Jensen	20.00	10.00
12 Bill Johnson	5.00	2.50
13 Ed Lopat	5.00	2.50
14 Cliff Mapes	5.00	2.50
15 Joe Page	5.00	2.50
16 Bob Porterfield	5.00	2.50
17 Vic Raschi	8.00	4.00
18 Allie Reynolds	8.00	4.00
19 Phil Rizzuto	30.00	15.00
20 Fred Sanford	5.00	2.50
21 Charlie Silvera	5.00	2.50
22 Casey Stengel MG	25.00	12.50
23 George Stirnweiss	5.00	2.50
24 Jim Turner CO	5.00	2.50
25 Gene Woodling	6.00	3.00

1953 Yankees Photos

Issued by one of the "stores" across the street from Yankee Stadium, these photos feature portrait photos of the Yankees on the front and the backs have the name, address and phone number of the store used to distribute the photos. It is possible that there might be more photos so any additions are appreciated. Since the cards are unnumbered, we have sequenced them in alphabetical order.

	NM	Ex
COMPLETE SET	100.00	50.00
1 Hank Bauer	10.00	5.00
2 Yogi Berra	20.00	10.00
3 Joe Collins	5.00	2.50
4 Whitey Ford	20.00	10.00
5 Billy Martin	15.00	7.50
6 Gil McDougal	8.00	4.00
7 Johnny Mize	12.00	6.00
8 Vic Raschi	8.00	4.00
9 Phil Rizzuto	15.00	7.50
10 Gene Woodling	6.00	3.00

1956 Yankees Jay Publishing

This 12-card set of the New York Yankees measures approximately 5 1/8" by 7". The fronts feature black-and-white posed player photos with the player's and team name printed below in the white border. These cards were packaged 12 to a packet and originally sold for 25 cents. The backs are blank. The cards are unnumbered and checklisted below in alphabetical order.

	NM	Ex
COMPLETE SET (12)	120.00	60.00
1 Hank Bauer	6.00	3.00
2 Larry Berra	15.00	7.50
3 Tommy Byrne	4.00	2.00
4 Andy Carey	4.00	2.00
5 Joe Collins	4.00	2.00
6 Whitey Ford	15.00	7.50
7 Elston Howard	8.00	4.00
8 Mickey Mantle	50.00	25.00
9 Billy Martin	12.00	6.00
10 Gil McDougald	6.00	3.00
11 Casey Stengel MG	15.00	7.50
12 Bob Turley	4.00	2.00

1956 Yankees Team Issue

This 24-card set of the New York Yankees features black-and-white player photos measuring approximately 6" by 9" with the player's name printed at the bottom. The cards are unnumbered and checklisted below in alphabetical order.

	NM	Ex
COMPLETE SET (24)	250.00	125.00
1 Hank Bauer	12.00	6.00
2 Yogi Berra	20.00	10.00
3 Tommy Byrne	8.00	4.00
4 Andy Carey	8.00	4.00
5 Bob Cerv	8.00	4.00
6 Gerry Coleman	8.00	4.00
7 Joe Collins	8.00	4.00
8 Whitey Ford	20.00	10.00
9 Bob Grim	8.00	4.00
10 Elston Howard	15.00	7.50
11 Johnny Kucks	8.00	4.00
12 Don Larsen	12.00	6.00
13 Jerry Lumpe	8.00	4.00
14 Mickey Mantle	50.00	25.00
15 Billy Martin	15.00	7.50
16 Mickey McDermott	8.00	4.00
17 Gil McDougald	10.00	5.00
18 Tom Morgan	8.00	4.00
19 Irv Noren	8.00	4.00
20 Phil Rizzuto	20.00	10.00
21 Eddie Robinson	8.00	4.00
22 Charley Silvera	8.00	4.00
23 Bill Skowron	12.00	6.00
24 Bob Turley	10.00	5.00

1957 Yankees Jay Publishing

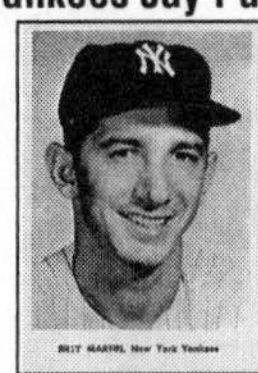

This 16-card set of the New York Yankees measures approximately 5" X 7". Since personnel changes were made during the season, there were more than just 12 cards issued. The fronts feature black-and-white posed player photos with the player's and team name printed below in the white border. These cards were packaged 12 to a packet and originally sold for 25 cents. The backs are blank. The cards are unnumbered and checklisted below in alphabetical order.

	NM	Ex
COMPLETE SET (12)	175.00	90.00
1 Hank Bauer	6.00	3.00
2 Larry Berra	25.00	12.50
3 Tommy Byrne	4.00	2.00
4 Jerry Coleman	4.00	2.00
5 Ed (Whitey) Ford	25.00	12.50
6 Elston Howard	8.00	4.00
7 Johnny Kucks	4.00	2.00
8 Don Larsen	5.00	2.50
9 Sal Maglie	5.00	2.50
10 Mickey Mantle	50.00	25.00
11 Billy Martin	8.00	4.00
12 Gil McDougald	5.00	2.50
13 Bill Skowron	6.00	3.00
14 Enos Slaughter	4.00	2.00
15 Casey Stengel MG	15.00	7.50
16 Tom Sturdivant	4.00	2.00

1957 Yankee Team Issue

These photos, which measure approximately 7 1/2" by 10" feature members of the 1957 New York Yankees. Since these photos are unnumbered, we have sequenced them in alphabetical order.

	NM	Ex
COMPLETE SET	175.00	90.00
1 Hank Bauer	15.00	7.50
2 Yogi Berra	20.00	10.00
3 Andy Carey	8.00	4.00
4 Joe Collins	8.00	4.00
5 Whitey Ford	20.00	10.00
6 Elston Howard	15.00	7.50
7 Don Larsen	10.00	5.00
8 Mickey Mantle	50.00	25.00
9 Gil McDougald	10.00	5.00
10 Bill Skowron	15.00	7.50
11 Casey Stengel MG	20.00	10.00
12 Bob Turley	10.00	5.00

1958 Yankees Jay Publishing

This 16-card set of the New York Yankees measures approximately 5" by 7" and features black-and-white player photos in a white border. These cards were packaged 12 to a packet. The backs are blank. The cards are unnumbered and checklisted below in alphabetical order. More than 12 cards are included in this set as they were released at different times during the season

	NM	Ex
COMPLETE SET	150.00	75.00
1 Hank Bauer	6.00	3.00
2 Larry "Yogi" Berra	15.00	7.50
3 Andy Carey	4.00	2.00
4 Whitey Ford	15.00	7.50
5 Elston Howard	8.00	4.00
6 Tony Kubek	8.00	4.00
7 Don Larsen	5.00	2.50
8 Jerry Lumpe	4.00	2.00
9 Mickey Mantle	50.00	25.00
10 Gil McDougald	4.00	2.00
11 Bobby Shantz	5.00	2.50
12 Bill Skowron	6.00	3.00
13 Casey Stengel MG	15.00	7.50
14 Tom Sturdivant	4.00	2.00
15 Bob Turley	4.00	2.00
16 Jim Turner CO Bill Dickey CO Frank Crosetti CO Casey Stengel MG	8.00	4.00

1959 Yankees Team Issue

These 12 black and white blank-backed photos measure 8" by 10" and feature a photo surrounded by white borders with the player's name printed in the lower left hand corner. As the photos are unnumbered, we have sequenced them in alphabetical order.

	NM	Ex
COMPLETE SET	120.00	60.00
1 Yogi Berra	15.00	7.50
2 Ryne Duren	4.00	2.00
3 Whitey Ford	15.00	7.50
4 Elston Howard	8.00	4.00
5 Tony Kubek	8.00	4.00
6 Mickey Mantle	50.00	25.00
7 Gil McDougald	5.00	2.50
8 Bobby Richardson	8.00	4.00
9 Bobby Shantz	4.00	2.00
10 Bill Skowron	6.00	3.00
11 Casey Stengel MG	10.00	5.00
12 Bob Turley	5.00	2.50

1959 Yankees Yoo-Hoo

These cards are black and white, with no printing on the back. They feature New York Yankee ballplayers, and were distributed as a premium in the New York area with a six-pack of Yoo-Hoo. There were six cards issued in the set. A facsimile signature of the player, along with the phrase "Me for Yoo-Hoo" appears on the front. The cards have a 15/16" tab at the bottom. The cards measure approximately 2 7/16" by 3 9/16" without the tab and 2 7/16" by 4 1/2" with the tab. The cards are valued below as being with tabs intact. The Mantle card is actually an advertising piece for Yoo-Hoo. Cards without tabs are valued between 50 and 75 percent of the full card.

	NM	Ex
COMPLETE SET (6)	2250.00	1100.00
1 Yogi Berra	500.00	250.00
2 Whitey Ford	200.00	100.00
3 Tony Kubek	125.00	60.00
4 Mickey Mantle SP Card is an advertisment for Yoo-Hoo Different size than other cards in set	2000.00	1000.00
5 Gil McDougald	100.00	50.00
6 Moose Skowron	125.00	60.00

1960 Yankees Jay Publishing

This 12-card set of the New York Yankees measures approximately 5" by 7" and features black-and-white player photos in a white border. These cards were packaged 12 to a packet. The backs are blank. The cards are unnumbered and checklisted below in alphabetical order.

	NM	Ex
COMPLETE SET (12)	100.00	40.00
1 Yogi Berra	15.00	6.00
2 Andy Carey	2.50	1.00
3 Whitey Ford	15.00	6.00
4 Elston Howard	5.00	2.00
5 Tony Kubek	5.00	2.00
6 Hector Lopez	2.50	1.00
7 Mickey Mantle	40.00	16.00
8 Roger Maris	12.00	4.80
9 Gil McDougald	2.50	1.00
10 Bill Skowron	3.00	1.20
11 Casey Stengel MG	10.00	4.00
12 Bob Turley	2.50	1.00

1960 Yankees Team Issue

These black and white cards, which measure approximately 6" by 8 1/2" featured members of the 1960 New York Yankees. Since these cards are unnumbered, we have sequenced them in alphabetical order.

	NM	Ex
COMPLETE SET	150.00	60.00
1 Yogi Berra	20.00	8.00
2 Andy Carey	5.00	2.00
3 Art Ditmar	5.00	2.00
4 Ryne Duren	5.00	2.00
5 Whitey Ford	20.00	8.00
6 Elston Howard	10.00	4.00
7 Tony Kubek	10.00	4.00
8 Mickey Mantle	40.00	16.00
9 Gil McDougald	6.00	2.40
10 Bobby Richardson	10.00	4.00
11 Bobby Shantz	5.00	2.00
12 Bill Skowron	10.00	4.00
13 Casey Stengel MG	12.00	4.80
14 Bob Turley	6.00	2.40

1961 Yankees Jay Publishing

This 12-card set of the New York Yankees measures approximately 5" by 7". The fronts feature black-and-white posed player photos with the player's and team name printed below in the white border. These cards were packaged 12 to a packet. The backs are blank. The cards are unnumbered and checklisted below in alphabetical order.

	NM	Ex
COMPLETE SET (12)	100.00	40.00
1 Yogi Berra	20.00	8.00
2 Clete Boyer	4.00	1.60
3 Art Ditmar	2.50	1.00
4 Whitey Ford	20.00	8.00
5 Ralph Houk MG	3.00	1.20
6 Elston Howard	5.00	2.00
7 Tony Kubek	5.00	2.00
8 Mickey Mantle	40.00	16.00
9 Roger Maris	20.00	8.00
10 Bobby Richardson	5.00	2.00
11 Bill Skowron	4.00	1.60
12 Bob Turley	2.50	1.00

1961 Yankees Team Issue

These 8" by 10" photos were issued to members of the press by the New York Yankees. These photos feature the player photo surrounded by white borders. Since these cards are not numbered, we have checklisted these cards in alphabetical order.

	NM	Ex
COMPLETE SET	150.00	60.00
1 Luis Arroyo	5.00	2.00
2 Yogi Berra	20.00	8.00
3 Jim Coates	5.00	2.00
4 Joe DeMaestri	5.00	2.00
5 Art Ditmar	5.00	2.00
6 Whitey Ford	20.00	8.00
7 Jesse Gonder	5.00	2.00
8 Ralph Houk MG	6.00	2.40
9 Deron Johnson	5.00	2.00
10 Tony Kubek	10.00	4.00
11 Mickey Mantle	40.00	16.00
12 Roger Maris	30.00	12.00
13 Bobby Richardson	10.00	4.00
14 Bill Skowron	8.00	3.20
15 Ralph Terry	5.00	2.00
16 Bob Turley	5.00	2.00

1962 Yankees Jay Publishing

This 12-card set of the New York Yankees measures approximately 5" by 7". The fronts feature black-and-white posed player photos with the player's and team name printed below in the white border. These cards were packaged 12 to a packet. The backs are blank. The cards are unnumbered and checklisted below in alphabetical order.

	NM	Ex
COMPLETE SET (12)	75.00	30.00
1 Luis Arroyo	2.50	1.00
2 Yogi Berra	20.00	8.00
3 John Blanchard	2.50	1.00
4 Cletis Boyer	4.00	1.60
5 Bud Daley	2.50	1.00
6 Whitey Ford	20.00	8.00
7 Ralph Houk MG	3.00	1.20
8 Elston Howard	5.00	2.00
9 Mickey Mantle	40.00	16.00
10 Roger Maris	20.00	8.00
11 Bobby Richardson	5.00	2.00
12 Bill Skowron	4.00	1.60

1962 Yankees Team Issue

These 5" by 7" blank backed photos feature members of the 1962 New York Yankees. The fronts feature black and white photos along with the players name printed in blank ink on the bottom. Since these photos are unnumbered we have sequenced them in alphabetical order

	NM	Ex
COMPLETE SET	125.00	50.00
1 Luis Arroyo	4.00	1.60
2 Yogi Berra	15.00	6.00
3 John Blanchard	4.00	1.60
4 Clete Boyer	5.00	2.00
5 Bob Cerv	4.00	1.60
6 Whitey Ford	15.00	6.00
7 Elston Howard	8.00	3.20
8 Tony Kubek	8.00	3.20
9 Hector Lopez	4.00	1.60
10 Mickey Mantle	40.00	16.00
11 Roger Maris	20.00	8.00
12 Bobby Richardson	8.00	3.20
13 Bill Skowron	5.00	2.00
14 Bob Turley	4.00	1.60

1963 Yankee Emblems

These seven patches which measure 3 1/2" by 4 1/2" feature members of the early 1960's Yankees. These patches have a player photo on the front and were issued in plastic-wrapped cardboard displays. Since these are unnumbered, we have sequenced them in alphabetical order.

	NM	Ex
COMPLETE SET	250.00	100.00
1 Yogi Berra	40.00	16.00
2 Clete Boyer	10.00	4.00
3 Elston Howard	25.00	10.00
4 Tony Kubek	25.00	10.00
5 Mickey Mantle	80.00	32.00
6 Roger Maris	60.00	24.00
7 Joe Pepitone	15.00	6.00
8 Bobby Richardson	25.00	10.00

1963 Yankees Jay Publishing

This 12-card set of the New York Yankees measures approximately 5" by 7". The fronts feature black-and-white posed player photos with the player's and team name printed below in the white border. These cards were packaged 12 to a packet. The backs are blank. The cards are unnumbered and checklisted below in alphabetical order.

	NM	Ex
COMPLETE SET (12)	80.00	32.00
1 Yogi Berra	15.00	6.00
2 Clete Boyer	4.00	1.60
3 Whitey Ford	15.00	6.00
4 Ralph Houk MG	3.00	1.20
5 Elston Howard	5.00	2.00
6 Tony Kubek	5.00	2.00
7 Mickey Mantle	40.00	16.00
8 Roger Maris	20.00	8.00
9 Joe Pepitone	5.00	2.00
10 Bobby Richardson	5.00	2.00
11 Ralph Terry	2.50	1.00
12 Tom Tresh	5.00	2.00

1963-67 Yankees Requena K Postcards

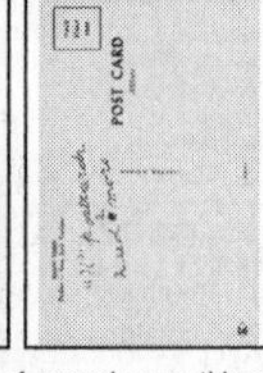

Issued over a period of several years this set features New York Yankee players only.The set features two types -- one in color, the other in black and white. Bridges only appears in black and white. We have sequenced this set in alphabetical order. Similar to the Dormand and Bill and Bob postcard, Requena postcards feature a K in the lower left of the reverse.

	NM	Ex
COMPLETE SET	500.00	200.00
1 Steve Barber	15.00	6.00
2A Yogi Berra Fascimile sig at top	50.00	20.00
2B Yogi Berra Facsimile Sig at bottom	50.00	20.00
2C Yogi Berra No signature	50.00	20.00
3 Johnny Blanchard	15.00	6.00
4 Jim Bouton	25.00	10.00
5 Clete Boyer	20.00	8.00
6 Marshall Bridges	15.00	6.00
7 Whitey Ford (2)	50.00	20.00
8 Elston Howard	30.00	12.00
9 Tony Kubek	30.00	12.00
10 Phil Linz	15.00	6.00
11 Fritz Peterson	15.00	6.00
12 Joe Pepitone	25.00	10.00
13 Pedro Ramos	15.00	6.00
14 Bobby Richardson	30.00	12.00
15 Bill Stafford	15.00	6.00
16 Mel Stottlemyre	25.00	10.00
18 Ralph Terry	15.00	6.00
19 Tom Tresh (2)	20.00	8.00

1964 Yankees Jay Publishing

This 12-card set of the New York Yankees measures approximately 5" by 7". The fronts feature black-and-white posed player photos with the player's and team name printed below in the white border. These cards were packaged 12 to a packet. The backs are blank. The cards are unnumbered and checklisted below in alphabetical order.

	NM	Ex
COMPLETE SET (12)	80.00	32.00
1 Yogi Berra MG	15.00	6.00
2 Clete Boyer	3.00	1.20
3 Al Downing	2.50	1.00
4 Whitey Ford	8.00	3.20
5 Elston Howard	5.00	2.00
6 Tony Kubek	5.00	2.00
7 Mickey Mantle	40.00	16.00
8 Roger Maris	20.00	8.00
9 Joe Pepitone	4.00	1.60
10 Bobby Richardson	5.00	2.00
11 Ralph Terry	2.50	1.00
12 Tom Tresh	4.00	1.60

1965 Yankees Jay Publishing

This 12-card set of the New York Yankees measures approximately 5" by 7". The fronts feature black-and-white posed player photos with the player's and team name printed below in the white border. These cards were packaged 12 to a packet. The backs are blank. The cards are unnumbered and checklisted below in alphabetical order.

	NM	Ex
COMPLETE SET (12)	100.00	40.00
1 Jim Bouton	5.00	2.00
2 Clete Boyer	4.00	1.60
3 Al Downing	2.50	1.00
4 Whitey Ford	15.00	6.00
5 Elston Howard	5.00	2.00
6 Tony Kubek	5.00	2.00
7 Mickey Mantle	40.00	16.00
8 Roger Maris	20.00	8.00
9 Joe Pepitone	4.00	1.60
10 Bobby Richardson	5.00	2.00
11 Mel Stottlemyre	4.00	1.60
12 Tom Tresh	4.00	1.60

1966 Yankees Team Issue

This 12-card set of the New York Yankees measures 4 7/8" by 7" and features black-and-white player photos in a white border with blank backs. These cards were originally packaged 12 to a packet with a price of 25 cents. The cards are unnumbered and checklisted below in alphabetical order. Changes in personnel are responsible for this checklist having more than 12 names.

	NM	Ex
COMPLETE SET (12)	60.00	24.00
1 Jim Bouton	4.00	1.60
2 Clete Boyer	3.00	1.20
3 Al Downing	2.00	.80
4 Whitey Ford	15.00	6.00
5 Ralph Houk MG	2.00	.80
6 Elston Howard	5.00	2.00
7 Johnny Keane MG	2.00	.80
8 Hector Lopez	2.00	.80
9 Mickey Mantle	30.00	12.00
10 Roger Maris	15.00	6.00
11 Joe Pepitone	4.00	1.60
12 Bobby Richardson	5.00	2.00
13 Mel Stottlemyre	4.00	1.60
14 Tom Tresh	4.00	1.60

1967 Yankees Photos SCFC

This 12-card set of the New York Yankees measures approximately 4" by 5" and features black-and-white player photos with white borders. The cards are listed below according to the numbers stamped on their white backs.

	NM	Ex
COMPLETE SET (12)	20.00	8.00
88 Team Photo	4.00	1.60
89 Ruben Amaro	2.00	.80
90 Steve Barber	2.00	.80
91 Steve Hamilton	2.00	.80
92 Bill Monbonquette	2.00	.80
93 Hal Reniff	2.00	.80
94 Tom Shopay	2.00	.80
95 Charlie Smith	2.00	.80
96 Thad Tillotson	2.00	.80
97 Dooley Womack	2.00	.80
98 Yankee Stadium	4.00	1.60
99 Jerry Coleman ANN	2.50	1.00

1968 Yankees Photos SCFC

This 29-card set of the New York Yankees measures approximately 4" by 5" and features black-and-white player photos with white borders. The cards are listed below according to the numbers stamped on their white backs.

	NM	Ex
COMPLETE SET (29)	60.00	24.00
59 Ruben Amaro	2.00	.80
60 Stan Bahnsen	2.00	.80
61 Steve Barber	2.00	.80
62 Horace Clarke	2.00	.80
63 Rocky Colavito	10.00	4.00
64 Al Downing	2.00	.80
65 Frank Fernandez	2.00	.80
66 Jake Gibbs	2.00	.80
67 Steve Hamilton	2.00	.80
68 Dick Howser	2.00	.80
69 Andy Kosco	2.00	.80
70 Lindy McDaniel	2.00	.80
71 Gene Michael	2.00	.80
72 Bill Monbouquette	2.00	.80
73 Joe Pepitone	3.00	1.20
74 Fritz Peterson (Autographed)	2.00	.80
75 Fritz Peterson (Closer Portrait)	2.00	.80
76 Bill Robinson	2.00	.80
77 Charlie Smith	2.00	.80
78 Fred Talbot	2.00	.80
79 Joe Verbanic	2.00	.80
80 Steve Whitaker	2.00	.80
81 Roy White	3.00	1.20
82 Dooley Womack	2.00	.80
83 Bobby Cox	8.00	3.20
84 Bill Dickey CO	4.00	1.60
85 Frank Fernandez	2.00	.80
86 Tom Tresh	3.00	1.20
87 Jim Turner CO	3.00	1.20

1969 Yankees Malanga

This 12-card set was issued in four strips of three cards each measuring approximately 8 1/2" by 3 3/4" and could be obtained from the artist. The fronts carry very crude black-and-white drawings of New York Yankee players by Rocco Malanga. The backs are blank. The cards are unnumbered and checklisted below in alphabetical order.

	NM	Ex
COMPLETE SET (12)	20.00	8.00
1 Horace Clarke	1.50	.60
2 Jake Gibbs	1.50	.60
3 Steve Hamilton UER (misspelled Hamiltom)	1.50	.60
4 Ralph Houk MG	2.00	.80
5 Mickey Mantle	10.00	4.00
6 Joe Pepitone	2.50	1.00
7 Bill Robinson	1.50	.60
8 Mel Stottemyre UER (misspelled Stottlemyre)	2.50	1.00
9 Fred Talbot	1.50	.60
10 Tom Tresh	2.50	1.00
11 Joe Verbanic	1.50	.60
12 Roy White	2.50	1.00

1969 Yankees Photos SCFC

This 22-card set of the New York Yankees measures approximately 4" by 5" and features black-and-white player photos with white borders. The cards are listed below according to the numbers stamped on their white backs.

	NM	Ex
COMPLETE SET (22)	25.00	10.00
37 Len Boehmer	1.50	.60
38 Bill Burbach	1.50	.60
39 Bobby Cox	3.00	1.20
40 Jimmie Hall	1.50	.60
41 Steve Hamilton	1.50	.60
42 Jack Kennedy	1.50	.60
43 Jerry Kenney	1.50	.60
44 Lindy McDaniel	1.50	.60
45 Bobby Murcer	3.00	1.20
46 Joe Pepitone	2.50	1.00
47 Fritz Peterson	1.50	.60
48 Bill Robinson	1.50	.60
49 Dick Simpson	1.50	.60
50 Mel Stottlemyre	2.50	1.00
51 Fred Talbot	1.50	.60
52 Joe Verbanic	1.50	.60
53 Ron Woods	1.50	.60
54 Jack Aker	1.50	.60
55 Horace Clarke	1.50	.60
56 Billy Cowan	1.50	.60
57 John Ellis	1.50	.60
58 Mike Kekich	1.50	.60

1970 Yankees Clinic Day Postcards

During the 1970 season, The New York Yankees had a promotion where fans could meet their favorite players before a game. These postcards were issued so the fans could have something to sign. These cards are sequenced in order of the player's appearance. Some cards are known to be in much shorter supply. The card of Roy White is extremely difficult since the game was rained out. The Murcer card was issued early in the season is difficult as well. Both cards are noted with a SP in the listings.

	NM	Ex
COMPLETE SET	50.00	20.00
COMMON CARD	1.00	.40
COMMON SP	5.00	2.00
1 Bobby Murcer SP	5.00	2.00
2 Roy White SP	25.00	10.00
3 Curt Blefary	1.00	.40
4 Fritz Peterson	1.00	.40
5 Danny Cater	1.00	.40
6 Horace Clarke	1.00	.40
7 Gene Michael	1.00	.40
8 Stan Bahnsen	1.00	.40
9 Thurman Munson	10.00	4.00
10 John Ellis	1.00	.40
11 Jerry Kenney	1.00	.40
12 Mel Stottlemyre	1.50	.60
13 Joe DiMaggio / Mickey Mantle	10.00	4.00

1970 Yankees Photos SCFC

This 36-card set of the New York Yankees measures approximately 4" by 5" and features black-and-white player photos with white borders. The cards are listed below according to the numbers stamped on their white backs.

	NM	Ex
COMPLETE SET (36)	50.00	20.00
1 Jack Aker	1.50	.60
2 Stan Bahnsen	1.50	.60
3 Frank Baker	1.50	.60
4 Curt Blefary	1.50	.60
5 Ron Blomberg	1.50	.60
6 Bill Burbach	1.50	.60
7 Danny Cater	1.50	.60
8 Horace Clarke	1.50	.60
9 John Cumberland	1.50	.60
10 John Ellis	1.50	.60
11 Jake Gibbs	1.50	.60
12 Steve Hamilton	1.50	.60
13 Ron Hansen	1.50	.60
14 Mike Hegan	1.50	.60
15 Ralph Houk MG	1.50	.60
16 Elston Howard CO	2.50	1.00
17 Dick Howser CO	1.50	.60
18 Mike Kekich	1.50	.60
19 Jerry Kenney	1.50	.60
20 Ron Klimkowski	1.50	.60
21 Steve Kline	1.50	.60
22 Jim Lyttle	1.50	.60
23 Mickey Mantle CO	10.00	4.00
24 Mike McCormick	1.50	.60
25 Lindy McDaniel	1.50	.60
26 Gene Michael	2.00	.80
27 Thurman Munson	5.00	2.00
28 Bobby Murcer	2.50	1.00
29 Fritz Peterson	1.50	.60
30 Mel Stottlemyre	2.50	1.00
31 Frank Tepedino	2.00	.80
32 Joe Verbanic	1.50	.60
33 Pete Ward	1.50	.60
34 Gary Waslewski	1.50	.60
35 Roy White	2.00	.80
36 Ron Woods	1.50	.60

1971 Yankees Arco Oil

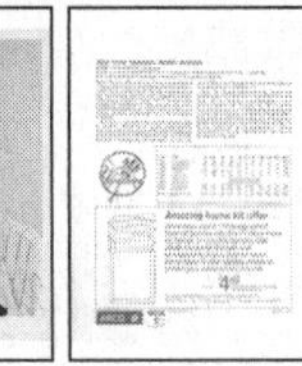

Sponsored by Arco Oil, these 12 pictures of the 1971 New York Yankees measure approximately 8" by 10" and feature on their fronts white-bordered posed color player photos. The player's name is shown in black lettering within the white margin below the photo. His facsimile autograph appears across the picture. The white back carries the team's and player's names at the top, followed below by position, biography, career highlights, and statistics. An ad at the bottom for picture frames rounds out the back. The cards are unnumbered and checklisted below in alphabetical order.

	NM	Ex
COMPLETE SET (12)	50.00	20.00
1 Jack Aker	4.00	1.60
2 Stan Bahnsen	4.00	1.60
3 Frank Baker	4.00	1.60
4 Danny Cater	4.00	1.60
5 Horace Clarke	6.00	2.40
6 John Ellis	4.00	1.60
7 Gene Michael	6.00	2.40
8 Thurman Munson	12.00	4.80
9 Bobby Murcer	8.00	3.20
10 Fritz Peterson	4.00	1.60
11 Mel Stottlemyre	8.00	3.20
12 Roy White	6.00	2.40

1971 Yankee Clinic Day Postcards

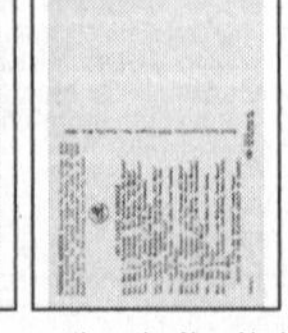

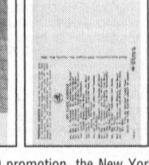

Similar to the 1970 promotion, the New York Yankees again had days where the fans could meet their favorite players before selected home games. These cards were issued so fans could have an item for the player to sign. We have sequenced this set in alphabetical order. These postcards were produced by Dexter Press.

	NM	Ex
COMPLETE SET (16)	50.00	20.00
1 Stan Bahnsen	1.00	.40
2 Curt Blefary	1.00	.40
3 Danny Cater	1.00	.40
4 Horace Clarke / Gene Michael	1.00	.40
5 John Ellis	1.00	.40
6 Jake Gibbs	1.00	.40
7 Ralph Houk MG	1.00	.40
8 Jerry Kenney / Frank Baker	1.00	.40
9 Jim Lyttle / Felipe Alou	1.00	.40
10 Mickey Mantle	25.00	10.00
11 Lindy McDaniel	1.00	.40
12 Thurman Munson	10.00	4.00
13 Bobby Murcer	3.00	1.20
14 Fritz Peterson	1.00	.40
15 Mel Stottlemyre	2.00	.80
16 Roy White	3.00	1.20

1972 Yankees Schedules

This eight card set was issued in very limited quantities. These cards have 1972 Yankees schedules on the back and are very difficult to obtain. These cards are unnumbered and we have sequenced them in alphabetical order.

	NM	Ex
COMPLETE SET (8)	600.00	240.00
1 Felipe Alou	100.00	40.00
2 Ron Blomberg	25.00	10.00
3 Thurman Munson	200.00	80.00
4 Bobby Murcer	100.00	40.00
5 Mel Stottlemyre	75.00	30.00
6 Ron Swoboda	50.00	20.00
7 Roy White	75.00	30.00
8 Bill White ANN / Phil Rizzuto / Frank Messer	100.00	40.00

1972 Yankees Team Issue

This six-card set of the 1972 New York Yankees measures approximately 4" by 6" and features color player photos with white borders. The backs are blank. The cards are unnumbered and checklisted below in alphabetical order.

	NM	Ex
COMPLETE SET (6)	25.00	10.00
1 Danny Cater	3.00	1.20
2 John Ellis	3.00	1.20
3 Thurman Munson	10.00	4.00
4 Bobby Murcer	5.00	2.00
5 Fritz Peterson	3.00	1.20
6 Roy White	5.00	2.00

1973 Yankees Team Issue

This six-card set of the New York Yankees measures approximately 7" by 8 3/4" and features color player photos in a white border. The player's name and team are printed in the wide bottom margin. The backs are blank. The cards are unnumbered and checklisted in alphabetical order.

	NM	Ex
COMPLETE SET (6)	25.00	10.00
1 Ron Blomberg	3.00	1.20
2 Sparky Lyle	5.00	2.00
3 Bobby Murcer	5.00	2.00
4 Graig Nettles	5.00	2.00
5 Fritz Peterson	3.00	1.20
6 Roy White	4.00	1.60

1975 Yankees 1927 TCMA

This 29-card set of the 1927 New York Yankees features black-and-white player photos in white borders. The backs carry player information and statistics. The cards are unnumbered and checklisted below in alphabetical order.

	NM	Ex
COMPLETE SET (29)	50.00	20.00
1 Walter Beall	1.00	.40
2 Benny Bengough	1.50	.60
3 Pat Collins	1.00	.40
4 Earle Combs	2.50	1.00
5 Joe Dugan	1.00	.40
6 Cedric Durst	1.00	.40
7 Mike Gazella	1.00	.40
8 Lou Gehrig	5.00	2.00
9 Joe Giard	1.00	.40
10 Johnny Grabowski	1.00	.40
11 Waite Hoyt	2.50	1.00
12 Miller Huggins MG	2.50	1.00
13 Mark Koenig	1.50	.60
14 Tony Lazzeri	2.50	1.00
15 Bob Meusel	2.00	.80
16 Wiley Moore	1.00	.40
17 Ray Morehart	1.00	.40
18 Ben Paschal	1.00	.40
19 Herb Pennock	2.50	1.00
20 George Pipgras	1.00	.40
21 Dutch Ruether	1.00	.40
22 Jacob Ruppert OWN	1.50	.60
23 Babe Ruth	8.00	3.20
24 Bob Shawkey	1.50	.60
25 Urban Shocker	1.00	.40
26 Myles Thomas	1.00	.40
27 Julie Wera	1.00	.40
28 Yankee Stadium	1.00	.40
29 Miller Huggins MG / Charlie O'Leary CO / Art Fletcher CO	1.50	.60
30 Lou Gehrig / Tony Lazzeri / Mark Koenig / Joe Dugan / Card measures 3 1/2" by 5"	3.00	1.20

1975 Yankees All-Time Team TCMA

This 12-card set features blue-and-white player photos of all-time great New York Yankees and measures approximately 2 1/2" by 3 3/4". The backs carry the checklist of the set. The cards are unnumbered and checklisted below in alphabetical order.

	NM	Ex
COMPLETE SET (12)	25.00	10.00
1 Bill Dickey	2.50	1.00
2 Joe DiMaggio	5.00	2.00
3 Whitey Ford	2.50	1.00
4 Lou Gehrig	5.00	2.00
5 Tony Lazzeri	2.50	1.00
6 Mickey Mantle	5.00	2.00
7 Johnny Murphy	1.00	.40
8 Phil Rizzuto	2.50	1.00
9 Red Rolfe	1.00	.40
10 Red Ruffing	2.00	.80
11 Babe Ruth	8.00	3.20
12 Casey Stengel MG	2.50	1.00

1975 Yankees Dynasty 1936-39 TCMA

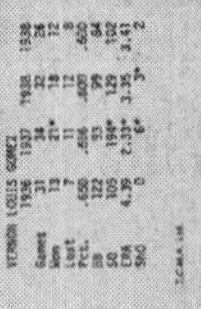

The first 49 cards in this set measure 2 3/4" by 4" and feature black-and-white player photos with white borders. The last five cards are 4" by 5 1/2" and feature photos of Yankees from 1936-39. The player's name and position are printed in blue below the picture. The phrase "1936-1939 Yankee Dynasty" is at the top except for card numbers 50-53, which have "World Champions -- 19XX" printed at the top. The backs carry statistics printed in blue. The cards are unnumbered and checklisted below in alphabetical order.

	NM	Ex
COMPLETE SET (55)	40.00	16.00
1 Ivy Paul Andrews	.50	.20
2 Joe Beggs	.50	.20
3 Marv Breuer	.50	.20
4 Johnny Broaca	.50	.20
5 Jumbo Brown	.50	.20
6 Spud Chandler	.75	.30
7 Ben Chapman	.50	.20
8 Earl Combs CO	1.50	.60
9 Frankie Crosetti	1.00	.40
10 Babe Dahlgren	.50	.20
11 Joe DiMaggio	6.00	2.40
12 Bill Dickey	1.50	.60
13 Atley Donald	.50	.20
14 Wes Farrell	.75	.30
15 Artie Fletcher CO	.50	.20
16 Lou Gehrig	6.00	2.40
17 Joe Glenn	.50	.20
18 Lefty Gomez	1.50	.60
19 Joe Gordon	1.00	.40
20 Bump Hadley	.50	.20
21 Don Heffner	.50	.20
22 Tommy Henrich	1.00	.40
23 Oral Hildebrand	.50	.20
24 Myril Hoag	.50	.20

25 Roy Johnson .50 .20
26 Art Jorgens .50 .20
27 Charlie Keller .75 .30
28 Ted Kleinhans .50 .20
29 Billy Knickerbocker .50 .20
30 Tony Lazzeri 1.50 .60
31 Frank Makosky .50 .20
32 Pat Malone .50 .20
33 Joe McCarthy MG 1.00 .40
Jacob Ruppert OWN
34 Johnny Murphy .75 .30
35 Monty Pearson .50 .20
36 Jake Powell .50 .20
37 Red Rolfe .75 .30
38 Buddy Rosar .50 .20
39 Red Ruffing 1.50 .60
40 Marius Russo .50 .20
41 Jack Saltzgaver .50 .20
42 Paul Schreiber .50 .20
43 Johnny Schulte .50 .20
44 Bob Seeds .50 .20
45 Twinkletoes Selkirk .75 .30
46 Steve Sundra .50 .20
47 Sandy Vance .50 .20
48 Dixie Walker .75 .30
49 Kemp Wicker .50 .20
50 World Champions 1936 4.00 1.60
(Team celebrating)
51 World Champions 1937 4.00 1.60
Joe DiMaggio
Frankie Crosetti
Tony Lazzeri
Bill Dickey
Lou Gehrig
Jake Powell
Twinkletoes Selkirk
52 World Champions 1938 1.50 .60
Red Rolfe
Tony Lazzeri
Lou Gehrig
Frankie Crosetti
53 World Champions 1939 4.00 1.60
Lou Gehrig
Joe DiMaggio
54 Lou Gehrig Hits Another 4.00 1.60

1975 Yankees SSPC

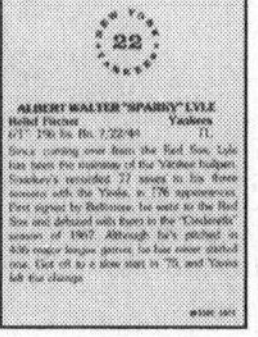

This 23-card standard-size set of New York Yankees features white-bordered posed color player photos on their fronts, which are free of any other markings. The white back carries the player's name in red lettering above his blue-lettered biography and career highlights. The cards are numbered on the back within a circle formed by the player's team name. A similar set of New York Mets was produced at the same time. This set is dated 1975 because that was Ed Brinkman's only season with the Yankees.

	NM	Ex
COMPLETE SET (23)	18.00	7.25
1 Jim Hunter	4.00	1.60
2 Bobby Bonds	1.00	.40
3 Ed Brinkman	.25	.10
4 Ron Blomberg	.50	.20
5 Thurman Munson	5.00	2.00
6 Roy White	.75	.30
7 Larry Gura	.25	.10
8 Ed Herrmann	.25	.10
9 Bill Virdon MG	.50	.20
10 Elliott Maddox	.25	.10
11 Lou Piniella	1.00	.40
12 Rick Dempsey	.75	.30
13 Fred Stanley	.25	.10
14 Chris Chambliss	1.00	.40
15 George Medich	.25	.10
16 Pat Dobson	.50	.20
17 Alex Johnson	.50	.20
18 Jim Mason	.25	.10
19 Sandy Alomar	.25	.10
20 Graig Nettles	1.00	.40
21 Walt Williams	.25	.10
22 Sparky Lyle	.75	.30
23 Dick Tidrow	.25	.10

1977 Yankees Burger King

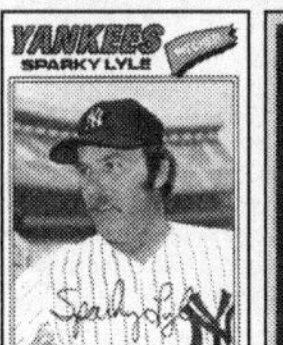

The cards in this 24-card set measure 2 1/2" by 3 1/2". The cards in this set marked with an asterisk have different poses than those cards in the regular 1977 Topps set. The checklist card is unnumbered and the Piniella card was issued subsequent to the original printing. The complete set price below refers to all 24 cards listed, including Piniella.

	NM	Ex
COMPLETE SET (24)	40.00	16.00
1 Yankees Team	1.00	.40
Billy Martin MG		
2 Thurman Munson* UER	8.00	3.20
Facsimile autograph misspelled		
3 Fran Healy	.25	.10
4 Jim Hunter	2.50	1.00
5 Ed Figueroa	.25	.10
6 Don Gullett*	.50	.20
Mouth closed		
7 Mike Torrez*	.50	.20
Shown as A's in 1977 Topps		
8 Ken Holtzman	.50	.20
9 Dick Tidrow	.25	.10
10 Sparky Lyle	.50	.20
11 Ron Guidry	.75	.30
12 Chris Chambliss	.50	.20
13 Willie Randolph*	.75	.30
No rookie trophy		
14 Bucky Dent*	.50	.20
Shown as White Sox in 1977 Topps		
15 Graig Nettles*	1.00	.40
Closer photo than in 1977 Topps		
16 Fred Stanley	.25	.10
17 Reggie Jackson*	12.00	4.80
Looking up with bat		
18 Mickey Rivers	.50	.20
19 Roy White	.50	.20
20 Jim Wynn*	.75	.30
Shown as Brave in 1977 Topps		
21 Paul Blair*	.75	.30
Shown as Oriole in 1977 Topps		
22 Carlos May *	.50	.20
(Shown as White Sox in 1977 Topps)		
23 Lou Piniella SP	20.00	8.00
NNO Checklist Card TP	.25	.10

1978 Yankees Burger King

The cards in this 23-card set measure 2 1/2" by 3 1/2". These cards were distributed in packs of three players plus a checklist at Burger King's New York area outlets. Cards with an asterisk have different poses than those in the Topps regular issue.

	NM	Ex
COMPLETE SET (23)	12.00	4.80
1 Billy Martin MG	1.00	.40
2 Thurman Munson	4.00	1.60
3 Cliff Johnson	.25	.10
4 Ron Guidry	1.00	.40
5 Ed Figueroa	.25	.10
6 Dick Tidrow	.25	.10
7 Jim Hunter	2.50	1.00
8 Don Gullett	.25	.10
9 Sparky Lyle	.75	.30
10 Goose Gossage *	1.00	.40
11 Rawly Eastwick *	.25	.10
12 Chris Chambliss	.75	.30
13 Willie Randolph	.75	.30
14 Graig Nettles	1.00	.40
15 Bucky Dent	.75	.30
16 Jim Spencer *	.25	.10
17 Fred Stanley	.25	.10
18 Lou Piniella	1.00	.40
19 Roy White	.75	.30
20 Mickey Rivers	.75	.30
21 Reggie Jackson	4.00	1.60
22 Paul Blair	.25	.10
NNO Checklist Card TP	.15	.06

1978 Yankees Photo Album

This 27-card set of the New York Yankees measures approximately 8" square and features a color player portrait in a white border with a facsimile autograph. The backs are blank. The cards are unnumbered and checklisted below in alphabetical order.

	NM	Ex
COMPLETE SET (27)	15.00	6.00
1 Jim Beattie	.25	.10
Brian Doyle		
Paul Lindblad		
Larry McCall		
Andy Messersmith		
2 Yogi Berra CO	1.00	.40
Art Fowler CO		
Elston Howard CO		
Dick Howser CO		
Gene Michael CO		
3 Paul Blair	.25	.10
4 Chris Chambliss	.75	.30
5 Kenny Clay	.25	.10
6 Bucky Dent	.75	.30
7 Ed Figueroa	.25	.10
8 Goose(Rich) Gossage	1.00	.40
9 Ron Guidry	1.00	.40
10 Don Gullett	.50	.20
11 Mike Heath	.25	.10
12 Catfish(Jim) Hunter	1.50	.60
13 Reggie Jackson	4.00	1.60
14 Cliff Johnson	.25	.10
15 Jay Johnstone	.50	.20
16 Bob Lemon MG	1.00	.40
17 Sparky Lyle	.50	.20
18 Thurman Munson	2.00	.80
19 Graig Nettles	1.00	.40
20 Lou Piniella	1.00	.40
21 Willie Randolph	.75	.30
22 Mickey Rivers	.50	.20
23 Jim Spencer	.25	.10
24 Fred Stanley	.25	.10
25 Gary Thomasson	.25	.10
26 Dick Tidrow	.25	.10
27 Roy White	.50	.20

1978 Yankees SSPC Diary

This 27 card standard-size set was inserted into the 1978 Yankees Yearbook and Diary of a Champion Yankee. These cards are full bleed and the backs have 1977 seasonal highlights.

	NM	Ex
COMPLETE SET (27)	10.00	4.00
1 Thurman Munson	3.00	1.20
2 Cliff Johnson	.10	.04
3 Lou Piniella	.75	.30
4 Dell Alston	.10	.04
5 Yankee Stadium	.10	.04
6 Ken Holtzman	.10	.04
7 Chris Chambliss	.25	.10
8 Roy White	.10	.04
9 Ed Figueroa	.10	.04
10 Dick Tidrow	.10	.04
11 Sparky Lyle	.25	.10
12 Fred Stanley	.10	.04
13 Mickey Rivers	.10	.04
14 Billy Martin MG	.25	.10
15 George Zeber	.10	.04
16 Ken Clay	.10	.04
17 Ron Guidry	.75	.30
18 Don Gullett	.10	.04
19 Fran Healy	.10	.04
20 Paul Blair	.10	.04
21 Mickey Klutts	.10	.04
22 Yankee Team	.10	.04
23 Catfish Hunter	2.00	.80
24 Bucky Dent	.25	.10
25 Graig Nettles	.75	.30
26 Reggie Jackson	3.00	1.20
27 Willie Randolph	.75	.30

1979 Yankees Burger King

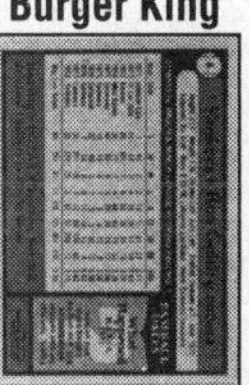

The cards in this 23-card set measure 2 1/2" by 3 1/2". There are 22 numbered cards and one unnumbered checklist in the 1979 Burger King Yankee set. The poses of Guidry, Tiant, John and Beniquez, each marked with an asterisk below, are different from their poses appearing in the regular Topps issue. The team card has the team leaders noted on the back.

	NM	Ex
COMPLETE SET (23)	12.00	4.80
1 Yankees Team:	1.00	.40
Bob Lemon MG		
2 Thurman Munson	4.00	1.60
3 Cliff Johnson	.25	.10
4 Ron Guidry*	.75	.30
Photo is from the 1979 Topps Record Breaker card		
5 Jay Johnstone	.50	.20
6 Jim Hunter	2.50	1.00
7 Jim Beattie	.25	.10
8 Luis Tiant *	1.00	.40
(Shown as Red Sox in 1979 Topps)		
9 Tommy John *	1.00	.40
(Shown as Dodgers in 1979 Topps)		
10 Goose Gossage	1.00	.40
11 Ed Figueroa	.25	.10
12 Chris Chambliss	.75	.30
13 Willie Randolph	1.00	.40
14 Bucky Dent	.75	.30
15 Graig Nettles	1.00	.40
16 Fred Stanley	.25	.10
17 Jim Spencer	.25	.10
18 Lou Piniella	1.00	.40
19 Roy White	.75	.30
20 Mickey Rivers	.75	.30
21 Reggie Jackson	4.00	1.60
22 Juan Beniquez *	.50	.20
Shown as Rangers in 1979 Topps		
NNO Checklist Card TP	.15	.06

1979 Yankees 1927 TCMA

This 32-card set features sepia tone pictures of the 1927 New York Yankees team. The fronts feature the player photo while the back has information about the featured player.

	NM	Ex
COMPLETE SET (32)	20.00	8.00
1 Babe Ruth	8.00	3.20
2 Lou Gehrig	5.00	2.00
3 Tony Lazzeri	1.00	.40
4 Mark Koenig	.50	.20
5 Julie Wera	.25	.10
6 Ray Morehart	.25	.10
7 Art Fletcher CO	.25	.10
8 Joe Dugan	.50	.20
9 Charlie O'Leary CO	.25	.10
10 Bob Meusel	.75	.30
11 Earle Combs	1.00	.40
12 Cedric Durst	.25	.10
13 John Grabowski	.25	.10
14 Mike Gazella	.25	.10
15 Pat Collins	.25	.10
16 Waite Hoyt	1.00	.40
17 Myles Thomas	.25	.10
18 Benny Bengough	.50	.20
19 Herb Pennock	1.00	.40
20 Wilcy Moore	.25	.10
21 Urban Shocker	.25	.10
22 Dutch Reuther	.25	.10
23 George Pipgras	.25	.10
24 Jacob Ruppert OWN	.50	.20
25 Eddie Bennett BB	.25	.10
26 Ed Barrow GM	.50	.20
27 Ben Paschal	.25	.10
28 Miller Huggins MG	1.00	.40
29 Joe Giard	.25	.10
30 Bob Shawkey	.50	.20
31 Walter Beall	.25	.10
32 Don Miller	.25	.10

1979 Yankees Picture Album

This 32-page Picture Album of the 1979 New York Yankees measures approximately 8" by 8" and features posed color player photos in white borders with a facsimile autograph across the bottom. The backs are blank. The cards are unnumbered and checklisted below in alphabetical order.

	NM	Ex
COMPLETE SET (34)	20.00	8.00
1 Jim Beattie	.50	.20
2 Juan Beniquez	.25	.10
3 Yogi Berra CO	2.00	.80
4 Bobby Brown	.25	.10
5 Ray Burris	.25	.10
6 Chris Chambliss	.50	.20
7 Ken Clay	.25	.10
8 Ron Davis	.25	.10
9 Bucky Dent	.50	.20
10 Brian Doyle	.25	.10
11 Mike Ferraro	.25	.10
12 Ed Figueroa	.25	.10
13 Art Fowler CO	.25	.10
14 Goose Gossage	1.00	.40
15 Ron Guidry	1.00	.40
16 Don Gullett	.25	.10
17 Jim Hegan CO	.25	.10
18 Don Hood	.25	.10
19 Jim Hunter	1.25	.50
20 Reggie Jackson	3.00	1.20
21 Tommy John	1.00	.40
22 Jim Kaat	.75	.30
23 Charley Lau CO	.25	.10
24 Billy Martin MG	1.00	.40
25 Thurman Munson	2.00	.80
26 Bobby Murcer	.75	.30
27 Jerry Narron	.25	.10
28 Graig Nettles	1.00	.40
29 Lou Piniella	.75	.30
30 Willie Randolph	1.00	.40
31 Jim Spencer	.25	.10
32 Fred Stanley	.25	.10
33 Luis Tiant	.75	.30
34 Roy White	.50	.20

1980 Yankees Greats TCMA

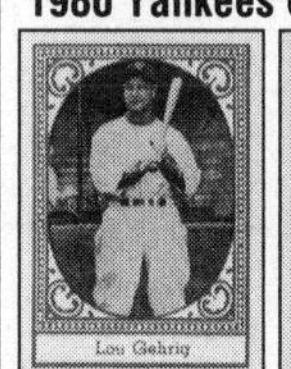
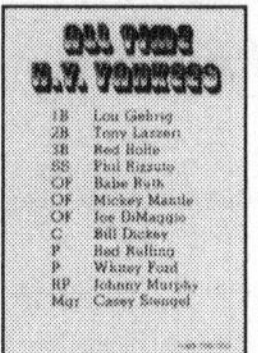

These 12 standard-size cards feature all-time Yankee greats. The fronts have a player photo and the backs display a checklist of who is in the set.

	NM	Ex
COMPLETE SET (12)	10.00	4.00
1 Lou Gehrig	2.50	1.00
2 Tony Lazzeri	.50	.20
3 Red Rolfe	.25	.10
4 Phil Rizzuto	1.00	.40
5 Babe Ruth	3.00	1.20
6 Mickey Mantle	3.00	1.20
7 Joe DiMaggio	2.50	1.00
8 Bill Dickey	.75	.30
9 Red Ruffing	.75	.30
10 Whitey Ford	1.00	.40
11 Johnny Murphy	.25	.10
12 Casey Stengel MG	.75	.30

1980 Yankees Photo Album

This 27-card set of the New York Yankees was distributed in a booklet measuring approximately 8" by 7 7/8". The fronts feature a color player portrait in a white border with a facsimile autograph. The backs are blank. The cards are unnumbered and checklisted below in alphabetical order.

	NM	Ex
COMPLETE SET (27)	12.00	4.80
1 Yogi Berra CO	1.00	.40
Mike Ferraro CO		
Jim Hegan CO		
Charley Lau CO		
Jeff Torborg CO		
Stan Williams CO		
2 Bobby Brown	.25	.10
3 Rick Cerone	.25	.10
4 Ron Davis	.25	.10
5 Bucky Dent	.75	.30
6 Ed Figueroa	.25	.10
7 Oscar Gamble	.50	.20
8 Goose(Rich) Gossage	1.00	.40
9 Ron Guidry	1.00	.40
10 Don Gullett	.25	.10
Johnny Oates		
11 Dick Howser MG	.25	.10
12 Reggie Jackson	2.00	.80
13 Tommy John	1.00	.40
14 Ruppert Jones	.25	.10
15 Joe Lefebvre	.25	.10
16 Rudy May	.25	.10
17 Bobby Murcer	1.00	.40
18 Graig Nettles	1.00	.40
19 Lou Piniella	1.00	.40
20 Willie Randolph	.75	.30
21 Eric Soderholm	.25	.10
22 Jim Spencer	.25	.10
23 Fred Stanley	.25	.10
24 Luis Tiant	.50	.20
25 Tom Underwood	.25	.10
26 Bob Watson	.50	.20
27 Dennis Werth	.25	.10

1981 Yankees Photo Album

This 26-card set of the New York Yankees was distributed in a booklet measuring approximately 8" square. The fronts feature a color player portrait in a white border with a facsimile autograph. The backs are blank. The cards are unnumbered and checklisted below in alphabetical order.

	Nm-Mt	Ex-Mt
COMPLETE SET (26)	15.00	6.00
1 Joe Altobelli CO	1.00	.40
Yogi Berra CO		
Mike Ferraro CO		
Clyde King CO		
Charley Lau CO		
Jeff Torborg CO		
2 Bobby Brown	.25	.10
3 Ron Davis	.25	.10
4 Bucky Dent	.75	.30
5 Barry Foote	.25	.10
6 Oscar Gamble	.50	.20
7 Goose(Rich) Gossage	1.00	.40
8 Ron Guidry	1.00	.40
9 Reggie Jackson	2.50	1.00
10 Tommy John	1.00	.40
11 Dave Laroche	.25	.10
12 Rudy May	.25	.10
13 Gene Michael MG	.25	.10
14 Larry Milbourne	.25	.10
15 Jerry Mumphrey	.25	.10
16 Bobby Murcer	1.00	.40
17 Gene Nelson	.25	.10
18 Graig Nettles	1.00	.40
19 Lou Piniella	1.00	.40
20 Willie Randolph	.75	.30
21 Rick Reuschel	.50	.20
22 Dave Revering	.25	.10
23 Dave Righetti	2.50	1.00
24 Aurelio Rodriguez	.25	.10
25 Bob Watson	.50	.20
26 Dave Winfield	2.50	1.00

1982 Yankees 1961 Black and White

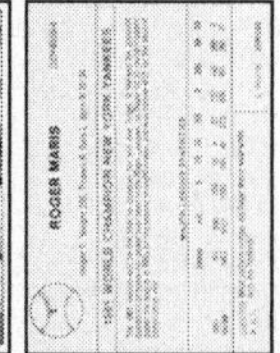

This 30-card set features black-and-white photos of the 1961 World Champion New York Yankees in white borders. The backs carry player information and career statistics. The last four cards are unnumbered and display photos of coaches. When placed together, the backs of these four cards form a blue-and-white photo of this championship team.

	Nm-Mt	Ex-Mt
COMPLETE SET (30)	8.00	3.20
1 Roger Maris	1.50	.60
2 Bobby Richardson	.50	.20
3 Tony Kubek	.50	.20
4 Elston Howard	.50	.20
5 Bill Skowron	.50	.20
6 Clete Boyer	.30	.12
7 Mickey Mantle	3.00	1.20
8 Yogi Berra	1.00	.40
9 Johnny Blanchard	.20	.08
10 Hector Lopez	.20	.08
11 Whitey Ford	1.50	.60
12 Ralph Terry	.20	.08
13 Bill Stafford	.10	.04
14 Bud Daley	.10	.04
15 Billy Gardner	.10	.04
16 Jim Coates	.10	.04
17 Luis Arroyo	.10	.04
18 Tex Clevenger	.10	.04
19 Bob Cerv	.10	.04
20 Art Ditmar	.10	.04

21 Bob Turley	.20	.08
22 Joe DeMaestri	.10	.04
23 Rollie Sheldon	.10	.04
24 Earl Torgeson	.10	.04
25 Hal Reniff	.10	.04
26 Ralph Houk MG	.20	.08
NNO Jim Hegan CO	.10	.04
NNO Wally Moses CO	.10	.04
NNO Johnny Sain CO	.20	.08
NNO Frank Crosetti CO	.20	.08

1982 Yankees 1961 Color

In addition to the black and white Yankees set Renata Galasso issued, they also issued a 37 card standard-size color set. The fronts have a player photo with the players name and position on the bottom and these are surrounded by white borders. The backs have some brief biographical information as well as an informational blurb and 1961 and career statistics.

	Nm-Mt	Ex-Mt
COMPLETE SET	20.00	8.00
1 Roger Maris	2.00	.80
2 Yogi Berra	1.50	.60
3 Whitey Ford	2.00	.80
4 Hector Lopez	.50	.20
5 Bob Turley	.50	.20
6 Frank Crosetti CO	.50	.20
7 Bob Cerv	.25	.10
8 Jack Reed	.25	.10
9 Luis Arroyo	.25	.10
10 Danny McDevitt	.25	.10
11 Duke Maas	.25	.10
12 Jesse Gonder	.25	.10
13 Ralph Terry	.50	.20
14 Deron Johnson	.25	.10
15 John Blanchard	.25	.10
16 Bill Stafford	.25	.10
17 Earl Torgeson	.25	.10
18 Tony Kubek	.75	.30
19 Rollie Sheldon	.25	.10
20 Tex Clevenger	.25	.10
21 Art Ditmar	.25	.10
22 Bud Daley	.25	.10
23 Jim Coates	.25	.10
24 Al Downing	.25	.10
25 Johnny Sain CO	.25	.10
26 Jim Hegan CO	.25	.10
27 Wally Moses CO	.25	.10
28 Ralph Houk MG	.25	.10
29 Bill Skowron	.75	.30
30 Bobby Richardson	1.00	.40
31 Johnny James	.25	.10
32 Hal Reniff	.25	.10
33 Mickey Mantle	4.00	1.60
34 Clete Boyer	.50	.20
35 Elston Howard	1.00	.40
36 Joe DeMaestri	.25	.10
37 Billy Gardner	.25	.10

1982 Yankees Photo Album

This 27-card set of the New York Yankees was distributed in a booklet measuring approximately 7 7/8" square. The fronts feature a color player portrait in a white border with a facsimile autograph. The backs are blank. The cards are unnumbered and checklisted below in alphabetical order.

	Nm-Mt	Ex-Mt
COMPLETE SET (27)	12.00	4.80
1 Doyle Alexander	.25	.10
Roger Erickson		
Barry Foote		
Dave LaRoche		
2 Joe Altobelli CO	1.00	.40
Yogi Berra CO		
Mike Ferraro CO		
Clyde King CO		
Joe Pepitone CO		
Jeff Torborg CO		
3 Rick Cerone	.25	.10
4 Dave Collins	.25	.10
5 Bucky Dent	.75	.30
6 George Frazier	.25	.10
7 Oscar Gamble	.50	.20
8 Goose(Rich) Gossage	1.00	.40
9 Ken Griffey	.50	.20
10 Ron Guidry	1.00	.40
11 Butch Hobson	.25	.10
12 Tommy John	1.00	.40
13 Rudy May	.25	.10
14 John Mayberry	.25	.10
15 Gene Michael MG	.25	.10
16 Mike Morgan	.25	.10
17 Jerry Mumphrey	.25	.10
18 Bobby Murcer	1.00	.40
19 Graig Nettles	1.00	.40
20 Lou Piniella	1.00	.40
21 Willie Randolph	.75	.30
22 Shane Rawley	.25	.10
23 Dave Righetti	1.00	.40
24 Andre Robertson	.25	.10
25 Roy Smalley	.25	.10
26 Dave Winfield	2.00	.80
27 Butch Wynegar	.25	.10

1983 Yankees A-S Fifty Years

With the great New York Yankee tradition, this set commemorates the first 50 years of Yankee All-Stars. Other than the Mickey Mantle checklist card, this set is sequenced in alphabetical order.

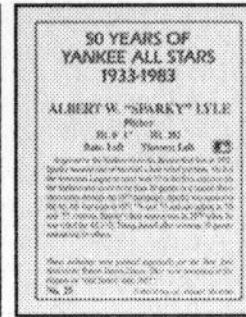

	Nm-Mt	Ex-Mt
COMPLETE SET (50)	12.50	5.00
1 Mickey Mantle CL	.75	.30
2 Luis Arroyo	.10	.04
3 Hank Bauer	.25	.10
4 Yogi Berra	.75	.30
5 Tommy Byrne	.10	.04
6 Spud Chandler	.10	.04
7 Ben Chapman	.10	.04
8 Jim Coates	.10	.04
9 Bill Dickey	.75	.30
10 Joe DiMaggio	1.50	.60
11 Al Downing	.10	.04
12 Ryne Duren	.10	.04
13 Whitey Ford PORT	.75	.30
14 Whitey Ford PIT	.75	.30
15 Lou Gehrig	1.50	.60
16 Lefty Gomez	.75	.30
17 Bob Grim	.10	.04
18 Tommy Henrich	.50	.20
20 Catfish Hunter	.75	.30
21 Billy Johnson	.10	.04
22 Charlie Keller	.25	.10
23 Johnny Kucks	.10	.04
24 Eddie Lopat	.25	.10
25 Sparky Lyle	.25	.10
26 Mickey Mantle	2.00	.80
27 Roger Maris	1.25	.50
28 Billy Martin	.75	.30
29 Johnny Mize	.75	.30
30 Bobby Murcer	.50	.20
31 Irv Noren	.10	.04
32 Joe Pepitone	.50	.20
33 Fritz Peterson	.10	.04
34 Vic Raschi	.10	.04
35 Allie Reynolds	.25	.10
36 Bobby Richardson	.50	.20
37 Phil Rizzuto	.75	.30
38 Marius Russo	.10	.04
40 Johnny Sain	.50	.20
41 George Selkirk	.10	.04
42 Bobby Shantz	.10	.04
43 Spec Shea	.10	.04
44 Moose Skowron	.50	.20
45 Casey Stengel	.75	.30
46 Mel Stottlemyre	.25	.10
47 Ralph Terry	.10	.04
48 Tom Tresh	.10	.04
49 Bob Turley	.10	.04
50 Roy White	.10	.04

1983 Yankees Photo Album

This 27-card set of the New York Yankees was sponsored by the New York Bus Service, the Bronx-Manhattan Express, and was distributed in a booklet measuring approximately 7 7/8" square. The fronts feature color player portraits in white borders with a facsimile autograph. The backs are blank. The cards are unnumbered and checklisted below in alphabetical order.

	Nm-Mt	Ex-Mt
COMPLETE SET (27)	12.00	4.80
1 Steve Balboni	4.00	1.60
Ray Fontenot		
Don Mattingly		
Bobby Meacham		
2 Don Baylor	.50	.20
3 Yogi Berra CO	1.00	.40
Sam Ellis CO		
Jeff Torborg CO		
Lee Walls CO		
Roy White CO		
Don Zimmer CO		
4 Bert Campaneris	.50	.20
5 Rick Cerone	.25	.10
6 George Frazier	.25	.10
7 Oscar Gamble	.50	.20
8 Goose Gossage	1.00	.40
9 Ken Griffey	.50	.20
10 Ron Guidry	1.00	.40
11 Jay Howell	.25	.10
12 Steve Kemp	.25	.10
13 Matt Keough	.25	.10
14 Billy Martin MG	.75	.30
15 Rudy May	.25	.10
16 Jerry Mumphrey	.25	.10
17 Dale Murray	.25	.10
18 Graig Nettles	1.00	.40
19 Lou Piniella	1.00	.40
20 Willie Randolph	.75	.30
21 Shane Rawley	.25	.10
22 Dave Righetti	.75	.30
23 Andre Robertson	.25	.10
24 Bob Shirley	.25	.10
25 Roy Smalley	.25	.10
26 David Winfield	1.00	.40
27 Butch Wynegar	.25	.10

1983 Yankee Yearbook Insert TCMA

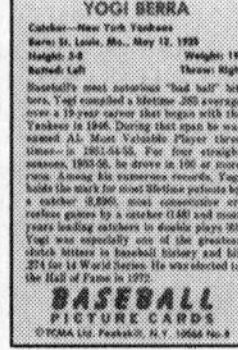

Subtitled Baseball Picture Cards, this uncut sheet produced by TCMA features 18 American League players of the past (nine Yankees and nine from other AL teams) and measures approximately 16 1/2" by 10 7/8". If cut into singles, each card would measure the standard size. The fronts feature white-bordered color drawings of the players. The player's name appears in white lettering within a black rectangle near the bottom. The back carries the player's name in red lettering at the top, followed below by biography and career highlights.

	Nm-Mt	Ex-Mt
COMPLETE SET (18)	10.00	4.00
1 Joe DiMaggio	2.50	1.00
2 Billy Pierce	.50	.20
3 Phil Rizzuto	1.00	.40
4 Ted Williams	2.50	1.00
5 Billy Martin	.75	.30
6 Mel Parnell	.25	.10
7 Harmon Killebrew	1.00	.40
8 Yogi Berra	1.00	.40
9 Roy Sievers	.25	.10
10 Bill Dickey	.75	.30
11 Hank Greenberg	.75	.30
12 Allie Reynolds	.50	.20
13 Joe Sewell	.75	.30
14 Virgil Trucks	.25	.10
15 Mickey Mantle	3.00	1.20
16 Boog Powell	.50	.20
17 Whitey Ford	1.50	.60
18 Lou Boudreau	.75	.30

1984 Yankees 1927 Galasso

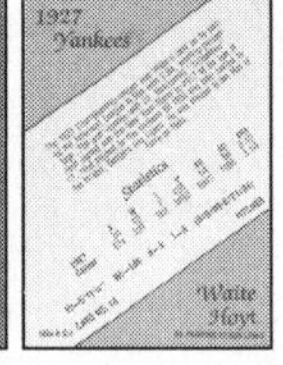

This 30-card set features replicas of oil paintings of the 1927 New York Yankees in blue borders by artist Ron Lewis. The backs carry player information and career statistics.

	Nm-Mt	Ex-Mt
COMPLETE SET (30)	8.00	3.20
1 Lou Gehrig	2.00	.80
2 Babe Ruth	3.00	1.20
3 Earle Combs	.50	.20
4 Ed Barrow GM	.20	.08
5 Bob Shawkey	.30	.12
6 Bob Meusel	.30	.12
7 Urban Shocker	.20	.08
8 Ben Paschal	.10	.04
9 John Grabowski	.10	.04
10 Jacob Ruppert OWN	.20	.08
11 Herb Pennock	.50	.20
12 Miller Huggins MG	.50	.20
13 Wiley Moore	.20	.08
14 Walter Beall	.10	.04
15 Cedric Durst	.10	.04
16 Tony Lazzeri	.50	.20
17 Mark Koenig	.20	.08
18 Waite Hoyt	.50	.20
19 Myles Thomas	.10	.04
20 Joe Dugan	.30	.12
21 Art Fletcher CO	.10	.04
22 Charlie O'Leary CO	.10	.04
23 Ray Morehart	.10	.04
24 Benny Bengough	.20	.08
25 Pat Collins	.10	.04
26 Dutch Ruether	.10	.04
27 George Pipgras	.10	.04
28 Mike Gazella	.10	.04
29 Julian Wera	.10	.04
30 Joe Giard	.10	.04

1985 Yankees TCMA Postcards

This 40-card set features color photos of the New York Yankees printed on postcard-size cards.

	Nm-Mt	Ex-Mt
COMPLETE SET (40)	10.00	4.00
1 Mike Connor CO	.10	.04
2 Yogi Berra MG	.75	.30
3 Stump Merrill CO	.10	.04
4 Gene Michael CO	.10	.04
5 Lou Piniella CO	.25	.10
6 Jeff Torborg CO	.10	.04
7 Mike Armstrong	.10	.04
8 Rich Bordi	.10	.04
9 Clay Christiansen	.10	.04
10 Joe Cowley	.10	.04
11 Jim Deshaies	.10	.04
12 Ron Guidry	.50	.20
13 John Montefusco	.10	.04
14 Dale Murray	.10	.04
15 Phil Niekro	1.00	.40
16 Alfonso Pulido	.10	.04
17 Dennis Rasmussen	.10	.04
18 Dave Righetti	.25	.10
19 Bob Shirley	.10	.04
20 Ed Whitson	.10	.04
21 Scott Bradley	.10	.04
22 Ron Hassey	.10	.04
23 Butch Wynegar	.10	.04
24 Dale Berra	.10	.04
25 Billy Sample	.10	.04
26 Rex Hudler	.25	.10
27 Don Mattingly	3.00	1.20
28 Bobby Meacham	.10	.04
29 Mike Pagliarulo	.10	.04
30 Willie Randolph	.75	.30
31 Andre Robertson	.10	.04
32 Henry Cotto	.10	.04
33 Don Baylor	.50	.20
34 Ken Griffey	.50	.20
35 Rickey Henderson	2.00	.80
36 Vic Mata	.10	.04
37 Omar Moreno	.10	.04
38 Dan Pasqua	.10	.04
39 Dave Winfield	1.50	.60
40 Brian Fisher	.10	.04

1986 Yankees TCMA

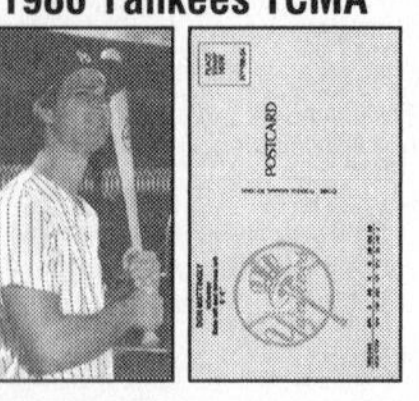

This 3 1/2" by 5 1/2" postcard set features members of the 1986 Yankees. The set has full-bleed color photographs. The backs have the players name and usually 1985 stats. The cards are numbered in the upper right corner with a "NYY86" prefix.

	Nm-Mt	Ex-Mt
COMPLETE SET (40)	12.00	4.80
1 Tommy John	.75	.30
2 Brad Arnsberg UER	.25	.10
Name spelled Arnsburg		
3 Al Holland UER	.25	.10
Name spelled All		
4 Mike Armstrong	.25	.10
5 Marty Bystrom	.25	.10
6 Doug Drabek	.75	.30
7 Brian Fisher	.25	.10
8 Stump Merrill CO	.25	.10
9 Ron Guidry	.75	.30
10 Joe Niekro	.50	.20
12 Dennis Rasmussen	.25	.10
13 Dave Righetti	.50	.20
14 Rod Scurry	.25	.10
15 Bob Shirley	.25	.10
16 Bob Tewksbury	.25	.10
17 Ed Whitson	.25	.10
18 Britt Burns	.25	.10
18 Gene Michael CO	.25	.10
19 Butch Wynegar	.25	.10
20 Ron Hassey	.25	.10
21 Dale Berra	.25	.10
22 Jeff Torborg CO	.25	.10
23 Mike Fischlin	.25	.10
24 Don Mattingly	4.00	1.60
25 Bobby Meacham	.25	.10
26 Mike Pagliarulo	.25	.10
27 Willie Randolph	.75	.30
28 Andre Robertson	.25	.10
29 Roy White CO	.50	.20
31 Henry Cotto	.25	.10
32 Ken Griffey	.75	.30
33 Rickey Henderson	1.50	.60
34 Vic Mata	.25	.10
35 Dan Pasqua	.25	.10
36 Dave Winfield	1.25	.50
37 Gary Roenicke	.25	.10
38 Lou Piniella MG	.75	.30
39 Joe Altobelli CO	.25	.10
40 Sammy Ellis CO	.25	.10
45 Mike Easler	.25	.10

1987 Yankees 1927 TCMA

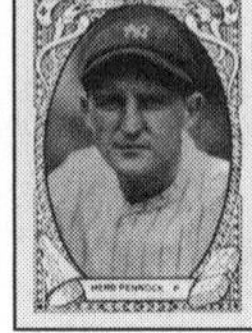

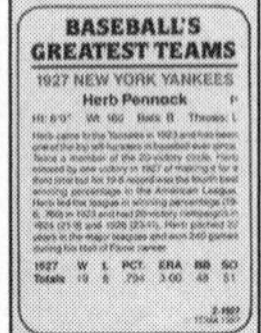

This nine-card standard-size set features key members of the 1927 Yankees. This team which had the famed "Murderers Row", is considered one of the all-time teams. The fronts feature black and white photographs. The backs have player information as well as stats from the 27 season.

	Nm-Mt	Ex-Mt
COMPLETE SET (9)	6.00	2.40
1 Miller Huggins MG	.50	.20
2 Herb Pennock	.75	.30
3 Tony Lazzeri	.75	.30
4 Waite Hoyt	.75	.30
5 Wilcy Moore	.25	.10
6 Earle Combs	.75	.30
7 Bob Meusel	.50	.20
8 Lou Gehrig	2.00	.80
9 Babe Ruth	2.50	1.00

1987 Yankees 1961 TCMA

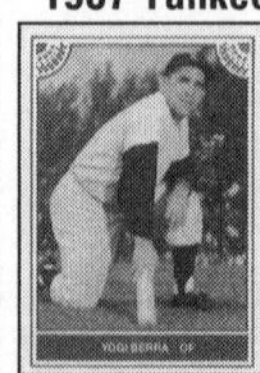

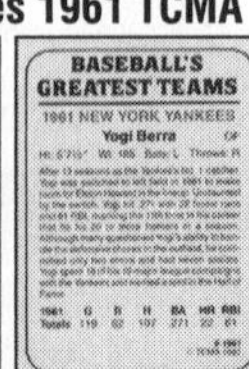

This nine-card standard-size set features members of the 1961 Yankees. This team set a major league record with 240 homers in a season and was led by Roger Maris and Mickey Mantle who combined for 115 of those blasts. The fronts display color photos, the player's name and position. The backs carry player information as well as more details about the 1961 season.

	Nm-Mt	Ex-Mt
COMPLETE SET (9)	6.00	2.40
1 Bill Skowron	.50	.20
2 Mickey Mantle	2.50	1.00
3 Bobby Richardson	.75	.30
4 Tony Kubek	.50	.20
5 Elston Howard	.75	.30
6 Yogi Berra	1.00	.40
7 Whitey Ford	1.00	.40
8 Roger Maris	1.00	.40
9 Ralph Houk MG	.25	.10

1988 Yankees Donruss Team Book

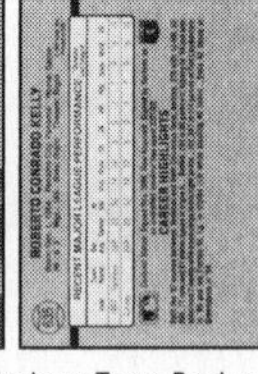

The 1988 Donruss Yankees Team Book set features 27 cards (three pages with nine cards on each page) plus a large full-page puzzle of Stan Musial. Cards are in full color and are standard size. The set was distributed as a four-page book; although the puzzle page was perforated, the card pages were not. The cover of the "Team Collection" book is primarily bright red. Card fronts are very similar in design to the 1988 Donruss regular issue. The card numbers on the backs are the same for those players that are the same as in the regular Donruss set; the new players pictured are numbered on the back as "NEW." The book is usually sold intact. When cut from the book into individual cards, these cards are distinguishable from the regular 1988 Donruss cards since these have a 1988 copyright on the back whereas the regular issue has a 1987 copyright on the back.

	Nm-Mt	Ex-Mt
COMPLETE SET (27)	4.00	1.60
43 Al Leiter RR	.75	.30
93 Dave Righetti	.25	.10
105 Mike Pagliarulo	.10	.04
128 Rick Rhoden	.10	.04
175 Ron Guidry	.25	.10
217 Don Mattingly	2.00	.80
228 Willie Randolph	.25	.10
251 Gary Ward	.10	.04
277 Rickey Henderson	1.00	.40
278 Dave Winfield	.75	.30
340 Claudell Washington	.10	.04
374 Charles Hudson	.10	.04
401 Tommy John	.50	.20
474 Joel Skinner	.10	.04
497 Tim Stoddard	.10	.04
545 Jay Buhner	.75	.30
616 Bobby Meacham	.10	.04
635 Roberto Kelly	.25	.10
NEW John Candelaria	.10	.04
NEW Jack Clark	.25	.10
NEW Jose Cruz	.25	.10
NEW Richard Dotson	.10	.04
NEW Cecilio Guante	.10	.04
NEW Lee Guetterman	.10	.04
NEW Rafael Santana	.10	.04
NEW Steve Shields	.10	.04
NEW Don Slaught	.10	.04

1989 Yankee Citgo All-Time Greats

These six cards feature great New York Yankees. Since the cards are unnumbered we have checklisted them below in alphabetical order.

	Nm-Mt	Ex-Mt
COMPLETE SET (6)	20.00	8.00
1 Whitey Ford	3.00	1.20
2 Lou Gehrig	5.00	2.00
3 Lefty Gomez	2.50	1.00
4 Phil Rizzuto	2.50	1.00
5 Babe Ruth	8.00	3.20
6 Casey Stengel	1.50	.60

1989 Yankees Score Nat West

The 1989 Score National Westminster Bank New York Yankees set features 33 standard-size cards. The fronts and backs are navy; the backs have color mug shots, 1988 and career stats. The set was given away at a 1989 Yankees' home game.

	Nm-Mt	Ex-Mt
COMPLETE SET (33)	20.00	8.00
1 Don Mattingly	8.00	3.20
2 Steve Sax	.50	.20
3 Alvaro Espinoza	.25	.10
4 Luis Polonia	.25	.10
5 Jesse Barfield	.25	.10
6 Dave Righetti	.50	.20
7 Dave Winfield	4.00	1.60
8 John Candelaria	.25	.10
9 Wayne Tolleson	.25	.10
10 Ken Phelps	.25	.10
11 Rafael Santana	.25	.10
12 Don Slaught	.25	.10
13 Mike Pagliarulo	.25	.10
14 Lance McCullers	.25	.10
15 Dave LaPoint	.25	.10
16 Dale Mohorcic	.25	.10
17 Steve Balboni	.25	.10
18 Roberto Kelly	.50	.20

19 Andy Hawkins .25 .10
20 Mel Hall .25 .10
21 Tom Brookens .25 .10
22 Deion Sanders 5.00 2.00
23 Richard Dotson .25 .10
24 Lee Guetterman .25 .10
25 Bob Geren .25 .10
26 Jimmy Jones .25 .10
27 Chuck Cary .25 .10
28 Ron Guidry 1.00 .40
29 Hal Morris .50 .20
30 Clay Parker .25 .10
31 Dallas Green MG .50 .20
32 Thurman Munson MEM 5.00 2.00
33 Yankees Team Card .50 .20

1990 Yankees Crown

This nine-card standard size set featuring Yankee greats was issued by Crown and is titled on the back "Jack Marcus favorite Yankee collection". The fronts have a player photo as well as a description about the photo while the back just mentions what the front is titled again.

	Nm-Mt	Ex-Mt
COMPLETE SET	20.00	6.00
1 Mickey Mantle	3.00	.90
2 Yogi Berra	1.00	.30
3 Phil Rizzuto	.25	.07
4 Babe Ruth Warren G Harding At the Polo Grounds, 1922	3.00	.90
5 Babe Ruth At the White house	4.00	1.20
6 Babe Ruth William Bendix 1948	3.00	.90
7 Babe Ruth At Yankee Stadium, 1924	3.00	.90
8 Babe Ruth Sammy Vick Ping Bodie 1920	3.00	.90
9 Lou Gehrig	2.00	.60

1990 Yankees Monument Park Rini Postcards

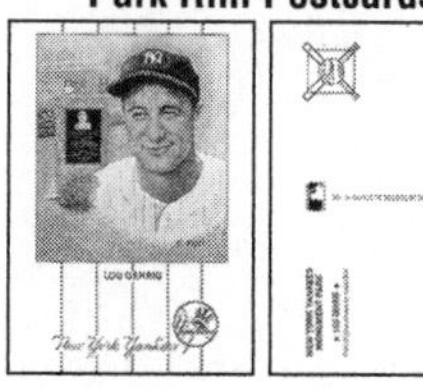

This set of 12 postcards measures 3 1/2" by 5 1/2". The fronts feature color drawings by Susan Rini.

	Nm-Mt	Ex-Mt
COMPLETE SET (12)	5.00	1.50
1 Lou Gehrig	2.00	.60
2 Babe Ruth	2.50	.75
3 Thurman Munson	.75	.23
4 Elston Howard	.25	.07
5 Phil Rizzuto	.75	.23
6 Mickey Mantle	2.50	.75
7 Bill Dickey	.75	.23
8 Lefty Gomez	.50	.15
9 Pope Paul VI	1.00	.30
10 Jacob Ruppert	.25	.07
11 Roger Maris	1.00	.30
12 Joe DiMaggio	2.00	.60

1990 Yankees Score Nat West

1990 Score National Westminster Bank Yankees is a 32-card, standard-size set featuring members of the 1990 New York Yankees. This set also has a special Billy Martin memorial card which honored the late Yankee manager who died in a truck accident on 12/25/89.

	Nm-Mt	Ex-Mt
COMPLETE SET (32)	15.00	4.50
1 Stump Merrill MG	.25	.07
2 Don Mattingly	8.00	2.40
3 Steve Sax	.50	.15
4 Alvaro Espinoza	.25	.07
5 Jesse Barfield	.50	.15
6 Roberto Kelly	.50	.15
7 Mel Hall	.25	.07
8 Claudell Washington	.25	.07
9 Bob Geren	.25	.07
10 Jim Leyritz	1.00	.30
11 Pascual Perez	.25	.07
12 Dave LaPoint	.25	.07
13 Tim Leary	.25	.07
14 Mike Witt	.25	.07
15 Chuck Cary	.25	.07
16 Dave Righetti	.50	.15
17 Lee Guetterman	.25	.07
18 Andy Hawkins	.25	.07
19 Greg Cadaret	.25	.07
20 Eric Plunk	.25	.07
21 Jimmy Jones	.25	.07
22 Deion Sanders	2.50	.75
23 Jeff D. Robinson	.25	.07
24 Matt Nokes	.25	.07
25 Steve Balboni	.25	.07
26 Wayne Tolleson	.25	.07
27 Randy Velarde	1.00	.30
28 Rick Cerone	.25	.07
29 Alan Mills	.25	.07
30 Billy Martin MEM	2.50	.75
31 Stadium Card	.50	.15
32 All-Time Yankee Record	.50	.15

1990 Yankees 61 Ron Lewis

These 42 oversized cards feature members of the 1961 New York Yankees. The fronts feature artwork by noted sports artist Ron Lewis.

	Nm-Mt	Ex-Mt
COMPLETE SET (42)	25.00	7.50
1 Team Photo	1.00	.30
2 Bobby Richardson	1.50	.45
3 Roger Maris	2.50	.75
4 Elston Howard	1.50	.45
5 Bill Skowron	1.50	.45
6 Clete Boyer	1.00	.30
7 Mickey Mantle	5.00	1.50
8 Yogi Berra	2.50	.75
9 Johnny Blanchard	.50	.15
10 Hector Lopez	.50	.15
11 Whitey Ford	2.50	.75
12 Ralph Terry	.50	.15
13 Bill Stafford	.50	.15
14 Bud Daley	.50	.15
15 Billy Gardner	.50	.15
16 Jim Coates	.50	.15
17 Luis Arroyo	.50	.15
18 Tex Clevenger	.50	.15
19 Bob Cerv	.50	.15
20 Art Ditmar	.50	.15
21 Bob Turley	1.00	.30
22 Joe DeMaestri	.50	.15
23 Rollie Sheldon	.50	.15
24 Earl Torgeson	.50	.15
25 Hal Reniff	.50	.15
26 Ralph Houk MG	1.00	.30
27 Johnny James	.50	.15
28 Bob Hale	.50	.15
29 Danny McDevitt	.50	.15
30 Duke Maas	.50	.15
31 Jim Hegan CO	.50	.15
32 Wally Moses CO	.50	.15
33 Frank Crosetti CO	1.00	.30
34 Lee Thomas	.50	.15
35 Al Downing	.50	.15
36 Jack Reed	.50	.15
37 Ryne Duren	.50	.15
38 Tom Tresh	1.00	.30
39 Johnny Sain CO	1.00	.30
40 Jesse Gonder	.50	.15
41 Deron Johnson	.50	.15
42 Tony Kubek	1.50	.45

1990 Yankees Topps TV

This Yankees team set contains 66 standard-size cards. Cards numbered 1-34 were with the parent club, while cards 35-66 were in the farm system. An early card of Deion Sanders is featured in this set.

	Nm-Mt	Ex-Mt
COMPLETE FACT. SET (66)	150.00	45.00
1 Bucky Dent MG	.50	.15
2 Mark Connor CO	.25	.07
3 Billy Connors CO	.25	.07
4 Mike Ferraro CO	.25	.07
5 Joe Sparks CO	.25	.07
6 Champ Summers CO	.25	.07
7 Greg Cadaret	.25	.07
8 Chuck Cary	.25	.07
9 Lee Guetterman	.25	.07
10 Andy Hawkins	.25	.07
11 Dave LaPoint	.25	.07
12 Tim Leary	.25	.07
13 Lance McCullers	.25	.07
14 Alan Mills	.25	.07
15 Clay Parker	.25	.07
16 Pascual Perez	.25	.07
17 Eric Plunk	.25	.07
18 Dave Righetti	.50	.15
19 Jeff D. Robinson	.25	.07
20 Rick Cerone	.25	.07
21 Bob Geren	.25	.07
22 Steve Balboni	.25	.07
23 Mike Blowers	.50	.15
24 Alvaro Espinoza	.25	.07
25 Don Mattingly	80.00	24.00
26 Steve Sax	.50	.15
27 Wayne Tolleson	.25	.07
28 Randy Velarde	.50	.15
29 Jesse Barfield	.50	.15
30 Mel Hall	.25	.07
31 Roberto Kelly	.50	.15
32 Luis Polonia	.25	.07
33 Deion Sanders	15.00	4.50
34 Dave Winfield	15.00	4.50
35 Steve Adkins	.25	.07
36 Oscar Azocar	.25	.07
37 Bob Brower	.25	.07
38 Britt Burns	.25	.07
39 Bob Davidson	.25	.07
40 Brian Dorsett	.25	.07
41 Dave Eiland	.25	.07
42 John Fishel	.25	.07
43 Andy Fox	.25	.07
44 John Habyan	.25	.07
45 Cullen Hartzog	.25	.07
46 Sterling Hitchcock	1.50	.45
47 Brian Johnson	.25	.07
48 Jimmy Jones	.25	.07
49 Scott Kamieniecki	.50	.15
50 Jim Leyritz	1.50	.45
51 Mark Leiter	.25	.07
52 Jason Maas	.25	.07
53 Kevin Maas	.50	.15
54 Hensley Meulens	.25	.07
55 Kevin Mmahat	.25	.07
56 Rich Monteleone	.25	.07
57 Vince Phillips	.25	.07
58 Carlos Rodriguez	.25	.07
59 Dave Sax	.25	.07
60 Willie Smith	.25	.07
61 Van Snider	.25	.07
62 Andy Stankiewicz	.25	.07
63 Wade Taylor	.25	.07
64 Ricky Torres	.25	.07
65 Jim Walewander	.25	.07
66 Bernie Williams	40.00	12.00

1991 Yankees Rini Postcards 1961 1

This set of 12 postcards measures 3 1/2" by 5 1/2" and showcases the 1961 New York Yankees. On a white background with blue stripes, the horizontal fronts feature color drawings by Susan Rini. The cards are numbered on the back as "X of 12."

	Nm-Mt	Ex-Mt
COMPLETE SET (12)	5.00	1.50
1 Yogi Berra	1.00	.30
2 Tom Tresh	.50	.15
3 Bill Skowron	.50	.15
4 Al Downing	.25	.07
5 Jim Coates	.25	.07
6 Luis Arroyo	.25	.07
7 Johnny Blanchard	.25	.07
8 Hector Lopez	.25	.07
9 Tony Kubek	.75	.23
10 Ralph Houk MG	.50	.15
11 Bobby Richardson	.75	.23
12 Clete Boyer	.50	.15

1991 Yankees Rini Postcards 1961 2

This set of 12 postcards measures 3 1/2" by 5 1/2" and showcases the 1961 New York Yankees. On a white background with blue stripes, the horizontal fronts feature color drawings by Susan Rini. The cards are numbered on the back as "X of 12."

	Nm-Mt	Ex-Mt
COMPLETE SET (12)	5.00	1.50
1 Roger Maris	1.00	.30
2 Jesse Gonder	.25	.07
3 Danny McDevitt	.25	.07
4 Lee Thomas	.25	.07
5 Billy Gardner	.25	.07
6 Ralph Terry	.50	.15
7 Hal Reniff	.25	.07
8 Earl Torgeson	.25	.07
9 Art Ditmar	.25	.07
10 Jack Reed	.25	.07
11 Johnny James	.25	.07
12 Elston Howard	.75	.23

1991 Yankees Rini Postcards 1961 3

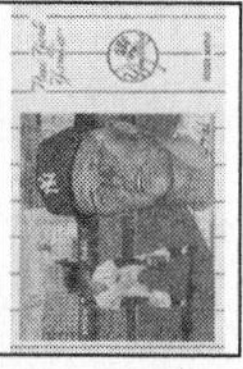

This set of 12 postcards measures 3 1/2" by 5 1/2" and showcases the 1961 New York Yankees. On a white background with blue stripes, the horizontal fronts feature color drawings by Susan Rini. The cards are numbered on the back as "X of 12."

	Nm-Mt	Ex-Mt
COMPLETE SET (12)	5.00	1.50
1 Mickey Mantle	2.00	.60
2 Deron Johnson	.25	.07
3 Bob Hale	.25	.07
4 Bill Stafford	.25	.07
5 Duke Maas	.25	.07
6 Bob Cerv	.25	.07
7 Roland Sheldon	.25	.07
8 Ryne Duren	.50	.15
9 Bob Turley	.50	.15
10 Whitey Ford	1.00	.30
11 Bud Daley	.25	.07
12 Joe DeMaestri	.25	.07

1992 Yankees WIZ 60s

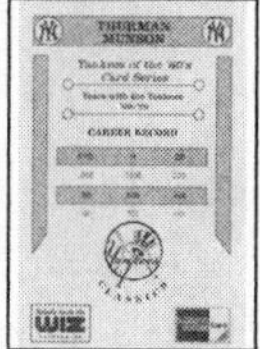

This 140-card set was sponsored by WIZ Home Entertainment Centers and American Express. The set was issued on 10" by 9" perforated sheets yielding cards measuring approximately 2" by 3". The cards are unnumbered and checklisted in alphabetical order.

	Nm-Mt	Ex-Mt
COMPLETE SET (140)	30.00	9.00
1 Jack Aker	.10	.03
2 Ruben Amaro	.10	.03
3 Luis Arroyo	.10	.03
4 Stan Bahnsen	.10	.03
5 Steve Barber	.10	.03
6 Ray Barker	.10	.03
7 Rich Beck	.10	.03
8 Yogi Berra	4.00	1.20
9 Johnny Blanchard	.25	.07
10 Gil Blanco	.10	.03
11 Ron Blomberg	.10	.03
12 Len Boehmer	.10	.03
13 Jim Bouton	.50	.15
14 Clete Boyer	.25	.07
15 Jim Brenneman	.10	.03
16 Marshall Bridges	.10	.03
17 Harry Bright	.10	.03
18 Hal Brown	.10	.03
19 Billy Bryan	.10	.03
20 Bill Burbach	.10	.03
21 Andy Carey	.25	.07
22 Duke Carmel	.10	.03
23 Bob Cerv	.25	.07
24 Horace Clarke	.10	.03
25 Tex Clevenger	.10	.03
26 Lu Clinton	.10	.03
27 Jim Coates	.10	.03
28 Rocky Colavito	2.00	.60
29 Billy Cowan	.10	.03
30 Bobby Cox	.50	.15
31 Jack Cullen	.10	.03
32 John Cumberland	.10	.03
33 Bud Daley	.10	.03
34 Joe DeMaestri	.10	.03
35 Art Ditmar	.10	.03
36 Al Downing	.25	.07
37 Ryne Duren	.25	.07
38 Doc Edwards	.10	.03
39 John Ellis	.10	.03
40 Frank Fernandez	.10	.03
41 Mike Ferraro	.10	.03
42 Whitey Ford	4.00	1.20
43 Bob Friend	.25	.07
44 John Gabler	.10	.03
45 Billy Gardner	.10	.03
46 Jake Gibbs	.25	.07
47 Jesse Gonder	.10	.03
48 Pedro Gonzalez	.10	.03
49 Eli Grba	.10	.03
50 Kent Hadley	.10	.03
51 Bob Hale	.10	.03
52 Jimmie Hall	.10	.03
53 Steve Hamilton	.10	.03
54 Mike Hegan	.10	.03
55 Bill Henry	.10	.03
56 Elston Howard	.75	.23
57 Dick Howser	.25	.07
58 Ken Hunt	.10	.03
59 Johnny James	.10	.03
60 Deron Johnson	.25	.07
61 Ken Johnson	.10	.03
62 Elvio Jimenez	.10	.03
63 Mike Jurewicz	.10	.03
64 Mike Kekich	.10	.03
65 John Kennedy	.10	.03
66 Jerry Kenney	.10	.03
67 Fred Kipp	.10	.03
68 Ron Klimkowski	.10	.03
69 Andy Kosco	.10	.03
70 Tony Kubek	.75	.23
71 Bill Kunkel	.10	.03
72 Phil Linz	.25	.07
73 Dale Long	.25	.07
74 Art Lopez	.10	.03
75 Hector Lopez	.25	.07
76 Jim Lyttle	.10	.03
77 Duke Maas	.10	.03
78 Mickey Mantle	10.00	3.00
79 Roger Maris	4.00	1.20
80 Lindy McDaniel	.25	.07
81 Danny McDevitt	.10	.03
82 Dave McDonald	.10	.03
83 Gil McDougald	.50	.15
84 Tom Metcalf	.10	.03
85 Bob Meyer	.10	.03
86 Gene Michael	.25	.07
87 Pete Mikkelsen	.10	.03
88 John Miller	.10	.03
89 Bill Monbouquette	.10	.03
90 Archie Moore	.10	.03
91 Ross Moschitto	.10	.03
92 Thurman Munson	2.00	.60
93 Bobby Murcer	.50	.15
94 Don Nottebart	.10	.03
95 Nate Oliver	.10	.03
96 Joe Pepitone	.25	.07
97 Cecil Perkins	.10	.03
98 Fritz Peterson	.10	.03
99 Jim Pisoni	.10	.03
100 Pedro Ramos	.10	.03
101 Jack Reed	.10	.03
102 Hal Reniff	.10	.03
103 Roger Repoz	.10	.03
104 Bobby Richardson	.75	.23
105 Dale Roberts	.10	.03
106 Bill Robinson	.25	.07
107 Ellie Rodriguez	.10	.03
108 Charlie Sands	.10	.03
109 Bob Schmidt	.10	.03
110 Dick Schofield	.10	.03
111 Billy Shantz	.10	.03
112 Bobby Shantz	.25	.07
113 Rollie Sheldon	.10	.03
114 Tom Shopay	.10	.03
115 Bill Short	.10	.03
116 Dick Simpson	.10	.03
117 Bill Skowron	.50	.15
118 Charley Smith	.10	.03
119 Tony Solaita	.10	.03
120 Bill Stafford	.10	.03
121 Mel Stottlemyre	.50	.15
122 Hal Stowe	.10	.03
123 Fred Talbot	.10	.03
124 Frank Tepedino	.25	.07
125 Ralph Terry	.25	.07
126 Lee Thomas	.10	.03
127 Bobby Tiefenauer	.10	.03
128 Bob Tillman	.10	.03
129 Thad Tillotson	.10	.03
130 Earl Torgeson	.10	.03
131 Tom Tresh	.25	.07
132 Bob Turley	.25	.07
133 Elmer Valo	.10	.03
134 Joe Verbanic	.10	.03
135 Steve Whitaker	.10	.03
136 Roy White	.25	.07
137 Stan Williams	.10	.03
138 Dooley Womack	.10	.03
139 Ron Woods	.10	.03
140 John Wyatt	.10	.03

1992 Yankees WIZ 70s

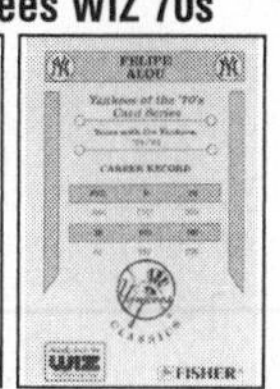

This 172-card set was sponsored by WIZ Home Entertainment Centers and Fisher. The set was issued on 10" by 9" perforated sheets yielding cards measuring approximately 2" by 3". The cards are unnumbered and checklisted in alphabetical order.

	Nm-Mt	Ex-Mt
COMPLETE SET (172)	30.00	9.00
1 Jack Aker	.10	.03
2 Doyle Alexander	.10	.03
3 Bernie Allen	.10	.03
4 Sandy Alomar	.25	.07
5 Felipe Alou	.50	.15
6 Matty Alou	.25	.07
7 Dell Alston	.10	.03
8 Rick Anderson	.10	.03
9 Stan Bahnsen	.10	.03
10 Frank Baker	.10	.03
11 Jim Beattie	.10	.03
12 Fred Beene	.10	.03
13 Juan Beniquez	.10	.03
14 Dave Bergman	.10	.03
15 Juan Bernhardt	.10	.03
16 Rick Bladt	.10	.03
17 Paul Blair	.25	.07
18 Wade Blasingame	.10	.03
19 Steve Blateric	.10	.03
20 Curt Blefary	.10	.03
21 Ron Blomberg	.25	.07
22 Len Boehmer	.10	.03
23 Bobby Bonds	.75	.23
24 Ken Brett	.10	.03
25 Ed Brinkman	.10	.03
26 Bobby Brown	.10	.03
27 Bill Burbach	.10	.03
28 Ray Burris	.10	.03
29 Tom Buskey	.10	.03
30 Johnny Callison	.25	.07
31 Danny Cater	.10	.03
32 Chris Chambliss	.50	.15
33 Horace Clarke	.10	.03
34 Ken Clay	.10	.03
35 Al Closter	.10	.03
36 Rich Coggins	.10	.03
37 Loyd Colson	.10	.03
38 Casey Cox	.10	.03
39 John Cumberland	.10	.03
40 Ron Davis	.10	.03
41 Jim Deidel	.10	.03
42 Rick Dempsey	.25	.07
43 Bucky Dent	.50	.15
44 Kerry Dineen	.10	.03
45 Pat Dobson	.10	.03
46 Brian Doyle	.10	.03
47 Rawly Eastwick	.10	.03
48 Dock Ellis	.10	.03
49 John Ellis	.10	.03
50 Ed Figueroa	.10	.03
51 Oscar Gamble	.25	.07
52 Damaso Garcia	.10	.03
53 Rob Gardner	.10	.03
54 Jake Gibbs	.25	.07
55 Fernando Gonzalez	.10	.03
56 Rich Gossage	.75	.23
57 Larry Gowell	.10	.03
58 Wayne Granger	.10	.03
59 Mike Griffin	.10	.03
60 Ron Guidry	.50	.15
61 Brad Gulden	.10	.03
62 Don Gullett	.25	.07
63 Larry Gura	.10	.03
64 Roger Hambright	.10	.03
65 Steve Hamilton	.10	.03
66 Ron Hansen	.10	.03
67 Jim Hardin	.10	.03
68 Jim Ray Hart	.10	.03
69 Fran Healy	.10	.03
70 Mike Heath	.10	.03
71 Mike Hegan	.10	.03
72 Elrod Hendricks	.10	.03
73 Ed Herrmann	.10	.03
74 Rich Hinton	.10	.03
75 Ken Holtzman	.25	.07
76 Don Hood	.10	.03
77 Catfish Hunter	1.50	.45
78 Grant Jackson	.10	.03
79 Reggie Jackson	5.00	1.50
80 Tommy John	.75	.23
81 Alex Johnson	.10	.03
82 Cliff Johnson	.25	.07
83 Jay Johnstone	.50	.15
84 Darryl Jones	.10	.03
85 Gary Jones	.10	.03
86 Jim Kaat	.75	.23
87 Bob Kammeyer	.10	.03
88 Mike Kekich	.10	.03
89 Jerry Kenney	.10	.03
90 Dave Kingman	.75	.23
91 Ron Klimkowski	.10	.03
92 Steve Kline	.10	.03

93 Mickey Klutts .10 .03
94 Hal Lanier .10 .03
95 Eddie Leon .10 .03
96 Terry Ley .10 .03
97 Paul Lindblad .10 .03
98 Gene Locklear .10 .03
99 Sparky Lyle .50 .15
100 Jim Lyttle .10 .03
101 Elliott Maddox .10 .03
102 Jim Magnuson .10 .03
103 Tippy Martinez .25 .07
104 Jim Mason .10 .03
105 Carlos May .10 .03
106 Rudy May .10 .03
107 Larry McCall .10 .03
108 Mike McCormick .10 .03
109 Lindy McDaniel .25 .07
110 Sam McDowell .25 .07
111 Rich McKinney .10 .03
112 George Medich .10 .03
113 Andy Messersmith .10 .03
114 Gene Michael .25 .07
115 Paul Mirabella .10 .03
116 Bobby Mitchell .10 .03
117 Gerry Moses .10 .03
118 Thurman Munson 2.50 .75
119 Bobby Murcer .75 .23
120 Larry Murray .10 .03
121 Jerry Narron .10 .03
122 Graig Nettles .75 .23
123 Bob Oliver .10 .03
124 Dave Pagan .10 .03
125 Gil Patterson .10 .03
126 Marty Perez .10 .03
127 Fritz Peterson .25 .07
128 Lou Piniella .50 .15
129 Dave Rajsich .10 .03
130 Domingo Ramos .10 .03
131 Lenny Randle .10 .03
132 Willie Randolph .75 .23
133 Dave Righetti .50 .15
134 Mickey Rivers .50 .15
135 Bruce Robinson .10 .03
136 Jim Roland .10 .03
137 Celerino Sanchez .10 .03
138 Rick Sawyer .10 .03
139 George Scott .25 .07
140 Duke Sims .10 .03
141 Roger Slagle .10 .03
142 Jim Spencer .10 .03
143 Charlie Spikes .10 .03
144 Roy Staiger .10 .03
145 Fred Stanley .10 .03
146 Bill Sudakis .10 .03
147 Ron Swoboda .25 .07
148 Frank Tepedino .25 .07
149 Stan Thomas .10 .03
150 Gary Thomasson .10 .03
151 Luis Tiant .75 .23
152 Dick Tidrow .10 .03
153 Rusty Torres .10 .03
154 Mike Torrez .10 .03
155 Cesar Tovar .10 .03
156 Cecil Upshaw .10 .03
157 Otto Velez .10 .03
158 Joe Verbanic .10 .03
159 Mike Wallace .10 .03
160 Danny Walton .10 .03
161 Pete Ward .10 .03
162 Gary Waslewski .10 .03
163 Dennis Werth .10 .03
164 Roy White .25 .07
165 Terry Whitfield .10 .03
166 Walt Williams .10 .03
167 Ron Woods .10 .03
168 Dick Woodson .10 .03
169 Ken Wright .10 .03
170 Jimmy Wynn .25 .07
171 Jim York .10 .03
172 George Zeber .10 .03

1992 Yankees WIZ 80s

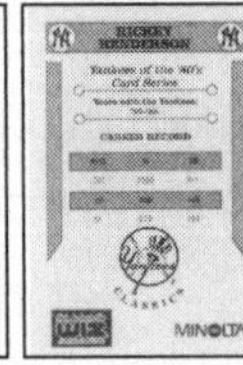

This 206-card set was sponsored by WIZ Home Entertainment Centers and Minolta. The set was issued on 10" by 9" perforated sheets yielding cards measuring approximately 2" by 3". The cards are unnumbered and checklisted in alphabetical order.

Nm-Mt Ex-Mt
COMPLETE SET (206) 30.00 9.00
1 Luis Aguayo .10 .03
2 Doyle Alexander .25 .07
3 Neil Allen .10 .03
4 Mike Armstrong .10 .03
5 Brad Arnsberg .10 .03
6 Tucker Ashford .10 .03
7 Steve Balboni .10 .03
8 Jesse Barfield .25 .07
9 Don Baylor .50 .15
10 Dale Berra .10 .03
11 Doug Bird .10 .03
12 Paul Blair .25 .07
13 Mike Blowers .10 .03
14 Juan Bonilla .10 .03
15 Rick Bordi .10 .03
16 Scott Bradley .10 .03
17 Marshall Brant .10 .03
18 Tom Brookens .10 .03
19 Bob Brower .10 .03
20 Bobby Brown .10 .03
21 Curt Brown .10 .03
22 Jay Buhner 2.00 .60
23 Marty Bystrom .10 .03
24 Greg Cadaret .10 .03
25 Bert Campaneris .25 .07
26 John Candelaria .25 .07
27 Chuck Cary .10 .03
28 Bill Castro .10 .03
29 Rick Cerone .10 .03
30 Chris Chambliss .25 .07
31 Clay Christiansen .10 .03
32 Jack Clark .25 .07
33 Pat Clements .10 .03
34 Dave Collins .10 .03
35 Don Cooper .10 .03
36 Henry Cotto .10 .03
37 Joe Cowley .10 .03
38 Jose Cruz .25 .07
39 Bobby Davidson .10 .03
40 Ron Davis .10 .03
41 Brian Dayett .10 .03
42 Ivan DeJesus .10 .03
43 Bucky Dent .25 .07
44 Jim Deshaies .10 .03
45 Orestes Destrade .10 .03
46 Brian Dorsett .10 .03
47 Richard Dotson .10 .03
48 Brian Doyle .10 .03
49 Doug Drabek .25 .07
50 Mike Easler .10 .03
51 Dave Eiland .10 .03
52 Roger Erickson .10 .03
53 Juan Espino .10 .03
54 Alvaro Espinoza .10 .03
55 Barry Evans .10 .03
56 Ed Figueroa .10 .03
57 Pete Filson .10 .03
58 Mike Fischlin .10 .03
59 Brian Fisher .10 .03
60 Tim Foli .10 .03
61 Ray Fontenot .10 .03
62 Barry Foote .10 .03
63 George Frazier .10 .03
64 Bill Fulton .10 .03
65 Oscar Gamble .25 .07
66 Bob Geren .10 .03
67 Rich Gossage .75 .23
68 Mike Griffin .10 .03
69 Ken Griffey .50 .15
70 Cecilio Guante .10 .03
71 Lee Guetterman .10 .03
72 Ron Guidry .50 .15
73 Brad Gulden .10 .03
74 Don Gullett .25 .07
75 Bill Gullickson .10 .03
76 Mel Hall .10 .03
77 Toby Harrah .10 .03
78 Ron Hassey .10 .03
79 Andy Hawkins .10 .03
80 Rickey Henderson 3.00 .90
81 Leo Hernandez .10 .03
82 Butch Hobson .10 .03
83 Al Holland .10 .03
84 Roger Holt .10 .03
85 Jay Howell .10 .03
86 Rex Hudler .25 .07
87 Charles Hudson .10 .03
88 Keith Hughes .10 .03
89 Reggie Jackson 3.00 .90
90 Stan Javier .10 .03
91 Stan Jefferson .10 .03
92 Tommy John .50 .15
93 Jimmy Jones .10 .03
94 Ruppert Jones .10 .03
95 Jim Kaat .75 .23
96 Curt Kaufman .10 .03
97 Roberto Kelly .50 .15
98 Steve Kemp .10 .03
99 Matt Keough .10 .03
100 Steve Kiefer .10 .03
101 Ron Kittle .10 .03
102 Dave LaPoint .10 .03
103 Marcus Lawton .10 .03
104 Joe Lefebvre .10 .03
105 Al Leiter .75 .23
106 Jim Lewis .10 .03
107 Bryan Little .10 .03
108 Tim Lollar .10 .03
109 Phil Lombardi .10 .03
110 Vic Mata .10 .03
111 Don Mattingly 10.00 3.00
112 Rudy May .10 .03
113 John Mayberry .10 .03
114 Lee Mazzilli .25 .07
115 Lance McCullers .10 .03
116 Andy McGaffigan .10 .03
117 Lynn McGlothen .10 .03
118 Bobby Meacham .10 .03
119 Hensley Meulens .10 .03
120 Larry Milbourne .10 .03
121 Kevin Mmahat .10 .03
122 Dale Mohorcic .10 .03
123 John Montefusco .10 .03
124 Omar Moreno .10 .03
125 Mike Morgan .10 .03
126 Jeff Moronko .10 .03
127 Hal Morris .10 .03
128 Jerry Mumphrey .10 .03
129 Bobby Murcer .50 .15
130 Dale Murray .10 .03
131 Gene Nelson .10 .03
132 Joe Niekro .25 .07
133 Phil Niekro .75 .23
134 Scott Nielsen .10 .03
135 Otis Nixon .10 .03
136 Johnny Oates .10 .03
137 Mike O'Berry .10 .03
138 Rowland Office .10 .03
139 John Pacella .10 .03
140 Mike Pagliarulo .25 .07
141 Clay Parker .10 .03
142 Dan Pasqua .10 .03
143 Mike Patterson .10 .03
144 Hipolito Pena .10 .03
145 Gaylord Perry .75 .23
146 Ken Phelps .10 .03
147 Lou Piniella .75 .23
148 Eric Plunk .10 .03
149 Luis Polonia .50 .15
150 Alfonso Pulido .10 .03
151 Jamie Quirk .10 .03
152 Bobby Ramos .10 .03
153 Willie Randolph .50 .15
154 Dennis Rasmussen .10 .03
155 Shane Rawley .10 .03
156 Rick Reuschel .25 .07
157 Dave Revering .10 .03
158 Rick Rhoden .10 .03
159 Dave Righetti .25 .07
160 Jose Rijo .10 .03
161 Andre Robertson .10 .03
162 Bruce Robinson .10 .03
163 Aurelio Rodriguez .10 .03
164 Edwin Rodriguez .10 .03
165 Gary Roenicke .10 .03
166 Jerry Royster .10 .03
167 Lenn Sakata .10 .03
168 Mark Salas .10 .03
169 Billy Sample .10 .03
170 Deion Sanders 3.00 .90
171 Rafael Santana .10 .03
172 Steve Sax .25 .07
173 Don Schulze .10 .03
174 Rodney Scott .10 .03
175 Rod Scurry .10 .03
176 Dennis Sherrill .10 .03
177 Steve Shields .10 .03
179 Bob Shirley .10 .03
180 Joel Skinner .10 .03
181 Don Slaught .25 .07
182 Roy Smalley .25 .07
183 Keith Smith .10 .03
184 Eric Soderholm .10 .03
185 Jim Spencer .10 .03
186 Fred Stanley .10 .03
187 Dave Stegman .10 .03
188 Tim Stoddard .10 .03
189 Walt Terrell .10 .03
190 Bob Tewksbury .10 .03
191 Luis Tiant .50 .15
192 Wayne Tolleson .10 .03
193 Steve Trout .10 .03
194 Tom Underwood .10 .03
195 Randy Velarde .10 .03
196 Gary Ward .10 .03
197 Claudell Washington .25 .07
198 Bob Watson .50 .15
199 Dave Wehrmeister .10 .03
200 Dennis Werth .10 .03
201 Stefan Wever .10 .03
202 Ed Whitson .10 .03
203 Ted Wilborn .10 .03
204 Dave Winfield 3.00 .90
205 Butch Wynegar .10 .03
206 Paul Zuvella .10 .03

1992 Yankees WIZ All-Stars

This 86-card set was sponsored by WIZ Home Entertainment Centers and American Express. The set was issued on five 15-card sheets and one 11-card title sheet, all measuring approximately 10" by 9". The perforated sheets yielded cards measuring approximately 2" by 3". The cards are unnumbered and checklisted in alphabetical order.

Nm-Mt Ex-Mt
COMPLETE SET (86) 30.00 9.00
1 Luis Arroyo .10 .03
2 Hank Bauer .25 .07
3 Yogi Berra 2.00 .60
4 Bobby Bonds .50 .15
5 Ernie Bonham .10 .03
6 Hank Borowy .10 .03
7 Jim Bouton .50 .15
8 Tommy Byrne .10 .03
9 Chris Chambliss .25 .07
10 Spud Chandler .25 .07
11 Ben Chapman .10 .03
12 Jim Coates .10 .03
13 Jerry Coleman .10 .03
14 Frank Crosetti .25 .07
15 Ron Davis .10 .03
16 Bucky Dent .25 .07
17 Bill Dickey .75 .23
18 Joe DiMaggio 5.00 1.50
19 Al Downing .10 .03
20 Ryne Duren .25 .07
21 Whitey Ford 2.00 .60
22 Lou Gehrig 5.00 1.50
23 Lefty Gomez .75 .23
24 Joe Gordon .25 .07
25 Rich Gossage .50 .15
26 Bob Grim .10 .03
27 Ron Guidry .50 .15
28 Rollie Hemsley .10 .03
29 Rickey Henderson 1.50 .45
30 Tommy Henrich .50 .15
31 Elston Howard .50 .15
32 Catfish Hunter .75 .23
33 Reggie Jackson 2.00 .60
34 Tommy John .50 .15
35 Billy Johnson .10 .03
36 Charlie Keller .25 .07
37 Tony Kubek .25 .07
38 Johnny Kucks .10 .03
39 Tony Lazzeri .75 .23
40 Johnny Lindell .10 .03
41 Ed Lopat .50 .15
42 Sparky Lyle .25 .07
43 Mickey Mantle 8.00 2.40
44 Roger Maris 2.00 .60
45 Billy Martin .75 .23
46 Don Mattingly 3.00 .90
47 Gil McDougald .25 .07
48 George McQuinn .10 .03
49 Johnny Mize .75 .23
50 Thurman Munson 1.50 .45
51 Bobby Murcer .25 .07
52 Johnny Murphy .10 .03
53 Graig Nettles .50 .15
54 Phil Niekro .75 .23
55 Irv Noren .10 .03
56 Joe Page .10 .03
57 Monte Pearson .10 .03
58 Joe Pepitone .25 .07
59 Fritz Peterson .10 .03
60 Willie Randolph .25 .07
61 Vic Raschi .25 .07
62 Allie Reynolds .50 .15
63 Bobby Richardson .50 .15
64 Dave Righetti .25 .07
65 Mickey Rivers .25 .07
66 Phil Rizzuto 1.50 .45
67 Aaron Robinson .10 .03
68 Red Rolfe .10 .03
69 Buddy Rosar .10 .03
70 Red Ruffing .75 .23
71 Marius Russo .10 .03
72 Babe Ruth 8.00 2.40
73 Johnny Sain .50 .15
74 Scott Sanderson .10 .03
75 Steve Sax .25 .07
76 George Selkirk .10 .03
77 Bobby Shantz .25 .07
78 Spec Shea .10 .03
79 Bill Skowron .25 .07
80 Snuffy Stirnweiss .10 .03
81 Mel Stottlemyre .25 .07
82 Ralph Terry .10 .03
83 Tom Tresh .25 .07
84 Bob Turley .25 .07
85 Roy White .25 .07
86 Dave Winfield 2.00 .60

1992 Yankees WIZ HOF

This 35-card set was sponsored by WIZ Home Entertainment Centers and Aiwa. The set was issued on two 15-card sheets and one five-card title sheet, all measuring approximately 10" by 9". The perforated sheets yielded cards measuring approximately 2" by 3". The cards are unnumbered and checklisted in alphabetical order.

Nm-Mt Ex-Mt
COMPLETE SET (35) 20.00 6.00
1 Home Run Baker .25 .07
2 Edward G. Barrow .25 .07
3 Yogi Berra 2.00 .60
4 Frank Chance .25 .07
5 Jack Chesbro .25 .07
6 Earle Combs .25 .07
7 Stan Coveleski .25 .07
8 Bill Dickey .75 .23
9 Joe DiMaggio 5.00 1.50
10 Whitey Ford 2.00 .60
11 Lou Gehrig 4.00 1.20
12 Lefty Gomez .50 .15
13 Clark C. Griffith .25 .07
14 Burleigh Grimes .25 .07
15 Bucky Harris .25 .07
16 Waite Hoyt .25 .07
17 Miller Huggins .25 .07
18 Catfish Hunter .50 .15
19 Willie Keeler .25 .07
20 Tony Lazzeri .25 .07
21 Larry MacPhail .25 .07
22 Mickey Mantle 5.00 1.50
23 Joe McCarthy MG .25 .07
24 Johnny Mize .50 .15
25 Herb Pennock .25 .07
26 Gaylord Perry .50 .15
27 Branch Rickey .25 .07
28 Red Ruffing .25 .07
29 Babe Ruth 5.00 1.50
30 Joe Sewell .25 .07
31 Enos Slaughter .50 .15
32 Casey Stengel .75 .23
33 Dazzy Vance .25 .07
34 Paul Waner .25 .07
35 George M. Weiss GM .25 .07

1993 Yankees Stadium Club

This 30-card standard-size set features the 1993 New York Yankees. The set was issued in hobby (plastic box) and retail (blister) form.

Nm-Mt Ex-Mt
COMP. FACT SET (30) 6.00 1.80
1 Don Mattingly 2.00 .60
2 Jim Abbott .25 .07
3 Matt Nokes .10 .03
4 Danny Tartabull .10 .03
5 Wade Boggs 1.00 .30
6 Melido Perez .10 .03
7 Steve Farr .10 .03
8 Kevin Maas .10 .03
9 Randy Velarde .10 .03
10 Mike Humphreys .10 .03
11 Mike Gallego .10 .03
12 Mike Stanley .10 .03
13 Jimmy Key .25 .07
14 Paul O'Neill .50 .15
15 Spike Owen .10 .03
16 Pat Kelly .10 .03
17 Sterling Hitchcock .10 .03
18 Mike Witt .10 .03
19 Scott Kamieniecki .10 .03
20 John Habyan .10 .03
21 Bernie Williams .75 .23
22 Brien Taylor .10 .03
23 Rick Monteleone .10 .03
24 Mark Hutton .10 .03
25 Robert Eenhoorn .10 .03
26 Gerald Williams .10 .03
27 Sam Militello .10 .03
28 Bob Wickman .75 .23
29 Andy Stankiewicz .10 .03
30 Domingo Jean .10 .03

1997 Yankees Score

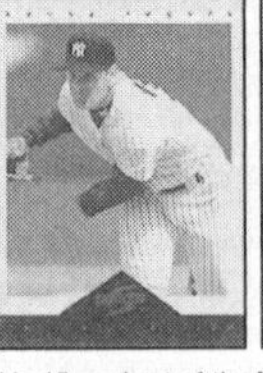

This 15-card set of the New York Yankees was issued in five-card packs with a suggested retail price of $1.30 each. The fronts feature color player photos with special team specific color foil stamping. The backs carry player information. Only 100 cases were made for each team. Platinum parallel cards were inserted at a rate of 1:6, Premier parallel cards at a rate of 1:31.

Nm-Mt Ex-Mt
COMPLETE SET (15) 8.00 2.40
*PLATINUM: 4X BASIC CARDS
*PREMIER: 20X BASIC CARDS
1 Bernie Williams .75 .23
2 Cecil Fielder .40 .12
3 Derek Jeter 4.00 1.20
4 Darryl Strawberry .40 .12
5 Andy Pettitte .60 .18
6 Ruben Rivera .25 .07
7 Mariano Rivera .75 .23
8 John Wetteland .40 .12
9 Paul O'Neill .75 .23
10 Wade Boggs 1.00 .30
11 Dwight Gooden .40 .12
12 David Cone .60 .18
13 Tino Martinez .60 .18
14 Kenny Rogers .25 .07
15 Andy Fox .25 .07

1998 Yankees Kodak Wells

This one-card set measuring approximately 5" by 3 3/4" was produced by Kodak commemorating the perfect game pitched by New York Yankees David Wells against the Minnesota Twins on May 17, 1998. The front features an action photo of the final strike for the final out printed on a lenticular card. The back is blank.

Nm-Mt Ex-Mt
1 David Wells 10.00 3.00

1998 Yankees Score

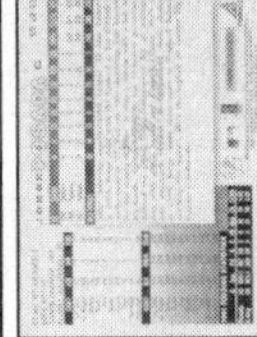

This 15-card set was issued in special retail packs and features color photos of the New York Yankees team. The backs carry player information. A special platinum parallel set was also issued and randomly inserted in packs.

Nm-Mt Ex-Mt
COMPLETE SET (15) 8.00 2.40
*PLATINUM: 5X BASIC CARDS
1 Hideki Irabu .25 .07
2 Derek Jeter 4.00 1.20
3 Tino Martinez .60 .18
4 David Cone .60 .18
5 Andy Pettitte .50 .12
6 Bernie Williams .75 .23
7 Charlie Hayes .25 .07
8 Pat Kelly .25 .07
9 Mariano Rivera .75 .23
10 Paul O'Neill .75 .23
11 Chad Curtis .25 .07
12 David Wells .60 .18
13 Cecil Fielder .40 .12
14 Wade Boggs 1.00 .30
15 Jorge Posada .75 .23

1998 Yankees 75th Anniversary

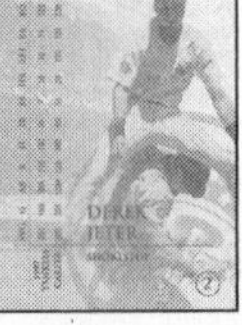

These 12 cards were issued by the New York Yankees and featured some of the stars of the team which celebrated the platinum anniversary since their move into Yankee stadium. The fronts have a player photo against the background of the big ball orchard in the Bronx. The back has an action photo and seasonal and career statistics. These cards were inserted into Yankee scorecards during the regular season.

	Nm-Mt	Ex-Mt
COMPLETE SET (12)	10.00	3.00
1 David Cone	.75	.23
2 Derek Jeter	5.00	1.50
3 Chili Davis	.50	.15
4 Joe Girardi	.25	.07
5 Hideki Irabu	.25	.07
6 Chuck Knoblauch	.50	.15
7 Tino Marinez	.75	.23
8 Paul O'Neill	1.00	.30
9 Andy Pettite	.75	.23
10 Mariano Rivera	1.00	.30
11 David Wells	.75	.23
12 Bernie Williams	1.00	.30

1998 Yankees Upper Deck

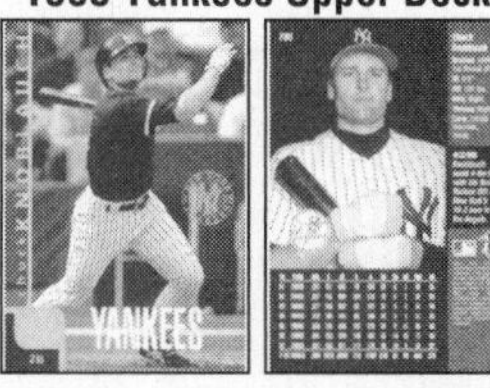
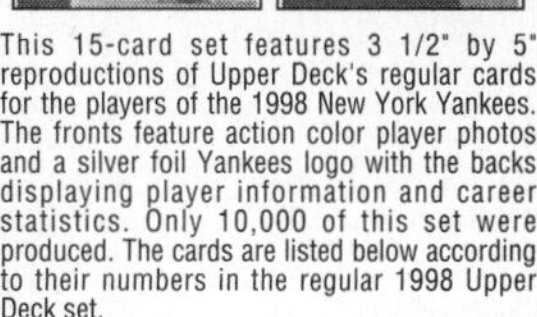

This 15-card set features 3 1/2" by 5" reproductions of Upper Deck's regular cards for the players of the 1998 New York Yankees. The fronts feature action color player photos and a silver foil Yankees logo with the backs displaying player information and career statistics. Only 10,000 of this set were produced. The cards are listed below according to their numbers in the regular 1998 Upper Deck set.

	Nm-Mt	Ex-Mt
COMPLETE FACT. SET (15)	15.00	4.50
169 Bernie Williams	1.50	.45
170 Andy Pettitte	.75	.23
172 Paul O'Neill	1.50	.45
175 David Cone	1.50	.45
176 Hideki Irabu	.50	.15
449 Tim Raines	.75	.23
450 Derek Jeter	8.00	2.40
460 Tino Martinez	1.25	.35
461 Chad Curtis	.50	.15
462 Ramiro Mendoza	.50	.15
464 David Wells	.75	.23
465 Mariano Rivera	1.50	.45
703 Chili Davis	.75	.23
704 Scott Brosius	.75	.23
705 Chuck Knoblauch	.75	.23

1998 Yankees Upper Deck WS Commemorative

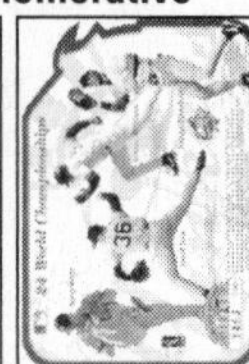

This one-card limited edition set commemorates the New York Yankees winning the 1998 World Series and has a suggested retail price of $19.95. The card features color action images of seven Yankees players on a die-cut card with a pin-striped background. Three players appear on the card front and four on the back. Only 9,800 of this card were produced and are serially numbered. The players are checklisted below as they appear on the card from left to right, front to back.

	Nm-Mt	Ex-Mt
1 Paul O'Neill	20.00	6.00
Tino Martinez		
Derek Jeter		
David Wells		
David Cone		
Bernie Williams		
Darryl Strawberry		

1999 Yankees Fleer

This 27-card set of the New York Yankees was distributed on three commemorative sheets each containing nine player cards, a title/checklist card, a sponsor card, and a 1999 Yankees schedule card. Each perforated sheet measures approximately 12 1/2" by 10 1/2".

	Nm-Mt	Ex-Mt
COMPLETE SET (30)	10.00	3.00
1 Derek Jeter	2.00	.60
2 Paul O'Neill	.75	.23
3 Scott Brosius	.25	.07
4 Mariano Rivera	.25	.07
5 Chuck Knoblauch	.25	.07
6 Graeme Lloyd	.10	.03
7 Joe Girardi	.10	.03
8 Orlando Hernandez	.25	.07
9 Tim Raines	.25	.07
10 Bernie Williams	.75	.23
11 Tino Martinez	.50	.15
12 Andy Pettitte	.25	.07
13 Hideki Irabu	.10	.03
14 Ramiro Mendoza	.10	.03
15 Jeff Nelson	.10	.03
16 Homer Bush	.10	.03
17 Darren Holmes	.10	.03
18 Yankees History	.10	.03
19 David Cone	.25	.07
20 David Wells	.50	.15
21 Chili Davis	.25	.07
22 Darryl Strawberry	.25	.07
23 Ricky Ledee	.10	.03
24 Jorge Posada	.50	.15
25 Luis Sojo	.10	.03
26 Chad Curtis	.10	.03
27 Mike Stanton	.10	.03
S1 Commemorative Sheet 1	5.00	1.50
S2 Commemorative Sheet 2	4.00	1.20
S3 Commemorative Sheet 3	4.00	1.20
NNO Sponsor Card	.10	.03
NNO 1999 Schedule Card	.10	.03
NNO Title Card CL	.10	.03

2000 Yankees Star Ledger

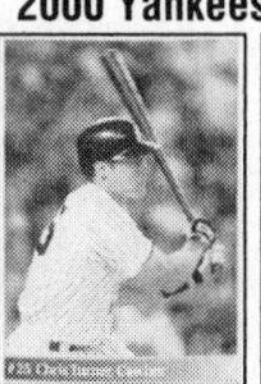
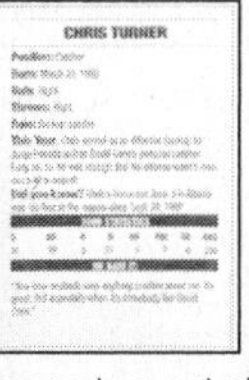

These small cards were sent as part of perforated sheets to only people who sold the Newark Star Ledger. The fronts have a color photo of the player with his name and position on the bottom. The backs have some biographical information, stats from 2000 and some personal information. Since these cards are unnumbered, we have sequenced them in alphabetical order.

	Nm-Mt	Ex-Mt
COMPLETE SET (24)	60.00	18.00
1 Clay Bellinger	1.50	.45
2 Scott Brosius	2.00	.60
3 Randy Choate	1.50	.45
4 Roger Clemens	8.00	2.40
5 David Cone	2.50	.75
6 Dwight Gooden	2.00	.60
7 Jason Grimsley	1.50	.45
8 Orlando Hernandez	1.50	.45
9 Glenallen Hill	1.50	.45
10 Derek Jeter	15.00	4.50
11 Chuck Knoblauch	2.00	.60
12 Ramiro Mendoza	1.50	.45
13 Jeff Nelson	1.50	.45
14 Paul O'Neill	3.00	.90
15 Andy Pettitte	2.50	.75
16 Jorge Posada	3.00	.90
17 Luis Rivera	1.50	.45
18 Mariano Rivera	3.00	.90
19 Luis Sojo	1.50	.45
20 Mike Stanton	1.50	.45
21 Joe Torre MG	3.00	.90
22 Chris Turner	1.50	.45
23 Jose Vizcaino	1.50	.45
24 Bernie Williams	3.00	.90

2002 Yankees Starting Five Fleer

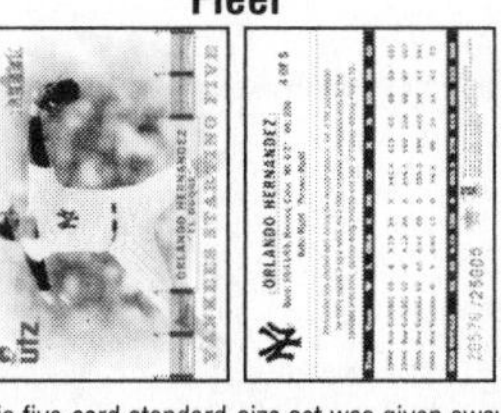

This five-card standard-size set was given away at a June 12, 2002 New York Yankee home game. These horizontal cards have an action photo of the pitcher in action along with their name and the words Yankee Starting Five on the bottom. The upper left has the "Utz" corporate sponsorship logo while the Fleer logo is in the upper right. The backs have biographical information, recent and career stats as well as the individual serial numbering for each card. This set was issued to a stated print run of 25,000 copies.

	Nm-Mt	Ex-Mt
COMPLETE SET	10.00	3.00
UNLISTED STARS	2.50	.75
1 Roger Clemens	5.00	1.50
2 David Wells	2.50	.75
3 Mike Mussina	2.50	.75
4 Orlando Hernandez	1.00	.30
5 Andy Pettitte	2.50	.75

2003 Yankees French Donruss

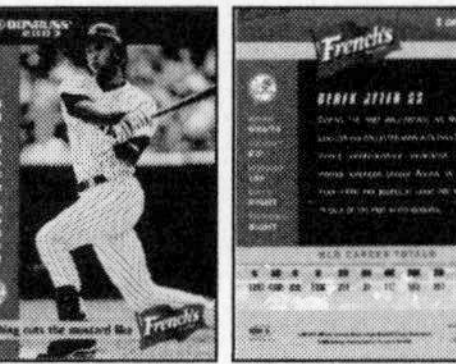

This six card set of some of the leading 2003 Yankees was produced by Donruss and sponsored by French's mustard.This set was given away at a Yankee game during the 2003 season.

	MINT	NRMT
COMPLETE SET	15.00	6.75
1 Derek Jeter	10.00	4.50
2 Alfonso Soriano	3.00	1.35
3 Jorge Posada	2.50	1.10
4 Jose Contreras	2.50	1.10
5 Jeff Weaver	1.00	.45
6 Steve Karsay	1.00	.45
NNO Hot Dog Info Card	.50	.23

2003 Yankees Greats Poland Springs

This five-card set was given away during a 2003 Yankees game. This set consists of four cards, which were also in the 2003 Flair Greats of the game set (but these have different numbering) and an ad card for Poland Springs bottled water

	MINT	NRMT
COMPLETE SET	5.00	2.20
1 Yogi Berra	1.50	.70
2 Whitey Ford	1.50	.70
3 Phil Rizzuto	1.50	.70
4 Reggie Jackson	1.50	.70
NNO Poland Springs Card	.25	.11

2003 Yankees McDonald's Upper Deck

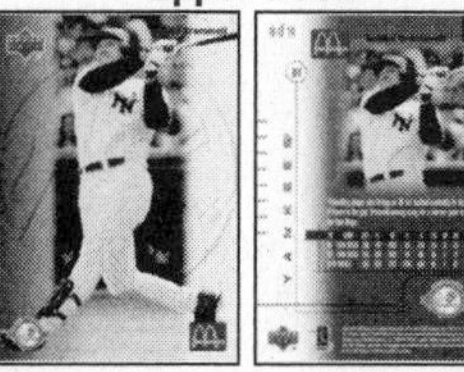

This 24-card standard-size set was issued as a promotion during the 2003 season. These cards were issued one per pack along with a contest card with the value of any "extra-value" meal.

	MINT	NRMT
COMPLETE SET	10.00	4.50
1 Juan Acevedo	.25	.11
2 Roger Clemens	2.00	.90
3 John Flaherty	.25	.11
4 Jason Giambi	1.25	.55
5 Chris Hammond	.25	.11
6 Sterling Hitchcock	.25	.11
7 Derek Jeter	4.00	1.80
8 Nick Johnson	1.00	.45
9 Steve Karsay	.25	.11
10 Hideki Matsui	4.00	1.80
11 Raul Mondesi	.50	.23
12 Mike Mussina	1.00	.45
13 Antonio Osuna	.25	.11
14 Andy Pettitte	.75	.35
15 Jorge Posada	1.00	.45
16 Mariano Rivera	1.00	.45
17 Alfonso Soriano	1.50	.70
18 Bubba Trammell	.25	.11
19 Robin Ventura	.50	.23
20 Jeff Weaver	.25	.11
21 David Wells	1.00	.45
22 Bernie Williams	1.00	.45
23 Enrique Wilson	.25	.11
24 Todd Zeile	.50	.23
XX Contest Card	.25	.11

1958 Yoo-Hoo Match Book Covers

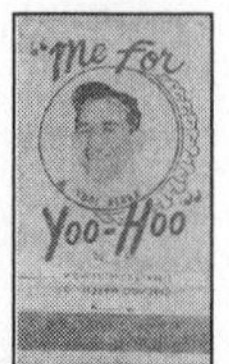

This yellow match book cover was issued by the Yoo-Hoo chocolate drink company and featured a photo of Yogi Berra on the back. The sepia, head shot photo is encircled with a bottle cap design and above and below the cap are the words "Me for Yoo-Hoo". Yogi Berra's name is printed on the lower portion of the picture. The inner portion of the match book cover carries an offer to mail in the empty cover with $2.50 and receive a book entitled "The Story of Yogi Berra". A matchbook was also made of Yankee great Mickey Mantle and that had offers inside for memorabilia from assorted New York Yankee.

	NM	Ex
COMPLETE SET	125.00	60.00
1 Yogi Berra	25.00	12.50
2 Mickey Mantle	100.00	50.00

1993 Yoo-Hoo

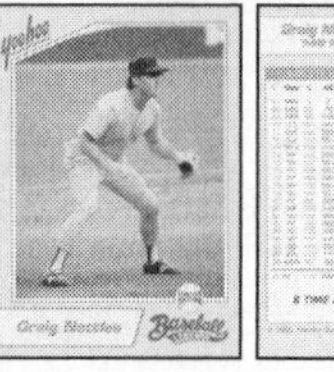

This standard-size 20-card set was issued by Yoo-Hoo Chocolate Beverage Corporation and celebrates some of baseball's legends. The cards are unnumbered and checklisted below in alphabetical order.

	Nm-Mt	Ex-Mt
COMPLETE SET (20)	10.00	3.00
1 Johnny Bench	.75	.23
2 Yogi Berra	1.00	.30
3 Lou Brock	.75	.23
4 Rod Carew	.75	.23
5 Bob Feller	1.00	.30
6 Whitey Ford	.75	.23
7 Steve Garvey	.25	.07
8 Al Kaline	1.00	.30
9 Willie McCovey	.50	.15
10 Joe Morgan	.50	.15
11 Stan Musial	1.00	.30
12 Gaylord Perry	.50	.15
13 Graig Nettles	.25	.07
14 Jim Rice	.25	.07
15 Phil Rizzuto	.75	.23
16 Brooks Robinson	1.00	.30
17 Pete Rose	1.00	.30
18 Tom Seaver	1.00	.30
19 Duke Snider	1.00	.30
20 Willie Stargell	.50	.15

1994 Yoo-Hoo

Issued in conjunction with Rawlings in two ten-card sets, each set consisting of eight player cards and two fact cards, this 20-card set features past winners of Rawlings Gold Glove Award. The first series was introduced in May, while the second series was released in August. The entire set could be received for proofs-of-purchase as well as postage and handling; a toll free number on Yoo-Hoo products could be called to obtain the details of the offer. The Fact Cards are numbered 1-4 on their fronts and backs, and have been arbitrarily assigned an "F" prefix below to distinguish them from the player cards. Interestingly, Don Mattingly appeared in this set although he was still active at time of issue. Some packs were sent out with Carl Yastrzemski's autographs. There is no certified mark or other way to verify that the card was specifically autographed.

	Nm-Mt	Ex-Mt
COMPLETE SET (20)	35.00	10.50
1 Luis Aparicio	2.00	.60
2 Bobby Bonds	1.00	.30
3 Bob Boone	1.00	.30
4 Steve Carlton	2.00	.60
5 Roberto Clemente	10.00	3.00
6 Bob Gibson	2.00	.60
7 Keith Hernandez	1.50	.45
8 Jim Kaat	1.50	.45
9 Roger Maris	5.00	1.50
10 Don Mattingly	8.00	2.40
11 Thurman Munson	2.00	.60
12 Phil Rizzuto	3.00	.90
13 Brooks Robinson	3.00	.90
14 Ryne Sandberg	8.00	2.40
15 Mike Schmidt	5.00	1.50
16 Carl Yastrzemski	3.00	.90
16A Carl Yastrzemski AU	20.00	6.00
Autograph is not certified		
F1 Fact Card 1	.25	.07
F2 Fact Card 2	.25	.07
F3 Fact Card 3	.25	.07
F4 Fact Card 4	.25	.07

1927 York Caramel E210

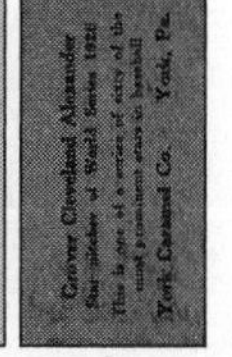

The cards in this 60-card set measure 1 3/8" by 2 1/2". This set contains numbered cards with black and white photos of baseball players in the series of "most prominent baseball stars" issued by the York Caramel Company. They were released to the public in 1927. Number 12 has been found with two spellings; number 58 appears with either Bell or Galloway; and numbers 9, 25, 31 and 46 have incorrect photos of players with the same last names. An interesting feature is the caption which appears under the players's name on back, e.g., Burleigh Grimes is dubbed "A Sterling National League Pitcher." The complete set price includes all variation cards listed in the checklist below.

	Ex-Mt	VG
COMPLETE SET (64)	6000.00	3000.00
1 Burleigh Grimes	100.00	50.00
2 Walter Reuther (sic& Ruether)	60.00	30.00
3A Joe Duggan ERR (sic, Dugan)	80.00	40.00
3B Joe Dugan COR	80.00	40.00
4 Red Faber	100.00	50.00
5 Gabby Hartnett	120.00	60.00
6 Babe Ruth	1500.00	750.00
7 Bob Meusel	80.00	40.00
8 Herb Pennock	100.00	50.00
9 George (H.) Burns (photo actually George J. Burns)	60.00	30.00
10 Joe Sewell	100.00	50.00
11 George Uhle	60.00	30.00
12A Bob O'Farrel ERR	80.00	40.00
12B Bob O'Farrell COR	80.00	40.00
13 Rogers Hornsby	250.00	125.00
14 Pie Traynor	120.00	60.00
15 Clarence Mitchell	60.00	30.00
16 Eppa Rixey	100.00	50.00
17 Carl Mays	80.00	40.00
18 Dolf Luque	60.00	30.00
19 Dave Bancroft	100.00	50.00
20 George Kelly	100.00	50.00
21 Ira Flagstead	60.00	30.00
22 Harry Heilmann	120.00	60.00
23 Ray Schalk	100.00	50.00
24 Johnny Mostil	60.00	30.00
25 Hack Wilson (photo actually Art Wilson)	200.00	100.00
26 Tom Zachary	60.00	30.00
27 Ty Cobb	1000.00	500.00
28 Tris Speaker	250.00	125.00
29 Ralph Perkins	60.00	30.00
30 Jess Haines (sic, Jesse)	100.00	50.00
31 Sherwood Smith (photo actually Jack Coombs)	60.00	30.00
32 Max Carey	100.00	50.00
33 Eugene Hargraves	60.00	30.00
34 Miguel L. Gonzales	60.00	30.00
35A Clifton Heathcot ERR	80.00	40.00
35B Clifton Heathcote COR	80.00	40.00
36 Sam Rice	100.00	50.00
37 Earl Sheely	60.00	30.00
38 Emory E. Rigney	60.00	30.00
39 Bib Falk	60.00	30.00
40 Nick Altrock	60.00	30.00
41 Stanley Harris	100.00	50.00
42 John J. McGraw MG	200.00	100.00
43 Wilbert Robinson MG	120.00	60.00
44 Grover C. Alexander	250.00	125.00
45 Walter Johnson	400.00	200.00
46 William H. Terry (photo actually Zeb Terry)	120.00	60.00
47 Eddie Collins	120.00	60.00
48 Marty McManus	60.00	30.00
49 Goose Goslin	120.00	60.00
50 Frankie Frisch	200.00	100.00
51 Jimmy Dykes	80.00	40.00
52 Cy Williams	80.00	40.00
53 Ed Roush	120.00	60.00
54 George Sisler	200.00	100.00
55 Ed Rommel	80.00	40.00
56 Rogers Peckinpaugh (sic, Roger)	80.00	40.00
57 Stan Coveleskie	100.00	50.00
58A Clarence Galloway	80.00	40.00
58B Lester Bell	80.00	40.00
59 Bob Shawkey	80.00	40.00
60 John P. McInnis	80.00	40.00

1974 Cy Young Museum Postcard

This one card postcard set was issued by TCMA to promote the Cy Young Museum in Newcomerstown, Ohio. The front has a picture of Young surrounded by the words "Cy Young Museum" on top and its location on the bottom. The back has some information about Young's career.

	NM	Ex
1 Cy Young	5.00	2.00

1994 Yount Ameritech

This credit card-sized (3 3/8" by 2 1/8") card was issued to fans at Milwaukee County Stadium on Robin Yount Tribute Day, May 29, 1994, to commemorate the retirement of his jersey number (19). It has rounded corners and features on its front a horizontal borderless color action shot of Yount. The card carries a value of 50 cents worth of pay telephone calls. The white back carries instructions for use and the production number out of 63,000 produced.

	Nm-Mt	Ex-Mt
1 Robin Yount	3.00	.90

1928 Yuenglings

The cards in this 60-card set measure approximately 1 3/8" by 2 9/16". This black and white, numbered set contains many Hall of Famers. The card backs are the same as those found in sets of E210 and W502. The Paul Waner card, number 45, actually contains a

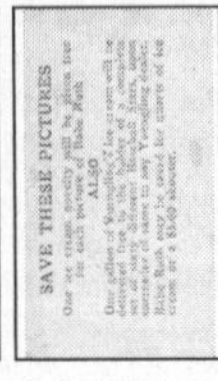

picture of Clyde Barnhardt. Each back contains an offer to redeem pictures of Babe Ruth for ice cream. The catalog designation for this set is F50.

	Ex-Mt	VG
COMPLETE SET (60)	3000.00	1500.00
1 Burleigh Grimes	30.00	15.00
2 Walter Reuther	15.00	7.50
3 Joe Dugan	20.00	10.00
4 Red Faber	30.00	15.00
5 Gabby Hartnett	30.00	15.00
6 Babe Ruth	800.00	400.00
7 Bob Meusel	25.00	12.50
8 Herb Pennock	30.00	15.00
9 George Burns	15.00	7.50
10 Joe Sewell	30.00	15.00
11 George Uhle	15.00	7.50
12 Bob O'Farrell	15.00	7.50
13 Rogers Hornsby	100.00	50.00
14 Pie Traynor	30.00	15.00
15 Clarence Mitchell	15.00	7.50
16 Eppa Rixey	30.00	15.00
17 Carl Mays	20.00	10.00
18 Adolfo Luque	20.00	10.00
19 Dave Bancroft	30.00	15.00
20 George Kelly	30.00	15.00
21 Earle Combs	30.00	15.00
22 Harry Heilmann	30.00	15.00
23 Ray Schalk	30.00	15.00
24 John Mostil	15.00	7.50
25 Hack Wilson	50.00	25.00
26 Lou Gehrig	500.00	250.00
27 Ty Cobb	500.00	250.00
28 Tris Speaker	80.00	40.00
29 Tony Lazzeri	30.00	15.00
30 Waite Hoyt	30.00	15.00
31 Sherwood Smith	15.00	7.50
32 Max Carey	30.00	15.00
33 Gene Hargrave	15.00	7.50
34 Miguel Gonzalez	20.00	10.00
35 Joe Judge	20.00	10.00
36 Sam Rice	30.00	15.00
37 Earl Sheely	15.00	7.50
38 Sam Jones	20.00	10.00
39 Bibb Falk	15.00	7.50
40 Willie Kamm	15.00	7.50
41 Bucky Harris	30.00	15.00
42 John McGraw MG	50.00	25.00
43 Art Nehf	20.00	10.00
44 Grover C. Alexander	100.00	50.00
45 Paul Waner	30.00	15.00
46 Bill Terry	60.00	30.00
47 Glenn Wright	15.00	7.50
48 Earl Smith	15.00	7.50
49 Goose Goslin	30.00	15.00
50 Frank Frisch	30.00	15.00
51 Joe Harris	15.00	7.50
52 Cy Williams	20.00	10.00
53 Eddie Roush	30.00	15.00
54 George Sisler	60.00	30.00
55 Ed Rommel	20.00	10.00
56 Roger Peckinpaugh	20.00	10.00
57 Stanley Coveleskie	30.00	15.00
58 Lester Bell	15.00	7.50
59 Lloyd Waner	30.00	15.00
60 John McInnis	20.00	10.00

1995 Zenith Samples

These nine cards were distributed to hobby media and dealers prior to the national release of 1995 Zenith. The cards parallel basic Zenith issues except for the bold "SAMPLE" text running diagonally across both the front and back.

	Nm-Mt	Ex-Mt
COMPLETE SET (9)	10.00	3.00
12 Cal Ripken	3.00	.90
20 Dante Bichette	.40	.12
51 Jim Thome	1.00	.30
70 Mark Grace	.75	.23
97 Ryan Klesko	.40	.12
111 Chipper Jones	1.50	.45
113 Curtis Goodwin	.20	.06
R7 Hideo Nomo	3.00	.90
NNO Information Card	.20	.06

1995 Zenith

The complete 1995 Zenith set consists of 150 standard-size cards. The cards are made of thick stock and are borderless. Included is a subset of 50 Rookies (111-150). The regular issued cards are in alphabetical order by first name. Rookie Cards in this set include Bobby Higginson and Hideo Nomo.

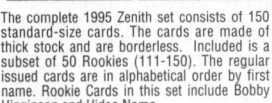

	Nm-Mt	Ex-Mt
COMPLETE SET (150)	40.00	12.00
1 Albert Belle	.40	.12
2 Alex Fernandez	.20	.06
3 Andy Benes	.20	.06
4 Barry Larkin	1.00	.30
5 Barry Bonds	2.50	.75
6 Ben McDonald	.20	.06
7 Bernard Gilkey	.20	.06
8 Billy Ashley	.20	.06
9 Bobby Bonilla	.40	.12
10 Bret Saberhagen	.40	.12
11 Brian Jordan	.40	.12
12 Cal Ripken	3.00	.90
13 Carlos Baerga	.20	.06
14 Carlos Delgado	.40	.12
15 Cecil Fielder	.40	.12
16 Chili Davis	.40	.12
17 Chuck Knoblauch	.40	.12
18 Craig Biggio	.60	.18
19 Danny Tartabull	.20	.06
20 Dante Bichette	.40	.12
21 Darren Daulton	.40	.12
22 David Justice	.40	.12
23 Dave Winfield	.40	.12
24 David Cone	.40	.12
25 Dean Palmer	.40	.12
26 Deion Sanders	.60	.18
27 Dennis Eckersley	.40	.12
28 Derek Bell	.20	.06
29 Don Mattingly	2.50	.75
30 Edgar Martinez	.60	.18
31 Eric Karros	.40	.12
32 James Mouton	.20	.06
33 Frank Thomas	1.00	.30
34 Fred McGriff	.60	.18
35 Gary Sheffield	.40	.12
36 Gary Gaetti	.40	.12
37 Greg Maddux	1.50	.45
38 Gregg Jefferies	.20	.06
39 Ivan Rodriguez	1.00	.30
40 Kenny Rogers	.40	.12
41 J.T. Snow	.40	.12
42 Hal Morris	.20	.06
43 E.Murray 3000th Hit	.60	.18
44 Javier Lopez	.40	.12
45 Jay Bell	.40	.12
46 Jeff Conine	.40	.12
47 Jeff Bagwell	.60	.18
48 Hideo Nomo Japanese	2.00	.60
49 Jeff Kent	.40	.12
50 Jeff King	.20	.06
51 Jim Thome	1.00	.30
52 Jimmy Key	.40	.12
53 Joe Carter	.40	.12
54 John Valentin	.20	.06
55 John Olerud	.40	.12
56 Jose Canseco	1.00	.30
57 Jose Rijo	.20	.06
58 Jose Offerman	.20	.06
59 Juan Gonzalez	1.00	.30
60 Ken Caminiti	.40	.12
61 Ken Griffey Jr.	1.50	.45
62 Kenny Lofton	.40	.12
63 Kevin Appier	.40	.12
64 Kevin Seitzer	.20	.06
65 Kirby Puckett	1.00	.30
66 Kirk Gibson	.40	.12
67 Larry Walker	.60	.18
68 Lenny Dykstra	.40	.12
69 Manny Ramirez	.40	.12
70 Mark Grace	.60	.18
71 Mark McGwire	2.50	.75
72 Marquis Grissom	.20	.06
73 Jim Edmonds	.40	.12
74 Matt Williams	.40	.12
75 Mike Mussina	1.00	.30
76 Mike Piazza	1.50	.45
77 Mo Vaughn	.40	.12
78 Moises Alou	.40	.12
79 Ozzie Smith	1.50	.45
80 Paul O'Neill	.60	.18
81 Paul Molitor	.60	.18
82 Rafael Palmeiro	.60	.18
83 Randy Johnson	1.00	.30
84 Raul Mondesi	.40	.12
85 Ray Lankford	.20	.06
86 Reggie Sanders	.40	.12
87 Rickey Henderson	1.00	.30
88 Rico Brogna	.20	.06
89 Roberto Alomar	1.00	.30
90 Robin Ventura	.40	.12
91 Roger Clemens	2.00	.60
92 Ron Gant	.40	.12
93 Rondell White	.40	.12
94 Royce Clayton	.20	.06
95 Ruben Sierra	.20	.06
96 Rusty Greer	.20	.06
97 Ryan Klesko	.40	.12
98 Sammy Sosa	1.50	.45
99 Shawon Dunston	.20	.06
100 Steve Ontiveros	.20	.06
101 Tim Naehring	.20	.06
102 Tim Salmon	.60	.18
103 Tino Martinez	.60	.18
104 Tony Gwynn	1.25	.35
105 Travis Fryman	.40	.12
106 Vinny Castilla	.40	.12
107 Wade Boggs	.60	.18
108 Wally Joyner	.40	.12
109 Wil Cordero	.20	.06
110 Will Clark	1.00	.30
111 Chipper Jones	1.00	.30
112 Armando Benitez	.40	.12
113 Curtis Goodwin	.20	.06
114 Gabe White	.20	.06
115 Vaughn Eshelman	.20	.06
116 Marty Cordova	.20	.06
117 Dustin Hermanson	.20	.06
118 Rich Becker	.20	.06
119 Ray Durham	.40	.12
120 Shane Andrews	.20	.06
121 Scott Ruffcorn	.20	.06
122 Mark Grudzielanek RC	.60	.18
123 James Baldwin	.20	.06
124 Carlos Perez RC	.40	.12
125 Julian Tavarez	.20	.06
126 Joe Vitiello	.20	.06
127 Jason Bates	.20	.06
128 Edgardo Alfonzo	.40	.12
129 Juan Acevedo RC	.20	.06
130 Bill Pulsipher	.20	.06
131 Bob Higginson RC	1.00	.30
132 Russ Davis	.20	.06
133 Charles Johnson	.40	.12
134 Derek Jeter	2.50	.75
135 Orlando Miller	.20	.06
136 LaTroy Hawkins	.20	.06
137 Brian L.Hunter	.20	.06
138 Roberto Petagine	.20	.06
139 Midre Cummings	.20	.06
140 Garret Anderson	.40	.12
141 Ugueth Urbina	.20	.06
142 Antonio Osuna	.20	.06
143 Michael Tucker	.20	.06
144 Benji Gil	.20	.06
145 Jon Nunnally	.20	.06
146 Alex Rodriguez	2.50	.75
147 Todd Hollandsworth	.20	.06
148 Alex Gonzalez	.20	.06
149 Hideo Nomo RC	2.00	.60
150 Shawn Green	.40	.12

1995 Zenith All-Star Salute

This 18-card set was randomly inserted in packs at a rate of one in six. The set commemorates many of the memorable plays of the 1995 All-Star Game played in Arlington, TX. The fronts have an action photo set out against the background of the game giving it a 3D look. The cards are numbered "X of 18."

	Nm-Mt	Ex-Mt
COMPLETE SET (18)	40.00	12.00
1 Cal Ripken	6.00	1.80
2 Frank Thomas	2.00	.60
3 Mike Piazza	3.00	.90
4 Kirby Puckett	2.00	.60
5 Manny Ramirez	.75	.23
6 Tony Gwynn	2.50	.75
7 Hideo Nomo	3.00	.90
8 Matt Williams	.75	.23
9 Randy Johnson	2.00	.60
10 Raul Mondesi	.75	.23
11 Albert Belle	.75	.23
12 Ivan Rodriguez	2.00	.60
13 Barry Bonds	5.00	1.50
14 Carlos Baerga	.40	.12
15 Ken Griffey Jr.	3.00	.90
16 Jeff Conine	.75	.23
17 Frank Thomas	2.00	.60
18 Cal Ripken Barry Bonds	6.00	1.80

1995 Zenith Rookie Roll Call

This 18-card, Dufex-designed standard-size set was randomly inserted in packs at a rate of one in 24. The set is comprised of 18 top rookies from 1995. Player information of previous accomplishments is also on the back and the cards are numbered "X of 18."

	Nm-Mt	Ex-Mt
COMPLETE SET (18)	40.00	12.00
1 Alex Rodriguez	10.00	3.00
2 Derek Jeter	10.00	3.00
3 Chipper Jones	4.00	1.20
4 Shawn Green	1.50	.45
5 Todd Hollandsworth	1.00	.30
6 Bill Pulsipher	1.00	.30
7 Hideo Nomo	5.00	1.50
8 Ray Durham	1.50	.45
9 Curtis Goodwin	1.00	.30
10 Brian L.Hunter	1.00	.30
11 Julian Tavarez	1.00	.30
12 Marty Cordova UER Kevin Maas pictured	1.00	.30
13 Michael Tucker	1.00	.30
14 Edgardo Alfonzo	1.50	.45
15 LaTroy Hawkins	1.00	.30
16 Carlos Perez	1.50	.45
17 Charles Johnson	1.50	.45
18 Benji Gil	1.00	.30

1995 Zenith Z-Team

This 18-card standard-size set was randomly inserted in packs at a rate of one in 72. The set is comprised of the best players in baseball and is done in 3-D Dufex. The backs also have player information and a "Z Team" emblem.

	Nm-Mt	Ex-Mt
COMPLETE SET (18)		
1 Cal Ripken	30.00	9.00
2 Ken Griffey Jr.	15.00	4.50
3 Frank Thomas	10.00	3.00
4 Matt Williams	4.00	1.20
5 Mike Piazza UER (Card says started at first base Piazza is a catcher)	15.00	4.50
6 Barry Bonds	25.00	7.50
7 Raul Mondesi	4.00	1.20
8 Greg Maddux	15.00	4.50
9 Jeff Bagwell	6.00	1.80
10 Manny Ramirez	4.00	1.20
11 Larry Walker	6.00	1.80
12 Tony Gwynn	12.00	3.60
13 Will Clark	10.00	3.00
14 Albert Belle	4.00	1.20
15 Kenny Lofton	4.00	1.20
16 Rafael Palmeiro	6.00	1.80
17 Don Mattingly	25.00	7.50
18 Carlos Baerga	2.00	.60

1996 Zenith

This 1996 Zenith set was issued in one series totalling 150 cards. The six-card packs retailed for $3.99 each. The set contains the subset: Honor Roll (131-150). The fronts feature a color player cutout over an arrangement of baseball bats on a black background. The backs carry a hit location chart and player statistics. Rookie Card include Darin Erstad.

	Nm-Mt	Ex-Mt
COMPLETE SET (150)	30.00	9.00
1 Ken Griffey Jr.	1.25	.35
2 Ozzie Smith	1.25	.35
3 Greg Maddux	1.25	.35
4 Rondell White	.30	.09
5 Mark McGwire	2.00	.60
6 Jim Thome	.75	.23
7 Ivan Rodriguez	.75	.23
8 Marc Newfield	.30	.09
9 Travis Fryman	.30	.09
10 Fred McGriff	.50	.15
11 Shawn Green	.30	.09
12 Mike Piazza	1.25	.35
13 Dante Bichette	.30	.09
14 Tino Martinez	.50	.15
15 Sterling Hitchcock	.30	.09
16 Ryne Sandberg	1.25	.35
17 Rico Brogna	.30	.09
18 Roberto Alomar	.75	.23
19 Barry Larkin	.75	.23
20 Bernie Williams	.50	.15
21 Gary Sheffield	.30	.09
22 Frank Thomas	.75	.23
23 Gregg Jefferies	.30	.09
24 Jeff Bagwell	.50	.15
25 Marty Cordova	.30	.09
26 Jim Edmonds	.30	.09
27 Jay Bell	.30	.09
28 Ben McDonald	.30	.09
29 Barry Bonds	2.00	.60
30 Mo Vaughn	.30	.09
31 Johnny Damon	.30	.09
32 Dean Palmer	.30	.09
33 Ismael Valdes	.30	.09
34 Manny Ramirez	.30	.09
35 Edgar Martinez	.50	.15
36 Cecil Fielder	.30	.09
37 Ryan Klesko	.30	.09
38 Ray Lankford	.30	.09
39 Tim Salmon	.50	.15
40 Joe Carter	.30	.09
41 Jason Isringhausen	.30	.09
42 Rickey Henderson	.75	.23
43 Lenny Dykstra	.30	.09
44 Andre Dawson	.30	.09
45 Paul O'Neill	.50	.15
46 Ray Durham	.30	.09
47 Raul Mondesi	.30	.09
48 Jay Buhner	.30	.09
49 Eddie Murray	.75	.23
50 Henry Rodriguez	.30	.09
51 Hal Morris	.30	.09
52 Mike Mussina	.75	.23
53 Wally Joyner	.30	.09
54 Will Clark	.75	.23
55 Chipper Jones	.75	.23
56 Brian Jordan	.30	.09
57 Larry Walker	.50	.15
58 Wade Boggs	.50	.15
59 Melvin Nieves	.30	.09
60 Charles Johnson	.30	.09
61 Juan Gonzalez	.75	.23
62 Carlos Delgado	.30	.09
63 Reggie Sanders	.30	.09
64 Brian L.Hunter	.30	.09
65 Edgardo Alfonzo	.30	.09
66 Kenny Lofton	.30	.09
67 Paul Molitor	.50	.15
68 Mike Bordick	.30	.09
69 Garret Anderson	.30	.09
70 Orlando Merced	.30	.09
71 Craig Biggio	.50	.15
72 Chuck Knoblauch	.30	.09
73 Mark Grace	.50	.15
74 Jack McDowell	.30	.09
75 Randy Johnson	.75	.23
76 Cal Ripken	2.50	.75
77 Matt Williams	.30	.09
78 Benji Gil	.30	.09
79 Moises Alou	.30	.09
80 Robin Ventura	.30	.09
81 Greg Vaughn	.30	.09
82 Carlos Baerga	.30	.09
83 Roger Clemens	1.50	.45
84 Hideo Nomo	.75	.23
85 Pedro Martinez	.75	.23
86 John Valentin	.30	.09
87 Andres Galarraga	.30	.09
88 Andy Pettitte	.50	.15
89 Derek Bell	.30	.09
90 Kirby Puckett	.75	.23
91 Tony Gwynn	1.00	.30
92 Brady Anderson	.30	.09
93 Derek Jeter	2.00	.60
94 Michael Tucker	.30	.09
95 Albert Belle	.30	.09
96 David Cone	.30	.09
97 J.T. Snow	.30	.09
98 Tom Glavine	.50	.15
99 Alex Rodriguez	1.50	.45
100 Sammy Sosa	1.25	.35
101 Karim Garcia	.30	.09
102 Alan Benes	.30	.09
103 Chad Mottola	.30	.09
104 Robin Jennings	.30	.09
105 Bob Abreu	.30	.09
106 Tony Clark	.30	.09
107 George Arias	.30	.09
108 Jermaine Dye	.30	.09
109 Jeff Suppan	.30	.09
110 Ralph Milliard RC	.30	.09
111 Ruben Rivera	.30	.09
112 Billy Wagner	.30	.09
113 Jason Kendall	.30	.09
114 Mike Grace RC	.30	.09
115 Edgar Renteria	.30	.09
116 Jason Schmidt	.30	.09
117 Paul Wilson	.30	.09
118 Rey Ordonez	.30	.09
119 Rocky Coppinger RC	.30	.09
120 Wilton Guerrero RC	.30	.09
121 Brooks Kieschnick	.30	.09
122 Raul Casanova	.30	.09
123 Alex Ochoa	.30	.09
124 Chan Ho Park	.30	.09
125 John Wasdin	.30	.09
126 Eric Owens	.30	.09
127 Justin Thompson	.30	.09
128 Chris Snopek	.30	.09
129 Terrell Wade	.30	.09
130 Darin Erstad RC	2.50	.75
131 Albert Belle HON	.30	.09
132 Cal Ripken HON	1.25	.35
133 Frank Thomas HON	.50	.15
134 Greg Maddux HON	.75	.23
135 Ken Griffey Jr. HON	.75	.23
136 Mo Vaughn HON	.30	.09
137 Chipper Jones HON	.50	.15
138 Mike Piazza HON	.75	.23
139 Ryan Klesko HON	.30	.09
140 Hideo Nomo HON	.50	.15
141 Roberto Alomar HON	.30	.09
142 Manny Ramirez HON	.30	.09
143 Gary Sheffield HON	.30	.09
144 Barry Bonds HON	.75	.23
145 Matt Williams HON	.30	.09
146 Jim Edmonds HON	.30	.09
147 Derek Jeter HON	1.00	.30
148 Sammy Sosa HON	.75	.23
149 Kirby Puckett HON	.50	.15
150 Tony Gwynn HON	.50	.15

1996 Zenith Artist's Proofs

Randomly inserted in packs at a rate of one in 35, this 150-card set is parallel to the regular Zenith set. The cards are distinguished from the regular set by the "Artist's Proof" all-gold, rainbow holographic foil stamp on the front.

Nm-Mt Ex-Mt

*STARS: 10X TO 25X BASIC CARDS ..

*ROOKIES: 4X TO 10X BASIC CARDS

1996 Zenith Diamond Club

Randomly inserted in packs at a rate of one in 24, cards from this 20-card set honor top performers on a Spectroetch card design printed on thick foil stock with etched highlights.

	Nm-Mt	Ex-Mt
COMPLETE SET (20)	120.00	36.00
*REAL DIAMOND: 2X TO 5X BASIC DIAMOND		
REAL DIAMOND STATED ODDS 1:350		
1 Albert Belle	2.50	.75
2 Mo Vaughn	2.50	.75
3 Ken Griffey Jr.	10.00	3.00
4 Mike Piazza	10.00	3.00
5 Cal Ripken	20.00	6.00
6 Jermaine Dye	2.50	.75
7 Jeff Bagwell	4.00	1.20
8 Frank Thomas	6.00	1.80
9 Alex Rodriguez	12.00	3.60
10 Ryan Klesko	2.50	.75
11 Roberto Alomar	6.00	1.80
12 Sammy Sosa	10.00	3.00
13 Matt Williams	2.50	.75
14 Gary Sheffield	2.50	.75
15 Ruben Rivera	2.50	.75
16 Darin Erstad	6.00	1.80
17 Randy Johnson	6.00	1.80
18 Greg Maddux	10.00	3.00
19 Karim Garcia	2.50	.75
20 Chipper Jones	6.00	1.80

1996 Zenith Mozaics

Randomly inserted in packs at a rate of one in 10, this 25-card set features three-player image cards of the hottest superstars. The fronts display multiple player images representing the core of each of the 28 teams and are printed on rainbow holographic foil.

	Nm-Mt	Ex-Mt
COMPLETE SET (25)	80.00	24.00
1 Greg Maddux Chipper Jones Ryan Klesko	6.00	1.80
2 Juan Gonzalez Will Clark Ivan Rodriguez	4.00	1.20
3 Frank Thomas Robin Ventura Ray Durham	4.00	1.20
4 Matt Williams Barry Bonds Osvaldo Fernandez	10.00	3.00
5 Ken Griffey Jr. Randy Johnson Alex Rodriguez	6.00	1.80
6 Sammy Sosa Ryne Sandberg Mark Grace	6.00	1.80
7 Jim Edmonds Tim Salmon Garret Anderson	1.50	.45
8 Cal Ripken Roberto Alomar Mike Mussina	12.00	3.60
9 Mo Vaughn Roger Clemens John Valentin	8.00	2.40
10 Barry Larkin Reggie Sanders Hal Morris	4.00	1.20
11 Ray Lankford Brian Jordan Ozzie Smith	6.00	1.80
12 Dante Bichette Larry Walker Andres Galarraga	2.50	.75
13 Mike Piazza Hideo Nomo Raul Mondesi	6.00	1.80
14 Ben McDonald Greg Vaughn Kevin Seitzer	1.50	.45
15 Joe Carter Carlos Delgado Alex Gonzalez	1.50	.45
16 Gary Sheffield Charles Johnson Jeff Conine	1.50	.45
17 Rondell White Moises Alou Henry Rodriguez	1.50	.45
18 Albert Belle Manny Ramirez Carlos Baerga	1.50	.45
19 Kirby Puckett Paul Molitor Chuck Knoblauch	4.00	1.20
20 Tony Gwynn Rickey Henderson Wally Joyner	5.00	1.50
21 Mark McGwire Mike Bordick Scott Brosius	10.00	3.00
22 Paul O'Neill Bernie Williams Wade Boggs	2.50	.75
23 Jay Bell Orlando Merced Jason Kendall	1.50	.45
24 Rico Brogna Paul Wilson Jason Isringhausen	1.50	.45
25 Jeff Bagwell Craig Biggio Derek Bell	2.50	.75

1996 Zenith Z-Team

Randomly inserted in packs at a rate of one in 72, this 18-card set features a color action player cutout on a clear micro-etched design with a gold foil Z-Team logo and a see-through green baseball field background. The backs carry player information printed on the back of the Z.

	Nm-Mt	Ex-Mt
COMPLETE SET (18)	200.00	60.00
1 Ken Griffey Jr.	20.00	6.00
2 Albert Belle	5.00	1.50
3 Cal Ripken	40.00	12.00
4 Frank Thomas	12.00	3.60
5 Greg Maddux	20.00	6.00
6 Mo Vaughn	5.00	1.50
7 Chipper Jones	12.00	3.60
8 Mike Piazza	20.00	6.00
9 Ryan Klesko	5.00	1.50
10 Hideo Nomo	12.00	3.60
11 Roberto Alomar	12.00	3.60
12 Manny Ramirez	5.00	1.50
13 Gary Sheffield	5.00	1.50
14 Barry Bonds	30.00	9.00
15 Matt Williams	5.00	1.50
16 Jim Edmonds	5.00	1.50
17 Kirby Puckett	12.00	3.60
18 Sammy Sosa	20.00	6.00

1997 Zenith

The 1997 Zenith set was issued in one series totalling 50 cards and was distributed in packs containing five standard-size cards and two 8" by 10" cards with a suggested retail price of $9.99. The fronts feature borderless color action player photos. The backs carry a black-and-white player photo with career statistics. The set contains 42 established player cards and eight rookie cards (43-50).

	Nm-Mt	Ex-Mt
COMPLETE SET (50)	25.00	7.50
1 Frank Thomas	1.00	.30
2 Tony Gwynn	1.25	.35
3 Jeff Bagwell	.60	.18
4 Paul Molitor	.60	.18
5 Roberto Alomar	1.00	.30
6 Mike Piazza	1.50	.45
7 Albert Belle	.40	.12
8 Greg Maddux	1.50	.45
9 Barry Larkin	1.00	.30
10 Tony Clark	.40	.12
11 Larry Walker	.60	.18
12 Chipper Jones	1.00	.30
13 Juan Gonzalez	1.00	.30
14 Barry Bonds	2.50	.75
15 Ivan Rodriguez	1.00	.30
16 Sammy Sosa	1.50	.45
17 Derek Jeter	2.50	.75
18 Hideo Nomo	1.00	.30
19 Roger Clemens	2.00	.60
20 Ken Griffey Jr.	1.50	.45
21 Andy Pettitte	.60	.18
22 Alex Rodriguez	1.50	.45
23 Tino Martinez	.60	.18
24 Bernie Williams	.60	.18
25 Ken Caminiti	.40	.12
26 John Smoltz	.60	.18
27 Javier Lopez	.40	.12
28 Mark McGwire	2.50	.75
29 Gary Sheffield	.40	.12
30 David Justice	.40	.12
31 Randy Johnson	1.00	.30
32 Chuck Knoblauch	.40	.12
33 Mike Mussina	1.00	.30
34 Deion Sanders	.60	.18
35 Cal Ripken	3.00	.90
36 Darin Erstad	.40	.12
37 Kenny Lofton	.40	.12
38 Jay Buhner	.40	.12
39 Brady Anderson	.40	.12
40 Edgar Martinez	.60	.18
41 Mo Vaughn	.40	.12
42 Ryne Sandberg	1.50	.45
43 Andruw Jones	.40	.12
44 Nomar Garciaparra	1.50	.45
45 Hideki Irabu RC	.40	.12
46 Wilton Guerrero	.40	.12
47 Jose Cruz Jr. RC	1.50	.45
48 Vladimir Guerrero	1.00	.30
49 Scott Rolen	.60	.18
50 Jose Guillen	.40	.12

1997 Zenith 8 x 10

Randomly inserted one in every pack, this 24-card set features 8" by 10" versions of the base set cards of the players listed below.

	Nm-Mt	Ex-Mt
COMPLETE SET (24)	25.00	7.50
*DUFEX: 1X TO 2.5X BASIC 8 X 10		
ONE DUFEX PER PACK		
1 Frank Thomas	1.25	.35
2 Tony Gwynn	1.50	.45
3 Jeff Bagwell	.75	.23
4 Ken Griffey Jr.	2.00	.60
5 Mike Piazza	2.00	.60
6 Greg Maddux	2.00	.60
7 Ken Caminiti	.50	.15
8 Albert Belle	.50	.15
9 Ivan Rodriguez	1.25	.35
10 Sammy Sosa	2.00	.60
11 Mark McGwire	3.00	.90
12 Roger Clemens	2.50	.75
13 Alex Rodriguez	2.00	.60
14 Chipper Jones	1.25	.35
15 Juan Gonzalez	1.25	.35
16 Barry Bonds	3.00	.90
17 Derek Jeter	3.00	.90
18 Hideo Nomo	1.25	.35
19 Cal Ripken	4.00	1.20
20 Hideki Irabu	.50	.15
21 Andruw Jones	.50	.15
22 Nomar Garciaparra	2.00	.60
23 Vladimir Guerrero	1.25	.35
24 Scott Rolen	.75	.23

1997 Zenith 8 x 10 Dufex Samples

These oversized Samples were distributed to dealers and hobby media several weeks prior to the shipping of 1997 Zenith to preview then then upcoming brand. The Samples are straight parallels of the basic issue 1997 Zenith 8 x 10 Dufex inserts except for the word "SAMPLE" running diagonally across the front and back of the card in bold black text.

	Nm-Mt	Ex-Mt
13 Alex Rodriguez	5.00	1.50

1997 Zenith the Big Picture

These six 8 by 10 photos were released as promos to demonstrate what the 1997 Zenith 8 by 10's would look like. They have the notation the Big Picture at the bottom of the card. The cards are skip-numbered and share the same number as the regular cards

	Nm-Mt	Ex-Mt
1 Frank Thomas	8.00	2.40
4 Ken Griffey Jr.	10.00	3.00
5 Mike Piazza	12.00	3.60
13 Alex Rodriguez	12.00	3.60
17 Derek Jeter	15.00	4.50
19 Cal Ripken Jr.	20.00	6.00

1997 Zenith V-2

Randomly inserted in packs at the rate of one in 47, this eight-card set features color action player photos produced with motion technology and state-of-the-art foil printing.

	Nm-Mt	Ex-Mt
COMPLETE SET (8)	150.00	45.00
1 Ken Griffey Jr.	20.00	6.00
2 Andruw Jones	5.00	1.50
3 Frank Thomas	12.00	3.60
4 Mike Piazza	20.00	6.00
5 Alex Rodriguez	20.00	6.00
6 Cal Ripken	40.00	12.00
7 Derek Jeter	30.00	9.00
8 Vladimir Guerrero	12.00	3.60

1997 Zenith Z-Team

Randomly inserted in packs, cards from this nine-card set feature color action photos of top players printed on full Mirror Gold Holographic Mylar foil card stock. Only 1,000 sets were produced and each card is sequentially numbered on back.

	Nm-Mt	Ex-Mt
COMPLETE SET (9)	150.00	45.00
1 Ken Griffey Jr.	20.00	6.00
2 Larry Walker	8.00	2.40
3 Frank Thomas	12.00	3.60
4 Alex Rodriguez	20.00	6.00
5 Mike Piazza	20.00	6.00
6 Cal Ripken	40.00	12.00
7 Derek Jeter	30.00	9.00
8 Andruw Jones	5.00	1.50
9 Roger Clemens	25.00	7.50

1998 Zenith Samples Large

One of these nine different 3 1/2" by 5" samples was inserted into dealer order forms to preview the upcoming 1998 Zenith baseball release. Each large sample card also contains a "hidden" standard size sample card inside. To get to the small sample card, however, one must tear the larger sample card in two - thereby destroying it. The cards were sent out around April, 1998. They're identical to regular issue large Zenith cards except for the bold "SAMPLE" text running diagonally across the back of the card. Prices below refer to mint untorn cards.

	Nm-Mt	Ex-Mt
COMPLETE SET (9)	25.00	7.50
Z1 Nomar Garciaparra	3.00	.90
Z3 Greg Maddux	3.00	.90
Z4 Frank Thomas	1.50	.45
Z9 Andruw Jones	1.25	.35
Z15 Derek Jeter	6.00	1.80
Z21 Mike Piazza	4.00	1.20
Z22 Tony Gwynn	3.00	.90
Z35 Ivan Rodriguez	1.50	.45
Z40 Ken Griffey Jr.	4.00	1.20

1998 Zenith Samples Small

One of these six different small (actually standard size 2 1/2" by 3 1/2") promo cards was "hidden" inside the larger 3 12/" by 5" Zenith Samples. The larger sample card had to be torn in two to get to this small card.

	Nm-Mt	Ex-Mt
COMPLETE SET (6)	15.00	4.50
2 Ken Griffey Jr.	4.00	1.20
12 Greg Maddux	3.00	.90
14 Mike Piazza	3.00	.90
17 Derek Jeter	6.00	1.80
18 Nomar Garciaparra	3.00	.90
19 Ivan Rodriguez	1.50	.45

1998 Zenith

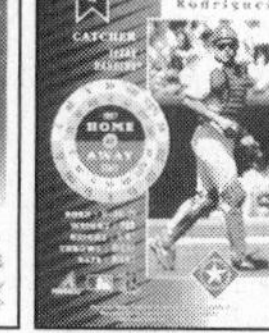

The 1998 Zenith set was issued in one series totalling 100 cards. The packs retailed for $5.99 each and contained three 5x7 Zenith cards each with one standard size card inside. The standard-size cards listed here had to be removed from the inside of the jumbo packs by tearing the large cards in half. This ill-conceived concept was entitled "Dare to Tear", thus collectors were faced with the dilemma of having to choose between the standard size card of the jumbo 5" by 7" card. Ultimately, collectors by and large chose to carefully slice the back of the jumbo cards and remove the small card. The fronts feature color action player photos. The backs carry player information and career statistic.

	Nm-Mt	Ex-Mt
COMPLETE SET (100)	50.00	15.00
1 Larry Walker	.75	.23
2 Ken Griffey Jr.	2.00	.60
3 Cal Ripken	4.00	1.20
4 Sammy Sosa	2.00	.60
5 Andruw Jones	.50	.15
6 Frank Thomas	1.25	.35
7 Tony Gwynn	1.50	.45
8 Rafael Palmeiro	.75	.23
9 Tim Salmon	.75	.23
10 Randy Johnson	1.25	.35
11 Juan Gonzalez	1.25	.35
12 Greg Maddux	2.00	.60
13 Vladimir Guerrero	1.25	.35
14 Mike Piazza	2.00	.60
15 Andres Galarraga	.50	.15
16 Alex Rodriguez	2.00	.60
17 Derek Jeter	3.00	.90
18 Nomar Garciaparra	2.00	.60
19 Ivan Rodriguez	1.25	.35
20 Chipper Jones	1.25	.35
21 Barry Larkin	1.25	.35
22 Mo Vaughn	.50	.15
23 Albert Belle	.50	.15
24 Scott Rolen	.75	.23
25 Sandy Alomar Jr.	.50	.15
26 Roberto Alomar	1.25	.35
27 Andy Pettitte	.75	.23
28 Chuck Knoblauch	.50	.15
29 Jeff Bagwell	.75	.23
30 Mike Mussina	1.25	.35
31 Fred McGriff	.75	.23
32 Roger Clemens	2.50	.75
33 Rusty Greer	.50	.15
34 Edgar Martinez	.75	.23
35 Paul Molitor	.75	.23
36 Mark Grace	.75	.23
37 Darin Erstad	.50	.15
38 Kenny Lofton	.50	.15
39 Tom Glavine	.75	.23
40 Javier Lopez	.50	.15
41 Will Clark	1.25	.35
42 Tino Martinez	.75	.23
43 Raul Mondesi	.50	.15
44 Brady Anderson	.50	.15
45 Chan Ho Park	.50	.15
46 Jason Giambi	1.25	.35
47 Manny Ramirez	.50	.15
48 Jay Buhner	.50	.15
49 Dante Bichette	.50	.15
50 Jose Cruz Jr.	.50	.15
51 Charles Johnson	.50	.15
52 Bernard Gilkey	.50	.15
53 Johnny Damon	.50	.15
54 David Justice	.50	.15
55 Justin Thompson	.50	.15
56 Bobby Higginson	.50	.15
57 Todd Hundley	.50	.15
58 Gary Sheffield	.50	.15
59 Barry Bonds	3.00	.90
60 Mark McGwire	3.00	.90
61 John Smoltz	.75	.23
62 Tony Clark	.50	.15
63 Brian Jordan	.50	.15
64 Jason Kendall	.50	.15
65 Mariano Rivera	.75	.23
66 Pedro Martinez	1.25	.35
67 Jim Thome	1.25	.35
68 Neifi Perez	.50	.15
69 Kevin Brown	.75	.23
70 Hideo Nomo	1.25	.35
71 Craig Biggio	.75	.23
72 Bernie Williams	.75	.23
73 Jose Guillen	.50	.15
74 Ken Caminiti	.50	.15
75 Livan Hernandez	.50	.15
76 Ray Lankford	.50	.15
77 Jim Edmonds	.50	.15
78 Matt Williams	.50	.15
79 Mark Kotsay	.50	.15
80 Moises Alou	.50	.15
81 Antone Williamson	.50	.15
82 Jaret Wright	.50	.15
83 Jacob Cruz	.50	.15
84 Abraham Nunez	.50	.15
85 Raul Ibanez	.50	.15
86 Miguel Tejada	.75	.23
87 Derrek Lee	.50	.15
88 Juan Encarnacion	.50	.15
89 Todd Helton	.75	.23
90 Travis Lee	.50	.15
91 Ben Grieve	.50	.15
92 Ryan McGuire	.50	.15
93 Richard Hidalgo	.50	.15
94 Paul Konerko	.50	.15
95 Shannon Stewart	.50	.15
96 Homer Bush	.50	.15
97 Lou Collier	.50	.15
98 Jeff Abbott	.50	.15
99 Brett Tomko	.50	.15
100 Fernando Tatis	.50	.15

1998 Zenith Z-Gold

Randomly inserted in packs, this 100 card set is a gold foil parallel version of the base set. Only 100 serially numbered sets were produced.

	Nm-Mt	Ex-Mt
*STARS: 6X TO 15X BASIC CARDS		

1998 Zenith Z-Silver

Randomly inserted in packs at the rate of one in seven, this 100-card set is a silver foil parallel version of the base set.

	Nm-Mt	Ex-Mt
*STARS: 2X TO 5X BASIC CARDS		

1998 Zenith 5 x 7

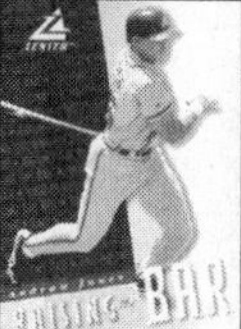

Inserted three per pack, this 80-card set features color action player photos printed on large 5x7 cards. Prices in our checklist refer to mint non-sliced (or "slit-back") cards. Each mint Zenith 5" by 7" card contains a standard-size (2 1/2" by 3 1/2") Zenith card inside it. Please see the 1998 Zenith listing for more details.

	Nm-Mt	Ex-Mt
COMPLETE SET (80)	80.00	24.00
*IMPULSE STARS: 2X TO 5X BASIC 5 X 7'S		
*IMPULSE SLIT-BACKS: .5X TO 1.25X BASIC 5 X 7'S		
IMPULSE STATED ODDS 1:7		
IMPULSE GOLD STATED ODDS 1:35		
1 Nomar Garciaparra	2.50	.75
2 Andres Galarraga	.60	.18
3 Greg Maddux	2.50	.75
4 Frank Thomas	1.50	.45
5 Mark McGwire	4.00	1.20
6 Rafael Palmeiro	1.00	.30
7 John Smoltz	1.00	.30
8 Jeff Bagwell	1.00	.30
9 Andruw Jones	.60	.18
10 Rusty Greer	.60	.18
11 Paul Molitor	1.00	.30
12 Bernie Williams	1.00	.30
13 Kenny Lofton	.60	.18
14 Alex Rodriguez	2.50	.75
15 Derek Jeter	4.00	1.20
16 Scott Rolen	1.00	.30
17 Albert Belle	.60	.18
18 Mo Vaughn	.60	.18
19 Chipper Jones	1.50	.45
20 Chuck Knoblauch	.60	.18
21 Mike Piazza	2.50	.75
22 Tony Gwynn	2.00	.60
23 Juan Gonzalez	1.50	.45
24 Andy Pettitte	1.00	.30
25 Tim Salmon	1.00	.30
26 Brady Anderson	.60	.18
27 Mike Mussina	1.50	.45
28 Edgar Martinez	1.00	.30
29 Jose Guillen	.60	.18
30 Hideo Nomo	1.50	.45
31 Jim Thome	1.50	.45
32 Mark Grace	1.00	.30
33 Darin Erstad	.60	.18
34 Bobby Higginson	.60	.18
35 Ivan Rodriguez	1.50	.45
36 Todd Hundley	.60	.18
37 Sandy Alomar Jr.	.60	.18
38 Gary Sheffield	.60	.18
39 David Justice	.60	.18
40 Ken Griffey Jr.	2.50	.75
41 Vladimir Guerrero	1.50	.45
42 Larry Walker	1.00	.30
43 Barry Bonds	4.00	1.20
44 Randy Johnson	1.50	.45
45 Roger Clemens	3.00	.90
46 Raul Mondesi	.60	.18
47 Tino Martinez	1.00	.30
48 Jason Giambi	1.50	.45
49 Matt Williams	.60	.18
50 Cal Ripken	5.00	1.50
51 Barry Larkin	1.50	.45
52 Jim Edmonds	.60	.18
53 Ken Caminiti	.60	.18
54 Sammy Sosa	2.50	.75
55 Tony Clark	.60	.18
56 Manny Ramirez	.60	.18
57 Bernard Gilkey	.60	.18
58 Jose Cruz Jr.	.60	.18
59 Brian Jordan	.60	.18
60 Kevin Brown	1.00	.30
61 Craig Biggio	1.00	.30
62 Javier Lopez	.60	.18
63 Jay Buhner	.60	.18
64 Roberto Alomar	1.50	.45
65 Justin Thompson	.60	.18
66 Todd Helton	1.00	.30
67 Travis Lee	.60	.18
68 Paul Konerko	.60	.18
69 Jaret Wright	.60	.18
70 Ben Grieve	.60	.18
71 Juan Encarnacion	.60	.18
72 Ryan McGuire	.60	.18
73 Derrek Lee	.60	.18
74 Abraham Nunez	.60	.18
75 Richard Hidalgo	.60	.18
76 Miguel Tejada	1.00	.30
77 Jacob Cruz	.60	.18
78 Homer Bush	.60	.18
79 Jeff Abbott	.60	.18
80 Lou Collier	.60	.18

1998 Zenith Raising the Bar

Randomly inserted in packs at the rate of one in 25, this 15-card set features color player photos of players with only a couple of years of big-league experience.

	Nm-Mt	Ex-Mt
COMPLETE SET (15)	100.00	30.00
1 Ken Griffey Jr.	10.00	3.00
2 Frank Thomas	6.00	1.80
3 Alex Rodriguez	10.00	3.00
4 Tony Gwynn	8.00	2.40
5 Mike Piazza	10.00	3.00
6 Ivan Rodriguez	6.00	1.80
7 Cal Ripken	20.00	6.00
8 Greg Maddux	10.00	3.00
9 Hideo Nomo	6.00	1.80
10 Mark McGwire	15.00	4.50
11 Juan Gonzalez	6.00	1.80
12 Andruw Jones	2.50	.75
13 Jeff Bagwell	4.00	1.20
14 Chipper Jones	6.00	1.80
15 Nomar Garciaparra	10.00	3.00

1998 Zenith Rookie Thrills

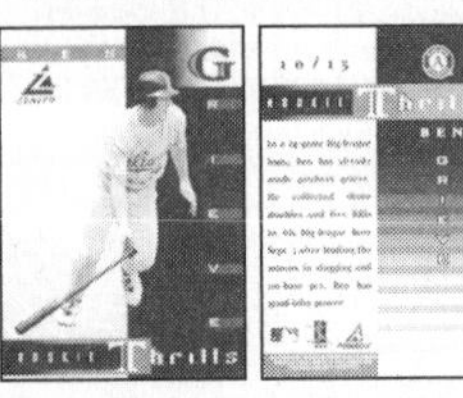

Randomly inserted in packs at the rate of one in 25, this 15-card set features color photos of top Rookie of the Year suspects.

	Nm-Mt	Ex-Mt
COMPLETE SET (15)	25.00	7.50
1 Travis Lee	2.00	.60
2 Juan Encarnacion	2.00	.60
3 Derrek Lee	2.00	.60
4 Raul Ibanez	2.00	.60
5 Ryan McGuire	2.00	.60
6 Todd Helton	3.00	.90
7 Jacob Cruz	2.00	.60
8 Abraham Nunez	2.00	.60
9 Paul Konerko	2.00	.60
10 Ben Grieve	2.00	.60
11 Jeff Abbott	2.00	.60
12 Richard Hidalgo	2.00	.60
13 Jaret Wright	2.00	.60
14 Lou Collier	2.00	.60
15 Miguel Tejada	3.00	.90

1998 Zenith Z-Team

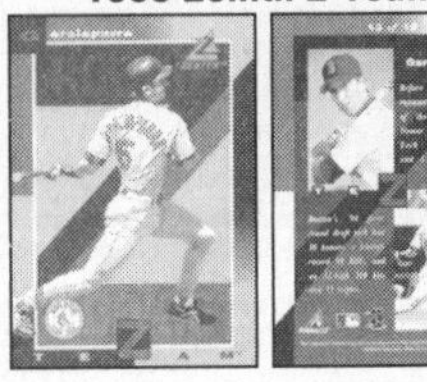

Randomly inserted in packs at the rate of 1:35 for cards 1-9 and 1:58 for cards 10-18, this 18-card set features action color photos of nine top veteran (1-9) and nine top rookie (10-18) players.

	Nm-Mt	Ex-Mt
COMPLETE SET (18)	120.00	36.00
*GOLD: 1.25X TO 3X BASIC Z-TEAM..		
GOLD STATED ODDS 1:175		
*5 x 7 STARS: .6X TO 1.5X BASIC Z-TEAM		
5 x 7 STATED ODDS 1:35		
1 Frank Thomas	8.00	2.40
2 Ken Griffey Jr.	12.00	3.60
3 Mike Piazza	12.00	3.60
4 Cal Ripken	25.00	7.50
5 Alex Rodriguez	12.00	3.60
6 Greg Maddux	12.00	3.60
7 Derek Jeter	20.00	6.00
8 Chipper Jones	8.00	2.40
9 Roger Clemens	15.00	4.50
10 Ben Grieve	3.00	.90
11 Derrek Lee	3.00	.90
12 Jose Cruz Jr.	3.00	.90
13 Nomar Garciaparra	12.00	3.60
14 Travis Lee	3.00	.90
15 Todd Helton	5.00	1.50
16 Paul Konerko	3.00	.90
17 Miguel Tejada	5.00	1.50
18 Scott Rolen	5.00	1.50

1998 Zenith Z-Team 5 x 7

Randomly inserted in packs at the rate of one in 35, this nine-card set is a partial parallel version of the first nine cards in the regular Zenith Z-Team insert set printed on large 5 x 7 cards.

	Nm-Mt	Ex-Mt
COMPLETE SET (9)	150.00	45.00
1 Frank Thomas	12.00	3.60
2 Ken Griffey Jr.	20.00	6.00
3 Mike Piazza	20.00	6.00
4 Cal Ripken	40.00	12.00
5 Alex Rodriguez	20.00	6.00
6 Greg Maddux	20.00	6.00
7 Derek Jeter	30.00	9.00
8 Chipper Jones	12.00	3.60
9 Roger Clemens	25.00	7.50

1992 Ziploc

This 11-card standard-size set features posed player photos of many of the game's all-time greats. The set was available via a mail-in offer for 50 cents and two UPC's from Ziploc sandwich bags. Individual cards were found one per specially marked package.

	Nm-Mt	Ex-Mt
COMPLETE SET (11)	10.00	3.00
1 Warren Spahn	1.00	.30
2 Bob Gibson	1.00	.30
3 Rollie Fingers	.50	.15
4 Carl Yastrzemski	1.00	.30
5 Brooks Robinson	1.50	.45
6 Pee Wee Reese	1.00	.30
7 Willie McCovey	1.00	.30
8 Willie Mays	1.50	.45
9 Nellie Fox	.50	.15
10 Yogi Berra	1.50	.45
11 Hank Aaron	1.50	.45

1977 Zip'z Discs

These discs are the second most common of the disc set issued in 1977. These discs have the Zip'z logo on the back.

	NM	Ex
COMPLETE SET (70)	125.00	50.00
1 Sal Bando	1.00	.40
2 Buddy Bell	2.00	.80
3 Johnny Bench	15.00	6.00
4 Lou Brock	10.00	4.00
5 Larry Bowa	2.00	.80
6 Steve Braun	1.00	.40
7 George Brett	25.00	10.00
8 Jeff Burroughs	1.00	.40
9 Campy Campaneris	2.00	.80
10 John Candelaria	1.00	.40
11 Jose Cardenal	1.00	.40
12 Rod Carew	10.00	4.00
13 Steve Carlton	10.00	4.00
14 Dave Cash	1.00	.40
15 Cesar Cedeno	1.00	.40
16 Ron Cey	2.00	.80
17 Dave Concepcion	3.00	1.20
18 Dennis Eckersley	10.00	4.00
19 Mark Fidrych	10.00	4.00
20 Rollie Fingers	8.00	3.20
21 Carlton Fisk	10.00	4.00
22 George Foster	3.00	1.20
23 Wayne Garland	1.00	.40
24 Ralph Garr	2.00	.80
25 Steve Garvey	6.00	2.40
26 Cesar Geronimo	1.00	.40
27 Bobby Grich	2.00	.80
28 Ken Griffey	3.00	1.20
29 Don Gullett	1.00	.40
30 Mike Hargrove	2.00	.80
31 Al Hrabosky	1.00	.40
32 Catfish Hunter	8.00	3.20
33 Reggie Jackson	15.00	6.00
34 Randy Jones	1.00	.40
35 Dave Kingman	4.00	1.60
36 Jerry Koosman	2.00	.80
37 Dave LaRoche	1.00	.40
38 Greg Luzinski	3.00	1.20
39 Fred Lynn	2.00	.80
40 Bill Madlock	2.00	.80
41 Rick Manning	1.00	.40
42 Jon Matlack	1.00	.40
43 John Mayberry	1.00	.40
44 Hal McRae	2.00	.80
45 Andy Messersmith	1.00	.40
46 Rick Monday	1.00	.40
47 John Montefusco	1.00	.40
48 Joe Morgan	8.00	3.20
49 Thurman Munson	6.00	2.40
50 Bobby Murcer	3.00	1.20
51 Bill North	1.00	.40
52 Jim Palmer	8.00	3.20
53 Tony Perez	8.00	3.20
54 Jerry Reuss	1.00	.40
55 Brooks Robinson	12.00	4.80
56 Pete Rose	15.00	6.00
57 Joe Rudi	1.00	.40
58 Nolan Ryan	30.00	12.00
59 Manny Sanguillen	1.00	.40
60 Mike Schmidt	15.00	6.00
61 Tom Seaver	15.00	6.00
62 Bill Singer	1.00	.40
63 Willie Stargell	8.00	3.20
64 Rusty Staub	3.00	1.20
65 Luis Tiant	2.00	.80
66 Bob Watson	2.00	.80
67 Butch Wynegar	1.00	.40
68 Carl Yastrzemski	12.00	4.80
69 Robin Yount	12.00	4.80
70 Richie Zisk	1.00	.40

1960 Bill Zuber Restaurant

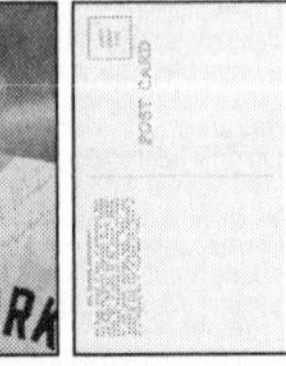

These items features retired Yankee Bill Zuber. The postcard is black-and-white borderless portrait in his New York Yankees uniform with a facsimile autograph. The back displays a postcard format with an advertisement for his restaurant in Homestead, Iowa. The matchbook has a small photo of Zuber and then complete informaiton about the restaurant as well as some details about his career.

	NM	Ex
COMPLETE SET (2)	30.00	12.00
1 Bill Zuber Postcard	15.00	6.00
2 Bill Zuber Matchbook	15.00	6.00

MINOR LEAGUE SINGLES

1883 California League Cabinets

These cabinets were recently discovered and feature members of the Haverlys, which played their games in San Francisco. The cabinets have the player photographed in their team uniforms with the player adding a fascimile signature on the bottom. Since these items are unnumbered we have sequenced them in alphabetical order. Any additions to this checklist are appreciated.

	Ex-Mt	VG
COMPLETE SET	3000.00	1500.00
1 Patsy Cahill	600.00	300.00
2 Frank Carrol	600.00	300.00
3 Peter Meegan	600.00	300.00
4 Tom McCord	600.00	300.00
5 A. Sohn	600.00	300.00

1886 Syracuse Stars Hancock

This three card set was issued by Hancock's Gents Furnishing Store and featured members of the 1886 Syracuse Stars. The fronts have a street clothes portrait of the featured player while the back has an advertisment for Hancock's. Interestingly the Photographer is noted as Goodwin, who would later in the decade produce more famous card sets. Since these cards are unnumbered, we have sequenced them in alphabetical order. It is possible that more cards exist so if there is any additional information we would appreciate it.

	Ex-Mt	VG
COMPLETE SET	15000.00	7500.00
1 Richard Buckley	5000.00	2500.00
2 Douglas Crothers	5000.00	2500.00
3 Philip Tomney	5000.00	2500.00

1888 S.F. Hess and Co. Creole N321

It is not known why S.F. Hess based in Rochester, N.Y., produced this set of regional ballplayers from the California League. Each card has a color drawing of a ballplayer and is copyrighted 1888. The teams represented are G and M's, Haverlys, Pioneers and Stocktons; in the checklist below these teams are coded GM, HAV, PIO and STOCK, respectively. There are 42 cards known (37 players and five variations) and all carry advertising for Creole cigarettes.

	Ex-Mt	VG
COMPLETE SET	80000.00	40000.00
1 Eddie Bennett HAV	2500.00	1250.00
2 George Borchers: GM	2500.00	1250.00
3 Tom Buckley HAV	2500.00	1250.00
4A Turk Burke STOCK pitching	2500.00	1250.00
4B Turk Burke STOCK batting	2500.00	1250.00
5 William Burnett: GM	2500.00	1250.00
6 Frank Carroll PIO	2500.00	1250.00
7 John Donahue PIO	2500.00	1250.00
8 Jack Donovan: GM	2500.00	1250.00
9 Michael Finn PIO	2500.00	1250.00
10 Charles Gagus HAV	2500.00	1250.00
11 George Hanley HAV	2500.00	1250.00
12A Pop Hardie: GM Catcher	2500.00	1250.00
12B Pop Hardie: GM Center Field	2500.00	1250.00
13 Jack Hayes STOCK	2500.00	1250.00
14 Jack Lawton HAV	2500.00	1250.00
15 Rube Levy HAV	5000.00	2500.00
16 Daniel Long: GM	2500.00	1250.00
17 Tom McCord: GM	2500.00	1250.00
18 McGinty	2500.00	1250.00
19 Peter Meegan HAV	2500.00	1250.00
20 Henry Moore STOCK	2500.00	1250.00
21 James Mullee PIO	2500.00	1250.00
22 Billy Newhart: GM	2500.00	1250.00
23 Joseph Noonan PIO	2500.00	1250.00
24 Harry O'Day STOCK	2500.00	1250.00
25 Hip Perrier PIO	2500.00	1250.00
26A Thomas Powers HAV first base	2500.00	1250.00
26B Thomas Powers HAV first base and Capt.	2500.00	1250.00
27 Jack Ryan: GM	2500.00	1250.00
28 Charles Selna STOCK	2500.00	1250.00
29 Joseph Shea: GM	2500.00	1250.00
30 Jack Sheridan Umpire	2500.00	1250.00
31 Big Smith PIO	2500.00	1250.00
32 Hugh Smith PIO	2500.00	1250.00
33 John Smith	2500.00	1250.00
34A Leonard Stockwell STOCK catching	2500.00	1250.00
34B Leonard Stockwell STOCK batting	2500.00	1250.00
35 Charles Sweeney HAV	2500.00	1250.00
36 Pop Swett HAV	2500.00	1250.00
37 Milton Whitehead STOCK	2500.00	1250.00

1905 Providence Clamdiggers Postcard

Little is known about this item. The front features a posed action shot of the featured player and the photo is credited to a photographer from the Providence Tribune. The back featured a baseball opinion. Any additional information would be appreciated.

	MINT	NRMT
1 Bob Peterson	100.00	45.00

1907 Newark Evening World Supplements

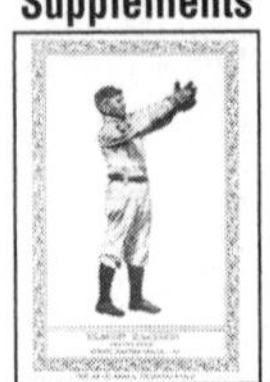

These fifteen 7 1/2" by 10 15/16" photos were printed as supplements to the Newark Evening World Newspaper. They feature players from the 1907 Newark franchise.

	Ex-Mt	VG
COMPLETE SET (15)	4500.00	2200.00
1 William Carrick	300.00	150.00
2 James Cockman	300.00	150.00
3 Clyde Engle	500.00	250.00
4 James Jones	300.00	150.00
5 Paul Krichell	500.00	250.00
6 Henry LaBelle	300.00	150.00
7 William Mahling	300.00	150.00
8 Chas. McCafferty	300.00	150.00
9 Thomas McCarthy	300.00	150.00
10 James Mullin	300.00	150.00
Sic, Mullen		
11 Al Pardee	300.00	150.00
12 Bayard Sharpe	300.00	150.00
13 John E. Shea	300.00	150.00
14 Oscar Stanage	400.00	200.00
15 Elmer Zacher	400.00	200.00

1908 Buffalo Bisons F.J. Offerman

This set was issued in 1908 by F.J. Offerman and bears remarkable similarities to the PC American League Publishing set. Like the PC 770 set, this set features a large action shot of the player plus a smaller street clothes shot enclosed in an oval on the front of the card. The set features Buffalo players only.

	Ex-Mt	VG
COMPLETE SET(19)	4000.00	2000.00
1 James Archer	300.00	150.00
2 James Cleary	250.00	125.00
3 Larry Hestefer	250.00	125.00
4 Hunter Hill	250.00	125.00
5 William H. Kester	250.00	125.00
6 Charles Kisinger	250.00	125.00
7 Leri Knapp	250.00	125.00
8 Lew McAllister	250.00	125.00
9 George N. McConnell	250.00	125.00
10 William J. Mulligan	250.00	125.00
11 James Murray	250.00	125.00
12 William H. Nattress	250.00	125.00
13 Ralph Parrott	250.00	125.00
14 John B. Ryan	250.00	125.00
15 George Schirm	250.00	125.00
16 George Smith	250.00	125.00
17 John H. Vowinkle	250.00	125.00
18 John White	250.00	125.00
19 Merton Whitney	250.00	125.00

1908 Indianapolis Postcards

These postcards feature members of the Indianapolis Team of the American Association. The fronts feature posed action shots while the backs have standard postcard backs. An extremely early card of Hall of Famer Rube Marquard is in this set.

	Ex-Mt	VG
COMPLETE SET (20)	2000.00	1000.00
1 Bert Briggs	100.00	50.00
2 Owen Bush	150.00	75.00
3 Charles Carr MG	100.00	50.00
4 James Cook	100.00	50.00
5 Chirs Coulter	100.00	50.00
6 Paul Davidson	100.00	50.00
7 Carl Druhot	100.00	50.00
8 Louis Durham	125.00	60.00
9 Claude Elliott	100.00	50.00
10 John Eubanks	100.00	50.00
11 John Hayden	100.00	50.00
12 William Hopke	100.00	50.00
13 Daniel Howley	125.00	60.00
14 Chris Lindsey	100.00	50.00
15 Patrick Livingston	100.00	50.00
16 Rube Marquard	500.00	250.00
17 Ed Siever	100.00	50.00
18 Walter Slagle	100.00	50.00
19 Perry Werden	100.00	50.00
20 Otto Williams	100.00	50.00

1909 Atlanta Crackers Postcard

This postcard, which measures approximately 4" by 6" features Dick Bayless who would lead the Southern Association in runs scored in 1909. The ornate front has "Atlanta-1909" on top and the player photo in an oval in the middle with his name and position on the bottom. This card was actually issued with rounded corners.

	MINT	NRMT
1 Dick Bayless	100.00	45.00

1909-11 Obak T212

The catalog designation T212 actually encompasses three separate minor league sets (listed in sequence in the checklist below). Each card measures 1 7/16" by 2 5/8". Set 1 (1-76) features 76 colored player cards representing six PCL teams and was issued in 1909. The obverse captions are stylized (slanted), and the word "Obak" on the reverse is

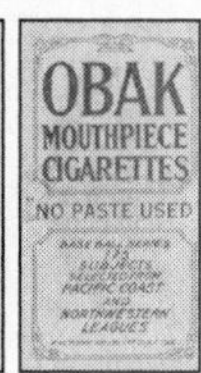

inscribed in "Old English" letters. Set 2 contains 175 colored cards (77-251) of players from six PCL and four NWL teams. The captions are not slanted, and "Obak" appears in large block letters on the back. Reverses advertise either "150" or "175" subjects, and some 35 different slogans exist. The backs of sets 1 and 2 are printed in blue. In contrast, the 1911 set of 175 colored cards has red-printed backs which contain a short biography and some statistics (252-426). The PCL and NWL are each represented by six teams in this set. Note that there is a Portland club in each league. The Obak brand was produced and distributed in California by a branch of the American Tobacco Company. Cards are ordered below alphabetically within team. Type 1 consists of Los Angeles (1-8), Oakland (9-20), Portland (23-33), Sacramento (34-46), San Francisco (47-62) and Vernon (63-76). Type 2 consists of Los Angeles (77-96), Oakland (97-113), Portland (114-132), Sacramento (133-151), San Francisco (152-172), Vernon (173-188), Seattle NWL (189-204), Spokane NWL (205-219), Tacoma NWL (220-235) and Vancouver NWL (236-251). Type 3 consists of Los Angeles (252-268), Oakland (269-287), Portland PCL (288-303), Sacramento (304-320), San Francisco (321-339), Vernon (340-358), Portland NWL (359-368), Seattle NWL (369-380), Spokane NWL (381-392), Tacoma NWL (393-403), Vancouver NWL (404-415), and Victoria NWL (416-426). While it is possible that it is unique; an album featuring 175 cards has surfaced.

	Ex-Mt	VG
COMPLETE SET	12000.00	6000.00
COMMON CARD (1-76)	80.00	40.00
COMMON CARD (77-251)	25.00	12.50
COMMON CARD (252-426)	25.00	12.50
1 John Beall	80.00	40.00
2 Bert Delmas	80.00	40.00
3 Frank Dillon	80.00	40.00
4 Ivon Howard	80.00	40.00
5 Walter Nagle	80.00	40.00
6 Jess Orendorff	80.00	40.00
7 Jud Smith	80.00	40.00
8 George Wheeler	80.00	40.00
9 George Boice	80.00	40.00
10 Donald Cameron	80.00	40.00
11 Frank Carrol	80.00	40.00
12 Tyler Christian	80.00	40.00
13 William Hogan	80.00	40.00
14 L.N. LaLonge	80.00	40.00
15 George Lewis	80.00	40.00
16 D. Lewis	80.00	40.00
17 Terry McKune	80.00	40.00
18 Howard Murphy	80.00	40.00
19 Harry Nelson	80.00	40.00
20 Ragan	80.00	40.00
20 James Wiggs	80.00	40.00
21 Bill Reidy	80.00	40.00
23 Richard Breen	80.00	40.00
24 Albert Carson	80.00	40.00
25 Gus Fisher	80.00	40.00
26 Jess Garrett	80.00	40.00
27 Jack Graney	100.00	50.00
28 Howard Guyn	80.00	40.00
29 Walt McCreedie	80.00	40.00
30 Ivy Olson	100.00	50.00
31 George Ort	80.00	40.00
32 Bud Ryan	80.00	40.00
33 William Speas	80.00	40.00
34 Charles Baum	80.00	40.00
35 Fred Brown	80.00	40.00
36 Jim Byrnes	80.00	40.00
37 Ehman	80.00	40.00
38 John Fitzgerald	80.00	40.00
39 Flannagan	80.00	40.00
40 Chick Gandil	300.00	150.00
41 Charlie Graham	80.00	40.00
42 John House	80.00	40.00
43 Henry Jansing	80.00	40.00
44 Fred Raymer	80.00	40.00
45 James Shinn	80.00	40.00
46 James Whalen	80.00	40.00
47 Claude Berry	80.00	40.00
48 Ping Bodie	100.00	50.00
49 Frank Browning	80.00	40.00
50 Frank Eastley	80.00	40.00
51 Edward Griffin	80.00	40.00
52 Clarence Henley	80.00	40.00
53 F. Lewis	80.00	40.00
54 Roy McArdle	80.00	40.00
55 Henry Melchior	80.00	40.00
56 Ernest Mohler	80.00	40.00
57 Rabbit Mundorff	80.00	40.00
58 Thomas Tennant	80.00	40.00
59 F. Williams	80.00	40.00
60 Nick Williams	80.00	40.00
61 Ralph Willis	80.00	40.00
62 Rollie Zeider	100.00	50.00
63 Claude Bernard	80.00	40.00
64 John Breckenridge	80.00	40.00
65 Norman Brashear	80.00	40.00
66 Drummond Brown	80.00	40.00
67 Bert Coy	80.00	40.00
68 Charles Eagan	80.00	40.00
69 Haley	80.00	40.00
70 Harkins	80.00	40.00
71 Roy Hitt	80.00	40.00
72 William Hogan	80.00	40.00
73 Felix Martinke	80.00	40.00
74 Anson Mott	80.00	40.00
75 Jesse Stoval	80.00	40.00
76 Ed Willett	80.00	40.00
77 James Agnew	25.00	12.50
78 Claude Bernard	25.00	12.50
79 Andrew Briswalter	25.00	12.50
80 Roy Castleton	25.00	12.50
81 Elmer Criger	25.00	12.50
82 Thomas Daley	25.00	12.50
83 Lee Delhi	25.00	12.50
84 Bert Delmas	25.00	12.50
85 Frank Dillon	25.00	12.50
86 Ivan Howard	25.00	12.50
87 Edward Klein	25.00	12.50
88 Howard Murphy	25.00	12.50
89 Walter Nagle	25.00	12.50
90 Jesse Ornsdorff	25.00	12.50
91 Roth	25.00	12.50
92 Hugh Smith	25.00	12.50
93 Jud Smith	25.00	12.50
94 Elmer Thorsen	25.00	12.50
95 Bill Tozer	25.00	12.50
96 Ted Waring	25.00	12.50
97 Donald Cameron	25.00	12.50
98 Frank Carroll	25.00	12.50
99 Tyler Christian	25.00	12.50
100 George Cutshaw	30.00	15.00
101 W.E. Harkins	25.00	12.50
102 Logan	25.00	12.50
103 Henry Lively	25.00	12.50
104 Heinie Manush	30.00	15.00
105 Carl Mitze	25.00	12.50
106 Walt Moser	25.00	12.50
107 Harry Nelson	25.00	12.50
108 M.J. Spiesman	25.00	12.50
109 Edward Swander	25.00	12.50
110 Chester Thomas	25.00	12.50
111 T.A. Tonnesen	25.00	12.50
112 Clyde Wares	25.00	12.50
113 Harry Wolverton	25.00	12.50
114 Charley Armbruster	25.00	12.50
115 Perle Casey	25.00	12.50
116 Gus Fisher	25.00	12.50
117 Jess Garrett	25.00	12.50
118 Sylveanus Gregg	30.00	15.00
119 August Hetling	25.00	12.50
120 Gene Krapp	25.00	12.50
121 Walt McCreedie	25.00	12.50
122 Milo Netzel	25.00	12.50
123 Ivy Olson	30.00	15.00
124 George Ort	25.00	12.50
125 Perrine	25.00	12.50
126 William Rapps	25.00	12.50
127 Dan Ryan	25.00	12.50
128 John "Buddy" Ryan	25.00	12.50
129 Tom Seaton	25.00	12.50
130 Joseph Smith	25.00	12.50
131 William Speas	25.00	12.50
132 Bill Steen	25.00	12.50
133 Charles Baum	25.00	12.50
134 Louis Boardman	25.00	12.50
135 Briggs	25.00	12.50
136 Fred Brown	25.00	12.50
137 Harold Danzig	25.00	12.50
138 Cliff Daringer	25.00	12.50
139 John Fitzgerald	25.00	12.50
140 John Fournier	25.00	12.50
141 Elwood Hiester	25.00	12.50
142 Hollis	25.00	12.50
143 Benjamin Hunt	25.00	12.50
144 L.N. LaLonge	25.00	12.50
145 Chester Nourse	25.00	12.50
146 Hank Perry	25.00	12.50
147 Persons	25.00	12.50
148 Fred Raymer	25.00	12.50
149 James Shinn	25.00	12.50
150 Edward Van Buren	25.00	12.50
151 James Whalen	25.00	12.50
152 Rex Ames	25.00	12.50
153 Claude Berry	25.00	12.50
154 Ping Bodie	30.00	15.00
155 Frank Browning	25.00	12.50
156 Byrd	25.00	12.50
157 Frank Eastley	25.00	12.50
158A Edward Griffin (175)	25.00	12.50
158B Edward Griffin (150)	25.00	12.50
159 Clarence Henley	25.00	12.50
160 James Lewis	25.00	12.50
161 Roy McArdle	25.00	12.50
162 Henry Melchoir	25.00	12.50
163 Frank Miller	25.00	12.50
164 Ernest Mohler	25.00	12.50
165 Rabbit Mundorff	120.00	60.00
166 Royal Shaw	25.00	12.50
167 Harry Stewart	25.00	12.50
168 Harry Suter	25.00	12.50
169 Thomas Tennant	25.00	12.50
170 Oscar Vitt	30.00	15.00
171 John Williams	25.00	12.50
172 Ralph Willis	25.00	12.50
173 John Breckenridge	25.00	12.50
174 Norman Brashear	25.00	12.50
175 Roy Brashear	25.00	12.50
176 Drummond Brown	25.00	12.50
177 Burrell	25.00	12.50
178 Walter Carlisle	25.00	12.50
179 Bert Coy	25.00	12.50
180 Robert Fisher	25.00	12.50
181 Arthur Hensling	25.00	12.50
182 Roy Hitt	25.00	12.50
183 Happy Hogan	25.00	12.50
184 William Lindsay	25.00	12.50
185 Felix Martinke	25.00	12.50
186 George Schafer	25.00	12.50
187 Jesse Stovell	25.00	12.50
188 Ed Willett	25.00	12.50
189 Akin	25.00	12.50
190 Bennett	25.00	12.50
191 Custer	25.00	12.50
192 Dretchko	25.00	12.50
193 John Frisk	25.00	12.50
194 Bert Hall	25.00	12.50
195 Hendrix	25.00	12.50
196 James Johnston	25.00	12.50
197 Mike Lynch	25.00	12.50
198 Frank Miller	25.00	12.50
199 George Pennington	25.00	12.50
200 Raymond	25.00	12.50
201 Tom Seaton	25.00	12.50
202 Shea	25.00	12.50
203 Gus Thompson	25.00	12.50
204 George Zackert	25.00	12.50
205 Jesse Baker	25.00	12.50
206 Bonner	25.00	12.50
207 Brooks	25.00	12.50
208 Cartwright	25.00	12.50
209 Phil Cooney	25.00	12.50
210 Davis	25.00	12.50
211 Flood	25.00	12.50
212 John Hickey	25.00	12.50
213 Holm	25.00	12.50
214 Keener	25.00	12.50
215 John Killilay	25.00	12.50
216 Ed Kippert	25.00	12.50
217 Louis Nordyke	25.00	12.50
218 Henry Ostdiek	25.00	12.50
219 Weed	25.00	12.50
220 Annis	25.00	12.50
221 Bassey	25.00	12.50
222 Cliff Blankenship	25.00	12.50
223 Byrnes	25.00	12.50
224 Curtis Coleman	25.00	12.50
225 Gaddy	25.00	12.50
226 Gurney	25.00	12.50
227 Bert Hall	25.00	12.50
228 Hartman	25.00	12.50
229 Jansing	25.00	12.50
230 Mott	25.00	12.50
231 Isaac Rockenfield	30.00	15.00
232 Schmutz	25.00	12.50
233 Starkell	25.00	12.50
234 Stevens	25.00	12.50
235 Warren	25.00	12.50
236 Breen	25.00	12.50
237 Bill Brinker	25.00	12.50
238 Drummond Brown	25.00	12.50
239 Capron	25.00	12.50
240 Chenault	25.00	12.50
241 Erickson	25.00	12.50
242 Flannagan	25.00	12.50
243 Harry Gardner	25.00	12.50
244 James	25.00	12.50
245 Jensen	25.00	12.50
246 Ed Kusel	25.00	12.50
247 Lewis	25.00	12.50
248 Scharnweber	25.00	12.50
249 Streib	25.00	12.50
250 Joe Sugden	25.00	12.50
251 Swain	25.00	12.50
252 Fred Abbott	25.00	12.50
253 James Agnew	25.00	12.50
254 Roy Akin	25.00	12.50
255 Curtis Bernard	25.00	12.50
256 Elmer Criger	25.00	12.50
257 T.F. Daley	25.00	12.50
258 Lee Delhi	25.00	12.50
259 Bert Delmas	25.00	12.50
260 Frank Dillon	25.00	12.50
261 Muriel Grindle	25.00	12.50
262 Ivan Howard	25.00	12.50
263 George Metzger	25.00	12.50
264 Charley Moore	25.00	12.50
265 Hugh Smith	25.00	12.50
266 Elmer Thorsen	25.00	12.50
267 Bill Tozer	25.00	12.50
268 George Wheeler	25.00	12.50
269 Harry Ables	25.00	12.50
270 Tyler Christian	25.00	12.50
271 Bert Coy	25.00	12.50
272 George Cutshaw	30.00	15.00
273 John Flater	25.00	12.50
274 August Hetling	25.00	12.50
275 Izzy Hoffman	25.00	12.50
276 Kittie Knight	25.00	12.50
277 Harl Maggert	25.00	12.50
278 Miller	25.00	12.50
279 Carl Mitze	25.00	12.50
280 William Pearce	25.00	12.50
281 Henry Pernoll	25.00	12.50
282 Monte Pfyl	25.00	12.50
283 John Tiedeman	25.00	12.50
284 Clyde Wares	25.00	12.50
285 James Wiggs	25.00	12.50
286 Harry Wolverton	25.00	12.50
287 Elmer Zacher	25.00	12.50
288 Shad Barry	25.00	12.50
289 Chester Chadbourne	25.00	12.50
290 Charles Fullerton	25.00	12.50
291 J. Henderson	25.00	12.50
292 Elmer Koestner	25.00	12.50
293 Arthur Krueger	25.00	12.50
294 Walter Kuhn	25.00	12.50
295 Walt McCreedie	25.00	12.50
296 Thomas Murray	25.00	12.50
297 Roger Peckinpaugh	40.00	20.00
298 William Rapps	25.00	12.50
299 Wilbur Rodgers	25.00	12.50
300 Bud Ryan	25.00	12.50
301 Tom Seaton	25.00	12.50
302 Tommy Sheehan	30.00	15.00
303 Bill Steen	25.00	12.50
304 Frank Arrelanes	25.00	12.50
305 Spider Baum	25.00	12.50
306 Herbert Byram	25.00	12.50
307 Harold Danzig	25.00	12.50
308 John Fitzgerald	25.00	12.50
309 Elwood Hiester	25.00	12.50
310 Benjamin Hunt	25.00	12.50
311 L.N. LaLonge	25.00	12.50
312 Bertram Lerchen	25.00	12.50
313 Chris Mahoney	25.00	12.50
314 Nourse	25.00	12.50
315 Patsy O'Rourke	25.00	12.50
316 James Shinn	25.00	12.50
317 Chester Thomas	25.00	12.50
318 Thompson	25.00	12.50
319 Frank Thornton	25.00	12.50
320 Edward Van Buren	25.00	12.50
321 Claude Berry	25.00	12.50
322 Frank Browning	25.00	12.50
323 Clarence Henley	25.00	12.50
324 Thomas Madden	25.00	12.50
325 Roy McArdle	25.00	12.50
326 Williard Meikle	25.00	12.50
327 Henry Melchoir	25.00	12.50
328 Frank Miller	25.00	12.50
329 Ernest Mohler	25.00	12.50
330 Doc Moskiman	25.00	12.50
331 Powell	25.00	12.50
332 William Ryan	25.00	12.50
333 Walter Schmidt	25.00	12.50
334 Royal Shaw	25.00	12.50
335 Harry Suter	25.00	12.50
336 Thomas Tennant	25.00	12.50
337 Oscar Vitt	30.00	15.00
338 Buck Weaver	250.00	125.00
339 Carl Zamloch	25.00	12.50
340 John Brackenridge	25.00	12.50
341 Roy Brashear	25.00	12.50
342 Drummond Brown	25.00	12.50
343 Burrell	25.00	12.50
344 Walter Carlisle	25.00	12.50
345 Albert Carson	25.00	12.50
346 Roy Castleton	25.00	12.50
347 Roy Hitt	25.00	12.50
348 Happy Hogan	25.00	12.50
349 Franz Hosp	25.00	12.50
350 John Kane	25.00	12.50
351 Clarence McDonnell	25.00	12.50
352 Ham Patterson	25.00	12.50
353 John Raleigh	25.00	12.50
354 Arthur Ross	25.00	12.50
355 Sheehan	25.00	12.50
356 Harry Stewart	25.00	12.50
357 George Stinson	25.00	12.50
358 Ed Willett	25.00	12.50
359 Bloomfield	25.00	12.50
360 Casey	25.00	12.50
361 Garrett	25.00	12.50
362 Harris	25.00	12.50
363 Fred Lamline	25.00	12.50
364 Edward Mensor	25.00	12.50
365 Mundorff	25.00	12.50
366 Speas	25.00	12.50
367 George Stovall	30.00	15.00
368 Williams	25.00	12.50
369 Art Bues	25.00	12.50
370 Butler	25.00	12.50
371 Cruikshank	25.00	12.50
372 John Kading	25.00	12.50
373 Bill Leard	25.00	12.50
374 Raymond	25.00	12.50
375 Seaton	25.00	12.50
376 Shea	25.00	12.50
377 David Skeels	25.00	12.50
378 Spencer	25.00	12.50
379 Weed	25.00	12.50
380 George Zackert	25.00	12.50
381 Bonner	25.00	12.50
382 Cartwright	25.00	12.50
383 Phil Cooney	25.00	12.50
384 John Frisk	25.00	12.50
385 Hasty	25.00	12.50
386 Holm	25.00	12.50
387 Ed Kippert	25.00	12.50
388 Milo Netzel	25.00	12.50
389 Louis Nordyke	25.00	12.50
390 Henry Ostdiek	25.00	12.50
391 Paul Strand	25.00	12.50
392 Zimmerman	25.00	12.50
393 Annis	25.00	12.50
394 Bassey	25.00	12.50
395 Burns	25.00	12.50
396 Curtis Coleman	25.00	12.50
397 Gordon	25.00	12.50
398 Hall	25.00	12.50
399 Eddie Higgins	25.00	12.50
400 Peter Morse	25.00	12.50
401 Isaac Rockenfield	30.00	15.00
402 Charlie Schmutz	25.00	12.50
403 Warren	25.00	12.50
404 Adams	25.00	12.50
405 Justin Bennett	25.00	12.50
406 Norman Brashear	25.00	12.50
407 Bill Brinker	25.00	12.50
408 Engel	25.00	12.50
409 Erickson	25.00	12.50
410 James	25.00	12.50
411 Jensen	25.00	12.50
412 Lewis	25.00	12.50
413 Scharnweber	25.00	12.50
414 Spiesman	25.00	12.50
415 Swain	25.00	12.50
416 Dashwood	25.00	12.50
417 Davis	25.00	12.50
418 Goodman	25.00	12.50
419 Ed Householder	25.00	12.50
420 Fred Raymer	25.00	12.50
421 Reddick	25.00	12.50
422 Jack Roche	25.00	12.50
423 Starkel	25.00	12.50
424 Ten Million	30.00	15.00
425 Blaine Thomas	25.00	12.50
426 Ward	25.00	12.50

1910 Bishop Coast League E99

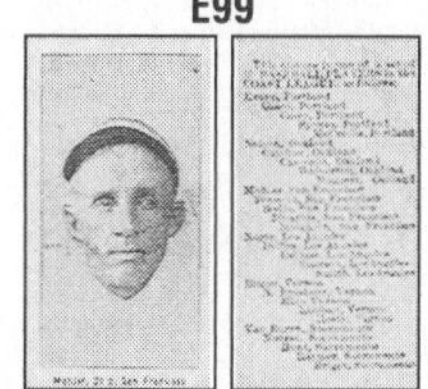

The cards in this 30-card set measure 1 1/2" by 2 3/4". Although there is no manufacturer's name to be found on the cards of this series, the similarities to set E100 almost certainly mark it as a product of Bishop and Co. The subjects are Coast League players, portrayed in black and white photos on solid color backgrounds. The cards are unnumbered but are back listed (starting with "Knapp"). The set was issued about 1910, and some players are found with more than one background color. The cards have been alphabetized and assigned numbers in the checklist below.

	Ex-Mt	VG
COMPLETE SET (30)	6000.00	3000.00
1 Ping Bodie	300.00	150.00
2 Norman Brashear	250.00	125.00
3 Hap Briggs	250.00	125.00
4 Jimmy Byones sic, Byrnes	250.00	125.00
5 Don Cameron	250.00	125.00
6 Pearl Casey	250.00	125.00
7 George Cutshaw	250.00	125.00
8 Bert Delmas	250.00	125.00
9 Frank Dillon	250.00	125.00
10 Tom Hasty	250.00	125.00
11 Roy Hitt	250.00	125.00
12 Wallace Hap. Hogan	250.00	125.00
13 Ben Hunt	250.00	125.00
14 Gene Krapp	250.00	125.00
15 John Lindsay	250.00	125.00
16 Harl Maggert	250.00	125.00
17 Harry McArdle	250.00	125.00
18 Walter McCredie sic, McCreedie	250.00	125.00
19 Henry Melchoir	250.00	125.00
20 Ernest Mohler	250.00	125.00
21 Walter Nagle	250.00	125.00
22 Slim Nelson	250.00	125.00
23 Chester Nourse	250.00	125.00
24 Ivy Olsen	300.00	150.00
25 Fred Raymer	250.00	125.00
26 Smith	250.00	125.00
27 Thomas Tennent sic, Tennant	250.00	125.00
28 Bill Thorsen	250.00	125.00
29 Edward Van Buren	250.00	125.00
30 Harry Wolverton	250.00	125.00

1910 Contentnea T209

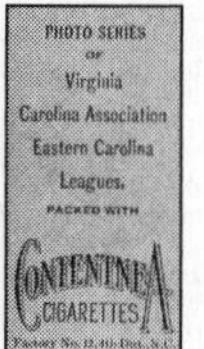

These baseball cards (each measuring 1 1/2" by 2 5/8") found as inserts in packs of Contentnea Cigarettes were released to the public in 1909 and 1910. Although both sets depict players from the Virginia, Carolina Association and Eastern Carolina leagues, they are otherwise dissimilar. The 16-card color series, known as Type I, is much tougher and more valuable. The obverse captions are printed in blue and are located in the white border at the bottom. The reverse is marked "First Series", but no subsequent printings are known. There are also 219 of the Type II black and white "Photo Series" listed below, although more are believed to exist. The captions on this type are printed in black and are found within a white panel inside the picture area. Both types are unnumbered. Type I cards are alphabetized below. while Type II cards are arranged in alphabetical order within team. Teams in Type II are Anderson (17-27), Charlotte (28-40), Danville (41-50), Fayetteville (51-58), Goldsboro (59-72), Greensboro (73-85), Greenville (86-98), Lynchburg (99-110), Norfolk (111-123), Portsmouth (124-134), Raleigh (135-153), Richmond (154-167), Roanoke (168-180), Rocky Mount (181-187), Spartanburg (188-199), Wilmington (200-210), Wilson (211-222), and Winston-Salem (223-235).

	Ex-Mt	VG
COMPLETE SET (236)	8000.00	4000.00
COMMON TYPE I (1-16)	200.00	100.00
COMMON TYPE II (17-236)	25.00	12.50
1 Armstrong (Wilson)	200.00	100.00
2 Booles (Raleigh)	200.00	100.00
3 Bourquise (Rocky Mount)	200.00	100.00
4 John Cooper (Wilson)	200.00	100.00
5 John Cowell (Wilson)	200.00	100.00
6 David Crockett (Goldsboro)	200.00	100.00
7 Fullenwider (Raleigh)	200.00	100.00
8 Gilmore (Winston-Salem)	200.00	100.00
9 H.H. Hoffman (Raleigh)	200.00	100.00
10 Lane (Wilson)	200.00	100.00
12 Daniel McGeehan (Wilson)	200.00	100.00
13 Pope (Raleigh)	200.00	100.00
14 Chris Sisson (Greensboro)	200.00	100.00
15 Charles Stubbe (Goldsboro)	200.00	100.00
16 Joseph Walsh (Goldsboro)	200.00	100.00
17 Byrd	25.00	12.50
18 Corbett	25.00	12.50
19 Farmer	25.00	12.50
20 Gorham	25.00	12.50
21 Harley	25.00	12.50
22 Kelly	25.00	12.50
23 A. McCarthy	25.00	12.50
24 J. McCarthy	25.00	12.50
25 Peloguin	25.00	12.50
26 Roth	25.00	12.50
27 Wehrell	25.00	12.50
28 Bausewein	25.00	12.50
29 Brazelle	25.00	12.50
30 Coutts	25.00	12.50
31 Cross	25.00	12.50
32 Dobard	25.00	12.50
33 Duvie	25.00	12.50
34 Francisco	25.00	12.50
35 Garman	25.00	12.50
36 Hargrave	25.00	12.50
37 Hemphrey	25.00	12.50
38 Leo McHugh	25.00	12.50
39 Taxis	25.00	12.50
40 Williams	25.00	12.50

41 Bussey 25.00 12.50
42 Callahan 25.00 12.50
43 Griffin 25.00 12.50
44 Hooker 25.00 12.50
45 Mayberry 25.00 12.50
46 Mullinix 25.00 12.50
47 Priest 25.00 12.50
48 Rickert 25.00 12.50
49 Schrader 25.00 12.50
50 Sullivan 25.00 12.50
51 Boyle 25.00 12.50
52 Crockett 25.00 12.50
53 Dobson 25.00 12.50
54 Galvin 25.00 12.50
55 Lavoia 25.00 12.50
56 Luyster 25.00 12.50
57 William Schumaker 25.00 12.50
58 Waters 25.00 12.50
59 Wamack 25.00 12.50
60 Dailey 25.00 12.50
61 Evans 25.00 12.50
62 Fulton 25.00 12.50
63 Gates 25.00 12.50
64 Oliver Gunderson 25.00 12.50
65 Handiboe 25.00 12.50
66 Kelly 25.00 12.50
67 Malcolm 25.00 12.50
68 Merchant 25.00 12.50
69 Morgan 25.00 12.50
70 Sharp 25.00 12.50
71 Stoehr 25.00 12.50
72 Webb 25.00 12.50
73 Wolf 25.00 12.50
74 Bentley 25.00 12.50
75 Beusse 25.00 12.50
76 Doak 25.00 12.50
77 Eldridge 25.00 12.50
78 Walter Hammersley 25.00 12.50
79 Hicks 25.00 12.50
80 Jackson 25.00 12.50
81 Martin 25.00 12.50
82 Pickard 25.00 12.50
83 Ridgeway 25.00 12.50
84 Springs 25.00 12.50
85 Walters 25.00 12.50
86 Weldon 25.00 12.50
87 Blackstone 25.00 12.50
88 F. Derrck 25.00 12.50
(sic& Derrick)
89 Claude Derrick 25.00 12.50
90 Drumm 25.00 12.50
91 Flowers 25.00 12.50
92 Jenkins 25.00 12.50
93 McFarlin 25.00 12.50
94 Noojin 25.00 12.50
95 Ochs 25.00 12.50
96 Redfern 25.00 12.50
97 Stouch 25.00 12.50
98 Wingo 25.00 12.50
99 Workman 25.00 12.50
100 Brandon 25.00 12.50
101 Griffin 25.00 12.50
102 Hoffman 25.00 12.50
103 Howedel 25.00 12.50
104 Levy 25.00 12.50
105 Lloyd 25.00 12.50
106 Lucia 25.00 12.50
107 Rawe 25.00 12.50
108 Sexton 25.00 12.50
109 A. Smith 25.00 12.50
110 D. Smith 25.00 12.50
111 Woolums 25.00 12.50
112 Armstrong 25.00 12.50
113 Banner 25.00 12.50
114 Busch 25.00 12.50
115 Chandler 25.00 12.50
116 Clark 25.00 12.50
117 Johnson 25.00 12.50
118 Mullany 25.00 12.50
119 Munsen 25.00 12.50
120 Murdock 25.00 12.50
121 Reggy 25.00 12.50
122 Tiedmann 25.00 12.50
123 Carl Walker 25.00 12.50
124 Walsh 25.00 12.50
125 Bowen 25.00 12.50
126 Clunk 25.00 12.50
127 Guiheen 25.00 12.50
128 Hamilton 25.00 12.50
129 Hannifen 25.00 12.50
130 Kunkle 25.00 12.50
131 McFarland 25.00 12.50
132 Smith 25.00 12.50
133 Toner 25.00 12.50
134 Vail 25.00 12.50
135 Welsher 25.00 12.50
136 Beatty 25.00 12.50
137 Biel 25.00 12.50
138 Frank Bigbie 25.00 12.50
139 Clemens 25.00 12.50
140 Daniel Hart 25.00 12.50
141 Hawkins 25.00 12.50
142 Hobbs 25.00 12.50
143 Jobson 25.00 12.50
144 Keating 25.00 12.50
145 King Kelly 25.00 12.50
146 Lathrop 25.00 12.50
147 McCormick 25.00 12.50
148 Mundell 25.00 12.50
149 Phoenix 25.00 12.50
150 Prim 25.00 12.50
151 Richardson 25.00 12.50
152 Simmons 25.00 12.50
153 Turner 25.00 12.50
154 Wright 25.00 12.50
155 Baker 25.00 12.50
156 Bigbie 25.00 12.50
157 Brown 25.00 12.50
158 Cowan 25.00 12.50
159 Hale 25.00 12.50
160 Irvine 25.00 12.50
161 Landgraff 25.00 12.50
162 Missitt 25.00 12.50
163 Morrissey 25.00 12.50
164 Salve 25.00 12.50
165 Shaw 25.00 12.50
166 Guy Titman 25.00 12.50
167 Verbout 25.00 12.50
168 Wallace 25.00 12.50
169 Andrada 25.00 12.50
170 Cafalu 25.00 12.50
171 Doyle 25.00 12.50
172 Fisher 25.00 12.50
173 Halland 25.00 12.50
174 Harry Jenkins 25.00 12.50
175 Eugene Newton 25.00 12.50
176 Powell 25.00 12.50
177 Presley and 25.00 12.50
Pritchard
(sic, Pressley)
178 Pritchard 25.00 12.50
179 Schmidt 25.00 12.50
180 Shanghnessy 25.00 12.50
181 Harry Spratt 25.00 12.50
182 Bonner 25.00 12.50
183 Creagan 25.00 12.50
184 Forque 25.00 12.50
185 Gatmeyer 25.00 12.50
186 James Gillespie 25.00 12.50
187 John Novak 25.00 12.50
188 Phealean 25.00 12.50
189 Abercrombie 25.00 12.50
190 Averett 25.00 12.50
191 Fairbanks 25.00 12.50
192 Gardin 25.00 12.50
193 F.J. Harrington 25.00 12.50
194 Harris 25.00 12.50
195 Jackson 25.00 12.50
196 Frank Thompson 25.00 12.50
197 Vickery 25.00 12.50
198 Tilly Walker 25.00 12.50
199 Robert Wood 25.00 12.50
200 Wynne 25.00 12.50
201 Bourquin 25.00 12.50
202 John Cooper 25.00 12.50
203 Doak 25.00 12.50
204 Ebinger 25.00 12.50
205 Foltz 25.00 12.50
206 Gehring 25.00 12.50
207 Howard 25.00 12.50
208 Hyames 25.00 12.50
209 Kelley 25.00 12.50
210 Kite 25.00 12.50
211 Tydeman 25.00 12.50
212 Charles Clapp 25.00 12.50
213 Cowells 25.00 12.50
214 Foreman 25.00 12.50
215 Bunn Hearne 25.00 12.50
216 Hudson 25.00 12.50
217 Lane 25.00 12.50
218 C. McGeehan 25.00 12.50
219 Dan McGeehan 25.00 12.50
220 Miller 25.00 12.50
221 Stewart 25.00 12.50
222 B.E. Thompson 25.00 12.50
223 James Westlake 25.00 12.50
224 Brent 25.00 12.50
225 Cote 25.00 12.50
226 John Ferrell 25.00 12.50
227 Fogarty 25.00 12.50
228 Frank King 25.00 12.50
229 William Loval 25.00 12.50
230 MacConachie 25.00 12.50
231 McKeavitt 25.00 12.50
232 Midkiff 25.00 12.50
233 Painter 25.00 12.50
234 Joshua Swindell 25.00 12.50
235 Templin 25.00 12.50
236 Willis 25.00 12.50

1910 Old Mill T210

At 640 cards, this is the largest 20th Century tobacco-issued baseball series, and it presents a formidable challenge to the collector. Each card measures 1 1/2" by 2 5/8". Eight minor leagues are each represented by a specific numbered series indicated on the reverse of each card. Each player's name and team are printed in black within the bottom white picture area. The list below is ordered alphabetically by player's name within team within series. Series 1 (South Atlantic League) teams are Augusta (1-13), Columbia (14-26), Columbus (27-39), Jacksonville (40-51), Macon (52-63) and Savannah (64-75). Series 2 (Virginia League) teams are Danville (76-88), Lynchburg (89-105), Norfolk (106-117), Portsmouth (118-132), Richmond (133-151), and Roanoke (152-162). Series 3 (Texas League) teams are Dallas (163-181), Ft. Worth (182-197), Galveston (198-204), Houston (205-216), Oklahoma City (217-221), San Antonio (222-230), Shreveport (231-243) and Waco (244-257). Series 4 (Virginia Valley League) teams are Charleston (258-272), Huntington (273-285), Montgomery (286-296) and Mt. Pleasant (297-306). Series 5 (Carolina Association) teams are Anderson (307-320), Charlotte (321-335), Greensboro (336-348), Greenville (349-364), Spartanburg (365-379) and Winston-Salem (380-393). Series 6 (Blue Grass League) teams are Frankfort (394-401), Lexington (402-414), Maysville (415-422), Paris (423-433), Richmond (434-443), Shelbyville (444-446) and Winchester (447-459). Series 7 (Eastern Carolina League) teams are Fayetteville (460-468), Goldsboro (469-490), Raleigh (491-504), Rocky Mount (505-519), Wilmington (520) and Wilson (521-526). Series 8 (Southern Association) teams are Atlanta (527-539), Birmingham (540-556), Chattanooga (557-566), Memphis (567-580), Mobile (581-592), Montgomery (593-608), Nashville (609-625) and New Orleans (626-640). The two key cards in the set are Casey Stengel and Joe Jackson.

Ex-Mt VG
COMPLETE SET (640) 20000.00 10000.00
COMMON SERIES 1 (1-75) 25.00 12.50
COMMON SERIES 2 (76-162) 20.00 10.00
COMMON SERIES 3 (163-257) 25.00 12.50
COMMON SERIES 4 (258-306) 25.00 12.50
COMMON SERIES 5 (307-393) 25.00 12.50
COMMON SERIES 6 (394-459) 20.00 10.00
COMMON SERIES 7 (460-526) 30.00 15.00
COMMON SERIES 8 (527-640) 25.00 12.50
1 Bagwell 25.00 12.50
2 Bierkorttle 25.00 12.50
3 Dudley 25.00 12.50
4 Edwards 25.00 12.50
5 Hannifan 25.00 12.50
6 Mike Hauser 25.00 12.50
7 McMahon 25.00 12.50
8 Frank Norcum 25.00 12.50
9 Pierce 25.00 12.50
10 Shields 25.00 12.50
11 Howard Smith 25.00 12.50
12 Viola 25.00 12.50
13 Louis Wagner 25.00 12.50
14 Breitenstein 25.00 12.50
15 Cavender 25.00 12.50
16 Joe Collins 25.00 12.50
17 Dwyer 25.00 12.50
18 Jones 25.00 12.50
19 Lewis 25.00 12.50
20 Marshall 25.00 12.50
21 Herbert Martin 25.00 12.50
22 John Massing 25.00 12.50
23 Mulldowney 25.00 12.50
24 Redfern 25.00 12.50
25 Schwietzka 25.00 12.50
26 Wohlleben 25.00 12.50
27 Becker 25.00 12.50
28 Bensen 25.00 12.50
29 James Fox 25.00 12.50
30 Harley 25.00 12.50
31 Hille 25.00 12.50
32 Krebs 25.00 12.50
33 Lewis 25.00 12.50
34 Arthur Long 25.00 12.50
35 McLeod 25.00 12.50
36 Radebaugh 25.00 12.50
37 Reynolds 25.00 12.50
38 Sisson 25.00 12.50
39 Toren 25.00 12.50
40 Bierman 25.00 12.50
41 Bremmerhoff 25.00 12.50
42 Robert Carter 25.00 12.50
43 DeFraites 25.00 12.50
44 Hoyt 25.00 12.50
45 Leo Huber 25.00 12.50
46 Lee 25.00 12.50
47 Manion 25.00 12.50
48 Mullaney 25.00 12.50
49 Pope 25.00 12.50
50 Taffee 25.00 12.50
51 Sahl 25.00 12.50
52 Benton 25.00 12.50
53 Carl Enbanks 25.00 12.50
54 Eubank 25.00 12.50
55 Ison 25.00 12.50
56 Kalkhoff 25.00 12.50
57 Lawrence 25.00 12.50
58 Lee 25.00 12.50
59 Perry Lipe 25.00 12.50
portrait
60 Perry Lipe 25.00 12.50
batting
61 Morse 25.00 12.50
62 Schulze 25.00 12.50
63 Weems 25.00 12.50
64 Balenti 25.00 12.50
65 Howard 25.00 12.50
66 Magoon 25.00 12.50
67 Joe Martina 25.00 12.50
68 Murch 25.00 12.50
69 Pelkey 25.00 12.50
70 Petit 25.00 12.50
71 Regan 25.00 12.50
72 Reynolds 25.00 12.50
73 Schulz 25.00 12.50
74 Hugh Sweeney 25.00 12.50
75 Wells 25.00 12.50
76 Bussey 20.00 10.00
77 Gaston 20.00 10.00
78 Henry Griffin 20.00 10.00
79 E.C. Hanks 20.00 10.00
80 Hooker 20.00 10.00
81 Kinkel 20.00 10.00
82 Larkins 20.00 10.00
83 Laughlin 20.00 10.00
84 Lloyd 20.00 10.00
85 Ivan Loos 20.00 10.00
86 Fleet Mayberry 20.00 10.00
87 August Schrader 20.00 10.00
88 Vincent Tydeman 20.00 10.00
89 Beham 20.00 10.00
90 Brandon 20.00 10.00
91 Breivogel 20.00 10.00
92 Eddowes 20.00 10.00
93 Louis Gehring 20.00 10.00
94 Griffen 20.00 10.00
95 H.H. Hoffman 20.00 10.00
96 Owen Jackson 20.00 10.00
97 Harry Levy 20.00 10.00
98 Lucia 20.00 10.00
99 Frank Michaels 20.00 10.00
100 William Rowe 20.00 10.00
101 James Sharp 20.00 10.00
102 Smith (at bat) 20.00 10.00
103 Smith (catching) 20.00 10.00
104 Bart Woolums 20.00 10.00
105 Zimmerman 20.00 10.00
106 J.P. Bonner 20.00 10.00
107 Busch 20.00 10.00
108 Robert Chandler 20.00 10.00
109 Clarke 20.00 10.00
110 John Fox 20.00 10.00
111 Jackson 20.00 10.00
112 Clarence Lovell 20.00 10.00
113 MacConachie 20.00 10.00
114 James Mullaney 20.00 10.00
115 Clarence Munson 20.00 10.00
116 Nimmo 20.00 10.00
117 Carl Walker 20.00 10.00
118 Bowen 20.00 10.00
119 Clunk 20.00 10.00
120 Henry Cote 20.00 10.00
121 Cowan 20.00 10.00
122 Foxen 20.00 10.00
123 Hamilton 20.00 10.00
124 Hannifan 20.00 10.00
125 Walter Jackson 20.00 10.00
126 Kirkpatrick 20.00 10.00
127 Herman McFarland 20.00 10.00
128 Norris 20.00 10.00
129 Smith 20.00 10.00
130 Spicer 20.00 10.00
131 Toner 20.00 10.00
132 Vail 20.00 10.00
133 Aaron Archer 20.00 10.00
134 William Baker 20.00 10.00
135 Harvey Brooks 20.00 10.00
136 Brown 20.00 10.00
137 Decker 20.00 10.00
138 Frank Hale 20.00 10.00
139 Irvine 20.00 10.00
140 Jackson 20.00 10.00
141 Keifel 20.00 10.00
142 Landgradd 20.00 10.00
143 J.J. Lawlor 20.00 10.00
144 Messitt 20.00 10.00
145 Peterson 20.00 10.00
146 Revelle 20.00 10.00
147 Shaw 20.00 10.00
148 Guy Titman 20.00 10.00
149 John Verbout 20.00 10.00
150 Arthur Wallace 20.00 10.00
151 Waymack 20.00 10.00
152 Frank Anrada 20.00 10.00
153 Frank Cefalu 20.00 10.00
154 Doyle 20.00 10.00
155 Fisher 20.00 10.00
156 Holland 20.00 10.00
157 Jenkins 20.00 10.00
158 Newton 20.00 10.00
159 Walt Powell 20.00 10.00
160 William Presley 20.00 10.00
161 Pritchard 20.00 10.00
162 Schmidt 20.00 10.00
163 Berlick 25.00 12.50
164 Dale 25.00 12.50
165 Doyle 25.00 12.50
166 Enos 25.00 12.50
167 Evans 25.00 12.50
168 Glawe 25.00 12.50
169 Hank Gowdy 40.00 20.00
170 Hicks 25.00 12.50
171 Walter Hirsch 25.00 12.50
172 Maloney 25.00 12.50
173 Meagher 25.00 12.50
174 Mullen 25.00 12.50
175 Halton Ogle 25.00 12.50
176 Jack Onslow 25.00 12.50
177 Robertson 25.00 12.50
178 Shindel 25.00 12.50
179 Shontz 25.00 12.50
180 Storch 25.00 12.50
181 Woodburn 25.00 12.50
182 Ash 25.00 12.50
183 Belew 25.00 12.50
184 Sandy Burke 25.00 12.50
185 Coyle 25.00 12.50
186 Deardoff 25.00 12.50
187 Fillman 25.00 12.50
188 Francis 25.00 12.50
189 Jolley 25.00 12.50
190 McKay 25.00 12.50
191 Morris 25.00 12.50
192 Pendelton 25.00 12.50
193 Powell 25.00 12.50
194 Ross Salazor 25.00 12.50
195 Weber 25.00 12.50
196 H.B. Weeks 25.00 12.50
197 Wertherford 25.00 12.50
198 Cable 25.00 12.50
199 Donnelley 25.00 12.50
200 Hise 25.00 12.50
201 Ely Kaphan 25.00 12.50
202 Dan Riley 25.00 12.50
203 Spangler 25.00 12.50
204 Stringer 25.00 12.50
205 Bell 25.00 12.50
206 Barney Burch 25.00 12.50
207 Tom Carlin 25.00 12.50
208 Corkhill 25.00 12.50
209 Hill 25.00 12.50
210 Hornsby 25.00 12.50
211 Malloy 25.00 12.50
212 Merritt 25.00 12.50
213 Norten 25.00 12.50
214 Rose 25.00 12.50
215 Roscoe Watson 25.00 12.50
216 Wickenhorf 25.00 12.50
217 Bandy 25.00 12.50
218 Davis 25.00 12.50
219 Nelson Jones 25.00 12.50
220 Alex Nagel 25.00 12.50
221 John Walsh 25.00 12.50
222 Alexander 25.00 12.50
223 Billiard 25.00 12.50
224 Blanding 25.00 12.50
225 Firestone 25.00 12.50
226 Joe Kipp 25.00 12.50
227 George Leidy 25.00 12.50
228 Slaven 25.00 12.50
229 George Stinson 25.00 12.50
230 George Yantz 25.00 12.50
231 Barenkamp 25.00 12.50
232 Cowans 25.00 12.50
233 Jim Galloway 25.00 12.50
234 Gardner 25.00 12.50
235 Dale Gear 25.00 12.50
236 Harper 25.00 12.50
237 Hinninger 25.00 12.50
238 Howell 25.00 12.50
239 Mills 25.00 12.50
240 Smith (Bat over 25.00 12.50
right shoulder)
241 Smith (Bat at 25.00 12.50
right hip)
242 Stadeli 25.00 12.50
243 Tesreau 25.00 12.50
244 Bennett 25.00 12.50
245 Barney Blue 25.00 12.50
246 Conoway 25.00 12.50
247 Curry 25.00 12.50
248 Drucke 25.00 12.50
249 Dugey 25.00 12.50
250 Gordon 25.00 12.50
251 Harbison 25.00 12.50
252 W.M. Hooks 25.00 12.50
253 Johnston 25.00 12.50
254 Munsell 25.00 12.50
255 Tony Thebo 25.00 12.50
256 Tullas 25.00 12.50
257 Williams 25.00 12.50
258 J. Benny 25.00 12.50
259 Carney 25.00 12.50
260 Conolly 25.00 12.50
261 Donnel 25.00 12.50
262 Erlewein 25.00 12.50
263 Ferrell 25.00 12.50
264 Heady 25.00 12.50
265 Dutch Hollis 25.00 12.50
266 Johnson 25.00 12.50
267 Ed Moore 25.00 12.50
268 Charles Pick 25.00 12.50
269 Joseph Stanley 25.00 12.50
270 Charles Stockum 25.00 12.50
271 Willis 25.00 12.50
272 Zurlage 25.00 12.50
273 Bonno 25.00 12.50
274 Brumfield 25.00 12.50
275 J.V. Campbell 25.00 12.50
276 Canepa 25.00 12.50
277 Edward Carter 25.00 12.50
278 Collier 25.00 12.50
279 Halterman 25.00 12.50
280 Howard Kane 25.00 12.50
281 Leonard 25.00 12.50
282 McClain 25.00 12.50
283 Walter Seaman 25.00 12.50
284 Frank Titlow 25.00 12.50
285 J.C. Young 25.00 12.50
286 Luther Aylor 25.00 12.50
287 Howard Cochrane 25.00 12.50
288 Davis 25.00 12.50
289 Geary 25.00 12.50
290 Lux 25.00 12.50
291 Moye 25.00 12.50
292 O'Connor 25.00 12.50
293 Orcutt 25.00 12.50
294 Spicer 25.00 12.50
295 Waldron 25.00 12.50
296 Womach 25.00 12.50
297 Best 25.00 12.50
298 Boshmer 25.00 12.50
299 Brown 25.00 12.50
300 Dougherty 25.00 12.50
301 F.M. Hunter 25.00 12.50
302 Edward Kuehn 25.00 12.50
303 Fred Mollenkamp 25.00 12.50
304 Chester Pickels 25.00 12.50
305 Ferdinand Schafer 25.00 12.50
306 Witter 25.00 12.50
307 Brannon 25.00 12.50
308 Corbett (3/4 pose) 25.00 12.50
309 Corbett (full pose) 25.00 12.50
310 Farmer 25.00 12.50
311 Finn 25.00 12.50
312 Gorham 25.00 12.50
313 Harley 25.00 12.50
314 Kelly 25.00 12.50
315 Lothrop 25.00 12.50
316 A. McCarthy 25.00 12.50
317 J. McCarthy 25.00 12.50
318 McEnvoe 25.00 12.50
319 Mangum 25.00 12.50
320 Wehrell 25.00 12.50
321 Bausewein 25.00 12.50
322 Brazell 25.00 12.50
323 L. Cross 25.00 12.50
324 Coutts 25.00 12.50
325 Leo Dobard 25.00 12.50
326 Duvie 25.00 12.50
327 Francisco 25.00 12.50
328 Gorman 25.00 12.50
329 Hargrave 25.00 12.50
330 Hayes 25.00 12.50
331 Humphrey 25.00 12.50
332 Johnson 25.00 12.50
333 Leo McHugh 25.00 12.50
334 Taxis 25.00 12.50
335 Williams 25.00 12.50
336 Bentley 25.00 12.50
337 C. Beusse 25.00 12.50
338 Fred Beusse 25.00 12.50
339 Eldridge 25.00 12.50
340 Walter Hammersley 25.00 12.50
341 Hicks 25.00 12.50
342 Jackson 25.00 12.50
343 Dudley James 25.00 12.50
344 Rickard 25.00 12.50
345 Smith 25.00 12.50
346 Thrasher 25.00 12.50
347 Walters 25.00 12.50
348 Weldon 25.00 12.50
349 Blackstone 25.00 12.50
350 Cashion 25.00 12.50
351 C. Derrick 25.00 12.50
352 F. Derrick 25.00 12.50
353 Drumm 25.00 12.50
354 Flowers 25.00 12.50
355 P.A. Jenkins 25.00 12.50
356 McFarlin 25.00 12.50
357 Noojin 25.00 12.50
358 Ochs 25.00 12.50
359 Redfern 25.00 12.50
360 Thomas Stouch 25.00 12.50
361 Trammel 25.00 12.50
362 Wingo 25.00 12.50
363 Workman 25.00 12.50
364 Wysong 25.00 12.50
365 Abercrombie 25.00 12.50
366 Avarett 25.00 12.50
367 Bigbee 25.00 12.50
368 Bullock 25.00 12.50
369 J.F. Crouch 25.00 12.50
370 Ehrhardt 25.00 12.50
371 Fairbanks 25.00 12.50
372 Gardin 25.00 12.50
373 Harrington 25.00 12.50
374 Harris 25.00 12.50
375 Roth (at bat) 25.00 12.50
376 Roth (fielding) 25.00 12.50
377 Springs 25.00 12.50
378 Walker 25.00 12.50
379 Wynne 25.00 12.50
380 Bievens 25.00 12.50
381 Buck Brent 25.00 12.50
382 John Ferrell 25.00 12.50

383 Fogarty 25.00 12.50
384 Gilmore 25.00 12.50
385 Guss 25.00 12.50
386 Laval 25.00 12.50
387 MacConachie 25.00 12.50
388 McKevitt 25.00 12.50
389 Midkiff 25.00 12.50
390 Moore 25.00 12.50
391 Painter 25.00 12.50
392 Reis 25.00 12.50
393 Templin 25.00 12.50
394 Angermeier 20.00 10.00
(sic& Angermeir)
395 Angermeir 20.00 10.00
396 Beard 20.00 10.00
397 Bohannon 20.00 10.00
398 Cornell 20.00 10.00
399 Hicks 20.00 10.00
400 Hoffman 20.00 10.00
401 McIlvain 20.00 10.00
402 Badger 20.00 10.00
403 Ellis 20.00 10.00
404 Endington 20.00 10.00
405 Haines 20.00 10.00
406 Hevevon 20.00 10.00
407 Keifel 20.00 10.00
408 Kinbrough 20.00 10.00
409 L'Heuveux 20.00 10.00
410 Meyers 20.00 10.00
411 Sinex 20.00 10.00
412 Fan Landingham 20.00 10.00
413 Viox 20.00 10.00
414 Yancy 20.00 10.00
415 Chase 20.00 10.00
416 Dailey 20.00 10.00
417 Everden 20.00 10.00
418 Gisler 20.00 10.00
419 Oyler 20.00 10.00
420 Ross 20.00 10.00
421 Schultz 20.00 10.00
422 Casey Stengel 1200.00 600.00
423 Barnett 20.00 10.00
424 Chapman 20.00 10.00
425 Goodman 20.00 10.00
426 Harold 20.00 10.00
427 Kaiser 20.00 10.00
428 Kuhlman 20.00 10.00
429 Kuhlmann 20.00 10.00
430 McKernon 20.00 10.00
431 Scheneberg (head 20.00 10.00
and shoulders)
432 Scheneberg (fielding) 20.00 10.00
433 Scott 20.00 10.00
434 Creager 20.00 10.00
435 Elgin 20.00 10.00
436 Moloney 20.00 10.00
437 Olson 20.00 10.00
438 Thoss 20.00 10.00
439 Tilford 20.00 10.00
440 Walden 20.00 10.00
441 Whitaker 20.00 10.00
442 Willis 20.00 10.00
443 Wright 20.00 10.00
444 Kircher 20.00 10.00
445 Van Landingham 20.00 10.00
446 Womble 20.00 10.00
447 Atwell 20.00 10.00
448 Barney 20.00 10.00
449 Callahan 20.00 10.00
450 Coleman 20.00 10.00
451 Cornell 20.00 10.00
452 Goostree (leaning 20.00 10.00
on bat)
453 Goostree (hands 20.00 10.00
behind back)
454 Horn 20.00 10.00
455 Kircher 20.00 10.00
456 Mullin 20.00 10.00
457 Reed 20.00 10.00
458 Toney 20.00 10.00
459 Yeager 20.00 10.00
460 Brandt 30.00 15.00
461 Cantwell 30.00 15.00
462 Dwyer 30.00 15.00
463 Galvin 30.00 15.00
464 Hartley 30.00 15.00
465 Luyster 30.00 15.00
466 Mayer 30.00 15.00
467 O'Halloran 30.00 15.00
468 Schumaker 30.00 15.00
469 Brown 30.00 15.00
470 Crockett 30.00 15.00
471 Dailey 30.00 15.00
472 Norman Evans 30.00 15.00
473 Fulton 30.00 15.00
474 Gates 30.00 15.00
475 Gunderson 30.00 15.00
476 Handibe 30.00 15.00
477 William Irving 30.00 15.00
478 Kaiser 30.00 15.00
479 Kelly 30.00 15.00
480 Kelly (Mascot) 30.00 15.00
481 MacDonald 30.00 15.00
482 Malcolm 30.00 15.00
483 Merchant 30.00 15.00
484 Morgan 30.00 15.00
485 Sharp 30.00 15.00
486 Steinback 30.00 15.00
487 Stoehr 30.00 15.00
488 Taylor 30.00 15.00
489 Webb 30.00 15.00
490 Wolf 30.00 15.00
491 Beatty 30.00 15.00
492 Biel 30.00 15.00
493 Carrol 30.00 15.00
494 Ham 30.00 15.00
495 Daniel Hart 30.00 15.00
496 Hobbs 30.00 15.00
497 George W. Kelly 30.00 15.00
498 McCormac 30.00 15.00
499 Newman 30.00 15.00
500 Prim 30.00 15.00
501 Richardson 30.00 15.00
502 Sherrill 30.00 15.00
503 Simmons 30.00 15.00
504 Wright 30.00 15.00
505 Bonner 30.00 15.00
506 Creagan 30.00 15.00
507 Cooney 30.00 15.00
508 Dobbs 30.00 15.00
509 Dussault 30.00 15.00
510 Forgue 30.00 15.00
511 Gastmeyer (batting) 30.00 15.00
512 Gastmeyer (fielding) 30.00 15.00
513 Gillespie 30.00 15.00
514 Griffin 30.00 15.00
515 Morris 30.00 15.00
516 Munson 30.00 15.00
517 Noval 30.00 15.00
518 Phelan 30.00 15.00
519 Reeves 30.00 15.00
520 Hyames 30.00 15.00
521 Armstrong 30.00 15.00
522 Cooper 30.00 15.00
523 Cowell 30.00 15.00
524 McGeehan 30.00 15.00
525 Mills 30.00 15.00
526 Whelan 30.00 15.00
527 Bartley 25.00 12.50
528 Bayless 25.00 12.50
529 Fisher 25.00 12.50
530 Griffin 25.00 12.50
531 Hanks 25.00 12.50
532 Hohnhorst 25.00 12.50
533 Jordan 25.00 12.50
534 Moran 25.00 12.50
535 Rogers 25.00 12.50
536 Seitz 25.00 12.50
537 Sid. Smith 25.00 12.50
538 Sweeney 25.00 12.50
539 Walker 25.00 12.50
540 Bauer 25.00 12.50
541 Elliott 25.00 12.50
542 Emery 25.00 12.50
543 Fleharty 25.00 12.50
544 Gygli 25.00 12.50
545 Kane 25.00 12.50
546 Larsen 25.00 12.50
547 Moxie Manuel 30.00 15.00
548 Marcan 25.00 12.50
549 McBride 25.00 12.50
550 McGilvray 25.00 12.50
551 McTigue 25.00 12.50
552 Molesworth 25.00 12.50
553 Newton 25.00 12.50
554 Owen 25.00 12.50
555 Schopp 25.00 12.50
556 Wagner 25.00 12.50
557 Carson 25.00 12.50
558 Collins 25.00 12.50
559 Demaree 25.00 12.50
560 Dobbs 25.00 12.50
561 McLaurin 25.00 12.50
562 Miller 25.00 12.50
563 Patterson 25.00 12.50
564 Rhodes 25.00 12.50
565 Schlitzer 25.00 12.50
566 Yerkes 25.00 12.50
567 Allen 25.00 12.50
568 Babb 25.00 12.50
569 Crandall 25.00 12.50
570 Cross 25.00 12.50
571 Davis 25.00 12.50
572 Dick 25.00 12.50
573 Dudley 25.00 12.50
574 Farrell 25.00 12.50
575 Fritz 25.00 12.50
576 Peters 25.00 12.50
577 Rementer 25.00 12.50
578 Steele 25.00 12.50
579 Wanner 25.00 12.50
580 Whitney 25.00 12.50
581 Allen 25.00 12.50
582 Berger 25.00 12.50
583 Bittroff 25.00 12.50
584 William Chappelle 25.00 12.50
585 Dunn 25.00 12.50
586 Hickman 25.00 12.50
587 Huelsman 25.00 12.50
588 Kerwin 25.00 12.50
589 Frank Rhoton 25.00 12.50
590 Swacina 25.00 12.50
591 Wagner 25.00 12.50
592 Wilder 25.00 12.50
593 Burnett 25.00 12.50
594 Daly 25.00 12.50
595 Graninger 25.00 12.50
596 Gribbin 25.00 12.50
597 Hart 25.00 12.50
598 McCreery 25.00 12.50
599 Miller 25.00 12.50
600 Nolley 25.00 12.50
601 Osteen 25.00 12.50
602 Joe Pepe 25.00 12.50
603 Phillips 25.00 12.50
604 Pratt 25.00 12.50
605 Manning Smith 25.00 12.50
606 Thomas (portrait) 25.00 12.50
607 Thomas (fielding) 25.00 12.50
608 Whiteman 25.00 12.50
609 Anderson 25.00 12.50
610 Bay 25.00 12.50
611 Bernard 25.00 12.50
612 Bronkie 25.00 12.50
613 Case 25.00 12.50
614 Harry Cohen 25.00 12.50
615 Erloff 25.00 12.50
616 Tim Flood 25.00 12.50
617 Kelly 25.00 12.50
618 Henry Keupper 25.00 12.50
619 Mike Lynch 25.00 12.50
620 Perdue 25.00 12.50
621 Seabough 25.00 12.50
622 Siegle 25.00 12.50
623 Vinson 25.00 12.50
624 Weif 25.00 12.50
625 Wiseman 25.00 12.50
626 Breitenstein 25.00 12.50
627 Brooks 25.00 12.50
628 Cafalu 25.00 12.50
629 DeMontreville 25.00 12.50
630 E. DeMontreville 25.00 12.50
631 Doster 25.00 12.50
632 Hess 25.00 12.50
633 Joe Jackson 6000.00 3000.00
634 James LaFitte 25.00 12.50
635 Lindsay 25.00 12.50
636 Frank Manush 25.00 12.50
637 Maxwell 25.00 12.50
638 Paige 25.00 12.50
639 Robertson 25.00 12.50
640 Rohe 25.00 12.50

1910 Red Sun T211

The green-bordered cards in this 75-card set measure approximately 1 1/2" by 2 5/8". The obverse design of this 1910 issue resembles that of the the T210 set except for the green borders surrounding the black and white picture area. All players in the set are from the Southern Association and all also appear in the T210 Series 8. The players have been alphabetized within team and numbered for reference in the checklist below. The teams are also ordered alphabetically: Atlanta (1-13), Birmingham (14-16), Memphis (17-22), Mobile (23-34), Montgomery (35-45), Nashville (46-62) and New Orleans (63-75).

Ex-Mt VG
COMPLETE SET (75) 3200.00 1600.00
1 Bartley 50.00 25.00
2 Bayless 50.00 25.00
3 Fisher 50.00 25.00
4 Griffin 50.00 25.00
5 Gornhorst 50.00 25.00
6 Hanks 50.00 25.00
7 Jordan 50.00 25.00
8 Moran 50.00 25.00
9 Rogers 50.00 25.00
10 Seitz 50.00 25.00
11 Sid Smith 50.00 25.00
12 Sweeney 50.00 25.00
13 Walker 50.00 25.00
14 Gygli 50.00 25.00
15 Kane 50.00 25.00
16 Molesworth 50.00 25.00
17 Babb 50.00 25.00
18 Cross 50.00 25.00
19 Davis 50.00 25.00
20 Dick 50.00 25.00
21 Fritz 50.00 25.00
22 Steele 50.00 25.00
23 Allen 50.00 25.00
24 Berger 50.00 25.00
25 Bittroff 50.00 25.00
26 Chappelle 50.00 25.00
27 Dunn 50.00 25.00
28 Hickman 50.00 25.00
29 Huelsman 50.00 25.00
30 Kerwin 50.00 25.00
31 Rhoton 50.00 25.00
32 Swacina 50.00 25.00
33 Wagner 50.00 25.00
34 Wilder 50.00 25.00
35 Jud Daly 50.00 25.00
36 Greminger 50.00 25.00
37 Gribbin 50.00 25.00
38 Hart 50.00 25.00
39 McCreary 50.00 25.00
40 Miller 50.00 25.00
41 Nolley 50.00 25.00
42 Pepe 50.00 25.00
43 Pratt 50.00 25.00
44 Smith 50.00 25.00
45 Thomas 50.00 25.00
46 Anderson 50.00 25.00
47 Bay 50.00 25.00
48 Bernard 50.00 25.00
49 Bronkie 50.00 25.00
50 Case 50.00 25.00
51 Cohen 50.00 25.00
52 Erloff 50.00 25.00
53 Flood 50.00 25.00
54 Kelly 50.00 25.00
55 Keupper 50.00 25.00
56 Lynch 50.00 25.00
57 Perdue 50.00 25.00
58 Seabrough 50.00 25.00
59 Siegel 50.00 25.00
60 Vinson 50.00 25.00
61 Wiseman 50.00 25.00
62 Welf 50.00 25.00
63 Breitenstein 50.00 25.00
64 Brooks 50.00 25.00
65 Cafalu 50.00 25.00
66 DeMontreville 50.00 25.00
67 E. DeMontreville 50.00 25.00
68 Foster 50.00 25.00
69 Hess 50.00 25.00
70 LaFitte 50.00 25.00
71 Lindsay 50.00 25.00
72 Manush 50.00 25.00
73 Paige 50.00 25.00
74 Robertson 50.00 25.00
75 Rohe 50.00 25.00

1911 Pacific Coast Biscuit D310

These cards, which measure approximately 2 1/2" by 4 1/2" feature players from the Pacific Coast League . Most of the cards were issued in black and white but a few were issued with a greenish sepia black and white.

Ex-Mt VG
COMPLETE SET 1200.00 600.00
1 Harry Ables 20.00 10.00
2 James Agnew 20.00 10.00
3 Roy Akin 20.00 10.00
4 Frank Arelanes 20.00 10.00
5 Charles Baum 20.00 10.00
6 Curtis Bernard 20.00 10.00
7 Claude Berry 20.00 10.00
8 Roy Brashear 20.00 10.00
9 Frank Browning 20.00 10.00
10 Leland Burrell 20.00 10.00
11 Herbert Byram 20.00 10.00
12 Walter Carlisle 20.00 10.00
13 Chester Chadbourne 20.00 10.00
14 Tyler Christian 20.00 10.00
15 George Cutshaw 20.00 10.00
16 Thomas Daley 20.00 10.00
17 Harold Danzig 20.00 10.00
18 Lee Delhi 20.00 10.00
19 Bert Delmas 20.00 10.00
20 Frank Dillon 20.00 10.00
21 Joseph Fitzgerald 20.00 10.00
22 Alva Gipe 20.00 10.00
23 Woody Heister 20.00 10.00
24 Ben Henderson 20.00 10.00
25 Clarence Henley 20.00 10.00
26 Roy Hitt 20.00 10.00
27 Harry Hoffman 20.00 10.00
28 Wallace Hogan 20.00 10.00
29 Joseph Holland 20.00 10.00
30 Franz Hosp 20.00 10.00
31 Ivon Howard 20.00 10.00
32 Elmer Kostner 20.00 10.00
33 Walter Kuhn 20.00 10.00
34 L.W. LaLonge 20.00 10.00
35 James Lewis 20.00 10.00
36 Thomas Madden 20.00 10.00
37 Harl Maggart 20.00 10.00
38 Harry McArdle 20.00 10.00
39 Walt McCredie 20.00 10.00
40 C. McDonnell 20.00 10.00
41 George Metzger 20.00 10.00
42 Carl Mitze 20.00 10.00
43 Ernest Mohler 20.00 10.00
44 Charles Moore 20.00 10.00
45 Daniel Murray 20.00 10.00
46 Chester Nourse 20.00 10.00
47 Joe O'Rourke 20.00 10.00
47 Ham Patterson 20.00 10.00
49 Roger Peckinpaugh 100.00 50.00
50 Hub Pernoll 20.00 10.00
51 M.C. Pfyl 20.00 10.00
52 John Raleigh 20.00 10.00
53 William Rapps 20.00 10.00
54 Arthur Ross 20.00 10.00
55 John Ryan 20.00 10.00
56 Tom Seaton 20.00 10.00
57 Tom Sheehan 20.00 10.00
58 Arthur Smith 20.00 10.00
59 Hughie Smith 20.00 10.00
60 William Steen 20.00 10.00
61 George Stinson 20.00 10.00
62 Harry Sutor 20.00 10.00
63 Thomas Tennant 20.00 10.00
64 Fuller Thompson 20.00 10.00
65 John Tiedeman 20.00 10.00
66 William Tozer 20.00 10.00
67 Edward Van Buren 20.00 10.00
68 Oscar Vitt 25.00 12.50
69 Clyde Wares 20.00 10.00
70 Buck Weaver 500.00 250.00
71 Harry Wolverton 20.00 10.00
72 Elmer Zacher 20.00 10.00

1911 Bishop Coast League E100

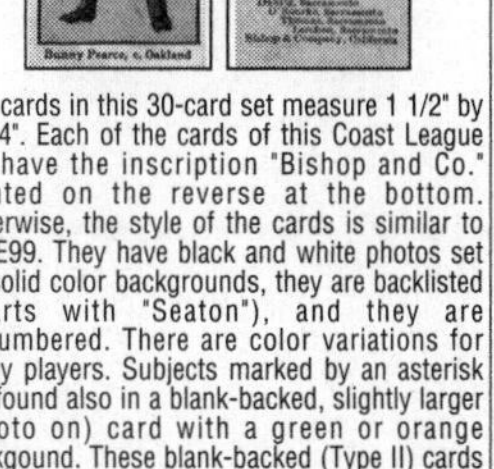

The cards in this 30-card set measure 1 1/2" by 2 3/4". Each of the cards of this Coast League set have the inscription "Bishop and Co." printed on the reverse at the bottom. Otherwise, the style of the cards is similar to set E99. They have black and white photos set on solid color backgrounds, they are backlisted (starts with "Seaton"), and they are unnumbered. There are color variations for many players. Subjects marked by an asterisk are found also in a blank-backed, slightly larger (photo on) card with a green or orange backgound. These blank-backed (Type II) cards are valued double the prices below. According to some hobbyists, there has never been a type two found in better than vg/ex condition. The cards in the set have been alphabetized and numbered in the checklist below. The set was produced around 1910.

Ex-Mt VG
COMPLETE SET (30) 6000.00 3000.00
1 Spider Baum 200.00 100.00
2 Len Burrell * 200.00 100.00
3 Walt Carlisle 200.00 100.00
4 George Cutshaw 200.00 100.00
5 Pete Daley 200.00 100.00
6 Babe Danzig * 200.00 100.00
7 Flame Delhi 200.00 100.00
8 Bert Delmas 200.00 100.00
9 Roy Hitt * 200.00 100.00
10 Happy Hogan 200.00 100.00
11 Dutch Lerchen 200.00 100.00
12 Walt McCreedie 200.00 100.00
13 Kid Mohler 200.00 100.00
14 Charlie Moore 200.00 100.00
15 Slim Nelson 200.00 100.00
16 Patsy O'Rourke 200.00 100.00
17 Ham Patterson 200.00 100.00
18 Ducky Pearce * 200.00 100.00
19 Roger Peckinpaugh 250.00 125.00
20 Monte Pfyle 200.00 100.00
sic, Pfyl *
21 Watt Powell 200.00 100.00
22 Bill Rapps 200.00 100.00
23 Tom Seaton * 200.00 100.00
24 Bill Steen 200.00 100.00
25 Harry Sutor 200.00 100.00
26 Tom Tennant 200.00 100.00
27 Pinch Thomas 200.00 100.00
28 Bill Tozer 200.00 100.00
29 Clyde Wares 200.00 100.00
30 Buck Weaver 800.00 400.00

1911 Big Eater E-Unc.

This 20-card set of the Pacific Coast League's team, the Sacramento Senators, features black-and-white player photos which measure approximately 2 1/8" by 4". Each card has a three line capiton giving the name of the player, the team as "SAC'TO" and the words, "HE EATS 'BIG EATER' " which is presumed to be the name of a candy. These cards are rarely found in a better condition than g-vg. There is speculation that these were issued by a candy company -- therefore the cards are listed with the "E" designation.

Ex-Mt VG
COMPLETE SET (20) 18000.00 9000.00
1 Frank Arellanes 1000.00 500.00
2 Charles Baum 1000.00 500.00
3 Herbert Byram 1000.00 500.00
4 Hal Danzig 1000.00 500.00
5 John Fitzgerald 1000.00 500.00
6 Gaddy 1000.00 500.00
(unidentified player)
7 Elwood Heister 1000.00 500.00
8 Hunt 1000.00 500.00
9 Henry Kerns 1000.00 500.00
10 Louis LaLonge 1000.00 500.00
11 Bertram Lerchen 1000.00 500.00
12 Jim Lewis 1000.00 500.00
13 Christopher Mahoney 1000.00 500.00
14 Richard Nebinger 1000.00 500.00
15 Joseph L. O'Rourke 1000.00 500.00
16 James Shinn 1000.00 500.00
17 Chester Thomas 1000.00 500.00
18 Cecil Thompson 1000.00 500.00
19 Frank Thornton 1000.00 500.00
20 Edward Van Buren 1000.00 500.00

1911 Mono T217

These 25 cards, which were issued as part of a far more inclusive set, including many famous actresses, feature players from the PCL. Since these cards are unnumbered, we have sequenced them in alphabetical order.

MINT NRMT
COMPLETE SET 70000.00 31500.00
1 Roy Akin 3000.00 1350.00
2 Curtis Bernard 3000.00 1350.00
3 Len Burrell 3000.00 1350.00
4 Chet Chadbourne 3000.00 1350.00
5 Bob Couchman 3000.00 1350.00
6 Elmer Criger 3000.00 1350.00
7 Pete Daley 3000.00 1350.00
8 Flame Delhi 3000.00 1350.00
Eyes Closed
9 Flame Delhi 3000.00 1350.00
Eyes Opened
10 Bert Delmas 3000.00 1350.00
11 Ivan Howard 3000.00 1350.00
12 Kitty Knight 3000.00 1350.00
13 Gene Krapp 3000.00 1350.00
Sic, Knapp
14 George Metzger 3000.00 1350.00
15 Carl Mitze 3000.00 1350.00
16 Patsy O'Rourke 3000.00 1350.00
17 Roger Peckinpaugh 4000.00 1800.00
18 Walter Schmidt 3000.00 1350.00
19 Hugh Smith 3000.00 1350.00
Batting
20 Hugh Smith 3000.00 1350.00
Fielding
21 William Stein 3000.00 1350.00
22 Elmer Thorsen 3000.00 1350.00
23 Oscar Vitt 4000.00 1800.00
24 Clyde Wares 3000.00 1350.00
25 George Wheeler 3000.00 1350.00

1911-12 Obak Premiums T4

Similar to the Pinkerton cabinets issued around the same time; this checklist is presented without prices. These cards are very scarce within the hobby as it originally took 50 coupons to receive one of these premiums. These cabinets measure approximately 5" by 7" are usually have a pencil marking in the back which correspond to the Obak listings of the 1911 set. In addition, subtle differences are known in every photo since they were enlarged from the original photo. It is believed that by 1913 only 25 coupons were needed for these and possibly less later in the decade. While there is not a lot of activity on these cards, a price of approximately $2500 for known copies in ex/mt condition is a good base to use for pricing.

Ex-Mt VG
COMPLETE SET (175)
1 Fred Abbott
2 James Agnew
3 Roy Akin
4 Curtis Bernard
5 Elmer Criger

6 T.F. Daley
7 Lee Delhi
8 Bert Delmas
9 Frank Dillon
10 Muriel Grindle
11 Ivan Howard
12 George Metzger
13 Charley Moore
14 Hugh Smith
15 Elmer Thorsen
16 Bill Tozer
17 George Wheeler
18 Harry Ables
19 Tyler Christian
20 Bert Coy
21 George Cutshaw
22 John Flater
23 August Hetling
24 Izzy Hoffman
25 Kittie Knight
26 Harl Maggert
27 Miller
28 Carl Mitze
29 William Pearce
30 Henry Pernoll
31 Monte Pfyl
32 John Tiedeman
33 Clyde Wares
34 James Wiggs
35 Harry Wolverton
36 Elmer Zacher
37 Shad Barry
38 Chester Chadbourne
39 Charles Fullerton
40 J. Henderson
41 Elmer Koestner
42 Arthur Krueger
43 Walter Kuhn
44 Walt McCreedie
45 Thomas Murray
46 Roger Peckinpaugh
47 William Rapps
48 Wilbur Rodgers
49 Bud Ryan
50 Tom Seaton
51 Tommy Sheehan
52 Bill Steen
53 Frank Arrelanes
54 Spider Baum
55 Herbert Byram
56 Harold Danzig
57 John Fitzgerald
58 Elwood Hiester
59 Benjamin Hunt
60 L.N. LaLonge
61 Bertram Lerchen
62 Chris Mahoney
63 Nourse
64 Patsy O'Rourke
65 James Shinn
66 Chester Thomas
67 Thompson
68 Frank Thornton
69 Edward Van Buren
70 Claude Berry
71 Frank Browning
72 Clarence Henley
73 Thomas Madden
74 Roy McArdle
75 Williard Meikle
76 Henry Melchoir
77 Frank Miller
78 Ernest Mohler
79 Doc Moskiman
80 Powell
81 William Ryan
82 Walter Schmidt
83 Royal Shaw
84 Harry Suter
85 Thomas Tennant
86 Oscar Vitt
87 Buck Weaver
88 Carl Zamloch
89 John Brackenridge
90 Roy Brashear
91 Drummond Brown
92 Burrell
93 Walter Carlisle
94 Albert Carson
95 Roy Castleton
96 Roy Hitt
97 Happy Hogan
98 Franz Hosp
99 John Kane
100 Clarence McDonnell
101 Ham Patterson
102 John Raleigh
103 Arhtur Ross
104 Sheehan
105 Harry Stewart
106 George Stinson
107 Ed Willett
108 Bloomfield
109 Casey
110 Garrett
111 Harris
112 Fred Lamline
113 Edward Mensor
114 Mundorff
115 Speas
116 George Stovall
117 Williams
118 Art Bues
119 Butler
120 Cruikshank
121 John Kading
122 Bill Leard
123 Raymond
124 Seaton
125 Shea
126 David Skeels
127 Spencer
128 Weed
129 George Zackert
130 Bonner
131 Cartwright
132 Phil Cooney
133 John Frisk
134 Hasty
135 Holm
136 Ed Kippert
137 Milo Netzel
138 Louis Nordyke
139 Henry Ostdiek
140 Paul Strand
141 Zimmerman
142 Annis
143 Bassey
144 Burns
145 Curtis Coleman
146 Gordon
147 Hall
148 Eddie Higgins
149 Peter Morse
150 Isaac Rockenfield
151 Charlie Schmutz
152 Warren
153 Adams
154 Justin Bennett
155 Norman Brashear
156 Bill Brinker
157 Engel
158 Erickson
159 James
160 Jensen
161 Lewis
162 Scharnweber
163 Spiesman
164 Swain
165 Dashwood
166 Davis
167 Goodman
168 Ed Householder
169 Fred Raymer
170 Reddick
171 Jack Roche
172 Starkel
173 Ten Million
174 Blaine Thomas
175 Ward

1911 Western Playground Assocation

These cards, which were issued as part of a redemption to help school kids, measure approximately 2 1/4" by 3 1/2". Each of these cards have the brown borders surrounding the player's photo. The backs of these cards feature certificates which could be used to recieive playground equipment. These cards were produced by Mysell-Rollins (a leading San Francisco turn of the century printer) and were used as give aways with students purchasing composition notebooks. The cards were then designed to be returned to teachers who would return them to the manufacturer for either playground equipment or other school supplies. These cards are unnumbered, so we have sequenced them in alphabetical order.

	MINT	NRMT
COMPLETE SET	40000.00	18000.00
1 Claude Berry	1000.00	450.00
2 Kitty Brashear	1000.00	450.00
3 Herb Byram	1000.00	450.00
4 Walt Carlisle	1000.00	450.00
5 Roy Castleton	1000.00	450.00
6 Chet Chadbourne	1000.00	450.00
7 Tyler Christian	1000.00	450.00
8 Bert Coy	1000.00	450.00
9 Pete Daley	1000.00	450.00
10 Cap Dillon	1000.00	450.00
11 Joe French	1000.00	450.00
12 Howie Gregory	1000.00	450.00
13 Spec Harkness	1000.00	450.00
14 Henie Heitmuller	1000.00	450.00
15 Ben Henderson	1000.00	450.00
16 Cack Henley	1000.00	450.00
17 Izzy Hoffman	1000.00	450.00
18 Happy Hogan	1000.00	450.00
19 Johnny Kane	1000.00	450.00
20 Jimmy Lewis	1000.00	450.00
21 Tom Madden	1000.00	450.00
22 Chris Mahoney	1000.00	450.00
23 George Metzger	1000.00	450.00
24 Frank Miller	1000.00	450.00
25 Kid Mohler	1000.00	450.00
26 Walter Nagle	1000.00	450.00
27 Patsy O'Rourke	1000.00	450.00
28 Ham Patterson	1000.00	450.00
29 Roger Peckinpaugh	1200.00	550.00
30 Bill Rapps	1000.00	450.00
31 Bill Rodgers Sic, Rogers	1000.00	450.00
32 Buddy Ryan	1000.00	450.00
33 Walter Schmidt Sic, Schmitt	1000.00	450.00
34 Tom Seaton	1000.00	450.00
35 Tommy Sheehan	1000.00	450.00
36 Harry Stewart	1000.00	450.00
37 George Stinson	1000.00	450.00
38 Harry Sutor Sic, Suter	1000.00	450.00
39 Harry Wolverton	1000.00	450.00
40 Elmer Zacher	1000.00	450.00

1911 Zeenuts

Zee-Nut cards were issued over a 28 year period. The cards measure a different size depending on when issued. 1911, 12 and Home Run Kisses have similar sizes. 1913, 14 and 15 have similar sizes. 1916 through 1918 are somewhat similar. 1919 through 1923 are somewhat similar. And 1924 through 1937 is somewhat similar. 1937's came with a coupon attached while 1938 came with a separate coupon. But once the coupon is taken off a 37

it is identical to a 38. Cards were issued one to a box in one of three 5 cent products; ZeeNuts, Rufneck and Home Run Kisses. These cards were made by Collins-McCarthy Candy Co. (And their successors). Most of the cards were marketed within a 100 mile radius of San Francisco. Cards are usually blank backed. Cards have been with printing on both sides. In this set, Card number 105 is a very early card of Buck Weaver. There is also a premium for Roger Peckinpaugh. Cards are priced without the coupon. There is currently an 100 percent premium for most cards if the coupon is attached. Complete set for each Zeenut yearly series is provided although completing almost any year set is a daunting task. Different dimensions are provided for each set; however all dimensions are approximate and cards can vary since printing was not as scientific pre-1940 as it is today. The 1911's measure approximately 2 1/8" by 4"

	Ex-Mt	VG
COMPLETE SET (122)	4500.00	2200.00
1 Frederick Abbott	40.00	20.00
2 James Agnew	40.00	20.00
3 Roy Akin	40.00	20.00
4 Curtis Bernard	40.00	20.00
5 Robert Couchman	40.00	20.00
6 Elmer Criger	40.00	20.00
7 Thomas Daley	40.00	20.00
8 Lee W. Delhi	40.00	20.00
9 Bert C. Delmas	40.00	20.00
10 Frank E. Dillon	40.00	20.00
11 Milton Driscoll	40.00	20.00
12 John A. Halla	40.00	20.00
13 William Heitmuller	40.00	20.00
14 Ivan Howard	40.00	20.00
15 Walter Leverenz	40.00	20.00
16 Elmer Lober	40.00	20.00
17 George Metzger	40.00	20.00
18 Charles W. Moore	40.00	20.00
19A Hugh Smith small	40.00	20.00
19B Hugh Smith Large	40.00	20.00
20 Harry Ables	40.00	20.00
21 Alex Arlett	40.00	20.00
22 Leo Bohen	40.00	20.00
23 J. Tyler Christian	40.00	20.00
24 Bert Coy	40.00	20.00
25 George Cutshaw	40.00	20.00
26 John Flater	40.00	20.00
27 William Gleason	40.00	20.00
28 Howard Gregory	40.00	20.00
29 August Hetling	40.00	20.00
30 Harry C. Hoffman	40.00	20.00
31 Orville Kilroy	40.00	20.00
32 Grover Knight	40.00	20.00
33 Harl Maggart	40.00	20.00
34 Elmer Martinoni	40.00	20.00
35 Carl Mitze	40.00	20.00
36 Lorenzo Patterson	40.00	20.00
37 William C. Pearce	40.00	20.00
38 Henry Pernoll	40.00	20.00
39 Meinhard Pfyl	40.00	20.00
40 John C. Tiedeman	40.00	20.00
41 Clyde Wares	40.00	20.00
42 Harry Wolverton MG	40.00	20.00
43 Elmer Zacher	40.00	20.00
44 John C. Barry	40.00	20.00
45 Chester Chadbourne	40.00	20.00
46 Charles Fullerton	40.00	20.00
47 Frederick Harkness	40.00	20.00
48 Elmer Koestner	40.00	20.00
49 Arthur Krueger	40.00	20.00
50 Walter Kuhn	40.00	20.00
51 William G. Lindsay	40.00	20.00
52 Walter McCredie	40.00	20.00
53 Terry W. McKune	40.00	20.00
54 Thomas J. Murray	40.00	20.00
55 Roger Peckinpaugh	60.00	30.00
56 William H. Rapps	40.00	20.00
57 Wilbur Rodgers	40.00	20.00
58 John B. Ryan	40.00	20.00
59 Thomas G. Seaton	40.00	20.00
60 Thomas H. Sheehan	60.00	30.00
61 William J. Steen	40.00	20.00
62 Frank Arellanes	40.00	20.00
63 Charles A. Baum	40.00	20.00
64 Herbert F. Byram	40.00	20.00
65 Harold Danzig	40.00	20.00
66 James Dulin	40.00	20.00
67 John P. Fitzgerald	40.00	20.00
68 Elwood Heister	40.00	20.00
69 Henry B. Kerns	40.00	20.00
70 Louis LaLonge	40.00	20.00
71 Bertram Lerchen	40.00	20.00
72 James J. Lewis	40.00	20.00
73 Christopher Mahoney	40.00	20.00
74 Richard Nebinger	40.00	20.00
75 Chester L. Nourse	40.00	20.00
76 Joseph L. O'Rourke	40.00	20.00
77 James E. Shinn	40.00	20.00
78 Chester Thomas	40.00	20.00
79 Cecil A. Thompson	40.00	20.00
80 Frank J. Thornton	40.00	20.00
81 Edward E. Van Buren	40.00	20.00
82 Claude E. Berry	40.00	20.00
83 Frank Browning	40.00	20.00
84 Fred Carman	40.00	20.00
85 Charles H. Fanning	40.00	20.00
86 Asa A. French	40.00	20.00
87 Clarence Henley	40.00	20.00
88 Joe G. Holland	40.00	20.00
89 Thomas J. Madden	40.00	20.00
90 Harry McArdle	40.00	20.00
91 Willard Meikle	40.00	20.00
92 Henry Melchoir	40.00	20.00
93 Frank L. Miller	40.00	20.00
94 Ernest F. Mohler	40.00	20.00
95 William B. Moskiman	40.00	20.00
96 Arthur E. Naylor	40.00	20.00
97 Winfield C. Noyes	40.00	20.00
98 Watt B. Powell	40.00	20.00
99 William Ryan	40.00	20.00
100 Royal N. Shaw	40.00	20.00
101 Arthur S. Smith	40.00	20.00
102 Harry R. Suter	40.00	20.00
103 Thomas F. Tennant	40.00	20.00
104 Oscar J. Vitt	60.00	30.00
105 George D. Weaver	500.00	250.00
106 Carl E. Zamloch	40.00	20.00
107 John Brackenridge	40.00	20.00
108 Roy P. Brashear	40.00	20.00
109A Drummond Brown small	40.00	20.00
109B Drummond Brown Medium	40.00	20.00
109C Drummond Brown Large	40.00	20.00
110 Leonard Burrell	40.00	20.00
111 Walter G. Carlisle	40.00	20.00
112A Alexander J. Carson Small	40.00	20.00
112B Albert Carson Medium	40.00	20.00
112C Albert Carson Large	40.00	20.00
113 Royal E. Castleton	40.00	20.00
114 Roy W. Hitt	40.00	20.00
115 Wallace L. Hogan	40.00	20.00
116 Franz P. Hosp	40.00	20.00
117 John F. Kane	40.00	20.00
118 Clarence M. McDonnell	40.00	20.00
119 Hamilton Patterson	40.00	20.00
120 John A. Raleigh	40.00	20.00
121 Harry L. Stewart	40.00	20.00
122A George C. Stinson Small	40.00	20.00
122B George Stinson Medium	40.00	20.00
122C George Stinson Large	40.00	20.00

1912 Imperial Tobacco C46

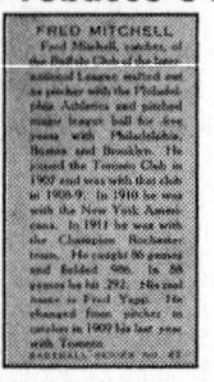

The cards in this 90-card set measure approximately 1 1/2" by 2 3/4". The 1912 C46 set features numbered cards which were issued with unidentified brands of cigarettes although there is speculation that Imperial Tobacco was the sponsor of the set. The set features International League players and is styled with a brown wood-grain look. Card backs feature brief biographical information.

	Ex-Mt	VG
COMPLETE SET (90)	4500.00	2200.00
1 William O'Hara	150.00	75.00
2 James McGinley	50.00	25.00
3 Geo.Frenchy LeClaire	50.00	25.00
4 John White	50.00	25.00
5 James Murray	50.00	25.00
6 Joe Ward	50.00	25.00
7 Whitey Alperman	50.00	25.00
8 Natty Nattress	50.00	25.00
9 Fred Sline	50.00	25.00
10 Royal Rock	50.00	25.00
11 Ray Demmitt	60.00	30.00
12 Butcher Boy Schmidt	50.00	25.00
13 Samuel Frock	50.00	25.00
14 Fred Burchell	50.00	25.00
15 Jack Kelley	50.00	25.00
16 Frank Barberich	50.00	25.00
17 Frank Corridon	50.00	25.00
18 Doc Adkins	50.00	25.00
19 Jack Dunn MG	60.00	30.00
20 James Walsh	50.00	25.00
21 Charles Handford	50.00	25.00
22 Dick Rudolph	60.00	30.00
23 Curt Elston	50.00	25.00
24 Carl Sitton	50.00	25.00
25 Charlie French	50.00	25.00
26 John Ganzel	50.00	25.00
27 Joe Kelley	200.00	100.00
28 Benny Meyers	50.00	25.00
29 George Schirm	50.00	25.00
30 William Purtell	50.00	25.00
31 Bayard Sharpe	50.00	25.00
32 Tony Smith	50.00	25.00
33 John Lush	50.00	25.00
34 William Collins	50.00	25.00
35 Art Phelan	50.00	25.00
36 Edward Phelps	50.00	25.00
37 Rube Vickers	60.00	30.00
38 Cy Seymour	80.00	40.00
39 Shadow Carroll	50.00	25.00
40 Jake Gettman	50.00	25.00
41 Luther Taylor	60.00	30.00
42 Walter Justis	50.00	25.00
43 Robert Fisher	50.00	25.00
44 Fred Parent	60.00	30.00
45 James Dygert	50.00	25.00
46 Johnnie Butler	50.00	25.00
47 Fred Mitchell	50.00	25.00
48 Heine Batch	50.00	25.00
49 Michael Corcoran	50.00	25.00
50 Edward Doescher	50.00	25.00
51 George Wheeler	50.00	25.00
52 Elijah Jones	50.00	25.00
53 Fred Truesdale	50.00	25.00
54 Fred Beebe	50.00	25.00
55 Louis Brockett	50.00	25.00
56 Robert Wells	50.00	25.00
57 Lew McAllister	50.00	25.00
58 Ralph Stroud	50.00	25.00
59 Vernon Manser	50.00	25.00
60 Ducky Holmes	50.00	25.00
61 Rube Dessau	50.00	25.00
62 Fred Jacklitsch	50.00	25.00
63 George Graham	50.00	25.00
64 Noah Henline	50.00	25.00
65 Chick Gandil	300.00	150.00
66 Tom Hughes	80.00	40.00
67 Joseph Delehanty	60.00	30.00
68 George Pierce	50.00	25.00
69 Gantt	50.00	25.00
70 Edward Fitzpatrick	50.00	25.00
71 Wyatt Lee	50.00	25.00
72 John Kissinger	50.00	25.00
73 William Malarkey	50.00	25.00
74 William Byers	50.00	25.00
75 George Simmons	50.00	25.00
76 Daniel Moeller	50.00	25.00
77 Joseph McGinnity	200.00	100.00
78 Alex Hardy	50.00	25.00
79 Bob Holmes	50.00	25.00
80 William Baxter	50.00	25.00
81 Edward Spencer	50.00	25.00
82 Bradley Kocher	50.00	25.00
83 Robert Shaw	50.00	25.00
84 Joseph Yeager	50.00	25.00
85 Carlo	50.00	25.00
86 William Abstein	60.00	30.00
87 Tim Jordan	50.00	25.00
88 Dick Breen	50.00	25.00
89 Tom McCarty	50.00	25.00
90 Ed Curtis	50.00	25.00

1912 Home Run Kisses E136-1

The cards in this 90-card set measure 2" by 4". This is perhaps the most distinctive of all the baseball series issued by the Collins-McCarthy company because of the clever product name and the distinctive ornate frame surrounding the picture area of the card. The players are from six different Pacific Coast League teams in the set. The name "Home Run Kisses" and the player's name and team are printed within the picture area; the picture itself is sepia. Some cards are found with premium advertising on the reverse but the great majority have only a simple easel design on the back. The cards have been alphabetized and numbered in the checklist below. These cards have been found with two different backs: Bardell Sepia Logo and a Premium Offer.

	Ex-Mt	VG
COMPLETE SET (90)	10000.00	5000.00
1 Walter Boles	120.00	60.00
2 Harvey Brooks	120.00	60.00
3 Charles Check	120.00	60.00
4 John Core	120.00	60.00
5 Thomas Daley	120.00	60.00
6 Frank Dillon MG	120.00	60.00
7 Milton Driscoll	175.00	90.00
8 John Flater	120.00	60.00
9 William Heitmuller	175.00	90.00
10 Walter Leverenz	175.00	90.00
11 Elmer Lober	120.00	60.00
12 George Metzger	175.00	90.00
13 Walter Nagle	120.00	60.00
14 William Page	120.00	60.00
15 Walter Slage	120.00	60.00
16 Hugh Smith	120.00	60.00
17 William Tozer	120.00	60.00
18 Harry Ables	120.00	60.00
19 Harvey Brooks	120.00	60.00
20 Bert Coy	120.00	60.00
21 Howard Gregory	120.00	60.00
22 Harry Hoffman	120.00	60.00
23 William Leard	120.00	60.00
24 William Malarkey	120.00	60.00
25 Elmer Martinoni	120.00	60.00
26 Henry Olmstead	120.00	60.00
27 Roy Parkins	120.00	60.00
28 Lorenzo Patterson	120.00	60.00
29 Henry Pernoll	120.00	60.00
30 John Tiedeman	120.00	60.00
31 Elmer Zacher	175.00	90.00
32 David Bancroft	300.00	150.00
33 Willie Butler	120.00	60.00
34 Chester Chadbourne	120.00	60.00
35 Walter Doane	120.00	60.00
36 August Fisher	120.00	60.00
37 David Gregg	120.00	60.00
38 Frederick Harkness	120.00	60.00
39 Daniel Howley	175.00	90.00
40 Albert Klawitter	120.00	60.00
41 Arthur Krueger	120.00	60.00
42 William Lindsay	120.00	60.00
43 Ward McDowell	120.00	60.00
44 Wilbur Rodgers	120.00	60.00
45 George Stone	120.00	60.00
46 Frank Arrelanes	120.00	60.00
47 George Gaddy	120.00	60.00
48 Elwood Heister	120.00	60.00
49 Harold Ireland	120.00	60.00
50 Ralph Kreitz	120.00	60.00
51 James Lewis	120.00	60.00
52 Joseph O'Rourke MG	120.00	60.00
53 Harry Price	120.00	60.00
54 Rudolph Schwenck	120.00	60.00
55 Thomas Sheehan	175.00	90.00
56 James Shinn	120.00	60.00
57 Charles Swain	120.00	60.00
58 Edward Van Buren	120.00	60.00
59 John Williams	250.00	125.00
60 Joseph Altman	120.00	60.00
61 Otto Auer	120.00	60.00
62 Claude Berry	120.00	60.00
63 Roy Corhan	120.00	60.00
64 Clarence Henley	120.00	60.00

65 William Johnson 120.00 60.00
66 Harry McArdle 120.00 60.00
67 William McCorry 120.00 60.00
68 Edward McIver 120.00 60.00
69 Frank Miller 120.00 60.00
70 Howard Mundorf 120.00 60.00
71 Winfield Noyes 120.00 60.00
72 Watt Powell 120.00 60.00
73 Thomas Raftery 120.00 60.00
74 Walter Schmidt 120.00 60.00
75 Willy Taylor 120.00 60.00
76 Thomas Toner 120.00 60.00
77 Samuel Agnew 120.00 60.00
78 Harry Bayless 120.00 60.00
79 Roy Brashear 120.00 60.00
80 Drummond Brown 120.00 60.00
81 Lenny Burrell 120.00 60.00
82 Walter Carlisle 175.00 90.00
83 Alexander Carson 120.00 60.00
84 Royal Castleton 120.00 60.00
85 Wallace Hogan MG 120.00 60.00
86 Frank Hosp 120.00 60.00
87 John Kane 120.00 60.00
88 Louis Litschi 120.00 60.00
89 Hamilton Patterson 120.00 60.00
90 John Raleigh 120.00 60.00

1912 Zeenuts

Counterfeit copies of certain Zeenuts have been produced in the last 10 years. A very early card of Dave "Beauty" Bancroft is in this set. Honolulu John Williams also has his first card in the set. Williams was the first player from Hawaii to play in the majors. The 1912's measure 2 1/8" by 4 1/16". Four different backs are known for this set: Bardell Sepia Logo -- small; Bardell Sepia Logo -- large; Premium Offer; Blank Back.

Ex-Mt VG
COMPLETE SET (158) 5000.00 2500.00
1 Joseph Berger 40.00 20.00
2 Walter Boles 40.00 20.00
3 Clarence Brooks 40.00 20.00
4 Charles Check 40.00 20.00
5 John Core 40.00 20.00
6 Thomas Daley 40.00 20.00
7 Frank Dillon 40.00 20.00
8 Milton Driscoll 40.00 20.00
9 John Flater 40.00 20.00
10 John Halla 40.00 20.00
11 William Heitmuller 40.00 20.00
12 Ivon Howard 40.00 20.00
13 Walter Leverenz 40.00 20.00
14 Elmer Lober 40.00 20.00
15 George Metzger 40.00 20.00
16 Charles Moore 40.00 20.00
17 Walter Nagle 40.00 20.00
18 William Page 40.00 20.00
19 Walter Slagle 40.00 20.00
20 Hugh Smith 40.00 20.00
21 William Tozer 40.00 20.00
22 Ody Abbott 40.00 20.00
23 Harry Ables 40.00 20.00
24 Leo Bohen 40.00 20.00
25 Harvey Brooks 40.00 20.00
26 Tyler Christian 40.00 20.00
27 Al Cook 40.00 20.00
28 Bert Coy 40.00 20.00
29 Blaine Durbin 40.00 20.00
30 James Frick 40.00 20.00
31 Howard Gregory 40.00 20.00
32 Joseph Hamilton 40.00 20.00
33 August Hetling 40.00 20.00
34 August Hetling 40.00 20.00
35 Harry Hoffman 40.00 20.00
36 John Killilay 40.00 20.00
37 William Leard 40.00 20.00
38 William Malarkey 40.00 20.00
39 Elmer Martinoni 40.00 20.00
40 Carl Mitze 40.00 20.00
41 Henry Olmstead 40.00 20.00
42 Roy Parkins 40.00 20.00
43 Lorenzo Patterson 40.00 20.00
44 Henry Pernoll 40.00 20.00
45 Ashley Pope 40.00 20.00
46 William Rohrer 40.00 20.00
47 Bayard Sharpe 40.00 20.00
48 John Tiedeman 40.00 20.00
49 Elmer Zacher 40.00 20.00
50 David Bancroft 250.00 125.00
51 John Burch 40.00 20.00
52 Henry Butcher 40.00 20.00
53 Willie Butler 40.00 20.00
54 Chester Chadbourne 40.00 20.00
55 Walter Doane 40.00 20.00
56 August Fisher 40.00 20.00
57 John Gilligan 40.00 20.00
58 Leo Girot 40.00 20.00
59 David Gregg 40.00 20.00
60 Frederick Harkness 40.00 20.00
61 Irving Higginbotham 40.00 20.00
62 Daniel Howley 40.00 20.00
63 Albert Klawitter 40.00 20.00
64 Elmer Koestner 40.00 20.00
65 Elmer Koestner 40.00 20.00
66 Arthur Krueger 40.00 20.00
67 Louis LaLonge 40.00 20.00
68 William Lindsay 40.00 20.00
69 Walter McCredie 40.00 20.00
70 Ward McDowell 40.00 20.00
71 William Rapps 40.00 20.00
72 William Rapps 40.00 20.00
73 Wilbur Rodgers 40.00 20.00
74 George Stone 40.00 20.00
75 Frank Arellanes 40.00 20.00
76 Charles Baum 40.00 20.00
77 Herbert Byram 40.00 20.00
78 Harry Cheek 40.00 20.00
79 John Fitzgerald 40.00 20.00
80 George Gaddy 40.00 20.00
81 Elwood Heister 40.00 20.00
82 Harold Ireland 40.00 20.00
83 Grover Knight 40.00 20.00
84 Ralph Kreitz 40.00 20.00
85 James Lewis 40.00 20.00
86 Thomas Madden 40.00 20.00
87 Christopher Mahoney 40.00 20.00
88 Hugh Miller 40.00 20.00
89 Joseph O'Rourke 40.00 20.00
90 William Orr 40.00 20.00
91 Harry Price 40.00 20.00
92 Rudolph Schwenck 40.00 20.00
93 Thomas Sheehan 40.00 20.00
94 James Shinn 40.00 20.00
95 Charles Swain 40.00 20.00
96 Edward Van Buren 40.00 20.00
97 John Williams 80.00 40.00
Honolulu
98 Joe Williams 40.00 20.00
99 Joseph Altman 40.00 20.00
100 Otto Auer 40.00 20.00
101 Jesse Baker 40.00 20.00
102 Jesse Baker 40.00 20.00
103 Claude Berry 40.00 20.00
104 Al Bonner 40.00 20.00
105 Breen 40.00 20.00
106 Roy Corhan 40.00 20.00
107 Lee Delhi 40.00 20.00
108 Charles Fanning 40.00 20.00
109 Albert Felts 40.00 20.00
110 Elmer Gedeon 40.00 20.00
111 Don Hamilton 40.00 20.00
112 Walter Hartley 40.00 20.00
113 Clarence Henley 40.00 20.00
114 William Jackson 40.00 20.00
115 William Johnson 40.00 20.00
116 Harry McArdle 40.00 20.00
117 George McAvoy 40.00 20.00
118 William McCorry 40.00 20.00
119 Edward McIver 40.00 20.00
120 Willard Meikle 40.00 20.00
121 Frank Miller 40.00 20.00
122 Ernest Mohler 40.00 20.00
123 Howard Mundorf 40.00 20.00
124 Howard Mundorf 40.00 20.00
125 Winfield Noyes 40.00 20.00
126 Watt Powell 40.00 20.00
127 Thomas Raftery 40.00 20.00
128 William Reidy 40.00 20.00
129 Walter Schmidt 40.00 20.00
130 Willy Taylor 40.00 20.00
131 Thomas Toner 40.00 20.00
132 Joseph Wagner 40.00 20.00
133 L. Williams 40.00 20.00
134 John Wuffli 40.00 20.00
135 Everette Zimmerman 40.00 20.00
136 Samuel Agnew 40.00 20.00
137 Harry Bayless 40.00 20.00
138 John Brackenridge 40.00 20.00
139 Roy Brashear 40.00 20.00
140 Drummond Brown 40.00 20.00
141 Leonard Burrell 40.00 20.00
142 Walter Carlisle 40.00 20.00
143 Alexander Carson 40.00 20.00
144 Royal Castleton 40.00 20.00
145 William Gray 40.00 20.00
146 Roy Hitt 40.00 20.00
147 Wallace Hogan 40.00 20.00
148 Franz Hosp 40.00 20.00
149 John Kane 40.00 20.00
150 Louis Litschi 40.00 20.00
151 Clarence McDonnell 40.00 20.00
152 Hamilton Patterson 40.00 20.00
153 John Raleigh 40.00 20.00
154 Harry Stewart 40.00 20.00
155 George Stinson 40.00 20.00
156 John Sullivan 40.00 20.00
157 William Temple 40.00 20.00
158 James Whalen 40.00 20.00

1913 Oakland Oaks Team Issue

This 20 card set, which measure approximately 2" by 3 5/8" features members of the 1913 Oakland Oaks. These blank-backed cards are sepia toned and have the player's last name and oakland on the bottom of the card. These cards are usually found with some trimming at either the top or the bottom.

Ex-Mt VG
COMPLETE SET 20000.00 10000.00
1 O.C. Abbott 1200.00 600.00
2 Harry Ables 1200.00 600.00
3 Jesse Becker 1200.00 600.00
4 W.W. Cook 1200.00 600.00
5 Bert Coy 1200.00 600.00
6 Rube Gardner 1200.00 600.00
7 Howard Gregory 1200.00 600.00
8 Gus Hetling 1200.00 600.00
9 Jack Killilay 1200.00 600.00
10 Bill Leard 1200.00 600.00
11 William John Malarkey 1200.00 600.00
12 Carl Mitze 1200.00 600.00
13 John Ness 1200.00 600.00
14 Henry Olmstead 1200.00 600.00
15 Cy Parkin 1200.00 600.00
16 W.J. Pearce 1200.00 600.00
17 Heine Pernoll 1200.00 600.00
18 Ashley Pope 1200.00 600.00
19 George Schirm 1200.00 600.00
20 Elmer Zacher 1200.00 600.00

1913 Zeenuts

Harry Heilmann has a very early card in this set. From 1913 through 1933 all measurements are given with coupons. These cards measure approximately 1 11/16" by 3 3/4".

Ex-Mt VG
COMPLETE SET (148) 6500.00 3200.00
1 Walter Boles 50.00 25.00
2 Clarence Brooks 50.00 25.00
3 James Byrnes 50.00 25.00
4 James Crabb 50.00 25.00
5 Frank Dillon 50.00 25.00
6 Milton Driscoll 50.00 25.00
7 George Ellis 50.00 25.00
8 Warren Gill 50.00 25.00
9 Claire Goodwin 50.00 25.00
10 John Halla 50.00 25.00
11 Ivon Howard 50.00 25.00
12 Charles Jackson 50.00 25.00
13 Ernest Johnson 50.00 25.00
14 Harl Maggart 50.00 25.00
15 George Metzger 50.00 25.00
16 Charles Moore 50.00 25.00
17 William Page 50.00 25.00
18 Madison Perritt 50.00 25.00
19 Brown Rogers 50.00 25.00
20 Jack Ryan 50.00 25.00
21 William Tozer 50.00 25.00
22 Michael Wotell 50.00 25.00
23 Ody Abbott 50.00 25.00
24 Harry Ables 50.00 25.00
25 Jesse Becker 50.00 25.00
26 Tyler Christian 50.00 25.00
27 Robert Clemons 50.00 25.00
28 Al Cook 50.00 25.00
29 Bert Coy 50.00 25.00
30 Joseph Crisp 50.00 25.00
31 L. Gardner 50.00 25.00
32 Howard Gregory 50.00 25.00
33 William Grey 50.00 25.00
34 Arthur Guest 50.00 25.00
35 August Hetling 50.00 25.00
36 Teddy Kaylor 50.00 25.00
37 John Killilay 50.00 25.00
38 William Leard 50.00 25.00
39 Claude Lohman 50.00 25.00
40 William Malarkey 50.00 25.00
41 Carl Mitze 50.00 25.00
42 John Ness 50.00 25.00
43 Roy Parkin 50.00 25.00
44 William Pearce 50.00 25.00
45 Henry Pernoll 50.00 25.00
46 Ashley Pope 50.00 25.00
47 Charles Pruitt 50.00 25.00
48 William Rohrer 50.00 25.00
49 George Schirm 50.00 25.00
50 Elmer Zacher 50.00 25.00
51 Claude Berry 50.00 25.00
52 Alexander Carson 50.00 25.00
53 Chester Chadbourne 50.00 25.00
54 Fred Derrick 50.00 25.00
55 Walter Doane 50.00 25.00
56 August Fisher 50.00 25.00
57 Justin Fitzgerald 50.00 25.00
58 Zeriah Hagerman 50.00 25.00
59 Harry Heilmann 500.00 250.00
Actually playing with Portland
in Northwest league
60 Irving Higginbotham 50.00 25.00
61 William James 50.00 25.00
62 Arthur Kores 50.00 25.00
63 Eugene Krapp 50.00 25.00
64 Harry Krause 50.00 25.00
65 Arthur Krueger 50.00 25.00
66 William Lindsay 50.00 25.00
67 Elmer Lober 50.00 25.00
68 Michael McCormick 50.00 25.00
69 Walter McCredie 50.00 25.00
70 James Riordan 50.00 25.00
71 Wilbur Rodgers 50.00 25.00
72 John Stanley 50.00 25.00
73 Harry Todd 50.00 25.00
74 James West 50.00 25.00
75 Frank Arellanes 50.00 25.00
76 John Bliss 50.00 25.00
77 Harry Cheek 50.00 25.00
78 Louis Drucke 50.00 25.00
79 Edward Hallinan 50.00 25.00
80 William Kenworthy 50.00 25.00
81 Albert Klawitter 50.00 25.00
82 James Lewis 50.00 25.00
83 Henry Lively 50.00 25.00
84A Hugh Miller 50.00 25.00
Full Glove
84B Hugh Miller 50.00 25.00
Part Glove
85 Roy Moran 50.00 25.00
86 Emmett Munsell 50.00 25.00
87 Paul Reitmyer 50.00 25.00
88 Joseph Schulz 50.00 25.00
89 James Shinn 50.00 25.00
90 Monroe Stark 50.00 25.00
91 Ralph Stroud 50.00 25.00
92 Thomas Tennant 50.00 25.00
93 Edward Van Buren 50.00 25.00
94 John Williams 100.00 50.00
95 Harry Wolverton 50.00 25.00
96 Ralph Young 50.00 25.00
97 Alex Arlett 50.00 25.00
98 Jesse Baker 50.00 25.00
99 William Cadreau 50.00 25.00
100 Walter Cartwright 50.00 25.00
101 Raymond Charles 50.00 25.00
102 Jay Clarke 50.00 25.00
103 Roy Corhan 50.00 25.00
104 Frank DeCanniere 50.00 25.00
105 Phillip Douglass 50.00 25.00
106 Jerome Downs 50.00 25.00
107 Charles Fanning 50.00 25.00
108 Clarence Henley 50.00 25.00
109 Harry Hoffman 50.00 25.00
110 William Hogan 50.00 25.00
111 George Howard 50.00 25.00
112 Harry Hughes 50.00 25.00
113 James Johnston 50.00 25.00
114 Albert Leifield 50.00 25.00
115 Harry McArdle 50.00 25.00
116 George McCarl 50.00 25.00
117 William McCorry 50.00 25.00
118 Howard Mundorf 50.00 25.00
119 Orval Overall 75.00 38.00
120 Walter Schaller 50.00 25.00
121 Walter Schmidt 50.00 25.00
122 Louis Sepulveda 50.00 25.00
123 Edward Spenger 50.00 25.00
124 Alfred Stanridge 50.00 25.00
125 Forrest Thomas 50.00 25.00
126 Charles Tonneman 50.00 25.00
127 Joseph Wagner 50.00 25.00
128 John Wuffli 50.00 25.00
129 Everette Zimmerman 50.00 25.00
130 Charles Baum 50.00 25.00
131 Harry Bayless 50.00 25.00
132 John Brackenridge 50.00 25.00
133 Roy Brashear 50.00 25.00
134 Walter Carlisle 50.00 25.00
135 Harold Elliott 50.00 25.00
136 Roy Hitt 50.00 25.00
137 Wallace Hogan 50.00 25.00
138 Franz Hosp 50.00 25.00
139 John Kane 50.00 25.00
140 Elmer Koestner 50.00 25.00
141 Ralph Kreitz 50.00 25.00
142 Louis Litschi 50.00 25.00
143 Clarence McDonnell 50.00 25.00
144 Paul Meloan 50.00 25.00
145 Joseph O'Rourke 50.00 25.00
146 Hamilton Patterson 50.00 25.00
147 John Raleigh 50.00 25.00
148 Clarence Sterritt 50.00 25.00

1914 Baltimore Orioles Schedules

These schedule/cards were issued during Babe Ruth's first season in professional baseball. The front has a picture of the Babe with his name and position in the lower left corner. The back has the 1914 Baltimore Orioles schedule. This list may be incomplete and any further additions are appreciated.

Ex-Mt VG
COMPLETE SET 35000.00 17500.00
1 Neal Ball 1500.00 750.00
2 Ensign Cottrell 1000.00 500.00
3 Birdie Cree 1000.00 500.00
4 Davidson 1000.00 500.00
5 Jack Dunn OWN 2000.00 1000.00
6 Babe Ruth 30000.00 15000.00
7 George Twombley 1000.00 500.00
8 Guy Zinn 1000.00 500.00

1914 Zeenuts

Jacinto Calvo has a card in this set. He was one of the early Cuban players in Professional Baseball. These cards measure approximately 2" by 4 1/16".

Ex-Mt VG
COMPLETE SET (146) 4500.00 2200.00
1 William Abstein 30.00 15.00
2 Carroll Barton 30.00 15.00
3 Walter Boles 30.00 15.00
4 Clarence Brooks 30.00 15.00
5 Jacinto Calvo 60.00 30.00
6 Charles Chech 30.00 15.00
7 James Crabb 30.00 15.00
8 Frank Dillon 30.00 15.00
9 Howard Ehmke 50.00 25.00
10 George Ellis 30.00 15.00
11 Elmer Gedeon 30.00 15.00
12 Thomas Hughes 30.00 15.00
13 Ernest Johnson 30.00 15.00
14 Edward Love 30.00 15.00
15 Harl Maggart 30.00 15.00
16 Herman Meek 30.00 15.00
17 George Metzger 30.00 15.00
18 Charles Moore 30.00 15.00
19 Paul Musser 30.00 15.00
20 William Page 30.00 15.00
21 Madison Perritt 30.00 15.00
22 Brown Rogers 30.00 15.00
23 Jack Ryan 30.00 15.00
24 Carl Sawyer 30.00 15.00
25 Harry Wolter 30.00 15.00
26 Harry Ables 30.00 15.00
27 Walter Alexander 30.00 15.00
28 Carl Arbogast 30.00 15.00
29 William Barrenkamp 30.00 15.00
30 Tyler Christian 30.00 15.00
31 Al Cook 30.00 15.00
32 Arthur Devlin 40.00 20.00
33 L. Gardner 30.00 15.00
34 Jacob Geyer 30.00 15.00
35 Arthur Guest 30.00 15.00
36 August Hettling 30.00 15.00
37 Teddy Kaylor 30.00 15.00
38 John Killilay 30.00 15.00
39 Albert Loomis 30.00 15.00
40 William Malarkey 30.00 15.00
41 William Menges 30.00 15.00
42 Robert Middleton 30.00 15.00
43 Carl Mitze 30.00 15.00
44 Rod Murphy 30.00 15.00
45 John Ness 30.00 15.00
46 Herschel Prough 30.00 15.00
47 Charles Pruiett 30.00 15.00
48A Thomas Quinlan 30.00 15.00
Small
48B Thomas Quinlan 30.00 15.00
Large
49 L. M. Ramey 30.00 15.00
50 Elmer Zacher 30.00 15.00
51 David Bancroft 300.00 150.00
52 Roy Brashear 30.00 15.00
53 Olaf Brenegan 30.00 15.00
54 Everett Brown 30.00 15.00
55 Robert Davis 30.00 15.00
56 Fred Derrick 30.00 15.00
57 Walter Doane 30.00 15.00
58 Evan Evans 30.00 15.00
59 August Fisher 30.00 15.00
60 Fred Frambach 30.00 15.00
61 Homer Haworth 30.00 15.00
62 Homer Haworth 30.00 15.00
63 Irving Higginbotham 30.00 15.00
64 Arthur Kores 30.00 15.00
65 Harry Krause 30.00 15.00
66 Elmer Lober 30.00 15.00
67 Elmer Martinoni 30.00 15.00
68 Walter McCredie 30.00 15.00
69 Lawrence Pape 30.00 15.00
70 Harold Peet 30.00 15.00
71A Floyd Perkins 30.00 15.00
Small
71B Floyd Perkins 30.00 15.00
Large
72 Elmer Rieger 30.00 15.00
73A Wilbur Rodgers 30.00 15.00
Small
73B Wilbur Rogers 30.00 15.00
Large
74 John Ryan 30.00 15.00
75 William Speas 30.00 15.00
76 James West 30.00 15.00
77 George Yantz 30.00 15.00
78 Frank Arellanes 30.00 15.00
79 Bert Coy 30.00 15.00
80 Joseph Gianini 30.00 15.00
81 Howard Gregory 30.00 15.00
82 Edward Hallinan 30.00 15.00
83 James Hannah 30.00 15.00
84 Sam Hern 30.00 15.00
85 Albert Klawitter 30.00 15.00
86 Remy Kramer 40.00 20.00
87 Byrd Lynn 30.00 15.00
88 Ernest Mohler 30.00 15.00
89 Roy Moran 30.00 15.00
90 William Orr 30.00 15.00
91 William Rohrer 30.00 15.00
92 James Shinn 30.00 15.00
93 Walter Slagle 30.00 15.00
94 Ralph Stroud 30.00 15.00
95 Thomas Tennant 30.00 15.00
96 Edward Van Buren 30.00 15.00
97 Harry Wolverton 30.00 15.00
98 Ralph Young 30.00 15.00
99 Alex Arlett 30.00 15.00
100 Wayne Barham 30.00 15.00
101 Charles Baum 30.00 15.00
102 Willie Butler 30.00 15.00
103 Walter Cartwright 30.00 15.00
104 Raymond Charles 30.00 15.00
105 Jay Clarke 30.00 15.00
106 Edward Colligan 30.00 15.00
107 Roy Corhan 30.00 15.00
108 Jerome Downs 30.00 15.00
109 Charles Fanning 30.00 15.00
110 Justin Fitzgerald 30.00 15.00
111 Ben Henderson 30.00 15.00
112 George Howard 30.00 15.00
113 Harry Hughes 30.00 15.00
114 Albert Liefield 30.00 15.00
115 Howard Mundorf 30.00 15.00
116 Charles O'Leary 40.00 20.00
117 Roy Parkin 30.00 15.00
118 Henry Pernoll 30.00 15.00
119 Walter Schaller 30.00 15.00
120 Walter Schmidt 30.00 15.00
121 Louis Sepulveda 30.00 15.00
122 Alfred Stanridge 30.00 15.00
123 Joseph Tobin 30.00 15.00
124 William Tozer 30.00 15.00
125 Zumwalt 30.00 15.00
126 Harry Bayless 30.00 15.00
127 John Bliss 30.00 15.00
128 William Borton 30.00 15.00
129 Walter Carlisle 30.00 15.00
130 Frank DeCannier 30.00 15.00
131 Earle Fleharty 30.00 15.00
132 Frederick Harkness 30.00 15.00
133 Clarence Henley 30.00 15.00
134 Roy Hitt 30.00 15.00
135 Wallace Hogan 30.00 15.00
136 Franz Hosp 30.00 15.00
137 John Kane 30.00 15.00
138 Edward Klepfer 30.00 15.00
139 William Leard 30.00 15.00
140 Louis Litschi 30.00 15.00
141 Harry McArdle 30.00 15.00
142 Clarence McDonald 30.00 15.00
143 Paul Meloan 30.00 15.00
144 John "Red" Powell 30.00 15.00
Small
144 Red Powell 30.00 15.00
Large
145 Guy White 30.00 15.00
146 Harold Elliott 30.00 15.00

1915 Zeenuts

Up to four variations per card are presently accounted for. These variations are in the sepia overlay. Cards were printed in black and white and the sepia overlay is where the variation is. Early cards of Fred McMullin (Only known card during his career), Swede Risberg, Lefty Williams and "Sleepy" Bill Burns are in this set. All four of those people had roles in the Black Sox Scandal of 1919. These cards measure approximately 2 by 3 3/4".

	Ex-Mt	VG
COMPLETE SET (133)	10000.00	5000.00
1 William Abstein	60.00	30.00
2 Justin Beatty	60.00	30.00
3 Albert Beumiller	60.00	30.00
4 Walter Boles	60.00	30.00
5 Clarence Brooks	60.00	30.00
6 Bill "Sleepy" Burns	120.00	60.00
7 Frank Dillon	60.00	30.00
8 George Ellis	60.00	30.00
9 Howard Harper	60.00	30.00
10 Thomas Hughes	60.00	30.00
11 Slim Love	60.00	30.00
12 Clarence McDonnell	60.00	30.00
13 Frederick McMullin	1500.00	750.00
Misspelled McMullen on card		
14 Harl Maggart	60.00	30.00
15 Herman Meek	60.00	30.00
16 George Metzger	60.00	30.00
17 Madison Perritt	60.00	30.00
18 Jack Ryan	60.00	30.00
19 Lynn Scoggins	60.00	30.00
20 Zebulon Terry	60.00	30.00
21 Harry Wolter	60.00	30.00
22 Harry Ables	60.00	30.00
23 John Alcock	60.00	30.00
24 Carl Arbogast	60.00	30.00
25 Samuel Beer	60.00	30.00
26 Raymond Boyd	60.00	30.00
27 Jack Bromley	60.00	30.00
28 Tyler Christian	60.00	30.00
29 William Daniels	60.00	30.00
30 Frank Elliott	60.00	30.00
31 Frank Elliott	60.00	30.00
32 L. Gardiner	60.00	30.00
33 Arthur Guest	60.00	30.00
34 George Howard	60.00	30.00
35 James Johnston	60.00	30.00
36 Albert Klawitter	60.00	30.00
37 Philip Koerner	60.00	30.00
38 Walter Kuhn	60.00	30.00
39 William Lindsay	60.00	30.00
40 Louis Litschi	60.00	30.00
41 Charles McAvoy	60.00	30.00
42 William Malarkey	60.00	30.00
43 Carl Manda	60.00	30.00
44 Arthur Marcan	60.00	30.00
45 Elmer Martinoni	60.00	30.00
46 Robert Middleton	60.00	30.00
47 Howard Mundorf	60.00	30.00
48 John Ness	60.00	30.00
49 Harry Price	60.00	30.00
50 Herschel Prough	60.00	30.00
51 Charles Prueitt	60.00	30.00
52 Alexander Remneas	60.00	30.00
53 John Russell	60.00	30.00
54 Ray Bates	60.00	30.00
55 Frederick Carrisch	60.00	30.00
56 Stanley Covaleski	500.00	250.00
57 Bob Davis	60.00	30.00
58 Fred Derrick	60.00	30.00
59 Walter Doane	60.00	30.00
60 Evan Evans	60.00	30.00
61 August Fisher	60.00	30.00
62 Irving Higginbotham	60.00	30.00
63 David Hilliard	60.00	30.00
64 George Kahler	60.00	30.00
65 Harry Krause	60.00	30.00
66 Elmer Lober	60.00	30.00
67 John Lush	60.00	30.00
68 Herbert Murphy	60.00	30.00
69 Walter McCredie	60.00	30.00
70 Milton Reed	60.00	30.00
71 William Speas	60.00	30.00
72 Bill Stumpf	60.00	30.00
73 Louis Barbour	60.00	30.00
74 Clifford Blankenship	60.00	30.00
75 Eddie Faye	60.00	30.00
76 Paul Fittery	60.00	30.00
77 Elmer Gedeon	60.00	30.00
78 Howard Gregory	60.00	30.00
79 Herbert Hall	60.00	30.00
80 John Halla	60.00	30.00
81 Edward Hallinan	60.00	30.00
82 James Hannah	60.00	30.00
83 Louis LaRoy	60.00	30.00
84 Willis Morgan	60.00	30.00
85 John Nutt	60.00	30.00
86 William Orr	60.00	30.00
87 William Rohrer	60.00	30.00
88 John Ryan	60.00	30.00
89 James Shinn	60.00	30.00
90 Thomas Tennant	60.00	30.00
91 Claude "Lefty" Williams	400.00	200.00
92 John Williams	120.00	60.00
93 Elmer Zacher	60.00	30.00
94 Rudolf Baerwald	60.00	30.00
95 Charles Baum	60.00	30.00
96 Arthur Benham	60.00	30.00
97 George Block	60.00	30.00
98 Frank Bodie	60.00	30.00
99 Charles Brown	60.00	30.00
100 Raymond Charles	60.00	30.00
101 Jay Clarke	60.00	30.00
102 John Couch	60.00	30.00
103 Elliott Dent	60.00	30.00
104 Jerome Downs	60.00	30.00
105 Charles Fanning	60.00	30.00
106 Justin Fitzgerald	60.00	30.00
107 Harry Heilmann	500.00	250.00
108 Robert Jones	60.00	30.00
109 Benjamin Karr	60.00	30.00
110 Jack Killilay	60.00	30.00
111 William Leard	60.00	30.00
112 Paul Meloan	60.00	30.00
113 Henry Pernoll	60.00	30.00
114 Jacob Reisigl	60.00	30.00
115 Walter Schaller	60.00	30.00
116 Walter Schmidt	60.00	30.00
117 Louis Sepulveda	60.00	30.00
118 Luther Smith	60.00	30.00
119 Joseph Tobin	60.00	30.00
120 Harry Wolverton	60.00	30.00
121 Harry Bayless	60.00	30.00
122 Joseph Berger	60.00	30.00
123 Walter Carlisle	60.00	30.00
124 Frank DeCanniere	60.00	30.00
125 Gustave Gleischmann	60.00	30.00
126 Clarence Henley	60.00	30.00
127 August Hetling	60.00	30.00
128 Roy Hitt	60.00	30.00
129 Roy Hitt	60.00	30.00
130 Wallace Hogan	60.00	30.00
131 Franz Hosp	60.00	30.00
132 John Kane	60.00	30.00
133 Carl Mitze	60.00	30.00
134 William Piercey	60.00	30.00
135 William Purtell	60.00	30.00
136 Charles Risberg	400.00	200.00
137 Charlie Chech	60.00	30.00
138 Arthur Fromme	60.00	30.00
139 Albert Mitchell	60.00	30.00
140 Edward Spencer	60.00	30.00
141 James West	60.00	30.00
142 Guy White	60.00	30.00

1916 Zeenuts

Jimmy Claxton in this set. That was the first regular card depicting a person of color marketed in the United States with a product. These cards measure 1 15/16" by 3 11/16".

	Ex-Mt	VG
COMPLETE SET (143)	6500.00	3200.00
1 John Bassler	30.00	15.00
2 Walter Boles	30.00	15.00
3 John Butler	30.00	15.00
4 Frank Chance	250.00	125.00
5 George Ellis	30.00	15.00
6 James Galloway	30.00	15.00
7 Carter Hogg	30.00	15.00
8 Oscar Horstman	30.00	15.00
9 George Kahler	30.00	15.00
10 John Kane	30.00	15.00
11 Philip Koerner	30.00	15.00
12 Frank Larsen	30.00	15.00
13 Howard McLarry	30.00	15.00
14 Harl Maggert	30.00	15.00
15 Jack Ryan	30.00	15.00
16 Lynn Scoggins	30.00	15.00
17 Alfred Stanridge	30.00	15.00
18 George Zabel	30.00	15.00
19 William Barbeau	30.00	15.00
20 Malcomb Barry	30.00	15.00
21 Samuel Beer	30.00	15.00
22 Joseph Berg	30.00	15.00
23 Joseph Berger	30.00	15.00
24 Raymond Boyd	30.00	15.00
25 James Claxton	2500.00	1250.00
26 Luther Cook	30.00	15.00
27 James Crandall	30.00	15.00
28 Robert Davis	30.00	15.00
29 Frank Elliott	30.00	15.00
30 Harold Elliott	30.00	15.00
31 L. Gardner	30.00	15.00
32 David Griffith	30.00	15.00
33 Irving Higginbotham	30.00	15.00
34 George Howard	30.00	15.00
35 William Kenworthy	30.00	15.00
36 Albert Klawitter	30.00	15.00
37 Edward Klein	30.00	15.00
38 Walter Kuhn	30.00	15.00
39 William Lane	30.00	15.00
40 James Manser	30.00	15.00
41 Elwood Martin	30.00	15.00
42 Robert Middleton	30.00	15.00
43 Herschel Prough	30.00	15.00
44 Charles Prueitt	30.00	15.00
45 Newton Randall	30.00	15.00
46 William Zimmerman	30.00	15.00
47 Frederick Carrisch	30.00	15.00
48 Fred Derrick	30.00	15.00
49 August Fisher	30.00	15.00
50 Louis Guisto	30.00	15.00
51 Zeriah Hagerman	30.00	15.00
52 Oscar Harstadt	30.00	15.00
53 Homer Haworth	30.00	15.00
54 Charles Hollocher	50.00	25.00
55 Byron Houck	30.00	15.00
56 Herbert Kelly	30.00	15.00
57 Harry Krause	30.00	15.00
58 John Lush	30.00	15.00
59 Walter McCredie	30.00	15.00
60 William Nixon	30.00	15.00
61 Winfield Noyes	30.00	15.00
62 Owen Quinn	30.00	15.00
63 John Roche	30.00	15.00
64 Clarence Smith	30.00	15.00
65 Allen Sothoron	30.00	15.00
66 William Southworth	50.00	25.00
67 Bill Speas	30.00	15.00
68 William Stumpf	30.00	15.00
69 Robert Vaughn	30.00	15.00
70 Charles Ward	30.00	15.00
71 Denny Wilie	30.00	15.00
72 Kenneth Williams	50.00	25.00
73 Harry Bayless	30.00	15.00
74 Clifford Blankenship	30.00	15.00
75 Anthony Brief	30.00	15.00
76 Stanley Dugan	30.00	15.00
77 Ross Eldred	30.00	15.00
78 Paul Fittery	30.00	15.00
79 Herbert Hall	30.00	15.00
80 Edward Hallinan	30.00	15.00
81 James Hannah	30.00	15.00
82 Thomas Hughes	30.00	15.00
83 William Menges	30.00	15.00
84 Emmett Munsell	30.00	15.00
85 Herbert Murphy	30.00	15.00
86 John Nutt	30.00	15.00
87 William Orr	30.00	15.00
88 Thomas Quinlan	30.00	15.00
89 Morris Rath	40.00	20.00
90 Jacob Reisegl	30.00	15.00
91 Walter Reuther	40.00	20.00
92 John Ryan	30.00	15.00
93 James Shinn	30.00	15.00
94 John Vann	30.00	15.00
95 Elmer Zacher	30.00	15.00
96 William Autrey	30.00	15.00
97 Charles Baum	30.00	15.00
98 George Block	30.00	15.00
99 Frank Bodie	50.00	25.00
100 Samuel Bohne	30.00	15.00
101 Clarence Brooks	30.00	15.00
102 Charles Brown	30.00	15.00
103 John Coffey	30.00	15.00
104 Joseph Corbett	30.00	15.00
105 John Couch	30.00	15.00
106 Talbot Dalton	30.00	15.00
107 Jerome Downs	30.00	15.00
108 Eric Erickson	30.00	15.00
109 Charles Fanning	30.00	15.00
110 Justin Fitzgerald	30.00	15.00
111 Frank Gay	30.00	15.00
112 Robert Jones	30.00	15.00
113 A.D. Machold	30.00	15.00
114 Frank O'Brien	30.00	15.00
115 John Oldham	30.00	15.00
116 Madison Perritt	30.00	15.00
117 Walter Schaller	30.00	15.00
118 Louis Sepulveda	30.00	15.00
119 Leslie Sheehan	30.00	15.00
120 William Steen	30.00	15.00
121 Harry Wolverton	30.00	15.00
122 John Wuffli	30.00	15.00
123 Donald Rader	30.00	15.00
124 Raymond Bates	30.00	15.00
125 C.H. Callahan	30.00	15.00
126 Frank DeCanniere	30.00	15.00
127 Walter Doane	30.00	15.00
128 Arthur Fromme	40.00	20.00
129 Gustave Gleischmann	30.00	15.00
130 Art Griggs	30.00	15.00
131 Otto Hess	30.00	15.00
132 Roy Hitt	30.00	15.00
133 Ellis Johnston	30.00	15.00
134 George Johnston	30.00	15.00
135 Mark McGaffigan	30.00	15.00
136 Walter Mattick	30.00	15.00
137 Albert Mitchell	30.00	15.00
138 Carl Mitze	30.00	15.00
139 Hamilton Patterson	30.00	15.00
140 John Quinn	50.00	25.00
141 Donald Rader	30.00	15.00
142 Charles Risberg	200.00	100.00
143 Edward Spencer	30.00	15.00
144 Albert Whalling	30.00	15.00
145 Dennis Wilie	30.00	15.00

1917 Zeenuts

These cards measure approximately 1 3/4" by 3 3/4".

	Ex-Mt	VG
COMPLETE SET (121)	3500.00	1800.00
1 John Bassler	40.00	20.00
2 Walter Boles	30.00	15.00
3 Charles Brown	30.00	15.00
4 Frank Chance	250.00	125.00
5 James Crandall	30.00	15.00
6 Robert Davis	30.00	15.00
7 Jacques Fournier	50.00	25.00
8 Frank Groehling	30.00	15.00
9 Charles Hall	30.00	15.00
10 Wade Killiffer	30.00	15.00
11 Peter Lapan	30.00	15.00
12 Harl Maggert	30.00	15.00
13 Emil Meusel	50.00	25.00
14 Jack Ryan	30.00	15.00
15 Joseph Schultz	30.00	15.00
16 Alfred Stanrdige	30.00	15.00
17 Zebulon Terry	30.00	15.00
18 Robert Vaughan	30.00	15.00
19 Alex Arlett	30.00	15.00
20 Samuel Beer	30.00	15.00
21 William Burns	30.00	15.00
22 F. Callan	30.00	15.00
23 Chester Chadbourne	30.00	15.00
24 Robert Coltrin	30.00	15.00
25 Richard Goodbred	30.00	15.00
26 George Howard	30.00	15.00
27 Joseph Kilhullen	30.00	15.00
28 Harry Krause	30.00	15.00
29 William Lane	30.00	15.00
30 William Lee	30.00	15.00
31 Edward Mensor	30.00	15.00
32 Robert Middleton	30.00	15.00
33 Lawrence Miller	30.00	15.00
34 Lawrence Miller	30.00	15.00
35 Rod Murphy	30.00	15.00
36 Daniel Murray	30.00	15.00
37 Oliver O'Mara	30.00	15.00
38 Herschel Prough	30.00	15.00
39 Charles Pruiett	30.00	15.00
40 John Roche	30.00	15.00
41 John Sheehan	30.00	15.00
42 Earl Baldwin	30.00	15.00
43 Lynn Brenton	30.00	15.00
44 Floyd Farmer	30.00	15.00
45 William Fincher	30.00	15.00
46 August Fisher	30.00	15.00
47 Oscar Harstad	30.00	15.00
48 Allan Helfrich	30.00	15.00
49 Charles Hollacher	40.00	20.00
50 Byron Houck	30.00	15.00
51 Albert Leake	30.00	15.00
52 Walter McCreedie	30.00	15.00
53 Frank O'Brien	30.00	15.00
54 Ralph Penelli	60.00	30.00
55 Kenneth Penner	30.00	15.00
56 Wesley Siglin	30.00	15.00
57 William Stumpf	30.00	15.00
58 Dennis Wilie	30.00	15.00
59 William Bernhard	30.00	15.00
60 Roy Bliss	30.00	15.00
61 Anthony Brief	30.00	15.00
62 Karl Crandall	30.00	15.00
63 Robert Cress	30.00	15.00
64 Stanley Dougan	30.00	15.00
65 Jean Dubuc	30.00	15.00
66 Evan Evans	30.00	15.00
67 Garde Gislason	30.00	15.00
68 James Hannah	30.00	15.00
69 Chester Hoff	30.00	15.00
70 Thomas Hughes	30.00	15.00
71 Walter Leverenz	30.00	15.00
72 William Orr	30.00	15.00
73 Thomas Quinlan	30.00	15.00
74 Morris Rath	40.00	20.00
75 John Ryan	30.00	15.00
76 Adolph Schinkle	30.00	15.00
77 Earl Sheeley	30.00	15.00
78 James Shinn	30.00	15.00
79 John Tobin	30.00	15.00
80 Delmer Baker	40.00	20.00
81 Delmer Baker	40.00	20.00
82 Charles Baum	30.00	15.00
83 Jacinto Calvo	60.00	30.00
84 Roy Corhan	30.00	15.00
85 Patrick Dougherty	30.00	15.00
86 Jerome Downs	30.00	15.00
87 George Ellis	30.00	15.00
88 Eric Erickson	30.00	15.00
89 Justin Fitzgerald	30.00	15.00
90 F. F. Hall	30.00	15.00
91 Leonard Hollywood	30.00	15.00
92 Philip Koerner	30.00	15.00
93 George Maisel	30.00	15.00
94 John Oldham	30.00	15.00
95 Charles Pick	30.00	15.00
96 Walter Schaller	30.00	15.00
97 Luther Smith	30.00	15.00
98 William Steen	30.00	15.00
99 Harry Wolverton	30.00	15.00
100 Frank Arellanes	30.00	15.00
101 C. H. Callahan	30.00	15.00
102 Barney Connifer	30.00	15.00
103 Frank DeCanniere	30.00	15.00
104 Walter Doane	30.00	15.00
105 Arthur Fromme	40.00	20.00
106 James Galloway	30.00	15.00
107 Art Griggs	30.00	15.00
108 Otto Hess	30.00	15.00
109 Roy Hitt	30.00	15.00
110 George Johnson	30.00	15.00
111 Howard McLarry	30.00	15.00
112 Walter Mattick	30.00	15.00
113 Albert Mitchell	30.00	15.00
114 Carl Mitze	30.00	15.00
115 John Quinn	50.00	25.00
116 Michael Simon	30.00	15.00
117 Robert Snyder	30.00	15.00
118 George Stovall	30.00	15.00
119 Joseph Sullivan	30.00	15.00
120 Ralph Valencia	30.00	15.00
121 Albert Whalling	30.00	15.00

1918 Zeenuts

These cards measure approximately 1 13/16" by 3 5/8".

	Ex-Mt	VG
COMPLETE SET (104)	6500.00	3200.00
1 Walter Boles	60.00	30.00
2 Charles Brown	60.00	30.00
3 Claude Cooper	60.00	30.00
4 James Crandall	60.00	30.00
5 Samuel Crawford	300.00	150.00
6 George Ellis	60.00	30.00
7 Paul Fittery	60.00	30.00
8 Jacques Fournier	80.00	40.00
9 Wade Killifer	60.00	30.00
10 Peter Lapan	60.00	30.00
11 Harold Leathers	60.00	30.00
12 Joseph Pepe	60.00	30.00
13 William Pertica	60.00	30.00
14 Alfred Stanbridge	60.00	30.00
15 Zebulon Terry	60.00	30.00
16 Ralph Valencia	60.00	30.00
17 Alex Arlett	60.00	30.00
18 Eugene Caldera	60.00	30.00
19 Paul Codington	60.00	30.00
20 Ralph Croll	60.00	30.00
21 L. Gardner	60.00	30.00
22 Nelson Hawkes	60.00	30.00
23 William Hollander	60.00	30.00
24 George Howard	60.00	30.00
25 Remy Kremer	80.00	40.00
26 Elmer Leifer	60.00	30.00
27 Elwood Martin	60.00	30.00
28 Edward Mensor	60.00	30.00
29 Robert Middleton	60.00	30.00
30 Lawrence Miller	60.00	30.00
31 Carl Mitze	60.00	30.00
32 Daniel Murray	60.00	30.00
33 Herschel Prough	60.00	30.00
34 George Shader	60.00	30.00
35 Robert Smale	60.00	30.00
36 Lynn Brenton	60.00	30.00
37 Jack Bromley	60.00	30.00
38 William Camm	60.00	30.00
39 D.K. Davis	60.00	30.00
40 Theodore Easterly	60.00	30.00
41 Ross Eldred	60.00	30.00
42 Carter Elliot	60.00	30.00
43 August Fisher	60.00	30.00
44 Frank Forsythe	60.00	30.00
45 Harry Gardner	60.00	30.00
46 Art Griggs	60.00	30.00
47 Albert Leake	60.00	30.00
48 J.M. McNulty	60.00	30.00
49 Ralph "Babe" Pinelli	120.00	60.00
50 Elton Prentice	60.00	30.00
51 Wilbur Rogers	60.00	30.00
52 James West	60.00	30.00
53 Dennis Wilie	60.00	30.00
54 Levi Arkenburg	60.00	30.00
55 Laverne Chappell	60.00	30.00
56 Allen Conwright	60.00	30.00
57 Elmer Cox	60.00	30.00
58 Karl Crandall	60.00	30.00
59 Jean Dubuc	60.00	30.00
60 John Dunn	60.00	30.00
61 Floyd Farmer	60.00	30.00
62 Michael Konnick	60.00	30.00
63 Walter Leverenz	60.00	30.00
64 Timothy McCabe	60.00	30.00
65 Walter McCredie	60.00	30.00
66 Ward Miller	60.00	30.00
67 Harry Morton	60.00	30.00
68 William Orr	60.00	30.00
69 Thomas Quinlan	60.00	30.00
70 John Ryan MG	60.00	30.00
71 John Sand	60.00	30.00
72 Earl Sheely	60.00	30.00
73 Wesley Siglin	60.00	30.00
74 Wallace Smith	60.00	30.00
75 Charles Baum	60.00	30.00
76 Clarence Brooks	60.00	30.00
77 Victor Dobbs	60.00	30.00
78 Jerome Downs	60.00	30.00
79 Jack Goldie	60.00	30.00
80 John Hummel	60.00	30.00
81 Herbert Hunter	60.00	30.00
82 George Johnson	60.00	30.00
83 George Johnson	60.00	30.00
84 Erving Kantlehner	60.00	30.00
85 Philip Koerner	60.00	30.00
86 William Llewlyn	60.00	30.00
87 Raymond McKee	60.00	30.00
88 Francis "Lefty" O'Doul	500.00	250.00
89 Andrew Phillips	60.00	30.00
90 Charles Pick	60.00	30.00
91 Peter Ritchie	60.00	30.00
92 Luther Smith	60.00	30.00
93 David Williams	60.00	30.00
94 John Alcock	60.00	30.00
95 William Borton	60.00	30.00
96 Albert DeVormer	80.00	40.00
97 Chester Chadbourne	60.00	30.00
98 William Essick	60.00	30.00
99 Arthur Fromme	80.00	40.00
100 Franz Hosp	60.00	30.00
101 John Mitchell	60.00	30.00
102 Roy Mitchell	60.00	30.00
103 Henry Moore	60.00	30.00
104 George Wisterzill	60.00	30.00

1919 Zeenuts

Some cards have been seen without sepia overlay. Fatty Arbuckle, the famous silent movie comedian has a card in this set. He was part owner of the Vernon Tigers which is how he ended up with a card. This card is considered among the keys in collecting Zeenuts. These cards measure approximately 1 3/4" by 3 5/8".

	Ex-Mt	VG
COMPLETE SET (144)	3500.00	1800.00
1 Walter Boles	20.00	10.00
2 Charles Brown	20.00	10.00
3 Claude Cooper	20.00	10.00
4 James Crandall	20.00	10.00
5 John Driscoll	20.00	10.00
6 George Ellis	20.00	10.00
7 Jacques Fournier	30.00	15.00
8 Fred Haney	30.00	15.00
9 William Kenworthy	20.00	10.00
10 Wade Killeffer	20.00	10.00
11 Peter Lapan	20.00	10.00
12 John Niehoff	20.00	10.00
13 Alex Arlett	20.00	10.00
14 Russ "Buzz" Arlett	40.00	20.00
15 Samuel Bohne	20.00	10.00
16 Claude Cooper	20.00	10.00
17 Ralph Croll	20.00	10.00
18 Harold Elliott	20.00	10.00
19 Carl Holling	20.00	10.00
20 George Howard MG	20.00	10.00
21 Remy Kramer	30.00	15.00
22 William Lane	20.00	10.00
23 William Lee	20.00	10.00
24 Carl Mitze MG	20.00	10.00
25 Rod Murphy	20.00	10.00
26 Chester Norse	20.00	10.00
27 John Roach	20.00	10.00
28 William Stumpf	20.00	10.00
29 Clyde Ware	20.00	10.00
30 Harry Weaver	20.00	10.00
31 Dennis Wilie	20.00	10.00
32 Delmer Baker	30.00	15.00
33 Luzurne Blue	30.00	15.00
34 Guy Cooper	20.00	10.00
35 Elmer Cox	20.00	10.00
36 Ernest Fallentine	20.00	10.00
37 Arthur Koehler	20.00	10.00
38 Walter McCreddie	20.00	10.00
39 George Maisel	20.00	10.00
40 John Oldham	20.00	10.00
41 Kenneth Penner	20.00	10.00
42 George Pennington	20.00	10.00
43 Donald Rader	20.00	10.00
44 Wesley Siglin	20.00	10.00
45 William Speas	20.00	10.00
46 Harvey Sutherland	20.00	10.00
47 Charles Walker	20.00	10.00
48 George Westerzil	20.00	10.00
49 Albert Zweifel	20.00	10.00
50 Ross Eldred	20.00	10.00
51 August Fisher	20.00	10.00
52 Art Griggs	20.00	10.00
53 Earl Larkin	20.00	10.00

54 Mark McGaffigan 20.00 10.00
55 Frank McHenry 20.00 10.00
56 J.M. McNulty 20.00 10.00
57 Robert Middleton 20.00 10.00
58 Daniel Murray 20.00 10.00
59 William Orr 20.00 10.00
60 William Piercy 20.00 10.00
61 Ralph Pinelli 40.00 20.00
62 Herschel Prough 20.00 10.00
63 Wilbur Rodgers 20.00 10.00
64 Clarence "Dazzy" Vance 200.00 100.00
65 Ally 20.00 10.00
66 Charles Byler 20.00 10.00
67 Eugene Caldera 20.00 10.00
68 Allen Conkwright 20.00 10.00
69 Raymond French 20.00 10.00
70 C.W. Henkle 20.00 10.00
71 Edward Herr 20.00 10.00
72 A.V. King 20.00 10.00
73 Emmet Mulory 20.00 10.00
74 William Rumler 20.00 10.00
75 John Sands 20.00 10.00
76 Earl Sheely 30.00 15.00
77 Kirby Sprangler 20.00 10.00
78 Edward Spencer 20.00 10.00
79 Pete Starasenich 20.00 10.00
80 Robert Willets 20.00 10.00
81 Earl Baldwin 20.00 10.00
82 Charles Baum 20.00 10.00
83 Clarence Brooks 20.00 10.00
84 James Cavaney 20.00 10.00
85 James Church 20.00 10.00
86 Jerry Coleman 20.00 10.00
87 Joseph Connolly 20.00 10.00
88 Roy Corhan 20.00 10.00
89 John Couch 20.00 10.00
90 Karl Crandall 20.00 10.00
91 Dell Crespi 20.00 10.00
92 Justin Fitzgerald 20.00 10.00
93 R. Flannigan 20.00 10.00
94 George Gibson 30.00 15.00
95 Howard Harper 20.00 10.00
96 Thomas Hickey 20.00 10.00
97 William Kamm 40.00 20.00
98 Philip Koerner 20.00 10.00
99 Remy Kramer 30.00 15.00
100 Maurice Schick 20.00 10.00
101 James Scott 20.00 10.00
102 Thomas Seaton 20.00 10.00
103 Bill Smith 20.00 10.00
104 Luther Smith 20.00 10.00
105 Snell 20.00 10.00
106 Carl Zamloch 20.00 10.00
107 Lyle Bigbee 20.00 10.00
108 Alvah Bowman 20.00 10.00
109 William Clymer 20.00 10.00
110 Pete Compton 20.00 10.00
111 William Cunningham 30.00 15.00
112 Frank Eastley 20.00 10.00
113 Albert Fabrique 20.00 10.00
114 Frederick Falkenberg 20.00 10.00
115 Grover Land 20.00 10.00
116 John Mails 30.00 15.00
117 Miles Mains 20.00 10.00
118 John Niehoff 20.00 10.00
119 Peter Ritchie 20.00 10.00
120 Wallace Schultz 20.00 10.00
121 James Walsh 20.00 10.00
122 Joseph Wilhoit 20.00 10.00
123 Roscoe "Fatty" Arbuckle 500.00 250.00
124 Zinn Beck 20.00 10.00
125 William Borton 20.00 10.00
126 Chester Chadbourne 20.00 10.00
127 Charles Chech 20.00 10.00
128 Lester Cook 20.00 10.00
129 Rexford Dawson 20.00 10.00
130 William Dell 20.00 10.00
131 Albert DeVormer 30.00 15.00
132 Jacob Edington 20.00 10.00
133 William Essick 30.00 15.00
134 Joseph Finneran 20.00 10.00
135 Robert Fisher 20.00 10.00
136 Arthur Fromme 30.00 15.00
137 Hugh High 20.00 10.00
138 Franz Hosp 20.00 10.00
139 Byron Houck 20.00 10.00
140 Thomas Long 20.00 10.00
141 Joseph Mathes 20.00 10.00
142 Bob Meusel 80.00 40.00
143 John Mitchell 20.00 10.00
144 Elmer Reigher 20.00 10.00

1920 Zeenuts

Some cards have been seen without grandstand. These cards measure approximately 1 3/4" by 3 5/8".

	Ex-Mt	VG
COMPLETE SET (151)	3000.00	1500.00
1 Victor Aldridge	30.00	15.00
2 Raymond Andrews	20.00	10.00
3 John Bassler	30.00	15.00
4 Charles Brown	20.00	10.00
5 James Crandall	20.00	10.00
6 Karl Crandall	20.00	10.00
7 Samuel Crawford	200.00	100.00
8 Nicholas Dumovich	20.00	10.00
9 George Ellis	20.00	10.00
10 Art Griggs	20.00	10.00
11 Fred Haney	20.00	10.00
12 Raymond Keating	20.00	10.00
13 Wade Killefer	20.00	10.00
14 James McAuley	20.00	10.00
15 John Niehoff	20.00	10.00
16 William Pertica	20.00	10.00
17 Alex Arlett	20.00	10.00
18 Russell Arlett	40.00	20.00
19 George Cunningham	20.00	10.00
20 Charles Dorman	20.00	10.00
21 Henry Gingiardi	20.00	10.00
22 Louis Guisto	20.00	10.00
23 William Hamilton	20.00	10.00
24 George Howard MG	20.00	10.00
25 John Knight	20.00	10.00
26 Remy Kremer	30.00	15.00
27 Don Lambert	20.00	10.00
28 William Lane	20.00	10.00
29 Lawrence Miller	20.00	10.00
30 Claude Mitchell	20.00	10.00
31 Carl Mitze	20.00	10.00
32 William Paull	20.00	10.00
33 George Petterson	20.00	10.00
34 Don Reagan	20.00	10.00
35 John Russell	20.00	10.00
36 Ed Spellman	20.00	10.00
37 Harry Weaver	20.00	10.00
38 Dennis Wilie	20.00	10.00
39 George Winn	20.00	10.00
40 Rollie Zeider	20.00	10.00
41 Delmer Baker	30.00	15.00
42 Luzurne Blue	30.00	15.00
43 Elmer Cox	20.00	10.00
44 Sylvester Johnson	30.00	15.00
45 Carroll Jones	20.00	10.00
46 Frank Juney	20.00	10.00
47 Rudolph Kallio	20.00	10.00
48 Wescott Kingdon	20.00	10.00
49 Arthur Koehler	20.00	10.00
50 Walter McCredie	20.00	10.00
51 George Maisel	20.00	10.00
52 Harold Polson	20.00	10.00
53 Samuel Ross	20.00	10.00
54 Walter Schaller	20.00	10.00
55 Clyde Schroeder	20.00	10.00
56 Wesley Siglin	20.00	10.00
57 Carl Spranger	20.00	10.00
58 Harvey Sutherland	20.00	10.00
59 George Wisterzill	20.00	10.00
60 Willie Butler	20.00	10.00
61 Pete Compton	20.00	10.00
62 Lester Cook	20.00	10.00
63 Ross Eldred	20.00	10.00
64 Guy Hodges	20.00	10.00
65 Jack Killeen	20.00	10.00
66 Earl Kunz	20.00	10.00
67 Earl Larkin	20.00	10.00
68 Mark McGaffigan	20.00	10.00
69 Walter Mails	30.00	15.00
70 Fred Mollwitz	20.00	10.00
71 Billy Orr	20.00	10.00
72 Kenneth Penner	20.00	10.00
73 Herschel Prough	20.00	10.00
74 Bill Rodgers MG	20.00	10.00
75 Robert Schang	20.00	10.00
76 William Stumpf	20.00	10.00
77 Charles Baum	20.00	10.00
78 Jack Bromley dark hat	20.00	10.00
79 Jack Bromley light hat	20.00	10.00
80 Norman Cullop	20.00	10.00
81 Charles Dylar	20.00	10.00
82 Russell James	20.00	10.00
83 Joe Jenkins	20.00	10.00
84 Ernest Johnson	20.00	10.00
85 Martin Krug	20.00	10.00
86 Walter Leverenz	20.00	10.00
87 Frank McHenry	20.00	10.00
88 Harl Maggart	20.00	10.00
89 Henry Matterson	20.00	10.00
90 Eddie Matteson	20.00	10.00
91 Elmer O'Shaughnessy	20.00	10.00
92 Elmer Reiger	20.00	10.00
93 Alex Reilly	20.00	10.00
94 Bill Rumler	20.00	10.00
95 John Sands	20.00	10.00
96 Earl Sheely	30.00	15.00
97 Ralph Stroud	20.00	10.00
98 Hollis Thurston dark hat	30.00	15.00
99 Hollis Thurston light hat	30.00	15.00
100 J.W. Worth	20.00	10.00
101 Samuel Agnew	20.00	10.00
102 Edward Anfinson	20.00	10.00
103 James Caveney	20.00	10.00
104 Joseph Connolly	20.00	10.00
105 Roy Corhan	20.00	10.00
106 Mario DeVitalus	20.00	10.00
107 Joseph Dooley	20.00	10.00
108 Justin Fitzgerald	20.00	10.00
109 John Gough	20.00	10.00
110 Bill Kamm	30.00	15.00
111 Phillip Koerner	20.00	10.00
112 Edward Love	20.00	10.00
113 Herbert McQuaid	20.00	10.00
114 Maurice Schick	20.00	10.00
115 James Scott	20.00	10.00
116 Thomas Seaton	20.00	10.00
117 Luther Smith	20.00	10.00
118 Michael Walsh	20.00	10.00
119 Archie Yelle	20.00	10.00
120 John Adams	20.00	10.00
121 Earl Baldwin	20.00	10.00
122 Samuel Bohne	20.00	10.00
123 Lynn Brenton	20.00	10.00
124 Harry Gardner	20.00	10.00
125 Bruce Hartford	20.00	10.00
126 William Kenworthy	20.00	10.00
127 Merlin Kopp	20.00	10.00
128 Rod Murphy	20.00	10.00
129 Robert Nixon	20.00	10.00
130 Arthur Rheinhart	20.00	10.00
131 Charles Schorr	20.00	10.00
132 Harry Siebold	20.00	10.00
133 Clyde Wares	20.00	10.00
134 Carl Zamlock	20.00	10.00
135 John Alcock	20.00	10.00
136 Chester Chadbourne	20.00	10.00
137 Albert DeVormer	30.00	15.00
138 Jacob Edington	20.00	10.00
139 William Essick	30.00	15.00
140 Robert Fisher	20.00	10.00
141 Arthur Fromme	30.00	15.00
142 Hugh High	20.00	10.00
143 Elmer Hill	20.00	10.00
144 Thomas Long	20.00	10.00
145 John Mitchell	20.00	10.00
146 Willie Mitchell	20.00	10.00
147 Moffitt	20.00	10.00
148 Harry Morse	20.00	10.00
149 Frank Schellenback	30.00	15.00
150 James Smith	20.00	10.00
151 James Sullivan	20.00	10.00

1921 Zeenuts

These cards measure 1 3/4" by 3 3/4".

	Ex-Mt	VG
COMPLETE SET (167)	3500.00	1800.00
1 Victor Aldridge	30.00	15.00
2 Earl Baldwin	20.00	10.00
3 Dorsey Carroll	20.00	10.00
4 Thomas Casey	20.00	10.00
5 Otis Crandall	20.00	10.00
6 Sam Crawford	200.00	100.00
7 Ken Douglas	20.00	10.00
8 Nick Dumovich	20.00	10.00
9 George Ellis	20.00	10.00
10 Arthur Griggs	20.00	10.00
11 Tom Hughes	20.00	10.00
12 Wade Killefer	20.00	10.00
13 Howard Lindimore	20.00	10.00
14 George Lyons	20.00	10.00
15 Jim McAuley	20.00	10.00
16 Bert Niehoff	20.00	10.00
17 Arthur Reinhardt	20.00	10.00
18 Oscar Stanage	20.00	10.00
19 Arnold Statz	40.00	20.00
20 Claude Thomas	20.00	10.00
21 Rollie Zeider	20.00	10.00
22 Allen Alton	20.00	10.00
23 Russell Arlett	40.00	20.00
24 Ray Brubaker	20.00	10.00
25 Ted Cather	20.00	10.00
26 Claude Cooper	20.00	10.00
27 Bernard Kearns	20.00	10.00
28 Eugene Kersten	20.00	10.00
29 Jack Knight	20.00	10.00
30 Arthur Koehler	20.00	10.00
31 Harry Krause	20.00	10.00
32 Ray Kremer	30.00	15.00
33 Lawrence Miller	20.00	10.00
34 Carl Mitze	20.00	10.00
35 Ralph Pinelli	40.00	20.00
36 Addison Read	20.00	10.00
37 Lane Shultis	20.00	10.00
38 Harry Siebold	20.00	10.00
39 Al White	20.00	10.00
40 Dennis Wilie	20.00	10.00
41 George Winn	20.00	10.00
42 Dale Baker	20.00	10.00
43 Art Bourg	20.00	10.00
44 Willie Butler	20.00	10.00
45 Fred Connel	20.00	10.00
46 Dick Cox	20.00	10.00
47 Gus Fisher	20.00	10.00
48 Walt Gennin	20.00	10.00
49 Sam Hale	20.00	10.00
50 Sylvester Johnson	30.00	15.00
51 Rudy Kallio	20.00	10.00
52 A.V. King	20.00	10.00
53 Wesley Kingdon	20.00	10.00
54 M.J. Krug	20.00	10.00
55 Walt McCredie	20.00	10.00
56 J.C. Nofziger	20.00	10.00
57 O'Malia	20.00	10.00
58 Hazen Paton	20.00	10.00
59 Herman Pillette	30.00	15.00
60 H.G. Polson	20.00	10.00
61 J.R. Poole	20.00	10.00
62 Sam Ross	20.00	10.00
63 M.J. Wolfer	20.00	10.00
64 Clyde Young	20.00	10.00
65 Ray Blossom	20.00	10.00
66 Pete Compton	20.00	10.00
67 Les Cook	20.00	10.00
68 Howard Elliott	20.00	10.00
69 Tony Faeth	20.00	10.00
70 Paul Fittery	20.00	10.00
71 Carroll Jones	20.00	10.00
72 Merlin Kopp	20.00	10.00
73 Earl Kunz	20.00	10.00
74 Mark McGaffigan	20.00	10.00
75 Fred Mollwitz	20.00	10.00
76 Dick Niehaus	20.00	10.00
77 Bill Orr	20.00	10.00
78 Ken Penner	20.00	10.00
79 Charley Pick	20.00	10.00
80 H.C. Prough	20.00	10.00
81 Wilbur Rodgers MG	20.00	10.00
82 Pete Rose	20.00	10.00
83 Sid Ross	20.00	10.00
84 Buddy Ryan	20.00	10.00
85 Bob Shang	20.00	10.00
86 Les Sheehan	20.00	10.00
87 Rich Berry	20.00	10.00
88 Harry Blacholder	20.00	10.00
89 Earl Brinley	20.00	10.00
90 John Bromley	20.00	10.00
91 Brown	20.00	10.00
92 C.A. Byler	20.00	10.00
93 Gavvy Cravath	40.00	20.00
94 A.F. Gould	20.00	10.00
95 A.J. Hesse	20.00	10.00
96 W.P. Jackson	20.00	10.00
97 P.W. Jacobs	20.00	10.00
98 Joe Jenkins	20.00	10.00
99 Ted Jourden	20.00	10.00
100 Jack Kifer	20.00	10.00
101 Walter Leverenz	20.00	10.00
102 Byrd Lynn	20.00	10.00
103 Mustain	20.00	10.00
104 Nickels	20.00	10.00
105 Harry Oliver	20.00	10.00
106 Elmer Rieger	20.00	10.00
107 Peter Rose	20.00	10.00
108 Heinie Sand	20.00	10.00
109 Paddy Siglin	20.00	10.00
110 Hollis Thurston	30.00	15.00
111 Hilliard Tyrell	20.00	10.00
112 Ed Van Osdoll	20.00	10.00
113 J.W. Wilhoit	20.00	10.00
114 Edwin Anfinson	20.00	10.00
115 Jim Caveney	20.00	10.00
116 Jack Couch	20.00	10.00
117 Roy Crumpler	20.00	10.00
118 Bert Ellison	20.00	10.00
119 Justin Fitzgerald	20.00	10.00
120 Ed Flaherty	20.00	10.00
121 Elmer Hansen	20.00	10.00
122 Bill Kamm	30.00	15.00
123 Joe Kelly	20.00	10.00
124 Sam Lewis	20.00	10.00
125 Willie Ludolph	20.00	10.00
126 Herb McQuaid	20.00	10.00
127 John Merritt	20.00	10.00
128 Jim O'Connell	20.00	10.00
129 Frank O'Doul	200.00	100.00
130 Morris Rath	30.00	15.00
131 Maurice Schick	20.00	10.00
132 Jim Scott	20.00	10.00
133 Shore	20.00	10.00
134 Tom Walsh	20.00	10.00
135 Archie Yelle	20.00	10.00
136 J.B. Adams	20.00	10.00
137 Ray Bates	20.00	10.00
138 Bill Cunningham	30.00	15.00
139 Joe Daley	20.00	10.00
140 Al Demaree	30.00	15.00
141 Ray Francis	20.00	10.00
142 Harry Gardner	20.00	10.00
143 Bob Geary	20.00	10.00
144 Elmer Jacobs	20.00	10.00
145 Bill Lane	20.00	10.00
146 Bob Middelton	20.00	10.00
147 Rod Murphy	20.00	10.00
148 Rube Oldring	30.00	15.00
149 Ernie Shorr	30.00	15.00
150 Ed Spencer	20.00	10.00
151 William Wtumpf	20.00	10.00
152 Forbes Alcock	20.00	10.00
153 Chester Chadbourne	20.00	10.00
154 Wheezer Dell	20.00	10.00
155 Bill Essick	30.00	15.00
156 Ray French	20.00	10.00
157 Arthur Fromme	30.00	15.00
158 Charles Gorman	20.00	10.00
159 James Hannah	20.00	10.00
160 Hugh High	20.00	10.00
161 Ham Hyatt	20.00	10.00
162 Ed Love	20.00	10.00
163 Bob McGraw	20.00	10.00
164 Willie Mitchell	20.00	10.00
165 Harry Morse	20.00	10.00
166 Dennis Murphy	20.00	10.00
167 Pete Schneider	20.00	10.00
168 Walter Smallwood	20.00	10.00
169 J.C. Smith	20.00	10.00

1922 Zeenuts

Cards seen with variations in Sepia tone overlay. A very early card of Hall of Famer Tony Lazzeri is in this set along with a card of Jim Thorpe. This is one of the few cards picturing Thorpe as a baseball player during his professional career. These cards measure 1 13/16" by 3 9/16".

	Ex-Mt	VG
COMPLETE SET (162)	5000.00	2500.00
1 Earle Baldwin	20.00	10.00
2 Dorsey Carroll	20.00	10.00
3 Otis Crandall	20.00	10.00
4 Tom Daly	20.00	10.00
5 Charles Deal	20.00	10.00
6 Nick Dumovich	20.00	10.00
7 Art Griggs	20.00	10.00
8 Tom Hughes	20.00	10.00
9 Wade Killefer	20.00	10.00
10 Howard Lindimore	20.00	10.00
11 George Lyons	20.00	10.00
12 Jim McAuley	20.00	10.00
13 Bill McCabe	20.00	10.00
14 Elmer Ponder	20.00	10.00
15 Harry Sullivan	20.00	10.00
16 Claude Thomas	20.00	10.00
17 Clarence Twombly	20.00	10.00
18 Bernie Viveros	20.00	10.00
19 Robert Wallace	20.00	10.00
20 Mark Wheat	20.00	10.00
21 Russ Arlett	40.00	20.00
22 Lynn Brenton	20.00	10.00
23 Don Brown	20.00	10.00
24 Ray Brubaker	20.00	10.00
25 Claude Cooper	20.00	10.00
26 Hod Eller	30.00	15.00
27 Ivan Howard	20.00	10.00
28 Gordon Jones	20.00	10.00
29 Earl Keiser	20.00	10.00
30 Jack Knight	20.00	10.00
31 Art Koehler	20.00	10.00
32 Ray Kremer	30.00	15.00
33 George Lafayette	20.00	10.00
34 Bill Marriott	20.00	10.00
35 Carl Mitze	20.00	10.00
36 Pat Monahan	20.00	10.00
37 Addison Read	20.00	10.00
38 Frank Schulte	25.00	12.50
39 Dennis Wilie	20.00	10.00
40 Dick Cox	20.00	10.00
41 Roy Crumpler	20.00	10.00
42 Howard Elliott	20.00	10.00
43 Harvey Freeman	20.00	10.00
44 Leroy Gressett	20.00	10.00
45 Charley High	20.00	10.00
46 Harry Kenworthy	20.00	10.00
47 Joseph Killhullen	20.00	10.00
48 A.V. King	20.00	10.00
49 Emmett McCann	20.00	10.00
50 J.R. Poole	20.00	10.00
51 Samuel Ross	20.00	10.00
52 J.A. Sargent	20.00	10.00
53 Harvey Sutherland	20.00	10.00
54 Jim Thorpe	2000.00	1000.00
55 Tom Turner	20.00	10.00
56 Carroll Canfield	20.00	10.00
57 Pete Compton	20.00	10.00
58 Les Cook	20.00	10.00
59 Paul Fittery	20.00	10.00
60 George Gibson	20.00	10.00
61 Hampton	20.00	10.00
62 Earl Kunz	20.00	10.00
63 Henry Hampton	20.00	10.00
64 Frederick Mollwitz	20.00	10.00
65 Dick Niehaus	20.00	10.00
66 Billy Orr	20.00	10.00
67 Walt Pearce	20.00	10.00
68 Charles Pick	20.00	10.00
69 Bill Prough	20.00	10.00
70 Buddy Ryan	20.00	10.00
71 Bob Schang	20.00	10.00
72 Elmer Shea	20.00	10.00
73 Les Sheehan	20.00	10.00
74 Oscar Stanage	20.00	10.00
75 Harry Blaeholder	20.00	10.00
76 Jack Bromley	20.00	10.00
77 C.A. Byler	20.00	10.00
78 Joseph Cartwright	20.00	10.00
79 A.F. Gould	20.00	10.00
80 Joe Jenkins	20.00	10.00
81 Rudy Kallio	20.00	10.00
82 Tony Lazzeri	200.00	100.00
83 Duffy Lewis	40.00	20.00
84 Sam Lewis	20.00	10.00
85 Lem Owen	20.00	10.00
86 Elmer Rieger	20.00	10.00
87 Heinie Sand	30.00	15.00
88 Maurice Schick	20.00	10.00
89 Paddy Siglin	20.00	10.00
90 Frank Soria	20.00	10.00
91 Paul Strand	20.00	10.00
92 Hollis Thurston	30.00	15.00
93 J.W. Wilhoit	20.00	10.00
94 Sam Agnew	30.00	15.00
95 Ed Anfinson	20.00	10.00
96 Fritz Coumbe	20.00	10.00
97 Bert Ellison	20.00	10.00
98 Justin Fitzgerald	20.00	10.00
99 Bob Geary	20.00	10.00
100 Bill Kamm	30.00	15.00
101 Pete Kilduff	30.00	15.00
102 Ross Lefevre	20.00	10.00
103 Herb McQuaid	20.00	10.00
104 John Miller	20.00	10.00
105 Oliver Mitchell	20.00	10.00
106 Jim O'Connell	30.00	15.00
107 Jim Scott	20.00	10.00
108 Charley See	20.00	10.00
109 Gene Valla	20.00	10.00
110 Andy Vargas	20.00	10.00
111 Tom Walsh	20.00	10.00
112 Lyle Wells	20.00	10.00
113 Richard Williams	20.00	10.00
114 Archie Yelle	20.00	10.00
115 Jack Adams	20.00	10.00
116 Spencer Adams	20.00	10.00
117 Ed Barney	20.00	10.00
118 L.T. Bell	20.00	10.00
119 George Brovold	20.00	10.00
120 George Burger	20.00	10.00
121 Thomas Connolly	20.00	10.00
122 Manuel Cueto	20.00	10.00
123 Joe Dailey	20.00	10.00
124 R.C. Eldred	20.00	10.00
125 Joe Finneran	20.00	10.00
126 Harry Gardner	20.00	10.00
127 Vean Gregg	30.00	15.00
128 Henry Henke	20.00	10.00
129 Elmer Jacobs	20.00	10.00
130 Reynolds Kelly	20.00	10.00
131 Bill Lane	20.00	10.00
132 Walter McCredie MG	20.00	10.00
133 Frank Mack	20.00	10.00
134 Herb May	20.00	10.00
135 Rod Murphy	20.00	10.00
136 James Richardson	20.00	10.00
137 Pete Ritchie	20.00	10.00
138 Ernie Schorr	20.00	10.00
139 Frank Schulte	25.00	12.50
140 Ed Spencer	20.00	10.00
141 William Stumpf	20.00	10.00
142 Frank Tobin	20.00	10.00
143 George Westersil	20.00	10.00
144 Ping Bodie	40.00	20.00
145 Chester Chadbourne	20.00	10.00
146 Wheezer Dell	20.00	10.00
147 Jesse Doyle	20.00	10.00
148 Bill Essick MG	30.00	15.00
149 Ray French	20.00	10.00
150 Ray Gilder	20.00	10.00
151 Harry Hannah	20.00	10.00
152 Nelson Hawks	20.00	10.00
153 Hugh High	20.00	10.00
154 Byron Houck	20.00	10.00
155 Ham Hyatt	20.00	10.00
156 William James	20.00	10.00
157 Dallas Locker	20.00	10.00
158 Dennis Murphy	20.00	10.00
159 Carl Sawyer	20.00	10.00
160 Pete Schneider	20.00	10.00
161 Red Smith	20.00	10.00
162 Rollie Zeider	20.00	10.00

1923 Kansas City Blues Baltimore Shirt

This 20 card set was issued as part of an "accordian-style" booklet. This set honored the pennant winning Kansas City Blues team as it was issued in an envelope from the Baltimore Shirt Co which then had four stores in the Kansas City area. Please note that since these cards are unnumbered, we have sequenced

them in alphabetical order.

	MINT	NRMT
COMPLETE SET	600.00	275.00
1 George Armstrong	30.00	13.50
2 Beals Becker	30.00	13.50
3 Lena Blackburne	30.00	13.50
4 Bunny Brief	30.00	13.50
5 Dudley Branom	30.00	13.50
6 Ray Caldwell	30.00	13.50
7 Nick Carter	30.00	13.50
8 Joe Dawson	30.00	13.50
9 Wilbur Good MG	30.00	13.50
10 Walter Hammond	30.00	13.50
11 Lew McCarty	30.00	13.50
12 George Muehlebach PRES	30.00	13.50
13 John Saladna	30.00	13.50
14 Ferd Schupp	30.00	13.50
15 Pete Scott	30.00	13.50
16 Bill Skiff	30.00	13.50
17 Herb Thormahlen	30.00	13.50
18 Roy Wilkinson	30.00	13.50
19 Glenn Wright	40.00	18.00
20 Jimmie Zinn	30.00	13.50
21 Dutch Zwilling	30.00	13.50

1923 Zeenuts

An early card of Hall of Famer Paul Waner is in this set. Cards measure approximately 1 7/8" by 3 9/16". Two different expiration dates have been noted for these cards. Cards with a sepia tint which were reissued from 1922 have an expiration date of April 1, 1923 while the regular black and white cards have an expiration date of April 1, 1924.

	Ex-Mt	VG
COMPLETE SET (198)	4000.00	2000.00
1 Earl Baldwin	20.00	10.00
2 Dorsey Carroll	20.00	10.00
3 Otis Crandall	20.00	10.00
4 Tom Daly	20.00	10.00
5 Charles Deal	20.00	10.00
6 Walter Golvin	20.00	10.00
7 Art Griggs	20.00	10.00
8 Roy Hannah	20.00	10.00
9 Wallace Hood	20.00	10.00
10 Percy Jones	20.00	10.00
11 Wade Killifer	20.00	10.00
12 Martin Krug	20.00	10.00
13 Howard Lindimore	20.00	10.00
14 George Lyons	20.00	10.00
15 Jim McAuley	20.00	10.00
16 James McAuliffe	20.00	10.00
17 Bill McCabe	20.00	10.00
18 Elmer Ponder	20.00	10.00
19 Lawrence Robertson	20.00	10.00
20 Claude Thomas	20.00	10.00
21 Clarence Twombly	20.00	10.00
22 Bob Wallace	20.00	10.00
23 Russ Arlett	40.00	20.00
24 Dale Baker	20.00	10.00
25 Lynn Brenton	20.00	10.00
26 Don Brown	20.00	10.00
27 Roy Brubaker	20.00	10.00
28 Ted Cather	20.00	10.00
29 Harold Chavez	20.00	10.00
30 Ira Colwell	20.00	10.00
31 Claude Cooper	20.00	10.00
32 Claude Cooper	20.00	10.00
33 Orville Eley	20.00	10.00
34 Horace Eller	30.00	15.00
35 Ivan Howard	20.00	10.00
36 Ivan Howard	20.00	10.00
37 Del Howard	20.00	10.00
38 Osborne Johnson	20.00	10.00
39 Gordon Jones	20.00	10.00
40 Earl Keiser	20.00	10.00
41 Jack Knight	20.00	10.00
42 Jack Knight	20.00	10.00
43 Art Koehler	20.00	10.00
44 Harry Krause	20.00	10.00
45 Ray Kremer	30.00	15.00
46 George Lafayette	20.00	10.00
47 George Lafayette	20.00	10.00
48 Mark McGaffigan	20.00	10.00
49 A.J. Maderas	20.00	10.00
50 Walt Mails	30.00	15.00
51 William Marriott	20.00	10.00
52 Carl Mitze	20.00	10.00
53 George Murchio	20.00	10.00
54 Addison Read	20.00	10.00
55 Addison Read	20.00	10.00
56 Marvin Smith	20.00	10.00
57 Chet Thomas	20.00	10.00
58 Lyle Wells	20.00	10.00
59 Dennis Wilie	20.00	10.00
60 Dennis Wilie	20.00	10.00
61 Frank Wetzel	20.00	10.00
62 Frank Brazil	20.00	10.00
63 Roy Crumpler	20.00	10.00
64 Tom Daly	20.00	10.00
65 Chas Eckert	20.00	10.00
66 Leroy Gressett	20.00	10.00
67 Charley High	20.00	10.00
68 John Jones	20.00	10.00
69 Lee King	20.00	10.00
70 Walt Leverenz	20.00	10.00
71 Emmett McCann	20.00	10.00
72 J.B. Middleton	20.00	10.00
73 Jack Onslow	20.00	10.00
74 Jim Poole	20.00	10.00
75 C.M. Schroeder	20.00	10.00
76 William Stumpf	20.00	10.00
77 Harvey Sutherland	20.00	10.00
78 M.J. Wolfer	20.00	10.00
79 B.W. Yarrison	20.00	10.00
80 Rollie Zeider	20.00	10.00
81 Harry Brown	20.00	10.00
82 Carroll Canfield	20.00	10.00
83 Charles Cochrane	20.00	10.00
84 Les Cook	20.00	10.00
85 Paul Fittery	20.00	10.00
86 Ed Hemingway	20.00	10.00
87 Hughes Houghs	20.00	10.00
88 Art Koehler	20.00	10.00
89 Merlin Kopp	20.00	10.00
90 George McGinnis	20.00	10.00
91 Earl McNeilly	20.00	10.00
92 Ken Penner	20.00	10.00
93 Charles Pick	20.00	10.00
94 Claude Rohwer	20.00	10.00
95 Buddy Ryan	20.00	10.00
96 Bob Schang	20.00	10.00
97 Merv Shea	20.00	10.00
98 Elmer Shea	20.00	10.00
99 Paddy Siglin	20.00	10.00
100 Moses Yellowhorse	40.00	20.00
101 Ed Anfinson	20.00	10.00
102 Fritz Coumbe	20.00	10.00
103 James Duchalsky	20.00	10.00
104 John Frederick	20.00	10.00
105 A.P. Gould	20.00	10.00
106 Rudy Kallio	20.00	10.00
107 Bernard Kearns	20.00	10.00
108 Lloyd Keller	20.00	10.00
109 Roy Leslie	20.00	10.00
110 Duffy Lewis	40.00	20.00
111 R.J. McCabe	20.00	10.00
112 Charles Matzen	20.00	10.00
113 Walt Pearce	20.00	10.00
114 John Peters	20.00	10.00
115 Les Sheehan	20.00	10.00
116 John Singleton	20.00	10.00
117 Paul Strand	20.00	10.00
118 Oscar Vitt	30.00	15.00
119 J.W. Wilhoit	20.00	10.00
120 Sam Agnew	20.00	10.00
121 Sam Agnew	20.00	10.00
122 Ernest Alten	20.00	10.00
123 Ed Anfinson	20.00	10.00
124 Timothy Buckley	20.00	10.00
125 Pete Compton	20.00	10.00
126 Henry Courtney	20.00	10.00
127 Bert Ellison	20.00	10.00
128 Bert Ellison	20.00	10.00
129 Ray Flashkamper	20.00	10.00
130 Robert Geary	20.00	10.00
131 Robert Geary	20.00	10.00
132 Timothy Hendryx	20.00	10.00
133 C.C. Hodge	20.00	10.00
134 Joe Kelly	20.00	10.00
135 Pete Kilduff	20.00	10.00
136 Alfred Lefevre	20.00	10.00
137 Doug McWeeney	20.00	10.00
138 John Miller	20.00	10.00
139 Oliver Mitchell	20.00	10.00
140 Oliver Mitchell	20.00	10.00
141 Edward Mulligan	20.00	10.00
142 Gus Noack	20.00	10.00
143 Hal Rhyne	20.00	10.00
144 Jim Scott	20.00	10.00
145 Charley See	20.00	10.00
146 Pat Shea	20.00	10.00
147 George Stanton	20.00	10.00
148 Gene Valla	20.00	10.00
149 Andy Vargas	20.00	10.00
150 Tom Dee Walsh	20.00	10.00
151 Paul Waner	300.00	150.00
152 Lyle Wells	20.00	10.00
153 Archie Yelle	20.00	10.00
154 Archie Yelle	20.00	10.00
155 Anderson	20.00	10.00
156 Ed Barney	20.00	10.00
157 Fred Blake	20.00	10.00
158 Sam Crane	20.00	10.00
159 Alvin Crowder	40.00	20.00
160 R.C. Eldred	20.00	10.00
161 Elmer Jacobs	20.00	10.00
162 Wheeler Johnston	20.00	10.00
163 Reynolds Kelly	20.00	10.00
164 Bill Lane	20.00	10.00
165 Alfred Levere	20.00	10.00
166 Bill Orr	20.00	10.00
167 Vic Pigg	20.00	10.00
168 William Plummer	20.00	10.00
169 W.C. Ramage	20.00	10.00
170 Pete Ritchie	20.00	10.00
171 Ray Rohwer	20.00	10.00
172 John Tesar	20.00	10.00
173 Frank Tobin	20.00	10.00
174 Tommy Walsh	20.00	10.00
175 Jim Welsh	20.00	10.00
176 Carl Williams	20.00	10.00
177 Harry Wolverton	20.00	10.00
178 Clarence Yaryan	20.00	10.00
179 Frank Bodie	40.00	20.00
180 Chester Chadbourne	20.00	10.00
181 Jesse Doyle	20.00	10.00
182 Bill Essick MG	30.00	15.00
183 Ray French	20.00	10.00
184 Ray Gilder	20.00	10.00
185 Charles Gorman	20.00	10.00
186 Harry Hannah	20.00	10.00
187 Hugh High	20.00	10.00
188 William James	20.00	10.00
189 James Jolly	20.00	10.00
190 Ed Kenna	20.00	10.00
191 Dallas Locker	20.00	10.00
192 Dennis Murphy	20.00	10.00
193 Rod Murphy	20.00	10.00
194 Perry O'Brien	20.00	10.00
195 Carl Sawyer	20.00	10.00
196 Pete Schneider	20.00	10.00
197 Frank Shellenback	30.00	15.00
198 Carlisle Smith	20.00	10.00

1924 Zeenuts

An early card of Hall of Famer Mickey Cochrane is in this set. These cards measure approximately 1 3/4" by 3 7/16".

	Ex-Mt	VG
COMPLETE SET (144)	3000.00	1500.00
1 Clyde Beck	20.00	10.00
2 Lyle Bigbee	20.00	10.00
3 John Billings	20.00	10.00
4 C.A. Byler	20.00	10.00
5 Otis Crandall	20.00	10.00
6 Ced Durst	20.00	10.00
7 Walt Golvin	20.00	10.00
8 Fred Gunther	20.00	10.00
9 Wally Hood	20.00	10.00
10 Tom Hughes	20.00	10.00
11 Ray Jacobs	20.00	10.00
12 Marty Krug	20.00	10.00
13 Jim McAuley	20.00	10.00
14 Elmer Meyers	20.00	10.00
15 Charley Root	40.00	20.00
16 C.E. Twombley	20.00	10.00
17 Robert Wallace	20.00	10.00
18 Bill Whaley	20.00	10.00
19 Spencer Adams	20.00	10.00
20 Russ Arlett	40.00	20.00
21 Del Baker	20.00	10.00
22 Ray Brubaker	20.00	10.00
23 Ted Cather	20.00	10.00
24 Claude Cooper	20.00	10.00
25 George Foster	20.00	10.00
26 Ed Goebel	20.00	10.00
27 Lou Guisto	20.00	10.00
28 Ivan Howard	20.00	10.00
29 Osborne Johnson	20.00	10.00
30 Harry Krause	20.00	10.00
31 Earl Kunz	20.00	10.00
32 George Lafayette	20.00	10.00
33 Leptich	20.00	10.00
34 Al Maderas	20.00	10.00
35 Walt Mails	20.00	10.00
36 Addison Read	20.00	10.00
37 Harry Siebold	20.00	10.00
38 Stan Benton	20.00	10.00
39 Frank Brazil	20.00	10.00
40 Mickey Cochrane	300.00	150.00
41 Dick Cox	20.00	10.00
42 Tom Daly	20.00	10.00
43 George Distel	20.00	10.00
44 Charley Eckert	20.00	10.00
45 LeRoy Gressett	20.00	10.00
46 Charley High	20.00	10.00
47 John Jones	20.00	10.00
48 Bill Kenworthy	20.00	10.00
49 Ed Lennon	20.00	10.00
50 Walt Leverenz	20.00	10.00
51 Emmett McCann	20.00	10.00
52 Jake Miller	20.00	10.00
53 Ted Pillette	20.00	10.00
54 Jim Poole	20.00	10.00
55 Wray Querry	20.00	10.00
56 C.M. Schroeder	20.00	10.00
57 Frank Wetzel	20.00	10.00
58 M.J. Wolfer	20.00	10.00
59 Harry Brown	20.00	10.00
60 Charles Cochrane	20.00	10.00
61 Sea Lion Hall	20.00	10.00
62 William Hughes	20.00	10.00
63 William James	20.00	10.00
64 Merlin Kopp	20.00	10.00
65 Earl McNeely	30.00	15.00
66 Harlan Peters	20.00	10.00
67 Charley Pick	20.00	10.00
68 Bill Prough	20.00	10.00
69 Claude Rowher	20.00	10.00
70 Bob Schang	20.00	10.00
71 Speck Shay	20.00	10.00
72 Merv Shea	30.00	15.00
73 Paddy Siglin	20.00	10.00
74 Art Smith	20.00	10.00
75 Moses Yellowhorse	40.00	20.00
76 Fred Coumbe	20.00	10.00
77 John Fredericks	20.00	10.00
78 Al Gould	20.00	10.00
79 Joe Jenkins	20.00	10.00
80 Roy Leslie	20.00	10.00
81 Duffy Lewis	40.00	20.00
82 John Peters	20.00	10.00
83 Oscar Vitt	25.00	12.50
84 Joseph Wilhoit	20.00	10.00
85 Sam Agnew	20.00	10.00
86 Timothy Buckley	20.00	10.00
87 George Burger	20.00	10.00
88 Bert Ellison	20.00	10.00
89 Raymond Flaskamper	20.00	10.00
90 Bob Geary	20.00	10.00
91 Martin Griffin	20.00	10.00
92 Tim Hendryx	20.00	10.00
93 C.C. Hodge	20.00	10.00
94 Joe Kelly	20.00	10.00
95 Pete Kilduff	30.00	15.00
96 Oliver Mitchell	20.00	10.00
97 Ed Mulligan	20.00	10.00
98 Norb Paynter	20.00	10.00
99 Hal Rhyne	20.00	10.00
100 Pete Ritchie	20.00	10.00
101 Charles Schorr	20.00	10.00
102 Jim Scott	20.00	10.00
103 Pat Shea	20.00	10.00
104 James Smith	20.00	10.00
105 George Stanton	20.00	10.00
106 Phillip Tanner	20.00	10.00
107 Gene Valla	20.00	10.00
108 Andy Vargas	20.00	10.00
109 Tom Dee Walsh	20.00	10.00
110 Paul Waner	250.00	125.00
111 Guy Williams	20.00	10.00
112 Archie Yelle	20.00	10.00
113 Earl Baldwin	20.00	10.00
114 Ted Baldwin	20.00	10.00
115 Cliff Brady	20.00	10.00
116 R.C. Eldred	20.00	10.00
117 Wade Killifer	20.00	10.00
118 Frank Osborne	20.00	10.00
119 Jim Welsh	20.00	10.00
120 Carl Williams	20.00	10.00
121 Andrew Bernard	20.00	10.00
122 Jim Blakesly	20.00	10.00
123 Leon Cadore	30.00	15.00
124 Chester Chadbourne	20.00	10.00
125 C.V. Christian	20.00	10.00
126 Charley Deal	20.00	10.00
127 Bill Essick	30.00	15.00
128 Charles Gorman	20.00	10.00
129 Wes Griffin	20.00	10.00
130 Harry Hannah	20.00	10.00
131 Frank Keck	20.00	10.00
132 Walt Kimmick	20.00	10.00
133 James McDowell	20.00	10.00
134 Mike Menosky	20.00	10.00
135 Dennis Murphy	20.00	10.00
136 Rod Murphy	20.00	10.00
137 Ken Penner	20.00	10.00
138 Pete Schneider	20.00	10.00
139 Alvy Sellers	20.00	10.00
140 Frank Shellenback	30.00	15.00
141 Oski Slade	20.00	10.00
142 Robert Vines	20.00	10.00
143 John Warner fielding	20.00	10.00
144 John Warner throwing	20.00	10.00

1925 Zeenuts

An early card of Hall of Famer Lloyd Waner is in this set. These cards measure approximately 1 3/4" by 3 7/16".

	Ex-Mt	VG
COMPLETE SET (162)	4000.00	2000.00
1 Clyde Beck	20.00	10.00
2 Otis Crandall	20.00	10.00
3 Russ Ennis	20.00	10.00
4 Ray Grimes	20.00	10.00
5 Wally Hood	20.00	10.00
6 Joe Horan	20.00	10.00
7 Ray Jacobs	20.00	10.00
8 Marty Krug	20.00	10.00
9 George Milstead	20.00	10.00
10 Elmer Phillips	20.00	10.00
11 Gus Sandberg	20.00	10.00
12 Ed Spencer	20.00	10.00
13 C.E. Twombly	20.00	10.00
14 Philip Weinert	20.00	10.00
15 Bill Whaley	20.00	10.00
16 Russ Arlett	40.00	20.00
17 Dale Baker	20.00	10.00
18 George Boehler	20.00	10.00
19 Joe Bratcher	20.00	10.00
20 Ray Brubaker	20.00	10.00
21 Ted Cather	20.00	10.00
22 Harold Chavez	20.00	10.00
23 Claude Cooper	20.00	10.00
24 Art Delaney	20.00	10.00
25 Mike Dempsey	20.00	10.00
26 Jake Flowers	30.00	15.00
27 Lon Guisto	20.00	10.00
28 Ivan Howard	20.00	10.00
29 Harry Krause	20.00	10.00
30 Earl Kunz	20.00	10.00
31 George Lafayette	20.00	10.00
32 William McCarren	20.00	10.00
33 Ron McDonald	20.00	10.00
34 George Makin	20.00	10.00
35 Urbane Pickering	20.00	10.00
36 Hub Pruett	20.00	10.00
37 Addison Read	20.00	10.00
38 Jim Reese	200.00	100.00
39 W.L. Crosby	20.00	10.00
40 Charles Deal	20.00	10.00
41 Charley High	20.00	10.00
42 Bill Hunnefield	20.00	10.00
43 Dave Keefe	20.00	10.00
44 Walt Leverenz	20.00	10.00
45 Duffy Lewis	40.00	20.00
46 Martin	20.00	10.00
47 Emmett McCann	20.00	10.00
48 George McGinnis	20.00	10.00
49 Fred Ortman	20.00	10.00
50 Ted Pillette	20.00	10.00
51 Reggie Rawlings	20.00	10.00
52 Harry Riconda	20.00	10.00
53 Ray Rohwer	20.00	10.00
54 Charles Rowland	20.00	10.00
55 Edward Sherling	20.00	10.00
56 Charles Thomas	20.00	10.00
57 Jess Winters	20.00	10.00
58 Arthur Woodring	20.00	10.00
59 Harry Brown	20.00	10.00
60 Carroll Canfield	20.00	10.00
61 Wallace Canfield	20.00	10.00
62 Charles Cockran	20.00	10.00
63 Wilbur Davis	20.00	10.00
64 E.M. Gorman	20.00	10.00
65 Clarence Hoffman	20.00	10.00
66 Vince Horton	20.00	10.00
67 William Hughes	20.00	10.00
68 W.J. James	20.00	10.00
69 Ray Keating	20.00	10.00
70 Art Koehler	20.00	10.00
71 Merlin Kopp	20.00	10.00
72 George McGinnis	20.00	10.00
73 Jim McLaughlin	20.00	10.00
74 Elwood Martin	20.00	10.00
75 Buddy Ryan	20.00	10.00
76 Bob Schang	20.00	10.00
77 Elmer Shea	20.00	10.00
78 Mervin Shea	30.00	15.00
79 Frank Shellenbach	30.00	15.00
80 Paddy Siglin	20.00	10.00
81 Harry Thompson	20.00	10.00
82 Lauri Vinci	20.00	10.00
83 Gene Wachenfeld	20.00	10.00
84 J.W. Watson	20.00	10.00
85 Chris Bahr	20.00	10.00
86 Joe Connolly	20.00	10.00
87 Les Cook	20.00	10.00
88 Fred Coumbe	20.00	10.00
89 John Frederick	20.00	10.00
90 Hensel Hulvey	20.00	10.00
91 Tony Lazzeri	200.00	100.00
92 Roy Leslie	20.00	10.00
93 Howard Lindemore	20.00	10.00
94 Rich McCabe	20.00	10.00
95 Mulcahy	20.00	10.00
96 Frank O'Doul	200.00	100.00
97 J.H. O'Neil	20.00	10.00
98 George Peery	20.00	10.00
99 Bill Piercey	20.00	10.00
100 Elmer Ponder	20.00	10.00
101 G.G. Steward	20.00	10.00
102 Oscar Vitt	30.00	15.00
103 James Aydelott	20.00	10.00
104 Sam Agnew	20.00	10.00
105 Frank Brower	20.00	10.00
106 J.W. Crockett	20.00	10.00
107 Bert Ellison	20.00	10.00
108 Bob Geary	20.00	10.00
109 Martin Griffin	20.00	10.00
110 Haughy	20.00	10.00
111 Tim Hendryx	20.00	10.00
112 Joe Kelly	20.00	10.00
113 Pete Kilduff	20.00	10.00
114 Oliver Mitchell	20.00	10.00
115 M.J. Moudy	20.00	10.00
116 Ed Mulligan	20.00	10.00
117 Norbi Paynter	20.00	10.00
118 Jeff Pfeffer	20.00	10.00
119 Hal Rhyne	20.00	10.00
120 Pete Ritchie	20.00	10.00
121 Vernon Stivers	20.00	10.00
122 Gus Suhr	30.00	15.00
123 Gene Valla	20.00	10.00
124 Paul Waner	200.00	100.00
125 Lloyd Waner	200.00	100.00
126 Guy Williams	20.00	10.00
127 Archie Yelle	20.00	10.00
128 Jim Bagby	40.00	20.00
129 Earl Baldwin	20.00	10.00
130 Cliff Brady	20.00	10.00
131 Ed Brandt	20.00	10.00
132 Frank Brazil	20.00	10.00
133 Sam Crane	20.00	10.00
134 George Cutshaw	20.00	10.00
135 Tom Daly	20.00	10.00
136 Nick Dumovich	20.00	10.00
137 R.C. Eldred	20.00	10.00
138 A.C. Elliott	20.00	10.00
139 Frank Emmer	20.00	10.00
140 Fred Fussell	20.00	10.00
141 Floyd Herman	200.00	100.00
142 Tom Daley	20.00	10.00
143 W.L. Plummer	20.00	10.00
144 Harvey Sutherland	20.00	10.00
145 Frank Tobin	20.00	10.00
146 James Yeargin	20.00	10.00
147 Clyde Barfoot	20.00	10.00
148 Beals Becker	20.00	10.00
149 Jim Blakesley	20.00	10.00
150 Ed Bryan	20.00	10.00
151 Carl Christain	20.00	10.00
152 Charles Eckert	20.00	10.00
153 William Essick	30.00	15.00
154 Neal Finn	20.00	10.00
155 Wes Griffin	20.00	10.00
156 Harry Hannah	20.00	10.00
157 Ed Hemingway	20.00	10.00
158 Willie Ludolph	20.00	10.00
159 Ken Penner	20.00	10.00
160 Gordon Slade	20.00	10.00
161 C.A. Thomas	20.00	10.00
162 Jack Warner	20.00	10.00
163 Rod Whitney	20.00	10.00
164 M.J. Wolfer	20.00	10.00

1926 Zeenuts

An early card of Hall of Famer Earl Averill is in this set. These cards measure approximately 1 3/4" by 3 7/16".

	Ex-Mt	VG
COMPLETE SET (172)	4000.00	2000.00
1 Joseph Connolly	20.00	10.00
2 Les Cook	20.00	10.00
3 Fred Coumbe	20.00	10.00
4 John Frederick	30.00	15.00
5 Malcolm Hillis	20.00	10.00
6 George Hollerson	20.00	10.00
7 Hensel Hulvey	20.00	10.00
8 John Kerr	20.00	10.00
9 Roy Leslie	20.00	10.00
10 Howard Lindemore	20.00	10.00
11 Walter McPhee	20.00	10.00
12 Phil Mulcahy	20.00	10.00
13 Frank O'Doul	200.00	100.00
14 Joseph O'Neill	20.00	10.00
15 John Peters	20.00	10.00
16 Augustus Redman	20.00	10.00
17 Leslie Sheehan	20.00	10.00
18 Frank Shellenbach	20.00	10.00
19 Ralph Stroud	20.00	10.00
20 Frank Zoellers	20.00	10.00
21 Frank Brazil	20.00	10.00
22 Charles Glazner	20.00	10.00
23 Earl Hamilton	20.00	10.00
24 Harry Hannah	20.00	10.00
25 Edson Hemingway	20.00	10.00
26 Lester Holmes	20.00	10.00
27 Wallace Hood	20.00	10.00
28 Ray Jacobs	20.00	10.00
29 Arthur Jahn	20.00	10.00
30 Martin Krug	20.00	10.00
31 John Mitchell	20.00	10.00
32 Gustave Sandberg	20.00	10.00
33 Herbert Sanders	20.00	10.00
34 George Staley	20.00	10.00

35 Arnold Statz 40.00 20.00
36 Arthur Weis 20.00 10.00
37 Wayne Wright 20.00 10.00
38 Byron Yarrison 20.00 10.00
39 Eugene Allen 20.00 10.00
40 Isaac Boone 40.00 20.00
41 Edwin Bryan 20.00 10.00
42 Clayton Carson 20.00 10.00
43 Carl Christian 20.00 10.00
44 Albert Cole 20.00 10.00
45 Ike Danning 20.00 10.00
46 Charles Eckert 20.00 10.00
47 Cornelius Finn 20.00 10.00
48 Bob Gillespie 20.00 10.00
49 Wes Griffin 20.00 10.00
50 Ducky Jones 20.00 10.00
51 William Ludolph 20.00 10.00
52 Walter McCredie MG 20.00 10.00
53 James McDowell 20.00 10.00
54 Denny Murphy 20.00 10.00
55 Joseph Oeschger 30.00 15.00
56 Thomas Oliver 30.00 15.00
57 Herman Pillette 20.00 10.00
58 William Rodda 20.00 10.00
59 Paddy Siglin 20.00 10.00
60 Gordon Slade 20.00 10.00
61 Evan Swanson 30.00 15.00
62 C.B. Thompson 20.00 10.00
63 Al Walters 20.00 10.00
64 Robert Whitney 20.00 10.00
65 Del Baker 30.00 15.00
66 Albert Bool 20.00 10.00
67 Ray Brubaker 20.00 10.00
68 Peter Daglia 20.00 10.00
69 Arthur Delaney 20.00 10.00
70 John Fenton 20.00 10.00
71 Jesse Fowler 20.00 10.00
72 Alex Freeman 20.00 10.00
73 Albert Gould 20.00 10.00
74 Antone Governor 20.00 10.00
75 Louis Guisto 20.00 10.00
76 Rex Hickok 20.00 10.00
77 Ivan Howard 20.00 10.00
78 Harry Krause 20.00 10.00
79 Earl Kunz 20.00 10.00
80 Lynford Lary 30.00 15.00
81 Frank McKenry 20.00 10.00
82 Earl McNally 20.00 10.00
83 George Makin 20.00 10.00
84 Lawrence Miller 20.00 10.00
85 Hubert Pruett 30.00 15.00
86 Addison Read 20.00 10.00
87 Jim Reese 200.00 100.00
88 John Stuart 20.00 10.00
89 William Bagwell 20.00 10.00
90 Charles Berry 20.00 10.00
91 Dennis Burns 20.00 10.00
92 John Couch 20.00 10.00
93 Eugene Elsh 20.00 10.00
94 Ernie Johnson 20.00 10.00
95 George Lafayette 20.00 10.00
96 Leo Mangum 20.00 10.00
97 Charles Meeker 20.00 10.00
98 Leonard Metz 20.00 10.00
99 Frederick Ortman 20.00 10.00
100 James Prothro 20.00 10.00
101 Max Rachac 20.00 10.00
102 Ray Rohwer 20.00 10.00
103 Elmer Smith 20.00 10.00
104 Marvin Smith 20.00 10.00
105 Charles Thomas 20.00 10.00
106 Frank Tobin 20.00 10.00
107 Daniel Alley 20.00 10.00
108 Carroll Canfield 20.00 10.00
109 William Canfield 20.00 10.00
110 Bill Cunningham 30.00 15.00
111 Wilbur Davis 20.00 10.00
112 Ray French 20.00 10.00
113 Dutch Hoffman 20.00 10.00
114 William Hughes 20.00 10.00
115 Rudolph Kallio 20.00 10.00
116 Raymond Keating 20.00 10.00
117 J.W. Knight 20.00 10.00
118 Arthur Koehler 20.00 10.00
119 Merlin Kopp 20.00 10.00
120 J.R. McLoughlin 20.00 10.00
121 Elwood Martin 20.00 10.00
122 John Monroe 20.00 10.00
123 Frank Osborn 20.00 10.00
124 Fred Pfahler 20.00 10.00
125 John Ryan 20.00 10.00
126 Elmer Shea 20.00 10.00
127 Mervin Shea 30.00 15.00
128 Bill Sweeney 20.00 10.00
129 Louri Vinci 20.00 10.00
130 Sam Agnew 20.00 10.00
131 Earl Averill 250.00 125.00
132 Francis Brower 20.00 10.00
133 James Crockett 20.00 10.00
134 Herbert Ellison 20.00 10.00
135 Raymond Flashkamper 20.00 10.00
136 Robert Geary 20.00 10.00
137 Martin Griffin 20.00 10.00
138 Sydney Hansen 20.00 10.00
139 Timothy Hendryx 20.00 10.00
140 Robert Hurst 20.00 10.00
141 James Jolly 20.00 10.00
142 Dick Kerr 40.00 20.00
143 Peter Kilduff 20.00 10.00
144 Bert Lang 20.00 10.00
145 Oliver Mitchell 20.00 10.00
146 Marvin Moudy 20.00 10.00
147 Edward Mulligan 20.00 10.00
148 Norbert Paynter 20.00 10.00
149 Edwin Rathjen 20.00 10.00
150 August Suhr 30.00 15.00
151 John Tadevich 20.00 10.00
152 Eugene Valla 20.00 10.00
153 Andrew Vargas 20.00 10.00
154 Lloyd Waner 200.00 100.00
155 Guy Williams 20.00 10.00
156 Archie Yelle 20.00 10.00
157 John Zaeffel 20.00 10.00
158 Ted Baldwin 20.00 10.00
159 Clifford Boyd 20.00 10.00
160 Cliff Brady 20.00 10.00
161 George Cutshaw 25.00 12.50
162 Ross Eldred 20.00 10.00
163 Jim Elliott 20.00 10.00
164 Floyd Ellsworth 20.00 10.00
165 Bob Hasty 20.00 10.00
166 Fuzzy Hufft 20.00 10.00
167 Joseph Jenkins 20.00 10.00
168 Wade Killifer 20.00 10.00
169 William Lane 20.00 10.00
170 William Plummer 20.00 10.00
171 C.A. Ramsey 20.00 10.00
172 Jack Sherlock 20.00 10.00

1927 Zeenuts

These cards measure approximately 1 3/4" by 3 3/8".

Ex-Mt VG
COMPLETE SET (144) 3500.00 1800.00
1 Les Cook 20.00 10.00
2 John Frederick 25.00 12.50
3 Curtis Fullerton 20.00 10.00
4 Charles Gooch 20.00 10.00
5 Rich McCabe 20.00 10.00
6 D.J. Murphy 20.00 10.00
7 Les Sheehan 20.00 10.00
8 James Tierney 20.00 10.00
9 Oscar Vitt 30.00 15.00
10 Dick Cox 20.00 10.00
11 Bruce Cunningham 20.00 10.00
12 Harry Hannah 20.00 10.00
13 Ed Hemingway 20.00 10.00
14 Wally Hood 20.00 10.00
15 Art Jahn 20.00 10.00
16 Martin Krug 20.00 10.00
17 Gustave Sandberg 20.00 10.00
18 Herbert Sanders 20.00 10.00
19 Arthur Weis 20.00 10.00
20 Wayne Wright 20.00 10.00
21 Eddie Bryan 20.00 10.00
22 Carl Christian 20.00 10.00
23 Nick Dumovitch 20.00 10.00
24 Charles Eckert 20.00 10.00
25 Cornelius Finn 20.00 10.00
26 Bob Gillespie 20.00 10.00
27 Harry Hooper 200.00 100.00
28 Ducky Jones 20.00 10.00
29 William Leard 20.00 10.00
30 Willie Ludolph 20.00 10.00
31 Osborne McDaniel 20.00 10.00
32 Tom Oliver 30.00 15.00
33 S.R. Parker 20.00 10.00
bat
34 S.R. Parker 20.00 10.00
throw
35 Herman Pillette 30.00 15.00
36 William Rodda 20.00 10.00
37 Edward Rose 20.00 10.00
38 Gordon Slade 20.00 10.00
39 Evan Swanson 30.00 15.00
40 Phil Weinert 20.00 10.00
41 Rodney Whitney 20.00 10.00
42 Russ Arlett 40.00 20.00
43 Delmer Baker 20.00 10.00
44 George Boehler 20.00 10.00
45 Albert Bool 20.00 10.00
46 Joseph Bratcher 20.00 10.00
47 Ray Brubaker 20.00 10.00
48 James Caveney 20.00 10.00
49 Wilbur Cooper 30.00 15.00
50 Pete Daglia 20.00 10.00
51 Leo Dickerman 20.00 10.00
52 John Fenton 20.00 10.00
53 Albert Gould 20.00 10.00
54 Antone Governor 20.00 10.00
55 Louis Guisto 20.00 10.00
56 Robert Hasty 20.00 10.00
57 Harry Krause 20.00 10.00
58 Lynford Lary 30.00 15.00
59 George Makin 20.00 10.00
60 Addison Read 20.00 10.00
61 Jim Reese 200.00 100.00
62A Shinners '27 20.00 10.00
62B Shinners 1927 20.00 10.00
63 Herman Sparks 20.00 10.00
64 Eugene Valla 20.00 10.00
65 William Bagwell 20.00 10.00
66 Stanwood Baumgartner 20.00 10.00
67 Bill Cissell 30.00 15.00
68 Bill Fischer 20.00 10.00
69 William Hughes 20.00 10.00
70 Ernie Johnson 20.00 10.00
71 Walter Kinney 20.00 10.00
72 Ray Lingrel 20.00 10.00
73 Al McCurdy 20.00 10.00
74 Leonard Metz 20.00 10.00
75 Parry O'Brien 20.00 10.00
76 Arthur Parker 20.00 10.00
77 Charles Ponder 20.00 10.00
78 James Prothro 25.00 12.50
79 Elmer Smith 20.00 10.00
80 Joe Storti 20.00 10.00
81 Lindo Storti 20.00 10.00
82 Paul Strand 20.00 10.00
83 Louis Wendell 20.00 10.00
84 Archie Yelle 20.00 10.00
85 Leonard Backer 20.00 10.00
86 Roy Brown 20.00 10.00
87 Claude Cooper 20.00 10.00
88 Ray French 20.00 10.00
89 Clarence Hoffman 20.00 10.00
90 Rudolph Kallio 20.00 10.00
91 Raymond Keating 20.00 10.00
92 David Keefe 20.00 10.00
93 J.W. Knight 20.00 10.00
94 Arthur Koehler 20.00 10.00
95 Merlin Kopp 20.00 10.00
96 Francis McGee 20.00 10.00
97 James McLaughlin 20.00 10.00
98 John Monroe 20.00 10.00
99 Frank Osborn 20.00 10.00
100 Max Rachac 20.00 10.00
101 Ray Rohwer 20.00 10.00
102 John Ryan MG 20.00 10.00
103 Henry Severeid 20.00 10.00
104 Elmer Shea 20.00 10.00
105 John Singleton 20.00 10.00
106 Peter Sunseri 20.00 10.00
107 Sam Agnew 20.00 10.00
108 Earl Averill 200.00 100.00
109 Loris Baker 20.00 10.00
110 Herbert Ellison 20.00 10.00
111 Robert Geary 20.00 10.00
112 Roy Johnson 20.00 10.00
113 James Jolly 20.00 10.00
114 Earl Kunz 20.00 10.00
115 Orville McMurtry 20.00 10.00
116 John Mails 20.00 10.00
117 Herb May 20.00 10.00
118 Oliver Mitchell 20.00 10.00
119 Marvin Moudy 20.00 10.00
120 Edward Mulligan 20.00 10.00
121 Frank O'Doul 200.00 100.00
122 John Sheehan 20.00 10.00
123 Al Stokes 20.00 10.00
124 August Suhr 30.00 15.00
125 Andrew Vargas 20.00 10.00
126 Nick Williams 20.00 10.00
127 Guy Williams 20.00 10.00
128 Burquist Woodson 20.00 10.00
129 Pellham Ballenger 20.00 10.00
130 Carson Bigbee 25.00 12.50
131 Charles Borreani 20.00 10.00
132 Clifford Brady 20.00 10.00
133 Herbert Brett 20.00 10.00
134 Martin Callaghan 20.00 10.00
135 Ross Eldred 20.00 10.00
136 James Hudgens 20.00 10.00
137 Irvin Hufft 20.00 10.00
138 Wade Killifer 20.00 10.00
139 Walter Kimmick 20.00 10.00
140 Sid Martin 20.00 10.00
141 John Miljus 30.00 15.00
142 Wilber Peters 20.00 10.00
143 C.A. Ramsey 20.00 10.00
144 Jack Sherlock 20.00 10.00

1928 Exhibits PCL

Exhibit card collectors speculate that this 32-card set, produced in 1928, was distributed regionally, in California only, in conjunction with the Exhibit Company's regular series of major league players. The cards are blue in color (as are the major league cards) and contain pictures of ball players from the six California teams of the PCL. There are no cards known for Portland and Seattle (and given that 32 cards is the exact length of a one-half sheet printing, none can be expected to appear. The cards have plain backs and carry a divided legend (two lines on each side) on the front. Several names are misspelled, several more are wrongly assigned ("Carl" instead of "Walter" Berger), and the Hollywood team name should read "Sheiks". Several of the cards are oriented horizontally (HOR). Each card measures 3 3/8" by 5 3/8". The catalog designation for this set is W465.

Ex-Mt VG
COMPLETE SET (32) 5000.00 2500.00
1 Buzz Arlett 200.00 100.00
2 Earl Averill 300.00 150.00
3 Carl Berger 200.00 100.00
Walter, sic
4 Ping Bodie 200.00 100.00
5 Carl Dittmar HOR 150.00 75.00
6 Jack Penton 150.00 75.00
7 Neal "Mickey" Finn 200.00 100.00
Cornelius, sic
8 Tony Governor 150.00 75.00
9 Truck Hannah HOR 200.00 100.00
10 Mickey Heath HOR 150.00 75.00
11 Wally Hood 150.00 75.00
12 Fuzzy Hufft 150.00 75.00
13 Snead Jolly (Smead 200.00 100.00
Jolley, sic)
14 Ducky Jones 150.00 75.00
15 Rudy Kallio 150.00 75.00
16 Johnny Kerr HOR 150.00 75.00
17 Harry Krause 150.00 75.00
18 Lynford H. Larry 200.00 100.00
(sic, Lary)
19 Dudley Lee 150.00 75.00
20 Walter "Duster" Mails 200.00 100.00
21 Jimmy Reese 250.00 125.00
22 Dusty Rhodes 150.00 75.00
23 Hal Rhyne 150.00 75.00
24 Hank Severied 150.00 75.00
Severeid, sic
25 Earl Sheely 200.00 100.00
26 Frank Shellenback 200.00 100.00
27 Gordon Slade 150.00 75.00
28 Hollis Thurston 200.00 100.00
29 Babe Twombly 150.00 75.00
30 Earl "Tex" Weathersby 150.00 75.00
31 Ray French 150.00 75.00
32 Ray Keating 150.00 75.00

1928-32 La Presse

These color retouched photos of Canadian ballplayers of the late '20s and early '30s were published in La Presse, a French-language newspaper of Montreal. The pictures measure approximately 10" by 16"; the player's name, followed by career highlights, appear within a rectangle below. The drawings are unnumbered and checklisted below in chronological order of publication.

Ex-Mt VG
COMPLETE SET (28) 650.00 325.00
1 Bob Shawkey 50.00 25.00
June 2, 1928
2 Lachine Club 25.00 12.50
June 9, 1928
3 Buckalew 25.00 12.50
Dunagan
Smith
Radwan
Fowler
Gulley
June 16, 1928
4 Seymour Bailey 25.00 12.50
June 23, 1928
5 Wilson Fewster 25.00 12.50
June 30, 1928
6 Tom Daly 25.00 12.50
July 14, 1928
7 Red Holt 25.00 12.50
August 11, 1928
8 Johnny Prud'homme 25.00 12.50
November 3, 1928
9 Walter Gautreau 25.00 12.50
April 13, 1929
10 Herb Thormahlen 25.00 12.50
April 27, 1929
11 Elon Hogsett 30.00 15.00
July 13, 1929
12 Del Bissonette 30.00 15.00
June 28, 1930
13 Smith 25.00 12.50
Thormalen
Griffin
Pomorski
May 31, 1930
14 Head 25.00 12.50
Jimmy Ripple
Conley
Celeran
June 7, 1930
15 Joe Hauser 50.00 25.00
July 12, 1930
16 Gowell Classet 25.00 12.50
September 13, 1930
17 Jimmy Ripple 25.00 12.50
July 4, 1930
18 Sol Mishkin 25.00 12.50
July 18, 1930
19 Walter Brown 25.00 12.50
August 15, 1931
20 Johnny Grabowski 25.00 12.50
May 28, 1932
21 John Clancy 25.00 12.50
June 25, 1932
22 Buck Walters 50.00 25.00
July 2, 1932
23 Bill McAfee 25.00 12.50
July 9, 1932
24 George Puccinelli 25.00 12.50
July 16, 1932
25 Buck Crouse 25.00 12.50
August 6, 1932
26 Olie Carnegie 25.00 12.50
August 13, 1932
27 Leo Mangum 25.00 12.50
August 20, 1932
28 Roy Parmalee 30.00 15.00
October 19, 1932

1928 Zeenuts

An early card of Ernie Lombardi is in this set. These cards measure approximately 1 3/4" by 3 3/8".

Ex-Mt VG
COMPLETE SET (168) 4000.00 2000.00
1 Samuel Agnew 20.00 10.00
2 John Bassler 30.00 15.00
3 Les Cook 20.00 10.00
4 Leo Fitterer 20.00 10.00
5 Curtis Fullerton 20.00 10.00
6 Charles Gooch 20.00 10.00
7 Mickey Heath 20.00 10.00
8 James Hulvey 20.00 10.00
9 Arthur Jacobs 20.00 10.00
10 John Kerr 20.00 10.00
11 Walter Kinney 20.00 10.00
12 Dudley Lee 20.00 10.00
13 Rich McCabe 20.00 10.00
14 Pat McNulty 20.00 10.00
15 Philip Mulcahy 20.00 10.00
16 Bill Murphy 20.00 10.00
17 Gordon Rhodes 20.00 10.00
18 Bob Roth 20.00 10.00
19 Frank Shellenback 30.00 15.00
20 James Sweeney 20.00 10.00
21 Clarence Twombly 20.00 10.00
22 Oscar Vitt MG 30.00 15.00
23 Julian Wera 20.00 10.00
24 Clyde Barfoot 20.00 10.00
25 Wally Berger 40.00 20.00
26 Carson Bigbee 25.00 12.50
27 Howard Burkett 20.00 10.00
28 Bruce Cunningham 20.00 10.00
29 Carl Dittmar 20.00 10.00
30 Glen Gabler 20.00 10.00
31 James Hannah 20.00 10.00
32 Wally Hood 20.00 10.00
33 Ducky Jones (bat) 20.00 10.00
34 Ducky Jones (throw) 20.00 10.00
35 Martin Krug MG 20.00 10.00
36 Bob Osborne 20.00 10.00
37 Wilbert Peters 20.00 10.00
38 Norman Plitt 20.00 10.00
39 Gustave Sandberg 20.00 10.00
40 Edward Schulmerich 20.00 10.00
41 Alfred Smith 20.00 10.00
42 George Staley 20.00 10.00
43 Earl Weathersby 20.00 10.00
44 Earl Baldwin 20.00 10.00
45 William Brenzel 20.00 10.00
46 Ed Bryan 20.00 10.00
47 Paul Downs 20.00 10.00
48 Charles Eckert 20.00 10.00
49 Cornelius Finn 30.00 15.00
50 Eugene Gomes 20.00 10.00
51 Carl Holling 20.00 10.00
52 William Hughes 20.00 10.00
53 Wade Killifer 20.00 10.00
54 Osborne McDaniel 20.00 10.00
55 Louis Martin 20.00 10.00
56 Merton Nelson 20.00 10.00
57 Herman Pillette 30.00 15.00
58 Bill Rodda 20.00 10.00
59 Edward Rose 20.00 10.00
60 Gordon Slade 20.00 10.00
61 Ernest Swanson 30.00 15.00
62 Arthur Weiss 20.00 10.00
63 Rodney Whitney 20.00 10.00
64 Del Baker 30.00 15.00
65 George Boehler 20.00 10.00
66 Albert Bool 20.00 10.00
67 Joseph Bratcher 20.00 10.00
68 Ray Brubaker 20.00 10.00
69 James Caveney 20.00 10.00
70 Wilburn Cooper 30.00 15.00
71 Howard Craghead 20.00 10.00
72 Peter Daglia 20.00 10.00
73 Monroe Dean 20.00 10.00
74 Cecil Duff 20.00 10.00
75 John Fenton 20.00 10.00
76 Foy Frazier 20.00 10.00
77 Al Gould 20.00 10.00
78 Antone Governor 20.00 10.00
79 Louis Guisto 20.00 10.00
80 Robert Hasty 20.00 10.00
81 Ivan Howard MG 20.00 10.00
82 Harry Krause 20.00 10.00
83 Lynford Lary 30.00 15.00
84 Ernie Lombardi 250.00 125.00
85 Emil Muesel 30.00 15.00
86 Addison Read 20.00 10.00
87 Jim Reese 200.00 100.00
88 Carson Bigbee 20.00 10.00
89 Isaac Boone 40.00 20.00
90 Ike Davis 20.00 10.00
91 Larry French 40.00 20.00
92 Ernie Johnson MG 20.00 10.00
93 James Keesey 20.00 10.00
94 W. E. Knothe 20.00 10.00
95 DeWitt LeBourveau 20.00 10.00
96 Joe Mellana 20.00 10.00
97 Charles Ponder 20.00 10.00
98 Tony Rego 30.00 15.00
99 Francis Sigafoos 20.00 10.00
100 John Warhop 20.00 10.00
101 Charles Wetzel 20.00 10.00
102 Carroll Yerkes 20.00 10.00
103 Leonard Backer 20.00 10.00
104 Wallace Canfield 20.00 10.00
105 Tom Flynn 20.00 10.00
106 Ray French 20.00 10.00
107 Andrew Harris 20.00 10.00
108 Dutch Hoffman 20.00 10.00
109 Rudolph Kallio 20.00 10.00
110 Ray Keating 20.00 10.00
111 David Keefe 20.00 10.00
112 Arthur Koehler 20.00 10.00
113 Merlin Kopp 20.00 10.00
114 Jim McLaughlin 20.00 10.00
115 John Monroe 20.00 10.00
116 Frank Osborn 20.00 10.00
117 Max Rachac 20.00 10.00
118 Ray Rohwer 20.00 10.00
119 John Ryan MG 20.00 10.00
120 Henry Severeid 20.00 10.00
121 Elmer Shea 20.00 10.00
122 Earl Sheely 20.00 10.00
123 John Singleton 20.00 10.00
124 Louri Vinci 20.00 10.00
125 Earl Averill 200.00 100.00
126 Frank Bodie 40.00 20.00
127 Adolph Camilli 40.00 20.00
128 Sid Cohen 20.00 10.00
129 Frank Crosetti 40.00 20.00
130 Jerry Donovan 20.00 10.00
131 Sydney Hansen 20.00 10.00
132 Roy Johnson 20.00 10.00
133 Smead Jolley 40.00 20.00
134 Francis McCrea 20.00 10.00
135 John Mails 20.00 10.00
136 William May 20.00 10.00
137 Solly Mishkin 20.00 10.00
138 Oliver Mitchell 20.00 10.00
139 Marvin Moudy 20.00 10.00
140 Edward Mulligan 20.00 10.00
141 Ralph Pinelli 40.00 20.00
142 Robert Reed 20.00 10.00
143 Hal Rhyne 20.00 10.00
144 Joe Sprinz 20.00 10.00
145 August Suhr 30.00 15.00
146 Andy Vargas 20.00 10.00
147 Frank Welch 20.00 10.00
148 Nick Williams MG 20.00 10.00
149 Charles Borreani 20.00 10.00
150 Ross Eldred 20.00 10.00
151 Fred Ellsworth 20.00 10.00
152 Kyle Graham 20.00 10.00
153 Kyle Graham 20.00 10.00
154 Andy House 20.00 10.00
155 James Hudgens 20.00 10.00
156 Irving Hufft 20.00 10.00
157 E. R. Knight 20.00 10.00
158 Elwood Martin 20.00 10.00
159 Jim Middleton 20.00 10.00
160 Fred Muller 20.00 10.00
161 Clyde Nance 20.00 10.00
162 Roy Parker 20.00 10.00
163 William Ruble 20.00 10.00
164 Jack Sherlock 20.00 10.00
165 Peter Sunseri 20.00 10.00
166 Arthur Teachout 20.00 10.00
167 Gomer Wilson 20.00 10.00
168 Merle Wolfer 20.00 10.00

1929 Zeenuts

Early cards of Ernie Nevers (Football Hall of Famer) and Lefty Gomez are in this set. These cards measure approximately 1 3/4" by 3 1/2".

	Ex-Mt	VG
COMPLETE SET (168)	4000.00	2000.00
1 William Albert	20.00	10.00
2 John Bassler	30.00	15.00
3 Cleo Carlyle	20.00	10.00
4 Minor Heath	20.00	10.00
5 Martin Krug MG	20.00	10.00
6 Dudley Lee	20.00	10.00
7 Rich McCabe	20.00	10.00
8 Mike Maloney	20.00	10.00
9 Leo Ostenberg	20.00	10.00
10 Wallace Ritter	20.00	10.00
11 Russ Rollings	20.00	10.00
12 William Rumler	20.00	10.00
13 Clyde Barfoot	20.00	10.00
14 Wally Berger	40.00	20.00
15 Howard Burkett	20.00	10.00
16 John Butler	20.00	10.00
17 Harry Childs	20.00	10.00
18 Carl Dittmar	20.00	10.00
19 Glen Gabler	20.00	10.00
20 James Hannah MG	20.00	10.00
21 Carl Holling	20.00	10.00
22 Ray Jacobs	20.00	10.00
23 Ducky Jones	20.00	10.00
24 Martin Krug MG	20.00	10.00
25 Russ Miller	20.00	10.00
26 W.A. Peters	20.00	10.00
27 Norman Plitt	20.00	10.00
28 Vaughn Roberts	20.00	10.00
29 Gustave Sandberg	20.00	10.00
30 Edward Schulmerich	20.00	10.00
31 Arnold Statz	40.00	20.00
32 Martin Tierney	20.00	10.00
33 Charles Tolson	20.00	10.00
34 August Walsh	20.00	10.00
35 Dallas Warren	20.00	10.00
36 Earl Webb	30.00	15.00
37 Earl Baldwin	20.00	10.00
38 Ike Boone	40.00	20.00
39 William Brenzel	20.00	10.00
40 Walter Christensen	20.00	10.00
41 Bert Cole	20.00	10.00
42 Neal Finn	20.00	10.00
43 Fred Hoffman	20.00	10.00
44 W. W. Hubbell	20.00	10.00
45 Irving Hufft	20.00	10.00
46 John Keane	20.00	10.00
47 Wade Killifer MG	20.00	10.00
48 John Knott	20.00	10.00
49 Harry Krause	20.00	10.00
50 Herbert McQuaid	20.00	10.00
51 Ed Mulligan	20.00	10.00
52 Clyde Nance	20.00	10.00
53 M. A. Nelson	20.00	10.00
54 Ernie Nevers	300.00	150.00
55 Herman Pillette	30.00	15.00
56 William Rodda	20.00	10.00
57 Pete Scott	20.00	10.00
58 Jack Sherlock	20.00	10.00
59 Gordon Slade	20.00	10.00
60 Leroy Anton	20.00	10.00
61 George Boehler	20.00	10.00
62 Mandy Brooks	20.00	10.00
63 Ray Brubaker	20.00	10.00
64 Joe Burns	20.00	10.00
65 Roy Carlyle	20.00	10.00
66 Howard Craghead	20.00	10.00
67 Peter Daglia	20.00	10.00
68 Monroe Dean	20.00	10.00
69 Martin Dumovich	20.00	10.00
70 John Fenton	20.00	10.00
71 Foy Frazier	20.00	10.00
72 Antone Governor	20.00	10.00
73 Ivan Howard MG	20.00	10.00
74 Bob Hurst	20.00	10.00
75 Charles Jeffcoat	20.00	10.00
76 Charles Kasich	20.00	10.00
77 Ernie Lombardi	200.00	100.00
78 Lou McEvoy	20.00	10.00
79 Gus McIsaacs	20.00	10.00
80 Addison Read	20.00	10.00
81 James Reese	200.00	100.00
82 John Vergez	20.00	10.00
83 Charles Bates	20.00	10.00
84 Leslie Bush	20.00	10.00
85 Joseph Cascarella	20.00	10.00
86 Guy Cooper	20.00	10.00
87 Jim Cronin	20.00	10.00
88 Ernest Hepting	20.00	10.00
89 Malcolm Hillis	20.00	10.00
90 Arthur Jahn	20.00	10.00
91 James Keesey	20.00	10.00
92 Jack Knight	20.00	10.00
93 W. E. Knothe	20.00	10.00
94 Leroy Mahaffey	30.00	15.00
95 Frederick Ortman	20.00	10.00
96 Tony Rego	40.00	20.00
97 Bill Rodgers MG	20.00	10.00
98 Robert Shanklin	20.00	10.00
99 Gale Staley	20.00	10.00
100 Edwin Tomlin	20.00	10.00
101 Raymond Volkman	20.00	10.00
102 George Weustling	20.00	10.00
103 Leonard Backer	20.00	10.00
104 Ed Bryan	20.00	10.00
105 William Burke	20.00	10.00
106 Adolph Camilli	40.00	20.00
107 J. O. Crandall	20.00	10.00
108 Tom Flynn	20.00	10.00
109 Antonio Freitas	25.00	12.50
110 Ray French	20.00	10.00
111 Albert Gould	20.00	10.00
112 Andrew Harris	20.00	10.00
113 Raymond Keating	20.00	10.00
114 Art Koehler	20.00	10.00
115 Anthony Krasovich	20.00	10.00
116 Earl Kunz	20.00	10.00
117 John Monroe	20.00	10.00
118 Frank Osborne	20.00	10.00
119 Max Rachac	20.00	10.00
120 Ray Rohwer	20.00	10.00
121 John Ryan	20.00	10.00
122 Henry Severeid	20.00	10.00
123 Louri Vinci	20.00	10.00
124 Loris Baker	20.00	10.00
125 James Caveney	20.00	10.00
126 John Couch	20.00	10.00
127 Frank Crosetti	40.00	20.00
128 Curt Davis	30.00	15.00
129 Jerry Donovan	20.00	10.00
130 Val Glynn	20.00	10.00
131 Lefty Gomez	250.00	125.00
132 Harvey Hand	20.00	10.00
133 Elmer Jacobs	20.00	10.00
134 Smead Jolley	25.00	12.50
135 Gordon Jones	20.00	10.00
136 Elton Langford	20.00	10.00
137 John Mails	20.00	10.00
138 Henry Oana	150.00	75.00
139 Ralph Pinelli	40.00	20.00
140 Fred Polvogt	20.00	10.00
141 Bob Reed	20.00	10.00
142 Stanley Schino	20.00	10.00
143 Walton Schmidt	20.00	10.00
144 August Suhr	30.00	15.00
145 Hollis Thurston	30.00	15.00
146 Nick Williams MG	20.00	10.00
147 Ab Wingo	20.00	10.00
148 Luis Almada	20.00	10.00
149 Andy Anderson	20.00	10.00
150 Dave Barbee	20.00	10.00
151 Charles Borreani	20.00	10.00
152 Earl Collard	20.00	10.00
153 Frank Cox	20.00	10.00
154 Oscar Eckhardt	40.00	20.00
155 Floyd Ellsworth	20.00	10.00
156 Elbert Fisch	20.00	10.00
157 Kyle Graham	20.00	10.00
158 Kyle Heatherly	20.00	10.00
159 Wally Hood	20.00	10.00
160 Andy Hood	20.00	10.00
161 Ernie Johnson MG	20.00	10.00
162 Rudolph Kallio	20.00	10.00
163 Osborne McDaniel	20.00	10.00
164 Fred Muller	20.00	10.00
165 Walter Olney	20.00	10.00
166 Fred Pipgras	20.00	10.00
167 William Steinecke	20.00	10.00
168 Harry Taylor	20.00	10.00

1930 Zeenuts

These cards measure approximately 1 13/16" by 3 1/2". Most of these cards have an expiration date of April 1, 1931; however, some have no expiration date featured on the coupons.

	Ex-Mt	VG
COMPLETE SET (186)	4000.00	2000.00
1 John Bassler	30.00	15.00
2 Otis Brannon	20.00	10.00
3 Howard Burkett	20.00	10.00
4 Cleo Carlyle	20.00	10.00
5 Michael Gazella	30.00	15.00
6 Ernest Kelly	20.00	10.00
7 Minor Heath	20.00	10.00
8 George Hollerson	20.00	10.00
9 Augustus Johns	20.00	10.00
10 Dudley Lee	20.00	10.00
11 Edwin Leishman	20.00	10.00
12 Mike Maloney	20.00	10.00
13 Vance Page	20.00	10.00
14 Walter Rehg	20.00	10.00
15 William Rumler	20.00	10.00
16 Henry Severeid	20.00	10.00
17 Jim Turner	40.00	20.00
18 Oscar Vitt MG	30.00	15.00
19 Frank Wetzel	20.00	10.00
20 Charles Wetzell	20.00	10.00
21 Edward Baecht	20.00	10.00
22 Noble Ballou	20.00	10.00
23 Clyde Barfoot	20.00	10.00
24 John Butler	20.00	10.00
25 Harry Childs	20.00	10.00
26 Carl Dittmar	20.00	10.00
27 Glen Gabler	20.00	10.00
28 Fred Haney	30.00	15.00
29 Roy Hannah	20.00	10.00
30 George Harper	20.00	10.00
31 Carl Holling	20.00	10.00
32 Berlyn Horn	20.00	10.00
33 Ray Jacobs	20.00	10.00
34 John Lelivelt	20.00	10.00
35 Johnny Moore	20.00	10.00
36 Art Parker	20.00	10.00
37 Wilbert Peters	20.00	10.00
38 Vaughn Roberts	20.00	10.00
39 Francis Sigafoos	20.00	10.00
40 Arnold Statz	40.00	20.00
41 August Walsh	20.00	10.00
42 Dallas Warren	20.00	10.00
43 Earl Webb	20.00	10.00
44 Earl Baldwin	20.00	10.00
45 Ike Boone	30.00	15.00
46 William Brenzel	20.00	10.00
47 George Burns	30.00	15.00
48 George Caster	20.00	10.00
49 Walter Christensen	20.00	10.00
50 Edwin Church	20.00	10.00
51 Bert Cole	20.00	10.00
52 Joe Coscarart	20.00	10.00
53 Ken Douglas	20.00	10.00
54 Fred Hoffman	20.00	10.00
55 Irving Hufft	20.00	10.00
56 Ernest Kelly	20.00	10.00
57 Wade Killifer MG	20.00	10.00
58 Charles Lieber	20.00	10.00
59 Herb McQuaide	20.00	10.00
60 John Monroe	20.00	10.00
61 Ed Mulligan	20.00	10.00
62 Merton Nelson	20.00	10.00
63 Ernie Nevers	250.00	125.00
64 Herman Pillette	20.00	10.00
65 Edward Pillette	20.00	10.00
66 William Rodda	20.00	10.00
67 Harry Rosenberg	40.00	20.00
68 Robert Shanklin	20.00	10.00
69 Charles Wallgren	20.00	10.00
70 Paul Andrews	20.00	10.00
71 Leroy Anton	20.00	10.00
72 Russ Arlett	40.00	20.00
73 Ray Brubaker	20.00	10.00
74 Harold Chamberlain	20.00	10.00
75 Howard Craghead	20.00	10.00
76 Pete Daglia	20.00	10.00
77 Monroe Dean	20.00	10.00
78 Bernard DeViveiros	20.00	10.00
79 Martin Dumovich	20.00	10.00
80 Jim Edwards	20.00	10.00
81 Antone Governor	20.00	10.00
82 Francis Griffin	20.00	10.00
83 Bob Hurst	20.00	10.00
84 Jack Jacobs	20.00	10.00
85 Charles Jeffcoat	20.00	10.00
86 Roy Joiner	20.00	10.00
87 Charles Kasich	20.00	10.00
88 Ernie Lombardi	200.00	100.00
89 Louis Martin	20.00	10.00
90 Joe Mellana	20.00	10.00
91 Monte Pearson	30.00	15.00
92 Walter Porter	20.00	10.00
93 Addison Read	20.00	10.00
94 Peter Ricci	20.00	10.00
95 Stanley Schino	20.00	10.00
96 Robert Stevenson	20.00	10.00
97 Bernard Uhalt	20.00	10.00
98 John Vergez	20.00	10.00
99 Carl Zamlach MG	20.00	10.00
100 Charles Bates	20.00	10.00
101 John Beck	20.00	10.00
102 Joe Bowman	20.00	10.00
103 Charles Chatham	20.00	10.00
104 Jim Cronin	20.00	10.00
105 Wally French	20.00	10.00
106 Malcolm Hillis	20.00	10.00
107 Bob Johnson	30.00	15.00
108 Frank Mulana	20.00	10.00
109 Ray Odell	20.00	10.00
110 Joseph Palmisano	20.00	10.00
111 Bill Pasedel	30.00	15.00
112 Joseph Trembly	20.00	10.00
113 Charles Woodall	20.00	10.00
114 Leonard Backer	20.00	10.00
115 Harry Brown	20.00	10.00
116 Ed Bryan	20.00	10.00
117 Dolph Camilli	40.00	20.00
118 Clem Coyle	20.00	10.00
119 Tom Flynn	20.00	10.00
120 Antonio Freitas	30.00	15.00
121 Ray French	20.00	10.00
122 Al Gould	20.00	10.00
123 Myril Hoag	30.00	15.00
124 Wally Hood	20.00	10.00
125 Ray Keating	20.00	10.00
126 Art Koehler	20.00	10.00
127 Jim McLaughlin	20.00	10.00
128 Frank Osborne	20.00	10.00
129 Ray Rohwer	20.00	10.00
130 John Ryan MG	20.00	10.00
131 Henry Steinbacker	20.00	10.00
132 Fay Thomas	20.00	10.00
133 Louri Vinci	20.00	10.00
134 Aaron Ward	30.00	15.00
135 Elwood Wirts	20.00	10.00
136 Loris Baker	20.00	10.00
137 James Caveney	20.00	10.00
138 Ed Coleman	20.00	10.00
139 Frank Crosetti	40.00	20.00
140 Curt Davis	30.00	15.00
141 Jerry Donovan	20.00	10.00
142 Alex Gaston	20.00	10.00
143 Elmer Jacobs	20.00	10.00
144 Arthur Jahn	20.00	10.00
145 E. R. Knight	20.00	10.00
146 Art McDougal	20.00	10.00
147 John Mails	30.00	15.00
148 John Miljus	30.00	15.00
149 John Miljus	30.00	15.00
150 Al Montgomery	20.00	10.00
151 Adolph Penebskey	20.00	10.00
152 Clyde Perry	20.00	10.00
153 Mel Petterson	20.00	10.00
154 Ralph Pinelli	40.00	20.00
155 George Powles	20.00	10.00
156 Bob Reed	20.00	10.00
157 Earl Sheely	20.00	10.00
158 Ernest Sulik	20.00	10.00
159 Milt Thomas	20.00	10.00
160 Hal Turpin	20.00	10.00
161 Nick Williams MG	20.00	10.00
162 Ab Wingo	20.00	10.00
163 James Zinn	20.00	10.00
164 William Allington	20.00	10.00
165 Luis Almada	20.00	10.00
166 David Barbee	20.00	10.00
167 Earl Brucker	20.00	10.00
168 Pat Collins	20.00	10.00
169 Frank Cox	20.00	10.00
170 Floyd Ellsworth	20.00	10.00
171 Charles Falk	20.00	10.00
172 Gilbert Fisch	20.00	10.00
173 Bob Holland	20.00	10.00
174 Andy House	20.00	10.00
175 W. W. Hubbell	20.00	10.00
176 Ernie Johnson MG	20.00	10.00
177 Rudolph Kallio	20.00	10.00
178 W. E. Knothe	20.00	10.00
179 Earl Kunz	20.00	10.00
180 Frank Lamanski	20.00	10.00
181 Bill Lawrence	20.00	10.00
182 Frederick Muller	20.00	10.00
183 Walter Olney	20.00	10.00
184 Fred Pipgrass	20.00	10.00
185 Harry Taylor	20.00	10.00
186 Gomer Wilson	20.00	10.00

1931 Zeenuts

These cards measure approximately 1 3/4" by 3 1/2".

	Ex-Mt	VG
COMPLETE SET (120)	2500.00	1250.00
1 David Barbee	20.00	10.00
2 John Bassler	30.00	15.00
3 Cleo Carlyle	20.00	10.00
4 Michael Gazella	30.00	15.00
5 Dudley Lee	20.00	10.00
6 Henry Severeid	20.00	10.00
7 Frank Shellenback	30.00	15.00
8 Jim Turner	40.00	20.00
9 Oscar Vitt MG	30.00	15.00
10 Charles Wetzel	20.00	10.00
11 Louis Baker	20.00	10.00
12 Vince Barton	20.00	10.00
13 Gilly Campbell	20.00	10.00
14 Eddie Farrell	20.00	10.00
15 Glen Gabler	20.00	10.00
16 Fred Haney	30.00	15.00
17 Roy Hannah	20.00	10.00
18 George Harper	20.00	10.00
19 Leroy Herrmann	20.00	10.00
20 John Lelivelt MG	20.00	10.00
21 Malcolm Moss	20.00	10.00
22 Art Parker	20.00	10.00
23 John Schulte	20.00	10.00
24 Carroll Yerkes	20.00	10.00
25 Fred Berger	20.00	10.00
26 Charles Biggs	20.00	10.00
27 William Brenzel	20.00	10.00
28 George Burns MG	30.00	15.00
29 Bert Cole	20.00	10.00
30 Joe Coscarart	20.00	10.00
31 Fred Hoffman	20.00	10.00
32 Carl Holling	20.00	10.00
33 Irving Hufft	20.00	10.00
34 John Knott	20.00	10.00
35 Charles Lieber	20.00	10.00
36 John Monroe	20.00	10.00
37 Ed Mulligan	20.00	10.00
38 Herman Pillette	20.00	10.00
39 Ted Pillette	20.00	10.00
40 William Sharpe	20.00	10.00
41 Augie Walsh	20.00	10.00
42 Paul Andrews	20.00	10.00
43 Leroy Anton	20.00	10.00
44 Monroe Dean	20.00	10.00
45 Hank DeBerry	30.00	15.00
46 Leonard Dondero	20.00	10.00
47 Bob Hurst	20.00	10.00
48 Fred Ortman	20.00	10.00
49 Harlen Pool	20.00	10.00
50 Ellis Powers	20.00	10.00
51 Addison Read	20.00	10.00
52 Andy Reese	20.00	10.00
53 Peter Ricci	20.00	10.00
54 Stanley Schino	20.00	10.00
55 Frank Tubbs	20.00	10.00
56 Bernard Uhalt	20.00	10.00
57 Charles Wade	20.00	10.00
58 Carl Zamlock	20.00	10.00
59 Spencer Abbott MG	20.00	10.00
60 Fred Berger	20.00	10.00
61 Joe Bowman	20.00	10.00
62 Ed Coleman	20.00	10.00
63 John Fenton	20.00	10.00
64 John Fitzpatrick	20.00	10.00
65 Ira Flagstead	20.00	10.00
66 Sam Hale	20.00	10.00
67 Rudy Kallio	20.00	10.00
68 Ray Keating	20.00	10.00
69 Edward Lipanovic	20.00	10.00
70 Hank McDonald	20.00	10.00
71 Oswald Orwoll	20.00	10.00
72 Bill Posedel	30.00	15.00
73 William Rhiel	20.00	10.00
74 Homer Summa	30.00	15.00
75 John Walters	20.00	10.00
76 Ken Williams	30.00	15.00
77 George Wise	20.00	10.00
78 Charles Woodall	20.00	10.00
79 Leonard Backer	20.00	10.00
80 Ed Bryan	20.00	10.00
81 Dolf Camilli	40.00	20.00
82 Roy Chesterfield	20.00	10.00
83 Frank Demaree	30.00	15.00
84 Tom Flynn	20.00	10.00
85 Tony Freitas	20.00	10.00
86 Ray French	20.00	10.00
87 Curtis Fullerton	20.00	10.00
88 Clarence Hamilton	20.00	10.00
89 W.W. Hubbell	20.00	10.00
90 Art Koehler	20.00	10.00
91 Jim McLaughlin	20.00	10.00
92 Ray Rohwer	20.00	10.00
93 John Ryan MG	20.00	10.00
94 William Simas	20.00	10.00
95 Henry Steinbacker	20.00	10.00
96 Louri Vinci	20.00	10.00
97 Elwood Wirts	20.00	10.00
98 Earl Baldwin	20.00	10.00
99 James Cavaney	20.00	10.00
100 Frank Crosetti	40.00	20.00
101 Curtis Davis	30.00	15.00
102 Art Delaney	20.00	10.00
103 Jerry Donovan	20.00	10.00
104 Ken Douglas	20.00	10.00
105 Foy Frazier	20.00	10.00
106 William Henderson	20.00	10.00
107 Elmer Jacobs	20.00	10.00
108 James Keesey	20.00	10.00
109 Art McDougall	20.00	10.00
110 Adolph Penebskey	20.00	10.00
111 Ralph Pinelli	40.00	20.00
112 Hal Turpin	20.00	10.00
113 Julian Wera	20.00	10.00
114 Nick Williams MG	20.00	10.00
115 Al Wingo	20.00	10.00
116 Jimmy Zinn	20.00	10.00
117 Floyd Ellsworth	20.00	10.00
118 Bob Holland	20.00	10.00
119 Fritz Knothe	20.00	10.00
120 Frank Lamanski	20.00	10.00

1932 Minneapolis Millers Wheaties

These blank backed cards, which measure approximately 5 7/16" by 3 7/16" feature members of the 1932 Minneapolis Millers. The cards feature player photos on the front in either black and white or sepia toned. Many players are not identified so one must tell who the player is from the signature.

	Ex-Mt	VG
COMPLETE SET	500.00	250.00
1 Dave Bancroft	40.00	20.00
2 Rube Benton	20.00	10.00
3 Donie Bush MG	20.00	10.00
4 Andy Cohen	20.00	10.00
5 Pea Ridge Day	20.00	10.00
6 Ray Fitzgerald	20.00	10.00
7 Fabian Gaffke	20.00	10.00
8 Babe Ganzel	20.00	10.00
9 Wes Griffin	20.00	10.00
10 Spencer Harris	20.00	10.00
11 Joe Hauser	25.00	12.50
12 Phil Hensick	20.00	10.00
13 Dutch Henry Minneapolis	20.00	10.00
14 Dutch Henry Chicago White Sox	20.00	10.00
15 Bunker Hill	20.00	10.00
16 Joe Mowry	20.00	10.00
17 Jess Petty	20.00	10.00
18 Bill Rodda	20.00	10.00
19 Harry Rice	20.00	10.00
20 Paul Richards	30.00	15.00
21 Art Ruble	20.00	10.00
22 Rosy Ryan	20.00	10.00
23 Al Sheehan ANN		
24 Eddie Sicking	20.00	10.00
25 Ernie Smith	20.00	10.00
26 E.R. Vangilder	20.00	10.00
27 Wally Tauscher	20.00	10.00
28 Hy VanDenburg	20.00	10.00

1932 Zeenuts

These cards measure approximately 1 3/4" by 3 1/2".

	Ex-Mt	VG
COMPLETE SET (120)	2500.00	1250.00
1 John Bassler	30.00	15.00
2 Otis Brannon	20.00	10.00
3 Martin Callaghan	20.00	10.00
4 Cleo Carlyle	20.00	10.00
5 Les Cook	20.00	10.00
6 Mike Gazella	30.00	15.00
7 Robert Hipps	20.00	10.00
8 Augustus Johns	20.00	10.00
9 Dudley Lee	20.00	10.00
10 Al McNeely	20.00	10.00
11 John Miljus	30.00	15.00
12 Vance Page	20.00	10.00
13 George Quellich	20.00	10.00
14 Tom Sheehan	20.00	10.00
15 Frank Shellenback	30.00	15.00
16 Jack Sherlock	20.00	10.00
17 Oscar Vitt MG	30.00	15.00
18 Emil Yde	30.00	15.00
19 Loris Baker	20.00	10.00
20 Noble Ballou	20.00	10.00
21 Gilly Campbell	20.00	10.00
22 Carl Dittmar	20.00	10.00
23 Fred Haney	30.00	15.00
24 James Hannah	20.00	10.00
25 Leroy Herrmann	20.00	10.00
26 Malcolm Moss	20.00	10.00
27 Arnold Statz	40.00	20.00
28 Homer Summa	20.00	10.00
29 Charles Briggs	20.00	10.00
30 George Caster	20.00	10.00
31 Bert Cole	20.00	10.00
32 Joe Coscarart	20.00	10.00
33 Babe Dahlgren	40.00	20.00
34 Joe Devine MG	20.00	10.00
35 Dan Hafey	20.00	10.00
36 Fred Hofman	20.00	10.00
37 Lloyd Johnson	20.00	10.00
38 Ernest Kelly	20.00	10.00
39 Charles Lieber	20.00	10.00
40 Jim Mosolf	20.00	10.00
41 Ed Mulligan	20.00	10.00
42 Herman Pillette	30.00	15.00
43 Peter Ricci	20.00	10.00
44 Ben Sankey	20.00	10.00
45 Vince Sherlock	20.00	10.00
46 Angie Walsh	20.00	10.00
47 Jim Welsh	20.00	10.00
48 Paul Zahniser	20.00	10.00
49 Leroy Anton	20.00	10.00
50 George Blackerby	20.00	10.00
51 Ray Brubaker	20.00	10.00
52 Pete Daglia	20.00	10.00
53 Monroe Dean	20.00	10.00
54 Arthur Delaney	20.00	10.00
55 Andy House	20.00	10.00

	Ex-Mt	VG
56 Irving Hufft	20.00	10.00
57 Robert Hurst	20.00	10.00
58 Roy Joiner	20.00	10.00
59 Charles Kasich	20.00	10.00
60 Arthur Koehler	20.00	10.00
61 Emil Mailho	20.00	10.00
62 Louis Martin	20.00	10.00
63 Ralph Pinelli	40.00	20.00
64 Harlin Poole	20.00	10.00
65 Addison Read	20.00	10.00
66 Fay Thomas	20.00	10.00
67 Bernard Uhalt	20.00	10.00
68 Ed Walsh Jr.	20.00	10.00
69 Carl Zamloch	20.00	10.00
70 Spencer Abbott MG	20.00	10.00
71 Fred Berger	20.00	10.00
72 John Fitzpatrick	20.00	10.00
73 Bob Johnson	40.00	20.00
74 John Monroe	20.00	10.00
75 Walter Shores	20.00	10.00
76 Ken Williams	30.00	15.00
77 George Wise	20.00	10.00
78 Leonard Backer	20.00	10.00
79 Stan Bordagaray	30.00	15.00
80 Adolph Camilli	40.00	20.00
81 Earl Collard	20.00	10.00
82 Jim Cronin	20.00	10.00
83 Frank Demaree	40.00	20.00
84 Bernard DeViveiros	20.00	10.00
85 Tony Freitas	30.00	15.00
86 Lawrence Gillick	20.00	10.00
87 Frank Osborn	20.00	10.00
88 Manuel Salvo	20.00	10.00
89 William Simas	20.00	10.00
90 Henry Steinbacker	20.00	10.00
91 Louri Vinci	20.00	10.00
92 Elwood Wirts	20.00	10.00
93 Charles Woodall	20.00	10.00
94 John Babich	30.00	15.00
95 James Caveney MG	20.00	10.00
96 Joseph Chamberlain	20.00	10.00
97 Curt Davis	30.00	15.00
98 Jerry Donovan	20.00	10.00
99 Foy Frazier	20.00	10.00
100 Art Garibaldi	20.00	10.00
101 William Henderson	20.00	10.00
102 Art Hunt	20.00	10.00
103 Elmer Jacobs	20.00	10.00
104 Jim Keesey	20.00	10.00
105 Heber Martin	20.00	10.00
106 Henry Oana	120.00	60.00
107 Adolph Penebsky	20.00	10.00
108 Ernie Sulik	20.00	10.00
109 Joe Ward	20.00	10.00
110 Julian Wera	20.00	10.00
111 Claude Willoughby	30.00	15.00
112 Luis Almada	20.00	10.00
113 Frank Cox	20.00	10.00
114 Floyd Ellsworth	20.00	10.00
115 Alex Gaston	30.00	15.00
116 Bob Holland	20.00	10.00
117 Ernie Johnson MG	20.00	10.00
118 Rudolph Kallio	20.00	10.00
119 Fred Muller	20.00	10.00
120 John Walters	20.00	10.00

1933 Minneapolis Millers Wheaties

These cards, which measure approximately 5 3/4" by 4" feature members of the 1933 Millers. The fronts have a player photo with his name and position on the bottom, while the postcard backs feature an advertisment for Wheaties. Since these cards are unnumbered, we have sequenced them in alphabetical order.

	Ex-Mt	VG
COMPLETE SET	2000.00	1000.00
1 Dave Bancroft MG	200.00	100.00
2 Rube Benton	100.00	50.00
3 Andy Cohen	120.00	60.00
4 Bob Fothergill	120.00	60.00
5 Babe Ganzel	100.00	50.00
6 Joe Glenn	100.00	50.00
7 Wes Griffin CO	100.00	50.00
8 Jack Hallett	100.00	50.00
9 Jerry Harrington ANN	100.00	50.00
10 Spencer Harris	100.00	50.00
11 Joe Hauser	150.00	75.00
12 Butch Henline	100.00	50.00
13 Walter Hilcher	100.00	50.00
14 Dutch Holland	100.00	50.00
15 Harry Holsclaw	100.00	50.00
16 Wes Kingdon	100.00	50.00
17 George Murray	100.00	50.00
18 Leo Norris	100.00	50.00
19 Jess Petty	100.00	50.00
20 Art Ruble	100.00	50.00
21 Al Sheehan ANN	100.00	50.00
22 Ernie Smith	100.00	50.00
23 Wally Tauscher	100.00	50.00
24 Hy VanDenburg	100.00	50.00

1933 Worch Cigar Minors

This is the companion set to the major league Worch issue. Please see that set for further details.

	Ex-Mt	VG
COMPLETE SET (103)	1000.00	500.00
1 Buzz Arlett	12.00	6.00
2 Dave Bancroft	20.00	10.00
With background		
3 Dave Bancroft	20.00	10.00
Without background		
4 Clyde Beck	10.00	5.00
5 Rube Benton	10.00	5.00
Throwing		
6 Otto Bluege	10.00	5.00
7 Bob Boken	10.00	5.00
8 Dudley Bramon	10.00	5.00
9 James Brown	10.00	5.00
10 Donie Bush	12.00	6.00
Printed name		
11 Donie Bush	12.00	6.00
In business suit		
12 Spurgeon Chandler	20.00	10.00
13 Tiny Chaplin	10.00	5.00
14 Gowell Claset	10.00	5.00
15 Andy Cohen	12.00	6.00
Fielding		
16 Bob Coleman MG	10.00	5.00
17 Nick Cullop	10.00	5.00
18 Robert Fenner	10.00	5.00
19 Lou Fetter	10.00	5.00
20 Bob Fothergill		
21 Fabian Gaffke	10.00	5.00
22 Denny Galehouse	10.00	5.00
23 Babe Ganzel	10.00	5.00
Batting with background)		
24 Babe Ganzel	10.00	1.00
Batting without background)		
25 Lou Garland	10.00	5.00
26 Johnny Gill	10.00	5.00
27 Joe Glenn	10.00	5.00
28 Berley Grimes	10.00	5.00
29 Pinky Hargrave	10.00	5.00
30 Bryan Harriss	10.00	5.00
31 Spencer Harris	10.00	5.00
Batting		
32 Joe Hauser	12.00	6.00
Batting		
33 Joe Hauser	12.00	6.00
Not batting		
34 Butch Henline		
35 Phil Hensick	10.00	5.00
Throwing		
36 Walter Hilcher	10.00	5.00
37 Jess Hill	10.00	5.00
38 Robert Holland	10.00	5.00
39 Harry Holsclaw	10.00	5.00
40 Meredith Hopkins	10.00	5.00
41 Irvine Jeffries		
41 Spike Hunter	10.00	5.00
42 Monk Joyner		
43 Ralph Judd	10.00	5.00
44 Ray Kolp	10.00	5.00
45 Eddie Leishman	10.00	5.00
46 Leitz	10.00	5.00
47 Chuck Morrow	10.00	5.00
48 Emmett McCann	10.00	5.00
49 Marty McManus	10.00	5.00
50 Bill McWilliams	10.00	5.00
51 Howard Mills	10.00	5.00
52 Joe Mowry	10.00	5.00
Batting)		
53 Leslie Munns	10.00	5.00
54 Floyd Newkirk	10.00	5.00
55 Leo Norris	10.00	5.00
56 Ben Paschal	10.00	5.00
57 Bill Perrin	10.00	5.00
58 Jess Petty		
Throwing, outfield wall visible		
59 Jess Petty	10.00	5.00
Throwing, clear background		
60 Ray Radcliff	10.00	5.00
61 Joe Rezotko	10.00	5.00
62 John Rigney	10.00	5.00
63 Lawrence Rosenthal	10.00	5.00
64 Art Ruble	10.00	5.00
Batting with background)		
65 Art Ruble	10.00	5.00
Batting without background)		
66 Ivy Shiver	10.00	5.00
67 Ernie Smith	10.00	5.00
Batting with background)		
68 Ernie Smith	10.00	5.00
Batting without background)		
69 Ray Starr	10.00	5.00
70 Lee Stine	10.00	5.00
71 Monty Stratton	20.00	10.00
72 Steve Sundra	10.00	5.00
73 Walt Tauscher	10.00	5.00
74 Miles Thomas	10.00	5.00
75 Phil Todt	10.00	5.00
76 Gene Trow	10.00	5.00
77 Russell Vanatta	10.00	5.00
78 Hy VanDenberg	10.00	5.00
Pitching, clear background		
79 Hy Vandenburg		
Pitching, wall visible		
80 Elam Vangilder	10.00	5.00
Pitching		
81 Jack Warner	10.00	5.00
82 Wolcyn	10.00	5.00
83 A.B. Wright	10.00	5.00
84 Russ Young	10.00	5.00

1933-36 Zeenuts (B and W)

Set includes: 1933, 1934, 1935, 1936. The reason they are grouped together is that once the coupon is removed there is no way to distinguish these cards. 1933 the coupons expiration date is April 1st, 1934. The 1934 cards coupons expire April 1st, 1935. The 1935 cards coupons expire April 1st, 1936. The 1936 cards have an expiration date of October 1st, 1936. However -- you need the coupons attached to be sure of what year your card is. If a player's name appears on 2 straight lines with the same card number it means the card was issued in 2 different sizes. These cards measure approximately 1 3/4" by 3 1/2".

	Ex-Mt	VG
COMPLETE SET (161)	10000.00	5000.00
1 Cleo Carlyle	20.00	10.00
2 Cedric Durst	30.00	15.00
3 Fred Haney	30.00	15.00
4 Gus Johns	20.00	10.00
5 Smead Jolley	40.00	20.00
6 Vance Page	20.00	10.00
7 Oscar Vitt MG	30.00	15.00
8 Carl Dittmar	20.00	10.00
9 Jim Oglesby	20.00	10.00
10 Jimmy Reese	200.00	100.00
Jimmy Reese		
11 Arnold Statz	40.00	20.00
12 Hal Stitzel	20.00	10.00
13 Louis Almada	20.00	10.00
Louis Almada		
14 John Babich	30.00	15.00
John Babich		
15 Clyde Beck	20.00	10.00
16 Clyde Beck	20.00	10.00
17 Walter Beck	30.00	15.00
18 Lincoln Blakely	20.00	10.00
19 Italo Chelini	20.00	10.00
20 Joseph Coscarart	20.00	10.00
21A M.Duggan	20.00	10.00
Small		
21B M. Duggan	20.00	10.00
Medium		
21C M.Duggan	20.00	10.00
Large		
22 Ox Eckhardt	40.00	20.00
Ox Eckhardt		
23 John Fitzpatrick	20.00	10.00
24 Mitchell Frankovich	20.00	10.00
25 Dan Hafey	20.00	10.00
Dan Hafey		
Dan Hafey		
26 Don Johnson	20.00	10.00
27 Lloyd Johnson	20.00	10.00
28 Edwin Joost	30.00	15.00
29 William Kamm MG	30.00	15.00
30 Charles Lieber	20.00	10.00
31 Clarence Mitchell	20.00	10.00
32 Roy Mort (throwing)	20.00	10.00
33 Roy Mort (batting)	20.00	10.00
34 Otho Nicholas	20.00	10.00
35 Otho Nitcholas	20.00	10.00
36 William Outen (throwing)	20.00	10.00
37 William Outen (batting)	20.00	10.00
38 Art Parker	20.00	10.00
39A Ted Pillette	20.00	10.00
Small		
39B Ted Pillette#[Large	20.00	10.00
40 Harry Rosenberg	40.00	20.00
41 Joe Sprinz	20.00	10.00
42 Walter Stewart	20.00	10.00
43 Hal Stitzel	20.00	10.00
44 John Stoneham	20.00	10.00
45 Charles Street MG	20.00	10.00
46 Hollis Thurston	30.00	15.00
47 Hollis Thurston	30.00	15.00
48 Bill Walters	20.00	10.00
49 Max West	30.00	15.00
50 Albert Wright	20.00	10.00
51 Albert Wright	20.00	10.00
52 Leroy Anton	20.00	10.00
Leroy Anton		
53 Merv Connors	30.00	15.00
54 Bernard DeViveiros	20.00	10.00
55 Ken Douglas	20.00	10.00
56 Henry Glaister	20.00	10.00
57 Hal Haid	20.00	10.00
58 Roy Joiner	20.00	10.00
59 Ernest Kelly	20.00	10.00
60 L.Kintana	20.00	10.00
L.Kintana		
61 Willie Ludolph	20.00	10.00
62 L.McEvoy	20.00	10.00
L.McEvoy		
63 Gene McIsaacs	20.00	10.00
64 Hugh McMullen	20.00	10.00
65 Emil Mailho	20.00	10.00
66 Fred Muller	20.00	10.00
Fred Muller		
67 Ed Mulligan	20.00	10.00
68 Ed Mulligan	20.00	10.00
69 Raymond Phebus	20.00	10.00
70 Harlin Poole	20.00	10.00
71 George Quellich	20.00	10.00
72 Albert Raimondi	20.00	10.00
Albert Raimondi		
73 Jimmy Rego	40.00	20.00
74 Michael Salinsen	20.00	10.00
75 Oscar Vitt MG	30.00	15.00
76 Ed Walsh Jr.	20.00	10.00
77 George Blackerby	20.00	10.00
78 Harold Brundin	20.00	10.00
79 Frank Cox	20.00	10.00
80 Arthur Jacobs	20.00	10.00
81 Rudy Kallio	20.00	10.00
82 Joe Palmisano	20.00	10.00
83 E.Sheely	20.00	10.00
E.Sheely		
84 Tony Borja	20.00	10.00
85 Jerry Donovan	20.00	10.00
86 Floyd Ellsworth	20.00	10.00
87 Daniel Hafey	20.00	10.00
88 William Hartwig	20.00	10.00
Willam Hartwig		
89 Berlyn Horne	20.00	10.00
90 Andy House	20.00	10.00
91 Alex Kampouris	30.00	15.00
92 Cal Lahman	20.00	10.00
93 Leo Ostenberg	20.00	10.00
94 Manuel Salvo	20.00	10.00
95 Henry Steinbacker	20.00	10.00
Henry Steinbacker		
96 James Stroner	20.00	10.00
97 Elwood Wirts	20.00	10.00
Elwood Wirts		
98 Leo Backer	20.00	10.00
99 William Ballou	20.00	10.00
William Ballou		
100 William Ballou	20.00	10.00
101 Steve Barath	20.00	10.00
102 Joe Becker	20.00	10.00
103 Tony Borja	20.00	10.00
104 James Cavaney MG	20.00	10.00
James Cavaney		
105 Albert Cole	20.00	10.00
106 Albert Cole	20.00	10.00
107 Curt Davis	30.00	15.00
108 Joe DiMaggio	3000.00	1500.00
THROW		
Spelled DeMaggio on the card		
109 Joe DiMaggio BAT	4000.00	2000.00
Spelled DeMaggio		
110 Vincent DiMaggio	500.00	250.00
Spelled DeMaggio on the card		
111 James Densmore	20.00	10.00
112 Ken Douglas	20.00	10.00
113 John Fenton	20.00	10.00
114 Elias Funk	20.00	10.00
115 A.Garibaldi	20.00	10.00
A.Garibaldi		
116 Sam Gibson	20.00	10.00
117 Sam Gibson	20.00	10.00
118 Gira	20.00	10.00
119 R. J. Graves	20.00	10.00
120 William Hartwig	20.00	10.00
121 Bill Henderson	20.00	10.00
122 Leroy Herrmann	20.00	10.00
123 Brooks Holder	20.00	10.00
124 Art Hunt	20.00	10.00
125 Karl Jorgensen	20.00	10.00
126 Ed Kenna	20.00	10.00
127 Hugh McMullen	20.00	10.00
128 W.Mails	30.00	15.00
W.Mails		
129 Joseph Marty	20.00	10.00
130 Joseph Marty	20.00	10.00
131 Tony Massuci	20.00	10.00
132 Tony Massuci	20.00	10.00
133 V.Monzo	20.00	10.00
V.Monzo		
134 Floyd Newkirk	20.00	10.00
135 T.Norbert	20.00	10.00
T.Norbert		
136 Frank O'Doul MG	200.00	100.00
137 Frank O'Doul MG	200.00	100.00
138 Les Powers	20.00	10.00
139A Harold Rhyne	20.00	10.00
Small		
139B Harold Rhyne	20.00	10.00
Large		
140 Harold Rhyne	20.00	10.00
141 Bill Salkeld	30.00	15.00
142 Carl Sever	20.00	10.00
143 Ken Sheehan	20.00	10.00
144 Ken Sheehan	20.00	10.00
145 Caesar Sinibaldi	20.00	10.00
146 Starritt	20.00	10.00
147 Hal Stitzel	20.00	10.00
148A Edward Stutz	20.00	10.00
Small		
148B Edward Stutz	20.00	10.00
Large		
149 Ernie Sulik	20.00	10.00
150 Charles Wallgren	20.00	10.00
151 Larry Woodall	20.00	10.00
Larry Woodall		
152 Larry Woodall	20.00	10.00
153 James Zinn	20.00	10.00
154 Nino Biongovanni	20.00	10.00
155 Joe Coscarart	20.00	10.00
156 Hal Haid	20.00	10.00
157 Bob Holland	20.00	10.00
158 Ernest Kelly	20.00	10.00
159 Fred Muller	20.00	10.00
160 Phil Page	20.00	10.00
161 William Radonitz	20.00	10.00

1933 Zeenuts (Sepia)

These cards measure 1 3/4" by 3 1/2."

	Ex-Mt	VG
COMPLETE SET (48)	800.00	400.00
1 John Bassler	30.00	15.00
2 Otis Brannan	20.00	10.00
3 Frank Shellenback	30.00	15.00
4 John Sherlock	20.00	10.00
5 Alan Strange	20.00	10.00
6 Oscar Vitt	30.00	15.00
7 William Cronin	20.00	10.00
8 John Lelivelt MG	20.00	10.00
9 Charles Moncrief	20.00	10.00
10 Lester Sweetland	20.00	10.00
11 Charles Wetzel	20.00	10.00
12 Louis Almada	20.00	10.00
13 Albert Cole	20.00	10.00
14 Ellsworth Dahlgren	40.00	20.00
15 Fred Hofmann	20.00	10.00
16 Paul Kelman	20.00	10.00
17 Wayne Osborne	20.00	10.00
18 Vincent Sherlock	20.00	10.00
19 Leroy Anton	20.00	10.00
20 Ray Brubaker	20.00	10.00
21 Myer Chozen	20.00	10.00
22 William Ludolph	20.00	10.00
23 Floyd Scott	20.00	10.00
24 Bernard Uhalt	20.00	10.00
25 Henry McDonald	20.00	10.00
26 James Petersen	20.00	10.00
27 Robert Reeves	20.00	10.00
28 Stanley Bordagary	30.00	15.00
29 Edwin Bryan	20.00	10.00
30 Adolph Camilli	40.00	20.00
31 Thomas Flynn	20.00	10.00
32 Raymond French	20.00	10.00
33 George McNeely MG	20.00	10.00
34 Herbert McQuaid	20.00	10.00
35 Henry Steinbacker	20.00	10.00
36 Louri Vinci	20.00	10.00
37 Charles Woodall	20.00	10.00
38 Gerald Donovan	20.00	10.00
39 Kenneth Douglas	20.00	10.00
40 August Galan	30.00	15.00
41 Lee Stine	20.00	10.00
42 Ernest Sulik	20.00	10.00
43 James Zinn	20.00	10.00
44 Richard Bonnelly	20.00	10.00
45 John Bottarini	20.00	10.00
46 George Burns MG	30.00	15.00
47 Richard Frietas	20.00	10.00
48 Lynn Nelson	20.00	10.00

1935 Pebble Beach

This seven-card extremely rare set features sepia tinted photos with autographs of players from the San Francisco-Oakland Bay Area Coast League minor league teams printed on postcard size cards. The set was offered on an evening sports show on radio station KYA in Oakland, sponsored by Pebble Beach clothier. The cards were issued periodically, and a collector could obtain them by sending in his name to the station when each new card was announced. The cards are unnumbered and checklisted below in alphabetical order. All cards seen in the marketplace have been signed in fountain pen ink.

	Ex-Mt	VG
COMPLETE SET (7)	2000.00	1000.00
1 Leroy Anton	100.00	50.00
2 Joe DiMaggio	1500.00	750.00
3 Wee Ludolph	100.00	50.00
4 Walter Mails	100.00	50.00
5 Lefty O'Doul	200.00	100.00
6 Gabby Street	100.00	50.00
7 Oscar Vitt MG	100.00	50.00

1937-38 Zeenuts

Set includes: 1937, 1938. 37's were issued with coupons. 38's with separate same size card that was a coupon. 37's and 38's are grouped together for when the coupon is cut off the 37's they measure the same as the 38's. When found, these cards along with 1911's are usually in better condition than other Zeenuts. 1937's without coupons measure approximately 1 11/16" by 3 1/2"; 1938's without coupons measure approximately 1 3/4" by 2 13/16".

	Ex-Mt	VG
COMPLETE SET (94)	3500.00	1800.00
1 Joe Coscarart	40.00	20.00
2 Harry Marble	40.00	20.00
3 Robert Mort	40.00	20.00
4 William Outen	40.00	20.00
5 Gordon Slade	40.00	20.00
6 Lou Tost	40.00	20.00
7 Joseph Vitter	40.00	20.00
8 Marv Gudat	40.00	20.00
9 Harry Hannah MG	40.00	20.00
10 Arnold Statz	80.00	40.00
11 Joe Annunzio	40.00	20.00
12 Walter Beck	50.00	25.00
13 Stewart Bolin	40.00	20.00
14 Mitchell Frankovich	40.00	20.00
15 Leroy Herrmann	40.00	20.00
16 Mark Koenig	60.00	30.00
17 Frank Lamanski	40.00	20.00
18 Harry Marble	40.00	20.00
19 Robert Mort	40.00	20.00
20 Otho Nitcholas	40.00	20.00
21 Wayne Osborne	40.00	20.00
22 William Outen	40.00	20.00
23 Willaim Outen	40.00	20.00
24 Albert Raimondi	40.00	20.00
25 Harry Rosenberg	80.00	40.00
26 Gordon Slade	40.00	20.00
27 Joseph Sprinz	40.00	20.00
28 Louis Tost	40.00	20.00
29 Max West	50.00	25.00
30 William Baker	40.00	20.00
31 C. Beck	40.00	20.00
32 Ken Douglas	40.00	20.00
33 Leonard Gabrielson	40.00	20.00
34 Hal Haid	40.00	20.00
35 Walt Judnich	50.00	25.00
36 Ed Leishman	40.00	20.00
37 Floyd Olds	40.00	20.00
38 Albert Raimondi	40.00	20.00
39 Ernie Koy	60.00	30.00
40 William Raimondi	40.00	20.00
41 Ken Sheehan	40.00	20.00
42 Sawyer	40.00	20.00
43 Anthony Bongiavanni	40.00	20.00
44 Harold Carson	40.00	20.00
45 Moose Clabaugh	40.00	20.00

	Ex-Mt	VG
46 William Cronin	40.00	20.00
47 John Fredericks	40.00	20.00
48 Bill Radonitz	40.00	20.00
49 Harry Rosenberg	80.00	40.00
50 Bill Sweeney	40.00	20.00
51 William Wilson	40.00	20.00
52 Henry Cullop	40.00	20.00
53 Tony Freitas	50.00	25.00
54 Art Garibaldi	40.00	20.00
55 Bob Klinger	40.00	20.00
56 George Murray	40.00	20.00
57 H. H. Newsome	40.00	20.00
58 Joe Orengo	40.00	20.00
59 Harry Pippin	40.00	20.00
60 Tom Seats	40.00	20.00
61 Sidney Stringfellow	40.00	20.00
62 John Vergez	40.00	20.00
63 Louis Vezelich	40.00	20.00
64 William Ballou	40.00	20.00
65 Harley Boss	40.00	20.00
66 Robert Cole	40.00	20.00
67 Neal Clifford	40.00	20.00
68 Pete Daglia	40.00	20.00
69 Dominic DiMaggio	400.00	200.00
70 Keith Frazier	40.00	20.00
71 Sam Gibson	40.00	20.00
72 John Gill	40.00	20.00
73 Graves	40.00	20.00
74 Larry Guay	40.00	20.00
75 Frank Hawkins	40.00	20.00
76 Brooks Holder	40.00	20.00
77 Ted Jennings	40.00	20.00
78 Lou Koupal	40.00	20.00
79 Gene Lillard	50.00	25.00
80 Gordon Mann	40.00	20.00
81 Oscar Miller	40.00	20.00
82 Pinckney Mills	40.00	20.00
83 Vincent Monzo	40.00	20.00
84 Lawrence Powell	40.00	20.00
85 Ernest Raimondi	40.00	20.00
86 Harold Rhyne	40.00	20.00
87 Ken Sheehan	40.00	20.00
88 William Shores	40.00	20.00
89 Joseph Sprinz	40.00	20.00
90 Harvey Storey	40.00	20.00
91 Ed Stutz	40.00	20.00
92 Francis Thomson	40.00	20.00
93 Joseph Vitter	40.00	20.00
94 Larry Woodall	40.00	20.00
95 Al Wright	40.00	20.00
96 Leonard Gabrielson	40.00	20.00
97 Ed Leishman	40.00	20.00
98 Fred Muller	40.00	20.00
99 Henry Ulrich	40.00	20.00

1938 Oakland Oaks Signal Oil Stamps

These stamps, which measure approximately 1 5/8" by 2 1/2" feature members of the 1938 Oakland Oaks. Since these stamps are unnumbered, we have sequenced them in alphabetical order.

	Ex-Mt	VG
COMPLETE SET	400.00	200.00
1 Joe Abreu	20.00	10.00
2 Pat Ambrose	20.00	10.00
3 Al Browne	20.00	10.00
4 Bill Conroy	20.00	10.00
5 Jerry Donovan	20.00	10.00
6 Ken Douglas	20.00	10.00
7 Bob Gibson	20.00	10.00
8 Jesse Hill	20.00	10.00
9 Delbert Holmes	20.00	10.00
10 Bob Joyce	20.00	10.00
11 Hugh Luby	20.00	10.00
12 Harry Martinez	20.00	10.00
13 Wilcy Moore	40.00	20.00
14 Floyd Newkirk	20.00	10.00
15 Floyd Olds	20.00	10.00
16 Bill Raimondi	20.00	10.00
17 Ken Sheehan	20.00	10.00
18 Holllis Thurston	30.00	15.00
19 George Turbeville	20.00	10.00
20 Lauri Vinci	20.00	10.00
21 Frank Volpi	20.00	10.00
22 Jackie Warner	20.00	10.00
23 Ed Yount	20.00	10.00
24 Dutch Zwilling	30.00	15.00

1940 Binghampton Crowley's Milk

These 3" by 5" blank-backed cards were issued to feature players on the Binghampton Eastern League team. The front have a blue-tinted player photo surrounded by a red-tinted illustrated baseball-scene border. The front also includes a facsimile player signature with their endorsement for Crowley's milk. Some backs with a stamped postcard back which are much tougher than the blank backs. This checklist could be incomplete so any additions are greatly appreciated.

	Ex-Mt	VG
1 Jimmy Adlam	100.00	50.00
2 Russ Bergman	100.00	50.00
3 Bruno Betzel	100.00	50.00
4 Vince DiBiassi	100.00	50.00
5 Jack Graham	100.00	50.00
6 Earl Reid	100.00	50.00
7 Frankie Slivanic	100.00	50.00

1940 San Francisco Seals Associated Station Stamps

These stamps, which measure approximately 2 1/4" by 1 3/4", and were in a blue on cream color, featured members of the 1940 San Francisco Seals. Since these stamps are unnumbered, we have sequenced them in alphabetical order.

	Ex-Mt	VG
COMPLETE SET	500.00	250.00
1 Win Ballou	20.00	10.00
2 John Barrett	20.00	10.00
3 Ed Botelho	20.00	10.00
4 Jack Burns	20.00	10.00
5 Frank Dasso	20.00	10.00
6 Al Epperly	20.00	10.00
7 Ferris Fain	40.00	20.00
8 Sam Gibson	20.00	10.00
9 Larry Guay	20.00	10.00
10 Brooks Holder	20.00	10.00
11 Ted Jennings	20.00	10.00
12 Bob Jensen	20.00	10.00
13 Orville Jorgens	20.00	10.00
14 Gene Kiley	20.00	10.00
15 Wilfred Lefebre	20.00	10.00
16 Wil Leonard	20.00	10.00
17 Ted Norbert	20.00	10.00
18 Lefty O'Doul MG	40.00	20.00
19 Larry Powell	20.00	10.00
20 Bob Price	20.00	10.00
21 Joe Sprinz	20.00	10.00
22 Harvey Storey	20.00	10.00
23 Ed Stutz	20.00	10.00
24 Jack Warner	20.00	10.00
25 Larry Woodall	20.00	10.00
26 Al Wright	20.00	10.00

1940 Solons Hughes

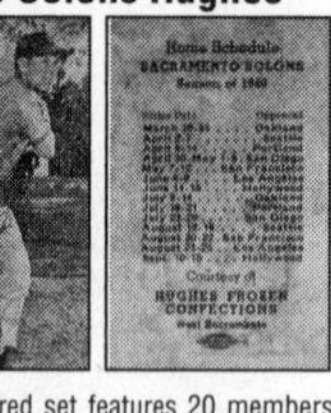

This unnumbered set features 20 members of the Sacramento Solons of the Pacific Coast League. The cards measure approximately 2" by 3" and are printed in black and white on rather thick card stock. Each card has a facsimile autograph on the front and a 1940 season home game schedule for the Sacramento Solons. The bottom of the reverse shows "Courtesy of Hughes Frozen Confections" and a tiny union label.

	Ex-Mt	VG
COMPLETE SET (20)	1800.00	900.00
1 Mel Almada	100.00	50.00
2 Frank Asbell	100.00	50.00
3 Larry Barton	100.00	50.00
4 Robert Blattner	100.00	50.00
5 Bennie Borgmann	100.00	50.00
6 Tony Freitas	100.00	50.00
7 Art Garibaldi	100.00	50.00
8 Jim Grilk	100.00	50.00
9 Gene Handley	100.00	50.00
10 Oscar Judd	100.00	50.00
11 Lynn King	100.00	50.00
12 Norbert Kleinke	100.00	50.00
13 Max Marshall	100.00	50.00
14 Wm. McLaughlin	100.00	50.00
15 Bruce Ogrodowski	100.00	50.00
16 Franich Riel	100.00	50.00
17 Bill Schmidt	100.00	50.00
18 Melvin Wasley	100.00	50.00
19 Chet Wieczorek	100.00	50.00
20 Deb Williams	100.00	50.00

1943 Centennial Flour

This set of 25 black and white cards features members of the Seattle Rainiers of the Pacific Coast League. The cards measure approximately 4" by 5" and contain a brief biographical sketch on the back. The cards are unnumbered and hence they are listed below alphabetically. This set can be distinguished from the other Centennial sets by looking at the obverse; Compliments of Centennial Flouring Mills is printed at the bottom.

	Ex-Mt	VG
COMPLETE SET (25)	950.00	475.00
1 John Babich	50.00	25.00
2 Nick Bonarigo	50.00	25.00
3 Eddie Carnett	50.00	25.00
4 Loyd Christopher	50.00	25.00
5 Joe Demoran	50.00	25.00
6 Joe Dobbins	50.00	25.00
7 Glenn Elliott	50.00	25.00
8 Carl Fischer	50.00	25.00
9 Leonard Gabrielson	50.00	25.00
10 Stanley Gray	50.00	25.00
11 Dick Gyselman	50.00	25.00
12 Jim Jewell	50.00	25.00
13 Sylvester Johnson	75.00	38.00
14 Pete Jonas	50.00	25.00
15 Bill Kats	50.00	25.00
16 Lynn King	50.00	25.00
17 Bill Lawrence	50.00	25.00
18 Clarence Marshall	50.00	25.00
19 Bill Matheson	50.00	25.00
20 Ford Mullen	50.00	25.00
21 Bill Skiff	50.00	25.00
22 Byron Speece	50.00	25.00
23 Hal Sueme	50.00	25.00
24 Hal Turpin	50.00	25.00
25 John Yelovic	50.00	25.00

1943 Milwaukee Brewers Team Issue

These 22 postcard-sized blank-backed photos, measuring 3 1/2" by 5" featuring members of the 1943 Milwaukee Brewers, were taken by Grand Studio and issued in a brown envelope as a complete team set. Since the cards are not numbered, we are sequencing them alphabetically.

	Ex-Mt	VG
COMPLETE SET (22)	400.00	200.00
1 Bob Bowman	20.00	10.00
2 Joe Berry	20.00	10.00
3 Earl Caldwell	20.00	10.00
4 Greg Clarke	20.00	10.00
5 Merv Connors	20.00	10.00
6 Paul Erickson	20.00	10.00
7 Charlie Grimm MG	40.00	20.00
8 Hank Helf	20.00	10.00
9 Don Johnson	20.00	10.00
10 Wes Livengood	20.00	10.00
11 Herschel Martin	20.00	10.00
12 Tommy Nelson	20.00	10.00
13 Bill Norman	20.00	10.00
14 Ted Norbert	20.00	10.00
15 Henry Oana	25.00	12.50
16 Jimmy Pruett	20.00	10.00
17 Bill Sahlin	20.00	10.00
18 Frank Secory	20.00	10.00
19 Red Smith	20.00	10.00
20 Charlie Sproull	20.00	10.00
21 Hugh Todd	20.00	10.00
22 Tony York	20.00	10.00

1943 Wilkes-Barre Barons

These six black and white blank-backed photos feature members of the Wilkes-Barre Barons. The photos were issued compliments of Golden Quality Ice Cream. The cards are unnumbered and we have sequenced them in alphabetical order. There may be more photos so any additions are appreciated.

	Ex-Mt	VG
COMPLETE SET	350.00	180.00
1 Alex Damaliton	50.00	25.00
2 Tony Lazzeri MG Batting Pose	100.00	50.00
3 Tony Lazzeri MG Hands on Knee	100.00	50.00
4 Jim McDonell	50.00	25.00
5 Joe Pennington	50.00	25.00
6 Ned Tryon	50.00	25.00

1944 Centennial Flour

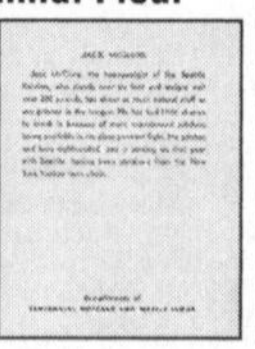

This set of 25 black and white cards features members of the Seattle Rainiers of the Pacific Coast League. The cards measure approximately 4" by 5" and contain a brief biographical sketch on the back. The cards are unnumbered and hence they are listed below alphabetically. This set can be distinguished from the other Centennial sets by looking at the obverse; Compliments of Centennial Hotcake and Waffle Flour is printed at the bottom.

	Ex-Mt	VG
COMPLETE SET (25)	1000.00	500.00
1 John Babich	50.00	25.00
2 Paul Carpenter	50.00	25.00
3 Loyd Christopher	50.00	25.00
4 Joe Demoran	50.00	25.00
5 Joe Dobbins	50.00	25.00
6 Glenn Elliott	50.00	25.00
7 Carl Fischer	50.00	25.00
8 Bob Garbould	50.00	25.00
9 Stanley Gray	50.00	25.00
10 Dick Gyselman	50.00	25.00
11 Gene Holt	50.00	25.00
12 Roy Johnson	50.00	25.00
13 Sylvester Johnson	75.00	38.00
14 Al Libke	50.00	25.00
15 Billy Lyman	50.00	25.00
16 Bill Matheson	50.00	25.00
17 Jack McClure	50.00	25.00
18 Jimmy Ripple	75.00	38.00
19 Sicks Stadium	50.00	25.00
20 Bill Skiff MG	50.00	25.00
21 Byron Speece	50.00	25.00
22 Hal Sueme	50.00	25.00
23 Frank Tincup	50.00	25.00
24 Jack Treece	50.00	25.00
25 Hal Turpin	50.00	25.00

1944 Milwaukee Brewers Team Issue

For the second straight year during World War II, these photos, which measure 3 1/2" by 5" were issued by the Triple AAA Milwaukee Brewers. These photos are unnumbered and are sequenced in alphabetical order.

	Ex-Mt	VG
COMPLETE SET	400.00	200.00
1 Julio Acosto	15.00	7.50
2 Heinz Becker	15.00	7.50
3 George Binks	15.00	7.50
4 Bob Bowman	15.00	7.50
5 Earl Caldwell	15.00	7.50
6 Dick Culler	15.00	7.50
7 Roy Eastwood	15.00	7.50
8 Jack Farmer	15.00	7.50
9 Charles Gassaway	15.00	7.50
10 Dick Hearn	15.00	7.50
11 Don Hendrickson	15.00	7.50
12 Ed Levy	15.00	7.50
13 Herschel Martin	15.00	7.50
14 Bill Nagel	15.00	7.50
15 Tommy Nelson	15.00	7.50
16 Bill Norman	15.00	7.50
17 Hal Peck	15.00	7.50
18 Jimmy Pruitt	15.00	7.50
19 Ken Raddant	15.00	7.50
20 Owen Scheetz	15.00	7.50
21 Eddie Scheive	15.00	7.50
22 Frank Secory	15.00	7.50
23 Red Smith	15.00	7.50
24 Floyd Speer	15.00	7.50
25 Charlie Sproull	15.00	7.50
26 Casey Stengel MG	50.00	25.00

1945 Centennial Flour

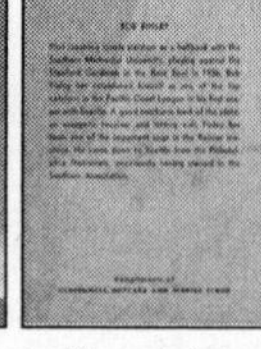

This set of 27 black and white cards features members of the Seattle Rainiers of the Pacific Coast League. The cards measure approximately 3 7/8" by 5 1/16" and contain a brief biographical sketch on the back. The picture of the player on the front is borderless and contains the player's name and team in a black strip at the bottom. The cards are unnumbered and hence they are listed below alphabetically.

	Ex-Mt	VG
COMPLETE SET (27)	900.00	450.00
1 Charley Aleno	40.00	20.00
2 Dick Briskey	40.00	20.00
3 John Carpenter	40.00	20.00
4 Joe Demoran	40.00	20.00
5 Joe Dobbins	40.00	20.00
6 Glenn Elliott	40.00	20.00
7 Bob Finley	40.00	20.00
8 Carl Fischer	40.00	20.00
9 Keith Frazier	40.00	20.00
10 Johnny Gill	40.00	20.00
11 Bob Gorbould	40.00	20.00
12 Chet Johnson	40.00	20.00
13 Sylvester Johnson	60.00	30.00
14 Bill Kats	40.00	20.00
15 Billy Lyman	40.00	20.00
16 Bill Matheson	40.00	20.00
17 George McDonald	40.00	20.00
18 Ted Norbert	40.00	20.00
19 Alex Palica	40.00	20.00
20 Joe Passero	40.00	20.00
21 Hal Patchett	40.00	20.00
22 Bill Skiff MG	40.00	20.00
23 Byron Speece	40.00	20.00
24 Hal Sueme	40.00	20.00
25 Eddie Taylor	40.00	20.00
26 Hal Turpin	40.00	20.00
27 Jack Whipple	40.00	20.00

1945 Milwaukee Brewers Team Issue

For the third and final season, the Brewers issued these 3 1/2" by 5" photos. These photos have blank-backed and are sequenced in alphabetical order.

	Ex-Mt	VG
COMPLETE SET	200.00	100.00
1 Julio Acosta	15.00	7.50
2 Arky Biggs	15.00	7.50
3 Bill Burgu	15.00	7.50
4 Nick Cullop MG	15.00	7.50
5 Peaches Davis	15.00	7.50
6 Otto Denning	15.00	7.50
7 Lew Flick	15.00	7.50
8 Don Hendrickson	15.00	7.50
9 Ed Kobesky	15.00	7.50
10 Carl Lindquist	15.00	7.50
11 Jack McGillen	15.00	7.50
12 Gene Nance	15.00	7.50
13 Bill Norman	15.00	7.50
14 Joe Rullo	15.00	7.50
15 Owen Scheetz	15.00	7.50
16 Floyd Speer	15.00	7.50

1946 Remar Bread

The 1946 Remar Bread set of 23 black and white cards was issued one player per week in stores carrying Remar Bread. The cards are easily identified by the "red loaf" of Remar bread on the back. The first cards issued were not numbered, but the rest were, beginning with No. 5. Raimondi was the first card issued and is scarce. The set depicts Oakland Oaks players only. Even though we have numbered the last five cards, they are actually unnumbered. The catalog designation is D317-1. Cards in this set measure approximately 2" by 3".

	Ex-Mt	VG
COMPLETE SET (23)	400.00	200.00
5 Herschel Martin	15.00	7.50
6 Bill Hart	15.00	7.50
7 Chuck Gassaway	15.00	7.50
8 Wally Westlake	20.00	10.00
9 Ora Burnett	15.00	7.50
10 Casey Stengel MG	120.00	60.00
11 Charles Metro	20.00	10.00
12 Tom Hafey	15.00	7.50
13 Tony Sabol	15.00	7.50
14 Ed Kearse	20.00	10.00
15 Bud Foster ANN	15.00	7.50
16 Johnny Price	15.00	7.50
17 Gene Bearden	20.00	10.00
18 Floyd Speer	15.00	7.50
19 Bryan Stephens	15.00	7.50
20 Rinaldo Ardizola	15.00	7.50
21 Ralph Buxton	15.00	7.50
22 Ambrose Palica	15.00	7.50
23 Brooks Holder	20.00	10.00
24 Henry Pippen	20.00	10.00
25 Bill Raimondi	60.00	30.00
26 Les Scarsella	20.00	10.00
27 Glen Stewart	20.00	10.00

1946 Sunbeam Bread

The 1946 Sunbeam Bread set of 21 black and white, unnumbered cards features the Sacramento Solons only. There is a reference to the "1946 Solons" on the fronts of the cards and small yellow and red bread loafs on the backs of the cards. The backs are in blue print and give a brief biography and a Sunbeam Bread ad. The catalog designation is D315-1. Cards in this set measure approximately 2" by 3".

	Ex-Mt	VG
COMPLETE SET (21)	800.00	400.00
1 Bud Beasley	30.00	15.00
2 Jack Calvey	30.00	15.00
3 Gene Corbett	30.00	15.00
4 Bill Conroy	30.00	15.00
5 Guy Fletcher	30.00	15.00
6 Tony Freitas	30.00	15.00
7 Ted Greenhalgh	30.00	15.00
8 Al Jarlett	30.00	15.00
9 Landrum	30.00	15.00
10 Gene Lillard	40.00	20.00
11 Garth Mann	30.00	15.00
12 Lilo Marcucci	40.00	20.00
13 Joe Marty	200.00	100.00
14 Steve Mesner	30.00	15.00
15 Herm Pillette	30.00	15.00
16 Earl Sheely	30.00	15.00
17 Al Smith	40.00	20.00
18 Gerald Staley	50.00	25.00
19 Averett Thompson	30.00	15.00
20 Jo Jo White	40.00	20.00
21 Bud Zipay	30.00	15.00

1947 Centennial Flour

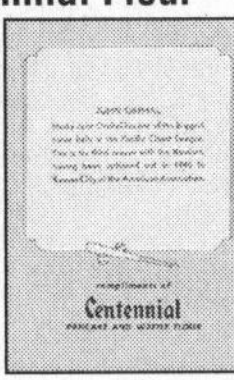

This set of 32 black and white cards features members of the Seattle Rainiers of the Pacific Coast League. The cards measure approximately 3 7/8" by 5 1/8" and contain a brief biographical sketch on the back. The picture of the player on the front is borderless and contains the player's name and team in a black strip at the bottom. The cards are unnumbered and hence they are listed below alphabetically. This set can be distinguished from the other Centennial sets by looking at the obverse; Compliments of Centennial Pancake and Waffle Flour is printed at the bottom.

	Ex-Mt	VG
COMPLETE SET (32)	750.00	375.00
1 Dick Barrett	40.00	20.00
2 Joe Buzas	25.00	12.50
3 Paul Carpenter	25.00	12.50
4 Rex Cecil	25.00	12.50
5 Tony Criscola	25.00	12.50
6 Walter Dubiel	25.00	12.50
7 Doug Ford	25.00	12.50
8 Rollie Hemsley	40.00	20.00
9 Jim Hill	25.00	12.50
10 Jim Hopper	25.00	12.50
11 Sigmund Jakucki	40.00	20.00
12 Bob Johnson	40.00	20.00
13 Pete Jonas	25.00	12.50
14 Joe Kaney	25.00	12.50
15 Hillis Layne	25.00	12.50
16 Lou Novikoff	40.00	20.00
17 Johnny O'Neil	25.00	12.50
18 John Orphal	25.00	12.50
19 Ike Pearson	25.00	12.50
20 Bill Posedel	40.00	20.00
21 Don Pulford	25.00	12.50
22 Tom Reis	25.00	12.50
23 Charley Ripple	25.00	12.50
24 Mickey Rocco	25.00	12.50
25 Johnny Rucker	25.00	12.50
26 Earl Sheely	25.00	12.50
27 Bob Stagg	25.00	12.50
28 Hal Sueme	25.00	12.50
29 Eddie Taylor	25.00	12.50
30 Edo Vanni	25.00	12.50
31 Jo Jo White	40.00	20.00
32 Tony York	25.00	12.50

1947 Padres Team Issue

This 24-card set of the San Diego Padres features black-and-white full-length player pictures with white borders. The set measures approximately 4 1/2" by 6 1/2" and was printed on linen finish paper. The backs are blank. The cards are unnumbered and checklisted below in alphabetical order.

	Ex-Mt	VG
COMPLETE SET (24)	250.00	125.00
1 John Barrett	10.00	5.00
2 Jim Brillheart CO	10.00	5.00
3 Dwain Clay	10.00	5.00
4 Jim(Rip) Collins MG	20.00	10.00
5 Pete Coscarart	10.00	5.00
6 Charles Eisenman	10.00	5.00
7 Dick Gyselman	10.00	5.00
8 Bob Hamilton	10.00	5.00
9 John Jensen	10.00	5.00
10 Vern Kennedy	15.00	7.50
11 Frank Kerr	10.00	5.00
12 Bob Kerrigan	10.00	5.00
13 Larry Lee	10.00	5.00
14 Jim McDonnell	10.00	5.00
15 John Olsen	10.00	5.00
16 Len Rice	10.00	5.00
17 Manuel Salvo	10.00	5.00
18 Tom Seats	10.00	5.00
19 Vince Shupe	10.00	5.00
20 Ray Tran	10.00	5.00
21 Al Triechel	10.00	5.00
22 Jim Triner	10.00	5.00
23 Ed Vitalich	10.00	5.00
24 Max West	15.00	7.50

1947 Remar Bread

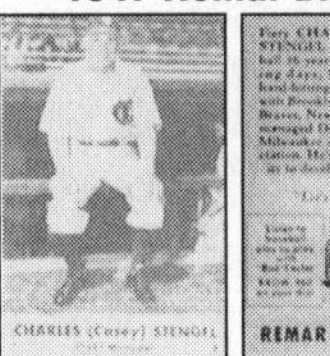

The 1947 Remar Bread set of 25 black and white, numbered cards features Oakland Oaks players only. Many cards are identical to the 1946 issue on the front except for the numbering. These cards are listed with an asterisk in the checklist. The backs are distinguishable from the 1946 issue by a "blue loaf" of Remar Bread. The backs are printed in blue and include player biographies and an ad for the Oakland Oaks radio station. The cards are on very thin stock. The catalog designation is D317-2. Cards in this set measure approximately 2" by 3".

	Ex-Mt	VG
COMPLETE SET	300.00	150.00
1 Bill Raimondi	10.00	5.00
2 Les Scarsella	10.00	5.00
3 Brooks Holder	10.00	5.00
4 Chuck Gassaway	10.00	5.00
5 Ora Burnett	10.00	5.00
6 Ralph Buxton	10.00	5.00
7 Ed Kearse	10.00	5.00
8 Casey Stengel MG	120.00	60.00
9 Bud Foster ANN	10.00	5.00
10 Ambrose Palica	10.00	5.00
11 Tom Hafey	10.00	5.00
12 Herschel Martin	10.00	5.00
13 Henry Pippen	10.00	5.00
14 Floyd Speer	10.00	5.00
15 Tony Sabol	10.00	5.00
16 Will Hafey	10.00	5.00
17 Ray Hamrick	10.00	5.00
18 Maurice Van Robays	10.00	5.00
19 Dario Lodigiani	10.00	5.00
20 Mel Duezabou	10.00	5.00
21 Damon Hayes	10.00	5.00
22 Gene Lillard	10.00	5.00
23 Al Wilkie	10.00	5.00
24 Tony Soriano	10.00	5.00
25 Glenn Crawford	10.00	5.00

1947 Royals Montreal

These cards measure approximately 4" by 6" and are printed on thick cardboard stock. The fronts feature black-and-white posed action photos bordered in white. Player information, including a brief biography, is printed in the wider bottom border. The backs are blank. The cards are unnumbered and checklisted below in alphabetical order.

	Ex-Mt	VG
COMPLETE SET (3)	25.00	12.50
1 Claude Corbitt	10.00	5.00
2 Roy Hughes	10.00	5.00
3 Don Ross	10.00	5.00

1947 Signal Oil

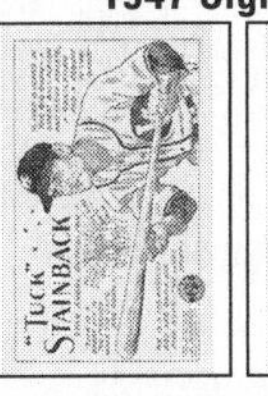

The 1947 Signal Oil set of 89 black and white, unnumbered drawings, by Al DeMaree, features Pacific Coast League players from five teams -- Hollywood Stars (1-20), Los Angeles Angels (21-38), Oakland Oaks (39-57), Sacramento Solons (58-73) and Seattle Rainiers (74-89). Numbers are assigned alphabetically within teams. The Sacramento player cards and to a greater extent the Seattle player cards are more difficult to obtain. The highlights of the careers of the players appear on the backgrounds of the cards as cartoons. Four players appear with two teams -- Frank Dasso, Guy Fletcher, Red Mann and Bill Ramsey. Woody Williams is considered quite scarce and Charles Ripple is somewhat less scarce. The catalog designation is UO11. Cards in this set measure approximately 5 1/2" by 3 1/2".

	Ex-Mt	VG
COMPLETE SET (89)	5000.00	2500.00
COMMON CARD (39-57)	20.00	10.00
COMMON CARD (58-73)	50.00	25.00
COMMON CARD (74-89)	100.00	50.00
1 Ed Albosta	30.00	15.00
2 Carl Cox	30.00	15.00
3 Frank Dasso	30.00	15.00
4 Tod Davis	30.00	15.00
5 Jimmy Delsing	40.00	20.00
6 Jimmy Dykes MG	60.00	30.00
7 Paul Gregory	30.00	15.00
8 Fred Haney GM	40.00	20.00
9 Francis Kelleher	30.00	15.00
10 Joe Krakauskas	30.00	15.00
11 Al Libke	30.00	15.00
12 Tony Lupien	40.00	20.00
13 Xavier Rescigno	30.00	15.00
14 Jack Sherman	30.00	15.00
15 Andy Skurski	30.00	15.00
16 Glen Stewart	30.00	15.00
17 Al Unser	40.00	20.00
18 Fred Vaughn	30.00	15.00
19 Woody Williams	800.00	400.00
20 Dutch Zernial	50.00	25.00
21 Red Adams	30.00	15.00
22 Larry Barton	30.00	15.00
23 Cliff Chambers	40.00	20.00
24 Lloyd Christopher	30.00	15.00
25 Cece Garriott	30.00	15.00
26 Al Glossops	30.00	15.00
27 Bill Kelly	30.00	15.00
28 Red Lynn	30.00	15.00
29 Eddie Malone	30.00	15.00
30 Dutch McCall	30.00	15.00
31 Don Osborn	30.00	15.00
32 John Ostrowski	30.00	15.00
33 Reggie Otero	30.00	15.00
34 Ray Prim	30.00	15.00
35 Ed Sauer	30.00	15.00
36 Bill Schuster	30.00	15.00
37 Tuck Stainback	40.00	20.00
38 Lou Stringer	30.00	15.00
39 Vic Buccola	20.00	10.00
40 Mickey Burnett	20.00	10.00
41 Ralph Buxton	20.00	10.00
42 Vince DiMaggio	100.00	50.00
43 Dizz Duezabou	20.00	10.00
44 Bud Foster ANN	20.00	10.00
45 Sherriff Gassaway	20.00	10.00
46 Tom Hafey	20.00	10.00
47 Brooks Holder	20.00	10.00
48 Gene Lillard	20.00	10.00
49 Dario Lodigiani	20.00	10.00
50 Hershel Martin	20.00	10.00
51 Cotton Pippen	20.00	10.00
52 Bill Raimondi	20.00	10.00
53 Tony Sabol	20.00	10.00
54 Les Scarsella	20.00	10.00
55 Floyd Speer	20.00	10.00
56 Casey Stengel MG	200.00	100.00
57 Maurice Van Robays	20.00	10.00
58 Bud Beasley	50.00	25.00
59 Frank Dasso	50.00	25.00
60 Ed Fitzgerald	50.00	25.00
61 Guy Fletcher	50.00	25.00
62 Tony Freitas	50.00	25.00
63 Red Mann	50.00	25.00
64 Joe Marty	50.00	25.00
65 Steve Mesner	50.00	25.00
66 Bill Ramsey	50.00	25.00
67 Chas. Ripple	400.00	200.00
68 John Rizzo	50.00	25.00
69 Al Smith	60.00	30.00
70 Ronnie Smith	50.00	25.00
71 Tommy Thompson	50.00	25.00
72 Jim Warner	60.00	30.00
73 Ed Zipay	50.00	25.00
74 Kewpie Barrett	120.00	60.00
75 Herman Besse	100.00	50.00
76 Guy Fletcher	100.00	50.00
77 Jack Jakucki	120.00	60.00
78 Bob Johnson	120.00	60.00
79 Pete Jonas	100.00	50.00
80 Hillis Layne	100.00	50.00
81 Red Mann	100.00	50.00
82 Lou Novikoff	120.00	60.00
83 John O'Neill	100.00	50.00
84 Bill Ramsey	100.00	50.00
85 Mickey Rocco	100.00	50.00
86 Geo. Scharein	100.00	50.00
87 Hal Sueme	100.00	50.00
88 Jo Jo White	120.00	60.00
89 Tony York	100.00	50.00

1947 Smith's Clothing

The 1947 Smith's Clothing set of 25 black and white, numbered cards features players from the Oakland Oaks only and is similar to the Remar Bread set. The backs give brief player biographies and a Smith's ad. The set is on very thin stock paper. The Max Marshall card is quite scarce, while the Gillespie, Hayes and Faria cards are tougher to find. The catalog designation is H801-3A. Cards in this set measure approximately 2" by 3".

	Ex-Mt	VG
COMPLETE SET (25)	800.00	400.00
1 Casey Stengel MG	200.00	100.00
2 Billy Raimondi	25.00	12.50
3 Les Scarsella	25.00	12.50
4 Brooks Holder	25.00	12.50
5 Ray Hamrick	25.00	12.50
6 Gene Lillard	25.00	12.50
7 Maurice Van Robays	25.00	12.50
8 Charlie Gassaway	25.00	12.50
9 Henry Pippen	25.00	12.50
10 James Arnold	25.00	12.50
11 Ralph Buxton	25.00	12.50
12 Ambrose Palica	25.00	12.50
13 Tony Sabol	25.00	12.50
14 Ed Kearse	25.00	12.50
15 Bill Hart	25.00	12.50
16 Snuffy Smith	25.00	12.50
17 Mickey Burnett	25.00	12.50
18 Tom Hafey	25.00	12.50
19 Will Hafey	25.00	12.50
20 Paul Gillespie	50.00	25.00
21 Damon Hayes	50.00	25.00
22 Max Marshall	120.00	60.00
23 Mel Duezabou	25.00	12.50
24 Mel Reeves	25.00	12.50
25 Joe Faria	50.00	25.00

1947 Sunbeam Bread Solons

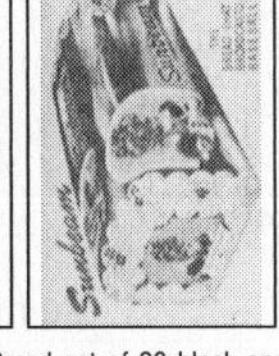

The 1947 Sunbeam Bread set of 26 black and white, unnumbered cards features the Sacramento Solons only. This set is distinguishable from the 1946 set by a reference to the "1947 Solons" on the fronts of the cards and a colored Sunbeam Bread loaf filling the entire back of the card. This issue is printed on very thin paper stock. The catalog designation is D315-2. Cards in this set measure approximately 2" by 3".

	Ex-Mt	VG
COMPLETE SET (26)	800.00	400.00
1 Gene Babbit	30.00	15.00
2 Bob Barthelson	30.00	15.00
3 Bud Beasley	30.00	15.00
4 Chuck Cronin	30.00	15.00
5 Eddie Fernandes	30.00	15.00
6 Ed Fitzgerald	30.00	15.00
7 Van Fletcher	30.00	15.00
8 Tony Freitas	30.00	15.00
9 Garth Mann	30.00	15.00
10 Joe Marty	60.00	30.00
11 Lou McCollum	30.00	15.00
12 Steve Mesner	30.00	15.00
13 Frank Nelson	30.00	15.00
14 Tommy Nelson	30.00	15.00
15 Joe Orengo	30.00	15.00
16 Hugh Orhan	30.00	15.00
17 Nick Pesut	30.00	15.00
18 Bill Ramsey	30.00	15.00
19 Johnny Rizzo	40.00	20.00
20 Mike Schemer	30.00	15.00
21 Al Smith	50.00	25.00
22 Tommy Thompson	30.00	15.00
23 Jim Warner	50.00	25.00
24 Mel Wasley	50.00	25.00
25 Leo Wells	30.00	15.00
26 Eddie Zipay	30.00	15.00

1948 Angels Team Issue

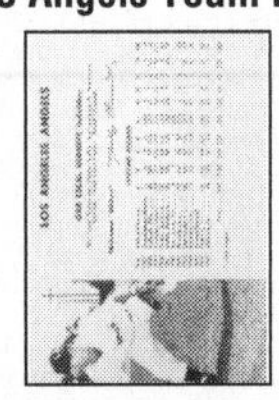

This 25-card set of the Los Angeles Angels features glossy black-and-white player photos printed on horizontal cards measuring approximately 6 3/4" by 4 3/4" with the player's autograph and complete playing record. The cards are unnumbered and checklisted below in alphabetical order.

	NM	Ex
COMPLETE SET (26)	250.00	125.00
1 Cliff Aberson	10.00	5.00
2 Charles Adams	10.00	5.00
3 John Adkins	10.00	5.00
4 Omer Anthony	10.00	5.00
5 Russell Bauers	10.00	5.00
6 Ora Escdal Burnett	10.00	5.00
7 Donald Carleen	10.00	5.00
8 Dom Dallessandro	12.00	6.00
9 Virgil Garriott	10.00	5.00
10 Paul Gillespie	10.00	5.00
11 Alban Glossop	10.00	5.00
12 Thomas Hafey	10.00	5.00
13 Donald Johnson	10.00	5.00
14 William Kelly MG	10.00	5.00
15 Harold Kleine	10.00	5.00
16 Walter Lanfranconi	10.00	5.00
17 Edward Lukon	10.00	5.00
18 Japhet Lynn	10.00	5.00
19 Edward Malone	10.00	5.00
20 Leonard Merullo	12.00	6.00
21 Ralph Novotney	10.00	5.00
22 John Ostrowski	12.00	6.00
23 John Sanford	10.00	5.00
24 Ed Sauer	10.00	5.00
25 William Schuster	10.00	5.00
26 John Warner CO	10.00	5.00

1948 Signal Oil

This set of 24 color photos of Oakland Oaks (Pacific Coast League) was given away at local gas stations. The cards are not numbered and are found with either blue or black printing on the back. Nicholas Etten and Brooks Holder are considered to be harder to find than the other cards in this set; they are notated with SP below. The catalog designation is U010. The cards are listed below in alphabetical order. The cards in this set measure approximately 2 3/8" by 3 1/2".

	NM	Ex
COMPLETE SET (24)	700.00	350.00
COMMON CARD (1-24)	20.00	10.00
COMMON SP	40.00	20.00
1 John Babich	20.00	10.00
2 Ralph Buxton	20.00	10.00
3 Loyd Christopher	20.00	10.00
4 Merrill Combs	20.00	10.00
5 Melvin Duezabou	20.00	10.00
6 Nicholas Etten SP	50.00	25.00
7 Bud Foster ANN	20.00	10.00
8 Charles Gassaway	20.00	10.00
9 Will Hafey	20.00	10.00
10 Ray Hamrick	20.00	10.00
11 Brooks Holder SP	40.00	20.00
12 Earl Jones	20.00	10.00
13 Cookie Lavagetto	40.00	20.00
14 Robert Lillard	20.00	10.00
15 Dario Lodigiani	20.00	10.00
16 Ernie Lombardi	80.00	40.00
17 Billy Martin	120.00	60.00
18 George Metkovich	25.00	12.50
19 William Raimondi	20.00	10.00
20 Les Scarsella	20.00	10.00
21 Floyd Speer	20.00	10.00
22 Casey Stengel MG	150.00	75.00
23 Maurice Van Robays	20.00	10.00
24 Aldon Wilkie	20.00	10.00

1948 Smith's Clothing

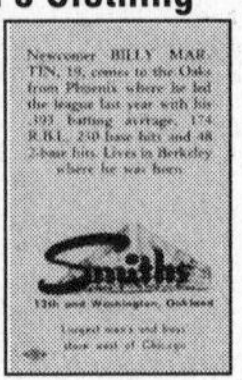

The 1948 Smith's Clothing set of 25 black and white numbered cards features Oakland Oaks players only and is printed on a much heavier stock than the 1947 Smith's set. The cards have a glossy finish. All cards feature full body shots showing players in either fielding, batting or pitching positions. The catalog designation is H801-3B. Cards in this set measure approximately 2" by 3".

	NM	Ex
COMPLETE SET (25)	650.00	325.00
1 Billy Raimondi	20.00	10.00
2 Brooks Holder	20.00	10.00
3 Will Hafey	30.00	15.00
4 Nick Etten	30.00	15.00
5 Loyd Christopher	20.00	10.00
6 Les Scarsella	20.00	10.00
7 Ray Hamrick	20.00	10.00
8 Gene Lillard	20.00	10.00
9 Maurice Van Robays	20.00	10.00
10 Charlie Gassaway	20.00	10.00
11 Ralph Buxton	20.00	10.00
12 Tom Hafey	20.00	10.00
13 Damon Hayes	20.00	10.00
14 Mel "Dizz" Duezabou	20.00	10.00
15 Dario Lodigiani	20.00	10.00
16 Vic Buccola	20.00	10.00
17 Billy Martin	120.00	60.00
18 Floyd Speer	20.00	10.00
19 Eddie Samcoff	20.00	10.00
20 Casey Stengel MG	150.00	75.00
21 Floyd Hittle	20.00	10.00
22 John Babich	20.00	10.00
23 Merrill Combs	20.00	10.00
24 Eddie Murphy	30.00	15.00
25 Bob Klinger	30.00	15.00

1948 Sommer and Kaufmann

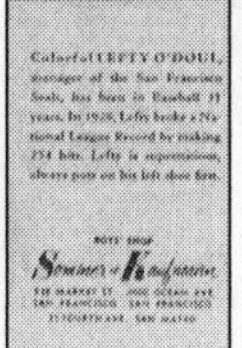

The 1948 Sommer and Kaufmann set of 30 numbered, black and white cards features players from the San Francisco Seals of the Pacific Coast League. The catalog designation is H801-4A. According to a recently rediscovered header card, these cards were given out three per week at the participating Sommer and Kaufmann Shoe Stores. The backs give brief player biographies and a Sommer and Kaufmann ad. The 1948 set can be distinguished from the 1949 set by the script writing of "Sommer and Kaufmann". The 1949 set has "Sommer and Kaufmann" in fancy print. Cards in this set measure approximately 2" by 3".

	NM	Ex
COMPLETE SET (30)	1400.00	700.00
1 Lefty O'Doul MG	80.00	40.00
2 Jack Brewer	40.00	20.00
3 Cornelius Dempsey	50.00	25.00
4 Tommy Fine	40.00	20.00
5 Kenneth Gables	40.00	20.00
6 Robert Joyce	40.00	20.00
7 Alfred Lien	40.00	20.00
8 Cliff Melton	50.00	25.00
9 Frank S. Shofner	40.00	20.00
10 Don Trower	40.00	20.00
11 Joe Brovia	40.00	20.00
12 Dino Restelli	50.00	25.00
13 Gene Woodling	60.00	30.00
14 Benjamin Guintini	40.00	20.00
15 Felix Mackiewicz	40.00	20.00
16 John Patrick Tobin	40.00	20.00
17 Manuel Perez Jr.	40.00	20.00
18 William Werle	40.00	20.00
19 Homer E. Howell Jr.	40.00	20.00
20 Wilfred Leonard	40.00	20.00
21 Bruce Ogrodowski	40.00	20.00
22 R. Dick Lajeskie	40.00	20.00
23 Hugh Luby	40.00	20.00
24 Roy Melvin Nicely	40.00	20.00
25 Raymond Orteig	40.00	20.00
26 Michael D. Rocco	40.00	20.00
27 Del Edward Young	40.00	20.00
28 Joe Sprinz	40.00	20.00
29 Leo Doc Hughes TR	40.00	20.00
30 Don Rode BB	40.00	20.00
Albert Bero BB		
Charlie Barnes BB		
NNO Header Card		
Salmon colored		

1949 Angels Team Issue

This 39-card set of the Los Angeles Angeles is similar to the 1948 Angels Team Issue set. The cards are unnumbered and checklisted below in alphabetical order. The blank-backed cards feature a player photo on the left and his career stats on the right side. This set was available at time of issue from the team for $1.

	NM	Ex
COMPLETE SET (39)	300.00	150.00
1 Clifford Aberson	8.00	4.00
2 Donald Alfano	8.00	4.00
3 Quentin Altizer	8.00	4.00
4 Omer Anthony	8.00	4.00
5 Nelson Burbrink	8.00	4.00
6 Forrest Burgess	12.00	6.00
7 Donald Carlsen	8.00	4.00
8 Joseph Damato	8.00	4.00
9 William Emmerich	8.00	4.00
10 Kenneth Gables	8.00	4.00
11 Virgil Garriott	8.00	4.00
12 Gordon Goldsberry	8.00	4.00
13 Alban Glossop	8.00	4.00
14 Frank Gustine	8.00	4.00
15 Lee Handley	8.00	4.00
16 Alan Ihde	8.00	4.00
17 Robert John Kelley ANN	8.00	4.00
18 Robert Edward Kelly	8.00	4.00
19 William Kelly MG	8.00	4.00
20 Walter Lanfranconi	8.00	4.00
21 Japhet Lynn	8.00	4.00
22 Clarence Maddern	8.00	4.00
23 Edward Malone	8.00	4.00
24 Carmen Mauro	8.00	4.00
25 Booker McDaniels	8.00	4.00
26 Calvin McLish	10.00	5.00
27 Cyril Moran	8.00	4.00
28 Ralph Novotney	8.00	4.00
29 John Ostrowski	8.00	4.00
30 Robert Rhawn	8.00	4.00
31 William Schuster	8.00	4.00
32 James Seerey	8.00	4.00
33 Bryan Stephens	8.00	4.00
34 Robert Sturgeon	8.00	4.00
35 W. Wayne Terwilliger	10.00	5.00
36 Gordon Van Dyke	8.00	4.00
37 John Warner CO	8.00	4.00
38 Don Watkins	8.00	4.00
39 The Trainers and Bat Boys	8.00	4.00

1949 Bowman PCL

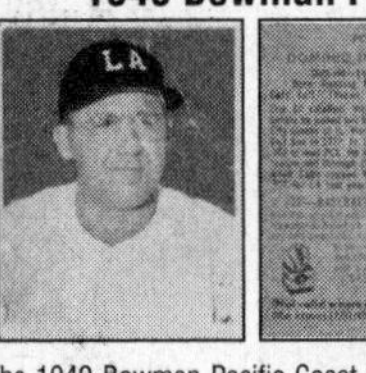
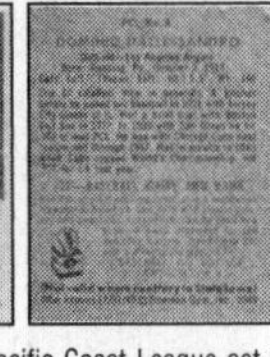

The 1949 Bowman Pacific Coast League set is recognized as one of the scarcest sets of the post-war period. Each card measures 2 1/16" by 2 1/2". Marketed regionally on the West Coast, it is thought that it may have been sold in sheets in candy and variety stores rather than in gum packs. The format of tinted photographs on colored backgrounds is identical to the regular 1949 Bowman issue.

	NM	Ex
COMPLETE SET (36)	8000.00	4000.00
1 Lee Anthony	250.00	125.00
2 George Metkovich	300.00	150.00
3 Ralph Hodgin	250.00	125.00
4 George Woods	250.00	125.00
5 Xavier Rescigno	250.00	125.00
6 Mickey Grasso	250.00	125.00
7 Johnny Rucker	250.00	125.00
8 Jack Brewer	250.00	125.00
9 Dom D'Allessandro	250.00	125.00
10 Charlie Gassaway	250.00	125.00
11 Tony Freitas	250.00	125.00
12 Gordon Maltzberger	250.00	125.00
13 John Jensen	250.00	125.00
14 Joyner White	250.00	125.00
15 Harvey Storey	250.00	125.00
16 Dick Lajeski	250.00	125.00
17 Albie Glossup	250.00	125.00
18 Bill Raimondi	250.00	125.00
19 Ken Holcombe	250.00	125.00
20 Don Ross	250.00	125.00
21 Pete Coscarart	250.00	125.00
22 Tony York	250.00	125.00
23 Jake Mooty	250.00	125.00
24 Charles Adams	250.00	125.00
25 Les Scarsella	250.00	125.00
26 Joe Marty	250.00	125.00
27 Frank Kelleher	250.00	125.00
28 Lee Handley	250.00	125.00
29 Herman Besse	250.00	125.00
30 John Lazor	250.00	125.00
31 Eddie Malone	250.00	125.00
32 Maurice Van Robays	250.00	125.00
33 Jim Tabor	250.00	125.00
34 Gene Handley	250.00	125.00
35 Tom Seats	250.00	125.00
36 Ora Burnett	250.00	125.00

1949 Fort Worth Cats

This 18 card set which was issued on heavy card stock and measures approximately 8" by 10" featured members of the 1949 Ft Worth Cats, which was a farm team of the Brooklyn Dodgers. Other than card numbers 1 and 9 -- this set is sequenced in alphabetical order.

	NM	Ex
COMPLETE SET	200.00	100.00
1 Sam DiBlasi Joe Landrum	10.00	5.00
2 Cal Abrams	12.00	6.00
3 Bob Austin	10.00	5.00
4 Carroll Berringer	12.00	6.00
5 Bobby Bragan	15.00	7.50
6 Bob Bundy	10.00	5.00
7 Eddie Chandler	10.00	5.00
8 Chris Van Cuyk	10.00	5.00
9 Sam DiBlasi Joe Landrum	10.00	5.00

10 George Dockins	10.00	5.00
11 Carl Erskine	20.00	10.00
12 Wally Fieta	10.00	5.00
13 Jack Lindsey	10.00	5.00
14 Bob Milliken	12.00	6.00
15 Walter Sessi	10.00	5.00
16 Ken Staples	10.00	5.00
17 Preston Ward	10.00	5.00
18 Dick Williams	20.00	10.00

1949 Remar Bread

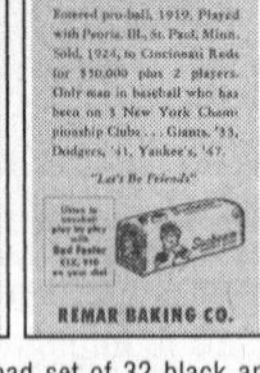

The 1949 Remar Bread set of 32 black and white picture cards depicts Oakland Oaks players only. The backs, in blue print on white stock, give vital statistics, 1948 records and show a Sunbeam bread loaf. Some cards were printed in limited quantities and the players have been placed in alphabetical order and numbered in the checklist, although the cards themselves are not numbered. The catalog designation is D317-4. Cards in this set measure approximately 2" by 3".

	NM	Ex
COMPLETE SET (32)	450.00	220.00
1 Ralph Buxton	8.00	4.00
2 Mario Candini	25.00	12.50
3 Rex Cecil	25.00	12.50
4 Loyd Christopher	8.00	4.00
5 Mel Duezabou	8.00	4.00
6 Chuck Dressen MG	25.00	12.50
7 Bud Foster ANN	8.00	4.00
8 Clarence Gassaway	8.00	4.00
9 Ray Hamrick	8.00	4.00
10 Jackie Jensen	50.00	25.00
11 Earl Jones	8.00	.65
12 George Kelly	25.00	12.50
13 Frank Kerr	25.00	12.50
14 Dick Kryhoski	25.00	12.50
15 Cookie Lavagetto	40.00	20.00
16 Dario Lodigiani	8.00	4.00
17 Billy Martin	100.00	50.00
18 George Metkovich	8.00	4.00
19 Frank Nelson	8.00	4.00
20 Don Padgett	8.00	4.00
21 Alonzo Perry	25.00	12.50
22 Bill Raimondi	8.00	4.00
23 Earl Rapp	8.00	4.00
24 Ed Samcoff	8.00	4.00
25 Les Scarsella	8.00	4.00
26 Forest Thompson	25.00	12.50
27 Earl Toolson	25.00	12.50
28 Louis Tost	25.00	12.50
29 Maurice Van Robays	10.00	5.00
30 Jim Wallace	8.00	4.00
31 Artie Wilson	10.00	5.00
32 Parnell Woods	30.00	15.00

1949 Solon Sunbeam/Pureta PC759

This set was co-issued by Sunbeam Bread and Pureta Sausage and features Sacramento Solons. The fronts feature the player and an microphone insert with station call letters printed on it. The backs feature ads for both Sunbeam Bread and Pureta Sausage. This is considered the toughest of the Remar-Sunbeam sets for these postcards were issued weekly and only through a special radio promotion.

	NM	Ex
COMPLETE SET (12)	550.00	275.00
1 Del Baker MG	50.00	25.00
2 Frankie Dasso	50.00	25.00
3 Walt Dropo	80.00	40.00
4 Joe Grace	50.00	25.00
5 Bob Gillespie	50.00	25.00
6 Ralph Hodgin	50.00	25.00
7 Freddie Marsh	50.00	25.00
8 Joe Marty	50.00	25.00
9 Len Ratto	50.00	25.00
10 Jim Tabor	50.00	25.00
11 Al White	50.00	25.00
12 Bill Wilson	50.00	25.00

1949 Sommer and Kaufmann

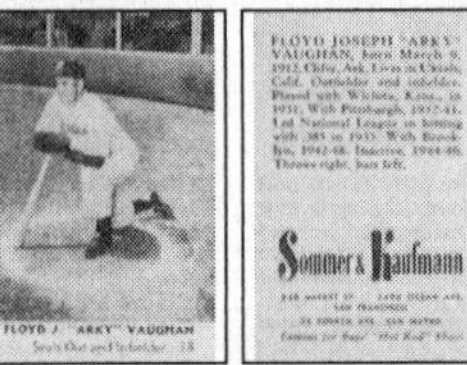

The 1949 Sommer and Kaufmann set of 28 numbered, black and white cards features players of the San Francisco Seals of the Pacific Coast League. Card No. 24 is not known to exist. The catalog designation is H801-4B. Cards in this set measure approximately 2" by 3".

	NM	Ex
COMPLETE SET (28)	1200.00	600.00
1 Lefty O'Doul MG	80.00	40.00
2 Jack Brewer	40.00	20.00
3 Kenneth H. Gables	40.00	20.00
4 Con Dempsey	50.00	25.00
5 Alfred Lien	40.00	20.00
6 Cliff Melton	50.00	25.00
7 Steve Nagy	40.00	20.00
8 Manny Perez	40.00	20.00
9 Roy Jarvis	40.00	20.00
10 Roy Partee	40.00	20.00
11 Reno Cheso	40.00	20.00
12 Dick Lajeskie	40.00	20.00
13 Roy M. Nicely	40.00	20.00
14 Mickey Rocco	40.00	20.00
15 Frank Shofner	40.00	20.00
16 Richard Holder	40.00	20.00
17 Dino Restelli	50.00	25.00
18 Arky Vaughan	80.00	40.00
19 Jackie Baccioccu	40.00	20.00
20 Robert F. Drilling	40.00	20.00
21 Del E. Young	40.00	20.00
22 Joseph D. Sprinz	40.00	20.00
23 Leo E.Doc Hughes TR Card Collector Dick Dobbins in background	40.00	20.00
25 Bert Singleton	40.00	20.00
26 John Gene Brocker	40.00	20.00
27 Jack Tobin	40.00	20.00
28 Walter Judnich	50.00	25.00
29 Harry (Hal) Foldman	40.00	20.00

1949 Hollywood Stars

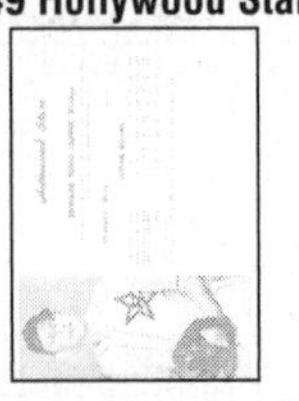

This 24 card set measures 7" by 4 3/4". The set was published by "Fan Pix" and the cards are set out in an horizontal format. The cards also had complete playing records and a space for autographs. This set was available for 60 cents from the Hollywood Stars at the time of issue.

	NM	Ex
COMPLETE SET	400.00	200.00
1 Jim Baxes	20.00	10.00
2 George Fallon	20.00	10.00
3 John Fitzpatrick	20.00	10.00
4 George Genovese	20.00	10.00
5 Hubert Gorman	20.00	10.00
6 Gene Handley	20.00	10.00
7 Fred Haney MG	20.00	10.00
8 James R. Hughes	20.00	10.00
9 Frank Kellerher	20.00	10.00
10 Gordon Maltzberger	20.00	10.00
11 Glen Moulder	20.00	10.00
12 Irv Noren	25.00	12.50
13 Edward Oliver	20.00	10.00
14 John O'Neil	20.00	10.00
15 Walter Olsen	20.00	10.00
16 Jack Paepke	20.00	10.00
17 Willard Ramsdell	20.00	10.00
18 Jack Salveson	20.00	10.00
19 Mike Sandlock	20.00	10.00
20 Art Schallock	20.00	10.00
21 Andy Skurski	20.00	10.00
22 Chuck Stevens	20.00	10.00
23 Al Unser	20.00	10.00
24 George Woods	20.00	10.00

1950 Ft Worth Cats

This set is similar to the 1949 Ft Worth Cats sets and feature players from the 1950 Ft Worth Cats. These cards are sequenced in alphabetical order. The Austin, Berringer, Van Cuyk and Landrum photos are the same ones used in 1949

	NM	Ex
COMPLETE SET	200.00	100.00
1 Bob Austin	10.00	5.00
2 Carroll Berringer	12.00	6.00
3 Frank Brown	10.00	5.00
4 Gene Clough	10.00	5.00
5 Chris Van Cuyk	10.00	5.00
6 Don Hoak	12.00	6.00
7 Wallace Jay	10.00	5.00
8 Jay Kelchner	10.00	5.00
9 Joe Landrum	10.00	5.00
10 Mike Lemish	10.00	5.00
11 Jack Lindsay	10.00	5.00
12 Ray Moore	10.00	5.00
13 John Reeves	10.00	5.00
14 Russ Rose	10.00	5.00
15 John Rutherford	10.00	5.00
16 Ken Staples	10.00	5.00
17 Fred Storck	10.00	5.00
18 Tommy Tatum	10.00	5.00
19 Joe Torpay	10.00	5.00
20 Mel Waters	10.00	5.00

1950 Remar Bread

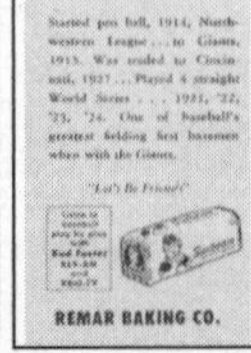

The 1950 Remar Bread set of 27 black and white, unnumbered cards features Oakland Oaks players only. The format is identical to the 1949 set except that the backs include 1949 records. The catalog designation is D317-5. The cards are listed below in alphabetical order. Cards in this set measure approximately 2" by 3".

	NM	Ex
COMPLETE SET (27)	250.00	125.00
1 George Bamberger	20.00	10.00
2 Hank Behrman	8.00	4.00
3 Loyd Christopher	8.00	4.00
4 Chuck Dressen MG	15.00	7.50
5 Mel Duezabou	8.00	4.00
6 Augie Galan	10.00	5.00
7 Clarence Gassaway	8.00	4.00
8 Allen Gettel	8.00	4.00
9 Ernie Groth	10.00	5.00
10 Ray Hamrick	8.00	4.00
11 Earl Harrist	8.00	4.00
12 Billy Herman	30.00	15.00
13 Bob Hofman	8.00	4.00
14 George Kelly MG	30.00	15.00
15 Cookie Lavagetto	15.00	7.50
16 Eddie Malone	8.00	4.00
17 George Metkovich	8.00	4.00
18 Frank Nelson	8.00	4.00
19 Ray Noble	8.00	4.00
20 Don Padgett	8.00	4.00
21 Earl Rapp	8.00	4.00
22 Clyde Shoun	8.00	4.00
23 Forest Thompson	8.00	4.00
24 Louis Tost	8.00	4.00
25 Dick Wakefield	15.00	7.50
26 Artie Wilson	10.00	5.00
27 Roy Zimmerman	8.00	4.00

1950 Stockton Ports Sunbeam D316-2

These 13 2" by 3" black and white cards were issued by Sunbeam bread to promote their product and features members of the 1950 Stockton Ports. Since the cards are unnumbered we have sequenced them in alphabetical order.

	NM	Ex
COMPLETE SET (13)	600.00	300.00
1 Dick Adams	50.00	25.00
2 Jim Brown	50.00	25.00
3 Harry Clements	50.00	25.00
4 John Goldborg	50.00	25.00
5 Jerry Haines	50.00	25.00
6 Al Heist	50.00	25.00
7 Don Masterson	50.00	25.00
8 Lauren Monroe	50.00	25.00
9 Frank Murray	50.00	25.00
10 Lauren Simon	50.00	25.00
11 George Stanich	50.00	25.00
12 Bob Stevens	50.00	25.00
13 Hal Zurcher	50.00	25.00

1950 Hollywood Stars

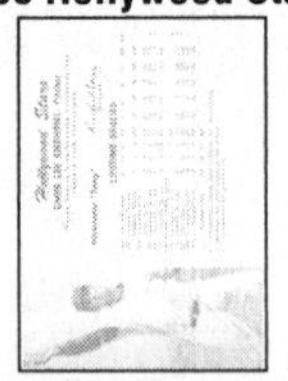

This set is very similar to the 1949 Hollywood Stars issue. The major difference is that there are fascimile autographs on the front. The photos are also totally different from the 1949 issue. This set was also issued by "Fan Pix".

	NM	Ex
COMPLETE SET	600.00	300.00
1 Lee Anthony	20.00	10.00
2 Bill Antonelle	20.00	10.00
3 Dick Barrett	20.00	10.00
5 Clint Conatser	20.00	10.00
6 Clifford Dapper	20.00	10.00
7 George Fallen	20.00	10.00
8 John Fitzpatrick	20.00	10.00
9 Murray Franklin	20.00	10.00
10 Herbert Gorman	20.00	10.00
11 Gene Handley	20.00	10.00
13 Clarence Hicks	20.00	10.00
14 Herb Karpel	20.00	10.00
15 Gene Kelleher	20.00	10.00
16 Ken Lehman	20.00	10.00
17 John Lindell	25.00	12.50
18 Gordon Maltzberger	20.00	10.00
19 Daniel Menendez	20.00	10.00
20 Larry Mondroff	20.00	10.00
21 Glenn Moulder	20.00	10.00
22 John O'Neil	20.00	10.00
23 Jack Paepke	20.00	10.00
24 Jean Pierre Roy	20.00	10.00
25 John Salveson, Jr.	20.00	10.00
26 Mike Sandlock	20.00	10.00
27 Edward Dauer	20.00	10.00
28 Art Schallock	20.00	10.00
29 George Schmees	20.00	10.00
30 Chuck Stevens	20.00	10.00
31 Ben Wade	20.00	10.00
32 George Woods	20.00	10.00

1950 World Wide Gum V362

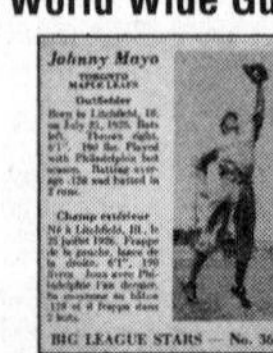

The cards in this 48-card set measure approximately 2 1/2" by 3 1/4". In 1950, long after its former parent company had disappeared from the card market, the World Wide Gum Company issued a set of blue printed cards depicting players from the International League. The fronts feature player photos with bilingual (French and English) biographies. The backs are blank. The series was entitled "Big League Stars". The catalog designation for this set is V362. The cards are numbered on the front. There is an early card of Hall of Fame manager Tommy Lasorda in this set.

	NM	Ex
COMPLETE SET (48)	4000.00	2000.00
1 Rocky Bridges	100.00	50.00
2 Chuck Connors	400.00	200.00
3 Jake Wade	80.00	40.00
4 Al Cihocki	80.00	40.00
5 John Simmons	80.00	40.00
6 Frank Trechock	80.00	40.00
7 Steve Lembo	80.00	40.00
8 Johnny Welaj	80.00	40.00
9 Seymour Block	80.00	40.00
10 Pat McGlothlin	80.00	40.00
11 Bryan Stephens	80.00	40.00
12 Clarence Podbielan	100.00	50.00
13 Clem Hausmann	80.00	40.00
14 Turk Lown	100.00	50.00
15 Joe Payne	80.00	40.00
16 Coaker Triplett	100.00	50.00
17 Nick Strincevich	80.00	40.00
18 Charlie Thompson	80.00	40.00
19 Eric Silverman	80.00	40.00
20 George Schmees	80.00	40.00
21 George Binks	80.00	40.00
22 Gino Cimoli	100.00	50.00
23 Marty Tabacheck	80.00	40.00
24 Al Gionfriddo	100.00	50.00
25 Ronnie Lee	80.00	40.00
26 Clyde King	100.00	50.00
27 Harry Heslet	80.00	40.00
28 Jerry Scala	80.00	40.00
29 Boris Woyt	80.00	40.00
30 Jack Collum	80.00	40.00
31 Chet Laabs	100.00	50.00
32 Carden Gillenwater	80.00	40.00
33 Irving Medlinger	80.00	40.00
34 Toby Atwell	80.00	40.00
35 Charlie Marshall	80.00	40.00
36 Johnny Mayo	80.00	40.00
37 Gene Markland	80.00	40.00
38 Russ Kerns	80.00	40.00
39 Jim Prendergast	80.00	40.00
40 Lou Welaj	80.00	40.00
41 Clyde Kluttz	100.00	50.00
42 Bill Glynn	80.00	40.00
43 Don Richmond	80.00	40.00
44 Hank Biasatti	80.00	40.00
45 Tommy Lasorda	500.00	250.00
46 Al Roberge	80.00	40.00
47 George Byam	80.00	40.00
48 Dutch Mele	100.00	50.00

1952 Dallas Eagles Team Issue

These cards, which measure approximately 2 1/2" by 3 1/2" feature members of the 1952 Dallas Eagles team. These black and white cards feature posed action shots surrounded by a white border which measured 1/8" all around. Since these photos are unnumbered, we have sequenced them in alphabetical order. There might be more cards in this set so all additions are appreciated.

	NM	Ex
COMPLETE SET	75.00	38.00
1 Ralph Albers	10.00	5.00
2 Bob Bundy	10.00	5.00
3 Dave Hoskins	10.00	5.00
4 Eddie Knoblauch	10.00	5.00
5 Walt Lanfranconi	10.00	5.00
6 Don Mossi	15.00	7.50
7 Clyde Perry	10.00	5.00
8 Harry Sullivan	10.00	5.00

1952 La Patrie

These posed color photos of Canadian baseball players of 1952 comprised an "Album Sportif" in La Patrie, a French-language Montreal newspaper. They are bordered in red, white and blue and measure approximately 11" by 15 1/4". The player's name appears at the upper right. The photos are unnumbered and checklisted below in alphabetical order.

	NM	Ex
COMPLETE SET (19)	350.00	180.00
1 Bob Alexander	10.00	5.00
2 Georges Carpentier	10.00	5.00
3 Hampton Coleman	10.00	5.00
4 Walter Fiala	10.00	5.00
5 Jim Gilliam UER (Gilliams printed on front)	50.00	25.00
6 Tom Hackett	10.00	5.00
7 Don Hoak	20.00	10.00
8 Tom Lasorda	100.00	50.00
9 Herbie Lash	10.00	5.00
10 Mal Mallette	10.00	5.00
11 Georges Maranda	10.00	5.00
12 Carmen Mauro	10.00	5.00
13 Solly Mohn	10.00	5.00
14 Jacques Monette	10.00	5.00
15 Johnny Podres	50.00	25.00
16 Ed Roebuck	15.00	7.50
17 Charlie Thompson	10.00	5.00
18 Don Thompson	10.00	5.00
19 John Wingo	10.00	5.00

1952 Laval Provinciale

Issued by Laval Dairies of Quebec, these 114 blank-backed cards measure approximately 1 1/4" by 2 1/2" and feature white-bordered black-and-white posed player photos. The player's name, team, position, birthplace and birthdate appear in the white margin below the photo. All text is in French. The cards are numbered on the front.

	NM	Ex
COMPLETE SET (114)	1000.00	500.00
1 Georges McQuinn	20.00	10.00
2 Cliff Statham	10.00	5.00
3 Frank Wilson	10.00	5.00
4 Frank Neri	10.00	5.00
5 Georges Maranda	15.00	7.50
6 Richard Cordeiro	10.00	5.00
7 Roger McCardell	10.00	5.00
8 Joseph Janiak	10.00	5.00
9 Herbert Shankman	10.00	5.00
10 Joe Subbiondo	10.00	5.00
11 Jack Brenner	10.00	5.00
12 Donald Buchanan	10.00	5.00
13 Bob Smith	15.00	7.50
14 Raymond Lague	10.00	5.00
15 Mike Fandozzi	10.00	5.00
16 Dick Moler	10.00	5.00
17 Edward Bazydlo	10.00	5.00
18 Danny Mazurek	10.00	5.00
19 Edwin Charles	15.00	7.50
20 Jack Mullaney	10.00	5.00
21 Bob Bolan	10.00	5.00
22 Bob Long	10.00	5.00
23 Cleo Lewright	10.00	5.00
24 Herb Taylor	10.00	5.00
25 Frank Gaeta	10.00	5.00
26 Bill Truitt	10.00	5.00
27 Jean Prats	10.00	5.00
28 Tex Taylor	10.00	5.00
29 Ronnie Delbianco	10.00	5.00
30 Joe Dilorenzo	10.00	5.00
31 John Paszek	10.00	5.00
32 Ken Suess	10.00	5.00
33 Harry Sims	10.00	5.00
34 William Jackson	10.00	5.00
35 Jerry Mayers	10.00	5.00
36 Gordon Maltzberger	15.00	7.50
37 Gerry Cabana	10.00	5.00
38 Gary Rutkay	10.00	5.00
39 Ken Hatcher	10.00	5.00
40 Vincent Cosenza	10.00	5.00
41 Edward Yaeger	10.00	5.00
42 Jimmy Orr	10.00	5.00
43 John Dimartino	10.00	5.00
44 Len Wisnaski	10.00	5.00
45 Pete Caniglia	10.00	5.00
46 Guy Coleman	10.00	5.00
47 Herb Fleischer	10.00	5.00
48 Charles Yahrling	10.00	5.00
49 Roger Bedard	10.00	5.00
50 Al Barillari	10.00	5.00
51 Hugh Mulcahy	15.00	7.50
52 Vincent Canepa	10.00	5.00
53 Bob Loranger	10.00	5.00
54 Georges Carpentier	10.00	5.00
55 Bill Hamilton	10.00	5.00
56 Hector Lopez	20.00	10.00
57 Joe Taylor	10.00	5.00
58 Alonso Brathwaite	10.00	5.00
59 Carl McQuillen	10.00	5.00
60 Robert Trice	15.00	7.50
61 John Dworak	10.00	5.00
62 Lal Pinkston	10.00	5.00
63 William Shannon	10.00	5.00
64 Stanley Watychowics	10.00	5.00
65 Roger Hebert	10.00	5.00
66 Troy Spencer	10.00	5.00
67 Johnny Rahan	10.00	5.00
68 John Sosh	10.00	5.00
69 Raymond Mason	10.00	5.00
70 Tom Smith	10.00	5.00
71 Douglas McBean	10.00	5.00
72 Bill Babik	10.00	5.00
73 Dante Cozzi	10.00	5.00
74 Melvil Doxtator	10.00	5.00
75 William(Bill) Gilday	10.00	5.00
76 Armando Diaz	10.00	5.00
77 Ackroyd Smith	10.00	5.00
78 Germain Pizarro	10.00	5.00
79 James Heap	10.00	5.00
80 Herbert B. Crompton	10.00	5.00
81 Howard J. Bodell	10.00	5.00
82 Andre Schreiser	10.00	5.00
83 John Wingo	10.00	5.00
84 Salvatore Arduini	10.00	5.00
85 Fred Paccito	10.00	5.00
86 Aaron Osofsky	10.00	5.00
87 Jack Digrace	10.00	5.00
88 Alfonzo Gerard	10.00	5.00
89 Manuel Trabous	10.00	5.00
90 Tom Barnes	10.00	5.00
91 Humberto Robinson	15.00	7.50
92 Jack Buxowatz	10.00	5.00
93 Marco Mainini	10.00	5.00
94 Claude St-Vincent	10.00	5.00
95 Fernand Brousseau	10.00	5.00
96 John Malangone	10.00	5.00
97 Pierre Nantel	10.00	5.00
98 Donald Stevens	10.00	5.00
99 Jim Prappas	10.00	5.00
100 Richard Fitzgerald	10.00	5.00
101 Yves Aubin	10.00	5.00
102 Frank Novosel	10.00	5.00
103 Tony Campos	10.00	5.00
104 Gelso Oviedo	10.00	5.00
105 July Becker	10.00	5.00
106 Aurelio Ala	10.00	5.00
107 Orlando Andux	10.00	5.00
108 Tom Hackett	10.00	5.00
109 Guillaume Vargas	10.00	5.00
110 Francisco Salfran	10.00	5.00
111 Jean-Marc Blais	10.00	5.00
112 Vince Pizzitola	10.00	5.00
113 John Olsen	10.00	5.00
114 Jacques Monette	10.00	5.00

1952 Miami Beach Flamingos Team Issue

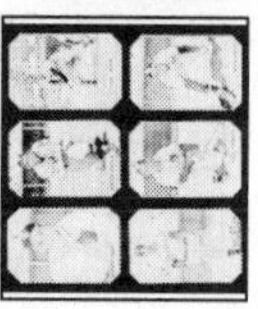

This 18 card set, which measures approximately 2 1/4" by 3 1/2" feature members of the 1952 Miami Beach Flamingos of the Florida International League. These cards were issued in an souvenir album. Since these cards are unnumbered, we have sequenced them in alphabetical order.

	Nm-Mt	Ex-Mt
COMPLETE SET (18)	150.00	70.00
1 Billy Barrett	10.00	4.50
2 Art Bosch	10.00	4.50
3 Jack Caro	10.00	4.50
4 George Handy	10.00	4.50
5 Clark Henry	10.00	4.50
6 Dario Jiminez	10.00	4.50
7 Jesse Levan	10.00	4.50
8 Bobby Lyons	10.00	4.50
9 Pepper Martin MG	20.00	9.00
10 Dick McMillin	10.00	4.50
11 Chico Morilla	10.00	4.50
12 Walt Nothe	10.00	4.50
13 Johnny Podgajny	10.00	4.50
14 Whitey Platt	10.00	4.50
15 Knobby Rosa	10.00	4.50
16 Mort Smith	10.00	4.50
17 Tommy Venn	10.00	4.50
18 Ray Williams	10.00	4.50

1952 Mothers Cookies

The cards in this 64-card set measure 2 3/16" by 3 1/2". The 1952 Mother's Cookies set contains numbered, full-color cards. They feature PCL players only and were distributed on the West Coast in bags of Mothers Cookies. Reported scarcities are 29 Peterson, 43 Erautt, 37 Welmaker, 11 MacCawley and 16 Talbot. Chuck Connors (4), the "Rifleman," is not scarce but is widely sought after. The catalog designation is D357-1. Johnny Lindell (#1) and Fred Haney (#13) are also known to exist with schedule backs. These backs are very scarce and are worth approximately 10 times the value of the regular cards.

	NM	Ex
COMPLETE SET (64)	2000.00	1000.00
COMMON CARD (1-64)	25.00	12.50
1 Johnny Lindell	30.00	15.00
2 Jim Davis	25.00	12.50
3 Al Gettel	25.00	12.50
4 Chuck Connors	250.00	125.00
5 Joe Grace	25.00	12.50
6 Eddie Basinski	25.00	12.50
7 Gene Handley	25.00	12.50
8 Walt Judnich	25.00	12.50
9 Jim Marshall	25.00	12.50
10 Max West	25.00	12.50
11 Bill MacCawley SP	50.00	25.00
12 Moreno Pieretti	25.00	12.50
13 Fred Haney MG	30.00	15.00
14 Earl Johnson	25.00	12.50
15 Dave Dahle	25.00	12.50
16 Bob Talbot SP	50.00	25.00
17 Smokey Singleton	25.00	12.50
18 Frank Austin	25.00	12.50
19 Joe Gordon MG	40.00	20.00
20 Joe Marty	25.00	12.50
21 Bob Gillespie	25.00	12.50
22 Red Embree	25.00	12.50
23 Lefty Olsen	25.00	12.50
24 Whitey Wietelmann	25.00	12.50
25 Lefty O'Doul MG	40.00	20.00
26 Memo Luna	25.00	12.50
27 John Davis	25.00	12.50
28 Dick Faber	25.00	12.50
29 Buddy Peterson SP	150.00	75.00
30 Hank Schenz	25.00	12.50
31 Tookie Gilbert	25.00	12.50
32 Mel Ott MG	100.00	50.00
33 Sam Chapman	30.00	15.00
34 John Ragni	25.00	12.50
35 Dick Cole	25.00	12.50
36 Tom Saffel	25.00	12.50
37 Roy Welmaker SP	100.00	50.00
38 Lou Stringer	25.00	12.50
39 Chuck Stevens	25.00	12.50
40 Artie Wilson	30.00	15.00
41 Charlie Schanz	25.00	12.50
42 Al Lyons	25.00	12.50
43 Joe Erautt SP	150.00	75.00
44 Clarence Maddern	25.00	12.50
45 Gene Baker	30.00	15.00
46 Tom Heath	25.00	12.50
47 Al Lien	25.00	12.50
48 Bill Reeder	25.00	12.50
49 Bob Thurman	30.00	15.00
50 Ray Orteig	25.00	12.50
51 Joe Brovia	25.00	12.50
52 Jim Russell	25.00	12.50
53 Fred Sanford	25.00	12.50
54 Jim Gladd	25.00	12.50
55 Clay Hopper MG	25.00	12.50
56 Bill Glynn	25.00	12.50
57 Mike McCormick	25.00	12.50
58 Richie Myers	25.00	12.50
59 Vinnie Smith	25.00	12.50
60 Stan Hack MG	30.00	15.00
61 Bob Spicer	25.00	12.50
62 Jack Hollis	25.00	12.50
63 Ed Chandler	25.00	12.50
64 Bill Moisan	25.00	12.50

1952 Parkhurst

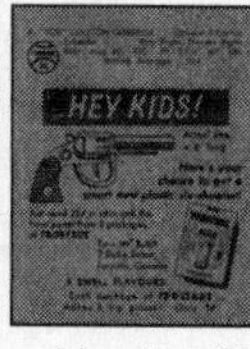

The 100 cards comprising the 1952 Parkhurst/Frostade set measure approximately 2" by 2 1/2" and depict players from three Canadian International League teams: Montreal Royals (49-76), Ottawa Athletics (77-100) and Toronto Maple Leafs (1-26). The fronts feature white-bordered black-and-white player photos. The plain backs have red print and carry the player's name, team, position and biography at the top; an ad for Frostade follows below. The set also includes a number of playing tip and play diagram cards (27-48). The catalog designation for this set is V338-1. Cards oriented horizontally are indicated below by HOR.

	NM	Ex
COMPLETE SET (100)	1650.00	800.00
COMMON CARD (1-25)	15.00	7.50
COMMON CARD (26-48)	10.00	5.00
COMMON CARD (49-100)	15.00	7.50
1 Joe Becker MG	20.00	10.00
2 Aaron Silverman	15.00	7.50
3 Bobby Rhawn HOR	15.00	7.50
4 Russ Bauers HOR	15.00	7.50
5 William Jennings HOR	15.00	7.50
6 Grover Bowers	15.00	7.50
7 Vic Lombardi	20.00	10.00
8 Billy DeMars	20.00	10.00
9 Frank Colman	15.00	7.50
10 Charles Grant	15.00	7.50
11 Irving Medlinger	15.00	7.50
12 Burke McLaughlin	15.00	7.50
13 Lew Morton	15.00	7.50
14 Red Barrett	20.00	10.00
15 Leon Foulk	15.00	7.50
16 Neil Sheridan	15.00	7.50
17 Ferrell(Andy) Anderson	15.00	7.50
18 Ray Shore	15.00	7.50
19 Duke Markell	15.00	7.50
20 Robert Balcena	15.00	7.50
21 Wilmer Fields	15.00	7.50
22 Charles White HOR	15.00	7.50
23 Gerald Fahr	15.00	7.50
24 Jose Bracho HOR	15.00	7.50
25 Edward Stevens HOR	20.00	10.00
26 Maple Leaf Stadium HOR	20.00	10.00
27 Throwing Home HOR	10.00	5.00
28 Regulation Baseball Diamond HOR	10.00	5.00
29 Gripping The Bat	10.00	5.00
30 Hiding Kind of Pitch	10.00	5.00
31 Catcher's Stance	10.00	5.00
32 Quiz Question How long does a batter have to see& swing at& and hit a fast ball	10.00	5.00
33 Finger and Arm Exercises HOR	10.00	5.00
34 First Baseman	10.00	5.00
35 Pitcher's Stance	10.00	5.00
36 Swinging Bats	10.00	5.00
37 Quiz Question HOR Can a player advance a base when a foul is caught	10.00	5.00
38 Watch the Ball HOR	10.00	5.00
39 Quiz Question HOR Can a team ever win a game with less runs than their opponents	10.00	5.00
40 Quiz Question Can a player put his own teammate out	10.00	5.00
41 How to Bunt	10.00	5.00
42 Wrist Snap	10.00	5.00
43 Pitching Practice	10.00	5.00
44 Stealing Bases	10.00	5.00
45 Pitching I	10.00	5.00
46 Pitching II	10.00	5.00
47 Signals	10.00	5.00
48 Regulation Baseballs	10.00	5.00
49 Albert Ronning	10.00	5.00
50 William C. Lane	15.00	7.50
51 William Samson	15.00	7.50
52 Charles Thompson	15.00	7.50
53 Ezra McGlothin	15.00	7.50
54 Forrest Jacobs	20.00	10.00
55 Arthur Fabbro	15.00	7.50
56 James Hughes	20.00	10.00
57 Don Hoak	25.00	12.50
58 Tommy Lasorda	200.00	100.00
59 Gilbert Mills	15.00	7.50
60 Malcolm Mallette	15.00	7.50
61 Glenn Nelson	15.00	7.50
62 John Simmons	15.00	7.50
63 R.S. Alex Alexander	15.00	7.50
64 Dan Bankhead	20.00	10.00
65 Solomon Coleman	15.00	7.50
66 Walter Alston MG	100.00	50.00
67 Walter Fiala	15.00	7.50
68 Jim Gilliam	60.00	30.00
69 Jim Pendleton	20.00	10.00
70 Gino Cimoli	20.00	10.00
71 Carmen Mauro	15.00	7.50
72 Walt Moryn	20.00	10.00
73 James Romano	15.00	7.50
74 Rollin Lutz	15.00	7.50
75 Ed Roebuck	20.00	10.00
76 John Podres	50.00	25.00
77 Walter Novick	15.00	7.50
78 Lefty Gohl	15.00	7.50
79 Thomas Kirk	15.00	7.50
80 Robert Betz	15.00	7.50
81 Bill Hockenbury	15.00	7.50
82 Albert Rubeling HOR	15.00	7.50
83 Julius Watlington	15.00	7.50
84 Frank Fanovich	15.00	7.50
85 Hank Foiles	20.00	10.00
86 Lou Limmer HOR	20.00	10.00
87 Edward Hrabcsak	15.00	7.50
88 Bob Gardner	15.00	7.50
89 John Metkovich	15.00	7.50
90 Jean-Pierre Roy	15.00	7.50
91 Frank Skaff MG	15.00	7.50
92 Harry Desert	15.00	7.50
93 Stan Jok	20.00	10.00
94 Russ Swingle	15.00	7.50
95 Bob Wellman	15.00	7.50
96 John Conway HOR	15.00	7.50
97 George Maskovich HOR	15.00	7.50
98 Charles Bishop	15.00	7.50
99 Joseph Murray	15.00	7.50
100 Mike Kume	20.00	10.00

1953 Fargo Moorehead

Roger Maris (spelled Maras) has an very early card in this set. Some players, including Maris, have two different cards. This checklist may be incomplete, so any additions are appreciated.

	NM	Ex
COMPLETE SET (16)	1200.00	600.00
1 Ken Braeseke	20.00	10.00
2 Zeke Bonura MG	30.00	15.00
3 Bob Borovica	20.00	10.00
4 Joe Camacho	20.00	10.00
5 Frank Gravino Hands at knees	20.00	10.00
6 Frank Gravino Hands at waist	20.00	10.00
7 Santo Luberto	20.00	10.00
8 Roger Maris Spelled Maras Fielding	500.00	250.00
9 Roger Maris Spelled Maras Batting	500.00	250.00
10 Jerry Mehlish	20.00	10.00
11 Ray Mendoza Hands outstretched for throw	20.00	10.00
12 Ray Mendoza Stretching for throw	20.00	10.00
13 Don Nance	20.00	10.00
14 Ray Seif	20.00	10.00
15 Will Sirois	20.00	10.00
16 Don Wolf	20.00	10.00

1953 Mothers Cookies

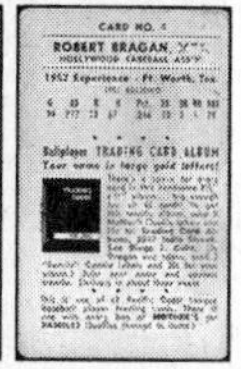

The cards in this 63-card set measure 2 3/16" by 3 1/2". The 1953 Mother's Cookies set features PCL players only. The cards are numbered and the corners are rounded in "playing-card" style. The set has different numbers than the 1952 series and carries a "trading card album" offer on the back. Eleven cards are marked with DP in the checklist below as they essentially were double printed and are more plentiful than the other numbers in the set. The catalog designation of the set is D357-2.

	NM	Ex
COMPLETE SET (63)	850.00	425.00
COMMON CARD (1-63)	15.00	7.50
COMMON CARD DP	8.00	4.00
1 Lee Winters	25.00	12.50
2 Joe Ostrowski	15.00	7.50
3 Willie Ramsdell	15.00	7.50
4 Bobby Bragan	25.00	12.50
5 Fletcher Robbe	15.00	7.50
6 Aaron Robinson	20.00	10.00
7 Augie Galan	20.00	10.00
8 Buddy Peterson	15.00	7.50
9 Lefty O'Doul MG	50.00	25.00
10 Walt Poceday	15.00	7.50
11 Nini Tornay	15.00	7.50
12 Jim Moran	15.00	7.50
13 George Schmees	15.00	7.50
14 Al Widmar	15.00	7.50
15 Richie Myers	15.00	7.50
16 Bill Howerton	15.00	7.50
17 Chuck Stevens	15.00	7.50
18 Joe Brovia	15.00	7.50
19 Max West	20.00	10.00
20 Eddie Malone	15.00	7.50
21 Gene Handley	15.00	7.50
22 William D. McCawley	15.00	7.50
23 Bill Sweeney	15.00	7.50
24 Tom Alston	20.00	10.00
25 George Vico	15.00	7.50
26 Hank Arft	15.00	7.50
27 Al Benton	20.00	10.00
28 Pete Milne	15.00	7.50
29 Jim Gladd	15.00	7.50
30 Earl Rapp	15.00	7.50
31 Ray Orteig	15.00	7.50
32 Eddie Basinski	15.00	7.50
33 Reno Cheso	15.00	7.50
34 Clarence Maddern	15.00	7.50
35 Marino Pieretti	15.00	7.50
36 Bill Raimondi	15.00	7.50
37 Frank Kelleher	15.00	7.50
38 George Bamberger	30.00	15.00
39 Dick Smith	15.00	7.50
40 Charley Schanz	15.00	7.50
41 John Van Cuyk	15.00	7.50
42 Lloyd Hittle	15.00	7.50
43 Tommy Heath	15.00	7.50
44 Frank Kalin	15.00	7.50
45 Jack Tobin DP	8.00	4.00
46 Jim Davis	15.00	7.50
47 Claude Christy	15.00	7.50
48 Elvin Tappe	15.00	7.50
49 Stan Hack MG	20.00	10.00
50 Fred Richards DP	8.00	4.00
51 Clay Hopper DP MG	8.00	4.00
52 Roy Welmaker	15.00	7.50
53 Red Adams DP	8.00	4.00
54 Piper Davis DP	8.00	4.00
55 Spider Jorgensen	20.00	10.00
56 Lee Walls	20.00	10.00
57 Jack Phillips DP	8.00	4.00
58 Red Lynn DP	8.00	4.00
59 Eddie Robinson DP	10.00	5.00
60 Gene Desautels DP	8.00	4.00
61 Bob Dillinger DP	15.00	7.50
62 Al Federoff	15.00	7.50
63 Bill Boemler DP	8.00	4.00

1953 San Francisco Seals Team Issue

This 24-card set measuring approximately 4" by 5" was issued by the club and features black-and-white player portraits with white borders. The player's autograph is printed on the picture. The backs are blank. The cards are unnumbered and checklisted below in alphabetical order.

	NM	Ex
COMPLETE SET (24)	125.00	60.00
1 Bill Boemler	8.00	4.00
2 Bill Bradford	8.00	4.00
3 Reno Cheso	8.00	4.00
4 Harland Clift CO	10.00	5.00
5 Walt Clough	8.00	4.00
6 Cliff Coggin	8.00	4.00
7 Tommy Heath MG	10.00	5.00
8 Leo Hughes TR	8.00	4.00
9 Frank Kalin	8.00	4.00
10 Al Lien	8.00	4.00
11 Al Lyons	8.00	4.00
12 John McCall	8.00	4.00
13 Bill McCawley	8.00	4.00
14 Jim Moran	8.00	4.00
15 Bob Muncrief	8.00	4.00
16 Leo Righetti	12.00	6.00
17 Ted Shandor	8.00	4.00
18 Elmer Singleton	8.00	4.00
19 Sal Taormina	8.00	4.00
20 Will Tiesiera	8.00	4.00
21 Nini Tornay	8.00	4.00
22 Lou Stringer	8.00	4.00
23 George Vico	8.00	4.00
24 Jerry Zuvela	8.00	4.00

1954 Charleston Senators Blossom Dairy

These blank-backed cards which measure 2 1/4" by 3 3/16" were sponsored by Blossom Dairy and featured members of the 1954 Charleston Senators. Since these cards are unnumbered, we have sequenced them in alphabetical order. There was also an album specially created for this set.

	NM	Ex
COMPLETE SET	2000.00	1000.00
1 Al Baro	100.00	50.00
2 Joe Becker	100.00	50.00
3 Joe Carroll	100.00	50.00
4 Gerald Red Fahr	100.00	50.00
5 Dick Fowler	100.00	50.00
6 Alex Garbowski	100.00	50.00
7 Gordon Goldsberry	100.00	50.00
8 Ross Grimsley	100.00	50.00
9 Sam Hairston	125.00	60.00
10 Phil Haugstad	100.00	50.00
11 Tom Hurd	100.00	50.00
12 Bob Killinger	100.00	50.00
13 John Kropf	100.00	50.00
14 Bob Masser	100.00	50.00
15 Danny Melendez	100.00	50.00
16 Bill Paolisso	100.00	50.00
17 Bill Pope	100.00	50.00
18 Lou Sleater	100.00	50.00
19 Dick Strahs	100.00	50.00
20 Joe Torpey	100.00	50.00
21 Bill Voiselle	125.00	60.00
22 Al Ware	100.00	50.00
XX Album		

1954 Seattle Popcorn

This 28-card set of the Seattle ballclub of the Pacific Coast League was distributed to the public as inserts in boxes of popcorn sold at Sicks' Stadium in Seattle. Only one card was inserted per box and measured approximately 2" by 3". The sets were produced by the Seattle ballclub and issued each season from 1954 through 1968. The fronts feature a black-and-white player photo with the player's name and position printed at the bottom. The backs are blank. All of the cards seem to have been cropped from a "premium" 8" by 10". All Popcorn cards may have part of a "premium". The cards are unnumbered and checklisted below in alphabetical order. Uncut sheets of these cards of any year of Seattle Popcorn should go for 1.5X to 2X the sum of any listed cards. All 1954 through 1968 Seattle Popcorn cards are expected to exist in a 8' by 10' "premium" form. All the photos are the same for the players each year but they may be cropped differently. These 8" by 10" single player photos of commons are currently valued at 1.5X to 2X the smaller player photos.

	NM	Ex
COMPLETE SET (23)	550.00	275.00
1 Gene Bearden	30.00	15.00
2 Al Brightman CO	20.00	10.00
3 Jack Burkowatz	20.00	10.00
4 Tommy Byrne	30.00	15.00
5 Merrill Combs	20.00	10.00
6 Joe Erautt	20.00	10.00
7 Bill Evans	20.00	10.00
8 Nanny Fernandez	20.00	10.00
9 Van Fletcher	20.00	10.00
10 Bob Hall	20.00	10.00
11 Pete Hernandez	20.00	10.00
12 Lloyd Jenney	20.00	10.00
13 Joe Joshua	20.00	10.00
14 Vern Kindsfather	20.00	10.00
15 Tom Lovrich	20.00	10.00
16 Clarence Maddern	20.00	10.00
17 Don Mallott	20.00	10.00
18 Loren Meyers	20.00	10.00
19 Steve Nagy	20.00	10.00
20 Ray Orteig	20.00	10.00
21 Gerry Priddy P/MG	30.00	15.00
22 George Schmees	20.00	10.00
23 Bill Schuster CO	20.00	10.00
24 Leo Thomas	20.00	10.00
25 Jack Tobin	20.00	10.00
26 Al Widmar	25.00	12.50
27 Artie Wilson	40.00	20.00
28 Al Zarilla	30.00	15.00

1955 Des Moines Homestead Bruins

ALWAYS A HIT
with your family
and guests
OLD HOMESTEAD
Products

This 21-card set features player portraits on cards measuring approximately 2 5/8" by 3 3/4" and was issued by the Iowa Packing Co. The cards were either distributed in packages of Old Homestead Franks or at Bruins ball games. The backs carry an ad for Old Homestead products. The cards are unnumbered and checklisted below alphabetically.

	NM	Ex
COMPLETE SET (21)	125.00	60.00
1 Bob Anderson	8.00	4.00
2 Ray Bellino	8.00	4.00
3 Don Biebel	8.00	4.00
4 Bobby Cooke	8.00	4.00
5 Dave Cunningham	8.00	4.00
6 Bert Flammini	8.00	4.00
7 Gene Fodge	8.00	4.00
8 Eddie Haas	8.00	4.00
9 Paul Hoffmeister	8.00	4.00
10 Pepper Martin MG	15.00	7.50
11 Jim McDaniel	8.00	4.00
12 Bob McKee	8.00	4.00
13 Paul Menking	8.00	4.00
14 Vern Morgan	8.00	4.00
15 Joe Pearson	8.00	4.00
16 John Pramesca	8.00	4.00
17 Joe Stanks	8.00	4.00
18 Jim Stoddard	8.00	4.00
19 Bob Thorpe	8.00	4.00
20 Burdy Thurlby	8.00	4.00
21 Don Watkins	8.00	4.00

1955 Seattle Popcorn

This 20-card set of the Seattle ballclub of the Pacific Coast League was distributed to the public as inserts in boxes of popcorn sold at Sicks' Stadium in Seattle. Only one card was inserted per box and measured approximately 2" by 3". The sets were produced by the Seattle ballclub and issued each season from 1954 through 1968. The fronts feature a black-and-white player photo with the player's name and position printed at the bottom. The backs are blank. No significant variations in these cards have been discovered. The cards are unnumbered and checklisted below in alphabetical order.

	NM	Ex
COMPLETE SET (20)	375.00	190.00
1 Bob Balcena	15.00	7.50
2 Monty Basgall	20.00	10.00
3 Ewell Blackwell	25.00	12.50
4 Bill Brenner	15.00	7.50
5 Jack Bukowatz	15.00	7.50
6 Van Fletcher	15.00	7.50
7 Joe Ginsberg	15.00	7.50
8 Jehosie Heard	15.00	7.50
9 Fred Hutchinson MG	50.00	25.00
10 Larry Jansen	25.00	12.50
11 Bob Kelly	15.00	7.50
12 Bill Kennedy	20.00	10.00
13 Lou Kretlow	15.00	7.50
14 Rocco Krsnich	15.00	7.50
15 Carmen Mauro	15.00	7.50
16 John Oldham	15.00	7.50
17 George Schmees	15.00	7.50
18 Elmer Singleton	15.00	7.50
19 Alan Strange CO	15.00	7.50
20 Gene Verble	15.00	7.50
21 Marv Williams	15.00	7.50
22 Harvey Zernia	15.00	7.50

1956 Lincon Chiefs Stuart Mutual Savings

This postcard sized card features slugging outfielder Dick Stuart, who was on his way to slugging 66 homers during the 1956 season. The top of the card has a posed action shot of Stuart while the bottom has information on who sponsored the photo as well the player's name and position

	MINT	NRMT
1 Dick Stuart	25.00	11.00

1956 Seattle Popcorn

This 27-card set of the Seattle Rainiers ballclub of the Pacific Coast League was distributed to the public as inserts in boxes of popcorn sold at Sicks' Stadium in Seattle. Only one card was inserted per box and measured approximately 2" by 3". The sets were produced by the ballclub and issued each season from 1954 through 1968. The fronts feature a black-and-white player photo with the player's name and position printed at the bottom. The backs are blank. The 1956's come either in blank back form or with 2 Gil's locations. The cards are unnumbered and checklisted below in alphabetical order.

	NM	Ex
COMPLETE SET (27)	400.00	200.00
1 Fred Baczewski	15.00	7.50
2 Bob Balcena	15.00	7.50
3 Bill Brenner	15.00	7.50
4 Sherry Dixon	15.00	7.50
5 Don Fracchia	15.00	7.50
6 Bill Glynn	15.00	7.50
7 Larry Jansen	25.00	12.50
8 Howie Judson	15.00	7.50
9 Bill Kennedy	15.00	7.50
10 Jack Lohrke	20.00	10.00
11 Vic Lombardi	20.00	10.00
12 Carmen Mauro	15.00	7.50
13 Ray Orteig	15.00	7.50
14 Bud Podbielan	15.00	7.50
15 Leo Righetti	20.00	10.00
16 Jim Robertson	15.00	7.50
17 Art Shallock UER (misspelled Schallock)	15.00	7.50
18 Art Schult	15.00	7.50
19 Luke Sewell MG	25.00	12.50
20 Elmer Singleton	15.00	7.50
21 Milt Smith (Action)	15.00	7.50
22 Milt Smith (Head)	15.00	7.50
23 Vern Stephens	20.00	10.00
24 Alan Strange CO	15.00	7.50
25 Joe Taylor	15.00	7.50
26 Artie Wilson	30.00	15.00
27 Harvey Zernia	15.00	7.50

1957 Chattanooga Lookouts Team Issue

These 8 1/2" by 11" blank-backed black and white photos feature members of the 1957 Chattanooga Lookouts. The players are in posed shots and the photos were taken by Hoss Photo Service in NY. Since these photos are unnumbered we have sequenced them in alphabetical order. An very early Harmon Killebrew card is in this set as well. It is possible that there are additional players so any additional information is appreciated.

	NM	Ex
COMPLETE SET	75.00	38.00
1 Bobby Brown	10.00	5.00
2 Harmon Killebrew	50.00	25.00
3 Ernie Ortavez	10.00	5.00
4 Stan Roseboro	10.00	5.00

1957 Hygrade Meats

This 12-card set features Seattle Rainiers of the Pacific Coast League (PCL) only. The cards measure 3 3/4" by 4 1/2" and they are unnumbered. The catalog designation for this scarce set is F178. These cards, along with Milwaukee Sausage and the Henry House issues were in direct contact with hot dog meats. Therefore, these cards are usually found in vg or less condition in these sets and a significant premium is attached for nm/mt cards or better.

	NM	Ex
COMPLETE SET (12)	2500.00	1250.00
1 Dick Aylward	200.00	100.00
2 Bob Balcena	200.00	100.00
3 Jim Dyck	200.00	100.00
4 Marion Fricano	200.00	100.00
5 Billy Glynn	200.00	100.00
6 Larry Jansen	250.00	125.00
7 Bill Kennedy	200.00	100.00
8 Jack Wayne (Lucky) Lohrke	200.00	100.00
9 Lefty O'Doul MG	300.00	150.00
10 Ray Orteig	200.00	100.00
11 Joe Taylor	200.00	100.00
12 Morrie Wills sic, Maury	400.00	200.00

1957 San Francisco Seals Golden State Dairy Stamps

These stamps, which measure approximately 2" by 2 1/2", which were in rust brown on orange, were designed to be glued into an album. Since these stamps are unnumbered, we have sequenced them in alphabetical order.

	NM	Ex
COMPLETE SET	400.00	200.00
1 Bill Abernathie	20.00	10.00
2 Ken Aspromonte	20.00	10.00
3 Harry Dorish	20.00	10.00
4 Joe Gordon MG	30.00	15.00
5 Grady Hatton	20.00	10.00
6 Tommy Hurd	20.00	10.00
7 Frank Kellert	20.00	10.00
8 Leo Kiely	20.00	10.00
9 Harry Malmberg	20.00	10.00
10 John McCall	20.00	10.00
11 Albie Pearson	25.00	12.50
12 Jack Phillips	20.00	10.00
13 Bill Renna	20.00	10.00
14 Ed Sadowski	20.00	10.00
15 Robert Smith	20.00	10.00
16 Jack Spring	20.00	10.00
17 Joe Tanner	20.00	10.00
18 Sal Taormina	20.00	10.00
19 Bert Thiel	20.00	10.00
20 Nini Tornay	20.00	10.00
21 Tommy Umphlett	20.00	10.00
22 Glenn Wright	20.00	10.00

1957 Seattle Popcorn

This 24-card set of the Seattle Rainiers ballclub of the Pacific Coast League was distributed to the public as inserts in boxes of popcorn sold at Sicks' Stadium in Seattle. Only one card was inserted per box and measured approximately 2" by 3". The sets were produced by the ballclub and issued each season from 1954 through 1968. The fronts feature a black-and-white player photo with the player's name and position printed at the bottom. The backs are either blank or note Gil's three drive in locations. The cards are unnumbered and checklisted below in alphabetical order.

	NM	Ex
COMPLETE SET (24)	350.00	180.00
1 Dick Aylward	12.00	6.00
2 Bob Balcena	12.00	6.00
3 Eddie Basinski	12.00	6.00
4 Hal Bevan	12.00	6.00
5 Joe Black	25.00	12.50
6 Juan Delis	12.00	6.00
7 Jim Dyck	12.00	6.00
8 Marion Fricano	12.00	6.00
9 Bill Glynn	12.00	6.00
10 Larry Jansen	15.00	7.50
11 Howie Judson	12.00	6.00
12 Bill Kennedy	12.00	6.00
13 Jack Lohrke	12.00	6.00
14 Carmen Mauro	12.00	6.00
15 George Munger	12.00	6.00
16 Lefty O'Doul MG	50.00	25.00
17 Ray Orteig	12.00	6.00
18 Duane Pillette	12.00	6.00
19 Bud Podbielan	12.00	6.00
20 Charley Rabe	12.00	6.00
21 Leo Righetti	15.00	7.50
22 Joe Taylor	12.00	6.00
23 Edo Vanni CO	12.00	6.00
24 Maury Willis UER misspelled Morrie	75.00	38.00

1958 Buffalo Bisons Bond Bread

This standard-size set black and white set features members of the 1958 Buffalo Bisons.

This set has the ACC designation of D301 and the cards feature an advertisment for the TV show "Casey Jones" at the bottom and a player bio with a blurb along with an ad for Bond Bread on the back.

	NM	Ex
COMPLETE SET (9)	200.00	100.00
1 Al Aber	20.00	10.00
2 Joe Caffie	20.00	10.00
3 Phil Cavaretta MG	40.00	20.00
4 Rip Coleman	20.00	10.00
5 Luke Easter	40.00	20.00
6 Ken Johnson	25.00	12.50
7 Lou Ortiz	20.00	10.00
8 Jack Phillips	20.00	10.00
9 Jim Small	20.00	10.00

1958 Omaha Cardinals Team Issue

This 24 card black and white blank-backed set, which measures approximately 3 3/'" by 4 3/8" features members of the Omaha Cardinals, who were a St Louis Cardinals farm club at that time. These cards are not numbered, so we have sequenced them in alphabetical order.

	NM	Ex
COMPLETE SET	600.00	300.00
1 Antonio Alomar	20.00	10.00
2 Dave Benedict	20.00	10.00
3 Bill Bergesch	20.00	10.00
4 Bob Blaylock	20.00	10.00
5 Pidge Browne	20.00	10.00
6 Chris Cannizzaro	25.00	12.50
7 Nels Chittum	20.00	10.00
8 Don Choate	20.00	10.00
9 Phil Clark	20.00	10.00
10 Jim Frey	25.00	12.50
11 Bob Gibson	200.00	100.00
12 Ev Joyner	20.00	10.00
13 Johnny Keane MG	20.00	10.00
14 Paul Kippels	20.00	10.00
15 Boyd Linker	20.00	10.00
16 Bob Mabe	20.00	10.00
17 Bernie Mateosky	20.00	10.00
18 Ron Plaza	20.00	10.00
19 Bill Queen	20.00	10.00
20 Bill Smith	20.00	10.00
21 Bobby Gene Smith	20.00	10.00
22 Lee Tate	20.00	10.00
23 Benny Valenzuela	20.00	10.00
24 Header Card	20.00	10.00

1958 Seattle Popcorn

This set is similar to the other Seattle Popcorn sets. The backs carry an advertisement for Ralph's Thriftway. Also mentioned was an offer of a free 8" by 10" player picture of the collector's choice for any nine cards. The nine cards were punched and returned to the collector along with the chosen 8" by 10" photo. The large photos were referred to as "Seattle Premiums." The cards are unnumbered and checklisted below in alphabetical order. Ralph's Thriftway took the place of Gil's Drive-In used in 1956 and 1957 for this promotion. No blank back Seattle cards were issued in 1958.

	NM	Ex
COMPLETE SET (19)	300.00	150.00
1 Bob Balcena	10.00	5.00
2 Eddie Basinski	10.00	5.00
3 Hal Bevan	10.00	5.00
4 Jack Bloomfield	10.00	5.00
5 Juan Delis	10.00	5.00
6 Dutch Dotterer	10.00	5.00
7 Jim Dyck	10.00	5.00
8 Al Federoff	10.00	5.00
9 Art Fowler	15.00	7.50
10 Bill Kennedy	10.00	5.00
11 Marty Kutyna	10.00	5.00
12 Ray Orteig	10.00	5.00
13 Duane Pillette	10.00	5.00
14 Vada Pinson	150.00	75.00
15 Connie Ryan MG	15.00	7.50
16 Phil Shartzer	10.00	5.00
17 Max Surkont	10.00	5.00
18 Gale Wade	10.00	5.00
19 Ted Wieand	10.00	5.00

1958 Union Oil

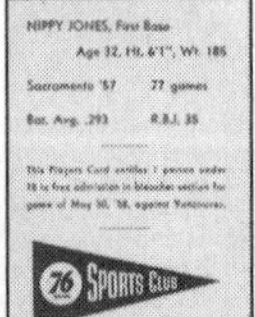

The 1958 Union Olil set of ten black and white, unnumbered cards depicts members of the Sacramento Solons. Each card has a white strip containing the player's name, team and position below the picture. The back has a pennant design advertising the "76 Sports Club" and states that the card is redeemable for free admission to a specific Solons game. The cards measure approximately 2 1/2" by 3 1/2".

	NM	Ex
COMPLETE SET (10)	200.00	100.00
1 Marshall Bridges	50.00	25.00
2 Dick Cole	15.00	7.50
3 Jim Greengrass	20.00	10.00
4 Al Heist	20.00	10.00
5 Nippy Jones	20.00	10.00
6 Carlos Paula	20.00	10.00
7 Kal Segrist	15.00	7.50
8 Sibbi Sisti	20.00	10.00
9 Joe Stanka	15.00	7.50
10 Bud Watkins	30.00	15.00

1959 Darigold Farms

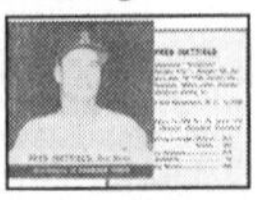

The cards in this 22-card set measure 2 1/2" by 2 3/8". Darigold Farms produced this 1959 set to spotlight the Spokane Indians baseball team. The cards are unnumbered and contain black and white photos set against colored backgrounds (1-8 have yellow, 9-16 have red and 17-22 have blue). The cards were attached to milk cartons by tabs and carry the catalog number F115-1. The cards have been alphabetized and assigned numbers in the checklist below.

	NM	Ex
COMPLETE SET (22)	600.00	300.00
1 Facundo Barragan	30.00	15.00
2 Steve Bilko	40.00	20.00
3 Bobby Bragan MG	40.00	20.00
4 Chuck Churn	30.00	15.00
5 Tommy Davis	60.00	30.00
6 Dom Domenichelli	30.00	15.00
7 Bob Giallombardo	30.00	15.00
8 Connie Grob	30.00	15.00
9 Fred Hatfield	30.00	15.00
10 Bob Lillis	40.00	20.00
11 Lloyd Merritt	30.00	15.00
12 Larry Miller	30.00	15.00
13 Chris Nicolosi	30.00	15.00
14 Allen Norris	30.00	15.00
15 Phil Ortega	30.00	15.00
16 Phillips Paine	30.00	15.00
17 Bill Parsons	30.00	15.00
18 Hisel Patrick	30.00	15.00
19 Tony Roig	30.00	15.00
20 Tom Saffell	30.00	15.00
21 Norm Sherry	40.00	20.00
22 Ben Wade	30.00	15.00

1959 Montreal Royals O'Keefe Ale

These 24 black and white photo stamps were issued by O'Keefe Ale and feature members of the 1959 Montreal Royals. The photos measure 3" by 4" and the stamps have a player photo. The bottom of the stamp has the players name and the position which is printed in English and French. Each of these stamps were designed to be mounted into an album.

	NM	Ex
COMPLETE SET (24)	250.00	125.00
1 Edmundo Amoros	15.00	7.50
2 Bob Aspromonte	12.00	6.00
3 Babe Birrer	10.00	5.00
4 Mike Brumley	10.00	5.00
5 Clay Bryant MG	10.00	5.00
6 Yvon Dunn TR	10.00	5.00
7 Bill George	10.00	5.00
8 Mike Goliat	10.00	5.00
9 John Gray	10.00	5.00
10 Billy Harris	10.00	5.00
11 Jim Koranda	10.00	5.00
12 Paul LaPalme	10.00	5.00
13 Tom Lasorda	30.00	15.00
14 Bob Lennon	10.00	5.00
15 Clyde Parris	10.00	5.00
16 Ed Rakow	10.00	5.00
17 Curt Roberts	10.00	5.00
18 Freddy Rodriguez	10.00	5.00
19 Harry Schwegman	10.00	5.00
20 Angel Scull	10.00	5.00
21 Dick Teed	10.00	5.00
22 Rene Valdes	10.00	5.00
23 Mid-Season Batting Averages	10.00	5.00
24 Mid-Season Pitching Averages	10.00	5.00
XX Album		

1959 Seattle Popcorn

This 38-card set of the Seattle Rainiers ballclub of the Pacific Coast League was distributed to the public as inserts in boxes of popcorn sold at Sicks' Stadium in Seattle. Only one card was inserted per box and measured approximately 2" by 3". The sets were produced by the ballclub and issued each season from 1954 through 1968. The fronts feature a black-and-white player photo with the player's name and position printed at the bottom. The backs are blank. Two separate releases were issued in

1959--one in the Spring in April using 1958 photos (1-13), and one in the Summer using 1959 photos (14-38). The cards are unnumbered and checklisted below in alphabetical order within the Spring or Summer season issues.

	NM	Ex
COMPLETE SET (38)	500.00	250.00
1 Frank Amaya	12.00	6.00
2 Hal Bevan	12.00	6.00
3 Jack Bloomfield	12.00	6.00
4 Clarence Churn	12.00	6.00
5 Eddie Kazak	12.00	6.00
6 Bill Kennedy	12.00	6.00
7 Harry Malmbeg	12.00	6.00
8 Claude Osteen	20.00	10.00
9 Charley Rabe	12.00	6.00
10 Max Surkont	12.00	6.00
11 Ted Tappe	12.00	6.00
12 Gale Wade	12.00	6.00
13 Bill Wight	12.00	6.00
14 Bobby Adams	12.00	6.00
15 Jack Dittmer	12.00	6.00
16 Jim Dyck	12.00	6.00
17 Dee Fondy	12.00	6.00
18 Mark Freeman	12.00	6.00
19 Dick Hanlon	12.00	6.00
20 Carroll Hardy	15.00	7.50
21 Bobby Henrich	12.00	6.00
22 Jay Hook	15.00	7.50
23 Fred Hutchinson MG	50.00	25.00
24 Jake Jenkins	12.00	6.00
25 Harry Lowren	12.00	6.00
26 Bob Mape UER (misspelled Mabe)	12.00	6.00
27 Harry Malmbeg UER (misspelled Malmberg	12.00	6.00
28 Darrell Martin	12.00	6.00
29 John McCall	12.00	6.00
30 Paul Pettit	20.00	10.00
31 Rudy Regalado	12.00	6.00
32 Eric Rodin	12.00	6.00
33 Don Rudolph	12.00	6.00
34 Lou Skizas	15.00	7.50
35 Dave Stenhouse	12.00	6.00
36 Alan Strange MG	12.00	6.00
37 Elmer Valo	20.00	10.00
38 Ed Winceniak	12.00	6.00

1960 Darigold Farms

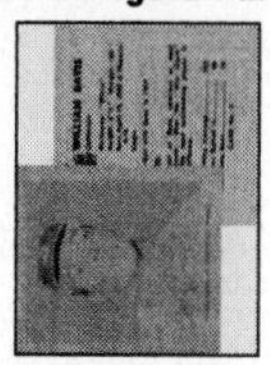

The cards in this 24-card set measure 2 3/8" by 2 9/16". The 1960 Darigold edition of the Spokane Indians has several distinguishing features which allow it to be separated from the similar set produced the year before. These cards are also cut similar to what a matchbook cover would be like. While the top half is basically just a white square, the bottom is where the picture is. In addition and most importantly, the cards are numbered and there are 24 in the set. The sequential use of color background was retained; with cards number 1-8 having a yellow background, cards 9-16 have a green background and 17-24 have a red background. A facsimile autograph was added to the front of each card. The catalog designation is F115-2.

	NM	Ex
COMPLETE SET (24)	800.00	325.00
1 Chris Nicolosi	30.00	12.00
2 Jim Pagliaroni	50.00	20.00
3 Roy Smalley	50.00	20.00
4 Bill Bethee	30.00	12.00
5 Joe Liscio TR	30.00	12.00
6 Curt Roberts	30.00	12.00
7 Ed Palmquist	30.00	12.00
8 Willie Davis	60.00	24.00
9 Bob Giallombardo	30.00	12.00
10 Pedro Gomez MG	50.00	20.00
11 Mel Nelson	30.00	12.00
12 Charlie Smith	40.00	16.00
13 Clarence Churn	30.00	12.00
14 Ramon Conde	30.00	12.00
15 George O'Donnell	30.00	12.00
16 Tony Roig	30.00	12.00
17 Frank Howard	60.00	24.00
18 Billy Harris	30.00	12.00
19 Mike Brumley	30.00	12.00
20 Earl Robinson	30.00	12.00
21 Ron Fairly	60.00	24.00
22 Joe Frazier	30.00	12.00
23 Allen Norris	30.00	12.00
24 Ford Young	30.00	12.00

1960 Henry House Wieners

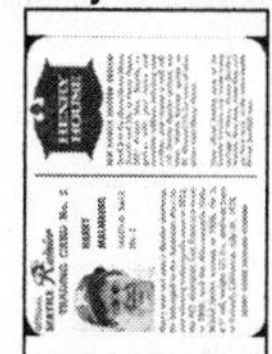

This 18-card set features Seattle Rainiers of the Pacific Coast League (PCL) only. The cards measure 3 3/4" by 4 1/2" and they are skip-numbered by uniform number. Cards are printed on stiff cardboard with red ink. The catalog designation for this scarce set is F171.

	NM	Ex
COMPLETE SET (18)	4000.00	1600.00
2 Harry Malmberg	250.00	100.00
3 Francisco Obregon	250.00	100.00
4 Johnny O'Brien	300.00	120.00
5 Gordon Coleman	300.00	120.00
6 Bill Hain	250.00	100.00
8 Dick Sisler	300.00	120.00
9 Jerry Zimmerman	250.00	100.00
10 Hal Bevan	250.00	100.00
14 Rudy Regalado	250.00	100.00
15 Paul Pettit	300.00	120.00
16 Buddy Gilbert	250.00	100.00
21 Erv Palica	250.00	100.00
22 Joe Taylor	250.00	100.00
25 Bill Kennedy	250.00	100.00
26 Dave Stenhouse	250.00	100.00
28 Ray Ripplemeyer	300.00	120.00
30 Charlie Beamon	250.00	100.00
33 Don Rudolph	250.00	100.00

1960 Maple Leafs Shopsy's Frankfurters

These 23 blank-backed cards measure approximately 2 3/16" by 3 1/4" and feature players from the Toronto Maple Leafs of the International League. The white-bordered cards carry posed black-and-white player photos. The player's name and position appear in black lettering within the bottom white margin; the words "Shopsy's Player Photo" appear in black lettering within the top white margin. The catalog designation for this set is FC35. The cards are unnumbered and checklisted below in alphabetical order.

	NM	Ex
COMPLETE SET (23)	900.00	350.00
1 Sparky Anderson	150.00	60.00
2 Bob Chakales	40.00	16.00
3 Al Cicotte	40.00	16.00
4 Rip Coleman	40.00	16.00
5 Steve Demeter	40.00	16.00
6 Don Dillard	40.00	16.00
7 Frank Funk	40.00	16.00
8 Russ Heman	40.00	16.00
9 Earl Hersh	40.00	16.00
10 Allen Jones	40.00	16.00
11 Jim King	40.00	16.00
12 Jack Kubiszyn	40.00	16.00
13 Mel McGaha CO	40.00	16.00
14 Bill Moran	40.00	16.00
15 Ron Negray	40.00	16.00
16 Herb Plews	40.00	16.00
17 Steve Ridzik	40.00	16.00
18 Pat Scantlebury	40.00	16.00
19 Bill Smith	40.00	16.00
20 Bob Smith	40.00	16.00
21 Tim Thompson	40.00	16.00
22 Jack Waters	40.00	16.00
23 Archie Wilson	40.00	16.00

1960 Seattle Popcorn

This 18-card set of the Seattle Rainiers ballclub of the Pacific Coast League was distributed to the public as inserts in boxes of popcorn sold at Sicks' Stadium in Seattle. Only one card was inserted per box and measured approximately 2" by 3". The sets were produced by the ballclub and issued each season from 1954 through 1968. The fronts feature a black-and-white player photo with the player's name and position printed at the bottom. The backs are blank. The cards are unnumbered and checklisted below in alphabetical order.

	NM	Ex
COMPLETE SET (18)	175.00	70.00
1 Charlie Beamon	10.00	4.00
2 Hal Bevan	10.00	4.00
3 Whammy Douglas	10.00	4.00
4 Buddy Gilbert	10.00	4.00
5 Hal Jeffcoat CO	10.00	4.00
6 Leigh Lawrence	10.00	4.00
7 Darrell Martin	10.00	4.00
8 Francisco Obregon	10.00	4.00
9 Johnny O'Brien	15.00	6.00
10 Paul Pettit	12.00	4.80
11 Ray Rippelmeyer	12.00	4.80
12 Don Rudolph	10.00	4.00
13 Willard Schmidt	10.00	4.00
14 Dick Sisler MG	15.00	6.00
15 Lou Skizas	10.00	4.00
16 Joe Taylor	10.00	4.00
17 Bob Thurman	10.00	4.00
18 Gerald Zimmerman	10.00	4.00

1960 Tacoma Bank

The Tacoma National Bank of Washington set features 21 large cards each measuring 3" by 5". The set exclusively features players from the Tacoma Giants of the Pacific Coast League (PCL). Several of the players went on to later play for the big league Giants. The catalog designation is H801-14. A pre-Rookie Card of Juan Marichal is in this set.

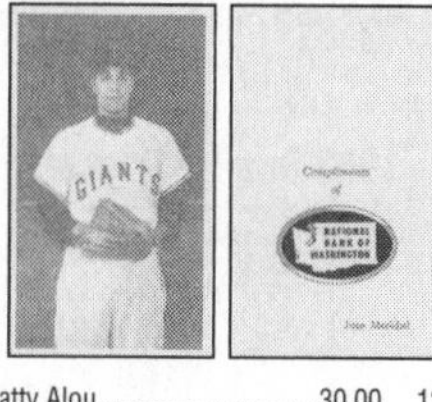

	NM	Ex
COMPLETE SET (21)	450.00	180.00
1 Matty Alou	30.00	12.00
2 Ossie Alvarez	20.00	8.00
3 Don Choate	20.00	8.00
4 Red Davis	20.00	8.00
5 Bob Farley	20.00	8.00
6 Eddie Fisher	25.00	10.00
7 Tom Haller	25.00	10.00
8 Sherman Jones	20.00	8.00
9 Juan Marichal	100.00	40.00
10 Ramon Monzant	20.00	8.00
11 Danny O'Connell	30.00	12.00
12 Jose Pagan	25.00	10.00
13 Bob Perry	20.00	8.00
14 Dick Phillips	20.00	8.00
15 Bobby Prescott	20.00	8.00
16 Marshall Renfroe	20.00	8.00
17 Frank Reveira	20.00	8.00
18 Dusty Rhodes	30.00	12.00
19 Sal Taormina	20.00	8.00
20 Verle Tiefenthaler	20.00	8.00
21 Dom Zanni	20.00	8.00

1960 Union Oil

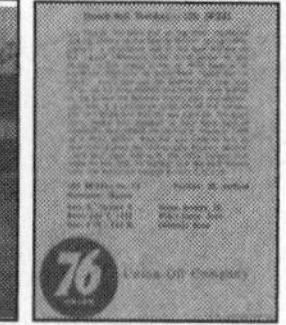

The 1960 Union Oil set consists of nine full-color, skip-numbered cards spotlighting the Seattle Rainers. These cards were given away by Union Oil stations in the Seattle area. The fronts contain full-length action photos taken at Sicks Stadium. Ripplemeyer and Obregon are considered the "scarcities" of the set. The biographical material on the back is entitled "Thumb Nail Sketches". Cards in this set measure approximately 3 1/8" by 4".

	NM	Ex
COMPLETE SET (9)	225.00	90.00
4 Francisco Obregon	25.00	10.00
6 Drew Gilbert	12.00	4.80
7 Bill Hain	12.00	4.80
10 Ray Ripplemeyer	125.00	50.00
13 Joe Taylor	12.00	4.80
15 Lou Skizas	12.00	4.80
17 Don Rudolph	15.00	6.00
19 Gordy Coleman	20.00	8.00
22 Hal Bevan	12.00	4.80

1961 Maple Leafs Bee Hive

These 24 blank-backed cards measure approximately 2 3/16" by 3 3/16" and are printed on thin stock. The set features white-bordered black-and-white photos of the 1961 Toronto Maple Leafs of the International League. The player's name and position appear in black lettering within the lower white margin. The catalog designation for this set is FC36. The cards are unnumbered and checklisted below in alphabetical order.

	NM	Ex
COMPLETE SET (24)	1000.00	400.00
1 Sparky Anderson	150.00	60.00
2 Fritzie Brickell	40.00	16.00
3 Ellis Burton	40.00	16.00
4 Bob Chakales	40.00	16.00
5 Rip Coleman	40.00	16.00
6 Steve Demeter	40.00	16.00
7 Joe Hannah	40.00	16.00
8 Earl Hersh	40.00	16.00
9 Lou Jackson	40.00	16.00
10 Ken Johnson	50.00	20.00
11 Lou Johnson	50.00	20.00
12 John Lipon	40.00	16.00
13 Carl Mathias	40.00	16.00
14 Bill Moran	40.00	16.00
15 Ron Negray	40.00	16.00
16 Herb Plews	40.00	16.00
17 Dave Pope	40.00	16.00
18 Steve Ridzik	40.00	16.00
19 Raul Sanchez	40.00	16.00
20 Pat Scantlebury	40.00	16.00
21 Bill Smith	40.00	16.00
22 Bob Smith	40.00	16.00
23 Chuck Tanner	60.00	24.00
24 Tim Thompson	40.00	16.00

1961 Seattle Popcorn

This 29-card set of the Seattle Rainiers ballclub of the Pacific Coast League was distributed to the public as inserts in boxes of popcorn sold at Sicks' Stadium in Seattle. Only one card was inserted per box and measured approximately 2" by 3". The sets were produced by the ballclub and issued each season from 1954 through 1968. The fronts feature a black-and-white player photo with the player's name and position printed at the bottom. The backs are blank. The cards are unnumbered and checklisted below in alphabetical order.

	NM	Ex
COMPLETE SET (29)	300.00	120.00
1 Galen Cisco	12.00	4.80
2 Marlin Coughtry	10.00	4.00
3 Marlin Coughtry (Batting)	10.00	4.00
4 Pete Cronin	10.00	4.00
5 Arnold Earley	10.00	4.00
6 Bob Heffner	10.00	4.00
7 Bob Heffner (Close-up)	10.00	4.00
8 Curt Jenson	10.00	4.00
9 Curt Jenson (Close-up)	10.00	4.00
10 Harry Malmberg P/CO	10.00	4.00
11 Harry Malmberg CO (Close-up)	10.00	4.00
12 Dave Mann	10.00	4.00
13 Darrell Martin	10.00	4.00
14 Erv Palica	10.00	4.00
15 Ervin Palica	10.00	4.00
16 Johnny Pesky MG	20.00	8.00
17 Johnny Pesky MG (Close-up)	20.00	8.00
18 Dick Radatz	15.00	6.00
19 Ted Schreiber	10.00	4.00
20 Ted Shreiber UER (misspelled Schreiber) (Batting)	10.00	4.00
21 Paul Smith	10.00	4.00
22 Paul Smith (Close-up)	10.00	4.00
23 Bob Tillman Marked as an infielder He played catcher Card says John Tillman	10.00	4.00
24 Bob Tillman Catcher	10.00	4.00
25 Bo Toft	10.00	4.00
26 Tom Umphlett	10.00	4.00
27 Tom Umphlett (Close-up)	10.00	4.00
28 Earl Wilson	15.00	6.00
29 Ken Wolfe	10.00	4.00

1961 Syracuse Chiefs Team Issue

These 5" by 7" cards photos were issued by the team to promote the players on the 1961 Syracuse Chiefs team. Since these photos are unnumbered, we have entered them in alphabetical order.

	NM	Ex
COMPLETE SET	60.00	24.00
1 Joe Bonikowski	5.00	2.00
2 Mike Cuellar	10.00	4.00
3 Ralph Lumenti	5.00	2.00
4 Dan Motta	5.00	2.00
5 Willie Miranda	5.00	2.00
6 Rip Repulski	6.00	2.40
7 Ted Sadowski	5.00	2.00
8 Woody Smith	5.00	2.00
9 Lee Stange	6.00	2.40
10 Ron Stillwell	5.00	2.00
11 Sandy Valdespino	5.00	2.00

1961 Tacoma Bank

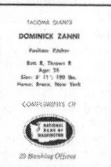

The Tacoma National Bank of Washington set again consists of 21 large (3" by 5") cards. The set exclusively features players from the Tacoma Giants of the Pacific Coast League (PCL). Several of the players went on to later play for the big league Giants. The catalog designation is H801-15. A pre-Rookie Card of Gaylord Perry is in this set.

	NM	Ex
COMPLETE SET (21)	300.00	120.00
1 Rafael Alomar	15.00	6.00
2 Ernie Bowman	15.00	6.00
3 Bud Byerly	15.00	6.00
4 Ray Daviault	15.00	6.00
5 Red Davis	15.00	6.00
6 Bob Farley	15.00	6.00
7 Gil Garrido	15.00	6.00
8 John Goetz	15.00	6.00
9 Bill Hain	15.00	6.00
10 Ronald Herbel	15.00	6.00
11 Lynn Lovenguth	15.00	6.00
12 Georges H. Maranda	15.00	6.00
13 Manny Mota	20.00	8.00
14 John Orsino	15.00	6.00
15 Gaylord Perry	50.00	20.00
16 Bob Perry	15.00	6.00
17 Dick Phillips	15.00	6.00
18 Frank Reveira	15.00	6.00
19 Dusty Rhodes	20.00	8.00
20 Verle Tiefenthaler	15.00	6.00
21 Dom Zanni	15.00	6.00

1961 Union Oil

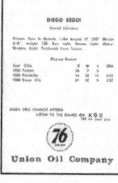

The cards in thie 67-card set measure 3" by 4". The 1961 Union Oil set of sepia, unnumbered cards contains players from six Pacific Coast League teams. Individual player cards were available only in their respective cities at Union 76 stations. The backs are in blue print and give player biographies and depict the Union 76 logo. Spokane players are more difficult to obtain than players from other teams. The Gomez and Prescott cards are scarce. The Mike Hershberger card actually depicts Bobby Knoop. Cards are numbered alphabetically with team (except Tacoma's uniform numbering) and have a prefix before the number indicating the team, i.e. Hawaii (H), Portland (P), San Diego (SD), Sacramento (S), Spokane (SP) and Tacoma (T). Later on in the 1961 season, some exhibition games were played between the Taiyo Whales of Japan and the Hawaii team. We are listing those cards at the end of our listing for this set.

	NM	Ex
COMPLETE SET (67)	1250.00	500.00
COMMON CARD (SD/T)	12.00	4.80
COMMON CARDS SD/T	15.00	6.00
H1 Ray Jablonski	30.00	12.00
H2 Jim McManus	25.00	10.00
H3 George Prescott	100.00	40.00
H4 Diego Segui	30.00	12.00
H5 Rachel Slider	25.00	10.00
H6 Jim Small	25.00	10.00
H7 Milt Smith	25.00	10.00
H8 Dave Thies	25.00	10.00
H9 Jay Ward	25.00	10.00
H10 Bill Werle	25.00	10.00
P1 Ed Bauta	12.00	4.80
P2 Vern Benson	12.00	4.80
P3 Jerry Buchek	12.00	4.80
P4 Bob Burda	12.00	4.80
P5 Duke Carmel	12.00	4.80
P6 Don Choate	12.00	4.80
P7 Phil Gagliano	12.00	4.80
P8 Jim Hickman	15.00	6.00
P9 Ray Katt	12.00	4.80
P10 Mel Nelson	12.00	4.80
P11 Jim Schaffer	12.00	4.80
P12 Mike Shannon	25.00	10.00
P13 Clint Stark	12.00	4.80
S1 Galen Cisco	12.00	4.80
S2 Lou Clinton	12.00	4.80
S3 Marlan Coughtry	12.00	4.80
S4 Harry Malmberg	12.00	4.80
S5 Dave Mann	12.00	4.80
S6 Derrell Martin	12.00	4.80
S7 Erv Palica	12.00	4.80
S8 John Pesky	20.00	8.00
S9 Bob Tillman	12.00	4.80
S10 Marv Toft	12.00	4.80
S11 Tom Umphlett	12.00	4.80
T10 Red Davis	12.00	4.80
T12 Dick Phillips	12.00	4.80
T17 Gil Garrido	12.00	4.80
T20 Georges Maranda	12.00	4.80
T25 John Orsino	12.00	4.80
T26 Dusty Rhodes	25.00	10.00
T28 Ron Herbel	12.00	4.80
T29 Gaylord Perry	150.00	60.00
T30 Rafael Alomar	12.00	4.80
T34 Bob Farley	12.00	4.80
SD1 Dick Barone	12.00	4.80
SD2 Jim Bolger	12.00	4.80
SD3 Kent Hadley	12.00	4.80
SD4 Mike Hershberger	12.00	4.80
SD5 Stan Johnson	12.00	4.80
SD6 Dick Lines	12.00	4.80
SD7 Jim Napier	12.00	4.80
SD8 Tony Roig	12.00	4.80
SD9 Herb Score	50.00	20.00
SD10 Harry Simpson	15.00	6.00
SD11 Joe Taylor	12.00	4.80
SD12 Ben Wade	12.00	4.80
SP1 Doug Camilli	25.00	10.00
SP2 Ramon Conde	25.00	10.00
SP3 Bob Giallombardo	25.00	10.00
SP4 Mike Goliat	25.00	10.00
SP5 Preston Gomez	100.00	40.00
SP6 Rod Graber	25.00	10.00
SP7 Tim Harkness	25.00	10.00
SP8 Jim Harwell	25.00	10.00
SP9 Howie Reed	25.00	10.00
SP10 Curt Roberts	25.00	10.00
SP11 Rene Valdes	25.00	10.00
TW1 Akihito Kondo		

TW2 Gentaro Shimada ....
TW3 Taiyo Whales ....

1962 Kahn's Atlanta

The cards in this 24-card set measure 3 1/4" X 4". The 1962 Kahn's Wieners Atlanta set features unnumbered, black and white cards of the Atlanta Crackers of the International League. The backs contain player statistical information as well as instructions on how to obtain free tickets. The catalog designation is F155-9. The cards are listed and numbered below in alphabetical order by the subject's name.

	NM	Ex
COMPLETE SET (24)	350.00	140.00
1 Jim Beauchamp	15.00	6.00
2 Gerry Buchek	12.00	4.80
3 Bob Burda	12.00	4.80
4 Dick Dietz	15.00	6.00
5 Bob Duliba	12.00	4.80
6 Harry Fanok	12.00	4.80
7 Phil Gagliano	15.00	6.00
8 John Glenn	12.00	4.80
9 Leroy Gregory	12.00	4.80
10 Dick Hughes	12.00	4.80
11 Johnny Kucks	15.00	6.00
12 Johnny Lewis	15.00	6.00
13 Tim McCarver	80.00	32.00
14 Bob Milliken	12.00	4.80
15 Joe M. Morgan	15.00	6.00
16 Ron Plaza	12.00	4.80
17 Bob Sadowski	12.00	4.80
18 Jim Saul	12.00	4.80
19 Willard Schmidt	12.00	4.80
20 Joe Schultz MG	15.00	6.00
21 Mike Shannon	30.00	12.00
22 Paul Toth	12.00	4.80
23 Lou Vickery	12.00	4.80
24 Fred Whitfield	15.00	6.00

1962 Omaha Dodgers Team Issue

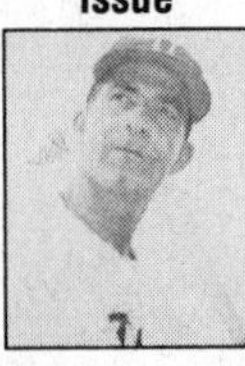

This 22 card blank backed set, which measured approximately 3 3/4" by 4 1/4" was issued by the team and featured members of the 1962 Omaha Dodgers. Each black and white photo features a facsimile autograph. Since these cards are unnumbered, we have sequenced them in alphabetical order.

	MINT	NRMT
COMPLETE SET	200.00	90.00
1 Joe Altobelli MG	10.00	4.50
2 Jim Barbieri	10.00	4.50
3 Scott Breeden	10.00	4.50
4 Mike Brumley	10.00	4.50
5 Jose Ceasar	10.00	4.50
6 Billy Hunter	10.00	4.50
7 Don LeJohn	10.00	4.50
8 Jack Lutz	10.00	4.50
9 Ken McMullen	12.00	5.50
10 Danny Ozark CO	10.00	4.50
11 Curt Roberts	10.00	4.50
12 Ernie Rodriguez	10.00	4.50
13 Dick Scarborough	10.00	4.50
14 Bart Shirley	10.00	4.50
15 Dick Smith	10.00	4.50
16 Jack Smith	10.00	4.50
17 Nate Smith	10.00	4.50
18 Gene Snyder	10.00	4.50
19 Burbon Wheeler	10.00	4.50
20 Nick Willhite	10.00	4.50
21 Jim Williams	10.00	4.50
22 Larry Williams	10.00	4.50

1962 Seattle Popcorn

This 19-card set of the Seattle Rainiers ballclub of the Pacific Coast League was distributed to the public as inserts in boxes of popcorn sold at Sicks' Stadium in Seattle. Only one card was inserted per box and measured approximately 2" by 3". The sets were produced by the ballclub and issued each season from 1954 through 1968. The fronts feature a black-and-white player photo with the player's name and position printed at the bottom. The backs are blank. The cards are unnumbered and checklisted below in alphabetical order.

	NM	Ex
COMPLETE SET (18)	175.00	70.00
1 Dave Hall	10.00	4.00
2 Billy Harrell	10.00	4.00
3 Curt Jenson UER	10.00	4.00
misspelled Jensen		
4 Stew MacDonald	10.00	4.00
5 Bill MacLeod	10.00	4.00
6 Dave Mann	10.00	4.00
7 Dave Mann	10.00	4.00
(Sliding)		
8 Dave Morehead	10.00	4.00
9 John Pesky MG	15.00	6.00
10 Ted Schreiber	10.00	4.00
(Position says Infielder)		
11 Ted Schreiber	10.00	4.00
(Position says Second Base)		
12 Elmer Singleton	10.00	4.00
13 Archie Skeen	10.00	4.00
14 Pete Smith	10.00	4.00
15 George Spencer	10.00	4.00
16 Bo Toft	10.00	4.00
17 Tom Umphlett	10.00	4.00
18 Ken Wolfe	10.00	4.00

1962 Tulsa Oilers Pepsi

Issued by Pepsi Cola to spotlight the 1962 Tulsa Oilers, these cards were originally distributed in two-card panels with a ring tab for attachment to a carton of soda. The cards are not numbered so we have sequenced them alphabetically and this set has a catalog number of F230-1. If a pair for any of the 1962, 63 or 66 sets is seen with the ring tab complete, add 25 percent to the combined values of the two players.

	NM	Ex
COMPLETE SET (24)	180.00	70.00
1 Bob Blaylock	8.00	3.20
2 Bud Bloomfield	8.00	3.20
3 Dick Hughes	8.00	3.20
4 Gary Kolb	8.00	3.20
5 Chris Krug	8.00	3.20
6 Hank Kuhlmann	8.00	3.20
7 Whitey Kurowski	12.00	4.80
8 Johnny Lewis	8.00	3.20
9 Elmer Lindsey	8.00	3.20
10 Jeoff Long	8.00	3.20
11 Pepper Martin	15.00	6.00
12 Jerry Marx	8.00	3.20
13 Weldon Mauldin	8.00	3.20
14 Dal Maxvill	8.00	3.20
15 Bill McNamee	8.00	3.20
16 Joe Patterson	8.00	3.20
17 Gordon Richardson	8.00	3.20
18 Daryl Robertson	8.00	3.20
19 Tommy Schwaner	8.00	3.20
20 Joe Shipley	8.00	3.20
21 Jon Smith BB	8.00	3.20
22 Clint Stark	8.00	3.20
23 Terry Tucker BB	8.00	3.20
24 Bill Wakefield	8.00	3.20

1963 Milwaukee Sausage

This 11-card set features Seattle Rainiers of the Pacific Coast League (PCL) only. The cards measure approximately 4 1/2" by 4 9/16" and they are unnumbered. Cards are printed on stiff cardboard with blue ink. The Milwaukee brand logo is featured in the upper right corner in red and yellow. The catalog designation for this scarce set is F180.

	NM	Ex
COMPLETE SET (11)	2200.00	900.00
1 Dave Hall	200.00	80.00
2 Bill Harrell	200.00	80.00
3 Pete Jernigan	200.00	80.00
4 Bill McLeod	200.00	80.00
5 Mel Parnell	250.00	100.00
6 Elmer Singleton	200.00	80.00
7 Archie Skeen	200.00	80.00
8 Paul Smith	250.00	100.00
9 Pete Smith	200.00	80.00
10 Bill Spanswick	200.00	80.00
11 George Spencer	200.00	80.00

1963 Rochester Red Wings Schieble Press W745

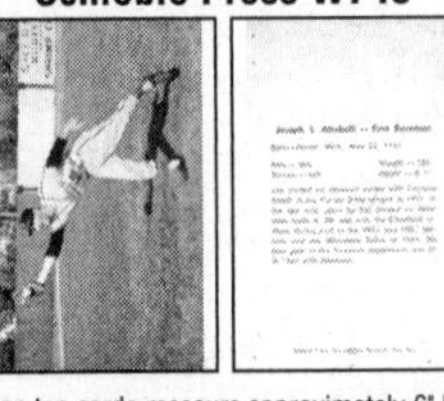

These ten cards measure approximately 6" by 3 3/4". The full-color borderless fronts feature a player photo along with a fascimile autograph. The horizontal backs feature player information along with a brief biography. The cards were produced by Scheible Press and their logo is listed on the bottom of the card. The Chittum card is made out of a thicker cardboard stock. The others are more of a thin paper stock. The cards were packaged in a envelope with nine cards indicating that there was a change in player selection later in the season.

	NM	Ex
COMPLETE SET (10)	100.00	40.00
1 Joe Altobelli HOR	15.00	6.00
2 Steve Bilko	12.00	4.80
3 Sam Bowens HOR	10.00	4.00
4 Don Brummer	10.00	4.00
5 Nelson Chittum	10.00	4.00
Thicker paper stock, no biography		
6 Luke Easter	20.00	8.00
7 Darrell Johnson MG	10.00	4.00
Chris Krug		
8 Fred Valentine	10.00	4.00
9 Ozzie Virgil	10.00	4.00
10 Ray Youngdahl	10.00	4.00

1963 Seattle Popcorn

This 15-card set of the Seattle Rainiers ballclub of the Pacific Coast League was distributed to the public as inserts in boxes of popcorn sold at Sicks' Stadium in Seattle. Only one card was inserted per box and measured approximately 2" by 3". The sets were produced by the ballclub and issued each season from 1954 through 1968. The fronts feature a black-and-white player photo with the player's name printed at the bottom. The backs are blank. The cards are unnumbered and checklisted below in alphabetical order.

	NM	Ex
COMPLETE SET (15)	150.00	60.00
1 Don Gile	10.00	4.00
2 Dave Hall	10.00	4.00
3 Billy Harrell	10.00	4.00
4 Pete Jernigan	10.00	4.00
5 Stan Johnson	10.00	4.00
6 Dalton Jones	10.00	4.00
7 Mel Parnell MG	15.00	6.00
8 Joe Pedrazzini	10.00	4.00
9 Elmer Singleton CO	10.00	4.00
10 Archie Skeen	10.00	4.00
11 Rac Slider	10.00	4.00
12 Pete Smith	10.00	4.00
13 Bill Spanswick	10.00	4.00
14 George Spencer	10.00	4.00
15 Wilbur Wood	20.00	8.00

1963 Tulsa Oilers Pepsi

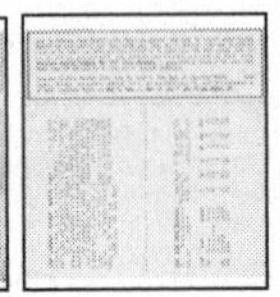

These sepia tone cards are unnumbered, as in the previous year, and depict Tulsa Oilers only. They are easily distinguished from the 1962 set by the Pepsi logo on the bottom right, which has "Pepsi-Cola" written over the bottle cap. The ring tab contains contest rules and an offer of free admission to an Oilers game. The catalog designation is F230-2.

	NM	Ex
COMPLETE SET (24)	180.00	70.00
1 Dennis Aust	8.00	3.20
2 Jim Beauchamp	8.00	3.20
3 Bud Bloomfield	8.00	3.20
4 Felix DeLeon	8.00	3.20
5 Don Dennis	8.00	3.20
6 Lamar Drummonds	8.00	3.20
7 Tom Hilgendorf	8.00	3.20
8 Gary Kolb	8.00	3.20
9 Chris Krug	8.00	3.20
10 Bee Lindsey	8.00	3.20
11 Roy Majtyka	8.00	3.20
12 Pepper Martin CO	15.00	6.00
13 Jerry Marx	8.00	3.20
14 Hunkey Mauldin	8.00	3.20
15 Joe Patterson	8.00	3.20
16 Grover Resinger	8.00	3.20
17 Gordon Richardson	8.00	3.20
18 Jon Smith BB	8.00	3.20
19 Chuck Taylor	8.00	3.20
20 Terry Tucker BB	8.00	3.20
21 Lou Vickery	8.00	3.20
22 Bill Wakefield	8.00	3.20
23 Harry Watts	8.00	3.20
24 Jerry Wild	8.00	3.20

1963-64 San Diego Padres Team Issue

These 8" by 10" blank-backed black and white photos feature members of the San Diego Padres, which were at that time a farm team for the Cincinnati Reds. The highlight of these photos is a pre-rookie photo of Hall of Famer Tony Perez. Since these photos are unnumbered, we have sequenced them in alphabetical order. It is possible that there are more photos so any additions are greatly appreciated.

	Nm-Mt	Ex-Mt
COMPLETE SET	80.00	36.00
1 Don Heffner MG	10.00	4.50
2 Tommy Helms	12.00	5.50
3 Tony Perez	50.00	22.00
4 Ray Rippelmeyer	10.00	4.50

1964 Seattle Popcorn

This 18-card set of the Seattle Rainiers ballclub of the Pacific Coast League was distributed to the public as inserts in boxes of popcorn sold at Sicks' Stadium in Seattle. Only one card was inserted per box and measured approximately 2" by 3". The sets were produced by the ballclub and issued each season from 1954 through 1968. The fronts feature a black-and-white player photo with the player's name printed at the bottom. The backs are blank. The cards are unnumbered and checklisted below in alphabetical order.

	NM	Ex
COMPLETE SET (18)	200.00	80.00
1 Earl Averill	20.00	8.00
2 Billy Gardner	20.00	8.00
3 Russ Gibson	12.00	4.80
4 Guido Grilli	12.00	4.80
5 Bob Guindon	12.00	4.80
6 Billy Harrell	12.00	4.80
7 Fred Holmes	12.00	4.80
8 Stan Johnson	12.00	4.80
9 Hal Kolstad	12.00	4.80
10 Gary Modrell	12.00	4.80
11 Felix Maldonado	12.00	4.80
12 Merlin Nippert	12.00	4.80
13 Rico Petrocelli	25.00	10.00
14 Jay Ritchie	12.00	4.80
15 Barry Shetrone	12.00	4.80
16 Pete Smith	12.00	4.80
17 Bill Tuttle	15.00	6.00
18 Edo Vanni MG	12.00	4.80

1964 Tulsa Oilers Pepsi

This eight-card set measures approximately 9" by 2 3/16" and was distributed by Pepsi-Cola. The fronts feature a facsimile player's autograph inside a baseball with player information printed below. These cards allowed a child under 12, when accompanied by an adult, free admission to Oiler Park on Pepsi-Oiler nights which were each Tuesday the Oilers were Home. The cards are unnumbered and checklisted below in alphabetical order.

	NM	Ex
COMPLETE SET	40.00	16.00
1 Bob Blaylock CO	5.00	2.00
2 Nelson Briles	10.00	4.00
3 Don Dennis	5.00	2.00
4 Bobby Dews	5.00	2.00
5 Dave Dowling	5.00	2.00
6 George Kernek	5.00	2.00
7 Chris Krug	5.00	2.00
8 Otto Meischner	5.00	2.00
9 Roy Majtyka	5.00	2.00
10 Grover Resinger MG	5.00	2.00
11 Rogers Robinson	5.00	2.00
12 Bobby Tolan	10.00	4.00
13 Lou Vickery	5.00	2.00
14 Harry Watts	5.00	2.00
15 Jerry Wild	5.00	2.00

1965 Seattle Popcorn

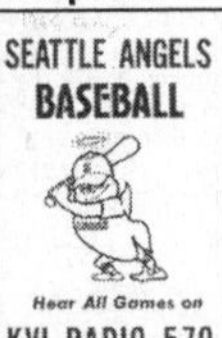

This 25-card set of the Seattle ballclub of the Pacific Coast League was distributed to the public as inserts in boxes of popcorn sold at Sicks' Stadium in Seattle. Only one card was inserted per box and measured approximately 2" by 3". The sets were produced by the ballclub and issued each season from 1954 through 1968. Since Seattle's major league affiliation switched from the Boston Red Sox to the California Angels, their name was changed from the "Rainiers" to the "Angels" for 1965. The fronts feature a black-and-white player photo with the player's name printed at the bottom. The backs carry an advertisement for radio station KVI 570 which carried Seattle's games. Since KVI is the only sponsor, this is how a collector can tell it is a 1965 card. Some cards are currently only known to exist in blank-back form. The cards are unnumbered and checklisted below in alphabetical order.

	NM	Ex
COMPLETE SET (24)	200.00	80.00
1 Earl Averill	10.00	4.00
2 Tom Burgmeier	8.00	3.20
3 Chuck Estrada	8.00	3.20
Blank Back		
Same pose and crop as 66		
4 Bob Guindon	8.00	3.20
5 Jack Hernandez	8.00	3.20
6 Fred Holmes	8.00	3.20
7 Ed Kirkpatrick	8.00	3.20
8 Hal Kolstad	8.00	3.20
9 Joe Koppe	8.00	3.20
10 Les Kuhnz	8.00	3.20
11 Bob Lemon MG	15.00	6.00
12 Bobby Locke	8.00	3.20
13 Jim McGlothlin	8.00	3.20
14 Bob Radovich	8.00	3.20
Blankback		
15 Bob Radovich	8.00	3.20
16 Merritt Ranew	8.00	3.20
17 Jimmie Reese CO	15.00	6.00
Blankback		
18 Rick Reichardt	8.00	3.20
Blankback		
19 Rick Reichardt	8.00	3.20
20 Tom Satriano	8.00	3.20
21 Dick Simpson	8.00	3.20
22 Jack Spring	8.00	3.20
Blankback		
23 Ed Sukla	8.00	3.20
24 Jackie Warner	8.00	3.20
25 Stan Williams	10.00	4.00

1966 Columbus Yankees Royal Crown

These cards, which measure the standard size when the coupon was detached, was issued by Royal Crown Cola in 1966. The black and white photos are only a small part of the card as the rest of the card is devoted to information about a contest in which a collector who completed the set was eligible for various prizes. Since this set is unnumbered, we have sequenced them in alphabetical order. Cards with tabs attached are worth 1.5X listed price. According to the tab, an album was also made for this set.

	NM	Ex
COMPLETE SET (20)	400.00	160.00
1 Gil Blanco	20.00	8.00
2 Ron Boyer	20.00	8.00
3 Jim Brenneman	20.00	8.00
4 Butch Cretara	20.00	8.00
5 Bill Henry	20.00	8.00
6 Joe Jeran	20.00	8.00
7 Jerry Kenney	20.00	8.00
8 Ron Kirk	20.00	8.00
9 Tom Kowalowski	20.00	8.00
10 Jim Marrujo	20.00	8.00
11 Dave McDonald	20.00	8.00
12 Ed Merritt	20.00	8.00
13 Jim Palma	20.00	8.00
14 Cecil Parkins	20.00	8.00
15 Jack Reed	20.00	8.00
16 Ellie Rodriguez	20.00	8.00
17 John Schroetpel	20.00	8.00
18 Dave Truelock	20.00	8.00
19 Steve Whitaker	20.00	8.00
20 Earl Willoughby	20.00	8.00
XX Album		

1966 Seattle Popcorn

This 30-card set of the Seattle Angels ballclub of the Pacific Coast League was distributed to the public as inserts in boxes of popcorn sold at Sicks' Stadium in Seattle. Only one card was inserted per box and measured approximately 2" by 3". The sets were produced by the ballclub and issued each season from 1954 through 1968. The fronts feature a black-and-white player photo with the player's name printed at the bottom. The backs carry an advertisement for radio station KVI 570 which carried Seattle's games. The 1966 cards list four other sponsors on the card. The cards are unnumbered and checklisted below in alphabetical order. John Olerud, father of future major league first baseman John Olerud, is believed to only have been released in a very scarce uncut sheet version. It is thought that less than five copies are known in the secondary market. Therefore, we are listing this card and not pricing it.

	NM	Ex
COMPLETE SET (29)	250.00	100.00
1 Del Bates	8.00	3.20
2 Tom Burgmeier	8.00	3.20
3 Jim Campanis	8.00	3.20
4 Jim Coates	8.00	3.20
5 Tony Cortopassi	8.00	3.20
6 Chuck Estrada	10.00	4.00
7 Ray Hernandez	8.00	3.20
8 Jay Johnstone	15.00	6.00
9 Bill Kelso	8.00	3.20
10 Vic LaRose	8.00	3.20
11 Bobby Locke	8.00	3.20
12 Rudy May	15.00	6.00
13 Andy Messersmith	15.00	6.00
14 Bubba Morton	8.00	3.20
15 Cotton Nash	12.00	4.80
16 John Olerud		
17 Marty Pattin	8.00	3.20
18 Merritt Ranew	8.00	3.20
19 Minnie Rojas	8.00	3.20
Blank-Back		
20 Minnie Rojas	8.00	3.20
21 George Rubio	8.00	3.20
22 Al Spangler	8.00	3.20
23 Ed Sukla	8.00	3.20
24 Felix Torres	8.00	3.20
25 Hector Torres	8.00	3.20
26 Ken Turner	8.00	3.20
27 Chuck Vinson	8.00	3.20

	NM	Ex
28 Don Wallace	8.00	3.20
29 Jack Warner	8.00	3.20
30 Mike White	8.00	3.20

1966 St. Petersburg Cardinals Team Issue

This 20-card set of the 1966 St. Petersburg Cardinals was sponsored by Foremost Milk and features black-and-white player portraits in white borders. The cards measure approximately 3 1/2" by 5". The backs are blank. The cards are unnumbered and checklisted below in alphabetical order.

	NM	Ex
COMPLETE SET (20)	80.00	32.00
1 Sparky Anderson	80.00	32.00
2 Dave Bakenhaster	1.00	.40
3 Leonard Boyer	1.00	.40
4 Ron Braddock	1.00	.40
5 Thomas"Chip" Coulter	1.00	.40
6 Ernest"Sweet Pea" Davis	1.00	.40
7 Phil Knuckles	1.00	.40
8 Doug Lukens	1.00	.40
9 Terry Milani	1.00	.40
10 Tim Morgan	1.00	.40
11 Harry Parker	1.00	.40
12 Jerry Robertson	1.00	.40
13 Francisco Rodriguez	1.00	.40
14 John"Sonny" Ruberto	1.00	.40
15 Charlie Stewart	1.00	.40
16 Gary L. Stone	1.00	.40
17 Charles"Tim" Thompson	1.00	.40
18 Jose Villar	1.00	.40
19 Archie L. Wade	1.00	.40
20 Jim Williamson	1.00	.40

1966 Toledo Mud Hens Team Issue

This 25-card set of the Toledo Mud Hens measures approximately 3 3/16" by 5" and features borderless black-and-white player photos. The backs are blank. The cards are unnumbered and checklisted below in alphabetical order.

	NM	Ex
COMPLETE SET (25)	100.00	40.00
1 Loren Babe MG	4.00	1.60
2 Jean Bahnsen	4.00	1.60
3 Bill Bethea	4.00	1.60
4 Wayne Comer	4.00	1.60
5 Jack Cullen	4.00	1.60
6 Jack Curtis	4.00	1.60
7 Jim Downs	4.00	1.60
8 Joe Faraci	4.00	1.60
9 Frank Fernandez	4.00	1.60
10 Mike Ferraro	4.00	1.60
11 Doc Foley	4.00	1.60
12 Mike Hegan	4.00	1.60
13 Jim Horsford	4.00	1.60
14 Dick Hughes	4.00	1.60
15 Elvis Jimenez	4.00	1.60
16 Tom Martz	4.00	1.60
17 Ed Merritt	4.00	1.60
18 Archie Moore	4.00	1.60
19 Bobby Murcer	20.00	8.00
20 Tony Przybycien	4.00	1.60
21 Bob Schmidt	4.00	1.60
22 Bill Shantz CO Charles Senger GM Loren Babe MG	4.00	1.60
23 Bill Shantz CO	4.00	1.60
24 Paul Toth	4.00	1.60
25 Jerry Walker	4.00	1.60

1966 Tulsa Oilers Pepsi

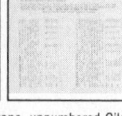

This set has 24 sepia tone, unnumbered Oilers cards, similar to previous issues but printed on thinner stock. Eight players were double printed (they are notated with a DP next to their names) and 16 two-card panels exist. Panel prices are 50 percent more than the sum of the individual prices.

	NM	Ex
COMPLETE SET (24)	250.00	100.00
COMMON CARD (1-24)	12.00	4.80
COMMON DP	8.00	3.20
1 Fritz Ackley	12.00	4.80
2 Dennis Aust	12.00	4.80
3 Elio Chacon DP	8.00	3.20
4 Jim Cosman	12.00	4.80
5 Mack Creager	12.00	4.80
6 Bobby Dews DP	8.00	3.20
7 Hal Gilson	12.00	4.80
8 Larry Jaster	12.00	4.80
9 Alex Johnson	15.00	6.00
10 George Kernek DP	8.00	3.20
11 Coco Laboy	12.00	4.80
12 Dick LeMay	12.00	4.80
13 Charlie Metro MG	12.00	4.80
14 Dave Pavlesic	12.00	4.80
15 Bobby Pfeil DP	8.00	3.20
16 Ron Piche	12.00	4.80
17 Bob Radovich	12.00	4.80
18 Dave Ricketts DP	8.00	3.20
19 Ted Savage DP	8.00	3.20
20 George Schultz	12.00	4.80
21 Ed Spiezio DP	8.00	3.20
22 Clint Stark	12.00	4.80
23 Bobby Tolan	15.00	6.00
24 Walt Williams	12.00	4.80

1967 Buffalo Bisons Jones Dairy

This one-card set was distributed by Jones Dairy on its milk cartons and features a 2 1/2" by 3" color photo of Duke Carmel of the Buffalo Bisons. The 1967 home schedule for the Bisons was also printed on the cartons.

	NM	Ex
1 Duke Carmel	25.00	10.00

1967 Seattle Popcorn

This 19-card set of the Seattle ballclub of the Pacific Coast League was distributed to the public as inserts in boxes of popcorn sold at Sicks' Stadium in Seattle. Only one card was inserted per box and measured approximately 2" by 3". The sets were produced by the ballclub and issued each season from 1954 through 1968. Since Seattle's major league affiliation switched from the Boston Red Sox to the California Angels, their name was changed from the "Rainiers" to the "Angels" for 1965. The fronts feature a black-and-white player photo with the player's name printed at the bottom. The backs carry an advertisement for radio station KVI 570 which carried Seattle's games. The 1967 cards have five listed sponsors. The cards are unnumbered and checklisted below in alphabetical order.

	NM	Ex
COMPLETE SET (19)	125.00	50.00
1 George Banks	8.00	3.20
2 Tom Burgmeier	8.00	3.20
3 Jim Coates	8.00	3.20
4 Chuck Cottier	8.00	3.20
5 Tony Curry	8.00	3.20
6 Vern Geishert	8.00	3.20
7 Jesse Hickman	8.00	3.20
8 Bill Kelso	8.00	3.20
9 Ed Kirkpatrick	8.00	3.20
10 Chris Krug	8.00	3.20
11 Bobby Locke	8.00	3.20
12 Bill Murphy	8.00	3.20
13 Marty Pattin	8.00	3.20
14 Merrit Ranew	8.00	3.20
15 Bob Sadowski	8.00	3.20
16 Ed Sukla	8.00	3.20
17 Hector Torres	8.00	3.20
18 Chuck Vinson	8.00	3.20
19 Don Wallace	8.00	3.20

1967 Tacoma Cubs Team Issue

These black and white photos, which measure approximately 3 1/2" by 3 1/4" were issued as part of the 1967 Clay Huntington's Pictorial Yearbook. These photos were given out a selected Tacoma Cubs game during the 1967 season. Since these photos are unnumbered, we have sequenced them in alphabetical order.

	NM	Ex
COMPLETE SET (23)	200.00	80.00
1 George Altman	12.00	4.80
2 Bob Barton	10.00	4.00
3 John Boccabella	12.00	4.80
4 Marv Breeding	10.00	4.00
5 Dick Calmus	10.00	4.00
6 Ron Campbell	10.00	4.00
7 Len Church	10.00	4.00
8 Billy Connors	12.00	4.80
9 Lee Elia	12.00	4.80
10 Chico Fernandez	10.00	4.00
11 Tom Fletcher	10.00	4.00
12 Dick James	10.00	4.00
14 Whitey Lockman MG	12.00	4.80
15 Tom Mandile	10.00	4.00
16 Bobby Mitchell	10.00	4.00
17 Joe Proski TR	10.00	4.00
18 Dick Radatz	12.00	4.80
19 Shorty Raudman	10.00	4.00
20 Gary Ross	10.00	4.00
21 Bob Scott	10.00	4.00
21 Elmer Singleton	10.00	4.00
22 Bobby Gene Smith	10.00	4.00
23 Gene Stephens	10.00	4.00

1967 Vancouver Mounties Standard Oil

Collect pictures of all the
1967 MOUNTIES
Supplied to you with the compliments of
CHEVRON DEALERS STANDARD STATIONS
and ...
GO SAFELY WITH
UNIROYAL

This 27-card set measures approximately 2" by 3" and features glossy black-and-white photos of the 1967 Pacific Coast League's Vancouver Mounties. The set was co-produced by Standard Oil (Chevron) and Uniroyal tires. This limited edition set is thought to have been distributed at participating service stations upon request with a fill-up.

	NM	Ex
COMPLETE SET (27)	100.00	40.00
1 Sal Bando	20.00	8.00
2 Frank Bastrire TR	3.00	1.20
3 Ossie Chavarria	3.00	1.20
4 Jim Dickson	3.00	1.20
5 John Donaldson	3.00	1.20
6 Jim Driscoll	3.00	1.20
7 Bob Duliba	3.00	1.20
8 Bill Edgerton	3.00	1.20
9 Larry Elliot	3.00	1.20
10 Ernie Foli	3.00	1.20
11 Joe Gaines	3.00	1.20
12 Vern Handrahan	3.00	1.20
13 Jim Hughes	3.00	1.20
14 Woody Huyke	3.00	1.20
15 Rene Lachemann	5.00	2.00
16 Bob Meyer	3.00	1.20
17 Wayne Norton	3.00	1.20
18 Gerry Reimer	3.00	1.20
19 Roberto Rodriquez	3.00	1.20
20 Ken Sanders	3.00	1.20
21 Randy Schwartz	3.00	1.20
22 Diego Segui	3.00	1.20
23 Paul Seitz	3.00	1.20
24 Ron Tompkins	3.00	1.20
25 Mickey Vernon MG	10.00	4.00
26 Jim Ward	3.00	1.20
27 Don Yingling	3.00	1.20

1968 Memphis Blues Red Barn

This set was issued by the Red Barn restaurant chain and featured members of the 1968 Memphis Blues. The fronts have the players photo located inside a "red barn" and the bottom has the player name and some biographical and career information. These cards are sequenced by uniform number and any additions to this checklist is appreciated. The Red Barn chain closed shortly after this set was issued.

	NM	Ex
COMPLETE SET	150.00	60.00
3 Mike Jorgensen	30.00	12.00
6 Joe Moock	25.00	10.00
9 Rod Gaspar	25.00	10.00
16 Barry Raziano	25.00	10.00
17 Curtis Brown	25.00	10.00
19 Ron Paul	25.00	10.00
24 Steve Christopher	25.00	10.00

1968 Seattle Popcorn

This 18-card set of the Seattle Angels ballclub of the Pacific Coast League was distributed to the public as inserts in boxes of popcorn sold at Sicks' Stadium in Seattle. Only one card was inserted per box and measured approximately 2" by 3". The sets were produced by the ballclub and issued each season from 1954 through 1968. The fronts feature a black-and-white player photo with the player's name printed at the bottom. The backs are blank. The cards are unnumbered and checklisted below in alphabetical order. The Overton is currently known to exist only in an uncut sheet. It is also not priced currently.

	NM	Ex
COMPLETE SET (18)	125.00	50.00
1 Ethan Blackaby	8.00	3.20
2 Jim Coates	8.00	3.20
3 Tom Egan	8.00	3.20
4 Larry Elliott	8.00	3.20
5 Jim Engelhardt	8.00	3.20
6 Gus Gil	8.00	3.20
7 Bill Harrelson	8.00	3.20
8 Steve Hovley	8.00	3.20
9 Jim Mahoney	8.00	3.20
10 Mickey McGuire	8.00	3.20
11 Joe Overton		
12 Marty Pattin	8.00	3.20
13 Larry Sherry	12.00	4.80
14 Marv Staehle	8.00	3.20
15 Ed Sukla	8.00	3.20
16 Jarvis Tatum	8.00	3.20
17 Hawk Taylor	8.00	3.20
18 Chuck Vinson	8.00	3.20

1970 Wichita Aeros McDonald's

This 18-card set features black-and-white photos of the Wichita Aeros printed on 2 1/2" by 3 1/4" cards with blank backs. The set was issued by McDonald's Restaurant. The cards are unnumbered and checklisted below in alphabetical order.

	NM	Ex
COMPLETE SET (18)	60.00	24.00
1 Ken Aspromonte MG	5.00	2.00
2 Frank Baker	4.00	1.60
3 Larry Burchart	4.00	1.60
4 Lou Camilli	4.00	1.60
5 Mike Carruthers	4.00	1.60
6 Chris Chambliss	15.00	6.00
7 Ed Farmer	4.00	1.60
8 Pedro Gonzales	4.00	1.60
9 Jerry Hinsley	4.00	1.60
10 Luis Isaac	4.00	1.60
11 John Lowenstein	5.00	2.00
12 Cap Peterson	4.00	1.60
13 Jim Rittwage	4.00	1.60
14 Bill Rohr	4.00	1.60
15 Richie Scheinblum	5.00	2.00
16 John Scruggs	4.00	1.60
17 Ken Suarez	4.00	1.60
18 Dick Tidrow	5.00	2.00

1971 Richmond Braves Team Issue

This 18-card black and white set was sponsored by Currie Press. The cards measure 3-3/8" X 5-5/16. A pre-Rookie Card of Dusty Baker is in this set.

	NM	Ex
COMPLETE SET (18)	75.00	30.00
1 Tommie Aaron	5.00	2.00
2 Sam Ayoub TR	3.00	1.20
3 Dusty Baker	20.00	8.00
4 Jim Breazeale	3.00	1.20
5 Jack Crist	3.00	1.20
6 Shaun Fitzmaurice	3.00	1.20
7 Jim French	3.00	1.20
8 Larry Jaster	6.00	2.40
9 Van Kelly	3.00	1.20
10 Rick Kester	3.00	1.20
11 Clyde King MG	5.00	2.00
12 Dave Lobb	3.00	1.20
13 Larry Maxie	3.00	1.20
14 Hank McGraw	3.00	1.20
15 Gary Neibauer	3.00	1.20
16 Guy Rose	3.00	1.20
17 Fred Velazquez	3.00	1.20
18 Bobby Young	3.00	1.20

1971 Syracuse Chiefs Postcards

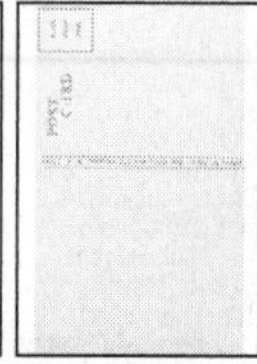

These eight postcards were produced by long time hobbyist and photographer Jeffrey Morey. These cards feature members of the 1971 Syracuse Chiefs and have the players photo along with his name on the front. The backs are in the standard postcard format.

	NM	Ex
COMPLETE SET (8)	40.00	16.00
1 Len Boehmer	5.00	2.00
2 Ozzie Chavarrio	5.00	2.00
3 Alan Closter	5.00	2.00
4 Fred Frazier	5.00	2.00
5 Rob Gardner	5.00	2.00
6 George Pena	5.00	2.00
7 Rusty Torres	5.00	2.00
8 Danny Walton	5.00	2.00

1972 Seattle Rainers Team Issue

Theser cards, issued in sheets of four players, were inserted in Seattle Rainier game programs. These sheets were issued on an irregular basis and since these cards are unnumbered, we have sequenced them in alphabetical order.

	NM	Ex
COMPLETE SET	30.00	12.00
1 Willy Adams	2.00	.80
2 Rafael Aniama	2.00	.80
3 Greg Brust	2.00	.80
4 Wade Carpenter	2.00	.80
5 Wes Dixon	2.00	.80
6 Ray Ewing	2.00	.80
7 Jose Gomez	2.00	.80
8 Rocky Hernandez	2.00	.80
9 Bill Kindall	2.00	.80
10 Kevin Kooyman	2.00	.80
11 Gene Lanthorn	2.00	.80
12 Jeff McKay	2.00	.80
13 Steve Mezich CO	2.00	.80
14 John Owens	2.00	.80
15 Tony Pepper	2.00	.80
16 Mike Peters	2.00	.80
17 Roger Rasmussen	2.00	.80
18 Ken Roll TR	2.00	.80
19 Rich Thompson	2.00	.80
20 Jesse Winchester	2.00	.80

1972 Tacoma Twins Team Issue

These cards, issued in the style of the Seattle "Popcorn" cards feature members of the 1972 Tacoma Twins. The fronts have a player photo with their name, position and some personal data on the bottom. Jim Strickland, Glenn Borgmann, Jerry Terrell and Ron Herbel are believed to be more difficult to obtain. We have notated those cards with an SP in our checklist. Since these cards are unnumbered, we have sequenced them in alphabetical order.

	NM	Ex
COMPLETE SET	40.00	16.00
SP COMMONS	5.00	2.00
1 Mike Adams	2.00	.80
2 Glenn Borgmann SP	5.00	2.00
3 Mike Brooks	2.00	.80
4 Ezell Carter	2.00	.80
5 Mike Derrick	2.00	.80
6 Glen Ezell	2.00	.80
7 Ken Gill	2.00	.80
8 Hal Haydel	2.00	.80
9 Ron Herbel SP	5.00	2.00
10 Jim Holt	2.00	.80
11 Tom Kelly	4.00	1.60
12 Steve Luebber	2.00	.80
13 Cap Peterson	2.00	.80
14 Dennis Saunders	2.00	.80
15 Jim Strickland SP	5.00	2.00
16 Jerry Terrell SP	5.00	2.00

1973 Syracuse Chiefs Team Issue

This 1973 Syracuse Chiefs team issued set features major league players as well as minor league players from the Yankee organization. The cards are black and white and measure 4" X 5". The cards were inserted one at a time inside the Syracuse Chiefs minor league programs. Card number 22 was a late addition to the set. The first six collectors who were able to show they had completed the set won a three speed bike.

	NM	Ex
COMPLETE SET (29)	150.00	60.00
COMPLETE SET W/PAZIK (30)	225.00	90.00
1 Felipe Alou		
2 Marty Alou		
3 Ron Blomberg		
4 John Callison		
5 Horace Clark		
6 Alan Closter		
7 Joe DiMaggio		
8 Lou Gehrig		
9 Larry Gowell		
10 Ralph Houk		
11 Mike Kekich		
12 Ron Klimkowski		
13 Steve Kline		
14 Sparky Lyle		
15 Mickey Mantle		
16 Lindy McDaniel		
17 George Medich		
18 Gene Michael		
19 Thurman Munson		
20 Bobby Murcer		
21 Graig Nettles		
22 Mike Pazik (Late Issue)		
23 Fritz Peterson		
24 Babe Ruth		
25 Cellie Sanchez		
26 Mel Stottlemyre		
27 Frank Tepedino		
28 Otto Velez		
29 Roy White		
30 George Zeber		

1974 Broder Popcorn

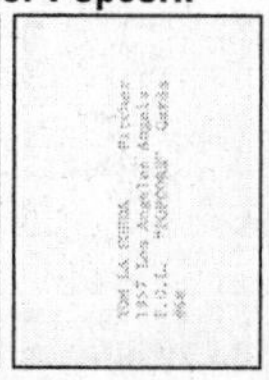

These more than 200 cards, issued over two series and designed in similar fashion to the old Seattle Popcorn cards were issued by collector Ed Broder and honors players from the 1957 PCL (The last year before major league teams moved out to the West Coast). This checklist is incomplete and additions and corrections are appreciated. Each series was available from Ed Broder for $5.75 each.

	NM	Ex
COMPLETE SET	200.00	80.00
1 Maury Wills	4.00	1.60
2 Joe Black	2.50	1.00
3 Mario Fricano	1.00	.40
4 Joe Taylor	1.00	.40
5 Dick Alyward	1.00	.40
6 Juan Delis	1.00	.40
7 Gene Hayden	1.00	.40
8 Babe Birrer	1.00	.40
9 Sparky Anderson	3.00	1.20
10 Connie Grob	1.00	.40
11 Walt Lammers	1.00	.40
12 Bert Hamric	1.00	.40
13 Steve Bilko	1.00	.40
14 Glen Mickens	1.00	.40
15 Frank Carswell	1.00	.40
16 Bobby Adams	1.00	.40
17 Billy DeMars	1.00	.40
18 Bill Sweeney MG	1.00	.40
19 Bob Alexander	1.00	.40
20 Sam Calderone	1.00	.40
21 Fred Besana	1.00	.40
22 Jim Archer	1.00	.40
23 Charlie White	1.00	.40
24 Spider Jorgensen	1.00	.40
25 Jim Marshall	1.00	.40
26 Charlie Beamon	1.00	.40
27 Bennie Daniels	1.00	.40
28 Clyde King MG	1.00	.40
29 Chuck Churn	1.00	.40
30 Bill Causion	1.00	.40
31 Ed White	1.00	.40
32 Tommy Heath MG	1.00	.40
33 Cuno Barragan	1.00	.40
34 Bud Watkins	1.00	.40
35 Al Heist	1.00	.40
36 Dick Cole	1.00	.40
37 Marshall Bridges	1.00	.40
38 Bob DiPietro	1.00	.40
39 Billy Harrell	1.00	.40
40 Gary Bell	1.50	.60
41 Jim Grant	1.50	.60
42 Catfish Metkovich MG	1.00	.40
43 Dolan Nichols	1.00	.40
44 Bob DePietro	1.00	.40
45 Sal Taormina	1.00	.40
46 Joe Gordon MG	2.00	.80
47 Marty Keough	1.00	.40
48 Joe Tanner	1.00	.40
49 Earl Wilson	1.00	.40
50 Leo Kiely	1.00	.40
51 Fred Bower	1.00	.40
52 Hal Groate	1.00	.40
53 Jim Konstanty	1.50	.60
54 Walt Masterson	1.00	.40
55 Unknown		
56 Bob Balcena	1.00	.40
57 Steve Watson	1.00	.40
58 Bill Glynn	1.00	.40
59 Lou Kretlow	1.00	.40
60 Glenn Isringhaus	1.00	.40
61 Larry Segovia	1.00	.40
62 Bob Borkowski	1.00	.40
63 Frank Ernaga	1.00	.40
64 Luis Marquez	1.00	.40
65 Joe Macko	1.00	.40
66 Elmer Singleton	1.00	.40
67 Jackie Warner	1.00	.40
68 Tom Lasorda	5.00	2.00
69 Dick Teed	1.00	.40

70 Tom Saffel 1.00 .40
71 Tony Barterone 1.00 .40
72 Fred Waters 1.00 .40
73 Carlos Bernier 1.00 .40
74 Bob Schakales 1.00 .40
75 Bill Abernathy 1.00 .40
76 Pumpsie Green 1.00 .40
77 Grady Hatton 1.00 .40
78 Harry Malmberg 1.00 .40
79 Ken Aspromonte 1.00 .40
80 Bill Prout 1.00 .40
81 Jerry Zimmerman 1.00 .40
82 Larry DiPippo 1.00 .40
83 Sandy Conseguera 1.00 .40
84 Joe Frasier 1.00 .40
85 Tito Francona 1.50 .60
86 Larry Webster 1.00 .40
87 Roger Osenbaugh 1.00 .40
88 Earl Harris 1.00 .40
89 Carl Duser 1.00 .40
90 Don Frailey 1.00 .40
91 Roger Bowman 1.00 .40
92 Earl Averill 1.00 .40
93 Dick Brodowski 1.00 .40
94 Billy Harrell 1.00 .40
95 Stan Locklin 1.00 .40
96 Billy Moran 1.00 .40
97 Billy Werle 1.00 .40
98 Tom Haller 1.50 .60
99 Dusty Rhodes 1.50 .60
100 Willie Kirkland 1.00 .40
101 Red Davis MG 1.00 .40
102 George Prescott 1.00 .40
103 Pete Burnside 1.00 .40
104 Jack Dittmar 1.00 .40
105 Winston Brown 1.00 .40
106 Terry Fox 1.00 .40
107 Bob Roselli 1.00 .40
108 Bob Schmidt 1.00 .40
109 Bud Watkins 1.00 .40
110 Jack Deitman 1.00 .40
111 Harry Fenn 1.00 .40
112 Doug Hubacek 1.00 .40
113 Bill Renna 1.00 .40
114 Al Schroll 1.00 .40
115 Unknown
116 Duane Pillette 1.00 .40
117 Clay Bryant 1.00 .40
118 Jim Fridley 1.00 .40
119 Vito Valentinetti 1.00 .40
120 Hal Bevan 1.00 .40
121 Jim Dyck 1.00 .40
122 Larry Jansen 1.50 .60
123 Edo Vanni 1.00 .40
124 Chuck Diering 1.00 .40
125 Lenny Green 1.00 .40
126 Ed Erautt 1.00 .40
127 Dan Baich 1.00 .40
128 Unknown
129 Ray Bauer 1.00 .40
130 Johnny Briggs 1.00 .40
131 Nini Tornay 1.00 .40
132 Frosty Morris 1.00 .40
133 Carl Greene 1.00 .40
134 Chico Heron 1.00 .40
135 Mike Kume 1.00 .40
136 Bob Ross 1.00 .40
137 Clay Dalrymple 1.00 .40
138 Gary Rushing 1.00 .40
139 Jim Greengrass 1.00 .40
140 Len Neal 1.00 .40
141 Curt Barclay 1.00 .40
142 Jim Brideweiser 1.00 .40
143 Owen Friend 1.00 .40
144 Gordon Jones 1.00 .40
145 Unknown
146 Dom Zanni 1.00 .40
147 Don Dillard 1.00 .40
148 Dee Fondy 1.00 .40
149 Ed Gasgue 1.00 .40
150 Catfish Metkovivch MG 1.00 .40
151 Bud Podbielan 1.00 .40
152 Ken Retzer 1.00 .40
153 Jim Bolger 1.00 .40
154 Roger Bowman 1.00 .40
155 Carl Greene 1.00 .40
156 Chuck Hickman 1.00 .40
157 Mike Krsinch 1.00 .40
158 Bob Perry 1.00 .40
159 Roger Osenbaugh 1.00 .40
160 Noel Mickkelson 1.00 .40
161 Tom Umphlett 1.00 .40
162 Heywood Sullivan 1.00 .40
163 Windy McCall 1.00 .40
164 Roy Tinney 1.00 .40
165 Jack Phillips 1.00 .40
166 Gale Wade 1.00 .40
167 Bob Cattora 1.00 .40
168 Bob Jenkins 1.00 .40
169 George Witt 1.00 .40
170 Don Rowe 1.00 .40
171 Al Federoff 1.00 .40
172 Unknown
173 Jack Lohrke 1.00 .40
174 Charlie Rabe 1.00 .40
175 Lou Righetti 1.00 .40
176 Unknown
177 Unknown
178 Carl Powis 1.00 .40
179 Solly Drake 1.00 .40
180 Dick Fielder 1.00 .40
181 Bob Thorpe 1.00 .40
182 Ray Shore 1.00 .40
183 Unknown
184 Ed Gasgue 1.00 .40
185 Bud Hardin 1.00 .40
186 Ed Kazak 1.00 .40
187 Kal Segrist 1.00 .40
188 Jim Westlake 1.00 .40
189 Jim Mangan 1.00 .40
190 Mike Coen 1.00 .40
191 Tom Bowers 1.00 .40
192 Mario Fricano 1.00 .40
193 Jake Jenkins 1.00 .40
194 Julio Navarro 1.00 .40
195 Sal Taormina 1.00 .40
196 Unknown
197 Rod Grabber 1.00 .40
198 Russ Heman 1.00 .40
199 Gene Leek 1.00 .40
200 Pete Mesa 1.00 .40
201 Dick Smith 1.00 .40
202 Pete Wojay 1.00 .40
203 Jim Davis 1.00 .40
204 Al Heist 1.00 .40
205 Whitey Wietelmann 1.00 .40
206 Clem Moore 1.00 .40
207 Ernie White 1.00 .40
208 Clay Dalrymple 1.00 .40
209 Milt Smith 1.00 .40
210 Nippy Jones 1.00 .40
211 Nippy Jones 1.00 .40
212 Don Hunter 1.00 .40
213 Bill Poesdel 1.00 .40
214 Carmen Mauro 1.00 .40
215 Jack Littrell 1.00 .40
216 Vic Lombardi 1.00 .40
217 Bob Dolan 1.00 .40
218 Bud Podbielan 1.00 .40
219 Dick Marlowe 1.00 .40
220 Kal Segrist 1.00 .40
221 Charlie Metro MG 1.00 .40
222 Unknown
223 Jay Van Noy 1.00 .40
224 Gene Fodge 1.00 .40
225 John Gray 1.00 .40
226 Ed Mickkelson 1.00 .40
227 Unkwown
228 Tom Hurd 1.00 .40
229 R.W. Smith 1.00 .40
230 Al Jones 1.00 .40
231 Stan Jankowski 1.00 .40
232 Dick Stigman 1.00 .40
233 Chuck Stevens 1.00 .40
234 Bob Roselli 1.00 .40
NNO Frank Kellert 1.00 .40
Pumpsie Green
Harry Malmberg
Grady Hatton
San Fransisco Seals Infield

1977 Pawtucket Red Sox Team Issue

These photos, which measure either 5" by 7" or 8" by 10" feature members of the 1977 Pawtucket Red Sox. We have sequenced this set in alphabetical order.

	NM	Ex
COMPLETE SET	30.00	12.00
1 Don Aase		
2 Jack Baker	2.00	.80
3 Rick Berg	2.00	.80
4 Dave Coleman	2.00	.80
5 Ted Cox	2.00	.80
6 Bo Diaz	3.00	1.20
7 Luis Delgado	2.00	.80
8 John Doherty	2.00	.80
9 Joel Finch	2.00	.80
10 Leo Frazier	2.00	.80
11 Wayne Harer	2.00	.80
12 Rick Krueger	2.00	.80
13 Mike Paxton	2.00	.80
14 John Poloni	2.00	.80
15 Bruce Poole	2.00	.80
16 Gary Purcell	2.00	.80
17 Jim Vosk	2.00	.80
18 Jim Wright	2.00	.80

1982 Anchorage Glacier Pilots Candaele

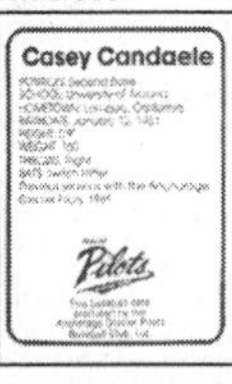

This unnumbered card, although dated 1982, was most likely produced at the same time as the Mark McGwire commemorative Glacier Pilots card. The card is blue and white-bordered and features a black and white photograph.

	Nm-Mt	Ex-Mt
1 Casey Candaele	10.00	4.00

1982 Anchorage Glacier Pilots McGwire

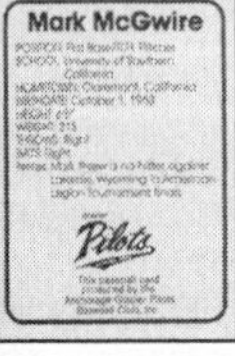
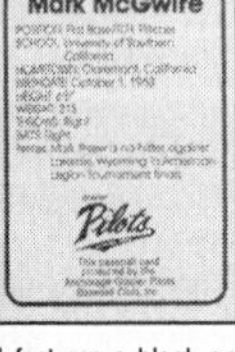

This blue-bordered card features a black and white photo of young Mark McGwire. Interestingly, McGwire was listed as both a first baseman and pitcher, and the card was issued to honor a no-hitter he threw in the American Legion finals against a Laramie, Wyoming team. The card was actually produced in two printings between 1988 and 1989. One printing for a California distributor resulted in mostly off-centered cards, while the second printing (for the team itself) was centered.

	Nm-Mt	Ex-Mt
1 Mark McGwire	120.00	47.50

1987 Vancouver Canadians Postcards

These blank backed postcards measure 5" by 7" and feature members of the 1987 Vancouver Canadians team. There might be more so any additions to this list is appreciated.

	Nm-Mt	Ex-Mt
COMPLETE SET (2)	5.00	2.00
1 Glenn Braggs	4.00	1.60
2 Sammy Haro	1.00	.40

1988 Bull Durham Movie

These four 4" by 5" cards were issued to promote the 1988 movie "Bull Durham". The fronts have the name of the character as well as two photos. The backs have some of the movie lines as uttered by the characters. Since the cards are unnumbered, we have identified them by their real identites and arranged the set in that order.

	Nm-Mt	Ex-Mt
COMPLETE SET (4)	5.00	2.00
1 Kevin Costner Crash Davis	2.00	.80
2 Tim Robbins Nuke LaLoosh	2.00	.80
3 Jenny Robertson Millie	.50	.20
4 Susan Sarandon Annie Savoy	2.00	.80

1988 Cape Cod Prospects P and L Promotions

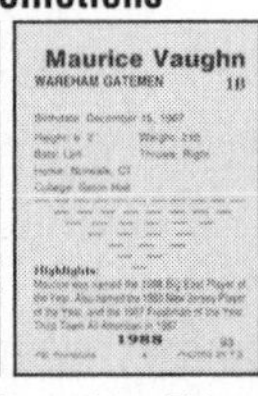

Issued by P and L Promotions. This set features 186 players from the Cape Cod league and includes first cards of Chuck Knoblauch, Jeff Bagwell, Tim Salmon and Mo Vaughn and early cards of Jeff Kent and Frank Thomas.

	Nm-Mt	Ex-Mt
COMPLETE SET (186)	50.00	20.00
1 Mark Johnson	.25	.10
2 John Valente	.25	.10
3 Warren Sawkiw	.25	.10
4 Ed Therrien	.25	.10
5 Lenny Richardson	.25	.10
6 Paul Ciaglo	.25	.10
7 Alex Alvarez	.25	.10
8 Richard Cordani	.25	.10
9 Chris Snyder	.25	.10
10 Michael Kelly	.25	.10
11 Keith Wiley	.25	.10
12 Brian Moure	.25	.10
13 David Flynn	.25	.10
14 Ed Cooney	.25	.10
15 Joe Conti	.25	.10
16 Joseph Delli Carri	.25	.10
17 Eamon Kingman	.25	.10
18 Tom Drell	.25	.10
19 Joe Logan	.25	.10
20 Jeff Borgese	.25	.10
21 John Byington	.25	.10
22 Brian Turang	.25	.10
23 Travis Tarchione	.25	.10
24 Mike Truschke	.25	.10
25 Rick Hirtensteiner	.25	.10
26 Pete Tsotsos	.25	.10
27 Harry Ball	.25	.10
28 Larry Russell	.25	.10
29 Alan Zinter	.25	.10
30 Brian Ahern	.25	.10
31 Chris Schaefer	.25	.10
32 Mike McNary	.25	.10
33 Chris Ebright	.25	.10
34 Darryl Scott	.25	.10
35 Russell Springer	.25	.10
36 Rafael Novoa	.25	.10
37 Ron Raper	.25	.10
38 Brian Shehan	.25	.10
39 Dave Wrona	.25	.10
40 Doug Shields	.25	.10
41 Stephen O'Donnell	.25	.10
42 Mike Mordecai	.25	.10
43 Steven Parris	.25	.10
44 Mike Zimmerman	.25	.10
45 Mitch Hannahs	.25	.10
46 Nolan Lane	.25	.10
47 Kurt Olson	.25	.10
48 Peter Altenberger	.25	.10
49 Rick Strickland	.25	.10
50 Bill Klenoshek Jr.	.25	.10
51 Eric Wedge	.25	.10
52 Larry Owens	.25	.10
53 Denny Neagle	1.00	.40
54 Preston Woods	.25	.10
55 Jim Dougherty	.25	.10
56 John Davis	.25	.10
57 Jeff Bagwell	5.00	2.00
58 Tom Riginos	.25	.10
59 Mark Sweeney	.25	.10
60 Scott Odierno	.25	.10
61 Michael LeBlanc	.25	.10
62 Michael Hinde	.25	.10
63 Scott Shockey	.25	.10
64 Brian Dour	.25	.10
65 Matt Dunbar	.25	.10
66 David Swartzbaugh	.25	.10
67 Curry Harden	.25	.10
68 Don Hutchinson	.25	.10
69 Mike Gardella	.25	.10
70 James Jones	.25	.10
71 Colin Ryan	.25	.10
72 Robert Rivell	.25	.10
73 Duane O'Hara	.25	.10
74 Bobby Kiser	.25	.10
75 Mike Trombley	.25	.10
76 John Farrell	.25	.10
77 Mark LaRosa	.25	.10
78 Scott Erwin	.25	.10
79 Thomas G. Raffo Jr.	.25	.10
80 George Tsamis	.25	.10
81 Alan Botkin	.25	.10
82 Bob McCreary	.25	.10
83 Jeff Cerqueira	.25	.10
84 Jim Jimaki	.25	.10
85 Mike McNamara	.25	.10
86 Tom Hickox	.25	.10
87 Scott Miller	.25	.10
88 Gary Scott	.25	.10
89 Brian Specyalski	.25	.10
90 Ron Frazier	.25	.10
91 Marcelino Sellas	.25	.10
92 Craig A. Cala	.25	.10
93 Mo Vaughn	2.00	.80
94 Chuck Knoblauch	1.00	.40
95 Dana Brown	.25	.10
96 Mike Weimerskirch	.25	.10
97 Darron Cox	.25	.10
98 Kevin Long	.25	.10
99 Kevin King	.25	.10
100 David Arendas	.25	.10
101 Burke Masters	.25	.10
102 Pat Leinan	.25	.10
103 Troy Bradford	.25	.10
104 Rich Samplinski	.25	.10
105 Sam Colarusso	.25	.10
106 John Thoden	.25	.10
107 Randy Pryor	.25	.10
108 John Kosenski	.25	.10
109 Keith Langston	.25	.10
110 Jody Hurst	.25	.10
111 Kevin Castleberry	.25	.10
112 Kyle Sanborn	.25	.10
113 Casey Waller	.25	.10
114 Brian Bark	.25	.10
115 Chris Barnes	.25	.10
116 Jesse Levis	.25	.10
117 George Sells	.25	.10
118 Tom Williams	.25	.10
119 Todd Mayo	.25	.10
120 Mathew Howard	.25	.10
121 Sam Taylor	.25	.10
122 Mike Grimes	.25	.10
123 Scott Centala	.25	.10
124 Drew Comeau	.25	.10
125 J.T. Snow	1.00	.40
126 Frank Thomas	5.00	2.00
127 Jason Klonoski	.25	.10
128 Marty Durkin	.25	.10
129 Tim Lata	.25	.10
130 Brian Barnes	.25	.10
131 Sam Drake	.25	.10
132 Tom Hardgrove	.25	.10
133 Lance Jones	.25	.10
134 Kirk Dressendorfer	.25	.10
135 Brad Myers	.25	.10
136 Gordon Tipton	.25	.10
137 Terry Taylor	.25	.10
138 John Valentin	1.00	.40
139 Kevin Morton	.25	.10
140 Ed Horowitz	.25	.10
141 Dave Tollison	.25	.10
142 Rick Kimball	.25	.10
143 Tim Williams	.25	.10
144 Tony Kounas	.25	.10
145 Jeromy Burnitz	1.00	.40
146 Mark Smith	.25	.10
147 Brad Beanblossom	.25	.10
148 Stewart Keyes	.25	.10
149 Will Vespe	.25	.10
150 Henry Manning	.25	.10
151 Dennis Burbank	.25	.10
152 Darryl Vice	.25	.10
153 Eric Bennett	.25	.10
154 Bob Gralewski	.25	.10
155 Michael Boyan	.25	.10
156 F.P. Santangelo	.25	.10
157 Bob Allen	.25	.10
158 Michael S. Myers	.25	.10
159 Andrew Albrecht	.25	.10
160 Robert Fazekas	.25	.10
161 Chris Slattery	.25	.10
162 Scott Morehouse	.25	.10
163 Robbie Katzaroff	.25	.10
164 Chris L. Jones	.25	.10
165 Bret Donovan	.25	.10
166 Tucker Hammagren	.25	.10
167 David Staton	.25	.10
168 Joseph Bruett	.25	.10
169 Jeff Kent	3.00	1.20
170 Troy Buckley	.25	.10
171 Garett Teel	.25	.10
172 Mark Carper	.25	.10
173 Joseph Kelly	.25	.10
174 Michael Wiseman	.25	.10
175 Howard Prager	.25	.10
176 Tim Salmon	3.00	1.20
177 Daniel Wilson	.25	.10
178 James Hoog	.25	.10
179 Trent Turner	.25	.10
180 David Krol	.25	.10
181 Steven Treadway	.25	.10
182 Patrick Varni	.25	.10
183 Troy Chacon	.25	.10
184 Roger Miller	.25	.10
185 Jeff Litzinger	.25	.10
186 Brian Shabosky	.25	.10

1988 Little Sun Minor League Legends

Titled "Legends of Minor League Baseball," this 11-card, standard-size set features color portraits by the artist Michael Guccione. The portraits are bordered with white and a thin inner black border. The backs contain the player's name, biography, career highlights and statistics in black print.

	Nm-Mt	Ex-Mt
COMPLETE SET (11)	8.00	3.20
1 Checklist	.50	.20
2 Pete Gray	1.50	.60
3 Ike Boone	.50	.20
4 Lou Novikoff	.50	.20
5 Luke Easter	.50	.20
6 Steve Bilko	.50	.20
7 Frank Shellenback	.50	.20
8 Smead Jolley	.50	.20
9 Jigger Statz	.50	.20
10 Joe Hauser	.50	.20
11 Fidel Castro	2.00	.80

1989 Little Sun High School Prospects

This 23-card standard size set features color photos of some of the top senior high school players. The card backs contain complete high school career stats and biographical notes. 5,000 sets were produced.

	Nm-Mt	Ex-Mt
COMPLETE SET (23)	10.00	4.00
*GLOSSY: .6X TO 1.5X BASIC CARDS		
GOLD PRINT RUN 1500 SETS		
1 Checklist Card	.50	.20
2 Earl Cunningham	.50	.20
3 Tom Engle	.50	.20
4 Bill Lott	.50	.20
5 Tyler Houston	.50	.20
6 Rod Walker	.50	.20
7 Bub Maietta	.50	.20
8 Andy Fox	.50	.20
9 Steve Proffitt	.50	.20
10 Paul Coleman	.50	.20
11 Bo Dodson	.50	.20
12 Richard Greenwell	.50	.20
13 Javier Delahoya	.50	.20
14 Jason Robertson	.50	.20
15 Billy Kostlich	.50	.20
16 Brant McCreadie	.50	.20
17 Jorge Jaime	.50	.20
18 John Hope	.50	.20
19 Edward Gerald	.50	.20
20 Ryan Klesko	4.00	1.60
21 Greg Blosser	.50	.20
22 Don Sheppard	.50	.20
23 Billy Reed CO Hillsborough High	.50	.20

1989 Star

This 200-card set was issued wax packs in two series; the first series featured different color bordered while the second series featured just red posed color player photos on its fronts. The player's name, team name, and position appear at the bottom. The yellow series one and white series two horizontal back carries the player's name at the top, followed by biography, career highlights, and statistics.

	Nm-Mt	Ex-Mt
COMPLETE SET (200)	15.00	6.00
COMP. SERIES 1 (100)	5.00	2.00
COMP. SERIES 2 (100)	10.00	4.00
1 Eric Anthony	.15	.06
2 David Rohde	.15	.06
3 Mike Simms	.15	.06
4 John Faccio	.15	.06
5 Oreste Marrero	.15	.06
6 Troy O'Leary	.50	.20
7 Rob Maurer	.15	.06
8 Rod Morris	.15	.06
9 Ed Ohman	.15	.06
10 Jim Byrd	.15	.06
11 Mark Cobb	.15	.06
12 Pat Combs	.15	.06
13 Tim Mauser	.15	.06
14 Jim Vatcher	.15	.06
15 Luis Gonzalez	1.00	.40
16 Andres Mota	.15	.06
17 Scott Servais	.15	.06
18 David Silvestri	.15	.06
19 Kevin Burdick	.15	.06
20 Tommy Shields	.15	.06
21 Mike York	.15	.06
22 Mike Anaya	.15	.06
23 Dale Plummer	.15	.06
24 Titi Roche	.15	.06
25 Vincent Zawaski	.15	.06
26 Anthony Barron	.15	.06
27 Rafael Bournigal	.15	.06
28 Albert Bustillos	.15	.06
29 Mark Griffin	.15	.06
30 Brett Magnussn	.15	.06
31 Mike Jones	.15	.06
32 Bret Barberie	.15	.06
33 Bert Echemendia	.15	.06
34 Mike Bell	.15	.06
35 Brian R. Hunter	.15	.06
36 Jim Lemasters	.15	.06
37 Rick Morris	.15	.06
38 Dominic Pierce	.15	.06
39 Joey Wardlow	.15	.06
40 Dera Clark	.15	.06
41 Stu Cole	.15	.06
42 Bob Hamelin	.15	.06

43 Deric Ladnier .15 .06
44 Brian McRae .50 .20
45 Mike Tresemer .15 .06
46 Steve Walker .15 .06
47 Greg Becker .15 .06
48 Art Calvert .15 .06
49 Todd Crosby .15 .06
50 Shawn Hathaway .15 .06
51 Rich Garces .15 .06
52 Todd McClure .15 .06
53 Steve Morris .15 .06
54 Tim Dell .15 .06
55 Antonio Linares .15 .06
56 John Marshall .15 .06
57 Mike Morandini .15 .06
58 Paul Fuller .15 .06
59 John Hudek .15 .06
60 Ron Stephens .15 .06
61 Scott Tedder .15 .06
62 Pete Alborano .15 .06
63 Kevin Shaw .15 .06
64 Antony Ariola .15 .06
65 James Buccheri .15 .06
66 William Love .15 .06
67 Steve Avery .50 .20
68 Rich Casarotti .15 .06
69 Brian Champion .15 .06
70 Wes Currin .15 .06
71 Biran Deak .15 .06
72 Ken Pennington .15 .06
73 Theron Todd .15 .06
74 Andy Tomberlin .15 .06
75 Richard Falkner .15 .06
76 Tommy Kramer .15 .06
77 Charles Nagy .50 .20
78 Chris Howard .15 .06
79 Mike Rhodes .15 .06
80 Gabriel Rodriguez .15 .06
81 Bob Zeihen .15 .06
82 Rod Beck .50 .20
83 Jamie Cooper .15 .06
84 Steve Decker .15 .06
85 Mark Dewey .15 .06
86 Juan Guerrero .15 .06
87 Andres Santana .15 .06
88 Pedro DeLeon .15 .06
89 Pat Kelly .15 .06
90 Bill Masse .15 .06
91 Jerry Neilson .15 .06
92 Mark Ohlms .15 .06
93 Moises Alou .50 .20
94 Ed Hartman .15 .06
95 Keith Richardson .15 .06
96 Royal Clayton .15 .06
97 Bobby Davidson .15 .06
98 Mitch Lyden .15 .06
99 Hensley Meulens .15 .06
100 John Ramos .15 .06
101 Robin Ventura 1.00 .40
102 Luis Mercedes .15 .06
103 Dave Miller .15 .06
104 Randy Berlin .15 .06
105 Mike Campas .15 .06
106 Jose Trujillo .15 .06
107 Lem Pilkenton .15 .06
108 Frank Bollick .15 .06
109 Bert Heffernan .15 .06
110 Chris Czarnik .15 .06
111 Andy Benes .50 .20
112 Skipper Wright .15 .06
113 Eric Alexander .15 .06
114 Manny Alexander .15 .06
115 Jimmy Roso .15 .06
116 Chris Donnels .15 .06
117 Jamie Roseboro .15 .06
118 Julian Yan .15 .06
119 Vicent Degifico .15 .06
120 Mickey Morandini .15 .06
121 Goose Gozzo .15 .06
122 Pedro Munoz .15 .06
123 Keith Helton .15 .06
124 Tino Martinez 1.00 .40
125 Sandy Alomar Jr. .50 .20
126 Scott Cooper .15 .06
127 Daryl Irvine .15 .06
128 Jim Orsag .15 .06
129 Mickey Pena .15 .06
130 Scott Sommers .15 .06
131 Ed Zambrano .15 .06
132 Dave Bettendorf .15 .06
133 Steve Allen .15 .06
134 Kevin Belcher .15 .06
135 Doug Cronk .15 .06
136 Tito Stewart .15 .06
137 Jeff Frye .15 .06
138 Trey McCoy .15 .06
139 Robb Nen .75 .30
140 Jim Hvizda .15 .06
141 Tommy Boyce .15 .06
142 Michael Maksudian .15 .06
143 Matt Current .15 .06
144 Tom Hardgrove .15 .06
145 Julio Vargas .15 .06
146 Dan Welch .15 .06
147 Steve Dunn .15 .06
148 Mike Misuraca .15 .06
149 Mike House .15 .06
150 Deion Sanders 1.00 .40
151 Willie Mota .15 .06
152 Tim Nedin .15 .06
153 Kerry Taylor .15 .06
154 Beau Allred .15 .06
155 Troy Neel .15 .06
156 Shawn Hare .15 .06
157 Chris Butterfield .15 .06
158 Tim Hines .15 .06
159 Pat Howell .15 .06
160 Paul Johnson .15 .06
161 Ryan Richmond .15 .06
162 Ernie Baker .15 .06
163 Pedro Castellano .15 .06
164 Eric Jaques .15 .06
165 Mark Willoughby .15 .06
166 Dan Segui .15 .06
167 Richard Shackle .15 .06
168 Mark Lewis .15 .06
169 John Johnstone .15 .06
170 Phil Plantier .15 .06
171 Wes Chamberlain .15 .06
172 James Harris .15 .06
173 Felix Antigua .15 .06
174 Bruce Schreiber .15 .06
175 Pete Rose Jr. .15 .06
176 Kelly Woods .15 .06
177 Anthony de la Cruz .15 .06
178 Charles Nagy .50 .20
179 Nolan Lane .15 .06
180 Fabio Gomez .15 .06
181 Chris Butler .15 .06
182 Brett Merriman .15 .06
183 Carlos Mota .15 .06
184 Doug Piatt .15 .06
185 Marc Tepper .15 .06
186 Dan Williams .15 .06
187 Maximo Aleys .15 .06
188 Ken Lewis .15 .06
189 Joey Vierra .15 .06
190 Ron Morton .15 .06
191 Brook Fordyce .15 .06
192 Steve McCarthy .15 .06
193 Steve Hosey .15 .06
194 Steve Foster .15 .06
195 Ron Crowe .15 .06
196 Steve Callahan .15 .06
197 Benny Colvard .15 .06
198 Adam Casillas .15 .06
199 Albert Belle 1.00 .40
200 Ben McDonald .15 .06

1989 Star Future Stars

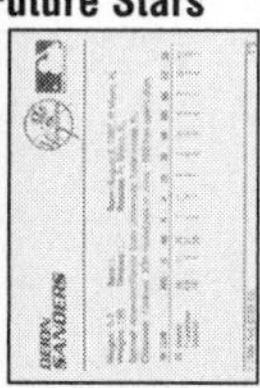

This 24-card minor league set features color photos of future star players of Major League Baseball with either red-and-gold or purple-and-yellow borders. The backs carry player information and statistics.

	Nm-Mt	Ex-Mt
COMPLETE SET (24)	10.00	4.00
1 Eric Anthony (Portrait holding bat)	.25	.10
2 Eric Anthony (At bat)	.25	.10
3 Mark Lewis (Portrait)	.25	.10
4 Mark Lewis (At bat)	.25	.10
5 Pete Rose Jr. (Portrait)	.25	.10
6 Pete Rose Jr. (Swinging bat)	.25	.10
7 Robin Ventura (On knee with bat)	1.50	.60
8 Robin Ventura (Playing his position)	1.50	.60
9 Beau Allred (Portrait with bat)	.25	.10
10 Beau Allred (Swinging bat)	.25	.10
11 Pat Combs (Portrait)	.25	.10
12 Pat Combs (With glove)	.25	.10
13 Deion Sanders (At bat)	1.50	.60
14 Deion Sanders (Swinging bat)	1.50	.60
15 Bob Hamelin (Portrait with bat)	.25	.10
16 Bob Hamelin (At bat)	.25	.10
17 Andy Benes (In dugout)	.75	.30
18 Andy Benes (Pitching)	.75	.30
19 Hensley Meulens (At bat)	.25	.10
20 Hensley Meulens (Playing his position)	.25	.10
21 Trey McCoy (Portrait with bat)	.25	.10
22 Trey McCoy (At bat)	.25	.10
23 Sandy Alomar Jr. (At bat)	.50	.20
24 Sandy Alomar Jr. (Catching)	.50	.20

1990 Best

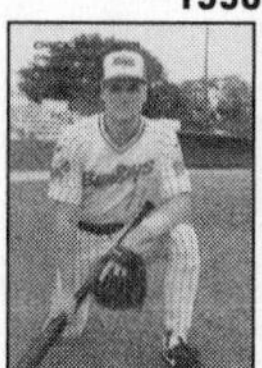

This 324-card set feature full color player shots with the player's name, team name and position appearing on the card fronts. The horizontal back carries the player's name and position at the top, followed by biography and statistics.

	Nm-Mt	Ex-Mt
COMPLETE SET (324)	40.00	12.00
1 Frank Thomas	3.00	.90
2 Eric Wedge	.25	.07
3 Willie Ansley	.25	.07
4 Mark Lewis	.25	.07
5 Greg Colbrunn	1.00	.30
6 David Staton	.25	.07
7 Ben McDonald	.25	.07
8 Brent Mayne	.25	.07
9 Ray Holbert	.25	.07
10 T.R. Lewis	.25	.07
11 Willie Banks	.25	.07
12 Steve Dunn	.25	.07
13 Juan Andujar	.25	.07
14 Roger Salkeld	.25	.07
15 Steve Hosey	.25	.07
16 Tyler Houston	1.00	.30
17 David Holdridge	.25	.07
18 Todd Malone	.25	.07
19 Tony Scruggs	.25	.07
20 Darron Cox	.25	.07
21 Mike Linskey	.25	.07
22 Darren Lewis	.25	.07
23 Eddie Zosky	.25	.07
24 Ramser Correa	.25	.07
25 Lee Upshaw	.25	.07
26 Bernie Williams	2.50	.75
27 Brian Harrison	.25	.07
28 Len Brutcher	.25	.07
29 Scott Centala	.25	.07
30 Kenny Morgan	.25	.07
31 Pedro Borbon Jr.	.25	.07
32 Lee Hancock	.25	.07
33 Clay Bellinger	.25	.07
34 Chris Myers	.25	.07
35 Russ Garside	.25	.07
36 Ron Plemmons	.25	.07
37 Jose LeBron	.25	.07
38 Tom Hardgrove	.25	.07
39 Alan Newman	.25	.07
40 Ramonb Jimenez	.25	.07
41 Ezequiel Herrera	.25	.07
42 Jason Satre	.25	.07
43 Bob Malloy	.25	.07
44 William Suero	.25	.07
45 Lenny Webster	.25	.07
46 Andy Ashby	1.00	.30
47 Darren Ritter	.25	.07
48 Andy Mota	.25	.07
49 Pat Gomez	.25	.07
50 Ron Stephens	.25	.07
51 Daniel Eskew	.25	.07
52 Joe Andrzejewski	.25	.07
53 Doug Robbins	.25	.07
54 Noel Velez	.25	.07
55 Dana Ridenour	.25	.07
56 Luis Martinez	.25	.07
57 Dave Fleming	.25	.07
58 Adell Davenport	.25	.07
59 Brent McCoy	.25	.07
60 Johnny Ard	.25	.07
61 Cal Eldred	1.00	.30
62 Tab Brown	.25	.07
63 Scott Kamieniecki	.25	.07
64 Scott Bryant	.25	.07
65 Brad Pennington	.25	.07
66 Bernie Jenkins	.25	.07
67 Frank Carey	.25	.07
68 Matt Witkowski	.25	.07
69 Checklist (1-48)	.25	.07
70 Josias Manzanillo	.25	.07
71 Checklist (49-96)	.25	.07
72 Andujar Cedeno UER Andvjar	.25	.07
73 Ricky Rojas	.25	.07
74 Scott Brosius	1.00	.30
75 Tom Redington	.25	.07
76 Kevin Rogers	.25	.07
77 Jerry Wolak	.25	.07
78 Rick Davis	.25	.07
79 Juan Guzman	1.00	.30
80 Cesar Bernhardt	.25	.07
81 Randy Simmons	.25	.07
82 Clyde Keller	.25	.07
83 Anthony Manahan	.25	.07
84 Tom Maynard	.25	.07
85 Ed Gustafson	.25	.07
86 Sean Berry	.25	.07
87 Brian Boltz	.25	.07
88 Shawn Gilbert	.25	.07
89 Rafael Novoa	.25	.07
90 John Vander Wal	1.00	.30
91 Scott Pose	.25	.07
92 Don Stanford	.25	.07
93 Joe Federico	.25	.07
94 Todd Watson	.25	.07
95 Luis Gonzalez	1.50	.45
96 Pat Leinen	.25	.07
97 Joel Estes	.25	.07
98 Troy O'Leary	.25	.07
99 Matt Stark	.25	.07
100 Tony Tarasco	.25	.07
101 Marc Lipson	.25	.07
102 Kevin Higgins	.25	.07
103 Jack Voigt	.25	.07
104 Steve Schrenk	.25	.07
105 Jonathan Hurst	.25	.07
106 Scott Erickson	1.00	.30
107 Javy Lopez	1.50	.45
108 Bob Zupcic	.25	.07
109 Edwin Marquez	.25	.07
110 Shawn Heiden	.25	.07
111 Mike Maksudian	.25	.07
112 Tony Eusebio	1.00	.30
113 Chris Hancock	.25	.07
114 Royce Clayton	1.00	.30
115 Tim Mauser	.25	.07
116 Checklist (97-144)	.25	.07
117 Carlos Maldonado	.25	.07
118 Rex De La Nunez	.25	.07
119 Mike Curtis	.25	.07
120 Roger Miller	.25	.07
121 Daryl Moore	.25	.07
122 Turk Wendell	1.00	.30
123 Dan Rambo	.25	.07
124 Scott Kimball	.25	.07
125 Willie Magallanes	.25	.07
126 Dannie Ray Harris	.25	.07
127 Joey James	.25	.07
128 Wil Cordero	.25	.07
129 Rob Taylor	.25	.07
130 Bryce Florie	.25	.07
131 Mike Mitchner	.25	.07
132 Jeff Bagwell	2.50	.75
133 Caesar Devares	.25	.07
134 Tim Gillis	.25	.07
135 Victor Hithe	.25	.07
136 Earl Steinmetz	.25	.07
137 Carl Keliipuleole	.25	.07
138 Ted Williams	.25	.07
139 Jorge Pedre	.25	.07
140 Amalio Carreno	.25	.07
141 Chris Gill	.25	.07
142 Dennis Wiseman	.25	.07
143 Checklist (145-192)	.25	.07
144 Derek Lee	.25	.07
145 Brett Synder	.25	.07
146 Chuck Knoblauch	1.00	.30
147 Rafael Quirico	.25	.07
148 Julian Yan	.25	.07
149 John Thelen	.25	.07
150 Checklist (193-240)	.25	.07
151 Darrin Reichle	.25	.07
152 John Ramos	.25	.07
153 Patrick Lennon	.25	.07
154 Wade Taylor	.25	.07
155 Mike Twardoski	.25	.07
156 Jeff Conine	1.00	.30
157 Kelly Mann	.25	.07
158 Gary Wilson	.25	.07
159 Chris Fye	.25	.07
160 Roger Hailey	.25	.07
161 Harold Allen	.25	.07
162 Ozzie Canseco	.25	.07
163 Checklist (241-288)	.25	.07
164 Rudy Seanez	.25	.07
165 John Zaksek	.25	.07
166 Roberto DeLeon	.25	.07
167 Matt Merullo	.25	.07
168 Checklist (289-324)	.25	.07
169 Terrell Hansen	.25	.07
170 Ron Crowe	.25	.07
171 Luis Galindez	.25	.07
172 Vilato Marrero	.25	.07
173 Scott Cepicky	.25	.07
174 Gary Resetar	.25	.07
175 Rich Scheid	.25	.07
176 Jimmy Rogers	.25	.07
177 Ken Pennington	.25	.07
178 Tom Martin	.25	.07
179 Mitch Lyden	.25	.07
180 Jorge Brito	.25	.07
181 Chris Gorton	.25	.07
182 Mark Sims	.25	.07
183 Jose Olmeda	.25	.07
184 Eddie Taubensee	1.00	.30
185 Steve Morris	.25	.07
186 Tim Pugh	.25	.07
187 Barry Winford	.25	.07
188 Allen Liebert	.25	.07
189 Kurt Brown	.25	.07
190 Kelly Lifgren	.25	.07
191 Mike Kelly	.25	.07
192 Roberto Munoz	.25	.07
193 Judd Johnson	.25	.07
194 Hector Wagner	.25	.07
195 Dave Reis	.25	.07
196 Isaiah Clark	.25	.07
197 William Schock	.25	.07
198 Ruben Gonzalez	.25	.07
199 Mike Eberle	.25	.07
200 Michael Arner	.25	.07
201 Raphael Bustamante	.25	.07
202 John Patterson	.25	.07
203 Jose Slusarski	.25	.07
204 Rodney McCray	.25	.07
205 Wally Trice	.25	.07
206 Edgar Caceres	.25	.07
207 Eugene Jones	.25	.07
208 Joey Wardlow	.25	.07
209 Steve Martin	.25	.07
210 Woody Williams	1.50	.45
211 Kevin Morton	.25	.07
212 Bobby DeJardin	.25	.07
213 Chris Bennett	.25	.07
214 Brian Johnson	.25	.07
215 Randy Snyder	.25	.07
216 Roberto Hernandez	1.00	.30
217 Glen Gardner	.25	.07
218 Fred Costello	.25	.07
219 Melvin Nieves	.25	.07
220 Al Martin UER All back information is wrong	1.00	.30
221 Kerry Knox	.25	.07
222 Michael Eatinger	.25	.07
223 Jim Myers	.25	.07
224 Jayhawk Owens	.25	.07
225 Jayson Best	.25	.07
226 Mike McDonald	.25	.07
226B Mike McDonald ERR	1.00	.30
227 Kim Batiste	.25	.07
228 Rich DeLucia	.25	.07
229 Chris Delarwelle	.25	.07
230 Jeff Hoffman	.25	.07
231 Bobby Moore	.25	.07
232 Dan Wilson	1.00	.30
233 Greg Pirkl	.25	.07
234 Craig Newkirk	.25	.07
235 Mike Hensley	.25	.07
236 Ryan Klesko	1.50	.45
237 Donald Sparks	.25	.07
238 J.D. Noland	.25	.07
239 Chris Howard	.25	.07
240 Stan Royer	.25	.07
241 Manny Alexander	.25	.07
242 Jeff Plympton	.25	.07
243 Jeff Juden	.25	.07
244 Charles Nagy	1.00	.30
245 Ryan Bowen	.25	.07
246 Scott Taylor	.25	.07
247 Tom Quinlan	.25	.07
248 Royal Thomas	.25	.07
249 Ricky Rhodes	.25	.07
250 Alex Fernandez	1.00	.30
251 Bruce Egloff	.25	.07
252 Greg Sparks	.25	.07
253 Brain Dour	.25	.07
254 John Byington	.25	.07
255 Stacey Burdick	.25	.07
256 Danny Matznick	.25	.07
257 Reed Olmstead	.25	.07
258 Jim Bowie	.25	.07
259 Jim Newlin	.25	.07
260 Ramon Caraballo	.25	.07
261 Brian Barnes	.25	.07
262 Mike Gardiner	.25	.07
263 Andy Fox	.25	.07
264 Brian McKeon	.25	.07
265 Andy Tomberlin	.25	.07
266 Frank Bellino	.25	.07
267 Tim Lata	.25	.07
268 Mike Burton	.25	.07
268B Mike Burton ERR	.25	.07
269 Jim Orsag	.25	.07
270 Scott Romano	.25	.07
271 Leon Glenn	.25	.07
272 Mike Misuraca	.25	.07
273 Randy Knorr	.25	.07
274 Eddie Tucker	.25	.07
275 Ken Powell	.25	.07
276 Brian McRae	.25	.07
277 Mark Merchant	.25	.07
278 Vinny Castilla	1.00	.30
279 Stephen Chitren	.25	.07
280 Marteese Robinson	.25	.07
281 Osvaldo Sanchez	.25	.07
282 Michael Mongiello	.25	.07
283 John Valentin	.25	.07
284 Timmie Morrow	.25	.07
285 Matt Murray	.25	.07
286 Darrell Sherman	.25	.07
287 Royal Clayton	.25	.07
288 Jason Robertson	.25	.07
289 John Kilner	.25	.07
290 Jeff Mutis	.25	.07
291 Gary Alexander	.25	.07
292 Oreste Marrero	.25	.07
293 Melvin Wearing	.25	.07
294 Scott Meadows	.25	.07
295 Pat Hentgen	1.00	.30
296 John Hudek	.25	.07
297 Tim Stargell	.25	.07
298 Tony Brown	.25	.07
299 Scott Plemmons	.25	.07
300 Chris Nabholz	.25	.07
301 Brian Romero	.25	.07
302 Vince Kindred	.25	.07
303 Robert Ayrault	.25	.07
304 Steve Stowell	.25	.07
305 Don Strange	.25	.07
306 Tim Nedin	.25	.07
307 Derek Livernois	.25	.07
308 Kerry Woodson	.25	.07
309 Sam Ferretti	.25	.07
310 Reuben Smiley	.25	.07
311 Jim Campbell	.25	.07
312 Al Osuna	.25	.07
313 Luis Mercedes	.25	.07
314 Billy Reed	.25	.07
315 Vince Harris	.25	.07
316 Jeff Carter	.25	.07
317 David Riddle	.25	.07
318 Frank Thomas BC	2.00	.60
319 Eric Wedge BC	.25	.07
320 Mark Lewis BC	.25	.07
321 Alex Fernandez BC	.25	.07
322 Chuck Knoblauch BC	1.50	.45
323 Charles Nagy BC	.25	.07
324 Tyler Houston BC	.25	.07

1990 Classic Draft Picks

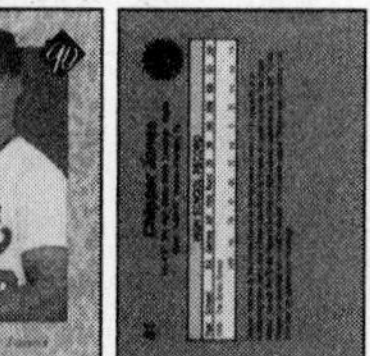

The 1990 Classic Draft Pick set is a standard-size 25-card set honoring the number one (first round) draft picks of 1990. According to the producer, the printing on this set was limited to 150,000 of each card. This was the first Classic set that was not a game set or trivia set. Card numbers 2 and 22 were not issued. An early Chipper Jones card is the highlight of this set.

	Nm-Mt	Ex-Mt
COMP.FACT.SET (25)	5.00	1.50
1 Chipper Jones	2.00	.60
3 Mike Lieberthal	.40	.12
4 Alex Fernandez	.10	.03
5 Kurt Miller	.10	.03
6 Marc Newfield UER	.10	.03
7 Dan Wilson	.40	.12
8 Tim Costo	.10	.03
9 Ron Walden	.10	.03
10 Carl Everett UER Evertt	.50	.15
11 Shane Andrews	.40	.12
12 Todd Ritchie	.40	.12
13 Donovan Osborne	.10	.03
14 Todd Van Poppel	.40	.12
15 Adam Hyzdu	.10	.03
16 Dan Smith	.10	.03
17 Jeromy Burnitz	.40	.12
18 Aaron Holbert	.10	.03
19 Eric Christopherson	.10	.03
20 Mike Mussina	1.00	.30
21 Tom Nevers	.10	.03
23 Lance Dickson	.10	.03
24 Rondell White	.40	.12
25 Robbie Beckett	.10	.03
26 Don Peters	.10	.03
P14 Todd Van Poppel Promo		
NNO Chipper Jones CL Rondell White CL	.50	.15

1990 CMC

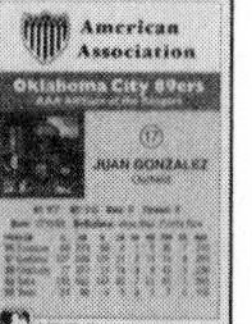

This 880-card set features Triple A cards of CMC and lower classification cards from ProCards. Both the CMC and ProCards , feature color player shots with the player's name, team name and position appearing on the card fronts. The CMC cards have a green and yellow combination border with the team logo in the lower corner while the ProCards feature a wood grain border with the words ProCards in the upper corner of the card. On the card backs, the CMC cards carries the league name, team name and affiliation folowed by the player's name, position, biography and statistics. The ProCards cards carries the player's name, position, biography and statistics.

	Nm-Mt	Ex-Mt
COMPLETE SET (880)	40.00	12.00
1 Stan Belinda	.15	.04
2 Gordon Dillard	.15	.04
3 Terry Collins MG	.15	.04
4 Mark Huismann	.15	.04
5 Hugh Kemp	.15	.04
6 Scott Medvin	.15	.04
7 Vicente Palacios	.15	.04
8 Rick Reed	.50	.15
9 Mark Ross	.15	.04
10 Dorn Taylor	.15	.04
11 Mike York	.15	.04
12 Jeff Richardson	.15	.04
13 Dann Bilardello	.15	.04
14 Tom Prince	.15	.04
15 Danny Sheaffer	.15	.04
16 Kevin Burdick	.15	.04
17 Steve Kiefer	.15	.04
18 Orlando Merced	.15	.04
19 Armando Moreno	.15	.04
20 Mark Ryal	.15	.04
21 Tommy Shields	.15	.04
22 Steve Carter	.15	.04
23 Wes Chamberlain	.15	.04
24 Jeff Cook	.15	.04
25 Scott Little	.15	.04
26 Jeff Peterek	.15	.04
27 Ed Puig	.15	.04
28 Tim Watkins	.15	.04
29 Tom Edens	.15	.04
30 Mike Capel	.15	.04
31 Darryel Walters	.15	.04
32 Joe Xavier	.15	.04
33 Tim Torricelli	.15	.04
34 Joe Redfield	.15	.04
35 D.L. Smith	.15	.04
36 Billy Moore	.15	.04
37 Joe Mitchell	.15	.04
38 Mario Monico	.15	.04
39 Frank Mattox	.15	.04
40 Tim McIntosh	.15	.04
41 Mark Higgins	.15	.04
42 George Canale	.15	.04
43 Don Gordon	.15	.04
44 Al Sadler	.15	.04
45 Don August	.15	.04
46 Mike Birkbeck	.15	.04
47 Dennis Powell	.15	.04
48 Chuck McGrath	.15	.04
49 Ruben Escalera	.15	.04
50 Dave Machemer MG	.15	.04
51 Steve Fireovid	.15	.04
52 Danny Clay	.15	.04
53 Howard Farmer	.15	.04
54 Travis Chambers	.15	.04
55 Chris Marchok	.15	.04
56 Dan Gakeler	.15	.04
57 Scott Anderson	.15	.04
58 Dale Mohorcic	.15	.04
59 Richard Thompson	.15	.04
60 Eddie Dixon	.15	.04
61 Jim Davins	.15	.04
62 Edwin Marquez	.15	.04
63 Jerry Goff	.15	.04
64 Dwight Lowry	.15	.04
65 Jim Steels	.15	.04
66 Quinn Mack	.15	.04
67 Eric Bullock	.15	.04
68 Otis Green	.15	.04
69 Randy Braun	.15	.04
70 Mel Houston	.15	.04
71 Jesus Paredes	.15	.04
72 Romy Cucjen	.15	.04
73 Jose Castro	.15	.04
74 Esteban Beltre	.15	.04
75 Tim Johnson MG	.15	.04
76 Shawn Boskie	.15	.04
77 Dave Masters	.15	.04
78 Kevin Blankenship	.15	.04
79 Greg Kallevig	.15	.04
80 Steve Parker	.15	.04
81 David Pavlas	.15	.04
82 Jeff Pico	.15	.04
83 Laddie Renfroe	.15	.04
84 Dean Wilkins	.15	.04
85 Paul Wilmet	.15	.04
86 Bob Bafia	.15	.04
87 Brian Guinn	.15	.04
88 Greg Smith	.15	.04
89 Derrick May	.15	.04
90 Glenn Sullivan	.15	.04
91 Bill Wrona	.15	.04
92 Erik Pappas	.15	.04
93 Hector Villanueva	.15	.04
94 Ced Landrum	.15	.04
95 Jeff Small	.15	.04
96 Gary Varsho	.15	.04
97 Brad Bierly	.15	.04
98 Jeff Hearron	.15	.04
99 Jim Essian MG	.15	.04
100 Brian McCann TR	.15	.04
101 Scott Arnold	.15	.04
102 Gibson Alba	.15	.04
103 Cris Carpenter	.15	.04
104 Stan Clarke	.15	.04
105 Mike Hinkle	.15	.04
106 Howard Hilton	.15	.04
107 Dave Osteen	.15	.04
108 Mike Perez	.15	.04
109 Bernard Gilkey	.50	.15
110 Dennis Carter	.15	.04
111 Julian Martinez	.15	.04
112 Rod Brewer	.15	.04
113 Ray Stephens	.15	.04
114 Ray Lankford	.50	.15
115 Craig Wilson	.15	.04
116 Roy Silver	.15	.04
117 Bien Figueroa	.15	.04
118 Jesus Mendez	.15	.04
119 Geronimo Pena	.15	.04
120 Omar Olivares	.15	.04
121 Mark Grater	.15	.04
122 Tim Sherrill	.15	.04
123 Pat Austin	.15	.04
124 Todd Crosby	.15	.04
125 Gary Nichols	.15	.04
126 Milt Hill	.15	.04
127 Robert Moore	.15	.04
128 Joey Vierra	.15	.04
129 Terry McGriff	.15	.04
130 Chris Hammond	.15	.04
131 Charlie Mitchell	.15	.04
132 Rodney Imes	.15	.04
133 Rob Lopez	.15	.04
134 Keith Brown	.15	.04
135 Scott Scudder	.15	.04
136 Bob Sebra	.15	.04
137 Donnie Scott	.15	.04
138 Skeeter Barnes	.15	.04
139 Paul Noce	.15	.04
140 Leo Garcia	.15	.04
141 Chris Jones	.15	.04
142 Kevin Pearson	.15	.04
143 Darryl Motley	.15	.04
144 Keith Lockhart	.15	.04
145 Brian Lane	.15	.04
146 Eddie Tanner	.15	.04
147 Reggie Jefferson	.15	.04
148 Neil Allen	.15	.04
149 Pete MacKanin MG	.15	.04
150 Ray Rippelmeyer CO	.15	.04
151 Jack Hardy	.15	.04
152 Steve Lankard	.15	.04
153 John Hoover	.15	.04
154 David Lynch	.15	.04
155 Mark Petkovsek	.15	.04
156 David Miller	.15	.04
157 Brad Arnsberg	.15	.04
158 Jeff Satzinger	.15	.04
159 John Barfield	.15	.04
160 Mike Berger	.15	.04
161 John Russell	.15	.04
162 Pat Garman	.15	.04
163 Gary Green	.15	.04
164 Brian House	.15	.04
165 Ron Washington	.15	.04
166 Nick Capra	.15	.04
167 Juan Gonzalez	3.00	.90
168 Gar Millay	.15	.04
169 Kevin Reimer	.15	.04
170 Bernie Tatis	.15	.04
171 Steve Smith MG	.15	.04
172 Dick Egan CO	.15	.04
173 Stan Hough CO	.15	.04
174 Ray Ramirez TR	.15	.04
175 Moe Drabowsky CO	.15	.04
176 Jay Baller	.15	.04
177 Ray Chadwick	.15	.04
178 Dera Clark	.15	.04
179 Luis Encarnacion	.15	.04
180 Jim LeMasters	.15	.04
181 Mike Magnante	.15	.04
182 Mel Stottlemyre Jr.	.15	.04
183 Tony Ferreira	.15	.04
184 Pete Filson	.15	.04
185 Andy McGaffigan	.15	.04
186 Luis de los Santos	.15	.04
187 Mike Loggins	.15	.04
188 Chito Martinez	.15	.04
189 Bobby Meacham	.15	.04
190 Russ Morman	.15	.04
191 Bill Pecota	.15	.04
192 Harvey Pulliam	.15	.04
193 Jeff Schulz	.15	.04
194 Gary Thurman	.15	.04
195 Thad Reece	.15	.04
196 Tim Spehr	.15	.04
197 Paul Zuvella	.15	.04
198 T.Poquette CO UER Rich Dubee CO Card misnumbered 199 on back	.15	.04
199 Bob Hamelin	.15	.04
200 Sal Rende	.15	.04
201 Steve Adkins	.15	.04
202 Dave Eiland	.15	.04
203 John Habyan	.15	.04
204 Mark Leiter	.15	.04
205 Kevin Mmahat	.15	.04
206 Hipolito Pena	.15	.04
207 Willie Smith	.15	.04
208 Rich Monteleone	.15	.04
209 Hensley Meulens	.15	.04
210 Andy Stankiewicz	.15	.04
211 Jim Leyritz	.50	.15
212 Jim Walewander	.15	.04
213 Oscar Azocar	.15	.04
214 John Fishel	.15	.04
215 Jason Maas	.15	.04
216 Van Snider	.15	.04
217 Kevin Maas	.15	.04
218 Ricky Torres	.15	.04
219 Dave Sax	.15	.04
220 Darrin Chapin	.15	.04
221 Rob Sepanek	.15	.04
222 Mark Wasinger	.15	.04
223 Jimmy Jones	.15	.04
224 Ken Rowe CO Stump Merrill MG Clete Boyer CO Mike Heifferon TR Troy Hillman CO	.15	.04
225 Carl (Stump) Merrill MG	.15	.04
226 Bob Davidson	.15	.04
227 Eric Boudreaux	.15	.04
228 Marvin Freeman	.15	.04
229 Jason Grimsley	.15	.04
230 Chuck Malone	.15	.04
231 Dickie Noles	.15	.04
232 Wally Ritchie	.15	.04
233 Bob Scanlan	.15	.04
234 Scott Service	.15	.04
235 Steve Sharts	.15	.04
236 John Gibbons	.15	.04
237 Sal Agostinelli	.15	.04
238 Jim Adduci	.15	.04
239 Kelly Heath	.15	.04
240 Mickey Morandini	.15	.04
241 Victor Rosario	.15	.04
242 Steve Stanicek	.15	.04
243 Jim Vatcher	.15	.04
244 Bill Dancy MG	.15	.04
245 Ron Jones	.15	.04
246 Chris Knabenshue	.15	.04
247 Keith Miller	.15	.04
248 Floyd Rayford CO	.15	.04
249 Jim Wright CO	.15	.04
250 Todd Frohwirth	.15	.04
251 Barney Nugent TR	.15	.04
252 Tito Stewart	.15	.04
253 John Trautwein	.15	.04
254 Mike Rochford	.15	.04
255 Larry Shikles	.15	.04
256 Daryl Irvine	.15	.04
257 John Leister	.15	.04
258 Joe Johnson	.15	.04
259 Mark Meleski CO	.15	.04
260 Steven Bast	.15	.04
261 Ed Nottle MG	.15	.04
262 John Flaherty	.15	.04
263 John Marzano	.15	.04
264 Gary Tremblay	.15	.04
265 Scott Cooper	.15	.04
266 Angel Gonzalez	.15	.04
267 Julius McDougal	.15	.04
268 Tim Naehring	.15	.04
269 Jim Pankovits	.15	.04
270 Rick Lancellotti	.15	.04
271 Mickey Pina	.15	.04
272 Phil Plantier	.15	.04
273 Jeff Stone	.15	.04
274 Scott Wade	.15	.04
275 Mike Dalton	.15	.04
276 Jeff Gray	.15	.04
277 Steve Avery	.50	.15
278 Leo Mazzone CO Sonny Jackson CO John Grubb CO	.15	.04
279 Dale Polley	.15	.04
280 Rusty Richards	.15	.04
281 Andy Nezelek	.15	.04
282 Ed Olwine	.15	.04
283 Jim Beauchamp MG	.15	.04
284 Paul Marak	.15	.04
285 David Justice	1.50	.45
286 Jimmy Kremers	.15	.04
287 Drew Denson	.15	.04
288 Barry Jones	.15	.04
289 Francisco Cabrera	.15	.04
290 Bruce Crabbe	.15	.04
291 Dennis Hood	.15	.04
292 Geronimo Berroa	.15	.04
293 Ed Whited	.15	.04
294 Sam Ayoub TR	.15	.04
295 Brian R. Hunter	.15	.04
296 Tommy Greene	.15	.04
297 John Mizerock	.15	.04
298 Ken Dowell	.15	.04
299 John Alva	.15	.04
300 Bill Laskey	.15	.04
301 Brian Snyder	.15	.04
302 Ben McDonald	.15	.04
303 Rob Woodward	.15	.04
304 Mickey Weston	.15	.04
305 Mike Jones	.15	.04
306 Curt Schilling	1.50	.45
307 Jay Aldrich	.15	.04
308 Paul Blair CO	.15	.04
309 Mike Smith	.15	.04
310 Jack Tackett	.15	.04
311 Leo Gomez	.15	.04
312 Juan Bell	.15	.04
313 Chris Hoiles	.15	.04
314 Donell Nixon	.15	.04
315 Steve Stanicek	.15	.04
316 Tim Dulin	.15	.04
317 Chris Padget	.15	.04
318 Greg Walker	.15	.04
319 Tony Chance	.15	.04
320 Jeff McKnight	.15	.04
321 J.J. Bautista	.15	.04
322 John Mitchell	.15	.04
323 Vic Hithe	.15	.04
324 Darrell Miller	.15	.04
325 Shane Turner	.15	.04
326 Greg Biagini	.15	.04
327 Alex Sanchez	.15	.04
328 Mauro Gozzo	.15	.04
329 Steve Cummings	.15	.04
330 Tom Gilles	.15	.04
331 Doug Linton	.15	.04
332 Mike Loynd	.15	.04
333 Bob Shirley	.15	.04
334 John Shea	.15	.04
335 Paul Kilgus	.15	.04
336 Carlos Diaz	.15	.04
337 Joe Szekely	.15	.04
338 Rick Lysander	.15	.04
339 Jim Eppard	.15	.04
340 Derek Bell	.50	.15
341 Jose Escobar	.15	.04
342 Webster Garrison	.15	.04
343 Paul Runge	.15	.04
344 Luis Sojo	.15	.04
345 Ed Sprague	.50	.15
346 Hector DeLaCruz	.15	.04
347 Rob Ducey	.15	.04
348 Ozzie Virgil	.15	.04
349 Stu Pederson	.15	.04
350 Mark Whiten	.15	.04
351 Andy Dziadkowiec	.15	.04
352 Shawn Barton	.15	.04
353 Kevin Brown	.15	.04
354 Rocky Childress	.15	.04
355 Brian Givens	.15	.04
356 Manny Hernandez	.15	.04
357 Jeff Innis	.15	.04
358 Cesar Mejia	.15	.04
359 Scott Nielsen	.15	.04
360 Dale Plummer	.15	.04
361 Ray Soff	.15	.04
362 Lou Thornton	.15	.04
363 Dave Trautwein	.15	.04
364 Julio Valera	.15	.04
365 Tim Bogar	.15	.04
366 Mike DeButch	.15	.04
367 Jeff Gardner	.15	.04
368 Denny Gonzalez	.15	.04
369 Chris Jelic	.15	.04
370 Roger Samuels	.15	.04
371 Dave Liddell	.15	.04
372 Orlando Mercado	.15	.04
373 Kelvin Torve	.15	.04
374 Alex Diaz	.15	.04
375 Keith Hughes	.15	.04
376 Darren Reed	.15	.04
377 Zolio Sanchez	.15	.04
378 Don Vesling	.15	.04
379 Scott Aldred	.15	.04
380 Dennis Burtt	.15	.04
381 Shawn Holman	.15	.04
382 Matt Kinzer	.15	.04
383 Randy Nosek	.15	.04
384 Jose Ramos	.15	.04
385 Kevin Ritz	.15	.04
386 Mike Schwabe	.15	.04
387 Steve Searcy	.15	.04
388 Eric Stone	.15	.04
389 Domingo Michel	.15	.04
390 Phil Ouellette	.15	.04
391 Shawn Hare	.15	.04
392 Jim Lindeman	.15	.04
393 Scott Livingstone	.15	.04
394 La Vel Freeman	.15	.04
395 Travis Fryman	.50	.15
396 Scott Lusader	.15	.04
397 Dean Decillis	.15	.04
398 Milt Cuyler	.15	.04
399 Jeff Jones CO UER (Card misnumbered 691 on back)	.15	.04
400 Phil Clark	.15	.04
401 Torey Lovullo	.15	.04
402 Aurelio Rodriguez CO	.15	.04
403 Mike Christopher	.15	.04
404 Jeff Bittiger	.15	.04
405 Jeff Fischer	.15	.04
406 Steve Davis	.15	.04
407 Morris Madden	.15	.04
408 Darren Holmes	.15	.04
409 Greg Mayberry	.15	.04
410 Mike Maddux	.15	.04
411 Tim Scott	.15	.04
412 Jim Neidlinger	.15	.04
413 Dave Walsh	.15	.04
414 Dennis Springer	.15	.04
415 Terry Wells	.15	.04
416 Adam Brown	.15	.04
417 Darrin Fletcher	.15	.04
418 Carlos Hernandez	.15	.04
419 Dave Hansen	.15	.04
420 Dan Henley	.15	.04
421 Jose Offerman	.50	.15
422 Jose Vizcaino	.50	.15
423 Luis Lopez	.15	.04
424 Butch Davis	.15	.04
425 Wayne Kirby	.15	.04
426 Mike Huff	.15	.04
427 Billy Bean	.15	.04
428 Pat Pacillo	.15	.04
429 Tony Blasucci	.15	.04
430 Mike Walker	.15	.04
431 Pat Rice	.15	.04
432 Terry Taylor	.15	.04
433 David Burba	.50	.15
434 Vance Lovelace	.15	.04
435 Ed Vande Berg	.15	.04
436 Greg Fulton	.15	.04
437 Ed Jurak	.15	.04
438 Dave Cochrane	.15	.04
439 Tino Martinez UER Edgar Martinez's name erroneously listed	.50	.15
440 Matt Sinatro	.15	.04
441 Bill McGuire	.15	.04
442 Mickey Brantley	.15	.04
443 Tom Dodd	.15	.04
444 Jim Weaver	.15	.04
445 Todd Haney	.15	.04
446 Casey Close	.15	.04
447 Theo Shaw	.15	.04
448 Keith Helton	.15	.04
449 Jose Melendez	.15	.04
450 Tom Jones MG	.15	.04
451 Dan Warthen CO	.15	.04
452 Randy Roetter TR	.15	.04
453 Mike Walker	.15	.04
454 Colby Ward	.15	.04
455 Joe Skalski	.15	.04
456 Efrain Valdez	.15	.04
457 Doug Robertson	.15	.04
458 Jeff Edwards	.15	.04
459 Greg McMichael	.15	.04
460 Carl Willis	.15	.04
461 Beau Allred	.15	.04
462 Jeff Kaiser	.15	.04
463 Ty Gainey	.15	.04
464 Tom Lampkin	.15	.04
465 Ever Magallanes	.15	.04
466 Tom Magrann	.15	.04
467 Jeff Manto	.15	.04
468 Luis Medina	.15	.04
469 Troy Neel	.15	.04
470 Steve Springer	.15	.04
471 Rick Adair CO UER (Card misnumbered 476 on back)	.15	.04
472 Turner Ward	.15	.04
473 Casey Webster	.15	.04
474 Jeff Wetherby	.15	.04
475 Alan Cockrell	.15	.04
476 Steve McInerney TR	.15	.04
477 Bobby Molinaro MG	.15	.04
478 Cliff Young	.15	.04
479 Mike Arner	.15	.04
480 Gary Buckels	.15	.04
481 Timothy Burcham	.15	.04
482 Sherman Corbett	.15	.04
483 Mike Erb	.15	.04
484 Mike Fetters	.15	.04
485 Chuck Hernandez CO	.15	.04
486 Jeff Heathcock	.15	.04
487 Scott Lewis	.15	.04
488 Rafael Montalvo	.15	.04
489 John Skurla	.15	.04
490 Lee Stevens	.50	.15
491 Nelson Rood	.15	.04
492 Bobby Rose	.50	.15
493 Dan Grunhard	.15	.04
494 Reed Peters	.15	.04
495 Doug Davis	.15	.04
496 Gary DiSarcina	.50	.15
497 Pete Coachman	.15	.04
498 Chris Cron	.15	.04
499 Karl Allaire	.15	.04
500 Ron Tingley	.15	.04
501 Chris Beasley	.15	.04
502 Max Oliveras MG	.15	.04
503 Roger Smithberg	.15	.04
504 Steve Peters	.15	.04
505 Matt Maysey	.15	.04
506 Terry Gilmore	.15	.04
507 Jeff Datz	.15	.04
508 Eric Nolte	.15	.04
509 Jim Lewis	.15	.04
510 Pete Roberts	.15	.04
511 Dan Murphy	.15	.04
512 Rich Rodriguez	.15	.04
513 Joe Lynch	.15	.04
514 Mike Basso	.15	.04
515 Ronn Reynolds	.15	.04
516 Jose Mota	.15	.04
517 Paul Faries	.15	.04
518 Warren Newson	.15	.04
519 Alex Cole	.15	.04
520 Tom LeVasseur	.15	.04
521 Charles Hillemann	.15	.04
522 Jeff Yurtin	.15	.04
523 Rafael Valdez	.15	.04
524 Brian Ohnoutka	.15	.04
525 Pat Kelly MG	.15	.04
526 Gary Lance CO	.15	.04
527 Tony Torchia CO	.15	.04
528 Paul McClellan	.15	.04
529 Randy McCament	.15	.04
530 Gil Heredia	.50	.15
531 George Bonilla	.15	.04
532 Russ Swan	.15	.04
533 Ed Vosberg	.15	.04
534 Eric Gunderson	.15	.04
535 Trevor Wilson	.15	.04
536 Greg Booker	.15	.04
537 Kirt Manwaring	.15	.04
538 Mike Kingery	.15	.04
539 Brian Brady	.15	.04
540 Mark Bailey	.15	.04
541 Gregg Ritchie	.15	.04
542 George Hinshaw	.15	.04
543 Craig Colbert	.15	.04
544 Kash Beauchamp	.15	.04
545 Jeff Carter	.15	.04
546 Mark Leonard	.15	.04
547 Tony Perezchica	.15	.04
548 Mike Laga	.15	.04
549 Mike Benjamin	.15	.04
550 Timber Mead	.15	.04
551 Duane Espy MG	.15	.04
552 Tim Ireland CO	.15	.04
553 Paul Abbott	.50	.15
554 Pat Bangtson	.15	.04
555 Larry Casian	.15	.04
556 Mike Cook	.15	.04
557 Pete Delkus	.15	.04
558 Mike Dyer	.15	.04
559 Charles Scott	.15	.04
560 Francisco Oliveras	.15	.04
561 Park Pittman	.15	.04
562 Jimmy Williams	.15	.04
563 Rich Yett	.15	.04
564 Vic Rodriguez	.15	.04
565 Jamie Nelson	.15	.04
566 Derek Parks	.15	.04
567 Ed Naveda	.15	.04
568 Scott Leius	.15	.04
569 Terry Jorgensen	.15	.04
570 Doug Baker	.15	.04
571 Chip Hale	.15	.04
572 Dave Jacas	.15	.04
573 Jim Shellenback CO	.15	.04
574 Rafael DeLima	.15	.04
575 Bernardo Brito	.15	.04
576 J.T. Bruett	.15	.04
577 Paul Sorrento	.50	.15
578 Ray Young	.15	.04
579 Dave Veres	.15	.04
580 Scott Chiamparino	.15	.04
581 Tony Ariola	.15	.04
582 Weston Weber	.15	.04
583 Bruce Walton	.15	.04
584 Dave Otto	.15	.04
585 Reese Lambert	.15	.04
586 Joe Bitker	.15	.04
587 Joe Law	.15	.04
588 Ed Wojna	.15	.04
589 Timothy Casey	.15	.04
590 Patrick Dietrick	.15	.04
591 Bruce Fields	.15	.04
592 Eric Fox	.15	.04
593 Scott Hemond	.15	.04
594 Steve Howard	.15	.04
595 Doug Jennings	.15	.04
596 Al Pedrique	.15	.04
597 Dann Howitt	.15	.04
598 Russ McGinnis	.15	.04
599 Troy Afenir	.15	.04
600 Larry Arndt	.15	.04
601 Dickie Scott CO	.15	.04
602 Kevin Ward	.15	.04
603 Ryan Bowen	.15	.04
604 Brian Meyer	.15	.04
605 Terry Clark	.15	.04
606 Darryl Kile	1.00	.30
607 Randy St. Claire	.15	.04
608 Randy Hennis	.15	.04
609 Lee Tunnell	.15	.04
610 William Brennan	.15	.04
611 Craig Smajstra	.15	.04
612 Gary Cooper	.15	.04
613 Carl Nichols	.15	.04
614 Louie Meadows	.15	.04
615 Josse Tolentino	.15	.04
616 Harry Spillman	.15	.04
617 Javier Ortiz	.15	.04
618 Doug Strange	.15	.04
619 Jim Olander	.15	.04
620 Karl Rhodes	.15	.04
621 Dave Rohde	.15	.04
622 Mike Simms	.15	.04
623 Scott Servais	.15	.04
624 Pedro Sanchez	.15	.04
625 Kevin Dean	.15	.04

626 Brian Fisher .15 .04
627 Bob Skinner MG .15 .04
628 Wilson Alvarez .50 .15
629 Adam Peterson .15 .04
630 Tom Drees .15 .04
631 Ravelo Manzanillo .15 .04
632 Marv Foley MG .15 .04
633 Grady Hall .15 .04
634 Mike Campbell .15 .04
635 Shawn Hillegas .15 .04
636 C.L. Penigar .15 .04
637 John Pawlowski .15 .04
638 Steve Rosenberg .15 .04
639 Jose Segura .15 .04
640 Rich Amaral .15 .04
641 Pete Dalena .15 .04
642 Ramon Sambo .15 .04
643 Marcus Lawton .15 .04
644 Orsino Hill .15 .04
645 Marlin McPhail .15 .04
646 Keith Smith .15 .04
647 Todd Trafton .15 .04
648 Norberto Martin .15 .04
649 Don Wakamatsu .15 .04
650 Jerry Willard .15 .04
651 Dana Williams .15 .04
652 Tracy Woodson .15 .04
653 Glenn Hoffman CO .15 .04
654 Tony Scruggs .15 .04
655 Reggie Sanders .50 .15
656 Rick Luecken .15 .04
657 Kent Mercker .15 .04
658 Claude Osteen CO .15 .04
Von Joshua CO
Walt McConnel CO
659 Scott Shockey .15 .04
660 Mario Brito .15 .04
661 Brian Barnes .15 .04
662 Ed Quijada .15 .04
663 Steve Wapnick .15 .04
664 Kevin Tahan .15 .04
665 Johnny Guzman .15 .04
666 Bronswell Patrick .15 .04
667 Kevin Kennedy MG .15 .04
668 Orlando Miller .15 .04
669 Mauricio Nunez .15 .04
670 Hector Rivera .15 .04
671 Roger LaFrancois CO .15 .04
672 Jackson Todd CO .15 .04
673 John Young TR .15 .04
674 Bob Bailor MG .15 .04
675 David Hajeck .15 .04
676 Ralph Wheeler CO .15 .04
677 Anthony Gutierrez .15 .04
678 Gaylen Pitts MG .15 .04
679 Mark Riggins CO .15 .04
680 Brad Bluestone TR .15 .04
681 Dick Bosman CO .15 .04
682 Wil Cordero .15 .04
683 Todd Hutcheson TR .15 .04
684 Steve Swisher MG .15 .04
685 John Cumberland CO .15 .04
686 Rich Miller CO .15 .04
687 Scott Lawrenson TR .15 .04
688 Larry Hardy CO .15 .04
689 Danny Boone .15 .04
690 Terrel Hansen .15 .04
691 Tom Gamboa MG .15 .04
692 Gavin Osteen .15 .04
693 Dave Riddle .15 .04
694 Tim Pugh .15 .04
695 Eugene Jones .15 .04
696 Scott Pose .15 .04
697 Ramon Jimenez .15 .04
698 Fred Russell .15 .04
699 Louis Talbert .15 .04
700 J.D. Noland .15 .04
701 Osvaldo Sanchez .15 .04
702 David Colon .15 .04
703 Jeff Hart .15 .04
704 Jeff Hoffman .15 .04
705 Sean Gilliam .15 .04
706 Al Pacheco .15 .04
707 Jason Satre .15 .04
708 Tim Cecil .15 .04
709 Phil Weise .15 .04
710 Larry Pardo .15 .04
711 Clemente Acosta .15 .04
712 Chris Johnson .15 .04
713 Frank Bolick .15 .04
714 Jose Garcia .15 .04
715 Adell Davenport .15 .04
716 Kevin Rogers .15 .04
717 Dan Rambo .15 .04
718 Vince Harris .15 .04
719 Darrell Sherman .15 .04
720 Isaiah Clark .15 .04
721 Miguel Sabino .15 .04
722 Frank Valdez .15 .04
723 Giovanni Miranda .15 .04
724 Dary Ratliff .15 .04
725 Michael Brewington .15 .04
726 Eric Parkinson .15 .04
727 Vinny Castilla .50 .15
728 Roger Hailey .15 .04
729 Earl Steinmetz .15 .04
730 Doug Gogolewski .15 .04
731 Andy Cook .15 .04
732 John Toale .15 .04
733 Mike Curtis .15 .04
734 Delwyn Young .15 .04
735 Scott Meadows .15 .04
736 Don Sparks .15 .04
737 Gary Wilson .15 .04
738 Blas Minor .15 .04
739 Jeff Bagwell 2.50 .75
740 Phil Bryant .15 .04
741 Felipe Castillo .15 .04
742 Craig Faulkner .15 .04
743 Jeff Conine .50 .15
744 Kevin Belcher .15 .04
745 Bill Haselman .15 .04
746 Matt Stark .15 .04
747 Todd Hall .15 .04
748 Scott Centala .15 .04
749 Doug Simons .15 .04
750 Shawn Gilbert .15 .04
751 Kenny Morgan .15 .04
752 Andy Mota .15 .04
753 Jeff Baldwin .15 .04
754 Reed Olmstead .15 .04
755 Basil Meyer .15 .04
756 Mark Razook .15 .04
757 Ken Pennington .15 .04
758 Shane Letterio .15 .04
759 Ted Williams .15 .04
760 Luis Gonzalez 1.50 .45
761 Carlos Garcia .15 .04
762 Terry Crowley .15 .04
763 Julio Peguero .15 .04
764 Francisco DeLaRosa .15 .04
765 Rodney Lofton .15 .04
766 Eric McCray .15 .04
767 Michael Wilkins .15 .04
768 John Kiely .15 .04
769 Derek Lee .15 .04
770 Bo Kennedy .15 .04
771 John Hudek .15 .04
772 Bernie Nunez .15 .04
773 Tom Quinlan .15 .04
774 Jimmy Tatum .15 .04
775 Casey Waller .15 .04
776 Doug Lindsey .15 .04
777 Roberto Zambrano .15 .04
778 Wade Taylor .15 .04
779 Carlos Maldonado .15 .04
780 Brent Mayne .15 .04
781 Jerry Rub .15 .04
782 Vince Phillips .15 .04
783 Eric Wedge .15 .04
784 Andy Ashby .50 .15
785 Royal Clayton .15 .04
786 Jeffrey Osborne .15 .04
787 Pat Kelly .15 .04
788 John Wehner .15 .04
789 Bernie Williams 2.50 .75
790 Moises Alou .50 .15
791 Mark Merchant .15 .04
792 Chris Myers .15 .04
793 Donald Harris .15 .04
794 Mike McDonald .15 .04
795 Jim Blueberg .15 .04
796 Jim Bowie .15 .04
797 Ruben Gonzalez .15 .04
798 Rob Maurer .15 .04
799 Monty Fariss .15 .04
800 Bob Ayrault .15 .04
801 Tim Mauser .15 .04
802 David Holdridge .15 .04
803 Kim Batiste .15 .04
804 Dan Peltier .15 .04
805 Derek Livernois .15 .04
806 Tom Fischer .15 .04
807 Chuck Knoblauch .50 .15
808 Willie Banks .15 .04
809 Johnny Ard .15 .04
810 Willie Ansley .15 .04
811 Andujar Cedeno .15 .04
812 Eddie Zosky .15 .04
813 Randy Knorr .15 .04
814 Juan Guzman .50 .15
815 Jimmy Rogers .15 .04
816 Nate Cromwell .15 .04
817 Aubrey Waggoner .15 .04
818 Frank Thomas 3.00 .90
819 Matt Merullo .15 .04
820 Roberto Hernandez .50 .15
821 Cesar Bernhardt .15 .04
822 Sterling Hitchcock .50 .15
823 Ricky Rhodes .15 .04
824 Todd Malone .15 .04
825 Andy Fox .15 .04
826 Ryan Klesko 1.50 .45
827 Tyler Houston .50 .15
828 Tab Brown .15 .04
829 Brian McRae .15 .04
830 Victor Cole .15 .04
831 Mark Lewis .15 .04
832 Rudy Seanez .15 .04
833 Charles Nagy .50 .15
834 Jeff Mutis .15 .04
835 Carl Keliipuleole .15 .04
836 Steve Pegues .15 .04
837 Mike Lumley .15 .04
838 Tim Leiper .15 .04
839 Dave Evans .15 .04
840 Darron Cox .15 .04
841 Tony Ochs .15 .04
842 Paul Coleman .15 .04
843 Rafael Novoa .15 .04
844 Clay Bellinger .15 .04
845 Jason McFarlin .15 .04
846 Craig Paquette .15 .04
847 Timmie Morrow .15 .04
848 Brian L. Hunter .15 .04
849 Willie Greene .15 .04
850 Austin Manahan .15 .04
851 Rich Aude .15 .04
852 Luis Lopez .15 .04
853 Darrin Reichle .15 .04
854 Tim Salmon 1.50 .45
855 Royce Clayton .50 .15
856 Steve Hosey .15 .04
857 Kerry Woodson .15 .04
858 Roger Salkeld .15 .04
859 Tim Stargell .15 .04
860 Greg Pirkl .15 .04
861 Pat Mahomes .15 .04
862 Denny Neagle .50 .15
863 Troy Buckley .15 .04
864 Ray Ortiz .15 .04
865 Leo Perez .15 .04
866 Cal Eldred .50 .15
867 Darin Kracl .15 .04
868 Lee Tinsley .15 .04
869 T.R. Lewis .15 .04
870 Jimmy Roso .15 .04
871 Tom Taylor .15 .04
872 Matt Anderson .15 .04
873 Kerwin Moore .15 .04
874 Rich Tunison .15 .04
875 Brian Ahern .15 .04
876 Eddie Taubensee .50 .15
877 Scott Bryant .15 .04
878 Steve Martin .15 .04
879 Josias Manzanillo .15 .04
880 Bob Zupcic .15 .04

1990 Little Sun High School Prospects

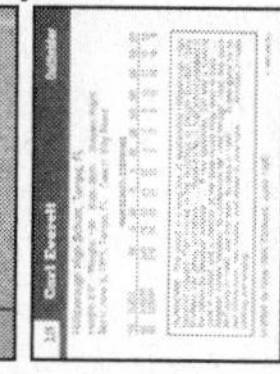

This 24-card standard size set features color photos of some of the top senior high school players. The card backs contain complete high school career stats and biographical notes. 6,000 regular sets were produced. Early cards of Garrett Anderson, Carl Everett and Mike Hampton are featured in this set.

	Nm-Mt	Ex-Mt
COMP.FACT.SET (24)	10.00	3.00
1 Checklist	.50	.15
2 Mike Lieberthal	1.50	.45
3 Lamar Cherry	.50	.15
4 Aaron Holbert	.50	.15
5 Sean Cheetham	.50	.15
6 Charles Poe	.50	.15
7 Gabriel White	.50	.15
8 Daniel Hernandez	.50	.15
9 Mark Anthony	.50	.15
10 Keith Tobey	.50	.15
11 Ronald Caridad	.50	.15
12 John Schulte	.50	.15
13 Carl Everett	2.50	.75
14 Shawn Wooten	.50	.15
15 Gary Hust	.50	.15
16 Vincent Bradford	.50	.15
17 Mark Lambert	.50	.15
18 Dan Tobin	.50	.15
19 Garret Anderson	4.00	1.20
20 Mike Hampton	2.00	.60
21 David Mowry	.50	.15
22 Jim Converse	.50	.15
23 Wade Fyock	.50	.15
24 Clyde Metcalf CO	.50	.15

1990 ProCards A and AA

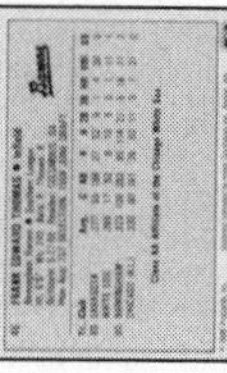

This 200-card set was issued wax packs and features orange bordered color player photos on its fronts. The player's name, position and team name appear at the bottom. The horizontal back carries the player's name and position at the top, followed by biography and statistics.

	Nm-Mt	Ex-Mt
COMPLETE SET (200)	20.00	6.00
1 Mike Linskey	.15	.04
2 Ben McDonald	.15	.04
3 Francisco DeLaRosa	.15	.04
4 Jose Mesa	.40	.12
5 Kevin Morton	.15	.04
6 Dan O'Neill	.15	.04
7 Dave Owen	.15	.04
8 Jeff Plympton	.15	.04
9 Charles Nagy	.40	.12
10 Rudy Seanez	.15	.04
11 Bruce Egloff	.15	.04
12 Joe Ausanio	.15	.04
13 Jim Tracy	.15	.04
14 Randy Tomlin	.15	.04
15 Jim Campbell	.15	.04
16 Mike Gardiner	.15	.04
17 Rusty Meacham	.15	.04
18 John Kiely	.15	.04
19 Darrin Chapin	.15	.04
20 Wade Taylor	.15	.04
21 Don Stanford	.15	.04
22 Andy Ashby	.40	.12
23 Bob Ayrault	.15	.04
24 Luis Mercedes	.15	.04
25 Scott Meadows	.15	.04
26 Jeff Bagwell	1.50	.45
27 Mark Lewis	.15	.04
28 Carlos Garcia	.15	.04
29 Moises Alou	.40	.12
30 Rico Brogna	.40	.12
31 Bernie Williams	1.50	.45
32 Pat Kelly	.15	.04
33 Mitch Lyden	.15	.04
34 Hector Wagner	.15	.04
35 Carlos Maldonado	.15	.04
36 Brian Barnes	.15	.04
37 Chris Nabholz	.15	.04
38 Jeff Carter	.15	.04
39 Johnny Ard	.15	.04
40 Willie Banks	.15	.04
41 Scott Erickson	.40	.12
42 Greg Johnson	.15	.04
43 Al Osuna	.15	.04
44 Bob MacDonald	.15	.04
45 Pat Hentgen	.40	.12
46 Frank Thomas	2.50	.75
47 Matt Stark	.15	.04
48 Jeff Conine	.40	.12
49 Sean Berry	.15	.04
50 Brian McRae	.15	.04
51 Bobby Moore	.15	.04
52 Brent Mayne	.15	.04
53 Greg Colbrunn	.40	.12
54 Terrel Hansen	.15	.04
55 Lenny Webster	.15	.04
56 Chuck Knoblauch	.40	.12
57 Willie Ansley	.15	.04
58 Andujar Cedeno	.15	.04
59 Luis Gonzalez	1.00	.30
60 Eddie Zosky	.15	.04
61 William Suero	.15	.04
62 Tom Quinlan	.15	.04
63 Kelly Mann	.15	.04
64 Mike Bell	.15	.04
65 Mark Dewey	.15	.04
66 Tom Hostetler	.15	.04
67 Kevin Belcher	.15	.04
68 Bill Haselman	.15	.04
69 Rob Maurer	.15	.04
70 Dan Rohrmeier	.15	.04
71 Dan Peltier	.15	.04
72 Steve Decker	.15	.04
73 Dave Patterson	.15	.04
74 Ed Zinter	.15	.04
75 David Bird	.15	.04
76 Willie Espinal	.15	.04
77 Dennis Fletcher	.15	.04
78 Travis Buckley	.15	.04
79 Brian Romero	.15	.04
80 Mike Arner	.15	.04
81 Brian Evans	.15	.04
82 John Graves	.15	.04
83 Randy Marshall	.15	.04
84 Mike Garcia	.15	.04
85 Jeff Braley	.15	.04
86 Ricky Rhodes	.15	.04
87 Jim Haller	.15	.04
88 Sterling Hitchcock	.40	.12
89 Rob Blumberg	.15	.04
90 Mike Ogliaruso	.15	.04
91 Gregg Martin	.15	.04
92 Tim Pugh	.15	.04
93 Roger Hailey	.15	.04
94 Don Strange	.15	.04
95 Robert Gaddy	.15	.04
96 Willie Greene	.15	.04
97 Austin Manahan	.15	.04
98 Tony Scruggs	.15	.04
99 Mike Burton	.15	.04
100 Shawn Holtzclaw	.15	.04
101 Orlando Miller	.15	.04
102 David Hajek	.15	.04
103 Scott Pose	.15	.04
104 Tyler Houston	.40	.12
105 Melvin Nieves	.15	.04
106 Ryan Klesko	1.00	.30
107 Daryl Moore	.15	.04
108 Skip Wiley	.15	.04
109 Brian McKeon	.15	.04
110 Rusty Kilgo	.15	.04
111 Chris Bushing	.15	.04
112 Alan Newman	.15	.04
113 Marc Lipson	.15	.04
114 Darin Karcl	.15	.04
115 Matt Grott	.15	.04
116 Rafael Novoa	.15	.04
117 Pat Rapp	.15	.04
118 Ed Gustafson	.15	.04
119 Chris Hancock	.15	.04
120 Mo Sanford	.15	.04
121 Bill Risley	.15	.04
122 Victor Garcia	.15	.04
123 Dave McAuliffe	.15	.04
124 Pedro Borbon Jr.	.15	.04
125 Rich Tunison	.15	.04
126 Fred Cooley	.15	.04
127 Joey James	.15	.04
128 Reggie Sanders	.40	.12
129 Scott Bryant	.15	.04
130 Brent McCoy	.15	.04
131 Ramon Caraballo	.15	.04
132 Javy Lopez	1.00	.30
133 Brian Harrison	.15	.04
134 Rich DeLucia	.15	.04
135 Roger Salkeld	.15	.04
136 Kerry Woodson	.15	.04
137 Chris Johnson	.15	.04
138 Cal Eldred	.40	.12
139 Angel Miranda	.15	.04
140 Rich Garces	.15	.04
141 Pat Mahomes	.15	.04
142 Denny Neagle	.40	.12
143 George Tsamis	.15	.04
144 Johnny Guzman	.15	.04
145 Dan Rambo	.15	.04
146 Jim Myers	.15	.04
147 Darrell Sherman	.15	.04
148 Dave Staton	.15	.04
149 Brian Turang	.15	.04
150 Bo Dodson	.15	.04
151 Dave Nilsson	.40	.12
152 Frank Bolick	.15	.04
153 Ray Ortiz	.15	.04
154 J.T. Bruett	.15	.04
155 John Patterson	.15	.04
156 Royce Clayton	.40	.12
157 Hilly Hathaway	.15	.04
158 Phil Leftwich	.15	.04
159 Randy Powers	.15	.04
160 Todd Van Poppel	.40	.12
161 Don Peters	.15	.04
162 Dave Zancanaro	.15	.04
163 Kirk Dressendorfer	.15	.04
164 Curtis Shaw	.15	.04
165 Joe Rosselli	.15	.04
166 Mark Dalesandro	.15	.04
167 Eric Helfand	.15	.04
168 Eric Booker	.15	.04
169 Adam Hyzdu	.15	.04
170 Eric Christopherson	.15	.04
171 Marcus Jensen	.40	.12
172 Derek Reid	.15	.04
173 Lance Dickson	.15	.04
174 Tim Parker	.15	.04
175 Jessie Hollins	.15	.04
176 Sam Militello	.15	.04
177 Darren Hodges	.15	.04
178 Kirt Ojala	.15	.04
179 Steve Karsay	.40	.12
180 Andrew Hartung	.15	.04
181 Kevin Jordan	.15	.04
182 Robert Eenhoorn	.15	.04
183 Jalal Leach	.15	.04
184 Carlos Delgado	1.50	.45
185 Sean Cheetham	.15	.04
186 J.J. Munoz	.15	.04
187 Jim Thome	2.50	.75
188 Tracy Sanders	.15	.04
189 Tony Clark	.40	.12
190 Jose Viera	.15	.04
191 Pat Dando	.15	.04
192 Brian Kowitz	.15	.04
193 Mike Lieberthal	.40	.12
194 Jeff Borgese	.15	.04
195 Mike Ferry	.15	.04
196 K.C. Gillum	.15	.04
197 Elliott Quinones	.15	.04
198 Grant Brittain	.15	.04
199 Checklist	.15	.04
200 Checklist	.15	.04

1990 ProCards AAA

This 700-card set was issued in wax packs and features white bordered color player photos on its fronts. The player's name, position and team name appear at the bottom. The horizontal back carries the player's name and position at the top, followed by biography and statistics.

	Nm-Mt	Ex-Mt
COMPLETE SET (700)	40.00	12.00
1 Terry Gilmore	.15	.04
2 Jim Lewis	.15	.04
3 Joe Lynch	.15	.04
4 Matt Maysey	.15	.04
5 Dan Murphy	.15	.04
6 Eric Nolte	.15	.04
7 Brian Ohnoutka	.15	.04
8 Steve Peters	.15	.04
9 Paul Quinzer	.15	.04
10 Pete Roberts	.15	.04
11 Rich Rodriguez	.15	.04
12 Roger Smithberg	.15	.04
13 Rafael Valdez	.15	.04
14 Mike Basso	.15	.04
15 Ronn Reynolds	.15	.04
16 Paul Faries	.15	.04
17 Tom LeVasseur	.15	.04
18 Jose Mota	.15	.04
19 Eddie Williams	.15	.04
20 Jeff Yurtin	.15	.04
21 Alex Cole	.15	.04
22 Charles Hillemann	.15	.04
23 Tom Howard	.15	.04
24 Warren Newson	.15	.04
25 Pat Kelly MG	.15	.04
26 Gary Lance CO	.15	.04
27 Tony Torchia CO	.15	.04
28 George Bonilla	.15	.04
29 Greg Booker	.15	.04
30 Rich Bordi	.15	.04
31 John Burkett	.15	.04
32 Gil Heredia	.50	.15
33 Bob Knepper	.15	.04
34 Randy McCament	.15	.04
35 Paul McClellan	.15	.04
36 Timber Mead	.15	.04
37 Ed Vosberg	.15	.04
38 Trevor Wilson	.15	.04
39 Mark Bailey	.15	.04
40 Kirt Manwaring	.15	.04
41 Mike Benjamin	.15	.04
42 Brian Brady	.15	.04
43 Jeff Carter	.15	.04
44 Craig Colbert	.15	.04
45 Erik Johnson	.15	.04
46 Greg Litton	.15	.04
47 Kash Beauchamp	.15	.04
48 George Hinshaw	.15	.04
49 Mike Kingery	.15	.04
50 Mark Leonard	.15	.04
51 Gregg Ritchie	.15	.04
52 Rick Parker	.15	.04
53 Duane Espy MG	.15	.04
54 Tim Ireland CO	.15	.04
55 Larry Hardy CO	.15	.04
56 Jeff Bittiger	.15	.04
57 Mike Christopher	.15	.04
58 Steve Davis	.15	.04
59 Jeff Fischer	.15	.04
60 Darren Holmes	.15	.04
61 Morris Madden	.15	.04
62 Mike Maddux	.15	.04
63 Greg Mayberry	.15	.04
64 Jim Neidlinger	.15	.04
65 Tim Scott	.15	.04
66 Dave Walsh	.15	.04
67 Terry Wells	.15	.04
68 Adam Brown	.15	.04
69 Darrin Fletcher	.15	.04
70 Carlos Hernandez	.15	.04
71 Dave Hansen	.15	.04
72 Dan Henley	.15	.04
73 Glenn Hoffman	.15	.04
74 Walt McConnell	.15	.04
75 Jose Offerman	.50	.15
76 Jose Vizcaino	.50	.15
77 Billy Bean	.15	.04
78 Butch Davis	.15	.04
79 Mike Huff	.15	.04
80 Wayne Kirby	.15	.04
81 Luis Lopez	.15	.04
82 Kevin Kennedy MG	.15	.04
83 Claude Osteen CO	.15	.04
84 Von Joshua CO	.15	.04
85 Chris Beasley	.15	.04
86 Gary Buckels	.15	.04
87 Tim Burcham	.15	.04
88 Sherman Corbett	.15	.04
89 Mike Erb	.15	.04
90 Mike Fetters	.15	.04
91 Jeff Heathcock	.15	.04
92 Scott Lewis	.15	.04
93 Rafael Montalvo	.15	.04
94 Cliff Young	.15	.04

95 Doug Davis .15 .04
96 Ron Tingley .15 .04
97 Karl Allaire .15 .04
98 Pete Coachman .15 .04
99 Chris Cron .15 .04
100 Gary DiSarcina .50 .15
101 Nelson Rood .15 .04
102 Bobby Rose .50 .15
103 Lee Stevens .50 .15
104 Dan Grunhard .15 .04
105 Reed Peters .15 .04
106 John Skurla .15 .04
107 Max Oliveras .15 .04
108 Chuck Hernandez .15 .04
109 Tony Blasucci .15 .04
110 Dave Burba .50 .15
111 Keith Helton .15 .04
112 Vance Lovelace .15 .04
113 Jose Melendez .15 .04
114 Pat Pacillo .15 .04
115 Pat Rice .15 .04
116 Terry Taylor .15 .04
117 Mike Walker .15 .04
118 Bill McGuire .15 .04
119 Matt Sinatro .15 .04
120 Mario Diaz .15 .04
121 Greg Fulton .15 .04
122 Todd Haney .15 .04
123 Ed Jurak .15 .04
124 Tino Martinez .50 .15
125 Jeff Schaefer .15 .04
126 Casey Close .15 .04
127 Tom Dodd .15 .04
128 Jim Weaver .15 .04
129 Tommy Jones .15 .04
130 Dan Warthen CO .15 .04
131 Tony Ariola .15 .04
132 Joe Bitker .15 .04
133 Scott Chiamparino .15 .04
134 Reese Lambert .15 .04
135 Joe Law .15 .04
136 Dave Otto .15 .04
137 Dave Veres .15 .04
138 Bruce Walton .15 .04
139 Wes Weber .15 .04
140 Ed Wojna .15 .04
141 Ray Young .15 .04
142 Troy Afenir .15 .04
143 Russ McGinnis .15 .04
144 Larry Arndt .15 .04
145 Mike Bordick .50 .15
146 Scott Hemond .15 .04
147 Dann Howitt .15 .04
148 Doug Jennings .15 .04
149 Al Pedrique .15 .04
150 Dick Scott .15 .04
151 Tim Casey .15 .04
152 Pat Dietrick .15 .04
153 Bruce Fields .15 .04
154 Eric Fox .15 .04
155 Steve Howard .15 .04
156 Kevin Ward .15 .04
157 Brad Fischer MG .15 .04
158 Chuck Estrada CO .15 .04
159 Wilson Alvarez .50 .15
160 Mike Campbell .15 .04
161 Tom Drees .15 .04
162 Grady Hall .15 .04
163 Shawn Hillegas .15 .04
164 Ravelo Manzanillo .15 .04
165 John Pawlowski .15 .04
166 Adam Peterson .15 .04
167 Steve Rosenberg .15 .04
168 Jose Segura .15 .04
169 Don Wakamatsu .15 .04
170 Jerry Willard .15 .04
171 Rich Amaral .15 .04
172 Pete Dalena .15 .04
173 Norberto Martin .15 .04
174 Keith Smith .15 .04
175 Todd Trafton .15 .04
176 Tracy Woodson .15 .04
177 Orsino Hill .15 .04
178 Marcus Lawton .15 .04
179 Marlin McPhail .15 .04
180 C.L. Penigar .15 .04
181 Ramon Sambo .15 .04
182 Dana Williams .15 .04
183 Marv Foley .15 .04
184 Moe Drabowsky CO .15 .04
185 Roger LaFrancois CO .15 .04
186 Ryan Bowen .15 .04
187 William Brennan .15 .04
188 Terry Clark .15 .04
189 Brian Fisher .15 .04
190 Randy Hennisaire .15 .04
191 Darryl Kile 1.00 .30
192 Brian Meyer .15 .04
193 Randy St. Claire .15 .04
194 Lee Tunnell .15 .04
195 Carl Nichols .15 .04
196 Scott Servais .15 .04
197 Pedro Sanchez .15 .04
198 Mike Simms .15 .04
199 Craig Smajstra .15 .04
200 Harry Spilman .15 .04
201 Doug Strange .15 .04
202 Jose Tolentino .15 .04
203 Gary Cooper .15 .04
204 Kevin Dean .15 .04
205 Louie Meadows .15 .04
206 Jim Olander .15 .04
207 Javier Ortiz .15 .04
208 Karl Rhodes .15 .04
209 Bob Skinner MG .15 .04
210 Brent Strom CO .15 .04
211 Tim Tolman CO .15 .04
212 Greg McMichael .15 .04
213 Doug Robertson .15 .04
214 Jeff Shaw .50 .15
215 Joe Skalski .15 .04
216 Efrain Valdez .15 .04
217 Mike Walker .15 .04
218 Colby Ward .15 .04
219 Carl Willis .15 .04
220 Tom Lampkin .15 .04
221 Tom Magrann .15 .04
222 Juan Castillo .15 .04
223 Ever Magallanes .15 .04
224 Jeff Manto .15 .04
225 Luis Medina .15 .04
226 Troy Neel .15 .04
227 Steve Springer .15 .04
228 Casey Webster .15 .04
229 Beau Allred .15 .04
230 Alan Cockrell .15 .04
231 Ty Gainey .15 .04
232 Dwight Taylor .15 .04
233 Turner Ward .15 .04
234 Jeff Wetherby .15 .04
235 Bobby Molinaro MG .15 .04
236 Buddy Bell CO .50 .15
237 Rick Adair CO .15 .04
238 Paul Abbott .50 .15
239 Pat Bangtson .15 .04
240 Larry Casian .15 .04
241 Mike Cook .15 .04
242 Pete Delkus .15 .04
243 Mike Dyer .15 .04
244 Mark Guthrie .15 .04
245 Orlando Lind .15 .04
246 Francisco Oliveras .15 .04
247 Park Pittman .15 .04
248 Charles Scott .15 .04
249 Jimmy Williams .15 .04
250 Jamie Nelson .15 .04
251 Derek Parks .15 .04
252 Doug Baker .15 .04
253 Chip Hale .15 .04
254 Terry Jorgensen .15 .04
255 Scott Leius .15 .04
256 Marty Lanoux .15 .04
257 Ed Naveda .15 .04
258 Victor Rodriguez .15 .04
259 Paul Sorrento .50 .15
260 Bernardo Brito .15 .04
261 Rafael Delima .15 .04
262 David Jacas .15 .04
263 Alonzo Powell .15 .04
264 Jim Shellenback MG .15 .04
265 Shawn Barton .15 .04
266 Kevin Brown .15 .04
267 Rocky Childress .15 .04
268 Brian Givens .15 .04
269 Manny Hernandez .15 .04
270 Jeff Innis .15 .04
271 Cesar Mejia .15 .04
272 Scott Nielsen .15 .04
273 Dale Plummer .15 .04
274 Roger Samuels .15 .04
275 Ray Soff .15 .04
276 Dave Trautwein .15 .04
277 Julio Valera .15 .04
278 Dave Liddell .15 .04
279 Orlando Mercado .15 .04
280 Tim Bogar .15 .04
281 Mike Debutch .15 .04
282 Jeff Gardner .15 .04
283 Denny Gonzalez .15 .04
284 Chris Jelic .15 .04
285 Kelvin Torve .15 .04
286 Alex Diaz .15 .04
287 Keith Hughes .15 .04
288 Darren Reed .15 .04
289 Zoilo Sanchez .15 .04
290 Lou Thornton .15 .04
291 Steve Swisher MG .15 .04
292 John Cumberland CO .15 .04
293 Rich Miller CO .15 .04
294 Jose DeJesus .15 .04
295 Marvin Freeman .15 .04
296 Todd Frohwirth .15 .04
297 Jason Grimsley .15 .04
298 Chuck Malone .15 .04
299 Brad Moore .15 .04
300 Wally Ritchie .15 .04
301 Bob Scanlan .15 .04
302 Scott Service .15 .04
303 Steve Sharts .15 .04
304 John Gibbons .15 .04
305 Tom Nieto .15 .04
306 Jim Adduci .15 .04
307 Kelly Heath .15 .04
308 Mickey Morandini .15 .04
309 Victor Rosario .15 .04
310 Steve Stanicek .15 .04
311 Greg Legg .15 .04
312 Ron Jones .15 .04
313 Chris Knabenshue .15 .04
314 Keith Miller .15 .04
315 Jim Vatcher .15 .04
316 Jim Wright CO .15 .04
317 Steve Adkins .15 .04
318 Darrin Chapin .15 .04
319 Bob Davidson .15 .04
320 Dave Eiland .15 .04
321 John Habyan .15 .04
322 Jimmy Jones .15 .04
323 Mark Leiter .15 .04
324 Kevin Mmahat .15 .04
325 Rich Monteleone .15 .04
326 Willie Smith .15 .04
327 Ricky Torres .15 .04
328 Jeff Datz .15 .04
329 Brian Dorsett .15 .04
330 Dave Sax .15 .04
331 Jim Leyritz .50 .15
332 Hensley Meulens .15 .04
333 Carlos Rodriguez .15 .04
334 Rob Sepanek .15 .04
335 Andy Stankiewicz .15 .04
336 Jim Walewander .15 .04
337 Mark Wasinger .15 .04
338 Oscar Azocar .15 .04
339 John Fishel .15 .04
340 Jason Maas .15 .04
341 Kevin Maas .15 .04
342 Van Snider .15 .04
343 Field Staff .15 .04
Clete Boyer
Stump Merrill MG
Ken Rowe
Trey Hillman
Mike Heifferon
344 Tom Gilles .15 .04
345 Maurio Gozzo .15 .04
346 Paul Kilgus .15 .04
347 Doug Linton .15 .04
348 Mike Loynd .15 .04
349 Rick Lysander .15 .04
350 Alex Sanchez .15 .04
351 John Shea .15 .04
352 Steve Wapnick .15 .04
353 Andy Dziadkowiec .15 .04
354 Joe Szekely .15 .04
355 Ozzie Virgil .15 .04
356 Jim Eppard .15 .04
357 Jose Escobar .15 .04
358 Webster Garrison .15 .04
359 Paul Runge .15 .04
360 Luis Sojo .15 .04
361 Ed Sprague .50 .15
362 Derek Bell .50 .15
363 Hector DeLaCruz .15 .04
364 Rob Ducey .15 .04
365 Pedro Munoz .15 .04
366 Stu Pederson .15 .04
367 Mark Whiten .15 .04
368 Bob Bailor MG .15 .04
369 Bob Shirley CO .15 .04
370 Rocket Wheeler CO .15 .04
371 Scott Aldred .15 .04
372 Dennis Burtt .15 .04
373 Shawn Holman .15 .04
374 Matt Kinzer .15 .04
375 Randy Nosek .15 .04
376 Jose Ramos .15 .04
377 Kevin Ritz .15 .04
378 Mike Schwabe .15 .04
379 Steve Searcy .15 .04
380 Eric Stone .15 .04
381 Don Vesling .15 .04
382 Phil Clark .15 .04
383 Phil Ouellette .15 .04
384 Dean DeCillis .15 .04
385 Travis Fryman .50 .15
386 Jim Lindeman .15 .04
387 Scott Livingstone .15 .04
388 Torey Lovullo .15 .04
389 Domingo Michel .15 .04
390 Milt Cuyler .15 .04
391 La Vel Freeman .15 .04
392 Shawn Hare .15 .04
393 Scott Lusader .15 .04
394 Tom Gamboa MG .15 .04
395 Jeff Jones CO .15 .04
396 Aurelio Rodriguez CO .15 .04
397 Steve Avery .50 .15
398 Tommy Greene .15 .04
399 Bill Laskey .15 .04
400 Paul Marak .15 .04
401 Andy Nezelek .15 .04
402 Ed Olwine .15 .04
403 Dale Polley .15 .04
404 Rusty Richards .15 .04
405 Brian Snyder .15 .04
406 Jimmy Kremers .15 .04
407 John Mizerock .15 .04
408 John Alva .15 .04
409 Francisco Cabrera .15 .04
410 Bruce Crabbe .15 .04
411 Drew Denson .15 .04
412 Ken Dowell .15 .04
413 Ed Whited .15 .04
414 Geronimo Berroa .15 .04
415 Dennis Hood .15 .04
416 Brian R. Hunter .15 .04
417 Barry Jones .15 .04
418 David Justice 1.50 .45
419 Jim Beauchamp MG .15 .04
420 John Grubb CO .15 .04
421 Leo Mazzone CO .15 .04
422 Sonny Jackson CO .15 .04
423 Rick Berg CO .15 .04
424 Steve Bast .15 .04
425 Tom Bolton .15 .04
426 Steve Curry .15 .04
427 Mike Dalton .15 .04
428 Jeff Gray .15 .04
429 Daryl Irvine .15 .04
430 Joe Johnson .15 .04
431 John Leister .15 .04
432 Mike Rochford .15 .04
433 Larry Shikles .15 .04
434 Tito Stewart .15 .04
435 John Trautwein .15 .04
436 John Flaherty .15 .04
437 John Marzano .15 .04
438 Gary Tremblay .15 .04
439 Scott Cooper .15 .04
440 Angel Gonzalez .15 .04
441 Tim Naehring .15 .04
442 Jim Pankovits .15 .04
443 Mo Vaughn 1.50 .45
444 Rick Lancellotti .15 .04
445 Mickey Pina .15 .04
446 Phil Plantier .15 .04
447 Jeff Stone .15 .04
448 Scott Wade .15 .04
449 Ed Nottle MG .15 .04
450 Mark Meleski CO .15 .04
451 Lee Stange CO .15 .04
452 Jay Aldrich .15 .04
453 Jose Bautista .15 .04
454 Eric Bell .15 .04
455 Dan Boone .15 .04
456 Ben McDonald .15 .04
457 John Mitchell .15 .04
458 Curt Schilling 1.50 .45
459 Mike Smith .15 .04
460 Rob Woodward .15 .04
461 Chris Hoiles .15 .04
462 Darrell Miller .15 .04
463 Jack Tackett .15 .04
464 Juan Bell .15 .04
465 Tim Dulin .15 .04
466 Leo Gomez .15 .04
467 Jeff McKnight .15 .04
468 Shane Turner .15 .04
469 Greg Walker .15 .04
470 Tony Chance .15 .04
471 Victor Hithe .15 .04
472 Donell Nixon .15 .04
473 Chris Padget .15 .04
474 Pete Stanicek .15 .04
475 Mike Linskey .15 .04
476 Joaquin Contreras .15 .04
477 Greg Biagini .15 .04
478 Dick Bosman .15 .04
479 Paul Blair CO .15 .04
480 Stan Belinda .15 .04
481 Gordon Dillard .15 .04
482 Mark Huismann .15 .04
483 Hugh Kemp .15 .04
484 Scott Medvin .15 .04
485 Vincente Palacios .15 .04
486 Rick Reed .50 .15
487 Mark Ross .15 .04
488 Dorn Taylor .15 .04
489 Mike York .15 .04
490 Dann Bilardello .15 .04
491 Tom Prince .15 .04
492 Danny Sheaffer .15 .04
493 Kevin Burdick .15 .04
494 Steve Kiefer .15 .04
495 Orlando Merced .15 .04
496 Armando Moreno .15 .04
497 Jeff Richardson .15 .04
498 Mark Ryal .15 .04
499 Tommy Shields .15 .04
500 Steve Carter .15 .04
501 Wes Chamberlain .15 .04
502 Jeff Cook .15 .04
503 Scott Little .15 .04
504 Terry Collins MG .15 .04
505 Jackie Brown CO .15 .04
506 Steve Henderson CO .15 .04
507 Gibson Alba .15 .04
508 Scott Arnold .15 .04
509 Cris Carpenter .15 .04
510 Stan Clarke .15 .04
511 Mark Grater .15 .04
512 Howard Hilton .15 .04
513 Mike Hinkle .15 .04
514 Omar Olivares .15 .04
515 Dave Osteen .15 .04
516 Mike Perez .15 .04
517 Tim Sherrill .15 .04
518 Scott Nichols .15 .04
519 Ray Stephens .15 .04
520 Pat Austin .15 .04
521 Red Brewer .15 .04
522 Todd Crosby .15 .04
523 Bien Figueroa .15 .04
524 Julian Martinez .15 .04
525 Jesus Mendez .15 .04
526 Geronimo Pena .15 .04
527 Craig Wilson .15 .04
528 Dennis Carter .15 .04
529 Bernard Gilkey .50 .15
530 Ray Lankford .50 .15
531 Mauricio Nunez .15 .04
532 Roy Silver .15 .04
533 Gaylen Pitts MG .15 .04
534 Mark Riggins CO .15 .04
535 Neil Allen .15 .04
536 Keith Brown .15 .04
537 Chris Hammond .15 .04
538 Milton Hill .15 .04
539 Rodney Imes .15 .04
540 Rob Lopez .15 .04
541 Charlie Mitchell .15 .04
542 Robert Moore .15 .04
543 Rosario Rodriguez .15 .04
544 Scott Scudder .15 .04
545 Bob Sebra .15 .04
546 Joey Vierra .15 .04
547 Tony DeFrancesco .15 .04
548 Terry McGriff .15 .04
549 Donnie Scott .15 .04
550 Reggie Jefferson .15 .04
551 Brian Lane .15 .04
552 Chris Lombardozzi .15 .04
553 Paul Noce .15 .04
554 Kevin Pearson .15 .04
555 Eddie Tanner .15 .04
556 Skeeter Barnes .15 .04
557 Leo Garcia .15 .04
558 Chris Jones .15 .04
559 Keith Lockhart .15 .04
560 Darryl Motley .15 .04
561 Pete MacKanin MG .15 .04
562 Ray Rippelmeyer CO .15 .04
563 Scott Anderson .15 .04
564 Esteban Beltre .15 .04
565 Travis Chambers .15 .04
566 Randy Braun .15 .04
567 Danny Clay .15 .04
568 Eric Bullock .15 .04
569 Jim Davins .15 .04
570 Jose Castro .15 .04
571 Eddie Dixon .15 .04
572 Romy Cucjen .15 .04
573 Howard Farmer .15 .04
574 Jerry Goff .15 .04
575 Steve Fireovid .15 .04
576 Otis Green .15 .04
577 Dan Gakeler .15 .04
578 Mel Houston .15 .04
579 Balvino Galvez .15 .04
580 Dwight Lowry .15 .04
581 Dale Mohorcic .15 .04
582 Quinn Mack .15 .04
583 Chris Marchok .15 .04
584 Edwin Marquez .15 .04
585 Mel Rojas .15 .04
586 Johnny Paredes .15 .04
587 Rich Thompson .15 .04
588 German Rivera .15 .04
589 James Steels .15 .04
590 Tim Johnson MG .15 .04
591 Gomer Hodge CO .15 .04
592 Joe Kerrigan CO .15 .04
593 Ray Chadwick .15 .04
594 Dera Clark .15 .04
595 Luis Encarnacion .15 .04
596 Tony Ferreira .15 .04
597 Pete Filson .15 .04
598 Jim LeMasters .15 .04
599 Mike Magnante .15 .04
600 Mike Tresemer .15 .04
601 Mel Stottlemyre Jr. .15 .04
602 Bill Wilkinson .15 .04
603 Kevin Burrell .15 .04
604 Tim Spehr .15 .04
605 Luis de los Santos .15 .04
606 Bob Hamelin .15 .04
607 Bobby Meacham .15 .04
608 Russ Morman .15 .04
609 Thad Reece .15 .04
610 Paul Zuvella .15 .04
611 Mike Loggins .15 .04
612 Chito Martinez .15 .04
613 Harvey Pulliam .15 .04
614 Jeff Schulz .15 .04
615 Sal Rende MG .15 .04
616 Tom Poquette CO .15 .04
617 Rich Dubee CO .15 .04
618 Kevin Blankenship .15 .04
619 Shawn Boskie .15 .04
620 Mark Bowden .15 .04
621 Greg Kallevig .15 .04
622 Dave Masters .15 .04
623 Steve Parker .15 .04
624 Dave Pavlas .15 .04
625 Laddie Renfroe .15 .04
626 Paul Wilmet .15 .04
627 Jeff Hearron .15 .04
628 Erik Pappas .15 .04
629 Hector Villanueva .15 .04
630 Bob Bafia .15 .04
631 Brian Guinn .15 .04
632 Jeff Small .15 .04
633 Greg Smith .15 .04
634 Glenn Sullivan .15 .04
635 Bill Wrona .15 .04
636 Brad Bierley .15 .04
637 Cedric Landrum .15 .04
638 Derrick May .15 .04
639 Gary Varsho .15 .04
640 Jim Essian MG .15 .04
641 Don August .15 .04
642 Mike Birkbeck .15 .04
643 Mike Capel .15 .04
644 Logan Easley .15 .04
645 Tom Edens .15 .04
646 Don Gordon .15 .04
647 Chuck McGrath .15 .04
648 Jeff Peterek .15 .04
649 Dennis Powell .15 .04
650 Ed Puig .15 .04
651 Al Sadler .15 .04
652 Tim Watkins .15 .04
653 Tim McIntosh .15 .04
654 Tim Torricelli .15 .04
655 George Canale .15 .04
656 Mark Higgins .15 .04
657 Frank Mattox .15 .04
658 Joe Mitchell .15 .04
659 Joe Redfield .15 .04
660 D.L. Smith .15 .04
661 Joe Xavier .15 .04
662 Ruben Escalera .15 .04
663 Mario Monico .15 .04
664 Billy Moore .15 .04
665 Darryel Walters .15 .04
666 Dave Machemer MG .15 .04
667 Jackson Todd CO .15 .04
668 Gerald Alexander .15 .04
669 Brad Arnsberg .15 .04
670 John Barfield .15 .04
671 Jack Hardy .15 .04
672 Ray Hayward .15 .04
673 John Hoover .15 .04
674 Steve Lankard .15 .04
675 David Lynch .15 .04
676 Craig McMurtry .15 .04
677 David Miller .15 .04
678 Mark Petkovsek .15 .04
679 Jeff Satzinger .15 .04
680 Mike Berger .15 .04
681 Dave Engle .15 .04
682 John Russell .15 .04
683 Pat Dodson .15 .04
684 Pat Garman .15 .04
685 Gary Green .15 .04
686 Brian House .15 .04
687 Dean Palmer .50 .15
688 Ron Washington .15 .04
689 Nick Capra .15 .04
690 Juan Gonzalez 4.00 1.20
691 Gar Millay .15 .04
692 Kevin Reimer .15 .04
693 Bernie Tatis .15 .04
694 Checklist .15 .04
695 Checklist .15 .04
696 Checklist .15 .04
697 Checklist .15 .04
698 Checklist .15 .04
699 Checklist .15 .04
700 Checklist .15 .04

1991 Classic Draft Picks

The premier edition of the 1991 Classic Draft Picks set contains 50 standard-size cards, plus a bonus card featuring Frankie Rodriguez. The production run was distributed between 330,000 hobby sets, 165,000 non-hobby sets, and 1,500 test sets. Each set includes a certificate of limited edition with a unique set number. This set includes Brien Taylor, the first pick of the '91 draft. The Frankie Rodriguez bonus card was only included in hobby sets. Cards were checklisted by Classic based on draft order. An early Manny Ramirez card is featured in this set.

	Nm-Mt	Ex-Mt
COMP.FACT.SET (50)	5.00	1.50
1 Brien Taylor	.40	.12
2 Mike Kelly	.15	.04
3 David McCarty	.40	.12
4 Dmitri Young	.40	.12
5 Joe Vitiello	.15	.04
6 Mark Smith	.15	.04
7 Tyler Green	.15	.04
8 Shawn Estes	.40	.12
9 Doug Glanville	.40	.12
10 Manny Ramirez	1.50	.45
11 Cliff Floyd	.75	.23
12 Tyrone Hill	.15	.04
13 Eduardo Perez	.15	.04

Card	Nm-Mt	Ex-Mt
14 Al Shirley	.15	.04
15 Benji Gil	.15	.04
16 Pokey Reese	.40	.12
17 Allen Watson	.15	.04
18 Brian Barber	.15	.04
19 Aaron Sele	.40	.12
20 John Farrell	.15	.04
21 Scott Ruffcorn	.15	.04
22 Brent Gates	.15	.04
23 Scott Stahoviak	.15	.04
24 Tom McKinnon	.15	.04
25 Shawn Livsey	.15	.04
26 Jason Pruitt	.15	.04
27 Greg Anthony	.15	.04
28 Justin Thompson	.15	.04
29 Steve Whitaker	.15	.04
30 Jorge Fabregas	.15	.04
31 Jeff Ware	.15	.04
32 Bobby Jones	.40	.12
33 J.J. Johnson	.15	.04
34 Mike Rossiter	.15	.04
35 Dan Cholowsky	.15	.04
36 Jimmy Gonzalez	.15	.04
37 Trevor Miller	.15	.04
38 Scott Hatteberg	.40	.12
39 Mike Groppuso	.15	.04
40 Ryan Long	.15	.04
41 Eddie Williams	.15	.04
42 Mike Durant	.15	.04
43 Buck McNabb	.15	.04
44 Jimmy Lewis	.15	.04
45 Eddie Ramos	.15	.04
46 Terry Horn	.15	.04
47 Jon Barnes	.15	.04
48 Shawn Curran	.15	.04
49 Tommy Adams	.15	.04
50 Trevor Mallory	.15	.04
NNO Frank Rodriguez BC	.15	.04

1991 Classic/Best

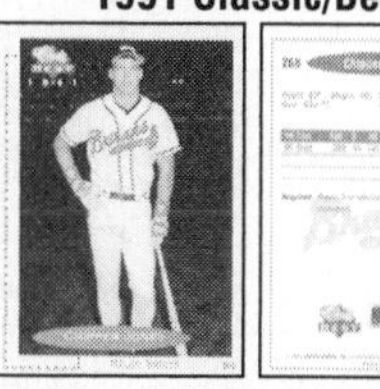

The 1991 Classic/Best baseball card set contains 450 standard-size cards. The cards were sold in factory sets and 12-card wax packs. A total of 2,100 autographed Mike Schmidt cards were randomly inserted in the wax packs only. Early cards of Carlos Delgado, Chipper Jones, Pedro Martinez and Ivan Rodriguez are featured in this set.

Card	Nm-Mt	Ex-Mt
COMP.FACT.SET (450)	20.00	6.00
COMPLETE SET (396)	10.00	3.00
1 Mike Schmidt	.50	.15
2 Kevin Roberson	.15	.04
3 Paul Rodgers	.15	.04
4 Marc Newfield	.15	.04
5 Marc Ronan	.15	.04
6 Marty Willis	.15	.04
7 Jason Hardtke	.15	.04
8 Matt Mieske	.15	.04
9 Brian Johnson	.15	.04
10 Alex Arias	.15	.04
11 Eric Young	.40	.12
12 Donald Harris	.15	.04
13 Bruce Chick	.15	.04
14 Brian Williams	.15	.04
15 Brian Cornelius	.15	.04
16 Brian Giles	1.00	.30
17 Brad Ausmus	.40	.12
18 Ivan Cruz	.15	.04
19 Kevin Flora	.15	.04
20 Robie Katzaroff	.15	.04
21 Randy Knorr	.15	.04
22 Micky Henson	.15	.04
23 Chris Haney	.15	.04
24 Jeff Mutis	.15	.04
25 Barry Winford	.15	.04
26 Ray Giannelli	.15	.04
27 Donovan Osborne	.15	.04
28 Ruben Gonzalez	.15	.04
29 Howard Battle	.15	.04
30 Greg O'Halloran	.15	.04
31 Ben Vanryn	.15	.04
32 Rick Huisman	.15	.04
33 Jose Valentin	.40	.12
34 Jose Zambrano	.15	.04
35 John Gross	.15	.04
36 Jessie Hollins	.15	.04
37 Kevin Scott	.15	.04
38 Kerwin Moore	.15	.04
39 Eric Albright	.15	.04
40 Ernesto Rodriguez	.15	.04
41 Reggie Sanders	.40	.12
42 Henry Werland	.15	.04
43 Boo Moore	.15	.04
44 Mike Messerly	.15	.04
45 Mike Lansing	.40	.12
46 Mike Gardella	.15	.04
47 Mo Sanford	.15	.04
48 Tavo Alvarez	.15	.04
49 Nick Davis	.15	.04
50 Charlie Hillemann	.15	.04
51 Jeff Darwin	.15	.04
52 Reid Cornelius	.15	.04
53 Matt Rambo	.15	.04
54 Rich Batchelor	.15	.04
55 Ricky Gutierrez	.15	.04
56 Rod Bolton	.15	.04
57 Pat Bryant	.15	.04
58 Hugh Walker	.15	.04
59 Keith Schmidt	.15	.04
60 Cesar Morillo	.15	.04
61 Gabe White	.15	.04
62 Javy Lopez UER	1.00	.30
63 Carlos Delgado	1.50	.45
64 John Johnstone	.15	.04
65 Andres Berumen	.15	.04
66 Brian Kowitz	.15	.04
67 Shane Reynolds	.40	.12
68 Jeromy Burnitz	.40	.12
69 Scott Bryant	.15	.04
70 Jason McFarlin	.15	.04
71 John Conner	.15	.04
72 Garrett Jenkins	.15	.04
73 Greg Kobza	.15	.04
74 Mark Swope	.15	.04
75 Jeronne Williams	.15	.04
76 Jeff Bonner	.15	.04
77 Jermaine Swinton	.15	.04
78 John Cohen	.15	.04
79 Johnny Calzado	.15	.04
80 Juan Andujar	.15	.04
81 Paul Ellis	.15	.04
82 Paul Gonzalez	.15	.04
83 Scott Taylor	.15	.04
84 Stan Spencer	.15	.04
85 Steve Martin	.15	.04
86 Scott Cepicky	.15	.04
87 Max Aleys	.15	.04
88 Michael Brown	.15	.04
89 Jim Waggoner	.15	.04
90 Mickey Rivers Jr.	.15	.04
91 Nate Cromwell	.15	.04
92 Carlos Perez	.15	.04
93 Matt Brown	.15	.04
94 Jose Hernandez	.40	.12
95 Johnny Ruffin	.15	.04
96 Kevin Jordan	.15	.04
97 Manny Alexander	.15	.04
98 Tony Longmire	.15	.04
99 Lonell Roberts	.15	.04
100 Doug Lindsey	.15	.04
101 Al Harley	.15	.04
102 Jerrey Thurston	.15	.04
103 Mike Williams	.15	.04
104 David Bell	.40	.12
105 Greg Johnson	.15	.04
106 Roger Salkeld	.15	.04
107 Mike Milchin	.15	.04
108 Jeff Kent	1.00	.30
109 Tim Stargell	.15	.04
110 Miah Bradbury	.15	.04
111 Paul Fletcher	.15	.04
112 Steve Rolen	.15	.04
113 Tony Spires	.15	.04
114 Kevin Tolar	.15	.04
115 Kevin Dattola	.15	.04
116 Sherman Obando	.15	.04
117 Sean Ryan	.15	.04
118 Carlos Mota	.15	.04
119 Steve Karsay	.40	.12
120 Kelly Lifgren	.15	.04
121 Damion Easley	.40	.12
122 Fred Russell	.15	.04
123 Freddie Davis Jr.	.15	.04
124 Dave Zancanaro	.15	.04
125 Jeff Jackson	.15	.04
126 Steve Pegues	.15	.04
127 Gerald Williams	.15	.04
128 Eric Helfand	.15	.04
129 Gary Painter	.15	.04
130 Colin Ryan	.15	.04
131 Randy Brown	.15	.04
132 Andy Fox	.15	.04
133 Mike Ogliaruso	.15	.04
134 Matt Franco	.15	.04
135 Willie Ansley	.15	.04
136 Ivan Rodriguez	2.00	.60
137 Anthony Lewis	.15	.04
138 Bill Wertz	.15	.04
139 Tom Kinney	.15	.04
140 Brad Hassinger	.15	.04
141 Elliot Gray	.15	.04
142 Clemente Alvarez	.15	.04
143 Mike Hankins	.15	.04
144 Jim Haller	.15	.04
145 Manny Martinez	.15	.04
146 Nilson Rolbedo	.15	.04
147 Rex De La Nuez	.15	.04
148 Steve Bethea	.15	.04
149 Oscar Munoz	.15	.04
150 Sam Militello	.15	.04
151 Phil Hiatt	.15	.04
152 Alberto DeLos Santos	.15	.04
153 Darrell Sherman	.15	.04
154 Henry Mercedes	.15	.04
155 David Holdridge	.15	.04
156 Sean Ross	.15	.04
157 Brandon Wilson	.15	.04
158 William Pennyfeather	.15	.04
159 Derek Parks	.15	.04
160 Troy O'Leary	.15	.04
161 Genaro Capusano	.15	.04
162 Robbie Beckett	.15	.04
163 Chris Burton	.15	.04
164 Jeff Williams	.15	.04
165 John Massarelli	.15	.04
166 John Kelly	.15	.04
167 Jim Wiley	.15	.04
168 Mark Mitchelson	.15	.04
169 Jeff McNeely	.15	.04
170 Keith Kimberlin	.15	.04
171 Mike DeKneef	.15	.04
172 Rusty Greer	.40	.12
173 Pete Castellano	.15	.04
174 Paul Torres	.15	.04
175 Rod McCall	.15	.04
176 Jim Bullinger	.15	.04
177 Brian Champion	.15	.04
178 Greg Hunter	.15	.04
179 Luis Galindez	.15	.04
180 Rodney Eldridge	.15	.04
181 Rudy Pemberton	.15	.04
182 Russ Davis	.40	.12
183 Cristobal Colon	.15	.04
184 Scott Bream	.15	.04
185 Tim Nedin	.15	.04
186 Joe Ausanio	.15	.04
187 Shannon Withem	.15	.04
188 Mike Oquist	.15	.04
189 Pete Young	.15	.04
190 Paul Carey	.15	.04
191 Chris Gies	.15	.04
192 Gar Finnvold	.15	.04
193 Greg Martin	.15	.04
194 Oreste Marrero	.15	.04
195 Jim Thome	2.00	.60
196 Bill Ostermeyer	.15	.04
197 David Hulse	.15	.04
198 Damon Buford	.15	.04
199 Jonathan Hurst	.15	.04
200 Rich Tunison	.15	.04
201 Tom Nevers	.15	.04
202 Tracy Sanders	.15	.04
203 Troy Buckley	.15	.04
204 Todd Guggiana	.15	.04
205 Tim Laker	.15	.04
206 Dean Locklear	.15	.04
207 Lee Tinsley	.15	.04
208 Jose Velez	.15	.04
209 Greg Zaun	.15	.04
210 Billy Ashley	.15	.04
211 Gary Caraballo	.15	.04
212 Kiki Jones	.15	.04
213 Dave Wrona	.15	.04
214 Michael Carter	.15	.04
215 Leon Glenn Jr.	.15	.04
216 Glenn Sutko	.15	.04
217 Pat Howell	.15	.04
218 Austin Manahan	.15	.04
219 Jon Jenkins	.15	.04
220 Brook Fordyce	.15	.04
221 Kevin Rogers	.15	.04
222 David Allen	.15	.04
223 Kurt Archer	.15	.04
224 Keith Mitchell	.15	.04
225 Bruce Schreiber	.15	.04
226 Greg Blosser	.15	.04
227 Dave Nilsson	.40	.12
228 Fred Cooley	.15	.04
229 Marc Lipson	.15	.04
230 Jay Gainer	.15	.04
231 Sean Cheetham	.15	.04
232 Tim Howard	.15	.04
233 Steve Hosey	.15	.04
234 Javier Ocasio	.15	.04
235 Ricky Rhodes	.15	.04
236 Mark Griffin	.15	.04
237 Scott Shockey	.15	.04
238 T.R. Lewis	.15	.04
239 Kevin Young	.40	.12
240 Robb Nen	.40	.12
241 Steve Dunn	.15	.04
242 Tommy Taylor	.15	.04
243 Keith Valrie	.15	.04
244 Mateo Ozuna	.15	.04
245 Scott Bullett	.15	.04
246 Anthony Brown	.15	.04
247 Phil Leftwich	.15	.04
248 Cliff Garrett	.15	.04
249 Wade Fyock	.15	.04
250 Shayne Rea	.15	.04
251 Royce Clayton	.40	.12
252 Martin Martinez	.15	.04
253 Dave Patterson	.15	.04
254 Robert Fitzpatrick	.15	.04
255 John Jackson	.15	.04
256 Enoch Simmons	.15	.04
257 Dave Proctor	.15	.04
258 Garret Anderson	1.00	.30
259 Mark Dalesandro	.15	.04
260 Ken Edenfield	.15	.04
261 Tom Raffo	.15	.04
262 Tim Cecil	.15	.04
263 Bobby Magallanes	.15	.04
264 Vince Castaldo	.15	.04
265 Terry Burrows	.15	.04
266 Victor Madrigal	.15	.04
267 Tyler Houston	.15	.04
268 Chipper Jones	2.00	.60
269 Terry Bradshaw	.15	.04
270 Jalal Leach	.15	.04
271 Jose Ventura	.15	.04
272 Derek Lee	.15	.04
273 Derek Reid	.15	.04
274 David Wilson	.15	.04
275 Pat Rapp	.15	.04
276 John Roper	.15	.04
277 Rogelio Nunez	.15	.04
278 Fred White	.15	.04
279 J.T. Snow	.40	.12
280 Pedro Astacio	.40	.12
281 Carey Thomas	.15	.04
282 Chris Johnson	.15	.04
283 Ignacio Duran	.15	.04
284 Dave Fleming	.15	.04
285 Wilson Alvarez	.15	.04
286 Eric Booker	.15	.04
287 John Ericks	.15	.04
288 Don Peters	.15	.04
289 Ed Ferm	.15	.04
290 Mike Lieberthal	.40	.12
291 John Jaha	.40	.12
292 Bryan Baar	.15	.04
293 Archie Corbin	.15	.04
294 Kevin Tatar	.15	.04
295 Shea Wardwell	.15	.04
296 Hipolito Pichardo	.15	.04
297 Curtis Leskanic	.15	.04
298 Sam August	.15	.04
299 Tim Pugh	.15	.04
300 Mike Huyler	.15	.04
301 Mark Parnell	.15	.04
302 Jeff Juden	.15	.04
303 Carl Sullivan	.15	.04
304 Tyrone Kingwood	.15	.04
305 Glenn Carter	.15	.04
306 Tom Fischer	.15	.04
307 Braulio Castillo	.15	.04
308 Bob McCreary	.15	.04
309 Ty Kovach	.15	.04
310 Troy Salvior	.15	.04
311 Mike Weimerskirch	.15	.04
312 Christopher Hatcher	.15	.04
313 Bryan Smith	.15	.04
314 John Patterson	.15	.04
315 Scooter Tucker	.15	.04
316 Ray Callari	.15	.04
317 Mike Moberg	.15	.04
318 Midre Cummings	.15	.04
319 Todd Ritchie	.40	.12
320 Eric Christopherson	.15	.04
321 Adam Hyzdu	.15	.04
322 Andres Duncan	.15	.04
323 Mike Myers	.15	.04
324 Salomon Torres	.15	.04
325 Tony Gilmore	.15	.04
326 Walter Trice	.15	.04
327 Tom Redington	.15	.04
328 Terry Taylor	.15	.04
329 Tim Salmon	1.00	.30
330 Dan Masteller	.15	.04
331 Mark Wohlers	.15	.04
332 Willie Smith	.15	.04
333 Todd Jones	.40	.12
334 Alan Zinter	.15	.04
335 Arthur Rhodes	.40	.12
336 Toby Borland	.15	.04
337 Shawn Whalen	.15	.04
338 Scott Sanders	.15	.04
339 Bill Meury	.15	.04
340 Amadoz Arias	.15	.04
341 Denny Hoppe	.15	.04
342 Dave Telgheder	.15	.04
343 Paul Bruno	.15	.04
344 Paul Russo	.15	.04
345 Rich Becker	.15	.04
346 Steve Vondran	.15	.04
347 Rich Langford	.15	.04
348 Ron Lockett	.15	.04
349 Sam Taylor	.15	.04
350 Willie Greene	.15	.04
351 Tom Houk	.15	.04
352 Lance Painter	.15	.04
353 Dan Wilson	.40	.12
354 John Keuhl	.15	.04
355 Pedro Martinez	2.00	.60
356 John Byington	.15	.04
357 Scott Freeman	.15	.04
358 Bo Dodson	.15	.04
359 Julian Vasquez	.15	.04
360 Rondell White	.40	.12
361 Aaron Small	.15	.04
362 Doug Fitzer	.15	.04
363 Billy White	.15	.04
364 Jeff Tuss	.15	.04
365 Jeff Barry	.15	.04
366 Craig Pueschner	.15	.04
367 Julio Bruno	.15	.04
368 Jamie Dismuke	.15	.04
369 K.C. Gillum	.15	.04
370 Jason Klonoski	.15	.04
371 Tim Persing	.15	.04
372 Mark Borcherding	.15	.04
373 Larry Luebbers	.15	.04
374 Carlos Fermin	.15	.04
375 Charlie Rogers	.15	.04
376 Ramon Caraballo	.15	.04
377 Orlando Miller	.15	.04
378 Joey James	.15	.04
379 Dan Rogers	.15	.04
380 Jon Shave	.15	.04
381 Frank Bolick	.15	.04
382 Frank Seminara	.15	.04
383 Mel Wearing Jr.	.15	.04
384 Zak Shinall	.15	.04
385 Sterling Hitchcock	.40	.12
386 Todd Van Poppel	.40	.12
387 D.J. Dozier	.15	.04
388 Ryan Klesko	1.00	.30
389 Tim Costo	.15	.04
390 Brad Pennington	.15	.04
391 Checklist	.15	.04
392 Checklist	.15	.04
393 Checklist	.15	.04
394 Checklist	.15	.04
395 Checklist	.15	.04
396 Checklist	.15	.04
397 Frank Rodriquez	.15	.04
398 Frank Jacobs	.15	.04
399 Mike Kelly	.15	.04
400 David McCarty	.40	.12
401 Scott Stahoviak	.15	.04
402 Doug Glanville	.40	.12
403 Curt Krippner	.15	.04
404 Joe Vitiello	.15	.04
405 Justin Thompson	.15	.04
406 Trevor Miller	.15	.04
407 Tarrick Brock	.15	.04
408 Eddie Williams	.15	.04
409 Scott Ruffcorn	.15	.04
410 Chris Durkin	.15	.04
411 Jim Lewis	.15	.04
412 Pokey Reese	.40	.12
413 Toby Rumfield	.15	.04
414 Brent Gates	.15	.04
415 Mike Neill	.15	.04
416 Tyler Green	.15	.04
417 Ron Allen	.15	.04
418 Larry Thomas Jr.	.15	.04
419 Chris Weinke	.40	.12
420 Matt Brewer	.15	.04
421 Dax Jones	.15	.04
422 Jon Farrell	.15	.04
423 Dan Jones	.15	.04
424 Eduardo Perez	.15	.04
425 Rodney Pedraza	.15	.04
426 Tom McKinnon	.15	.04
427 Al Watson	.15	.04
428 Herbert Perry	.40	.12
429 Shawn Estes	.40	.12
430 Tommy Adams	.15	.04
431 Mike Grace	.15	.04
432 Tyson Godfrey	.15	.04
433 Andy Hartung	.15	.04
434 Shawn Livsey	.15	.04
435 Earl Cunningham	.15	.04
436 Scott Lydy	.15	.04
437 Aaron Sele	.40	.12
438 Tim Costo	.15	.04
439 Tanyon Sturtze	.15	.04
440 Ed Ramos	.15	.04
441 Buck McNabb	.15	.04
442 Scott Hatteberg	.40	.12
443 Brian Barber	.15	.04
444 Julian Heredia	.15	.04
445 Chris Pritchett	.15	.04
446 Bubba Smith	.15	.04
447 Shawn Purdy	.15	.04
448 Jeff Borski	.15	.04
449 Jamie Gonzalez	.15	.04
450 Checklist (397-450)	.15	.04
AU1 M.Schmidt AU/2100	40.00	12.00

1991 Classic/Best Gold Bonus

The 1991 Classic/Best Gold Bonus card set contains 20 standard-size cards. These cards

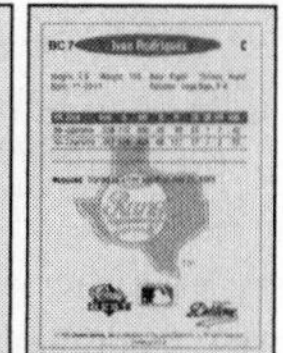

were inserted at a rate of one per jumbo pack. The card design is the same as the 1991 Classic/Best regular issued set except for the gold foil stamp on the player's name.

Card	Nm-Mt	Ex-Mt
COMPLETE SET (20)	10.00	3.00
BC1 Mike Schmidt	1.00	.30
BC2 Marc Newfield	.25	.07
BC3 Matt Mieske	.25	.07
BC4 Reggie Sanders	.50	.15
BC5 Jeromy Burnitz	.50	.15
BC6 Todd Van Poppel	.50	.15
BC7 Ivan Rodriguez	2.00	.60
BC8 Sam Militello	.25	.07
BC9 Jim Thome	2.00	.60
BC10 Brook Fordyce	.25	.07
BC11 Dave Nilsson	.50	.15
BC12 Royce Clayton	.50	.15
BC13 Mark Wohlers	.25	.07
BC14 Arthur Rhodes	.50	.15
BC15 Ryan Klesko	1.00	.30
BC16 Mike Kelly	.25	.07
BC17 Frank Rodriguez	.25	.07
BC18 David McCarty	.50	.15
BC19 Tyler Green	.25	.07
BC20 Eduardo Perez	.25	.07

1991 Front Row Draft Picks

This 50-card premier edition set includes 27 of the top 40 eligible players from the 1991 Baseball Draft. The cards measure the standard size and 240,000 sets were produced. Each set contains a numbered card registering the set and one card from a limited Draft Pick subset as a bonus card. In exchange for returning the bonus card, the collector received card number 50 (Benji Gil), a mini-update set (51-54; sent to the first 120,000 respondents), and one card from a five-card Frankie Rodriguez bonus set. An early Manny Ramirez card is featured in this set.

Card	Nm-Mt	Ex-Mt
COMP.FACT.SET (50)	3.00	.90
COMMON CARD (1-49)	.15	.04
COMMON EXCH (50-54)	.50	.15
1 Frank Rodriguez	.15	.04
2 Aaron Sele	.40	.12
3 Chad Schoenvogel	.15	.04
4 Scott Ruffcorn	.15	.04
5 Dan Cholowsky	.15	.04
6 Gene Schall	.15	.04
7 Trever Miller	.15	.04
8 Chris Durkin	.15	.04
9 Mike Neill	.15	.04
10 Kevin Stocker	.15	.04
11 Bobby Jones	.40	.12
12 Jon Farrell	.15	.04
13 Ron Allen	.15	.04
14 Mike Rossiter	.15	.04
15 Scott Hatteberg	.40	.12
16 Rod Pedraza	.15	.04
17 Mike Durant	.15	.04
18 Ryan Long	.15	.04
19 Greg Anthony	.15	.04
20 Jon Barnes	.15	.04
21 Brian Barber	.15	.04
22 Brent Gates	.15	.04
23 Pokey Reese	.40	.12
24 Terry Horn	.15	.04
25 Scott Stahoviak	.15	.04
26 Jason Pruitt	.15	.04
27 Shawn Curran	.15	.04
28 Jimmy Lewis	.15	.04
29 Alex Ochoa	.40	.12
30 Joe DeBerry	.15	.04
31 Justin Thompson	.15	.04
32 Jimmy Gonzalez	.15	.04
33 Edward Ramos	.15	.04
34 Tyler Green	.15	.04
35 Toby Rumfield	.15	.04
36 Dave Doorneweerd	.15	.04
37 Jeff Hostetler	.15	.04
38 Shawn Livsey	.15	.04
39 Mike Groppuso	.15	.04
40 Steve Whitaker	.15	.04
41 Tom McKinnon	.15	.04
42 Buck McNabb	.15	.04
43 Al Shirley	.15	.04
44 Allan Watson	.15	.04
45 Bill Bliss	.15	.04
46 Todd Hollandsworth	.40	.12
47 Manny Ramirez	1.50	.45
48 J.J. Johnson	.15	.04
49 Cliff Floyd	.75	.23
50 Benji Gil EXCH	.50	.15
51 Herbert Perry EXCH	.60	.18
52 Tarrik Brock EXCH	.50	.15
53 Trevor Mallory EXCH	.50	.15
54 Chris Pritchett EXCH	.50	.15

1991 Front Row Draft Picks Gold

This is a parallel to the regular 1991 Front Row Draft Pick set

Nm-Mt Ex-Mt
*GOLD: 1.5X TO 4X VALUE

1991 Front Row Draft Picks Silver

This is also a parallel to the regular Front Row Draft Pick set.

Nm-Mt Ex-Mt
*SILVER: .75X TO 2X BASIC CARDS ..

1991 Front Row Draft Picks Autographs

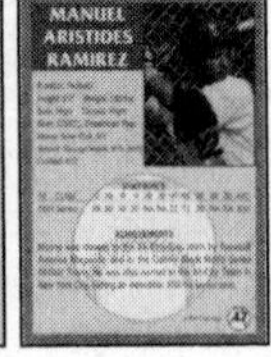

These cards feature autographs of some of the leading players in the Front Row set.

Nm-Mt Ex-Mt
NNO Cliff Floyd /1500 10.00 3.00
NNO Manny Ramirez/1900 20.00 6.00

1991 Front Row Frankie Rodriguez

Nm-Mt Ex-Mt
COMPLETE SET (4) 2.00 .60
COMMON PLAYER (1-4) .50 .15

1991 Line Drive Previews

This six-card standard-size set was issued as a preview of the 1991 Line Drive Pre-Rookie set. The cards have glossy color action player photos bordered in white. The player's name appears in either red or blue lettering at the card top, with team logo in the upper right corner. The team name and position are given below the picture. The backs are printed in black on either blue and white or red and white, and feature biography and statistics.

Nm-Mt Ex-Mt
COMPLETE SET (6) 5.00 1.50
47 Greg Tubbs .50 .15
79 Tim Costo .50 .15
167 Reggie Sanders .75 .23
221 Rick Wilkins .50 .15
422 Hugh Walker .50 .15
573 Anthony Young .50 .15

1991 Line Drive AA

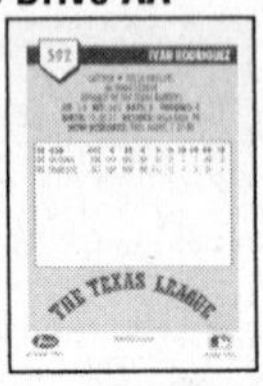

This 650-card standard-size set has glossy color action player photos bordered in white. Early cards of Jeff Kent, Ivan Rodriguez and Jim Thome are featured in this set.

Nm-Mt Ex-Mt
COMPLETE SET (650) 25.00 7.50
1 Andy Cook .15 .04
2 Russ Davis .50 .15
3 Bobby DeJardin .15 .04
4 Mike Draper .15 .04
5 Victor Garcia .15 .04
6 Mike Gardella .15 .04
7 Cullen Hartzog .15 .04
8 Jay Knoblauh .15 .04
9 Billy Masse .15 .04
10 Jeff Livesey .15 .04
11 Edward Martel .15 .04
12 Vince Phillips .15 .04
13 Tom Popplewell .15 .04
14 Jerry Rub .15 .04
15 Dave Silvestri .15 .04
16 Tom Newell .15 .04
17 Willie Smith .15 .04
18 J.T. Snow .50 .15
19 Don Stanford .15 .04
20 Larry Stanford .15 .04
21 John Toale .15 .04
22 Hector Vargas .15 .04
23 Gerald Williams .15 .04
24 Dan Radison MGR .15 .04
25 Dave Jorn CO .15 .04
Bob Mariano CO
26 Frank Abreau .15 .04
27 Cliff Brannon .15 .04
28 Greg Carmona .15 .04
29 Ric Christian .15 .04
30 John Ericks .15 .04
31 Steve Fanning .15 .04
32 Joey Fernandez .15 .04
33 Jose Fernandez .15 .04
34 Mike Fiore .15 .04
35 David Grimes .15 .04
36 Dale Kisten .15 .04
37 John Lepley .15 .04
38 Luis Martinez .15 .04
39 Mike Milchin .15 .04
40 Donovan Osborne .15 .04
41 Gabriel Ozuna .15 .04
42 Lee Plemel .15 .04
43 Don Prybylinski .15 .04
44 John Sellick .15 .04
45 Jeff Shireman .15 .04
46 Brian Stone .15 .04
47 Charlie White .15 .04
48 Dennis Wiseman .15 .04
49 Joe Pettini MG .15 .04
50 Scott Melvin CO .15 .04
Marty Mason CO
51 Wilson Alvarez .15 .04
52 Wayne Busby .15 .04
53 Darrin Campbell .15 .04
54 Mark Chasey .15 .04
55 Ron Coomer .50 .15
56 Argenis Cortez .15 .04
57 Mike Davino .15 .04
58 Lindsay Foster .15 .04
59 Ramon Garcia .15 .04
60 Kevin Garner .15 .04
61 Jeff Gay .15 .04
62 Chris Howard .15 .04
63 John Hudek .15 .04
64 Scott Jaster .15 .04
65 Bo Kennedy .15 .04
66 Derek Lee .15 .04
67 Frank Merigliano .15 .04
68 Scott Middaugh .15 .04
69 Javier Ocasio .15 .04
70 Kinnis Pledger .15 .04
71 Greg Roth .15 .04
72 Aubrey Waggoner .15 .04
73 Jose Ventura .15 .04
74 Tony Franklin MG .15 .04
75 Rick Peterson CO .15 .04
Pat Roessler CO
Sam Hairston CO
76 Ramon Bautista .15 .04
77 Eric Bell .15 .04
78 Jim Bruske .15 .04
79 Tim Costo .15 .04
80 Mike Curtis .15 .04
81 Jerry DiPoto .15 .04
82 Daren Epley .15 .04
83 Sam Ferretti .15 .04
84 Garland Kiser .15 .04
85 Ty Kovach .15 .04
86 Tom Kramer .15 .04
87 Nolan Lane .15 .04
88 Jesse Levis .15 .04
89 Carlos Martinez .15 .04
90 Jeff Mutis .15 .04
91 Rouglas Odor .15 .04
92 Gary Resetar .15 .04
93 Greg Roscoe .15 .04
94 Miguel Sabino .15 .04
95 Bernie Tatis .15 .04
96 Jim Thome 2.50 .75
97 Ken Ramos .15 .04
98 Ken Whitfield .15 .04
99 Ken Bolek MG .15 .04
100 Dave Keller CO .15 .04
101 Steve Adams .15 .04
102 Stan Fansler .15 .04
103 Mandy Romero .15 .04
104 Terry Crowley Jr. .15 .04
105 Chip Duncan .15 .04
106 Greg Edge .15 .04
107 Chris Estep .15 .04
108 Carl Hamilton .15 .04
109 Lee Hancock .15 .04
110 Tim Hines .15 .04
111 Mike Huyler .15 .04
112 Paul Miller .15 .04
113 Pete Murphy .15 .04
114 Darwin Pennye .15 .04
115 Mike Roesler .15 .04
116 Bruce Schreiber .15 .04
117 Greg Sparks .15 .04
118 Dennis Tafoya .15 .04
119 Tim Wakefield .75 .23
120 Ben Webb .15 .04
121 John Wehner .15 .04
122 Ed Yacopino .15 .04
123 Eddie Zambrano .15 .04
124 Marc Bombard MGR .15 .04
125 Trent Jewett CO .15 .04
Spin Williams CO
126 Alex Arias .15 .04
127 Paul Blair .15 .04
128 Jim Bullinger .15 .04
129 Dick Canan .15 .04
130 Rusty Crockett .15 .04
131 Steve DiBartolomeo .15 .04
132 John Gardner .15 .04
133 Henry Gomez .15 .04
134 Ty Griffin .15 .04
135 Shannon Jones .15 .04
136 Mike Knapp .15 .04
137 Tim Parker .15 .04
138 Elvin Paulino .15 .04
139 Fernando Ramsey .15 .04
140 Kevin Roberson .15 .04
141 John Salles .15 .04
142 Mike Sodders .15 .04
143 Bill St. Peter .15 .04
144 Julio Strauss .15 .04
145 Scott Taylor .15 .04
146 Tim Watkins .15 .04
147 Doug Welch .15 .04
148 Billy White .15 .04
149 Jay Loviglio MG .15 .04
150 Rick Kranitz CO .15 .04
151 Rick Allen .15 .04
152 Mike Anderson .15 .04
153 Bobby Ayala .15 .04
154 Pete Beeler .15 .04
155 Jeff Branson .15 .04
156 Scott Bryant .15 .04
157 Bill Dodd .15 .04
158 Steve Foster .15 .04
159 Victor Garcia .15 .04
160 Frank Kremblas .15 .04
161 Greg Lonigro .15 .04
162 Dave Mcauliffe .15 .04
163 Steve McCarthy .15 .04
164 Scott Pose .15 .04
165 Tim Pugh .15 .04
166 Bill Risley .15 .04
167 Reggie Sanders .50 .15
168 Mo Sanford .15 .04
169 Scott Sellner .15 .04
170 Jerry Spradlin .15 .04
171 Glenn Sutko .15 .04
172 Todd Trafton .15 .04
173 Bernie Walker .15 .04
174 Jim Tracy MGR .15 .04
175 Mike Griffin CO .15 .04
176 Shon Ashley .15 .04
177 John Byington .15 .04
178 Mark Chapman .15 .04
179 Jim Czajkowski .15 .04
180 Ruben Escalera .15 .04
181 Craig Faulkner .15 .04
182 Tim Fortugno .15 .04
183 Don Gordon .15 .04
184 Mitch Hannahs .15 .04
185 Steve Lienhard .15 .04
186 Dave Jacas .15 .04
187 Kenny Jackson .15 .04
188 John Jaha .50 .15
189 Chris Johnson .15 .04
190 Mark Kiefer .15 .04
191 Pat Listach .15 .04
192 Tom McGraw .15 .04
193 Angel Miranda .15 .04
194 Dave Nilsson .50 .15
195 Jeff Schwarz .15 .04
196 Steve Sparks .50 .15
197 Jim Tatum .15 .04
198 Brandy Vann .15 .04
199 Dave Huppert MGR .15 .04
200 Paul Lindblad CO .15 .04
201 Rich Casarotti .15 .04
202 Vinny Castilla .50 .15
203 Brian Champion .15 .04
204 Popeye Cole .15 .04
205 Johnny Cuevas .15 .04
206 Brian Deak .15 .04
207 Pat Gomez .15 .04
208 Judd Johnson .15 .04
209 Ryan Klesko 1.00 .30
210 Rich Maloney .15 .04
211 Al Martin .50 .15
212 Keith Mitchell .15 .04
213 Rick Morris .15 .04
214 Ben Rivera .15 .04
215 Napoleon Robinson .15 .04
216 Boi Rodriguez .15 .04
217 Sean Ross .15 .04
218 Earl Sanders .15 .04
219 Scott Taylor .15 .04
220 Lee Upshaw .15 .04
221 Preston Watson .15 .04
222 Turk Wendell .15 .04
223 Mark Wohlers .15 .04
224 Chris Chambliss MGR .50 .15
225 Terry Harper CO .15 .04
Bill Slack CO
Randy Ingle CO
226 Jeff Bumgarner .15 .04
227 Stacey Burdick .15 .04
228 Paul Carey .15 .04
229 Bobby Dickerson .15 .04
230 Roy Gilbert .15 .04
231 Ricky Gutierrez .15 .04
232 Tim Holland .15 .04
233 Stacy Jones .15 .04
234 Tyrone Kingwood .15 .04
235 Mike Lehman .15 .04
236 Rod Lofton .15 .04
237 Kevin Hickey .15 .04
238 Joel McKeon .15 .04
239 Scott Meadows .15 .04
240 Steve Luebber CO .15 .04
241 Mike Oquist .15 .04
242 Oswald Peraza .15 .04
243 Tim Raley .15 .04
244 Arthur Rhodes .50 .15
245 Doug Robbins .15 .04
246 Ken Shamburg .15 .04
247 Todd Stephan .15 .04
248 Jack Voigt .15 .04
249 Jerry Narron MGR .15 .04
250 Joe Durham CO .15 .04
251 Chris Cassels .15 .04
252 Arcie Cianfrocco .15 .04
253 Dan Freed .15 .04
254 Greg Fulton .15 .04
255 Chris Haney .15 .04
256 Cesar Hernandez .15 .04
257 Richard Holsman .15 .04
258 Rob Katzaroff .15 .04
259 Bryn Kosco .15 .04
260 Ken Lake .15 .04
261 Hector Rivera .15 .04
262 Chris Marchok .15 .04
263 Chris Martin .15 .04
264 Matt Maysey .15 .04
265 Omer Munoz .15 .04
266 Bob Natal .15 .04
267 Chris Pollack .15 .04
268 F.P. Santangelo .15 .04
269 Joe Siddall .15 .04
270 Stan Spencer .15 .04
271 Matt Stairs .15 .04
272 David Wainhouse .15 .04
273 Pete Young .15 .04
274 Mike Quade MG .15 .04
275 Joe Kerrigan CO .15 .04
Pete Dalena CO
276 Marco Armas .15 .04
277 Bob Bafia .15 .04
278 Dean Borrelli .15 .04
279 John Briscoe .15 .04
280 James Buccheri .15 .04
281 Tom Carcione .15 .04
282 Joel Chimelis .15 .04
283 Fred Cooley .15 .04
284 Russ Cormier .15 .04
285 Matt Grott .15 .04
286 Dwayne Hosey .15 .04
287 Chad Kuhn .15 .04
288 Dave Latter .15 .04
289 Francisco Matos .15 .04
290 Gavin Osteen .15 .04
291 Tim Peek .15 .04
292 Don Peters .15 .04
293 Scott Shockey .15 .04
294 Will Tejada .15 .04
295 Lee Tinsley .15 .04
296 Todd Van Poppel .50 .15
297 Darryl Vice .15 .04
298 Dave Zancanaro .15 .04
299 Casey Parsons MGR .15 .04
300 Bert Bradley CO .15 .04
301 Frank Carey .15 .04
302 Larry Carter .15 .04
303 Jim McNamara .15 .04
304 Tom Ealy .15 .04
305 Juan Guerrero .15 .04
306 Bryan Hickerson .15 .04
307 Steve Hosey .15 .04
308 Tom Hostetler .15 .04
309 Erik Johnson .15 .04
310 Dan Lewis .15 .04
311 Paul McClellan .15 .04
312 Jim McNamara .15 .04
313 Kevin Meier .15 .04
314 Jim Myers .15 .04
315 Dave Patterson .15 .04
316 John Patterson .15 .04
317 Jim Pena .15 .04
318 Dan Rambo .15 .04
319 Steve Reed .15 .04
320 Kevin Rogers .15 .04
321 Reuben Smiley .15 .04
322 Scooter Tucker .15 .04
323 Pete Weber .15 .04
324 Bill Evers MGR .15 .04
325 Tony Taylor CO .15 .04
Todd Oakes CO
326 Fernando Arguelles .15 .04
327 Shawn Barton .15 .04
328 Jim Blueberg .15 .04
329 Frank Bolick .15 .04
330 Bret Boone 1.00 .30
331 Jim Bowie .15 .04
332 Jim Campanis .15 .04
333 Gary Eave .15 .04
334 David Evans .15 .04
335 Fernando Figueroa .15 .04
336 Dave Fleming .15 .04
337 Ruben Gonzalez .15 .04
338 Mike McDonald .15 .04
339 Jeff Nelson .50 .15
340 Jim Newlin .15 .04
341 Ken Pennington .15 .04
342 Mike Pitz .15 .04
343 Dave Richards .15 .04
344 Roger Salkeld .15 .04
345 Jack Smith .15 .04
346 Tim Stargell .15 .04
347 Brian Turang .15 .04
348 Ted Williams .15 .04
349 Jim Nettles MGR .15 .04
350 Bobby Cuellar CO .15 .04
Lem Pilkinton CO
351 Pete Blohm .15 .04
352 Domingo Cedeno .15 .04
353 Nate Cromwell .15 .04
354 Jesse Cross .15 .04
355 Juan DeLaRosa .15 .04
356 Bobby Deloach .15 .04
357 Ray Giannelli .15 .04
358 Darren Hall .15 .04
359 Mark Young .15 .04
360 Jeff Kent 1.00 .30
361 Randy Knorr .15 .04
362 Jose Monzon .15 .04
363 Bernie Nunez .15 .04
364 Paul Rodgers .15 .04
365 Jimmy Rogers .15 .04
366 Mike Taylor .15 .04
367 Ryan Thompson .15 .04
368 Jason Townley .15 .04
369 Rick Trlicek .15 .04
370 Anthony Ward .15 .04
371 Dave Weathers .15 .04
372 Woody Williams .75 .23
373 Julian Yan .15 .04
374 John Stearns MGR .15 .04
375 Mike McAlpin CO .15 .04
Steve Mingori CO
376 Doyle Balthazar .15 .04
377 Basilio Cabrera .15 .04
378 Ron Cook .15 .04
379 Ivan Cruz .15 .04
380 Dean Decillis .15 .04
381 John DeSilva .15 .04
382 John Doherty .15 .04
383 Lou Frazier .15 .04
384 Luis Galindo .15 .04
385 Greg Gohr .15 .04
386 Buddy Groom .15 .04
387 Darren Hursey .15 .04
388 Riccardo Ingram .15 .04
389 Keith Kimberlin .15 .04
390 Todd Krumm .15 .04
391 Randy Marshall .15 .04
392 Domingo Michel .15 .04
393 Steve Pegues .15 .04
394 Jose Ramos .15 .04
395 Bob Reimink .15 .04
396 Ruben Rodriguez .15 .04
397 Eric Stone .15 .04
398 Marty Willis .15 .04
399 Gene Roof MGR .15 .04
400 Jeff Jones CO .15 .04
Dan Raley CO
401 Pete Alborano .15 .04
402 Jim Baxter .15 .04
403 Tony Clements .15 .04
404 Archie Corbin .15 .04
405 Andres Cruz .15 .04
406 Jeff Garber .15 .04
407 David Gonzalez .15 .04
408 Kevin Koslofski .15 .04
409 Deric Ladnier .15 .04
410 Mark Parnell .15 .04
411 Jorge Pedre .15 .04
412 Doug Peters .15 .04
413 Hipolito Pichardo .15 .04
414 Eddie Pierce .15 .04
415 Mike Poehl .15 .04
416 Darryl Robinson .15 .04
417 Steve Shifflett .15 .04
418 Jim Smith .15 .04
419 Lou Talbert .15 .04
420 Terry Taylor .15 .04
421 Rich Tunison .15 .04
422 Hugh Walker .15 .04
423 Darren Watkins .15 .04
424 Jeff Cox MGR .15 .04
425 Brian Peterson CO .15 .04
Mike Alvarez CO
426 Clemente Acosta .15 .04
427 Jeff Barns .15 .04
428 Mike Butcher .15 .04
429 Glenn Carter .15 .04
430 Marvin Cobb .15 .04
431 Sherman Corbett .15 .04
432 Kevin Davis .15 .04
433 Damion Easley .50 .15
434 Kevin Flora .15 .04
435 Larry Gonzalez .15 .04
436 Mark Howie .15 .04
437 Todd James .15 .04
438 Bobby Jones .50 .15
439 Steve King .15 .04
440 Marcus Lawton .15 .04
441 Ken Rivers .15 .04
442 Doug Robertson .15 .04
443 Tim Salmon 1.50 .45
444 Ramon Sambo .15 .04
445 Daryl Sconiers .15 .04
446 Dave Shotkoski .15 .04
447 Terry Taylor .15 .04
448 Mark Zappelli .15 .04
449 Don Long MGR .15 .04
450 Kernan Ronan CO .15 .04
Gene Richards CO
451 Michael Beams .15 .04
452 Greg Blosser .15 .04
453 Brian Conroy .15 .04
454 Freddie Davis .15 .04
455 Colin Dixon .15 .04
456 Peter Estrada .15 .04
457 Ray Fagnant .15 .04
458 Tom Fischer .15 .04
459 John Flaherty .15 .04
460 Donald Florence .15 .04
461 Blane Fox .15 .04
462 Steve Hendricks .15 .04
463 Wayne Housie .15 .04
464 Peter Hoy .15 .04
465 Thomas Kane .15 .04
466 David Milstien .15 .04
467 Juan Paris .15 .04
468 Scott Powers .15 .04
469 Paul Quantrill .15 .04
470 Randy Randle .15 .04
471 Al Sanders .15 .04
472 Scott Taylor .15 .04
473 John Valentin .15 .04
474 Gary Allenson MGR .15 .04
475 Rick Wise CO .15 .04
476 Pat Bangtson .15 .04
477 Carlos Capellan .15 .04
478 Rafael DeLima .15 .04
479 Frank Valdez .15 .04
480 Cheo Garcia .15 .04
481 Shawn Gilbert .15 .04
482 Greg Johnson .15 .04
483 Jay Kvasnicka .15 .04
484 Orlando Lind .15 .04
485 Pat Mahomes .15 .04
486 Jose Marzan .15 .04
487 Dan Masteller .15 .04
488 Bob McCreary .15 .04
489 Steve Muh .15 .04
490 Reed Olmstead .15 .04
491 Ray Ortiz .15 .04
492 Derek Parks .15 .04
493 Joe Siwa .15 .04
494 Steve Stowell .15 .04
495 Mike Trombley .15 .04
496 Jim Shellenback CO .15 .04
497 Rob Wassenaar .15 .04
498 Phil Wiese .15 .04
499 Scott Ullger MGR .15 .04
500 Mark Funderburk CO .15 .04
501 Jason Backs .15 .04
502 Toby Borland .15 .04
503 Cliff Brantley .15 .04
504 Dana Brown .15 .04
505 John Burgos .15 .04
506 Andy Carter .15 .04
507 Bruce Dostal .15 .04
508 Rick Dunnum .15 .04
509 John Martin CO .15 .04
510 David Holdridge .15 .04
511 Darrell Lindsey .15 .04
512 Doug Lindsey .15 .04
513 Tony Longmire .15 .04
514 Tom Marsh .15 .04
515 Rod Robertson .15 .04
516 Edwin Rosado .15 .04
517 Sean Ryan .15 .04
518 Steve Scarsone .15 .04
519 Mark Sims .15 .04
520 Jeff Tabaka .15 .04
521 Tony Trevino .15 .04
522 Casey Waller .15 .04
523 Cary Williams .15 .04
524 D.McCormack MGR .15 .04
525 Al LeBoeuf CO .15 .04
526 Steve Allen .15 .04
527 Jorge Alvarez .15 .04
528 Bryan Baar .15 .04
529 Tim Barker .15 .04
530 Tony Barron .15 .04
531 Cam Biberdorf .15 .04
532 Jason Brosnan .15 .04
533 Braulio Castillo .15 .04
534 Steve Finken .15 .04
535 Freddy Gonzalez .15 .04
536 Mike James .15 .04
537 Brett Magnusson .15 .04
538 Jose Munoz .15 .04
539 Lance Rice .15 .04
540 Zak Shinall .15 .04
541 Dennis Springer .15 .04
542 Ramon Taveras .15 .04
543 Jimmy Terrill .15 .04
544 Brian Taxler .15 .04
545 Jody Treadwell .15 .04
546 Mike White .15 .04
547 Mike Wilkins .15 .04
548 Eric Young .15 .04
549 J.Shoemaker MGR .15 .04
550 James Wray .15 .04
551 Willie Ansley .15 .04
552 Sam August .15 .04
553 Jeff Baldwin .15 .04
554 Pete Bauer .15 .04
555 Kevin Coffman .15 .04
556 Kevin Dean .15 .04
557 Tony Eusebio .15 .04
558 Dean Freeland .15 .04
559 Rusty Harris .15 .04
560 Dean Hartgraves .15 .04

561 Trent Hubbard .15 .04
562 Bert Hunter .15 .04
563 Bernie Jenkins .15 .04
564 Richie Simon .15 .04
565 Keith Kaiser .15 .04
566 Steve Larose .15 .04
567 Lance Madsen .15 .04
568 Scott Makarewicz .15 .04
569 Rob Mallicoat .15 .04
570 Joe Mikulik .15 .04
571 Orlando Miller .15 .04
572 Shane Reynolds .50 .15
573 Richie Simon .15 .04
574 Rick Sweet MGR .15 .04
575 Don Reynolds CO .15 .04
Charlie Taylor CO
576 Rob Brown .15 .04
577 Mike Burton .15 .04
578 Everett Cunningham .15 .04
579 Jeff Frye .15 .04
580 Pat Garman .15 .04
581 Bryan Gore .15 .04
582 David Green .15 .04
583 Donald Harris .15 .04
584 Jose Hernandez .50 .15
585 Greg Iavarone .15 .04
586 Barry Manuel .15 .04
587 Trey McCoy .15 .04
588 Rod Morris .15 .04
589 Robb Nen .50 .15
590 David Perez .15 .04
591 Bobby Reed .15 .04
592 Ivan Rodriguez 2.00 .60
593 Dan Rohrmeier .15 .04
594 Brian Romero .15 .04
595 Luke Sable .15 .04
596 Frederic Samson .15 .04
597 Cedric Shaw .15 .04
598 Chris Shiflett .15 .04
599 Bobby Jones MGR .15 .04
600 Oscar Acosta CO .15 .04
Jeff Hubbard CO
601 Mike Basso .15 .04
602 Doug Brocail .15 .04
603 Rafael Chavez .15 .04
604 Brian Cisarik .15 .04
605 Greg David .15 .04
606 Rick Davis .15 .04
607 Vince Harris .15 .04
608 Charles Hillemann .15 .04
609 Kerry Knox .15 .04
610 Pete Kuld .15 .04
611 Jim Lewis .15 .04
612 Luis Lopez .15 .04
613 Pedro A. Martinez .15 .04
614 Tim McWilliam .15 .04
615 Tom Redington .15 .04
616 Darrin Reichle .15 .04
617 A.J. Sager .15 .04
618 Frank Seminara .15 .04
619 Darrell Sherman .15 .04
620 Jose Valentin .50 .15
621 Guillermo Velasquez .15 .04
622 Tim Wallace .15 .04
623 Brian Wood .15 .04
624 Steve Lubratich MGR .15 .04
625 John Cumberland CO .15 .04
Jack Maloof CO
626 Tim Bogar .15 .04
627 Jeromy Burnitz .50 .15
628 Hernan Cortes .15 .04
629 Steve Davis .15 .04
630 Joe Delli Carri .15 .04
631 D.J. Dozier .15 .04
632 Javier Gonzalez .15 .04
633 Rudy Hernandez .15 .04
634 Chris Hill .15 .04
635 John Johnstone .15 .04
636 Doug Kline .15 .04
637 Loy McBride .15 .04
638 Joel Horlen CO .15 .04
639 Tito Navarro .15 .04
640 Toby Nivens .15 .04
641 Bryan Rogers .15 .04
642 David Sommer .15 .04
643 Greg Talamantez .15 .04
644 Dave Telgheder .15 .04
645 Jose Vargas .15 .04
646 Aguedo Vasquez .15 .04
647 Paul Williams .15 .04
648 Alan Zinter .15 .04
649 Clint Hurdle MGR .15 .04
650 Jim Eschen CO .15 .04

1991 Line Drive AAA

This 650-card standard-size set has glossy color action player photos bordered in white. Early cards of Jeff Kent and Mike Mussina are featued in this set.

	Nm-Mt	Ex-Mt
COMPLETE SET (650)	25.00	7.50
COMP.FACT.SET (650)	30.00	9.00

1 Billy Bean .15 .04
2 Jerry Brooks .15 .04
3 Mike Christopher .15 .04
4 Dennis Cook .15 .04
5 Butch Davis .15 .04
6 Tom Goodwin .15 .04
7 Dave Hansen .15 .04
8 Jeff Hartsock .15 .04
9 Bert Heffernan .15 .04
10 Carlos Hernandez .15 .04
11 Chris Jones .15 .04
12 Eric Karros .50 .15
13 Dave Lynch .15 .04
14 Luis Martinez .15 .04
15 Jamie McAndrew .15 .04
16 Jim Neidlinger .15 .04
17 Jose Offerman .50 .15
18 Eddie Pye .15 .04
19 Henry Rodriguez .50 .15
20 Greg Smith .15 .04
21 Dave Veres .15 .04
22 Dave Walsh .15 .04
23 John Wetteland .50 .15
24 Kevin Kennedy MG .15 .04
25 Von Joshua CO .15 .04
Claude Osteen CO
26 Jeff Banister .15 .04
27 Cecil Espy .15 .04
28 Steve Fireovid .15 .04
29 Carlos Garcia .15 .04
30 Mark Huismann .15 .04
31 Scott Little .15 .04
32 Tom Magrann .15 .04
33 Roger Mason .15 .04
34 Tim Meeks .15 .04
35 Orlando Merced .15 .04
36 Joey Meyer .15 .04
37 Keith Miller .15 .04
38 Blas Minor .15 .04
39 Armando Moreno .15 .04
40 Jeff Neely .15 .04
41 Joe Redfield .15 .04
42 Rick Reed .50 .15
43 Jeff Richardson .15 .04
44 Rosario Rodriguez .15 .04
45 Jeff Schulz .15 .04
46 Jim Tracy .15 .04
47 Greg Tubbs .15 .04
48 Mike York .15 .04
49 Terry Collins MG .15 .04
50 Jackie Brown CO .15 .04
51 Rich Amaral .15 .04
52 Rick Balabon .15 .04
53 Dave Brundage .15 .04
54 Dave Burba .50 .15
55 Dave Cochrane .15 .04
56 Alan Cockrell .15 .04
57 Mike Cook .15 .04
58 Keith Helton .15 .04
59 Dennis Hood .15 .04
60 Chris Howard .15 .04
61 Chuck Jackson .15 .04
62 Calvin Jones .15 .04
63 Pat Lennon .15 .04
64 Shane Letterio .15 .04
65 Vance Lovelace .15 .04
66 Tino Martinez .50 .15
67 John Mitchell .15 .04
68 Dennis Powell .15 .04
69 Alonzo Powell .15 .04
70 Pat Rice .15 .04
71 Ricky Rojas .15 .04
72 Steve Springer .15 .04
73 Ed Vande Berg .15 .04
74 Keith Bodie MG .15 .04
75 Ross Grimsley CO .15 .04
76 Eddie Taubensee .50 .15
77 Jeff Bittiger .15 .04
78 Willie Blair .15 .04
79 Marty Brown .15 .04
80 Kevin Burdick .15 .04
81 Steve Cummings .15 .04
82 Mauro Gozzo .15 .04
83 Ricky Horton .15 .04
84 Stan Jefferson .15 .04
85 Brian Johnson .15 .04
86 Barry Jones .15 .04
87 Wayne Kirby .15 .04
88 Mark Lewis .15 .04
89 Rudy Seanez .15 .04
90 Luis Lopez .15 .04
91 Ever Magallanes .15 .04
92 Luis Medina .15 .04
93 Dave Otto .15 .04
94 Roberto Zambrano .15 .04
95 Jeff Shaw .50 .15
96 Efrain Valdez .15 .04
97 Sergio Valdez .15 .04
98 Kevin Wickander .15 .04
99 Charlie Manuel MG .15 .04
100 Rick Adair CO .15 .04
Jim Gabella CO
101 Steve Adkins .15 .04
102 Daven Bond .15 .04
103 Darrin Chapin .15 .04
104 Royal Clayton .15 .04
105 Steve Howe .15 .04
106 Keith Hughes .15 .04
107 Mike Humphreys .15 .04
108 Jeff Johnson .15 .04
109 Scott Kamieniecki .15 .04
110 Pat Kelly .15 .04
111 Jason Maas .15 .04
112 Alan Mills .15 .04
113 Rich Monteleone .15 .04
114 Hipolito Pena .15 .04
115 John Ramos .15 .04
116 Carlos Rodriguez .15 .04
117 Dave Sax .15 .04
118 Van Snider .15 .04
119 Don Sparks .15 .04
120 Andy Stankiewicz .15 .04
121 Wade Taylor .15 .04
122 Jim Walewander .15 .04
123 Bernie Williams .50 .15
124 Rick Down MG .15 .04
125 Gary Denbo CO .15 .04
Clete Boyer CO
Russ Meyer CO
126 D.L. Smith .15 .04
127 Jim Austin .15 .04
128 Esteban Beltre .15 .04
129 Mickey Brantley .15 .04
130 George Canale .15 .04
131 Matias Carrillo .15 .04
132 Juan Castillo .15 .04
133 Jim Davins .15 .04
134 Carlos Diaz .15 .04
135 Cal Eldred .15 .04
136 Narciso Elvira .15 .04
137 Brian Fisher .15 .04
138 Chris George .15 .04
139 Sandy Guerrero .15 .04
140 Doug Henry .15 .04
141 Darren Holmes .15 .04
142 Mike Ignasiak .15 .04
143 Jeff Kaiser .15 .04
144 Joe Kmak .15 .04
145 Tim McIntosh .15 .04
146 Charlie Montoyo .15 .04
147 Jim Olander .15 .04
148 Ed Puig .15 .04
149 Tony Muser MGR .15 .04
150 Lamar Johnson CO .15 .04
Don Rowe CO
151 Kyle Abbott .15 .04
152 Ruben Amaro .15 .04
153 Kent Anderson .15 .04
154 Mike Erb .15 .04
155 Randy Bockus .15 .04
156 Gary Buckels .15 .04
157 Tim Burcham .15 .04
158 Chris Cron .15 .04
159 Chad Curtis .50 .15
160 Doug Davis .15 .04
161 Mark Davis .15 .04
162 Gary DiSarcina .15 .04
163 Mike Fetters .15 .04
164 Joe Grahe .15 .04
165 Dan Grunhard .15 .04
166 Dave Leiper .15 .04
167 Rafael Montalvo .15 .04
168 Reed Peters .15 .04
169 Bobby Rose .50 .15
170 Lee Stevens .15 .04
171 Ron Tingley .15 .04
172 Ed Vosberg .15 .04
173 Mark Wasinger .15 .04
174 Max Oliveras MG .15 .04
175 Lenn Sakata CO .15 .04
Gary Ruby CO
176 Bret Barberie .15 .04
177 Kevin Bearse .15 .04
178 Kent Bottenfield .50 .15
179 Wil Cordero .15 .04
180 Mike Davis .15 .04
181 Alex Diaz .15 .04
182 Eddie Dixon .15 .04
183 Jeff Fassero .50 .15
184 Jerry Goff .15 .04
185 Todd Haney .15 .04
186 Steve Hecht .15 .04
187 Jimmy Kremers .15 .04
188 Quinn Mack .15 .04
189 David Masters .15 .04
190 Marlin McPhail .15 .04
191 Doug Piatt .15 .04
192 Dana Ridenour .15 .04
193 Scott Service .15 .04
194 Razor Shines .15 .04
195 Tito Stewart .15 .04
196 Mel Houston .15 .04
197 John Vander Wal .50 .15
198 Darrin Winston .15 .04
199 Jerry Manuel MG .15 .04
200 Gomer Hodge CO .15 .04
Nardi Contreras CO
201 Brad Bierley .15 .04
202 Steve Carter .15 .04
203 Frank Castillo .50 .15
204 Lance Dickson .15 .04
205 Craig Smajstra .15 .04
206 Brian Guinn .15 .04
207 Joe Kraemer .15 .04
208 Cedric Landrum .15 .04
209 Derrick May .15 .04
210 Scott May .15 .04
211 Russ McGinnis .15 .04
212 Chuck Mount .15 .04
213 Dave Pavlas .15 .04
214 Laddie Renfroe .15 .04
215 David Rosario .15 .04
216 Rey Sanchez .15 .04
217 Dan Simonds .15 .04
218 Jeff Small .15 .04
219 Doug Strange .15 .04
220 Glenn Sullivan .15 .04
221 Rick Wilkins .15 .04
222 Steve Wilson .15 .04
223 Bob Scanlan .15 .04
224 Jim Essian MG .15 .04
225 Grant Jackson CO .15 .04
226 Luis Alicea .50 .15
227 Rob Brewer .15 .04
228 Nick Castaneda .15 .04
229 Stan Clarke .15 .04
230 Marty Clary .15 .04
231 Fidel Compres .15 .04
232 Todd Crosby .15 .04
233 Bob Davidson .15 .04
234 Bien Figueroa .15 .04
235 Ed Fulton .15 .04
236 Mark Grater .15 .04
237 Omar Olivares .15 .04
238 Brian Jordan .50 .15
239 Lonnie Maclin .15 .04
240 Julian Martinez .15 .04
241 Al Nipper .15 .04
242 Dave Osteen .15 .04
243 Leny Picota .15 .04
244 Dave Richardson .15 .04
245 Mike Ross .15 .04
246 Stan Royer .15 .04
247 Tim Sherrill .15 .04
248 Carl Ray Stephens .15 .04
249 Mark DeJohn MG .15 .04
250 Mark Riggins CO .15 .04
251 Billy Bates .15 .04
252 Freddie Benavides .15 .04
253 Keith Brown .15 .04
254 Adam Casillas .15 .04
255 Tony DeFrancesco .15 .04
256 Leo Garcia .15 .04
257 Angel Gonzalez .15 .04
258 Denny Gonzalez .15 .04
259 Kip Gross .15 .04
260 Charlie Mitchell .15 .04
261 Milton Hill .15 .04
262 Rodney Imes .15 .04
263 Reggie Jefferson .15 .04
264 Keith Lockhart .15 .04
265 Manny Jose .15 .04
266 Terry Lee .15 .04
267 Rob Lopez .15 .04
268 Gino Minutelli .15 .04
269 Kevin Pearson .15 .04
270 Ross Powell .15 .04
271 Donnie Scott .15 .04
272 Luis Vasquez .15 .04
273 Joey Vierra .15 .04
274 Pete MacKanin MG .15 .04
275 Don Gullett CO .15 .04
Jim Lett CO
276 Oscar Azocar .15 .04
277 Dann Bilardello .15 .04
278 Ricky Bones .15 .04
279 Brian Dorsett .15 .04
280 Scott Coolbaugh .15 .04
281 John Costello .15 .04
282 Terry Gilmore .15 .04
283 Jeremy Hernandez .15 .04
284 Kevin Higgins .15 .04
285 Chris Jelic .15 .04
286 Dean Kelley .15 .04
287 Derek Lilliquist .15 .04
288 Jose Melendez .15 .04
289 Jose Mota .15 .04
290 Adam Peterson .15 .04
291 Ed Romero .15 .04
292 Steven Rosenberg .15 .04
293 Tim Scott .15 .04
294 Dave Staton .15 .04
295 Will Taylor .15 .04
296 Jim Vatcher .15 .04
297 Dan Walters .15 .04
298 Kevin Ward .15 .04
299 Jim Riggleman MG .15 .04
300 Jon Matlack CO .15 .04
Tony Torchia CO
301 Gerald Alexander .15 .04
302 Kevin Belcher .15 .04
303 Jeff Andrews .15 .04
304 Tony Scruggs .15 .04
305 Jeff Bronkey .15 .04
306 Paco Burgos .15 .04
307 Nick Capra .15 .04
308 Monty Fariss .15 .04
309 Darrin Garner .15 .04
310 Bill Haselman .50 .15
311 Terry Mathews .15 .04
312 Rob Maurer .15 .04
313 Gar Millay .15 .04
314 Dean Palmer .50 .15
315 Roger Pavlik .15 .04
316 Dan Peltier .15 .04
317 Steve Peters .15 .04
318 Mark Petkovsek .15 .04
319 Jim Poole .15 .04
320 Paul Postier .15 .04
321 Wayne Rosenthal .15 .04
322 Dan Smith .15 .04
323 Terry Wells .15 .04
324 T.Thompson MG .15 .04
325 Stan Hough CO .15 .04
326 Sean Berry .15 .04
327 Jacob Brumfield .15 .04
328 Bob Buchanan .15 .04
329 Kevin Burrell .15 .04
330 Stu Cole .15 .04
331 Victor Cole .15 .04
332 Jeff Conine .50 .15
333 Tommy Dunbar .15 .04
334 Luis Encarnacion .15 .04
335 Greg Everson .15 .04
336 Bob Hamelin .15 .04
337 Joel Johnston .15 .04
338 Frank Laureano .15 .04
339 Jim LeMasters .15 .04
340 Mike Magnante .15 .04
341 Carlos Maldonado .15 .04
342 Andy McGaffigan .15 .04
343 Bobby Moore .15 .04
344 Harvey Pulliam .15 .04
345 Daryl Smith .15 .04
346 Tim Spehr .15 .04
347 Hector Wagner .15 .04
348 Paul Zuvella .15 .04
349 Sal Rende MG .15 .04
350 Brian Poldberg CO .15 .04
Guy Hansen CO
351 Luis Aguayo .15 .04
352 Tom Barrett .15 .04
353 Mike Brumley .15 .04
354 Scott Cooper .15 .04
355 Mike Gardiner .15 .04
356 Eric Hetzel .15 .04
357 Mike Twardoski .15 .04
358 Rick Lancellotti .15 .04
359 Derek Livernois .15 .04
360 Mark Meleski .15 .04
361 Kevin Morton .15 .04
362 Dan O'Neill .15 .04
363 Jim Pankovits .15 .04
364 Mickey Pina .15 .04
365 Phil Plantier .15 .04
366 Jeff Plympton .15 .04
367 Todd Pratt .15 .04
368 Larry Shikles .15 .04
369 Jeff Stone .15 .04
370 Mo Vaughn .50 .15
371 David Walters .15 .04
372 Eric Wedge .15 .04
373 Bob Zupcic .15 .04
374 Butch Hobson MG .15 .04
375 Rich Gale CO .15 .04
376 Rich Aldrete .15 .04
377 Mark Bailey .15 .04
378 Rod Beck .50 .15
379 Jeff Carter .15 .04
380 Craig Colbert .15 .04
381 Darnell Coles .15 .04
382 Mark Dewey .15 .04
383 Gil Heredia .50 .15
384 Darren Lewis .15 .04
385 Johnny Ard .15 .04
386 Rafael Novoa .15 .04
387 Francisco Oliveras .15 .04
388 Tony Perezchica .15 .04
389 Mark Thurmond .15 .04
390 Mike Remlinger .15 .04
391 Greg Ritchie .15 .04
392 Rick Rodriguez .15 .04
393 Andres Santana .15 .04
394 Jose Segura .15 .04
395 Stuart Tate .15 .04
396 Jimmy Williams .15 .04
397 Jim Wilson .15 .04
398 Ted Wood .15 .04
399 Duane Espy MG .15 .04
400 Alan Bannister CO .15 .04
Larry Hardy CO
401 Paul Abbott .50 .15
402 Willie Banks .15 .04
403 Bernardo Brito .15 .04
404 Jarvis Brown .15 .04
405 J.T. Bruett .15 .04
406 Tim Drummond .15 .04
407 Tom Edens .15 .04
408 Rich Garces .15 .04
409 Chip Hale .15 .04
410 Terry Jorgensen .15 .04
411 Kenny Morgan .15 .04
412 Pedro Munoz .15 .04
413 Edgar Naveda .15 .04
414 Denny Neagle .50 .15
415 Jeff Reboulet .15 .04
416 Victor Rodriguez .15 .04
417 Jack Savage .15 .04
418 Dan Sheaffer .15 .04
419 Charles Scott .15 .04
420 Paul Sorrento .15 .04
421 George Tsamis .15 .04
422 Lenny Webster .15 .04
423 Carl Willis .15 .04
424 Russ Nixon MG .15 .04
425 Jim Dwyer CO .15 .04
Gorman Heimueller CO
Paul Kirsch CO
426 John Alva .15 .04
427 Mike Bell .15 .04
428 Tony Castillo .15 .04
429 Bruce Crabbe .15 .04
430 John Davis .15 .04
431 Brian R. Hunter .15 .04
432 Randy Kramer .15 .04
433 Mike Loggins .15 .04
434 Kelly Mann .15 .04
435 Tom McCarthy .15 .04
436 Yorkis Perez .15 .04
437 Dale Polley .15 .04
438 Armando Reynoso .50 .15
439 Rusty Richards .15 .04
440 Victor Rosario .15 .04
441 Mark Ross .15 .04
442 Rico Rossy .15 .04
443 Randy St. Claire .15 .04
444 Joe Szekely .15 .04
445 Andy Tomberlin .15 .04
446 Matt Turner .15 .04
447 Glenn Wilson .15 .04
448 Tracy Woodson .15 .04
449 Phil Niekro MG .50 .15
450 Bruce Dal Canton CO .15 .04
Sonny Jackson CO
451 Tony Chance .15 .04
452 Joaquin Contreras .15 .04
453 Francisco DeLaRosa .15 .04
454 Benny Distefano .15 .04
455 Mike Eberle .15 .04
456 Todd Frohwirth .15 .04
457 Steve Jeltz .15 .04
458 Chito Martinez .15 .04
459 Dave Martinez .15 .04
460 Jeff McKnight .15 .04
461 Luis Mercedes .15 .04
462 Mike Mussina 2.50 .75
463 Chris Myers .15 .04
464 Joe Price .15 .04
465 Israel Sanchez .15 .04
466 David Segui .50 .15
467 Tommy Shields .15 .04
468 Mike Linskey .15 .04
469 Jack Tackett .15 .04
470 Anthony Telford .15 .04
471 Shane Turner .15 .04
472 Jeff Wetherby .15 .04
473 Rob Woodward .15 .04
474 Greg Biagini MG .15 .04
475 Mike Young CO .15 .04
Dick Bosman CO
476 Sal Agostinelli .15 .04
477 Gary Alexander .15 .04
478 Andy Ashby .50 .15
479 Bob Ayrault .15 .04
480 Kim Batiste .15 .04
481 Amalio Carreno .15 .04
482 Rocky Elli .15 .04
483 Darrin Fletcher .15 .04
484 Jeff Grotewold .15 .04
485 Chris Knabenshue .15 .04
486 Greg Legg .15 .04
487 Jim Lindeman .15 .04
488 Chuck Malone .15 .04
489 Tim Mauser .15 .04
490 Louie Meadows .15 .04
491 Mickey Morandini .15 .04
492 Julio Peguero .15 .04
493 Wally Ritchie .15 .04
494 Bruce Ruffin .15 .04
495 Rick Schu .15 .04
496 Ray Searage .15 .04
497 Scott Wade .15 .04
498 Gary Wilson .15 .04
499 Bill Dancy MG .15 .04
500 Floyd Rayford CO .15 .04
Jim Wright CO
501 Derek Bell .50 .15
502 Rob Ducey .15 .04
503 Julius McDougal .15 .04
504 Juan Guzman .50 .15
505 Pat Hentgen .50 .15
506 Shawn Jeter .15 .04
507 Doug Linton .15 .04
508 Bob MacDonald .15 .04
509 Mike Maksudian .15 .04
510 Ravelo Manzanillo .15 .04
511 Domingo Martinez .15 .04
512 Stu Pederson .15 .04
513 Marty Pevey .15 .04
514 Tom Quinlan .15 .04
515 Alex Sanchez .15 .04
516 Jerry Schunk .15 .04
517 John Shea .15 .04
518 Ed Sprague .15 .04
519 William Suero .15 .04

520 Steve Wapnick .15 .04
521 Mickey Weston .15 .04
522 John Poloni .15 .04
523 Eddie Zosky .15 .04
524 Bob Bailor MGR .15 .04
525 Rocket Wheeler CO .15 .04
526 Troy Afenir .15 .04
527 Mike Bordick .50 .15
528 Jorge Brito .15 .04
529 Scott Brosius .50 .15
530 Kevin Campbell .15 .04
531 Pete Coachman .15 .04
532 Dan Eskew .15 .04
533 Eric Fox .15 .04
534 Apolinar Garcia .15 .04
535 Webster Garrison .15 .04
536 Johnny Guzman .15 .04
537 Jeff Pico .15 .04
538 Dann Howitt .15 .04
539 Doug Jennings .15 .04
540 Brad Komminsk .15 .04
541 Tim McCoy .15 .04
542 Jeff Musselman .15 .04
543 Troy Neel .15 .04
544 Will Schock .15 .04
545 Nelson Simmons .15 .04
546 Bruce Walton .15 .04
547 Pat Wernig .15 .04
548 Ron Witmeyer .15 .04
549 Jeff Newman MG .15 .04
550 Glenn Abbott CO .15 .04
551 Kevin Baez .15 .04
552 Blaine Beatty .15 .04
553 Doug Cinnella .15 .04
554 Chris Donnels .15 .04
555 Jeff Gardner .15 .04
556 Terrel Hansen .15 .04
557 Manny Hernandez .15 .04
558 Eric Hillman .15 .04
559 Todd Hundley .50 .15
560 Alex Jimenez .15 .04
561 Tim Leiper .15 .04
562 Lee May Jr. .15 .04
563 Orlando Mercado .15 .04
564 Brad Moore .15 .04
565 Al Pedrique .15 .04
566 Dale Plummer .15 .04
567 Rich Sauveur .15 .04
568 Ray Soff .15 .04
569 Kelvin Torve .15 .04
570 Dave Trautwein .15 .04
571 Julio Valera .15 .04
572 Robbie Wine .15 .04
573 Anthony Young .15 .04
574 Steve Swisher MG .15 .04
575 Ron Washington CO .15 .04
Bob Apodaca CO
576 Scott Aldred .15 .04
577 Karl Allaire .15 .04
578 Skeeter Barnes .15 .04
579 Arnie Beyeler .15 .04
580 Rico Brogna .50 .15
581 Phil Clark .15 .04
582 Mike Dalton .15 .04
583 Curt Ford .15 .04
584 Dan Gakeler .15 .04
585 David Haas .15 .04
586 Shawn Hare .15 .04
587 John Kiely .15 .04
588 Mark Leiter .15 .04
589 Scott Livingstone .15 .04
590 Mitch Lyden .15 .04
591 Eric Mangham .15 .04
592 Rusty Meacham .15 .04
593 Mike Munoz .15 .04
594 Randy Nosek .15 .04
595 Johnny Paredes .15 .04
596 Kevin Ritz .15 .04
597 Rich Rowland .15 .04
598 Don Vesling .15 .04
599 Joe Sparks MG .15 .04
600 Mark Wagner CO .15 .04
Ralph Treuel CO
601 Harold Allen .15 .04
602 Eric Anthony .15 .04
603 Doug Baker .15 .04
604 Ryan Bowen .15 .04
605 Mike Capel .15 .04
606 Andujar Cedeno .15 .04
607 Terry Clark .15 .04
608 Carlo Colombino .15 .04
609 Gary Cooper .15 .04
610 Calvin Schiraldi .15 .04
611 Randy Hennis .15 .04
612 Butch Henry .15 .04
613 Blaise Ilsley .15 .04
614 Kenny Lofton 1.00 .30
615 Terry McGriff .15 .04
616 Andy Mota .15 .04
617 Javier Ortiz .15 .04
618 Scott Servais .15 .04
619 Mike Simms .15 .04
620 Jose Tolentino .15 .04
621 Lee Tunnell .15 .04
622 Brent Strom .15 .04
623 Gerald Young .15 .04
624 Bob Skinner MG .15 .04
625 Dave Engle CO .15 .04
626 Cesar Bernhardt .15 .04
627 Mario Brito .15 .04
628 Kurt Brown .15 .04
629 John Cangelosi .15 .04
630 Jeff Carter .15 .04
631 Tom Drees .15 .04
632 Grady Hall .15 .04
633 Joe Hall .15 .04
634 Curt Hasler .15 .04
635 Danny Heep .15 .04
636 Dan Henley .15 .04
637 Roberto Hernandez .50 .15
638 Orsino Hill .15 .04
639 Jerry Kutzler .15 .04
640 Norberto Martin .15 .04
641 Rod McCray .15 .04
642 Rob Nelson .15 .04
643 Warren Newson .15 .04
644 Greg Perschke .15 .04
645 Rich Scheid .15 .04
646 Matt Stark .15 .04
647 Ron Stephens .15 .04
648 Don Wakamatsu .15 .04
649 Marv Foley MG .15 .04
650 Roger LaFrancois CO .15 .04
Moe Drabowsky CO

1991 Little Sun High School Prospects

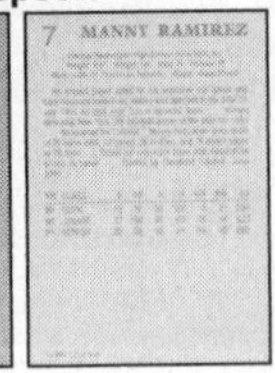

This 36-card standard-size set highlights outstanding high school prospects for 1991 that were drafted by major league teams. According to the first card, only 10,000 sets were produced. The set also included a coupon that could be redeemed for an 8" X 10" uncut sheet featuring the four players included in Little Sun's 1991 Gold Prospects Club, Al Shirley, Benji Gil, Shawn Estes and Cliff Floyd. Early Cards of Manny Ramirez and Mike Sweeney are featured in this set.

	Nm-Mt	Ex-Mt
COMP.FACT.SET (36)	15.00	4.50
1 Title Card	.25	.07
2 Al Shirley	.25	.07
3 Tyrone Hill	.25	.07
4 Justin Thompson	.25	.07
5 Mike Sweeney	4.00	1.20
6 Jimmy Haynes	1.00	.30
7 Manny Ramirez	8.00	2.40
8 Tarrik Brock	.25	.07
9 Vince Jackson	.25	.07
10 Jon Barnes	.25	.07
11 Shawn Estes	1.00	.30
12 Johnny Walker	.25	.07
13 O'Brian Cunningham	.25	.07
14 Mike Busby	.25	.07
15 Khary Heidelberg	.25	.07
16 Tom McKinnon	.25	.07
17 Billy Stephens	.25	.07
18 Jon Barnes Pep Harris	.25	.07
19 Cliff Floyd	4.00	1.20
20 Rick Gorecki	.25	.07
21 Mike Rossiter	.25	.07
22 Mike Walkden	.25	.07
23 Dwayne Gerald	.25	.07
24 Terry Horn	.25	.07
25 Shawn Curran	.25	.07
26 Pep Harris	.25	.07
27 Benji Gil	.25	.07
28 Jon Pitts	.25	.07
29 Maceo Houston	.25	.07
30 Ryan Long	.25	.07
31 Jason Pruitt	.25	.07
32 Eddie Williams	.25	.07
33 Steve Mandl CO	.25	.07
34 Al Berry CO	.25	.07
35 George Genovese SC	.25	.07
36 Checklist Prep Baseball Facts and Figures	.25	.07

1991 Little Sun High School Prospects Autographs

One Autograph card was distributed in each of the 2,000 Glossy/Gold factory sets. All four players listed below signed 500 cards each though the cards are not actually serial numbered.

	Nm-Mt	Ex-Mt
AU1 Shawn Estes	10.00	3.00
AU2 Cliff Floyd	15.00	4.50
AU3 Benji Gil	5.00	1.50
AU4 Al Shirley	5.00	1.50

1991-92 ProCards Tomorrow's Heroes

This 360-card standard size set features white bordered color player photos of the minor league top prospects. The player's name, position, and team name appear at the bottom. The back carries the player's name and position, followed by biography and statistics. The cards were issued in 12-card wax packs. 1,009 cases were produced. Early cards of Carlos Delgado, Chipper Jones, Pedro Martinez, Mike Mussina, Manny Ramirez and Ivan Rodriguez are featured in this set.

	Nm-Mt	Ex-Mt
COMPLETE SET (360)	40.00	12.00
1 Mike Mussina	2.50	.75
2 Luis Mercedes	.15	.04
3 Todd Frohwirth	.15	.04
4 Chito Martinez	.15	.04
5 David Segui	.50	.15
6 Arthur Rhodes	.50	.15
7 Stacy Jones	.15	.04
8 Darryl Moore	.15	.04
9 Manny Alexander	.15	.04
10 Jeff Williams	.15	.04
11 Matt Anderson	.15	.04
12 Chris Lemp	.15	.04
13 Rick Krivda	.15	.04
14 Phil Plantier	.15	.04
15 Mo Vaughn	.50	.15
16 Scott Cooper	.15	.04
17 Mike Gardiner	.50	.15
18 Kevin Morton	.15	.04
19 Jeff Plympton	.15	.04
20 Jeff McNeely	.15	.04
21 Willie Tatum	.15	.04
22 Tim Smith	.15	.04
23 Frank Rodriguez	.15	.04
24 Chris Davis	.15	.04
25 Cory Bailey	.15	.04
26 Rob Henkel	.15	.04
27 Kyle Abbott	.15	.04
28 Lee Stevens	.15	.04
29 Chad Curtis	.50	.15
30 Ruben Amaro	.15	.04
31 Mark Howie	.15	.04
32 Tim Salmon	1.00	.30
33 Kevin Flora	.15	.04
34 Garret Anderson	1.00	.30
35 Darryl Scott	.15	.04
36 Don Vidmar	.15	.04
37 Korey Keling	.15	.04
38 Troy Percival	.75	.23
39 Eduardo Perez	.15	.04
40 Julian Heredia	.15	.04
41 Wilson Alvarez	.15	.04
42 Ramon Garcia	.15	.04
43 Johnny Ruffin	.15	.04
44 Scott Cepicky	.15	.04
45 Rod Bolton	.15	.04
46 Rogelio Nunez	.15	.04
47 Brandon Wilson	.15	.04
48 Marc Kubicki	.15	.04
49 Mark Lewis	.15	.04
50 Jim Thome	2.50	.75
51 Tim Costo	.15	.04
52 Jeff Mutis	.15	.04
53 Tracy Sanders	.15	.04
54 Mike Soper	.15	.04
55 Miguel Flores	.15	.04
56 Brian Giles	1.00	.30
57 Curtis Leskanic	.15	.04
58 Kyle Washington	.15	.04
59 Jason Hardtke	.15	.04
60 Albie Lopez	.50	.15
61 Oscar Resendez	.15	.04
62 Manny Ramirez	1.50	.45
63 Rico Brogna	.50	.15
64 Scott Livingstone	.15	.04
65 Greg Gohr	.15	.04
66 Scott Aldred	.15	.04
67 Brian Warren	.15	.04
68 Bob Undorf	.15	.04
69 Rob Grable	.15	.04
70 Tom Mezzanotte	.15	.04
71 Justin Thompson	.15	.04
72 Trever Miller	.15	.04
73 Joel Johnston	.15	.04
74 Kevin Koslofski	.15	.04
75 Archie Corbin	.15	.04
76 Phil Hiatt	.15	.04
77 Danny Miceli	.15	.04
78 Joe Randa	.50	.15
79 Mark Johnson	.15	.04
80 Joe Vitiello	.15	.04
81 Cal Eldred	.15	.04
82 Doug Henry	.15	.04
83 Dave Nilsson	.50	.15
84 John Jaha	.50	.15
85 Shon Ashley	.15	.04
86 Jim Tatum	.15	.04
87 Bo Dodson	.15	.04
88 Otis Green	.15	.04
89 Denny Neagle	.50	.15
90 Checklist (1-90)	.15	.04
91 Pedro Munoz	.15	.04
92 Jarvis Brown	.15	.04
93 Pat Mahomes	.15	.04
94 Cheo Garcia	.15	.04
95 David McCarty	.50	.15
96 Chris Delawelle	.15	.04
97 Scott Stahoviak	.15	.04
98 Midre Cummings	.15	.04
99 Todd Ritchie	.50	.15
100 Dave Sartain	.15	.04
101 Pedro Grifol	.15	.04
102 Eddie Guardado	.50	.15
103 Bob Carlson	.15	.04
104 Sandy Diaz	.15	.04
105 John Ramos	.15	.04
106 Bernie Williams	.50	.15
107 Wade Taylor	.15	.04
108 Pat Kelly	.15	.04
109 Jeff Johnson	.15	.04
110 Scott Kamieniecki	.15	.04
111 Dave Silvestri	.15	.04
112 Ed Martel	.15	.04
113 Willie Smith	.15	.04
114 J.T. Snow	.50	.15
115 Gerald Williams	.15	.04
116 Larry Stanford	.15	.04
117 Bruce Prybylinski	.15	.04
118 Rey Noriega	.15	.04
119 Rich Batchelor	.15	.04
120 Brad Ausmus	.50	.15
121 Robert Eenhoorn	.15	.04
122 Sam Militello	.15	.04
123 Jason Robertson	.15	.04
124 Carl Everett	.75	.23
125 Kiki Hernandez	.15	.04
126 Rafael Quirico	.15	.04
127 Lyle Mouton	.15	.04
128 Tim Flannelly	.15	.04
129 Todd Van Poppel	.50	.15
130 Tim Peek	.15	.04
131 Henry Mercedes	.15	.04
132 Todd Smith	.15	.04
133 Brent Gates	.15	.04
134 Gary Hust	.15	.04
135 Mike Neill	.15	.04
136 Russ Brock	.15	.04
137 Ricky Kimball	.15	.04
138 Tino Martinez		
139 Calvin Jones	.15	.04
140 Roger Salked	.15	.04
141 Dave Fleming	.15	.04
142 Bret Boone	1.00	.30
143 Jim Campanis	.15	.04
144 Marc Newfield	.15	.04
145 Mike Hampton	.50	.15
146 Shawn Estes	.50	.15
147 David Lisiecki	.15	.04
148 Dean Palmer	.50	.15
149 Rob Maurer	.15	.04
150 Jim Poole	.15	.04
151 Terry Mathews	.15	.04
152 Monty Fariss	.15	.04
153 Ivan Rodriguez	2.00	.60
154 Barry Manuel	.15	.04
155 Donald Harris	.15	.04
156 Rusty Greer	.50	.15
157 Matt Whiteside	.15	.04
158 Derek Bell	.50	.15
159 Eddie Zosky	.15	.04
160 Domingo Martinez	.15	.04
161 Juan Guzman	.50	.15
162 Ed Sprague	.15	.04
163 Rob Ducey	.15	.04
164 Vince Horsman	.15	.04
165 Darren Hall	.15	.04
166 Rick Trlicek	.15	.04
167 Dave Weathers	.15	.04
168 Robert Perez	.15	.04
169 Nigel Wilson	.15	.04
170 Carlos Delgado	1.50	.45
171 Steve Karsay	.50	.15
172 Howard Battle	.15	.04
173 Huck Flener	.15	.04
174 Robert Butler	.15	.04
175 Giovanni Carrara	.15	.04
176 Michael Taylor	.15	.04
177 Brian R. Hunter	.15	.04
178 Turk Wendell	.50	.15
179 Mark Wohlers	.15	.04
180 Checklist (91-180)	.15	.04
181 Ryan Klesko	1.00	.30
182 Keith Mitchell	.15	.04
183 Vinny Castilla	.50	.15
184 Napoleon Robinson	.15	.04
185 Mike Kelly	.15	.04
186 Javy Lopez	1.00	.30
187 Ramon Caraballo	.15	.04
188 David Nied	.15	.04
189 Don Strange	.15	.04
190 Chipper Jones	3.00	.90
191 Troy Hughes	.15	.04
192 Don Robinson	.15	.04
193 Lance Marks	.15	.04
194 Manuel Jimenez	.15	.04
195 Tony Graffanino	.15	.04
196 Brad Woodall	.15	.04
197 Kevin Grijak	.15	.04
198 Dario Paulino	.15	.04
199 Lance Dickson	.15	.04
200 Rey Sanchez	.15	.04
201 Elvin Paulino	.15	.04
202 Alex Arias	.15	.04
203 Fernando Ramsey	.15	.04
204 Pete Castellano	.15	.04
205 Ryan Hawblitzel	.15	.04
206 John Jensen	.15	.04
207 Jerrone Williams	.15	.04
208 Earl Cunningham	.15	.04
209 Phil Dauphin	.15	.04
210 Doug Glanville	.50	.15
211 Jim Robinson	.15	.04
212 Ken Arnold	.15	.04
213 Reggie Jefferson	.15	.04
214 Reggie Sanders	.50	.15
215 Mo Sanford	.15	.04
216 Steve Foster	.15	.04
217 Dan Wilson	.50	.15
218 John Roper	.15	.04
219 Trevor Hoffman	1.00	.30
220 Pokey Reese	.50	.15
221 John Hrusovsky	.15	.04
222 Andy Mota	.15	.04
223 Kenny Lofton	1.00	.30
224 Andujar Cedeno	.15	.04
225 Ryan Bowen	.15	.04
226 Jeff Juden	.15	.04
227 Chris Gardner	.15	.04
228 Brian Williams	.15	.04
229 Ed Ponte	.15	.04
230 Chris Hatcher	.15	.04
231 Fletcher Thompson	.15	.04
232 Wally Trice	.15	.04
233 Donne Wall	.15	.04
234 Tom Nevers	.15	.04
235 Jim Daugherty	.15	.04
236 Mark Loughlin	.15	.04
237 Jose Offerman	.50	.15
238 Dave Hansen	.15	.04
239 Carlos Hernandez	.15	.04
240 Eric Karros	.50	.15
241 Henry Rodriguez	.50	.15
242 Jamie McAndrew	.15	.04
243 Tom Goodwin	.15	.04
244 Pedro Martinez	3.00	.90
245 Braulio Castillo	.15	.04
246 Matt Howard	.15	.04
247 Michael Mimbs	.15	.04
248 Murph Proctor	.15	.04
249 Vernon Spearman	.15	.04
250 Jason Kerr	.15	.04
251 Mike Sharp	.15	.04
252 Pedro Osuna	.15	.04
253 Doug Piatt	.15	.04
254 Wil Cordero	.15	.04
255 John Vander Wal	.50	.15
256 Bret Barberie	.15	.04
257 Todd Haney	.15	.04
258 Chris Haney	.15	.04
259 Matt Stairs	.15	.04
260 David Wainhouse	.15	.04
261 Bob Natal	.15	.04
262 Rob Katzaroff	.15	.04
263 Willie Greene	.15	.04
264 Reid Cornelius	.15	.04
265 Glenn Murray	.15	.04
266 Rondell White	.50	.15
267 Tavo Alvarez	.15	.04
268 Gabe White	.15	.04
269 Brian Looney		
270 Checklist (181-270)	.15	.04
271 Derrick White	.15	.04
272 Heath Haynes	.15	.04
273 Mike Daniel	.15	.04
274 Jim Austin	.15	.04
275 Chris Donnels	.15	.04
276 Julio Valera	.15	.04
277 Todd Hundley	.50	.15
278 Anthony Young	.15	.04
279 Jeff Gardner	.15	.04
280 Jeromy Burnitz	.50	.15
281 Tito Navarro	.15	.04
282 D.J. Dozier	.15	.04
283 Julian Vasquez	.15	.04
284 Pat Howell	.15	.04
285 Brook Fordyce	.15	.04
286 Todd Douma	.15	.04
287 Jose Martinez	.15	.04
288 Ricky Otero	.15	.04
289 Quilvio Veras	.50	.15
290 Joe Crawford	.15	.04
291 Todd Fiegel	.15	.04
292 Jason Jacome	.15	.04
293 Kim Batiste	.15	.04
294 Andy Ashby	.50	.15
295 Wes Chamberlain	.15	.04
296 Dave Hollins	.15	.04
297 Tony Longmire	.15	.04
298 Nikco Riesgo	.15	.04
299 Cliff Brantley	.15	.04
300 Troy Paulsen	.15	.04
301 Elliott Gray	.15	.04
302 Mike Lieberthal	.50	.15
303 Tyler Green	.15	.04
304 Dan Brown	.15	.04
305 Carlos Garcia	.15	.04
306 John Wehner	.15	.04
307 Paul Miller	.15	.04
308 Tim Wakefield	.75	.23
309 Kurt Miller	.15	.04
310 Joe Sondrini	.15	.04
311 Hector Fajardo	.15	.04
312 Scott Bullett	.15	.04
313 Jon Farrell	.15	.04
314 Marc Pisciotta	.15	.04
315 Rheal Cormier	.15	.04
316 Omar Olivares	.15	.04
317 Donovan Osborne	.15	.04
318 Clyde Keller	.15	.04
319 John Kelly	.15	.04
320 Terry Bradshaw	.15	.04
321 Brian Eversgerd	.15	.04
322 Dmitri Young	.50	.15
323 Eddie Williams	.15	.04
324 Brian Barber	.15	.04
325 Andy Bruce	.15	.04
326 Tom McKinnon	.15	.04
327 Jamie Cochran	.15	.04
328 Steve Jones	.15	.04
329 Jerry Santos	.15	.04
330 Allen Watson	.15	.04
331 John Mabry	.50	.15
332 Jose Melendez	.15	.04
333 Dave Staton	.15	.04
334 Frank Seminara	.15	.04
335 Matt Mieske	.15	.04
336 Jay Gainer	.15	.04
337 J.D. Noland	.15	.04
338 Roberto Arredondo	.15	.04
339 Lance Painter	.15	.04
340 Darren Lewis	.15	.04
341 Ted Wood	.15	.04
342 Johnny Ard	.15	.04
343 Royce Clayton	.50	.15
344 Paul McClellan	.15	.04
345 John Patterson	.15	.04
346 Steve Hosey	.15	.04
347 Larry Carter	.15	.04
348 Juan Guerrero	.15	.04
349 Bryan Hickerson	.15	.04
350 Rich Huisman	.15	.04
351 Kevin McGehee	.15	.04
352 Gary Sharko	.15	.04
353 Salomon Torres	.15	.04
354 Eric Christopherson	.15	.04
355 Rod Huffman	.15	.04
356 Will VanLandingham	.15	.04
357 Frank Charles	.15	.04
358 Ken Grundt	.15	.04
359 Matt Brewer	.15	.04
360 Checklist (271-360)	.15	.04

1992 Classic/Best

The 1992 Classic/Best Minor League set features top prospects from Double-A and Single-A teams. The cards were sold in a reusable card box initially containing 12 cards but capable of holding a larger quantity. Classic issued a transferable Certificate of Registration to owners mailing in pictures taken showing their autograph card. Classic announced a production run of 20,000 numbered cases. Early cards of Bob Abreu, Johnny Damon, Carlos Delgado, Jim Edmonds, Shawn Green, Derek Jeter (issued only in the high series), Mike Piazza and Manny Ramirez are featured in this set.

	Nm-Mt	Ex-Mt
COMP.FACT.SET (450)	25.00	7.50
COMPLETE LO SET (400)	15.00	4.50
COMP.HI.FACT.SET (50)	15.00	4.50
1 Nolan Ryan	1.00	.30
2 Darius Gash	.15	.04
3 Brad Ausmus	.40	.12
4 Mike Gardella	.15	.04
5 Mark Hutton	.15	.04
6 Bobby Munoz	.15	.04
7 Don Sparks	.15	.04
8 Shane Andrews	.15	.04
9 Gary Hymel	.15	.04
10 Roberto Arredondo	.15	.04
11 Joe Randa	.40	.12
12 Pedro Grifol	.15	.04
13 Steve Dixon	.15	.04
14 John Thomas	.15	.04

15 Chris Durkin .15 .04
16 Jeff Conger .15 .04
17 John Farrell .15 .04
18 Antonio Mitchell .15 .04
19 Matt Ruebel .15 .04
20 Darren Burton .15 .04
21 Lance Jennings .15 .04
22 Kerwin Moore .15 .04
23 Julio Bruno .15 .04
24 Joe Vitiello .15 .04
25 Brook Fordyce .15 .04
26 Rob Katzaroff .15 .04
27 Julian Vasquez .15 .04
28 Alan Zinter .15 .04
29 Clemente Alvarez .15 .04
30 Scott Cepicky .15 .04
31 Mike Mongiello .15 .04
32 Tom Redington .15 .04
33 Johnny Ruffin .15 .04
34 Eric Booker .15 .04
35 Manny Martinez .15 .04
36 Mike Grimes .15 .04
37 Paul Byrd .40 .12
38 Brian Giles 1.00 .30
39 David Mlicki .15 .04
40 Tracy Sanders .15 .04
41 Kyle Washington .15 .04
42 Scott Bullett .15 .04
43 Steve Cooke .15 .04
44 Austin Manahan .15 .04
45 Ben Shelton .15 .04
46 Joe DeBerry .15 .04
47 Steve Gibralter .15 .04
48 Willie Greene .15 .04
49 Brian Koelling .15 .04
50 Larry Luebbers .15 .04
51 Greg Pepper Anthony .15 .04
52 Homer Bush .40 .12
53 Manny Cora .15 .04
54 Joey Hamilton .15 .04
55 David Mowry .15 .04
56 Bobby Perna .15 .04
57 Jamie Dismuke .15 .04
58 Kenneth Gillum .15 .04
59 Pokey Reese .40 .12
60 Phil Dauphin .15 .04
61 Ryan Hawblitzel .15 .04
62 Tim Parker .15 .04
63 Dave Swartzbaugh .15 .04
64 Billy White .15 .04
65 Terry Burrows .15 .04
66 Chris Gies .15 .04
67 Kurt Miller .15 .04
68 Timmie Morrow .15 .04
69 Benny Colvard .15 .04
70 Tim Costo .15 .04
71 Mica Lewis .15 .04
72 John Roper .15 .04
73 Kevin Tatar .15 .04
74 Joel Adamson .15 .04
75 Mike Farmer .15 .04
76 Kevin Stocker .15 .04
77 David Tokheim .15 .04
78 Ray Jackson .15 .04
79 Dax Jones .15 .04
80 Randy Curtis .15 .04
81 Eric Reichenbach .15 .04
82 Jerome Tolliver .15 .04
83 Quilvio Veras .40 .12
84 George Evangelista .15 .04
85 Pat Bryant .15 .04
86 Willie Canate .15 .04
87 Brian Lane .15 .04
88 Howard Battle .15 .04
89 Rob Butler .15 .04
90 Carlos Delgado 1.50 .45
91 Tyler Houston .15 .04
92 Troy Hughes .15 .04
93 Chipper Jones 1.00 .30
94 Mel Nieves .15 .04
95 Jose Olmeda .15 .04
96 John Finn .15 .04
97 Mike Guerrero .15 .04
98 Troy O'Leary .15 .04
99 Ben Blomdahl .15 .04
100 Mike Schmidt .50 .15
101 Carlos Burguillos .15 .04
102 Kiki Hernandez .15 .04
103 Brian DuBose .15 .04
104 Kevin Morgan .15 .04
105 Justin Thompson .15 .04
106 Jason Alstead .15 .04
107 Matt Anderson .15 .04
108 Brad Pennington .15 .04
109 Brad Tyler .15 .04
110 Jovino Carvajal .15 .04
111 Roger Luce .15 .04
112 Ken Powell .15 .04
113 Steve Sadecki .15 .04
114 Craig Clayton .15 .04
115 Russell Davis .40 .12
116 Mike Kelly .15 .04
117 Javy Lopez .40 .12
118 Doug Piatt .15 .04
119 Manny Alexander .15 .04
120 Damon Buford .15 .04
121 Erik Schullstrom .15 .04
122 Mark Smith .15 .04
123 Jeff Williams .15 .04
124 Reid Cornelius .15 .04
125 Tim Laker .15 .04
126 Chris Martin .15 .04
127 Mike Mathile .15 .04
128 Derrick White .15 .04
129 Luis Galindez .15 .04
130 John Kuehl .15 .04
131 Ray McDavid .15 .04
132 Sean Mulligan .15 .04
133 Tookie Spann .15 .04
134 Marcos Armas .15 .04
135 Scott Erwin .15 .04
136 Johnny Guzman .15 .04
137 Mike Mohler .15 .04
138 Craig Paquette .15 .04
139 Dean Tatarian .15 .04
140 Orlando Miller .15 .04
141 Tow Maynard .15 .04
142 Marc Newfield .15 .04
143 Greg Pirkl .15 .04
144 Jesus Tavarez .15 .04
145 Tom Smith .15 .04
146 Brad Seitzer .15 .04
147 Brent Brede .15 .04
148 Elston Hansen .15 .04
149 Jamie Ogden .15 .04
150 Rogelio Nunez .15 .04
151 Manny Cervantes .15 .04
152 David Sartain .15 .04
153 Shawn Bryant .15 .04
154 Chad Ogea .15 .04
155 Manny Ramirez 1.50 .45
156 Darrell Whitmore .15 .04
157 Greg O'Halloran .15 .04
158 Tim Brown .15 .04
159 Curtis Pride .40 .12
160 Marcus Moore .15 .04
161 Robert Perez .15 .04
162 Aaron Small .15 .04
163 David Tollison .15 .04
164 Nigel Wilson .15 .04
165 Jim Givens .15 .04
166 Dennis McNamara .15 .04
167 Kelley O'Neal .15 .04
168 Rudy Pemberton .15 .04
169 Joe Perona .15 .04
170 Brian Cornelius .15 .04
171 Ivan Cruz .15 .04
172 Frank Gonzales .15 .04
173 Mike Lumley .15 .04
174 Brian Warren .15 .04
175 Aaron Sele .40 .12
176 Gary Carballo .15 .04
177 Creighton Gubanich .15 .04
178 Brad Parker .15 .04
179 Scott Sheldon .15 .04
180 Archie Corbin .15 .04
181 Phil Hiatt .15 .04
182 Domingo Mota .15 .04
183 Dan Carlson .15 .04
184 Hugh Walker .15 .04
185 Joe Ciccarella .15 .04
186 John Jackson .15 .04
187 Brent Gates .15 .04
188 Eric Helfand .15 .04
189 Damon Mashore .15 .04
190 Curtis Shaw .15 .04
191 Jason Wood .15 .04
192 Terry Powers .15 .04
193 Steve Karsay .15 .04
194 Greg Blosser .15 .04
195 Gar Finnvold .15 .04
196 Scott Hatteberg .40 .12
197 Derek Livernois .15 .04
198 Jeff McNeely .15 .04
199 Rex DeLaNuez .15 .04
200 Ken Griffey Jr. 1.00 .30
201 Pat Meares .15 .04
202 Alan Newman .15 .04
203 Paul Russo .15 .04
204 Anthony Collier .15 .04
205 Roberto Petagine .15 .04
206 Brian L. Hunter .40 .12
207 James Mouton .15 .04
208 Tom Nevers .15 .04
209 Garret Anderson 1.00 .30
210 Clifton Garrett .15 .04
211 Eduardo Perez .15 .04
212 Shawn Purdy .15 .04
213 Darren Bragg .15 .04
214 Glenn Murray .15 .04
215 Ruben Santana .15 .04
216 Charles(Bubba) Smith .15 .04
217 Terry Adams .15 .04
218 William (Bill) Bliss .15 .04
219 German Diaz .15 .04
220 Willie Gardner .15 .04
221 Ed Larregui .15 .04
222 Tim Garland .15 .04
223 Kevin Jordan .15 .04
224 Tim Rumer .15 .04
225 Jason Robertson .15 .04
226 Todd Claus .15 .04
227 Julian Heredia .15 .04
228 Mark Sweeney .15 .04
229 Robert Eenhoorn .15 .04
230 Tyler Green .15 .04
231 Mike Lieberthal .40 .12
232 Ron Lockett .15 .04
233 Tom Nuneviller .15 .04
234 Sean Ryan .15 .04
235 Alvaro Benavides .15 .04
236 Kevin Bellomo .15 .04
237 Tony Bridges .15 .04
238 Eric Whitford .15 .04
239 James Bishop .15 .04
240 Midre Cummings .15 .04
241 Tom Green .15 .04
242 Marcus Hanel .15 .04
243 Billy Ashley .15 .04
244 Matt Howard .15 .04
245 Tommy Adams .15 .04
246 Craig Bryant .15 .04
247 Ron Pezzoni .15 .04
248 Barry Miller .15 .04
249 Jason McFarlin .15 .04
250 Joe Rosselli .15 .04
251 Billy Van Landingham .15 .04
252 Christopher Seelbach .15 .04
253 Jason Bere .40 .12
254 Eric Christopherson .15 .04
255 Rick Huisman .15 .04
256 Kevin McGehee .15 .04
257 Salomon Torres .15 .04
258 Brian Boehringer .15 .04
259 Glenn DiSarcina .15 .04
260 Jason Schmidt 1.50 .45
261 Charles Poe .15 .04
262 Ricky Bottalico .40 .12
263 Tommy Eason .15 .04
264 Joel Gilmore .15 .04
265 Pat Ruth .15 .04
266 Gene Schall .15 .04
267 Jim Campbell .15 .04
268 Brian Barber .15 .04
269 Allen Battle .15 .04
270 Marc Ronan .15 .04
271 Scott Simmons .15 .04
272 Dmitri Young .40 .12
273 Butch Huskey .15 .04
274 Frank Jacobs .15 .04
275 Aaron Ledesma .15 .04
276 Jose Martinez .15 .04
277 Andy Beasley .15 .04
278 Paul Ellis .15 .04
279 John Kelly .15 .04
280 Jeremy McGarity .15 .04
281 Mateo Ozuna .15 .04
282 Allen Watson .15 .04
283 Francisco Gamez .15 .04
284 Leon Glenn .15 .04
285 Duane Singleton .15 .04
286 Andy Pettitte 1.00 .30
287 Donald Harris .15 .04
288 Robb Nen .40 .12
289 Jose Oliva .15 .04
290 Keith Garagozzo .15 .04
291 Dan Smith .15 .04
292 Kiki Jones .15 .04
293 Rich Becker .15 .04
294 Mike Durant .15 .04
295 Denny Hocking .15 .04
296 Mike Lewis .15 .04
297 Troy Ricker .15 .04
298 Todd Ritchie .15 .04
299 Scott Stahoviak .15 .04
300 Brien Taylor .15 .04
301 Jim Austin .15 .04
302 Mike Daniel .15 .04
303 Joseph Eischen .15 .04
304 Ranbir Grewal .15 .04
305 Rondell White .40 .12
306 Mark Hubbard .15 .04
307 Tate Seefried .15 .04
308 Tom Wilson .15 .04
309 Benji Gil .15 .04
310 Mike Edwards .15 .04
311 J.D. Noland .15 .04
312 Jay Gainer .15 .04
313 Lance Painter .15 .04
314 Tim Worrell .15 .04
315 Sean Cheetham .15 .04
316 Earl Cunningham .15 .04
317 Brad Erdman .15 .04
318 Paul Torres .15 .04
319 Jose Vierra .15 .04
320 Chris Gambs .15 .04
321 Brandon Wilson .15 .04
322 Bret Donovan .15 .04
323 Larry Thomas .15 .04
324 Brian Griffiths .15 .04
325 Chad Schoenvogel .15 .04
326 Mandy Romero .15 .04
327 Chris Curtis .15 .04
328 Jim Campanis .15 .04
329 Anthony Manahan .15 .04
330 Jason Townley .15 .04
331 Fidel Compres .15 .04
332 John Ericks .15 .04
333 Don Prybylinski .15 .04
334 Jason Best .15 .04
335 Rob Wishnevski .15 .04
336 John Byington .15 .04
337 Omar Garcia .15 .04
338 Tony Eusebio .15 .04
339 Paul Swingle .15 .04
340 Mark Zappelli .15 .04
341 Bobby Jones .40 .12
342 J.R. Phillips .15 .04
343 Jim Edmonds 1.00 .30
344 Greg Hansell .15 .04
345 Mike Piazza 2.50 .75
346 Mike Busch .15 .04
347 Darrell Sherman .15 .04
348 Shawn Green 1.50 .45
349 Willie Mota .15 .04
350 David McCarty .15 .04
351 James Dougherty .15 .04
352 Fernando Vina .40 .12
353 Ken Huckaby .15 .04
354 Joe Vitko .15 .04
355 Roberto (Diaz) Mejia .15 .04
356 Willis Otanez .15 .04
357 Billy Lott .15 .04
358 Jason Pruitt .15 .04
359 Jorge Fabregas .15 .04
360 Mike Stefanski .15 .04
361 Robert Saitz .15 .04
362 Scott Talanoa .15 .04
363 LaRue Baber .15 .04
364 Tyrone Hill .15 .04
365 Rick Mediavilla .15 .04
366 Eddie Williams .15 .04
367 Rigo Beltran .15 .04
368 Doug VanderWeele .15 .04
369 Donnie Elliott .15 .04
370 Dan Cholowsky .15 .04
371 Derrell Rumsey .15 .04
372 Tony Graffanino .15 .04
373 Scott Ruffcorn .15 .04
374 Mike Rossiter .15 .04
375 Mike Robertson .15 .04
376 P.J. Forbes .15 .04
377 Doug Brady .15 .04
378 Rick Clelland .15 .04
379 Ugueth Urbina .40 .12
380 Cliff Floyd .75 .23
381 Danny Young .15 .04
382 Eddie Ramos .15 .04
383 Bob Abreu 1.00 .30
384 Gary Mota .15 .04
385 Tony Womack .40 .12
386 Jeff Motuzas .15 .04
387 Desi Relaford .40 .12
388 John Elerman .15 .04
389 Walt McKeel .15 .04
390 Tim VanEgmond .15 .04
391 Frank Rodriguez .15 .04
392 Paul Carey .15 .04
393 Michael Matheny .40 .12
394 George Glinatsis .15 .04
395 Checklist 1-69 .15 .04
396 Checklist 70-138 .15 .04
397 Checklist 139-207 .15 .04
398 Checklist 208-276 .15 .04
399 Checklist 277-345 .15 .04
400 Checklist 346-400 .15 .04
401 Paul Shuey .15 .04
402 Derek Jeter 4.00 1.20
403 Derek Wallace .15 .04
404 Sean Lowe .40 .12
405 Jim Pittsley .15 .04
406 Shannon Stewart .40 .12
407 Jamie Arnold .15 .04
408 Jason Kendall .40 .12
409 Eddie Pearson .15 .04
410 Todd Steverson .15 .04
411 Dan Serafini .15 .04
412 John Burke .15 .04
413 Jeff Schmidt .15 .04
414 Sherard Clinkscales .15 .04
UER (Name misspelled
Sherrard on both sides)
415 Shon Walker .15 .04
416 Brandon Cromer .15 .04
417 Johnny Damon 1.00 .30
418 Michael Moore .15 .04
419 Michael Matthews .15 .04
420 Brian Sackinsky .15 .04
421 Jon Lieber .40 .12
422 Danny Clyburn .15 .04
423 Chris Smith .15 .04
424 Dwain Bostic .15 .04
425 Bob Wolcott .15 .04
426 Mike Gulan .15 .04
427 Yuri Sanchez .15 .04
428 Tony Sheffield .15 .04
429 Ritchie Moody .15 .04
430 Andy Hartung .15 .04
431 Trey Beamon .15 .04
432 Tim Crabtree .15 .04
433 Mark Thompson .15 .04
434 John Lynch .50 .15
435 Adell Davenport .15 .04
436 Juan DeLaRosa .15 .04
437 Ben Gonzalez .15 .04
438 Lew Hill .15 .04
439 Tavo Alvarez .15 .04
440 Kevin Meier .15 .04
441 Troy Penix .15 .04
442 Scott Pose .15 .04
443 Scott Samuels .15 .04
444 Mark Voisard .15 .04
445 Jon Shave .15 .04
446 Joel Chimelis .15 .04
447 Jesus Martinez .15 .04
448 Elgin Bobo .15 .04
449 Chad Fonville .15 .04
450 Checklist (401-450) .15 .04

1992 Classic/Best Autographs

According to Classic, 14,000 numbered and autographed cards of five different superstars were randomly inserted in packs; the players and their quantities are Nolan Ryan (3,000), Mike Schmidt (4,000), Ken Griffey Jr. (3,000), Brien Taylor (3,000) and David McCarty (1,000). The sixth autograph card, that of Royce Clayton (2,000) was randomingly in white jumbo packs.Please note, these cards are not serial numbered, nor is there a stamp of authenticity on the cards and no message stating that is a real autographed card.

	Nm-Mt	Ex-Mt
AU1 Ken Griffey Jr./3100	100.00	30.00
AU2 David McCarty/1000	3.00	.90
AU3 Nolan Ryan/3100	100.00	30.00
AU4 Mike Schmidt/4100	40.00	12.00
AU5 Brien Taylor/3100	3.00	.90
AU6 Royce Clayton/2000	3.00	.90

1992 Classic/Best Blue Bonus

The 30 standard-size cards were inserted one per 1992 Classic/Best Black Jumbo Packs. The cards are numbered on the back with a "BC" prefix. A signed version of the Carlos Delgado card was distributed by Treat Entertainment in special retail packs.

	Nm-Mt	Ex-Mt
COMPLETE SET (30)	25.00	7.50
BC1 Nolan Ryan	2.50	.75
BC2 Mark Hutton	.25	.07
BC3 Shane Andrews	.25	.07
BC4 Scott Bullett	.25	.07
BC5 Kurt Miller	.25	.07
BC6 Carlos Delgado	2.50	.75
BC7 Chipper Jones	2.00	.60
BC8 Dmitri Young	1.00	.30
BC9 Mike Kelly	.25	.07
BC10 Javy Lopez	1.00	.30
BC11 Aaron Sele	1.00	.30
BC12 Ken Griffey Jr.	2.00	.60
BC13 Midre Cummings	.25	.07
BC14 Salomon Torres	.25	.07
BC15 Brien Taylor	.25	.07
BC16 Mike Piazza	6.00	1.80
BC17 David McCarty	.25	.07
BC18 Scott Ruffcorn	.25	.07
BC19 Cliff Floyd	1.50	.45
BC20 Frank Rodriguez	.25	.07
BC21 Paul Shuey	.25	.07
BC22 Derek Jeter	10.00	3.00
BC23 Derek Wallace	.25	.07
BC24 Shannon Stewart	1.00	.30
BC25 Jamie Arnold	.25	.07
BC26 Jason Kendall	1.00	.30
BC27 Todd Steverson	.25	.07
BC28 Dan Serafini	.25	.07
BC29 John Burke	.25	.07
BC30 Michael Moore	.25	.07
A-BC6 Carlos Delgado AU	15.00	4.50

1992 Classic/Best Red Bonus

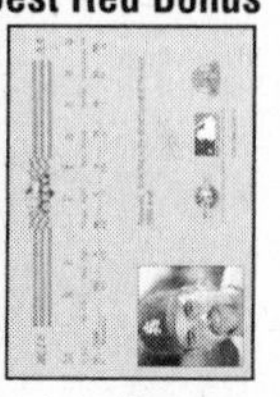

The 20 standard-size cards in this set were inserted one per 1992 Classic/Best Black Jumbo Packs. The Classic/ Best logo and red stripes appear at the top. The cards are numbered on the back with a "BC" prefix. A Chipper Jones autograph card was distributed by Treat Entertainment.

	Nm-Mt	Ex-Mt
COMPLETE SET (20)	15.00	4.50
BC1 Nolan Ryan	2.50	.75
BC2 Mark Hutton	.25	.07
BC3 Shane Andrews	.25	.07
BC4 Scott Bullett	.25	.07
BC5 Kurt Miller	.25	.07
BC6 Carlos Delgado	2.50	.75
BC7 Chipper Jones	2.00	.60
BC8 Dmitri Young	1.00	.30
BC9 Mike Kelly	.25	.07
BC10 Javy Lopez	1.00	.30
BC11 Aaron Sele	1.00	.30
BC12 Ken Griffey Jr.	2.00	.60
BC13 Midre Cummings	.25	.07
BC14 Salomon Torres	.25	.07
BC15 Brien Taylor	.25	.07
BC16 Mike Piazza	6.00	1.80
BC17 David McCarty	.25	.07
BC18 Scott Ruffcorn	.25	.07
BC19 Cliff Floyd	1.50	.45
BC20 Frank Rodriguez	.25	.07
A-BC6 Carlos Delgado AU	15.00	4.50
A-BC7 Chipper Jones AU	25.00	7.50

1992 Classic Draft Picks Previews

These five baseball draft preview standard-size cards were inserted into Classic basketball draft pick foil packs. According to the backs, only 11,200 of each card were produced. The fronts display glossy color action player photos with white borders. The player's name appears in a teal stripe beneath the picture. This stripe intersects the Classic logo at the lower left corner, and the word "Preview" wraps around the top of the logo. The brightly colored backs display a drawing of a batter clad in a red-and-purple uniform with a stadium in the background. This picture is accented by two series of short purple diagonal stripes on the left and right. The picture is overprinted with silver foil lettering.

	Nm-Mt	Ex-Mt
COMPLETE SET (5)	2.00	.60
BB1 Phil Nevin	.50	.15
BB2 Paul Shuey	.50	.15
BB3 B.J. Wallace	.50	.15
BB4 Jeffrey Hammonds	.50	.15
BB5 Chad Mottola	.50	.15

1992 Classic Draft Picks Promos

These three standard-size cards were sealed in a cello pack and show the design of the 1992 Classic Draft Picks issues. All three cards have color player photos on the fronts; card numbers 1-2 have white borders while card number 3 has a silver foil border. The player's name appears in a teal stripe beneath the picture with the Classic logo at the lower left corner. On a forest green background, the backs have a second color photo, biography, and player profile. The backs of card numbers 1-2 are glossy while that of number 3 is not. The cards are marked "For Promotional Purposes Only" on the back. The cards are unnumbered and checklisted below in alphabetical order.

	Nm-Mt	Ex-Mt
COMPLETE SET (3)	6.00	1.80
1 Jeffrey Hammonds UER (Misspelled Jeffery on card front)	2.00	.60
2 Phil Nevin	2.50	.75
3 Brien Taylor	1.50	.45

1992 Classic Draft Picks

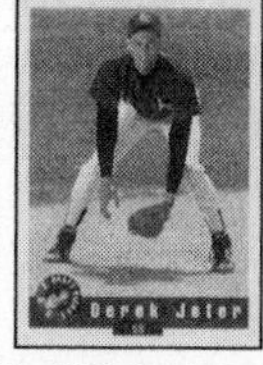

The 1992 Classic Draft Picks set consists of 125 standard-size cards. The set was sold in 16-card jumbo packs only to the hobby and periodical industries. The production run was reported to be 5,000 individually number cases, and no factory sets were produced. A ten-card flashback subset (cards 86-95) features Mike Mussina, Brien Taylor, and Mike Kelly. A Derek

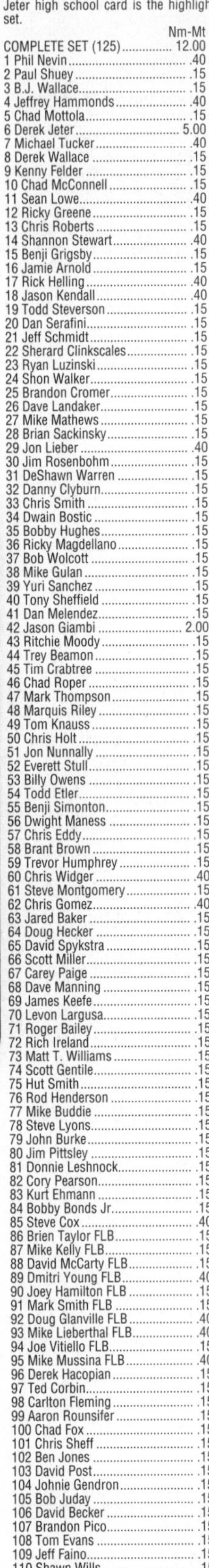

Jeter high school card is the highlight of this set.

Nm-Mt Ex-Mt
COMPLETE SET (125) 12.00 3.60
1 Phil Nevin .40 .12
2 Paul Shuey .15 .04
3 B.J. Wallace .15 .04
4 Jeffrey Hammonds .40 .12
5 Chad Mottola .15 .04
6 Derek Jeter 5.00 1.50
7 Michael Tucker .40 .12
8 Derek Wallace .15 .04
9 Kenny Felder .15 .04
10 Chad McConnell .15 .04
11 Sean Lowe .40 .12
12 Ricky Greene .15 .04
13 Chris Roberts .15 .04
14 Shannon Stewart .40 .12
15 Benji Grigsby .15 .04
16 Jamie Arnold .15 .04
17 Rick Helling .40 .12
18 Jason Kendall .40 .12
19 Todd Steverson .15 .04
20 Dan Serafini .15 .04
21 Jeff Schmidt .15 .04
22 Sherard Clinkscales .15 .04
23 Ryan Luzinski .15 .04
24 Shon Walker .15 .04
25 Brandon Cromer .15 .04
26 Dave Landaker .15 .04
27 Mike Mathews .15 .04
28 Brian Sackinsky .15 .04
29 Jon Lieber .40 .12
30 Jim Rosenbohm .15 .04
31 DeShawn Warren .15 .04
32 Danny Clyburn .15 .04
33 Chris Smith .15 .04
34 Dwain Bostic .15 .04
35 Bobby Hughes .15 .04
36 Ricky Magdellano .15 .04
37 Bob Wolcott .15 .04
38 Mike Gulan .15 .04
39 Yuri Sanchez .15 .04
40 Tony Sheffield .15 .04
41 Dan Melendez .15 .04
42 Jason Giambi 2.00 .60
43 Ritchie Moody .15 .04
44 Trey Beamon .15 .04
45 Tim Crabtree .15 .04
46 Chad Roper .15 .04
47 Mark Thompson .15 .04
48 Marquis Riley .15 .04
49 Tom Knauss .15 .04
50 Chris Holt .15 .04
51 Jon Nunnally .15 .04
52 Everett Stull .15 .04
53 Billy Owens .15 .04
54 Todd Etler .15 .04
55 Benji Simonton .15 .04
56 Dwight Maness .15 .04
57 Chris Eddy .15 .04
58 Brant Brown .15 .04
59 Trevor Humphrey .15 .04
60 Chris Widger .40 .12
61 Steve Montgomery .15 .04
62 Chris Gomez .40 .12
63 Jared Baker .15 .04
64 Doug Hecker .15 .04
65 David Spykstra .15 .04
66 Scott Miller .15 .04
67 Carey Paige .15 .04
68 Dave Manning .15 .04
69 James Keefe .15 .04
70 Levon Largusa .15 .04
71 Roger Bailey .15 .04
72 Rich Ireland .15 .04
73 Matt T. Williams .15 .04
74 Scott Gentile .15 .04
75 Hut Smith .15 .04
76 Rod Henderson .15 .04
77 Mike Buddie .15 .04
78 Steve Lyons .15 .04
79 John Burke .15 .04
80 Jim Pittsley .15 .04
81 Donnie Leshnock .15 .04
82 Cory Pearson .15 .04
83 Kurt Ehmann .15 .04
84 Bobby Bonds Jr. .15 .04
85 Steve Cox .40 .12
86 Brien Taylor FLB .15 .04
87 Mike Kelly FLB .15 .04
88 David McCarty FLB .15 .04
89 Dmitri Young FLB .40 .12
90 Joey Hamilton FLB .15 .04
91 Mark Smith FLB .15 .04
92 Doug Glanville FLB .40 .12
93 Mike Lieberthal FLB .40 .12
94 Joe Vitiello FLB .15 .04
95 Mike Mussina FLB .40 .12
96 Derek Hacopian .15 .04
97 Ted Corbin .15 .04
98 Carlton Fleming .15 .04
99 Aaron Rounsifer .15 .04
100 Chad Fox .15 .04
101 Chris Sheff .15 .04
102 Ben Jones .15 .04
103 David Post .15 .04
104 Johnie Gendron .15 .04
105 Bob Juday .15 .04
106 David Becker .15 .04
107 Brandon Pico .15 .04
108 Tom Evans .15 .04
109 Jeff Faino .15 .04
110 Shawn Wills .15 .04
111 Derrick Cantrell .15 .04
112 Steve Rodriguez .15 .04
113 Ray Suplee .15 .04
114 Pat Leahy .15 .04
115 Matt Luke .15 .04
116 Jon McMullen .15 .04
117 Preston Wilson .75 .23
118 Gus Gandarillas .15 .04
119 Pete Janicki .15 .04
120 Byron Mathews .15 .04
121 Eric Owens .40 .12
122 John Lynch .50 .15
123 Mike Hickey .15 .04
124 Checklist 1-64 .15 .04
125 Checklist 65-125 .15 .04

1992 Classic Draft Picks Foil Bonus

One of these twenty foil bonus standard-size cards was inserted in each 1992 Classic Draft Picks jumbo pack. The photos and text of these bonus cards are identical to the regular issues, except that a silver foil coating has created a metallic sheen on the front, and the forest green backs have a faded look. A three-card flashback subset (cards BC18-BC20) features Brien Taylor, Mike Kelly, and Mike Mussina.

Nm-Mt Ex-Mt
COMPLETE SET (20) 20.00 6.00
BC1 Phil Nevin .75 .23
BC2 Paul Shuey .25 .07
BC3 B.J. Wallace .25 .07
BC4 Jeffrey Hammonds .75 .23
BC5 Chad Mottola .25 .07
BC6 Derek Jeter 8.00 2.40
BC7 Michael Tucker .75 .23
BC8 Derek Wallace .25 .07
BC9 Kenny Felder .25 .07
BC10 Chad McConnell .25 .07
BC11 Sean Lowe .75 .23
BC12 Chris Roberts .25 .07
BC13 Shannon Stewart .75 .23
BC14 Benji Grigsby .25 .07
BC15 Jamie Arnold .25 .07
BC16 Ryan Luzinski .25 .07
BC17 Bobby Bonds Jr. .25 .07
BC18 Brien Taylor FLB .25 .07
BC19 Mike Kelly FLB .25 .07
BC20 Mike Mussina FLB .75 .23

1992 Front Row Draft Picks Promos

These unnumbered cards were issued to preview the 1992 Front Row card set featuring some of the leading high school players in the country. Each card front parallels the corresponding basic issue card. The promo card backs, however, feature a large Front Row logo.

Nm-Mt Ex-Mt
COMPLETE SET (2) 5.00 1.50
NNO Derek Jeter 5.00 1.50
NNO Chad Mottola 1.00 .30

1992 Front Row Draft Picks

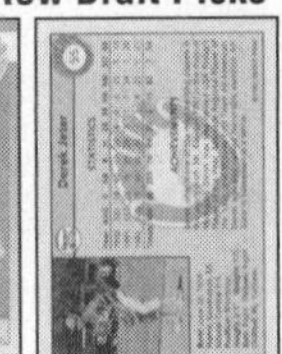

This 100-card standard-size set features color action player photos. According to Front Row, the production run was 10,000 wax cases and 2,500 30-set factory cases (both were individually numbered). Gold and silver foil stamped cards were randomly inserted into wax packs. A Derek Jeter high school card is the highlight of this set.

Nm-Mt Ex-Mt
COMPLETE SET (100) 10.00 3.00
COMP.FACT.SET (100) 10.00 3.00
1 Dan Melendez .15 .04
2 Billy Owens .15 .04
3 Sherard Clinkscales .15 .04
4 Tim Moore .15 .04
5 Mike Hickey .15 .04
6 Ken Carlyle .15 .04
7 Todd Steverson .15 .04
8 Ted Corbin .15 .04
9 Tim Crabtree .15 .04
10 Jason Angel .15 .04
11 Mike Gulan .15 .04
12 Jared Baker .15 .04
13 Mike Buddie .15 .04
14 Brandon Pico .15 .04
15 Jon Nunnally .15 .04
16 Scott Patton .15 .04
17 Tony Sheffield .15 .04
18 Danny Clyburn .15 .04
19 Tom Knauss .15 .04
20 Carey Paige .15 .04
21 Keith Johnson .15 .04
22 Larry Mitchell .15 .04
23 Tim Leger .15 .04
24 Doug Hecker .15 .04
25 Aaron Thatcher .15 .04
26 Marquis Riley .15 .04
27 Jamie Taylor .15 .04
28 Don Wengert .15 .04
29 Jason Moler .15 .04
30 Kevin Kloek .15 .04
31 Kevin Pearson .15 .04
32 David Mysel .15 .04
33 Chris Holt .15 .04
34 Chris Gomez .40 .12
35 Joe Hamilton .15 .04
36 Brandon Cromer .15 .04
37 Lloyd Peever .15 .04
38 Gordon Sanchez .15 .04
39 Bonus Card .15 .04
40 Jason Giambi 2.00 .60
41 Sean Runyan .15 .04
42 Jamie Keefe .15 .04
43 Scott Gentile .15 .04
44 Michael Tucker .40 .12
45 Scott Klingenbeck .15 .04
46 Ed Christian .15 .04
47 Scott Miller .15 .04
48 Rick Navarro .15 .04
49 Bill Selby .15 .04
50 Chris Roberts .15 .04
51 John Dillinger .15 .04
52 Keith Johns .15 .04
53 Matt Williams .15 .04
54 Garvin Alston .15 .04
55 Derek Jeter 5.00 1.50
56 Chris Eddy .15 .04
57 Jeff Schmidt .15 .04
58 Chris Petersen .15 .04
59 Chris Sheff .15 .04
60 Chad Roper .15 .04
61 Rich Ireland .15 .04
62 Tibor Brown .15 .04
63 Todd Etler .15 .04
64 John Turlais .15 .04
65 Shawn Holcomb .15 .04
66 Ben Jones .15 .04
67 Marcel Galligani .15 .04
68 Troy Penix .15 .04
69 Matt Luke .15 .04
70 David Post .15 .04
71 Mike Warner .15 .04
72 Alexis Aranzamendi .15 .04
73 Larry Hingle .15 .04
74 Shon Walker .15 .04
75 Mark Thompson .15 .04
76 Jon Lieber .40 .12
77 Wes Weger .15 .04
78 Mike Smith .15 .04
79 Ritchie Moody .15 .04
80 B.J. Wallace .15 .04
81 Rick Helling .40 .12
82 Chad Mottola .15 .04
83 Brant Brown .15 .04
84 Steve Rodriguez .15 .04
85 John Vanhof .15 .04
86 Brian Wolf .15 .04
87 Steve Montgomery .15 .04
88 Eric Owens .40 .12
89 Jason Kendall .40 .12
90 Bob Bennett .15 .04
91 Joe Petcka .15 .04
92 Jim Rosenbohm .15 .04
93 David Manning .15 .04
94 David Landaker .15 .04
95 Dan Kyslinger .15 .04
96 Roger Bailey .15 .04
97 Jon Zuber .15 .04
98 Steve Cox .40 .12
99 Chris Widger .40 .12
100 Checklist 1-100 .15 .04

1992 Front Row Draft Picks Gold

This is a parallel of the 1992 Front Row Draft Pick set. The cards were distributed in factory set format within a clear 100-ct plastic snap case. Each snap case was sealed with a large green sticker with the words 'Factory Sealed' printed on it. The cards within feature an attractive gold foil treatment running across the top of each card front.

Nm-Mt Ex-Mt
COMP.FACT.SET (100) 50.00 15.00
*GOLD: 2.5X TO 6X BASIC CARDS

1992 Front Row Draft Picks Silver

This Silver parallel of the 1992 Front Row Draft Pick set was issued in factory set form. Each set came in a 100-card plastic snap-case that was sealed with a green factory sticker. Unlike the basic cards, each Silver parallel featured a strip of silver foil running across the top of the card containing the Front Row logo.

Nm-Mt Ex-Mt
COMP.FACT.SET (100) 50.00 15.00
*SILVER: 2.5X TO 6X BASIC CARDS

1992 Front Row Draft Picks Autographs

This 20-card set was issued in sealed factory set form only. Though the cards are not serial-numbered, each set included a certificate of authenticity of which was serial numbered of 500. The cards were signed by the athletes in blue ink and a sticker was placed on back identifying it as a certified autograph.

MINT NRMT
COMP.FACT.SET (20) 300.00 135.00
SEALED FACTORY SET DISTRIBUTION
STATED PRINT RUN 500 SETS
1 Sherard Clinkscales 5.00 2.20
2 Brandon Cromer 5.00 2.20
3 Jason Giambi 40.00 18.00
4 Mike Gulan 5.00 2.20
5 Rick Helling 8.00 3.60
6 Derek Jeter 200.00 90.00
7 Jason Kendall 15.00 6.75
8 David Landaker 5.00 2.20
9 Jon Lieber 8.00 3.60
10 Dan Melendez 5.00 2.20
11 Jason Moler 5.00 2.20
12 Chad Mottola 5.00 2.20
13 Chris Roberts 5.00 2.20
14 Jim Rosenbohm 5.00 2.20
15 Jeff Schmidt 5.00 2.20
16 Tony Sheffield 5.00 2.20
17 Todd Steverson 5.00 2.20
18 Michael Tucker 8.00 3.60
19 Shon Walker 5.00 2.20
20 B.J. Wallace 5.00 2.20

1992 Little Sun High School Prospects

This 30-card set features a selection of top high school ballplayers including future star Derek Jeter. 3,000 sets were produced and each set was distributed in a sticker-sealed, plastic snap case with a serial numbered checklist card. In addition, each youngster featured in the set received a limited number of special 31-card sets that included the basic 30 cards plus an unsigned version of their Autograph insert card.

Nm-Mt Ex-Mt
COMP.OPEN SET (30) 80.00 24.00
COMP.SEALED SET (31) 150.00 45.00
1 Logo Card 1.00 .30
2 Derek Jeter 60.00 18.00
3 William Urbina 1.00 .30
4 Mike Rennhack 1.00 .30
5 Tony Sheffield 1.00 .30
6 Ryan Wilson 1.00 .30
7 Todd Etler 1.00 .30
8 Brendan Hause 1.00 .30
9 Carey Paige 1.00 .30
10 Chris Dean 1.00 .30
11 Jason Kendall 2.50 .75
12 Scott Patton 1.00 .30
13 John Bowles 1.00 .30
14 Sean Runyan 1.00 .30
15 Jason Lowe 1.00 .30
16 David Post 1.00 .30
17 Rick Talbott 1.00 .30
18 Hut Smith 1.00 .30
19 Dave Landaker 1.00 .30
20 Tim Adkins 1.00 .30
21 Tray Nelson 1.00 .30
22 Chad Roper 1.00 .30
23 Steve Lackey 1.00 .30
24 Tom Evans 1.00 .30
25 Damon Hollins 1.00 .30
26 Jeff Patzke 1.00 .30
27 Preston Wilson 8.00 2.40
28 Tyrone Domingo 1.00 .30
29 Rich Hofman 1.00 .30
30 Did You Know 1.00 .30

1992 Little Sun High School Prospects Proofs

These cards were issued to the players that signed autographs for the Little Sun High School prospect set. These cards are unsigned but otherwise are the same as the autographed cards. No pricing is available due to market scarcity.

Nm-Mt Ex-Mt
NNO Derek Jeter
NNO Jason Kendall
NNO Dave Landaker
NNO Chad Roper

1992 Little Sun High School Prospects Autographs

Issued at a rate of one every three factory sets, these four cards feature autographs of four of the players in the Little Sun set. The most important of these cards is a very early autographed card of New York Yankee superstar Derek Jeter. Each player signed 250 cards, although they lack serial numbering.

Nm-Mt Ex-Mt
NNO Derek Jeter 400.00 120.00
NNO Jason Kendall 25.00 7.50
NNO Dave Landaker 10.00 3.00
NNO Chad Roper 10.00 3.00

1992 SkyBox AA

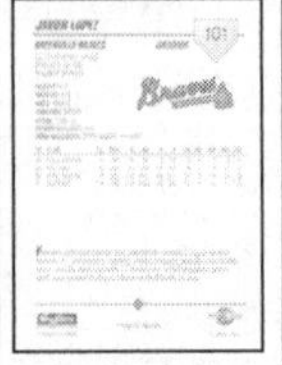

This 310-card standard-size set has glossy color action player photos bordered in white. Early cards of Jim Edmonds, Brian Giles and Mike Piazza are featured in this set.

Nm-Mt Ex-Mt
COMPLETE SET (310) 20.00 6.00
1 Rich Batchelor .15 .04
2 Russ Davis .50 .15
3 Kiki Hernandez .15 .04
4 Sterling Hitchcock .50 .15
5 Darren Hodges .15 .04
6 Jeff Hoffman .15 .04
7 Mark Hutton .15 .04
8 Bobby Munoz .15 .04
9 Rey Noriega .15 .04
10 Sherman Obando .15 .04
11 John Viera .15 .04
12 Cliff Brannon .15 .04
13 Chuck Carr .15 .04
14 Fidel Compres .15 .04
15 Tripp Cromer .15 .04
16 John Ericks .15 .04
17 Gabby Ozuna .15 .04
18 Don Prybylinski .15 .04
19 John Sellick .15 .04
20 John Thomas .15 .04
21 Tom Urbani .15 .04
22 Chris Butterfield .15 .04
23 Todd Douma .15 .04
24 Brook Fordyce .15 .04
25 Tim Howard .15 .04
26 John Johnstone .15 .04
27 Bobby Jones .50 .15
28 Rob Katzaroff .15 .04
29 Gregg Langbehn .15 .04
30 Curtis Pride .50 .15
31 Julian Vasquez .15 .04
32 Joe Vitko .15 .04
33 Tom Wegmann .15 .04
34 Mike White .15 .04
35 Alan Zinter .15 .04
36 Clemente Alvarez .15 .04
37 Cesar Bernhardt .15 .04
38 Wayne Busby .15 .04
39 Scott Cepicky .15 .04
40 John Hudek .15 .04
41 Scott Jaster .15 .04
42 Bo Kennedy .15 .04
43 Mike Mongiello .15 .04
44 Kinnis Pledger .15 .04
45 Johnny Ruffin .15 .04
46 Jose Ventura .15 .04
47 Paul Byrd .50 .15
48 Colin Charland .15 .04
49 Miguel Flores .15 .04
50 Brian Giles 1.00 .30
51 Jose Hernandez .50 .15
52 Nolan Lane .15 .04
53 David Mlicki .15 .04
54 Tracy Sanders .15 .04
55 Mike Soper .15 .04
56 Kelly Stinnett .15 .04
57 Joe Turek .15 .04
58 Kyle Washington .15 .04
59 Dave Bird .15 .04
60 Scott Bullett .15 .04
61 Steve Cooke .15 .04
62 Alberto De Los Santos .15 .04
63 Stan Fansler .15 .04
64 Austin Manahan .15 .04
65 Daryl Ratliff .15 .04
66 Mandy Romero .15 .04
67 Ben Shelton .15 .04
68 Paul Wagner .15 .04
69 Mike Zimmerman .15 .04
70 Phil Dauphin .15 .04
71 Chris Ebright .15 .04
72 Mike Grace .15 .04
73 Ryan Hawblitzel .15 .04
74 Jessie Hollins .15 .04
75 Tim Parker .15 .04
76 Dave Swartzbaugh .15 .04
77 Steve Trachsel .15 .04
78 Billy White .15 .04
79 Bobby Ayala .15 .04
80 Tim Costo .15 .04
81 Ty Griffin .15 .04
82 Cesar Hernandez .15 .04
83 Trevor Hoffman 1.00 .30
84 Brian Lane .15 .04
85 Scott Pose .15 .04
86 Johnny Ray .15 .04
87 John Roper .15 .04
88 Glenn Sutko .15 .04
89 Kevin Tatar .15 .04
90 John Byington .15 .04
91 Tony Diggs .15 .04
92 Bo Dodson .15 .04
93 Craig Faulkner .15 .04
94 Jim Hunter .15 .04
95 Oreste Marrero .15 .04
96 Troy O'Leary .15 .04
97 Brian Bark .15 .04
98 Dennis Burlingame .15 .04
99 Ramon Caraballo .15 .04
100 Mike Kelly .15 .04
101 Javy Lopez .50 .15
102 Don Strange .15 .04
103 Tony Tarasco .15 .04
104 Manny Alexander .15 .04
105 Damon Buford .15 .04
106 Cesar Devares .15 .04
107 Rodney Lofton .15 .04
108 Brent Miller .15 .04
109 David Miller .15 .04
110 Daryl Moore .15 .04
111 John O'Donoghue .15 .04
112 Erik Schullstrom .15 .04
113 Mark Smith .15 .04
114 Mel Wearing .15 .04
115 Jeff Williams .15 .04
116 Kip Yaughn .15 .04
117 Doug Bochtler .15 .04
118 Travis Buckley .15 .04
119 Reid Cornelius .15 .04
120 Chris Johnson .15 .04
121 Tim Laker .15 .04
122 Chris Martin .15 .04
123 Mike Mathile .15 .04
124 Darwin Pennye .15 .04
125 Doug Piatt .15 .04
126 Kurt Abbott .50 .15
127 Marcos Armas .15 .04
128 James Buccheri .15 .04
129 Kevin Dettola .15 .04
130 Scott Erwin .15 .04
131 Johnny Guzman .15 .04
132 David Jacas .15 .04

Card	Nm-Mt	Ex-Mt
33 Francisco Matos	.15	.04
34 Mike Mohler	.15	.04
35 Craig Paquette	.15	.04
36 Todd Revenig	.15	.04
37 Todd Smith	.15	.04
38 Ricky Strebeck	.15	.04
39 Sam August	.15	.04
40 Tony Eusebio	.15	.04
41 Brian Griffiths	.15	.04
42 Todd Jones	.50	.15
43 Orlando Miller	.15	.04
44 Howard Prager	.15	.04
45 Matt Rambo	.15	.04
46 Lee Sammons	.15	.04
47 Richie Simon	.15	.04
48 Frank Bolick	.15	.04
49 Jim Campanis	.15	.04
50 Jim Converse	.15	.04
51 Bobby Holley	.15	.04
52 Troy Kent	.15	.04
53 Brent Knackert	.15	.04
54 Anthony Manahan	.15	.04
55 Tow Maynard	.15	.04
56 Mike McDonald	.15	.04
57 Marc Newfield	.15	.04
58 Greg Pirkl	.15	.04
59 Jesus Tavarez	.15	.04
60 Kerry Woodson	.15	.04
61 Graeme Lloyd	.15	.04
62 Paul Menhart	.15	.04
63 Marcus Moore	.15	.04
64 Greg O'Halloran	.15	.04
65 Mark Ohlms	.15	.04
66 Robert Perez	.15	.04
67 Aaron Small	.15	.04
68 Nigel Wilson	.15	.04
69 Julian Yan	.15	.04
70 Jeff Braley	.15	.04
71 Brian Cornelius	.15	.04
72 Ivan Cruz	.15	.04
73 Lou Frazier	.15	.04
74 Frank Gonzalez	.15	.04
75 Tyrone Kingwood	.15	.04
76 Leo Torres	.15	.04
77 Brian Warren	.15	.04
78 Brian Ahern	.15	.04
79 Tony Bridges	.15	.04
80 Paco Burgos	.15	.04
81 Adam Casillas	.15	.04
82 Archie Corbin	.15	.04
83 Phil Hiatt	.15	.04
84 Marcus Lawton	.15	.04
85 Domingo Mota	.15	.04
86 Mark Parnell	.15	.04
87 Ed Pierce	.15	.04
88 Rich Tunison	.15	.04
89 Hugh Walker	.15	.04
90 Skip Wiley	.15	.04
91 Dave Adams	.15	.04
92 Mick Billmeyer	.15	.04
93 Marvin Cobb	.15	.04
94 Jim Edmonds	1.00	.30
95 Corey Kapano	.15	.04
96 Jeff Kipila	.15	.04
97 Joe Kraemer	.15	.04
98 Rey Martinez	.15	.04
99 J.R. Phillips	.15	.04
00 Darryl Scott	.15	.04
01 Paul Swingle	.15	.04
02 Mark Zapelli	.15	.04
03 Greg Blosser	.15	.04
04 Bruce Chick	.15	.04
05 Colin Dixon	.15	.04
06 Gar Finnvold	.15	.04
07 Scott Hatteberg	.50	.15
08 Derek Livernois	.15	.04
09 Jeff McNeely	.15	.04
10 Tony Mosley	.15	.04
11 Bill Norris	.15	.04
12 Ed Riley	.15	.04
13 Ken Ryan	.15	.04
14 Tim Smith	.15	.04
15 Willie Tatum	.15	.04
16 Rex De La Nuez	.15	.04
17 Rich Garces	.15	.04
18 Curtis Leskanic	.15	.04
19 Mica Lewis	.15	.04
20 David McCarty	.15	.04
21 Pat Meares	.15	.04
22 Alan Newman	.15	.04
23 Jayhawk Owens	.15	.04
24 Carlos Pulido	.15	.04
25 Rusty Richards	.15	.04
26 Paul Russo	.15	.04
27 Brad Brink	.15	.04
28 Andy Carter	.15	.04
29 Tyler Green	.15	.04
30 Mike Lieberthal	.50	.15
31 Chris Limbech	.15	.04
32 Ron Lockett	.15	.04
33 Tom Nuneviller	.15	.04
34 Troy Paulson	.15	.04
35 Todd Pratt	.15	.04
36 Sean Ryan	.15	.04
37 Matt Stevens	.15	.04
38 Sam Taylor	.15	.04
39 Casey Waller	.15	.04
40 Mike Williams	.15	.04
41 Jorge Alvarez	.15	.04
42 Billy Ashley	.15	.04
43 Tim Barker	.15	.04
44 Bill Bene	.15	.04
45 John Deutsch	.15	.04
46 Greg Hansell	.15	.04
47 Matt Howard	.15	.04
48 Ron Maurer	.15	.04
49 Mike Mimbs	.15	.04
50 Chris Morrow	.15	.04
51 Mike Piazza	6.00	1.80
52 Dennis Springer	.15	.04
53 Clay Bellinger	.15	.04
54 Dan Carlson	.15	.04
55 Eric Christopherson	.15	.04
56 Adell Davenport	.15	.04
57 Steve Finken	.15	.04
58 Rick Huisman	.15	.04
59 Kevin McGehee	.15	.04
60 Dan Rambo	.15	.04
61 Steve Reed	.15	.04
62 Kevin Rogers	.15	.04
263 Salomon Torres	.15	.04
264 Pete Weber	.15	.04
265 Brian Romero	.15	.04
266 Cris Colon	.15	.04
267 Rusty Greer	.50	.15
268 Donald Harris	.15	.04
269 David Hulse	.15	.04
270 Pete Kidd	.15	.04
271 Robb Nen	.50	.15
272 Jose Oliva	.15	.04
273 Steve Rowley	.15	.04
274 Jon Shave	.15	.04
275 Cedric Shaw	.15	.04
276 Dan Smith	.15	.04
277 Matt Whiteside	.15	.04
278 Scott Fredrickson	.15	.04
279 Jay Gainer	.15	.04
280 Paul Gonzalez	.15	.04
281 Vince Harris	.15	.04
282 Ray Holbert	.15	.04
283 Dwayne Hosey	.15	.04
284 J.D. Noland	.15	.04
285 Lance Painter	.15	.04
286 Scott Sanders	.15	.04
287 Darrell Sherman	.15	.04
288 Brian Wood	.15	.04
289 Tim Worrell	.15	.04
290 John Jaha	.50	.15
291 Jim Bowie	.15	.04
292 Mark Howie	.15	.04
293 Matt Stairs	.15	.04
294 Larry Carter	.15	.04
295 Pat Mahomes	.15	.04
296 Jeff Mutis	.15	.04
297 Municipal Stadium	.15	.04
298 Knights Castle	.15	.04
299 Engel Stadium	.15	.04
300 T.McCarver Stadium	.15	.04
301 Beehive Field	.15	.04
302 Tinker Field	.15	.04
303 Checklist Alpha 1	.15	.04
304 Checklist Alpha 2	.15	.04
305 Checklist Alpha 3	.15	.04
306 Checklist Alpha 4	.15	.04
307 Checklist Numeric 1	.15	.04
308 Checklist Numeric 2	.15	.04
309 Checklist Numeric 3	.15	.04
310 Checklist Numeric 4	.15	.04

1992 SkyBox AAA

This 310-card standard-size set has glossy color action player photos bordered in white. Please note that a few Tim Salmon error cards packed out into the product as card number 165 (it is unclear as to how many of these cards packed out). An early card of Pedro Martinez is featured in this set.

Card	Nm-Mt	Ex-Mt
COMPLETE SET (310)	15.00	4.50
1 Pedro Astacio	.50	.15
2 Bryan Baar	.15	.04
3 Tom Goodwin	.15	.04
4 Jeff Hamilton	.15	.04
5 Pedro Martinez	3.00	.90
6 Jamie McAndrew	.15	.04
7 Mark Mimbs	.15	.04
8 Raul Mondesi	.50	.15
9 Jose Munoz	.15	.04
10 Henry Rodriguez	.15	.04
11 Eric Young	.50	.15
12 Joe Ausanio	.15	.04
13 Victor Cole	.15	.04
14 Carlos Garcia	.15	.04
15 Blas Minor	.15	.04
16 William Pennyfeather	.15	.04
17 Mark Petkovsek	.15	.04
18 Jeff Richardson	.15	.04
19 Rosario Rodriguez	.15	.04
20 Tim Wakefield	.75	.23
21 John Wehner	.15	.04
22 Kevin Young	.50	.15
23 Mike Blowers	.15	.04
24 Bret Boone	.50	.15
25 Jim Bowie	.15	.04
26 Dave Brundage	.15	.04
27 Randy Kramer	.15	.04
28 Patrick Lennon	.15	.04
29 Jim Newlin	.15	.04
30 Jose Nunez	.15	.04
31 Mike Remlinger	.15	.04
32 Pat Rice	.15	.04
33 Roger Salkeld	.15	.04
34 Beau Allred	.15	.04
35 Denis Boucher	.15	.04
36 Mike Christopher	.15	.04
37 Daren Epley	.15	.04
38 Tom Kramer	.15	.04
39 Jerry DiPoto	.15	.04
40 Jeff Mutis	.15	.04
41 Jeff Shaw	.50	.15
42 Lee Tinsley	.15	.04
43 Kevin Wickander	.15	.04
44 Royal Clayton	.15	.04
45 Bobby DeJardin	.15	.04
46 Mike Draper	.15	.04
47 Mike Humphreys	.15	.04
48 Torey Lovullo	.15	.04
49 Ed Martel	.15	.04
50 Billy Masse	.15	.04
51 Hensley Meulens	.15	.04
52 Sam Militello	.15	.04
53 John Ramos	.15	.04
54 David Rosario	.15	.04
55 David Silvestri	.15	.04
56 J.T. Snow	.50	.15
57 Russ Springer	.15	.04
58 Larry Stanford	.15	.04
59 Wade Taylor	.15	.04
60 Gerald Williams	.15	.04
61 Cal Eldred	.15	.04
62 Chris George	.15	.04
63 Otis Green	.15	.04
64 Mike Ignasiak	.15	.04
65 John Jaha	.50	.15
66 Mark Kiefer	.15	.04
67 Matt Mieske	.15	.04
68 Angel Miranda	.15	.04
69 Dave Nilsson	.50	.15
70 Jim Olander	.15	.04
71 Jim Tatum	.15	.04
72 Jose Valentin	.50	.15
73 Don Barbara	.15	.04
74 Chris Beasley	.15	.04
75 Mike Butcher	.15	.04
76 Damion Easley	.50	.15
77 Kevin Flora	.15	.04
78 Tim Fortugno	.15	.04
79 Larry Gonzalez	.15	.04
80 Todd James	.15	.04
81 Tim Salmon	.50	.15
82 Don Vidmar	.15	.04
83 Cliff Young	.15	.04
84 Shon Ashley	.15	.04
85 Brian Barnes	.15	.04
86 Blaine Beatty	.15	.04
87 Kent Bottenfield	.50	.15
88 Wil Cordero	.15	.04
89 Jerry Goff	.15	.04
90 Jon Hurst	.15	.04
91 Jim Kremers	.15	.04
92 Matt Maysey	.15	.04
93 Rob Natal	.15	.04
94 Matt Stairs	.15	.04
95 David Wainhouse	.15	.04
96 Alex Arias	.15	.04
97 Scott Bryant	.15	.04
98 Jim Bullinger	.15	.04
99 Pedro Castellano	.15	.04
100 Lance Dickson	.15	.04
101 John Gardner	.15	.04
102 Jeff Hartsock	.15	.04
103 Elvin Paulino	.15	.04
104 Fernando Ramsey	.15	.04
105 Laddie Renfroe	.15	.04
106 Kevin Roberson	.15	.04
107 John Salles	.15	.04
108 Derrick May	.15	.04
109 Turk Wendell	.50	.15
110 Doug Brocail	.15	.04
111 Terry Bross	.15	.04
112 Scott Coolbaugh	.15	.04
113 Rick Davis	.15	.04
114 Jeff Gardner	.15	.04
115 Steve Pegues	.15	.04
116 Frank Seminara	.15	.04
117 Dave Staton	.15	.04
118 Will Taylor	.15	.04
119 Jim Vatcher	.15	.04
120 Guillermo Velasquez	.15	.04
121 Dan Walters	.15	.04
122 Rene Arocha	.50	.15
123 Rod Brewer	.15	.04
124 Ozzie Canseco	.15	.04
125 Mark Clark	.15	.04
126 Joey Fernandez	.15	.04
127 Lonnie Maclin	.15	.04
128 Mike Milchin	.15	.04
129 Stan Royer	.15	.04
130 Tracy Woodson	.15	.04
131 Bob Buchanan	.15	.04
132 Mark Howie	.15	.04
133 Tony Menendez	.15	.04
134 Gino Minutelli	.15	.04
135 Tim Pugh	.15	.04
136 Mo Sanford	.15	.04
137 Joey Vierra	.15	.04
138 Dan Wilson	.50	.15
139 Kevin Blankenship	.15	.04
140 Todd Burns	.15	.04
141 Tom Drees	.15	.04
142 Jeff Frye	.15	.04
143 Chuck Jackson	.15	.04
144 Rob Maurer	.15	.04
145 Russ McGinnis	.15	.04
146 Dan Peltier	.15	.04
147 Wayne Rosenthal	.15	.04
148 Bob Sebra	.15	.04
149 Sean Berry	.15	.04
150 Stu Cole	.15	.04
151 Jeff Conine	.50	.15
152 Kevin Koslofski	.15	.04
153 Kevin Long	.15	.04
154 Carlos Maldonado	.15	.04
155 Dennis Moeller	.15	.04
156 Harvey Pulliam	.15	.04
157 Luis Medina	.15	.04
158 Steve Shifflett	.15	.04
159 Tim Spehr	.15	.04
160 Brian Conroy	.15	.04
161 Wayne Housie	.15	.04
162 Daryl Irvine	.15	.04
163 Dave Milstien	.15	.04
164 Jeff Plympton	.15	.04
165 Tim Salmon ERR	.50	.15
165 Paul Quantrill	.15	.04
166 Larry Shikles	.15	.04
167 Scott Taylor	.15	.04
168 Mike Twardoski	.15	.04
169 John Valentin	.15	.04
170 David Walters	.15	.04
171 Eric Wedge	.15	.04
172 Bob Zupcic	.15	.04
173 Johnny Ard	.15	.04
174 Larry Carter	.15	.04
175 Steve Decker	.15	.04
176 Steve Hosey	.15	.04
177 Paul McClellan	.15	.04
178 Jim Myers	.15	.04
179 Jamie Cooper	.15	.04
180 Pat Rapp	.15	.04
181 Ted Wood	.15	.04
182 Willie Banks	.15	.04
183 Bernardo Brito	.15	.04
184 J.T. Bruett	.15	.04
185 Larry Casian	.15	.04
186 Shawn Gilbert	.15	.04
187 Greg Johnson	.15	.04
188 Terry Jorgensen	.15	.04
189 Edgar Naveda	.15	.04
190 Derek Parks	.15	.04
191 Danny Sheaffer	.15	.04
192 Mike Trombley	.15	.04
193 George Tsamis	.15	.04
194 Rob Wessenaar	.50	.15
195 Vinny Castilla	.50	.15
196 Pat Gomez	.15	.04
197 Ryan Klesko	.50	.15
198 Keith Mitchell	.15	.04
199 Bobby Moore	.15	.04
200 David Nied	.15	.04
201 Armando Reynoso	.50	.15
202 Napoleon Robinson	.15	.04
203 Boi Rodriguez	.15	.04
204 Randy St. Claire	.15	.04
205 Mark Wohlers	.15	.04
206 Ricky Gutierrez	.15	.04
207 Mike Lehman	.15	.04
208 Richie Lewis	.15	.04
209 Scott Meadows	.15	.04
210 Mike Oquist	.15	.04
211 Arthur Rhodes	.15	.04
212 Ken Shamburg	.15	.04
213 Todd Stephan	.15	.04
214 Anthony Telford	.15	.04
215 Jack Voigt	.15	.04
216 Bob Ayrault	.15	.04
217 Toby Borland	.15	.04
218 Braulio Castillo	.15	.04
219 Darrin Chapin	.15	.04
220 Bruce Dostal	.15	.04
221 Tim Mauser	.15	.04
222 Steve Scarsone	.15	.04
223 Rick Schu	.15	.04
224 Butch Davis	.15	.04
225 Ray Giannelli	.15	.04
226 Randy Knorr	.15	.04
227 Al Leiter	.50	.15
228 Doug Linton	.15	.04
229 Domingo Martinez	.15	.04
230 Tom Quinlan	.15	.04
231 Jerry Schunk	.15	.04
232 Ed Sprague	.15	.04
233 David Weathers	.15	.04
234 Eddie Zosky	.15	.04
235 John Briscoe	.15	.04
236 Kevin Campbell	.15	.04
237 Jeff Carter	.15	.04
238 Steve Chitren	.15	.04
239 Reggie Harris	.15	.04
240 Dann Howitt	.15	.04
241 Troy Neel	.15	.04
242 Gavin Osteen	.15	.04
243 Tim Peek	.15	.04
244 Todd Van Poppel	.15	.04
245 Ron Witmeyer	.15	.04
246 David Zancanaro	.15	.04
247 Kevin Baez	.15	.04
248 Jeromy Burnitz	.50	.15
249 Chris Donnels	.15	.04
250 D.J. Dozier	.15	.04
251 Terrel Hansen	.15	.04
252 Eric Hillman	.15	.04
253 Pat Howell	.15	.04
254 Lee May Jr.	.15	.04
255 Pete Schourek	.15	.04
256 David Telgheder	.15	.04
257 Julio Valera	.15	.04
258 Rico Brogna	.15	.04
259 Steve Carter	.15	.04
260 Steve Cummings	.15	.04
261 Greg Gohr	.15	.04
262 David Haas	.15	.04
263 Shawn Hare	.15	.04
264 Riccardo Ingram	.15	.04
265 John Kiely	.15	.04
266 Kurt Knudsen	.15	.04
267 Victor Rosario	.15	.04
268 Rich Rowland	.15	.04
269 John DeSilva	.15	.04
270 Gary Cooper	.15	.04
271 Chris Gardner	.15	.04
272 Jeff Juden	.15	.04
273 Rob Mallicoat	.15	.04
274 Andy Mota	.15	.04
275 Shane Reynolds	.50	.15
276 Mike Simms	.15	.04
277 Scooter Tucker	.15	.04
278 Brian Williams	.15	.04
279 Rod Bolton	.15	.04
280 Ron Coomer	.50	.15
281 Chris Cron	.15	.04
282 Ramon Garcia	.15	.04
283 Chris Howard	.15	.04
284 Roberto Hernandez	.50	.15
285 Derek Lee	.15	.04
286 Ever Magallanes	.15	.04
287 Norberto Martin	.15	.04
288 Greg Perschke	.15	.04
289 Ron Stephens	.15	.04
290 Derek Bell POY	.50	.15
291 Rich Amaral	.15	.04
292 Derek Bell BC	.50	.15
293 Jim Olander	.15	.04
294 Gil Heredia	.50	.15
295 Rick Reed	.50	.15
296 Armando Reynoso	.50	.15
297 Charlotte NC	.15	.04
298 Ottawa Ontario	.15	.04
299 Pilot Field	.15	.04
300 H.Cooper Stadium	.15	.04
301 Bush Stadium	.15	.04
302 Silver Stadium	.15	.04
303 Checklist Alpha 1	.15	.04
304 Checklist Alpha 2	.15	.04
305 Checklist Alpha 3	.15	.04
306 Checklist Alpha 4	.15	.04
307 Checklist Numeric 1	.15	.04
308 Checklist Numeric 2	.15	.04
309 Checklist Numeric 3	.15	.04
310 Checklist Numeric 4	.15	.04

1992 Upper Deck Minors

The 1992 Upper Deck Minor League set consists of 330 standard-size cards highlighting top prospects and stand out players from Triple-A, Double-A and Single-A teams. No factory sets were produced and the foil packs featured a 26-card Organizational Players of the Year insert set and a nine-card Top Prospect Holograms insert set. The set commences with three subsets: 1992 Draft Picks (1-23), Team Checklists (24-49) and Diamond Skills (50-70). The remainder of the set (260 cards) highlights the top ten players in each of the 26 minor league organizations. Early cards of Johnny Damon, Carlos Delgado, Jason Giambi, Shawn Green, Derek Jeter, Chipper Jones, Manny Ramirez and Shannon Stewart are featured in this set.

Card	Nm-Mt	Ex-Mt
COMPLETE SET (330)	30.00	9.00
1 Johnny Damon CL Michael Tucker FDP CL	.50	.15
2 B.J. Wallace FDP	.15	.04
3 Jeffrey Hammonds FDP	.50	.15
4 Chad Mottola FDP	.15	.04
5 Derek Jeter FDP	15.00	4.50
6 Michael Tucker FDP	.50	.15
7 Derek Wallace FDP	.15	.04
8 Chad McConnell FDP	.15	.04
9 Rick Greene FDP	.15	.04
10 Shannon Stewart FDP	.50	.15
11 Benji Grigsby FDP	.15	.04
12 Jamie Arnold FDP	.15	.04
13 Rick Helling FDP	.50	.15
14 Jason Kendall FDP	.50	.15
15 Eddie Pearson FDP	.15	.04
16 Todd Steverson FDP	.15	.04
17 John Burke FDP	.15	.04
18 Brandon Cromer FDP	.15	.04
19 Johnny Damon FDP	1.00	.30
20 Jason Giambi FDP	4.00	1.20
21 John Lynch FDP	3.00	.90
22 Jared Baker FDP	.15	.04
23 Roger Bailey FDP	.15	.04
24 Eduardo Perez TC	.15	.04
25 Gary Mota TC	.15	.04
26 Mike Neill TC	.15	.04
27 Howard Battle TC	.15	.04
28 Mike Kelly TC	.15	.04
29 Tyrone Hill TC	.15	.04
30 Dmitri Young TC	.50	.15
31 Ryan Hawblitzel TC	.15	.04
32 Raul Mondesi TC	.50	.15
33 Rondell White TC	.15	.04
34 Salomon Torres TC	.15	.04
35 Manny Ramirez TC	.50	.15
36 Marc Newfield TC	.15	.04
37 Butch Huskey TC	.15	.04
38 Mark Smith TC	.15	.04
39 Joey Hamilton TC	.15	.04
40 Tyler Green TC	.15	.04
41 Midre Cummings TC	.15	.04
42 Kurt Miller TC	.15	.04
43 Frank Rodriguez TC	.15	.04
44 John Roper TC	.15	.04
45 Phil Hiatt TC	.15	.04
46 Justin Thompson TC	.15	.04
47 David McCarty TC	.15	.04
48 Mike Robertson TC	.15	.04
49 Brien Taylor TC	.15	.04
50 Carlos Delgado CL Rondell White CL	.75	.23
51 Damon Buford DS	.15	.04
52 Mike Neill DS	.15	.04
53 Carlos Delgado DS	1.00	.30
54 Frank Rodriguez DS	.15	.04
55 Manny Ramirez DS	1.00	.30
56 Carl Everett DS	.50	.15
57 Brien Taylor DS	.15	.04
58 Kurt Miller DS	.15	.04
59 Alex Ochoa DS	.15	.04
60 Alex Gonzalez DS	.50	.15
61 Darrell Sherman DS	.15	.04
62 Dmitri Young DS	.50	.15
63 Cliff Floyd DS	.50	.15
64 Ray McDavid DS	.15	.04
65 Rondell White DS	.50	.15
66 Chipper Jones DS	.75	.23
67 Allen Watson DS	.15	.04
68 Tyler Green DS	.15	.04
69 Steve Gibralter DS	.15	.04
70 Pokey Reese DS	.15	.04
71 Scott Burrell	.50	.15
72 Julian Vasquez	.15	.04
73 Juan Delarosa	.15	.04
74 Lance Dickson	.15	.04
75 Todd Van Poppel	.15	.04
76 Joey Hamilton	.15	.04
77 Mark Mimbs	.15	.04
78 Austin Manahan	.15	.04
79 Mike Milchin	.15	.04
80 David Bell	.50	.15
81 Terrell Lowery	.15	.04
82 Tony Tarasco	.15	.04
83 Shon Walker	.15	.04
84 Robb Nen	.50	.15
85 Turk Wendell	.50	.15
86 John Byington	.15	.04
87 Derek Reid	.15	.04
88 Lee Heath	.15	.04
89 Matt Anderson	.15	.04
90 Joe Perona	.15	.04
91 Tito Navarro	.15	.04
92 Scott Erwin	.15	.04
93 Jim Pittsley	.15	.04
94 Chris Seelbach	.15	.04
95 Skeets Thomas	.15	.04
96 Kevin Flora	.15	.04
97 Scott Pose	.15	.04
98 Jason Hardtke	.15	.04
99 Joe Ciccarella	.15	.04
100 Les Norman	.15	.04

101 Joe Calder .15 .04
102 Willie Otanez .15 .04
103 Ray Holbert .15 .04
104 Dan Serafini .15 .04
105 Trevor Hoffman 1.50 .45
106 Todd Ritchier .15 .04
107 Lance Jennings .15 .04
108 Jon Farrell .15 .04
109 Rick Gorecki .15 .04
110 Kevin Stocker .15 .04
111 Joe Caruso .15 .04
112 Tom Nuneviller .15 .04
113 Matt Mieske .15 .04
114 Luis Ortiz .15 .04
115 Marty Cordova .50 .15
116 Rikkert Faneyte .15 .04
117 Rodney Bolton .15 .04
118 Steve Trachsel .15 .04
119 Sean Lowe .50 .15
120 Sean Ryan .15 .04
121 Tim Vanegmond .15 .04
122 Craig Paquette .15 .04
123 Andre Keene .15 .04
124 Kevin Roberson .15 .04
125 Mark Anthony .15 .04
126 Joe DeBerry .15 .04
127 Tracy Sanders .15 .04
128 Eric Christopherson .15 .04
129 Steve Dreyer .15 .04
130 Jeromy Burnitz .50 .15
131 Mike Lansing .50 .15
132 Russ Davis .50 .15
133 Pedro Castellano .15 .04
134 Troy Percival 1.00 .30
135 Tyrone Hill .15 .04
136 Rene Arocha .50 .15
137 John DeSilva .15 .04
138 Donne Wall .15 .04
139 Justin Mashore .15 .04
140 Miguel Flores .15 .04
141 John Finn .15 .04
142 Paul Shuey .15 .04
143 Gabby Martinez .15 .04
144 Ryan Luzinski .15 .04
145 Brent Gates .15 .04
146 Manny Ramirez 3.00 .90
147 Mark Hutton .15 .04
148 Derek Lee .15 .04
149 Scott Pisciotta .15 .04
150 Greg Hansell .15 .04
151 Tyler Houston .15 .04
152 Chris Pritchett .15 .04
153 Allen Watson .15 .04
154 Steve Karsay .15 .04
155 Carl Everett .50 .15
156 Mike Robertson .15 .04
157 Fausto Cruz .15 .04
158 Kiki Hernandez .15 .04
159 Bill Bliss .15 .04
160 Todd Hollandsworth .50 .15
161 Justin Thompson .15 .04
162 Ozzie Timmons .15 .04
163 Raul Mondesi .50 .15
164 Shawn Estes .50 .15
165 Chipper Jones 2.00 .60
166 Kurt Miller .15 .04
167 Tyler Green .15 .04
168 Jimmy Haynes .50 .15
169 Dave Doorneweerd .15 .04
170 Bubba Smith .15 .04
171 Scott Lydy .15 .04
172 Aaron Holbert .15 .04
173 Doug Glanville .50 .15
174 Benji Gil .15 .04
175 Eddie Williams .15 .04
176 Phil Hiatt .15 .04
177 Chris Durkin .15 .04
178 Brian Barber .15 .04
179 John Cummings .15 .04
180 Frank Campos .15 .04
181 Tim Worrell .15 .04
182 Tony Clark .50 .15
183 T.R. Lewis .15 .04
184 Mike Lieberthal .50 .15
185 Keith Mitchell .15 .04
186 Rick Huisman .15 .04
187 Quilvio Veras .50 .15
188 Brian Hancock .15 .04
189 Tarrik Brock .15 .04
190 Herbert Perry .50 .15
191 Dave Staton .15 .04
192 Derek Lowe 1.50 .45
193 Joel Wolfe .15 .04
194 Lyle Mouton .15 .04
195 Greg Gohr .15 .04
196 Duane Singleton .15 .04
197 Jamie McAndrew .15 .04
198 Brad Pennington .15 .04
199 Pork Chop Pough .15 .04
200 Boo Moore .15 .04
201 Henry Blanco .15 .04
202 Gabe White .15 .04
203 Manny Cora .15 .04
204 Keith Gordon .15 .04
205 John Jackson .15 .04
206 Mike Hostetler .15 .04
207 Jeff McCurry .15 .04
208 Steve Olsen .15 .04
209 Roberto Mejia .15 .04
210 Ramon Caraballo .15 .04
211 Matt Whisenant .15 .04
212 Mike Bovee .15 .04
213 Riccardo Ingram .15 .04
214 Mike Rossiter .15 .04
215 Andres Duncan .15 .04
216 Steve Dunn .15 .04
217 Mike Grace .15 .04
218 Tim Howard .15 .04
219 Todd Jones .50 .15
220 Tyrone Kingwood .15 .04
221 Damon Buford .15 .04
222 Bobby Munoz .15 .04
223 Jim Campanis .15 .04
224 Johnny Ruffin .15 .04
225 Shawn Green 3.00 .90
226 Pokey Reese .50 .15
227 Kevin McGehee .15 .04
228 J.R. Phillips .15 .04
229 Rafael Quirico .15 .04
230 Mike Zimmerman .15 .04
231 Ron Lockett .15 .04
232 Bobby Reed .15 .04
233 John Roper .15 .04
234 John Mabry .50 .15
235 Chris Martin .15 .04
236 Ricky Otero .15 .04
237 Orlando Miller .15 .04
238 Scott Hatteberg .50 .15
239 Toby Borland .15 .04
240 Alan Newman .15 .04
241 Ivan Cruz .15 .04
242 Paul Byrd .50 .15
243 Daryl Henderson .15 .04
244 Adam Hyzdu .15 .04
245 Rich Becker .15 .04
246 Scott Ruffcorn .15 .04
247 Tommy Adams .15 .04
248 Jose Martinez .15 .04
249 Darrell Sherman .15 .04
250 Tom Nevers .15 .04
251 Brandon Wilson .15 .04
252 Mike Hampton .50 .15
253 Mo Sanford .15 .04
254 Alex Ochoa .50 .15
255 David McCarty .15 .04
256 Ray McDavid .15 .04
257 Roger Salkeld .15 .04
258 Jeff McNeely .15 .04
259 Jim Converse .15 .04
260 Greg Blosser .15 .04
261 Salomon Torres .15 .04
262 Tavo Alvarez .15 .04
263 Marc Newfield .15 .04
264 Carlos Delgado 3.00 .90
265 Brien Taylor .15 .04
266 Frank Rodriguez .15 .04
267 Cliff Floyd 1.25 .35
268 Troy O'Leary .15 .04
269 Butch Huskey .15 .04
270 Michael Carter .15 .04
271 Eduardo Perez .15 .04
272 Gary Mota .15 .04
273 Mike Neill .15 .04
274 Dmitri Young .50 .15
275 Mike Kelly .15 .04
276 Rondell White .50 .15
277 Midre Cummings .15 .04
278 Kerwin Moore .15 .04
279 Derrick White .15 .04
280 Howard Battle .15 .04
281 Mark Smith .15 .04
282 Ben Shelton .15 .04
283 Jose Oliva .15 .04
284 Steve Gibralter .15 .04
285 Billy Hall .15 .04
286 Nigel Wilson .15 .04
287 Brook Fordyce .15 .04
288 Mike Durant .15 .04
289 Gary Caraballo .15 .04
290 Shane Andrews .15 .04
291 Aaron Sele .50 .15
292 Garret Anderson 2.00 .60
293 Oscar Munoz .15 .04
294 Bobby Jones .50 .15
295 Joe Rosselli .15 .04
296 Chad Ogea .15 .04
297 Ugueth Urbina .50 .15
298 Ryan Hawblitzel .15 .04
299 Dennis Burlingame .15 .04
300 Damon Mashore .15 .04
301 Jeff Jackson .15 .04
302 Glenn Murray .15 .04
303 Darren Burton .15 .04
304 Scott Cepicky .15 .04
305 Phil Dauphin .15 .04
306 Kevin Tatar .15 .04
307 Domingo Jean .15 .04
308 Darren Oliver .50 .15
309 Joe Vitiello .15 .04
310 John Johnstone .15 .04
311 Bo Dodson .15 .04
312 Jon Shave .15 .04
313 Roberto Petagine .15 .04
314 Clifton Garrett .15 .04
315 Rob Butler .15 .04
316 Jermaine Swinton .15 .04
317 Alex Gonzalez .50 .15
318 Jeff Williams .15 .04
319 James Baldwin .50 .15
320 Scott Stahoviak .15 .04
321 John Cotton .15 .04
322 Jim Wawruck .15 .04
323 Jeff Ware .15 .04
324 Brian L. Hunter .15 .04
325 Joe Randa .50 .15
326 Robert Eenhoorn .15 .04
327 Rod Lofton .15 .04
328 Buck McNabb .15 .04
329 Jorge Fabregas .15 .04
330 Brian Koelling .15 .04
P1 Brien Taylor PROMO

1992 Upper Deck Minors Player of the Year

These twenty-six standard-size Player of the Year cards were randomly inserted in 1992 Upper Deck Minor League foil packs and features each Major League club's minor league player of the year. These card have a "PY" numbering prefix.

Nm-Mt Ex-Mt
COMPLETE SET (26) 40.00 12.00
PY1 Garret Anderson 5.00 1.50
PY2 Gary Mota 2.00 .60
PY3 Scott Lydy 2.00 .60
PY4 Carlos Delgado 8.00 2.40
PY5 Chipper Jones 10.00 3.00
PY6 Troy O'Leary 2.00 .60
PY7 Dmitri Young 2.50 .75
PY8 Ozzie Timmons 2.00 .60
PY9 Todd Hollandsworth 2.50 .75
PY10 Cliff Floyd 3.00 .90
PY11 Joe Rosselli 2.00 .60
PY12 Chad Ogea 2.00 .60
PY13 Tommy Adams 2.00 .60
PY14 Bobby Jones 2.50 .75
PY15 Mark Smith 2.00 .60
PY16 Ray McDavid 2.00 .60
PY17 Mike Lieberthal 2.50 .75
PY18 Midre Cummings 2.00 .60
PY19 Kurt Miller 2.00 .60
PY20 Aaron Sele 2.50 .75
PY21 Steve Gibralter 2.00 .60
PY22 Phil Hiatt 2.00 .60
PY23 Ivan Cruz 2.00 .60
PY24 Marty Cordova 2.50 .75
PY25 Brandon Wilson SP 2.00 .60
PY26 Brien Taylor SP 2.00 .60

1992 Upper Deck Minors Top Prospect Holograms

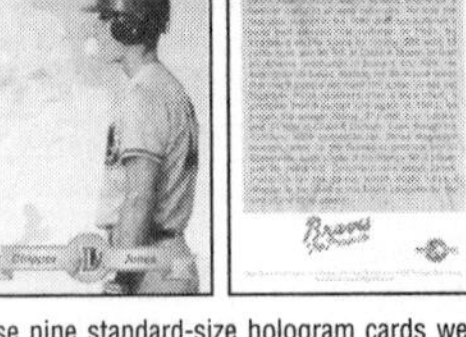

These nine standard-size hologram cards were randomly inserted in 1992 Upper Deck Minor League foil packs. These cards have a "TP" numbering prefix.

Nm-Mt Ex-Mt
COMPLETE SET (9) 15.00 4.50
TP1 Midre Cummings 1.50 .45
TP2 Cliff Floyd 3.00 .90
TP3 Chipper Jones 8.00 2.40
TP4 Mike Kelly 1.50 .45
TP5 David McCarty 1.50 .45
TP6 Frank Rodriguez 1.50 .45
TP7 Brien Taylor 1.50 .45
TP8 Rondell White 2.50 .75
TP9 Dmitri Young 2.50 .75

1992-93 Excel

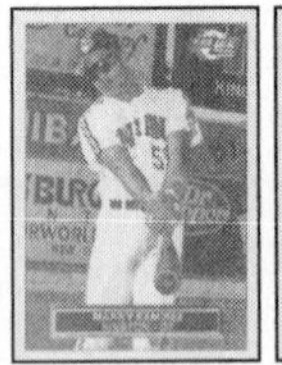

The 1992-93 Excel Minor League set consists of 250 cards featuring minor league players from AAA, AA and A teams. The cards are numbered and checklisted alphabetically within and according to major league teams for the NL and AL. Early cards of Edgardo Alfonzo, Carlos Delgado, Jim Edmonds, Derek Jeter and Chipper Jones are featured in this set.

Nm-Mt Ex-Mt
COMPLETE SET (250) 25.00 7.50
1 Mike D'Andrea .15 .04
2 Chipper Jones 1.50 .45
3 Mike Kelly .15 .04
4 Brian Kowitz .15 .04
5 Napoleon Robinson .15 .04
6 Tony Tarasco .15 .04
7 Pedro Castellano .15 .04
8 Doug Glanville .50 .15
9 Andy Hartung .15 .04
10 Jay Hassel .15 .04
11 Ryan Hawblitzel .15 .04
12 Kevin Roberson .15 .04
13 Chad Tredaway .15 .04
14 Jose Vierra .15 .04
15 Matt Wallbeck .15 .04
16 Tim Belk .15 .04
17 Jamie Dismuke .15 .04
18 Chad Fox .15 .04
19 Micah Franklin .15 .04
20 Dan Frye .15 .04
21 Steve Gibralter .15 .04
22 Demetrish Jenkins .15 .04
23 Jason Kummerfeldt .15 .04
24 Bo Loftin .15 .04
25 Chad Mottola .15 .04
26 Bobby Perna .15 .04
27 Scott Pose .15 .04
28 Pokey Reese .50 .15
29 John Roper .15 .04
30 Jerry Spradlin .15 .04
31 Roger Bailey .15 .04
32 Jason Bates .15 .04
33 John Burke .15 .04
34 Jason Hutchins .15 .04
35 Troy Ricker .15 .04
36 Mark Thompson .15 .04
37 Lou Lucca .15 .04
38 John Lynch .75 .23
39 Todd Pridy .15 .04
40 Gary Cooper .15 .04
41 Jim Dougherty .15 .04
42 Tony Eusebio .15 .04
43 Chris Hatcher .15 .04
44 Chris Hill .15 .04
45 Trent Hubbard .15 .04
46 Todd Jones .50 .15
47 Jeff Juden .15 .04
48 James Mouton .15 .04
49 Tom Nevers .15 .04
50 Jim Waring .15 .04
51 Chris Abbe .15 .04
52 Jay Kirkpatrick .15 .04
53 Raul Mondesi .50 .15
54 Vernon Spearman .15 .04
55 Tavo Alvarez .15 .04
56 Shane Andrews .15 .04
57 Yamil Benitez .15 .04
58 Cliff Floyd .75 .23
59 Antonio Grissom .15 .04
60 Tyrone Horne .15 .04
61 Mike Lansing .50 .15
62 Edgar Tovar .15 .04
63 Ugueth Urbina .50 .15
64 David Wainhouse .15 .04
65 Derrick White .15 .04
66 Gabe White .15 .04
67 Rondell White .50 .15
68 Edgardo Alfonzo .50 .15
69 Jeromy Burnitz .50 .15
70 Jay Davis .15 .04
71 Cesar Diaz .15 .04
72 Todd Douma .15 .04
73 Brook Fordyce .15 .04
74 Butch Huskey .15 .04
75 Bobby J.Jones .50 .15
76 Jose Martinez .15 .04
77 Ricky Otero .15 .04
78 Jim Popoff .15 .04
79 Al Shirley .15 .04
80 Julian Vasquez .15 .04
81 Quilvio Veras .50 .15
82 Fernando Vina .50 .15
83 Ron Blazier .15 .04
84 Tommy Eason .15 .04
85 Tyler Green .15 .04
86 Mike Lieberthal .50 .15
87 Tom Nuneviller .15 .04
88 Matt Whisenant .15 .04
89 Jon Zuber .15 .04
90 Midre Cummings .15 .04
91 Jon Farrell .15 .04
92 Ramon Martinez .15 .04
93 Antonio Mitchell .15 .04
94 Keith Thomas .15 .04
95 Rene Arocha .50 .15
96 Brian Barber .15 .04
97 Jamie Cochran .15 .04
98 Mike Gulan .15 .04
99 Keith Johns .15 .04
100 John Kelly .15 .04
101 Anthony Lewis .15 .04
102 T.J. Mathews .15 .04
103 Kevin Meier .15 .04
104 David Oehrlein .15 .04
105 Gerry Santos .15 .04
106 Basil Shabazz .15 .04
107 Eddie Williams .15 .04
108 Dmitri Young .50 .15
109 Jay Gainer .15 .04
110 Pedro A.Martinez .15 .04
111 Dave Staton .15 .04
112 Tim Worrell .15 .04
113 Dan Carlson .15 .04
114 Joel Chimelis .15 .04
115 Eric Christopherson .15 .04
116 Adell Davenport .15 .04
117 Ken Grundt .15 .04
118 Rick Huisman .15 .04
119 Andre Keene .15 .04
120 Kevin McGehee .15 .04
121 Salomon Torres .15 .04
122 Damon Buford .15 .04
123 Stanton Cameron .15 .04
124 Rick Krivda .15 .04
125 Alex Ochoa .50 .15
126 Brad Pennington .15 .04
127 Mark Smith .15 .04
128 Mel Wearing .15 .04
129 Cory Bailey .15 .04
130 Greg Blosser .15 .04
131 Joe Caruso .15 .04
132 Jason Friedman .15 .04
133 Jose Malave .15 .04
134 Jeff McNeely .15 .04
135 Luis Ortiz .15 .04
136 Ed Riley .15 .04
137 Frank Rodriguez .15 .04
138 Aaron Sele .50 .15
139 Garret Anderson 1.50 .45
140 Ron Correia .15 .04
141 Jim Edmonds 1.50 .45
142 John Fritz .15 .04
143 Brian Grebeck .15 .04
144 Jeff Kipila .15 .04
145 Orlando Palmeiro .15 .04
146 Eduardo Perez .15 .04
147 John Pricher .15 .04
148 Chris Pritchett .15 .04
149 James Baldwin .50 .15
150 Rod Bolton .15 .04
151 Essex Burton .15 .04
152 Scott Cepicky .15 .04
153 Steve Olsen .15 .04
154 Scott Ruffcorn .15 .04
155 Steve Schrenk .15 .04
156 Larry Thomas .15 .04
157 Brandon Wilson .15 .04
158 Paul Byrd .50 .15
159 Willie Canate .15 .04
160 Marc Marini .15 .04
161 Jon Nunnally .15 .04
162 Chad Ogea .15 .04
163 Herb Perry .50 .15
164 Manny Ramirez 2.50 .75
165 Omar Ramirez .15 .04
166 Ken Ramos .15 .04
167 Tracy Sanders .15 .04
168 Paul Shuey .15 .04
169 Kyle Washington .15 .04
170 Ivan Cruz .15 .04
171 Lou Frazier .15 .04
172 Brian Bevil .15 .04
173 Shane Halter .15 .04
174 Phil Hiatt .15 .04
175 Lance Jennings .15 .04
176 Les Norman .15 .04
177 Joe Randa .50 .15
178 Dan Rohmeier .15 .04
179 Larry Sutton .15 .04
180 Joe Vitiello .15 .04
181 John Byington .15 .04
182 Edgar Caceres .15 .04
183 Jeff Cirillo .50 .15
184 Mike Farrell .15 .04
185 Kenny Felder .15 .04
186 Tyrone Hill .15 .04
187 Brian Hostetler .15 .04
188 Danan Hughes .15 .04
189 Scott Karl .15 .04
190 Joe Kmak .15 .04
191 Rob Lukachyk .15 .04
192 Matt Mieske .15 .04
193 Troy O'Leary .15 .04
194 Cecil Rodriguez .15 .04
195 Tim Unroe .15 .04
196 Wes Weger .15 .04
197 Rich Becker .15 .04
198 Marty Cordova .50 .15
199 Steve Dunn .15 .04
200 Mike Durant .15 .04
201 Denny Hocking .15 .04
202 David McCarty .15 .04
203 Damian Miller .50 .15
204 Scott Stahoviak .15 .04
205 Russ Davis .50 .15
206 Mike Draper .15 .04
207 Carl Everett .50 .15
208 Lew Hill .15 .04
209 Mark Hutton .15 .04
210 Derek Jeter 6.00 1.80
211 Kevin Jordan .15 .04
212 Lyle Mouton .15 .04
213 Bobby Munoz .15 .04
214 Andy Pettitte 1.50 .45
215 Brien Taylor .15 .04
216 Brent Gates .15 .04
217 Eric Helfand .15 .04
218 Curtis Shaw .15 .04
219 Todd Van Poppel .15 .04
220 Miah Bradbury .15 .04
221 Darren Bragg .15 .04
222 Jim Converse .15 .04
223 John Cummings .15 .04
224 Shawn Estes .50 .15
225 Mike Hampton .50 .15
226 Derek Lowe 1.25 .35
227 Ellerton Maynard .15 .04
228 Fred McNair .15 .04
229 Marc Newfield .15 .04
230 Desi Relaford .50 .15
231 Ruben Santana .15 .04
232 Bubba Smith .15 .04
233 Brian Turang .15 .04
234 Benji Gil .15 .04
235 Jose Oliva .15 .04
236 Jon Shave .15 .04
237 Travis Baptist .15 .04
238 Howard Battle .15 .04
239 Rob Butler .15 .04
240 Tim Crabtree .15 .04
241 Juan DeLaRosa .15 .04
242 Carlos Delgado 2.50 .75
243 Alex Gonzalez .50 .15
244 Steve Karsay .15 .04
245 Paul Spoljaric .15 .04
246 Todd Steverson .15 .04
247 Nigel Wilson .15 .04
248 Checklist (1-82) .15 .04
249 Checklist (83-164) .15 .04
250 Checklist (165-250) .15 .04

1992-93 Excel All-Stars

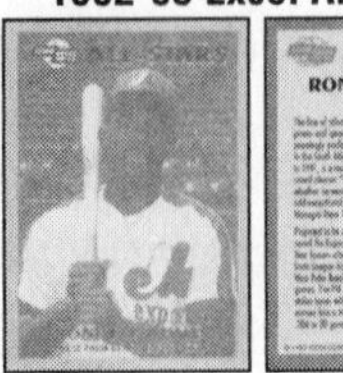
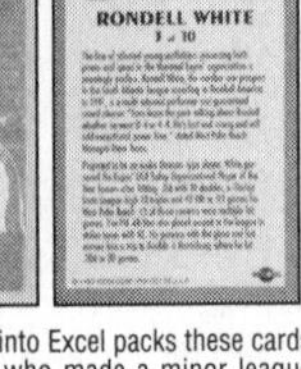

Randomly inserted into Excel packs these cards feature 10 players who made a minor league All-Star team.

Nm-Mt Ex-Mt
COMPLETE SET (10) 20.00 6.00
1 Brien Taylor 1.00 .30
2 Chipper Jones 5.00 1.50
3 Rondell White 2.00 .60
4 Mike Lieberthal 2.00 .60
5 Bobby J.Jones 2.00 .60
6 Carlos Delgado 5.00 1.50
7 Aaron Sele 2.00 .60
8 Brent Gates 1.00 .30
9 Phil Hiatt 1.00 .30
10 Brandon Wilson 1.00 .30

1992-93 Excel League Leaders

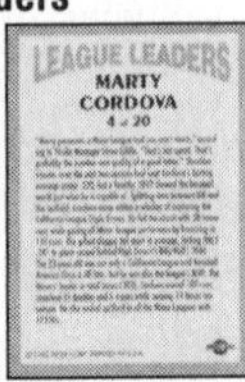

Inserted at a rate of one per jumbo pack, these 20 cards feature players who led a minor league in any category.

Nm-Mt Ex-Mt
COMPLETE SET (20) 8.00 2.40
1 Travis Baptist .25 .07
2 Bubba Smith .25 .07
3 Rob Butler .25 .07
4 Marty Cordova 1.00 .30
5 John Fritz .25 .07
6 Quilvio Veras 1.00 .30
7 Cliff Floyd 1.50 .45
8 Denny Hocking .25 .07
9 Rich Becker .25 .07
10 Jim Popoff .25 .07
11 John Kelly .25 .07
12 Tavo Alvarez .25 .07
13 Scott Pose .25 .07
14 Steve Gibralter .25 .07

15 Joe Caruso .25 .07
16 Chad Ogea .25 .07
17 Troy O'Leary .25 .07
18 Russ Davis 1.00 .30
19 John Cummings .25 .07
20 Ken Ramos .25 .07

1993 Classic/Best Promos

These four standard-size cards were issued to promote the 1993 Classic/Best product. The fronts are similar to what the regular Classic/Best cards would look like while the backs clearly state that these are promotional cards.

	Nm-Mt	Ex-Mt
COMPLETE SET (4)	8.00	2.40
1 Derek Jeter	6.00	1.80
2 Carlos Delgado	1.50	.45
3 Rick Helling	.75	.23
4 Derek Wallace	.50	.15

1993 Classic/Best

The 1993 Classic/Best Minor League set features top prospects from Double-A and Single-A teams. The standard size cards feature on fronts a color player photo bordered in gray. The Classic/Best logo, the player's name, position and team name also appear. The backs have biography, statistics and a photo. Early cards of Edgardo Alfonzo, Derek Jeter and Jose Vidro are featured in this set.

	Nm-Mt	Ex-Mt
COMPLETE SET (300)	10.00	3.00
1 Paul Shuey	.15	.04
2 Brad Clontz	.15	.04
3 Phil Dauphin	.15	.04
4 Kevin Flora	.15	.04
5 Doug Glanville	.40	.12
6 Hilly Hathaway	.15	.04
7 Scott Hatteberg	.15	.04
8 Ryan Hawblitzel	.15	.04
9 Bob Henkel	.15	.04
10 Mike Kelly	.15	.04
11 Jose Malave	.15	.04
12 Jeff McNeely	.15	.04
13 Roberto Mejia	.15	.04
14 Kevin Roberson	.15	.04
15 Chad Roper	.15	.04
16 John Roper	.15	.04
17 Pete Rose Jr.	.15	.04
18 Paul Russo	.15	.04
19 John Salles	.15	.04
20 Tracy Sanders	.15	.04
21 Chris Saunders	.15	.04
22 Jason Schmidt	1.50	.45
23 Aaron Sele	.15	.04
24 Bob Abreu	1.00	.30
25 Don Sparks	.15	.04
26 Scott Stahoviak	.15	.04
27 Matt Stairs	.15	.04
28 Todd Steverson	.15	.04
29 Ozzie Timmons	.15	.04
30 Michael Tucker	.15	.04
31 Jose Viera	.15	.04
32 B.J. Wallace	.15	.04
33 Mark Wohlers	.15	.04
34 Gabe White	.15	.04
35 Rick White	.15	.04
36 Rondell White	.40	.12
37 Todd Williams	.15	.04
38 Mike Williams	.15	.04
39 Gerald Williams	.15	.04
40 Desi Wilson	.15	.04
41 Johnny Ard	.15	.04
42 Jamie Arnold	.15	.04
43 Howard Battle	.15	.04
44 Greg Blosser	.15	.04
45 Rob Butler	.15	.04
46 Dan Carlson	.15	.04
47 Joe Caruso	.15	.04
48 Bobby Chouinard	.15	.04
49 Adell Davenport	.15	.04
50 Juan De La Rosa	.15	.04
51 Alex Gonzalez	.40	.12
52 Steve Hosey	.15	.04
53 Rick Krivda	.15	.04
54 T.R. Lewis	.15	.04
55 Jose Mercedes	.15	.04
56 Melvin Nieves	.15	.04
57 Luis Ortiz	.15	.04
58 Joe Rosselli	.15	.04
59 Brian Sackinsky	.15	.04
60 Salomon Torres	.15	.04
61 James Baldwin	.40	.12
62 Travis Baptist	.15	.04
63 Bret Boone	.40	.12
64 Mike Buddie	.15	.04
65 Paul Carey	.15	.04
66 Tim Crabtree	.15	.04
67 Tony Longmire	.15	.04
68 Robert Eenhoorn	.15	.04
69 Paul Ellis	.15	.04
70 Shawn Estes	.15	.04
71 Andy Fox	.15	.04
72 Shawn Green UER Front photo is Alex Gonzalez	1.00	.30
73 Jimmy Haynes	.40	.12
74 Sterling Hitchcock	.40	.12
75 Mark Hutton	.15	.04
76 Domingo Jean	.15	.04
77 Kevin Jordan	.15	.04
78 Steve Karsay	.15	.04
79 Paul Fletcher	.15	.04
80 Mike Milchin	.15	.04
81 Lyle Mouton	.15	.04
82 Bobby Munoz	.15	.04
83 Alex Ochoa	.15	.04
84 Steve Olsen	.15	.04
85 Billy Owens	.15	.04
86 Eddie Pearson	.15	.04
87 Mike Robertson	.15	.04
88 Johnny Ruffin	.15	.04
89 Mark Smith	.15	.04
90 Brandon Wilson	.15	.04
91 Derek Jeter	5.00	1.50
92 Edgardo Alfonzo	.40	.12
93 Jeff Alkire	.15	.04
94 Roger Bailey	.15	.04
95 Jeff Barry	.15	.04
96 Terrell Buckley	.15	.04
97 Hector Carrasco	.15	.04
98 Danny Clyburn	.15	.04
99 Darren Burton	.15	.04
100 Scott Eyre	.15	.04
101 Chad Fox	.15	.04
102 Joe Hudson	.15	.04
103 Jason Hutchins	.15	.04
104 Bobby Jones	.15	.04
105 Jason Kendall	.40	.12
106 Ricky Magdaleno	.15	.04
107 Buck McNabb	.15	.04
108 Doug Mlicki	.15	.04
109 Chris Eddy	.15	.04
110 Jon Lieber	.40	.12
111 Ken Powell	.15	.04
112 Todd Pridy	.15	.04
113 Marquis Riley	.15	.04
114 Steve Rodriguez	.15	.04
115 Brian Rupp	.15	.04
116 Yuri Sanchez	.15	.04
117 Al Shirley	.15	.04
118 Paul Spoljaric	.15	.04
119 Amaury Telemaco	.15	.04
120 Shon Walker	.15	.04
121 Tavo Alvarez	.15	.04
122 Shane Andrews	.15	.04
123 Billy Ashley	.15	.04
124 Brian Barber	.15	.04
125 Trey Beamon	.15	.04
126 Scott Bryant	.15	.04
127 Scott Bullett	.15	.04
128 Ozzie Canseco	.15	.04
129 Brian Carpenter	.15	.04
130 Roger Cedeno	.40	.12
131 Randy Curtis	.15	.04
132 A.De Los Santos	.15	.04
133 Steve Dixon	.15	.04
134 Joey Eischen	.15	.04
135 Brook Fordyce	.15	.04
136 Rick Gorecki	.15	.04
137 Lee Hancock	.15	.04
138 Todd Hollandsworth	.15	.04
139 Frank Jacobs	.15	.04
140 Mark Johnson	.15	.04
141 Albie Lopez	.40	.12
142 Dan Melendez	.15	.04
143 William Pennyfeather	.15	.04
144 Scott Lydy	.15	.04
145 Chris Snopek	.15	.04
146 Quilvio Veras	.40	.12
147 Jose Vidro	1.00	.30
148 Allen Watson	.15	.04
149 Matt Whisenant	.15	.04
150 Craig Wilson	.15	.04
151 Rich Becker	.15	.04
152 Mike Durant	.15	.04
153 Brad Ausmus	.40	.12
154 Robbie Beckett	.15	.04
155 Steve Dunn	.15	.04
156 Paul Byrd	.15	.04
157 Jason Bere	.15	.04
158 Ben Blomdahl	.15	.04
159 John Brothers	.15	.04
160 Tim Costo	.15	.04
161 Joel Chimelis	.15	.04
162 Kenny Carlyle	.15	.04
163 Garvin Alston	.15	.04
164 Sean Bergman	.15	.04
165 Marshall Boze	.15	.04
166 Terry Burrows	.15	.04
167 Danny Bautista	.40	.12
168 Jason Bates	.15	.04
169 Brent Bowers	.15	.04
170 Rico Brogna	.15	.04
171 Armann Brown	.15	.04
172 Brant Brown	.15	.04
173 Julio Bruno	.15	.04
174 Mike DeJean	.15	.04
175 Nick Delvecchio	.15	.04
176 Bobby Bonds Jr.	.15	.04
177 Miguel Castellano	.15	.04
178 Tommy Adams	.15	.04
179 Alan Burke	.15	.04
180 John Burke	.15	.04
181 Ivan Cruz	.15	.04
182 Johnny Damon	1.00	.30
183 Carl Everett	.40	.12
184 Jorge Fabregas	.15	.04
185 John Fantauzzi	.15	.04
186 Mike Farmer	.15	.04
187 Mike Farrell	.15	.04
188 Omar Garcia	.15	.04
189 Brent Gates	.15	.04
190 Jason Giambi	1.50	.45
191 K.C. Gillum	.15	.04
192 Chris Gomez	.40	.12
193 Ricky Greene	.15	.04
194 Willie Greene	.15	.04
195 Benji Grigsby	.15	.04
196 Mike Groppuso	.15	.04
197 Johnny Guzman	.15	.04
198 Bob Hamelin	.15	.04
199 Joey Hamilton	.15	.04
200 Chris Haney	.15	.04
201 Donald Harris	.15	.04
202 Andy Hartung	.15	.04
203 Chris Hatcher	.15	.04
204 Rick Helling	.15	.04
205 Edgar Herrera	.15	.04
206 Aaron Holbert	.15	.04
207 Ray Holbert	.15	.04
208 Tyler Houston	.15	.04
209 Brian L. Hunter	.15	.04
210 Miguel Jimenez	.15	.04
211 Charles Johnson	.40	.12
212 Corey Kapano	.15	.04
213 Tom Knauss	.15	.04
214 Brian Koelling	.15	.04
215 Brian Lane	.15	.04
216 Kevin Legault	.15	.04
217 Mark Lewis	.15	.04
218 Luis Lopez	.15	.04
219 Jose Martinez	.15	.04
220 Mitch Meluskey	.40	.12
221 Casey Mendenhall	.15	.04
222 Danny Miceli	.15	.04
223 Tony Mitchell	.15	.04
224 Ritchie Moody	.15	.04
225 James Mouton	.15	.04
226 Steve Murphy	.15	.04
227 Mike Neill	.15	.04
228 Tom Nevers	.15	.04
229 Alan Newman	.15	.04
230 Tom Neneviller	.15	.04
231 Jon Nunnally	.15	.04
232 Chad Ogea	.15	.04
233 Ray Ortiz	.15	.04
234 Orlando Palmeiro	.15	.04
235 Craig Paquette	.15	.04
236 Troy Percival	.40	.12
237 Bobby Perna	.15	.04
238 John Pricher	.15	.04
239 Ken Ramos	.15	.04
240 Joe Randa	.15	.04
241 Ron Blazier	.15	.04
242 Terry Bradshaw	.15	.04
243 Jason Hisey	.15	.04
244 Sean Lowe	.15	.04
245 Chad McConnell	.15	.04
246 Jackie Nickell	.15	.04
247 Pat Rapp	.15	.04
248 Pokey Reese	.15	.04
249 Desi Relaford	.15	.04
250 Troy Ricker	.15	.04
251 Todd Ritchie	.15	.04
252 Chris Roberts	.15	.04
253 Scott Sanders	.15	.04
254 Ruben Santana	.15	.04
255 Chris Seelbach	.15	.04
256 Dan Serafini	.15	.04
257 Curtis Shaw	.15	.04
258 Kennie Steenstra	.15	.04
259 Kevin Stocker	.15	.04
260 Tanyon Sturtze	.15	.04
261 Tim Stutheit	.15	.04
262 Jamie Taylor	.15	.04
263 Chad Townsend	.15	.04
264 Steve Trachsel	.15	.04
265 Jose Valentin	.40	.12
266 K.C. Waller	.15	.04
267 Chris Weinke	.40	.12
268 Darrell Whitmore	.15	.04
269 Juan Williams	.15	.04
270 Tim Worrell	.15	.04
271 Tim Belk	.15	.04
272 London Bradley	.15	.04
273 Tilson Brito	.15	.04
274 Felipe Crespo	.15	.04
275 Kenny Felder	.15	.04
276 Billy Hall	.15	.04
277 Terrell Hansen	.15	.04
278 Rod Henderson	.15	.04
279 Bobby Holley	.15	.04
280 Bobby Hughes	.15	.04
281 Rick Huisman	.15	.04
282 Jack Johnson	.15	.04
283 Gabby Martinez	.15	.04
284 Jose Millares	.15	.04
285 Jason Moler	.15	.04
286 Willie Mota	.15	.04
287 Marty Neff	.15	.04
288 Eric Owens	.40	.12
289 Daryl Ratliff	.15	.04
290 Ozzie Sanchez	.15	.04
291 Dave Silvestri	.15	.04
292 Chris Stynes	.15	.04
293 Aubrey Waggoner	.15	.04
294 Jimmy White	.15	.04
295 Jim Campanis	.15	.04
296 Tony Womack	.40	.12
297 Checklist	.15	.04
298 Checklist	.15	.04
299 Checklist	.15	.04
300 Checklist	.15	.04

1993 Classic/Best Autographs

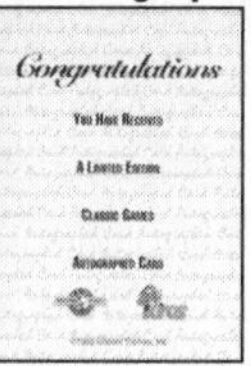

According to Classic, 9,600 numbered and autographed cards of eight different prospects were randomly inserted in packs with each player signing 1,200 cards; the players are Carlos Delgado, Cliff Floyd, Jeffrey Hammonds, Derek Jeter, Mike Kelly, Phil Nevin, Paul Shuey and Dmitri Young. All the cards were individually numbered to 1,200. The backs give a congratulations for receiving a Classic Autographed card. The cards are unnumbered so we have sequenced them in alphabetical order.

	Nm-Mt	Ex-Mt
AU1 Carlos Delgado	15.00	4.50
AU2 Cliff Floyd	8.00	2.40
AU3 Jeffrey Hammonds	5.00	1.50
AU4 Derek Jeter	100.00	30.00
AU5 Mike Kelly	3.00	.90
AU6 Phil Nevin	5.00	1.50
AU7 Paul Shuey	3.00	.90
AU8 Dmitri Young	5.00	1.50

1993 Classic/Best Expansion #1 Picks

These two standard-size cards depict 1992 number 1 draft picks for the 1993 expansion

teams Colorado Rockies and Florida Marlins. The cards were randomly inserted in 1993 Classic/Best foil packs. The cards are numbered on the back with the prefix "EP."

	Nm-Mt	Ex-Mt
EP1 John Burke	1.00	.30
EP2 Charles Johnson	4.00	1.20

1993 Classic/Best MVPs

This ten-card standard-size set features minor league MVPs in color photos framed on the lower and right side by a team color-coded stripe. The cards are numbered on the back with an "MVP" prefix. The cards were randomly inserted in 1993 Classic/Best foil packs.

	Nm-Mt	Ex-Mt
COMPLETE SET (10)	6.00	1.80
1 Bubba Smith	.50	.15
2 Javy Lopez	1.00	.30
3 Marty Cordova	1.00	.30
4 Troy O'Leary	.50	.15
5 Steve Gibralter	.50	.15
6 Gary Mota	.50	.15
7 Larry Sutton	.50	.15
8 Dan Frye	.50	.15
9 Russ Davis	1.00	.30
10 Carlos Delgado	1.00	.30

1993 Classic/Best Player and Manager of the Year

This set of two standard-size cards displays Manager of the Year Marc Hill and Player of the Year Carlos Delgado holding their trophies in waist up color portraits. The cards are numbered on the back with a "PM" prefix. The cards were randomly inserted in 1993 Classic/Best foil packs.

	Nm-Mt	Ex-Mt
PM1 Carlos Delgado	2.00	.60
PM2 Marc Hill	1.00	.30

1993 Classic/Best Young Guns

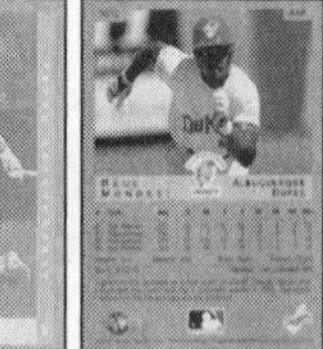

This set consists of 28 standard-size cards featuring high-gloss full-action photos enclosed by silver foil borders. The cards are numbered on the back with a "YG" prefix. The cards were randomly inserted in 1993 Classic/Best foil packs at an average of two or three per box.

	Nm-Mt	Ex-Mt
COMPLETE SET (28)	30.00	9.00
YG1 Midre Cummings	.50	.15
YG2 Carlos Delgado	1.00	.30
YG3 Cliff Floyd	1.00	.30
YG4 Jeffrey Hammonds	.50	.15
YG5 Tyrone Hill	.50	.15
YG6 Butch Huskey	.50	.15
YG7 Chipper Jones	5.00	1.50
YG8 Mike Lieberthal	1.00	.30
YG9 David McCarty	.50	.15
YG10 Ray McDavid	.50	.15
YG11 Kurt Miller	.50	.15
YG12 Raul Mondesi	1.00	.30
YG13 Chad Mottola	.50	.15
YG14 Calvin Murray	.50	.15
YG15 Phil Nevin	1.00	.30
YG16 Marc Newfield	.50	.15
YG17 Eduardo Perez	.50	.15
YG18 Manny Ramirez	1.00	.30
YG19 Edgar Renteria	3.00	.90
YG20 Frank Rodriguez	.50	.15
YG21 Scott Ruffcorn	.50	.15
YG22 Brien Taylor	.50	.15
YG23 Justin Thompson	.50	.15
YG24 Mark Thompson	.50	.15
YG25 Todd Van Poppel	.50	.15
YG26 Joe Vitiello	.50	.15
YG27 Derek Wallace	.50	.15
YG28 Dmitri Young	1.00	.30

1993 Classic/Best Fisher Nuts

This 20-card set features color action photos in white borders of some of Minor League Baseball's hottest prospects. The backs carry player information and career statistics. The set was available only for a short time from Fisher for a certain amount of money with proof of purchase. This set is also referred to as "Stars of the Future".

	Nm-Mt	Ex-Mt
COMPLETE SET (20)	30.00	9.00
1 Joe Vitiello	1.00	.30
2 Steve Gibralter	1.00	.30
3 Rob Butler	1.00	.30
4 Carlos Delgado	4.00	1.20
5 Chipper Jones	6.00	1.80
6 Mike Kelly	1.00	.30
7 Marc Newfield	1.00	.30
8 Aaron Sele	2.50	.75
9 Brent Gates	1.00	.30
10 Eduardo Perez	1.50	.45
11 Mike Lieberthal	1.50	.45
12 Midre Cummings	1.00	.30
13 Dmitri Young	1.50	.45
14 Brien Taylor	1.00	.30
15 David McCarty	1.00	.30
16 Scott Ruffcorn	1.00	.30
17 Cliff Floyd	2.50	.75
18 Rondell White	3.00	.90
19 Paul Shuey	1.50	.45
20 Checklist	1.00	.30

1993 Classic/Best Gold Promos

These four standard-size promo cards were issued to preview the innovative design of the 1993 Classic/Best Minor League Gold set. The fronts feature glossy color player photos tilted slightly to the right so that the picture's corners extend off the card edges. The color of the front border varies from card to card. The player's name and team name are printed in gold foil lettering and the oversized first letter of the player's name is scripted. The backs have a larger version of the player's name in gold foil and display two smaller player photos, biography and in a color-coded bar statistics. The cards are marked as promos by the disclaimer "For Promotional Use Only" in gold foil immediately above the statistics. The cards are unnumbered and checklisted below in alphabetical order.

	Nm-Mt	Ex-Mt
COMPLETE SET (4)	5.00	1.50
1 Mike Kelly	1.50	.45
2 David McCarty	1.50	.45
3 Brien Taylor	1.50	.45
4 Joe Vitiello	1.50	.45

1993 Classic/Best Gold

The 1993 Classic/Best Minor League Gold set consists of 220 standard-size cards featuring 216 cards of players in Double A, Class A and Rookie Leagues plus four checklist cards. The production run was 6,000 sequentially numbered ten-box cases. The foil packs included randomly inserted autograph cards of Barry Bonds and Gary Sheffield. Early cards of Edgardo Alfonzo, Carlos Delgado, Derek Jeter, Chipper Jones and Manny Ramirez are featured in this set.

	Nm-Mt	Ex-Mt
COMPLETE SET (220)	15.00	4.50
1 Barry Bonds	1.50	.45
2 Mark Hutton	.15	.04
3 Lyle Mouton	.15	.04
4 Don Sparks	.15	.04
5 Joe Randa	.15	.04
6 Dave Mlicki	.15	.04
7 Ken Ramos	.15	.04
8 Bill Wertz	.15	.04
9 Jon Shave	.15	.04
10 Dan Smith	.15	.04
11 William Canate	.15	.04
12 Albie Lopez	.50	.15
13 Rod McCall	.15	.04
14 Paul Shuey	.15	.04
15 Ian Doyle	.15	.04
16 Marc Marini	.15	.04
17 Brien Taylor	.15	.04
18 Mike Kelly	.15	.04
19 Andy Nezelek	.15	.04
20 Marcos Armas	.15	.04
21 Chad Ogea	.15	.04
22 Frank Rodriguez	.15	.04
23 Aaron Sele	.15	.04
24 Tim Vanegmond	.15	.04
25 Phil Hiatt	.15	.04
26 Dan Rohrmeier	.15	.04
27 Greg Blosser	.15	.04
28 Scott Hatteberg	.15	.04
29 Ed Riley	.15	.04
30 Edgar Alfonzo	.15	.04
31 Jorge Fabregas	.15	.04
32 Eduardo Perez	.15	.04
33 John Cummings	.15	.04
34 Bubba Smith	.15	.04
35 Kevin Jordan	.15	.04
36 Tyler Green	.15	.04
37 Heath Haynes	.15	.04
38 Gabe White	.15	.04

1993 Classic/Best Gold

39 Doug Glanville .50 .15
40 Jose Viera .15 .04
41 Rich Becker .15 .04
42 Marty Cordova .50 .15
43 Mike Durant .15 .04
44 Todd Ritchie .15 .04
45 Scott Stahoviak .15 .04
46 Tavo Alvarez .15 .04
47 Chris Malinoski .15 .04
48 Rondell White .50 .15
49 Tim Worrell .15 .04
50 Benji Gil .15 .04
51 Ben Blomdahl .15 .04
52 Rich Kelly .15 .04
53 Justin Thompson .15 .04
54 Scott Pose .15 .04
55 John Roper .15 .04
56 Rafael Chaves .15 .04
57 Billy Hall .15 .04
58 Ray McDavid .15 .04
59 Mark Smith .15 .04
60 Jeff Williams .15 .04
61 Bobby J.Jones .15 .04
62 Stanton Cameron .15 .04
63 Mike Lumley .15 .04
64 Troy Buckley .15 .04
65 James Dougherty .15 .04
66 Chris Hill .15 .04
67 Tom Nevers .15 .04
68 Joe Rosselli .15 .04
69 Steve Whitaker .15 .04
70 Butch Huskey .15 .04
71 Shane Andrews .15 .04
72 Cliff Floyd .50 .15
73 Alex Ochoa .15 .04
74 Brent Gates .15 .04
75 Curtis Shaw .15 .04
76 Midre Cummings .15 .04
77 Steve Olsen .15 .04
78 Mike Robertson .15 .04
79 Scott Ruffcorn .15 .04
80 Brandon Wilson .15 .04
81 Darren Burton .15 .04
82 Kerwin Moore .15 .04
83 Joe Vitiello .15 .04
84 Hugh Walker .15 .04
85 Howard Battle .15 .04
86 Rob Butler .15 .04
87 Carlos Delgado .50 .15
88 Jeff Ware .15 .04
89 Mike Hostetler .15 .04
90 Brian Kowitz .15 .04
91 Ryan Hawblitzel .15 .04
92 Juan De La Rosa .15 .04
93 David McCarty .15 .04
94 Paul Russo .15 .04
95 Dan Cholowsky .15 .04
96 Dmitri Young .50 .15
97 Paul Ellis .15 .04
98 Jay Kirkpatrick .15 .04
99 Jeff Jackson .15 .04
100 Duane Singleton .15 .04
101 Kiki Hernandez .15 .04
102 Raul Herrera .15 .04
103 Brian Bevil .15 .04
104 Mark Johnson .15 .04
105 Bob Abreu 1.00 .30
106 Gary Mota .15 .04
107 Jose Cabrera .15 .04
108 Jeff Runion .15 .04
109 B.J. Wallace .15 .04
110 Jim Arnold .15 .04
111 Dwight Maness .15 .04
112 Fernando DaSilva .15 .04
113 Chris Burr .15 .04
114 Dan Serafini .15 .04
115 Derek Jeter 8.00 2.40
116 Lew Hill .15 .04
117 Andy Pettitte 1.00 .30
118 Keith Johns .15 .04
119 Sean Lowe .15 .04
120 T.J. Mathews .15 .04
121 Ricardo Medina .15 .04
122 Scott Gentile .15 .04
123 Everett Stull .15 .04
124 Manny Ramirez .50 .15
125 Archie Corbin .15 .04
126 Matt Karchner .15 .04
127 Domingo Mota .15 .04
128 Alex Gonzalez .50 .15
129 Joe Lis Jr. .15 .04
130 Paul Spoljaric .15 .04
131 Clifton Garrett .15 .04
132 Marc Hill .15 .04
133 Jesus Martinez .15 .04
134 Salomon Torres .15 .04
135 Tommy Eason .15 .04
136 Matt Whisenant .15 .04
137 Jon Zuber .15 .04
138 Luis Martinez .15 .04
139 Glenn Murray .15 .04
140 John Saffer .15 .04
141 Tommy Adams .15 .04
142 Manny Cervantes .15 .04
143 George Glinatsis .15 .04
144 Chris Dessellier .15 .04
145 Joe Pomierski .15 .04
146 John Vanhof .15 .04
147 Matt T. Williams .15 .04
148 Maurice Christmas .15 .04
149 Damon Hollins .15 .04
150 Sean Smith .15 .04
151 Doug Hecker .15 .04
152 Jamie Sepeda .15 .04
153 Steve Solomon .15 .04
154 Jeff Tabaka .15 .04
155 Greg Elliott .15 .04
156 Jim Waring .15 .04
157 Omar Garcia .15 .04
158 Ricky Otero .15 .04
159 Jamie Brewington .15 .04
160 Chad Fonville .15 .04
161 Sean Runyan .15 .04
162 Jim Givens .15 .04
163 Dennis McNamara .15 .04
164 Rudy Pemberton .15 .04
165 Brian Raabe .15 .04
166 Jeffrey Hammonds .15 .04
167 Chris Hatcher .15 .04
168 Chris Saunders .15 .04
169 Aaron Fultz .15 .04
170 Mike Freitas .15 .04
171 Tim Adkins .15 .04
172 Chipper Jones 1.00 .30
173 Brandon Cromer .15 .04
174 Shannon Stewart .50 .15
175 David Tollison .15 .04
176 Rob Adkins .15 .04
177 Todd Steverson .15 .04
178 Dennis Konuszewski .15 .04
179 Marty Neff .15 .04
180 Vernon Spearman .15 .04
181 Don Wengert .15 .04
182 Allen Battle .15 .04
183 Michael Moore .15 .04
184 Sherard Clinkscales .15 .04
185 Jamie Dismuke .15 .04
186 Tucker Hammargren .15 .04
187 John Hrusovsky .15 .04
188 Elliott Quinones .15 .04
189 Pokey Reese .15 .04
190 Rich Ireland .15 .04
191 Shawn Estes .15 .04
192 Greg Shockey .15 .04
193 Mike Zimmerman .15 .04
194 Danny Clyburn .15 .04
195 Jason Kendall .50 .15
196 Shon Walker .15 .04
197 Gary Wilson .15 .04
198 John Dillinger .15 .04
199 Jim Keefe .15 .04
200 Eddie Pearson .15 .04
201 Johnny Damon 1.00 .30
202 Jim Pittsley .15 .04
203 Jason Bere .15 .04
204 James Baldwin .50 .15
205 John Burke .15 .04
206 Scot Sealy .15 .04
207 Ken Carlyle .15 .04
208 Tim Crabtree .15 .04
209 Quilvio Veras .50 .15
210 Edgardo Alfonzo .50 .15
211 Adell Davenport .15 .04
212 Dan Frye .15 .04
213 Derek Lowe .50 .15
214 Steve Gibralter .15 .04
215 Troy O'Leary .15 .04
216 Gary Sheffield .50 .15
217 Checklist (1-55) .15 .04
218 Checklist (56-110) .15 .04
219 Checklist (111-165) .15 .04
220 Checlklist (166-220) .15 .04

1993 Classic/Best Gold Autographs

Randomly inserted into packs, these cards feature autographs of leading major league players that Classic had under contract to sign autographs. Please note that in our checklist the print run is listed after the player's name.

	Nm-Mt	Ex-Mt
AU1 Barry Bonds AU/2050	120.00	36.00
AU2 G.Sheffield AU/2050	20.00	6.00

1993 Classic/Best Gold LPs

Randomly inserted in 1992 Classic/Best retail white jumbo packs, this limited-print five-card set measures the standard size. The fronts are identical to the regular series featuring glossy color player photos tilted slightly to the right so that the picture's corners extend off the card edges. The color of the front border varies from card to card. The player's name and team name are printed in gold foil lettering and the oversized first letter of the player's name is scripted. The background of the full-bleed photo on the horizontal back is out of focus to make the player stand out. Each card has a message congratulating the collector on receiving this limited print card.

	Nm-Mt	Ex-Mt
COMPLETE SET(5)	5.00	1.50
1 David McCarty	1.00	.30
2 Brien Taylor	1.00	.30
3 Joe Vitiello	1.00	.30
4 Mike Kelly	1.00	.30
5 Carlos Delgado	2.00	.60

1993-94 Excel

The 1993-94 Excel Minor League set consists of 300 cards featuring minor league players from AAA, AA and A teams. The cards are numbered and checklisted alphabetically within and according to major league teams for the NL and AL. Early card of Bob Abreu, Edgardo Alfonzo, Johnny Damon, Jason Giambi and Derek Jeter are featured in this set.

	Nm-Mt	Ex-Mt
COMPLETE SET (300)	20.00	6.00

1 Armando Benitez .50 .15
2 Stanton Cameron .15 .04
3 Eric Chavez .15 .04
4 Rick Forney .15 .04
5 Jim Foster .15 .04
6 Curtis Goodwin .15 .04
7 Jimmy Haynes .50 .15
8 Scott Klingenbeck .15 .04
9 Rick Krivda .15 .04
10 T.R. Lewis .15 .04
11 Brian Link .15 .04
12 Scott McClain .15 .04
13 Alex Ochoa .15 .04
14 Jay Powell .15 .04
15 Brian Sackinsky .15 .04
16 Brad Tyler .15 .04
17 Gregg Zaun .15 .04
18 Joel Bennett .15 .04
19 Felix Colon .15 .04
20 Ryan McGuire .15 .04
21 Frankie Rodriguez .15 .04
22 Tim Vanegmond .15 .04
23 Garret Anderson .50 .15
24 Jorge Fabregas .15 .04
25 P.J. Forbes .15 .04
26 John Fritz .15 .04
27 Todd Greene .15 .04
28 Jose Musset .15 .04
29 Orlando Palmeiro .15 .04
30 Jon Pricher .15 .04
31 Chris Pritchett .15 .04
32 Marquis Riley .15 .04
33 Luis Andujar .15 .04
34 James Baldwin .50 .15
35 Brian Boehringer .15 .04
36 Ron Coomer .50 .15
37 Ray Durham .50 .15
38 Robert Ellis .15 .04
39 Jeff Pierce .15 .04
40 Olmedo Saenz .15 .04
41 Brandon Wilson .15 .04
42 Ian Doyle .15 .04
43 Jason Fronio .15 .04
44 Derek Hacopian .15 .04
45 Daron Kirkreit .15 .04
46 Mike Neal .15 .04
47 Chad Ogea .15 .04
48 Cesar Perez .15 .04
49 Omar Ramirez .15 .04
50 J.J. Thobe .15 .04
51 Casey Whitten .15 .04
52 Eric Danapilis .15 .04
53 Brian Edmondson .15 .04
54 Tony Fuduric .15 .04
55 Ricky Greene .15 .04
56 Bob Higginson .50 .15
57 Felipe Lira .15 .04
58 Joshua Neese .15 .04
59 Shannon Penn .15 .04
60 John Rosengren .15 .04
61 Phil Stidham .15 .04
62 Justin Thompson .15 .04
63 Shawn Wooten .15 .04
64 Brian Bevil .15 .04
65 Mel Bunch .15 .04
66 Johnny Damon 1.00 .30
67 Chris Eddy .15 .04
68 Jon Lieber .50 .15
69 Les Norman .15 .04
70 Jim Pittsley .15 .04
71 Kris Ralston .15 .04
72 Joe Randa .15 .04
73 Kevin Rawitzer .15 .04
74 Chris Sheehan .15 .04
75 Robert Toth .15 .04
76 Michael Tucker .15 .04
77 Brian Banks .15 .04
78 Marshall Boze .15 .04
79 Jeff Cirillo .50 .15
80 Bo Dodson .15 .04
81 Bobby Hughes .15 .04
82 Scott Karl .15 .04
83 Mike Matheny .50 .15
84 Kevin Riggs .15 .04
85 Sid Roberson .15 .04
86 Charlie Rogers .15 .04
87 Mike Stefanski .15 .04
88 Scott Talanoa .15 .04
89 Derek Wachter .15 .04
90 Wes Weger .15 .04
91 Anthony Byrd .15 .04
92 Marty Cordova .50 .15
93 Steve Dunn .15 .04
94 Gus Gandarillos .15 .04
95 LaTroy Hawkins .50 .15
96 Oscar Munoz .15 .04
97 Dan Perkins .15 .04
98 Dan Serafini UER .15 .04
Name spelled Ken on card
99 Ken Tirpack .15 .04
100 Russ Davis .50 .15
101 Nick Delvecchio .15 .04
102 Robert Eenhoorn .15 .04
103 Ron Frazier .15 .04
104 Kraig Hawkins .15 .04
105 Keith Heberling .15 .04
106 Derek Jeter 5.00 1.50
107 Kevin Jordan .15 .04
108 Ryan Karp .15 .04
109 Matt Luke .15 .04
110 Lyle Mouton .15 .04
111 Andy Pettitte 1.00 .30
112 Jorge Posada 1.50 .45
113 Ruben Rivera .15 .04
114 Tate Seefried .15 .04
115 Brien Taylor .15 .04
116 Mark Acre .15 .04
117 Jim Bowie .15 .04
118 Russ Brock .15 .04
119 Fausto Cruz .15 .04
120 Jason Giambi 2.00 .60
121 Izzy Molina .15 .04
122 George Williams .15 .04
123 Joel Wolfe .15 .04
124 Ernie Young .15 .04
125 Tim Davis .15 .04
126 Jackie Nickell .15 .04
127 Ruben Santana .15 .04
128 Mac Suzuki .50 .15
129 Ron Villone .15 .04
130 Rich Aurilia .75 .23
131 John Dettmer .15 .04
132 Scott Eyre .15 .04
133 Dave Geeve .15 .04
134 Rick Helling .15 .04
135 Kerry Lacy .15 .04
136 Trey McCoy .15 .04
137 Wes Shook .15 .04
138 Howard Battle .15 .04
139 D.J. Boston .15 .04
140 Rick Butler .15 .04
141 Brad Cornett .15 .04
142 Jesse Cross .15 .04
143 Alex Gonzalez .50 .15
144 Kurt Heble .15 .04
145 Jose Herrera .15 .04
146 Ryan Jones .15 .04
147 Robert Perez .15 .04
148 Jose Silva .15 .04
149 Shannon Stewart .50 .15
150 Chris Weinke .50 .15
151 Jamie Arnold .15 .04
152 Chris Brock .15 .04
153 Tony Graffanino .15 .04
154 Damon Hollins .15 .04
155 Mike Hostetler .15 .04
156 Mike Kelly .15 .04
157 Andre King .15 .04
158 Darrell May .15 .04
159 Vince Moore .15 .04
160 Don Strange .15 .04
161 Dominic Therrien .15 .04
162 Terrell Wade .15 .04
163 Brant Brown .15 .04
164 Matt Franco .15 .04
165 Brooks Kieschnick .15 .04
166 Jon Ratliff .15 .04
167 Kennie Steenstra .15 .04
168 Amaury Telemaco .15 .04
169 Ozzie Timmons .15 .04
170 Hector Trinidad .15 .04
171 Travis Willis .15 .04
172 Tim Belk .15 .04
173 Jamie Dismuke .15 .04
174 Mike Ferry .15 .04
175 Chris Hook .15 .04
176 John Hrusovsky .15 .04
177 Cleveland Ladell .15 .04
178 Martin Lister .15 .04
179 Chad Mottola .15 .04
180 Eric Owens .50 .15
181 Scott Sullivan .15 .04
182 Pat Watkins .15 .04
183 Jason Bates .15 .04
184 John Burke .15 .04
185 Quinton McCracken .50 .15
186 Neifi Perez .50 .15
187 Bryan Rekar .15 .04
188 Mark Thompson .15 .04
189 Tim Clark .15 .04
190 Vic Darensbourg .15 .04
191 Charles Johnson .50 .15
192 Bryn Kosco .15 .04
193 Reynol Mendoza .15 .04
194 Kerwin Moore .15 .04
195 John Toale .15 .04
196 Bob Abreu 1.00 .30
197 Jim Bruske .15 .04
198 Jim Dougherty .15 .04
199 Tony Eusebio .15 .04
200 Kevin Gallaher .15 .04
201 Chris Holt .15 .04
202 Brian L. Hunter .15 .04
203 Orlando Miller .15 .04
204 Donovan Mitchell .15 .04
205 Alvin Morman .15 .04
206 James Mouton .15 .04
207 Phil Nevin .50 .15
208 Roberto Petagine .15 .04
209 Billy Wagner .75 .23
210 Mike Busch .15 .04
211 Roger Cedeno .50 .15
212 Chris Demetral .15 .04
213 Rick Gorecki .15 .04
214 Ryan Henderson .15 .04
215 Todd Hollandsworth .15 .04
216 Ken Huckaby .15 .04
217 Rich Linares .15 .04
218 Ryan Luzinski .15 .04
219 Doug Newstrom .15 .04
220 Ben Van Ryn .15 .04
221 Todd Williams .15 .04
222 Shane Andrews .15 .04
223 Reid Cornelius .15 .04
224 Joey Eischen .15 .04
225 Heath Haynes .15 .04
226 Rod Henderson .15 .04
227 Mark LaRosa .15 .04
228 Glenn Murray .15 .04
229 Ugueth Urbina .15 .04
230 B.J. Wallace .15 .04
231 Gabe White .15 .04
232 Edgardo Alfonzo .50 .15
233 Randy Curtis .15 .04
234 Omar Garcia .15 .04
235 Jason Isringhausen .50 .15
236 Eric Ludwick .15 .04
237 Bill Pulsipher .15 .04
238 Chris Roberts .15 .04
239 Quilvio Veras .50 .15
240 Pete Walker .15 .04
241 Mike Welch .15 .04
242 Preston Wilson 1.00 .30
243 Ricky Bottalico .50 .15
244 Alan Burke .15 .04
245 Phil Geisler .15 .04
246 Mike Lieberthal .50 .15
247 Jason Moler .15 .04
248 Gene Schall .15 .04
249 Mark Tranberg .15 .04
250 Jermaine Allensworth .15 .04
251 Michael Brown .15 .04
252 Jason Kendall .50 .15
253 Jeff McCurry .15 .04
254 Jeff Alkire .15 .04
255 Mike Badorek .15 .04
256 Brian Barber .15 .04
257 Alan Benes .15 .04
258 Jeff Berblinger .15 .04
259 Joe Biasucci .15 .04
260 Terry Bradshaw .15 .04
261 Duff Brumley .15 .04
262 Kirk Bullinger .15 .04
263 Mike Busby .15 .04
264 Jamie Cochran .15 .04
265 Clint Davis .15 .04
266 Mike Gulan .15 .04
267 Aaron Holbert .15 .04
268 John Kelly .15 .04
269 John Mabry .50 .15
270 Frankie Martinez .15 .04
271 T.J. Mathews .15 .04
272 Aldo Pecorilli .15 .04
273 Doug Radziewicz .15 .04
274 Brian Rupp .15 .04
275 Gerald Witasick .15 .04
276 Dmitri Young .50 .15
277 Homer Bush .50 .15
278 Glenn Dishman .15 .04
279 Sean Drinkwater .15 .04
280 Bryce Florie .15 .04
281 Billy Hall .15 .04
282 Jason Hardtke .15 .04
283 Ray Holbert .15 .04
284 Brian Johnson .15 .04
285 Ray McDavid .15 .04
286 Ira Smith .15 .04
287 Steve Day .15 .04
288 Kurt Ehmann .15 .04
289 Chad Fonville .15 .04
290 Kris Franko .15 .04
291 Aaron Fultz .15 .04
292 Marcus Jensen .15 .04
293 Calvin Murray .15 .04
294 Jeff Richey .15 .04
295 Bill VanLandingham .15 .04
296 Keith Williams .15 .04
297 Chris Wimmer .15 .04
298 Checklist .15 .04
299 Checklist .15 .04
300 Checklist .15 .04

1993-94 Excel All-Stars

Randomly inserted into packs, these 10 cards feature players who earned spots on minor-league All-Stars teams.

	Nm-Mt	Ex-Mt
COMPLETE SET (10)	8.00	2.40
1 Charles Johnson	1.00	.30
2 Roberto Petagine	.50	.15
3 James Mouton	.50	.15
4 Russ Davis	1.00	.30
5 Alex Gonzalez	1.00	.30
6 Johnny Damon	2.00	.60
7 Garret Anderson	1.00	.30
8 Brian L. Hunter	.50	.15
9 D.J. Boston	.50	.15
10 Terrell Wade	.50	.15

1993-94 Excel First Year Phenoms

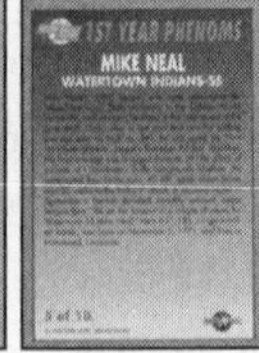

Randomly inserted into packs, these 10 cards feature players who made their minor league debuts in 1993.

	Nm-Mt	Ex-Mt
COMPLETE SET (10)	4.00	1.20
1 Jim Foster	.50	.15
2 Brian Link	.50	.15
3 Jeff Berblinger	.50	.15
4 Doug Newstrom	.50	.15
5 Mike Neal	.50	.15
6 Jermaine Allensworth	.50	.15
7 Todd Greene	.50	.15
8 Keith Williams	.50	.15
9 Shawn Wooten	.50	.15
10 Joshua Neese	.50	.15

1993-94 Excel League Leaders

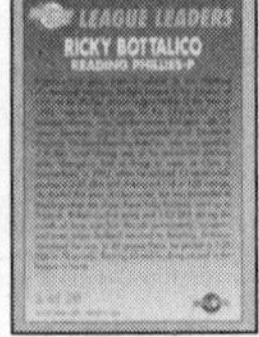

Inserted at a rate of one every two packs, these 20 cards feature players who a minor league in any category.

	Nm-Mt	Ex-Mt
COMPLETE SET (20)	15.00	4.50
1 James Baldwin	1.00	.30
2 Joel Bennett	.50	.15
3 Ricky Bottalico	1.00	.30
4 Mike Busch	.50	.15
5 Duff Brumley	.50	.15
6 Jamie Cochran	.50	.15
7 John Dettmer	.50	.15
8 Joey Eischen	.50	.15
9 LaTroy Hawkins	1.00	.30
10 Derek Jeter	10.00	3.00
11 Ryan Karp	.50	.15
12 Rick Krivda	.50	.15
13 Trey McCoy	.50	.15
14 Jason Moler	.50	.15
15 Chad Mottola	.50	.15
16 Jose Silva	.50	.15
17 Brien Taylor	.50	.15
18 Michael Tucker	.50	.15
19 Ugueth Urbina	.50	.15
20 Ben Van Ryn	.50	.15

1994 Action Packed Prototypes

These three standard-size promo cards were issued to preview the design of the 72-card

1994 Action Packed Scouting Report series. Card number 1, representing a regular issue card, features a full-bleed embossed color player photo on its front, with the player's name in a baseball at the upper left. Card numbers 2-3, which represent Franchise Gems, also have a full-bleed color embossed photo on their fronts with a Franchise Gem logo at the upper left. The cards are numbered on the back and marked "Prototype" near the bottom edge.

	Nm-Mt	Ex-Mt
COMPLETE SET (3)	5.00	1.50
1 Trot Nixon	2.00	.60
2 Alex Gonzalez	2.00	.60
3 Russ Davis	2.00	.60

1994 Action Packed

The 1994 Action Packed Scouting Report set consists of 72 standard-size cards featuring top AAA, AA, and A prospects picked by Action Packed's scouts. 24K gold versions of selected cards were randomly inserted in the foil packs as chase cards. The 12-card Franchise Gems subset feature a heat sensitive graphic that reveals Action Packed's prediction of the player's impact year. Special cards reveal a prize-winning message and become exchange cards which could be redeemed for genuine diamond-studded collector versions of the card. Early cards of Derek Jeter, Michael Jordan (as a baseball player) and Alex Rodriguez are featured in this set.

	Nm-Mt	Ex-Mt
COMPLETE SET (72)	20.00	6.00
COMMON CARD (1-66)	.25	.07
COMMON (67-71)	.50	.15
1 Alex Rodriguez	5.00	1.50
2 Trot Nixon	1.00	.30
3 Chan Ho Park	.75	.23
4 Brooks Kieschnick	.25	.07
5 Matt Brunson	.25	.07
6 Wayne Gomes	.25	.07
7 Charles Johnson	.75	.23
8 Kirk Presley	.25	.07
9 Daron Kirkreit	.25	.07
10 Curtis Goodwin	.25	.07
11 Alex Ochoa	.25	.07
12 Midre Cummings	.25	.07
13 Russ Davis	.25	.07
14 Phil Nevin	.75	.23
15 J.R. Phillips	.25	.07
16 Jeff Granger	.25	.07
17 Mac Suzuki	.75	.23
18 Johnny Damon	.75	.23
19 Chad Mottola	.25	.07
20 Scott Ruffcorn	.25	.07
21 Brian Barber	.25	.07
22 Frank Rodriguez	.25	.07
23 Michael Jordan	4.00	1.20
24 Michael Tucker	.25	.07
25 Rondell White	.75	.23
26 Ugueth Urbina	.25	.07
27 Tyrone Hill	.25	.07
28 Dmitri Young	.75	.23
29 Marshall Boze	.25	.07
30 Marc Newfield	.25	.07
31 James Baldwin	.25	.07
32 Terrell Wade	.25	.07
33 Curtis Pride	.75	.23
34 Gabe White	.25	.07
35 Derrek Lee	1.00	.30
36 Bill Pulsipher	.25	.07
37 Butch Huskey	.25	.07
38 Nigel Wilson	.25	.07
39 Tim Clark	.25	.07
40 Ozzie Timmons	.25	.07
41 Brien Taylor	.25	.07
42 J.T. Snow	.75	.23
43 Derek Jeter	3.00	.90
44 Rick Krivda	.25	.07
45 Kevin Millar	1.00	.30
46 Matt Franco	.25	.07
47 Jose Silva	.25	.07
48 Benji Gil	.25	.07
49 Pokey Reese	.25	.07
50 Todd Hollandsworth	.25	.07
51 Robert Ellis	.25	.07
52 Brian L. Hunter	.25	.07
53 Ryan Luzinski	.25	.07
54 Kurt Miller	.25	.07
55 Alex Rodriguez FG	5.00	1.50
56 Chan Ho Park FG	.75	.23
57 Brooks Kieschnick FG	.25	.07
58 Charles Johnson FG	.75	.23
59 Alex Ochoa FG	.25	.07
60 Michael Tucker FG	.25	.07
61 Phil Nevin FG	.75	.23
62 Jose Silva FG	.25	.07
63 James Baldwin FG	.25	.07
64 Rondell White FG	.75	.23
65 Trot Nixon FG	1.00	.30
66 Todd Hollandsworth FG	.25	.07
67 Roberto Clemente Hidden Talent	.50	.15
68 Roberto Clemente Four-time batting champ	.50	.15
69 Roberto Clemente 1966 NL MVP	.50	.15
70 Roberto Clemente 3,000-Hit Club	.50	.15
71 Roberto Clemente 1973 Hall of Fame	.50	.15
72 Checklist (1-72)	.25	.07
AU1 F.Rodriguez AU/2500	5.00	1.50

1994 Action Packed 24K Gold

Issued at a rate of one every 96 packs, these 13 cards feature the words "24K" on the front.

	Nm-Mt	Ex-Mt
*GOLD DIAMOND:2X TO 5X BASIC 24K		
GD STATED ODDS: 1:1920 PACKS		
1G Alex Rodriguez	50.00	15.00
2G Chan Ho Park	8.00	2.40
3G Brooks Kieschnick	5.00	1.50
4G Charles Johnson	8.00	2.40
5G Alex Ochoa	5.00	1.50
6G Michael Tucker	5.00	1.50
7G Phil Nevin	8.00	2.40
8G Jose Silva	5.00	1.50
9G James Baldwin	5.00	1.50
10G Rondell White	8.00	2.40
11G Trot Nixon	10.00	3.00
12G Todd Hollandsworth	5.00	1.50
13G Checklist	5.00	1.50

1994 Classic

This 200-card set features a selection of minor league prospects. The cards were distributed in packs and sold nationwide. Key cards include Alex Rodriguez and Michael Jordan. In addition, two separate Cal Ripken cards were randomly seeded into packs to commemorate his 2000th consecutive game played. Ripken signed 2000 copies of the scarcer version, each of which is serial numbered in blue ink on front.

	Nm-Mt	Ex-Mt
COMPLETE SET (200)	15.00	4.50
1 Michael Jordan	3.00	.90
2 Felipe Lira	.15	.04
3 Jose Silva	.15	.04
4 Turi Sanchez	.15	.04
5 Marcus Jensen	.15	.04
6 Julio Santana	.15	.04
7 Angel Martinez	.15	.04
8 Jose Herrera	.15	.04
9 D.J. Boston	.15	.04
10 Trot Nixon	.75	.23
11 Trey Beamon	.15	.04
12 Danny Clyburn	.15	.04
13 John Wasdin	.15	.04
14 Vince Moore	.15	.04
15 Vic Darensbourg	.15	.04
16 Kevin Gallaher	.15	.04
17 Julio Bruno	.15	.04
18 Terrell Lowery	.15	.04
19 Phil Geisler	.15	.04
20 Chan Ho Park	.50	.15
21 Chad McConnell	.15	.04
22 Ricky Bottalico	.50	.15
23 Jim Pittsley	.15	.04
24 Gabe Martinez	.15	.04
25 Johnny Damon	.50	.15
26 Basil Shabazz	.15	.04
27 Billy Ashley	.15	.04
28 Andy Pettitte		
29 Robert Ellis	.15	.04
30 Mike Zolecki	.15	.04
31 AS League Card #1	.15	.04
32 John Burke	.15	.04
33 Chris Snopek	.15	.04
34 Mark Thompson	.15	.04
35 Jimmy Haynes	.15	.04
36 Ron Villone	.15	.04
37 Curtis Goodwin	.15	.04
38 Tim Belk	.15	.04
39 Rod Henderson	.15	.04
40 Butch Huskey	.15	.04
41 Chris Smith	.15	.04
42 B.J. Wallace	.15	.04
43 Guillermo Mercedes	.15	.04
44 Ugueth Urbina	.15	.04
45 Fausto Cruz	.15	.04
46 Julian Tavarez	.15	.04
47 Scott Lydy	.15	.04
48 Darren Burton	.15	.04
49 Mac Suzuki	.50	.15
50 Kirk Presley	.15	.04
51 Alex Rodriguez CL	1.50	.45
52 Armando Benitez	.50	.15
53 Rodney Pedraza	.15	.04
54 LaTroy Hawkins	.50	.15
55 Rick Forney	.15	.04
56 Tripp Cromer	.15	.04
57 Andres Berumen	.15	.04
58 Terry Bradshaw	.15	.04
59 Omar Ramirez	.15	.04
60 Derek Jeter	3.00	.90
61 Kerwin Moore	.15	.04
62 Andy Larkin	.15	.04
63 Neifi Perez	.50	.15
64 Casey Whitten	.15	.04
65 Jon Ratliff	.15	.04
66 J.J. Johnson	.15	.04
67 Preston Wilson	.50	.15
68 Jason Isringhausen	.50	.15
69 Adam Meinershagen	.15	.04
70 Rondell White	.50	.15
71 Shannon Stewart	.50	.15
72 Keith Heberling	.15	.04
73 Ruben Rivera	.15	.04
74 Mike Lieberthal	.50	.15
75 Damon Hollins	.15	.04
76 Jason Jacome	.15	.04
77 Amaury Telemaco	.15	.04
78 Scott Talanoa	.15	.04
79 Dave Stevens	.15	.04
80 Brien Taylor	.15	.04
81 AS League Card #2	.15	.04
82 Brian Barber	.15	.04
83 Ray Durham	.50	.15
84 Brent Bowers	.15	.04
85 Shane Andrews	.15	.04
86 Gabe White	.15	.04
87 Midre Cummings	.15	.04
88 Brad Radke	.50	.15
89 Joe Randa	.15	.04
90 Phil Nevin	.50	.15
91 Joe Vitiello	.15	.04
92 Ray McDavid	.15	.04
93 Robbie Beckett	.15	.04
94 Frank Rodriguez	.15	.04
95 Marc Newfield	.15	.04
96 Joey Eischen	.15	.04
97 Manny Alexander	.15	.04
98 Jeff McNeely	.15	.04
99 Mark Smith	.15	.04
100 Alex Rodriguez	5.00	1.50
101 Todd Hollandsworth	.15	.04
102 Scott Ruffcorn	.15	.04
103 Kurt Miller	.15	.04
104 Justin Mashore	.15	.04
105 Garret Anderson	.50	.15
106 Nigel Wilson	.15	.04
107 Howard Battle	.15	.04
108 Pokey Reese	.15	.04
109 Orlando Miller	.15	.04
110 Bill Pulsipher	.15	.04
111 Edgar Renteria	1.50	.45
112 Steve Gibralter	.15	.04
113 Gene Schall	.15	.04
114 John Roper	.15	.04
115 Alvin Morman	.15	.04
116 Doug Glanville	.50	.15
117 Mark Hutton	.15	.04
118 Glenn Murray	.15	.04
119 Curtis Shaw	.15	.04
120 Alex Ochoa	.15	.04
121 Michael Moore	.15	.04
122 Joey Hamilton	.15	.04
123 James Baldwin	.15	.04
124 Chad Ogea	.15	.04
125 Rikkert Faneyte	.15	.04
126 Benji Gil	.15	.04
127 Kenny Felder	.15	.04
128 Brant Brown	.15	.04
129 Eddie Pearson	.15	.04
130 Derrek Lee	.75	.23
131 AS League Card #3	.15	.04
132 Dan Serafini	.15	.04
133 Ramon Caraballo	.15	.04
134 Derek Wallace	.15	.04
135 Jamie Arnold	.15	.04
136 Domingo Jean	.15	.04
137 Jose Malave	.15	.04
138 Derek Lowe	.50	.15
139 Marshall Boze	.15	.04
140 Billy Wagner	.75	.23
141 Matt Franco	.15	.04
142 Roger Cedeno	.15	.04
143 Russ Davis	.15	.04
144 Kevin Flora	.15	.04
145 Rick Gorecki	.15	.04
146 Rick Greene	.15	.04
147 Brian L. Hunter	.15	.04
148 Rich Aurilia	.75	.23
149 Jason Moler	.15	.04
150 Michael Tucker	.15	.04
151 Alex Rodriguez CL	1.50	.45
152 Chad Mottola	.15	.04
153 Calvin Murray	.15	.04
154 Melvin Nieves	.15	.04
155 Luis Ortiz	.15	.04
156 Chris Roberts	.15	.04
157 Todd Williams	.15	.04
158 Tony Phillips	.15	.04
159 DeShawn Warren	.15	.04
160 Paul Shuey	.15	.04
161 Dmitri Young	.50	.15
162 Jermaine Allensworth	.15	.04
163 Daron Kirkreit	.15	.04
164 Scott Christman	.15	.04
165 Steve Soderstrom	.15	.04
166 J.R. Phillips	.15	.04
167 Karim Garcia	.50	.15
168 Marc Acre	.15	.04
169 Jose Paniagua	.50	.15
170 Terrell Wade	.15	.04
171 Mike Bell	.15	.04
172 Alan Benes	.15	.04
173 Jeff D'Amico	.50	.15
174 Tate Seefried	.15	.04
175 Wayne Gomes	.15	.04
176 Chris Singleton	.50	.15
177 Marc Valdes	.15	.04
178 Jamey Wright	.50	.15
179 Jay Powell	.15	.04
180 Charles Johnson	.50	.15
181 Mitch House	.15	.04
182 Torii Hunter	1.00	.30
183 Jeff Suppan	.50	.15
184 Roberto Petagine	.15	.04
185 Ryan McGuire	.15	.04
186 Andrew Lorraine	.15	.04
187 Matt Brunson	.15	.04
188 Eduardo Perez	.15	.04
189 Jay Witasick	.15	.04
190 Shawn Green	.50	.15
191 Cleveland Ladell	.15	.04
192 Paul Bako	.15	.04
193 Brook Fordyce	.15	.04
194 Kym Ashworth	.15	.04
195 Tony Mitchell	.15	.04
196 Tony Clark	.50	.15
197 Curtis Pride	.50	.15
198 Arquimedez Pozo	.15	.04
199 Rey Ordonez	.50	.15
200 Brooks Kieschnick	.15	.04
CB1 A.Rodriguez Promo	5.00	1.50
CR1 Cal Ripken Special	5.00	1.50
AU1 Cal Ripken AU/2000	120.00	36.00

1994 Classic Autographs

These cards were randomly inserted into packs. Each player signed a different amount of cards and we have put the number signed after the players name in our checklist. The fronts of the card have the signature along with a serial number while the back has a congratulations message from Classic.

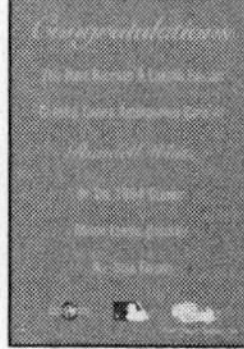

	Nm-Mt	Ex-Mt
AU1 Alex Rodriguez/2100	200.00	60.00
AU2 Terrell Wade/2080	3.00	.90
AU3 B.Kieschnick/3400	3.00	.90
AU4 Rondell White/2880	5.00	1.50
AU5 Michael Tucker/2400	5.00	1.50
AU6 Kirk Presley/1300	3.00	.90
AUTN Trot Nixon/1700		

1994 Classic Bonus Baby

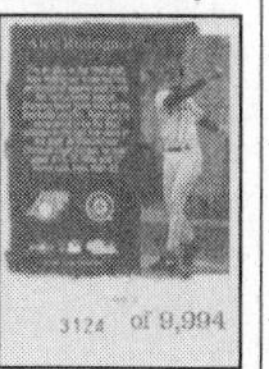

This set is numbered to 9994. There is also autographed cards found, so far, at least of Alex Rodriguez, numbered to 435. No pricing is yet available on the Rodriguez autograph but it is believed the card was initially offered for sale via television on the Home Shopping Network.

	Nm-Mt	Ex-Mt
COMPLETE SET (5)	25.00	7.50
BB1 Trot Nixon	3.00	.90
BB2 Kirk Presley	1.00	.30
BB3 Alex Rodriguez	20.00	6.00
BB4 Brooks Kieschnick	1.00	.30
BB5 Michael Tucker	1.00	.30
BB3A A.Rodriguez AU/435	350.00	105.00

1994 Classic Cream of the Crop

Inserted at a rate of one per pack, these 25 cards feature the players Classic thought were the leading prospects in their 1994 minor league product. Cards of Derek Jeter and Alex Rodriguez are the key cards in this set.

	Nm-Mt	Ex-Mt
COMPLETE SET (25)	25.00	7.50
C1 Trot Nixon	.75	.23
C2 Kirk Presley	.50	.15
C3 Mac Suzuki	.50	.15
C4 Brooks Kieschnick	.50	.15
C5 Johnny Damon	.50	.15
C6 Howard Battle	.50	.15
C7 Michael Tucker	.50	.15
C8 Todd Hollandsworth	.50	.15
C9 J.R. Phillips	.50	.15
C10 Shannon Stewart	.50	.15
C11 Alex Rodriguez	2.50	.75
C12 Terrell Wade	.50	.15
C13 Rondell White	.50	.15
C14 James Baldwin	.50	.15
C15 Shane Andrews	.50	.15
C16 Chan Ho Park	.50	.15
C17 Derek Jeter	2.50	.75
C18 Charles Johnson	.50	.15
C19 Bill Pulsipher	.50	.15
C20 Phil Nevin	.50	.15
C21 Scott Ruffcorn	.50	.15
C22 Midre Cummings	.50	.15
C23 Frank Rodriguez	.50	.15
C24 Dmitri Young	.50	.15
C25 Shawn Green	.50	.15

1994 Classic #1 Draft Pick Mail-In

One set per mail-in wrapper offer.

	Nm-Mt	Ex-Mt
COMPLETE SET (5)	4.00	1.20
DD1 Paul Wilson	1.00	.30
DD2 Ben Grieve	.75	.23
DD3 Dustin Hermanson	.75	.23
DD4 Antone Williamson	1.00	.30
DD5 Josh Booty	.75	.23

1994 Classic Tri-Cards

This 28-card insert features a selection of three prospects from each major league team's farm system. Production was stated by the manufacturer at 8,000 sets. The cards were randomly seeded into packs.

	Nm-Mt	Ex-Mt
COMPLETE SET (28)	60.00	18.00
T1 Jamie Arnold T2 Terrell Wade T3 Ramon Caraballo	1.00	.30
T4 Jay Powell T5 Alex Ochoa T6 Manny Alexander	1.50	.45
T7 Trot Nixon T8 Jose Malave T9 Frank Rodriguez	2.00	.60
T10 DeShawn Warren T11 Chris Smith T12 Andrew Lorraine	1.00	.30
T13 Jon Ratliff T14 Brooks Kieschnick T15 Matt Franco	1.00	.30
T16 Eddie Pearson T17 Chris Snopek T18 James Baldwin	1.00	.30
T19 Paul Bako T20 Chad Mottola T21 John Roper	1.00	.30
T22 Daron Kirkreit T23 Tony Mitchell T24 Chad Ogea	1.00	.30
T25 Mike Zolecki T26 Rodney Pedraza T27 Mark Thompson	1.00	.30
T28 Matt Brunson T29 Tony Clark T30 Felipe Lira	1.50	.45
T31 Edgar Renteria T32 Charles Johnson T33 Kurt Miller	3.00	.90
T34 Billy Wagner T35 Kevin Gallaher T36 Phil Nevin	2.00	.60
T37 Johnny Damon T38 Darren Burton T39 Michael Tucker	1.50	.45
T40 Kym Ashworth T41 Chan Ho Park T42 Todd Hollandsworth	1.50	.45
T43 Gabe Martinez T44 Scott Talanoa T45 Marshall Boze	1.00	.30
T46 LaTroy Hawkins T47 Brad Radke T48 Dave Stevens	1.50	.45
T49 Jose Paniagua T50 Ugueth Urbina T51 Rondell White	1.50	.45
T52 Bill Pulsipher T53 Butch Huskey T54 Kirk Presley	1.00	.30
T55 Derek Jeter T56 Brien Taylor T57 Russ Davis	8.00	2.40
T58 Jose Herrera T59 Curtis Shaw T60 Mark Acre	1.00	.30
T61 Wayne Gomes T62 Jason Moler T63 Phil Geisler	1.00	.30
T64 Mitch House T65 Jermaine Allensworth T66 Midre Cummings	1.00	.30
T67 Derrek Lee T68 Robbie Beckett T69 Ray McDavid	2.00	.60
T70 Chris Singleton T71 Calvin Murray T72 J.R. Phillips	1.50	.45
T73 Alex Rodriguez T74 Mac Suzuki T75 Marc Newfield	10.00	3.00
T76 Basil Shabazz T77 Dmitri Young T78 Brian Barber	1.50	.45
T79 Mike Bell T80 Terrell Lowery T81 Benji Gil	1.00	.30
T82 Jose Silva T83 Brent Bowers T84 Shawn Green	1.50	.45

1994 Classic Update Cream of the Crop

Inserted as a rate of one per Classic Update pack, these 20 cards feature the players Classic thought were the best players in their 1994 Update set. An early Nomar Garciaparra card is the key card in this set.

	Nm-Mt	Ex-Mt
COMPLETE SET (20)	25.00	7.50
CC1 Paul Wilson	.50	.15
CC2 Ben Grieve	.50	.15
CC3 Dustin Hermanson	.50	.15
CC4 Antone Williamson	.50	.15
CC5 Josh Booty	.50	.15
CC6 Doug Million	.50	.15
CC7 Todd Walker	.75	.23
CC8 C.J. Nitkowski	.50	.15
CC9 Jaret Wright	.50	.15
CC10 Mark Farris	.50	.15
CC11 Nomar Garciaparra	5.00	1.50
CC12 Paul Konerko	1.50	.45
CC13 Jayson Peterson	.50	.15
CC14 Matt Smith	.50	.15
CC15 Ramon Castro	.50	.15
CC16 Cade Gaspar	.50	.15
CC17 Terrence Long	1.00	.30
CC18 Hiram Bocachica	.50	.15

CC19 Dante Powell .50 .15
CC20 Brian Buchanan .50 .15

1994 Classic/Best Gold Promos

These two standard-size promos were issued to herald the release of the 200-card 1994 Classic/Best Minor League Gold set. The front features a borderless color player photo, with the player's name appearing vertically in gold foil at the upper right. The player's team name appears vertically up the right side. The back carries an oblique, horizontally oriented color player photo. To its right are the player's name, team name, position, and stats; all vertically oriented and stamped in gold foil. The player's biography appears horizontally oriented to the photo's left. The cards are numbered on the back with a "PR" prefix.

Nm-Mt Ex-Mt
1 Brien Taylor .50 .15
2 Phil Nevin 1.00 .30

1994 Classic/Best Gold

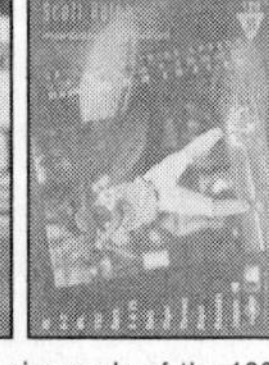

These 200 standard-size cards of the 1994 Classic Best Minor League Gold set feature players from Triple A, Double A, Single A, Short Season, and the Rookie League. Randomly inserted in the foil packs were a 19-card number one Picks set, five acetate cards, and autographed cards by David Justice. An early Scott Rolen card is featured in this set. Justice signed 4,000 cards which were randomly seeded into packs.

Nm-Mt Ex-Mt
COMPLETE SET (200) 15.00 4.50
1 Brien Taylor .15 .04
2 Jeff D'Amico .50 .15
3 Trot Nixon .75 .23
4 Clayton Byrne .15 .04
5 Eric Chavez .15 .04
6 Matt Jarvis .15 .04
7 Billy Owens .15 .04
8 Jay Powell .15 .04
9 Robert Eenhoorn .15 .04
10 Trey Beamon .15 .04
11 Todd Williams .15 .04
12 Tim Davis .15 .04
13 Brian Barber .15 .04
14 Jeff Shireman .15 .04
15 Melvin Mora .75 .23
16 Phil Nevin .50 .15
17 Kendall Rhine .15 .04
18 Billy Wagner .75 .23
19 Jason Kendall .50 .15
20 Kelly Wunsch .15 .04
21 D.J. Boston .15 .04
22 Shannon Stewart .50 .15
23 Anthony Manahan .15 .04
24 Dwight Robinson .15 .04
25 Alan Benes .15 .04
26 Dennis Slininger .15 .04
27 John Burke .15 .04
28 Jamey Wright .50 .15
29 Scott Eyre .15 .04
30 Jack Kimel .15 .04
31 Kerry Lacy .15 .04
32 Rich Aurilia .75 .23
33 Dave Giberti .15 .04
34 Daryl Henderson .15 .04
35 Stanley Evans .15 .04
36 Wayne Gomes .15 .04
37 Rob Grable .15 .04
38 Mike Juhl .15 .04
39 Jason Moler .15 .04
40 Jon Zuber .15 .04
41 Chad Fonville .15 .04
42 Mark Thompson .15 .04
43 Billy Masse .15 .04
44 Derek Hacopian .15 .04
45 J.J. Thobe .15 .04
46 Charles York .15 .04
47 Jamie Howard .15 .04
48 Andre King .15 .04
49 Tim Delgado .15 .04
50 Mike Hubbard .15 .04
51 Bernie Nunez .15 .04
52 Jon Ratliff .15 .04
53 Pedro Valdez .15 .04
54 Rich Butler .15 .04
55 Felipe Crespo .15 .04
56 Randy Phillips .15 .04
57 Todd Steverson .15 .04
58 Chris Stynes .15 .04
59 Ben Weber .50 .15
60 Chris Weinke .50 .15
61 Rob Lukachyk .15 .04
62 Brett King .15 .04
63 Chris Singleton .50 .15
64 Brian Bright .15 .04
65 Brent Brede .15 .04
66 Steve Hazlett .15 .04
67 Dan Serafini .15 .04
68 Matt Farner .15 .04
69 Jeremy Lee .15 .04
70 Anthony Medrano .15 .04
71 Josue Estrada .15 .04
72 Martin Mainville .15 .04
73 Chris Schwab .15 .04
74 John Roskos .15 .04
75 Charles Peterson .15 .04
76 Kevin Pickford .15 .04
77 Charles Rice .15 .04
78 Mike Bell .15 .04
79 Ed Diaz .15 .04
80 Torii Hunter 1.50 .45
81 Kelcey Mucker .15 .04
82 Nick Delvecchio .15 .04
83 Derek Jeter 3.00 .90
84 Ryan Karp .15 .04
85 Matt Luke .15 .04
86 Ray Suplee .15 .04
87 Tyler Houston .15 .04
88 Brad Cornett .15 .04
89 Kris Harmes .15 .04
90 Shane Andrews .15 .04
91 Ugueth Urbina .15 .04
92 Chris Mader .15 .04
93 Eddie Pearson .15 .04
94 Tim Clark .15 .04
95 Chris Malinoski .15 .04
96 John Toale .15 .04
97 Mark Acre .15 .04
98 Ernie Young .15 .04
99 Jeff Schmidt .15 .04
100 Roberto Petagine .15 .04
101 Eddy Diaz .15 .04
102 Ruben Santana .15 .04
103 Ron Villone .15 .04
104 Nate Dishington .15 .04
105 Charles Johnson .50 .15
106 Preston Wilson .50 .15
107 Paul Shuey .15 .04
108 Howard Battle .15 .04
109 Tim Hyers .15 .04
110 Rick Greene .15 .04
111 Justin Thompson .15 .04
112 Frank Rodriguez .15 .04
113 Jamie Arnold .15 .04
114 Marty Malloy .15 .04
115 Darrell May .15 .04
116 Leo Ramirez .15 .04
117 Tom Thobe .15 .04
118 Terrell Wade .15 .04
119 Marc Valdes .15 .04
120 Scott Rolen 3.00 .90
121 Les Norman .15 .04
122 Michael Tucker .15 .04
123 Joe Vitiello .15 .04
124 Chris Roberts .15 .04
125 Jason Giambi 1.50 .45
126 Izzy Molina .15 .04
127 Scott Shockey .15 .04
128 John Wasdin .15 .04
129 Joel Wolfe .15 .04
130 Brooks Kieschnick .15 .04
131 Kennie Steenstra .15 .04
132 Hector Trinidad .15 .04
133 Derek Wallace .15 .04
134 Kevin Lane .15 .04
135 Buck McNabb .15 .04
136 James Mouton .15 .04
137 Joey Eischen .15 .04
138 Todd Haney .15 .04
139 John Pricher .15 .04
140 Jeff Brown .15 .04
141 Jason Hardtke .15 .04
142 Derrek Lee .75 .23
143 Ira Smith .15 .04
144 Mike Kelly .15 .04
145 Mark Smith .15 .04
146 Sherard Clinkscales .15 .04
147 Ben Van Ryn .15 .04
148 Tim Cooper .15 .04
149 Manny Martinez .15 .04
150 Kurt Ehmann .15 .04
151 Doug Mirabelli .15 .04
152 Chris Wimmer .15 .04
153 Scott Christman .15 .04
154 Kevin Coughlin .15 .04
155 Troy Fryman .15 .04
156 Sean Johnston .15 .04
157 Jeff Alkire .15 .04
158 Mike Busby .15 .04
159 John O'Brien .15 .04
160 Brian Rupp .15 .04
161 Steve Soderstrom .15 .04
162 Craig Wilson .15 .04
163 Alan Burke .15 .04
164 Mike Murphy .15 .04
165 T.J. Mathews .15 .04
166 Edgardo Alfonzo .50 .15
167 Randy Curtis .15 .04
168 Bernie Millan .15 .04
169 Mike Cantu .15 .04
170 Clint Davis .15 .04
171 Jason Hisey .15 .04
172 Aldo Pecorilli .15 .04
173 Dmitri Young .50 .15
174 Marshall Boze .15 .04
175 Bill Hardwick .15 .04
176 Kevin Riggs .15 .04
177 Lee Stevens .15 .04
178 Webster Garrison .15 .04
179 Wally Ritchie .15 .04
180 Cris Colon .15 .04
181 Rick Helling .15 .04
182 Trey McCoy .15 .04
183 Marc Barcelo .15 .04
184 Chris Demetral .15 .04
185 Rich Linares .15 .04
186 Daron Kirkreit .15 .04
187 Casey Whitten .15 .04
188 Shon Walker .15 .04
189 Rod Henderson .15 .04
190 Tyrone Horne .15 .04
191 B.J. Wallace .15 .04
192 Louis Maberry .15 .04
193 Brian Boehringer .15 .04
194 Glenn DiSarcina .15 .04
195 Melvin Bunch .15 .04
196 Chad Mottola .15 .04
197 Ryan Luzinski .15 .04
198 Tom Wilson .15 .04
199 Checklist (1-100) .15 .04
200 Checklist (101-200) .15 .04
AU1 D.Justice AU/4000 15.00 4.50

1994 Classic/Best Gold Acetates

These glow-in-the-dark, illustrated, acetate cards were inserted at the rate of four per case. They were designed by comic artist Neal Adams, featured a common background, and are numbered on the back with an "SH" prefix.

Nm-Mt Ex-Mt
COMPLETE SET (5) 20.00 6.00
SH1 Brien Taylor 2.00 .60
SH2 Dmitri Young 3.00 .90
SH3 Derek Jeter 15.00 4.50
SH4 Phil Nevin 3.00 .90
SH5 Frank Rodriguez 2.00 .60

1994 Classic/Best Gold #1 Pick LPs

These limited-print, chromium effect (reflective texture, shiny/glossy glass look) cards feature 19 first round picks from the 1993 June Major League Baseball Draft. Average insert ratio was 30 per case. The cards are numbered on the back with an "LP" prefix.

Nm-Mt Ex-Mt
COMPLETE SET (19) 20.00 6.00
LP1 Alan Benes 1.00 .30
LP2 Scott Christman 1.00 .30
LP3 Jeff D'Amico 1.50 .45
LP4 Wayne Gomes 1.00 .30
LP5 Torii Hunter 4.00 1.20
LP6 Brooks Kieschnick 1.00 .30
LP7 Daron Kirkreit 1.00 .30
LP8 Derrek Lee 2.00 .60
LP9 Trot Nixon 2.00 .60
LP10 Charles Peterson 1.00 .30
LP11 Jay Powell 1.00 .30
LP12 Jon Ratliff 1.00 .30
LP13 Chris Schwab 1.00 .30
LP14 Steve Soderstrom 1.00 .30
LP15 Marc Valdes 1.00 .30
LP16 Billy Wagner 2.00 .60
LP17 John Wasdin 1.00 .30
LP18 Jamey Wright 1.50 .45
LP19 Kelly Wunsch 1.00 .30

1994 Classic/Best Gold Rookie Express

Randomly inserted into packs, these 20 cards feature some of the leading prospects from the Classic/Best gold set.

Nm-Mt Ex-Mt
COMPLETE SET (20) 6.00 1.80
RE1 Alan Benes .50 .15
RE2 Scott Ruffcorn .50 .15
RE3 Jeff D'Amico .50 .15
RE4 Wayne Gomes .50 .15
RE5 Torii Hunter 2.50 .75
RE6 Brooks Kieschnick .50 .15
RE7 Daron Kirkreit .50 .15
RE8 Derrek Lee .75 .23
RE9 Trot Nixon .75 .23
RE10 Charles Peterson .50 .15
RE11 Jay Powell .50 .15
RE12 Jon Ratliff .50 .15
RE13 Chris Schwab .50 .15
RE14 Steve Soderstrom .50 .15
RE15 Marc Valdes .50 .15
RE16 Billy Wagner .75 .23
RE17 John Wasdin .50 .15
RE18 Jamey Wright .50 .15
RE19 Kelly Wunsch .50 .15
RE20 B.Kieschnick GLOW .50 .15

1994 Signature Rookies

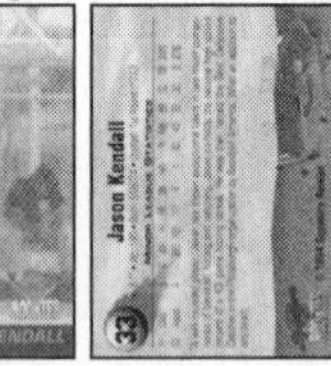

Issued early in 1994, this product is important in the sports card collecting field as it was the first product to include a signed card in every pack. This would presage some of the products later issued by major league licensed companies. These cards listed in our checklist were the non-autographed cards also included in every pack. An early Derek Jeter card is included in this set.

Nm-Mt Ex-Mt
COMPLETE SET (50) 8.00 2.40
1 Russ Davis .15 .04
2 Brant Brown .15 .04
3 Ricky Bottalico .40 .12
4 Brian Bevil .15 .04
5 Garret Anderson .40 .12
6 Rod Henderson .15 .04
7 Keith Herling .15 .04
8 Scott Hatteberg UER .15 .04
Spelled Hatteburg on front
9 Brook Fordyce .15 .04
10 Joey Eischen .15 .04
11 Orlando Miller .15 .04
12 Ray McDavid .15 .04
13 Andre King .15 .04
14 Todd Hollandsworth .15 .04
15 Tyrone Hill .15 .04
16 Paul Spoljaric .15 .04
17 Todd Ritchie .15 .04
18 Herbert Perry .40 .12
19 Alex Ochoa .15 .04
20 Mike Neill .15 .04
21 John Burke .15 .04
22 Alan Benes .15 .04
23 Robbie Beckett .15 .04
24 Brian Barber .15 .04
25 Justin Thompson .15 .04
26 Joey Hamilton .15 .04
27 Rick Greene .15 .04
28 Wayne Gomes .15 .04
29 Matt Drews .15 .04
30 Jeff D'Amico .40 .12
31 Bryn Kosco .15 .04
32 Brooks Kieschnick .15 .04
33 Jason Kendall .40 .12
34 Mike Kelly .15 .04
35 Derek Jeter 3.00 .90
36 Jay Powell .15 .04
37 Phil Nevin .40 .12
38 Kurt Miller .15 .04
39 Chad McConnell .15 .04
40 Sean Lowe .15 .04
41 Michael Tucker .15 .04
42 Paul Shuey .15 .04
43 Dan Smith .15 .04
44 Pokey Reese .15 .04
45 Kirk Presley .15 .04
46 Jamey Wright .40 .12
47 Gabe White .15 .04
48 John Wasdin .15 .04
49 Billy Wagner .50 .15
50 Joe Vitiello .15 .04

1994 Signature Rookies Signatures

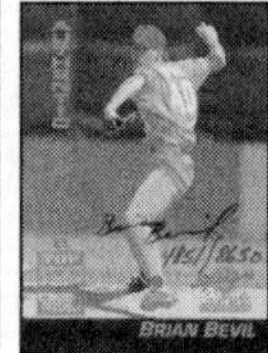

Each card is sequentially serial numbered out of 8650.

Nm-Mt Ex-Mt
1 Russ Davis 2.00 .60
2 Brant Brown 2.00 .60
3 Ricky Bottalico 3.00 .90
4 Brian Bevil 2.00 .60
5 Garret Anderson 10.00 3.00
6 Rod Henderson 2.00 .60
7 Keith Herling 2.00 .60
8 Scott Hatteberg UER 3.00 .90
Name spelled Hatteburg on front
9 Brook Fordyce 2.00 .60
10 Joey Eischen 2.00 .60
11 Orlando Miller 2.00 .60
12 Ray McDavid 2.00 .60
13 Andre King 2.00 .60
14 Todd Hollandsworth 3.00 .90
15 Tyrone Hill 2.00 .60
16 Paul Spoljaric 2.00 .60
17 Todd Ritchie 3.00 .90
18 Herbert Perry 3.00 .90
19 Alex Ochoa 3.00 .90
20 Mike Neill 2.00 .60
21 John Burke 2.00 .60
22 Alan Benes 2.00 .60
23 Robbie Beckett 2.00 .60
24 Brian Barber 2.00 .60
25 Justin Thompson 2.00 .60
26 Joey Hamilton 3.00 .90
27 Rick Greene 2.00 .60
28 Wayne Gomes 2.00 .60
29 Matt Drews 2.00 .60
30 Jeff D'Amico 3.00 .90
31 Bryn Kosco 2.00 .60
32 Brooks Kieschnick 3.00 .90
33 Jason Kendall 3.00 .90
34 Mike Kelly 2.00 .60
35 Derek Jeter 60.00 18.00
36 Jay Powell 2.00 .60
37 Phil Nevin 3.00 .90
38 Kurt Miller 2.00 .60
39 Chad McConnell 2.00 .60
40 Sean Lowe 2.00 .60
41 Michael Tucker 3.00 .90
42 Paul Shuey 2.00 .60
43 Dan Smith 2.00 .60
44 Pokey Reese 3.00 .90
45 Kirk Presley 2.00 .60
46 Jamey Wright 3.00 .90
47 Gabe White 2.00 .60
48 John Wasdin 2.00 .60
49 Billy Wagner 10.00 3.00
50 Joe Vitiello 2.00 .60

1994 Signature Rookies Bonus Signatures Draft Picks

Randomly inserted in packs, this five-card set measures the standard size. The fronts feature glossy color player photos that are full-bleed except at the bottom where the picture is edged by a black stripe carrying the player's name. The words "Tuff Stuff Promo" and the production figures "1 of 10,000" are stamped in gold foil and run down the left edge. The cards are signed on the front in blue ink, with each card individually numbered out of 1,562. A gold foil "Bonus Signature" logo in the lower left rounds out the front. On a background consisting of a blue sky, green grass and a baseball stadium, the horizontal backs present biography, statistics and player profile. Unsigned promo versions of these cards were also issued.

Nm-Mt Ex-Mt
COMPLETE SET (5) 10.00 3.00
P1 Rick Helling 2.00 .60
P2 C.Johnson SP1000 3.00 .90
P3 Chad Mottola 2.00 .60
P4 J.R. Phillips 2.00 .60
P5 Glenn Williams UER 2.00 .60
Name spelled Glen on card

1994 Signature Rookies Cliff Floyd

Randomly inserted in packs, this five-card set measures the standard size. The fronts feature glossy color player photos that are full-bleed, except at the bottom where the picture is edged by a black stripe carrying the player's name. The production figures "1 of 10,000" is stamped in gold foil and runs down the left edge. A gold foil "Hottest Rookie" logo in the lower left rounds out the front. On a background consisting of a blue sky, green grass and a baseball stadium, the horizontal backs present player profile, statistics, and other information. Floyd also signed 225 of each card which were randomly inserted into packs..

Nm-Mt Ex-Mt
COMPLETE SET (5) 1.00 .30
COMMON CARD (BB1-BB5) .50 .15

1994 Signature Rookies Cliff Floyd Signatures

Cliff Floyd signed all five of his special cards. He signed 225 of each card.

Nm-Mt Ex-Mt
COMMON CARD (BB1-BB5) 5.00 1.50

1994 Signature Rookies Hottest Prospects

Randomly inserted in packs, this 12-card set measures the standard size. The fronts feature glossy color player photos that are full-bleed except at the bottom, where the picture is edged by a black stripe carrying the player's name. The production figures "1 of 5,000" is stamped in gold foil and runs down the left edge. A gold foil "Hottest Prospect" logo in the lower left rounds out the front. On a background consisting of a blue sky, green grass and a baseball stadium, the horizontal backs present biography, statistics and player profile.

Nm-Mt Ex-Mt
COMPLETE SET (12) 8.00 2.40
S1 John Burke .25 .07
S2 Russ Davis .25 .07
S3 Todd Hollandsworth .25 .07
S4 Derek Jeter 5.00 1.50
S5 Mike Kelly .25 .07
S6 Ray McDavid .25 .07
S7 Kurt Miller .25 .07
S8 Phil Nevin .50 .15
S9 Alex Ochoa .25 .07
S10 Justin Thompson .25 .07
S11 Michael Tucker .25 .07
S12 Gabe White .25 .07

1994 Signature Rookies Hottest Prospects Mail-In Promos

This five-card standard-size set was offered by Signature Rookies to collectors as a mail-in promotion. The fronts have full-color photos bleeding to the upper corners. The bottom of the card features the player's name in red against a black background. The Hottest Prospect logo is above the lower left corner while the Signature Rookies logo is above the lower right corner. The backs have a line of vital stats, followed by minor league statistics and a brief biography. The cards are numbered out of 3,000.

Nm-Mt Ex-Mt
COMPLETE SET (5) 10.00 3.00
S1 John Burke .50 .15
S2 Russ Davis .50 .15
S3 Todd Hollandsworth .50 .15
S4 Derek Jeter 10.00 3.00
S5 Mike Kelly .50 .15

1994 Signature Rookies Hottest Prospects Mail-In Promos Signatures

These cards are numbered out of 1,000 and are signed.

	Nm-Mt	Ex-Mt
S1 John Burke	2.00	.60
S2 Russ Davis	2.00	.60
S3 Todd Hollandsworth	2.00	.60
S4 Derek Jeter	80.00	24.00
S5 Mike Kelly	2.00	.60
S6 Kurt Miller	2.00	.60
S7 Phil Nevin	3.00	.90
S8 Alex Ochoa	3.00	.90
S9 Justin Thompson	2.00	.60
S10 Gabe White	2.00	.60

1994 Signature Rookies Hottest Prospects Signatures

These cards are numbered to 1000.

	Nm-Mt	Ex-Mt
S1 John Burke	2.00	.60
S2 Russ Davis	2.00	.60
S3 Todd Hollandsworth	2.00	.60
S4 Derek Jeter	80.00	24.00
S5 Mike Kelly	2.00	.60
S6 Ray McDavid	2.00	.60
S7 Kurt Miller	2.00	.60
S8 Phil Nevin	3.00	.90
S9 Alex Ochoa	3.00	.90
S10 Justin Thompson	2.00	.60
S11 Michael Tucker	2.00	.60
S12 Gabe White	2.00	.60

1994 Signature Rookies Draft Picks

The 1994 Signature Rookies Draft Picks set consists of 100 standard-size cards. The fronts feature full-bleed color action shots. Marbleized green stripes accent the pictures on the left and bottom. In these green stripes appear the production figures ("1 of 45,000") and the player's name, both in gold foil. On a background consisting of a ghosted version of the front photo, the backs have a color headshot in the upper left corner, with the remainder of the back filled with biography, statistics, and player profile. Early cards of Nomar Garciaparra, Ben Grieve, Paul Konerko, Terrence Long and Jay Payton are included in this set.

	Nm-Mt	Ex-Mt
COMPLETE SET (100)	10.00	3.00
1 Josh Booty	.40	.12
2 Paul Wilson	.15	.04
3 Ben Grieve	.40	.12
4 Dustin Hermanson	.40	.12
5 Antone Williamson	.15	.04
6 McKay Christensen	.15	.04
7 Doug Million	.15	.04
8 Todd Walker	.50	.15
9 C.J. Nitkowski	.15	.04
10 Jaret Wright	.40	.12
11 Mark Farris	.15	.04
12 Nomar Garciaparra	4.00	1.20
13 Paul Konerko	1.00	.30
14 Jason Varitek	.40	.12
15 Jayson Peterson	.15	.04
16 Matt Smith	.15	.04
17 Ramon Castro	.15	.04
18 Cade Gaspar	.15	.04
19 Bret Wagner	.15	.04
20 Terrence Long	.75	.23
21 Hiram Bocachica	.40	.12
22 Dante Powell	.15	.04
23 Brian Buchanan	.15	.04
24 Scott Elarton	.40	.12
25 Mark Johnson	.15	.04
26 Jacob Shumate	.15	.04
27 Kevin Witt	.15	.04
28 Jay Payton	.40	.12
29 Mike Thurman	.15	.04
30 Jacob Cruz	.15	.04
31 Chris Clemons	.15	.04
32 Travis Miller	.15	.04
33 Sean Johnston	.15	.04
34 Brad Rigby	.15	.04
35 Doug Webb	.15	.04
36 John Ambrose	.15	.04
37 Cletus Davidson	.15	.04
38 Tony Terry	.15	.04
39 Jason Camilli	.15	.04
40 Roger Goedde	.15	.04
41 Corey Pointer	.15	.04
42 Trey Moore	.15	.04
43 Brian Stephenson	.15	.04
44 Dan Lock	.15	.04
45 Mike Darr	.15	.04
46 Carl Dale	.15	.04
47 Tommy Davis	.15	.04
48 Kevin L.Brown	.15	.04
49 Ryan Nye	.15	.04
50 Rodriguez Smith	.15	.04
51 Andy Taulbee	.15	.04
52 Jerry Whittaker	.15	.04
53 John Crowther	.15	.04
54 Bryon Gainey	.15	.04
55 Bill King	.15	.04
56 Heath Murray	.15	.04
57 Larry Barnes	.15	.04
58 Todd Cadey	.15	.04
59 Paul Failla	.15	.04
60 Brian Meadows	.15	.04
61 A.J. Pierzynski	1.00	.30
62 Aaron Boone	1.00	.30
63 Mike Metcalfe	.15	.04
64 Matt Wagner	.15	.04
65 Jaime Bluma	.15	.04
66 Oscar Robles	.15	.04
67 Greg Whiteman	.15	.04
68 Roger Worley	.15	.04
69 Paul Ottavinia	.15	.04
70 Joe Giuliano	.15	.04
71 Chris McBride	.15	.04
72 Jason Beverlin	.15	.04
73 Gordon Amerson	.15	.04
74 Tom Mott	.15	.04
75 Rob Welch	.15	.04
76 Jason Kelly	.15	.04
77 Matt Treanor	.15	.04
78 Jason Sikes	.15	.04
79 Steve Shoemaker	.15	.04
80 Troy Brohawn	.15	.04
81 Jeff Abbott	.40	.12
82 Steve Woodard	.15	.04
83 Greg Morris	.15	.04
84 John Slamka	.15	.04
85 John Schroeder	.15	.04
86 Clay Caruthers	.15	.04
87 Eddie Brooks	.15	.04
88 Tim Byrdak	.15	.04
89 Bob Howry	.40	.12
90 Midre Cummings	.15	.04
91 John Dettmer	.15	.04
92 Gar Finnvold	.15	.04
93 Dwayne Hosey	.15	.04
94 Jason Jacome	.15	.04
95 Doug Jennings	.15	.04
96 Luis Lopez	.15	.04
97 John Mabry	.40	.12
98 Rondell White	.40	.12
99 J.T. Snow	.40	.12
100 Vic Darensbourg	.15	.04

1994 Signature Rookies Draft Picks Signatures

The 1994 Signature Rookies Draft Picks Signature set consists of 100 standard-size cards. An autographed card or a trade coupon was seeded in each pack. The trade coupon could be mailed in and redeemed for an autograph card. The card design is identical to the regular issue series. These cards differ in that an autograph in blue ink is inscribed across the picture and the cards are individually numbered out "of 7,750." Early autographed cards of Nomar Garciaparra, Ben Grieve, Paul Konerko, Terrence Long and Jay Payton are included in this set.

	Nm-Mt	Ex-Mt
COMPLETE SET (100)	200.00	60.00
1 Josh Booty	1.50	.45
2 Paul Wilson	3.00	.90
3 Ben Grieve	3.00	.90
4 Dustin Hermanson	3.00	.90
5 Antone Williamson	1.50	.45
6 McKay Christensen	1.50	.45
7 Doug Million	1.50	.45
8 Todd Walker	5.00	1.50
9 C.J. Nitkowski	1.50	.45
10 Jaret Wright	3.00	.90
11 Mark Farris	1.50	.45
12 Nomar Garciaparra	50.00	15.00
13 Paul Konerko	8.00	2.40
14 Jason Varitek	10.00	3.00
15 Jayson Peterson	1.50	.45
16 Matt Smith	1.50	.45
17 Ramon Castro	1.50	.45
18 Cade Gaspar	1.50	.45
19 Bret Wagner	1.50	.45
20 Terrence Long	5.00	1.50
21 Hiram Bocachica	3.00	.90
22 Dante Powell	1.50	.45
23 Brian Buchanan	1.50	.45
24 Scott Elarton	3.00	.90
25 Mark Johnson	1.50	.45
26 Jacob Shumate	1.50	.45
27 Kevin Witt	1.50	.45
28 Jay Payton	3.00	.90
29 Mike Thurman	1.50	.45
30 Jacob Cruz	1.50	.45
31 Chris Clemons	1.50	.45
32 Travis Miller	1.50	.45
33 Sean Johnston	1.50	.45
34 Brad Rigby	1.50	.45
35 Doug Webb	1.50	.45
36 John Ambrose	1.50	.45
37 Cletus Davidson	1.50	.45
38 Tony Terry	1.50	.45
39 Jason Camilli	1.50	.45
40 Roger Goedde	1.50	.45
41 Corey Pointer	1.50	.45
42 Trey Moore	1.50	.45
43 Brian Stephenson	1.50	.45
44 Dan Lock	1.50	.45
45 Mike Darr	3.00	.90
46 Carl Dale	1.50	.45
47 Tommy Davis	1.50	.45
48 Kevin L.Brown	1.50	.45
49 Ryan Nye	1.50	.45
50 Rodriguez Smith	1.50	.45
51 Andy Taulbee	1.50	.45
52 Jerry Whittaker	1.50	.45
53 John Crowther	1.50	.45
54 Bryon Gainey	1.50	.45
55 Bill King	1.50	.45
56 Heath Murray	1.50	.45
57 Larry Barnes	1.50	.45
58 Todd Cadey	1.50	.45
59 Paul Failla	1.50	.45
60 Brian Meadows	1.50	.45
61 A.J. Pierzynski	8.00	2.40
62 Aaron Boone	8.00	2.40
63 Mike Metcalfe	1.50	.45
64 Matt Wagner	1.50	.45
65 Jaime Bluma	1.50	.45
66 Oscar Robles	1.50	.45
67 Greg Whiteman	1.50	.45
68 Roger Worley	1.50	.45
69 Paul Ottavinia	1.50	.45
70 Joe Giuliano	1.50	.45
71 Chris McBride	1.50	.45
72 Jason Beverlin	1.50	.45
73 Gordon Amerson	1.50	.45
74 Tom Mott	1.50	.45
75 Rob Welch	1.50	.45
76 Jason Kelly	1.50	.45
77 Matt Treanor	1.50	.45
78 Jason Sikes	1.50	.45
79 Steve Shoemaker	1.50	.45
80 Troy Brohawn	1.50	.45
81 Jeff Abbott	1.50	.45
82 Steve Woodard	1.50	.45
83 Greg Morris	1.50	.45
84 John Slamka	1.50	.45
85 John Schroeder	1.50	.45
86 Clay Caruthers	1.50	.45
87 Eddie Brooks	1.50	.45
88 Tim Byrdak	1.50	.45
89 Bob Howry	3.00	.90
90 Midre Cummings	1.50	.45
91 John Dettmer	1.50	.45
92 Gar Finnvold	1.50	.45
93 Dwayne Hosey	1.50	.45
94 Jason Jacome	1.50	.45
95 Doug Jennings	1.50	.45
96 Luis Lopez	1.50	.45
97 John Mabry	3.00	.90
98 Rondell White	3.00	.90
99 J.T. Snow	3.00	.90
100 Vic Darensbourg	1.50	.45

1994 Signature Rookies Draft Picks Bonus Signatures

Randomly inserted in packs, this 10-card standard-size set features on its fronts full-bleed color action shots. Marbleized green stripes accent the pictures on the left and bottom. In the bottom green stripe appears the player's name in gold foil. The autograph is inscribed across the picture in blue ink. On a background consisting of a ghosted version of the front photo, the backs have a color headshot in the upper left corner, with the remainder of the back filled with biography, statistics, and player profile.

	Nm-Mt	Ex-Mt
COMPLETE SET (10)	25.00	7.50
1 Matt Beaumont	3.00	.90
2 Yates Hall	3.00	.90
3 Jed Hansen	3.00	.90
4 Ryan Helms	3.00	.90
5 Russ Johnson/3250	3.00	.90
6 Carlton Loewer	3.00	.90
7 Darrell Nicholas	3.00	.90
8 Paul O'Malley	3.00	.90
9 Jeremy Powell	3.00	.90
10 Scott Shores	3.00	.90

1994 Signature Rookies Draft Picks Flip Cards

Randomly inserted in packs, this five-card standard-size set features full-bleed color action shots on both sides. Marbleized green stripes accent the pictures on the left and bottom. In these green stripes appear the production figures ("1 of 15,000") and the player's name, both in gold foil. The cards are unnumbered and checklisted below alphabetically according to the first player listed.

	Nm-Mt	Ex-Mt
COMPLETE SET (5)	6.00	1.80
1 Craig Griffey Ken Griffey Sr.	.50	.15
2 Craig Griffey Ken Griffey Jr.	1.50	.45
3 Ken Griffey Jr. Ken Griffey Sr.	1.50	.45
4 Reid Ryan Nolan Ryan	2.00	.60
5 Paul Wilson Phil Nevin	.50	.15

1994 Signature Rookies Draft Picks Flip Cards Signatures

Randomly inserted in Signature Rookie Draft Picks baseball packs, this nine-card standard-size autograph set features full-bleed color action shots on both sides. Marbleized green stripes accent the pictures on the left and bottom. Individual autographs appear across the photo. Instead of inserting an autographed card, a individually numbered certificate was inserted to be redeemed for those cards featuring the autographs of Nolan Ryan and Ken Griffey Jr. Ryan signed 1,000 of the Nolan/Reid cards and Ken Jr. signed 500 picturing him with Ken Sr.and 500 with brother Craig. Phil Nevin signed 1,050 cards, Reid Ryan 2,100, Craig Griffey signed 2,000 (1000 with Ken Jr. and 1000 with Ken Sr.) and Ken Sr. signed 2000 (1000 with Craig and 1000 with Ken Jr.). The cards are unnumbered and checklisted below alphabetically according to the first player listed.

	Nm-Mt	Ex-Mt
AU1 Craig Griffey AU2000 Ken Griffey Sr.	5.00	1.50
AU2 Craig Griffey AU1000 Ken Griffey Jr.	5.00	1.50
AU3 Ken Griffey Sr. Craig Griffey AU1000	10.00	3.00
AU4 Ken Griffey Sr. Ken Griffey Jr. AU1000	10.00	3.00
AU5 Ken Griffey Jr. AU500 Craig Griffey	100.00	30.00
AU6 Ken Griffey Jr. AU500 Ken Griffey Sr.	100.00	30.00
AU7 Nolan Ryan AU1000 Reid Ryan	100.00	30.00
AU8 Reid Ryan AU2100 Nolan Ryan	5.00	1.50
AU9 Phil Nevin AU1050 Paul Wilson	8.00	2.40

1994 Signature Rookies Draft Picks Top Prospects

These five standard-size cards feature on their fronts color player action shots that are borderless, except at the bottom where the black border carries the player's name in red lettering. The player's signature appears in blue ink across the card face. The words "Authentic Signature" appear in gold-foil lettering to the left. Each card is also stated as "1 of 20,000" on front. On a cartoonlike background of a baseball rocketing skyward from a ballpark, the horizontal backs carry the player's name, biography, statistics and highlights in black lettering.

	Nm-Mt	Ex-Mt
COMPLETE SET (5)	1.00	.30
T1 Scott Ruffcorn	.25	.07
T2 Brad Woodall	.25	.07
T3 Andrew Lorraine	.25	.07
T4 LaTroy Hawkins	.50	.15
T5 Alan Benes	.25	.07

1994 Upper Deck Minors

Issued late in 1994, this standard-size set features the leading prospects in the minor leagues at that point. Subsets in this set include All-Star (91-100) and MLE (146-160). An early Richard Hidalgo card is in the set and special cards of Michael Jordan utilizing Gold and Silver foil were also inserted in this set.

	Nm-Mt	Ex-Mt
COMPLETE SET (270)	15.00	4.50
1 Alex Gonzalez	.50	.15
2 Brooks Kieschnick	.15	.04
3 Michael Tucker	.15	.04
4 Trot Nixon	.75	.23
5 Brien Taylor	.15	.04
6 Quinton McCracken	.15	.04
7 Terrell Wade	.15	.04
8 Brandon Wilson	.15	.04
9 Roberto Petagine	.15	.04
10 Chad Mottola	.15	.04
11 T.R. Lewis	.15	.04
12 Herbert Perry	.50	.15
13 Bob Abreu	1.00	.30
14 Jorge Fabregas	.15	.04
15 Mike Kelly	.15	.04
16 Ryan McGuire	.15	.04
17 Alan Zinter	.15	.04
18 Troy Hughes	.15	.04
19 Brook Fordyce	.15	.04
20 Alex Ochoa	.15	.04
21 Chris Wimmer	.15	.04
22 Jason Hardtke	.15	.04
23 Richard Hidalgo	1.00	.30
24 Greg Zaun	.15	.04
25 Roger Cedeno	.15	.04
26 Curtis Shaw	.15	.04
27 Brian Giles	1.00	.30
28 Felix Rodriguez	.15	.04
29 Motor-Boat Jones	.15	.04
30 Dmitri Young	.50	.15
31 Justin Mashore	.15	.04
32 Curtis Goodwin	.15	.04
33 Marquis Riley	.15	.04
34 Les Norman	.15	.04
35 Billy Hall	.15	.04
36 Jamie Arnold	.15	.04
37 Mike Farmer	.15	.04
38 Brent Bowers	.15	.04
39 Chad McConnell	.15	.04
40 Mike Robertson	.15	.04
41 Brent Cookson	.15	.04
42 Dan Cholowsky	.15	.04
43 Justin Thompson	.15	.04
44 Joe Vitiello	.15	.04
45 Todd Steverson	.15	.04
46 Brian Bevil	.15	.04
47 Paul Shuey	.15	.04
48 Scott Eyre	.15	.04
49 Rick Greene	.15	.04
50 Jose Silva	.15	.04
51 Kurt Miller	.15	.04
52 Ron Villone	.15	.04
53 Darren Bragg	.15	.04
54 Mike Lieberthal	.50	.15
55 Gabe White	.15	.04
56 Vince Moore	.15	.04
57 Tony Clark	.50	.15
58 Chris Eddy	.15	.04
59 Ray Durham	.50	.15
60 Todd Hollandsworth	.15	.04
61 Andres Berumen	.15	.04
62 Quilvio Veras	.15	.04
63 Wayne Gomes	.15	.04
64 Ryan Karp	.15	.04
65 Randy Curtis	.15	.04
66 Steve Rodriguez	.15	.04
67 Jason Schmidt	3.00	.90
68 Mark Acre	.15	.04
69 B.J. Wallace	.15	.04
70 Alvin Morman	.15	.04
71 Travis Baptist	.15	.04
72 Jim Wawruck	.15	.04
73 Marty Cordova	.15	.04
74 Jamie Dismuke	.15	.04
75 Joe Randa	.15	.04
76 Danny Clyburn	.15	.04
77 Joey Eischen	.15	.04
78 Chris Seelbach	.15	.04
79 Izzy Molina	.15	.04
80 Chris Roberts	.15	.04
81 Rod Henderson	.15	.04
82 Kennie Steenstra	.15	.04
83 Ugueth Urbina	.15	.04
84 Stanton Cameron	.15	.04
85 Doug Glanville	.50	.15
86 Billy Wagner	.75	.23
87 Tate Seefried	.15	.04
88 Tyler Houston	.15	.04
89 Derek Lowe	.50	.15
90 Alan Benes	.15	.04
91 Terrell Wade AS FOIL	.15	.04
92 R.Henderson AS FOIL	.15	.04
93 C.Johnson AS FOIL	.50	.15
94 D.J. Boston AS FOIL	.15	.04
95 R.Santana AS FOIL	.15	.04
96 Joe Randa AS FOIL	.15	.04
97 Alex Gonzalez AS FOIL	.50	.15
98 Tim Clark AS FOIL	.15	.04
99 Randy Curtis AS FOIL	.15	.04
100 Brian L. Hunter AS FOIL	.15	.04
101 Jose Lima	.50	.15
102 Ray Holbert	.15	.04
103 Karim Garcia	.50	.15
104 Chris Martin	.15	.04
105 David Bell	.50	.15
106 Tim Clark	.15	.04
107 Matt Drews	.15	.04
108 Dan Serafini	.15	.04
109 Demetrish Jenkins	.15	.04
110 Charles Johnson	.50	.15
111 Jason Moler	.15	.04
112 Bret Backlund	.15	.04
113 Kevin Jordan	.15	.04
114 Jesus Tavarez	.15	.04
115 Frank Rodriguez	.15	.04
116 Derrek Lee	.75	.23
117 Pokey Reese	.15	.04
118 Dave Stevens	.15	.04
119 Julio Bruno	.15	.04
120 D.J. Boston	.15	.04
121 Jim Dougherty	.15	.04
122 Daron Kirkreit	.15	.04
123 Kerwin Moore	.15	.04
124 Jason Kendall	.50	.15
125 Johnny Damon	.50	.15
126 Andre King	.15	.04
127 Raul Gonzalez	.15	.04
128 Eddie Pearson	.15	.04
129 Yuri Sanchez	.15	.04
130 Russ Davis	.15	.04
131 Arquimedez Pozo	.15	.04
132 Jon Lieber	.15	.04
133 Glenn Murray	.15	.04
134 Brant Brown	.15	.04
135 Brian L. Hunter	.15	.04
136 Mike Gulan	.15	.04
137 Tim Vanegmond	.15	.04
138 Will VanLandingham	.15	.04
139 Robert Ellis	.15	.04
140 Calvin Murray	.15	.04
141 Kurt Ehmann	.15	.04
142 Brian DuBose	.15	.04
143 Robert Eenhoorn	.15	.04
144 Howard Battle	.15	.04
145 Jason Giambi	1.50	.45
146 James Baldwin MLE	.15	.04
147 Rick Helling MLE	.15	.04
148 Ricky Bottalico MLE	.50	.15
149 Paul Spoljaric MLE	.15	.04
150 Alex Gonzalez MLE	.50	.15
151 Tavo Alvarez MLE	.15	.04
152 Joey Eischen MLE	.15	.04
153 Shane Andrews MLE	.15	.04
154 James Mouton MLE	.15	.04
155 Russ Davis MLE	.15	.04
156 Phil Nevin MLE	.50	.15
157 Garret Anderson MLE	.50	.15
158 Gabe White MLE	.15	.04
159 Brian L. Hunter MLE	.15	.04
160 Ray McDavid MLE	.15	.04
161 Mike Durant	.15	.04
162 Eric Owens	.15	.04
163 Rick Gorecki	.15	.04
164 Lyle Mouton	.15	.04
165 Ray McDavid	.15	.04
166 Tony Graffanino	.15	.04
167 Todd Ritchie	.15	.04
168 Jose Herrera	.15	.04
169 Steve Dunn	.15	.04
170 Tavo Alvarez	.15	.04
171 Jon Farrell	.15	.04
172 Omar Ramirez	.15	.04
173 Ruben Santana	.15	.04
174 Tracy Sanders	.15	.04
175 Shane Andrews	.15	.04
176 Rob Henkel	.15	.04
177 Joel Wolfe	.15	.04
178 Chris Schwab	.15	.04
179 Chris Weinke	.50	.15
180 Ozzie Timmons	.15	.04
181 Jason Bates	.15	.04
182 Matt Brunson	.15	.04
183 Garret Anderson	.50	.15

Card	Nm-Mt	Ex-Mt
184 Brian Rupp	.15	.04
185 Derek Jeter	4.00	1.20
186 Desi Relaford	.15	.04
187 Darren Burton	.15	.04
188 David Mysel	.15	.04
189 Steve Soderstrom	.15	.04
190 Steve Gibralter	.15	.04
191 Brian Sackinsky	.15	.04
192 Marc Pisciotta	.15	.04
193 Gene Schall	.15	.04
194 Jimmy Haynes	.15	.04
195 Shannon Stewart	.50	.15
196 Neifi Perez	.50	.15
197 Chris Colon	.15	.04
198 Trey Beamon	.15	.04
199 Jon Zuber	.15	.04
200 John Burke	.15	.04
201 Derek Wallace	.15	.04
202 Chad Ogea	.15	.04
203 Ernie Young	.15	.04
204 Jose Malave	.15	.04
205 Bill Pulsipher	.15	.04
206 Leon Glenn	.15	.04
207 Scott Sullivan	.15	.04
208 Orlando Miller	.15	.04
209 John Wasdin	.15	.04
210 Paul Spoljaric	.15	.04
211 Charles Peterson	.15	.04
212 Ben Van Ryn	.15	.04
213 Chris Sexton	.15	.04
214 Bobby Bonds Jr.	.15	.04
215 James Mouton	.15	.04
216 Terrell Lowery	.15	.04
217 Oscar Munoz	.15	.04
218 Mike Bell	.15	.04
219 Preston Wilson	.50	.15
220 Mark Thompson	.15	.04
221 Aaron Holbert	.15	.04
222 Tommy Adams	.15	.04
223 Ramon D. Martinez	.15	.04
224 Tim Davis	.15	.04
225 Ricky Bottalico	.50	.15
226 Rick Krivda	.15	.04
227 Troy Percival	.50	.15
228 Mark Sweeney	.15	.04
229 Joey Hamilton	.15	.04
230 Phil Nevin	.50	.15
231 Jon Ratliff	.15	.04
232 Mark Smith	.15	.04
233 Tyrone Hill	.15	.04
234 Kevin Riggs	.15	.04
235 John Dettmer	.15	.04
236 Brian Barber	.15	.04
237 Hector Trinidad	.15	.04
238 Jeff Alkire	.15	.04
239 Phil Geisler	.15	.04
240 Rick Helling	.15	.04
241 Edgardo Alfonzo	.50	.15
242 Matt Franco	.15	.04
243 Chad Roper	.15	.04
244 Basil Shabazz	.15	.04
245 James Baldwin	.15	.04
246 Scott Hatteberg	.15	.04
247 Glenn DiSarcina	.15	.04
248 LaTroy Hawkins	.50	.15
249 Marshall Boze	.15	.04
250 Michael Moore	.15	.04
251 Brien Taylor FOIL	.15	.04
252 Johnny Damon FOIL	.50	.15
253 Curtis Goodwin FOIL	.15	.04
254 Jose Silva FOIL	.15	.04
255 Terrell Wade FOIL	.15	.04
256 Dmitri Young FOIL	.50	.15
257 Roger Cedeno FOIL	.15	.04
258 Alex Ochoa FOIL	.15	.04
259 D.J. Boston FOIL	.15	.04
260 Michael Tucker FOIL	.15	.04
261 Calvin Murray FOIL	.15	.04
262 Frank Rodriguez FOIL	.15	.04
263 Michael Moore FOIL	.15	.04
264 Ugueth Urbina FOIL	.15	.04
265 Chad Mottola FOIL	.15	.04
266 T.Hollandsworth FOIL	.15	.04
267 Rod Henderson FOIL	.15	.04
268 R.Petagine FOIL	.15	.04
269 Charles Johnson FOIL	.50	.15
270 Trot Nixon FOIL	.75	.23
P10 Chad Mottola Promo	1.00	.30
MJ23 M.Jordan GOLD	10.00	3.00
MJ23 M.Jordan SILVER	5.00	1.50

1994 Upper Deck Minors Player of the Year

Inserted in packs at stated odds of one in nine, these 29 cards feature players who had won player of the year awards at various minor leagues during their career.

	Nm-Mt	Ex-Mt
COMPLETE SET (28)	15.00	4.50
PY1 Marquis Riley	.50	.15
PY2 Roberto Petagine	.50	.15
PY3 Ernie Young	.50	.15
PY4 Alex Gonzalez	1.50	.45
PY5 Terrell Wade	.50	.15
PY6 Marshall Boze	.50	.15
PY7 Mike Gulan	.50	.15
PY8 Brant Brown	.50	.15
PY9 Roger Cedeno	.50	.15
PY10 Rod Henderson	.50	.15
PY11 Calvin Murray	.50	.15
PY12 Omar Ramirez	.50	.15
PY13 Ruben Santana	.50	.15
PY14 Charles Johnson	1.50	.45
PY15 Bill Pulsipher	.50	.15
PY16 Alex Ochoa	.50	.15
PY17 Ray McDavid	.50	.15
PY18 Jason Moler	.50	.15
PY19 Danny Clyburn	.50	.15
PY20 Rick Helling	.50	.15
PY21 Frank Rodriguez	.50	.15
PY22 Chad Mottola	.50	.15
PY23 John Burke	.50	.15
PY24 Michael Tucker	.50	.15
PY25 Brian DuBose	.50	.15
PY26 LaTroy Hawkins	1.50	.45
PY27 James Baldwin	.50	.15
PY28 Ryan Karp	.50	.15

1994 Upper Deck Minors Top 10 Prospects

These sets were mailed to collectors who sent in 15 Upper Deck Minor wrappers back to Upper Deck. These sets were sent in sealed plastic wrappers. The key card in this set is an early Alex Rodriguez insert card.

	Nm-Mt	Ex-Mt
COMP. FACT SET (10)	30.00	9.00
1 Roger Cedeno	1.50	.45
2 Johnny Damon	2.00	.60
3 Alex Gonzalez	2.00	.60
4 Charles Johnson	2.00	.60
5 Chad Mottola	1.50	.45
6 Phil Nevin	2.00	.60
7 Alex Ochoa	1.50	.45
8 Alex Rodriguez	25.00	7.50
9 Jose Silva	1.50	.45
10 Michael Tucker	1.50	.45

1994 Upper Deck Minors Trade Cards

Inserted in packs at stated odds of one in 135, these cards were good for a exchange card of either Alex Rodriguez or Kirk Presley. These cards could be exchanged until December 31, 1994.

	Nm-Mt	Ex-Mt
TC1 Alex Rodriguez	50.00	15.00
TC2 Kirk Presley	1.00	.30
NNO Expired Trade Card 1	1.00	.30
NNO Expired Trade Card 2	1.00	.30

1994 Wilson Jordan

This one-card set features a color action photo of Michael Jordan in a Birmingham Barons uniform with a facsimile autograph. Only a limited number of this card was produced and obtained free with the purchase of a bat and ball each also printed with Jordan's name and facsimile autograph.

	Nm-Mt	Ex-Mt
1 Michael Jordan	5.00	1.50

1994-95 Excel

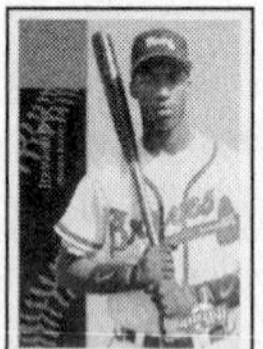

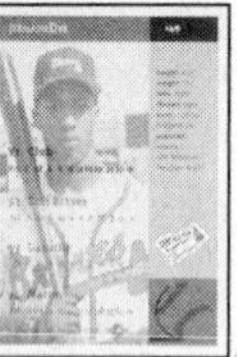

The 1994-95 Excel Minor League set consists of 300 cards featuring minor league players from AAA, AA and A teams. The cards are numbered and checklisted alphabetically within and according to major league teams for the NL and AL. Early cards of Edgardo Alfonzo, Tony Batista, Nomar Garciaparra, Ben Grieve, Richard Hidalgo, Jermaine Dye and Scott Rolen are featured in this set.

	Nm-Mt	Ex-Mt
COMPLETE SET (300)	25.00	7.50
1 Kim Bartee	.15	.04
2 Harry Berrios	.15	.04
3 Tommy Davis	.15	.04
4 Cesar Devarez	.15	.04
5 Curtis Goodwin	.15	.04
6 Jimmy Haynes	.15	.04
7 Chris Lemp	.15	.04
8 Alex Ochoa	.15	.04
9 B.J. Waszgis	.15	.04
10 Nomar Garciaparra	5.00	1.50
11 Jose Malave	.15	.04
12 Glenn Murray	.15	.04
13 Trot Nixon	.75	.23
14 Frank Rodriguez	.15	.04
15 Bill Selby	.15	.04
16 Jeff Suppan	.50	.15
17 George Arias	.15	.04
18 Todd Blyleven	.15	.04
19 John Donati	.15	.04
20 Todd Greene	.15	.04
21 Bret Hemphill	.15	.04
22 Michael Holtz	.15	.04
23 Troy Percival	.50	.15
24 Luis Raven	.15	.04
25 James Baldwin	.15	.04
26 Mike Bertotti	.15	.04
27 Ben Boulware	.15	.04
28 Ray Durham	.50	.15
29 Jimmy Hurst	.15	.04
30 Rich Pratt	.15	.04
31 Mike Sirotka	.50	.15
32 Archie Vazquez	.15	.04
33 Harold Williams	.15	.04
34 Chris Woodfin	.15	.04
35 David Bell	.50	.15
36 Todd Betts	.15	.04
37 Jim Betzsold	.15	.04
38 Einar Diaz	.15	.04
39 Travis Driskill	.50	.15
40 Damian Jackson	.50	.15
41 Daron Kirkreit	.15	.04
42 Steve Kline	.15	.04
43 Tony Mitchell	.15	.04
44 Enrique Wilson	.15	.04
45 Jaret Wright	.50	.15
46 Matt Brunson	.15	.04
47 Tony Clark	.50	.15
48 Cade Gaspar	.15	.04
49 John Grimm	.15	.04
50 Bob Higginson	.50	.15
51 Shannon Penn	.15	.04
52 John Rosengren	.15	.04
53 Jaime Bluma	.15	.04
54 Mike Bovee	.15	.04
55 Nevin Brewer	.15	.04
56 Johnny Damon	.50	.15
57 Lino Diaz	.15	.04
58 Bart Evans	.15	.04
59 Sal Fasano	.15	.04
60 Tim Grieve	.15	.04
61 Jim Pittsley	.15	.04
62 Joe Randa	.15	.04
63 Ken Ray	.15	.04
64 Glendon Rusch	.50	.15
65 Larry Sutton	.15	.04
66 Dilson Torres	.15	.04
67 Michael Tucker	.15	.04
68 Joe Vitiello	.15	.04
69 James Cole	.15	.04
70 Danny Klassen	.15	.04
71 Jeff Kramer	.15	.04
72 Mark Loretta	.50	.15
73 Danny Perez	.15	.04
74 Sid Roberson	.15	.04
75 Scott Talanoa	.15	.04
76 Tim Unroe	.15	.04
77 Antone Williamson	.15	.04
78 Marc Barcelo	.15	.04
79 Trevor Cobb	.15	.04
80 Marty Cordova	.15	.04
81 Javier DeJesus	.15	.04
82 Darren Fidge	.15	.04
83 Troy Fortin	.15	.04
84 Gus Gandarillas	.15	.04
85 Adrian Gordon	.15	.04
86 LaTroy Hawkins	.50	.15
87 Jake Patterson	.15	.04
88 Brad Radke	.50	.15
89 Todd Walker	.75	.23
90 Brian Boehringer	.15	.04
91 Brian Buchanan	.15	.04
92 Andy Croghan	.15	.04
93 Chris Cumberland	.15	.04
94 Matt Drews	.15	.04
95 Keith Heberling	.15	.04
96 Jason Jarvis	.15	.04
97 Derek Jeter	3.00	.90
98 Ricky Ledee	.50	.15
99 Matt Luke	.15	.04
100 James Musselwhite	.15	.04
101 Andy Pettitte		
102 Mariano Rivera	.50	.15
103 Ruben Rivera	.15	.04
104 Tate Seefried	.15	.04
105 Scott Standish	.15	.04
106 Jim Banks	.15	.04
107 Tony Batista	.75	.23
108 Ben Grieve	.50	.15
109 Jose Herrera	.15	.04
110 Steve Lemke	.15	.04
111 Eric Martins	.15	.04
112 Scott Spiezio	.75	.23
113 John Wasdin	.15	.04
114 Scott Davison	.15	.04
115 Chris Dean	.15	.04
116 Giomar Guevara	.15	.04
117 Tim Harikkala	.15	.04
118 Brett Hinchliffe	.15	.04
119 Matt Mantei	.50	.15
120 Arquimedez Pozo	.15	.04
121 Marino Santana	.15	.04
122 John Vanhof	.15	.04
123 Chris Widger	.15	.04
124 Mike Bell	.15	.04
125 Mark Brandenburg	.15	.04
126 Kevin L.Brown	.15	.04
127 Bucky Buckles	.15	.04
128 Jaime Escamilla	.15	.04
129 Terrell Lowery	.15	.04
130 Jerry Martin	.15	.04
131 Reid Ryan	.15	.04
132 Julio Santana	.15	.04
133 Howard Battle	.15	.04
134 D.J. Boston	.15	.04
135 Chris Carpenter	.50	.15
136 Freddy Adrian Garcia	.15	.04
137 Aaron Jersild	.15	.04
138 Ricardo Jordan	.15	.04
139 Angel Martinez	.15	.04
140 Jose Pett	.15	.04
141 Jose Silva	.15	.04
142 David Sinnes	.15	.04
143 Rob Steinert	.15	.04
144 Chris Stynes	.15	.04
145 Mike Toney	.15	.04
146 Chris Weinke	.50	.15
147 Kevin Witt	.15	.04
148 Brad Clontz	.15	.04
149 Jermaine Dye	1.00	.30
150 Tony Graffanino	.15	.04
151 Kevin Grijak	.15	.04
152 Damon Hollins	.15	.04
153 Marcus Hostetler	.15	.04
154 Darrell May	.15	.04
155 Wonderful Monds	.15	.04
156 Carl Schutz	.15	.04
157 Chris Seelbach	.15	.04
158 Jacob Shumate	.15	.04
159 Terrell Wade	.15	.04
160 Glenn Williams	.15	.04
161 Alex Cabrera	.50	.15
162 Gabe Duross	.15	.04
163 Shawn Hill	.15	.04
164 Mike Hubbard	.15	.04
165 Dave Hutcheson	.15	.04
166 Brooks Kieschnick	.15	.04
167 Bobby Morris	.15	.04
168 Jayson Peterson	.15	.04
169 Jason Ryan	.15	.04
170 Ozzie Timmons	.15	.04
171 Cedric Allen	.15	.04
172 Aaron Boone	1.50	.45
173 Ray Brown	.15	.04
174 Damon Callahan	.15	.04
175 Decomba Conner	.15	.04
176 Emiliano Giron	.15	.04
177 James Lofton	.15	.04
178 Nick Morrow	.15	.04
179 C.J. Nitkowski	.15	.04
180 Eddie Priest	.15	.04
181 Pokey Reese	.15	.04
182 Jason Robbins	.15	.04
183 Scott Sullivan	.15	.04
184 Pat Watkins	.15	.04
185 Juan Acevedo	.15	.04
186 Derrick Gibson	.15	.04
187 Pookie Jones	.15	.04
188 Terry Jones	.15	.04
189 Doug Million	.15	.04
190 Lloyd Peever	.15	.04
191 Jacob Viano	.15	.04
192 Mark Voisard	.15	.04
193 Josh Booty	.50	.15
194 Will Cunnane	.15	.04
195 Andy Larkin	.15	.04
196 Billy McMillon	.15	.04
197 Kevin Millar	1.00	.30
198 Marc Valdes	.15	.04
199 Bob Abreu	1.00	.30
200 Jamie Daspit	.15	.04
201 Scott Elarton	.50	.15
202 Kevin Gallaher	.15	.04
203 Richard Hidalgo	1.00	.30
204 Chris Holt	.15	.04
205 Rick Huisman	.15	.04
206 Doug Mlicki	.15	.04
207 Julien Tucker	.15	.04
208 Billy Wagner	.75	.23
209 Juan Castro	.15	.04
210 Roger Cedeno	.15	.04
211 Ron Coomer	.50	.15
212 Karim Garcia	.50	.15
213 Todd Hollandsworth	.15	.04
214 Paul Konerko	1.00	.30
215 Antonio Osuna	.15	.04
216 Willis Otanez	.15	.04
217 Dan Ricabal	.15	.04
218 Ken Sikes	.15	.04
219 Yamil Benitez	.15	.04
220 Geoff Blum	.50	.15
221 Scott Gentile	.15	.04
222 Mark Grudzielanek	.50	.15
223 Kevin Northrup	.15	.04
224 Carlos Perez	.50	.15
225 Matt Raleigh	.15	.04
226 Al Reyes	.15	.04
227 Everett Stull	.15	.04
228 Ugueth Urbina	.15	.04
229 Neil Weber	.15	.04
230 Edgardo Alfonzo	.50	.15
231 Jason Isringhausen	.50	.15
232 Terrence Long	.75	.23
233 Rey Ordonez	.50	.15
234 Ricky Otero	.15	.04
235 Jay Payton	.50	.15
236 Kirk Presley	.15	.04
237 Bill Pulsipher	.15	.04
238 Chris Roberts	.15	.04
239 Jeff Tam	.15	.04
240 Paul Wilson	.15	.04
241 David Doster	.15	.04
242 Wayne Gomes	.15	.04
243 Jeremey Kendall	.15	.04
244 Ryan Nye	.15	.04
245 Shane Pullen	.15	.04
246 Scott Rolen	3.00	.90
247 Gene Schall	.15	.04
248 Brian Stumpf	.15	.04
249 Jake Austin	.15	.04
250 Trey Beamon	.15	.04
251 Danny Clyburn	.15	.04
252 Louis Collier	.15	.04
253 Mark Farris	.15	.04
254 Mark Johnson	.15	.04
255 Jason Kendall	.50	.15
256 Esteban Loaiza	1.50	.45
257 Joe Maskivish	.15	.04
258 Ramon Morel	.15	.04
259 Gary Wilson	.15	.04
260 Matt Arrandale	.15	.04
261 Allen Battle	.15	.04
262 Alan Benes	.15	.04
263 Jeff Berblinger	.15	.04
264 Terry Bradshaw	.15	.04
265 Darrell Deak	.15	.04
266 Criag Grasser	.15	.04
267 Yates Hall	.15	.04
268 Kevin Lovingier	.15	.04
269 Eli Marrero	.50	.15
270 Jeff Matulevich	.15	.04
271 Joe McEwing	.50	.15
272 Eric Miller	.15	.04
273 Tom Minor	.15	.04
274 Scott Simmons	.15	.04
275 Chris Stewart	.15	.04
276 Bret Wagner	.15	.04
277 Travis Welch	.15	.04
278 Jay Witasick	.15	.04
279 Homer Bush	.50	.15
280 Raul Casanova	.15	.04
281 Glenn Dishman	.15	.04
282 Gary Dixon	.15	.04
283 Devohn Duncan	.15	.04
284 Dustin Hermanson	.50	.15
285 Earl Johnson	.15	.04
286 Derrek Lee	.75	.23
287 Todd Schmitt	.15	.04
288 Ira Smith	.15	.04
289 Jason Thompson	.15	.04
290 Bryan Wolff	.15	.04
291 Jeff Martin	.15	.04
292 Dante Powell	.15	.04
293 Jeff Richey	.15	.04
294 Joe Rosselli	.15	.04
295 Benji Simonton	.15	.04
296 Steve Whitaker	.15	.04
297 Keith Williams	.15	.04
298 Checklist 1-113	.15	.04
299 Checklist 114-226	.15	.04
300 Checklist 227-300	.15	.04

1994-95 Excel All-Stars

Randomly inserted into packs, these 10 card feature players who earned spots on various minor-league all-star teams.

	Nm-Mt	Ex-Mt
COMPLETE SET (10)	12.00	3.60
1 Raul Casanova	.50	.15
2 Tony Clark	1.00	.30
3 Ray Durham	1.00	.30
4 Ron Coomer	1.00	.30
5 Derek Jeter	5.00	1.50
6 Trey Beamon	.50	.15
7 Johnny Damon	1.00	.30
8 Ruben Rivera	.50	.15
9 Todd Greene	.50	.15
10 Alan Benes	.50	.15

1994-95 Excel First Year Phenoms

Randomly inserted into packs, these 10 cards feature players who made their professional debut in 1994.

	Nm-Mt	Ex-Mt
COMPLETE SET (10)	10.00	3.00
1 Paul Konerko	2.00	.60
2 Ray Brown	.50	.15
3 Chris Dean	.50	.15
4 Aaron Boone	3.00	.90
5 Rey Ordonez	1.00	.30
6 Decomba Conner	.50	.15
7 Ben Grieve	1.00	.30
8 Jay Payton	1.00	.30
9 Dante Powell	.50	.15
10 Dustin Hermanson	1.00	.30

1994-95 Excel League Leaders

Randomly inserted into packs, these 20 cards feature players who led a minor-league in any category in 1994.

	Nm-Mt	Ex-Mt
COMPLETE SET (20)	12.00	3.60
1 Juan Acevedo	.50	.15
2 James Baldwin	.50	.15
3 Allen Battle	.50	.15
4 Harry Berrios	.50	.15
5 Brad Clontz	.50	.15
6 Will Cunnane	.50	.15
7 Glenn Dishman	.50	.15
8 LaTroy Hawkins	1.00	.30
9 Jimmy Haynes	.50	.15
10 Richard Hidalgo	2.00	.60
11 Earl Johnson	.50	.15
12 Jim Pittsley	.50	.15
13 Bill Pulsipher	.50	.15
14 Benji Simonton	.50	.15
15 Larry Sutton	.50	.15
16 Michael Tucker	.50	.15
17 Tim Unroe	.50	.15
18 Joe Vitiello	.50	.15
19 Billy Wagner	1.50	.45
20 Harold Williams	.50	.15

1995 Action Packed

The 1995 Action Packed Scouting Report set consists of standard-size cards featuring top AAA, AA, and A prospects picked by Action Packed's scouts. 24K gold versions of selected cards were randomly inserted in the foil packs as chase cards. The 12-card Franchise Gems subset feature a heat sensitive graphic that reveals Action Packed's prediction of the player's impact year. Hobby foil packs were randomly seeded with autographed 24K Gold and Diamond version Franchise Gem cards of minor league Player of the Year Derek Jeter. Hot packs, which contained six 24K Gold cards, were seeded one per 480 packs. Topical subsets featured include No. 1 Draft Picks (52-61) and Franchise Gems (62-79). Each card in the second subset was highlighted with gold foil accents in every groove and die cut. Also each card features a scouting report of each player's strengths and weaknesses. Minor league cards of Ben Grieve, Nomar Garciaparra and Derek Jeter are featured in this set.

	Nm-Mt	Ex-Mt
COMPLETE SET (83)	20.00	6.00
1 Derek Jeter POY	3.00	.90
2 Trot Nixon	.50	.15
3 Charles Johnson	.50	.15
4 Chan Ho Park	.50	.15
5 Terrell Wade	.25	.07
6 Carlos Delgado	.50	.15

Card	Nm-Mt	Ex-Mt
7 Brian L. Hunter	.25	.07
8 Tony Clark	.25	.07
9 Russ Davis	.25	.07
10 Derek Jeter	3.00	.90
11 Alex Gonzalez	.50	.15
12 Scott Ruffcorn	.25	.07
13 Todd Hollandsworth	.25	.07
14 Phil Nevin	.50	.15
15 Marc Newfield	.25	.07
16 Jose Silva	.25	.07
17 Willie Greene	.25	.07
18 Billy Ashley	.25	.07
19 James Baldwin	.25	.07
20 Jeff Granger	.25	.07
21 Michael Tucker	.25	.07
22 Johnny Damon	.50	.15
23 Roger Cedeno	.25	.07
24 Mac Suzuki	.25	.07
25 Curtis Goodwin	.25	.07
26 Frank Rodriguez	.25	.07
27 Roberto Mejia	.25	.07
28 LaTroy Hawkins	.25	.07
29 Alex Ochoa	.25	.07
30 Jose Oliva	.25	.07
31 Ruben Rivera	.25	.07
32 Ray Durham	.50	.15
33 Eduardo Perez	.25	.07
34 Jose Malave	.25	.07
35 Jeromy Burnitz	.50	.15
36 Brad Woodall	.25	.07
37 Joe Vitiello	.25	.07
38 Daron Kirkreit	.25	.07
39 Jimmy Haynes	.25	.07
40 Andrew Lorraine	.25	.07
41 Arquimedez Pozo	.25	.07
42 Armando Benitez	.50	.15
43 Alan Benes	.25	.07
44 Julian Tavarez	.25	.07
45 Curtis Pride	.25	.07
46 Homer Bush	.25	.07
47 Pokey Reese	.25	.07
48 Billy Wagner	.50	.15
49 Richard Hidalgo	.50	.15
50 Allen Battle	.25	.07
51 Kevin Millar	1.00	.30
52 Paul Wilson FDP	.25	.07
53 Ben Grieve FDP	.50	.15
54 Dustin Hermanson FDP	.25	.07
55 Antone Williamson FDP	.25	.07
56 Josh Booty FDP	.50	.15
57 Doug Million FDP	.25	.07
58 Jaret Wright FDP	.50	.15
59 Todd Walker FDP	.50	.15
60 N.Garciaparra FDP	3.00	.90
61 C.J. Nitkowski FDP	.25	.07
62 Charles Johnson FG	.25	.07
63 Marc Newfield FG	.25	.07
64 Ray Durham FG	.50	.15
65 Carlos Delgado FG	.50	.15
66 Alex Gonzalez FG	.50	.15
67 Derek Jeter FG	3.00	.90
68 Jose Oliva FG	.25	.07
69 Billy Ashley FG	.25	.07
70 Brian L. Hunter FG	.25	.07
71 Ruben Rivera FG	.25	.07
72 Alan Benes FG	.25	.07
73 Willie Greene FG	.25	.07
74 Russ Davis FG	.25	.07
75 Jose Malave FG	.25	.07
76 LaTroy Hawkins FG	.50	.15
77 Frank Rodriguez FG	.25	.07
78 Scott Ruffcorn FG	.25	.07
79 Ben Grieve FG	.50	.15
80 Max Patkin With Glove	.50	.15
81 Max Patkin Grinning	.50	.15
82 Max Patkin Tounge Sticking Out	.50	.15
83 Checklist	.25	.07

1995 Action Packed 24K Gold

Randomly inserted into packs, these 20 cards feature the words "24K" on the front.

Card	Nm-Mt	Ex-Mt
COMPLETE SET (18)	100.00	30.00
1G Charles Johnson	5.00	1.50
2G Marc Newfield	5.00	1.50
3G Ray Durham	5.00	1.50
4G Carlos Delgado	5.00	1.50
5G Alex Gonzalez	5.00	1.50
6G Derek Jeter	15.00	4.50
7G Jose Oliva	5.00	1.50
8G Billy Ashley	5.00	1.50
9G Brian L. Hunter	5.00	1.50
10G Ruben Rivera	5.00	1.50
11G Alan Benes	5.00	1.50
12G Willie Greene	5.00	1.50
13G Russ Davis	5.00	1.50
14G Jose Malave	5.00	1.50
15G LaTroy Hawkins	5.00	1.50
16G Frank Rodriguez	5.00	1.50
17G Scott Ruffcorn	5.00	1.50
18G Ben Grieve	5.00	1.50
1A Derek Jeter AU	80.00	24.00
1D Derek Jeter DIAM AU	80.00	24.00

1995 Best

This 135-card set was issued in two parts; the first part (1-100) featured the Top 100 Prospects with the second part featuring the Top Draft Picks (101-133) from the 1995 Draft. The first series of cards was available in both hobby and retail packs while the final 34 cards were only available in retail packs. Early cards of Bob Abreu, Darin Erstad, Vladimir Guerrero, Todd Helton, Andruw Jones, Scott Rolen and Kerry Wood are featured in this set.

Card	Nm-Mt	Ex-Mt
COMPLETE SET (135)	50.00	15.00
COMP.HOBBY SET (101)	15.00	4.50
COMMON (1-100/CL)	.15	.04
COMMON (101-133/CL)	2.00	.60
1 Rocky Coppinger	.15	.04
2 Rafael Orellano	.15	.04
3 Nomar Garciaparra	2.50	.75
4 Ryan McGuire	.15	.04
5 Pork Chop Pough	.15	.04
6 Trot Nixon	.40	.12
7 Donnie Sadler	.15	.04
8 Chris Allison	.15	.04
9 Todd Greene	.15	.04
10 George Arias	.15	.04
11 Matt Beaumont	.15	.04
12 Jeff Abbott	.40	.12
13 Tom Fordham	.15	.04
14 Damian Jackson	.40	.12
15 Richie Sexson	2.00	.60
16 Bartolo Colon	1.25	.35
17 David Roberts	.40	.12
18 Daryle Ward	.40	.12
19 Brandon Reed	.15	.04
20 Juan Encarnacion	.40	.12
21 Eddy Gaillard	.15	.04
22 Derek Hacopian	.15	.04
23 Glendon Rusch	.40	.12
24 Lino Diaz	.15	.04
25 Tim Byrdak	.15	.04
26 Antone Williamson	.15	.04
27 Jonas Hamlin	.15	.04
28 Todd Walker	.40	.12
29 Dan Serafini	.15	.04
30 Kim Bartee	.15	.04
31 Shane Bowers	.15	.04
32 Tyrone Horne	.15	.04
33 Nick DelVecchio	.15	.04
34 Mike Figga	.15	.04
35 Matt Drews	.15	.04
36 Ray Ricken	.15	.04
37 Ben Grieve	.40	.12
38 Steve Cox	.15	.04
39 Scott Spiezio	.40	.12
40 Desi Relaford	.15	.04
41 Matt Wagner	.15	.04
42 James Bonnici	.15	.04
43 Osvaldo Fernandez	.15	.04
44 Marino Santana	.15	.04
45 Julio Santana	.15	.04
46 Jeff Davis	.15	.04
47 Trey Beamon	.15	.04
48 Jose Pett	.15	.04
49 Chris Carpenter	.40	.12
50 Andruw Jones	4.00	1.20
51 Damon Hollins	.15	.04
52 Jermaine Dye	.40	.12
53 Aldo Pecorilli	.15	.04
54 Carey Paige	.15	.04
55 Damian Moss	.40	.12
56 Ron Wright	.15	.04
57 Brooks Kieschnick	.15	.04
58 Pedro Valdes	.15	.04
59 Scott Samuels	.15	.04
60 Bobby Morris	.15	.04
61 Amaury Telemaco	.15	.04
62 Steve Gibralter	.15	.04
63 Pokey Reese	.15	.04
64 Pat Watkins	.15	.04
65 Aaron Boone	1.00	.30
66 Jamey Wright	.15	.04
67 Derrick Gibson	.15	.04
68 Brent Crowther	.15	.04
69 Ralph Milliard	.15	.04
70 Edgar Renteria	.40	.12
71 Billy McMillon	.15	.04
72 Clemente Nunez	.15	.04
73 Bob Abreu	1.00	.30
74 Eric Ludwick	.15	.04
75 Tony Mounce	.15	.04
76 Chris Latham	.15	.04
77 Wilton Guerrero	.15	.04
78 Adam Riggs	.15	.04
79 Paul Konerko	.40	.12
80 Vladimir Guerrero	4.00	1.20
81 Brad Fullmer	.40	.12
82 Hiram Bocachica	.40	.12
83 Paul Wilson	.15	.04
84 Jay Payton	.40	.12
85 Rey Ordonez	.40	.12
86 Wendell Magee	.15	.04
87 Wayne Gomes	.15	.04
88 Carlton Loewer	.15	.04
89 Scott Rolen	2.50	.75
90 Rich Hunter	.15	.04
91 Jason Kendall	.40	.12
92 Micah Franklin	.15	.04
93 Elmer Dessens	.15	.04
94 Matt Ruebel	.15	.04
95 Mike Gulan	.15	.04
96 Jay Witasick	.15	.04
97 Bret Wagner	.15	.04
98 Greg LaRocca	.15	.04
99 Jason Thompson	.15	.04
100 Derrek Lee	.40	.12
101 Jason Kendall BB SP	2.00	.60
102 Derrek Lee BB SP	2.00	.60
103 Todd Walker BB SP	.40	.12
104 Edgar Renteria BB SP	2.00	.60
105 Scott Rolen BB SP	5.00	1.50
106 Andruw Jones BB SP	8.00	2.40
107 Jay Payton BB SP	2.00	.60
108 Derrick Gibson BB SP	2.00	.60
109 Paul Wilson BB SP	2.00	.60
110 Brandon Reed BB SP	2.00	.60
111 Ben Davis SP	2.00	.60
112 Chad Hermansen SP	2.00	.60
113 Corey Jenkins SP	2.00	.60
114 Geoff Jenkins SP	3.00	.90
115 Ryan Jaroncyk SP	2.00	.60
116 Andy Yount SP	2.00	.60
117 Reggie Taylor SP	2.00	.60
118 Joe Fontenot SP	2.00	.60
119 Mike Drumright SP	2.00	.60
120 David Yocum SP	2.00	.60
121 Jonathan Johnson SP	2.00	.60
122 Jaime Jones SP	2.00	.60
123 Tony McKnight SP	2.00	.60
124 Michael Barrett SP	2.00	.60
125 Roy Halladay SP	6.00	1.80
126 Todd Helton SP	5.00	1.50
127 Juan LeBron SP	2.00	.60
128 Darin Erstad SP	3.00	.90
129 Jose Cruz Jr. SP	3.00	.90
130 Kerry Wood SP	10.00	3.00
131 Shea Morenz SP	2.00	.60
132 Mark Redman SP	2.00	.60
133 Matt Morris SP	3.00	.90
NNO Checklist (1-100)	.15	.04
NNO CL SP (101-133)	2.00	.60

1995 Best Autographs

Randomly inserted into packs, these four cards feature autographs of some of the leading prospects on the 1995 Best set. A first year autograph of Andruw Jones is the highlight of this set.

Card	Nm-Mt	Ex-Mt
AU1 Todd Greene	2.00	.60
AU2 Andruw Jones	25.00	7.50
AU3 Jay Payton	3.00	.90
AU4 Paul Wilson	2.00	.60

1995 Best Franchise

Inserted at an average of one per four boxes. The first six-cards were available only in retail packs with the remaining six available only in hobby packs.

Card	Nm-Mt	Ex-Mt
COMPLETE SET (12)	80.00	24.00
F1 Darin Erstad	8.00	2.40
F2 Nomar Garciaparra	15.00	4.50
F3 Rocky Coppinger	3.00	.90
F4 Matt Drews	3.00	.90
F5 Ben Grieve	5.00	1.50
F6 Todd Walker	5.00	1.50
F7 Edgar Renteria	5.00	1.50
F8 Derrick Gibson	3.00	.90
F9 Andruw Jones	15.00	4.50
F10 Derrek Lee	5.00	1.50
F11 Jason Kendall	5.00	1.50
F12 Paul Wilson	3.00	.90

1995 Hutchinson Popcorn

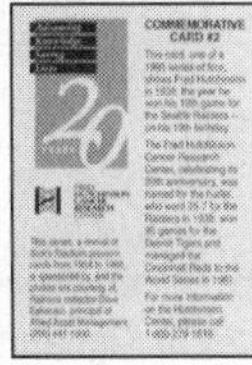

This four-card set was distributed one per bag of free popcorn handed out to attendees at the Tacoma Rainers ball game in 1995 celebrating the 20th anniversary of the Fred Hutchinson Cancer Research Center. The set measures approximately 2" by 3" and is a revival of cards distributed in popcorn bags at Sicks' Seattle Stadium from 1954 to 1968. The fronts feature black-and-white photos of Fred Hutchinson at various phases of his career. The backs carry information about the photo.

Card	Nm-Mt	Ex-Mt
COMPLETE SET (4)	10.00	3.00
COMMON CARD (1-4)	2.50	.75
3 Fred Hutchinson Bob Feller	5.00	1.50

1995 Signature Rookies Previews

Randomly inserted into packs, these cards have a stated print run of 25,000 sets.

Card	Nm-Mt	Ex-Mt
COMPLETE SET (38)	5.00	1.50
1 Tavo Alvarez	.25	.07
2 Rich Batchelor	.25	.07
3 Doug Bochtler	.25	.07
4 Jerry Brooks	.25	.07
5 Scott Bryant	.25	.07
6 Mike Busby	.25	.07
7 Fred Costello	.25	.07
8 Glenn Dishman	.25	.07
9 James Foster	.25	.07
10 Webster Garrison	.25	.07
11 Tony Graffanino	.75	.23
12 Billy Hall	.25	.07
13 Mike Hubbard	.25	.07
14 Jason Hutchins	.25	.07
15 Rick Kelley	.25	.07
16 Jerry Koller	.25	.07
17 Ryan Luzinski	.25	.07
18 Anthony Manahan	.25	.07
19 Mike Matthews	.25	.07
20 Greg McCarthy	.25	.07
21 Jeff McCurry	.25	.07
22 Gino Minutelli	.25	.07
23 Izzy Molina	.25	.07
24 Scott Moten	.25	.07
25 Peter Munro	.75	.23
26 Willis Otanez	.25	.07
27 Rodney Pedraza	.25	.07
28 Brandon Pico	.25	.07
29 Brian Raabe	.25	.07
30 Eddie Rios	.25	.07
31 Toby Rumfield	.25	.07
32 Andy Sheets	.25	.07
33 Larry Sutton	.25	.07
34 Brian Thomas	.25	.07
35 Hector Trinidad	.25	.07
36 Jim Waring	.25	.07
37 Mike Welch	.25	.07
38 Steve Wojciechowski	.25	.07

1995 Signature Rookies Previews Signatures

Randomly inserted into packs, these 38 card parallel the regular Signature Rookies Previews cards. Each card had a stated print run of 6,000 serial numbered sets.

Card	Nm-Mt	Ex-Mt
1 Tavo Alvarez	1.00	.30
2 Rich Batchelor	1.00	.30
3 Doug Bochtler	1.00	.30
4 Jerry Brooks	1.00	.30
5 Scott Bryant	1.00	.30
6 Mike Busby	1.00	.30
7 Fred Costello	1.00	.30
8 Glenn Dishman	1.00	.30
9 James Foster	1.00	.30
10 Webster Garrison	1.00	.30
11 Tony Graffanino	3.00	.90
12 Billy Hall	1.00	.30
13 Mike Hubbard	1.00	.30
14 Jason Hutchins	1.00	.30
15 Rick Kelley	1.00	.30
16 Jerry Koller	1.00	.30
17 Ryan Luzinski	1.00	.30
18 Anthony Manahan	1.00	.30
19 Mike Matthews	1.00	.30
20 Greg McCarthy	1.00	.30
21 Jeff McCurry	1.00	.30
22 Gino Minutelli	1.00	.30
23 Izzy Molina	1.00	.30
24 Scott Moten	1.00	.30
25 Peter Munro	3.00	.90
26 Willis Otanez	1.00	.30
27 Rodney Pedraza	1.00	.30
28 Brandon Pico	1.00	.30
29 Brian Raabe	1.00	.30
30 Eddie Rios	1.00	.30
31 Toby Rumfield	1.00	.30
32 Andy Sheets	1.00	.30
33 Larry Sutton	1.00	.30
34 Brian Thomas	1.00	.30
35 Hector Trinidad	1.00	.30
36 Jim Waring	1.00	.30
37 Mike Welch	1.00	.30
38 Steve Wojciechowski	1.00	.30

1995 Signature Rookies Preview '95 Promos

This five-card standard-size set was issued to promote the 1995 Signature Rookies Preview '95 series. The fronts feature full-bleed color action photos, except at the lower left and upper right, where a gold foil edged black marbleized geometric design accents the picture. "Promo 1 of 7,500" is gold foil stamped across the bottom. On a second player photo with black marbleized borders, the backs have overprinted a color headshot, career highlights, and statistics.

Card	Nm-Mt	Ex-Mt
COMPLETE SET (5)	3.00	.90
P1 Brad Woodall	.25	.07
P2 Ruben Rivera	.25	.07
P3 Karim Garcia	1.00	.30
P4 Ray Durham	1.00	.30
P5 Juan Acevedo	.50	.15

1995 Signature Rookies

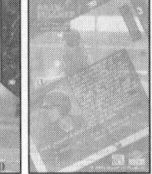

Each card in this set has a stated print run of 25,000 cards.

Card	Nm-Mt	Ex-Mt
COMPLETE SET (50)	4.00	1.20
1 Mark Acre	.15	.04
2 Edgar Alfonzo	.15	.04
3 Ivan Arteaga	.15	.04
4 Rich Aude	.15	.04
5 Joe Ausanio	.15	.04
6 Marc Barcelo	.15	.04
7 Allen Battle	.15	.04
8 Rigo Beltran	.15	.04
9 Darren Bragg	.15	.04
10 Rico Brogna	.15	.04
11 Mike Busch	.15	.04
12 Juan Castillo	.15	.04
13 Joe Ciccarella	.15	.04
14 Darrell Deak	.15	.04
15 Steve Dunn	.15	.04
16 Vaughn Eshelman	.15	.04
17 Bart Evans	.15	.04
18 Rikkert Faneyte	.15	.04
19 Kenny Felder	.15	.04
20 Micah Franklin	.15	.04
21 Brad Fullmer	.40	.12
22 Willie Greene	.15	.04
23 Greg Hansell	.15	.04
24 Phil Hiatt	.15	.04
25 Todd Hollandsworth	.15	.04
26 Damon Hollins	.15	.04
27 Chris Hook	.15	.04
28 Kerry Lacy	.15	.04
29 Todd LaRocca	.15	.04
30 Sean Lawrence	.15	.04
31 Aaron Ledesma	.15	.04
32 Esteban Loaiza	.40	.12
33 Albie Lopez	.15	.04
34 Luis Lopez	.15	.04
35 Marc Marini	.15	.04
36 Nate Minchey	.15	.04
37 Doug Mlicki	.15	.04
38 Glenn Murray	.15	.04
39 Troy O'Leary	.15	.04
40 Eric Owens	.15	.04
41 Orlando Palmeiro	.15	.04
42 Todd Pridy	.15	.04
43 Joe Randa	.15	.04
44 Jason Schmidt	.75	.23
45 Basil Shabazz	.15	.04
46 Paul Spoljaric	.15	.04
47 J.J. Thobe	.15	.04
48 Sean Whiteside	.15	.04
49 Gary Wilson	.15	.04
50 Shannon Withem	.15	.04

1995 Signature Rookies Signatures

Randomly inserted into packs, these 48 cards are a parallel to the 1995 Signature Rookie set. These cards, which are autographed, have a stated print run of 5,750 sets. Neither Kerry Lacy (card number 28) nor Basil Shabazz (card number 45) signed or returned their cards. It's also believed that Willie Greene (card number 22) and Albie Lopez (card number 33) failed to return their cards.

Card	Nm-Mt	Ex-Mt
1 Mark Acre	2.00	.60
2 Edgar Alfonzo	2.00	.60
3 Ivan Arteaga	2.00	.60
4 Rich Aude	2.00	.60
5 Joe Ausanio	2.00	.60
6 Marc Barcelo	2.00	.60
7 Allen Battle	2.00	.60
8 Rigo Beltran	2.00	.60
9 Darren Bragg	2.00	.60
10 Rico Brogna	3.00	.90
11 Mike Busch	2.00	.60
12 Juan Castillo	2.00	.60
13 Joe Ciccarella	2.00	.60
14 Darrell Deak	2.00	.60
15 Steve Dunn	2.00	.60
16 Vaughn Eshelman	2.00	.60
17 Bart Evans	2.00	.60
18 Rikkert Faneyte	2.00	.60
19 Kenny Felder	2.00	.60
20 Micah Franklin	2.00	.60
21 Brad Fullmer	3.00	.90
23 Greg Hansell	2.00	.60
24 Phil Hiatt	2.00	.60
25 Todd Hollandsworth	3.00	.90
26 Damon Hollins	2.00	.60
27 Chris Hook	2.00	.60
29 Todd LaRocca	2.00	.60
30 Sean Lawrence	2.00	.60
31 Aaron Ledesma	2.00	.60
32 Esteban Loaiza	8.00	2.40
34 Luis Lopez	2.00	.60
35 Marc Marini	2.00	.60
36 Nate Minchey	2.00	.60
37 Doug Mlicki	2.00	.60
38 Glenn Murray	2.00	.60
39 Troy O'Leary	3.00	.90
40 Eric Owens	3.00	.90
41 Orlando Palmeiro	2.00	.60
42 Todd Pridy	2.00	.60
43 Joe Randa	3.00	.90
44 Jason Schmidt	10.00	3.00
46 Paul Spoljaric	2.00	.60
47 J.J. Thobe	2.00	.60
48 Sean Whiteside	2.00	.60
49 Gary Wilson	2.00	.60
50 Shannon Withem	2.00	.60

1995 Signature Rookies Draft Day Stars

Randomly inserted into packs, these five cards feature players recently drafted.

Card	Nm-Mt	Ex-Mt
COMPLETE SET (5)	3.00	.90
DD1 Matt Beaumont	.50	.15
DD2 Josh Booty	1.00	.30
DD3 Russ Johnson	.50	.15
DD4 Todd Walker	1.00	.30
DD5 Jaret Wright	1.00	.30

1995 Signature Rookies Draft Day Stars Signatures

These are the signed card parallels to the Draft Day Stars insert set. Each card is numbered out of 2100.

	Nm-Mt	Ex-Mt
DD1 Matt Beaumont	2.00	.60
DD2 Josh Booty	5.00	1.50
DD3 Russ Johnson	2.00	.60
DD4 Todd Walker	5.00	1.50
DD5 Jaret Wright	5.00	1.50

1995 Signature Rookies Future Dynasty

Randomly inserted into packs, this five-card set features some of the leading prospects who were not yet in the majors.

	Nm-Mt	Ex-Mt
COMPLETE SET (5)	4.00	1.20
FD1 Billy Ashley	.50	.15
FD2 Ben Grieve	1.00	.30
FD3 Derek Jeter	3.00	.90
FD4 Ruben Rivera	.50	.15
FD5 Antone Williamson	.50	.15

1995 Signature Rookies Future Dynasty Signatures

These are the signed card parallels to the Future Dynasty insert set. Each card is numbered out of 1050.

	Nm-Mt	Ex-Mt
FD1 Billy Ashley	2.00	.60
FD2 Ben Grieve	5.00	1.50
FD3 Derek Jeter	60.00	18.00
FD4 Ruben Rivera	2.00	.60
FD5 Antone Williamson	2.00	.60

1995 Signature Rookies Major Rookies

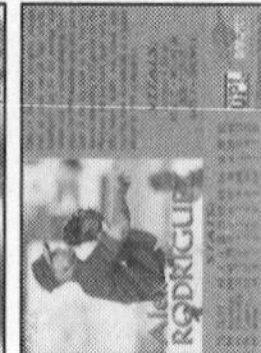

Randomly inserted into packs, these five cards feature players that Signature Rookies thought were ready for the major leagues in 1995.

	Nm-Mt	Ex-Mt
COMPLETE SET (5)	6.00	1.80
MR1 Marty Cordova	.50	.15
MR2 Benji Gil	.50	.15
MR3 Charles Johnson	1.00	.30
MR4 Manny Ramirez	1.00	.30
MR5 Alex Rodriguez	3.00	.90

1995 Signature Rookies Major Rookies Signatures

These are the signed card parallels to the Major Rookies insert set. Each card numbered out of 750.

	Nm-Mt	Ex-Mt
MR1 Marty Cordova	2.00	.60
MR2 Benji Gil	2.00	.60
MR3 Charles Johnson	5.00	1.50
MR4 Manny Ramirez	20.00	6.00
MR5 Alex Rodriguez	60.00	18.00

1995 Signature Rookies Organizational Player of the Year

Randomly inserted into packs, these five cards feature players selected as the organizational player of the year for 1994.

	Nm-Mt	Ex-Mt
COMPLETE SET (5)	3.00	.90
OP1 Juan Acevedo	.50	.15
OP2 Johnny Damon	1.00	.30
OP3 Ray Durham	1.00	.30
OP4 LaTroy Hawkins	.50	.15
OP5 Brad Woodall	.50	.15

1995 Signature Rookies Organizational Player of the Year Signatures

These are the signed card parallels to the Organizational Player of the Year set. Each card is numbered out of 1000. Johnny Damon (Card number OP2) did not sign or return his cards.

	Nm-Mt	Ex-Mt
OP1 Juan Acevedo	2.00	.60
OP3 Ray Durham	5.00	1.50
OP4 LaTroy Hawkins	2.00	.60
OP5 Brad Woodall	2.00	.60

1995 Signature Rookies Fame and Fortune Erstad

Random inserts in the football/basketball Fame and Fortune product. Cards feature Erstad in his University of Nebraska days as a dual sport football/baseball star.

	Nm-Mt	Ex-Mt
COMPLETE SET (5)	8.00	2.40
COMMON CARD (E1-E5)	2.00	.60

1995 Signature Rookies Members Only Preview

This 10-card standard-size set was issued by Signature Rookies to club members. The fronts feature a 95 preview in the upper left corner, while the lower right corner identifies the card as a 1995 issue. The Signature Rookies logo is in the lower left corner while player identification is located in the upper right corner. The backs include information about vital stats, a brief biography, and a 1994 and career stat line.

	Nm-Mt	Ex-Mt
COMPLETE SET (10)	3.00	.90
P1 Andrew Lorraine	.25	.07
P2 LaTroy Hawkins	.50	.15
P3 Brad Woodall	.25	.07
P4 Jeremy Powell	.25	.07
P5 Charles Johnson	1.00	.30
P6 Jed Hansen	.25	.07
P7 Yates Hall	.25	.07
P8 Russ Johnson	.25	.07
P9 Scott Shores	.25	.07
P10 Matt Beaumont	.25	.07

1995 Signature Rookies Members Only Preview Signatures

This 10-card standard-size set was issued by Signature Rookies to club members. The fronts feature a 95 preview in the upper left corner, while the lower right corner identifies the card as a 1995 issue. The signature Rookies logo is in the lower left corner while player identification is located in the upper right corner. The backs include information about vital stats, a brief biography, and a 1994 and career stat line. A Signature Rookies authentic signature logo is stamped on the card.

	Nm-Mt	Ex-Mt
COMPLETE SET (10)	20.00	6.00
P1 Andrew Lorraine	2.00	.60
P2 LaTroy Hawkins	3.00	.90
P3 Brad Woodall	2.00	.60
P4 Jeremy Powell	2.00	.60
P5 Charles Johnson	5.00	1.50
P6 Jed Hansen	2.00	.60
P7 Yates Hall	2.00	.60
P8 Russ Johnson	2.00	.60
P9 Scott Shores	2.00	.60
P10 Matt Beaumont	2.00	.60

1995 Signature Rookies Old Judge

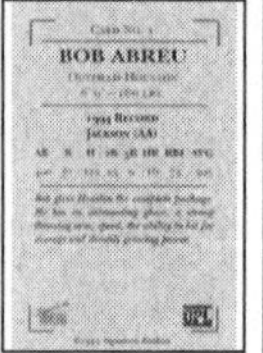

This set was issued in six card packs. The packs contained four Old Judge cards, one chase set card and one autographed card. This specially designed series emulates the original size and styling of the early 1900's Old Judge Tobacco cards and features 35 of today's top minor league baseball players. Each player hand signed 3,750 cards.

	Nm-Mt	Ex-Mt
COMPLETE SET (36)	5.00	1.50
1 Bob Abreu	1.00	.30
2 Kym Ashworth	.10	.03
3 Jared Baker	.10	.03
4 Paul Bako	.10	.03
5 Jason Bates	.10	.03
6 Yamil Benitez	.10	.03
7 Marshall Boze	.10	.03
8 Rich Butler	.10	.03
9 John Carter	.10	.03
10 Jeff Cirillo	.40	.12
11 Randy Curtis	.10	.03
12 Sal Fasano	.10	.03
13 Aaron Fultz	.10	.03
14 Karim Garcia	.40	.12
15 Kevin Grijak	.10	.03
16 Wilton Guerrero	.10	.03
17 Stacy Hollins	.10	.03
18 Bobby Hughes	.10	.03
19 Jimmy Hurst	.10	.03
20 Jason Isringhausen	.40	.12
21 Ryan Karp	.10	.03
22 Derek Lowe	.40	.12
23 Matt Luke	.10	.03
24 Lyle Mouton	.10	.03
25 David Mysel	.10	.03
26 Marc Newfield	.10	.03
27 Jim Pittsley	.10	.03
28 Chris Scheff	.10	.03
29 Tate Seefried	.10	.03
30 Shawn Senior	.10	.03
31 Andy Stewart	.10	.03
32 Ozzie Timmons	.10	.03
33 Quilvio Veras	.10	.03
34 Donny White	.10	.03
35 Mike Zimmerman	.10	.03
36 Ruben Rivera CL	.10	.03

1995 Signature Rookies Old Judge Signatures

Each card is serially numbered out of 3750. The fronts just have an autograph on them while the backs are the same as the regular cards.

	Nm-Mt	Ex-Mt
1 Bob Abreu	10.00	3.00
2 Kym Ashworth	3.00	.90
3 Jared Baker	3.00	.90
4 Paul Bako	3.00	.90
5 Jason Bates	3.00	.90
6 Yamil Benitez	3.00	.90
7 Marshall Boze	3.00	.90
8 Rich Butler	3.00	.90
9 John Carter	3.00	.90
10 Jeff Cirillo	5.00	1.50
11 Randy Curtis	3.00	.90
12 Sal Fasano	3.00	.90
13 Aaron Fultz	3.00	.90
14 Karim Garcia	5.00	1.50
15 Kevin Grijak	3.00	.90
16 Wilton Guerrero	3.00	.90
17 Stacy Hollins	3.00	.90
18 Bobby Hughes	3.00	.90
19 Jimmy Hurst	3.00	.90
20 Jason Isringhausen	5.00	1.50
21 Ryan Karp	3.00	.90
22 Derek Lowe	8.00	2.40
23 Matt Luke	3.00	.90
24 Lyle Mouton	3.00	.90
25 David Mysel	3.00	.90
26 Marc Newfield	3.00	.90
27 Jim Pittsley	3.00	.90
28 Chris Scheff	3.00	.90
29 Tate Seefried	3.00	.90
30 Shawn Senior	3.00	.90
31 Andy Stewart	3.00	.90
32 Ozzie Timmons	3.00	.90
33 Quilvio Veras	5.00	1.50
34 Donny White	3.00	.90
35 Mike Zimmerman	3.00	.90

1995 Signature Rookies Old Judge All-Stars

Unsigned ratio 1:12; signed ratio 1:24.

	Nm-Mt	Ex-Mt
COMPLETE SET (5)	2.00	.60
AS1 Trey Beamon	.50	.15
AS2 Tim Belk	.50	.15
AS3 Jimmy Haynes	.50	.15
AS4 Mark Johnson	.50	.15
AS5 Chris Stynes	.50	.15

1995 Signature Rookies Old Judge All-Stars Signatures

Each card numbered out of 2100.

	Nm-Mt	Ex-Mt
AS1 Trey Beamon	2.00	.60
AS2 Tim Belk	2.00	.60
AS3 Jimmy Haynes	2.00	.60
AS4 Mark Johnson	2.00	.60
AS5 Chris Stynes	2.00	.60

1995 Signature Rookies Old Judge Hot Prospects

Unsigned ratio 1:10; signed ratio 1:30.

	Nm-Mt	Ex-Mt
COMPLETE SET (5)	2.00	.60
HP1 Billy Ashley	.50	.15
HP2 Brad Clontz	.50	.15
HP3 Andrew Lorraine	.50	.15
HP4 Ruben Rivera	.50	.15
HP5 Jason Thompson	.50	.15

1995 Signature Rookies Old Judge Hot Prospects Signatures

Each card numbered out of 1550.

	Nm-Mt	Ex-Mt
HP1 Billy Ashley	2.00	.60
HP2 Brad Clontz	2.00	.60
HP3 Andrew Lorraine	2.00	.60
HP4 Ruben Rivera	2.00	.60
HP5 Jason Thompson	2.00	.60

1995 Signature Rookies Old Judge Joe DiMaggio

Only 5,000 cards; 250 signed cards; unsigned card ratio 1 in every 3 boxes; signed card ratio 1 in every 3 cases.

	Nm-Mt	Ex-Mt
JD1 Joe DiMaggio	5.00	1.50
JD2 Joe DiMaggio AU/250	250.00	75.00

1995 Signature Rookies Old Judge Preview '95

Featuring 35 of today's top minor league baseball players, the Old Judge T-95 series emulates the original size (2" by 3") and styling of the early 1900's Old Judge Tobacco cards. This preview set differs from the regular Old Judge T-95 in gold stamping, multiple photos and UV coating. Just 500 of these are signed, ratio 1:14.

	Nm-Mt	Ex-Mt
COMPLETE SET (35)	15.00	4.50
1 Bob Abreu	1.50	.45
2 Kym Ashworth	.40	.12
3 Jared Baker	.40	.12
4 Paul Bako	.40	.12
5 Jason Bates	.40	.12
6 Yamil Benitez	.40	.12
7 Marshall Boze	.40	.12
8 Rich Butler	.40	.12
9 John Carter	.40	.12
10 Jeff Cirillo	.75	.23
11 Randy Curtis	.40	.12
12 Sal Fasano	.40	.12
13 Aaron Fultz	.40	.12
14 Karim Garcia	.75	.23
15 Kevin Grijak	.40	.12
16 Wilton Guerrero	.40	.12
17 Stacy Hollins	.40	.12
18 Bobby Hughes	.40	.12
19 Jimmy Hurst	.40	.12
20 Jason Isringhausen	.75	.23
21 Ryan Karp	.40	.12
22 Derek Lowe	.75	.23
23 Matt Luke	.40	.12
24 Lyle Mouton	.40	.12
25 David Mysel	.40	.12
26 Marc Newfield	.40	.12
27 Jim Pittsley	.40	.12
28 Chris Scheff	.40	.12
29 Tate Seefried	.40	.12
30 Shawn Senior	.40	.12
31 Andy Stewart	.40	.12
32 Ozzie Timmons	.40	.12
33 Quilvio Veras	.40	.12
34 Donny White	.40	.12
35 Mike Zimmerman	.40	.12

1995 Signature Rookies Old Judge Preview '95 Signatures

Each card numbered out of 500.

	Nm-Mt	Ex-Mt
1 Bob Abreu	10.00	3.00
2 Kym Ashworth	3.00	.90
3 Jared Baker	3.00	.90
4 Paul Bako	3.00	.90
5 Jason Bates	3.00	.90
6 Yamil Benitez	3.00	.90
7 Marshall Boze	3.00	.90
8 Rich Butler	3.00	.90
9 John Carter	3.00	.90
10 Jeff Cirillo	5.00	1.50
11 Randy Curtis	3.00	.90
12 Sal Fasano	3.00	.90
13 Aaron Fultz	3.00	.90
14 Karim Garcia	5.00	1.50
15 Kevin Grijak	3.00	.90
16 Wilton Guerrero	3.00	.90
17 Stacy Hollins	3.00	.90
18 Bobby Hughes	3.00	.90
19 Jimmy Hurst	3.00	.90
20 Jason Isringhausen	5.00	1.50
21 Ryan Karp	3.00	.90
22 Derek Lowe	8.00	2.40
23 Matt Luke	3.00	.90
24 Lyle Mouton	3.00	.90
25 David Mysel	3.00	.90
26 Marc Newfield	3.00	.90
27 Jim Pittsley	3.00	.90
28 Chris Scheff	3.00	.90
29 Tate Seefried	3.00	.90
30 Shawn Senior	3.00	.90
31 Andy Stewart	3.00	.90
32 Ozzie Timmons	3.00	.90
33 Quilvio Veras	5.00	1.50
34 Donny White	3.00	.90
35 Mike Zimmerman	3.00	.90

1995 Signature Rookies Old Judge Star Squad

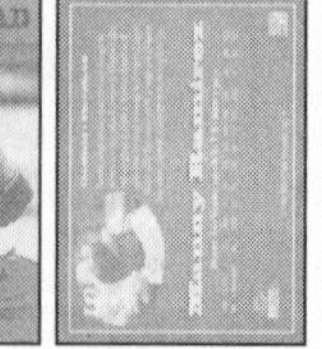

Randomly inserted in packs, these 10 cards feature some of the leading prospects in the minors. These cards are serial numbered to 1000.

	Nm-Mt	Ex-Mt
COMPLETE SET (10)	8.00	2.40
1 Ruben Rivera	.50	.15
2 Charles Johnson	1.00	.30
3 Derek Jeter	5.00	1.50
4 Todd Hollandsworth	.50	.15
5 Billy Ashley	.50	.15
6 Benji Gil	.50	.15
7 Vaughn Eshelman	.50	.15
8 Ray Durham	1.00	.30
9 Marty Cordova	.50	.15
10 Manny Ramirez	1.00	.30

1995 Signature Rookies Old Judge Star Squad Signatures

This is an autographed parallel to the basic Star Squad inserts. Each card is numbered out of 525 on front in blue ink sharpie. An additional Derek Jeter card signed and numbered to 250 copies also exists. Unlike the basic autos numbered to 525 (which confusingly each say 1 of 10,000 in foil), this card incorporates the serial numbering directly into the foil stamping "X of 250" on front.

	Nm-Mt	Ex-Mt
1 Ruben Rivera	4.00	1.20
2 Charles Johnson	10.00	3.00
3 Derek Jeter	80.00	24.00
3A Derek Jeter/250	100.00	30.00
4 Todd Hollandsworth	4.00	1.20
5 Billy Ashley	4.00	1.20
6 Benji Gil	4.00	1.20
7 Vaughn Eshelman	4.00	1.20
8 Ray Durham	10.00	3.00
9 Marty Cordova	4.00	1.20
10 Manny Ramirez	20.00	6.00

1995 SP Top Prospects Promos

It's believed that unnumbered promotional cards were created for all twenty-six of the SP Top Prospect Autograph inserts. The cards were distributed to dealers (one per order form) and hobby media several weeks prior to the product's shipping date. The cards parallel the Autograph inserts design and photos but are NOT signed by the athlete (and also lack the hologram stickers present on the real Autographs). The text "For promotional use only - This is not a Signature card" runs diagonally across each card back. Pricing information is limited due to the infrequency that these cards surface in the secondary market. The cards are checklisted below in alphabetical order by player's last name.

	Nm-Mt	Ex-Mt
COMPLETE SET (26)		
1 Bob Abreu		
2 Gabe Alvarez		
3 George Arias		
4 Trey Beamon		
5 Aaron Boone		
6 Raul Casanova		
7 Bartolo Colon		
8 Jermaine Dye		
9 Nomar Garciaparra		
10 Ben Grieve		
11 Vladimir Guerrero		
12 Richard Hidalgo		
13 Andruw Jones		
14 Michael Jordan		
15 Jason Kendall		
16 Brooks Kieschnick		
17 Derrek Lee		
18 Wonderful Monds		
19 Rey Ordonez		
20 Jay Payton		
21 Adam Riggs		
22 Scott Rolen		
23 Jason Thompson		
24 Paul Wilson		
25 Jaret Wright		
26 Todd Greene		
27 Todd Helton Card never released		

1995 SP Top Prospects

This 165-card set with 140 silver metallic die-cut cards features the top prospects in the minors. The set includes two subsets; Top Ten Prospects (1-10) featuring the cream of the crop and 1995 Draft Class subset (100-114) featuring 15-players who were selected in the 1995 amateur draft. Early cards of Darin Erstad, Andruw Jones, Vladimir Guerrero, Todd Helton and Scott Rolen are featured in this set.

	Nm-Mt	Ex-Mt
COMPLETE SET (165)	40.00	12.00
1 Andruw Jones TOP	4.00	1.20
2 Brooks Kieschnick TOP	.40	.12
3 Nomar Garciaparra TOP	3.00	.90
4 Adam Riggs TOP	.40	.12
5 Paul Wilson TOP	.40	.12
6 Trey Beamon TOP	.40	.12
7 Vladimir Guerrero TOP	5.00	1.50
8 Ben Grieve TOP	1.00	.30
9 Jay Payton TOP	1.00	.30
10 Todd Walker TOP	1.00	.30
11 Jermaine Dye	1.00	.30
12 Damon Hollins	.40	.12
13 Wonderful Monds	.40	.12
14 Damian Moss	1.00	.30
15 Andruw Jones	8.00	2.40
16 Danny Clyburn	.40	.12
17 Billy Percibal	.40	.12
18 Rocky Coppinger	.40	.12
19 Tommy Davis	.40	.12
20 Nomar Garciaparra	6.00	1.80
21 Trot Nixon	1.00	.30
22 Jose Malave	.40	.12
23 Ryan McGuire	.40	.12
24 Rafael Orellano	.40	.12

5 Darin Erstad 2.00 .60
6 George Arias .40 .12
7 Matt Beaumont .40 .12
8 Jason Dickson .40 .12
9 Greg Shockey .40 .12
0 Brooks Kieschnick .40 .12
1 Jon Ratliff .40 .12
2 Amaury Telemaco .40 .12
3 Bob Morris .40 .12
4 Charles Poe .40 .12
5 Harold Williams .40 .12
6 Jeff Abbott 1.00 .30
7 Tom Fordham .40 .12
8 Pokey Reese .40 .12
9 Pat Watkins .40 .12
0 Aaron Boone 2.00 .60
1 Chad Mottola .40 .12
2 Jason Robbins .40 .12
3 Jaret Wright 1.00 .30
4 Casey Whitten .40 .12
5 Bartolo Colon 2.00 .60
6 Richie Sexson 2.00 .60
7 Enrique Wilson .40 .12
8 Doug Million .40 .12
9 Joel Moore .40 .12
0 Derrick Gibson .40 .12
1 Neifi Perez .40 .12
2 Jamey Wright .40 .12
3 Juan Encarnacion 1.00 .30
4 Cade Gaspar .40 .12
5 Justin Thompson .40 .12
6 Bubba Trammell 1.00 .30
7 Daryle Ward 1.00 .30
8 Clemente Nunez .40 .12
9 Will Cunnane .40 .12
0 Billy McMillon .40 .12
1 Matt Whisenant .40 .12
2 Edgar Renteria 1.00 .30
3 Josh Booty 1.00 .30
4 Bob Abreu 2.00 .60
5 Richard Hidalgo 1.00 .30
6 Ramon Castro .40 .12
7 Scott Elarton 1.00 .30
8 Jhonny Perez .40 .12
9 Mendy Lopez .40 .12
70 Glendon Rusch 1.00 .30
71 Sal Fasano .40 .12
72 Sergio Nunez .40 .12
73 Matt Smith .40 .12
74 Chris Latham .40 .12
75 Adam Riggs .40 .12
76 Wilton Guerrero .40 .12
77 Paul Konerko 1.00 .30
78 Gary Rath .40 .12
79 Jim Cole .40 .12
80 Jeff D'Amico .40 .12
81 Antone Williamson .40 .12
82 Todd Dunn .40 .12
83 Brian Banks .40 .12
84 Shane Bowers .40 .12
85 Todd Walker 1.00 .30
86 Troy Carrasco .40 .12
87 Travis Miller .40 .12
88 Kim Bartee .40 .12
89 Dan Serafini .40 .12
90 Vladimir Guerrero 10.00 3.00
91 Hiram Bocachica 1.00 .30
92 Brad Fullmer 1.00 .30
93 Geoff Blum 1.00 .30
94 Israel Alcantara .40 .12
95 Jay Payton 1.00 .30
96 Rey Ordonez 1.00 .30
97 Paul Wilson 1.00 .30
98 Preston Wilson 1.00 .30
99 Terrence Long 1.00 .30
100 Darin Erstad DRAFT 2.00 .60
101 Gabe Alvarez DRAFT .40 .12
102 J.Johnson DRAFT .40 .12
103 Adam Benes DRAFT .40 .12
104 D.Martinez Jr. DRAFT .40 .12
105 Jaime Jones DRAFT .40 .12
106 C.Hermansen DRAFT .40 .12
107 Geoff Jenkins DRAFT 2.00 .60
108 Juan LeBron DRAFT .40 .12
109 Mark Redman DRAFT 1.00 .30
110 Jose Cruz Jr. DRAFT 2.00 .60
111 Carlos Beltran DRAFT 8.00 2.40
112 Todd Helton DRAFT 4.00 1.20
113 Andy Yount DRAFT .40 .12
114 Ryan Jaroncyk DRAFT .40 .12
115 Sean Johnston .40 .12
116 Scott Romano .40 .12
117 Brian Buchanan .40 .12
118 Nick Delvecchio .40 .12
119 Ramiro Mendoza 1.00 .30
120 Matt Drews .40 .12
121 Shane Spencer 1.00 .30
122 Jason McDonald .40 .12
123 Scott Spiezio 1.00 .30
124 Brad Rigby 1.00 .30
125 Ben Grieve 1.00 .30
126 Steve Cox .40 .12
127 Willie Morales .40 .12
128 Wayne Gomes .40 .12
129 Larry Wimberly .40 .12
130 Scott Rolen 4.00 1.20
131 Carlton Loewer .40 .12
132 Wendell Magee .40 .12
133 Charles Peterson .40 .12
134 Lou Collier .40 .12
135 Trey Beamon .40 .12
136 Micah Franklin .40 .12
137 Jason Kendall 1.00 .30
138 Homer Bush .40 .12
139 Dickie Woodridge .40 .12
140 Derrek Lee 1.00 .30
141 Raul Casanova .40 .12
142 Greg LaRocca .40 .12
143 Jason Thompson .40 .12
144 Jacob Cruz .40 .12
145 Jesus Ibarra .40 .12
146 Jay Canizaro .40 .12
147 Steve Soderstrom .40 .12
148 Dante Powell .40 .12
149 James Bonnici .40 .12
150 Raul Ibanez 1.00 .30
151 Trey Moore .40 .12
152 Desi Relaford .40 .12
153 Jason Varitek 1.00 .30
154 Jay Witasick .40 .12
155 Bret Wagner .40 .12
156 Aaron Holbert .40 .12
157 Fernando Tatis 1.00 .30
158 Mike Bell .40 .12
159 Jeff Davis .40 .12
160 Julio Santana .40 .12
161 Kevin Brown C .40 .12
162 Felipe Crespo .40 .12
163 Kevin Witt .40 .12
164 Mark Sievert .40 .12
165 Jose Pett .40 .12

1995 SP Top Prospects Autographs

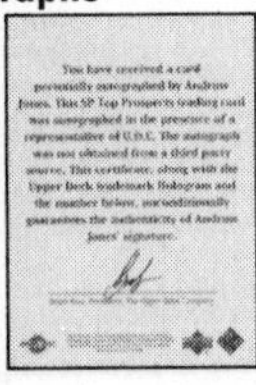

This 26-card insert set features autographs of the top prospects in the minors and a rare Michael Jordan. There are estimated to be between 25 and 50 Michael Jordan autograph cards produced for this set. The autographs are inserted at a rate of one per box. All of the cards are diecut. Besides Jordan, the set is loaded with stars like Nomar Garciaparra, Vladimir Guerrero and Andruw Jones.

	Nm-Mt	Ex-Mt
1 Bob Abreu	30.00	9.00
2 Gabe Alvarez	15.00	4.50
3 George Arias	15.00	4.50
4 Trey Beamon	15.00	4.50
5 Aaron Boone	30.00	9.00
6 Raul Casanova	15.00	4.50
7 Bartolo Colon	30.00	9.00
8 Jermaine Dye	25.00	7.50
9 Nomar Garciaparra	120.00	36.00
10 Ben Grieve	20.00	6.00
11 Vladimir Guerrero	150.00	45.00
12 Richard Hidalgo	25.00	7.50
13 Andruw Jones	100.00	30.00
14 Michael Jordan SP		
15 Jason Kendall	20.00	6.00
16 Brooks Kieschnick	15.00	4.50
17 Derrek Lee	25.00	7.50
18 Wonderful Monds	15.00	4.50
19 Rey Ordonez	20.00	6.00
20 Jay Payton	20.00	6.00
21 Adam Riggs	15.00	4.50
22 Scott Rolen	60.00	18.00
23 Jason Thompson	15.00	4.50
24 Paul Wilson	15.00	4.50
25 Jaret Wright	20.00	6.00
26 Todd Greene	15.00	4.50

1995 SP Top Prospects Destination the Show

This 20-card insert set features the high-profile Minor League players expected to make their major league debut by 1996. The Destination the Show inserts were inserted at a rate of one in 63 packs.

	Nm-Mt	Ex-Mt
COMPLETE SET (20)	600.00	180.00
DS1 Andruw Jones	80.00	24.00
DS2 Richard Hidalgo	10.00	3.00
DS3 Paul Wilson	10.00	3.00
DS4 Brooks Kieschnick	10.00	3.00
DS5 Ben Grieve	10.00	3.00
DS6 Adam Riggs	10.00	3.00
DS7 Vladimir Guerrero	100.00	30.00
DS8 Paul Konerko	10.00	3.00
DS9 Jose Cruz Jr.	20.00	6.00
DS10 Todd Walker	10.00	3.00
DS11 Darin Erstad	30.00	9.00
DS12 Derrek Lee	10.00	3.00
DS13 Scott Rolen	50.00	15.00
DS14 Trey Beamon	10.00	3.00
DS15 Nomar Garciaparra	80.00	24.00
DS16 Jason Kendall	10.00	3.00
DS17 Aaron Boone	20.00	6.00
DS18 Matt Drews	10.00	3.00
DS19 Derrick Gibson	10.00	3.00
DS20 Jay Payton	10.00	3.00

1995 SP Top Prospects Michael Jordan Time Capsule

This four-card set recaps Michael Jordan's Minor League career. Time Capsules are inserted at a rate of one per nine packs.

	Nm-Mt	Ex-Mt
COMPLETE SET (4)	30.00	9.00
COMMON (TC1-TC4)	8.00	2.40

1995 Upper Deck Minors

The set can be subdivided into regular cards (1-100, 116-160, 170-214), Season Highlights (101-106), International Flavor (107-115), Road To The Show (161-169), and Draft Class (215-224). Card 225 was a special card of the Durham Bulls Athletic Park. An early Vladimir Guerrero card is the highlight of this set.

	Nm-Mt	Ex-Mt
COMPLETE SET (225)	25.00	7.50
1 Derek Jeter	3.00	.90

2 Michael Tucker .15 .04
3 Alex Ochoa .15 .04
4 Bill Pulsipher .15 .04
5 Terrell Wade .15 .04
6 Johnny Damon .50 .15
7 LaTroy Hawkins .15 .04
8 Ruben Rivera .15 .04
9 Jason Giambi 1.25 .35
10 Todd Hollandsworth .15 .04
11 Alan Benes .15 .04
12 John Wasdin .15 .04
13 Roger Cedeno .15 .04
14 Karim Garcia .50 .15
15 Brooks Kieschnick .15 .04
16 David Bell .15 .04
17 Trot Nixon .50 .15
18 Jose Malave .15 .04
19 Rey Ordonez .50 .15
20 Raul Casanova .15 .04
21 Chad Mottola .15 .04
22 Phil Nevin .50 .15
23 Jim Pittsley .15 .04
24 Frank Rodriguez .15 .04
25 Todd Greene .15 .04
26 Mike Bell .15 .04
27 Jason Kendall .50 .15
28 Pokey Reese .15 .04
29 Jose Silva .15 .04
30 Kirk Presley .15 .04
31 Joe Randa .15 .04
32 Shannon Stewart .50 .15
33 Danny Clyburn .15 .04
34 Glenn Williams .15 .04
35 Terry Bradshaw .15 .04
36 Jimmy Hurst .15 .04
37 Scott Spiezio .50 .15
38 Richard Hidalgo .50 .15
39 Matt Brunson .15 .04
40 Juan Acevedo .15 .04
41 Trey Beamon .15 .04
42 Kim Bartee .15 .04
43 James Baldwin .15 .04
44 Matt Arrandale .15 .04
45 Michael Jordan 2.00 .60
46 Tony Graffanino .15 .04
47 Wonderful Monds .15 .04
48 Bob Abreu 1.00 .30
49 Edgardo Alfonzo .50 .15
50 Damon Hollins .15 .04
51 Marc Barcelo .15 .04
52 D.J. Boston .15 .04
53 Einar Diaz .15 .04
54 Matt Drews .15 .04
55 Benji Simonton .15 .04
56 Bart Evans .15 .04
57 Micah Franklin .15 .04
58 Curtis Goodwin .15 .04
59 Craig Griffey .15 .04
60 Billy Wagner .50 .15
61 Jimmy Haynes .15 .04
62 Jose Herrera .15 .04
63 Greg Keagle .15 .04
64 Andy Larkin .15 .04
65 Jason Isringhausen .50 .15
66 Derrek Lee .50 .15
67 Terrell Lowery .15 .04
68 Ryan Luzinski .15 .04
69 Angel Martinez .15 .04
70 Tony Clark .15 .04
71 Ryan McGuire .15 .04
72 Damian Moss .50 .15
73 Hugo Pivaral .15 .04
74 Arquimedez Pozo .15 .04
75 Daron Kirkreit .15 .04
76 Luis Raven .15 .04
77 Desi Relaford .15 .04
78 Scott Rolen 2.00 .60
79 Joe Rosselli .15 .04
80 Chris Roberts .15 .04
81 Giomar Guevara .15 .04
82 Gene Schall .15 .04
83 Jeff Suppan .15 .04
84 Mac Suzuki .15 .04
85 Jason Thompson .15 .04
86 Marc Valdes .15 .04
87 Pat Watkins .15 .04
88 Jay Witasick .15 .04
89 Ray Durham .50 .15
90 Brad Fullmer .50 .15
91 Roger Bailey .15 .04
92 DeShawn Warren .15 .04
93 Jermaine Dye .50 .15
94 Scott Romano .15 .04
95 Aaron Boone 1.00 .30
96 Tate Seefried .15 .04
97 Chris Stynes .15 .04
98 Chris Widger .15 .04
99 Desi Wilson .15 .04
100 Dante Powell .15 .04
101 Neifi Perez SH .15 .04
102 Alex Ochoa SH .15 .04
103 Kelly Wunsch SH .15 .04
104 Jason Robbins SH .15 .04
105 Kevin Coughlin SH .15 .04
106 Bill Pulsipher SH .15 .04
107 Roger Cedeno IF .15 .04
108 Jose Herrera IF .15 .04
109 Andre King IF .15 .04
110 Rey Ordonez IF .15 .04
111 Jose Pett IF .15 .04
112 Ruben Rivera IF .15 .04
113 Jose Silva IF .15 .04
114 Mac Suzuki IF .15 .04
115 Glenn Williams IF .15 .04
116 Will Cunnane .15 .04
117 Neifi Perez .15 .04
118 Andre King .15 .04
119 Quinton McCracken .15 .04
120 Brian Giles 1.00 .30
121 Kenny Felder .15 .04
122 Jermaine Allensworth .15 .04
123 Allen Battle .15 .04
124 Howard Battle .15 .04
125 Doug Million .15 .04
126 Geoff Blum .50 .15
127 Vladimir Guerrero 5.00 1.50
128 Torii Hunter .50 .15
129 Doug Glanville .15 .04
130 Dustin Hermanson .15 .04
131 Mark Grudzielanek .50 .15
132 Phil Geisler .15 .04
133 Chris Carpenter .50 .15
134 Brain Sackinsky .15 .04
135 Josh Booty .50 .15
136 Shane Andrews .15 .04
137 Scott Eyre .15 .04
138 Chad Fox .15 .04
139 George Arias .15 .04
140 Scott Sullivan .15 .04
141 Todd Dunn .15 .04
142 Nate Holdren .15 .04
143 Gus Gandarillas .15 .04
144 Scott Talanoa .15 .04
145 Sal Fasano .15 .04
146 Stoney Briggs .15 .04
147 Yamil Benitez .15 .04
148 Chris Wimmer .15 .04
149 M.De los Santos .15 .04
150 Ben Grieve .50 .15
151 Homer Bush .15 .04
152 Wilton Guerrero .15 .04
153 Benji Grigsby .15 .04
154 Cade Gaspar .15 .04
155 Hiram Bocachica .50 .15
156 Dave Vanhof .15 .04
157 Frank Catalanotto .50 .15
158 Marcus Jensen .15 .04
159 Jamie Arnold .15 .04
160 Cesar Devarez .15 .04
161 Alan Benes RTS .15 .04
162 Johnny Damon RTS .50 .15
163 LaTroy Hawkins RTS .15 .04
164 D.Hermanson RTS .15 .04
165 Derek Jeter RTS 1.50 .45
166 Terrell Wade RTS .15 .04
167 Todd Walker RTS .50 .15
168 John Wasdin RTS .15 .04
169 Paul Wilson RTS .15 .04
170 Todd Walker .50 .15
171 Danny Klassen .15 .04
172 Bob Morris .15 .04
173 Kelly Wunsch .15 .04
174 Fletcher Thompson .15 .04
175 Terrence Long .50 .15
176 Andy Pettitte .75 .23
177 Lou Pote .15 .04
178 Steve Kline .15 .04
179 Damian Jackson .50 .15
180 Matt Smith .15 .04
181 Tim Unroe .15 .04
182 Jim Cole .15 .04
183 Bill McMillon .15 .04
184 Matt Luke .15 .04
185 Sergio Nunez .15 .04
186 Edgar Renteria .50 .15
187 Bill Selby .15 .04
188 Jamey Wright .15 .04
189 Steve Whitaker .15 .04
190 Joe Vitiello .15 .04
191 Jacob Shumate .15 .04
192 C.J. Nitkowski .15 .04
193 Mark Johnson .15 .04
194 Paul Konerko .50 .15
195 Jay Payton .50 .15
196 Jayson Peterson .15 .04
197 Brian Buchanan .15 .04
198 Ramon Castro .15 .04
199 Antone Williamson .15 .04
200 Paul Wilson .15 .04
201 Jaret Wright .50 .15
202 Carlton Loewer .15 .04
203 Jon Zuber .15 .04
204 Ugueth Urbina .15 .04
205 Nomar Garciaparra 2.50 .75
206 Yuri Sanchez .15 .04
207 Jason Moler .15 .04
208 Lyle Mouton .15 .04
209 Mark P. Johnson .15 .04
210 Matt Raleigh .15 .04
211 Julio Santana .15 .04
212 Willis Ontanez .15 .04
213 Ozzie Timmons .15 .04
214 Victor Rodriguez .15 .04
215 Paul Wilson DC .15 .04
216 Ben Grieve DC .50 .15
217 Dustin Hermanson DC .15 .04
218 A.Williamson DC .15 .04
219 Josh Booty DC .15 .04
220 Todd Walker DC .50 .15
221 Jaret Wright DC .15 .04
222 Paul Konerko DC .50 .15
223 Doug Million DC .15 .04
224 Hiram Bocachica DC .15 .04
225 Durham Athletic Park .15 .04

1995 Upper Deck Minors Future Stock

Issued at a rate of one per pack, this set is a parallel of the 1995 Upper Deck Minors set. The words "Future Stock" printed on the front differentiate these cards from the regular cards.

	Nm-Mt	Ex-Mt
COMPLETE SET (225)	50.00	15.00

*FUT.STOCK: .75X TO 2X BASIC CARDS

1995 Upper Deck Minors Autographs

Autographed cards were issued to the first dealers who ordered the 1995 Upper Deck Minor League product. The fronts feature full-bleed color action photos, with the player's autograph inscribed across the picture. The backs carry a congratulatory message. Each player signed 1,000 of his cards. Depending on

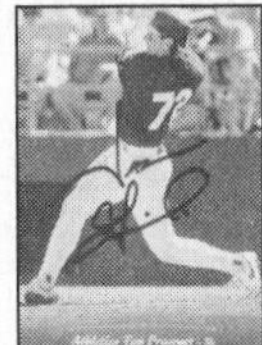

the size of the order, dealers received from one to four cards.

	Nm-Mt	Ex-Mt
1 Mike Bell	10.00	3.00
2 Alan Benes	10.00	3.00
3 Johnny Damon	15.00	4.50
4 Jason Giambi	30.00	9.00
5 LaTroy Hawkins	10.00	3.00
6 Todd Hollandsworth	10.00	3.00
7 Derek Jeter	80.00	24.00
8 Alex Ochoa	10.00	3.00
9 Terrell Wade	10.00	3.00
10 Paul Wilson	10.00	3.00

1995 Upper Deck Minors Michael Jordan Jumbos

This oversize set, was available from Upper Deck in return for a mail-in wrapper offer.

	Nm-Mt	Ex-Mt
COMPLETE SET (5)	25.00	7.50
COMMON (MJ1-MJ5)	5.00	1.50

1995 Upper Deck Minors Michael Jordan One On One

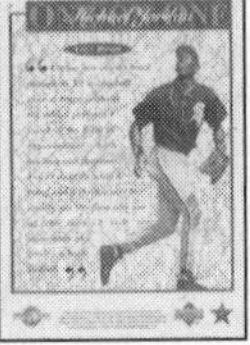

Issued one per four-card retail pack.

	Nm-Mt	Ex-Mt
COMPLETE SET (10)	15.00	4.50
COMMON CARD (1-10)	1.50	.45

1995 Upper Deck Minors Michael Jordan Scrapbook

Inserted at a rate of one in 35, these 10 cards feature highlights of Michael Jordan's 1994 Minor League season.

	Nm-Mt	Ex-Mt
COMPLETE SET (10)	100.00	30.00
COMMON (MJ1-MJ10)	10.00	3.00

1995 Upper Deck Minors Organizational Profiles

Inserted at a rate of one every 10 packs, these 28 cards feature a leading player from each major league organization. The set is sequenced alphabetically by major league organization.

	Nm-Mt	Ex-Mt
COMPLETE SET (28)	40.00	12.00
OP1 Terrell Wade	1.00	.30
OP2 Alex Ochoa	1.00	.30
OP3 Nomar Garciaparra	8.00	2.40
OP4 Todd Greene	1.00	.30
OP5 Brooks Kieschnick	1.00	.30
OP6 Michael Jordan	10.00	3.00
OP7 C.J. Nitkowski	1.00	.30
OP8 Daron Kirkreit	1.00	.30
OP9 Juan Acevedo	1.00	.30
OP10 Tony Clark	1.00	.30
OP11 Josh Booty	2.00	.60
OP12 Billy Wagner	2.00	.60
OP13 Johnny Damon	2.00	.60
OP14 Paul Konerko	2.00	.60
OP15 Antone Williamson	1.00	.30
OP16 Todd Walker	2.00	.60
OP17 Ugueth Urbina	1.00	.30
OP18 Bill Pulsipher	1.00	.30
OP19 Ruben Rivera	1.00	.30
OP20 John Wasdin	1.00	.30
OP21 Scott Rolen	10.00	3.00
OP22 Trey Beamon	1.00	.30
OP23 Alan Benes	1.00	.30
OP24 Raul Casanova	1.00	.30
OP25 Dante Powell	1.00	.30
OP26 Arquimedez Pozo	1.00	.30
OP27 Julio Santana	1.00	.30
OP28 Jose Silva	1.00	.30

1995 Upper Deck Minors Top 10 Prospects

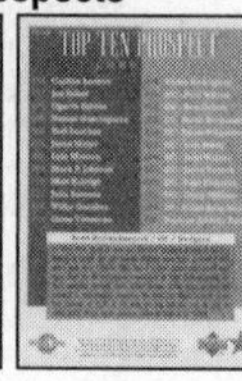

Issued at a rate of one every 10 packs, these 10 cards feature some of the leading prospects in the minors in 1995.

Nm-Mt Ex-Mt
COMPLETE SET (10) 15.00 4.50
1 Derek Jeter 10.00 3.00
2 James Baldwin 1.00 .30
3 Johnny Damon 2.00 .60
4 Ruben Rivera 1.00 .30
5 Bill Pulsipher 1.00 .30
6 Jose Silva 1.00 .30
7 Roger Cedeno 1.00 .30
8 Alan Benes 1.00 .30
9 Michael Tucker 1.00 .30
10 Todd Hollandsworth 1.00 .30

1996 Best

This 100-card set features color player photo shots on white borders. The team logo, player's name and position appear across the bottom of the card. The back carry a color photo along with player information.

Nm-Mt Ex-Mt
COMPLETE SET (100) 10.00 3.00
1 Winston Abreu .15 .04
2 Antonio Alfonseca .40 .12
3 Richard Almanzar .15 .04
4 Gabe Alvarez .15 .04
5 Marlon Anderson .40 .12
6 Kym Ashworth .15 .04
7 Marc Barcelo .15 .04
8 Brian Barkley .15 .04
9 Mike Bell .15 .04
10 Carlos Beltran .75 .23
11 Shayne Bennett .15 .04
12 Jeremy Blevins .15 .04
13 Kevin Brown .15 .04
14 Ray Brown .15 .04
15 Homer Bush .15 .04
16 Jay Canizaro .15 .04
17 Troy Carrasco .15 .04
18 Raul Casanova .15 .04
19 Luis Castillo .50 .15
20 Ramon Castro .15 .04
21 Gary Coffee .15 .04
22 Decomba Conner .15 .04
23 Kevin Coughlin .15 .04
24 Jacob Cruz .15 .04
25 Jeff D'Amico .15 .04
26 Tommy Davis .15 .04
27 Edwin Diaz .15 .04
28 Einar Diaz .15 .04
29 David Doster .15 .04
30 Derrin Ebert .15 .04
31 Bobby Estalella .40 .12
32 Alex Gonzalez .40 .12
33 Kevin Grijak .15 .04
34 Jose Guillen 1.00 .30
35 Tim Harkrider .15 .04
36 Dan Held .15 .04
37 Wes Helms .40 .12
38 Erik Hiljus .15 .04
39 Aaron Holbert .15 .04
40 Raul Ibanez .40 .12
41 Jesse Ibarra .15 .04
42 Marty Janzen .15 .04
43 Robin Jennings .15 .04
44 Sean Johnston .15 .04
45 Randy Jorgensen .15 .04
46 Marc Kroon .15 .04
47 Mike Kusiewicz .15 .04
48 Carlos Lee .75 .23
49 Brian Lesher .15 .04
50 George Lombard .15 .04
51 Roberto Lopez .15 .04
52 Fernando Lunar .15 .04
53 Len Manning .15 .04
54 Eddy Martinez .15 .04
55 Jesus Martinez .15 .04
56 Onan Masaoka .15 .04
57 Joe Maskavish .15 .04
58 Jeff Matulevich .15 .04
59 Brian Meadows .15 .04
60 Mike Metcalfe .15 .04
61 Doug Mlicki .15 .04
62 Steve Montgomery .15 .04
63 Trey Moore .15 .04
64 Nick Morrow .15 .04
65 Bryant Nelson .15 .04
66 Sergio Nunez .15 .04
67 Hector Ortega .15 .04
68 Russ Ortiz 1.00 .30
69 Eric Owens .15 .04
70 Billy Percibal .15 .04
71 Charles Peterson .15 .04
72 A.J. Pierzynski .75 .23
73 Charles Poe .15 .04
74 Dante Powell .15 .04
75 Kenny Pumphrey .15 .04
76 Angel Ramirez .15 .04
77 Julio Ramirez .15 .04
78 Gary Rath .15 .04
79 Jon Ratliff .15 .04
80 Brad Rigby .15 .04
81 Benj Sampson .15 .04
82 Greg Shockey .15 .04
83 Steve Shoemaker .15 .04
84 Demond Smith .15 .04
85 Robert Smith .40 .12
86 Steve Soderstrom .15 .04
87 Fernando Tatis .40 .12
88 Jose Texidor .15 .04
89 Brett Tomko .40 .12
90 Javier Valentin .15 .04
91 Jason Varitek .40 .12
92 Andrew Vessel .15 .04
93 Casey Whitten .15 .04
94 Enrique Wilson .15 .04
95 Preston Wilson .40 .12
96 Larry Wimberly .15 .04
97 Jaret Wright .40 .12
98 Dmitri Young .40 .12
99 Joe Young .15 .04
100 Checklist .15 .04

1996 Best Autographs

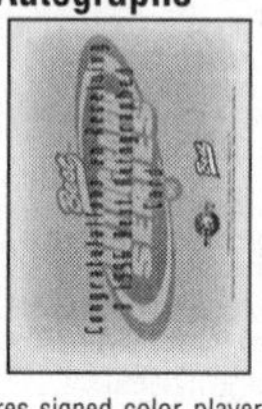

This 91-card set features signed color player photos on a white background. The autographs were inserted at a rate of one per pack.

Nm-Mt Ex-Mt
1 Israel Alcantera 2.00 .60
2 Richard Almanzar 2.00 .60
3 Brian Banks 2.00 .60
4 Marc Barcelo 2.00 .60
5 Kimera Bartee 2.00 .60
6 Jeremy Blevins 2.00 .60
7 Jamie Bluma 2.00 .60
8 D.J. Boston 2.00 .60
9 Kevin Brown 2.00 .60
10 Homer Bush 2.00 .60
11 Jay Canizaro 2.00 .60
12 Luis Castillo 5.00 1.50
13 Dave Coggin 2.00 .60
14 Bartolo Colon 5.00 1.50
15 Jacob Cruz 2.00 .60
16 Lino Diaz 2.00 .60
17 Todd Dunn 2.00 .60
18 Jermaine Dye 3.00 .90
19 Bobby Estalella 3.00 .90
20 Tom Fordham 2.00 .60
21 Karim Garcia 3.00 .90
22 Todd Greene 2.00 .60
23 Ben Grieve 3.00 .90
24 Mike Gulan 2.00 .60
25 Derek Hacopian 2.00 .60
26 Wes Helms 5.00 1.50
27 Brett Herbison 2.00 .60
28 Chad Hermansen 2.00 .60
29 Aaron Holbert 2.00 .60
30 Damon Hollins 2.00 .60
31 Ryan Jaroncyk 2.00 .60
32 Geoff Jenkins 5.00 1.50
33 Earl Johnson 2.00 .60
34 Andruw Jones 20.00 6.00
35 Jason Kendall 3.00 .90
36 Brooks Kieschnick 2.00 .60
37 Andre King 2.00 .60
38 Paul Konerko 3.00 .90
39 Todd Landry 2.00 .60
40 Mendy Lopez 2.00 .60
41 Roberto Lopez 2.00 .60
42 Eric Ludwick 2.00 .60
43 Mike Maurer 2.00 .60
44 Brian Meadows 2.00 .60
45 Ralph Milliard 2.00 .60
46 Doug Mlicki 2.00 .60
47 Julio Mosquera 2.00 .60
48 Tony Mounce 2.00 .60
49 Sergio Nunez 2.00 .60
50 Russ Ortiz 8.00 2.40
51 Carey Paige 2.00 .60
52 Jay Payton 3.00 .90
53 Charles Peterson 2.00 .60
54 Tommy Phelps 2.00 .60
55 Hugo Pivaral 2.00 .60
56 Dante Powell 2.00 .60
57 Angel Ramirez 2.00 .60
58 Gary Rath 2.00 .60
59 Mark Redman 3.00 .90
60 Adam Riggs 2.00 .60
61 Lonell Roberts 2.00 .60
62 Scott Rolen 15.00 4.50
63 Glendon Rusch 3.00 .90
64 Matt Sachse 2.00 .60
65 Donnie Sadler 2.00 .60
66 William Santamaria 2.00 .60
67 Todd Schmidt 2.00 .60
68 Richie Sexson 10.00 3.00
69 Alvie Shepherd 2.00 .60
70 Steve Shoemaker 2.00 .60
71 Brian Sikorski 2.00 .60
72 Randall Simon 3.00 .90
73 Matt Smith 2.00 .60
74 Scott Spiezio 3.00 .90
75 Everett Stull 2.00 .60
76 Jose Texidor 2.00 .60
77 Mike Thurman 2.00 .60
78 Brett Tomko 3.00 .90
79 Hector Trinidad 2.00 .60
80 Pedro Valdes 2.00 .60
81 Andrew Vessel 2.00 .60
82 Jacob Viano 2.00 .60
83 Terrell Wade 2.00 .60
84 Bret Wagner 2.00 .60
85 Todd Walker 3.00 .90
86 Travis Welch 2.00 .60
87 Casey Whitten 2.00 .60
88 Paul Wilson 2.00 .60
89 Preston Wilson 5.00 1.50
90 Kevin Witt 2.00 .60
91 Jamey Wright 2.00 .60

1996 Best 1st Round Picks

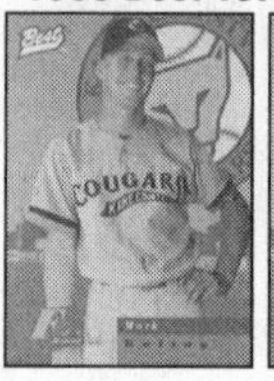
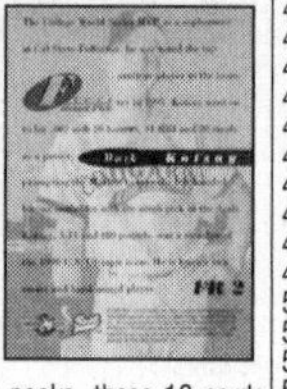

Randomly inserted into packs, these 16 cards feature some of the leading prospects selected in the 1996 draft.

Nm-Mt Ex-Mt
COMPLETE SET (16) 30.00 9.00
FR1 Chad Green 1.50 .45
FR2 Mark Kotsay 3.00 .90
FR3 Robert Stratton 3.00 .90
FR4 Dee Brown 3.00 .90
FR5 Matt Halloran 1.50 .45
FR6 Joe Lawrence 3.00 .90
FR7 Todd Noel 1.50 .45
FR8 Jake Westbrook 3.00 .90
FR9 Gil Meche 8.00 2.40
FR10 Damian Rolls 1.50 .45
FR11 John Oilver 1.50 .45
FR12 Josh Garrett 1.50 .45
FR13 A.J. Zapp 1.50 .45
FR14 Danny Peoples 1.50 .45
FR15 Paul Wilder 1.50 .45
FR16 Nick Bierbrodt 1.50 .45

1996 Best Player of the Year Andruw Jones

Inserted one per retail box.

Nm-Mt Ex-Mt
COMPLETE SET (5) 20.00 6.00
COMMON CARD (1-5) 5.00 1.50

1996 Best Player of the Year Andruw Jones Autographs

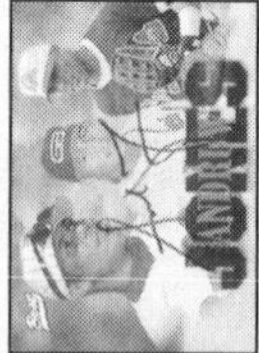
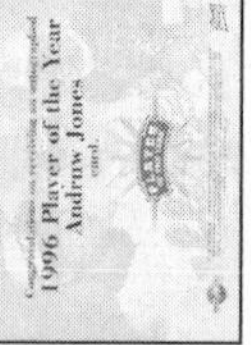

Randomly inserted into retail packs, these five cards features signatgures from Andruw Jones. Jones signed 500 of each of these cards.

Nm-Mt Ex-Mt
COMMON CARD (1-5) 25.00 7.50

1996 Excel

The 1996 Excel Minor League set consists of 250 cards featuring minor league players from AAA, AA and A teams. The cards are numbered and checklisted alphabetically within and according to major league teams for the NL and AL. Early cards of Russell Branyan, Darin Erstad and Geoff Jenkins are included in this set. An unnumbered Wendell Magee sample card was distributed to dealers to preview the set.

Nm-Mt Ex-Mt
COMPLETE SET (250) 20.00 6.00
1 Kim Bartee .15 .04
2 Carlos Chavez .15 .04
3 Rocky Coppinger .15 .04
4 Tommy Davis .15 .04
5 Eddy Martinez .15 .04
6 Billy Owens .15 .04
7 Billy Percibal .15 .04
8 Garrett Stephenson .50 .15
9 Rachaad Stewart .15 .04
10 Chris Allison .15 .04
11 Virgil Chevalier .15 .04
12 Nomar Garciaparra 3.00 .90
13 Jose Malave .15 .04
14 Ryan McGuire .15 .04
15 Trot Nixon .50 .15
16 Rafael Orellano .15 .04
17 Pork Chop Pough .15 .04
18 Donnie Sadler .15 .04
19 Bill Selby .15 .04
20 Nathan Tebbs .15 .04
21 George Arias .15 .04
22 Matt Beaumont .15 .04
23 Danny Buxbaum .15 .04
24 Jovino Carvajal .15 .04
25 Geoff Edsell .15 .04
26 Darin Erstad 1.25 .35
27 Aaron Guiel .15 .04
28 Mike Holtz .15 .04
29 Ryan Kane .15 .04
30 Jeff Abbott .15 .04
31 Kevin Coughlin .15 .04
32 Tom Fordham .15 .04
33 Carlos Lee .75 .23
34 Frank Menechino .15 .04
35 Charles Poe .15 .04
36 Nilson Robledo .15 .04
37 Juan Thomas .15 .04
38 Archie Vazquez .15 .04
39 Bruce Aven .15 .04
40 Russell Branyan .50 .15
41 Bartolo Colon .50 .15
42 Einar Diaz .15 .04
43 Mike Glavine .15 .04
44 Ricky Gutierrez .15 .04
45 Rick Heiserman .15 .04
46 Richie Sexson .50 .15
47 Enrique Wilson .15 .04
48 Jaret Wright .50 .15
49 Bryan Corey .15 .04
50 Mike Drumright .15 .04
51 Juan Encarnacion .15 .04
52 Brandon Reed .15 .04
53 Bubba Trammell .50 .15
54 Daryle Ward .50 .15
55 Jaime Bluma .15 .04
56 Tim Byrdak .15 .04
57 Gary Coffee .15 .04
58 Lino Diaz .15 .04
59 Sal Fasano .15 .04
60 Jed Hansen .15 .04
61 Juan LeBron .15 .04
62 Sean McNally .15 .04
63 Anthony Medrano .15 .04
64 Rodolfo Mendez .15 .04
65 Sergio Nunez .15 .04
66 Mandy Romero .15 .04
67 Glendon Rusch .15 .04
68 Ryan Banks .15 .04
69 Jeff D'Amico .15 .04
70 Jonas Hamlin .15 .04
71 Geoff Jenkins .75 .23
72 Roberto Lopez .15 .04
73 Gerald Parent .15 .04
74 Doug Webb .15 .04
75 Antone Williamson .15 .04
76 Shane Bowers .15 .04
77 Shane Gunderson .15 .04
78 Corey Koskie .50 .15
79 Jake Patterson .15 .04
80 A.J. Pierzynski 1.00 .30
81 Mark Redman .50 .15
82 Dan Serafini .15 .04
83 Todd Walker .50 .15
84 Chris Corn .15 .04
85 Nick Delvecchio .15 .04
86 Dan Donato .15 .04
87 Matt Drews .15 .04
88 Mike Figga .15 .04
89 Ben Ford .15 .04
90 Marty Janzen .15 .04
91 Shea Morenz .15 .04
92 Ray Ricken .15 .04
93 Shane Spencer .50 .15
94 Bob St.Pierre .15 .04
95 Jay Tessmer .15 .04
96 Chris Wilcox .15 .04
97 Steve Cox .15 .04
98 Ben Grieve .15 .04
99 Jason McDonald .15 .04
100 Brad Rigby .15 .04
101 Demond Smith .15 .04
102 Jim Bonnici .15 .04
103 Jose Cruz Jr. 1.00 .30
104 Osvaldo Fernandez .15 .04
105 Raul Ibanez .50 .15
106 Desi Relaford .15 .04
107 Marino Santana .15 .04
108 Kevin Brown .15 .04
109 Jeff Davis .15 .04
110 Edwin Diaz .15 .04
111 Jonathan Johnson .15 .04
112 Fernando Tatis .50 .15
113 Andrew Vessel .15 .04
114 John Curl .15 .04
115 Ryan Jones .15 .04
116 Julio Mosquera .15 .04
117 Jeff Patzke .15 .04
118 Mike Peeples .15 .04
119 Mark Sievert .15 .04
120 Joe Young .15 .04
121 Winston Abreu .15 .04
122 Anthony Briggs .15 .04
123 Matt Byrd .15 .04
124 Jermaine Dye .50 .15
125 Derrin Ebert .15 .04
126 Wes Helms .50 .15
127 Damon Hollins .15 .04
128 Ryan Jacobs .15 .04
129 Andruw Jones 1.50 .45
130 Gus Kennedy .15 .04
131 George Lombard .15 .04
132 Damian Moss .15 .04
133 Robert Smith .50 .15
134 Pedro Swann .15 .04
135 Ron Wright .15 .04
136 Pat Cline .15 .04
137 Robin Jennings .15 .04
138 Brooks Kieschnick .15 .04
139 Ed Larregui .15 .04
140 Jason Maxwell .15 .04
141 Bobby Morris .15 .04
142 Amaury Telemaco .15 .04
143 Pedro Valdes .15 .04
144 Cedric Allen .15 .04
145 Justin Atchley .15 .04
146 Aaron Boone .50 .15
147 Steve Goodhart .15 .04
148 Chris Murphy .15 .04
149 Christian Rojas .15 .04
150 Terry Wright .15 .04
151 Brent Crowther .15 .04
152 Angel Echevarria .15 .04
153 Derrick Gibson .15 .04
154 Todd Helton 2.00 .60
155 Terry Jones .15 .04
156 David Kennedy .15 .04
157 Mike Kusiewicz .15 .04
158 Joel Moore .15 .04
159 Jacob Viano .15 .04
160 Jamey Wright .15 .04
161 Todd Dunwoody .15 .04
162 Ryan Jackson .15 .04
163 Billy McMillon .15 .04
164 Ralph Milliard .15 .04
165 Clemente Nunez .15 .04
166 Edgar Renteria .50 .15
167 Chris Sheff .15 .04
168 Matt Whisenant .15 .04
169 Bob Abreu .50 .15
170 Ramon Castro .15 .04
171 Richard Hidalgo .50 .15
172 Tony McKnight .15 .04
173 Tony Mounce .15 .04
174 Roberto Duran .15 .04
175 Wilton Guerrero .15 .04
176 Joe Jacobsen .15 .04
177 Paul Konerko .50 .15
178 Chris Latham .15 .04
179 Onan Masaoka .15 .04
180 Mike Metcalfe .15 .04
181 Kevin Pincavitch .15 .04
182 Adam Riggs .15 .04
183 David Yocum .15 .04
184 Jake Benz .15 .04
185 Hiram Bocachica .50 .15
186 Brad Fullmer .50 .15
187 Vladimir Guerrero 2.50 .75
188 Eric Ludwick .15 .04
189 Carlos Mendoza .15 .04
190 Jarrod Patterson .15 .04
191 Jay Payton .15 .04
192 Paul Wilson .15 .04
193 Julio Zorrilla .15 .04
194 Marlon Anderson .50 .15
195 Ron Blazier .15 .04
196 Steve Carver .15 .04
197 Blake Doolan .15 .04
198 David Doster .15 .04
199 Tommy Eason .15 .04
200 Zach Elliott .15 .04
201 Bobby Estalella .50 .15
202 Rob Grable .15 .04
203 Bronson Heflin .15 .04
204 Dan Held .15 .04
205 Kevin Hooker .15 .04
206 Rich Hunter .15 .04
207 Carlton Loewer .15 .04
208 Wendell Magee .15 .04
209 Len Manning .15 .04
210 Fred McNair .15 .04
211 Ryan Nye .15 .04
212 Scott Rolen 2.00 .60
213 Brian Stumpf .15 .04
214 Reggie Taylor .15 .04
215 Larry Wimberly .15 .04
216 Micah Franklin .15 .04
217 Chad Hermansen .15 .04
218 Jason Kendall .50 .15
219 Garrett Long .15 .04
220 Joe Maskivish .15 .04
221 Chris Peters .15 .04
222 Charles Peterson .15 .04
223 Charles Rice .15 .04
224 Reed Secrist .15 .04
225 Derek Swafford .15 .04
226 Mike Busby .15 .04
227 Mike Gulan .15 .04
228 Chris Haas .15 .04
229 Jeff Matulevich .15 .04
230 Steve Montgomery .15 .04
231 Matt Morris 1.50 .45
232 Bret Wagner .15 .04
233 Gabe Alvarez .15 .04
234 Raul Casanova .15 .04
235 Ben Davis .15 .04
236 Bubba Dixon .15 .04
237 Greg LaRocca .15 .04
238 Derrek Lee .50 .15
239 Jason Thompson .15 .04
240 Darin Blood .15 .04
241 Jay Canizaro .15 .04
242 Edwin Corps .15 .04
243 Jacob Cruz .15 .04
244 Joe Fontenot .15 .04
245 Jesse Ibarra .15 .04
246 Dante Powell .15 .04
247 Keith Williams .15 .04
248 Checklist .15 .04
249 Checklist .15 .04
250 Checklist .15 .04
SAMP W.Magee Sample .50 .15

1996 Excel All-Stars

Inserted at a rate of one per 13 packs, these 10 cards feature players who made minor-league all-star teams.

Nm-Mt Ex-Mt
COMPLETE SET (10) 20.00 6.00
1 Jason Kendall 1.50 .45
2 Steve Cox 1.00 .30
3 Adam Riggs 1.00 .30
4 George Arias 1.00 .30
5 Wilton Guerrero 1.00 .30
6 Vladimir Guerrero 5.00 1.50
7 Andruw Jones 4.00 1.20
8 Jay Payton 1.00 .30
9 Raul Ibanez 1.50 .45
10 Paul Wilson 1.00 .30

1996 Excel Climbing

Inserted at a rate of one per six packs, these 10 cards feature players who were making quick progress through a minor league system.

Nm-Mt Ex-Mt
COMPLETE SET (10) 8.00 2.40
1 Jeff Abbott .50 .15
2 Rocky Coppinger .50 .15
3 Brent Crowther .50 .15
4 Rich Hunter .50 .15
5 Chris Latham .50 .15
6 Wendell Magee .50 .15
7 Jay Payton .50 .15

8 Ray Ricken	.50	.15
9 Scott Rolen	3.00	.90
10 Paul Wilson	.50	.15

1996 Excel First Year Phenoms

Inserted a rate of one per three packs, these 10 cards feature players who had made their professional debut in 1995.

	Nm-Mt	Ex-Mt
COMPLETE SET (10)	12.00	3.60
1 Gabe Alvarez	.50	.15
2 Jose Cruz Jr.	2.00	.60
3 Ben Davis	.50	.15
4 Darin Erstad	2.00	.60
5 Todd Helton	2.50	.75
6 Chad Hermansen	.50	.15
7 Geoff Jenkins	1.25	.35
8 Carlton Loewer	.50	.15
9 Shea Morenz	.50	.15
10 Matt Morris	2.50	.75

1996 Excel Season Crowns

Inserted at a rate of one of four packs, these 10 cards feature players who led a minor league in a category in 1995.

	Nm-Mt	Ex-Mt
COMPLETE SET (10)	15.00	4.50
1 Matt Beaumont	.50	.15
2 Bartolo Colon	1.00	.30
3 Matt Drews	.50	.15
4 Derrick Gibson	.50	.15
5 Vladimir Guerrero	5.00	1.50
6 Andruw Jones	4.00	1.20
7 Brandon Reed	.50	.15
8 Glendon Rusch	.50	.15
9 Richie Sexson	1.00	.30
10 Shane Spencer	1.00	.30

1996 Excel Team Leaders

Inserted at a rate of one per 35 packs, these 10 cards feature some leading players for minor league teams.

	Nm-Mt	Ex-Mt
COMPLETE SET (10)	15.00	4.50
1 George Arias	2.00	.60
2 Kevin Coughlin	2.00	.60
3 Wilton Guerrero	2.00	.60
4 Dan Held	2.00	.60
5 Brooks Kieschnick	2.00	.60
6 Wendell Magee	2.00	.60
7 Jason McDonald	2.00	.60
8 Adam Riggs	2.00	.60
9 Juan Thomas	2.00	.60
10 Ron Wright	2.00	.60

1996 Hutchinson Popcorn

This four-card set was distributed one per bag of free popcorn handed out to attendees at the Fred Hutchinson Day Tacoma Rainers ball game in 1996. The set measures approximately 2" by 3" and is a revival of cards distributed in popcorn bags at Sicks' Seattle Stadium from 1954 to 1968. The fronts feature black-and-white photos of Fred Hutchinson at various phases of his career. The backs carry information about the photo.

	Nm-Mt	Ex-Mt
COMPLETE SET (4)	10.00	3.00
COMMON CARD (1-4)	2.50	.75
2 Fred Hutchinson Dick(Kewpie) Barrett Alice Brougham(Mascot)	3.00	.90

1996 Signature Rookies Old Judge

The SR Old Judge T-96 set was issued in one series totalling 38 cards.

	Nm-Mt	Ex-Mt
COMPLETE SET (38)	5.00	1.50
1 Tommy Adams	.25	.07
2 Travis Baptist	.25	.07
3 Mike Birkbeck	.25	.07
4 Jim Bowie	.25	.07
5 Duff Brumley	.25	.07
6 Scott Bullett	.25	.07
7 Frank Catalanotto	.50	.15
8 Chris Cumberland	.25	.07
9 Travis Driskill	.50	.15
10 John Frascatore	.25	.07
11 Brian Giles	1.00	.30
12 Vladimir Guerrero	2.50	.75
13 Butch Huskey	.25	.07
14 Greg Keagle	.25	.07
15 Jay Kirkpatrick	.25	.07
16 Ed Larregui	.25	.07
17 Mitch Lyden	.25	.07
18 T.J. Mathews	.25	.07
19 Brian Maxcy	.25	.07
20 Jeff McNeely	.25	.07
21 Tony Mitchell	.25	.07
22 Kerwin Moore	.25	.07
23 Oscar Munoz	.25	.07
24 Les Norman	.25	.07
25 Jayhawk Owens	.25	.07
26 Mark Petkovsek	.25	.07
27 Hugo Pivaral	.25	.07
28 Chad Renfroe	.25	.07
29 Victor Rodriguez UER Alex Rodriguez pictured	.25	.07
30 Matt Rundels	.25	.07
31 Willie Smith	.25	.07
32 Amaury Telemaco	.25	.07
33 Robert Toth	.25	.07
34 Ben Van Ryn	.25	.07
35 Wes Weger	.25	.07
36 Don Wengert	.25	.07
37 Kelly Wunsch	.25	.07
NNO Checklist	.25	.07

1996 Signature Rookies Old Judge Signatures

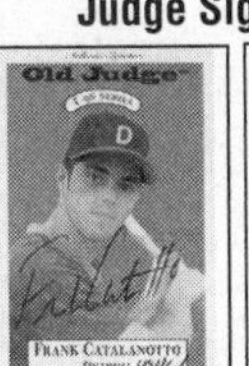

Each card is numbered out of 6000. Vladimir Guerrero and Victor Rodriguez did not sign/return their cards.

	Nm-Mt	Ex-Mt
1 Tommy Adams	2.00	.60
2 Travis Baptist	2.00	.60
3 Mike Birkbeck	2.00	.60
4 Jim Bowie	2.00	.60
5 Duff Brumley	2.00	.60
6 Scott Bullett	2.00	.60
7 Frank Catalanotto	3.00	.90
8 Chris Cumberland	2.00	.60
9 Travis Driskill	3.00	.90
10 John Frascatore	2.00	.60
11 Brian Giles	10.00	3.00
13 Butch Huskey	2.00	.60
14 Greg Keagle	2.00	.60
15 Jay Kirkpatrick	2.00	.60
16 Ed Larregui	2.00	.60
17 Mitch Lyden	2.00	.60
18 T.J. Mathews	2.00	.60
19 Brian Maxcy	2.00	.60
20 Jeff McNeely	2.00	.60
21 Tony Mitchell	2.00	.60
22 Kerwin Moore	2.00	.60
23 Oscar Munoz	2.00	.60
24 Les Norman	2.00	.60
25 Jayhawk Owens	2.00	.60
26 Mark Petkovsek	2.00	.60
27 Hugo Pivaral	2.00	.60
28 Chad Renfroe	2.00	.60
30 Matt Rundels	2.00	.60
31 Willie Smith	2.00	.60
32 Amaury Telemaco	2.00	.60
33 Robert Toth	2.00	.60
34 Ben Van Ryn	2.00	.60
35 Wes Weger	2.00	.60
36 Don Wengert	2.00	.60
37 Kelly Wunsch	2.00	.60

1996 Signature Rookies Old Judge Marty Cordova

This five-card set, featuring 1995 AL Rookie of the Year Marty Cordova, was randomly inserted into packs.

	Nm-Mt	Ex-Mt
COMPLETE SET (5)	2.00	.60
COMMON (RY1-RY5)	.50	.15

1996 Signature Rookies Old Judge Marty Cordova Signatures

Randomly inserted into packs, these five cards feature signatures from Marty Cordova, who earned the 1995 AL Rookie of the Year award.

	Nm-Mt	Ex-Mt
COMMON (RY1-RY5)	3.00	.90

1996 Signature Rookies Old Judge Ken Griffey Jr.

Randomly inserted into packs, these cards feature superstar Ken Griffey Jr.

	Nm-Mt	Ex-Mt
COMMON CARD (J1-J5)	1.00	.30

1996 Signature Rookies Old Judge Ken Griffey Jr. Signatures

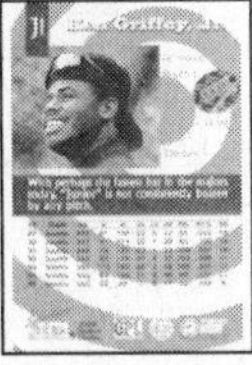

Randomly inserted into packs, these five cards feature signatures of Ken Griffey Jr. These cards have a stated print run of 250 serial numbered sets.

	Nm-Mt	Ex-Mt
COMMON CARD (J1-J5)	80.00	24.00

1996 Signature Rookies Old Judge Major Respect

Randomly inserted into packs, this five-card set features players on the cusp of making it big in the majors.

	Nm-Mt	Ex-Mt
COMPLETE SET (5)	6.00	1.80
M1 Alex Rodriguez	4.00	1.20
M2 Johnny Damon	1.00	.30
M3 Karim Garcia	.50	.15
M4 Garret Anderson	1.00	.30
M5 Bill Pulsipher	.50	.15

1996 Signature Rookies Old Judge Major Respect Signatures

Randomly inserted into packs, these five cards feature not only players who are on the cusp of making it in the majors but also have authentic signatures of those players.

	Nm-Mt	Ex-Mt
M1 Alex Rodriguez	80.00	24.00
M2 Johnny Damon	5.00	1.50
M3 Karim Garcia	2.00	.60
M4 Garret Anderson	10.00	3.00
M5 Bill Pulsipher	2.00	.60

1996 Signature Rookies Old Judge Peak Picks

Randomly inserted in packs, these 10 cards feature some of the leading prospects who had recently been drafted.

	Nm-Mt	Ex-Mt
COMPLETE SET (10)	15.00	4.50
P1 Darin Erstad	2.50	.75
P2 Jose Cruz Jr.	2.00	.60
P3 Jonathan Johnson	.50	.15
P4 Todd Helton	3.00	.90
P5 Matt Morris	3.00	.90
P6 Tony McKnight	.50	.15
P7 Reggie Taylor	.50	.15
P8 David Yocum	.50	.15
P9 Shea Morenz	.50	.15
P10 Ben Davis	.50	.15

1996 Signature Rookies Old Judge Peak Picks Signatures

Randomly inserted into packs, these 10 cards feature not only players who had been recently drafted but also feature authentic signatures of those players.

	Nm-Mt	Ex-Mt
P1 Darin Erstad	8.00	2.40
P2 Jose Cruz Jr.	8.00	2.40
P3 Jonathan Johnson	2.00	.60
P4 Todd Helton	25.00	7.50
P5 Matt Morris	15.00	4.50
P6 Tony McKnight	2.00	.60
P7 Reggie Taylor	5.00	1.50
P8 David Yocum	2.00	.60
P9 Shea Morenz	2.00	.60
P10 Ben Davis	2.00	.60

1996 Signature Rookies Old Judge Rising Stars

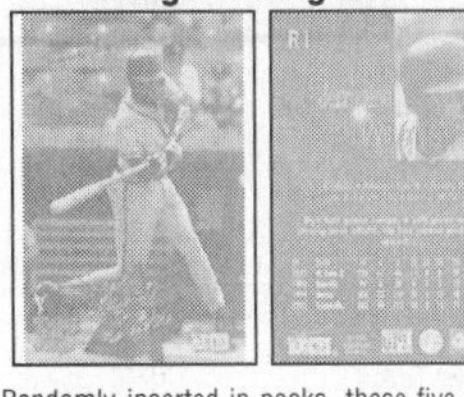

Randomly inserted in packs, these five cards feature players who are making quick progress through the minor leagues.

	Nm-Mt	Ex-Mt
COMPLETE SET (5)	3.00	.90
R1 Jermaine Dye	1.00	.30
R2 Ben Grieve	.50	.15
R3 Ryan Helms	.50	.15
R4 Jeff Darwin	.50	.15
R5 Alan Benes	.50	.15

1996 Signature Rookies Old Judge Rising Stars Signatures

Randomly inserted in packs, these five cards feature not only players making a quick rise through the minors but also authentic autographs of these players.

	Nm-Mt	Ex-Mt
R1 Jermaine Dye	5.00	1.50
R2 Ben Grieve	5.00	1.50
R3 Ryan Helms	2.00	.60
R4 Jeff Darwin	2.00	.60
R5 Alan Benes	2.00	.60

1996 Signature Rookies Old Judge Top Prospect

Randomly inserted into packs, these 10 cards feature players considered to be among the leading prospects in baseball.

	Nm-Mt	Ex-Mt
COMPLETE SET (10)	3.00	.90
T1 Juan Acevedo	.50	.15
T2 Mike Bovee	.25	.07
T3 Mark Hubbard	.25	.07
T4 Luis Raven	.25	.07
T5 Desi Relaford	.50	.15
T6 Antone Williamson	.25	.07
T7 Nick Delvecchio	.25	.07
T8 Andy Larkin	.25	.07
T9 Kris Ralston	.25	.07
T10 Jeff Suppan	.25	.07

1996 Signature Rookies Old Judge Top Prospect Signatures

Randomly inserted into packs, these 10 cards not only feature players considered to be among the leading prospects in baseball but also contain authentic signatures of those players.

	Nm-Mt	Ex-Mt
T1 Juan Acevedo	2.00	.60
T2 Mike Bovee	1.00	.30
T3 Mark Hubbard	1.00	.30
T4 Luis Raven	1.00	.30
T5 Desi Relaford	2.00	.60
T6 Antone Williamson	1.00	.30
T7 Nick Delvecchio	1.00	.30
T8 Andy Larkin	1.00	.30
T9 Kris Ralston	1.00	.30
T10 Jeff Suppan	2.00	.60

1997 Best

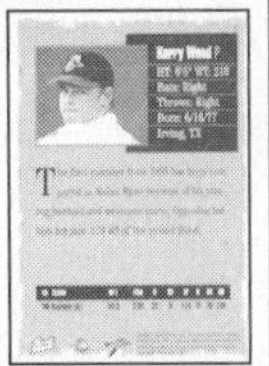

This 100 standard-size set feature leading minor league players. Key cards in this set include Adrian Beltre, Kris Benson, Eric Chavez, Magglio Ordonez, Miguel Tejada and Kerry Wood.

	Nm-Mt	Ex-Mt
COMPLETE SET (100)	20.00	6.00
COMP.PROSPECTS (50)	10.00	3.00
COMP.AUTO.SERIES (50)	10.00	3.00
1 Kerry Wood	4.00	1.20
2 Matt White	.40	.12
3 Travis Lee	.40	.12
4 Miguel Tejada	2.00	.60
5 Kris Benson	.40	.12
6 Paul Konerko	.40	.12
7 Jose Cruz Jr.	.75	.23
8 Derrek Lee	.40	.12
9 Todd Helton	1.00	.30
10 Carl Pavano	.15	.04
11 Ben Grieve	.15	.04
12 Richard Hidalgo	.40	.12
13 Chad Hermansen	.15	.04
14 Jaret Wright	.40	.12
15 Roy Halladay	1.50	.45
16 Hideki Irabu	.40	.12
17 Matt Morris	.40	.12
18 Aramis Ramirez	1.00	.30
19 Robinson Checo	.15	.04
20 Chris Carpenter	.15	.04
21 Adrian Beltre	.75	.23
22 Braden Looper	.15	.04
23 Rolando Arrojo	.15	.04
24 Juan Melo	.15	.04
25 Eli Marrero	.15	.04
26 Kevin McGlinchy	.15	.04
27 Sidney Ponson	.60	.18
28 John Patterson	.40	.12
29 Brian Rose	.15	.04
30 Joe Fontenot	.15	.04
31 Chris Reitsma	.40	.12
32 Paul Wilder	.15	.04
33 Ron Wright	.15	.04
34 A.J. Zapp	.15	.04
35 Donnie Sadler	.15	.04
36 Valerio De Los Santos	.15	.04
37 Eric Chavez	2.00	.60
38 Jake Westbrook	.40	.12
39 Seth Greisinger	.15	.04
40 Derrick Gibson	.15	.04
41 Ben Davis	.15	.04
42 Rafael Medina	.15	.04
43 Britt Reames	.15	.04
44 Ben Petrick	.15	.04
45 Josh Paul	.40	.12
46 Brad Fullmer	.40	.12
47 Jarrod Washburn	.40	.12
48 Kelvim Escobar	.15	.04
49 Manuel Aybar	.15	.04
50 Wes Helms	.15	.04
51 Mike Stoner	.15	.04
52 George Lombard	.15	.04
53 Calvin Pickering	.15	.04
54 Tony Armas Jr.	.40	.12
55 John Barnes	.15	.04
56 Russell Branyan	.15	.04
57 Sean Casey	.40	.12
58 E.Velazquez-Clemente	.15	.04
59 Mike Vavrek	.15	.04
60 Magglio Ordonez	1.00	.30
61 Mike Caruso	.15	.04
62 Pat Cline	.15	.04
63 Courtney Duncan	.15	.04
64 Juan Encarnacion	.15	.04
65 Jason Varitek	.40	.12
66 Alex Gonzalez	.50	.15
67 Ryan Jackson	.15	.04
68 Kevin Miller	.15	.04
69 John Roskos	.15	.04
70 Daryle Ward	.15	.04
71 Dee Brown	.40	.12
72 Ted Lilly	.40	.12
73 Chad Green	.15	.04
74 David Ortiz	1.00	.30
75 Jacque Jones	.60	.18
76 Luis Rivas	.40	.12
77 Orlando Cabrera	.40	.12
78 Javier Vazquez	1.50	.45
79 Jesus Sanchez	.15	.04
80 Eric Milton	.50	.15
81 Ricky Ledee	.40	.12
82 Ramon Hernandez	.15	.04
83 A.J. Hinch	.15	.04
84 Marlon Anderson	.15	.04
85 Ryan Brannan	.15	.04
86 Abraham Nunez	.15	.04
87 Matt Clement	.60	.18
88 Kerry Robinson	.15	.04
89 Cliff Politte	.15	.04
90 Pablo Ortega	.15	.04
91 Aramis Ramirez	1.00	.30
92 Eric Chavez	2.00	.60
93 Brent Butler	.40	.12
94 Cole Liniak	.15	.04
95 Travis Lee	.40	.12
96 Adrian Beltre	.75	.23
97 Paul Konerko	.40	.12
98 Brad Fullmer	.40	.12
99 Jeremy Giambi	.40	.12
100 Gil Meche	.75	.23

1997 Best All-Stars

Inserted at a rate of one per six packs, these 15 cards feature players who made a minor-league all-star team.

	Nm-Mt	Ex-Mt
COMPLETE SET (15)	25.00	7.50
1 Seth Greisinger	1.00	.30
2 Hideki Irabu	1.00	.30
3 Josh Paul	1.00	.30
4 Jaret Wright	1.00	.30
5 Norm Hutchins	1.00	.30
6 Miguel Tejada	4.00	1.20
7 Ruben Mateo	1.00	.30
8 Matt White	1.00	.30
9 Marc Lewis	1.00	.30
10 Jose Cruz Jr.	2.00	.60

11 Quincy Carter .... 2.00 .60
12 Kris Benson .... 1.00 .30
13 Ben Petrick .... 1.00 .30
14 Adrian Beltre .... 1.50 .45
15 Travis Lee .... 1.00 .30

1997 Best Autographs Autograph Series

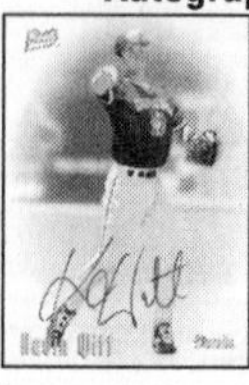

These autograph cards were inserted one per autograph series packs. These cards are unnumbered so we have sequenced them in alphabetical order.

	Nm-Mt	Ex-Mt
1 Israel Alcantara	2.00	.60
2 Richard Almanzar	2.00	.60
3 Marc Barcelo	2.00	.60
4 Tim Belk	2.00	.60
5 Jeremy Blevins	2.00	.60
6 James Bonnici	2.00	.60
7 Homer Bush	2.00	.60
8 Davey Coggin	2.00	.60
9 Bartolo Colon	3.00	.90
10 Lee Daniels	2.00	.60
11 Ryan Dempster	3.00	.90
12 Lino Diaz	2.00	.60
13 Tom Fordham	2.00	.60
14 Ben Grieve	3.00	.90
15 Mike Gulan	2.00	.60
16 Ryan Hancock	2.00	.60
17 Wes Helms	2.00	.60
18 Brett Herbison	2.00	.60
19 Chad Hermansen	2.00	.60
20 Damon Hollins	2.00	.60
21 Ryan Jaroncyk	2.00	.60
22 Geoff Jenkins	3.00	.90
23 Earl Johnson	2.00	.60
24 Andre King	2.00	.60
25 Paul Konerko	3.00	.90
26 Todd Landry	2.00	.60
27 Jeff Liefer	2.00	.60
28 Mendy Lopez	2.00	.60
29 Roberto Lopez	2.00	.60
30 Johnny Martinez	2.00	.60
31 Mike Maurer	2.00	.60
32 Brian Meadows	2.00	.60
33 Doug Mlicki	2.00	.60
34 Tony Mounce	2.00	.60
35 Sergio Nunez	2.00	.60
36 Russ Ortiz	3.00	.90
37 Carey Paige	2.00	.60
38 Jay Payton	2.00	.60
39 Ben Petrick	2.00	.60
40 Tommy Phelps	2.00	.60
41 Hugo Pivaral	2.00	.60
42 Angel Ramirez	2.00	.60
43 Gary Rath	2.00	.60
44 Mark Redman	3.00	.90
45 Adam Riggs	2.00	.60
46 Lonell Roberts	2.00	.60
47 Glendon Rusch	3.00	.90
48 Matt Ryan	2.00	.60
49 Donnie Sadler	2.00	.60
50 William Santamaria	2.00	.60
51 Todd Schmitt	2.00	.60
52 Richie Sexson	8.00	2.40
53 Alvie Sheperd	2.00	.60
54 Steve Shoemaker	2.00	.60
55 Brian Sikorski	2.00	.60
56 Randall Simon	3.00	.90
57 Bobby Smith	2.00	.60
58 Matt Smith	2.00	.60
59 Jose Texidor	2.00	.60
60 Jason Thompson	2.00	.60
61 Mike Thurman	2.00	.60
62 Brett Tomko	3.00	.90
63 Hector Trinidad	2.00	.60
64 Andrew Vessel	2.00	.60
65 Jacob Viano	2.00	.60
66 Jarrod Washburn	3.00	.90
67 Travis Welch	2.00	.60
68 Casey Whitten	2.00	.60
69 Shad Williams	2.00	.60
70 Paul Wilson	2.00	.60
71 Preston Wilson	5.00	1.50
72 Randy Winn	3.00	.90
73 Kevin Witt	2.00	.60

1997 Best Autographs Prospect Series

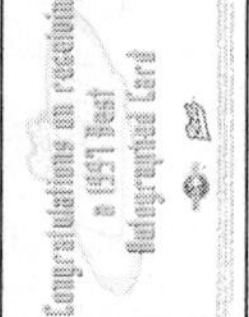

Inserte at a rate of one every 19 packs, these cards feature some of the leading prospects,.

	Nm-Mt	Ex-Mt
H1 Ben Grieve	3.00	.90
H2 Wes Helms	2.00	.60
H3 Brett Herbison	2.00	.60
H4 Chad Hermansen	2.00	.60
H5 Geoff Jenkins	3.00	.90
H6 Paul Konerko	3.00	.90
H7 Ben Petrick	2.00	.60
H8 Donnie Sadler	2.00	.60
H9 Randall Simon	3.00	.90
H10 Brett Tomko	3.00	.90
R1 Richard Almanzar	2.00	.60
R2 Tim Belk	2.00	.60
R3 Homer Bush	2.00	.60
R4 Bartolo Colon	3.00	.90
R5 Tom Fordham	2.00	.60
R6 Damon Hollins	2.00	.60
R7 Mendy Lopez	2.00	.60
R8 Doug Mlicki	2.00	.60
R9 Jay Payton	2.00	.60
R10 Mark Redman	3.00	.90
R11 Adam Riggs	2.00	.60
R12 Lonell Roberts	2.00	.60
R13 Glendon Rusch	3.00	.90
R14 Richie Sexson	8.00	2.40
R15 Alvie Shepherd	2.00	.60
R16 Mike Thurman	2.00	.60
R17 Andrew Vessel	2.00	.60
R18 Casey Whitten	2.00	.60
R19 Preston Wilson	5.00	1.50

1997 Best Bets Preview

These cards were inserted at a rate of one per 90 packs and feature players who seem closest to playing in the major leagues.

	Nm-Mt	Ex-Mt
COMPLETE SET (10)	60.00	18.00
1 Miguel Tejada	15.00	4.50
2 Adrian Beltre	6.00	1.80
3 Hideki Irabu	4.00	1.20
4 Kris Benson	4.00	1.20
5 Matt White	4.00	1.20
6 Travis Lee	4.00	1.20
7 Corey Erickson	4.00	1.20
8 Jose Cruz Jr.	6.00	1.80
9 Marc Lewis	4.00	1.20
10 Rolando Arrojo	4.00	1.20

1997 Best Case Topper

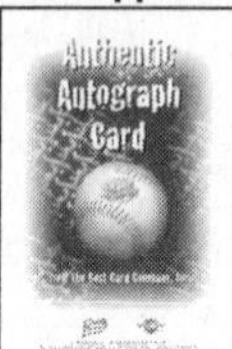

These 4" by 6" over-sized cards were distributed one per 1998 Best Signature Series hobby case. The cards were packed on top of the sealed boxes but within the sealed case. Each card is serial-numbered to 500 on front and carries the text "Auto Best" in cursive silver lettering.

	Nm-Mt	Ex-Mt
1 Kris Benson	4.00	1.20
2 Sean Casey Akron	4.00	1.20
3 Sean Casey Buffalo	4.00	1.20
4 Seth Greisinger	4.00	1.20
5 Ben Grieve	4.00	1.20
6 Chad Hermansen	4.00	1.20
7 Paul Konerko	4.00	1.20
8 Britt Reames	4.00	1.20
9 Jake Westbrook	4.00	1.20
10 Paul Wilder	4.00	1.20
11 Kerry Wood	25.00	7.50
12 A.J. Zapp	4.00	1.20

1997 Best Cornerstone

Inserted at a rate of one in 49 auto series cards, these 12 cards feature players who promise to be the future cornerstones of their major league teams.

	Nm-Mt	Ex-Mt
COMPLETE SET (12)	50.00	15.00
1 Travis Lee	3.00	.90
2 Adrian Beltre	6.00	1.80
3 Ben Grieve	2.00	.60
4 Paul Konerko	3.00	.90
5 Ricky Ledee	3.00	.90
6 Brad Fullmer	3.00	.90
7 Alex Gonzalez	4.00	1.20
8 Russell Branyan	2.00	.60
9 Eric Milton	5.00	1.50
10 Jaret Wright	3.00	.90
11 Derrek Lee	3.00	.90
12 Kris Benson	3.00	.90

1997 Best Diamond Best

Inserted at a rate of one in 19 prospect hobby packs and one in 25 auto series packs, these cards feature 20 of the leading minor league prospects.

	Nm-Mt	Ex-Mt
COMP.PROSP.SER.(10)	60.00	18.00
COMP.AUTO.SER. (10)	40.00	12.00
1 Hideki Irabu	1.00	.30
2 Kerry Wood	12.00	3.60
3 Matt White	1.00	.30
4 Travis Lee	1.00	.30
5 Miguel Tejada	8.00	2.40
6 Kris Benson	1.00	.30
7 Paul Konerko	1.00	.30
8 Jose Cruz Jr.	4.00	1.20
9 Derrek Lee	1.00	.30
10 Todd Helton	5.00	1.50
11 Dee Brown	1.00	.30
12 Aramis Ramirez	5.00	1.50
13 Ramon Hernandez	1.00	.30
14 Eric Chavez	6.00	1.80
15 A.J. Zapp	1.00	.30
16 A.J. Hinch	1.00	.30
17 Juan Melo	1.00	.30
18 Cole Liniak	1.00	.30
19 David Ortiz	5.00	1.50
20 Russell Branyan	1.00	.30

1997 Best Five

These five cards, which feature some of the leading minor league prospects of 1997, were inserted at a rate of one per prospects hobby box.

	Nm-Mt	Ex-Mt
COMPLETE SET (5)	15.00	4.50
1 Kris Benson	1.00	.30
2 Kerry Wood	10.00	3.00
3 Travis Lee	1.00	.30
4 Hideki Irabu	1.00	.30
5 Matt White	1.00	.30

1997 Best Full Count Autographs

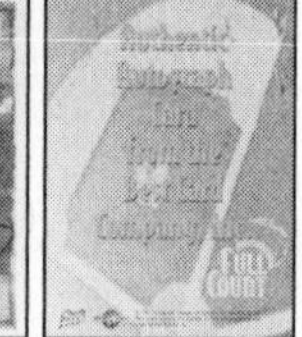

These cards were randomly seeded into packs of 1998 Best Signature Series baseball. The cards are copyrighted as 1997 issues and share the exact same front design as the basic 1997 Best cards. In all likelihood, there may've been complications or delays to finish these cards in time for the 1997 packout and they were thrown into 1998 packs rather than being destroyed, sitting in a warehouse forever or being sold individually by the manufacturer. In addition, a standard-sized mail-in offer card featuring a copy of Kerry Wood's 1997 Full Count autograph on front (whereby the collector could obtain the featured card for $49.99) was made available.

	Nm-Mt	Ex-Mt
1 Kris Benson	3.00	.90
2 Dee Brown	3.00	.90
3 Eric Chavez	15.00	4.50
4 Chad Green	2.00	.60
5 Ben Grieve	3.00	.90
6 Todd Helton	25.00	7.50
7 Chad Hermansen	2.00	.60
8 Paul Konerko	3.00	.90
9 Mark Kotsay	3.00	.90
10 Braden Looper	2.00	.60
11 Gil Meche	8.00	2.40
12 Juan Melo	2.00	.60
13 Eric Milton	8.00	2.40
14 Abraham Nunez	2.00	.60
15 John Patterson	3.00	.90
16 Carl Pavano	3.00	.90
17 Sidney Ponson	5.00	1.50
18 Aramis Ramirez	8.00	2.40
19 Britt Reames	2.00	.60
20 Kerry Robinson	2.00	.60
21 Jake Westbrook	3.00	.90
22 Paul Wilder	2.00	.60
23 Kerry Wood	30.00	9.00
24 A.J. Zapp	2.00	.60
NNO K. Wood Mail-In Offer	.50	.15

1997 Best Guns

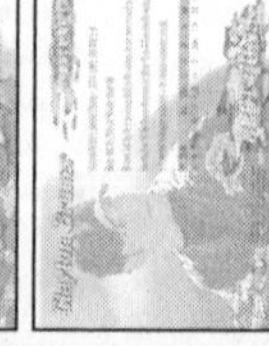

Inserted one per retail box, these five cards featue leading pitching prospects.

	Nm-Mt	Ex-Mt
COMPLETE SET (10)	20.00	6.00
1 Robinson Checo	1.00	.30
2 Rolando Arrojo	1.00	.30
3 Clayton Bruner	1.00	.30
4 Grant Roberts	1.00	.30
5 Brian Rose	1.00	.30
6 Carl Pavano	1.00	.30
7 Kerry Wood	10.00	3.00
8 Kris Benson	1.00	.30
9 Jaret Wright	1.00	.30
10 Cliff Politte	1.00	.30

1997 Best International Best

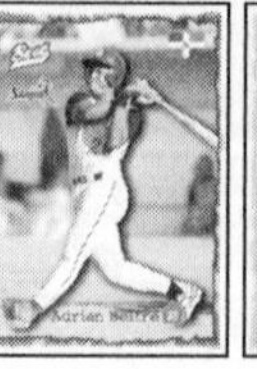
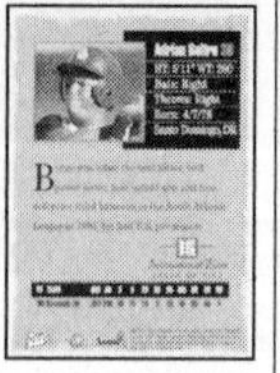

Inserted one per sealed hobby boxes that were produced late in the Best run, these five cards feature leading prospects born in various foreign countries.

	Nm-Mt	Ex-Mt
COMPLETE SET (5)	15.00	4.50
IB1 Miguel Tejada	8.00	2.40
IB2 Hideki Irabu	1.00	.30
IB3 Adrian Beltre	3.00	.90
IB4 Rolando Arrojo	1.00	.30
IB5 Robinson Checo	1.00	.30

1997 Best Limited Autographs

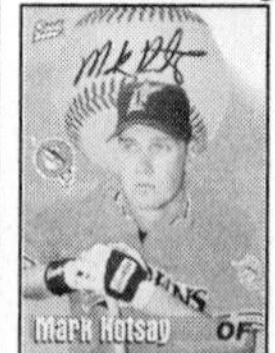

These signed cards were randomly inserted into autograph series packs. Since these cards are unnumbered we have sequenced them in alphabetical order. These cards are serial numbered to 250.

	Nm-Mt	Ex-Mt
1 Richard Almanzar	8.00	2.40
2 Kris Benson	10.00	3.00
3 Darin Blood	8.00	2.40
4 Adrian Brown	8.00	2.40
5 Dee Brown	10.00	3.00
6 Kevin Brown	8.00	2.40
7 Eric Chavez	40.00	12.00
8 D.T. Cromer	8.00	2.40
9 Lorenzo De La Cruz	8.00	2.40
10 Adam Eaton	10.00	3.00
11 Nelson Figueroa	10.00	3.00
12 Juan E.Gonzalez	8.00	2.40
13 Chad Green	8.00	2.40
14 Seth Greisinger	8.00	2.40
15 Ben Grieve	10.00	3.00
16 Matt Halloran	8.00	2.40
17 Chad Hermansen	8.00	2.40
18 Mark Johnson	8.00	2.40
19 Billy Koch	10.00	3.00
20 Paul Konerko	10.00	3.00
21 Mark Kotsay	10.00	3.00
22 Joe Lawrence	10.00	3.00
23 Braden Looper	8.00	2.40
24 Gil Meche	20.00	6.00
25 Eric Milton	20.00	6.00
26 Abraham Nunez	8.00	2.40
27 John Oliver	8.00	2.40
28 Russ Ortiz	10.00	3.00
29 John Patterson	10.00	3.00
30 Carl Pavano	10.00	3.00
31 Elvis Pena	8.00	2.40
32 Danny Peoples	8.00	2.40
33 Neifi Perez	10.00	3.00
34 Sidney Ponson	20.00	6.00
35 Aramis Ramirez	25.00	7.50
36 Britt Reames	8.00	2.40
37 Kerry Robinson	8.00	2.40
38 Bubba Trammell	10.00	3.00
39 Mike Villano	8.00	2.40
40 Jake Westbrook	10.00	3.00
41 Paul Wilder	8.00	2.40
42 Enrique Wilson	8.00	2.40
43 Kerry Wood	60.00	18.00
44 A.J. Zapp	8.00	2.40
AJ Andruw Jones	25.00	7.50

1997 Best Lumber

Inserted at a rate of one per 90 prospects retail packs, these 10 cards feature some of the leading minor league hitters.

	Nm-Mt	Ex-Mt
COMPLETE SET (10)	80.00	24.00
1 Adrian Beltre	8.00	2.40
2 Russell Branyan	4.00	1.20
3 Derrek Lee	5.00	1.50
4 Brad Fullmer	5.00	1.50
5 Ben Grieve	4.00	1.20
6 Mike Stoner	4.00	1.20
7 A.J. Hinch	4.00	1.20
8 Paul Konerko	5.00	1.50
9 Ricky Ledee	5.00	1.50
10 Travis Lee	5.00	1.50

1997 Best Premium Autographs

These cards are unnumbered and checklisted below alphabetically by last name. The cards were inserted in retail boxes only, and are serial

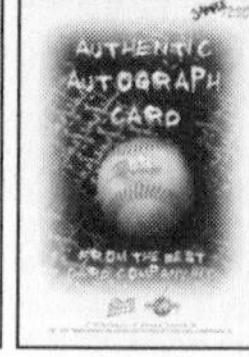

numbered to 250.

	Nm-Mt	Ex-Mt
1 Richard Almanzar	5.00	1.50
2 Kris Benson	8.00	2.40
3 Darin Blood	5.00	1.50
4 Adrian Brown	5.00	1.50
5 Dee Brown	8.00	2.40
6 Kevin Brown C	5.00	1.50
7 Eric Chavez	25.00	7.50
8 D.T. Cromer	5.00	1.50
9 Lorenzo DeLeCruz	5.00	1.50
10 Adam Eaton	8.00	2.40
11 Nelson Figueroa	8.00	2.40
12 Juan E.Gonzalez	5.00	1.50
13 Chad Green	5.00	1.50
14 Seth Greisinger	5.00	1.50
15 Ben Grieve	8.00	2.40
16 Matt Halloran	5.00	1.50
17 Chad Hermansen	5.00	1.50
18 Mark Johnson	5.00	1.50
19 Billy Koch	8.00	2.40
20 Paul Konerko	8.00	2.40
21 Mark Kotsay	8.00	2.40
22 Joe Lawrence	8.00	2.40
23 Braden Looper	5.00	1.50
24 Kevin McGlinchy	5.00	1.50
25 Gil Meche	12.00	3.60
26 Juan Melo	5.00	1.50
27 Eric Milton	12.00	3.60
28 John Nicholson	5.00	1.50
29 Todd Noel	5.00	1.50
30 Abraham Nunez	5.00	1.50
31 Russ Ortiz	8.00	2.40
32 Yudith Ozario	5.00	1.50
33 John Patterson	8.00	2.40
34 Carl Pavano	8.00	2.40
35 Elvis Pena	5.00	1.50
36 Danny Peoples	5.00	1.50
37 Neifi Perez	8.00	2.40
38 Sidney Ponson	12.00	3.60
39 Aramis Ramirez	15.00	4.50
40 Britt Reames	5.00	1.50
41 Kerry Robinson	5.00	1.50
42 Jeff Sexton	5.00	1.50
43 Bubba Trammell	8.00	2.40
44 Mike Villano	5.00	1.50
45 Jake Westbrook	8.00	2.40
46 Paul Wilder	5.00	1.50
47 Enrique Wilson	5.00	1.50
48 Kerry Wood	40.00	12.00
49 A.J. Zapp	5.00	1.50

1997 Best Premium Preview

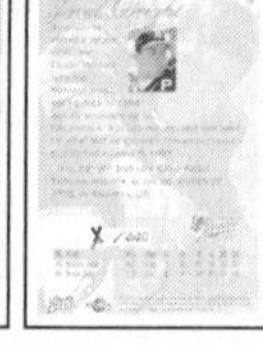

Inserted one per auto series box these cards have a stated print run of 200 serial numbered sets.

	Nm-Mt	Ex-Mt
COMPLETE SET (50)	150.00	45.00
1 Jaret Wright	4.00	1.20
2 Damian Jackson	2.50	.75
3 Kerry Wood	20.00	6.00
4 Adrian Beltre	8.00	2.40
5 Sean Casey	4.00	1.20
6 Paul Konerko	4.00	1.20
7 Ben Grieve	2.50	.75
8 Hideki Irabu	4.00	1.20
9 Rolando Arrojo	2.50	.75
10 Robinson Checo	2.50	.75
11 Donnie Sadler	2.50	.75
12 Todd Helton	15.00	4.50
13 Jose Cruz Jr.	6.00	1.80
14 Ricky Ledee	4.00	1.20
15 Calvin Pickering	2.50	.75
16 Alex Gonzalez	5.00	1.50
17 Alvie Shepherd	2.50	.75
18 Michael Coleman	2.50	.75
19 Derrek Lee	4.00	1.20
20 Brad Fullmer	4.00	1.20
21 Derrick Gibson	2.50	.75
22 A.J. Hinch	2.50	.75
23 Juan Melo	2.50	.75
24 David Ortiz	8.00	2.40
25 Ramon Hernandez	2.50	.75
26 Mike Stoner	2.50	.75
27 George Lombard	2.50	.75
28 Chad Hermansen	2.50	.75
29 Mark Fischer	2.50	.75
30 Trot Nixon	4.00	1.20
31 Kevin Nicholson	2.50	.75
32 Kevin Millar	8.00	2.40
33 John Roskos	2.50	.75
34 Aramis Ramirez	8.00	2.40
35 Randall Simon	4.00	1.20
36 Carl Pavano	2.50	.75
37 Brian Rose	2.50	.75
38 Enrique Wilson	2.50	.75
39 Russell Branyan	2.50	.75
40 Chan Perry	2.50	.75
41 Juan Encarnacion	2.50	.75
42 Grant Roberts	4.00	1.20
43 Marlon Anderson	2.50	.75
44 Matt White	4.00	1.20
45 Jason Varitek	4.00	1.20
46 Cole Liniak	2.50	.75

	Nm-Mt	Ex-Mt
47 Roy Halladay	12.00	3.60
48 Maggio Ordonez	8.00	2.40
49 Richie Sexson	4.00	1.20
50 Travis Lee	4.00	1.20

1997 Best Wheels

Issued one per retail prospects packs, these five cards feature some of the leading speedsters in the minor leagues.

	Nm-Mt	Ex-Mt
COMPLETE SET (5)	6.00	1.80
1 Donnie Sadler	1.00	.30
2 Juan Encarnacion	1.00	.30
3 Damian Jackson	1.00	.30
4 Chad Green	1.00	.30
5 Mark Kotsay	1.00	.30

1997 Best Carolina Classic Show Promos

This 10-card set features card fronts adapted from the 1997 Best minor league regular issue set and Diamond Best inserts with the addition of show sponsor Tuff Stuff's logo. The backs feature the show logo and date. Each card is numbered out of 10, and individually hand numbered out of 1000. The cards were distributed via wrapper redemption at the show held Oct. 17-19, 1997.

	Nm-Mt	Ex-Mt
COMPLETE SET (10)	50.00	15.00
1 Travis Lee	10.00	3.00
2 Jose Cruz Jr.	8.00	2.40
3 Ben Grieve	10.00	3.00
4 Todd Helton DB	8.00	2.40
5 Travis Lee DB	8.00	2.40
6 Kerry Wood	8.00	2.40
7 Hideki Irabu	3.00	.90
8 Matt White	2.00	.60
9 Jaret Wright	2.00	.60
10 Derrek Lee DB	4.00	1.20

1997 Hutchinson Popcorn

This four-card set was distributed one per bag of free popcorn handed out to attendees at the Fred Hutchinson Day Tacoma Rainers ball game in 1997. The set measures approximately 2" by 3" and is a revival of cards distributed in popcorn bags at Sicks' Seattle Stadium from 1954 to 1968. The fronts feature black-and-white photos of Fred Hutchinson at various phases of his career. The backs carry information about the photo.

	Nm-Mt	Ex-Mt
COMPLETE SET (4)	10.00	3.00
COMMON CARD (1-4)	2.50	.75

1998 Best Promos Player of the Year

These five cards were issued to promote the 1998 Best Player of the Year product.

	Nm-Mt	Ex-Mt
COMPLETE SET (5)	4.00	1.20
NNO T.Helton POY Cont.	1.50	.45
NNO Paul Konerko POY	.50	.15
NNO M.Kotsay Diam.Best	.50	.15
NNO Darnell McDonald	.50	.15
NNO K.Wood Possibilities	1.00	.30

1998 Best Promos Signature Series

Cards are unnumbered and checklisted below in alphabetical order.

	Nm-Mt	Ex-Mt
COMPLETE SET (5)	8.00	2.40
1 Rick Ankiel Diam.Best	1.50	.45
2 Bruce Chen	.50	.15
3 J.D. Drew No.1 Pick	1.50	.45
4 Troy Glaus No.1 Pick	4.00	1.20
5 Ryan Minor Cornerstone	.50	.15

1998 Best

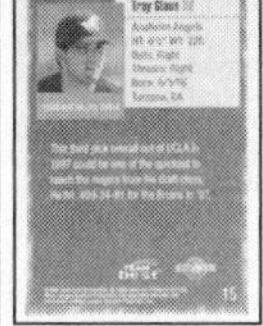

These 100 cards were issued over two series. Cards number 1 through 50 were issued in Player of the Year packs and cards numbered 51-100 were issued in signature series packs. Early cards of Rick Ankiel, J.D. Drew and Troy Glaus are featured in this set.

	Nm-Mt	Ex-Mt
COMPLETE SET (100)	30.00	9.00
COMP.POY SET (50)	10.00	3.00
COMP.SIG.SER.SET (50)	20.00	6.00
1 Ryan Anderson	.40	.12
2 Lorenzo Barcelo	.15	.04
3 Hiram Bocachica	.15	.04
4 Dave Borkowski	.15	.04
5 Russ Branyan	.15	.04
6 Dermal Brown	.15	.04
7 Brent Butler	.15	.04
8 Enrique Calero	.15	.04
9 Bruce Chen	.15	.04
10 Ryan Christenson	.15	.04
11 Pat Cline	.15	.04
12 Scott Elarton	.15	.04
13 Mario Encarnacion	.15	.04
14 Mark Fischer	.15	.04
15 Troy Glaus	2.00	.60
16 Alex Hernandez	.15	.04
17 Norm Hutchins	.15	.04
18 Geoff Jenkins	.40	.12
19 Adam Kennedy	.15	.04
20 Corey Koskie	.40	.12
21 Mark Kotsay	.15	.04
22 Ricky Ledee	.15	.04
23 Carlos Lee	.50	.15
24 Corey Lee	.15	.04
25 Mike Lowell	1.00	.30
26 T.R. Marcinczyk	.15	.04
27 Willie Martinez	.15	.04
28 Darnell McDonald	.40	.12
29 Jackson Melian	.40	.12
30 Chad Meyers	.15	.04
31 Ryan Minor	.15	.04
32 Kenderick Moore	.15	.04
33 Julio Moreno	.15	.04
34 Rod Myers	.15	.04
35 Abraham Nunez	.15	.04
36 Vladimir Nunez	.15	.04
37 Ramon Ortiz	.40	.12
38 Chan Perry	.15	.04
39 Ben Petrick	.15	.04
40 Aramis Ramirez	.40	.12
41 Grant Roberts	.15	.04
42 Alex Sanchez	.15	.04
43 Jared Sandberg	.15	.04
44 Scott Schoeneweis	.15	.04
45 Steve Shoemaker	.15	.04
46 Matt White	.40	.12
47 Paul Wilder	.15	.04
48 Preston Wilson	.40	.12
49 Kevin Witt	.15	.04
50 Jay Yennaco	.15	.04
51 Matt Anderson	.40	.12
52 Rick Ankiel	.40	.12
53 Tony Armas Jr.	.40	.12
54 John Barnes	.15	.04
55 Robbie Bell	.15	.04
56 Kris Benson	.15	.04
57 Lance Berkman	.40	.12
58 Russell Branyan	.15	.04
59 Brent Butler	.15	.04
60 Troy Cameron	.15	.04
61 Eric Chavez	.40	.12
62 Bruce Chen	.15	.04
63 Matt Clement	.40	.12
64 Ben Davis	.15	.04
65 J.D. Drew	1.25	.35
66 Tim Drew	.15	.04
67 Derrick Gibson	.15	.04
68 Troy Glaus	2.00	.60
69 Chad Hermansen	.15	.04
70 Ramon Hernandez	.15	.04
71 Gabe Kapler	.40	.12
72 Mike Kinkade	.15	.04
73 Scott Krause	.15	.04
74 Mike Lowell	1.00	.30
75 Willie Martinez	.15	.04
76 Donzell McDonald	.15	.04
77 Gil Meche	.40	.12
78 Juan Melo	.15	.04
79 Wade Miller	.60	.18
80 Ryan Minor	.15	.04
81 Abraham Nunez	.15	.04
82 Pablo Ozuna	.15	.04
83 John Patterson	.15	.04
84 Josh Paul	.15	.04
85 Ben Petrick	.15	.04
86 Calvin Pickering	.15	.04
87 Placido Polanco	.40	.12
88 Aramis Ramirez	.40	.12
89 Julio Ramirez	.15	.04
90 Luis Rivas	.40	.12
91 Luis Rivera	.15	.04
92 Ruben Rivera	.15	.04
93 Grant Roberts	.15	.04
94 Jimmy Rollins	.60	.18
95 Bobby Seay	.40	.12
96 Jason Standridge	.15	.04
97 Dernell Stenson	.40	.12
98 Vernon Wells	.40	.12
99 Matt White	.40	.12
100 Ed Yarnall	.15	.04

1998 Best Autographs Player of the Year

Inserted at a rate of one per 19 Player of the Year hobby packs, these 22 cards feature some of the leading minor league prospects. It's believed that the Adam Eaton card was distributed in Signature Series packs but hails from the Player of the Year set.

	Nm-Mt	Ex-Mt
1 Kris Benson	5.00	1.50
2 Dermal Brown	3.00	.90
3 Eric Chavez	10.00	3.00
4 Adam Eaton	3.00	.90
5 Chad Green	3.00	.90
6 Seth Greisinger	3.00	.90
7 Ben Grieve	5.00	1.50
8 Chad Hermansen	3.00	.90
9 Billy Koch	5.00	1.50
10 Braden Looper	3.00	.90
11 Gil Meche	8.00	2.40
12 Eric Milton	3.00	.90
13 John Patterson	3.00	.90
14 Carl Pavano	5.00	1.50
15 Danny Peoples	3.00	.90
16 Sidney Ponson	5.00	1.50
17 Brian Rose	3.00	.90
18 Bubba Trammell '96 Design	3.00	.90
19 Jake Westbrook	3.00	.90
20 Paul Wilder	3.00	.90
21 Kerry Wood	25.00	7.50
22 A.J. Zapp	3.00	.90

1998 Best Autographs Signature Series

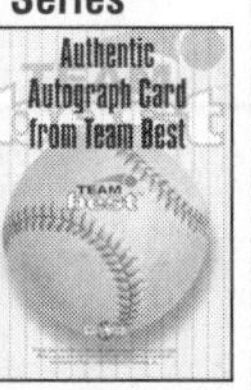

Issued at an approximate rate of five autographs per signature series hobby boxes and one autograph per retail box, these cards feature signed cards of leading prospects. The first certified autograph card of Troy Glaus is featured in this set. A Brian Rose card surfaced in the secondary market featuring an alternate front-card design yet with the same beige background tones and linear pinstripes.

	Nm-Mt	Ex-Mt
1 John Bale	2.50	.75
2 Kevin Barker	2.50	.75
3 Todd Belitz	2.50	.75
4 Aaron Bond	2.50	.75
5 A.J. Burnett	5.00	1.50
6 Brent Butler	2.50	.75
7 Buddy Carlyle	2.50	.75
8 Ramon Castro	2.50	.75
9 Frank Catalanotto	4.00	1.20
10 Giuseppe Chiaramonte	2.50	.75
11 Alex Cora	4.00	1.20
12 Francisco Cordero	4.00	1.20
13 David Cortes	2.50	.75
14 Dean Crow	2.50	.75
15 Doug Davis	4.00	1.20
16 Glenn Davis	2.50	.75
17 Gookie Dawkins	2.50	.75
18 Matt DeWitt	2.50	.75
19 Octavio Dotel	4.00	1.20
20 Mike Duvall	2.50	.75
21 Troy Glaus	20.00	6.00
22 Geoff Goetz	2.50	.75
23 Jason Grilli	2.50	.75
24 Al Hawkins	2.50	.75
25 Bryan Hebson	2.50	.75
26 Alex Hernandez	2.50	.75
27 Doug Johnston	2.50	.75
28 Juan Lebron	2.50	.75
29 John Leroy	2.50	.75
30 Randi Mallard	2.50	.75
31 Sam Marsonek	2.50	.75
32 Ramon E.Martinez	2.50	.75
33 Ruben Mateo	4.00	1.20
34 Joe Mays	4.00	1.20
35 David Melendez	2.50	.75
36 Justin Miller	2.50	.75
37 Ryan Minor	2.50	.75
38 Warren Morris	2.50	.75
39 Pablo Ozuna	2.50	.75
40 Brian Passini	2.50	.75
41 Santiago Perez	2.50	.75
42 Marc Pisciotta	2.50	.75
43 Rob Ramsay	2.50	.75
44 Grant Roberts	2.50	.75
45 John Roskos	2.50	.75
46 Luis de los Santos	2.50	.75
47 Brian Simmons	2.50	.75
48 Reggie Taylor	2.50	.75
49 Andy Thompson	2.50	.75
50 Chris Tynan	2.50	.75
51 Jose Vidro	5.00	1.50
52 Jayson Werth	2.50	.75
53 Ed Yarnall	2.50	.75
NNO Brian Rose Alternate Front	2.50	.75

1998 Best Bets

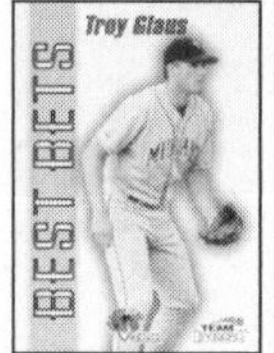

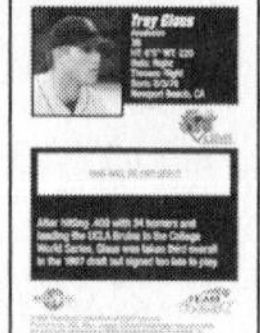

Inserted one every 90 retail packs, these 12 cards are unnumbered and checklisted below in alphabetical order.

	Nm-Mt	Ex-Mt
COMPLETE SET (12)	60.00	18.00
1 Matt Anderson	5.00	1.50
2 Lance Berkman	5.00	1.50
3 Eric Chavez	5.00	1.50
4 Bruce Chen	3.00	.90
5 Matt Clement	5.00	1.50
6 J.D. Drew	8.00	2.40
7 Troy Glaus	10.00	3.00
8 George Lombard	3.00	.90
9 Ryan Minor	3.00	.90
10 Dernell Stenson	5.00	1.50
11 Jayson Werth	3.00	.90
12 Ed Yarnall	3.00	.90

1998 Best Cornerstone

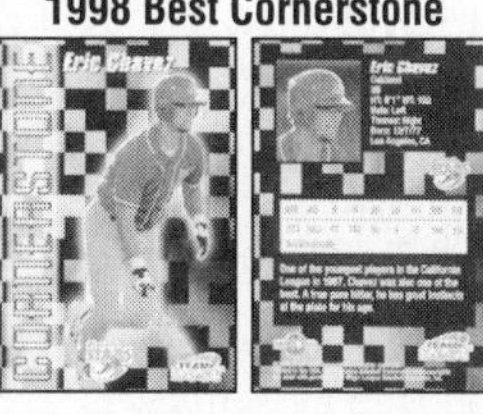

Issued at a rate of one every 90 signature series hobby packs, these 12 cards feature players believed to be the key player in their minor league system.

	Nm-Mt	Ex-Mt
COMPLETE SET (12)	60.00	18.00
1 Matt Anderson	5.00	1.50
2 Lance Berkman	5.00	1.50
3 Eric Chavez	5.00	1.50
4 Bruce Chen	5.00	1.50
5 Matt Clement	5.00	1.50
6 J.D. Drew	8.00	2.40
7 Troy Glaus	10.00	3.00
8 George Lombard	5.00	1.50
9 Ryan Minor	5.00	1.50
10 Dernell Stenson	5.00	1.50
11 Jayson Werth	5.00	1.50
12 Ed Yarnall	5.00	1.50

1998 Best Diamond Best

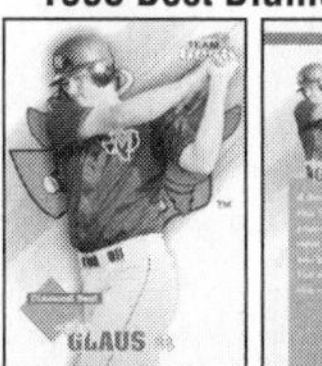

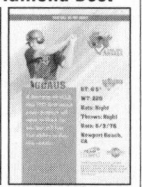

Inserted at a rate of one in 19 hobby packs in either series, these 20 cards feature some of the leading prospects in the minors. Cards numbered 1-10 were included in the POY hobby packs and cards numbered 11-20 were included in signature series packs.

	Nm-Mt	Ex-Mt
COMP.POY SET (10)	30.00	9.00
COMP.SIG.SER.SET (10)	50.00	15.00
1 Darnell McDonald	2.00	.60
2 Adrian Beltre	2.00	.60
3 Derrick Gibson	1.00	.30
4 Mark Kotsay	1.00	.30
5 Braden Looper	1.00	.30
6 Carl Pavano	1.00	.30
7 Brian Rose	1.00	.30
8 Jared Sandberg	1.00	.30
9 Vernon Wells	2.00	.60
10 Sean Casey	2.00	.60
11 Rick Ankiel	2.00	.60
12 Michael Barrett	1.00	.30
13 Matt Clement	2.00	.60
14 J.D. Drew	5.00	1.50
15 Bobby Estalella	2.00	.60
16 Troy Glaus	8.00	2.40
17 Alex Gonzalez	1.00	.30
18 George Lombard	1.00	.30
19 Mike Lowell	5.00	1.50
20 Dernell Stenson	2.00	.60

1998 Best Diamond Best Autographs

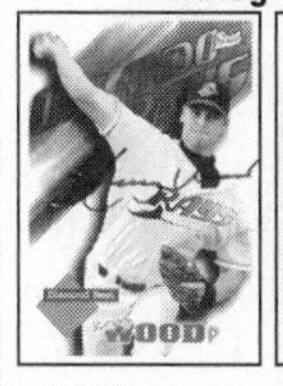

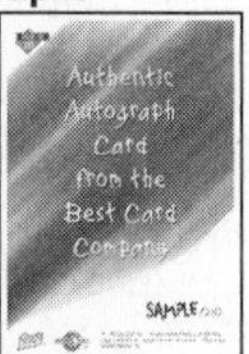

Inserted at a rate of one every 180 player of the year hobby packs, these eight cards feature signed cards of the diamond best cards. Cards numbered 5 and 6 do not exist. These cards have a stated print run of 250 sets.

	Nm-Mt	Ex-Mt
1 Kris Benson	10.00	3.00
2 Dermal Brown	10.00	3.00
3 Eric Chavez	15.00	4.50
4 Todd Helton	25.00	7.50
7 Braden Looper	10.00	3.00
8 Juan Melo	10.00	3.00
9 Kerry Wood	30.00	9.00
10 A.J. Zapp	10.00	3.00

1998 Best Paul Konerko

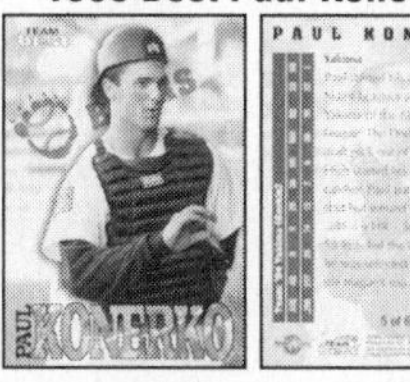

Inserted at a rate of one every 36 player of the year packs, this six card set features leading prospect Paul Konerko. Thre are also autograph parallels of these cards issued, these cards were random inserts in player of the year packs and were also available via a redemption program.

	Nm-Mt	Ex-Mt
COMMON CARD (1-6)	1.00	.30
COMMON AUTO (1-6)	10.00	3.00

AUTOS RANDOM INSERTS IN POY HOBBY
AUTOS ALSO AVAIL.VIA REDEMPTION

1998 Best Number One Pick

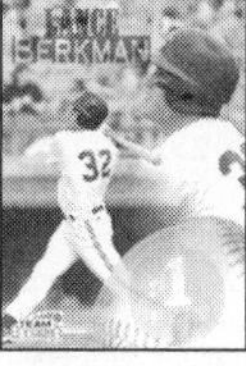

Issued one per signature series hobby box, these cards feature players taken as their teams number one pick. Each card has a stated print run of 900 sets.

	Nm-Mt	Ex-Mt
COMPLETE SET (42)	120.00	36.00
1 Aaron Akin	2.50	.75
2 Matt Anderson	4.00	1.20
3 Ryan Anderson	4.00	1.20
4 Shane Arthurs	2.50	.75
5 Michael Barrett	2.50	.75
6 Kris Benson	2.50	.75
7 Lance Berkman	4.00	1.20
8 Rocky Biddle	2.50	.75
9 Ryan Bradley	2.50	.75
10 Dermal Brown	2.50	.75
11 Troy Cameron	2.50	.75
12 Brett Caradonna	2.50	.75
13 Eric Chavez	4.00	1.20
14 Michael Cuddyer	4.00	1.20
15 John Curtice	2.50	.75
16 Glenn Davis	2.50	.75
17 J.J. Davis	2.50	.75
18 Jason Dellaero	2.50	.75
19 J.D. Drew	6.00	1.80
20 Tim Drew	2.50	.75
21 Eric DuBose	4.00	1.20
22 Mark Fischer	2.50	.75
23 Troy Glaus	10.00	3.00
24 Geoff Goetz	2.50	.75
25 Jason Grilli	2.50	.75
26 Nathan Haynes	2.50	.75
27 Bryan Hebson	2.50	.75
28 Geoff Jenkins	4.00	1.20
29 Adam Kennedy	2.50	.75
30 Billy Koch	4.00	1.20
31 Matt LeCroy	2.50	.75
32 Mark Mangum	2.50	.75
33 Darnell McDonald	4.00	1.20
34 Kevin Nicholson	2.50	.75
35 John Patterson	2.50	.75
36 Danny Peoples	2.50	.75
37 Dan Reichert	2.50	.75
38 Jason Romano	2.50	.75
39 Jason Standridge	2.50	.75
40 Vernon Wells	4.00	1.20
41 Jayson Werth	2.50	.75
42 Matt White	4.00	1.20

1998 Best Player of the Year Contenders

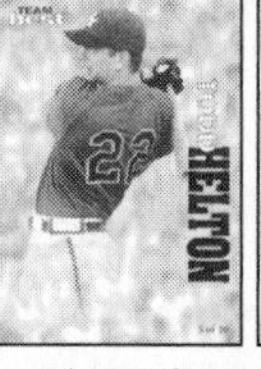

Inserted a rate of one per 90 player of the year hobby packs, these 10 cards feature leading players for the "player of the year" award. 400 serial #'d sets were produced and the cards are hand-numbered as such on back.

	Nm-Mt	Ex-Mt
COMPLETE SET (10)	40.00	12.00
1 Derrick Gibson	2.00	.60
2 Ben Grieve VERT	2.00	.60
3 Ben Grieve	2.00	.60
4 Todd Helton VERT	10.00	3.00
5 Todd Helton	10.00	3.00
6 Mark Kotsay VERT	2.00	.60
7 Mark Kotsay	2.00	.60
8 Carl Pavano	2.00	.60
9 Brian Rose VERT	2.00	.60
10 Brian Rose	2.00	.60

1998 Best Possibilities

Inserted at a rate of one per 19 player of the year hobby packs, these five cards feature a pitcher and a hitter who both are thought to have a chance to be leading major leaguers.

	Nm-Mt	Ex-Mt
COMPLETE SET (5)	20.00	6.00
1 Kris Benson Mark Kotsay	1.00	.30
2 Braden Looper Sean Casey	2.00	.60

3 Brian Rose 1.00 .30
Dermal Brown
4 Matt White 2.00 .60
Ben Grieve
5 Kerry Wood 8.00 2.40
Todd Helton

1998 Best Young Guns

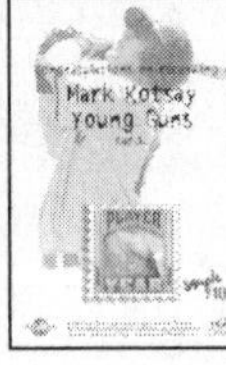

Inserted only in retail packs at the rate of one in 90, these cards are individually numbered to 100. The cards closely parallel the 1998 Best Player of the Contender inserts. Young Guns feature pure white backgrounds on the front of each card. Player of the Year Contenders feature a muted grey image of a crowd in the background.

	Nm-Mt	Ex-Mt
COMPLETE SET (10)	100.00	30.00
1 Derrick Gibson	4.00	1.20
2 Ben Grieve	4.00	1.20
3 Ben Grieve VERT	4.00	1.20
4 Todd Helton	15.00	4.50
5 Todd Helton VERT	15.00	4.50
6 Mark Kotsay	4.00	1.20
7 Mark Kotsay VERT	4.00	1.20
8 Carl Pavano	4.00	1.20
9 Brian Rose	4.00	1.20
10 Brian Rose VERT	4.00	1.20

1998 Hutchinson Popcorn

In a departure from the first few Hutchinson Popcorn sets issues, these cards are slightly oversized. Collector Dave Eskenazi is instrumental in putting all these sets together

	Nm-Mt	Ex-Mt
COMPLETE SET	12.00	3.60
COMMON CARD	2.50	.75
3 Fred Hutchinson MG Elmer Singleton Roy Orteig Al Somers UMP	3.00	.90
4 Fred Hutchinson MG Frank Robinson	5.00	1.50

1998 SP Top Prospects

The 1998 SP set was issued in one series totalling 126 cards and was distributed in eight-card packs with a suggested retail price of $4.39. The fronts feature color photos of top Minor League players. The backs carry player information. The set contains the topical subset: Top 10 Prospects (1-10). An early card of Ruben Mateo is featured in this set.

	Nm-Mt	Ex-Mt
COMPLETE SET (126)	15.00	4.50
1 Travis Lee T10	.25	.07
2 Paul Konerko T10	.75	.23
3 Ben Grieve T10	.25	.07
4 Kerry Wood T10	1.00	.30
5 Miguel Tejada T10	.75	.23
6 Juan Encarnacion T10	.25	.07
7 Jackson Melian T10	.75	.23
8 Chad Hermansen T10	.25	.07
9 Aramis Ramirez T10	.25	.07
10 Russell Branyan T10	.25	.07
11 Norm Hutchins	.25	.07
12 Jarrod Washburn	.75	.23
13 Larry Barnes	.25	.07
14 Scott Schoeneweis	.25	.07
15 Travis Lee	.25	.07
16 Mike Stoner	.25	.07
17 Nick Bierbrodt	.25	.07
18 Vladimir Nunez	.25	.07
19 Wes Helms	.25	.07
20 Jason Marquis	.25	.07
21 George Lombard	.25	.07
22 Bruce Chen	.25	.07
23 Rob Bell	.25	.07
24 Adam Johnson	.25	.07
25 Ryan Minor	.25	.07
26 Sidney Ponson	.75	.23
27 Calvin Pickering	.25	.07
28 Donnie Sadler	.25	.07
29 Cole Liniak	.25	.07
30 Carl Pavano	.25	.07
31 Kerry Wood	2.50	.75
32 Pat Cline	.25	.07
33 Jason Maxwell	.25	.07
34 Jason Dellaero	.25	.07
35 Mike Caruso	.25	.07
36 Jeff Liefer	.25	.07
37 Brian Simmons	.25	.07
38 Carlos Lee	1.00	.30
39 Jeff Inglin	.25	.07
40 Darron Ingram	.25	.07
41 Justin Towle	.25	.07
42 Pat Watkins	.25	.07
43 Richie Sexson	.75	.23
44 Danny Peoples	.25	.07
45 Russell Branyan	.25	.07
46 Scott Morgan	.25	.07
47 Mike Glavine	.25	.07
48 Willie Martinez	.25	.07
49 Jake Westbrook	.25	.07
50 Derrick Gibson	.25	.07
51 Ben Petrick	.25	.07
52 Mike Drumright	.25	.07
53 Seth Greisinger	.25	.07
54 Robert Fick	1.00	.30
55 Dave Borkowski	.25	.07
56 Jesse Ibarra	.25	.07
57 Nate Rolison	.25	.07
58 Jaime Jones	.25	.07
59 Aaron Akin	.25	.07
60 Alex Gonzalez	.25	.07
61 Richard Hidalgo	.75	.23
62 Scott Elarton	.75	.23
63 Daryle Ward	.25	.07
64 Jeremy Giambi	.75	.23
65 Dermal Brown	.25	.07
66 Enrique Calero	.25	.07
67 Glenn Davis	.25	.07
68 Adrian Beltre	.75	.23
69 Alex Cora	.75	.23
70 Paul Konerko	.75	.23
71 Mike Kinkade	.25	.07
72 Danny Klassen	.25	.07
73 Chad Green	.25	.07
74 Kevin Barker	.25	.07
75 David Ortiz	.75	.23
76 Jacque Jones	.75	.23
77 Luis Rivas	.75	.23
78 Hiram Bocachica	.25	.07
79 Javier Vazquez	.75	.23
80 Brad Fullmer	.75	.23
81 Preston Wilson	.75	.23
82 Octavio Dotel	.25	.07
83 Fletcher Bates	.25	.07
84 Grant Roberts	.25	.07
85 Jackson Melian	.75	.23
86 Katsuhiro Maeda	.25	.07
87 Ricky Ledee	.25	.07
88 Eric Milton	.25	.07
89 Eric Chavez	.75	.23
90 Ben Grieve	.25	.07
91 Miguel Tejada	1.50	.45
92 A.J. Hinch	.25	.07
93 Ramon Hernandez	.25	.07
94 Chris Enochs	.25	.07
95 Marlon Anderson	.25	.07
96 Reggie Taylor	.25	.07
97 Steve Carver	.25	.07
98 Ron Wright	.25	.07
99 Kris Benson	.25	.07
100 Chad Hermansen	.25	.07
101 Aramis Ramirez	.75	.23
102 Adam Kennedy	.25	.07
103 Braden Looper	.25	.07
104 Cliff Politte	.25	.07
105 Brent Butler	.25	.07
106 Juan Melo	.25	.07
107 Ben Davis	.25	.07
108 Kevin Nicholson	.25	.07
109 Gary Matthews Jr.	.25	.07
110 Matt Clement	.75	.23
111 Jason Brester	.25	.07
112 Joe Fontenot	.25	.07
113 Darin Blood	.25	.07
114 Greg Wooten	.25	.07
115 Jeff Farnsworth	.25	.07
116 Robert Luce	.25	.07
117 Rolando Arrojo	.25	.07
118 Doug Johnson	.25	.07
119 James Manias	.25	.07
120 Alex Sanchez	.25	.07
121 Warren Morris	.25	.07
122 Ruben Mateo	.75	.23
123 Corey Lee	.25	.07
124 Roy Halladay	.75	.23
125 Kevin Witt	.25	.07
126 Tom Evans	.25	.07

1998 SP Top Prospects Autographs

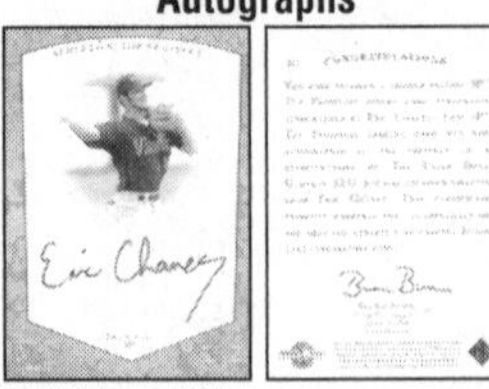

Randomly inserted in packs at the rate of one in 16, this 27-card set features color player photos with the player's signature below. The backs carry player information.

	Nm-Mt	Ex-Mt
AB Adrian Beltre	8.00	2.40
BB Brent Butler	4.00	1.20
BD Ben Davis	4.00	1.20
BG Ben Grieve	8.00	2.40
CH Chad Hermansen	4.00	1.20
CL Corey Lee	4.00	1.20
DK Derrick Gibson	4.00	1.20
DP Danny Peoples	4.00	1.20
DW Daryle Ward	4.00	1.20
EC Eric Chavez	15.00	4.50
GM Gary Matthews Jr.	4.00	1.20
GR Grant Roberts	4.00	1.20
JJ Jacque Jones	8.00	2.40
JM Juan Melo	4.00	1.20
JT Justin Towle	4.00	1.20
KB Kris Benson	8.00	2.40
KM Katsuhiro Maeda	4.00	1.20
KW Kerry Wood	40.00	12.00
MT Miguel Tejada	20.00	6.00
PK Paul Konerko	8.00	2.40
RB Russell Branyan	4.00	1.20
RF Robert Fick	10.00	3.00
RH Ramon Hernandez	8.00	2.40
RL Ricky Ledee	4.00	1.20
SM Scott Morgan	4.00	1.20
TL Travis Lee	4.00	1.20
WM Warren Morris	4.00	1.20

1998 SP Top Prospects Destination The Show

Randomly inserted in packs at the rate of one in 90, this 30-card set features color photos of some of the most talented minor league players who hope to make the major league. The backs carry player information.

	Nm-Mt	Ex-Mt
COMPLETE SET (30)	400.00	120.00
PRES.ED: RANDOM INSERTS IN PACKS		
PRES.ED PRINT RUN 10 SERIAL #'d SETS		
PRES.ED NOT PRICED DUE TO SCARCITY		
DS1 Travis Lee	10.00	3.00
DS2 Eric Chavez	15.00	4.50
DS3 Ramon Hernandez	15.00	4.50
DS4 Daryle Ward	10.00	3.00
DS5 Jackson Melian	15.00	4.50
DS6 Ben Grieve	10.00	3.00
DS7 Brent Butler	10.00	3.00
DS8 Rolando Arrojo	10.00	3.00
DS9 Ryan Minor	10.00	3.00
DS10 Adrian Beltre	15.00	4.50
DS11 Sidney Ponson	15.00	4.50
DS12 Gary Matthews Jr.	10.00	3.00
DS13 Ron Wright	10.00	3.00
DS14 Warren Morris	10.00	3.00
DS15 Russell Branyan	10.00	3.00
DS16 Paul Konerko	15.00	4.50
DS17 Mike Caruso	10.00	3.00
DS18 Jacque Jones	15.00	4.50
DS19 Preston Wilson	15.00	4.50
DS20 Chad Hermansen	10.00	3.00
DS21 Aramis Ramirez	15.00	4.50
DS22 Kerry Wood	50.00	15.00
DS23 Corey Lee	10.00	3.00
DS24 Carl Pavano	15.00	4.50
DS25 Kris Benson	15.00	4.50
DS26 Derrick Gibson	10.00	3.00
DS27 Mike Stoner	10.00	3.00
DS28 Juan Melo	10.00	3.00
DS29 Mike Kinkade	10.00	3.00
DS30 Alex Gonzalez	15.00	4.50

1998 SP Top Prospects Small Town Heroes

Randomly inserted in packs at the rate of one in five, this 30-card set celebrates the hometowns of 30 minor league teams with color photos of some of the promising players from those teams.

	Nm-Mt	Ex-Mt
COMPLETE SET (30)	25.00	7.50
PRES.ED: RANDOM INSERTS IN PACKS		
PRES.ED PRINT RUN 10 SERIAL #'d SETS		
PRES.ED NOT PRICED DUE TO SCARCITY		
H1 Travis Lee	1.00	.30
H2 Eric Chavez	1.00	.30
H3 Mike Caruso	1.00	.30
H4 Adrian Beltre	1.00	.30
H5 Jackson Melian	1.00	.30
H6 Adam Johnson	1.00	.30
H7 Carlos Lee	1.50	.45
H8 Kris Benson	1.00	.30
H9 Jacque Jones	1.00	.30
H10 Russell Branyan	1.00	.30
H11 John Patterson	1.00	.30
H12 Ryan Minor	1.00	.30
H13 Dermal Brown	1.00	.30
H14 Mike Stoner	1.00	.30
H15 Derrick Gibson	1.00	.30
H16 Ben Davis	1.00	.30
H17 Kevin Witt	1.00	.30
H18 Justin Towle	1.00	.30
H19 Doug Johnson	1.00	.30
H20 Chad Hermansen	1.00	.30
H21 Sidney Ponson	1.00	.30
H22 Marlon Anderson	1.00	.30
H23 Kerry Wood	1.50	.45
H24 Alex Gonzalez	1.00	.30
H25 Carl Pavano	1.00	.30
H26 A.J. Hinch	1.00	.30
H27 Juan Melo	1.00	.30
H28 Dave Borkowski	1.00	.30
H29 Jake Westbrook	1.00	.30
H30 Daryle Ward	1.00	.30

1999 Baseball America Promos

These cards were given out to dealers and hobby media in five-card complete set form. These unnumbered cards parallel a selection of basic issue and insert cards from the then-upcoming 1999 Baseball America brand issued by Team Best. The backs of the cards make them easy to identify from their basic issue counterparts in that each card states "for promotional purposes only", featuring a large Baseball America Top Prospects brand logo.

	Nm-Mt	Ex-Mt
NNO Rick Ankiel	.75	.23
NNO Lance Berkman	1.00	.30
NNO Pat Burrell Possibilities	1.50	.45
NNO Marcus Giles MVP	1.00	.30
NNO Ryan Minor Scout's Choice	.50	.15

1999 Baseball America

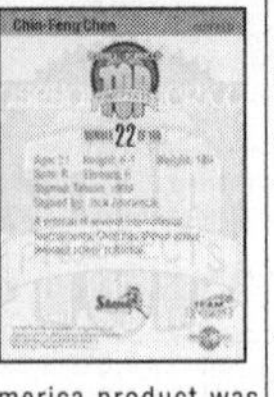

The 1999 Baseball America product was released in June, 2000 and featured a 100-card base set. Each box contained 18 packs and six cards per pack. Key cards include Rick Ankiel, Pat Burrell, Chin-Feng Chen, Joe Crede and Corey Patterson.

	Nm-Mt	Ex-Mt
COMPLETE SET (100)	10.00	3.00
1 Paul Ah Yat	.25	.07
2 Efrain Alamo	.25	.07
3 Chip Alley	.25	.07
4 Ryan Anderson	.25	.07
5 Rick Ankiel	.40	.12
6 Tony Armas Jr.	.25	.07
7 Bronson Arroyo Jr.	.25	.07
8 Mike Bacsik	.25	.07
9 Kevin Barker	.25	.07
10 Fletcher Bates	.25	.07
11 Rob Bell	.25	.07
12 Ron Belliard	.25	.07
13 Peter Bergeron	.40	.12
14 Lance Berkman	.40	.12
15 Nick Bierbrodt	.25	.07
16 Milton Bradley	.40	.12
17 Russ Branyan	.25	.07
18 Pat Burrell	2.50	.75
19 Sean Burroughs	1.50	.45
20 Brent Butler	.25	.07
21 Bruce Chen	.25	.07
22 Chin-Feng Chen	.60	.18
23 Giuseppe Chiaramonte	.25	.07
24 Jin Ho Cho	.25	.07
25 Francis Collins	.25	.07
26 Joe Crede	.50	.15
27 Cesar Crespo	.40	.12
28 Bubba Crosby	.50	.15
29 Michael Cuddyer	.25	.07
30 Ben Davis	.25	.07
31 Tim DeCinces	.25	.07
32 Tomas De La Rosa	.25	.07
33 Octavio Dotel	.25	.07
34 Kelly Dransfeldt	.25	.07
35 Tim Drew	.25	.07
36 Matt Drews	.25	.07
37 Mike Drumright	.25	.07
38 Todd Dunn	.25	.07
39 Chad Durham	.25	.07
40 Alex Eckelman	.25	.07
41 Chris Enochs	.25	.07
42 Cordell Farley	.25	.07
43 Franky Figueroa	.25	.07
44 Joe Fontenot	.25	.07
45 Eric Gillespie	.25	.07
46 Mike Glavine	.25	.07
47 Jason Grote	.25	.07
48 Jerry Hairston Jr.	.25	.07
49 Toby Hall	.40	.12
50 Chad Harville	.25	.07
51 Alex Hernandez	.25	.07
52 Junior Herndon	.40	.12
53 Mike Huelsmann	.25	.07
54 Aubrey Huff	1.25	.35
55 Chad Hutchinson	.40	.12
56 Jamie Jones	.25	.07
57 Kenny Kelly	.40	.12
58 Scott Krause	.25	.07
59 Jason LaRue	.25	.07
60 Carlos Lee	.40	.12
61 Corey Lee	.25	.07
62 Willie Martinez	.25	.07
63 Ruben Mateo	.25	.07
64 Darnell McDonald	.25	.07
65 Cody McKay	.25	.07
66 Dan McKinley	.25	.07
67 Jackson Melian	.40	.12
68 Jason Middlebrook	.40	.12
69 Ryan Minor	.25	.07
70 Mark Mulder	2.00	.60
71 Vladimir Nunez	.25	.07
72 Pablo Ozuna	.25	.07
73 Corey Patterson	2.00	.60
74 John Patterson	.25	.07
75 Josh Paul	.25	.07
76 Angel Pena	.25	.07
77 Carlos Pena	.60	.18
78 Juan Pena	.25	.07
79 Brad Penny	.25	.07
80 Kyle Peterson	.25	.07
81 Ben Petrick	.25	.07
82 Calvin Pickering	.25	.07
83 Arquimedez Pozo	.25	.07
84 Paul Rigdon	.25	.07
85 Grant Roberts	.25	.07
86 Nate Rolison	.25	.07
87 Damian Rolls	.25	.07
88 Ryan Rupe	.25	.07
89 Jose Santos	.25	.07
90 Todd Sears	.40	.12
91 Fernando Seguignol	.25	.07
92 Brett Taft	.25	.07
93 Chris Truby	.25	.07
94 Jayson Werth	.25	.07
95 Matt White	.40	.12
96 Todd Williams	.25	.07
97 Cliff Wilson	.25	.07
98 Randy Wolf	.40	.12
99 Kelly Wunsch	.25	.07
100 Mike Zywica	.25	.07

1999 Baseball America Gold

This parallel insert to the regular Baseball America set were randomly inserted into packs. These cards have a stated print run of 50 sets.

	Nm-Mt	Ex-Mt
*GOLD: 5X TO 12X BASIC CARDS		

1999 Baseball America Silver

Inserted as a one per Baseball American chiptopper, these cards parallel the regular Baseball America set. These cards have a stated print run of 150 sets.

	Nm-Mt	Ex-Mt
*SILVER: 2.5X TO 6X BASIC CARDS		

1999 Baseball America Diamond Best

This 100 card set was produced by Team Best and all cards are a straight parallel of the basic 1999 Baseball America set except that all Diamond Best cards have silver foil logos on front.

	Nm-Mt	Ex-Mt
COMPLETE SET (100)	25.00	7.50

1999 Baseball America Diamond Best Gold

Randomly inserted into packs, these cards parallel the Baseball American Diamond Best cards.

	Nm-Mt	Ex-Mt
*GOLD: .6X TO 1.5X BASIC CARDS		

1999 Baseball America League MVPs

Inserted at a rate of one per 19 Baseball America and Baseball America Diamond Best packs, these 10 cards feature players who won various minor-league MVP awards.

	Nm-Mt	Ex-Mt
COMPLETE SET (10)	10.00	3.00
1 Brian August	1.00	.30
2 Joe Crede	1.50	.45
3 Shawn Gallagher	1.00	.30
4 Jay Gibbons	2.00	.60
5 Marcus Giles	1.50	.45
6 Jason Hart	1.50	.45
7 Tyrone Horne	1.00	.30
8 Pablo Ozuna	1.00	.30
9 Brad Penny	1.50	.45
10 Calvin Pickering	1.00	.30

1999 Hutchinson Popcorn

Staying with the trend begun with the 1998 set, these cards are also slightly oversized and feature highlights from the life and career of Fred Hutchinson.

	Nm-Mt	Ex-Mt
COMPLETE SET (4)	10.00	3.00
COMMON CARD (1-4)	2.50	.75
4 Fred Hutchinson MG Casey Stengel MG Walter Alston MG	4.00	1.20

1999 Just Promos

These 12 cards were issued to promote the various brands of cards the Just company would produce in 1999.

	Nm-Mt	Ex-Mt
COMPLETE SET (12)	12.00	3.60
NNO Jeff Austin Debuts	.50	.15
NNO Pat Burrell Nine IM	1.50	.45
NNO Sean Casey Longshots	1.00	.30
NNO Sean Casey Stars IM	1.00	.30
NNO John Elway IM	1.50	.45
NNO John Elway Horizontal	1.50	.45
NNO Jody Gerut Debuts IM	1.00	.30
NNO Josh Hamilton Debuts JF	.50	.15
NNO Nick Johnson Longshots	1.00	.30
NNO Gabe Kapler Power IM	.50	.15
NNO Aramis Ramirez Nine IM	1.00	.30
NNO Alfonso Soriano Stars IM	2.00	.60
NNO Pat Burrell Facts JF	1.50	.45
NNO Adam Piatt Spotlight JF	.50	.15
NNO Ben Sheets Drafted JF	1.00	.30

1999 Just

The Just base set was released in three separate series entitled Just Imagine, Just the

Start and Justifiable in 1999. The set features 250-player cards.

	Nm-Mt	Ex-Mt
COMPLETE SET (250)	50.00	15.00
COMP.START (50)	10.00	3.00
COMP.IMAGINE (100)	25.00	7.50
COMP.JUSTIFIABLE (100)	15.00	4.50
1 Hector Almonte	.25	.07
2 Wes Anderson	.40	.12
3 Ryan Anderson	.25	.07
4 Clayton Andrews	.25	.07
5 Rick Ankiel	.40	.12
6 Brad Baisley	.40	.12
7 Kevin Barker	.25	.07
8 Michael Barrett	.25	.07
9 Kris Benson	.25	.07
10 Peter Bergeron	.40	.12
11 Lance Berkman	.40	.12
12 Nate Bump	.40	.12
13 Eric Byrnes	.50	.15
14 Giuseppe Chiaramonte	.25	.07
15 Glenn Davis	.25	.07
16 Juan Dilone	.25	.07
17 Eric Dubose	.25	.07
18 Rick Elder	.40	.12
19 Alex Escobar	.40	.12
20 Rafael Furcal	.75	.23
21 Shawn Gallagher	.25	.07
22 Marcus Giles	.75	.23
23 Geoff Goetz	.25	.07
24 Jason Grilli	.25	.07
25 Cristian Guzman	.40	.12
26 Mark Harriger	.25	.07
27 Nick Johnson	.75	.23
28 Gabe Kapler	.25	.07
29 Kenny Kelly	.40	.12
30 Adam Kennedy	.25	.07
31 Corey Lee	.25	.07
32 Kevin McGlinchy	.25	.07
33 Gil Meche	.40	.12
34 Jackson Melian	.40	.12
35 Warren Morris	.25	.07
36 Ricky Williams	.75	.23
37 Pablo Ozuna	.25	.07
38 Ben Petrick	.25	.07
39 Scott Pratt	.40	.12
40 Chris Reinike	.25	.07
41 Zach Sorenson	.25	.07
42 Dernell Stenson	.25	.07
43 Andy Thompson	.25	.07
44 Luis Vizcaino	.25	.07
45 Daryle Ward	.25	.07
46 Vernon Wells	.40	.12
47 Jayson Werth	.25	.07
48 Jake Westbrook	.25	.07
49 Ricky Williams FB	.75	.23
50 Randy Wolf	.40	.12
51 Paul Ah Yat	.40	.12
52 Israel Alcantara	.25	.07
53 Erick Almonte	.40	.12
54 Gabe Alvarez	.25	.07
55 Tony Armas Jr.	.25	.07
56 Jeff Austin	.40	.12
57 Benito Baez	.25	.07
58 Kevin Beirne	.40	.12
59 Ron Belliard	.25	.07
60 Micah Bowie	.25	.07
61 Russell Branyan	.25	.07
62 Antone Brooks	.25	.07
63 A.J. Burnett	.50	.15
64 Pat Burrell	2.00	.60
65 Brent Butler	.25	.07
66 Troy Cameron	.25	.07
67 Sean Casey	.40	.12
68 Bruce Chen	.40	.12
69 Chin-Feng Chen	.50	.15
70 Jin Ho Cho	.25	.07
71 Jesus Colome	.25	.07
72 Carl Crawford	.75	.23
73 Bubba Crosby	.50	.15
74 Jack Cust	.25	.07
75 Mike Darr	.25	.07
76 Ben Davis	.25	.07
77 Octavio Dotel	.25	.07
78 Kelly Dransfeldt	.25	.07
79 Adam Dunn	2.50	.75
80 Erubiel Durazo	.50	.15
81 John Elway	.75	.23
82 John Elway	.75	.23
83 Mario Encarnacion	.25	.07
84 Seth Etherton	.40	.12
85 Adam Everett	.40	.12
86 Franky Figueroa	.25	.07
87 Mike Frank	.25	.07
88 Jon Garland	.25	.07
89 Chris George	.40	.12
90 Jody Gerut	1.00	.30
91 Derrick Gibson	.25	.07
92 Jerry Hairston Jr.	.25	.07
93 Josh Hamilton	.50	.15
94 Jason Hart	.40	.12
95 Chad Harville	.40	.12
96 Nathan Haynes	.25	.07
97 Junior Herndon	.40	.12
98 Shea Hillenbrand	.75	.23
99 Matt Holliday	.40	.12
100 Brandon Inge	.40	.12
101 Jacque Jones	.40	.12
102 Gabe Kapler	.25	.07
103 Austin Kearns	2.00	.60
104 Brandon Larson	.40	.12
105 Jason Larue	.25	.07
106 Carlos Lee	.40	.12
107 Corey Lee	.25	.07
108 Donny Leon	.25	.07
109 George Lombard	.25	.07
110 Julio Lugo	.25	.07
111 Chris Magruder	.25	.07
112 Mark Mangum	.25	.07
113 Jason Marquis	.25	.07
114 Ruben Mateo	.25	.07
115 Luis Matos	.75	.23
116 Gary Matthews Jr.	.25	.07
117 Juan Melo	.25	.07
118 Orber Moreno	.25	.07
119 Mark Mulder	1.50	.45
120 Corey Patterson	1.50	.45
121 Angel Pena	.25	.07
122 Elvis Pena	.25	.07
123 Kyle Peterson	.25	.07
124 Adam Piatt	.40	.12
125 Calvin Pickering	.25	.07
126 Jeremy Powell	.25	.07
127 Luke Prokopec	.40	.12
128 Aramis Ramirez	.40	.12
129 Julio Ramirez	.25	.07
130 Matt Riley	.75	.23
131 Luis Rivera	.25	.07
132 Grant Roberts	.25	.07
133 Ryan Rupe	.25	.07
134 C.C. Sabathia	.50	.15
135 Luis Saturria	.25	.07
136 Fernando Seguignol	.25	.07
137 Alfonso Soriano	3.00	.90
138 Pat Strange	.40	.12
139 Robert Stratton	.25	.07
140 Reggie Taylor	.25	.07
141 Jorge Toca	.25	.07
142 Tony Torcato	.40	.12
143 Bubba Trammell	.25	.07
144 T.J. Tucker	.25	.07
145 Juan Uribe	.40	.12
146 Kip Wells	.40	.12
147 Ricky Williams	.75	.23
148 Ricky Williams	.75	.23
149 Kevin Witt	.25	.07
150 Ed Yarnall	.25	.07
151 Winston Abreu	.25	.07
152 Chris Aguila	.40	.12
153 Bronson Arroyo	.25	.07
154 Robert Averette	.25	.07
155 Mike Bacsik	.25	.07
156 Andrew Beinbrink	.25	.07
157 Matt Belisle	.40	.12
158 Matt Blank	.25	.07
159 Jung Bong	.40	.12
160 Milton Bradley	.40	.12
161 Ryan Bradley	.25	.07
162 Dermal Brown	.25	.07
163 Sean Burroughs	1.25	.35
164 Chance Caple	.40	.12
165 Hee Seop Choi	1.25	.35
166 Mike Christensen	.25	.07
167 Doug Clark	.25	.07
168 Javier Colina	.25	.07
169 Brian Cooper	.25	.07
170 Pat Daneker	.25	.07
171 Randey Dorame	.25	.07
172 Ryan Drese	.40	.12
173 Chris Duncan	.40	.12
174 Adam Dunn	2.50	.75
175 David Eckstein	.40	.12
176 Alex Fernandez	.40	.12
177 Choo Freeman	.40	.12
178 Neil Frendling	.40	.12
179 Eddy Furniss	.40	.12
180 B.J. Garbe	.40	.12
181 Yon German	.25	.07
182 Esteban German	.25	.07
183 Dan Grummitt	.40	.12
184 Will Hartley	.40	.12
185 Jesus Hernandez	.25	.07
186 Alex Hernandez	.25	.07
187 James Hood	.25	.07
188 Aubrey Huff	1.00	.30
189 Chad Hutchinson	.40	.12
190 Jason Jennings	.40	.12
191 Jaime Jones	.40	.12
192 David Kelton	.40	.12
193 Mike Lamb	.40	.12
194 Jacques Landry	.25	.07
195 Ryan Langerhans	.40	.12
196 Nelson Lara	.25	.07
197 Nick Leach	.40	.12
198 Steve Lomasney	.25	.07
199 Felipe Lopez	.40	.12
200 Ryan Ludwick	.40	.12
201 Pat Manning	.40	.12
202 T.R. Marcinczyk	.40	.12
203 Hipolito Martinez	.25	.07
204 Tony McKnight	.25	.07
205 Tydus Meadows	.25	.07
206 Corky Miller	.25	.07
207 Frank Moore	.25	.07
208 Scott Morgan	.25	.07
209 Tony Mota	.25	.07
210 Ntema Ndungidi	.25	.07
211 David Noyce	.40	.12
212 Franklin Nunez	.40	.12
213 Jose Ortiz	.40	.12
214 Jimmy Osting	.25	.07
215 Jorge Padilla	.40	.12
216 Mike Paradis	.25	.07
217 Brandon Parker	.25	.07
218 Jarrod Patterson	.25	.07
219 John Patterson	.25	.07
220 Jay Payton	.25	.07
221 Juan Pena	.25	.07
222 Brad Penny	.25	.07
223 Danny Peoples	.40	.12
224 Paul Phillips	.40	.12
225 Josh Pressley	.40	.12
226 Tim Raines Jr.	.40	.12
227 Paul Rigdon	.25	.07
228 Jimmy Rollins	.40	.12
229 J.C. Romero	.25	.07
230 Marcos Scutaro	.25	.07
231 Sammy Serrano	.25	.07
232 Wascar Serrano	.40	.12
233 Ben Sheets	.50	.15
234 Carlos Silva	.40	.12
235 Scott Sobkowiak	.25	.07
236 Ramon Soler	.25	.07
237 Shawn Sonnier	.25	.07
238 Jovanny Sosa	.40	.12
239 Jason Standridge	.25	.07
240 Brent Stentz	.25	.07
241 Seth Taylor	.40	.12
242 Jason Tyner	.40	.12
243 Brant Ust	.25	.07
244 Eric Valent	.40	.12
245 Ismael Villegas	.25	.07
246 David Walling	.40	.12
247 Rico Washington	.25	.07
248 Brad Wilkerson	.40	.12
249 Patrick Williams	.40	.12
250 Barry Zito	2.00	.60

1999 Just Black

Randomly inserted into all Just products at stated odds of one in 240 packs, this 250-card insert is a complete parallel of the Just base set. The set features a black border, and each card is individually serial numbered to 50.

	Nm-Mt	Ex-Mt
*JUST BLACK: 8X TO 20X BASIC CARDS		

1999 Just Autographs

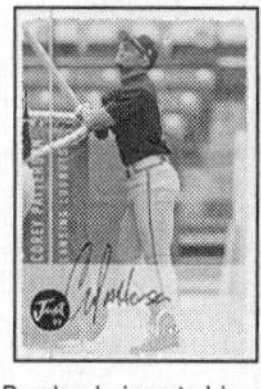

Randomly inserted in a wide array of 1999 and 2000 Just products at a rate of 1:12, this large insert set features autographed cards of top minor league prospects. Note the following abbreviations to specify distribution: IM for 1999 Just Imagine, IM '00 for 2000 Just Imagine, JF for 1999 Justifiable, JF '00 for 2000 Justifiable, ST for 1999 Just the Start and PV for 2000 Just the Preview 2K. These cards are unnumbered and have been checklisted below alphabetically by player's last name.

	Nm-Mt	Ex-Mt
1 Israel Alcantara IM	2.00	.60
2 Erick Almonte PV	3.00	.90
3 Hector Almonte IM	2.00	.60
4 Hector Almonte ST	2.00	.60
5 Wes Anderson PV	3.00	.90
6 Rick Ankiel IM	3.00	.90
7 Rick Ankiel JF	3.00	.90
8 Tony Armas Jr. IM '00	2.00	.60
9 Jeff Austin IM	3.00	.90
10 Benito Baez IM	2.00	.60
11 Brad Baisley ST	3.00	.90
12 Kevin Barker IM	2.00	.60
13 Kevin Barker PV	2.00	.60
14 Michael Barrett ST	3.00	.90
15 Kevin Beirne IM	3.00	.90
16 Matt Belisle PV	3.00	.90
17 Kris Benson ST	3.00	.90
18 Brent Billingsley ST	2.00	.60
19 Casey Blake ST	3.00	.90
20 Micah Bowie IM	2.00	.60
21 Antone Brooks IM	2.00	.60
22 A.J. Burnett PV	5.00	1.50
23 Sean Burroughs JF	10.00	3.00
24 Eric Byrnes JF	5.00	1.50
25 Troy Cameron JF	2.00	.60
26 Sean Casey IM	3.00	.90
27 Jesus Colome IM	2.00	.60
28 Bubba Crosby IM	5.00	1.50
29 Jack Cust IM	2.00	.60
30 Jack Cust PV	2.00	.60
31 Pat Daneker PV	2.00	.60
32 Mike Darr PV	2.00	.60
33 Ben Davis IM	2.00	.60
34 Glenn Davis PV	2.00	.60
35 Glenn Davis ST	2.00	.60
36 Juan Dilone JF	2.00	.60
37 Juan Dilone ST	2.00	.60
38 Rick Elder ST	3.00	.90
39 Mario Encarnacion PV	2.00	.60
40 Seth Etherton IM	3.00	.90
41 Franky Figueroa PV	2.00	.60
42 Mark Fischer ST	2.00	.60
43 Mike Frank IM	2.00	.60
44 Rafael Furcal JF	10.00	3.00
45 Rafael Furcal ST	10.00	3.00
46 Jon Garland IM	2.00	.60
47 Chris George IM	3.00	.90
48 Jody Gerut PV	10.00	3.00
49 Geoff Goetz ST	2.00	.60
50 Jason Grilli IM	2.00	.60
51 Jason Grilli ST	2.00	.60
52 Mark Harriger ST	2.00	.60
53 Jason Hart JF	3.00	.90
54 Nathan Haynes PV	2.00	.60
55 Junior Herndon IM	3.00	.90
56 Shea Hillenbrand JF	8.00	2.40
57 Heath Honeycutt ST	2.00	.60
58 Jay Hood PV	2.00	.60
59 Nick Johnson JF	10.00	3.00
60 Jaime Jones PV	2.00	.60
61 Gabe Kapler IM	2.00	.60
62 Gabe Kapler PV	2.00	.60
63 Gabe Kapler ST	2.00	.60
64 Austin Kearns PV	15.00	4.50
65 David Kelton PV	3.00	.90
66 Adam Kennedy JF	3.00	.90
67 Adam Kennedy ST	3.00	.90
68 Nelson Lara PV	2.00	.60
69 Brandon Larson JF '00	3.00	.90
70 Jason Larue PV	2.00	.60
71 Corey Lee IM	2.00	.60
72 Donny Leon IM	2.00	.60
73 Steve Lomasney PV	2.00	.60
74 George Lombard IM	2.00	.60
75 Julio Lugo IM	2.00	.60
76 Chris Magruder IM	2.00	.60
77 Mark Mangum IM	2.00	.60
78 Jason Marquis IM	2.00	.60
79 Luis Matos IM	8.00	2.40
80 Gil Meche PV	5.00	1.50
81 Jackson Melian IM '00	3.00	.90
82 Juan Melo IM	2.00	.60
83 Juan Melo ST	2.00	.60
84 Orber Moreno IM	2.00	.60
85 Guillermo Mota PV	2.00	.60
86 Tony Mota PV	2.00	.60
87 Mark Mulder JF	15.00	4.50
88 Mark Mulder ST	15.00	4.50
89 Pablo Ozuna IM	2.00	.60
90 Pablo Ozuna IM '00	2.00	.60
91 Pablo Ozuna JF	2.00	.60
92 Corey Patterson JF	10.00	3.00
93 Corey Patterson JF '00	10.00	3.00
94 Corey Patterson PV	10.00	3.00
95 Jay Payton PV	2.00	.60
96 Angel Pena JF	2.00	.60
97 Kyle Peterson IM	2.00	.60
98 Ben Petrick IM	2.00	.60
99 Calvin Pickering IM	2.00	.60
100 Aramis Ramirez IM	3.00	.90
101 Aramis Ramirez PV	3.00	.90
102 Julio Ramirez JF	2.00	.60
103 Matt Riley JF	5.00	1.50
104 Luis Rivera PV	2.00	.60
105 Grant Roberts JF	2.00	.60
106 Luis Saturria PV	2.00	.60
107 Zach Sorensen IM	2.00	.60
108 Alfonso Soriano IM	40.00	12.00
109 A.Soriano IM '00	40.00	12.00
110 Jovanny Sosa IM '00	3.00	.90
111 Pat Strange IM	3.00	.90
112 Reggie Taylor IM	2.00	.60
113 Andy Thompson ST	2.00	.60
114 Jorge Toca IM	2.00	.60
115 Jorge Toca IM '00	2.00	.60
116 Tony Torcato JF	3.00	.90
117 Bubba Trammell IM	2.00	.60
118 Pete Tucci ST	2.00	.60
119 T.J. Tucker IM	2.00	.60
120 T.J. Tucker ST	2.00	.60
121 Juan Uribe IM	3.00	.90
122 Ismael Villegas PV	2.00	.60
123 Kip Wells IM	3.00	.90
124 Jayson Werth PV	2.00	.60
125 Jayson Werth ST	2.00	.60
126 Jake Westbrook PV	2.00	.60
127 Jake Westbrook ST	2.00	.60
128 Ricky Williams ST	30.00	9.00
129 Enrique Wilson PV	2.00	.60
130 Randy Wolf IM	3.00	.90
131 Barry Zito IM '00	20.00	6.00
132 Barry Zito PV	20.00	6.00

1999 Just Autographs Black

These autographs were randomly inserted into the 2000 Just Gold factory sets. Each card features a black border, and is serial numbered to 50.

	Nm-Mt	Ex-Mt
1 Rick Ankiel JG '00	12.00	3.60
2 Tony Armas Jr. JG '00	8.00	2.40
3 Matt Belisle JG '00	12.00	3.60
4 Jacob Cruz JG '00	8.00	2.40
5 Jack Cust JG '00	8.00	2.40
6 Pat Daneker JG '00	8.00	2.40
7 M.Encarnacion JG '00	8.00	2.40
8 Robert Fick JG '00	12.00	3.60
9 Nick Johnson JG '00	30.00	9.00
10 Jaime Jones JG '00	8.00	2.40
11 Austin Kearns JG '00	50.00	15.00
12 David Kelton JG '00	12.00	3.60
13 Nelson Lara JG '00	8.00	2.40
14 Brandon Larson JG '00	12.00	3.60
15 Steve Lomasney JG '00	8.00	2.40
16 Gil Meche JG '00	20.00	6.00
17 Guillermo Mota JG '00	8.00	2.40
18 Tony Mota JG '00	8.00	2.40
19 Pablo Ozuna JG '00	8.00	2.40
20 Pablo Ozuna JG '00	8.00	2.40
21 Corey Patterson JG '00	30.00	9.00
22 Corey Patterson JG '00	30.00	9.00
23 Corey Patterson JG '00	30.00	9.00
24 Jay Payton JG '00	8.00	2.40
25 Aramis Ramirez JG '00	12.00	3.60
26 Ryan Rupe JG '00	8.00	2.40
27 Alfonso Soriano JG '00	120.00	36.00
28 Jovanny Sosa JG '00	12.00	3.60
29 Jorge Toca JG '00	8.00	2.40
30 Jorge Toca JG '00	8.00	2.40
31 Enrique Wilson JG '00	8.00	2.40
32 Barry Zito JG '00	60.00	18.00
33 Barry Zito JG '00	60.00	18.00

1999 Just Autographs Die Cuts

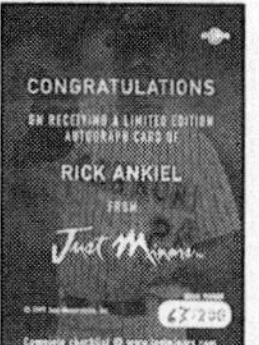

In addition to the regular autograph cards inserted in the 1999 Just Imagine, Just the Start and Justifiable and 2000 Just Imagine and Just the Preview 2K wax products, there were die-cut versions produced that were hand-numbered of 200. Cards seeded into separate boxes are tagged with suffixes after the player's name as follows: IM for 1999 Just Imagine, ST for 1999 Just the Start, JF for 1999 Justifiable, IM '00 for 2000 Just Imagine and PV for 2000 Just the Preview 2K. Cards are unnumbered on back and are checklisted below alphabetically by each player's last name.

	Nm-Mt	Ex-Mt
COMPLETE SET (52)		
1 Hector Almonte ST	4.00	1.20
2 Rick Ankiel IM	6.00	1.80
3 Rick Ankiel JF	6.00	1.80
4 Rick Ankiel PV	6.00	1.80
5 Tony Armas Jr. IM '00	4.00	1.20
6 Jeff Austin IM	6.00	1.80
7 Brad Baisley ST	6.00	1.80
8 Kevin Barker PV	4.00	1.20
9 Michael Barrett ST	6.00	1.80
10 Kevin Beirne IM	6.00	1.80
11 Matt Belisle JF	6.00	1.80
12 Kris Benson ST	6.00	1.80
13 Casey Blake ST	6.00	1.80
14 Micah Bowie IM	4.00	1.20
15 Sean Burroughs JF	20.00	6.00
16 Troy Cameron IM	4.00	1.20
17 Jacob Cruz PV	4.00	1.20
18 Jack Cust PV	4.00	1.20
19 Glenn Davis ST	4.00	1.20
20 Rick Elder ST	6.00	1.80
21 Seth Etherton IM	6.00	1.80
22 Robert Fick PV	6.00	1.80
23 Mike Frank IM	4.00	1.20
24 Chris George IM	6.00	1.80
25 Geoff Goetz ST	4.00	1.20
26 Jason Grilli ST	4.00	1.20
27 Mark Harriger ST	4.00	1.20
28 Gabe Kapler IM	4.00	1.20
29 Gabe Kapler PV	4.00	1.20
30 Gabe Kapler ST	4.00	1.20
31 Austin Kearns PV	30.00	9.00
32 George Lombard IM	4.00	1.20
33 Jason Marquis IM	4.00	1.20
34 Gil Meche JF	12.00	3.60
35 Jackson Melian	4.00	1.20
36 Tony Mota PV	4.00	1.20
37 Mark Mulder JF	30.00	9.00
38 Mark Mulder ST	30.00	9.00
39 Pablo Ozuna IM	4.00	1.20
40 Corey Patterson JF-JS-2K1	20.00	6.00
41 Corey Patterson PV	20.00	6.00
42 Elvis Pena PV	4.00	1.20
43 Calvin Pickering IM	4.00	1.20
44 Matt Riley JF	10.00	3.00
45 Ryan Rupe PV	4.00	1.20
46 Zach Sorensen IM	4.00	1.20
47 Jorge Toca IM	4.00	1.20
48 T.J. Tucker IM	4.00	1.20
49 Jayson Werth ST	4.00	1.20
50 Jake Westbrook ST	4.00	1.20
51 Ricky Williams ST	40.00	12.00
52 Randy Wolf IM	6.00	1.80
53 Barry Zito PV	40.00	12.00

1999 Just Debuts Imagine

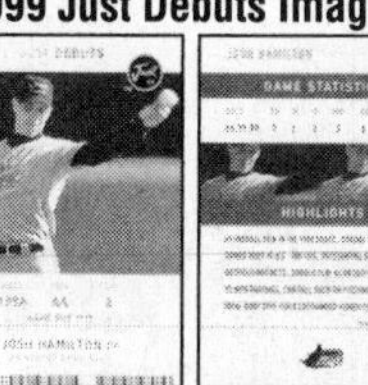

Randomly inserted as a "box-topper" in Imagine boxes, this insert features 10 prospects that look to make their major league debut in 1999.

	Nm-Mt	Ex-Mt
COMPLETE SET (10)	25.00	7.50
1 Jeff Austin	1.00	.30
2 Chin-Feng Chen	1.50	.45
3 Erubiel Durazo	1.50	.45
4 Jody Gerut	2.00	.60
5 Josh Hamilton	1.50	.45
6 Corey Patterson	5.00	1.50
7 Alfonso Soriano	6.00	1.80
8 Jorge Toca	1.00	.30
9 Kip Wells	1.00	.30
10 Brad Wilkerson	1.00	.30

1999 Just Debuts Justifiable

Randomly inserted in Justifiable packs at one in 240, this 10-card insert set features 10 up and coming prospects.

	Nm-Mt	Ex-Mt
COMPLETE SET (10)	150.00	45.00
1 B.J. Garbe	5.00	1.50
2 Ben Sheets	6.00	1.80
3 Jeff Austin	5.00	1.50
4 Chin-Feng Chen	8.00	2.40
5 Jody Gerut	15.00	4.50
6 Josh Hamilton	8.00	2.40
7 Corey Patterson	20.00	6.00
8 Alfonso Soriano	25.00	7.50
9 Jorge Toca	5.00	1.50
10 Kip Wells	5.00	1.50

1999 Just Diamond Autographs

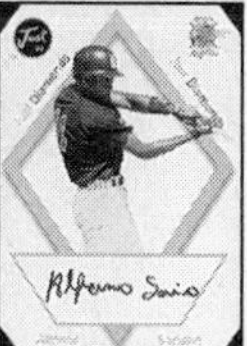

Randomly inserted in packs of 1999 Justifiable and 2000 Just the Preview 2K, this 18-card insert parallels a selection of the base autographs. Each card is serial numbered to 100 by hand.

	Nm-Mt	Ex-Mt
1 Rick Ankiel JF	8.00	2.40
2 Matt Belisle JF	8.00	2.40
3 Sean Burroughs JF	25.00	7.50

	Nm-Mt	Ex-Mt
4 Troy Cameron JF	5.00	1.50
5 Sean Casey PV	8.00	2.40
6 Dionys Cesar JF	5.00	1.50
7 Jacob Cruz PV	5.00	1.50
8 Jack Cust PV	5.00	1.50
9 Rafael Furcal JF	25.00	7.50
10 Nick Johnson JF	25.00	7.50
11 David Kelton PV	8.00	2.40
12 Pablo Ozuna JF	5.00	1.50
13 Corey Patterson JF	25.00	7.50
14 Jay Payton PV	5.00	1.50
15 Aramis Ramirez JF	8.00	2.40
16 Alfonso Soriano PV	100.00	30.00
17 Kip Wells JF	8.00	2.40
18 Enrique Wilson PV	5.00	1.50

1999 Just Drafted

These 10 cards were inserted as a box-topper and featured players who had been recently drafted.

	Nm-Mt	Ex-Mt
COMPLETE SET (10)	15.00	4.50
1 Larry Bigbie	1.00	.30
2 Chance Caple	1.00	.30
3 Chris Duncan	1.00	.30
4 B.J. Garbe	1.00	.30
5 Josh Hamilton	1.50	.45
6 Will Hartley	1.00	.30
7 Mike Paradis	1.00	.30
8 Ben Sheets	1.50	.45
9 David Walling	1.00	.30
10 Barry Zito	6.00	1.80

1999 Just Due

Randomly inserted into Just the Start product at one in six, this insert focuses on minor leaguer's that are due for a shot at the major leagues.

	Nm-Mt	Ex-Mt
COMPLETE SET (10)	6.00	1.80
1 Michael Barrett	.50	.15
2 Kris Benson	.50	.15
3 Peter Bergeron	.50	.15
4 Lance Berkman	.50	.15
5 Nick Johnson	1.25	.35
6 Gabe Kapler	.50	.15
7 Corey Lee	.50	.15
8 Jackson Melian	.50	.15
9 Dernell Stenson	.50	.15
10 Randy Wolf	.50	.15

1999 Just Facts

Randomly inserted in Justifiable packs at one in 24, this 10-card insert features 10 prospects and various facts about them.

	Nm-Mt	Ex-Mt
COMPLETE SET (10)	25.00	7.50
1 Pat Burrell	6.00	1.80
2 Sean Burroughs	4.00	1.20
3 Adam Eaton	1.00	.30
4 Marcus Giles	2.50	.75
5 Josh Hamilton	1.50	.45
6 Nick Johnson	2.50	.75
7 Corey Patterson	5.00	1.50
8 Jason Standridge	1.00	.30
9 Jorge Toca	1.00	.30
10 Eric Valent	1.00	.30

1999 Just Imagine Autographs

Randomly inserted in packs, this insert is a partial parallel of the Just Autographs set. Each card is numbered "X/200" on back except John Elway of whom only 100 copies were produced.

	Nm-Mt	Ex-Mt
1 Israel Alcantara	3.00	.90
2 Rick Ankiel	5.00	1.50
3 Jeff Austin	5.00	1.50
4 Micah Bowie	3.00	.90
5 Troy Cameron	3.00	.90
6 Sean Casey	5.00	1.50
7 Sean Casey	5.00	1.50
8 Jack Cust	3.00	.90
9 John Elway	120.00	36.00
10 Mike Frank	3.00	.90
11 Rafael Furcal	15.00	4.50
12 Jon Garland	3.00	.90
13 Gabe Kapler	3.00	.90
14 Julio Lugo	3.00	.90
15 Jason Marquis	3.00	.90
16 Pablo Ozuna	3.00	.90
17 Kyle Peterson	3.00	.90
18 Julio Ramirez	3.00	.90
19 Matt Riley	8.00	2.40
20 Alfonso Soriano	60.00	18.00
21 Jorge Toca	3.00	.90
22 T.J. Tucker	3.00	.90
23 Kip Wells	5.00	1.50
24 Ricky Williams	40.00	12.00
25 Ricky Williams	40.00	12.00

1999 Just Longshots

Randomly inserted in Just Imagine packs at one in eight, this insert features 10 major league prospects.

	Nm-Mt	Ex-Mt
COMPLETE SET (10)	5.00	1.50
1 Wes Anderson	.75	.23
2 David Eckstein	.75	.23
3 Marcus Giles	2.00	.60
4 Kevin Haverbusch	.50	.15
5 Gabe Kapler	.50	.15
6 Julio Lugo	.50	.15
7 Gary Matthews Jr.	.50	.15
8 Ryan Minor	.50	.15
9 Jason Regan	.50	.15
10 Daryle Ward	.50	.15

1999 Just News

Randomly inserted into Just the Start product at one in 240, this insert focuses on minor leaguer's that have made news with their performances at the minor league level.

	Nm-Mt	Ex-Mt
COMPLETE SET (6)	50.00	15.00
JN1 Rick Ankiel Alex Escobar	5.00	1.50
JN2 Marcus Giles Mark Harriger	15.00	4.50
JN3 Gabe Kapler Kevin McGlinchy	5.00	1.50
JN4 Jackson Melian Warren Morris	5.00	1.50
JN5 Dernell Stenson Vernon Wells	5.00	1.50
JN6 Ricky Williams Ricky Williams	15.00	4.50

1999 Just Nine Imagine

Randomly inserted in Just Imagine packs at one in 240, this nine-card insert set features only the brightest minor league prospects.

	Nm-Mt	Ex-Mt
COMPLETE SET (9)	120.00	36.00
1 Rick Ankiel	5.00	1.50
2 Ron Belliard	5.00	1.50
3 Pat Burrell	25.00	7.50
4 Lance Berkman	5.00	1.50
5 Ben Davis	5.00	1.50
6 Ruben Mateo	5.00	1.50
7 Corey Patterson	20.00	6.00
8 Aramis Ramirez	5.00	1.50
9 Alfonso Soriano	30.00	9.00

1999 Just Nine The Start

Randomly inserted into Just the Start product at one in 24, this insert focuses on minor leaguer's that are just starting their professional careers.

	Nm-Mt	Ex-Mt
COMPLETE SET (9)	15.00	4.50
1 Rick Ankiel	1.00	.30
2 Michael Barrett	1.00	.30
3 Lance Berkman	1.00	.30
4 Alex Escobar	1.00	.30
5 Nick Johnson	2.50	.75
6 Gabe Kapler	1.00	.30
7 Warren Morris	1.00	.30
8 Pablo Ozuna	1.00	.30
9 Ben Petrick	1.00	.30

1999 Just Power

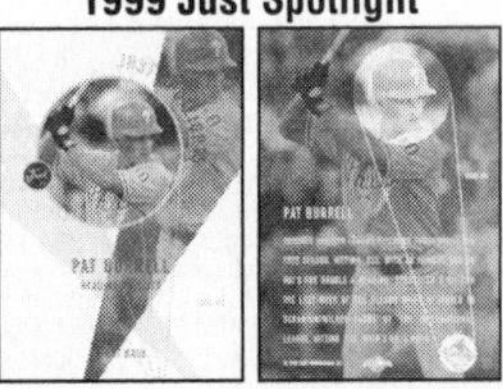

Randomly inserted into Just the Start product at one in 24, this insert focuses on minor league power hitters and pitchers.

	Nm-Mt	Ex-Mt
COMPLETE SET (10)	10.00	3.00
1 Ryan Anderson	1.00	.30
2 Wes Anderson	1.00	.30
3 Lance Berkman	1.00	.30
4 Juan Dilone	1.00	.30
5 Marcus Giles	2.50	.75
6 Gabe Kapler	1.00	.30
7 Kevin McGlinchy	1.00	.30
8 Gil Meche	1.00	.30
9 Dernell Stenson	1.00	.30
10 Ricky Williams	3.00	.90

1999 Just Spotlight

Randomly inserted in Justifiable packs at one in 24, this 10-card insert features 10 prospects that are in the spotlight this season.

	Nm-Mt	Ex-Mt
COMPLETE SET (10)	25.00	7.50
1 Dee Brown	1.00	.30
2 Pat Burrell	6.00	1.80
3 Josh Hamilton	1.50	.45
4 Nick Johnson	2.50	.75
5 Jason Marquis	1.00	.30
6 Pablo Ozuna	1.00	.30
7 John Patterson	1.00	.30
8 Adam Piatt	1.00	.30
9 Matt Riley	2.00	.60
10 Alfonso Soriano	6.00	1.80

1999 Just Stars

Randomly inserted in Imagine packs at one in 24, this insert set features 10 players that made themselves stars in the minor leagues.

	Nm-Mt	Ex-Mt
COMPLETE SET (10)	25.00	7.50
1 Rick Ankiel	1.00	.30
2 Pat Burrell	6.00	1.80
3 Sean Casey	1.00	.30
4 Erubiel Durazo	1.50	.45
5 Nick Johnson	2.50	.75
6 Jacque Jones	1.00	.30
7 Ruben Mateo	1.00	.30
8 Gary Matthews Jr.	1.00	.30
9 Adam Piatt	1.00	.30
10 Alfonso Soriano	6.00	1.80

1999 SP Top Prospects

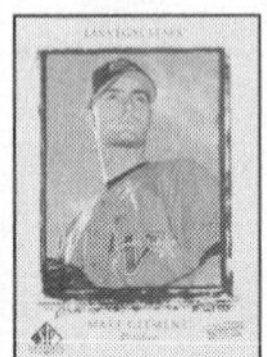

The 1999 SP Top Prospects set was released as a 126-card set that featured 116 player cards and 10 "top ten" player checklists. There was only one series offered. Each pack contained eight cards and carried a suggested retail price of 4.99. Early cards of Rick Ankiel, Pat Burrell, Drew Henson and Heisman Award winner Ricky Williams are featured in this set. The Henson card was "pulled" because of issues with his college eligibility; however, it is estimated that most of the Henson cards were released before that issue came up.

	Nm-Mt	Ex-Mt
COMPLETE SET (126)	20.00	6.00
1 J.D. Drew T10	.40	.12
2 Matt Clement T10	.40	.12
3 Alex Gonzalez T10	.40	.12
4 Rick Ankiel T10	.75	.23
5 Alex Escobar T10	.75	.23
6 Eric Chavez T10	.75	.23
7 Lance Berkman T10	.75	.23
8 Russell Branyan T10	.40	.12
9 Gabe Kapler T10	.40	.12
10 Bruce Chen T10	.40	.12
11 Chuck Abbott	.40	.12
12 Ryan Anderson	.40	.12
13 Rick Ankiel UER	.75	.23
14 Michael Barrett	.40	.12
15 Carlos Beltran	.75	.23
16 Bucky Jacobsen	.75	.23
17 Kris Benson	.40	.12
18 Lance Berkman	.75	.23
19 Ryan Brannan	.40	.12
20 Russell Branyan	.40	.12
21 Dermal Brown	.40	.12
22 Roosevelt Brown	.75	.23
23 Juan LeBron	.40	.12
24 Brent Butler	.40	.12
25 Ross Gload	.40	.12
26 Eric Chavez	.75	.23
27 Bruce Chen	.40	.12
28 Matt Clement	.75	.23
29 Adonis Harrison	.40	.12
30 Francisco Cordero	.40	.12
31 David Cortes	.40	.12
32 Paxton Crawford	.75	.23
33 Joe Crede	1.00	.30
34 Bobby Cripps	.40	.12
35 Michael Cuddyer	.40	.12
36 John Curtice	.40	.12
37 Mike Darr	.40	.12
38 Ben Davis	.40	.12
39 Glenn Davis	.40	.12
40 Matt DeWitt	.40	.12
41 Shea Hillenbrand	2.00	.60
42 Adam Eaton	.40	.12
43 Mario Encarnacion	.40	.12
44 Chris Enochs	.40	.12
45 Pat Burrell	5.00	1.50
46 Kyle Farnsworth	1.00	.30
47 Nelson Figueroa	.40	.12
48 Shawn Gallagher	.40	.12
49 Chad Hutchinson	.75	.23
50 Marcus Giles	2.00	.60
51 J.D. Drew	.75	.23
52 Alex Gonzalez	.40	.12
53 Chad Green	.40	.12
54 Jason Grilli	.40	.12
55 Seth Etherton	.75	.23
56 Roy Halladay	.75	.23
57 Tyrone Hartshorn	.40	.12
58 Al Hawkins	.40	.12
59 Chad Hermansen	.40	.12
60 Ramon Hernandez	.40	.12
61 Mark Johnson	.40	.12
62 Doug Johnston	.40	.12
63 Jacque Jones	.75	.23
64 Adam Kennedy	.40	.12
65 Cesar King	.40	.12
66 Brendan Kingman	.40	.12
67 Mike Kinkade	.40	.12
68 Corey Koskie	.75	.23
69 Mike Kusiewicz	.40	.12
70 Mike Colangelo	.40	.12
71 Jason LaRue	.40	.12
72 Joe Lawrence	.40	.12
73 Carlos Lee	.75	.23
74 Jeff Liefer	.40	.12
75 Mike Lincoln	.40	.12
76 George Lombard	.40	.12
77 Mike Lowell	.75	.23
78 Alex Escobar	.75	.23
79 Sam Marsonek	.40	.12
80 Ruben Mateo	.40	.12
81 Brian Benefield	.40	.12
82 Gary Matthews Jr.	.40	.12
83 Joe Mays	.75	.23
84 Jackson Melian	.75	.23
85 Juan Melo	.40	.12
86 Chad Meyers	.40	.12
87 Matt Miller	.75	.23
88 Damon Minor	.40	.12
89 Ryan Minor	.40	.12
90 Mike Mitchell	.40	.12
91 Shea Morenz	.40	.12
92 Warren Morris	.40	.12
93 Drew Henson	5.00	1.50
94 Todd Noel	.40	.12
95 Pablo Ozuna	.40	.12
96 John Patterson	.40	.12
97 Josh Paul	.40	.12
98 Angel Pena	.40	.12
99 Juan Pena	.40	.12
100 Danny Peoples	.40	.12
101 Santiago Perez	.40	.12
102 Tommy Peterman	.40	.12
103 Ben Petrick	.40	.12
104 Calvin Pickering	.40	.12
105 John Powers	.40	.12
106 Gabe Kapler	.40	.12
107 Rob Ramsay	.40	.12
108 Luis Figueroa	.40	.12
109 Grant Roberts	.40	.12
110 Fernando Seguignol	.40	.12
111 Juan Sosa	.40	.12
112 Dernell Stenson	.40	.12
113 John Stephens	.75	.23
114 Mike Stoner	.40	.12
115 Reggie Taylor	.40	.12
116 Justin Towle	.40	.12
117 Carlos Villalobos	.75	.23
118 Vernon Wells	.75	.23
119 Jayson Werth	.40	.12
120 Jake Westbrook	.40	.12
121 Matt White	.75	.23
122 Ricky Williams	3.00	.90
123 Kevin Witt	.40	.12
124 Dewayne Wise	.40	.12
125 Ed Yarnall	.40	.12
126 Mike Zywica	.40	.12

1999 SP Top Prospects Chirography

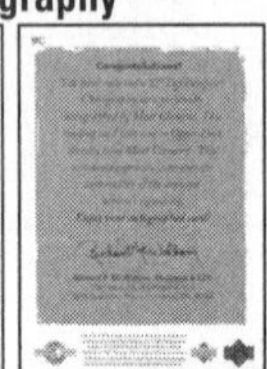

Randomly inserted in packs at one in eight, this 30-card insert features autographed cards from some of the hottest up and coming prospects. Card backs are numbered with the player's initials. The backs have a congratulatory message from Upper Deck boss Richard McWilliam that this is a real signed card. An early Rick Ankiel autograph card is featured in this set.

	Nm-Mt	Ex-Mt
BB Brent Butler	5.00	1.50
BC Bruce Chen	5.00	1.50
BP Ben Petrick	5.00	1.50
CE Chris Enochs	5.00	1.50
CH Chad Hermansen	5.00	1.50
CK Cesar King	5.00	1.50
CL Carlos Lee	10.00	3.00
DB Dermal Brown	5.00	1.50
DC David Cortes	5.00	1.50
EC Eric Chavez	15.00	4.50
EY Ed Yarnall	5.00	1.50
FC Francisco Cordero	5.00	1.50
GL George Lombard	5.00	1.50
GM Gary Matthews Jr.	5.00	1.50
JM Juan Melo	5.00	1.50
JP John Patterson	5.00	1.50
JW Jayson Werth	5.00	1.50
LB Lance Berkman	15.00	4.50
MC Matt Clement	10.00	3.00
MD Mike Darr	5.00	1.50
MK Mike Kinkade	5.00	1.50
ML Mike Lowell	10.00	3.00
MW Matt White	10.00	3.00
RA Ryan Anderson	5.00	1.50
RH Ramon Hernandez	10.00	3.00
RM Ruben Mateo	5.00	1.50
WM Warren Morris	5.00	1.50
JAM Jackson Melian	10.00	3.00
RIA Rick Ankiel	10.00	3.00
RYM Ryan Minor	5.00	1.50

1999 SP Top Prospects Destination the Show

Randomly inserted in packs at one in 92, this 30-card insert set serial numbered to 100 features only the brightest stars on a super-premium design. Card backs carry a "D" prefix.

	Nm-Mt	Ex-Mt
D1 Ryan Anderson	8.00	2.40
D2 Rick Ankiel	10.00	3.00
D3 Lance Berkman	10.00	3.00
D4 Russell Branyan	8.00	2.40
D5 Juan Melo	8.00	2.40
D6 Alex Gonzalez	10.00	3.00
D7 Eric Chavez	10.00	3.00
D8 Bruce Chen	8.00	2.40
D9 Matt Clement	10.00	3.00
D10 Ed Yarnall	8.00	2.40
D11 Dernell Stenson	8.00	2.40
D12 Corey Koskie	10.00	3.00
D13 J.D. Drew	10.00	3.00
D14 Chad Hermansen	8.00	2.40
D15 Ramon Hernandez	10.00	3.00
D16 Cesar King	8.00	2.40
D17 Mike Kinkade	8.00	2.40
D18 Carlos Lee	10.00	3.00
D19 George Lombard	8.00	2.40
D20 Ruben Mateo	8.00	2.40
D21 Gary Matthews Jr.	8.00	2.40
D22 Pat Burrell	40.00	12.00
D23 Ryan Minor	8.00	2.40
D24 Warren Morris	8.00	2.40
D25 Gabe Kapler	8.00	2.40
D26 Mike Lowell	10.00	3.00
D27 Jayson Werth	8.00	2.40
D28 Matt White	10.00	3.00
D29 Pablo Ozuna	8.00	2.40
D30 Mike Stoner	8.00	2.40

1999 SP Top Prospects Great Futures

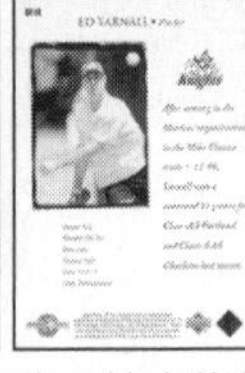

Randomly inserted in packs at 1 in 4, this 30 card insert set features 30 top minor league players who will undoubtedly have an outstanding future in the big leagues. Card backs carry a "GF" prefix.

	Nm-Mt	Ex-Mt
COMPLETE SET (30)	25.00	7.50
GF1 Ryan Anderson	1.00	.30
GF2 Rick Ankiel	1.00	.30
GF3 Lance Berkman	1.00	.30
GF4 Russell Branyan	1.00	.30
GF5 Dermal Brown	1.00	.30
GF6 Brent Butler	1.00	.30
GF7 Eric Chavez	1.00	.30
GF8 Bruce Chen	1.00	.30
GF9 Matt Clement	1.00	.30
GF10 Ed Yarnall	1.00	.30
GF11 Mike Darr	1.00	.30
GF12 Chris Enochs	1.00	.30
GF13 J.D. Drew	1.00	.30
GF14 Chad Hermansen	1.00	.30
GF15 Ramon Hernandez	1.00	.30
GF16 Cesar King	1.00	.30
GF17 Mike Kinkade	1.00	.30
GF18 Carlos Lee	1.00	.30
GF19 George Lombard	1.00	.30
GF20 Ruben Mateo	1.00	.30
GF21 Gary Matthews Jr.	1.00	.30
GF22 Jackson Melian	1.00	.30
GF23 Ryan Minor	1.00	.30
GF24 Warren Morris	1.00	.30
GF25 John Patterson	1.00	.30
GF26 Ben Petrick	1.00	.30
GF27 Jayson Werth	1.00	.30
GF28 Matt White	1.00	.30
GF29 Francisco Cordero	1.00	.30
GF30 Mike Stoner	1.00	.30

1999 SP Top Prospects Retrospectives

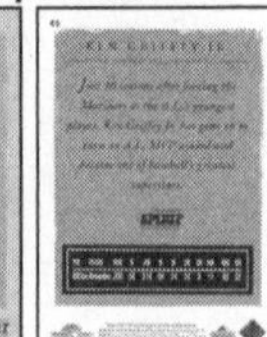

Randomly inserted in packs at one in 13, this 10-card set features 5 cards of Ken Griffey Jr., and 5 cards of Michael Jordan. Card backs carry a "R" prefix.

	Nm-Mt	Ex-Mt
COMMON GRIFFEY (R1-R5)	1.50	.45
COMMON JORDAN (R6-R10)	3.00	.90
NNO Ken Griffey Jr. AU/10		
NNO Michael Jordan AU/10		

1999 Team Best Player of the Year

The 1999 Team Best Player of the Year product was released in November,1999 as 50-card set. The product features some of the brightest young stars in major league baseball. Card packs contained six cards and carried a suggested retail price of 2.99. Early cards of Rick Ankiel, Pat Burrell, Chin-Feng Chen, Rafael Furcal, Josh Hamilton and Corey Patterson are

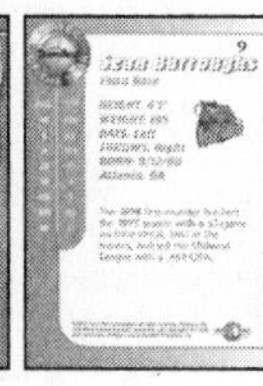

featured in this set.

	Nm-Mt	Ex-Mt
COMPLETE SET (50)	15.00	4.50
1 Ryan Anderson	.25	.07
2 Rick Ankiel	.40	.12
3 Jeff Austin	.40	.12
4 Kurt Bierek	.25	.07
5 Jung Bong	.40	.12
6 Dee Brown	.25	.07
7 Nate Bump	.40	.12
8 Pat Burrell	2.50	.75
9 Sean Burroughs	1.50	.45
10 Brent Butler	.25	.07
11 Chin-Feng Chen	.60	.18
12 Hee Seop Choi	1.50	.45
13 Joe Crede	.50	.15
14 Jack Cust	.25	.07
15 Gookie Dawkins	.25	.07
16 Trent Durrington	.25	.07
17 Seth Etherton	.40	.12
18 Vince Faison	.40	.12
19 Choo Freeman	.40	.12
20 Rafael Furcal	1.00	.30
21 Jay Gibbons	.60	.18
22 Marcus Giles	.75	.23
23 J.M. Gold	.25	.07
24 Jeff Goldbach	.25	.07
25 Josh Hamilton	.60	.18
26 Kevin Haverbusch	.25	.07
27 D'Angelo Jimenez	.25	.07
28 Nick Johnson	1.00	.30
29 Adam Kennedy	.25	.07
30 Steve Lomasney	.25	.07
31 George Lombard	.25	.07
32 Felipe Lopez	.40	.12
33 Jason Marquis	.25	.07
34 Tydus Meadows	.25	.07
35 Aaron Myette	.40	.12
36 Corey Patterson	2.00	.60
37 Carlos Pena	.60	.18
38 Adam Piatt	.40	.12
39 Julio Ramirez	.25	.07
40 Matt Riley	.75	.23
41 Juan Rivera	.40	.12
42 Jason Romano	.25	.07
43 Aaron Rowand	.40	.12
44 C.C. Sabathia	.60	.18
45 Alfonso Soriano	5.00	1.50
46 Jason Standridge	.25	.07
47 Dernell Stenson	.25	.07
48 Jorge Toca	.25	.07
49 Eric Valent	.40	.12
50 Jayson Werth	.25	.07

1999 Team Best Player of the Year Gold

Randomly inserted in packs, this insert is a complete parallel of the Player of the Year base set. Each card is serial numbered to 50.

Nm-Mt Ex-Mt

*GOLD: 5X TO 12X BASIC CARDS......

1999 Team Best Player of the Year Silver

Randomly inserted in packs, this insert is a complete parallel of the Player of the Year base set. Each card is serial numbered to 150.

Nm-Mt Ex-Mt

*SILVER: 2.5X TO 6X BASIC CARDS ..

1999 Team Best Player of the Year Contenders

Randomly inserted in packs at one in 90, this insert set features 10 of the minor league's brightest stars.

	Nm-Mt	Ex-Mt
COMPLETE SET (10)	80.00	24.00
1 Dee Brown	4.00	1.20
2 Pat Burrell	12.00	3.60
3 Chin-Feng Chen	5.00	1.50
4 Rafael Furcal	6.00	1.80
5 Nick Johnson	6.00	1.80
6 Ramon Ortiz	4.00	1.20
7 Aramis Ramirez	4.00	1.20
8 Matt Riley	5.00	1.50
9 Jason Standridge	4.00	1.20
10 Vernon Wells	4.00	1.20

1999 Team Best Player of the Year Past Player Autographs

Randomly inserted in packs, this insert set features the autographs of Andruw Jones, Paul Konerko, and Eric Chavez.

	Nm-Mt	Ex-Mt
1 Andruw Jones	15.00	4.50
2 Paul Konerko	10.00	3.00
3 Eric Chavez	10.00	3.00

1999 Team Best Player of the Year POY

Randomly inserted in packs at one in 19, this 10-card insert set features cards of the two 1999 Player of the Year winners; Rick Ankiel and Adam Piatt.

	Nm-Mt	Ex-Mt
COMMON ANKIEL (1-6)	1.50	.45
COMMON PIATT (7-10)	1.00	.30

1999 Team Best Player of the Year Young Guns

Randomly inserted into retail packs at one in 90, this 10-card insert set features some of the best prospects in baseball.

	Nm-Mt	Ex-Mt
1 Dee Brown	5.00	1.50
2 Pat Burrell	25.00	7.50
3 Chen-Feng Chen	25.00	7.50
4 Rafael Furcal	20.00	6.00
5 Nick Johnson	15.00	4.50
6 Ramon Ortiz	8.00	2.40
7 Aramis Ramirez	10.00	3.00
8 Matt Riley	5.00	1.50
9 Jason Standridge	5.00	1.50
10 Vernon Wells	15.00	4.50

1999 Team Best Rookies Promos

These five standard-size cards were issued to promote the 1999 Team Best Rookies set.

	Nm-Mt	Ex-Mt
NNO Alex Escobar Wheels	.50	.15
NNO Adam Everett	.50	.15
NNO Marcus Giles Lumber	.50	
NNO Ryan Bradley	.50	.15
NNO J.D.Drew	1.00	.30
Pablo Ozuna Future		

1999 Team Best Rookies

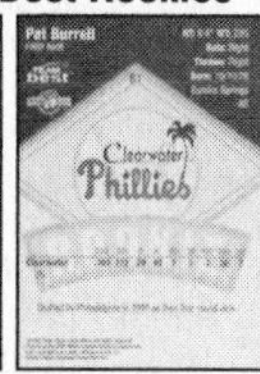

This 100 card set, issued in packs, features the leading new players to professional baseball in 1999. Card number 32, Josh Hancock, was pulled early in production because of a wrong photo. The card was corrected and mailed out to collectors who contact Team Best via mail or the internet.

	Nm-Mt	Ex-Mt
COMPLETE SET (99)	15.00	4.50
1 Chip Ambres	.40	.12
2 Scott Barrett	.25	.07
3 Todd Belhorn	.25	.07
4 Darren Blakely	.25	.07
5 Matt Borne	.25	.07
6 Nate Bump	.40	.12
7 Ryan Bundy	.25	.07
8 Eric Byrnes	.50	.15
9 David Callahan	.40	.12
10 Rob Castelli	.25	.07
11 Doug Clark	.25	.07
12 Greg Clark	.25	.07
13 Darryl Conyer	.40	.12
14 Jeremy Cotten	.25	.07
15 Bubba Crosby	.50	.15
16 Mike Curry	.40	.12
17 Mike Dean	.25	.07
18 David Diaz	.25	.07
19 Jeremy Dodson	.40	.12
20 Ryan Drese	.40	.12
21 J.D. Drew	.40	.12
22 Morgan Ensberg	.50	.15
23 Adam Everett	.40	.12
24 Mike Fischer	.40	.12
25 Pete Fisher	.25	.07
26 Josh Fogg	.40	.12
27 Brad Freeman	.25	.07
28 Nate Frese	.25	.07
29 Eddy Furniss	.25	.07
30 Keith Ginter	.25	.07
31 Eric Good	.25	.07
32 Josh Hancock ERR SP		
32A Josh Hancock COR		
33 Ryan Harber	.25	.07
34 Jason Hart	.40	.12
35 Jason Hill	.25	.07
36 Heath Honeycutt	.25	.07
37 Aubrey Huff	1.25	.35
38 Chad Hutchinson	.40	.12
39 Brandon Inge	.40	.12
40 Brett Jodie	.25	.07
41 Gabe Johnson	.40	.12
42 Clint Johnston	.40	.12
43 Jesse Joyce	.25	.07
44 Randy Keisler	.40	.12
45 Jarrod Kingrey	.25	.07
46 Craig Kuzmic	.25	.07
47 Tim Lemon	.25	.07
48 Ryan Lentz	.25	.07
49 Neil Longo	.25	.07
50 Felipe Lopez	.40	.12
51 Javier A.Lopez	.25	.07
52 Phil Lowery	.40	.12
53 Chris Magruder	.25	.07
54 Mike Maroth	.40	.12
55 Kennon McArthur	.25	.07
56 Shawn McCorkle	.40	.12
57 Arturo McDowell	.40	.12
58 Josh McKinley	.40	.12
59 Jason Michaels	.25	.07
60 Ryan Moskau	.25	.07
61 Mark Mulder	2.00	.60
62 Will Ohman	.25	.07
63 Todd Ozias	.25	.07
64 Matt Padgett	.25	.07
65 Corey Patterson	2.00	.60
66 Adam Pettyjohn	.40	.12
67 Brad Piercy	.25	.07
68 Scott Pratt	.40	.12
69 Kris Rayborn	.25	.07
70 Chris Reinike	.25	.07
71 Billy Rich	.25	.07
72 Ryan Ridenour	.25	.07
73 Brian Rogers	.40	.12
74 Aaron Rowand	.40	.12
75 Ryan Rupe	.25	.07
76 C.C. Sabathia	.60	.18
77 Jason Saenz	.40	.12
78 Aaron Sams	.40	.12
79 Sammy Serrano	.25	.07
80 Clint Smith	.25	.07
81 Pat Burrell	2.50	.75
82 Zach Sorensen	.25	.07
83 Steve Stemle	.25	.07
84 John Stewart	.25	.07
85 Tyler Thompson	.25	.07
86 Matt Thornton	.40	.12
87 Tony Torcato	.40	.12
88 Keola de la Tori	.25	.07
89 Andres Torres	.40	.12
90 Jason Tyner	.40	.12
91 Jeff Urban	.40	.12
92 Eric Valent	.40	.12
93 Derek Wathan	.40	.12
94 Jeff Weaver	.40	.12
95 Jake Weber	.25	.07
96 Ken Westmoreland	.25	.07
97 Brad Wilkerson	.40	.12
98 Clyde Williams	.25	.07
99 Jeff Winchester	.25	.07
100 Mitch Wylie	.25	.07

1999 Team Best Rookies Gold

Randomly inserted into packs, this 100-card insert is a complete parallel of the base set. These cards feature gold foil, and are individually serial numbered to 50.

Nm-Mt Ex-Mt

*GOLD: 5X TO 12X BASIC CARDS......

1999 Team Best Rookies Silver

Randomly inserted into packs, this 100-card insert is a complete parallel of the base set. These cards feature silver foil, and are individually serial numbered to 125.

Nm-Mt Ex-Mt

*SILVER: 2.5X TO 6X BASIC CARDS ..

1999 Team Best All-Stars

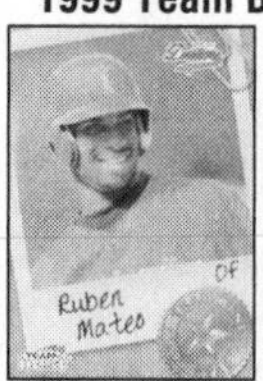

Randomly inserted in Baseball America Top Prospects retail packs at one in 90, this retail only insert set features ten all-star caliber minor league players.

	Nm-Mt	Ex-Mt
COMPLETE SET (10)	50.00	15.00
1 Rick Ankiel	5.00	1.50
2 Lance Berkman	5.00	1.50
3 Pat Burrell	12.00	3.60
4 Octavio Dotel	5.00	1.50
5 Alex Escobar	5.00	1.50
6 George Lombard	5.00	1.50
7 Ruben Mateo	5.00	1.50
8 Ryan Minor	5.00	1.50
9 Pablo Ozuna	5.00	1.50
10 Dernell Stenson	5.00	1.50

1999 Team Best Autographs

Randomly inserted into Baseball America Team Best Player of the Year packs at a rate of approximately two per box, this 67-card insert features autographed cards of some of the hottest prospects in baseball. Early autographed cards of Rick Ankiel and Corey Patterson are featured in this set.

	Nm-Mt	Ex-Mt
1 Rick Ankiel BA-TP-TR	5.00	1.50
2 Tony Armas Jr. TP	2.00	.60
3 Michael Barrett BA-TR	5.00	1.50
4 Lance Berkman BA-TR	10.00	3.00
5 Nick Bierbrodt TP	2.00	.60
6 Jamie Brown TP	2.00	.60
7 A.J. Burnett BA-TR	8.00	2.40
8 Steve Carver BA	2.00	.60
9 Bruce Chen BA-TR	2.00	.60
10 Jesus Colome TP	2.00	.60
11 M.Cuddyer BA-TR	2.00	.60
12 Octavio Dotel TP	5.00	1.50
13 Kelly Dransfeldt TP	2.00	.60
14 J.D. Drew BA-TR	10.00	3.00
15 Tim Drew BA	2.00	.60
16 Alex Escobar BA-TR	5.00	1.50
17 Seth Etherton BA-TR	5.00	1.50
18 Adam Everett TP	5.00	1.50
19 Vince Faison TP	5.00	1.50
20 Brian Falkenborg BA	2.00	.60
21 Robert Fick BA	5.00	1.50
22 Mark Fischer BA-TR	2.00	.60
23 Eddy Furniss BA	2.00	.60
24 Troy Glaus BA-TP-TR	15.00	4.50
25 Nathan Haynes BA-TR	2.00	.60
26 Chad Hermansen BA	2.00	.60
27 Junior Herndon TP	5.00	1.50
28 S.Hillenbrand BA-TR	8.00	2.40
29 Aubrey Huff TP	10.00	3.00
30 Mark Johnson BA	2.00	.60
31 Adam Kennedy BA	5.00	1.50
32 Jason LaRue BA	2.00	.60
33 Matt LeCroy BA-TR	5.00	1.50
34 Carlos Lee BA	5.00	1.50
35 Corey Lee BA-TP-TR	2.00	.60
36 Felipe Lopez BA	5.00	1.50
37 Jason Marquis TP	2.00	.60
38 Willie Martinez TP	2.00	.60
39 Ruben Mateo TP	2.00	.60
40 Darnell McDonald BA	2.00	.60
41 Ryan Minor TP	2.00	.60
42 Warren Morris TP	2.00	.60
43 Mark Mulder BA	15.00	4.50
44 Trot Nixon BA-TR	10.00	3.00
45 Todd Noel BA-TR	2.00	.60
46 Pablo Ozuna BA-TR	2.00	.60
47 Corey Patterson TP	10.00	3.00
48 Carlos Pena TP	8.00	2.40
49 Brad Penny BA-TR	5.00	1.50
50 Ben Petrick TP	2.00	.60
51 Calvin Pickering BA-TR	2.00	.60
52 Paul Rigdon TP	2.00	.60
53 Matt Riley BA-TR	8.00	2.40
54 Grant Roberts TP	2.00	.60
55 Jason Romano BA-TR	2.00	.60
56 Ryan Rupe BA	2.00	.60
57 C.C. Sabathia TP	8.00	2.40
58 Randall Simon BA	5.00	1.50
59 Jason Standridge BA	2.00	.60
60 Nathan Teut BA	2.00	.60
61 Pete Tucci BA-TR	2.00	.60
62 Jason Tyner TP	5.00	1.50
63 Eric Valent BA-TR	5.00	1.50
64 Vernon Wells BA	10.00	3.00
65 Jake Westbrook BA-TR	2.00	.60
66 Randy Wolf BA	5.00	1.50
67 Ed Yarnall TP	2.00	.60

1999 Team Best Diamond Best

Randomly inserted into Team Best Diamond Best Edition at one in 30, this insert focuses on the best minor league players.

	Nm-Mt	Ex-Mt
COMPLETE SET (10)	20.00	6.00
1 Ryan Anderson	1.50	.45
2 Pat Burrell	8.00	2.40
3 Bruce Chen	1.00	.30
4 Mike Darr	1.00	.30
5 Octavio Dotel	1.00	.30
6 Jason LaRue	1.00	.30
7 Damon Minor	1.00	.30
8 Kyle Peterson	1.00	.30
9 Fernando Seguignol	1.00	.30
10 Alfonso Soriano	15.00	4.50

1999 Team Best Future Stars

Randomly inserted in Team Best Rookies at one in 18, this 25-card insert features future major league baseball players.

	Nm-Mt	Ex-Mt
COMPLETE SET (25)	100.00	30.00
1 Darryl Conyer	1.00	.30
Javier Lopez		
2 Troy Cameron	1.00	.30
Luis Rivera		
3 Troy Glaus	2.50	.75
Darren Blakely		
4 Jayson Werth	1.00	.30
Darnell McDonald		
5 Adam Everett	1.00	.30
Mike Maroth		
6 Aaron Rowand	1.00	.30
Josh Fogg		
7 Corey Patterson	8.00	2.40
Aaron Sams		
8 C.C. Sabathia	2.50	.75
Zach Sorensen		
9 Jeff Weaver	1.00	.30
Brandon Inge		
10 Chip Ambres	1.00	.30
Derek Wathan		
11 Bubba Crosby	2.00	.60
Ryan Moskau		
12 Josh McKinley	1.00	.30
Brad Wilkerson		
13 Randy Keisler	1.00	.30
Ryan Bradley		
14 Jason Tyner	1.00	.30
Jason Saenz		
15 Mark Mulder	8.00	2.40
Jason Hart		
16 Eric Valent	1.00	.30
Jason Michaels		
17 Clint Johnston	1.00	.30
Eddy Furniss		
18 Pablo Ozuna	1.00	.30
J.D. Drew		
19 Rick Ankiel	1.00	.30
Chad Hutchinson		
20 J.D. Drew	1.00	.30
Tim Drew		
21 Darnell McDonald	1.00	.30
Donzell McDonald		
22 Tony Torcato	1.00	.30
Nate Bump		
23 Matt Thornton	1.00	.30
Ryan Anderson		
24 Felipe Lopez	1.00	.30
Vernon Wells		
25 Ryan Bundy	1.00	.30
Jarrod Kingrey		

1999 Team Best Guns

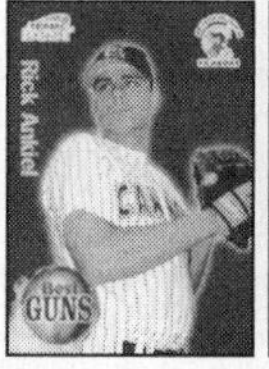
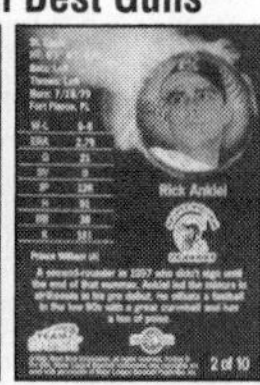

Randomly inserted in Team Best Rookies at one in 19, this 10-card insert features players with terrific throwing arms.

	Nm-Mt	Ex-Mt
COMPLETE SET (10)	10.00	3.00
1 Ryan Anderson	1.00	.30
2 Rick Ankiel	1.00	.30
3 Ryan Bradley	1.00	.30
4 Bruce Chen	1.00	.30
5 Matt Clement	1.00	.30
6 Octavio Dotel	1.00	.30
7 John Patterson	1.00	.30
8 Matt Riley	2.00	.60
9 Brent Stentz	1.00	.30
10 Ed Yarnall	1.00	.30

1999 Team Best League Leaders

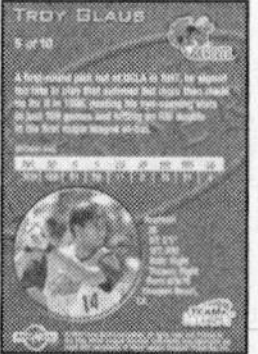

Randomly inserted in packs at one in 90, this retail only insert set features ten prospects that were among the league leaders in various categories.

	Nm-Mt	Ex-Mt
COMPLETE SET (10)	80.00	24.00
1 Michael Barrett	5.00	1.50
2 Lance Berkman	8.00	2.40
3 J.D. Drew	8.00	2.40
4 Marcus Giles	8.00	2.40
5 Troy Glaus	10.00	3.00
6 George Lombard	5.00	1.50
7 Doug Mientkiewicz	8.00	2.40
8 Trot Nixon	8.00	2.40
9 Calvin Pickering	5.00	1.50
10 Pete Tucci	5.00	1.50

1999 Team Best Lumber

Randomly inserted in Team Best Rookies at one in 90, this 10-card insert features minor leagues players that have proven that they can hit in the major leagues.

	Nm-Mt	Ex-Mt
COMPLETE SET (10)	50.00	15.00
1 Michael Barrett	5.00	1.50
2 Lance Berkman	8.00	2.40
3 J.D. Drew	8.00	2.40
4 Marcus Giles	8.00	2.40
5 Troy Glaus	10.00	3.00
6 George Lombard	5.00	1.50
7 Doug Mientkiewicz	8.00	2.40
8 Trot Nixon	8.00	2.40
9 Calvin Pickering	5.00	1.50
10 Pete Tucci	5.00	1.50

1999 Team Best Possibilities

Inserrted at a rate of one in 19 Team Best Baseball America packs, these five double-sided cards each feature two leading prospects in the minor leagues.

Nm-Mt Ex-Mt
COMPLETE SET (5) 6.00 1.80
1 Ryan Anderson 1.00 .30
Calvin Pickering
2 Rick Ankiel 1.00 .30
Chad Hermansen
3 Ryan Bradley 1.00 .30
Ryan Minor
4 John Patterson 1.00 .30
Lance Berkman
5 Brad Penny 5.00 1.50
Pat Burrell

1999 Team Best Rookie Bammers

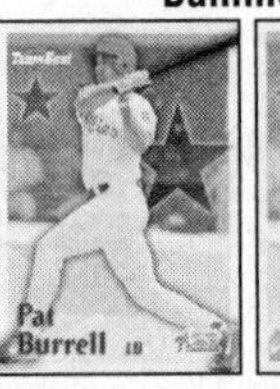

Randomly inserted as a box-topper in the 1999 Team Best Diamond Best Edition product at one per box, this insert features one "Bammer Bear" and a trading card of the corresponding player.

Nm-Mt Ex-Mt
COMPLETE SET (6) 10.00 3.00
1 Ryan Anderson .75 .23
2 Rick Ankiel 1.00 .30
3 Lance Berkman 1.00 .30
4 Pat Burrell 4.00 1.20
5 J.D. Drew Arkansas 1.00 .30
6 J.D. Drew Memphis 1.00 .30

1999 Team Best Scouts Choice

Inserted at a rate of one in 90 Team Best Baseball America packs, these 10 cards feature players projected by baseball scouts to have all the tools needed to make it big in the majors.

Nm-Mt Ex-Mt
COMPLETE SET (10) 80.00 24.00
1 Rick Ankiel 5.00 1.50
2 Lance Berkman 5.00 1.50
3 Pat Burrell 12.00 3.60
4 Octavio Dotel 5.00 1.50
5 Alex Escobar 5.00 1.50
6 George Lombard 5.00 1.50
7 Ruben Mateo 5.00 1.50
8 Ryan Minor 5.00 1.50
9 Pablo Ozuna 5.00 1.50
10 Dernell Stenson 5.00 1.50

1999 Team Best Wheels

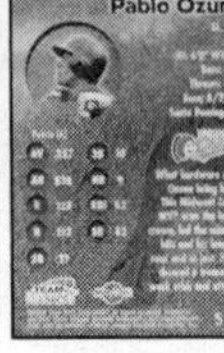

Randomly inserted into Team Best Rookies at one in 19, this 5-card set features some of the fastest prospects in baseball.

Nm-Mt Ex-Mt
COMPLETE SET (5) 4.00 1.20
1 Alex Escobar 1.00 .30
2 Cordell Farley 1.00 .30
3 Carlos Febles 1.00 .30
4 Nathan Haynes 1.00 .30
5 Pablo Ozuna 1.00 .30

1999-00 Just Debuts Autographs

These autograph cards parallel the basic Debut inserts. The cards were distributed as part of the 1999 and 2000 Just Stuff mail-in program. Each card was hand-numbered on back to 100. Cards were distributed in 2000 based on a 1999 sales promotion, they also exhibit altered Just logos from its regular issue. The 1999 issue has the "Just 99" logo while these autographs has the "Just 2K" logo, prompting the split year.

Nm-Mt Ex-Mt
7 Alfonso Soriano IM 60.00 18.00
8 Jorge Toca IM 3.00 .90
9 Kip Wells IM 5.00 1.50

1999-00 Just Drafted Autographs

This autograph card parallels the basic Drafted insert. This card was distributed as part of the 1999 and 2000 Just Stuff mail-in program. This card was hand-numbered on back to 100. Card

was distributed in 2000 based on a 1999 sales promotion, it also exhibits an altered Just logo from its regular issue. The 1999 issue has the "Just 99" logo while this autograph has the "Just" logo, prompting the split year. This card is not numbered.

Nm-Mt Ex-Mt
1 Barry Zito 40.00 12.00

1999-00 Just Due Autographs

These autograph cards parallel the basic Due inserts. The cards were distributed as part of the 1999 and 2000 Just Stuff mail-in program. Each card was hand-numbered on back to 100. These unnumbered cards are checklisted alphabetically by player last name. Cards were distributed in 2000 based on a 1999 sales promotion, they also exhibit altered Just logos from its regular issue. The 1999 issue has the "Just 99" logo while these autographs has the "Just 2K" logo, prompting the split year.

Nm-Mt Ex-Mt
1 N.Johnson Due AU 15.00 4.50
2 Gabe Kapler 3.00 .90

1999-00 Just Facts Autographs

This autograph card parallels the basic Facts insert. This card was distributed as part of the 1999 and 2000 Just Stuff mail-in program. This card was hand-numbered on back to 100. Card was distributed in 2000 based on a 1999 sales promotion, it also exhibits an altered Just logo from its regular issue. The 1999 issue has the "Just 99" logo while this autograph has the "Just" logo, prompting the split year. This card is not numbered.

Nm-Mt Ex-Mt
1 Rafael Furcal 15.00 4.50

1999-00 Just News Autographs

These autograph cards parallel the basic News inserts. The cards were distributed as part of the 1999 and 2000 Just Stuff mail-in program. Each card was hand-numbered on back to 100. Cards were distributed in 2000 based on a 1999 sales promotion, they also exhibit altered Just logos from its regular issue. The 1999 issue has the "Just 99" logo while these autographs has the "Just 2K" logo, prompting the split year.

Nm-Mt Ex-Mt
1 Rick Ankiel 5.00 1.50
3 Gabe Kapler 3.00 .90

1999-00 Just Nine Autographs

These autograph cards parallel the basic Just Nine inserts. The cards were distributed as part of the 1999 and 2000 Just Stuff mail-in program. Each card was hand-numbered on back to 100. These unnumbered cards are checklisted alphabetically by player last name. Cards were distributed in 2000 based on a 1999 sales promotion, they also exhibit altered Just logos from its regular issue. The 1999 issue has the "Just 99" logo while these autographs has several variations, "Just 2K", "Just" and "Just 99" logos, but the key is that they were distributed in 2000 via 1999 sales promotion prompting the split year.

Nm-Mt Ex-Mt
1 Rick Ankiel 5.00 1.50
2 Rafael Furcal 15.00 4.50
3 Gabe Kapler 3.00 .90
4 C.Patterson Nine AU 15.00 4.50
5 A.Ramirez Nine AU 5.00 1.50
6 Alfonso Soriano 60.00 18.00

1999-00 Just Power Autographs

This autograph card parallels the basic Power insert. This card was distributed as part of the 1999 and 2000 Just Stuff mail-in program. This card was hand-numbered on back to 100. Card was distributed in 2000 based on a 1999 sales promotion prompting the split year. This card is not numbered.

Nm-Mt Ex-Mt
1 Gil Meche 10.00 3.00

1999-00 Just Spotlight Autographs

These autograph cards parallel the basic Spotlightt inserts. The cards were distributed as part of the 1999 and 2000 Just Stuff mail-in program. Each card was hand-numbered on back to 100. Cards were distributed in 2000 based on a 1999 sales promotion, they also exhibit altered Just logos from its regular issue. The 1999 issue has the "Just 99" logo while these autographs has the "Just 2K" logo, prompting the split year.

Nm-Mt Ex-Mt
4 Nick Johnson 15.00 4.50
Spot '99 AU
10 Alfonso Soriano 60.00 18.00

1999-00 Just Stars Autographs

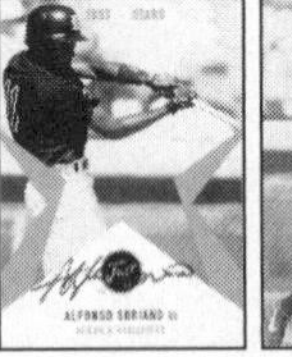

These autograph cards parallel the basic Debut inserts. The cards were distributed as part of the 1999 and 2000 Just Stuff mail-in program. Each card was hand-numbered on back to 100. These unnumbered cards are checklisted alphabetically by player last name. Cards were distributed in 2000 based on a 1999 sales promotion, they also exhibit altered Just logos from its regular issue. The 1999 issue has the "Just 99" logo while these autographs has the "Just 2K" logo, prompting the split year.

Nm-Mt Ex-Mt
1 Rick Ankiel 5.00 1.50
2 Sean Casey 5.00 1.50
3 Nick Johnson 15.00 4.50
4 Alfonso Soriano 60.00 18.00
Stars '99 AU

2000 Diamond Authentics Autographs

The 2000 Diamond Authentics product was released in May,2000 as a 31-card autograph set. Each base card was individually serial numbered to 3,250. Each pack carried a suggested retail price of $9.99.

Nm-Mt Ex-Mt
COMPLETE SET (31) 50.00 15.00
1 Fletcher Bates 2.00 .60
2 Mark Harriger 2.00 .60
3 Jesse Ibarra 2.00 .60
4 Keith Glauber 2.00 .60
5 Melvin Rosario 2.00 .60
6 Mike Rodriguez 2.00 .60
7 Paul Avery 2.00 .60
8 Larry Barnes 3.00 .90
9 Eric Gillespie 2.00 .60
10 Mike Glendenning 2.00 .60
11 Josh Goldfield 2.00 .60
12 Dan Phillips 2.00 .60
13 Josh Reding 2.00 .60
14 Jon Schaeffer 2.00 .60
15 Kevin Sheredy 2.00 .60
16 Julio Lugo Jr. 3.00 .90
17 Tonayne Brown 2.00 .60
18 Jon Hamilton 2.00 .60
19 Vince LaCorte 2.00 .60
20 Ruddy Lugo 3.00 .90
21 Danny Ardoin 2.00 .60
22 Jermaine Clark 3.00 .90
23 Jason Sekany 2.00 .60
24 Mike Villano 2.00 .60
25 Justin Albertson 2.00 .60
26 Jesse Garcia 2.00 .60
27 Rikki Johnston 2.00 .60
28 Roosevelt Brown 2.00 .60
29 Rickey Cradle 2.00 .60
30 Shea Hillenbrand 5.00 1.50
31 Chris Richard 3.00 .90

2000 Diamond Authentics Magnificent 7 Autographs

Randomly inserted into packs this 7-card insert set features autographed cards of some of the hottest minor league players. There were only 1,250 serial-numbered sets of this insert produced. Card backs carry a "MS" prefix.

Nm-Mt Ex-Mt
COMPLETE SET (7) 40.00 12.00
*REDEMPTION: .04X TO .1X BASIC AUTOS
REDEMPTION SET AVAIL.VIA INFO CARD
REDEMPTION CARDS ARE NOT SIGNED!
MS1 Eric Gagne 10.00 3.00
MS2 Luis Rivera 3.00 .90
MS3 D'Angelo Jimenez 8.00 2.40
MS4 Jackson Melian 5.00 1.50
MS5 Barry Zito 15.00 4.50
MS6 Scott Comer 3.00 .90
MS7 Jeff DaVanon 5.00 1.50

2000 Diamond Authentics Adam Piatt Triple Crown Autographs

Randomly inserted into packs, this three-card insert features the 1999 Texas League Triple Crown winner Adam Piatt. There were only 500 serial numbered sets of this insert produced. Card backs carry a "TC" prefix.

Nm-Mt Ex-Mt
COMPLETE SET (3) 25.00 7.50
COMMON CARD (TC1-TC3) 8.00 2.40
*REDEMPTION: .075X TO .2X BASIC AUTOS
REDEMPTION SET AVAIL.VIA INFO CARD
REDEMPTION CARDS ARE NOT SIGNED!

2000 Diamond Authentics Redemptions

This 31-card parallel was made available on a special card offer within 2000 Diamond Authentics packs. Each card parallels the base autographed version except for the fact that NONE of the redemptions are signed nor serial-numbered in any manner.

Nm-Mt Ex-Mt
COMPLETE SET (31) 10.00 3.00
*REDEMPTIONS: .075X TO .2X BASIC AUTOS

2000 High School All-Americans

This 10 card set, printed to a quantity of 10,000, was issued by Sean Moore. These cards feature player photos surrounded by white borders. The back has a biography. Among the prospects included in this set were Rocco Baldelli, Laynce Nix and Jason Stokes.

Nm-Mt Ex-Mt
COMPLETE SET (10) 15.00 4.50
1 Jason Stokes 3.00 .90
2 Laynce Nix 2.00 .60
3 Rocco Baldelli 5.00 1.50
4 Justin Hileman .75 .23
5 Jason Kaanoi .75 .23
6 Derek Thompson .75 .23
7 David Espinosa .75 .23
8 Dustin McGowan 1.25 .35
9 Rocco Baldelli POY 5.00 1.50
10 Checklist .50 .15

2000 High School All-Americans Foil

This 10 card set is a complete parallel of the 2000 High School All American set, printed to a quantity of 1000, was issued by Sean Moore. These cards feature player photos on a silver foiled card. The back has a biography.

Nm-Mt Ex-Mt
COMPLETE SET (10) 25.00 7.50
*FOIL: 1X TO 2.5X BASIC CARDS

2000 High School All-Americans Autograph Promo

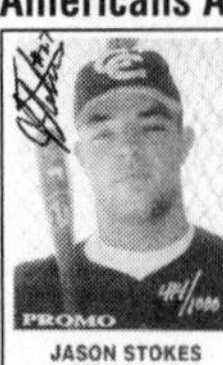
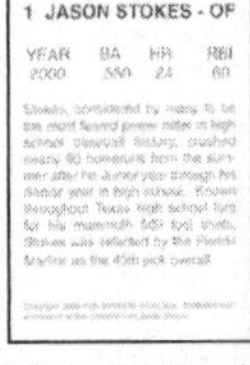

Jason Stokes and David Espinosa autographs were inserted into one in every five sets. Each card was individually serial numbered to 1000, and each card had a "PROMO" foil stamp on the front.

Nm-Mt Ex-Mt
1 Jason Stokes/1000 40.00 12.00
7 David Espinosa/1000 5.00 1.50

2000 Hutchinson Popcorn

This four card set honoring the career of Fred Hutchinson, was issues for the sixth consecutive season. These cards mention that this is the 25th anniversary of the creation of the Fred Hutchinson Cancer Research Center.

Nm-Mt Ex-Mt
COMPLETE SET (4) 10.00 3.00
COMMON CARD (1-4) 2.50 .75
3 Fred Hutchinson MG 3.00 .90
Bobby Gene Smith
Hal Smith
Milt Smith
Robert Smith
4 Fred Hutchinson MG 3.00 .90
Leo Lassen ANN

2000 Just Promos Imagine

Given out to hobby dealers and members of the media, this five-card set was issued in a cello wrapper with press information about the product.

Nm-Mt Ex-Mt
COMPLETE SET (5) 5.00 1.50
NNO Rick Ankiel .50 .15
NNO Mark Mulder 1.00 .30
Debuts
NNO Corey Patterson 1.00 .30
Tools
NNO Vernon Wells 1.00 .30
Dominant
NNO Nick Johnson 2.00 .60
Alfonso Soriano Gems

2000 Just Promos The Preview 2K

Given out to hobby dealers and members of the media, this five-card set was issued in a cello wrapper with press information about the product.

Nm-Mt Ex-Mt
COMPLETE SET (5) 3.00 .90
1 Brian Daubach .50 .15
2 Ben Broussard Debuts .50 .15
3 Josh Hamilton Drafted .50 .15
4 Rick Ankiel The One .75 .23
5 Pat Burrell Tools 1.50 .45

2000 Just

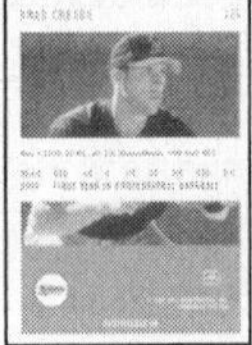

The 2000 Just product was released in several series as follows: Just the Preview 2K (cards 1-100) in May, 2000, Just Imagine (cards 101-200) in July, 2000 and Justifiable (cards 201-300) in October, 2000. The set features some of the hottest young talent in minor league baseball. Each pack contained six cards and carried a suggested retail price of $1.99. Each box contained 24 packs and two Autograph cards graded and sealed by USA Grading Services. The graded Autograph cards were placed on top of the sealed packs within the cello wrapped box. Key cards within the basic set include Wilson Betemit, Tony Blanco, Joe Borchard, Chin-Feng Chen, Brad Cresse, Adrian Gonzalez, J.R. House, Kevin Mench, Luis Montanez and Jon Rauch.

	Nm-Mt	Ex-Mt
COMPLETE SET (300)	50.00	15.00
COMP.PREVIEW (100)	15.00	4.50
COMP.IMAGINE (100)	15.00	4.50
COMP.JUSTIFIABLE(100)	20.00	6.00
1 Andy Abad	.25	.07
2 Brent Abernathy	.40	.12
3 Luke Allen	.25	.07
4 Ryan Anderson	.25	.07
5 Wes Anderson	.40	.12
6 Rod Bair	.25	.07
7 Larry Barnes	.25	.07
8 Rob Bell	.25	.07
9 Darren Blakely	.25	.07
10 Lesli Brea	.25	.07
11 Ben Broussard	.40	.12
12 Nate Bump	.25	.07
13 Morgan Burkhart	.25	.07
14 Brent Butler	.25	.07
15 Eric Byrnes	.50	.15
16 Eric Cammack	.40	.12
17 Marcos Castillo	.40	.12
18 Jim Chamblee	.25	.07
19 Carlos Chantres	.25	.07
20 Chin-Feng Chen	.50	.15
21 Jermaine Clark	.40	.12
22 Pasqual Coco	.25	.07
23 Eric Cole	.40	.12
24 Steve Colyer	.25	.07
25 Joe Crede	.40	.12
26 Cesar Crespo	.40	.12
27 Michael Cuddyer	.25	.07
28 John Curl	.25	.07
29 Brian Daubach	.25	.07
30 Luis De Los Santos	.25	.07
31 Jason Dewey	.25	.07
32 Alejandro Diaz	.25	.07
33 R.A. Dickey	.25	.07
34 Tim Drew	.25	.07
35 Trent Durrington	.25	.07
36 Josue Espada	.40	.12
37 Ben Ford	.25	.07
38 Rafael Furcal	.40	.12
39 Jay Gibbons	.60	.18
40 Marcus Giles	.40	.12
41 Jeff Goldbach	.40	.12
42 Jimmy H.Gonzalez	.40	.12
43 Jason Grabowski	.40	.12
44 Junior Guerrero	.25	.07
45 Rick Guttormson	.25	.07
46 Josh Hamilton	.25	.07
47 Chad Harville	.25	.07
48 Kevin Haverbusch	.25	.07
49 Eric Ireland	.25	.07
50 Cesar Izturis	.40	.12
51 Nick Johnson	.40	.12
52 Josh Kalinowski	.40	.12
53 Mike Lamb	.40	.12
54 Matt LeCroy	.25	.07
55 Garry Maddox Jr.	.25	.07
56 Willie Martinez	.25	.07
57 Shawn McCorkle	.40	.12
58 Darnell McDonald	.40	.12
59 Donzell McDonald	.25	.07
60 Sean McGowan	.25	.07
61 Aaron McNeal	.40	.12
62 Steve Medrano	.25	.07
63 Todd Mensik	.25	.07
64 Phil Merrell	.40	.12
65 Mike Meyers	.40	.12
66 Ryan Mills	.25	.07
67 Ryan Moskau	.25	.07
68 Abraham Nunez	.25	.07
69 Jorge Nunez	.40	.12
70 Talmadge Nunnari	.40	.12
71 Jeremy Owens	.40	.12
72 Pablo Ozuna	.25	.07
73 Corey Patterson	.40	.12
74 Kit Pellow	.25	.07
75 Carlos Pena	.25	.07
76 Wynter Phoenix	.25	.07
77 Adam Piatt	.25	.07
78 Juan Pierre	.75	.23
79 Rob Pugmire	.40	.12
80 Tim Redding	.40	.12
81 Brian Reith	.40	.12
82 Michael Restovich	.40	.12
83 Damian Rolls	.25	.07
84 Aaron Rowand	.40	.12
85 Ruben Salazar	.40	.12
86 Alex Sanchez	.25	.07
87 Jared Sandberg	.25	.07
88 Jason Sekany	.25	.07
89 Pat Strange	.40	.12
90 David Therneau	.25	.07
91 Chris Truby	.25	.07
92 T.J. Tucker	.25	.07
93 Jeff Urban	.25	.07
94 Scott Vieira	.25	.07
95 Matt Wade	.40	.12
96 Jake Weber	.25	.07
97 Jayson Werth	.25	.07
98 Matt White	.40	.12
99 Jack Wilson	.40	.12
100 Mike Zywica	.25	.07
101 Rick Ankiel	.25	.07
102 Ricardo Aramboles	.25	.07
103 Rick Asadoorian	.40	.12
104 Jeff Austin	.40	.12
105 Danys Baez	.40	.12
106 Brad Baisley	.40	.12
107 Matt Belisle	.25	.07
108 Lance Berkman	.40	.12
109 Wilson Betemit	.40	.12
110 Nick Bierbrodt	.25	.07
111 Casey Blake	.25	.07
112 Josh Bonifay	.40	.12
113 Bobby Bradley	.40	.12
114 Milton Bradley	.40	.12
115 Junior Brignac	.25	.07
116 Roosevelt Brown	.25	.07
117 Pat Burrell	.40	.12
118 Sean Burroughs	.40	.12
119 Ben Christensen	.40	.12
120 Ryan Christianson	.40	.12
121 Michael Coleman	.25	.07
122 Jesus Colome	.25	.07
123 Jesus Cordero	.25	.07
124 Nate Cornejo	.25	.07
125 Robbie Crabtree	.25	.07
126 Jack Cust	.25	.07
127 Casey Daigle	.40	.12
128 Ben Davis	.25	.07
129 Travis Dawkins	.25	.07
130 Choo Freeman	.25	.07
131 Chris George	.25	.07
132 Gary Glover	.25	.07
133 Jerry Hairston Jr.	.25	.07
134 Ken Harvey	.50	.15
135 Jeff Heaverlo	.40	.12
136 Elvin Hernandez	.25	.07
137 J.R. House	.40	.12
138 Ty Howington	.40	.12
139 Aubrey Huff	.40	.12
140 Norm Hutchins	.40	.12
141 Chad Hutchinson	.25	.07
142 Brandon Inge	.40	.12
143 Jason Jennings	.25	.07
144 Ben Johnson	.40	.12
145 Jaime Jones	.40	.12
146 Jason Jones	.40	.12
147 Ryan Kibler	.40	.12
148 Bobby Kielty	.40	.12
149 Hong-Chih Kuo	.50	.15
150 John Lackey	.40	.12
151 Gerald Laird	.50	.15
152 Allen Levrault	.25	.07
153 Steve Lomasney	.25	.07
154 George Lombard	.25	.07
155 Felipe Lopez	.25	.07
156 Pat Manning	.40	.12
157 Luis Matos	.75	.23
158 Matt McClendon	.40	.12
159 Brian McNichol	.25	.07
160 Chris Mears	.40	.12
161 Jackson Melian	.40	.12
162 Ryan Minor	.25	.07
163 Chad Moeller	.25	.07
164 Scott Morgan	.25	.07
165 Tony Mota	.25	.07
166 Eric Munson	.25	.07
167 Corey Myers	.40	.12
168 Miguel Olivo	.40	.12
169 Ramon Ortiz	.40	.12
170 Jarrod Patterson	.25	.07
171 Alex Pena	.25	.07
172 Wily Mo Pena	.25	.07
173 Ben Petrick	.25	.07
174 Paul Phillips	.25	.07
175 Calvin Pickering	.25	.07
176 Guillermo Quiroz	.60	.18
177 Tim Raines Jr.	.25	.07
178 Aramis Ramirez	.40	.12
179 Julio Ramirez	.25	.07
180 Matt Riley	.25	.07
181 David Riske	.25	.07
182 Juan Rivera	.25	.07
183 Luis Rivera	.25	.07
184 J.P. Roberge	.25	.07
185 Grant Roberts	.25	.07
186 C.C. Sabathia	.40	.12
187 Brian Sanches	.40	.12
188 Bobby Seay	.40	.12
189 Wascar Serrano	.40	.12
190 Juan Silvestre	.40	.12
191 Chris Snelling	.50	.15
192 Kyle Snyder	.25	.07
193 Alfonso Soriano	.50	.15
194 Jason Standridge	.25	.07
195 Andy Thompson	.25	.07
196 Luis Torres	.25	.07
197 Roberto Vaz	.25	.07
198 Rico Washington	.25	.07
199 Peanut Williams	.25	.07
200 Kevin Witt	.25	.07
201 Kurt Ainsworth	.50	.15
202 Tony Alvarez	.40	.12
203 Craig Anderson	.40	.12
204 Robert Averette	.25	.07
205 Josh Beckett	1.25	.35
206 Adam Bernero	.25	.07
207 Tony Blanco	.40	.12
208 Willie Bloomquist	.75	.23
209 Joe Borchard	.60	.18
210 Danny Borrell	.40	.12
211 Shaun Boyd	.40	.12
212 Donnie Bridges	.25	.07
213 Dee Brown	.25	.07
214 Eric Bruntlett	.40	.12
215 Sean Burnett	.60	.18
216 A.J. Burnett	.25	.07
217 Matt Butler	.25	.07
218 Marlon Byrd	1.00	.30
219 Alex Cabrera	.40	.12
220 Hee Seop Choi	1.25	.35
221 Alex Cintron	.75	.23
222 Brian Cole	.40	.12
223 Carl Crawford	.40	.12
224 Brad Cresse	.40	.12
225 Chuck Crowder	.40	.12
226 Daniel Curtis	.40	.12
227 Zach Day	.40	.12
228 Mario Encarnacion	.25	.07
229 Alex Escobar	.25	.07
230 Eric Gagne	.25	.07
231 Jon Garland	.25	.07
232 Jay Gehrke	.25	.07
233 David Gil	.40	.12
234 Keith Ginter	.40	.12
235 Matt Ginter	.40	.12
236 Josh Girdley	.25	.07
237 Adrian Gonzalez	.75	.23
238 Ryan Gripp	.40	.12
239 Matt Guerrier	.40	.12
240 Elpidio Guzman	.40	.12
241 Geraldo Guzman	.25	.07
242 Toby Hall	.40	.12
243 Jason Hart	.40	.12
244 Shane Heams	.25	.07
245 Adrian Hernandez	.40	.12
246 Aaron Herr	.40	.12
247 Bobby Hill	.40	.12
248 Eric Johnson	.40	.12
249 Gary Johnson	.25	.07
250 Kelly Johnson	.40	.12
251 Tripper Johnson UER	.40	.12
252 Austin Kearns	.40	.12
253 Randy Keisler	.40	.12
254 David Kelton	.25	.07
255 Bob Keppel	.40	.12
256 Matt Kinney	.40	.12
257 Brandon Larson	.40	.12
258 Gary Majewski	.25	.07
259 Kevin Mench	.40	.12
260 Luis Montanez	.40	.12
261 Brett Myers	1.25	.35
262 Tomo Ohka	.25	.07
263 Bill Ortega	.40	.12
264 Omar Ortiz	.25	.07
265 Christian Parra	.40	.12
266 David Parrish	.40	.12
267 Chad Petty	.40	.12
268 Jon Rauch	.40	.12
269 Keith Reed	.40	.12
270 Dominic Rich	.40	.12
271 Francisco Rodriguez	.75	.23
272 Nate Rolison	.25	.07
273 Vince Rooi	.40	.12
274 B.J. Ryan	.25	.07
275 Mike Schultz	.40	.12
276 Jacobo Sequea	.25	.07
277 Bud Smith	.40	.12
278 Corey Smith	.40	.12
279 Seung Song	.50	.15
280 John Stephens	.40	.12
281 Mike Stodolka	.50	.15
282 Robert Stratton	.25	.07
283 Jason Stumm	.40	.12
284 Brian Tallet	.40	.12
285 Derek Thompson	.40	.12
286 Scott Thorman	.40	.12
287 Tony Torcato	.25	.07
288 Torre Tyson	.25	.07
289 Eric Valent	.25	.07
290 Luis Vizcaino	.25	.07
291 Adam Wainwright	.75	.23
292 Chris Wakeland	.25	.07
293 Tiger Wang	.75	.23
294 David Watkins	.40	.12
295 Brian West	.40	.12
296 Jake Westbrook	.25	.07
297 Dan Wheeler	.25	.07
298 Brad Wilkerson	.40	.12
299 Blake Williams	.40	.12
300 Carlos Zambrano	1.00	.30

2000 Just Black

Randomly inserted into packs, this 300-card insert set parallels the Just base set. There were only 50 serial numbered sets produced of this black bordered parallel. Each card is hand numbered "X/50" on back in blue ink sharpie. Please note that cards 1-100 were released in 2000 Just the Preview 2K, cards 101-200 were released in 2000 Just Imagine and cards 201-300 were released in Justifiable.

Nm-Mt Ex-Mt

*JUST BLACK: 8X TO 20X BASIC CARDS

2000 Just Gold

The 2000 Just Gold factory set was released in November, 2000 as a 300-card set. Each set also incuded eight random autographs. Each set carried a suggested retail price of 49.95. There were 5000 sets produced.

	Nm-Mt	Ex-Mt
COMP.FACT.SET (308)	50.00	15.00
COMPLETE SET (300)	40.00	12.00

*GOLD: .6X TO 1.5X BASIC CARDS

2000 Just Autographs

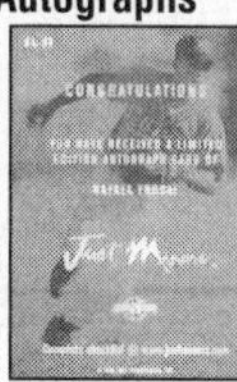

Inserted at a rate of two per hobby box into Just Imagine, Just Graded 2K (graded cards in packs), and Justifiable as a chip-topper (aka the cards were placed on top of the packs within the sealed box), this set features autograph cards of minor league prospects. The hobby box chip-topper cards were all professionally graded and encased by USA grading services. The cards were also randomly seeded into retail packs in non-graded form. The card fronts are a straight parallel from the basic issue 2000 Just set (except of course for the player's autograph - signed in blue ink sharpie). The borderless card backs feature the same photo used on the front, but with a single tone dark blue-purple hue with "congrataultions" text overlaid. Each card carries a "BA" prefix. A few cards are not priced due to market scarcity.

Nm-Mt Ex-Mt

GR SUFFIX ON JUST GRADED 2K DIST.
IM SUFFIX ON IMAGINE DISTRIBUTION
JF SUFFIX ON JUSTIFIABLE DISTRIBUTION
JG SUFFIX ON JUST GOLD DISTRIBUTION
JS SUFFIX ON JUST STUFF DISTRIBUTION

	Nm-Mt	Ex-Mt
BA1 Brent Abernathy IM	3.00	.90
BA2 Roosevelt Brown IM	2.00	.60
BA3 A.J. Burnett JF	3.00	.90
BA5 Joe Crede IM	3.00	.90
BA6 Brian Daubach JF	2.00	.60
BA8 Alex Escobar IM	2.00	.60
BA9 Rafael Furcal IM	5.00	1.50
BA10 Eric Gagne JF	15.00	4.50
BA11 K.Haverbusch JG	2.00	.60
BA12 Aubrey Huff IM	5.00	1.50
BA13 Brandon Inge JF	3.00	.90
BA14 Nick Johnson GR	5.00	1.50
BA15 Josh Kalinowski IM	2.00	.60
BA16 Steve Lomasney JF	2.00	.60
BA17 Mike Meyers IM	3.00	.90
BA18 T.Nunnari IM	2.00	.60
BA19 Jose Ortiz IM	3.00	.90
BA20 Ramon Ortiz JG	3.00	.90
BA21 Pablo Ozuna JF	2.00	.60
BA22 Adam Piatt GR	2.00	.60
BA23 Julio Ramirez IM	2.00	.60
BA24 Chris Reinike JF	2.00	.60
BA25 Matt Riley JG	3.00	.90
BA26 Ruben Salazar IM	3.00	.90
BA27 T.J. Tucker IM	2.00	.60
BA28 Eric Valent JG	2.00	.60
BA29 Rico Washington JG	2.00	.60
BA30 Kevin Witt IM	2.00	.60
BA31 Wes Anderson JG	3.00	.90
BA35 Casey Blake	2.00	.60
BA36 Bobby Bradley GR	3.00	.90
BA37 Ben Broussard JG	3.00	.90
BA38 Jesus Colome JG	2.00	.60
BA40 Nate Cornejo JG	2.00	.60
BA41 Robbie Crabtree JG	2.00	.60
BA42 Cesar Crespo JG	3.00	.90
BA46 Tim Drew JF	2.00	.60
BA47 Chad Harville JG	2.00	.60
BA48 Elvin Hernandez JG	2.00	.60
BA49 Aubrey Huff JF	5.00	1.50
BA50 Norm Hutchins JG	2.00	.60
BA52 Eric Ireland JG	2.00	.60
BA55 Jaime Jones JS-2K1	2.00	.60
BA56 Bobby Kielty JF	3.00	.90
BA57 Bobby Kielty JG	3.00	.90
BA58 Matthew LeCroy JG	2.00	.60
BA59 Matthew LeCroy JG	2.00	.60
BA60 Allen Levrault JF	2.00	.60
BA61 Pat Manning JG	3.00	.90
BA62 Hipolito Martinez JG	2.00	.60
BA63 D.McDonald JG	2.00	.60
BA64 Brian McNichol JG	2.00	.60
BA65 Jackson Melian JS-2K1	3.00	.90
BA66 Mike Meyers JF	3.00	.90
BA67 Mark Mulder JG	10.00	3.00
BA69 Pablo Ozuna JS-2K1	2.00	.60
BA70 Alex Pena JF	2.00	.60
BA71 Alex Pena JG	2.00	.60
BA72 Juan Pierre JG	10.00	3.00
BA74 Juan Rivera JG	2.00	.60
BA75 Luis Rivera JF	2.00	.60
BA76 J.P. Roberge JG	2.00	.60
BA77 Grant Roberts JG	2.00	.60
BA79 Bobby Seay JG	2.00	.60
BA80 Juan Silvestre JF	3.00	.90
BA84 Matt White JG	3.00	.90
BA85 Matt White JF	3.00	.90
BA86 Peanut Williams JG	2.00	.60
BA87 Jack Wilson JF	3.00	.90

2000 Just Autographs Black

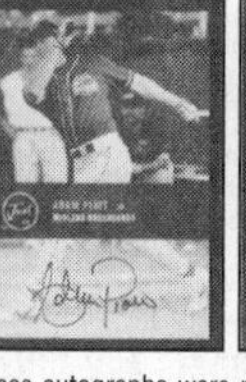

These autographs were randomly inserted into the 2000 Just Gold factory sets. Each card features a black border, and is serial numbered to 50.

	Nm-Mt	Ex-Mt
BA1 Brent Abernathy JG	12.00	3.60
BA3 A.J. Burnett JG	12.00	3.60
BA4 Sean Burroughs JG	20.00	6.00
BA5 Joe Crede JG	12.00	3.60
BA6 Brian Daubach JG	8.00	2.40
BA8 Alex Escobar JG	8.00	2.40
BA9 Rafael Furcal JG	20.00	6.00
BA10 Eric Gagne JG	50.00	15.00
BA12 Aubrey Huff JG	20.00	6.00
BA13 Brandon Inge JG	12.00	3.60
BA14 Nick Johnson JG	20.00	6.00
BA15 Josh Kalinowski JG	8.00	2.40
BA16 Steve Lomasney JG	8.00	2.40
BA17 Mike Meyers JG	12.00	3.60
BA18 T.Nunnari JG	8.00	2.40
BA19 Jose Ortiz JG	12.00	3.60
BA20 Ramon Ortiz JG	12.00	3.60
BA21 Pablo Ozuna JG	8.00	2.40
BA22 Adam Piatt JG	8.00	2.40
BA23 Julio Ramirez JG	8.00	2.40
BA24 Chris Reinike JG	8.00	2.40
BA27 T.J. Tucker JG	8.00	2.40
BA29 Rico Washington JG	8.00	2.40
BA30 Kevin Witt JG	8.00	2.40
BA31 Wes Anderson JG	12.00	3.60
BA32 Tony Armas Jr. JG	8.00	2.40
BA33 Brad Baisley JG	12.00	3.60
BA34 Matt Belisle JG	8.00	2.40
BA35 Casey Blake JG	8.00	2.40
BA36 Bobby Bradley JG	12.00	3.60
BA37 Ben Broussard JG	12.00	3.60
BA38 Jesus Colome JG	8.00	2.40
BA40 Nate Cornejo JG	8.00	2.40
BA41 Robbie Crabtree JG	8.00	2.40
BA47 Chad Harville JG	8.00	2.40
BA48 Elvin Hernandez JG	8.00	2.40
BA49 Aubrey Huff JG	20.00	6.00
BA50 Norm Hutchins JG	8.00	2.40
BA51 Brandon Inge JG	12.00	3.60
BA61 Pat Manning JG	12.00	3.60
BA62 Hipolito Martinez JG	8.00	2.40
BA63 D.McDonald JG	8.00	2.40
BA64 Brian McNichol JG	8.00	2.40
BA66 Mike Meyers JG	12.00	3.60
BA67 Mark Mulder JG	30.00	9.00
BA69 Pablo Ozuna JG	8.00	2.40
BA72 Juan Pierre JG	30.00	9.00
BA73 Aramis Ramirez JG	12.00	3.60
BA74 Juan Rivera JG	8.00	2.40
BA75 Luis Rivera JG	8.00	2.40
BA76 J.P. Roberge JG	8.00	2.40
BA77 Grant Roberts JG	8.00	2.40
BA78 C.C. Sabathia JG	12.00	3.60
BA80 Juan Silvestre JG	12.00	3.60
BA81 Chris Snelling JG	20.00	6.00
BA83 Jayson Werth JG	8.00	2.40
BA86 Peanut Williams JG	8.00	2.40
BA87 Jack Wilson JG	12.00	3.60

2000 Just Autographs Die Cut

Randomly inserted into Just Imagine, Just Gold, Just Graded 2K (inserted into packs), and Justifiable hobby boxes. Most of the cards were encased and graded by USA and then placed into boxes as a chip-topper. A limited number of cards were randomly seeded into retail packs and also included as part of the Just Stuff direct mail program in non-graded form. This set parallels the standard Just Autographs. Both sets utilize the same photography (of which hails from the standard set), but the Autographs Die Cut cards feature a dramatic borderless photo design on front, rounded corners (similar to a playing card) and a rectangular white area at the base of the card front for the player's autograph. Card backs feature a horizontal white and purple design and carry a "DC" prefix. Each card is numbered "X/200" on back.

Nm-Mt Ex-Mt

GR SUFFIX ON JUST GRADED 2K DIST.
IM SUFFIX ON IMAGINE DISTRIBUTION
JF SUFFIX ON JUSTIFIABLE DISTRIBUTION
JG SUFFIX ON JUST GOLD DISTRIBUTION
JS SUFFIX ON JUST STUFF DISTRIBUTION

	Nm-Mt	Ex-Mt
DC1 Roosevelt Brown IM	4.00	1.20
DC2 A.J. Burnett GR	6.00	1.80
DC3 Sean Burroughs JS	10.00	3.00
DC4 Wilson Castillo JG	4.00	1.20
DC5 Brian Daubach	4.00	1.20
DC8 Rafael Furcal IM	10.00	3.00
DC9 Eric Gagne GR	25.00	7.50
DC10 Nick Johnson IM	10.00	3.00
DC11 Steve Lomasney IM	4.00	1.20
DC12 Mike Meyers IM	6.00	1.80
DC13 T.Nunnari IM	4.00	1.20
DC14 Ramon Ortiz JS-2K1	6.00	1.80
DC15 Pablo Ozuna IM	4.00	1.20
DC16 Adam Piatt JG	4.00	1.20
DC17 Julio Ramirez IM	4.00	1.20
DC18 Matt Riley GR	6.00	1.80
DC19 Ruben Salazar IM	6.00	1.80
DC20 T.J. Tucker JF	4.00	1.20
DC21 Eric Valent JG	4.00	1.20
DC22 Wes Anderson JF	6.00	1.80
DC23 Tony Armas Jr. JF	4.00	1.20
DC24 Brad Baisley JF	6.00	1.80
DC25 Matt Belisle JG	4.00	1.20
DC26 Bobby Bradley GR	6.00	1.80
DC27 Ben Broussard GR	6.00	1.80
DC28 Jesus Colome GR	4.00	1.20
DC29 Cesar Crespo JG	6.00	1.80
DC32 Brian Daubach GR	4.00	1.20
DC33 Tim Drew JF	4.00	1.20
DC34 Aubrey Huff GR	10.00	3.00
DC35 Brandon Inge GR	6.00	1.80
DC36 Nick Johnson JS	10.00	3.00
DC37 Nick Johnson JS	10.00	3.00
DC38 D.McDonald JF	4.00	1.20
DC39 J. Melian JG-JS	6.00	1.80
DC40 Mike Meyers JF	6.00	1.80
DC41 Mark Mulder JF	15.00	4.50
DC43 Pablo Ozuna JG	4.00	1.20
DC44 Juan Pierre GR	15.00	4.50
DC45 Aramis Ramirez JF	6.00	1.80
DC46 Luis Rivera JF	4.00	1.20
DC47 Grant Roberts GR	4.00	1.20
DC48 C.C. Sabathia JG	6.00	1.80
DC49 Bobby Seay JG	4.00	1.20
DC50 Juan Silvestre GR	6.00	1.80
DC51 Chris Snelling JF	10.00	3.00
DC52 Francisco Trejo JS	4.00	1.20
DC53 Jayson Werth JG	4.00	1.20
DC54 Matt White JF	6.00	1.80
DC55 Matt White GR	6.00	1.80
DC56 Jack Wilson GR	6.00	1.80

2000 Just Autographs Gold

Randomly inserted as chiptoppers into 2000 Just products, this insert features autographed cards of top minor league prospects. Each card features a gold bordered frame on front, is signed by the athlete and individually serial numbered 1 of 1. No pricing is available due to scarcity.

Nm-Mt Ex-Mt

JF SUFFIX ON JUSTIFIABLE DISTRIBUTION
JG SUFFIX ON JUST GOLD DISTRIBUTION

2000 Just Candidates

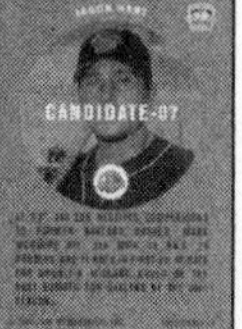

2000 Just Candidates

Randomly inserted into packs of 2000 Justifiable at one in 24, this 10-card insert features some of the Minor League's most promising talent. Card backs carry a "JC" prefix.

	Nm-Mt	Ex-Mt
COMPLETE SET (10)	10.00	3.00
JC1 Ryan Anderson	1.00	.30
JC2 Bobby Bradley	1.00	.30
JC3 Pat Burrell	1.00	.30
JC4 Alex Cabrera	1.00	.30
JC5 Keith Ginter	1.00	.30
JC6 Josh Hamilton	1.00	.30
JC7 Jason Hart	1.00	.30
JC8 Adam Piatt	1.00	.30
JC9 Juan Silvestre	1.00	.30
JC10 Chin-Hui Tsao	2.50	.75

2000 Just Debuts

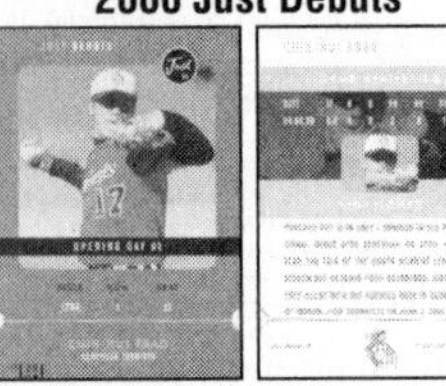

This insert set features minor leaguers that look to make their rookie debuts in 2000. Cards 1-10 were inserted into Preview 2K packs. Cards 11-20 were inserted into Imagine packs. Both products had seeding rates of 1:24.

	Nm-Mt	Ex-Mt
COMP.2K SET (10)	15.00	4.50
COMP.IMAGINE (10)	15.00	4.50
COMP.JUSTIFIABLE (10)	15.00	4.50
JD1 Kurt Ainsworth	1.50	.45
JD2 Ben Broussard	1.00	.30
JD3 Ben Christensen	1.00	.30
JD4 Alejandro Diaz	1.00	.30
JD5 Corey Myers	1.00	.30
JD6 Omar Ortiz	1.00	.30
JD7 Lyle Overbay	1.00	.30
JD8 Brian Roberts	1.00	.30
JD9 Jerome Williams	3.00	.90
JD10 Barry Zito	6.00	1.80
JD11 Casey Burns	1.00	.30
JD12 Donovan Graves	1.00	.30
JD13 Ty Howington	1.00	.30
JD14 Ben Johnson	1.00	.30
JD15 Bobby Kielty	1.00	.30
JD16 Hong-Chih Kuo	1.50	.45
JD17 Sean McGowan	1.00	.30
JD18 Mark Mulder	1.50	.45
JD19 Eric Munson	1.00	.30
JD20 Chin-Hui Tsao	2.50	.75
JD21 Rick Asadoorian	1.00	.30
JD22 Danys Baez	1.00	.30
JD23 Josh Beckett	3.00	.90
JD24 Shaun Boyd	1.00	.30
JD25 Bobby Bradley	1.00	.30
JD26 Jace Brewer	1.00	.30
JD27 Brad Cresse	1.00	.30
JD28 Adrian Gonzalez	2.00	.60
JD29 Adrian Hernandez	1.00	.30
JD30 Corey Smith	1.00	.30

2000 Just Dominant

Randomly inserted into Just Imagine at a rate of one 24 packs, this 10-card insert features players that were very dominanting at the minor league level. Card backs carry a "JD" prefix.

	Nm-Mt	Ex-Mt
COMPLETE SET (10)	12.00	3.60
JD1 Rick Ankiel	1.00	.30
JD2 Lance Berkman	1.00	.30
JD3 Ben Broussard	1.00	.30
JD4 Pat Burrell	1.00	.30
JD5 Chin-Feng Chen	1.50	.45
JD6 Carl Crawford	1.00	.30
JD7 Josh Hamilton	1.00	.30
JD8 Eric Munson	1.00	.30
JD9 Corey Patterson	1.00	.30
JD10 Vernon Wells	1.00	.30

2000 Just Drafted

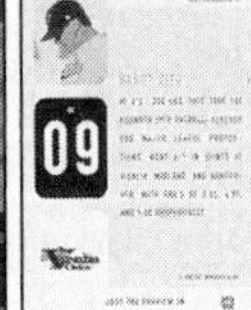

Randomly inserted into packs at one in 240, this insert features 10 players that were recently drafted by major league ballclubs. Card backs carry the player's initials as prefixes.

	Nm-Mt	Ex-Mt
COMPLETE SET (10)	50.00	15.00
BG5 B.J. Garbe	5.00	1.50
BS10 Ben Sheets	8.00	2.40
BZ9 Barry Zito	30.00	9.00
CC30 Chance Caple	5.00	1.50
CD46 Chris Duncan	5.00	1.50
DW27 David Walling	5.00	1.50
JH1 Josh Hamilton	5.00	1.50
LB21 Larry Bigbie	5.00	1.50
MP13 Mike Paradis	5.00	1.50
WH74 Will Hartley	5.00	1.50

2000 Just Gamers

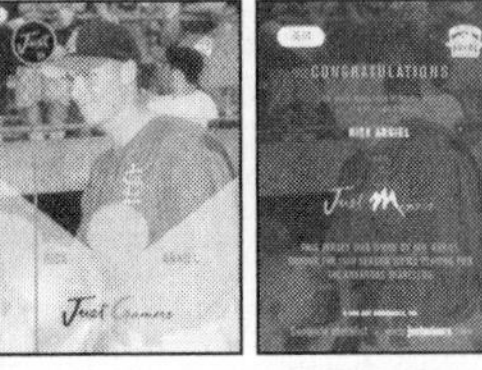

Randomly inserted into Just Imagine and Justifiable packs at a rate of one in 260, this 5-card set features game used bat and jersey cards.

	Nm-Mt	Ex-Mt
JG1 Rick Ankiel Jersey IM	10.00	3.00
JG2 Rafael Furcal Bat IM	10.00	3.00
JG3 Pat Burrell Jersey JF	15.00	4.50
JG4 Sean Burroughs Bat JF	15.00	4.50
JG5 Corey Patterson Bat JF	10.00	3.00

2000 Just Gamers Autograph

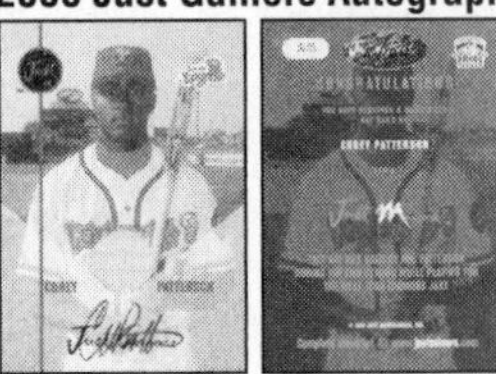

Randomly seeded into packs of Imagine and Justifiable, these four cards are an upgraded parallel of the Just Gamers inserts. Each card features either a game used bat chip or jersey swatch and was signed on front by the player in blue ink sharpie. Only 24 copies of each card was produced. Each card is affixed with a holofoil sticker on back of which is hand numbered "X/24" in blue ink sharpie. Card number JG3 does not exist as Pat Burrell did not participate in the autograph program.

	Nm-Mt	Ex-Mt
JG1 Rick Ankiel Jersey IM		
JG2 Rafael Furcal Bat IM		
JG4 Sean Burroughs Bat JF		
JG5 Corey Patterson Bat JF		

2000 Just Gamers Die Cuts

Randomly inserted into packs of Just Imagine and Justifiable, this five-card insert set is an upgraded parallel of the Just Gamers insert. Each card features either a game used bat chip or jersey swatch. Unlike the basic Gamers inserts, each of these cards features rounded die cut corners (similar to a playing card) and are individually hand-numbered on back "X/100" in blue ink sharpie. The hand-numbering "of 100" can be confusing because, in truth, only the first 90 copies of each card were utilized for this set. The last ten copies of each card (serial #'d copies 91-100) were all set aside for use in the Die Cuts Autograph parallel cards.

	Nm-Mt	Ex-Mt
JGDC1 Rick Ankiel Jersey IM	15.00	4.50
JGDC2 Rafael Furcal Bat IM	15.00	4.50
JGDC3 Pat Burrell Jersey JF	25.00	7.50
JGDC4 Sean Burroughs Bat JF	20.00	6.00
JGDC5 Corey Patterson Bat JF	25.00	7.50

2000 Just Gamers Die Cuts Autograph

Randomly inserted into packs of Just Imagine and Justifiable, this four-card insert set is an upgraded parallel of the Just Gamers Die Cuts insert. Each card features either a game used bat chip or jersey swatch plus a player autograph signed on front in blue ink sharpie. Each card back features two different sets of serial numbering - a rectangular white box at the base of the card and a holofoil sticker at the top of the card. The last ten copies of each basic Gamers Die Cuts card was set aside to create this upgraded parallel. Thus, the serial numbering within the white rectangle at the base of each card back will read as "X/100" but will contain numbers exclusively between 91-100. The cards are again numbered using the holofoil stickers, but this time using an "X/10" system. Card number JGDC3 does not exist as Pat Burrell did not participate in the autograph program.

	Nm-Mt	Ex-Mt
JGDC1 Rick Ankiel Jersey IM		
JGDC2 Rafael Furcal Bat IM		
JGDC4 Sean Burroughs Bat JF		
JGDC5 Corey Patterson Bat JF		

2000 Just Gems Imagine

Randomly inserted into packs of Just Imagine 2k at one in 24, this 10-card insert set features players that are a "Gem" on the playing field. Card backs carry a "JG" prefix.

	Nm-Mt	Ex-Mt
COMPLETE SET (10)	15.00	4.50
JG1 Ryan Anderson	1.00	.30
JG2 Pat Burrell	1.00	.30
JG3 Sean Burroughs	1.00	.30
JG4 Chin-Feng Chen	1.50	.45
JG5 Gookie Dawkins	1.00	.30
JG6 Marcus Giles	1.00	.30
JG7 Josh Hamilton	1.00	.30
JG8 Corey Patterson	1.00	.30
JG9 Adam Piatt	1.00	.30
JG10 Nick Johnson Alfonso Soriano	1.50	.45

2000 Just Gems Justifiable

Randomly inserted into Justifiable packs at one in 240, this 10-card insert features players that look to make the Major Leagues in the next few years. Card backs carry a "J" prefix.

	Nm-Mt	Ex-Mt
COMPLETE SET (10)	60.00	18.00
J1 Ryan Anderson	5.00	1.50
J2 Pat Burrell	8.00	2.40
J3 Sean Burroughs	10.00	3.00
J4 Chin-Feng Chen	8.00	2.40
J5 Gookie Dawkins	5.00	1.50
J6 Marcus Giles	5.00	1.50
J7 Josh Hamilton	5.00	1.50
J8 Corey Patterson	5.00	1.50
J9 Adam Piatt	5.00	1.50
J10 Nick Johnson Alfonso Soriano	15.00	4.50

2000 Just Graphs

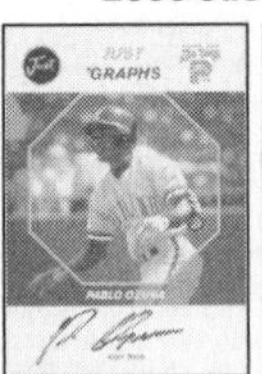

These autographs were randomly inserted into Just Gold factory sets and 2000 Just Graded 2K packs. Each card is individually serial numbered to 100. Please note that cards with a "JG" suffix were inserted into Just Gold Factory sets, while cards with a "GR" suffix were inserted into Just Graded 2K packs, and were all graded by the U.S.A. grading company.

GR SUFFIX ON JUST GRADED 2K DIST.
JG SUFFIX ON JUST GOLD DISTRIBUTION
JS SUFFIX ON JUST STUFF DISTRIBUTION

	Nm-Mt	Ex-Mt
JG2 Wes Anderson GR	8.00	2.40
JG3 Rick Ankiel GR	5.00	1.50
JG4 Tony Armas Jr. GR	5.00	1.50
JG5 Matt Belisle JG	5.00	1.50
JG6 Ben Broussard GR	8.00	2.40
JG7 Sean Burroughs GR	15.00	4.50
JG8 Jesus Colome GR	5.00	1.50
JG12 Rafael Furcal GR	15.00	4.50
JG14 Aubrey Huff GR	15.00	4.50
JG15 Nick Johnson JS	15.00	4.50
JG16 Brandon Larson JS	8.00	2.40
JG17 Mike Meyers GR	8.00	2.40
JG18 Mark Mulder GR	30.00	9.00
JG20 Pablo Ozuna JG	5.00	1.50
JG21 Adam Piatt GR	5.00	1.50
JG22 Juan Pierre GR	20.00	6.00
JG23 Julio Ramirez GR	5.00	1.50
JG24 Luis Rivera GR	5.00	1.50
JG25 Juan Silvestre GR	8.00	2.40
JG26 Chris Snelling JG	12.00	3.60
JG27 Jayson Werth JG	5.00	1.50
JG28 Matt White GR	8.00	2.40
JG29 Peanut Williams GR	5.00	1.50
JG30 Barry Zito JS	50.00	15.00

2000 Just Justinkt Autographs

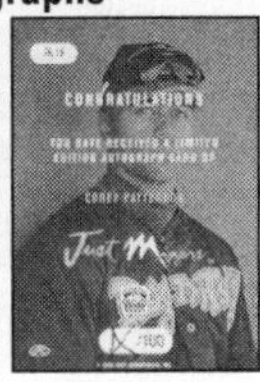

Randomly inserted as USA professionally graded chiptoppers in hobby boxes and standard inserts in retail boxes in various 2000 Just products, this insert set features autographed cards of some of the hottest minor league prospects. Please note that these cards are individually serial numbered to 100. Cards backs carry a "JK" prefix.

	Nm-Mt	Ex-Mt
JK1 Tony Armas Jr. IM	6.00	1.80
JK2 Jeff Austin IM	10.00	3.00
JK3 A.J. Burnett JF	10.00	3.00
JK4 Sean Burroughs JS	15.00	4.50
JK5 Jack Cust JF	6.00	1.80
JK6 Brian Daubach JF	6.00	1.80
JK8 Rafael Furcal IM	15.00	4.50
JK9 Jon Garland IM	6.00	1.80
JK10 Aubrey Huff IM	15.00	4.50
JK11 Nick Johnson IM	15.00	4.50
JK12 Steve Lomasney IM	6.00	1.80
JK14 T.Nunnari IM	6.00	1.80
JK15 Pablo Ozuna IM	6.00	1.80
JK16 Corey Patterson JF	15.00	4.50
JK17 Adam Piatt JF	6.00	1.80
JK18 Julio Ramirez IM	6.00	1.80
JK19 Matt Riley JF	10.00	3.00
JK21 T.J. Tucker JF	6.00	1.80

2000 Just Mystery Gamers

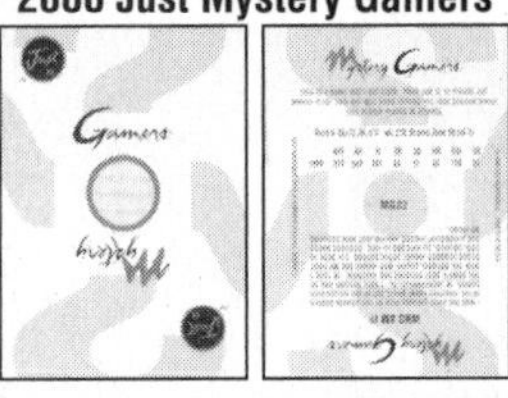

These two cards were randomly inserted into Just Imagine and Justifiable packs, this insert features actual chips from game-used bats of Ken Griffey Jr. and Chipper Jones. Card backs carry a "MG" prefix.

	Nm-Mt	Ex-Mt
MG1 Ken Griffey Jr. Bat IM	20.00	6.00
MG2 Chipper Jones Bat JF	15.00	4.50

2000 Just Mystery Gamers Die Cut

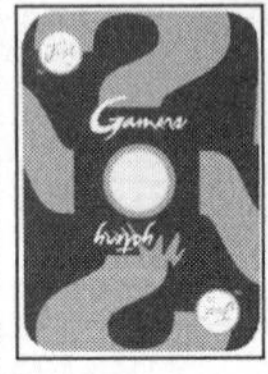

These two cards were randomly inserted into Just Imagine and Justifiable packs, this insert is a complete die cut parallel of the Mystery Gamers insert. Card backs carry a "MGDC" prefix.

	Nm-Mt	Ex-Mt
MGDC1 Ken Griffey Jr. Bat IM	30.00	9.00
MGDC2 Chipper Jones Bat JF	25.00	7.50

2000 Just Mystery Signatures

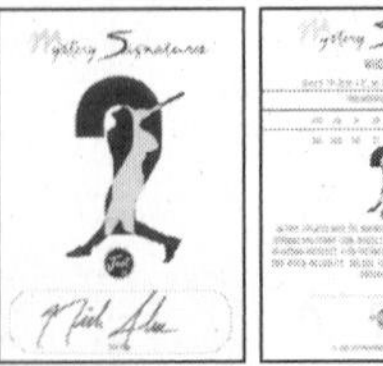

Randomly inserted primarily into various 2000 Just products, this insert set features mystery autographs of various minor league players. Card backs carry a "MS" prefix. Cards with an "IM" suffix were distributed in Just Imagine 2k, cards with a "JG" prefix were inserted into the 2000 Just Gold factory set, cards with a "GR" prefix were inserted into the 2000 Just Graded 2K product and cards with a JS prefix were included in the Just Stuff direct mail program. Please note that all of the Gabe Kapler Mystery Signatures (and most of the Miguel Cabrera's) were graded by U.S.A. grading service.

Nm-Mt Ex-Mt

*USA 10: .6X TO 1.5X HI COLUMN....
GR SUFFIX ON JUST GRADED 2K DIST.
IM SUFFIX ON IMAGINE DISTRIBUTION
JG SUFFIX ON JUST GOLD DISTRIBUTION
JS SUFFIX ON JUST STUFF DISTRIBUTION

	Nm-Mt	Ex-Mt
MS1 Miguel Cabrera IM	25.00	7.50
MS2 Guillermo Quiroz IM	5.00	1.50
MS4 Ramon Ortiz JG	3.00	.90
MS6 Nick Johnson IM	5.00	1.50
MS7 Placido Polanco IM	2.00	.60
MS8 Wily Mo Pena JG	2.00	.60
MS9 Jim Parque JS	2.00	.60
MS10 Odalis Perez JG	3.00	.90
MS11 Gabe Kapler GR	2.00	.60
MS13 Wilfredo Rodriguez JS	3.00	.90

2000 Just Nine

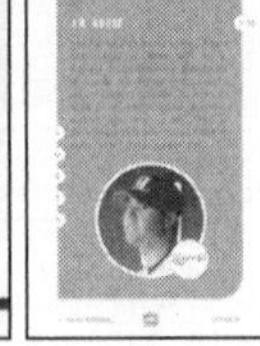

These cards were randomly inserted into Justifiable packs at one in 24, this insert features nine Minor League players that could be a starter in the Major Leagues by season's end. Card backs carry a "J" prefix.

	Nm-Mt	Ex-Mt
COMPLETE SET (9)	10.00	3.00
J1 Josh Beckett	3.00	.90
J2 Sean Burroughs	1.00	.30
J3 Jack Cust	1.00	.30
J4 Marcus Giles	1.00	.30
J5 Josh Hamilton	1.00	.30
J6 J.R. House	1.00	.30
J7 Nick Johnson	1.00	.30
J8 Corey Patterson	1.00	.30
J9 Alfonso Soriano	1.50	.45

2000 Just the One

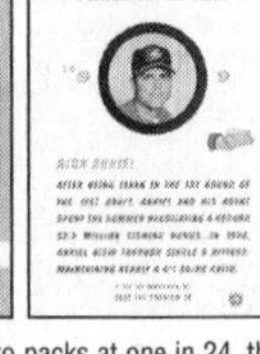

Randomly inserted into packs at one in 24, this insert set features five cards of pitching prospect Rick Ankiel. Card backs carry a "TORA" prefix.

	Nm-Mt	Ex-Mt
COMPLETE SET (5)	5.00	1.50
COMMON ANKIEL (1-5)	1.00	.30

2000 Just Tools Imagine

Randomly inserted into Just Imagine packs at one in 240, this 10-card set is a complete parallel of the Just Tools insert found in the Just the Preview 2K product.

	Nm-Mt	Ex-Mt
COMPLETE SET (10)	50.00	15.00
1 Ryan Anderson	5.00	1.50
2 Rick Ankiel	5.00	1.50
3 Pat Burrell	8.00	2.40
4 Chin-Feng Chen	8.00	2.40
5 Rafael Furcal	5.00	1.50
6 B.J. Garbe	5.00	1.50
7 Josh Hamilton	5.00	1.50
8 Nick Johnson	5.00	1.50
9 Pablo Ozuna	5.00	1.50
10 Corey Patterson	5.00	1.50

2000 Just Tools Preview 2K

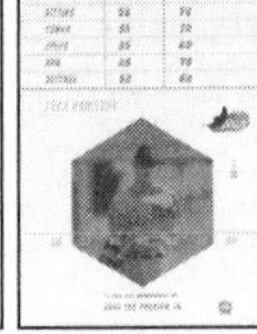

Randomly inserted into packs of Just the Preview 2K at one in 24, this 10-card insert features some of the most talented minor league ballplayers.

	Nm-Mt	Ex-Mt
COMPLETE SET (10)	10.00	3.00
1 Ryan Anderson	1.00	.30
2 Rick Ankiel	1.00	.30
3 Pat Burrell	1.00	.30
4 Chin-Feng Chen	1.50	.45
5 Rafael Furcal	1.00	.30
6 B.J. Garbe	1.00	.30
7 Josh Hamilton	1.00	.30
8 Nick Johnson	1.00	.30
9 Pablo Ozuna	1.00	.30
10 Corey Patterson	1.00	.30

2000 Just Graded 2k

The 2000 Just Graded 2k set was released in early January, 2001 and features a 50-card base set. Each card in the set is graded by U.S.A. grading company. Prices listed below refer to all grades except for Gem Mint 10. Please see multiplier listed below for Gem Mint 10 premiums. Each pack contained one card, and carried a suggested retail price of $14.99. Please note that there were only 500 of each graded base-card produced.

	Nm-Mt	Ex-Mt
*USA 10: .75X TO 2X HI COLUMN		
1 Ryan Anderson	4.00	1.20
2 Rick Asadoorian	4.00	1.20
3 Danys Baez	4.00	1.20
4 Josh Beckett	12.00	3.60
5 Boof Bonser	4.00	1.20
6 Chris Bootcheck	4.00	1.20
7 Joe Borchard	6.00	1.80
8 Shaun Boyd	4.00	1.20
9 Bobby Bradley	4.00	1.20
10 Sean Burroughs	4.00	1.20
11 Hee Seop Choi	15.00	4.50
12 Joe Crede	4.00	1.20
13 Brad Cresse	4.00	1.20
14 Ben Diggins	4.00	1.20
15 Adrian Gonzalez	8.00	2.40
16 Cristian Guerrero	4.00	1.20
17 Josh Hamilton	4.00	1.20
18 Adrian Hernandez	4.00	1.20
19 Aaron Herr	4.00	1.20
20 J.R. House	4.00	1.20
21 Adam Johnson	4.00	1.20
22 Kelly Johnson	4.00	1.20
23 Tripper Johnson	4.00	1.20
24 Deivi Mendez	4.00	1.20
25 Luis Montanez	4.00	1.20
26 Eric Munson	4.00	1.20
27 Xavier Nady	8.00	2.40
28 Lance Niekro	4.00	1.20
29 David Parrish	4.00	1.20
30 Corey Patterson	4.00	1.20
31 Carlos Pena	4.00	1.20
32 Jon Rauch	4.00	1.20
33 C.C. Sabathia	4.00	1.20
34 Mike Schultz	4.00	1.20
35 Ben Sheets	6.00	1.80
36 Corey Smith	4.00	1.20
37 Seung Song	5.00	1.50
38 Alfonso Soriano	5.00	1.50
39 Robert Stiehl	4.00	1.20
40 Mike Stodolka	4.00	1.20
41 Derek Thompson	4.00	1.20
42 Joe Torres	4.00	1.20
43 Chin-Hui Tsao	10.00	3.00
44 Chase Utley	10.00	3.00
45 Adam Wainwright	8.00	2.40
46 Tiger Wang	10.00	3.00
47 Vernon Wells	4.00	1.20
48 Matt Wheatland	4.00	1.20
49 Blake Williams	4.00	1.20
50 Barry Zito	25.00	7.50

2000 Just Graded 2K Black

Randomly inserted into packs at one in 16, this 50-card insert set parallels the Just Graded 2K base set. There were only 50 serial numbered sets produced of this black bordered parallel. Each card is hand numbered "X/50" on the back in blue ink sharpie. Please note that all of these cards were graded by the U.S.A. grading company.

	Nm-Mt	Ex-Mt
*BLACK USA 8-USA 9.5: .75X TO 2X BASIC		
*BLACK USA 10: 1X TO 2.5X BASIC		

2000 Royal Rookies

The 2000 Royal Rookies product was released as a 40-card set that featured some of the minor league's top prospects. Each pack contained 6 cards and carried an approximate retail price of $2-$3. Each pack contained one autographed card. Each box contained 12 packs.

	Nm-Mt	Ex-Mt
COMPLETE SET (40)	5.00	1.50
1 Fletcher Bates	.15	.04
2 Eddy Garabito	.15	.04
3 Juan Aracena	.15	.04
4 Andrew Beinbrink	.15	.04
5 Ed Rogers	.15	.04
6 Jason Sekany	.15	.04
7 Juan Guzman	.15	.04
8 Howie Clark	.15	.04
9 Jody Gerut	.50	.15
10 Chris Snelling	.50	.15
11 Nick Theodorou	.15	.04
12 Jermaine Clark	.25	.07
13 Chris Richard	.15	.04
14 Brent Hoard	.15	.04
15 Josh Reding	.15	.04
16 Mike Glendenning	.15	.04
17 Dan Phillips	.15	.04
18 Eric Gillespie	.15	.04
19 Larry Barnes	.15	.04
20 Chris Barski	.15	.04
21 Julio Zuleta	.15	.04
22 Damon Minor	.15	.04
23 Brian Cooper	.15	.04
24 Adam Eaton	.25	.07
25 Carlos Casimiro UER	.15	.04
Last name misspelled Casamiro		
26 Jeremy Blevins	.15	.04
27 Jon Schaeffer	.15	.04
28 Mark Lukasiewicz	.15	.04
29 Norm Hutchins UER	.15	.04
Name misspelled Hutchinson		
30 Mark Harriger	.15	.04
31 Rikki Johnston	.15	.04
32 Jon Tucker	.15	.04
33 Brett Caradonna	.15	.04
34 Adam Piatt	.15	.04
Rick Ankiel		
35 Mark Seaver	.15	.04
36 Mike Villano	.15	.04
37 Danny Ardoin	.15	.04
38 J.J. Sherrill	.15	.04
39 Ryan Drese UER	.25	.07
Wrong statistics on back		
40 Ken Griffey Jr. CL	.40	.12

2000 Royal Rookies Autographs

These autograph cards parallel the base set (excluding card 38 and 40) and were seeded at a rate of one per pack. Each card is serial numbered of 4950 on front.

	Nm-Mt	Ex-Mt
1 Fletcher Bates	2.00	.60
2 Eddy Garabito	2.00	.60
3 Juan Aracena	2.00	.60
4 Andrew Beinbrink	2.00	.60
5 Ed Rogers	2.00	.60
6 Jason Sekany	2.00	.60
7 Juan Guzman	2.00	.60
8 Howie Clark	2.00	.60
9 Jody Gerut	5.00	1.50
10 Chris Snelling	3.00	.90
11 Nick Theodorou	2.00	.60
12 Jermaine Clark	3.00	.90
13 Chris Richard	2.00	.60
14 Brent Hoard	2.00	.60
15 Josh Reding	2.00	.60
16 Mike Glendenning	2.00	.60
17 Dan Phillips	2.00	.60
18 Eric Gillespie	2.00	.60
19 Larry Barnes	2.00	.60
20 Chris Barski	2.00	.60
21 Julio Zuleta	2.00	.60
22 Damon Minor	2.00	.60
23 Brian Cooper	2.00	.60
24 Adam Eaton	3.00	.90
25 Carlos Casimiro UER	2.00	.60
Last name misspelled Casamiro		
26 Jeremy Blevins	2.00	.60
27 Jon Schaeffer	2.00	.60
28 Mark Lukasiewicz	2.00	.60
29 Norm Hutchins UER	2.00	.60
Name misspelled Hutchinson		
30 Mark Harriger	2.00	.60
31 Rikki Johnston	2.00	.60
32 Jon Tucker	2.00	.60
33 Brett Caradonna	2.00	.60
35 Mark Seaver	2.00	.60
36 Mike Villano	2.00	.60
37 Danny Ardoin	2.00	.60
38 J.J. Sherrill	2.00	.60
39 Ryan Drese UER	3.00	.90
Wrong statistics on back		

2000 Royal Rookies Rick Ankiel Pitcher of the Year

This three-card set commemorates top prospect Rick Ankiel. The cards were seeded into packs at an approximate rate of 1:12.

	Nm-Mt	Ex-Mt
COMPLETE SET (3)	1.50	.45
COMMON CARD (1-3)	.50	.15

2000 Royal Rookies Rick Ankiel Pitcher of the Year Autographs

These autographed cards parallel the basic Ankiel inserts. Each card is serial numbered of 500 on front.

	Nm-Mt	Ex-Mt
COMMON CARD (1-3)	3.00	.90

2000 Royal Rookies Elite Eight

This 8-card set features a selection of top prospects. The cards were randomly seeded

into packs at an approximate rate of 1:6.

	Nm-Mt	Ex-Mt
COMPLETE SET (8)	5.00	1.50
1 Roosevelt Brown	.40	.12
2 Travis Dawkins	.40	.12
3 Barry Zito	2.00	.60
4 Eric Gagne	.75	.23
5 Jeff DaVanon	.40	.12
6 Brett Myers	1.00	.30
7 Julio Lugo	.40	.12
8 Shea Hillenbrand	.40	.12

2000 Royal Rookies Elite Eight Autographs

These autographed cards parallel the basic Elite Eight inserts and were randomly seeded into packs at an approximate rate of one per box. Each card is serial numbered of 2500 on front.

	Nm-Mt	Ex-Mt
1 Roosevelt Brown	2.00	.60
2 Travis Dawkins	2.00	.60
3 Barry Zito	15.00	4.50
4 Eric Gagne	10.00	3.00
5 Jeff DaVanon	2.00	.60
6 Brett Myers	5.00	1.50
7 Julio Lugo	2.00	.60
8 Shea Hillenbrand	3.00	.90

2000 Royal Rookies Ken Griffey Jr.

This 5-card set commemorates Cincinnati Reds slugger Ken Griffey Jr. The cards were randomly seeded into packs at an approximate rate of 1:12.

	Nm-Mt	Ex-Mt
COMPLETE SET (5)	5.00	1.50
COMMON CARD (1-5)	1.00	.30

2000 Royal Rookies Adam Piatt Player of the Year

Randomly inserted into packs at a rate of 1:12, this 3-card set features the 1999 minor league player of the year, Adam Piatt.

	Nm-Mt	Ex-Mt
COMPLETE SET (3)	1.50	.45
COMMON CARD (1-3)	.50	.15

2000 Royal Rookies Adam Piatt Player of the Year Autographs

Randomly inserted into packs at an approximate rate of 1:12, this 3-card insert is a complete parallel of the Adam Piatt Player of the Year insert. Each card is autographed by Adam Piatt

	Nm-Mt	Ex-Mt
COMMON CARD (1-3)	3.00	.90

2000 Royal Rookies Futures

The 2000 Royal Rookies Futures product was released September,2000 as a 36-card set. The set features minor league prospects and Ken Griffey Jr. checklist card.

	Nm-Mt	Ex-Mt
COMPLETE SET (36)	5.00	1.50
1 Ramon Soler	.15	.04
2 Aron Weston	.25	.07
3 Alex Requena	.25	.07
4 Eric Johnson	.15	.04
5 Tony Mota	.15	.04
6 Miguel Cabrera	5.00	1.50
7 Jovanny Cedeno UER	.25	.07
Last name misspelled Cedano		
8 Jose Morban	.25	.07
9 Enrique Ramirez	.15	.04
10 Steve Goodson	.15	.04
11 Carlos Silva	.15	.04
12 Jovanny Sosa	.25	.07
13 Jeff Bailey	.15	.04
14 Eric Byrnes	.50	.15
15 Rob Pugmire	.15	.04
16 Frederick Torres	.15	.04
17 Jeff Inglin	.15	.04
18 Jermaine Clark	.25	.07
19 Adam Melhuse	.15	.04
20 Dustin Carr	.15	.04
21 Paul Hoover	.15	.04
22 Christian Parker	.15	.04
23 Paul Ottavinia	.15	.04
24 Maxim St. Pierre	.15	.04
25 Tony Pena Jr.	.25	.07
26 Jay Gehrke	.15	.04
27 Scott Seal	.15	.04
28 J.J. Putz	.25	.07
29 Jesus Medrano	.15	.04
30 Bret Prinz	.15	.04
31 Derrick Cook	.15	.04
32 Mark Roberts	.15	.04
33 Napoleon Calzado	.15	.04
34 Francisco Rodriguez	1.00	.30
35 Brant Ust	.15	.04
36 Ken Griffey Jr. CL	.25	.07

2000 Royal Rookies Futures Autographs

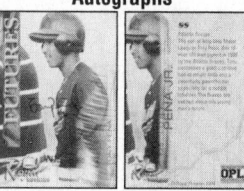

Inserted at one per pack, this 35-card insert is in fact, an autographed parallel of the base set. Please note that the Ken Griffey Jr. checklist was not included in this set. An very early Miguel Cabrera autograph card was included in this set.

	Nm-Mt	Ex-Mt
STATED ODDS 1:1		
STATED PRINT RUN 4950 SERIAL #'d SETS		
1 Ramon Soler	2.00	.60
2 Aron Weston	3.00	.90
3 Alex Requena	3.00	.90
4 Eric Johnson	2.00	.60
5 Tony Mota	2.00	.60
6 Miguel Cabrera	30.00	9.00
7 Jovanny Cedeno UER	3.00	.90
Misspelled Cedano		
8 Jose Morban	3.00	.90
9 Enrique Ramirez	2.00	.60
10 Steve Goodson	2.00	.60
11 Carlos Silva	2.00	.60
12 Jovanny Sosa	3.00	.90
13 Jeff Bailey	2.00	.60
14 Eric Byrnes	3.00	.90
15 Rob Pugmire	2.00	.60
16 Frederick Torres	2.00	.60
17 Jeff Inglin	2.00	.60
18 Jermaine Clark	3.00	.90
19 Adam Melhuse	2.00	.60
20 Dustin Carr	2.00	.60
21 Paul Hoover	2.00	.60
22 Christian Parker	2.00	.60
23 Paul Ottavinia	2.00	.60
24 Maxim St. Pierre	2.00	.60
25 Tony Pena Jr.	3.00	.90
26 Jay Gehrke	2.00	.60
27 Scott Seal	2.00	.60
28 J.J. Putz	3.00	.90
29 Jesus Medrano	2.00	.60
30 Bret Prinz	2.00	.60
31 Derrick Cook	2.00	.60
32 Mark Roberts	2.00	.60
33 Napoleon Calzado	2.00	.60
34 Francisco Rodriguez	5.00	1.50
35 Brant Ust	2.00	.60

2000 Royal Rookies Futures Blue Chips

Randomly inserted into packs, this 10-cards insert features blue chip prospects.

	Nm-Mt	Ex-Mt
1 Rick Ankiel	.25	.07
2 C.C. Sabathia	.40	.12
3 Jayson Werth	.25	.07
4 Brad Baisley	.25	.07
5 Adam Piatt	.25	.07
6 Travis Dawkins	.25	.07
7 Jeremy Ward	.25	.07
8 Luis Rivera	.25	.07
9 Eric Gagne	.50	.15
10 Alex Escobar	.25	.07

2000 Royal Rookies Futures Blue Chips Autographs

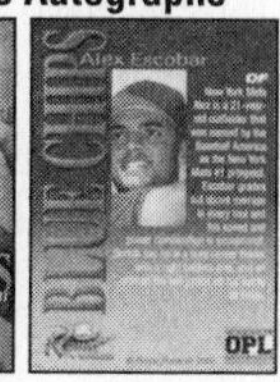

Randomly inserted into packs, this 10-cards insert is an autographed parallel of the Blue Chips insert. Each card is individually serial numbered to 1995.

	Nm-Mt	Ex-Mt
1 Rick Ankiel	2.00	.60
2 C.C. Sabathia	3.00	.90
3 Jayson Werth	2.00	.60
4 Brad Baisley	2.00	.60
5 Adam Piatt	2.00	.60
6 Travis Dawkins	2.00	.60
7 Jeremy Ward	2.00	.60
8 Luis Rivera	2.00	.60
9 Eric Gagne	10.00	3.00
10 Alex Escobar	2.00	.60

2000 Royal Rookies Futures High Yield

Randomly inserted into packs, this 10-card insert features prospects that look to produce high yields for their ballclubs.

	Nm-Mt	Ex-Mt
1 Ty Howington	.40	.12
2 Brennan King	.25	.07
3 Jason Stumm	.25	.07
4 Roosevelt Brown	.25	.07
5 Julio Lugo	.25	.07
6 Colby Lewis	.40	.12
7 Jamie Brown	.25	.07
8 Julio Ramirez	.25	.07
9 Jorge Toca	.25	.07
10 Nathan Haynes	.25	.07

2000 Royal Rookies Futures High Yield Autographs

Randomly inserted into packs, this 10-cards insert is an autographed parallel of the High Yield insert. Each card is individually serial numbered to 2500.

	Nm-Mt	Ex-Mt
1 Ty Howington	3.00	.90
2 Brennan King	2.00	.60
3 Jason Stumm	2.00	.60
4 Roosevelt Brown	2.00	.60
5 Julio Lugo	2.00	.60
6 Colby Lewis	3.00	.90
7 Jamie Brown	2.00	.60
8 Julio Ramirez	2.00	.60
9 Jorge Toca	2.00	.60
10 Nathan Haynes	2.00	.60

2000 Royal Rookies Futures Wall Street Alex Rodriguez

Randomly inserted into packs, this insert features five cards of hitting star Alex Rodriguez.

	Nm-Mt	Ex-Mt
COMPLETE SET (5)	5.00	1.50
COMMON CARD (1-5)	1.00	.30

2000 SP Top Prospects

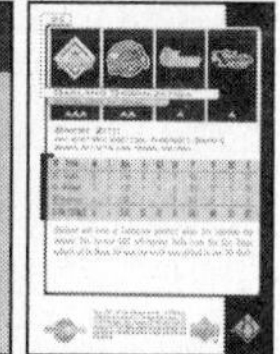

The 2000 SP Top Prospects set was released in late December, 1999 as a 135-card set. The set features many of major league baseball's top prospects. Each pack contained eight cards and carried a suggested retail price of 4.99. Notable Cards include Chin-Feng Chen and Barry Zito.

	Nm-Mt	Ex-Mt
COMPLETE SET (135)	25.00	7.50
1 Rick Ankiel T10	.40	.12

2 Brad Penny T10 .40 .12
3 Ryan Anderson T10 .40 .12
4 Pablo Ozuna T10 .40 .12
5 Alex Escobar T10 .40 .12
6 John Patterson T10 .40 .12
7 Corey Patterson T10 .75 .23
8 Nick Johnson T10 .75 .23
9 Pat Burrell T10 .75 .23
10 Matt Riley T10 .40 .12
11 Larry Barnes .40 .12
12 Brian Cooper .40 .12
13 E.J. t'Hoen .40 .12
14 Oscar Salazar .75 .23
15 Mark Mulder .75 .23
16 Roberto Vaz .40 .12
17 Eric DuBose .40 .12
18 Jacques Landry .40 .12
19 Adam Piatt .40 .12
20 Josue Espada .75 .23
21 Jesus Colome .40 .12
22 Barry Zito 6.00 1.80
23 Eric Byrnes 1.00 .30
24 Jason Hart .75 .23
25 Felipe Lopez .40 .12
26 Pasqual Coco .40 .12
27 Vernon Wells .75 .23
28 John Sneed .40 .12
29 Jorge Nunez .75 .23
30 Cameron Reimers .40 .12
31 Jung Bong .40 .12
32 Rafael Furcal .75 .23
33 Jason Marquis .40 .12
34 Derrin Ebert .40 .12
35 Troy Cameron .40 .12
36 Chad Green .40 .12
37 Rick Ankiel .40 .12
38 Chad Hutchinson .40 .12
39 Chris Haas .40 .12
40 Brent Butler .40 .12
41 Adam Kennedy .40 .12
42 Donovan Graves .75 .23
43 Ben Christensen .75 .23
44 Corey Patterson .75 .23
45 Eric Hinske 1.25 .35
46 Tydus Meadows .40 .12
47 Micah Bowie .40 .12
48 Todd Belitz .40 .12
49 Matt White .75 .23
50 Kenny Kelly .75 .23
51 Josh Hamilton .40 .12
52 Aubrey Huff .75 .23
53 Abraham Nunez .40 .12
54 John Patterson .40 .12
55 Bubba Crosby .40 .12
56 Chin-Feng Chen 1.50 .45
57 David Ross .75 .23
58 Guillermo Mota .40 .12
59 Milton Bradley .75 .23
60 Peter Bergeron .40 .12
61 Josh McKinley .40 .12
62 Tony Armas Jr. .40 .12
63 Josh Reding .40 .12
64 Tony Torcato UER .40 .12
Card numbered 66
65 Mike Glendenning .40 .12
66 Jesus Hernandez .40 .12
67 C.C. Sabathia .75 .23
68 Mike Edwards .40 .12
69 Kevin Gryboski .40 .12
70 Harvey Hargrove .40 .12
71 Ryan Anderson .40 .12
72 Peanut Williams .40 .12
73 Brad Penny .40 .12
74 Pablo Ozuna .40 .12
75 Jason Grilli .40 .12
76 Julio Ramirez .40 .12
77 A.J. Burnett .40 .12
78 Nate Bump .40 .12
79 Wes Anderson .75 .23
80 Grant Roberts .40 .12
81 Alex Escobar .40 .12
82 Jason Tyner .75 .23
83 Jorge Toca .40 .12
84 Robert Stratton .40 .12
85 Rick Elder .40 .12
86 Keith Reed .75 .23
87 Darnell McDonald .40 .12
88 Jayson Werth .40 .12
89 Matt Riley .40 .12
90 Wascar Serrano .75 .23
91 Vince Faison .75 .23
92 Omar Ortiz .40 .12
93 Junior Herndon .40 .12
94 Sean Burroughs .75 .23
95 Eric Valent .40 .12
96 Pat Burrell .75 .23
97 Reggie Taylor .40 .12
98 Eddy Furniss .40 .12
99 Chad Hermansen .40 .12
100 Kevin Haverbusch .40 .12
101 Carlos Pena .40 .12
102 Adam Everett .40 .12
103 Dernell Stenson .40 .12
104 David Eckstein .40 .12
105 John Curtice .40 .12
106 Travis Dawkins .40 .12
107 Jacobo Sequea .40 .12
108 Eric LeBlanc .40 .12
109 Rob Bell .40 .12
110 Austin Kearns .75 .23
111 Jeff Winchester .40 .12
112 Choo Freeman .40 .12
113 Ben Petrick .40 .12
114 Jody Gerut 2.00 .60
115 Josh Kalinowski .40 .12
116 Travis Thompson .40 .12
117 Jeff Austin .75 .23
118 Junior Guerrero .40 .12
119 Eric Munson .40 .12
120 Eric Gillespie .40 .12
121 Michael Cuddyer .40 .12
122 Jason Ryan .40 .12
123 Luis Rivas .40 .12
124 Ryan Mills .40 .12
125 Michael Restovich .40 .12
126 Josh Fogg .75 .23
127 Luis Raven .40 .12
128 Joe Crede .75 .23
129 Aaron Rowand .75 .23
130 Kip Wells .40 .12
131 Nick Johnson .75 .23
132 Ryan Bradley .40 .12
133 Andy Brown .40 .12
134 Donny Leon .40 .12
135 Jackson Melian .75 .23

2000 SP Top Prospects Premium Edition

Randomly inserted in packs, this insert is a complete parallel of the SP Top Prospects base set. Each card is serial numbered to 175.

Nm-Mt Ex-Mt
*PREM.ED: 2.5X TO 6X BASIC CARDS

2000 SP Top Prospects Big Town Dreams

Randomly inserted in packs at 1 in 11, this 10-card insert features ten major league hopefuls on super-premium holo-foil cards. Card backs carry a "B" prefix.

Nm-Mt Ex-Mt
COMPLETE SET (10) 10.00 3.00
B1 Jorge Toca 1.00 .30
B2 Josh Hamilton 1.00 .30
B3 Alex Escobar 1.00 .30
B4 Joe Crede 1.00 .30
B5 Eric Munson 1.00 .30
B6 Chin-Feng Chen 2.00 .60
B7 Dernell Stenson 1.00 .30
B8 Pat Burrell 1.00 .30
B9 Corey Patterson 1.00 .30
B10 Donny Leon 1.00 .30

2000 SP Top Prospects Chirography

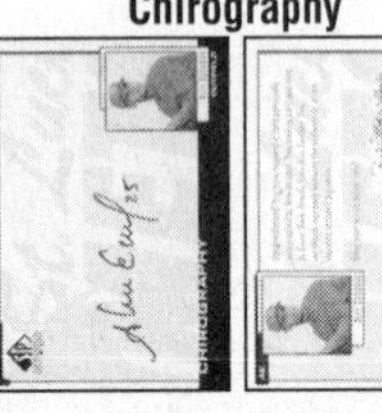
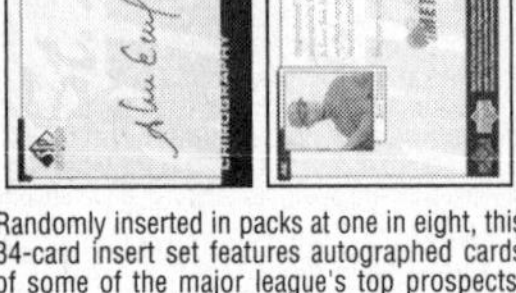

Randomly inserted in packs at one in eight, this 34-card insert set features autographed cards of some of the major league's top prospects. Card backs are numbered using the player's initials.

Nm-Mt Ex-Mt
GOLD CHIR: RANDOM INSERTS IN PACKS
GOLD CHIR.PRINT RUN 25 SERIAL #'d SETS
GOLD CHIR: NO PRICING DUE TO SCARCITY
AE Alex Escobar 5.00 1.50
AEV Adam Everett 5.00 1.50
AH Aubrey Huff 10.00 3.00
AK Austin Kearns 10.00 3.00
BEN Ben Christensen 8.00 2.40
BP Brad Penny 8.00 2.40
CH Chris Haas 5.00 1.50
CH Chad Hermansen 5.00 1.50
CHU Chad Hutchinson 8.00 2.40
DS Dernell Stenson 8.00 2.40
EM Eric Munson 8.00 2.40
FL Felipe Lopez 5.00 1.50
GR Grant Roberts 5.00 1.50
JG Jody Gerut 15.00 4.50
JGR Jason Grilli 5.00 1.50
JH Josh Hamilton 5.00 1.50
JHE Junior Herndon 5.00 1.50
JM Josh McKinley 8.00 2.40
JMA Jason Marquis 5.00 1.50
JR Julio Ramirez 5.00 1.50
JTO Jorge Toca 5.00 1.50
JW Jayson Werth 5.00 1.50
MM Mark Mulder 15.00 4.50
MR Matt Riley 8.00 2.40
NJ Nick Johnson 10.00 3.00
PB Pat Burrell 15.00 4.50
PBE Peter Bergeron 5.00 1.50
PC Pasqual Coco 5.00 1.50
PO Pablo Ozuna 5.00 1.50
RB Ryan Bradley 5.00 1.50
ROB Rob Bell 5.00 1.50
RT Reggie Taylor 5.00 1.50
SB Sean Burroughs 10.00 3.00
TT Tony Torcato 5.00 1.50

2000 SP Top Prospects Destination the Show

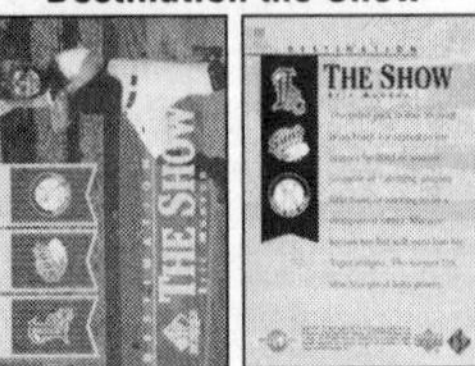

Randomly inserted in packs at one in 92, this 20-card insert set features only the brightest stars on super-premium design. Each card carries a "D" prefix.

Nm-Mt Ex-Mt
COMPLETE SET (20) 150.00 45.00
D1 Rick Ankiel 10.00 3.00
D2 Brad Penny 10.00 3.00
D3 John Patterson 10.00 3.00
D4 Rob Bell 10.00 3.00
D5 Mark Mulder 10.00 3.00
D6 Corey Patterson 10.00 3.00
D7 Eric Munson 10.00 3.00
D8 Nick Johnson 10.00 3.00
D9 Dernell Stenson 10.00 3.00
D10 Ryan Bradley 10.00 3.00
D11 Alex Escobar 10.00 3.00
D12 Matt White 10.00 3.00
D13 Michael Cuddyer 10.00 3.00
D14 Ryan Anderson 10.00 3.00
D15 Pablo Ozuna 10.00 3.00
D16 Pat Burrell 10.00 3.00
D17 A.J. Burnett 10.00 3.00
D18 Josh Hamilton 10.00 3.00
D19 Jason Grilli 10.00 3.00
D20 Matt Riley 10.00 3.00

2000 SP Top Prospects Game Used Bats

Randomly inserted in packs at one in 288, this 10-card insert set features game-used bat cards of top prospects and players like Michael Jordan and Ken Griffey Jr. Card backs carry a "G" prefix. Ken Griffey Jr. and Michael Jordan also signed a very limited number of these cards.

Nm-Mt Ex-Mt
GEM Eric Munson 8.00 2.40
GJH Josh Hamilton 8.00 2.40
GJR Ken Griffey Jr. 25.00 7.50
GJT Jorge Toca 8.00 2.40
GJW Jayson Werth 8.00 2.40
GMJ Michael Jordan 40.00 12.00
GNJ Nick Johnson 10.00 3.00
GPB Peter Bergeron 8.00 2.40
GPO Pablo Ozuna 8.00 2.40
GRF Rafael Furcal 10.00 3.00
JRAU K. Griffey Jr.
AU/24
MJAU Michael Jordan AU/45

2000 SP Top Prospects Great Futures

Randomly inserted in packs at one in four, this insert set features 20 prospects that have a great future in the major leagues. Card backs carry a "F" prefix.

Nm-Mt Ex-Mt
COMPLETE SET (20) 20.00 6.00
F1 Jorge Toca 1.00 .30
F2 Ryan Anderson 1.00 .30
F3 Eric Munson 1.00 .30
F4 Rick Ankiel 1.00 .30
F5 Rob Bell 1.00 .30
F6 Matt Riley 1.00 .30
F7 Pat Burrell 1.00 .30
F8 Nick Johnson 1.00 .30
F9 Jody Gerut 2.50 .75
F10 Sean Burroughs 1.00 .30
F11 Austin Kearns 1.00 .30
F12 Corey Patterson 1.00 .30
F13 Josh Hamilton 1.00 .30
F14 Rafael Furcal 1.00 .30
F15 Donny Leon 1.00 .30
F16 Peter Bergeron 1.00 .30
F17 A.J. Burnett 1.00 .30
F18 Alex Escobar 1.00 .30
F19 Brad Penny 1.00 .30
F20 Chin-Feng Chen 2.00 .60

2000 SP Top Prospects Minor Memories

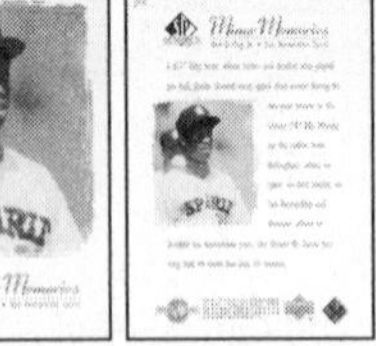

Randomly inserted in packs at one in 11, this insert features cards of Ken Griffey Jr. and Michael Jordan. Card backs carry "JR" and "MJ" prefixes.

Nm-Mt Ex-Mt
COMPLETE SET (10) 15.00 4.50
COMMON GRIFFEY (5) 1.50 .45
COMMON JORDAN (5) 3.00 .90

2000 SP Top Prospects Prospective Superstars

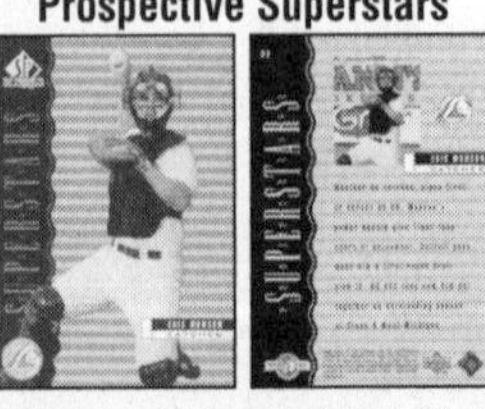

Randomly inserted in packs at one in 24, this insert set features 12 of the major leagues prospective superstars. Card backs carry a "P" prefix.

Nm-Mt Ex-Mt
COMPLETE SET (12) 25.00 7.50
P1 Pat Burrell 2.00 .60
P2 Eric Munson 2.00 .60
P3 Rick Ankiel 2.00 .60
P4 Brad Penny 2.00 .60
P5 Ben Petrick 2.00 .60
P6 Josh Hamilton 2.00 .60
P7 Adam Piatt 2.00 .60
P8 A.J. Burnett 2.00 .60
P9 Rafael Furcal 2.00 .60
P10 Sean Burroughs 2.00 .60
P11 Chin-Feng Chen 4.00 1.20
P12 Nick Johnson 2.00 .60

2000 SP Top Prospects Small Town Heroes

Randomly inserted in packs at one in 11, this 12-card insert set features the "small-town" feel of minor league baseball. Card backs carry a "S" prefix.

Nm-Mt Ex-Mt
COMPLETE SET (12) 10.00 3.00
S1 Josh Hamilton 1.00 .30
S2 Jorge Toca 1.00 .30
S3 John Patterson 1.00 .30
S4 Jacques Landry 1.00 .30
S5 Felipe Lopez 1.00 .30
S6 Choo Freeman 1.00 .30
S7 Eric Valent 1.00 .30
S8 Jody Gerut 3.00 .90
S9 Michael Restovich 1.00 .30
S10 Pablo Ozuna 1.00 .30
S11 Kip Wells 1.00 .30
S12 Michael Cuddyer 1.00 .30

2000 Team Best Rookies Promos

These cards were distributed in complete set form (within a plastic snap case) to dealers and hobby media to preview the upcoming 2000 Team Best Rookies brand. The card fronts are identical to basic 2000 Team Best Rookies cards but each card back features a large brand logo and states "for promotional purposes only".

Nm-Mt Ex-Mt
NNO Cover Card .25 .07
NNO Pat Burrell Bomber 1.50 .45
NNO Sean Burroughs .75 .23
NNO Corey Myers .50 .15
NNO Corey Patterson 1st 1.00 .30

2000 Team Best Rookies Extended Promos

These three cards were given out to hobby dealers and members of the media, to promote the 2000 Team Best Rookies Extended product. Each card features minor league prospect Josh Hamilton.

Nm-Mt Ex-Mt
COMPLETE SET (3) 3.00 .90
COMMON CARD (1-3) 1.00 .30

2000 Team Best Rookies

The 2000 Team Best Rookies first series product was released in May, 2000 as a 225-card set followed by a 25-card Extended set in November, 2000. There were some problems when the product was in production, and many of the first series cards were misnumbered. The manufacturer offered to replace all misnumbered cards through a mail-in redemption process in addition to seeding corrected versions into extended packs. Each first series and extended series pack contained six-cards and carried a suggested retail price of $2.99. Notable cards in this set include J.R. House, Ben Sheets and Barry Zito.

Nm-Mt Ex-Mt
COMPLETE SET (250) 120.00 36.00
COMP. SERIES 1 (225) 100.00 30.00
COMP. SERIES 2 (25) 20.00 6.00
1 Kurt Ainsworth 1.25 .35
2 Travis Anderson .50 .15
3 Ryan Baerlocher .50 .15
3 Chris Sampson ERR75 .50 .15
4 Andrew Beinbrink COR .50 .15
5 Jonathan Berry .50 .15
6 Larry Bigbie .75 .23
7 Josh Bonifay COR .50 .15
7 Josh Bonifay ERR .50 .15
Text on back refers to J.R. House
8 Casey Burns .50 .15
9 Mike Bynum COR .50 .15
10 Marlon Byrd 2.50 .75
11 Terry Byron COR .50 .15
12 Chance Caple .50 .15
13 Matt Cepicky .50 .15
14 Ryan Christianson .50 .15
14 Joe Thurston ERR85 1.25 .35
15 B.R. Cook .50 .15
16 Carl Crawford .50 .15
17 Chuck Crowder .50 .15
18 Jeremy Cunningham .50 .15
19 Chris Curry .50 .15
19 Mike Bynum ERR9 .50 .15
20 Phil Devey .50 .15
20 A.Beinbrink ERR4 .50 .15
21 Grant Dorn .50 .15
21 Chris Testa ERR83 .50 .15
22 Mike Dwyer COR .50 .15
23 Mike Dzurilla .50 .15
23 Barry Zito ERR99 6.00 1.80
24 Vince Faison .50 .15
25 Carlos Figeroa .50 .15
26 Aaron Franke .50 .15
27 Charlie Frazier .50 .15
28 B.J. Garbe .50 .15
29 Curtis Gay .50 .15
30 Jay Gehrke .50 .15
31 Scott Goodman .50 .15
32 Alex Graman .50 .15
33 Ryan Gripp .50 .15
33 Robb Quinlan ERR70 .50 .15
34 Josh Hamilton COR .50 .15
35 Ken Harvey 1.50 .45
36 Jeff Heaverlo .50 .15
37 Ben Hickman .50 .15
38 Mike Hill COR .50 .15
39 Josh Holliday .50 .15
40 Kevin Hooper .50 .15
41 Ryan Jamison .50 .15
41 Josh Hamilton ERR34 .50 .15
42 Eric Johnson .50 .15
43 Jake Joseph .50 .15
44 Ryan Kibler COR .50 .15
45 John Lackey .50 .15
46 Jake Laidlaw .50 .15
47 Jay Landreth COR .50 .15
48 Jason Lane .75 .23
49 Jay Langston .50 .15
50 Peyton Lewis .50 .15
50 M.Thompson ERR84 .50 .15
51 Mike MacDougal .75 .23
51 Ben Sheets ERR78 1.50 .45
Card was intended to be number 78, also text on back refers to Mike McDougald
52 Mike Mallory .50 .15
53 Justin Martin .50 .15
54 Lamont Matthews .50 .15
55 Matt McClendon .50 .15
56 Sean McGowan .50 .15
57 Todd Mitchell .50 .15
57 Terry Byron ERR11 .50 .15
58 Matt Mize .50 .15
58 Matt Watson ERR94 .50 .15
59 Jason Moore .50 .15
60 Corey Myers .50 .15
61 Derrick Nunley .50 .15
62 Rodney Nye .50 .15
63 Mike Paradis .50 .15
63 Mike Dwyer ERR22 .50 .15
64 Val Pascucci .50 .15
65 Dustin Pate .50 .15
66 Mike Patten .50 .15
67 Brad Pautz .50 .15
68 Josh Pearce .50 .15
68 Ryan Kibler ERR44 .50 .15
69 Andy Phillips .50 .15
70 Robb Quinlan COR .50 .15
71 G.J. Raymundo .50 .15
71 Dominic Woody ERR97 .50 .15
72 Justin Reid .50 .15
72 M.Rosamond ERR74 .50 .15
73 Nate Robertson .50 .15
74 Mike Rosamond COR .50 .15
75 Chris Sampson COR .50 .15
76 Matt Schneider .50 .15
77 Shawn Schumacher .50 .15
UER First name misspelled Sean
78 Ben Sheets COR 1.50 .45
79 Jeremy Sickles .50 .15
80 Kyle Snyder .50 .15
80 Mike Hill ERR38 .50 .15
81 Jack Taschner .50 .15
82 Seth Taylor .50 .15
82 C. Williams ERR95 .50 .15
83 Chris Testa COR .50 .15
84 Mike Thompson COR .50 .15
85 Joe Thurston COR 1.25 .35
86 Jon Topolski .50 .15
86 J.Williams ERR96 3.00 .90
87 Dan Tosca .50 .15
87 Jay Landreth ERR47 .50 .15
88 Nick Trzesniak COR .50 .15
88 Nick Trzesniak ERR .50 .15
Last name misspelled Trzeniak
89 Brant Ust .50 .15
90 Josh Vitek .50 .15
91 David Walling .50 .15
92 Jeremy Ward .50 .15
93 Anthony Ware .50 .15
94 Matt Watson COR .50 .15
95 Charles Williams COR .50 .15
96 Jerome Williams COR 3.00 .90
97 Dominic Woody COR .50 .15
98 Shane Wright .50 .15
99 Barry Zito COR 6.00 1.80
100 Alec Zumwalt .50 .15
101 Chip Ambres 1ST .50 .15
102 Jeff Austin 1ST .50 .15
103 Pat Burrell 1ST .75 .23
104 Sean Burroughs 1ST .50 .15
105 Bubba Crosby 1ST .50 .15
106 Choo Freeman 1ST .50 .15
107 Josh Hamilton 1ST .50 .15
108 Mark Mulder 1ST .75 .23
109 Corey Patterson 1ST .50 .15
110 Carlos Pena 1ST .50 .15
111 Eric Valent 1ST .50 .15
112 Kip Wells 1ST .50 .15
113 Kurt Ainsworth ERR 1.25 .35
Misnumbered 1 on front
113 Kurt Ainsworth COR 1.25 .35
114 Travis Anderson .50 .15
115 Ryan Baerlocher ERR .50 .15
Misnumbered 3 on front
115 Ryan Baerlocher COR .50 .15
116 Andrew Beinbrink .50 .15
117 Jonathan Berry .50 .15
118 Larry Bigbie .75 .23

119 Josh Bonifay ERR .50 .15
Card back text refers to J.R. House
119 Josh Bonifay COR .50 .15
120 Ben Broussard .50 .15
121 Casey Burns ERR .50 .15
Misnumbered 8 on front
121 Casey Burns COR .50 .15
122 Mike Bynum .50 .15
123 Marlon Byrd 2.50 .75
124 Terry Byron .50 .15
125 Chance Caple .50 .15
126 Matt Cepicky .50 .15
127 Ryan Christianson .50 .15
128 B.R. Cook .50 .15
129 Carl Crawford .50 .15
130 Chuck Crowder .50 .15
131 Jeremy Cunningham .50 .15
132 Chris Curry .50 .15
133 Phil Devey .50 .15
134 Grant Dorn .50 .15
135 Mike Dwyer .50 .15
136 Mike Dzurilla .50 .15
137 Vince Faison .50 .15
138 Carlos Figeroa .50 .15
139 Aaron Franke .50 .15
140 Charlie Frazier .50 .15
141 B.J. Garbe .50 .15
142 Curtis Gay .50 .15
143 Jay Gehrke .50 .15
144 Scott Goodman .50 .15
145 Alex Graman .50 .15
146 Ryan Gripp .50 .15
147 Josh Hamilton .50 .15
148 Ken Harvey 1.50 .45
149 Jeff Heaverlo .50 .15
150 Ben Hickman .50 .15
151 Mike Hill .50 .15
152 Josh Holliday .50 .15
153 Kevin Hooper ERR .50 .15
Misnumbered 202 on front
153 Kevin Hooper COR .50 .15
154 Ryan Jamison .50 .15
155 Eric Johnson .50 .15
156 Jake Joseph .50 .15
157 Ryan Kibler .50 .15
158 John Lackey .50 .15
159 Jake Laidlaw .50 .15
160 Jay Landreth .50 .15
161 Jason Lane .75 .23
162 Jay Langston .50 .15
163 Peyton Lewis .50 .15
164 Mike MacDougal .75 .23
165 Mike Mallory .50 .15
166 Justin Martin .50 .15
167 Lamont Matthews .50 .15
168 Matt McClendon .50 .15
169 Sean McGowan .50 .15
170 Todd Mitchell .50 .15
171 Matt Mize .50 .15
172 Jason Moore .50 .15
173 Corey Myers .50 .15
174 Derrick Nunley .50 .15
175 Rodney Nye .50 .15
176 Mike Paradis .50 .15
177 Val Pascucci .50 .15
178 Dustin Pate .50 .15
179 Mike Patten .50 .15
180 Brad Pautz .50 .15
181 Josh Pearce .50 .15
182 Andy Phillips .50 .15
183 Robb Quinlan .50 .15
184 G.J. Raymundo .50 .15
185 Justin Reid .50 .15
186 Nate Robertson .50 .15
187 Mike Rosamond .50 .15
188 Chris Sampson .50 .15
189 Matt Schneider .50 .15
190 Shawn Schumacher .50 .15
UER Sean
191 Ben Sheets 1.50 .45
192 Jeremy Sickles .50 .15
193 Kyle Snyder ERR .50 .15
Font for name on front is over-sized
193 Kyle Snyder COR .50 .15
Font is normal
194 Jack Taschner .50 .15
195 Seth Taylor .50 .15
196 Chris Testa .50 .15
197 Mike Thompson .50 .15
198 Joe Thurston 1.25 .35
199 Jon Topolski .50 .15
200 Dan Tosca .50 .15
201 Nick Trzesniak ERR .50 .15
Last name misspelled Trezniak
201 Nick Trzesniak COR .50 .15
202 Brant Ust .50 .15
203 Josh Vitek .50 .15
204 David Walling .50 .15
205 Jeremy Ward .50 .15
206 Anthony Ware .50 .15
207 Matt Watson .50 .15
208 Charles Williams .50 .15
209 Jerome Williams 3.00 .90
210 Dominic Woody ERR .50 .15
Font for name on front is over-sized
210 Dominic Woody COR .50 .15
Font is normal
211 Shane Wright .50 .15
212 Barry Zito 6.00 1.80
213 Alec Zumwalt .50 .15
214 Chip Ambres 1ST .50 .15
215 Jeff Austin 1ST .50 .15
216 Pat Burrell 1ST .75 .23
217 Sean Burroughs 1ST .50 .15
218 Bubba Crosby 1ST .50 .15
219 Choo Freeman 1ST .50 .15
220 Josh Hamilton 1ST .50 .15
221 Mark Mulder 1ST .75 .23
222 Corey Patterson 1ST .50 .15
223 Carlos Pena 1ST .50 .15
224 Eric Valent 1ST .50 .15
225 Kip Wells 1ST .50 .15
226 Danys Baez .50 .15
227 Josh Beckett 2.00 .60
228 Willie Bloomquist 2.50 .75
229 Bobby Bradley .50 .15
230 Ben Broussard .50 .15
231 Ben Christensen .50 .15
232 Brian Cole .50 .15
233 Enrique Cruz .50 .15
234 Matt Ginter .50 .15
235 J.R. House .50 .15
236 Ty Howington .50 .15
237 Russ Jacobson .50 .15
238 Neil Jenkins .50 .15
239 Jason Jennings .50 .15
240 Colby Lewis .75 .23
241 Ryan Ludwick .50 .15
242 Mike Maroth .50 .15
243 Eric Munson .50 .15
244 Neal Musser .50 .15
245 Brett Myers 3.00 .90
246 Wily Mo Pena .50 .15
247 Brian Sanches .50 .15
248 Ramon Santiago .50 .15
249 Jason Stumm .50 .15
250 Dan Wright .50 .15

2000 Team Best Rookies Bronze

Randomly inserted into packs of 2000 Team Best Extended, this 125-card set is a parallel of the first 125 cards in the 2000 Team Best base set. Each card was produced using a bronze foil stamping.

Nm-Mt Ex-Mt
*BRONZE: .5X TO 1.2X BASIC CARDS

2000 Team Best Rookies Gold

Randomly inserted into packs of 2000 Team Best Extended, this 125-card set is a parallel of the first 125 cards in the 2000 Team Best base set. Each card was produced using a gold foil stamping.

Nm-Mt Ex-Mt
*GOLD: 1.5X TO 4X BASIC CARDS

2000 Team Best Rookies Silver

Randomly inserted into packs of 2000 Team Best Extended, this 125-card set is a parallel of the first 125 cards in the 2000 Team Best base set. Each card was produced using a silver foil stamping.

Nm-Mt Ex-Mt
*SILVER: .75X TO 2X BASIC CARDS

2000 Team Best Rookies Autographs

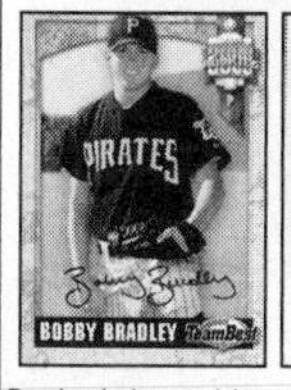

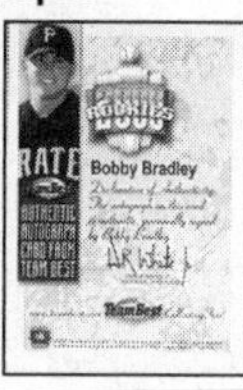

Randomly inserted into packs at one in three, this 50-card set features certified autographs of some of the hottest young talent in major league baseball. Ty Howington's card was not available for insertion into packs of Team Best Rookies and was mailed to collectors several months later.

Nm-Mt Ex-Mt
1 Kurt Ainsworth 8.00 2.40
2 Chad Allen 2.50 .75
3 Chip Ambres 2.50 .75
4 Ryan Anderson 2.50 .75
5 Rick Asadoorian UER 4.00 1.20
Asadoorian is misspelled on the card
6 Jeff Austin 4.00 1.20
7 Peter Bergeron 2.50 .75
8 Bobby Bradley 4.00 1.20
9 Milton Bradley 4.00 1.20
10 Ben Broussard 4.00 1.20
11 Andy Brown 2.50 .75
12 Roosevelt Brown 2.50 .75
13 Sean Burroughs 10.00 3.00
14 Brian Cooper 2.50 .75
15 Francisco Cordero 2.50 .75
16 Bubba Crosby 8.00 2.40
17 Jack Cust 2.50 .75
18 Ryan Dempster 4.00 1.20
19 Rick Elder 2.50 .75
20 Choo Freeman 2.50 .75
21 B.J. Garbe 4.00 1.20
22 Jon Garland 2.50 .75
23 Marcus Giles 4.00 1.20
24 Keith Ginter 2.50 .75
25 Jeff Goldbach 2.50 .75
26 Josh Hamilton 2.50 .75
27 Jason Hart 4.00 1.20
28 Chad Harville 2.50 .75
29 Shane Heams 2.50 .75
30 Jeff Heaverlo 4.00 1.20
31 Ty Howington MAIL 4.00 1.20
32 Cesar Izturis 4.00 1.20
33 Austin Kearns 10.00 3.00
34 Mike Lincoln 2.50 .75
35 George Lombard 2.50 .75
36 Julio Lugo 2.50 .75
37 Matt McClendon 4.00 1.20
38 Mike Meyers 2.50 .75
39 Jim Morris 25.00 7.50
40 Brett Myers 10.00 3.00
41 Danny Peoples 2.50 .75
42 Luis Rivera 2.50 .75
43 Nate Rolison 2.50 .75
44 B.J. Ryan 2.50 .75
45 Kyle Snyder 2.50 .75
46 Pat Strange 4.00 1.20
47 Jason Stumm 4.00 1.20
48 Tyler Walker 2.50 .75
49 Brad Wilkerson 4.00 1.20
50 Barry Zito 25.00 7.50

2000 Team Best Rookies Babbitt's Bombers

Randomly inserted into packs at one in 72, this eight-card set features some of the top young power hitters in the minor leagues.

Nm-Mt Ex-Mt
COMPLETE SET (8) 30.00 9.00
*SILVER: .6X TO 1.5X BASIC BABBITT
SILVER PRINT RUN 150 SERIAL #'d SETS
*GOLD: .75X TO 2X BASIC BABBITT
GOLD PRINT RUN 100 SERIAL #'d SETS
GOLD/SILVER RANDOM INSERTS IN PACKS
1 Russell Branyan 3.00 .90
2 Morgan Burkhart 3.00 .90
3 Pat Burrell 5.00 1.50
4 Josh Hamilton 3.00 .90
5 Nick Johnson 5.00 1.50
6 George Lombard 3.00 .90
7 Carlos Pena 3.00 .90
8 Dernell Stenson 3.00 .90

2000 Team Best Rookies Diamond Best

Randomly inserted into Extended packs at one in 90, this 10-card insert features some of the best minor league talent.

Nm-Mt Ex-Mt
COMPLETE SET (10) 50.00 15.00
1 Josh Beckett 10.00 3.00
2 Russell Branyan 5.00 1.50
3 Pat Burrell 6.00 1.80
4 Michael Cuddyer 5.00 1.50
5 Alex Escobar 5.00 1.50
6 Josh Hamilton 5.00 1.50
7 Steve Lomasney 5.00 1.50
8 Tomo Ohka 5.00 1.50
9 Adam Piatt 5.00 1.50
10 Jimmy Rollins 6.00 1.80

2000-01 Just Candidates Autographs

These autograph cards parallel the basic Candidates inserts. The cards were distributed as part of the 1999 and 2000 Just Stuff mail-in program. Each card was hand-numbered on back to 100. These unnumbered cards are checklisted alphabetically by player last name

Nm-Mt Ex-Mt
1 Josh Beckett 40.00 12.00
2 Bobby Bradley 5.00 1.50
3 Josh Hamilton 3.00 .90

2000-01 Just Debuts Autographs

These autograph cards parallel the basic Debuts inserts. The cards were distributed as part of the 1999, 2000 and 2001 Just Stuff mail-in program. Each card was hand-numbered on back to 100.

Nm-Mt Ex-Mt
2 Ben Broussard 5.00 1.50
10 Barry Zito 25.00 7.50

2000-01 Just Diamonds Autographs

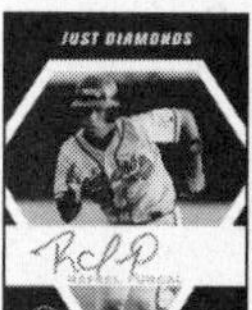

This autograph card of Rafael Furcal was distributed as part of the 1999 and 2000 Just Stuff mail-in program. The card is serial numbered of 100 on back. Unlike most other Just Stuff autograph cards, this Furcal issue does not parallel a more common unsigned version of the card.

Nm-Mt Ex-Mt
1 Rafael Furcal 5.00 1.50

2000-01 Just Dominant Autographs

Some of these autographed cards parallel the basic Dominant inserts, however, some players are exclusive through the "Stuff" program. These players include Tim Hudson, Sean Burroughs and Josh Hamilton.. The cards were distributed as part of the 1999 and 2000 Just Stuff mail-in program. Each card was hand-numbered on back to 100. These unnumbered cards are checklisted alphabetically by player last name

Nm-Mt Ex-Mt
1 Ben Broussard 5.00 1.50
2 Sean Burroughs 5.00 1.50
3 Rafael Furcal 5.00 1.50
4 Josh Hamilton 5.00 1.50
5 Tim Hudson 5.00 1.50
6 Corey Patterson 5.00 1.50

2000-01 Just Nine Autographs

These autograph cards parallel the basic Just Nine inserts. The cards were distributed as part of the 1999 and 2000 Just Stuff mail-in program. Each card was hand-numbered on back to 100. These unnumbered cards are checklisted alphabetically by player last name

Nm-Mt Ex-Mt
1 Josh Beckett 40.00 12.00
2 Nick Johnson 5.00 1.50

2000-01 Just Stuff

Cards from this 11-card set were available only by participating in the Just Stuff program whereby collectors purchased a selection of collectible cards, figurines and equipment directly from the manufacturer via mail order in six different "Stuff" packages. Card backs for the equipment cards carry a "JS" prefix and the autograph cards are all unnumbered (but checklisted below alphabetically by player's last name). Package number 2 carried an initial direct cost of $29.95 and for that each participant received a random selection of one signed card (out of a possible ten different cards), 10 packs of 2000 Just and a 5-card promo set. Package number 6 carried an initial direct cost of $79.95 and participants received a random selection of one autograph card (out of a possible four different cards) and one equipment card (out of a possible four different cards). Participants for package number 6 were not allowed to select their specific card unless they ordered four packages at once ensuring one of each card from the manufacturer. Packages 1, 3 and 5 contained a selection of mini-helmets (signed by the player), a Rick Ankiel figurine and autographed baseballs. These items are not checklisted below because they fall outside of the realm of sportscards. Many of the other sets including the 1999-00 Just Autographs (ie; Debuts, Due, Facts, News, etc) and a few 2001 insert autographs (ie; Dominant, Debuts, Candidates, etc.) were also available in this promotion, however, were broken up for readers convenience and accurately distinguish some as split years.

Nm-Mt Ex-Mt
JS6-01 Rick Ankiel Jsy 8.00 2.40
JS6-01 Rick Ankiel Jsy AU/10
JS6-01 Mystery Bat 25.00 7.50
Ken Griffey Jr.
JS6-02 Rafael Furcal Bat 5.00 1.50
JS6-02 Rafael Furcal Bat AU/10
JS6-03 Pat Burrell Jsy 20.00 6.00
JS6-04 Sean Burroughs Bat 10.00 3.00
JS6-04 Sean Burroughs Bat AU/10
JS6-05 Corey Patterson Bat 8.00 2.40
JS6-05 Corey Patterson Bat AU/10
JS6-06 Mystery Bat/C.Jones 15.00 4.50

2000-01 Just the One Autographs

These autograph cards parallel the basic Just the One inserts. The cards were distributed as part of the 1999 and 2000 Just Stuff mail-in program. Each card was hand-numbered on back to 100.

Nm-Mt Ex-Mt
RA Rick Ankiel Potomac 5.00 1.50
RA Rick Ankiel Peoria 5.00 1.50
RA Rick Ankiel Arkansas 5.00 1.50
TORA4 Rick Ankiel 5.00 1.50
TORA5 Rick Ankiel 5.00 1.50

2000-01 Just Tools Autographs

These autograph cards parallel the basic Tools inserts. The cards were distributed as part of the 1999, 2000 and 2001 Just Stuff mail-in program. Each card was hand-numbered on back to 100.

Nm-Mt Ex-Mt
1 Sean Burroughs 5.00 1.50
2 Corey Patterson 5.00 1.50
3 Adam Piatt 3.00 .90

2001 Just 2k1 Top Prospect Promos

This 13-card set was distributed in complete set form via the 2001 Just Stuff mail program (whereby consumers could purchase a selection of different packages containing various signed memorabilia and trading cards). It's believed the cards were intended to preview an upcoming brand entitled Just 2k1, but for various reasons, the manufacturer never released the set.

Nm-Mt Ex-Mt
COMPLETE SET (13) 30.00 9.00
TPP-1 Wilson Betemit 3.00 .90
TPP-2 Joe Borchard 4.00 1.20
TPP-3 Cristian Guerrero 1.25 .35
TPP-4 J.R. House 1.00 .30
TPP-5 Hee Seop Choi 3.00 .90
TPP-6 Tiger Wang 1.25 .35
TPP-7 Justin Morneau 3.00 .90
TPP-8 Tony Blanco 4.00 1.20
TPP-9 Luis Montanez 2.00 .60
TPP-10 Drew Henson 4.00 1.20
TPP-11 Adrian Gonzalez 2.00 .60
TPP-12 Bobby Hill 3.00 .90
BONUS Drew Henson Bonus 6.00 1.80

2001 Just Autographs

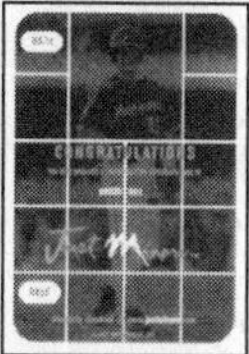

These cards were distributed via mail as part of the Just Stuff program (whereby consumers could purchase a selection of different packages of material (often a mixture of signed memorabilia and trading cards) directly from the manufacturer. The cards that have been verified to exist create a skip-numbered checklist, but it's believed additional cards were produced and distributed. The cards share a similar design to the 2001 Just 2k1 Top

Prospect Promos and may have been produced as insert cards for a Just 2k1 branded product that never managed to reach final production stages. Bobby Hill's first certified autograph cards are featured within this set.

	Nm-Mt	Ex-Mt
A SUFFIX ON JUST STUFF 2K1.2		
B SUFFIX ON JUST STUFF 2K1.3		
BA2 Bobby Bradley		
BA4 Ben Broussard		
BA6 Alex Cintron B	2.00	.60
BA7 Alex Cole		
BA8 Michael Coleman A	2.00	.60
BA9 Jesus Colome		
BA10 Carl Crawford A	5.00	1.50
BA11 Jack Cust		
BA14 Chris George		
BA15 Marcus Giles		
BA16 Matt Ginter B	2.00	.60
BA18 Jeff Goldbach B	2.00	.60
BA19 Toby Hall B	3.00	.90
BA20 Jason Hart		
BA22 Bobby Hill Portrait B	15.00	4.50
BA23 J.R. House B	2.00	.60
BA25 Ben Johnson B	2.00	.60
BA26 Austin Kearns B	10.00	3.00
BA28 Colby Lewis B	2.00	.60
BA30 Jackson Melian		
BA32 Pablo Ozuna A	2.00	.60
BA33 Carlos Pena		
BA36 Keith Reed		
BA37 Jason Repko Great Falls A	2.00	.60
BA38 Luis Rivas B	2.00	.60
BA39 Luis Rivera B	2.00	.60
BA41 B.J. Ryan		
BA42 C.C. Sabathia		
BA47 Tony Torcato		
BA48 Luis Torres B	2.00	.60
BA49 Jeremy Ward B	2.00	.60
BA50 Carlos Zambrano		
BA51 Barry Zito		
BA52 Bobby Bradley		
BA53 Carl Crawford		
BA54 Jack Cust A	3.00	.90
BA56 Jason Hart		
BA56 Jason Hart		
BA57 J.R. House		
BA60 Carlos Zambrano		
BA62 Winston Abreu B	2.00	.60
BA63 Brad Baisley A	2.00	.60
BA64 Matt Belisle B	2.00	.60
BA65 Casey Burns A	2.00	.60
BA66 Travis Dawkins Rockford		
BA67 Scott Downs B	2.00	.60
BA68 Tim Drew B	2.00	.60
BA70 Vince Faison B	2.00	.60
BA71 Keith Ginter		
BA72 Cristian Guerrero		
BA74 Bobby Hill Batting A	10.00	3.00
BA77 Brandon Larson		
BA78 Matt LeCroy Portrait A	2.00	.60
BA80 Nick Neugebauer Portrait		
BA84 Jon Rauch		
BA85 Jason Repko Yakima B	2.00	.60
BA88 Nick Stocks Portrait A	2.00	.60
BA89 Tony Torcato		
BA90 Eric Valent		
BA91 Jayson Werth B	3.00	.90
BA92 Jerome Williams		
BA93 Travis Dawkins Lookouts		
BA95 Brandon Larson		
BA96 Matt LeCroy Batting B	2.00	.60
BA97 Nick Neugebauer		
BA98 Nick Stocks Kneeling	2.00	.60

2001 Royal Rookies

	Nm-Mt	Ex-Mt
COMPLETE SET (44)	5.00	1.50
1 Mark Brownson	.15	.04
2 Jason Woolf	.15	.04
3 Enrique Cruz	.15	.04
4 Jose Mieses	.15	.04
5 Erick Almonte	.25	.07
6 Randey Dorame	.15	.04
7 Alex Hernandez	.15	.04
8 Marlon Byrd	.75	.23
9 Kevin Connacher	.15	.04
10 Asdrubal Orapeza	.15	.04
11 Seth McClung	.25	.07
12 Delvin James	.15	.04
13 Albenis Machado	.15	.04
14 Jose Leon	.15	.04
15 Randy Meadows	.15	.04
16 Luke Allen	.15	.04
17 Hector Almonte	.15	.04
18 Peter Bauer	.15	.04
19 Todd Betts	.15	.04
20 Adrian Burnside	.15	.04
21 Angel Berroa	.75	.23
22 Cesar Saba	.15	.04
23 Luis Garcia	.15	.04
24 Ron Paulino	.15	.04
25 Alexis Gomez	.25	.07
26 Ryan Ballard	.15	.04
27 Enemencio Pacheco	.15	.04
28 Michael Napoli	.15	.04
29 Francis Finnerty	.15	.04
30 Javier Calzada	.15	.04
31 Shawn Sonnier	.15	.04
32 Mike Porzio	.15	.04
33 Rafael Pujols	.15	.04
34 Pedro Santana	.15	.04
35 Carlos Urquiola	.15	.04
36 Ty Howington / Jason Stumm	.15	.04
37 Brennan King / Jorge Toca	.15	.04
38 Alex Escobar / Jeremy Ward	.15	.04
39 C.C. Sabathia / Brad Baisley	.25	.07
40 Nathan Haynes / Julio Ramirez	.15	.04
41 Colby Lewis / Jamie Brown	.15	.04
42 Roosevelt Brown / Eric Byrnes	.25	.07
43 Todd Helton Base CL	.25	.07
44 Todd Helton Insert CL	.25	.07

2001 Royal Rookies Autographs

	Nm-Mt	Ex-Mt
1 Mark Brownson	2.00	.60
2 Jason Woolf	2.00	.60
3 Enrique Cruz	2.00	.60
4 Jose Mieses	2.00	.60
5 Erick Almonte	3.00	.90
6 Randey Dorame	2.00	.60
7 Alex Hernandez	2.00	.60
8 Marlon Byrd	5.00	1.50
9 Kevin Connacher	2.00	.60
10 Asdrubal Orapeza	2.00	.60
11 Seth McClung	3.00	.90
12 Delvin James	2.00	.60
13 Albenis Machado	2.00	.60
14 Jose Leon	2.00	.60
15 Randy Meadows	2.00	.60
16 Luke Allen	2.00	.60
17 Hector Almonte	2.00	.60
18 Peter Bauer	2.00	.60
19 Todd Betts	2.00	.60
20 Adrian Burnside	2.00	.60
21 Angel Berroa	5.00	1.50
22 Cesar Saba	2.00	.60
23 Luis Garcia	2.00	.60
24 Ron Paulino	2.00	.60
25 Alexis Gomez	3.00	.90
26 Ryan Ballard	2.00	.60
27 Enemencio Pacheco	2.00	.60
28 Michael Napoli	2.00	.60
29 Francis Finnerty	2.00	.60
30 Javier Calzada	2.00	.60
31 Shawn Sonnier	2.00	.60
32 Mike Porzio	2.00	.60
33 Rafael Pujols	2.00	.60
34 Pedro Santana	2.00	.60
35 Carlos Urquiola	2.00	.60

2001 Royal Rookies Amazing Todd Helton

	Nm-Mt	Ex-Mt
COMPLETE SET (5)	2.50	.75
COMMON CARD (1-5)	.50	.15

2001 Royal Rookies Amazing Todd Helton Autographs

	Nm-Mt	Ex-Mt
COMMON CARD (1-5)	15.00	4.50

2001 Royal Rookies Barnstormers

	Nm-Mt	Ex-Mt
1 Brian Wolfe	.25	.07
2 Garett Gentry	.25	.07
3 Corey Spencer	.25	.07
4 Alfredo Amezaga	.40	.12
5 Vince Faison	.25	.07
6 Darron Cox	.25	.07
7 Luis Martinez	.25	.07
8 Junior Herndon	.25	.07
9 Kenny Nelson	.50	.15
10 Jay Sitzman	.25	.07

2001 Royal Rookies Barnstormers Autographs

	Nm-Mt	Ex-Mt
1 Brian Wolfe	2.00	.60
2 Garett Gentry	2.00	.60
3 Corey Spencer	2.00	.60
4 Alfredo Amezaga	3.00	.90
5 Vince Faison	2.00	.60
6 Darron Cox	2.00	.60
7 Luis Martinez	2.00	.60
8 Junior Herndon	2.00	.60
9 Kenny Nelson	3.00	.90
10 Jay Sitzman	2.00	.60

2001 Royal Rookies Boys of Summer

	Nm-Mt	Ex-Mt
COMPLETE SET (10)	2.50	.75
1 Luke Prokopec	.25	.07
2 Tim Drew	.25	.07
3 Joe Crede	.40	.12
4 Dan Wheeler	.25	.07
5 Horacio Estrada	.25	.07
6 Andy Beal	.25	.07
7 Ted Rose	.25	.07
8 Bert Snow	.25	.07
9 Kevin Burford	.25	.07
10 Brett Weber	.25	.07

2001 Royal Rookies Boys of Summer Autographs

	Nm-Mt	Ex-Mt
1 Luke Prokopec	2.00	.60
2 Tim Drew	2.00	.60
3 Joe Crede	3.00	.90
4 Dan Wheeler	2.00	.60
5 Horacio Estrada	2.00	.60
6 Andy Beal	2.00	.60
7 Ted Rose	2.00	.60
8 Bert Snow	2.00	.60
9 Kevin Burford	2.00	.60
10 Brett Weber	2.00	.60

2001 Royal Rookies Futures

	Nm-Mt	Ex-Mt
COMPLETE SET (40)	5.00	1.50
1 Steve Torrealba	.15	.04
2 Jack Taschner	.15	.04
3 Lee Gardner	.15	.04
4 Jared Abruzzo	.25	.07
5 Bryant Nelson	.15	.04
6 Scott Stewart	.15	.04
7 Hank Blalock	2.00	.60
8 Todd Rizzo	.15	.04
9 Ryan Hankins	.15	.04
10 Jeff Andrews	.15	.04
11 Simon Pond	.40	.12
12 Dave Post	.15	.04
13 Steve Minus	.15	.04
14 Brian Wiese	.15	.04
15 Sean Burnett	.25	.07
16 Miguel Cabrera	1.00	.30
17 Jose Castillo	.60	.18
18 Anderson Machado	.25	.07
19 Ranier Olmedo	.15	.04
20 Aaron McNeal	.15	.04
21 Brett Jodie	.15	.04
22 Mike Lockwood	.15	.04
23 Aaron Sledd	.15	.04
24 Jorge DeLeon	.15	.04
25 Luis Saturria	.15	.04
26 Roberto Machado	.15	.04
27 Ricky Stone	.15	.04
28 Jesus Feliciano	.15	.04
29 Earl Snyder	.15	.04
30 Brian Schmack	.25	.07
31 Eric Johnson	.15	.04
32 Brian Wolfe	.15	.04
33 Sheldon Fulse	.15	.04
34 Scott Barber	.25	.07
35 Aron Weston	.25	.07
36 Kenny Nelson	.40	.12
37 Ryan Drese	.25	.07
38 J.J. Putz	.15	.04
39 Scot Shields	.15	.04
40 Ryan Carter	.15	.04

2001 Royal Rookies Futures Limited Edition

	Nm-Mt	Ex-Mt
COMPLETE SET (40)	15.00	4.50
*LTD.ED: .75X TO 2X BASIC CARDS ..		
RANDOM INSERTS IN PACKS		

2001 Royal Rookies Futures Autographs

	Nm-Mt	Ex-Mt
1 Steve Torrealba	2.00	.60
2 Jack Taschner	2.00	.60
3 Lee Gardner	2.00	.60
4 Jared Abruzzo	3.00	.90
5 Bryant Nelson	2.00	.60
6 Scott Stewart	2.00	.60
7 Hank Blalock	15.00	4.50
8 Todd Rizzo	2.00	.60
9 Ryan Hankins	2.00	.60
10 Jeff Andrews	2.00	.60
11 Simon Pond	3.00	.90
12 Dave Post	2.00	.60
13 Steve Minus	2.00	.60
14 Brian Wiese	2.00	.60
15 Sean Burnett	3.00	.90
16 Miguel Cabrera	20.00	6.00
17 Jose Castillo	5.00	1.50
18 Anderson Machado	3.00	.90
19 Ranier Olmedo	2.00	.60
20 Aaron McNeal	2.00	.60
21 Brett Jodie	2.00	.60
22 Mike Lockwood	2.00	.60
23 Aaron Sledd	2.00	.60
24 Jorge DeLeon	2.00	.60
25 Luis Saturria	2.00	.60
26 Roberto Machado	2.00	.60
27 Ricky Stone	2.00	.60
28 Jesus Feliciano	2.00	.60
29 Earl Snyder	2.00	.60
30 Brian Schmack	3.00	.90
31 Eric Johnson	2.00	.60
32 Brian Wolfe	2.00	.60
33 Sheldon Fulse	2.00	.60
34 Scott Barber	2.00	.60
35 Aron Weston	3.00	.90
36 Kenny Nelson	3.00	.90
37 Ryan Drese	3.00	.90
38 J.J. Putz	2.00	.60
39 Scot Shields	2.00	.60
40 Ryan Carter	2.00	.60

2001 Royal Rookies Futures Blue Chips

	Nm-Mt	Ex-Mt
COMPLETE SET (5)	2.50	.75
BC1 Jerome Williams	1.50	.45
BC2 Brett Myers	.40	.12
BC3 Wilson Betemit	.40	.12
BC4 Billy Traber	.40	.12
BC5 Jose Ortiz	.25	.07

2001 Royal Rookies Futures Blue Chips Autographs

	Nm-Mt	Ex-Mt
BC1 Jerome Williams	8.00	2.40
BC2 Brett Myers	3.00	.90
BC3 Wilson Betemit	3.00	.90
BC4 Billy Traber	3.00	.90
BC5 Jose Ortiz	2.00	.60

2001 Royal Rookies Futures High Yield

	Nm-Mt	Ex-Mt
COMPLETE SET (5)	2.00	.60
HY1 Chris Snelling	.75	.23
HY2 Bret Prinz	.25	.07
HY3 Orlando Woodards	.25	.07
HY4 Nick Neugebauer	.25	.07
HY5 Jake Peavy	.75	.23

2001 Royal Rookies Futures High Yield Autographs

	Nm-Mt	Ex-Mt
HY1 Chris Snelling	3.00	.90
HY2 Bret Prinz	2.00	.60
HY3 Orlando Woodards	2.00	.60
HY4 Nick Neugebauer	2.00	.60
HY5 Jake Peavy	5.00	1.50

2001 SP Top Prospects

The 2001 SP Top Prospects product went live in December, 2000. The set features 90 of the Minor Leagues most coveted prospects. Please

note that cards 88-90 are player/checklist cards. Each pack contained 5 cards and carried a suggested retail price of $2.99.

	Nm-Mt	Ex-Mt
COMPLETE SET (90)	20.00	6.00
1 Nathan Haynes	.40	.12
2 Francisco Rodriguez	.75	.23
3 Joe Torres	.40	.12
4 Mario Encarnacion	.40	.12
5 Justin Miller	.40	.12
6 Jason Hart	.40	.12
7 Miguel Olivo	.40	.12
8 Felipe Lopez	.40	.12
9 Vernon Wells	.75	.23
10 Cesar Izturis	.40	.12
11 Kenny Kelly	.40	.12
12 Josh Hamilton	.40	.12
13 Jesus Colome	.40	.12
14 Aubrey Huff	.75	.23
15 Toby Hall	.40	.12
16 Danys Baez	.40	.12
17 C.C. Sabathia	.75	.23
18 Ryan Anderson	.40	.12
19 Ryan Christianson	.40	.12
20 Richard Stahl	.40	.12
21 Matt Riley	.40	.12
22 Jayson Werth	.40	.12
23 Tripper Johnson	.40	.12
24 Jason Grabowski	.40	.12
25 Jason Romano	.40	.12
26 Carlos Pena	.40	.12
27 Rick Asadoorian	.40	.12
28 Steve Lomasney	.40	.12
29 Sun Woo Kim	.40	.12
30 Phillip Dumatrait	.40	.12
31 Chris George	.40	.12
32 Dee Brown	.40	.12
33 Jeff Austin	.75	.23
34 Ramon Santiago	.40	.12
35 Chris Wakeland	.40	.12
36 Brandon Inge	.40	.12
37 Michael Cuddyer	.40	.12
38 Michael Restovich	.40	.12
39 Ruben Salazar	.40	.12
40 Joe Crede	.40	.12
41 Aaron Rowand	.40	.12
42 Wily Mo Pena	.40	.12
43 Nick Johnson	.75	.23
44 Aaron McNeal	.40	.12
45 Wilfredo Rodriguez	.40	.12
46 Keith Ginter	.40	.12
47 Pat Manning	.40	.12
48 George Lombard	.40	.12
49 Marcus Giles	.75	.23
50 Nick Neugebauer	.40	.12
51 Ben Sheets	.75	.23
52 Ben Johnson	.40	.12
53 Chad Hutchinson	.40	.12
54 Luis Saturria	.40	.12
55 Corey Patterson	.75	.23
56 Hee Seop Choi	3.00	.90
57 Ben Christensen	.40	.12
58 John Patterson	.40	.12
59 Jack Cust	.40	.12
60 Hong-Chih Kuo	1.00	.30
61 Chin-Feng Chen	.75	.23
62 Justin Wayne	.75	.23
63 Brad Wilkerson	.40	.12
64 Kurt Ainsworth	.40	.12
65 Tony Torcato	.40	.12
66 Michael Byas	.40	.12
67 Julio Ramirez	.40	.12
68 Josh Beckett	.75	.23
69 Abraham Nunez	.40	.12
70 Adrian Gonzalez	.75	.23
71 Alex Escobar	.40	.12
72 Pat Strange	.40	.12
73 Brian Cole	.40	.12
74 Sean Burroughs	.75	.23
75 Wascar Serrano	.40	.12
76 Vince Faison	.40	.12
77 Dennis Tankersley	.75	.23
78 Brad Baisley	.40	.12
79 Jimmy Rollins	.75	.23
80 Eric Valent	.40	.12
81 J.J. Davis	.40	.12
82 Bobby Bradley	.40	.12
83 Adam Dunn	.75	.23
84 Drew Henson	1.50	.45
85 Jackson Melian	.75	.23
86 Choo Freeman	.40	.12
87 Jason Jennings	.40	.12
88 Corey Patterson CL	.75	.23
89 Josh Hamilton CL	.40	.12
90 Sean Burroughs CL	.75	.23

2001 SP Top Prospects Big Town Dreams

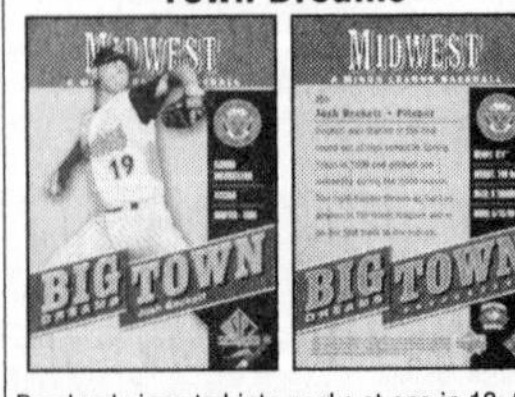

Randomly inserted into packs at one in 12, this 15-card insert features players that that have always dreamed of playing in the Major Leagues. Card backs carry a "BD" prefix.

	Nm-Mt	Ex-Mt
COMPLETE SET (15)	25.00	7.50
BD1 Vernon Wells	2.00	.60
BD2 Corey Patterson	2.00	.60
BD3 Michael Cuddyer	1.00	.30
BD4 Aaron McNeal	1.00	.30
BD5 Josh Beckett	2.00	.60
BD6 Drew Henson	2.50	.75
BD7 Sean Burroughs	2.00	.60
BD8 Alex Escobar	1.00	.30
BD9 C.C. Sabathia	2.00	.60
BD10 Josh Hamilton	1.00	.30
BD11 John Patterson	1.00	.30
BD12 Aaron Rowand	1.00	.30
BD13 Dee Brown	1.00	.30
BD14 Choo Freeman	1.00	.30
BD15 Nick Johnson	2.00	.60

2001 SP Top Prospects Chirography

Randomly inserted into packs at one in 11, this 26-card insert features authentic autographs from some of the Minor Leagues most prized prospects. Card backs carry the players initials as numbering. Please note that Jackson Melian packed out as an exchange card with a redemption deadline of 8/07/01.

	Nm-Mt	Ex-Mt
GOLD: RANDOM INSERTS IN PACKS .		
GOLD PRINT RUN 25 SERIAL #'d SETS		
GOLD NO PRICING DUE TO SCARCITY		
AE Alex Escobar	5.00	1.50
AG Adrian Gonzalez	8.00	2.40
AH Aubrey Huff	8.00	2.40
AM Aaron McNeal	5.00	1.50
BC Ben Christensen	5.00	1.50
BC Brian Cole	8.00	2.40
BI Brandon Inge	5.00	1.50
BS Ben Sheets	8.00	2.40
CC Chin-Feng Chen	60.00	18.00
CS C.C. Sabathia	8.00	2.40
CW Chris Wakeland	5.00	1.50
GR Keith Ginter	5.00	1.50
JB Josh Beckett	40.00	12.00
JH Josh Hamilton	5.00	1.50
JM Justin Miller	5.00	1.50
JT Joe Torres	5.00	1.50
KA Kurt Ainsworth	5.00	1.50
KK Kenny Kelly	5.00	1.50
MC Michael Cuddyer	5.00	1.50
MG Marcus Giles	15.00	4.50
PS Pat Strange	5.00	1.50
RS Ramon Santiago	5.00	1.50
TH Toby Hall	5.00	1.50
TJ Tripper Johnson	5.00	1.50
JCO Jesus Colome	5.00	1.50
JME Jackson Melian	8.00	2.40

2001 SP Top Prospects Destination the Show

Randomly inserted into packs at one in 18, this 12-card insert features players that look to make the Major League roster in the very near future. Card backs carry a "S" prefix.

	Nm-Mt	Ex-Mt
COMPLETE SET (12)	50.00	15.00
S1 Corey Patterson	3.00	.90
S2 Drew Henson	5.00	1.50
S3 Chin-Feng Chen	3.00	.90
S4 Josh Hamilton	2.00	.60
S5 Nick Johnson	3.00	.90
S6 Ben Sheets	3.00	.90
S7 Sean Burroughs	3.00	.90
S8 C.C. Sabathia	3.00	.90
S9 Ryan Anderson	2.00	.60
S10 Michael Cuddyer	2.00	.60
S11 Vernon Wells	3.00	.90
S12 Josh Beckett	3.00	.90

2001 SP Top Prospects Game Used Bat

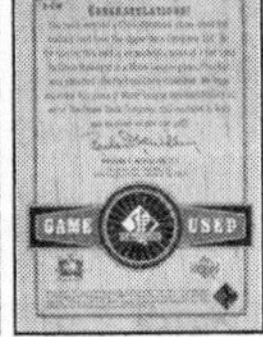

Randomly inserted into packs at one in 23, this 17-card insert features actual chips from game-used bats. Card backs carry a "B" prefix followed by the players initials.

	Nm-Mt	Ex-Mt
B-AES Alex Escobar	8.00	2.40
B-AH Aubrey Huff	10.00	3.00
B-BC Brian Cole	8.00	2.40
B-BI Brandon Inge	8.00	2.40
B-CW Chris Wakeland	8.00	2.40

B-JCR Joe Crede 8.00 2.40
B-JH Josh Hamilton 8.00 2.40
B-JJ J.J. Davis 8.00 2.40
B-JM Jackson Melian 10.00 3.00
B-JR Jason Romano 8.00 2.40
B-JW Jayson Werth 8.00 2.40
B-KG Ken Griffey Jr. 30.00 9.00
B-KK Kenny Kelly 8.00 2.40
B-MC Michael Cuddyer 8.00 2.40
B-MG Marcus Giles 10.00 3.00
B-MJ Michael Jordan 40.00 12.00
B-TH Toby Hall 8.00 2.40

2001 SP Top Prospects Great Futures

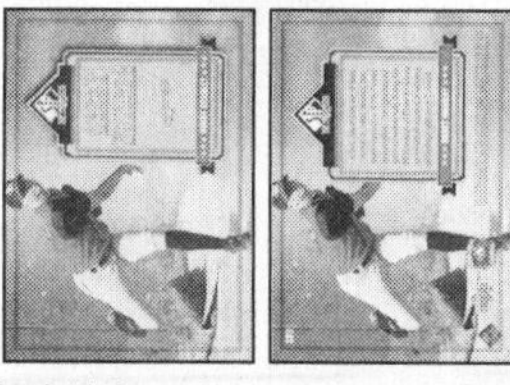

Randomly inserted into packs at one in 12, this 15-card insert features players that look forward to having a great future in the Major Leagues. Card backs carry a "GF" prefix.

Nm-Mt Ex-Mt
COMPLETE SET (15) 25.00 7.50
GF1 Josh Beckett 2.00 .60
GF2 Josh Hamilton 1.00 .30
GF3 Bobby Bradley 1.00 .30
GF4 Ben Sheets 2.00 .60
GF5 Nick Johnson 2.00 .60
GF6 Corey Patterson 2.00 .60
GF7 Sean Burroughs 2.00 .60
GF8 Alex Escobar 1.00 .30
GF9 Chin-Feng Chen 2.00 .60
GF10 Ryan Anderson 1.00 .30
GF11 Drew Henson 3.00 .90
GF12 Rick Asadoorian 1.00 .30
GF13 Aaron Rowand 1.00 .30
GF14 C.C. Sabathia 2.00 .60
GF15 John Patterson 1.00 .30

2001 Team Best

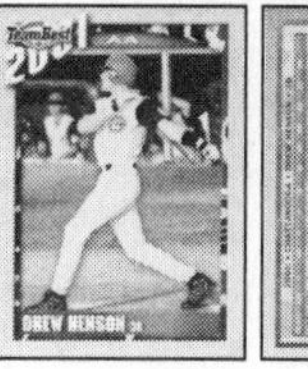

The 2001 Team Best product was released in early May, 2001 and features a 102-card base set which contains many top prospects and young stars. Please note that cards 13 and 14 of Joe Borchard were issued as exchange cards. Each pack contained five cards and carried a suggested retail price of $2.99.

Nm-Mt Ex-Mt
COMPLETE SET (102) 40.00 12.00
1 Brent Abernathy .50 .15
2 Kurt Ainsworth .50 .15
3 Israel Alcantara .50 .15
4 Marlon Anderson .50 .15
5 Ryan Anderson .50 .15
6 Robert Averette .50 .15
7 Brad Baisley .50 .15
8 Lorenzo Barcelo .50 .15
9 Josh Beckett 1.00 .30
10 Rob Bell .50 .15
11 Todd Betts .50 .15
12 Willie Bloomquist .75 .23
13 Joe Borchard Hogs EXCH 1.50 .45
14 Joe Borchard Barons EXCH 1.50 .45
15 Bobby Bradley .50 .15
16 Milton Bradley .75 .23
17 Ben Broussard .50 .15
18 Mark Buehrle .75 .23
19 Pat Burrell .75 .23
20 Sean Burroughs .75 .23
21 Mike Bynum .50 .15
22 Ramon Castro .50 .15
23 Chin-Feng Chen .75 .23
24 Hee Seop Choi 4.00 1.20
25 Ryan Christianson .50 .15
26 Brian Cole .50 .15
27 Jesus Colome .50 .15
28 Paxton Crawford .50 .15
29 Joe Crede .50 .15
30 Brad Cresse .50 .15
31 Michael Cuddyer .50 .15
32 Jack Cust .50 .15
33 Travis Dawkins .50 .15
34 Zach Day .75 .23
35 Tim Drew .50 .15
36 Adam Dunn .75 .23
37 Alex Escobar .50 .15
38 Casey Fossum .75 .23
39 Mike Frank .50 .15
40 Choo Freeman .50 .15
41 B.J. Garbe .50 .15
42 Jon Garland .50 .15
43 Marcus Giles .75 .23
44 Keith Ginter .50 .15
45 Elpidio Guzman .75 .23
46 Josh Hamilton .50 .15
47 Jason Hart .50 .15
48 Jeff Heaverlo .50 .15
49 Drew Henson 2.00 .60
50 J.R. House .50 .15
51 Aubrey Huff .75 .23
52 Brandon Inge .50 .15
53 Cesar Izturis .50 .15
54 Jason Jennings .50 .15
55 Kenny Kelly .50 .15
56 Sun Woo Kim .50 .15

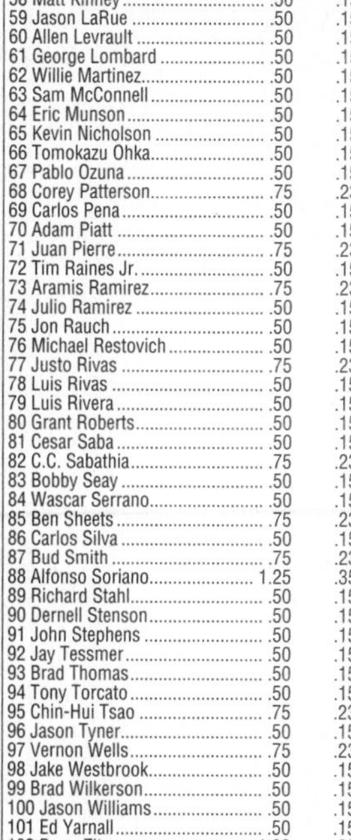

57 Mike Kinkade .50 .15
58 Matt Kinney .50 .15
59 Jason LaRue .50 .15
60 Allen Levrault .50 .15
61 George Lombard .50 .15
62 Willie Martinez .50 .15
63 Sam McConnell .50 .15
64 Eric Munson .50 .15
65 Kevin Nicholson .50 .15
66 Tomokazu Ohka .50 .15
67 Pablo Ozuna .50 .15
68 Corey Patterson .75 .23
69 Carlos Pena .50 .15
70 Adam Piatt .50 .15
71 Juan Pierre .75 .23
72 Tim Raines Jr. .50 .15
73 Aramis Ramirez .75 .23
74 Julio Ramirez .50 .15
75 Jon Rauch .50 .15
76 Michael Restovich .50 .15
77 Justo Rivas .75 .23
78 Luis Rivas .50 .15
79 Luis Rivera .50 .15
80 Grant Roberts .50 .15
81 Cesar Saba .50 .15
82 C.C. Sabathia .75 .23
83 Bobby Seay .50 .15
84 Wascar Serrano .50 .15
85 Ben Sheets .75 .23
86 Carlos Silva .50 .15
87 Bud Smith .75 .23
88 Alfonso Soriano 1.25 .35
89 Richard Stahl .50 .15
90 Dernell Stenson .50 .15
91 John Stephens .50 .15
92 Jay Tessmer .50 .15
93 Brad Thomas .50 .15
94 Tony Torcato .50 .15
95 Chin-Hui Tsao .75 .23
96 Jason Tyner .50 .15
97 Vernon Wells .75 .23
98 Jake Westbrook .50 .15
99 Brad Wilkerson .50 .15
100 Jason Williams .50 .15
101 Ed Yarnall .50 .15
102 Barry Zito 1.00 .30
NNO J.Borchard EXCH Card .50 .15

2001 Team Best Autographs

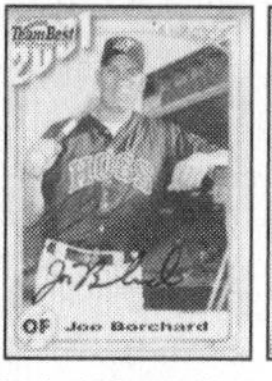

Randomly inserted into packs at one in eight, this 21-card insert set features authentic autographs of players like Joe Borchard, Josh Hamilton, and Barry Zito. Please note that the cards have been listed below in alphabetical order for convenience.

Nm-Mt Ex-Mt
1 Andrew Beinbrink 4.00 1.20
2 Joe Borchard Hogs 10.00 3.00
3 Joe Borchard Barons 10.00 3.00
4 Mike Bynum 4.00 1.20
5 Ryan Christianson 4.00 1.20
6 Adam Dunn 15.00 4.50
7 Casey Fossum 6.00 1.80
8 Josh Hamilton 4.00 1.20
9 J.R. House 4.00 1.20
10 Kenny Kelly 4.00 1.20
11 Matt Kinney 4.00 1.20
12 John Lackey 6.00 1.80
13 Kevin Nicholson 4.00 1.20
14 Tomo Ohka 10.00 3.00
15 Juan Pierre 6.00 1.80
16 Jon Rauch 4.00 1.20
17 Ben Sheets 6.00 1.80
18 Bud Smith 6.00 1.80
19 Richard Stahl 4.00 1.20
20 Barry Zito 15.00 4.50

2001 Team Best Babbitt's Bombers

Randomly inserted into packs at one in 48, this 11-card insert set features players that have a knack for hitting the longball.

Nm-Mt Ex-Mt
COMPLETE SET (11) 40.00 12.00
1 Sean Burroughs 5.00 1.50
2 Michael Cuddyer 4.00 1.20
3 Jack Cust 4.00 1.20
4 Choo Freeman 4.00 1.20
5 Marcus Giles 5.00 1.50
6 Keith Ginter 4.00 1.20
7 Jason Hart 4.00 1.20
8 Danny Peoples 4.00 1.20
9 Keith Reed 4.00 1.20
10 Vernon Wells 5.00 1.50
11 Brad Wilkerson 4.00 1.20

2001 Team Best Lumber

Randomly inserted into packs at one in 96, this 10-card insert features some of the purest hitters in the Minor Leagues.

Nm-Mt Ex-Mt
COMPLETE SET (10) 60.00 18.00
1 Russell Branyan 5.00 1.50

2 Morgan Burkhart 5.00 1.50
3 Pat Burrell 5.00 1.50
4 Sean Burroughs 5.00 1.50
5 Drew Henson 10.00 3.00
Sean Burroughs
6 Josh Hamilton 5.00 1.50
7 Nick Johnson 5.00 1.50
8 George Lombard 5.00 1.50
9 Carlos Pena 5.00 1.50
10 Dernell Stenson 5.00 1.50

2001 Upper Deck Minors Centennial

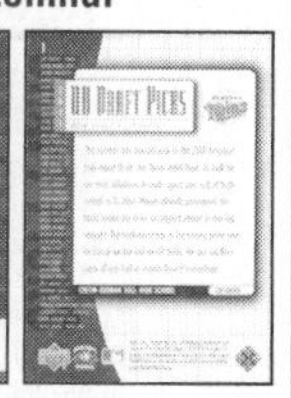

This product was released in mid-December 2001, and featured a 100-card base set consisting of top Minor League talents. Each pack contained 5-cards, and carried a suggested retail price of $2.99.

Nm-Mt Ex-Mt
COMPLETE SET (100) 20.00 6.00
1 Joe Mauer 4.00 1.20
2 Jake Gautreau .25 .07
3 Mike Jones .40 .12
4 Bobby Crosby 1.50 .45
5 Chris Smith .25 .07
6 John VanBenschoten .75 .23
7 Colt Griffin .60 .18
8 Chris Burke .40 .12
9 Kenny Baugh .25 .07
10 Casey Kotchman 2.00 .60
11 Joe Torres .25 .07
12 Alfredo Amezaga .40 .12
13 Chris Bootcheck .40 .12
14 Jason Hart .25 .07
15 Ryan Ludwick .25 .07
16 Mario Ramos .40 .12
17 Tyrell Godwin .25 .07
18 Orlando Hudson .40 .12
19 Josh Hamilton .25 .07
20 Toe Nash .25 .07
21 Carl Crawford .25 .07
22 Roger Maris 1.50 .45
23 J.D. Martin .25 .07
24 Alex Herrera .25 .07
25 Rafael Soriano .60 .18
26 Antonio Perez .25 .07
27 Jamal Strong .25 .07
28 Eddie Murray .60 .18
29 Keith Reed .25 .07
30 John Stephens .25 .07
31 Hank Blalock 2.00 .60
32 Wade Boggs .40 .12
33 Freddy Sanchez .25 .07
34 Seung Song .50 .15
35 George Brett 1.50 .45
36 Corey Thurman .25 .07
37 Omar Infante .50 .15
38 Matt Wheatland .25 .07
39 Justin Morneau 1.50 .45
40 Michael Restovich .25 .07
41 Joe Borchard .75 .23
42 Corwin Malone .25 .07
43 Jon Rauch .25 .07
44 Joe DiMaggio 2.00 .60
45 Deivi Mendez .25 .07
46 Drew Henson .60 .18
47 Jason Lane .40 .12
48 Mike Nannini .25 .07
49 Garett Gentry .25 .07
50 Trey Hodges .25 .07
51 Kelly Johnson .25 .07
52 Dave Krynzel .25 .07
53 Bill Hall .25 .07
54 Blake Williams .25 .07
55 John Gall .25 .07
56 Joe Carter .25 .07
57 Ryne Sandberg 1.50 .45
58 Hee Seop Choi 1.50 .45
59 Nic Jackson .25 .07
60 Bobby Hill .50 .15
61 Brad Cresse .25 .07
62 Corey Myers .25 .07
63 Steve Garvey .25 .07
64 Chin-Feng Chen .25 .07
65 Ben Diggins .25 .07
66 Willy Aybar .75 .23
67 Andre Dawson .25 .07
68 Brandon Phillips .25 .07
69 Justin Wayne .40 .12
70 Brandon Watson .25 .07
71 Willie McCovey .25 .07
72 Jerome Williams 1.25 .35
73 Boof Bonser .40 .12
74 Lance Niekro .25 .07
75 Adrian Gonzalez .25 .07
76 Will Smith .25 .07
77 Miguel Cabrera 2.50 .75
78 Nolan Ryan 2.00 .60
79 Pat Strange .25 .07
80 Jae Seo .25 .07
81 Ozzie Smith 1.00 .30
82 Sean Burroughs .25 .07
83 Dennis Tankersley .25 .07
84 Jake Peavy .75 .23
85 Gary Burnham .25 .07
86 Marlon Byrd 1.00 .30
87 Brett Myers .25 .07
88 Adam Walker .25 .07
89 Dave Parker .25 .07
90 J.R. House .25 .07
91 Bobby Bradley .25 .07
92 Sean Burnett .25 .07
93 Austin Kearns .25 .07
94 Ty Howington .25 .07
95 Chin-Hui Tsao .25 .07
96 Joe DiMaggio .50 .15
Josh Hamilton
97 Ozzie Smith .50 .15
Bobby Hill
98 George Brett .50 .15
Sean Burroughs
99 Willie McCovey .25 .07
Adrian Gonzalez
100 Nolan Ryan 1.00 .30
Dennis Tankersley UER
Josh Beckett is pictured on the card

2001 Upper Deck Minors Centennial Combo Game Bat/Jersey

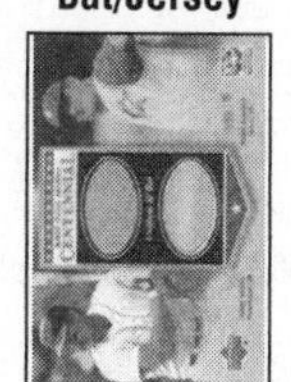

Randomly inserted into packs, this 4-card insert features swatches of both game-jerseys and game-bats. Card backs carry a "C" prefix.

Nm-Mt Ex-Mt
GOLD RANDOM INSERTS IN PACKS
GOLD PRINT RUN 25 SERIAL #'d SETS
NO GOLD PRICING DUE TO SCARCITY
C-BB George Brett 80.00 24.00
Sean Burroughs
C-BBL Wade Boggs 80.00 24.00
Hank Blalock
C-DH Joe DiMaggio
Josh Hamilton
C-MG Willie McCovey
Adrian Gonzalez

2001 Upper Deck Minors Centennial Combo Signatures

Randomly inserted into packs, this 5-card insert features dual-signatures from greats like McCovey/Gonzalez. Card backs carry a "CS" prefix.

Nm-Mt Ex-Mt
GOLD RANDOM INSERTS IN PACKS
GOLD PRINT RUN 25 SERIAL #'d SETS
NO PRICING DUE TO SCARCITY
CS-BBL Wade Boggs
Hank Blalock
CS-CL Joe Carter
Jason Lane
CS-MG Willie McCovey
Adrian Gonzalez
CS-PN Dave Parker
Toe Nash
CS-SH Ryne Sandberg
Bobby Hill

2001 Upper Deck Minors Centennial Game Bat

Randomly inserted into packs, this 9-card insert features chips from authentic game-used bats. Card backs carry a "B" prefix. Please note that either one bat or jersey card was issued per box.

Nm-Mt Ex-Mt
GOLD RANDOM INSERTS IN PACKS
GOLD PRINT RUN 25 SERIAL #'d SETS
GOLD NO PRICING DUE TO SCARCITY
B-AG Adrian Gonzalez 8.00 2.40
B-BC Brad Cresse 8.00 2.40
B-BP Brandon Phillips 8.00 2.40
B-HB Hank Blalock 15.00 4.50
B-JB Joe Borchard 10.00 3.00
B-JH Josh Hamilton 8.00 2.40
B-JL Jason Lane 8.00 2.40
B-JR J.R. House 8.00 2.40
B-SB Sean Burroughs 8.00 2.40

2001 Upper Deck Minors Centennial Game Jersey

Randomly inserted into packs, this 14-card insert features swatches from authentic game-used jerseys. Card backs carry a "J" prefix. Please note that either one bat or jersey card was issued per box.

Nm-Mt Ex-Mt
GOLD RANDOM INSERTS IN PACKS
GOLD PRINT RUN 25 SERIAL #'d SETS
GOLD NO PRICING DUE TO SCARCITY
J-AD Andre Dawson 15.00 4.50
J-DP Dave Parker 15.00 4.50
J-EM Eddie Murray 20.00 6.00
J-GB George Brett 40.00 12.00
J-JC Joe Carter 15.00 4.50
J-JD Joe DiMaggio SP
J-NR Nolan Ryan 50.00 15.00
J-OS Ozzie Smith 25.00 7.50
J-RM Roger Maris SP
J-RS Ryne Sandberg 40.00 12.00
J-SG Steve Garvey 15.00 4.50
J-TL Tommy Lasorda 15.00 4.50
J-WB Wade Boggs 15.00 4.50
J-WM Willie McCovey 15.00 4.50

2001 Upper Deck Minors Centennial Legendary Signatures

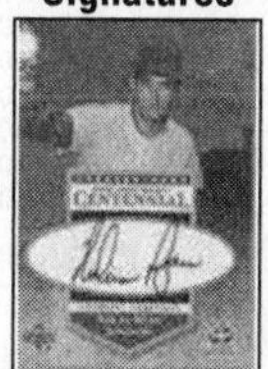

Randomly inserted into packs, this nine-card insert features authentic signatures from legendary players like Nolan Ryan and Ryne Sandberg. Card backs carry a "L" prefix.

Nm-Mt Ex-Mt
GOLD RANDOM INSERTS IN PACKS
GOLD PRINT RUN 25 SERIAL #'d SETS
GOLD NO PRICING DUE TO SCARCITY
L-DP Dave Parker 40.00 12.00
L-JC Joe Carter 40.00 12.00
L-NR Nolan Ryan 150.00 45.00
L-OS Ozzie Smith 80.00 24.00
L-RS Ryne Sandberg 120.00 36.00
L-SG Steve Garvey 40.00 12.00
L-TL Tommy Lasorda/50 EXCH. 40.00 12.00
L-WB Wade Boggs 50.00 15.00
L-WM Willie McCovey 50.00 15.00

2001 Upper Deck Minors Centennial MJ Game Bat

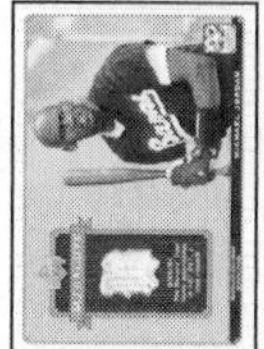

Randomly inserted into packs a 1:24, this 12-card insert features game-used bat chips from Michael Jordan. Card backs carry a "MJ" prefix.

Nm-Mt Ex-Mt
COMMON CARD 15.00 4.50
GOLD RANDOM INSERTS IN PACKS
GOLD PRINT RUN 25 SERIAL #'d SETS
NO GOLD PRICING DUE TO SCARCITY

2001 Upper Deck Minors Centennial MJ Memorabilia

Randomly inserted into packs, this 7-card insert features swatches of game-used memorabilia from the legendary Michael Jordan. Card backs carry a "MJ" prefix.

Nm-Mt Ex-Mt
GOLD RANDOM INSERTS IN PACKS
GOLD PRINT RUN 25 SERIAL #'d SETS
NO GOLD PRICING DUE TO SCARCITY
MJC Michael Jordan Cleats/100 100.00 30.00
MJJ1 Michael Jordan Jsy 40.00 12.00
MJJ2 Michael Jordan Jsy 40.00 12.00
MJJ3 Michael Jordan Jsy 40.00 12.00
MJBG Michael Jordan Btg Glv/100 100.00 30.00
MJBJ M.Jordan Bat-Jsy 80.00 24.00
MJGJ Michael Jordan Btg Glv-Jsy/25

2001 Upper Deck Minors Centennial Signatures

Randomly inserted into packs, this 22-card insert features authentic signatures from future stars like Josh Hamilton and Hank Blalock. Card backs carry a "S" prefix.

	Nm-Mt	Ex-Mt
GOLD RANDOM INSERTS IN PACKS..		
GOLD PRINT RUN 25 SERIAL #'d SETS		
GOLD NO PRICING DUE TO SCARCITY		
S-AG Adrian Gonzalez	15.00	4.50
S-BBO Boof Bonser	15.00	4.50
S-BBR Bobby Bradley	15.00	4.50
S-BC Brad Cresse	15.00	4.50
S-BH Bobby Hill	25.00	7.50
S-BP Brandon Phillips	15.00	4.50
S-DT Dennis Tankersley	10.00	3.00
S-HB Hank Blalock	60.00	18.00
S-JBO Joe Borchard	25.00	7.50
S-JHA Josh Hamilton	15.00	4.50
S-JHO J.R. House	15.00	4.50
S-JL Jason Lane	15.00	4.50
S-JM J.D. Martin	10.00	3.00
S-JR Jon Rauch	15.00	4.50
S-JT Joe Torres	15.00	4.50
S-JWA Justin Wayne	15.00	4.50
S-JWI Jerome Williams	30.00	9.00
S-KJ Kelly Johnson	10.00	3.00
S-RS Rafael Soriano	25.00	7.50
S-SB Sean Burroughs	15.00	4.50
S-TN Toe Nash	10.00	3.00
S-WA Willy Aybar	20.00	6.00

2002 Just Prospects

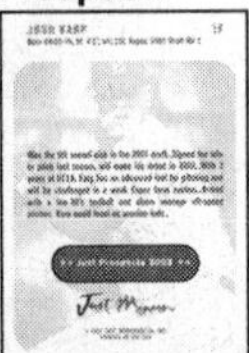

Issued in factory set form, this is a 50 card set. Each factory set contained 40 basic cards along with a selected autographed card numbered from 41-50. In addition, about half of the factory sets had one autograph card parallel of cards numbered 1 through 40.

	Nm-Mt	Ex-Mt
COMP.FACT.SET (41)	20.00	6.00
COMP.SET w/o SP'S (40)	8.00	2.40
COMMON CARD (1-40)	.25	.07
COMMON AUTO (41-50)	5.00	1.50
1 Willy Aybar	.25	.07
2 Angel Berroa	.25	.07
3 Wilson Betemit	.25	.07
4 Hank Blalock	.40	.12
5 Tony Blanco	.25	.07
6 Boof Bonser	.25	.07
7 Joe Borchard	.25	.07
8 Carl Crawford	.25	.07
9 Juan Cruz	.25	.07
10 Nelson Cruz UER	.25	.07
Birthdate should be July 1st, 1981		
11 Domingo Cuello	.25	.07
12 Gavin Floyd	.75	.23
13 Franklyn German	.25	.07
14 Adrian Gonzalez	.25	.07
15 Danny Gonzalez	.25	.07
16 Gabe Gross	.25	.07
17 Angel Guzman	1.50	.45
18 Joel Guzman	.25	.07
19 Josh Karp	.25	.07
20 Austin Kearns	.25	.07
21 Joe Mauer	1.50	.45
22 Yadier Molina	.25	.07
23 Justin Morneau	.25	.07
24 Xavier Nady	.25	.07
25 Chris Narveson	.25	.07
26 Miguel Negron	.25	.07
27 Bubba Nelson	.40	.12
28 Nick Neugebauer	.25	.07
29 Jake Peavy	.25	.07
30 Carlos Pena	.25	.07
31 Antonio Perez	.25	.07
32 Jon Rauch	.25	.07
33 Jose Rojas	.40	.12
34 Felix Sanchez	.25	.07
35 Chris Snelling	.50	.15
36 Rafael Soriano	.25	.07
37 Dennis Tankersley	.25	.07
38 Mark Teixeira	.40	.12
39 Josh Thigpen	.25	.07
40 Billy Traber	.50	.15
41 Taggert Bozied AU	8.00	2.40
42 Aaron Cook AU	5.00	1.50
43 Carlos Duran AU	5.00	1.50
44 Mike Fontenot AU	5.00	1.50
45 Jimmy Gobble AU	8.00	2.40
46 Jonny Gomes AU	5.00	1.50
47 Matt Harrington AU	5.00	1.50
48 Bobby Jenks AU	8.00	2.40
49 Todd Linden AU	8.00	2.40
50 Clint Nageotte AU	6.00	1.80

2002 Just Prospects Black

Inserted in factory sets at a stated rate of one per 10 sets this is a parallel to the Just Prospects set. These cards were issued to a stated print run of 50 serial numbered sets. The cards numbered from 41 through 50 were not signed by the players.

	Nm-Mt	Ex-Mt
*BLACK 1-40: 5X TO 12X BASIC		
*BLACK 41-50: .4X TO 1X BASIC		

2002 Just Prospects Gold

This is a parallel to the Just Prospect set. These cards were issued in Just Prospect Gold factory sets. Cards numbered 41 through 50 were issued one per gold factory set.

	Nm-Mt	Ex-Mt
*GOLD 1-40: .4X TO 1X BASIC 02 JUST		
41 Taggert Bozied SP	2.50	.75
42 Aaron Cook SP	1.50	.45
43 Carlos Duran SP	1.00	.30
44 Mike Fontenot SP	1.50	.45
45 Jimmy Gobble SP	1.50	.45
46 Jonny Gomes SP	3.00	.90
47 Matt Harrington SP	1.00	.30
48 Bobby Jenks SP	1.50	.45
49 Todd Linden SP	3.00	.90
50 Clint Nageotte SP	1.50	.45

2002 Just Prospects Autographs

Issued at a stated rate of one in two factory sets, this is a parallel to the Just Prospect set. These cards were issued to differing print runs and we have noted that information next to the player's name in our checklist. Card number 34 does not exist. Cards 28 and 30 were distributed only in late factory sets due to both athletes returning their cards late.

	Nm-Mt	Ex-Mt
BLACK RANDOM INSERTS IN SETS ...		
BLACK PRINT RUN 25 SERIAL #'d SETS		
NO BLACK PRICING DUE TO SCARCITY		
1 Willy Aybar/200	8.00	2.40
2 Angel Berroa/50	15.00	4.50
3 Wilson Betemit/50	15.00	4.50
4 Hank Blalock/50	25.00	7.50
5 Tony Blanco/50	15.00	4.50
6 Boof Bonser/200	8.00	2.40
7 Joe Borchard/50	15.00	4.50
8 Carl Crawford/50	15.00	4.50
9 Juan Cruz/200	8.00	2.40
10 Nelson Cruz/200	10.00	3.00
11 Domingo Cuello/200	8.00	2.40
12 Gavin Floyd/50	30.00	9.00
13 Franklyn German/200	8.00	2.40
14 Adrian Gonzalez/75	15.00	4.50
15 Danny Gonzalez/200	8.00	2.40
16 Gabe Gross/200	8.00	2.40
17 Angel Guzman/200	20.00	6.00
18 Joel Guzman/200	8.00	2.40
19 Josh Karp/200	8.00	2.40
20 Austin Kearns/50	15.00	4.50
21 Joe Mauer/50	50.00	15.00
22 Yadier Molina/200	10.00	3.00
23 Justin Morneau/50	25.00	7.50
24 Xavier Nady/50	15.00	4.50
25 Chris Narveson/200	10.00	3.00
26 Miguel Negron/200	8.00	2.40
27 Bubba Nelson/200	10.00	3.00
28 Nick Neugebauer/50	15.00	4.50
29 Jake Peavy/200	8.00	2.40
30 Carlos Pena/50	15.00	4.50
31 Antonio Perez/200	8.00	2.40
32 Jon Rauch/200	8.00	2.40
33 Jose Rojas/200	10.00	3.00
35 Chris Snelling/200	10.00	3.00
36 Rafael Soriano/50	25.00	7.50
37 Dennis Tankersley/50	15.00	4.50
38 Mark Teixeira/50	25.00	7.50
39 Josh Thigpen/200	8.00	2.40
40 Billy Traber/200	10.00	3.00

2002 Just Prospects Gold Autographs

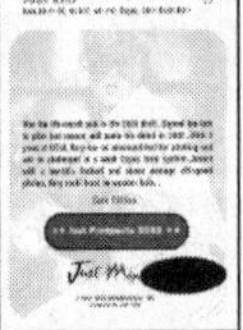

These 36 cards were inserted two per Gold Factory set. These cards were basically issued to a print run of 300 cards except for a few which were only issued to 50. Cards numbered 30 and 34 did not make it back in time for packing into these sets.

	Nm-Mt	Ex-Mt
1 Willy Aybar/300	5.00	1.50
2 Angel Berroa/300	5.00	1.50
3 Wilson Betemit/50	15.00	4.50
4 Hank Blalock/300	8.00	2.40
5 Tony Blanco/300	5.00	1.50
7 Joe Borchard/300	5.00	1.50
9 Juan Cruz/300	5.00	1.50
10 Nelson Cruz/300	5.00	1.50
11 Domingo Cuello/300	5.00	1.50
12 Gavin Floyd/300	15.00	4.50
13 Franklyn German/300	5.00	1.50
14 Adrian Gonzalez/300	5.00	1.50
15 Danny Gonzalez/300	5.00	1.50
16 Gabe Gross/300	5.00	1.50
17 Angel Guzman/300	20.00	6.00
18 Joel Guzman/300	5.00	1.50
19 Josh Karp/300	5.00	1.50
20 Austin Kearns/300	5.00	1.50
21 Joe Mauer/50	60.00	18.00
22 Yadier Molina/300	5.00	1.50
23 Justin Morneau/300	8.00	2.40
24 Xavier Nady/300	5.00	1.50
25 Chris Narveson/300	5.00	1.50
26 Miguel Negron/300	5.00	1.50
27 Bubba Nelson/300	8.00	2.40
28 Nick Neugebauer/300	5.00	1.50
29 Jake Peavy/275	5.00	1.50
31 Antonio Perez/300	5.00	1.50
32 Jon Rauch/300	5.00	1.50
33 Jose Rojas/300	8.00	2.40
35 Chris Snelling/300	10.00	3.00
36 Rafael Soriano/300	8.00	2.40
37 Dennis Tankersley/50	15.00	4.50
38 Mark Teixeira/50	20.00	6.00
39 Josh Thigpen/300	5.00	1.50
40 Billy Traber/300	10.00	3.00

2002 UD Minor League

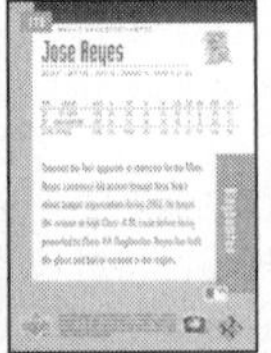

This 400 card set was released in November, 2002. It was issued in six card packs which came 18 packs to a box and had an SRP of $2.99 per pack. Cards numbered 201 through 230 belong to the On the Fast Track subset while cards numbered 231 through 240 are Draft Day Gem subset cards. Cards numbered 241 through 400 feature Minor League team logos along with a profile of the team.

	Nm-Mt	Ex-Mt
COMPLETE SET (400)	150.00	45.00
1 Bobby Jenks	2.00	.60
2 Chris Bootcheck	.75	.23
3 Francisco Rodriguez	.50	.15
4 Ervin-Johan Santana	3.00	.90
5 Casey Kotchman	4.00	1.20
6 Jeff Mathis	.50	.15
7 Joe Torres	.50	.15
8 Anthony Pluta	.50	.15
9 John Buck	.50	.15
10 Chris Burke	1.00	.30
11 Rodrigo Rosario	.75	.23
12 Chad Qualls	.75	.23
13 Tommy Whiteman	1.50	.45
14 Bobby Crosby	1.00	.30
15 Chris Tritle	.75	.23
16 Mike Wood	.75	.23
17 Freddie Bynum	.50	.15
18 John-Ford Griffin	.50	.15
19 Nick Swisher	2.50	.75
20 Gabe Gross	.50	.15
21 Tracy Thorpe	1.00	.30
22 Alexis Rios	15.00	4.50
23 Ramon Castro	.50	.15
24 Richard Lewis	.50	.15
25 Bryan Digby	.50	.15
26 Brett Evert	.50	.15
27 Matt Belisle	.50	.15
28 Carlos Duran	.75	.23
29 Zach Miner	1.00	.30
30 Gonzalo Lopez	.75	.23
31 Adam Wainwright	.50	.15
32 Kelly Johnson	.50	.15
33 Bubba Nelson	1.50	.45
34 Wilson Betemit	.50	.15
35 Mike Jones	.50	.15
36 Ben Hendrickson	.50	.15
37 Corey Hart	2.50	.75
38 David Krynzel	.50	.15
39 Cristian Guerrero	.50	.15
40 Matt Yeatman	.75	.23
41 Prince Fielder	8.00	2.40
42 Cristobal Correa	.75	.23
43 Jimmy Journell	.50	.15
44 Scotty Layfield	.75	.23
45 Justin Pope	.50	.15
46 B.R. Cook	.50	.15
47 Yadier Molina	1.00	.30
48 Dan Haren	1.50	.45
49 Chris Duncan	.75	.23
50 Luis Montanez	.50	.15
51 Angel Guzman	8.00	2.40
52 J.J. Johnson	.50	.15
53 Nic Jackson	.75	.23
54 David Kelton	.50	.15
55 Ben Christensen	.50	.15
56 Felix Sanchez	.75	.23
57 Rocco Baldelli	2.00	.60
58 Josh Hamilton	.50	.15
59 Jon Switzer	.75	.23
60 Jace Brewer	.50	.15
61 Jorge Cantu	.50	.15
62 Chad Tracy	2.50	.75
63 Luis Terrero	.50	.15
64 Mike Gosling	.75	.23
65 Brad Cresse	.50	.15
66 Jesus Cota	.75	.23
67 Scott Hairston	2.50	.75
68 Lino Garcia	.75	.23
69 Jason Bulger	.75	.23
70 Oscar Villarreal	.75	.23
71 Beltran Perez	.75	.23
72 Jose Rojas	.75	.23
73 Brennan King	.75	.23
74 Koyie Hill	.50	.15
75 Hong-Chih Kuo	1.50	.45
76 Willy Aybar	.50	.15
77 Joel Guzman	.50	.15
78 Josh Karp	.75	.23
79 Rich Rundles	.50	.15
80 Luke Lockwood	.50	.15
81 Donnie Bridges	.50	.15
82 Eric Good	.50	.15
83 Claudio Vargas	.50	.15
84 Seung Song	.50	.15
85 Jerome Williams	1.00	.30
86 Boof Bonser	.50	.15
87 Erick Threets	1.00	.30
88 Jesse Foppert	2.50	.75
89 Lance Niekro	.50	.15
90 Julian Benavidez	.75	.23
91 Francisco Liriano	1.00	.30
92 Grady Sizemore	.75	.23
93 Ryan Church	1.00	.30
94 Travis Foley	.75	.23
95 Brian Tallet	1.00	.30
96 Billy Traber	1.50	.45
97 Dan Denham	.50	.15
98 J.D. Martin	.50	.15
99 Corey Smith	.50	.15
100 Derek Thompson	.50	.15
101 Michael Garciaparra	1.50	.45
102 Ryan Christianson	.50	.15
103 Jamal Strong	.50	.15
104 Matt Thornton	.75	.23
105 Rett Johnson	1.00	.30
106 Clint Nageotte	1.50	.45
107 Shin-Soo Choo	2.50	.75
108 Allen Baxter	.75	.23
109 Adrian Gonzalez	.50	.15
110 Denny Bautista	.50	.15
111 Miguel Cabrera	2.00	.60
112 Josh Wilson	.75	.23
113 Rob Henkel	.75	.23
114 Craig Brazell	1.00	.30
115 Enrique Cruz	.50	.15
116 Aaron Heilman	.50	.15
117 David Wright	3.00	.90
118 Justin Huber	1.50	.45
119 Jose Reyes	1.00	.30
120 Neal Musser	.75	.23
121 Keith Reed	.50	.15
122 Richard Stahl	.50	.15
123 Matt Riley	.50	.15
124 Mike Fontenot	.75	.23
125 Tim Raines Jr.	.50	.15
126 Beau Hale	.50	.15
127 Josh Barfield	4.00	1.20
128 Tagg Bozied	2.50	.75
129 Mark Phillips	1.50	.45
130 Jake Gautreau	.50	.15
131 Ben Johnson	.50	.15
132 Xavier Nady	.50	.15
133 Taylor Buchholz	1.00	.30
134 Gavin Floyd	3.00	.90
135 Anderson Machado	.75	.23
136 Jorge Padilla	.75	.23
137 Yoel Hernandez	1.00	.30
138 Chase Utley	.50	.15
139 J.R. House	.50	.15
140 Justin Reid	.75	.23
141 Jon VanBenschoten	.75	.23
142 Chris Young	.75	.23
143 Sean Burnett	.50	.15
144 Jose Castillo	2.50	.75
145 Mario Ramos	.75	.23
146 Patrick Boyd	.75	.23
147 Jason Bourgeois	.50	.15
148 Mark Teixeira	1.00	.30
149 Mauricio Lara	.75	.23
150 Manny Delcarmen	.75	.23
151 Phil Dumatrait	.50	.15
152 Josh Thigpen	.75	.23
153 Tony Blanco	.50	.15
154 Rene Miniel	1.50	.45
155 Kevin Huang	1.50	.45
156 Anastacio Martinez	.75	.23
157 Ty Howington	.50	.15
158 Dane Sardinha	.50	.15
159 Ranier Olmedo	.50	.15
160 Dustin Moseley	1.00	.30
161 Ryan Snare	.75	.23
162 Justin Gillman	.75	.23
163 Choo Freeman	.50	.15
164 Jayson Nix	.50	.15
165 Garrett Atkins	1.50	.45
166 Javier Colina	.50	.15
167 Rene Reyes	.75	.23
168 Ching-Lung Lo	1.50	.45
169 Chin-Hui Tsao	.50	.15
170 Brad Hawpe	.50	.15
171 Jason Young	.75	.23
172 Cory Vance	.50	.15
173 Matt Holliday	.50	.15
174 Mike Stodolka	.50	.15
175 Colt Griffin	1.50	.45
176 Alejandro Machado	.75	.23
177 Kenny Baugh	.50	.15
178 Charley Carter	.75	.23
179 Preston Larrison	1.00	.30
180 Cody Ross	.50	.15
181 Nook Logan	.75	.23
182 Jeremy Bonderman	1.50	.45
183 David Espinosa	.50	.15
184 Michael Restovich	.50	.15
185 Rob Bowen	.75	.23
186 B.J. Garbe	.75	.23
187 Justin Morneau	.75	.23
188 Joe Mauer	8.00	2.40
189 Jon McDonald	.75	.23
190 Franklin Francisco	.75	.23
191 Corwin Malone	.75	.23
192 Felix Diaz	.50	.15
193 Tim Hummel	.75	.23
194 Kris Honel	.50	.15
195 Matt Smith	.75	.23
196 Alex Graman	.50	.15
197 Brandon Claussen	1.00	.30
198 Erick Almonte	.50	.15
199 Bronson Sardinha	.50	.15
200 Danny Borrell	.50	.15
201 Casey Kotchman OFT	2.00	.60
202 John Buck OFT	.50	.15
203 Bobby Crosby OFT	1.00	.30
204 Gabe Gross OFT	.50	.15
205 Wilson Betemit OFT	.50	.15
206 David Krynzel OFT	.50	.15
207 Jimmy Journell OFT	.50	.15
208 David Kelton OFT	.50	.15
209 Josh Hamilton OFT	.50	.15
210 Luis Terrero OFT	.50	.15
211 Joel Guzman OFT	.50	.15
212 Seung Song OFT	.50	.15
213 Jerome Williams OFT	.75	.23
214 J.D. Martin OFT	.50	.15
215 Clint Nageotte OFT	1.00	.30
216 Miguel Cabrera OFT	1.00	.30
217 Aaron Heilman OFT	.50	.15
218 Richard Stahl OFT	.50	.15
219 Jake Gautreau OFT	.50	.15
220 Taylor Buchholz OFT	.75	.23
221 J.R. House OFT	.50	.15
222 Mark Teixeira OFT	1.00	.30
223 Tony Blanco OFT	.50	.15
224 Ty Howington OFT	.50	.15
225 Chin-Hui Tsao OFT	.50	.15
226 Colt Griffin OFT	1.00	.30
227 Kenny Baugh OFT	.50	.15
228 Joe Mauer OFT	4.00	1.20
229 Corwin Malone OFT	.50	.15
230 Brandon Claussen OFT	.50	.15
231 Scott Kazmir DG	8.00	2.40
232 Zach Greinke DG	8.00	2.40
233 Scott Moore DG	1.50	.45
234 Drew Meyer DG	.75	.23
235 Khalil Greene DG	5.00	1.50
236 Chris Gruler DG	1.00	.30
237 Prince Fielder DG	8.00	2.40
238 Jeff Francis DG	.75	.23
239 Jeremy Hermida DG	4.00	1.20
240 Nick Swisher DG	2.50	.75
241 Salt Lake Stingers TM	.50	.15
242 Arkansas Travelers TM	.50	.15
243 Rancho Cucamonga Quakes TM	.50	.15
244 Cedar Rapids Kernels TM	.50	.15
245 Provo Angels TM	.50	.15
246 New Orleans Zephyrs TM	.50	.15
247 Round Rock Express TM	.50	.15
248 Lexington Legends TM	.50	.15
249 Michigan Battle Cats TM	.50	.15
250 Tri-City ValleyCats TM	.50	.15
251 Sacramento River Cats TM	.50	.15
252 Midland Rockhounds TM	.50	.15
253 Modesto A's TM	.50	.15
254 Visalia Oaks TM	.50	.15
255 Vancouver Canadians TM	.50	.15
256 Syracuse Skychiefs TM	.50	.15
257 Tennessee Smokies TM	.50	.15
258 Dunedin Blue Jays TM	.50	.15
259 Charleston WV Alleycats TM	.50	.15
260 Auburn Doubledays TM	.50	.15
261 Richmond Braves TM	.50	.15
262 Greenville Braves TM	.50	.15
263 Macon Braves TM	.50	.15
264 Myrtle Beach Pelicans TM	.50	.15
265 Danville Braves TM	.50	.15
266 Gulf Coast Braves TM	.50	.15
267 Indianapolis Indians TM	.50	.15
268 Huntsville Stars TM	.50	.15
269 High Desert Mavericks TM	.50	.15
270 Beloit Snappers TM	.50	.15
271 Ogden RaptorsTM	.50	.15
272 Memphis Redbirds TM	.50	.15
273 New Haven Ravens TM	.50	.15
274 Potomac Cannons TM	.50	.15
275 Peoria Chiefs TM	.50	.15
276 New Jersey Cardinals TM	.50	.15
277 Johnson City CardinalsTM	.50	.15
278 Iowa Cubs TM	.50	.15
279 West Tenn Diamond Jaxx TM	.50	.15
280 Daytona Cubs TM	.50	.15
281 Lansing Lugnuts TM	.50	.15
282 Boise Hawks TM	.50	.15
283 Mesa Cubs TM	.50	.15
284 Durham Bulls TM	.50	.15
285 Orlando Rays TM	.50	.15
286 Bakersfield Blaze TM	.50	.15
287 Charleston SC River Dogs TM	.50	.15
288 Hudson Valley Renegades TM	.50	.15
289 Tucson Sidewinders TM	.50	.15
290 El Paso Diablos TM	.50	.15
291 Lancaster JetHawks TM	.50	.15
292 South Bend Silver Hawks TM	.50	.15
293 Yakima Bears TM	.50	.15
294 Missoula Osprey TM	.50	.15
295 Las Vegas 51s TM	.50	.15
296 Jacksonville Suns TM	.50	.15
297 Vero Beach Dodgers TM	.50	.15
298 South Georgia Waves TM	.50	.15
299 Great Falls Dodgers TM	.50	.15
300 Gulf Coast DodgersTM	.50	.15
301 Ottawa Lynx TM	.50	.15
302 Harrisburg Senators TM	.50	.15
303 Brevard County Manatees TM	.50	.15
304 Clinton Lumberkings TM	.50	.15
305 Vermont Expos TM	.50	.15
306 Fresno Grizzlies TM	.50	.15
307 Shreveport Sw.Dragons TM	.50	.15
308 San Jose Giants TM	.50	.15
309 Hagerstown Suns TM	.50	.15
310 Salem-Keizer Volcanoes TM	.50	.15
311 Arizona GiantsTM	.50	.15
312 Buffalo Bisons TM	.50	.15
313 Akron Aeros TM	.50	.15
314 Kinston Indians TM	.50	.15
315 Columbus RedStixx TM	.50	.15
316 Mahoning Valley Scrappers TM	.50	.15
317 Burlington NC Indians TM	.50	.15
318 Tacoma Rainiers TM	.50	.15
319 San Antonio Missions TM	.50	.15
320 San Bernardino Stampede TM	.50	.15
321 Wisconsin Timber Rattlers TM	.50	.15
322 Everett Aqua Sox TM	.50	.15
323 Calgary Cannons TM	.50	.15
324 Portland Sea Dogs TM	.50	.15
325 Jupiter Hammerheads TM	.50	.15

326 Kane County Cougars TM....... .50 .15
327 Jamestown Jammers TM....... .50 .15
328 Norfolk Tides TM................ .50 .15
329 Binghamton Mets TM............ .50 .15
330 St. Lucie TM....................... .50 .15
331 Capital City Bombers TM........ .50 .15
332 Brooklyn Cyclones TM.......... .50 .15
333 Kingsport Mets TM............... .50 .15
334 Rochester Red Wings TM...... .50 .15
335 Bowie Baysox TM................. .50 .15
336 Frederick Keys TM............... .50 .15
337 Delmarva Shorebirds TM....... .50 .15
338 Bluefield Orioles TM............ .50 .15
339 Portland Beavers TM............ .50 .15
340 Mobile BayBears TM............ .50 .15
341 Lake Elsinore Storm TM........ .50 .15
342 Ft. Wayne Wizards TM.......... .50 .15
343 Eugene Emeralds TM............ .50 .15
344 SWB Red Barons TM............. .50 .15
345 Reading Phillies TM.............. .50 .15
346 Clearwater Phillies TM.......... .50 .15
347 Lakewood BlueClaws TM....... .50 .15
348 Batavia Muckdogs TM........... .50 .15
349 Nashville Sounds TM............ .50 .15
350 Altoona Curve TM................ .50 .15
351 Hickory Crawdads TM........... .50 .15
352 Lynchburg Hillcats TM.......... .50 .15
353 Williamsport Crosscutters TM .50 .15
354 Oklahoma RedHawks TM....... .50 .15
355 Tulsa Drillers TM................. .50 .15
356 Charlotte Rangers TM........... .50 .15
357 Savannah Sand Gnats TM...... .50 .15
358 Pulaski Rangers TM............. .50 .15
359 Pawtucket Red Sox TM......... .50 .15
360 Trenton Thunder TM............. .50 .15
361 Sarasota Red Sox TM........... .50 .15
362 Augusta GreenJackets TM...... .50 .15
363 Lowell Spinners TM.............. .50 .15
364 Gulf Coast Red SoxTM.......... .50 .15
365 Louisville Bats TM............... .50 .15
366 Chattanooga Lookouts TM..... .50 .15
367 Stockton Ports TM............... .50 .15
368 Dayton Dragons TM.............. .50 .15
369 Billings Mustangs TM........... .50 .15
370 Colorado Springs Sky Sox TM .50 .15
371 Carolina Mudcats TM............ .50 .15
372 Salem Avalanche TM............ .50 .15
373 Tri City Dust Devils TM......... .50 .15
374 Asheville Tourists TM........... .50 .15
375 Omaha Royals TM................ .50 .15
376 Wichita Wranglers TM........... .50 .15
377 Wilmington Blue Rocks TM.... .50 .15
378 Burlington Bees TM.............. .50 .15
379 Spokane Indians TM............. .50 .15
380 Toledo Mud Hens TM............ .50 .15
381 Erie Seawolves TM............... .50 .15
382 Lakeland Tigers TM.............. .50 .15
383 West Michigan Whitecaps TM .50 .15
384 Oneonta Tigers TM............... .50 .15
385 Edmonton Trappers TM......... .50 .15
386 New Britain Rock Cats TM...... .50 .15
387 Ft. Myers Miracle TM............ .50 .15
388 Quad City River Bandits TM... .50 .15
389 Elizabethton TwinsTM........... .50 .15
390 Charlotte Knights TM............ .50 .15
391 Birmingham Barons TM......... .50 .15
392 Winston-Salem Warthogs TM .50 .15
393 Kannapolis Intimidators TM... .50 .15
394 Bristol White Sox TM............ .50 .15
395 Columbus Clippers TM.......... .50 .15
396 Norwich Navigators TM......... .50 .15
397 Tampa Yankees TM.............. .50 .15
398 Greensboro Bats TM............ .50 .15
399 Staten Island Yankees TM...... .50 .15
400 Gulf Coast Yankees TM......... .50 .15

2002 UD Minor League Game Jerseys

Inserted into packs at a stated rate of one in 18, these 10 cards feature game-used jersey pieces of some of the leading prospects in baseball.

Nm-Mt Ex-Mt
STATED PRINT RUN 850 SETS
CARDS ARE NOT SERIAL NUMBERED
PRINT RUN INFO PROVIDED BY UPPER DECK
JAH Aaron Heilman.................... 8.00 2.40
JBU Chris Burke...................... 10.00 3.00
JCR Bobby Crosby.................... 15.00 4.50
JCT Chad Tracy........................ 10.00 3.00
JDK David Krynzel..................... 8.00 2.40
JJB Jeremy Bonderman.............. 10.00 3.00
JJH Josh Hamilton...................... 8.00 2.40
JJJ Jimmy Journell..................... 8.00 2.40
JMT Mark Teixeira.................... 15.00 4.50
JRB Rocco Baldelli.................... 20.00 6.00

2002 UD Minor League MJ Game-Worn Flashbacks

Inserted into packs at a stated rate of one in 144 for the Scorpions piece and randomly inserted for the other cards, these five cards feature game-worn jersey pieces of Michael Jordan. The cards which are numbered from WS1 through WS4 are all issued to a stated print run of 25 or fewer and no pricing is provided for these cards due to market scarcity.

Nm-Mt Ex-Mt
SS M.Jordan Scorpions/1490... 40.00 12.00
WS1 Michael Jordan Black/25............
WS2 Michael Jordan White/10............
WS3 Michael Jordan Silver/5.............
WS4 Michael Jordan Gold/1...............

2002 UD Minor League Signature Collection

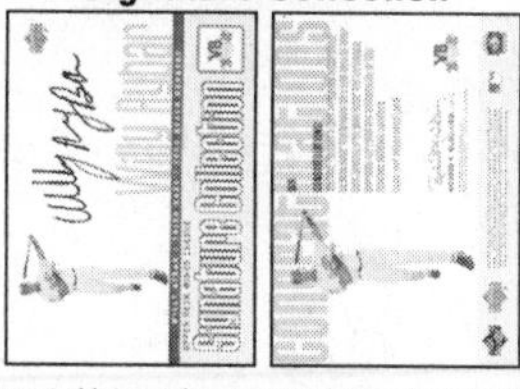

Inserted into packs at a stated rate of one in 18, these 34 cards feature autographs from some of the leading prospects in the minor league set.

Nm-Mt Ex-Mt
GOLD RANDOM INSERTS IN PACKS..
GOLD PRINT RUN 10 SERIAL #'d SETS
SILVER RANDOM INSERTS IN PACKS
SILVER PRINT RUN 25 SERIAL #'d SETS
NO GOLD/SILVER PRICES DUE TO SCARCITY
AG Adrian Gonzalez................... 15.00 4.50
AH Aaron Heilman..................... 10.00 3.00
BB Brian Bass.......................... 10.00 3.00
BC Brad Cresse........................ 10.00 3.00
BT Billy Traber......................... 15.00 4.50
CB Chris Burke......................... 15.00 4.50
CG Colt Griffin.......................... 15.00 4.50
CK Casey Kotchman.................. 25.00 7.50
CL Brandon Claussen................. 15.00 4.50
CM Corwin Malone.................... 10.00 3.00
CT Chad Tracy.......................... 15.00 4.50
DK David Krynzel...................... 10.00 3.00
GF Gavin Floyd......................... 25.00 7.50
GG Gabe Gross......................... 10.00 3.00
JB John Buck........................... 10.00 3.00
JE Jerome Williams................... 20.00 6.00
JF John-Ford Griffin.................. 10.00 3.00
JG Jake Gautreau...................... 10.00 3.00
JH Josh Hamilton...................... 10.00 3.00
JJ Jimmy Journell..................... 10.00 3.00
JM J.D. Martin......................... 10.00 3.00
JO Joe Mauer........................... 40.00 12.00
JS Jason Stokes........................ 30.00 9.00
JU Justin Huber........................ 15.00 4.50
KB Kenny Baugh........................ 10.00 3.00
MC Miguel Cabrera.................... 40.00 12.00
MG Michael Garciaparra.............. 15.00 4.50
MJ Mike Jones........................... 10.00 3.00
MT Mark Teixeira...................... 20.00 6.00
PF Prince Fielder...................... 40.00 12.00
SB Sean Burnett........................ 10.00 3.00
TH Ty Howington....................... 10.00 3.00
WA Willy Aybar......................... 10.00 3.00
DKE David Kelton..................... 10.00 3.00

2002 Upper Deck USA Baseball

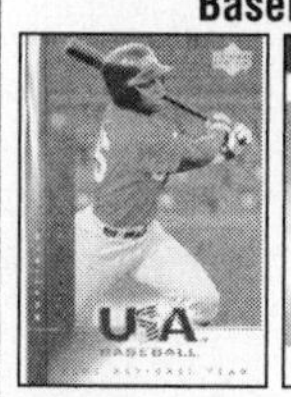

This 32 card set, which was issued as a fund raiser for USA baseball was available through the USA baseball web site for an SRP of $19.99. Each factory set contained regular issue cards and one autograph and one jersey card. According to USA Baseball, no more than 10,000 sets were printed.

Nm-Mt Ex-Mt
COMP.FACT.SET (32).................. 60.00 18.00
COMPLETE SET (30)................... 25.00 7.50
1 Chad Cordero.......................... .75 .23
2 Philip Humber......................... 1.00 .30
3 Grant Johnson.......................... .75 .23
4 Wes Littleton........................... 1.50 .45
5 Kyle Sleeth.............................. 3.00 .90
6 Huston Street........................... 1.00 .30
7 Brad Sullivan........................... 1.50 .45
8 Bob Zimmermann....................... .75 .23
9 Abe Alvarez.............................. 1.00 .30
10 Kyle Bakker............................. .75 .23
11 Clint Sammons......................... .75 .23
12 Landon Powell.......................... .75 .23
13 Michael Aubrey........................ 4.00 1.20
14 Aaron Hill................................ 2.00 .60
15 Conor Jackson......................... 2.50 .75
16 Eric Patterson........................... 1.00 .30
17 Dustin Pedroia........................... .75 .23
18 Rickie Weeks........................... 8.00 2.40
19 Shane Costa............................. 1.00 .30
20 Mark Jurich................................ .75 .23
21 Sam Fuld................................... .75 .23
22 Carlos Quentin.......................... 2.00 .60
23 Ryan Garko................................ .75 .23
24 Lelo Prado................................. .75 .23
25 Terry Alexander.......................... .75 .23
26 Sunny Golloway.......................... .75 .23
27 Terry Rupp CO............................ .50 .15
28 Team USA.................................. .50 .15
29 Team USA w/Flag........................ .50 .15
30 Team USA Checklist..................... .50 .15

2002 Upper Deck USA Baseball Jerseys

Inserted one per Team USA factory set, these 22 cards featured game worn swatches from members of Team USA. Each of these cards were issued to a stated print run of 475 serial numbered sets.

Nm-Mt Ex-Mt
AA Abe Alvarez........................ 15.00 4.50
AH Aaron Hill........................... 20.00 6.00
BS Brad Sullivan....................... 15.00 4.50
BZ Bob Zimmermann.................. 10.00 3.00
CC Chad Cordero...................... 10.00 3.00
CJ Conor Jackson..................... 20.00 6.00
CQ Carlos Quentin..................... 15.00 4.50
CS Clint Sammons..................... 10.00 3.00
DP Dustin Pedroia...................... 10.00 3.00
EP Eric Patterson....................... 15.00 4.50
GJ Grant Johnson...................... 10.00 3.00
HS Huston Street....................... 15.00 4.50
KB Kyle Bakker......................... 10.00 3.00
KS Kyle Sleeth.......................... 25.00 7.50
LP Landon Powell...................... 10.00 3.00
MA Michael Aubrey................... 40.00 12.00
MJ Mark Jurich......................... 10.00 3.00
PH Philip Humber....................... 15.00 4.50
RW Rickie Weeks...................... 60.00 18.00
SC Shane Costa......................... 15.00 4.50
SF Sam Fuld............................. 10.00 3.00
WL Wes Littleton....................... 15.00 4.50

2002 Upper Deck USA Baseball Signatures

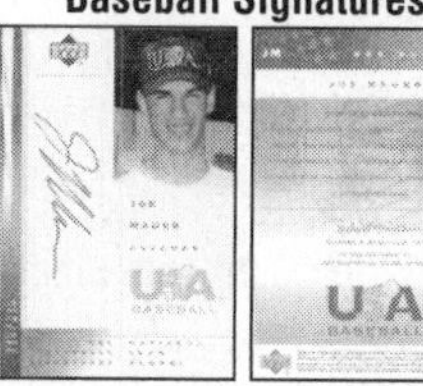

Inserted one per Team USA factory set, these 27 cards feature signatures of Team USA alumni. Each of these cards were issued to a stated print run of 375 serial numbered sets.

Nm-Mt Ex-Mt
BC Bobby Crosby...................... 80.00 24.00
BD Ben Diggins......................... 15.00 4.50
CE Clint Everts.......................... 30.00 9.00
CK Casey Kotchman................... 80.00 24.00
DK David Krynzel...................... 15.00 4.50
JB Josh Bard............................ 15.00 4.50
JF Jeff Francoeur...................... 80.00 24.00
JH J.J. Hardy........................... 60.00 18.00
JJ Jacque Jones........................ 15.00 4.50
JK Josh Karp............................ 15.00 4.50
JL James Loney........................ 80.00 24.00
JM Joe Mauer.......................... 100.00 30.00
JS Jason Stanford...................... 15.00 4.50
JW Justin Wayne....................... 15.00 4.50
KD Keoni DeRenne.................... 15.00 4.50
KH Koyie Hill............................ 15.00 4.50
LD Lenny Dinardo...................... 15.00 4.50
MG Mike Gosling....................... 15.00 4.50
MH Matt Holliday...................... 15.00 4.50
MP Mark Prior......................... 150.00 45.00
MW Matt Whitney..................... 25.00 7.50
PS Phil Seibel........................... 15.00 4.50
RH Ryan Howard....................... 25.00 7.50
SB Sean Burnett........................ 15.00 4.50
SN Shane Nance........................ 15.00 4.50
WB Willie Bloomquist................. 40.00 12.00
ZS Zack Segovia........................ 15.00 4.50

2002-03 Just Rookies Black Test

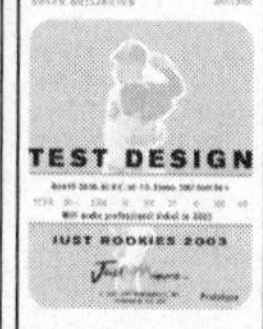

These cards were made available as Test Design prototypes to dealers. The cards are not particularly scarce, which could be misleading given the typical nature of test issue cards. Card fronts feature a solid black background.

Nm-Mt Ex-Mt
COMPLETE SET (2).................... 2.50 .75
BB1 Bryan Bullington.................. 1.50 .45
RG1 Rudy Guillen....................... 1.00 .30

2002-03 Just Rookies

This 40 card set was issued in January 2003 and these cards were directly available from the manufacturer.

Nm-Mt Ex-Mt
COMPLETE SET (40)................ 10.00 3.00
1 B.J. Upton............................. 1.50 .45
2 Khalil Greene......................... 1.25 .35
3 Jeremy Hermida...................... 1.00 .30
4 Chad Tracy............................. .60 .18

5 Francisco Cruceta...................... .25 .07
6 Hanley Ramirez......................... .60 .18
7 Jeff Francoeur.......................... 1.50 .45
8 Kyle Pawelczyk.......................... .25 .07
9 Justin Huber............................. .50 .15
10 Gregor Blanco.......................... .25 .07
11 Andy Marte............................ 1.00 .30
12 Taggert Bozied.......................... .60 .18
13 Felix Pie................................. 1.00 .30
14 Dontrelle Willis........................ 1.50 .45
15 Jason Stokes............................ 1.50 .45
16 Corey Hart................................ .60 .18
17 Sergio Santos............................ .75 .23
18 John-Ford Griffin....................... .25 .07
19 Shin-Soo Choo........................... .60 .18
20 Todd Linden.............................. .60 .18
21 Jonathan Figueroa....................... .40 .12
22 James Loney............................ 1.25 .35
23 Jason Pridie................................ .50 .15
24 Denard Span............................... .40 .12
25 Matt Whitney............................. .50 .15
26 Dan Meyer................................. .40 .12
27 Rudy Guillen............................... .60 .18
28 Micah Schilling............................ .40 .12
29 Wes Bankston............................. .60 .18
30 Travis Ishikawa............................ .25 .07
31 Jake Blalock................................ .75 .23
32 C.J. Wilson................................. .25 .07
33 Laynce Nix................................ 1.00 .30
34 Brian Bruney................................ .25 .07
35 Chris Gruler................................. .40 .12
36 Merkin Valdez-Mateo..................... .75 .23
37 Clint Everts.................................. .50 .15
38 Scott Moore.................................. .40 .12
39 Bryan Bullington............................ .60 .18
40 Zach Parker.................................. .25 .07

2002-03 Just Rookies Black

Available directly from Just, this is a parallel to the Just Rookies set. These cards have black borders and were issued to a stated print run of 50 serial numbered sets.

Nm-Mt Ex-Mt
*BLACK: 5X TO 12X BASIC CARDS....

2002-03 Just Rookies Gold

Available directly from Just, this is a parallel to the Just Rookies set. These cards have gold borders, were issued only in factory set form and were issued to a stated print run of 1000 sets.

Nm-Mt Ex-Mt
*GOLD: 1.5X TO 4X BASIC...............
DISTRIBUTED IN FACTORY SET FORM
INITIALLY AVAIL.ONLY TO CLUB MEMBERS
STATED PRINT RUN 1000 SETS.........

2002-03 Just Rookies Silver

Available directly from Just, this is a parallel to the Just Rookies set. These cards have silver borders, were issued only in factory set form and were issued to a stated print run of 5000 sets.

Nm-Mt Ex-Mt
COMP.FACT.SET (40)................ 25.00 7.50
*SILVER: .6X TO 1.5X BASIC CARDS .

2002-03 Just Rookies Autographs

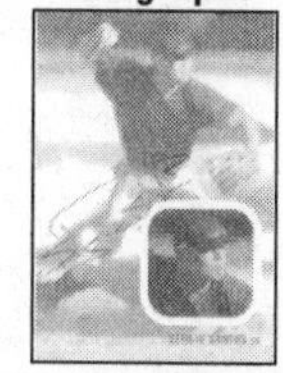

These cards were issued directly to the collector by Just. These cards were issued to stated print runs between 50 and 400 copies and we have notated that information in our checklist.

Nm-Mt Ex-Mt
1 Wes Bankston/200................ 12.00 3.60
2 Jake Blalock/400.................. 10.00 3.00
3 Gregor Blanco/400................. 5.00 1.50
4 Taggert Bozied/100.............. 12.00 3.60
5 Brian Bruney/500................... 8.00 2.40
6 Bryan Bullington/50.............. 25.00 7.50
7 Shin-Soo Choo/500............... 25.00 7.50
8 Francisco Cruceta/400............. 5.00 1.50
9 Clint Everts/400................... 10.00 3.00
10 Jonathan Figueroa/400........... 8.00 2.40
11 Jeff Francoeur/400.............. 25.00 7.50
12 Khalil Greene/50................. 40.00 12.00
13 John-Ford Griffin/400............. 5.00 1.50
14 Chris Gruler/400.................... 8.00 2.40
15 Rudy Guillen/200................. 12.00 3.60
16 Corey Hart/400.................... 10.00 3.00
17 Jeremy Hermida/200............. 15.00 4.50
18 Justin Huber/50................... 20.00 6.00
19 Travis Ishikawa/400................ 8.00 2.40
20 Todd Linden/50.................... 25.00 7.50
21 James Loney/200.................. 20.00 6.00
22 Andy Marte/50..................... 40.00 12.00
23 Merkin Valdez-Mateo/400...... 12.00 3.60
24 Dan Meyer/300..................... 10.00 3.00
25 Scott Moore/500.................... 8.00 2.40
26 Laynce Nix/400.................... 15.00 4.50
27 Zach Parker/400..................... 5.00 1.50
28 Kyle Pawelczyk/400................ 5.00 1.50
29 Felix Pie/200....................... 15.00 4.50
30 Jason Pridie/400.................. 10.00 3.00
31 Hanley Ramirez/200.............. 15.00 4.50
32 Sergio Santos/200................. 15.00 4.50
33 Micah Schilling/400................. 5.00 1.50
34 Denard Span/400.................... 5.00 1.50
35 Jason Stokes/100.................. 30.00 9.00
36 Chad Tracy/400.................... 10.00 3.00
37 B.J. Upton/50...................... 50.00 15.00
38 Matt Whitney/200................. 10.00 3.00
39 Dontrelle Willis/100.............. 25.00 7.50
40 C.J. Wilson/400..................... 5.00 1.50

2002-03 Just Rookies Autographs Gold

Available directly from Just, this is a parallel to the Just Rookies Autograph set. Each of these cards was issued to a stated print run of 100 serial numbered sets. These cards were originally available only toe Just Rookies Club members.

Nm-Mt Ex-Mt
*GOLD: .6X TO 1.5X BASIC p/r 400-500
*GOLD: .5X TO 1.2X BASIC p/r 200-300
*GOLD: .4X TO 1X BASIC p/r 100
*GOLD: .3X TO .8X BASIC p/r 50......

2002-03 Just Rookies Autographs Silver

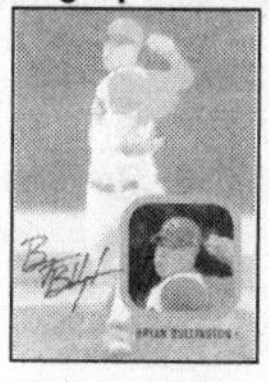

Available directly from Just, this is a parallel to the Just Rookies Autograph set. Each of these cards was issued to a stated print run of 375 serial numbered sets.

Nm-Mt Ex-Mt
*SILVER: .4X TO 1X BASIC p/r 400-500
*SILVER: .3X TO .8X BASIC p/r 200-300
*SILVER: .25X TO .6X BASIC p/r 100 .
*SILVER: .2X TO .5X BASIC p/r 50....

2003-04 Just Rookies

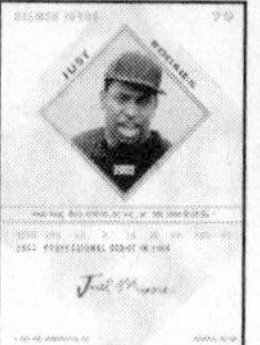

MINT NRMT
COMPLETE SET (80)................ 20.00 9.00
ISSUED DIRECTLY FROM MANUFACTURER
STATED PRINT RUN 15,000 SETS......
1 Anderson Amador...................... .75 .35
2 Luis Atilano............................. .50 .23
3 Paul Bacot............................... .50 .23
4 Aaron Baldiris........................... .75 .35
5 Jimmy Barthmaier...................... .40 .18
6 Daric Barton........................... 1.00 .45
7 Chad Billingsley........................ .75 .35
8 Andres Blanco.......................... .40 .18
9 Larry Broadway........................ .40 .18
10 Robinson Cano......................... .50 .23
11 Matt Chico............................... .75 .35
12 Hu Chin-Lung......................... 1.00 .45
13 Jesse Crain............................... .40 .18
14 Juan Dominguez........................ .40 .18
15 Dennis Dove............................. .50 .23
16 Eric Duncan............................ 1.00 .45
17 Jesse English............................ .40 .18
18 Brian Finch............................... .40 .18
19 Enrique Gonzalez....................... .40 .18
20 Tom Gorzelanny........................ .50 .23
21 Franklin Gutierrez.................... 1.50 .70
22 Anthony Gwynn....................... 1.00 .45
23 Josh Hall.................................. .50 .23
24 Mickey Hall............................... .75 .35
25 Ryan Hannaman......................... .40 .18
26 Matt Harrison............................ .50 .23
27 Felix Hernandez....................... 1.50 .70
28 Shawn Hill................................ .50 .23
29 Jason Hirsh.............................. .50 .23
30 James Houser............................ .75 .35
31 Kevin Howard........................... .40 .18
32 Edwin Jackson......................... 1.50 .70
33 Blair Johnson............................ .40 .18
34 Kody Kirkland............................ .50 .23
35 Jason Kubel.............................. .50 .23
36 Andy LaRoche......................... 1.00 .45
37 Donald Levinski......................... .40 .18
38 Kenny Lewis............................. .75 .35
39 Bobby Livingston....................... .50 .23
40 Adam Loewen......................... 1.50 .70
41 Chris Lubanski......................... 1.00 .45
42 Luis Martinez............................ .40 .18
43 Macay McBride......................... .40 .18
44 Brian McCann........................... .75 .35

45 Dallas McPherson .50 .23
46 Lastings Milledge 1.50 .70
47 Greg Miller .50 .23
48 Daniel Moore .40 .18
49 Steve Moss .40 .18
50 David Murphy .75 .35
51 Darin Naatjes .40 .18
52 Dioner Navarro 1.00 .45
53 Ramon Nivar .75 .35
54 David Pauley .40 .18
55 Elizardo Ramirez .60 .25
56 Jeremy Reed .50 .23
57 Jo Jo Reyes .75 .35
58 Tony Richie .40 .18
59 Alexis Rios 1.00 .45
60 Arturo Rivas .40 .18
61 Jarrod Saltalamacchia .75 .35
62 Dennis Sarfate .50 .23
63 Chris Seddon .40 .18
64 Alexander Smit 1.00 .45
65 Sean Smith .50 .23
66 Brad Snyder .75 .35
67 Brian Snyder .50 .23
68 Edgar Soto .40 .18
69 Tim Stauffer .75 .35
70 Jake Stevens .50 .23
71 Brad Sullivan .75 .35
72 Kazuhito Tadano 1.00 .45
73 Anderson Tavarez .50 .23
74 James Tomlin .50 .23
75 Rusty Tucker .50 .23
76 Doug Waechter .50 .23
77 Ryan Wagner .75 .35
78 Brandon Weeden .40 .18
79 Delmon Young 2.00 .90
80 Joel Zumaya .75 .35

2003-04 Just Rookies Black

MINT NRMT
*BLACK: 5X TO 12X BASIC
ISSUED DIRECTLY FROM MANUFACTURER
STATED PRINT RUN 50 SERIAL #'d SETS

2003-04 Just Rookies Gold

MINT NRMT
*GOLD: 1.5X TO 4X BASIC
DISTRIBUTED IN FACTORY SET FORM
STATED PRINT RUN 1000 SERIAL #'d SETS

2003-04 Just Rookies Silver

MINT NRMT
COMP.FACT.SET (80) 25.00 11.00
*SILVER: .6X TO 1.5X BASIC
DISTRIBUTED IN FACTORY SET FORM
STATED PRINT RUN 5000 SETS

2003-04 Just Rookies Autographs

MINT NRMT
ISSUED DIRECTLY FROM MANUFACTURER
PRINT RUNS B/WN 50-875 COPIES PER
1 Anderson Amador/50 20.00 9.00
2 Luis Atilano/375 10.00 4.50
3 Paul Bacot/375 10.00 4.50
4 Aaron Baldiris/375 10.00 4.50
5 Jimmy Barthmaier/875 5.00 2.20
6 Daric Barton/375 10.00 4.50
7 Chad Billingsley/375 10.00 4.50
8 Andres Blanco/375 8.00 3.60
9 Larry Broadway/875 5.00 2.20
10 Robinson Cano/50 20.00 9.00
11 Matt Chico/375 10.00 4.50
12 Hu Chin-Lung/50 25.00 11.00
13 Jesse Crain/375 8.00 3.60
14 Juan Dominguez/375 8.00 3.60
15 Dennis Dove/375 10.00 4.50
16 Eric Duncan/350 15.00 6.75
17 Jesse English/375 8.00 3.60
18 Brian Finch/375 8.00 3.60
19 Enrique Gonzalez/375 8.00 3.60
20 Tom Gorzelanny/875 8.00 3.60
21 Franklin Gutierrez/50 30.00 13.50
22 Anthony Gwynn/100 15.00 6.75
23 Josh Hall/875 8.00 3.60
24 Mickey Hall/875 8.00 3.60
26 Matt Harrison/375 10.00 4.50
27 Felix Hernandez/350 10.00 4.50
28 Shawn Hill/375 10.00 4.50
29 Jason Hirsh/375 10.00 4.50
30 James Houser/875 8.00 3.60
31 Kevin Howard/375 8.00 3.60
32 Edwin Jackson/50 40.00 18.00
33 Blair Johnson/375 8.00 3.60
34 Kody Kirkland/375 10.00 4.50
35 Jason Kubel/375 10.00 4.50
36 Andy LaRoche/375 10.00 4.50
37 Donald Levinski/375 8.00 3.60
38 Kenny Lewis/375 10.00 4.50
39 Bobby Livingston/875 8.00 3.60
40 Adam Loewen/50 30.00 13.50
41 Chris Lubanski/350 15.00 6.75
42 Luis Martinez/375 8.00 3.60
43 Macay McBride/375 8.00 3.60
44 Brian McCann/375 10.00 4.50
45 Dallas McPherson/50 25.00 11.00
46 Lastings Milledge/350 20.00 9.00
47 Greg Miller/50 25.00 11.00
48 Daniel Moore/375 8.00 3.60
49 Steve Moss/375 8.00 3.60
50 David Murphy/200 15.00 6.75
51 Darin Naatjes/875 5.00 2.20
52 Dioner Navarro/200 15.00 6.75
53 Ramon Nivar/375 10.00 4.50
54 David Pauley/375 8.00 3.60
55 Elizardo Ramirez/375 10.00 4.50
56 Jeremy Reed/375 10.00 4.50
57 Jo Jo Reyes/375 10.00 4.50
58 Tony Richie/375 8.00 3.60
59 Alexis Rios/50 40.00 18.00
60 Arturo Rivas/875 5.00 2.20
61 Jarrod Saltalamacchia/375 10.00 4.50
62 Dennis Sarfate/375 10.00 4.50
63 Chris Seddon/375 8.00 3.60
64 Alexander Smit/375 10.00 4.50
65 Sean Smith/375 10.00 4.50
66 Brad Snyder/875 10.00 4.50
67 Brian Snyder/875 8.00 3.60
68 Edgar Soto/375 8.00 3.60
69 Tim Stauffer/875 8.00 3.60
70 Jake Stevens/375 10.00 4.50
71 Brad Sullivan/350 10.00 4.50
72 Kazuhito Tadano/50 40.00 18.00
73 Anderson Tavarez/875 8.00 3.60
74 James Tomlin/375 10.00 4.50
75 Rusty Tucker/375 10.00 4.50
76 Doug Waechter/375 10.00 4.50
77 Ryan Wagner/375 10.00 4.50
79 Delmon Young/50 50.00 22.00
80 Joel Zumaya/375 10.00 4.50

2003-04 Just Rookies Autographs Black

MINT NRMT
ISSUED DIRECTLY FROM MANUFACTURER
STATED PRINT RUN 25 SERIAL #'d SETS
NO PRICING DUE TO SCARCITY

2003-04 Just Rookies Autographs Gold

MINT NRMT
*GOLD: .6X TO 1.5X p/r 875
*GOLD: .5X TO 1.2X p/r 200-375
*GOLD: .4X TO 1X p/r 100
*GOLD: .3X TO .8X p/r 50
DISTRIBUTED IN FACTORY SET FORM
STATED PRINT RUN 100 SERIAL #'d SETS

2003-04 Just Rookies Autographs Silver

MINT NRMT
*SILVER: .3X TO .8X BASIC p/r 200-375
*SILVER: .25X TO .6X BASIC p/r 100 .
*SILVER: .2X TO .5X BASIC p/r 50
AVAIL.THROUGH RETAIL DISTRIBUTION
STATED PRINT RUN 375 SERIAL #'d SETS

2003-04 Just Rookies '04 Preview

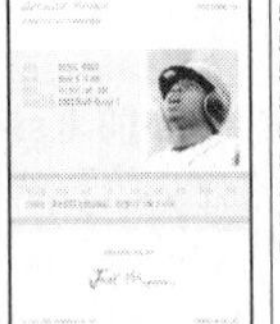

Nm-Mt Ex-Mt
COMPLETE SET (10) 5.00 1.50
ISSUED ONLY TO DISTRIBUTORS
STATED PRINT RUN 15,000 SETS
*BLACK: 5X TO 12X BASIC 04 PREVIEW
BLACK ISSUED ONLY TO DISTRIBUTORS
BLACK PRINT RUN 50 SERIAL #'d SETS
*GOLD: 1.5X TO 4X BASIC 04 PREVIEW
GOLD ISSUED IN FACTORY SET FORM
GOLD INITIALLY AVAIL.TO CLUB MEMBERS
GOLD PRINT RUN 1000 SERIAL #'d SETS
*SILVER: .6X TO 1.5X BASIC 04 PREVIEW
SILVER ISSUED ONLY TO DISTRIBUTORS
SILVER PRINT RUN 5000 SETS
1 Anderson Amador .75 .23
2 Eric Duncan 1.00 .30
3 Anthony Gwynn 1.00 .30
4 Cole Hamels .75 .23
5 Andy LaRoche 1.00 .30
6 Adam Loewen 1.50 .45
7 David Murphy .75 .23
8 Mark Prior 3.00 .90
9 Alexis Rios 1.00 .30
10 Delmon Young 2.00 .60

2003-04 Just Rookies '04 Preview Autographs

Nm-Mt Ex-Mt
ISSUED DIRECTLY FROM MANUFACTURER
STATED PRINT RUN 50 SERIAL #'d SETS
BLACK ISSUED FROM MANUFACTURER
BLACK PRINT RUN 25 SERIAL #'d SETS
NO BLACK PRICING DUE TO SCARCITY
*GOLD: X TO X BASIC AUTO
GOLD ISSUED IN FACTORY SET FORM
GOLD INITIALLY AVAIL.TO CLUB MEMBERS
GOLD PRINT RUN 100 SERIAL #'d SETS
1 Anderson Amador
2 Eric Duncan
3 Anthony Gwynn
4 Cole Hamels
5 Andy LaRoche
6 Adam Loewen
7 David Murphy
8 Mark Prior
9 Alexis Rios
10 Delmon Young

2002-03 Justifiable

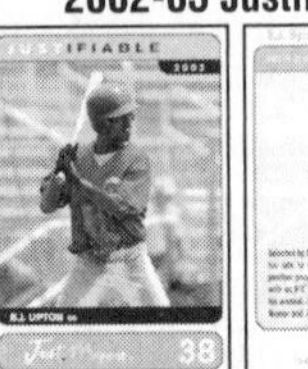
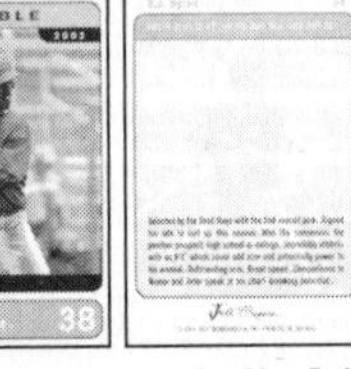

Nm-Mt Ex-Mt
COMP.SET w/o AU's (39) 10.00 3.00
COMMON CARD (2-40) .25 .07
COMMON CARD (41-50) 5.00 1.50
1 Russ Adams SP
2 Travis Blackley .60 .18
3 Matt Cain .60 .18
4 Travis Chapman .25 .07
5 Kyle Davies .40 .12
6 Carlos Duran .25 .07
7 Gavin Floyd .75 .23
8 Jesse Foppert .60 .18
9 Choo Freeman .25 .07
10 Jimmy Gobble .50 .15
11 Jonny Gomes .40 .12
12 Khalil Greene 1.25 .35
13 Joel Guzman .25 .07
14 Luke Hagerty .25 .07
15 Jack Hannahan .25 .07
16 Rich Harden 1.50 .45
17 J.J. Hardy .75 .23
18 Jeremy Hermida 1.00 .30
19 Kris Honel .25 .07
20 Casey Kotchman 1.00 .30
21 Cliff Lee .40 .12
22 Francisco Liriano .25 .07
23 Jose Lopez 1.00 .30
24 Andy Marte 1.00 .30
25 Victor Martinez .25 .07
26 Joe Mauer 1.50 .45
27 Drew Meyer .25 .07
28 Dustin Moseley .25 .07
29 Clint Nageotte .40 .12
30 Rhett Parrott .25 .07
31 Josh Phelps .25 .07
32 Brandon Phillips .25 .07
33 Jose Reyes .40 .12
34 Felix Sanchez .25 .07
35 Sergio Santos .75 .23
36 Mark Teixeira .40 .12
37 Andres Torres .25 .07
38 B.J. Upton 1.50 .45
39 Shane Victorino .25 .07
40 David Wright .75 .23
41 Joseph Blanton AU/1000 15.00 4.50
42 Shin Soo Choo AU/500 12.00 3.60
43 Jason Cooper AU/1000 5.00 1.50
44 Jeff Francis AU/1000 5.00 1.50
45 Jeff Francoeur AU/500 25.00 7.50
46 Joey Gomes AU/1000 5.00 1.50
47 Corey Hart AU/500 12.00 3.60
48 Justin Huber AU/500 8.00 2.40
49 Dan Meyer AU/500 5.00 1.50
50 Dontrelle Willis AU/500 20.00 6.00
51 Scott Hairston AU/1000
52 Anthony Lerew AU/1000
53 Jeff Mathis AU/1000
54 Felix Pie AU/500
55 Jason Pridie AU/500
56 Hanley Ramirez AU/500
57 Joe Saunders AU/1000
58 Jason Stokes AU/500
59 Brian Tallet AU/1000
60 Chad Tracy AU/1000

2002-03 Justifiable Black

Nm-Mt Ex-Mt
*BLACK 1-40: 5X TO 12X BASIC

2002-03 Justifiable Gold

Nm-Mt Ex-Mt
COMP.FACT.SET (60)
*GOLD 1-40: X TO X BASIC

2002-03 Justifiable Silver

Nm-Mt Ex-Mt
COMP.FACT.SET (60) 25.00 7.50
*SILVER 1-40: .6X TO 1.5X BASIC
*SILVER 41-50: X TO X BASIC
*SILVER 51-60: X TO X BASIC

2002-03 Justifiable Autographs

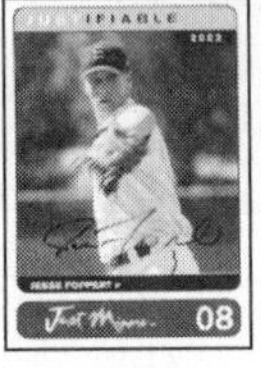
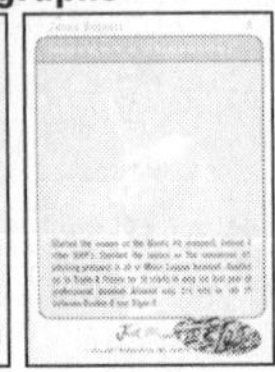

Nm-Mt Ex-Mt
1 Russ Adams SP
2 Travis Blackley/400 12.00 3.60
3 Matt Cain/400 12.00 3.60
4 Travis Chapman/400 5.00 1.50
5 Kyle Davies/400 8.00 2.40
6 Carlos Duran/50 15.00 4.50
7 Gavin Floyd/50 30.00 9.00
8 Jesse Foppert/400 12.00 3.60
9 Choo Freeman/400 5.00 1.50
10 Jimmy Gobble/50 25.00 7.50
11 Jonny Gomes/50 20.00 6.00
12 Khalil Greene/50 40.00 12.00
13 Joel Guzman/50 15.00 4.50
14 Luke Hagerty/400 5.00 1.50
15 Jack Hannahan/400 5.00 1.50
16 Rich Harden/400 20.00 6.00
17 J.J. Hardy/400 15.00 4.50
18 Jeremy Hermida/50 30.00 9.00
19 Kris Honel/400 5.00 1.50
20 Casey Kotchman/400 20.00 6.00
21 Cliff Lee/400 8.00 2.40
22 Francisco Liriano/400 5.00 1.50
23 Jose Lopez/50 40.00 12.00
24 Andy Marte/50 40.00 12.00
25 Victor Martinez/50 15.00 4.50
26 Joe Mauer/50 50.00 15.00
27 Drew Meyer/400 5.00 1.50
28 Dustin Moseley/400 8.00 2.40
29 Clint Nageotte/50 20.00 6.00
30 Rhett Parrott/400 5.00 1.50
31 Josh Phelps/50 15.00 4.50
32 Brandon Phillips/75 15.00 4.50
33 Jose Reyes/50 25.00 7.50
34 Felix Sanchez/400 5.00 1.50
35 Sergio Santos/400 12.00 3.60
36 Mark Teixeira/50 25.00 7.50
37 Andres Torres/400 5.00 1.50
38 B.J. Upton/50 50.00 15.00
39 Shane Victorino/400 5.00 1.50
40 David Wright/500 15.00 4.50

2002-03 Justifiable Autographs Gold

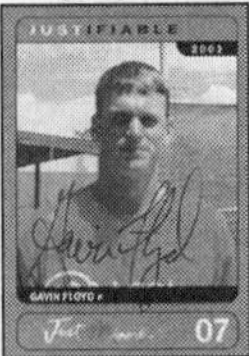

Nm-Mt Ex-Mt
*GOLD: .6X TO 1.5X BASIC AU p/r 400-500
*GOLD: .3X TO .8X BASIC p/r 50-75

2003 Just Stars

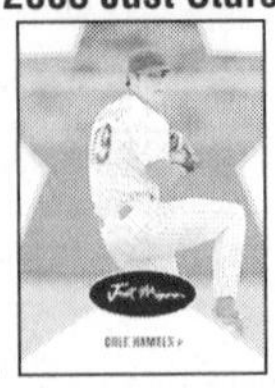

MINT NRMT
COMPLETE SET (50) 15.00 6.75
ISSUED DIRECTLY FROM MANUFACTURER
STATED PRINT RUN 10,000 SETS
1 Joaquin Arias .50 .23
2 Eric Aybar .50 .23
3 Josh Barfield .50 .23
4 Bobby Basham .75 .35
5 Ronald Belisario .50 .23
6 Bobby Brownlie .75 .35
7 Miguel Cabrera 1.50 .70
8 Alberto Callaspo 1.00 .45
9 Jose Capellan .50 .23
10 Fausto Carmona .75 .35
11 Jose Castillo .40 .18
12 Hu Chin-Lung 1.00 .45
13 Jose Rafael Diaz .50 .23
14 Zach Duke .50 .23
15 Elijah Dukes .50 .23
16 J.D. Durbin .75 .35
17 Justin Germano .50 .23
18 Byron Gettis .50 .23
19 Alfredo Gonzalez .50 .23
20 Edgar Gonzalez .50 .23
21 Derek Grigsby UER .50 .23
Should be Derick
22 Jeremy Guthrie .40 .18
23 Franklin Gutierrez 1.50 .70
24 Cole Hamels .75 .35
25 Zach Hammes .40 .18
26 Dan Haren .75 .35
27 Brendan Harris .50 .23
28 Blake Hawksworth .75 .35
29 Trevor Hutchinson .50 .23
30 Edwin Jackson 1.50 .70
31 Kevin Jepsen .40 .18
32 Adam Loewen 1.50 .70
33 John Maine 1.25 .55
34 John McCurdy .40 .18
35 Dustin McGowan .50 .23
36 Brian Miller .50 .23
37 Dustin Nippert .50 .23
38 Leo Nunez .50 .23
39 Vince Perkins .50 .23
40 Mark Schramek .40 .18
41 Kelly Shoppach .75 .35
42 Andy Sisco .75 .35
43 Grady Sizemore .50 .23
44 Chris Snyder .40 .18
45 Kazuhito Tadano 1.25 .55
46 Ferdin Tejeda .50 .23
47 Jose Valdez .50 .23
48 Joe Valentine .50 .23
49 Adam Wainwright .40 .18
50 Matt Yeatman .50 .23

2003 Just Stars Autographs

MINT NRMT
ISSUED DIRECTLY FROM MANUFACTURER
PRINT RUNS B/WN 50-875 COPIES PER
1 Joaquin Arias/375 8.00 3.60
2 Eric Aybar/375 8.00 3.60
3 Josh Barfield/50 25.00 11.00
4 Bobby Basham/375 8.00 3.60
5 Ronald Belisario/875 8.00 3.60
6 Bobby Brownlie/50 20.00 9.00
7 Miguel Cabrera/50 50.00 22.00
8 Alberto Callaspo/375 10.00 4.50
9 Jose Capellan/375 8.00 3.60
10 Fausto Carmona/875 8.00 3.60
11 Jose Castillo/875 5.00 2.20
12 Hu Chin-Lung/50 25.00 11.00
13 Jose Rafael Diaz/375 5.00 2.20
14 Zach Duke/375 8.00 3.60
15 Elijah Dukes/500 5.00 2.20
16 J.D. Durbin/375 5.00 2.20
17 Justin Germano/375 5.00 2.20
18 Byron Gettis/375 5.00 2.20
19 Alfredo Gonzalez/875 5.00 2.20
20 Edgar Gonzalez/375 5.00 2.20
21 Derek Grigsby UER/375 5.00 2.20
Should be Derick
22 Jeremy Guthrie/50 15.00 6.75
23 Franklin Gutierrez/500 15.00 6.75
24 Cole Hamels/250 15.00 6.75
25 Zach Hammes/375 5.00 2.20
26 Dan Haren/50 20.00 9.00
27 Brendan Harris/375 8.00 3.60
28 Blake Hawksworth/500 8.00 3.60
29 Trevor Hutchinson/875 8.00 3.60
30 Edwin Jackson/500 15.00 6.75
31 Kevin Jepsen/375 5.00 2.20
32 Adam Loewen/50 30.00 13.50
33 John Maine/500 15.00 6.75
34 John McCurdy/375 5.00 2.20
35 Dustin McGowan/375 8.00 3.60
36 Brian Miller/375 8.00 3.60
37 Dustin Nippert/375 8.00 3.60
38 Leo Nunez/375 8.00 3.60
39 Vince Perkins/50 20.00 9.00
40 Mark Schramek/875 5.00 2.20
41 Kelly Shoppach/375 10.00 4.50
42 Andy Sisco/375 10.00 4.50
43 Grady Sizemore/50 40.00 18.00
44 Chris Snyder/375 5.00 2.20
45 Kazuhito Tadano/875 15.00 6.75
46 Ferdin Tejeda/375 5.00 2.20
47 Jose Valdez/375 5.00 2.20
48 Joe Valentine/375 5.00 2.20
49 Adam Wainwright/50 15.00 6.75
50 Matt Yeatman/375 8.00 3.60

2003 Just Stars Autographs Black

MINT NRMT
ISSUED DIRECTLY FROM MANUFACTURER
STATED PRINT RUN 25 SERIAL #'d SETS
NO PRICING DUE TO SCARCITY

2003 Just Stars Autographs Gold

MINT NRMT
*GOLD: .6X TO 1.5X BASIC AU p/r 250+
*GOLD: .3X TO .8X BASIC AU p/r 50 ..
DISTRIBUTED IN FACTORY SET FORM
INITIALLY AVAIL.ONLY TO CLUB MEMBERS
STATED PRINT RUN 100 SERIAL #'d SETS

2003 Just Stars Autographs Silver

MINT NRMT
*SILVER: .4X TO 1X BASIC AU p/r 250+
*SILVER: .2X TO .5X BASIC AU p/r 50
AVAIL.THROUGH RETAIL DISTRIBUTION
STATED PRINT RUN 375 SERIAL #'d SETS

2003 Just Stars Black

MINT NRMT
*BLACK: 5X TO 12X BASIC
ISSUED DIRECTLY FROM MANUFACTURER
STATED PRINT RUN 50 SERIAL #'d SETS

2003 Just Stars Gold

MINT NRMT
*GOLD: 1.5X TO 4X BASIC
DISTRIBUTED IN FACTORY SET FORM
INITIALLY AVAIL.ONLY TO CLUB MEMBERS
STATED PRINT RUN 1000 SERIAL #'d SETS

2003 Just Stars Silver

MINT NRMT
*SILVER: .6X TO 1.5X BASIC
DISTRIBUTED IN FACTORY SET FORM
STATED PRINT RUN 5000 SETS

2003 Just Stars ME 8 x 10 Autographs

MINT NRMT
ONE PER SEALED ME BOX
1 Michael Barrett
2 Hank Blalock
3 Tony Blanco
4 Brian Bruney
5 Miguel Cabrera
6 Carl Crawford
7 Juan Cruz
8 Jesse Foppert
9 Jeff Francoeur
10 Choo Freeman
11 Eric Gagne
12 Marcus Giles
13 Gabe Gross
14 Chris Gruler
15 Anthony Gwynn
16 Rich Harden
17 Wes Helms
18 Austin Kearns
19 David Kelton
20 Casey Kotchman
21 Joe Kennedy
22 James Loney
23 Victor Martinez
24 Xavier Nady
25 Nick Neugebauer
26 Laynce Nix
27 Lyle Overbay
28 Carlos Pena
29 Josh Phelps
30 Brandon Phillips
31 Jon Rauch
32 Alexis Rios
33 Nolan Ryan
34 Chris Snelling
35 Tim Spooneybarger
36 Dennis Tankersley
37 Mark Teixeira
38 Adam Wainwright
39 Dontrelle Willis

2003 Upper Deck USA Baseball

This 30-card factory set was issued at a SRP of $30 and featured 27 player cards along with two signature cards and one signed jersey card per factory set. This set honored players who were involved with the 2003 USA baseball team

as well as the coaches.

	MINT	NRMT
COMP.FACT.SET (30)	35.00	16.00
COMPLETE SET (27)	15.00	6.75
1 Justin Orenduff	.75	.35
2 Micah Owings	.75	.35
3 Steven Register	.75	.35
4 Huston Street	.75	.35
5 Justin Verlander	1.50	.70
6 Jered Weaver	5.00	2.20
7 Matt Campbell	.50	.23
8 Stephen Head	1.00	.45
9 Mark Romanczuk	.50	.23
10 Jeff Clement	2.00	.90
11 Mike Nickeas	.50	.23
12 Tyler Greene	.75	.35
13 Paul Janish	.50	.23
14 Jeff Larish	1.50	.70
15 Eric Patterson	.75	.35
16 Dustin Pedroia	.50	.23
17 Michael Griffin	.50	.23
18 Brent Lillibridge	.50	.23
19 Danny Putnam	.75	.35
20 Seth Smith	.75	.35
21 Ray Tanner CO	.50	.23
22 Dick Cooke CO	.50	.23
23 Mark Scalf CO	.50	.23
24 Mike Weathers CO	.50	.23
25 Team Card	.50	.23
26 Commemorative Card	.50	.23
27 Checklist	.50	.23

2003 Upper Deck USA Baseball Signatures Blue

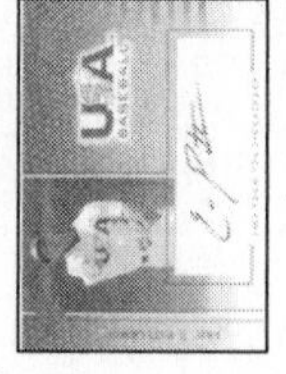

	MINT	NRMT
*BLUE AU: .75X TO 2X RED AU		
TWO BLUE/RED AUTOS PER FACTORY SET		
STATED PRINT RUN 250 SERIAL #'d SETS		
6 Jered Weaver	120.00	55.00

2003 Upper Deck USA Baseball Signatures Red

	MINT	NRMT
TWO BLUE/RED AUTOS PER FACTORY SET		
STATED PRINT RUN 750 SERIAL #'d SETS		
1 Justin Orenduff	10.00	4.50
2 Micah Owings	10.00	4.50
3 Steven Register	10.00	4.50
4 Huston Street	10.00	4.50
5 Justin Verlander	20.00	9.00
6 Jered Weaver	50.00	22.00
7 Matt Campbell	8.00	3.60
8 Stephen Head	15.00	6.75
9 Mark Romanczuk	8.00	3.60
10 Jeff Clement	25.00	11.00
11 Mike Nickeas	8.00	3.60
12 Tyler Greene	10.00	4.50
13 Paul Janish	8.00	3.60
14 Jeff Larish	20.00	9.00
15 Eric Patterson	10.00	4.50
16 Dustin Pedroia	8.00	3.60
17 Michael Griffin	8.00	3.60
18 Brent Lillibridge	8.00	3.60
19 Danny Putnam	10.00	4.50
20 Seth Smith	10.00	4.50

2003 Upper Deck USA Baseball Signed Jersey Blue

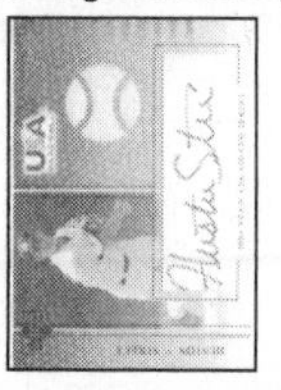

	MINT	NRMT
*BLUE JSY: .75X TO 2X RED JSY		
ONE BLUE/RED AU JSY PER FACTORY SET		
STATED PRINT RUN 150 SERIAL #'d SETS		
6 Jered Weaver	200.00	90.00

2003 Upper Deck USA Baseball Signed Jersey Red

	MINT	NRMT
ONE BLUE/RED AU JSY PER FACTORY SET		
STATED PRINT RUN 350 SERIAL #'d SETS		
1 Justin Orenduff	15.00	6.75
2 Micah Owings	15.00	6.75
3 Steven Register	15.00	6.75
4 Huston Street	15.00	6.75
5 Justin Verlander	25.00	11.00
6 Jered Weaver	80.00	36.00
7 Matt Campbell	10.00	4.50
8 Stephen Head	20.00	9.00
9 Mark Romanczuk	10.00	4.50
10 Jeff Clement	40.00	18.00
11 Mike Nickeas	10.00	4.50
12 Tyler Greene	15.00	6.75
13 Paul Janish	10.00	4.50
14 Jeff Larish	25.00	11.00
15 Eric Patterson	15.00	6.75
16 Dustin Pedroia	10.00	4.50
17 Michael Griffin	10.00	4.50
18 Brent Lillibridge	10.00	4.50
19 Danny Putnam	15.00	6.75
20 Seth Smith	15.00	6.75

2003-04 Just Prospects '04 Preview

	Nm-Mt	Ex-Mt
COMPLETE SET (10)	5.00	1.50
ISSUED ONLY TO DISTRIBUTORS		
STATED PRINT RUN 15,000 SETS		
*BLACK: 5X TO 12X BASIC 04 PREVIEW		
BLACK ISSUED ONLY TO DISTRIBUTORS		
BLACK PRINT RUN 50 SERIAL #'d SETS		
*GOLD: 1.5X TO 4X BASIC 04 PREVIEW		
GOLD ISSUED IN FACTORY SET FORM		
GOLD INITIALLY AVAIL.TO CLUB MEMBERS		
GOLD PRINT RUN 1000 SERIAL #'d SETS		
*SILVER: .6X TO 1.5X BASIC 04 PREVIEW		
SILVER ISSUED ONLY TO DISTRIBUTORS		

SILVER PRINT RUN 5000 SETS		
1 Robinson Cano	.50	.15
2 Franklin Gutierrez	1.50	.45
3 Felix Hernandez	1.50	.45
4 Edwin Jackson	1.50	.45
5 Chris Lubanski	1.00	.30
6 Lastings Milledge	1.50	.45
7 Greg Miller	.50	.15
8 Dioner Navarro	1.00	.30
9 Mark Prior	3.00	.90
10 Brad Sullivan	.75	.23

2003-04 Just Prospects '04 Preview Autographs

Nm-Mt Ex-Mt

ISSUED DIRECTLY FROM MANUFACTURER
STATED PRINT RUN 50 SERIAL #'d SETS
BLACK ISSUED FROM MANUFACTURER
BLACK PRINT RUN 25 SERIAL #'d SETS
NO BLACK PRICING DUE TO SCARCITY
GOLD ISSUED IN FACTORY SET FORM
GOLD INITIALLY AVAIL.TO CLUB MEMBERS
GOLD PRINT RUN 100 SERIAL #'d SETS
1 Robinson Cano
2 Franklin Gutierrez
3 Felix Hernandez
4 Edwin Jackson
5 Chris Lubanski
6 Lastings Milledge
7 Greg Miller
8 Dioner Navarro
9 Mark Prior
10 Brad Sullivan

MINOR LEAGUE TEAM SETS

1972 Cedar Rapids Cardinals TCMA

This set is considered complete at 29 cards. The team photo card number 30 was a late issue and is very scarce. The regular cards in the set measure 2-1/8" X 3-1/4" and are black and white. The team photo card measures 4-15/16" X 3-7/16" and is also black and white. We have priced the set with and without the team card.

COMPLETE SET (29) 250.00 100.00

1972 San Francisco Seals 1954 Aldama

These cards were drawn by sports artist Carl Aldana and honored members of the 1954 San Francisco Seals. According to published reports at the time, only 100 sets were produced and they were available from the artist for $2 per set.

COMPLETE SET 25.00 10.00

1973 Cedar Rapids Astros TCMA

The cards measure 2-3/16" X 3-5/8" and are black and white.

COMPLETE SET (28) 110.00 45.00

1973 Tacoma Twins Caruso

These cards measure 2-3/8" X 3-1/8" and have blank backs.

COMPLETE SET (21) 20.00 8.00

1973 Trois-Rivieres Aigles

These cards which measure 7" by 8 3/4" are black and white and are blankbacked. The set features members of the Cincinnati Reds farm system and we have sequenced them in alphabetical order.

COMPLETE SET 30.00 12.00

1973 Wichita Aeros J.P. Kelly Bank

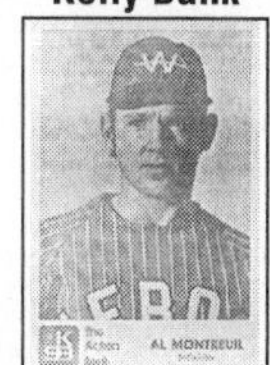

These cards measure 3-3/4"X 5" and are black and white. Variation cards of Jim Hibbs number 4 and Ron Tompkins number 17 exist with their names printed with both small and large lettering.

COMPLETE SET (19) 100.00 40.00
COMPLETE SET (21) 125.00 50.00

1974 Albuquerque Dukes Caruso

COMPLETE SET (16) 25.00 10.00

1974 Albuquerque Dukes Team Issue

These cards which measure 2 1/2" by 4" feature members of the 1974 Albuquerque Dukes and were given away at the June 1st, 1974 game. According to published reports, 2,000 sets were produced.

COMPLETE SET (23) 400.00 160.00

1974 Cedar Rapids Astros TCMA

COMPLETE SET (28) 150.00 60.00

1974 Gastonia Rangers TCMA

Approximately 1,100 sets were produced. Black and White

COMPLETE SET (24) 150.00 60.00

1974 Hawaii Islanders Caruso

COMPLETE SET (8) 20.00 8.00

1974 Phoenix Giants Caruso

COMPLETE SET (11) 18.00 7.25

1974 Sacramento Solons Caruso

COMPLETE SET (18) 20.00 8.00

1974 Salt Lake City Angels Caruso

COMPLETE SET (10) 20.00 8.00

1974 Spokane Indians Caruso

COMPLETE SET (18) 20.00 8.00

1974 Syracuse Chiefs Team Issue

This 1974 Syracuse Chiefs team issued set features major league players as well as minor league players from the Yankee organization. The cards are black and white and measure 4" X 5". The cards were inserted one at a time inside the Syracuse Chiefs minor league programs. Card number 7 was a late addition to the set.

COMPLETE SET (29) 150.00 60.00
COMPLETE SET (30) 200.00 80.00

1974 Tacoma Twins Caruso

COMPLETE SET (27) 20.00 8.00

1974 Wichita Aeros One Day Film

COMPLETE SET (29) 125.00 50.00
COMPLETE SET (28) 100.00 40.00

1975 Albuquerque Dukes Caruso

Any of the 1975 minor league sets issued by Caruso were originally available for $5 per.

COMPLETE SET (21) 28.00 11.00

1975 Anderson Rangers TCMA

Any 1975 TCMA set was available direct from TCMA for $3 in 1975.

COMPLETE SET (25) 60.00 24.00

1975 Appleton Foxes TCMA

COMPLETE SET (29) 50.00 20.00

1975 Burlington Bees TCMA

COMPLETE SET (29) 60.00 24.00

1975 Cedar Rapids Giants TCMA

COMPLETE SET (32) 75.00 30.00

1975 Clinton Pilots TCMA

COMPLETE SET (30) 100.00 40.00

1975 Dubuque Packers TCMA

COMPLETE SET (32) 60.00 24.00

1975 Fort Lauderdale Yanks Sussman

This set is considered complete at 29 cards. Card number 22, Jesus Figueroa, is a short-print as it was used as the key card for collectors to win the prizes offered. These were inserted into progams.

COMPLETE SET (29) 75.00 30.00

1975 Hawaii Islanders Caruso

COMPLETE SET (21) 25.00 10.00

1975 International League All Stars Broder

COMPLETE SET (36) 50.00 20.00

1975 International League All-Stars TCMA

COMPLETE SET (31) 25.00 10.00

1975 Iowa Oaks TCMA

This set was issued for photo ball night on May 20, 1975.

COMPLETE SET (21) 150.00 60.00

1975 Lafayette Drillers TCMA

COMPLETE SET (32) 150.00 60.00

1975 Lynchburg Rangers TCMA

COMPLETE SET (26) 50.00 20.00

1975 Oakland Oaks 20th Anniversary

This 36-card set features black-and-white photos of Minor League players. The cards are unnumbered and checklisted below in alphabetical order. Doug McWilliams, who did the original photography for this set, also produced it 20 years later.

COMPLETE SET (36) 30.00 12.00

1975 Oklahoma City 89ers Team Issue

5,000 sets were printed. Cards were black and white and measured 2 1/2" by 3 1/2".

COMPLETE SET (24) 25.00 10.00

1975 Omaha Royals Team Issue

COMPLETE SET (18) 100.00 40.00

1975 Pacific Coast League All-Stars Broder

COMPLETE SET (36) 100.00 40.00
COMPLETE SET (37) 125.00 50.00

1975 Phoenix Giants Caruso

COMPLETE SET (21) 25.00 10.00

1975 Phoenix Giants Circle K

Noted sports hobbyist Mike Cramer printed this set. It was originally available from the team for $4. These cards measure the standard-size.

COMPLETE SET (26) 10.00 4.00

1975 Quad City Angels TCMA

COMPLETE SET (34) 75.00 30.00

1975 Sacramento Solons Caruso

COMPLETE SET (22) 30.00 12.00

1975 Salt Lake City Caruso

COMPLETE SET (20) 25.00 10.00

1975 San Antonio Brewers TCMA

COMPLETE SET (22) 40.00 16.00

1975 Shreveport Captains TCMA

COMPLETE SET (23) 60.00 24.00

1975 Spokane Indians Caruso

COMPLETE SET (21) 20.00 8.00

1975 Syracuse Chiefs Team Issue

This 1975 Syracuse Chiefs team issued set features major league players as well as minor league players from the Yankee organization. The cards are black and white and measure 2'1/2" X 3'1/2". The cards were inserted one at a time inside the Syracuse Chiefs minor league programs. Rich Bladt was a late addition to the set.

COMPLETE SET (24) 100.00 40.00
COMPLETE SET (25) 150.00 60.00

1975 Tacoma Twins KMMO

COMPLETE SET (21) 20.00 8.00

1975 Tidewater Tides Team Issue

COMPLETE SET (24) 150.00 60.00

1975 Tucson Toros Caruso

COMPLETE SET (21) 25.00 10.00

1975 Tucson Toros Team Issue

This set was produced by long time hobbyist Wayne Grove. The cards measure 2 1/2" by 3 1/2.

COMPLETE SET (24) 40.00 16.00

1975 Tulsa Oilers 7-11

These were available either from local 7-11 stores on a one per week basis or from the team directly for $4. A placemat featuring all 24 players in this set was also issued.
COMPLETE SET (24)............. 100.00 40.00

1975 Waterbury Dodgers TCMA

Approximately 1,100 sets were produced. Black and White
COMPLETE SET (22)............... 80.00 32.00

1975 Waterloo Royals TCMA

COMPLETE SET (34)............. 100.00 40.00
COMPLETE SET (35)............. 175.00 70.00

1975 West Palm Beach Expos Sussman

This 32-card standard-size set of the 1975 West Palm Beach Expos, a Class A Florida State League affiliate of the Montreal Expos, features white-bordered posed black-and-white player photos on its fronts. The team name appears above the photo, while the player's name and position are printed on the bottom. The backs are blank. The cards are numbered on the front in the upper left corner.
COMPLETE SET (29)............... 30.00 12.00
COMPLETE SET (32)............... 40.00 16.00

1976 Appleton Foxes TCMA

COMPLETE SET (29)............... 60.00 24.00

1976 Arkansas Travelers TCMA

Approximately 1,100 sets were produced. Black and White.
COMPLETE SET (12)............. 175.00 70.00

1976 Asheville Tourists TCMA

COMPLETE SET (25)............... 75.00 30.00

1976 Batavia Trojans Team Issue

COMPLETE SET (29)............. 150.00 60.00

1976 Baton Rouge Cougars TCMA

COMPLETE SET (21)............... 80.00 32.00

1976 Burlington Bees TCMA

COMPLETE SET (33)............... 50.00 20.00

1976 Cedar Rapids Giants TCMA

COMPLETE SET (37)............... 40.00 16.00
COMPLETE SET (39)............... 80.00 32.00

1976 Clinton Pilots TCMA

COMPLETE SET (35)............. 125.00 50.00
COMPLETE SET (37)............. 150.00 60.00

1976 Dubuque Packers TCMA

COMPLETE SET (40)............... 75.00 30.00

1976 Fort Lauderdale Yanks Sussman

This set was available from the team for $4.
COMPLETE SET (30)............... 80.00 32.00

1976 Hawaii Islanders Caruso

All the 1976 sets produced for PCL teams by Frank Caruso were available from him for $5 each.
COMPLETE SET (21)............... 30.00 12.00

1976 Indianapolis Indians Team Issue

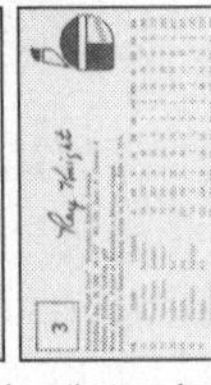

This set was available from the team for $3.25 when it was orginally issued.
COMPLETE SET (26)............... 40.00 16.00

1976 Oklahoma City 89ers Team Issue

These 2 1/2" by 3 1/2" black and white cards were issued at the Oklahoma City 89ers game on July 26th to the first 2,000 attendees. The backs have vital stats, career highlights and the player's record.
COMPLETE SET (24)............. 120.00 47.50

1976 Omaha Royals Top Trophies

COMPLETE SET (27)............. 100.00 40.00

1976 Phoenix Giants Caruso

COMPLETE SET (20)............... 30.00 12.00

1976 Phoenix Giants Coca Cola

This set was available from the Phoenix Giants for $4. These larger premium photos were also available for five coke caps and 25 cents each.
COMPLETE SET (24)............... 15.00 6.00

1976 Phoenix Giants Cramer

3,000 of these sets were printed. This set was originially available from the producer for $3.50 per set.
COMPLETE SET (24)............... 30.00 12.00

1976 Phoenix Giants Valley National Bank

These cards are slightly oversized.
COMPLETE SET (24)............... 25.00 10.00

1976 Quad City Angels TCMA

Card number 21 Manuel Mercedes is a scarce late issue.
COMPLETE SET (39)............. 125.00 50.00
Card number 21 Manuel Mercedes is a scarce late issue.
COMPLETE SET (40)............. 175.00 70.00

1976 Sacramento Solons Caruso

COMPLETE SET (23)............... 30.00 12.00

1976 Salt Lake City Gulls Caruso

COMPLETE SET (22)............... 15.00 6.00

1976 San Antonio Brewers Team Issue

COMPLETE SET (26)............... 80.00 32.00

1976 Seattle Rainiers Cramer

B/W cards; measure 2" by 3", blank backs.
COMPLETE SET (20)............... 20.00 8.00

1976 Shreveport Captains TCMA

Card number 23 Barry Weinberg was a late issue. The oversized team photo card (5 3/8" by 3 1/2") is considered very scarce.
COMPLETE SET (23)............... 50.00 20.00
COMPLETE SET (24)............. 100.00 40.00
COMPLETE SET (25)............. 200.00 80.00

1976 Spokane Indians Caruso

COMPLETE SET (21)............... 30.00 12.00

1976 Tacoma Twins Dairy Queen

Frank Caruso produced this set for the Tacoma Twins. At the end of the season, these sets were available from the producer for $4.50 a set.
COMPLETE SET (24)............... 30.00 12.00

1976 Tucson Toros Caruso

COMPLETE SET (20)............... 15.00 6.00

1976 Tucson Toros Team Issue

This set was produced by long time hobbyist Wayne Grove. These black and white cards measure 2 1/2" by 3 1/2". These cards were given out on May 28th and the players were made available to autograph these cards.
COMPLETE SET (24)............... 20.00 8.00

1976 Tulsa Oilers Goof's Pants

This set was originally available from the Tulsa Oilers for $5.
COMPLETE SET (26)............. 250.00 100.00

1976 Waterloo Royals TCMA

COMPLETE SET (33)............... 75.00 30.00

1976 Wausau Mets TCMA

COMPLETE SET (25)............... 80.00 32.00

1976 Williamsport Tomahawks TCMA

1,000 sets were produced. According to published reports at the time: Mike Dolf, Tim Norrid and Bob Servoss may have been produced in smaller quantities than the other cards.
COMPLETE SET (23)............... 60.00 24.00

1977 Appleton Foxes TCMA

This 30-card standard-size set of the 1977 Appleton Foxes, a Class A Midwest League affiliate of the Chicago White Sox, features white-bordered posed black-and-white player photos on its fronts. The player's name, position and Foxes logo appear in the orange section near the bottom. The league affiliation appears across an upper corner. The plain white back carries the McDonalds logo and the words "Appleton Foxes" in bold letters. The cards are unnumbered and checklisted below in alphabetical order. Card number 16B Orestes Minoso Jr. is a late issue.
COMPLETE SET (30)............. 100.00 40.00
COMPLETE SET (29)............... 60.00 24.00

1977 Arkansas Travelers TCMA

This 21-card standard-size set of the 1977 Arkansas Travelers, a Class AA Texas League affiliate of the St. Louis Cardinals, features white-bordered posed black-and-white player photos on its fronts. The player's name, position and Travelers logo appear in the orange section near the bottom. The league affiliation appears across an upper corner. The plain white back carries the player's name, position and biography. The cards are unnumbered and checklisted below in alphabetical order. Several of the players below have variations.
COMPLETE SET (12)............... 80.00 32.00
COMPLETE SET (21)............. 200.00 80.00

1977 Asheville Tourists TCMA

This 29-card standard-size set of the 1977 Asheville Tourists, a Class A Western Carolinas League affiliate of the Texas Rangers, features white-bordered posed black-and-white player photos on its fronts. The player's name, position and Tourists logo appear in the orange section near the bottom. The league affiliation appears across an upper corner. The plain white back carries the player's name, position and biography. The cards are unnumbered and checklisted below in alphabetical order.
COMPLETE SET (29)............... 30.00 12.00

1977 Bristol Red Sox TCMA

This 20-card standard-size set of the 1977 Bristol Red Sox, a Class AA Eastern League affiliate of the Boston Red Sox, features white-bordered posed black-and-white player photos on its fronts. The player's name, position and Red Sox logo appear in the orange section near the bottom. The league affiliation appears across an upper corner. The plain white back carries the words "Bristol Red Sox" in large letters along with the player's name, position and biography. The cards are unnumbered and checklisted below in alphabetical order.
COMPLETE SET (20)............. 200.00 80.00

1977 Burlington Bees TCMA

This 27-card standard-size set of the 1977 Burlington Bees, a Class A Midwest League affiliate of the Milwaukee Brewers, features white-bordered posed black-and-white player photos on its fronts. The player's name, position and Bees logo appear in the orange section near the bottom. The league affiliation appears across an upper corner. The plain white back carries the player's name, position and biography. The cards are unnumbered and checklisted below in alphabetical order. Card #12 Gary Halls and #17 Candy Mercado are late issues.
COMPLETE SET (25)............... 60.00 24.00
COMPLETE SET (27)............. 100.00 40.00

1977 Cedar Rapids Giants TCMA

This 25-card standard-size set of the 1977 Cedar Rapids Giants, a Class A Midwest League affiliate of the San Francisco Giants, features white-bordered posed black-and-white player photos on its fronts. The player's name, position and Giants logo appear in the orange section near the bottom. The league affiliation appears across an upper corner. The plain white back carries the player's name, position and biography. The cards are unnumbered and checklisted below in alphabetical order. John Laubhan was a late addition to the set.
COMPLETE SET (24)............... 75.00 30.00
COMPLETE SET (25)............. 150.00 60.00

1977 Charleston Patriots TCMA

This 25-card standard-size set of the 1977 Charleston Patriots, a Class A Western Carolinas League affiliate of the Pittsburgh Pirates, features white-bordered posed black-and-white player photos on its fronts. The player's name, position and Patriots logo appear in the orange section near the bottom. The league affiliation appears across an upper corner. The plain white back carries the words "Charleston Patriots" in large letters followed by the player's name, position and biography. The cards are unnumbered and checklisted below in alphabetical order.
COMPLETE SET (25)............... 50.00 20.00

1977 Clinton Dodgers TCMA

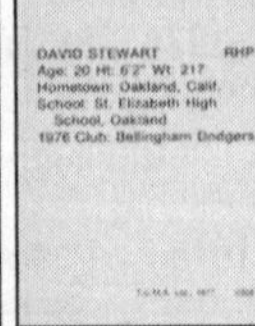

This 29-card standard-size set of the 1977 Clinton Dodgers, a Class A Midwest League affiliate of the Los Angeles Dodgers, features white-bordered posed black-and-white player photos on its fronts. The player's name, position and Dodgers logo appear in the orange section near the bottom. The league affiliation appears across an upper corner. The plain white back carries the player's name, position and biography. The cards are unnumbered and checklisted below in alphabetical order. Approximately 1,100 sets were produced.
COMPLETE SET (29)............. 120.00 47.50

1977 Cocoa Astros TCMA

This 25-card standard-size set of the 1977 Cocoa Astros, a Class A Florida State League affiliate of the Houston Astros, features white-bordered posed black-and-white player photos on its fronts. The player's name, position and Astros logo appear in the orange section near the bottom. The league affiliation appears across an upper corner. The cards are unnumbered and checklisted below in alphabetical order.
COMPLETE SET (25)............... 40.00 16.00

1977 Columbus Clippers TCMA

This 24-card standard-size set of the 1977 Columbus Clippers, a Class AAA International League affiliate of the New York Yankees, features white-bordered posed black-and-white player photos on its fronts. The player's name and Clippers logo appear in the orange section near the bottom. The league affiliation appears across an upper corner. The plain white back carries the 1977 Clippers home schedule. The cards are unnumbered and checklisted below in alphabetical order. Approximately 1,100 sets were produced.
COMPLETE SET (22)............. 250.00 100.00
COMPLETE SET W/COR (24) . 300.00 120.00

1977 Daytona Beach Islanders TCMA

This 27-card standard-size set of the 1977 Daytona Beach Islanders, a Class A Florida State League affiliate of the Kansas City Royals, features white-bordered posed black-and-white player photos on its fronts. The player's name, position and Islanders logo appear in the orange section near the bottom. The league affiliation appears across an upper corner. The plain white back carries the words "Daytona Beach Islanders" in large letters followed by the player's name, position and biography. The cards are unnumbered and checklisted below in alphabetical order.
COMPLETE SET (27)............... 40.00 16.00

1977 Evansville Triplets TCMA

This 25-card standard-size set of the 1977 Evansville Triplets, a Class AAA American Association affiliate of the Detroit Tigers, features white-bordered posed black-and-white player photos on its fronts. The player's name, position and Triplets logo appear in the orange section near the bottom. The league affiliation appears across an upper corner. The plain white back carries the player's name, position and biography along with the words "Evansville Triplets" across the top of the card. The cards are unnumbered and checklisted below in alphabetical order.
COMPLETE SET (25)............. 400.00 160.00

1977 Fort Lauderdale Yankees Sussman

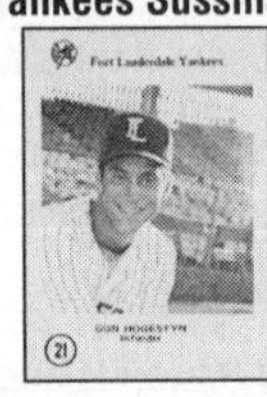

COMPLETE SET (31)............... 80.00 32.00

1977 Holyoke Millers TCMA

This 26-card standard-size set of the 1977 Holyoke Millers, a Class AA Eastern League affiliate of the Milwaukee Brewers, features white-bordered posed black-and-white player photos on its fronts. The player's name, position and Millers logo appear in the orange section near the bottom. The league affiliation appears across an upper corner. The cards are unnumbered and checklisted below in alphabetical order.
COMPLETE SET (26)............... 25.00 10.00

1977 Indianapolis Indians Team Issue

This set was originally available from the team for $3.50 each. Uncut sheets were also issued and these were available for $7 at time of issue.
COMPLETE SET (27)............... 20.00 8.00

1977 Jacksonville Suns TCMA

This 22-card standard-size set of the 1977 Jacksonville Suns, a Class AA Southern League affiliate of the Kansas City Royals, features white-bordered posed black-and-white player photos on its fronts. The player's name, position and Suns logo appear in the orange section near the bottom. The league affiliation appears across an upper corner. The plain white back carries the words "Jacksonville Suns" logo in bold letters. The cards are unnumbered and checklisted below in alphabetical order.
COMPLETE SET (22)............... 75.00 30.00

1977 Lodi Dodgers TCMA

This 25-card standard-size set of the 1977 Lodi Dodgers, a Class A Carolina League affiliate of the Los Angeles Dodgers, features white-bordered posed black-and-white player photos on its fronts. The player's name, position and Dodgers logo appear in the orange section near the bottom. The league affiliation appears across an upper corner. The plain white back carries the player's name, position and biography along with the "Lodi Dodgers" logo in bold letters. The cards are unnumbered and checklisted below in alphabetical order.
COMPLETE SET (25)............... 80.00 32.00

1977 Lynchburg Mets TCMA

This 34-card standard-size set of the 1977 Lynchburg Mets, a Class A Carolina League affiliate of the New York Mets, features white-bordered posed black-and-white player photos on its fronts. The player's name, position and Mets logo appear in the orange section near the bottom. The league affiliation appears across an upper corner. The cards are unnumbered and checklisted below in alphabetical order. This set contains a few of variations; including one recently discovered of Bob Healy without a position or name.
COMPLETE SET (32)............. 200.00 80.00
COMPLETE SET (33)............. 300.00 120.00
COMPLETE SET (34)............. 400.00 160.00
COMPLETE SET (35).........................
COMPLETE SET (30)............. 100.00 40.00

1977 Modesto A's Chong

This 22-card blank-backed set of the 1977 Modesto A's, a Class A California League affiliate of the Oakland Athletics, features white-bordered posed black-and-white player photos on its fronts. This issue includes the minor league card debut of Rickey Henderson. Approximately 400 sets were produced.
COMPLETE SET (22)........... 1200.00 475.00

1977 Newark Co-Pilots TCMA

This 29-card standard-size set of the 1977 Newark Co-Pilots, a Class A New York-Penn League affiliate of the Milwaukee Brewers, features white-bordered posed black-and-white player photos on its fronts. The player's name, position and Pilots logo appear in the orange section near the bottom. The league affiliation appears across an upper corner. The plain white back carries the words "Newark Co-Pilots" in large letters followed by the player's name, position and biography. The cards are unnumbered and checklisted below in alphabetical order. Approximately 1,100 sets were produced.
COMPLETE SET (29)............... 50.00 20.00

1977 Orlando Twins TCMA

This 24-card standard-size set of the 1977 Orlando Twins, a Class AA Southern League affiliate of the Minnesota Twins, features white-bordered posed black-and-white player photos on its fronts. The player's name, position and Twins logo appear in the orange section near the bottom. The league affiliation appears across an upper corner. The plain white back carries the words "Orlando Twins" in large letters followed by the player's name, position and biography. The cards are unnumbered and checklisted below in alphabetical order. Both Terry Felton variation cards number 9A and number 9B are late issues.
COMPLETE SET (22)............... 50.00 20.00
COMPLETE SET W/ONE FELTON (23) 80.00 32.00
COMPLETE SET W/BOTH FELTON (24) 100.0040.00

1977 Phoenix Giants Coke Premium

COMPLETE SET (24)............... 25.00 10.00

1977 Phoenix Giants Cramer Coke

The four sets Mike Cramer produced for PCL teams in 1977 were available upon issue fo $9.50 for the group.
COMPLETE SET (24)............... 10.00 4.00

1977 Phoenix Giants Valley National Bank

COMPLETE SET (24)............... 30.00 12.00

1977 Quad City Angels TCMA

This 29-card standard-size set of the 1977 Quad City Angels, a Class A Midwest League affiliate of the California Angels, features white bordered posed black-and-white player photos on its fronts. The player's name, position and Angels logo appear in the orange section near the bottom. The league affiliation appears across an upper corner. The plain white back carries the player's name, position, biography and the words "Quad City Angels" in bold letters. The cards are unnumbered and checklisted below in alphabetical order.
COMPLETE SET (29)............... 50.00 20.00

1977 Reading Phillies TCMA

This 23-card standard-size set of the 1977 Reading Phillies, a Class AA Eastern League

affiliate of the Philadelphia Phillies, features white-bordered posed black-and-white player photos on its fronts. The player's name, position and Phillies logo appear in the orange section near the bottom. The league affiliation appears across an upper corner. The plain white back carries the words "Reading Phillies" in large letters followed by the player's name, position and biography. The cards are unnumbered and checklisted below in alphabetical order.
COMPLETE SET (23)............. 300.00 120.00

1977 Rochester Red Wings McCurdy's

COMPLETE SET (24)............. 150.00 60.00

1977 Salem Pirates TCMA

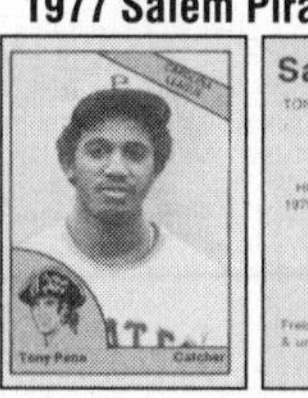

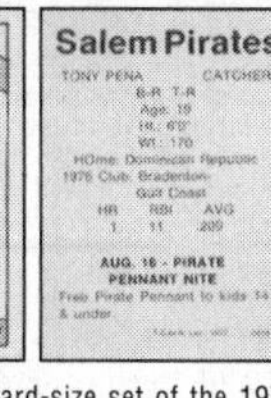

This 35-card standard-size set of the 1977 Salem Pirates, a Class A Carolina League affiliate of the Pittsburgh Pirates, features white-bordered posed black-and-white player photos on its fronts. The player's name, position and Pirates logo appear in the orange section near the bottom. The league affiliation appears across an upper corner. The plain white back carries the words "Salem Pirates" in large letters followed by the player's name, position and biography. The cards are unnumbered and checklisted below in alphabetical order. This set contains numerous variations which are listed below.
COMPLETE SET (24)............. 150.00 60.00

1977 Salt Lake City Gulls Cramer

This set was available from the team at the time of issue for $4.
COMPLETE SET (24)............... 10.00 4.00

1977 San Jose Missions Mr. Chef's

Long time hobbyist Barry Colla produced this set and upon issue this set was available for $5.50.
COMPLETE SET (25)............... 25.00 10.00

1977 Shreveport Captains TCMA

This 23-card standard-size set of the 1977 Shreveport Captains, a Class AA Texas League affiliate of the Pittsburgh Pirates, features white-bordered posed black-and-white player photos on its fronts. The player's name, position and Captains logo appear in the orange section near the bottom. The league affiliation appears across an upper corner. The cards are unnumbered and checklisted below in alphabetical order.
COMPLETE SET (23)............. 120.00 47.50

1977 Spartanburg Phillies TCMA

This 24-card standard-size set of the 1977 Spartanburg Phillies, a Class A Western Carolinas League affiliate of the Philadelphia Phillies, features white-bordered posed black-and-white player photos on its fronts. The player's name, position and Phillies logo appear in the orange section near the bottom. The league affiliation appears across an upper corner. The plain white back carries the Spartanburg Phillies 1977 schedule.
COMPLETE SET (24)............. 125.00 50.00

1977 Spokane Indians Cramer

These sets were originally available from the team for $3.75.
COMPLETE SET (24)............. 15.00 6.00

1977 St. Petersburg Cardinals TCMA

This 26-card standard-size set of the 1977 St. Petersburg Cardinals, a Class A Florida State League affiliate of the St. Louis Cardinals, features white-bordered posed black-and-white player photos on its fronts. The player's name, position and Cardinals logo appear in the orange section near the bottom. The league affiliation appears across an upper corner. The plain white back carries the St. Petersburg Cardinals 1977 home games schedule. NNO Mike Nagle was a late issue to the set.
COMPLETE SET (25)............... 80.00 32.00
COMPLETE SET (26)............. 150.00 60.00

1977 Tacoma Twins Dairy Queen

The cards measure 2 3/4" by 3 9/16" and have blank backs. Card numbers 8 Tim Loiberg, 16B Rob Wilfong and 24B Jeff Holly were not issued with the original set and thus not considered part of the regular set. The duplication of numbers have to do with the consideration that uniforms numbers were used to Identify the cards in this set. This set, without the unissued cards, were available upon issue from the team for $5.
COMPLETE SET (27)............... 30.00 12.00
COMPLETE SET (30)............... 50.00 20.00

1977 Tucson Toros Cramer

These sets were available from the team in year of issue for $3.
COMPLETE SET (24)............... 10.00 4.00

1977 Visalia Oaks TCMA

This 17-card standard-size set of the 1977 Visalia Oaks, a Class A California League affiliate of the Minnesota Twins, features white-bordered posed black-and-white player photos on its fronts. The player's name, position and Oaks logo appear in the orange section near the bottom. The league affiliation appears across an upper corner. The plain white back carries the words "Visalia Oaks" in large letters followed by the player's name, position and biography. The cards are unnumbered and checklisted below in alphabetical order.
COMPLETE SET (17)............... 30.00 12.00

1977 Waterloo Indians TCMA

This 32-card standard-size set of the 1977 Waterloo Indians, a Class A Midwest League affiliate of the Cleveland Indians, features white-bordered posed black-and-white player photos on its fronts. The player's name, position and Indians logo appear in the orange section near the bottom. The league affiliation appears across an upper corner. The plain white back carries the player's name and position followed by a biography. The cards are unnumbered and checklisted below in alphabetical order. Card numbers 2 John Arnold and 23 Dave Strickfaden are late issues. Card number 3B Thomas Brennan with the corrected Midwest League affiliation on front is considered scarce.
COMPLETE SET (29)............... 60.00 24.00

1977 Wausau Mets TCMA

This 24-card standard-size set of the 1977 Wausau Mets, a Class A Midwest League Independent, features white-bordered posed black-and-white player photos on its fronts. The player's name, position and Mets logo appear in the orange section near the bottom. The league affiliation appears across an upper corner. The plain white back carries the words "Wausau Mets" in large letters followed by the player's name, position and biography. The cards are unnumbered and checklisted below in alphabetical order.
COMPLETE SET (24)............... 60.00 24.00

1977 West Haven Yankees TCMA

This 25-card standard-size set of the 1977 West Haven Yankees, a Class AA Eastern League affiliate of the Oakland Athletics, features white-bordered posed black-and-white player photos on its fronts. The player's name, position and Yankees logo appear in the orange section near the bottom. The league affiliation appears across an upper corner. The plain white back carries the words "West Haven Yankees" in big letters across the top. The cards are unnumbered and checklisted below in alphabetical order.
COMPLETE SET (25)............. 150.00 60.00

1978 Appleton Foxes TCMA

This 25-card standard-size set of the 1978 Appleton Foxes, a Class A Midwest League affiliate of the Chicago White Sox, features white-bordered posed black-and-white player photos on its fronts. The player's name and Foxes logo appear in the green section near the bottom. The league affiliation appears across an upper corner. The plain white horizontal back carries the words "The Minors - 1978 Appleton Foxes" at the top. The cards are unnumbered and checklisted below in alphabetical order.
COMPLETE SET (25)............... 50.00 20.00

1978 Arkansas Travelers TCMA

This 23-card standard-size set of the 1978 Arkansas Travelers, a Class AA Texas League affiliate of the St. Louis Cardinals, features white-bordered posed black-and-white player photos on its fronts. The player's name and Cardinals logo appear in the green section near the bottom. The league affiliation appears across an upper corner. The plain white horizontal back carries the words "The Minors - 1978 Arkansas Travelers" at the top. The cards are unnumbered and checklisted below in alphabetical order. Approximately 1,100 sets were produced.
COMPLETE SET (23)............. 250.00 100.00

1978 Asheville Tourists TCMA

This 29-card standard-size set of the 1978 Asheville Tourists, a Class A Western Carolinas League affiliate of the Texas Rangers, features white-bordered posed black-and-white player photos on its fronts. The player's name and Tourists logo appear in the green section near the bottom. The league affiliation appears across an upper corner. The plain white horizontal back carries the words "The Minors - 1978 Asheville Tourists" at the top. The cards are unnumbered and checklisted below in alphabetical order.
COMPLETE SET (29)............... 40.00 16.00

1978 Burlington Bees TCMA

This 28-card standard-size set of the 1978 Burlington Bees, a Class A Midwest League affiliate of the Milwaukee Brewers, features white-bordered posed black-and-white player photos on its fronts. The player's name and Bees logo appear in the green section near the bottom. The league affiliation appears across an upper corner. The plain white horizontal back carries the words "The Minors - 1978 Burlington Bees" at the top. The cards are unnumbered and checklisted below in alphabetical order.
COMPLETE SET (28)............... 50.00 20.00

1978 Cedar Rapids Giants TCMA

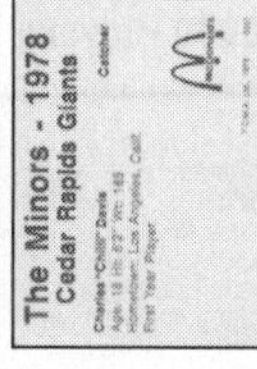

This 29-card standard-size set of the 1978 Cedar Rapids Giants, a Class A Midwest League affiliate of the San Francisco Giants, features white-bordered posed black-and-white player photos on its fronts. The player's name and Giants logo appear in the green section near the bottom. The league affiliation appears across an upper corner. The plain white horizontal back carries the words "The Minors - 1978 Cedar Rapids Giants" at the top. The cards are unnumbered and checklisted below in alphabetical order.
COMPLETE SET (29)............. 120.00 47.50

1978 Charleston Charlies TCMA

This 20-card standard-size set of the 1978 Charleston Charlies, a Class AAA International League affiliate of the Houston Astros, features white-bordered posed color player photos on its fronts. The white back carries the year, league, team name, the player's name, position, biography and statistics. The cards are unnumbered and checklisted below in alphabetical order.
COMPLETE SET (20)............... 20.00 8.00

1978 Charleston Pirates TCMA

This 24-card standard-size set of the 1978 Charleston Pirates, a Class A Western Carolinas League affiliate of the Pittsburgh Pirates, features white-bordered posed black-and-white player photos on its fronts. The player's name and Pirates logo appear in the green section near the bottom. The league affiliation appears across an upper corner. The plain white horizontal back carries the words "The Minors - 1978 Charleston Pirates" at the top. The cards are unnumbered and checklisted below in alphabetical order.
COMPLETE SET (24)............... 30.00 12.00

1978 Clinton Dodgers TCMA

This 33-card standard-size set of the 1978 Clinton Dodgers, a Class A Midwest League affiliate of the Los Angeles Dodgers, features white-bordered posed black-and-white player photos on its fronts. The player's name and Dodgers logo appear in the green section near the bottom. The league affiliation appears across an upper corner. The plain white horizontal back carries the words "The Minors - 1978 Clinton Dodgers" at the top. The cards are unnumbered and checklisted below in alphabetical order. Approximately 1,100 sets were produced.
COMPLETE SET (33)............... 50.00 20.00

1978 Columbus Clippers TCMA

This 27-card standard-size set of the 1978 Columbus Clippers, a Class AAA International League affiliate of the Pittsburgh Pirates, features white-bordered posed color player photos on its fronts. The white back carries the year, league, team name, the player's name, position, biography and statistics. The cards are unnumbered and checklisted below in alphabetical order.
COMPLETE SET (27)............... 30.00 12.00

1978 Daytona Beach Astros TCMA

This 26-card standard-size set of the 1978 Daytona Beach Astros, a Class A Florida State League affiliate of the Houston Astros, features white-bordered posed black-and-white player photos on its fronts. The player's name and Astros logo appear in the green section near the bottom. The league affiliation appears across an upper corner. The plain white horizontal back carries the words "The Minors - 1978 Daytona Beach Astros" at the top. The cards are unnumbered and checklisted below in alphabetical order.
COMPLETE SET (26)............... 25.00 10.00

1978 Dunedin Blue Jays TCMA

This 27-card standard-size set of the 1978 Dunedin Blue Jays, a Class A Florida State League affiliate of the Toronto Blue Jays, features white-bordered posed black-and-white player photos on its fronts. The player's name and Blue Jays logo appear in the green section near the bottom. The league affiliation appears across an upper corner. The plain white horizontal back carries the words "The Minors - 1978 Dunedin Blue Jays" at the top. This issue includes the first minor league appearance of Jesse Barfield. The cards are unnumbered and checklisted below in alphabetical order.
COMPLETE SET (27)............. 125.00 50.00

1978 Greenwood Braves TCMA

This 29-card standard-size set of the 1978 Greenwood Braves, a Class A Western Carolinas League affiliate of the Atlanta Braves, features white-bordered posed black-and-white player photos on its fronts. The player's name and Braves logo appear in the green section near the bottom. The league affiliation appears across an upper corner. The plain white horizontal back carries the words "The Minors - 1978 Greenwood Braves" at the top. The cards are unnumbered and checklisted below in alphabetical order.
COMPLETE SET (29)............... 30.00 12.00

1978 Holyoke Millers TCMA

This 24-card standard-size set of the 1978 Holyoke Millers, a Class AA Eastern League affiliate of the Milwaukee Brewers, features white-bordered posed color player photos on its fronts. The white back carries the year, league, team name, the player's name, position, biography and statistics. The cards are unnumbered and checklisted below in alphabetical order. Approximately 5,000 sets were produced.
COMPLETE SET (24)............... 20.00 8.00

1978 Indianapolis Indians Team Issue

This set was available from the team at time of issue for $3.50.
COMPLETE SET (27)............... 30.00 12.00

1978 Knoxville Knox Sox TCMA

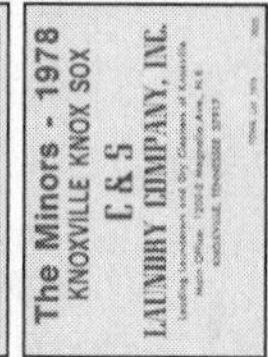

This 25-card standard-size set of the 1978 Knoxville Knox Sox, a Class AA Southern League affiliate of the Chicago White Sox, features white-bordered posed black-and-white player photos on its fronts. The player's name and Knox Sox logo appear in the green section near the bottom. The league affiliation appears across an upper corner. The plain white horizontal back carries the words "The Minors - 1978 Knoxville Knox Sox" at the top. The cards are unnumbered and checklisted below in alphabetical order. Approximately 1,100 sets were produced. The key card in this set is Harold Baines first card issue.
COMPLETE SET (25)............. 250.00 100.00

1978 Lodi Dodgers TCMA

This 26-card standard-size set of the 1978 Lodi Dodgers, a Class A California League affiliate of the Los Angeles Dodgers, features white-bordered posed black-and-white player photos on its fronts. The player's name and Dodgers logo appear in the green section near the bottom. The league affiliation appears across an upper corner. The plain white horizontal back carries the words "The Minors - 1978 Lodi Dodgers" at the top. The cards are unnumbered and checklisted below in alphabetical order.
COMPLETE SET (25)............... 30.00 12.00
COMPLETE SET (26)............... 60.00 24.00

1978 Memphis Chicks Britling Cafeterias

Printed on thin card stock, this 10-card set of the 1978 Memphis Chicks, a Class AA Southern League affiliate of the Montreal Expos, measures 2 3/4" by 3 7/8" and features white-bordered and blue-screened posed player photos on its fronts. The player's name and logos for the Chicks and Britling appear within the wide white bottom margin. The red, white, and blue horizontal back carries the player's name and biography at the top, followed by career highlights and statistics. Although some cards are numbered on the back (e.g., #1 Perez; #2 Hemm; #3 McMullen; #4 Goldetsky), the rest carry no card numbers. Therefore, the cards are listed below alphabetically by player's last name.
COMPLETE SET (10)............... 25.00 10.00

1978 Newark Wayne Co-Pilots TCMA

This 45-card standard-size set of the 1978 Newark Wayne Co-Pilots, a Class A New York-Penn League affiliate of the Milwaukee Brewers, features white-bordered posed black-and-white player photos on its fronts. The player's name and Co-Pilots logo appear in the green section near the bottom. The league affiliation appears across an upper corner. The plain white horizontal back carries the words "The Minors - 1978 Newark Wayne Co-Pilots" at the top. The cards are unnumbered and checklisted below in alphabetical order.
COMPLETE SET (45)............... 30.00 12.00

1978 Orlando Twins TCMA

This 23-card standard-size set of the 1978 Orlando Twins, a Class AA Southern League affiliate of the Minnesota Twins, features white-bordered posed black-and-white player photos on its fronts. The player's name and Twins logo appear in the green section near the bottom. The league affiliation appears across an upper corner. The plain white horizontal back carries the words "The Minors - 1978 Orlando Twins" at the top. The cards are unnumbered and checklisted below in alphabetical order.
COMPLETE SET (23)............... 25.00 10.00

1978 Phoenix Giants Cramer

This set was originally available from the team for $2.95.
COMPLETE SET (25)............... 10.00 4.00

1978 Quad City Angels TCMA

This 30-card standard-size set of the 1978 Quad City Angels, a Class A Midwest League affiliate of the California Angels, features white-bordered posed black-and-white player photos on its fronts. The player's name and Angels logo appear in the green section near the bottom. The league affiliation appears across an upper corner. The plain white horizontal back carries the words "The Minors - 1978 Quad City Angels" at the top. The cards are unnumbered and checklisted below in alphabetical order.
COMPLETE SET (30)............... 80.00 32.00

1978 Richmond Braves TCMA

This 20-card standard-size set of the 1978 Richmond Braves, a Class AAA International League affiliate of the Atlanta Braves, features white-bordered posed color player photos on its fronts. The white back carries the year, league, team name, the player's name, position, biography and statistics. The cards are unnumbered and checklisted below in alphabetical order.
COMPLETE SET (20)............... 20.00 8.00

1978 Rochester Red Wings TCMA

This 17-card standard-size set of the 1978 Rochester Red Wings, a Class AAA International League affiliate of the Baltimore Orioles, features white-bordered posed color player photos on its fronts. The white back carries the year, league, team name, the player's name, position, biography and statistics. The cards are unnumbered and checklisted below in alphabetical order.
COMPLETE SET (17)............... 30.00 12.00

1978 Salem Pirates TCMA

This 18-card standard-size set of the 1978 Salem Pirates, a Class A Carolina League affiliate of the Pittsburgh Pirates, features white-bordered posed black-and-white player photos on its fronts. The player's name and Pirates logo appear in the green section near the bottom. The league affiliation appears across an upper corner. The plain white horizontal back carries the words "The Minors - 1978 Salem Pirates" at the top. The cards are unnumbered and checklisted below in alphabetical order.
COMPLETE SET (18)............... 30.00 12.00

1978 Salt Lake City Gulls Cramer

COMPLETE SET (24)............... 10.00 4.00

1978 San Jose Missions Mr. Chef's

COMPLETE SET (24)............... 40.00 16.00

1978 Spokane Indians Cramer

This set was originally available from the team for $3.75.
COMPLETE SET (24)............... 10.00 4.00

1978 Springfield Redbirds Wiener King

COMPLETE SET (24)............. 100.00 40.00

1978 St. Petersburg Cardinals TCMA

This 29-card standard-size set of the 1978 St. Petersburg Cardinals, a Class A Florida State League affiliate of the St. Louis Cardinals, features white-bordered posed black-and-white player photos on its fronts. The player's name and Cardinals logo appear in the green section near the bottom. The league affiliation appears across an upper corner. The plain white horizontal back carries the words "The Minors - 1978 St. Petersburg Cardinals" at the top. The cards are unnumbered and checklisted below in alphabetical order.
COMPLETE SET (29)............... 40.00 16.00

1978 Syracuse Chiefs TCMA

This 22-card standard-size set of the 1978 Syracuse Chiefs, a Class AAA International League affiliate of the Toronto Blue Jays, features white-bordered posed color player photos on its fronts. The white back carries the year, league, team name, the player's name, position, biography and statistics. This issue includes Danny Ainge's first appearance on a minor league card. The cards are unnumbered and checklisted below in alphabetical order.
COMPLETE SET (22) 50.00 20.00

1978 Tacoma Yankees Cramer

Dell Alston was traded before this set was released and the only way that card was available was through Cramer Sports Promotions.
COMPLETE SET (25) 8.00 3.20

1978 Tidewater Tides TCMA

This 27-card standard-size set of the 1978 Tidewater Tides, a Class AAA International League affiliate of the New York Mets, features white-bordered posed color player photos on its fronts. The white back carries the year, league, team name, the player's name, position, biography and statistics. The cards are unnumbered and checklisted below in alphabetical order.
COMPLETE SET (27) 30.00 12.00

1978 Tucson Toros Cramer

Rusty Torres was not issued with the team set and the only this card was available was through Cramer Sports Productions.
COMPLETE SET (25) 10.00 4.00

1978 Waterloo Indians TCMA

This 26-card standard-size set of the 1978 Waterloo Indians, a Class A Midwest League affiliate of the Cleveland Indians, features white-bordered posed black-and-white player photos on its fronts. The player's name and Indians logo appear in the green section near the bottom. The league affiliation appears across an upper corner. The plain white horizontal back carries the words "The Minors - 1978 Waterloo Indians" at the top. The cards are unnumbered and checklisted below in alphabetical order.
COMPLETE SET (26) 20.00 8.00

1978 Wausau Mets TCMA

This 25-card standard-size set of the 1978 Wausau Mets, a Class A Midwest League affiliate of the New York Mets, features white-bordered posed black-and-white player photos on its fronts. The player's name and Mets logo appear in the green section near the bottom. The league affiliation appears across an upper corner. The plain white horizontal back carries the words "The Minors - 1978 Wausau Mets" at the top. The cards are unnumbered and checklisted below in alphabetical order.
COMPLETE SET (25) 60.00 24.00

1978 Wisconsin Rapids Twins TCMA

This 18-card standard-size set of the 1978 Wisconsin Rapids Twins, a Class A Midwest League affiliate of the Minnesota Twins, features white-bordered posed black-and-white player photos on its fronts. The player's name and Twins logo appear in the green section near the bottom. The league affiliation appears across an upper corner. The plain white horizontal back carries the words "The Minors - 1978 Wisconsin Rapids Twins" at the top. The cards are unnumbered and checklisted below in alphabetical order.
COMPLETE SET (18) 30.00 12.00

1979 Albuquerque Dukes TCMA

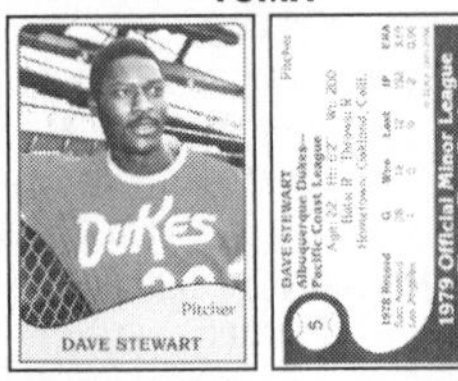

This 23-card standard-size set of the 1979 Albuquerque Dukes, a Class AAA Pacific Coast League affiliate of the Los Angeles Dodgers, features white-bordered posed color player photos on its fronts. The player's name and position appear in the lower yellow portion of the front. The horizontal back carries the player's name, position, team, and league at the top, followed by biography and statistics. Any TCMA team set in 1979 was available for $2.50 from the manufacturer.
COMPLETE SET (23) 250.00 100.00

1979 Albuquerque Dukes University Volkswagen

This blank-backed set, which measure approximately 8 1/2" by 11" and features members of the 1979 Albuquerque Dukes, was sponsored by University Volkswagen. The cards have a player photo, biographical information, a blurb about the player and career stats until that point. Since the cards are unnumbered, we have sequenced them in alphabetical order.
COMPLETE SET 150.00 60.00

1979 Appleton Foxes TCMA

This 25-card standard-size set of the 1979 Appleton Foxes, a Class A Midwest League affiliate of the Chicago White Sox, features white-bordered posed black-and-white player photos on its fronts. The player's name and position appear in the lower orange portion of the front. The horizontal back carries the player's name, position, team, and league at the top, followed by biography and statistics.
COMPLETE SET (25) 50.00 20.00

1979 Arkansas Travelers TCMA

This 23-card standard-size set of the 1979 Arkansas Travelers, a Class AA Texas League affiliate of the St. Louis Cardinals, features white-bordered posed color player photos on its fronts. The player's name and position appear in the lower yellow portion of the front. The horizontal back carries the player's name, position, team, and league at the top, followed by biography and statistics.
COMPLETE SET (23) 20.00 8.00

1979 Asheville Tourists TCMA

This 28-card standard-size set of the 1979 Asheville Tourists, a Class A Western Carolinas League affiliate of the Texas Rangers, features white-bordered posed black-and-white player photos on its fronts. The player's name and position appear in the lower orange portion of the front. The horizontal back carries the player's name, position, team, and league at the top, followed by biography and statistics.
COMPLETE SET (28) 150.00 60.00

1979 Buffalo Bisons TCMA

This 21-card standard-size set of the 1979 Buffalo Bisons, a Class AA Eastern League affiliate of the Pittsburgh Pirates, features white-bordered posed color player photos on its fronts. The player's name and position appear in the lower orange portion of the front. The horizontal back carries the player's name, position, team, and league at the top, followed by biography and statistics.
COMPLETE SET (21) 100.00 40.00

1979 Burlington Bees TCMA

This 25-card standard-size set of the 1979 Burlington Bees, a Class A Midwest League affiliate of the Milwaukee Brewers, features white-bordered posed black-and-white player photos on its fronts. The player's name and position appear in the lower orange portion of the front. The horizontal back carries the player's name, position, team, and league at the top, followed by biography and statistics.
COMPLETE SET (25) 25.00 10.00

1979 Cedar Rapids Giants TCMA

This 32-card standard-size set of the 1979 Cedar Rapids Giants, a Class A Midwest League affiliate of the San Francisco Giants, features white-bordered posed black-and-white player photos on its fronts. The player's name and position appear in the lower orange portion of the front. The horizontal back carries the player's name, position, team, and league at the top, followed by biography and statistics.
COMPLETE SET (32) 75.00 30.00

1979 Charleston Charlies TCMA

This 21-card standard-size set of the 1979 Charleston Charlies, a Class AAA International League affiliate of the Houston Astros, features white-bordered posed color player photos on its fronts. The player's name and position appear in the lower yellow portion of the front. The horizontal back carries the player's name, position, team, and league at the top, followed by biography and statistics.
COMPLETE SET (19) 15.00 6.00
COMPLETE SET (21) 40.00 16.00

1979 Clinton Dodgers TCMA

This 28-card standard-size set of the 1979 Clinton Dodgers, a Class A Midwest League affiliate of the Los Angeles Dodgers, features white-bordered posed black-and-white player photos on its fronts. The player's name and position appear in the lower orange portion of the front. The horizontal back carries the player's name, position, team, and league at the top, followed by biography and statistics.
COMPLETE SET (28) 50.00 20.00

1979 Columbus Clippers TCMA

This 29-card standard-size set of the 1979 Columbus Clippers, a Class AAA International League affiliate of the New York Yankees, features white-bordered posed color player photos on its fronts. The player's name and position appear in the lower yellow portion of the front. The horizontal back carries the player's name, position, team, and league at the top, followed by biography and statistics.
COMPLETE SET (29) 20.00 8.00

1979 Elmira Pioneer Red Sox TCMA

This 28-card standard-size set of the 1979 Elmira Pioneer Red Sox, a Class A New York-Penn League affiliate of the Boston Red Sox, features white-bordered posed black-and-white player photos on its fronts. The player's name and position appear in the lower orange portion of the front. The horizontal back carries the player's name, position, team, and league at the top, followed by biography and statistics.
COMPLETE SET (28) 100.00 40.00

1979 Hawaii Islanders Cramer

2 3/8" by 3 1/2" color cards.
COMPLETE SET (24) 10.00 4.00

1979 Hawaii Islanders TCMA

This 24-card standard-size set of the 1979 Hawaii Islanders, a Class AAA Pacific Coast affiliate of the San Diego Padres, features white-bordered posed color player photos on its fronts. The player's name and position appear in the lower yellow portion of the front. The horizontal back carries the player's name, position, team, and league at the top, followed by biography and statistics.
COMPLETE SET (24) 15.00 6.00

1979 Holyoke Millers TCMA

This 30-card standard-size set of the 1979 Holyoke Millers, a Class AA Eastern League affiliate of the Milwaukee Brewers, features white-bordered posed color player photos on its fronts. The player's name and position appear in the lower yellow portion of the front. The horizontal back carries the player's name, position, team, and league at the top, followed by biography and statistics.
COMPLETE SET (30) 15.00 6.00

1979 Indianapolis Indians Team Issue

2,000 sets printed. Cards were written by collector Tom Akins and Max Schumacher, who was president of the team. Original issue price was $3.25.
COMPLETE SET (32) 30.00 12.00

1979 Iowa Oaks Police

Black and White. 2 5/8" by 4 1/8". 230,000 of each card were issued. Kevin Bell comes with or without a star on the back. Cards are unnumbered so we have sequenced them in alphabetical order.
COMPLETE SET (15) 200.00 80.00

1979 Jackson Mets TCMA

This 25-card standard-size set of the 1979 Jackson Mets, a Class AA Texas League affiliate of the New York Mets, features white-bordered posed color player photos on its fronts. The player's name and position appear in the lower yellow portion of the front. The horizontal back carries the player's name, position, team, and league at the top, followed by biography and statistics. Card #22B of the Front Office Staff is a late issue; we have priced the set with and without this card. Approximately 2,500 sets were produced.
COMPLETE SET (24) 15.00 6.00

1979 Knoxville Knox Sox TCMA

This 26-card standard-size set of the 1979 Knoxville Knox Sox, a Class AA Southern League affiliate of the Chicago White Sox, features white-bordered posed black-and-white player photos on its fronts. The player's name and position appear in the lower orange portion of the front. The horizontal back carries the player's name, position, team, and league at the top, followed by biography and statistics.
COMPLETE SET (26) 60.00 24.00

1979 Lodi Dodgers TCMA

This 21-card standard-size set of the 1979 Lodi Dodgers, a Class A California League affiliate of the Los Angeles Dodgers, features white-bordered posed black-and-white player photos on its fronts. The player's name and position appear in the lower orange portion of the front. The horizontal back carries the player's name, position, team, and league at the top, followed by biography and statistics.
COMPLETE SET (21) 125.00 50.00

1979 Memphis Chicks TCMA

This 24-card standard-size set of the 1979 Memphis Chicks, a Class AA Southern League affiliate of the Montreal Expos, features white-bordered posed black-and-white player photos on its fronts. The player's name and position appear within an orange area near the bottom. The white and black horizontal back carries the player's name and position at the top, followed by biography, career highlights, and statistics. This issue includes the only minor league card appearance of Tim Raines. Approximately 1,500 sets were produced.
COMPLETE SET (24) 200.00 80.00

1979 Nashville Sounds Team Issue

COMPLETE SET (25) 30.00 12.00

1979 Newark Co-Pilots TCMA

This 24-card standard-size set of the 1979 Newark Co-Pilots, a Class A New York-Penn League Independent, features white-bordered posed black-and-white player photos on its fronts. The player's name and position appear in the lower orange portion of the front. The horizontal back carries the player's name, position, team, and league at the top, followed by biography and statistics.
COMPLETE SET (24) 25.00 10.00

1979 Ogden A's TCMA

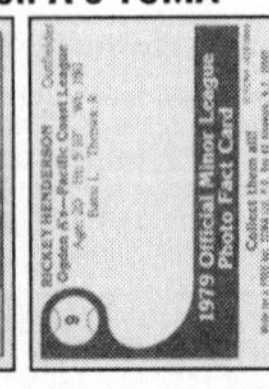

This 26-card standard-size set of the 1979 Ogden A's, a Class AAA Pacific Coast League affiliate of the Oakland Athletics, features white-bordered posed color player photos on its fronts. The player's name and position appear in the lower yellow portion of the front. The horizontal back carries the player's name, position, team, and league at the top, followed by biography and statistics. Approximately 3,000 sets were produced. An early Rickey Henderson card is the key to this set.
COMPLETE SET (26) 100.00 40.00

1979 Phoenix Giants Valley National Bank

COMPLETE SET (24) 8.00 3.20

1979 Portland Beavers TCMA

This 24-card standard-size set of the 1979 Portland Beavers, a Class AAA Pacific Coast League affiliate of the Pittsburgh Pirates, features white-bordered posed color player photos on its fronts. The player's name and position appear in the lower yellow portion of the front. The horizontal back carries the player's name, position, team, and league at the top, followed by biography and statistics.
COMPLETE SET (24) 20.00 8.00

1979 Quad City Cubs TCMA

This 27-card standard-size set of the 1979 Quad City Cubs, a Class A Midwest League affiliate of the Chicago Cubs, features white-bordered posed black-and-white player photos on its fronts. The player's name and position appear in the lower orange portion of the front. The horizontal back carries the player's name, position, team, and league at the top, followed by biography and statistics.
COMPLETE SET (27) 50.00 20.00

1979 Richmond Braves TCMA

This 25-card standard-size set of the 1979 Richmond Braves, a Class AAA International League affiliate of the Atlanta Braves, features white-bordered posed color player photos on its fronts. The player's name and position appear in the lower yellow portion of the front. The horizontal back carries the player's name, position, team, and league at the top, followed by biography and statistics.
COMPLETE SET (25) 15.00 6.00

1979 Rochester Red Wings TCMA

This 20-card standard-size set of the 1979 Rochester Red Wings, a Class AAA International League affiliate of the Baltimore Orioles, features white-bordered posed color player photos on its fronts. The player's name and position appear in the lower yellow portion of the front. The horizontal back carries the player's name, position, team, and league at the top, followed by biography and statistics.
COMPLETE SET (20) 10.00 4.00

1979 Salt Lake City Gulls TCMA

This 23-card standard-size set of the 1979 Salt Lake City Gulls, a Class AAA Pacific Coast League affiliate of the California Angels, features white-bordered posed color player photos on its fronts. The player's name and position appear in the lower yellow portion of the front. The horizontal back carries the player's name, position, team, and league at the top, followed by biography and statistics.
COMPLETE SET (23) 15.00 6.00

1979 Savannah Braves TCMA

This 26-card standard-size set of the 1979 Savannah Braves, a Class AA Southern League affiliate of the Atlanta Braves, features white-bordered posed color player photos on its fronts. The player's name and position appear in the lower yellow portion of the front. The horizontal back carries the player's name, position, team, and league at the top, followed by biography and statistics.
COMPLETE SET (26) 25.00 10.00

1979 Spokane Indians TCMA

This 25-card standard-size set of the 1979 Spokane Indians, a Class AAA Pacific Coast League affiliate of the Seattle Mariners, features white-bordered posed color player photos on its fronts. The player's name and position appear in the lower yellow portion of the front. The horizontal back carries the player's name, position, team, and league at the top, followed by biography and statistics.
COMPLETE SET (25) 10.00 4.00

1979 Syracuse Chiefs TCMA

This 20-card standard-size set of the 1979 Syracuse Chiefs, a Class AAA International League affiliate of the Toronto Blue Jays, features white-bordered posed color player photos on its fronts. The player's name and position appear in the lower yellow portion of the front. The horizontal back carries the player's name, position, team, and league at the top, followed by biography and statistics.
COMPLETE SET (20) 25.00 10.00

1979 Syracuse Chiefs Team Issue

COMPLETE SET (24) 80.00 32.00

1979 Tacoma Tugs TCMA

This 26-card standard-size set of the 1979 Tacoma Tugs, a Class AAA Pacific Coast League affiliate of the Cleveland Indians, features white-bordered posed color player photos on its fronts. The player's name and position appear in the lower yellow portion of the front. The horizontal back carries the player's name, position, team, and league at the top, followed by biography and statistics.
COMPLETE SET (26) 20.00 8.00

1979 Tidewater Tides TCMA

This 25-card standard-size set of the 1979 Tidewater Tides, a Class AAA International League affiliate of the New York Mets, features white-bordered posed color player photos on its fronts. The player's name and position appear in the lower yellow portion of the front. The horizontal back carries the player's name, position, team, and league at the top, followed by biography and statistics. Approximately 4,000 sets were produced.
COMPLETE SET (25) 60.00 24.00

1979 Toledo Mud Hens TCMA

This 22-card standard-size set of the 1979 Toledo Mud Hens, a Class AAA International League affiliate of the Minnesota Twins, features white-bordered posed color player photos on its fronts. The player's name and position appear in the lower yellow portion of the front. The horizontal back carries the player's name, position, team, and league at the top, followed by biography and statistics.
COMPLETE SET (22) 10.00 4.00

1979 Tucson Toros TCMA

This 24-card standard-size set of the 1979 Tucson Toros, a Class AAA Pacific Coast League affiliate of the Texas Rangers, features white-bordered posed color player photos on its fronts. The player's name and position appear in the lower yellow portion of the front. The horizontal back carries the player's name, position, team, and league at the top, followed by biography and statistics.
COMPLETE SET (24) 10.00 4.00

1979 Tulsa Drillers TCMA

This 24-card standard-size set of the 1979 Tulsa Drillers, a Class AA Texas League affiliate of the Texas Rangers, was available at time of issue from the team for $2.25.
COMPLETE SET (24) 20.00 8.00

1979 Vancouver Canadians TCMA

This 25-card standard-size set of the 1979 Vancouver Canadians, a Class AAA Pacific Coast League affiliate of the Milwaukee Brewers, features white-bordered posed color player photos on its fronts. The player's name and position appear in the lower yellow portion of the front. The horizontal back carries the player's name, position, team, and league at the top, followed by biography and statistics. It is possible that all cards numbered higher than 21 were late additions to the set.
COMPLETE SET (25) 15.00 6.00

1979 Waterbury A's TCMA

This 25-card standard-size set of the 1979 Waterbury A's, a Class AA Eastern League affiliate of the Oakland Athletics, features white-bordered posed black-and-white player photos on its fronts. The player's name and position appear in the lower orange portion of the front. The horizontal back carries the player's name, position, team, and league at the top, followed by biography and statistics.
COMPLETE SET (25) 100.00 40.00

1979 Waterloo Indians TCMA

This 36-card standard-size set of the 1979 Waterloo Indians, a Class A Midwest League affiliate of the Cleveland Indians, features

white-bordered posed black-and-white player photos on its fronts. The player's name and position appear in the lower orange portion of the front. The horizontal back carries the player's name, position, team, and league at the top, followed by biography and statistics.
COMPLETE SET (36)................ 80.00 32.00

1979 Wausau Timbers TCMA

This 25-card standard-size set of the 1979 Wausau Timbers, a Class A Midwest League Independent, features white-bordered posed black-and-white player photos on its fronts. The player's name and position appear in the lower orange portion of the front. The horizontal back carries the player's name, position, team, and league at the top, followed by biography and statistics. Approximately 1,100 sets were produced.
COMPLETE SET (25)................ 25.00 10.00

1979 West Haven Yankees TCMA

This 30-card standard-size set of the 1979 West Haven Yankees, a Class AA Eastern League affiliate of the New York Yankees, features white-bordered posed color player photos on its fronts. The player's name and position appear in the lower yellow portion of the front. The horizontal back carries the player's name, position, team, and league at the top, followed by biography and statistics. Approximately 2,000 sets were produced.
COMPLETE SET (30)................ 60.00 24.00

1979 Wisconsin Rapids Twins TCMA

This 23-card standard-size set of the 1979 Wisconsin Rapids Twins, a Class A Midwest League affiliate of the Minnesota Twins, features white-bordered posed black-and-white player photos on its fronts. The player's name and position appear in the lower orange portion of the front. The horizontal back carries the player's name, position, team, and league at the top, followed by biography and statistics.
COMPLETE SET (23)................ 40.00 16.00

1980 Albuquerque Dukes TCMA

This 27-card standard-size set of the 1980 Albuquerque Dukes, a Class AAA Pacific Coast League affiliate of the Los Angeles Dodgers, features red-bordered posed color player photos with rounded corners on its fronts. The player's name and position appear in a white bar under the photo, and the team name is printed under this bar. The horizontal back carries the player's name, position, team, league, and biography.
COMPLETE SET (27)................ 50.00 20.00

1980 Anderson Braves TCMA

This 29-card standard-size set of the 1980 Anderson Braves, a Class A South Atlantic League affiliate of the Atlanta Braves, features red-bordered posed color player photos with rounded corners on its fronts. The player's name and position appear in a white bar under the photo, and the team name is printed under this bar. The horizontal back carries the player's name, position, team, league, and biography.
COMPLETE SET (29)................ 30.00 12.00

1980 Appleton Foxes TCMA

This 30-card standard-size set of the 1980 Appleton Foxes, a Class A Midwest League affiliate of the Chicago White Sox, features red-bordered posed black-and-white player photos with rounded corners on its fronts. The player's name and position appear in a white bar under the photo, and the team name is printed under this bar. The horizontal back carries the player's name, position, team, league, and biography.
COMPLETE SET (30)................ 125.00 50.00

1980 Arkansas Travelers TCMA

This 25-card standard-size set of the 1980 Arkansas Travelers, a Class AA Texas League affiliate of the St. Louis Cardinals, features red-bordered posed color player photos with rounded corners on its fronts. The player's name and position appear in a white bar under the photo, and the team name is printed under this bar. The horizontal back carries the player's name, position, team, league, and biography.
COMPLETE SET (25)................ 15.00 6.00

1980 Asheville Tourists TCMA

This 28-card standard-size set of the 1980 Asheville Tourists, a Class A South Atlantic League affiliate of the Texas Rangers, features red-bordered posed color player photos with rounded corners on its fronts. The player's name and position appear in a white bar under the photo, and the team name is printed under this bar. The horizontal back carries the player's name, position, team, league, and biography. Approximately 2,500 sets were produced.
COMPLETE SET (28)................ 30.00 12.00

1980 Batavia Trojans TCMA

This 30-card standard-size set of the 1980 Batavia Trojans, a Class A New York-Penn League affiliate of the Cleveland Indians, features red-bordered posed black-and-white player photos with rounded corners on its fronts. The player's name and position appear in a white bar under the photo, and the team name is printed under this bar. The horizontal back carries the player's name, position, team, league, and biography.
COMPLETE SET (30)................ 125.00 50.00

1980 Buffalo Bisons TCMA

This 16-card standard-size set of the 1980 Buffalo Bisons, a Class AA Eastern League affiliate of the Pittsburgh Pirates, features red-bordered posed color player photos with rounded corners on its fronts. The player's name and position appear in a white bar under the photo, and the team name is printed under this bar. The horizontal back carries the player's name, position, team, league, and biography.
COMPLETE SET (16)................ 30.00 12.00

1980 Burlington Bees TCMA

This 29-card standard-size set of the 1980 Burlington Bees, a Class A Midwest League affiliate of the Milwaukee Brewers, features red-bordered posed black-and-white player photos with rounded corners on its fronts. The player's name and position appear in a white bar under the photo, and the team name is printed under this bar. The horizontal back carries the player's name, position, team, league, and biography.
COMPLETE SET (29)................ 40.00 16.00

1980 Cedar Rapids Reds TCMA

This 26-card standard-size set of the 1980 Cedar Rapids Reds, a Class A Midwest League affiliate of the Cincinnati Reds, features red-bordered posed color player photos with rounded corners on its fronts. The player's name and position appear in a white bar under the photo, and the team name is printed under this bar. The horizontal back carries the player's name, position, team, league, and biography.
COMPLETE SET (26)................ 10.00 4.00

1980 Charleston Charlies TCMA

This 17-card standard-size set of the 1980 Charleston Charlies, a Class AAA International League affiliate of the Texas Rangers, features red-bordered posed color player photos with rounded corners on its fronts. The player's name and position appear in a white bar under the photo, and the team name is printed under this bar. The horizontal back carries the player's name, position, team, league, and biography.
COMPLETE SET (17)................ 15.00 6.00

1980 Charlotte O's Police

This 28-card standard-size set of the 1980 Charlotte O's, a Class AA Southern League affiliate of the Baltimore Orioles, features orange-bordered posed color player photos. The player's name and position appear in white letters across the bottom of the card with the team's logo printed on the right. The back carries player tips and crime prevention tips. Single cards from the set were given out one or two at a time to local school children. Less than a dozen complete sets are known to exist. This issue features the minor league card debut of Cal Ripken Jr.
COMPLETE SET (25)........... 3500.00 1400.00

1980 Charlotte O's W3TV

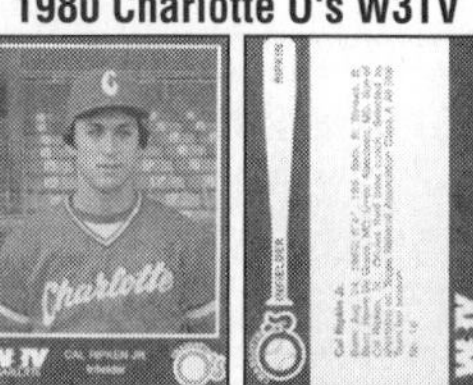

This 28-card standard-size set of the 1980 Charlotte O's, a Class AA Southern League affiliate of the Baltimore Orioles, features blue-bordered posed color player photos. The player's name and position appear in white letters across the bottom of the card with the team's logo printed on the right and the sponsor's logo printed on the left. The back carries the player's name, position, team, league, and biography. This issue features the minor league card debut of Cal Ripken Jr.
COMPLETE SET (28)........... 1500.00 400.00

1980 Clinton Giants TCMA

This 27-card standard-size set of the 1980 Clinton Giants, a Class A Midwest League affiliate of the San Francisco Giants, features red-bordered posed black-and-white player photos with rounded corners on its fronts. The player's name and position appear in a white bar under the photo, and the team name is printed under this bar. The horizontal back carries the player's name, position, team, league, and biography.
COMPLETE SET (27)................ 80.00 32.00

1980 Columbus Astros TCMA

This 22-card standard-size set of the 1980 Columbus Astros, a Class AA Southern League affiliate of the Houston Astros, features red-bordered posed black-and-white player photos with rounded corners on its fronts. The player's name and position appear in a white bar under the photo, and the team name is printed under this bar. The horizontal back carries the player's name, position, team, league, and biography.
COMPLETE SET (22)................ 50.00 20.00

1980 Columbus Clippers Police

According to sources near the time of issue, 50,000 sets were produced.
COMPLETE SET (25)................ 25.00 10.00

1980 Columbus Clippers TCMA

This 28-card standard-size set of the 1980 Columbus Clippers, a Class AAA International League affiliate of the New York Yankees, features red-bordered posed color player photos with rounded corners on its fronts. The player's name and position appear in a white bar under the photo, and the team name is printed under this bar. The horizontal back carries the player's name, position, team, league, and biography.
COMPLETE SET (28)................ 50.00 20.00

1980 El Paso Diablos TCMA

This 24-card standard-size set of the 1980 El Paso Diablos, a Class AA Texas League affiliate of the Milwaukee Brewers, features red-bordered posed color player photos with rounded corners on its fronts. The player's name and position appear in a white bar under the photo, and the team name is printed under this bar. The horizontal back carries the player's name, position, team, league, and biography.
COMPLETE SET (24)................ 20.00 8.00

1980 Elmira Pioneer Red Sox TCMA

This 44-card standard-size set of the 1980 Elmira Pioneer, a Class A New York-Penn League affiliate of the Boston Red Sox, features red-bordered posed black-and-white player photos with rounded corners on its fronts. The player's name and position appear in a white bar under the photo, and the team name is printed under this bar. The horizontal back carries the player's name, position, team, league, and biography. Approximately 1,100 sets were produced.
COMPLETE SET (44)............. 120.00 47.50

1980 Evansville Triplets TCMA

This 24-card standard-size set of the 1980 Evansville Triplets, a Class AAA American Association affiliate of the Detroit Tigers, features red-bordered posed color player photos with rounded corners on its fronts. The player's name and position appear in a white bar under the photo, and the team name is printed under this bar. The horizontal back carries the player's name, position, team, league, and biography.
COMPLETE SET (24)................ 15.00 6.00

1980 Glens Falls White Sox B/W TCMA

This 29-card standard-size set of the 1980 Glens Falls White Sox, a Class AA Eastern League affiliate of the Chicago White Sox, features red-bordered posed black-and-white player photos with rounded corners on its fronts. The player's name and position appear in a white bar under the photo, and the team name is printed under this bar. The horizontal back carries the player's name, position, team, league, and biography.
COMPLETE SET (29)............. 150.00 60.00

1980 Glens Falls White Sox Color TCMA

This 30-card standard-size set of the 1980 Glens Falls White Sox, a Class AA Eastern League affiliate of the Chicago White Sox, features red-bordered posed color player photos with rounded corners on its fronts. The player's name and position appear in a white bar under the photo, and the team name is printed under this bar. The horizontal back carries the player's name, position, team, league, and biography.
COMPLETE SET (30)................ 30.00 12.00

1980 Hawaii Islanders TCMA

This 25-card standard-size set of the 1980 Hawaii Islanders, a Class AAA Pacific Coast League affiliate of the San Diego Padres, features red-bordered posed color player photos with rounded corners on its fronts. The player's name and position appear in a white bar under the photo, and the team name is printed under this bar. The horizontal back carries the player's name, position, team, league, and biography.
COMPLETE SET (25)................ 15.00 6.00

1980 Holyoke Millers TCMA

This 25-card standard-size set of the 1980 Holyoke Millers, a Class AA Eastern League affiliate of the Milwaukee Brewers, features red-bordered posed color player photos with rounded corners on its fronts. The player's name and position appear in a white bar under the photo, and the team name is printed under this bar. The horizontal back carries the player's name, position, team, league, and biography.
COMPLETE SET (25)................ 15.00 6.00

1980 Indianapolis Indians Team Issue

This 32 card set measured 2 5/8" by 3 5/8" and was issued by the team and sold directly upon release for $3.25.
COMPLETE SET (..................... 30.00 12.00

1980 Iowa Oaks Police

Included in this 16-card set of the White Sox Class AAA affiliate are two scarce cards (number 2B and number 12B). The set has been priced both with and without these late issues. According to sources at the time of issue, 200,000 total cards were produced.
COMPLETE SET (14)............. 250.00 100.00
Included in this 16-card set of the White Sox Class AAA affiliate are two scarce cards (number 2B and number 12B). The set has been priced both with and without these late issues. According to sources at the time of issue, 200,000 total cards were produced.
COMPLETE SET W/VAR (16) . 400.00 160.00

1980 Knoxville Blue Jays TCMA

This 28-card standard-size set of the 1980 Knoxville Blue Jays, a Class AA Southern League affiliate of the Toronto Blue Jays, features red-bordered posed black-and-white player photos with rounded corners on its fronts. The player's name and position appear in a white bar under the photo, and the team name is printed under this bar. The horizontal back carries the player's name, position, team, league, and biography.
COMPLETE SET (28)............. 120.00 47.50

1980 Lynn Sailors TCMA

This 23-card standard-size set of the 1980 Lynn Sailors, a Class AAA Eastern League affiliate of the Seattle Mariners, features red-bordered posed color player photos with rounded corners on its fronts. The player's name and position appear in a white bar under the photo, and the team name is printed under this bar. The horizontal back carries the player's name, position, team, league, and biography.
COMPLETE SET (23)................ 15.00 6.00

1980 Memphis Chicks TCMA

This 30-card standard-size set of the 1980 Memphis Chicks, a Class AA Southern League affiliate of the Montreal Expos, features red-bordered posed black-and-white player photos on its fronts. The player's name and position appear near the bottom. The white and blue horizontal back carries the player's name and position at the top, followed by biography, career highlights, and statistics. This set includes the first minor league card of Tony Phillips.
COMPLETE SET (30)................ 60.00 24.00

1980 Nashville Sounds Team Issue

COMPLETE SET (25)................ 25.00 10.00

1980 Ogden A's TCMA

This 23-card standard-size set of the 1980 Ogden A's, a Class AAA Pacific Coast League affiliate of the Oakland Athletics, features red-bordered posed color player photos with rounded corners on its fronts. The player's name and position appear in a white bar under the photo, and the team name is printed under this bar. The horizontal back carries the player's name, position, team, league, and biography.
COMPLETE SET (23)................ 15.00 6.00

1980 Omaha Royals Police

COMPLETE SET (24)................ 80.00 32.00

1980 Orlando Twins TCMA

This 22-card standard-size set of the 1980 Orlando Twins, a Class AA Southern League affiliate of the Minnesota Twins, features red-bordered posed black-and-white player photos with rounded corners on its fronts. The player's name and position appear in a white bar under the photo, and the team name is printed under this bar. The horizontal back carries the player's name, position, team, league, and biography.
COMPLETE SET (22)............. 120.00 47.50

1980 Peninsula Pilots B/W TCMA

This 27-card standard-size set of the 1980 Peninsula Pilots, a Class A Carolina League affiliate of the Philadelphia Phillies, features red-bordered posed black-and-white player photos with rounded corners on its fronts. The player's name and position appear in a white bar under the photo, and the team name is printed under this bar. The horizontal back carries the player's name, position, team, league, and biography. Approximately 1,100 sets were produced.
COMPLETE SET (27)................ 80.00 32.00

1980 Peninsula Pilots Color TCMA

This 27-card standard-size set of the 1980 Peninsula Pilots, a Class A Carolina League affiliate of the Philadelphia Phillies, features red-bordered posed color player photos with rounded corners on its fronts. The player's name and position appear in a white bar under the photo, and the team name is printed under this bar. The horizontal back carries the player's name, position, team, league, and biography. Approximately 2,500 sets were produced.
COMPLETE SET (27)................ 60.00 24.00

1980 Phoenix Giants Valley National Bank

COMPLETE SET (26)................ 15.00 6.00

1980 Portland Beavers TCMA

This 26-card standard-size set of the 1980 Portland Beavers, a Class AAA Pacific Coast League affiliate of the Pittsburgh Pirates, features red-bordered posed color player photos with rounded corners on its fronts. The player's name and position appear in a white bar under the photo, and the team name is printed under this bar. The horizontal back carries the player's name, position, team, league, and biography.
COMPLETE SET (26)................ 20.00 8.00

1980 Quad City Cubs TCMA

This 32-card standard-size set of the 1980 Quad City Cubs, a Class A Midwest League affiliate of the Chicago Cubs, features red-bordered posed black-and-white player photos with rounded corners on its fronts. The player's name and position appear in a white bar under the photo, and the team name is printed under this bar. The horizontal back carries the player's name, position, team, league, and biography.
COMPLETE SET (32)................ 80.00 32.00

1980 Reading Phillies TCMA

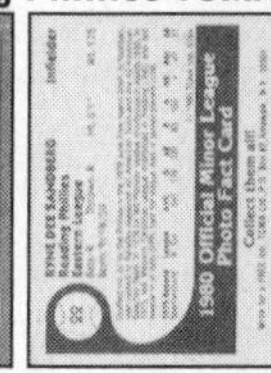

This 24-card standard-size set of the 1980 Reading Phillies, a Class AA Eastern League affiliate of the Philadelphia Phillies, features red-bordered posed black-and-white player photos with rounded corners on its fronts. The player's name and position appear in a white bar under the photo, and the team name is printed under this bar. The horizontal back carries the player's name, position, team, league, and biography. This issue inlcudes the minor league card debuts of Ryne Sandberg and George Bell. Approximately 1,100 sets were produced.
COMPLETE SET (24)........... 1000.00 400.00

1980 Richmond Braves TCMA

This 23-card standard-size set of the 1980 Richmond Braves, a Class AAA International League affiliate of the Atlanta Braves, features red-bordered posed color player photos with rounded corners on its fronts. The player's name and position appear in a white bar under the photo, and the team name is printed under this bar. The horizontal back carries the player's name, position, team, league, and biography.
COMPLETE SET (23)................ 15.00 6.00

1980 Rochester Red Wings TCMA

This 21-card standard-size set of the 1980 Rochester Red Wings, a Class AAA International League affiliate of the Baltimore Orioles, features red-bordered posed color player photos with rounded corners on its fronts. The player's name and position appear in a white bar under the photo, and the team name is printed under this bar. The horizontal back carries the player's name, position, team, league, and biography.
COMPLETE SET (21)................ 15.00 6.00

1980 Salt Lake City Gulls TCMA

This 26-card standard-size set of the 1980 Salt Lake City Gulls, a Class AAA Pacific Coast League affiliate of the California Angels, features red-bordered posed color player photos with rounded corners on its fronts. The player's name and position appear in a white bar under the photo, and the team name is printed under this bar. The horizontal back carries the player's name, position, team, league, and biography.
COMPLETE SET (26)................ 10.00 4.00

1980 San Jose Missions Jack in the Box

This 21 card set measured 2" by 3" and was sponsored by Jack in the Box restaurant chain.
COMPLETE SET (21)................ 75.00 30.00

1980 Spokane Indians TCMA

This 24-card standard-size set of the 1980 Spokane Indians, a Class AAA Pacific Coast League affiliate of the Seattle Mariners, features red-bordered posed color player photos with rounded corners on its fronts. The player's name and position appear in a white bar under the photo, and the team name is printed under this bar. The horizontal back carries the player's name, position, team, league, and biography.
COMPLETE SET (24)................ 25.00 10.00

1980 Syracuse Chiefs TCMA

This 23-card standard-size set of the 1980 Syracuse Chiefs, a Class AAA International League affiliate of the Toronto Blue Jays, features red-bordered posed color player photos on its fronts. The player's name and position appear in a white bar under the photo, and the team name is printed under this bar. The horizontal back carries the player's name, position, team, and league at the top, followed by biography and statistics.
COMPLETE SET (23)................ 30.00 12.00

1980 Syracuse Chiefs Team Issue

This 24-card set of the 1980 Syracuse Chiefs, a Class AAA International League affiliate of the Toronto Blue Jays, measures about 3 1/4" by 5" and features white-bordered posed black-and-white photos on its fronts. The player's uniform number and name appear in the bottom wider border. The backs are blank. The cards are unnumbered and checklisted below in alphabetical order.
COMPLETE SET (24)................ 80.00 32.00

1980 Tacoma Tigers TCMA

This 28-card standard-size set of the 1980 Tacoma Tigers, a Class AAA Pacific Coast League affiliate of the Cleveland Indians, features red-bordered posed color player photos with rounded corners on its fronts. The player's name and position appear in a white bar under the photo, and the team name is printed under this bar. The horizontal back carries the player's name, position, team, league, and biography.
COMPLETE SET (28)................ 15.00 6.00

1980 Tidewater Tides TCMA

This 24-card standard-size set of the 1980 Tidewater Tides, a Class AAA International League affiliate of the New York Mets, features red-bordered posed color player photos with rounded corners on its fronts. The player's name and position appear in a white bar under the photo, and the team name is printed under this bar. The horizontal back carries the player's name, position, team, league, and biography.
COMPLETE SET (24)................ 40.00 16.00

1980 Toledo Mud Hens TCMA

This 20-card standard-size set of the 1980 Toledo Mud Hens, a Class AAA International League affiliate of the Minnesota Twins, features red-bordered posed color player photos with rounded corners on its fronts. The player's name and position appear in a white bar under the photo, and the team name is printed under this bar. The horizontal back carries the player's name, position, team, league, and biography.
COMPLETE SET (20)................ 15.00 6.00

1980 Tucson Toros TCMA

This 24-card standard-size set of the 1980 Tucson Toros, a Class AAA Pacific Coast League affiliate of the Houston Astros, features red-bordered posed color player photos with rounded corners on its fronts. The player's name and position appear in a white bar under the photo, and the team name is printed under this bar. The horizontal back carries the player's name, position, team, league, and biography.
COMPLETE SET (24)................ 10.00 4.00

1980 Tulsa Drillers TCMA

This 26-card standard-size set of the 1980 Tulsa Drillers, a Class AA Texas League affiliate of the Texas Rangers, features red-bordered posed color player photos with rounded corners on its fronts. The player's name and position appear in a white bar under the photo, and the team name is printed under this bar. The horizontal back carries the player's name, position, team, league, and biography.
COMPLETE SET (26)................ 10.00 4.00

1980 Utica Blue Jays TCMA

This 33-card standard-size set of the 1980 Utica Blue Jays, a Class A New York-Penn League affiliate of the Toronto Blue Jays, features red-bordered posed black-and-white player photos with rounded corners on its fronts. The player's name and position appear in a white bar under the photo, and the team name is printed under this bar. The horizontal back carries the player's name, position, team, league, and biography.
COMPLETE SET (33)................ 60.00 24.00

1980 Vancouver Canadians TCMA

This 22-card standard-size set of the 1980 Vancouver Canadians, a Class AAA Pacific Coast League affiliate of the Milwaukee Brewers, features red-bordered posed color player photos with rounded corners on its fronts. The player's name and position appear in a white bar under the photo, and the team name is printed under this bar. The horizontal back carries the player's name, position, team, league, and biography.
COMPLETE SET (22)................ 15.00 6.00

1980 Waterbury Reds TCMA

This 22-card standard-size set of the 1980 Waterbury Reds, a Class AA Eastern League affiliate of the Cincinnati Reds, features red-bordered posed black-and-white player photos with rounded corners on its fronts. The player's name and position appear in a white bar under the photo, and the team name is printed under this bar. The horizontal back carries the player's name, position, team, league, and biography.
COMPLETE SET (22)................ 125.00 50.00

1980 Waterloo Indians TCMA

This 35-card standard-size set of the 1980 Waterloo Indians, a Class A Midwest League affiliate of the Cleveland Indians, features red-bordered posed black-and-white player photos with rounded corners on its fronts. The player's name and position appear in a white bar under the photo, and the team name is printed under this bar. The horizontal back carries the player's name, position, team, league, and biography.
COMPLETE SET (35)................ 120.00 47.50

1980 Wausau Timbers TCMA

This 23-card standard-size set of the 1980 Wausau Timbers, a Class A Midwest League Independent, features red-bordered posed black-and-white player photos with rounded corners on its fronts. The player's name and position appear in a white bar under the photo, and the team name is printed under this bar. The horizontal back carries the player's name, position, team, league, and biography.
COMPLETE SET (23)................ 75.00 30.00

1980 West Haven White Caps TCMA

This 31-card standard-size set of the 1980 West Haven White Caps, a Class AA Eastern League affiliate of the Oakland Athletics, features red-bordered posed color player photos with rounded corners on its fronts. The player's name and position appear in a white bar under the photo, and the team name is printed under this bar. The horizontal back carries the player's name, position, team, league, and biography.
COMPLETE SET (31)................ 15.00 6.00

1980 Wichita Aeros TCMA

This 22-card standard-size set of the 1980 Wichita Aeros, a Class AAA American Association affiliate of the Chicago Cubs, features red-bordered posed color player photos with rounded corners on its fronts. The player's name and position appear in a white bar under the photo, and the team name is printed under this bar. The horizontal back carries the player's name, position, team, league, and biography. Approximately 2,500 sets were produced.
COMPLETE SET (22)................ 80.00 32.00

1980 Wisconsin Rapids Twins TCMA

This 27-card standard-size set of the 1980 Wisconsin Rapids Twins, a Class A Midwest League affiliate of the Minnesota Twins, features red-bordered posed black-and-white player photos with rounded corners on its fronts. The player's name and position appear in a white bar under the photo, and the team name is printed under this bar. The horizontal back carries the player's name, position, team, league, and biography.
COMPLETE SET (27)................ 150.00 60.00

1981 Albuquerque Dukes TCMA

This 26-card standard-size set of the 1981 Albuquerque Dukes, a Class AAA Pacific Coast League affiliate of the Los Angeles Dodgers, features white-bordered posed color player photos on its fronts. The player's name and position appear in red letters below the photo. The horizontal back carries the player's name, position, team, and league at the top, followed by biography and statistics.
COMPLETE SET (26)................ 60.00 24.00

1981 Appleton Foxes TCMA

This 29-card standard-size set of the 1981 Appleton Foxes, a Class A Midwest League affiliate of the Chicago White Sox, features white-bordered posed color player photos on its fronts. The player's name and position appear in red letters below the photo. The horizontal back carries the player's name, position, team, and league at the top, followed by biography and statistics.
COMPLETE SET (29)................ 20.00 8.00

1981 Arkansas Travelers TCMA

This 23-card standard-size set of the 1981 Arkansas Travelers, a Class AA Texas League affiliate of the St. Louis Cardinals, features white-bordered posed black-and-white player photos on its fronts. The player's name and position appear in black letters below the photo. The horizontal back carries the player's name, position, team, and league at the top, followed by biography and statistics.
COMPLETE SET (23)................ 30.00 12.00

1981 Batavia Trojans TCMA

This 30-card standard-size set of the 1981 Batavia Trojans, a Class A New York-Penn League affiliate of the Cleveland Indians, features white-bordered posed black-and-white player photos on its fronts. The player's name and position appear in black letters below the photo. The horizontal back carries the player's name, position, team, and league at the top, followed by biography and statistics. Approximately 1,100 sets were produced.
COMPLETE SET (30)................ 25.00 10.00

1981 Birmingham Barons TCMA

This 25-card standard-size set of the 1981 Birmingham Barons, a Class AA Southern League affiliate of the Detroit Tigers, features white-bordered posed black-and-white color player photos on its fronts. The player's name and position appear in black letters below the photo. The horizontal back carries the player's name, position, team, and league at the top, followed by biography and statistics.
COMPLETE SET (25)................ 75.00 30.00

1981 Bristol Red Sox TCMA

This 22-card standard-size set of the 1981 Bristol Red Sox, a Class AA Eastern League affiliate of the Boston Red Sox, features white-bordered posed color player photos on its fronts. The player's name and position appear in red letters below the photo. The horizontal back carries the player's name, position, team, and league at the top, followed by biography and statistics.
COMPLETE SET (22)................ 20.00 8.00

1981 Buffalo Bisons TCMA

This 25-card standard-size set of the 1981 Buffalo Bisons, a Class AA Eastern League affiliate of the Pittsburgh Pirates, features white-bordered posed color player photos on its fronts. The player's name and position appear in red letters below the photo. The horizontal back carries the player's name, position, team, and league at the top, followed by biography and statistics.
COMPLETE SET (25)................ 15.00 6.00

1981 Burlington Bees TCMA

This 29-card standard-size set of the 1981 Burlington Bees, a Class A Midwest League affiliate of the Milwaukee Brewers, features white-bordered posed black-and-white player photos on its fronts. The player's name and position appear in black letters below the photo. The horizontal back carries the player's name, position, team, and league at the top, followed by biography and statistics.
COMPLETE SET (29)................ 30.00 12.00

1981 Cedar Rapids Reds TCMA

This 26-card standard-size set of the 1981 Cedar Rapids Reds, a Class A Midwest League affiliate of the Cincinnati Reds, features white-bordered posed color player photos on its fronts. The player's name and position appear in red letters below the photo. The horizontal back carries the player's name, position, team, and league at the top, followed by biography and statistics.
COMPLETE SET (26)................ 30.00 12.00

1981 Charleston Charlies TCMA

This 24-card standard-size set of the 1981 Charleston Charlies, a Class AAA International League affiliate of the Cleveland Indians, features white-bordered posed color player photos on its fronts. The player's name and position appear in red letters below the photo. The horizontal back carries the player's name, position, team, and league at the top, followed by biography and statistics.
COMPLETE SET (24)................ 25.00 10.00

1981 Charleston Royals TCMA

This 26-card standard-size set of the 1981 Charleston Royals, a Class A South Atlantic League affiliate of the Kansas City Royals, features white-bordered posed black-and-white player photos on its fronts. The player's name and position appear in black letters below the photo. The horizontal back carries the player's name, position, team, and league at the top, followed by biography and statistics.
COMPLETE SET (26)................ 20.00 8.00

1981 Chattanooga Lookouts TCMA

This 25-card standard-size set of the 1981 Chattanooga Lookouts, a Class AA Southern League affiliate of the Cleveland Indians, features white-bordered posed black-and-white player photos on its fronts. The player's name and position appear in black letters below the photo. The horizontal back carries the player's name, position, team, and league at the top, followed by biography and statistics. Approximately 1,100 sets were produced.
COMPLETE SET (25)................ 25.00 10.00

1981 Clinton Giants TCMA

This 29-card standard-size set of the 1981 Clinton Giants, a Class A Midwest League affiliate of the San Francisco Giants, features white-bordered posed black-and-white player photos on its fronts. The player's name and position appear in black letters below the photo. The horizontal back carries the player's name, position, team, and league at the top, followed by biography and statistics.
COMPLETE SET (29)................ 30.00 12.00

1981 Columbus Clippers Police

The Dick Hoover card was issued to honor his career and to memoralize him.
COMPLETE SET (25)................ 15.00 6.00

1981 Columbus Clippers TCMA

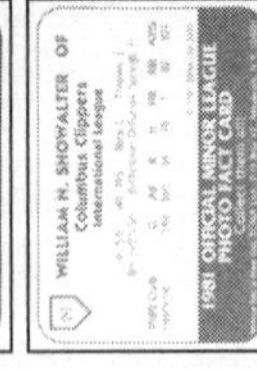

This 28-card standard-size set of the 1981 Columbus Clippers, a Class AAA International League affiliate of the New York Yankees, features white-bordered posed color player photos on its fronts. The player's name and position appear in red letters below the photo. The horizontal back carries the player's name, position, team, and league at the top, followed by biography and statistics.
COMPLETE SET (28)................ 50.00 20.00

1981 Durham Bulls TCMA

This 24-card standard-size set of the 1981 Durham Bulls, a Class A Carolina League affiliate of the Atlanta Braves, features white-bordered posed black-and-white player photos on its fronts. The player's name and position appear in black letters below the photo. The horizontal back carries the player's name, position, team, and league at the top, followed by biography and statistics.
COMPLETE SET (24)................ 25.00 10.00

1981 Edmonton Trappers Red Rooster

COMPLETE SET (24)................ 20.00 8.00

1981 El Paso Diablos TCMA

This 24-card standard-size set of the 1981 El Paso Diablos, a Class AA Texas League affiliate of the Milwaukee Brewers, features white-bordered posed color player photos on its fronts. The player's name and position appear in red letters below the photo. The horizontal back carries the player's name, position, team, and league at the top, followed by biography and statistics.
COMPLETE SET (24)................ 20.00 8.00

1981 Evansville Triplets TCMA

This 22-card standard-size set of the 1981 Evansville Triplets, a Class AAA American Association affiliate of the Detroit Tigers, features white-bordered posed color player photos on its fronts. The player's name and position appear in red letters below the photo. The horizontal back carries the player's name, position, team, and league at the top, followed by biography and statistics.
COMPLETE SET (22)................ 15.00 6.00

1981 Glens Falls White Sox TCMA

This 24-card standard-size set of the 1981 Glens Falls White Sox, a Class AA Eastern League affiliate of the Chicago White Sox, features white-bordered posed color player photos on its fronts. The player's name and position appear in red letters below the photo. The horizontal back carries the player's name, position, team, and league at the top, followed by biography and statistics.
COMPLETE SET(24)................ 40.00 16.00

1981 Hawaii Islanders TCMA

This 23-card standard-size set of the 1981 Hawaii Islanders, a Class AAA Pacific Coast League affiliate of the San Diego Padres, features white-bordered posed color player photos on its fronts. The player's name and position appear in red letters below the photo. The horizontal back carries the player's name, position, team, and league at the top, followed by biography and statistics.
COMPLETE SET (23)................ 10.00 4.00

1981 Holyoke Millers TCMA

This 26-card standard-size set of the 1981 Holyoke Millers, a Class AA Eastern League affiliate of the California Angels, features white-bordered posed color player photos on its fronts. The player's name and position appear in red letters below the photo. The horizontal back carries the player's name, position, team, and league at the top, followed by biography and statistics.
COMPLETE SET (26)................ 15.00 6.00

1981 Indianapolis Indians Team Issue

These sets were available from the team for $5 upon issue.
COMPLETE SET (32)................ 30.00 12.00

1981 Lynn Sailors TCMA

This 29-card standard-size set of the 1981 Lynn Sailors, a Class AA Eastern League affiliate of the Seattle Mariners, features white-bordered posed color player photos on its fronts. The player's name and position appear in red letters below the photo. The horizontal back carries the player's name, position, team, and league at the top, followed by biography and statistics.
COMPLETE SET (29)................ 30.00 12.00

1981 Miami Orioles TCMA

This 23-card standard-size set of the 1981 Miami Orioles, a Class A Florida State League affiliate of the Baltimore Orioles, features white-bordered posed black-and-white player photos on its fronts. The player's name and position appear in black letters below the photo. The horizontal back carries the player's name, position, team, and league at the top, followed by biography and statistics.
COMPLETE SET (21)................ 15.00 6.00
COMPLETE SET W/22/23 (23) 125.00 50.00

1981 Nashville Sounds Team Issue

COMPLETE SET (25)................ 25.00 8.00

1981 Oklahoma City 89ers TCMA

This 26-card standard-size set of the 1981 Oklahoma City 89ers, a Class AAA American Association affiliate of the Philadelphia Phillies, features white-bordered posed color player photos on its fronts. The player's name and position appear in red letters below the photo. The horizontal back carries the player's name, position, team, and league at the top, followed by biography and statistics. This issue includes a second year card of Ryne Sandberg. Approximately 3,500 sets were produced.
COMPLETE SET (26)................ 100.00 40.00

1981 Omaha Royals TCMA

This 24-card standard-size set of the 1981 Omaha Royals, a Class AAA American Association affiliate of the Kansas City Royals, features white-bordered posed color player photos on its fronts. The player's name and position appear in red letters below the photo. The horizontal back carries the player's name, position, team, and league at the top, followed by biography and statistics.
COMPLETE SET (24)................ 20.00 8.00

1981 Pawtucket Red Sox TCMA

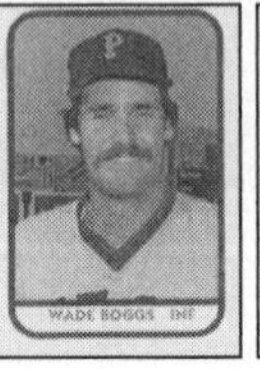

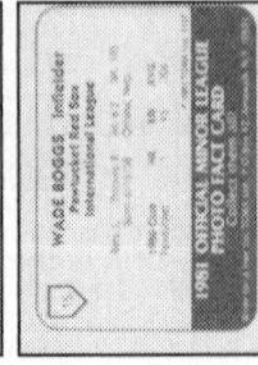

This 24-card standard-size set of the 1981 Pawtucket Red Sox, a Class AAA International League affiliate of the Boston Red Sox, features white-bordered posed color player photos on its fronts. The player's name and position appear in red letters below the photo. The horizontal back carries the player's name, position, team, and league at the top, followed by biography and statistics. This issue includes the only minor league card of Wade Boggs. Approximately 3,500 sets were produced.
COMPLETE SET (24)................ 60.00 24.00

1981 Phoenix Giants Valley National Bank

Hobbyists Lou Chericoni, Miles Locke and Stan Marks were involved in producing this set. This set was available upon issue for $3.
COMPLETE SET (27)................ 15.00 6.00

1981 Portland Beavers TCMA

This 27-card standard-size set of the 1981 Portland Beavers, a Class AAA Pacific Coast League affiliate of the Pittsburgh Pirates, features white-bordered posed color player photos on its fronts. The player's name and position appear in red letters below the photo. The horizontal back carries the player's name, position, team, and league at the top, followed by biography and statistics.
COMPLETE SET (27)................ 15.00 6.00

1981 Quad City Cubs TCMA

This 33-card standard-size set of the 1981 Quad City Cubs, a Class A Midwest League affiliate of the Chicago Cubs, features white-bordered posed black-and-white player photos on its fronts. The player's name and position

appear in black letters below the photo. The horizontal back carries the player's name, position, team, and league at the top, followed by biography and statistics.
COMPLETE SET (33)............... 10.00 4.00

1981 Reading Phillies TCMA

This 24-card standard-size set of the 1981 Reading Phillies, a Class AA Eastern League affiliate of the Philadelphia Phillies, features white-bordered posed black-and-white player photos on its fronts. The player's name and position appear in black letters below the photo. The horizontal back carries the player's name, position, team, and league at the top, followed by biography and statistics.
COMPLETE SET (24)............ 120.00 47.50

1981 Redwood Pioneers TCMA

This 30-card standard-size set of the 1981 Redwood Pioneers, a Class A California League affiliate of the California Angels, features white-bordered posed black-and-white photos on its fronts. The player's name and position appear in black letters below the photo. The horizontal back carries the player's name, position, team, and league at the top, followed by biography and statistics.
COMPLETE SET (30)............... 20.00 8.00

1981 Richmond Braves TCMA

This 25-card standard-size set of the 1981 Richmond Braves, a Class AAA International League affiliate of the Atlanta Braves, features white-bordered posed color player photos on its fronts. The player's name and position appear in red letters below the photo. The horizontal back carries the player's name, position, team, and league at the top, followed by biography and statistics.
COMPLETE SET (25)............... 30.00 12.00

1981 Rochester Red Wings TCMA

This 23-card standard-size set of the 1981 Rochester Red Wings, a Class AAA International League affiliate of the Baltimore Orioles, features white-bordered posed color player photos on its fronts. The player's name and position appear in red letters below the photo. The horizontal back carries the player's name, position, team, and league at the top, followed by biography and statistics. This issue includes a second year card of Cal Ripken Jr. Approximately 3,500 sets were produced.
COMPLETE SET (25)............ 350.00 140.00

1981 Rochester Red Wings WTF

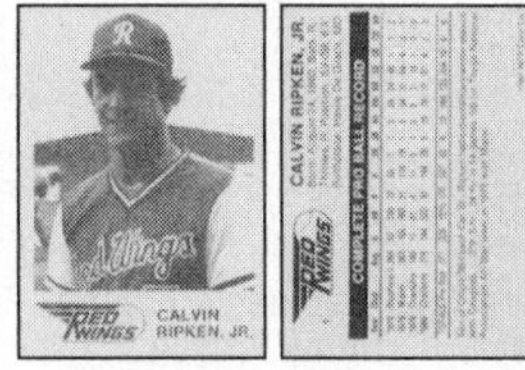

This 25-card standard-size set of the 1981 Rochester Red Wings, a Class AAA International League affiliate of the Baltimore Orioles, features white-bordered posed black-and-white player photos on its fronts. This issue includes a second year card of Cal Ripken Jr.
COMPLETE SET (25)............ 500.00 160.00

1981 Salt Lake City Gulls TCMA

This 26-card standard-size set of the 1981 Salt Lake City Gulls, a Class AAA Pacific Coast League affiliate of the Seattle Mariners, features white-bordered posed color player photos on its fronts. The player's name and position appear in red letters below the photo. The horizontal back carries the player's name, position, team, and league at the top, followed by biography and statistics.
COMPLETE SET (26)............... 15.00 6.00

1981 Shreveport Captains TCMA

This 23-card standard-size set of the 1981 Shreveport Captains, a Class AA Texas League affiliate of the San Francisco Giants, features white-bordered posed black-and-white player photos on its fronts. The player's name and position appear in black letters below the photo. The horizontal back carries the player's name, position, team, and league at the top, followed by biography and statistics.
COMPLETE SET (23)............... 30.00 12.00

1981 Spokane Indians TCMA

This 32-card standard-size set of the 1981 Spokane Indians, a Class AAA Pacific Coast League affiliate of the Seattle Mariners, features white-bordered posed color player photos on its fronts. The player's name and position appear in red letters below the photo. The horizontal back carries the player's name, position, team, and league at the top, followed by biography and statistics.
COMPLETE SET (32)............... 15.00 6.00

1981 Syracuse Chiefs TCMA

This 24-card standard-size set of the 1981 Syracuse Chiefs, a Class AAA International League affiliate of the Toronto Blue Jays, features white-bordered posed color player photos on its fronts. The player's name and position appear in red letters below the photo. The horizontal back carries the player's name, position, team, and league at the top, followed by biography and statistics.
COMPLETE SET (24)............... 15.00 6.00

1981 Syracuse Chiefs Team Issue

Cards measure 3 1/2" by 5" and the backs are blank.
COMPLETE SET (24)............... 75.00 30.00

1981 Tacoma Tigers TCMA

This 32-card standard-size set of the 1981 Tacoma Tigers, a Class AAA Pacific Coast League affiliate of the Oakland Athletics, features white-bordered posed color player photos on its fronts. The player's name and position appear in red letters below the photo. The horizontal back carries the player's name, position, team, and league at the top, followed by biography and statistics.
COMPLETE SET (32)............... 15.00 6.00

1981 Tidewater Tides TCMA

This 29-card standard-size set of the 1981 Tidewater Tides, a Class AAA International League affiliate of the New York Mets, features white-bordered posed color player photos on its fronts. The player's name and position appear in red letters below the photo. The horizontal back carries the player's name, position, team, and league at the top, followed by biography and statistics. Approximately 3,000 sets were produced.
COMPLETE SET (29)............... 20.00 8.00

1981 Toledo Mud Hens TCMA

This 22-card standard-size set of the 1981 Toledo Mud Hens, a Class AAA International League affiliate of the Minnesota Twins, features white-bordered posed color player photos on its fronts. The player's name and position appear in red letters below the photo. The horizontal back carries the player's name, position, team, and league at the top, followed by biography and statistics.
COMPLETE SET (22)............... 15.00 6.00

1981 Tucson Toros TCMA

This 26-card standard-size set of the 1981 Tucson Toros, a Class AAA Pacific Coast League affiliate of the Houston Astros, features white-bordered posed color player photos on its fronts. The player's name and position appear in red letters below the photo. The horizontal back contains safety tips.
COMPLETE SET (26)............... 20.00 8.00

1981 Tulsa Drillers TCMA

This 30-card standard-size set of the 1981 Tulsa Drillers, a Class AA Texas League affiliate of the Texas Rangers, features white-bordered posed color player photos on its fronts. The player's name and position appear in red letters below the photo. The horizontal back carries the player's name, position, team, and league at the top, followed by biography and statistics.
COMPLETE SET (30)............... 20.00 8.00

1981 Vancouver Canadians TCMA

This 25-card standard-size set of the 1981 Vancouver Canadians, a Class AAA Pacific Coast League affiliate of the Milwaukee Brewers, features white-bordered posed color player photos on its fronts. The player's name and position appear in red letters below the photo. The horizontal back carries the player's name, position, team, and league.
COMPLETE SET (25)............... 15.00 6.00

1981 Vero Beach Dodgers TCMA

This 27-card standard-size set of the 1981 Vero Beach Dodgers, a Class A Florida State League affiliate of the Los Angeles Dodgers, features white-bordered posed black-and-white player photos on its fronts. The player's name and position appear in black letters below the photo. The horizontal back carries the player's name, position, team, and league at the top, followed by biography and statistics.
COMPLETE SET (27)............... 15.00 6.00

1981 Waterbury Reds TCMA

This 23-card standard-size set of the 1981 Waterbury Reds, a Class AA Eastern League affiliate of the Cincinnati Reds, features white-bordered posed black-and-white player photos on its fronts. The player's name and position appear in black letters below the photo. The horizontal back carries the player's name, position, team, and league at the top, followed by biography and statistics.
COMPLETE SET (23)............... 40.00 16.00

1981 Waterloo Indians TCMA

This 34-card standard-size set of the 1981 Waterloo Indians, a Class A Midwest League affiliate of the Cleveland Indians, features white-bordered posed black-and-white player photos on its fronts. The player's name and position appear in black letters below the photo. The horizontal back carries the player's name, position, team, and league at the top, followed by biography and statistics.
COMPLETE SET (34)............... 30.00 12.00

1981 Wausau Timbers TCMA

This 29-card standard-size set of the 1981 Wausau Timbers, a Class A Midwest League affiliate of the Seattle Mariners, features white-bordered posed black-and-white player photos on its fronts. The player's name and position appear in black letters below the photo. The horizontal back carries the player's name, position, team, and league at the top, followed by biography and statistics.
COMPLETE SET (29)............... 40.00 16.00

1981 West Haven A's TCMA

This 23-card standard-size set of the 1981 West Haven A's, a Class AA Eastern League affiliate of the Oakland Athletics, features white-bordered posed color player photos on its fronts. The player's name and position appear in red letters below the photo. The horizontal back carries the player's name, position, team, and league at the top, followed by biography and statistics.
COMPLETE SET (23)............... 30.00 12.00

1981 Wisconsin Rapids Twins TCMA

This 23-card standard-size set of the 1981 Wisconsin Rapids Twins, a Class A Midwest League affiliate of the Minnesota Twins, features white-bordered posed black-and-white player photos on its fronts. The player's name and position appear in black letters below the photo. The horizontal back carries the player's name, position, team, and league at the top, followed by biography and statistics.
COMPLETE SET (23)............... 30.00 12.00

1982 Albuquerque Dukes TCMA

This 27-card standard-size set of the 1982 Albuquerque Dukes, a Class AAA Pacific Coast League affiliate of the Los Angeles Dodgers, features white-bordered posed color player photos on its fronts. Most are horizontally oriented. The player's name and position appear at the (vertical) bottom. The white and black back carries the team name at the top, followed below by the league affiliation, and then the player's name, biography and statistics. This issue includes the minor league card debut of Orel Hershiser.
COMPLETE SET (27)............... 40.00 16.00

1982 Alexandria Dukes TCMA

This 27-card standard-size set of the 1982 Alexandria Dukes, a Class A Carolina League affiliate of the Pittsburgh Pirates, features white-bordered posed black-and-white player photos on its fronts. The player's name and position appear at the bottom. The white and black back carries the team name at the top, followed below by the league affiliation, and then the player's name, biography and statistics.
COMPLETE SET (27)............... 30.00 12.00

1982 Amarillo Gold Sox TCMA

This 25-card standard-size set of the 1982 Amarillo Gold Sox, a Class AA Texas League affiliate of the San Diego Padres, features white-bordered posed black-and-white player photos on its fronts. The player's name and position appear at the bottom. The white and black back carries the team name at the top, followed below by the league affiliation, and then the player's name, biography and statistics.
COMPLETE SET (25)............... 30.00 12.00

1982 Appleton Foxes Fritsch

All the Midwest league sets issued by Larry Fritsch were available upon issue at $3.75 per set.
COMPLETE SET (31)............... 10.00 4.00

1982 Arkansas Travelers TCMA

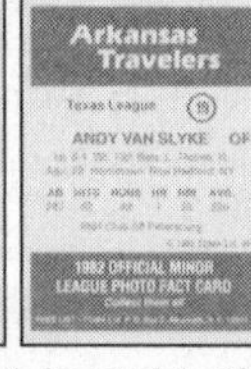

This 24-card standard-size set of the 1982 Arkansas Travelers, a Class AA Texas League affiliate of the St. Louis Cardinals, features white-bordered posed black-and-white player photos on its fronts. The player's name and position appear at the bottom. The white and black back carries the team name at the top, followed below by the league affiliation, and then the player's name, biography and statistics.
COMPLETE SET (24)............. 120.00 47.50

1982 Auburn Astros TCMA

This 19-card standard-size set of the 1982 Auburn Astros, a Class A New York-Penn League affiliate of the Houston Astros, features white-bordered posed black-and-white player photos on its fronts. The player's name and position appear at the bottom. The white and black back carries the team name at the top, followed below by the league affiliation, and then the player's name, biography and statistics.
COMPLETE SET (19)............... 15.00 6.00

1982 Beloit Brewers Fritsch

COMPLETE SET (27)............... 10.00 4.00

1982 Birmingham Barons TCMA

This 24-card standard-size set of the 1982 Birmingham Barons, a Class AA Southern League affiliate of the Detroit Tigers, features white-bordered posed color player photos on its fronts. Most are horizontally oriented. The player's name and position appear at the (vertical) bottom. The white and black back carries the team name at the top, followed below by the league affiliation, and then the player's name, biography and statistics.
COMPLETE SET (24)............... 15.00 6.00

1982 Buffalo Bisons TCMA

This 18-card standard-size set of the 1982 Buffalo Bisons, a Class AA Eastern League affiliate of the Pittsburgh Pirates, features white-bordered posed color player photos on its fronts. Most are horizontally oriented. The player's name and position appear at the (vertical) bottom. The white and black back carries the team name at the top, followed below by the league affiliation, and then the player's name, biography and statistics.
COMPLETE SET (18)............... 20.00 8.00

1982 Burlington Rangers Fritsch

COMPLETE SET (30)................. 8.00 3.20

1982 Burlington Rangers TCMA

This 27-card standard-size set of the 1982 Burlington Rangers, a Class A Midwest League affiliate of the Texas Rangers, features white-bordered posed black-and-white player photos on its fronts. The player's name and position appear at the bottom. The white and black back carries the team name at the top, followed below by the league affiliation, and then the player's name, biography and statistics.
COMPLETE SET (26)............... 25.00 10.00

1982 Cedar Rapids Reds TCMA

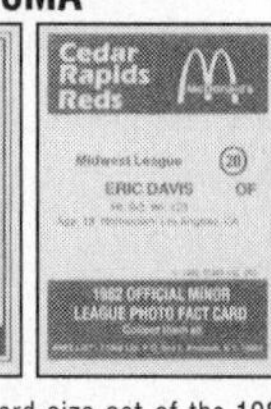

This 27-card standard-size set of the 1982 Cedar Rapids Reds, a Class A Midwest League affiliate of the Cincinnati Reds, features white-bordered posed color player photos on its fronts. Most are horizontally oriented. The player's name and position appear at the (vertical) bottom. The white and black back carries the team name at the top, followed below by the league affiliation, and then the player's name, biography and statistics. This issue includes the minor league card debut of Eric Davis. Approximately 3,000 sets were produced.
COMPLETE SET (27)............... 60.00 24.00

1982 Charleston Charlies TCMA

This 24-card standard-size set of the 1982 Charleston Charlies, a Class AAA International League affiliate of the Cleveland Indians, features white-bordered posed color player photos on its fronts. Most are horizontally oriented. The player's name and position appear at the (vertical) bottom. The white and black back carries the team name at the top, followed below by the league affiliation, and then the player's name, biography and statistics.
COMPLETE SET (24)............... 15.00 6.00

1982 Charleston Royals TCMA

This 24-card standard-size set of the 1982 Charleston Royals, a Class A South Atlantic League affiliate of the Kansas City Royals, features white-bordered posed black-and-white player photos on its fronts. The player's name and position appear at the bottom. The white and black back carries the team name at the top, followed below by the league affiliation, and then the player's name, biography and statistics. This issue includes the minor league card debut of David Cone.
COMPLETE SET (24)............... 75.00 30.00

1982 Chattanooga Lookouts TCMA

This 25-card standard-size set of the 1982 Chattanooga Lookouts, a Class AA Southern League affiliate of the Cleveland Indians, features white-bordered posed black-and-white player photos on its fronts. The player's name and position appear at the bottom. The white and black back carries the team name at the top, followed below by the league affiliation, and then the player's name, biography and statistics.
COMPLETE SET (25)............... 50.00 20.00

1982 Clinton Giants Fritsch

COMPLETE SET (32)............... 25.00 10.00

1982 Columbus Clippers Police

A second year minor league card of Don Mattingly is in this set.
COMPLETE SET (25)............... 30.00 12.00

1982 Columbus Clippers TCMA

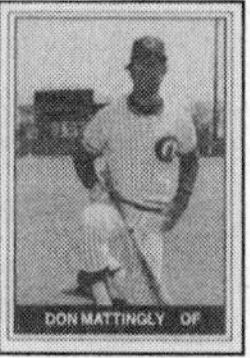

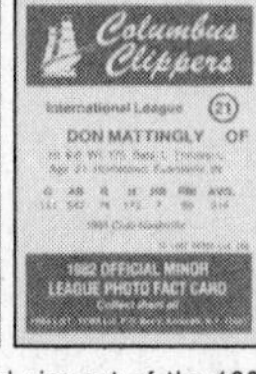

This 26-card standard-size set of the 1982 Columbus Clippers, a Class AAA International League affiliate of the New York Yankees, features white-bordered posed color player photos on its fronts. Most are horizontally oriented. The player's name and position appear at the (vertical) bottom. The white and black back carries the team name at the top, followed below by the league affiliation, and then the player's name, biography and statistics. This issue includes a second year minor league card of Don Mattingly. Approximately 3,500 sets were produced.
COMPLETE SET (26)............. 100.00 40.00

1982 Danville Suns Fritsch

COMPLETE SET (28)............... 25.00 10.00

1982 Daytona Beach Astros TCMA

This 25-card standard-size set of the 1982 Daytona Beach Astros, a Class A Florida State League affiliate of the Houston Astros, features white-bordered posed black-and-white player photos on its fronts. The player's name and position appear at the bottom. The white and black back carries the team name at the top, followed below by the league affiliation, and then the player's name, biography and statistics. Approximately 1,100 sets were produced.
COMPLETE SET (25)............... 30.00 12.00

1982 Durham Bulls TCMA

This 25-card standard-size set of the 1982 Durham Bulls, a Class A Carolina League affiliate of the Atlanta Braves, features white-bordered posed black-and-white player photos on its fronts. The player's name and position appear at the bottom. The white and black back carries the team name at the top, followed below by the league affiliation, and then the player's name, biography and statistics.
COMPLETE SET (25)............... 50.00 20.00

1982 Edmonton Trappers TCMA

This 25-card standard-size set of the 1982 Edmonton Trappers, a Class AAA Pacific Coast League affiliate of the Chicago White Sox, features white-bordered posed color player photos on its fronts. Most are horizontally oriented. The player's name and position appear at the (vertical) bottom. The white and black back carries the team name at the top, followed below by the league affiliation, and then the player's name, biography and statistics.
COMPLETE SET (25)............... 30.00 12.00

1982 El Paso Diablos TCMA

This 24-card standard-size set of the 1982 El Paso Diablos, a Class AA Texas League affiliate of the Milwaukee Brewers, features white-bordered posed color player photos on its fronts. The player's name and position appear at the bottom. The white and black back carries the team name at the top, followed below by the league affiliation, and then the player's name, biography and statistics.
COMPLETE SET (24)............... 20.00 8.00

1982 Evansville Triplets TCMA

This 25-card standard-size set of the 1982 Evansville Triplets, a Class AAA American Association affiliate of the Detroit Tigers, features white-bordered posed color player photos on its fronts. The player's name and position appear at the bottom. The white and black back carries the team name at the top, followed below by the league affiliation, and

then the player's name, biography and statistics.
COMPLETE SET (25)................ 15.00 6.00

1982 Fort Myers Royals TCMA

This 23-card standard-size set of the 1982 Fort Myers Royals, a Class A Florida State League affiliate of the Kansas City Royals, features white-bordered posed black-and-white player photos on its fronts. The player's name and position appear at the bottom. The white and black back carries the team name at the top, followed below by the league affiliation, and then the player's name, biography and statistics.
COMPLETE SET (23)................ 20.00 8.00

1982 Glens Falls White Sox TCMA

This 23-card standard-size set of the 1982 Glens Falls White Sox, a Class AA Eastern League affiliate of the Chicago White Sox, features white-faced fronts bordered by two thin red lines framing posed black-and-white player portraits. A red stripe below the photo carries the player's name and position. The white back carries the team name at the top, followed by the player's name, position, biography and statistics.
COMPLETE SET (23)............. 150.00 60.00

1982 Hawaii Islanders TCMA

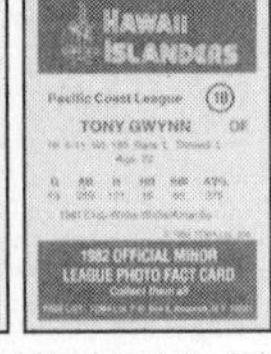

This 25-card standard-size set of the 1982 Hawaii Islanders, a Class AAA Pacific Coast League affiliate of the San Diego Padres, features white-bordered posed color player photos on its fronts. The player's name and position appear at the bottom. The white and black back carries the team name at the top, followed below by the league affiliation, and then the player's name, biography and statistics. This issue includes the only minor league card of Tony Gwynn.
COMPLETE SET (25)............. 250.00 100.00

1982 Holyoke Millers TCMA

This 26-card standard-size set of the 1982 Holyoke Millers, a Class AA Eastern League affiliate of the California Angels, features white-bordered posed color player photos on its fronts. The player's name and position appear at the bottom. The white and black back carries the team name at the top, followed below by the league affiliation, and then the player's name, biography and statistics.
COMPLETE SET (26)................ 10.00 4.00

1982 Idaho Falls Athletics TCMA

This 33-card standard-size set of the 1982 Idaho Falls Athletics, a Rookie Class Pioneer League affiliate of the Oakland Athletics, features white-faced fronts bordered by two thin red lines framing posed black-and-white player portraits. A red stripe below the photo carries the player's name and position. The white back carries the team name at the top, followed by the player's name, position, biography and statistics.
COMPLETE SET (33)................ 20.00 8.00

1982 Indianapolis Indians Team Issue

1,200 sets were produced.
COMPLETE SET (32)................ 20.00 8.00

1982 Iowa Cubs TCMA

This 32-card standard-size set of the 1982 Iowa Cubs, a Class AAA American Association affiliate of the Chicago Cubs, features white-bordered posed color player photos on its fronts. The player's name and position appear at the bottom. The white and black back carries the team name at the top, followed below by the league affiliation, and then the player's name, biography and statistics.
COMPLETE SET (32)................ 30.00 12.00

1982 Jackson Mets TCMA

This 25-card standard-size set of the 1982 Jackson Mets, a Class AA Texas League affiliate of the New York Mets, features white-bordered posed color player photos on its fronts. The player's name and position appear at the bottom. The white and black back carries the team name at the top, followed below by the league affiliation, and then the player's name, biography and statistics. This issue includes the minor league card debut of Darryl Strawberry. Approximately 2,500 sets were produced.
COMPLETE SET (25)................ 40.00 16.00

1982 Kinston Blue Jays Kelly Studio

These cards feature members of the 1982 Kinston Blue Jays that feature future NFL quarterback Jay Schroeder. Since these cards are unnumbered, we have sequenced them in alphabetical order.
COMPLETE SET 20.00 9.00

1982 Knoxville Blue Jays TCMA

This 23-card standard-size set of the 1982 Knoxville Blue Jays, a Class AA Southern League affiliate of the Toronto Blue Jays, features white-faced fronts bordered by two thin red lines framing posed black-and-white player portraits. A red stripe below the photo carries the player's name and position. The white back carries the team name at the top, followed by the player's name, position, biography and statistics.
COMPLETE SET (23)................ 15.00 6.00

1982 Louisville Redbirds Ehrlers

COMPLETE SET (30)................ 30.00 12.00

1982 Lynchburg Mets TCMA

This 23-card standard-size set of the 1982 Lynchburg Mets, a Class A Carolina League affiliate of the New York Mets, features white-bordered posed black-and-white player photos on its fronts. The player's name and position appear at the bottom. The white and black back carries the team name at the top, followed below by the league affiliation, and then the player's name, biography and statistics.
COMPLETE SET (20)................ 50.00 20.00

1982 Lynn Sailors TCMA

This 18-card standard-size set of the 1982 Lynn Sailors, a Class AA Eastern League affiliate of the Seattle Mariners, features white-bordered posed black-and-white player photos on its fronts. The player's name and position appear at the bottom. The white and black back carries the team name at the top, followed below by the league affiliation, and then the player's name, biography and statistics.
COMPLETE SET (18)................ 30.00 12.00

1982 Madison Muskies Fritsch

COMPLETE SET (34).................. 8.00 3.20

1982 Miami Marlins TCMA

This 22-card standard-size set of the 1982 Miami Marlins, a Class A Florida State League affiliate of the San Diego Padres, features white-bordered posed black-and-white player photos on its fronts. The player's name and position appear at the bottom. The white and black back carries the team name at the top, followed below by the league affiliation, and then the player's name, biography and statistics.
COMPLETE SET (22)................ 15.00 6.00

1982 Nashville Sounds Team Issue

COMPLETE SET (28).................. 8.00 3.20

1982 Oklahoma City 89ers TCMA

This 25-card standard-size set of the 1982 Oklahoma City 89ers, a Class AAA American Association affiliate of the Texas Rangers, features white-bordered posed color player photos on its fronts. The player's name and position appear at the bottom. The white and black back carries the team name at the top, followed below by the league affiliation, and then the player's name, biography and statistics.
COMPLETE SET (25)................ 50.00 20.00

1982 Omaha Royals TCMA

This 29-card standard-size set of the 1982 Omaha Royals, a Class AAA American Association affiliate of the Kansas City Royals, features white-bordered posed color player photos on its fronts. The player's name and position appear at the bottom. The white and black back carries the team name at the top, followed below by the league affiliation, and then the player's name, biography and statistics.
COMPLETE SET (27)................ 20.00 8.00
COMPLETE SET (29)................ 60.00 24.00

1982 Oneonta Yankees TCMA

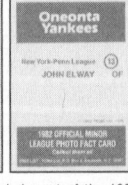

This 17-card standard-size set of the 1982 Oneonta Yankees, a Class A New York-Penn League affiliate of the New York Yankees, features white-bordered posed black-and-white player photos on its fronts. The player's name and position appear at the bottom. The white and black back carries the team name at the top, followed below by the league affiliation, and then the player's name, biography and statistics. This issue includes the only minor league card of Denver Broncos' quarterback John Elway. Approximately 1,100 sets were produced.
COMPLETE SET (17)............. 400.00 160.00

1982 Orlando Twins 81 SL Champs TCMA

This 24-card standard-size set of the 1982 Orlando Twins, a Class AA Southern League affiliate of the Minnesota Twins, features white-bordered posed black-and-white player photos on its fronts. The player's name and position appear at the bottom. The white and black back carries the team name at the top, followed below by the league affiliation, and then the player's name, biography and statistics. The words Southern League Champs is printed on the front of each card.
COMPLETE SET (24)................ 60.00 24.00

1982 Orlando Twins TCMA

This 24-card standard-size set of the 1982 Orlando Twins, a Class AA Southern League affiliate of the Minnesota Twins, features white-bordered posed black-and-white player photos on its fronts. The player's name and position appear at the bottom. The white and black back carries the team name at the top, followed below by the league affiliation, and then the player's name, biography and statistics.
COMPLETE SET (24)................ 40.00 16.00

1982 Phoenix Giants Valley National Bank

COMPLETE SET (27)................ 15.00 6.00

1982 Portland Beavers TCMA

This 25-card standard-size set of the 1982 Portland Beavers, a Class AAA Pacific Coast League affiliate of the Pittsburgh Pirates, features white-bordered posed color player photos on its fronts. The player's name and position appear at the bottom. The white and black back carries the team name at the top, followed below by the league affiliation, and then the player's name, biography and statistics.
COMPLETE SET (25)................ 20.00 8.00

1982 Quad City Cubs TCMA

This 28-card standard-size set of the 1982 Quad City Cubs, a Class A Midwest League affiliate of the Chicago Cubs, features white-bordered posed black-and-white player photos on its fronts. The player's name and position appear at the bottom. The white and black back carries the team name at the top, followed below by the league affiliation, and then the player's name, biography and statistics.
COMPLETE SET (28)................ 20.00 8.00

1982 Reading Phillies TCMA

This 22-card standard-size set of the 1982 Reading Phillies, a Class AA Eastern League affiliate of the Philadelphia Phillies, features white-bordered posed black-and-white player photos on its fronts. The player's name and position appear at the bottom. The white and black back carries the team name at the top, followed below by the league affiliation, and then the player's name, biography and statistics.
COMPLETE SET (22)................ 30.00 12.00

1982 Redwood Pioneers TCMA

This 27-card standard-size set of the 1982 Redwood Pioneers, a Class A California League affiliate of the California Angels, features white-bordered posed black-and-white player photos on its fronts. The player's name and position appear at the bottom. The white and black back carries the team name at the top, followed below by the league affiliation, and then the player's name, biography and statistics.
COMPLETE SET (27)................ 20.00 8.00

1982 Richmond Braves TCMA

This 32-card standard-size set of the 1982 Richmond Braves, a Class AAA International League affiliate of the Atlanta Braves, features white-bordered posed color player photos on its fronts. The player's name and position appear at the bottom. The white and black back carries the team name at the top, followed below by the league affiliation, and then the player's name, biography and statistics.
COMPLETE SET (31)................ 25.00 10.00
COMPLETE SET (32)............. 100.00 40.00

1982 Rochester Red Wings TCMA

This 22-card standard-size set of the 1982 Rochester Red Wings, a Class AAA International League affiliate of the Baltimore Orioles, features white-bordered posed color player photos on its fronts. The player's name and position appear at the bottom. The white and black back carries the team name at the top, followed below by the league affiliation, and then the player's name, biography and statistics.
COMPLETE SET (22)................ 20.00 8.00

1982 Salt Lake City Gulls TCMA

This 25-card standard-size set of the 1982 Salt Lake City Gulls, a Class AAA Pacific Coast League affiliate of the Seattle Mariners, features white-bordered posed color player photos on its fronts. The player's name and position appear at the bottom. The white and black back carries the team name at the top, followed below by the league affiliation, and then the player's name, biography and statistics.
COMPLETE SET (25)................ 15.00 6.00

1982 Spokane Indians TCMA

This 26-card standard-size set of the 1982 Spokane Indians, a Class AAA Pacific Coast League affiliate of the California Angels, features white-bordered posed color player photos on its fronts. The player's name and position appear at the bottom. The white and black back carries the team name at the top, followed below by the league affiliation, and then the player's name, biography and statistics.
COMPLETE SET (26)................ 15.00 6.00

1982 Springfield Cardinals Fritsch

COMPLETE SET (24).................. 8.00 3.20

1982 Syracuse Chiefs TCMA

This 29-card standard-size set of the 1982 Syracuse Chiefs, a Class AAA International League affiliate of the Toronto Blue Jays, features white-bordered posed color player photos on its fronts. The player's name and position appear at the bottom. The white and black back carries the team name at the top, followed below by the league affiliation, and then the player's name, biography and statistics. This issue includes Tony Fernandez' minor league debut. Two cards were issued bearing number 27; those and number 28 were late issues.
COMPLETE SET (26)................ 40.00 16.00

1982 Syracuse Chiefs Team Issue

This issue includes Tony Fernandez' minor league card debut.
COMPLETE SET (24)............. 100.00 40.00

1982 Tacoma Tigers TCMA

This 39-card standard-size set of the 1982 Tacoma Tigers, a Class AAA Pacific Coast League affiliate of the Oakland Athletics, features white-bordered posed color player photos on its fronts. The player's name and position appear at the bottom. The white and black back carries the team name at the top, followed below by the league affiliation, and then the player's name, biography and statistics.
COMPLETE SET (37)................ 15.00 6.00

1982 Tidewater Tides TCMA

This 26-card standard-size set of the 1982 Tidewater Tides, a Class AAA International League affiliate of the New York Mets, features white-bordered posed color player photos on its fronts. The player's name and position appear at the bottom. The white and black back carries the team name at the top, followed below by the league affiliation, and then the player's name, biography and statistics.
COMPLETE SET (25)................ 25.00 10.00

1982 Toledo Mud Hens TCMA

This 27-card standard-size set of the 1982 Toledo Mud Hens, a Class AAA International League affiliate of the Minnesota Twins, features white-bordered posed color player photos on its fronts. The player's name and position appear at the bottom. The white and black back carries the team name at the top, followed below by the league affiliation, and then the player's name, biography and statistics.
COMPLETE SET (24)................ 30.00 12.00

1982 Tucson Toros TCMA

This 28-card standard-size set of the 1982 Tucson Toros, a Class AAA Pacific Coast League affiliate of the Houston Astros, features white-bordered posed color player photos on its fronts. The player's name and position appear at the bottom. The white and black back carries safety tips.
COMPLETE SET (28)................ 25.00 10.00

1982 Tulsa Drillers TCMA

This 28-card standard-size set of the 1982 Tulsa Drillers, a Class AA Texas League affiliate of the Texas Rangers, features white-bordered posed color player photos on its fronts. The player's name and position appear at the bottom. The white and black back carries the team name at the top, followed below by the league affiliation, and then the player's name, biography and statistics.
COMPLETE SET (24)................ 30.00 12.00

1982 Vancouver Canadians TCMA

This 24-card standard-size set of the 1982 Vancouver Canadians, a Class AAA Pacific Coast League affiliate of the Milwaukee Brewers, features white-bordered posed color player photos on its fronts. The player's name and position appear at the bottom. The white and black back carries the team name at the top, followed below by the league affiliation, and then the player's name, biography and statistics.
COMPLETE SET (24)................ 15.00 6.00

1982 Vero Beach Dodgers TCMA

This 29-card standard-size set of the 1982 Vero Beach Dodgers, a Class A Florida State League affiliate of the Los Angeles Dodgers, features white-bordered posed black-and-white player photos on its fronts. The player's name and position appear at the bottom. The white and black back carries the team name at the top, followed below by the league affiliation, and then the player's name, biography and statistics.
COMPLETE SET (29)................ 50.00 20.00

1982 Waterbury Reds TCMA

This 23-card standard-size set of the 1982 Waterbury Reds, a Class AA Eastern League affiliate of the Cincinnati Reds, features white-bordered posed color photos on its fronts. The player's name and position appear at the bottom. The white and black back carries the team name at the top, followed below by the league affiliation, and then the player's name, biography and statistics. This issue includes the minor league card debut of Danny Tartabull. Approximately 1,600 sets were produced.
COMPLETE SET (23)................ 50.00 20.00

1982 Waterloo Indians Fritsch

COMPLETE SET (28).................. 8.00 3.20

1982 Waterloo Indians TCMA

This 28-card standard-size set of the 1982 Waterloo Indians, a Class A Midwest League affiliate of the Cleveland Indians, features white-bordered posed black-and-white player photos on its fronts. The player's name and position appear at the bottom. The white and black back carries the team name at the top, followed below by the league affiliation, and then the player's name, biography and statistics.
COMPLETE SET (25)................ 15.00 6.00

1982 Wausau Timbers Fritsch

COMPLETE SET (31)................ 15.00 6.00

1982 West Haven A's TCMA

This 29-card standard-size set of the 1982 West Haven A's, a Class AA Eastern League affiliate of the Oakland Athletics, features white-bordered posed black-and-white player photos on its fronts. The player's name and position appear at the bottom. The white and black back carries the team name at the top, followed below by the league affiliation, and then the player's name, biography and statistics.
COMPLETE SET (29)................ 20.00 8.00

1982 Wichita Aeros Team Issue

This 20-card standard-size set of the 1982 Wichita Aeros, a Class AAA American Association affiliate of the Montreal Expos, features white-bordered posed color player photos on its fronts. The player's name, team, and position appear at the bottom. The white back carries the Aeros All Time Single Season Batting Records. The cards are unnumbered and checklisted below in alphabetical order.
COMPLETE SET (20)................ 25.00 10.00

1982 Wisconsin Rapids Twins Fritsch

COMPLETE SET (27)................ 15.00 6.00

1983 Albany-Colonie A's TCMA

This 20-card standard-size set of the 1983 Albany A's, a Class AA Eastern League affiliate of the Oakland Athletics, features white-bordered posed color player photos on its fronts. The player's name and position appear within a blue stripe at the bottom. The plain back carries the team name at the top, followed below by the league affiliation, and then the player's name, biography and statistics.
COMPLETE SET (20)................ 50.00 20.00

1983 Albuquerque Dukes TCMA

This 25-card standard-size set of the 1983 Albuquerque Dukes, a Class AAA Pacific Coast League affiliate of the Los Angeles Dodgers, features white-bordered posed color player photos on its fronts. The player's name and position appear within a blue stripe at the bottom. The plain back carries the team name at the top, followed below by the league affiliation, and then the player's name, biography and statistics. This issue includes a second year card of Orel Hershiser.
COMPLETE SET (25)................ 40.00 16.00

1983 Alexandria Dukes TCMA

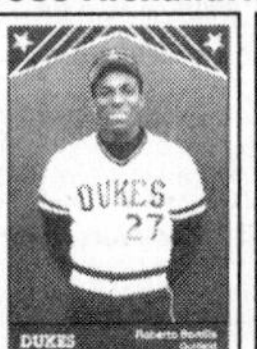
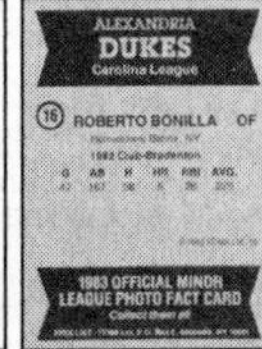

This 31-card standard-size set of the 1983 Alexandria Dukes, a Class A Carolina League affiliate of the Pittsburgh Pirates, features white-bordered posed color player photos on its fronts. The player's name and position appear within a blue stripe at the bottom. The plain back carries the team name at the top,

followed below by the league affiliation, and then the player's name, biography and statistics. This issue includes the minor league card debut of Bobby Bonilla. Approximately 1,100 sets were produced.
COMPLETE SET (31)............... 30.00 12.00

1983 Anderson Braves TCMA

This 33-card standard-size set of the 1983 Anderson Braves, a Class A South Atlantic League affiliate of the Atlanta Braves, features white-bordered posed color player photos on its fronts. The player's name and position appear within a blue stripe at the bottom. The plain back carries the team name at the top, followed below by the league affiliation, and then the player's name, biography and statistics.
COMPLETE SET (33)............... 25.00 10.00

1983 Appleton Foxes Fritsch

COMPLETE SET (30)............... 15.00 6.00

1983 Arkansas Travelers TCMA

This 25-card standard-size set of the 1983 Arkansas Travelers, a Class AA Texas League affiliate of the St. Louis Cardinals, features white-bordered posed color player photos on its fronts. The player's name and position appear within a blue stripe at the bottom. The plain back carries the team name at the top, followed below by the league affiliation, and then the player's name, biography and statistics.
COMPLETE SET (25)............... 60.00 24.00

1983 Beaumont Golden Gators TCMA

This 23-card standard-size set of the 1983 Beaumont Golden Gators, a Class AA Texas League affiliate of the San Diego Padres, features white-bordered posed color player photos on its fronts. The player's name and position appear within a blue stripe at the bottom. The plain back carries the team name at the top, followed below by the league affiliation, and then the player's name, biography and statistics.
COMPLETE SET (23)............... 60.00 24.00

1983 Beloit Brewers Fritsch

COMPLETE SET (30)............... 15.00 6.00

1983 Birmingham Barons TCMA

This 25-card standard-size set of the 1983 Birmingham Barons, a Class AA Southern League affiliate of the DetroitTigers, features white-bordered posed color player photos on its fronts. The player's name and position appear within a blue stripe at the bottom. The plain back carries the team name at the top, followed below by the league affiliation, and then the player's name, biography and statistics.
COMPLETE SET (25)............... 15.00 6.00

1983 Buffalo Bisons TCMA

This 25-card standard-size set of the 1983 Buffalo Bisons, a Class AA Eastern League affiliate of the Cleveland Indians, features white-bordered posed color player photos on its fronts. The player's name and position appear within a blue stripe at the bottom. The plain back carries the team name at the top, followed below by the league affiliation, and then the player's name, biography and statistics.
COMPLETE SET (25)............... 30.00 12.00

1983 Burlington Rangers Fritsch

COMPLETE SET (30)............... 10.00 4.00

1983 Burlington Rangers TCMA

This 28-card standard-size set of the 1983 Burlington Rangers, a Class A Midwest League affiliate of the Texas Rangers, features white-bordered posed color player photos on its fronts. The player's name and position appear within a blue stripe at the bottom. The plain back carries the team name at the top, followed below by the league affiliation, and then the player's name, biography and statistics.
COMPLETE SET (28)............... 20.00 8.00

1983 Butte Copper Kings TCMA

This 33-card standard-size set of the 1983 Butte Copper Kings, a Rookie Class Pioneer League affiliate of the Kansas City Royals, features white-bordered posed color player photos on its fronts. The player's name and position appear within a blue stripe at the bottom. The plain back carries the team name at the top, followed below by the league affiliation, and then the player's name, biography and statistics. Approximately 1,100 sets were produced.
COMPLETE SET (33)............... 30.00 12.00

1983 Cedar Rapids Reds Fritsch

COMPLETE SET (26)............... 15.00 6.00

1983 Cedar Rapids Reds TCMA

This 28-card standard-size set of the 1983 Cedar Rapids Reds, a Class A Midwest League affiliate of the Cincinnati Reds, features white-bordered posed color player photos on its fronts. The player's name and position appear within a blue stripe at the bottom. The plain back carries the team name at the top, followed below by the league affiliation, and then the player's name, biography and statistics.
COMPLETE SET (28)............... 30.00 12.00

1983 Charleston Charlies TCMA

This 22-card standard-size set of the 1983 Charleston Royals, a Class AAA International League affiliate of the Cleveland Indians, features white-bordered posed color player photos on its fronts. The player's name and position appear within a blue stripe at the bottom. The plain back carries the team name at the top, followed below by the league affiliation, and then the player's name, biography and statistics.
COMPLETE SET (22)............... 10.00 4.00

1983 Charleston Royals TCMA

This 26-card standard-size set of the 1983 Charleston Royals, a Class A South Atlantic League affiliate of the Kansas City Royals, features white-bordered posed color player photos on its fronts. The player's name and position appear within a blue stripe at the bottom. The plain back carries the team name at the top, followed below by the league affiliation, and then the player's name, biography and statistics.
COMPLETE SET (26)............... 15.00 6.00

1983 Chattanooga Lookouts TCMA

This 28-card standard-size set of the 1983 Chattanooga Lookouts, a Class AA Southern League affiliate of the Seattle Mariners, features white-bordered posed color player photos on its fronts. The player's name and position appear within a blue stripe at the bottom. The plain back carries the team name at the top, followed below by the league affiliation, and then the player's name, biography and statistics. This issue includes the minor league card debut of Mark Langston.
COMPLETE SET (28)............ 150.00 60.00

1983 Clinton Giants Fritsch

COMPLETE SET (30)................. 8.00 3.20

1983 Columbus Astros TCMA

This 24-card standard-size set of the 1983 Columbus Astros, a Class AA Southern League affiliate of the Houston Astros, features white-bordered posed color player photos on its fronts. The player's name and position appear within a blue stripe at the bottom. The plain back carries the team name at the top, followed below by the league affiliation, and then the player's name, biography and statistics.
COMPLETE SET (24)............... 50.00 20.00

1983 Columbus Clippers TCMA

This 27-card standard-size set of the 1983 Columbus Clippers, a Class AAA International League affiliate of the New York Yankees, features white-bordered posed color player photos on its fronts. The player's name and position appear within a blue stripe at the bottom. The plain back carries the team name at the top, followed below by the league affiliation, and then the player's name, biography and statistics.
COMPLETE SET (27)............... 50.00 20.00

1983 Daytona Beach Astros TCMA

This 27-card standard-size set of the 1983 Daytona Beach Astros, a Class A Florida State League affiliate of the Houston Astros, features white-bordered posed color player photos on its fronts. The player's name and position appear within a blue stripe at the bottom. The plain back carries the team name at the top, followed below by the league affiliation, and then the player's name, biography and statistics.
COMPLETE SET (27)............... 15.00 6.00

1983 Durham Bulls TCMA

This 29-card standard-size set of the 1983 Durham Bulls, a Class A Carolina League affiliate of the Atlanta Braves, features white-bordered posed color player photos on its fronts. The player's name and position appear within a blue stripe at the bottom. The plain back carries the team name at the top, followed below by the league affiliation, and then the player's name, biography and statistics.
COMPLETE SET (29)............... 25.00 10.00

1983 El Paso Diablos TCMA

This 25-card standard-size set of the 1983 El Paso Diablos, a Class AA Texas League affiliate of the Milwaukee Brewers, features white-bordered posed color player photos on its fronts. The player's name and position appear within a blue stripe at the bottom. The plain back carries the team name at the top, followed below by the league affiliation, and then the player's name, biography and statistics.
COMPLETE SET (25)............... 15.00 6.00

1983 Erie Cardinals TCMA

This 25-card standard-size set of the 1983 Erie Cardinals, a Class A New York-Penn League affiliate of the St. Louis Cardinals, features white-bordered posed color player photos on its fronts. The player's name and position appear within a blue stripe at the bottom. The plain back carries the team name at the top, followed below by the league affiliation, and then the player's name, biography and statistics.
COMPLETE SET (25)............... 25.00 10.00

1983 Evansville Triplets TCMA

This 25-card standard-size set of the 1983 Evansville Triplets, a Class AAA American Association affiliate of the Detroit Tigers, features white-bordered posed color player photos on its fronts. The player's name and position appear within a blue stripe at the bottom. The plain back carries the team name at the top, followed below by the league affiliation, and then the player's name, biography and statistics.
COMPLETE SET (25)............... 15.00 6.00

1983 Glen Falls White Sox TCMA

This 24-card standard-size set of the 1983 Glen Falls White Sox, a Class AA Eastern League affiliate of the Chicago White Sox, features white-bordered posed color player photos on its fronts. The player's name and position appear within a blue stripe at the bottom. The plain back carries the team name at the top, followed below by the league affiliation, and then the player's name, biography and statistics.
COMPLETE SET (24)............... 75.00 30.00

1983 Greensboro Hornets TCMA

This 30-card standard-size set of the 1983 Greensboro Hornets, a Class A South Atlantic League affiliate of the New York Yankees, features white-bordered posed color player photos on its fronts. The player's name and position appear within a blue stripe at the bottom. The plain back carries the team name at the top, followed below by the league affiliation, and then the player's name, biography and statistics.
COMPLETE SET (30)............... 50.00 20.00

1983 Idaho Falls Athletics TCMA

This 34-card standard-size set of the 1983 Idaho Falls Athletics, a Rookie Class A Pioneer League affiliate of the Oakland Athletics, features white-bordered posed color player photos on its fronts. The player's name and position appear within a blue stripe at the bottom. The plain back carries the team name at the top, followed below by the league affiliation, and then the player's name, biography and statistics.
COMPLETE SET (34)............... 15.00 6.00

1983 Indianapolis Indians Team Issue

1,200 sets were produced.
COMPLETE SET (32)............... 15.00 6.00

1983 Iowa Cubs TCMA

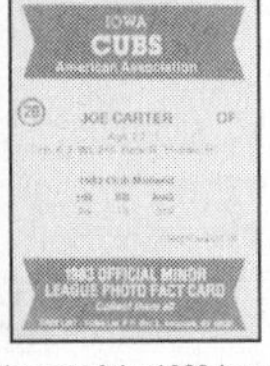

This 31-card standard-size set of the 1983 Iowa Cubs, a Class AAA American Association affiliate of the Chicago Cubs, features white-bordered posed color player photos on its fronts. The player's name and position appear within a blue stripe at the bottom. The plain back carries the team name at the top, followed below by the league affiliation, and then the player's name, biography and statistics. This issue includes the minor league card debut of Joe Carter. Interstingly, these cards feature grey backs unlike the normal white backs of a TCMA minor league set.
COMPLETE SET (30)............... 40.00 16.00

1983 Kinston Blue Jays Team Issue

This 28-card standard size unnumbered set of the 1983 Kinston Blue Jays was issued by Tony Kelly's Studio. This set includes a card of former Washington Redskins' quarterback Jay Schroeder. David Wells also has his first minor league card in this set.
COMPLETE SET (28)............ 100.00 40.00

1983 Knoxville Blue Jays TCMA

This 22-card standard-size set of the 1983 Knoxville Blue Jays, a Class AA Southern League affiliate of the Toronto Blue Jays, features white-bordered posed color player photos on its fronts. The player's name and position appear within a blue stripe at the bottom. The plain back carries the team name at the top, followed below by the league affiliation, and then the player's name, biography and statistics.
COMPLETE SET (22)............... 25.00 10.00

1983 Las Vegas Stars Baseball Hobby News

This set was produced by long term hobbyists Frank and Vivian Barning.
COMPLETE SET (22)............... 20.00 8.00

1983 Louisville Redbirds Riley's

COMPLETE SET (30)............... 25.00 10.00

1983 Lynchburg Mets TCMA

This 23-card standard-size set of the 1983 Lynchburg Mets, a Class A Carolina League affiliate of the New York Mets, features white-bordered posed color player photos on its fronts. The player's name and position appear within a blue stripe at the bottom. The plain back carries the team name at the top, followed below by the league affiliation, and then the player's name, biography and statistics. This issue includes the minor league card debuts of Lenny Dykstra and Dwight Gooden. Approximately 4,000 sets were produced.
COMPLETE SET (23)............... 30.00 12.00

1983 Lynn Pirates TCMA

This 27-card standard-size set of the 1983 Lynn Pirates, a Class AA Eastern League affiliate of the Pittsburgh Pirates, features white-bordered posed color player photos on its fronts. The player's name and position appear within a blue stripe at the bottom. The plain back carries the team name at the top, followed below by the league affiliation, and then the player's name, biography and statistics.
COMPLETE SET (27)............... 50.00 20.00

1983 Madison Muskies Fritsch

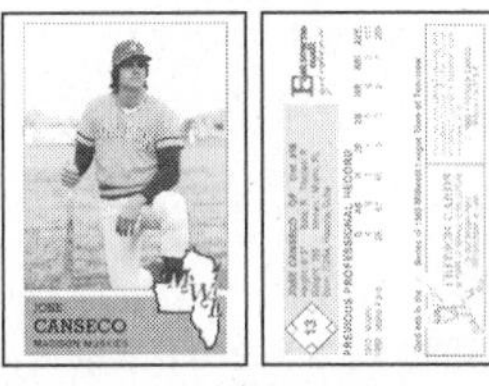

This issue include the minor league card debut of Jose Canseco.
COMPLETE SET (32)............... 25.00 12.00

1983 Memphis Chicks TCMA

This 24-card standard-size set of the 1983 Memphis Chicks, a Class AA Southern League affiliate of the Montreal Expos, features white-bordered posed color player photos on its fronts. The player's name and position appear within a blue stripe at the bottom. The plain back carries the team name at the top, followed below by the league affiliation, and then the player's name, biography and statistics.
COMPLETE SET (24)............... 30.00 12.00

1983 Miami Marlins TCMA

This 28-card standard-size set of the 1983 Miami Marlins, a Class A Florida State League affiliate of the San Diego Padres, features white-bordered posed color player photos on its fronts. The player's name and position appear within a blue stripe at the bottom. The plain back carries the team name at the top, followed below by the league affiliation, and then the player's name, biography and statistics. This issue includes the minor league card debut of Benito Santiago.
COMPLETE SET (28)............... 80.00 32.00

1983 Midland Cubs TCMA

This 26-card standard-size set of the 1983 Midland Angels, a Class AA Texas League affiliate of the Chicago Cubs, features white-bordered posed color player photos on its fronts. The player's name and position appear within a blue stripe at the bottom. The plain back carries the team name at the top, followed below by the league affiliation, and then the player's name, biography and statistics.
COMPLETE SET (26)............... 25.00 10.00

1983 Nashua Angels TCMA

This 27-card standard-size set of the 1983 Nashua Angels, a Class AA Eastern League affiliate of the California Angels, features white-bordered posed color player photos on its fronts. The player's name and position appear within a blue stripe at the bottom. The plain back carries the team name at the top, followed below by the league affiliation, and then the player's name, biography and statistics.
COMPLETE SET (27)............... 10.00 4.00

1983 Nashville Sounds Team Issue

COMPLETE SET (25)............... 15.00 6.00

1983 Oklahoma City 89ers TCMA

This 24-card standard-size set of the 1983 Oklahoma City 89ers, a Class AAA American Association affiliate of the Texas Rangers, features white-bordered posed color player photos on its fronts. The player's name and position appear within a blue stripe at the bottom. The plain back carries the team name at the top, followed below by the league affiliation, and then the player's name, biography and statistics.
COMPLETE SET (24)............... 25.00 10.00

1983 Omaha Royals TCMA

This 26-card standard-size set of the 1983 Omaha Royals, a Class AAA American Association affiliate of the Kansas City Royals, features white-bordered posed color player photos on its fronts. The player's name and position appear within a blue stripe at the bottom. The plain back carries the team name at the top, followed below by the league affiliation, and then the player's name, biography and statistics.
COMPLETE SET (26)............... 30.00 12.00

1983 Orlando Twins TCMA

This 23-card standard-size set of the 1983 Orlando Twins, a Class AA Southern League affiliate of the Minnesota Twins, features white-bordered posed color player photos on its fronts. The player's name and position appear within a blue stripe at the bottom. The plain back carries the team name at the top, followed below by the league affiliation, and then the player's name, biography and statistics.
COMPLETE SET (22)............... 12.00 4.80

1983 Pawtucket Red Sox TCMA

This 26-card standard-size set of the 1983 Pawtucket Red Sox, a Class AAA International League affiliate of the Boston Red Sox, features white-bordered posed color player photos on its fronts. The player's name and position appear within a blue stripe at the bottom. The plain back carries the team name at the top, followed below by the league affiliation, and then the player's name, biography and statistics.
COMPLETE SET (26)............... 40.00 16.00

1983 Peoria Suns Fritsch

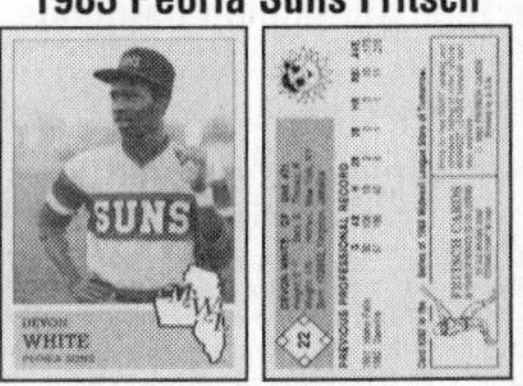

COMPLETE SET (30)............... 15.00 6.00

1983 Phoenix Giants Baseball Hobby News

COMPLETE SET (28)............... 25.00 10.00

1983 Portland Beavers TCMA

This 25-card standard-size set of the 1983 Portland Beavers, a Class AAA Pacific Coast League affiliate of the Philadelphia Phillies, features white-bordered posed color player photos on its fronts. The player's name and position appear within a blue stripe at the bottom. The plain back carries the team name at the top, followed below by the league affiliation, and then the player's name, biography and statistics.
COMPLETE SET (25)............ 100.00 40.00
COMPLETE SET (22)............... 60.00 24.00

1983 Quad City Cubs TCMA

This 27-card standard-size set of the 1983 Quad City Cubs, a Class A Midwest League affiliate of the Chicago Cubs, features white-bordered posed color player photos on its fronts. The player's name and position appear within a blue stripe at the bottom. The plain back carries the team name at the top, followed below by the league affiliation, and then the player's name, biography and statistics. This issue includes the minor league card debut of Shawon Dunston.
COMPLETE SET (27)............... 30.00 12.00

1983 Reading Phillies TCMA

This 24-card standard-size set of the 1983 Reading Phillies, a Class AA Eastern League affiliate of the Philadelphia Phillies, features white-bordered posed color player photos on its fronts. The player's name and position appear within a blue stripe at the bottom. The plain back carries the team name at the top, followed below by the league affiliation, and then the player's name, biography and statistics. This issue includes the minor league card debut of Darren Daulton.
COMPLETE SET (24)............ 150.00 60.00

1983 Redwood Pioneers TCMA

This 32-card standard-size set of the 1983 Redwood Pioneers, a Class A California League affiliate of the California Angels, features white-bordered posed color player photos on its fronts. The player's name and position appear

within a blue stripe at the bottom. The plain back carries the team name at the top, followed below by the league affiliation, and then the player's name, biography and statistics.
COMPLETE SET (32)............... 15.00 6.00

1983 Richmond Braves TCMA

This 25-card standard-size set of the 1983 Richmond Braves, a Class AAA International League affiliate of the Atlanta Braves, features white-bordered posed color player photos on its fronts. The player's name and position appear within a blue stripe at the bottom. The plain back carries the team name at the top, followed below by the league affiliation, and then the player's name, biography and statistics.
COMPLETE SET (25)............... 25.00 10.00

1983 Rochester Red Wings TCMA

This 25-card standard-size set of the 1983 Rochester Red Wings, a Class AAA International League affiliate of the Baltimore Orioles, features white-bordered posed color player photos on its fronts. The player's name and position appear within a blue stripe at the bottom. The plain back carries the team name at the top, followed below by the league affiliation, and then the player's name, biography and statistics.
COMPLETE SET (25)............... 20.00 8.00

1983 Salt Lake City Gulls TCMA

This 26-card standard-size set of the 1983 Salt Lake City Gulls, a Class AAA Pacific Coast League affiliate of the Seattle Mariners, features white-bordered posed color player photos on its fronts. The player's name and position appear within a blue stripe at the bottom. The plain back carries the team name at the top, followed below by the league affiliation, and then the player's name, biography and statistics.
COMPLETE SET (26)............... 25.00 10.00

1983 San Jose Bees Colla

This standard size set of the San Jose Bees, a Class A California League Co-op team of the Baltimore Orioles and Seibu Lions was produced by collector Barry Colla.
COMPLETE SET (26)............... 15.00 6.00

1983 Springfield Cardinals Fritsch

COMPLETE SET (26)............... 15.00 6.00

1983 St. Petersburg Cardinals TCMA

This 30-card standard-size set of the 1983 St. Petersburg Cardinals, a Class A Florida State League affiliate of the St. Louis Cardinals, features white-bordered posed color player photos on its fronts. The player's name and position appear within a blue stripe at the bottom. The plain back carries the team name at the top, followed below by the league affiliation, and then the player's name, biography and statistics.
COMPLETE SET (30)............... 30.00 12.00

1983 Syracuse Chiefs TCMA

This 26-card standard-size set of the 1983 Syracuse Chiefs, a Class AAA International League affiliate of the Toronto Blue Jays, features white-bordered posed color player photos on its fronts. The player's name and position appear within a blue stripe at the bottom. The plain back carries the team name at the top, followed below by the league affiliation, and then the player's name, biography and statistics.
COMPLETE SET (26)............... 50.00 20.00

1983 Tacoma Tigers TCMA

This 36-card standard-size set of the 1983 Tacoma Tigers, a Class AAA Pacific Coast League affiliate of the Oakland Athletics, features white-bordered posed color player photos on its fronts. The player's name and position appear within a blue stripe at the bottom. The plain back carries the team name at the top, followed below by the league affiliation, and then the player's name, biography and statistics.
COMPLETE SET (31)............... 15.00 6.00
COMPLETE SET (36)............... 100.00 40.00

1983 Tampa Tarpons TCMA

This 29-card standard-size set of the 1983 Tampa Tarpons, a Class A Florida State League affiliate of the Cincinnati Reds, features white-bordered posed color player photos on its fronts. The player's name and position appear within a blue stripe at the bottom. The plain back carries the team name at the top, followed below by the league affiliation, and then the player's name, biography and statistics.
COMPLETE SET (29)............... 40.00 16.00

1983 Tidewater Tides TCMA

This 29-card standard-size set of the 1983 Tidewater Tides, a Class AAA International League affiliate of the New York Mets, features white-bordered posed color player photos on its fronts. The player's name and position appear within a blue stripe at the bottom. The plain back carries the team name at the top, followed below by the league affiliation, and then the player's name, biography and statistics. Approximately 4,000 sets were

produced.
COMPLETE SET (29)............... 40.00 16.00

1983 Toledo Mud Hens TCMA

This 29-card standard-size set of the 1983 Toledo Mud Hens, a Class AAA International League affiliate of the Minnesota Twins, features white-bordered posed color player photos on its fronts. The player's name and position appear within a blue stripe at the bottom. The plain back carries the team name at the top, followed below by the league affiliation, and then the player's name, biography and statistics.
COMPLETE SET (25)............... 20.00 8.00
COMPLETE SET (29)............... 100.00 40.00

1983 Tri-Cities Triplets TCMA

This 28-card standard-size set of the 1983 Tri-Cities Triplets, a Class A Northwest League affiliate of the Texas Rangers, features white-bordered posed color player photos on its fronts. The player's name and position appear within a blue stripe at the bottom. The plain back carries the team name at the top, followed below by the league affiliation, and then the player's name, biography and statistics.
COMPLETE SET (28)............... 15.00 6.00

1983 Tucson Toros TCMA

This 26-card standard-size set of the 1983 Tucson Toros, a Class AAA Pacific Coast League affiliate of the Houston Astros, features white-bordered posed color player photos on its fronts. The player's name and position appear within a blue stripe at the bottom. The back contains safety tips.
COMPLETE SET (25)............... 12.00 4.80

1983 Tulsa Drillers TCMA

This 25-card standard-size set of the 1983 Tulsa Drillers, a Class AA Texas League affiliate of the Texas Rangers, features white-bordered posed color player photos on its fronts. The player's name and position appear within a blue stripe at the bottom. The plain back carries the team name at the top, followed below by the league affiliation, and then the player's name, biography and statistics.
COMPLETE SET (25)............... 20.00 8.00

1983 Vero Beach Dodgers TCMA

This 29-card standard-size set of the 1983 Vero Beach Dodgers, a Class A Florida State League affiliate of the Los Angeles Dodgers, features white-bordered posed color player photos on its fronts. The player's name and position appear within a blue stripe at the bottom. The plain back carries the team name at the top, followed below by the league affiliation, and then the player's name, biography and statistics.
COMPLETE SET (29)............... 30.00 12.00

1983 Visalia Oaks Fritsch

This 25-card set of the 1983 Visalia Oaks, a Class A California League affiliate of the Minnesota Twins, features the only minor league card of Kirby Puckett.
COMPLETE SET (25)............... 250.00 80.00

1983 Waterbury Reds TCMA

This 19-card standard-size set of the 1983 Waterbury Reds, a Class AA Eastern League affiliate of the Cincinnati Reds, features white-bordered posed color player photos on its fronts. The player's name and position appear within a blue stripe at the bottom. The plain back carries the team name at the top, followed below by the league affiliation, and then the player's name, biography and statistics. This issue includes a second year card of Eric Davis. Approximately 1,600 sets were produced.
COMPLETE SET (19)............... 30.00 12.00

1983 Waterloo Indians Fritsch

COMPLETE SET (29)............... 8.00 3.20

1983 Wausau Timbers Fritsch

COMPLETE SET (31)............... 8.00 3.20

1983 Wichita Aeros Dog'n Shake

Sponsored by Dog'n'Shake and produced by Rock's Dugout, this 24-card standard-size set of the 1983 Wichita Aeros, a Class AAA American Association affiliate of the Montreal Expos, features white-bordered posed color player photos on its fronts. The player's name and position, and team and sponsor's logos, appear at the bottom. The white horizontal back carries the player's name, biography and statistics.
COMPLETE SET (24)............... 30.00 12.00

1983 Wisconsin Rapids Twins Fritsch

COMPLETE SET (28)............... 8.00 3.20

1984 Albany A's TCMA

This 26-card standard-size set of the 1984 Albany A's, a Class AA Eastern League affiliate of the Oakland Athletics, features green-bordered posed color player shots on its fronts. The player's position, player's name and the team name are printed below the photo in white lettering. The white back carries the team name and year at the top, followed by the league, player's name, position, and biography.
COMPLETE SET (26)............... 30.00 12.00

1984 Albuquerque Dukes Cramer

This 27-card standard-size set of the 1984 Albuquerque Dukes, a Class AAA Pacific Coast League affiliate of the Los Angeles Dodgers, features white-bordered posed color player photos on its fronts. The player's name, position, and team name appear at the bottom. The gray horizontal back carries the player's name and position within a baseball bat icon at the top, followed below by biography and statistics, some enhanced by a cartoon. All 1984 Cramer minor league sets were also issued in a "tiffany" or glossy style as well. They were issued as complete sets of all the teams and each are valued at 2X the regular minor league cards.
COMPLETE SET (27)............... 8.00 3.20

1984 Arizona Wildcats Police

COMPLETE SET (21)............... 15.00 6.00

1984 Arkansas Travelers TCMA

This 26-card standard-size set of the 1984 Arkansas Travelers, a Class AA Texas League affiliate of the St. Louis Cardinals, features green-bordered posed color player shots on its fronts. The player's position, player's name and the team name are printed below the photo in white lettering. The white back carries the team name and year at the top, followed by the league, player's name, position, and biography. Approximately 3,000 sets were produced.
COMPLETE SET (26)............... 25.00 10.00

1984 Beaumont Golden Gators TCMA

This 25-card standard-size set of the 1984 Beaumont Golden Gators, a Class AA Texas League affiliate of the San Diego Padres, features green-bordered posed color player shots on its fronts. The player's position, player's name and the team name are printed below the photo in white lettering. The white back carries the team name and year at the top, followed by the league, player's name, position, and biography.
COMPLETE SET (25)............... 15.00 6.00

1984 Buffalo Bisons TCMA

This 25-card standard-size set of the 1984 Buffalo Bisons, a Class AA Eastern League affiliate of the Cleveland Indians, features green-bordered posed color player shots on its fronts. The player's position, player's name and the team name are printed below the photo in white lettering. The white back carries the team name and year at the top, followed by the league, player's name, position, and biography.
COMPLETE SET (25)............... 15.00 6.00

1984 Butte Copper Kings TCMA

This 27-card standard-size set of the 1984 Butte Copper Kings, a Rookie Class Pioneer League affiliate of the Seattle Mariners, features green-bordered posed color player shots on its fronts. The player's position, player's name and the team name are printed below the photo in white lettering. The white back carries the team name and year at the top, followed by the league, player's name, position, and biography. Approximately 2,000 sets were produced.
COMPLETE SET (27)............... 15.00 6.00

1984 Cedar Rapids Reds TCMA

This 28-card standard-size set of the 1984 Cedar Rapids Reds, a Class A Midwest League affiliate of the Cincinnati Reds, features green-bordered posed color player shots on its fronts. The player's position, player's name and the team name are printed below the photo in white lettering. The white back carries the team name and year at the top, followed by the league, player's name, position, and biography.
COMPLETE SET (28)............... 20.00 8.00

1984 Charlotte O's TCMA

This 27-card standard-size set of the 1984 Charlotte O's, a Class AA Southern League affiliate of the Baltimore Orioles, features green-bordered posed color player shots on its fronts. The player's position, player's name and the team name are printed below the photo in white lettering. The white back carries the team name and year at the top, followed by the league, player's name, position, and biography.
COMPLETE SET (27)............... 15.00 6.00

1984 Chattanooga Lookouts TCMA

This 29-card standard-size set of the 1984 Chattanooga Lookouts, a Class A California League affiliate of the Seattle Mariners, features green-bordered posed color player shots on its fronts. The player's position, player's name and the team name are printed below the photo in white lettering. The white back carries the team name and year at the top, followed by the league, player's name, position, and biography.
COMPLETE SET (29)............... 15.00 6.00

1984 Columbus Clippers Police

COMPLETE SET (25)............... 8.00 3.20

1984 Columbus Clippers TCMA

This 25-card standard-size set of the 1984 Columbus Clippers, a Class AAA International League affiliate of the New York Yankees, features green-bordered posed color player shots on its fronts. The player's position, player's name and the team name are printed below the photo in white lettering. The white back carries the team name and year at the top, followed by the league, player's name, position, and biography.
COMPLETE SET (25)............... 20.00 8.00

1984 Durham Bulls TCMA

This 30-card standard-size set of the 1984 Durham Bulls, a Class A Carolina League affiliate of the Atlanta Braves, features green-bordered posed color player shots on its fronts. The player's position, player's name and the team name are printed below the photo in white lettering. The white back carries the team name and year at the top, followed by the league, player's name, position, and biography.
COMPLETE SET (30)............... 20.00 8.00

1984 Edmonton Trappers Cramer

This 26-card standard-size set of the 1984 Edmonton Trappers, a Class AAA Pacific Coast League affiliate of the California Angels, features white-bordered posed color player photos on its fronts. The player's name, position, and team name appear at the bottom. The gray horizontal back carries the player's name and position within a baseball bat icon at the top, followed below by biography and statistics. .
COMPLETE SET (26)............... 8.00 3.20

1984 El Paso Diablos TCMA

This 25-card standard-size set of the 1984 El Paso Diablos, a Class AA Texas League affiliate of the Milwaukee Brewers, features green-bordered posed color player shots on its fronts. The player's position, player's name and the team name are printed below the photo in white lettering. The white back carries the team name and year at the top, followed by the league, player's name, position, and biography.
COMPLETE SET (25)............... 20.00 8.00

1984 Evansville Triplets TCMA

This 22-card standard-size set of the 1984 Evansville Triplets, a Class AAA American Association affiliate of the Detroit Tigers, features green-bordered posed color player shots on its fronts. The player's position, player's name and the team name are printed below the photo in white lettering. The white back carries the team name and year at the top, followed by the league, player's name, position, and biography.
COMPLETE SET (22)............... 15.00 6.00

1984 Everett Giants Cramer

This 35-card standard-size set of the 1984 Everett Giants, a Class A Northwest League affiliate of the San Francisco Giants, features white-bordered posed color player photos on its fronts. The player's name, position, and team name appear at the bottom. The gray horizontal back carries the player's name and position within a baseball bat icon at the top, followed below by biography and statistics, some enhanced by a cartoon. Card numbers 6B, 10B, 13B, 22B, and 30B were all late issues.
COMPLETE SET (30)............... 15.00 6.00

1984 Greensboro Hornets TCMA

This 26-card standard-size set of the 1984 Greensboro Hornets, a Class A South Atlantic League affiliate of the New York Yankees, features green-bordered posed color player shots on its fronts. The player's position, player's name and the team name are printed below the photo in white lettering. The white back carries the team name and year at the top, followed by the league, player's name, position, and biography.
COMPLETE SET (26)............... 30.00 12.00

1984 Hawaii Islanders Cramer

This 26-card standard-size set of the 1984 Hawaii Islanders, a Class AAA Pacific Coast League affiliate of the Pittsburgh Pirates, features white-bordered posed color player photos on its fronts. The player's name, position, and team name appear at the bottom. The gray horizontal back carries the player's name and position within a baseball bat icon at the top, followed below by biography and statistics, some enhanced by a cartoon.
COMPLETE SET (26)............... 8.00 3.20

1984 Idaho Falls A's Team Issue

Less than 500 sets were produced and given away at the ballpark.
COMPLETE SET (30)............... 75.00 30.00

1984 Indianapolis Indians Team Issue

This 32-card set of the 1984 Indianapolis Indians, a Class AAA American Association affiliate of the Montreal Expos, features borderless posed color player shots on its fronts, and measures approximately 2 1/2" by 3 3/4". A blue arc above the photo carries the player's name, position, and team name. The white horizontal back carries the player's autograph facsimile at the top, followed by biography, statistics, and career highlights. 1,200 sets were produced.
COMPLETE SET (32)............... 15.00 6.00

1984 Iowa Cubs TCMA

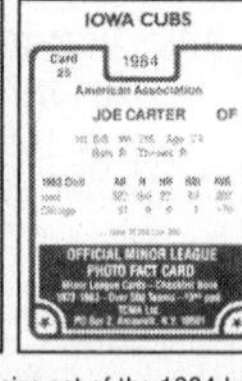

This 31-card standard-size set of the 1984 Iowa Cubs, a Class AAA American Association affiliate of the Chicago Cubs, features green-bordered posed color player shots on its fronts. The player's position, player's name and the team name are printed below the photo in white lettering. The white back carries the team name and year at the top, followed by the league, player's name, position, and biography. This issue includes a second year card of Joe Carter.
COMPLETE SET (31)............... 40.00 16.00

1984 Jackson Mets Feder

COMPLETE SET (15)............... 40.00 16.00

1984 Jackson Mets TCMA

This 25-card standard-size set of the 1984 Jackson Mets, a Class AA Texas League affiliate of the New York Mets, features green-bordered posed color player shots on its fronts. The player's position, player's name and the team name are printed below the photo in white lettering. The white back carries the team name and year at the top, followed by the league, player's name, position, and biography.
COMPLETE SET (25)............... 40.00 16.00

1984 Las Vegas Stars Cramer

This 25-card standard-size set of the 1984 Las Vegas Stars, a Class AAA Pacific Coast League affiliate of the San Diego Padres, features white-bordered posed color player photos on its fronts. The player's name, position, and team name appear at the bottom. The gray horizontal back carries the player's name and position within a baseball bat icon at the top, followed below by biography and statistics, some enhanced by a cartoon.
COMPLETE SET (25)............... 20.00 8.00

1984 Little Falls Mets TCMA

This 26-card standard-size set of the 1984 Little Falls Mets, a Class A New York-Penn League affiliate of the New York Mets, features green-bordered posed color player shots on its fronts. The player's position, player's name and the team name are printed below the photo in white lettering. The white back carries the team name and year at the top, followed by the league, player's name, position, and biography. Approximately 1,600 sets were produced.
COMPLETE SET (26)............... 30.00 12.00

1984 Louisville Redbirds Riley's

COMPLETE SET (30)............... 20.00 8.00

1984 Madison Muskies Police

COMPLETE SET (25)............... 25.00 10.00

1984 Maine Guides TCMA

This 23-card standard-size set of the 1984 Maine Guides, a Class AAA International League affiliate of the Cleveland Indians, features green-bordered posed color player shots on its fronts. The player's position, player's name and the team name are printed below the photo in white lettering. The white back carries the team name and year at the top, followed by the league, player's name, position, and biography.
COMPLETE SET (23)............... 10.00 4.00

1984 Memphis Chicks TCMA

This 25-card standard-size set of the 1984 Memphis Chicks, a Class AA Southern League affiliate of the Kansas City Royals, features green-bordered posed color player shots on its fronts. The player's position, player's name and the team name are printed below the photo in white lettering. The white back carries the team name and year at the top, followed by the league, player's name, position, and biography. This issue includes a second year minor league card of David Cone.
COMPLETE SET (25)................ 40.00 16.00

1984 Midland Cubs TCMA

This 24-card standard-size set of the 1984 Midland Cubs, a Class AA Texas League affiliate of the Chicago Cubs, features green-bordered posed color player shots on its fronts. The player's position, player's name and the team name are printed below the photo in white lettering. The white back carries the team name and year at the top, followed by the league, player's name, position, and biography.
COMPLETE SET (24)................ 30.00 12.00

1984 Modesto A's Chong

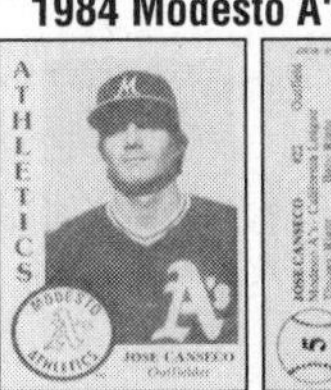

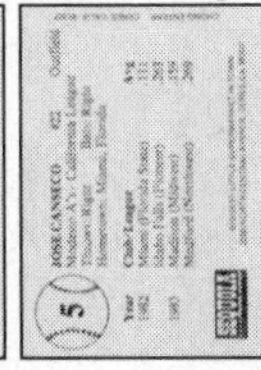

This set was issued in Black and White and includes a second year card of Jose Canseco.
COMPLETE SET (28).............. 150.00 60.00

1984 Nashville Sounds Team Issue

COMPLETE SET (25)................ 10.00 4.00

1984 Newark Orioles TCMA

This 25-card standard-size set of the 1984 Newark Orioles, a Class A New York-Penn League affiliate of the Baltimore Orioles, features green-bordered posed color player shots on its fronts. The player's position, player's name and the team name are printed below the photo in white lettering. The white back carries the team name and year at the top, followed by the league, player's name, position, and biography.
COMPLETE SET (25)................ 15.00 6.00

1984 Oklahoma City 89ers TCMA

This 24-card standard-size set of the 1984 Oklahoma City 89ers, a Class AAA American Association affiliate of the Texas Rangers, features green-bordered posed color player shots on its fronts. The player's position, player's name and the team name are printed below the photo in white lettering. The white back carries the team name and year at the top, followed by the league, player's name, position, and biography.
COMPLETE SET (24)................ 25.00 10.00

1984 Omaha Royals TCMA

This 30-card standard-size set of the 1984 Omaha Royals, a Class AAA American Association League affiliate of the Kansas City Royals, features green-bordered posed color player shots on its fronts. The player's position, player's name and the team name are printed below the photo in white lettering. The white back carries the team name and year at the top, followed by the league, player's name, position, and biography.
COMPLETE SET (30)................ 15.00 6.00

1984 Pawtucket Red Sox TCMA

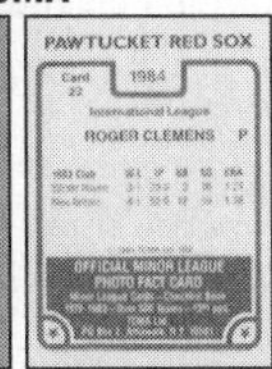

This 25-card standard-size set of the 1984 Pawtucket Red Sox, a Class AAA International League affiliate of the Boston Red Sox, features green-bordered posed color player shots on its fronts. The player's position, player's name and the team name are printed below the photo in white lettering. The white back carries the team name and year at the top, followed by the league, player's name, position, and biography. This issue includes the minor league card debut of Roger Clemens. Approximately 4,000 sets were produced. The photos of Tony Herron and Paul Hundhammer were reversed in this sets first printing.
COMPLETE SET (25).............. 200.00 80.00
COMPLETE SET (29).............. 250.00 100.00

1984 Phoenix Giants Cramer

This 25-card standard-size set of the 1984 Phoenix Giants, a Class AAA Pacific Coast League affiliate of the San Francisco Giants, features white-bordered posed color player photos on its fronts. The player's name, position, and team name appear at the bottom. The gray horizontal back carries the player's name and position within a baseball bat icon at the top, followed below by biography and statistics, some enhanced by a cartoon.
COMPLETE SET (25)................ 15.00 6.00

1984 Portland Beavers Cramer

This 22-card standard-size set of the 1984 Portland Beavers, a Class AAA Pacific Coast League affiliate of the Philadelphia Phillies, features white-bordered posed color player photos on its fronts. The player's name, position, and team name appear at the bottom. The gray horizontal back carries the player's name and position within a baseball bat icon at the top, followed below by biography and statistics, some enhanced by a cartoon.
COMPLETE SET (22)................ 20.00 8.00

1984 Prince William Pirates TCMA

This 34-card standard-size set of the 1984 Prince William Pirates, a Class A Carolina League affiliate of the Pittsburgh Pirates, features green-bordered posed color player shots on its fronts. The player's position, player's name and the team name are printed below the photo in white lettering. The white back carries the team name and year at the top, followed by the league, player's name, position, and biography.
COMPLETE SET (34)................ 15.00 6.00

1984 Richmond Braves TCMA

This 27-card standard-size set of the 1984 Richmond Braves, a Class AAA International League affiliate of the Atlanta Braves, features green-bordered posed color player shots on its fronts. The player's position, player's name and the team name are printed below the photo in white lettering. The white back carries the team name and year at the top, followed by the league, player's name, position, and biography.
COMPLETE SET (27)................ 10.00 4.00

1984 Rochester Red Wings TCMA

This 19-card standard-size set of the 1984 Rochester Red Wings, a Class AAA International League affiliate of the Baltimore Orioles, features green-bordered posed color player shots on its fronts. The player's position, player's name and the team name are printed below the photo in white lettering. The white back carries the team name and year at the top, followed by the league, player's name, position, and biography.
COMPLETE SET (19)................ 15.00 6.00

1984 Salt Lake City Gulls Cramer

This 24-card standard-size set of the 1984 Salt Lake City Gulls, a Class AAA Pacific Coast League affiliate of the Seattle Mariners, features white-bordered posed color player photos on its fronts. The player's name, position, and team name appear at the bottom. The gray horizontal back carries the player's name and position within a baseball bat icon at the top, followed below by biography and statistics, some enhanced by a cartoon.
COMPLETE SET (24)................ 20.00 8.00

1984 Savannah Cardinals TCMA

This 26-card standard-size set of the 1984 Savannah Cardinals, a Class A South Atlantic League affiliate of the St. Louis Cardinals, features green-bordered posed color player shots on its fronts. The player's position, player's name and the team name are printed below the photo in white lettering. The white back carries the team name and year at the top, followed by the league, player's name, position, and biography.
COMPLETE SET (26)................ 15.00 6.00

1984 Shreveport Captains First Base

COMPLETE SET (24)................ 25.00 10.00

1984 Spokane Indians Newspaper

This set contains Sandy Alomar Jr's first ever card.
COMPLETE SET (25)................ 50.00 20.00

1984 Syracuse Chiefs TCMA

This 32-card standard-size set of the 1984 Syracuse Chiefs, a Class AAA International League affiliate of the Toronto Blue Jays, features green-bordered posed color player shots on its fronts. The player's position, player's name and the team name are printed below the photo in white lettering. The white back carries the team name and year at the top, followed by the league, player's name, position, and biography.
COMPLETE SET (32)................ 30.00 12.00

1984 Tacoma Tigers Cramer

This 25-card standard-size set of the 1984 Tacoma Tigers, a Class AAA Pacific Coast League affiliate of the Oakland Athletics, features white-bordered posed color player photos on its fronts. The player's name, position, and team name appear at the bottom. The gray horizontal back carries the player's name and position within a baseball bat icon at the top, followed below by biography and statistics, some enhanced by a cartoon.
COMPLETE SET (25)................ 8.00 3.20

1984 Tidewater Tides TCMA

This 28-card standard-size set of the 1984 Tidewater Tides, a Class AAA International League affiliate of the New York Mets, features green-bordered posed color player shots on its fronts. The player's position, player's name and the team name are printed below the photo in white lettering. The white back carries the team name and year at the top, followed by the league, player's name, position, and biography. Approximately 4,000 sets were produced. Although it's not considered part of the set, a late issue card of Darryl Strawberry was released.
COMPLETE SET (28)................ 25.00 10.00

1984 Toledo Mud Hens TCMA

This 24-card standard-size set of the 1984 Toledo Mud Hens, a Class AAA International League affiliate of the Minnesota Twins, features green-bordered posed color player shots on its fronts. The player's position, player's name and the team name are printed below the photo in white lettering. The white back carries the team name and year at the top, followed by the league, player's name, position, and biography.
COMPLETE SET (24)................ 15.00 6.00

1984 Tucson Toros Cramer

This 25-card standard-size set of the 1984 Tucson Toros, a Class AAA Pacific Coast League affiliate of the Houston Astros, features white-bordered posed color player photos on its fronts. The player's name, position, and team name appear at the bottom. The gray horizontal back carries the player's name and position within a baseball bat icon at the top, followed below by biography and statistics, some enhanced by a cartoon.
COMPLETE SET (25)................ 8.00 3.20

1984 Tulsa Drillers Team Issue

2,000 sets were produced.
COMPLETE SET (22)................ 20.00 8.00

1984 Vancouver Canadians Cramer

Sponsored by Orange Crush, this 25-card standard-size set of the 1984 Vancouver Canadians, a Class AAA Pacific Coast League affiliate of the Milwaukee Brewers, features white-bordered posed color player photos on its fronts. The player's name, position, and team name appear at the bottom. The gray horizontal back carries the player's name and position within a baseball bat icon at the top, followed below by biography and statistics, some enhanced by a cartoon.
COMPLETE SET (25)................ 15.00 6.00

1984 Visalia Oaks TCMA

This 25-card standard-size set of the 1984 Visalia Oaks, a Class A California League affiliate of the Minnesota Twins, features green-bordered posed color player shots on its fronts. The player's position, player's name and the team name are printed below the photo in white lettering. The white back carries the team name and year at the top, followed by the league, player's name, position, and biography.
COMPLETE SET (25)................ 20.00 8.00

1984 Wichita Aeros Rock's Dugout

COMPLETE SET (23)................ 40.00 16.00

1985 Albany Yankees TCMA

This 35-card standard-size set of the 1985 Albany Yankees, a Class AA Eastern League affiliate of the New York Yankees, features blue-bordered posed color player shots on its fronts. The team name is printed at the top with the player's name and position appearing vertically on the lower left edge. The white back carries the team name and league at the top, followed by the player's name, position, and biography.
COMPLETE SET (33)................ 40.00 16.00

1985 Albuquerque Dukes Cramer

This 25-card standard-size set of the 1985 Albuquerque Dukes, a Class AAA Pacific Coast League affiliate of the Los Angeles Dodgers, features white-bordered posed color player photos on its fronts. The player's name, position, and team name appear at the bottom. The light blue horizontal back carries the player's name and position within a baseball bat icon at the top, followed below by biography and statistics, some enhanced by a cartoon.
COMPLETE SET (25)................ 6.00 2.40

1985 Anchorage Glacier Pilots Team Issue

COMPLETE SET (45)................ 25.00 10.00

1985 Beaumont Golden Gators TCMA

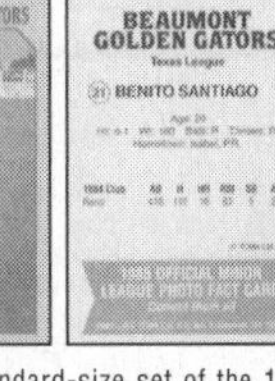

This 25-card standard-size set of the 1985 Beaumont Golden Gators, a Class AA Texas League affiliate of the San Diego Padres, features blue-bordered posed color player shots on its fronts. The team name is printed at the top with the player's name and position appearing vertically on the lower left edge. The white back carries the team name and league at the top, followed by the player's name, position, and biography.
COMPLETE SET (25)................ 30.00 12.00

1985 Beloit Brewers TCMA

This 26-card standard-size set of the 1985 Beloit Brewers, a Class A Midwest League affiliate of the Milwaukee Brewers, features blue-bordered posed color player shots on its fronts. The team name is printed at the top with the player's name and position appearing vertically on the lower left edge. The white back carries the team name and league at the top, followed by the player's name, position, and biography.
COMPLETE SET (26)................ 12.00 4.80

1985 Bend Phillies Cramer

COMPLETE SET (24)................ 10.00 4.00

1985 Buffalo Bisons TCMA

This 26-card standard-size set of the 1985 Buffalo Bisons, a Class AAA American Association affiliate of the Chicago White Sox, features blue-bordered posed color player shots on its fronts. The team name is printed at the top with the player's name and position appearing vertically on the lower left edge. The white back carries the team name and league at the top, followed by the player's name, position, and biography.
COMPLETE SET (26)................ 10.00 4.00

1985 Burlington Rangers TCMA

This 28-card standard-size set of the 1985 Burlington Rangers, a Class A Midwest League affiliate of the Texas Rangers, features blue-bordered posed color player shots on its fronts. The team name is printed at the top with the player's name and position appearing vertically on the lower left edge. The white back carries the team name and league at the top, followed by the player's name, position, and biography.
COMPLETE SET (28)................ 10.00 4.00

1985 Calgary Cannons Cramer

This 25-card standard-size set of the 1985 Calgary Cannons, a Class AAA Pacific Coast League affiliate of the Seattle Mariners, features white-bordered posed color player photos on its fronts. The player's name, position, and team name appear at the bottom. The blue horizontal back carries the player's name and position within a baseball bat icon at the top, followed below by biography and statistics.
COMPLETE SET (25)................ 18.00 7.25

1985 Cedar Rapids Reds TCMA

This 32-card standard-size set of the 1985 Cedar Rapids Reds, a Class A Midwest League affiliate of the Cincinnati Reds, features blue-bordered posed color player shots on its fronts. The team name is printed at the top with the player's name and position appearing vertically on the lower left edge. The white back carries the team name and league at the top, followed by the player's name, position, and biography.
COMPLETE SET (32)................ 30.00 12.00

1985 Charlotte O's TCMA

This 31-card standard-size set of the 1985 Charlotte O's, a Class AA Southern League affiliate of the Baltimore Orioles, features blue-bordered posed color player shots on its fronts. The team name is printed at the top with the player's name and position appearing vertically on the lower left edge. The white back carries the team name and league at the top, followed by the player's name, position, and biography.
COMPLETE SET (29)................ 10.00 4.00

1985 Clovis HS Smokey

COMPLETE SET (44)................ 10.00 4.00

1985 Columbus Clippers Police

COMPLETE SET (25)................ 10.00 4.00

1985 Columbus Clippers TCMA

This 28-card standard-size set of the 1985 Columbus Clippers, a Class AAA International League affiliate of the New York Yankees, features blue-bordered posed color player shots on its fronts. The team name is printed at the top with the player's name and position appearing vertically on the lower left edge. The white back carries the team name and league at the top, followed by the player's name, position, and biography.
COMPLETE SET (26)................ 15.00 6.00
COMPLETE SET (28)................ 20.00 8.00

1985 Durham Bulls TCMA

This 31-card standard-size set of the 1985 Durham Bulls, a Class A Carolina League affiliate of the Atlanta Braves, features blue-bordered posed color player shots on its fronts. The team name is printed at the top with the player's name and position appearing vertically on the lower left edge. The white back carries the team name and league at the top, followed by the player's name, position, and biography.
COMPLETE SET (31)................ 15.00 6.00

1985 Edmonton Trappers Cramer

This 25-card standard-size set of the 1985 Edmonton Trappers, a Class AAA Pacific Coast League affiliate of the California Angels, features white-bordered posed color player photos on its fronts. The player's name, position, and team name appear at the bottom. The blue horizontal back carries the player's name and position within a baseball bat icon at the top, followed below by biography and statistics. This issue includes Wally Joyner's first and only minor league card appearance. Approximately 5,000 sets were produced.
COMPLETE SET (25)................ 20.00 8.00

1985 Elmira Pioneers TCMA

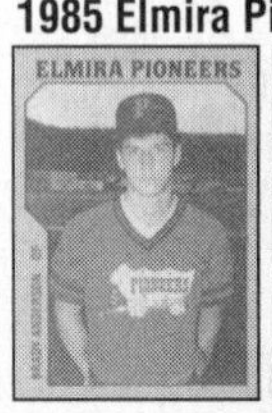

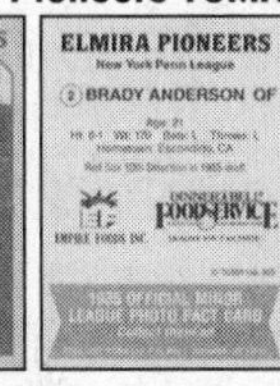

This 25-card standard-size set of the 1985 Elmira Pioneers, a Class A New York-Penn League affiliate of the Boston Red Sox, features blue-bordered posed color player shots on its fronts. The team name is printed at the top with the player's name and position appearing vertically on the lower left edge. The white back carries the team name and league at the top, followed by the player's name, position, and biography. This issue includes the minor league card debut of Brady Anderson.
COMPLETE SET (25)................ 30.00 12.00

1985 Everett Giants Cramer

COMPLETE SET (24)................ 10.00 4.00

1985 Everett Giants II Cramer

COMPLETE SET (24)................ 15.00 6.00

1985 Fresno Giants Smokey Bear

COMPLETE SET (32)................ 80.00 32.00

1985 Ft. Myers Royals TCMA

This 30-card standard-size set of the 1985 Ft. Myers Royals, a Class A Florida State League affiliate of the Kansas City Royals, features blue-bordered posed color player shots on its fronts. The team name is printed at the top with the player's name and position appearing vertically on the lower left edge. The white back carries the team name and league at the top, followed by the player's name, position, and biography.
COMPLETE SET (30)................ 30.00 12.00

1985 Greensboro Hornets TCMA

This 28-card standard-size set of the 1985 Greensboro Hornets, a Class A South Atlantic League affiliate of the Boston Red Sox, features blue-bordered posed color player shots on its fronts. The team name is printed at the top with the player's name and position appearing vertically on the lower left edge. The white back carries the team name and league at the top, followed by the player's name, position, and biography.
COMPLETE SET (28)................ 10.00 4.00

1985 Greenville Braves Team Issue

COMPLETE SET (26)................ 60.00 24.00

1985 Hawaii Islanders Cramer

This 25-card standard-size set of the 1985 Hawaii Islanders, a Class AAA Pacific Coast League affiliate of the Pittsburgh Pirates, features white-bordered posed color player photos on its fronts. The player's name, position, and team name appear at the bottom. The light blue horizontal back carries the player's name and position within a baseball bat icon at the top, followed below by biography and statistics, some enhanced by a cartoon.
COMPLETE SET (25)................. 8.00 3.20

1985 Huntsville Stars Jennings

COMPLETE SET (25)................ 25.00 10.00

1985 Indianapolis Indians Team Issue

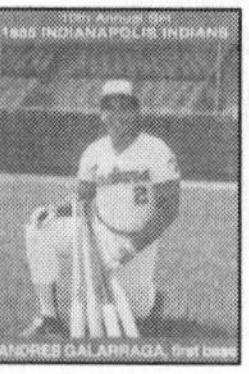

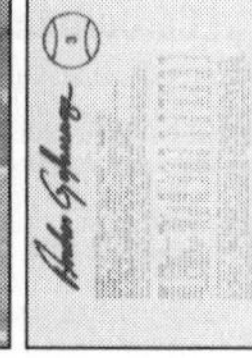

Produced by Tom Aikens, this 36-card 10th Annual Set of the 1985 Indianapolis Indians, a Class AAA American Association affiliate of the Montreal Expos, features posed color player shots on its fronts, and measures approximately 2 1/2" by 3 5/8". A brown stripe above the photo carries the team name; another below the picture carries the player's name and position. The white horizontal back carries the player's autograph facsimile at the top, followed by biography, statistics, and career highlights. This issue includes Andres Galarraga's only minor league card appearance. Cards 28-36 are authorized reproductions from each of the nine previous Indians sets. Each of these cards is denoted in the checklist below by the year of the set from which it was reproduced. 1,200 sets were produced.
COMPLETE SET (36)................ 60.00 24.00

1985 International League All-Stars TCMA

Sets with cards numbers18, 44 and 45 demand a premium, since they were pulled from most sets. Approximately 2,500 sets were produced.
COMPLETE SET (42)................ 40.00 16.00
Sets with cards numbers18, 44 and 45 demand a premium, since they were pulled from most sets. Approximately 2,500 sets were produced.
COMPLETE SET (45)................ 60.00 24.00

1985 Iowa Cubs TCMA

This 34-card standard-size set of the 1985 Iowa Cubs, a Class AAA American Association affiliate of the Chicago Cubs, features blue-bordered posed color player shots on its fronts. The team name is printed at the top with the player's name and position appearing vertically on the lower left edge. The white back carries the team name and league at the top, followed by the player's name, position, and biography.
COMPLETE SET (34)................ 15.00 6.00

1985 Kinston Blue Jays TCMA

This 26-card standard-size set of the 1985 Kinston Blue Jays, a Class A Carolina League affiliate of the Toronto Blue Jays, features blue-bordered posed color player shots on its fronts. The team name is printed at the top with the player's name and position appearing vertically on the lower left edge. The white back carries the team name and league at the top, followed by the player's name, position, and biography. The Howard and Carter Funeral Home sponsored the set. This issue includes the debuts of Pat Borders, Jose Mesa and Glenallen Hill.
COMPLETE SET (26)................ 30.00 12.00

1985 Las Vegas Stars Cramer

This 25-card standard-size set of the 1985 Las Vegas Stars, a Class AAA Pacific Coast League affiliate of the San Diego Padres, features white-bordered posed color player photos on its fronts. The player's name, position, and team name appear at the bottom. The light blue horizontal back carries the player's name and position within a baseball bat icon at the top, followed below by biography and statistics, some enhanced by a cartoon.
COMPLETE SET (25)................ 20.00 8.00

1985 Little Falls Mets TCMA

This 27-card standard-size set of the 1985 Little Falls Mets, a Class A New York-Penn League affiliate of the New York Mets, features blue-bordered posed color player shots on its fronts. The team name is printed at the top with the player's name and position appearing vertically on the lower left edge. The white back carries the team name and league at the top, followed by the player's name, position, and biography.
COMPLETE SET (27)................ 10.00 4.00

1985 Louisville Redbirds Riley's

COMPLETE SET (30)................ 15.00 6.00

1985 Lynchburg Mets TCMA

This 27-card standard-size set of the 1985 Lynchburg Mets, a Class A Carolina League affiliate of the New York Mets, features blue-bordered posed color player shots on its fronts. The team name is printed at the top with the player's name and position appearing vertically on the lower left edge. The white back carries the team name and league at the top, followed by the player's name, position, and biography. Approximately 2,500 sets were produced.
COMPLETE SET (27)................ 15.00 6.00

1985 Madison Muskies Police

COMPLETE SET (25)................ 30.00 12.00

1985 Madison Muskies TCMA

This 25-card standard-size set of the 1985 Madison Muskies, a Class A Midwest League affiliate of the Oakland Athletics, features blue-bordered posed color player shots on its fronts. The team name is printed at the top with the player's name and position appearing vertically on the lower left edge. The white back carries the team name and league at the top, followed by the player's name, position, and biography.
COMPLETE SET (25)................ 30.00 12.00

1985 Maine Guides TCMA

This 30-card standard-size set of the 1985 Maine Guides, a Class AAA International League affiliate of the Cleveland Indians, features blue-bordered posed color player shots on its fronts. The team name is printed at the top with the player's name and position appearing vertically on the lower left edge. The white back carries the team name and league at the top, followed by the player's name, position, and biography.
COMPLETE SET (30)................ 15.00 6.00

1985 Mexico City Tigers TCMA

This 29-card standard-size set of the 1985 Mexico City Tigers, a Class AAA Mexican League Independent, features blue-bordered posed color player shots on its fronts. The team name is printed at the top with the player's name and position appearing vertically on the lower left edge. The white back carries the team name and league at the top, followed by the player's name, position, and biography.
COMPLETE SET (29)................ 15.00 6.00

1985 Miami Hurricanes

The cards have black or orange border variations. The black version is much more difficult. Those cards are valued at approximately 2 to 3 times the values of the orange borders.
COMPLETE SET (16)................ 15.00 6.00

1985 Midland Angels TCMA

This 25-card standard-size set of the 1985 Midland Angels, a Class AA Texas League affiliate of the California Angels, features blue-bordered posed color player shots on its fronts. The team name is printed at the top with the player's name and position appearing vertically on the lower left edge. The white back carries the team name and league at the top, followed by the player's name, position, and biography.
COMPLETE SET (25)................ 25.00 10.00

1985 Modesto A's Chong

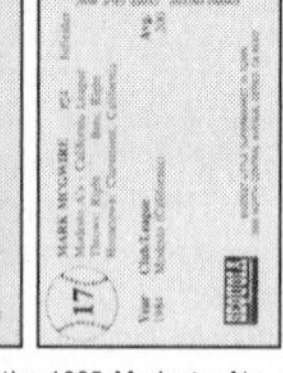

This 28-card set of the 1985 Modesto A's, a Class A California League affiliate of the Oakland Athletics, features white-bordered posed black-and-white player photos on its fronts. The player's name and position is printed at the bottom. The white back carries the player's name, position and biography. This issue includes the minor league card team set debut of Mark McGwire. Sets have either a correct spelling Mark McGwire or an error Mark McGuire. According to the printer, three printings were made of this set. Approximately 500 error sets were made, with another 500 corrected sets; both are commonly found slightly off center. A subsequent, centered printing of about 700 corrected sets was then printed from an uncut sheet (not the printing plates), making these cards noticeably lighter. Both corrected versions are valued equally. It has since been alledged that there are many more than the announced number of Mark McGwire corrected cards on the marketplace due to reprinting the McGwire correction.
COMPLETE COR SET (28)........ 80.00 32.00
COMPLETE ERR SET (34)....... 800.00 325.00

1985 Nashua Pirates TCMA

This 29-card standard-size set of the 1985 Nashua Pirates, a Class AA Eastern League affiliate of the Pittsburgh Pirates, features blue-bordered posed color player shots on its fronts. The team name is printed at the top with the player's name and position appearing vertically on the lower left edge. The white back carries the team name and league at the top, followed by the player's name, position, and biography.
COMPLETE SET (29)................ 20.00 8.00

1985 Nashville Sounds Team Issue

COMPLETE SET (25)................. 8.00 3.20

1985 Newark Orioles TCMA

This 25-card standard-size set of the 1985 Newark Orioles, a Class A New York-Penn League affiliate of the Baltimore Orioles, features blue-bordered posed color player shots on its fronts. The team name is printed at the top with the player's name and position appearing vertically on the lower left edge. The white back carries the team name and league at the top, followed by the player's name, position, and biography.
COMPLETE SET (25)................ 10.00 4.00

1985 Oklahoma City 89ers TCMA

This 30-card standard-size set of the 1985 Oklahoma City 89ers, a Class AAA American Association affiliate of the Texas Rangers, features blue-bordered posed color player shots on its fronts. The team name is printed at the top with the player's name and position appearing vertically on the lower left edge. The white back carries the team name and league at the top, followed by the player's name, position, and biography. Approximately 2,500 sets were produced.
COMPLETE SET (30)................ 25.00 10.00

1985 Omaha Royals TCMA

This 31-card standard-size set of the 1985 Omaha Royals, a Class AAA American Association affiliate of the Kansas City Royals, features blue-bordered posed color player shots on its fronts. The team name is printed at the top with the player's name and position appearing vertically on the lower left edge. The white back carries the team name and league at the top, followed by the player's name, position, and biography. This issue includes a third year minor league card of David Cone.
COMPLETE SET (31)................ 30.00 12.00

1985 Orlando Twins TCMA

This 26-card standard-size set of the 1985 Orlando Twins, a Class AA Southern League affiliate of the Minnesota Twins, features blue-bordered posed color player shots on its fronts. The team name is printed at the top with the player's name and position appearing vertically on the lower left edge. The white back carries the team name and league at the top, followed by the player's name, position, and biography.
COMPLETE SET (26)................ 10.00 4.00

1985 Osceola Astros Team Issue

This 30-card set of the 1985 Osceola Astros, a Class A Florida State League affiliate of the Houston Astros, features the minor league card debut of Ken Caminiti.
COMPLETE SET (30).............. 100.00 40.00

1985 Pawtucket Red Sox TCMA

This 20-card standard-size set of the 1985 Pawtucket Red Sox, a Class AAA International League affiliate of the Boston Red Sox, features blue-bordered posed color player shots on its fronts. The team name is printed at the top with the player's name and position appearing vertically on the lower left edge. The white back carries the team name and league at the top, followed by the player's name, position, and biography.
COMPLETE SET (20)................ 30.00 12.00

1985 Phoenix Giants Cramer

This 25-card standard-size set of the 1985 Phoenix Giants, a Class AAA Pacific Coast League affiliate of the San Francisco Giants, features white-bordered posed color player photos on its fronts. The player's name, position, and team name appear at the bottom. The light blue horizontal back carries the player's name and position within a baseball bat icon at the top, followed below by biography and statistics, some enhanced by a cartoon.
COMPLETE SET (25)................. 8.00 3.20

1985 Portland Beavers Cramer

This 25-card standard-size set of the 1985 Portland Beavers, a Class AAA Pacific Coast League affiliate of the Philadelphia Phillies, features white-bordered posed color player photos on its fronts. The player's name, position, and team name appear at the bottom. The light blue horizontal back carries the player's name and position within a baseball bat icon at the top, followed below by biography and statistics, some enhanced by a cartoon.
COMPLETE SET (25)................ 30.00 12.00

1985 Prince William Pirates TCMA

This 31-card standard-size set of the 1985 Prince William Pirates, a Class A Carolina League affiliate of the Pittsburgh Pirates, features blue-bordered posed color player shots on its fronts. The team name is printed at the top with the player's name and position appearing vertically on the lower left edge. The white back carries the team name and league at the top, followed by the player's name, position, and biography. This issue includes the minor league card debut of John Smiley.
COMPLETE SET (31)................ 20.00 8.00

1985 Reading Phillies ProCards

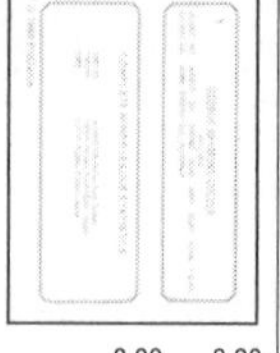

COMPLETE SET (26)................. 8.00 3.20

1985 Red Wing Aces/Scarlets

COMPLETE SET (25)................. 5.00 2.00

1985 Richmond Braves TCMA

This 26-card standard-size set of the 1985 Richmond Braves, a Class AAA International League affiliate of the Atlanta Braves, features blue-bordered posed color player shots on its fronts. The team name is printed at the top with the player's name and position appearing vertically on the lower left edge. The white back carries the team name and league at the top, followed by the player's name, position, and biography.
COMPLETE SET (26)................ 15.00 6.00

1985 Rochester Red Wings TCMA

This 31-card standard-size set of the 1985 Rochester Red Wings, a Class AAA International League affiliate of the Baltimore Orioles, features blue-bordered posed color player shots on its fronts. The team name is printed at the top with the player's name and position appearing vertically on the lower left edge. The white back carries the team name and league at the top, followed by the player's name, position, and biography.
COMPLETE SET (29)................ 10.00 4.00

1985 Spokane Indians Cramer

COMPLETE SET (24)................ 10.00 4.00

1985 Spokane Indians Greats Cramer

COMPLETE SET (24)................ 10.00 4.00

1985 Springfield Cardinals TCMA

This 25-card standard-size set of the 1985 Springfield Cardinals, a Class A Midwest League affiliate of the St. Louis Cardinals, features blue-bordered posed color player shots on its fronts. The team name is printed at the top with the player's name and position appearing vertically on the lower left edge. The white back carries the team name and league at the top, followed by the player's name, position, and biography. This issue includes the minor league card debut of Jeff Fassero.
COMPLETE SET (25)................ 15.00 6.00

1985 Syracuse Chiefs TCMA

This 31-card standard-size set of the 1985 Syracuse Chiefs, a Class AAA International League affiliate of the Toronto Blue Jays, features blue-bordered posed color player shots on its fronts. The team name is printed at the top with the player's name and position appearing vertically on the lower left edge. The white back carries the team name and league at the top, followed by the player's name, position, and biography. This issue includes the minor league card debut of Fred McGriff. Approximately 3,000 sets were produced.
COMPLETE SET (31)................ 80.00 16.00

1985 Tacoma Tigers Cramer

This 25-card standard-size set of the 1985 Tacoma Tigers, a Class AAA Pacific Coast League affiliate of the Oakland Athletics, features white-bordered posed color player photos on its fronts. The player's name, position, and team name appear at the bottom. The light blue horizontal back carries the player's name and position within a baseball bat icon at the top, followed below by biography and statistics, some enhanced by a cartoon.
COMPLETE SET (25)................ 15.00 6.00

1985 Tidewater Tides TCMA

This 28-card standard-size set of the 1985 Tidewater Tides, a Class AAA International League affiliate of the New York Mets, features blue-bordered posed color player shots on its fronts. The team name is printed at the top with the player's name and position appearing vertically on the lower left edge. The white back carries the team name and league at the top, followed by the player's name, position, and biography. Approximately 4,000 sets were produced.
COMPLETE SET (27)................ 60.00 24.00
COMPLETE SET W/COR (28) ... 75.00 30.00

1985 Toledo Mud Hens TCMA

This 26-card standard-size set of the 1985 Toledo Mud Hens, a Class AAA International League affiliate of the Detroit Tigers, features blue-bordered posed color player shots on its fronts. The team name is printed at the top with the player's name and position appearing vertically on the lower left edge. The white back carries the team name and league at the top, followed by the player's name, position, and biography.
COMPLETE SET (25)................ 15.00 6.00
COMPLETE SET (26)................ 20.00 8.00

1985 Tucson Toros Cramer

This 25-card standard-size set of the 1985 Tucson Toros, a Class AAA Pacific Coast League affiliate of the Houston Astros, features white-bordered posed color player photos on its fronts. The player's name, position, and team name appear at the bottom. The light blue horizontal back carries the player's name and position within a baseball bat icon at the top, followed below by biography and statistics, some enhanced by a cartoon.
COMPLETE SET (25)................ 10.00 4.00

1985 Tulsa Drillers Team Issue

This issue includes the minor league card debut of Ruben Sierra.
COMPLETE SET (27)................ 60.00 24.00
COMPLETE SET (28)................ 80.00 32.00

1985 Utica Blue Sox TCMA

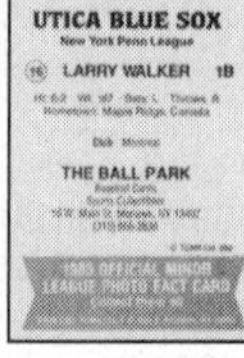

This 26-card standard-size set of the 1985 Utica Blue Sox, a Class A New York-Penn League Independent, features blue-bordered posed color player shots on its fronts. The team name is printed at the top with the player's name and position appearing vertically on the lower left edge. The white back carries the team name and league at the top, followed by the player's name, position, and biography. This issue includes the minor league card debut of Larry Walker.
COMPLETE SET (26)................ 50.00 24.00

1985 Vancouver Canadians Cramer

This 25-card standard-size set of the 1985 Vancouver Canadians, a Class AAA Pacific Coast League affiliate of the Milwaukee Brewers, features white-bordered posed color player photos on its fronts. The player's name, position, and team name appear at the bottom. The light blue horizontal back carries the player's name and position within a baseball bat icon at the top, followed below by biography and statistics, some enhanced by a cartoon.
COMPLETE SET (25)................. 8.00 3.20

1985 Vero Beach Dodgers TCMA

This 27-card standard-size set of the 1985 Vero Beach Dodgers, a Class A Florida State League affiliate of the Los Angeles Dodgers, features blue-bordered posed color player shots on its fronts. The team name is printed at the top with the player's name and position appearing vertically on the lower left edge. The white back carries the team name and league at the top, followed by the player's name, position, and biography.
COMPLETE SET (27)................ 15.00 6.00

1985 Visalia Oaks TCMA

This 25-card standard-size set of the 1985 Visalia Oaks, a Class A California League affiliate of the Minnesota Twins, features blue-bordered posed color player shots on its fronts. The team name is printed at the top with the player's name and position appearing vertically on the lower left edge. The white back carries the team name and league at the top, followed by the player's name, position, and biography. This issue includes the minor league card debut of Jay Bell.
COMPLETE SET (25)................ 20.00 8.00

1985 Waterbury Indians TCMA

This 25-card standard-size set of the 1985 Waterbury Indians, a Class AA Eastern League affiliate of the Cleveland Indians, features blue-bordered posed color player shots on its fronts. The team name is printed at the top with the player's name and position appearing vertically on the lower left edge. The white back carries the team name and league at the top, followed by the player's name, position, and biography.
COMPLETE SET (25)................ 20.00 8.00

1986 Albany-Colonie Yankees TCMA

This 32-card standard-size set of the 1986 Albany Yankees, a Class AA Eastern League affiliate of the New York Yankees, features

ite-bordered posed color player shots set on hsia backgrounds. The team name is printed hin the fuchsia area below the photo. A ck stripe at the bottom carries the player's ne and position. The white back carries the m name and league at the top, followed by e player's name, positon, biography and tistics.
MPLETE SET (32)................ 15.00 6.00

1986 Albuquerque Dukes ProCards

is 28-card standard-size set of the 1986 uquerque Dukes, a Class AAA Pacific Coast ague affiliate of the Los Angeles Dodgers, atures white-bordered posed color player otos on its fronts. The player's name, team, d position appear at the bottom. The white rizontal back carries the player's name and sition at the top, followed by biography and atistics. The cards are unnumbered and ecklisted below in alphabetical order.
MPLETE SET (28).................. 5.00 2.00

1986 Anchorage Glacier Pilots Team Issue

MPLETE SET (42)................ 15.00 6.00

1986 Appleton Foxes ProCards

is 28-card standard-size set of the 1986 pleton Foxes, a Class A Midwest League iliate of the Chicago White Sox, features ite-bordered posed color player photos on fronts. The player's name, team, and sition appear at the bottom. The white rizontal back carries the player's name and sition at the top, followed by biography and atistics. The cards are unnumbered and ecklisted below in alphabetical order.
MPLETE SET (28).................. 5.00 2.00

986 Arizona Wildcats Police

MPLETE SET (20)................ 20.00 8.00

1986 Arkansas Travelers ProCards

is 26-card standard-size set of the 1986 kansas Travelers, a Class AA Texas League filiate of the St. Louis Cardinals, features hite-bordered posed color player photos on fronts. The player's name, team, and osition appear at the bottom. The white orizontal back carries the player's name and osition at the top, followed by biography and atistics. The cards are unnumbered and ecklisted below in alphabetical order. This sue includes the minor league card debut of ance Johnson.
OMPLETE SET (26)................ 15.00 6.00

1986 Asheville Tourists ProCards

his 29-card standard-size set of the 1986 sheville Tourists, a Class A South Atlantic eague affiliate of the Houston Astros, features hite-bordered posed color player photos on s fronts. The player's name, team, and osition appear at the bottom. The white orizontal back carries the player's name and osition at the top, followed by biography and atistics. The cards are unnumbered and ecklisted below in alphabetical order.
OMPLETE SET (29).................. 5.00 2.00

1986 Auburn Astros ProCards

his 27-card standard-size set of the 1986 uburn Astros, a Class A New York-Penn eague affiliate of the Houston Astros, features hite-bordered posed color player photos on s fronts. The player's name, team, and osition appear at the bottom. The white orizontal back carries the player's name and osition at the top, followed by biography and tatistics. The cards are unnumbered and hecklisted below in alphabetical order.
OMPLETE SET (27).................. 5.00 2.00

1986 Bakersfield Dodgers ProCards

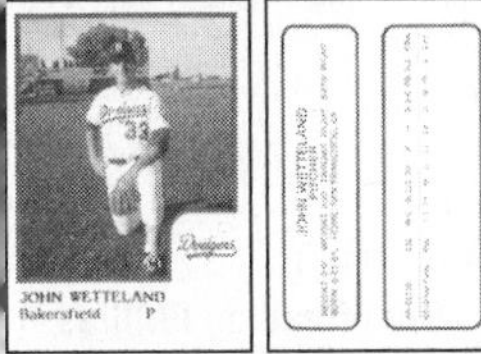

his 29-card standard-size set of the 1986 akersfield Dodgers, a Class A California eague affiliate of the Los Angeles Dodgers, eatures white-bordered posed color player hotos on its fronts. The player's name, team, nd position appear at the bottom. The white orizontal back carries the player's name and osition at the top, followed by biography and tatistics. The cards are unnumbered and hecklisted below in alphabetical order. This ssue includes the minor league card debuts of amon Martinez and John Wetteland.
OMPLETE SET (29)................ 20.00 8.00

1986 Beaumont Golden Gators ProCards

his 25-card standard-size set of the 1986 eaumont Golden Gators, a Class AA Texas League affiliate of the San Diego Padres, features white-bordered posed color player photos on its fronts. The player's name, team, and position appear at the bottom. The white horizontal back carries the player's name and position at the top, followed by biography and statistics. The cards are unnumbered and checklisted below in alphabetical order.
COMPLETE SET (25)................ 15.00 6.00

1986 Bellingham Mariners Cramer

COMPLETE SET (29).................. 5.00 2.00

1986 Beloit Brewers ProCards

This 26-card standard-size set of the 1986 Beloit Brewers, a Class A Midwest League affiliate of the Milwaukee Brewers, features white-bordered posed color player photos on its fronts. The player's name, team, and position appear at the bottom. The white horizontal back carries the player's name and position at the top, followed by biography and statistics. The cards are unnumbered and checklisted below in alphabetical order.
COMPLETE SET (26).................. 5.00 2.00

1986 Bend Phillies Cramer

This issue includes the minor league card debut of Andy Ashby.
COMPLETE SET (25).................. 8.00 3.20

1986 Birmingham Barons Team Issue

COMPLETE SET (28)................ 60.00 24.00

1986 Buffalo Bisons ProCards

This 26-card standard-size set of the 1986 Buffalo Bisons, a Class AAA American Association affiliate of the Chicago White Sox, features white-bordered posed color player photos on its fronts. The player's name, team, and position appear at the bottom. The white horizontal back carries the player's name and position at the top, followed by biography and statistics. The cards are unnumbered and checklisted below in alphabetical order.
COMPLETE SET (26).................. 5.00 2.00

1986 Burlington Expos ProCards

This 28-card standard-size set of the 1986 Burlington Expos, a Class A Midwest League affiliate of the Montreal Expos, features white-bordered posed color player photos on its fronts. The player's name, team, and position appear at the bottom. The white horizontal back carries the player's name and position at the top, followed by biography and statistics. The cards are unnumbered and checklisted below in alphabetical order. This issue includes a second year card of Larry Walker.
COMPLETE SET (28)................ 20.00 8.00

1986 Calgary Cannons ProCards

This 26-card standard-size police set of the 1986 Calgary Cannons, a Class AAA Pacific Coast League affiliate of the Seattle Mariners, features white-bordered posed color player photos on its fronts. The player's name, team, and position appear at the bottom. The white horizontal back carries the player's name at the top, followed by biography, statistics, and safety tips. The cards are unnumbered and checklisted below in alphabetical order.
COMPLETE SET (26).................. 5.00 2.00

1986 Cedar Rapids Reds TCMA

This 28-card standard-size set of the 1986 Cedar Rapids Reds, a Class A Midwest League affiliate of the Cincinnati Reds, features white-bordered posed color player photos on its fronts. The player's name, team, and position appear at the bottom. The white horizontal back carries the player's name and position at the top, followed by biography and statistics. The cards are unnumbered and checklisted below in alphabetical order.
COMPLETE SET (28).................. 5.00 2.00

1986 Charleston Rainbows ProCards

This 30-card standard-size set of the 1986 Charleston Rainbows, a Class A South Atlantic League affiliate of the San Diego Padres, features white-bordered posed color player photos on its fronts. The player's name, team, and position appear at the bottom. The white horizontal back carries the player's name and position at the top, followed by biography and statistics. The cards are unnumbered and checklisted below in alphabetical order. This issue includes the minor league card debut of Carlos Baerga.
COMPLETE SET W/VAR (31) ... 40.00 16.00
COMPLETE SET (29)................ 30.00 12.00

1986 Charlotte Orioles WBTV

Cards are unnumbered.
COMPLETE SET (30)................ 30.00 12.00

1986 Chattanooga Lookouts ProCards

This 25-card standard-size set of the 1986 Chattanooga Lookouts, a Class AA Southern League affiliate of the Seattle Mariners, features white-bordered posed color player photos on its fronts. The player's name, team, and position appear at the bottom. The white horizontal back carries the player's name and position at the top, followed by biography and statistics. The cards are unnumbered and checklisted below in alphabetical order. This issue includes the minor league card debut of Edgar Martinez.
COMPLETE SET (25)................ 20.00 8.00

1986 Clearwater Phillies ProCards

This 26-card standard-size set of the 1986 Clearwater Phillies, a Class A Florida State League affiliate of the Philadelphia Phillies, features white-bordered posed color player photos on its fronts. The player's name, team, and position appear at the bottom. The white horizontal back carries the player's name and position at the top, followed by biography and statistics. The cards are unnumbered and checklisted below in alphabetical order.
COMPLETE SET (26).................. 5.00 2.00

1986 Clinton Giants ProCards

This 29-card standard-size set of the 1986 Clinton Giants, a Class A Midwest League affiliate of the San Francisco Giants, features white-bordered posed color player photos on its fronts. The player's name, team, and position appear at the bottom. The white horizontal back carries the player's name and position at the top, followed by biography and statistics. The cards are unnumbered and checklisted below in alphabetical order.
COMPLETE SET (29).................. 5.00 2.00

1986 Columbia Mets ProCards

This 29-card standard-size set of the 1986 Columbia Mets, a Class A South Atlantic League affiliate of the New York Mets, features white-bordered posed color player photos on its fronts. The player's name, team, and position appear at the bottom. The white horizontal back carries the player's name and position at the top, followed by biography and statistics. The cards are unnumbered and checklisted below in alphabetical order. This issue includes the minor league card debut of Gregg Jefferies.
COMPLETE SET (28)................ 20.00 8.00
COMPLETE SET (29)................ 30.00 12.00

1986 Columbus Astros ProCards

This 25-card standard-size set of the 1986 Columbus Astros, a Class AA Southern League affiliate of the Houston Astros, features white-bordered posed color player photos on its fronts. The player's name, team, and position appear at the bottom. The white horizontal back carries the player's name and position at the top, followed by biography and statistics. The cards are unnumbered and checklisted below in alphabetical order. This issue includes a second year card of Ken Caminiti.
COMPLETE SET (25)................ 20.00 8.00

1986 Columbus Clippers Police

This 25-card standard-size set of the 1986 Columbus Clippers, a Class AAA International League affiliate of the New York Yankees.
COMPLETE SET (25)................ 10.00 4.00

1986 Columbus Clippers ProCards

This 26-card standard-size set of the 1986 Columbus Clippers, a Class AAA International League affiliate of the New York Yankees, features white-bordered posed color player photos on its fronts. The player's name, team, and position appear at the bottom. The white horizontal back carries the player's name and position at the top, followed by biography and statistics. The cards are unnumbered and checklisted below in alphabetical order.
COMPLETE SET (26).................. 8.00 3.20

1986 David Lipscomb Bisons

COMPLETE SET (24)................ 15.00 6.00

1986 Daytona Beach Islanders ProCards

This 29-card standard-size set of the 1986 Daytona Beach Islanders, a Class A Florida State League Independent, features white-bordered posed color player photos on its fronts. The player's name, team, and position appear at the bottom. The white horizontal back carries the player's name and position at the top, followed by biography and statistics. The cards are unnumbered and checklisted below in alphabetical order.
COMPLETE SET (29).................. 5.00 2.00

1986 Durham Bulls ProCards

This 27-card standard-size set of the 1986 Durham Bulls, a Class A Carolina League affiliate of the Atlanta Braves, features white-bordered posed color player photos on its fronts. The player's name, team, and position appear at the bottom. The white horizontal back carries the player's name and position at the top, followed by biography and statistics. The cards are unnumbered and checklisted below in alphabetical order. This issue includes the minor league card debut of Ron Gant.
COMPLETE SET (27)................ 15.00 6.00

1986 Edmonton Trappers ProCards

This 27-card standard-size set of the 1986 Edmonton Trappers, a Class AAA Pacific Coast League affiliate of the California Angels, features white-bordered posed color player photos on its fronts. The player's name, team, and position appear at the bottom. The white horizontal back carries the player's name and position at the top, followed by biography and statistics. The cards are unnumbered and checklisted below in alphabetical order.
COMPLETE SET (27)................ 10.00 4.00

1986 El Paso Diablos ProCards

This 23-card standard-size set of the 1986 El Paso Diablos, a Class AA Texas League affiliate of the Milwaukee Brewers, features white-bordered posed color player photos on its fronts. The player's name, team, and position appear at the bottom. The white horizontal back carries the player's name and position at the top, followed by biography and statistics. The cards are unnumbered and checklisted below in alphabetical order.
COMPLETE SET (23).................. 5.00 2.00

1986 Elmira Pioneers ProCards

This 30-card standard-size set of the 1986 Elmira Pioneer Red Sox, a Class A New York-Penn League affiliate of the Boston Red Sox, features white-bordered posed color player photos on its fronts. The player's name, team, and position appear at the bottom. The white horizontal back carries the player's name and position at the top, followed by biography and statistics. The cards are unnumbered and checklisted below in alphabetical order. This set contains the first card of Curt Schilling.
COMPLETE SET (30)................ 100.00 32.00

1986 Erie Cardinals ProCards

This 31-card standard-size set of the 1986 Erie Cardinals, a Class A New York-Penn League affiliate of the St. Louis Cardinals, features white-bordered posed color player photos on its fronts. The player's name, team, and position appear at the bottom. The white horizontal back carries the player's name and position at the top, followed by biography and statistics. The cards are unnumbered and checklisted below in alphabetical order. The unnumbered William Hershman card is not included in all sets. This issue includes the minor league card debut of Todd Zeile.
COMPLETE SET (30)................ 15.00 6.00
COMPLETE SET (31)................ 25.00 10.00

1986 Eugene Emeralds Cramer

This issue includes the minor league card debut of Brian McRae.
COMPLETE SET (25)................ 10.00 4.00

1986 Everett Giants Cramer

This issue includes the minor league card debut of Matt Williams.
COMPLETE SET (32)................ 30.00 12.00

1986 Everett Giants Popcorn Cramer

COMPLETE SET (36)................ 10.00 4.00

1986 Florida State League All-Stars ProCards

This 50-card standard-size set of the 1986 Florida State League All-Stars features white-bordered posed color player photos on its fronts. The player's name, team, and position appear at the bottom. The white horizontal back carries the player's name and position at the top, followed by biography and statistics. The cards are unnumbered and checklisted below in alphabetical order. This issue includes a second year card of Brady Anderson.
COMPLETE SET (50)................ 25.00 10.00

1986 Fresno Giants Smokey Bear

This 32-card set features black and white photos framed with an orange lined border and a dark blue background. The team name and the player's last name appear across the top with the words "wildfire prevention" appearing across the bottom.
COMPLETE SET (32)................ 30.00 12.00

1986 Ft. Lauderdale Yankees ProCards

This 23-card standard-size set of the 1986 Ft. Lauderdale Yankees, a Class A Florida State League affiliate of the New York Yankees, features white-bordered posed color player photos on its fronts. The player's name, team, and position appear at the bottom. The white horizontal back carries the player's name and position at the top, followed by biography and statistics. The cards are unnumbered and checklisted below in alphabetical order.
COMPLETE SET (23).................. 5.00 2.00

1986 Ft. Myers Royals ProCards

This 29-card standard-size set of the 1986 Ft. Myers Royals, a Class A Florida State League affiliate of the Kansas City Royals, features white-bordered posed color player photos on its fronts. The player's name, team, and position appear at the bottom. The white horizontal back carries the player's name and position at the top, followed by biography and statistics. The cards are unnumbered and checklisted below in alphabetical order.
COMPLETE SET (29).................. 5.00 2.00

1986 Geneva Cubs ProCards

This 27-card standard-size set of the 1986 Geneva Cubs, a Class A New York-Penn League affiliate of the Chicago Cubs, features white-bordered posed color player photos on its fronts. The player's name, team, and position appear at the bottom. The white horizontal back carries the player's name and position at the top, followed by biography and statistics. The cards are unnumbered and checklisted below in alphabetical order.
COMPLETE SET (27).................. 5.00 2.00

1986 Glen Falls Tigers ProCards

This 24-card standard-size set of the 1986 Glen Falls Tigers, a Class AA Eastern League affiliate of the Detroit Tigers, features white-bordered posed color player photos on its fronts. The player's name, team, and position appear at the bottom. The white horizontal back carries the player's name and position at the top, followed by biography and statistics. The cards are unnumbered and checklisted below in alphabetical order.
COMPLETE SET (24).................. 5.00 2.00

1986 Greensboro Hornets ProCards

This 27-card standard-size set of the 1986 Greensboro Hornets, a Class A South Atlantic League affiliate of the Boston Red Sox, features white-bordered posed color player photos on its fronts. The player's name, team, and position appear at the bottom. The white horizontal back carries the player's name and position at the top, followed by biography and statistics. The cards are unnumbered and checklisted below in alphabetical order.
COMPLETE SET (27).................. 5.00 2.00

1986 Greenville Braves ProCards

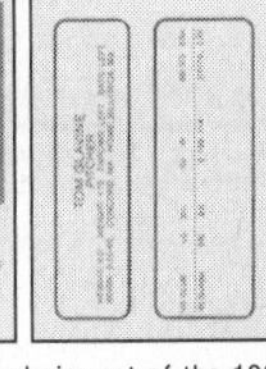

This 23-card standard-size set of the 1986 Greenville Braves, a Class AA Southern League affiliate of the Greenville Braves, features white-bordered posed color player photos on its fronts. The player's name, team, and position appear at the bottom. The white horizontal back carries the player's name and position at the top, followed by biography and statistics. The cards are unnumbered and checklisted below in alphabetical order. This issue includes the minor league card debut of Tom Glavine.
COMPLETE SET (23)................ 50.00 20.00

1986 Hagerstown Suns ProCards

This 29-card standard-size set of the 1986 Hagerstown Suns, a Class A Carolina League affiliate of the Baltimore Orioles, features white-bordered posed color player photos on its fronts. The player's name, team, and position appear at the bottom. The white horizontal back carries the player's name and position at the top, followed by biography and statistics. The cards are unnumbered and checklisted below in alphabetical order.
COMPLETE SET (29).................. 5.00 2.00

1986 Hawaii Islanders ProCards

This 23-card standard-size set of the 1986 Hawaii Islanders, a Class AAA Pacific Coast League affiliate of the Pittsburgh Pirates, features white-bordered posed color player photos on its fronts. The player's name, team, and position appear at the bottom. The white horizontal back carries the player's name and position at the top, followed by biography and

statistics. The cards are unnumbered and checklisted below in alphabetical order.
COMPLETE SET (23)................. 5.00 2.00

1986 Huntsville Stars Jennings

This issue includes a second year card of Mark McGwire.
COMPLETE SET (25)................ 25.00 10.00

1986 Indianapolis Indians Team Issue

This 36-card set of the 1986 Indianapolis Indians, a Class AAA American Association affiliate of the Montreal Expos, features posed color player shots on its fronts, and measures approximately 2 1/2" by 3 5/8". A gold stripe appears above and below the photo. The upper gold stripe carries the team name; the player's name and position are printed within a brown baseball bat icon in the bottom gold margin. The white horizontal back carries the player's autograph facsimile at the top, followed by biography, statistics, and career highlights. The cards are numbered on the back. Card nos. 2, 5, 8, 11, 14, 18, 21, 24 and 29 depict players or teams from the past.
COMPLETE SET (36)................. 8.00 3.20

1986 Iowa Cubs ProCards

This 26-card standard-size set of the 1986 Iowa Cubs, a Class AAA American Association affiliate of the Chicago Cubs, features white-bordered posed color player photos on its fronts. The player's name, team, and position appear at the bottom. The white horizontal back carries the player's name and position at the top, followed by biography and statistics. The cards are unnumbered and checklisted below in alphabetical order.
COMPLETE SET (26)................. 5.00 2.00

1986 Jackson Mets TCMA

This 27-card standard-size set of the 1986 Jackson Mets, a Class AA Texas League affiliate of the New York Mets, features white-bordered posed color player shots set on fuchsia backgrounds. The team name is printed within the fuchsia area below the photo. A black stripe at the bottom carries the player's name and position. The white back carries the team name and league at the top, followed by the player's name, positon, biography and statistics.
COMPLETE SET (27)................. 8.00 3.20

1986 Jacksonville Expos TCMA

This 26-card standard-size set of the 1986 Jacksonville Expos, a Class AA Southern League affiliate of the Montreal Expos, features white-bordered posed color player shots set on fuchsia backgrounds. The team name is printed within the fuchsia area below the photo. A black stripe at the bottom carries the player's name and position. The white back carries the team name and league at the top, followed by the player's name, positon, biography and statistics. The set was sponsored by Golden Glove, a local sports card store.
COMPLETE SET (26)................. 8.00 3.20

1986 Jamestown Expos ProCards

This 30-card standard-size set of the 1986 Jamestown Expos, a Class A New York-Penn League affiliate of the Montreal Expos, features white-bordered posed color player photos on its fronts. The player's name, team, and position appear at the bottom. The white horizontal back carries the player's name and position at the top, followed by biography and statistics. The cards are unnumbered and checklisted below in alphabetical order.
COMPLETE SET (30)................. 5.00 2.00

1986 Kenosha Twins ProCards

This 25-card standard-size set of the 1986 Kenosha Twins, a Class A Midwest League affiliate of the Minnesota Twins, features white-bordered posed color player photos on its fronts. The player's name, team, and position appear at the bottom. The white horizontal back carries the player's name and position at the top, followed by biography and statistics. The cards are unnumbered and checklisted below in alphabetical order.
COMPLETE SET (25)................. 5.00 2.00

1986 Kinston Eagles ProCards

This 25-card standard-size set of the 1986 Kinston Eagles, a Class A Carolina League Independent, features white-bordered posed color player photos on its fronts. The player's name, team, and position appear at the bottom. The white horizontal back carries the player's name and position at the top, followed by biography and statistics. The cards are unnumbered and checklisted below in alphabetical order.
COMPLETE SET (25)................. 5.00 2.00

1986 Knoxville Blue Jays ProCards

Sponsored by Smokey Mountain Collectibles, this 27-card standard-size set of the 1986 Knoxville Blue Jays, a Class A Southern League affiliate of the Toronto Blue Jays, features white-bordered posed color player photos on its fronts. The player's name, team, and position appear at the bottom. The white horizontal back carries the player's name and position at the top, followed by biography and statistics. The cards are unnumbered and checklisted below in alphabetical order.
COMPLETE SET (27)................. 5.00 2.00

1986 Lakeland Tigers ProCards

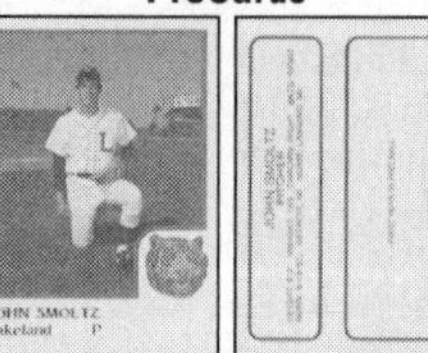

This 25-card standard-size set of the 1986 Lakeland Tigers, a Class A Florida State League affiliate of the Detroit Tigers, features white-bordered posed color player photos on its fronts. The player's name, team, and position appear at the bottom. The white horizontal back carries the player's name and position at the top, followed by biography and statistics. The cards are unnumbered and checklisted below in alphabetical order. This issue includes the minor league card debut of John Smoltz.
COMPLETE SET (25)................ 25.00 10.00

1986 Las Vegas Stars ProCards

This 26-card standard-size set of the 1986 Las Vegas Stars, a Class AAA Pacific Coast League affiliate of the San Diego Padres, features white-bordered posed color player photos on its fronts. The player's name, team, and position appear at the bottom. The white horizontal back carries the player's name and position at the top, followed by biography and statistics. The cards are unnumbered and checklisted below in alphabetical order.
COMPLETE SET (24)................. 5.00 2.00
COMPLETE SET W/Bowa (26).. 10.00 4.00

1986 Little Falls Mets ProCards

This 29-card standard-size set of the 1986 Little Falls Mets, a Class A New York-Penn League affiliate of the New York Mets, features white-bordered posed color player photos on its fronts. The player's name, team, and position appear at the bottom. The white horizontal back carries the player's name and position at the top, followed by biography and statistics. The cards are unnumbered and checklisted below in alphabetical order.
COMPLETE SET (29)................. 5.00 2.00

1986 Louisville Redbirds Team Issue

COMPLETE SET (30)................ 10.00 4.00

1986 Lynchburg Mets ProCards

This 28-card standard-size set of the 1986 Lynchburg Mets, a Class A Carolina League affiliate of the New York Mets, features white-bordered posed color player photos on its fronts. The player's name, team, and position appear at the bottom. The white horizontal back carries the player's name and position at the top, followed by biography and statistics. The cards are unnumbered and checklisted below in alphabetical order.
COMPLETE SET (28)................. 5.00 2.00

1986 Macon Pirates ProCards

This 27-card standard-size set of the 1986 Macon Pirates, a Class A South Atlantic League affiliate of the Pittsburgh Pirates, features white-bordered posed color player photos on its fronts. The player's name, team, and position appear at the bottom. The white horizontal back carries the player's name and position at the top, followed by biography and statistics. The cards are unnumbered and checklisted below in alphabetical order. This issue includes the minor league card debut of Orlando Merced.
COMPLETE SET (27)................ 10.00 4.00

1986 Madison Muskies Police

COMPLETE SET (27)................ 10.00 4.00

1986 Madison Muskies ProCards

This 28-card standard-size set of the 1986 Madison Muskies, a Class A Midwest League affiliate of the Oakland Athletics, features white-bordered posed color player photos on its fronts. The player's name, team, and position appear at the bottom. The white horizontal back carries the player's name and position at the top, followed by biography and statistics. The cards are unnumbered and checklisted below in alphabetical order.
COMPLETE SET (28)................. 5.00 2.00

1986 Maine Guides ProCards

This 26-card standard-size set of the 1986 Maine Guides, a Class AAA International League affiliate of the Cleveland Indians, features white-bordered posed color player photos on its fronts. The player's name, team, and position appear at the bottom. The white horizontal back carries the player's name and position at the top, followed by biography and statistics. The cards are unnumbered and checklisted below in alphabetical order.
COMPLETE SET (26)................. 5.00 2.00

1986 Medford A's Cramer

COMPLETE SET (25)................. 8.00 3.20

1986 Memphis Chicks Time Out Sports

This 26-card standard-size set of the 1986 Memphis Chicks features gold-bordered posed color player photos on its fronts. The player's name, team logo, and position appear at the bottom. The sets were produced by Time Out Sports Productions (Peter Kass) and come with a certificate of authenticity. 10,000 gold border and 5,000 silver border sets were produced. This issue includes the only minor league card of Bo Jackson.
COMPLETE GOLD SET (26)...... 15.00 6.00
COMPLETE SILVER SET (26)... 30.00 12.00

1986 Miami Marlins ProCards

This 29-card standard-size set of the 1986 Miami Marlins, a Class A Florida State League Independent, features white-bordered posed color player photos on its fronts. The player's name, team, and position appear at the bottom. The white horizontal back carries the player's name and position at the top, followed by biography and statistics. The cards are unnumbered and checklisted below in alphabetical order.
COMPLETE SET (29)................. 5.00 2.00

1986 Midland Angels ProCards

This 26-card standard-size set of the 1986 Midland Angels, a Class AA Texas League affiliate of the California Angels, features white-bordered posed color player photos on its fronts. The player's name, team, and position appear at the bottom. The white horizontal back carries the player's name and position at the top, followed by biography and statistics. The cards are unnumbered and checklisted below in alphabetical order.
COMPLETE SET (26)................. 5.00 2.00

1986 Modesto A's Chong

COMPLETE SET (27)................ 15.00 6.00

1986 Modesto A's ProCards

This 27-card standard-size set of the 1986 Modesto A's, a Class A California League affiliate of the Oakland Athletics, features white-bordered posed color player photos on its fronts. The player's name, team, and position appear at the bottom. The white horizontal back carries the player's name and position at the top, followed by biography and statistics. The cards are unnumbered and checklisted below in alphabetical order.
COMPLETE SET (26)................. 5.00 2.00
COMPLETE SET (27)................ 10.00 4.00

1986 Nashua Pirates ProCards

This 28-card standard-size set of the 1986 Nashua Pirates, a Class AA Eastern League affiliate of the Pittsburgh Pirates, features white-bordered posed color player photos on its fronts. The player's name, team, and position appear at the bottom. The white horizontal back carries the player's name and position at the top, followed by biography and statistics. The cards are unnumbered and checklisted below in alphabetical order.
COMPLETE SET (28)................. 5.00 2.00

1986 Nashville Sounds Team Issue

COMPLETE SET (24)................. 8.00 3.20

1986 New Britain Red Sox ProCards

This 25-card standard-size set of the 1986 New Britain Red Sox, a Class AA Eastern League affiliate of the Boston Red Sox, features white-bordered posed color player photos on its fronts. The player's name, team, and position appear at the bottom. The white horizontal back carries the player's name and position at the top, followed by biography and statistics. The cards are unnumbered and checklisted below in alphabetical order. This issue includes the minor league card debut of Ellis Burks.
COMPLETE SET (25)................ 15.00 6.00

1986 Oklahoma City 89ers ProCards

This 26-card standard-size set of the 1986 Oklahoma City 89ers, a Class AAA American Association affiliate of the Texas Rangers, features white-bordered posed color player photos on its fronts. The player's name, team, and position appear at the bottom. The white horizontal back carries the player's name and position at the top, followed by biography and statistics. The cards are unnumbered and checklisted below in alphabetical order.
COMPLETE SET (26)................. 8.00 3.20

1986 Omaha Royals ProCards

This 29-card standard-size set of the 1986 Omaha Royals, a Class AAA American Association affiliate of the Kansas City Royals, features white-bordered posed color player photos on its fronts. The player's name, team, and position appear at the bottom. The white horizontal back carries the player's name and position at the top, followed by biography and statistics. The cards are unnumbered and checklisted below in alphabetical order.
COMPLETE SET (29)................ 20.00 8.00

1986 Omaha Royals TCMA

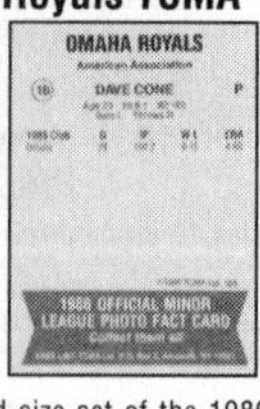

This 25-card standard-size set of the 1986 Omaha Royals, a Class AAA American Association affiliate of the Kansas City Royals, features white-bordered posed color player shots set on fuchsia backgrounds. The team name is printed within the fuchsia area below the photo. A black stripe at the bottom carries the player's name and position. The white back carries the team name and league at the top, followed by the player's name, positon, biography and statistics.
COMPLETE SET (25)................ 20.00 8.00

1986 Orlando Twins ProCards

This 24-card standard-size set of the 1986 Orlando Twins, a Class AA Southern League affiliate of the Minnesota Twins, features white-bordered posed color player photos on its fronts. The player's name, team, and position appear at the bottom. The white horizontal back carries the player's name and position at the top, followed by biography and statistics. The cards are unnumbered and checklisted below in alphabetical order.
COMPLETE SET (24)................. 5.00 2.00

1986 Osceola Astros ProCards

This 29-card standard-size set of the 1986 Osceola Astros, a Class A Florida State League affiliate of the Houston Astros, features white-bordered posed color player photos on its fronts. The player's name, team, and position appear at the bottom. The white horizontal back carries the player's name and position at the top, followed by biography and statistics. The cards are unnumbered and checklisted below in alphabetical order.
COMPLETE SET (29)................. 5.00 2.00

1986 Palm Springs Angels ProCards

This 29-card standard-size set of the 1986 Palm Springs Angels, a Class A California League affiliate of the California Angels, features white-bordered posed color player photos on its fronts. The player's name, team, and position appear at the bottom. The white horizontal back carries the player's name and position at the top, followed by biography and statistics. The cards are unnumbered and checklisted below in alphabetical order. This issue includes the minor league card debut of Dante Bichette.
COMPLETE SET (29)................ 15.00 6.00

1986 Palm Springs Angels Smokey

Black and White Posed shots with Smokey the Bear. These are not standad-size cards, they are a little bit larger.
COMPLETE SET (28)................ 20.00 8.00

1986 Pawtucket Red Sox ProCards

This 28-card standard-size set of the 1986 Pawtucket Red Sox, a Class AAA International League affiliate of the Boston Red Sox, features white-bordered posed color player photos on its fronts. The player's name, team, and position appear at the bottom. The white horizontal back carries the player's name and position at the top, followed by biography and statistics. The cards are unnumbered and checklisted below in alphabetical order.
COMPLETE SET (28)................. 5.00 2.00

1986 Peninsula White Sox ProCards

This 28-card standard-size set of the 1986 Peninsula White Sox, a Class A Carolina League affiliate of the Chicago White Sox, features white-bordered posed color player photos on its fronts. The player's name, team, and position appear at the bottom. The white horizontal back carries the player's name and position at the top, followed by biography and statistics. The cards are unnumbered and checklisted below in alphabetical order.
COMPLETE SET (28)................. 5.00 2.00

1986 Peoria Chiefs ProCards

This 27-card standard-size set of the 1986 Peoria Chiefs, a Class A Midwest League affiliate of the Chicago Cubs, features white-bordered posed color player photos on its fronts. The player's name, team, and position appear at the bottom. The white horizontal back carries the player's name and position at the

top, followed by biography and statistics. T cards are unnumbered and checklisted below alphabetical order. This issue includes minor league card debut of Mark Grace.
COMPLETE SET (27)................ 50.00 20.

1986 Phoenix Firebirds ProCards

This 26-card standard-size set of the 19 Phoenix Firebirds, a Class AAA Pacific Co League affiliate of the San Francisco Gian features white-bordered posed color pla photos on its fronts. The player's name, tea and position appear at the bottom. The wh horizontal back carries the player's name a position at the top, followed by biography a statistics. The cards are unnumbered a checklisted below in alphabetical order.
COMPLETE SET (26)................. 5.00 2.

1986 Pittsfield Cubs ProCard

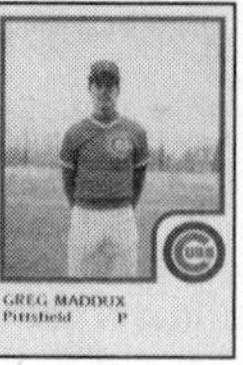

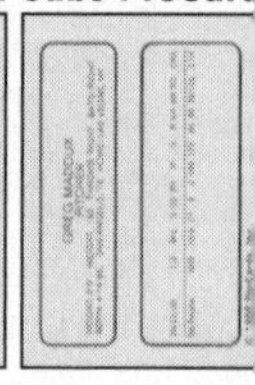

This 25-card standard-size set of the 19 Pittsfield Cubs, a Class AA Eastern Leag affiliate of the Chicago Cubs, features whi bordered posed color player photos on fronts. The player's name, team, and positi appear at the bottom. The white horizontal ba carries the player's name and position at t top, followed by biography and statistics. T cards are unnumbered and checklisted below alphabetical order. This issue includes t minor league card debut of Greg Maddux a Rafael Palmeiro.
COMPLETE SET (25)............. 225.00 80.0

1986 Portland Beavers ProCards

This 23-card standard-size set of the 19 Portland Beavers, a Class AAA Pacific Co League affiliate of the Philadelphia Phillie features white-bordered posed color pla photos on its fronts. The player's name, tea and position appear at the bottom. The wh horizontal back carries the player's name a position at the top, followed by biography a statistics. The cards are unnumbered a checklisted below in alphabetical order.
COMPLETE SET (23)................. 5.00 2.0

1986 Prince William Pirates ProCards

This 27-card standard-size set of the 19 Prince William Pirates, a Class A Caroli League affiliate of the Pittsburgh Pirate features white-bordered posed color play photos on its fronts. The player's name, tea and position appear at the bottom. The wh horizontal back carries the player's name a position at the top, followed by biography a statistics. The cards are unnumbered a checklisted below in alphabetical order.
COMPLETE SET (27)................. 5.00 2.0

1986 Quad City Angels ProCards

This 33-card standard-size set of the 198 Quad City Angels, a Class A Midwest Leag affiliate of the California Angels, features wh bordered posed color player photos on i fronts. The player's name, team, and positi appear at the bottom. The white horizontal ba carries the player's name and position at t top, followed by biography and statistics. T cards are unnumbered and checklisted below alphabetical order. This issue includes t minor league card debut of Chuck Finley.
COMPLETE SET (33)................ 15.00 6.0

1986 Reading Phillies ProCards

This 26-card standard-size set of the 198 Reading Phillies, a Class AA Eastern Leag affiliate of the Philadelphia Phillies, featur white-bordered posed color player photos o its fronts. The player's name, team, a position appear at the bottom. The whi horizontal back carries the player's name a position at the top, followed by biography a statistics. The cards are unnumbered a checklisted below in alphabetical order.
COMPLETE SET (26)................. 5.00 2.0

1986 Red Wing Aces/Scarlet

Sponsored by the Red Wing Police Departme and various local businesses, this 25-ca standard-size set features the 1986 Red Wi Aces/Scarlets. The fronts feature black-an white posed player photos with dark blu

borders. The team name is printed in a red bar above the photo, while the player's name, position and number, along with the team logo, appear in a red bar below the photo. The backs carry a player profile, safety tips and advertisements for various sponsors.
COMPLETE SET (25)................. 5.00 2.00

1986 Richmond Braves ProCards

This 26-card standard-size set of the 1986 Richmond Braves, a Class AAA International League affiliate of the Atlanta Braves, features white-bordered posed color player photos on its fronts. The player's name, team, and position appear at the bottom. The white horizontal back carries the player's name and position at the top, followed by biography and statistics. The cards are unnumbered and checklisted below in alphabetical order.
COMPLETE SET (26)................. 5.00 2.00

1986 Rochester Red Wings ProCards

This 26-card standard-size set of the 1986 Rochester Red Wings, a Class AAA International League affiliate of the Baltimore Orioles, features white-bordered posed color player photos on its fronts. The player's name, team, and position appear at the bottom. The white horizontal back carries the player's name and position at the top, followed by biography and statistics. The cards are unnumbered and checklisted below in alphabetical order.
COMPLETE SET (26)................. 5.00 2.00

1986 Salem Angels Cramer

COMPLETE SET (25)................. 8.00 3.20

1986 Salem Red Birds ProCards

This 29-card standard-size set of the 1986 Salem Red Birds, a Class A Carolina League affiliate of the Texas Rangers, features white-bordered posed color player photos on its fronts. The player's name, team, and position appear at the bottom. The white horizontal back carries the player's name and position at the top, followed by biography and statistics. The cards are unnumbered and checklisted below in alphabetical order.
COMPLETE SET (29)................. 5.00 2.00

1986 San Jose Bees ProCards

This 25-card standard-size set of the 1986 San Jose Bees, a Class A California League Independent, features white-bordered posed color player photos on its fronts. The player's name, team, and position appear at the bottom. The white horizontal back carries the player's name and position at the top, followed by biography and statistics. The cards are unnumbered and checklisted below in alphabetical order.
COMPLETE SET (25)................. 5.00 2.00

1986 Shreveport Captains ProCards

This 28-card standard-size set of the 1986 Shreveport Captains, a Class AA Texas League affiliate of the San Francisco Giants, features white-bordered posed color player photos on its fronts. The player's name, team, and position appear at the bottom. The white horizontal back carries the player's name and position at the top, followed by biography and statistics. The cards are unnumbered and checklisted below in alphabetical order.
COMPLETE SET (28)................. 8.00 3.20

1986 Southern League All-Stars Jennings

COMPLETE SET (25)............... 25.00 10.00

1986 Spokane Indians Cramer

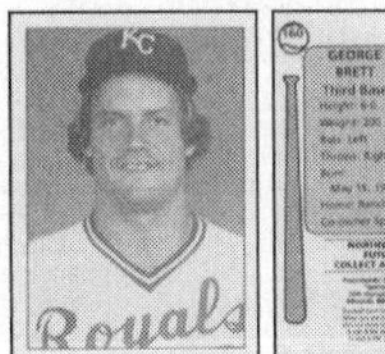

COMPLETE SET (25)............... 30.00 12.00

1986 St. Petersburg Cardinals ProCards

This 29-card standard-size set of the 1986 St. Petersburg Cardinals, a Class A Florida State League affiliate of the St. Louis Cardinals, features white-bordered posed color player photos on its fronts. The player's name, team, and position appear at the bottom. The white horizontal back carries the player's name and position at the top, followed by biography and statistics. The cards are unnumbered and checklisted below in alphabetical order.
COMPLETE SET (29)................. 8.00 3.20

1986 Stars of the Future TCMA

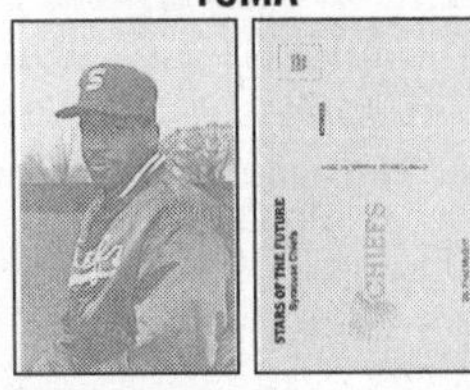

COMPLETE SET (40)............... 30.00 12.00

1986 Stockton Ports ProCards

This 26-card standard-size set of the 1986 Stockton Ports, a Class A California League affiliate of the Milwaukee Brewers, features white-bordered posed color player photos on its fronts. The player's name, team, and position appear at the bottom. The white horizontal back carries the player's name and position at the top, followed by biography and statistics. The cards are unnumbered and checklisted below in alphabetical order.
COMPLETE SET (26)................. 5.00 2.00

1986 Sumter Braves ProCards

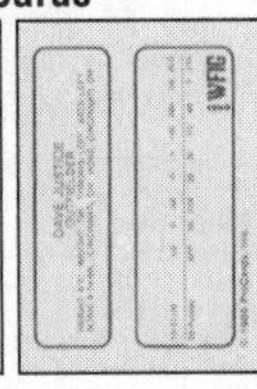

This 30-card standard-size set of the 1986 Sumter Braves, a Class A South Atlantic League affiliate of the Atlanta Braves, features white-bordered posed color player photos on its fronts. The player's name, team, and position appear at the bottom. The white horizontal back carries the player's name and position at the top, followed by biography and statistics. The cards are unnumbered and checklisted below in alphabetical order. This issue includes the minor league card debuts of Dave Justice and Al Martin.
COMPLETE SET (30)............... 25.00 10.00

1986 Syracuse Chiefs ProCards

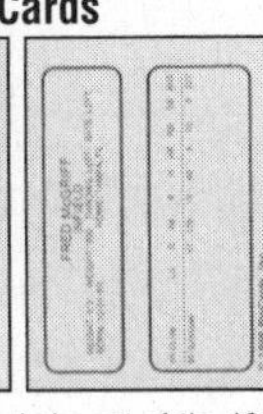

This 27-card standard-size set of the 1986 Syracuse Chiefs, a Class AAA International League affiliate of the Toronto Blue Jays, features white-bordered posed color player photos on its fronts. The player's name, team name, and position appear at the bottom. The white horizontal back carries the player's name and position at the top, followed by biography and statistics. The cards are unnumbered and checklisted below in alphabetical order. This issue includes a second year card of Fred McGriff.
COMPLETE SET (27)............... 20.00 8.00

1986 Tacoma Tigers ProCards

This 25-card standard-size set of the 1986 Tacoma Tigers, a Class AAA Pacific Coast League affiliate of the Oakland Athletics, features white-bordered posed color player photos on its fronts. The player's name, team, and position appear at the bottom. The white horizontal back carries the player's name and position at the top, followed by biography and statistics. The cards are unnumbered and checklisted below in alphabetical order.
COMPLETE SET (25)................. 5.00 2.00

1986 Tampa Tarpons ProCards

This 27-card standard-size set of the 1986 Tampa Tarpons, a Class A Florida State League affiliate of the Cincinnati Reds, features white-bordered posed color player photos on its fronts. The player's name, team, and position appear at the bottom. The white horizontal back carries the player's name and position at the top, followed by biography and statistics. The cards are unnumbered and checklisted below in alphabetical order.
COMPLETE SET (27)................. 5.00 2.00

1986 Tidewater Tides ProCards

This 28-card standard-size set of the 1986 Tidewater Tides, a Class AAA International League affiliate of the New York Mets, features white-bordered posed color player photos on its fronts. The player's name, team, and position appear at the bottom. The white horizontal back carries the player's name and position at the top, followed by biography and statistics. The cards are unnumbered and checklisted below in alphabetical order.
COMPLETE SET (28)................. 8.00 3.20

1986 Toledo Mud Hens ProCards

This 24-card standard-size set of the 1986 Toledo Mud Hens, a Class AAA International League affiliate of the Minnesota Twins, features white-bordered posed color player photos on its fronts. The player's name, team, and position appear at the bottom. The white horizontal back carries the player's name and position at the top, followed by biography and statistics. The cards are unnumbered and checklisted below in alphabetical order.
COMPLETE SET (24)................. 5.00 2.00

1986 Tri-Cities Triplets Cramer

COMPLETE SET (14)................. 8.00 3.20

1986 Tucson Toros ProCards

This 26-card standard-size set of the 1986 Tucson Toros, a Class AAA Pacific Coast League affiliate of the Houston Astros, features white-bordered posed color player photos on its fronts. The player's name, team, and position appear at the bottom. The white horizontal back carries the player's name and position at the top, followed by biography and statistics. The cards are unnumbered and checklisted below in alphabetical order.
COMPLETE SET (26)................. 5.00 2.00

1986 Tulsa Drillers Team Issue

COMPLETE SET (27)............... 15.00 6.00

1986 Vancouver Canadians ProCards

This 27-card standard-size set of the 1986 Vancouver Canadians, a Class AAA Pacific Coast League affiliate of Milwaukee Brewers, features white-bordered posed color player photos on its fronts. The player's name, team name, and position appear at the bottom. The white horizontal back carries the player's name and position at the top, followed by biography and statistics. There have been reports of scarce error cards of Steve Kiefer, Joe Meyer, Charlie O'Brien, and Rick Waits that carry Buffalo Bisons logos. The cards are unnumbered and checklisted below in alphabetical order. This issue includes the minor league card debut of B.J. Surhoff.
COMPLETE SET (27)............... 15.00 6.00

1986 Ventura Gulls ProCards

This 28-card standard-size set of the 1986 Ventura Gulls, a Class A affiliate of the Toronto Blue Jays, features white-bordered posed color player photos on its fronts. The player's name, team, and position appear at the bottom. The white horizontal back carries the player's name and position at the top, followed by biography and statistics. The cards are unnumbered and checklisted below in alphabetical order. This issue includes the minor league card debut of Todd Stottlemyre.
COMPLETE SET (28)............... 15.00 6.00

1986 Vermont Reds ProCards

This 24-card standard-size set of the 1986 Vermont Reds, a Class AA Eastern League affiliate of the Cincinnati Reds, features white-bordered posed color player photos on its fronts. The player's name, team, and position appear at the bottom. The white horizontal back carries the player's name and position at the top, followed by biography and statistics. The cards are unnumbered and checklisted below in alphabetical order.
COMPLETE SET (24)................. 5.00 2.00

1986 Vero Beach Dodgers ProCards

This 27-card standard-size set of the 1986 Vero Beach Dodgers, a Class A Florida State League affiliate of the Los Angeles Dodgers, features white-bordered posed color player photos on its fronts. The player's name, team, and position appear at the bottom. The white horizontal back carries the player's name and position at the top, followed by biography and statistics. The cards are unnumbered and checklisted below in alphabetical order. This issue includes the minor league card debut of Juan Guzman.
COMPLETE SET (27)................. 8.00 3.20

1986 Visalia Oaks ProCards

This 24-card standard-size set of the 1986 Visalia Oaks, a Class A California League affiliate of the Minnesota Twins, features white-bordered posed color player photos on its fronts. The player's name, team, and position appear at the bottom. The white horizontal back carries the player's name and position at the top, followed by biography and statistics. The cards are unnumbered and checklisted below in alphabetical order.
COMPLETE SET (24)................. 5.00 2.00

1986 Waterbury Indians ProCards

This 26-card standard-size set of the 1986 Waterbury Indians, a Class AA Eastern League affiliate of the Cleveland Indians, features white-bordered posed color player photos on its fronts. The player's name, team, and position appear at the bottom. The white horizontal back carries the player's name and position at the top, followed by biography and statistics. The cards are unnumbered and checklisted below in alphabetical order.
COMPLETE SET (26)............... 15.00 6.00

1986 Waterloo Indians ProCards

This 32-card standard-size set of the 1986 Waterloo Indians, a Class A Midwest League affiliate of the Cleveland Indians, features white-bordered posed color player photos on its fronts. The player's name, team, and position appear at the bottom. The white horizontal back carries the player's name and position at the top, followed by biography and statistics. The cards are unnumbered and checklisted below in alphabetical order.
COMPLETE SET (32)................. 5.00 2.00

1986 Watertown Pirates ProCards

This 27-card standard-size set of the 1986 Watertown Pirates, a Class A New York-Penn League affiliate of the Pittsburgh Pirates, features white-bordered posed color player photos on its fronts. The player's name, team, and position appear at the bottom. The white horizontal back carries the player's name and position at the top, followed by biography and statistics. The cards are unnumbered and checklisted below in alphabetical order. This issue includes the minor league card debut of Moises Alou.
COMPLETE SET (27)............... 20.00 8.00

1986 Wausau Timbers ProCards

This 29-card standard-size set of the 1986 Wausau Timbers, a Class A Midwest League affiliate of the Seattle Mariners, features white-bordered posed color player photos on its fronts. The player's name, team, and position appear at the bottom. The white horizontal back carries the player's name and position at the top, followed by biography and statistics. The cards are unnumbered and checklisted below in alphabetical order. This issue includes the minor league card debut of Omar Vizquel.
COMPLETE SET (29)............... 20.00 8.00

1986 West Palm Beach Expos ProCards

This 28-card standard-size set of the 1986 West Palm Beach Expos, a Class A Florida State League affiliate of the Montreal Expos, features white-bordered posed color player photos on its fronts. The player's name, team and position appear at the bottom. The white horizontal back carries the player's name, position and biography. This issue includes Randy Johnson's minor league card debut. The cards are unnumbered and checklisted below in alphabetical order.
COMPLETE SET (28)............. 125.00 50.00

1986 Winston-Salem Spirits ProCards

This 29-card standard-size set of the 1986 Winston-Salem Spirits, a Class A Carolina League affiliate of the Chicago Cubs, features white-bordered posed color player photos on its fronts. The player's name, team, and position appear at the bottom. The white horizontal back carries the player's name and position at the top, followed by biography and statistics. The cards are unnumbered and checklisted below in alphabetical order.
COMPLETE SET (29)................. 5.00 2.00

1986 Winter Haven Red Sox ProCards

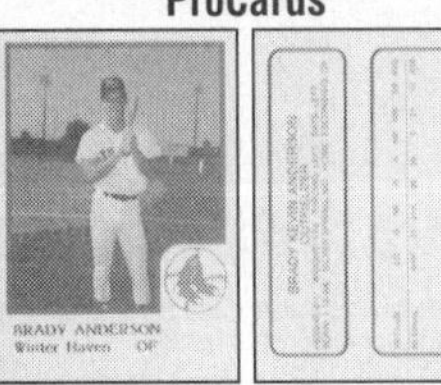

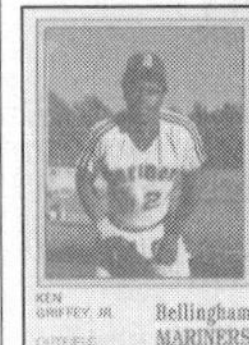

This 27-card standard-size set of the 1986 Winter Haven Red Sox, a Class A Florida State League affiliate of the Boston Red Sox, features white-bordered posed color player photos on its fronts. The player's name, team, and position appear at the bottom. The white horizontal back carries the player's name and position at the top, followed by biography and statistics. The cards are unnumbered and checklisted below in alphabetical order. This issue includes a second year card of Brady Anderson.
COMPLETE SET (27)............... 15.00 6.00

1987 Albany Yankees ProCards

This 23-card standard-size set of the 1987 Albany Yankees, a Class AA Eastern League affiliate of the New York Yankees, features white-bordered posed color player photos on its fronts. The player's name and position appear at the bottom. The white horizontal back is framed by a black line and carries the player's name at the top, followed by biography and statistics.
COMPLETE SET (23)................. 5.00 2.00

1987 Albuquerque Dukes DARE

Set was apparently produced and distributed by the team. At the bottom of the reverse on each card is an anti-drug message from the Dukes and the local police departments.
COMPLETE SET (30)................. 8.00 3.20

1987 Anchorage Glacier Pilots

COMPLETE SET (42)............... 15.00 6.00

1987 Appleton Foxes ProCards

This 30-card standard-size set of the 1987 Appleton Foxes, a Class A Midwest League affiliate of the Kansas City Royals, features white-bordered posed color player photos on its fronts. The player's name and position appear at the bottom. The white horizontal back is framed by a black line and carries the player's name at the top, followed by biography and statistics.
COMPLETE SET (30)................. 5.00 2.00

1987 Arizona Wildcats Police

COMPLETE SET (20)............... 25.00 10.00

1987 Arkansas Travelers ProCards

This 25-card standard-size set of the 1987 Arkansas Travelers, a Class AA Texas League affiliate of the St. Louis Cardinals, features white-bordered posed color player photos on its fronts. The player's name and position appear at the bottom. The white horizontal back is framed by a black line and carries the player's name at the top, followed by biography and statistics. This issue includes the minor league card debut of Ken Hill.
COMPLETE SET (25)............... 10.00 4.00

1987 Asheville Tourists ProCards

This 28-card standard-size set of the 1987 Asheville Tourists, a Class A South Atlantic League affiliate of the Houston Astros, features white-bordered posed color player photos on its fronts. The player's name and position appear at the bottom. The white horizontal back is framed by a black line and carries the player's name at the top, followed by biography and statistics.
COMPLETE SET (28)................. 5.00 2.00

1987 Auburn Astros ProCards

This 25-card standard-size set of the 1987 Auburn Astros, a Class A New York-Penn League affiliate of the Houston Astros, features white-bordered posed color player photos on its fronts. The player's name and position appear at the bottom. The white horizontal back is framed by a black line and carries the player's name at the top, followed by biography and statistics.
COMPLETE SET (25)................. 5.00 2.00

1987 Bakersfield Dodgers ProCards

This 29-card standard-size set of the 1987 Bakersfield Dodgers, a Class A California League affiliate of the Los Angeles Dodgers, features white-bordered posed color player photos on its fronts. The player's name and position appear at the bottom. The white horizontal back is framed by a black line and carries the player's name at the top, followed by biography and statistics.
COMPLETE SET (29)................. 5.00 2.00

1987 Bellingham Mariners Team Issue

This 34-card standard-size set of the 1987 Bellingham Mariners, a Class A Northwest League affiliate of the Seattle Mariners, features white-bordered posed color player photos in a square yellow bordered box on its fronts. The player's name, position and team name appear across the bottom. The back carries the player's name at the top, followed by biography and statistics. This issue includes the minor league card debut of Ken Griffey Jr. 15,000 sets were produced.
COMPLETE SET (34).............. 120.00 47.50

1987 Beloit Brewers ProCards

This 26-card standard-size set of the 1987 Beloit Brewers, a Class A Midwest League affiliate of the Milwaukee Brewers, features white-bordered posed color player photos on its fronts. The player's name and position appear at the bottom. The white horizontal back is framed by a black line and carries the player's name at the top, followed by biography and statistics. This issue includes the minor league card debut of Greg Vaughn.
COMPLETE SET (26)............... 15.00 6.00

1987 Birmingham Barons Best

COMPLETE SET (28)................. 5.00 2.00

1987 Brigham Young Cougars

This 22-card set featues color photos of BYU's Baseball team. Produced by Utah Sports Card Co.
COMPLETE SET (22)............... 10.00 4.00

1987 Buffalo Bisons Pucko

5,000 sets were produced.
COMPLETE SET (29)................. 5.00 2.00

1987 Burlington Expos ProCards

This 29-card standard-size set of the 1987 Burlington Expos, a Class A Midwest League affiliate of the Montreal Expos, features white-bordered posed color player photos on its fronts. The player's name and position appear at the bottom. The white horizontal back is framed by a black line and carries the player's name at the top, followed by biography and statistics. This issue includes the first team set appearance of Mel Rojas.
COMPLETE SET (29)................. 5.00 2.00

1987 Calgary Cannons ProCards

This 24-card standard-size set of the 1987 Calgary Cannons, a Class AAA Pacific Coast League affiliate of the Seattle Mariners, features white-bordered posed color player photos on its fronts. The player's name and position appear at the bottom. The white horizontal back is framed by a black line and carries the player's name at the top, followed by biography and statistics. This issue includes a second year card of Edgar Martinez.
COMPLETE SET (24)............... 15.00 6.00

1987 Cedar Rapids Reds ProCards

This 28-card standard-size set of the 1987 Cedar Rapids Reds, a Class A Midwest League affiliate of the Cincinnati Reds, features white-bordered posed color player photos on its fronts. The player's name and position appear at the bottom. The white horizontal back is framed by a black line and carries the player's name at the top, followed by biography and statistics.
COMPLETE SET (28)................. 5.00 2.00

1987 Charleston Rainbows ProCards

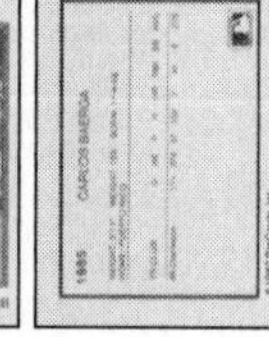

This 23-card standard-size set of the 1987 Charleston Rainbows, a Class A South Atlantic League affiliate of the San Diego Padres, features white-bordered posed color player photos on its fronts. The player's name and position appear at the bottom. The white horizontal back is framed by a black line and carries the player's name at the top, followed by biography and statistics. This issue includes a second year card of Carlos Baerga.
COMPLETE SET (23)............... 15.00 6.00

1987 Charleston Wheelers ProCards

This 28-card standard-size set of the 1987 Charleston Wheelers, a Class A South Atlantic League Independent, features white-bordered posed color player photos on its fronts. The player's name and position appear at the bottom. The white horizontal back is framed by a black line and carries the player's name at the top, followed by biography and statistics.
COMPLETE SET (28)................. 5.00 2.00

1987 Charlotte O's WBTV

COMPLETE SET (30)................. 8.00 3.20

1987 Chattanooga Lookouts Best

COMPLETE SET (26)................. 8.00 3.20

1987 Clearwater Phillies ProCards

This 27-card standard-size set of the 1987 Philadelphia Phillies, a Class A Florida State League affiliate of the Philadelphia Phillies, features white-bordered posed color player photos on its fronts. The player's name and position appear at the bottom. The white horizontal back is framed by a black line and carries the player's name at the top, followed by biography and statistics.
COMPLETE SET (27)................. 5.00 2.00

1987 Clinton Giants ProCards

This 29-card standard-size set of the 1987 Clinton Giants, a Class A Midwest League affiliate of the San Francisco Giants, features white-bordered posed color player photos on its fronts. The player's name and position appear at the bottom. The white horizontal back is framed by a black line and carries the player's name at the top, followed by biography and statistics.
COMPLETE SET (29)................. 5.00 2.00

1987 Columbia Mets ProCards

This 29-card standard-size set of the 1987 Columbia Mets, a Class A South Atlantic League affiliate of the New York Mets, features white-bordered posed color player photos on its fronts. The player's name and position appear at the bottom. The white horizontal back is framed by a black line and carries the player's name at the top, followed by biography and statistics.
COMPLETE SET (29)................. 5.00 2.00

1987 Columbus Astros ProCards

This 25-card standard-size set of the 1987 Columbus Astros, a Class AA Southern League affiliate of the Houston Astros, features white-bordered posed color player photos on its fronts. The player's name and position appear at the bottom. The white horizontal back is framed by a black line and carries the player's name at the top, followed by biography and statistics. This issue includes a third year card of Ken Caminiti.
COMPLETE SET (25)............... 15.00 6.00

1987 Columbus Clippers Police

This 25-card standard-size set of the 1987 Columbus Clippers, a Class AAA International affiliate of the New York Yankees, features the minor league card debut of Jay Buhner.
COMPLETE SET (25)............... 15.00 6.00

1987 Columbus Clippers ProCards

This 27-card standard-size set of the 1987 Columbus Clippers, a Class AAA International affiliate of the New York Yankees, features white-bordered posed color player photos on its fronts. The player's name and position appear at the bottom. The white horizontal back is framed by a black line and carries the player's name at the top, followed by biography and statistics. This issue includes the minor league card debut of Jay Buhner.
COMPLETE SET (27)............... 20.00 8.00

1987 Columbus Clippers TCMA

This 25-card standard-size set of the 1987 Columbus Clippers, a Class AAA International affiliate of the New York Yankees, features the minor league card debut of Jay Buhner.
COMPLETE SET (25)............... 10.00 4.00

1987 David Lipscomb

This set was released in 1987 as a 25-card set at David Lipscomb college. The set features all of the players and coaches from that year's team. Please note that these cards are a little smaller than average-sized cards.
COMPLETE SET (25)............... 10.00 4.00

1987 Daytona Beach Admirals ProCards

This 26-card standard-size set of the 1987 Daytona Beach Admirals, a Class A Florida State League affiliate of the Chicago White Sox, features white-bordered posed color player photos on its fronts. The player's name and position appear at the bottom. The white horizontal back is framed by a black line and carries the player's name at the top, followed by biography and statistics.
COMPLETE SET (26)................. 5.00 2.00

1987 Denver Zephyrs ProCards

This 27-card standard-size set of the 1987 Denver Zephyrs, a Class AAA American Association affiliate of the Milwaukee Brewers, features white-bordered posed color player photos on its fronts. The player's name and position appear at the bottom. The white horizontal back is framed by a black line and carries the player's name at the top, followed by biography and statistics.
COMPLETE SET (27)................. 5.00 2.00

1987 Dunedin Blue Jays ProCards

This 29-card standard-size set of the 1987 Dunedin Blue Jays, a Class A Florida State League affiliate of the Toronto Blue Jays, features white-bordered posed color player photos on its fronts. The player's name and position appear at the bottom. The white horizontal back is framed by a black line and carries the player's name at the top, followed by biography and statistics.
COMPLETE SET (29)................. 5.00 2.00

1987 Durham Bulls ProCards

This 28-card standard-size set of the 1987 Durham Bulls, a Class A Carolina League affiliate of the Atlanta Braves, features white-bordered posed color player photos on its fronts. The player's name and position appear at the bottom. The white horizontal back is framed by a black line and carries the player's name at the top, followed by biography and statistics.
COMPLETE SET (28)................. 5.00 2.00

1987 Edmonton Trappers ProCards

This 23-card standard-size set of the 1987 Edmonton Trappers, a Class AAA Pacific Coast League affiliate of the California Angels, features white-bordered posed color player photos on its fronts. The player's name and position appear at the bottom. The white horizontal back is framed by a black line and carries the player's name at the top, followed by biography and statistics.
COMPLETE SET (23)................. 5.00 2.00

1987 El Paso Diablos ProCards

This 27-card standard-size set of the 1987 El Paso Diablos, a Class AA Texas League affiliate of the Milwaukee Brewers, features white-bordered posed color player photos on its fronts. The player's name and position appear at the bottom. The white horizontal back is framed by a black line and carries the player's name at the top, followed by biography and statistics.
COMPLETE SET (27)................. 5.00 2.00

1987 Elmira Pioneers (Black) Cain

This 34-card set of the 1987 Elmira Pioneers, a Class A New York-Penn League affiliate of the Boston Red Sox, features black and white player photos. The cards measure 41/2" x 3 1/2" and are horizontal. 2,500 sets were produced.
COMPLETE SET (34)................. 5.00 2.00

1987 Elmira Pioneers (Red) Cain

This 35-card set of the 1987 Elmira Pioneers, a Class A New York-Penn League affiliate of the Boston Red Sox, features black and white player photos with a red border. The cards measure 3 3/4" x 2 1/2" and are horizontal. 1,500 sets were produced.
COMPLETE SET (35)............... 50.00 20.00

1987 Erie Cardinals ProCards

This 29-card standard-size set of the 1987 Erie Cardinals, a Class A New York-Penn League affiliate of the St. Louis Cardinals, features white-bordered posed color player photos on its fronts. The player's name and position appear at the bottom. The white horizontal back is framed by a black line and carries the player's name at the top, followed by biography and statistics.
COMPLETE SET (29)................. 5.00 2.00

1987 Eugene Emeralds Procards

This 30-card standard-size set of the 1987 Eugene Emeralds, a Class A Northwest League affiliate of the Kansas City Royals, features white-bordered posed color player photos on its fronts. The player's name and position appear at the bottom. The white horizontal back is framed by a black line and carries the player's name at the top, followed by biography and statistics. This issue includes the minor league card debuts of Kevin Appier and Tom Gordon.
COMPLETE SET (30)............... 10.00 4.00

1987 Everett Giants Cramer

COMPLETE SET (34)................. 5.00 2.00

1987 Fayetteville Generals ProCards

This 27-card standard-size set of the 1987 Fayetteville Generals, a Class A South Atlantic League affiliate of the Detroit Tigers, features white-bordered posed color player photos on its fronts. The player's name and position appear at the bottom. The white horizontal back is framed by a black line and carries the player's name at the top, followed by biography and statistics.
COMPLETE SET (27)................. 5.00 2.00

1987 Ft. Lauderdale Yankees ProCards

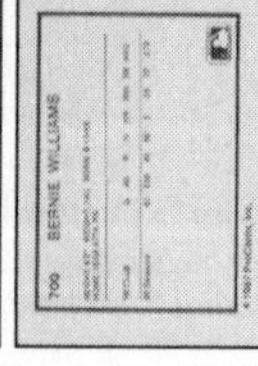

This 30-card standard-size set of the 1987 Ft. Lauderdale Yankees, a Class A Florida State League affiliate of the New York Yankees, features white-bordered posed color player photos on its fronts. The player's name and position appear at the bottom. The white horizontal back is framed by a black line and carries the player's name at the top, followed by biography and statistics. This issue includes the minor league card debut of Bernie Williams.
COMPLETE SET (30)............... 30.00 12.00

1987 Ft. Myers Royals ProCards

This 34-card standard-size set of the 1987 Ft. Myers Royals, a Class A Florida State League affiliate of the Kansas City Royals, features white-bordered posed color player photos on its fronts. The player's name and position appear at the bottom. The white horizontal back is framed by a black line and carries the player's name at the top, followed by biography and statistics. This issue includes the minor league card debut of Tom Gordon and a second year card of Brian McRae.
COMPLETE SET (34)............... 15.00 6.00

1987 Gastonia Rangers ProCards

This 29-card standard-size set of the 1987 Gastonia Rangers, a Class A South Atlantic League affiliate of the Texas Rangers, features white-bordered posed color player photos on its fronts. The player's name and position appear at the bottom. The white horizontal back is framed by a black line and carries the player's name at the top, followed by biography and statistics. This issue includes the minor league card debuts of Juan Gonzalez, Sammy Sosa and Dean Palmer.
COMPLETE SET (29)............. 200.00 80.00

1987 Geneva Cubs ProCards

This 26-card standard-size set of the 1987 Geneva Cubs, a Class A New York-Penn League affiliate of the Chicago Cubs, features white-bordered posed color player photos on its fronts. The player's name and position appear at the bottom. The white horizontal back is framed by a black line and carries the player's name at the top, followed by biography and statistics.
COMPLETE SET (26)................. 5.00 2.00

1987 Glens Falls Tigers ProCards

This 25-card standard-size set of the 1987 Glens Falls Tigers, a Class AA Eastern League affiliate of the Detroit Tigers, features white-bordered posed color player photos on its fronts. The player's name and position appear at the bottom. The white horizontal back is framed by a black line and carries the player's name at the top, followed by biography and statistics. This issue includes the minor league card debut of Chris Hoiles and a second year card of John Smoltz.
COMPLETE SET (25)............... 15.00 6.00

1987 Greensboro Hornets ProCards

This 26-card standard-size set of the 1987 Greensboro Hornets, a Class A South Atlantic League affiliate of the Boston Red Sox, features white-bordered posed color player photos on its fronts. The player's name and position appear at the bottom. The white horizontal back is framed by a black line and carries the player's name at the top, followed by biography and statistics. A second year card of Curt Schilling is in this set.
COMPLETE SET (26)............... 40.00 12.00

1987 Greenville Braves Best

This issue includes second year cards of Dave Justice and Ron Gant.
COMPLETE SET (28)............... 30.00 12.00

1987 Hagerstown Suns ProCards

This 29-card standard-size set of the 1987 Hagerstown Suns, a Class A Carolina League affiliate of the Baltimore Orioles, features white-bordered posed color player photos on its fronts. The player's name and position appear at the bottom. The white horizontal back is framed by a black line and carries the player's name at the top, followed by biography and statistics.
COMPLETE SET (29)................. 5.00 2.00

1987 Harrisburg Senators ProCards

This 26-card standard-size set of the 1987 Harrisburg Senators, a Class AA Eastern League affiliate of the Pittsburgh Pirates, features white-bordered posed color player photos on its fronts. The player's name and position appear at the bottom. The white horizontal back is framed by a black line and carries the player's name at the top, followed by biography and statistics.
COMPLETE SET (26)................. 5.00 2.00

1987 Hawaii Islanders ProCards

This 27-card standard-size set of the 1987 Hawaii Islanders, a Class AAA Pacific Coast League affiliate of the Chicago White Sox, features white-bordered posed color player photos on its fronts. The player's name and position appear at the bottom. The white horizontal back is framed by a black line and carries the player's name at the top, followed by biography and statistics.
COMPLETE SET (27)................. 5.00 2.00

1987 Hawaii Rainbows

COMPLETE SET (30)............... 10.00 4.00

1987 Huntsville Stars Team Issue

COMPLETE SET (25)................. 5.00 2.00

1987 Idaho Falls Braves ProCards

This 27-card standard-size set of the 1987 Idaho Falls Braves, a Rookie Class Pioneer League affiliate of the Atlanta Braves, features white-bordered posed color player photos on its fronts. The player's name and position appear at the bottom. The white horizontal back is framed by a black line and carries the player's name at the top, followed by biography and statistics.
COMPLETE SET (27)................. 5.00 2.00

1987 Indianapolis Indians Team Issue

Sponsored by Pepsi, this 36-card set of the 1987 Indianapolis Indians, a Class AAA American Association affiliate of the Montreal Expos, features posed color player shots on its fronts, and measures approximately 2 1/2" by 3 5/8". The team name appears within the blue stripe across the top; in the blue stripe below the picture is the player's name and position. The white horizontal back carries the player's name at the top, followed by biography, statistics, and career highlights.
COMPLETE SET (36)............... 15.00 6.00

1987 International League All-Stars TCMA

COMPLETE SET (45)............... 18.00 7.25

1987 Iowa Cubs Team Issue

This issue includes a second year card of Rafael Palmeiro.
COMPLETE SET (25)............... 30.00 12.00

1987 Jackson Mets Feder

COMPLETE SET (25)............... 10.00 4.00

1987 Jacksonville Expos ProCards

This 29-card standard-size set of the 1987 Jacksonville Expos, a Class AA Southern League affiliate of the Montreal Expos, features white-bordered posed color player photos on its fronts. The player's name and position appear at the bottom. The white horizontal back is framed by a black line and carries the player's name at the top, followed by biography and statistics. This issue includes a second year card of Randy Johnson and a third year card of Larry Walker.
COMPLETE SET (29)............... 60.00 24.00

1987 Jamestown Expos ProCards

Sponsored by Roach Photography, this 30-card standard-size set of the 1987 Jamestown Expos, a Class A New York-Penn League affiliate of the Montreal Expos, features white-bordered posed color player photos on its fronts. The player's name appears at the bottom. The white horizontal back is framed by a black line and carries the player's name at the top, followed by biography and the sponsor's logo.
COMPLETE SET (30)................. 5.00 2.00

1987 Kenosha Twins ProCards

This 29-card standard-size set of the 1987 Kenosha Twins, a Class A Midwest League affiliate of the Minnesota Twins, features white-bordered posed color player photos on its fronts. The player's name and position appear at the bottom. The white horizontal back is framed by a black line and carries the player's name at the top, followed by biography and statistics.
COMPLETE SET (29) 5.00 2.00

1987 Kinston Indians ProCards

This 24-card standard-size set of the 1987 Kinston Indians, a Class A Carolina League affiliate of the Cleveland Indians, features white-bordered posed color player photos on its fronts. The player's name and position appear at the bottom. The white horizontal back is framed by a black line and carries the player's name at the top, followed by biography and statistics.
COMPLETE SET (24) 5.00 2.00

1987 Knoxville Blue Jays ProCards

This 27-card standard-size set of the 1987 Knoxville Blue Jays, a Class AA Southern League affiliate of the Toronto Blue Jays, features white-bordered posed color player photos on its fronts. The player's name and position appear at the bottom. The white horizontal back is framed by a black line and carries the player's name at the top, followed by biography and statistics.
COMPLETE SET (27) 5.00 2.00

1987 Lakeland Tigers ProCards

This 26-card standard-size set of the 1987 Lakeland Tigers, a Class A Florida State League affiliate of the Detroit Tigers, features white-bordered posed color player photos on its fronts. The player's name and position appear at the bottom. The white horizontal back is framed by a black line and carries the player's name at the top, followed by biography and statistics.
COMPLETE SET (26) 5.00 2.00

1987 Las Vegas Stars ProCards

This 27-card standard-size set of the 1987 Las Vegas Stars, a Class AAA Pacific Coast League affiliate of the San Diego Padres, features white-bordered posed color player photos on its fronts. The player's name and position appear at the bottom. The white horizontal back is framed by a black line and carries the player's name at the top, followed by biography and statistics.
COMPLETE SET (27) 5.00 2.00

1987 Little Falls Mets ProCards

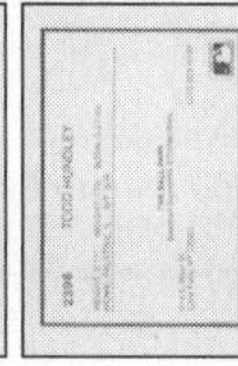

This 29-card standard-size set of the 1987 Little Falls Mets, a Class A New York-Penn affiliate of the New York Mets, features white-bordered posed color player photos on its fronts. The player's name and position appear at the bottom. The white horizontal back is framed by a black line and carries the player's name at the top, followed by biography and statistics. This issue includes the minor league card debut of Todd Hundley.
COMPLETE SET (29) 10.00 4.00

1987 Louisville Redbirds Team Issue

COMPLETE SET (30) 15.00 6.00

1987 LSU Tigers Police

The cards are unnumbered and checklisted below in alphabetical order. Joey Belle is known today as Albert Belle.
COMPLETE SET (8) 25.00 10.00

1987 Lynchburg Mets ProCards

This 28-card standard-size set of the 1987 Lynchburg Mets, a Class A Carolina League affiliate of the New York Mets, features white-bordered posed color player photos on its fronts. The player's name and position appear at the bottom. The white horizontal back is framed by a black line and carries the player's name at the top, followed by biography and statistics.
COMPLETE SET (28) 5.00 2.00

1987 Macon Pirates ProCards

This 25-card standard-size set of the 1987 Macon Pirates, a Class A South Atlantic League affiliate of the Pittsburgh Pirates, features white-bordered posed color player photos on its fronts. The player's name and position appear at the bottom. The white horizontal back is framed by a black line and carries the player's name at the top, followed by biography and statistics.
COMPLETE SET (25) 5.00 2.00

1987 Madison Muskies Police

COMPLETE SET (23) 8.00 3.20

1987 Madison Muskies ProCards

This 25-card standard-size set of the 1987 Madison Muskies, a Class A Midwest League affiliate of the Oakland Athletics, features white-bordered posed color player photos on its fronts. The player's name and position appear at the bottom. The white horizontal back is framed by a black line and carries the player's name at the top, followed by biography and statistics.
COMPLETE SET (25) 5.00 2.00

1987 Maine Guides ProCards

This 23-card standard-size set of the 1987 Maine Guides, a Class AAA International League affiliate of the Philadelphia Phillies, features white-bordered posed color player photos on its fronts. The player's name and position appear at the bottom. The white horizontal back is framed by a black line and carries the player's name at the top, followed by biography and statistics.
COMPLETE SET (23) 5.00 2.00

1987 Maine Guides TCMA

COMPLETE SET (25) 10.00 4.00

1987 Memphis Chicks Best

COMPLETE SET (27) 8.00 3.20

1987 Memphis Chicks ProCards

This 27-card standard-size set of the 1987 Memphis Chicks, a Class AA Southern affiliate of the Kansas City Royals, features white-bordered posed color player photos on its fronts. The player's name and position appear at the bottom. The white horizontal back is framed by a black line and carries the player's name at the top, followed by biography and statistics.
COMPLETE SET (27) 5.00 2.00

1987 Miami Marlins ProCards

This 25-card standard-size set of the 1987 Miami Marlins, a Class A Florida State League Independent, features white-bordered posed color player photos on its fronts. The player's name and position appear at the bottom. The white horizontal back is framed by a black line and carries the player's name at the top, followed by biography and statistics.
COMPLETE SET (25) 5.00 2.00

1987 Midland Angels ProCards

This 30-card standard-size set of the 1987 Midland Angels, a Class AA Texas League affiliate of the California Angels, features white-bordered posed color player photos on its fronts. The player's name and position appear at the bottom. The white horizontal back is framed by a black line and carries the player's name at the top, followed by biography and statistics.
COMPLETE SET (30) 5.00 2.00

1987 Modesto A's Chong

The last four cards in the set feature Modesto A's alumni and are numbered 1-4; the prefix A has been added in the checklist below for clarity. Cards are black and white with green print on the back and are printed on thin card stock.
COMPLETE SET (32) 8.00 3.20

1987 Modesto A's ProCards

This 25-card standard-size set of the 1987 Modesto A's, a Class A California League affiliate of the Oakland Athletics, features white-bordered posed color player photos on its fronts. The player's name and position appear at the bottom. The white horizontal back is framed by a black line and carries the player's name at the top, followed by biography and statistics.
COMPLETE SET (25) 5.00 2.00

1987 Myrtle Beach Blue Jays ProCards

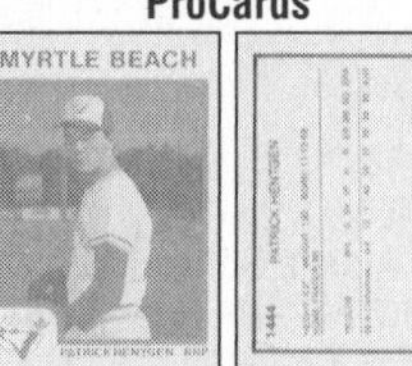

This 30-card standard-size set of the 1987 Myrtle Beach Blue Jays, a Class A South Atlantic League affiliate of the Toronto Blue Jays, features white-bordered posed color player photos on its fronts. The player's name and position appear at the bottom. The white horizontal back is framed by a black line and carries the player's name at the top, followed by biography and statistics. This issue includes the debut of Pat Hentgen.
COMPLETE SET (30) 25.00 10.00

1987 Nashville Sounds Team Issue

COMPLETE SET (25) 5.00 2.00

1987 New Britain Red Sox ProCards

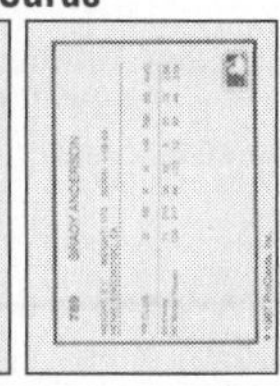

This 25-card standard-size set of the 1987 New Britain Red Sox, a Class AA Eastern League affiliate of the Boston Red Sox, features white-bordered posed color player photos on its fronts. The player's name and position appear at the bottom. The white horizontal back is framed by a black line and carries the player's name at the top, followed by biography and statistics. This issue includes a third year card of Brady Anderson.
COMPLETE SET (25) 15.00 6.00

1987 Newark Orioles ProCards

This 29-card standard-size set of the 1987 Newark Orioles, a Class A New York-Penn affiliate of the Baltimore Orioles, features white-bordered posed color player photos on its fronts. The player's name and position appear at the bottom. The white horizontal back is framed by a black line and carries the player's name at the top, followed by biography and statistics. This issue includes the minor league card debut of Steve Finley.
COMPLETE SET (29) 15.00 6.00

1987 Oklahoma City 89ers ProCards

This 27-card standard-size set of the 1987 Oklahoma City 89ers, a Class AAA American Association affiliate of the Texas Rangers, features white-bordered posed color player photos on its fronts. The player's name and position appear at the bottom. The white horizontal back is framed by a black line and carries the player's name at the top, followed by biography and statistics.
COMPLETE SET (27) 8.00 3.20

1987 Omaha Royals ProCards

This 26-card standard-size set of the 1987 Omaha Royals, a Class AAA American Association affiliate of the Kansas City Royals, features white-bordered posed color player photos on its fronts. The player's name and position appear at the bottom. The white horizontal back is framed by a black line and carries the player's name at the top, followed by biography and statistics.
COMPLETE SET (26) 5.00 2.00

1987 Oneonta Yankees ProCards

This 33-card standard-size set of the 1987 Oneonta Yankees, a Class A New York-Penn League affiliate of the New York Yankees, features white-bordered posed color player photos on its fronts. The player's name and position appear at the bottom. The white horizontal back is framed by a black line and carries the player's name at the top, followed by biography and statistics. This issue includes the minor league card debut of Bernie Williams.
COMPLETE SET (33) 30.00 12.00

1987 Orlando Twins ProCards

This 26-card standard-size set of the 1987 Orlando Twins, a Class AA Southern League affiliate of the Minnesota Twins, features white-bordered posed color player photos on its fronts. The player's name and position appear at the bottom. The white horizontal back is framed by a black line and carries the player's name at the top, followed by biography and statistics.
COMPLETE SET (26) 5.00 2.00

1987 Osceola Astros ProCards

This 29-card standard-size set of the 1987 Osceola Astros, a Class A Florida State League affiliate of the Houston Astros, features white-bordered posed color player photos on its fronts. The player's name and position appear at the bottom. The white horizontal back is framed by a black line and carries the player's name at the top, followed by biography and statistics.
COMPLETE SET (29) 5.00 2.00

1987 Palm Springs ProCards

This 32-card standard-size set of the 1987 Palm Springs Angels, a Class A California League affiliate of the California Angels, features white-bordered posed color player photos on its fronts. The player's name and position appear at the bottom. The white horizontal back is framed by a black line and carries the player's name at the top, followed by biography and statistics.
COMPLETE SET (32) 5.00 2.00

1987 Pan Am Team USA Blue BDK

This issue includes the first card of Frank Thomas.
COMPLETE SET (34) 100.00 40.00
COMPLETE SET (35) 120.00 47.50

1987 Pawtucket Red Sox ProCards

This 27-card standard-size set of the 1987 Pawtucket Red Sox, a Class AAA International League affiliate of the Boston Red Sox, features white-bordered posed color player photos on its fronts. The player's name and position appear at the bottom. The white horizontal back is framed by a black line and carries the player's name at the top, followed by biography and statistics. This issue includes a second year card of Ellis Burks.
COMPLETE SET (27) 5.00 2.00

1987 Pawtucket Red Sox TCMA

COMPLETE SET (28) 4.00 1.60

1987 Peninsula White Sox ProCards

This 29-card standard-size set of the 1987 Peninsula White Sox, a Class A Carolina affiliate of the Chicago White Sox, features white-bordered posed color player photos on its fronts. The player's name and position appear at the bottom. The white horizontal back is framed by a black line and carries the player's name at the top, followed by biography and statistics.
COMPLETE SET (29) 5.00 2.00

1987 Peoria Chiefs Pizza World

This six-card promotional set was distributed through the Pizza World restaurant. One card per each Pizza World pizza ordered. The set was also sponsored by radio station WWCT 106. The cards measure 4'1/2" X 5'1/2" and feature black and white photos with blue borders.
COMPLETE SET (6) 25.00 10.00

1987 Peoria Chiefs ProCards

This 29-card standard-size set of the 1987 Peoria Chiefs, a Class A Midwest League affiliate of the Chicago Cubs, features white-bordered posed color player photos on its fronts. The player's name and position appear at the bottom. The white horizontal back is framed by a black line and carries the player's name at the top, followed by biography and statistics.
COMPLETE SET (29) 5.00 2.00

1987 Phoenix Firebirds ProCards

This 28-card standard-size set of the 1987 Phoenix Firebirds, a Class AAA Pacific Coast League affiliate of the San Francisco Giants, features white-bordered posed color player photos on its fronts. The player's name and position appear at the bottom. The white horizontal back is framed by a black line and carries the player's name at the top, followed by biography and statistics. This issue includes a second year card of Matt Williams.
COMPLETE SET (28) 15.00 6.00

1987 Pittsfield Cubs ProCards

This 26-card standard-size set of the 1987 Pittsfield Cubs, a Class AA Eastern League affiliate of the Chicago Cubs, features white-bordered posed color player photos on its fronts. The player's name and position appear at the bottom. The white horizontal back is framed by a black line and carries the player's name at the top, followed by biography and statistics. This issue includes a second year card of Mark Grace.
COMPLETE SET (26) 20.00 8.00

1987 Pocatello Giants The Bon

The 32-card standard-szie set featuring the 1987 Pocatello Giants set was sponsored by The Bon clothing store. The fronts have posed player photos (from the waist up), with a stripe below the picture, as well as sponsor and team logos. The horizontally oriented backs have a picture of a bat and baseball at the top, with biography and career information below. Less than 1,000 sets were produced.
COMPLETE SET (32) 30.00 12.00

1987 Port Charlotte Rangers ProCards

This 27-card standard-size set of the 1987 Port Charlotte Rangers, a Class A Florida State League affiliate of the Texas Rangers, features white-bordered posed color player photos on its fronts. The player's name and position appear at the bottom. The white horizontal back is framed by a black line and carries the player's name at the top, followed by biography and statistics.
COMPLETE SET (27) 5.00 2.00

1987 Portland Beavers ProCards

This 25-card standard-size set of the 1987 Portland Beavers, a Class AAA Pacific Coast League affiliate of the Minnesota Twins, features white-bordered posed color player photos on its fronts. The player's name and position appear at the bottom. The white horizontal back is framed by a black line and carries the player's name at the top, followed by biography and statistics.
COMPLETE SET (25) 5.00 2.00

1987 Prince William Yankees ProCards

This 29-card standard-size set of the 1987 Prince William Yankees, a Class A Carolina League affiliate of the New York Yankees, features white-bordered posed color player photos on its fronts. The player's name and position appear at the bottom. The white horizontal back is framed by a black line and carries the player's name at the top, followed by biography and statistics.
COMPLETE SET (29) 5.00 2.00

1987 Quad City Angels ProCards

This 31-card standard-size set of the 1987 Quad City Angels, a Class A Midwest League affiliate of the California Angels, features white-bordered posed color player photos on its fronts. The player's name and position appear at the bottom. The white horizontal back is framed by a black line and carries the player's name at the top, followed by biography and statistics.
COMPLETE SET (31) 5.00 2.00

1987 Reading Phillies ProCards

This 26-card standard-size set of the 1987 Reading Phillies, a Class AA Eastern League affiliate of the Philadelphia Phillies, features white-bordered posed color player photos on its fronts. The player's name and position appear at the bottom. The white horizontal back is framed by a black line and carries the player's name at the top, followed by biography and statistics.
COMPLETE SET (26) 5.00 2.00

1987 Richmond Braves Bob's Camera

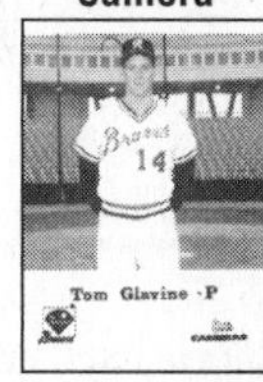

This 29-card team set of the 1989 Richmond Braves, a Class AAA International League affiliate of the Atlanta Braves, was sponsored by Bob's Camera. The fronts feature borderless color player photos with sponsors' and team's logos in the wide bottom margin. The backs are blank. This issue includes a second year card of Tom Glavine. 500 sets were produced.
COMPLETE SET (24) 100.00 40.00

1987 Richmond Braves Crown

This issue includes a second year card of Tom Glavine.
COMPLETE SET (30) 30.00 12.00

1987 Richmond Braves TCMA

This issue includes a second year card of Tom Glavine.
COMPLETE SET (29) 20.00 8.00

1987 Rochester Red Wings ProCards

This 27-card standard-size set of the 1987 Rochester Red Wings, a Class AAA International League affiliate of the Baltimore Orioles, features white-bordered posed color player photos on its fronts. The player's name and position appear at the bottom. The white horizontal back is framed by a black line and carries the player's name at the top, followed by biography and statistics.
COMPLETE SET (27) 5.00 2.00

1987 Rochester Red Wings TCMA

COMPLETE SET (29) 4.00 1.60

1987 Salem Angels ProCards

This 34-card standard-size set of the 1987 Salem Angels, a Class A Northwest League affiliate of the California Angels, features white-bordered posed color player photos on its fronts. The player's name and position appear at the bottom. The white horizontal back is framed by a black line and carries the player's name at the top, followed by biography and statistics.
COMPLETE SET (34)................. 5.00 2.00

1987 Salem Buccaneers ProCards

This 30-card standard-size set of the 1987 Salem Buccaneers, a Class A Carolina League affiliate of the Pittsburgh Pirates, features white-bordered posed color player photos on its fronts. The player's name and position appear at the bottom. The white horizontal back is framed by a black line and carries the player's name at the top, followed by biography and statistics. This issue includes the minor league card debut of Jeff King.
COMPLETE SET (30)............... 10.00 4.00

1987 Salinas Spurs Smokey

This issue includes a second year card of Omar Vizquel.
COMPLETE SET (32)............... 80.00 32.00

1987 Salt Lake Trappers Taco Time

COMPLETE SET (30)................. 8.00 3.20

1987 San Antonio Dodgers Team Issue

COMPLETE SET W/LOGO (25)... 6.00 2.40
COMPLETE SET (24)................. 5.00 2.00

1987 San Bernardino Spirit ProCards

This 23-card standard-size set of the 1987 San Bernardino Spirit, a Class A California League Independent, features white-bordered posed color player photos on its fronts. The player's name and position appear at the bottom. The white horizontal back is framed by a black line and carries the player's name at the top, followed by biography and statistics.
COMPLETE SET (23)................. 5.00 2.00

1987 San Jose Bees ProCards

This 30-card standard-size set of the 1987 San Jose Bees, a Class A California League Independent, features white-bordered posed color player photos on its fronts. The player's name and position appear at the bottom. The white horizontal back is framed by a black line and carries the player's name at the top, followed by biography and statistics.
COMPLETE SET (30)................. 5.00 2.00

1987 Savannah Cardinals ProCards

This 26-card standard-size set of the 1987 Savannah Cardinals, a Class A South Atlantic League affiliate of the St. Louis Cardinals, features white-bordered posed color player photos on its fronts. The player's name and position appear at the bottom. The white horizontal back is framed by a black line and carries the player's name at the top, followed by biography and statistics.
COMPLETE SET (26)................. 5.00 2.00

1987 Shreveport Captains ProCards

This 25-card standard-size set of the 1987 Shreveport Captains, a Class AA Texas League affiliate of the San Francisco Giants, features white-bordered posed color player photos on its fronts. The player's name and position appear at the bottom. The white horizontal back is framed by a black line and carries the player's name at the top, followed by biography and statistics.
COMPLETE SET (25)................. 5.00 2.00

1987 Southern League All-Stars Jennings

COMPLETE SET (25)............... 25.00 10.00

1987 Spartanburg Phillies ProCards

This 28-card standard-size set of the 1987 Spartanburg Phillies, a Class A South Atlantic League affiliate of the Philadelphia Phillies, features white-bordered posed color player photos on its fronts. The player's name and position appear at the bottom. The white horizontal back is framed by a black line and carries the player's name at the top, followed by biography and statistics.
COMPLETE SET (28)................. 5.00 2.00

1987 Spokane Indians ProCards

This 25-card standard-size set of the 1987 Spokane Indians, a Class A Northwest League affiliate of the San Diego Padres, features white-bordered posed color player photos on its fronts. The player's name and position appear at the bottom. The white horizontal back is framed by a black line and carries the player's name at the top, followed by biography and statistics. This issue includes the minor league card debut of Jose Valentin.
COMPLETE SET (25)................. 8.00 3.20

1987 Springfield Cardinals Best

This issue includes the minor league card debut of Bernard Gilkey and a second year card of Todd Zeile.
COMPLETE SET (28)............... 15.00 6.00

1987 St. Petersburg Cardinals ProCards

This 27-card standard-size set of the 1987 St. Petersburg Cardinals, a Class A Florida State League affiliate of the St. Louis Cardinals, features white-bordered posed color player photos on its fronts. The player's name and position appear at the bottom. The white horizontal back is framed by a black line and carries the player's name at the top, followed by biography and statistics.
COMPLETE SET (27)................. 5.00 2.00

1987 Stockton Ports ProCards

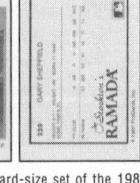

This 26-card standard-size set of the 1987 Stockton Ports, a Class A California League affiliate of the Milwaukee Brewers, features white-bordered posed color player photos on its fronts. The player's name and position appear at the bottom. The white horizontal back is framed by a black line and carries the player's name at the top, followed by biography and statistics. This issue includes the minor league card debut of Gary Sheffield.
COMPLETE SET (26)............... 25.00 10.00

1987 Sumter Braves ProCards

This 30-card standard-size set of the 1987 Sumter Braves, a Class A South Atlantic League affiliate of the Atlanta Braves, features white-bordered posed color player photos on its fronts. The player's name and position appear at the bottom. The white horizontal back is framed by a black line and carries the player's name at the top, followed by biography and statistics.
COMPLETE SET (30)................. 8.00 3.20

1987 Syracuse Chiefs 10th Anniversary

1978-87 Souvenir Ticket set, unnumbered
COMPLETE SET (12)............... 10.00 4.00

1987 Syracuse Chiefs ProCards

This 23-card standard-size set of the 1987 Syracuse Chiefs, a Class AAA International League affiliate of the Toronto Blue Jays, features white-bordered posed color player photos on its fronts. The player's name and position appear at the bottom. The white horizontal back is framed by a black line and carries the player's name at the top, followed by biography and statistics.
COMPLETE SET (23)................. 5.00 2.00

1987 Syracuse Chiefs TCMA

This 33-card set of the 1987 Syracuse Chiefs, a Class AAA International League affiliate of the Toronto Blue Jays, measures about 2 1/2" by 3 3/4" and features white-bordered posed color player photos on its fronts. The player's name and position appear at the bottom. The white back carries the league and team names at the top, followed by the player's name, position, biography, and statistics.
COMPLETE SET (33)............... 10.00 4.00

1987 Tacoma Tigers ProCards

This 23-card standard-size set of the 1987 Tacoma Tigers, a Class AAA Pacific Coast League affiliate of the Oakland Athletics, features white-bordered posed color player photos on its fronts. The player's name and position appear at the bottom. The white horizontal back is framed by a black line and carries the player's name at the top, followed by biography and statistics.
COMPLETE SET (23)................. 5.00 2.00

1987 Tampa Tarpons ProCards

This 30-card standard-size set of the 1987 Tampa Tarpons, a Class A Florida State League affiliate of the Cincinnati Reds, features white-bordered posed color player photos on its fronts. The player's name and position appear at the bottom. The white horizontal back is framed by a black line and carries the player's name at the top, followed by biography and statistics.
COMPLETE SET (30)................. 5.00 2.00

1987 Texas League All-Stars Feder

COMPLETE SET (36)............... 20.00 8.00

1987 Tidewater Tides ProCards

This 33-card standard-size set of the 1987 Tidewater Tides, a Class AAA International League affiliate of the New York Mets, features white-bordered posed color player photos on its fronts. The player's name and position appear at the bottom. The white horizontal back is framed by a black line and carries the player's name at the top, followed by biography and statistics.
COMPLETE SET (33)................. 8.00 3.20

1987 Tidewater Tides TCMA

COMPLETE SET (30)................. 5.00 2.00

1987 Toledo Mud Hens ProCards

This 30-card standard-size set of the 1987 Toledo Mud Hens, a Class AAA International League affiliate of the Detroit Tigers, features white-bordered posed color player photos on its fronts. The player's name and position appear at the bottom. The white horizontal back is framed by a black line and carries the player's name at the top, followed by biography and statistics.
COMPLETE SET (30)................. 5.00 2.00

1987 Toledo Mud Hens TCMA

COMPLETE SET (25)................. 4.00 1.60

1987 Tucson Toros ProCards

This 25-card standard-size set of the 1987 Tucson Toros, a Class AAA Pacific Coast League affiliate of the Houston Astros, features white-bordered posed color player photos on its fronts. The player's name and position appear at the bottom. The white horizontal back is framed by a black line and carries the player's name at the top, followed by biography and statistics.
COMPLETE SET (25)................. 5.00 2.00

1987 Utica Blue Sox ProCards

This 33-card standard-size set of the 1987 Utica Blue Sox, a Class A New York-Penn League affiliate of the Philadelphia Phillies, features white-bordered posed color player photos on its fronts. The player's name and position appear at the bottom. The white horizontal back is framed by a black line and carries the player's name at the top, followed by biography and statistics.
COMPLETE SET (33)................. 5.00 2.00

1987 Vancouver Canadians ProCards

This 25-card standard-size set of the 1987 Vancouver Canadians, a Class AAA Pacific Coast League affiliate of the Pittsburgh Pirates, features white-bordered posed color player photos on its fronts. The player's name and position appear at the bottom. The white horizontal back is framed by a black line and carries the player's name at the top, followed by biography and statistics.
COMPLETE SET (25)................. 5.00 2.00

1987 Vermont Reds ProCards

This 26-card standard-size set of the 1987 Vermont Reds, a Class AA Eastern League affiliate of the Cincinnati Reds, features white-bordered posed color player photos on its fronts. The player's name and position appear at the bottom. The white horizontal back is framed by a black line and carries the player's name at the top, followed by biography and statistics.
COMPLETE SET (26)................. 5.00 2.00

1987 Vero Beach Dodgers ProCards

This 31-card standard-size set of the 1987 Vero Beach Dodgers, a Class A Florida State League affiliate of the Los Angeles Dodgers, features white-bordered posed color player photos on its fronts. The player's name and position appear at the bottom. The white horizontal back is framed by a black line and carries the player's name at the top, followed by biography and statistics.
COMPLETE SET (31)................. 8.00 3.20

1987 Visalia Oaks ProCards

This 27-card standard-size set of the 1987 Visalia Oaks, a Class A California League affiliate of the Minnesota Twins, features white-bordered posed color player photos on its fronts. The player's name and position appear at the bottom. The white horizontal back is framed by a black line and carries the player's name at the top, followed by biography and statistics.
COMPLETE SET (27)................. 5.00 2.00

1987 Waterloo Indians ProCards

This 29-card standard-size set of the 1987 Waterloo Indians, a Class A Midwest League affiliate of the Cleveland Indians, features white-bordered posed color player photos on its fronts. The player's name and position appear at the bottom. The white horizontal back is framed by a black line and carries the player's name at the top, followed by biography and statistics.
COMPLETE SET (29)................. 5.00 2.00

1987 Watertown Pirates ProCards

This 31-card standard-size set of the 1987 Watertown Pirates, a Class A New York-Penn League affiliate of the Pittsburgh Pirates, features white-bordered posed color player photos on its fronts. The player's name and position appear at the bottom. The white horizontal back is framed by a black line and carries the player's name at the top, followed by biography and statistics. This issue includes a second year card of Moises Alou.
COMPLETE SET (31)............... 15.00 6.00

1987 Wausau Timbers ProCards

This 28-card standard-size set of the 1987 Wausau Timbers, a Class A Midwest League affiliate of the Seattle Mariners, features white-bordered posed color player photos on its fronts. The player's name and position appear at the bottom. The white horizontal back is framed by a black line and carries the player's name at the top, followed by biography and statistics.
COMPLETE SET (28)................. 5.00 2.00

1987 West Palm Beach Expos ProCards

This 28-card standard-size set of the 1987 West Palm Beach Expos, a Class A Florida State League affiliate of the Montreal Expos, features white-bordered posed color player photos on its fronts. The player's name and position appear at the bottom. The white horizontal back is framed by a black line and carries the player's name at the top, followed by biography and statistics.
COMPLETE SET (28)................. 5.00 2.00

1987 Wichita Pilots Rock's Dugout

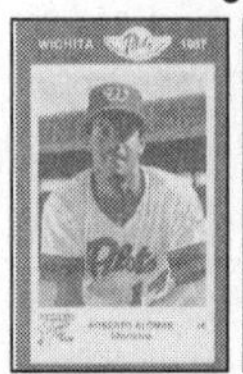

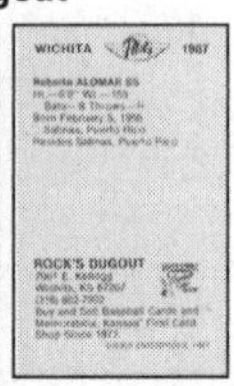

This issue includes the minor league card debut of Roberto Alomar.
COMPLETE SET (25)............... 50.00 20.00

1987 Williamsport Bills ProCards

This 27-card standard-size set of the 1987 Williamsport Bills, a Class AA Eastern League affiliate of the Cleveland Indians, features white-bordered posed color player photos on its fronts. The player's name and position appear at the bottom. The white horizontal back is framed by a black line and carries the player's name at the top, followed by biography and statistics.
COMPLETE SET (27)................. 5.00 2.00

1987 Winston-Salem Spirits ProCards

This 27-card standard-size set of the 1987 Winston-Salem Spirits, a Class A Carolina League affiliate of the Chicago Cubs, features white-bordered posed color player photos on its fronts. The player's name and position appear at the bottom. The white horizontal back is framed by a black line and carries the player's name at the top, followed by biography and statistics.
COMPLETE SET (27)................. 5.00 2.00

1987 Winter Haven Red Sox ProCards

This 30-card standard-size set of the 1987 Winter Haven Red Sox, a Class A Florida State league affiliate of the Boston Red Sox, features white-bordered posed color player photos on its fronts. The player's name and position appear at the bottom. The white horizontal back is framed by a black line and carries the player's name at the top, followed by biography and statistics.
COMPLETE SET (30)................. 5.00 2.00

1987 Wytheville Cubs ProCards

This 31-card standard-size set of the 1987 Wytheville Cubs, a Rookie Class Appalachian League affiliate of the Chicago Cubs, features white-bordered posed color player photos on its fronts. The player's name and position appear at the bottom. The white horizontal back is framed by a black line and carries the player's name at the top, followed by biography and statistics.
COMPLETE SET (31)................. 5.00 2.00

1988 Alaska Goldpanners All-Time AS '60s Team Issue

Set features alumni of the Goldpanners who played in the '60s. According to the team there were only 5000 sets produced for this series
COMPLETE SET (12)............... 20.00 8.00

1988 Alaska Goldpanners All-Time AS '70s Team Issue

Set features alumni of the Goldpanners who played in the '70s. According to the team there were only 10,000 sets produced for this series.
COMPLETE SET (12)............... 20.00 8.00

1988 Alaska Goldpanners Team Issue

COMPLETE SET (20)............... 25.00 10.00

1988 Albany Yankees ProCards

This 27-card standard-size set of the 1988 Albany Yankees, a Class AA Eastern League affiliate of the New York Yankees, features silver-bordered posed color player photos on its fronts. The player's name, position, and team name appear at the bottom. The plain white back carries the player's name at the top, followed by biography and statistics.
COMPLETE SET (27)................. 5.00 2.00

1988 Albuquerque Dukes CMC

10,000 sets were produced.
COMPLETE SET (25)................. 4.00 1.60

1988 Albuquerque Dukes ProCards

This 29-card standard-size set of the 1988 Albuquerque Dukes, a Class AAA Pacific Coast League affiliate of the Los Angeles Dodgers, features bronze-bordered posed color player photos on its fronts. The player's name, position, and team name appear at the bottom. The plain white back carries the player's name at the top, followed by biography and statistics.
COMPLETE SET (29)................. 5.00 2.00

1988 Appleton Foxes ProCards

This 30-card standard-size set of the 1988 Appleton Foxes, a Class A Midwest League affiliate of the Kansas City Royals, features bronze-bordered posed color player photos on its fronts. The player's name, position, and team name appear at the bottom. The plain white back carries the player's name at the top, followed by biography and statistics.
COMPLETE SET (30)................. 5.00 2.00

1988 Arizona Wildcats Police

COMPLETE SET (16)............... 20.00 8.00

1988 Arkansas Travelers Grand Slam

COMPLETE SET (25)................. 5.00 2.00

1988 Asheville Tourists ProCards

This 31-card standard-size set of the 1988 Asheville Tourists, a Class A South Atlantic League affiliate of the Houston Astros, features bronze-bordered posed color player photos on its fronts. The player's name, position, and team name appear at the bottom. The plain white back carries the player's name at the top, followed by biography and statistics.
COMPLETE SET (31)................. 5.00 2.00

1988 Auburn Astros ProCards

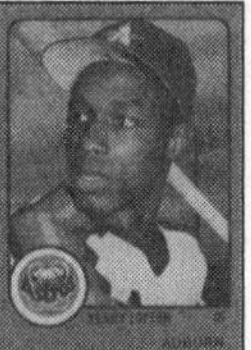
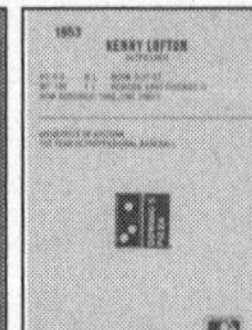

This 29-card standard-size set of the 1988 Auburn Astros, a Class A New York-Penn League affiliate of the Houston Astros, features bronze-bordered posed color player photos on its fronts. The player's name, position, and team name appear at the bottom. The plain white back carries the player's name at the top, followed by biography and statistics. This issue includes the minor league card debut of Kenny Lofton.
COMPLETE SET (29)............... 40.00 16.00

1988 Augusta Pirates ProCards

This 33-card standard-size set of the 1988 Augusta Pirates, a Class A South Atlantic League affiliate of the Pittsburgh Pirates, features bronze-bordered posed color player photos on its fronts. The player's name, position, and team name appear at the bottom. The plain white back carries the player's name at the top, followed by biography and statistics.
COMPLETE SET (33)............... 15.00 6.00

1988 Bakersfield Dodgers Cal League Cards

COMPLETE SET (34)................. 5.00 2.00

1988 Baseball America AA All-Stars Best

Produced by Best Cards and as selected by Baseball America. 7,000 sets were produced.
COMPLETE SET (30)............... 15.00 6.00

1988 Baseball City Royals Star

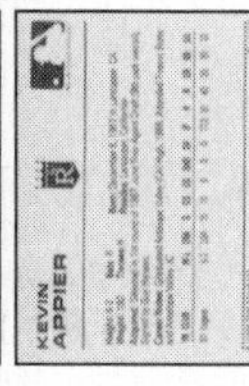

This issue includes the minor league card debut of Jeff Conine.
COMPLETE SET (25) 15.00 6.00

1988 Batavia Clippers ProCards

This 31-card standard-size set of the 1988 Batavia Clippers, a Class A New York-Penn League affiliate of the Philadelphia Phillies, features bronze-bordered posed color player photos on its fronts. The player's name, position, and team name appear at the bottom. The plain white back carries the player's name at the top, followed by biography and statistics.
COMPLETE SET (31) 5.00 2.00

1988 Bellingham Mariners Legoe

COMPLETE SET (32) 5.00 2.00

1988 Beloit Brewers Grand Slam

COMPLETE SET (25) 5.00 2.00

1988 Bend Bucks Legoe

This issue includes the minor league card debut of Jim Edmonds.
COMPLETE SET (36) 30.00 12.00

1988 Billings Mustangs ProCards

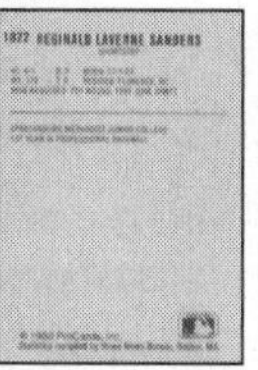

This 31-card standard-size set of the 1988 Billings Mustangs, a Rookie Class Pioneer League affiliate of the Cincinnati Reds, features bronze-bordered posed color player photos on its fronts. The player's name, position, and team name appear at the bottom. The plain white back carries the player's name at the top, followed by biography and statistics. This issue includes the minor league card debut of Reggie Sanders.
COMPLETE SET (31) 20.00 8.00

1988 Birmingham Barons Best

This 29-card standard-size set of the 1988 Birmingham Barons, a Class AA Southern League affiliate of the Chicago White Sox, features red and black bordered posed color player photos on its fronts. The team name appears at the top, and below the picture is the player's name and position. The horizontal gray back carries the player's name and position at the top, followed by biography, career highlights, and statistics. The set is printed on thin card stock.
COMPLETE SET (29) 5.00 2.00

1988 Boise Hawks ProCards

This 29-card standard-size set of the 1988 Boise Hawks, a Class A Northwest League Independent, features bronze-bordered posed color player photos on its fronts. The player's name, position, and team name appear at the bottom. The plain white back carries the player's name at the top, followed by biography and statistics.
COMPLETE SET (29) 5.00 2.00

1988 Bristol Tigers ProCards

This 32-card standard-size set of the 1988 Bristol Tigers, a Rookie Class Appalachian League League affiliate of the Detroit Tigers, features bronze-bordered posed color player photos on its fronts. The player's name, position, and team name appear at the bottom. The plain white back carries the player's name at the top, followed by biography and statistics.
COMPLETE SET (32) 5.00 2.00

1988 Buffalo Bisons CMC

10,000 sets were produced.
COMPLETE SET (25) 4.00 1.60

1988 Buffalo Bisons ProCards

This 31-card standard-size set of the 1988 Buffalo Bisons, a Class AAA American Association affiliate of the Pittsburgh Pirates, features gold-bordered posed color player photos on its fronts. The player's name, position, and team name appear at the bottom. The plain white back carries the player's name at the top, followed by biography and statistics.
COMPLETE SET (31) 5.00 2.00

1988 Buffalo Bisons Team Issue

This nine-card set of the 1988 Buffalo Bisons, a Class AAA American Association affiliate of the Pittsburgh Pirates, features eight color player cards along with a team photo. The set was sponsored by Polaroid and distributed on a special promotional Polaroid Camera Day at the ballpark.
COMPLETE SET (9) 25.00 10.00

1988 Burlington Braves ProCards

This 31-card standard-size set of the 1988 Burlington Braves, a Class A Midwest League affiliate of the Atlanta Braves, features bronze-bordered posed color player photos on its fronts. The player's name, position, and team name appear at the bottom. The plain white back carries the player's name at the top, followed by biography and statistics.
COMPLETE SET (31) 5.00 2.00

1988 Burlington Indians ProCards

This 31-card standard-size set of the 1988 Burlington Indians, a Rookie Class Appalachian League affiliate of the Cleveland Indians, features bronze-bordered posed color player photos on its fronts. The player's name, position, and team name appear at the bottom. The plain white back carries the player's name at the top, followed by biography and statistics. This issue includes the minor league card debut of Mark Lewis.
COMPLETE SET (31) 10.00 4.00

1988 Butte Copper Kings Sports Pro

COMPLETE SET (29) 5.00 2.00

1988 Calgary Cannons CMC

This 25-card standard-size set of the 1988 Calgary Cannons, a Class AAA Pacific Coast League affiliate of the Seattle Mariners, features on its fronts black-bordered posed color player photos framed by a green line. The team's name, the player's name, and his position appear at the bottom. The white back is framed by a black line and carries the team's name and league at the top, followed by the player's name, biography and statistics.
COMPLETE SET (25) 10.00 4.00

1988 Calgary Cannons ProCards

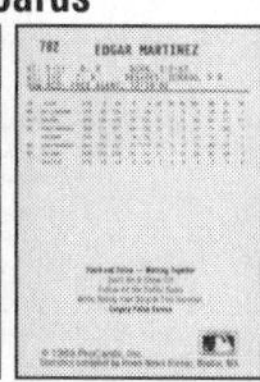

This 28-card standard-size set of the 1988 Calgary Cannons, a Class AAA Pacific Coast League affiliate of the Seattle Mariners, features gold-bordered posed color player photos on its fronts. The player's name, position, and team name appear at the bottom. The plain white back carries the player's name at the top, followed by biography and statistics.
COMPLETE SET (28) 15.00 6.00

1988 California League All-Stars Cal League

This 50 card set features the leading prospects in the California league in 1988. An early card of Ken Griffey Jr. highlights this set.
COMPLETE SET (50) 40.00 16.00

1988 Cape Cod Prospects Ballpark

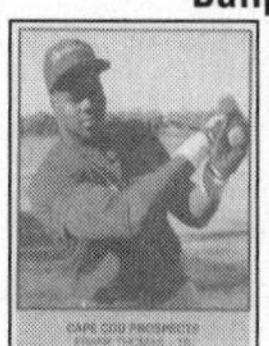

Issued and produced by collector/dealer Fred Suzman, this set features twenty of the Cape Cod League's top players and ten team cards. This issue includes first cards of Chuck Knoblauch, Jeff Bagwell and Mo Vaughn and a second card issue of Frank Thomas.
COMPLETE SET (30) 50.00 20.00

1988 Carolina League All-Stars Star

COMPLETE SET (40) 15.00 6.00

1988 Cedar Rapids Reds ProCards

This 31-card standard-size set of the 1988 Cedar Rapids Reds, a Class A Midwest League affiliate of the Cincinnati Reds, features bronze-bordered posed color player photos on its fronts. The player's name, position, and team name appear at the bottom. The plain white back carries the player's name at the top, followed by biography and statistics.
COMPLETE SET (31) 5.00 2.00

1988 Charleston Rainbows ProCards

This 30-card standard-size set of the 1988 Charleston Rainbows, a Class A California League affiliate of the San Diego Padres, features bronze-bordered posed color player photos on its fronts. The player's name, position, and team name appear at the bottom. The plain white back carries the player's name at the top, followed by biography and statistics.
COMPLETE SET (30) 5.00 2.00

1988 Charleston Wheelers Best

This 28-card standard-size set of the 1988 Charleston Wheelers, a Class A South Atlantic League affiliate of the Chicago Cubs, features blue and black bordered posed color player photos on its fronts. The team name appears at the top, and below the picture is the player's name and position. The horizontal gray back carries the player's name and position at the top, followed by biography, career highlights, and statistics. The set is printed on thin card stock.
COMPLETE SET (28) 5.00 2.00

1988 Charlotte Knights Team Issue

COMPLETE SET (25) 10.00 4.00

1988 Charlotte Rangers Star

This 25-card standard-size set of the 1988 Charlotte Rangers, a Class A Florida State League affiliate of the Texas Rangers, features orange-bordered posed color player photos on its fronts. The player's name, team name, and position appear at the bottom. The yellowish horizontal back carries the player's name at the top, followed by biography, career highlights, and statistics. This issue inlcudes second year cards of Juan Gonzalez, Sammy Sosa and Dean Palmer.
COMPLETE SET (23) 50.00 20.00

1988 Chattanooga Lookouts Best

This 26-card standard-size set of the 1988 Chattanooga Lookouts, a Class AA Southern League affiliate of the Cincinnati Reds, features red and black bordered posed color player photos on its fronts. The team name appears at the top, and below the picture is the player's name and position. The horizontal gray back carries the player's name and position at the top, followed by biography, career highlights, and statistics. The set is printed on thin card stock.
COMPLETE SET (26) 5.00 2.00

1988 Chattanooga Lookouts Legends Team Issue

COMPLETE SET (32) 30.00 12.00

1988 Clearwater Phillies Star

COMPLETE SET (26) 5.00 2.00

1988 Clinton Giants ProCards

This 29-card standard-size set of the 1988 Clinton Giants, a Class A Midwest League affiliate of the San Francisco Giants, features bronze-bordered posed color player photos on its fronts. The player's name, position, and team name appear at the bottom. The plain white back carries the player's name at the top, followed by biography and statistics.
COMPLETE SET (29) 5.00 2.00

1988 Colorado Springs Sky Sox CMC

10,000 sets were produced.
COMPLETE SET (25) 4.00 1.60

1988 Colorado Springs Sky Sox ProCards

This 29-card standard-size set of the 1988 Colorado Springs Sky Sox, a Class AAA Pacific Coast League affiliate of the Cleveland Indians, features gold-bordered posed color player photos on its fronts. The player's name, position, and team name appear at the bottom. The plain white back carries the player's name at the top, followed by biography and statistics.
COMPLETE SET (29) 5.00 2.00

1988 Columbia Mets Grand Slam

COMPLETE SET (27) 5.00 2.00

1988 Columbus Astros Best

This 28-card standard-size set of the 1988 Columbus Astros, a Class AA Southern League affiliate of the Houston Astros, features orange and black bordered posed color player photos on its fronts. The team name appears at the top, and below the picture is the player's name and position. The horizontal gray back carries the player's name and position at the top, followed by biography, career highlights, and statistics. The set is printed on thin card stock.
COMPLETE SET (28) 5.00 2.00

1988 Columbus Clippers CMC

10,000 sets were produced. This issue includes a second year card of Jay Buhner.
COMPLETE SET (26) 5.00 2.00

1988 Columbus Clippers Police

This issue includes a second year card of Jay Buhner.
COMPLETE SET (25) 10.00 4.00

1988 Columbus Clippers ProCards

This 29-card standard-size set of the 1988 Columbus Clippers, a Class AAA International League affiliate of the New York Yankees, features gold-bordered posed color player photos on its fronts. The player's name, position, and team name appear at the bottom. The plain white back carries the player's name at the top, followed by biography and statistics. This issue includes a second year card of Jay Buhner.
COMPLETE SET (29) 10.00 4.00

1988 Denver Zephyrs CMC

10,000 sets were produced.
COMPLETE SET (25) 4.00 1.60

1988 Denver Zephyrs ProCards

This 30-card standard-size set of the 1988 Denver Zephyrs, a Class AAA American Association affiliate of the Milwaukee Brewers, features gold-bordered posed color player photos on its fronts. The player's name, position, and team name appear at the bottom. The plain white back carries the player's name at the top, followed by biography and statistics.
COMPLETE SET (30) 5.00 2.00

1988 Dunedin Blue Jays Star

This 25-card standard-size set of the 1988 Dunedin Blue Jays, a Class A Florida State League affiliate of the Toronto Blue Jays, features blue-bordered posed color player photos on its fronts. The player's name, team name, and position appear at the bottom. The yellowish horizontal back carries the player's name at the top, followed by biography, career highlights, and statistics. Doug Ault's manager card (number 25) was a late issue. This issue includes a second year card of Pat Hentgen.
COMPLETE SET (25) 15.00 6.00

1988 Durham Bulls Star

COMPLETE SET (24) 4.00 1.60
COMPLETE ORANGE SET (26). 10.00 4.00

1988 Eastern League All-Stars ProCards

COMPLETE SET (52) 8.00 3.20

1988 Edmonton Trappers CMC

This 25-card standard-size set of the 1988 Edmonton Trappers, a Class AAA Pacific Coast League affiliate of the California Angels, features on its fronts black-bordered posed color player photos framed by a green line. The team's name, the player's name, and his position appear at the bottom. The white back is framed by a black line and carries the team's name and league at the top, followed by the player's name, position, biography and statistics. This issue includes a second year card of Dante Bichette. 10,000 sets were produced.
COMPLETE SET (25) 10.00 4.00

1988 Edmonton Trappers ProCards

This 31-card standard-size set of the 1988 Edmonton Trappers, a Class AAA Pacific Coast League affiliate of the California Angels, features gold-bordered posed color player photos on its fronts. The player's name, position, and team name appear at the bottom. The plain white back carries the player's name at the top, followed by biography and statistics. This issue includes a second year card of Dante Bichette.
COMPLETE SET (31) 15.00 6.00

1988 El Paso Diablos Best

This 30-card standard-size set of the 1988 El Paso Diablos, a Class AA Texas League affiliate of the Milwaukee Brewers, features red and black bordered posed color player photos on its fronts. The team name appears at the top, and below the picture is the player's name and position. The horizontal gray back carries the player's name and position at the top, followed by biography, career highlights, and statistics. The set is printed on thin card stock. Only 1300 of the platinum version were produced. This

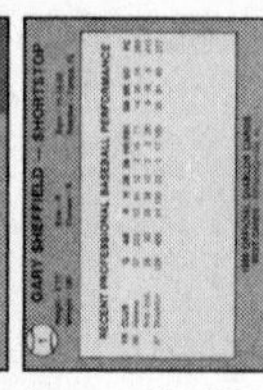

issue includes second year cards of Gary Sheffield and Greg Vaughn.
COMPLETE SET (30) 25.00 10.00

1988 Elmira Pioneers 100th Cain

This 12-card set of the 1988 Elmira Pioneers, a Class A New York-Penn League affiliate of the Boston Red Sox, features black and white player photos with a blue star white border. 200 sets were produced.
COMPLETE SET (12) 30.00 12.00

1988 Elmira Pioneers Cain

This 30-card set of the 1988 Elmira Pioneers, a Class A New York-Penn League affiliate of the Boston Red Sox, features black and white player photos with a red star white border. The cards measure 3 3/4" x 2 1/2" and are horizontal. This issue includes the minor league card debut of Tim Naehring. 4,800 sets were produced.
COMPLETE SET (30) 8.00 3.20

1988 Eugene Emeralds Best

This 30-card standard-size set of the 1988 Eugene Emeralds, a Class A Northwest League affiliate of the Kansas City Royals, features blue and black bordered posed color player photos on its fronts. The team name appears at the top, and below the picture is the player's name and position. The horizontal gray back carries the player's name and position at the top, followed by biography, career highlights, and statistics. The set is printed on thin card stock.
COMPLETE SET (30) 5.00 2.00

1988 Fayetteville Generals ProCards

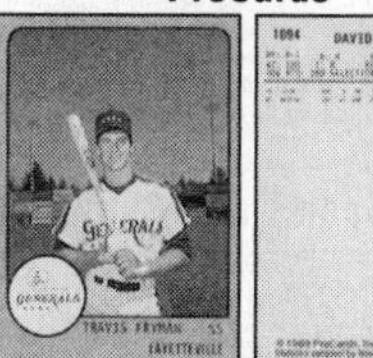

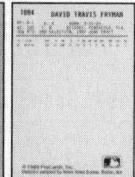

This 28-card standard-size set of the 1988 Fayetteville Generals, a Class A South Atlantic League affiliate of the Detroit Tigers, features bronze-bordered posed color player photos on its fronts. The player's name, position, and team name appear at the bottom. The plain white back carries the player's name at the top, followed by biography and statistics. This issue includes the minor league card debut of Travis Fryman.
COMPLETE SET (28) 30.00 12.00

1988 Florida State League All-Stars Star

COMPLETE SET (52) 10.00 4.00

1988 Fresno Suns Cal League Cards

COMPLETE SET (27) 5.00 2.00

1988 Fresno Suns ProCards

This 29-card standard-size set of the 1988 Fresno Suns, a Class A California League Independent, features bronze-bordered posed color player photos on its fronts. The player's name, position, and team name appear at the bottom. The plain white back carries the player's name at the top, followed by biography and statistics.
COMPLETE SET (29) 5.00 2.00

1988 Ft. Lauderdale Yankees Star

COMPLETE SET (24) 5.00 2.00

1988 Gastonia Rangers ProCards

This 30-card standard-size set of the 1988 Gastonia Rangers, a Class A South Atlantic League affiliate of the Texas Rangers, features bronze-bordered posed color player photos on its fronts. The player's name, position, and team name appear at the bottom. The plain white back carries the player's name at the top, followed by biography and statistics.
COMPLETE SET (30) 20.00 8.00

1988 Geneva Cubs ProCards

This 30-card standard-size set of the 1988 Geneva Cubs, a Class A New York-Penn League affiliate of the Chicago Cubs, features bronze-bordered posed color player photos on its fronts. The player's name, position, and team name appear at the bottom. The plain white back carries the player's name at the top, followed by biography and statistics.
COMPLETE SET (30) 5.00 2.00

1988 Glens Falls Tigers ProCards

This 27-card standard-size set of the 1988 Glens Falls Tigers, a Class AA Eastern League affiliate of the Detroit Tigers, features silver-bordered posed color player photos on its fronts. The player's name, position, and team name appear at the bottom. The plain white back carries the player's name at the top, followed by biography and statistics.
COMPLETE SET (27).................. 5.00 2.00

1988 Great Falls Dodgers Sports Pro

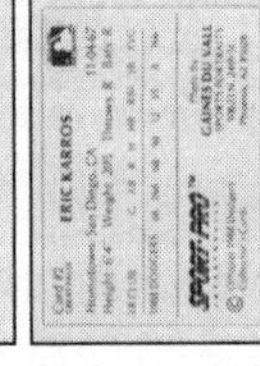

This issue includes the minor league card debut of Eric Karros. 4,000 sets were produced.
COMPLETE SET (27)............... 20.00 8.00

1988 Greensboro Hornets ProCards

This 26-card standard-size set of the 1988 Greensboro Hornets, a Class A South Atlantic League affiliate of the Cincinnati Reds, features bronze-bordered posed color player photos on its fronts. The player's name, position, and team name appear at the bottom. The plain white back carries the player's name at the top, followed by biography and statistics.
COMPLETE SET (26).................. 5.00 2.00

1988 Greenville Braves Best

This 24-card standard-size set of the 1988 Greenville Braves, a Class AA Southern League affiliate of the Atlanta Braves, features blue and black bordered posed color player photos on its fronts. The team name appears at the top, and below the picture is the player's name and position. The horizontal gray back carries the player's name and position at the top, followed by biography, career highlights, and statistics. The set is printed on thin card stock.
COMPLETE SET (24).................. 5.00 2.00

1988 Hagerstown Suns Star

COMPLETE SET (25).................. 5.00 2.00

1988 Hamilton Redbirds ProCards

This 30-card standard-size set of the 1988 Hamilton Redbirds, a Class A New York-Penn League affiliate of the St. Louis Cardinals, features bronze-bordered posed color player photos on its fronts. The player's name, position, and team name appear at the bottom. The plain white back carries the player's name at the top, followed by biography and statistics.
COMPLETE SET (30).................. 5.00 2.00

1988 Harrisburg Senators ProCards

This 30-card standard-size set of the 1988 Harrisburg Senators, a Class AA Eastern Coast League affiliate of the Pittsburgh Pirates, features silver-bordered posed color player photos on its fronts. The player's name, position, and team name appear at the bottom. The plain white back carries the player's name at the top, followed by biography and statistics.
COMPLETE SET (30).................. 8.00 3.20

1988 Huntsville Stars Team Issue

COMPLETE SET (25).................. 5.00 2.00

1988 Idaho Falls Braves ProCards

This 31-card standard-size set of the 1988 Idaho Falls Braves, a Rookie Class Pioneer League affiliate of the Atlanta Braves, features bronze-bordered posed color player photos on its fronts. The player's name, position, and team name appear at the bottom. The plain white back carries the player's name at the top, followed by biography and statistics.
COMPLETE SET (31).................. 5.00 2.00

1988 Indianapolis Indians CMC

10,000 sets were produced.
COMPLETE SET (25)............... 20.00 8.00

1988 Indianapolis Indians ProCards

This 31-card standard-size set of the 1988 Indianapolis Indians, a Class AAA American Association affiliate of the Montreal Expos, features gold-bordered posed color player photos on its fronts. The player's name, position, and team name appear at the bottom. The plain white back carries the player's name at the top, followed by biography and statistics.
COMPLETE SET (31)............... 25.00 10.00

1988 Iowa Cubs CMC

10,000 sets were produced.
COMPLETE SET (25)............... 10.00 4.00

1988 Iowa Cubs ProCards

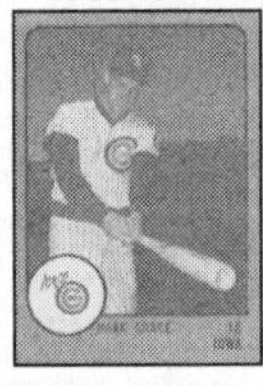
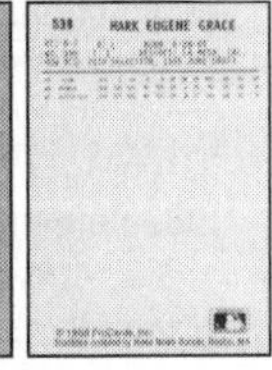

This 30-card standard-size set of the 1988 Iowa Cubs, a Class AAA American Association affiliate of the Chicago Cubs, features gold-bordered posed color player photos on its fronts. The player's name, position, and team name appear at the bottom. The plain white back carries the player's name at the top, followed by biography and statistics.
COMPLETE SET (30)............... 15.00 6.00

1988 Jackson Mets Grand Slam

COMPLETE SET (25).................. 5.00 2.00

1988 Jacksonville Expos Best

This 29-card standard-size set of the 1988 Jacksonville Expos, a Class AA Southern League affiliate of the Montreal Expos, features red and black bordered posed color player photos on its fronts. The team name appears at the top, and below the picture is the player's name and position. The horizontal gray back carries the player's name and position at the top, followed by biography, career highlights, and statistics. The set is printed on thin card stock.
COMPLETE SET (29).................. 5.00 2.00

1988 Jacksonville Expos ProCards

This 32-card standard-size set of the 1988 Jacksonville Expos, a Class AA Southern League affiliate of the Montreal Expos, features silver-bordered posed color player photos on its fronts. The player's name, position, and team name appear at the bottom. The plain white back carries the player's name at the top, followed by position, biography, and statistics. The set was sponsored by Golden Glove, a baseball card and sports memorabilia store.
COMPLETE SET (32).................. 5.00 2.00

1988 Jamestown Expos ProCards

This 31-card standard-size set of the 1988 Jamestown Expos, a Class A New York-Penn League affiliate of the Montreal Expos, features copper-bordered posed color player photos on its fronts. The player's name, position, and team name appear at the bottom. The plain white back carries the player's name and position at the top, followed by biography and statistics. The set was sponsored by Roach Photography. This issue includes the first cards of Marquis Grissom and Wil Cordero.
COMPLETE SET (31)............... 20.00 8.00

1988 Kenosha Twins ProCards

This 29-card standard-size set of the 1988 Kenosha Twins, a Class A Midwest League affiliate of the Minnesota Twins, features bronze-bordered posed color player photos on its fronts. The player's name, position, and team name appear at the bottom. The plain white back carries the player's name at the top, followed by biography and statistics.
COMPLETE SET (29).................. 5.00 2.00

1988 Kinston Indians Star

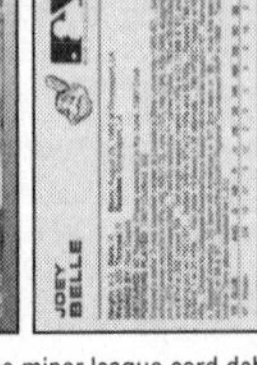

This issue includes the minor league card debut of Albert "Joey" Belle.
COMPLETE SET (24)............... 30.00 12.00

1988 Knoxville Blue Jays Best

This 26-card standard-size set of the 1988 Knoxville Blue Jays, a Class AA Southern League affiliate of the Toronto Blue Jays, features blue- and black- bordered posed color player photos on its fronts. The team name appears at the top, and below the picture is the player's name and position. The horizontal gray back carries the player's name and position at the top, followed by biography, career highlights, and statistics. The set is printed on thin card stock.
COMPLETE SET (26).................. 5.00 2.00

1988 Lakeland Tigers Star

COMPLETE SET (25).................. 5.00 2.00

1988 Las Vegas Stars CMC

This 25-card standard-size set of the 1988 Las Vegas Stars, a Class AAA Pacific Coast League affiliate of the San Diego Padres, features a second year card of Roberto Alomar. 10,000 sets were produced.
COMPLETE SET (25)............... 10.00 4.00

1988 Las Vegas Stars ProCards

This 28-card standard-size set of the 1988 Las Vegas Stars, a Class AAA Pacific Coast League affiliate of the San Diego Padres, features gold-bordered posed color player photos on its fronts. The player's name, position, and team name appear at the bottom. The plain white back carries the player's name at the top, followed by biography and statistics. This issue includes a second year card of Roberto Alomar.
COMPLETE SET (28)............... 15.00 6.00

1988 Little Falls Mets Pucko

This issue includes a second year card of Todd Hundley. 3,500 sets produced.
COMPLETE SET (29)............... 15.00 6.00

1988 Louisville Red Birds CMC

10,000 sets were produced.
COMPLETE SET (25).................. 4.00 1.60

1988 Louisville Red Birds ProCards

This 26-card standard-size set of the 1988 Louisville Red Birds, a Class AAA American Association affiliate of the St. Louis Cardinals, features gold-bordered posed color player photos on its fronts. The player's name, position, and team name appear at the bottom. The plain white back carries the player's name at the top, followed by biography and statistics.
COMPLETE SET (26).................. 5.00 2.00

1988 Louisville Red Birds Team Issue

COMPLETE SET (54).................. 5.00 2.00

1988 Lynchburg Red Sox Star

COMPLETE SET (27).................. 5.00 2.00

1988 Madison Muskies Police

Set was sponsored by T and J Cards and WKOW-TV.
COMPLETE SET (25).................. 8.00 3.20

1988 Maine Phillies CMC

10,000 sets were produced.
COMPLETE SET (25).................. 4.00 1.60

1988 Maine Phillies ProCards

This 27-card standard-size set of the 1988 Maine Phillies, a Class AAA International League affiliate of the Philadelphia Phillies, features gold-bordered posed color player photos on its fronts. The player's name, position, and team name appear at the bottom. The plain white back carries the player's name at the top, followed by biography and statistics.
COMPLETE SET (27).................. 5.00 2.00

1988 Martinsville Phillies Star

This set was issued with either blue borders or a scarcer, red-bordered version.
COMPLETE BLUE SET (32)........ 5.00 2.00
COMPLETE RED SET (32)........ 10.00 4.00

1988 Martinsville Phillies Star Red

COMPLETE RED SET (32).................. 4.50

1988 Memphis Chicks Best

This 27-card standard-size set of the 1988 Memphis Chicks, a Class AA Southern League affiliate of the Kansas City Royals, features blue and black bordered posed color player photos on its fronts. The team name appears at the top, and below the picture is the player's name and position. The horizontal gray back carries the player's name and position at the top, followed by biography, career highlights, and statistics. The set is printed on thin card stock.
COMPLETE SET (27).................. 5.00 2.00

1988 Miami Marlins Star

COMPLETE SET (24).................. 5.00 2.00

1988 Midland Angels Grand Slam

COMPLETE SET (25).................. 5.00 2.00

1988 Midwest League All-Stars Grand Slam

COMPLETE SET (59)............... 10.00 4.00

1988 Mississippi State Bulldogs

COMPLETE SET (39)............... 20.00 8.00

1988 Modesto A's Cal League Cards

COMPLETE SET (28).................. 5.00 2.00

1988 Modesto A's Team Issue

COMPLETE SET (36).................. 5.00 2.00

1988 Myrtle Beach Blue Jays ProCards

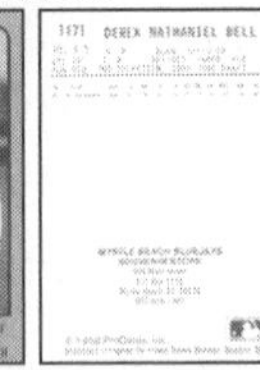

This 28-card standard-size set of the 1988 Myrtle Beach Blue Jays, a Class A South Atlantic League affiliate of the Toronto Blue Jays, features copper-bordered posed color player photos on its fronts. The player's name, position, and team name appear at the bottom. The plain white back carries the player's name at the top, followed by biography and statistics. The set was sponsored by Myrtle Beach Blue Jays Souvenir Store. This issue includes the first minor league card appearance of Derek Bell.
COMPLETE SET (28)............... 10.00 4.00

1988 Nashville Sounds CMC

10,000 sets were produced.
COMPLETE SET (25).................. 4.00 1.60

1988 Nashville Sounds ProCards

This 26-card standard-size set of the 1988 Nashville Sounds, a Class AAA American Association affiliate of the Cincinnati Reds, features gold-bordered posed color player photos on its fronts. The player's name, position, and team name appear at the bottom. The plain white back carries the player's name at the top, followed by biography and statistics.
COMPLETE SET (26).................. 5.00 2.00

1988 Nashville Sounds Team Issue

COMPLETE SET (25).................. 5.00 2.00

1988 Nebraska Cornhuskers

COMPLETE SET (27)............... 15.00 6.00

1988 New Britain Red Sox ProCards

This 25-card standard-size set of the 1988 New Britain Red Sox, a Class AA Eastern League affiliate of the Boston Red Sox, features silver-bordered posed color player photos on its fronts. The player's name, position, and team name appear at the bottom. The plain white back carries the player's name at the top, followed by biography and statistics. A third year card of Curt Schilling is in this set.
COMPLETE SET (25)............... 25.00 10.00

1988 Oklahoma City 89ers CMC

10,000 sets were produced.
COMPLETE SET (25).................. 5.00 2.00

1988 Oklahoma City 89ers ProCards

This 27-card standard-size set of the 1988 Oklahoma City 89ers, a Class AAA American Association affiliate of the Texas Rangers, features gold-bordered posed color player photos on its fronts. The player's name, position, and team name appear at the bottom. The plain white back carries the player's name at the top, followed by biography and statistics.
COMPLETE SET (27).................. 5.00 2.00

1988 Oklahoma Sooners

COMPLETE SET (24)............... 15.00 6.00

1988 Omaha Royals CMC

10,000 sets were produced.
COMPLETE SET (25).................. 5.00 2.00

1988 Omaha Royals ProCards

This 29-card standard-size set of the 1988 Omaha Royals, a Class AAA American Association affiliate of the Kansas City Royals, features gold-bordered posed color player photos on its fronts. The player's name, position, and team name appear at the bottom. The plain white back carries the player's name at the top, followed by biography and statistics.
COMPLETE SET (29).................. 5.00 2.00

1988 Oneonta Yankees ProCards

This 34-card standard-size set of the 1988 Oneonta Yankees, a Class A New York-Penn League affiliate of the New York Yankees, features bronze-bordered posed color player photos on its fronts. The player's name, position, and team name appear at the bottom. The plain white back carries the player's name at the top, followed by biography and statistics.
COMPLETE SET (34).................. 5.00 2.00

1988 Orlando Twins Best

This 29-card standard-size set of the 1988 Orlando Twins, a Class AA Southern League affiliate of the Minnesota Twins, features red and black bordered posed color player photos on its fronts. The team name appears at the top, and below the picture is the player's name and position. The horizontal gray back carries the player's name and position at the top, followed by biography, career highlights, and statistics. The set is printed on thin card stock.
COMPLETE SET (29).................. 5.00 2.00

1988 Osceola Astros Star

COMPLETE SET (25).................. 5.00 2.00

1988 Palm Springs Angels Cal League Cards

COMPLETE SET (31).................. 5.00 2.00

1988 Palm Springs Angels ProCards

This 32-card standard-size set of the 1988 Palm Springs Angels, a Class A California League affiliate of the California Angels, features bronze-bordered posed color player photos on its fronts. The player's name, position, and team name appear at the bottom. The plain white back carries the player's name at the top, followed by biography and statistics.
COMPLETE SET (32).................. 5.00 2.00

1988 Pawtucket Red Sox CMC

10,000 sets were produced.
COMPLETE SET (25).................. 4.00 1.60

1988 Pawtucket Red Sox ProCards

This 26-card standard-size set of the 1988 Pawtucket Red Sox, a Class AAA International League affiliate of the Boston Red Sox, features gold-bordered posed color player photos on its fronts. The player's name, position, and team name appear at the bottom. The plain white back carries the player's name at the top, followed by biography and statistics.
COMPLETE SET (26).................. 5.00 2.00

1988 Peninsula Oilers

This 31-card set of the 1988 Peninsula Oilers of the Alaska Central Baseball League features borderless color player photos printed on thick card stock. The backs carry player information. The cards are unnumbered and checklisted below in alphabetical order. An early card of John Olerud is featured in this set.
COMPLETE SET (31)............... 25.00 10.00

1988 Peoria Chiefs Team Issue

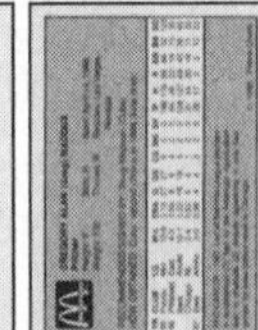

This issue includes third year cards of Mark Grace, Greg Maddux and Rafael Palmeiro. There is also a card of star Basketball player Hersey Hawkins, who attended Bradley University and led the nation in scoring.
COMPLETE SET (35)............... 40.00 16.00

1988 Phoenix Firebirds CMC

10,000 sets were produced.
COMPLETE SET (25)............... 10.00 4.00

1988 Phoenix Firebirds ProCards

This 29-card standard-size set of the 1988 Phoenix Firebirds, a Class AAA Pacific Coast League affiliate of the San Francisco Giants, features gold-bordered posed color player photos on its fronts. The player's name, position, and team name appear at the bottom. The plain white back carries the player's name at the top, followed by biography and statistics.
COMPLETE SET (29)............... 10.00 4.00

1988 Pittsfield Cubs ProCards

This 25-card standard-size set of the 1988 Pittsfield Cubs, a Class AA Eastern League affiliate of the Chicago Cubs, features silver-bordered posed color player photos on its fronts. The player's name, position, and team name appear at the bottom. The plain white back carries the player's name at the top, followed by biography and statistics.
COMPLETE SET (25)................. 5.00 2.00

1988 Pocatello Giants ProCards

This 31-card standard-size set of the 1988 Pocatello Giants, a Rookie Class Pioneer League affiliate of the San Francisco Giants, features bronze-bordered posed color player photos on its fronts. The player's name, position, and team name appear at the bottom. The plain white back carries the player's name at the top, followed by biography and statistics.
COMPLETE SET (31)................. 5.00 2.00

1988 Portland Beavers CMC

10,000 sets were produced.
COMPLETE SET (25)................. 4.00 1.60

1988 Portland Beavers ProCards

This 27-card standard-size set of the 1988 Portland Beavers, a Class AAA Pacific Coast League affiliate of the Minnesota Twins, features gold-bordered posed color player photos on its fronts. The player's name, position, and team name appear at the bottom. The plain white back carries the player's name at the top, followed by biography and statistics.
COMPLETE SET (27)................. 5.00 2.00

1988 Prince William Yankees Star

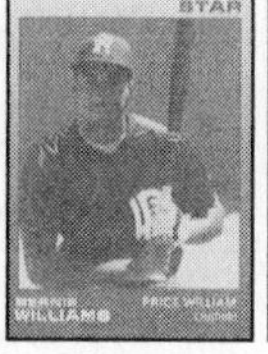

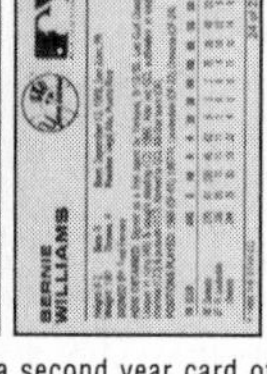

This issue includes a second year card of Bernie Williams.
COMPLETE SET (25)................ 20.00 8.00

1988 Pulaski Braves ProCards

This 25-card standard-size set of the 1988 Pulaski Braves, a Rookie Class Appalachian League affiliate of the Atlanta Braves, features bronze-bordered posed color player photos on its fronts. The player's name, position, and team name appear at the bottom. The plain white back carries the player's name at the top, followed by biography and statistics.
COMPLETE SET (25)................. 5.00 2.00

1988 Quad City Angels Grand Slam

COMPLETE SET (30)................. 5.00 2.00

1988 Reading Phillies ProCards

This 27-card standard-size set of the 1988 Reading Phillies, a Class AA Eastern League affiliate of the Philadelphia Phillies, features silver-bordered posed color player photos on its fronts. The player's name, position, and team name appear at the bottom. The plain white back carries the player's name at the top, followed by biography and statistics.
COMPLETE SET (27)................. 5.00 2.00

1988 Reno Silver Sox Cal League Cards

COMPLETE SET (24)................. 5.00 2.00

1988 Richmond Braves Bob's Camera

This 29-card team set of the 1989 Richmond Braves, a Class AAA International League affiliate of the Atlanta Braves, was sponsored by Bob's Camera. The fronts feature borderless color player photos with sponsors' and team's logos in the wide bottom margin. The backs are blank. This issue includes third year cards of Dave Justice, Ron Gant and John Smoltz. 500 sets were produced.
COMPLETE SET (25).............. 100.00 40.00

1988 Richmond Braves CMC

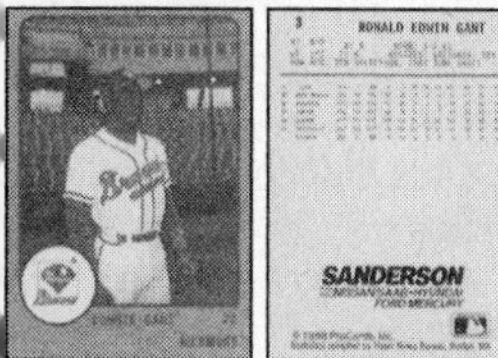

This issue includes third year cards of Dave Justice, Ron Gant and John Smoltz.
COMPLETE SET (25)................ 10.00 4.00

1988 Richmond Braves ProCards

This 27-card standard-size set of the 1988 Richmond Braves, a Class AAA International League affiliate of the Atlanta Braves, features gold-bordered posed color player photos on its fronts. The player's name, position, and team name appear at the bottom. The plain white back carries the player's name at the top, followed by biography and statistics. This issue includes third year cards of Dave Justice, Ron Gant and John Smoltz.
COMPLETE SET (27)................ 25.00 10.00

1988 Riverside Red Wave Cal League Cards

COMPLETE SET (28)................. 5.00 2.00

1988 Riverside Red Wave ProCards

This 27-card standard-size set of the 1988 Riverside Red Wave, a Class A California League affiliate of the San Diego Padres, features gold-bordered posed color player photos on its fronts. The player's name, position, and team name appear at the bottom. The plain white back carries the player's name at the top, followed by biography and statistics.
COMPLETE SET (27)................. 5.00 2.00

1988 Rochester Red Wings CMC

10,000 sets were produced.
COMPLETE SET (25)................. 4.00 1.60

1988 Rochester Red Wings Governor's Cup Pucko

1,200 sets were produced.
COMPLETE SET (36)................ 15.00 6.00

1988 Rochester Red Wings ProCards

This 30-card standard-size set of the 1988 Rochester Red Wings, a Class AAA International League affiliate of the Baltimore Orioles, features gold-bordered posed color player photos on its fronts. The player's name, position, and team name appear at the bottom. The plain white back carries the player's name at the top, followed by biography and statistics.
COMPLETE SET (30)................. 5.00 2.00

1988 Rochester Red Wings Team Issue

COMPLETE SET (26)................ 10.00 4.00

1988 Rockford Expos Litho Center

Printed by Rockford Litho Center, this 34-card standard-size set of the 1988 Rockford Expos, a Class A Midwest League affiliate of the Montreal Expos, features on its white-bordered fronts posed color player photos set on red backgrounds. The player's name and position appear within a yellow diagonal stripe at the lower right. The white horizontal back is framed by a black line and carries the player's name and uniform number at the top, followed by biography and the name of the sponsor, Rockford Magazine. This issue includes Delino DeShields' first team set appearance. The cards are unnumbered and checklisted below in alphabetical order.
COMPLETE SET (34)................. 5.00 2.00

1988 Salem Buccaneers Star

COMPLETE SET (25)................. 5.00 2.00

1988 Salt Lake City Trappers Team Issue

COMPLETE SET (31)................. 8.00 3.20

1988 San Antonio Missions Best

This 28-card standard-size set of the 1988 San Antonio Missions, a Class AA Texas League affiliate of the Los Angeles Dodgers, features blue and black bordered posed color player photos on its fronts. The team name appears at the top, and below the picture is the player's name and position. The horizontal gray back carries the player's name and position at the top, followed by biography, career highlights, and statistics. The set is printed on thin card stock. Only 1300 platinum sets were produced.
COMPLETE SET (28)................. 5.00 2.00
COMPLETE PLATINUM SET (28) 12.00 4.80

1988 San Bernardino Spirit Best

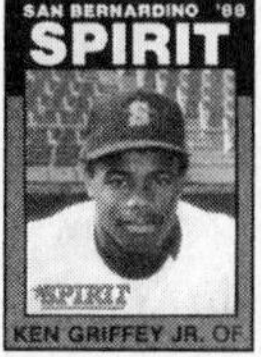

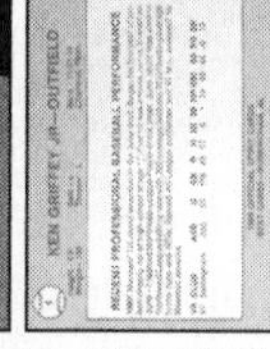

This 28-card standard-size set of the 1988 San Bernardino Spirit, a Class A California League affiliate of the Seattle Mariners, features blue and black bordered posed color player photos on its fronts. The team name appears at the top, and below the picture is the player's name and position. The horizontal gray back carries the player's name and position at the top, followed by biography, career highlights, and statistics. The set is printed on thin card stock. 5,000 sets were produced. Only 1300 platinum sets were produced. This issue includes a second year card of Ken Griffey Jr.
COMPLETE SET (28)............. 120.00 70.00

1988 San Bernardino Spirit Cal League Cards

This 28-card standard-size set of the 1988 San Bernardino Spirit, a Class A California League affiliate of the Seattle Mariners, features a second year card of Ken Griffey Jr. 10,000 sets were produced.
COMPLETE SET (28)............... 30.00 16.00

1988 San Diego State Aztecs All-Time Greats

Honoring the best players from San Diego State, standard size, black inner border and white outer border with "SDSU" and school mascot in red at top. Cards are unnumbered but are ordered below alphabetically for reference.
COMPLETE SET (22)............... 20.00 8.00

1988 San Jose Giants Cal League Cards

COMPLETE SET (29)................. 5.00 2.00

1988 San Jose Giants ProCards

This 30-card standard-size set of the 1988 San Jose Giants, a Class A California League affiliate of the San Francisco Giants, features bronze-bordered posed color player photos on its fronts. The player's name, position, and team name appear at the bottom. The plain white back carries the player's name at the top, followed by biography and statistics.
COMPLETE SET (30)................. 5.00 2.00

1988 Savannah Cardinals ProCards

This 29-card standard-size set of the 1988 Savannah Cardinals, a Class A South Atlantic League affiliate of the St. Louis Cardinals, features bronze-bordered posed color player photos on its fronts. The player's name, position, and team name appear at the bottom. The plain white back carries the player's name at the top, followed by biography and statistics.
COMPLETE SET (29)................. 5.00 2.00

1988 Shreveport Captains ProCards

This 25-card standard-size set of the 1988 Shreveport Captains, a Class AA Texas League affiliate of the San Francisco Giants, features silver-bordered posed color player photos on its fronts. The player's name, position, and team name appear at the bottom. The plain white back carries the player's name at the top, followed by biography and statistics.
COMPLETE SET (25)................. 5.00 2.00

1988 South Atlantic League All-Stars Grand Slam

COMPLETE SET (28)................. 8.00 3.20

1988 South Bend White Sox Grand Slam

COMPLETE SET (28)................. 5.00 2.00

1988 Southern League All-Stars Jennings

COMPLETE SET (40)................. 5.00 2.00

1988 Southern Oregon A's ProCards

This 28-card standard-size set of the 1988 Southern Oregon A's, a Class A Northwest League affiliate of the Oakland Athletics, features bronze-bordered posed color player photos on its fronts. The player's name, position, and team name appear at the bottom. The plain white back carries the player's name at the top, followed by biography and statistics.
COMPLETE SET (28)................. 5.00 2.00

1988 Spartanburg Phillies ProCards

This 26-card standard-size set of the 1988 Spartanburg Phillies, a Class A South Atlantic League affiliate of the Philadelphia Phillies, features bronze-bordered posed color player photos on its fronts. The player's name, position, and team name appear at the bottom. The plain white back carries the player's name at the top, followed by biography and statistics.
COMPLETE SET (26)................. 5.00 2.00

1988 Spartanburg Phillies Star

This set was issued with either red borders or a scarcer, blue-bordered version. 2,500 sets were produced.
COMPLETE RED SET (24).......... 4.00 1.60
COMPLETE BLUE SET (24)...... 10.00 4.00

1988 Spokane Indians ProCards

This 26-card standard-size set of the 1988 Spokane Indians, a Class A Northwest League affiliate of the San Diego Padres, features bronze-bordered posed color player photos on its fronts. The player's name, position, and team name appear at the bottom. The plain white back carries the player's name at the top, followed by biography and statistics.
COMPLETE SET (26)................. 5.00 2.00

1988 Springfield Cardinals Best

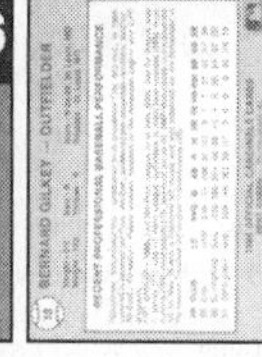

This 28-card standard-size set of the 1988 Springfield Cardinals, a Class A Midwest League affiliate of the St. Louis Cardinals, features red and black bordered posed color player photos on its fronts. The team name appears at the top, and below the picture is the player's name and position. The horizontal gray back carries the player's name and position at the top, followed by biography, career highlights, and statistics. The set is printed on thin card stock. This issue includes the minor league card debut of Ray Lankford and a second year card of Bernard Gilkey.
COMPLETE SET (28)................ 20.00 8.00

1988 St. Catharines Blue Jays ProCards

Sponsored by The Standard, this 35-card standard-size set of the 1988 St. Catharines Blue Jays, a Class A New York-Penn League affiliate of the Toronto Blue Jays, features bronze-bordered posed color player photos on its fronts. The player's name, position, and team name appear at the bottom. The plain white back carries the player's name and position at the top, followed by biography and statistics.
COMPLETE SET (35)................. 5.00 2.00

1988 St. Lucie Mets Star

COMPLETE SET (25)................. 5.00 2.00

1988 St. Petersburg Cardinals Star

COMPLETE SET (25)................. 5.00 2.00

1988 Stockton Ports Cal League Cards

COMPLETE SET (31)................. 5.00 2.00

1988 Stockton Ports ProCards

This 33-card standard-size set of the 1988 Stockton Ports, a Class A California League affiliate of the Milwaukee Brewers, features bronze-bordered posed color player photos on its fronts. The player's name, position, and team name appear at the bottom. The plain white back carries the player's name at the top, followed by biography and statistics.
COMPLETE SET (33)................. 5.00 2.00

1988 Sumter Braves ProCards

This 32-card standard-size set of the 1988 Sumter Braves, a Class A South Atlantic League affiliate of the Atlanta Braves, features bronze-bordered posed color player photos on its fronts. The player's name, position, and team name appear at the bottom. The plain white back carries the player's name at the top, followed by biography and statistics.
COMPLETE SET (32)................. 5.00 2.00

1988 Syracuse Chiefs CMC

This 25-card standard-size set of the 1988 Syracuse Chiefs, a Class AAA International League affiliate of the Toronto Blue Jays, features on its fronts black-bordered posed color player photos framed by a red line. The team's name, the player's name, and his position appear at the bottom. The white back is framed by a black line and carries the team's name and league at the top, followed by the player's name, biography and statistics. 10,000 sets were produced.
COMPLETE SET (25)................. 4.00 1.60

1988 Syracuse Chiefs ProCards

This 30-card standard-size set of the 1988 Syracuse Chiefs, a Class AAA International League affiliate of the Toronto Blue Jays, features gold-bordered posed color player photos on its fronts. The player's name, position, and team name appear at the bottom. The plain white back carries the player's name at the top, followed by biography and statistics.
COMPLETE SET (30)................. 5.00 2.00

1988 Tacoma Tigers CMC

10,000 sets were produced.
COMPLETE SET (25)................. 4.00 1.60

1988 Tacoma Tigers ProCards

This 28-card standard-size set of the 1988 Tacoma Tigers, a Class AAA Pacific Coast League affiliate of the Oakland A's, features bronze-bordered posed color player photos on its fronts. The player's name, position, and team name appear at the bottom. The plain white back carries the player's name at the top, followed by biography and statistics.
COMPLETE SET (28)................. 5.00 2.00

1988 Tampa Tarpons Star

COMPLETE SET (24)................. 4.00 1.60
COMPLETE SET (26)................. 6.00 2.40

1988 Texas League All-Stars Grand Slam

COMPLETE SET (39)................ 15.00 6.00

1988 Tidewater Tides Candl

Set was produced as a perforated sheet with a team photo at the top.
COMPLETE SET (30)................ 15.00 6.00

1988 Tidewater Tides CMC

10,000 sets were produced. Approximately, 2,000 of the sets contain the Gregg Jefferies error card.
COMPLETE SET (25)................. 8.00 3.20
COMPLETE SET W/ERROR (25) 15.00 6.00

1988 Tidewater Tides ProCards

This 29-card standard-size set of the 1988 Tidewater Tides, a Class AAA International League affiliate of the New York Mets, features gold-bordered posed color player photos on its fronts. The player's name, position, and team name appear at the bottom. The plain white back carries the player's name at the top, followed by biography and statistics.
COMPLETE SET (29)................. 8.00 3.20

1988 Toledo Mud Hens CMC

10,000 sets were produced.
COMPLETE SET (25)................. 4.00 1.60

1988 Toledo Mud Hens ProCards

This 28-card standard-size set of the 1988 Toledo Mud Hens, a Class AAA International League affiliate of the Detroit Tigers, features gold-bordered posed color player photos on its fronts. The player's name, position, and team name appear at the bottom. The plain white back carries the player's name at the top, followed by biography and statistics.
COMPLETE SET (28)................. 5.00 2.00

1988 Triple A All-Stars CMC

These cards have a copyright date of 1989.
COMPLETE SET (45)................ 10.00 4.00

1988 Triple A All-Stars ProCards

COMPLETE SET (55)................ 10.00 4.00

1988 Tucson Toros CMC

This issue includes the minor league card debut of Craig Biggio and a fourth year card of Ken Caminiti. 10,000 sets were produced.
COMPLETE SET (25)................ 10.00 4.00

1988 Tucson Toros Jones Photo

Produced by Jones Photo. The cards are unnumbered so they are ordered below in alphabetical order. A complete set could only be obtained by attending all five promotional giveaway nights at the ballpark. The cards measure 5" by 7" and are full color photos of the players. This issue includes the minor league card debut of Craig Biggio and a fourth year card of Ken Caminiti. 400 sets were produced.
COMPLETE SET (24)................ 80.00 32.00

1988 Tucson Toros ProCards

This 28-card standard-size set of the 1988 Tucson Toros, a Class AAA Pacific Coast League affiliate of the Houston Astros, features gold-bordered posed color player photos on its fronts. The player's name, position, and team name appear at the bottom. The plain white back carries the player's name at the top, followed by biography and statistics. This issue includes the minor league card debut of Craig Biggio and a fourth year card of Ken Caminiti.
COMPLETE SET (28)................ 15.00 6.00

1988 Tulsa Drillers Team Issue

COMPLETE SET (28)................ 20.00 8.00

1988 Utica Blue Sox Pucko

3,500 sets were produced.
COMPLETE SET (29)................. 5.00 2.00

1988 Vancouver Canadians CMC

This 25-card standard-size set of the 1988 Vancouver Canadians, a Class AAA Pacific

Coast League affiliate of the Chicago White Sox, features on its fronts black-bordered posed color player photos framed by a green line. The team's name, the player's name, and his position appear at the bottom. The white back is framed by a black line and carries the team's name and league at the top, followed by the player's name, biography and statistics. 10,000 sets were produced.
COMPLETE SET (25)................. 4.00 1.60

1988 Vancouver Canadians ProCards

This 27-card standard-size set of the 1988 Vancouver Canadians, a Class AAA Pacific Coast League affiliate of the Chicago White Sox, features gold-bordered posed color player photos on its fronts. The player's name, position, and team name appear at the bottom. The plain white back carries the player's name at the top, followed by biography and statistics.
COMPLETE SET (27)................. 5.00 2.00

1988 Vermont Mariners ProCards

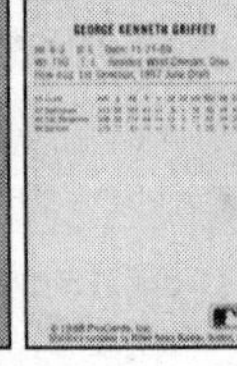

This 27-card standard-size set of the 1988 Vermont Mariners, a Class AA Eastern League affiliate of the Seattle Mariners, features silver-bordered posed color player photos on its fronts. The player's name, position, and team name appear at the bottom. The plain white back carries the player's name at the top, followed by biography and statistics. A late issue promotional card of Ken Griffey Jr. was also produced by ProCards in 1988 but is not considered part of this set. The Griffey card has a red border and was printed off center. Perfectly centered counterfeit copies exist.
COMPLETE SET (27)................. 10.00 4.00

1988 Vero Beach Dodgers Star

COMPLETE SET (26)................. 4.00 1.60
COMPLETE SET (27)................. 6.00 2.40

1988 Virginia Generals Star

COMPLETE SET (23)................. 5.00 2.00

1988 Visalia Oaks Cal League Cards

COMPLETE SET (30)................. 5.00 2.00

1988 Visalia Oaks ProCards

This 28-card standard-size set of the 1988 Visalia Oaks, a Class A California League affiliate of the Minnesota Twins, features bronze-bordered posed color player photos on its fronts. The player's name, position, and team name appear at the bottom. The plain white back carries the player's name at the top, followed by biography and statistics.
COMPLETE SET (28)................. 5.00 2.00

1988 Waterloo Indians ProCards

This 29-card standard-size set of the 1988 Waterloo Indians, a Class A Midwest League affiliate of the Cleveland Indians, features bronze-bordered posed color player photos on its fronts. The player's name, position, and team name appear at the bottom. The plain white back carries the player's name at the top, followed by biography and statistics.
COMPLETE SET (29)................. 5.00 2.00

1988 Watertown Pirates Pucko

3,500 sets were produced.
COMPLETE SET (35)................. 5.00 2.00

1988 Wausau Timbers Grand Slam

COMPLETE SET (28)................. 5.00 2.00

1988 West Palm Beach Expos Star

This 27-card standard-size set of the 1988 West Palm Beach Expos, a Class A Florida State League affiliate of the Montreal Expos, features turquoise-bordered posed color player photos on its fronts. The player's name, team name, and position appear at the bottom. The yellowish horizontal back carries the player's name at the top, followed by biography, career highlights, and statistics. The Felipe Alou card was a late issue.
COMPLETE SET (27)................. 5.00 2.00

1988 Wichita Pilots Rock's Dugout

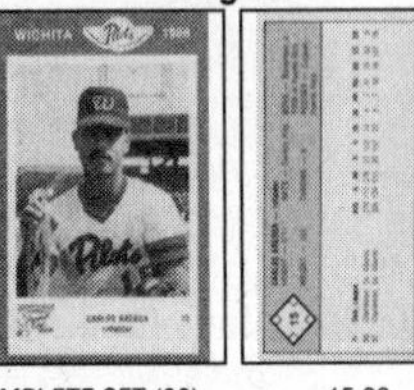

COMPLETE SET (30)................ 15.00 6.00

1988 Williamsport Bills ProCards

This 27-card standard-size set of the 1988 Williamsport Bills, a Class AA Eastern League affiliate of the Cleveland Indians, features silver-bordered posed color player photos on its fronts. The player's name, position, and team name appear at the bottom. The plain white back carries the player's name at the top, followed by biography and statistics.
COMPLETE SET (27)................. 5.00 2.00

1988 Winston-Salem Spirits Star

COMPLETE SET (22)................. 5.00 2.00

1988 Winter Haven Red Sox Star

COMPLETE SET (27)................. 5.00 2.00

1988 Wytheville Cubs ProCards

This 31-card standard-size set of the 1988 Wytheville Cubs, a Rookie Class Appalachian League affiliate of the Chicago Cubs, features bronze-bordered posed color player photos on its fronts. The player's name, position, and team name appear at the bottom. The plain white back carries the player's name at the top, followed by biography and statistics.
COMPLETE SET (31)................. 5.00 2.00

1989 Alaska Goldpanners

COMPLETE SET (20)................. 8.00 3.20

1989 Alaska Goldpanners All-Time AS '80s Team Issue

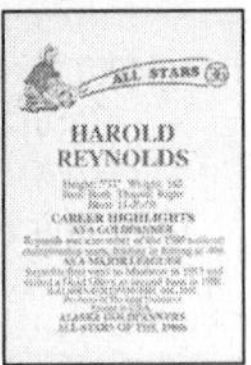

This 12-card blue-bordered set features 12 players from the Alaska Goldpanners that made the Major Leagues during the 1980's. Please note that these cards are numbered 25-36.
COMPLETE SET (12)

1989 Albany Yankees Best

The 1989 Albany Yankees set contains 30 standard-size cards. The fronts have posed color player photos with white borders. The year "1989" and the city are written vertically on the left side of the card, and the player's name and position are given below the picture. In a horizontal format, the backs have biography, recent professional baseball performance summary (including statistics), and a color headshot, all in a yellow rectangular box. This issue includes the minor league card debut of Deion Sanders.
COMPLETE SET (30)................ 15.00 6.00

1989 Albany Yankees ProCards

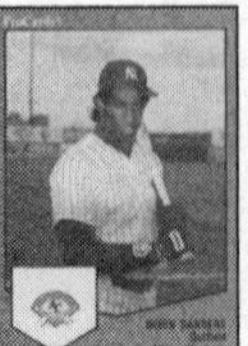
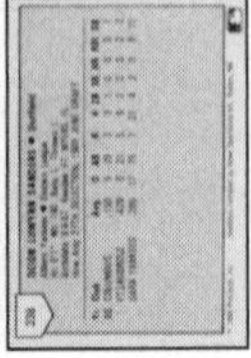

This 29-card standard-size set of the 1989 Albany Yankees, a Class AA Eastern League affiliate of the New York Yankees, features red-bordered posed color player photos on its fronts. The player's name, position, and team name appear at the bottom. The horizontal gray back carries the player's name and position at the top, followed by biography and statistics. This issue includes the minor league card debut of Deion Sanders.
COMPLETE SET (29)................ 15.00 6.00

1989 Albany Yankees Star

The 1989 Albany-Colonie Yankees set contains 23 standard-size cards. The fronts have posed color player photos, with purple borders on the top portion of the card fading to yellow as one moves down the card face. In purple print on a

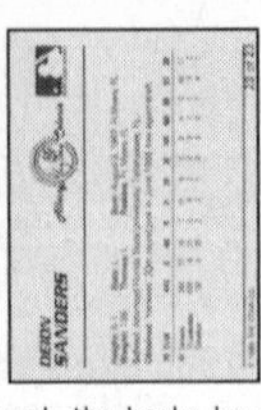

pale yellow background, the backs have biography and statistics. The Sanders card was not delivered with the original set; it has black in place of purple and appears out of alphabetical order. This issue includes the minor league card debut of Deion Sanders. 5,000 sets produced.
COMPLETE SET (23)................ 15.00 6.00

1989 Albuquerque Dukes CMC

COMPLETE SET (25)................. 5.00 2.00

1989 Albuquerque Dukes ProCards

This 30-card standard-size set of the 1989 Albuquerque Dukes, a Class AAA Pacific Coast League affiliate of the Los Angeles Dodgers, features blue-bordered posed color player photos on its fronts. The player's name, position, and team name appear at the bottom. The horizontal gray back carries the player's name and position at the top, followed by biography and statistics.
COMPLETE SET (30)................. 5.00 2.00

1989 Anchorage Bucs Team Issue

Produced by the Anchorage Bucs Baseball Club Inc., this 29-card standard-size set features the 1989 Bucs team. On a yellow ochre card face, the fronts feature color player portraits with a thin black border. The team name is printed above the photo, while the player's name and number appear below the photo. The backs carry a short player biography and the team logo.
COMPLETE SET (29)................. 8.00 3.20

1989 Anchorage Glacier Pilots

COMPLETE SET (35)................. 8.00 3.20

1989 Appleton Foxes ProCards

This 31-card standard-size set of the 1989 Appleton Foxes, a Class A Midwest League affiliate of the Kansas City Royals, features orange-bordered posed color player photos on its fronts. The player's name, position, and team name appear at the bottom. The horizontal gray back carries the player's name and position at the top, followed by biography and statistics.
COMPLETE SET (31)................. 5.00 2.00

1989 Arizona State Boosters

COMPLETE SET (30)................ 10.00 4.00

1989 Arkansas Travelers Grand Slam

COMPLETE SET (25)................ 10.00 4.00

1989 Asheville Tourists ProCards

This 30-card standard-size set of the 1989 Asheville Tourists, a Class A South Atlantic League affiliate of the Houston Astros, features orange-bordered posed color player photos on its fronts. The player's name, position, and team name appear at the bottom. The horizontal gray back carries the player's name and position at the top, followed by biography and statistics.
COMPLETE SET (30)................. 5.00 2.00

1989 Auburn Astros ProCards

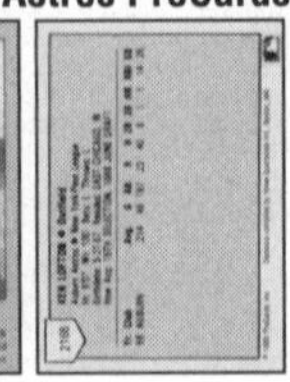

This 31-card standard-size set of the 1989 Auburn Astros, a Class A New York-Penn League affiliate of the Houston Astros, features orange-bordered posed color player photos on its fronts. The player's name, position, and team name appear at the bottom. The horizontal gray back carries the player's name and position at the top, followed by biography and statistics. This issue includes a second year card of Kenny Lofton.
COMPLETE SET (31)................ 15.00 6.00

1989 Augusta Pirates ProCards

This 32-card standard-size set of the 1989 Augusta Pirates, a Class A South Atlantic League affiliate of the Pittsburgh Pirates, features orange-bordered posed color player photos on its fronts. The player's name, position, and team name appear at the bottom. The horizontal gray back carries the player's name and position at the top, followed by biography and statistics.
COMPLETE SET (32)................. 5.00 2.00

1989 Bakersfield Dodgers Cal League Cards

This issue includes a second year card of Eric Karros.
COMPLETE SET (29)................. 5.00 2.00

1989 Baseball America AA Prospects Best

This 31-card standard-size set features top AA prospects from the Eastern League, the Southern League, and the Texas League. The fronts of the cards feature posed color player photos, with a red border on the top half of the card and a white border on the bottom half. Player information appears in black print below the picture. The words "1989 Top AA Prospects" in red lettering round out the card face at the bottom. The horizontally oriented backs have black print on gray and white, and present biography and statistics. Future major league stars in the set include Sammy Sosa, Juan Gonzalez, Robin Ventura, and Marquis Grissom.
COMPLETE SET (31)................ 40.00 16.00

1989 Baseball City Royals Star

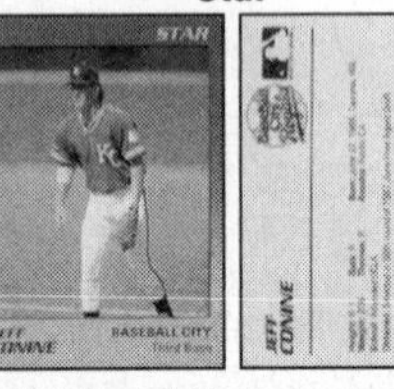

The 1989 Baseball City Royals set contains 26 standard-size cards. The fronts have posed color player photos, with purple borders on the top portion of the card fading to gray as one moves down the card face. In purple print on a gray background, the backs have biography and statistics. Card number 25 was never issued. This issue includes a second year card of Jeff Conine. 5,000 sets produced.
COMPLETE SET (26)................ 10.00 4.00

1989 Batavia Clippers ProCards

This 31-card standard-size set of the 1989 Batavia Clippers, a Class A New York-Penn League affiliate of the Philadelphia Phillies, features orange-bordered posed color player photos on its fronts. The player's name, position, and team name appear at the bottom. The horizontal gray back carries the player's name and position at the top, followed by biography and statistics.
COMPLETE SET (31)................. 5.00 2.00

1989 Bellingham Mariners Legoe

The 1989 Bellingham Mariners set consists of 37 standard-size cards. The glossy color player photos are enframed by yellow and blue borders, while the card face itself is light blue. On a light blue background decorated with white baseballs across the top, the horizontally oriented backs have biography, complete Minor League record, and a "Did You Know?" trivia feature.
COMPLETE SET (37)................. 5.00 2.00

1989 Beloit Brewers I Star

The 1989 Beloit Brewers set contains 26 standard-size cards. The fronts have posed color player photos, with blue borders on the top portion of the card fading to yellow as one moves down the card face. In blue print on a pale yellow background, the backs have biography and statistics. 5,000 sets produced.
COMPLETE SET (26)................. 5.00 2.00

1989 Beloit Brewers II Star

The 1989 Beloit Brewers set contains 25 standard-size cards. The fronts have posed color player photos, with yellow borders on the top portion of the card fading to blue as one moves down the card face. In blue print on a pale yellow background, the backs have biography and statistics. 5,000 sets produced.
COMPLETE SET (25)................. 5.00 2.00

1989 Bend Bucks Legoe

The 1989 Bend Bucks set consists of 30 standard-size cards. The front design features a mix of posed or action color player photos, with a thin black border on a white card face. In black print on white, the backs have brief

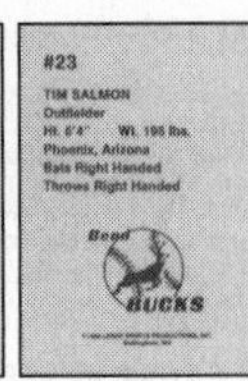

biographical information and the team logo. This issue includes the minor league card debut of Tim Salmon.
COMPLETE SET (30)................ 20.00 8.00

1989 Billings Mustangs ProCards

This 31-card standard-size set of the 1989 Billings Mustangs, a Rookie Class Pioneer League affiliate of the Cincinnati Reds, features orange-bordered posed color player photos on its fronts. The player's name, position, and team name appear at the bottom. The horizontal gray back carries the player's name and position at the top, followed by biography and statistics.
COMPLETE SET (31)................. 8.00 3.20

1989 Birmingham Barons All Decade Best

COMPLETE SET (34)................. 8.00 3.20

1989 Birmingham Barons Best

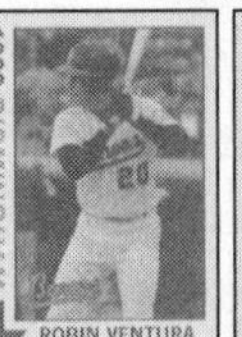

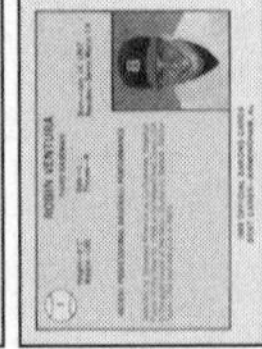

This 30-card standard-size set features the 1989 Birmingham Barons, a farm club for the Chicago White Sox. The fronts have posed color player photos with white borders. The year "1989" and the city are written vertically on the left side of the card, and the player's name and position are given below the picture. In horizontal format, the backs have biography recent professional baseball performance summary (including statistics), and a color headshot, all in a yellow rectangular box. The Platinum version sets were limited to production run of 1,500.
COMPLETE SET (30)............... 15.00 6.00

1989 Birmingham Barons ProCards

This 31-card standard-size set of the 198 Birmingham Barons, a Class AA Southern League affiliate of the Chicago White Sox features red-bordered posed color player photos on its fronts. The player's name position, and team name appear at the bottom The horizontal gray back carries the player' name and position at the top, followed by biography and statistics.
COMPLETE SET (31)............... 10.00 4.00

1989 Bluefield Orioles Star

The 1989 Bluefield Orioles set contains 3 standard-size cards. The fronts have posed color player photos, with black borders on the top portion of the card fading to orange as one moves down the card face. In black print on pale orange background, the backs have brief biographical information. Card numbers 26-3 were issued later, and the color of their border is reversed (orange at top fading to black). The cards are arranged alphabetically and numbered on the back "X of 31." Card number 31 was never issued. 5,000 sets produced.
COMPLETE SET (30)................. 5.00 2.00

1989 Boise Hawks ProCards

This 31-card standard-size set of the 198 Boise Hawks, a Class A Northwest League Independent, features orange-bordered posed color player photos on its fronts. The player' name, position, and team name appear at the bottom. The horizontal gray back carries the player's name and position at the top, followed by biography and statistics.
COMPLETE SET (31)................. 5.00 2.00

1989 Bristol Tigers Star

The 1989 Bristol Tigers set contains 3 standard-size cards. The fronts have posed color player photos, with blue borders on the top portion of the card fading to orange as one moves down the card face. In blue print on pale orange background, the backs have biography and statistics. 5,000 sets produced.
COMPLETE SET (31)................. 5.00 2.00

1989 Buffalo Bisons CMC

COMPLETE SET (25)................. 5.00 2.00

1989 Buffalo Bisons ProCards

This 27-card standard-size set of the 198 Buffalo Bisons, a Class AAA American Association affiliate of the Pittsburgh Pirates features orange-bordered posed color player photos on its fronts. The player's name

position, and team name appear at the bottom. The horizontal gray back carries the player's name and position at the top, followed by biography and statistics.
COMPLETE SET (27).................. 5.00 2.00

1989 Bull Durham Orion Set

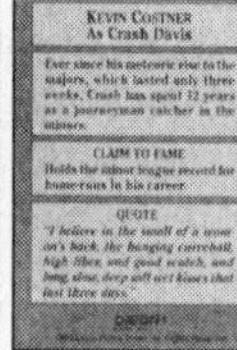

This six-card set features color photos of the cast of the movie, "Bull Durham." The backs carry information about the character, his "Claim to Fame" according to the movie, one of his lines from the movie, and the name of the performer who plays the character. The cards are unnumbered and checklisted below in alphabetical order.
COMPLETE SET (6).................. 10.00 4.00

1989 Burlington Braves ProCards

This 32-card standard-size set of the 1989 Burlington Braves, a Class A Midwest League affiliate of the Atlanta Braves, features orange-bordered posed color player photos on its fronts. The player's name, position, and team name appear at the bottom. The horizontal gray back carries the player's name and position at the top, followed by biography and statistics.
COMPLETE SET (32).................. 5.00 2.00

1989 Burlington Braves Star

The 1989 Burlington Braves set contains 29 standard-size cards. The fronts have posed color player photos, with red borders on the top portion of the card fading to purple as one moves down the card face. In purple print on a pale pink background, the backs have personal information, how the player was obtained, and statistics. Card numbers 26-29 have different color lettering on the fronts than the other cards. The cards are arranged alphabetically and numbered on the back "X of 30." Card number 30 was never issued. 5,000 sets produced.
COMPLETE SET (29).................. 5.00 2.00

1989 Burlington Indians Star

The 1989 Burlington Indians set contains 29 standard-size cards. The fronts have posed color player photos, with blue borders on the top portion of the card fading to red as one moves down the card face. In blue print on a pink background, the backs have biography and statistics. 5,000 sets produced.
COMPLETE SET (29).................. 5.00 2.00

1989 Butte Copper Kings Sports Pro

The 1989 Butte Copper Kings set consists of 30 standard-size cards. The front design has posed color player photos (shot from the waist up), with a thin black border on a white card face. The team logo adorns the card above the picture, and the player's name and position appear at the card bottom. In a horizontal format, the backs provide brief biographical information.
COMPLETE SET (30).................. 5.00 2.00

1989 Calgary Cannons CMC

This 25-card standard-size set of the 1989 Calgary Cannons, a Class AAA Pacific Coast League affiliate of the Seattle Mariners, features on its fronts white-bordered posed color player photos framed by a black line. The team's name, the player's name, and his position appear at the bottom. The white back is framed by a black line and carries the team's name and league at the top, followed by the player's name, biography and statistics. Cards 13, 24, and 25 bear incorrect copyright dates, 1988.
COMPLETE SET (25).................. 5.00 2.00

1989 Calgary Cannons ProCards

This 24-card standard-size set of the 1989 Calgary Cannons, a Class AAA Pacific Coast League affiliate of the Seattle Mariners, features blue-bordered posed color player photos on its fronts. The player's name, position, and team name appear at the bottom. The horizontal gray back carries the player's name at the top, followed by biography and statistics.
COMPLETE SET (24).................. 8.00 3.20

1989 California League All-Stars Cal League Cards

COMPLETE SET (56).................. 5.00 2.00

1989 Canton-Akron Indians Best

The 1989 Canton Indians set contains 28 standard-size cards. The fronts have posed color player photos with white borders. The year "1989" and the city are written vertically on the left side of the card, and the player's name and position are given below the picture. In a horizontal format, the backs have biography, recent professional baseball performance statistics, and a color headshot, all in a yellow rectangular box.
COMPLETE SET (28).................. 5.00 2.00

1989 Canton-Akron Indians ProCards

This 28-card standard-size set of the 1989 Canton-Akron Indians, a Class AA Eastern League affiliate of the Cleveland Indians, features red-bordered posed color player photos on its fronts. The player's name, position, and team name appear at the bottom. The horizontal gray back carries the player's name and position at the top, followed by biography and statistics. .
COMPLETE SET (28).................. 5.00 2.00

1989 Canton-Akron Indians Star

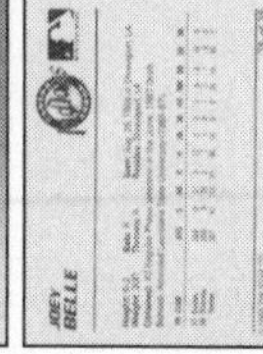

The 1989 Canton-Akron Indians set contains 25 standard-size cards. The fronts have posed color player photos, with purple borders on the top portion of the card fading to yellow as one moves down the card face. In purple print on a pale yellow background, the backs have biography and statistics. 5,000 sets produced. This issue includes a second year card of Albert "Joey" Belle.
COMPLETE SET (25).................. 20.00 8.00

1989 Carson Newman Eagles

Sponsored by Havoline Motor Oil, this 27-card standard-size set features the 1989 Carson Newman Eagles. The cards measure the standard size. On a light blue card face, the fronts feature color action player photos with thin black borders. The player's name, number, position and the team logo appear below the photo. On a light blue background, the horizontal backs carry player biography and statistics.
COMPLETE SET (27).................. 10.00 4.00

1989 Cedar Rapids Reds All-Decade Best

COMPLETE SET (36).................. 5.00 2.00

1989 Cedar Rapids Reds Best

The 1989 Cedar Rapids Reds set contains 30 standard-size cards. The fronts have posed color player photos with white borders. The year "1989" and the city are written vertically on the left side of the card, and the player's name and position are given below the picture. In a horizontal format, the backs have biography, recent professional baseball performance summary (including statistics), and a color headshot, all in a yellow rectangular box.
COMPLETE SET (30).................. 5.00 2.00

1989 Cedar Rapids Reds ProCards

This 29-card standard-size set of the 1989 Cedar Rapids Reds, a Class A Midwest League affiliate of the Cincinnati Reds, features orange-bordered posed color player photos on its fronts. The player's name, position, and team name appear at the bottom. The horizontal gray back carries the player's name and position at the top, followed by biography and statistics.
COMPLETE SET (29).................. 5.00 2.00

1989 Cedar Rapids Reds Star

The 1989 Cedar Rapids Reds set contains 30 standard-size cards. The fronts have posed color player photos, with red borders on the top portion of the card fading to yellow as one moves down the card face. In red print on a pale yellow background, the backs have biography and statistics. 5,000 sets produced.
COMPLETE SET (30).................. 5.00 2.00

1989 Charleston Rainbows ProCards

This 28-card standard-size set of the 1989 Charleston Rainbows, a Class A South Atlantic League affiliate of the San Diego Padres, features orange-bordered posed color player photos on its fronts. The player's name, position, and team name appear at the bottom. The horizontal gray back carries the player's name and position at the top, followed by biography and statistics.
COMPLETE SET (28).................. 5.00 2.00

1989 Charleston Wheelers Best

This 27-card standard-size set features the 1989 Charleston Wheelers, a farm club for the Chicago Cubs. The fronts have posed color player photos with white borders. The year "1989" and the city are written vertically on the left side of the card, and the player's name and position are given below the picture. In a horizontal format, the backs have biography, recent professional baseball performance summary (including statistics), and a color headshot, all in a yellow rectangular box.
COMPLETE SET (27).................. 5.00 2.00

1989 Charleston Wheelers ProCards

This 28-card standard-size set of the 1989 Charleston Wheelers, a Class A South Atlantic League affiliate of the Chicago Cubs, features orange-bordered posed color player photos on its fronts. The player's name, position, and team name appear at the bottom. The horizontal gray back carries the player's name and position at the top, followed by biography and statistics.
COMPLETE SET (28).................. 5.00 2.00

1989 Charlotte Knights Team Issue

The 1989 Charlotte Knights set consists of 25 standard-size cards. The glossy color player photos are trimmed in black and have the player's name in a salmon-colored banner across the top of the picture. The team logo is superimposed at the lower right corner. In a horizontal format, the backs present biography and statistics.
COMPLETE SET (25).................. 5.00 2.00

1989 Charlotte Rangers Star

The 1989 Charlotte Rangers set contains 28 standard-size cards. The fronts have posed color player photos, with blue borders on the top portion of the card fading to red as one moves down the card face. In blue print on a pink background, the backs have biography and statistics. The card numbers were inadvertently omitted from cards 10, 11, and 15. 5,000 sets produced.
COMPLETE SET (28).................. 5.00 2.00

1989 Chattanooga Lookouts Best

This 26-card standard-size set features the 1989 Chattanooga Lookouts, a farm club for the Cincinnati Reds. The fronts have posed color player photos with white borders. The year "1989" and the city are written vertically on the left side of the card, and the player's name and position are given below the picture. In a horizontal format, the backs have biography, recent professional baseball performance summary (including statistics), and a color headshot, all in a yellow rectangular box.
COMPLETE SET (26).................. 5.00 2.00

1989 Chattanooga Lookouts Grand Slam

COMPLETE SET (25).................. 5.00 2.00

1989 Chattanooga Lookouts Legends II Team Issue

This 33-card standard-size set features outstanding players who later went on to play in the Majors. The fronts have black and white mugshots, with red borders on a white card face. The words "Lookouts Legends II" and the Coke logo adorn the top of the front. The horizontally oriented backs present career summaries. The unnumbered checklist card has a photo of the Chatanooga Regional History Museum.
COMPLETE SET (33).................. 10.00 4.00

1989 Clearwater Phillies Star

The 1989 Clearwater Phillies set contains 26 standard-size cards. The fronts have posed color player photos, with red borders on the top portion of the card fading to gray as one moves down the card face. In red print on a gray background, the backs have biography and statistics. The unnumbered Royal Thomas card was a late production; it has a different photo and a white background on the back. 5,000 sets produced.
COMPLETE SET (26).................. 5.00 2.00

1989 Clinton Giants ProCards

This 31-card standard-size set of the 1989 Clinton Giants, a Class A Midwest League affiliate of the San Francisco Giants, features orange-bordered posed color player photos on its fronts. The player's name, position, and team name appear at the bottom. The horizontal gray back carries the player's name and position at the top, followed by biography and statistics.
COMPLETE SET (31).................. 5.00 2.00

1989 Colorado Springs Sky Sox CMC

COMPLETE SET (25).................. 5.00 2.00

1989 Colorado Springs Sky Sox ProCards

This 28-card standard-size set of the 1989 Colorado Springs Sky Sox, a Class AAA Pacific Coast League affiliate of the Cleveland Indians, features blue-bordered posed color player photos on its fronts. The player's name, position, and team name appear at the bottom. The horizontal gray back carries the player's name and position at the top, followed by biography and statistics.
COMPLETE SET (28).................. 5.00 2.00

1989 Columbia Mets Best

The 1989 Columbia Mets set contains 30 standard-size cards. The fronts have posed color player photos with white borders. The year "1989" and the city are written vertically on the left side of the card, and the player's name and position are given below the picture. In a horizontal format, the backs have biography, recent professional baseball performance summary (including statistics), and a color headshot, all in a yellow rectangular box. This issue includes a third year card of Todd Hundley.
COMPLETE SET (30).................. 15.00 6.00

1989 Columbia Mets Grand Slam

The 1989 Columbia Mets set contains 29 standard-size cards. This issue includes a third year card of Todd Hundley.
COMPLETE SET (29).................. 15.00 6.00

1989 Columbus Clippers CMC

This 30-card standard-size set of the 1989 Columbus Clippers, a Class AAA International League affiliate of the New York Yankees, features a third year card of Bernie Williams.
COMPLETE SET (30).................. 12.00 4.80

1989 Columbus Clippers Police

This 25-card standard-size set of the 1989 Columbus Clippers, a Class AAA International League affiliate of the New York Yankees, features a third year card of Bernie Williams.
COMPLETE SET (25).................. 12.00 4.80

1989 Columbus Clippers ProCards

This 28-card standard-size set of the 1989 Columbus Clippers, a Class AAA International League affiliate of the New York Yankees, features blue-bordered posed color player photos on its fronts. The player's name, position, and team name appear at the bottom. The horizontal gray back carries the player's name and position at the top, followed by biography and statistics.
COMPLETE SET (28).................. 15.00 6.00

1989 Columbus Mudcats Best

This 28-card standard-size set features the 1989 Columbus Mudcats, a farm club for the Houston Astros. The fronts have posed color player photos with white borders. The year "1989" and the city are written vertically on the left side of the card, and the player's name and position are given below the picture. In a horizontal format, the backs have biography, recent professional baseball performance summary (including statistics), and a color headshot, all in a yellow rectangular box.
COMPLETE SET (28).................. 5.00 2.00

1989 Columbus Mudcats ProCards

This 31-card standard-size set of the 1989 Columbus Mudcats, a Class AA Southern League affiliate of the Houston Astros, features red-bordered posed color player photos on its fronts. The player's name, position, and team name appear at the bottom. The horizontal gray back carries the player's name and position at the top, followed by biography and statistics.
COMPLETE SET (31).................. 5.00 2.00

1989 Columbus Mudcats Star

This 24-card standard-size set features the 1989 Columbus Mudcats, a farm club for the Houston Astros. The fronts have posed color player photos, with red borders on the top portion of the card fading to gray as one moves down the card face. In red print on a gray background, the backs have biography and statistics. 5,000 sets produced.
COMPLETE SET (24).................. 5.00 2.00

1989 Denver Zephyrs CMC

COMPLETE SET (25).................. 5.00 2.00

1989 Denver Zephyrs ProCards

This 28-card standard-size set of the 1989 Denver Zephyrs, a Class AAA Pacific Coast League affiliate of the Milwaukee Brewers, features blue-bordered posed color player photos on its fronts. The player's name, position, and team name appear at the bottom. The horizontal gray back carries the player's name and position at the top, followed by biography and statistics.
COMPLETE SET (28).................. 5.00 2.00

1989 Dunedin Blue Jays Star

This 26-card standard-size set of the 1989 Dunedin Blue Jays, a Class A Florida State League affiliate of the Toronto Blue Jays, features indigo-bordered posed color player photos on its fronts. The player's name, team name, and position appear at the bottom. The white horizontal back carries the player's name at the top, followed by biography and statistics. The coaching staff card (number 26) was a late issue. 5,000 sets produced.
COMPLETE SET (25).................. 8.00 3.20

1989 Durham Bulls I Star

This 29-card first series standard-size set features the 1989 Durham Bulls, a farm club for the Atlanta Braves. The fronts have posed color player photos, with aqua borders on the top portion of the card fading to orange as one moves down the card face. In blue print on a pale orange background, the backs have biography and statistics. Card numbers 26-29 have white backs; also Costner's card has an orange front border fading to blue. The cards are arranged alphabetically and numbered on the back. 5,000 sets produced.
COMPLETE SET (29).................. 10.00 4.00

1989 Durham Bulls II Star

This 29-card second series standard-size set features the 1989 Durham Bulls, a farm club for the Atlanta Braves. The fronts have the same posed color player photos as on the first series, but with orange borders on the top portion of the card fading to blue as one moves down the card face. In blue print on a white background, the backs have biography and statistics. The cards are arranged alphabetically and numbered on the back. 5,000 sets produced.
COMPLETE SET (29).................. 20.00 8.00

1989 Durham Bulls Team Issue

This 28-card second series set features the 1989 Durham Bulls, a farm club for the Atlanta Braves, was issued in one large sheet featuring six perforated strips with a large team photo in the wide top strip. Sponsored by Kodak, the fronts carry color player photos while the backs display player career statistics. The cards are unnumbered and checklisted below in alphabetical order.
COMPLETE SET (28).................. 10.00 4.00

1989 Eastern League All-Stars ProCards

COMPLETE SET (26).................. 15.00 6.00

1989 Eastern League Diamond Diplomacy ProCards

COMPLETE SET (50).................. 5.00 2.00

1989 Edmonton Trappers CMC

This 25-card standard-size set of the 1989 Edmonton Trappers, a Class AAA Pacific Coast League affiliate of the California Angels, features on its fronts white-bordered posed color player photos framed by a black line. The team's name, the player's name, and his position appear at the bottom. The white back is framed by a black line and carries the team's name and league at the top, followed by the player's name, position, biography and statistics.
COMPLETE SET (25).................. 5.00 2.00

1989 Edmonton Trappers ProCards

This 25-card standard-size set of the 1989 Edmonton Trappers, a Class AAA Pacific Coast League affiliate of the California Angels, features blue-bordered posed color player photos on its fronts. The player's name, position, and team name appear at the bottom. The horizontal gray back carries the player's name and position at the top, followed by biography and statistics.
COMPLETE SET (25).................. 5.00 2.00

1989 El Paso Diablos Grand Slam

COMPLETE SET (30).................. 5.00 2.00

1989 Elizabethton Twins Star

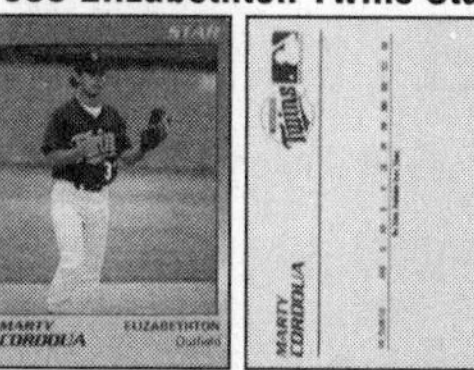

The 1989 Elizabethton Twins set contains 31 standard-size cards. The fronts have posed color player photos, with purple borders on the top portion of the card fading to red as one moves down the card face. In purple print on a pink background, the backs have biography and statistics. Card numbers 26-31 have blue rather than purple borders. The cards are arranged alphabetically and numbered on the back. This issue includes the minor league card debuts of Marty Cordova and Denny Neagle. 5,000 sets produced.
COMPLETE SET (31).................. 15.00 6.00

1989 Elmira Pioneers Pucko

The 1989 Elmira Pioneer set was first issued with 28 standard-size cards; later 4 cards (29-32) were added to the set, bringing the total to 32. The front design features color player photos bordered in red; the four update cards, however, have black and white photos. The team logo appears in a circle at the lower left corner of the picture. The back has biography

and professional record (where appropriate). 3,750 sets were produced.
COMPLETE SET (32)................. 5.00 2.00

1989 Erie Orioles Star

The 1989 Erie Orioles set contains 29 standard-size cards. The fronts have posed color player photos, with black borders on the top portion of the card fading to orange as one moves down the card face. In black print on a pale orange background, the backs have biography and statistics. 5,000 sets produced.
COMPLETE SET (29)................. 8.00 3.20

1989 Eugene Emeralds Best

This 25-card standard-size set features the 1989 Eugene Emeralds, a farm club for the Kansas City Royals. The fronts have posed color player photos with white borders. The year "1989" and the city are written vertically on the left side of the card, and the player's name and position are given below the picture. In a horizontal format, the backs have biography, recent professional baseball performance summary (including statistics), and a color headshot, all in a yellow rectangular box.
COMPLETE SET (25)................. 5.00 2.00

1989 Everett Giants Star

The 1989 Everett Giants set contains 32 standard-size cards. The fronts have posed color player photos, with black borders on the top portion of the card fading to orange as one moves down the card face. In black print on a pale orange background, the backs have biographical information. 5,000 sets produced.
COMPLETE SET (32)................. 5.00 2.00

1989 Fayetteville Generals ProCards

This 29-card standard-size set of the 1989 Fayetteville Generals, a Class A South Atlantic League affiliate of the Detroit Tigers, features orange-bordered posed color player photos on its fronts. The player's name, position, and team name appear at the bottom. The horizontal gray back carries the player's name and position at the top, followed by biography and statistics.
COMPLETE SET (29)................. 5.00 2.00

1989 Frederick Keys Star

This 27-card standard-size set features the 1989 Frederick Keys, a farm club for the Baltimore Orioles. The fronts have posed color player photos, with black borders on the top portion of the card fading to orange as one moves down the card face. In black print on a pale orange background, the backs have biography and statistics. Card numbers 26-27 were late productions; card number 26 has purple print on the reverse. 5,000 sets produced.
COMPLETE SET (27)................. 8.00 3.20

1989 Fresno State Bulldogs Smokey

This 24-card standard-size set features the 1989 Fresno State Bulldog baseball team. The fronts feature either posed or action color player photos. Beneath the photo, the player's name, position, and "Bulldogs" is printed between the Smokey the Bear and team logos. The backs have biographical information and a fire prevention cartoon starring Smokey. The cards are unnumbered and checklisted below in alphabetical order.
COMPLETE SET (24)................ 10.00 4.00

1989 Ft. Lauderdale Yankees Star

The 1989 Fort Lauderdale Yankees set contains 29 standard-size cards. The fronts have posed color player photos, with purple borders on the top portion of the card fading to gray as one moves down the card face. In purple print on a gray background, the backs have biography and statistics. Card numbers 26-29 have different colors and appear to be late productions. 5,000 sets produced.
COMPLETE SET (29)................. 5.00 2.00

1989 Gastonia Rangers ProCards

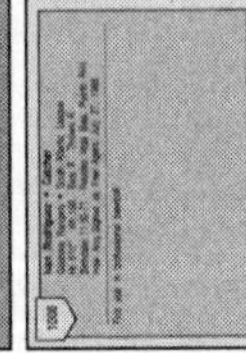

This 30-card standard-size set of the 1989 Gastonia Rangers, a Class A South Atlantic League affiliate of the Texas Rangers, features orange-bordered posed color player photos on its fronts. The player's name, position, and team name appear at the bottom. The horizontal gray back carries the player's name and position at the top, followed by biography and statistics. This issue includes the minor league card debut of Ivan Rodriguez.
COMPLETE SET (30)................ 60.00 24.00

1989 Gastonia Rangers Star

The 1989 Gastonia Rangers set contains 26 standard-size cards. The fronts have posed color player photos, with blue borders on the top portion of the card fading to gray as one moves down the card face. In blue print on a white background, the backs have biography and statistics. The cards are arranged alphabetically and numbered on the back. The Coaching Staff card has no number. This issue includes the minor league card debut of Ivan Rodriguez. 5,000 sets produced.
COMPLETE SET (26)................ 20.00 8.00

1989 Geneva Cubs ProCards

This 31-card standard-size set of the 1989 Geneva Cubs, a Class A New York-Penn League affiliate of the Chicago Cubs, features orange-bordered posed color player photos on its fronts. The player's name, position, and team name appear at the bottom. The horizontal gray back carries the player's name and position at the top, followed by biography and statistics.
COMPLETE SET (31)................. 5.00 2.00

1989 Georgia College Colonials

COMPLETE SET (36)................ 10.00 4.00

1989 Great Falls Dodgers Sports Pro

This 33-card standard-size set of the 1989 Great Falls Dodgers, a Rookie Class Pioneer League affiliate of the Los Angeles Dodgers, features posed color head-and-shoulders shots, with thin black borders on a white card face. The horizontally oriented backs have biographical information.
COMPLETE SET (33)................. 5.00 2.00

1989 Greensboro Hornets ProCards

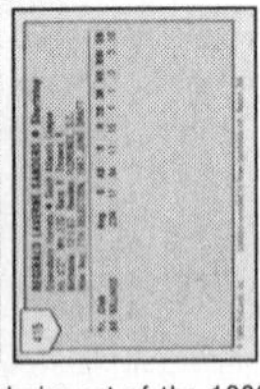

This 29-card standard-size set of the 1989 Greensboro Hornets, a Class A South Atlantic League affiliate of the Cincinnati Reds, features orange-bordered posed color player photos on its fronts. The player's name, position, and team name appear at the bottom. The horizontal gray back carries the player's name and position at the top, followed by biography and statistics. This issue includes a second year card of Reggie Sanders.
COMPLETE SET (29)................ 10.00 4.00

1989 Greenville Braves Best

The 1989 Greenville Braves set contains 29 standard-size cards. The fronts have posed color player photos with white borders. The year "1989" and the city are written vertically on the left side of the card, and the player's name and position are given below the picture. In a horizontal format, the backs have biography, recent professional baseball performance summary (including statistics), and a color headshot, all in a yellow rectangular box.
COMPLETE SET (29)................ 10.00 4.00

1989 Greenville Braves ProCards

This 30-card standard-size set of the 1989 Greenville Braves, a Class AA Southern League affiliate of the Atlanta Braves, features red-bordered posed color player photos on its fronts. The player's name, position, and team name appear at the bottom. The horizontal gray back carries the player's name and position at the top, followed by biography and statistics.
COMPLETE SET (30)................. 5.00 2.00

1989 Greenville Braves Star

The 1989 Greenville Braves set contains 25 standard-size cards. The fronts have posed color player photos, with blue borders on the top portion of the card fading to red as one moves down the card face. In blue print on a pink background, the backs have biography and statistics. 5,000 sets produced.
COMPLETE SET (25)................. 5.00 2.00

1989 Hagerstown Suns Best

This 29-card standard-size set features the 1989 Hagerstown Suns, a farm club for the Baltimore Orioles. The fronts have posed color player photos with white borders. The year "1989" and the city are written vertically on the left side of the card, and the player's name and position are given below the picture. In a horizontal format, the backs have biography, recent professional baseball performance summary (including statistics), and a color headshot, all in a yellow rectangular box.
COMPLETE SET (29)................. 5.00 2.00

1989 Hagerstown Suns ProCards

This 26-card standard-size set of the 1989 Hagerstown Suns, a Class AA Eastern League affiliate of the Baltimore Orioles, features red-bordered posed color player photos on its fronts. The player's name, position, and team name appear at the bottom. The horizontal gray back carries the player's name and position at the top, followed by biography and statistics.
COMPLETE SET (26)................. 5.00 2.00

1989 Hagerstown Suns Star

This 22-card standard-size set features the 1989 Hagerstown Suns, a farm club of the Baltimore Orioles. The fronts have posed color player photos, with black borders on the top portion of the card fading to orange as one moves down the card face. In black print on a pale orange background, the backs have biography and statistics. 5,000 sets produced.
COMPLETE SET (22)................. 5.00 2.00

1989 Hamilton Redbirds Star

This 29-card standard-size set features the 1989 Hamilton Redbirds, a farm club for the St. Louis Cardinals. The fronts have posed color player photos, with red borders on the top portion of the card fading to yellow as one moves down the card face. In red print on a pale yellow background, the backs have biography and statistics. 5,000 sets produced.
COMPLETE SET (29)................. 5.00 2.00

1989 Harrisburg Senators ProCards

This 26-card standard-size set of the 1989 Harrisburg Senators, a Class AA Eastern League affiliate of the Pittsburgh Pirates, features red-bordered posed color player photos on its fronts. The player's name, position, and team name appear at the bottom. The horizontal gray back carries the player's name and position at the top, followed by biography and statistics.
COMPLETE SET (26)................. 5.00 2.00

1989 Harrisburg Senators Star

This 23-card standard-size set features the 1989 Harrisburg Senators, a farm club for the Pittsburgh Pirates. The fronts have posed color player photos, with red borders on the top portion of the card fading to gray as one moves down the card face. In red print on a gray background, the backs have biography and statistics. 5,000 sets produced.
COMPLETE SET (23)................. 5.00 2.00

1989 Helena Brewers Sports Pro

The 1989 Helena Brewers set consists of 27 standard-size cards. The front design has posed color head-and-shoulders shots, with thin black borders on a white card face. A black sticker with the words "1st Helena Set Ever!" is superimposed on the player photos and detracts from the cards' appearance. The horizontally oriented backs have brief biographical information.
COMPLETE SET (27)................. 5.00 2.00

1989 Huntsville Stars Best

This 29-card standard-size set features the 1989 Huntsville Stars, a farm club for the Oakland Athletics. The fronts have posed color player photos with white borders. The year "1989" and the city are written vertically on the left side of the card, and the player's name and position are given below the picture. In a horizontal format, the backs have biography, recent professional baseball performance summary (including statistics), and a color headshot, all in a yellow rectangular box.
COMPLETE SET (29)................. 5.00 2.00

1989 Idaho Falls Braves ProCards

This 31-card standard-size set of the 1989 Idaho Falls Braves, a Rookie Class Pioneer League affiliate of the Atlanta Braves, features orange-bordered posed color player photos on its fronts. The player's name, position, and team name appear at the bottom. The horizontal gray back carries the player's name and position at the top, followed by biography and statistics.
COMPLETE SET (31)................. 5.00 2.00

1989 Indianapolis Indians CMC

This 25-card standard-size set of the 1989 Indianapolis Indians, a Class AAA American Association affiliate of the Montreal Expos, features on its fronts white-bordered posed color player photos framed by a black line. The team's name, the player's name, and his position appear at the bottom. The white back is framed by a black line and carries the team's name and league at the top, followed by the player's name, position, biography and statistics. Hook's and Pepsi co-sponsored the set.
COMPLETE SET (25)................ 10.00 4.00

1989 Indianapolis Indians ProCards

This 32-card standard-size set of the 1989 Indianapolis Indians, a Class AAA American Association affiliate of the Montreal Expos, features blue-bordered posed color player photos on its fronts. The player's name, position, and team name appear at the bottom. The horizontal gray back carries the player's name and position at the top, followed by biography and statistics. The set was co-sponsored by Pepsi and Hook's.
COMPLETE SET (32)................ 15.00 6.00

1989 Iowa Cubs CMC

COMPLETE SET (25)................. 5.00 2.00

1989 Iowa Cubs ProCards

This 28-card standard-size set of the 1989 Iowa Cubs, a Class AAA American Association affiliate of the Chicago Cubs, features blue-bordered posed color player photos on its fronts. The player's name, position, and team name appear at the bottom. The horizontal gray back carries the player's name and position at the top, followed by biography and statistics.
COMPLETE SET (28)................. 5.00 2.00

1989 Jackson Mets Grand Slam

COMPLETE SET (30)................. 5.00 2.00

1989 Jacksonville Expos Best

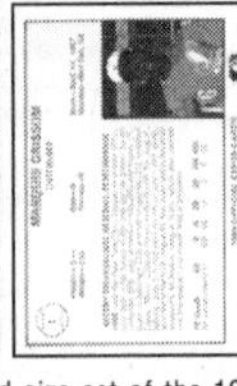

This 29-card standard-size set of the 1989 Jacksonville Expos, a Class AA Southern League affiliate of the Montreal Expos, features white-bordered posed color player photos on its fronts. The year "1989" and the city are written vertically on the left side, and the player's name and position are given below the picture. In a horizontal format, the yellow backs carry the player's name and position at the top, followed by biography, career highlights, statistics, and a color headshot.
COMPLETE SET (29)................ 15.00 6.00

1989 Jacksonville Expos ProCards

This 29-card standard-size set of the 1989 Jacksonville Expos, a Class AA Southern League affiliate of the Montreal Expos, features red-bordered posed color player photos on its fronts. The player's name, position, and team name appear at the bottom. The horizontal gray back carries the player's name and position at the top, followed by biography and statistics. The set was sponsored by Kool-Aid.
COMPLETE SET (29)................ 10.00 4.00

1989 Jamestown Expos ProCards

This 30-card standard-size set of the 1989 Jamestown Expos, a Class A New York-Penn League affiliate of the Montreal Expos, features orange-bordered posed color player photos on its fronts. The player's name, position, and team name appear at the bottom. The horizontal gray back carries the player's name and position at the top, followed by biography and statistics. The set was co-sponsored by McDonald's and Coca-Cola.
COMPLETE SET (30)................. 5.00 2.00

1989 Johnson City Cardinals Star

The 1989 Johnson City Cardinals set contains 26 standard-size cards. The fronts have posed color player photos, with red borders on the top portion of the card fading to yellow as one moves down the card face. In red print on a pale yellow background, the backs have biography and statistics. The reverse of card number 26 is a slighter darker shade of yellow than the other cards. 5,000 sets produced.
COMPLETE SET (26)................. 5.00 2.00

1989 Kenosha Twins ProCards

This 29-card standard-size set of the 1989 Kenosha Twins, a Class A Midwest League affiliate of the Minnesota Twins, features orange-bordered posed color player photos on its fronts. The player's name, position, and team name appear at the bottom. The horizontal gray back carries the player's name and position at the top, followed by biography and statistics.
COMPLETE SET (29)................. 5.00 2.00

1989 Kenosha Twins Star

The 1989 Kenosha Twins set contains 27 standard-size cards. The fronts have posed color player photos, with blue borders on the top portion of the card fading to red as one moves down the card face. In dark blue print on a medium blue background, the backs have biography and statistics. Card numbers 26-27 have a light blue background on the reverse. 5,000 sets produced.
COMPLETE SET (27)................. 5.00 2.00

1989 Kingsport Mets Star

The 1989 Kingsport Mets set contains 30 standard-size cards. The fronts have posed color player photos, with blue borders on the top portion of the card fading to orange as one moves down the card face. In blue print on a pale orange background, the backs have biography and statistics. The fronts of card numbers 26-30 have a lighter shade of orange than the other cards. 5,000 sets produced.
COMPLETE SET (30)................. 5.00 2.00

1989 Kinston Indians Star

The 1989 Kinston Indians set contains 27 standard-size cards. The fronts have posed color player photos, with purple borders on the top portion of the card fading to yellow as one moves down the card face. In purple print on a pale yellow background, the backs have biography and statistics. This issue includes the minor league card debut of Charles Nagy. 5,000 sets produced.
COMPLETE SET (27)................ 15.00 6.00

1989 Knoxville Blue Jays Best

This 31-card standard-size 10th Anniversary set of the 1989 Knoxville Blue Jays, a Class AA Southern League affiliate of the Toronto Blue Jays, features white-bordered posed and action color player photos on its fronts. The year "1989" and the city are written vertically on the left side of the card, and the player's name and position are given below the picture. In a horizontal format, the backs have biography, statistics, career highlights, and a color headshot, all in a yellow rectangular box. The backs of the Rogers and Schunk cards were reversed.
COMPLETE SET (31)................ 15.00 6.00

1989 Knoxville Blue Jays ProCards

This 31-card standard-size set of the 1989 Knoxville Blue Jays, a Class AA Southern League affiliate of the Toronto Blue Jays, features red-bordered posed color player photos on its fronts. The player's name, position, and team name appear at the bottom. The horizontal gray back carries the player's name and position at the top, followed by biography and statistics. The set was sponsored by the Knoxville Coin Exchange.
COMPLETE SET (31)................ 10.00 4.00

1989 Knoxville Blue Jays Star

This 25-card standard-size set of the 1989 Knoxville Blue Jays, a Class AA Southern League affiliate of the Toronto Blue Jays, features blue-bordered posed color player photos on its fronts. The player's name, team name, and position appear at the bottom. The light blue horizontal back carries the player's name at the top, followed by biography and statistics. 5,000 sets produced.
COMPLETE SET (25)................ 10.00 4.00

1989 Lakeland Tigers Star

The 1989 Lakeland Tigers set contains 28 standard-size cards. The fronts have posed color player photos, with blue borders on the top portion of the card fading to orange as one moves down the card face. In blue print on a pale orange background, the backs have biography and statistics. The cards are arranged alphabetically and numbered on the back. 5,000 sets produced.
COMPLETE SET (28)................. 5.00 2.00

1989 Las Vegas Stars CMC

COMPLETE SET (25)................ 10.00 4.00

1989 Las Vegas Stars ProCards

This 29-card standard-size set of the 1989 Las Vegas Stars, a Class AAA Pacific Coast League affiliate of the San Diego Padres, features blue-bordered posed color player photos on its fronts. The player's name, position, and team name appear at the bottom. The horizontal gray back carries the player's name and position at the top, followed by biography and statistics.
COMPLETE SET (29)................ 15.00 6.00

1989 London Tigers ProCards

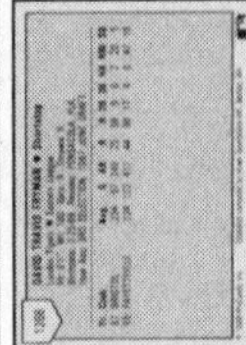

This 32-card standard-size set of the 1989 London Tigers, a Class AA Eastern League affiliate of the Detroit Tigers, features red-bordered posed color player photos on its fronts. The player's name, position, and team name appear at the bottom. The horizontal gray back carries the player's name and position at the top, followed by biography and statistics.
COMPLETE SET (32)................ 20.00 8.00

1989 Louisville Red Birds CMC

COMPLETE SET (25)................. 5.00 2.00

1989 Louisville Red Birds ProCards

This 28-card standard-size set of the 1989 Louisville Red Birds, a Class AAA American Association affiliate of the St. Louis Cardinals, features blue-bordered posed color player photos on its fronts. The player's name, position, and team name appear at the bottom. The horizontal gray back carries the player's name and position at the top, followed by biography and statistics. 7,500 sets were produced.
COMPLETE SET (28)................. 8.00 3.20

1989 Louisville Red Birds Team Issue

This set contains 38 standard-size cards. The color action player photos adorning the fronts have rounded corners and white borders. The team logo is superimposed at the lower left corner of the picture. The backs present biographical and statistical information.
COMPLETE SET (38)................ 10.00 4.00

1989 Lynchburg Red Sox Star

The 1989 Lynchburg Red Sox set contains 29 standard-size cards. The fronts have posed color player photos, with red borders on the top portion of the card fading to blue as one moves down the card face. In blue print on a pink background, the backs have biography and statistics. Card numbers 26-29 have blue background on the reverse. 5,000 sets produced.
COMPLETE SET (29).................. 5.00 2.00

1989 Madison Muskies Star

This 26-card standard-size set features the 1989 Madison Muskies, a farm club for the Oakland Athletics. The fronts have posed color player photos, with green borders on the top portion of the card fading to yellow as one moves down the card face. In green print on a pale yellow background, the backs have biography and statistics. Card numbers 23-25 were apparently never issued. 5,000 sets produced.
COMPLETE SET (26).................. 5.00 2.00

1989 Martinsville Phillies Star

The 1989 Martinsville Phillies set contains 35 standard-size cards. The fronts have posed color player photos, with aqua borders on the top portion of the card fading to red as one moves down the card face. In red print on a white background, the backs have biography and statistics. 5,000 sets produced.
COMPLETE SET (35).................. 5.00 2.00

1989 Medford Athletics Best

The 1989 Medford Athletics set contains 31 standard-size cards. The fronts have posed color player photos with white borders. The year "1989" and the city are written vertically on the left side of the card, and the player's name and position are given below the picture. In a horizontal format, the backs have biography, recent professional baseball performance summary (including statistics), and a color headshot, all in a yellow rectangular box.
COMPLETE SET (31).................. 5.00 2.00

1989 Memphis Chicks Best

This 28-card standard-size set features the 1989 Memphis Chicks, a farm club for the Kansas City Royals. The fronts have posed color player photos with white borders. The year "1989" and the city are written vertically on the left side of the card, and the player's name and position are given below the picture. In a horizontal format, the backs have biography, recent professional baseball performance summary (including statistics), and a color headshot, all in a yellow rectangular box.
COMPLETE SET (28).................. 5.00 2.00

1989 Memphis Chicks ProCards

This 28-card standard-size set of the 1989 Memphis Chicks, a Class AA Southern League affiliate of the Kansas City Royals, features red-bordered posed color player photos on its fronts. The player's name, position, and team name appear at the bottom. The horizontal gray back carries the player's name and position at the top, followed by biography and statistics.
COMPLETE SET (28).................. 5.00 2.00

1989 Memphis Chicks Star

This 24-card standard-size set features the 1989 Memphis Chicks, a farm club for the Kansas City Royals. The fronts have posed color player photos, with blue borders on the top portion of the card fading to sky blue as one moves down the card face. In blue print on a pale blue background, the backs have biography and statistics. 5,000 sets produced.
COMPLETE SET (24).................. 5.00 2.00

1989 Miami Miracle I Star

The 1989 Miami Miracle I set contains 25 standard-size cards. The fronts have posed color player photos, with turquoise borders on the top portion of the card fading to yellow as one moves down the card face. In turquoise print on a pale yellow background, the backs have biography and statistics. 5,000 sets produced.
COMPLETE SET (25).................. 5.00 2.00

1989 Miami Miracle II Star

The 1989 Miami Miracle II set contains 22 standard-size cards. The fronts have posed color player photos, with aqua borders on the top portion of the card fading to yellow as one moves down the card face. In blue print on a white background, the backs have biography and statistics. The card number was left off of card number 3. 5,000 sets produced.
COMPLETE SET (22).................. 5.00 2.00

1989 Michigan State Pepsi

This set, features the current players from the 1989 Michigan State team along with some of

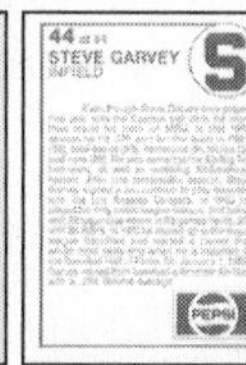

the best players they had up to that time as well. The first part of the set is devoted to the current players and the second half includes cards of many all-time Spartan greats. The backs have information about the player and the "Pepsi" sponsorship logo.
COMPLETE SET (54)................ 20.00 8.00

1989 Midland Angels Grand Slam

COMPLETE SET (30).................. 5.00 2.00

1989 Mississippi State Bulldogs

COMPLETE SET (45)................ 15.00 6.00

1989 Modesto A's Cal League Cards

COMPLETE SET (25).................. 5.00 2.00

1989 Modesto A's Chong

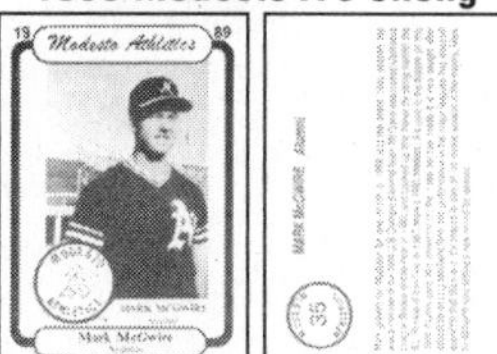

COMPLETE SET (35)................ 50.00 20.00

1989 Myrtle Beach Blue Jays ProCards

This 30-card standard-size set of the 1989 Myrtle Beach Blue Jays, a Class A South Atlantic League affiliate of the Toronto Blue Jays, features orange-bordered posed color player photos on its fronts. The player's name, position, and team name appear at the bottom. The horizontal gray back carries the player's name and position at the top, followed by biography and statistics. The set was sponsored by the Myrtle Beach Blue Jays Souvenir Store.
COMPLETE SET (30).................. 5.00 2.00

1989 Nashville Sounds CMC

COMPLETE SET (25).................. 5.00 2.00

1989 Nashville Sounds ProCards

This 28-card standard-size set of the 1989 Nashville Sounds, a Class AAA American Association affiliate of the Cincinnati Reds, features blue-bordered posed color player photos on its fronts. The player's name, position, and team name appear at the bottom. The horizontal gray back carries the player's name and position at the top, followed by biography and statistics.
COMPLETE SET (28).................. 5.00 2.00

1989 Nashville Sounds Team Issue

COMPLETE SET (30).................. 6.00 2.40

1989 New Britain Red Sox ProCards

This 27-card standard-size set of the 1989 New Britain Red Sox, a Class AA Eastern League affiliate of the Boston Red Sox, features red-bordered posed color player photos on its fronts. The player's name, position, and team name appear at the bottom. The horizontal gray back carries the player's name and position at the top, followed by biography and statistics.
COMPLETE SET (27).................. 5.00 2.00

1989 New Britain Red Sox Star

The 1989 New Britain Red Sox set contains 25 standard-size cards. The fronts have posed color player photos, with red borders on the top portion of the card fading to gray as one moves down the card face. In red print on a gray background, the backs have biography and statistics. 5,000 sets produced.
COMPLETE SET (25).................. 5.00 2.00

1989 Niagara Falls Rapids Pucko

The 1989 Niagara Falls set contains 31 standard-size cards. The front features color action player photos bordered in red. The team name and player's name appear in white stripes above and below the picture respectively, with the team logo in the lower left corner. The backs have biography, the circumstances of the player's signing or drafting, and an advertisement for a baseball card shop. A peculiarity of the set is the two number 5 cards.
3,750 sets were produced.
COMPLETE SET (31).................. 6.00 2.40

1989 Oklahoma City 89ers CMC

COMPLETE SET (25).................. 5.00 2.00

1989 Oklahoma City 89ers ProCards

This 29-card standard-size set of the 1989 Oklahoma City 89ers, a Class AAA American Association affiliate of the Texas Rangers, features blue-bordered posed color player photos on its fronts. The player's name, position, and team name appear at the bottom. The horizontal gray back carries the player's name and position at the top, followed by biography and statistics.
COMPLETE SET (29).................. 5.00 2.00

1989 Oklahoma Sooners

COMPLETE SET (24)................ 10.00 4.00

1989 Omaha Royals CMC

COMPLETE SET (25).................. 8.00 3.20

1989 Omaha Royals ProCards

This 27-card standard-size set of the 1989 Omaha Royals, a Class AAA American Association affiliate of the Kansas City Royals, features blue-bordered posed color player photos on its fronts. The player's name, position, and team name appear at the bottom. The horizontal gray back carries the player's name and position at the top, followed by biography and statistics.
COMPLETE SET (27).................. 8.00 3.20

1989 Oneonta Yankees ProCards

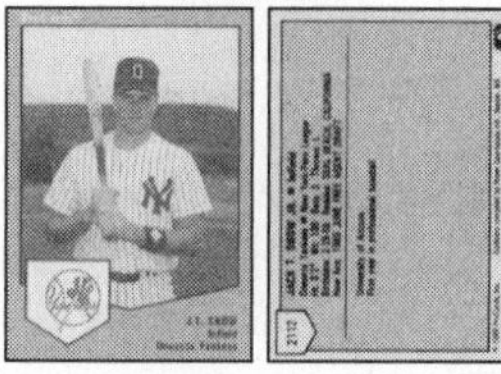

This 32-card standard-size set of the 1989 Oneonta Yankees, a Class A New York-Penn League affiliate of the New York Yankees, features orange-bordered posed color player photos on its fronts. The player's name, position, and team name appear at the bottom. The horizontal gray back carries the player's name and position at the top, followed by biography and statistics.
COMPLETE SET (32)................ 10.00 4.00

1989 Orlando Twins Best

The 1989 Orlando Twins set contains 31 standard-size cards. The fronts have posed color player photos with white borders. The year "1989" and the city are written vertically on the left side of the card, and the player's name and position are given below the picture. In a horizontal format, the backs have biography, recent professional baseball performance summary (including statistics), and a color headshot, all in a yellow rectangular box.
COMPLETE SET (31).................. 5.00 2.00

1989 Orlando Twins ProCards

This 30-card standard-size set of the 1989 Orlando Twins, a Class AA Southern League affiliate of the Minnesota Twins, features red-bordered posed color player photos on its fronts. The player's name, position, and team name appear at the bottom. The horizontal gray back carries the player's name and position at the top, followed by biography and statistics.
COMPLETE SET (30).................. 5.00 2.00

1989 Osceola Astros Star

The 1989 Osceola Astros set contains 27 standard-size cards. The fronts have posed color player photos, with orange borders on the top portion of the card fading to blue as one moves down the card face. In blue print on a pale yellow background, the backs have biography and statistics. 5,000 sets produced.
COMPLETE SET (27)................ 15.00 6.00

1989 Palm Springs Angels Cal League Cards

COMPLETE SET (32).................. 5.00 2.00

1989 Palm Springs Angels ProCards

This 28-card standard-size set of the 1989 Palm Springs Angels, a Class A California League affiliate of the California Angels, features orange-bordered posed color player photos on its fronts. The player's name, position, and team name appear at the bottom. The horizontal gray back carries the player's name and position at the top, followed by biography and statistics.
COMPLETE SET (28).................. 5.00 2.00

1989 Pawtucket Red Sox CMC

COMPLETE SET (25).................. 5.00 2.00

1989 Pawtucket Red Sox Dunkin' Donuts

This 30-card set of the Pawtucket Red Sox, a Class AAA International League affiliate of the Boston Red Sox, was issued in one large sheet featuring six perforated five-card strips with a large team photo in the wide top strip. Sponsored by Dunkin' Donuts, the fronts carry color player photos while the backs display player career statistics. The cards are unnumbered and checklisted below in alphabetical order. 5,000 sets were produced with the majority of them given away at the ballpark.
COMPLETE SET (29)................ 30.00 12.00

1989 Pawtucket Red Sox ProCards

This 28-card standard-size set of the 1989 Pawtucket Red Sox, a Class AAA International League affiliate of the Boston Red Sox, features blue-bordered posed color player photos on its fronts. The player's name, position, and team name appear at the bottom. The horizontal gray back carries the player's name and position at the top, followed by biography and statistics.
COMPLETE SET (28).................. 5.00 2.00

1989 Peninsula Oilers Team Issue

This 29-card set of the 1989 Peninsula Oilers of the Alaska Central Baseball League features color player portraits in black-and-white borders. The backs carry player information. An early Jeff Cirillo card is in this set.
COMPLETE SET (29)................ 15.00 6.00

1989 Peninsula Pilots Star

The 1989 Peninsula Pilots set contains 26 standard-size cards. The fronts have posed color player photos, with blue borders on the top portion of the card fading to sky blue as one moves down the card face. In blue print on a light blue background, the backs have biography and statistics. Card number 26 has blue-fading-to-red borders on the front and a pink background on the back. 5,000 sets produced.
COMPLETE SET (26).................. 5.00 2.00

1989 Peoria Chiefs Team Issue

This 35-card standard-size set was cosponsored by McDonald's restaurants and Kodak, and logos for these sponsors adorn the top of the card face. A coupon redeemable at McDonald's was included in the set. The front design features a mix of posed or action color player photos, with black borders on a white card face. A Chiefs' baseball hat and a baseball icon appear at the lower corners of the picture. In black print on gray and white, the horizontally oriented backs have biography, statistics, and a brief summary of the player's pro career (where appropriate). 7,000 of these sets were produced.
COMPLETE SET (35)................ 12.00 4.80
COMPLETE GOLD 200 SET (35) 20.00 8.00

1989 Phoenix Firebirds CMC

COMPLETE SET (25)................ 10.00 4.00

1989 Phoenix Firebirds ProCards

This 29-card standard-size set of the 1989 Phoenix Firebirds, a Class AAA Pacific Coast League affiliate of the San Francisco Giants, features blue-bordered posed color player photos on its fronts. The player's name, position, and team name appear at the bottom. The horizontal gray back carries the player's name and position at the top, followed by biography and statistics.
COMPLETE SET (29)................ 10.00 4.00

1989 Pittsfield Mets Star

The 1989 Pittsfield Mets set contains 29 standard-size cards. The fronts have posed color player photos, with blue borders on the top portion of the card fading to orange as one moves down the card face. In blue print on a pale orange background, the backs have biography and statistics. 5,000 sets produced.
COMPLETE SET (29).................. 5.00 2.00

1989 Portland Beavers CMC

COMPLETE SET (25).................. 5.00 2.00

1989 Portland Beavers ProCards

This 26-card standard-size set of the 1989 Portland Beavers, a Class AAA Pacific Coast League affiliate of the Minnesota Twins, features blue-bordered posed color player photos on its fronts. The player's name, position, and team name appear at the bottom. The horizontal gray back carries the player's name and position at the top, followed by biography and statistics.
COMPLETE SET (26).................. 5.00 2.00

1989 Prince William Cannons Star

This 29-card standard-size set features the 1989 Prince William Cannons, a farm club for the New York Yankees. The fronts have posed color player photos, with blue borders on the top portion of the card fading to red as one moves down the card face. In blue print on a pink background, the backs have biography and statistics. The backs of card numbers 26-29 are a lighter shade of pink than the other cards. 5,000 sets produced.
COMPLETE SET (29).................. 5.00 2.00

1989 Princeton Pirates Star

The 1989 Princeton Pirates set contains 28 standard-size cards. The fronts have posed color player photos, with black borders on the top portion of the card fading to yellow as one moves down the card face. In black print on a pale yellow background, the backs have biography and statistics. 5,000 sets produced.
COMPLETE SET (28).................. 5.00 2.00

1989 Pulaski Braves ProCards

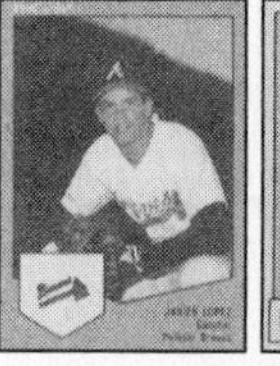

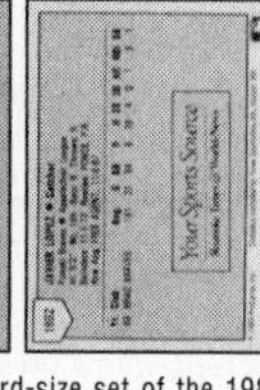

This 28-card standard-size set of the 1989 Pulaski Braves, a Rookie Class Appalachian League affiliate of the Atlanta Braves, features orange-bordered posed color player photos on its fronts. The player's name, position, and team name appear at the bottom. The horizontal gray back carries the player's name and position at the top, followed by biography and statistics. This issue includes the minor league card debuts of Javy Lopez and Melvin Nieves.
COMPLETE SET (28)................ 25.00 10.00

1989 Quad City Angels Best

The 1989 Quad City Angels set contains 31 standard-size cards. The fronts have posed color player photos with white borders. The year "1989" and the city are written vertically on the left side of the card, and the player's name and position are given below the picture. In a horizontal format, the backs have biography, recent professional baseball performance summary (including statistics), and a color headshot, all in a yellow rectangular box. This issue includes a second year card of Jim Edmonds.
COMPLETE SET (31)................ 15.00 6.00

1989 Quad City Angels Grand Slam

COMPLETE SET (30)................ 10.00 4.00

1989 Reading Phillies Best

The 1989 Reading Phillies set contains 27 standard-size cards. The fronts have posed color player photos with white borders. The year "1989" and the city are written vertically on the left side of the card, and the player's name and position are given below the picture. In a horizontal format, the backs have biography, recent professional baseball performance summary (including statistics), and a color headshot, all in a yellow rectangular box.
COMPLETE SET (27).................. 5.00 2.00

1989 Reading Phillies ProCards

This 27-card standard-size set of the 1989 Reading Phillies, a Class AA Eastern League affiliate of the Philadelphia Phillies, features red-bordered posed color player photos on its fronts. The player's name, position, and team name appear at the bottom. The horizontal gray back carries the player's name and position at the top, followed by biography and statistics.
COMPLETE SET (27).................. 5.00 2.00

1989 Reading Phillies Star

The 1989 Reading Phillies set contains 28 standard-size cards. The fronts have posed color player photos, with red borders on the top portion of the card fading to gray as one moves down the card face. In red print on a gray background, the backs have biography and statistics. Card number 27 has a white rather than a gray background, and there are two different cards with the number 26. 5,000 sets produced.
COMPLETE SET (28).................. 5.00 2.00

1989 Reno Silver Sox Cal League Cards

COMPLETE SET (27).................. 5.00 2.00

1989 Richmond Braves Bob's Camera

This 29-card team set of the 1989 Richmond Braves, a Class AAA International League affiliate of the Atlanta Braves, was sponsored

by Bob's Camera. The fronts feature borderless color player photos with sponsors' and team's logos in the wide bottom margin. The backs are blank. 500 sets were produced.
COMPLETE SET (29)............... 60.00 24.00

1989 Richmond Braves CMC

COMPLETE SET (25)............... 10.00 4.00

1989 Richmond Braves ProCards

This 31-card standard-size set of the 1989 Richmond Braves, a Class AAA International League affiliate of the Atlanta Braves, features blue-bordered posed color player photos on its fronts. The player's name, position, and team name appear at the bottom. The horizontal gray back carries the player's name and position at the top, followed by biography and statistics.
COMPLETE SET (31)............... 10.00 4.00

1989 Richmond Braves Team Issue

COMPLETE SET (25)............... 15.00 6.00

1989 Riverside Red Wave Best

This 30-card standard-size set features the 1989 Riverside Red Waves, a farm club for the San Diego Padres. The fronts have posed color player photos with white borders. The year "1989" and the city are written vertically on the left side of the card, and the player's name and position are given below the picture. In a horizontal format, the backs have biography, recent professional baseball performance summary (including statistics), and a color headshot, all in a yellow rectangular box.
COMPLETE SET (30)................. 5.00 2.00

1989 Riverside Red Wave Cal League Cards

COMPLETE SET (31)................. 5.00 2.00

1989 Riverside Red Wave ProCards

This 31-card standard-size set of the 1989 Riverside Red Wave, a Class A California League affiliate of the San Diego Padres, features orange-bordered posed color player photos on its fronts. The player's name, position, and team name appear at the bottom. The horizontal gray back carries the player's name and position at the top, followed by biography and statistics.
COMPLETE SET (31)................. 5.00 2.00

1989 Rochester Red Wings CMC

COMPLETE SET (25)............... 20.00 6.00

1989 Rochester Red Wings ProCards

This 30-card standard-size set of the 1989 Rochester Red Wings, a Class AAA International League affiliate of the Baltimore Orioles, features blue-bordered posed color player photos on its fronts. The player's name, position, and team name appear at the bottom. The horizontal gray back carries the player's name and position at the top, followed by biography and statistics.
COMPLETE SET (30)............... 25.00 8.00

1989 Rockford Expos Litho Center

Printed by Rockford Litho Center, this 31-card standard-size set of the 1989 Rockford Expos, a Class A Midwest League affiliate of the Montreal Expos, features on its white-bordered fronts posed color player photos set on red backgrounds. The player's name and position appear within a yellow diagonal stripe at the lower right. The white horizontal back carries the player's name, uniform number, and position at the top, followed by biography and the name of the sponsor, Sports Wearhouse. The cards are unnumbered and checklisted below in alphabetical order.
COMPLETE SET (31)................. 5.00 2.00

1989 Salem Buccaneers Star

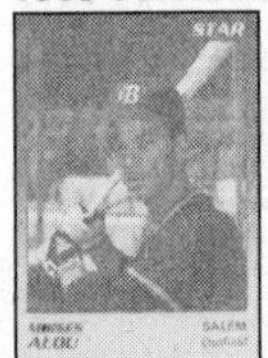
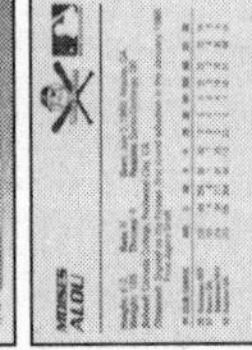

This 29-card standard-size set features the 1989 Salem Buccaneers, a farm club for the Pittsburgh Pirates. The fronts have posed color player photos, with black borders on the top portion of the card fading to yellow as one moves down the card face. In black print on a pale yellow background, the backs have biography and statistics. The Harris card is a late issue and has a white background on the reverse. 5,000 sets produced.
COMPLETE SET (29)................. 5.00 2.00

1989 Salem Dodgers Team Issue

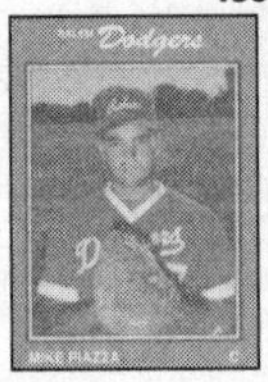

This 30-card set standard size set of the 1989 Salem Buccaneers, a farm club for the Los Angeles Dodgers, feature blue borders with color photos. 2,500 sets were produced. This issue includes the minor league card debut of Mike Piazza.
COMPLETE SET (30)............ 100.00 40.00

1989 Salinas Spurs Cal League Cards

COMPLETE SET (27)................. 5.00 2.00

1989 Salinas Spurs ProCards

This 30-card standard-size set of the 1989 Salinas Spurs, a Class A California League Independent, features orange-bordered posed color player photos on its fronts. The player's name, position, and team name appear at the bottom. The horizontal gray back carries the player's name and position at the top, followed by biography and statistics.
COMPLETE SET (30)................. 5.00 2.00

1989 Salt Lake Trappers Team Issue

This 30-card standard-size set was sponsored by Baseball Cards, etc. and Magic 107.5 radio station. The fronts feature glossy posed color photos (some of which are rather comical), bordered in red on a white card face. The team name appears in red print on the card face, while player information is given in a yellow stripe below the picture. In black print on white and orange, the backs present biography, player profile, and a Baseball Cards, etc. advertisement. Card number 29 features Bill Murray, the well-known actor and comedian.
COMPLETE SET (30)................. 5.00 2.00

1989 San Antonio Missions Best

This 28-card standard-size set features the 1989 San Antonio Missions, a farm club for the Los Angeles Dodgers. The fronts have posed color player photos with white borders. The year "1989" and the city are written vertically on the left side of the card, and the player's name and position are given below the picture. In a horizontal format, the backs have biography, recent professional baseball performance summary (including statistics), and a color headshot, all in a yellow rectangular box. The cards are numbered in a baseball icon on the back.
COMPLETE SET (28)................. 5.00 2.00

1989 San Bernardino Spirit Best

This 29-card standard-size set features the 1989 San Bernardino Spirit, a farm club for the Seattle Mariners. The fronts have posed color player photos with white borders. The year "1989" and the city are written vertically on the left side of the card, and the player's name and position are given below the picture. In a horizontal format, the backs have biography, recent professional baseball performance summary (including statistics), and a color headshot, all in a yellow rectangular box. The owner of the team is Mark Harmon, the well-known actor.
COMPLETE SET (29)................. 5.00 2.00

1989 San Bernardino Spirit Cal League Cards

COMPLETE SET (32)................. 5.00 2.00

1989 San Diego State All-Time Greats

Honoring the best players from San Diego State, standard size, black inner border and white outer border with "SDSU" and school mascot in red at top
COMPLETE SET (21)............... 15.00 6.00

1989 San Diego State Aztecs Smokey

COMPLETE SET (28)............... 10.00 4.00

1989 San Jose Giants Best

The 1989 San Jose Giants set contains 31 standard-size cards. The fronts have posed color player photos with white borders. The year "1989" and the city are written vertically on the left side of the card, and the player's name and position are given below the picture. In a horizontal format, the backs have biography, recent professional baseball performance summary (including statistics), and a color headshot, all in a yellow rectangular box.
COMPLETE SET (31)................. 5.00 2.00

1989 San Jose Giants Cal League Cards

COMPLETE SET (30)................. 5.00 2.00

1989 San Jose Giants ProCards

This 30-card standard-size set of the 1989 San Jose Giants, a Class A California League affiliate of the San Francisco Giants, features orange-bordered posed color player photos on its fronts. The player's name, position, and team name appear at the bottom. The horizontal gray back carries the player's name and position at the top, followed by biography and statistics.
COMPLETE SET (30)................. 5.00 2.00

1989 San Jose Giants Star

The 1989 San Jose Giants set contains 28 standard-size cards. The fronts have posed color player photos, with orange borders on the top portion of the card fading to black as one moves down the card face. In black print on a pale orange background, the backs have biography and statistics. The color scheme of the front borders on card numbers 26-28 is reversed; also these cards have blue instead of black print on the back. 5,000 sets produced.
COMPLETE SET (28)................. 5.00 2.00

1989 Sarasota White Sox Star

The 1989 Sarasota White Sox set contains 25 standard-size cards. The fronts have posed color player photos, with blue borders on the top portion of the card fading to red as one moves down the card face. In blue print on a light blue background, the backs have biography and statistics. 5,000 sets produced.
COMPLETE SET (25)................. 5.00 2.00

1989 Savannah Cardinals ProCards

This 30-card standard-size set of the 1989 Savannah Cardinals, a Class A South Atlantic affiliate of the St. Louis Cardinals, features orange-bordered posed color player photos on its fronts. The player's name, position, and team name appear at the bottom. The horizontal gray back carries the player's name and position at the top, followed by biography and statistics.
COMPLETE SET (30)................. 5.00 2.00

1989 Scranton Red Barons CMC

COMPLETE SET (25)................. 5.00 2.00

1989 Scranton Red Barons ProCards

This 28-card standard-size set of the 1989 Scranton Red Barons, a Class AAA International League affiliate of the Philadelphia Phillies, features blue-bordered posed color player photos on its fronts. The player's name, position, and team name appear at the bottom. The horizontal gray back carries the player's name and position at the top, followed by biography and statistics.
COMPLETE SET (28)................. 5.00 2.00

1989 Shreveport Captains ProCards

This 27-card standard-size set of the 1989 Shreveport Captains, a Class AA Texas League affiliate of the San Francisco Giants, features red-bordered posed color player photos on its fronts. The player's name, position, and team name appear at the bottom. The horizontal gray back carries the player's name and position at the top, followed by biography and statistics.
COMPLETE SET (27)................. 5.00 2.00

1989 South Atlantic League All-Stars Grand Slam

COMPLETE SET (46)............... 25.00 10.00

1989 South Bend White Sox Grand Slam

COMPLETE SET (30)................. 5.00 2.00

1989 Southern League All-Stars Jennings

This 25-card standard-size set showcases Southern League All-Stars. The front design has a mix of posed or action color player photos, with white and purple borders on a light blue card face. The year "1989" appears in a row of stars at the card top, and the Southern League logo is superimposed at the lower left corner. The horizontally oriented backs have biography, statistics, and the player's regular team.
COMPLETE SET (25)................. 5.00 2.00

1989 Spartanburg Phillies ProCards

This 30-card standard-size set of the 1989 Spartanburg Phillies, a Class A South Atlantic League affiliate of the Philadelphia Phillies, features orange-bordered posed color player photos on its fronts. The player's name, position, and team name appear at the bottom. The horizontal gray back carries the player's name and position at the top, followed by biography and statistics.
COMPLETE SET (30)................. 5.00 2.00

1989 Spartanburg Phillies Star

The 1989 Spartanburg Phillies set contains 26 standard-size cards. The fronts have posed color player photos, with red borders on the top portion of the card fading to gray as one moves down the card face. In red print on a gray background, the backs have biography and statistics. The back of card number 26 has a white background. The cards are arranged alphabetically and numbered on the back. 5,000 sets produced.
COMPLETE SET (26)................. 5.00 2.00

1989 Spokane Indians Sports Pro

The 1989 Spokane Indians set was sponsored by Sport Pro and University City. The 26 standard-size cards have on the fronts posed color player photos with white borders. The team name and logo appear in a black stripe at the top of the card. In a horizontal format, the backs have brief biographical information and sponsors' advertisements.
COMPLETE SET (26)................. 5.00 2.00

1989 Springfield Cardinals Best

The 1989 Springfield Cardinals set contains 30 standard-size cards. The fronts have posed color player photos with white borders. The year "1989" and the city are written vertically on the left side of the card, and the player's name and position are given below the picture. In a horizontal format, the backs have biography, recent professional baseball performance summary (including statistics), and a color headshot, all in a yellow rectangular box.
COMPLETE SET (30)................. 5.00 2.00

1989 St. Catharines Blue Jays ProCards

Sponsored by The Standard, this 28-card standard-size set of the 1989 St. Catharines Blue Jays, a Class A New York-Penn League affiliate of the Toronto Blue Jays, features orange-bordered posed color player photos on its fronts. The player's name, position, and team name appear at the bottom. The horizontal gray back carries the player's name and position at the top, followed by biography and statistics. This issue includes the minor league card debut of Carlos Delgado and Jeff Kent.
COMPLETE SET (28)............... 40.00 16.00

1989 St. Lucie Mets Star

The 1989 St. Lucie Mets set contains 27 standard-size cards. The fronts have posed color player photos, with blue borders on the top portion of the card fading to orange as one moves down the card face. In blue print on a pale orange background, the backs have biography and statistics. The cards are arranged alphabetically and numbered on the back. 5,000 sets produced.
COMPLETE SET (27)................. 5.00 2.00

1989 St. Petersburg Cardinals Star

The 1989 St. Petersburg Cardinals set contains 29 standard-size cards. The fronts have posed color player photos, with red borders on the top portion of the card fading to yellow as one moves down the card face. In red print on a pale yellow background, the backs have biography and statistics. 5,000 sets produced.
COMPLETE SET (29)................. 5.00 2.00

1989 Stockton Ports Best

This 32-card standard-size set features the 1989 Stockton Ports, a farm club for the Milwaukee Brewers. The fronts have posed color player photos with white borders. The year "1989" and the city are written vertically on the left side of the card, and the player's name and position are given below the picture. In a horizontal format, the backs have biography, recent professional baseball performance summary (including statistics), and a color headshot, all in a yellow rectangular box.
COMPLETE SET (32)................. 5.00 2.00

1989 Stockton Ports Cal League Cards

COMPLETE SET (30)................. 5.00 2.00

1989 Stockton Ports ProCards

This 31-card standard-size set of the 1989 Stockton Ports, a Class A California League affiliate of the Milwaukee Brewers, features orange-bordered posed color player photos on its fronts. The player's name, position, and team name appear at the bottom. The horizontal gray back carries the player's name and position at the top, followed by biography and statistics. Card number 376 Kent Hetrick has the wrong back. The card back is number 466 Jeffrey Gay of the Palm Springs Angels. A second card in the set also has a wrong back. Card number 372 Leo Perez has Palm Springs Angels player James Townsend number 463 on the back.
COMPLETE SET (31)................. 5.00 2.00

1989 Stockton Ports Star

This 28-card standard-size set features the 1989 Stockton Ports, a farm club for the Milwaukee Brewers. The fronts have posed color player photos, with blue borders on the top portion of the card fading to yellow as one moves down the card face. In blue print on a pale yellow background, the backs have biography and statistics. 5,000 sets produced.
COMPLETE SET (28)................. 5.00 2.00

1989 Sumter Braves ProCards

This 33-card standard-size set of the 1989 Sumter Braves, a Class A South Atlantic League affiliate of the Atlanta Braves, features orange-bordered posed color player photos on its fronts. The player's name, position, and team name appear at the bottom. The horizontal gray back carries the player's name and position at the top, followed by biography and statistics.
COMPLETE SET (33)................. 5.00 2.00

1989 Syracuse Chiefs CMC

This 25-card standard-size set of the 1989 Syracuse Chiefs, a Class AAA International League affiliate of the Toronto Blue Jays, features on its fronts white-bordered posed color player photos framed by a black line. The team's name, the player's name, and his position appear at the bottom. The white back is framed by a black line and carries the team's name and league at the top, followed by the player's name, biography and statistics.
COMPLETE SET (25)................. 5.00 2.00

1989 Syracuse Chiefs Merchants Bank

Sponsored by Merchants Bank and WIXT Channel 9, this photo album features the 1989 Syracuse Chiefs, a Class AAA International League affiliate of the Toronto Blue Jays. The photo album unfolds to reveal three 11" by 8 1/4" sheets. The first sheet displays a color team photo, with player identification immediately below. The second panel carries fifteen player cards in three rows of five each. The third panel has ten player cards in its top two rows, with the third row consisting of Merchant Bank advertisements. The perforated player cards measure 2 1/4" by 2 1/2". The fronts display white-bordered color posed player portraits; player identification and sponsor logos are below the pictures. The horizontal backs carry biography and statistics. The cards are unnumbered and checklisted below in alphabetical order.
COMPLETE SET (25)................. 8.00 3.20

1989 Syracuse Chiefs ProCards

This 27-card standard-size set of the 1989 Syracuse Chiefs, a Class AAA International League affiliate of the Toronto Blue Jays, features blue-bordered posed color player photos on its fronts. The player's name, position, and team name appear at the bottom. The horizontal gray back carries the player's name and position at the top, followed by biography and statistics.
COMPLETE SET (27)................. 5.00 2.00

1989 Tacoma Tigers CMC

COMPLETE SET (25)................. 5.00 2.00

1989 Tacoma Tigers ProCards

This 32-card standard-size set of the 1989 Tacoma Tigers, a Class AAA Pacific Coast League affiliate of the Oakland Athletics, features blue-bordered posed color player photos on its fronts. The player's name, position, and team name appear at the bottom. The horizontal gray back carries the player's name and position at the top, followed by biography and statistics.
COMPLETE SET (32)............... 30.00 12.00

1989 Tennessee Tech Golden Eagles

COMPLETE SET (36)............... 10.00 4.00

1989 Texas League All-Stars Grand Slam

COMPLETE SET (40)............... 20.00 8.00

1989 Tidewater Tides Candl

Set features leading players in Tidewater history.
COMPLETE SET (15)............... 10.00 4.00

1989 Tidewater Tides CMC

COMPLETE SET (29)................. 5.00 2.00

1989 Tidewater Tides ProCards

This 30-card standard-size set of the 1989 Tidewater Tides, a Class AAA International League affiliate of the New York Mets, features blue-bordered posed color player photos on its fronts. The player's name, position, and team name appear at the bottom. The horizontal gray back carries the player's name and position at the top, followed by biography and statistics.
COMPLETE SET (30).................. 5.00 2.00

1989 Toledo Mud Hens CMC

COMPLETE SET (25).................. 5.00 2.00

1989 Toledo Mud Hens ProCards

This 30-card standard-size set of the 1989 Toledo Mud Hens, a Class AAA International League affiliate of the Detroit Tigers, features blue-bordered posed color player photos on its fronts. The player's name, position, and team name appear at the bottom. The horizontal gray back carries the player's name and position at the top, followed by biography and statistics.
COMPLETE SET (30).................. 5.00 2.00

1989 Triple A All-Stars CMC

COMPLETE SET (45)............... 10.00 4.00

1989 Triple A All-Stars ProCards

COMPLETE SET (55)............... 10.00 4.00

1989 Tucson Toros CMC

COMPLETE SET (25).................. 5.00 2.00

1989 Tucson Toros Jones Photo

Produced by Jones Photo. The cards are unnumbered so they are ordered below in alphabetical order. A complete set could only be obtained by attending all five promotional giveaway nights at the ballpark. The cards measure 5" by 7" and are full color photos of the players. 400 sets were produced. Less than 100 of each of the late issue cards exist.
COMPLETE SET (24)............... 40.00 16.00

1989 Tucson Toros ProCards

This 28-card standard-size set of the 1989 Tucson Toros, a Class AAA Pacific Coast League affiliate of the Houston Astros, features blue-bordered posed color player photos on its fronts. The player's name, position, and team name appear at the bottom. The horizontal gray back carries the player's name and position at the top, followed by biography and statistics.
COMPLETE SET (28).................. 5.00 2.00

1989 Tulsa Drillers Grand Slam

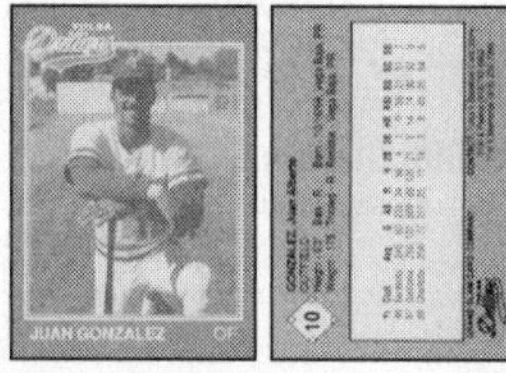

This issue includes third year cards of Juan Gonzalez, Dean Palmer and Sammy Sosa.
COMPLETE SET (26)............... 50.00 20.00

1989 Tulsa Drillers Team Issue

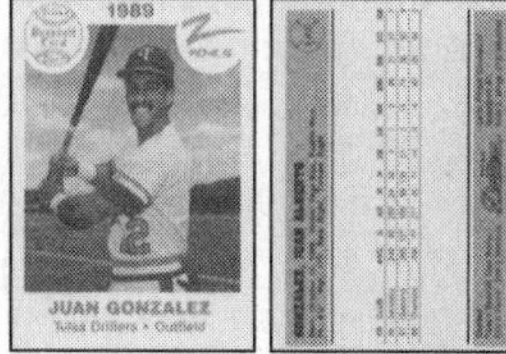

This issue includes third year cards of Juan Gonzalez, Dean Palmer and Sammy Sosa.
COMPLETE SET (27)............. 100.00 40.00

1989 Utica Blue Sox Pucko

The 1989 Utica Blue Sox set contains 34 standard-size cards. The front design features glossy color player photos with purple borders. The team logo is superimposed at the lower left corner. The backs have brief biography, the circumstances under which the player was drafted, and statistics (where appropriate). Most of the players (2-27) are arranged alphabetically. 3,750 sets were produced.
COMPLETE SET (34).................. 5.00 2.00

1989 Vancouver Canadians CMC

This 25-card standard-size set of the 1989 Vancouver Canadians, a Class AAA Pacific Coast League affiliate of the Chicago White Sox, features on its fronts white-bordered posed color player photos framed by a black line. The team's name, the player's name, and his position appear at the bottom. The white back is framed by a black line and carries the team's name and league at the top, followed by the player's name, biography and statistics.
COMPLETE SET (25).................. 5.00 2.00

1989 Vancouver Canadians ProCards

This 27-card standard-size set of the 1989 Vancouver Canadians, a Class AAA Pacific Coast League affiliate of the Chicago White Sox, features blue-bordered posed color player photos on its fronts. The player's name, position, and team name appear at the bottom. The horizontal gray back carries the player's name and position at the top, followed by biography and statistics. This issue includes Jack McDowell's only minor league card.
COMPLETE SET (27)................ 10.00 4.00

1989 Vero Beach Dodgers Star

The 1989 Vero Beach set contains 29 standard-size cards. The fronts have posed color player photos, with blue borders on the top portion of the card fading to yellow as one moves down the card face. In blue print on a cream-colored background, the backs have biography and statistics. The backs of card numbers 26-29 have a pale yellow background. 5,000 sets produced.
COMPLETE SET (29)............... 15.00 6.00

1989 Visalia Oaks Cal League Cards

COMPLETE SET (29).................. 5.00 2.00

1989 Visalia Oaks ProCards

This 31-card standard-size set of the 1989 Visalia Oaks, a Class A Cal League affiliate of the Minnesota Twins, features orange-bordered posed color player photos on its fronts. The player's name, position, and team name appear at the bottom. The horizontal gray back carries the player's name and position at the top, followed by biography and statistics.
COMPLETE SET (31).................. 5.00 2.00

1989 Waterloo Diamonds ProCards

This 28-card standard-size set of the 1989 Waterloo Diamonds, a Class A Midwest League Independent, features orange-bordered posed color player photos on its fronts. The player's name, position, and team name appear at the bottom. The horizontal gray back carries the player's name and position at the top, followed by biography and statistics.
COMPLETE SET (28).................. 5.00 2.00

1989 Waterloo Diamonds Star

The 1989 Waterloo Diamonds set contains 32 standard-size cards. The fronts have posed color player photos, with blue borders on the top portion of the card fading to sky blue as one moves down the card face. In blue print on a white background, the backs have biography and statistics. 5,000 sets produced.
COMPLETE SET (32).................. 5.00 2.00

1989 Watertown Indians Star

The 1989 Waterloo Diamonds set contains 29 standard-size cards. The fronts have posed color player photos, with blue borders on the top portion of the card fading to sky blue as one moves down the card face. In blue print on a pale blue background, the backs have biography and statistics. Card numbers 26-29 have a white background on the reverse. 5,000 sets produced.
COMPLETE SET (29).................. 5.00 2.00

1989 Wausau Timbers Grand Slam

COMPLETE SET (28).................. 5.00 2.00

1989 Welland Pirates Pucko

This 35-card standard-size set of the 1989 Welland Pirates, a Class A New York-Penn League affiliate of the Pittsburgh Pirates, features glossy player photos with mustard-colored borders on its fronts. The team name is printed in a white bar above the photo, while the player's name and position and the team logo appear on the bottom. The backs carry a brief biography, the circumstances under which the player was drafted, and statistics (where appropriate). 3,750 sets were produced.
COMPLETE SET (35).................. 5.00 2.00

1989 West Palm Beach Expos Star

This 31-card standard-size set of the 1989 West Palm Beach Expos, a Class A Florida State League affiliate of the Montreal Expos, features posed color player photos, with blue borders on the top portion of the card, fading to red as one moves down the card face. The player's name, team name, and position appear at the bottom. In blue print on a pink background, the backs carry biography and statistics. There are two cards numbered 26. The last seven cards listed below were late issues. 5,000 sets produced.
COMPLETE SET (31).................. 5.00 2.00

1989 Wichita Bonus Rock

These two bonus cards were produced by Rock's Dugout. They are of the same size and design as the 1989 Wichita Champions regular issue, except they have orange borders on the front and red print on the back.
COMPLETE SET (2).................... 8.00 3.20

1989 Wichita Champions Rock

The 1989 Wichita Wranglers Champion Highlight set was produced by Rock's Dugout and contains 20 standard-size cards. The front features a glossy color player photo bordered in purple, with the team name and player's name in yellow lettering. The horizontally oriented backs have a caption printed in purple and a rope serving as a border.
COMPLETE SET (20).................. 8.00 3.20

1989 Wichita Stadium Rock

The 1989 Wichita Wranglers Stadium set was produced by Rock's Dugout and contains 30 standard-size cards. The front design of these cards is unique; it features color posed player photos cut out and superimposed on unfocused black and white shots of the baseball stadium. The lettering and numbering on the card fronts is in red. The backs are blank. The set also includes four advertisement cards for baseball card shops in Wichita. This set includes an early card of '88 Olympic star and veteran major league pitcher Andy Benes.
COMPLETE SET (30)............... 10.00 4.00

1989 Wichita Update Rock

The 1989 Wichita Wranglers Update set was produced by Rock's Dugout and contains 20 standard-size cards. The front features a glossy color player photo bordered in red, with the team name and player's name in black lettering. The horizontally oriented backs have a caption printed in red and a rope serving as a border.
COMPLETE SET (20).................. 8.00 3.20

1989 Wichita Wranglers Rock

The 1989 Wichita Wranglers set was produced by Rock's Dugout and contains 30 standard-size cards. The fronts feature posed color player photos (from the waist up), with white borders on a red card face. In black lettering on gray and white, the horizontally oriented backs present biography, career record, and an advertisement for a baseball cardshop. The cards are skip-numbered on both sides by uniform number, and checklisted below accordingly.
COMPLETE SET (30)............... 10.00 4.00

1989 Williamsport Bills ProCards

This 25-card standard-size set of the 1989 Williamsport Bills, a Class AA Eastern League affiliate of the Seattle Mariners, features red-bordered posed color player photos on its fronts. The player's name, position, and team name appear at the bottom. The horizontal gray back carries the player's name and position at the top, followed by biography and statistics. This issue includes the minor league card debut of Tino Martinez.
COMPLETE SET (25)............... 15.00 6.00

1989 Williamsport Bills Star

The 1989 Williamsport Bills set contains 25 standard-size cards. The fronts have posed color player photos, with blue borders on the top portion of the card fading to yellow as one moves down the card face. In blue print on a white background, the backs have biography and statistics. Card number 25 has a pale yellow background on the reverse. This issue includes the minor league card debut of Tino Martinez. 5,000 sets produced.
COMPLETE SET (25)............... 15.00 6.00

1989 Winston-Salem Spirits Star

The 1989 Winston-Salem Spirits set contains 26 standard-size cards. The fronts have posed color player photos, with blue borders on the top portion of the card fading to gray as one moves down the card face. In blue print on a pale green background, the backs have biography and statistics. The last four cards have white background on the reverse, and the front borders of the Julio Strauss card fade from blue to white. 5,000 sets produced.
COMPLETE SET (26).................. 5.00 2.00

1989 Winter Haven Red Sox Star

The 1989 Winter Haven set contains 29 standard-size cards. The fronts have posed color player photos, with blue borders on the top portion of the card fading to gray as one moves down the card face. In blue print on a light gray background, the backs have biography and statistics. This issue includes the minor league card debut of John Valentin. 5,000 sets produced.
COMPLETE SET (29)............... 10.00 4.00

1989 Wytheville Cubs Star

The 1989 Wytheville Cubs set contains 30 standard-size cards. The fronts have posed color player photos, with blue borders on the top portion of the card fading to red as one moves down the card face. In blue print on a pink background, the backs have biography and statistics. 5,000 sets produced.
COMPLETE SET (30).................. 5.00 2.00

1990 Alaska Goldpanners Stars of the '90s Team Issue

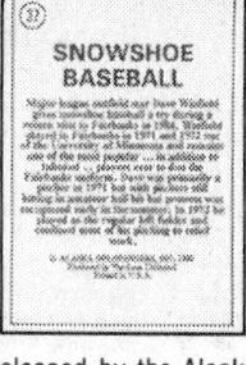

This 12-card set was released by the Alaska Goldpanner in 1990, and features yellow-bordered player cards from Goldpanner players that made it to the major leagues in the eighties. The set is numbered 37-48.
COMPLETE SET (12)............... 15.00 4.50

1990 Alaska Goldpanners Team Issue

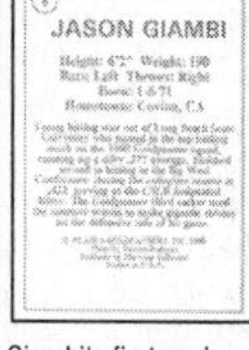

This set contains Jason Giambi's first card.
COMPLETE SET (16)............... 30.00 12.00

1990 Albany Yankees All Decade Best

This 36-card standard-size set of the 1990 Albany Yankees, a Class AA Eastern League affiliate of the New York Yankees, features white-bordered posed and action color player photos on its fronts. The player's name and position appear vertically on the left side. The words "All Decade" appear across the top. The yellow horizontal back carries the player's name and years played at the top, followed by player's history, highlights, and statistics. 2,500 sets were produced.
COMPLETE SET (36)............... 10.00 3.00

1990 Albany Yankees Best

This 26-card standard-size set of the 1990 Albany Yankees, a Class AA Eastern League affiliate of the New York Yankees, features white-bordered posed and action color player photos on its fronts. The player's name and position appear vertically on the left side. The yellow horizontal back carries the player's name and position at the top, followed by biography, career highlights, and statistics. A player head shot appears in the lower right corner.
COMPLETE SET (26)............... 10.00 3.00

1990 Albany Yankees ProCards

This 29-card standard-size set of the 1990 Albany Yankees, a Class AA Eastern League affiliate of the New York Yankees, features on its white-bordered fronts posed color player photos set on simulated wood-grain backgrounds. The player's name, position, and team appear within a gold-colored rectangle below the photo. The tan horizontal back is bordered in white and carries the player's name at the top, followed by biography and statistics.
COMPLETE SET (29)............... 10.00 3.00

1990 Albany Yankees Star

This 28-card standard-size set of the 1990 Albany Yankees, a Class AA Eastern League affiliate of the New York Yankees, features purple bordered posed color player photos on its fronts. The player's name, team name, and position appear at the bottom. The white horizontal back carries the player's name at the top, followed by biography, career highlights, and statistics.
COMPLETE SET (28)............... 10.00 3.00

1990 Albuquerque Dukes CMC

This 28-card standard-size set of the 1990 Albuquerque Dukes, a Class AAA Pacific Coast League affiliate of the Los Angeles Dodgers, features white-bordered posed color player photos on its fronts. The player's name and position appear at the bottom; the team name appears vertically on the left. The back carries the league emblem in the white area at the top, the team name in the green stripe below, and player's name, position, biography, and statistics in the yellow area at the bottom. 1,100 sets were produced.
COMPLETE SET (28).................. 5.00 1.50

1990 Albuquerque Dukes ProCards

This 30-card standard-size set of the 1990 Albuquerque Dukes, a Class AAA Pacific Coast League affiliate of the Los Angeles Dodgers, features on its white-bordered fronts posed color player photos set on simulated wood-grain backgrounds. The player's name, position, and team appear within a gold-colored rectangle below the photo. The tan horizontal back is bordered in white and carries the player's name at the top, followed by biography and statistics.
COMPLETE SET (30).................. 5.00 1.50

1990 Albuquerque Dukes Tribune

This 31-card standard-size set was sponsored by the Albuquerque Tribune, and its logo appears at the bottom of the reverse. The cards feature on the observe a posed color player photo. No information is provided on the card fronts. The back lists biography and 1989 statistics. The cards are unnumbered and checklisted below in alphabetical order.
COMPLETE SET (31)............... 10.00 3.00

1990 Appleton Foxes Box Scores

COMPLETE SET (30).................. 5.00 1.50

1990 Appleton Foxes ProCards

This 29-card standard-size set of the 1990 Appleton Foxes, a Class A Midwest League affiliate of the Kansas City Royals, features on its white-bordered fronts posed color player photos set on simulated wood-grain backgrounds. The player's name, position, and team appear within a gold-colored rectangle below the photo. The tan horizontal back is bordered in white and carries the player's name at the top, followed by biography and statistics.
COMPLETE SET (29).................. 5.00 1.50

1990 Arizona Wildcats Police

COMPLETE SET (18)............... 10.00 3.00

1990 Arkansas Razorbacks

COMPLETE SET (33)............... 10.00 3.00

1990 Arkansas Travelers Grand Slam

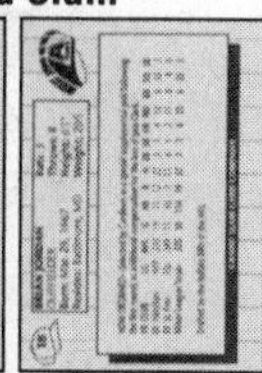

Brian Jordan is the featured player in this set.
COMPLETE SET (30)............... 10.00 3.00

1990 Asheville Tourists ProCards

This 28-card standard-size set of the 1990 Asheville Tourists, a Class A South Atlantic League affiliate of the Houston Astros, features on its white-bordered fronts posed color player photos set on simulated wood-grain backgrounds. The player's name, position, and team appear within a gold-colored rectangle below the photo. The tan horizontal back is bordered in white and carries the player's name at the top, followed by biography and statistics. This issue includes the minor league card debut of Brian L. Hunter.
COMPLETE SET (28)............... 10.00 3.00

1990 Auburn Astros Best

This 25-card standard-size set of the 1990 Auburn Astros, a Class A New York-Penn League affiliate of the Houston Astros, features white-bordered posed and action color player photos on its fronts. The player's name and position appear vertically on the left side. The yellow horizontal back carries the player's name and position at the top, followed by biography, career highlights, and statistics. A player head shot appears in the lower right corner.
COMPLETE SET (25).................. 5.00 1.50

1990 Auburn Astros ProCards

This 26-card standard-size set of the 1990 Auburn Astros, a Class A New York-Penn League affiliate of the Houston Astros, features on its white-bordered fronts posed color player photos set on simulated wood-grain backgrounds. The player's name, position, and team appear within a gold-colored rectangle below the photo. The tan horizontal back is bordered in white and carries the player's name at the top, followed by biography and statistics.
COMPLETE SET (26).................. 5.00 1.50

1990 Augusta Pirates ProCards

This 27-card standard-size set of the 1990 Augusta Pirates, a Class A South Atlantic League affiliate of the Augusta Pirates, features on its white-bordered fronts posed color player photos set on simulated wood-grain

backgrounds. The player's name, position, and team appear within a gold-colored rectangle below the photo. The tan horizontal back is bordered in white and carries the player's name at the top, followed by biography and statistics.
COMPLETE SET (27).................. 5.00 1.50

1990 Bakersfield Dodgers Cal League Cards

COMPLETE SET (32).................. 5.00 1.50

1990 Baseball City Royals Star

This 31-card standard-size set of the 1990 Baseball City Royals, a Class A Florida State League affiliate of the Kansas City Royals, features blue bordered posed color player photos on its fronts. The player's name, team name, and position appear at the bottom. The white horizontal back carries the player's name at the top, followed by biography, career highlights, and statistics.
COMPLETE SET (31).................. 5.00 1.50

1990 Batavia Clippers ProCards

This 30-card standard-size set of the 1990 Batavia Clippers, a Class A New York-Penn League affiliate of the Philadelphia Phillies, features on its white-bordered fronts posed color player photos set on simulated wood-grain backgrounds. The player's name, position, and team appear within a gold-colored rectangle below the photo. The tan horizontal back is bordered in white and carries the player's name at the top, followed by biography and statistics.
COMPLETE SET (30).................. 5.00 1.50

1990 Beloit Brewers Best

This 27-card standard-size set of the 1990 Beloit Brewers, a Class A Midwest League affiliate of the Milwaukee Brewers, features white-bordered posed and action color player photos on its fronts. The player's name and position appear vertically on the left side. The yellow horizontal back carries the player's name and position at the top, followed by biography, career highlights, and statistics. A player head shot appears in the lower right corner.
COMPLETE SET (27).................. 5.00 1.50

1990 Beloit Brewers Star

This 27-card standard-size set of the 1990 Beloit Brewers, a Class A Midwest League affiliate of the Milwaukee Brewers, features yellow bordered posed color player photos on its fronts. The player's name, team name, and position appear at the bottom. The white horizontal back carries the player's name at the top, followed by biography, career highlights, and statistics.
COMPLETE SET (27).................. 5.00 1.50

1990 Bend Bucks Legoe

COMPLETE SET (32).................. 5.00 1.50

1990 Billings Mustangs ProCards

This 30-card standard-size set of the 1990 Billings Mustangs, a Rookie Class Pioneer League affiliate of the Cincinnati Reds, features on its white-bordered fronts posed color player photos set on simulated wood-grain backgrounds. The player's name, position, and team appear within a gold-colored rectangle below the photo. The tan horizontal back is bordered in white and carries the player's name at the top, followed by biography and statistics.
COMPLETE SET (30).................. 5.00 1.50

1990 Birmingham Barons All Decade Best

This 34-card standard-size set of the 1990 Birmingham Barons, a Class AA Southern League affiliate of the Chicago White Sox, features white-bordered posed and action color player photos on its fronts. The player's name and position appear vertically on the left side. The words "All Decade" appear across the top. The yellow horizontal back carries the player's name and years played at the top, followed by player's history, highlights, and statistics. 2,500 sets were produced.
COMPLETE SET (34).................. 8.00 2.40

1990 Birmingham Barons Best

This 30-card standard-size set of the 1990 Birmingham Barons, a Class AA Southern League affiliate of the Chicago White Sox, features white-bordered posed and action color player photos on its fronts. The player's name and position appear vertically on the left side. The yellow horizontal back carries the player's name and position at the top, followed by biography, career highlights, and statistics. A player head shot appears in the lower right corner. This issue includes the minor league card debut of Frank Thomas.
COMPLETE SET (30).................. 30.00 9.00

1990 Birmingham Barons ProCards

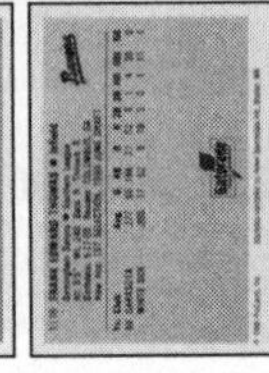

This 28-card standard-size set of the 1990 Birmingham Barons, a Class AA Southern League affiliate of the Chicago White Sox, features on its white-bordered fronts posed color player photos set on simulated wood-grain backgrounds. The player's name, position, and team appear within a gold-colored rectangle below the photo. The tan horizontal back is bordered in white and carries the player's name at the top, followed by biography and statistics. This issue includes the minor league card debut of Frank Thomas.
COMPLETE SET (28)................ 20.00 6.00

1990 Boise Hawks ProCards

This 33-card standard-size set of the 1990 Boise Hawks, a Class A Northwest League affiliate of the California Angels, features on its white-bordered fronts posed color player photos set on simulated wood-grain backgrounds. The player's name, position, and team appear within a gold-colored rectangle below the photo. The tan horizontal back is bordered in white and carries the player's name at the top, followed by biography and statistics.
COMPLETE SET (33).................. 5.00 1.50

1990 Bristol Tigers ProCards

This 29-card standard-size set of the 1990 Bristol Tigers, a Rookie Class Appalachian League affiliate of the Detroit Tigers, features on its white-bordered fronts posed color player photos set on simulated wood-grain backgrounds. The player's name, position, and team appear within a gold-colored rectangle below the photo. The tan horizontal back is bordered in white and carries the player's name at the top, followed by biography and statistics. This issue includes the minor league card debut of Tony Clark.
COMPLETE SET (29).................. 8.00 2.40

1990 Bristol Tigers Star

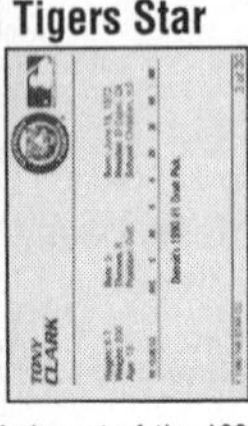

This 30-card standard-size set of the 1990 Bristol Tigers, a Rookie Class Appalachian League affiliate of the Detroit Tigers, features orange bordered posed color player photos on its fronts. The player's name, team name, and position appear at the bottom. The white horizontal back carries the player's name at the top, followed by biography, career highlights, and statistics. This issue includes the minor league card debut of Tony Clark.
COMPLETE SET (30).................. 8.00 2.40

1990 Buffalo Bisons CMC

This 25-card standard-size set of the 1990 Buffalo Bisons, a Class AAA American Association League affiliate of the Pittsburgh Pirates, features white-bordered posed color player photos on its fronts. The player's name and position appear at the bottom; the team name appears vertically on the left. The back carries the league emblem in the white area at the top, the team name in the green stripe below, and player's name, position, biography, and statistics in the yellow area at the bottom. 1,100 sets were produced.
COMPLETE SET (25).................. 5.00 1.50

1990 Buffalo Bisons ProCards

This 28-card standard-size set of the 1990 Buffalo Bisons, a Class AAA American Association League affiliate of the Pittsburgh Pirates, features on its white-bordered fronts posed color player photos set on simulated wood-grain backgrounds. The player's name, position, and team appear within a gold-colored rectangle below the photo. The tan horizontal back is bordered in white and carries the player's name at the top, followed by biography and statistics.
COMPLETE SET (28).................. 5.00 1.50

1990 Buffalo Bisons Team Issue

This 27 card was issued only to fans attending a Buffalo Bisons game. These cards, which measure approximately 2 5/8" by 3 5/8" when perforated, were in an album entitled "Stars of the Future". The entire folder measures 10" by 13 1/2". This set was sponsored by WNY Lincoln-Mercury dealers.
COMPLETE SET (27)................ 10.00 3.00

1990 Burlington Braves Best

This 30-card standard-size set of the 1990 Burlington Braves, a Class A Midwest League affiliate of the Atlanta Braves, features white-bordered posed and action color player photos on its fronts. The player's name and position appear vertically on the left side. The yellow horizontal back carries the player's name and position at the top, followed by biography, career highlights, and statistics. A player head shot appears in the lower right corner. This issue includes a second year card of Javy Lopez.
COMPLETE SET (30)................ 15.00 4.50

1990 Burlington Braves ProCards

This 30-card standard-size set of the 1990 Burlington Braves, a Class A Midwest League affiliate of the Atlanta Braves, features on its white-bordered fronts posed color player photos set on simulated wood-grain backgrounds. The player's name, position, and team appear within a gold-colored rectangle below the photo. The tan horizontal back is bordered in white and carries the player's name at the top, followed by biography and statistics. This issue includes a second year card of Javy Lopez.
COMPLETE SET (30)................ 12.00 3.60

1990 Burlington Braves Star

This 31-card standard-size set of the 1990 Burlington Braves, a Class A Midwest League affiliate of the Atlanta Braves, features red bordered posed color player photos on its fronts. The player's name, team name, and position appear at the bottom. The white horizontal back carries the player's name at the top, followed by biography, career highlights, and statistics. This issue includes a second year card of Javy Lopez.
COMPLETE SET (31)................ 15.00 4.50

1990 Burlington Indians ProCards

This 28-card standard-size set of the 1990 Burlington Indians, a Rookie Class Appalachian League affiliate of the Cleveland Indians, features on its white-bordered fronts posed color player photos set on simulated wood-grain backgrounds. The player's name, position, and team appear within a gold-colored rectangle below the photo. The tan horizontal back is bordered in white and carries the player's name at the top, followed by biography and statistics. This issue includes the minor league card debut of Jim Thome.
COMPLETE SET (28)................ 40.00 12.00

1990 Butte Copper Kings Sports Pro

This 30-card standard-size set of the 1990 Butte Copper Kings, a Rookie Class A Pioneer League affiliate of the Texas Rangers, features posed color head-and-shoulders shots, with thin black borders on a white card face. The horizontally oriented backs have biographical information. This issue includes the minor league card debut of Rusty Greer.
COMPLETE SET (30)................ 15.00 4.50

1990 Calgary Cannons CMC

This 25-card standard-size set of the 1990 Calgary Cannons, a Class AAA Pacific Coast League affiliate of the Seattle Mariners, features white-bordered posed color player photos on its fronts. The player's name and position appear at the bottom; the team name appears vertically on the left. The back carries the league emblem in the white area at the top, the team name in the green stripe below, and player's name, position, biography, and statistics in the yellow area at the bottom. 1,100 sets were produced.
COMPLETE SET (25)................ 15.00 4.50

1990 Calgary Cannons ProCards

This 23-card standard-size set of the 1990 Calgary Cannons, a Class AAA Pacific Coast League affiliate of the Seattle Mariners, features on its white-bordered fronts posed color player photos set on simulated wood-grain backgrounds. The player's name, position, and team appear within a gold-colored rectangle below the photo. The tan horizontal back is bordered in white and carries the player's name at the top, followed by biography and statistics.
COMPLETE SET (23).................. 5.00 1.50

1990 California League All-Stars Cal League Cards

COMPLETE SET (56)................ 10.00 3.00

1990 Canton-Akron Indians Best

This 28-card standard-size set of the 1990 Canton-Akron Indians, a Class AA Eastern League affiliate of the Cleveland Indians, features white-bordered posed and action color player photos on its fronts. The player's name and position appear vertically on the left side. The yellow horizontal back carries the player's name and position at the top, followed by biography, career highlights, and statistics. A player head shot appears in the lower right corner.
COMPLETE SET (28)................ 10.00 3.00

1990 Canton-Akron Indians ProCards

This 27-card standard-size set of the 1990 Canton-Akron Indians, a Class AA Eastern League affiliate of the Cleveland Indians, features on its white-bordered fronts posed color player photos set on simulated wood-grain backgrounds. The player's name, position, and team appear within a gold-colored rectangle below the photo. The tan horizontal back is bordered in white and carries the player's name at the top, followed by biography and statistics.
COMPLETE SET (27).................. 8.00 2.40

1990 Canton-Akron Indians Star

This 21-card standard-size set of the 1990 Canton-Akron Indians, a Class AA Eastern League affiliate of the Cleveland Indians, features light purple bordered posed color player photos on its fronts. The player's name, team name, and position appear at the bottom. The white horizontal back carries the player's name at the top, followed by biography, career highlights, and statistics.
COMPLETE SET (21)................ 10.00 3.00

1990 Carolina League All-Stars

COMPLETE SET (52).................. 5.00 1.50

1990 Cedar Rapids Reds All Decade Best

This 36-card standard-size set of the 1990 Cedar Rapids Reds, a Class A Midwest League affiliate of the Cincinnati Reds, features white-bordered posed and action color player photos on its fronts. The player's name and position appear vertically on the left side. The words "All Decade" appear across the top. The yellow horizontal back carries the player's name and years played at the top, followed by player's history, highlights, and statistics. 2,500 sets were produced.
COMPLETE SET (36).................. 5.00 1.50

1990 Cedar Rapids Reds Best

This 27-card standard-size set of the 1990 Cedar Rapids Reds, a Class A Midwest League affiliate of the Cincinnati Reds, features white-bordered posed and action color player photos on its fronts. The player's name and position appear vertically on the left side. The yellow horizontal back carries the player's name and position at the top, followed by biography, career highlights, and statistics. A player head shot appears in the lower right corner.
COMPLETE SET (27).................. 8.00 2.40

1990 Cedar Rapids Reds ProCards

This 27-card standard-size set of the 1990 Cedar Rapids Reds, a Class A Midwest League affiliate of the Cincinnati Reds, features on its white-bordered fronts posed color player photos set on simulated wood-grain backgrounds. The player's name, position, and team appear within a gold-colored rectangle below the photo. The tan horizontal back is bordered in white and carries the player's name at the top, followed by biography and statistics.
COMPLETE SET (27).................. 5.00 1.50

1990 Charleston Rainbows Best

This 28-card standard-size set of the 1990 Charleston Rainbows, a Class A South Atlantic League affiliate of the San Diego Padres, features white-bordered posed and action color player photos on its fronts. The player's name and position appear vertically on the left side. The yellow horizontal back carries the player's name and position at the top, followed by biography, career highlights, and statistics. A player head shot appears in the lower right corner.
COMPLETE SET (28).................. 5.00 1.50

1990 Charleston Rainbows ProCards

This 28-card standard-size set of the 1990 Charleston Rainbows, a Class A South Atlantic League affiliate of the San Diego Padres, features on its white-bordered fronts posed color player photos set on simulated wood-grain backgrounds. The player's name, position, and team appear within a gold-colored rectangle below the photo. The tan horizontal back is bordered in white and carries the player's name at the top, followed by biography and statistics.
COMPLETE SET (28).................. 5.00 1.50

1990 Charleston Wheelers Best

This 29-card standard-size set of the 1990 Charleston Wheelers, a Class A South Atlantic League affiliate of the Cincinnati Reds, features white-bordered posed and action color player photos on its fronts. The player's name and position appear vertically on the left side. The yellow horizontal back carries the player's name and position at the top, followed by biography, career highlights, and statistics. A player head shot appears in the lower right corner.
COMPLETE SET (29).................. 5.00 1.50

1990 Charleston Wheelers ProCards

This 28-card standard-size set of the 1990 Charleston Wheelers, a Class A South Atlantic League affiliate of the Cincinnati Reds, features on its white-bordered fronts posed color player photos set on simulated wood-grain backgrounds. The player's name, position, and team appear within a gold-colored rectangle below the photo. The tan horizontal back is bordered in white and carries the player's name at the top, followed by biography and statistics.
COMPLETE SET (28).................. 5.00 1.50

1990 Charlotte Knights Team Issue

COMPLETE SET (25).................. 8.00 2.40

1990 Charlotte Rangers Star

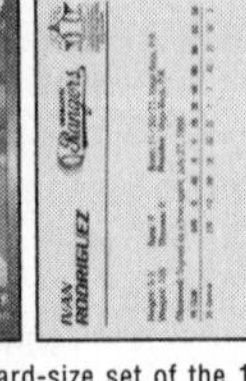

This 30-card standard-size set of the 1990 Charlotte Rangers, a Class A Florida State League affiliate of the Texas Rangers, features blue bordered posed color player photos on its fronts. The player's name, team name, and position appear at the bottom. The white horizontal back carries the player's name at the top, followed by biography, career highlights, and statistics.This issue includes a second year card of Ivan Rodriguez.
COMPLETE SET (30)................ 30.00 9.00

1990 Chattanooga Lookouts Grand Slam

COMPLETE SET (27).................. 5.00 1.50

1990 Clearwater Phillies Star

This 27-card standard-size set of the 1990 Clearwater Phillies; a Class A Florida State League affiliate of the Philadelphia Phillies, features red bordered posed color player photos on its fronts. The player's name, team name, and position appear at the bottom. The white horizontal back carries the player's name at the top, followed by biography, career highlights, and statistics.
COMPLETE SET (27).................. 5.00 1.50

1990 Clinton Giants Best

This 29-card standard-size set of the 1990 Clinton Giants, a Class A Midwest League affiliate of the San Francisco Giants, features white-bordered posed and action color player photos on its fronts. The player's name and position appear vertically on the left side. The yellow horizontal back carries the player's name and position at the top, followed by biography, career highlights, and statistics. A player head shot appears in the lower right corner.
COMPLETE SET (29).................. 5.00 1.50

1990 Clinton Giants ProCards

This 29-card standard-size set of the 1990 Clinton Giants, a Class A Midwest League affiliate of the San Francisco Giants, features on its white-bordered fronts posed color player photos set on simulated wood-grain backgrounds. The player's name, position, and team appear within a gold-colored rectangle below the photo. The tan horizontal back is bordered in white and carries the player's name at the top, followed by biography and statistics.
COMPLETE SET (29).................. 5.00 1.50

1990 Clinton Giants Update Team Issue

This 12-card standard-size update set of the 1990 Clinton Giants, a Class A Midwest League affiliate of the San Francisco Giants, features white-bordered posed and action color player photos on its fronts. The player's name and position appear vertically on the left side. The yellow horizontal back carries the player's name and position at the top, followed by biography, career highlights, and statistics. A player head shot appears in the lower right corner. 1,000 sets were produced.
COMPLETE SET (12).................. 5.00 1.50

1990 Colorado Springs Sky Sox CMC

This 24-card standard-size set of the 1990 Colorado Springs Sky Sox, a Class AAA Pacific Coast League affiliate of the Cleveland Indians, features white-bordered posed color player photos on its fronts. The player's name and position appear at the bottom; the team name appears vertically on the left. The back carries

the league emblem in the white area at the top, the team name in the green stripe below, and player's name, position, biography, and statistics in the yellow area at the bottom. 1,100 sets were produced.
COMPLETE SET (24)................. 5.00 1.50

1990 Colorado Springs Sky Sox ProCards

This 27-card standard-size set of the 1990 Colorado Springs Sky Sox, a Class AAA Pacific Coast League affiliate of the Cleveland Indians, features on its white-bordered fronts posed color player photos set on simulated wood-grain backgrounds. The player's name, position, and team appear within a gold-colored rectangle below the photo. The tan horizontal back is bordered in white and carries the player's name at the top, followed by biography and statistics.
COMPLETE SET (27)................. 5.00 1.50

1990 Columbia Mets Grand Slam

COMPLETE SET (30)................. 5.00 1.50

1990 Columbia Mets Postcards Play II

This 27-card set was issued in 4 series, with 7 cards in Series I, III-IV, and 6 in Series II. Play II produced 2,000 sets and 100 uncut sheets; 500 sets were given away at Mets games during the summer of '90. The cards measure 3 1/2" by 5" and are in the postcard format. The front design has posed glossy color player photos, with interlocking orange and navy blue borders. The player's name and team logo appear in blue and white stripes respectively below the picture. The backs are printed in dark blue. On the left half appears biography and player profile, while the right half has space for the address and stamp. The cards are numbered on the back within each series.
COMPLETE SET (27)................ 15.00 4.50

1990 Columbus Clippers CMC

This 27-card standard-size set of the 1990 Columbus Clippers, a Class AAA International League affiliate of the New York Yankees, features on its white-bordered fronts posed color player photos on its fronts. The player's name and position appear at the bottom; the team name appears vertically on the left. The back carries the league emblem in the white area at the top, the team name in the green stripe below, and player's name, position, biography, and statistics in the yellow area at the bottom. 1,100 sets were produced.
COMPLETE SET (27)................. 5.00 1.50

1990 Columbus Clippers Police

COMPLETE SET (25)................. 5.00 1.50

1990 Columbus Clippers ProCards

This 28-card standard-size set of the 1990 Columbus Clippers, a Class AAA International League affiliate of the New York Yankees, features on its white-bordered fronts posed color player photos set on simulated wood-grain backgrounds. The player's name, position, and team appear within a gold-colored rectangle below the photo. The tan horizontal back is bordered in white and carries the player's name at the top, followed by biography and statistics.
COMPLETE SET (28)................. 5.00 1.50

1990 Columbus Mudcats Best

This 26-card standard-size set of the 1990 Columbus Mudcats, a Class AA Southern League affiliate of the Houston Astros, features white-bordered posed and action color player photos on its fronts. The player's name and position appear vertically on the left side. The yellow horizontal back carries the player's name and position at the top, followed by biography, career highlights, and statistics. A player head shot appears in the lower right corner.
COMPLETE SET (26)................ 15.00 4.50

1990 Columbus Mudcats ProCards

This 27-card standard-size set of the 1990 Columbus Mudcats, a Class AA Southern League affiliate of the Houston Astros, features on its white-bordered fronts posed color player photos set on simulated wood-grain backgrounds. The player's name, position, and team appear within a gold-colored rectangle below the photo. The tan horizontal back is bordered in white and carries the player's name at the top, followed by biography and statistics.
COMPLETE SET (27)................ 15.00 4.50

1990 Columbus Mudcats Star

This 29-card standard-size set of the 1990 Columbus Mudcats, a Class AA Southern League affiliate of the Houston Astros, features red bordered posed color player photos on its fronts. The player's name, team name, and position appear at the bottom. The white horizontal back carries the player's name at the top, followed by biography, career highlights, and statistics.
COMPLETE SET (29)................ 15.00 4.50

1990 David Lipscomb

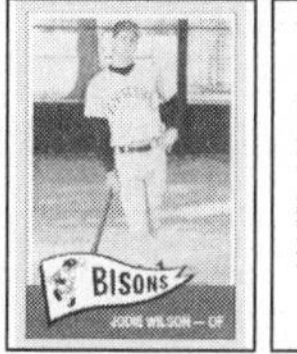

This set was released in 1990 as a 25-card set at David Lipscomb college. The set features all of the players and coaches from that year's team. Please note that these cards are a little smaller than average-sized cards.
COMPLETE SET (25)................ 10.00 3.00

1990 Denver Zephyrs CMC

This 26-card standard-size set of the 1990 Denver Zephyrs, a Class AAA American Association affiliate of the Milwaukee Brewers, features white-bordered posed color player photos on its fronts. The player's name and position appear at the bottom; the team name appears vertically on the left. The back carries the league emblem in the white area at the top, the team name in the green stripe below, and player's name, position, biography, and statistics in the yellow area at the bottom. 1,100 sets were produced.
COMPLETE SET (26)................. 5.00 1.50

1990 Denver Zephyrs ProCards

This 28-card standard-size set of the 1990 Denver Zephyrs, a Class AAA American Association affiliate of the Milwaukee Brewers, features on its white-bordered fronts posed color player photos set on simulated wood-grain backgrounds. The player's name, position, and team appear within a gold-colored rectangle below the photo. The tan horizontal back is bordered in white and carries the player's name at the top, followed by biography and statistics.
COMPLETE SET (28)................. 5.00 1.50

1990 Dunedin Blue Jays Star

This 28-card standard-size set of the 1990 Dunedin Blue Jays, a Class A Florida State League affiliate of the Toronto Blue Jays, features blue bordered posed color player photos on its fronts. The player's name, team name, and position appear at the bottom. The white horizontal back carries the player's name at the top, followed by biography, career highlights, and statistics.
COMPLETE SET (28)................ 12.00 3.60

1990 Durham Bulls Team Issue

This 29-card set of the 1990 Durham Bulls, a Class A Carolina League affiliate of the Atlanta Braves, features team colors with classic head shots of each player. The set was sponsored by the Herald Sun and printed by SportsPrint in Atlanta on a high-gloss 14 pt. card stock and measure 2 3/8" X 3 1/2".
COMPLETE SET (29)................. 5.00 1.50

1990 Durham Bulls Update Team Issue

This eight-card update set of the 1990 Durham Bulls, a Class A Carolina League affiliate of the Atlanta Braves, features team colors with classic head shots of each player. The set was sponsored by the Herald Sun and printed by SportsPrint in Atlanta on a high-gloss 14 pt. card stock and measure 2 3/8" X 3 1/2". This issue includes a first year minor league card of Ryan Klesko.
COMPLETE SET (8)................. 25.00 7.50

1990 Eastern League All-Stars ProCards

Early cards of Jeff Bagwell and Bernie Williams highlight this set.
COMPLETE SET (48)................ 20.00 6.00

1990 Edmonton Trappers CMC

This 24-card standard-size set of the 1990 Edmonton Trappers, a Class AAA Pacific Coast League affiliate of the California Angels, features white-bordered posed color player photos on its fronts. The player's name and position appear at the bottom; the team name appears vertically on the left. The back carries the league emblem in the white area at the top, the team name in the green stripe below, and player's name, position, biography, and statistics in the yellow area at the bottom. 1,100 sets were produced.
COMPLETE SET (24)................. 5.00 1.50

1990 Edmonton Trappers ProCards

This 25-card standard-size set of the 1990 Edmonton Trappers, a Class AAA Pacific Coast League affiliate of the California Angels, features on its white-bordered fronts posed color player photos set on simulated wood-grain backgrounds. The player's name, position, and team appear within a gold-colored rectangle below the photo. The tan horizontal back is bordered in white and carries the player's name and position at the top, followed by biography and statistics.
COMPLETE SET (25)................. 5.00 1.50

1990 El Paso Diablos All-Time Greats Team Issue

COMPLETE SET (45)................ 25.00 7.50

1990 El Paso Diablos Grand Slam

COMPLETE SET (25)................. 5.00 1.50

1990 Elizabethton Twins Star

This 26-card standard-size set of the 1990 Elizabethton Twins, a Rookie Class Appalachian League affiliate of the Minnesota Twins, features blue bordered posed color player photos on its fronts. The player's name, team name, and position appear at the bottom. The white horizontal back carries the player's name at the top, followed by biography, career highlights, and statistics.
COMPLETE SET (26)................. 5.00 1.50

1990 Elmira Pioneers Pucko

COMPLETE SET (27)................. 5.00 1.50

1990 Erie Sailors Star

This 31-card standard-size set of the 1990 Erie Sailors, a Class A New York-Penn League Independent, features purple bordered posed color player photos on its fronts. The player's name, team name, and position appear at the bottom. The white horizontal back carries the player's name at the top, followed by biography, career highlights, and statistics.
COMPLETE SET (31)................. 5.00 1.50

1990 Eugene Emeralds Grand Slam

COMPLETE SET (30)................. 5.00 1.50

1990 Everett Giants Best

This 28-card standard-size set of the 1990 Everett Giants, a Class A Northwest League affiliate of the San Francisco Giants, features white-bordered posed and action color player photos on its fronts. The player's name and position appear vertically on the left side. The yellow horizontal back carries the player's name and position at the top, followed by biography, career highlights, and statistics. A player head shot appears in the lower right corner.
COMPLETE SET (28)................. 5.00 1.50

1990 Everett Giants ProCards

This 32-card standard-size set of the 1990 Everett Giants, a Class A Northwest League affiliate of the San Francisco Giants, features on its white-bordered fronts posed color player photos set on simulated wood-grain backgrounds. The player's name, position, and team appear within a gold-colored rectangle below the photo. The tan horizontal back is bordered in white and carries the player's name at the top, followed by biography and statistics.
COMPLETE SET (32)................. 5.00 1.50

1990 Fayetteville Generals ProCards

This 28-card standard-size set of the 1990 Fayetteville Generals, a Class A South Atlantic League affiliate of the Detroit Tigers, features on its white-bordered fronts posed color player photos set on simulated wood-grain backgrounds. The player's name, position, and team appear within a gold-colored rectangle below the photo. The tan horizontal back is bordered in white and carries the player's name at the top, followed by biography and statistics.
COMPLETE SET (28)................. 5.00 1.50

1990 Florida State League All-Stars Star

Early cards of Jeff Kent and Ivan Rodriguez highlight this set
COMPLETE SET (50)................ 20.00 6.00

1990 Frederick Keys Team Issue

COMPLETE SET (30)................. 5.00 1.50

1990 Fresno State Smokey

This 16-card set features posed color photos of the 1990 Fresno State Bulldog baseball team with Smokey the Bear printed on perferated cards from an uncut sheet. The backs carry player information and a fire prevention cartoon starring Smokey. The cards are unnumbered and checklisted below in alphabetical order.
COMPLETE SET (16)................ 10.00 3.00

1990 Ft. Lauderdale Yankees Star

This 27-card standard-size set of the 1990 Ft. Lauderdale Yankees, a Class A Florida State League affiliate of the New York Yankees, features purple bordered posed color player photos on its fronts. The player's name, team name, and position appear at the bottom. The white horizontal back carries the player's name at the top, followed by biography, career highlights, and statistics.
COMPLETE SET (27)................. 5.00 1.50

1990 Gastonia Rangers Best

This 30-card standard-size set of the 1990 Gastonia Rangers, a Class A South Atlantic League affiliate of the Texas Rangers, features white-bordered posed and action color player photos on its fronts. The player's name and position appear vertically on the left side. The yellow horizontal back carries the player's name and position at the top, followed by biography, career highlights, and statistics. A player head shot appears in the lower right corner.
COMPLETE SET (30)................. 5.00 1.50

1990 Gastonia Rangers ProCards

This 29-card standard-size set of the 1990 Gastonia Rangers, a Class A South Atlantic League affiliate of the Texas Rangers, features on its white-bordered fronts posed color player photos set on simulated wood-grain backgrounds. The player's name, position, and team appear within a gold-colored rectangle below the photo. The tan horizontal back is bordered in white and carries the player's name at the top, followed by biography and statistics.
COMPLETE SET (29)................. 5.00 1.50

1990 Gastonia Rangers Star

This 29-card standard-size set of the 1990 Gastonia Rangers, a Class A South Atlantic League affiliate of the Texas Rangers, features blue bordered posed color player photos on its fronts. The player's name, team name, and position appear at the bottom. The white horizontal back carries the player's name at the top, followed by biography, career highlights, and statistics.
COMPLETE SET (29)................. 5.00 1.50

1990 Gate City Pioneers ProCards

This 27-card standard-size set of the 1990 Gate City Pioneers, a Rookie Class Pioneer League Independent, features on its white-bordered fronts posed color player photos set on simulated wood-grain backgrounds. The player's name, position, and team appear within a gold-colored rectangle below the photo. The tan horizontal back is bordered in white and carries the player's name at the top, followed by biography and statistics.
COMPLETE SET (27)................. 5.00 1.50

1990 Gate City Pioneers Sports Pro

This 30-card standard-size set of the 1990 Gate City Pioneers, a Rookie Class A Pioneer League Independent, features posed color head-and-shoulders shots, with thin black borders on a white card face. The horizontally oriented backs have biographical information.
COMPLETE SET (24)................. 5.00 1.50

1990 Geneva Cubs ProCards

This 27-card standard-size set of the 1990 Geneva Cubs, a Class A New York-Penn League affiliate of the Chicago Cubs, features on its white-bordered fronts posed color player photos set on simulated wood-grain backgrounds. The player's name, position, and team appear within a gold-colored rectangle below the photo. The tan horizontal back is bordered in white and carries the player's name at the top, followed by biography and statistics.
COMPLETE SET (27)................. 5.00 1.50

1990 Geneva Cubs Star

This 26-card standard-size set of the 1990 Geneva Cubs, a Class A New York-Penn League affiliate of the Chicago Cubs, features light orange bordered posed color player photos on its fronts. The player's name, team name, and position appear at the bottom. The white horizontal back carries the player's name at the top, followed by biography, career highlights, and statistics.
COMPLETE SET (26)................. 5.00 1.50

1990 Georgia College Colonials

COMPLETE SET (35)................ 10.00 3.00

1990 Great Falls Dodgers Sports Pro

This 30-card standard-size set of the 1990 Great Falls Dodgers, a Rookie Class A Pioneer League affiliate of the Los Angeles Dodgers,

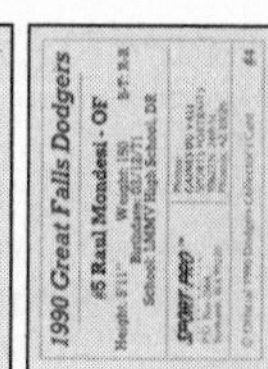

features posed color head-and-shoulders shots, with thin black borders on a white card face. The horizontally oriented backs have biographical information. This issue includes the minor league card debuts of Pedro Martinez and Raul Mondesi.
COMPLETE SET (30)............. 100.00 30.00

1990 Greensboro Hornets Best

This 30-card standard-size set of the 1990 Greensboro Hornets, a Class A South Atlantic League affiliate of the New York Yankees, features white-bordered posed and action color player photos on its fronts. The player's name and position appear vertically on the left side. The yellow horizontal back carries the player's name and position at the top, followed by biography, career highlights, and statistics. A player head shot appears in the lower right corner.
COMPLETE SET (30)................. 5.00 1.50

1990 Greensboro Hornets ProCards

This 31-card standard-size set of the 1990 Greensboro Hornets, a Class A South Atlantic League affiliate of the New York Yankees, features on its white-bordered fronts posed color player photos set on simulated wood-grain backgrounds. The player's name, position, and team appear within a gold-colored rectangle below the photo. The tan horizontal back is bordered in white and carries the player's name at the top, followed by biography and statistics. .
COMPLETE SET (31)................. 5.00 1.50

1990 Greensboro Hornets Star

This 26-card standard-size set of the 1990 Greensboro Hornets, a Class A South Atlantic League affiliate of the New York Yankees, features green bordered posed color player photos on its fronts. The player's name, team name, and position appear at the bottom. The white horizontal back carries the player's name at the top, followed by biography, career highlights, and statistics.
COMPLETE SET (26)................. 5.00 1.50

1990 Greenville Braves Best

This 22-card standard-size set of the 1990 Greenville Braves, a Class AA Southern League affiliate of the Atlanta Braves, features white-bordered posed and action color player photos on its fronts. The player's name and position appear vertically on the left side. The yellow horizontal back carries the player's name and position at the top, followed by biography, career highlights, and statistics. A player head shot appears in the lower right corner.
COMPLETE SET (22)................. 5.00 1.50

1990 Greenville Braves ProCards

This 26-card standard-size set of the 1990 Greenville Braves, a Class AA Southern League affiliate of the Atlanta Braves, features on its white-bordered fronts posed color player photos set on simulated wood-grain backgrounds. The player's name, position, and team appear within a gold-colored rectangle below the photo. The tan horizontal back is bordered in white and carries the player's name at the top, followed by biography and statistics.
COMPLETE SET (26)................. 5.00 1.50

1990 Greenville Braves Star

This 24-card standard-size set of the 1990 Greenville Braves, a Class AA Southern League affiliate of the Atlanta Braves, features blue bordered posed color player photos on its fronts. The player's name, team name, and position appear at the bottom. The white horizontal back carries the player's name at the top, followed by biography, career highlights, and statistics.
COMPLETE SET (24)................. 5.00 1.50

1990 Hagerstown Suns All Decade Best

This 36-card standard-size set of the 1990 Hagerstown Suns, a Class AA Eastern League affiliate of the Baltimore Orioles,features white-bordered posed and action color player photos on its fronts. The player's name and position appear vertically on the left side. The words "All Decade" appear across the top. The yellow horizontal back carries the player's name and years played at the top, followed by player's history, highlights, and statistics. 2,500 sets were produced.
COMPLETE SET (36)................. 5.00 1.50

1990 Hagerstown Suns Best

This 30-card standard-size set of the 1990 Hagerstown Suns, a Class AA Eastern League affiliate of the Baltimore Orioles, features white-

bordered posed and action color player photos on its fronts. The player's name and position appear vertically on the left side. The yellow horizontal back carries the player's name and position at the top, followed by biography, career highlights, and statistics. A player head shot appears in the lower right corner.
COMPLETE SET (30)................. 5.00 1.50

1990 Hagerstown Suns ProCards

This 33-card standard-size set of the 1990 Hagerstown Suns, a Class AA Eastern League affiliate of the Baltimore Orioles, features on its white-bordered fronts posed color player photos set on simulated wood-grain backgrounds. The player's name, position, and team appear within a gold-colored rectangle below the photo. The tan horizontal back is bordered in white and carries the player's name at the top, followed by biography and statistics.
COMPLETE SET (33)................. 5.00 1.50

1990 Hagerstown Suns Star

This 28-card standard-size set of the 1990 Hagerstown Suns, a Class AA Eastern League affiliate of the Baltimore Orioles, features blue bordered posed color player photos on its fronts. The player's name, team name, and position appear at the bottom. The white horizontal back carries the player's name at the top, followed by biography, career highlights, and statistics.
COMPLETE SET (28)................. 5.00 1.50

1990 Hamilton Redbirds Best

This 28-card standard-size set of the 1990 Hamilton Redbirds, a Class A New York-Penn League affiliate of the St. Louis Cardinals, features white-bordered posed and action color player photos on its fronts. The player's name and position appear vertically on the left side. The yellow horizontal back carries the player's name and position at the top, followed by biography, career highlights, and statistics. A player head shot appears in the lower right corner.
COMPLETE SET (28)................. 5.00 1.50

1990 Hamilton Redbirds Star

This 28-card standard-size set of the 1990 Hamilton Redbirds, a Class A New York-Penn League affiliate of the St. Louis Cardinals, features yellow bordered posed color player photos on its fronts. The player's name, team name, and position appear at the bottom. The white horizontal back carries the player's name at the top, followed by biography, career highlights, and statistics.
COMPLETE SET (28)................. 5.00 1.50

1990 Harrisburg Senators ProCards

This 26-card standard-size set of the 1990 Harrisburg Senators, a Class AA Eastern League affiliate of the Pittsburgh Pirates, features on its white-bordered fronts posed color player photos set on simulated wood-grain backgrounds. The player's name, position, and team appear within a gold-colored rectangle below the photo. The tan horizontal back is bordered in white and carries the player's name at the top, followed by biography and statistics.
COMPLETE SET (26)................. 5.00 1.50

1990 Harrisburg Senators Star

This 25-card standard-size set of the 1990 Harrisburg Senators, a Class AA Eastern League affiliate of the Pittsburgh Pirates, features red bordered posed color player photos on its fronts. The player's name, team name, and position appear at the bottom. The white horizontal back carries the player's name at the top, followed by biography, career highlights, and statistics.
COMPLETE SET (25)................. 5.00 1.50

1990 Helena Brewers Sports Pro

This 29-card standard-size set of the 1990 Helena Brewers, a Rookie Class Pioneer League affiliate of the Milwaukee Brewers, features posed color head-and-shoulders shots, with thin black borders on a white card face. The horizontally oriented backs have biographical information.
COMPLETE SET (29)................. 5.00 1.50

1990 Huntington Cubs ProCards

This 32-card standard-size set of the 1990 Huntington Cubs, a Rookie Class Appalachian League affiliate of the Chicago Cubs, features on its white-bordered fronts posed color player photos set on simulated wood-grain backgrounds. The player's name, position, and team appear within a gold-colored rectangle below the photo. The tan horizontal back is bordered in white and carries the player's name at the top, followed by biography and statistics. Jason Sehorn, star cornerback for the New York Football Giants, has his only Baseball card in this set
COMPLETE SET (32)................. 8.00 2.40

1990 Huntsville Stars Best

This 27-card standard-size set of the 1990 Huntsville Stars, a Class AA Southern League affiliate of the Oakland A's, features white-bordered posed and action color player photos on its fronts. The player's name and position appear vertically on the left side. The yellow horizontal back carries the player's name and position at the top, followed by biography, career highlights, and statistics. A player head shot appears in the lower right corner.
COMPLETE SET (27)................. 5.00 1.50

1990 Idaho Falls Braves ProCards

This 31-card standard-size set of the 1990 Idaho Falls Braves, a Rookie Class Pioneer League affiliate of the Atlanta Braves, features on its white-bordered fronts posed color player photos set on simulated wood-grain backgrounds. The player's name, position, and team appear within a gold-colored rectangle below the photo. The tan horizontal back is bordered in white and carries the player's name at the top, followed by biography and statistics.
COMPLETE SET (31)................. 5.00 1.50

1990 Indianapolis Indians CMC

This 25-card standard-size set of the 1990 Indianapolis Indians, a Class AAA American Association affiliate of the Montreal Expos, features white-bordered posed color player photos on its fronts. The player's name and position appear at the bottom; the team name appears vertically on the left. The back carries the league emblem in the white area at the top, the team name in the green stripe below, and player's name, position, biography, and statistics in the yellow area at the bottom. 1,100 sets were produced.
COMPLETE SET (25)................. 5.00 1.50

1990 Indianapolis Indians ProCards

This 31-card standard-size set of the 1990 Indianapolis Indians, a Class AAA American Association affiliate of the Montreal Expos, features on its white-bordered fronts posed color player photos set on simulated wood-grain backgrounds. The player's name, position, and team appear within a gold-colored rectangle below the photo. The tan horizontal back is bordered in white and carries the player's name and position at the top, followed by biography and statistics. The set was co-sponsored by Pepsi and Hook's.
COMPLETE SET (31)................. 5.00 1.50

1990 Iowa Cubs CMC

This 25-card standard-size set of the 1990 Iowa Cubs, a Class AAA American Association affiliate of the Chicago Cubs, features white-bordered posed color player photos on its fronts. The player's name and position appear at the bottom; the team name appears vertically on the left. The back carries the league emblem in the white area at the top, the team name in the green stripe below, and player's name, position, biography, and statistics in the yellow area at the bottom. 1,100 sets were produced.
COMPLETE SET (25)................. 5.00 1.50

1990 Iowa Cubs ProCards

This 24-card standard-size set of the 1990 Iowa Cubs, a Class AAA American Association affiliate of the Chicago Cubs, features on its white-bordered fronts posed color player photos set on simulated wood-grain backgrounds. The player's name, position, and team appear within a gold-colored rectangle below the photo. The tan horizontal back is bordered in white and carries the player's name at the top, followed by biography and statistics.
COMPLETE SET (24)................. 5.00 1.50

1990 Jackson Mets Grand Slam

COMPLETE SET (29)................. 8.00 2.40

1990 Jacksonville Expos Best

This 30-card standard-size set of the 1990 Jacksonville Expos, a Class AA Southern League affiliate of the Montreal Expos, features white-bordered posed and action color player photos on its fronts. The player's name and position appear vertically on the left side. The yellow horizontal back carries the player's name and position at the top, followed by biography, career highlights, and statistics. A player head shot appears in the lower right corner.
COMPLETE SET (30)................. 5.00 1.50

1990 Jacksonville Expos ProCards

This 29-card standard-size set of the 1990 Jacksonville Expos, a Class AA Southern League affiliate of the Montreal Expos, features on its white-bordered fronts posed color player photos set on simulated wood-grain backgrounds. The player's name, position, and team appear within a gold-colored rectangle below the photo. The tan horizontal back is bordered in white and carries the player's name and position at the top, followed by biography and statistics.
COMPLETE SET (29)................. 5.00 1.50

1990 Jamestown Expos Pucko

This 34-card standard-size set of the 1990 Jamestown Expos, a Class A New York-Penn League affiliate of the Montreal Expos, features gray-bordered posed color player shots on its fronts. A red stripe below the photo carries the team name; a white stripe above, the player's name and position. The white back carries the player's name at the top, followed by biography, player profile, and statistics.
COMPLETE SET (34)................. 7.00 2.10

1990 Johnson City Cardinals Star

This 30-card standard-size set of the 1990 Johnson City Cardinals, a Rookie Class Appalachian League affiliate of the St. Louis Cardinals, features red bordered posed color player photos on its fronts. The player's name, team name, and position appear at the bottom. The white horizontal back carries the player's name at the top, followed by biography, career highlights, and statistics.
COMPLETE SET (30)................. 5.00 1.50

1990 Kenosha Twins Best

This 30-card standard-size set of the 1990 Kenosha Twins, a Class A Midwest League affiliate of the Minnesota Twins, features white-bordered posed and action color player photos on its fronts. The player's name and position appear vertically on the left side. The yellow horizontal back carries the player's name and position at the top, followed by biography, career highlights, and statistics. A player head shot appears in the lower right corner.
COMPLETE SET (30)................. 5.00 1.50

1990 Kenosha Twins ProCards

This 27-card standard-size set of the 1990 Kenosha Twins, a Class A Midwest League affiliate of the Minnesota Twins, features on its white-bordered fronts posed color player photos set on simulated wood-grain backgrounds. The player's name, position, and team appear within a gold-colored rectangle below the photo. The tan horizontal back is bordered in white and carries the player's name at the top, followed by biography and statistics.
COMPLETE SET (27)................. 5.00 1.50

1990 Kenosha Twins Star

This 29-card standard-size set of the 1990 Kenosha Twins, a Class A Midwest League affiliate of the Minnesota Twins, features purple bordered posed color player photos on its fronts. The player's name, team name, and position appear at the bottom. The white horizontal back carries the player's name at the top, followed by biography, career highlights, and statistics.
COMPLETE SET (29)................. 5.00 1.50

1990 Kingsport Mets Best

This 28-card standard-size set of the 1990 Kingsport Mets, a Rookie Class Appalachian League affiliate of the New York Mets, features white-bordered posed and action color player photos on its fronts. The player's name and position appear vertically on the left side. The yellow horizontal back carries the player's name and position at the top, followed by biography, career highlights, and statistics. A player head shot appears in the lower right corner.
COMPLETE SET (28)................. 5.00 1.50

1990 Kingsport Mets Star

This 30-card standard-size set of the 1990 Kingsport Mets, a Rookie Class Appalachian League affiliate of the New York Mets, features orange bordered posed color player photos on its fronts. The player's name, team name, and position appear at the bottom. The white horizontal back carries the player's name at the top, followed by biography, career highlights, and statistics.
COMPLETE SET (30)................. 10.00 3.00

1990 Kinston Indians Team Issue

NNO Tim Costo was a late addition to the set.
COMPLETE SET (30)................. 5.00 1.50
COMPLETE SET (31)................. 6.00 1.80

1990 Kissimmee Dodgers Diamond

COMPLETE SET (29)................. 5.00 1.50

1990 Knoxville Blue Jays Best

This 28-card standard-size set of the 1990 Knoxville Blue Jays, a Class AA Southern League affiliate of the Toronto Blue Jays, features white-bordered posed and action color player photos on its fronts. The player's name and position appear vertically on the left side. The yellow horizontal back carries the player's name and position at the top, followed by biography and statistics. A player head shot appears in the lower right corner.
COMPLETE SET (28)................. 8.00 2.40

1990 Knoxville Blue Jays ProCards

This 25-card standard-size set of the 1990 Knoxville Smokies, a Class AA Southern League affiliate of the Toronto Blue Jays, features on its white-bordered fronts posed color player photos set on simulated wood-grain backgrounds. The player's name, position, and team appear within a gold-colored rectangle below the photo. The tan horizontal back is bordered in white and carries the player's name at the top, followed by biography and statistics.
COMPLETE SET (25)................. 8.00 2.40

1990 Knoxville Blue Jays Star

This 26-card standard-size set of the 1990 Knoxville Blue Jays, a Class AA Southern League affiliate of the Toronto Blue Jays, features yellow-bordered posed color player photos on its fronts. The player's name, team name, and position appear at the bottom. The white horizontal back carries the player's name at the top, followed by biography and statistics.
COMPLETE SET (26)................. 8.00 2.40

1990 Lakeland Tigers Star

This 28-card standard-size set of the 1990 Lakeland Tigers, a Class A Florida State League affiliate of the Detroit Tigers, features orange bordered posed color player photos on its fronts. The player's name, team name, and position appear at the bottom. The white horizontal back carries the player's name at the top, followed by biography, career highlights, and statistics.
COMPLETE SET (28)................. 5.00 1.50

1990 Las Vegas Stars CMC

This 25-card standard-size set of the 1990 Las Vegas Stars, a Class AAA Pacific Coast League affiliate of the San Diego Padres, features white-bordered posed color player photos on its fronts. The player's name and position appear at the bottom; the team name appears vertically on the left. The back carries the league emblem in the white area at the top, the team name in the green stripe below, and player's name, position, biography, and statistics in the yellow area at the bottom. 1,100 sets were produced.
COMPLETE SET (25)................. 5.00 1.50

1990 Las Vegas Stars ProCards

This 28-card standard-size set of the 1990 Las Vegas Stars, a Class AAA Pacific Coast League affiliate of the San Diego Padres, features on its white-bordered fronts posed color player photos set on simulated wood-grain backgrounds. The player's name, position, and team appear within a gold-colored rectangle below the photo. The tan horizontal back is bordered in white and carries the player's name at the top, followed by biography and statistics.
COMPLETE SET (28)................. 5.00 1.50

1990 London Tigers ProCards

This 22-card standard-size set of the 1990 London Tigers, a Class AA Eastern League affiliate of the Detroit Tigers, features on its white-bordered fronts posed color player photos set on simulated wood-grain backgrounds. The player's name, position, and team appear within a gold-colored rectangle below the photo. The tan horizontal back is bordered in white and carries the player's name at the top, followed by biography and statistics.
COMPLETE SET (22)................. 5.00 1.50

1990 Louisville Red Birds CMC

This 29-card standard-size set of the 1990 Louisville Red Birds, a Class AAA American Association affiliate of the St. Louis Cardinals, features white-bordered posed color player photos on its fronts. The player's name and position appear at the bottom; the team name appears vertically on the left. The back carries the league emblem in the white area at the top, the team name in the green stripe below, and player's name, position, biography, and statistics in the yellow area at the bottom. 1,100 sets were produced.
COMPLETE SET (29)................. 10.00 3.00

1990 Louisville Red Birds Louisville Baseball Club

COMPLETE SET (42)................. 10.00 3.00

1990 Louisville Red Birds ProCards

This 29-card standard-size set of the 1990 Louisville Red Birds, a Class AAA American Association affiliate of the St. Louis Cardinals, features on its white-bordered fronts posed color player photos set on simulated wood-grain backgrounds. The player's name, position, and team appear within a gold-colored rectangle below the photo. The tan horizontal back is bordered in white and carries the player's name at the top, followed by biography and statistics.
COMPLETE SET (29)................. 8.00 2.40

1990 LSU Tigers Anheuser-Busch

Sponsored by Anheuser-Busch, this 16-card set measures the standard size. On a white card face, the fronts feature color action player photos with rounded corners. The team and sponsor logos appear above the photo, while the player's name and position are printed inside a baseball in the lower left corner. The backs carry player profiles and a message from Anheuser-Busch to drink responsibly.
COMPLETE SET (16)................. 10.00 3.00

1990 LSU Tigers Ben McDonald McDag

This 16-card standard-size set was produced by McDag Productions in honor of LSU All-American baseball pitcher Ben McDonald. Ten thousand sets were produced. The color photos on the card fronts capture various moments in McDonald's career, from childhood to his college days. The pictures are bordered in white. In blue print, the horizontally oriented backs summarize McDonald's career and present a "question and answer" trivia feature. A drawing of the Big Ben clock appears on both sides of the card.
COMPLETE SET (16)................. 5.00 1.50

1990 LSU Tigers Greats McDag

COMPLETE SET (16)................. 10.00 3.00

1990 LSU Tigers Police

COMPLETE SET (16)................. 10.00 3.00

1990 Lynchburg Red Sox Team Issue

COMPLETE SET (27)................. 5.00 1.50

1990 Madison Muskies Best

This 29-card standard-size set of the 1990 Madison Muskies, a Class A Midwest League affiliate of the Oakland Athletics, features white-bordered posed and action color player photos on its fronts. The player's name and position appear vertically on the left side. The yellow horizontal back carries the player's name and position at the top, followed by biography, career highlights, and statistics. A player head shot appears in the lower right corner.
COMPLETE SET (29)................. 5.00 1.50

1990 Madison Muskies ProCards

This 26-card standard-size set of the 1990 Madison Muskies, a Class A Midwest League affiliate of the Oakland Athletics, features on its white-bordered fronts posed color player photos set on simulated wood-grain backgrounds. The player's name, position, and team appear within a gold-colored rectangle below the photo. The tan horizontal back is bordered in white and carries the player's name at the top, followed by biography and statistics.
COMPLETE SET (26)................. 5.00 1.50

1990 Martinsville Phillies ProCards

This 34-card standard-size set of the 1990 Martinsville Phillies, a Rookie Class Appalachian League affiliate of the Philadelphia Phillies, features on its white-bordered fronts posed color player photos set on simulated wood-grain backgrounds. The player's name, position, and team appear within a gold-colored rectangle below the photo. The tan horizontal back is bordered in white and carries the player's name at the top, followed by biography and statistics.
COMPLETE SET (34)................. 8.00 2.40

1990 Medicine Hat Blue Jays Best

This 28-card standard-size set of the 1990 Medicine Hat Blue Jays, a Class A Pioneer League affiliate of the Toronto Blue Jays, features white-bordered posed color player photos on its fronts. The player's name and position appear vertically on the left side. The yellow horizontal back carries the player's name and position at the top, followed by biography. A player head shot appears in the lower right corner.
COMPLETE SET (28)................. 5.00 1.50

1990 Memphis Chicks Best

This 29-card standard-size set of the 1990 Memphis Chicks, a Class AA Southern League affiliate of the Kansas City Royals, features white-bordered posed and action color player photos on its fronts. The player's name and position appear vertically on the left side. The yellow horizontal back carries the player's name and position at the top, followed by biography, career highlights, and statistics. A player head shot appears in the lower right corner.
COMPLETE SET (29)................. 8.00 2.40

1990 Memphis Chicks ProCards

This 28-card standard-size set of the 1990 Memphis Chicks, a Class AA Southern League affiliate of the Kansas City Royals, features on its white-bordered fronts posed color player photos set on simulated wood-grain backgrounds. The player's name, position, and team appear within a gold-colored rectangle below the photo. The tan horizontal back is bordered in white and carries the player's name at the top, followed by biography and statistics.
COMPLETE SET (28)................. 5.00 1.50

1990 Memphis Chicks Star

This 27-card standard-size set of the 1990 Memphis Chicks, a Class AA Southern League

affiliate of the Kansas City Royals, features blue bordered posed color player photos on its fronts. The player's name, team name, and position appear at the bottom. The white horizontal back carries the player's name at the top, followed by biography, career highlights, and statistics.
COMPLETE SET (27).................. 5.00 1.50

1990 Miami Miracle I Star

This 31-card standard-size set of the 1990 Miami Miracle, a Class A Florida State League Independent, features yellow bordered posed color player photos on its fronts. The player's name, team name, and position appear at the bottom. The white horizontal back carries the player's name at the top, followed by biography, career highlights, and statistics.
COMPLETE SET (31)................ 15.00 4.50

1990 Miami Miracle II Star

This 31-card standard-size set of the 1990 Miami Miracle, a Class A Florida State League Independent, features green bordered posed color player photos on its fronts. The player's name, team name, and position appear at the bottom. The white horizontal back carries the player's name at the top, followed by biography, career highlights, and statistics.
COMPLETE SET (31).................. 5.00 1.50

1990 Midland Angels Grand Slam

COMPLETE SET (30).................. 5.00 1.50

1990 Midwest League All-Stars Grand Slam

COMPLETE SET (58)................ 10.00 3.00

1990 Mississippi State Bulldogs

COMPLETE SET (44)................ 15.00 4.50

1990 Modesto A's Cal League Cards

COMPLETE SET (25).................. 5.00 1.50

1990 Modesto A's Chong

COMPLETE SET (35).................. 5.00 1.50

1990 Modesto A's ProCards

This 29-card standard-size set of the 1990 Modesto A's, a Class A California League affiliate of the Oakland Athletics, features on its white-bordered fronts posed color player photos set on simulated wood-grain backgrounds. The player's name, position, and team appear within a gold-colored rectangle below the photo. The tan horizontal back is bordered in white and carries the player's name at the top, followed by biography and statistics.
COMPLETE SET (29).................. 5.00 1.50

1990 Myrtle Beach Blue Jays ProCards

This 29-card standard-size set of the 1990 Myrtle Beach Blue Jays, a Class A South Atlantic League affiliate of the Toronto Blue Jays, features on its white-bordered fronts posed color player photos set on simulated wood-grain backgrounds. The player's name, position, and team appear within a gold-colored rectangle below the photo. The tan horizontal back is bordered in white and carries the player's name and position at the top, followed by biography and statistics.
COMPLETE SET (29).................. 5.00 1.50

1990 Nashville Sounds CMC

This 26-card standard-size set of the 1990 Nashville Sounds, a Class AAA American Association affiliate of the Cincinnati Reds, features white-bordered posed color player photos on its fronts. The player's name and position appear at the bottom; the team name appears vertically on the left. The back carries the league emblem in the white area at the top, the team name in the green stripe below, and player's name, position, biography, and statistics in the yellow area at the bottom. 1,100 sets were produced.
COMPLETE SET (26).................. 5.00 1.50

1990 Nashville Sounds ProCards

This 29-card standard-size set of the 1990 Nashville Sounds, a Class AAA American Association affiliate of the Cincinnati Reds, features on its white-bordered fronts posed color player photos set on simulated wood-grain backgrounds. The player's name, position, and team appear within a gold-colored rectangle below the photo. The tan horizontal back is bordered in white and carries the player's name at the top, followed by biography and statistics.
COMPLETE SET (29).................. 5.00 1.50

1990 Nebraska Cornhuskers

COMPLETE SET (28)................ 10.00 3.00

1990 New Britain Red Sox Best

This 29-card standard-size set of the 1990 New Britain Red Sox, a Class AA Eastern League affiliate of the Boston Red Sox, features white-bordered posed and action color player photos on its fronts. The player's name and position

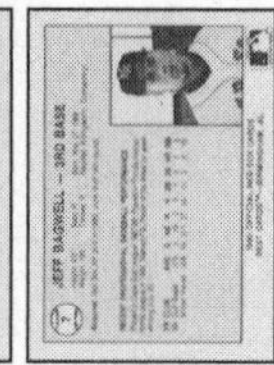

appear vertically on the left side. The yellow horizontal back carries the player's name and position at the top, followed by biography, career highlights, and statistics. A player head shot appears in the lower right corner. This issue includes the minor league card debut of Jeff Bagwell.
COMPLETE SET (29)................ 25.00 7.50

1990 New Britain Red Sox ProCards

This 26-card standard-size set of the 1990 New Britain Red Sox, a Class AA Eastern League affiliate of the Boston Red Sox, features on its white-bordered fronts posed color player photos set on simulated wood-grain backgrounds. The player's name, position, and team appear within a gold-colored rectangle below the photo. The tan horizontal back is bordered in white and carries the player's name at the top, followed by biography and statistics. This issue includes the minor league card debut of Jeff Bagwell.
COMPLETE SET (26)................ 20.00 6.00

1990 New Britain Red Sox Star

This 27-card standard-size set of the 1990 New Britain Red Sox, a Class AA Eastern League affiliate of the Boston Red Sox, features blue bordered posed color player photos on its fronts. The player's name, team name, and position appear at the bottom. The white horizontal back carries the player's name at the top, followed by biography, career highlights, and statistics. This issue includes the minor league card debut of Jeff Bagwell.
COMPLETE SET (27)................ 15.00 4.50

1990 Niagara Falls Rapids Pucko

COMPLETE SET (33).................. 5.00 1.50

1990 Oklahoma City 89ers CMC

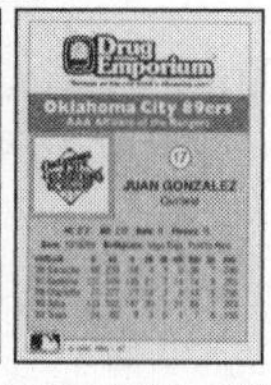

This 24-card standard-size set of the 1990 Oklahoma City 89ers, a Class AAA American Association affiliate of the Texas Rangers, features white-bordered posed color player photos on its fronts. The player's name and position appear at the bottom; the team name appears vertically on the left. The back carries the league emblem in the white area at the top, the team name in the green stripe below, and player's name, position, biography, and statistics in the yellow area at the bottom. This issue includes a fourth year card of Juan Gonzalez. 1,100 sets were produced.
COMPLETE SET (24)................ 20.00 6.00

1990 Oklahoma City 89ers ProCards

This 30-card standard-size set of the 1990 Oklahoma City 89ers, a Class AAA American Association affiliate of the Texas Rangers, features on its white-bordered fronts posed color player photos set on simulated wood-grain backgrounds. The player's name, position, and team appear within a gold-colored rectangle below the photo. The tan horizontal back is bordered in white and carries the player's name at the top, followed by biography and statistics. This issue includes fourth year cards of Juan Gonzalez and Dean Palmer.
COMPLETE SET (30)................ 20.00 6.00

1990 Oklahoma Sooners

COMPLETE SET (24)................ 10.00 3.00

1990 Omaha Royals CMC

This 25-card standard-size set of the 1990 Omaha Royals, a Class AAA American Association affiliate of the Kansas City Royals, features white-bordered posed color player photos on its fronts. The player's name and position appear at the bottom; the team name appears vertically on the left. The back carries the league emblem in the white area at the top, the team name in the green stripe below, and player's name, position, biography, and statistics in the yellow area at the bottom. 1,100 sets were produced.
COMPLETE SET (25).................. 5.00 1.50

1990 Omaha Royals ProCards

This 26-card standard-size set of the 1990 Omaha Royals, a Class AAA American Association affiliate of the Kansas City Royals, features on its white-bordered fronts posed color player photos set on simulated wood-grain backgrounds. The player's name, position, and team appear within a gold-colored rectangle below the photo. The tan horizontal back is bordered in white and carries the player's name at the top, followed by biography and statistics.
COMPLETE SET (26).................. 5.00 1.50

1990 Oneonta Yankees ProCards

This 29-card standard-size set of the 1990 Oneonta Yankees, a Class A New York-Penn League affiliate of the New York Yankees, features on its white-bordered fronts posed color player photos set on simulated wood-grain backgrounds. The player's name, position, and team appear within a gold-colored rectangle below the photo. The tan horizontal back is bordered in white and carries the player's name at the top, followed by biography and statistics.
COMPLETE SET (29).................. 5.00 1.50

1990 Orlando Sun Rays Best

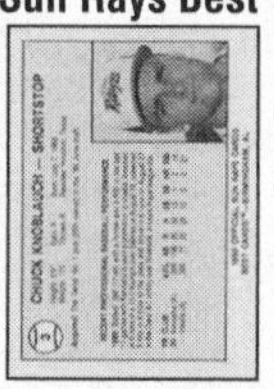

This 30-card standard-size set of the 1990 Orlando Sun Rays, a Class AA Southern League affiliate of the Minnesota Twins, features white-bordered posed and action color player photos on its fronts. The player's name and position appear vertically on the left side. The yellow horizontal back carries the player's name and position at the top, followed by biography, career highlights, and statistics. A player head shot appears in the lower right corner. This issue includes the minor league card debuts of Chuck Knoblauch and Scott Erickson.
COMPLETE SET (30)................ 10.00 3.00

1990 Orlando Sun Rays ProCards

This 27-card standard-size set of the 1990 Orlando Sun Rays, a Class AA Southern League affiliate of the Minnesota Twins, features on its white-bordered fronts posed color player photos set on simulated wood-grain backgrounds. The player's name, position, and team appear within a gold-colored rectangle below the photo. The tan horizontal back is bordered in white and carries the player's name at the top, followed by biography and statistics. This issue includes the minor league card debuts of Chuck Knoblauch and Scott Erickson.
COMPLETE SET (27).................. 8.00 2.40

1990 Orlando Sun Rays Star

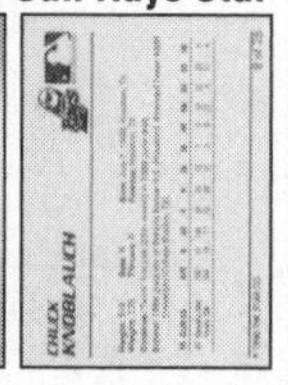

This 28-card standard-size set of the 1990 Orlando Sun Rays, a Class AA Southern League affiliate of the Minnesota Twins, features blue bordered posed color player photos on its fronts. The player's name, team name, and position appear at the bottom. The white horizontal back carries the player's name at the top, followed by biography, career highlights, and statistics. This issue includes the minor league card debuts of Chuck Knoblauch and Scott Erickson.
COMPLETE SET (28)................ 25.00 7.50

1990 Osceola Astros Star

This 30-card standard-size set of the 1990 Osceola Astros, a Class A Florida State League affiliate of the Houston Astros, features orange bordered posed color player photos on its fronts. The player's name, team name, and position appear at the bottom. The white horizontal back carries the player's name at the top, followed by biography, career highlights, and statistics. This issue includes a third year card of Kenny Lofton.
COMPLETE SET (30)................ 10.00 3.00

1990 Palm Springs Angels Cal League Cards

COMPLETE SET (27)................ 10.00 3.00

1990 Palm Springs Angels ProCards

This 28-card standard-size set of the 1990 Palm Springs Angels, a Class A California League affiliate of the California Angels, features on its white-bordered fronts posed color player photos set on simulated wood-grain backgrounds. The player's name, position, and team appear within a gold-colored rectangle below the photo. The tan horizontal back is bordered in white and carries the player's name at the top, followed by biography and statistics.
COMPLETE SET (28)................ 18.00 5.50

1990 Pan Am Team USA Red BDK

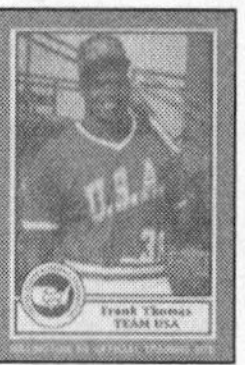

These red-bordered cards were a redesigned, 1990 re-issue of the 1987 Pan Am set. Even though the design is the same as the 1987 cards, we are now calling them 1990 cards. As designated by the copyright on the back.
COMPLETE SET (26)................ 12.00 3.60

1990 Pawtucket Red Sox CMC

This 31-card set of the Pawtucket Red Sox, a Class AAA International League affiliate of the Boston Red Sox, features white-bordered posed color player photos on its fronts. The player's name and position appear at the bottom; the team name appears vertically on the left. The back carries the league emblem in the white area at the top, the team name in the green stripe below, and player's name, position, biography, and statistics in the yellow area at the bottom. 1,100 sets were produced.
COMPLETE SET (25).................. 5.00 1.50

1990 Pawtucket Red Sox Dunkin' Donuts

This 31-card set of the Pawtucket Red Sox, a Class AAA International League affiliate of the Boston Red Sox, was issued in one large sheet featuring six perforated five-card strips with a large team photo in the wide top strip. Sponsored by Dunkin' Donuts, the fronts carry color player photos while the backs display player career statistics. The cards are unnumbered and checklisted below in alphabetical order. This issue includes the minor league card debut of Mo Vaughn.
COMPLETE SET (31)................ 50.00 15.00

1990 Pawtucket Red Sox ProCards

This 29-card standard-size set of the 1990 Pawtucket Red Sox, a Class AAA International League affiliate of the Boston Red Sox, features on its white-bordered fronts posed color player photos set on simulated wood-grain backgrounds. The player's name, position, and team appear within a gold-colored rectangle below the photo. The tan horizontal back is bordered in white and carries the player's name at the top, followed by biography and statistics. This issue includes the minor league card debut of Mo Vaughn.
COMPLETE SET (29)................ 15.00 4.50

1990 Peninsula Oilers Team Issue

This 24-card set of the 1990 Peninsula Oilers of the Alaska Central Baseball League features color player portraits in black-and-white borders. The backs carry player information. The cards are checklisted below according to where they appear on the Checklist card.
COMPLETE SET (24).................. 5.00 1.50

1990 Peninsula Pilots Star

This 27-card standard-size set of the 1990 Peninsula Pilots, a Class A Carolina League affiliate of the Seattle Mariners, features red bordered posed color player photos on its fronts. The player's name, team name, and position appear at the bottom. The white horizontal back carries the player's name at the top, followed by biography, career highlights and statistics.
COMPLETE SET (27).................. 5.00 1.50

1990 Peoria Chiefs Earl Cunningham Team Issue

COMPLETE SET (4).................. 10.00 3.00

1990 Peoria Chiefs Team Issue

COMPLETE SET (38)................ 15.00 4.50

1990 Peoria Chiefs Update Team Issue

COMPLETE SET (7).................. 5.00 1.50

1990 Phoenix Firebirds CMC

This 26-card standard-size set of the 1990 Phoenix Firebirds, a Class AAA Pacific Coast League affiliate of the San Francisco Giants, features white-bordered posed color player photos on its fronts. The player's name and position appear at the bottom; the team name appears vertically on the left. The back carries the league emblem in the white area at the top, the team name in the green stripe below, and player's name, position, biography, and statistics in the yellow area at the bottom. 1,100 sets were produced.
COMPLETE SET (26).................. 5.00 1.50

1990 Phoenix Firebirds ProCards

This 29-card standard-size set of the 1990 Phoenix Firebirds, a Class AAA Pacific Coast League affiliate of the San Francisco Giants, features on its white-bordered fronts posed color player photos set on simulated wood-grain backgrounds. The player's name, position, and team appear within a gold-colored rectangle below the photo. The tan horizontal back is bordered in white and carries the player's name at the top, followed by biography and statistics.
COMPLETE SET (29).................. 5.00 1.50

1990 Pittsfield Mets Pucko

COMPLETE SET (32).................. 8.00 2.40

1990 Portland Beavers CMC

This 25-card standard-size set of the 1990 Portland Beavers, a Class AAA Pacific Coast League affiliate of the Minnesota Twins, features white-bordered posed color player photos on its fronts. The player's name and position appear at the bottom; the team name appears vertically on the left. The back carries the league emblem in the white area at the top, the team name in the green stripe below, and player's name, position, biography, and statistics in the yellow area at the bottom. 1,100 sets were produced.
COMPLETE SET (25).................. 5.00 1.50

1990 Portland Beavers ProCards

This 28-card standard-size set of the 1990 Portland Beavers, a Class AAA Pacific Coast League affiliate of the Minnesota Twins, features on its white-bordered fronts posed color player photos set on simulated wood-grain backgrounds. The player's name, position, and team appear within a gold-colored rectangle below the photo. The tan horizontal back is bordered in white and carries the player's name at the top, followed by biography and statistics.
COMPLETE SET (28).................. 5.00 1.50

1990 Prince William Cannons Team Issue

COMPLETE SET (30).................. 5.00 1.50

1990 Princeton Patriots Diamond

COMPLETE SET (30).................. 5.00 1.50

1990 Pulaski Braves Best

This 29-card standard-size set of the 1990 Pulaski Braves, a Rookie Class Appalachian League affiliate of the Atlanta Braves, features white-bordered posed and action color player photos on its fronts. The player's name and position appear vertically on the left side. The yellow horizontal back carries the player's name and position at the top, followed by biography, career highlights, and statistics. A player head shot appears in the lower right corner.
COMPLETE SET (29).................. 5.00 1.50

1990 Pulaski Braves ProCards

This 31-card standard-size set of the 1990 Pulaski Braves, a Rookie Class Appalachian League affiliate of the Atlanta Braves, features on its white-bordered fronts posed color player photos set on simulated wood-grain backgrounds. The player's name, position, and team appear within a gold-colored rectangle below the photo. The tan horizontal back is bordered in white and carries the player's name at the top, followed by biography and statistics.
COMPLETE SET (31).................. 5.00 1.50

1990 Quad City Angels Grand Slam

COMPLETE SET (30).................. 5.00 1.50

1990 Reading Phillies Best

This 26-card standard-size set of the 1990 Reading Phillies, a Class AA Eastern League affiliate of the Philadelphia Phillies, features white-bordered posed and action color player photos on its fronts. The player's name and

position appear vertically on the left side. The yellow horizontal back carries the player's name and position at the top, followed by biography, career highlights, and statistics. A player head shot appears in the lower right corner.
COMPLETE SET (26)................. 5.00 1.50

1990 Reading Phillies ProCards

This 27-card standard-size set of the 1990 Reading Phillies, a Class AA Eastern League affiliate of the Philadelphia Phillies, features on its white-bordered fronts posed color player photos set on simulated wood-grain backgrounds. The player's name, position, and team appear within a gold-colored rectangle below the photo. The tan horizontal back is bordered in white and carries the player's name at the top, followed by biography and statistics.
COMPLETE SET (27)................. 5.00 1.50

1990 Reading Phillies Star

This 28-card standard-size set of the 1990 Reading Phillies, a Class AA Eastern League affiliate of the Philadelphia Phillies, features blue bordered posed color player photos on its fronts. The player's name, team name, and position appear at the bottom. The white horizontal back carries the player's name at the top, followed by biography, career highlights, and statistics.
COMPLETE SET (28)................. 5.00 1.50

1990 Reno Silver Sox Cal League Cards

COMPLETE SET (31)................. 5.00 1.50

1990 Richmond Braves 25th Anniversary Team Issue

COMPLETE SET (23)................ 20.00 6.00

1990 Richmond Braves Bob's Camera

This 22-card team set of the 1990 Richmond Braves, a Class AAA International League affiliate of the Atlanta Braves, was sponsored by Bob's Camera. The fronts feature borderless color player photos with sponsors' and team's logos in the wide bottom margin. The backs are blank. 500 sets were produced.
COMPLETE SET (22)............... 40.00 12.00

1990 Richmond Braves CMC

This 27-card standard-size set of the 1990 Richmond Braves, a Class AAA International League affiliate of the Atlanta Braves, features white-bordered posed color player photos on its fronts. The player's name and position appear at the bottom; the team name appears vertically on the left. The back carries the league emblem in the white area at the top, the team name in the green stripe below, and player's name, position, biography, and statistics in the yellow area at the bottom. 1,100 sets were produced.
COMPLETE SET (27)............... 15.00 4.50

1990 Richmond Braves ProCards

This 28-card standard-size set of the 1990 Richmond Braves, a Class AAA International League affiliate of the Atlanta Braves, features on its white-bordered fronts posed color player photos set on simulated wood-grain backgrounds. The player's name, position, and team appear within a gold-colored rectangle below the photo. The tan horizontal back is bordered in white and carries the player's name at the top, followed by biography and statistics.
COMPLETE SET (28)............... 10.00 3.00

1990 Richmond Braves Team Issue

This 30-card set of the Richmond Braves, a Class AAA International League affiliate of the Atlanta Braves, was issued in one large sheet featuring six perforated five-card strips with a large team photo in the wide top strip. Sponsored by Richmond Comix and Cards and WRNL Radio, the fronts carry color player photos. 5,000 sets were produced with 3,000 of them given away on a promotional night at the ballpark.
COMPLETE SET (30)............... 20.00 6.00

1990 Riverside Red Wave Best

This 27-card standard-size set of the 1990 Riverside Red Wave, a Class A California League affiliate of the San Diego Padres, features white-bordered posed and action color player photos on its fronts. The player's name and position appear vertically on the left side. The yellow horizontal back carries the player's name and position at the top, followed by biography, career highlights, and statistics. A player head shot appears in the lower right corner.
COMPLETE SET (27)................. 5.00 1.50

1990 Riverside Red Wave Cal League Cards

COMPLETE SET (27)................. 5.00 1.50

1990 Riverside Red Wave ProCards

This 28-card standard-size set of the 1990 Riverside Red Wave, a Class A California League affiliate of the San Diego Padres, features on its white-bordered fronts posed color player photos set on simulated wood-grain backgrounds. The player's name, position, and team appear within a gold-colored rectangle below the photo. The tan horizontal back is bordered in white and carries the player's name at the top, followed by biography and statistics.
COMPLETE SET (28)................. 5.00 1.50

1990 Rochester Red Wings CMC

This 27-card standard-size set of the 1990 Rochester Red Wings, a Class AAA International League affiliate of the Baltimore Orioles, features white-bordered posed color player photos on its fronts. The player's name and position appear at the bottom; the team name appears vertically on the left. The back carries the league emblem in the white area at the top, the team name in the green stripe below, and player's name, position, biography, and statistics in the yellow area at the bottom. 1,100 sets were produced.
COMPLETE SET (27)............... 15.00 4.50

1990 Rochester Red Wings Governor's Cup

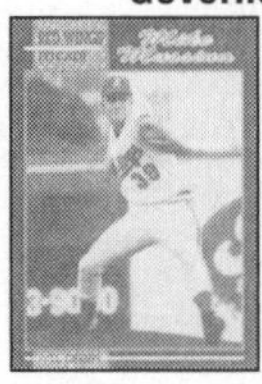

This issue includes the minor league card debut of Mike Mussina as well as an early card of Curt Schilling. 2,000 sets were produced.
COMPLETE SET (36)............... 50.00 12.00

1990 Rochester Red Wings ProCards

This 29-card standard-size set of the 1990 Rochester Red Wings, a Class AAA International League affiliate of the Baltimore Orioles, features on its white-bordered fronts posed color player photos set on simulated wood-grain backgrounds. The player's name, position, and team appear within a gold-colored rectangle below the photo. The tan horizontal back is bordered in white and carries the player's name at the top, followed by biography and statistics.
COMPLETE SET (29)............... 20.00 6.00

1990 Rockford Expos Litho Center

Printed by Rockford Litho Center, this 30-card standard-size set of the 1990 Rockford Expos, a Class A Midwest League affiliate of the Montreal Expos, features on its white-bordered fronts posed color player photos set on red backgrounds. The player's name and position appear within a yellow diagonal stripe at the lower right. The white horizontal back is framed by a black line and carries the player's name, uniform number, and position at the top, followed by biography and the names of the sponsors, WROK radio and Tomorrow is Yesterday. The cards are unnumbered and checklisted below in alphabetical order.
COMPLETE SET (30)................. 5.00 1.50

1990 Rockford Expos ProCards

This 29-card standard-size set of the 1990 Rockford Expos, a Class A Midwest League affiliate of the Montreal Expos, features on its white-bordered fronts posed color player photos set on simulated wood-grain backgrounds. The player's name, position, and team appear within a gold-colored rectangle below the photo. The tan horizontal back is bordered in white and carries the player's name and position at the top, followed by biography and statistics.
COMPLETE SET (29)................. 5.00 1.50

1990 Salem Buccaneers Star

This 27-card standard-size set of the 1990 Salem Buccaneers, a Class A Carolina League affiliate of the Pittsburgh Pirates, features yellow bordered posed color player photos on its fronts. The player's name, team name, and position appear at the bottom. The white horizontal back carries the player's name at the top, followed by biography, career highlights, and statistics.
COMPLETE SET (27)................. 5.00 1.50

1990 Salinas Spurs Cal League Cards

COMPLETE SET (32)................. 5.00 1.50

1990 Salinas Spurs ProCards

This 26-card standard-size set of the 1990 Salinas Spurs, a Class A California League Independent, features on its white-bordered fronts posed color player photos set on simulated wood-grain backgrounds. The player's name, position, and team appear within a gold-colored rectangle below the photo. The tan horizontal back is bordered in white and carries the player's name at the top, followed by biography and statistics.
COMPLETE SET (26)................. 5.00 1.50

1990 San Antonio Missions Grand Slam

COMPLETE SET (30)................ 10.00 3.00

1990 San Bernardino Spirit Best

This 28-card standard-size set of the 1990 San Bernardino Spirit, a Class A California League affiliate of the Seattle Mariners, features white-bordered posed and action color player photos on its fronts. The player's name and position appear vertically on the left side. The yellow horizontal back carries the player's name and position at the top, followed by biography, career highlights, and statistics. A player head shot appears in the lower right corner.
COMPLETE SET (28)................. 5.00 1.50

1990 San Bernardino Spirit Cal League Cards

COMPLETE SET (32)................. 5.00 1.50

1990 San Bernardino Spirit ProCards

This 28-card standard-size set of the 1990 San Bernardino Spirit, a Class A California League affiliate of the Seattle Mariners, features on its white-bordered fronts posed color player photos set on simulated wood-grain backgrounds. The player's name, position, and team appear within a gold-colored rectangle below the photo. The tan horizontal back is bordered in white and carries the player's name at the top, followed by biography and statistics.
COMPLETE SET (28)................. 5.00 1.50

1990 San Diego State Aztecs 3D/Autograph Pro Image

COMPLETE SET (10)................ 25.00 7.50

1990 San Jose Giants Best

This 30-card standard-size set of the 1990 San Jose Giants, a Class A California League affiliate of the San Francisco Giants, features white-bordered posed and action color player photos on its fronts. The player's name and position appear vertically on the left side. The yellow horizontal back carries the player's name and position at the top, followed by biography, career highlights, and statistics. A player head shot appears in the lower right corner.
COMPLETE SET (30)................. 5.00 1.50

1990 San Jose Giants Cal League Cards

COMPLETE SET (28)................. 5.00 1.50

1990 San Jose Giants ProCards

This 30-card standard-size set of the 1990 San Jose Giants, a Class A California League affiliate of the San Francisco Giants, features on its white-bordered fronts posed color player photos set on simulated wood-grain backgrounds. The player's name, position, and team appear within a gold-colored rectangle below the photo. The tan horizontal back is bordered in white and carries the player's name at the top, followed by biography and statistics.
COMPLETE SET (30)................. 5.00 1.50

1990 San Jose Giants Star

This 30-card standard-size set of the 1990 San Jose Giants, a Class A California League affiliate of the San Francisco Giants, features orange bordered posed color player photos on its fronts. The player's name, team name, and position appear at the bottom. The white horizontal back carries the player's name at the top, followed by biography, career highlights, and statistics.
COMPLETE SET (30)................. 5.00 1.50

1990 Sarasota White Sox Star

This 30-card standard-size set of the 1990 Sarasota White Sox, a Class A Florida State League affiliate of the Chicago White Sox, features blue bordered posed color player photos on its fronts. The player's name, team name, and position appear at the bottom. The white horizontal back carries the player's name at the top, followed by biography, career highlights, and statistics.
COMPLETE SET (30)................. 5.00 1.50

1990 Savannah Cardinals ProCards

This 28-card standard-size set of the 1990 Savannah Cardinals, a Class A South Atlantic League affiliate of the St. Louis Cardinals, features on its white-bordered fronts posed color player photos set on simulated wood-grain backgrounds. The player's name, position, and team appear within a gold-colored rectangle below the photo. The tan horizontal back is bordered in white and carries the player's name at the top, followed by biography and statistics.
COMPLETE SET (28)................. 5.00 1.50

1990 Scranton Red Barons CMC

This 25-card standard-size set of the 1990 Scranton Red Barons, a Class AAA International League affiliate of the Philadelphia Phillies, features white-bordered posed color player photos on its fronts. The player's name and position appear at the bottom; the team name appears vertically on the left. The back carries the league emblem in the white area at the top, the team name in the green stripe below, and player's name, position, biography, and statistics in the yellow area at the bottom. 1,100 sets were produced.
COMPLETE SET (25)................. 5.00 1.50

1990 Scranton Red Barons ProCards

This 24-card standard-size set of the 1990 Scranton Red Barons, a Class AAA International League affiliate of the Philadelphia Phillies, features on its white-bordered fronts posed color player photos set on simulated wood-grain backgrounds. The player's name, position, and team appear within a gold-colored rectangle below the photo. The tan horizontal back is bordered in white and carries the player's name at the top, followed by biography and statistics.
COMPLETE SET (24)................. 5.00 1.50

1990 Shreveport Captains ProCards

This 27-card standard-size set of the 1990 Shreveport Captains, a Class AA Texas League affiliate of the San Francisco Giants, features on its white-bordered fronts posed color player photos set on simulated wood-grain backgrounds. The player's name, position, and team appear within a gold-colored rectangle below the photo. The tan horizontal back is bordered in white and carries the player's name at the top, followed by biography and statistics.
COMPLETE SET (27)................. 5.00 1.50

1990 Shreveport Captains Star

This 27-card standard-size set of the 1990 Shreveport Captains, a Class AA Texas League affiliate of the San Francisco Giants, features purple bordered posed color player photos on its fronts. The player's name, team name, and position appear at the bottom. The white horizontal back carries the player's name at the top, followed by biography, career highlights, and statistics.
COMPLETE SET (27)................. 5.00 1.50

1990 South Atlantic League All-Stars Star

COMPLETE SET (48)............... 10.00 3.00

1990 South Bend White Sox Best

This 29-card standard-size set of the 1990 South Bend White Sox, a Class A Midwest League affiliate of the Chicago White Sox,features white-bordered posed and action color player photos on its fronts. The player's name and position appear vertically on the left side. The yellow horizontal back carries the player's name and position at the top, followed by biography, career highlights, and statistics. A player head shot appears in the lower right corner.
COMPLETE SET (29)................. 5.00 1.50

1990 South Bend White Sox Grand Slam

COMPLETE SET (30)................. 5.00 1.50

1990 Southern Cal Trojans Smokey

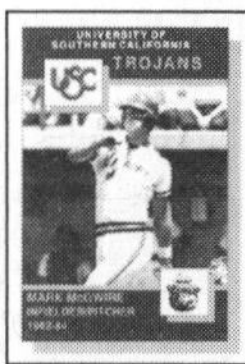

This 12-card set was sponsored by the USDA Forest Service in conjunction with other federal agencies. The standard-size cards have on their fronts black and white photos of outstanding players (except for legendary coach Rod Dedeaux) from past USC baseball teams who went on to play in the major Leagues. The team name and player information appear in maroon stripes above and below the picture. A yellow stripe on the bottom and right side of the picture serve as a shadow border. School and Smokey logos superimposed on the picture round out the card face. In black lettering on white, each back has career summary and a fire prevention cartoon starring Smokey. The cards are unnumbered and checklisted below in alphabetical order. The set was also issued as a an uncut sheet, with three rows of four cards each. The card sets were given away to the first 1,000 fans who attended any game during a series between USC and Stanford, February 23-25, at Dedeaux Field. The key card in this set is of Mark McGwire, who would set the single-season Home Run record during the summer of 1998.
COMPLETE SET (12)............. 100.00 30.00

1990 Southern League All-Stars Don Jennings

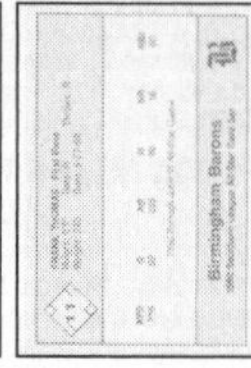

Early cards of Luis Gonzalez and Frank Thomas are in this set.
COMPLETE SET (50)................ 15.00 4.50

1990 Southern Oregon A's Best

This 30-card standard-size set of the 1990 Southern Oregon A's, a Class A South Atlantic League affiliate of the Oakland Athletics, features white-bordered posed and action color player photos on its fronts. The player's name and position appear vertically on the left side. The yellow horizontal back carries the player's name and position at the top, followed by biography, career highlights, and statistics. A player head shot appears in the lower right corner.
COMPLETE SET (30)................. 5.00 1.50

1990 Southern Oregon A's ProCards

This 30-card standard-size set of the 1990 Southern Oregon A's, a Class A South Atlantic League affiliate of the Oakland Athletics, features on its white-bordered fronts posed color player photos set on simulated wood-grain backgrounds. The player's name, position, and team appear within a gold-colored rectangle below the photo. The tan horizontal back is bordered in white and carries the player's name at the top, followed by biography and statistics.
COMPLETE SET (30)................. 5.00 1.50

1990 Spartanburg Phillies Best

This 30-card standard-size set of the 1990 Spartanburg Phillies, a Class A South Atlantic League affiliate of the Philadelphia Phillies, features white-bordered posed and action color player photos on its fronts. The player's name and position appear vertically on the left side. The yellow horizontal back carries the player's name and position at the top, followed by biography, career highlights, and statistics. A player head shot appears in the lower right corner.
COMPLETE SET (30)................. 5.00 1.50

1990 Spartanburg Phillies ProCards

This 29-card standard-size set of the 1990 Spartanburg Phillies, a Class A South Atlantic League affiliate of the Philadelphia Phillies, features on its white-bordered fronts posed color player photos set on simulated wood-grain backgrounds. The player's name, position, and team appear within a gold-colored rectangle below the photo. The tan horizontal back is bordered in white and carries the player's name at the top, followed by biography and statistics.
COMPLETE SET (29)................. 5.00 1.50

1990 Spartanburg Phillies Star

This 29-card standard-size set of the 1990 Spartanburg Phillies, a Class A South Atlantic League affiliate of the Philadelphia Phillies, features red bordered posed color player photos on its fronts. The player's name, team name, and position appear at the bottom. The white horizontal back carries the player's name at the top, followed by biography, career highlights, and statistics.
COMPLETE SET (29)................. 5.00 1.50

1990 Spokane Indians Sports Pro

This 28-card standard-size set of the 1990 Spokane Indians, a Class A Northwest League affiliate of the San Diego Padres, features posed color head-and-shoulders shots, with thin black borders on a white card face. The horizontally oriented backs have biographical information.
COMPLETE SET (28)................. 5.00 1.50

1990 Springfield Cardinals All Decade Best

This 36-card standard-size set of the 1990 Springfield Cardinals, a Class A Midwest League affiliate of the St. Louis Cardinals, features white-bordered posed and action color player photos on its fronts. The player's name and position appear vertically on the left side. The words "All Decade" appear across the top. The yellow horizontal back carries the player's name and years played at the top, followed by player's history, highlights, and statistics. 2,500 sets were produced.
COMPLETE SET (36)................. 8.00 2.40

1990 Springfield Cardinals Best

This 29-card standard-size set of the 1990 Springfield Cardinals, a Class A Midwest League affiliate of the St. Louis Cardinals, features white-bordered posed and action color player photos on its fronts. The player's name and position appear vertically on the left side. The yellow horizontal back carries the player's name and position at the top, followed by biography, career highlights, and statistics. A player head shot appears in the lower right corner.
COMPLETE SET (29)................. 5.00 1.50

1990 St. Catharines Blue Jays ProCards

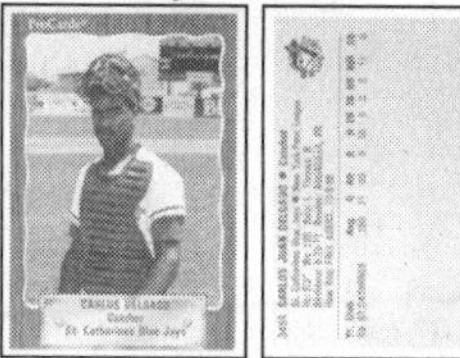

This 34-card standard-size set of the 1990 St. Catharines Blue Jays, a Class A New York-Penn League affiliate of the Toronto Blue Jays, features on its white-bordered fronts posed color player photos set on simulated wood-grain backgrounds. The player's name, position, and team appear within a gold-colored rectangle below the photo. The tan horizontal back is bordered in white and carries the player's name and position at the top, followed by biography and statistics. This issue includes Steve Karsay's minor league team set debut.
COMPLETE SET (34)............... 15.00 4.50

1990 St. Lucie Mets Star

This 31-card standard-size set of the 1990 St. Lucie Mets, a Class A Florida State League affiliate of the New York Mets, features blue bordered posed color player photos on its fronts. The player's name, team name, and position appear at the bottom. The white horizontal back carries the player's name at the top, followed by biography, career highlights, and statistics.
COMPLETE SET (31)................. 5.00 1.50

1990 St. Pete Cardinals Star

This 26-card standard-size set of the 1990 St. Pete Cardinals, a Class A Florida State League affiliate of the St. Louis Cardinals, features red bordered posed color player photos on its fronts. The player's name, team name, and position appear at the bottom. The white horizontal back carries the player's name at the top, followed by biography, career highlights, and statistics.
COMPLETE SET (26)................. 5.00 1.50

1990 Stockton Ports Best

This 29-card standard-size set of the 1990 Stockton Ports, a Class A California League affiliate of the Milwaukee Brewers, features white-bordered posed and action color player photos on its fronts. The player's name and position appear vertically on the left side. The yellow horizontal back carries the player's name and position at the top, followed by biography, career highlights, and statistics. A player head shot appears in the lower right corner.
COMPLETE SET (29)................. 5.00 1.50

1990 Stockton Ports Cal League Cards

COMPLETE SET (29)................. 5.00 1.50

1990 Stockton Ports ProCards

This 29-card standard-size set of the 1990 Stockton Ports, a Class A California League affiliate of the Milwaukee Brewers, features on its white-bordered fronts posed color player photos set on simulated wood-grain backgrounds. The player's name, position, and team appear within a gold-colored rectangle below the photo. The tan horizontal back is bordered in white and carries the player's name at the top, followed by biography and statistics.
COMPLETE SET (29)................. 5.00 1.50

1990 Sumter Braves Best

This 30-card standard-size set of the 1990 Sumter Braves, a Class A South Atlantic League affiliate of the Atlanta Braves, features white-bordered posed and action color player photos on its fronts. The player's name and position appear vertically on the left side. The yellow horizontal back carries the player's name and position at the top, followed by biography, career highlights, and statistics. A player head shot appears in the lower right corner. This issue includes the minor league card debuts of Ryan Klesko and Vinny Castilla.
COMPLETE SET (30)............... 10.00 3.00

1990 Sumter Braves ProCards

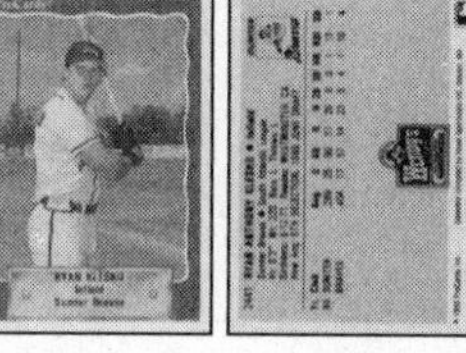

This 30-card standard-size set of the 1990 Sumter Braves, a Class A South Atlantic League affiliate of the Atlanta Braves, features on its white-bordered fronts posed color player photos set on simulated wood-grain backgrounds. The player's name, position, and team appear within a gold-colored rectangle below the photo. The tan horizontal back is bordered in white and carries the player's name at the top, followed by biography and statistics. This issue includes the minor league card debuts of Ryan Klesko and Vinny Castilla.
COMPLETE SET (30)............... 10.00 3.00

1990 Syracuse Chiefs CMC

This 28-card standard-size set of the 1990 Syracuse Chiefs, a Class AAA International League affiliate of the Toronto Blue Jays, features white-bordered posed color player photos on its fronts. The player's name and position appear at the bottom; the team name appears vertically on the left. The back carries the league emblem in the white area at the top, the team name in the green stripe below, and player's name, position, biography, and statistics in the yellow area at the bottom. 1,100 sets were produced.
COMPLETE SET (28)............... 10.00 3.00

1990 Syracuse Chiefs Merchants Bank

Sponsored by Merchants Bank and WIXT Channel 9, this photo album features the 1990 Syracuse Chiefs, a Class AAA International League affiliate of the Toronto Blue Jays. The photo album unfolds to reveal three 11" by 9 1/2" sheets. The first sheet displays a color team photo, with player identification and a Merchants Bank advertisement beneath the picture. The second and third panels each consist of three rows with five cards per row. The perforated player cards measure roughly 2 1/4" by 3 1/4". The fronts display white-bordered color posed player pictures shot from the waist up; player identification and sponsor logos are below the pictures. In blue lettering, the horizontal backs carry biography and statistics. A facsimile autograph in red ink rounds out the back. The cards are unnumbered and checklisted below in alphabetical order.
COMPLETE SET (30)............... 10.00 3.00

1990 Syracuse Chiefs ProCards

This 28-card standard-size set of the 1990 Syracuse Chiefs, a Class AAA International League affiliate of the Toronto Blue Jays, features on its white-bordered fronts posed color player photos set on simulated wood-grain backgrounds. The player's name, position, and team appear within a gold-colored rectangle below the photo. The tan horizontal back is bordered in white and carries the player's name at the top, followed by biography and statistics.
COMPLETE SET (28)................. 8.00 2.40

1990 Tacoma Tigers CMC

This 25-card standard-size set of the 1990 Tacoma Tigers, a Class AAA Pacific Coast League affiliate of the Oakland Athletics, features white-bordered posed color player photos on its fronts. The player's name and position appear at the bottom; the team name appears vertically on the left. The back carries the league emblem in the white area at the top, the team name in the green stripe below, and player's name, position, biography, and statistics in the yellow area at the bottom. 1,100 sets were produced.
COMPLETE SET (25)................. 5.00 1.50

1990 Tacoma Tigers ProCards

This 29-card standard-size set of the 1990 Tacoma Tigers, a Class AAA Pacific Coast League affiliate of the Oakland Athletics, features on its white-bordered fronts posed color player photos set on simulated wood-grain backgrounds. The player's name, position, and team appear within a gold-colored rectangle below the photo. The tan horizontal back is bordered in white and carries the player's name at the top, followed by biography and statistics.
COMPLETE SET (29)................. 5.00 1.50

1990 Tampa Yankees Diamond

Mariano Rivera's first card is in this set.
COMPLETE SET (28)............... 25.00 7.50

1990 Texas League All-Stars Grand Slam

COMPLETE SET (38)............... 10.00 3.00

1990 Tidewater Tides CMC

This 30-card standard-size set of the 1990 Tidewater Tides, a Class AAA International League affiliate of the New York Mets, features white-bordered posed color player photos on its fronts. The player's name and position appear at the bottom; the team name appears vertically on the left. The back carries the league emblem in the white area at the top, the team name in the green stripe below, and player's name, position, biography, and statistics in the yellow area at the bottom. 1,100 sets were produced.
COMPLETE SET (30)................. 5.00 1.50

1990 Tidewater Tides ProCards

This 30-card standard-size set of the 1990 Tidewater Tides, a Class AAA International League affiliate of the New York Mets, features on its white-bordered fronts posed color player photos set on simulated wood-grain backgrounds. The player's name, position, and team appear within a gold-colored rectangle below the photo. The tan horizontal back is bordered in white and carries the player's name at the top, followed by biography and statistics.
COMPLETE SET (30)................. 5.00 1.50

1990 Toledo Mud Hens CMC

This 27-card standard-size set of the 1990 Toledo Mud Hens, a Class AAA International League affiliate of the Detroit Tigers, features white-bordered posed color player photos on its fronts. The player's name and position appear at the bottom; the team name appears vertically on the left. The back carries the league emblem in the white area at the top, the team name in the green stripe below, and player's name, position, biography, and statistics in the yellow area at the bottom. 1,100 sets were produced.
COMPLETE SET (27)............... 10.00 3.00

1990 Toledo Mud Hens ProCards

This 27-card standard-size set of the 1990 Toledo Mud Hens, a Class AAA International League affiliate of the Detroit Tigers, features on its white-bordered fronts posed color player photos set on simulated wood-grain backgrounds. The player's name, position, and team appear within a gold-colored rectangle below the photo. The tan horizontal back is bordered in white and carries the player's name at the top, followed by biography and statistics.
COMPLETE SET (27)............... 15.00 4.50

1990 Triple A All-Stars CMC

COMPLETE SET (45)............... 10.00 3.00

1990 Triple A All-Stars ProCards

COMPLETE SET (54)............... 15.00 4.50

1990 Tucson Toros CMC

This 25-card standard-size set of the 1990 Tucson Toros, a Class AAA Pacific Coast League affiliate of the Houston Astros, features white-bordered posed color player photos on its fronts. The player's name and position appear at the bottom; the team name appears vertically on the left. The back carries the league emblem in the white area at the top, the team name in the green stripe below, and player's name, position, biography, and statistics in the yellow area at the bottom. 1,100 sets were produced.
COMPLETE SET (25)................. 5.00 1.50

1990 Tucson Toros ProCards

This 27-card standard-size set of the 1990 Tucson Toros, a Class AAA Pacific Coast League affiliate of the Houston Astros, features on its white-bordered fronts posed color player photos set on simulated wood-grain backgrounds. The player's name, position, and team appear within a gold-colored rectangle below the photo. The tan horizontal back is bordered in white and carries the player's name at the top, followed by biography and statistics.
COMPLETE SET (27)................. 5.00 1.50

1990 Tulsa Drillers All Decade Best

This 28-card standard-size set of the 1990 Tulsa Drillers, a Class AA Texas League affiliate of the Texas Rangers, features white-bordered posed and action color player photos on its fronts. The player's name and position appear vertically on the left side. The words "All Decade" appear across the top. The yellow horizontal back carries the player's name and years played at the top, followed by player's history, highlights, and statistics. 2,500 sets were produced. Cards of Juan Gonzalez and Sammy Sosa highlight this set.
COMPLETE SET (36)............... 40.00 12.00

1990 Tulsa Drillers ProCards

This 28-card standard-size set of the 1990 Tulsa Drillers, a Class AA Texas League affiliate of the Texas Rangers, features on its white-bordered fronts posed color player photos set on simulated wood-grain backgrounds. The player's name, position, and team appear within a gold-colored rectangle below the photo. The tan horizontal back is bordered in white and carries the player's name at the top, followed by biography and statistics.
COMPLETE SET (28)................. 8.00 2.40

1990 Tulsa Drillers Team Issue

COMPLETE SET (28)............... 10.00 3.00

1990 UNLV Smokey

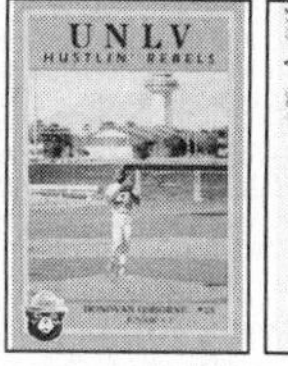

16 cards, Perforated on one sheet. Donovan Osborne key player in set.
COMPLETE SET (16)............... 10.00 3.00

1990 Utica Blue Sox Pucko

COMPLETE SET (30)................. 5.00 1.50

1990 Vancouver Canadians CMC

This 27-card standard-size set of the 1990 Vancouver Canadians, a Class AAA Pacific Coast League affiliate of the Chicago White Sox, features white-bordered posed color player photos on its fronts. The player's name and position appear at the bottom; the team name appears vertically on the left. The back carries the league emblem in the white area at the top, the team name in the green stripe below, and player's name, position, biography, and statistics in the yellow area at the bottom. 1,100 sets were produced.
COMPLETE SET (27)................. 5.00 1.50

1990 Vancouver Canadians ProCards

This 28-card standard-size set of the 1990 Vancouver Canadians, a Class AAA Pacific Coast League affiliate of the White Sox, features on its white-bordered fronts posed color player photos set on simulated wood-grain backgrounds. The player's name, position, and team appear within a gold-colored rectangle below the photo. The tan horizontal back is bordered in white and carries the player's name and position at the top, followed by biography and statistics.
COMPLETE SET (28)................. 5.00 1.50

1990 Vero Beach Dodgers Star

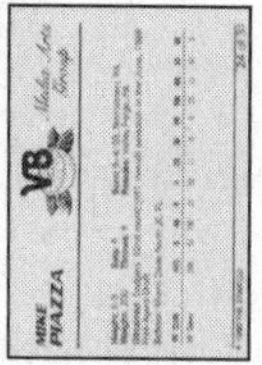

This 31-card standard-size set of the 1990 Vero Beach Dodgers, a Class A Florida State League affiliate of the Los Angeles Dodgers, features blue bordered posed color player photos on its fronts. The player's name, team name, and position appear at the bottom. The white horizontal back carries the player's name at the top, followed by biography, career highlights, and statistics. This issue includes a second year card of Mike Piazza.
COMPLETE SET (31)............... 40.00 12.00

1990 Visalia Oaks Cal League Cards

COMPLETE SET (30)................. 5.00 1.50

1990 Visalia Oaks ProCards

This 26-card standard-size set of the 1990 Visalia Oaks, a Class A California League affiliate of the Minnesota Twins, features on its white-bordered fronts posed color player photos set on simulated wood-grain backgrounds. The player's name, position, and team appear within a gold-colored rectangle below the photo. The tan horizontal back is bordered in white and carries the player's name at the top, followed by biography and statistics.
COMPLETE SET (26)................. 5.00 1.50

1990 Waterloo Diamonds Best

This 28-card standard-size set of the 1990 Waterloo Diamonds, a Class A Midwest League affiliate of the San Diego Padres, features white-bordered posed and action color player photos on its fronts. The player's name and position appear vertically on the left side. The yellow horizontal back carries the player's name and position at the top, followed by biography, career highlights, and statistics. A player head shot appears in the lower right corner.
COMPLETE SET (28)................. 5.00 1.50

1990 Waterloo Diamonds ProCards

This 27-card standard-size set of the 1990 Waterloo Diamonds, a Class A Midwest League affiliate of the San Diego Padres, features on its white-bordered fronts posed color player photos set on simulated wood-grain backgrounds. The player's name, position, and team appear within a gold-colored rectangle below the photo. The tan horizontal back is bordered in white and carries the player's name at the top, followed by biography and statistics.
COMPLETE SET (27)................. 5.00 1.50

1990 Watertown Indians Star

This 28-card standard-size set of the 1990 Watertown Indians, a Class A New York-Penn League affiliate of the Cleveland Indians, features red bordered posed color player photos on its fronts. The player's name, team name, and position appear at the bottom. The white horizontal back carries the player's name at the top, followed by biography, career highlights and statistics. Brian Giles first card is in this set.
COMPLETE SET (28)............... 15.00 4.50

1990 Wausau Timbers Best

This 28-card standard-size set of the 1990 Wausau Timbers, a Class A Midwest League affiliate of the Baltimore Orioles, features white-bordered posed and action color player photos on its fronts. The player's name and position appear vertically on the left side. The yellow horizontal back carries the player's name and position at the top, followed by biography, career highlights, and statistics. A player head shot appears in the lower right corner.
COMPLETE SET (28)................. 5.00 1.50

1990 Wausau Timbers ProCards

This 32-card standard-size set of the 1990 Wausau Timbers, a Class A Midwest League affiliate of the Baltimore Orioles, features on its white-bordered fronts posed color player photos set on simulated wood-grain backgrounds. The player's name, position, and team appear within a gold-colored rectangle below the photo. The tan horizontal back is bordered in white and carries the player's name at the top, followed by biography and statistics.
COMPLETE SET (32)................. 5.00 1.50

1990 Wausau Timbers Star

This 29-card standard-size set of the 1990 Wausau Timbers, a Class A Midwest League affiliate of the Baltimore Orioles, features orange bordered posed color player photos on its fronts. The player's name, team name, and position appear at the bottom. The white horizontal back carries the player's name at the top, followed by biography, career highlights, and statistics.
COMPLETE SET (29)................. 5.00 1.50

1990 Welland Pirates Pucko

This 36-card standard-size set of the 1990 Welland Pirates, a Class A New York-Penn League affiliate of the Pittsburgh Pirates, features posed color player photos on a gray background with black and white dots. The player's name and position are printed in a white bar above the photo, while the team name and logo appear on the bottom. The backs carry a brief biography, the circumstances under which the player was drafted, and statistics (where appropriate). The set was sponsored by Farr and Fuss Lincoln Mercury in Welland.
COMPLETE SET (36)................. 5.00 1.50

1990 West Palm Beach Expos Star

This 32-card standard-size set of the 1990 West Palm Beach Expos, a Class A Florida State League affiliate of the Montreal Expos, features red-bordered posed color player photos on its fronts. The player's name, team name, and position appear at the bottom. In red letters on a white background, the horizontal back carries the player's name at the top, followed by biography, career highlights, and statistics.
COMPLETE SET (32)................. 5.00 1.50

1990 Wichita State Shockers Game Day

COMPLETE SET (46)............... 20.00 6.00

1990 Wichita Wranglers Rock's Dugout

COMPLETE SET (28)................. 5.00 1.50

1990 Williamsport Bills Best

This 27-card standard-size set of the 1990 Williamsport Bills, a Class AA Eastern League affiliate of the Seattle Mariners, features white-bordered posed and action color player photos on its fronts. The player's name and position appear vertically on the left side. The yellow horizontal back carries the player's name and position at the top, followed by biography, career highlights, and statistics. A player head shot appears in the lower right corner.
COMPLETE SET (27)................. 5.00 1.50

1990 Williamsport Bills ProCards

This 26-card standard-size set of the 1990 Williamsport Bills, a Class AA Eastern League

affiliate of the Seattle Mariners, features on its white-bordered fronts posed color player photos set on simulated wood-grain backgrounds. The player's name, position, and team appear within a gold-colored rectangle below the photo. The tan horizontal back is bordered in white and carries the player's name at the top, followed by biography and statistics.
COMPLETE SET (26) 5.00 1.50

1990 Williamsport Bills Star

This 27-card standard-size set of the 1990 Williamsport Bills, a Class AA Eastern League affiliate of the Seattle Mariners, features blue bordered posed color player photos on its fronts. The player's name, team name, and position appear at the bottom. The white horizontal back carries the player's name at the top, followed by biography, career highlights, and statistics.
COMPLETE SET (27) 5.00 1.50

1990 Winston-Salem Spirits Team Issue

COMPLETE SET (30) 5.00 1.50

1990 Winter Haven Red Sox Star

This 28-card standard-size set of the 1990 Winter Haven Red Sox, a Class A Florida State League affiliate of the Boston Red Sox, features blue bordered posed color player photos on its fronts. The player's name, team name, and position appear at the bottom. The white horizontal back carries the player's name at the top, followed by biography, career highlights, and statistics.
COMPLETE SET (28) 5.00 1.50

1990 Yakima Bears Team Issue

COMPLETE SET (37) 5.00 1.50

1991 Albany Yankees Classic/Best Kraft

This six-card set features white-bordered posed color player photos on its fronts. The player's name, team, and position appear at the bottom. A Classic and Kraft logo also appear on the front of the card. The white back is framed by a thin black line and carries the player's name and position at the top, followed by biography, statistics and team logos.
COMPLETE SET (6) 8.00 2.40

1991 Albany Yankees Line Drive

COMPLETE SET (26) 5.00 1.50

1991 Albany Yankees ProCards

This 28-card standard-size set of the 1991 Albany Yankees, a Class AA Eastern League affiliate of the New York Yankees, features on its white-bordered fronts posed color player photos set on simulated spiral-bound yellow notebooks. The player's name, position, and team appear within a green rectangle below the photo. The yellow horizontal back is bordered in white and carries the player's name at the top, followed by biography and statistics.
COMPLETE SET (28) 5.00 1.50

1991 Albuquerque Dukes Line Drive

COMPLETE SET (26) 10.00 3.00

1991 Albuquerque Dukes ProCards

This 27-card standard-size set of the 1991 Albuquerque Dukes, a Class AAA Pacific Coast League affiliate of the Los Angeles Dodgers, features on its white-bordered fronts posed color player photos set on simulated spiral-bound yellow notebooks. The player's name, position, and team appear within a green rectangle below the photo. The yellow horizontal back is bordered in white and carries the player's name at the top, followed by biography and statistics. This issue includes a third year card of Henry Rodriguez and a fourth year card of Eric Karros.
COMPLETE SET (27) 10.00 3.00

1991 Appleton Foxes Classic/Best

This 29-card standard-size set of the 1991 Appleton Foxes, a Class A Midwest League affiliate of the Kansas City Royals, features white-bordered posed color player photos on its fronts. The player's name, team, and position appear at the bottom. The white back is framed by a thin black line and carries the player's name and position at the top, followed by biography, statistics and team logos.
COMPLETE SET (29) 5.00 1.50

1991 Appleton Foxes ProCards

This 28-card standard-size set of the 1991 Appleton Foxes, a Class A Midwest League affiliate of the Kansas City Royals, features on its white-bordered fronts posed color player photos set on simulated spiral-bound yellow notebooks. The player's name, position, and team appear within a green rectangle below the photo. The yellow horizontal back is bordered in white and carries the player's name at the top, followed by biography and statistics.
COMPLETE SET (28) 5.00 1.50

1991 Arkansas Travelers Line Drive

COMPLETE SET (26) 5.00 1.50

1991 Arkansas Travelers ProCards

This 29-card standard-size set of the 1991 Arkansas Travelers, a Class AA Texas League affiliate of the St. Louis Cardinals, features on its white-bordered fronts posed color player photos set on simulated spiral-bound yellow notebooks. The player's name, position, and team appear within a green rectangle below the photo. The yellow horizontal back is bordered in white and carries the player's name at the top, followed by biography and statistics.
COMPLETE SET (29) 5.00 1.50

1991 Asheville Tourists Classic/Best

This 29-card standard-size set of the 1991 Asheville Tourists, a Class A South Atlantic League affiliate of the Houston Astros, features white-bordered posed color player photos on its fronts. The player's name, team, and position appear at the bottom. The white back is framed by a thin black line and carries the player's name and position at the top, followed by biography, statistics and team logos.
COMPLETE SET (29) 5.00 1.50

1991 Asheville Tourists ProCards

This 29-card standard-size set of the 1991 Asheville Tourists, a Class A South Atlantic League affiliate of the Houston Astros, features on its white-bordered fronts posed color player photos set on simulated spiral-bound yellow notebooks. The player's name, position, and team appear within a green rectangle below the photo. The yellow horizontal back is bordered in white and carries the player's name at the top, followed by biography and statistics.
COMPLETE SET (29) 5.00 1.50

1991 Auburn Astros Classic/Best

This 29-card standard-size set of the 1991 Auburn Astros, a Class A New York-Penn League affiliate of the Houston Astros, features white-bordered posed color player photos on its fronts. The player's name, team, and position appear at the bottom. The white back is framed by a thin black line and carries the player's name and position at the top, followed by biography, statistics and team logos.
COMPLETE SET (29) 5.00 1.50

1991 Auburn Astros ProCards

This 26-card standard-size set of the 1991 Auburn Astros, a Class A New York-Penn League affiliate of the Houston Astros, features on its white-bordered fronts posed color player photos set on simulated spiral-bound yellow notebooks. The player's name, position, and team appear within a green rectangle below the photo. The yellow horizontal back is bordered in white and carries the player's name at the top, followed by biography and statistics.
COMPLETE SET (26) 5.00 1.50

1991 Augusta Pirates Classic/Best

This 30-card standard-size set of the 1991 Augusta Pirates, a Class A South Atlantic League affiliate of the Pittsburgh Pirates, features white-bordered posed color player photos on its fronts. The player's name, team, and position appear at the bottom. The white back is framed by a thin black line and carries the player's name and position at the top, followed by biography, statistics and team logos.
COMPLETE SET (30) 5.00 1.50

1991 Augusta Pirates ProCards

This 31-card standard-size set of the 1991 Augusta Pirates, a Class A South Atlantic League affiliate of the Pittsburgh Pirates, features on its white-bordered fronts posed color player photos set on simulated spiral-bound yellow notebooks. The player's name, position, and team appear within a green rectangle below the photo. The yellow horizontal back is bordered in white and carries the player's name at the top, followed by biography and statistics.
COMPLETE SET (31) 5.00 1.50

1991 Bakersfield Dodgers Cal League

This issue includes a second year card of Raul Mondesi and a third year card of Mike Piazza.
COMPLETE SET (32) 30.00 9.00

1991 Baseball City Royals Classic/Best

This 30-card standard-size set of the 1991 Baseball City Royals, a Class A Florida State League affiliate of the Kansas City Royals, features white-bordered posed color player photos on its fronts. The player's name, team, and position appear at the bottom. The white back is framed by a thin black line and carries the player's name and position at the top, followed by biography, statistics and team logos.
COMPLETE SET (30) 5.00 1.50

1991 Baseball City Royals ProCards

This 29-card standard-size set of the 1991 Baseball City Royals, a Class A Florida State League affiliate of the Kansas City Royals, features on its white-bordered fronts posed color player photos set on simulated spiral-bound yellow notebooks. The player's name, position, and team appear within a green rectangle below the photo. The yellow horizontal back is bordered in white and carries the player's name at the top, followed by biography and statistics.
COMPLETE SET (29) 5.00 1.50

1991 Batavia Clippers Classic/Best

This 30-card standard-size set of the 1991 Batavia Clippers, a Class A New York-Penn League affiliate of the Philadelphia Phillies, features white-bordered posed color player photos on its fronts. The player's name, team, and position appear at the bottom. The white back is framed by a thin black line and carries the player's name and position at the top, followed by biography, statistics and team logos.
COMPLETE SET (30) 5.00 1.50

1991 Batavia Clippers ProCards

This 30-card standard-size set of the 1991 Batavia Clippers, a Class A New York-Penn League affiliate of the Philadelphia Phillies, features on its white-bordered fronts posed color player photos set on simulated spiral-bound yellow notebooks. The player's name, position, and team appear within a green rectangle below the photo. The yellow horizontal back is bordered in white and carries the player's name at the top, followed by biography and statistics.
COMPLETE SET (30) 5.00 1.50

1991 Bellingham Mariners Classic/Best

This 30-card standard-size set of the 1991 Bellingham Mariners, a Class A Northwest League affiliate of the Seattle Mariners, features white-bordered posed color player photos on its fronts. The player's name, team, and position appear at the bottom. The white back is framed by a thin black line and carries the player's name and position at the top, followed by biography, statistics and team logos.
COMPLETE SET (30) 10.00 3.00

1991 Bellingham Mariners ProCards

This 32-card standard-size set of the 1991 Bellingham Mariners, a Class A Northwest League affiliate of the Seattle Mariners, features on its white-bordered fronts posed color player photos set on simulated spiral-bound yellow notebooks. The player's name, position, and team appear within a green rectangle below the photo. The yellow horizontal back is bordered in white and carries the player's name at the top, followed by biography and statistics
COMPLETE SET (32) 8.00 2.40

1991 Beloit Brewers Classic/Best

This 28-card standard-size set of the 1991 Beloit Brewers, a Class A Midwest League affiliate of the Milwaukee Brewers, features white-bordered posed color player photos on its fronts. The player's name, team, and position appear at the bottom. The white back is framed by a thin black line and carries the player's name and position at the top, followed by biography, statistics and team logos.
COMPLETE SET (28) 5.00 1.50

1991 Beloit Brewers ProCards

This 28-card standard-size set of the 1991 Beloit Brewers, a Class A Midwest League affiliate of the Milwaukee Brewers, features on its white-bordered fronts posed color player photos set on simulated spiral-bound yellow notebooks. The player's name, position, and team appear within a green rectangle below the photo. The yellow horizontal back is bordered in white and carries the player's name at the top, followed by biography and statistics.
COMPLETE SET (28) 5.00 1.50

1991 Bend Bucks Classic/Best

This 29-card standard-size set of the 1991 Bend Bucks, a Class A Northwest League Independent, features white-bordered posed color player photos on its fronts. The player's name, team, and position appear at the bottom. The white back is framed by a thin black line and carries the player's name and position at the top, followed by biography, statistics and team logos.
COMPLETE SET (29) 5.00 1.50

1991 Bend Bucks ProCards

This 29-card standard-size set of the 1991 Bend Bucks, a Class A Northwest League Independent, features on its white-bordered fronts posed color player photos set on simulated spiral-bound yellow notebooks. The player's name, position, and team appear within a green rectangle below the photo. The yellow horizontal back is bordered in white and carries the player's name at the top, followed by biography and statistics.
COMPLETE SET (29) 5.00 1.50

1991 Billings Mustangs ProCards

This 28-card standard-size set of the 1991 Billings Mustangs, a Rookie Class Pioneer League affiliate of the Cincinnati Reds, features on its white-bordered fronts posed color player photos set on simulated spiral-bound yellow notebooks. The player's name, position, and team appear within a green rectangle below the photo. The yellow horizontal back is bordered in white and carries the player's name at the top, followed by biography and statistics.
COMPLETE SET (28) 5.00 1.50

1991 Billings Mustangs Sports Pro

This 30-card standard-size set of the 1991 Billings Mustangs, a Rookie Class Pioneer League affiliate of the Cincinnati Reds, features posed color head-and-shoulders shots, with thin black borders on a white card face. The horizontally oriented backs have biographical information.
COMPLETE SET (30) 5.00 1.50

1991 Birmingham Barons Line Drive

This issue includes a fourth year card of Wilson Alvarez.
COMPLETE SET (26) 5.00 1.50

1991 Birmingham Barons ProCards

This 28-card standard-size set of the 1991 Birmingham Barons, a Class AA Southern League affiliate of the Chicago White Sox, features on its white-bordered fronts posed color player photos set on simulated spiral-bound yellow notebooks. The player's name, position, and team appear within a green rectangle below the photo. The yellow horizontal back is bordered in white and carries the player's name at the top, followed by biography and statistics. This issue includes a fourth year card of Wilson Alvarez.
COMPLETE SET (28) 5.00 1.50

1991 Bluefield Orioles Classic/Best

This 26-card standard-size set of the 1991 Bluefield Orioles, a Rookie Class Appalachian League affiliate of the Baltimore Orioles, features white-bordered posed color player photos on its fronts. The player's name, team, and position appear at the bottom. The white back is framed by a thin black line and carries the player's name and position at the top, followed by biography, statistics and team logos.
COMPLETE SET (26) 5.00 1.50

1991 Bluefield Orioles ProCards

This 26-card standard-size set of the 1991 Bluefield Orioles, a Rookie Class Appalachian League affiliate of the Baltimore Orioles, features on its white-bordered fronts posed color player photos set on simulated spiral-bound yellow notebooks. The player's name, position, and team appear within a green rectangle below the photo. The yellow horizontal back is bordered in white and carries the player's name at the top, followed by biography and statistics.
COMPLETE SET (26) 5.00 1.50

1991 Boise Hawks Classic/Best

This 30-card standard-size set of the 1991 Boise Hawks, a Class A Northwest League affiliate of the California Angels, features white-bordered posed color player photos on its fronts. The player's name, team, and position appear at the bottom. The white back is framed by a thin black line and carries the player's name and position at the top, followed by biography, statistics and team logos.
COMPLETE SET (30) 5.00 1.50

1991 Boise Hawks ProCards

This 35-card standard-size set of the 1991 Boise Hawks, a Class A Northwest League affiliate of the California Angels, features on its white-bordered fronts posed color player photos set on simulated spiral-bound yellow notebooks. The player's name, position, and team appear within a green rectangle below the photo. The yellow horizontal back is bordered in white and carries the player's name at the top, followed by biography and statistics.
COMPLETE SET (35) 5.00 1.50

1991 Bristol Tigers Classic/Best

This 30-card standard-size set of the 1991 Bristol Tigers, a Rookie Class Appalachian League affiliate of the Detroit Tigers, features white-bordered posed color player photos on its fronts. The player's name, team, and position appear at the bottom. The white back is framed by a thin black line and carries the player's name and position at the top, followed by biography, statistics and team logos.
COMPLETE SET (30) 10.00 3.00

1991 Bristol Tigers ProCards

This 30-card standard-size set of the 1991 Bristol Tigers, a Rookie Class Appalachian League affiliate of the Detroit Tigers, features on its white-bordered fronts posed color player photos set on simulated spiral-bound yellow notebooks. The player's name, position, and team appear within a green rectangle below the photo. The yellow horizontal back is bordered in white and carries the player's name at the top, followed by biography and statistics. This issue includes the minor league card debut of Justin Thompson.
COMPLETE SET (30) 8.00 2.40

1991 Buffalo Bisons Line Drive

COMPLETE SET (26) 5.00 1.50

1991 Buffalo Bisons ProCards

This 26-card standard-size set of the 1991 Buffalo Bisons, a Class AAA American Association affiliate of the Pittsburgh Pirates, features on its white-bordered fronts posed color player photos set on simulated spiral-bound yellow notebooks. The player's name, position, and team appear within a green rectangle below the photo. The yellow horizontal back is bordered in white and carries the player's name at the top, followed by biography and statistics.
COMPLETE SET (26) 5.00 1.50

1991 Burlington Astros Classic/Best

This 29-card standard-size set of the 1991 Burlington Astros, a Class A Midwest League affiliate of the Houston Astros, features white-bordered posed color player photos on its fronts. The player's name, team, and position appear at the bottom. The white back is framed by a thin black line and carries the player's name and position at the top, followed by biography, statistics and team logos.
COMPLETE SET (29) 5.00 1.50

1991 Burlington Astros ProCards

This 28-card standard-size set of the 1991 Burlington Astros, a Class A Midwest League affiliate of the Houston Astros, features on its white-bordered fronts posed color player photos set on simulated spiral-bound yellow notebooks. The player's name, position, and team appear within a green rectangle below the photo. The yellow horizontal back is bordered in white and carries the player's name at the top, followed by biography and statistics.
COMPLETE SET (28) 5.00 1.50

1991 Burlington Indians ProCards

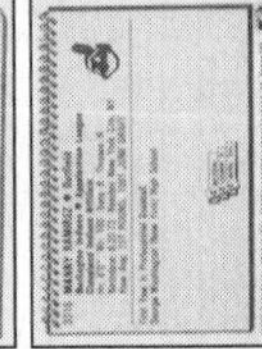

This 34-card standard-size set of the 1991 Burlington Indians, a Rookie Class Appalachian League affiliate of the Cleveland Indians, features on its white-bordered fronts posed color player photos set on simulated spiral-bound yellow notebooks. The player's name, position, and team appear within a green rectangle below the photo. The yellow horizontal back is bordered in white and carries the player's name at the top, followed by biography and statistics. This issue includes the minor league card debut of Manny Ramirez.
COMPLETE SET (34) 40.00 12.00

1991 Butte Copper Kings Sports Pro

This 30-card standard-size set of the 1991 Butte Copper Kings, a Rookie Class Pioneer League affiliate of the Texas Rangers, features posed color head-and-shoulders shots, with thin black borders on a white card face. The horizontally oriented backs have biographical information.
COMPLETE SET (30) 5.00 1.50

1991 Calgary Cannons Line Drive

This 26-card standard-size set of the 1991 Calgary Cannons, a Class AAA Pacific Coast League affiliate of the Seattle Mariners, features posed color player photos on its white-bordered fronts. The player's name appears in red lettering at the top; his position and team

name appear in red lettering below the photo. The back carries the player's name within a red stripe at the top, followed by position, team name and affiliation, biography and statistics.
COMPLETE SET (26) 5.00 1.50

1991 Calgary Cannons ProCards

This 25-card standard-size set of the 1991 Calgary Cannons, a Class AAA Pacific Coast League affiliate of the Seattle Mariners, features on its white-bordered fronts posed color player photos set on simulated spiral-bound yellow notebooks. The player's name, position, and team appear within a green rectangle below the photo. The yellow horizontal back is bordered in white and carries the player's name at the top, followed by biography and statistics.
COMPLETE SET (25) 5.00 1.50

1991 California League All-Stars

The 1991 California League All-Stars contains 56 standard-size cards. The fronts feature mostly posed color player photos with silver borders. The words "All Star" are printed in red across the bottom of the picture, with the player's name below and to the right. In black print on white background, the horizontally oriented backs present biography and career statistics. Early cards of Pedro Martinez and Mike Piazza are in this set.
COMPLETE SET (56) 30.00 9.00

1991 Canton-Akron Indians Line Drive

COMPLETE SET (26) 20.00 6.00

1991 Canton-Akron Indians ProCards

This 28-card standard-size set of the 1991 Canton-Akron Indians, a Class AA Eastern League affiliate of the Cleveland Indians, features on its white-bordered fronts posed color player photos set on simulated spiral-bound yellow notebooks. The player's name, position, and team appear within a green rectangle below the photo. The yellow horizontal back is bordered in white and carries the player's name at the top, followed by biography and statistics. This issue includes Jim Thome's second year minor league card.
COMPLETE SET (28) 20.00 6.00

1991 Carolina League All-Stars ProCards

COMPLETE SET (47) 10.00 3.00

1991 Carolina Mudcats Line Drive

COMPLETE SET (26) 5.00 1.50

1991 Carolina Mudcats ProCards

This 26-card standard-size set of the 1991 Carolina Mudcats, a Class AA Southern League affiliate of the Pittsburgh Pirates, features on its white-bordered fronts posed color player photos set on simulated spiral-bound yellow notebooks. The player's name, position, and team appear within a green rectangle below the photo. The yellow horizontal back is bordered in white and carries the player's name at the top, followed by biography and statistics.
COMPLETE SET (26) 5.00 1.50

1991 Cedar Rapids Reds Classic/Best

This 30-card standard-size set of the 1991 Cedar Rapids Reds, a Class A Midwest League affiliate of the Cincinnati Reds, features white-bordered posed color player photos on its fronts. The player's name, team, and position appear at the bottom. The white back is framed by a thin black line and carries the player's name and position at the top, followed by biography, statistics and team logos.
COMPLETE SET (30) 5.00 1.50

1991 Cedar Rapids Reds ProCards

This 30-card standard-size set of the 1991 Cedar Rapids Reds, a Class A Midwest League affiliate of the Cincinnati Reds, features on its white-bordered fronts posed color player photos set on simulated spiral-bound yellow notebooks. The player's name, position, and team appear within a green rectangle below the photo. The yellow horizontal back is bordered in white and carries the player's name at the top, followed by biography and statistics.
COMPLETE SET (30) 5.00 1.50

1991 Charleston Rainbows Classic/Best

This 29-card standard-size set of the 1991 Charleston Rainbows, a Class A South Atlantic League affiliate of the San Diego Padres, features white-bordered posed color player photos on its fronts. The player's name, team, and position appear at the bottom. The white back is framed by a thin black line and carries the player's name and position at the top, followed by biography, statistics and team logos.
COMPLETE SET (29) 5.00 1.50

1991 Charleston Rainbows ProCards

This 27-card standard-size set of the 1991 Charleston Rainbows, a Class A South Atlantic League affiliate of the San Diego Padres, features on its white-bordered fronts posed color player photos set on simulated spiral-bound yellow notebooks. The player's name, position, and team appear within a green rectangle below the photo. The yellow horizontal back is bordered in white and carries the player's name at the top, followed by biography and statistics.
COMPLETE SET (27) 5.00 1.50

1991 Charleston Wheelers Classic/Best

This 28-card standard-size set of the 1991 Charleston Wheelers, a Class A South Atlantic League affiliate of the Cincinnati Reds, features white-bordered posed color player photos on its fronts. The player's name, team, and position appear at the bottom. The white back is framed by a thin black line and carries the player's name and position at the top, followed by biography, statistics and team logos.
COMPLETE SET (28) 5.00 1.50

1991 Charleston Wheelers ProCards

This 27-card standard-size set of the 1991 Charleston Wheelers, a Class A South Atlantic League affiliate of the Cincinnati Reds, features on its white-bordered fronts posed color player photos set on simulated spiral-bound yellow notebooks. The player's name, position, and team appear within a green rectangle below the photo. The yellow horizontal back is bordered in white and carries the player's name at the top, followed by biography and statistics.
COMPLETE SET (27) 5.00 1.50

1991 Charlotte Knights Line Drive

COMPLETE SET (26) 5.00 1.50

1991 Charlotte Knights ProCards

This 26-card standard-size set of the 1991 Charlotte Knights, a Class AA Southern League affiliate of the Chicago Cubs, features on its white-bordered fronts posed color player photos set on simulated spiral-bound yellow notebooks. The player's name, position, and team appear within a green rectangle below the photo. The yellow horizontal back is bordered in white and carries the player's name at the top, followed by biography and statistics.
COMPLETE SET (26) 5.00 1.50

1991 Charlotte Rangers Classic/Best

This 30-card standard-size set of the 1991 Charlotte Rangers, a Class A Florida State League affiliate of the Texas Rangers, features white-bordered posed color player photos on its fronts. The player's name, team, and position appear at the bottom. The white back is framed by a thin black line and carries the player's name and position at the top, followed by biography, statistics and team logos.
COMPLETE SET (30) 8.00 2.40

1991 Charlotte Rangers ProCards

This 28-card standard-size set of the 1991 Charlotte Rangers, a Class A Florida State League affiliate of the Texas Rangers, features on its white-bordered fronts posed color player photos set on simulated spiral-bound yellow notebooks. The player's name, position, and team appear within a green rectangle below the photo. The yellow horizontal back is bordered in white and carries the player's name at the top, followed by biography and statistics.
COMPLETE SET (28) 5.00 1.50

1991 Chattanooga Lookouts Line Drive

This issue contains a fourth year card of Reggie Sanders.
COMPLETE SET (26) 5.00 1.50

1991 Chattanooga Lookouts ProCards

This 27-card standard-size set of the 1991 Chattanooga Lookouts, a Class AA Southern League affiliate of the Cincinnati Reds, features on its white-bordered fronts posed color player photos set on simulated spiral-bound yellow notebooks. The player's name, position, and team appear within a green rectangle below the photo. The yellow horizontal back is bordered in white and carries the player's name at the top, followed by biography and statistics. This issue includes a fourth year card of Reggie Sanders.
COMPLETE SET (27) 5.00 1.50

1991 Clearwater Phillies Classic/Best

This 27-card standard-size set of the 1991 Clearwater Phillies, a Class A Florida State League affiliate of the Philadelphia Phillies, features white-bordered posed color player photos on its fronts. The player's name, team, and position appear at the bottom. The white back is framed by a thin black line and carries the player's name and position at the top, followed by biography, statistics and team logos.
COMPLETE SET (27) 5.00 1.50

1991 Clearwater Phillies ProCards

This 29-card standard-size set of the 1991 Clearwater Phillies, a Class A Florida State League affiliate of the Philadelphia Phillies, features on its white-bordered fronts posed color player photos set on simulated spiral-bound yellow notebooks. The player's name, position, and team appear within a green rectangle below the photo. The yellow horizontal back is bordered in white and carries the player's name at the top, followed by biography and statistics.
COMPLETE SET (29) 5.00 1.50

1991 Clinton Giants Classic/Best

This 29-card standard-size set of the 1991 Clinton Giants, a Class A Midwest League affiliate of the San Francisco Giants, features white-bordered posed color player photos on its fronts. The player's name, team, and position appear at the bottom. The white back is framed by a thin black line and carries the player's name and position at the top, followed by biography, statistics and team logos.
COMPLETE SET (29) 5.00 1.50

1991 Clinton Giants ProCards

This 29-card standard-size set of the 1991 Clinton Giants, a Class A Midwest League affiliate of the San Francisco Giants, features on its white-bordered fronts posed color player photos set on simulated spiral-bound yellow notebooks. The player's name, position, and team appear within a green rectangle below the photo. The yellow horizontal back is bordered in white and carries the player's name at the top, followed by biography and statistics.
COMPLETE SET (29) 5.00 1.50

1991 Colorado Springs Sky Sox Line Drive

COMPLETE SET (26) 5.00 1.50

1991 Colorado Springs Sky Sox ProCards

This 28-card standard-size set of the 1991 Colorado Springs Sky Sox, a Class AAA Pacific Coast League affiliate of the Cleveland Indians, features on its white-bordered fronts posed color player photos set on simulated spiral-bound yellow notebooks. The player's name, position, and team appear within a green rectangle below the photo. The yellow horizontal back is bordered in white and carries the player's name at the top, followed by biography and statistics.
COMPLETE SET (28) 5.00 1.50

1991 Columbia Mets Play II

The 32 cards in this Columbia Mets set measure 2 3/8" by 3 1/2". Play II produced 3,000 sets; 1,000 sets were intended for distribution by the Columbia Mets at the ballpark in late August. In addition, 150 uncut sheets were made. The fronts feature posed color player photos with rounded corners. The card face is primarily white, with diagonal blue streaks visible at the top and bottom of the card. Player information is given in the lower left corner, and the Mets' team logo appears in the lower right corner. The horizontally oriented backs are printed in black and gray on white, and present biographical as well as statistical information.
COMPLETE SET (33) 15.00 4.50

1991 Columbia Mets Postcards Play II

This 28-card set was issued in 4 series, with 7 cards per series. Play II produced 1,500 sets and 150 uncut sheets; 500 sets were given out at Mets park. The cards measure 5" by 3 9/16" and are in the postcard format. The front design has posed color player photos, with thin red borders in purple, white, and red on a black card face. The player's name is written vertically in yellow block lettering in a purple stripe on the left side of the picture. The backs are printed in dark blue. On the left half appears biography and player profile, while the right half has space for the address and stamp. The cards are numbered on the back 1-7 within series I-IV.
COMPLETE SET (28) 25.00 7.50

1991 Columbus Clippers Line Drive

This set includes a fifth year issue of Bernie Williams.
COMPLETE SET (26) 10.00 3.00

1991 Columbus Clippers Police

This issue includes a fifth year card of Bernie Williams.
COMPLETE SET (24) 10.00 3.00

1991 Columbus Clippers ProCards

This 29-card standard-size set of the 1991 Columbus Clippers, a Class AAA International League affiliate of the New York Yankees, features on its white-bordered fronts posed color player photos set on simulated spiral-bound yellow notebooks. The player's name, position, and team appear within a green rectangle below the photo. The yellow horizontal back is bordered in white and carries the player's name at the top, followed by biography and statistics. This issue includes a fifth year card of Bernie Williams.
COMPLETE SET (29) 10.00 3.00

1991 Columbus Indians Classic/Best

This 30-card standard-size set of the 1991 Columbus Indians, a Class A South Atlantic League affiliate of the Cleveland Indians, features white-bordered posed color player photos on its fronts. The player's name, team, and position appear at the bottom. The white back is framed by a thin black line and carries the player's name and position at the top, followed by biography, statistics and team logos.
COMPLETE SET (30) 5.00 1.50

1991 Columbus Indians ProCards

This 32-card standard-size set of the 1991 Columbus Indians, a Class A South Atlantic League affiliate of the Cleveland Indians, features on its white-bordered fronts posed color player photos set on simulated spiral-bound yellow notebooks. The player's name, position, and team appear within a green rectangle below the photo. The yellow horizontal back is bordered in white and carries the player's name at the top, followed by biography and statistics.
COMPLETE SET (32) 5.00 1.50

1991 Denver Zephyrs Line Drive

COMPLETE SET (26) 5.00 1.50

1991 Denver Zephyrs ProCards

This 27-card standard-size set of the 1991 Denver Zephyrs, a Class AAA American Association affiliate of the Milwaukee Brewers, features on its white-bordered fronts posed color player photos set on simulated spiral-bound yellow notebooks. The player's name, position, and team appear within a green rectangle below the photo. The yellow horizontal back is bordered in white and carries the player's name at the top, followed by biography and statistics.
COMPLETE SET (27) 5.00 1.50

1991 Dunedin Blue Jays Classic/Best

This 30-card standard-size set of the 1991 Dunedin Blue Jays, a Class A Florida State League affiliate of the Toronto Blue Jays, features white-bordered posed color player photos on its fronts. The player's name, position, and team name appear within a black stripe below the photo. The white back is framed by a black line and carries the player's name and position at the top, followed by biography and statistics.
COMPLETE SET (30) 5.00 1.50

1991 Dunedin Blue Jays ProCards

This 29-card standard-size set of the 1991 Dunedin Blue Jays, a Class A Florida State League affiliate of the Toronto Blue Jays, features on its white-bordered fronts posed color player photos set on simulated spiral-bound yellow notebooks. The player's name, position, and team appear within a green rectangle below the photo. The yellow horizontal back is bordered in white and carries the player's name at the top, followed by biography and statistics.
COMPLETE SET (29) 5.00 1.50

1991 Durham Bulls Classic/Best

This 26-card standard-size set of the 1991 Durham Bulls, a Class A Carolina League affiliate of the Atlanta Braves, features white-bordered posed color player photos on its fronts. The player's name, team, and position appear at the bottom. The white back is framed by a thin black line and carries the player's name and position at the top, followed by biography, statistics and team logos. This issue includes a third year card of Javy Lopez.
COMPLETE SET (26) 10.00 3.00

1991 Durham Bulls ProCards

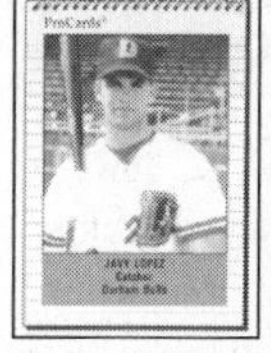

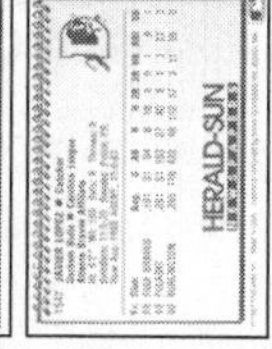

This 26-card standard-size set of the 1991 Durham Bulls, a Class A Carolina League affiliate of the Atlanta Braves, features on its white-bordered fronts posed color player photos set on simulated spiral-bound yellow notebooks. The player's name, position, and team appear within a green rectangle below the photo. The yellow horizontal back is bordered in white and carries the player's name at the top, followed by biography and statistics. This issue includes a third year card of Javy Lopez.
COMPLETE SET (33) 8.00 2.40

1991 Durham Bulls Update ProCards

This nine-card standard-size set of the 1991 Durham Bulls, a Class A Carolina League affiliate of the Atlanta Braves, features on its white-bordered fronts posed color player photos set on simulated spiral-bound yellow notebooks. The player's name, position, and team appear within a green rectangle below the photo. The yellow horizontal back is bordered in white and carries the player's name at the top, followed by biography and statistics.
COMPLETE SET (9) 5.00 1.50

1991 Edmonton Trappers Line Drive

This 26-card standard-size set of the 1991 Edmonton Trappers, a Class AAA Pacific Coast League affiliate of the California Angels, features posed color player photos on its white-bordered fronts. The player's name appears in red lettering at the top; his position and team name appear in red lettering below the photo. The back carries the player's name within a red stripe at the top, followed by position, team name and affiliation, biography and statistics.
COMPLETE SET (26) 5.00 1.50

1991 Edmonton Trappers ProCards

This 28-card standard-size set of the 1991 Edmonton Trappers, a Class AAA Pacific Coast League affiliate of the California Angels, features on its white-bordered fronts posed color player photos set on simulated spiral-bound yellow notebooks. The player's name, position, and team appear within a green rectangle below the photo. The yellow horizontal back is bordered in white and carries the player's name at the top, followed by biography and statistics.
COMPLETE SET (28) 5.00 1.50

1991 El Paso Diablos Line Drive

COMPLETE SET (26) 5.00 1.50

1991 El Paso Diablos ProCards

This 26-card standard-size set of the 1991 El Paso Diablos, a Class AA Texas League affiliate of the Milwaukee Brewers, features on its white-bordered fronts posed color player photos set on simulated spiral-bound yellow notebooks. The player's name, position, and team appear within a green rectangle below the photo. The yellow horizontal back is bordered in white and carries the player's name at the top, followed by biography and statistics.
COMPLETE SET (26) 5.00 1.50

1991 Elizabethton Twins ProCards

This 26-card standard-size set of the 1991 Elizabethton Twins, a Rookie Class Appalachian League affiliate of the Minnesota Twins, features on its white-bordered fronts posed color player photos set on simulated spiral-bound yellow notebooks. The player's name, position, and team appear within a green rectangle below the photo. The yellow horizontal back is bordered in white and carries the player's name at the top, followed by biography and statistics.
COMPLETE SET (26) 5.00 1.50

1991 Elmira Pioneers Classic/Best

This 30-card standard-size set of the 1991 Elmira Pioneers, a Class A New York-Penn League affiliate of the Boston Red Sox, features white-bordered posed color player photos on its fronts. The player's name, team, and position appear at the bottom. The white back is framed by a thin black line and carries the player's name and position at the top, followed by biography, statistics and team logos. This issue includes the minor league card debut of Frank Rodriguez.
COMPLETE SET (30) 5.00 1.50

1991 Elmira Pioneers ProCards

This 29-card standard-size set of the 1991 Elmira Pioneers, a Class A New York-Penn League affiliate of the Boston Red Sox, features on its white-bordered fronts posed color player photos set on simulated spiral-bound yellow notebooks. The player's name, position, and team appear within a green rectangle below the photo. The yellow horizontal back is bordered in white and carries the player's name at the top, followed by biography and statistics.
COMPLETE SET (29) 5.00 1.50

1991 Erie Sailors Classic/Best

This issue along with the Fleer/PC issue features NFL Safety John Lynch.
COMPLETE SET (29) 20.00 1.50

1991 Erie Sailors ProCards

This 30-card standard-size set of the 1991 Erie Sailors, a Class A New York-Penn League Independent, features on its white-bordered fronts posed color player photos set on simulated spiral-bound yellow notebooks. The player's name, position, and team appear within a green rectangle below the photo. The yellow horizontal back is bordered in white and carries the player's name at the top, followed by biography and statistics.
COMPLETE SET (30)................ 12.00 1.50

1991 Eugene Emeralds Classic/Best

This 30-card standard-size set of the 1991 Eugene Emeralds, a Class A Northwest League affiliate of the Kansas City Royals, features white-bordered posed color player photos on its fronts. The player's name, team, and position appear at the bottom. The white back is framed by a thin black line and carries the player's name and position at the top, followed by biography, statistics and team logos.
COMPLETE SET (30).................. 5.00 1.50

1991 Eugene Emeralds ProCards

This 30-card standard-size set of the 1991 Eugene Emeralds, a Class A Northwest League affiliate of the Kansas City Royals, features on its white-bordered fronts posed color player photos set on simulated spiral-bound yellow notebooks. The player's name, position, and team appear within a green rectangle below the photo. The yellow horizontal back is bordered in white and carries the player's name at the top, followed by biography and statistics.
COMPLETE SET (30).................. 5.00 1.50

1991 Everett Giants Classic/Best

This 30-card standard-size set of the 1991 Everett Giants, a Class A Northwest League affiliate of the San Francisco Giants, features white-bordered posed color player photos on its fronts. The player's name, team, and position appear at the bottom. The white back is framed by a thin black line and carries the player's name and position at the top, followed by biography, statistics and team logos.
COMPLETE SET (30).................. 5.00 1.50

1991 Everett Giants ProCards

This 33-card standard-size set of the 1991 Everett Giants, a Class A Northwest League affiliate of the San Francisco Giants, features on its white-bordered fronts posed color player photos set on simulated spiral-bound yellow notebooks. The player's name, position, and team appear within a green rectangle below the photo. The yellow horizontal back is bordered in white and carries the player's name at the top, followed by biography and statistics.
COMPLETE SET (33).................. 5.00 1.50

1991 Fayetteville Generals Classic/Best

This 30-card standard-size set of the 1991 Fayetteville Generals, a Class A South Atlantic League affiliate of the Detroit Tigers, features white-bordered posed color player photos on its fronts. The player's name, team, and position appear at the bottom. The white back is framed by a thin black line and carries the player's name and position at the top, followed by biography, statistics and team logos.
COMPLETE SET (30).................. 5.00 1.50

1991 Fayetteville Generals ProCards

This 29-card standard-size set of the 1991 Fayetteville Generals, a Class A South Atlantic League affiliate of the Detroit Tigers, features on its white-bordered fronts posed color player photos set on simulated spiral-bound yellow notebooks. The player's name, position, and team appear within a green rectangle below the photo. The yellow horizontal back is bordered in white and carries the player's name at the top, followed by biography and statistics.
COMPLETE SET (29).................. 5.00 1.50

1991 Florida State League All-Stars ProCards

COMPLETE SET (46).................. 5.00 1.50

1991 Frederick Keys Classic/Best

This 30-card standard-size set of the 1991 Frederick Keys, a Class A Carolina League affiliate of the Baltimore Orioles, features white-bordered posed color player photos on its fronts. The player's name, team, and position appear at the bottom. The white back is framed by a thin black line and carries the player's name and position at the top, followed by biography, statistics and team logos.
COMPLETE SET (30).................. 5.00 1.50

1991 Frederick Keys ProCards

This 29-card standard-size set of the 1991 Frederick Keys, a Class A Carolina League affiliate of the Baltimore Orioles, features on its white-bordered fronts posed color player photos set on simulated spiral-bound yellow notebooks. The player's name, position, and team appear within a green rectangle below the photo. The yellow horizontal back is bordered in white and carries the player's name at the top, followed by biography and statistics.
COMPLETE SET (29).................. 5.00 1.50

1991 Fresno State Bulldogs Smokey

The Fresno State Bulldogs set was sponsored by Grandy's in cooperation USDA Forest Service and other agencies. The set was issued as a unperforated sheet with four rows of four cards each. If the cards were cut, they would measure the standard size. The fronts feature glossy color player photos, with blue borders on a red card face. Player information appears below the picture, between the Smokey and Grandy's logos. The backs present college statistics and a fire prevention cartoon starring Smokey. The cards are unnumbered and checklisted below in alphabetical order.
COMPLETE SET (16)................ 10.00 3.00

1991 Fresno State Lady Bulldogs Smokey

COMPLETE SET (14)................ 10.00 3.00

1991 Ft. Lauderdale Yankees Classic/Best

This 30-card standard-size set of the 1991 Ft. Lauderdale Yankees, a Class A Florida State League affiliate of the New York Yankees, features white-bordered posed color player photos on its fronts. The player's name, team, and position appear at the bottom. The white back is framed by a thin black line and carries the player's name and position at the top, followed by biography, statistics and team logos.
COMPLETE SET (30).................. 5.00 1.50

1991 Ft. Lauderdale Yankees ProCards

This 31-card standard-size set of the 1991 Ft. Lauderdale Yankees, a Class A Florida State League affiliate of the New York Yankees, features on its white-bordered fronts posed color player photos set on simulated spiral-bound yellow notebooks. The player's name, position, and team appear within a green rectangle below the photo. The yellow horizontal back is bordered in white and carries the player's name at the top, followed by biography and statistics.
COMPLETE SET (31).................. 5.00 1.50

1991 Gastonia Rangers Classic/Best

This 30-card standard-size set of the 1991 Gastonia Rangers, a Class A South Atlantic League affiliate of the Texas Rangers, features white-bordered posed color player photos on its fronts. The player's name, team, and position appear at the bottom. The white back is framed by a thin black line and carries the player's name and position at the top, followed by biography, statistics and team logos. Both Dell Curry, the NBA 6th Man Award winner of 1994; and Muggsy Bogues, star NBA guard; are also included in this set.
COMPLETE SET (30).................. 5.00 1.50

1991 Gastonia Rangers ProCards

This 31-card standard-size set of the 1991 Gastonia Rangers, a Class A South Atlantic League affiliate of the Texas Rangers, features on its white-bordered fronts posed color player photos set on simulated spiral-bound yellow notebooks. The player's name, position, and team appear within a green rectangle below the photo. The yellow horizontal back is bordered in white and carries the player's name at the top, followed by biography and statistics.
COMPLETE SET (31).................. 5.00 1.50

1991 Geneva Cubs Classic/Best

This 30-card standard-size set of the 1991 Geneva Cubs, a Class A New York-Penn League affiliate of the Chicago Cubs, features white-bordered posed color player photos on its fronts. The player's name, team, and position appear at the bottom. The white back is framed by a thin black line and carries the player's name and position at the top, followed by biography, statistics and team logos.
COMPLETE SET (30).................. 5.00 1.50

1991 Geneva Cubs ProCards

This 30-card standard-size set of the 1991 Geneva Cubs, a Class A New York-Penn League affiliate of the Chicago Cubs, features on its white-bordered fronts posed color player photos set on simulated spiral-bound yellow notebooks. The player's name, position, and team appear within a green rectangle below the photo. The yellow horizontal back is bordered in white and carries the player's name at the top, followed by biography and statistics.
COMPLETE SET (30).................. 5.00 1.50

1991 Great Falls Dodgers Sports Pro

This 30-card standard-size set of the 1991 Great Falls Dodgers, a Rookie Class Pioneer League affiliate of the Los Angeles Dodgers, features posed color head-and-shoulders shots, with thin black borders on a white card face. The horizontally oriented backs have biographical information.
COMPLETE SET (30).................. 5.00 1.50

1991 Greensboro Hornets ProCards

This 29-card standard-size set of the 1991 Greensboro Hornets, a Class A South Atlantic League affiliate of the New York Yankees, features on its white-bordered fronts posed color player photos set on simulated spiral-bound yellow notebooks. The player's name, position, and team appear within a green rectangle below the photo. The yellow horizontal back is bordered in white and carries the player's name at the top, followed by biography and statistics. This issue includes an early card of Mariano Rivera.
COMPLETE SET (29)................ 15.00 4.50

1991 Greenville Braves Classic/Best

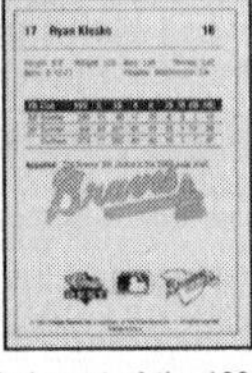

This 29-card standard-size set of the 1991 Greenville Braves, a Class AA Southern League affiliate of the Atlanta Braves, features white-bordered posed color player photos on its fronts. The player's name, team, and position appear at the bottom. The white back is framed by a thin black line and carries the player's name and position at the top, followed by biography, statistics and team logos. Second year cards of Vinny Castilla and Ryan Klesko are in this set.
COMPLETE SET (29)................ 10.00 3.00

1991 Greenville Braves Line Drive

Second year cards of Vinny Castilla and Ryan Klesko are in this set.
COMPLETE SET (26)................ 10.00 3.00

1991 Greenville Braves ProCards

This 27-card standard-size set of the 1991 Greenville Braves, a Class AA Southern League affiliate of the Atlanta Braves, features on its white-bordered fronts posed color player photos set on simulated spiral-bound yellow notebooks. The player's name, position, and team appear within a green rectangle below the photo. The yellow horizontal back is bordered in white and carries the player's name at the top, followed by biography and statistics. Second year cards of Vinny Castilla and Ryan Klesko are in this set.
COMPLETE SET (27)................ 10.00 3.00

1991 Gulf Coast Rangers Sports Pro

This 30-card standard-size set of the 1991 Gulf Coast Rangers, a Rookie Class Gulf Coast League affiliate of the Texas Rangers, features posed color head-and-shoulders shots, with thin black borders on a white card face. The horizontally oriented backs have biographical information.
COMPLETE SET (30).................. 5.00 1.50

1991 Hagerstown Suns Line Drive

This 26-card standard-size set of the 1991 Hagerstown Suns, a Class AA Eastern League affiliate of the Baltimore Orioles, features posed color player photos on its white-bordered fronts. The player's name appears in blue lettering at the top; his position and team name appear in blue lettering below the photo. The back carries the player's name within a blue stripe at the top, followed by position, team name and affiliation, biography and statistics.
COMPLETE SET (26).................. 5.00 1.50

1991 Hagerstown Suns ProCards

This 28-card standard-size set of the 1991 Hagerstown Suns, a Class AA Eastern League affiliate of the Baltimore Orioles, features on its white-bordered fronts posed color player photos set on simulated spiral-bound yellow notebooks. The player's name, position, and team appear within a green rectangle below the photo. The yellow horizontal back is bordered in white and carries the player's name at the top, followed by biography and statistics.
COMPLETE SET (28).................. 5.00 1.50

1991 Hamilton Redbirds Classic/Best

This 30-card standard-size set of the 1991 Hamilton Redbirds, a Class A New York-Penn League affiliate of the St. Louis Cardinals, features white-bordered posed color player photos on its fronts. The player's name, team, and position appear at the bottom. The white back is framed by a thin black line and carries the player's name and position at the top, followed by biography, statistics and team logos. This set features the minor league card debut of John Mabry.
COMPLETE SET (30).................. 8.00 2.40

1991 Hamilton Redbirds ProCards

This 33-card standard-size set of the 1991 Hamilton Redbirds, a Class A New York-Penn League affiliate of the St. Louis Cardinals, features on its white-bordered fronts posed color player photos set on simulated spiral-bound yellow notebooks. The player's name, position, and team appear within a green rectangle below the photo. The yellow horizontal back is bordered in white and carries the player's name at the top, followed by biography and statistics. This issue includes the minor league card debut of John Mabry.
COMPLETE SET (33).................. 5.00 1.50

1991 Harrisburg Senators Line Drive

This 26-card standard-size set of the 1991 Harrisburg Senators, a Class AA Eastern League affiliate of the Montreal Expos, features posed color player photos on its white-bordered fronts. The player's name appears in blue lettering at the top; his position and team name appear in blue lettering below the photo. The back carries the player's name within a blue stripe at the top, followed by position, team name and affiliation, biography and statistics.
COMPLETE SET (26).................. 5.00 1.50

1991 Harrisburg Senators ProCards

This 29-card standard-size set of the 1991 Harrisburg Senators, a Class AA Eastern League affiliate of the Montreal Expos, features on its white-bordered fronts posed color player photos set on simulated spiral-bound yellow notebooks. The player's name, position, and team appear within a green rectangle below the photo. The yellow horizontal back is bordered in white and carries the player's name and position at the top, followed by biography and statistics.
COMPLETE SET (29).................. 5.00 1.50

1991 Helena Brewers Sports Pro

This 30-card standard-size set of the 1991 Helena Brewers, a Rookie Class Pioneer League affiliate of the Milwaukee Brewers, features posed color head-and-shoulders shots, with thin black borders on a white card face. The horizontally oriented backs have biographical information.
COMPLETE SET (30)................ 10.00 3.00

1991 High Desert Mavericks Classic/Best

This 30-card standard-size set of the 1991 High Desert Mavericks, a Class A California League affiliate of the San Diego Padres, features white-bordered posed color player photos on its fronts. The player's name, team, and position appear at the bottom. The white back is framed by a thin black line and carries the player's name and position at the top, followed by biography, statistics and team logos.
COMPLETE SET (30).................. 5.00 1.50

1991 High Desert Mavericks ProCards

This 32-card standard-size set of the 1991 High Desert Mavericks, a Class A California League affiliate of the San Diego Padres, features on its white-bordered fronts posed color player photos set on simulated spiral-bound yellow notebooks. The player's name, position, and team appear within a green rectangle below the photo. The yellow horizontal back is bordered in white and carries the player's name at the top, followed by biography and statistics.
COMPLETE SET (32).................. 5.00 1.50

1991 Huntington Cubs Classic/Best

This 30-card standard-size set of the 1991 Huntington Cubs, a Rookie Class Appalachian League affiliate of the Chicago Cubs, features white-bordered posed color player photos on its fronts. The player's name, team, and position appear at the bottom. The white back is framed by a thin black line and carries the player's name and position at the top, followed by biography, statistics and team logos.
COMPLETE SET (30).................. 5.00 1.50

1991 Huntington Cubs ProCards

This 32-card standard-size set of the 1991 Huntington Cubs, a Rookie Class Appalachian League affiliate of the Chicago Cubs, features on its white-bordered fronts posed color player photos set on simulated spiral-bound yellow notebooks. The player's name, position, and team appear within a green rectangle below the photo. The yellow horizontal back is bordered in white and carries the player's name at the top, followed by biography and statistics.
COMPLETE SET (32).................. 5.00 1.50

1991 Huntsville Stars Classic/Best

This 26-card standard-size set of the 1991 Huntsville Stars, a Class AA Southern League affiliate of the Oakland Athletics, features white-bordered posed color player photos on its fronts. The player's name, team, and position appear near the bottom. The white back is framed by a black line and carries the player's name and position at the top, followed by biography and statistics.
COMPLETE SET (26).................. 5.00 1.50

1991 Huntsville Stars Line Drive

COMPLETE SET (26).................. 5.00 1.50

1991 Huntsville Stars ProCards

This 26-card standard-size set of the 1991 Huntsville Stars, a Class AA Southern League affiliate of the Oakland Athletics, features on its white-bordered fronts posed color player photos set on simulated spiral-bound yellow notebooks. The player's name, position, and team appear within a green rectangle below the photo. The yellow horizontal back is bordered in white and carries the player's name at the top, followed by biography and statistics.
COMPLETE SET (26).................. 5.00 1.50

1991 Huntsville Stars Team Issue

COMPLETE SET (25).................. 5.00 1.50

1991 Idaho Falls Braves ProCards

This 29-card standard-size set of the 1991 Idaho Falls Braves, a Rookie Class Pioneer League affiliate of the Atlanta Braves, features on its white-bordered fronts posed color player photos set on simulated spiral-bound yellow notebooks. The player's name, position, and team appear within a green rectangle below the photo. The yellow horizontal back is bordered in white and carries the player's name at the top, followed by biography and statistics.
COMPLETE SET (29).................. 5.00 1.50

1991 Idaho Falls Braves Sports Pro

This 30-card standard-size set of the 1991 Idaho Falls Braves, a Rookie Class Pioneer League affiliate of the Atlanta Braves, features posed color head-and-shoulders shots, with thin black borders on a white card face. The horizontally oriented backs have biographical information.
COMPLETE SET (30).................. 7.00 2.10

1991 Indianapolis Indians Line Drive

This 26-card standard-size set of the 1991 Indianapolis Indians, a Class AAA American Association affiliate of the Montreal Expos, features posed color player photos on its white-bordered fronts. The player's name appears in red lettering at the top; his position and team name appear in red lettering below the photo. The back carries the player's name within a red stripe at the top, followed by position, team name and affiliation, biography and statistics.
COMPLETE SET (26).................. 5.00 1.50

1991 Indianapolis Indians ProCards

This 28-card standard-size set of the 1991 Indianapolis Indians, a Class AAA American Association affiliate of the Montreal Expos, features on its white-bordered fronts posed color player photos set on simulated spiral-bound yellow notebooks. The player's name, position, and team appear within a green rectangle below the photo. The yellow horizontal back is bordered in white and carries the player's name and position at the top, followed by biography and statistics. The logos for Pepsi and Hook's Drug Stores round out the back.
COMPLETE SET (28).................. 5.00 1.50

1991 Iowa Cubs Line Drive

COMPLETE SET (26).................. 5.00 1.50

1991 Iowa Cubs ProCards

This 26-card standard-size set of the 1991 Iowa Cubs, a Class AAA American Association affiliate of the Chicago Cubs, features on its white-bordered fronts posed color player photos set on simulated spiral-bound yellow notebooks. The player's name, position, and team appear within a green rectangle below the photo. The yellow horizontal back is bordered in white and carries the player's name at the top, followed by biography and statistics.
COMPLETE SET (26).................. 5.00 1.50

1991 Jackson Generals Line Drive

COMPLETE SET (26).................. 5.00 1.50

1991 Jackson Generals ProCards

This 28-card standard-size set of the 1991 Jackson Generals, a Class AA Texas League affiliate of the Houston Astros, features on its white-bordered fronts posed color player photos set on simulated spiral-bound yellow notebooks. The player's name, position, and team appear within a green rectangle below the photo. The yellow horizontal back is bordered in white and carries the player's name at the top, followed by biography and statistics.
COMPLETE SET (28).................. 5.00 1.50

1991 Jacksonville Suns Line Drive

COMPLETE SET (26)................ 15.00 4.50

1991 Jacksonville Suns ProCards

This 29-card standard-size set of the 1991 Jacksonville Suns, a Class AA Southern League affiliate of the Seattle Mariners, features on its white-bordered fronts posed color player photos set on simulated spiral-bound yellow notebooks. The player's name, position, and team appear within a green rectangle below the photo. The yellow horizontal back is bordered in white and carries the player's name at the top, followed by biography and statistics.
COMPLETE SET (29)................ 15.00 4.50

1991 Jamestown Expos Classic/Best

This 30-card standard-size set of the 1991 Jamestown Expos, a Class A New York-Penn League affiliate of the Montreal Expos, features white-bordered posed color player photos on its fronts. The player's name, team, and position appear near the bottom. The white back is framed by a black line and carries the player's name and position at the top, followed by biography and statistics. This issue includes the minor league card debut of Mark Grudzielanek.
COMPLETE SET (30)................ 10.00 3.00

1991 Jamestown Expos ProCards

This 29-card standard-size set of the 1991 Jamestown Expos, a Class A New York-Penn League affiliate of the Montreal Expos, features on its white-bordered fronts posed color player photos set on simulated spiral-bound yellow notebooks. The player's name, position, and team appear within a green rectangle below the photo. The yellow horizontal back is bordered in white and carries the player's name and position at the top, followed by biography and statistics. This issue includes the minor league card debut of Mark Grudzielanek.
COMPLETE SET (29).................. 8.00 2.40

1991 Jesuit HS Alumni

This 8-card set was issued to commemorate the 1,000th baseball game in the history of Jesuit High School (in New Orleans) and to honor alumni who played in the Majors. The cards were given away to those attending ceremonies on April 13-14. They measure 2 11/16" by 3 13/16". The fronts have black and white pictures of the players in their high school uniforms. The pictures are enframed by black borders on a white card face. The player's name, year of graduating class, and his stints in the Majors are listed below the picture. In a horizontal format, the backs have player information and a "Did You Know?" feature, which presents the outstanding achievements of the player. The cards are unnumbered and checklisted below in chronological order of high school graduating class.
COMPLETE SET (8).................. 10.00 3.00

1991 Johnson City Cardinals Classic/Best

This 30-card standard-size set of the 1991 Johnson City Cardinals, a Rookie Class Appalachian League affiliate of the St. Louis Cardinals, features white-bordered posed color player photos on its fronts. The player's name, team, and position appear at the bottom. The white back is framed by a thin black line and carries the player's name and position at the top, followed by biography, statistics and team logos. This issue includes the minor league card debut of Dmitri Young.
COMPLETE SET (30)................ 10.00 3.00

1991 Johnson City Cardinals ProCards

This 29-card standard-size set of the 1991 Johnson City Cardinals, a Rookie Class Appalachian League affiliate of the St. Louis Cardinals, features on its white-bordered fronts posed color player photos set on simulated spiral-bound yellow notebooks. The player's name, position, and team appear within a green rectangle below the photo. The yellow horizontal back is bordered in white and carries the player's name at the top, followed by biography and statistics. This issue includes the minor league card debut of Dmitri Young.
COMPLETE SET (29)................ 10.00 3.00

1991 Kane County Cougars Classic/Best

This 30-card standard-size set of the 1991 Kane County Cougars, a Class A Midwest League affiliate of the Baltimore Orioles, features white-bordered posed color player photos on its fronts. The player's name, team, and position appear at the bottom. The white back is framed by a thin black line and carries the player's name and position at the top, followed by biography, statistics and team logos.
COMPLETE SET (30).................. 5.00 1.50

1991 Kane County Cougars ProCards

This 28-card standard-size set of the 1991 Kane County Cougars, a Class A Midwest League affiliate of the Baltimore Orioles, features on its white-bordered fronts posed color player photos set on simulated spiral-bound yellow notebooks. The player's name, position, and team appear within a green rectangle below the photo. The yellow horizontal back is bordered in white and carries the player's name at the top, followed by biography and statistics.
COMPLETE SET (28).................. 5.00 1.50

1991 Kane County Cougars Team Issue

This 27-card set measures the standard size. On a black card face, the glossy color action player photos are bordered in white and green. The player's name and position appear in white lettering above the picture, with the team name on a diagonal stripe in the lower right corner. In a horizontal format,the back has biography, statistics, and a question-and-answer trivia feature. The cards are unnumbered and checklisted below in alphabetical order, with the uniform number after the name.
COMPLETE SET (27).................. 5.00 1.50

1991 Kenosha Twins Classic/Best

This 28-card standard-size set of the 1991 Kenosha Twins, a Class A Midwest League affiliate of the Minnesota Twins, features white-bordered posed color player photos on its fronts. The player's name, team, and position appear at the bottom. The white back is framed by a thin black line and carries the player's name and position at the top, followed by biography, statistics and team logos.
COMPLETE SET (28).................. 5.00 1.50

1991 Kenosha Twins ProCards

This 28-card standard-size set of the 1991 Kenosha Twins, a Class A Midwest League affiliate of the Minnesota Twins, features on its white-bordered fronts posed color player photos set on simulated spiral-bound yellow notebooks. The player's name, position, and team appear within a green rectangle below the photo. The yellow horizontal back is bordered in white and carries the player's name at the top, followed by biography and statistics.
COMPLETE SET (28).................. 5.00 1.50

1991 Kingsport Mets Classic/Best

This 29-card standard-size set of the 1991 Kingsport Mets, a Rookie Class Appalachian League affiliate of the New York Mets, features white-bordered posed color player photos on its fronts. The player's name, team, and position appear at the bottom. The white back is framed by a thin black line and carries the player's name and position at the top, followed by biography, statistics and team logos.
COMPLETE SET (29).................. 5.00 1.50

1991 Kingsport Mets ProCards

This 28-card standard-size set of the 1991 Kingsport Mets, a Rookie Class Appalachian League affiliate of the New York Mets, features on its white-bordered fronts posed color player photos set on simulated spiral-bound yellow notebooks. The player's name, position, and team appear within a green rectangle below the photo. The yellow horizontal back is bordered in white and carries the player's name at the top, followed by biography and statistics.
COMPLETE SET (28).................. 5.00 1.50

1991 Kinston Indians Classic/Best

This 30-card standard-size set of the 1991 Kinston Indians, a Class A Carolina League affiliate of the Cleveland Indians, features white-bordered posed color player photos on its fronts. The player's name, team, and position appear at the bottom. The white back is framed by a thin black line and carries the player's name and position at the top, followed by biography, statistics and team logos.
COMPLETE SET (30).................. 5.00 1.50

1991 Kinston Indians ProCards

This 31-card standard-size set of the 1991 Kinston Indians, a Class A Carolina League affiliate of the Cleveland Indians, features on its white-bordered fronts posed color player photos set on simulated spiral-bound yellow notebooks. The player's name, position, and team appear within a green rectangle below the photo. The yellow horizontal back is bordered in white and carries the player's name at the top, followed by biography and statistics.
COMPLETE SET (31).................. 5.00 1.50

1991 Kissimmee Dodgers ProCards

This 32-card standard-size set of the 1991 Kissimmee Dodgers, a Rookie Class Gulf Coast League affiliate of the Los Angeles Dodgers, features on its white-bordered fronts posed color player photos set on simulated spiral-bound yellow notebooks. The player's name, position, and team appear within a green rectangle below the photo. The yellow horizontal back is bordered in white and carries the player's name at the top, followed by biography and statistics. This issue includes the minor league card debut of Ismael Valdes.
COMPLETE SET (32).................. 8.00 2.40

1991 Knoxville Blue Jays Line Drive

This 26-card standard-size set of the 1991 Knoxville Blue Jays, a Class AA Southern League affiliate of the Toronto Blue Jays, features posed color player photos on its white-bordered fronts. The player's name appears in blue lettering at the top; his position and team name appear in blue lettering below the photo. The back carries the player's name within a blue stripe at the top, followed by position, team name and affiliation, biography and statistics.
COMPLETE SET (26)................ 12.00 3.60

1991 Knoxville Blue Jays ProCards

This 28-card standard-size set of the 1991 Knoxville Blue Jays, a Class AA Southern League affiliate of the Toronto Blue Jays, features on its white-bordered fronts posed color player photos set on simulated spiral-bound yellow notebooks. The player's name, position, and team appear within a green rectangle below the photo. The yellow horizontal back is bordered in white and carries the player's name and position at the top, followed by biography and statistics.
COMPLETE SET (28)................ 10.00 3.00

1991 Lakeland Tigers Classic/Best

This 30-card standard-size set of the 1991 Lakeland Tigers, a Class A Florida State League affiliate of the Detroit Tigers, features white-bordered posed color player photos on its fronts. The player's name, team, and position appear at the bottom. The white back is framed by a thin black line and carries the player's name and position at the top, followed by biography, statistics and team logos.
COMPLETE SET (30).................. 5.00 1.50

1991 Lakeland Tigers ProCards

This 29-card standard-size set of the 1991 Lakeland Tigers, a Class A Florida State League affiliate of the Detroit Tigers, features on its white-bordered fronts posed color player photos set on simulated spiral-bound yellow notebooks. The player's name, position, and team appear within a green rectangle below the photo. The yellow horizontal back is bordered in white and carries the player's name at the top, followed by biography and statistics.
COMPLETE SET (29).................. 5.00 1.50

1991 Las Vegas Stars Line Drive

COMPLETE SET (26).................. 5.00 1.50

1991 Las Vegas Stars ProCards

This 31-card standard-size set of the 1991 Las Vegas Stars, a Class AAA Pacific Coast League affiliate of the San Diego Padres, features on its white-bordered fronts posed color player photos set on simulated spiral-bound yellow notebooks. The player's name, position, and team appear within a green rectangle below the photo. The yellow horizontal back is bordered in white and carries the player's name at the top, followed by biography and statistics.
COMPLETE SET (31).................. 5.00 1.50

1991 London Tigers Line Drive

COMPLETE SET (26).................. 5.00 1.50

1991 London Tigers ProCards

This 27-card standard-size set of the 1991 London Tigers, a Class AA Eastern League affiliate of the Detroit Tigers, features on its white-bordered fronts posed color player photos set on simulated spiral-bound yellow notebooks. The player's name, position, and team appear within a green rectangle below the photo. The yellow horizontal back is bordered in white and carries the player's name at the top, followed by biography and statistics.
COMPLETE SET (27).................. 5.00 1.50

1991 Louisville Redbirds Line Drive

COMPLETE SET (26)................ 10.00 3.00

1991 Louisville Redbirds ProCards

This 29-card standard-size set of the 1991 Louisville Redbirds, a Class AAA American Association affiliate of the Louisville Redbirds, features on its white-bordered fronts posed color player photos set on simulated spiral-bound yellow notebooks. The player's name, position, and team appear within a green rectangle below the photo. The yellow horizontal back is bordered in white and carries the player's name at the top, followed by biography and statistics. This issue includes the second year card of Brian Jordan.
COMPLETE SET (29)................ 10.00 3.00

1991 Louisville Redbirds Team Issue

Brian Jordan has a second year card and an autographed card in this set.
COMPLETE SET (34)................ 40.00 12.00

1991 LSU Tigers Police

This 16-card standard-size set was sponsored by law enforcement agencies in conjunction with other sponsors in honor of the 1991 NCAA National Champion LSU Tigers. Production quantities were limited to 5,000 sets. The fronts have color action photos, accented in purple on mustard-colored borders. A banner with the words "National Champions" overlays the upper left corner of the picture, and the sponsors' logos appear across the card bottom. The backs have either a caption to the picture or player profile, as well as "Tips from the National Champions" in the form of anti-drug and alcohol messages.
COMPLETE SET (16)................ 10.00 3.00

1991 Lynchburg Red Sox Classic/Best

This 29-card standard-size set of the 1991 Lynchburg Red Sox, a Class A Carolina League affiliate of the Boston Red Sox, features white-bordered posed color player photos on its fronts. The player's name, team, and position appear at the bottom. The white back is framed by a thin black line and carries the player's name and position at the top, followed by biography, statistics and team logos.
COMPLETE SET (29).................. 5.00 1.50

1991 Lynchburg Red Sox ProCards

This 28-card standard-size set of the 1991 Lynchburg Red Sox, a Class A Carolina League affiliate of the Boston Red Sox, features on its white-bordered fronts posed color player photos set on simulated spiral-bound yellow notebooks. The player's name, position, and team appear within a green rectangle below the photo. The yellow horizontal back is bordered in white and carries the player's name at the top, followed by biography and statistics.
COMPLETE SET (28).................. 5.00 1.50

1991 Macon Braves Classic/Best

This 30-card standard-size set of the 1991 Macon Braves, a Class A South Atlantic League affiliate of the Atlanta Braves, features white-bordered posed color player photos on its fronts. The player's name, team, and position appear near the bottom. The white back is framed by a black line and carries the player's name and position at the top, followed by biography and statistics. This issue includes the minor league card debut of Chipper Jones.
COMPLETE SET (30)................ 40.00 12.00

1991 Macon Braves ProCards

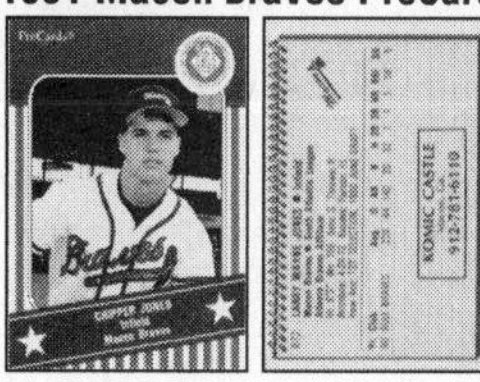

This 31-card standard-size set of the 1991 Macon Braves, a Class A South Atlantic League affiliate of the Atlanta Braves, features on its white-bordered fronts posed color player photos set on simulated spiral-bound yellow notebooks. The player's name, position, and team appear within a green rectangle below the photo. The yellow horizontal back is bordered in white and carries the player's name and position at the top, followed by biography and statistics. This issue includes the minor league card debut of Chipper Jones.
COMPLETE SET (31)................ 40.00 12.00

1991 Madison Muskies Classic/Best

This 30-card standard-size set of the 1991 Madison Muskies, a Class A Midwest League affiliate of the Oakland Athletics, features white-bordered posed color player photos on its fronts. The player's name, team, and position appear at the bottom. The white back is framed by a thin black line and carries the player's name and position at the top, followed by biography, statistics and team logos.
COMPLETE SET (30).................. 5.00 1.50

1991 Madison Muskies ProCards

This 27-card standard-size set of the 1991 Madison Muskies, a Class A Midwest League affiliate of the Oakland Athletics, features on its white-bordered fronts posed color player photos set on simulated spiral-bound yellow notebooks. The player's name, position, and team appear within a green rectangle below the photo. The yellow horizontal back is bordered in white and carries the player's name at the top, followed by biography and statistics.
COMPLETE SET (27).................. 5.00 1.50

1991 Martinsville Phillies Classic/Best

This 30-card standard-size set of the 1991 Martinsville Phillies, a Rookie Class Appalachian League affiliate of the Philadelphia Phillies, features white-bordered posed color player photos on its fronts. The player's name, team, and position appear at the bottom. The white back is framed by a thin black line and carries the player's name and position at the top, followed by biography, statistics and team logos.
COMPLETE SET (30).................. 5.00 1.50

1991 Martinsville Phillies ProCards

This 31-card standard-size set of the 1991 Martinsville Phillies, a Rookie Class Appalachian League affiliate of the Philadelphia Phillies, features on its white-bordered fronts posed color player photos set on simulated spiral-bound yellow notebooks. The player's name, position, and team appear within a green rectangle below the photo. The yellow horizontal back is bordered in white and carries the player's name at the top, followed by biography and statistics.
COMPLETE SET (31).................. 5.00 1.50

1991 Medicine Hat Blue Jays ProCards

This 31-card standard-size set of the 1991 Medicine Hat Blue Jays, a Class A Pioneer League affiliate of the Toronto Blue Jays, features on its white-bordered fronts posed color player photos set on simulated spiral-bound yellow notebooks. The player's name, position, and team appear within a green rectangle below the photo. The yellow horizontal back is bordered in white and carries the player's name and position at the top, followed by biography.
COMPLETE SET (31).................. 5.00 1.50

1991 Medicine Hat Blue Jays Sports Pro

This 30-card standard-size set of the 1991 Medicine Hat Blue Jays, a Class A Pioneer League affiliate of the Toronto Blue Jays, features white-bordered posed color player photos on its fronts. The team name appears above the picture; the player's name appears below. The white horizontal back is framed by a black line and carries the player's name and position followed by biography. The set was sponsored by Monarch Cable TV Ltd. and printed on thin card stock.
COMPLETE SET (30).................. 5.00 1.50

1991 Memphis Chicks Line Drive

COMPLETE SET (26).................. 5.00 1.50

1991 Memphis Chicks ProCards

This 27-card standard-size set of the 1991 Memphis Chicks, a Class AA Southern League affiliate of the Kansas City Royals, features on its white-bordered fronts posed color player photos set on simulated spiral-bound yellow notebooks. The player's name, position, and team appear within a green rectangle below the photo. The yellow horizontal back is bordered in white and carries the player's name at the top, followed by biography and statistics.
COMPLETE SET (27).................. 5.00 1.50

1991 Miami Hurricanes Bumble Bee

The University of Miami Hurricane baseball team is featured on this sheet measuring approximately 10" by 10 1/2". After perforation, the cards measure the standard size. The fronts have color action player photos, with orange borders on a green card face. The school and team name appear above in white lettering, while player information appears between the logos beneath the picture. The backs have

player profile (in English and Spanish), statistics, and a "Hurricanes Just Say No to Drugs" public service message. The cards are unnumbered and checklisted below in alphabetical order.
COMPLETE SET (12)................ 10.00 3.00

1991 Miami Miracle Classic/Best

This 30-card standard-size set of the 1991 Miami Miracles, a Class A Florida State League Independent, features white-bordered posed color player photos on its fronts. The player's name, team, and position appear at the bottom. The white back is framed by a thin black line and carries the player's name and position at the top, followed by biography, statistics and team logos.
COMPLETE SET (30)................ 5.00 1.50

1991 Miami Miracle ProCards

This 27-card standard-size set of the 1991 Miami Miracle, a Class A Florida State League Independent, features on its white-bordered fronts posed color player photos set on simulated spiral-bound yellow notebooks. The player's name, position, and team appear within a green rectangle below the photo. The yellow horizontal back is bordered in white and carries the player's name at the top, followed by biography and statistics.
COMPLETE SET (27)................ 5.00 1.50

1991 Midland Angels Line Drive

This issue includes a fourth year card of Tim Salmon.
COMPLETE SET (26)................ 8.00 2.40

1991 Midland Angels One Hour Photo

This 32-card set of the 1991 Midland Angels, a Class AA Texas League affiliate of the California Angels, features color player photos. The set measures approximately 5 1/2" by 5". The backs are blank. The cards are unnumbered and checklisted below in alphabetical order. 500 sets were produced. This issue includes a fourth year card of Tim Salmon.
COMPLETE SET (32)................ 60.00 18.00

1991 Midland Angels ProCards

This 27-card standard-size set of the 1991 Midland Angels, a Class AA Texas League affiliate of the California Angels, features on its white-bordered fronts posed color player photos set on simulated spiral-bound yellow notebooks. The player's name, position, and team appear within a green rectangle below the photo. The yellow horizontal back is bordered in white and carries the player's name at the top, followed by biography and statistics. This issue includes the fourth year card of Tim Salmon.
COMPLETE SET (27)................ 8.00 2.40

1991 Midwest League All-Stars ProCards

COMPLETE SET (51)................ 5.00 1.50

1991 Mississippi State Bulldogs

COMPLETE SET (55)................ 15.00 4.50

1991 Modesto A's Classic/Best

This 27-card standard-size set of the 1991 Modesto A's, a Class A California League affiliate of the Oakland Athletics, features white-bordered posed color player photos on its fronts. The player's name, team, and position appear at the bottom. The white back is framed by a thin black line and carries the player's name and position at the top, followed by biography, statistics and team logos.
COMPLETE SET (27)................ 5.00 1.50

1991 Modesto A's ProCards

This 30-card standard-size set of the 1991 Modesto A's, a Class A California League affiliate of the Oakland Athletics, features on its white-bordered fronts posed color player photos set on simulated spiral-bound yellow notebooks. The player's name, position, and team appear within a green rectangle below the photo. The yellow horizontal back is bordered in white and carries the player's name at the top, followed by biography and statistics.
COMPLETE SET (30)................ 5.00 1.50

1991 Myrtle Beach Hurricanes Classic/Best

This 30-card standard-size set of the 1991 Myrtle Beach Hurricanes, a Class A South Atlantic League affiliate of the Toronto Blue Jays, features white-bordered posed color player photos on its fronts. The player's name, team, and position appear near the bottom. The white back is framed by a black line and carries the player's name and position at the top, followed by biography and statistics. This issue includes a third year card of Carlos Delgado.
COMPLETE SET (30)................ 15.00 4.50

1991 Myrtle Beach Hurricanes ProCards

This 30-card standard-size set of the 1991 Myrtle Beach Hurricanes, a Class A South Atlantic League affiliate of the Toronto Blue Jays, features on its white-bordered fronts posed color player photos set on simulated spiral-bound yellow notebooks. The player's name, position, and team appear within a green rectangle below the photo. The yellow horizontal back is bordered in white and carries the player's name at the top, followed by biography and statistics. This issue includes a third year card of Carlos Delgado.
COMPLETE SET (30)................ 15.00 4.50

1991 Nashville Sounds Line Drive

COMPLETE SET (26)................ 5.00 1.50

1991 Nashville Sounds ProCards

This 27-card standard-size set of the 1991 Nashville Sounds, a Class AAA American Association affiliate of the Cincinnati Reds, features on its white-bordered fronts posed color player photos set on simulated spiral-bound yellow notebooks. The player's name, position, and team appear within a green rectangle below the photo. The yellow horizontal back is bordered in white and carries the player's name at the top, followed by biography and statistics.
COMPLETE SET (27)................ 5.00 1.50

1991 New Britain Red Sox Line Drive

COMPLETE SET (26)................ 5.00 1.50

1991 New Britain Red Sox ProCards

This 26-card standard-size set of the 1991 New Britain Red Sox, a Class AA Eastern League affiliate of the Boston Red Sox, features on its white-bordered fronts posed color player photos set on simulated spiral-bound yellow notebooks. The player's name, position, and team appear within a green rectangle below the photo. The yellow horizontal back is bordered in white and carries the player's name at the top, followed by biography and statistics.
COMPLETE SET (26)................ 5.00 1.50

1991 Niagara Falls Rapids Classic/Best

This 30-card standard-size set of the 1991 Niagara Falls Rapids, a Class A New York-Penn League affiliate of the Detroit Tigers, features white-bordered posed color player photos on its fronts. The player's name, team, and position appear at the bottom. The white back is framed by a thin black line and carries the player's name and position at the top, followed by biography, statistics and team logos. This issue includes the second year card of Tony Clark.
COMPLETE SET (30)................ 10.00 3.00

1991 Niagara Falls Rapids ProCards

This 30-card standard-size set of the 1991 Niagara Falls Rapids, a Class A New York-Penn League affiliate of the Detroit Tigers, features on its white-bordered fronts posed color player photos set on simulated spiral-bound yellow notebooks. The player's name, position, and team appear within a green rectangle below the photo. The yellow horizontal back is bordered in white and carries the player's name at the top, followed by biography and statistics. This issue includes the second year card of Tony Clark.
COMPLETE SET (30)................ 8.00 2.40

1991 Oklahoma City 89ers Line Drive

This set includes the fifth year card of Dean Palmer.
COMPLETE SET (26)................ 5.00 1.50

1991 Oklahoma City 89ers ProCards

This 27-card standard-size set of the 1991 Oklahoma City 89ers, a Class AAA American Association affiliate of the Texas Rangers, features on its white-bordered fronts posed color player photos set on simulated spiral-bound yellow notebooks. The player's name, position, and team appear within a green rectangle below the photo. The yellow horizontal back is bordered in white and carries the player's name at the top, followed by biography and statistics. This issue includes the fifth year card of Dean Palmer.
COMPLETE SET (27)................ 5.00 1.50

1991 Oklahoma State Cowboys

COMPLETE SET (32)................ 10.00 3.00

1991 Omaha Royals Line Drive

COMPLETE SET (26)................ 5.00 1.50

1991 Omaha Royals ProCards

This 26-card standard-size set of the 1991 Omaha Royals, a Class AAA American Association affiliate of the Kansas City Royals, features on its white-bordered fronts posed color player photos set on simulated spiral-bound yellow notebooks. The player's name, position, and team appear within a green rectangle below the photo. The yellow horizontal back is bordered in white and carries the player's name at the top, followed by biography and statistics. This issue includes the fourth year card of Jeff Conine.
COMPLETE SET (26)................ 5.00 1.50

1991 Oneonta Yankees ProCards

This 27-card standard-size set of the 1991 Oneonta Yankees, a Class A New York-Penn League affiliate of the New York Yankees, features on its white-bordered fronts posed color player photos set on simulated spiral-bound yellow notebooks. The player's name, position, and team appear within a green rectangle below the photo. The yellow horizontal back is bordered in white and carries the player's name at the top, followed by biography and statistics.
COMPLETE SET (27)................ 25.00 7.50

1991 Orlando Sun Rays Line Drive

COMPLETE SET (26)................ 5.00 1.50

1991 Orlando Sun Rays ProCards

This 27-card standard-size set of the 1991 Orlando Sun Rays, a Class AA Southern League affiliate of the Minnesota Twins, features on its white-bordered fronts posed color player photos set on simulated spiral-bound yellow notebooks. The player's name, position, and team appear within a green rectangle below the photo. The yellow horizontal back is bordered in white and carries the player's name at the top, followed by biography and statistics.
COMPLETE SET (27)................ 5.00 1.50

1991 Osceola Astros Classic/Best

This 29-card standard-size set of the 1991 Osceola Astros, a Class A Florida State League affiliate of the Houston Astros, features white-bordered posed color player photos on its fronts. The player's name, team, and position appear at the bottom. The white back is framed by a thin black line and carries the player's name and position at the top, followed by biography, statistics and team logos.
COMPLETE SET (29)................ 5.00 1.50

1991 Osceola Astros ProCards

This 29-card standard-size set of the 1991 Osceola Astros, a Class A Florida State League affiliate of the Houston Astros, features on its white-bordered fronts posed color player photos set on simulated spiral-bound yellow notebooks. The player's name, position, and team appear within a green rectangle below the photo. The yellow horizontal back is bordered in white and carries the player's name at the top, followed by biography and statistics. This issue includes the second year card of Brian L. Hunter.
COMPLETE SET (29)................ 5.00 1.50

1991 Palm Springs Angels ProCards

This 30-card standard-size set of the 1991 Palm Springs Angels, a Class A California League affiliate of the California Angels, features on its white-bordered fronts posed color player photos set on simulated spiral-bound yellow notebooks. The player's name, position, and team appear within a green rectangle below the photo. The yellow horizontal back is bordered in white and carries the player's name at the top, followed by biography and statistics. This issue includes the fourth year card of Jim Edmonds.
COMPLETE SET (30)................ 10.00 3.00

1991 Pawtucket Red Sox Dunkin' Donuts

This 31-card set of the Pawtucket Red Sox, a Class AAA International League affiliate of the Boston Red Sox, was issued in one large sheet featuring six perforated five-card strips with a large team photo in the wide top strip. Sponsored by Channel 10 and Dunkin' Donuts, the fronts carry color player photos while the backs display player career statistics. The cards are unnumbered and checklisted below in alphabetical order. This issue includes a second minor league year card of Mo Vaughn.
COMPLETE SET (31)................ 50.00 15.00

1991 Pawtucket Red Sox Line Drive

This issue includes a second year minor league card of Mo Vaughn.
COMPLETE SET (26)................ 10.00 3.00

1991 Pawtucket Red Sox ProCards

This 27-card standard-size set of the 1991 Pawtucket Red Sox, a Class AAA International League affiliate of the Boston Red Sox, features on its white-bordered fronts posed color player photos set on simulated spiral-bound yellow notebooks. The player's name, position, and team appear within a green rectangle below the photo. The yellow horizontal back is bordered in white and carries the player's name at the top, followed by biography and statistics. This issue includes a second year minor league card of Mo Vaughn.
COMPLETE SET (27)................ 10.00 3.00

1991 Peninsula Oilers

This 29-card set of the 1991 Peninsula Oilers of the Alaska Central Baseball League features color player head circular photos on a red-and-white, black-striped background. The backs carry player information. The cards are unnumbered and checklisted below in alphabetical order.
COMPLETE SET (29)................ 10.00 3.00

1991 Peninsula Pilots Classic/Best

This 25-card standard-size set of the 1991 Peninsula Pilots, a Class A Carolina League affiliate of the Seattle Mariners, features white-bordered posed color player photos on its fronts. The player's name, team, and position appear at the bottom. The white back is framed by a thin black line and carries the player's name and position at the top, followed by biography, statistics and team logos.
COMPLETE SET (25)................ 5.00 1.50

1991 Peninsula Pilots ProCards

This 28-card standard-size set of the 1991 Peninsula Pilots, a Class A Carolina League affiliate of the Seattle Mariners, features on its white-bordered fronts posed color player photos set on simulated spiral-bound yellow notebooks. The player's name, position, and team appear within a green rectangle below the photo. The yellow horizontal back is bordered in white and carries the player's name at the top, followed by biography and statistics.
COMPLETE SET (28)................ 5.00 1.50

1991 Peoria Chiefs Classic/Best

This 29-card standard-size set of the 1991 Peoria Cubs, a Class A Midwest League affiliate of the Chicago Cubs, features white-bordered posed color player photos on its fronts. The player's name, team, and position appear at the bottom. The white back is framed by a thin black line and carries the player's name and position at the top, followed by biography, statistics and team logos.
COMPLETE SET (29)................ 5.00 1.50

1991 Peoria Chiefs ProCards

This 29-card standard-size set of the 1991 Peoria Cubs, a Class A Midwest League affiliate of the Chicago Cubs, features on its white-bordered fronts posed color player photos set on simulated spiral-bound yellow notebooks. The player's name, position, and team appear within a green rectangle below the photo. The yellow horizontal back is bordered in white and carries the player's name at the top, followed by biography and statistics.
COMPLETE SET (29)................ 5.00 1.50

1991 Peoria Chiefs Team Issue

COMPLETE SET (34)................ 5.00 1.50

1991 Phoenix Firebirds Line Drive

COMPLETE SET (26)................ 5.00 1.50

1991 Phoenix Firebirds ProCards

This 29-card standard-size set of the 1991 Phoenix Firebirds, a Class AAA Pacific Coast League affiliate of the San Francisco Giants, features on its white-bordered fronts posed color player photos set on simulated spiral-bound yellow notebooks. The player's name, position, and team appear within a green rectangle below the photo. The yellow horizontal back is bordered in white and carries the player's name at the top, followed by biography and statistics.
COMPLETE SET (29)................ 5.00 1.50

1991 Pittsfield Mets Classic/Best

This 28-card standard-size set of the 1991 Pittsfield Mets, a Class A New York-Penn League affiliate of the New York Mets, features white-bordered posed color player photos on its fronts. The player's name, team, and position appear at the bottom. The white back is framed by a thin black line and carries the player's name and position at the top, followed by biography, statistics and team logos.
COMPLETE SET (28)................ 5.00 1.50

1991 Pittsfield Mets ProCards

This 28-card standard-size set of the 1991 Pittsfield Mets, a Class A New York-Penn League affiliate of the New York Mets, features on its white-bordered fronts posed color player photos set on simulated spiral-bound yellow notebooks. The player's name, position, and team appear within a green rectangle below the photo. The yellow horizontal back is bordered in white and carries the player's name at the top, followed by biography and statistics.
COMPLETE SET (28)................ 5.00 1.50

1991 Pocatello Pioneers ProCards

This 31-card standard-size set of the 1991 Pocatello Pioneers, a Rookie Class Pioneer League Independent, features on its white-bordered fronts posed color player photos set on simulated spiral-bound yellow notebooks. The player's name, position, and team appear within a green rectangle below the photo. The yellow horizontal back is bordered in white and carries the player's name at the top, followed by biography and statistics.
COMPLETE SET (31)................ 5.00 1.50

1991 Pocatello Pioneers Sports Pro

This 30-card standard-size set of the 1991 Pocatello Pioneers, a Rookie Class Pioneer League Independent, features posed color head-and-shoulders shots, with thin black borders on a white card face. The horizontally oriented backs have biographical information.
COMPLETE SET (30)................ 5.00 1.50

1991 Portland Beavers Line Drive

COMPLETE SET (26)................ 5.00 1.50

1991 Portland Beavers ProCards

This 28-card standard-size set of the 1991 Portland Beavers, a Class AAA Pacific Coast League affiliate of the Minnesota Twins, features on its white-bordered fronts posed color player photos set on simulated spiral-bound yellow notebooks. The player's name, position, and team appear within a green rectangle below the photo. The yellow horizontal back is bordered in white and carries the player's name at the top, followed by biography and statistics.
COMPLETE SET (28)................ 5.00 1.50

1991 Prince William Cannons Classic/Best

This 30-card standard-size set of the 1991 Prince William Cannons, a Class A Carolina League affiliate of the New York Yankees, features white-bordered posed color player photos on its fronts. The player's name, team, and position appear at the bottom. The white back is framed by a thin black line and carries the player's name and position at the top, followed by biography, statistics and team logos.
COMPLETE SET (30)................ 5.00 1.50

1991 Prince William Cannons ProCards

This 29-card standard-size set of the 1991 Prince William Cannons, a Class A Carolina League affiliate of the New York Yankees, features on its white-bordered fronts posed color player photos set on simulated spiral-bound yellow notebooks. The player's name, position, and team appear within a green rectangle below the photo. The yellow horizontal back is bordered in white and carries the player's name at the top, followed by biography and statistics.
COMPLETE SET (29)................ 5.00 1.50

1991 Princeton Reds Classic/Best

This 30-card standard-size set of the 1991 Princeton Reds, a Rookie Class Appalachian League affiliate of the Cincinnati Reds, features white-bordered posed color player photos on its fronts. The player's name, team, and position appear at the bottom. The white back is framed by a thin black line and carries the player's name and position at the top, followed by biography, statistics and team logos.
COMPLETE SET (30)................ 5.00 1.50

1991 Princeton Reds ProCards

This 30-card standard-size set of the 1991 Princeton Reds, a Rookie Class Appalachian League affiliate of the Cincinnati Reds, features on its white-bordered fronts posed color player photos set on simulated spiral-bound yellow notebooks. The player's name, position, and team appear within a green rectangle below the photo. The yellow horizontal back is bordered in white and carries the player's name at the top, followed by biography and statistics.
COMPLETE SET (30)................ 5.00 1.50

1991 Pulaski Braves Classic/Best

This 30-card standard-size set of the 1991 Pulaski Braves, a Rookie Class Appalachian League affiliate of the Atlanta Braves, features white-bordered posed color player photos on its fronts. The player's name, team, and position appear at the bottom. The white back is framed by a thin black line and carries the player's name and position at the top, followed by biography, statistics and team logos.
COMPLETE SET (30).................. 5.00 1.50

1991 Pulaski Braves ProCards

This 31-card standard-size set of the 1991 Pulaski Braves, a Rookie Class Appalachian League affiliate of the Atlanta Braves, features on its white-bordered fronts posed color player photos set on simulated spiral-bound yellow notebooks. The player's name, position, and team appear within a green rectangle below the photo. The yellow horizontal back is bordered in white and carries the player's name at the top, followed by biography and statistics.
COMPLETE SET (31).................. 5.00 1.50

1991 Quad City Angels Classic/Best

This 29-card standard-size set of the 1991 Quad City Angels, a Class A Midwest League affiliate of the California Angels, features white-bordered posed color player photos on its fronts. The player's name, team, and position appear at the bottom. The white back is framed by a thin black line and carries the player's name and position at the top, followed by biography, statistics and team logos. This issue includes the minor league card debut of Garret Anderson.
COMPLETE SET (29)................ 20.00 6.00

1991 Quad City Angels ProCards

This 31-card standard-size set of the 1991 Quad City Angels, a Class A Midwest League affiliate of the California Angels, features on its white-bordered fronts posed color player photos set on simulated spiral-bound yellow notebooks. The player's name, position, and team appear within a green rectangle below the photo. The yellow horizontal back is bordered in white and carries the player's name at the top, followed by biography and statistics. This issue includes the minor league card debut of Garret Anderson.
COMPLETE SET (31)................ 20.00 6.00

1991 Reading Phillies Line Drive

COMPLETE SET (26).................. 5.00 1.50

1991 Reading Phillies ProCards

This 27-card standard-size set of the 1991 Reading Phillies, a Class AA Eastern League affiliate of the Philadelphia Phillies, features on its white-bordered fronts posed color player photos set on simulated spiral-bound yellow notebooks. The player's name, position, and team appear within a green rectangle below the photo. The yellow horizontal back is bordered in white and carries the player's name at the top, followed by biography and statistics.
COMPLETE SET (27).................. 5.00 1.50

1991 Reno Silver Sox Cal League Cards

COMPLETE SET (29).................. 5.00 1.50

1991 Richmond Braves Bob's Camera

This 42-card team set of the 1991 Richmond Braves, a Class AAA International League affiliate of the Atlanta Braves, was sponsored by Bob's Camera. The fronts feature borderless color player photos with sponsors' and team's logos in the wide bottom margin. The backs are blank. 500 sets were produced.
COMPLETE SET (42)................ 80.00 24.00

1991 Richmond Braves Line Drive

COMPLETE SET (26)................ 15.00 4.50

1991 Richmond Braves ProCards

This 30-card standard-size set of the 1991 Richmond Braves, a Class AAA International League affiliate of the Atlanta Braves, features on its white-bordered fronts posed color player photos set on simulated spiral-bound yellow notebooks. The player's name, position, and team appear within a green rectangle below the photo. The yellow horizontal back is bordered in white and carries the player's name at the top, followed by biography and statistics.
COMPLETE SET (30)................ 15.00 4.50

1991 Richmond Braves Team Issue

This 28-card standard-size set of the 1991 Richmond Braves, a Class AAA International League affiliate of the Atlanta Braves, was issued in seven strips that included four cards and a Pepsi coupon. The set was sponsored by Ukrop's. One strip was inserted in every 24 packs of Pepsi.
COMPLETE SET (28).................. 5.00 1.50

1991 Rochester Red Wings Line Drive

This issue includes a second year card of Mike Mussina.
COMPLETE SET (26)................ 15.00 4.50

1991 Rochester Red Wings ProCards

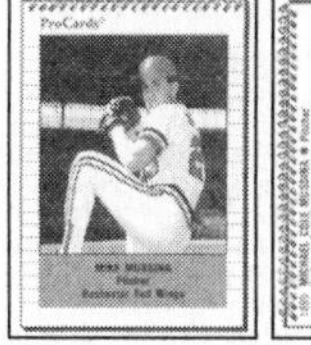

This 27-card standard-size set of the 1991 Rochester Red Wings, a Class AAA International League affiliate of the Baltimore Orioles, features on its white-bordered fronts posed color player photos set on simulated spiral-bound yellow notebooks. The player's name, position, and team appear within a green rectangle below the photo. The yellow horizontal back is bordered in white and carries the player's name at the top, followed by biography and statistics. This issue includes a second year card of Mike Mussina.
COMPLETE SET (27)................ 15.00 4.50

1991 Rockford Expos Classic/Best

This 30-card standard-size set of the 1991 Rockford Expos, a Class A Midwest League affiliate of the Montreal Expos, features white-bordered posed color player photos on its fronts. The player's name, team, and position appear at the bottom. The white back is framed by a thin black line and carries the player's name and position at the top, followed by biography, statistics and team logos.
COMPLETE SET (30).................. 5.00 1.50

1991 Rockford Expos ProCards

This 29-card standard-size set of the 1991 Rockford Expos, a Class A Midwest League affiliate of the Montreal Expos, features on its white-bordered fronts posed color player photos set on simulated spiral-bound yellow notebooks. The player's name, position, and team appear within a green rectangle below the photo. The yellow horizontal back is bordered in white and carries the player's name and position at the top, followed by biography and statistics.
COMPLETE SET (29).................. 5.00 1.50

1991 Salem Buccaneers Classic/Best

This 26-card standard-size set of the 1991 Salem Buccaneers, a Class A Carolina League affiliate of the Pittsburgh Pirates, features white-bordered posed color player photos on its fronts. The player's name, team, and position appear at the bottom. The white back is framed by a thin black line and carries the player's name and position at the top, followed by biography, statistics and team logos.
COMPLETE SET (26).................. 5.00 1.50

1991 Salem Buccaneers ProCards

This 27-card standard-size set of the 1991 Salem Buccaneers, a Class A Carolina League affiliate of the Pittsburgh Pirates, features on its white-bordered fronts posed color player photos set on simulated spiral-bound yellow notebooks. The player's name, position, and team appear within a green rectangle below the photo. The yellow horizontal back is bordered in white and carries the player's name at the top, followed by biography and statistics.
COMPLETE SET (27).................. 5.00 1.50

1991 Salinas Spurs Classic/Best

This 30-card standard-size set of the 1991 Salinas Spurs, a Class A California League Independent, features white-bordered posed color player photos on its fronts. The player's name, team, and position appear at the bottom. The white back is framed by a thin black line and carries the player's name and position at the top, followed by biography, statistics and team logos.
COMPLETE SET (30).................. 5.00 1.50

1991 Salinas Spurs ProCards

This 31-card standard-size set of the 1991 Salinas Spurs, a Class A California League Independent, features on its white-bordered fronts posed color player photos set on simulated spiral-bound yellow notebooks. The player's name, position, and team appear within a green rectangle below the photo. The yellow horizontal back is bordered in white and carries the player's name at the top, followed by biography and statistics.
COMPLETE SET (31).................. 5.00 1.50

1991 Salt Lake Trappers ProCards

This 30-card standard-size set of the 1991 Salt Lake Trappers, a Rookie Class Pioneer League Independent, features on its white-bordered fronts posed color player photos set on simulated spiral-bound yellow notebooks. The player's name, position, and team appear within a green rectangle below the photo. The yellow horizontal back is bordered in white and carries the player's name at the top, followed by biography and statistics.
COMPLETE SET (30).................. 5.00 1.50

1991 Salt Lake Trappers Sports Pro

This 30-card standard-size set of the 1991 Salt Late Trappers, a Rookie Class Pioneer League Independent, features posed color head-and-shoulders shots, with thin black borders on a white card face. The horizontally oriented backs have biographical information.
COMPLETE SET (30).................. 5.00 1.50

1991 San Antonio Missions Line Drive

COMPLETE SET (26).................. 5.00 1.50

1991 San Antonio Missions ProCards

This 30-card standard-size set of the 1991 San Antonio Missions, a Class AA Texas League affiliate of the Los Angeles Dodgers, features on its white-bordered fronts posed color player photos set on simulated spiral-bound yellow notebooks. The player's name, position, and team appear within a green rectangle below the photo. The yellow horizontal back is bordered in white and carries the player's name at the top, followed by biography and statistics. This issue includes the second year card of Pedro J. Martinez.
COMPLETE SET (30)................ 30.00 9.00

1991 San Bernardino Spirit Classic/Best

This 28-card standard-size set of the 1991 San Bernardino Spirit, a Class A California League affiliate of the Seattle Mariners, features white-bordered posed color player photos on its fronts. The player's name, team, and position appear at the bottom. The white back is framed by a thin black line and carries the player's name and position at the top, followed by biography, statistics and team logos. This issue includes the minor league card debut of and Mike Hampton.
COMPLETE SET (28)................ 15.00 4.50

1991 San Bernardino Spirit ProCards

This 30-card standard-size set of the 1991 San Bernardino Spirit, a Class A California League affiliate of the Seattle Mariners, features on its white-bordered fronts posed color player photos set on simulated spiral-bound yellow notebooks. The player's name, position, and team appear within a green rectangle below the photo. The yellow horizontal back is bordered in white and carries the player's name at the top, followed by biography and statistics. This issue includes the minor league card debut of Mike Hampton.
COMPLETE SET (30)................ 15.00 4.50

1991 San Jose Giants Classic/Best

This 30-card standard-size set of the 1991 San Jose Giants, a Class A California League affiliate of the San Francisco Giants, features white-bordered posed color player photos on its fronts. The player's name, team, and position appear at the bottom. The white back is framed by a thin black line and carries the player's name and position at the top, followed by biography, statistics and team logos.
COMPLETE SET (30).................. 5.00 1.50

1991 San Jose Giants ProCards

This 30-card standard-size set of the 1991 San Jose Giants, a Class A California League affiliate of the San Francisco Giants, features on its white-bordered fronts posed color player photos set on simulated spiral-bound yellow notebooks. The player's name, position, and team appear within a green rectangle below the photo. The yellow horizontal back is bordered in white and carries the player's name at the top, followed by biography and statistics.
COMPLETE SET (30).................. 5.00 1.50

1991 Sarasota White Sox Classic/Best

This 29-card standard-size set of the 1991 Sarasota White Sox, a Class A Florida State League affiliate of the Chicago White Sox, features white-bordered posed color player photos on its fronts. The player's name, team, and position appear at the bottom. The white back is framed by a thin black line and carries the player's name and position at the top, followed by biography, statistics and team logos.
COMPLETE SET (29).................. 5.00 1.50

1991 Sarasota White Sox ProCards

This 30-card standard-size set of the 1991 Sarasota White Sox, a Class A Florida State League affiliate of the Chicago White Sox, features on its white-bordered fronts posed color player photos set on simulated spiral-bound yellow notebooks. The player's name, position, and team appear within a green rectangle below the photo. The yellow horizontal back is bordered in white and carries the player's name at the top, followed by biography and statistics.
COMPLETE SET (30).................. 5.00 1.50

1991 Savannah Cardinals Classic/Best

This 29-card standard-size set of the 1991 Savannah Cardinals, a Class A South Atlantic League affiliate of the St. Louis Cardinals, features white-bordered posed color player photos on its fronts. The player's name, team, and position appear at the bottom. The white back is framed by a thin black line and carries the player's name and position at the top, followed by biography, statistics and team logos.
COMPLETE SET (29).................. 5.00 1.50

1991 Savannah Cardinals ProCards

This 29-card standard-size set of the 1991 Savannah Cardinals, a Class A South Atlantic League affiliate of the St. Louis Cardinals, features on its white-bordered fronts posed color player photos set on simulated spiral-bound yellow notebooks. The player's name, position, and team appear within a green rectangle below the photo. The yellow horizontal back is bordered in white and carries the player's name at the top, followed by biography and statistics.
COMPLETE SET (29).................. 5.00 1.50

1991 Scranton Red Barons Line Drive

COMPLETE SET (26).................. 5.00 1.50

1991 Scranton Red Barons ProCards

This 29-card standard-size set of the 1991 Scranton Red Barons, a Class AAA International League affiliate of the Philadelphia Phillies, features on its white-bordered fronts posed color player photos set on simulated spiral-bound yellow notebooks. The player's name, position, and team appear within a green rectangle below the photo. The yellow horizontal back is bordered in white and carries the player's name at the top, followed by biography and statistics.
COMPLETE SET (29).................. 5.00 1.50

1991 Shreveport Captains Line Drive

COMPLETE SET (26).................. 5.00 1.50

1991 Shreveport Captains ProCards

This 28-card standard-size set of the 1991 Shreveport Captains, a Class AA Texas League affiliate of the San Francisco Giants, features on its white-bordered fronts posed color player photos set on simulated spiral-bound yellow notebooks. The player's name, position, and team appear within a green rectangle below the photo. The yellow horizontal back is bordered in white and carries the player's name at the top, followed by biography and statistics.
COMPLETE SET (28).................. 5.00 1.50

1991 South Atlantic League All-Stars ProCards

Early cards of Carlos Delgado and Chipper Jones are featured in this set.
COMPLETE SET (48)................ 25.00 7.50

1991 South Bend White Sox Classic/Best

This 29-card standard-size set of the 1991 South Bend White Sox, a Class A Midwest League affiliate of the Chicago White Sox, features white-bordered posed color player photos on its fronts. The player's name, team, and position appear at the bottom. The white back is framed by a thin black line and carries the player's name and position at the top, followed by biography, statistics and team logos. This issue includes the minor league card debut of Jason Bere.
COMPLETE SET (29).................. 5.00 1.50

1991 South Bend White Sox ProCards

This 30-card standard-size set of the 1991 South Bend White Sox, a Class A Midwest League affiliate of the Chicago White Sox, features on its white-bordered fronts posed color player photos set on simulated spiral-bound yellow notebooks. The player's name, position, and team appear within a green rectangle below the photo. The yellow horizontal back is bordered in white and carries the player's name at the top, followed by biography and statistics. This issue includes the minor league card debut of Jason Bere.
COMPLETE SET (30).................. 5.00 1.50

1991 Southern Oregon A's Anniversary ProCards

This 36-card tenth anniversary set of the 1991 Southern Oregon A's features on its white-bordered fronts posed color player photos printed on simulated spiral-bound yellow notebooks. The player's name, position, and team appear within a green rectangle below the photo. The yellow horizontal back is bordered in white and carries the player's name at the top, followed by biography and statistics.
COMPLETE SET (36)................ 15.00 4.50

1991 Southern Oregon A's Classic/Best

This 30-card standard-size set of the 1991 Southern Oregon A's, a Class A Northwest League affiliate of the Oakland Athletics, features white-bordered posed color player photos on its fronts. The player's name, team, and position appear at the bottom. The white back is framed by a thin black line and carries the player's name and position at the top, followed by biography, statistics and team logos.
COMPLETE SET (30).................. 5.00 1.50

1991 Southern Oregon A's ProCards

This 37-card standard-size set of the 1991 Southern Oregon A's, a Class A Northwest League affiliate of the Oakland Athletics, features on its white-bordered fronts posed color player photos set on simulated spiral-bound yellow notebooks. The player's name, position, and team appear within a green rectangle below the photo. The yellow horizontal back is bordered in white and carries the player's name at the top, followed by biography and statistics.
COMPLETE SET (37).................. 5.00 1.50

1991 Spartanburg Phillies Classic/Best

This 30-card standard-size set of the 1991 Spartanburg Phillies, a Class A South Atlantic League affiliate of the Philadelphia Phillies, features white-bordered posed color player photos on its fronts. The player's name, team, and position appear at the bottom. The white back is framed by a thin black line and carries the player's name and position at the top, followed by biography, statistics and team logos.
COMPLETE SET (30).................. 5.00 1.50

1991 Spartanburg Phillies ProCards

This 30-card standard-size set of the 1991 Spartanburg Phillies, a Class A South Atlantic League affiliate of the Philadelphia Phillies, features on its white-bordered fronts posed color player photos set on simulated spiral-bound yellow notebooks. The player's name, position, and team appear within a green rectangle below the photo. The yellow horizontal back is bordered in white and carries the player's name at the top, followed by biography and statistics.
COMPLETE SET (30).................. 5.00 1.50

1991 Spokane Indians Classic/Best

This 30-card standard-size set of the 1991 Spokane Indians, a Class A Northwest League affiliate of the San Diego Padres, features white-bordered posed color player photos on its fronts. The player's name, team, and position appear at the bottom. The white back is framed by a thin black line and carries the player's name and position at the top, followed by biography, statistics and team logos.
COMPLETE SET (30).................. 5.00 1.50

1991 Spokane Indians ProCards

This 31-card standard-size set of the 1991 Spokane Indians, a Class A Northwest League affiliate of the San Diego Padres, features on its white-bordered fronts posed color player photos set on simulated spiral-bound yellow notebooks. The player's name, position, and team appear within a green rectangle below the photo. The yellow horizontal back is bordered in white and carries the player's name at the top, followed by biography and statistics.
COMPLETE SET (31).................. 5.00 1.50

1991 Springfield Cardinals Classic/Best

This 30-card standard-size set of the 1991 Springfield Cardinals, a Class A Midwest League affiliate of the St. Louis Cardinals, features white-bordered posed color player photos on its fronts. The player's name, team, and position appear at the bottom. The white back is framed by a thin black line and carries the player's name and position at the top, followed by biography, statistics and team logos.
COMPLETE SET (30).................. 5.00 1.50

1991 Springfield Cardinals ProCards

This 31-card standard-size set of the 1991 Springfield Cardinals, a Class A Midwest League affiliate of the St. Louis Cardinals, features on its white-bordered fronts posed color player photos set on simulated spiral-bound yellow notebooks. The player's name, position, and team appear within a green rectangle below the photo. The yellow horizontal back is bordered in white and carries the player's name at the top, followed by biography and statistics.
COMPLETE SET (31)................. 5.00 1.50

1991 St. Catharines Blue Jays Classic/Best

This 30-card standard-size set of the 1991 St. Catharines Blue Jays, a Class A New York-Penn League affiliate of the Montreal Expos, features white-bordered posed color player photos on its fronts. The player's name, team, and position appear at the bottom. The white back is framed by a thin black line and carries the player's name and position at the top, followed by biography, statistics and team logos.
COMPLETE SET (30)................. 5.00 1.50

1991 St. Catharines Blue Jays ProCards

This 28-card standard-size set of the 1991 St. Catharines Blue Jays, a Class A New York-Penn League affiliate of the Toronto Blue Jays, features on its white-bordered fronts posed color player photos set on simulated spiral-bound yellow notebooks. The player's name, position, and team appear within a green rectangle below the photo. The yellow horizontal back is bordered in white and carries the player's name and position at the top, followed by biography and statistics.
COMPLETE SET (28)................. 5.00 1.50

1991 St. Lucie Mets Classic/Best

This 30-card standard-size set of the 1991 St. Lucie Mets, a Class A Florida State League affiliate of the New York Mets, features white-bordered posed color player photos on its fronts. The player's name, team, and position appear at the bottom. The white back is framed by a thin black line and carries the player's name and position at the top, followed by biography, statistics and team logos.
COMPLETE SET (30)................. 5.00 1.50

1991 St. Lucie Mets ProCards

This 29-card standard-size set of the 1991 St. Lucie Mets, a Class A Florida State League affiliate of the New York Mets, features on its white-bordered fronts posed color player photos set on simulated spiral-bound yellow notebooks. The player's name, position, and team appear within a green rectangle below the photo. The yellow horizontal back is bordered in white and carries the player's name at the top, followed by biography and statistics.
COMPLETE SET (29)................. 5.00 1.50

1991 St. Petersburg Cardinals Classic/Best

This 30-card standard-size set of the 1991 St. Petersburg Cardinals, a Class A Florida State League affiliate of the St. Louis Cardinals, features white-bordered posed color player photos on its fronts. The player's name, team, and position appear at the bottom. The white back is framed by a thin black line and carries the player's name and position at the top, followed by biography, statistics and team logos.
COMPLETE SET (30)................. 5.00 1.50

1991 St. Petersburg Cardinals ProCards

This 30-card standard-size set of the 1991 St. Petersburg Cardinals, a Class A Florida State League affiliate of the St. Louis Cardinals, features on its white-bordered fronts posed color player photos set on simulated spiral-bound yellow notebooks. The player's name, position, and team appear within a green rectangle below the photo. The yellow horizontal back is bordered in white and carries the player's name at the top, followed by biography and statistics.
COMPLETE SET (30)................. 5.00 1.50

1991 Stockton Ports Classic/Best

This 26-card standard-size set of the 1991 Stockton Ports, a Class A California League affiliate of the Milwaukee Brewers, features white-bordered posed color player photos on its fronts. The player's name, team, and position appear at the bottom. The white back is framed by a thin black line and carries the player's name and position at the top, followed by biography, statistics and team logos.
COMPLETE SET (26)................. 5.00 1.50

1991 Stockton Ports ProCards

This 27-card standard-size set of the 1991 Stockton Ports, a Class A California League affiliate of the Milwaukee Brewers, features on its white-bordered fronts posed color player photos set on simulated spiral-bound yellow notebooks. The player's name, position, and team appear within a green rectangle below the photo. The yellow horizontal back is bordered in white and carries the player's name at the top, followed by biography and statistics.
COMPLETE SET (27)................. 5.00 1.50

1991 Sumter Flyers Classic/Best

This 30-card standard-size set of the 1991 Sumter Flyers, a Class A South Atlantic League affiliate of the Montreal Expos, features white-bordered posed color player photos on its fronts. The player's name, team, and position appear at the bottom. The white back is framed by a thin black line and carries the player's name and position at the top, followed by biography, statistics and team logos. This issue includes the team set debuts of Rondell White and Shane Andrews.
COMPLETE SET (30)............... 10.00 3.00

1991 Sumter Flyers ProCards

This 31-card standard-size set of the 1991 Sumter Flyers, a Class A South Atlantic League affiliate of the Montreal Expos, features on its white-bordered fronts posed color player photos set on simulated spiral-bound yellow notebooks. The player's name, position, and team appear within a green rectangle below the photo. The yellow horizontal back is bordered in white and carries the player's name and position at the top, followed by biography and statistics. This issue includes the team set debuts of Rondell White and Shane Andrews.
COMPLETE SET (31)................. 8.00 2.40

1991 Syracuse Chiefs Kraft

This five-card set of the 1991 Syracuse Chiefs, a Class AAA International League affiliate of the Toronto Blue Jays, measures 2 3/8" by 3 1/2" and features on its white-bordered fronts posed color player photos set on backgrounds consisting of diagonal blue lines. The player's name, team name, and uniform number appear within a blue diamond at the lower right. The white horizontal back carries the player's name, uniform number, and position at the top, followed by biography and statistics. The cards are unnumbered and checklisted below in alphabetical order. This issue includes the fourth year card of Derek Bell.
COMPLETE SET (5)................. 10.00 3.00

1991 Syracuse Chiefs Line Drive

This 26-card standard-size set of the 1991 Syracuse Chiefs, a Class AAA International League affiliate of the Toronto Blue Jays, features posed color player photos on its white-bordered fronts. The player's name appears in red lettering at the top; his position and team name appear in red lettering below the photo. The back carries the player's name within a red stripe at the top, followed by position, team name and affiliation, biography and statistics. This issue includes the fourth year card of Derek Bell.
COMPLETE SET (26)................. 5.00 1.50

1991 Syracuse Chiefs Merchants Bank

Sponsored by Merchants Bank and WIXT Channel 9, this photo album features the 1991 Syracuse Chiefs, a Class AAA International League affiliate of the Toronto Blue Jays. The photo album unfolds to reveal three 9 3/8 by 10 5/8" sheets. The first sheet displays a montage of five color action player photos, with a Merchants Bank advertisement beneath the picture. The second and third panels each consist of five rows with three cards per row. The perforated player cards are horizontally oriented and measure 3 1/8" by 2 1/8". Inside a light blue border, the fronts display white-bordered color posed or action player pictures, with player identification immediately below. Sponsor logos and the team logo appear to the right of the photos on a wide white stripe. In blue print, the horizontal backs carry biography and statistics. A facsimile autograph in red ink rounds out the back. The cards are unnumbered and checklisted below in alphabetical order. This issue includes the fourth year card of Derek Bell.
COMPLETE SET (30)............... 10.00 3.00

1991 Syracuse Chiefs ProCards

This 25-card standard-size set of the 1991 Syracuse Chiefs, a Class AAA International League affiliate of the Toronto Blue Jays, features on its white-bordered fronts posed color player photos set on simulated spiral-bound yellow notebooks. The player's name, position, and team appear within a green rectangle below the photo. The yellow horizontal back is bordered in white and carries the player's name and position at the top, followed by biography and statistics. This issue includes the fourth year card of Derek Bell.
COMPLETE SET (25)................. 5.00 1.50

1991 Tacoma Tigers Line Drive

COMPLETE SET (26)................. 5.00 1.50

1991 Tacoma Tigers ProCards

This 29-card standard-size set of the 1991 Tacoma Tigers, a Class AAA Pacific Coast League affiliate of the Oakland Athletics, features on its white-bordered fronts posed color player photos set on simulated spiral-bound yellow notebooks. The player's name, position, and team appear within a green rectangle below the photo. The yellow horizontal back is bordered in white and carries the player's name at the top, followed by biography and statistics.
COMPLETE SET (29)................. 5.00 1.50

1991 Tidewater Tides Line Drive

This issue includes the fourth year card of Todd Hundley.
COMPLETE SET (26)................. 8.00 2.40

1991 Tidewater Tides ProCards

This 30-card standard-size set of the 1991 Tidewater Tides, a Class AAA International League affiliate of the New York Mets, features on its white-bordered fronts posed color player photos set on simulated spiral-bound yellow notebooks. The player's name, position, and team appear within a green rectangle below the photo. The yellow horizontal back is bordered in white and carries the player's name at the top, followed by biography and statistics. This issue includes the fourth year card of Todd Hundley.
COMPLETE SET (30)................. 5.00 1.50

1991 Toledo Mud Hens Line Drive

COMPLETE SET (26)................. 5.00 1.50

1991 Toledo Mud Hens ProCards

This 28-card standard-size set of the 1991 Toledo Mud Hens, a Class AAA International League affiliate of the Detroit Tigers, features on its white-bordered fronts posed color player photos set on simulated spiral-bound yellow notebooks. The player's name, position, and team appear within a green rectangle below the photo. The yellow horizontal back is bordered in white and carries the player's name at the top, followed by biography and statistics.
COMPLETE SET (28)................. 5.00 1.50

1991 Triple A All-Stars ProCards

COMPLETE SET (55)............... 15.00 4.50

1991 Tucson Toros Line Drive

COMPLETE SET (26)................. 8.00 2.40

1991 Tucson Toros ProCards

This 28-card standard-size set of the 1991 Tucson Toros, a Class AAA Pacific Coast League affiliate of the Houston Astros, features on its white-bordered fronts posed color player photos set on simulated spiral-bound yellow notebooks. The player's name, position, and team appear within a green rectangle below the photo. The yellow horizontal back is bordered in white and carries the player's name at the top, followed by biography and statistics. This issue includes the fourth year card of Kenny Lofton.
COMPLETE SET (28)................. 8.00 2.40

1991 Tulsa Drillers Line Drive

COMPLETE SET (26)............... 20.00 6.00

1991 Tulsa Drillers ProCards

This 27-card standard-size set of the 1991 Tulsa Drillers, a Class AA Texas League affiliate of the Texas Rangers, features on its white-bordered fronts posed color player photos set on simulated spiral-bound yellow notebooks. The player's name, position, and team appear within a green rectangle below the photo. The yellow horizontal back is bordered in white and carries the player's name at the top, followed by biography and statistics. This issue includes a third year card of Ivan Rodriguez.
COMPLETE SET (27................ 20.00 6.00

1991 Tulsa Drillers Team Issue

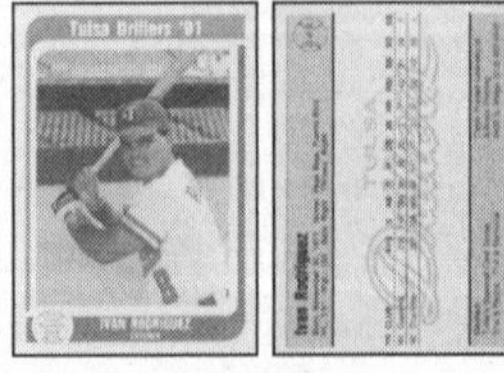

This issue includes a third year card of Ivan Rodriguez.
COMPLETE SET (30)............... 40.00 12.00

1991 Utica Blue Sox Classic/Best

This 30-card standard-size set of the 1991 Utica Blue Sox, a Class A New York-Penn League affiliate of the Chicago White Sox, features white-bordered posed color player photos on its fronts. The player's name, team, and position appear at the bottom. The white back is framed by a thin black line and carries the player's name and position at the top, followed by biography, statistics and team logos. This issue includes the minor league card debut of Ray Durham.
COMPLETE SET (30)............... 12.00 3.60

1991 Utica Blue Sox ProCards

This 29-card standard-size set of the 1991 Utica Blue Sox, a Class A New York-Penn League affiliate of the Chicago White Sox, features on its white-bordered fronts posed color player photos set on simulated spiral-bound yellow notebooks. The player's name, position, and team appear within a green rectangle below the photo. The yellow horizontal back is bordered in white and carries the player's name at the top, followed by biography and statistics. This issue includes the minor league card debut of Ray Durham.
COMPLETE SET (29)............... 10.00 3.00

1991 Vancouver Canadians Line Drive

This 26-card standard-size set of the 1991 Vancouver Canadians, a Class AAA Pacific Coast League affiliate of the Chicago White Sox, features posed color player photos on its white-bordered fronts. The player's name appears in red lettering at the top; his position and team name appear in red lettering below the photo. The back carries the player's name within a red stripe at the top, followed by position, team name and affiliation, biography and statistics.
COMPLETE SET (26)................. 5.00 1.50

1991 Vancouver Canadians ProCards

This 27-card standard-size set of the 1991 Vancouver Canadians, a Class AAA Pacific Coast League affiliate of the Chicago White Sox, features on its white-bordered fronts posed color player photos set on simulated spiral-bound yellow notebooks. The player's name, position, and team appear within a green rectangle below the photo. The yellow horizontal back is bordered in white and carries the player's name and position at the top, followed by biography and statistics.
COMPLETE SET (27)................. 5.00 1.50

1991 Vero Beach Dodgers Classic/Best

This 30-card standard-size set of the 1991 Vero Beach Dodgers, a Class A Florida State League affiliate of the Los Angeles Dodgers, features white-bordered posed color player photos on its fronts. The player's name, team, and position appear at the bottom. The white back is framed by a thin black line and carries the player's name and position at the top, followed by biography, statistics and team logos.
COMPLETE SET (30)................. 5.00 1.50

1991 Vero Beach Dodgers ProCards

This 33-card standard-size set of the 1991 Vero Beach Dodgers, a Class A Florida State League affiliate of the Los Angeles Dodgers, features on its white-bordered fronts posed color player photos set on simulated spiral-bound yellow notebooks. The player's name, position, and team appear within a green rectangle below the photo. The yellow horizontal back is bordered in white and carries the player's name at the top, followed by biography and statistics.
COMPLETE SET (33)................. 5.00 1.50

1991 Visalia Oaks Classic/Best

This 27-card standard-size set of the 1991 Visalia Oaks, a Class A California League affiliate of the Minnesota Twins, features white-bordered posed color player photos on its fronts. The player's name, team, and position appear at the bottom. The white back is framed by a thin black line and carries the player's name and position at the top, followed by biography, statistics and team logos.
COMPLETE SET (27)................. 5.00 1.50

1991 Visalia Oaks ProCards

This 25-card standard-size set of the 1991 Visalia Oaks, a Class A California League affiliate of the Minnesota Twins, features on its white-bordered fronts posed color player photos set on simulated spiral-bound yellow notebooks. The player's name, position, and team appear within a green rectangle below the photo. The yellow horizontal back is bordered in white and carries the player's name at the top, followed by biography and statistics.
COMPLETE SET (25)................. 5.00 1.50

1991 Visalia Oaks Update ProCards

This three-card standard-size set of the 1991 Visalia Oaks, a Class A California League affiliate of the Minnesota Twins, features on its white-bordered fronts posed color player photos set on simulated spiral-bound yellow notebooks. The player's name, position, and team appear within a green rectangle below the photo. The yellow horizontal back is bordered in white and carries the player's name at the top, followed by biography and statistics.
COMPLETE SET (3)................... 5.00 1.50

1991 Waterloo Diamonds Classic/Best

This 29-card standard-size set of the 1991 Waterloo Diamonds, a Class A Midwest League affiliate of the San Diego Padres, features white-bordered posed color player photos on its fronts. The player's name, team, and position appear at the bottom. The white back is framed by a thin black line and carries the player's name and position at the top, followed by biography, statistics and team logos.
COMPLETE SET (29)................. 5.00 1.50

1991 Waterloo Diamonds ProCards

This 28-card standard-size set of the 1991 Waterloo Diamonds, a Class A Midwest League affiliate of the San Diego Padres, features on its white-bordered fronts posed color player photos set on simulated spiral-bound yellow notebooks. The player's name, position, and team appear within a green rectangle below the photo. The yellow horizontal back is bordered in white and carries the player's name at the top, followed by biography and statistics.
COMPLETE SET (28)................. 5.00 1.50

1991 Watertown Indians Classic/Best

This 30-card standard-size set of the 1991 Watertown Indians, a Class A New York-Penn League affiliate of the Cleveland Indians, features white-bordered posed color player photos on its fronts. The player's name, team, and position appear at the bottom. The white back is framed by a thin black line and carries the player's name and position at the top, followed by biography, statistics and team logos.
COMPLETE SET (30)................. 5.00 1.50

1991 Watertown Indians ProCards

This 31-card standard-size set of the 1991 Watertown Indians, a Class A New York-Penn League affiliate of the Cleveland Indians, features on its white-bordered fronts posed color player photos set on simulated spiral-bound yellow notebooks. The player's name, position, and team appear within a green rectangle below the photo. The yellow horizontal back is bordered in white and carries the player's name at the top, followed by biography and statistics.
COMPLETE SET (31)................. 5.00 1.50

1991 Welland Pirates Classic/Best

This 30-card standard-size set of the 1991 Welland Pirates, a Class A New York-Penn League affiliate of the Pittsburgh Pirates, features white-bordered posed color player photos on its fronts. The player's name, team, and position appear at the bottom. The white back is framed by a thin black line and carries the player's name and position at the top, followed by biography, statistics and team logos.
COMPLETE SET (30)................. 5.00 1.50

1991 Welland Pirates ProCards

This 31-card standard-size set of the 1991 Welland Pirates, a Class A New York-Penn League affiliate of the Pittsburgh Pirates, features on its white-bordered fronts posed color player photos set on simulated spiral-bound yellow notebooks. The player's name, position, and team appear within a green rectangle below the photo. The yellow horizontal back is bordered in white and carries the player's name and position at the top, followed by biography and statistics.
COMPLETE SET (31)................. 5.00 1.50

1991 West Palm Beach Expos Classic/Best

This 30-card standard-size set of the 1991 West Palm Beach Expos, a Class A Florida State League affiliate of the Montreal Expos, features white-bordered posed color player photos on its fronts. The player's name, team, and position appear at the bottom. The white back is framed by a thin black line and carries the player's name and position at the top, followed by biography, statistics and team logos.
COMPLETE SET (30)................. 5.00 1.50

1991 West Palm Beach Expos ProCards

This 30-card standard-size set of the 1991 West Palm Beach Expos, a Class A Florida State League affiliate of the Montreal Expos, features on its white-bordered fronts posed color player photos set on simulated spiral-bound yellow notebooks. The player's name, position, and team appear within a green rectangle below the photo. The yellow horizontal back is bordered in white and carries the player's name and position at the top, followed by biography and statistics.
COMPLETE SET (30)................. 5.00 1.50

1991 Wichita Wranglers Line Drive

COMPLETE SET (26) 5.00 1.50

1991 Wichita Wranglers ProCards

This 28-card standard-size set of the 1991 Wichita Wranglers, a Class AA Texas League affiliate of the San Diego Padres, features on its white-bordered fronts posed color player photos set on simulated spiral-bound yellow notebooks. The player's name, position, and team appear within a green rectangle below the photo. The yellow horizontal back is bordered in white and carries the player's name at the top, followed by biography and statistics.
COMPLETE SET (28) 5.00 1.50

1991 Wichita Wranglers Rock's Dugout

COMPLETE SET (27) 5.00 1.50

1991 Williamsport Bills Line Drive

COMPLETE SET (26) 5.00 1.50

1991 Williamsport Bills ProCards

This 27-card standard-size set of the 1991 Williamsport Bills, a Class AA Eastern League affiliate of the New York Mets, features on its white-bordered fronts posed color player photos set on simulated spiral-bound yellow notebooks. The player's name, position, and team appear within a green rectangle below the photo. The yellow horizontal back is bordered in white and carries the player's name at the top, followed by biography and statistics.
COMPLETE SET (27) 5.00 1.50

1991 Winston-Salem Spirits Classic/Best

This 29-card standard-size set of the 1991 Winston Salem Spirits, a Class A Carolina League affiliate of the Chicago Cubs, features white-bordered posed color player photos on its fronts. The player's name, team, and position appear at the bottom. The white back is framed by a thin black line and carries the player's name and position at the top, followed by biography, statistics and team logos.
COMPLETE SET (29) 5.00 1.50

1991 Winston-Salem Spirits ProCards

This 28-card standard-size set of the 1991 Winston Salem Spirits, a Class A Carolina League affiliate of the Chicago Cubs, features on its white-bordered fronts posed color player photos set on simulated spiral-bound yellow notebooks. The player's name, position, and team appear within a green rectangle below the photo. The yellow horizontal back is bordered in white and carries the player's name at the top, followed by biography and statistics.
COMPLETE SET (28) 5.00 1.50

1991 Winter Haven Red Sox Classic/Best

This 30-card standard-size set of the 1991 Winter Haven Red Sox, a Class A Florida State League affiliate of the Boston Red Sox, features white-bordered posed color player photos on its fronts. The player's name, team, and position appear at the bottom. The white back is framed by a thin black line and carries the player's name and position at the top, followed by biography, statistics and team logos.
COMPLETE SET (30) 5.00 1.50

1991 Winter Haven Red Sox ProCards

This 27-card standard-size set of the 1991 Winter Haven Red Sox, a Class A Florida State League affiliate of the Boston Red Sox, features on its white-bordered fronts posed color player photos set on simulated spiral-bound yellow notebooks. The player's name, position, and team appear within a green rectangle below the photo. The yellow horizontal back is bordered in white and carries the player's name at the top, followed by biography and statistics.
COMPLETE SET (27) 5.00 1.50

1991 Yakima Bears Classic/Best

This 30-card standard-size set of the 1991 Yakima Bears, a Class A Northwest League affiliate of the Los Angeles Dodgers, features white-bordered posed color player photos on its fronts. The player's name, team, and position appear at the bottom. The white back is framed by a thin black line and carries the player's name and position at the top, followed by biography, statistics and team logos.
COMPLETE SET (30) 5.00 1.50

1991 Yakima Bears ProCards

This 30-card standard-size set of the 1991 Yakima Bears, a Class A Northwest League affiliate of the Los Angeles Dodgers, features on its white-bordered fronts posed color player photos set on simulated spiral-bound yellow notebooks. The player's name, position, and team appear within a green rectangle below the photo. The yellow horizontal back is bordered in white and carries the player's name at the top, followed by biography and statistics.
COMPLETE SET (30) 5.00 1.50

1991-92 Hawaii-Hilo Women's Softball

This 15-card set measures 2 1/4" by 3 1/2" and was sponsored by Mauna Loa. The fronts feature posed player shots framed by a thin blue inner border and a thin red outer border on a blue background. The school logo is in the lower left corner and the player's name and position are along the right side of the photo. The backs carry the player's name, position, and jersey number in a white stripe with biographical information and career highlights below on a blue blackground. The cards are unnumbered and checklisted below in alphabetical order.
COMPLETE SET (15) 8.00 2.40

1991-92 Washington Viacom

COMPLETE SET (4) 5.00 1.50

1992 Albany Polecats Classic/Best

This 30-card standard-size set of the 1992 Albany Polecats, a Class A South Atlantic League affiliate of the Montreal Expos, features white-bordered posed color player photos on its fronts. The player's name, position, and team name appear at the lower right. The white back is framed by a red line and carries the player's name and position at the top, followed by biography and statistics. This issue includes the first Classic/Best team set appearances of Cliff Floyd and Ugueth Urbina.
COMPLETE SET (30) 25.00 7.50

1992 Albany Polecats Fleer/ProCards

This 27-card standard-size set of the 1992 Albany Polecats, a Class A South Atlantic League affiliate of the Montreal Expos, features brown-bordered posed color player photos on its fronts. The player's name appears in an upper corner; his team and position appear in a lower corner. The white back is framed by a black line and carries the player's name at the top, followed by biography and statistics. This issue includes the first Fleer/ProCards team set appearances of Cliff Floyd and Ugueth Urbina.
COMPLETE SET (27) 15.00 4.50

1992 Albany Yankees Fleer/ProCards

This 28-card standard-size set of the 1992 Albany Yankees, a Class AA Eastern League affiliate of the New York Yankees, features brown-bordered posed color player photos on its fronts. The player's name appears in an upper corner; his team and position appear in a lower corner. The white back is framed by a black line and carries the player's name at the top, followed by biography and statistics.
COMPLETE SET(28) 5.00 1.50

1992 Albany Yankees SkyBox

COMPLETE SET(26) 5.00 1.50

1992 Albuquerque Dukes Fleer/ProCards

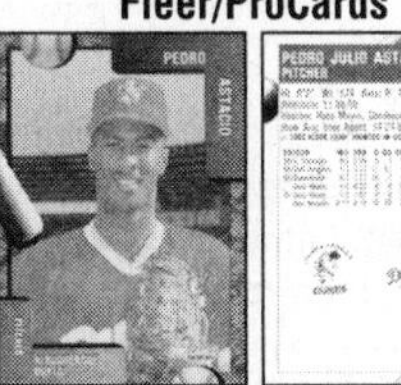

This 32-card standard-size set of the 1992 Albuquerque Dukes, a Class AAA Pacific Coast League affiliate of the Los Angeles Dodgers, features brown-bordered posed color player photos on its fronts. The player's name appears in an upper corner; his team and position appear in a lower corner. The white back is framed by a black line and carries the player's name at the top, followed by biography and statistics. This set includes a third year card of Pedro Martinez and a fourth year card of Mike Piazza.
COMPLETE SET(32) 40.00 12.00

1992 Albuquerque Dukes SkyBox

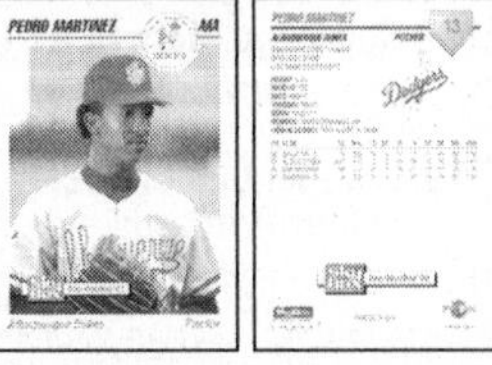

A third year card of Pedro Martinez highlights this set.
COMPLETE SET (26) 25.00 7.50

1992 Appleton Foxes Classic/Best

This 30-card standard-size set of the 1992 Appleton Foxes, a Class A Midwest League affiliate of the Kansas City Royals, features white-bordered posed color player photos on its fronts. The player's name, team, and position appear at the bottom. The white back is framed by a thin red line and carries the player's name and position at the top, followed by biography, statistics and team logos.
COMPLETE SET (30) 5.00 1.50

1992 Appleton Foxes Fleer/ProCards

This 32-card standard-size set of the 1992 Appleton Foxes, a Class A Midwest League affiliate of the Kansas City Royals, features brown-bordered posed color player photos on its fronts. The player's name appears in an upper corner; his team and position appear in a lower corner. The white back is framed by a black line and carries the player's name at the top, followed by biography and statistics.
COMPLETE SET (32) 5.00 1.50

1992 Arizona Wildcats Police

COMPLETE SET (20) 10.00 3.00

1992 Arkansas Travelers Fleer/ProCards

This 27-card standard-size set of the 1992 Arkansas Travelers, a Class AA Texas League affiliate of the St. Louis Cardinals, features brown-bordered posed color player photos on its fronts. The player's name appears in an upper corner; his team and position appear in a lower corner. The white back is framed by a black line and carries the player's name at the top, followed by biography and statistics.
COMPLETE SET(27) 5.00 1.50

1992 Arkansas Travelers SkyBox

COMPLETE SET (26) 5.00 1.50

1992 Asheville Tourists Classic/Best

This 30-card standard-size set of the 1992 Asheville Tourists, a Class A South Atlantic League affiliate of the Houston Astros, features white-bordered posed color player photos on its fronts. The player's name, team, and position appear at the bottom. The white back is framed by a thin red line and carries the player's name and position at the top, followed by biography, statistics and team logos. This issue includes the minor league card debut of Bob Abreu.
COMPLETE SET (30) 20.00 6.00

1992 Auburn Astros Classic/Best

This 30-card standard-size set of the 1992 Auburn Astros, a Class A New York-Penn League affiliate of the Houston Astros, features white-bordered posed color player photos on its fronts. The player's name, team, and position appear at the bottom. The white back is framed by a thin red line and carries the player's name and position at the top, followed by biography, statistics and team logos.
COMPLETE SET (30) 5.00 1.50

1992 Auburn Astros Fleer/ProCards

This 31-card standard-size set of the 1992 Auburn Astros, a Class A New York-Penn League affiliate of the Houston Astros, features brown-bordered posed color player photos on its fronts. The player's name appears in an upper corner; his team and position appear in a lower corner. The white back is framed by a black line and carries the player's name at the top, followed by biography and statistics.
COMPLETE SET(31) 5.00 1.50

1992 Augusta Pirates Classic/Best

This 28-card standard-size set of the 1992 Augusta Pirates, a Class A South Atlantic League affiliate of the Pittsburgh Pirates, features white-bordered posed color player photos on its fronts. The player's name, team, and position appear at the bottom. The white back is framed by a thin red line and carries the player's name and position at the top, followed by biography, statistics and team logos.
COMPLETE SET (28) 5.00 1.50

1992 Augusta Pirates Fleer/ProCards

This 29-card standard-size set of the 1992 Augusta Pirates, a Class A South Atlantic League affiliate of the Pittsburgh Pirates, features brown-bordered posed color player photos on its fronts. The player's name appears in an upper corner; his team and position appear in a lower corner. The white back is framed by a black line and carries the player's name at the top, followed by biography and statistics.
COMPLETE SET(29) 5.00 1.50

1992 Bakersfield Dodgers Cal League Cards

This issue includes the minor league card debut of Todd Hollandsworth.
COMPLETE SET(32) 5.00 1.50

1992 Baseball City Royals Classic/Best

This 30-card standard-size set of the 1992 Baseball City Royals, a Class A Florida State League affiliate of the Kansas City Royals, features white-bordered posed color player photos on its fronts. The player's name, team, and position appear at the bottom. The white back is framed by a thin red line and carries the player's name and position at the top, followed by biography, statistics and team logos.
COMPLETE SET (30) 5.00 1.50

1992 Baseball City Royals Fleer/ProCards

This 27-card standard-size set of the 1992 Baseball City Royals, a Class A Florida State League affiliate of the Kansas City Royals, features brown-bordered posed color player photos on its fronts. The player's name appears in an upper corner; his team and position appear in a lower corner. The white back is framed by a black line and carries the player's name at the top, followed by biography and statistics.
COMPLETE SET(27) 5.00 1.50

1992 Batavia Clippers Classic/Best

This 30-card standard-size set of the 1992 Batavia Clippers, a Class A New York-Penn League affiliate of the Philadelphia Phillies, features white-bordered posed color player photos on its fronts. The player's name, team, and position appear at the bottom. The white back is framed by a thin red line and carries the player's name and position at the top, followed by biography, statistics and team logos.
COMPLETE SET (30) 5.00 1.50

1992 Batavia Clippers Fleer/ProCards

This 32-card standard-size set of the 1992 Batavia Clippers, a Class A New York-Penn League affiliate of the Philadelphia Phillies, features brown-bordered posed color player photos on its fronts. The player's name appears in an upper corner; his team and position appear in a lower corner. The white back is framed by a black line and carries the player's name at the top, followed by biography and statistics.
COMPLETE SET(32) 5.00 1.50

1992 Bellingham Mariners Classic/Best

This 30-card standard-size set of the 1992 Bellingham Mariners, a Class A Northwest League affiliate of the Seattle Mariners, features white-bordered posed color player photos on its fronts. The player's name, team, and position appear at the bottom. The white back is framed by a thin red line and carries the player's name and position at the top, followed by biography, statistics and team logos.
COMPLETE SET (30) 25.00 7.50

1992 Bellingham Mariners Fleer/ProCards

This 33-card standard-size set of the 1992 Bellingham Mariners, a Class A Northwest League affiliate of the Seattle Mariners, features brown-bordered posed color player photos on its fronts. The player's name appears in an upper corner; his team and position appear in a lower corner. The white back is framed by a black line and carries the player's name at the top, followed by biography and statistics.
COMPLETE SET(33) 18.00 5.50

1992 Beloit Brewers Classic/Best

This 30-card standard-size set of the 1992 Beloit Brewers, a Class A Midwest League affiliate of the Milwaukee Brewers, features white-bordered posed color player photos on its fronts. The player's name, team, and position appear at the bottom. The white back is framed by a thin red line and carries the player's name and position at the top, followed by biography, statistics and team logos.
COMPLETE SET (30) 5.00 1.50

1992 Beloit Brewers Fleer/ProCards

This 30-card standard-size set of the 1992 Beloit Brewers, a Class A Midwest League affiliate of the Milwaukee Brewers, features brown-bordered posed color player photos on its fronts. The player's name appears in an upper corner; his team and position appear in a lower corner. The white back is framed by a black line and carries the player's name at the top, followed by biography and statistics.
COMPLETE SET(30) 5.00 1.50

1992 Bend Rockies Classic/Best

This 30-card standard-size set of the 1992 Bend Rockies, a Class A Northwest League affiliate of the Colorado Rockies, features white-bordered posed color player photos on its fronts. The player's name, team, and position appear at the bottom. The white back is framed by a thin red line and carries the player's name and position at the top, followed by biography, statistics and team logos.
COMPLETE SET (30) 5.00 1.50

1992 Bend Rockies Fleer/ProCards

This 27-card standard-size set of the 1992 Bend Rockies, a Class A Northwest League affiliate of the Colorado Rockies, features brown-bordered posed color player photos on its fronts. The player's name appears in an upper corner; his team and position appear in a lower corner. The white back is framed by a black line and carries the player's name at the top, followed by biography and statistics.
COMPLETE SET (27) 5.00 1.50

1992 Billings Mustangs Fleer/ProCards

This 30-card standard-size set of the 1992 Billings Mustangs, a Rookie Class Pioneer League affiliate of the Cincinnati Reds, features brown-bordered posed color player photos on its fronts. The player's name appears in an upper corner; his team and position appear in a lower corner. The white back is framed by a black line and carries the player's name at the top, followed by biography and statistics.
COMPLETE SET(30) 5.00 1.50

1992 Billings Mustangs Sports Pro

COMPLETE SET (30) 5.00 1.50

1992 Binghamton Mets Fleer/ProCards

This 28-card standard-size set of the 1992 Binghamton Mets, a Class AA Eastern League affiliate of the New York Mets, features brown-bordered posed color player photos on its fronts. The player's name appears in an upper corner; his team and position appear in a lower corner. The white back is framed by a black line and carries the player's name at the top, followed by biography and statistics. This set includes Bobby Jones' first team set card.
COMPLETE SET(28) 5.00 1.50

1992 Binghamton Mets SkyBox

This issue includes the minor league card debut of Bobby Jones.
COMPLETE SET (26) 5.00 1.50

1992 Birmingham Barons Fleer/ProCards

This 28-card standard-size set of the 1992 Birmingham Barons, a Class AA Southern League affiliate of the Chicago White Sox, features brown-bordered posed color player photos on its fronts. The player's name appears in an upper corner; his team and position appear in a lower corner. The white back is framed by a black line and carries the player's name at the top, followed by biography and statistics.
COMPLETE SET(28) 5.00 1.50

1992 Birmingham Barons SkyBox

COMPLETE SET (26) 5.00 1.50

1992 Bluefield Orioles Classic/Best

This 30-card standard-size set of the 1992 Bluefield Orioles, a Rookie Class Appalachian League affiliate of the Baltimore Orioles, features white-bordered posed color player photos on its fronts. The player's name, team, and position appear at the bottom. The white back is framed by a thin red line and carries the player's name and position at the top, followed by biography, statistics and team logos.
COMPLETE SET (30) 5.00 1.50

1992 Bluefield Orioles Fleer/ProCards

This 26-card standard-size set of the 1992 Bluefield Orioles, a Rookie Class Appalachian League affiliate of the Baltimore Orioles, features brown-bordered posed color player photos on its fronts. The player's name appears in an upper corner; his team and position appear in a lower corner. The white back is framed by a black line and carries the player's name at the top, followed by biography and statistics.
COMPLETE SET(26) 5.00 1.50

1992 Boise Hawks Classic/Best

This 30-card standard-size set of the 1992 Boise Hawks, a Class A Northwest League affiliate of the California Angels, features white-bordered posed color player photos on its fronts. The player's name, team, and position appear at the bottom. The white back is framed by a thin red line and carries the player's name and position at the top, followed by biography, statistics and team logos.
COMPLETE SET (30) 5.00 1.50

1992 Boise Hawks Fleer/ProCards

This 33-card standard-size set of the 1992 Boise Hawks, a Class A Northwest League affiliate of the California Angels, features brown-bordered posed color player photos on its fronts. The player's name appears in an upper corner; his team and position appear in a lower corner. The white back is framed by a

black line and carries the player's name at the top, followed by biography and statistics.
COMPLETE SET(33) 5.00 1.50

1992 Bristol Tigers Classic/Best

This 30-card standard-size set of the 1992 Bristol Tigers, a Rookie Class Appalachian League affiliate of the Detroit Tigers, features white-bordered posed color player photos on its fronts. The player's name, team, and position appear at the bottom. The white back is framed by a thin red line and carries the player's name and position at the top, followed by biography, statistics and team logos.
COMPLETE SET (30) 5.00 1.50

1992 Bristol Tigers Fleer/ProCards

This 33-card standard-size set of the 1992 Bristol Tigers, a Rookie Class Appalachian League affiliate of the Detroit Tigers, features brown-bordered posed color player photos on its fronts. The player's name appears in an upper corner; his team and position appear in a lower corner. The white back is framed by a black line and carries the player's name at the top, followed by biography and statistics.
COMPLETE SET(33) 5.00 1.50

1992 Buffalo Bisons Blue Shield

This 28-card set subtitled "Stars of the Future" is sponsored by Blue Shield of Western New York, and is produced on a tri-fold sheet containing perforated cards. The first panel displays a Blue Shield logo, the second panel contains four rows of 4 cards, and the third panel contains four rows of 3 cards. The cards measure approximately 2 1/2" x 3 7/16" and are edged in royal blue. The fronts display a color action shot of the player with the Buffalo Bison's team logo in the upper left corner, the Blue Shield logo in a white box on the lower left corner and to the side, a gold box with the player's name and team number. The horizontal backs contain biography and career statistics printed in black on a white background. The cards are unnumbered and checklisted below alphabetically.
COMPLETE SET (28) 10.00 3.00

1992 Buffalo Bisons Fleer/ProCards

This 27-card standard-size set of the 1992 Buffalo Bisons, a Class AAA American Association affiliate of the Pittsburgh Pirates, features brown-bordered posed color player photos on its fronts. The player's name appears in an upper corner; his team and position appear in a lower corner. The white back is framed by a black line and carries the player's name at the top, followed by biography and statistics.
COMPLETE SET(27) 5.00 1.50

1992 Buffalo Bisons SkyBox

COMPLETE SET (26) 5.00 1.50

1992 Burlington Astros Classic/Best

This 30-card standard-size set of the 1992 Burlington Astros, a Class A Midwest League affiliate of the Houston Astros, features white-bordered posed color player photos on its fronts. The player's name, team, and position appear at the bottom. The white back is framed by a thin red line and carries the player's name and position at the top, followed by biography, statistics and team logos.
COMPLETE SET (30) 5.00 1.50

1992 Burlington Astros Fleer/ProCards

This 30-card standard-size set of the 1992 Burlington Astros, a Class A Midwest League affiliate of the Houston Astros, features brown-bordered posed color player photos on its fronts. The player's name appears in an upper corner; his team and position appear in a lower corner. The white back is framed by a black line and carries the player's name at the top, followed by biography and statistics.
COMPLETE SET(30) 5.00 1.50

1992 Burlington Indians Classic/Best

This 30-card standard-size set of the 1992 Burlington Indians, a Rookie Class Appalachian League affiliate of the Cleveland Indians, features white-bordered posed color player photos on its fronts. The player's name, team, and position appear at the bottom. The white back is framed by a thin red line and carries the player's name and position at the top, followed by biography, statistics and team logos. This issue includes the minor league card debut of Damian Jackson.
COMPLETE SET (30) 5.00 1.50

1992 Burlington Indians Fleer/ProCards

This 32-card standard-size set of the 1992 Burlington Indians, a Rookie Class Appalachian League affiliate of the Cleveland Indians, features brown-bordered posed color player photos on its fronts. The player's name appears in an upper corner; his team and position appear in a lower corner. The white back is framed by a black line and carries the player's name at the top, followed by biography and statistics. This set includes the minor league card debut of Damian Jackson.
COMPLETE SET(32) 5.00 1.50

1992 Butte Copper Kings Sports Pro

COMPLETE SET (30) 20.00 6.00

1992 Calgary Cannons Fleer/ProCards

This 22-card standard-size set of the 1992 Calgary Cannons, a Class AAA Pacific Coast League affiliate of the Seattle Mariners, features brown-bordered posed color player photos on its fronts. The player's name appears in an upper corner; his team and position appear in a lower corner. The white back is framed by a black line and carries the player's name and position at the top, followed by biography and statistics.
COMPLETE SET (22) 5.00 1.50

1992 Calgary Cannons SkyBox

This 26-card standard-size set of the 1992 Calgary Cannons, a Class AAA Pacific Coast League affiliate of the Seattle Mariners, features white-bordered posed color player photos on its fronts. The player's name appears at the top; his team and position appear at the bottom. The white back carries the player's name, team name, and position at the top, followed by biography and statistics.
COMPLETE SET (26) 5.00 1.50

1992 California League All-Stars Cal League Cards

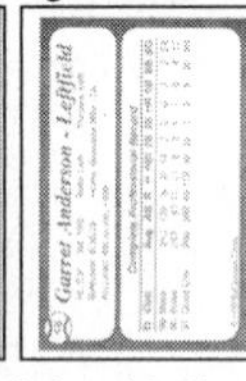

An early card of Garrett Anderson is in this set.
COMPLETE SET (53) 8.00 2.40

1992 Canton-Akron Indians Fleer/ProCards

This 28-card standard-size set of the 1992 Canton-Akron Indians, a Class AA Eastern League affiliate of the Cleveland Indians, features brown-bordered posed color player photos on its fronts. The player's name appears in an upper corner; his team and position appear in a lower corner. The white back is framed by a black line and carries the player's name at the top, followed by biography and statistics.
COMPLETE SET(28) 5.00 1.50

1992 Canton-Akron Indians SkyBox

COMPLETE SET (26) 5.00 1.50

1992 Carolina Mudcats Fleer/ProCards

This 26-card standard-size set of the 1992 Carolina Mudcats, a Class AA Southern League affiliate of the Pittsburgh Pirates, features brown-bordered posed color player photos on its fronts. The player's name appears in an upper corner; his team and position appear in a lower corner. The white back is framed by a black line and carries the player's name at the top, followed by biography and statistics.
COMPLETE SET(26) 5.00 1.50

1992 Carolina Mudcats SkyBox

COMPLETE SET (26) 5.00 1.50

1992 Cedar Rapids Reds Classic/Best

This 31-card standard-size set of the 1992 Cedar Rapids Reds, a Class A Midwest League affiliate of the Cincinnati Reds, features white-bordered posed color player photos on its fronts. The player's name, team, and position appear at the bottom. The white back is framed by a thin red line and carries the player's name and position at the top, followed by biography, statistics and team logos.
COMPLETE SET (31) 5.00 1.50

1992 Cedar Rapids Reds Fleer/ProCards

This 30-card standard-size set of the 1992 Cedar Rapids Reds, a Class A Midwest League affiliate of the Cincinnati Reds, features brown-bordered posed color player photos on its fronts. The player's name appears in an upper corner; his team and position appear in a lower corner. The white back is framed by a black line and carries the player's name at the top, followed by biography and statistics.
COMPLETE SET(30) 5.00 1.50

1992 Charleston (WV) Wheelers Classic/Best

This 30-card standard-size set of the 1992 Charleston Wheelers, a Class A South Atlantic League affiliate of the Cincinnati Reds, features white-bordered posed color player photos on its fronts. The player's name, team, and position appear at the bottom. The white back is framed by a thin red line and carries the player's name and position at the top, followed by biography, statistics and team logos.
COMPLETE SET (30) 5.00 1.50

1992 Charleston Rainbows Classic/Best

This 30-card standard-size set of the 1992 Charleston Rainbows, a Class A South Atlantic League affiliate of the San Diego Padres, features white-bordered posed color player photos on its fronts. The player's name, team, and position appear at the bottom. The white back is framed by a thin red line and carries the player's name and position at the top, followed by biography, statistics and team logos. This issue includes the minor league card debut of Joey Hamilton.
COMPLETE SET (30) 5.00 1.50

1992 Charleston Rainbows Fleer/ProCards

This 28-card standard-size set of the 1992 Charleston Rainbows, a Class A South Atlantic League affiliate of the San Diego Padres, features brown-bordered posed color player photos on its fronts. The player's name appears in an upper corner; his team and position appear in a lower corner. The white back is framed by a black line and carries the player's name at the top, followed by biography and statistics.
COMPLETE SET(28) 5.00 1.50

1992 Charleston Wheelers Fleer/ProCards

This 25-card standard-size set of the 1992 Charleston Wheelers, a Class A South Atlantic League affiliate of the Cincinnati Reds, features brown-bordered posed color player photos on its fronts. The player's name appears in an upper corner; his team and position appear in a lower corner. The white back is framed by a black line and carries the player's name at the top, followed by biography and statistics.
COMPLETE SET(25) 5.00 1.50

1992 Charlotte Knights Fleer/ProCards

This 25-card standard-size set of the 1992 Charlotte Knights, a Class AA Southern League affiliate of the Chicago Cubs, features brown-bordered posed color player photos on its fronts. The player's name appears in an upper corner; his team and position appear in a lower corner. The white back is framed by a black line and carries the player's name at the top, followed by biography and statistics.
COMPLETE SET(25) 5.00 1.50

1992 Charlotte Knights SkyBox

COMPLETE SET (26) 5.00 1.50

1992 Charlotte Rangers Classic/Best

This 30-card standard-size set of the 1992 Charlotte Rangers, a Class A Florida State League affiliate of the Texas Rangers, features white-bordered posed color player photos on its fronts. The player's name, team, and position appear at the bottom. The white back is framed by a thin red line and carries the player's name and position at the top, followed by biography, statistics and team logos.
COMPLETE SET (30) 5.00 1.50

1992 Charlotte Rangers Fleer/ProCards

This 27-card standard-size set of the 1992 Charlotte Rangers, a Class A Florida State League affiliate of the Texas Rangers, features brown-bordered posed color player photos on its fronts. The player's name appears in an upper corner; his team and position appear in a lower corner. The white back is framed by a black line and carries the player's name at the top, followed by biography and statistics.
COMPLETE SET(27) 5.00 1.50

1992 Chattanooga Lookouts Fleer/ProCards

This 27-card standard-size set of the 1992 Chattanooga Lookouts, a Class AA Southern League affiliate of the Cincinnati Reds, features brown-bordered posed color player photos on its fronts. The player's name appears in an upper corner; his team and position appear in a lower corner. The white back is framed by a black line and carries the player's name at the top, followed by biography and statistics.
COMPLETE SET(27) 5.00 1.50

1992 Chattanooga Lookouts SkyBox

COMPLETE SET (26) 5.00 1.50

1992 Clearwater Phillies Classic/Best

This 30-card standard-size set of the 1992 Clearwater Phillies, a Class A Florida State League affiliate of the Philadelphia Phillies, features white-bordered posed color player photos on its fronts. The player's name, team, and position appear at the bottom. The white back is framed by a thin red line and carries the player's name and position at the top, followed by biography, statistics and team logos.
COMPLETE SET (30) 5.00 1.50

1992 Clearwater Phillies Fleer/ProCards

This 32-card standard-size set of the 1992 Clearwater Phillies, a Class A Florida State League affiliate of the Philadelphia Phillies, features brown-bordered posed color player photos on its fronts. The player's name appears in an upper corner; his team and position appear in a lower corner. The white back is framed by a black line and carries the player's name at the top, followed by biography and statistics.
COMPLETE SET(32) 5.00 1.50

1992 Clinton Giants Classic/Best

This 30-card standard-size set of the 1992 Clinton Giants, a Class A Midwest League affiliate of the San Francisco Giants, features white-bordered posed color player photos on its fronts. The player's name, team, and position appear at the bottom. The white back is framed by a thin red line and carries the player's name and position at the top, followed by biography, statistics and team logos.
COMPLETE SET (30) 5.00 1.50

1992 Clinton Giants Fleer/ProCards

This 29-card standard-size set of the 1992 Clinton Giants, a Class A Midwest League affiliate of the San Francisco Giants, features brown-bordered posed color player photos on its fronts. The player's name appears in an upper corner; his team and position appear in a lower corner. The white back is framed by a black line and carries the player's name at the top, followed by biography and statistics.
COMPLETE SET(29) 5.00 1.50

1992 Colorado Springs Sky Sox Fleer/ProCards

This 28-card standard-size set of the 1992 Colorado Springs Sky Sox, a Class AAA Pacific Coast League affiliate of the Cleveland Indians, features brown-bordered posed color player photos on its fronts. The player's name appears in an upper corner; his team and position appear in a lower corner. The white back is framed by a black line and carries the player's name at the top, followed by biography and statistics.
COMPLETE SET(28) 5.00 1.50

1992 Colorado Springs Sky Sox SkyBox

COMPLETE SET (26) 5.00 1.50

1992 Columbia Mets Classic/Best

This 30-card standard-size set of the 1992 Columbia Mets, a Class A South Atlantic League affiliate of the New York Mets, features white-bordered posed color player photos on its fronts. The player's name, team, and position appear at the bottom. The white back is framed by a thin red line and carries the player's name and position at the top, followed by biography, statistics and team logos.
COMPLETE SET (30) 5.00 1.50

1992 Columbia Mets Fleer/ProCards

This 27-card standard-size set of the 1992 Columbia Mets, a Class A South Atlantic League affiliate of the New York Mets, features brown-bordered posed color player photos on its fronts. The player's name appears in an upper corner; his team and position appear in a lower corner. The white back is framed by a black line and carries the player's name at the top, followed by biography and statistics. This includes the first team set card of Raul Casanova.
COMPLETE SET(27) 5.00 1.50

1992 Columbia Mets Insert Set PLAY II

Inserted one per 1992 Columbia Mets PLAY II sets. 250 sets were produced.
COMPLETE SET(9) 100.00 30.00

1992 Columbia Mets PLAY II

1,500 sets were produced.
COMPLETE SET(42) 25.00 7.50

1992 Columbus Clippers Fleer/ProCards

This 28-card standard-size set of the 1992 Columbus Clippers, a Class AAA International League affiliate of the New York Yankees, features brown-bordered posed color player photos on its fronts. The player's name appears in an upper corner; his team and position appear in a lower corner. The white back is framed by a black line and carries the player's name at the top, followed by biography and statistics. This set includes a sixth year card of Bernie Williams.
COMPLETE SET(28) 5.00 1.50

1992 Columbus Clippers Police

This set includes a sixth year card of Bernie Williams.
COMPLETE SET (25) 5.00 1.50

1992 Columbus Clippers SkyBox

This set includes a sixth year card of Bernie Williams.
COMPLETE SET (26) 8.00 2.40

1992 Columbus RedStixx Classic/Best

This 30-card standard-size set of the 1992 Columbus Redstixx, a Class A South Atlantic League affiliate of the Cleveland Indians, features white-bordered posed color player photos on its fronts. The player's name, team, and position appear at the bottom. The white back is framed by a thin red line and carries the player's name and position at the top, followed by biography, statistics and team logos.
COMPLETE SET (30) 5.00 1.50

1992 Columbus Redstixx Fleer/ProCards

This 32-card standard-size set of the 1992 Columbus Redstixx, a Class A South Atlantic League affiliate of the Cleveland Indians, features brown-bordered posed color player photos on its fronts. The player's name appears in an upper corner; his team and position appear in a lower corner. The white back is framed by a black line and carries the player's name at the top, followed by biography and statistics.
COMPLETE SET(32) 5.00 1.50

1992 David Lipscomb Bisons

COMPLETE SET (25) 10.00 3.00

1992 Denver Zephyrs Fleer/ProCards

This 28-card standard-size set of the 1992 Denver Zephyrs, a Class AAA American Association affiliate of the Milwaukee Brewers, features brown-bordered posed color player photos on its fronts. The player's name appears in an upper corner; his team and position appear in a lower corner. The white back is framed by a black line and carries the player's name at the top, followed by biography and statistics.
COMPLETE SET(28) 5.00 1.50

1992 Denver Zephyrs SkyBox

COMPLETE SET (26) 5.00 1.50

1992 Dunedin Blue Jays Classic/Best

This 30-card standard-size set of the 1992 Dunedin Blue Jays, a Class A Florida State League affiliate of the Toronto Blue Jays, features white-bordered posed color player photos on its fronts. The player's name, position, and team name appear at the lower right. The white back is framed by a red line and carries the player's name and position at the top, followed by biography and statistics. This issue includes Shawn Green's first Classic/Best team set appearance as well as a fourth year card of Carlos Delgado.
COMPLETE SET (30) 30.00 9.00

1992 Dunedin Blue Jays Fleer/ProCards

This 27-card standard-size set of the 1992 Dunedin Blue Jays, a Class A Florida State League affiliate of the Toronto Blue Jays, features brown-bordered posed color player photos on its fronts. The player's name appears in an upper corner; his team and position appear in a lower corner. The white back is framed by a black line and carries the player's name and position at the top, followed by biography and statistics. This issue includes Shawn Green's first team set card appearance and a fourth year card of Carlos Delgado.
COMPLETE SET (27) 20.00 6.00

1992 Dunedin Blue Jays St Petersburg Times

So far, the only card known from this oversized set is Carlos Delgado. It is presumed that there are other cards in this set. Any additional information is appreciated.
COMPLETE SET 10.00 3.00

1992 Durham Bulls Classic/Best

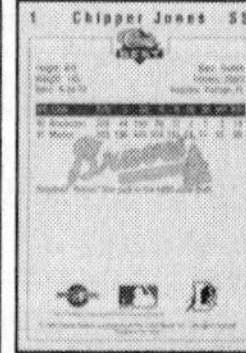

This 30-card standard-size set of the 1992 Durham Bulls, a Class A Carolina League affiliate of the Atlanta Braves, features white-bordered posed color player photos on its fronts. The player's name, team, and position

appear at the bottom. The white back is framed by a thin red line and carries the player's name and position at the top, followed by biography, statistics and team logos. This issue includes a second year minor league card of Chipper Jones.
COMPLETE SET (30)................ 30.00 9.00

1992 Durham Bulls Fleer/ProCards

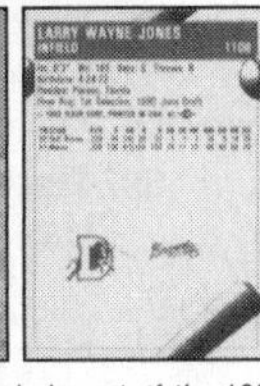

This 28-card standard-size set of the 1992 Durham Bulls, a Class A Carolina League affiliate of the Atlanta Braves, features brown-bordered posed color player photos on its fronts. The player's name appears in an upper corner; his team and position appear in a lower corner. The white back is framed by a black line and carries the player's name at the top, followed by biography and statistics. This set includes a second year minor league card of Chipper Jones.
COMPLETE SET(28)................ 20.00 6.00

1992 Durham Bulls Team Issue

This 28-card standard-size set of the 1992 Durham Bulls, a Class A Carolina League affiliate of the Atlanta Braves features a second year minor league card of Chipper Jones.
COMPLETE SET(29)................ 25.00 7.50

1992 Edmonton Trappers Fleer/ProCards

This 24-card standard-size set of the 1992 Edmonton Trappers, a Class AAA Pacific Coast League affiliate of the California Angels, features brown-bordered posed color player photos on its fronts. The player's name appears in an upper corner; his team and position appear in a lower corner. The white back is framed by a black line and carries the player's name and position at the top, followed by biography and statistics. This set inlcudes a fifth year card of Tim Salmon.
COMPLETE SET (24)................ 8.00 2.40

1992 Edmonton Trappers SkyBox

This 26-card standard-size set of the 1992 Edmonton Trappers, a Class AAA Pacific Coast League affiliate of the California Angels, features white-bordered posed color player photos on its fronts. The player's name appears at the top; his team and position appear at the bottom. The white back carries the player's name at the top, followed by biography and statistics. This set includes a fifth year card of Tim Salmon.
COMPLETE SET (26)................ 8.00 2.40

1992 El Paso Diablos Fleer/ProCards

This 27-card standard-size set of the 1992 El Paso Diablos, a Class AA Texas League affiliate of the Milwaukee Brewers, features brown-bordered posed color player photos on its fronts. The player's name appears in an upper corner; his team and position appear in a lower corner. The white back is framed by a black line and carries the player's name at the top, followed by biography and statistics.
COMPLETE SET(27)................ 5.00 1.50

1992 El Paso Diablos SkyBox

COMPLETE SET (26)................ 5.00 1.50

1992 Elizabethton Twins Classic/Best

This 30-card standard-size set of the 1992 Elizabethton Twins, a Rookie Class Appalachian League affiliate of the Minnesota Twins, features white-bordered posed color player photos on its fronts. The player's name, team, and position appear at the bottom. The white back is framed by a thin red line and carries the player's name and position at the top, followed by biography, statistics and team logos.
COMPLETE SET (30)................ 5.00 1.50

1992 Elizabethton Twins Fleer/ProCards

This 28-card standard-size set of the 1992 Elizabethton Twins, a Rookie Class Appalachian League affiliate of the Minnesota Twins, features brown-bordered posed color player photos on its fronts. The player's name appears in an upper corner; his team and position appear in a lower corner. The white back is framed by a black line and carries the player's name at the top, followed by biography and statistics.
COMPLETE SET(28)................ 5.00 1.50

1992 Elmira Pioneers Classic/Best

This 30-card standard-size set of the 1992 Elmira Pioneers, a Class A New York-Penn League affiliate of the Boston Red Sox, features white-bordered posed color player photos on its fronts. The player's name, team, and position appear at the bottom. The white back is framed by a thin red line and carries the player's name and position at the top, followed by biography, statistics and team logos.
COMPLETE SET (30)................ 5.00 1.50

1992 Elmira Pioneers Fleer/ProCards

This 25-card standard-size set of the 1992 Elmira Pioneers, a Class A New York-Penn League affiliate of the Boston Red Sox, features brown-bordered posed color player photos on its fronts. The player's name appears in an upper corner; his team and position appear in a lower corner. The white back is framed by a black line and carries the player's name at the top, followed by biography and statistics.
COMPLETE SET(25)................ 5.00 1.50

1992 Erie Sailors Classic/Best

This 30-card standard-size set of the 1992 Erie Sailors, a Class A New York-Penn League affiliate of the Florida Marlins, features white-bordered posed color player photos on its fronts. The player's name, team, and position appear at the bottom. The white back is framed by a thin red line and carries the player's name and position at the top, followed by biography, statistics and team logos.
COMPLETE SET (30)................ 5.00 1.50

1992 Erie Sailors Fleer/ProCards

This 33-card standard-size set of the 1992 Erie Sailors, a Class A New York-Penn League affiliate of the Florida Marlins, features brown-bordered posed color player photos on its fronts. The player's name appears in an upper corner; his team and position appear in a lower corner. The white back is framed by a black line and carries the player's name at the top, followed by biography and statistics.
COMPLETE SET(33)................ 5.00 1.50

1992 Eugene Emeralds Classic/Best

This 30-card standard-size set of the 1992 Eugene Emeralds, a Class A Northwest League affiliate of the Kansas City Royals, features white-bordered posed color player photos on its fronts. The player's name, team, and position appear at the bottom. The white back is framed by a thin red line and carries the player's name and position at the top, followed by biography, statistics and team logos. Mike Sweeney's first team set card is in a highlight of this set.
COMPLETE SET (30)................ 25.00 7.50

1992 Eugene Emeralds Fleer/ProCards

This 30-card standard-size set of the 1992 Eugene Emeralds, a Class A Northwest League affiliate of the Kansas City Royals, features brown-bordered posed color player photos on its fronts. The player's name appears in an upper corner; his team and position appear in a lower corner. The white back is framed by a black line and carries the player's name at the top, followed by biography and statistics. This set inlcudes the first team set card of Mike Sweeney.
COMPLETE SET(30)................ 15.00 4.50

1992 Everett Giants Classic/Best

This 30-card standard-size set of the 1992 Everett Giants, a Class A Northwest League affiliate of the San Francisco Giants, features white-bordered posed color player photos on its fronts. The player's name, team, and position appear at the bottom. The white back is framed by a thin red line and carries the player's name and position at the top, followed by biography, statistics and team logos.
COMPLETE SET (30)................ 5.00 1.50

1992 Everett Giants Fleer/ProCards

This 32-card standard-size set of the 1992 Everett Giants, a Class A Northwest League affiliate of the San Francisco Giants, features brown-bordered posed color player photos on its fronts. The player's name appears in an upper corner; his team and position appear in a lower corner. The white back is framed by a black line and carries the player's name at the top, followed by biography and statistics.
COMPLETE SET(32)................ 5.00 1.50

1992 Fayetteville Generals Classic/Best

This 30-card standard-size set of the 1992 Fayetteville Generals, a Class A South Atlantic League affiliate of the Detroit Tigers, features white-bordered posed color player photos on its fronts. The player's name, team, and position appear at the bottom. The white back is framed by a thin red line and carries the player's name and position at the top, followed by biography, statistics and team logos.
COMPLETE SET (30)................ 5.00 1.50

1992 Fayetteville Generals Fleer/ProCards

This 29-card standard-size set of the 1992 Fayetteville Generals, a Class A South Atlantic League affiliate of the Detroit Tigers, features brown-bordered posed color player photos on its fronts. The player's name appears in an upper corner; his team and position appear in a lower corner. The white back is framed by a black line and carries the player's name at the top, followed by biography and statistics.
COMPLETE SET(29)................ 5.00 1.50

1992 Fort Lauderdale Yankees Classic/Best

This 30-card standard-size set of the 1992 Fort Lauderdale Yankees, a Class A Florida State League affiliate of the New York Yankees, features white-bordered posed color player photos on its fronts. The player's name, team, and position appear at the bottom. The white back is framed by a thin red line and carries the player's name and position at the top, followed by biography, statistics and team logos.
COMPLETE SET (30)................ 5.00 1.50

1992 Fort Lauderdale Yankees Fleer/ProCards

This 31-card standard-size set of the 1992 Fort Lauderdale Yankees, a Class A Florida State League affiliate of the New York Yankees, features brown-bordered posed color player photos on its fronts. The player's name appears in an upper corner; his team and position appear in a lower corner. The white back is framed by a black line and carries the player's name at the top, followed by biography and statistics. This set includes a third year card of Mariano Rivera.
COMPLETE SET(31)................ 15.00 4.50

1992 Fort Lauderdale Yankees Team Issue

COMPLETE SET (32)................ 12.00 3.60

1992 Fort Myers Miracle Classic/Best

This 30-card standard-size set of the 1992 Fort Myers Miracle, a Class A Florida State League Independent, features white-bordered posed color player photos on its fronts. The player's name, team, and position appear at the bottom. The white back is framed by a thin red line and carries the player's name and position at the top, followed by biography, statistics and team logos.
COMPLETE SET (30)................ 5.00 1.50

1992 Fort Myers Miracle Fleer/ProCards

This 27-card standard-size set of the 1992 Fort Myers Miracle, a Class A Florida State League Independent, features brown-bordered posed color player photos on its fronts. The player's name appears in an upper corner; his team and position appear in a lower corner. The white back is framed by a black line and carries the player's name at the top, followed by biography and statistics.'
COMPLETE SET(27)................ 5.00 1.50

1992 Frederick Keys Classic/Best

This 30-card standard-size set of the 1992 Frederick Keys, a Class A Carolina League affiliate of the Baltimore Orioles, features white-bordered posed color player photos on its fronts. The player's name, team, and position appear at the bottom. The white back is framed by a thin red line and carries the player's name and position at the top, followed by biography, statistics and team logos.
COMPLETE SET (30)................ 5.00 1.50

1992 Frederick Keys Fleer/ProCards

This 29-card standard-size set of the 1992 Frederick Keys, a Class A Carolina League affiliate of the Baltimore Orioles, features brown-bordered posed color player photos on its fronts. The player's name appears in an upper corner; his team and position appear in a lower corner. The white back is framed by a black line and carries the player's name at the top, followed by biography and statistics.
COMPLETE SET(29)................ 5.00 1.50

1992 Gastonia Rangers Classic/Best

This 30-card standard-size set of the 1992 Gastonia Rangers, a Class A South Atlantic League affiliate of the Texas Rangers, features white-bordered posed color player photos on its fronts. The player's name, team, and position appear at the bottom. The white back is framed by a thin red line and carries the player's name and position at the top, followed by biography, statistics and team logos.
COMPLETE SET (30)................ 5.00 1.50

1992 Gastonia Rangers Fleer/ProCards

This 29-card standard-size set of the 1992 Gastonia Rangers, a Class A South Atlantic League affiliate of the Texas Rangers, features brown-bordered posed color player photos on its fronts. The player's name appears in an upper corner; his team and position appear in a lower corner. The white back is framed by a black line and carries the player's name at the top, followed by biography and statistics.
COMPLETE SET(29)................ 5.00 1.50

1992 Geneva Cubs Classic/Best

This 30-card standard-size set of the 1992 Geneva Cubs, a Class A New York-Penn League affiliate of the Chicago Cubs, features white-bordered posed color player photos on its fronts. The player's name, team, and position appear at the bottom. The white back is framed by a thin red line and carries the player's name and position at the top, followed by biography, statistics and team logos.
COMPLETE SET (30)................ 5.00 1.50

1992 Geneva Cubs Fleer/ProCards

This 28-card standard-size set of the 1992 Geneva Cubs, a Class A New York-Penn League affiliate of the Chicago Cubs, features brown-bordered posed color player photos on its fronts. The player's name appears in an upper corner; his team and position appear in a lower corner. The white back is framed by a black line and carries the player's name at the top, followed by biography and statistics.
COMPLETE SET(28)................ 5.00 1.50

1992 Great Falls Dodgers Sports Pro

This issue includes the minor league card debut of Roger Cedeno.
COMPLETE SET (30)................ 10.00 3.00

1992 Greensboro Hornets Classic/Best

This 30-card standard-size set of the 1992 Greensboro Hornets, a Class A South Atlantic League affiliate of the New York Yankees, features white-bordered posed color player photos on its fronts. The player's name, team, and position appear at the bottom. The white back is framed by a thin red line and carries the player's name and position at the top, followed by biography, statistics and team logos. This issue includes the minor league card debut of Andy Pettitte.
COMPLETE SET (30)................ 50.00 12.00

1992 Greensboro Hornets Fleer/ProCards

This 30-card standard-size set of the 1992 Greensboro Hornets, a Class A South Atlantic League affiliate of the New York Yankees, features brown-bordered posed color player photos on its fronts. The player's name appears in an upper corner; his team and position appear in a lower corner. The white back is framed by a black line and carries the player's name at the top, followed by biography and statistics. This set includes the first team set card of Andy Pettitte.
COMPLETE SET(30)................ 30.00 7.50

1992 Greenville Braves Fleer/ProCards

This 25-card standard-size set of the 1992 Greenville Braves, a Class AA Southern League affiliate of the Atlanta Braves, features brown-bordered posed color player photos on its fronts. The player's name appears in an upper corner; his team and position appear in a lower corner. The white back is framed by a black line and carries the player's name at the top, followed by biography and statistics. This set includes a fourth year card of Javy Lopez.
COMPLETE SET(25)................ 8.00 2.40

1992 Greenville Braves SkyBox

This set includes a fourth year card of Javy Lopez.
COMPLETE SET (26)................ 8.00 2.40

1992 Gulf Coast Dodgers Fleer/ProCards

This 31-card standard-size set of the 1992 Gulf Coast Dodgers, a Rookie Class A Gulf Coast League affiliate of the Los Angeles Dodgers, features brown-bordered posed color player photos on its fronts. The player's name appears in an upper corner; his team and position appear in a lower corner. The white back is framed by a black line and carries the player's name at the top, followed by biography and statistics.
COMPLETE SET(31)................ 5.00 1.50

1992 Gulf Coast Mets Fleer/ProCards

This 31-card standard-size set of the 1992 Gulf Coast Mets, a Rookie Class Gulf Coast League affiliate of the New York Mets, features brown-bordered posed color player photos on its fronts. The player's name appears in an upper corner; his team and position appear in a lower corner. The white back is framed by a black line and carries the player's name at the top, followed by biography and statistics. This set includes the first team set card of Jason Isringhausen.
COMPLETE SET(31)................ 8.00 2.40

1992 Gulf Coast Rangers Sports Pro

COMPLETE SET (30)................ 5.00 1.50

1992 Gulf Coast Yankees Fleer/ProCards

This 30-card standard-size set of the 1992 Gulf Coast Yankees, a Rookie Class Gulf Coast League affiliate of the New York Yankees, features brown-bordered posed color player photos on its fronts. The player's name appears in an upper corner; his team and position appear in a lower corner. The white back is framed by a black line and carries the player's name at the top, followed by biography and statistics. This issue includes the first year cards of Derek Jeter and Ricky Ledee.
COMPLETE SET(30)................ 150.00 45.00

1992 Hagerstown Suns Fleer/ProCards

This 25-card standard-size set of the 1992 Hagerstown Suns, a Class AA Eastern League affiliate of the Baltimore Orioles, features brown-bordered posed color player photos on its fronts. The player's name appears in an upper corner; his team and position appear in a lower corner. The white back is framed by a black line and carries the player's name at the top, followed by biography and statistics.
COMPLETE SET (25)................ 5.00 1.50

1992 Hagerstown Suns SkyBox

COMPLETE SET (26)................ 5.00 1.50

1992 Hamilton Redbirds Classic/Best

This 30-card standard-size set of the 1992 Hamilton Redbirds, a Class A New York-Penn League affiliate of the St. Louis Cardinals, features white-bordered posed color player photos on its fronts. The player's name, team, and position appear at the bottom. The white back is framed by a thin red line and carries the player's name and position at the top, followed by biography, statistics and team logos.
COMPLETE SET (30)................ 5.00 1.50

1992 Hamilton Redbirds Fleer/ProCards

This 32-card standard-size set of the 1992 Hamilton Redbirds, a Class A New York-Penn League affiliate of the St. Louis Cardinals, features brown-bordered posed color player photos on its fronts. The player's name appears in an upper corner; his team and position appear in a lower corner. The white back is framed by a black line and carries the player's name at the top, followed by biography and statistics.
COMPLETE SET (32)................ 5.00 1.50

1992 Harrisburg Senators Fleer/ProCards

This 27-card standard-size set of the 1992 Harrisburg Senators, a Class AA Eastern League affiliate of the Montreal Expos, features brown-bordered posed color player photos on its fronts. The player's name appears in an upper corner; his team and position appear in a lower corner. The white back is framed by a black line and carries the player's name at the top, followed by biography and statistics.
COMPLETE SET (27)................ 5.00 1.50

1992 Harrisburg Senators SkyBox

This 26-card standard-size set of the 1992 Harrisburg Senators, a Class AA Eastern League affiliate of the Montreal Expos, features white-bordered posed color player photos on its fronts. The player's name appears at the top; his team and position appear at the bottom. The white back carries the player's name at the top, followed by team name, position, biography, and statistics.
COMPLETE SET (26)................ 5.00 1.50

1992 Helena Brewers Fleer/ProCards

This 27-card standard-size set of the 1992 Helena Brewers, a Rookie Class Pioneer League affiliate of the Milwaukee Brewers, features brown-bordered posed color player photos on its fronts. The player's name appears in an upper corner; his team and position appear in a lower corner. The white back is framed by a black line and carries the player's name at the top, followed by biography and statistics.
COMPLETE SET (27)................ 5.00 1.50

1992 Helena Brewers Sports Pro

COMPLETE SET (30)................. 6.00 1.80

1992 High Desert Mavericks Classic/Best

This 30-card standard-size set of the 1992 High Desert Mavericks, a Class A California League affiliate of the San Diego Padres, features white-bordered posed color player photos on its fronts. The player's name, team, and position appear at the bottom. The white back is framed by a thin red line and carries the player's name and position at the top, followed by biography, statistics and team logos.
COMPLETE SET (30)................. 5.00 1.50

1992 Huntington Cubs Classic/Best

This 30-card standard-size set of the 1992 Huntsville Stars, a Class AA Southern League affiliate of the Oakland Athletics, features white-bordered posed color player photos on its fronts. The player's name, team, and position appear at the bottom. The white back is framed by a thin red line and carries the player's name and position at the top, followed by biography, statistics and team logos.
COMPLETE SET (30)................. 5.00 1.50

1992 Huntington Cubs Fleer/ProCards

This 32-card standard-size set of the 1992 Huntington Cubs, a Rookie Class A Appalachian League affiliate of the Chicago Cubs, features brown-bordered posed color player photos on its fronts. The player's name appears in an upper corner; his team and position appear in a lower corner. The white back is framed by a black line and carries the player's name at the top, followed by biography and statistics.
COMPLETE SET (32)................. 5.00 1.50

1992 Huntsville Stars Fleer/ProCards

This 27-card standard-size set of the 1992 Huntsville Stars, a Class AA Southern League affiliate of the Oakland Athletics, features brown-bordered posed color player photos on its fronts. The player's name appears in an upper corner; his team and position appear in a lower corner. The white back is framed by a black line and carries the player's name at the top, followed by biography and statistics.
COMPLETE SET (27)................. 5.00 1.50

1992 Huntsville Stars SkyBox

COMPLETE SET (26)................. 5.00 1.50

1992 Idaho Falls Gems Fleer/ProCards

This 32-card standard-size set of the 1992 Idaho Falls Gems, a Rookie Class Pioneer League affiliate of the Atlanta Braves, features brown-bordered posed color player photos on its fronts. The player's name appears in an upper corner; his team and position appear in a lower corner. The white back is framed by a black line and carries the player's name at the top, followed by biography and statistics.
COMPLETE SET (32)................. 5.00 1.50

1992 Idaho Falls Gems Sports Pro

This 30-card standard-size set of the 1992 Idaho Falls Gems, a Rookie Class Pioneer League affiliate of the Atlanta Braves.
COMPLETE SET (30)................. 5.00 1.50

1992 Indianapolis Indians Fleer/ProCards

This 29-card standard-size set of the 1992 Indianapolis Indians, a Class AAA American Association affiliate of the Montreal Expos, features brown-bordered posed color player photos on its fronts. The player's name appears in an upper corner; his team and position appear in a lower corner. The white back is framed by a black line and carries the player's name and position at the top, followed by biography and statistics.
COMPLETE SET (29)................. 5.00 1.50

1992 Indianapolis Indians SkyBox

This 26-card standard-size set of the 1992 Indianapolis Indians, a Class AAA American Association affiliate of the Montreal Expos, features white-bordered posed color player photos on its fronts. The player's name appears at the top; his team and position appear at the bottom. The white back carries the player's name at the top, followed by his team's name, position, biography and statistics. The set was co-sponsored by Pepsi and Hood's Drug Stores.
COMPLETE SET (26)................. 5.00 1.50

1992 Iowa Cubs Fleer/ProCards

This 24-card standard-size set of the 1992 Iowa Cubs, a Class AAA American Association affiliate of the Chicago Cubs, features brown-bordered posed color player photos on its fronts. The player's name appears in an upper corner; his team and position appear in a lower corner. The white back is framed by a black line and carries the player's name at the top, followed by biography and statistics.
COMPLETE SET (24)................. 5.00 1.50

1992 Iowa Cubs SkyBox

COMPLETE SET (26)................. 5.00 1.50

1992 Jackson Generals Fleer/ProCards

This 27-card standard-size set of the 1992 Jackson Generals, a Class AA Texas League affiliate of the Houston Astros, features brown-bordered posed color player photos on its fronts. The player's name appears in an upper corner; his team and position appear in a lower corner. The white back is framed by a black line and carries the player's name at the top, followed by biography and statistics.
COMPLETE SET (27)................. 5.00 1.50

1992 Jackson Generals SkyBox

COMPLETE SET (26)................. 5.00 1.50

1992 Jacksonville Suns Fleer/ProCards

This 26-card standard-size set of the 1992 Jacksonville Suns, a Class AA Southern League affiliate of the Seattle Mariners, features brown-bordered posed color player photos on its fronts. The player's name appears in an upper corner; his team and position appear in a lower corner. The white back is framed by a black line and carries the player's name at the top, followed by biography and statistics.
COMPLETE SET (26)................. 5.00 1.50

1992 Jacksonville Suns SkyBox

COMPLETE SET (26)................. 5.00 1.50

1992 Jamestown Expos Classic/Best

This 30-card standard-size set of the 1992 Jamestown Expos, a Class A New York-Penn League affiliate of the Montreal Expos, features white-bordered posed color player photos on its fronts. The player's name, team, and position appear near the bottom. The white back is framed by a orange line and carries the player's name and position at the top, followed by biography and statistics.
COMPLETE SET (30)................. 5.00 1.50

1992 Jamestown Expos Fleer/ProCards

This 28-card standard-size set of the 1992 Jamestown Expos, a Class A New York-Penn League affiliate of the Montreal Expos, features brown-bordered posed color player photos on its fronts. The player's name appears in an upper corner; his team and position appear in a lower corner. The white back is framed by a black line and carries the player's name and position at the top, followed by biography and statistics.
COMPLETE SET (28)................. 5.00 1.50

1992 Johnson City Cardinals Classic/Best

This 30-card standard-size set of the 1992 Johnson City Cardinals, a Rookie Class Appalachian League affiliate of the St. Louis Cardinals, features white-bordered posed color player photos on its fronts. The player's name, team, and position appear at the bottom. The white back is framed by a thin red line and carries the player's name and position at the top, followed by biography, statistics and team logos.
COMPLETE SET (30)................. 5.00 1.50

1992 Johnson City Cardinals Fleer/ProCards

This 31-card standard-size set of the 1992 Johnson City Cardinals, a Rookie Class Appalachian League affiliate of the St. Louis Cardinals, features brown-bordered posed color player photos on its fronts. The player's name appears in an upper corner; his team and position appear in a lower corner. The white back is framed by a black line and carries the player's name at the top, followed by biography and statistics.
COMPLETE SET (31)................. 5.00 1.50

1992 Kane County Cougars Classic/Best

This 30-card standard-size set of the 1992 Kane County Cougars, a Class A Midwest League affiliate of the Baltimore Orioles, features white-bordered posed color player photos on its fronts. The player's name, team, and position appear at the bottom. The white back is framed by a thin red line and carries the player's name and position at the top, followed by biography, statistics and team logos. This issue includes the minor league card debut of Alex Ochoa.
COMPLETE SET (30)................. 8.00 2.40

1992 Kane County Cougars Fleer/ProCards

This 29-card standard-size set of the 1992 Kane County Cougars, a Class A Midwest League affiliate of the Baltimore Orioles, features brown-bordered posed color player photos on its fronts. The player's name appears in an upper corner; his team and position appear in a lower corner. The white back is framed by a black line and carries the player's name at the top, followed by biography and statistics. This issue includes the minor league card debut of Alex Ochoa.
COMPLETE SET (29)................. 8.00 2.40

1992 Kane County Cougars Team Issue

This 30-card standard-size set of the 1992 Kane County Cougars, a Class A Midwest League affiliate of the Baltimore Orioles, features the minor league card debut of Alex Ochoa.
COMPLETE SET (30)................. 8.00 2.40

1992 Kenosha Twins Classic/Best

This 27-card standard-size set of the 1992 Kenosha Twins, a Class A Midwest League affiliate of the Minnesota Twins, features white-bordered posed color player photos on its fronts. The player's name, team, and position appear at the bottom. The white back is framed by a thin red line and carries the player's name and position at the top, followed by biography, statistics and team logos. This issue features the minor league card debut of Brad Radke.
COMPLETE SET (27)................. 8.00 2.40

1992 Kenosha Twins Fleer/ProCards

This 28-card standard-size set of the 1992 Kenosha Twins, a Class A Midwest League affiliate of the Minnesota Twins, features brown-bordered posed color player photos on its fronts. The player's name appears in an upper corner; his team and position appear in a lower corner. The white back is framed by a black line and carries the player's name at the top, followed by biography and statistics. This issue includes the minor league card debut of Brad Radke.
COMPLETE SET (28)................. 8.00 2.40

1992 Kingsport Mets Classic/Best

This 30-card standard-size set of the 1992 Kingsport Mets, a Rookie Class Appalachian League affiliate of the New York Mets, features white-bordered posed color player photos on its fronts. The player's name, team, and position appear at the bottom. The white back is framed by a thin red line and carries the player's name and position at the top, followed by biography, statistics and team logos.
COMPLETE SET (30)................. 5.00 1.50

1992 Kingsport Mets Fleer/ProCards

This 31-card standard-size set of the 1992 Kingsport Mets, a Rookie Class Appalachian League affiliate of the New York Mets, features brown-bordered posed color player photos on its fronts. The player's name appears in an upper corner; his team and position appear in a lower corner. The white back is framed by a black line and carries the player's name at the top, followed by biography and statistics.
COMPLETE SET (31)................. 5.00 1.50

1992 Kinston Indians Classic/Best

This 30-card standard-size set of the 1992 Kinston Indians, a Class A Carolina League affiliate of the Cleveland Indians, features white-bordered posed color player photos on its fronts. The player's name, team, and position appear at the bottom. The white back is framed by a thin red line and carries the player's name and position at the top, followed by biography, statistics and team logos.
COMPLETE SET (30)................. 5.00 1.50

1992 Kinston Indians Fleer/ProCards

This 29-card standard-size set of the 1992 Kinston Indians, a Class A Carolina League affiliate of the Cleveland Indians, features brown-bordered posed color player photos on its fronts. The player's name appears in an upper corner; his team and position appear in a lower corner. The white back is framed by a black line and carries the player's name at the top, followed by biography and statistics. This issue includes a second year card of Manny Ramirez.
COMPLETE SET (29)................. 25.00 7.50

1992 Knoxville Blue Jays Fleer/ProCards

This 29-card standard-size set of the 1992 Knoxville Blue Jays, a Class AA Southern League affiliate of the Toronto Blue Jays, features brown-bordered posed color player photos on its fronts. The player's name appears in an upper corner; his team and position appear in a lower corner. The white back is framed by a black line and carries the player's name and position at the top, followed by biography and statistics.
COMPLETE SET (29)................. 5.00 1.50

1992 Knoxville Blue Jays SkyBox

This 26-card standard-size set of the 1992 Knoxville Blue Jays, a Class AA Southern League affiliate of the Toronto Blue Jays, features white-bordered posed color player photos on its fronts. The player's name appears at the top; his team and position appear at the bottom. The white back carries the player's name at the top, followed by biography and statistics.
COMPLETE SET (26)................. 5.00 1.50

1992 Lakeland Tigers Classic/Best

This 30-card standard-size set of the 1992 Lakeland Tigers, a Class A Florida State League affiliate of the Detroit Tigers, features white-bordered posed color player photos on its fronts. The player's name, team, and position appear at the bottom. The white back is framed by a thin red line and carries the player's name and position at the top, followed by biography, statistics and team logos.
COMPLETE SET (30)................. 5.00 1.50

1992 Lakeland Tigers Fleer/ProCards

This 26-card standard-size set of the 1992 Lakeland Tigers, a Class A Florida State League affiliate of the Detroit Tigers, features brown-bordered posed color player photos on its fronts. The player's name appears in an upper corner; his team and position appear in a lower corner. The white back is framed by a black line and carries the player's name at the top, followed by biography and statistics.
COMPLETE SET (26)................. 5.00 1.50

1992 Las Vegas Stars Fleer/ProCards

This 24-card standard-size set of the 1992 Las Vegas Stars, a Class AAA Pacific Coast League affiliate of the San Diego Padres, features brown-bordered posed color player photos on its fronts. The player's name appears in an upper corner; his team and position appear in a lower corner. The white back is framed by a black line and carries the player's name at the top, followed by biography and statistics.
COMPLETE SET (24)................. 5.00 1.50

1992 Las Vegas Stars SkyBox

COMPLETE SET (26)................. 5.00 1.50

1992 Lethbridge Mounties Sports Pro

COMPLETE SET (30)................. 5.00 1.50

1992 London Tigers Fleer/ProCards

This 29-card standard-size set of the 1992 London Tigers, a Class AA Eastern League affiliate of the Detroit Tigers, features brown-bordered posed color player photos on its fronts. The player's name appears in an upper corner; his team and position appear in a lower corner. The white back is framed by a black line and carries the player's name at the top, followed by biography and statistics.
COMPLETE SET (29)................. 5.00 1.50

1992 London Tigers SkyBox

COMPLETE SET (26)................. 5.00 1.50

1992 Louisville Redbirds Fleer/ProCards

This 26-card standard-size set of the 1992 Louisville Redbirds, a Class AAA American Association affiliate of the St. Louis Cardinals, features brown-bordered posed color player photos on its fronts. The player's name appears in an upper corner; his team and position appear in a lower corner. The white back is framed by a black line and carries the player's name at the top, followed by biography and statistics.
COMPLETE SET (26)................. 5.00 1.50

1992 Louisville Redbirds SkyBox

COMPLETE SET (26)................. 5.00 1.50

1992 LSU Tigers McDag

An early card of Todd Walker is in this set.
COMPLETE SET (16)................ 15.00 4.50

1992 Lynchburg Red Sox Classic/Best

This 30-card standard-size set of the 1992 Lynchburg Red Sox, a Class A Carolina League affiliate of the Boston Red Sox, features white-bordered posed color player photos on its fronts. The player's name, team, and position appear at the bottom. The white back is framed by a thin red line and carries the player's name and position at the top, followed by biography, statistics and team logos. This issue includes the minor league card debut of Aaron Sele.
COMPLETE SET (30)................. 8.00 2.40

1992 Lynchburg Red Sox Fleer/ProCards

This 26-card standard-size set of the 1992 Lynchburg Red Sox, a Class A Carolina League affiliate of the Boston Red Sox, features brown-bordered posed color player photos on its fronts. The player's name appears in an upper corner; his team and position appear in a lower corner. The white back is framed by a black line and carries the player's name at the top, followed by biography and statistics. This issue includes the minor league card debut of Aaron Sele.
COMPLETE SET (26)................. 8.00 2.40

1992 Macon Braves Classic/Best

This 30-card standard-size set of the 1992 Macon Braves, a Class A South Atlantic League affiliate of the Atlanta Braves, features white-bordered posed color player photos on its fronts. The player's name, team, and position appear at the bottom. The white back is framed by a thin red line and carries the player's name and position at the top, followed by biography, statistics and team logos. This issue includes the minor league card debut of Jason Schmidt.
COMPLETE SET (30)................ 20.00 1.50

1992 Macon Braves Fleer/ProCards

This 30-card standard-size set of the 1992 Macon Braves, a Class A South Atlantic League affiliate of the Atlanta Braves, features brown-bordered posed color player photos on its fronts. The player's name appears in an upper corner; his team and position appear in a lower corner. The white back is framed by a black line and carries the player's name at the top, followed by biography and statistics. This issue includes the minor league card debut of Jason Schmidt.
COMPLETE SET (30)................ 20.00 1.50

1992 Madison Muskies Classic/Best

This 30-card standard-size set of the 1992 Madison Muskies, a Class A Midwest League affiliate of the Oakland Athletics, features white-bordered posed color player photos on its fronts. The player's name, team, and position appear at the bottom. The white back is framed by a thin red line and carries the player's name and position at the top, followed by biography, statistics and team logos.
COMPLETE SET (30)................. 5.00 1.50

1992 Madison Muskies Fleer/ProCards

This 29-card standard-size set of the 1992 Madison Muskies, a Class A Midwest League affiliate of the Oakland Athletics, features brown-bordered posed color player photos on its fronts. The player's name appears in an upper corner; his team and position appear in a lower corner. The white back is framed by a black line and carries the player's name at the top, followed by biography and statistics.
COMPLETE SET (29)................. 5.00 1.50

1992 Martinsville Phillies Classic/Best

This 30-card standard-size set of the 1992 Martinsville Phillies, a Rookie Class Appalachian League affiliate of the Philadelphia Phillies, features white-bordered posed color player photos on its fronts. The player's name, team, and position appear at the bottom. The white back is framed by a thin red line and carries the player's name and position at the top, followed by biography, statistics and team logos.
COMPLETE SET (30)................. 5.00 1.50

1992 Martinsville Phillies Fleer/ProCards

This 32-card standard-size set of the 1992 Martinsville Phillies, a Rookie Class Appalachian League affiliate of the Philadelphia Phillies, features brown-bordered posed color player photos on its fronts. The player's name appears in an upper corner; his team and position appear in a lower corner. The white back is framed by a black line and carries the player's name at the top, followed by biography and statistics.
COMPLETE SET (32)................. 5.00 1.50

1992 Medicine Hat Blue Jays Fleer/ProCards

This 24-card standard-size set of the 1992 Medicine Hat Blue Jays, a Class A Pioneer League affiliate of the Toronto Blue Jays, features brown-bordered posed color player photos on its fronts. The player's name appears in an upper corner; his team and position appear in a lower corner. The white back is framed by a black line and carries the player's name and position at the top, followed by biography and statistics.
COMPLETE SET (24)................. 5.00 1.50

1992 Medicine Hat Blue Jays Sports Pro

This 29-card standard-size set of the 1992 Medicine Hat Blue Jays, a Class A Pioneer League affiliate of the Toronto Blue Jays, features on its fronts white-bordered posed color player photos framed by double black lines. The white-on-black team name appears at

the top. The white back is framed by double black lines and carries the year and team name at the top, followed by the player's name, uniform number, position, and biography. The sponsor's name, Safeway, appears near the bottom.
COMPLETE SET (29)................. 5.00 1.50

1992 Memphis Chicks Fleer/ProCards

This 29-card standard-size set of the 1992 Memphis Chicks, a Class AA Southern League affiliate of the Kansas City Royals, features brown-bordered posed color player photos on its fronts. The player's name appears in an upper corner; his team and position appear in a lower corner. The white back is framed by a black line and carries the player's name and position at the top, followed by biography and statistics.
COMPLETE SET (29)................. 5.00 1.50

1992 Memphis Chicks SkyBox

COMPLETE SET (26)................. 5.00 1.50

1992 Midland Angels Fleer/ProCards

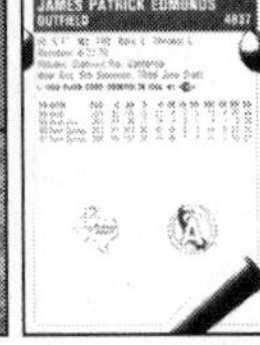

This 26-card standard-size set of the 1992 Midland Angels, a Class AA Texas League affiliate of the California Angels, features brown-bordered posed color player photos on its fronts. The player's name appears in an upper corner; his team and position appear in a lower corner. The white back is framed by a black line and carries the player's name and position at the top, followed by biography and statistics. This issue includes a fifth year card of Jim Edmonds.
COMPLETE SET (26)............... 10.00 3.00

1992 Midland Angels One Hour Photo

This 28-card set of the 1992 Midland Angels, a Class AA Texas League affiliate of the California Angels, features color player photos. The set measures approximately 5 1/2" by 5". The backs are blank. The cards are unnumbered and checklisted below in alphabetical order. 500 sets were produced. This set includes a fifth year card of Jim Edmonds.
COMPLETE SET (28)............... 60.00 18.00

1992 Midland Angels SkyBox

This issue includes a fifth year card of Jim Edmonds.
COMPLETE SET (26)............... 10.00 3.00

1992 Midwest League All-Stars Team Issue

Early cards of James Baldwin, Jeff Cirillo and Dmitri Young
COMPLETE SET (54)................. 8.00 2.40

1992 Minnesota

COMPLETE SET (22)............... 10.00 3.00

1992 Mississippi State Bulldogs

COMPLETE SET (50)............... 15.00 4.50

1992 Modesto A's Classic/Best

This 30-card standard-size set of the 1992 Modesto A's, a Class A California League affiliate of the Oakland Athletics, features white-bordered posed color player photos on its fronts. The player's name, team, and position appear at the bottom. The white back is framed by a thin red line and carries the player's name and position at the top, followed by biography, statistics and team logos.
COMPLETE SET (30)................. 5.00 1.50

1992 Modesto A's Fleer/ProCards

This 22-card standard-size set of the 1992 Modesto A's, a Class A California League affiliate of the Oakland Athletics, features brown-bordered posed color player photos on its fronts. The player's name appears in an upper corner; his team and position appear in a lower corner. The white back is framed by a black line and carries the player's name and position at the top, followed by biography and statistics.
COMPLETE SET (22)................. 5.00 1.50

1992 Myrtle Beach Hurricanes Classic/Best

This 30-card standard-size set of the 1992 Myrtle Beach Hurricanes, a Class A South Atlantic League affiliate of the Toronto Blue Jays, features white-bordered posed color player photos on its fronts. The player's name, team, and position appear near the bottom. The white back is framed by an orange line and carries the player's name and position at the top, followed by biography and statistics. This issue includes the minor league debut of Alex Gonzalez.
COMPLETE SET (30)................. 5.00 1.50

1992 Myrtle Beach Hurricanes Fleer/ProCards

This 29-card standard-size set of the 1992 Myrtle Beach Hurricanes, a Class A South Atlantic League affiliate of the Toronto Blue Jays, features brown-bordered posed color player photos on its fronts. The player's name appears in an upper corner; his team and position appear in a lower corner. The white back is framed by a black line and carries the player's name and position at the top, followed by biography and statistics. This issue includes the minor league card debut of Alex Gonzalez.
COMPLETE SET (29)................. 5.00 1.50

1992 Nashville Sounds Fleer/ProCards

This 26-card standard-size set of the 1992 Nashville Sounds, a Class AAA American Association affiliate of the Cincinnati Reds, features brown-bordered posed color player photos on its fronts. The player's name appears in an upper corner; his team and position appear in a lower corner. The white back is framed by a black line and carries the player's name and position at the top, followed by biography and stats.
COMPLETE SET (26)................. 5.00 1.50

1992 Nashville Sounds SkyBox

COMPLETE SET (26)................. 5.00 1.50

1992 New Britain Red Sox Fleer/ProCards

This 27-card standard-size set of the 1992 New Britain Red Sox, a Class AA Eastern League affiliate of the Boston Red Sox, features brown-bordered posed color player photos on its fronts. The player's name appears in an upper corner; his team and position appear in a lower corner. The white back is framed by a black line and carries the player's name and position at the top, followed by biography and statistics.
COMPLETE SET (27)................. 5.00 1.50

1992 New Britain Red Sox SkyBox

COMPLETE SET (26)................. 5.00 1.50

1992 Niagara Falls Rapids Classic/Best

This 30-card standard-size set of the 1992 Niagara Falls, a Class A New York-Penn League affiliate of the Detroit Tigers, features white-bordered posed color player photos on its fronts. The player's name, team, and position appear at the bottom. The white back is framed by a thin red line and carries the player's name and position at the top, followed by biography, statistics and team logos. This issue includes the minor league card debut of Bobby Higginson and a third year card of Tony Clark.
COMPLETE SET (30)............... 15.00 4.50

1992 Niagara Falls Rapids Fleer/ProCards

This 32-card standard-size set of the 1992 Niagara Falls, a Class A New York-Penn League affiliate of the Detroit Tigers, features brown-bordered posed color player photos on its fronts. The player's name appears in an upper corner; his team and position appear in a lower corner. The white back is framed by a black line and carries the player's name and position at the top, followed by biography and statistics. This issue inlcudes the minor league card debut of Bobby Higginson and a third year card of Tony Clark.
COMPLETE SET (32)............... 10.00 3.00

1992 Oklahoma City 89ers Fleer/ProCards

This 28-card standard-size set of the 1992 Oklahoma City 89ers, a Class AAA American Association League affiliate of the Texas Rangers, features brown-bordered posed color player photos on its fronts. The player's name appears in an upper corner; his team and position appear in a lower corner. The white back is framed by a black line and carries the player's name and position at the top, followed by biography and statistics.
COMPLETE SET (28)................. 5.00 1.50

1992 Oklahoma City 89ers SkyBox

COMPLETE SET (26)................. 5.00 1.50

1992 Oklahoma State Cowboys

COMPLETE SET (32)............... 10.00 3.00

1992 Omaha Royals Fleer/ProCards

This 29-card standard-size set of the 1992 Omaha Royals, a Class AAA American Association affiliate of the Kansas City Royals, features brown-bordered posed color player photos on its fronts. The player's name appears in an upper corner; his team and position appear in a lower corner. The white back is framed by a black line and carries the player's name and position at the top, followed by biography and statistics. This issue includes a fifth year card of Jeff Conine.
COMPLETE SET (29)................. 5.00 1.50

1992 Omaha Royals Shurfine

COMPLETE SET (2)................... 5.00 1.50

1992 Omaha Royals SkyBox

This set inclueds a fifth year card of Jeff Conine.
COMPLETE SET (26)................. 5.00 1.50

1992 Oneonta Yankees Classic/Best

This 30-card standard-size set of the 1992 Oneonta Yankees, a Class A New York-Penn League affiliate of the New York Yankees, features white-bordered posed color player photos on its fronts. The player's name, team, and position appear at the bottom. The white back is framed by a thin red line and carries the player's name and position at the top, followed by biography, statistics and team logos.
COMPLETE SET (30)................. 5.00 1.50

1992 Orlando Sun Rays Fleer/ProCards

This 26-card standard-size set of the 1992 Orlando Sun Rays, a Class AA Southern League affiliate of the Minnesota Twins, features brown-bordered posed color player photos on its fronts. The player's name appears in an upper corner; his team and position appear in a lower corner. The white back is framed by a black line and carries the player's name and position at the top, followed by biography and statistics.
COMPLETE SET (26)................. 5.00 1.50

1992 Orlando Sun Rays SkyBox

COMPLETE SET (26)................. 5.00 1.50

1992 Osceola Astros Classic/Best

This 30-card standard-size set of the 1992 Osceola Astros, a Class A Florida State League affiliate of the Houston Astros, features white-bordered posed color player photos on its fronts. The player's name, team, and position appear at the bottom. The white back is framed by a thin red line and carries the player's name and position at the top, followed by biography, statistics and team logos.
COMPLETE SET (30)................. 5.00 1.50

1992 Osceola Astros Fleer/ProCards

This 28-card standard-size set of the 1992 Osceola Astros, a Class A Florida State League affiliate of the Houston Astros, features brown-bordered posed color player photos on its fronts. The player's name appears in an upper corner; his team and position appear in a lower corner. The white back is framed by a black line and carries the player's name and position at the top, followed by biography and statistics.
COMPLETE SET (28)................. 5.00 1.50

1992 Palm Springs Angels Classic/Best

This 30-card standard-size set of the 1992 Palm Springs Angels, a Class A California League affiliate of the California Angels, features white-bordered posed color player photos on its fronts. The player's name, team, and position appear at the bottom. The white back is framed by a thin red line and carries the player's name and position at the top, followed by biography, statistics and team logos. This issue includes a third year card of Garret Anderson.
COMPLETE SET (30)................. 8.00 2.40

1992 Palm Springs Angels Fleer/ProCards

This 29-card standard-size set of the 1992 Palm Springs Angels, a Class A California League affiliate of the California Angels, features brown-bordered posed color player photos on its fronts. The player's name appears in an upper corner; his team and position appear in a lower corner. The white back is framed by a black line and carries the player's name and position at the top, followed by biography and statistics. This issue includes a third year card of Garret Anderson.
COMPLETE SET (29)................. 8.00 2.40

1992 Pawtucket Red Sox Dunkin' Donuts

This 31-card set of the Pawtucket Red Sox, a Class AAA International League affiliate of the Boston Red Sox, was issued in one large sheet featuring six perforated five-card strips with a large team photo in the wide top strip. Sponsored by Channel 10 and Dunkin' Donuts, the fronts carry color player photos while the backs display player career statistics. The cards are unnumbered and checklisted below in alphabetical order. This issue includes a fourth year card of Mo Vaughn.
COMPLETE SET (31)............... 50.00 15.00

1992 Pawtucket Red Sox Fleer/ProCards

This 28-card standard-size set of the 1992 Pawtucket Red Sox, a Class AAA International League affiliate of the Boston Red Sox, features brown-bordered posed color player photos on its fronts. The player's name appears in an upper corner; his team and position appear in a lower corner. The white back is framed by a black line and carries the player's name and position at the top, followed by biography and statistics. This issue includes a fourth year card of Mo Vaughn.
COMPLETE SET (28)............... 10.00 3.00

1992 Pawtucket Red Sox SkyBox

COMPLETE SET (26)................. 5.00 1.50

1992 Peninsula Oilers Team Issue

This 28-card set of the 1992 Peninsula Oilers of the Alaska Central Baseball League features color player portraits in black-and-white borders. The backs carry player information. The cards are listed below according to where they are on the set checklist.
COMPLETE SET (29)................. 5.00 1.50

1992 Peninsula Pilots Classic/Best

This 30-card standard-size set of the 1992 Peninsula Pilots, a Class A Carolina League affiliate of the Seattle Mariners, features white-bordered posed color player photos on its fronts. The player's name, team, and position appear at the bottom. The white back is framed by a thin red line and carries the player's name and position at the top, followed by biography, statistics and team logos.
COMPLETE SET (30)................. 5.00 1.50

1992 Peninsula Pilots Fleer/ProCards

This 28-card standard-size set of the 1992 Peninsula Pilots, a Class A Carolina League affiliate of the Seattle Mariners, features brown-bordered posed color player photos on its fronts. The player's name appears in an upper corner; his team and position appear in a lower corner. The white back is framed by a black line and carries the player's name and position at the top, followed by biography and statistics.
COMPLETE SET (28)................. 5.00 1.50

1992 Peoria Chiefs Classic/Best

This 30-card standard-size set of the 1992 Peoria Chiefs, a Class A Midwest League affiliate of the Chicago Cubs, features white-bordered posed color player photos on its fronts. The player's name, team, and position appear at the bottom. The white back is framed by a thin red line and carries the player's name and position at the top, followed by biography, statistics and team logos.
COMPLETE SET (30)................. 5.00 1.50

1992 Peoria Chiefs Team Issue

COMPLETE SET (31)................. 5.00 1.50

1992 Phoenix Firebirds Fleer/ProCards

This 26-card standard-size set of the 1992 Phoenix Firebirds, a Class AAA Pacific Coast League affiliate of the San Francisco Giants, features brown-bordered posed color player photos on its fronts. The player's name appears in an upper corner; his team and position appear in a lower corner. The white back is framed by a black line and carries the player's name and position at the top, followed by biography and statistics.
COMPLETE SET (26)................. 5.00 1.50

1992 Phoenix Firebirds SkyBox

COMPLETE SET (26)................. 5.00 1.50

1992 Pittsfield Mets Classic/Best

This 28-card standard-size set of the 1992 Pittsfield Mets, a Class A New York-Penn League affiliate of the New York Mets, features white-bordered posed color player photos on its fronts. The player's name, team, and position appear at the bottom. The white back is framed by a thin red line and carries the player's name and position at the top, followed by biography, statistics and team logos. This issue includes the minor league card debut of Edgardo Alfonzo.
COMPLETE SET (30)............... 20.00 6.00

1992 Pittsfield Mets Fleer/ProCards

This 28-card standard-size set of the 1992 Pittsfield Mets, a Class A New York-Penn League affiliate of the New York Mets, features brown-bordered posed color player photos on its fronts. The player's name appears in an upper corner; his team and position appear in a lower corner. The white back is framed by a black line and carries the player's name and position at the top, followed by biography and statistics. This issue includes the minor league card debut of Edgardo Alfonzo.
COMPLETE SET (28)............... 12.00 3.60

1992 Portland Beavers Fleer/ProCards

This 26-card standard-size set of the 1992 Portland Beavers, a Class AAA Pacific Coast League affiliate of the Minnesota Twins, features brown-bordered posed color player photos on its fronts. The player's name appears in an upper corner; his team and position appear in a lower corner. The white back is framed by a black line and carries the player's name and position at the top, followed by biography and statistics.
COMPLETE SET (26)................. 5.00 1.50

1992 Portland Beavers SkyBox

COMPLETE SET (26)................. 5.00 1.50

1992 Prince William Cannons Classic/Best

This 30-card standard-size set of the 1992 Prince William Cannons, a Class A Carolina League affiliate of the New York Yankees, features white-bordered posed color player photos on its fronts. The player's name, team, and position appear at the bottom. The white back is framed by a thin red line and carries the player's name and position at the top, followed by biography, statistics and team logos.
COMPLETE SET (30)................. 5.00 1.50

1992 Prince William Cannons Fleer/ProCards

This 29-card standard-size set of the 1992 Prince William Cannons, a Class A Carolina League affiliate of the New York Yankees, features brown-bordered posed color player photos on its fronts. The player's name appears in an upper corner; his team and position appear in a lower corner. The white back is framed by a black line and carries the player's name and position at the top, followed by biography and statistics.
COMPLETE SET (29)................. 5.00 1.50

1992 Princeton Reds Classic/Best

This 30-card standard-size set of the 1992 Princeton Reds, a Rookie Class Appalachian League affiliate of the Cincinnati Reds, features white-bordered posed color player photos on its fronts. The player's name, team, and position appear at the bottom. The white back is framed by a thin red line and carries the player's name and position at the top, followed by biography, statistics and team logos.
COMPLETE SET (30)................. 5.00 1.50

1992 Princeton Reds Fleer/ProCards

This 29-card standard-size set of the 1992 Princeton Reds, a Rookie Class Appalachian League affiliate of the Cincinnati Reds, features brown-bordered posed color player photos on its fronts. The player's name appears in an upper corner; his team and position appear in a lower corner. The white back is framed by a black line and carries the player's name and position at the top, followed by biography and statistics.
COMPLETE SET (29)................. 5.00 1.50

1992 Pulaski Braves Classic/Best

This 30-card standard-size set of the 1992 Pulaski Braves, a Rookie Class Appalachian League affiliate of the Atlanta Braves, features white-bordered posed color player photos on its fronts. The player's name, team, and position appear at the bottom. The white back is framed by a thin red line and carries the player's name and position at the top, followed by biography, statistics and team logos.
COMPLETE SET (30)................. 5.00 1.50

1992 Pulaski Braves Fleer/ProCards

This 32-card standard-size set of the 1992 Pulaski Braves, a Rookie Class Appalachian League affiliate of the Atlanta Braves, features brown-bordered posed color player photos on its fronts. The player's name appears in an upper corner; his team and position appear in a lower corner. The white back is framed by a black line and carries the player's name and position at the top, followed by biography and statistics.
COMPLETE SET (32)................. 5.00 1.50

1992 Quad City River Bandits Classic/Best

This 30-card standard-size set of the 1992 Quad City River Bandits, a Class A Midwest League affiliate of the California Angels, features white-bordered posed color player photos on its fronts. The player's name, team, and position appear at the bottom. The white back is framed by a thin red line and carries the player's name and position at the top, followed by biography, statistics and team logos.
COMPLETE SET (30)................. 5.00 1.50

1992 Quad City River Bandits Fleer/ProCards

This 30-card standard-size set of the 1992 Quad City River Bandits, a Class A Midwest League affiliate of the California Angels, features brown-bordered posed color player photos on its fronts. The player's name appears in an upper corner; his team and position appear in a lower corner. The white back is framed by a black line and carries the player's name and position at the top, followed by biography and statistics.
COMPLETE SET (30)................. 5.00 1.50

1992 Reading Phillies Fleer/ProCards

This 29-card standard-size set of the 1992 Reading Phillies, a Class AA Eastern League affiliate of the Philadelphia Phillies, features brown-bordered posed color player photos on its fronts. The player's name appears in an upper corner; his team and position appear in a lower corner. The white back is framed by a black line and carries the player's name and position at the top, followed by biography and statistics.
COMPLETE SET (29)................. 5.00 1.50

1992 Reading Phillies SkyBox

COMPLETE SET (26)................. 5.00 1.50

1992 Reno Silver Sox Cal League Cards

COMPLETE SET (29)................. 5.00 1.50

1992 Richmond Braves Bleacher Bums

3,500 sets were produced. This set includes a fourth year card of Ryan Klesko.
COMPLETE SET (26)................. 15.00 4.50

1992 Richmond Braves Bob's Camera

This 26-card team set of the 1992 Richmond Braves, a Class AAA International League affiliate of the Atlanta Braves, was sponsored by Bob's Camera and measures approximately 4" by 4 7/8". The fronts feature borderless color player photos with sponsors' and team's logos in the wide bottom margin. This issue includes a fourth year card of Ryan Klesko. The backs are blank. 500 sets were produced.
COMPLETE SET (26)............... 50.00 15.00

1992 Richmond Braves Fleer/ProCards

This 28-card standard-size set of the 1992 Richmond Braves, a Class AAA International League affiliate of the Atlanta Braves, features brown-bordered posed color player photos on its fronts. The player's name appears in an upper corner; his team and position appear in a lower corner. The white back is framed by a black line and carries the player's name and position at the top, followed by biography and statistics. This issue includes a fourth year card of Ryan Klesko.
COMPLETE SET (28)................. 8.00 2.40

1992 Richmond Braves Richmond Comix

This issue includes a fourth year card of Ryan Klesko.
COMPLETE SET (26)............... 25.00 7.50

1992 Richmond Braves SkyBox

This issue inlcudes a fourth year card of Ryan Klesko.
COMPLETE SET (26)................. 8.00 2.40

1992 Richmond Braves Ukrops

This 50 card standard-size set was issued in two card strips. The player featured on the left side of the strip was a current Richmond Brave while the player on the right side was a player show who had passed through Richmond while on his way to the majors These cards feature the player's photo in the middle with his name and position in the lower left and the Ukrop logo on the bottom right. The back has statistics as well as an advertisement for the sponsors which also includes Pepsi.
COMPLETE SET 20.00 6.00

1992 Rochester Red Wings Fleer/ProCards

This 26-card standard-size set of the 1992 Rochester Red Wings, a Class AAA International League affiliate of the Baltimore Orioles, features brown-bordered posed color player photos on its fronts. The player's name appears in an upper corner; his team and position appear in a lower corner. The white back is framed by a black line and carries the player's name and position at the top, followed by biography and statistics.
COMPLETE SET (26)................. 5.00 1.50

1992 Rochester Red Wings SkyBox

COMPLETE SET (26)................. 5.00 1.50

1992 Rochester Red Wings Team Issue

This 31-card set of the Rochester Red Wings, a Class AAA International League affiliate of the Baltimore Orioles, was sponsored by Wegmans Photo Center and Channel 13 WOKR. The set was distributed on a three-page fold out with 15 perforated cards on two pages and the team picture on the third page. The backs carry player information, a facsimile autograph and career statistics. The cards are unnumbered and checklisted below in alphabetical order.
COMPLETE SET (30)............... 10.00 3.00

1992 Rockford Expos Classic/Best

This 30-card standard-size set of the 1992 Rockford Expos, a Class A Midwest League affiliate of the Montreal Expos, features white-bordered posed color player photos on its fronts. The player's name, team, and position appear at the bottom. The white back is framed by a thin red line and carries the player's name and position at the top, followed by biography, statistics and team logos.
COMPLETE SET (30)................. 5.00 1.50

1992 Rockford Expos Fleer/ProCards

This 28-card standard-size set of the 1992 Rockford Expos, a Class A Midwest League affiliate of the Montreal Expos, features brown-bordered posed color player photos on its fronts. The player's name appears in an upper corner; his team and position appear at a lower corner. The white back is framed by a black line and carries the player's name and position at the top, followed by biography and statistics.
COMPLETE SET (28)................. 5.00 1.50

1992 Salem Buccaneers Classic/Best

This 30-card standard-size set of the 1992 Salem Buccaneers, a Class A Carolina League affiliate of the Pittsburgh Pirates, features white-bordered posed color player photos on its fronts. The player's name, team, and position appear at the bottom. The white back is framed by a thin red line and carries the player's name and position at the top, followed by biography, statistics and team logos.
COMPLETE SET (30)................. 5.00 1.50

1992 Salem Buccaneers Fleer/ProCards

This 28-card standard-size set of the 1992 Salem Buccaneers, a Class A Carolina League affiliate of the Pittsburgh Pirates, features brown-bordered posed color player photos on its fronts. The player's name appears in an upper corner; his team and position appear in a lower corner. The white back is framed by a black line and carries the player's name and position at the top, followed by biography and statistics.
COMPLETE SET (28)................. 5.00 1.50

1992 Salinas Spurs Classic/Best

This 30-card standard-size set of the 1992 Salinas Spurs, a Class A California League Independent, features white-bordered posed color player photos on its fronts. The player's name, team, and position appear at the bottom. The white back is framed by a thin red line and carries the player's name and position at the top, followed by biography, statistics and team logos.
COMPLETE SET (30)................. 5.00 1.50

1992 Salinas Spurs Fleer/ProCards

This 31-card standard-size set of the 1992 Salinas Spurs, a Class A California League Independent, features brown-bordered posed color player photos on its fronts. The player's name appears in an upper corner; his team and position appear in a lower corner. The white back is framed by a black line and carries the player's name and position at the top, followed by biography and statistics.
COMPLETE SET (31)................. 5.00 1.50

1992 Salt Lake Trappers Sports Pro

COMPLETE SET (30)................. 5.00 1.50

1992 San Antonio Missions Fleer/ProCards

This 24-card standard-size set of the 1992 San Antonio Missions, a Class AA Texas League affiliate of the Los Angeles Dodgers, features brown-bordered posed color player photos on its fronts. The player's name appears in an upper corner; his team and position appear in a lower corner. The white back is framed by a black line and carries the player's name and position at the top, followed by biography and statistics. This issue includes a third year card of Raul Mondesi.
COMPLETE SET (24)................. 10.00 3.00

1992 San Antonio Missions SkyBox

An early card of Mike Piazza is in this set.
COMPLETE SET (26)............... 30.00 9.00

1992 San Bernardino Spirit Classic/Best

This 30-card standard-size set of the 1992 San Bernardino Spirit, a Class A California League affiliate of the Seattle Mariners, features white-bordered posed color player photos on its fronts. The player's name, team, and position appear at the bottom. The white back is framed by a thin red line and carries the player's name and position at the top, followed by biography, statistics and team logos.
COMPLETE SET (30)................. 5.00 1.50

1992 San Bernardino Spirit Fleer/ProCards

This 33-card standard-size set of the 1992 San Bernardino Spirit, a Class A California League affiliate of the Seattle Mariners, features brown-bordered posed color player photos on its fronts. The player's name appears in an upper corner; his team and position appear in a lower corner. The white back is framed by a black line and carries the player's name and position at the top, followed by biography and statistics.
COMPLETE SET (33)................. 5.00 1.50

1992 San Jose Giants Classic/Best

This 30-card standard-size set of the 1992 San Jose Giants, a Class A California League affiliate of the San Francisco Giants, features white-bordered posed color player photos on its fronts. The player's name, team, and position appear at the bottom. The white back is framed by a thin red line and carries the player's name and position at the top, followed by biography, statistics and team logos.
COMPLETE SET (30)................. 5.00 1.50

1992 Sarasota White Sox Classic/Best

This 30-card standard-size set of the 1992 Sarasota White Sox, a Class A Florida State League affiliate of the Chicago White Sox, features white-bordered posed color player photos on its fronts. The player's name, team, and position appear at the bottom. The white back is framed by a thin red line and carries the player's name and position at the top, followed by biography, statistics and team logos.
COMPLETE SET (30)................. 5.00 1.50

1992 Sarasota White Sox Fleer/ProCards

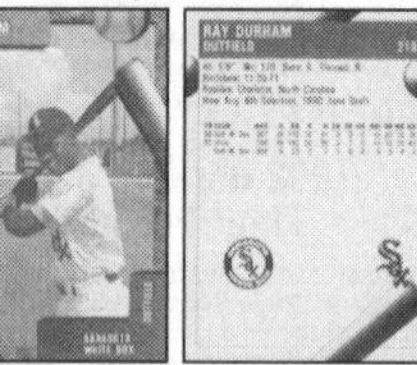

This 30-card standard-size set of the 1992 Sarasota White Sox, a Class A Florida State League affiliate of the Chicago White Sox, features brown-bordered posed color player photos on its fronts. The player's name appears in an upper corner; his team and position appear in a lower corner. The white back is framed by a black line and carries the player's name and position at the top, followed by biography and statistics. This issue includes the second year card of Ray Durham.
COMPLETE SET (30)................. 8.00 2.40

1992 Savannah Cardinals Classic/Best

This 30-card standard-size set of the 1992 Savannah Cardinals, a Class A South Atlantic League affiliate of the St. Louis Cardinals, features white-bordered posed color player photos on its fronts. The player's name, team, and position appear at the bottom. The white back is framed by a thin red line and carries the player's name and position at the top, followed by biography, statistics and team logos.
COMPLETE SET (30)................. 5.00 1.50

1992 Savannah Cardinals Fleer/ProCards

This 30-card standard-size set of the 1992 Savannah Cardinals, a Class A South Atlantic League affiliate of the St. Louis Cardinals, features brown-bordered posed color player photos on its fronts. The player's name appears in an upper corner; his team and position appear in a lower corner. The white back is framed by a black line and carries the player's name and position at the top, followed by biography and statistics.
COMPLETE SET (30)................. 5.00 1.50

1992 Scranton/Wilkes-Barre Red Barons Fleer/ProCards

This 27-card standard-size set of the 1992 Scranton/Wilkes-Barre Red Barons, a Class AAA International League affiliate of the Philadelphia Phillies, features brown-bordered posed color player photos on its fronts. The player's name appears in an upper corner; his team and position appear in a lower corner. The white back is framed by a black line and carries the player's name and position at the top, followed by biography and statistics.
COMPLETE SET (27)................. 5.00 1.50

1992 Scranton/Wilkes-Barre Red Barons SkyBox

This 26-card standard-size set of the 1992 Scranton/Wilkes-Barre Red Barons, a Class AAA International League affiliate of the Philadelphia Phillies, features white-bordered posed color player photos on its fronts. The player's name, team, and position appear at the bottom. The white back is framed by a thin red line and carries the player's name and position at the top, followed by biography, statistics and team logos.
COMPLETE SET (26)................. 5.00 1.50

1992 Shreveport Captains Fleer/ProCards

This 27-card standard-size set of the 1992 Shreveport Captains, a Class AA Texas League affiliate of the San Francisco Giants, features brown-bordered posed color player photos on its fronts. The player's name appears in an upper corner; his team and position appear in a lower corner. The white back is framed by a black line and carries the player's name and position at the top, followed by biography and statistics.
COMPLETE SET (27)................. 5.00 1.50

1992 Shreveport Captains SkyBox

COMPLETE SET (26)................. 5.00 1.50

1992 South Bend White Sox Classic/Best

This 30-card standard-size set of the 1992 South Bend White Sox, a Class A Midwest League affiliate of the Chicago White Sox, features white-bordered posed color player photos on its fronts. The player's name, team, and position appear at the bottom. The white back is framed by a thin red line and carries the player's name and position at the top, followed by biography, statistics and team logos.
COMPLETE SET (30)................. 5.00 1.50

1992 South Bend White Sox Fleer/ProCards

This 30-card standard-size set of the 1992 South Bend White Sox, a Class A Midwest League affiliate of the Chicago White Sox, features brown-bordered posed color player photos on its fronts. The player's name appears in an upper corner; his team and position appear in a lower corner. The white back is framed by a black line and carries the player's name and position at the top, followed by biography and statistics. This issue includes the minor league card debut of James Baldwin.
COMPLETE SET (30)................. 8.00 2.40

1992 Southern Oregon A's Classic/Best

This 30-card standard-size set of the 1992 Southern Oregon A's, a Class A Northwest League affiliate of the Oakland Athletics, features white-bordered posed color player photos on its fronts. The player's name, team, and position appear at the bottom. The white back is framed by a thin red line and carries the player's name and position at the top, followed by biography, statistics and team logos.
COMPLETE SET (30)................. 5.00 1.50

1992 Southern Oregon A's Fleer/ProCards

This 33-card standard-size set of the 1992 Southern Oregon A's, a Class A Northwest League affiliate of the Oakland Athletics, features brown-bordered posed color player photos on its fronts. The player's name appears in an upper corner; his team and position appear in a lower corner. The white back is framed by a black line and carries the player's name and position at the top, followed by biography and statistics.
COMPLETE SET (33)................. 5.00 1.50

1992 Spartanburg Phillies Classic/Best

This 30-card standard-size set of the 1992 Spartanburg Phillies, a Class A South Atlantic League affiliate of the Philadelphia Phillies, features white-bordered posed color player photos on its fronts. The player's name, team, and position appear at the bottom. The white back is framed by a thin red line and carries the player's name and position at the top, followed by biography, statistics and team logos.
COMPLETE SET (30)................. 5.00 1.50

1992 Spartanburg Phillies Fleer/ProCards

This 29-card standard-size set of the 1992 Spartanburg Phillies, a Class A South Atlantic League affiliate of the Philadelphia Phillies features brown-bordered posed color player photos on its fronts. The player's name appears in an upper corner; his team and position appear in a lower corner. The white back is framed by a black line and carries the player's name and position at the top, followed by biography and statistics.
COMPLETE SET (29)................. 5.00 1.50

1992 Spokane Indians Classic/Best

This 30-card standard-size set of the 1992 Spokane Indians, a Class A Northwest League affiliate of the San Diego Padres, features white-bordered posed color player photos on its fronts. The player's name, team, and position appear at the bottom. The white back is framed by a thin red line and carries the player's name and position at the top, followed by biography, statistics and team logos.
COMPLETE SET (30)................. 5.00 1.50

1992 Spokane Indians Fleer/ProCards

This 30-card standard-size set of the 1992 Spokane Indians, a Class A Northwest League affiliate of the San Diego Padres, features brown-bordered posed color player photos on its fronts. The player's name appears in an upper corner; his team and position appear in a lower corner. The white back is framed by a black line and carries the player's name and position at the top, followed by biography and statistics.
COMPLETE SET (30)................. 5.00 1.50

1992 Springfield Cardinals Classic/Best

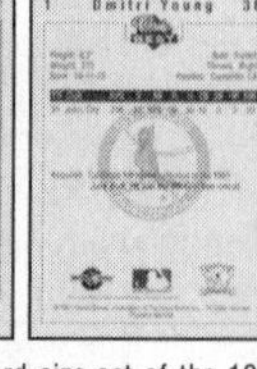

This 30-card standard-size set of the 1992 Springfield Cardinals, a Class A Midwest League affiliate of the St. Louis Cardinals, features white-bordered posed color player photos on its fronts. The player's name, team, and position appear at the bottom. The white back is framed by a thin red line and carries the player's name and position at the top, followed by biography, statistics and team logos. This issue includes a second year card of Dmitri Young. In addition, a Dmitri Young promo card was distributed to dealers and hobby media to preview the 1992 run of Classic/Best team sets. The set price does not include this promo card.
COMPLETE SET (30)................. 8.00 2.40

1992 Springfield Cardinals Fleer/ProCards

This 29-card standard-size set of the 1992 Springfield Cardinals, a Class A Midwest League affiliate of the St. Louis Cardinals, features brown-bordered posed color player photos on its fronts. The player's name appears in an upper corner; his team and position appear in a lower corner. The white back is framed by a black line and carries the player's name and position at the top, followed by biography and statistics. This issue includes a second year card of Dmitri Young.
COMPLETE SET (29)................. 8.00 2.40

1992 St. Catharines Blue Jays Classic/Best

This 30-card standard-size set of the 1992 St. Catharines Blue Jays, a Class A New York-Penn League affiliate of the Montreal Expos, features white-bordered posed color player photos on its fronts. The player's name, team, and position appear at the bottom. The white back is framed by a thin red line and carries the player's name and position at the top, followed by biography, statistics and team logos.
COMPLETE SET (30)................. 5.00 1.50

1992 St. Catharines Blue Jays Fleer/ProCards

This 29-card standard-size set of the 1992 St. Catharines Blue Jays, a Class A New York-Penn League affiliate of the Toronto Blue Jays, features brown-bordered posed color player photos on its fronts. The player's name appears in an upper corner; his team and position appear in a lower corner. The white back is framed by a black line and carries the player's name and position at the top, followed by biography and statistics.
COMPLETE SET (29)................. 5.00 1.50

1992 St. Lucie Mets Classic/Best

This 30-card standard-size set of the 1992 St. Lucie Mets, a Class A Florida State League affiliate of the New York Mets, features white-bordered posed color player photos on its fronts. The player's name, team, and position

ppear at the bottom. The white back is framed by a thin red line and carries the player's name and position at the top, followed by biography, statistics and team logos.
COMPLETE SET (30) 5.00 1.50

1992 St. Lucie Mets Fleer/ProCards

This 30-card standard-size set of the 1992 St. Lucie Mets, a Class A Florida State League affiliate of the New York Mets, features brown-bordered posed color player photos on its fronts. The player's name appears in an upper corner; his team and position appear in a lower corner. The white back is framed by a black line and carries the player's name and position at the top, followed by biography and statistics.
COMPLETE SET (30) 5.00 1.50

1992 St. Petersburg Cardinals Classic/Best

This 30-card standard-size set of the 1992 St. Petersburg Cardinals, a Class A Florida State League affiliate of the St. Louis Cardinals, features white-bordered posed color player photos on its fronts. The player's name, team, and position appear at the bottom. The white back is framed by a thin red line and carries the player's name and position at the top, followed by biography, statistics and team logos.
COMPLETE SET (30) 5.00 1.50

1992 St. Petersburg Cardinals Fleer/ProCards

This 26-card standard-size set of the 1992 St. Petersburg Cardinals, a Class A Florida State League affiliate of the St. Louis Cardinals, features brown-bordered posed color player photos on its fronts. The player's name appears in an upper corner; his team and position appear in a lower corner. The white back is framed by a black line and carries the player's name and position at the top, followed by biography and statistics.
COMPLETE SET (26) 5.00 1.50

1992 Stockton Ports Classic/Best

This 30-card standard-size set of the 1992 Stockton Ports, a Class A California League affiliate of the Milwaukee Brewers, features white-bordered posed color player photos on its fronts. The player's name, team, and position appear at the bottom. The white back is framed by a thin red line and carries the player's name and position at the top, followed by biography, statistics and team logos.
COMPLETE SET (30) 5.00 1.50

1992 Stockton Ports Fleer/ProCards

This 28-card standard-size set of the 1992 Stockton Ports, a Class A California League affiliate of the Milwaukee Brewers, features brown-bordered posed color player photos on its fronts. The player's name appears in an upper corner; his team and position appear in a lower corner. The white back is framed by a black line and carries the player's name and position at the top, followed by biography and statistics.
COMPLETE SET (28) 5.00 1.50

1992 Syracuse Chiefs Fleer/ProCards

This 31-card standard-size set of the 1992 Syracuse Chiefs, a Class AAA International League affiliate of the Toronto Blue Jays, features brown-bordered posed color player photos on its fronts. The player's name appears in an upper corner; his team and position appear in a lower corner. The white back is framed by a black line and carries the player's name and position at the top, followed by biography and statistics. This issue includes a sixth year card of Pat Hentgen.
COMPLETE SET (31) 5.00 1.50

1992 Syracuse Chiefs Merchants Bank

This set includes a sixth year card of Pat Hentgen.
COMPLETE SET (30) 10.00 3.00

1992 Syracuse Chiefs SkyBox

This 26-card standard-size set of the 1992 Syracuse Chiefs, a Class AAA International League affiliate of the Toronto Blue Jays, features white-bordered posed color player photos on its fronts. The player's name appears at the top; his team and position appear at the bottom. The white back carries the player's name at the top, followed by biography and statistics.
COMPLETE SET (26) 5.00 1.50

1992 Syracuse Chiefs Tallmadge Tire

Printed on thin card stock, this five-card set features former Syracuse Chiefs who've gone on to major league careers. Each card measures about 2 3/8" by 3 1/2" and features on its front a posed color player photo with a white outer border and blue inner border. The player's name appears within a baseball diamond design at the lower right; below is the sponsor's name, Tallmadge Tire, and the set's subtitle, Former Chiefs Collectibles. The horizontal white back carries the player's name and position at the top, followed by biography and statistics, all in blue lettering. The cards are unnumbered and checklisted below in alphabetical order. Several coupon cards for Tallmadge Tire's products and services were also issued with the set.
COMPLETE SET (5) 15.00 4.50

1992 Tacoma Tigers Fleer/ProCards

This 26-card standard-size set of the 1992 Tacoma Tigers, a Class AAA Pacific Coast League affiliate of the Oakland Athletics, features brown-bordered posed color player photos on its fronts. The player's name appears in an upper corner; his team and position appear in a lower corner. The white back is framed by a black line and carries the player's name and position at the top, followed by biography and statistics.
COMPLETE SET (26) 5.00 1.50

1992 Tacoma Tigers SkyBox

COMPLETE SET (26) 5.00 1.50

1992 Texas Longhorns

This set features leading players in University of Texas history. The first 41 cards feature players and they are sequenced in alphabetical order. The last four cards highlight special events.
COMPLETE SET (45) 15.00 4.50

1992 Tidewater Tides Fleer/ProCards

This 28-card standard-size set of the 1992 Tidewater Tides, a Class AAA International League affiliate of the New York Mets, features brown-bordered posed color player photos on its fronts. The player's name appears in an upper corner; his team and position appear in a lower corner. The white back is framed by a black line and carries the player's name and position at the top, followed by biography and statistics.
COMPLETE SET (28) 5.00 1.50

1992 Tidewater Tides SkyBox

COMPLETE SET (26) 5.00 1.50

1992 Toledo Mud Hens Fleer/ProCards

This 29-card standard-size set of the 1992 Toledo Mud Hens, a Class AAA International League affiliate of the Detroit Tigers, features brown-bordered posed color player photos on its fronts. The player's name appears in an upper corner; his team and position appear in a lower corner. The white back is framed by a black line and carries the player's name and position at the top, followed by biography and statistics.
COMPLETE SET (29) 5.00 1.50

1992 Toledo Mud Hens SkyBox

COMPLETE SET (26) 5.00 1.50

1992 Triple A All-Stars SkyBox

COMPLETE SET (38) 15.00 4.50

1992 Tucson Toros Fleer/ProCards

This 30-card standard-size set of the 1992 Tucson Toros, a Class AAA Pacific Coast League affiliate of the Houston Astros, features brown-bordered posed color player photos on its fronts. The player's name appears in an upper corner; his team and position appear in a lower corner. The white back is framed by a black line and carries the player's name and position at the top, followed by biography and statistics.
COMPLETE SET (30) 5.00 1.50

1992 Tucson Toros SkyBox

COMPLETE SET (26) 5.00 1.50

1992 Tulsa Drillers Fleer/ProCards

This 27-card standard-size set of the 1992 Tulsa Drillers, a Class AA Texas League affiliate of the Texas Rangers, features brown-bordered posed color player photos on its fronts. The player's name appears in an upper corner; his team and position appear in a lower corner. The white back is framed by a black line and carries the player's name and position at the top, followed by biography and statistics.
COMPLETE SET (27) 5.00 1.50

1992 Tulsa Drillers SkyBox

COMPLETE SET (26) 5.00 1.50

1992 Utica Blue Sox Classic/Best

This 26-card standard-size set of the 1992 Utica Blue Sox, a Class A New York-Penn League affiliate of the Chicago White Sox, features white-bordered posed color player photos on its fronts. The player's name, team, and position appear at the bottom. The white back is framed by a thin red line and carries the player's name and position at the top, followed by biography, statistics and team logos. This issue includes the minor league card debut of Mike Cameron.
COMPLETE SET (26) 25.00 7.50

1992 Vancouver Canadians Fleer/ProCards

This 24-card standard-size set of the 1992 Vancouver Canadians, a Class AAA Pacific Coast League affiliate of the Chicago White Sox, features brown-bordered posed color player photos on its fronts. The player's name appears in an upper corner; his team and position appear in a lower corner. The white back is framed by a black line and carries the player's name and position at the top, followed by biography and statistics.
COMPLETE SET (24) 5.00 1.50

1992 Vancouver Canadians SkyBox

This 26-card standard-size set of the 1992 Vancouver Canadians, a Class AAA Pacific Coast League affiliate of the Chicago White Sox, features white-bordered posed color player photos on its fronts. The player's name appears at the top; his team and position appear at the bottom. The white back carries the player's name at the top, followed by biography and statistics.
COMPLETE SET (26) 5.00 1.50

1992 Vero Beach Dodgers Classic/Best

This 30-card standard-size set of the 1992 Vero Beach Dodgers, a Class A Florida State League affiliate of the Los Angeles Dodgers, features white-bordered posed color player photos on its fronts. The player's name, team, and position appear at the bottom. The white back is framed by a thin red line and carries the player's name and position at the top, followed by biography, statistics and team logos.
COMPLETE SET (30) 5.00 1.50

1992 Vero Beach Dodgers Fleer/ProCards

This 32-card standard-size set of the 1992 Vero Beach Dodgers, a Class A Florida State League affiliate of the Los Angeles Dodgers, features brown-bordered posed color player photos on its fronts. The player's name appears in an upper corner; his team and position appear in a lower corner. The white back is framed by a black line and carries the player's name and position at the top, followed by biography and statistics.
COMPLETE SET (32) 5.00 1.50

1992 Visalia Oaks Classic/Best

This 30-card standard-size set of the 1992 Visalia Oaks, a Class A California League affiliate of the Minnesota Twins, features white-bordered posed color player photos on its fronts. The player's name, team, and position appear at the bottom. The white back is framed by a thin red line and carries the player's name and position at the top, followed by biography, statistics and team logos.
COMPLETE SET (30) 5.00 1.50

1992 Visalia Oaks Fleer/ProCards

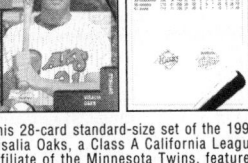

This 28-card standard-size set of the 1992 Visalia Oaks, a Class A California League affiliate of the Minnesota Twins, features brown-bordered posed color player photos on its fronts. The player's name appears in an upper corner; his team and position appear in a lower corner. The white back is framed by a black line and carries the player's name and position at the top, followed by biography and statistics.
COMPLETE SET (28) 5.00 1.50

1992 Waterloo Diamonds Classic/Best

This 30-card standard-size set of the 1992 Waterloo Diamonds, a Class A Midwest League affiliate of the San Diego Padres, features white-bordered posed color player photos on its fronts. The player's name, team, and position appear at the bottom. The white back is framed by a thin red line and carries the player's name and position at the top, followed by biography, statistics and team logos.
COMPLETE SET (30) 5.00 1.50

1992 Waterloo Diamonds Fleer/ProCards

This 27-card standard-size set of the 1992 Waterloo Diamonds, a Class A Midwest League affiliate of the San Diego Padres, features brown-bordered posed color player photos on its fronts. The player's name appears in an upper corner; his team and position appear in a lower corner. The white back is framed by a black line and carries the player's name and position at the top, followed by biography and statistics.
COMPLETE SET (27) 5.00 1.50

1992 Watertown Indians Classic/Best

This 30-card standard-size set of the 1992 Watertown Indians, a Class A New York-Penn League affiliate of the Cleveland Indians, features white-bordered posed color player photos on its fronts. The player's name, team, and position appear at the bottom. The white back is framed by a thin red line and carries the player's name and position at the top, followed by biography and statistics.
COMPLETE SET (30) 5.00 1.50

1992 Watertown Indians Fleer/ProCards

This 29-card standard-size set of the 1992 Watertown Indians, a Class A New York-Penn League affiliate of the Cleveland Indians, features brown-bordered posed color player photos on its fronts. The player's name appears in an upper corner; his team and position appear in a lower corner. The white back is framed by a black line and carries the player's name and position at the top, followed by biography and statistics.
COMPLETE SET (29) 5.00 1.50

1992 Welland Pirates Classic/Best

This 30-card standard-size set of the 1992 Welland Pirates, a Class A New York-Penn League affiliate of the Pittsburgh Pirates, features white-bordered posed color player photos on its fronts. The player's name, team, and position appear at the bottom. The white back is framed by a thin red line and carries the player's name and position at the top, followed by biography, statistics and team logos.
COMPLETE SET (30) 5.00 1.50

1992 Welland Pirates Fleer/ProCards

This 30-card standard-size set of the 1992 Welland Pirates, a Class A New York-Penn League affiliate of the Pittsburgh Pirates, features brown-bordered posed color player photos on its fronts. The player's name appears in an upper corner; his team and position appear in a lower corner. The white back is framed by a black line and carries the player's name and position at the top, followed by biography and statistics.
COMPLETE SET (30) 5.00 1.50

1992 West Palm Beach Expos Classic/Best

This 30-card standard-size set of the 1992 West Palm Beach Expos, a Class A Florida State League affiliate of the Montreal Expos, features white-bordered posed color player photos on its fronts. The player's name, team, and position appear at the bottom. The white back is framed by a thin red line and carries the player's name and position at the top, followed by biography, statistics and team logos. This issue includes a second year card of Rondell White.
COMPLETE SET (30) 8.00 2.40

1992 West Palm Beach Expos Fleer/ProCards

This 29-card standard-size set of the 1992 West Palm Beach Expos, a Class A Florida State League affiliate of the Montreal Expos, features brown-bordered posed color player photos on its fronts. The player's name appears in an upper corner; his team and position appear in a lower corner. The white back is framed by a black line and carries the player's name and position at the top, followed by biography and statistics. This issue includes a second year card of Rondell White.
COMPLETE SET (29) 8.00 2.40

1992 Wichita Wranglers Fleer/ProCards

This 21-card standard-size set of the 1992 Wichita Wrnaglers, a Class AA Texas League affiliate of the San Diego Padres, features brown-bordered posed color player photos on its fronts. The player's name appears in an upper corner; his team and position appear in a lower corner. The white back is framed by a black line and carries the player's name and position at the top, followed by biography and statistics.
COMPLETE SET (21) 5.00 1.50

1992 Wichita Wranglers SkyBox

COMPLETE SET (26) 5.00 1.50

1992 Winston-Salem Spirits Classic/Best

This 29-card standard-size set of the 1992 Winston-Salem Spirits, a Class A Carolina League affiliate of the Chicago Cubs, features white-bordered posed color player photos on its fronts. The player's name, team, and position appear at the bottom. The white back is framed by a thin red line and carries the player's name and position at the top, followed by biography, statistics and team logos.
COMPLETE SET (29) 5.00 1.50

1992 Winston-Salem Spirits Fleer/ProCards

This 28-card standard-size set of the 1992 Winston-Salem Spirits, a Class A Carolina League affiliate of the Chicago Cubs, features brown-bordered posed color player photos on its fronts. The player's name appears in an upper corner; his team and position appear in a lower corner. The white back is framed by a black line and carries the player's name and position at the top, followed by biography and statistics.
COMPLETE SET (28) 5.00 1.50

1992 Winter Haven Red Sox Classic/Best

This 30-card standard-size set of the 1992 Winter Haven Red Sox, a Class A Florida State League affiliate of the Boston Red Sox, features white-bordered posed color player photos on its fronts. The player's name, team, and position appear at the bottom. The white back is framed by a thin red line and carries the player's name and position at the top, followed by biography, statistics and team logos.
COMPLETE SET (30) 5.00 1.50

1992 Winter Haven Red Sox Fleer/ProCards

This 30-card standard-size set of the 1992 Winter Haven Red Sox, a Class A Florida State League affiliate of the Boston Red Sox, features brown-bordered posed color player photos on its fronts. The player's name appears in an upper corner; his team and position appear in a lower corner. The white back is framed by a black line and carries the player's name and position at the top, followed by biography and statistics.
COMPLETE SET (30) 5.00 1.50

1992 Yakima Bears Classic/Best

This 27-card standard-size set of the 1992 Yakima Bears, a Class A Northwest League affiliate of the Los Angeles Dodgers, features white-bordered posed color player photos on its fronts. The player's name, team, and position appear at the bottom. The white back is framed by a thin red line and carries the player's name and position at the top, followed by biography, statistics and team logos.
COMPLETE SET (27) 5.00 1.50

1992 Yakima Bears Fleer/ProCards

This 32-card standard-size set of the 1992 Yakima Bears, a Class A Northwest League affiliate of the Los Angeles Dodgers, features brown-bordered posed color player photos on its fronts. The player's name appears in an upper corner; his team and position appear in a lower corner. The white back is framed by a black line and carries the player's name and position at the top, followed by biography and statistics.
COMPLETE SET (32) 5.00 1.50

1993 Albany Polecats Classic/Best

This 30-card standard-size set of the 1993 Albany Polecats, a Class A South Atlantic League affiliate of the Baltimore Orioles, features white-bordered posed color player shots on its fronts. A team-color-coded stripe below the photo carries the player's name; another above, his position and team name. On a ghosted team-logo, the white back carries the player's name at the top, followed by biography and statistics..
COMPLETE SET (30) 5.00 1.50

1993 Albany Polecats Fleer/ProCards

This 28-card standard-size set of the 1993 Albany Polecats, a Class A South Atlantic League affiliate of the Baltimore Orioles, features white-bordered posed color player photos on its fronts. The player's name, team, and position appear near the bottom. The white horizontal back is framed by a blue line and carries the player's name at the top, followed by biography and statistics. A drawing of a ballplayer in action appears on the left.
COMPLETE SET (28) 5.00 1.50

1993 Albany Yankees Fleer/ProCards

This 29-card standard-size set of the 1993 Albany Yankees, a Class AA Eastern League affiliate of the New York Yankees, features white-bordered posed color player photos on its fronts. The player's name, team, and position appear near the bottom. The white horizontal back is framed by a blue line and carries the player's name at the top, followed by biography and statistics. A drawing of a ballplayer in action appears on the left.
COMPLETE SET (29) 5.00 1.50

1993 Albuquerque Dukes Fleer/ProCards

This 31-card standard-size set of the 1993 Albuquerque Dukes, a Class AAA Pacific Coast League affiliate of the Los Angeles Dodgers, features white-bordered posed color player photos on its fronts. The player's name, team, and position appear near the bottom. The white horizontal back is framed by a blue line and carries the player's name at the top, followed by biography and statistics. A drawing of a ballplayer in action appears on the left.
COMPLETE SET (31) 8.00 2.40

1993 Appleton Foxes Classic/Best

This 30-card standard-size set of the 1993 Appleton Foxes, a Class A Midwest League affiliate of the Seattle Mariners, features white-bordered posed color player shots on its fronts. A team-color-coded stripe below the photo carries the player's name; another above, his position and team name. On a ghosted team-logo, the white back carries the player's name at the top, followed by biography and statistics.
COMPLETE SET (30) 5.00 1.50

1993 Appleton Foxes Fleer/ProCards

This 29-card standard-size set of the 1993 Appleton Foxes, a Class A Midwest League affiliate of the Seattle Mariners, features white-bordered posed color player photos on its fronts. The player's name, team, and position appear near the bottom. The white horizontal back is framed by a blue line and carries the player's name at the top, followed by biography and statistics. A drawing of a ballplayer in action appears on the left.
COMPLETE SET (29) 5.00 1.50

1993 Arkansas Travelers Fleer/ProCards

This 27-card standard-size set of the 1993 Arkansas Travelers, a Class AA Texas League affiliate of the St. Louis Cardinals, features white-bordered posed color player photos on its fronts. The player's name, team, and position appear near the bottom. The white horizontal back is framed by a blue line and carries the player's name at the top, followed by biography and statistics. A drawing of a ballplayer in action appears on the left.
COMPLETE SET (27) 5.00 1.50

1993 Asheville Tourists Classic/Best

This 30-card standard-size set of the 1993 Asheville Tourists, a Class A South Atlantic League affiliate of the Houston Astros, features white-bordered posed color player shots on its fronts. A team-color-coded stripe below the photo carries the player's name; another above, his position and team name. On a ghosted team-logo, the white back carries the player's name at the top, followed by biography and statistics. This issue includes the minor league card debut of Richard Hidalgo.
COMPLETE SET (30) 15.00 7.50

1993 Asheville Tourists Fleer/ProCards

This 30-card standard-size set of the 1993 Asheville Tourists, a Class A South Atlantic League affiliate of the Houston Astros, features white-bordered posed color player photos on its fronts. The player's name, team, and position appear near the bottom. The white horizontal back is framed by a blue line and carries the player's name at the top, followed by biography and statistics. A drawing of a ballplayer in action appears on the left. This set includes Richard Hidalgo's first team set card.
COMPLETE SET (30) 12.00 6.00

1993 Auburn Astros Classic/Best

This 30-card standard-size set of the 1993 Auburn Astros, a Class A New York-Penn League affiliate of the Houston Astros, features white-bordered posed color player shots on its fronts. A team-color-coded stripe below the photo carries the player's name; another above, his position and team name. On a ghosted team-logo, the white back carries the player's name at the top, followed by biography and statistics. This issue includes the minor league card debut of Billy Wagner.
COMPLETE SET (30) 10.00 3.00

1993 Auburn Astros Fleer/ProCards

This 30-card standard-size set of the 1993 Auburn Astros, a Class A New York-Penn League affiliate of the Houston Astros, features white-bordered posed color player photos on its fronts. The player's name, team, and position appear near the bottom. The white horizontal back is framed by a blue line and carries the player's name at the top, followed by biography and statistics. A drawing of a ballplayer in action appears on the left. This set includes Billy Wagner's first team set card.
COMPLETE SET (30) 8.00 2.40

1993 Augusta Pirates Classic/Best

This 30-card standard-size set of the 1993 Augusta Pirates, a Class A South Atlantic League affiliate of the Pittsburgh Pirates, features white-bordered posed color player shots on its fronts. A team-color-coded stripe below the photo carries the player's name; another above, his position and team name. On a ghosted team-logo, the white back carries the player's name at the top, followed by biography and statistics. This issue includes the minor league card debut of Jason Kendall.
COMPLETE SET (30) 15.00 4.50

1993 Augusta Pirates Fleer/ProCards

This 27-card standard-size set of the 1993 Augusta Pirates, a Class A South Atlantic League affiliate of the Pittsburgh Pirates, features white-bordered posed color player photos on its fronts. The player's name, team, and position appear near the bottom. The white horizontal back is framed by a blue line and carries the player's name at the top, followed by biography and statistics. A drawing of a ballplayer in action appears on the left. This set includes the first minor league team set card of Jason Kendall.
COMPLETE SET (27) 12.00 3.60

1993 Bakersfield Dodgers Cal League Cards

This issue includes the minor league card debut of Karim Garcia.
COMPLETE SET (32) 5.00 1.50

1993 Batavia Clippers Classic/Best

This 30-card standard-size set of the 1993 Batavia Clippers, a Class A New York-Penn League affiliate of the Philadelphia Phillies, features white-bordered posed color player shots on its fronts. A team-color-coded stripe below the photo carries the player's name; another above, his position and team name. On a ghosted team-logo, the white back carries the player's name at the top, followed by biography and statistics.
COMPLETE SET (30) 5.00 1.50

1993 Batavia Clippers Fleer/ProCards

This 30-card standard-size set of the 1993 Batavia Clippers, a Class A New York-Penn League affiliate of the Philadelphia Phillies, features white-bordered posed color player photos on its fronts. The player's name, team, and position appear near the bottom. The white horizontal back is framed by a blue line and carries the player's name at the top, followed by biography and statistics. A drawing of a ballplayer in action appears on the left.
COMPLETE SET (30) 5.00 1.50

1993 Bellingham Mariners Classic/Best

This 30-card standard-size set of the 1993 Bellingham Mariners, a Class A Northwest League affiliate of the Seattle Mariners, features white-bordered posed color player shots on its fronts. A team-color-coded stripe below the photo carries the player's name; another above, his position and team name. On a ghosted team-logo, the white back carries the player's name at the top, followed by biography and statistics.
COMPLETE SET (30) 5.00 1.50

1993 Bellingham Mariners Fleer/ProCards

This 30-card standard-size set of the 1993 Bellingham Mariners, a Class A Northwest League affiliate of the Seattle Mariners, features white-bordered posed color player photos on its fronts. The player's name, team, and position appear near the bottom. The white horizontal back is framed by a blue line and carries the player's name at the top, followed by biography and statistics. A drawing of a ballplayer in action appears on the left.
COMPLETE SET (30) 5.00 1.50

1993 Beloit Brewers Classic/Best

This 30-card standard-size set of the 1993 Beloit Brewers, a Class A Midwest League affiliate of the Milwaukee Brewers, features white-bordered posed color player shots on its fronts. A team-color-coded stripe below the photo carries the player's name; another above, his position and team name. On a ghosted team-logo, the white back carries the player's name at the top, followed by biography and statistics.
COMPLETE SET (30) 5.00 1.50

1993 Beloit Brewers Fleer/ProCards

This 30-card standard-size set of the 1993 Beloit Brewers, a Class A Midwest League affiliate of the Milwaukee Brewers, features white-bordered posed color player photos on its fronts. The player's name, team, and position appear near the bottom. The white horizontal back is framed by a blue line and carries the player's name at the top, followed by biography and statistics. A drawing of a ballplayer in action appears on the left.
COMPLETE SET (30) 5.00 1.50

1993 Bend Rockies Classic/Best

This 30-card standard-size set of the 1993 Bend Rockies, a Class A Northwest League affiliate of the Colorado Rockies, features white-bordered posed color player shots on its fronts. A team-color-coded stripe below the photo carries the player's name; another above, his position and team name. On a ghosted team-logo, the white back carries the player's name at the top, followed by biography and statistics. This issue includes the minor league card debut of Neifi Perez.
COMPLETE SET (30) 10.00 3.00

1993 Bend Rockies Fleer/ProCards

This 30-card standard-size set of the 1993 Bend Rockies, a Class A Northwest League affiliate of the Colorado Rockies, features white-bordered posed color player photos on its fronts. The player's name, team, and position appear near the bottom. The white horizontal back is framed by a blue line and carries the player's name at the top, followed by biography and statistics. A drawing of a ballplayer in action appears on the left. This set includes Neifi Perez first team set card.
COMPLETE SET (30) 8.00 2.40

1993 Billings Mustangs Fleer/ProCards

This 30-card standard-size set of the 1993 Billings Mustangs, a Rookie Class Pioneer League affiliate of the Cincinnati Reds, features white-bordered posed color player photos on its fronts. The player's name, team, and position appear near the bottom. The white horizontal back is framed by a blue line and carries the player's name at the top, followed by biography and statistics. A drawing of a ballplayer in action appears on the left.
COMPLETE SET (30) 5.00 1.50

1993 Billings Mustangs Sports Pro

COMPLETE SET (28) 8.00 2.40

1993 Binghamton Mets Fleer/ProCards

This 26-card standard-size set of the 1993 Binghamton Mets, a Class AA Eastern League affiliate of the New York Mets, features white-bordered posed color player photos on its fronts. The player's name, team, and position appear near the bottom. The white horizontal back is framed by a blue line and carries the player's name at the top, followed by biography and statistics. A drawing of a ballplayer in action appears on the left.
COMPLETE SET (26) 5.00 1.50

1993 Birmingham Barons Fleer/ProCards

This 27-card standard-size set of the 1993 Birmingham Barons, a Class AA Southern League affiliate of the Chicago White Sox, features white-bordered posed color player photos on its fronts. The player's name, team, and position appear near the bottom. The white horizontal back is framed by a blue line and carries the player's name at the top, followed by biography and statistics. A drawing of a ballplayer in action appears on the left. This set includes a second year team set card of Ray Durham.
COMPLETE SET (27) 5.00 1.50

1993 Bluefield Orioles Classic/Best

This 30-card standard-size set of the 1993 Bluefield Orioles, a Rookie Class Appalachian League affiliate of the Baltimore Orioles, features white-bordered posed color player shots on its fronts. A team-color-coded stripe below the photo carries the player's name; another above, his position and team name. On a ghosted team-logo, the white back carries the player's name at the top, followed by biography and statistics.
COMPLETE SET (30) 5.00 1.50

1993 Bluefield Orioles Fleer/ProCards

This 27-card standard-size set of the 1993 Bluefield Orioles, a Rookie Class Appalachian League affiliate of the Baltimore Orioles, features white-bordered posed color player photos on its fronts. The player's name, team, and position appear near the bottom. The white horizontal back is framed by a blue line and carries the player's name at the top, followed by biography and statistics. A drawing of a ballplayer in action appears on the left.
COMPLETE SET (27) 5.00 1.50

1993 Boise Hawks Classic/Best

This 30-card standard-size set of the 1993 Boise Hawks, a Class A Northwest League affiliate of the California Angels, features white-bordered posed color player shots on its fronts. A team-color-coded stripe below the photo carries the player's name; another above, his position and team name. On a ghosted team-logo, the white back carries the player's name at the top, followed by biography and statistics.
COMPLETE SET (30) 5.00 1.50

1993 Boise Hawks Fleer/ProCards

This 31-card standard-size set of the 1993 Boise Hawks, a Class A Northwest League affiliate of the California Angels, features white-bordered posed color player photos on its fronts. The player's name, team, and position appear near the bottom. The white horizontal back is framed by a blue line and carries the player's name at the top, followed by biography and statistics. A drawing of a ballplayer in action appears on the left.
COMPLETE SET (31) 5.00 1.50

1993 Bowie Baysox Fleer/ProCards

This 24-card standard-size set of the 1993 Bowie Baysox, a Class AA Eastern League affiliate of the Baltimore Orioles, features white-bordered posed color player photos on its fronts. The player's name, team, and position appear near the bottom. The white horizontal back is framed by a blue line and carries the player's name at the top, followed by biography and statistics. A drawing of a ballplayer in action appears on the left. This set includes Jeffrey Hammonds' first team set card.
COMPLETE SET (24) 8.00 2.40

1993 Bristol Tigers Classic/Best

This 30-card standard-size set of the 1993 Bristol Tigers, a Rookie Class Appalachian League affiliate of the Detroit Tigers, features white-bordered posed color player shots on its fronts. A team-color-coded stripe below the photo carries the player's name; another above, his position and team name. On a ghosted team-logo, the white back carries the player's name at the top, followed by biography and statistics.
COMPLETE SET (30) 5.00 1.50

1993 Bristol Tigers Fleer/ProCards

This 30-card standard-size set of the 1993 Bristol Tigers, a Rookie Class Appalachian League affiliate of the Detroit Tigers, features white-bordered posed color player photos on its fronts. The player's name, team, and position appear near the bottom. The white horizontal back is framed by a blue line and carries the player's name at the top, followed by biography and statistics. A drawing of a ballplayer in action appears on the left.
COMPLETE SET (30) 5.00 1.50

1993 Buffalo Bisons Fleer/ProCards

This 27-card standard-size set of the 1993 Buffalo Bisons, a Class AAA American Association affiliate of the Pittsburgh Pirates, features white-bordered posed color player photos on its fronts. The player's name, team, and position appear near the bottom. The white horizontal back is framed by a blue line and carries the player's name at the top, followed by biography and statistics. A drawing of a ballplayer in action appears on the left.
COMPLETE SET (27) 5.00 1.50

1993 Burlington Bees Classic/Best

This 30-card standard-size set of the 1993 Burlington Bees, a Class A Midwest League affiliate of the Montreal Expos, features white-bordered posed color player shots on its fronts. A team-color-coded stripe below the photo carries the player's name; another above, his position and team name. The white back carries the player's name at the top, followed by biography and statistics. This set includes Jose Vidro's first team set card.
COMPLETE SET (30) 15.00 4.50

1993 Burlington Bees Fleer/ProCards

This 28-card standard-size set of the 1993 Burlington Bees, a Class A Midwest League affiliate of the Montreal Expos, features white-bordered posed color player photos on its fronts. The player's name, team, and position appear near the bottom. The white horizontal back is framed by a blue line and carries the player's name at the top, followed by biography and statistics. A drawing of a ballplayer in action appears on the left. This issue includes the minor league card debut of Jose Vidro.
COMPLETE SET (28) 10.00 3.00

1993 Burlington Indians Classic/Best

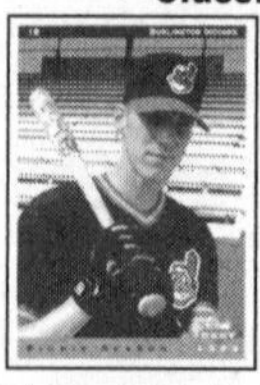

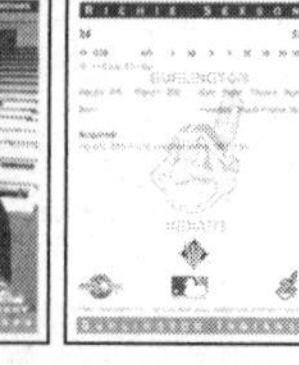

This 30-card standard-size set of the 1993 Burlington Indians, a Rookie Class Appalachian League affiliate of the Cleveland Indians, features white-bordered posed color player shots on its fronts. A team-color-coded stripe below the photo carries the player's name; another above, his position and team name. On a ghosted team-logo, the white back carries the player's name at the top, followed by biography and statistics. This issue includes the minor league card debut of Richie Sexson.
COMPLETE SET (30) 30.00 9.00

1993 Burlington Indians Fleer/ProCards

This 31-card standard-size set of the 1993 Burlington Indians, a Rookie Class Appalachian League affiliate of the Cleveland Indians, features white-bordered posed color player photos on its fronts. The player's name, team, and position appear near the bottom. The white horizontal back is framed by a blue line and carries the player's name at the top, followed by biography and statistics. A drawing of a ballplayer in action appears on the left. This set includes the first team set cards of Richie Sexson and Alex Ramirez.
COMPLETE SET (31) 20.00 6.00

1993 Butte Copper Kings Sports Pro

COMPLETE SET (24) 5.00 1.50

1993 Calgary Cannons Fleer/ProCards

This 29-card standard-size set of the 1993 Calgary Cannons, a Class AAA Pacific Coast League affiliate of the Seattle Mariners, features white-bordered posed color player photos on its fronts. The player's name, team, and position appear near the bottom. The white horizontal back is framed by a blue line and carries the player's name at the top, followed by biography and statistics. A drawing of a ballplayer in action appears on the left.
COMPLETE SET (29) 5.00 1.50

1993 Canton-Akron Indians Fleer/ProCards

This 26-card standard-size set of the 1993 Canton-Akron Indians, a Class AA Eastern League affiliate of the Cleveland Indians, features white-bordered posed color player photos on its fronts. The player's name, team, and position appear near the bottom. The white horizontal back is framed by a blue line and carries the player's name at the top, followed by biography and statistics. A drawing of a ballplayer in action appears on the left. This set includes a third year team set card of Manny Ramirez.
COMPLETE SET (26) 20.00 6.00

1993 Capital City Bombers Classic/Best

This 30-card standard-size set of the 1993 Capital City Bombers, a Class A South Atlantic League affiliate of the New York Mets, features white-bordered posed color player shots on its fronts. A team-color-coded stripe below the photo carries the player's name; another above, his position and team name. On a ghosted team-logo, the white back carries the player's name at the top, followed by biography and statistics.
COMPLETE SET (30) 5.00 1.50

1993 Capital City Bombers Fleer/ProCards

This 26-card standard-size set of the 1993 Capital City Bombers, a Class A South Atlantic League affiliate of the New York Mets, features white-bordered posed color player photos on its fronts. The player's name, team, and position appear near the bottom. The white horizontal back is framed by a blue line and carries the player's name at the top, followed by biography and statistics. A drawing of a ballplayer in action appears on the left.
COMPLETE SET (26) 5.00 1.50

1993 Carolina League All-Stars Fleer/ProCards

An early card of Jorge Posada is in this set.
COMPLETE SET (52) 15.00 4.50

1993 Carolina Mudcats Fleer/ProCards

This 30-card standard-size set of the 1993 Carolina Mudcats, a Class AA Southern League affiliate of the Pittsburgh Pirates, features white-bordered posed color player photos on its fronts. The player's name, team, and position appear near the bottom. The white horizontal back is framed by a blue line and carries the player's name at the top, followed by biography and statistics. A drawing of a ballplayer in action appears on the left.
COMPLETE SET (30) 5.00 1.50

1993 Carolina Mudcats Team Issue

COMPLETE SET (24) 5.00 1.50

1993 Cedar Rapids Kernels Classic/Best

This 30-card standard-size set of the 1993 Cedar Rapids Kernels, a Class A Midwest League affiliate of the California Angels, features white-bordered posed color player shots on its fronts. A team-color-coded stripe below the photo carries the player's name; another above, his position and team name. On a ghosted team-logo, the white back carries the player's name at the top, followed by biography and statistics.
COMPLETE SET (30) 5.00 1.50

1993 Cedar Rapids Kernels Fleer/ProCards

This 28-card standard-size set of the 1993 Cedar Rapids Kernels, a Class A Midwest League affiliate of the California Angels, features white-bordered posed color player photos on its fronts. The player's name, team, and position appear near the bottom. The white horizontal back is framed by a blue line and carries the player's name at the top, followed by biography and statistics. A drawing of a ballplayer in action appears on the left.
COMPLETE SET (28)................. 5.00 1.50

1993 Central Valley Rockies Classic/Best

This 30-card standard-size set of the 1993 Central Valley Rockies, a Class A California League affiliate of the Colorado Rockies, features white-bordered posed color player shots on its fronts. A team-color-coded stripe below the photo carries the player's name; another above, his position and team name. On a ghosted team-logo, the white back carries the player's name at the top, followed by biography and statistics.
COMPLETE SET (30)................. 5.00 1.50

1993 Central Valley Rockies Fleer/ProCards

This 29-card standard-size set of the 1993 Central Valley Rockies, a Class A California League affiliate of the Colorado Rockies, features white-bordered posed color player photos on its fronts. The player's name, team, and position appear near the bottom. The white horizontal back is framed by a blue line and carries the player's name at the top, followed by biography and statistics. A drawing of a ballplayer in action appears on the left.
COMPLETE SET (29)................. 5.00 1.50

1993 Charleston Rainbows Classic/Best

This 30-card standard-size set of the 1993 Charleston Rainbows, a Class A South Atlantic League affiliate of the Texas Rangers, features white-bordered posed color player shots on its fronts. A team-color-coded stripe below the photo carries the player's name; another above, his position and team name. On a ghosted team-logo, the white back carries the player's name at the top, followed by biography and statistics.
COMPLETE SET (30)................. 5.00 1.50

1993 Charleston Rainbows Fleer/ProCards

This 31-card standard-size set of the 1993 Charleston Rainbows, a Class A South Atlantic League affiliate of the Texas Rangers, features white-bordered posed color player photos on its fronts. The player's name, team, and position appear near the bottom. The white horizontal back is framed by a blue line and carries the player's name at the top, followed by biography and statistics. A drawing of a ballplayer in action appears on the left.
COMPLETE SET (31)................. 5.00 1.50

1993 Charlotte Knights Fleer/ProCards

This 28-card standard-size set of the 1993 Charlotte Knights, a Class AAA International League affiliate of the Cleveland Indians, features white-bordered posed color player photos on its fronts. The player's name, team, and position appear near the bottom. The white horizontal back is framed by a blue line and carries the player's name at the top, followed by biography and statistics. A drawing of a ballplayer in action appears on the left. This set includes Jim Thome's third team set card.
COMPLETE SET (28)................. 8.00 2.40

1993 Charlotte Rangers Classic/Best

This 30-card standard-size set of the 1993 Charlotte Rangers, a Class A Florida State League affiliate of the Texas Rangers, features white-bordered posed color player shots on its fronts. A team-color-coded stripe below the photo carries the player's name; another above, his position and team name. On a ghosted team-logo, the white back carries the player's name at the top, followed by biography and statistics.
COMPLETE SET (30)................ 10.00 3.00

1993 Charlotte Rangers Fleer/ProCards

This 28-card standard-size set of the 1993 Charlotte Rangers, a Class A Florida State League affiliate of the Texas Rangers, features white-bordered posed color player photos on its fronts. The player's name, team, and position appear near the bottom. The white horizontal back is framed by a blue line and carries the player's name at the top, followed by biography and statistics. A drawing of a ballplayer in action appears on the left.
COMPLETE SET (28)................ 10.00 3.00

1993 Chattanooga Lookouts Fleer/ProCards

This 26-card standard-size set of the 1993 Chattanooga Lookouts, a Class AA Southern League affiliate of the Cincinnati Reds, features white-bordered posed color player photos on its fronts. The player's name, team, and position appear near the bottom. The white horizontal back is framed by a blue line and carries the player's name at the top, followed by biography and statistics. A drawing of a ballplayer in action appears on the left.
COMPLETE SET (26)................. 5.00 1.50

1993 Clearwater Phillies Classic/Best

This 30-card standard-size set of the 1993 Clearwater Phillies, a Class A Florida State League affiliate of the Philadelphia Phillies, features white-bordered posed color player shots on its fronts. A team-color-coded stripe below the photo carries the player's name; another above, his position and team name. On a ghosted team-logo, the white back carries the player's name at the top, followed by biography and statistics.
COMPLETE SET (30)................. 5.00 1.50

1993 Clearwater Phillies Fleer/ProCards

This 27-card standard-size set of the 1993 Clearwater Phillies, a Class A Florida State League affiliate of the Philadelphia Phillies, features white-bordered posed color player photos on its fronts. The player's name, team, and position appear near the bottom. The white horizontal back is framed by a blue line and carries the player's name at the top, followed by biography and statistics. A drawing of a ballplayer in action appears on the left.
COMPLETE SET (27)................. 5.00 1.50

1993 Clinton Giants Classic/Best

This 30-card standard-size set of the 1993 Clinton Giants, a Class A Midwest League affiliate of the San Francisco Giants, features white-bordered posed color player shots on its fronts. A team-color-coded stripe below the photo carries the player's name; another above, his position and team name. On a ghosted team-logo, the white back carries the player's name at the top, followed by biography and statistics.
COMPLETE SET (30)................. 5.00 1.50

1993 Clinton Giants Fleer/ProCards

This 28-card standard-size set of the 1993 Clinton Giants, a Class A Midwest League affiliate of the San Francisco Giants, features white-bordered posed color player photos on its fronts. The player's name, team, and position appear near the bottom. The white horizontal back is framed by a blue line and carries the player's name at the top, followed by biography and statistics. A drawing of a ballplayer in action appears on the left.
COMPLETE SET (28)................. 5.00 1.50

1993 Colorado Springs Sky Sox Fleer/ProCards

This 25-card standard-size set of the 1993 Colorado Springs Sky Sox, a Class AAA Pacific Coast League affiliate of the Colorado Rockies, features white-bordered posed color player photos on its fronts. The player's name, team, and position appear near the bottom. The white horizontal back is framed by a blue line and carries the player's name at the top, followed by biography and statistics. A drawing of a ballplayer in action appears on the left.
COMPLETE SET (25)................. 5.00 1.50

1993 Columbus Clippers Fleer/ProCards

This 27-card standard-size set of the 1993 Columbus Clippers, a Class AAA International League affiliate of the New York Yankees, features white-bordered posed color player photos on its fronts. The player's name, team, and position appear near the bottom. The white horizontal back is framed by a blue line and carries the player's name at the top, followed by biography and statistics. A drawing of a ballplayer in action appears on the left.
COMPLETE SET (27)................. 5.00 1.50

1993 Columbus Clippers Police

COMPLETE SET (25)................. 5.00 1.50

1993 Columbus Clippers Team Issue

This 26 card standard-size set features members of the 1993 Columbus Clippers. The fronts feature player portraits surrounded the white borders. The players name is above the photo and the 1993 Columbus Clippers name is below the picture. The horizontal backs have the players vital stats as well as statistics. Since the cards are unnumbered, we have sequenced them in alphabetical order.
COMPLETE SET (26)................ 20.00 6.00

1993 Columbus RedStixx Classic/Best

This 30-card standard-size set of the 1993 Columbus RedStixx, a Class A South Atlantic League affiliate of the Cleveland Indians, features white-bordered posed color player shots on its fronts. A team-color-coded stripe below the photo carries the player's name; another above, his position and team name. On a ghosted team-logo, the white back carries the player's name at the top, followed by biography and statistics.
COMPLETE SET (30)................. 5.00 1.50

1993 Columbus RedStixx Fleer/ProCards

This 30-card standard-size set of the 1993 Columbus RedStixx, a Class A South Atlantic League affiliate of the Cleveland Indians, features white-bordered posed color player photos on its fronts. The player's name, team, and position appear near the bottom. The white horizontal back is framed by a blue line and carries the player's name at the top, followed by biography and statistics. A drawing of a ballplayer in action appears on the left.
COMPLETE SET (30)................. 5.00 1.50

1993 Danville Braves Classic/Best

This 30-card standard-size set of the 1993 Danville Braves, a Rookie Class Appalachian League affiliate of the Atlanta Braves, features white-bordered posed color player shots on its fronts. A team-color-coded stripe below the photo carries the player's name; another above, his position and team name. On a ghosted team-logo, the white back carries the player's name at the top, followed by biography and statistics.
COMPLETE SET (30)................. 5.00 1.50

1993 Danville Braves Fleer/ProCards

This 31-card standard-size set of the 1993 Danville Braves, a Rookie Class Appalachian League affiliate of the Atlanta Braves, features white-bordered posed color player photos on its fronts. The player's name, team, and position appear near the bottom. The white horizontal back is framed by a blue line and carries the player's name at the top, followed by biography and statistics. A drawing of a ballplayer in action appears on the left.
COMPLETE SET (31)................. 5.00 1.50

1993 David Lipscomb Bisons

COMPLETE SET (25)................ 10.00 3.00

1993 Daytona Cubs Classic/Best

This 30-card standard-size set of the 1993 Daytona Cubs, a Class A Florida State League affiliate of the Chicago Cubs, features white-bordered posed color player shots on its fronts. A team-color-coded stripe below the photo carries the player's name; another above, his position and team name. On a ghosted team-logo, the white back carries the player's name at the top, followed by biography and statistics.
COMPLETE SET (30)................. 5.00 1.50

1993 Daytona Cubs Fleer/ProCards

This 26-card standard-size set of the 1993 Daytona Cubs, a Class A Florida State League affiliate of the Chicago Cubs, features white-bordered posed color player photos on its fronts. The player's name, team, and position appear near the bottom. The white horizontal back is framed by a blue line and carries the player's name at the top, followed by biography and statistics. A drawing of a ballplayer in action appears on the left.
COMPLETE SET (26)................. 5.00 1.50

1993 Dunedin Blue Jays Classic/Best

This 30-card standard-size set of the 1993 Dunedin Blue Jays, a Class A Florida State League affiliate of the Toronto Blue Jays, features white-bordered posed color player shots on its fronts. A team-color-coded stripe below the photo carries the player's name; another above, his position and team name. The white back carries the player's name at the top, followed by biography and statistics. An early card of Heisman trophy winner Chris Weinke is in this set.
COMPLETE SET (30)................. 5.00 1.50

1993 Dunedin Blue Jays Family Fun Night

An early card of Heisman Trophy winner Chris Weinke is in this set.
COMPLETE SET (30)................ 20.00 6.00

1993 Dunedin Blue Jays Fleer/ProCards

This 27-card standard-size set of the 1993 Dunedin Blue Jays, a Class A Florida State League affiliate of the Toronto Blue Jays, features white-bordered posed color player photos on its fronts. The player's name, team, and position appear near the bottom. The white horizontal back is framed by a blue line and carries the player's name at the top, followed by biography and statistics. A drawing of a ballplayer in action appears on the left. An early card of Heisman Trophy winner Chris Weinke is in this set.
COMPLETE SET (27)................. 5.00 1.50

1993 Durham Bulls Classic/Best

This 30-card standard-size set of the 1993 Durham Bulls, a Class A Carolina League affiliate of the Atlanta Braves, features white-bordered posed color player shots on its fronts. A team-color-coded stripe below the photo carries the player's name; another above, his position and team name. On a ghosted team-logo, the white back carries the player's name at the top, followed by biography and statistics.
COMPLETE SET (30)................. 5.00 1.50

1993 Durham Bulls Fleer/ProCards

This 31-card standard-size set of the 1993 Durham Bulls, a Class A Carolina League affiliate of the Atlanta Braves, features white-bordered posed color player photos on its fronts. The player's name, team, and position appear near the bottom. The white horizontal back is framed by a blue line and carries the player's name at the top, followed by biography and statistics. A drawing of a ballplayer in action appears on the left.
COMPLETE SET (310................. 5.00 1.50

1993 Durham Bulls Team Issue

COMPLETE SET (31)................. 5.00 1.50

1993 Edmonton Trappers Fleer/ProCards

This 27-card standard-size set of the 1993 Edmonton Trappers, a Class AAA Pacific Coast League affiliate of the Florida Marlins, features white-bordered posed color player photos on its fronts. The player's name, team, and position appear near the bottom. The white horizontal back is framed by a blue line and carries the player's name at the top, followed by biography and statistics. A drawing of a ballplayer in action appears on the left.
COMPLETE SET (27)................. 5.00 1.50

1993 El Paso Diablos Fleer/ProCards

This 30-card standard-size set of the 1993 El Paso Brewers, a Class AA Texas Laegue League affiliate of the Milwaukee Brewers, features white-bordered posed color player photos on its fronts. The player's name, team, and position appear near the bottom. The white horizontal back is framed by a blue line and carries the player's name at the top, followed by biography and statistics. A drawing of a ballplayer in action appears on the left.
COMPLETE SET (30)................. 5.00 1.50

1993 Elizabethton Twins Classic/Best

This 30-card standard-size set of the 1993 Elizabethton Twins, a Rookie Class Appalachian League affiliate of the Minnesota Twins, features white-bordered posed color player shots on its fronts. A team-color-coded stripe below the photo carries the player's name; another above, his position and team name. On a ghosted team-logo, the white back carries the player's name at the top, followed by biography and statistics.
COMPLETE SET (30)................. 5.00 1.50

1993 Elizabethton Twins Fleer/ProCards

This 25-card standard-size set of the 1993 Elizabethton Twins, a Rookie Class Appalachian League affiliate of the Minnesota Twins, features white-bordered posed color player photos on its fronts. The player's name, team, and position appear near the bottom. The white horizontal back is framed by a blue line and carries the player's name at the top, followed by biography and statistics. A drawing of a ballplayer in action appears on the left.
COMPLETE SET (25)................. 5.00 1.50

1993 Elmira Pioneers Classic/Best

This 30-card standard-size set of the 1993 Elmira Pioneers, a Class A New York-Penn League affiliate of the Florida Marlins, features white-bordered posed color player shots on its fronts. A team-color-coded stripe below the photo carries the player's name; another above, his position and team name. On a ghosted team-logo, the white back carries the player's name at the top, followed by biography and statistics. Erick Strickland, who went on to become an NBA player, is also in this set.
COMPLETE SET (30)................. 6.00 1.80

1993 Elmira Pioneers Fleer/ProCards

This 29-card standard-size set of the 1993 Elmira Pioneers, a Class A New York-Penn League affiliate of the Florida Marlins, features white-bordered posed color player photos on its fronts. The player's name, team, and position appear near the bottom. The white horizontal back is framed by a blue line and carries the player's name at the top, followed by biography and statistics. A drawing of a ballplayer in action appears on the left. This set includes the first team set cards of Andy Larkin and Billy McMillon. Erick Strickland, who went on to become an NBA player, is also in this set.
COMPLETE SET (29)................. 5.00 1.50

1993 Erie Sailors Classic/Best

This 30-card standard-size set of the 1993 Erie Sailors, a Class A New York-Penn League affiliate of the Texas Rangers, features white-bordered posed color player shots on its fronts. A team-color-coded stripe below the photo carries the player's name; another above, his position and team name. On a ghosted team-logo, the white back carries the player's name at the top, followed by biography and statistics.
COMPLETE SET (30)................. 5.00 1.50

1993 Erie Sailors Fleer/ProCards

This 30-card standard-size set of the 1993 Erie Sailors, a Class A New York-Penn League affiliate of the Texas Rangers, features white-bordered posed color player photos on its fronts. The player's name, team, and position appear near the bottom. The white horizontal back is framed by a blue line and carries the player's name at the top, followed by biography and statistics. A drawing of a ballplayer in action appears on the left.
COMPLETE SET (30)................. 5.00 1.50

1993 Eugene Emeralds Classic/Best

This 30-card standard-size set of the 1993 Eugene Emeralds, a Class A Northwest League affiliate of the Kansas City Royals, features white-bordered posed color player shots on its fronts. A team-color-coded stripe below the photo carries the player's name; another above, his position and team name. On a ghosted team-logo, the white back carries the player's name at the top, followed by biography and statistics. An early card of Mike Sweeney is in this set.
COMPLETE SET (30)................ 15.00 4.50

1993 Eugene Emeralds Fleer/ProCards

This 29-card standard-size set of the 1993 Eugene Emeralds, a Class A Northwest League affiliate of the Kansas City Royals, features white-bordered posed color player photos on its fronts. The player's name, team, and position appear near the bottom. The white horizontal back is framed by a blue line and carries the player's name at the top, followed by biography and statistics. A drawing of a ballplayer in action appears on the left. An early card of Mike Sweeney is in this set.
COMPLETE SET (29)................ 10.00 3.00

1993 Everett Giants Classic/Best

This 30-card standard-size set of the 1993 Everett Giants, a Class A Northwest League affiliate of the San Francisco Giants, features white-bordered posed color player shots on its fronts. A team-color-coded stripe below the photo carries the player's name; another above, his position and team name. On a ghosted team-logo, the white back carries the player's name at the top, followed by biography and statistics.
COMPLETE SET (30)................. 5.00 1.50

1993 Everett Giants Fleer/ProCards

This 31-card standard-size set of the 1993 Everett Giants, a Class A Northwest League affiliate of the San Francisco Giants, features white-bordered posed color player photos on its fronts. The player's name, team, and position appear near the bottom. The white horizontal back is framed by a blue line and carries the player's name at the top, followed by biography and statistics. A drawing of a ballplayer in action appears on the left.
COMPLETE SET (31)................. 5.00 1.50

1993 Fayetteville Generals Classic/Best

This 30-card standard-size set of the 1993 Fayetteville Generals, a Class A South Atlantic League affiliate of the Detroit Tigers, features white-bordered posed color player shots on its fronts. A team-color-coded stripe below the photo carries the player's name; another above, his position and team name. On a ghosted team-logo, the white back carries the player's name at the top, followed by biography and statistics.
COMPLETE SET (30)................. 5.00 1.50

1993 Fayetteville Generals Fleer/ProCards

This 29-card standard-size set of the 1993 Fayetteville Generals, a Class A South Atlantic League affiliate of the Detroit Tigers, features white-bordered posed color player photos on its fronts. The player's name, team, and position appear near the bottom. The white horizontal back is framed by a blue line and carries the player's name at the top, followed by biography and statistics. A drawing of a ballplayer in action appears on the left.
COMPLETE SET (29)................. 5.00 1.50

1993 Florida State League All-Stars Fleer/ProCards

An early card of Edgardo Alfonzo is in this set.
COMPLETE SET (51)............... 15.00 4.50

1993 Fort Lauderdale Red Sox Classic/Best

This 30-card standard-size set of the 1993 Ft. Lauderdale Red Sox, a Class A Florida State League affiliate of the Boston Red Sox, features white-bordered posed color player shots on its fronts. A team-color-coded stripe below the photo carries the player's name; another above, his position and team name. On a ghosted team-logo, the white back carries the player's name at the top, followed by biography and statistics.
COMPLETE SET (30)................. 5.00 1.50

1993 Fort Lauderdale Red Sox Fleer/ProCards

This 30-card standard-size set of the 1993 Ft. Lauderdale Red Sox, a Class A Florida State League affiliate of the Boston Red Sox, features white-bordered posed color player photos on its fronts. The player's name, team, and position appear near the bottom. The white horizontal back is framed by a blue line and carries the player's name at the top, followed by biography and statistics. A drawing of a ballplayer in action appears on the left.
COMPLETE SET (30)................. 5.00 1.50

1993 Fort Myers Miracle Classic/Best

This 30-card standard-size set of the 1993 Fort Myers Miracle, a Class A Florida State League affiliate of the Minnesota Twins, features white-bordered posed color player shots on its fronts. A team-color-coded stripe below the photo carries the player's name; another above, his position and team name. On a ghosted team-logo, the white back carries the player's name at the top, followed by biography and statistics.
COMPLETE SET (30)................. 8.00 2.40

1993 Fort Myers Miracle Fleer/ProCards

This 28-card standard-size set of the 1993 Fort Myers Miracle, a Class A Florida State League affiliate of the Minnesota Twins, features white-bordered posed color player photos on its fronts. The player's name, team, and position appear near the bottom. The white horizontal back is framed by a blue line and carries the player's name at the top, followed by biography and statistics. A drawing of a ballplayer in action appears on the left..
COMPLETE SET (28)................. 5.00 1.50

1993 Fort Wayne Wizards Classic/Best

This 30-card standard-size set of the 1993 Fort Wayne Wizards, a Class A Midwest League affiliate of the Minnesota Twins, features white-bordered posed color player shots on its fronts. A team-color-coded stripe below the photo carries the player's name; another above, his position and team name. On a ghosted team-logo, the white back carries the player's name at the top, followed by biography and statistics.
COMPLETE SET (30)................. 5.00 1.50

1993 Fort Wayne Wizards Fleer/ProCards

This 28-card standard-size set of the 1993 Fort Wayne Wizards, a Class A Midwest League affiliate of the Minnesota Twins, features white-bordered posed color player photos on its fronts. The player's name, team, and position appear near the bottom. The white horizontal back is framed by a blue line and carries the player's name at the top, followed by biography and statistics. A drawing of a ballplayer in action appears on the left.
COMPLETE SET (28)................. 5.00 1.50

1993 Frederick Keys Classic/Best

This 30-card standard-size set of the 1993 Frederick Keys, a Class A Carolina League affiliate of the Baltimore Orioles, features white-bordered posed color player shots on its fronts. A team-color-coded stripe below the photo carries the player's name; another above, his position and team name. On a ghosted team-logo, the white back carries the player's name at the top, followed by biography and statistics.
COMPLETE SET (30)................. 5.00 1.50

1993 Frederick Keys Fleer/ProCards

This 30-card standard-size set of the 1993 Frederick Keys, a Class A Carolina League affiliate of the Baltimore Orioles, features white-bordered posed color player photos on its fronts. The player's name, team, and position appear near the bottom. The white horizontal back is framed by a blue line and carries the player's name at the top, followed by biography and statistics. A drawing of a ballplayer in action appears on the left.
COMPLETE SET (30)................. 5.00 1.50

1993 Geneva Cubs Classic/Best

This 30-card standard-size set of the 1993 Geneva Cubs, a Class A New York-Penn League affiliate of the Chicago Cubs, features white-bordered posed color player shots on its fronts. A team-color-coded stripe below the photo carries the player's name; another above, his position and team name. On a ghosted team-logo, the white back carries the player's name at the top, followed by biography and statistics.
COMPLETE SET (30)................. 5.00 1.50

1993 Geneva Cubs Fleer/ProCards

This 31-card standard-size set of the 1993 Geneva Cubs, a Class A New York-Penn League affiliate of the Chicago Cubs, features white-bordered posed color player photos on its fronts. The player's name, team, and position appear near the bottom. The white horizontal back is framed by a blue line and carries the player's name at the top, followed by biography and statistics. A drawing of a ballplayer in action appears on the left.
COMPLETE SET (31)................. 5.00 1.50

1993 Glens Falls Redbirds Classic/Best

This 30-card standard-size set of the 1993 Glens Falls Redbirds, a Class A New York-Penn League affiliate of the St. Louis Cardinals, features white-bordered posed color player shots on its fronts. A team-color-coded stripe below the photo carries the player's name; another above, his position and team name. On a ghosted team-logo, the white back carries the player's name at the top, followed by biography and statistics.
COMPLETE SET (30)................. 5.00 1.50

1993 Glens Falls Redbirds Fleer/ProCards

This 31-card standard-size set of the 1993 Glens Falls Redbirds, a Class A New York-Penn League affiliate of the St. Louis Cardinals, features white-bordered posed color player photos on its fronts. The player's name, team, and position appear near the bottom. The white horizontal back is framed by a blue line and carries the player's name at the top, followed by biography and statistics. A drawing of a ballplayer in action appears on the left.
COMPLETE SET (31)................. 5.00 1.50

1993 Great Falls Dodgers Sports Pro

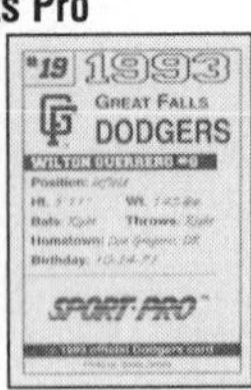

This issue includes the minor league card debut of Wilton Guerrero.
COMPLETE SET (30)................. 8.00 2.40

1993 Greensboro Hornets Classic/Best

This 30-card standard-size set of the 1993 Greensboro Hornets, a Class A South Atlantic League affiliate of the New York Yankees, features white-bordered posed color player shots on its fronts. A team-color-coded stripe below the photo carries the player's name; another above, his position and team name. On a ghosted team-logo, the white back carries the player's name at the top, followed by biography and statistics. This issue includes a second year card of Derek Jeter.
COMPLETE SET(30)................. 100.00 30.00

1993 Greensboro Hornets Fleer/ProCards

This 31-card standard-size set of the 1993 Greensboro Hornets, a Class A South Atlantic League affiliate of the New York Yankees, features white-bordered posed color player photos on its fronts. The player's name, team, and position appear near the bottom. The white horizontal back is framed by a blue line and carries the player's name at the top, followed by biography and statistics. A drawing of a ballplayer in action appears on the left. This set includes a second year card of Derek Jeter.
COMPLETE SET(31)................. 60.00 18.00

1993 Greenville Braves Fleer/ProCards

This 28-card standard-size set of the 1993 Greenville Braves, a Class AA Southern League affiliate of the Atlanta Braves, features white-bordered posed color player photos on its fronts. The player's name, team, and position appear near the bottom. The white horizontal back is framed by a blue line and carries the player's name at the top, followed by biography and statistics. A drawing of a ballplayer in action appears on the left.
COMPLETE SET (28)................. 5.00 1.50

1993 Hagerstown Suns Classic/Best

This 30-card standard-size set of the 1993 Hagerstown Suns, a Class A South Atlantic League affiliate of the Toronto Blue Jays, features white-bordered posed color player shots on its fronts. A team-color-coded stripe below the photo carries the player's name; another above, his position and team name. The white back carries the player's name at the top, followed by statistics and biography.
COMPLETE SET (30)................. 5.00 1.50

1993 Hagerstown Suns Fleer/ProCards

This 30-card standard-size set of the 1993 Hagerstown Suns, a Class A South Atlantic League affiliate of the Toronto Blue Jays, features white-bordered posed color player photos on its fronts. The player's name, team, and position appear near the bottom. The white horizontal back is framed by a blue line and carries the player's name at the top, followed by biography and statistics. A drawing of a ballplayer in action appears on the left.
COMPLETE SET (30)................. 5.00 1.50

1993 Harrisburg Senators Fleer/ProCards

This 28-card standard-size set of the 1993 Harrisburg Senators, a Class AA Eastern League affiliate of the Montreal Expos, features white-bordered posed color player photos on its fronts. The player's name, team, and position appear near the bottom. The white horizontal back is framed by a blue line and carries the player's name at the top, followed by biography and statistics. A drawing of a ballplayer in action appears on the left. This set includes Rondell White's third year team set card.
COMPLETE SET (28)................. 8.00 2.40

1993 Helena Brewers Fleer/ProCards

This 31-card standard-size set of the 1993 Helena Brewers, a Class A Pioneer League affiliate of the Milwaukee Brewers, features white-bordered posed color player photos on its fronts. The player's name, team, and position appear near the bottom. The white horizontal back is framed by a blue line and carries the player's name at the top, followed by biography and statistics. A drawing of a ballplayer in action appears on the left.
COMPLETE SET (31)................. 5.00 1.50

1993 Helena Brewers Sports Pro

COMPLETE SET (28)................. 5.00 1.50

1993 Hickory Crawdads Classic/Best

This 30-card standard-size set of the 1993 Hickory Crawdads, a Class A South Atlantic League affiliate of the Chicago White Sox, features white-bordered posed color player shots on its fronts. A team-color-coded stripe below the photo carries the player's name; another above, his position and team name. On a ghosted team-logo, the white back carries the player's name at the top, followed by biography and statistics. This issue includes the minor league card debut of Maggilo Ordonez.
COMPLETE SET (30)................ 25.00 7.50

1993 Hickory Crawdads Fleer/ProCards

This 30-card standard-size set of the 1993 Hickory Crawdads, a Class A South Atlantic League affiliate of the Chicago White Sox, features white-bordered posed color player photos on its fronts. The player's name, team, and position appear near the bottom. The white horizontal back is framed by a blue line and carries the player's name at the top, followed by biography and statistics. A drawing of a ballplayer in action appears on the left. This set includes the first card of Magglio Ordonez.
COMPLETE SET (30)................ 15.00 4.50

1993 High Desert Mavericks Classic/Best

This 30-card standard-size set of the 1993 High Desert Mavericks, a Class A California League affiliate of the Florida Marlins, features white-bordered posed color player shots on its fronts. A team-color-coded stripe below the photo carries the player's name; another above, his position and team name. On a ghosted team-logo, the white back carries the player's name at the top, followed by biography and statistics.
COMPLETE SET (30)................ 10.00 3.00

1993 High Desert Mavericks Fleer/ProCards

This 31-card standard-size set of the 1993 High Desert Mavericks, a Class A California League affiliate of the Florida Marlins, features white-bordered posed color player photos on its fronts. The player's name, team, and position appear near the bottom. The white horizontal back is framed by a blue line and carries the player's name at the top, followed by biography and statistics. A drawing of a ballplayer in action appears on the left.
COMPLETE SET (31)................. 5.00 1.50

1993 Hollywood Legends

This 20-card set of the Hollywood Legends Baseball team in the Barnstorming Baseball Club features white bordered color action player photos and was produced by Star Sports Cards, Inc. The backs carry player information. The cards are unnumbered and checklisted below in alphabetical order.
COMPLETE SET (20)................ 10.00 3.00

1993 Huntington Cubs Classic/Best

This 30-card standard-size set of the 1993 Huntington Cubs, a Rookie Class Appalachian League affiliate of the Chicago Cubs, features white-bordered posed color player shots on its fronts. A team-color-coded stripe below the photo carries the player's name; another above, his position and team name. On a ghosted team-logo, the white back carries the player's name at the top, followed by biography and statistics.
COMPLETE SET (30)................. 5.00 1.50

1993 Huntington Cubs Fleer/ProCards

This 30-card standard-size set of the 1993 Huntington Cubs, a Rookie Class Appalachian League affiliate of the Chicago Cubs, features white-bordered posed color player photos on its fronts. The player's name, team, and position appear near the bottom. The white horizontal back is framed by a blue line and carries the player's name at the top, followed by biography and statistics. A drawing of a ballplayer in action appears on the left.
COMPLETE SET (30)................. 5.00 1.50

1993 Huntsville Stars Fleer/ProCards

This 26-card standard-size set of the 1993 Huntsville Stars, a Class AA Southern League affiliate of the Oakland Athletics, features white-bordered posed color player photos on its fronts. The player's name, team, and position appear near the bottom. The white horizontal back is framed by a blue line and carries the player's name at the top, followed by biography and statistics. A drawing of a ballplayer in action appears on the left.
COMPLETE SET (26)................. 5.00 1.50

1993 Idaho Falls Braves Fleer/ProCards

This 31-card standard-size set of the 1993 Idaho Falls Braves, a Class A Pioneer League affiliate of the Atlanta Braves, features white-bordered posed color player photos on its fronts. The player's name, team, and position appear near the bottom. The white horizontal back is framed by a blue line and carries the player's name at the top, followed by biography and statistics. A drawing of a ballplayer in action appears on the left.
COMPLETE SET (31)................. 5.00 1.50

1993 Idaho Falls Braves Sports Pro

COMPLETE SET (30)................. 5.00 1.50

1993 Indianapolis Indians Fleer/ProCards

This 25-card standard-size set of the 1993 Indianapolis Indians, a Class AAA American Association affiliate of the Cincinnati Reds, features white-bordered posed color player photos on its fronts. The player's name, team, and position appear near the bottom. The white horizontal back is framed by a blue line and carries the player's name at the top, followed by biography and statistics. A drawing of a ballplayer in action appears on the left.
COMPLETE SET (25)................. 5.00 1.50

1993 Iowa Cubs Fleer/ProCards

This 24-card standard-size set of the 1993 Iowa Cubs, a Class AAA American Association affiliate of the Chicago Cubs, features white-bordered posed color player photos on its fronts. The player's name, team, and position appear near the bottom. The white horizontal back is framed by a blue line and carries the player's name at the top, followed by biography and statistics. A drawing of a ballplayer in action appears on the left.
COMPLETE SET (24)................. 5.00 1.50

1993 Jackson Generals Fleer/ProCards

This 27-card standard-size set of the 1993 Jackson Generals, a Class AA Texas League affiliate of the Houston Astros, features white-bordered posed color player photos on its fronts. The player's name, team, and position appear near the bottom. The white horizontal back is framed by a blue line and carries the player's name at the top, followed by biography and statistics. A drawing of a ballplayer in action appears on the left.
COMPLETE SET (27)................. 5.00 1.50

1993 Jacksonville Suns Fleer/ProCards

This 22-card standard-size set of the 1993 Jacksonville Suns, a Class AA Southern League affiliate of the Seattle Mariners, features white-bordered posed color player photos on its fronts. The player's name, team, and position appear near the bottom. The white horizontal back is framed by a blue line and carries the player's name at the top, followed by biography and statistics. A drawing of a ballplayer in action appears on the left.
COMPLETE SET (22)................. 5.00 1.50

1993 Jamestown Expos Classic/Best

This 30-card standard-size set of the 1993 Jamestown Expos, a Class A New York-Penn League affiliate of the Montreal Expos, features white-bordered posed color player shots on its fronts. A team-color-coded stripe below the photo carries the player's name; another above, his position and team name. The white back carries the player's name at the top, followed by biography and statistics.
COMPLETE SET (30)................. 5.00 1.50

1993 Jamestown Expos Fleer/ProCards

This 28-card standard-size set of the 1993 Jamestown Expos, a Class A New York-Penn League affiliate of the Montreal Expos, features white-bordered posed color player photos on its fronts. The player's name, team, and position appear near the bottom. The white horizontal back is framed by a blue line and carries the player's name at the top, followed by biography and statistics. A drawing of a ballplayer in action appears on the left.
COMPLETE SET (28)................. 5.00 1.50

1993 Johnson City Cardinals Classic/Best

This 30-card standard-size set of the 1993 Johnson City Cardinals, a Rookie Class Appalachian League affiliate of the St. Louis Cardinals, features white-bordered posed color player shots on its fronts. A team-color-coded stripe below the photo carries the player's name; another above, his position and team name. On a ghosted team-logo, the white back carries the player's name at the top, followed by biography and statistics.
COMPLETE SET (30)................. 5.00 1.50

1993 Johnson City Cardinals Fleer/ProCards

This 31-card standard-size set of the 1993 Johnson City Cardinals, a Rookie Class Appalachian League affiliate of the St. Louis Cardinals, features white-bordered posed color player photos on its fronts. The player's name, team, and position appear near the bottom. The white horizontal back is framed by a blue line and carries the player's name at the top, followed by biography and statistics. A drawing of a ballplayer in action appears on the left.
COMPLETE SET (31)................. 5.00 1.50

1993 Kane County Cougars Classic/Best

This 30-card standard-size set of the 1993 Kane County Cougars, a Class A Midwest League affiliate of the Florida Marlins, features white-bordered posed color player shots on its fronts. A team-color-coded stripe below the photo carries the player's name; another above, his position and team name. On a ghosted team-logo, the white back carries the player's name at the top, followed by biography and statistics. This issue includes the minor league card debuts of Charles Johnson and Edgar Renteria.
COMPLETE SET (30)............... 15.00 4.50

1993 Kane County Cougars Fleer/ProCards

This 28-card standard-size set of the 1993 Kane County Cougars, a Class A Midwest League affiliate of the Florida Marlins, features white-bordered posed color player photos on its fronts. The player's name, team, and position appear near the bottom. The white horizontal back is framed by a blue line and carries the player's name at the top, followed by biography and statistics. A drawing of a ballplayer in action appears on the left. This set includes the first year cards of Charles Johnson and Edgar Renteria.
COMPLETE SET (28)............... 20.00 6.00

1993 Kane County Cougars Team Issue

This 30-card standard-size set of the 1993 Kane County Cougars, a Class A Midwest League affiliate of the Florida Marlins, features the minor league card debuts of Charles Johnson and Edgar Renteria.
COMPLETE SET (30).............. 25.00 7.50

1993 Kingsport Mets Classic/Best

This 30-card standard-size set of the 1993 Kingsport Mets, a Rookie Class Appalachian League affiliate of the New York Mets, features white-bordered posed color player shots on its fronts. A team-color-coded stripe below the photo carries the player's name; another above, his position and team name. On a ghosted team-logo, the white back carries the player's name at the top, followed by biography and statistics. This issue includes the minor league card debut of Preston Wilson.
COMPLETE SET (30)............... 10.00 3.00

1993 Kingsport Mets Fleer/ProCards

This 27-card standard-size set of the 1993 Kingsport Mets, a Rookie Class Appalachian League affiliate of the New York Mets, features white-bordered posed color player photos on its fronts. The player's name, team, and position appear near the bottom. The white horizontal back is framed by a blue line and carries the player's name at the top, followed by biography and statistics. A drawing of a ballplayer in action appears on the left. This set includes the first year card of Preston Wilson.
COMPLETE SET (27)............... 10.00 3.00

1993 Kinston Indians Classic/Best

This 30-card standard-size set of the 1993 Kinston Indians, a Class A Carolina League affiliate of the Cleveland Indians, features white-bordered posed color player shots on its fronts. A team-color-coded stripe below the photo carries the player's name; another above, his position and team name. On a ghosted team-logo, the white back carries the player's name at the top, followed by biography and statistics.
COMPLETE SET (30)................. 5.00 1.50

1993 Kinston Indians Fleer/ProCards

This 30-card standard-size set of the 1993 Kinston Indians, a Class A Carolina League affiliate of the Cleveland Indians, features white-bordered posed color player photos on its fronts. The player's name, team, and position appear near the bottom. The white horizontal back is framed by a blue line and carries the player's name at the top, followed by biography and statistics. A drawing of a ballplayer in action appears on the left.
COMPLETE SET (30)................. 5.00 1.50

1993 Kinston Indians Team Issue

COMPLETE SET (30)................. 5.00 1.50

1993 Knoxville Smokies Fleer/ProCards

This 29-card standard-size set of the 1993 Knoxville Smokies, a Class AA Southern League affiliate of the Toronto Blue Jays, features white-bordered posed color player photos on its fronts. The player's name, team, and position appear near the bottom. The white horizontal back is framed by a blue line and carries the player's name at the top, followed by biography and statistics. A drawing of a ballplayer in action appears on the left. This set includes the second year card of Shawn Green and a third year card of Carlos Delgado.
COMPLETE SET (29)............... 20.00 6.00

1993 Lakeland Tigers Classic/Best

This 30-card standard-size set of the 1993 Lakeland Tigers, a Class A Florida State League affiliate of the Detroit Tigers, features white-bordered posed color player shots on its fronts. A team-color-coded stripe below the photo carries the player's name; another above, his position and team name. On a ghosted team-logo, the white back carries the player's name at the top, followed by biography and statistics.
COMPLETE SET (30)................. 5.00 1.50

1993 Lakeland Tigers Fleer/ProCards

This 31-card standard-size set of the 1993 Lakeland Tigers, a Class A Florida State League affiliate of the Detroit Tigers, features white-bordered posed color player photos on its fronts. The player's name, team, and position appear near the bottom. The white horizontal back is framed by a blue line and carries the player's name at the top, followed by biography and statistics. A drawing of a ballplayer in action appears on the left. .
COMPLETE SET (31)................. 5.00 1.50

1993 Las Vegas Stars Fleer/ProCards

This 29-card standard-size set of the 1993 Las Vegas Stars, a Class AAA Pacific Coast League affiliate of the San Diego Padres, features white-bordered posed color player photos on its fronts. The player's name, team, and position appear near the bottom. The white horizontal back is framed by a blue line and carries the player's name at the top, followed by biography and statistics. A drawing of a ballplayer in action appears on the left.
COMPLETE SET (29)................. 5.00 1.50

1993 Lethbridge Mounties Fleer/ProCards

This 26-card standard-size set of the 1993 Lethbridge Mounties, a Rookie Class Pioneer League Independent, features white-bordered posed color player photos on its fronts. The player's name, team, and position appear near the bottom. The white horizontal back is framed by a blue line and carries the player's name at the top, followed by biography and statistics. A drawing of a ballplayer in action appears on the left.
COMPLETE SET (26)................. 5.00 1.50

1993 Lethbridge Mounties Sports Pro

COMPLETE SET (26)................. 5.00 1.50

1993 London Tigers Fleer/ProCards

This 29-card standard-size set of the 1993 London Tigers, a Class AA Eastern League affiliate of the Detroit Tigers, features white-bordered posed color player photos on its fronts. The player's name, team, and position appear near the bottom. The white horizontal back is framed by a blue line and carries the player's name at the top, followed by biography and statistics. A drawing of a ballplayer in action appears on the left.
COMPLETE SET (29)................. 5.00 1.50

1993 Louisville Redbirds Fleer/ProCards

This 26-card standard-size set of the 1993 Louisville Redbirds, a Class AAA American Association affiliate of the St. Louis Cardinals, features white-bordered posed color player photos on its fronts. The player's name, team, and position appear near the bottom. The white horizontal back is framed by a blue line and carries the player's name at the top, followed by biography and statistics. A drawing of a ballplayer in action appears on the left.
COMPLETE SET (26)................. 5.00 1.50

1993 LSU Tigers McDag

COMPLETE SET (16)............... 12.00 3.60

1993 Lynchburg Red Sox Classic/Best

This 30-card standard-size set of the 1993 Lynchburg Red Sox, a Class A Carolina League affiliate of the Boston Red Sox, features white-bordered posed color player shots on its fronts. A team-color-coded stripe below the photo carries the player's name; another above, his position and team name. On a ghosted team-logo, the white back carries the player's name at the top, followed by biography and statistics.
COMPLETE SET (30)................. 5.00 1.50

1993 Lynchburg Red Sox Fleer/ProCards

This 29-card standard-size set of the 1993 Lynchburg Red Sox, a Class A Carolina League affiliate of the Boston Red Sox, features white-bordered posed color player photos on its fronts. The player's name, team, and position appear near the bottom. The white horizontal back is framed by a blue line and carries the player's name at the top, followed by biography and statistics. A drawing of a ballplayer in action appears on the left.
COMPLETE SET (29)................. 5.00 1.50

1993 Macon Braves Classic/Best

This 30-card standard-size set of the 1993 Macon Braves, a Class A South Atlantic League affiliate of the Atlanta Braves, features white-bordered posed color player shots on its fronts. A team-color-coded stripe below the photo carries the player's name; another above, his position and team name. On a ghosted team-logo, the white back carries the player's name at the top, followed by biography and statistics.
COMPLETE SET(30)................. 5.00 1.50

1993 Macon Braves Fleer/ProCards

This 30-card standard-size set of the 1993 Macon Braves, a Class A South Atlantic League affiliate of the Atlanta Braves, features white-bordered posed color player photos on its fronts. The player's name, team, and position appear near the bottom. The white horizontal back is framed by a blue line and carries the player's name at the top, followed by biography and statistics. A drawing of a ballplayer in action appears on the left.
COMPLETE SET(30)................. 5.00 1.50

1993 Madison Muskies Classic/Best

This 30-card standard-size set of the 1993 Madison Muskies, a Class A Midwest League affiliate of the Oakland Athletics, features white-bordered posed color player shots on its fronts. A team-color-coded stripe below the photo carries the player's name; another above, his position and team name. On a ghosted team-logo, the white back carries the player's name at the top, followed by biography and statistics.
COMPLETE SET (30)................. 5.00 1.50

1993 Madison Muskies Fleer/ProCards

This 27-card standard-size set of the 1993 Madison Muskies, a Class A Midwest League affiliate of the Oakland Athletics, features white-bordered posed color player photos on its fronts. The player's name, team, and position appear near the bottom. The white horizontal back is framed by a blue line and carries the player's name at the top, followed by biography and statistics. A drawing of a ballplayer in action appears on the left.
COMPLETE SET (27)................. 5.00 1.50

1993 Martinsville Phillies Classic/Best

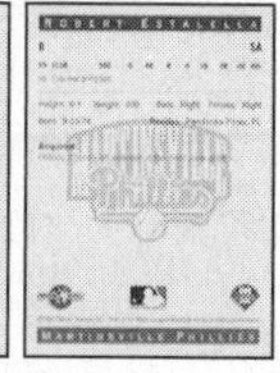

This 30-card standard-size set of the 1993 Martinsville Phillies, a Rookie Class Appalachian League affiliate of the Philadelphia Phillies, features white-bordered posed color player shots on its fronts. A team-color-coded stripe below the photo carries the player's name; another above, his position and team name. On a ghosted team-logo, the white back carries the player's name at the top, followed by biography and statistics. This issue includes the minor league card debuts of Bobby Estalella.
COMPLETE SET (30)................. 8.00 2.40

1993 Martinsville Phillies Fleer/ProCards

This 31-card standard-size set of the 1993 Martinsville Phillies, a Rookie Class Appalachian League affiliate of the Philadelphia Phillies, features white-bordered posed color player photos on its fronts. The player's name, team, and position appear near the bottom. The white horizontal back is framed by a blue line and carries the player's name at the top, followed by biography and statistics. A drawing of a ballplayer in action appears on the left. This set includes the first year cards of Bobby Estalella.
COMPLETE SET (31)................. 8.00 2.40

1993 Medicine Hat Blue Jays Fleer/ProCards

This 27-card standard-size set of the 1993 Medicine Hat Blue Jays, a Class A Pioneer League affiliate of the Toronto Blue Jays, features white-bordered posed color player photos on its fronts. The player's name, team, and position appear near the bottom. The white horizontal back is framed by a blue line and carries the player's name at the top, followed by biography and statistics. A drawing of a ballplayer in action appears on the left.
COMPLETE SET (27)................. 5.00 1.50

1993 Medicine Hat Blue Jays Sports Pro

This 25-card standard-size set of the 1992 Medicine Hat Blue Jays, a Class A Pioneer League affiliate of the Toronto Blue Jays, features on its fronts white-bordered posed color player photos framed by a black line. The player's name and position appear in white lettering within a black stripe near the bottom. The blue-on-black team name appears near the left margin. The white back is framed by a black line and carries the year and team name at the top, followed by the player's name, uniform number, position, and hometown. The sponsor's name, One Hour Photo, appears near the bottom.
COMPLETE SET (25)................. 6.00 1.80

1993 Memphis Chicks Fleer/ProCards

This 25-card standard-size set of the 1993 Memphis Chicks, a Class AA Southern League affiliate of the Kansas City Royals, features white-bordered posed color player photos on its fronts. The player's name, team, and position appear near the bottom. The white horizontal back is framed by a blue line and carries the player's name at the top, followed by biography and statistics. A drawing of a ballplayer in action appears on the left.
COMPLETE SET (25)................. 5.00 1.50

1993 Midland Angels Fleer/ProCards

This 27-card standard-size set of the 1993 Midland Angels, a Class AA Texas League affiliate of the California Angels, features white-bordered posed color player photos on its fronts. The player's name, team, and position appear near the bottom. The white horizontal back is framed by a blue line and carries the player's name at the top, followed by biography and statistics. A drawing of a ballplayer in action appears on the left.
COMPLETE SET (27)................. 5.00 1.50

1993 Midland Angels One Hour Photo

This 33-card set of the 1993 Midland Angels, a Class AA Texas League affiliate of the California Angels, features color player photos. The set measures approximately 5 1/2" by 5". The backs are blank. The cards are unnumbered and checklisted below in alphabetical order. 500 sets were produced.
COMPLETE SET (33)............... 40.00 12.00

1993 Midwest League All-Stars Fleer/ProCards

COMPLETE SET (56)............... 10.00 3.00

1993 Mississippi State Bulldogs

COMPLETE SET (49)............... 10.00 3.00

1993 Modesto A's Classic/Best

This 30-card standard-size set of the 1993 Modesto A's, a Class A California League affiliate of the Oakland Athletics, features white-bordered posed color player shots on its fronts. A team-color-coded stripe below the photo carries the player's name; another above, his position and team name. On a ghosted team-logo, the white back carries the player's name at the top, followed by biography and statistics. This issue includes the minor league team set card debut of Jason Giambi.
COMPLETE SET(30)................. 40.00 12.00

1993 Modesto A's Fleer/ProCards

This 28-card standard-size set of the 1993 Modesto A's, a Class A California League affiliate of the Oakland Athletics, features white-bordered posed color player photos on its fronts. The player's name, team, and position appear near the bottom. The white horizontal back is framed by a blue line and carries the player's name at the top, followed by biography and statistics. A drawing of a ballplayer in action appears on the left. This set includes the first team set card of Jason Giambi.
COMPLETE SET(28)................. 25.00 7.50

1993 Nashville Sounds Fleer/ProCards

This 25-card standard-size set of the 1993 Nashville Sounds, a Class AAA American Association affiliate of the Chicago White Sox, features white-bordered posed color player photos on its fronts. The player's name, team, and position appear near the bottom. The white horizontal back is framed by a blue line and carries the player's name at the top, followed by biography and statistics. A drawing of a ballplayer in action appears on the left.
COMPLETE SET (25)................. 5.00 1.50

1993 Nashville Xpress Fleer/ProCards

This 27-card standard-size set of the 1993 Nashville Xpress, a Class AA Southern League affiliate of the Minnesota Twins, features white-bordered posed color player photos on its fronts. The player's name, team, and position appear near the bottom. The white horizontal back is framed by a blue line and carries the player's name at the top, followed by biography and statistics. A drawing of a ballplayer in action appears on the left.
COMPLETE SET (27)................. 5.00 1.50

1993 New Britain Red Sox Fleer/ProCards

This 28-card standard-size set of the 1993 New Britain Red Sox, a Class AA Eastern League affiliate of the Boston Red Sox, features white-bordered posed color player photos on its fronts. The player's name, team, and position appear near the bottom. The white horizontal back is framed by a blue line and carries the player's name at the top, followed by biography and statistics. A drawing of a ballplayer in action appears on the left.
COMPLETE SET (28)................. 5.00 1.50

1993 New Orleans Zephyrs Fleer/ProCards

This 26-card standard-size set of the 1993 New Orleans Zephyrs, a Class AAA American Association affiliate of the Milwaukee Brewers, features white-bordered posed color player photos on its fronts. The player's name, team, and position appear near the bottom. The white horizontal back is framed by a blue line and carries the player's name at the top, followed by biography and statistics. A drawing of a ballplayer in action appears on the left.
COMPLETE SET (26)................. 5.00 1.50

1993 Niagara Falls Rapids Fleer/ProCards

This 31-card standard-size set of the 1993 Niagara Falls Rapids, a Class A New York-Penn League affiliate of the Detroit Tigers, features white-bordered posed color player photos on its fronts. The player's name, team, and position appear near the bottom. The white horizontal back is framed by a blue line and carries the player's name at the top, followed by biography and statistics. A drawing of a ballplayer in action appears on the left.
COMPLETE SET (31)................. 5.00 1.50

1993 Norfolk Tides Fleer/ProCards

This 27-card standard-size set of the 1993 Norfolk Tides, a Class AAA International League affiliate of the New York Mets, features white-bordered posed color player photos on its fronts. The player's name, team, and position appear near the bottom. The white horizontal back is framed by a blue line and carries the player's name at the top, followed by biography and statistics. A drawing of a ballplayer in action appears on the left.
COMPLETE SET (27)................. 5.00 1.50

1993 Oklahoma City 89ers Fleer/ProCards

This 26-card standard-size set of the 1993 Oklahoma City 89ers, a Class AAA American Association affiliate of the Texas Rangers, features white-bordered posed color player photos on its fronts. The player's name, team, and position appear near the bottom. The white horizontal back is framed by a blue line and carries the player's name at the top, followed by biography and statistics. A drawing of a ballplayer in action appears on the left.
COMPLETE SET (26)................. 5.00 1.50

1993 Oklahoma State

This 32-card set of the 1993 Oklahoma State Baseball team features action color player photos in orange borders. The backs carry player information. The cards are unnumbered and checklisted
COMPLETE SET (32)............... 10.00 3.00

1993 Omaha Royals Fleer/ProCards

This 29-card standard-size set of the 1993 Omaha Royals, a Class AAA American Association affiliate of the Kansas City Royals, features white-bordered posed color player photos on its fronts. The player's name, team, and position appear near the bottom. The white horizontal back is framed by a blue line and carries the player's name at the top, followed by biography and statistics. A drawing of a ballplayer in action appears on the left.
COMPLETE SET (29)................. 5.00 1.50

1993 Oneonta Yankees Classic/Best

This 30-card standard-size set of the 1993 Oneonta Yankees, a Class A New York-Penn League affiliate of the New York Yankees, features white-bordered posed color player shots on its fronts. A team-color-coded stripe below the photo carries the player's name; another above, his position and team name. On a ghosted team-logo, the white back carries the player's name at the top, followed by biography and statistics.
COMPLETE SET (30)................. 8.00 2.40

1993 Oneonta Yankees Fleer/ProCards

This 31-card standard-size set of the 1993 Oneonta Yankees, a Class A New York-Penn League affiliate of the New York Yankees, features white-bordered posed color player photos on its fronts. The player's name, team, and position appear near the bottom. The white horizontal back is framed by a blue line and carries the player's name at the top, followed by biography and statistics. A drawing of a ballplayer in action appears on the left.
COMPLETE SET (31)................. 8.00 2.40

1993 Orlando Cubs Fleer/ProCards

This 26-card standard-size set of the 1993 Orlando Cubs, a Class AA Southern League affiliate of the Chicago Cubs, features white-bordered posed color player photos on its fronts. The player's name, team, and position appear near the bottom. The white horizontal back is framed by a blue line and carries the player's name at the top, followed by biography and statistics. A drawing of a ballplayer in action appears on the left.
COMPLETE SET (26)................. 5.00 1.50

1993 Osceola Astros Classic/Best

This 30-card standard-size set of the 1993 Osceola Astros, a Class A Florida State League affiliate of the Houston Astros, features white-bordered posed color player shots on its fronts. A team-color-coded stripe below the photo carries the player's name; another above, his position and team name. On a ghosted team-logo, the white back carries the player's name at the top, followed by biography and statistics. This issue includes a second year card of Bob Abreu.
COMPLETE SET (30)............... 15.00 4.50

1993 Osceola Astros Fleer/ProCards

This 29-card standard-size set of the 1993 Osceola Astros, a Class A Florida State League affiliate of the Houston Astros, features white-bordered posed color player photos on its fronts. The player's name, team, and position appear near the bottom. The white horizontal back is framed by a blue line and carries the player's name at the top, followed by biography and statistics. A drawing of a ballplayer in action appears on the left. This set includes a second year card of Bob Abreu.
COMPLETE SET (29)............... 10.00 3.00

1993 Ottawa Lynx Fleer/ProCards

This 23-card standard-size set of the 1993 Ottawa Lynx, a Class AAA International League affiliate of the Montreal Expos, features white-bordered posed color player photos on its fronts. The player's name, team, and position appear near the bottom. The white horizontal back is framed by a blue line and carries the player's name at the top, followed by biography and statistics. A drawing of a ballplayer in action appears on the left.
COMPLETE SET (23).................. 5.00 1.50

1993 Palm Springs Angels Classic/Best

This 30-card standard-size set of the 1993 Palm Springs Angels, a Class A California League affiliate of the California Angels, features white-bordered posed color player shots on its fronts. A team-color-coded stripe below the photo carries the player's name; another above, his position and team name. On a ghosted team-logo, the white back carries the player's name at the top, followed by biography and statistics.
COMPLETE SET (30).................. 5.00 1.50

1993 Palm Springs Angels Fleer/ProCards

This 29-card standard-size set of the 1993 Palm Springs Angels, a Class A California League affiliate of the California Angels, features white-bordered posed color player photos on its fronts. The player's name, team, and position appear near the bottom. The white horizontal back is framed by a blue line and carries the player's name at the top, followed by biography and statistics. A drawing of a ballplayer in action appears on the left.
COMPLETE SET (29).................. 5.00 1.50

1993 Pawtucket Red Sox Dunkin' Donuts

This 31-card set of the Pawtucket Red Sox, a Class AAA International League affiliate of the Boston Red Sox, was issued in one large sheet featuring six perforated five-card strips with a large team photo in the wide top strip. Sponsored by Channel 10 and Dunkin' Donuts, the fronts carry color player photos while the backs display player career statistics. The cards are unnumbered and checklisted below in alphabetical order. This issue includes a second year card of Aaron Sele.
COMPLETE SET (31)................ 40.00 12.00

1993 Pawtucket Red Sox Fleer/ProCards

This 29-card standard-size set of the 1993 Pawtucket Red Sox, a Class AAA International League affiliate of the Boston Red Sox, features white-bordered posed color player photos on its fronts. The player's name, team, and position appear near the bottom. The white horizontal back is framed by a blue line and carries the player's name at the top, followed by biography and statistics. A drawing of a ballplayer in action appears on the left. This set includes a second year card of Aaron Sele.
COMPLETE SET (29).................. 8.00 2.40

1993 Pawtucket Red Sox Team Issue

This set includes a second year card of Aaron Sele.
COMPLETE SET (25).................. 8.00 2.40

1993 Peninsula Oilers Team Issue

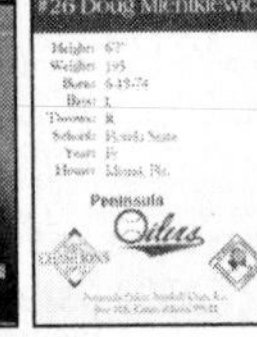

This 28-card set features color portraits of the 1993 Peninsula Oilers of the Alaska Central Baseball League on a red-and-black background. The backs carry player information. (There is no number 26.)
COMPLETE SET (27)................ 20.00 6.00

1993 Peoria Chiefs Classic/Best

This 30-card standard-size set of the 1993 Peoria Chiefs, a Class A Midwest League affiliate of the Chicago Cubs, features white-bordered posed color player shots on its fronts. A team-color-coded stripe below the photo carries the player's name; another above, his position and team name. On a ghosted team-logo, the white back carries the player's name at the top, followed by biography and statistics.
COMPLETE SET (30).................. 5.00 1.50

1993 Peoria Chiefs Fleer/ProCards

This 27-card standard-size set of the 1993 Peoria Chiefs, a Class A Midwest League affiliate of the Chicago Cubs, features white-bordered posed color player photos on its fronts. The player's name, team, and position appear near the bottom. The white horizontal back is framed by a blue line and carries the player's name at the top, followed by biography and statistics. A drawing of a ballplayer in action appears on the left.
COMPLETE SET (27).................. 5.00 1.50

1993 Peoria Chiefs Team Issue

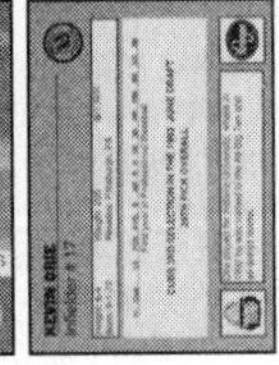

This 30-card standard-size set of the 1993 Peoria Chiefs, a Class A Midwest League affiliate of the Chicago Cubs.
COMPLETE SET (30)................ 10.00 3.00

1993 Phoenix Firebirds Fleer/ProCards

This 29-card standard-size set of the 1993 Phoenix Firebirds, a Class AAA Pacific Coast League affiliate of the San Francisco Giants, features white-bordered posed color player photos on its fronts. The player's name, team, and position appear near the bottom. The white horizontal back is framed by a blue line and carries the player's name at the top, followed by biography and statistics. A drawing of a ballplayer in action appears on the left.
COMPLETE SET (29).................. 5.00 1.50

1993 Pittsfield Mets Classic/Best

This 30-card standard-size set of the 1993 Pittsfield Mets, a Class A New York-Penn League affiliate of the New York Mets, features white-bordered posed color player shots on its fronts. A team-color-coded stripe below the photo carries the player's name; another above, his position and team name. On a ghosted team-logo, the white back carries the player's name at the top, followed by biography and statistics. This issue includes early cards of Benny Agbayani and Jason Isringhausen.
COMPLETE SET (30)................ 20.00 6.00

1993 Pittsfield Mets Fleer/ProCards

This 30-card standard-size set of the 1993 Pittsfield Mets, a Class A New York-Penn League affiliate of the New York Mets, features white-bordered posed color player photos on its fronts. The player's name, team, and position appear near the bottom. The white horizontal back is framed by a blue line and carries the player's name at the top, followed by biography and statistics. A drawing of a ballplayer in action appears on the left. This set includes early cards of Benny Agbayani and Jason Isringhausen.
COMPLETE SET (30)................ 15.00 4.50

1993 Pocatello Posse Fleer/ProCards

This 25-card standard-size set of the 1993 Pocatello Posse, a Rookie Class Pioneer League Independent, features white-bordered posed color player photos on its fronts. The player's name, team, and position appear near the bottom. The white horizontal back is framed by a blue line and carries the player's name at the top, followed by biography and statistics. A drawing of a ballplayer in action appears on the left.
COMPLETE SET (25).................. 5.00 1.50

1993 Pocatello Posse Sports Pro

COMPLETE SET (26).................. 5.00 1.50

1993 Portland Beavers Fleer/ProCards

This 21-card standard-size set of the 1993 Portland Beavers, a Class AAA Pacific Coast League affiliate of the Minnesota Twins, features white-bordered posed color player photos on its fronts. The player's name, team, and position appear near the bottom. The white horizontal back is framed by a blue line and carries the player's name at the top, followed by biography and statistics. A drawing of a ballplayer in action appears on the left.
COMPLETE SET (21).................. 5.00 1.50

1993 Prince William Cannons Classic/Best

This 30-card standard-size set of the 1993 Prince William Cannons, a Class A Carolina League affiliate of the New York Yankees, features white-bordered posed color player shots on its fronts. A team-color-coded stripe below the photo carries the player's name; another above, his position and team name. On a ghosted team-logo, the white back carries the player's name at the top, followed by biography and statistics.
COMPLETE SET (30)................ 20.00 6.00

1993 Prince William Cannons Fleer/ProCards

This 30-card standard-size set of the 1993 Prince William Cannons, a Class A Carolina League affiliate of the New York Yankees, features white-bordered posed color player photos on its fronts. The player's name, team, and position appear near the bottom. The white horizontal back is framed by a blue line and carries the player's name at the top, followed by biography and statistics. A drawing of a ballplayer in action appears on the left.
COMPLETE SET (30)................ 12.00 3.60

1993 Princeton Reds Classic/Best

This 30-card standard-size set of the 1993 Princeton Reds, a Rookie Class Appalachian League affiliate of the Cincinnati Reds, features white-bordered posed color player shots on its fronts. A team-color-coded stripe below the photo carries the player's name; another above, his position and team name. On a ghosted team-logo, the white back carries the player's name at the top, followed by biography and statistics.
COMPLETE SET (30).................. 5.00 1.50

1993 Princeton Reds Fleer/ProCards

This 31-card standard-size set of the 1993 Princeton Reds, a Rookie Class Appalachian League affiliate of the Cincinnati Reds, features white-bordered posed color player photos on its fronts. The player's name, team, and position appear near the bottom. The white horizontal back is framed by a blue line and carries the player's name at the top, followed by biography and statistics. A drawing of a ballplayer in action appears on the left.
COMPLETE SET (31).................. 5.00 1.50

1993 Quad City River Bandits Classic/Best

This 30-card standard-size set of the 1993 Quad City River Bandits, a Class A Midwest League affiliate of the Houston Astros, features white-bordered posed color player shots on its fronts. A team-color-coded stripe below the photo carries the player's name; another above, his position and team name. On a ghosted team-logo, the white back carries the player's name at the top, followed by biography and statistics.
COMPLETE SET (30).................. 5.00 1.50

1993 Quad City River Bandits Fleer/ProCards

This 30-card standard-size set of the 1993 Quad City River Bandits, a Class A Midwest League affiliate of the Houston Astros, features white-bordered posed color player photos on its fronts. The player's name, team, and position appear near the bottom. The white horizontal back is framed by a blue line and carries the player's name at the top, followed by biography and statistics. A drawing of a ballplayer in action appears on the left.
COMPLETE SET (30).................. 5.00 1.50

1993 Rancho Cucamonga Quakes Classic/Best

This 30-card standard-size set of the 1993 Rancho Cucamonga Quakes, a Class A California League affiliate of the San Diego Padres, features white-bordered posed color player shots on its fronts. A team-color-coded stripe below the photo carries the player's name; another above, his position and team name. On a ghosted team-logo, the white back carries the player's name at the top, followed by biography and statistics.
COMPLETE SET (30).................. 5.00 1.50

1993 Rancho Cucamonga Quakes Fleer/ProCards

This 32-card standard-size set of the 1993 Rancho Cucamonga Quakes, a Class A California League affiliate of the San Diego Padres, features white-bordered posed color player photos on its fronts. The player's name, team, and position appear near the bottom. The white horizontal back is framed by a blue line and carries the player's name at the top, followed by biography and statistics. A drawing of a ballplayer in action appears on the left. This set includes a second year card of Joey Hamilton.
COMPLETE SET (32).................. 5.00 1.50

1993 Reading Phillies Fleer/ProCards

This 26-card standard-size set of the 1993 Reading Phillies, a Class AA Eastern League affiliate of the Philadelphia Phillies, features white-bordered posed color player photos on its fronts. The player's name, team, and position appear near the bottom. The white horizontal back is framed by a blue line and carries the player's name at the top, followed by biography and statistics. A drawing of a ballplayer in action appears on the left.
COMPLETE SET (26).................. 5.00 1.50

1993 Richmond Braves Bleacher Bums

This 26-card standard-size set of the 1993 Richmond Braves, a Class AAA International League affiliate of the Atlanta Braves features a third year card of Chipper Jones. Two

prototype issues were issued to preview this set. These cards feature Chipper Jones and Ryan Klesko
COMPLETE SET (26)................ 30.00 9.00
COMPLETE GOLD SET (26).... 100.00 30.00

1993 Richmond Braves Bleacher Bums Gold

COMPLETE SET (26)........................ 13.50
COMPLETE GOLD SET (26)................. 55.00

1993 Richmond Braves Fleer/ProCards

This 30-card standard-size set of the 1993 Richmond Braves, a Class AAA International League affiliate of the Atlanta Braves, features white-bordered posed color player photos on its fronts. The player's name, team, and position appear near the bottom. The white horizontal back is framed by a blue line and carries the player's name at the top, followed by biography and statistics. A drawing of a ballplayer in action appears on the left. This set includes a third year card of Chipper Jones.
COMPLETE SET (30)................ 20.00 6.00

1993 Richmond Braves Pepsi

This 25-card standard-size set of the 1993 Richmond Braves, a Class AAA International League affiliate of the Atlanta Braves features a third year card of Chipper Jones.
COMPLETE SET (25)................ 30.00 9.00

1993 Richmond Braves Richmond Camera

This 25-card team set of the 1993 Richmond Braves, a Class AA International League affiliate of the Atlanta Braves, measures approximately 4" by 4 7/8". The fronts feature borderless color player photos with sponsors' and team's logos in the wide bottom margin. The backs are blank. This set includes a third year card of Chipper Jones. 500 sets were produced.
COMPLETE SET (25)................ 80.00 24.00

1993 Richmond Braves Richmond Comix

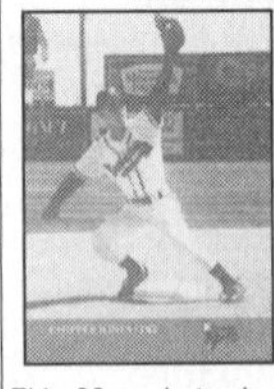

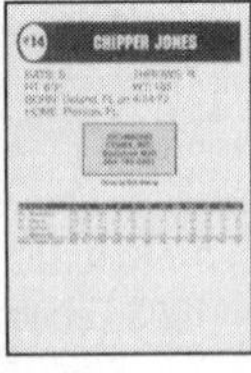

This 30-card standard-size set of the 1993 Richmond Braves, a Class AAA International League affiliate of the Atlanta Braves features a third year card of Chipper Jones.
COMPLETE SET (30)................ 30.00 9.00

1993 Riverside Pilots Cal League Cards

COMPLETE SET (32).................. 8.00 2.40

1993 Rochester Red Wings Fleer/ProCards

This 29-card standard-size set of the 1993 Rochester Red Wings, a Class AAA International League affiliate of the Baltimore Orioles, features white-bordered posed color player photos on its fronts. The player's name, team, and position appear near the bottom. The white horizontal back is framed by a blue line and carries the player's name at the top, followed by biography and statistics. A drawing of a ballplayer in action appears on the left. This set includes a first year minor league card of Jeffrey Hammonds.
COMPLETE SET (29).................. 8.00 2.40

1993 Rockford Royals Classic/Best

This 30-card standard-size set of the 1993 Rockford Royals, a Class A Midwest League affiliate of the Kansas City Royals, features white-bordered posed color player shots on its fronts. A team-color-coded stripe below the photo carries the player's name; another above, his position and team name. On a ghosted team-logo, the white back carries the player's name at the top, followed by biography and statistics. This issue includes Johnny Damon.
COMPLETE SET(30)................ 20.00 6.00

1993 Rockford Royals Fleer/ProCards

This 31-card standard-size set of the 1993 Rockford Royals, a Class A Midwest League affiliate of the Kansas City Royals, features white-bordered posed color player photos on its fronts. The player's name, team, and position appear near the bottom. The white

horizontal back is framed by a blue line and carries the player's name at the top, followed by biography and statistics. A drawing of a ballplayer in action appears on the left. This set includes Johnny Damon.
COMPLETE SET (31)................ 12.00 3.60

1993 Salem Buccaneers Classic/Best

This 30-card standard-size set of the 1993 Salem Buccaneers, a Class A Carolina League affiliate of the Pittsburgh Pirates, features white-bordered posed color player shots on its fronts. A team-color-coded stripe below the photo carries the player's name; another above, his position and team name. On a ghosted team-logo, the white back carries the player's name at the top, followed by biography and statistics.
COMPLETE SET (30).................. 5.00 1.50

1993 Salem Buccaneers Fleer/ProCards

This 29-card standard-size set of the 1993 Salem Buccaneers, a Class A Carolina League affiliate of the Pittsburgh Pirates, features white-bordered posed color player photos on its fronts. The player's name, team, and position appear near the bottom. The white horizontal back is framed by a blue line and carries the player's name at the top, followed by biography and statistics. A drawing of a ballplayer in action appears on the left.
COMPLETE SET (29).................. 5.00 1.50

1993 San Antonio Missions Fleer/ProCards

This 28-card standard-size set of the 1993 San Antonio Missions, a Class AA Texas League affiliate of the Los Angeles Dodgers, features white-bordered posed color player photos on its fronts. The player's name, team, and position appear near the bottom. The white horizontal back is framed by a blue line and carries the player's name at the top, followed by biography and statistics. A drawing of a ballplayer in action appears on the left. This set includes the second year cards of Todd Hollandsworth and Roger Cedeno.
COMPLETE SET (28).................. 8.00 2.40

1993 San Bernardino Spirit Classic/Best

This 30-card standard-size set of the 1993 San Bernardino Spirit, a Class A California League Independent, features white-bordered posed color player shots on its fronts. A team-color-coded stripe below the photo carries the player's name; another above, his position and team name. On a ghosted team-logo, the white back carries the player's name at the top, followed by biography and statistics.
COMPLETE SET (30).................. 5.00 1.50

1993 San Bernardino Spirit Fleer/ProCards

This 26-card standard-size set of the 1993 San Bernardino Spirit, a Class A California League Independent, features white-bordered posed color player photos on its fronts. The player's name, team, and position appear near the bottom. The white horizontal back is framed by a blue line and carries the player's name at the top, followed by biography and statistics. A drawing of a ballplayer in action appears on the left.
COMPLETE SET (26).................. 5.00 1.50

1993 San Jose Giants Classic/Best

This 30-card standard-size set of the 1993 San Jose Giants, a Class A California League affiliate of the San Francisco Giants, features white-bordered posed color player shots on its fronts. A team-color-coded stripe below the photo carries the player's name; another above, his position and team name. On a ghosted team-logo, the white back carries the player's name at the top, followed by biography and statistics.
COMPLETE SET (30).................. 5.00 1.50

1993 San Jose Giants Fleer/ProCards

This 30-card standard-size set of the 1993 San Jose Giants, a Class A California League affiliate of the San Francisco Giants, features white-bordered posed color player photos on its fronts. The player's name, team, and position appear near the bottom. The white horizontal back is framed by a blue line and carries the player's name at the top, followed by biography and statistics. A drawing of a ballplayer in action appears on the left.
COMPLETE SET (30).................. 5.00 1.50

1993 Sarasota White Sox Classic/Best

This 30-card standard-size set of the 1993 Sarasota White Sox, a Class A Florida State League affiliate of the Chicago White Sox, features white-bordered posed color player shots on its fronts. A team-color-coded stripe below the photo carries the player's name; another above, his position and team name. On a ghosted team-logo, the white back carries the player's name at the top, followed by biography and statistics.
COMPLETE SET (30)................. 5.00 1.50

1993 Sarasota White Sox Fleer/ProCards

This 30-card standard-size set of the 1993 Sarasota White Sox, a Class A Florida State League affiliate of the Chicago White Sox, features white-bordered posed color player photos on its fronts. The player's name, team, and position appear near the bottom. The white horizontal back is framed by a blue line and carries the player's name at the top, followed by biography and statistics. A drawing of a ballplayer in action appears on the left.
COMPLETE SET (30)................. 5.00 1.50

1993 Savannah Cardinals Classic/Best

This 30-card standard-size set of the 1993 Savannah Cardinals, a Class A South Atlantic League affiliate of the St. Louis Cardinals, features white-bordered posed color player shots on its fronts. A team-color-coded stripe below the photo carries the player's name; another above, his position and team name. On a ghosted team-logo, the white back carries the player's name at the top, followed by biography and statistics.
COMPLETE SET (30)................. 5.00 1.50

1993 Savannah Cardinals Fleer/ProCards

This 27-card standard-size set of the 1993 Savannah Cardinals, a Class A South Atlantic League affiliate of the St. Louis Cardinals, features white-bordered posed color player photos on its fronts. The player's name, team, and position appear near the bottom. The white horizontal back is framed by a blue line and carries the player's name at the top, followed by biography and statistics. A drawing of a ballplayer in action appears on the left.
COMPLETE SET (27)................. 5.00 1.50

1993 Scranton/Wilkes-Barre Red Barons Fleer/ProCards

This 25-card standard-size set of the 1993 Scranton/Wilkes-Barre Red Barons, a Class AAA International League affiliate of the Philadelphia Phillies, features white-bordered posed color player photos on its fronts. The player's name, team, and position appear near the bottom. The white horizontal back is framed by a blue line and carries the player's name at the top, followed by biography and statistics. A drawing of a ballplayer in action appears on the left.
COMPLETE SET (25)................. 5.00 1.50

1993 Scranton/Wilkes-Barre Red Barons Team Issue

COMPLETE SET (30)................. 5.00 1.50

1993 Shreveport Captains Fleer/ProCards

This 27-card standard-size set of the 1993 Shreveport Captains, a Class AA Texas League affiliate of the San Francisco Giants, features white-bordered posed color player photos on its fronts. The player's name, team, and position appear near the bottom. The white horizontal back is framed by a blue line and carries the player's name at the top, followed by biography and statistics. A drawing of a ballplayer in action appears on the left.
COMPLETE SET (27)................. 5.00 1.50

1993 South Atlantic League All-Stars Fleer/ProCards

Early cards of Richard Hidalgo, Derek Jeter and Jason Kendall highlight this set.
COMPLETE SET (57)............... 40.00 12.00

1993 South Atlantic League All-Stars Inserts Play II

COMPLETE SET (18)............... 80.00 24.00

1993 South Atlantic League All-Stars Play II

COMPLETE SET (42)............... 25.00 7.50

1993 South Bend White Sox Classic/Best

This 30-card standard-size set of the 1993 South Bend White Sox, a Class A Midwest League affiliate of the Chicago White Sox, features white-bordered posed color player shots on its fronts. A team-color-coded stripe below the photo carries the player's name; another above, his position and team name. On a ghosted team-logo, the white back carries the player's name at the top, followed by biography and statistics. This issue includes a second year card of Mike Cameron.
COMPLETE SET (30)................ 20.00 6.00

1993 South Bend White Sox Fleer/ProCards

This 30-card standard-size set of the 1993 South Bend White Sox, a Class A Midwest League affiliate of the Chicago White Sox, features white-bordered posed color player photos on its fronts. The player's name, team, and position appear near the bottom. The white horizontal back is framed by a blue line and carries the player's name at the top, followed by biography and statistics. A drawing of a ballplayer in action appears on the left. This set includes a second year card of Mike Cameron.
COMPLETE SET (30)............... 12.00 3.60

1993 Southeastern

COMPLETE SET (15)............... 10.00 3.00

1993 Southern Oregon A's Classic/Best

This 30-card standard-size set of the 1993 Southern Oregon A's, a Class A Northwest League affiliate of the Oakland Athletics, features white-bordered posed color player shots on its fronts. A team-color-coded stripe below the photo carries the player's name; another above, his position and team name. On a ghosted team-logo, the white back carries the player's name at the top, followed by biography and statistics. This issue includes the minor league card debuts of Scott Spiezio and Steve Cox.
COMPLETE SET (30)............... 15.00 4.50

1993 Southern Oregon A's Fleer/ProCards

This 30-card standard-size set of the 1993 Southern Oregon A's, a Class A Northwest League affiliate of the Oakland Athletics, features white-bordered posed color player photos on its fronts. The player's name, team, and position appear near the bottom. The white horizontal back is framed by a blue line and carries the player's name at the top, followed by biography and statistics. A drawing of a ballplayer in action appears on the left. This set includes the first year cards of Scott Spiezio and Steve Cox.
COMPLETE SET (30)............... 12.00 3.60

1993 Spartanburg Phillies Classic/Best

This 30-card standard-size set of the 1993 Spartanburg Phillies, a Class A South Atlantic League affiliate of the Philadelphia Phillies, features white-bordered posed color player shots on its fronts. A team-color-coded stripe below the photo carries the player's name; another above, his position and team name. On a ghosted team-logo, the white back carries the player's name at the top, followed by biography and statistics.
COMPLETE SET (30)................. 5.00 1.50

1993 Spartanburg Phillies Fleer/ProCards

This 29-card standard-size set of the 1993 Spartanburg Phillies, a Class A South Atlantic League affiliate of the Philadelphia Phillies, features white-bordered posed color player photos on its fronts. The player's name, team, and position appear near the bottom. The white horizontal back is framed by a blue line and carries the player's name at the top, followed by biography and statistics. A drawing of a ballplayer in action appears on the left.
COMPLETE SET (29)................. 5.00 1.50

1993 Spokane Indians Classic/Best

This 30-card standard-size set of the 1993 Spokane Indians, a Class A Northwest League affiliate of the San Diego Padres, features white-bordered posed color player shots on its fronts. A team-color-coded stripe below the photo carries the player's name; another above, his position and team name. On a ghosted team-logo, the white back carries the player's name at the top, followed by biography and statistics.
COMPLETE SET (30)................. 5.00 1.50

1993 Spokane Indians Fleer/ProCards

This 27-card standard-size set of the 1993 Spokane Indians, a Class A Northwest League affiliate of the San Diego Padres, features white-bordered posed color player photos on its fronts. The player's name, team, and position appear near the bottom. The white horizontal back is framed by a blue line and carries the player's name at the top, followed by biography and statistics. A drawing of a ballplayer in action appears on the left.
COMPLETE SET (27)................. 5.00 1.50

1993 Springfield Cardinals Classic/Best

This 30-card standard-size set of the 1993 Springfield Cardinals, a Class A Midwest League affiliate of the St. Louis Cardinals, features white-bordered posed color player shots on its fronts. A team-color-coded stripe below the photo carries the player's name; another above, his position and team name. On a ghosted team-logo, the white back carries the player's name at the top, followed by biography and statistics.
COMPLETE SET (30)................. 5.00 1.50

1993 Springfield Cardinals Fleer/ProCards

This 29-card standard-size set of the 1993 Springfield Cardinals, a Class A Midwest League affiliate of the St. Louis Cardinals, features white-bordered posed color player photos on its fronts. The player's name, team, and position appear near the bottom. The white horizontal back is framed by a blue line and carries the player's name at the top, followed by biography and statistics. A drawing of a ballplayer in action appears on the left.
COMPLETE SET (29)................. 5.00 1.50

1993 St. Catharines Blue Jays Classic/Best

This 30-card standard-size set of the 1993 St. Catharines Blue Jays, a Class A New York-Penn League affiliate of the Toronto Blue Jays, features white-bordered posed color player shots on its fronts. A team-color-coded stripe below the photo carries the player's name; another above, his position and team name. On a ghosted team-logo, the white back carries the player's name at the top, followed by biography and statistics. This set includes Shannon Stewart's first team set card.
COMPLETE SET (30)............... 10.00 3.00

1993 St. Catharines Blue Jays Fleer/ProCards

This 27-card standard-size set of the 1993 St. Catharines Blue Jays, a Class A New York-Penn League affiliate of the Toronto Blue Jays, features white-bordered posed color player photos on its fronts. The player's name, team, and position appear near the bottom. The white horizontal back is framed by a blue line and carries the player's name at the top, followed by biography and statistics. A drawing of a ballplayer in action appears on the left. This set includes Shannon Stewart's first team set card.
COMPLETE SET (27)............... 10.00 3.00

1993 St. Lucie Mets Classic/Best

This 30-card standard-size set of the 1993 St. Lucie Mets, a Class A Florida State League affiliate of the New York Mets, features white-bordered posed color player shots on its fronts. A team-color-coded stripe below the photo carries the player's name; another above, his position and team name. On a ghosted team-logo, the white back carries the player's name at the top, followed by biography and statistics. An early card of Edgardo Alfonzo is in this set.
COMPLETE SET (30)............... 20.00 6.00

1993 St. Lucie Mets Fleer/ProCards

This 28-card standard-size set of the 1993 St. Lucie Mets, a Class A Florida State League affiliate of the New York Mets, features white-bordered posed color player photos on its fronts. The player's name, team, and position appear near the bottom. The white horizontal back is framed by a blue line and carries the player's name at the top, followed by biography and statistics. A drawing of a ballplayer in action appears on the left. An early card of Edgardo Alfonzo is in this set.
COMPLETE SET (28)............... 15.00 4.50

1993 St. Petersburg Cardinals Classic/Best

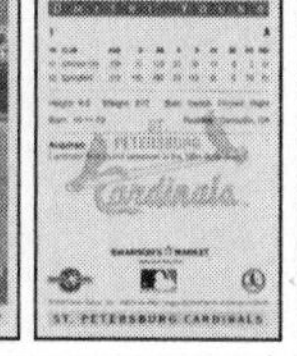

This 30-card standard-size set of the 1993 St. Petersburg Cardinals, a Class A Florida State League affiliate of the St. Louis Cardinals, features white-bordered posed color player shots on its fronts. A team-color-coded stripe below the photo carries the player's name; another above, his position and team name. On a ghosted team-logo, the white back carries the player's name at the top, followed by biography and statistics.
COMPLETE SET (30)................. 5.00 1.50

1993 St. Petersburg Cardinals Fleer/ProCards

This 30-card standard-size set of the 1993 St. Petersburg Cardinals, a Class A Florida State League affiliate of the St. Louis Cardinals, features white-bordered posed color player photos on its fronts. The player's name, team, and position appear near the bottom. The white horizontal back is framed by a blue line and carries the player's name at the top, followed by biography and statistics. A drawing of a ballplayer in action appears on the left.
COMPLETE SET (30)................. 5.00 1.50

1993 Stockton Ports Classic/Best

This 30-card standard-size set of the 1993 Stockton Ports, a Class A California League affiliate of the Milwaukee Brewers, features white-bordered posed color player shots on its fronts. A team-color-coded stripe below the photo carries the player's name; another above, his position and team name. On a ghosted team-logo, the white back carries the player's name at the top, followed by biography and statistics.
COMPLETE SET (30)................. 5.00 1.50

1993 Stockton Ports Fleer/ProCards

This 29-card standard-size set of the 1993 Stockton Ports, a Class A California League affiliate of the Milwaukee Brewers, features white-bordered posed color player photos on its fronts. The player's name, team, and position appear near the bottom. The white horizontal back is framed by a blue line and carries the player's name at the top, followed by biography and statistics. A drawing of a ballplayer in action appears on the left.
COMPLETE SET (29)................. 5.00 1.50

1993 Syracuse Chiefs Fleer/ProCards

This 27-card standard-size set of the 1993 Syracuse Chiefs, a Class AAA International League affiliate of the Toronto Blue Jays, features white-bordered posed color player photos on its fronts. The player's name, team, and position appear near the bottom. The white horizontal back is framed by a blue line and carries the player's name at the top, followed by biography and statistics. A drawing of a ballplayer in action appears on the left.
COMPLETE SET (27)................. 5.00 1.50

1993 Tacoma Tigers Fleer/ProCards

This 27-card standard-size set of the 1993 Tacoma Tigers, a Class AAA Pacific Coast League affiliate of the Oakland Athletics, features white-bordered posed color player photos on its fronts. The player's name, team, and position appear near the bottom. The white horizontal back is framed by a blue line and carries the player's name at the top, followed by biography and statistics. A drawing of a ballplayer in action appears on the left.
COMPLETE SET (27)................. 5.00 1.50

1993 Tennessee Tech

This 36-card set of the Tennessee Tech Baseball team features color player photos in light beige borders. The backs carry player information and career statistics. The cards are unnumbered and checklisted below in the order as they appear on the printed checklist. Cards 30 through 36 feature highlights of Tennesse Tech's baseball history.
COMPLETE SET (36)............... 10.00 3.00

1993 Texas Longhorns

University of Texas college set
COMPLETE SET (9)................. 15.00 4.50

1993 Toledo Mud Hens Fleer/ProCards

This 28-card standard-size set of the 1993 Toledo Mud Hens, a Class AAA International League affiliate of the Detroit Tigers, features white-bordered posed color player photos on its fronts. The player's name, team, and position appear near the bottom. The white horizontal back is framed by a blue line and carries the player's name at the top, followed by biography and statistics. A drawing of a ballplayer in action appears on the left.
COMPLETE SET (28)................. 5.00 1.50

1993 Triple A All-Stars Fleer/ProCards

This 55-card standard-size set of the 1993 Triple A All-Stars features white-bordered posed color player photos on its fronts. The player's name, team, and position appear near the bottom. The white horizontal back is framed by a blue line and carries the player's name at the top, followed by biography and statistics. A drawing of a ballplayer in action appears on the left. This issue includes third year cards of Chipper Jones and Jim Thome.
COMPLETE SET (55)............... 25.00 7.50

1993 Tucson Toros Fleer/ProCards

This 29-card standard-size set of the 1993 Tucson Toros, a Class AAA Pacific Coast League affiliate of the Houston Astros, features white-bordered posed color player photos on its fronts. The player's name, team, and position appear near the bottom. The white horizontal back is framed by a blue line and carries the player's name at the top, followed by biography and statistics. A drawing of a ballplayer in action appears on the left.
COMPLETE SET (29)................. 5.00 1.50

1993 Tulsa Drillers Fleer/ProCards

This 27-card standard-size set of the 1993 Tulsa Drillers, a Class AA Texas League affiliate of the Texas Rangers, features white-bordered posed color player photos on its fronts. The player's name, team, and position appear near the bottom. The white horizontal back is framed by a blue line and carries the player's name at the top, followed by biography and statistics. A drawing of a ballplayer in action appears on the left.
COMPLETE SET (27)................. 5.00 1.50

1993 Tulsa Drillers Team Issue

A card of Sammy Sosa highlights this set.
COMPLETE SET (30)............... 25.00 7.50

1993 Utica Blue Sox Classic/Best

This 30-card standard-size set of the 1993 Utica Blue Sox, a Class A New York-Penn League affiliate of the Boston Red Sox, features white-bordered posed color player shots on its fronts. A team-color-coded stripe below the photo carries the player's name; another above, his position and team name. On a ghosted team-logo, the white back carries the player's name at the top, followed by biography and statistics.
COMPLETE SET (30)................. 5.00 1.50

1993 Utica Blue Sox Fleer/ProCards

This 26-card standard-size set of the 1993 Utica Blue Sox, a Class A New York-Penn League affiliate of the Boston Red Sox, features white-bordered posed color player photos on its fronts. The player's name, team, and position appear near the bottom. The white horizontal back is framed by a blue line and carries the player's name at the top, followed by biography and statistics. A drawing of a ballplayer in action appears on the left.
COMPLETE SET (26)................. 5.00 1.50

1993 Vancouver Canadians Fleer/ProCards

This 28-card standard-size set of the 1993 Vancouver Canadians, a Class AAA Pacific Coast League affiliate of the California Angels, features white-bordered posed color player photos on its fronts. The player's name, team, and position appear near the bottom. The white horizontal back is framed by a blue line and carries the player's name at the top, followed by biography and statistics. A drawing of a ballplayer in action appears on the left. This set includes a fourth year card of Garret Anderson and a sixth year card of Jim Edmonds.
COMPLETE SET (28)............... 10.00 3.00

1993 Vero Beach Dodgers Classic/Best

This 30-card standard-size set of the 1993 Vero Beach Dodgers, a Class A Florida State League affiliate of the Los Angeles Dodgers, features white-bordered posed color player shots on its fronts. A team-color-coded stripe below the photo carries the player's name; another above, his position and team name. On a ghosted team-logo, the white back carries the player's name at the top, followed by biography and statistics.
COMPLETE SET (30)................. 5.00 1.50

1993 Vero Beach Dodgers Fleer/ProCards

This 31-card standard-size set of the 1993 Vero Beach Dodgers, a Class A Florida State League affiliate of the Los Angeles Dodgers, features white-bordered posed color player photos on its fronts. The player's name, team, and position appear near the bottom. The white horizontal back is framed by a blue line and carries the player's name at the top, followed by biography and statistics. A drawing of a ballplayer in action appears on the left.
COMPLETE SET (31)................. 5.00 1.50

1993 Waterloo Diamonds Classic/Best

This 30-card standard-size set of the 1993 Waterloo Diamonds, a Class A Midwest League affiliate of the San Diego Padres, features white-bordered posed color player shots on its fronts. A team-color-coded stripe below the photo carries the player's name; another above, his position and team name. On a ghosted team-logo, the white back carries the player's name at the top, followed by biography and statistics.
COMPLETE SET (30)................. 5.00 1.50

1993 Waterloo Diamonds Fleer/ProCards

This 29-card standard-size set of the 1993 Waterloo Diamonds, a Class A Midwest League affiliate of the San Diego Padres, features white-bordered posed color player photos on its fronts. The player's name, team, and position appear near the bottom. The white horizontal back is framed by a blue line and carries the player's name at the top, followed by biography and statistics. A drawing of a ballplayer in action appears on the left.
COMPLETE SET (29)................. 5.00 1.50

1993 Watertown Indians Classic/Best

This 30-card standard-size set of the 1993 Watertown Indians, a Class A New York-Penn League affiliate of the Cleveland Indians, features white-bordered posed color player shots on its fronts. A team-color-coded stripe below the photo carries the player's name; another above, his position and team name. On a ghosted team-logo, the white back carries the player's name at the top, followed by biography and statistics.
COMPLETE SET (30)................. 5.00 1.50

1993 Watertown Indians Fleer/ProCards

This 30-card standard-size set of the 1993 Watertown Indians, a Class A New York-Penn League affiliate of the Cleveland Indians, features white-bordered posed color player photos on its fronts. The player's name, team, and position appear near the bottom. The white horizontal back is framed by a blue line and carries the player's name at the top, followed by biography and statistics. A drawing of a ballplayer in action appears on the left.
COMPLETE SET (30)................. 5.00 1.50

1993 Welland Pirates Classic/Best

This 30-card standard-size set of the 1993 Welland Pirates, a Class A New York-Penn League affiliate of the Pittsburgh Pirates, features white-bordered posed color player shots on its fronts. A team-color-coded stripe below the photo carries the player's name; another above, his position and team name. On a ghosted team-logo, the white back carries the player's name at the top, followed by biography and statistics.
COMPLETE SET (30)................. 5.00 1.50

1993 Welland Pirates Fleer/ProCards

This 31-card standard-size set of the 1993 Welland Pirates, a Class A New York-Penn League affiliate of the Pittsburgh Pirates, features white-bordered posed color player photos on its fronts. The player's name, team, and position appear near the bottom. The white horizontal back is framed by a blue line and carries the player's name at the top, followed by biography and statistics. A drawing of a ballplayer in action appears on the left.
COMPLETE SET (31)................. 5.00 1.50

1993 West Palm Beach Expos Classic/Best

This 30-card standard-size set of the 1993 West Palm Beach Expos, a Class A Florida State League affiliate of the Montreal Expos, features white-bordered posed color player shots on its fronts. A team-color-coded stripe below the photo carries the player's name; another above, his position and team name. On a ghosted team logo, the white back carries the player's name at the top, followed by statistics and biography.
COMPLETE SET (30)................. 5.00 1.50

1993 West Palm Beach Expos Fleer/ProCards

This 30-card standard-size set of the 1993 West Palm Beach Expos, a Class A Florida State League affiliate of the Montreal Expos, features white-bordered posed color player photos on its fronts. The player's name, team, and position appear near the bottom. The white horizontal back is framed by a blue line and carries the player's name at the top, followed by biography and statistics. A drawing of a ballplayer in action appears on the left.
COMPLETE SET (30)................. 5.00 1.50

1993 West Virginia Wheelers Classic/Best

This 30-card standard-size set of the 1993 West Virginia Wheelers, a Class A South Atlantic League affiliate of the Cincinnati Reds, features white-bordered posed color player shots on its fronts. A team-color-coded stripe below the photo carries the player's name; another above, his position and team name. On a ghosted team logo, the white back carries the player's name at the top, followed by statistics and biography.
COMPLETE SET (30)................. 5.00 1.50

1993 West Virginia Wheelers Fleer/ProCards

This 27-card standard-size set of the 1993 West Virginia Wheelers, a Class A South Atlantic League affiliate of the Cincinnati Reds, features white-bordered posed color player photos on its fronts. The player's name, team, and position appear near the bottom. The white horizontal back is framed by a blue line and carries the player's name at the top, followed by biography and statistics. A drawing of a ballplayer in action appears on the left.
COMPLETE SET (27)................. 5.00 1.50

1993 Wichita Wranglers Fleer/ProCards

This 26-card standard-size set of the 1993 Wichita Wranglers, a Class AA Texas League affiliate of the San Diego Padres, features white-bordered posed color player photos on its fronts. The player's name, team, and position appear near the bottom. The white horizontal back is framed by a blue line and carries the player's name at the top, followed by biography and statistics. A drawing of a ballplayer in action appears on the left.
COMPLETE SET (26)................. 5.00 1.50

1993 Wilmington Blue Rocks Classic/Best

This 30-card standard-size set of the 1993 Wilmington Blue Rocks, a Class A Carolina League affiliate of the Kansas City Royals, features white-bordered posed color player shots on its fronts. A team-color-coded stripe below the photo carries the player's name; another above, his position and team name. On a ghosted team logo, the white back carries the player's name at the top, followed by statistics and biography. This set includes the minor league card debut of Michael Tucker. In addition, a Michael Tucker promo card was distributed to dealers and hobby media to preview the 1993 run of Classic/Best team sets. This promo card is not considered part of the complete set.
COMPLETE SET (30)................. 8.00 2.40

1993 Wilmington Blue Rocks Fleer/ProCards

This 30-card standard-size set of the 1993 Wilmington Blue Rocks, a Class A Carolina League affiliate of the Kansas City Royals, features white-bordered posed color player photos on its fronts. The player's name, team, and position appear near the bottom. The white horizontal back is framed by a blue line and carries the player's name at the top, followed by biography and statistics. A drawing of a ballplayer in action appears on the left. This set includes the first year minor league card of Michael Tucker.
COMPLETE SET (30)................. 8.00 2.40

1993 Winston-Salem Spirits Classic/Best

This 30-card standard-size set of the 1993 Winston-Salem Spirits, a Class A Carolina League affiliate of the Cincinnati Reds, features white-bordered posed color player shots on its fronts. A team-color-coded stripe below the photo carries the player's name; another above, his position and team name. On a ghosted team logo, the white back carries the player's name at the top, followed by statistics and biography.
COMPLETE SET (30)................. 5.00 1.50

1993 Winston-Salem Spirits Fleer/ProCards

This 25-card standard-size set of the 1993 Winston-Salem Spirits, a Class A Carolina League affiliate of the Cincinnati Reds, features white-bordered posed color player photos on its fronts. The player's name, team, and position appear near the bottom. The white horizontal back is framed by a blue line and carries the player's name at the top, followed by biography and statistics. A drawing of a ballplayer in action appears on the left.
COMPLETE SET (25)................. 5.00 1.50

1993 Yakima Bears Classic/Best

This 30-card standard-size set of the 1993 Yakima Bears, a Class A Northwest League affiliate of the Los Angeles Dodgers, features white-bordered posed color player shots on its fronts. A team-color-coded stripe below the photo carries the player's name; another above, his position and team name. On a ghosted team logo, the white back carries the player's name at the top, followed by statistics and biography.
COMPLETE SET (30)................. 5.00 1.50

1993 Yakima Bears Fleer/ProCards

This 31-card standard-size set of the 1993 Yakima Bears, a Class A Northwest League affiliate of the Los Angeles Dodgers, features white-bordered posed color player photos on its fronts. The player's name, team, and position appear near the bottom. The white horizontal back is framed by a blue line and carries the player's name at the top, followed by biography and statistics. A drawing of a ballplayer in action appears on the left.
COMPLETE SET (31)................. 5.00 1.50

1994 Albany Polecats Classic

This 30-card standard-size set of the 1994 Albany Polecats, a Class A South Atlantic League affiliate of the Baltimore Orioles, features white-bordered posed color player shots on its fronts with the player's name and position, team name, logo and Classic logo appearing across the bottom of each card. On a ghosted team logo, the white back carries the player's name at the top, followed by biography and statistics.
COMPLETE SET (30)................. 5.00 1.50

1994 Albany Polecats Fleer/ProCards

This 30-card standard-size set of the 1994 Albany Polecats, a Class A South Atlantic League affiliate of the Baltimore Orioles, features white-bordered posed color player photos on its fronts with the player's name, position, team name and Fleer/ProCards logo across the bottom of each card. The white back with vertical light blue stripes carries the player's name at the top, followed by biography and statistics.
COMPLETE SET (30)................. 5.00 1.50

1994 Albany Yankees Fleer/ProCards

This 31-card standard size set of the 1994 Albany Yankees, a Class AA Eastern League affiliate of the New York Yankees, features white-bordered posed color player photos on its fronts with the player's name, position, team name and Fleer/ProCards logo across the bottom of each card. The white back with vertical light blue stripes carries the player's name at the top, followed by biography and statistics.
COMPLETE SET (31)................. 5.00 1.50

1994 Albany Yankees Yearbook Team Issue

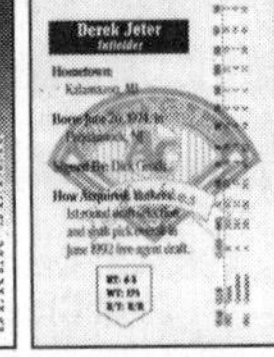

Issued as a three card panel in the 1994 Albany-Colonie Yankees Souvenir Yearbooks. This issue features a third year card of Derek Jeter.
COMPLETE SET (3)............... 120.00 36.00

1994 Albuquerque Dukes Fleer/ProCards

This 27-card standard size set of the 1994 Albuquerque Dukes, a Class AAA Pacific Coast League affiliate of the Los Angeles, features white-bordered posed color player photos on its fronts with the player's name, position, team name and Fleer/ProCards logo across the bottom of each card. The white back with vertical light blue stripes carries the player's name at the top, followed by biography and statistics.
COMPLETE SET (27)............... 10.00 3.00

1994 Alexandria Aces McDag

This 12-card standard-size set features a member of the Alexandria Aces along with a police officer. The backs of the card give information on the Ace along with identifying the police officer and giving a safety tip.
COMPLETE SET 5.00 1.50

1994 Appleton Foxes Classic

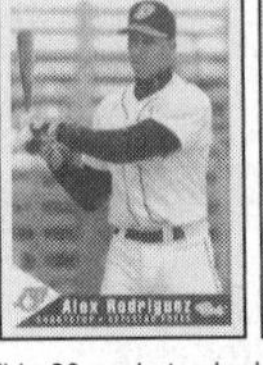

This 30-card standard-size set of the 1994 Appleton Foxes, a Class A Midwest League affiliate of the Seattle Mariners, features white-bordered posed color player shots on its fronts with the player's name and position, team name and logo and Classic logo appearing across the bottom of each card. On a ghosted team logo, the white back carries the player's name at the top, followed by biography and statistics. This issue includes the minor league card debut of Alex Rodriguez.
COMPLETE SET (30)............. 250.00 75.00

1994 Appleton Foxes Fleer/ProCards

This 28-card standard size set of the 1994 Appleton Foxes, a Class A Midwest League affiliate of the Seattle Mariners, features white-bordered posed color player photos on its fronts with the player's name, position, team name and Fleer/ProCards logo across the bottom of each card. The white back with vertical light blue stripes carries the player's name at the top, followed by biography and statistics. This issue includes the minor league card debut of Alex Rodriguez.
COMPLETE SET (28)............... 50.00 15.00

1994 Arizona Fall League SplitSecond

Manufactured and distributed by Jessen Associates, Inc.
COMPLETE SET (21)............... 15.00 4.50

1994 Arkansas Travelers Fleer/ProCards

This 26-card standard size set of the 1994 Arkansas Travelers, a Class AA Texas League affiliate of the St. Louis Cardinals, features white-bordered posed color player photos on its fronts with the player's name, position, team name and Fleer/ProCards logo across the bottom of each card. The white back with vertical light blue stripes carries the player's name at the top, followed by biography and statistics.
COMPLETE SET (26)................. 5.00 1.50

1994 Asheville Tourists Classic

This 30-card standard size set of the 1994 Asheville Tourists, a Class A South Atlantic League affiliate of the Colorado Rockies, features white-bordered posed color player shots on its fronts with the player's name and position, team name and logo and Classic logo appearing across the bottom of each card. On a ghosted team logo, the white back carries the player's name at the top, followed by biography and statistics.
COMPLETE SET (30)................. 8.00 2.40

1994 Asheville Tourists Fleer/ProCards

This 30-card standard size set of the 1994 Asheville Tourists, a Class A South Atlantic League affiliate of the Colorado Rockies, features white-bordered posed color player photos on its fronts with the player's name, position, team name and Fleer/ProCards logo across the bottom of each card. The white back with vertical light blue stripes carries the player's name at the top, followed by biography and statistics.
COMPLETE SET (30)................. 5.00 1.50

1994 Auburn Astros Classic

This 30-card standard size set of the 1994 Auburn Astros, a Class A New York-Penn League affiliate of the Houston Astros, features white-bordered posed color player shots on its fronts with the player's name and position, team name and logo and Classic logo appearing across the bottom of each card. On a ghosted team logo, the white back carries the player's name at the top, followed by biography and statistics.
COMPLETE SET (30)................. 8.00 2.40

1994 Auburn Astros Fleer/ProCards

This 29-card standard size set of the 1994 Auburn Astros, a Class A New York-Penn League affiliate of the Houston Astros, features white-bordered posed color player photos on its fronts with the player's name, position, team name and Fleer/ProCards logo across the bottom of each card. The white back with vertical light blue stripes carries the player's name at the top, followed by biography and statistics.
COMPLETE SET (29)................. 5.00 1.50

1994 Augusta Greenjackets Classic

This 30-card standard size set of the 1994 Augusta GreenJackets, a Class A South Atlantic League affiliate of the Pittsburgh Pirates, features white-bordered posed color player shots on its fronts with the player's name and position, team name and logo and Classic logo appearing across the bottom of each card. On a ghosted team logo, the white back carries the player's name at the top, followed by biography and statistics.
COMPLETE SET (30)................. 8.00 2.40

1994 Augusta GreenJackets Fleer/ProCards

This 28-card standard size set of the 1994 Augusta GreenJackets, a Class A South Atlantic League affiliate of the Pittsburgh Pirates, features white-bordered posed color player photos on its fronts with the player's name, position, team name and Fleer/ProCards logo across the bottom of each card. The white back with vertical light blue stripes carries the player's name at the top, followed by biography and statistics.
COMPLETE SET (28)................. 5.00 1.50

1994 Bakersfield Dodgers Classic

This 30-card standard size set of the 1994 Bakersfield Dodgers, a Class A California League affiliate of the Los Angeles Dodgers, features white-bordered posed color player shots on its fronts with the player's name and position, team name and logo and Classic logo appearing across the bottom of each card. On a ghosted team logo, the white back carries the player's name at the top, followed by biography and statistics.
COMPLETE SET (30)............... 20.00 6.00

1994 Batavia Clippers Classic

This 30-card standard size set of the 1994 Batavia Clippers, a Class A New York-Penn League affiliate of the Philadelphia Phillies, features white-bordered posed color player shots on its fronts with the player's name and position, team name and logo and Classic logo appearing across the bottom of each card. On a ghosted team logo, the white back carries the player's name at the top, followed by biography and statistics.
COMPLETE SET (30)................. 8.00 2.40

1994 Batavia Clippers Fleer/ProCards

This 32-card standard size set of the 1994 Batavia Clippers, a Class A New York-Penn League affiliate of the Philadelphia Phillies, features white-bordered posed color player photos on its fronts with the player's name, position, team name and Fleer/ProCards logo across the bottom of each card. The white back with vertical light blue stripes carries the player's name at the top, followed by biography and statistics.
COMPLETE SET (32)................. 5.00 1.50

1994 Bellingham Mariners Classic

This 30-card standard size set of the 1994 Bellingham Mariners, a Class A Northwest League affiliate of the Seattle Mariners, features white-bordered posed color player shots on its fronts with the player's name and position, team name and logo and Classic logo appearing across the bottom of each card. On a ghosted team logo, the white back carries the player's name at the top, followed by biography and statistics.
COMPLETE SET (30)................. 8.00 2.40

1994 Bellingham Mariners Fleer/ProCards

This 31-card standard size set of the 1994 Bellingham Mariners, a Class A Northwest League affiliate of the Seattle Mariners, features white-bordered posed color player photos on its fronts with the player's name, position, team name and Fleer/ProCards logo across the bottom of each card. The white back with vertical light blue stripes carries the player's name at the top, followed by biography and statistics.
COMPLETE SET (31)................. 5.00 1.50

1994 Beloit Brewers Classic

This 30-card standard size set of the 1994 Beloit Brewers, a Class A Midwest League affiliate of the Milwaukee Brewers, features white-bordered posed color player shots on its fronts with the player's name and position, team name and logo and Classic logo appearing across the bottom of each card. On a ghosted team logo, the white back carries the player's name at the top, followed by biography and statistics.
COMPLETE SET (30)................. 8.00 2.40

1994 Beloit Brewers Fleer/ProCards

This 30-card standard size set of the 1994 Beloit Brewers, a Class A Midwest League affiliate of the Milwaukee Brewers, features white-bordered posed color player photos on its fronts with the player's name, position, team name and Fleer/ProCards logo across the bottom of each card. The white back with vertical light blue stripes carries the player's name at the top, followed by biography and statistics.
COMPLETE SET (30)................. 5.00 1.50

1994 Bend Rockies Classic

This 30-card standard size set of the 1994 Bend Rockies, a Class A Northwest League affiliate of the Colorado Rockies,features white-bordered posed color player shots on its fronts with the player's name and position, team name and logo and Classic logo appearing across the bottom of each card. On a ghosted team logo, the white back carries the player's name at the top, followed by biography and statistics.
COMPLETE SET (30)................. 8.00 2.40

1994 Bend Rockies Fleer/ProCards

This 31-card standard size set of the 1994 Bend Rockies, a Class A Northwest League affiliate of the Colorado Rockies, features white-bordered posed color player photos on its fronts with the player's name, position, team name and Fleer/ProCards logo across the bottom of each card. The white back with vertical light blue stripes carries the player's name at the top, followed by biography and statistics.
COMPLETE SET (31)................. 5.00 1.50

1994 Billings Mustangs Fleer/ProCards

This 27-card standard size set of the 1994 Billings Mustangs, a Rookie Class Pioneer League affiliate of the Cincinnati Reds, features white-bordered posed color player photos on its fronts with the player's name, position, team name and Fleer/ProCards logo across the bottom of each card. The white back with vertical light blue stripes carries the player's name at the top, followed by biography and statistics. This issue features the minor league card debut of Aaron Boone.
COMPLETE SET (27)................. 15.00 2.40

1994 Billings Mustangs Sports Pro

This 27-card standard size set of the 1994 Billings Mustangs, a Rookie Class Pioneer League affiliate of the Cincinnati Reds features

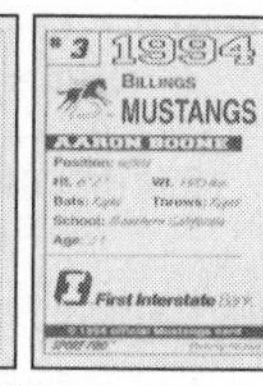

the minor league card debut of Aaron Boone.
COMPLETE SET (30) 20.00 3.00

1994 Binghamton Mets Fleer/ProCards

This 28-card standard size set of the 1994 Binghamton Mets, a Class AA Eastern League affiliate of the New York Mets, features white-bordered posed color player photos on its fronts with the player's name, position, team name and Fleer/ProCards logo across the bottom of each card. The white back with vertical light blue stripes carries the player's name at the top, followed by biography and statistics. An early card of Edgardo Alfonzo is an highlight of this set.
COMPLETE SET (28) 15.00 4.50

1994 Birmingham Barons Classic

This 30-card standard size set of the 1994 Birmingham Barons, a Class AA Southern League affiliate of the Chicago White Sox, features white-bordered posed color player shots on its fronts with the player's name and position, team name and logo and Classic logo appearing across the bottom of each card. On a ghosted team logo, the white back carries the player's name at the top, followed by biography and statistics. This issue features the minor league card debut of Michael Jordan.
COMPLETE SET (30) 30.00 9.00

1994 Birmingham Barons Fleer/ProCards

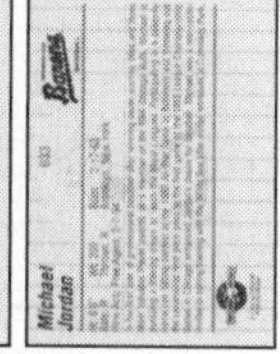

This 28-card standard size set of the 1994 Birmingham Barons, a Class AA Southern League affiliate of the Chicago White Sox, features white-bordered posed color player photos on its fronts with the player's name, position, team name and Fleer/ProCards logo across the bottom of each card. The white back with vertical light blue stripes carries the player's name at the top, followed by biography and statistics. This issue features the minor league card debut of Michael Jordan.
COMPLETE SET (28) 20.00 6.00

1994 Bluefield Orioles Classic

This 30-card standard size set of the 1994 Bluefield Orioles, a Rookie Class Appalachian League affiliate of the Baltimore Orioles, features white-bordered posed color player shots on its fronts with the player's name and position, team name and logo and Classic logo appearing across the bottom of each card. On a ghosted team logo, the white back carries the player's name at the top, followed by biography and statistics.
COMPLETE SET (30) 8.00 2.40

1994 Bluefield Orioles Fleer/ProCards

This 30-card standard size set of the 1994 Bluefield Orioles, a Rookie Class Appalachian League affiliate of the Baltimore Orioles, features white-bordered posed color player photos on its fronts with the player's name, position, team name and Fleer/ProCards logo across the bottom of each card. The white back with vertical light blue stripes carries the player's name at the top, followed by biography and statistics.
COMPLETE SET (30) 5.00 1.50

1994 Boise Hawks Classic

This 30-card standard size set of the 1994 Boise Hawks, a Class A Northwest League affiliate of the California Angels, features white-bordered posed color player shots on its fronts with the player's name and position, team name and logo and Classic logo appearing across the bottom of each card. On a ghosted team logo, the white back carries the player's name at the top, followed by biography and statistics.
COMPLETE SET (30) 8.00 2.40

1994 Boise Hawks Fleer/ProCards

This 31-card standard size set of the 1994 Boise Hawks, a Class A Northwest League affiliate of the California Angels, features white-bordered posed color player photos on its fronts with the player's name, position, team name and Fleer/ProCards logo across the bottom of each card. The white back with vertical light blue stripes carries the player's name at the top, followed by biography and statistics.
COMPLETE SET (31) 5.00 1.50

1994 Bowie Baysox Fleer/ProCards

This 27-card standard size set of the 1994 Bowie Baysox, a Class AA Eastern League affiliate of the Baltimore Orioles, features white-bordered posed color player photos on its fronts with the player's name, position, team name and Fleer/ProCards logo across the bottom of each card. The white back with vertical light blue stripes carries the player's name at the top, followed by biography and statistics.
COMPLETE SET (27) 5.00 1.50

1994 Brevard County Manatees Classic

This 30-card standard size set of the 1994 Brevard County Manatees, a Class A Florida State League affiliate of the Florida Marlins, features white-bordered posed color player shots on its fronts with the player's name and position, team name and logo and Classic logo appearing across the bottom of each card. On a ghosted team logo, the white back carries the player's name at the top, followed by biography and statistics.
COMPLETE SET (30) 8.00 2.40

1994 Brevard County Manatees Fleer/ProCards

This 30-card standard size set of the 1994 Brevard County Manatees, a Class A Florida State League affiliate of the Florida Marlins, features white-bordered posed color player photos on its fronts with the player's name, position, team name and Fleer/ProCards logo across the bottom of each card. The white back with vertical light blue stripes carries the player's name at the top, followed by biography and statistics.
COMPLETE SET (30) 5.00 1.50

1994 Bristol Tigers Classic

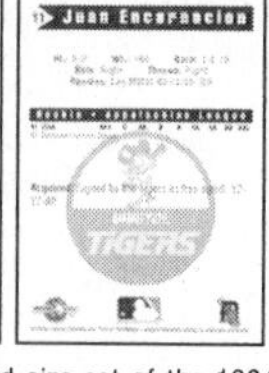

This 30-card standard size set of the 1994 Bristol Tigers, a Rookie Class Appalachian League affiliate of the Detroit Tigers, features white-bordered posed color player shots on its fronts with the player's name and position, team name and logo and Classic logo appearing across the bottom of each card. On a ghosted team logo, the white back carries the player's name at the top, followed by biography and statistics. This issue includes the minor league card debuts of Juan Encarnacion.
COMPLETE SET (30) 20.00 6.00

1994 Bristol Tigers Fleer/ProCards

This 30-card standard size set of the 1994 Bristol Tigers, a Rookie Class Appalachian League affiliate of the Detroit Tigers, features white-bordered posed color player photos on its fronts with the player's name, position, team name and Fleer/ProCards logo across the bottom of each card. The white back with vertical light blue stripes carries the player's name at the top, followed by biography and statistics. This issue includes the minor league card debuts of Juan Encarnacion, Daryle Ward and Willis Roberts.
COMPLETE SET (30) 15.00 4.50

1994 Buffalo Bisons Fleer/ProCards

This 27-card standard size set of the 1994 Buffalo Bisons, a Class AAA American Association affiliate of the Pittsburgh Pirates, features white-bordered posed color player photos on its fronts with the player's name, position, team name and Fleer/ProCards logo across the bottom of each card. The white back with vertical light blue stripes carries the player's name at the top, followed by biography and statistics.
COMPLETE SET (28) 5.00 1.50

1994 Burlington Bees Classic

This 30-card standard size set of the 1994 Burlington Bees, a Class A Midwest League affiliate of the Montreal Expos, features white-bordered posed color player shots on its fronts with the player's name and position, team name and logo and Classic logo appearing across the bottom of each card. On a ghosted team logo, the white back carries the player's name at the top, followed by biography and statistics.
COMPLETE SET (30) 8.00 2.40

1994 Burlington Bees Fleer/ProCards

This 29-card standard size set of the 1994 Burlington Bees, a Class A Midwest League affiliate of the Montreal Expos, features white-bordered posed color player photos on its fronts with the player's name, position, team name and Fleer/ProCards logo across the bottom of each card. The white back with vertical light blue stripes carries the player's name at the top, followed by biography and statistics.
COMPLETE SET (29) 5.00 1.50

1994 Burlington Indians Classic

This 30-card standard size set of the 1994 Burlington Indians, a Rookie Class Appalachian League affiliate of the Cleveland Indians, features white-bordered posed color player shots on its fronts with the player's name and position, team name and logo and Classic logo appearing across the bottom of each card. On a ghosted team logo, the white back carries the player's name at the top, followed by biography and statistics. This issue includes the minor league card debut of Russ Branyan.
COMPLETE SET (30) 15.00 4.50

1994 Burlington Indians Fleer/ProCards

This 31-card standard size set of the 1994 Burlington Indians, a Rookie Class Appalachian League affiliate of the Cleveland Indians, features white-bordered posed color player photos on its fronts with the player's name, position, team name and Fleer/ProCards logo across the bottom of each card. The white back with vertical light blue stripes carries the player's name at the top, followed by biography and statistics. This issue includes the minor league card debuts of Russ Branyan and Bartolo Colon.
COMPLETE SET (31) 12.00 3.60

1994 Butte Copper Kings Sports Pro

COMPLETE SET (30) 5.00 1.50

1994 Calgary Cannons Fleer/ProCards

This 27-card standard size set of the 1994 Calgary Cannons, a Class AAA Pacific Coast League affiliate of the Seattle Mariners, features white-bordered posed color player photos on its fronts with the player's name, position, team name and Fleer/ProCards logo across the bottom of each card. The white back with vertical light blue stripes carries the player's name at the top, followed by biography and statistics.
COMPLETE SET (27) 5.00 1.50

1994 Canton-Akron Indians Fleer/ProCards

This 30-card standard size set of the 1994 Canton-Akron Indians, a Class AA Eastern League affiliate of the Cleveland Indians, features white-bordered posed color player photos on its fronts with the player's name, position, team name and Fleer/ProCards logo across the bottom of each card. The white back with vertical light blue stripes carries the player's name at the top, followed by biography and statistics.
COMPLETE SET (30) 5.00 1.50

1994 Capital City Bombers Classic

This 30-card standard size set of the 1994 Capital City Bombers, a Class A South Atlantic affiliate of the New York Mets, features white-bordered posed color player shots on its fronts with the player's name and position, team name and logo and Classic logo appearing across the bottom of each card. On a ghosted team logo, the white back carries the player's name at the top, followed by biography and statistics.
COMPLETE SET (30) 8.00 2.40

1994 Capital City Bombers Fleer/ProCards

This 29-card standard size set of the 1994 Capital City Bombers, a Class A South Atlantic affiliate of the New York Mets, features white-bordered posed color player photos on its fronts with the player's name, position, team name and Fleer/ProCards logo across the bottom of each card. The white back with vertical light blue stripes carries the player's name at the top, followed by biography and statistics.
COMPLETE SET (29) 5.00 1.50

1994 Carolina League All-Stars Fleer/ProCards

An early card of Jason Kendall is in this set.
COMPLETE SET (53) 15.00 4.50

1994 Carolina League All-Time

COMPLETE SET (36) 10.00 3.00

1994 Carolina Mudcats Fleer/ProCards

This 28-card standard size set of the 1994 Carolina Mudcats, a Class AA Southern League affiliate of the Pittsburgh Pirates, features white-bordered posed color player photos on its fronts with the player's name, position, team name and Fleer/ProCards logo across the bottom of each card. The white back with vertical light blue stripes carries the player's name at the top, followed by biography and statistics.
COMPLETE SET (28) 5.00 1.50

1994 Cedar Rapids Kernels Classic

This 30-card standard size set of the 1994 Cedar Rapids Kernels, a Class A Midwest League affiliate of the California Angels, features white-bordered posed color player shots on its fronts with the player's name and position, team name and logo and Classic logo appearing across the bottom of each card. On a ghosted team logo, the white back carries the player's name at the top, followed by biography and statistics.
COMPLETE SET (30) 8.00 2.40

1994 Cedar Rapids Kernels Fleer/ProCards

This 27-card standard size set of the 1994 Cedar Rapids Kernels, a Class A Midwest League affiliate of the California Angels, features white-bordered posed color player photos on its fronts with the player's name, position, team name and Fleer/ProCards logo across the bottom of each card. The white back with vertical light blue stripes carries the player's name at the top, followed by biography and statistics.
COMPLETE SET (27) 5.00 1.50

1994 Central Valley Rockies Classic

This 30-card standard size set of the 1994 Central Valley Rockies, a Class A California League affiliate of the Colorado Rockies, features white-bordered posed color player shots on its fronts with the player's name and position, team name and logo and Classic logo appearing across the bottom of each card. On a ghosted team logo, the white back carries the player's name at the top, followed by biography and statistics.
COMPLETE SET (30) 8.00 2.40

1994 Central Valley Rockies Fleer/ProCards

This 30-card standard size set of the 1994 Central Valley Rockies, a Class A California League affiliate of the Colorado Rockies, features white-bordered posed color player photos on its fronts with the player's name, position, team name and Fleer/ProCards logo across the bottom of each card. The white back with vertical light blue stripes carries the player's name at the top, followed by biography and statistics.
COMPLETE SET (30) 5.00 1.50

1994 Charleston Riverdogs Classic

This 30-card standard size set of the 1994 Charleston RiverDogs, a Class A South Atlantic League affiliate of the Texas Rangers, features white-bordered posed color player shots on its fronts with the player's name and position, team name and logo and Classic logo appearing across the bottom of each card. On a ghosted team logo, the white back carries the player's name at the top, followed by biography and statistics.
COMPLETE SET (30) 8.00 2.40

1994 Charleston RiverDogs Fleer/ProCards

This 29-card standard size set of the 1994 Charleston RiverDogs, a Class A South Atlantic League affiliate of the Texas Rangers, features white-bordered posed color player photos on its fronts with the player's name, position, team name and Fleer/ProCards logo across the bottom of each card. The white back with vertical light blue stripes carries the player's name at the top, followed by biography and statistics.
COMPLETE SET (29) 5.00 1.50

1994 Charleston Wheelers Classic

This 30-card standard size set of the 1994 Charleston Wheelers, a Class A South Atlantic League affiliate of the Cincinnati Reds, features white-bordered posed color player shots on its fronts with the player's name and position, team name and logo and Classic logo appearing across the bottom of each card. On a ghosted team logo, the white back carries the player's name at the top, followed by biography and statistics.
COMPLETE SET (30) 8.00 2.40

1994 Charleston Wheelers Fleer/ProCards

This 28-card standard size set of the 1994 Charleston Wheelers, a Class A South Atlantic League affiliate of the Cincinnati Reds, features white-bordered posed color player photos on its fronts with the player's name, position, team name and Fleer/ProCards logo across the bottom of each card. The white back with vertical light blue stripes carries the player's name at the top, followed by biography and statistics.
COMPLETE SET (28) 5.00 1.50

1994 Charlotte Knights Fleer/ProCards

This 26-card standard size set of the 1994 Charlotte Knights, a Class AAA International League affiliate of the Cleveland Indians, features white-bordered posed color player photos on its fronts with the player's name, position, team name and Fleer/ProCards logo across the bottom of each card. The white back with vertical light blue stripes carries the player's name at the top, followed by biography and statistics.
COMPLETE SET (26) 5.00 1.50

1994 Charlotte Rangers Fleer/ProCards

This 27-card standard size set of the 1994 Charlotte Rangers, a Class A Florida State League affiliate of the Texas Rangers, features white-bordered posed color player photos on its fronts with the player's name, position, team name and Fleer/ProCards logo across the bottom of each card. The white back with vertical light blue stripes carries the player's name at the top, followed by biography and statistics.
COMPLETE SET (27) 5.00 1.50

1994 Chattanooga Lookouts Fleer/ProCards

This 27-card standard size set of the 1994 Chattanooga Lookouts, a Class AA Southern League affiliate of the Cincinnati Reds, features white-bordered posed color player photos on its fronts with the player's name, position, team name and Fleer/ProCards logo across the bottom of each card. The white back with vertical light blue stripes carries the player's name at the top, followed by biography and statistics.
COMPLETE SET (27) 5.00 1.50

1994 Clearwater Phillies Classic

This 30-card standard size set of the 1994 Clearwater Phillies, a Class A Florida State League affiliate of the Philadelphia Phillies, features white-bordered posed color player shots on its fronts with the player's name and position, team name and logo and Classic logo appearing across the bottom of each card. On a ghosted team logo, the white back carries the player's name at the top, followed by biography and statistics.
COMPLETE SET (30) 8.00 2.40

1994 Clearwater Phillies Fleer/ProCards

This 30-card standard size set of the 1994 Clearwater Phillies, a Class A Florida State League affiliate of the Philadelphia Phillies, features white-bordered posed color player photos on its fronts with the player's name, position, team name and Fleer/ProCards logo across the bottom of each card. The white back with vertical light blue stripes carries the player's name at the top, followed by biography and statistics.
COMPLETE SET (30) 5.00 1.50

1994 Clinton Lumberkings Classic

This 30-card standard size set of the 1994 Clinton LumberKings, a Class A Midwest League affiliate of the San Francisco Giants, features white-bordered posed color player shots on its fronts with the player's name and position, team name and logo and Classic logo appearing across the bottom of each card. On a ghosted team logo, the white back carries the player's name at the top, followed by biography and statistics.
COMPLETE SET (30) 8.00 2.40

1994 Clinton LumberKings Fleer/ProCards

This 30-card standard size set of the 1994 Clinton LumberKings, a Class A Midwest League affiliate of the San Francisco Giants, features white-bordered posed color player photos on its fronts with the player's name, position, team name and Fleer/ProCards logo across the bottom of each card. The white back with vertical light blue stripes carries the player's name at the top, followed by biography and statistics.
COMPLETE SET (30) 5.00 1.50

1994 Colorado Silver Bullets Coors

COMPLETE SET (9) 10.00 3.00

1994 Colorado Springs Sky Sox Fleer/ProCards

This 28-card standard size set of the 1994 Colorado Springs Sky Sox, a Class AAA Pacific Coast League affiliate of the Colorado Rookies, features white-bordered posed color player photos on its fronts with the player's name, position, team name and Fleer/ProCards logo across the bottom of each card. The white back with vertical light blue stripes carries the player's name at the top, followed by biography and statistics.
COMPLETE SET (28) 5.00 1.50

1994 Columbus Clippers Fleer/ProCards

This 30-card standard size set of the 1994 Columbus Clippers, a Class AAA International League affiliate of the New York Yankees, features white-bordered posed color player photos on its fronts with the player's name, position, team name and Fleer/ProCards logo across the bottom of each card. The white back with vertical light blue stripes carries the player's name at the top, followed by biography and statistics.
COMPLETE SET (30) 15.00 4.50

1994 Columbus Clippers Police

COMPLETE SET (25) 15.00 4.50

1994 Columbus Clippers Team Issue

These 27 standard-size cards feature members of the 1994 Columbus Clippers. The cards are surrounded by thin white borders with the words "Columbus Clippers" in large white letter on the top and the players name printed in red on the bottom. The back has biographical information and career stats. Since the cards are unnumbered we have checklisted them in alphabetical order. The cards were printed by Metro Media Marketing, Inc.
COMPLETE SET (28) 20.00 6.00

1994 Columbus Redstixx Classic

This 30-card standard size set of the 1994 Columbus RedStixx, a Class A South Atlantic League affiliate of the Cleveland Indians, features white-bordered posed color player shots on its fronts with the player's name and position, team name and logo and Classic logo appearing across the bottom of each card. On a ghosted team logo, the white back carries the player's name at the top, followed by biography and statistics. This issue includes a second year card of Richie Sexson.
COMPLETE SET (30) 25.00 7.50

1994 Columbus RedStixx Fleer/ProCards

This 31-card standard size set of the 1994 Columbus RedStixx, a Class A South Atlantic League affiliate of the Cleveland Indians, features white-bordered posed color player photos on its fronts with the player's name, position, team name and Fleer/ProCards logo across the bottom of each card. The white back with vertical light blue stripes carries the player's name at the top, followed by biography and statistics. This issue includes a second year card of Richie Sexson.
COMPLETE SET (31) 15.00 4.50

1994 Danville Braves Classic

This 30-card standard size set of the 1994 Danville Braves, a Class A Appalachian League affiliate of the Atlanta Braves, features white-bordered posed color player shots on its fronts with the player's name and position, team name and logo and Classic logo appearing across the bottom of each card. On a ghosted team logo, the white back carries the player's name at the top, followed by biography and statistics. This issue includes early cards of Kevin Millwood, Damian Moss and John Rocker.
COMPLETE SET (30) 20.00 6.00

1994 Danville Braves Fleer/ProCards

This 30-card standard size set of the 1994 Danville Braves, a Class A Appalachian League affiliate of the Atlanta Braves, features white-bordered posed color player photos on its fronts with the player's name, position, team name and Fleer/ProCards logo across the bottom of each card. The white back with vertical light blue stripes carries the player's name at the top, followed by biography and statistics. This issue includes early cards of Damian Moss, Kevin Millwood and John Rocker.
COMPLETE SET (30) 12.00 3.60

1994 David Lipscomb Bisons

This 25-card standard-size set features the 1994 Bisons. On a light blue background, the fronts feature posed color player photos with rounded corners. The team name appears above the picture, while the player's name and position, and the team logo are printed under the picture. The white backs carry the player's name, number, and position, a short biography and a summary of accomplishments. The cards are unnumbered and checklisted below in alphabetical order.
COMPLETE SET (25) 10.00 3.00

1994 Daytona Cubs Classic

This 30-card standard size set of the 1994 Daytona Cubs, a Class A Florida State League affiliate of the Chicago Cubs, features white-bordered posed color player shots on its fronts with the player's name and position, team name and logo and Classic logo appearing across the bottom of each card. On a ghosted team logo, the white back carries the player's name at the top, followed by biography and statistics.
COMPLETE SET (30) 8.00 2.40

1994 Daytona Cubs Fleer/ProCards

This 29-card standard size set of the 1994 Daytona Cubs, a Class A Florida State League affiliate of the Chicago Cubs, features white-bordered posed color player photos on its fronts with the player's name, position, team name and Fleer/ProCards logo across the bottom of each card. The white back with vertical light blue stripes carries the player's name at the top, followed by biography and statistics.
COMPLETE SET (29) 5.00 1.50

1994 Dunedin Blue Jays Classic

This 30-card standard size set of the 1994 Dunedin Blue Jays, a Class A Florida State League affiliate of the Toronto Blue Jays, features white-bordered posed color player shots on its fronts with the player's name and position, team name and logo and Classic logo appearing across the bottom of each card. On a ghosted team logo, the white back carries the player's name at the top, followed by biography and statistics.
COMPLETE SET (30) 8.00 2.40

1994 Dunedin Blue Jays Fleer/ProCards

This 30-card standard size set of the 1994 Dunedin Blue Jays, a Class A Florida State League affiliate of the Toronto Blue Jays, features white-bordered posed color player photos on its fronts with the player's name, position, team name and Fleer/ProCards logo across the bottom of each card. The white back with vertical light blue stripes carries the player's name at the top, followed by biography and statistics.
COMPLETE SET (30) 5.00 1.50

1994 Durham Bulls Classic

This 30-card standard size set of the 1994 Durham Bulls, a Class A Carolina League affiliate of the Atlanta Braves, features white-bordered posed color player shots on its fronts with the player's name and position, team name and logo and Classic logo appearing across the bottom of each card. On a ghosted team logo, the white back carries the player's name at the top, followed by biography and statistics.
COMPLETE SET (30) 10.00 3.00

1994 Durham Bulls Fleer/ProCards

This 30-card standard size set of the 1994 Durham Bulls, a Class A Carolina League affiliate of the Atlanta Braves, features white-bordered posed color player photos on its fronts with the player's name, position, team name and Fleer/ProCards logo across the bottom of each card. The white back with vertical light blue stripes carries the player's name at the top, followed by biography and statistics.
COMPLETE SET (30) 8.00 2.40

1994 Durham Bulls Team Issue

The cards are unnumbered and checklisted below in alphabetical order.
COMPLETE SET (32) 8.00 2.40

1994 Edmonton Trappers Fleer/ProCards

This 27-card standard size set of the 1994 Edmonton Trappers, a Class AAA Pacific Coast League affiliate of the Florida Marlins, features white-bordered posed color player photos on its fronts with the player's name, position, team name and Fleer/ProCards logo across the bottom of each card. The white back with vertical light blue stripes carries the player's name at the top, followed by biography and statistics.
COMPLETE SET (27) 8.00 2.40

1994 El Paso Diablos Fleer/ProCards

This 28-card standard size set of the 1994 El Paso Diablos, a Class AA Texas League affiliate of the Milwaukee Brewers, features white-bordered posed color player photos on its fronts with the player's name, position, team name and Fleer/ProCards logo across the bottom of each card. The white back with vertical light blue stripes carries the player's name at the top, followed by biography and statistics.
COMPLETE SET (28) 5.00 1.50

1994 Elizabethton Twins Classic

This 30-card standard size set of the 1994 Elizabethton Twins, a Rookie Class Appalachian League affiliate of the Minnesota Twins, features white-bordered posed color player shots on its fronts with the player's name and position, team name and logo and Classic logo appearing across the bottom of each card. On a ghosted team logo, the white back carries the player's name at the top, followed by biography and statistics. This issue includes the minor league card debut of Jose Valentin.
COMPLETE SET (30) 10.00 3.00

1994 Elizabethton Twins Fleer/ProCards

This 29-card standard size set of the 1994 Elizabethton Twins, a Rookie Class Appalachian League affiliate of the Minnesota Twins, features white-bordered posed color player photos on its fronts with the player's name, position, team name and Fleer/ProCards logo across the bottom of each card. The white back with vertical light blue stripes carries the player's name at the top, followed by biography and statistics. This issue includes the minor league card debut of Jose Valentin.
COMPLETE SET (29) 8.00 2.40

1994 Elmira Pioneers Classic

This 29-card standard size set of the 1994 Elmira Pioneers, a Class A New York-Penn League affiliate of the Florida Marlins, features white-bordered posed color player shots on its fronts with the player's name and position, team name and logo and Classic logo appearing across the bottom of each card. On a ghosted team logo, the white back carries the player's name at the top, followed by biography and statistics.
COMPLETE SET (29) 8.00 2.40

1994 Elmira Pioneers Fleer/ProCards

This 27-card standard size set of the 1994 Elmira Pioneers, a Class A New York-Penn League affiliate of the Florida Marlins, features white-bordered posed color player photos on its fronts with the player's name, position, team name and Fleer/ProCards logo across the bottom of each card. The white back with vertical light blue stripes carries the player's name at the top, followed by biography and statistics.
COMPLETE SET (27) 5.00 1.50

1994 Eugene Emeralds Classic

This 30-card standard size set of the 1994 Eugene Emeralds, a Class A Northwest League affiliate of the Kansas City Royals, eatures white-bordered posed color player shots on its fronts with the player's name and position, team name and logo and Classic logo appearing across the bottom of each card. On a ghosted team logo, the white back carries the player's name at the top, followed by biography and statistics.
COMPLETE SET (30) 8.00 2.40

1994 Eugene Emeralds Fleer/ProCards

This 28-card standard size set of the 1994 Eugene Emeralds, a Class A Northwest League affiliate of the Kansas City Royals, features white-bordered posed color player photos on its fronts with the player's name, position, team name and Fleer/ProCards logo across the bottom of each card. The white back with vertical light blue stripes carries the player's name at the top, followed by biography and statistics.
COMPLETE SET (28) 5.00 1.50

1994 Everett Giants Classic

This 30-card standard size set of the 1994 Everett Giants, a Class A Northwest League affiliate of the San Francisco Giants, features white-bordered posed color player shots on its fronts with the player's name and position, team name and logo and Classic logo appearing across the bottom of each card. On a ghosted team logo, the white back carries the player's name at the top, followed by biography and statistics.
COMPLETE SET (30) 8.00 2.40

1994 Everett Giants Fleer/ProCards

This 31-card standard size set of the 1994 Everett Giants, a Class A Northwest League affiliate of the San Francisco Giants, features white-bordered posed color player photos on its fronts with the player's name, position, team name and Fleer/ProCards logo across the bottom of each card. The white back with vertical light blue stripes carries the player's name at the top, followed by biography and statistics.
COMPLETE SET (31) 10.00 3.00

1994 Fayetteville Generals Classic

This 30-card standard size set of the 1994 Fayetteville Generals, a Class A South Atlantic League affiliate of the Detroit Tigers, features white-bordered posed color player shots on its fronts with the player's name and position, team name and logo and Classic logo appearing across the bottom of each card. On a ghosted team logo, the white back carries the player's name at the top, followed by biography and statistics. This issue includes a minor league card debut of Juan Encarnacion.
COMPLETE SET (30) 15.00 4.50

1994 Fayetteville Generals Fleer/ProCards

This 29-card standard size set of the 1994 Fayetteville Generals, a Class A South Atlantic League affiliate of the Detroit Tigers, features white-bordered posed color player photos on its fronts with the player's name, position, team name and Fleer/ProCards logo across the bottom of each card. The white back with vertical light blue stripes carries the player's name at the top, followed by biography and statistics. This issue includes a minor league card debut of Juan Encarnacion.
COMPLETE SET (29) 12.00 3.60

1994 Florida State League All-Stars Fleer/ProCards

An early Derek Jeter card highlights this set.
COMPLETE SET (52) 50.00 15.00

1994 Fort Myers Miracle Classic

This 30-card standard size set of the 1994 Fort Myers Miracle, a Class A Florida State League affiliate of the Minnesota Twins, features white-bordered posed color player shots on its fronts with the player's name and position, team name and logo and Classic logo appearing across the bottom of each card. On a ghosted team logo, the white back carries the player's name at the top, followed by biography and statistics.
COMPLETE SET (30) 8.00 2.40

1994 Fort Myers Miracle Fleer/ProCards

This 28-card standard size set of the 1994 Fort Myers Miracle, a Class A Florida State League affiliate of the Minnesota Twins, features white-bordered posed color player photos on its fronts with the player's name, position, team name and Fleer/ProCards logo across the bottom of each card. The white back with vertical light blue stripes carries the player's name at the top, followed by biography and statistics.
COMPLETE SET (28) 5.00 1.50

1994 Fort Wayne Wizards Classic

This 30-card standard size set of the 1994 Fort Wayne Wizards, a Class A Midwest League affiliate of the Minnesota Twins, features white-bordered posed color player shots on its fronts with the player's name and position, team name and logo and Classic logo appearing across the bottom of each card. On a ghosted team logo, the white back carries the player's name at the top, followed by biography and statistics.
COMPLETE SET (30) 8.00 2.40

1994 Fort Wayne Wizards Fleer/ProCards

This 28-card standard size set of the 1994 Fort Wayne Wizards, a Class A Midwest League affiliate of the Minnesota Twins, features white-bordered posed color player photos on its fronts with the player's name, position, team name and Fleer/ProCards logo across the bottom of each card. The white back with vertical light blue stripes carries the player's name at the top, followed by biography and statistics.
COMPLETE SET (28) 5.00 1.50

1994 Frederick Keys Classic

This 30-card standard size set of the 1994 Frederick Keys, a Class A Carolina League affiliate of the Baltimore Orioles, features white-bordered posed color player shots on its fronts with the player's name and position, team name and logo and Classic logo appearing across the bottom of each card. On a ghosted team logo, the white back carries the player's name at the top, followed by biography and statistics.
COMPLETE SET (30) 8.00 2.40

1994 Frederick Keys Fleer/ProCards

This 29-card standard size set of the 1994 Frederick Keys, a Class A Carolina League affiliate of the Baltimore Orioles, features white-bordered posed color player photos on its fronts with the player's name, position, team name and Fleer/ProCards logo across the bottom of each card. The white back with vertical light blue stripes carries the player's name at the top, followed by biography and statistics.
COMPLETE SET (29) 5.00 1.50

1994 Great Falls Dodgers Sports Pro

COMPLETE SET (30) 8.00 2.40

1994 Greensboro Bats Classic

This 30-card standard size set of the 1994 Greensboro Bats, a Class A South Atlantic League affiliate of the New York Yankees, features white-bordered posed color player shots on its fronts with the player's name and position, team name and logo and Classic logo appearing across the bottom of each card. On a ghosted team logo, the white back carries the player's name at the top, followed by biography and statistics.
COMPLETE SET (30) 8.00 2.40

1994 Greensboro Bats Fleer/ProCards

This 31-card standard size set of the 1994 Greensboro Bats, a Class A South Atlantic League affiliate of the New York Yankees, features white-bordered posed color player photos on its fronts with the player's name, position, team name and Fleer/ProCards logo across the bottom of each card. The white back with vertical light blue stripes carries the player's name at the top, followed by biography and statistics.
COMPLETE SET (31) 5.00 1.50

1994 Greenville Braves Fleer/ProCards

This 28-card standard size set of the 1994 Greenville Braves, a Class AA Southern League affiliate of the Atlanta Braves, features white-bordered posed color player photos on its fronts with the player's name, position, team name and Fleer/ProCards logo across the bottom of each card. The white back with vertical light blue stripes carries the player's name at the top, followed by biography and statistics.
COMPLETE SET (28) 5.00 1.50

1994 Greenville Braves Team Issue

Sponsored by Super Stars and Rock 101 (WROQ), this 30-card set was issued as an uncut, perforated sheet. It consists of three panels (each measuring approximately 10 5/8" by 9 3/8") joined together to form one continuous sheet. The first panel features sponsors' logos and a game photo. The second panel features 15 player cards, while the third panel has 13 player cards and two logo cards. After perforation, the cards measure approximately 2 1/8" by 3 1/8". On a white card face, the fronts have color player portraits with red and blue borders. The player's name and position appear below the picture with the sponsor logos immediately below. The horizontal backs carry a short player biography and career stats. The cards are unnumbered and arranged alphabetical, with the manager and coaches listed before the players.
COMPLETE SET (30) 8.00 2.40

1994 Hagerstown Suns Classic

This 30-card standard size set of the 1994 Hagerstown Suns, a Class A South Atlantic League affiliate of the Toronto Blue Jays, features white-bordered posed color player shots on its fronts with the player's name and position, team name and logo and Classic logo appearing across the bottom of each card. On a ghosted team logo, the white back carries the player's name at the top, followed by biography and statistics.
COMPLETE SET (30) 8.00 2.40

1994 Hagerstown Suns Fleer/ProCards

This 29-card standard size set of the 1994 Hagerstown Suns, a Class A South Atlantic League affiliate of the Toronto Blue Jays, features white-bordered posed color player photos on its fronts with the player's name, position, team name and Fleer/ProCards logo across the bottom of each card. The white back with vertical light blue stripes carries the player's name at the top, followed by biography and statistics.
COMPLETE SET (29) 5.00 1.50

1994 Harrisburg Senators Fleer/ProCards

This 29-card standard size set of the 1994 Harrisburg Senators, a Class AA Eastern League affiliate of the Montreal Expos, features white-bordered posed color player photos on its fronts with the player's name, position, team name and Fleer/ProCards logo across the bottom of each card. The white back with vertical light blue stripes carries the player's name at the top, followed by biography and statistics.
COMPLETE SET (29) 5.00 1.50

1994 Hawaii Rainbows

This 30-card set of the University of Hawaii Rainbows Baseball team features color player photos in white borders. The set was produced for 7-11 stores and sponsored by Pepsi, Bank of America, and Oscar Mayer. The backs carry player information and career statistics. The cards are unnumbered and checklisted below in alphabetical order.
COMPLETE SET (30) 10.00 3.00

1994 Helena Brewers Fleer/ProCards

This 27-card standard size set of the 1994 Helena Brewers, a Rookie Class Pioneer League affiliate of the Milwaukee Brewers, features white-bordered posed color player photos on its fronts with the player's name, position, team name and Fleer/ProCards logo across the bottom of each card. The white back with vertical light blue stripes carries the player's name at the top, followed by biography and statistics.

COMPLETE SET (27) 5.00 1.50

1994 Helena Brewers Sports Pro

COMPLETE SET (30) 8.00 2.40

1994 Hickory Crawdads Classic

This 30-card standard size set of the 1994 Hickory Crawdads, a Class A South Atlantic League affiliate of the Chicago White Sox, features white-bordered posed color player shots on its fronts with the player's name and position, team name and logo and Classic logo appearing across the bottom of each card. On a ghosted team logo, the white back carries the player's name at the top, followed by biography and statistics. An early card of Magglio Ordonez is a highlight of this set.

COMPLETE SET (30) 25.00 7.50

1994 Hickory Crawdads Fleer/ProCards

This 30-card standard size set of the 1994 Hickory Crawdads, a Class A South Atlantic League affiliate of the Chicago White Sox, features white-bordered posed color player photos on its fronts with the player's name, position, team name and Fleer/ProCards logo across the bottom of each card. The white back with vertical light blue stripes carries the player's name at the top, followed by biography and statistics. An early card of Magglio Ordonez is a featured card in this set.

COMPLETE SET (30) 15.00 4.50

1994 High Desert Mavericks Classic

This 30-card standard size set of the 1994 High Desert Mavericks, a Class A California League Independent, features white-bordered posed color player shots on its fronts with the player's name and position, team name and logo and Classic logo appearing across the bottom of each card. On a ghosted team logo, the white back carries the player's name at the top, followed by biography and statistics.

COMPLETE SET (30) 8.00 2.40

1994 High Desert Mavericks Fleer/ProCards

This 30-card standard size set of the 1994 High Desert Mavericks, a Class A California League Independent, features white-bordered posed color player photos on its fronts with the player's name, position, team name and Fleer/ProCards logo across the bottom of each card. The white back with vertical light blue stripes carries the player's name at the top, followed by biography and statistics.

COMPLETE SET (30) 5.00 1.50

1994 Hudson Valley Renegades Classic

This 30-card standard size set of the 1994 Hudson Valley Renegades, a Class A New York-Penn League affiliate of the Texas Rangers, features white-bordered posed color player shots on its fronts with the player's name and position, team name and logo and Classic logo appearing across the bottom of each card. On a ghosted team logo, the white back carries the player's name at the top, followed by biography and statistics.

COMPLETE SET (30) 8.00 2.40

1994 Hudson Valley Renegades Fleer/ProCards

This 30-card standard size set of the 1994 Hudson Valley Renegades, a Class A New York-Penn League affiliate of the Texas Rangers, features white-bordered posed color player photos on its fronts with the player's name, position, team name and Fleer/ProCards logo across the bottom of each card. The white back with vertical light blue stripes carries the player's name at the top, followed by biography and statistics.

COMPLETE SET (30) 5.00 1.50

1994 Huntington Cubs Classic

This 30-card standard size set of the 1994 Huntington Cubs, a Rookie Class Appalachian League affiliate of the Chicago Cubs, features white-bordered posed color player shots on its fronts with the player's name and position, team name and logo and Classic logo appearing across the bottom of each card. On a ghosted team logo, the white back carries the player's name at the top, followed by biography and statistics.

COMPLETE SET (30) 8.00 2.40

1994 Huntington Cubs Fleer/ProCards

This 31-card standard size set of the 1994 Huntington Cubs, a Rookie Class Appalachian League affiliate of the Chicago Cubs, features white-bordered posed color player photos on its fronts with the player's name, position, team name and Fleer/ProCards logo across the bottom of each card. The white back with vertical light blue stripes carries the player's name at the top, followed by biography and statistics.

COMPLETE SET (31) 5.00 1.50

1994 Huntsville Stars Team Issue

This 27-card standard size set of the 1994 Huntsville Stars, a Class AA Southern League affiliate of the Oakland Athletics, was sponsored by Burger King. An early card of Jason Giambi is in this set.

COMPLETE SET (27) 20.00 6.00

1994 Idaho Falls Braves Fleer/ProCards

This 31-card standard size set of the 1994 Idaho Falls Braves, a Rookie Class Pioneer League affiliate of the Atlanta Braves, features white-bordered posed color player photos on its fronts with the player's name, position, team name and Fleer/ProCards logo across the bottom of each card. The white back with vertical light blue stripes carries the player's name at the top, followed by biography and statistics.

COMPLETE SET (31) 5.00 1.50

1994 Idaho Falls Braves Sports Pro

COMPLETE SET (30) 8.00 2.40

1994 Indianapolis Indians Fleer/ProCards

This 27-card standard size set of the 1994 Indianapolis Indians, a Class AAA American Association League affiliate of the Cincinnati Reds, features white-bordered posed color player photos on its fronts with the player's name, position, team name and Fleer/ProCards logo across the bottom of each card. The white back with vertical light blue stripes carries the player's name at the top, followed by biography and statistics.

COMPLETE SET (27) 5.00 1.50

1994 Iowa Cubs Fleer/ProCards

This 26-card standard size set of the 1994 Iowa Cubs, a Class AAA American Association affiliate of the Chicago Cubs, features white-bordered posed color player photos on its fronts with the player's name, position, team name and Fleer/ProCards logo across the bottom of each card. The white back with vertical light blue stripes carries the player's name at the top, followed by biography and statistics.

COMPLETE SET (26) 5.00 1.50

1994 Jackson Generals Fleer/ProCards

This 27-card standard size set of the 1994 Jackson Generals, a Class AA Texas League affiliate of the Houston Astros, features white-bordered posed color player photos on its fronts with the player's name, position, team name and Fleer/ProCards logo across the bottom of each card. The white back with vertical light blue stripes carries the player's name at the top, followed by biography and statistics. An early card of Bob Abreu is in this set.

COMPLETE SET (27) 10.00 3.00

1994 Jacksonville Suns Fleer/ProCards

This 27-card standard size set of the 1994 Jacksonville Suns, a Class AA Southern League affiliate of the Seattle Mariners, features white-bordered posed color player photos on its fronts with the player's name, position, team name and Fleer/ProCards logo across the bottom of each card. The white back with vertical light blue stripes carries the player's name at the top, followed by biography and statistics.

COMPLETE SET (27) 5.00 1.50

1994 Jamestown Jammers Classic

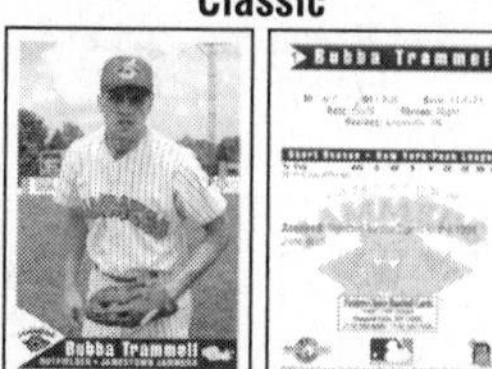

This 30-card standard size set of the 1994 Jamestown Jammers, a Class A New York-Penn League affiliate of the Detroit Tigers, features white-bordered posed color player shots on its fronts with the player's name and position, team name and logo and Classic logo appearing across the bottom of each card. On a ghosted team logo, the white back carries the player's name at the top, followed by biography and statistics. This issue includes the minor league card debut of Bubba Trammell.

COMPLETE SET (30) 10.00 3.00

1994 Jamestown Jammers Fleer/ProCards

This 30-card standard size set of the 1994 Jamestown Jammers, a Class A New York-Penn League affiliate of the Detroit Tigers, features white-bordered posed color player photos on its fronts with the player's name, position, team name and Fleer/ProCards logo across the bottom of each card. The white back with vertical light blue stripes carries the player's name at the top, followed by biography and statistics. This issue includes the minor league card debut of Bubba Trammell.

COMPLETE SET (30) 8.00 2.40

1994 Johnson City Cardinals Classic

This 30-card standard size set of the 1994 Johnson City Cardinals, a Rookie Class Appalachian League affiliate of the St. Louis Cardinals, features white-bordered posed color player shots on its fronts with the player's name and position, team name and logo and Classic logo appearing across the bottom of each card. On a ghosted team logo, the white back carries the player's name at the top, followed by biography and statistics.

COMPLETE SET (30) 8.00 2.40

1994 Johnson City Cardinals Fleer/ProCards

This 31-card standard size set of the 1994 Johnson City Cardinals, a Rookie Class Appalachian League affiliate of the St. Louis Cardinals, features white-bordered posed color player photos on its fronts with the player's name, position, team name and Fleer/ProCards logo across the bottom of each card. The white back with vertical light blue stripes carries the player's name at the top, followed by biography and statistics.

COMPLETE SET (31) 5.00 1.50

1994 Kane County Cougars Classic

This 30-card standard size set of the 1994 Kane County Cougars, a Class A Midwest League affiliate of the Florida Marlins, features white-bordered posed color player shots on its fronts with the player's name and position, team name and logo and Classic logo appearing across the bottom of each card. On a ghosted team logo, the white back carries the player's name at the top, followed by biography and statistics.

COMPLETE SET (30) 12.00 2.40

1994 Kane County Cougars Fleer/ProCards

This 30-card standard size set of the 1994 Kane County Cougars, a Class A Midwest League affiliate of the Florida Marlins, features white-bordered posed color player photos on its fronts with the player's name, position, team name and Fleer/ProCards logo across the bottom of each card. The white back with vertical light blue stripes carries the player's name at the top, followed by biography and statistics.

COMPLETE SET (30) 5.00 1.50

1994 Kane County Cougars Team Issue

This 30-card standard size set features members of the 1994 Kane County Cougars, a Class A Midwest League affiliate of the Florida Marlins.

COMPLETE SET (30) 5.00 1.50

1994 Kingsport Mets Classic

This 30-card standard size set of the 1994 Kingsport Mets, a Rookie Class Appalachian League affiliate of the New York Mets, features white-bordered posed color player shots on its fronts with the player's name and position, team name and logo and Classic logo appearing across the bottom of each card. On a ghosted team logo, the white back carries the player's name at the top, followed by biography and statistics. This issue includes the minor league card debut of Terrence Long.

COMPLETE SET (30) 20.00 6.00

1994 Kingsport Mets Fleer/ProCards

This 29-card standard size set of the 1994 Kingsport Mets, a Rookie Class Appalachian League affiliate of the New York Mets, features white-bordered posed color player photos on its fronts with the player's name, position, team name and Fleer/ProCards logo across the bottom of each card. The white back with vertical light blue stripes carries the player's name at the top, followed by biography and statistics. This issue includes the minor league card debut of Terrence Long.

COMPLETE SET (29) 10.00 3.00

1994 Kinston Indians Classic

This 30-card standard size set of the 1994 Kinston Indians, a Class A Carolina League affiliate of the Cleveland Indians, features white-bordered posed color player shots on its fronts with the player's name and position, team name and logo and Classic logo appearing across the bottom of each card. On a ghosted team logo, the white back carries the player's name at the top, followed by biography and statistics.

COMPLETE SET (30) 8.00 2.40

1994 Kinston Indians Fleer/ProCards

This 29-card standard size set of the 1994 Kinston Indians, a Class A Carolina League affiliate of the Cleveland Indians, features white-bordered posed color player photos on its fronts with the player's name, position, team name and Fleer/ProCards logo across the bottom of each card. The white back with vertical light blue stripes carries the player's name at the top, followed by biography and statistics.

COMPLETE SET (29) 5.00 1.50

1994 Knoxville Smokies Fleer/ProCards

This 28-card standard size set of the 1994 Knoxville Smokies, a Class AA Southern League affiliate of the Toronto Blue Jays, features white-bordered posed color player photos on its fronts with the player's name, position, team name and Fleer/ProCards logo across the bottom of each card. The white back with vertical light blue stripes carries the player's name at the top, followed by biography and statistics.

COMPLETE SET (28) 5.00 1.50

1994 Lake Elsinore Storm Classic

This 30-card standard size set of the 1994 Lake Elsinore Storm, a Class A California League affiliate of the California Angels, features white-bordered posed color player shots on its fronts with the player's name and position, team name and logo and Classic logo appearing across the bottom of each card. On a ghosted team logo, the white back carries the player's name at the top, followed by biography and statistics.

COMPLETE SET (30) 8.00 2.40

1994 Lake Elsinore Storm Fleer/ProCards

This 29-card standard size set of the 1994 Lake Elsinore Storm, a Class A California League affiliate of the California Angels, features white-bordered posed color player photos on its fronts with the player's name, position, team name and Fleer/ProCards logo across the bottom of each card. The white back with vertical light blue stripes carries the player's name at the top, followed by biography and statistics.

COMPLETE SET (29) 5.00 1.50

1994 Lakeland Tigers Classic

This 30-card standard size set of the 1994 Lakeland Tigers, a Class A Florida State League affiliate of the Detroit Tigers, features white-bordered posed color player shots on its fronts with the player's name and position, team name and logo and Classic logo appearing across the bottom of each card. On a ghosted team logo, the white back carries the player's name at the top, followed by biography and statistics.

COMPLETE SET (30) 8.00 2.40

1994 Lakeland Tigers Fleer/ProCards

This 28-card standard size set of the 1994 Lakeland Tigers, a Class A Florida State League affiliate of the Detroit Tigers, features white-bordered posed color player photos on its fronts with the player's name, position, team name and Fleer/ProCards logo across the bottom of each card. The white back with vertical light blue stripes carries the player's name at the top, followed by biography and statistics.

COMPLETE SET (28) 5.00 1.50

1994 Las Vegas Stars Fleer/ProCards

This 25-card standard size set of the 1994 Las Vegas Stars, a Class AAA Pacific Coast League affiliate of the San Diego Padres, features white-bordered posed color player photos on its fronts with the player's name, position, team name and Fleer/ProCards logo across the bottom of each card. The white back with vertical light blue stripes carries the player's name at the top, followed by biography and statistics.

COMPLETE SET (25) 5.00 1.50

1994 Lethbridge Mounties Fleer/ProCards

This 30-card standard size set of the 1994 Lethbridge Mounties, a Rookie Class Pioneer League Independent, features white-bordered posed color player photos on its fronts with the player's name, position, team name and Fleer/ProCards logo across the bottom of each card. The white back with vertical light blue stripes carries the player's name at the top, followed by biography and statistics.

COMPLETE SET (30) 5.00 1.50

1994 Lethbridge Mounties Sports Pro

COMPLETE SET (30) 8.00 2.40

1994 Louisville Redbirds Fleer/ProCards

This 29-card standard size set of the 1994 Louisville Redbirds, a Class AAA American Association affiliate of the St. Louis Cardinals, features white-bordered posed color player photos on its fronts with the player's name, position, team name and Fleer/ProCards logo across the bottom of each card. The white back with vertical light blue stripes carries the player's name at the top, followed by biography and statistics.

COMPLETE SET (29) 5.00 1.50

1994 LSU Tigers

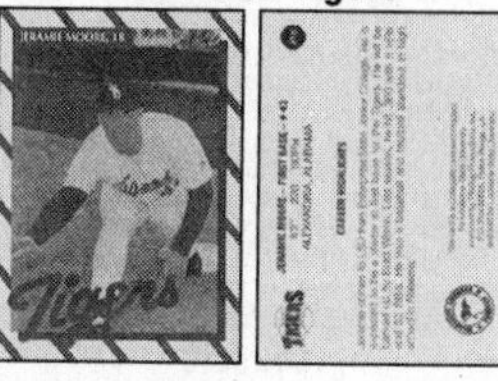

These 16 standard-size cards feature on their fronts posed color player photos of the 1994 LSU Tigers. The cards' white borders are highlighted by diagonal purple lines. Most cards carry the players name at the top of the photo and the team name at the bottom, but a few have this arrangement reversed. The white horizontal back carries the player's name, position, and uniform number at the top, followed below by biography and career highlights. All text is in purple lettering.

COMPLETE SET (16) 10.00 3.00

1994 LSU Tigers McDag Purple

These cards, featuring members of the 1994 LSU Tigers, features purple borders on the front with full-color action photos. The logo on the front says "LSU 1893-1993".

COMPLETE SET (16) 10.00 3.00

1994 Lynchburg Red Sox Classic

This 30-card standard size set of the 1994 Lynchburg Red Sox, a Class A Carolina League affiliate of the Boston Red Sox, features white-bordered posed color player shots on its fronts with the player's name and position, team name and logo and Classic logo appearing across the bottom of each card. On a ghosted team logo, the white back carries the player's name at the top, followed by biography and statistics. This issue includes the minor league card debut of Trot Nixon.

COMPLETE SET (30) 12.00 3.60

1994 Lynchburg Red Sox Fleer/ProCards

This 29-card standard size set of the 1994 Lynchburg Red Sox, a Class A Carolina League affiliate of the Boston Red Sox, features white-bordered posed color player photos on its fronts with the player's name, position, team name and Fleer/ProCards logo across the bottom of each card. The white back with vertical light blue stripes carries the player's name at the top, followed by biography and statistics. This issue includes the minor league card debut of Trot Nixon.

COMPLETE SET (29) 15.00 4.50

1994 Macon Braves Classic

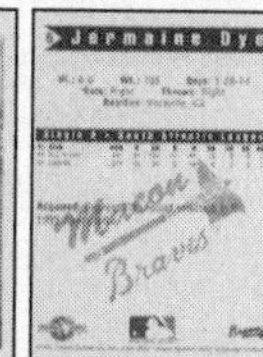

This 30-card standard size set of the 1994 Macon Braves, a Class A South Atlantic League affiliate of the Atlanta Braves, features white-bordered posed color player shots on its fronts with the player's name and position, team name and logo and Classic logo appearing across the bottom of each card. On a ghosted team logo, the white back carries the player's name at the top, followed by biography and statistics. This issue includes the minor league card debut of Jermaine Dye.

COMPLETE SET (30) 25.00 7.50

1994 Macon Braves Fleer/ProCards

This 31-card standard size set of the 1994 Macon Braves, a Class A South Atlantic League affiliate of the Atlanta Braves, features white-bordered posed color player photos on its fronts with the player's name, position, team name and Fleer/ProCards logo across the bottom of each card. The white back with vertical light blue stripes carries the player's name at the top, followed by biography and statistics. This issue includes the minor league card debut of Jermaine Dye.

COMPLETE SET (31) 15.00 4.50

1994 Madison Hatters Classic

This 30-card standard size set of the 1994 Madison Hatters, a Class A Midwest League affiliate of the St. Louis Cardinals, features white-bordered posed color player shots on its fronts with the player's name and position, team name and logo and Classic logo

appearing across the bottom of each card. On a ghosted team logo, the white back carries the player's name at the top, followed by biography and statistics.
COMPLETE SET (30) 8.00 2.40

1994 Madison Hatters Fleer/ProCards

This 30-card standard size set of the 1994 Madison Hatters, a Class A Midwest League affiliate of the St. Louis Cardinals, features white-bordered posed color player photos on its fronts with the player's name, position, team name and Fleer/ProCards logo across the bottom of each card. The white back with vertical light blue stripes carries the player's name at the top, followed by biography and statistics.
COMPLETE SET (30) 5.00 1.50

1994 Martinsville Phillies Classic

This 30-card standard size set of the 1994 Martinsville Phillies, a Class A Appalachian League affiliate of the Philadelphia Phillies, features white-bordered posed color player shots on its fronts with the player's name and position, team name and logo and Classic logo appearing across the bottom of each card. On a ghosted team logo, the white back carries the player's name at the top, followed by biography and statistics.
COMPLETE SET (30) 8.00 2.40

1994 Martinsville Phillies Fleer/ProCards

This 31-card standard size set of the 1994 Martinsville Phillies, a Class A Appalachian League affiliate of the Philadelphia Phillies, features white-bordered posed color player photos on its fronts with the player's name, position, team name and Fleer/ProCards logo across the bottom of each card. The white back with vertical light blue stripes carries the player's name at the top, followed by biography and statistics.
COMPLETE SET (31) 5.00 1.50

1994 Medicine Hat Blue Jays Fleer/ProCards

This 29-card standard size set of the 1994 Medicine Hat Blue Jays, a Rookie Class Pioneer League affiliate of the Toronto Blue Jays, features white-bordered posed color player photos on its fronts with the player's name, position, team name and Fleer/ProCards logo across the bottom of each card. The white back with vertical light blue stripes carries the player's name at the top, followed by biography and statistics. This issue includes the minor league card debuts of Chris Carpenter.
COMPLETE SET (29) 10.00 3.00

1994 Medicine Hat Blue Jays Sports Pro

This 30-card standard size set of the 1994 Medicine Hat Blue Jays, a Rookie Class Pioneer League affiliate of the Toronto Blue Jays, features the minor league card debuts of Chris Carpenter.
COMPLETE SET (30) 10.00 3.00

1994 Memphis Chicks Fleer/ProCards

This 28-card standard size set of the 1994 Memphis Chicks, a Class AA Southern League affiliate of the Kansas City Royals, features white-bordered posed color player photos on its fronts with the player's name, position, team name and Fleer/ProCards logo across the bottom of each card. The white back with vertical light blue stripes carries the player's name at the top, followed by biography and statistics.
COMPLETE SET (28) 5.00 1.50

1994 Midland Angels Fleer/ProCards

This 27-card standard size set of the 1994 Midland Angels, a Class AA Texas League affiliate of the California Angels, features white-bordered posed color player photos on its fronts with the player's name, position, team name and Fleer/ProCards logo across the bottom of each card. The white back with vertical light blue stripes carries the player's name at the top, followed by biography and statistics.
COMPLETE SET (27) 5.00 1.50

1994 Midland Angels One Hour Photo

This 33-card set of the 1994 Midland Angels, a Class AA Texas League affiliate of the California Angels, features color player photos. The set measures approximately 5 1/2" by 5". The backs are blank. The cards are unnumbered and checklisted below in alphabetical order. 500 sets were produced.
COMPLETE SET (33) 40.00 12.00

1994 Midwest League All-Stars Fleer/ProCards

This 59-card standard size set of the 1994 Midwest League All-Stars features white-bordered posed color player photos on its fronts with the player's name, position, team name and Fleer/ProCards logo across the bottom of each card. The white back with vertical light blue stripes carries the player's

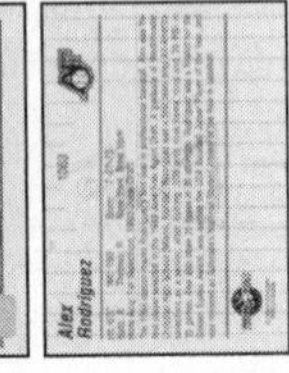

name at the top, followed by biography and statistics. This issue includes a first year card of Alex Rodriguez and an early card of Richard Hidalgo.
COMPLETE SET (59) 60.00 18.00

1994 Mississippi State Bulldogs

Checklisted by uniform number.
COMPLETE SET 20.00 6.00

1994 Modesto A's Classic

This 30-card standard size set of the 1994 Modesto A's, a Class A California League affiliate of the Oakland Athletics, features white-bordered posed color player shots on its fronts with the player's name and position, team name and logo and Classic logo appearing across the bottom of each card. On a ghosted team logo, the white back carries the player's name at the top, followed by biography and statistics. Tony Batista's first card is in this set.
COMPLETE SET (30) 20.00 6.00

1994 Modesto A's Fleer/ProCards

This 26-card standard size set of the 1994 Modesto A's, a Class A California League affiliate of the Oakland Athletics, features white-bordered posed color player photos on its fronts with the player's name, position, team name and Fleer/ProCards logo across the bottom of each card. The white back with vertical light blue stripes carries the player's name at the top, followed by biography and statistics. Tony Batista's first card is in this set.
COMPLETE SET (26) 15.00 4.50

1994 Nashville Sounds Fleer/ProCards

This 27-card standard size set of the 1994 Nashville Sounds, a Class AAA American Association League affiliate of the Chicago White Sox, features white-bordered posed color player photos on its fronts with the player's name, position, team name and Fleer/ProCards logo across the bottom of each card. The white back with vertical light blue stripes carries the player's name at the top, followed by biography and statistics.
COMPLETE SET (27) 5.00 1.50

1994 Nashville Xpress Fleer/ProCards

This 28-card standard size set of the 1994 Nashville Xpress, a Class AA Southern League affiliate of the Minnesota Twins, features white-bordered posed color player photos on its fronts with the player's name, position, team name and Fleer/ProCards logo across the bottom of each card. The white back with vertical light blue stripes carries the player's name at the top, followed by biography and statistics.
COMPLETE SET (28) 5.00 1.50

1994 New Britain Red Sox Fleer/ProCards

This 27-card standard size set of the 1994 New Britain Red Sox, a Class AA Eastern League affiliate of the Boston Red Sox, features white-bordered posed color player photos on its fronts with the player's name, position, team name and Fleer/ProCards logo across the bottom of each card. The white back with vertical light blue stripes carries the player's name at the top, followed by biography and statistics.
COMPLETE SET (27) 5.00 1.50

1994 New Haven Ravens Fleer/ProCards

This 29-card standard size set of the 1994 New Haven Ravens, a Class AA Eastern League affiliate of the Colorado Rockies, features white-bordered posed color player photos on its fronts with the player's name, position, team name and Fleer/ProCards logo across the bottom of each card. The white back with vertical light blue stripes carries the player's name at the top, followed by biography and statistics.
COMPLETE SET (29) 5.00 1.50

1994 New Jersey Cardinals Classic

This 30-card standard size set of the 1994 New Jersey Cardinals, a Class A New York-Penn League affiliate of the St. Louis Cardinals, features white-bordered posed color player shots on its fronts with the player's name and position, team name and logo and Classic logo appearing across the bottom of each card. On a ghosted team logo, the white back carries the player's name at the top, followed by biography and statistics.
COMPLETE SET (30) 8.00 2.40

1994 New Jersey Cardinals Fleer/ProCards

This 31-card standard size set of the 1994 New Jersey Cardinals, a Class A New York-Penn League affiliate of the St. Louis Cardinals, features white-bordered posed color player photos on its fronts with the player's name, position, team name and Fleer/ProCards logo across the bottom of each card. The white back with vertical light blue stripes carries the player's name at the top, followed by biography and statistics.
COMPLETE SET (31) 5.00 1.50

1994 New Orleans Zephyrs Fleer/ProCards

This 27-card standard size set of the 1994 New Orleans Zephyrs, a Class AAA American Association affiliate of the Milwaukee Brewers, features white-bordered posed color player photos on its fronts with the player's name, position, team name and Fleer/ProCards logo across the bottom of each card. The white back with vertical light blue stripes carries the player's name at the top, followed by biography and statistics.
COMPLETE SET (27) 5.00 1.50

1994 Norfolk Tides Fleer/ProCards

This 27-card standard size set of the 1994 Norfolk Tides, a Class AAA International League affiliate of the New York Mets, features white-bordered posed color player photos on its fronts with the player's name, position, team name and Fleer/ProCards logo across the bottom of each card. The white back with vertical light blue stripes carries the player's name at the top, followed by biography and statistics.
COMPLETE SET (27) 5.00 1.50

1994 Ogden Raptors Fleer/ProCards

This 24-card standard size set of the 1994 Ogden Raptors, a Rookie Class Pioneer League Independent, features white-bordered posed color player photos on its fronts with the player's name, position, team name and Fleer/ProCards logo across the bottom of each card. The white back with vertical light blue stripes carries the player's name at the top, followed by biography and statistics.
COMPLETE SET (24) 5.00 1.50

1994 Ogden Raptors Sports Pro

COMPLETE SET (30) 8.00 2.40

1994 Oklahoma City 89ers Fleer/ProCards

This 25-card standard size set of the 1994 Oklahoma City 89ers, a Class AAA American Association affiliate of the Texas Rangers, features white-bordered posed color player photos on its fronts with the player's name, position, team name and Fleer/ProCards logo across the bottom of each card. The white back with vertical light blue stripes carries the player's name at the top, followed by biography and statistics.
COMPLETE SET (25) 5.00 1.50

1994 Omaha Royals Fleer/ProCards

This 27-card standard size set of the 1994 Omaha Royals, a Class AAA American Association affiliate of the Kansas City Royals, features white-bordered posed color player photos on its fronts with the player's name, position, team name and Fleer/ProCards logo across the bottom of each card. The white back with vertical light blue stripes carries the player's name at the top, followed by biography and statistics.
COMPLETE SET (27) 5.00 1.50

1994 Oneonta Yankees Classic

This 30-card standard size set of the 1994 Oneonta Yankees, a Class A New York-Penn League affiliate of the New York Yankees, features white-bordered posed color player shots on its fronts with the player's name and position, team name and logo and Classic logo appearing across the bottom of each card. On a ghosted team logo, the white back carries the player's name at the top, followed by biography and statistics.
COMPLETE SET (30) 8.00 2.40

1994 Oneonta Yankees Fleer/ProCards

This 31-card standard size set of the 1994 Oneonta Yankees, a Class A New York-Penn League affiliate of the New York Yankees, features white-bordered posed color player photos on its fronts with the player's name, position, team name and Fleer/ProCards logo across the bottom of each card. The white back with vertical light blue stripes carries the player's name at the top, followed by biography and statistics.
COMPLETE SET (31) 5.00 1.50

1994 Orlando Cubs Fleer/ProCards

This 26-card standard size set of the 1994 Orlando Cubs, a Class AA Southern League affiliate of the Chicago Cubs, features white-bordered posed color player photos on its fronts with the player's name, position, team name and Fleer/ProCards logo across the bottom of each card. The white back with vertical light blue stripes carries the player's name at the top, followed by biography and statistics.
COMPLETE SET (26) 5.00 1.50

1994 Osceola Astros Anniversary Team Issue

These 30 cards feature some of the leading players in Osceola Astros history. 1,000 of these sets were produced.
COMPLETE SET 10.00 3.00

1994 Osceola Astros Classic

This 30-card standard size set of the 1994 Osceola Astros, a Class A Florida State League affiliate of the Houston Astros, features white-bordered posed color player shots on its fronts with the player's name and position, team name and logo and Classic logo appearing across the bottom of each card. On a ghosted team logo, the white back carries the player's name at the top, followed by biography and statistics.
COMPLETE SET (30) 8.00 2.40

1994 Osceola Astros Fleer/ProCards

This 30-card standard size set of the 1994 Osceola Astros, a Class A Florida State League affiliate of the Houston Astros, features white-bordered posed color player photos on its fronts with the player's name, position, team name and Fleer/ProCards logo across the bottom of each card. The white back with vertical light blue stripes carries the player's name at the top, followed by biography and statistics.
COMPLETE SET (30) 5.00 1.50

1994 Ottawa Lynx Fleer/ProCards

This 19-card standard size set of the 1994 Ottawa Lynx, a Class AAA International League affiliate of the Montreal Expos, features white-bordered posed color player photos on its fronts with the player's name, position, team name and Fleer/ProCards logo across the bottom of each card. The white back with vertical light blue stripes carries the player's name at the top, followed by biography and statistics.
COMPLETE SET (19) 5.00 1.50

1994 Pawtucket Red Sox Dunkin' Donuts

This 31-card set of the Pawtucket Red Sox, a Class AAA International League affiliate of the Boston Red Sox, was issued in one large sheet featuring six perforated five-card strips with a large team photo in the wide top strip. Sponsored by Channel 10 and Dunkin' Donuts, the fronts carry color player photos while the backs display player career statistics. The cards are unnumbered and checklisted below in alphabetical order.
COMPLETE SET (31) 40.00 12.00

1994 Pawtucket Red Sox Fleer/ProCards

This 25-card standard size set of the 1994 Pawtucket Red Sox, a Class AAA International League affiliate of the Boston Red Sox, features white-bordered posed color player photos on its fronts with the player's name, position, team name and Fleer/ProCards logo across the bottom of each card. The white back with vertical light blue stripes carries the player's name at the top, followed by biography and statistics.
COMPLETE SET (25) 5.00 1.50

1994 Peoria Chiefs Classic

This 30-card standard size set of the 1994 Peoria Chiefs, a Class A Midwest League affiliate of the Chicago Cubs, features white-bordered posed color player shots on its fronts with the player's name and position, team name and logo and Classic logo appearing across the bottom of each card. On a ghosted team logo, the white back carries the player's name at the top, followed by biography and statistics.
COMPLETE SET (30) 8.00 2.40

1994 Peoria Chiefs Fleer/ProCards

This 29-card standard size set of the 1994 Peoria Chiefs, a Class A Midwest League affiliate of the Chicago Cubs, features white-bordered posed color player photos on its fronts with the player's name, position, team name and Fleer/ProCards logo across the bottom of each card. The white back with vertical light blue stripes carries the player's name at the top, followed by biography and statistics.
COMPLETE SET (29) 5.00 1.50

1994 Phoenix Firebirds Fleer/ProCards

This 27-card standard size set of the 1994 Phoenix Firebirds, a Class AAA Pacific Coast League affiliate of the San Francisco Giants, features white-bordered posed color player photos on its fronts with the player's name, position, team name and Fleer/ProCards logo across the bottom of each card. The white back with vertical light blue stripes carries the player's name at the top, followed by biography and statistics.
COMPLETE SET (27) 5.00 1.50

1994 Pittsfield Mets Classic

This 30-card standard size set of the 1994 Pittsfield Mets, a Class A New York-Penn League affiliate of the New York Mets, features white-bordered posed color player shots on its fronts with the player's name and position, team name and logo and Classic logo appearing across the bottom of each card. On a ghosted team logo, the white back carries the player's name at the top, followed by biography and statistics. This issue includes the minor league card debut of Jay Payton.
COMPLETE SET (30) 20.00 6.00

1994 Pittsfield Mets Fleer/ProCards

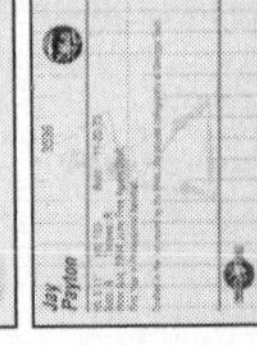

This 27-card standard size set of the 1994 Pittsfield Mets, a Class A New York-Penn League affiliate of the New York Mets, features white-bordered posed color player photos on its fronts with the player's name, position, team name and Fleer/ProCards logo across the bottom of each card. The white back with vertical light blue stripes carries the player's name at the top, followed by biography and statistics. This issue includes the minor league card debut of Jay Payton.
COMPLETE SET (27) 10.00 3.00

1994 Portland Sea Dogs Fleer/ProCards

This 27-card standard size set of the 1994 Portland Sea Dogs, a Class AA Eastern League affiliate of the Florida Marlins, features white-bordered posed color player photos on its fronts with the player's name, position, team name and Fleer/ProCards logo across the bottom of each card. The white back with vertical light blue stripes carries the player's name at the top, followed by biography and statistics. This issue includes a second year card of Charles Johnson.
COMPLETE SET (27) 8.00 2.40

1994 Portland Sea Dogs Team Issue

This 31-card standard size set of the 1994 Portland Sea Dogs, a Class AA Eastern League affiliate of the Florida Marlins, features a second year card of Charles Johnson.
COMPLETE SET (31) 8.00 2.40

1994 Prince William Cannons Classic

This 30-card standard size set of the 1994 Prince William Cannons, a Class A Carolina League affiliate of the Chicago White Sox features white-bordered posed color player shots on its fronts with the player's name and position, team name and logo and Classic logo appearing across the bottom of each card. On a ghosted team logo, the white back carries the player's name at the top, followed by biography and statistics.
COMPLETE SET (30) 20.00 6.00

1994 Prince William Cannons Fleer/ProCards

This 28-card standard size set of the 1994 Prince William Cannons, a Class A Carolina League affiliate of the Chicago White Sox, features white-bordered posed color player photos on its fronts with the player's name, position, team name and Fleer/ProCards logo across the bottom of each card. The white back with vertical light blue stripes carries the player's name at the top, followed by biography and statistics.
COMPLETE SET (28)................ 12.00 3.60

1994 Princeton Reds Classic

This 30-card standard size set of the 1994 Princeton Reds, a Rookie Class Appalachian League affiliate of the Cincinnati Reds, features white-bordered posed color player shots on its fronts with the player's name and position, team name and logo and Classic logo appearing across the bottom of each card. On a ghosted team logo, the white back carries the player's name at the top, followed by biography and statistics.
COMPLETE SET (30).................. 8.00 2.40

1994 Princeton Reds Fleer/ProCards

This 29-card standard size set of the 1994 Princeton Reds, a Rookie Class Appalachian League affiliate of the Cincinnati Reds, features white-bordered posed color player photos on its fronts with the player's name, position, team name and Fleer/ProCards logo across the bottom of each card. The white back with vertical light blue stripes carries the player's name at the top, followed by biography and statistics.
COMPLETE SET (29).................. 5.00 1.50

1994 Quad City River Bandits Classic

This 30-card standard size set of the 1994 Quad City River Bandits, a Class A Midwest League affiliate of the Houston Astros, features white-bordered posed color player shots on its fronts with the player's name and position, team name and logo and Classic logo appearing across the bottom of each card. On a ghosted team logo, the white back carries the player's name at the top, followed by biography and statistics. This issue includes second year cards of Billy Wagner and Richard Hidalgo.
COMPLETE SET (30).................. 20.00 6.00

1994 Quad City River Bandits Fleer/ProCards

This 29-card standard size set of the 1994 Quad City River Bandits, a Class A Midwest League affiliate of the Houston Astros, features white-bordered posed color player photos on its fronts with the player's name, position, team name and Fleer/ProCards logo across the bottom of each card. The white back with vertical light blue stripes carries the player's name at the top, followed by biography and statistics. This issue includes second year cards of Billy Wagner and Richard Hidalgo.
COMPLETE SET (29)................ 10.00 3.00

1994 Rancho Cucamonga Quakes Classic

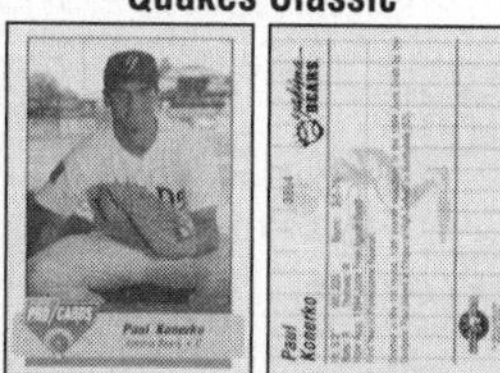

This 30-card standard size set of the 1994 Rancho Cucamonga Quakes, a Class A California League affiliate of the San Diego Padres, features white-bordered posed color player shots on its fronts with the player's name and position, team name and logo and Classic logo appearing across the bottom of each card. On a ghosted team logo, the white back carries the player's name at the top, followed by biography and statistics. This issue includes the minor league card debut of Derrek Lee.
COMPLETE SET (30)................ 10.00 3.00

1994 Rancho Cucamonga Quakes Fleer/ProCards

This 29-card standard size set of the 1994 Rancho Cucamonga Quakes, a Class A California League affiliate of the San Diego Padres, features white-bordered posed color player photos on its fronts with the player's name, position, team name and Fleer/ProCards logo across the bottom of each card. The white back with vertical light blue stripes carries the player's name at the top, followed by biography and statistics. This issue includes the minor league card debut of Derrek Lee.
COMPLETE SET (29).................. 8.00 2.40

1994 Reading Phillies Fleer/ProCards

This 27-card standard size set of the 1994 Reading Phillies, a Class AA Eastern League affiliate of the Philadelphia Phillies, features white-bordered posed color player photos on its fronts with the player's name, position, team name and Fleer/ProCards logo across the bottom of each card. The white back with vertical light blue stripes carries the player's name at the top, followed by biography and statistics.
COMPLETE SET (27).................. 5.00 1.50

1994 Richmond Braves Fleer/ProCards

This 30-card standard size set of the 1994 Richmond Braves, a Class AAA International League affiliate of the Atlanta Braves, features white-bordered posed color player photos on its fronts with the player's name, position, team name and Fleer/ProCards logo across the bottom of each card. The white back with vertical light blue stripes carries the player's name at the top, followed by biography and statistics.
COMPLETE SET (30).................. 5.00 1.50

1994 Riverside Pilots Cal League Cards

COMPLETE SET (32).................. 5.00 1.50

1994 Rochester Red Wings Fleer/ProCards

This 27-card standard size set of the 1994 Rochester Red Wings, a Class AAA International League affiliate of the Baltimore Orioles, features white-bordered posed color player photos on its fronts with the player's name, position, team name and Fleer/ProCards logo across the bottom of each card. The white back with vertical light blue stripes carries the player's name at the top, followed by biography and statistics.
COMPLETE SET (27).................. 8.00 2.40

1994 Rochester Red Wings Team Issue

COMPLETE SET (30).................. 8.00 2.40

1994 Rockford Royals Classic

This 30-card standard size set of the 1994 Rockford Royals, a Class A Midwest League affiliate of the Kansas City Royals, features white-bordered posed color player shots on its fronts with the player's name and position, team name and logo and Classic logo appearing across the bottom of each card. On a ghosted team logo, the white back carries the player's name at the top, followed by biography and statistics. This issue includes the minor league card debut of Glendon Rusch and a third year minor league card of Mike Sweeney.
COMPLETE SET (30)................ 10.00 3.00

1994 Rockford Royals Fleer/ProCards

This 31-card standard size set of the 1994 Rockford Royals, a Class A Midwest League affiliate of the Kansas City Royals, features white-bordered posed color player photos on its fronts with the player's name, position, team name and Fleer/ProCards logo across the bottom of each card. The white back with vertical light blue stripes carries the player's name at the top, followed by biography and statistics. This issue includes the minor league card debut of Glendon Rusch.
COMPLETE SET (31).................. 8.00 2.40

1994 Salem Buccaneers Classic

This 30-card standard size set of the 1994 Salem Buccaneers, a Class A Carolina League affiliate of the Pittsburgh Pirates, features white-bordered posed color player shots on its fronts with the player's name and position, team name and logo and Classic logo appearing across the bottom of each card. On a ghosted team logo, the white back carries the player's name at the top, followed by biography and statistics.
COMPLETE SET (30).................. 8.00 2.40

1994 Salem Buccaneers Fleer/ProCards

This 28-card standard size set of the 1994 Salem Buccaneers, a Class A Carolina League affiliate of the Pittsburgh Pirates, features white-bordered posed color player photos on its fronts with the player's name, position, team name and Fleer/ProCards logo across the bottom of each card. The white back with vertical light blue stripes carries the player's name at the top, followed by biography and statistics.
COMPLETE SET (28).................. 5.00 1.50

1994 Salt Lake Buzz Fleer/ProCards

This 27-card standard size set of the 1994 Salt Lake Buzz, a Class AAA Pacific Coast League affiliate of the Minnesota Twins, features white-bordered posed color player photos on its fronts with the player's name, position, team name and Fleer/ProCards logo across the bottom of each card. The white back with vertical light blue stripes carries the player's name at the top, followed by biography and statistics.
COMPLETE SET (27).................. 5.00 1.50

1994 San Antonio Missions Fleer/ProCards

This 31-card standard size set of the 1994 San Antonio Missions, a Class AA Texas League

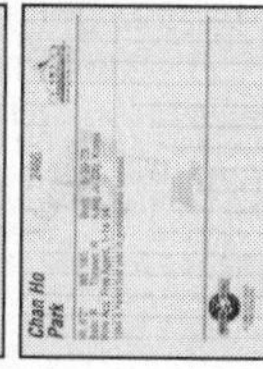

affiliate of the Los Angeles Dodgers, features white-bordered posed color player photos on its fronts with the player's name, position, team name and Fleer/ProCards logo across the bottom of each card. The white back with vertical light blue stripes carries the player's name at the top, followed by biography and statistics. This issue includes the minor league card debut of Chan Ho Park.
COMPLETE SET (31)................ 15.00 4.50

1994 San Bernardino Spirit Classic

This 30-card standard size set of the 1994 San Bernardino Spirit, a Class A California League Independent, features white-bordered posed color player shots on its fronts with the player's name and position, team name and logo and Classic logo appearing across the bottom of each card. On a ghosted team logo, the white back carries the player's name at the top, followed by biography and statistics.
COMPLETE SET (30).................. 8.00 2.40

1994 San Bernardino Spirit Fleer/ProCards

This 28-card standard size set of the 1994 San Bernardino Spirit, a Class A California League Independent, features white-bordered posed color player photos on its fronts with the player's name, position, team name and Fleer/ProCards logo across the bottom of each card. The white back with vertical light blue stripes carries the player's name at the top, followed by biography and statistics.
COMPLETE SET (28).................. 5.00 1.50

1994 San Jose Giants Classic

This 30-card standard size set of the 1994 San Jose Giants, a Class A California League affiliate of the San Francisco Giants, features white-bordered posed color player shots on its fronts with the player's name and position, team name and logo and Classic logo appearing across the bottom of each card. On a ghosted team logo, the white back carries the player's name at the top, followed by biography and statistics.
COMPLETE SET (30).................. 8.00 2.40

1994 San Jose Giants Fleer/ProCards

This 29-card standard size set of the 1994 San Jose Giants, a Class A California League affiliate of the San Francisco Giants, features white-bordered posed color player photos on its fronts with the player's name, position, team name and Fleer/ProCards logo across the bottom of each card. The white back with vertical light blue stripes carries the player's name at the top, followed by biography and statistics.
COMPLETE SET (29).................. 5.00 1.50

1994 Sarasota Red Sox Classic

This 30-card standard size set of the 1994 Sarasota Red Sox, a Class A Florida State League affiliate of the Boston Red Sox, features white-bordered posed color player shots on its fronts with the player's name and position, team name and logo and Classic logo appearing across the bottom of each card. On a ghosted team logo, the white back carries the player's name at the top, followed by biography and statistics.
COMPLETE SET (30).................. 8.00 2.40

1994 Sarasota Red Sox Fleer/ProCards

This 30-card standard size set of the 1994 Sarasota Red Sox, a Class A Florida State League affiliate of the Boston Red Sox, features white-bordered posed color player photos on its fronts with the player's name, position, team name and Fleer/ProCards logo across the bottom of each card. The white back with vertical light blue stripes carries the player's name at the top, followed by biography and statistics.
COMPLETE SET (30).................. 5.00 1.50

1994 Savannah Cardinals Classic

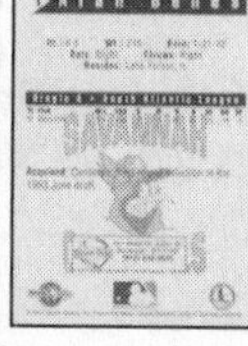

This 30-card standard size set of the 1994 Savannah Cardinals, a Class A South Atlantic League affiliate of the St. Louis Cardinals, features white-bordered posed color player shots on its fronts with the player's name and position, team name and logo and Classic logo appearing across the bottom of each card. On a ghosted team logo, the white back carries the player's name at the top, followed by biography and statistics.
COMPLETE SET (30).................. 8.00 2.40

1994 Savannah Cardinals Fleer/ProCards

This 31-card standard size set of the 1994 Savannah Cardinals, a Class A South Atlantic League affiliate of the St. Louis Cardinals, features white-bordered posed color player photos on its fronts with the player's name, position, team name and Fleer/ProCards logo across the bottom of each card. The white back with vertical light blue stripes carries the player's name at the top, followed by biography and statistics.
COMPLETE SET (31).................. 5.00 1.50

1994 Scranton/Wilkes-Barre Red Barons Fleer/ProCards

This 26-card standard size set of the 1994 Scranton/Wilkes-Barre Red Barons, a Class AAA International League affiliate of the Philadelphia Phillies, features white-bordered posed color player photos on its fronts with the player's name, position, team name and Fleer/ProCards logo across the bottom of each card. The white back with vertical light blue stripes carries the player's name at the top, followed by biography and statistics.
COMPLETE SET (26).................. 5.00 1.50

1994 Shreveport Captains Fleer/ProCards

This 29-card standard size set of the 1994 Shreveport Captains, a Class AA Texas League affiliate of the San Francisco Giants, features white-bordered posed color player photos on its fronts with the player's name, position, team name and Fleer/ProCards logo across the bottom of each card. The white back with vertical light blue stripes carries the player's name at the top, followed by biography and statistics.
COMPLETE SET (29).................. 5.00 1.50

1994 South Atlantic League All-Stars Fleer/ProCards

Early cards of Jermaine Dye, Maggio Ordonez and Richie Sexson are featured in this set.
COMPLETE SET (57).................. 25.00 7.50

1994 South Bend Silver Hawks Classic

This 30-card standard size set of the 1994 South Bend Silver Hawks, a Class A Midwest League affiliate of the Chicago White Sox, features white-bordered posed color player shots on its fronts with the player's name and position, team name and logo and Classic logo appearing across the bottom of each card. On a ghosted team logo, the white back carries the player's name at the top, followed by biography and statistics.
COMPLETE SET (30).................. 8.00 2.40

1994 South Bend Silver Hawks Fleer/ProCards

This 29-card standard size set of the 1994 South Bend Silver Hawks, a Class A Midwest League affiliate of the Chicago White Sox, features white-bordered posed color player photos on its fronts with the player's name, position, team name and Fleer/ProCards logo across the bottom of each card. The white back with vertical light blue stripes carries the player's name at the top, followed by biography and statistics.
COMPLETE SET (29).................. 5.00 1.50

1994 Southern Oregon A's Classic

This 30-card standard size set of the 1994 Southern Oregon Athletics, a Class AAA International League affiliate of the Montreal Expos, features white-bordered posed color player shots on its fronts with the player's name and position, team name and logo and Classic logo appearing across the bottom of each card. On a ghosted team logo, the white back carries the player's name at the top, followed by biography and statistics. This issue includes the minor league card debut of Ben Grieve.
COMPLETE SET (30)................ 15.00 4.50

1994 Southern Oregon A's Fleer/ProCards

This 29-card standard size set of the 1994 Southern Oregon Athletics, a Class AAA International League affiliate of the Montreal Expos, features white-bordered posed color player photos on its fronts with the player's name, position, team name and Fleer/ProCards logo across the bottom of each card. The white back with vertical light blue stripes carries the player's name at the top, followed by biography and statistics. This issue includes the minor league card debut of Ben Grieve.
COMPLETE SET (29)................ 10.00 3.00

1994 Spartanburg Phillies Classic

This 30-card standard size set of the 1994 Spartanburg Phillies, a Class A South Atlantic

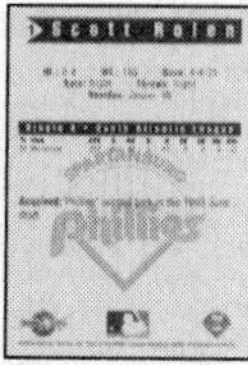

League affiliate of the Philadelphia Phillies, features white-bordered posed color player shots on its fronts with the player's name and position, team name and logo and Classic logo appearing across the bottom of each card. On a ghosted team logo, the white back carries the player's name at the top, followed by biography and statistics. This issue includes the minor league card debut of Scott Rolen.
COMPLETE SET (28)................ 40.00 12.00

1994 Spartanburg Phillies Fleer/ProCards

This 30-card standard size set of the 1994 Spartanburg Phillies, a Class A South Atlantic League affiliate of the Philadelphia Phillies, features white-bordered posed color player photos on its fronts with the player's name, position, team name and Fleer/ProCards logo across the bottom of each card. The white back with vertical light blue stripes carries the player's name at the top, followed by biography and statistics. This issue includes the minor league card debut of Scott Rolen.
COMPLETE SET (30)................ 25.00 7.50

1994 Spokane Indians Classic

This 30-card standard size set of the 1994 Spokane Indians, a Class A Northwest League affiliate of the San Diego Padres, features white-bordered posed color player shots on its fronts with the player's name and position, team name and logo and Classic logo appearing across the bottom of each card. On a ghosted team logo, the white back carries the player's name at the top, followed by biography and statistics.
COMPLETE SET (30).................. 5.00 1.50

1994 Spokane Indians Fleer/ProCards

This 30-card standard size set of the 1994 Spokane Indians, a Class A Northwest League affiliate of the San Diego Padres, features white-bordered posed color player photos on its fronts with the player's name, position, team name and Fleer/ProCards logo across the bottom of each card. The white back with vertical light blue stripes carries the player's name at the top, followed by biography and statistics.
COMPLETE SET (30).................. 5.00 1.50

1994 Springfield Sultans Classic

This 30-card standard size set of the 1994 Springfield Sultans, a Class A Midwest League affiliate of the San Diego Padres, features white-bordered posed color player shots on its fronts with the player's name and position, team name and logo and Classic logo appearing across the bottom of each card. On a ghosted team logo, the white back carries the player's name at the top, followed by biography and statistics.
COMPLETE SET (30).................. 8.00 2.40

1994 Springfield Sultans Fleer/ProCards

This 27-card standard size set of the 1994 Springfield Sultans, a Class A Midwest League affiliate of the San Diego Padres, features white-bordered posed color player photos on its fronts with the player's name, position, team name and Fleer/ProCards logo across the bottom of each card. The white back with vertical light blue stripes carries the player's name at the top, followed by biography and statistics.
COMPLETE SET (27).................. 5.00 1.50

1994 St. Catharines Blue Jays Classic

This 30-card standard size set of the 1994 St. Catherines Blue Jays, a Class A New York-Penn League affiliate of the Toronto Blue Jays, features white-bordered posed color player shots on its fronts with the player's name and position, team name and logo and Classic logo appearing across the bottom of each card. On a ghosted team logo, the white back carries the player's name at the top, followed by biography and statistics.
COMPLETE SET (30).................. 8.00 2.40

1994 St. Catharines Blue Jays Fleer/ProCards

This 30-card standard size set of the 1994 St. Catherines Blue Jays, a Class A New York-Penn League affiliate of the Toronto Blue Jays, features white-bordered posed color player photos on its fronts with the player's name, position, team name and Fleer/ProCards logo across the bottom of each card. The white back with vertical light blue stripes carries the player's name at the top, followed by biography and statistics.
COMPLETE SET (30).................. 5.00 1.50

1994 St. Lucie Mets Classic

This 30-card standard size set of the 1994 St. Lucie Mets, a Class A Florida State League affiliate of the New York Mets, features white-bordered posed color player shots on its fronts with the player's name and position, team name and logo and Classic logo appearing across the bottom of each card. On a ghosted team logo, the white back carries the player's name at the top, followed by biography and statistics. Early cards of Benny Agbayani, Jason Isringhausen and Rey Ordonez are featured in this set.

COMPLETE SET (30)............... 10.00 3.00

1994 St. Lucie Mets Fleer/ProCards

This 29-card standard size set of the 1994 St. Lucie Mets, a Class A Florida State League affiliate of the New York Mets, features white-bordered posed color player photos on its fronts with the player's name, position, team name and Fleer/ProCards logo across the bottom of each card. The white back with vertical light blue stripes carries the player's name at the top, followed by biography and statistics. Early cards of Benny Agbayani, Jason Isringhausen and Rey Ordonez are included in this set.

COMPLETE SET (29)................. 8.00 2.40

1994 St. Petersburg Cardinals Classic

This 30-card standard size set of the 1994 St. Petersburg Cardinals, a Class A Florida State League affiliate of the St. Louis Cardinals, features white-bordered posed color player shots on its fronts with the player's name and position, team name and logo and Classic logo appearing across the bottom of each card. On a ghosted team logo, the white back carries the player's name at the top, followed by biography and statistics.

COMPLETE SET (30)................. 8.00 2.40

1994 St. Petersburg Cardinals Fleer/ProCards

This 29-card standard size set of the 1994 St. Petersburg Cardinals, a Class A Florida State League affiliate of the St. Louis Cardinals, features white-bordered posed color player photos on its fronts with the player's name, position, team name and Fleer/ProCards logo across the bottom of each card. The white back with vertical light blue stripes carries the player's name at the top, followed by biography and statistics.

COMPLETE SET (29)................. 5.00 1.50

1994 Stockton Ports Classic

This 30-card standard size set of the 1994 Stockton Ports, a Class A California League affiliate of the Milwaukee Brewers, features white-bordered posed color player shots on its fronts with the player's name and position, team name and logo and Classic logo appearing across the bottom of each card. On a ghosted team logo, the white back carries the player's name at the top, followed by biography and statistics.

COMPLETE SET (30)................. 8.00 2.40

1994 Stockton Ports Fleer/ProCards

This 28-card standard size set of the 1994 Stockton Ports, a Class A California League affiliate of the Milwaukee Brewers, features white-bordered posed color player photos on its fronts with the player's name, position, team name and Fleer/ProCards logo across the bottom of each card. The white back with vertical light blue stripes carries the player's name at the top, followed by biography and statistics.

COMPLETE SET (28)................. 5.00 1.50

1994 Syracuse Chiefs Fleer/ProCards

This 26-card standard size set of the 1994 Syracuse Chiefs, a Class AAA International League affiliate of the Toronto Blue Jays, features white-bordered posed color player photos on its fronts with the player's name, position, team name and Fleer/ProCards logo across the bottom of each card. The white back with vertical light blue stripes carries the player's name at the top, followed by biography and statistics. An early card of Shawn Green is a highlight of this set.

COMPLETE SET (26)............... 15.00 4.50

1994 Syracuse Chiefs Team Issue

Sponsored by Kool-Aid, Post and WIXT, this 30-card set was issued as an uncut, perforated sheet. It consists of three panels (each measuring approximately 10 5/8" by 9 3/8") joined together to form one continuous sheet. The first panel features sponsors' logos and a large player photo. The second and third panels feature 15 player cards each. After perforation, the cards measure approximately 2 1/8" by 3 1/8". On a red card face, the fronts have posed color player photos. The player's name and position appear in a blue bar below the picture with the sponsor logos immediately below. The horizontal backs carry a short player biography and career stats. An early card of Shawn Green is a highlight in this set.

COMPLETE SET (30)............... 25.00 7.50

1994 Tacoma Tigers Fleer/ProCards

This 28-card standard size set of the 1994 Tacoma Tigers, a Class AAA Pacific Coast League affiliate of the Oakland Athletics, features white-bordered posed color player photos on its fronts with the player's name, position, team name and Fleer/ProCards logo across the bottom of each card. The white back with vertical light blue stripes carries the player's name at the top, followed by biography and statistics.

COMPLETE SET (28)................. 5.00 1.50

1994 Tampa Yankees Classic

This 30-card standard size set of the 1994 Tampa Yankees, a Class A Florida State League affiliate of the New York Yankees, features white-bordered posed color player shots on its fronts with the player's name and position, team name and logo and Classic logo appearing across the bottom of each card. On a ghosted team logo, the white back carries the player's name at the top, followed by biography and statistics. This issue includes a third year card of Derek Jeter.

COMPLETE SET (30)............... 50.00 15.00

1994 Tampa Yankees Fleer/ProCards

This 32-card standard size set of the 1994 Tampa Yankees, a Class A Florida State League affiliate of the New York Yankees, features white-bordered posed color player photos on its fronts with the player's name, position, team name and Fleer/ProCards logo across the bottom of each card. The white back with vertical light blue stripes carries the player's name at the top, followed by biography and statistics. This issue includes a third year card of Derek Jeter.

COMPLETE SET (32)............... 30.00 9.00

1994 Toledo Mud Hens Fleer/ProCards

This 27-card standard size set of the 1994 Toledo Mud Hens, a Class AAA International League affiliate of the Detroit Tigers, features white-bordered posed color player photos on its fronts with the player's name, position, team name and Fleer/ProCards logo across the bottom of each card. The white back with vertical light blue stripes carries the player's name at the top, followed by biography and statistics.

COMPLETE SET (27)................. 5.00 1.50

1994 Trenton Thunder Fleer/ProCards

This 27-card standard size set of the 1994 Trenton Thunder, a Class AA Eastern League affiliate of the Detroit Tigers, features white-bordered posed color player photos on its fronts with the player's name, position, team name and Fleer/ProCards logo across the bottom of each card. The white back with vertical light blue stripes carries the player's name at the top, followed by biography and statistics.

COMPLETE SET (27)................. 5.00 1.50

1994 Triple A All-Stars Fleer/ProCards

COMPLETE SET (47)............... 10.00 3.00

1994 Tucson Toros Fleer/ProCards

This 29-card standard size set of the 1994 Tucson Toros, a Class AAA Pacific Coast affiliate of the Houston Astros, features white-bordered posed color player photos on its fronts with the player's name, position, team name and Fleer/ProCards logo across the bottom of each card. The white back with vertical light blue stripes carries the player's name at the top, followed by biography and statistics.

COMPLETE SET (29)................. 5.00 1.50

1994 Tulsa Drillers Fleer/ProCards

This 27-card standard size set of the 1994 Tulsa Drillers, a Class AA Texas League affiliate of the Texas Rangers, features white-bordered posed color player photos on its fronts with the player's name, position, team name and Fleer/ProCards logo across the bottom of each card. The white back with vertical light blue stripes carries the player's name at the top, followed by biography and statistics.

COMPLETE SET (27)............... 10.00 3.00

1994 Tulsa Drillers Team Issue

COMPLETE SET (30)................. 5.00 1.50

1994 Utica Blue Sox Classic

This 29-card standard size set of the 1994 Utica Blue Sox, a Class A New York-Penn League affiliate of the Boston Red Sox, features white-bordered posed color player shots on its fronts with the player's name and position, team name and logo and Classic logo appearing across the bottom of each card. On a ghosted team logo, the white back carries the player's name at the top, followed by biography and statistics.

COMPLETE SET (30)................. 8.00 2.40

1994 Utica Blue Sox Fleer/ProCards

This 29-card standard size set of the 1994 Utica Blue Sox, a Class A New York-Penn League affiliate of the Boston Red Sox, features white-bordered posed color player photos on its fronts with the player's name, position, team name and Fleer/ProCards logo across the bottom of each card. The white back with vertical light blue stripes carries the player's name at the top, followed by biography and statistics.

COMPLETE SET (29)................. 5.00 1.50

1994 Vancouver Canadians Fleer/ProCards

This 26-card standard size set of the 1994 Vancouver Canadians, a Class AAA Pacific Coast League affiliate of the California Angels, features white-bordered posed color player photos on its fronts with the player's name, position, team name and Fleer/ProCards logo across the bottom of each card. The white back with vertical light blue stripes carries the player's name at the top, followed by biography and statistics.

COMPLETE SET (26)................. 8.00 2.40

1994 Vermont Expos Classic

This 28-card standard size set of the 1994 Vermont Expos, a Class A New York-Penn League affiliate of the Montreal Expos, features white-bordered posed color player shots on its fronts with the player's name and position, team name and logo and Classic logo appearing across the bottom of each card. On a ghosted team logo, the white back carries the player's name at the top, followed by biography and statistics.

COMPLETE SET (28)................. 8.00 2.40

1994 Vermont Expos Fleer/ProCards

This 28-card standard size set of the 1994 Vermont Expos, a Class A New York-Penn League affiliate of the Montreal Expos, features white-bordered posed color player photos on its fronts with the player's name, position, team name and Fleer/ProCards logo across the bottom of each card. The white back with vertical light blue stripes carries the player's name at the top, followed by biography and statistics.

COMPLETE SET (28)................. 5.00 1.50

1994 Vero Beach Dodgers Classic

This 30-card standard size set of the 1994 Vero Beach Dodgers, a Class A Florida State League affiliate of the Los Angeles Dodgers, features white-bordered posed color player shots on its fronts with the player's name and position, team name and logo and Classic logo appearing across the bottom of each card. On a ghosted team logo, the white back carries the player's name at the top, followed by biography and statistics.

COMPLETE SET (30)................. 8.00 2.40

1994 Vero Beach Dodgers Fleer/ProCards

This 31-card standard size set of the 1994 Vero Beach Dodgers, a Class A Florida State League affiliate of the Los Angeles Dodgers, features white-bordered posed color player photos on its fronts with the player's name, position, team name and Fleer/ProCards logo across the bottom of each card. The white back with vertical light blue stripes carries the player's name at the top, followed by biography and statistics.

COMPLETE SET (31)................. 5.00 1.50

1994 Watertown Indians Classic

This 30-card standard size set of the 1994 Watertown Indians, a Class A New York-Penn League affiliate of the Cleveland Indians, features white-bordered posed color player shots on its fronts with the player's name and position, team name and logo and Classic logo appearing across the bottom of each card. On a ghosted team logo, the white back carries the player's name at the top, followed by biography and statistics.

COMPLETE SET (30)................. 8.00 2.40

1994 Watertown Indians Fleer/ProCards

This 30-card standard size set of the 1994 Watertown Indians, a Class A New York-Penn League affiliate of the Cleveland Indians, features white-bordered posed color player photos on its fronts with the player's name, position, team name and Fleer/ProCards logo across the bottom of each card. The white back with vertical light blue stripes carries the player's name at the top, followed by biography and statistics.

COMPLETE SET (30)................. 5.00 1.50

1994 Welland Pirates Classic

This 30-card standard size set of the 1994 Welland Pirates, a Class A New York-Penn League affiliate of the Pittsburgh Pirates, features white-bordered posed color player shots on its fronts with the player's name and position, team name and logo and Classic logo appearing across the bottom of each card. On a ghosted team logo, the white back carries the player's name at the top, followed by biography and statistics.

COMPLETE SET (30)................. 8.00 2.40

1994 Welland Pirates Fleer/ProCards

This 31-card standard size set of the 1994 Welland Pirates, a Class A New York-Penn League affiliate of the Pittsburgh Pirates, features white-bordered posed color player photos on its fronts with the player's name, position, team name and Fleer/ProCards logo across the bottom of each card. The white back with vertical light blue stripes carries the player's name at the top, followed by biography and statistics.

COMPLETE SET (31)................. 5.00 1.50

1994 West Michigan Whitecaps Classic

This 30-card standard size set of the 1994 West Michigan Whitecaps, a Class A Midwest League affiliate of the Oakland Athletics, features white-bordered posed color player shots on its fronts with the player's name and position, team name and logo and Classic logo appearing across the bottom of each card. On a ghosted team logo, the white back carries the player's name at the top, followed by biography and statistics.

COMPLETE SET (30)................. 8.00 2.40

1994 West Michigan Whitecaps Fleer/ProCards

This 28-card standard size set of the 1994 West Michigan Whitecaps, a Class A Midwest League affiliate of the Oakland Athletics, features white-bordered posed color player photos on its fronts with the player's name, position, team name and Fleer/ProCards logo across the bottom of each card. The white back with vertical light blue stripes carries the player's name at the top, followed by biography and statistics.

COMPLETE SET (28)................. 5.00 1.50

1994 West Palm Beach Expos Classic

This 30-card standard size set of the 1994 West Palm Beach Expos, a Class A Florida State League affiliate of the Montreal Expos, features white-bordered posed color player shots on its fronts with the player's name and position, team name and logo and Classic logo appearing across the bottom of each card. On a ghosted team logo, the white back carries the player's name at the top, followed by biography and statistics. An early card of Jose Vidro is an highlight of this set.

COMPLETE SET (30)............... 15.00 4.50

1994 West Palm Beach Expos Fleer/ProCards

This 30-card standard size set of the 1994 West Palm Beach Expos, a Class A Florida State League affiliate of the Montreal Expos, features white-bordered posed color player photos on its fronts with the player's name, position, team name and Fleer/ProCards logo across the bottom of each card. The white back with vertical light blue stripes carries the player's name at the top, followed by biography and statistics. An early card of Jose Vidro is featured within this set.

COMPLETE SET (30)............... 10.00 3.00

1994 Wichita Wranglers Fleer/ProCards

This 26-card standard size set of the 1994 Wichita Wranglers, a Class AA Texas League affiliate of the San Diego Padres, features white-bordered posed color player photos on its fronts with the player's name, position, team name and Fleer/ProCards logo across the bottom of each card. The white back with vertical light blue stripes carries the player's name at the top, followed by biography and statistics.

COMPLETE SET (26)................. 5.00 1.50

1994 Williamsport Cubs Classic

This 30-card standard size set of the 1994 Williamsport Cubs, a Class A New York-Penn League affiliate of the Chicago Cubs, features white-bordered posed color player shots on its fronts with the player's name and position, team name and logo and Classic logo appearing across the bottom of each card. On a ghosted team logo, the white back carries the player's name at the top, followed by biography and statistics.

COMPLETE SET (30)................. 8.00 2.40

1994 Williamsport Cubs Fleer/ProCards

This 30-card standard size set of the 1994 Williamsport Cubs, a Class A New York-Penn League affiliate of the Chicago Cubs, features white-bordered posed color player photos on its fronts with the player's name, position, team name and Fleer/ProCards logo across the bottom of each card. The white back with vertical light blue stripes carries the player's name at the top, followed by biography and statistics.

COMPLETE SET (30)................. 5.00 1.50

1994 Wilmington Blue Rocks Classic

This 30-card standard size set of the 1994 Wilmington Blue Rocks, a Class A Carolina League affiliate of the Kansas City Royals, features white-bordered posed color player shots on its fronts with the player's name and position, team name and logo and Classic logo appearing across the bottom of each card. On a ghosted team logo, the white back carries the player's name at the top, followed by biography and statistics. This issue includes a second year card of Johnny Damon.

COMPLETE SET (30)............... 10.00 3.00

1994 Wilmington Blue Rocks Fleer/ProCards

This 29-card standard size set of the 1994 Wilmington Blue Rocks, a Class A Carolina League affiliate of the Kansas City Royals, features white-bordered posed color player photos on its fronts with the player's name, position, team name and Fleer/ProCards logo across the bottom of each card. The white back with vertical light blue stripes carries the player's name at the top, followed by biography and statistics. This issue includes a second year card of Johnny Damon.

COMPLETE SET (29)................. 8.00 2.40

1994 Winston-Salem Spirits Classic

This 30-card standard size set of the 1994 Winston-Salem Spirits, a Class A Carolina League affiliate of the Cincinnati Reds, features white-bordered posed color player shots on its fronts with the player's name and position, team name and logo and Classic logo appearing across the bottom of each card. On a ghosted team logo, the white back carries the player's name at the top, followed by biography and statistics.

COMPLETE SET (30)................. 8.00 2.40

1994 Winston-Salem Spirits Fleer/ProCards

This 28-card standard size set of the 1994 Winston-Salem Spirits, a Class A Carolina League affiliate of the Cincinnati Reds, features white-bordered posed color player photos on its fronts with the player's name, position, team name and Fleer/ProCards logo across the bottom of each card. The white back with vertical light blue stripes carries the player's name at the top, followed by biography and statistics.

COMPLETE SET (28)................. 5.00 1.50

1994 Yakima Bears Classic

This 30-card standard size set of the 1994 Yakima Bears, a Class A Northwest League affiliate of the Los Angeles Dodgers, features white-bordered posed color player shots on its fronts with the player's name and position, team name and logo and Classic logo appearing across the bottom of each card. On a ghosted team logo, the white back carries the player's name at the top, followed by biography and statistics. This issue includes the minor league card debut of Paul Konerko.

COMPLETE SET (30)............... 30.00 9.00

1994 Yakima Bears Fleer/ProCards

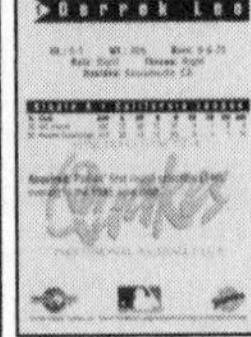

This 30-card standard size set of the 1994 Yakima Bears, a Class A Northwest League affiliate of the Los Angeles Dodgers, features white-bordered posed color player photos on its fronts with the player's name, position, team name and Fleer/ProCards logo across the bottom of each card. The white back with vertical light blue stripes carries the player's name at the top, followed by biography and statistics. This issue includes the minor league card debut of Paul Konerko.

COMPLETE SET (30)............... 20.00 6.00

1995 Arizona Fall League SplitSecond

This 22-card set of the Arizona Fall League honors some of the all-stars of the League's

1995 season. These cards were manufactured and distributed by Jessen Associates, Inc. The fronts feature color action player photos with clouds over a mountain top as the bottom border. The backs carry player biographical information and career statistics. The cards are unnumbered and checklisted below in alphabetical order. This issue features the first year cards of Todd Walker and Darin Erstad.
COMPLETE SET (22)................ 25.00 7.50

1995 Arkansas Travelers Team Issue

This 30-card set was produced by Multi-Ad Services and sponsored by Sonic Drive-Ins and features borderless color player photos of the 1995 Arkansas Travelers, a Class AA Texas League affiliate of the St. Louis Cardinals. The backs carry player biographical information and career statistics. The cards are unnumbered and checklisted below in alphabetical order. 500 sets were produced.
COMPLETE SET (29)................ 15.00 4.50

1995 Asheville Tourists Team Issue

This 30-card set of the 1995 Asheville Tourists, a Class A South Atlantic League affiliate of the Colorado Rockies, features color player photos with a white border and thin gold inner border. The backs carry player information and career statistics. The cards are unnumbered and checklisted below according to the player's jersey number.
COMPLETE SET (30)................ 8.00 2.40

1995 Asheville Tourists Update Team Issue

This 15-card set is an update of the 30-card 1995 Asheville Tourists team set, A Class A South Atlantic League affiliate of the Colorado Rockies, features the same format and design as the original set. The cards are unnumbered and checklisted below according to the player's jersey number. This issue features the minor league card debut of Todd Helton.
COMPLETE SET (15)................ 75.00 22.00

1995 Auburn Astros Team Issue

This 30-card set of the Auburn Astros, a Class A New York-Penn League affiliate of the Houston Astros, was sponsored by Multi-Ad Services Inc. and features borderless posed color player photos on the fronts. The backs carry player information. 750 sets were produced.
COMPLETE SET (30)................ 10.00 3.00

1995 Bakersfield Blaze Team Issue

This 32-card set of the 1995 Bakersfield Blaze, a Class A California League Independent, features color player photos in a blue outer border with a thin white inner border. The backs carry player information and statistics. 8,000 sets were produced and each checklist is sequentially numbered. This issue includes the minor league card debut of Hideo Nomo.
COMPLETE SET (32)................ 15.00 4.50

1995 Batavia Clippers Team Issue

This 33-card set of the Batavia Clippers, a Class A New York-Penn League of the Philadelphia Phillies, was produced by Multi-Ad Services Inc. and features color player posed photos with a two-sided white triangular border. The backs display player information and career statistics. The cards are unnumbered and checklisted below in alphabetical order. This issue includes the minor league card debuts of Marlon Anderson. 1,500 sets were produced.
COMPLETE SET (33)................ 8.00 2.40

1995 Bellingham Giants Team Issue

This 36-card set of the 1995 Bellingham Giants, A Class A Northwest League affiliate of the San Francisco Giants, features posed color player photos by Greenleaf Photography with a black, white, and orange border. The backs carry player information. The cards are unnumbered and checklisted below according to the player's jersey number as listed on the card back. This issue includes the minor league card debut of Russ Ortiz.
COMPLETE SET (36)................ 20.00 6.00

1995 Beloit Snappers Team Issue

This 31-card set of the 1995 Beloit Snappers, a Class A Midwest League affiliate of the Milwaukee Brewers, features borderless color action player photos on the fronts. The backs carry player information and career statistics. This issue includes the minor league card debut of Ron Belliard. 1,000 sets were produced.
COMPLETE SET (31)................ 10.00 3.00

1995 Billings Mustangs Team Issue

This 29-card set of the 1995 Billings Mustangs, a Rookie Class Pioneer League affiliate of the Cincinnati Reds, was sponsored by First Interstate Bank and features borderless black-and-white player photos by Dennis R. Clark. The backs carry player information.
COMPLETE SET (29)................ 40.00 12.00

1995 Binghamton Mets Team Issue

This 28-card set of the 1995 Binghamton Mets, a Class AA Eastern League affiliate of the New York Mets, features color player photos in a wide blue border with red and thin white inner borders. The backs carry player information and career statistics. The cards are unnumbered and checklisted below according to the player's jersey number. 2,500 sets were produced.
COMPLETE SET (28)................ 10.00 3.00

1995 Boise Hawks Team Issue

This 35-card set of the 1995 Boise Hawks, a Class A Northwest League affiliate of the California Angels, features color player photos in a marblized blue border. The backs carry player information and career statistics. The cards are unnumbered and checklisted below alphabetically. 1,000 sets were produced.
COMPLETE SET (35)................ 18.00 5.50

1995 Bowie Baysox Team Issue

This 31-card set of the 1995 Bowie Baysox, a Class AA Eastern League affiliate of the Baltimore Orioles, was produced by Choice Marketing, Inc. and features posed borderless color player photos by Ben Koeber and Greg L'Heureux. The backs carry player information and career statistics. The cards are unnumbered and checklisted below according to the player's jersey number. 4,000 sets were produced.
COMPLETE SET (31)................ 8.00 2.40

1995 Brevard County Manatees Fleer/ProCards

This 30-card set of the 1995 Brevard County Manatees, a Class A Florida State League affiliate of the Florida Marlins, was produced by the Fleer Corp and features posed color player photos in a white border on the card fronts. The backs carry player information and career statistics.
COMPLETE SET (30)................ 8.00 2.40

1995 Burlington Bees Team Issue

This 36-card set of the 1995 Burlington Bees, a Class A Midwest League affiliate of the San Francisco Giants, features color action player photos on the fronts. The backs carry a small black-and-white player head photo with player information and career statistics. This issue includes the only minor league card ever issued of Paul Molitor. 2,000 sets were produced.
COMPLETE SET (36)................ 15.00 4.50

1995 Butte Copper Kings Team Issue

This 32-card set of the 1995 Butte Copper Kings, a Rookie Class Pioneer League Independent, features posed color photos of the players each sitting beside his locker with his name and jersey number printed on the locker shelf. A facsimile autograph is printed in a red bar down the left. The backs carry player information. 2,000 sets were produced.
COMPLETE SET (32)................ 8.00 2.40

1995 Carolina Mudcats Fleer/ProCards

This 30-card set of the1995 Carolina Mudcats, a Class AA Southern League affiliate of the Pittsburgh Pirates, was produced by the Fleer Corp. and feature posed color player photos in a white border on the card fronts. The backs carry player information and career statistics.
COMPLETE SET (30)................ 8.00 2.40

1995 Cedar Rapids Kernels Team Issue

This 32-card set of the 1995 Cedar Rapids Kernels, a Class A Midwest League affiliate of the California Angels, was sponsored by McDonald's and features borderless color action player photos by Jim Tevis. The backs carry player information and statistics. The cards are unnumbered and checklisted below according to the player's jersey number printed on the card back.
COMPLETE SET (32)................ 8.00 2.40

1995 Charleston Riverdogs Team Issue

This 30-card set of the 1995 Charleston Riverdogs, a Class A South Atlantic League affiliate of the Texas Rangers, was produced by Multi-Ad Services Inc. and sponsored by Kinko's, Charleston Classic Rock and Roll Radio Station 98ROCK. The fronts feature borderless color player photos with the player's name and team's name in team colored bars at the bottom. The backs carry player information and career statistics. This issue includes the minor league card debut of Fernando Tatis. 2,000 sets were produced.
COMPLETE SET (30)................ 25.00 7.50

1995 Charleston Riverdogs Update Team Issue

This nine-card set is an update of the 30-card 1995 Charleston Riverdogs team set and features the same format and design as the original set with a continuation of the card numbers. 1,000 sets were produced. An early card of Fernando Tatis highlights this set.
COMPLETE SET (9)................ 25.00 7.50

1995 Charlotte Knights Team Issue

This 30-card set of the 1995 Charlotte Knights, a Class AAA International League affiliate of the Florida Marlins, was produced by Coastal Forms and Data Products and features color player photos with a white outside border and team colored inner borders. The backs carry player career statistics. 5,000 sets were produced.
COMPLETE SET (30)................ 10.00 3.00

1995 Chattanooga Lookouts Team Issue

This 31-card set of the 1995 Chattanooga Lookouts, a Class AA Southern League affiliate of the Cincinnati Reds, features posed color player photos with empty stadium seats as the background and a black border. The backs carry player information and career statistics.
COMPLETE SET (31)................ 10.00 3.00

1995 Clearwater Phillies Fleer/ProCards

This 30-card set of the 1995 Clearwater Phillies, a Class A Florida State League affiliate of the Philadelphia Phillies, was produced by the Fleer Corp. and features posed and action color player photos in a white border on the card fronts. The backs carry player information and career statistics.
COMPLETE SET (30)................ 8.00 2.40

1995 Colorado Silver Bullets

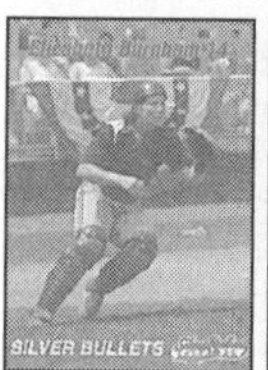

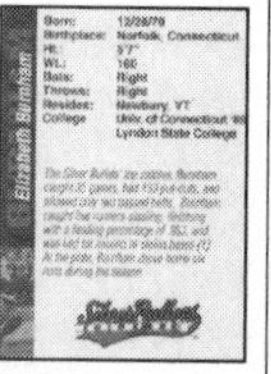

This 28-card set measures the standard size. The fronts feature borderless action player photos with the player's name and jersey number printed in blue at the top over the player's position which is in red. The team name and logo are at the bottom. The backs carry a vertical blue stripe on the left with a small, partial version of the front photo and the player's name printed in white over the light blue last name. Biographical information and other personal information are printed in blue on a white background. The team logo appears at the bottom. The cards are unnumbered and checklisted below in alphabetical order.
COMPLETE SET (28)................ 15.00 4.50

1995 Colorado Silver Bullets Update

COMPLETE SET (9)................ 8.00 2.40

1995 Columbus Clippers Milk Caps Team Issue

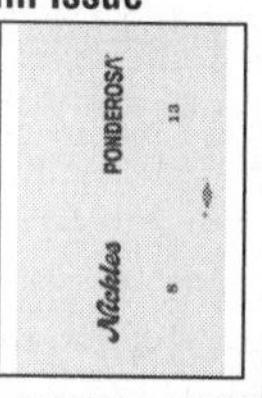

This 12-card set featuring 24 Milk Caps of 1995 Columbus Clippers. One card was given out to children 12 and under at each Monday home game during the1995 season. The set includes milk caps of Derek Jeter and Andy Pettitte. 2,750 sets were produced.
COMPLETE SET (12)................ 40.00 12.00

1995 Columbus Clippers Police

This 32-card set of the 1995 Columbus Clippers, a Class AAA International League affiliate of the New York Yankees, was sponsored by the Columbus Police Department and features color player photos in a blue border. The backs carry player statistics and various messages from area elementary school students about the dangers of using drugs. The cards are unnumbered and checklisted below in alphabetical order. 1,500 sets were produced. Cards of Derek Jeter, Andy Pettitte and Jorge Posada are included in this set.
COMPLETE SET (32)................ 80.00 24.00

1995 Columbus Clippers Team Issue

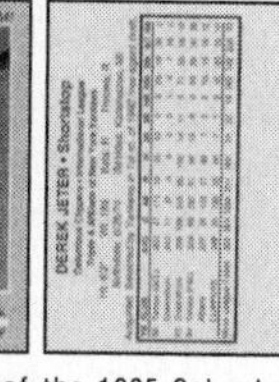

This 32-card set of the 1995 Columbus Clippers, a Class AAA International League affiliate of the New York Yankees, features color player photos in a gray border. The backs carry player information and career statistics. The cards are unnumbered and checklisted below alphabetically. 2,500 sets were produced. Minor league cards of Derek Jeter, Andy Pettitte and Jorge Posada are included in this set.
COMPLETE SET (32)................ 60.00 18.00

1995 Danville Braves Team Issue

This 30-card set of the Danville Braves, a Rookie Class Appalachian League affiliate of the Atlanta Braves, was issued in six strips of six perforated cards each and was distributed by McDonald's restaurants. Each strip features five player cards with a sixth card being a "buy one get one free" coupon for a Big Mac Sandwich redeemable at a specific McDonald's. The fronts feature color player photos with player information and statistics on the backs. The cards are unnumbered and checklisted below in alpabetical order. This issue includes the minor league card debut of Bruce Chen. Only 1,000 sets were produced.
COMPLETE SET (30)................ 40.00 12.00

1995 David Lipscomb Bisons

The cards are unnumbered and checklisted below in alphabetical order.
COMPLETE SET (25)................ 10.00 3.00

1995 Dunedin Blue Jays Team Issue

This 30-card set of the 1995 Dunedin Blue Jays, a Class A Florida State League affiliate of the Toronto Blue Jays, features color player portraits in a white border. The player's name and position are printed in white in a bottom black bar. The backs carry player information, career statistics, and sponsor logos. The cards are unnumbered and checklisted below in alphabetical order. An early card of Chris Carpenter highlights this set.
COMPLETE SET (30)................ 50.00 15.00

1995 Durham Bulls Team Issue

This 42-card set of the 1995 Durham Bulls, a Class A Carolina League affiliate of the Atlanta Braves, was sponsored by Crystal Springs and the Herald-Sun Newpapers. The fronts feature color player photos in a thin maroon, gold, or brown frame with the player's name and position printed in white in the wide maroon, gold, or brown margin at the top. The backs carry player information and career statistics. The cards are unnumbered and checklisted below in alphabetical order. 2,000 sets were produced.
COMPLETE SET (42)................ 10.00 3.00

1995 Edmonton Trappers Team Issue

This 30-card set of the 1995 Edmonton Trappers, a Class AAA Pacific Coast League affiliate of the Oakland Athletics, was produced by Macri Photographic Design and features borderless color player portraits with the player's name and position printed in a white bar at the bottom. The backs carry player information and career statistics. The cards are unnumbered and checklisted below in alphabetical order. A minor league card of Jason Giambi is featured in this set.
COMPLETE SET (30)................ 25.00 7.50

1995 El Paso Diablos Team Issue

This 24-card set of the 1995 El Paso Diablos, a Class AA Texas League affiliate of the Milwaukee Brewers, was produced by Multi-Ad Services Inc. and features borderless color player photos with the player's name printed across the small gold and red bars at the bottom. The backs carry player information and career statistics. The cards are unnumbered and checklisted below in alphabetical order. 1,000 sets were produced.
COMPLETE SET (24)................ 10.00 3.00

1995 Elmira Pioneers Team Issue

This 30-card set of the 1995 Elmira Pioneers, a Class A New York-Penn League affiliate of the Florida Marlins, was produced by Multi-Ad Services Inc. and features color player portraits with the player's name printed in a bar down the left. The backs carry player information and career statistics. The cards are unnumbered and checklisted below in alphabetical order. This issue inlcudes the minor league card debut of Josh Booty. 1,000 sets were produced.
COMPLETE SET (30)................ 10.00 3.00

1995 Elmira Pioneers Update Team Issue

This 31-card set of the 1995 Elmira Pioneers, a Class A New York-Penn League affiliate of the Florida Marlins, was produced by Multi-Ad Services Inc. and features color player portraits with the player's name printed in a bar down the left. The backs carry player information and career statistics. The cards are unnumbered and checklisted below in alphabetical order. 500 sets were produced.
COMPLETE SET (31)................ 20.00 6.00

1995 Eugene Emeralds Team Issue

This 32-card set of the 1995 Eugene Emeralds, a Class A Northwest League affiliate of the Atlanta Braves, features color player photos in a white border. The backs carry player information and career statistics along with a police safety message printed at the bottom. This issue includes the minor league card debut of George Lombard and an early card of John Rocker. 3,000 sets were produced.
COMPLETE SET (32)................ 20.00 6.00

1995 Everett Aquasox Team Issue

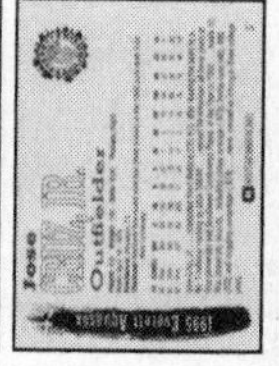

This 30-card set of the 1995 Everett Aquasox, a Class A Northwest League affiliate of the Seattle Mariners, was produced by Multi-Ad Services Inc. and features borderless color player portaits with the player's name in an orange bar at the bottom. The backs carry player information and career statistics. This issue includes the minor league card debut of Jose Cruz Jr. 2,000 sets were produced.
COMPLETE SET (30)................ 25.00 7.50

1995 Fayetteville Generals Team Issue

This 30-card set of the 1995 Fayetteville Generals, a Class South Atlantic League affiliate of the Detroit Tigers, was produced by Multi-Ad Services Inc. and features borderless color player photos with the player's name printed on an orange bar at the bottom. The backs carry player information and career statistics. 4,000 sets were produced with 3,600 given away at the ballpark. Early cards of Juan Encarnacion and Daryle Ward are included in this set.
COMPLETE SET (30)................ 25.00 7.50

1995 Fort Myers Miracle Team Issue

This 32-card set of the 1995 Fort Myers Miracle, a Class A Florida State League affiliate of the Minnesota Twins, features color player photos in a white border with the player's name and team name printed in a vertical bar down the left. The backs carry player information and statistics. This issue includes the minor league card debuts of Torii Hunter and Mark Redman. 1,000 sets were produced.
COMPLETE SET (32)................ 30.00 9.00

1995 Fort Wayne Wizards Team Issue

This 32-card set of the 1995 Fort Wayne Wizards, a Class A Midwest League affiliate of the Minnesota Twins, features borderless color player photos with the player's name and position printed on a small blue triangle in the bottom left corner. The backs carry player information and career statistics. 1,000 sets were produced.
COMPLETE SET (32)................ 15.00 4.50

1995 Great Falls Dodgers Team Issue

This 40-card set of the 1995 Great Falls Dodgers, a Rookie Class Pioneer League affiliate of the Los Angeles Dodgers, features black-and-white borderless player photos and measures approximately 3 5/8" by 6". The team's logo, player's name, and player's position are printed in the wide bottom margin. The backs carry a postcard format with player information printed in the top left corner. Only 200 complete collated sets were produced.
COMPLETE SET (40)................ 60.00 18.00

1995 Greensboro Bats Team Issue

This 33-card set of the 1995 Greensboro Bats, a Class A South Atlantic League affiliate of the New York Yankees, was produced by Multi-Ad Services Inc. and features color player photos with a black outside border and thin red inside border. The backs carry player information and career statistics.
COMPLETE SET (33)................ 10.00 3.00

1995 Greenville Braves Team Issue

This 28-card set of the 1995 Greenville Braves, a Class AA Southern League affiliate of the Atlanta Braves, features color player photos in a blue-and-white border with the player's last name running continuously down one side. The Coca-Cola logo is printed in a red-framed blue bar at the bottom. The backs carry player information and career statistics. The cards are unnumbered and checklisted below according to the player's jersey number printed in red in a blue circle at the bottom on the card's front.
COMPLETE SET (28)................ 10.00 3.00

1995 Hagerstown Suns Fleer/ProCards

This 30-card set of the 1995 Hagerstown Suns, a Class A South Atlantic League affiliate of the Toronto Blue Jays, was produced by the Fleer Corp. and features posed color player photos in a white border on the card fronts. The backs carry player information and career statistics.
COMPLETE SET (30).................. 8.00 2.40

1995 Hardware City Rock Cats Team Issue

This 29-card set of the 1995 Hardware City Rock Cats, a Class AA Eastern League affiliate of the Minnesota Twins, was produced by Multi-Ad Services Inc. and features color player photos in a white pin-striped frame. The backs carry player information and career statistics. This issue includes the minor league card debuts of Matt Lawton and Todd Walker. 1,000 sets were produced.
COMPLETE SET (29)................ 25.00 7.50

1995 Harrisburg Senators Team Issue

This 28-card set of the 1995 Harrisburg Senators, a Class AA Eastern League affiliate of the Montreal Expos, features color player photos in a blue border with thin red and thinner white inner borders. The player's name, team name, and position are printed in a light yellow bar at the bottom. The backs carry player information and career statistics. The cards are unnumbered and checklisted below according to the player's jersey number printed on the back of the card. 2,000 sets were produced.
COMPLETE SET (28)................ 10.00 3.00

1995 Helena Brewers Team Issue

This 32-card set of the 1995 Helena Brewers, a Rookie Class Pioneer League affiliate of the Milwaukee Brewers, features borderless color player photos with the player's name and position printed on purple mountains at the bottom. The backs carry player information.
COMPLETE SET (32)................ 10.00 3.00

1995 Hudson Valley Renegades Team Issue

This 30-card set of the 1995 Hudson Valley Renegades, a Class A New York-Penn League affiliate of the Texas Rangers, was produced by Multi-Ad Services Inc. and features color player photos framed at the top in violet and at the bottom in green with a thin gray inner border. The backs display player information. 1,500 sets were produced. This issue includes the minor league card debut of Scott Podsednik.
COMPLETE SET (30)................ 20.00 3.00

1995 Huntsville Stars Team Issue

This 29-card set of the 1995 Huntsville Stars, a Class AA Southern League affiliate of the Oakland Athletics, was sponsored by Burger King and features color player portraits in a thin red border and a red, white, blue, and black or yellow wider outside border. The backs carry player information and statistics. The cards are unnumbered and checklisted below in alphabetical order.
COMPLETE SET (29)................ 10.00 3.00

1995 Idaho Falls Braves Team Issue

This 29-card set of the 1995 Idaho Falls Braves, a Rookie Class Pioneer League affiliate of the San Diego Padres, was sponsored by Hardee's, the Post Register, and KIFI-TV. The fronts feature color player portraits with various shades and widths of red, white, and blue borders. The backs display player information and statistics. The set also contains two smaller cards of first round draft pick Ben Davis, which were issued later as singles. The backs of these two cards carry a message from Ben Davis to Little Leaguers along with player information. The cards are unnumbered and checklisted below according to the jersey number of the player printed on the card front. 2,000 sets were produced. The complete set of 27 cards includes an unnumbered card of John Maxwell.
COMPLETE SET (27)................ 12.00 3.60
COMPLETE SET W/UPDATES (29) 6.00 1.80

1995 Indianapolis Indians Fleer/ProCards

This 30-card set of the 1995 Indianapolis Indians, a Class AAA American Association affiliate of the Cincinnati Reds, was produced by the Fleer Corp. and features posed color player photos in a white border on the card fronts. The backs carry player information and career statistics.
COMPLETE SET (30).................. 8.00 2.40

1995 Iowa Cubs Team Issue

This 25-card set of the 1995 Iowa Cubs, a Class AAA American Association affiliate of the Chicago Cubs, was produced by Multi-Ad Services Inc. and features borderless color player photos with the player's name. The backs carry player information and career statistics. The cards are unnumbered and checklisted below in alphabetical order. 1,000 sets were produced.
COMPLETE SET (25)................ 10.00 3.00

1995 Jackson Generals Smokey

This 26-card set of the 1995 Jackson Generals was sponsored by the USDA Forest Service. The fronts feature color action player photos in blue borders. The backs carry a Smokey the Bear cartoon and a warning to be careful with fire. The cards are unnumbered and checklisted below in alphabetical order.
COMPLETE SET (26)................ 15.00 4.50

1995 Jackson Generals Team Issue

This 27-card set of the 1995 Jackson Generals, a Class AA Texas League affiliate of the Houston Astros, was produced by Multi-Ad Services Inc. and features borderless color player photos. The backs carry player information and career statistics. 1,000 sets were produced.
COMPLETE SET (27)................ 15.00 4.50

1995 Jacksonville Suns Team Issue

This 28-card set of the 1995 Jacksonville Suns, a Class AA Southern League affiliate of the Detroit Tigers, features color player photos in white borders. The backs carry player information and career statistics. The cards are unnumbered and checklisted below in alphabetical order. 700 sets were produced.
COMPLETE SET (28)................ 10.00 3.00

1995 Kane County Cougars Legends Team Issue

This 15-card set features borderless color player photos of some of the 1993, 1994, and 1995 Cougars Alumni and Prospects. The backs carry information about the player and career statistics. The cards are unnumbered and checklisted below in alphabetical order. 2,000 sets were produced. A first year card of Luis Castillo highlights this set.
COMPLETE SET (15)................ 10.00 3.00

1995 Kane County Cougars Team Issue

This 32-card set of the 1995 Kane County Cougars, a Class A Midwest League affiliate of the Florida Marlins, features color player photos with a thin gold inner border around the player's image. The backs carry information about the player and career statistics. 3,000 sets were produced. The cards are unnumbered and checklisted below according to the player's jersey number. This issue includes the minor league card debut of Luis Castillo. A local sponsor, Eckrich also produced 1,000 of these sets.
COMPLETE SPONSOR SET (32) 15.00 4.50
COMPLETE SET (32)................ 12.00 3.60

1995 Kane County Cougars Team Issue Eckrich

1,000 of these sets which were sponsored by Eckrich were produced.
COMPLETE SET (32)................ 20.00 6.75
COMPLETE SPONSOR SET (32) 15.00 4.50

1995 Kinston Indians Team Issue

This 30-card set of the 1995 Kinston Indians, a Class A Carolina League affiliate of the Cleveland Indians, was produced by Multi-Ad Services Inc. and features borderless color player photos. The backs carry player information and career statistics. The cards are unnumbered and checklisted below in alphabetical order. This issue includes the minor league card debut of Danny Graves.
COMPLETE SET (30)................ 15.00 4.50

1995 Knoxville Smokies Fleer/ProCards

This 29-card set of the 1995 Knoxville Smokies, a Class AA Southern League affiliate of the Toronto Blue Jays, was produced by the Fleer Corp. and features posed color player photos in a white border on the card fronts. The backs carry player information and career statistics.
COMPLETE SET (29).................. 8.00 2.40

1995 Lake Elsinore Storm Team Issue

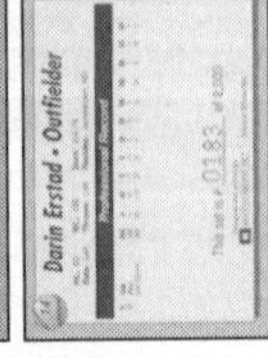

This 30-card set of the 1995 Lake Elsinore Storm, a Class A California League affiliate of the California Angels, was produced by Multi-Ad Services Inc. and features color player photos with blue borders. The backs carry player information and career statistics. This issue includes the minor league card debut of Darin Erstad. 2,000 sets were produced.
COMPLETE SET (30)................ 30.00 9.00

1995 Louisville Redbirds Fleer/ProCards

This 30-card set of the 1995 Louisville Redbirds, a Class AAA American Association affiliate of the St. Louis Cardinals, was produced by the Fleer Corp. and features posed color player photos in a white border on the card fronts. The backs carry player information and career statistics.
COMPLETE SET (30).................. 8.00 2.40

1995 LSU Tigers

These 16 standard-size cards feature on their fronts posed color player photos of the 1995 LSU Tigers. The cards' yellow borders are highlighted by vertical black lines. Cards carry the players name at the bottom of the photo and the team name at the top.
COMPLETE SET (16)................ 20.00 6.00

1995 Lynchburg Hillcats Team Issue

This 30-card set of the 1995 Lynchburg Hillcats, a Class A Carolina League affiliate of the Pittsburgh Pirates, was produced by Multi-Ad Services Inc. and features borderless color player photos. The backs carry player information and Minor League statistics. The cards are unnumbered and checklisted below in alphabetical order.
COMPLETE SET (30).................. 8.00 2.40

1995 Macon Braves Team Issue

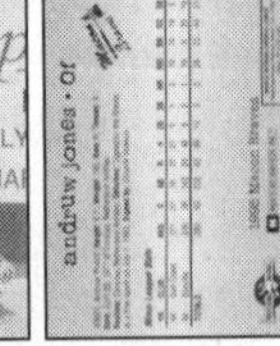

This 30-card set of the 1995 Macon Braves, a Class A South Atlantic League affiliate of the Atlanta Braves, was produced by Multi-Ad Services and features borderless color player photos. The backs carry player information and career statistics. The cards are unnumbered and checklisted below in alphabetical order. This issue includes the minor league card debuts of Andruw Jones and Wes Helms. 1,000 sets were produced.
COMPLETE SET (30).............. 175.00 52.50

1995 Macon Braves Update Team Issue

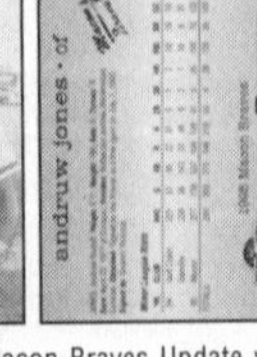

This six-card set Macon Braves Update was produced by Multi-Ad Services Inc. and carried a retail price of $5, features borderless color player photos of Macon Braves 1995 All-Stars with a limited addition Andruw Jones Player of the Year card. The backs carry player information and career statistics. The cards are unnumbered and checklisted below in alphabetical order. Andruw Jones is the key player in this set.
COMPLETE SET (6).................. 60.00 18.00

1995 Martinsville Phillies Team Issue

This 30-card set of the Martinsville Phillies, a Rookie Class Appalachian League affiliate of the Philadelphia Phillies, was issued in six strips of five perforated cards each and was produced by Multi-Ad Services Inc. and sponsored by Nabisco and Acme Markets. Each card features color action player photos on the front with player information and statistics on the back. The cards are unnumbered and checklisted below in alphabetical order. This issue includes the minor league card debuts of Reggie Taylor and Texas Longhorns' running back and Heisman Trophy winner, Ricky Williams. 1,000 sets were produced.
COMPLETE SET (30)................ 80.00 24.00

1995 Memphis Chicks Team Issue

This 27-card set of the 1995 Memphis Chicks, A Class AA Southern League affiliate of the San Diego Padres, was produced by Multi-Ad Services Inc. and features borderless color player photos. The backs carry player information and career statistics. 1,000 sets were produced.
COMPLETE SET (27)................ 10.00 3.00

1995 Michigan Battle Cats Team Issue

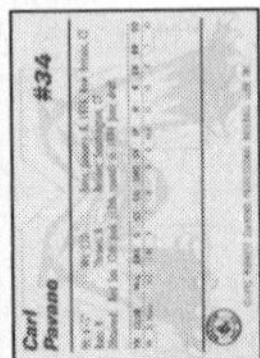

This 30-card set of the 1995 Michigan Battle Cats, a Class A Midwest League affiliate of the Boston Red Sox, features borderless color player photos with the player's name and position printed in a black bar at the bottom. The backs carry player information and career statistics. The cards are unnumbered and checklisted below in alphabetical order. This issue includes the minor league card debuts of Michael Coleman and Carl Pavano. 10,000 sets were produced.
COMPLETE SET (30)................ 15.00 4.50

1995 Midland Angels One Hour Photo

This 36-card set of the 1995 Midland Angels, a Class AA Texas League affiliate of the California Angels, features color player photos. The set measures approximately 5 1/2" by 5". The backs are blank. The cards are unnumbered and checklisted below in alphabetical order. 500 sets were produced.
COMPLETE SET (36)................ 60.00 18.00

1995 Midland Angels Team Issue

This 30-card set of the 1995 Midland Angels, a Class AA Texas League affiliate of the California Angels, was produced by Multi-Ad Services Inc. and features borderless color player portraits. The backs carry player information and career statistics. The cards are unnumbered and checklisted below in alphabetical order. 1,000 sets were produced.
COMPLETE SET (30)................ 10.00 3.00

1995 Midwest League All-Stars

This 58-card set honors the Midwest Minor League's 1995 All-Stars and features color player photos in a pastel star-design border. The backs carry player information and career statistics with the player's team logo. The cards are unnumbered and checklisted below in alphabetical order.
COMPLETE SET (58)................ 10.00 3.00

1995 Modesto A's Team Issue

This 32-card set of the 1995 Modesto A's, a Class A California League affiliate of the Oakland Athletics, was sponsored by McDonalds Restaurants and features black-and-white player portraits. The backs carry player information and career statistics. The cards are unnumbered and checklisted below in alphabetical order. This issue includes a second year card of Ben Grieve.
COMPLETE SET (32)................ 20.00 6.00

1995 Nashville Sounds Team Issue

This 30-card set of the Nashville Sounds, a Class AAA American Association affiliate of the Chicago White Sox, was issued in one large sheet measuring approximately 14 3/8" by 24 1/2" and was sponsored by Nabisco and H.G. Hill Food Stores. Each sheet consists of five perforated six-card player strips with the sponsors' names and team logo printed in a wide strip at the top. The fronts feature color player photos with the backs displaying player information printed over a very light team logo as background.
COMPLETE SET (30).................. 8.00 2.40

1995 New Haven Ravens Team Issue

This 34-card set of the 1995 New Haven Ravens, a Class AA Eastern League affiliate of the Colorado Rockies, was produced by Choice Marketing and features color player portraits. The backs carry player information and career statistics. 3,000 sets were produced.
COMPLETE SET (34)................ 10.00 3.00

1995 New Jersey Cardinals Team Issue

This 30-card set of the 1995 New Jersey Cardinals, a Class A New York-Penn League affiliate of the St. Louis Cardinals, was produced by Multi-Ad Services Inc. and features color player photos with a thin white border around the player's image. The backs carry player information and career statistics. The cards are unnumbered and checklisted below in alphabetical order. This issue includes the minor league card debut of Matt Morris. 3,000 sets were produced.
COMPLETE SET (30)................ 25.00 7.50

1995 Norfolk Tides Team Issue

This 30-card set of the 1995 Norfolk Tides, a Class AAA International League affiliate of the New York Mets, features color player photos in a white frame with a blue inner border. The backs carry another player photo at the side of the player information and career statistics box. 10,000 sets were produced.
COMPLETE SET (30)................ 10.00 3.00

1995 Norwich Navigators Team Issue

This 42-card set of the 1995 Norwich Navigators, a Class AA Eastern League affiliate of the New York Yankees, was produced by Choice Marketing. The fronts feature borderless color player photos. The backs carry player information and career statistics. The cards are checklisted below according to the players' jersey numbers printed on the backs of the cards.
COMPLETE SET (42)................ 10.00 3.00

1995 Norwich Navigators Update Team Issue

These 11 cards are an update to the original 1995 Norwich Navigators Team Set and feature the same design as the original set. The cards are checklisted below according to the player's jersey number as listed on the back of the card.
COMPLETE SET (11).................. 8.00 2.40

1995 Ogden Raptors Team Issue

This 30-card set of the 1995 Ogden Raptors, a Rookie Class Pioneer League Independent, was produced by Multi-Ad Services Inc. and features borderless color player photos. The backs carry player information. The cards are unnumbered and checklisted below in alphabetical order.
COMPLETE SET (30)................ 10.00 3.00

1995 Omaha Royals Team Issue

This 29-card set of the 1995 Omaha Royals, a Class AAA American Association affiliate of the Kansas City Royals, was produced by Multi-Ad Services Inc. and features color player photos with a thin white border around the player's image. The backs carry player information and career statistics.
COMPLETE SET (29)................ 10.00 3.00

1995 Orlando Cubs Fleer/ProCards

This 30-card set of the 1995 Orlando Cubs, a Class AA Southern League affiliate of the Chicago Cubs, was produced by the Fleer Corp. and features posed color player photos in a white border on the card fronts. The backs carry player information and career statistics.
COMPLETE SET (30).................. 8.00 2.40

1995 Pawtucket Red Sox Dunkin' Donuts

This 31-card Pawtucket Red Sox set, a Class AAA International League affiliate of the Boston Red Sox, was issued in one large sheet featuring six perforated five-card strips with a large team photo in the wide top strip. Sponsored by WJAR Newschannel 10 and Dunkin' Donuts, the fronts carry color player photos while the backs display player career statistics. The cards are unnumbered and checklisted below in alphabetical order.
COMPLETE SET (31)................ 50.00 15.00

1995 Pawtucket Red Sox Team Issue

This 30-card set of the 1995 Pawtucket Red Sox, a Class AAA International League affiliate of the Boston Red Sox, features color player portraits on the front with a fading yellow border of various widths. The backs carry player information and career statistics. 4,500 sets were produced.
COMPLETE SET (30)............... 10.00 3.00

1995 Peoria Chiefs Team Issue

This 31-card set of the 1995 Peoria Chiefs, a Class A Midwest League affiliate of the St. Louis Cardinals, was sponsored by Kitchen Cooked Potato Chips and Kroger Food Stores. The fronts feature color player photos with a fading blue to red border on two sides. The backs carry player information and career statistics.
COMPLETE SET (31)............... 10.00 3.00

1995 Phoenix Firebirds Team Issue

This 30-card set of the 1995 Phoenix Firebirds, a Class AAA Pacific Coast League affiliate of the San Francisco Giants, was sponsored by Keebler, Smitty's and KVRY 104.7 FM. The fronts feature color player photos with a blue border imprinted with the team logo. The backs carry sponsor logos and a small black-and-white player head photo with player information and career statistics. 4,000 sets were produced.
COMPLETE SET (30)................ 8.00 2.40

1995 Piedmont Phillies Fleer/ProCards

This 28-card set of the 1995 Piedmont Phillies, a Class A South Atlantic League affiliate of the Philadelphia Phillies, was produced by the Fleer Corp. and features posed color player photos in a white border on the card fronts. The backs carry player information and career statistics.
COMPLETE SET (28)................ 8.00 2.40

1995 Pittsfield Mets Team Issue

This 32-card set of the 1995 Pittsfield Mets, a Class A New York-Penn League affiliate of the New York Mets, was produced by Multi-Ad Services Inc. and features color player photos with a thin white border around the player's image. The backs carry player information and career statistics. The cards are unnumbered and checklisted below according to the player's jersey number. 1,000 sets were produced. This issue includes a second year card of Terrence Long.
COMPLETE SET (32)............... 12.00 3.60

1995 Port City Roosters Team Issue

This 29-card set of the 1995 Port City Roosters, a Class AA Southern League affiliate of the Seattle Mariners, was produced by Multi-Ad Services Inc. and features color player photos with a thin white border around the player's image. The backs carry player information and career statistics. The cards are unnumbered and checklisted below in alphabetical order. This issue includes the minor league card debut of Jason Varitek.
COMPLETE SET (29)............... 10.00 3.00

1995 Portland Sea Dogs Team Issue

This 30-card set of the 1995 Portland Sea Dogs, a Class AA Eastern League affiliate of the Florida Marlins, features color player photos in a black border. The backs carry a small color player head photo with player information and career statistics. The cards are unnumbered and checklisted below in alphabetical order.
COMPLETE SET (30)............... 10.00 3.00

1995 Prince William Cannons Team Issue

This 30-card set of the 1995 Prince William Cannons, a Class A Carolina League affiliate of the Chicago White Sox, was produced by Multi-Ad Services Inc. and features borderless color player photos. The backs carry player information and career statistics.
COMPLETE SET (30)............... 12.00 3.60

1995 Quad City River Bandits Team Issue

This 30-card set of the 1995 Quad City River Bandits, a Class A Midwest League affiliate of the Houston Astros, features color player photos over a background of baseballs. The backs carry player information and career statistics. The cards are unnumbered and checklisted below in alphabetical order. This issue includes the minor league card debut of Scott Elarton. 500 sets were produced.
COMPLETE SET (30)............... 20.00 6.00

1995 Rancho Cucamonga Quakes Team Issue

This 30-card set of the 1995 Rancho Cucamonga Quakes, a Class A California League affiliate of the San Diego Padres, was produced by Sport Shots and features borderless color player photos with the player's name, jersey number, and position in a bar near the bottom. The backs carry information about the player and career statistics. The cards are unnumbered and checklisted below according to the player's jersey number. This issue includes a first year card of Matt Clement and a second year card of Derrek Lee. 1,000 sets were produced.
COMPLETE SET (30)............... 25.00 7.50

1995 Reading Phillies Eastern League Champions Team Issue

This 36-card set of the 1995 Reading Phillies, a Class AA Eastern League affiliate of the Philadelphia Phillies, honors the 1995 Easter League Champions and was sponsored by Nabisco. The fronts feature borderless player photos. The backs carry player information and career statistics. The cards are unnumbered and checklisted below in alphabetical order. This issue includes a second year card of Scott Rolen.
COMPLETE SET (36)............... 40.00 12.00

1995 Reading Phillies Team Issue

This 28-card set of the 1995 Reading Phillies, a Class AA Eastern League affiliate of the Philadelphia Phillies, features color player action photos in a blue border with thin red and thinner white inner borders. The backs carry player information and career statistics. The cards are unnumbered and checklisted below in alphabetical order. Issued in conjunction with Nabisco.
COMPLETE SET (28)............... 50.00 15.00

1995 Richmond Braves Richmond Camera

This 29-card team set of the 1995 Richmond Braves, a Class AAA International League affiliate of the Atlanta Braves, was sponsored by Richmond Camera and measures approximately 4" by 4 7/8". The fronts feature borderless color player photos with sponsors' and team's logos in the wide bottom margin. The backs are blank. The cards are unnumbered and checklisted below in alphabetical order. 500 sets were produced.
COMPLETE SET (29)............... 60.00 18.00

1995 Richmond Braves Team Issue

This 30-card set of the 1995 Richmond Braves, a Class AAA International League affiliate of the Atlanta Braves, was sponsored by Pepsi Cola and features color art work of the players. The backs carry the player's name, postion, and statistics with the sponsor logo printed at the bottom. 7,500 sets were produced.
COMPLETE SET (30)................ 8.00 2.40

1995 Rochester Red Wings Team Issue

This 48-card set of the 1995 Rochester Red Wings, a Class AAA International League affiliate of the Baltimore Orioles, was produced by Bill Pucko Cards and features borderless color player photos by Barbara Jean Germano. The backs carry player information and career statistics.
COMPLETE SET (48)................ 8.00 2.40

1995 Rockford Cubs Team Issue

This 32-card set of the 1995 Rockford Cubs, a Class A Midwest League affiliate of the Chicago Cubs, was sponsored by AM radio station WROK 1440 and Eagle Country Market. The fronts feature color player photos with the player's name and position in a red bar at the bottom. The backs carry player information and career statistics with the sponsor logos printed below. 1,000 sets were produced.
COMPLETE SET (32)............... 15.00 4.50

1995 Salem Avalanche Team Issue

This 30-card set of the 1995 Salem Avalanche, a Class A Carolina League affiliate of the Colorado Rockies, was produced by Multi-Ad Services Inc. and features borderless color player photos. The backs carry player information and career statistics.
COMPLETE SET (30)............... 10.00 3.00

1995 San Antonio Missions Team Issue

This 30-card set of the 1995 San Antonio Missions, a Class AA Texas League affiliate of the Los Angeles Dodgers, was produced by Multi-Ad Services Inc. and features borderless color player photos. The backs carry player information and career statistics. The cards are unnumbered and checklisted below according to the player's jersey number as listed on the card back.
COMPLETE SET (30)............... 15.00 4.50

1995 San Bernardino Spirit Team Issue

This 32-card set of the 1995 San Bernardino Spirit, a Class A California League affiliate of the Los Angeles Dodgers, was produced by Multi-Ad Services Inc. and features borderless color player posed and action photos. The backs carry player information and career statistics. This issue includes a second year card of Paul Konerko.
COMPLETE SET (32)............... 20.00 6.00

1995 Scranton/Wilkes-Barre Red Barons Dunkin' Donuts

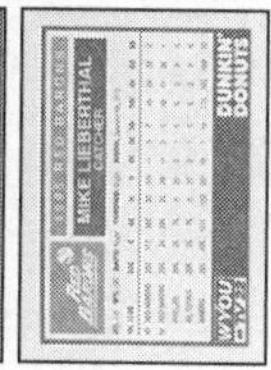

This 30-card set features members of the Scranton Wilkes-Barre Red Barons (a triple-A affiliate of the Philadelphia Phillies). The cards were issued as a perforated sheet that folds out to poster size. Each card features a truly crude full color painted image on front, surrounded by a dark purple border. The set was sponsored by Dunkin' Donuts and WYOU-22 TV. The cards are unnumbered and checklisted below in alphabetical order. Hitting coach Dave Cash and catcher Mike Lieberthal are the only players of note.
COMPLETE SET (30)............... 40.00 12.00

1995 Scranton/Wilkes-Barre Red Barons Team Issue

This 30-card set of the 1995 Scranton/Wilkes-Barre Red Barons, a Class AAA International League affiliate of the Philadelphia Phillies, features color player photos in a blue frame with thin red outside and inside borders. The teams name is printed in white around the frame with the player's name and position at the bottom. The backs carry player information and career statistics. The cards are unnumbered and checklisted below in alphabetical order.
COMPLETE SET (30)............... 20.00 6.00

1995 Spokane Indians Team Issue

This 32-card set of the 1995 Spokane Indians, a Class A Northwest League affiliate of the Kansas City Royals, was sponsored by First Seafirst Bank and features color player photos with a thin red inner border and blue marblized frame. The backs carry player information and career statistics with the sponsor's logo printed at the bottom. The cards are unnumbered and checklisted below in alphabetical order. Mark Quinn's first card is included in this set.
COMPLETE SET (32)............... 15.00 4.50

1995 Springfield Sultans Team Issue

This 30-card set of the 1995 Springfield Sultans, a Class A Midwest League affiliate of the Kansas City Royals, was produced by Multi-Ad Services Inc. and features borderless color player photos. The backs carry player information and career statistics. 1,500 sets were produced.
COMPLETE SET (30)............... 10.00 3.00

1995 St. Catherines Stompers Team Issue

This 36-card set of the 1995 St. Catherines Stompers, a Class A New York-Penn League affiliate of the Toronto Blue Jays, features color player photos with a thin yellow inner border and a purple frame with yellow corner stripes. The backs carry player information and a team safety tip.
COMPLETE SET (36)............... 50.00 15.00

1995 St. Lucie Mets Team Issue

This 36-card set of the 1995 St. Lucie Mets, a Class A Florida State League affiliate of the New York Mets, was sponsored by Publix Super Markets and features color player photos with different colored borders. The backs carry player information, career statistics, and the sponsor's logo.
COMPLETE SET (36)................ 8.00 2.40

1995 Syracuse Chiefs Team Issue

This 29-card set of the 1995 Syracuse Chiefs team was sponsored by George's Sports Cards and features color player photos with a purple, blue, and white border. The backs carry player information and career statistics with the sponsor logo printed at the bottom. The cards are unnumbered and checklisted below in alphabetical order. An minor league card of Carlos Delgado is featured in this set.
COMPLETE SET (29)............... 15.00 4.50

1995 Tacoma Rainiers Team Issue

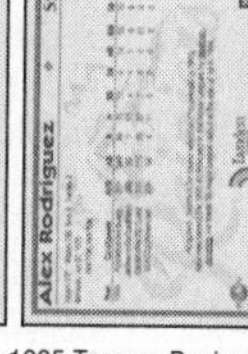

This 30-card set of the 1995 Tacoma Raniers, a Class AAA Pacific Coast League affiliate of the Seattle Mariners, was sponsored by Lynden Farms and features color player photos in a white frame with a red inner border. The backs carry player information and 1994 season statistics. This issue includes a second year card of Alex Rodriguez. 5,000 sets were produced.
COMPLETE SET (30)............... 60.00 18.00

1995 Tampa Yankees Team Issue

This 30-card set of the 1995 Tampa Yankees, a Class A Florida State League affiliate of the New York Yankees, was sponsored by Multi-Ad Services Inc. and features borderless color player photos by Cliff Welch. The backs carry player information and career statistics.
COMPLETE SET (30)................ 8.00 2.40

1995 Tennessee Volunteers Wendy's

The cards are unnumbered and checklisted below in alphabetical order. Issued in two eight-card sheets. Two cards of future batting champion Todd Helton are the key cards in this set.
COMPLETE SET (16)............... 25.00 7.50

1995 Toledo Mud Hens Team Issue

This 30-card team set of the 1995 Toledo Mud Hens, a Class AAA International League affiliate of the Detroit Tigers, features posed color player photos with blue, white, and two-sided thin red borders. The backs carry player biographical information and career statistics. 5,000 sets were produced.
COMPLETE SET (30)................ 8.00 2.40

1995 Trenton Thunder Team Issue

This 31-card set of the 1995 Trenton Thunder, a Class AA Eastern League affiliate of the Boston Red Sox, features posed color player portraits with a white and thin green-striped border. The team logo and player's name and position are printed in the wide bottom margin. The backs carry player biographical information and career statistics. This issue includes the minor league card set debut of Nomar Garciaparra. This set was issued both in set and in uncut sheet form.
COMPLETE SET (31)............ 150.00 45.00

1995 Tucson Toros Team Issue

This 29-card team set of the 1995 Tucson Toros, a Class AAA Pacific Coast League affiliate of the Houston Astros, features color player images on a transparent light gray background over a wood simulated background with the team's name and logo running througout. The backs display a black-and-white player's head photo with biographical information and career statistics. The cards are unnumbered and checklisted below in alphabetical order. 3,000 sets were produced. An early card of Bob Abreu is featured in this set.
COMPLETE SET (29)............... 10.00 3.00

1995 Tulsa Drillers Team Issue

This 30-card set of the 1995 Tulsa Drillers, a Class AA Texas League affiliate of the Texas Rangers, features borderless color player photos on the fronts with the player's name, position, and team logo printed in a red bar across the bottom. The backs carry player information and career statistics with sponsor logo and an Oklahoma Highway Safety message printed at the bottom.
COMPLETE SET (30)............... 10.00 3.00

1995 Vero Beach Dodgers Team Issue

This 30-card set of the Vero Beach Dodgers, a Class A Florida State League affiliate of the Los Angeles Dodgers, was issued in one sheet consisting of five perforated six-card strips. The fronts feature color player photos while the backs carry player information and career statistics. The cards are unnumbered and checklisted below in alphabetical order. 750 sets were produced.
COMPLETE SET (30).............. 15.00 4.50

1995 Watertown Indians Team Issue

This 30-card set of the 1995 Watertown Indians, a Class A New York-Penn League affiliate of the Cleveland Indians, features color player action photos by Jim Thwaits in a white border. The backs carry player information and career statistics. The cards are unnumbered and checklisted below in alphabetical order.

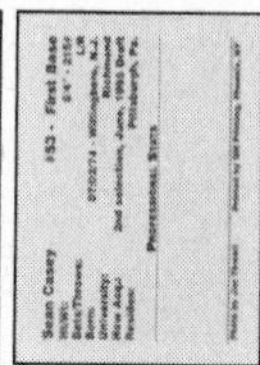

This issue includes the minor league card debut of Sean Casey.
COMPLETE SET (30)............... 50.00 15.00

1995 West Michigan Whitecaps Team Issue

This 30-card set of the 1995 West Mighigan Whitecaps, a Class A Midwest League affiliate of the Oakland Athletics, features color player photos with a team color and logo border. The backs carry a small black-and-white player head photo with biographical information and career statistics. The cards are unnumbered and checklisted below according to the player's jersey number. This issue includes a second year card of Ben Grieve.
COMPLETE SET (30)............... 10.00 3.00

1995 Wichita Wranglers Team Issue

This 30-card set of the 1995 Wichita Wranglers, a Class AA Texas League affiliate of the Kansas City Royals, was produced by Multi-Ad Services Inc. and features borderless color player photos on the fronts. The backs carry player biographical information and career statistics. The cards are unnumbered and checklisted below according to the player's jersey number.
COMPLETE SET (30)............... 10.00 3.00

1995 Wilmington Blue Rocks Team Issue

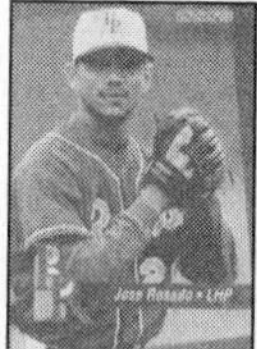

This 30-card set of the 1995 Wilmington Blue Rocks, a Class A Carolina League affiliate of the Kansas City Royals, was produced by Choice Marketing Inc. and features color player photos on the fronts. The backs carry player biographical information and career statistics. The cards are unnumbered and checklisted below according to the player's jersey number. Early cards of Glendon Rusch and Mike Sweeney are included in this set.
COMPLETE SET (30)............... 20.00 6.00

1995 Yakima Bears Team Issue

This 36-card set of the 1995 Yakima Bears, a Class A Northwest League affiliate of the Los Angeles Dodgers, features color player photos on the fronts with a white and thin-gold border. The backs carry player information and career statistics. The cards are unnumbered and checklisted below in alphabetical order. 1,500 sets were produced.
COMPLETE SET (36)............... 15.00 4.50

1996 Appalachian League All-Stars Best

An early Jimmy Rollins card highlights this set.
COMPLETE SET (30)............... 15.00 4.50

1996 Arkansas Travelers Best

This 29-card set of the 1996 Arkansas Travelers, a Class AA Texas League affiliate of the St. Louis Cardinals, was produced by Best Cards, Inc. and features color action player photos in a white border. The backs carry player information and career statistics.
COMPLETE SET (29)............... 20.00 6.00

1996 Asheville Tourists Best

This 30-card set of the 1996 Asheville Tourists, a Class A South Atlantic League affiliate of the Colorado Rockies, was produced by Best Cards, Inc. and features color action player photos in a white border. The backs carry player information and career statistics. This issue includes the minor league card debut of Ben Petrick.
COMPLETE SET (30)............... 10.00 3.00

1996 Auburn Doubledays Best

This 30-card set of the 1996 Auburn Doubledays, a Class A New York-Penn League affiliate of the Houston Astros, was produced by Best Cards, Inc. and features color action player photos in a white border. The backs carry player information and career statistics.
COMPLETE SET (30)............... 10.00 3.00

1996 Augusta Greenjackets Best

This 29-card set of the 1996 Augusta Greenjackets, a Class A South Atlantic League

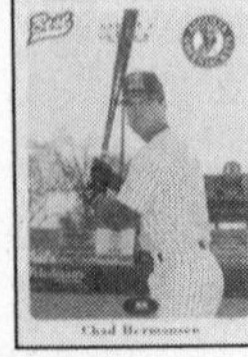
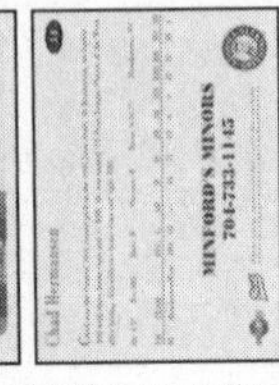

affiliate of the Pittsburgh Pirates, was produced by Best Cards, Inc. and features color action player photos in a white border. The backs carry player information and career statistics.This issue includes the minor league team set card debuts of Chad Hermansen and Bronson Arroyo.
COMPLETE SET (29)................ 30.00 9.00

1996 Batavia Clippers Team Issue

This 34-card set of the 1996 Batavia Clippers, a Class A New York-Penn League affiliate of the Philadelphia Phillies, features color player portraits with white borders. The backs carry player information and career statistics.
COMPLETE SET (34)................ 10.00 3.00

1996 Bellingham Giants Team Issue

This 36-card set of the 1996 Bellingham Giants, a Class A Northwest League affiliate of the San Francisco Giants, was produced by Grandstand Cards and sponsored by various area companies. The fronts feature color player photos with white frames and a two-sided fading orange inner border. The backs carry player information and interesting player notes with a sponsor name at the bottom.
COMPLETE SET (36)................ 15.00 4.50

1996 Beloit Snappers Team Issue

This 36-card set of the 1996 Beloit Snappers, a Class A Midwest League affiliate of the Milwaukee Brewers, was produced by Raging Color Classics and sponsored by radio station 97ZOK and the Beloit Memorial Hospital. The fronts feature color player photos in white borders. The backs carry a small black-and-white player portrait with player information and career statistics. The cards are unnumbered and checklisted below in alphabetical order.
COMPLETE SET (36)................ 10.00 3.00

1996 Billings Mustangs Team Issue

This 31-card set of the 1996 Billings Mustangs, a Rookie Class Pioneer League affiliate of the Cincinnati Reds, was sponsored by the First Interstate Bank and features black-and-white borderless color player photos by Dennis Clark. The backs carry player information and statistics. The cards are unnumbered and checklisted below in alphabetical order.
COMPLETE SET (31)................ 40.00 12.00

1996 Binghamton Mets Best

This 30-card set of the 1996 Binghamton Bees, a Class AA Eastern League affiliate of the New York Mets, was produced by Best Cards, Inc. and features color action player photos in a white border. The backs carry player information and career statistics. Early cards of Benny Agbayani and Brian Daubach highlight this set.
COMPLETE SET (30)................ 15.00 4.50

1996 Birmingham Barons Best

This 30-card set of the 1996 Birmingham Barons, a Class AA Southern League affiliate of the Chicago White Sox, was produced by Best Cards, Inc. and features color action player photos in a white border. The backs carry player information and career statistics. Early cards of Mike Cameron and Magglio Ordonez highlight this set.
COMPLETE SET (30)................ 15.00 4.50

1996 Bluefield Orioles Best

This 27-card set of the 1996 Bluefield Orioles, a Rookie Class Appalachian League affiliate of the Baltimore Orioles, was produced by Best Cards, Inc. and features color action player photos in a white border. The backs carry player information and career statistics.
COMPLETE SET (30)................ 10.00 3.00

1996 Boise Hawks Best

This 30-card set of the 1996 Boise Hawks, a Class A Northwest League affiliate of the California Angels, was produced by Best Cards, Inc. and features color action player photos in a white border. The backs carry player information and career statistics.
COMPLETE SET (30)................ 10.00 3.00

1996 Bowie Baysox Best

This 27-card set of the 1996 Bowie Baysox, a Class AA Eastern League affiliate of the Baltimore Orioles, was produced by Best Cards, Inc. and features color action player photos in a white border. The backs carry player information and career statistics.
COMPLETE SET (27)................ 8.00 2.40

1996 Brevard County Manatees Best

This 30-card set of the 1996 Brevard County Manatees, a Class A Florida State League affiliate of the Florida Marlins, was produced by Best Cards, Inc. and features color action player photos in a white border. The backs carry player information and career statistics.
COMPLETE SET (30)................ 10.00 3.00

1996 Bristol White Sox Best

This 30-card set of the 1996 Bristol White Sox, a Rookie Class Appalachian League affiliate of the Chicago White Sox, was produced by Best Cards, Inc. and features color action player photos in a white border. The backs carry player information and career statistics.
COMPLETE SET (30)................ 10.00 3.00

1996 Buffalo Bisons Best

This 24-card set of the 1996 Buffalo Bisons, a Class AAA American Association affiliate of the Cleveland Indians, was produced by Best Cards, Inc. and features color action player photos in a white border. The backs carry player information and career statistics. An early card of Brian Giles highlights this set.
COMPLETE SET (24)................ 10.00 3.00

1996 Burlington Bees Team Issue

This 33-card set of the 1996 Burlington Bees, a Class A Midwest League affiliate of the San Francisco Giants, features borderless color player photos. The backs carry a small black-and-white player portrait with player information and career statistics. The cards are unnumbered and checklisted below according to the way they are listed on the checklist card.
COMPLETE SET (33)................ 40.00 12.00

1996 Burlington Indians Best

This 30-card set of the 1996 Burlington Indians, a Rookie Class Appalachian League affiliate of the Cleveland Indians, was produced by Best Cards, Inc. and features color action player photos in a white border. The backs carry player information and career statistics.
COMPLETE SET (30)................ 10.00 3.00

1996 Butte Copper Kings Best

This 30-card set of the 1996 Butte Copper Kings, a Class Rookie Class Pioneer League affiliate of the Tampa Bay Devil Rays, was produced by Best Cards, Inc. and features color action player photos in a white border. The backs carry player information and career statistics.
COMPLETE SET (30)................ 8.00 2.40

1996 Canton-Akron Indians Best

This 30-card set of the 1996 Canton-Akron Indians, a Class AA Eastern League affiliate of the Cleveland Indians, was produced by Best Cards, Inc. and features color action player photos in a white border. The backs carry player information and career statistics.
COMPLETE SET (30)................ 10.00 3.00

1996 Carolina League All-Stars 1 Best

This 24-card set of the 1996 Carolina League's All-Star team was produced by Best Cards, Inc. and sponsored by Minford's Minors. The cards are printed on thin card stock. The fronts feature color player photos in a white border. The backs carry player information. The set features early cards of Sean Casey, Jose Guillen and Andruw Jones. 1,582 sets were produced.
COMPLETE SET (24)................ 25.00 7.50

1996 Carolina League All-Stars 2 Best

This 26-card set of the 1996 Carolina League's All-Star team was produced by Best Cards, Inc. and sponsored by Minford's Minors. The fronts feature color player photos in white borders. The backs carry player information. This set was printed on a thicker card stock. The features first year cards of Jose Guillen and Miquel Tejada and second year cards of Andruw Jones and Wes Helms. 1,110 sets were produced.
COMPLETE SET (26)................ 40.00 12.00

1996 Carolina League All-Stars Insert Best

This 10-card set was produced by Best Cards, Inc. and sponsored by Minford's Minors. The fronts feature borderless color player photos of some of the most notable All-Stars of the 1996 Carolina League's All-Star team. The backs carry a statement about why the player was picked for this set. Only a limited number of this set was produced and each set is sequentially numbered. Key players in this set include Andruw Jones and Miguel Tejada.
COMPLETE SET (10)................ 80.00 24.00

1996 Carolina Mudcats Best

This 30-card set of the 1996 Carolina Mudcats, a Class AA Southern League affiliate of the Pittsburgh Pirates, was produced by Best Cards, Inc. and features color action player photos in a white border. The backs carry player information and career statistics.
COMPLETE SET (30)................ 10.00 3.00

1996 Cedar Rapids Kernels Team Issue

This 32-card set of the 1996 Cedar Rapids Kernels, a Class A Midwest League affiliate of the California Angels, was sponsored by McDonald's Restaurants and features color player photos by Jim Tevis. The backs carry player information and statistics. The cards are unnumbered and checklisted below according to the way they are listed on the checklist card.
COMPLETE SET (32)................ 10.00 3.00

1996 Charleston Riverdogs Team Issue

This 32-card set of the 1996 Charleston Riverdogs, a Class A South Atlantic League affiliate of the Texas Rangers, features color player photos in white borders. The backs carry player information and career statistics. This issue includes the minor league card debuts of Ruben Mateo and Ryan Dempster.
COMPLETE SET (32)................ 25.00 7.50

1996 Charlotte Knights Best

This 29-card set of the 1996 Charlotte Knights, a Class AAA International League affiliate of the Florida Marlins, was produced by Best Cards, Inc. and features color action player photos in a white border. The backs carry player information and career statistics. This issue includes the minor league card debut Livan Hernandez.
COMPLETE SET (29)................ 10.00 3.00

1996 Chattanooga Lookouts Best

This 30-card set of the 1996 Chattanooga Lookouts, a Class AA Southern League affiliate of the Cincinnati Reds, was produced by Best Cards, Inc. and features color action player photos in a white border. The backs carry player information and career statistics. This issue includes the minor league card debut of Brett Tomko.
COMPLETE SET (30)................ 10.00 3.00

1996 Clinton Lumber Kings Team Issue

This 29-card set of lthe 1996 Clinton Lumber Kings, a Class A Midwest League affiliate of the San Diego Padres, features color player photos with a vertical green bar on the left. The backs carry a small black-and-white head photo with player information and career statistics. The cards are unnumbered and checklisted below in alphabetical order. An early card of Matt Clement is included in this set.
COMPLETE SET (29)................ 25.00 7.50

1996 Colorado Silver Bullets

This 28-card set features color action player photos with white, red and purple borders. The backs carry player information. The cards are unnumbered and checklisted below in alphabetical order.
COMPLETE SET (28)................ 10.00 3.00

1996 Colorado Springs Sky Sox Team Issue

This 33-card set of the 1996 Colorado Springs Sky Sox, a Class AAA Pacific Coast League affiliate of the Colorado Rockies, features borderless color player photos with the player's name and position printed in a black bar at the bottom. The backs carry player information and career statistics.
COMPLETE SET (33)................ 10.00 3.00

1996 Columbus Clippers Best

This 30-card set of the 1996 Columbus Clippers, a Class AAA International League affiliate of the New York Yankees, was produced by Best Cards, Inc. and features color action player photos in a white border. The backs carry player information and career statistics.
COMPLETE SET (30)................ 8.00 2.40

1996 Danville Braves Best

This 30-card set of the 1996 Danville Braves, a Rookie Class Appalachian League affiliate of the Atlanta Braves, was produced by Best Cards, Inc. and features color action player photos in a white border. The backs carry player information and career statistics. This issue includes the minor league card debuts of Kevin McGlinchy and Delvis Pacheco.
COMPLETE SET (30)................ 30.00 9.00

1996 Daytona Cubs Best

This 30-card set of the 1996 Daytona Cubs, a Class A Florida State League affiliate of the Chicago Cubs, was produced by Best Cards, Inc. and features color action player photos in a white border. The backs carry player information and career statistics. This issue includes the minor league card debut of Kerry Wood.
COMPLETE SET (30)................ 30.00 9.00

1996 Delmarva Shorebirds Best

This 30-card set of the 1996 Delmarva Shorebirds, a Class A South Atlantic League affiliate of the Montreal Expos, was produced by Best Cards, Inc. and features color action player photos in a white border. The backs carry player information and career statistics. An early card of Javier Vazquez is included in this set.
COMPLETE SET (30)................ 25.00 3.60

1996 Delmarva Shorebirds Update Best

This six-card strip was issued in late 1996 as an update.
COMPLETE SET (6).................... 5.00 1.50

1996 Double-A All-Stars Best

Cards of Vladimir Guerrero, Todd Helton and Richard Hidalgo are the highlights of this set.
COMPLETE SET (56)................ 25.00 7.50

1996 Dunedin Blue Jays Best

This 30-card set of the 1996 Dunedin Blue Jays, a Class A Florida State League affiliate of the Toronto Blue Jays, was produced by Best Cards, Inc. and features color action player photos in a white border. The backs carry player information and career statistics. This issue includes the minor league card debut of Kelvim Escobar.
COMPLETE SET (30)................ 15.00 4.50

1996 Dunedin Blue Jays Team Issue

This 30-card set of the 1996 Dunedin Blue Jays, a Class A Florida State League affiliate of the Toronto Blue Jays, was sponsored by the Times, Perkins Family Restaurant and Bakery, and ABC Station 28. The fronts feature color player portraits in a white border. The player's name and position is printed in a black bar at the bottom. The backs carry player information and career statistics. The cards are unnumbered and checklisted below in alphabetical order. This issue includes the minor league card debut of Kelvim Escobar.
COMPLETE SET (30)................ 30.00 9.00

1996 Dunedin Blue Jays Update Team Issue

This 18-card set is an update to the regular 1996 Dunedin Blue Jays team and features color player photos in a white border. The backs carry player information. The cards are unnumbered and checklisted below in alphabetical order.
COMPLETE SET (18)................ 30.00 9.00

1996 Durham Bulls Blue Best

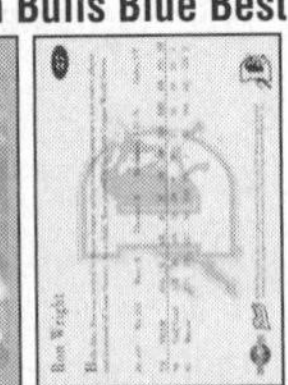

This 30-card set of the 1996 Durham Bulls, a Class A Carolina League affiliate of the Atlanta Braves, was produced by Best Cards, Inc. and features color action player photos in a blue border. The backs carry player information and career statistics. This issue features the second year card of Andruw Jones.
COMPLETE SET (30)................ 50.00 15.00

1996 Durham Bulls Brown Best

This 30-card set of the 1996 Durham Bulls, a Class A Carolina League affiliate of the Atlanta Braves, honors the Carolina League's Southern Division First Half Champions and the team's All-Star players. The set was produced by Best Cards, Inc. and features color action player photos in a brown border. The backs carry player information and career statistics. This issue features the second year card of Andruw Jones.
COMPLETE SET (30)................ 30.00 9.00

1996 El Paso Diablos Best

This 30-card set of the 1996 El Paso Diablos, a Class AA Texas League affiliate of the Milwaukee Brewers, was produced by Best Cards, Inc. and features color player photos in a white border. The backs carry player information and career statistics. This issue includes the minor league card debut of Geoff Jenkins.
COMPLETE SET (30)................ 15.00 4.50

1996 Erie Seawolves Best

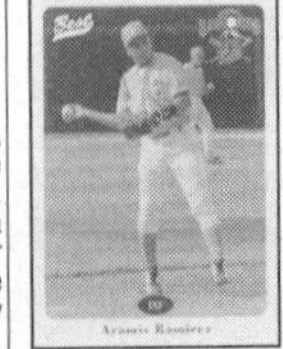
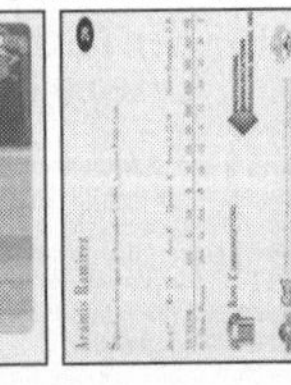

This 25-card set of the 1996 Erie Seawolves, a Class A New York-Penn League affiliate of the Pittsburgh Pirates, was produced by Best Cards, Inc. and features color player photos in a white border. The backs carry player information and career statistics. This issue includes the minor league card debut of Aramis Ramirez.
COMPLETE SET (25)................ 15.00 4.50

1996 Eugene Emeralds Best

This 27-card set of the 1996 Eugene Emeralds, a Class A Northwest League affiliate of the Atlanta Braves, was produced by Best Cards, Inc. and features color player photos in a white border. The backs carry player information and career statistics.
COMPLETE SET (27)................ 15.00 4.50

1996 Everett Aquasox Best

This 30-card set of the 1996 Everett Aquasox, a Class A Northwest League affiliate of the Seattle Mariners, was produced by Best Cards, Inc. and features color player photos in a white border. The backs carry player information and career statistics.
COMPLETE SET (30)................ 10.00 3.00

1996 Fayetteville Generals Best

This 30-card set of the 1996 Fort Myers Miracle, a Class A South Atlantic League affiliate of the Detroit Tigers, was produced by Best Cards, Inc. and features color player photos in a white border. The backs carry player information and career statistics. This issue includes the minor league card debuts of Gabe Kapler and David Borkowski.
COMPLETE SET (30)................ 40.00 12.00

1996 Fort Myers Miracle Best

This 30-card set of the 1996 Fort Myers Miracle, a Class A Florida State League affiliate of the Minnesota Twins, was produced by Best Cards, Inc. and features color player photos in a white border. The backs carry player information and career statistics.
COMPLETE SET (30)................ 10.00 3.00

1996 Fort Wayne Wizards Best

This 31-card set of the 1996 Fort Wayne Wizards, a Class A Midwest League affiliate of the Minnesota Twins, was produced by Best Cards, Inc. and features color player photos in a white border. The backs carry player information and career statistics.
COMPLETE SET (31)................ 10.00 3.00

1996 Frederick Keys Best

This 30-card set of the 1996 Frederick Keys, a Class A Carolina League affiliate of the Baltimore Orioles, was produced by Best Cards, Inc. and features color player photos in a white border. The backs carry player information and career statistics.
COMPLETE SET (30)................ 10.00 3.00

1996 Great Falls Dodgers Best

This Minor Miracles 30-card set of the 1996 Great Falls Dodgers team was produced by Best Cards, Inc. and features color player photos in a blue border. The backs carry player information and career statistics. Each set is numbered out of 1,000 and indicated on Card #30.
COMPLETE SET (30)................ 15.00 4.50

1996 Great Falls Dodgers Team Issue

This 36-card set of the 1996 Great Falls Dodgers, a Rookie Class Pioneer League affiliate of the Los Angeles Dodgers, features color player photos with a black shadow in gray and blue borders. The backs carry a small black-and-white player head photo with player information and career highlights. The cards are unnumbered and checklisted below according to the way they are listed on the checklist.
COMPLETE SET (36)................ 10.00 3.00

1996 Greensboro Bats Best

This 30-card set of the 1996 Greensboro Bats, a Class A South Atlantic League affiliate of the New York Yankees, was produced by Best Cards, Inc. and features color player photos in a white border. The backs carry player information and career statistics. This issue includes the minor league card debut of D'Angelo Jimenez.
COMPLETE SET (30)................ 20.00 6.00

1996 Greenville Braves Best

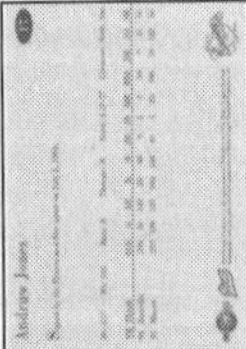

This 30-card set of the 1996 Greenville Braves, a Class AA Southern League affiliate of the Atlanta Braves, was produced by Best Cards, Inc. and features color player photos in a white

border. The backs carry player information and career statistics. This issue features the second year card of Andruw Jones.
COMPLETE SET (30)................ 30.00 9.00

1996 Greenville Braves Team Issue

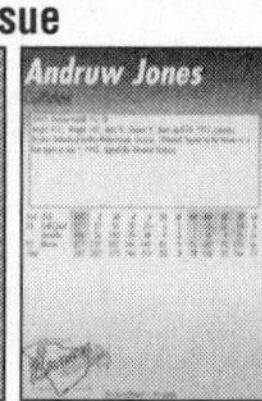

This 30-card set of the 1996 Greenville Braves, a Class AA Southern League affiliate of the Atlanta Braves, was sponsored by Coca-Cola and features color player photos in a blue striped frame with a thin red inner border. The backs carry player information and career statistics. This issue features the second year card of Andruw Jones.
COMPLETE SET (30)................ 30.00 9.00

1996 Hagerstown Suns Best

This 30-card set of the 1996 Hagerstown Suns, a Class A South Atlantic League affiliate of the Toronto Blue Jays, was produced by Best Cards, Inc. and features color player photos in a white border. The backs carry player information and career statistics.
COMPLETE SET (30)................ 10.00 3.00

1996 Hardware City Rock Cats Best

This 30-card set of the 1996 Hardware City Rock Cats, a Class AA Eastern League affiliate of the Minnesota Twins, was produced by Best Cards, Inc. and features color player photos in a white border. The backs carry player information and career statistics.
COMPLETE SET (30)................ 10.00 3.00

1996 Harrisburg Senators Best

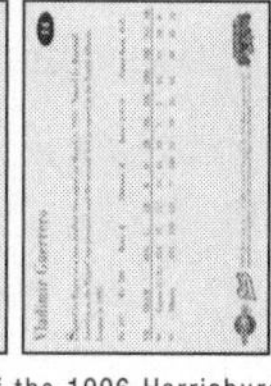

This 29-card set of the 1996 Harrisburg Senators, a Class AA Eastern League affiliate of the Montreal Expos, was produced by Best Cards, Inc. and features color player photos in a white border. The backs carry player information and career statistics. This issue includes the minor league team set card debut of Vladimir Guerrero.
COMPLETE SET (29)................ 60.00 18.00

1996 Helena Brewers Team Issue

This 34-card set of the 1996 Helena Brewers, a Rookie Class Pioneer League affiliate of the Milwaukee Brewers, was sponsored by TV station KTVH Channel 12 and Shodair Children's Hospital. The fronts feature borderless color player photos with the player's name and position printed in red at the bottom above purple snow-capped mountain tops. The backs carry a small black-and-white player portrait with player information and sponsors' logos.
COMPLETE SET (34)................ 40.00 12.00

1996 Hickory Crawdads Best

This 30-card set of the 1996 Hickory Crawdads team was produced by Best Cards, Inc. and features color player photos. The backs carry player information and statistics. Only 1,000 of this set were produced and is sequentially numbered on Card number 30. This issue includes the minor league card debut of Carlos Lee.
COMPLETE SET (30)................ 30.00 9.00

1996 High Desert Mavericks Best

This 30-card set of the 1996 High Desert Mavericks, a Class A California League affiliate of the Baltimore Orioles, was produced by Best Cards, Inc. and features color player photos in a white border. The backs carry player information and career statistics.
COMPLETE SET (30)................ 10.00 3.00

1996 High Desert Mavericks Police

This 24-card set of the 1996 High Desert Mavericks, a Class A California League affiliate of the Baltimore Orioles, was sponsored by the California Highway Patrol. The fronts feature color player photos in a black border. The backs carry player information and a safety message from the Designated Driver Program.
COMPLETE SET (24)................ 15.00 4.50

1996 Hilo Stars Hawaii Winter Ball

This 36-card set of the 1996 Hilo Stars team was produced by Trade Publishing and features borderless color player portraits by Reed Takaaze. The backs carry player information and player statistics. Early cards of Benny Agbayani and Terrence Long are included in this set.
COMPLETE SET (36)................ 25.00 7.50

1996 Honolulu Sharks Hawaii Winter Ball

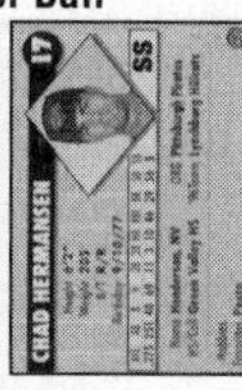

This 36-card set of the 1996 Honolulu Sharks team was produced by Trade Publishing and features borderless action color player photos by Jay Metzger. The backs carry a small black-and-white player headshot by Ray Wong with player information and statistics. This issue includes first year cards of Chad Hermansen and Brad Fullmer.
COMPLETE SET (36)................ 20.00 6.00

1996 Hudson Valley Renegades Best

This 30-card set of the 1996 Hudson Valley Renegades, a Class A New York-Penn League Co-op, was produced by Best Cards, Inc. and features color player photos in a white border. The backs carry player information and career statistics.
COMPLETE SET (30)................ 10.00 3.00

1996 Huntsville Stars Team Issue

This 28-card set of the 1996 Huntsville Stars, a Class AA Southern League affiliate of the Oakland Athletics, was sponsored by Burger King and features color player portraits with a thin red and a wider blue border. The backs carry player information and career statistics. The cards are unnumbered and checklisted below in alphabetical order. A minor league card of Ben Grieve is included in this set.
COMPLETE SET (28)................ 80.00 24.00

1996 Idaho Falls Braves Team Issue

This 32-card set of the 1996 Idaho Falls Braves, a Rookie Class Pioneer League affiliate of the San Diego Padres, was sponsored by C-A-L Ranch Stores, United Furniture Warehouse, Radio Station Z103 and KIFI-TV Channel 8. The fronts feature color player portraits in a fading blue, white, and salmon border. The backs carry player information, career statistics, and sponsor logos. The cards are unnumbered and checklisted below in alphabetical order.
COMPLETE SET (32)................ 18.00 5.50

1996 Indianapolis Indians Best

This 30-card set of the 1996 Indianapolis Indians, a Class AAA American Association affiliate of the Cincinnati Reds, was produced by Best Cards, Inc. and features color player photos in a white border. The backs carry player information and career statistics.
COMPLETE SET (30)................. 8.00 2.40

1996 Iowa Cubs Best

This 30-card set of the 1996 Iowa Cubs, a Class AAA American Association affiliate of the Chicago Cubs, was produced by Best Cards, Inc. and features color player photos in a white border. The backs carry player information and career statistics.
COMPLETE SET (30)................. 8.00 2.40

1996 Jackson Generals Best

This 27-card set of the 1996 Jackson Generals, a Class AA Texas League affiliate of the Houston Astros, was produced by Best Cards, Inc. and features color player photos in a white border. The backs carry player information and career statistics. A minor league card of Richard Hidalgo is a highlight of this set.
COMPLETE SET (27)................ 15.00 4.50

1996 Jackson Generals Smokey

This 27-card set of the 1996 Jackson Generals was sponsored by the USDA Forest Service. The fronts feature color action player photos in black-and-white borders. The backs carry a Smokey the Bear cartoon and a warning to be careful with fire. The cards are unnumbered and checklisted below in alphabetical order. A minor league card of Richard Hidalgo highlights this set.
COMPLETE SET (27)................ 20.00 6.00

1996 Jacksonville Suns Best

This 30-card set of the 1996 Jacksonville Suns, a Class AA Southern League affiliate of the Detroit Tigers, was produced by Best Cards, Inc. and features color player photos in a white border. The backs carry player information and career statistics.
COMPLETE SET (30)................ 10.00 3.00

1996 Johnson City Cardinals Team Issue

This 35-card set of the 1996 Johnson City Cardinals, a Rookie Class Pioneer League affiliate of the St. Louis Cardinals, was produced and sponsored by Interstate Graphics, Inc. and co-sponsored by Fox TV station, WEMT-TV 39. The fronts feature color player portraits in a white border. The backs carry information about the player. The cards are unnumbered and checklisted below in alphabetical order. This issue includes the minor league card debut of Brent Butler.
COMPLETE SET (35)................ 15.00 4.50

1996 Kane County Cougars Team Issue

This 31-card set of the 1996 Kane County Cougars, a Class A Midwest League affiliate of the Florida Marlins, features color player photos with the player's name and team logo printed in a green vertical bar on the left. The backs carry a small black-and-white player head photo with player information and career statistics. A parallel set was produced that was a little bit larger in size and printed on heavier card stock. The team logo was printed in gold foil. A limited number of this set was produced and each card is sequentially numbered. A second parallel set was produced for a Connies Pizza Giveaway and was printed on somewhat thinner card stock. The cards are unnumbered and checklisted below in alphabetical order. 3,500 regular sets were produced.
COMPLETE SET (31)................ 12.00 3.60
COMPLETE GOLD SET (31)...... 18.00 5.50
COMPLETE SPONSOR SET (31) 30.00 9.00

1996 Kane County Cougars Team Issue Connie's Pizza

1,100 sets were produced.
COMPLETE SET (31)................................ 5.50
COMPLETE GOLD SET (31)........................ 8.00
COMPLETE SPONSOR SET (31) 30.00 9.00

1996 Kane County Cougars Team Issue Gold

1,500 sets were produced.
COMPLETE SET (31)................................ 5.50
COMPLETE GOLD SET (31)...... 18.00 5.50
COMPLETE SPONSOR SET (31) 13.50

1996 Kane County Cougars Update Team Issue

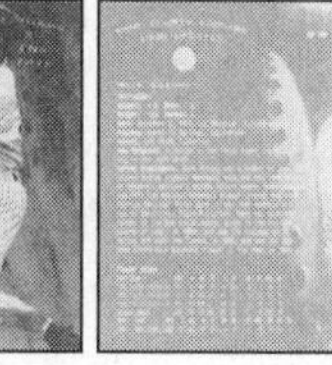

This 13-card set is printed on heavy card stock and features color player images on a simulated wood background with the words "Pro Stock" made to look burned into the background. The backs carry player information with career highlights and statistics. Only 750 of this set were produced and each card is sequentially numbered. The cards are unnumbered and checklisted below in alphabetical order. This set includes the minor league card debuts of Ryan Dempster, Mark Kotsay and Alex Gonzalez.
COMPLETE SET (13)................ 25.00 7.50

1996 Kinston Indians Best

This 30-card set of the 1996 Kinston Indians, a Class A Carolina League affiliate of the Cleveland Indians, was produced by Best Cards, Inc. and features color player photos in a white border. The backs carry player information and career statistics. This issue includes an early card of Sean Casey.
COMPLETE SET (30)................ 25.00 7.50

1996 Kissimmee Cobras Best

This 30-card set of the 1996 Kissimmee Cobras, a Class A Florida State League affiliate of the Houston Astros, was produced by Best Cards, Inc. and features color player photos in a white border. The backs carry player information and career statistics.
COMPLETE SET (30)................ 10.00 3.00

1996 Knoxville Smokies Best

This 30-card set of the 1996 Knoxville Smokies, a Class AA Southern League affiliate of the Toronto Blue Jays, was produced by Best Cards, Inc. and features color player photos in a white border. The backs carry player information and career statistics.
COMPLETE SET (25)................ 10.00 3.00

1996 Lake Elsinore Storm Best

This 30-card set of the 1996 Lake Elsinore Storm, a Class A California League affiliate of the California Angels, was produced by Best Cards, Inc. and features color player photos in a white border. The backs carry player information and career statistics.
COMPLETE SET (30)................ 10.00 3.00

1996 Lakeland Tigers Best

This 30-card set of the 1996 Lakeland Tigers, a Class A Florida State League affiliate of the Detroit Tigers, was produced by Best Cards, Inc. and features color player photos in a white border. The backs carry player information and career statistics. Early cards of Juan Encarnacion and Daryle Ward are included in this set.
COMPLETE SET (30)................ 10.00 3.00

1996 Lancaster Jethawks Best

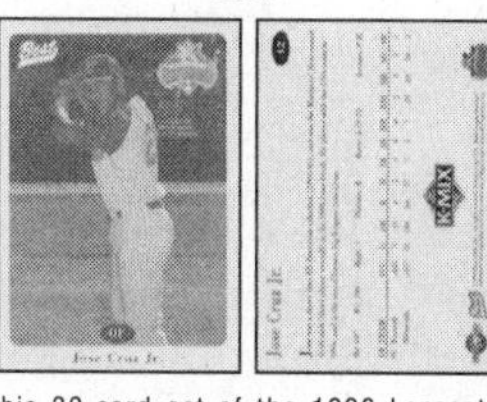

This 30-card set of the 1996 Lancaster Jethawks, a Class A California League affiliate of the Seattle Mariners, was produced by Best Cards, Inc. and features color player photos in a white border. The backs carry player information and career statistics. This issue includes a second year card of Jose Cruz Jr.
COMPLETE SET (30)................ 15.00 4.50

1996 Lansing Lugnuts Best

This 30-card set of the 1996 Lansing Lugnuts, a Class A Midwest League affiliate of the Kansas City Royals, was produced by Best Cards, Inc. and features color player photos in a white border. The backs carry player information and career statistics. This issue includes the minor league card debut of Carlos Beltran and Carlos Febles as well as an early card of Mark Quinn.
COMPLETE SET (30)................ 50.00 15.00

1996 Las Vegas Stars Best

This 30-card set of the 1996 Las Vegas Stars, a Class AAA Pacific Coast League affiliate of the San Diego Padres, was produced by Best Cards, Inc. and features color player photos in a white border. The backs carry player information and career statistics.
COMPLETE SET (30)................ 10.00 3.00

1996 Lethbridge Black Diamonds Best

This 33-card set of the 1996 Lethbridge Black Diamonds, a Rookie Class Pioneer League affiliate of the Arizona Diamondbacks, was produced by Best Cards, Inc. and features color player photos in a white border. The backs carry player information and career statistics
COMPLETE SET (33)................ 10.00 3.00

1996 Louisville Redbirds Best

This 30-card set of the 1996 Louisville Redbirds, a Class AAA American Association affiliate of the St. Louis Cardinals, was produced by Best Cards, Inc. and features color player photos in a white border. The backs carry player information and career statistics.
COMPLETE SET (28)................ 10.00 3.00

1996 Lowell Spinners Best

This 30-card set of the 1996 Lowell Spinners, a Class A New York-Penn League affiliate of the Boston Red Sox, was produced by Best Cards, Inc. and features color player photos in a white border. The backs carry player information and career statistics. This issue includes the minor league card debut of both Corey Jenkins and Matt Kinney.
COMPLETE SET (30)................ 50.00 15.00

1996 LSU Tigers

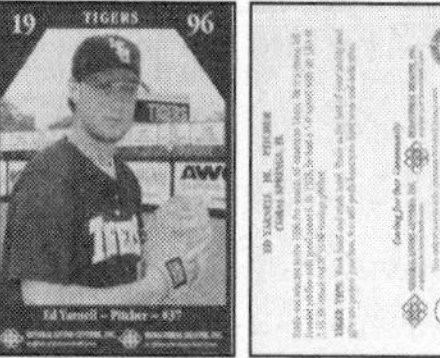

These 16 standard-size cards feature on their fronts posed color player photos of the 1996 LSU Tigers. The cards' have purple borders, and carry the players name at the bottom of the photo and the team name at the top.
COMPLETE SET (16)................ 20.00 6.00

1996 Lynchburg Hillcats Best

This 30-card set of the 1996 Lynchburg Hillcats, a Class A Carolina League affiliate of the Pittsburgh Pirates, was produced by Best Cards, Inc. and features color player photos in a white border. The backs carry player information and career statistics. This issue includes the minor league card debuts of Jose Guillen and Jimmy Anderson.
COMPLETE SET (30)................ 30.00 9.00

1996 Lynchburg Hillcats Update Best

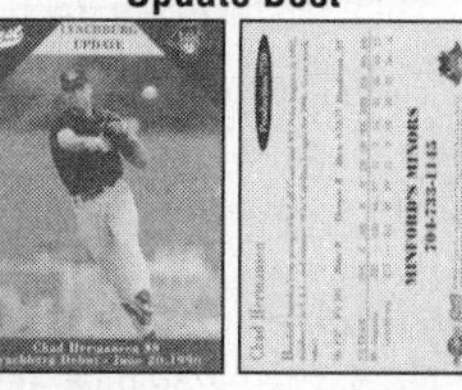

COMPLETE SET (1).................... 5.00 1.50

1996 Macon Braves Best

This 30-card set of the 1996 Macon Braves, a Class A South Atlantic League affiliate of the Atlanta Braves, was produced by Best Cards, Inc. and features color player photos in a white border. The backs carry player information and career statistics. An early card of John Rocker highlights this set.
COMPLETE SET (30)................ 15.00 4.50

1996 Martinsville Phillies Best

This 30-card set of the 1996 Martinsville Phillies, a Rookie Class Appalachian League affiliate of the Philadelphia Phillies, was produced by Best Cards, Inc. and features color player photos in a white border. The backs carry player information and career statistics. An early card of Jimmy Rollins is the highlight of this set.
COMPLETE SET (30)................ 18.00 5.50

1996 Maui Stingrays Hawaii Winter Ball

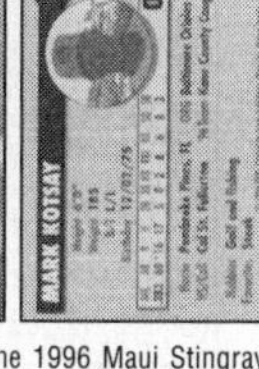

This 36-card set of the 1996 Maui Stingrays team was produced by Trade Publishing and features borderless color player portraits by Wayne Tanaka. The backs carry a small circular black-and-white player head photo with player information and statistics. This issue includes a first year card of Mark Kotsay and a second year card of Jaime Jones.
COMPLETE SET (36)................ 20.00 6.00

1996 Medicine Hat Blue Jays Team Issue

This 33-card set of the 1996 Medicine Hat Blue Jays, a Rookie Class Pioneer League affiliate of the Toronto Blue Jays, was sponsored by CSC Collectables and Prime Printing. The fronts feature color player posed photos in a white border. The backs carry player information. The cards are unnumbered and checklisted below in alphabetical order.
COMPLETE SET (33)................ 60.00 18.00

1996 Memphis Chicks Best

This 30-card set of the 1996 Memphis Chicks, a Class AA Southern League affiliate of the San Diego Padres, was produced by Best Cards, Inc. and features color player photos in a white border. The backs carry player information and career statistics.
COMPLETE SET (30)................ 10.00 3.00

1996 Michigan Battle Cats Best

This 29-card set of the 1996 Michigan Battle Cats, a Class A Midwest League affiliate of the Boston Red Sox, was produced by Best Cards, Inc. and features color player photos in a white border. The backs carry player information and career statistics.
COMPLETE SET (30)................ 10.00 3.00

1996 Midland Angels Best

This 29-card set of the 1996 Midland Angels, a Class AA Texas League affiliate of the California Angels, was produced by Best Cards, Inc. and

features color player photos in a white border. The backs carry player information and career statistics.
COMPLETE SET (30)................ 10.00 3.00

1996 Midland Angels One Hour Photo

This 23-card set of the 1996 Midland Angels, a Class AA Texas League affiliate of the California Angels, was sponsored by the Leukemia Society of America and features color player photos. The set measures approximately 5 1/2" by 5". The backs are blank. The cards are unnumbered and checklisted below in alphabetical order. 500 sets were produced.
COMPLETE SET (23)................ 50.00 15.00

1996 Midwest League All-Stars Best

Early cards of Matt Clement, David Ortiz and Mark Quinn are the featured players in this set.
COMPLETE SET (58)................ 10.00 3.00

1996 Modesto A's Best

This 30-card set of the 1996 Modesto A's team was produced by Best Cards, Inc. and sponsored by Krier's Cards and Comics. The fronts feature black-and-white player portraits in a white border. The backs carry player information and career statistics. This issue includes the minor league card debut of Miquel Tejada and a third year card of Ben Grieve. 1,000 sets were produced.
COMPLETE SET (30)................ 40.00 12.00

1996 Nashville Sounds Best

This 30-card set of the 1996 Nashville Sounds, a Class AAA American Association affiliate of the Chicago White Sox, was produced by Best Cards, Inc. and features color player photos in a white border. The backs carry player information and career statistics.
COMPLETE SET (30)................ 8.00 2.40

1996 New Haven Raven Uncut Sheet Team Issue

This nine-card set of the 1996 New Haven Ravens, a Class AA Eastern League affiliate of the Colorado Rockies, was issued in one perforated sheet measuring approximately 8 1/2" by 11 1/2" and sponsored by the Herlin Press. The fronts feature color player portraits, while the backs display player information and career statistics. The ninth card was a raffle card that could be sent into the team with a dollar donation to be eligible for a drawing for prizes. This issue includes a second year card of Todd Helton.
COMPLETE UNCUT SHEET (9). 30.00 9.00

1996 New Haven Ravens Best

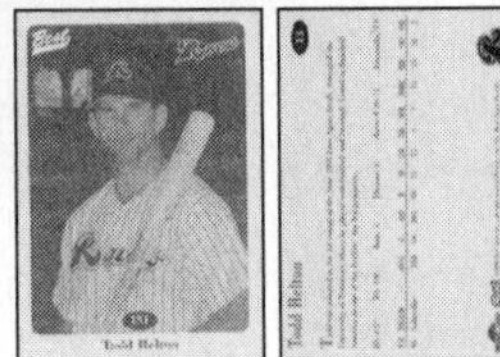

This 30-card set of the 1996 New Haven Ravens, a Class AA Eastern League affiliate of the Colorado Rockies, was produced by Best Cards, Inc. and features color player photos in a white border. The backs carry player information and career statistics. This issue includes a second year card of Todd Helton.
COMPLETE SET (31)................ 30.00 9.00

1996 New Jersey Cardinals Best

This 30-card set of the 1996 New Jersey Cardinals, a Class A New York-Penn League affiliate of the St. Louis Cardinals, was produced by Best Cards, Inc. and features color player photos in a white border. The backs carry player information and career statistics.
COMPLETE SET (30)................ 8.00 2.40

1996 Norfolk Tides Best

This 30-card set of the 1996 Norfolk Tides, a Class AAA International League affiliate of the New York Mets, was produced by Best Cards, Inc. and features color player photos in a white border. The backs carry player information and career statistics.
COMPLETE SET (30)................ 10.00 3.00

1996 Norwich Navigators Best

This 28-card set of the 1996 Norwich Navigators, a Class AA Eastern League affiliate of the New York Yankees, was produced by Best Cards, Inc. and features color player photos in a white border. The backs carry player information and career statistics.
COMPLETE SET (28)................ 8.00 2.40

1996 Norwich Navigators Team Issue

This 12-card set of the 1996 Norwich Navigators, a Class AA Eastern League affiliate of the New York Yankees, was produced by Choice Marketing and sponsored by Old Saybrook Shopping Center. The set was distributed in one sheet measuring approximately 10 5/16" by 10 11/16". The fronts feature color action player photos. The backs carry player biographical information and career statistics. The cards are unnumbered and checklisted below in alphabetical order.
COMPLETE SET (12)................ 10.00 3.00

1996 Ogden Raptors Team Issue

This 39-card set of the 1996 Ogden Raptors, a Rookie Class Pioneer League affiliate of the Milwaukee Brewers, was sponsored by Warrens Restaurant and features color action player photos in a gray border. The backs carry player information and sponsor logo. The cards are checklisted below according to the player's jersey number.
COMPLETE SET (39)................ 10.00 3.00

1996 Oklahoma City 89ers Best

This 28-card set of the 1996 Oklahoma City 89ers, a Class AAA American Association affiliate of the Texas Rangers, was produced by Best Cards, Inc. and features color player photos in a white border. The backs carry player information and career statistics.
COMPLETE SET (28)................ 8.00 2.40

1996 Omaha Royals Best

This 30-card set of the 1996 Omaha Royals, a Class AAA American Association affiliate of the Kansas City Royals, was produced by Best Cards, Inc. and features color player photos in a white border. The backs carry player information and career statistics.
COMPLETE SET (30)................ 10.00 3.00

1996 Orlando Cubs Best

This 30-card set of the 1996 Orlando Cubs, a Class AA Southern League affiliate of the Chicago Cubs, was produced by Best Cards, Inc. and features color player photos in a white border. The backs carry player information and career statistics.
COMPLETE SET (30)................ 10.00 3.00

1996 Pawtucket Red Sox Dunkin' Donuts

This 30-card set of the 1996 Pawtucket Red Sox, a Class AAA International League affiliate of the Boston Red Sox, was issued in one large sheet featuring six perforated five-card strips with a large team photo in the wide top strip. Sponsored by Channel 10 and Dunkin' Donuts, the fronts carry color player photos while the backs display player career statistics. The cards are unnumbered and checklisted below in alphabetical order.
COMPLETE SET (30)................ 40.00 12.00

1996 Peoria Chiefs Best

This 30-card set of the 1996 Peoria Chiefs, a Class A Midwest League affiliate of the St. Louis Cardinals, was produced by Best Cards, Inc. and features color player photos in a white border. The backs carry player information and career statistics.
COMPLETE SET (30)................ 15.00 4.50

1996 Phoenix Firebirds Best

This 30-card set of the 1996 Phoenix Firebirds, a Class AAA Pacific Coast League affiliate of the San Francisco Giants, was produced by Best Cards, Inc. and features color player photos in a white border. The backs carry player information and career statistics.
COMPLETE SET (30)................ 15.00 4.50

1996 Piedmont Boll Weevils Best

This 30-card set of the 1996 Piedmont Boll Weevils, a Class A South Atlantic League affiliate of the Philadelphia Phillies, was produced by Best Cards, Inc. and features color player photos in a white border. The backs carry player information and career statistics. This issue includes two cards of Texas Longhorns' runningback Ricky Williams; including a posed Heisman shot.
COMPLETE SET (30)................ 80.00 24.00

1996 Pittsfield Mets Best

This 30-card set of the 1996 Pittsfield Mets, a Class A New York-Penn League affiliate of the New York Mets, was produced by Best Cards, Inc. and features color player photos in a white border. The backs carry player information and career statistics.
COMPLETE SET (30)................ 8.00 2.40

1996 Port City Roosters Best

This 29-card set of the 1996 Port City Roosters, a Class AA Southern League affiliate of the Seattle Mariners, was produced by Best Cards, Inc. and features color player photos in a white border. The backs carry player information and career statistics.
COMPLETE SET (29)................ 8.00 2.40

1996 Portland Rockies Best

This 30-card set of the 1996 Portland Rockies, a Class A Northwest League affiliate of the Colorado Rockies, was produced by Best Cards, Inc. and features color player photos in a white border. The backs carry player information and career statistics.
COMPLETE SET (30)................ 10.00 3.00

1996 Portland Sea Dogs Best

This 29-card set of the 1996 Portland Sea Dogs, a Class AA Eastern League affiliate of the Florida Marlins, was produced by Best Cards, Inc. and features color player photos in a white border. The backs carry player information and career statistics. A card of Luis Castillo highlights this set.
COMPLETE SET (29)................ 50.00 15.00

1996 Prince William Cannons Best

This 30-card set of the 1996 Prince William Cannons, a Class A Carolina League affiliate of the Chicago White Sox, was produced by Best Cards, Inc. and features color player photos in a white border. The backs carry player information and career statistics.
COMPLETE SET (30)................ 10.00 3.00

1996 Quad City River Bandits Best

This 29-card set of the 1996 Quad City River Bandits, a Class A Midwest League affiliate of the Houston Astros, was produced by Best Cards, Inc. and features color player photos in a white border. The backs carry player information and career statistics. An early card of Freddy Garcia highlights this set.
COMPLETE SET (29)................ 25.00 7.50

1996 Rancho Cucamonga Quakes Best

This 30-card set of the 1996 Rancho Cucamonga Quakes, a Class A California League affiliate of the San Diego Padres, was produced by Best Cards, Inc. and features color player photos in a white border. The backs carry player information and career statistics.
COMPLETE SET (30)................ 10.00 3.00

1996 Reading Phillies Best

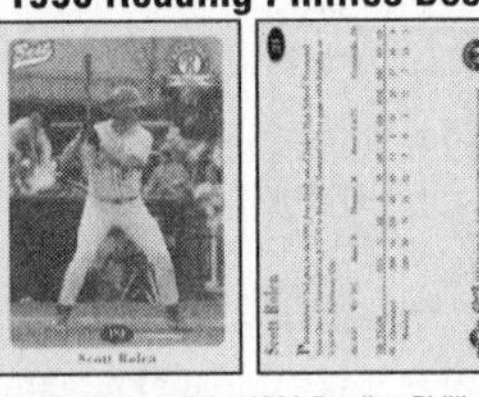

This 29-card set of the 1996 Reading Phillies, a Class AA Eastern League affiliate of the Philadelphia Phillies, was produced by Best Cards, Inc. and features color player photos in a white border. The backs carry player information and career statistics. This issue includes a third year card of Scott Rolen.
COMPLETE SET (29)................ 25.00 7.50

1996 Richmond Braves Best

This 30-card set of the 1996 Richmond Braves, a Class AAA International League affiliate of the Atlanta Braves, was produced by Best Cards, Inc. and features color player photos in a white border. The backs carry player information and career statistics.
COMPLETE SET (30)................ 10.00 3.00

1996 Richmond Braves Richmond Camera

This 26-card team set of the 1996 Richmond Braves, a Class AAA International League affiliate of the Atlanta Braves, was sponsored by Richmond Camera and Benjamin Moore Paints and measures approximately 4" by 4 7/8". The fronts feature borderless color player photos with sponsors' and team's logos in the wide bottom margin. This issue includes a second year card of Andruw Jones. The backs are blank. 500 sets were produced.
COMPLETE SET (26)............. 100.00 30.00

1996 Richmond Braves Update Best

This 30-card set of the 1996 Richmond Braves team features color player photos in red borders. The backs carry player information and career statistics. This issue includes a second year card of Andruw Jones. Card #1 of Andruw Jones is numbered out of 1,000.
COMPLETE SET (30)................ 40.00 12.00

1996 Richmond Roosters Grandstand

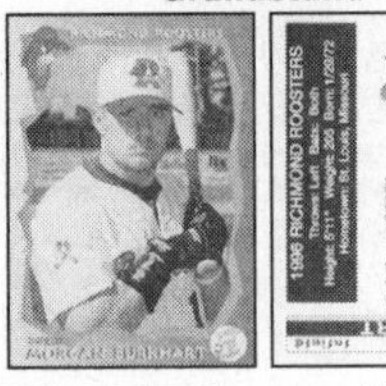

COMPLETE SET (25)................ 10.00 3.00

1996 Rochester Red Wings Best

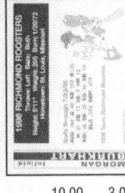

This 30-card set of the 1996 Rochester Red Wings, a Class AAA International League affiliate of the Baltimore Orioles, was produced by Best Cards, Inc. and features color player photos in a white border. The backs carry player information and career statistics.
COMPLETE SET (30)................ 10.00 3.00

1996 Rockford Cubs Team Issue

This 32-card set of the 1996 Rockford Cubs, a Class A Midwest League affiliate of the Chicago Cubs, was sponsored by AM radio station WROK 1440 and TV station WREX channel 13. The fronts feature color player photos with a red side and a blue bottom border. The backs carry player information and sponsor logos. The cards are unnumbered and checklisted below in alphabetical order.
COMPLETE SET (32)................ 10.00 3.00

1996 Salem Avalanche Best

This 30-card set of the 1996 Salem Avalanche, a Class A Carolina League affiliate of the Colorado Rockies, was produced by Best Cards, Inc. and features color player photos in a white border. The backs carry player information and career statistics.
COMPLETE SET (30)................ 10.00 3.00

1996 San Antonio Missions Best

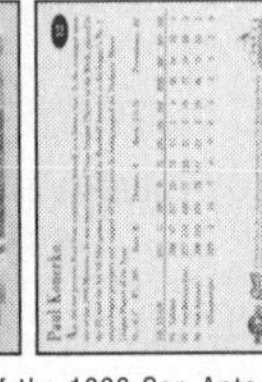

This 30-card set of the 1996 San Antonio Missions, a Class AA Texas League affiliate of the Los Angeles Dodgers, was produced by Best Cards, Inc. and features color player photos with a yellow border. The backs carry player information and career statistics. This issue includes a third year card of Paul Konerko.
COMPLETE SET (30)................ 10.00 3.00

1996 San Bernardino Stampede Best

This 30-card set of the 1996 San Bernardino Stampede, a Class A California League affiliate of the Los Angeles Dodgers, was produced by Best Cards, Inc. and features color player photos in a white border. The backs carry player information and career statistics.
COMPLETE SET (30)................ 8.00 2.40

1996 San Jose Giants Best

This 30-card set of the 1996 San Jose Giants, a Class A California League affiliate of the San Francisco Giants, was produced by Best Cards, Inc. and features color player photos in a white border. The backs carry player information and career statistics.
COMPLETE SET (30)................ 10.00 3.00

1996 Sarasota Red Sox Best

This 30-card set of the 1996 Sarasota Red Sox, a Class A Florida State League affiliate of the Boston Red Sox, was produced by Best Cards, Inc. and features color player photos in a white border. The backs carry player information and career statistics.
COMPLETE SET (30)................ 10.00 3.00

1996 Savannah Sandgnats Best

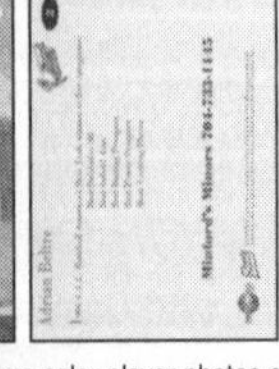

This 30-card set features color player photos of the 1996 Savannah Sandgnats team. The backs carry player information and career statistics. Card number 30 in each set is individually numbered out of 750. This issue includes the minor league card debuts of Adrian Beltre and Eric Gagne.
COMPLETE SET (30)................ 40.00 6.00

1996 Scranton/Wilkes-Barre Red Barons Best

This 30-card set of the 1996 Scranton/Wilkes-Barre Red Barons, a Class AAA International League affiliate of the Philadelphia Phillies, was produced by Best Cards, Inc. and features color player photos in a white border. The backs carry player information and career statistics.
COMPLETE SET (30)................ 10.00 3.00

1996 South Bend Silver Hawks Best

This 28-card set of the 1996 South Bend Silver Hawks, a Class A Midwest League affiliate of the Chicago White Sox, was produced by Best Cards, Inc. and features color player photos in a white border. The backs carry player information and career statistics. This issue includes the minor league card debuts of Jeff Liefer and Mario Valdez.
COMPLETE SET (28)................ 10.00 3.00

1996 Southern Oregon Timberjacks Grandstand

This 28-card set of the 1996 Southern Oregon Timberjacks, a Class A Northwest League affiliate of the Oakland Athletics, was produced by Grandstand Cards and sponsored by various area companies. The fronts feature color player photos with white frames and a two-sided fading green inner border. The backs carry player information and interesting player notes with a sponsor name at the bottom. This issue includes the minor league card debut of Miquel Tejada.
COMPLETE SET (28)................ 60.00 18.00

1996 Spokane Indians Best

This 30-card set of the 1996 Spokane Indians, a Class A Northwest League affiliate of the Kansas City Royals, was produced by Best Cards, Inc. and features color player photos in a white border. The backs carry player information and career statistics. This issue includes the minor league card debut of Carlos Beltran.
COMPLETE SET (30)................ 30.00 9.00

1996 St. Catharines Stompers Best

This 30-card set of the 1996 St. Catherines Stompers, a Class A New York-Penn League affiliate of the Toronto Blue Jays, was produced by Best Cards, Inc. and features color player photos in a white border. The backs carry player information and career statistics.
COMPLETE SET (30)................ 10.00 3.00

1996 St. Lucie Mets Team Issue

This 34-card set of the St. Luice Mets, a Class A Florida State League affiliate of the New York Mets, was issued in six perforated strips with four strips containing six player cards and two strips containing five player cards and a sponsor ad card. The set was sponsored by Publix Super Markets. The player cards feature color player portraits on the fronts and player information and statistics on the backs.
COMPLETE SET (34)................ 10.00 3.00

1996 St. Petersburg Cardinals Best

This 30-card set of the 1996 St. Petersburg Cardinals, a Class A Florida State League affiliate of the St. Louis Cardinals, was produced by Best Cards, Inc. and features color player photos in a white border. The backs carry player information and career statistics.
COMPLETE SET (30)................ 20.00 6.00

1996 Stockton Ports Best

This 30-card set of the 1996 Stockton Ports, a Class A California League affiliate of the Milwaukee Brewers, was produced by Best Cards, Inc. and features color player photos in a white border. The backs carry player information and career statistics.
COMPLETE SET (30)................ 10.00 3.00

1996 Syracuse Chiefs Team Issue

This 30-card set of the 1996 Syracuse Chiefs, a Class AAA International League affiliate of the Toronto Blue Jays, features color player photos on a facsimile stone background with a black border. The backs carry player information and career statistics. The cards are unnumbered and checklisted below in alphabetical order.
COMPLETE SET (30)................ 10.00 3.00

1996 Tacoma Rainiers Best

This 30-card set of the 1996 Tacoma Rainers, a Class AAA Pacific Coast League affiliate of the Seattle Mariners, was produced by Best Cards,

Inc. and features color player photos in a white border. The backs carry player information and career statistics.
COMPLETE SET (30)................. 8.00 2.40

1996 Tampa Yankees Best

This 29-card set of the 1996 Tampa Yankees, a Class A Florida State League affiliate of the New York Yankees, was produced by Best Cards, Inc. and features color player photos in a white border. The backs carry player information and career statistics.
COMPLETE SET (29)............... 10.00 3.00

1996 Texas League All-Stars Best

Cards of Richard Hidalgo, Paul Konerko and Mike Sweeney are the key cards in this set.
COMPLETE SET (36)................ 15.00 4.50

1996 Toledo Mud Hens Best

This 30-card set of the 1996 Toledo Mud Hens, a Class AAA International League affiliate of the Detroit Tigers, was produced by Best Cards, Inc. and features color player photos in a white border. The backs carry player information and career statistics.
COMPLETE SET (30)................. 8.00 2.40

1996 Trenton Thunder Best

This 30-card set of the 1996 Trenton Thunder, a Class AA Eastern League affiliate of the Boston Red Sox, was produced by Best Cards, Inc. and features color player photos in a white border. The backs carry player information and career statistics.
COMPLETE SET (30)............... 10.00 3.00

1996 Tucson Toros Best

This 29-card set of the 1996 Tucson Toros, a Class AAA Pacific Coast League affiliate of the Houston Astros, was produced by Best Cards, Inc. and features color player photos in a white border. The backs carry player information and career statistics. An early card of Bob Abreu highlights this set.
COMPLETE SET (29)............... 15.00 4.50

1996 Tulsa Drillers Team Issue

This 30-card set of the 1996 Tulsa Drillers, a Class AA Texas League affiliate of the Texas Rangers, was sponsored by radio station K95FM and the Oklahoma Highway Patrol. The fronts feature borderless color player photos. The backs carry player information and career statistics.
COMPLETE SET (30)............... 10.00 3.00

1996 Vancouver Canadians Best

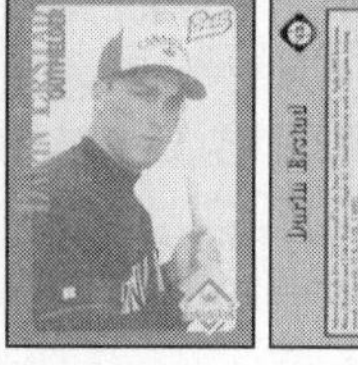

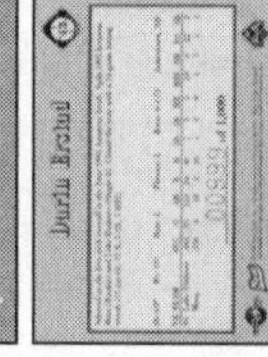

This 30-card set of the 1996 Vancouver Canadians, a Class AAA Pacific Coast League affiliate of the California Angels, was produced by Best Cards, Inc. and features color player photos in a blue border. The backs carry player information and career statistics. This issue includes a second year card of Darin Erstad. Each set is numbered out of 1,000.
COMPLETE SET (30)............... 40.00 12.00

1996 Vermont Expos Best

This 30-card set of the 1996 Vermont Expos, a Class A New York-Penn League affiliate of the Montreal Expos, was produced by Best Cards, Inc. and features color player photos in a white border. The backs carry player information and career statistics.
COMPLETE SET (30)............... 10.00 3.00

1996 Vero Beach Dodgers Best

This 30-card set of the 1996 Vero Beach Dodgers, a Class A Florida State League affiliate of the Los Angeles Dodgers, was produced by Best Cards, Inc. and features color player photos in a white border. The backs carry player information and career statistics.
COMPLETE SET (30)............... 25.00 7.50

1996 Watertown Indians Team Issue

This 36-card set of the 1996 Watertown Indians, a Class A New York-Penn League affiliate of the Cleveland Indians, was sponsored by Cablesystems of Watertown and features color player action photos by Jim Thwaits in a white border. The backs carry player information and career statistics. The cards are unnumbered and checklisted below in alphabetical order.
COMPLETE SET (36)............... 10.00 3.00

1996 West Michigan Whitecaps Best

This 30-card set of the 1996 West Michigan Whitecaps, a Class A Midwest League affiliate of the Oakland Athletics, was produced by Best Cards, Inc. and features color player photos in a white border. The backs carry player information and career statistics.
COMPLETE SET (30)............... 10.00 3.00

1996 West Oahu Canefires Hawaii Winter Ball

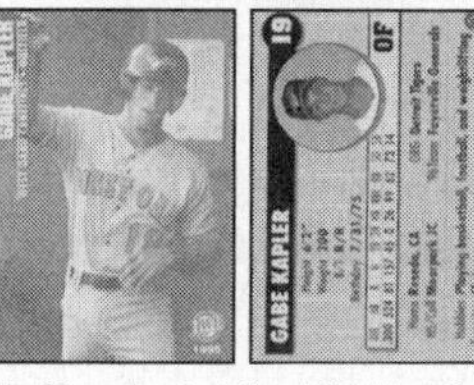

This 36-card set of the 1996 West Oahu Canefires team was produced by Trade Publishing and features borderless color action player photos by Jay Metzger. The backs carry a small black-and-white player headshot by Ray Wong with player information and statistics. The cards are unnumbered and checklisted below according to the player's jersey number. This issue includes a first year card of Gabe Kapler.
COMPLETE SET (36)............... 25.00 7.50

1996 West Palm Beach Expos Best

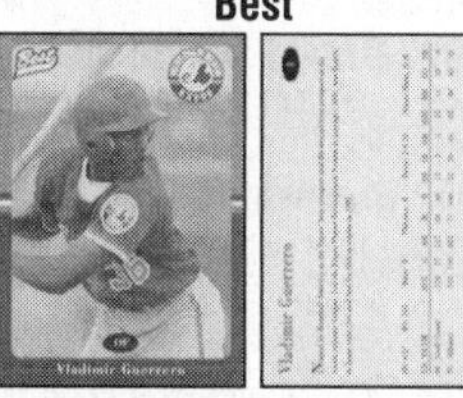

This 31-card set of the 1996 West Palm Beach Expos, a Class A Florida State League affiliate of the Montreal Expos, was produced by Best Cards, Inc. and features color player photos with red top borders and bottom blue ones. The backs carry player information and career statistics. Card number 31 in each set is individually numbered out of 2,000. This issue includes the minor league team set card debuts of Vladimir Guerrer, Brad Fullmer and Hiram Bocachica.
COMPLETE SET (31)............. 150.00 45.00

1996 Wichita Wranglers Best

This 30-card set of the 1996 Wichita Wranglers, a Class AA Texas League affiliate of the Kansas City Royals, was produced by Best Cards, Inc. and features color player photos in a white border. The backs carry player information and career statistics. An early card of Mike Sweeney is a highlight of this set.
COMPLETE SET (30)............... 10.00 3.00

1996 Wichita Wranglers Jiffy Print

An early card of Mike Sweeney highlights this set.
COMPLETE SET (18)............... 10.00 3.00

1996 Wilmington Blue Rocks Best

This 30-card set of the 1996 Wilmington Blue Rocks, a Class A Carolina League affiliate of the Kansas City Royals, was produced by Best Cards, Inc. and features color player photos in a white border. The backs carry player information and career statistics.
COMPLETE SET (30)............... 10.00 3.00

1996 Wisconsin Timber Rattlers Best

This 30-card set of the 1996 Wisconsin Timber Rattlers, a Class A Midwest League affiliate of the Seattle Mariners, was produced by Best Cards, Inc. and features color player photos in a white border. The backs carry player information and career statistics. This issue includes the minor league card debut of David Arias-Ortiz.
COMPLETE SET (30)............... 15.00 4.50

1996 Yakima Bears Team Issue

This 35-card set of lthe 1996 Yakima Bears, a Class A Northwest League affiliate of the Los Angeles Dodgers, was sponsored by TV station KIMA channel 29 and features color player action photos in a white border. The backs carry a small black-and-white player head photo with player information and statistics. The cards are unnumbered and checklisted below according to the player's jersey number as printed on the card back. This issue includes the minor league card debuts of Peter Bergeron.
COMPLETE SET (35)............... 10.00 3.00

1997 Akron Aeros Best

This 30-card set of the 1997 Akron Aeros, a Class AA team affiliate of the Cleveland Indians, was produced by Best Cards, Inc. and features color player photos in a one-sided, ball-laces border. The backs carry player information and career statistics. An early card of Sean Casey highlights this set.
COMPLETE SET (30)............... 15.00 4.50

1997 Albuquerque Dukes Grandstand

This set of the Albuquerque Dukes Minor League team was produced by Grandstand Cards and features color player portraits. The backs carry player information and career statistics. The cards are unnumbered and checklisted below in alphabetical order. Key players include Paul Konerko and Karim Garcia.
COMPLETE SET (30)............... 10.00 3.00

1997 Albuquerque Dukes Update Grandstand

This set updates the Albuquerque Dukes Minor League team set produced by Grandstand Cards and features color portraits of additional Dukes players. The backs carry player information and career statistics. The cards are unnumbered and checklisted below in alphabetical order.
COMPLETE SET (5)................... 5.00 1.50

1997 Appalachian League Top Prospects Best

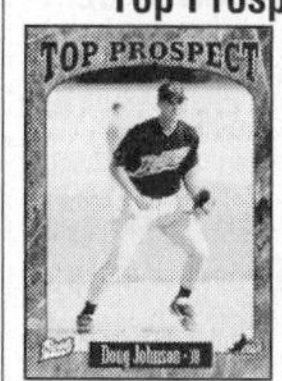

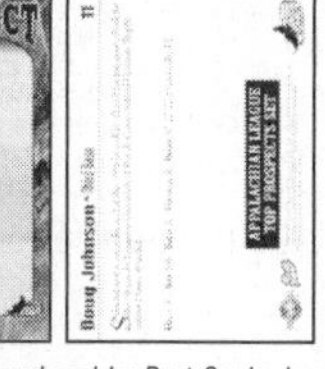

This 30-card set, produced by Best Cards, Inc. features color photos of the top prospects from the teams in the Appalachian League printed on a facsimile marble background. The backs carry information about the player. NFL Quarterback Doug Johnson is featured in this set.
COMPLETE SET (30)............... 15.00 3.00

1997 Arizona State Baseball Greats

This 23-card set features maroon-and-orange bordered black-and-white photos of great players who played for Arizona State University. The set is printed on heavy, laminated card stock. The backs carry player information and statistics. The best players in this set are Barry Bonds and Reggie Jackson.
COMPLETE SET (23)............... 40.00 12.00

1997 Arkansas Travelers Best

This 30-card set of the 1997 Arkansas Travelers, a Class AA Texas League affiliate of the St. Louis Cardinals, was produced by Best Cards, Inc. and features color action player photos in a one-sided ball-laces border. The backs carry player information and career statistics.
COMPLETE SET (30)............... 10.00 3.00

1997 Asheville Tourists Best

This 30-card set of the 1997 Asheville Tourists, a Class A South Atlantic League affiliate of the Colorado Rockies, was produced by Best Cards, Inc. and features color player photos in a one-sided ball laces border. The backs carry player information and career statistics.
COMPLETE SET (30)............... 10.00 3.00

1997 Auburn Doubledays Team Issue

This 30-card set of the 1997 Auburn Doubledays features color player photos with a light blue top and left border. The backs carry player information. (There is no card number 18.). Roy Oswalt is the key player in this set.
COMPLETE SET (30)............... 60.00 18.00

1997 Auburn Tigers College Issue

Please note that these cards need to say "All-Time Great" in the upper right hand corner to be a legititmate card. If the cards do not have this logo, the card was reproduced later and was not issued by the University.
COMPLETE SET 10.00 3.00

1997 Augusta Greenjackets Best

This 30-card set of the 1997 Augusta Greenjackets, a Class A South Atlantic League affiliate of the Pittsburgh Pirates, was produced by Best Cards, Inc. and features color action player photos in a two-sided green border. The backs carry player information and career statistics.
COMPLETE SET (30)................. 8.00 2.40

1997 Bakersfield Blaze Best

This 30-card set of the 1997 Bakersfield Blaze, a Class A affiliate of the San Francisco Giants, was produced by Best Cards, Inc. and features color player photos in a blue border. The backs carry player information and career statistics.
COMPLETE SET (30)................. 8.00 2.40

1997 Bakersfield Blaze Team Issue

This 30-card set of the 1997 Bakersfield Blaze, a Class A affiliate of the San Francisco Giants, was sponsored by Pepsi and features color player photos in a blue border. The backs carry player information and career statistics.
COMPLETE SET (30)................. 8.00 2.40

1997 Batavia Clippers Team Issue

This 32-card set of the 1997 Batavia Clippers features color action player photos with red top and left borders. The backs carry player information. Randy Wolf is the key player in this set.
COMPLETE SET (32)............... 10.00 3.00

1997 Beloit Snappers Best

This 30-card set of the 1997 Beloit Snappers, a Class A Midwest League affiliate of the Milwaukee Brewers, was produced by Best Card, Inc. and features color player photos in a two-sided, blue zigzag border. The backs carry player information and career statistics.
COMPLETE SET (30)............... 10.00 3.00

1997 Billings Mustangs Team Issue

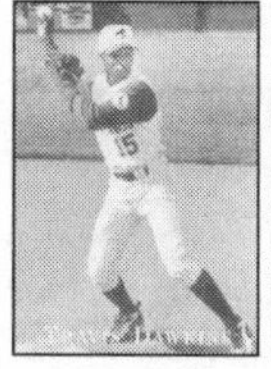

Travis Dawkins and Scott Williamson are the key players in this set.
COMPLETE SET (36)............... 80.00 24.00

1997 Binghamton Mets Best

This 32-card set of the 1997 Binghamton Bees, a Class AA Eastern League affiliate of the New York Mets, was produced by Best Cards, Inc. and features color action player photos in a one sided, ball-laces border. The backs carry player information and career statistics. Octavio Dotel is the key player in this set.
COMPLETE SET (32)............... 10.00 3.00

1997 Birmingham Barons Best

This 30-card set of the 1997 Birmingham Barons, a Class AA Southern League affiliate of the Chicago White Sox, was produced by Best Cards, Inc. and features color action player photos in a two-sided white and blue zigzag border. The backs carry player information and career statistics.
COMPLETE SET (30)............... 10.00 3.00

1997 Boise Hawks Grandstand

This set of the Boise Hawks Minor League team was produced by Grandstand Cards and features color player portraits. The backs carry player information and career statistics. The cards are unnumbered and checklisted below in alphabetical order.
COMPLETE SET (32)............... 10.00 3.00

1997 Bowie Baysox Best

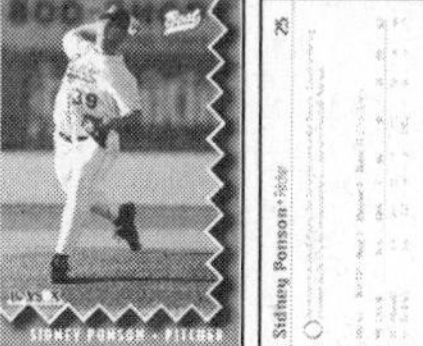

This 29-card set of the 1997 Bowie Baysox, a Class AA Eastern League affiliate of the Baltimore Orioles, was produced by Best Cards, Inc. and features color action player photos in a white and aqua zigzag border. The backs carry player information and career statistics. Sidney Ponson is the key player in this set.
COMPLETE SET (29)............... 10.00 3.00

1997 Brevard County Manatees Best

This 31-card set of the 1997 Brevard County Manatees, a Class A Florida State League affiliate of the Florida Marlins, was produced by Best Cards, Inc. and features color action player photos in a two-sided, zigzag border. The backs carry player information and career statistics.
COMPLETE SET (31)................. 8.00 2.40

1997 Bristol White Sox Best

This 30-card set of the 1997 Bristol White Sox, a Rookie Class Appalachian League affiliate of the Chicago White Sox, was produced by Best Cards, Inc. and features color action player photos on a black-and-gray background. The backs carry player information and career statistics. Aaron Myette is the key player in this set.
COMPLETE SET (30)............... 10.00 3.00

1997 Buffalo Bisons Best

This 30-card set of the 1997 Buffalo Bisons, a Class AAA American Association affiliate of the Cleveland Indians, was produced by Best Cards, Inc. and features color action player photos in a one-sided, ball-laces border. The backs carry player information and career statistics.
COMPLETE SET (30)................. 8.00 2.40

1997 Burlington Bees Best

This 30-card set of the 1997 Burlington Bees, a Class A Midwest League affiliate of the San Francisco Giants, was produced by Best Cards, Inc. and features color player photos. The backs carry player information and career statistics.
COMPLETE SET (30)................. 8.00 2.40

1997 Burlington Indians Grandstand

This set of the Burlington Indians Minor League team was produced by Grandstand Cards and features color player portraits. The backs carry player information and career statistics. The cards are unnumbered and checklisted below in alphabetical order.
COMPLETE SET (30)............... 10.00 3.00

1997 Butte Copper Kings Best

This 30-card set of the 1997 Butte Copper Kings, a Class A affiliate of the Anaheim Angels, was produced by Best Card, Inc. and features color player photos. The backs carry player information and career statistics.
COMPLETE SET (30)............... 10.00 3.00

1997 Butte Copper Kings KBOW

This 30-card set of the 1997 Butte Copper Kings, a Class A affiliate of the Anaheim Angels, was produced by Best Card, Inc. and sponsored by AM Country Radio Station KBOW 550, Taco John's, and Gaines Du Vall Sports Portraits. The fronts feature posed color player photos. The backs carry player information and career statistics.
COMPLETE SET (30)............... 10.00 3.00

1997 Calgary Cannons Best

This 30-card set of the 1997 Calgary Cannons, a Class AAA affiliate of the Pittsburgh Pirates, was produced by Best Cards, Inc. and features color player photos in a two-sided blue border. The backs carry player information and career statistics.
COMPLETE SET (30)............... 30.00 9.00

1997 California League Top Prospects Best

This 31-card set, produced by Best Cards, Inc. features color photos of the top prospects from the teams in the California League printed on a facsimile marble background. The backs carry information about the player. Eric Chavez and Jose Ortiz are the key players in this set.
COMPLETE SET (31)............... 20.00 6.00

1997 California/Carolina League All-Stars Team Issue

This 50-card set features color photos of the All-Star players from the California and Carolina Leagues printed diagonally with a one side and bottom red and green borders. The backs carry player information and career statistics. The

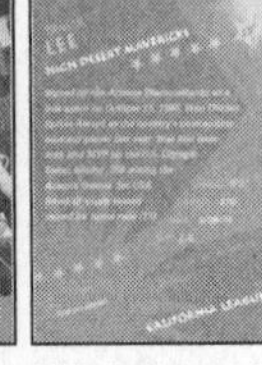

first 25 cards are the California League All-Stars, while the last 25 cards are the All-Stars from the Carolina League. Key players in this set include Kris Benson, Carlos Lee, Jose Ortiz and Mark Quinn.
COMPLETE SET (50)............... 25.00 7.50

1997 Capital City Bombers Best

This 30-card set of the 1997 Capital City Bombers, a Class A team affiliate of the New York Mets, was produced by Best Cards, Inc. and features color player photos in black borders. The backs carry player information and career statistics. Octavio Dotel is the key player in this set.
COMPLETE SET (30)............... 10.00 3.00

1997 Carolina League Top Prospects Best

This 31-card set, produced by Best Cards, Inc. features color photos of the top prospects from the teams in the Carolina League printed on a facsimile marble background. The backs carry information about the player. Kris Benson, Carlos Lee and Aramis Ramirez are the key players in this set.
COMPLETE SET (31)............... 20.00 6.00

1997 Carolina Mud Cats Best

This 29-card set of the 1997 Carolina Mudcats, a Class AA Southern League affiliate of the Pittsburgh Pirates, was produced by Best Cards, Inc. and features color action player photos in a thin black border. The backs carry player information and career statistics.
COMPLETE SET (29)............... 10.00 3.00

1997 Cedar Rapids Kernels Grandstand

This set of the Cedar Rapids Kernels Minor League team was produced by Grandstand Cards and features color player portraits. The backs carry player information and career statistics. The cards are unnumbered and checklisted below in alphabetical order. Ramon Ortiz is the key player in this set.
COMPLETE SET (30)............... 15.00 4.50

1997 Charleston RiverDogs Grandstand

This set of the Charleston RiverDogs Minor League team was produced by Grandstand Cards and features color player portraits. The backs carry player information and career statistics. The cards are unnumbered and checklisted below in alphabetical order.
COMPLETE SET (28)................ 8.00 2.40

1997 Charlotte Knights Best

This 30-card set of the 1997 Charlotte Knights, a Class AAA International League affiliate of the Florida Marlins, was produced by Best Cards, Inc. and features color action player photos in a white border on an aqua and black background. The backs carry player information and career statistics.
COMPLETE SET (30)............... 10.00 3.00

1997 Chattanooga Lookouts Best

This 27-card set of the 1997 Chattanooga Lookouts, a Class AA Southern League affiliate of the Cincinnati Reds, was produced by Best Cards, Inc. and features color action player photos in a white border. The backs carry player information and career statistics.
COMPLETE SET (27)............... 8.00 2.40

1997 Clearwater Phillies Best

This 30-card set of the 1997 Clearwater Phillies, a Class A Minor League team affiliate of the Philadelphia Phillies, was produced by Best Cards, Inc. and features color player photos in a one-sided, ball-laces border. The backs carry player information and career statistics.
COMPLETE SET (30)................ 8.00 2.40

1997 Clinton LumberKings Grandstand

This set of the Clinton LumberKings Minor League team was produced by Grandstand Cards and features color player portraits. The backs carry player information and career statistics. The cards are unnumbered and checklisted below in alphabetical order.
COMPLETE SET (30)............... 15.00 4.50

1997 Colorado Springs SkySox All-Time Team Issue

This 32-card set was sponsored by Bill's Sports Collectibles and Sports Radio station KRDO 1240 AM to celebrate the teams 10th Anniversary. The fronts feature black-and-white photos of top players from 1988-1997. The backs carry player information and sponsor logos.
COMPLETE SET (32)............... 15.00 4.50

1997 Colorado Springs SkySox Team Issue

This 29-card set of the Colorado Springs SkySox Team was sponsored by Bill's Sports Collectibles, 98.9 FM Radio Station, KOAA-TV Station and the Colorado Springs Independent. The fronts feature borderless color player photos. The backs carry the sponsor logos and a small black-and-white player head photo with player information and career statistics. The cards are unnumbered and checklisted below in alphabetical order. Todd Helton is the key player in this set.
COMPLETE SET (29)............... 25.00 7.50

1997 Columbus Clippers Best

This 30-card set of the 1997 Columbus Clippers, a Class AAA International League affiliate of the New York Yankees, was produced by Best Cards, Inc. and features color player photos in a two-sided, zigzag blue border. The backs carry player information and career statistics.
COMPLETE SET (30)................ 8.00 2.40

1997 Columbus Clippers D.A.R.E.

This 29-card set of the 1997 Columbus Clippers was sponsored by Drug Abuse Resistance Education (D.A.R.E.), Galyan's Trading Company, and McDonalds. The fronts feature color player portraits in white-and-black borders. The backs carry player information and sponsor logos. The cards are unnumbered and checklisted below in alphabetical order.
COMPLETE SET (29)............... 10.00 3.00

1997 Danville Braves Best

This 30-card set of the 1997 Danville Braves, a Rookie Class Appalachian League affiliate of the Atlanta Braves, was produced by Best Cards, Inc. and features color action player photos in a one-sided, ball-laces border. The backs carry player information and career statistics. Marcus Giles is the key player in this set.
COMPLETE SET (30)............... 20.00 4.50

1997 Delmarva Shorebirds Best

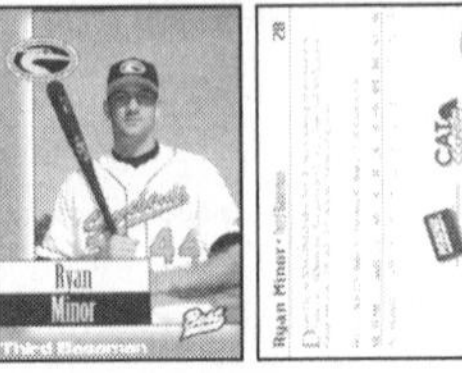

This 30-card set of the 1997 Delmarva Shorebirds, a Class A Minor League team, was produced by Best Cards, Inc. and features color action player photos in a two-sided orange border. The backs carry player information and career statistics. Ryan Minor makes his minor league team set debut in this set.
COMPLETE SET (30)............... 40.00 12.00

1997 Double-A All-Stars Multi-Ad

This 60-card set features color action photos and portraits of players who played in the AA All-Star game on July 7, 1997, in San Antonio, Texas. The backs carry player information and career statistics. (There is no card number 12.) Mark Kotsay, Fernando Tatis and Daryle Ward are the key players in this set.
COMPLETE SET (59)............... 10.00 3.00

1997 Dunedin Blue Jays Team Issue

This 34-card team issue set of the 1997 Dunedin Blue Jays, a Florida State League Class A Baseball Club, was sponsored by the "Times" and printed by Pinellas Press. The fronts freature posed color player photos with white borders and thin red inner borders. The backs carry player information and career statistics. Only 1,000 of the sets were made and serially numbered. The cards are unnumbered and checklisted below in alphabetical order. Billy Koch is the key player in this set.
COMPLETE SET (34)............... 15.00 4.50

1997 Durham Bulls ATG Team Issue

This 10-card set commemorates the 18-yr. partnership between the Durham Bulls and the Atlanta Braves. The fronts feature color photos of players who have all played for the Bulls as a part of the Braves organization. The backs carry information about the player. The cards are unnumbered and checklisted below as they appear on the Checklist card. This set was sponsored by Bellsouth Mobility. Chipper Jones is the best player in this set.
COMPLETE SET (10)............... 15.00 4.50

1997 Durham Bulls Team Issue

This 30-card set of the 1997 Durham Bulls, a Class A Carolina League affiliate of the Atlanta Braves, was produced by Best Cards, Inc. and features borderless color player photos. The backs carry player information and career statistics. There is no information on the card as to either set producer or sponsorship. An early card of John Rocker highlights this set.
COMPLETE SET (30)............... 40.00 12.00

1997 Eastern League Top Prospects Best

This 31-card set, produced by Best Cards, Inc. features color photos of the top prospects from the teams in the Eastern League printed on a facsimile marble background. The backs carry information about the player.
COMPLETE SET (31)............... 10.00 3.00

1997 El Paso Diablos Best

This 30-card set of the 1997 El Paso Diablos, a Class AA Texas League affiliate of the Milwaukee Brewers, was produced by Best Cards, Inc. and features color player photos on a blue background. The backs carry player information and career statistics.
COMPLETE SET (30)................ 8.00 2.40

1997 Erie Sea Wolves Best

This 30-card set of the 1997 Erie Seawolves, a Class A New York-Penn League affiliate of the Pittsburgh Pirates, was produced by Best Cards, Inc. and features color player photos. The backs carry player information and career statistics.
COMPLETE SET (30)............... 10.00 3.00

1997 Eugene Emeralds Best

This 30-card set of the 1997 Eugene Emeralds, a Class A Northwest League affiliate of the Atlanta Braves, was produced by Best Cards, Inc. and features color player photos in a two-sided, blue zigzag border. The backs carry player information and career statistics.
COMPLETE SET (30)................ 8.00 2.40

1997 Everett AquaSox Grandstand

This set of the Everett AquaSox Grandstand Minor League team was produced by Grandstand Cards and features color player portraits. The backs carry player information and career statistics. The cards are unnumbered and checklisted below in alphabetical order.
COMPLETE SET (30)............... 10.00 3.00

1997 Florida State League Top Prospects Best

This 31-card set, produced by Best Cards, Inc. features color photos of the top prospects from the teams in the Florida State League printed on a facsimile marble background. The backs carry player information. Adrian Beltre, Jacques Jones, Gabe Kapler and Ruben Mateo are the key players in this set.
COMPLETE SET (31)............... 15.00 4.50

1997 Fort Myers Miracle Best

This 30-card set of the 1997 Fort Myers Miracle, a Class A Florida State League affiliate of the Minnesota Twins, was produced by Best Cards, Inc. and features color player photos in a one-sided, ball laces border. The backs carry player information and career statistics. Cards

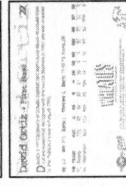

of Jacque Jones and David Ortiz highlight this set.
COMPLETE SET (30)............... 15.00 4.50

1997 Fort Wayne Wizards Best

This 30-card set of the 1997 Fort Wayne Wizards, a Class A Midwest League affiliate of the Minnesota Twins, was produced by Best Cards, Inc. and features color player photos in a one-sided ball laces border. The backs carry player information and career statistics.
COMPLETE SET (30)............... 10.00 3.00

1997 Frederick Keys Best

This 30-card set of the 1997 Frederick Keys, a Class A Carolina League affiliate of the Baltimore Orioles, was produced by Best Cards, Inc. and features color player photos in a two-sided orange border. The backs carry player information and career statistics.
COMPLETE SET (30)................ 8.00 2.40

1997 Great Falls Dodgers Team Issue

COMPLETE SET (31)............... 15.00 4.50

1997 Greensboro Bats Best

This 30-card set of the 1997 Greensboro Bats, a Class A South Atlantic League affiliate of the New York Yankees, was produced by Best Cards, Inc. and features color player photos. The backs carry player information and career statistics. Early cards of Tony Armas Jr and Nick Johnson are the keys to this set.
COMPLETE SET (30)............... 100.00 30.00

1997 Greenville Braves Grandstand

This set of the Greenville Braves Minor League team was produced by Grandstand Cards and features color player portraits. The backs carry player information and career statistics. The cards are unnumbered and checklisted below in alphabetical order. An early card of Kevin Millwood highlights this set.
COMPLETE SET (28)............... 15.00 4.50

1997 Hagerstown Suns Best

This 30-card set of the 1997 Hagerstown Suns, a Class A South Atlantic League affiliate of the Toronto Blue Jays, was produced by Best Cards, Inc. and features color player photos. The backs carry player information and career statistics.
COMPLETE SET (30)............... 25.00 7.50

1997 Harrisburg Senators Best

This 28-card set of the 1997 Harrisburg Senators, a Class AA Eastern League affiliate of the Montreal Expos, was produced by Best Cards, Inc. and features color player photos in a white border. The backs carry player information and career statistics.
COMPLETE SET (28)............... 10.00 3.00

1997 Helena Brewers Best

This 30-card set of the 1997 Helena Brewers, a Rookie Class Pioneer League affiliate of the Milwaukee Brewers, was produced by Best Cards, Inc. and features color player photos in a one-sided, ball-laces border. The backs carry player information and career statistics.
COMPLETE SET (30)................ 8.00 2.40

1997 Hickory Crawdads Beige Best

This 30-card set of the 1997 Hickory Crawdads team, a Class A affiliate of the Chicago White Sox, was produced by Best Cards, Inc. and features color player photos with a one-sided, ball-laces border. The backs carry player information and statistics. An early card of Joe Crede highlights this set.
COMPLETE SET (30)............... 15.00 4.50

1997 Hickory Crawdads Red Best

This 30-card set of the 1997 Hickory Crawdads team, a Class A affiliate of the Chicago White Sox, was produced by Best Cards, Inc. and features color player photos with a two-sided red border. The backs carry player information and statistics. Joe Crede is the key player in this set.
COMPLETE SET (30)............... 15.00 4.50

1997 High Desert Mavericks Grandstand

This set of the High Desert Mavericks Minor League team was produced by Grandstand Cards and features color player portraits. The backs carry player information and career statistics. The cards are unnumbered and checklisted below in alphabetical order. Travis Lee makes his minor league team set debut in this set.
COMPLETE SET (30)............... 30.00 9.00

1997 High Desert Mavericks Update Grandstand

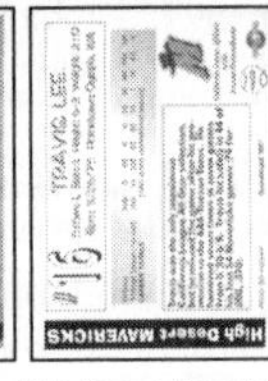

This set updates the High Desert Mavericks Minor League team set produced by Grandstand Cards and features color player portraits. The backs carry player information and career statistics. The cards are unnumbered and checklisted below in alphabetical order. Travis Lee makes his minor league team set debut in this set.
COMPLETE SET (18)................ 8.00 2.40

1997 Hudson Valley Renegades Best

This 30-card set of the 1997 Hudson Valley Renegades, a Class A New York-Penn League Co-op, was produced by Best Cards, Inc. and features color player photos in a one-sided, ball-laces border. The backs carry player information and career statistics.
COMPLETE SET (30)................ 8.00 2.40

1997 Huntsville Stars Team Issue

This 28-card set of the Huntsville Stars was sponsored by Burger King and features color player portraits. The backs carry player information and career statistics. The cards are unnumbered and checklisted below in alphabetical order. Ben Grieve and Miguel Tejada are the key cards in this set.
COMPLETE SET (28)............... 20.00 6.00

1997 Idaho Falls Braves Team Issue

This 32-card set of the 1997 Idaho Falls Braves was sponsored by C-A-L Ranch Stores, United Furniture Warehouse, Z103, and KPVI-TV Channel 6. The fronts feature color player photos with a thin white inner and thicker green outer border. The backs carry player information, career statistics, and sponsor logos. The cards are unnumbered and checklisted below in alphabetical order.
COMPLETE SET (32)............... 10.00 3.00

1997 Indianapolis Indians Best

This 30-card set of the 1997 Indianapolis Indians, a Class AAA American Association affiliate of the Cincinnati Reds, was produced by Best Cards, Inc. and features color player photos in a thin black border. The backs carry player information and career statistics.
COMPLETE SET (30)................ 8.00 2.40

1997 Iowa Cubs Best

This 29-card set of the 1997 Iowa Cubs, a Class AAA American Association affiliate of the Chicago Cubs, was produced by Best Cards, Inc. and features color player photos in a two-sided, zigzag white-and-blue border. The backs carry player information and career statistics.
COMPLETE SET (29)................ 8.00 2.40

1997 Jackson Generals Best

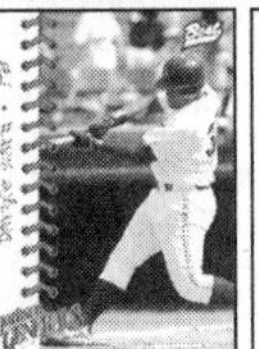

This 28-card set of the 1997 Jackson Generals, a Class AA Texas League affiliate of the Houston Astros, was produced by Best Cards, Inc. and features color player photos in a one-sided, ball laces border. The backs carry player information and career statistics. Scott Elarton

and Daryle Ward are the key players in this set.
COMPLETE SET (28)................ 10.00 3.00

1997 Jackson Generals Smokey

This perforated 26-card set of the Jackson Generals was sponsored by the USDA Forest Service and features color player photos in blue borders. The backs carry a drawing of Smokey the Bear and friends. The cards are unnumbered and checklisted below in alphabetical order. Cards of Scott Elarton and Daryle Ward highlight this set.
COMPLETE SET (26)................ 15.00 4.50

1997 Jacksonville Suns Best

This 27-card set of the 1997 Jacksonville Suns, a Class AA Southern League affiliate of the Detroit Tigers, was produced by Best Cards, Inc. and features color player photos in a thin black border. The backs carry player information and career statistics.
COMPLETE SET (27)................ 8.00 2.40

1997 Johnson City Cardinals Team Issue

This 37-card set of the 1997 Johnson City Cardinals was sponsored by Interstate Graphics, Inc. The fronts feature color player portraits in white borders. The backs carry player information. The cards are unnumbered and checklisted below in alphabetical order.
COMPLETE SET (37)................ 10.00 3.00

1997 Kinston Indians Best

This 30-card set of the 1997 Kinston Indians, a Class A Carolina League affiliate of the Cleveland Indians, was produced by Best Cards, Inc. and features color player photos in a two-sided, blue zigzag border. The backs carry player information and career statistics.
COMPLETE SET (30)................ 10.00 3.00

1997 Kissimmee Cobras Best

This 30-card set of the 1996 Kissimmee Cobras, a Class A Florida State League affiliate of the Houston Astros, was produced by Best Cards, Inc. and features color player photos in a two-sided red-and-white zigzag border. The backs carry player information and career statistics. An early card of Freddy Garcia highlights this set.
COMPLETE SET (30)................ 20.00 6.00

1997 Knoxville Smokies Best

This 28-card set of the 1997 Knoxville Smokies, a Class AA Southern League affiliate of the Toronto Blue Jays, was produced by Best Cards, Inc. and features color player photos in a white-and-blue zigzag border. The backs carry player information and career statistics.
COMPLETE SET (28)................ 8.00 2.40

1997 Lake Elsinore Storm Grandstand

This set of the Lake Elsinore Storm Minor League team was produced by Grandstand Cards and features color player portraits. The backs carry player information and career statistics. The cards are unnumbered and checklisted below in alphabetical order.
COMPLETE SET (30)................ 8.00 2.40

1997 Lakeland Tigers Best

This 30-card set of the 1997 Lakeland Tigers, a Class A Florida State League affiliate of the Detroit Tigers, was produced by Best Cards, Inc. and features color player photos in a one-sided ball-laces border. The backs carry player information and career statistics. An early card of Gabe Kapler is the highlight of this set.
COMPLETE SET (30)................ 15.00 4.50

1997 Lancaster Jethawks Best

This 30-card set of the 1997 Lancaster Jethawks, a Class A California League affiliate of the Seattle Mariners, was produced by Best Cards, Inc. and features color player photos in a two-sided red border. The backs carry player information and career statistics.
COMPLETE SET (30)................ 8.00 2.40

1997 Lansing Lugnuts Team Issue

This 30-card set of the 1997 Lansing Lugnuts, a Class A Midwest League affiliate of the Kansas City Royals features color action player photos in red-and-white borders. The backs carry player biographical information and career statistics. The set was distributed on five sheets with six different perforated cards on each sheet. The cards are unnumbered and checklisted below in alphabetical order.
COMPLETE SET (30)................ 12.00 3.60

1997 Las Vegas Stars 15th Anniversary Best

This 30-card set of the 1997 Las Vegas Stars, a Class AAA Pacific Coast League affiliate of the San Diego Padres, was produced by Best Cards, Inc. and commemorates the team's 15th Anniversary. The fronts feature color player photos in a white and blue zigzag border. The backs carry player information and career statistics.
COMPLETE SET (30)................ 8.00 2.40

1997 Lethbridge Black Diamonds Best

This 30-card set of the 1997 Lethbridge Black Diamonds, a Rookie Class Pioneer League affiliate of the Arizona Diamondbacks, was produced by Best Cards, Inc. and features color player photos in a two-sided, blue zigzag border. The backs carry player information and career statistics.
COMPLETE SET (30)................ 8.00 2.40

1997 Louisville Redbirds Best

This 30-card set of the 1997 Louisville Redbirds, a Class AAA American Association affiliate of the St. Louis Cardinals, was produced by Best Cards, Inc. and features color player photos in a two-sided zigzag border. The backs carry player information and career statistics.
COMPLETE SET (30)................ 10.00 3.00

1997 Lowell Spinners Best

This 30-card set of the 1997 Lowell Spinners, a Class A New York-Penn League affiliate of the Boston Red Sox, was produced by Best Cards, Inc. and features color player photos. The backs carry player information and career statistics.
COMPLETE SET (30)................ 15.00 4.50

1997 LSU Tigers

These 16 standard-size cards feature on their fronts posed color player photos of the 1997 LSU Tigers. The cards' have purple borders with yellow stripes that run vertically in the background, and carry the players name at the bottom of the photo and the team name at the top.
COMPLETE SET (16)................ 18.00 5.50

1997 Lynchburg Hillcats Best

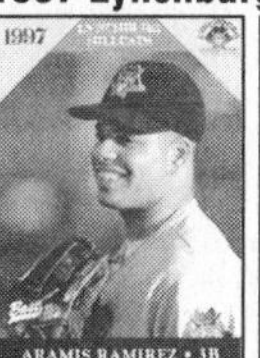

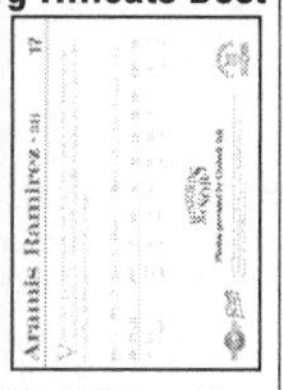

This 30-card set of the 1997 Lynchburg Hillcats, a Class A Carolina League affiliate of the Pittsburgh Pirates, was produced by Best Cards, Inc. and features color player photos. The backs carry player information and career statistics. Kris Benson and Aramis Ramirez are the key players in this set.
COMPLETE SET (30)................ 20.00 6.00

1997 Macon Braves Best

This 30-card set of the 1997 Macon Braves, a Class A South Atlantic League affiliate of the Atlanta Braves, was produced by Best Cards, Inc. and features color player photos in a white and red zigzag border. The backs carry player information and career statistics. Early cards of Bruce Chen and Jason Marquis highlight this set.
COMPLETE SET (30)................ 20.00 6.00

1997 Michigan Battle Cats Best

This 30-card set of the 1997 Michigan Battle Cats, a Class A Midwest League affiliate of the Boston Red Sox, was produced by Best Cards, Inc. and features color player photos in a two-sided green border. The backs carry player information and career statistics. An early card of Dernell Stenson is the key to this set.
COMPLETE SET (30)................ 25.00 7.50

1997 Midland Angels Best

This 30-card set of the 1997 Midland Angels, a Class AA Texas League affiliate of the California Angels, was produced by Best Cards, Inc. and features color player photos in a white border. The backs carry player information and career statistics. Card No. 29 was not available and listed on the checklist as "TBA."
COMPLETE SET (30)................ 8.00 2.40

1997 Midwest League Top Prospects Best

This 30-card set, produced by Best Cards, Inc. features color photos of the top prospects from the teams in the Midwest League printed on a facsimile marble background. The backs carry player information.
COMPLETE SET (30)................ 15.00 4.50

1997 Mobile Bay Bears Best

This 30-card set of the 1997 Mobile Bay Bears, a Class AA team affiliate of the San Diego Padres, was produced by Best Cards, Inc. and features color player photos with a one-sided, ball-laces border. The backs carry player information and career statistics. A card of Hank Aaron, all time home run king, highlights this set.
COMPLETE SET (30)................ 15.00 4.50

1997 Modesto A's Grandstand

This set of the Modesto A's Minor League team was produced by Grandstand Cards and features color player portraits. The backs carry player information and career statistics. The cards are unnumbered and checklisted below in alphabetical order. Jose Ortiz first card is the key card in this set.
COMPLETE SET (30)................ 20.00 6.00

1997 New Britain Rock Cats Best

This 30-card set of the 1997 New Britain Rock Cats, a Class AA team affiliate of the Minnesota Twins, was produced by Best Cards, Inc. and features color player photos in a thin black border. The backs carry player information and career statistics.
COMPLETE SET (30)................ 10.00 3.00

1997 New Haven Ravens Best

This 30-card set of the 1997 New Haven Ravens, a Class AA Eastern League affiliate of the Colorado Rockies, was produced by Best Cards, Inc. and features color player photos. The backs carry player information and career statistics.
COMPLETE SET (30)................ 8.00 2.40

1997 New Jersey Cardinals Best

This 30-card set of the 1997 New Jersey Cardinals, a Class A New York-Penn League affiliate of the St. Louis Cardinals, was produced by Best Cards, Inc. and sponsored by Chase. The fronts feature borderless posed player photos. The backs carry player information and career statistics. An early card of Adam Kennedy highlights this set.
COMPLETE SET (30)................ 12.00 3.60

1997 New Jersey Cardinals Strips

This six-card set of the 1997 New Jersey Cardinals, a Class A New York-Penn League affiliate of the St. Louis Cardinals, was produced by Best Cards, Inc. and distributed in one strip measuring approximately 16 1/4" by 3 1/2". The front features color photos of the team's six 1997 Top Prospects. The back displays player information and career statistics. Adam Kennedy is the key player in this set.
COMPLETE SET (6)................ 15.00 4.50

1997 Norfolk Tides Best

This 34-card set of the 1997 Norfolk Tides, a Class AAA International League affiliate of the New York Mets, was produced by Best Card, Inc. and sponsored by All Sport Body Quencher. The fronts feature posed color player photos in a two-sided zig-zag design blue border. The backs carry player information and career statistics.
COMPLETE SET (34)................ 8.00 2.40

1997 Norfolk Tides Team Issue

COMPLETE SET (34)................ 8.00 2.40

1997 Norwich Navigators Best

This 32-card set of the 1997 Norwich Navigators, a Class AA Eastern League affiliate of the New York Yankees, was produced by Best Cards, Inc. and features color player photos in a two-sided purple border. The backs carry player information and career statistics.
COMPLETE SET (32)................ 8.00 2.40

1997 Norwich Navigators Team Issue

This 30-card set of the 1997 Norwich Navigators, a Class AA Eastern League affiliate of the New York Yankees, was sponsored by Don Mallon Chevrolet and features color action player photos in gold borders. The backs carry player biographical information and career statistics. The set was distributed in two large sheets with 15 cards on each sheet. The cards are unnumbered and checklisted below alphabetically.
COMPLETE SET (30)................ 10.00 3.00

1997 Oklahoma City 89ers Best

This 25-card set of the 1997 Oklahoma City 89ers, a Class AAA American Association affiliate of the Texas Rangers, was produced by Best Cards, Inc. and features color player photos in a white border. The backs carry player information, career statistics and a safety message.
COMPLETE SET (25)................ 8.00 2.40

1997 Omaha Royals Best

This 36-card set of the 1997 Omaha Royals, a Class AAA American Association affiliate of the Kansas City Royals, was produced by Best Cards, Inc. and features color player photos in a blue border. The backs carry player information and career statistics.
COMPLETE SET (36)................ 8.00 2.40

1997 Orlando Rays Best

This 30-card set of the 1997 Orlando Rays, a Class AA Southern League affiliate of the Chicago Cubs, was produced by Best Cards, Inc. and features color player photos in a partial zigzag green border. The backs carry player information and career statistics. Kerry Wood has a card in this set.
COMPLETE SET (30)................ 25.00 7.50

1997 Pawtucket Red Sox All-Time Greats Dunkin' Donuts

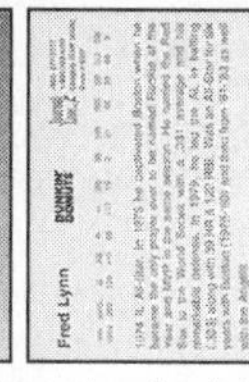

This 30-card set features a dynamic selection of All-Time Greats that played for the Pawtucket Red Sox throughout the years. The set was issued as a perforated sheet that folds out to poster size. Each unnumbered standard size card features a full color photo (with some amazing vintage minor league shots of stars like Wade Boggs, Fred Lynn and Jim Rice) surrounded by a light purple border. The set was sponsored by Dunkin' Donuts, projo.com and the Providence Journal. The cards have been checklisted below in alphabetical order.
COMPLETE SET (30)................ 70.00 21.00

1997 Pawtucket Red Sox All-Time Greats Team Issue

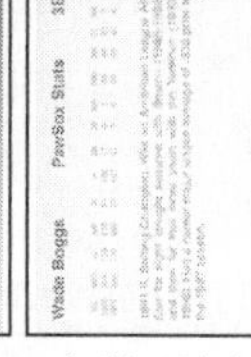

Some of the best players in this set include Wade Boggs, Roger Clemens and Jim Rice.
COMPLETE SET (31)................ 30.00 9.00

1997 Pawtucket Red Sox Best

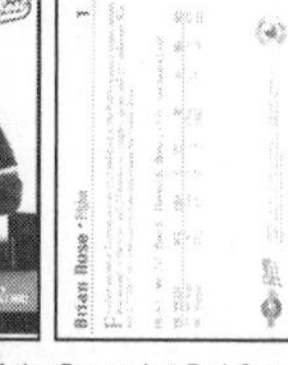

This 30-card set of the Pawtucket Red Sox, a Class AAA International League affiliate of the Boston Red Sox, was produced by Best Cards, Inc. and features color player portraits in a thin black border
COMPLETE SET (30)................ 10.00 3.00

1997 Peoria Chiefs Best

This 30-card set of the 1997 Peoria Chiefs, a Class A Midwest League affiliate of the St. Louis Cardinals, was produced by Best Cards, Inc. and features color player photos in a one-sided, ball laces border. The backs carry player information and career statistics.
COMPLETE SET (30)................ 8.00 2.40

1997 Phoenix Firebirds Team Issue

This 30-card set of the 1997 Phoenix Firebirds was sponsored by Tony's Pizza. The fronts feature color player photos with a flame-style border. The backs carry player information and career statistics. The cards are unnumbered and checklisted below in alphabetical order.
COMPLETE SET (30)................ 10.00 3.00

1997 Phoenix Firebirds/Giants Dream Team Issue

This 29-card set features black-and-white photos of all-time great Phoenix Giants and Firebirds players in orange-and-navy borders. The backs carry player information.
COMPLETE SET (29)................ 20.00 6.00

1997 Piedmont Boll Weevils Best

This 30-card set of the 1997 Piedmont Boll Weevils, a Class A South Atlantic League affiliate of the Philadelphia Phillies, was produced by Best Cards, Inc. and features color player photos with a one-sided ball-laces border on a ball park background. The backs carry player information and career statistics. Early cards of Adam Eaton and Jimmy Rollins highlight this set.
COMPLETE SET (30)................ 10.00 3.00

1997 Pittsfield Mets Best

This 30-card set of the 1997 Pittsfield Mets, a Class A New York-Penn League affiliate of the New York Mets, was produced by Best Cards, Inc. and features color player photos. The backs carry player information and career statistics. This issue includes the minor league card debut of Corey Erickson.
COMPLETE SET (30)................ 8.00 2.40

1997 Portland Rockies Grandstand

This set of the Portland Rockies Minor League team was produced by Grandstand Cards and features color player portraits. The backs carry player information and career statistics. The cards are unnumbered and checklisted below in alphabetical order.
COMPLETE SET (30)................ 8.00 2.40

1997 Portland Sea Dogs Best

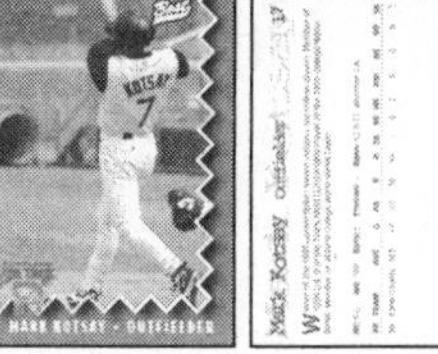

This 30-card set of the 1997 Portland Sea Dogs, a Class AA Eastern League affiliate of the Florida Marlins, was produced by Best Cards, Inc. and features color player photos in a two-sided, white and aqua border. The backs carry player information and career statistics. An early card of Mark Kotsay highlights this set.
COMPLETE SET (30)................ 10.00 3.00

1997 Prince William Cannons Best

This 30-card set of the 1997 Prince William Cannons, a Class A team affiliate of the St. Louis Cardinals, was produced by Best Cards, Inc. and features color player photos in a one-sided ball laces border. The backs carry player information and career statistics.
COMPLETE SET (30)................ 10.00 3.00

1997 Princeton Devil Rays Team Issue

NFL Quarterback Doug Johnson is featured in this set.
COMPLETE SET (30)................ 15.00 4.50

1997 Quad City River Bandits Best

This 30-card set of the 1997 Quad City River Bandits, a Class A Midwest League affiliate of the Houston Astros, was produced by Best Cards, Inc. and features color player photos in a blue border. The backs carry player information and career statistics.
COMPLETE SET (30)................ 20.00 6.00

1997 Rancho Cucamonga Quakes Grandstand

This set of the Rancho Cucamonga Quakes Minor League team was produced by Grandstand Cards and features color player portraits. The backs carry player information and career statistics. The cards are unnumbered and checklisted below in alphabetical order. An early card of Matt Clement highlights this set.
COMPLETE SET (30)................ 8.00 2.40

1997 Rancho Cucamonga Quakes Update Grandstand

This set updates the Rancho Cucamonga Quakes Minor League team set produced by Grandstand Cards and features color player portraits. The backs carry player information and career statistics.
COMPLETE SET (7)................ 4.00 1.20

1997 Reading Phillies Best

This 27-card set of the 1997 Reading Phillies, a Class AA Eastern League affiliate of the Philadelphia Phillies, was produced by Best Cards, Inc. and features color player photos in a white border. The backs carry player information and career statistics.
COMPLETE SET (27)................ 8.00 2.40

1997 Richmond Braves Best

This 30-card set of the 1997 Richmond Braves, a Class AAA International League affiliate of the Atlanta Braves, was produced by Best Cards, Inc. and features color player photos in a white-and-blue zigzag border. The backs carry player information and career statistics.
COMPLETE SET (30)................ 8.00 2.40

1997 Rochester Red Wings Best

This 30-card set of the 1997 Rochester Red Wings, a Class AAA International League affiliate of the Baltimore Orioles, was produced by Best Cards, Inc. and features color player photos in a red border. The backs carry player information and career statistics.
COMPLETE SET (30)................ 8.00 2.40

1997 Rockford Cubs Best

This 30-card set of the 1997 Rockford Cubs, a Class A Midwest League affiliate of the Chicago Cubs, was produced by Best Cards, Inc. and features color player portraits in a blue border. The backs carry player information and career statistics. Quincy Carter, the football player, is the key player in this set.
COMPLETE SET (30)................ 30.00 12.00

1997 Salem Avalanche Team Issue

This 38-card set of the 1997 Salem Avalanche, a Carolina League Class A affiliate of the Colorado Rockies, was sponsored by Kroger and Van de Kamp's and features color player portraits on a purple and thin gray-striped background. The backs carry small black-and-white player portraits with player information and career statistics. A set of 10 cards was produced later in the season to update the original set with the added new players. This set displays the same design except the background on front is gray with thin purple stripes. The cards are checklisted at the end with the letter, "U" before their numbers.
COMPLETE SET (38)................ 15.00 4.50

1997 Salem Avalanche Team Issue Update

These 10 cards updated the 1997 Salem Avalanche Team Issue
COMPLETE SET (10).................. 5.00 1.50

1997 Salem-Keizer Volcanoes Grandstand

This set of the Salem-Keizer Volcanoes Minor League team was produced by Grandstand Cards and features color player portraits. The backs carry player information and career statistics. The cards are unnumbered and checklisted below in alphabetical order.
COMPLETE SET (42).................. 8.00 2.40

1997 Salt Lake Buzz Best

This 29-card set of the 1997 Salt Lake Buzz, a Class AAA team affiliate of the Minnesota Twins, was produced by Best Cards, Inc. and features color player photos in thin black borders. The backs carry player information and career statistics.
COMPLETE SET (29).................. 8.00 2.40

1997 San Antonio Missions Best

This 30-card set of the 1997 San Antonio Missions, a Class AA Texas League affiliate of the Los Angeles Dodgers, was produced by Best Cards, Inc. and features color player photos. The backs carry player information and career statistics.
COMPLETE SET (30).................. 8.00 2.40

1997 San Bernadino Stampede Best

This 30-card set of the 1997 San Bernardino Stampede, a Class A California League affiliate of the Los Angeles Dodgers, was produced by Best Cards, Inc. and features color player photos in a thin black border. The backs carry player information and career statistics.
COMPLETE SET (30).................. 8.00 2.40

1997 San Jose Giants Best

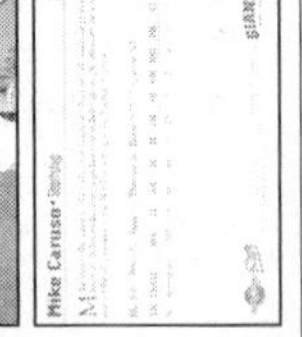

This 30-card set of the 1997 San Jose Giants, a Class A California League affiliate of the San Francisco Giants, was produced by Best Cards, Inc. and features color player photos in a one-sided, ball-laces border. The backs carry player information and career statistics.
COMPLETE SET (30).................. 8.00 2.40

1997 Sarasota Red Sox Best

This 30-card set of the 1997 Sarasota Red Sox, a Class A Florida State League affiliate of the Boston Red Sox, was produced by Best Cards, Inc. and features color player photos in a thin blue border. The backs carry player information and career statistics. Nomar Garciaparra is the key player in this set.
COMPLETE SET (30)............... 30.00 9.00

1997 Scranton/Wilkes-Barre Red Barons Best

This 30-card set of the 1997 Scranton/Wilkes-Barre Red Barons, a Class A affiliate of the Philadelphia Phillies, was produced by Best Cards, Inc. and features color player photos in a one-sided, ball-laces border. The backs carry player information and career statistics.
COMPLETE SET (30).................. 8.00 2.40

1997 Shreveport Captains Best

This 28-card set of the 1997 Shreveport Captains, a Class AA team affiliate of the San Francisco Giants, was produced by Best Cards, Inc. The fronts feature color player photos in a two-sided blue border with a thin black inner border. The backs carry player information and career statistics.
COMPLETE SET (29).................. 8.00 2.40

1997 Shreveport Captains Willis-Knighton SportsCare

This 29-card set of the 1997 Shreveport Captains, a Class AA team affiliate of the San Francisco Giants, was produced by Best Cards, Inc. and sponsored by Willis-Knighton SportsCare. The fronts feature color player photos in a two-sided blue border with a thin black inner border. The backs carry player information and career statistics.
COMPLETE SET (29).................. 8.00 2.40

1997 South Atlantic League Top Prospects Best

This 31-card set, produced by Best Cards, Inc. features color photos of the top prospects from the teams in the South Atlantic League printed on a facsimile marble background. The backs carry player information. Early cards of Joe Crede and Nick Johnson highlight this set.
COMPLETE SET (31)................ 25.00 7.50

1997 South Bend Silver Hawks Best

This 30-card set of the 1997 South Bend Silver Hawks, a Class A Midwest League affiliate of the Chicago White Sox, was produced by Best Cards, Inc. and features color player photos in a one-sided ball-laces border. The backs carry player information and career statistics. Brad Penny is the key player in this set.
COMPLETE SET (30)................ 10.00 3.00

1997 Southern League Top Prospects Best

This 31-card set, produced by Best Cards, Inc. features color photos of the top prospects from the teams in the Southern League printed on a facsimile marble background. The backs carry player information. Leading prospects in this set include Ben Grieve, Kevin Millwood, Miguel Tejada and Kerry Wood.
COMPLETE SET (31)................ 25.00 7.50

1997 Southern Oregon Timberjacks Best

This 29-card set of the 1997 Southern Oregon Timberjacks, a Class A Northwest League affiliate of the Oakland Athletics, was produced by Best Cards, Inc. and features color player photos. The backs carry player information and career statistics. Tim Hudson's first minor league team set card highlights this set.
COMPLETE SET (29)................ 20.00 6.00

1997 Spokane Indians Grandstand

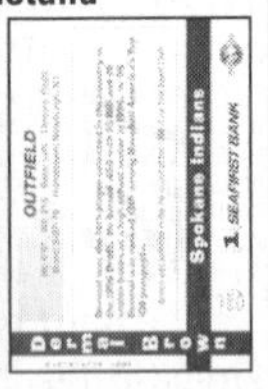

This set of the Spokane Indians Grandstand Minor League team was produced by Grandstand Cards and features color player portraits. The backs carry player information and career statistics. The cards are unnumbered and checklisted below in alphabetical order.
COMPLETE SET (31)............... 15.00 4.50

1997 St. Catharines Stompers Best

This 30-card set of the 1997 St. Catherines Stompers, a Class A New York-Penn League affiliate of the Toronto Blue Jays, was produced by Best Cards, Inc. and features color player photos. The backs carry player information and career statistics. Early cards of Vernon Wells and Michael Young highlight this set.
COMPLETE SET (30)............... 20.00 6.00

1997 St. Lucie Mets Best

This 30-card set of the 1997 St. Lucie Mets, a Class A Florida State League affiliate of the New York Mets, was produced by Best Cards, Inc. and features color player photos with a blue border. The backs carry player information and career statistics. Early cards of Terrence Long and Preston Wilson are the keys to this set.
COMPLETE SET (30)............... 10.00 3.00

1997 St. Paul Saints Team Issue

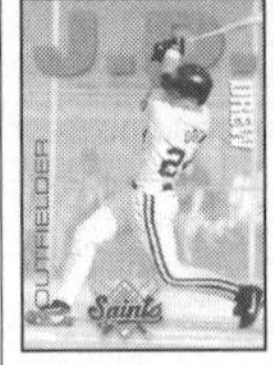

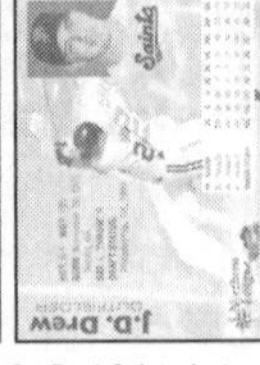

This 32-card set of the St. Paul Saints features borderless color player photos. The backs carry a small black-and-white player head photo with player information and career statistics printed on a black-and-white action player photo background. The cards are unnumbered and checklisted below in alphabetical order. An early card of J.D. Drew is in this set.
COMPLETE SET (32)............... 60.00 18.00

1997 St. Petersburg Devil Rays Best

This 30-card set of the 1997 St. Petersburg Devil Rays, a Class A Minor League Team, was produced by Best Cards, Inc. and features color player photos. The backs carry player information and career statistics.
COMPLETE SET (30).................. 8.00 2.40

1997 St. Petersburg Devil Rays Update Best

This 30-card update set of the Tampa Bay Devil Rays' Class A Minor League Team, produced by Best Cards, Inc., includes the minor league card debut of Rolando Arrojo.
COMPLETE SET (30).................. 8.00 2.40

1997 Stockton Ports Best

This 30-card set of the 1997 Stockton Ports, a Class A California League affiliate of the Milwaukee Brewers, was produced by Best Cards, Inc. and features color player photos in a thin black border. The backs carry player information and career statistics.
COMPLETE SET (30).................. 8.00 2.40

1997 Syracuse Sky Chiefs Best

This 30-card set of the 1997 Syracuse Sky Chiefs, a Class AAA International League affiliate of the Toronto Blue Jays, features color player photos. The backs carry player information and career statistics.
COMPLETE SET (30).................. 8.00 2.40

1997 Tacoma Rainiers Best

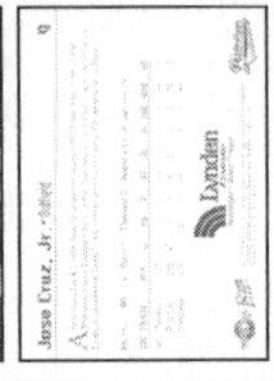

This 30-card set of the 1997 Tacoma Rainers, a Class AAA Pacific Coast League affiliate of the Seattle Mariners, was produced by Best Cards, Inc. and features color player photos in a thin black border. The backs carry player information and career statistics. An early card of Jose Cruz, Jr. highlights this set.
COMPLETE SET (30)............... 15.00 4.50

1997 Tampa Yankees Best

This 33-card set of the 1997 Tampa Yankees, a Class A Florida State League affiliate of the New York Yankees, was produced by Best Cards, Inc. and features color player photos in a white border. The backs carry player information and career statistics. Key cards in this set include Hideki Irabu and Eric Milton.
COMPLETE SET (33)............... 10.00 3.00

1997 Texas League Top Prospects Best

This 31-card set, produced by Best Cards, Inc. features color photos of the top prospects from the teams in the Texas League printed on a facsimile marble background. The backs carry player information. Scott Elarton and Fernando Tatis are the keys to this set.
COMPLETE SET (31)............... 10.00 3.00

1997 Toledo Mud Hens Best

This 36-card set of the 1997 Toledo Mud Hens, a Class AAA International League affiliate of the Detroit Tigers, was produced by Best Cards, Inc. and features color player photos in a two-sided, red zigzag border. The backs carry player information and career statistics.
COMPLETE SET (36).................. 8.00 2.40

1997 Trenton Thunder Best

This 30-card set of the 1997 Trenton Thunder, a Class AA Eastern League affiliate of the Boston Red Sox, was produced by Best Cards, Inc. and sponsored by Blockbuster. The fronts feature color player photos in a two-sided green border. The backs carry player information and career statistics. The last five cards of the set were unnumbered with the sponsor logo on the fronts and video rental promotions on the backs.
COMPLETE SET (30).................. 8.00 2.40

1997 Tucson Toros Best

This 29-card set of the 1997 Tucson Toros, a Class AAA Pacific Coast League affiliate of the Houston Astros, was produced by Best Cards, Inc. and features color player photos in a two-sided red zigzag border. The backs carry player information and career statistics. Travis Lee has a minor league team set card in this, his first season in professional baseball.
COMPLETE SET (29).................. 8.00 2.40

1997 Tulsa Drillers Team Issue

This 30-card set features color photos of the Tulsa Drillers and was sponsored by 106.9 FM Radio Station and the Oklahoma Highway Safety Office. The backs carry player information and career statistics along with a safety message. The key player in this set is Fernando Tatis.
COMPLETE SET (30)............... 10.00 3.00

1997 UCLA Bruins Team Issue

College cards of major leaguers Troy Glaus, Jim Parque and Eric Valent are in this set.
COMPLETE SET (31)............. 300.00 90.00

1997 Vancouver Canadians Best

This 30-card set of the 1997 Vancouver Canadians, a Class AAA Pacific Coast League affiliate of the California Angels, was produced by Best Cards, Inc. and features color player photos. The backs carry player information and career statistics.
COMPLETE SET (30).................. 8.00 2.40

1997 Vermont Expos Best

This 30-card set of the 1997 Vermont Expos, a Class A New York-Penn League affiliate of the Montreal Expos, was produced by Best Cards, Inc. and features color player photos in a one-sided, ball-laces border. The backs carry player information and career statistics. Milton Bradley's card highlights this set.
COMPLETE SET (30)............... 10.00 3.00

1997 Vero Beach Dodgers Best

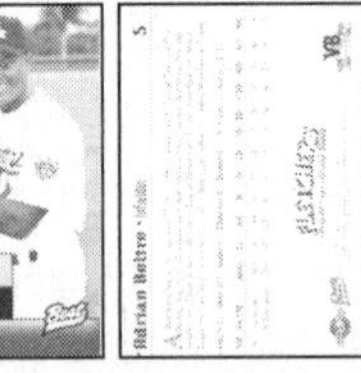

This 30-card set of the 1997 Vero Beach Dodgers, a Class A Florida State League affiliate of the Los Angeles Dodgers, was produced by Best Cards, Inc. and features color player photos in a two-sided blue border. The backs carry player information and career statistics. An early card of Adrian Beltre is the key to this set.
COMPLETE SET (30)............... 15.00 4.50

1997 Visalia Oaks Grandstand

This set of the Visalia Oaks Minor League team was produced by Grandstand Cards and features color player portraits. The backs carry player information and career statistics. The cards are unnumbered and checklisted below in alphabetical order. Eric Chavez's first minor league team set card is included in this set.
COMPLETE SET (30)............... 40.00 12.00

1997 Watertown Indians Team Issue

This 34-card set of the 1997 Watertown Indians sponsored by Time Warner Cable features color player photos in white borders. The backs carry player information and career statistics. The cards are unnumbered and checklisted below in alphabetical order.
COMPLETE SET (34)............... 12.00 3.60

1997 West Michigan Whitecaps Best

This 30-card set of the 1997 West Michigan Whitecaps, a class A team affiliate of the Detroit Tigers, was produced by Best Cards, Inc. and features color player photos in blue borders. The backs carry player information and career statistics.
COMPLETE SET (30)............... 15.00 4.50

1997 Wichita Wranglers Best

This 30-card set of the 1997 Wichita Wranglers, a Class AA Texas League affiliate of the Kansas City Royals, was produced by Best Cards, Inc. and features color player photos in a white border. The backs carry player information and career statistics.
COMPLETE SET (30).................. 8.00 2.40

1997 Williamsport Cubs Best

This 30-card set of the 1997 Williamsport Cubs, a Class A team affiliate of the Chicago Cubs, was produced by Best Cards, Inc. and features color player photos in a one-sided, ball-laces border. The backs carry player information and career statistics.
COMPLETE SET (30).................. 8.00 2.40

1997 Wilmington Blue Rocks Team Issue

Key players in this set include Carlos Beltran, Carlos Febles and Mark Quinn.
COMPLETE SET (30)............... 10.00 3.00

1997 Winnipeg Goldeyes Team Issue

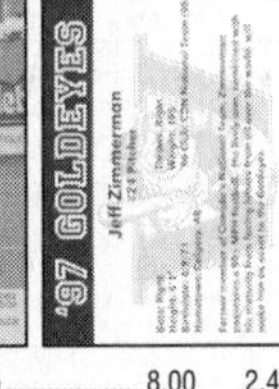

COMPLETE SET (30).................. 8.00 2.40

1997 Wisconsin Timber Rattlers Best

This 29-card set of the 1996 Wisconsin Timber Rattlers, a Class A Midwest League affiliate of the Seattle Mariners, was produced by Best Cards, Inc. and features color player photos in a zigzag maroon-and-white border. The backs carry player information and career statistics.
COMPLETE SET (29)............... 15.00 4.50

1997 Yakima Bears Grandstand

This set of the Yakima Bears Minor League team was produced by Grandstand Cards and features color player portraits. The backs carry player information and career statistics. The cards are unnumbered and checklisted below in alphabetical order.
COMPLETE SET (36).................. 8.00 2.40

1998 Akron Aeros Multi-Ad

This 30-card set of the 1998 Akron Aeros, a Class AA team affiliate of the Cleveland Indians, was produced by Multi-Ad Sports, Inc. and features posed color player photos with a two-sided purple border. The backs carry player information and career statistics.
COMPLETE SET (30)............... 10.00 3.00

1998 Albuquerque Dukes Grandstand

This set of the Albuquerque Dukes Minor League team was produced by Grandstand Cards and features color player portraits. The backs carry player information and career statistics. The cards are unnumbered and checklisted below in alphabetical order.
COMPLETE SET (30).................. 8.00 2.40

1998 Appalachian League Prospect Q-Cards

This 31-card set of the Appalachain Minor League team was produced by Blueline Communications and features color player photos in a green border. The backs carry player information and career statistics. C.C. Sabathia is the key player in this set.
COMPLETE SET (31)............... 18.00 5.50

1998 Arizona Fall League Prospects

This 25-card set features color action photos of the top prospects from the teams in the Arizona Fall League printed inside white borders. The backs carry information about the player and statistics. Early cards of J.D. Drew and Alfonso Soriano highlight this set.
COMPLETE SET (25)............... 50.00 12.00

1998 Arizona Fall League Prospects Gold

COMPLETE SET (25)............... 50.00 12.00

1998 Arkansas Travelers Highlights Team Issue

This 10-card set of the 1998 Arkansas Travelers, a Class AA Texas League affiliate of

the St. Louis Cardinals, features color player photos. The backs carry player information. Two card of J.D. Drew are the keys to this set.
COMPLETE SET (10)................ 25.00 12.00

1998 Arkansas Travelers Multi-Ad

This 30-card set of the 1998 Arkansas Travelers, a Class AA Texas League affiliate of the St. Louis Cardinals, was produced by Multi-Ad Services, Inc. and features posed color player photos in a two-sided red border. The backs carry player information and career statistics along with sponsor logos.
COMPLETE SET (30)................ 30.00 15.00

1998 Arkansas Travelers Update Multi-Ad

This one-card update to the Arkansas Travelers set features super prospect J. D. Drew. It was available singly or as a package with the regular set.
COMPLETE SET (1).................. 15.00 6.00

1998 Asheville Tourists Multi-Ad

This 30-card set of the 1998 Asheville Tourists, a Class A South Atlantic League affiliate of the Colorado Rockies, was produced by Multi-Ad Services, Inc. and features color player photos in a red facsimile textured border. The backs carry player information and career statistics along with team and sponsor logos.
COMPLETE SET (30).................. 8.00 2.40

1998 Auburn Doubledays Team Issue

This 34-card set of the Auburn Doubledays Minor League team features color player photos with green borders. The backs carry player information and career statistics. The cards are unnumbered and checklisted below in alphabetical order. Early cards of Keith Ginter, Roy Oswalt and Tim Redding highlight this set.
COMPLETE SET (34)................ 30.00 9.00

1998 Augusta Greenjackets Multi-Ad

This 30-card set of the Albuquerque Dukes Minor League team was produced by Multi-AD Sports and features color player photos with a facsimile ball-laces border on one side. The backs carry player information and career statistics.
COMPLETE SET (30).................. 8.00 2.40

1998 Batavia Muckdogs Team Issue

This 35-card set of the 1998 Batavia Muckdogs, a Minor League team, features color player photos in white borders. The backs display player information. The cards are unnumbered and checklisted below in alphabetical order. A card of Ricky Williams, first draft pick of the New Orleans Saints in 1999, is in this set.
COMPLETE SET (35)................ 20.00 6.00

1998 Beloit Snappers Multi-Ad

This 30-card set of the 1998 Beloit Snappers, a Class A Midwest League affiliate of the Milwaukee Brewers, was produced by Multi-Ad Services, Inc. and features color player photos with the player's name printed in the one-sided blue border. The backs carry player information and career statistics along with team and sponsor logos. Only 1,000 of this set were produced and are sequentially numbered.
COMPLETE SET (30)................ 15.00 4.50

1998 Billings Mustangs Team Issue

This set of the Billings Mustangs Minor League team features borderless black-and-white player photos. The backs carry player information and career statistics. The cards are unnumbered and checklisted below in alphabetical order. First cards of Adam Dunn and Austin Kearns are the highlights of this set.
COMPLETE SET (38).............. 175.00 45.00

1998 Binghamton Mets Q-Cards

This 30-card set of the Binghamton Mets Minor League team was produced by Blueline Communications and features color player photos in blue borders. The backs carry player information and career statistics.
COMPLETE SET (30).................. 8.00 2.40

1998 Birmingham Barons Grandstand

This set of the Birmingham Barons Minor League team was produced by Grandstand Cards and features color player photos with white borders. The backs carry player information and career statistics. The cards are unnumbered and checklisted below in alphabetical order. A card of Jim Abbott was issued late in the year and was not inserted in many sets. It is listed at the end of these listings as a SP. In addition, an early card of Carlos Lee was issued in this set.
COMPLETE SET (30)................ 10.00 3.00

1998 Bluefield Orioles Q-Cards

This set of the Bluefield Orioles Minor League team was produced by Blueline Communications and was sponsored by Grant's Supermarkets, A.J.'s and Nash-Finch Co. The fronts feature color player photos. The backs carry player information and career statistics.
COMPLETE SET (32)................ 10.00 3.00

1998 Boise Hawks Grandstand

COMPLETE SET 10.00 3.00

1998 Bowie Baysox Multi-Ad

This set of the Bowie Baysox Minor League team was produced by Multi-Ad Sports and features color player photos with a three-sided black border. The backs carry player information and career statistics.
COMPLETE SET (30)................ 20.00 6.00

1998 Bowie Nationals On Deck

COMPLETE SET 8.00 2.40

1998 Bridgeport Bluefish Multi-Ad

This set of the Bridgeport Bluefish Minor League team was produced by Multi-Ad Sports and features color player photos with a one-sided green border. The backs carry player information and career statistics.
COMPLETE SET (30).................. 8.00 2.40

1998 Bristol White Sox Q-Cards

This set of the Bristol White Sox Minor League team was produced by Blueline Communications and features color player photos with white borders. The backs carry player information and career statistics.
COMPLETE SET (30)................ 10.00 3.00

1998 Buffalo Bisons Grandstand

This set of the Buffalo Bisons Minor League team was produced by Grandstand Cards and features color player photos with a one-sided green border. The backs carry player information and career statistics. The cards are unnumbered and checklisted below in alphabetical order.
COMPLETE SET (30)................ 10.00 3.00

1998 Burlington Bees Multi-Ad

This set of the Burlington Bees Minor League team was produced by Multi-Ad Sports and features color player photos. The backs carry player information and career statistics.
COMPLETE SET (30)................ 10.00 3.00

1998 Butte Copper Kings Grandstand

This 34-card set of the 1998 Butte Copper Kings, a Class A affiliate of the Anaheim Angels, was produced by Grandstand Cards and features color player photos. The backs carry player information, career statistics, and sponsor logos.
COMPLETE SET (34).................. 8.00 2.40

1998 Cape Fear Crocs Multi-Ad

This set of the Cape Fear Crocs Minor League team was produced by Multi-Ad Sports and features color player photos with dark blue borders. The backs carry player information and career statistics.
COMPLETE SET (30)................ 10.00 3.00

1998 Capital City Bombers Fox 57

This set of the Capital City Bombers Fox 57 Minor League team was produced by sponsored by WACH Fox 57 and features color player photos. The backs carry player information and career statistics. Alex Escobar is the key player in this set.
COMPLETE SET (30)................ 15.00 4.50

1998 Capital City Bombers Multi-Ad

This set of the Capital City Bombers Minor League team was produced by Multi-Ad Sports and features color player photos with black-and-red borders. The backs carry player information and career statistics. Alex Escobar is the key player in this set.
COMPLETE SET (30)................ 25.00 7.50

1998 Capital City Bombers SAL Championship Multi-Ad

This 31-card set commemorates the Capital City Bombers as the 1998 South Atlantic League (SAL) Champions and was produced by Multi-Ad Sports. The fronts features color player action and posed photos with the title "1998 SAL Champions" printed above the picture and the player's name and position in the red bar at the bottom. The backs carry player information and '98 statistics. Only 750 of these sets were made and sequentially numbered on the back of card number 31. Two cards of Alex Escobar highlight this set.
COMPLETE SET (31)................ 25.00 7.50

1998 Carolina League All-Stars Choice

This set of the Carolina League All-Stars team was produced by Choice Marketing, Inc. and features color player photos. The backs carry player information and career statistics. The cards are unnumbered and checklisted below in alphabetical order. Early cards of Carlos Beltran and Joe Crede highlight this set.
COMPLETE SET (42)................ 40.00 12.00

1998 Carolina League Prospects Q-Cards

This 32-card set of the Carolina League's Top Prospects was produced by Blueline Communications and features color action player photos in red and blue borders. The back carry player information and career statistics. Early cards of Rick Ankiel, Carlos Beltran and Joe Crede are the key players in this set.
COMPLETE SET (32)................ 15.00 4.50

1998 Carolina Mudcats Multi-Ad

This set of the Carolina Mudcats Minor League team was produced by Multi-Ad Sports and features color player photos with a ball lace facsimile border on one side. The backs carry player information and career statistics.
COMPLETE SET (30).................. 8.00 2.40

1998 Cedar Rapids Kernels Team Issue

This 31-card set of the Cedar Rapids Kernels Minor League team features color player photos in white borders. The backs carry player information and career statistics. The cards are unnumbered and checklisted below in alphabetical order.
COMPLETE SET (31).................. 8.00 2.40

1998 Charleston Alley Cats Multi-Ad

This 31-card set of the Charleston Alley Cats Minor League team was produced by Multi-Ad Sports and features color player photos with a red border on one side. The backs carry player information and career statistics.
COMPLETE SET (31).................. 8.00 2.40

1998 Charleston River Dogs Grandstand

This 34-card set of the Charleston River Dogs Minor League team was produced by Grandstand Cards and features borderless color action player photos. The backs carry player information and career statistics. The cards are unnumbered and checklisted below in alphabetical order.
COMPLETE SET (34)................ 15.00 4.50

1998 Charlotte Knights Q-Cards

This 30-card set of the Charlotte Knights Minor League team was produced by Blueline Communications and features color player photos with green borders. The backs carry player information and career statistics.
COMPLETE SET (30).................. 8.00 2.40

1998 Charlotte Rangers Multi-Ad

This 30-card set of the Charlotte Rangers Minor League team was produced by Multi-Ad Sports and features color player photos in red borders. The backs carry player information and career statistics. Ivan Rodriguez is the key player in this set.
COMPLETE SET (30)................ 15.00 4.50

1998 Chattanooga Lookouts Grandstand

This 30-card set of the Chattanooga Lookouts Minor League team was produced by Grandstand Cards and features color player photos with a black border on one side. The backs carry player information and career statistics. The cards are unnumbered and checklisted below in alphabetical order.
COMPLETE SET (30).................. 8.00 2.40

1998 Clearwater Phillies Multi-Ad

This 30-card set of the Clearwater Phillies Minor League team was produced by Multi-Ad Sports and features color player photos with a blue border on one side. The backs carry player information and career statistics. Early cards of Adam Eaton and Jimmy Rollins highlight this set.
COMPLETE SET (30)................ 10.00 3.00

1998 Clearwater Phillies Update Multi-Ad

This 30-card set is an updated version of the Clearwater Phillies Minor League team was produced by Multi-Ad Sports. The fronts feature color player photos with a blue border on one side. The backs carry player information and career statistics. Pat Burrell's first card is in this set.
COMPLETE SET (30)................ 25.00 7.50

1998 Clinton LumberKings Grandstand

This 30-card set of the Clinton LumberKings Minor League team was produced by Grandstand Cards and features color player photos with white borders. The backs carry player information and career statistics.
COMPLETE SET (30)................ 10.00 3.00

1998 Colorado Springs Sky Sox

COMPLETE SET (27).................. 8.00 2.40

1998 Columbus Clippers Multi-Ad

This 30-card set of the Columbus Clippers Minor League team was produced by Multi-Ad Sports and features posed color player photos with a blue border on one side. The backs carry player information and career statistics. Cards of Orlando Hernandez and Mike Lowell highlight this set.
COMPLETE SET (30)................ 15.00 4.50

1998 Columbus Clippers Police

This 25-card set of the Columbus Clippers Minor League was produced for the Drug Abuse Resistance Education program features and borderless color player portraits. The backs carry player information and career statistics. The cards are unnumbered and checklisted below in alphabetical order. Early cards of Orlando Hernandez and Mike Lowell highlight this set.
COMPLETE SET (25)................ 25.00 7.50

1998 Columbus Red Stixx Multi-Ad

This 30-card set of the Columbus Red Stixx Minor League team was produced by Multi-Ad Sports and features color player photos with red borders. The backs carry player information and career statistics.
COMPLETE SET (30)................ 10.00 3.00

1998 Danville 97s Q-Cards

This 31-card set of the Danville 97s Minor League team was produced by Blueline Communications and features color player photos with red-and-yellow borders. The backs carry player information and career statistics.
COMPLETE SET (31)................ 12.00 3.60

1998 Danville Braves Q-Cards

This 31-card set of the Danville Braves Minor League team was produced by Blueline Communications and features color player photos with inner red and outer blue borders. The backs carry player information and career statistics. Rafael Furcal's first card is in this set.
COMPLETE SET (31)................ 25.00 7.50

1998 Daytona Cubs Grandstand

COMPLETE SET (21)................ 10.00 3.00

1998 Delaware Stars Team Issue

Cards of Dermal Brown and Eric Valent highlight this set.
COMPLETE SET (29)................ 15.00 4.50

1998 Delmarva Rockfish Team Issue

COMPLETE SET (30)................ 15.00 4.50

1998 Delmarva Shorebirds Multi-Ad

This 30-card set of the Delmarva Shorebirds Minor League team was produced by Multi-Ad Sports and features color player photos in black-and-red borders. The backs carry player information and career statistics.
COMPLETE SET (30)................ 10.00 3.00

1998 Duluth Superior Dukes Grandstand

COMPLETE SET (27).................. 8.00 2.40

1998 Dunedin Blue Jays Stickers Team Issue

This 24-sticker team issue set of the 1998 Dunedin Blue Jays, a Florida State League Class A Baseball Club, features color player head photos measuring approximately 2" by 2". The stickers were made to be placed in a two-page 8 1/2" by 11" Blue Jays Family Night Sticker Album. The back of the album displays the dates for the Dunedin Blue Jays Family nights and sponsor logos
COMPLETE SET (24)................ 25.00 7.50

1998 Dunedin Blue Jays Team Issue

This 33-card team issue set of the 1998 Dunedin Blue Jays, a Florida State League Class A Baseball Club, was printed by Pinellas Press. The fronts freature posed color player photos with a gray-and-white striped background. The backs carry player information and career statistics. Only 1,000 of the sets were made and serially numbered. (There is no card number 1)
COMPLETE SET (33).................. 8.00 2.40

1998 Durham Bulls Team Issue

This 30-card set of the Durham Bulls Minor League team was sponsored by Radio Station 105.1 (G105) and The Herald Sun. The fronts feature color player photos with a one-sided circular border. The backs carry player information and career statistics. The cards are unnumbered and checklisted below in alphabetical order.
COMPLETE SET (30)................ 15.00 4.50

1998 Eastern League Top Prospects Multi-Ad

This 30-card set of the Eastern Minor League's Top Prospects was produced by Multi-Ad Sports and features posed color player photos with circular borders. The backs carry player information and career statistics. A card of Dernell Stenson highlights this set.
COMPLETE SET (30)................ 10.00 3.00

1998 El Paso Diablos Grandstand

This 29-card set of the El Paso Diablos Minor League team was produced by Grandstand Cards and features posed color player photos with a gray-and-black border on the bottom and one side. The backs carry player information and career statistics. The cards are unnumbered and checklisted below in alphabetical order.
COMPLETE SET (29).................. 8.00 2.40

1998 Erie Sea Wolves Multi-Ad

This 30-card set of the Erie Sea Wolves Minor League team was produced by Multi-Ad Sports and features color player photos in blue borders. The backs carry player information and career statistics.
COMPLETE SET (30)................ 10.00 3.00

1998 Eugene Emeralds Grandstand

This 32-card set of the Eugene Emeralds Minor League team was produced by Grandstand Cards and afeatures action color player photos with a blue border on one side. The backs carry player information, career statistics, and a safety message. The cards are unnumbered and checklisted below in alphabetical order.
COMPLETE SET (32)................ 10.00 3.00

1998 Everett AquaSox Grandstand

This 30-card set of the Everett AquaSox Minor League team was produced by Grandstand and features color player portraits. The backs carry player information and career statistics. The cards are unnumbered and checklisted below in alphabetical order.
COMPLETE SET (30).................. 8.00 2.40

1998 Fargo Red Hawks Multi-Ad

This 30-card set of the Fargo Red Hawks Independent Minor League team was produced by Multi-Ad Sports and sponsored by Domino's Pizza. The fronts feature color action player photos. The backs carry player information and career statistics. The cards are unnumbered and checklisted below in alphabetical order.
COMPLETE SET (30).................. 8.00 2.40

1998 Fort Myers Miracle Team Issue

This 32-card set of the Fort Myers Miracle Minor League team features color action player photos with a two-sided red-and-blue border. The backs display a small black-and-white player head photo with player information and career statistics on a faint black-and-white player photo background. The cards are unnumbered and checklisted below in alphabetical order.
COMPLETE SET (32)................ 10.00 3.00

1998 Fort Wayne Wizards Q-Cards

This 30-card set of the Fort Wayne Wizards Minor League team was produced by Blueline Communications and features color action player photos in blue borders with stars. The backs carry player information and career statistics.
COMPLETE SET (30)................ 12.00 3.60

1998 Frederick Keys Multi-Ad

This 30-card set of the Frederick Keys Minor League team was produced by Multi-Ad Sports and features color action player photos with a one-sided facsimile ball laces border. The

backs carry player information and career statistics.
COMPLETE SET (30)............... 10.00 3.00

1998 Frederick Regiment Team Issue

COMPLETE SET (31)............... 10.00 3.00

1998 Fresno Grizzlies Grandstand

This 30-card set of the Fresno Grizzlies Minor League team was produced by Grandstand Cards and features color action player photos with a purple border on one side. The backs carry player information and career statistics. The cards are unnumbered and checklisted below in alphabetical order.
COMPLETE SET (30)................. 8.00 2.40

1998 Grays Harbor Gulls Grandstand

COMPLETE SET (30)................. 8.00 2.40

1998 Great Falls Dodgers Grandstand

This 31-card set of the Great Falls Dodgers Minor League team was produced by Grandstand Cards and features posed color player photos with a blue border on one side. The backs carry player information and career statistics. The card are unnumbered and checklisted below in alphabetical order.
COMPLETE SET (31)................. 8.00 2.40

1998 Greensboro Bats Multi-Ad

This 30-card set of the Greensboro Bats Minor League team was produced by Multi-Ad Sports and features color player photos with a purple-and-black border. The backs carry player information and career statistics.
COMPLETE SET (30)............... 10.00 3.00

1998 Greenville Braves Grandstand

This 28-card set of the Greelnville Braves Minor League team was produced by Grandstand and features color player photos with a blue border on one side. The backs carry player information and career statistics. The cards are unnumbered and checklisted below in alphabetical order.
COMPLETE SET (28)................. 8.00 2.40

1998 Hagerstown Suns Multi-Ad

This 30-card set of the Hagerstown Suns Minor League team was produced by Multi-Ad Sports and features color player photos with a blue border on one side. The backs carry player information and career statistics. An early card of Vernon Wells highlights this set.
COMPLETE SET (30)............... 25.00 7.50

1998 Harrisburg Senators Multi-Ad

This 30-card set of the Harrisburg Senators Minor League team was produced by Multi-Ad Sports and features color player photos with a red-and-black border. The backs carry player information and career statistics.
COMPLETE SET (30)................. 8.00 2.40

1998 Harrisburg Senators WINK 104

This 30-card set of the Harrisburg Senators Minor League team was produced by Multi-Ad Sports and sponsored by Radio Station WINK 104. The fronts feature color player photos with a red-and-black border. The backs carry player information and career statistics.
COMPLETE SET (30)............... 15.00 4.50

1998 Helena Brewers Multi-Ad

This 33-card set of the Helena Brewers Minor League team was produced by Multi-Ad Sports and features color player photos with a blue border on two sides. The backs carry player information and career statistics.
COMPLETE SET (30)............... 10.00 3.00

1998 Hickory Crawdads Multi-Ad

This 30-card set of the Hickory Crawdads Minor League team was produced by Multi-Ad Sports and features color player photos with a red-and-black border. The backs carry player information and career statistics.
COMPLETE SET (30)................. 8.00 2.40

1998 Hickory Crawdads Update OSP

This 30-card updated set of the Hickory Crawdads Minor League team was produced by Original Smith Printing Sports and features color player photos with a red-and-black border. The backs carry player information and career statistics. Jon Garland is the key player in this set.
COMPLETE SET (30)............... 15.00 4.50

1998 High Desert Mavericks Grandstand

This 30-card set of the High Desert Mavericks Minor League team was produced by Grandstand and features color player photos in a white border. The backs carry player information and career statistics. The cards are unnumbered and checklisted below in alphabetical order.
COMPLETE SET (30)............... 20.00 6.00

1998 Hudson Valley Renegades OSP

This 30-card set of the Hudson Valley Renegades Minor League team was produced by Original Smith Printing Sports and features color player photos with a violet border on one side. The backs carry player information and career statistics.
COMPLETE SET (30)............... 10.00 3.00

1998 Huntsville Stars Team Issue

This 25-card set of the Huntsville Stars Minor League team was sponsored by Burger King and features color player photos in a white border. The backs carry player information and career statistics. Eric Chavez and Tim Hudson are the key players in this set.
COMPLETE SET (25)............... 20.00 6.00

1998 Indianapolis Indians Q-Cards

This 36-card set of the Indianapolis Indians Minor League team was produced by Blueline Communications and features color player photos in a red border. The backs carry player information and career statistics. An early card of Sean Casey highlights this set.
COMPLETE SET (36)............... 15.00 4.50

1998 Iowa Cubs Q-Cards

This 30-card set of the Iowa Cubs Minor League team was produced by Blueline Communications and features color player photos. The backs carry player information and career statistics. An early card of Kerry Wood is the key to this set.
COMPLETE SET (30)............... 15.00 4.50

1998 Jackson Generals Multi-Ad

This 28-card set of the Jackson Generals Minor League team was produced by Multi-Ad Sports and features color player photos in a blue border. The backs carry player information and career statistics. Early cards of Lance Berkman and Freddy Garcia highlight this set.
COMPLETE SET (28)............... 40.00 12.00

1998 Jacksonville Suns Multi-Ad

This 28-card set of the Jacksonville Suns Minor League team was produced by Multi-Ad Sports and features color player photos with a blue border on one side. The backs carry player information and career statistics. An early card of Gabe Kapler is the key to this set.
COMPLETE SET (28)............... 15.00 4.50

1998 Jacksonville Suns Update Grandstand

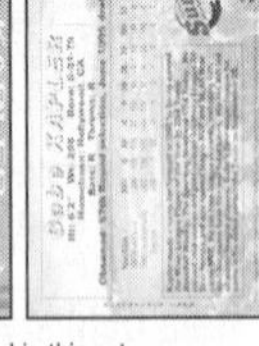

Gabe Kapler is included in this set.
COMPLETE SET 30.00 9.00

1998 Johnson City Cardinals Interstate Graphics

This 36-card set of the Johnson City Cardinals Minor League team was sponsorsed by Interstate Graphics and features color player photos in a white border. The backs carry player information and career statistics. The cards are unnumbered and checklisted below in alphabetical order. Bud Smith's first team set card is included in this set.
COMPLETE SET (36)............... 15.00 4.50

1998 Jupiter Hammerheads Q-Cards

This 30-card set of the Jupiter Hammerheads Minor League team was produced by Blueline Communications and features color player photos in a gray border. The backs carry player information and career statistics. Tony Armas Jr. is the key player in this set.
COMPLETE SET (30)............... 10.00 3.00

1998 Kane County Cougars Connie's Pizza

This 32-card set of the Kane County Cougars Minor League team was sponsored by Connie's Pizza and features borderless action color player photos. The backs carry player information and career statistics. The cards are unnumbered and checklisted below in alphabetical order.
COMPLETE SET (32)............... 15.00 4.50

1998 Kane County Cougars Team Issue

This 32-card set of the Kane County Cougars Minor League team features borderless action color player photos. The backs carry player information and career statistics. The cards are unnumbered and checklisted below in alphabetical order.
COMPLETE SET (32)............... 10.00 3.00

1998 Kinston Indians Q-Cards

This 30-card set of the Kinston Indians Minor League team was produced by Blueline Communications and features color player photos with a thin yellow inner border and thin blue outer border. The backs carry player information and career statistics.
COMPLETE SET (30)................. 8.00 2.40

1998 Kissimmee Cobras Q-Cards

This 30-card set of the Kissimmee Cobras Minor League team was produced by Blueline Communications and features color player photos in a green border. The backs carry player information and career statistics.
COMPLETE SET (30)................. 8.00 2.40

1998 Knoxville Smokies Grandstand

This 27-card set of the Knoxville Smokies Minor League team was produced by Grandstand and features color player photos with a green border on one side. The backs carry player information and career statistics. The cards are unnumbered and checklisted below in alphabetical order.
COMPLETE SET (27)................. 8.00 2.40

1998 Lafayette Leopards Grandstand

COMPLETE SET (30)................. 8.00 2.40

1998 Lake Elsinore Storm Grandstand

This 30-card set of the Lake Elsinore Storm Minor League team was produced by Grandstand and features color player photos in a white border. The backs carry player information and career statistics. The cards are unnumbered and checklisted below in alphabetical order.
COMPLETE SET (30)................. 8.00 2.40

1998 Lakeland Tigers Multi-Ad

This 30-card set of the Lakeland Tigers Minor League team was produced by Multi-Ad Sports and features color player photos with a blue border on one side. The backs carry player information and career statistics.
COMPLETE SET (30)................. 8.00 2.40

1998 Lancaster Jethawks Grandstand

This 30-card set of the High Desert Mavericks Minor League team was produced by Grandstand and features color player photos in a white border. The backs carry player information and career statistics. The cards are unnumbered and checklisted below in alphabetical order.
COMPLETE SET (30)................. 8.00 2.40

1998 Lansing Lugnuts Q-Cards

This 31-card set of the Lansing Lugnuts Minor League team was produced by Blueline Communications and features borderless color player photos. The backs carry player information and career statistics.
COMPLETE SET (31)............... 10.00 3.00

1998 Las Vegas Stars Multi-Ad

This 28-card set of the Las Vegas Stars Minor League team was produced by Multi-Ad Sports and features color player photos with a dark blue border on one side. The backs carry player information and career statistics.
COMPLETE SET (28)................. 8.00 2.40

1998 Lethbridge Black Diamonds Grandstand

This 30-card set of the Lethbridge Black Diamonds Minor League team was produced by Grandstand and features color player photos in a white border. The backs carry player information and career statistics. The cards are unnumbered and checklisted below in alphabetical order. Jack Cust's first minor league team set card is included in this set.
COMPLETE SET (30)............... 15.00 4.50

1998 Louisville Redbirds Q-Cards

This 36-card set of the Louisville Redbirds Minor League team was produced by Blueline Communications and features action color player photos. The backs carry player information and career statistics. An early card of Geoff Jenkins is included in this set.
COMPLETE SET (36)............... 20.00 6.00

1998 Louisville Redbirds Team Issue Update

COMPLETE SET 20.00 7.50

1998 Lowell Spinners Multi-Ad

This 31-card set of the Lowell Spinners Minor League team was produced by Multi-Ad Sports and features color player photos with a facsimile ball-laces border on one side. The backs carry player information and career statistics.
COMPLETE SET (31)................. 8.00 2.40

1998 LSU Tigers

These 16 standard-size cards feature on their fronts posed color player photos of the 1998 LSU Tigers. The cards' have purple borders with lines that run horizontal across the middle of the card, and carry the players name at the top of the photo and the team name in the middle. Brad Cresse's first card is included in this set.
COMPLETE SET (16)............... 25.00 7.50

1998 Lynchburg Hillcats Q-Cards

This 29-card set of the Lynchburg Hillcats Minor League team was produced by Blueline Communications and features color player photos in a green-and-yellow border. The backs carry player information and career statistics.
COMPLETE SET (29)................. 8.00 2.40

1998 Macon Braves Multi-Ad

This 29-card set of the Macon Braves Minor League team was produced by Multi-Ad Sports and features color player photos. The backs carry player information and career statistics. An early card of Marcus Giles highlights this set.
COMPLETE SET (29)............... 25.00 7.50

1998 Madison Black Wolf Multi-Ad

This 25-card set of the Madison Black Wolf, an Independent Minor League team, was produced by Multi-Ad Sports and features color player photos in a blue-and-black border. The backs carry player information and career statistics.
COMPLETE SET (25)................. 8.00 2.40

1998 Martinsville Phillies Grandstand

This 29-card set of the Martinsville Phillies Minor League team was produced by Grandstand and features color player photos with a red border on one side. The backs carry player information and career statistics. The cards are unnumbered and checklisted below in alphabetical order.
COMPLETE SET (29............... 10.00 3.00

1998 Memphis Redbirds Grandstand

This 25-card set of the Memphis Redbirds Minor League team was produced by Grandstand and features color player photos. The backs carry player information and career statistics. The cards are unnumbered and checklisted below in alphabetical order.
COMPLETE SET (25)................. 8.00 2.40

1998 Memphis Redbirds Update Team Issue

One card set, featuring phenom J.D. Drew
COMPLETE SET 15.00 6.00

1998 Michigan Battle Cats Multi-Ad

This 30-card set of the Michigan Battle Cats Minor League team was produced by Grandstand and features color player photos with diagonal top and bottom green borders. The backs carry player information and career statistics.
COMPLETE SET (30)............... 25.00 7.50

1998 Midland Angels Grandstand

This 28-card set of the Midland Angels Minor League team was produced by Grandstand and features color player photos with a red border on one side. The backs carry player information and career statistics. The cards are unnumbered and checklisted below in alphabetical order. The key cards in the set are Troy Glaus and Ramon Ortiz.
COMPLETE SET (28)............... 30.00 9.00

1998 Midland Angels OHP

This 28-card set of the Midland Angels Minor League team was produced for the Leukemia Society of America and sponsored by Panther Canyon Oil and Gas. The fronts feature 3 1/2" by 5" posed color player photos printed on cards measuring approximately 5 1/2" by 5". The backs are blank. The cards are unnumbered and checklisted below in alphabetical order. Troy Glaus is the key player in this set.
COMPLETE SET (28)............ 120.00 36.00

1998 Midwest League Prospects Multi-Ad

This 28-card set of the Midwest Minor League Top Prospects was produced by Multi-Ad Sports and features color player photos with an oval frame-style border. The backs carry player information and career statistics. Among the prospects in this set is Rick Ankiel.
COMPLETE SET (28)............... 18.00 5.50

1998 Mobile Bay Bears Southern League Champions Grandstand

This 25-card set of the 1998 Southern League Champions, the Mobile Bay Bears, was produced by Grandstand and features color player photos with the set name printed in the transparent right border. The backs carry player information and 1998 statistics. The cards are unnumbered and checklisted below in alphabetical order.
COMPLETE SET (25)............... 12.00 3.60

1998 Mobile Bay Bears Team Issue

This 31-card set of the Mobile Bay Bears Minor League team features color player photos with white outer, blue middle, and thin red inner borders. The backs carry player information and career statistics. The cards are unnumbered and checklisted below in alphabetical order.
COMPLETE SET (31)............... 10.00 3.00

1998 Modesto A's Grandstand

This 30-card set of the Modesto A's Minor League team was produced by Grandstand and features color player photos in a white border. The backs carry player information and career statistics. The cards are unnumbered and checklisted below in alphabetical order. Cards of Tim Hudson and Adam Piatt highlight this set.
COMPLETE SET (30)............... 25.00 7.50

1998 Nashville Sounds Team Issue

This 33-card set of the Nashville Sounds Minor League team features borderless color player photos. The backs carry player information and career statistics. A limited number of this set was produced and sequentially numbered. The cards are unnumbered and checklisted below in alphabetical order. An early card of Kris Benson highlights this set.
COMPLETE SET (33)............... 20.00 6.00

1998 Nashville Sounds Team Issue Stadium Set

This 31-card set of the Nashville Sounds Minor League team features borderless color player photos. The backs carry player information and career statistics. The cards are unnumbered and checklisted below in alphabetical order. The key player in this set is Kris Benson.
COMPLETE SET (31)............... 25.00 7.50

1998 New Britain Rock Cats Multi-Ad

This 27-card set of the New Britain Rock Cats Minor League team was produced by Multi-Ad Sports and features color player photos with red borders. The backs carry player information and career statistics.
COMPLETE SET (27)............... 15.00 4.50

1998 New Haven Ravens Maritime Aquarium

This 31-card set of the New Haven Ravens Minor League team was produced by Multi-Ad Sports and sponsored by the Maritime Aquarium. The fronts feature color player photos with a ball lace facsimile border on one side. The backs carry player information and career statistics.
COMPLETE SET (31)................. 8.00 2.40

1998 New Haven Ravens Multi-Ad

This 31-card set of the New Haven Ravens Minor League team was produced by Multi-Ad Sports and features color player photos with a ball lace facsimile border on one side. The backs carry player information and career statistics.
COMPLETE SET (31)................. 8.00 2.40

1998 New Jersey Cardinals Multi-Ad

This 32-card set of lthe New Jersey Cardinals Minor League team was produced by Multi-Ad Sports and features color player photos in black-and-white borders. The backs carry player information and career statistics. (There is no card number 24.)
COMPLETE SET (32)................ 10.00 3.00

1998 New Orleans Zephyrs Multi-Ad

This 28-card set of the New Haven Ravens Minor League team was produced by Multi-Ad Sports and features color player photos with blue borders on two sides. The backs carry player information and career statistics.
COMPLETE SET (28).................. 8.00 2.40

1998 Norfolk Tides Police/Fox33

This 30-card set of the Norfolk Tides Minor League team was produced by Blueline Communications and sponsored by Fox 33 Kids Club and Chartway Federal Credit Union. The fronts feature color player photos in blue borders. The backs carry player information and career statistics as well as a safety message. The cards are unnumbered and checklisted below in alphabetical order.
COMPLETE SET (30).................. 8.00 2.40

1998 Norfolk Tides Q-Cards

This 36-card set of the Norfolk Tides Minor League team was produced by Blueline Communications and features borderless color player photos. The backs carry player information and career statistics.
COMPLETE SET (36)................ 10.00 3.00

1998 Norwich Navigators Q-Cards

This 30-card set of the Norwich Navigators Minor League team was produced by Blueline Communications and features color player photos with black outer and thin yellow inner borders. The backs carry player information and career statistics.
COMPLETE SET (30).................. 8.00 2.40

1998 Odgen Raptors Team Issue

COMPLETE SET 8.00 2.40

1998 Oklahoma Redhawks Multi-Ad

This 30-card set of the Oklahoma Redhawks Minor League team was produced by Multi-Ad Sports and features color player photos with a ball lace facsimile border on one side. The backs carry player information and career statistics.
COMPLETE SET (30).................. 8.00 2.40

1998 Omaha Royals Multi-Ad

This 30-card set of the Omaha Royals Minor League team was produced by Multi-Ad Sports and features color player photos with a ball lace facsimile border on one side. The backs carry player information and career statistics.
COMPLETE SET (30).................. 8.00 2.40

1998 Oneonta Yankees Grandstand

This 32-card set of the Oneonta Yankees Minor League team was produced by Grandstand and features color player photos. The backs carry player information and career statistics. The cards are unnumbered and checklisted below in alphabetical order.
COMPLETE SET (32).................. 8.00 2.40

1998 Orlando Rays Multi-Ad

This 29-card set of the Orlando Rays Minor League team was produced by Multi-Ad Sports and features color player photos. The backs carry player information and career statistics.
COMPLETE SET (29).................. 8.00 2.40

1998 Pawtucket Red Sox Q-Cards

This 30-card set of the Pawtucket Red Sox Minor League team was produced by Blueline Communications and features color player photos with gray inner and navy outer borders. The backs carry player information and career statistics.
COMPLETE SET (30)................ 10.00 3.00

1998 Peoria Chiefs Multi-Ad

This 30-card set of the Peoria Chiefs Minor League team was produced by Multi-Ad Sports and features color player photos. The backs

carry player information and career statistics. Rick Ankiel is in this set.
COMPLETE SET (30)................ 50.00 15.00

1998 Piedmont Boll Weevils Multi-Ad

This 29-card set of the Piedmont Boll Weevils Minor League team was produced by Multi-Ad Sports and features color player photos with blue borders on two sides. The backs carry player information and career statistics.
COMPLETE SET (29)................ 15.00 4.50

1998 Pittsfield Mets Multi-Ad

This 34-card set of the New Haven Ravens Minor League team was produced by Multi-Ad Sports and features color player photos with blue borders. The backs carry player information and career statistics.
COMPLETE SET (34).................. 8.00 2.40

1998 Portland Rockies Grandstand

This 30-card set of the Portland Rockies was produced by Grandstand and features color player photos. The backs carry player information and career statistics. The cards are unnumbered and checklisted below in alphabetical order. Juan Pierre is the key player in this set.
COMPLETE SET (30)................ 15.00 4.50

1998 Portland Sea Dogs 5th Anniversary Q-Cards

This 36-card set of the Portland Sea Dogs was produced by Blueline Communications and features color player photos. The backs carry player information and career statistics.
COMPLETE SET (36)................ 10.00 3.00

1998 Portland Sea Dogs Q-Cards

This 30-card set of the Portland Sea Dogs Minor League team was produced by Blueline Communications and features borderless color player photos. The backs carry player information and career statistics.
COMPLETE SET (30).................. 8.00 2.40

1998 Prince William Cannons Anniversary Set Multi-Ad

This 30-card set of the Prince William Cannons Minor League team was produced by Multi-Ad Sports and features color player photos with black outer and thin white inner borders. The backs carry player information and career statistics. Magglio Ordonez is the best player in this set.
COMPLETE SET (30)................ 15.00 4.50

1998 Prince William Cannons Q-Cards

This 30-card set of the Prince William Cannons Minor League team was produced by Blueline Communications and features color player photos with gray-and-purple borders. The backs carry player information and career statistics. Rick Ankiel is the key player in this set.
COMPLETE SET (30)................ 12.00 7.50

1998 Princeton Devil Rays Q-Cards

This 30-card set of the Princeton Devil Rays Minor League team was produced by Blueline Communications and was sponsored by Princeton Community Hospital. The fronts feature color player photos with a purple border. The backs carry player information and career statistics.
COMPLETE SET (30)................ 10.00 3.00

1998 Quad City River Bandits Grandstand

This 30-card set of the Quad City River Bandits Minor League team was produced by Grandstand and features color player photos in white borders. The backs carry player information and career statistics. The cards are unnumbered and checklisted below in alphabetical order.
COMPLETE SET (30)................ 10.00 3.00

1998 Rancho Cucamonga Quakes Grandstand

This 31-card set of the Rancho Cucamonga Quakes Minor League team was produced by Grandstand and features borderless color player photos. The backs carry player information and career statistics. The cards are unnumbered and checklisted below in alphabetical order.
COMPLETE SET (31)................ 10.00 3.00

1998 Rancho Cucamonga Quakes GTE

This 31-card set of the Rancho Cucamonga Quakes Minor League team was produced by Multi-Ad Sports and sponsored by GTE Superpages Interactive Services. The fronts feature borderless color player photos. The backs carry player information and career statistics. This set was a Stadium giveaway. The cards are unnumbered and checklisted below in alphabetical order.
COMPLETE SET (31)................ 15.00 4.50

1998 Reading Phillies Multi-Ad

This 28-card set of the Reading Phillies Minor League team was produced by Multi-Ad Sports and features color player photos. The backs carry player information and career statistics. Only 2,000 of this set were made.
COMPLETE SET(28)................ 10.00 3.00

1998 Reading Phillies Update Multi-Ad

This 30-card set of the Reading Phillies Minor League team was an updated version and was produced by Multi-Ad Sports. The fronts feature color player photos while the backs carry player information and career statistics. Only 1,000 of this set were made.
COMPLETE SET (30)................ 10.00 3.00

1998 Richmond Braves Q-Cards

This 30-card set of the Richmond Braves Minor League team was produced by Blueline Communications and features color player photos with aqua borders. The backs carry player information and career statistics.
COMPLETE SET (30).................. 8.00 2.40

1998 Rochester Red Wings Q-Cards

This 30-card set of the Rochester Red Wings Minor League team was produced by Blueline Communications and features color player photos with yellow-and-red borders. The backs carry player information and career statistics.
COMPLETE SET (30)................ 10.00 3.00

1998 Rockford Cubbies Multi-Ad

This 30-card set of the Rockford Cubbies Minor League team was produced by Multi-Ad Sports and features color player photos with a ball-laces facsimile border on one side. The backs carry player information and career statistics. The cards are unnumbered and checklisted below in alphabetical order. An early card of Jon Garland highlights this set.
COMPLETE SET (30)................ 15.00 4.50

1998 Rockford Cubbies Team Issue

This 30-card set of the Rockford Cubbies Minor League team was printed by Rockford Litho Center and features color player photos. The backs carry player information and career statistics. The cards are unnumbered and checklisted below in alphabetical order. The key player in this set is Jon Garland.
COMPLETE SET (30)................ 15.00 4.50

1998 Salem Avalanche Choice

This 30-card set of the Salem Avalanche Choice Minor League team was produced by Choice Marketing and features borderless color player photos. The backs carry player information and career statistics.
COMPLETE SET (30).................. 8.00 2.40

1998 Salem-Keizer Volcanoes Grandstand

This 36-card set of the Salem-Keizer Volcanoes Minor League team was produced by Grandstand and features color player photos. The backs carry player information and career statistics. The cards are unnumbered and checklisted below in alphabetical order. Tony Torcato's first minor league team set card is included in this set.
COMPLETE SET (36)................ 12.00 3.60

1998 Salt Lake Buzz OSP

This 30-card set of the Salt Lake Buzz Minor League team was produced by OSP Sports and features color player photos with blue borders on two sides. The backs carry player information and career statistics.
COMPLETE SET (30)................ 10.00 3.00

1998 San Antonio Missions Grandstand

This 30-card set of the San Antonio Missions Minor League team was produced by Grandstand and features color player photos. The backs carry player information and career statistics.The cards are unnumbered and checklisted below in alphabetical order. Early cards of Adrian Beltre and Peter Bergeron highlight this set.
COMPLETE SET (30)................ 10.00 3.00

1998 San Antonio Missions Multi-Ad

This 30-card set of the San Antonio Missions Minor League team was produced by Multi-Ad Sports and features color player photos. The backs carry player information and career statistics.
COMPLETE SET (30).................. 8.00 2.40

1998 San Bernardino Stampede Grandstand

This 32-card set of the San Bernardino Stampede Minor League Team was produced by Grandstand and features color player photos. The backs carry player information and career statistics. The cards are unnumbered and checklisted below in alphabetical order.
COMPLETE SET (32).................. 8.00 2.40

1998 San Bernardino Stampede Team Issue Strips

This 29-card set of the San Bernardino Stampede Minor League Team was distributed in seven five-card perforated strips and was sponsored by Radio Station KOLA 99.9 and Round Table Pizza. Each strip featured four player cards and one sponsor coupon card. The fronts display color action player photos. The backs carry player information and career statistics. The cards are unnumbered and checklisted below in alphabetical order.
COMPLETE SET (29)................ 25.00 7.50

1998 San Jose Giants Q-Cards

This 30-card set of the San Jose Giants Minor League team was produced by Blueline Communications and features color player photos with black outer and orange inner borders. The backs carry player information and career statistics.
COMPLETE SET (30).................. 8.00 2.40

1998 Savannah Sand Gnats Multi-Ad

This 30-card set of the Savannah Sand Gnats Minor League team was produced by Multi-Ad Sports and features color player photos with black-and-burgundy borders. The backs carry player information and career statistics.
COMPLETE SET (30)................ 10.00 3.00

1998 Scranton/Wilkes-Barre Red Barons 10th Anniversary Team Issue

This 20-card set of the Scranton/Wilkes-Barre Red Barons Minor League team was produced by the Team to commemorate its 10th anniversary. The fronts freature color player photos with a blue border on two sides. The backs carry player information and career statistics. The cards are unnumbered and checklisted below in alphabetical order.
COMPLETE SET (20).................. 8.00 2.40

1998 Scranton/Wilkes-Barre Red Barons Q-Cards

This 30-card set of the Scranton/Wilkes-Barre Red Barons Minor League team was produced by Blueline Communications and features color player photos with black outer and thin red inner borders. The backs carry player information and career statistics.
COMPLETE SET (30)................ 10.00 3.00

1998 Shreveport Captains Multi-Ad

This 29-card set of the Shreveport Captains Minor League team was produced by Multi-Ad Sports and features color player photos with black-and-red borders. The backs carry player information and career statistics.
COMPLETE SET (29).................. 8.00 2.40

1998 Shreveport Captains WK SportsCare

This 30-card set of the Shreveport Captains Minor League team was produced by Multi-Ad Sports and sponsored by Willis-Knighton SportsCare. The fronts features color player photos with black-and-red borders. The backs carry player information and career statistics.
COMPLETE SET (30).................. 8.00 2.40

1998 Sioux City Explorers Grandstand

COMPLETE SET (25).................. 8.00 2.40

1998 South Atlantic League Prospects Multi-Ad

This 30-card set of the South Atlantic League Minor League Teams' top prospects for the Major League was produced by Multi-Ad Sports and features posed color player photos. The backs carry player information and career statistics.
COMPLETE SET (30)................ 10.00 3.00

1998 South Bend Silver Hawks Multi-Ad

This 27-card set of the South Bend Silver Hawks Minor League team was produced by Multi-Ad Sports and features color player photos. The backs carry player information and career statistics. Abraham Nunez first team set card is in this set.
COMPLETE SET (27)................ 10.00 3.00

1998 Southern League Top Prospects Grandstand

This 32-card set of the Southern League Minor League Teams' Top Prospects for the Major League was produced by Grandstand and features color player photos. The backs carry player information and career statistics. Eric Chavez and Carlos Lee are the key players in this set.
COMPLETE SET (32)................ 12.00 3.60

1998 Southern Oregon Timberjacks Grandstand

This 33-card set of lthe Southern Oregon Timberjacks Minor League team was produced by Grandstand and features borderless color player photos. The backs carry player information and career statistics. The cards are unnumbered and checklisted below in alphabetical order. Jason Hart's first team set card is included in this set.
COMPLETE SET (33)................ 15.00 4.50

1998 Spokane Indians Grandstand

This 33-card set of the Spokane Indians Minor League team was produced by Grandstand and features color player photos. The backs carry player information and career statistics. The cards are unnumbered and checklisted below in alphabetical order.
COMPLETE SET (33).................. 8.00 2.40

1998 St. Catharines Stompers Multi-Ad

This 31-card set of the St. Catharines Stompers Minor League team was produced by Multi-Ad Sports and features color player photos. The backs carry player information and career statistics.
COMPLETE SET (31).................. 8.00 2.40

1998 St. Lucie Mets Multi-Ad

This 30-card set of the St. Lucie Mets Minor League team was produced by Multi-Ad Sports and features color player photos with blue borders. The backs carry player information and career statistics.
COMPLETE SET (30)................ 10.00 3.00

1998 St. Paul Saints Team Issue

This 32-card set of the St. Paul Saints, a Northern League minor league team, features borderless color player photos. The black-and-white backs carry another player photo, a small head shot, player information and career statistics. The cards are unnumbered and checklisted below in alphabetical order. J.D. Drew has an early card in this set.
COMPLETE SET (32)................ 20.00 6.00

1998 St. Petersburg Devil Rays Multi-Ad

This 30-card set of the St. Petersburg Devil Rays Minor League team was produced by Multi-Ad Sports and features color player photos. The backs carry player information and career statistics.
COMPLETE SET (30).................. 8.00 2.40

1998 Stockton Ports Grandstand

This 30-card set of the Stockton Ports Minor League team was produced by Grandstand and features color player photos in white borders. The backs carry player information and career statistics. The cards are unnumbered and checklisted below in alphabetical order.
COMPLETE SET (30)................ 10.00 3.00

1998 Stockton Ports Update Grandstand

This six-card set features additional players added to the 1998 Stockton Ports Grandstand set.
COMPLETE SET (6)................... 10.00 3.00

1998 Syracuse Skychiefs Grandstand

This 31-card set of the Syracuse Skychiefs Minor League team was produced by Grandstand and features color player photos in white borders. The backs carry player information and career statistics. The cards are unnumbered and checklisted below in alphabetical order. Carlos Delgado is the key player in this set.
COMPLETE SET (31)................ 10.00 3.00

1998 Tacoma Rainiers Q-Cards

This 30-card set of the Tacoma Rainiers Minor League team was produced by Blueline Communications and features color player photos in blue borders. The backs carry player

information and career statistics.
COMPLETE SET (30) 10.00 3.00

1998 Tampa Yankees Multi-Ad

This 30-card set of the Tampa Yankees Minor League team was produced by Multi-Ad Sports and features color player photos in gray-and-blue borders. The backs carry player information and career statistics. An early card of Nick Johnson highlights this set.
COMPLETE SET (30) 25.00 7.50

1998 Tennessee Volunteers Krystal Multi-Ad

COMPLETE SET (18) 8.00 2.40

1998 Texas League Top Prospects Grandstand

This 30-card set of the Texas League Minor Leagues' Top Prospects was produced by Grandstand and features color player photos in white borders. The backs carry player information and career statistics. The cards are unnumbered and checklisted below in alphabetical order. Troy Glaus is the key player in this set.
COMPLETE SET (30) 20.00 6.00

1998 Toledo Mud Hens Q-Cards

This 33-card set of the Toledo Mud Hens Minor League team was produced by Blueline Communications and features color action player photos with the team name printed in a marbleized blue bar at the top. The backs carry player information and career statistics.
COMPLETE SET (33) 10.00 3.00

1998 Trenton Thunder Multi-Ad

This 29-card set of the Trenton Thunder was produced by Multi-Ad and features color player photos with a facsimile ball-laces border on one side. The backs carry player information and career statistics. (There is no card number 15.)
COMPLETE SET (29) 10.00 3.00

1998 Tucson Sidewinders Multi-Ad

This 29-card set of the Tucson Sidewinders Minor League team was produced by Multi-Ad Sports and features color player photos in black-and-tan borders. The backs carry player information and career statistics.
COMPLETE SET (29) 8.00 2.40

1998 Tulsa Drillers Team Issue

This 27-card set of the Tulsa Drillers was sponsored by FM radio station KICK99 and the Oklahoma Highway Safety Office. The fronts feature borderless color player photos. The backs carry player information and career statistics. An early card of Ruben Mateo is the key to this set.
COMPLETE SET (27) 15.00 4.50

1998 Tulsa Drillers Texas League Champions Team Issue

This 32-card set of the 1998 Texas League Champions, the Tulsa Drillers, features color player portraits outlined with a thin red line. The backs carry a black-and-white photo of the Championship Trophy. The cards are unnumbered and checklisted below in alphabetical order. An early card of Ruben Mateo highlights this set.
COMPLETE SET (32) 20.00 6.00

1998 Vancouver Canadians Grandstand

This 30-card set of the Vancouver Canadians Minor League team was produced by Grandstand and features color player portraits in white borders. The backs carry player information and career statistics. The cards are unnumbered and checklisted below in alphabetical order. An early card of Troy Glaus is the key to this set.
COMPLETE SET (30) 50.00 15.00

1998 Vancouver Canadians Grandstand w/Glaus Auto

According to dealers, Troy Glaus was supposed to sign 100 cards for this promotion but only signed 50 cards.
COMPLETE SET (31) 60.00 18.00

1998 Vermont Expos OSP

This 35-card set of the Vermont Expos Minor League team was produced by OSP Sports and features color player photos with blue borders on two sides. The backs carry player information and career statistics. Donnie Bridges first team set card is the highlight of this set.
COMPLETE SET (35) 10.00 3.00

1998 Vero Beach Dodgers Multi-Ad

This 31-card set of the Vero Beach Dodgers Minor League team was produced by Multi-Ad Sports and features color player photos with blue borders. The backs carry player information and career statistics.
COMPLETE SET (31) 10.00 3.00

1998 Visalia Oaks Grandstand

This 31-card set of the Visalia Oaks Minor League team was produced by Grandstand and features borderless color player photos. The backs carry player information and career statistics. The cards are unnumbered and checklisted below in alphabetical order.
COMPLETE SET (31) 10.00 3.00

1998 Watertown Indians Team Issue

This 35-card set of the Watertown Indians Minor League team was sponosred by Time Warner Cable and printed by QM Printing of Phoenix NY. The fronts feature color player photos with white borders. The backs carry player information and career statistics. The cards are unnumbered and checklisted below in alphabetical order.
COMPLETE SET (35) 10.00 3.00

1998 West Michigan Whitecaps Multi-Ad

This 30-card set of the West Michigan Whitecaps Minor League team was produced by Multi-Ad Sports and features color player photos with a one-sided blue border. The backs carry player information and career statistics. The cards are unnumbered and checklisted below in alphabetical order.
COMPLETE SET (30) 8.00 2.40

1998 West Tennessee Diamond Jaxx Multi-Ad

This 30-card set of the West Tennessee Diamond Jaxx Minor League team was produced by Multi-Ad Sports and features posed color player photos. The backs carry player information and career statistics.
COMPLETE SET (30) 8.00 2.40

1998 Wichita Wranglers Multi-Ad

This 30-card set of the Wichita Wranglers Minor League team was produced by Multi-Ad Sports and features color player photos with a facsimile ball-laces border on one side. The backs carry player information and career statistics. An early card of Mark Quinn highlights this set.
COMPLETE SET (30) 10.00 3.00

1998 Williamsport Cubs Jeremi Gonzalez Team Issue

This one-card set of Jeremi Gonzalez of the Williamsport Cubs Minor League Team was produced by Sport Shots and features a borderless action color player photos. The back displays player information and career statistics.
COMPLETE SET (1) 5.00 2.20

1998 Williamsport Cubs Kerry Wood Phone Card Team Issue

This one-card limited edition prepaid phone card set of Kerry Woods of the 1995 Williamsport Cubs Minor League team measures approximately 2 1/8" by 3 3/8" and features a borderless color player photo. The back displays the card's worth of two minutes calling time with instructions on how to use the card which expires on 8/31/99. Only 1500 cards were produced and are sequentially numbered.
COMPLETE SET (1) 10.00 3.00

1998 Williamsport Cubs Kerry Wood Team Issue

This limited edition one-card set of Kerry Wood of the 1995 Williamsport Cubs Minor League Team was produced by Sport Shots and features a borderless action color player photos. The back displays player information and career statistics. Only 2000 cards were produced.
COMPLETE SET (1) 8.00 2.40

1998 Williamsport Cubs Multi-Ad

This 30-card set of the Williamsport Cubs Minor League team was produced by Multi-Ad Sports and features color player photos with a red border down one side. The backs carry player information and career statistics.
COMPLETE SET (30) 30.00 9.00

1998 Wilmington Blue Rocks Choice

This 30-card set of the Wilmington Blue Rocks Minor League team was produced by Choice Marketing and features borderless color action player photos. The backs carry player information and career statistics. The cards are unnumbered and checklisted below in alphabetical order.
COMPLETE SET (30) 10.00 3.00

1998 Winston-Salem Warthogs Q-Cards

This 30-card set of the Winston-Salem Warthogs Minor League team was produced by Blueline Communications and features color action player photos in a gray-and-red border. The black-and-white backs carry player information and career statistics. Joe Crede is the key to this set.
COMPLETE SET (30) 12.00 3.60

1998 Wisconsin Timber Rattlers Multi-Ad

This 30-card set of the Wisconsin Timber Rattlers Minor League team was produced by Multi-Ad Sports and features color action player photos with a dark maroon bar down one side. The backs carry player information and career statistics. Ryan Anderson's first team set is the highlight of this set.
COMPLETE SET (30) 25.00 7.50

1998 Yakima Bears Grandstand

This 34-card set of the Yakima Bears Minor League team was produced by Grandstand and features color player photos in white borders. The backs carry player information. The cards are unnumbered and checklisted below in alphabetical order.
COMPLETE SET (34) 8.00 2.40

1999 Akron Aeros Multi-Ad

COMPLETE SET (30) 8.00 2.40

1999 Albuquerque Dukes Grandstand

COMPLETE SET (30) 10.00 3.00

1999 Altoona Curve Grandstand

COMPLETE SET (31) 10.00 3.00

1999 Appalachian League Prospects Multi-Ad

Among the prospects in this set are Josh Hamilton and Jon Rauch.
COMPLETE SET 20.00 6.00

1999 Arizona Fall League Prospects

This 30 card standard-size set features the leading prospects who participated in the 1999 Arizona Fall League. Important prospects in this set include Pat Burrell and Corey Patterson.
COMPLETE SET (30) 20.00 6.00

1999 Arkansas Travelers Multi-Ad

This 30-card set of the Arkansas Travelers Minor League team was produced by Multi-Ad Sports and features color player photos with a white border. The backs carry player information and career statistics. An early card of Rick Ankiel highlights this set.
COMPLETE SET (30) 10.00 3.00

1999 Asheville Tourists Multi-Ad

This 30-card set of the Asheville Tourists Minor League team was produced by Multi-Ad and features color player photos with a blue border on the bottom. The backs carry player information and career statistics. An early card of Juan Pierre highlights this set.
COMPLETE SET (30) 15.00 4.50

1999 Asheville Tourists Update Grandstand

Juan Pierre is included in this set.
COMPLETE SET (10) 18.00 5.50

1999 Auburn Doubledays Grandstand

COMPLETE SET (33) 15.00 4.50

1999 Augusta Greenjackets Multi-Ad

This 30-card set of the Augusta Greenjackets Minor League team was produced by Multi-Ad Sports and features color player photos with a green border on one side which has the player name. The backs carry player information and career statistics.
COMPLETE SET (30) 10.00 3.00

1999 Bakersfield Blaze Team Issue

COMPLETE SET 10.00 3.00

1999 Batavia Muckdogs Team Issue

COMPLETE SET (41) 25.00 7.50

1999 Beloit Snappers Multi-Ad

Nick Neugebauer is the key player in this set.
COMPLETE SET 12.00 3.60

1999 Billings Mustangs Grandstand

COMPLETE SET (32) 12.00 3.60

1999 Binghamton Mets Blueline

COMPLETE SET(30) 10.00 3.00

1999 Binghamton Mets Press and Sun-Bulletin

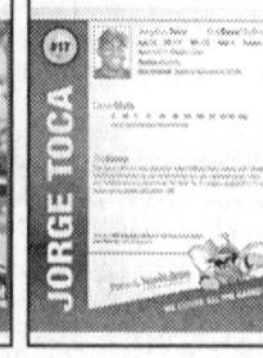

This 12-card set features members of the Binghamton Mets (a double-A affiliate of the New York Mets). The jumbo sized cards (approximately 8 1/2" by 11") were printed on thin cardboard stock and each feature a full color photo on front with the player's name and uniform number boldly running down the left side, framed by a royal blue border. Card backs feature a color headshot, full statistics and skill breakdowns called "The Scoop". The cards were sponsored by The Press and Sun-Bulletin newspaper. The set is skip-numbered due to the fact that card numbering is based upon player jerseys. Noteworthy players include Cuban slugger Jorge Toca and outfield prospect Jason Tyner.
COMPLETE SET (11) 50.00 15.00

1999 Birmingham Barons Grandstand

An early card of Joe Crede highlights this set.
COMPLETE SET (30) 10.00 3.00

1999 Bluefield Orioles Grandstand

COMPLETE SET (30) 10.00 3.00

1999 Boise Hawks Grandstand

COMPLETE SET (34) 20.00 6.00

1999 Bowie Baysox Multi-Ad

COMPLETE SET 10.00 3.00

1999 Brevard County Manatees Multi-Ad

COMPLETE SET 8.00 2.40

1999 Bristol Sox Grandstand

Jon Rauch's first team set card is the key to this set.
COMPLETE SET (30) 15.00 4.50

1999 Bristol Sox Update Grandstand

COMPLETE SET 15.00 4.50

1999 Buffalo Bisons Blueline

COMPLETE SET (30) 10.00 3.00

1999 Burlington Bees Multi-Ad

This 34-card set of the Burlington Bees Minor League team was produced by Multi-Ad and features color player photos with a red lace border on the left side. The backs carry player information and career statistics.
COMPLETE SET 10.00 3.00

1999 Burlington Indians Grandstand

COMPLETE SET (32) 8.00 2.40

1999 Butte Copper Kings Grandstand

Fransisco Rodriguez is the key card in this set.
COMPLETE SET 30.00 9.00

1999 Cape Fear Crocs Team Issue

COMPLETE SET (30) 8.00 2.40

1999 Capital City Bombers Multi-Ad

Pat Strange's first team set card is the key to this set.
COMPLETE SET (30) 15.00 4.50

1999 Carolina League Prospects Choice

COMPLETE SET (30) 15.00 4.50

1999 Carolina Mudcats Team Issue

COMPLETE SET (31) 8.00 2.40

1999 Cedar Rapids Kernels Multi-Ad

COMPLETE SET (34) 8.00 2.40

1999 Charleston Alley Cats Multi-Ad

This 30-card set of the Charleston Alley Cats Minor League Team was produced by Multi-Ad Sports and features color player photos with black borders. The backs carry player information and career statistics.
COMPLETE SET (30) 8.00 2.40

1999 Charleston Riverdogs Multi-Ad

COMPLETE SET (32) 8.00 2.40

1999 Charlotte Knights Blueline

This 30-card set of the Charlotte Knights Minor League team was produced by Blueline Communications. The cards features color player photos with a grey border on one side. The backs carry player information and career statistics.
COMPLETE SET (30) 10.00 3.00

1999 Chattanooga Lookouts Grandstand

COMPLETE SET (30) 10.00 3.00

1999 Chico Heat Grandstand

COMPLETE SET 8.00 2.40

1999 Chillicothe Paints Grandstand

COMPLETE SET (26) 10.00 3.00

1999 Clearwater Phillies Multi-Ad

COMPLETE SET 10.00 3.00

1999 Clinton Lumber Kings Grandstand

COMPLETE SET (32) 10.00 3.00

1999 Colorado Springs Sky Sox Team Issue

COMPLETE SET (28) 5.00 1.50

1999 Columbus Clippers Blueline

COMPLETE SET (31) 10.00 3.00

1999 Columbus Reddstixx Multi-Ad

COMPLETE SET 8.00 2.40

1999 Danville Braves Grandstand

Wilson Betemit's first team set card highlights this set.
COMPLETE SET 18.00 5.50

1999 Daytona Cubs Roox

COMPLETE SET (30) 30.00 9.00

1999 Delmarva Shorebirds Multi-Ad

This 29-card set of the Delmarva Shorebirds Minor League team was produced by Multi-Ad Sports and features borderless color player photos. The backs carry player information and career statistics. The cards are unnumbered and checklisted below in alphabetical order.
COMPLETE SET (29) 10.00 3.00

1999 Dunedin Blue Jays Multi-Ad

This 30-card set of the Dunedin Blue Jays Minor League team was produced by Multi-Ad and features color player photos in a white

border. The backs carry player information and career statistics. In addition, approximately 1000 sets were issued in uncut sheet form.
COMPLETE SET (30)................ 30.00 9.00

1999 Dunedin Blue Jays Multi-Ad Uncut

COMPLETE SET (30)................ 30.00 9.00

1999 Durham Bulls Blueline

COMPLETE SET (30)................. 8.00 2.40

1999 El Paso Diablos Grandstand

COMPLETE SET (30)................ 20.00 6.00

1999 Elizabethton Twins Roox

COMPLETE SET (31)................ 25.00 7.50

1999 Erie Seawolves Multi-Ad

This 28-card set of the Erie Seawolves Minor League team was produced by Multi-Ad and features color player photos with a black and blue border at the bottom. The backs carry player information and career statistics.
COMPLETE SET (28)................ 10.00 3.00

1999 Eugene Emeralds Grandstand

Juan Cruz's first team set card highlights this set.
COMPLETE SET 15.00 4.50

1999 Everett Aquasox Grandstand

COMPLETE SET (31)................ 18.00 5.50

1999 Fort Myers Miracle Team Issue

This 31-card set of the Fort Myers Miracle Minor League team features color action player photos with a two-sided red-and-blue thin inner border and a purple outer border. The backs display a small black-and-white player head photo with player information and career statistics on a faint black-and-white player photo background. The cards are unnumbered and checklisted below in alphabetical order.
COMPLETE SET (31)................ 10.00 3.00

1999 Fort Wayne Wizards Multi-Ad

This set included Sean Burrough's first team set card.
COMPLETE SET (30)................ 25.00 7.50

1999 Frederick Keys Grandstand

This 28-card set of the 1999 Frederick Keys was produced by Grandstand and features color player portraits in a white border. The backs carry player information and career statistics. The cards are unnumbered and checklisted below in alphabetical order. There is also a separate version with a Pepsi logo on the front. These cards sell for 2X the regular cards.
COMPLETE SET (28)................ 10.00 3.00

1999 Fresno Grizzlies Grandstand

This 30-card set of the Fresno Grizzlies Minor League team was produced by Grandstand and features color action player photos with the team name printed in a transparent purple border on the right and the player's name and positon at the bottom. The backs carry player information and career statistics. The cards are unnumbered and checklisted below in alphabetical order.
COMPLETE SET (30)................ 10.00 3.00

1999 Great Falls Dodgers Multi-Ad

COMPLETE SET (30)................ 10.00 3.00

1999 Greensboro Bats Multi-Ad

COMPLETE SET (30)................ 10.00 3.00

1999 Greenville Braves Grandstand

COMPLETE SET 8.00 2.40

1999 Hagerstown Suns Multi-Ad

This 30-card set of the Hagerstown Suns Minor League team was produced my Multi-Ad Sports and features color players photos with a right blue border with their name. The backs carry player information and career statistics.
COMPLETE SET (30)................ 25.00 7.50

1999 Harrisburg Senators Multi-Ad

This 30-card set of the Harrisburg Senators Minor League team was produced by Multi-Ad Sports and features color player photos in a white border. The backs carry player information and career statistics.
COMPLETE SET (30)................ 10.00 3.00

1999 Helena Brewers Multi-Ad

COMPLETE SET (30)................... 8.00 2.40

1999 Hickory Crawdads Multi-Ad

This 30-card set of the Hickory Crawdads Minor League Team was produced by Multi-Ad and features color player photos in a white border. The backs carry player information and career statistics.
COMPLETE SET (30)................ 12.00 3.60

1999 Hickory Crawdads Update Multi-Ad

COMPLETE SET (30)................ 10.00 3.00

1999 High Desert Mavericks Grandstand

COMPLETE SET (27)................ 10.00 3.00

1999 Hudson Valley Renegades Grandstand

COMPLETE SET (32)................ 10.00 3.00

1999 Hudson Valley Renegades Update Autograph Grandstand

One card set, featuring Josh Hamilton's autograph.
COMPLETE SET (1)................... 40.00 12.00

1999 Hudson Valley Renegades Update Grandstand

This one card set was issued to take advantage of prospect Josh Hamilton's popularity.
COMPLETE SET 10.00 3.00

1999 Huntsville Stars Team Issue Burger King

COMPLETE SET (29)................... 8.00 2.40

1999 Indianapolis Indians Blueline

This 31-card set of the Indianapolis Indians Minor League team was produced by Blueline Communications and features color player photos in a grey border. The backs carry player information and career statistics.
COMPLETE SET (31)................... 8.00 2.40

1999 International League Prospects

COMPLETE SET (30)................ 10.00 3.00

1999 Iowa Cubs Multi-Ad

COMPLETE SET (30)................ 15.00 4.50

1999 Jackson Generals Multi-Ad

This 30-card set of the Jackson Generals Mult-Ad Minor League team was produced by Multi-Ad Sports and features color player photos with a red border on the bottom. The backs carry player information and career statistics.
COMPLETE SET (30)................... 8.00 2.40

1999 Jacksonville Suns Grandstand

COMPLETE SET (28)................ 10.00 3.00

1999 Johnson City Cardinals Team Issue

COMPLETE SET(35).................... 8.00 2.40

1999 Kane County Cougars Team Issue

These cards also come with a Connie's Pizza logo on the back. These cards sell for 4X the regular cards.
COMPLETE SET (30)................ 10.00 3.00

1999 Kinston Indians Choice

COMPLETE SET (30)................... 8.00 2.40

1999 Kissimmee Cobras Multi-Ad

COMPLETE SET (30)................ 12.00 3.60

1999 Knoxville Smokies Grandstand

COMPLETE SET (27)................... 8.00 2.40

1999 Lake Elsinore Land Sharks Grandstand

COMPLETE SET (33)................ 12.00 3.60

1999 Lake Elsinore Storm Grandstand

COMPLETE SET (30)................... 8.00 2.40

1999 Lakeland Tigers Multi-Ad

This 30 card standard-size set was issued by Multi-Ad and features members of the Lakeland Tigers team. This set is notable as it features an early card of Eric Munson
COMPLETE SET (30)................ 20.00 6.00

1999 Lancaster Jethawks Grandstand

COMPLETE SET (31)................ 12.00 3.60

1999 Lancaster Stealth Grandstand

COMPLETE SET 15.00 4.50

1999 Lansing Lugnuts Grandstand

This 31-card set features members of the Lansing Lugnuts. An early card of Corey Patterson is featured in this set
COMPLETE SET (31)................ 25.00 7.50

1999 Las Vegas Stars Multi-Ad

COMPLETE SET (30)................... 8.00 2.40

1999 Legends of Bowman

Given out one per selected home games at Bowman Field.
COMPLETE SET (5)................. 30.00 9.00

1999 Louisville Riverbats Blueline

COMPLETE SET (34)................... 8.00 2.40

1999 Lowell Spinners Multi-Ad

COMPLETE SET (32)................ 10.00 3.00

1999 Lynchburg Hillcats Choice

COMPLETE SET (30)................ 10.00 3.00

1999 Macon Braves 1 Multi-Ad

An early card of Rafael Furcal highlights this set.
COMPLETE SET (30)................ 20.00 6.00

1999 Mahoning Valley Scrappers Multi-Ad

COMPLETE SET (30)................ 25.00 7.50

1999 Martinsville Astros Grandstand

COMPLETE SET (30)................ 20.00 6.00

1999 Memphis Redbirds Team Issue

This 30-card set of the Memphis Redbirds features color player photos in a white border. The backs carry player information and career statistics. An early card of Rick Ankiel is the key to this set.
COMPLETE SET (30)................ 15.00 4.50

1999 Michigan Battlecats Multi-Ad

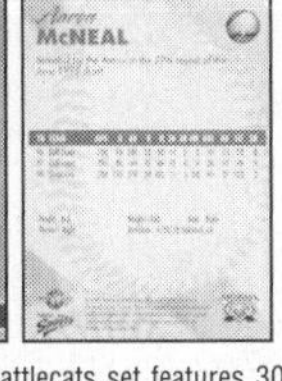

The 1999 Michigan Battlecats set features 30 cards of top Houston Astros prospects. Please note that cards 31-36 were issued in a special update set at the end of the year. It is rumored that card number 34 was missing from many of the update sets, and may be in shorter supply.
COMPLETE SET (30)................ 25.00 7.50

1999 Midland Rockhounds Grandstand

An early card of Tim Hudson is included in this set.
COMPLETE SET (30)................ 25.00 7.50

1999 Midland Rockhounds One Hour Photo

This 27-card set featuring members of the Midland Rockhounds (a affiliate of the Oakland A's). Each blank-backed, oversize card is printed on thin Kodak film stock and features a full color photo on front with the team logo and player name at the base. The set was sponsored by One Hour Photo though there's no mention of the company on the cards themselves. The set is skip-numbered due to the fact that card numbers are based on player jerseys. Three cards are unnumbered and run at the end of our checklist. Key cards include Mario Encarnacion and Adam Piatt.
COMPLETE SET 40.00 12.00

1999 Midwest League Prospects Multi-Ad

This 29-card set features color photos with red borders of the top player prospects from the teams in the Midwest Minor League. The backs carry player information and career statistics. Please note that early in 2000 an Update set was released that contained cards 30-35. These six cards were only available in the Update set. Among the key prospects in the basic set are Sean Burroughs, Austin Kearns and Corey Patterson. A card of Hee Seop Choi is included in the update set.
COMPLETE SET (29)................ 20.00 6.00

1999 Missoula Osprey Grandstand

COMPLETE SET (31)................ 15.00 4.50

1999 Mobile Baybears Team Issue

COMPLETE SET (32)................... 8.00 2.40

1999 Modesto A's Grandstand

This 30-card set of the Modesto A's Minor League team was produced by Grandstand and features color player photos in a white border. The backs carry player information and career statistics. The cards are unnumberd and checklisted below in alphabetical order.
COMPLETE SET (30)................ 15.00 4.50

1999 Myrtle Beach Pelicans Multi-Ad

COMPLETE SET (30)................ 25.00 7.50

1999 Nashville Sounds Team Issue

COMPLETE SET (30)................ 10.00 3.00

1999 New Britain Rock Cats Multi-Ad

COMPLETE SET (27)................ 10.00 3.00

1999 New Haven Ravens BlueLine

COMPLETE SET 20.00 6.00

1999 New Jersey Cardinals Multi-Ad

COMPLETE SET (32)................ 20.00 3.00

1999 New Jersey Cardinals Star-Ledger

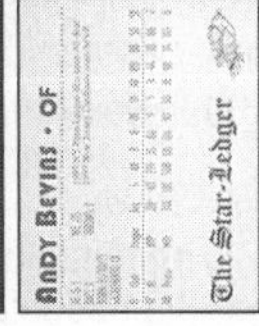

This six card set of the New Jersey Cardinals (a single A affiliate of the St.Louis Cardinals) was issued as an unperforated strip of standard-size (2 1/2" by 3 1/2") unnumbered cards and sponsored by The Star-Ledger newspaper. Each card features a full color posed photo surrounded a flat black and marbled red border. The cards are checklisted below in the order they appear on the strip.
COMPLETE SET (6).................... 5.00 1.50

1999 New Orleans Zephyrs Multi-Ad

This 28-card set of the New Orleans Zephyrs Minor League team was produced by Multi-Ad Sports and features color player photos with a blue and black border on the bottom. The backs carry player information and career statistics.
COMPLETE SET (28)................ 15.00 4.50

1999 Newark Bears Multi-Ad

COMPLETE SET (25)................... 8.00 2.40

1999 Norfolk Tides All Sport Blueline

Standard card design, sponsored by All Sport.
COMPLETE SET (35)................ 10.00 3.00

1999 Norfolk Tides Fox 33 Blueline

Issued in conjunction with Chartway Credit Union, Safety Set. Horizontal Design
COMPLETE SET (30)................ 10.00 3.00

1999 Northeastern University Carlos Pena

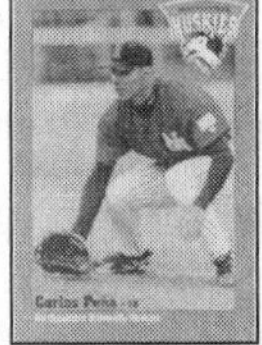

This one card set was given away at the FanFest in Boston in July, 1999. It features star prospect Carlos Pena and has a picture of Pena on the front and personal information on the back. Pena was a Northeastern University player before turning professional.
COMPLETE SET (1).................... 5.00 1.50

1999 Norwich Navigators Blueline

This 30-card set of the Norwich Navigators Minor League team was produced by Blueline Communications and features color player photos with a purple border on one side with the player's name. The backs carry player information and career statistics. Among the prosepects in this set are Nick Johnson and Alfonso Soriano.
COMPLETE SET (30)................ 30.00 9.00

1999 Ogden Raptors Team Issue

Cristian Guerrero and Olympic Hero Ben Sheets have their first minor league team set cards in this set.
COMPLETE SET (36)................ 20.00 6.00

1999 Oklahoma Redhawks Multi-Ad

This 30-card set of the Oklahoma Redhawks Minor League team was produced by Multi-Ad Sports and features oval-shaped color player photos with gold marbleized borders. The backs carry player information, career statistics, and a safety message.
COMPLETE SET (30)................ 15.00 4.50

1999 Omaha Golden Spikes Multi-Ad

COMPLETE SET (29)................ 10.00 3.00

1999 Orlando Rays Multi-Ad

This 30-card set of the Orlando Rays Minor League team was produced by Multi-Ad Sports and features borderless color player photos. The backs carry player information and career statistics.
COMPLETE SET (30)................ 15.00 4.50

1999 Pawtucket Red Sox BlueLine

COMPLETE SET (32)................ 15.00 4.50

1999 Pawtucket Red Sox Dunkin' Donuts

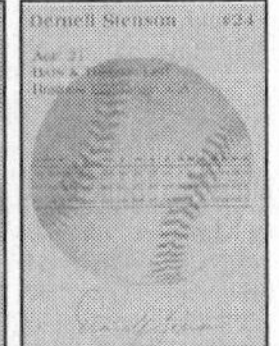

This 30-card set of the Pawtucket Red Sox (a triple-A affiliate of the Boston Red Sox) was issued as a perforated sheet of cards that folds out to poster-size. The cards were sponsored by Dunkin' Donuts (continuing a long-standing tradition) in addition to the Providence Journal. Jin Ho Cho, Tomokazu Ohka, Juan Pena and Dernell Stenson are the featured players. The set is skip-numbered because each card number is derived from the players jersey. Three cards are actually unnumbered as those

players did not have jersey numbers assigned to them at the time this set was printed.
COMPLETE SET (30)................ 30.00 9.00

1999 Peoria Chiefs Multi-Ad

This 30-card set of the Peoria Chiefs Minor League team was produced by Multi-Ad Sports and features color player photos with the player's name and position printed in a black bar on the right side. The backs carry a small black-and-white player head photo with player information and statistics.
COMPLETE SET (30)................ 12.00 3.60

1999 Piedmont Boll Weevils Multi-Ad

COMPLETE SET (30)................ 10.00 3.00

1999 Pittsfield Mets Multi-Ad

COMPLETE SET (30)................. 8.00 2.40

1999 Portland Sea Dogs Grandstand

COMPLETE SET (30)................ 20.00 6.00

1999 Potomac Cannons Choice

COMPLETE SET (30)................ 10.00 3.00

1999 Princeton Devil Rays Grandstand

Josh Hamilton's first team set card is part of this set.
COMPLETE SET (30)................ 30.00 12.00

1999 Princeton Devil Rays Update Grandstand

This 30 card update standard-size set was issued so cards of young phenom, Josh Hamilton could be included. Please note there are three different versions of Hamilton in this set. 1500 sets were produced.
COMPLETE SET (30)................ 15.00 6.00

1999 Pulaski Rangers Grandstand

Kevin Mench's first minor league team set card is included in this set.
COMPLETE SET (30)................ 15.00 4.50

1999 Quad City River Bandits Roox

COMPLETE SET (31)................ 15.00 4.50

1999 Rancho Cucamonga Quakes Grandstand

This 30-card set of the Rancho Cucamonga Quakes Minor League team features color player photos with a black-and-aqua two-side border. The backs carry player information and career statistics. The cards are unnumbered and checklisted below in alphabetical order. Sean Burroughs has an early card in this set.
COMPLETE SET (30)................ 8.00 2.40
COMPLETE SET (31)................ 25.00 7.50

1999 Reading Phillies Bonus Multi-Ad

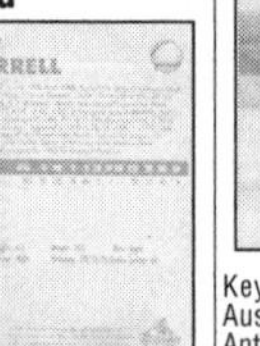

COMPLETE SET (1)................. 10.00 3.00

1999 Reading Phillies Multi-Ad

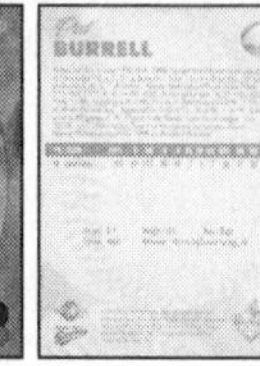

This 28-card set of the Reading Phillies Minor League team was produced by Multi-Ad Sports and features color player photos with a photo action shot and a red border. The backs carry player information and career statistics. Young slugger Pat Burrell is featured in this set. He has a card that is almost identical to this one issued in the 1999 Reading Phillies Multi-Ad Update set. The two cards feature identical fronts, but fortunately do differ in the design on the card back. This first card features highlights and awards information packed very tightly into the top half of the card back. The Update Burrell features the same information, but it's flowed out in larger text and takes up the bulk of the space on the card back.
COMPLETE SET (28)................ 20.00 6.00

1999 Reading Phillies Update Multi-Ad

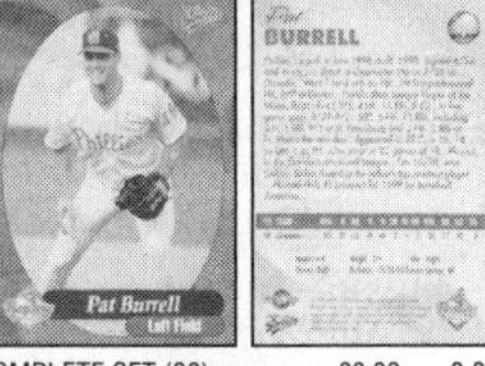

COMPLETE SET (28)................ 20.00 6.00

1999 Richmond Braves Blueline

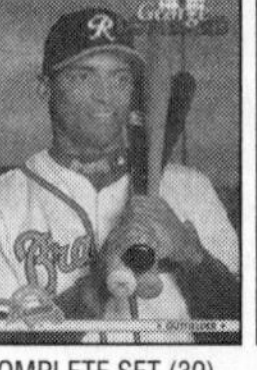
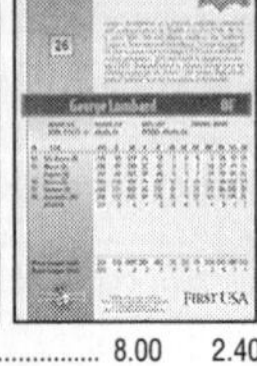

COMPLETE SET (30)................. 8.00 2.40

1999 Richmond Braves Richmond Camera

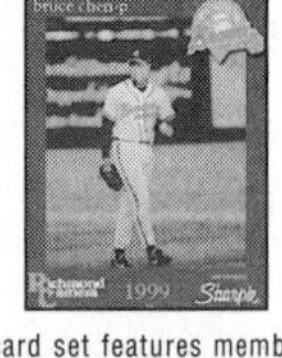

This 20-card set features members of the Richmond Braves, a AAA affiliate of the Atlanta Braves. The oversized cards (measuring approximately 4" x 5") are sponsored by Richmond Camera, Sharpie and Sanford and are actually printed on thin AGFA film stock rather than actual cardboard. Each card features a full color photo surrounded by a royal blue border. The card backs are blank except for the text AGFA running across diagonally.
COMPLETE SET (20)................ 40.00 12.00

1999 Rio Grande Valley Grandstand

COMPLETE SET (25)................. 8.00 2.40

1999 River City Rascals Team Issue

COMPLETE SET (36)................. 8.00 2.40

1999 Rochester Red Wings BlueLine

COMPLETE SET (30)................. 8.00 2.40

1999 Rockford Reds Roox

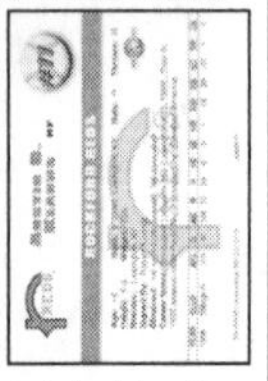

Key cards in this set include Adam Dunn, Austin Kearns and the first team set card of Antonio Perez.
COMPLETE SET (28)................ 25.00 7.50

1999 Salem Avalanche Choice

COMPLETE SET (30)................. 8.00 2.40

1999 Salem-Keizer Volcanoes Grandstand

Jerome Williams' first team set card is part of this set.
COMPLETE SET (36)................ 20.00 6.00

1999 Salt Lake Buzz Multi-Ad

COMPLETE SET (30)................. 8.00 2.40

1999 San Antonio Missions Grandstand

COMPLETE SET (31)................ 10.00 3.00

1999 San Bernardino Stampede County Sun

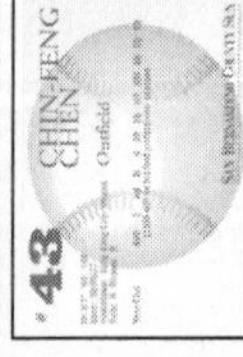

This 23-card oversized set was released by the County Sun newspaper in 1999. The set features all of the 1999 San Bernardino players and coaches. Each card measures approximately 4x6. Chin-Feng Chen has a card in this set.
COMPLETE SET (23)................ 25.00 7.50

1999 San Bernardino Stampede Grandstand

Chin-Feng Chen's first team set card is part of this set.
COMPLETE SET (31)................ 20.00 6.00

1999 San Jose Giants BlueLine

COMPLETE SET (30)................. 8.00 2.40

1999 Sarasota Red Sox Team Issue

COMPLETE SET (28)................ 10.00 3.00

1999 Savannah Sand Gnats Multi-Ad

COMPLETE SET (29)................ 10.00 3.00

1999 Schaumburg Flyers Team Issue

COMPLETE SET (30)................. 5.00 1.50

1999 Scranton/Wilkes-Barre Red Barons Blueline

This 32-card set of the 1999 Scranton/Wilkes-Barre Red Barons Minor League team was produced by Blueline Communications and features color player photos with red-and-white borders. The backs carry player information and career statistics.
COMPLETE SET (32)................. 8.00 2.40

1999 Shreveport Captains Multi-Ad

COMPLETE SET (28)................ 10.00 3.00

1999 Sioux City Explorers Grandstand

COMPLETE SET (30)................. 8.00 2.40

1999 Sioux Falls Canaries Multi-Ad

COMPLETE SET (24)................. 8.00 2.40

1999 Somerset Patriots Multi-Ad

COMPLETE SET (30)................. 8.00 2.40

1999 South Atlantic League Top Prospects Multi-Ad

An early card of Rafael Furcal highlights this set.
COMPLETE SET (30)................ 20.00 6.00

1999 South Bend Silver Hawks Multi-Ad

COMPLETE SET (31)................. 8.00 2.40

1999 Southern League Top Prospects Grandstand

This 31-card set of the Southern League Minor League Teams' Top Prospects for the Major League was produced by Grandstand and features color player photos, action and portraits, with white borders. The backs carry player information and career statistics. The cards are unnumbered and checklisted below in alphabetical order.
COMPLETE SET (31)................ 10.00 3.00

1999 Southern Oregon Timberjacks Grandstand

COMPLETE SET (29)................ 40.00 12.00

1999 Southern Oregon Timberjacks Update Grandstand

COMPLETE SET (8)................. 10.00 3.00

1999 Southern Oregon Timberjacks Wonder Bread

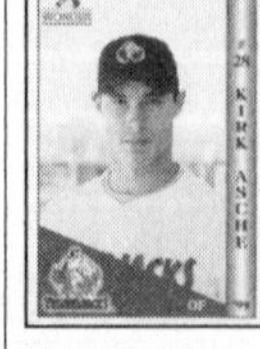
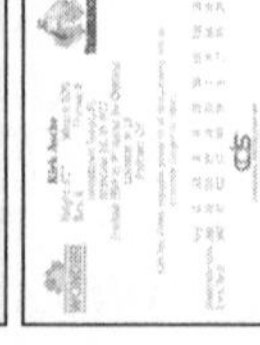

500 sets produced.
COMPLETE SET (10)................ 40.00 12.00

1999 Spokane Indians Grandstand

COMPLETE SET (35)................ 18.00 5.50

1999 St. Catherines Stompers Multi-Ad

COMPLETE SET (36)................. 8.00 2.40

1999 St. Lucie Mets Grandstand

COMPLETE SET (31)................ 20.00 6.00

1999 St. Paul Saints Team Issue

COMPLETE SET (32)................. 8.00 2.40

1999 St. Petersburg Devil Rays Multi-Ad

COMPLETE SET (30)................ 15.00 4.50

1999 Staten Island Yankees Multi-Ad

COMPLETE SET (33)................ 10.00 3.00

1999 Stockton Ports Grandstand

COMPLETE SET (30)................. 8.00 2.40

1999 Syracuse Skychiefs Blueline

This 28-card set of the Syracuse Skychiefs Minor League team was produced by Blueline Communications and features color player photos in a grey border. The backs carry player information and career statistics.
COMPLETE SET (28)................ 10.00 3.00

1999 Tacoma Rainiers Blue Line

COMPLETE SET (30)................. 8.00 2.40

1999 Tampa Yankees Multi-Ad

This 28-card set of the Tampa Yankees Minor League team was produced by Multi-Ad Sports and features color player photos with a red lace border on the left side. The backs carry player information and career statistics. Two sport star Drew Henson has a card in this set.
COMPLETE SET (28)................ 40.00 12.00

1999 Tampa Yankees Update Multi-Ad

An early card of Drew Henson highlights this set.
COMPLETE SET (30)................ 20.00 6.00

1999 Tennessee Volunteers Multi-Ad/Krystal

This 32-card set of the 1999 University of Tennessee's Baseball team was produced by Multi-Ad Sports, sponsored by Krystal Restaurants, and features color player photos with a ball lace facsimile border on one side. The backs carry player information and statistics.
COMPLETE SET (32)................ 10.00 3.00

1999 Texas League Prospects Grandstand

Among the prospects in this set are Rick Ankiel, Eric Gagne and Tim Hudson.
COMPLETE SET (32)................ 20.00 6.00

1999 Toledo Mudhens Grandstand

COMPLETE SET (32)................. 8.00 2.40

1999 Trenton Thunder Multi-Ad

COMPLETE SET (30)................ 20.00 6.00

1999 Tucson Sidewinders Multi-Ad

COMPLETE SET (29)................ 20.00 6.00

1999 Tulsa Drillers Team Issue

COMPLETE SET (30)................ 10.00 3.00

1999 Vancouver Canadians Grandstand

An early card of Tim Hudson highlights this set.
COMPLETE SET (30)................ 25.00 7.50

1999 Vermont Expos Grandstand

COMPLETE SET (35)................. 8.00 2.40

1999 Vero Beach Dodgers Multi-Ad

COMPLETE SET (30)................. 8.00 2.40

1999 Visalia Oaks Grandstand

Barry Zito's first team set card is a highlight of this set.
COMPLETE SET (27)................ 30.00 9.00

1999 Waterbury Spirit Warning Track

COMPLETE SET (25)................. 8.00 2.40

1999 West Michigan Whitecaps 5th Anniversary Multi-Ad

This 30-card set of the West Michigan Whitecaps celebrates the fifth anniversary of the team and was produced by Multi-Ad Sports. The fronts feature color photos of star players from the five years of the team's existence. The backs carry a small black-and-white head photo with the player's star year on the team under the photo, player information and career statistics. The cards are unnumbered and checklisted below in alphabetical order.
COMPLETE SET (30)................ 10.00 3.00

1999 West Michigan Whitecaps Multi-Ad

COMPLETE SET (30)................ 12.00 3.60

1999 West Michigan Whitecaps Update Multi-Ad

COMPLETE SET (12)................ 12.00 3.60

1999 West Tennessee Diamond Jaxx Grandstand

COMPLETE SET (30)................ 10.00 3.00

1999 Wichita Wranglers Choice

COMPLETE SET (30)................. 8.00 2.40

1999 Wichita Wranglers Choice Zoo

COMPLETE SET (30)................. 8.00 2.40

1999 Williamsport Crosscutters Multi-Ad

COMPLETE SET (34)................. 8.00 2.40

1999 Wilmington Blue Rocks Choice

This 30-card set of the Wilmington Blue Rocks Minor League team was produced by Choice Marketing and features color player photos with a blue border on one side and at the top. The backs carry player information and career statistics.
COMPLETE SET (30)................ 10.00 3.00

1999 Wilmington Blue Rocks In the Show Choice

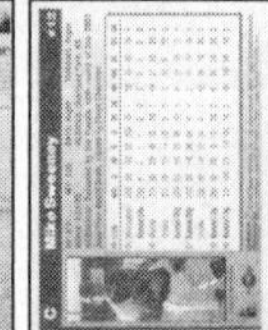

COMPLETE SET (41)................ 15.00 4.50

1999 Winnipeg Goldeyes Team Issue

COMPLETE SET (30)................. 8.00 2.40

1999 Winston-Salem Warthogs Choice

COMPLETE SET (30)................ 15.00 4.50

1999 Yakima Bears Grandstand

COMPLETE SET (32)................. 8.00 2.40

2000 Adirondack Lumberjacks Warning Track

COMPLETE SET (30)................. 8.00 2.40

2000 Akron Aeros Multi-Ad

This set includes early cards of Danys Baez and C.C. Sabathia.
COMPLETE SET (30)................ 15.00 4.50

2000 Albany-Colonie Diamond Dogs Warning Track

COMPLETE SET (30).................. 8.00 2.40

2000 Albuquerque Dukes Grandstand

COMPLETE SET (30)................ 10.00 3.00

2000 Alexandria Aces Team Issue

COMPLETE SET (24)................ 10.00 3.00

2000 Allentown Ambassadors Warning Track

COMPLETE SET (26).................. 8.00 2.40

2000 Altoona Curve Grandstand

COMPLETE SET (30)................ 10.00 3.00

2000 Appalachian League Top Prospect Grandstand

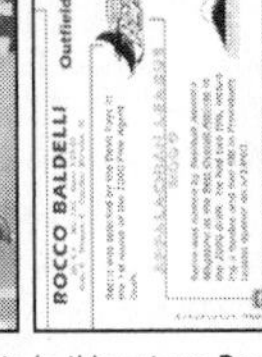

Among the prospects in this set are Rocco Baldelli, Shaun Boyd, Enrique Cruz and Corey Smith.
COMPLETE SET (30)................ 25.00 7.50

2000 Arizona Fall League Prospects

Among the prospects in this set are Joe Borchard, Chin-Feng Chen, Hee Seop Choi, Brad Cresse, Jason Hart and Kevin Mench.
COMPLETE SET (30)................ 20.00 6.00

2000 Arkansas Travelers Multi-Ad

An early card of Bud Smith is the key to this set.
COMPLETE SET (30)................ 10.00 3.00

2000 Asheville Tourists Grandstand

This set is highlighted by Chin-Hui Tsao's first team set card.
COMPLETE SET (25)................ 15.00 4.50

2000 Auburn Doubledays Grandstand

COMPLETE SET (29)................ 12.00 3.60

2000 Augusta Greenjackets Multi-Ad

Brad Baker is included in this set.
COMPLETE SET (30)................ 15.00 4.50

2000 Bakersfield Blaze Pizza Hut/Pepsi

COMPLETE SET (31)................ 10.00 3.00

2000 Batavia Muckdogs Team Issue

This set is highlighted by the first team set card of Chase Utley.
COMPLETE SET (39)................ 10.00 3.00

2000 Beloit Snappers Rockford Litho

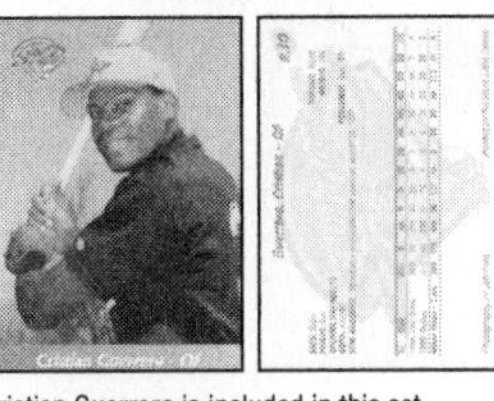

Cristian Guerrero is included in this set.
COMPLETE SET (33)................ 25.00 7.50

2000 Billings Mustangs Grandstand

COMPLETE SET (34)................ 12.00 3.60

2000 Binghamton Mets Blueline

An early card of Alex Escobar is the key to this set.
COMPLETE SET (30)................ 10.00 3.00

2000 Birmingham Barons Grandstand

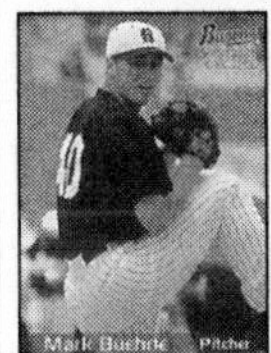

Prospects in this set include Mark Buehrle, Joe Crede, Josh Fogg, Matt Ginter and Aaron Rowand.
COMPLETE SET (31)................ 25.00 7.50

2000 Birmingham Barons Grandstand Update

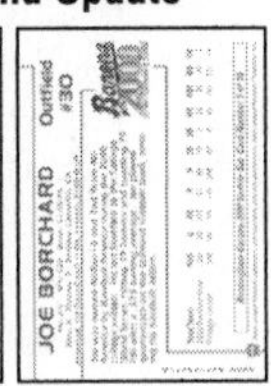

These sets were issued and the collector received one of the two Borchard autographs in his set.
COMPLETE SET (10)................ 80.00 24.00

2000 Bluefield Orioles Grandstand

COMPLETE SET (34)................ 10.00 3.00

2000 Boise Hawks Grandstand

COMPLETE SET (34)................ 15.00 4.50

2000 Bowie Baysox Grandstand

COMPLETE SET (28)................ 10.00 3.00

2000 Brevard County Manatees Multi-Ad

COMPLETE SET (30)................ 10.00 3.00

2000 Bridgeport Bluefish Multi-Ad

COMPLETE SET (31)................ 10.00 3.00

2000 Bristol White Sox Grandstand

COMPLETE SET (30).................. 8.00 2.40

2000 Buffalo Bisons Blueline

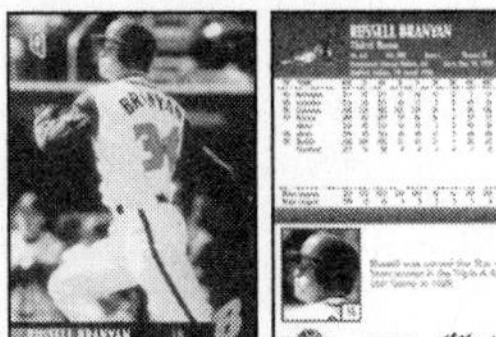

COMPLETE SET (30)................ 10.00 3.00

2000 Burlington Bees Multi-Ad

COMPLETE SET (30)................ 10.00 3.00

2000 Burlington Indians Grandstand

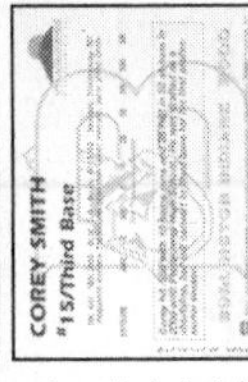

Corey Smith's first team set card is included in this set.
COMPLETE SET (31)................ 15.00 4.50

2000 Butte Copper Kings Grandstand

COMPLETE SET (32)................ 15.00 4.50

2000 Calgary Cannons Bell Intrigna

COMPLETE SET (34)................ 10.00 3.00

2000 California League Prospects Grandstand

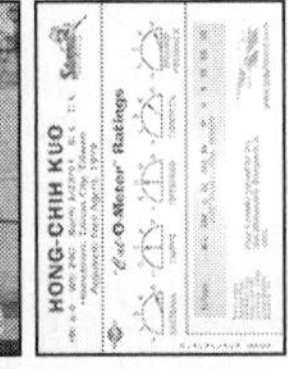

Some of the prospects in this set include Willie Bloomquist, Hong-Chih Huo, Nick Neugebauer, Antonio Perez and Jerome Williams.
COMPLETE SET (29)................ 15.00 4.50

2000 Cape Fear Crocs Multi-Ad

Very scarce set. Brandon Phillips and Wilkan Ruan are in this set.
COMPLETE SET (30)............. 120.00 18.00

2000 Capital City Bombers Multi-Ad

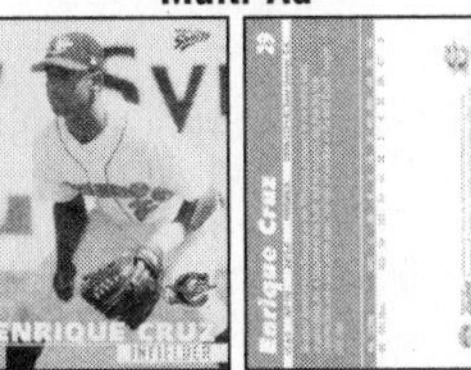

An early card of Enrique Cruz highlights this set.
COMPLETE SET (30)................ 10.00 3.00

2000 Capitales De Quebec Subway

COMPLETE SET (24).................. 8.00 2.40

2000 Carolina League Prospects Choice

An early card of C.C. Sabathia highlights this set.
COMPLETE SET (35)................ 15.00 4.50

2000 Carolina Mudcats Grandstand

A card of Juan Pierre is the key card in this set.
COMPLETE SET (30)................ 12.00 3.60

2000 Cedar Rapids Kernels Multi-Ad

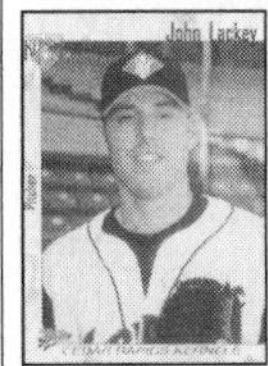

John Lackey is the featured player in this set.
COMPLETE SET (30)................ 15.00 4.50

2000 Charleston Alley Cats Multi-Ad

COMPLETE SET (30).................. 8.00 2.40

2000 Charleston RiverDogs Multi-Ad

Early cards of Carl Crawford and Josh Hamilton is included in this set.
COMPLETE SET (30)................ 12.00 3.60

2000 Charlotte Knights Blueline

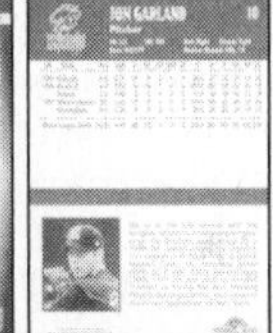

COMPLETE SET (30)................ 10.00 3.00

2000 Charlotte Rangers Multi-Ad

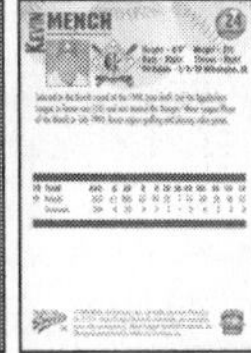

An early card of Kevin Mench is a highlight of this set.
COMPLETE SET (30)................ 12.00 3.60

2000 Chattanooga Lookouts Grandstand

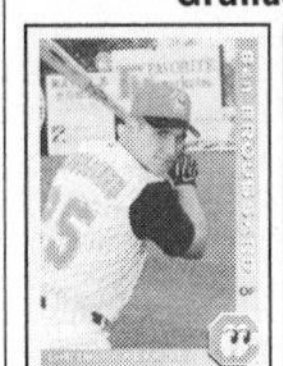

COMPLETE SET (30)................ 10.00 3.00

2000 Chattanooga Lookouts Update Grandstand

Several cards of Drew Henson are included in this set.
COMPLETE SET (9).................. 30.00 9.00

2000 Chico Heat Grandstand

COMPLETE SET (25).................. 5.00 1.50

2000 Clearwater Phillies Multi-Ad

COMPLETE SET (30)................ 20.00 6.00

2000 Clinton Lumber Kings Grandstand

COMPLETE SET (30).................. 8.00 2.40

2000 Colorado Springs Sky Sox Team Issue

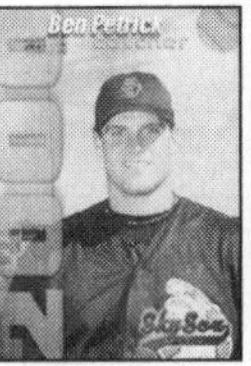

COMPLETE SET (31).................. 8.00 2.40

2000 Columbus Clippers Police Sheet Nubix

An early card of Alfonso Soriano is a key to this set.
COMPLETE SET (25)................ 30.00 9.00

2000 Columbus Clippers Q-Cards/Blueline

An early card of Alfonso Soriano highlights this set.
COMPLETE SET (36)................ 40.00 9.00

2000 Columbus Redstixx Multi-Ad

COMPLETE SET (32)................ 10.00 3.00

2000 Danville Braves Grandstand

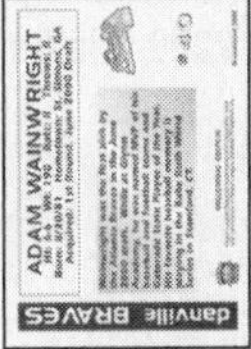

Adam Wainwright's first team set card is the key to this set.
COMPLETE SET (35)................ 15.00 4.50

2000 Dayton Dragons Krogers

Early cards of Adam Dunn and Austin Kearns highlight this set.
COMPLETE SET (30)................ 30.00 9.00

2000 Daytona Cubs Grandstand

Hee Seop Choi and Kerry Wood are the featured players in this set.
COMPLETE SET (32)................ 20.00 6.00

2000 Delmarva Shorebirds Multi-Ad

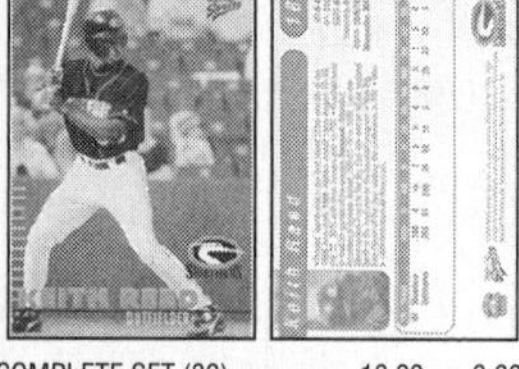

COMPLETE SET (30)................ 10.00 3.00

2000 Duluth-Superior Dukes Warning Track

COMPLETE SET (29)................ 8.00 2.40

2000 Dunedin Blue Jays Grandstand

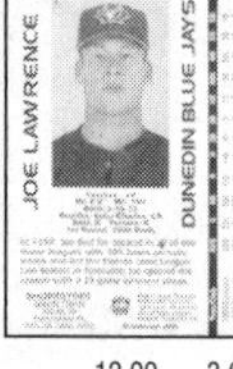

COMPLETE SET (30)................ 12.00 3.60

2000 Edmonton Trappers Team Issue

COMPLETE SET (30)................ 10.00 3.00

2000 El Paso Diablos Grandstand

COMPLETE SET (30)................ 10.00 3.00

2000 Erie Seawolves Multi-Ad

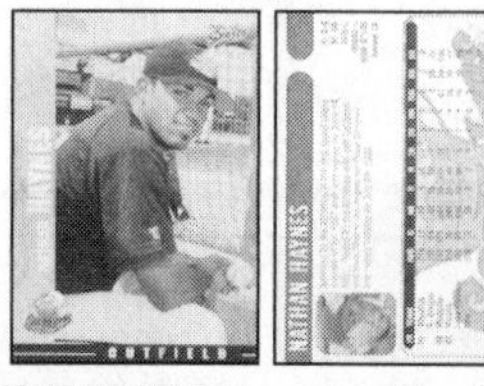

COMPLETE SET (30)................ 8.00 2.40

2000 Eugene Emeralds Grandstand

COMPLETE SET (31)................ 15.00 4.50

2000 Evansville Otters Warning Track

COMPLETE SET (25)................ 8.00 2.40

2000 Everett Aquasox Grandstand

COMPLETE SET (31)................ 12.00 3.60

2000 Fargo-Moorhead Redhawks Domino's Pizza

COMPLETE SET (30)................ 8.00 2.40

2000 Fort Myers Miracle Multi-Ad

COMPLETE SET (30)................ 15.00 4.50

2000 Fort Wayne Wizards Team Issue

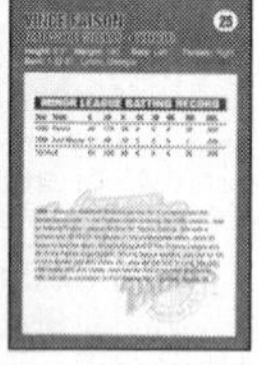

This set was issued and distributed in two formats: standard 2 1/2" by 3 1/2" cards and an uncut sheet. The value for the sheet is listed below. Cards of Sean Burroughs, Eric Cyr and Jacob Peavy are the highlights of this set.
COMPLETE SET (34)................ 20.00 6.00
COMPLETE SHEET (34)................ 40.00 12.00

2000 Frederick Keys Grandstand

COMPLETE SET (31)................ 10.00 3.00

2000 Fresno Grizzlies Grandstand

An early card of Pedro Feliz highlights this set.
COMPLETE SET (26)................ 10.00 3.00

2000 Great Falls Dodgers Grandstand

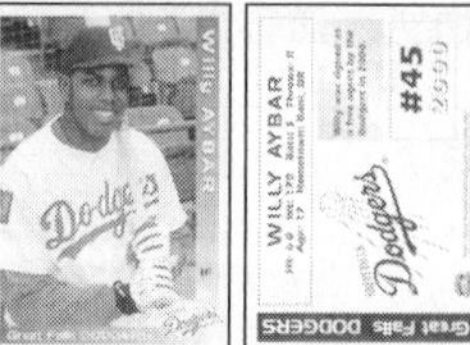

COMPLETE SET (29)................ 15.00 4.50

2000 Greensboro Bats Multi-Ad

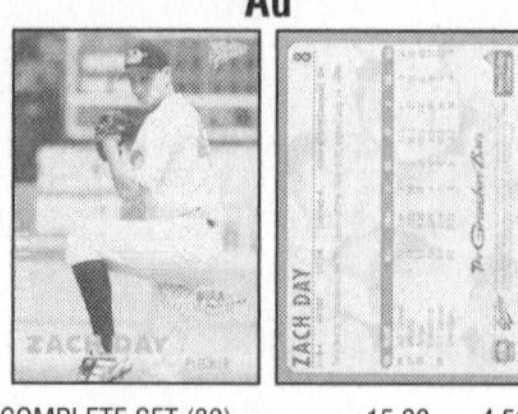

COMPLETE SET (30)................ 15.00 4.50

2000 Greenville Braves Grandstand

COMPLETE SET (29)................ 10.00 3.00

2000 Hagerstown Suns Multi-Ad

COMPLETE SET (30)................ 10.00 3.00

2000 Harrisburg Senators Commemorative Set

This 17-card set was produced by Cheez-it in 2000 to Commemorate the 1996 Championship Harrisburg Senators. Key cards in the set include Vladimir Guerrero, Jose Vidro, and Brad Fullmer.
COMPLETE SET (17)................ 15.00 4.50

2000 Harrisburg Senators Multi-Ad

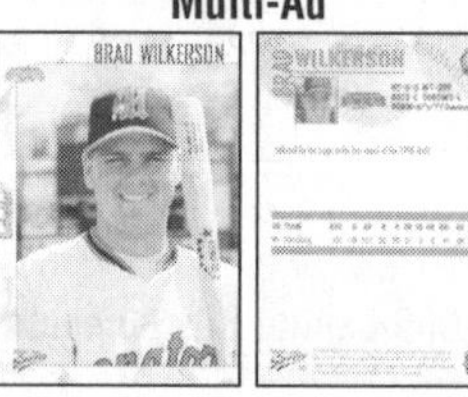

Brad Wilkerson is the key player in this set.
COMPLETE SET (28)................ 15.00 4.50

2000 Helena Brewers Multi-Ad

COMPLETE SET (30)................ 10.00 3.00

2000 Hickory Crawdads Multi-Ad

Early cards of Bobby Bradley and J.R. House highlight this set.
COMPLETE SET (30)................ 15.00 4.50

2000 Hickory Crawdads Update Multi-Ad

COMPLETE SET (30)................ 15.00 4.50

2000 High Desert Mavericks Grandstand

COMPLETE SET (30)................ 10.00 3.00

2000 Hudson Valley Renegades Grandstand

COMPLETE SET (33)................ 10.00 3.00

2000 Huntsville Stars Burger King

An early card of Ben Sheets highlights this set.
COMPLETE SET (29)................ 15.00 4.50

2000 Idaho Falls Padres Grandstand

COMPLETE SET (30)................ 15.00 4.50

2000 Indianapolis Indians Q-Cards/Blueline

COMPLETE SET (30)................ 8.00 2.40

2000 Iowa Cubs Multi-Ad

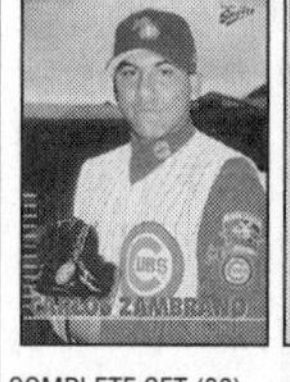
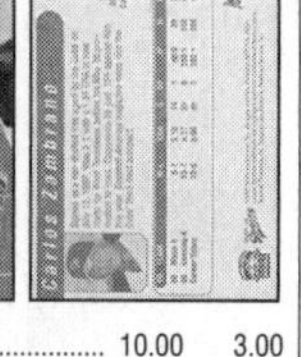

COMPLETE SET (30)................ 10.00 3.00

2000 Jacksonville Suns Grandstand

COMPLETE SET (31)................ 10.00 3.00

2000 Jamestown Jammers Grandstand

COMPLETE SET (28)................ 15.00 4.50

2000 Johnson City Cardinals Interstate Graphics

COMPLETE SET (40)................ 10.00 3.00

2000 Jupiter Hammerheads Team Issue

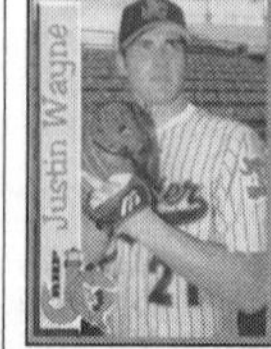
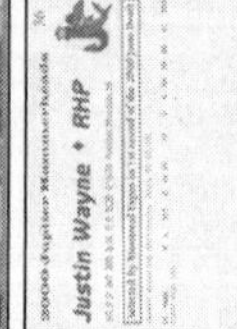

Early cards of Valentino Pascucci and Justin Wayne highlight this set.
COMPLETE SET (40)................ 18.00 5.50

2000 Kane County Cougars Active Graphics

The 2000 Kane County Active Graphics set was released in July,2000 as a 32-card set. The set parallels the 2000 Connie's Pizza Kane County Cougars set. However, this set was produced on a very thick stock, and the cards are topped with a glossy covering. The back of the cards state that they were produced by Active Graphics. This set also features prospect cards of Chip Ambres and Josh Beckett that were not included in the Connie's Pizza set.
COMPLETE SET (32)................ 30.00 6.00

2000 Kane County Cougars Connie's Pizza

The 2000 Kane County Connie's Pizza set was released in June,2000 as a 32-card set. The set parallels the 2000 Active Graphics Kane County Cougars set. However, this set was produced on a thinner stock, and the cards are not topped with a glossy covering. The back of the cards state that they were produced by Connie's Pizza. This set includes two cards that were not found in the Active Graphics set: a team checklist card and an Ozzie the Cougar mascot card.

2000 Kane County Cougars Old Navy

The 2000 Kane County Old Navy set was released in June, 2000 as a 32-card set. The set parallels the 2000 Connie's Pizza Kane County Cougars set in that both are produced on thin stock, making them condition sensitive. The back of the cards feature a black and white oval Old Navy logo. Similar to the Connie's Pizza issue, a team checklist and an Ozzie the Cougar mascot card are included. Only 750 sets were produced all of which were distributed in loosely-sealed, clear, plastic bags.
COMPLETE SET (32)................ 60.00 22.00

2000 Kinston Indians Choice

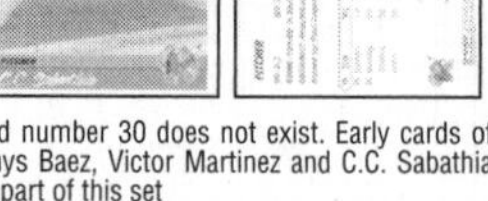

Card number 30 does not exist. Early cards of Danys Baez, Victor Martinez and C.C. Sabathia are part of this set
COMPLETE SET (30)................ 15.00 4.50

2000 Kissimmee Cobras Multi-Ad

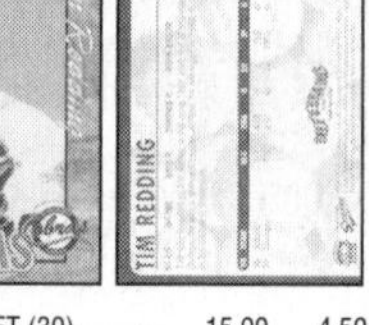

COMPLETE SET (30)................ 15.00 4.50

2000 Lake Elsinore Storm Grandstand

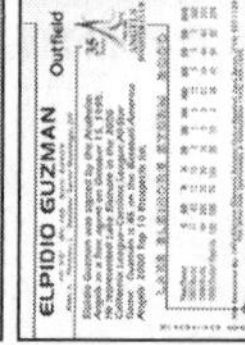

Key cards in this set include Alfredo Amezaga, John Lackey, Robb Quinlan and Francisco Rodriguez.
COMPLETE SET (36)................ 20.00 6.00

2000 Lakeland Tigers Multi-Ad

OMPLETE SET (30)............... 15.00 4.50

2000 Lancaster Jethawks Grandstand

OMPLETE SET (30)............... 10.00 3.00

2000 Lansing Lugnuts Grandstand

ın early card of Juan Cruz highlights this set.
OMPLETE SET (31)............... 15.00 4.50

2000 Las Vegas Stars Multi-Ad

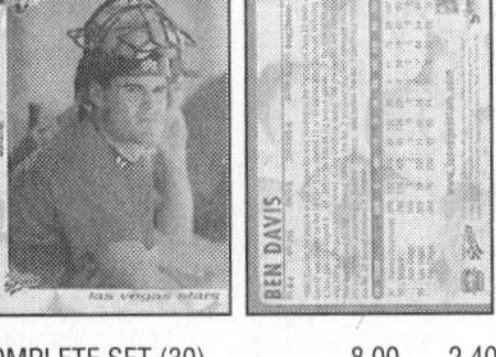

COMPLETE SET (30)................ 8.00 2.40

2000 Legends of Bowman

Given out one per selected game at Bowman Field.
COMPLETE SET (5)................ 30.00 9.00

2000 Long Island Ducks Multi-Ad

COMPLETE SET (30)................ 8.00 2.40

2000 Louisville Riverbats Q-Cards/Blueline

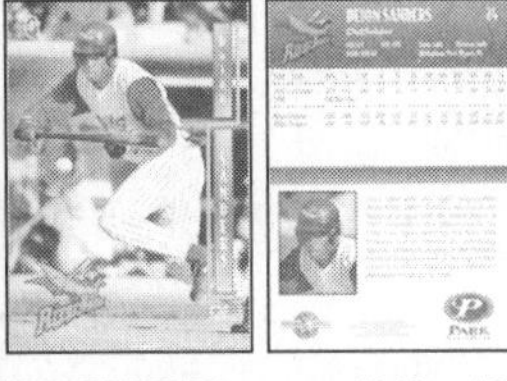

COMPLETE SET (36)............... 15.00 4.50

2000 Lowell Spinners Multi-Ad

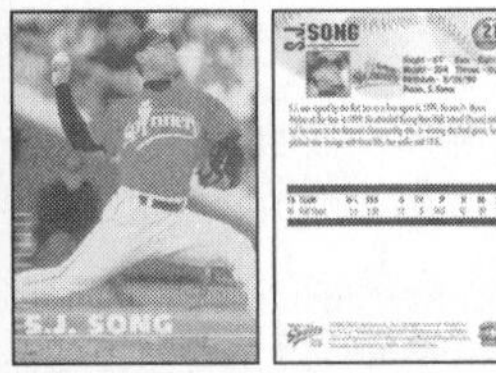

COMPLETE SET (30)............... 12.00 3.60

2000 Lowell Spinners Update Grandstand

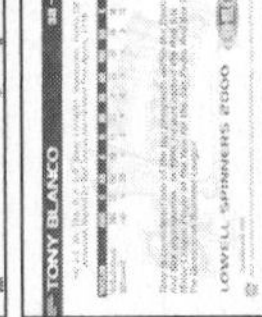

750 sets produced. Key cards in this set include Tony Blanco, Julio Guerrero and Freddy Sanchez.
COMPLETE SET (12)............... 25.00 7.50

2000 LSU Tigers

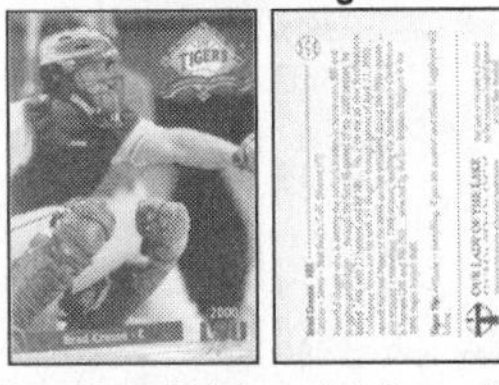

These 16 standard-size cards feature on their fronts posed color player photos of the 2000 LSU Tigers. The cards' carry the players name at the bottom of the photo and the team name in the top right corner. Key players in this set include Brad Cresse, Brad Hawpe and Brian Tallet.
COMPLETE SET (16)............... 25.00 7.50

2000 Lynchburg Hillcats Choice

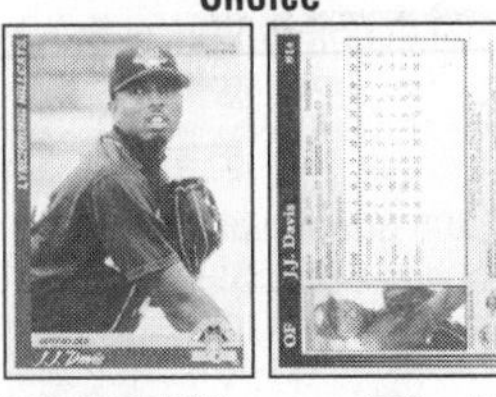

COMPLETE SET (32)............... 10.00 3.00

2000 Macon Braves Multi-Ad

COMPLETE SET (30)............... 12.00 3.60

2000 Mahoning Valley Scrappers Multi-Ad

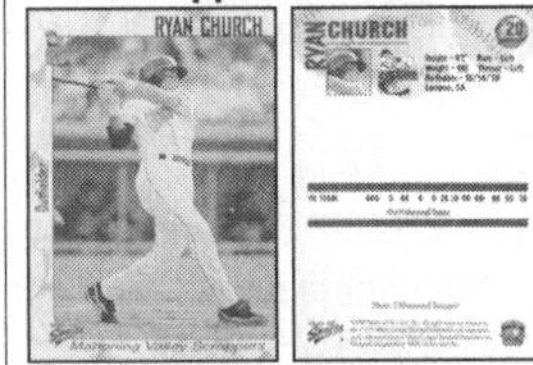

COMPLETE SET (30)............... 15.00 4.50

2000 Martinsville Astros Grandstand

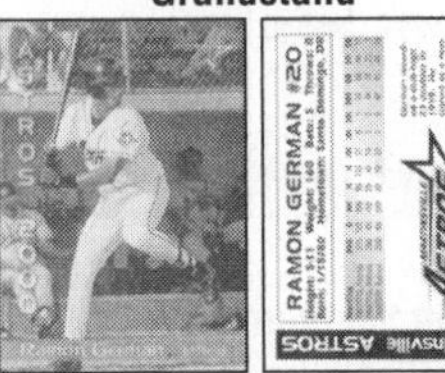

COMPLETE SET (30)............... 10.00 3.00

2000 Memphis Redbirds Team Issue

J.D. Drew is included in this set.
COMPLETE SET (30)............... 15.00 4.50

2000 Michigan Battlecats Multi-Ad

COMPLETE SET (30)............... 15.00 4.50

2000 Midland Rockhounds Grandstand

Jason Hart has an early card in this set.
COMPLETE SET (28)............... 10.00 3.00

2000 Midwest League All-Stars Active Graphics

Among the prospects in this set are Jacob Peavy, Albert Pujols (his first minor league team set card), and Chris Snelling.
COMPLETE SET (57)............... 40.00 12:00

2000 Midwest League Top Prospects Multi-Ad

Among the prospects are Jacob Peavy, Albert Pujols (his first minor league team set card) and Chris Snelling. The Albert Pujols card can be differentiated from the Peoria Chiefs card by the words "top prospect" near the bottom left corner.
COMPLETE SET (29)............... 20.00 6.00

2000 Missoula Osprey Grandstand

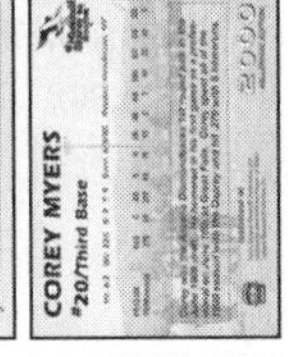

COMPLETE SET (31)............... 10.00 3.00

2000 Mobile Baybears Grandstand

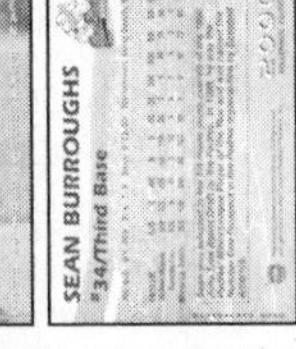

This set is highlighted by early cards of Sean Burroughs and Adam Eaton.
COMPLETE SET (30)............... 10.00 3.00

2000 Modesto A's Grandstand

COMPLETE SET (30)............... 10.00 3.00

2000 Mudville Nine Grandstand

An early card of Nick Neugebauer is the highlight of this set.
COMPLETE SET (30)............... 10.00 3.00

2000 Myrtle Beach Pelicans Multi-Ad

Christian Parra is the key player in this set.
COMPLETE SET (30)............... 10.00 3.00

2000 Nashville Sounds Multi-Ad

COMPLETE SET (30)............... 10.00 3.00

2000 New Britain Rock Cats Blueline

Bobby Kielty is the key player in this set.
COMPLETE SET (30)............... 10.00 3.00

2000 New Haven Ravens Herlin Press

COMPLETE SET (31)............... 15.00 4.50

2000 New Jersey Cardinals Grandstand

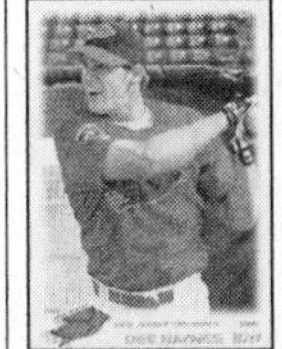

COMPLETE SET (33)............... 15.00 4.50

2000 New Jersey Cardinals Star-Ledger Uncut Sheet

COMPLETE SET (1)............... 10.00 3.00

2000 New Jersey Cardinals Update Grandstand

COMPLETE SET (3)............... 5.00 1.50

2000 New Jersey Jackals Warning Track

COMPLETE SET (31)............... 8.00 2.40

2000 New Orleans Zephyrs Multi-Ad

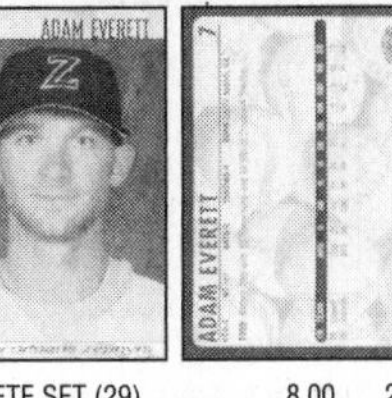

COMPLETE SET (29)............... 8.00 2.40

2000 Newark Bears Citation Graphics

The set is unnumbered and listed below in alphabetical order.
COMPLETE SET (29)............... 15.00 4.50

2000 Norfolk Tides Q-Cards/Blueline

Timo Perez, 2000 Post-Season Hero, has an early card in this set.
COMPLETE SET (36)............... 10.00 3.00

2000 Norwich Navigators Q-Cards/Blueline

COMPLETE SET (30)............... 15.00 4.50

2000 Ogden Raptors Team Issue

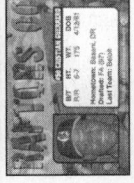

Key cards in this set include Cristan Guerrero, Corey Hart and Dave Krynzel.
COMPLETE SET (40)............... 25.00 7.50

2000 Oklahoma Redhawks Multi-Ad

COMPLETE SET (29)............... 10.00 3.00

2000 Omaha Golden Spikes Multi-Ad

COMPLETE SET (35)............... 10.00 3.00

2000 Oneonta Tigers Grandstand

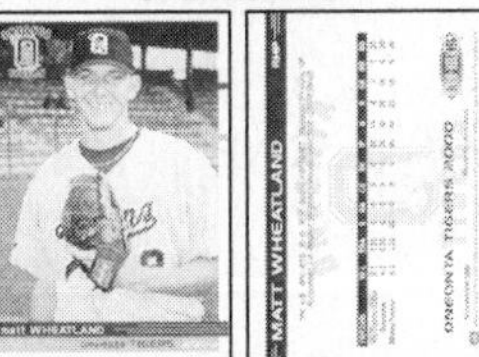

COMPLETE SET (29)............... 15.00 4.50

2000 Orlando Rays Multi-Ad

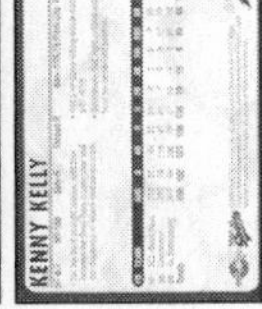

COMPLETE SET (30)............... 10.00 3.00

2000 Ottawa Lynx Blueline

COMPLETE SET (30)............... 10.00 3.00

2000 Pawtucket PawSox Blueline

COMPLETE SET (30)............... 10.00 3.00

2000 Pawtucket PawSox Dunkin' Donuts

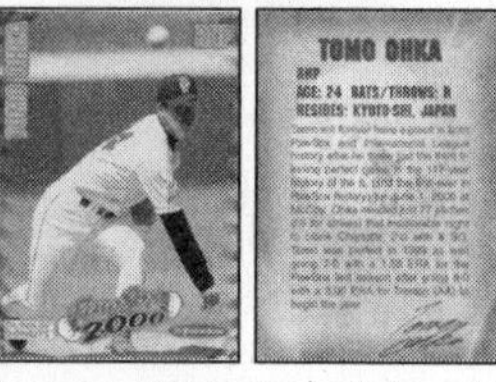

Please note that the Team Photo card is oversized and measures 12 in. x 7 in.
COMPLETE SET (31)............... 30.00 9.00

2000 Peoria Chiefs Multi-Ad

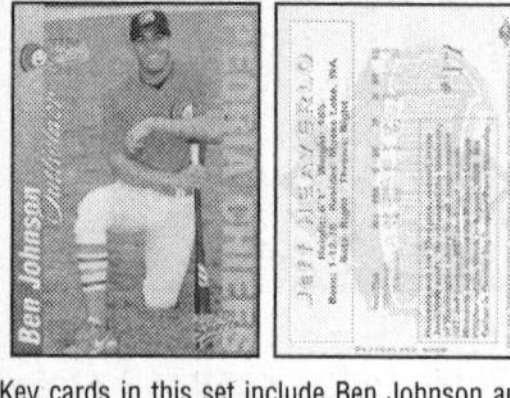

Key cards in this set include Ben Johnson and Albert Pujols.
COMPLETE SET (30)............... 50.00 15.00

2000 Piedmont Boll Weevils Multi-Ad

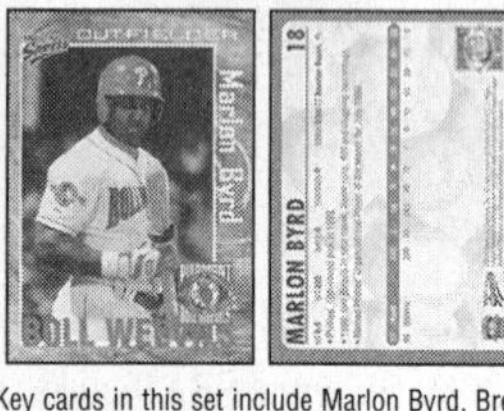

Key cards in this set include Marlon Byrd, Brett Myers and Jorge Padilla.
COMPLETE SET (30)............... 50.00 15.00

2000 Pittsfield Mets Multi-Ad

COMPLETE SET (32)............... 10.00 3.00

2000 Portland Sea Dogs Grandstand

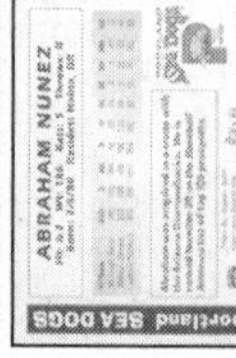

COMPLETE SET (33)............... 10.00 3.00

2000 Potomac Cannons Choice

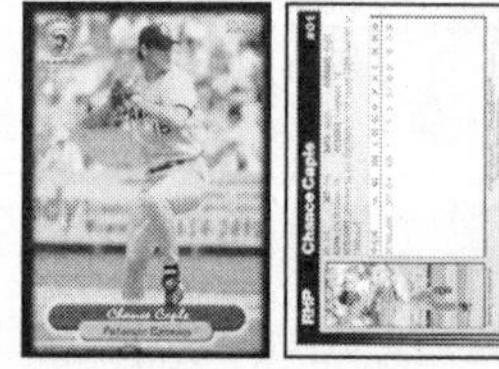

COMPLETE SET (30)............... 10.00 3.00

2000 Princeton Devil Rays Grandstand

Rocco Baldelli's first team set card is part of this set.
COMPLETE SET (30)............... 40.00 12.00

2000 Pulaski Rangers Grandstand

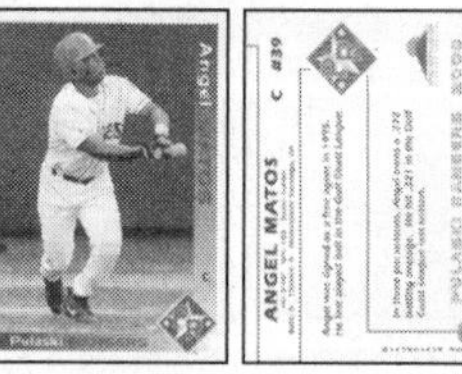

COMPLETE SET (29)............... 10.00 3.00

2000 Quad City River Bandits Roox

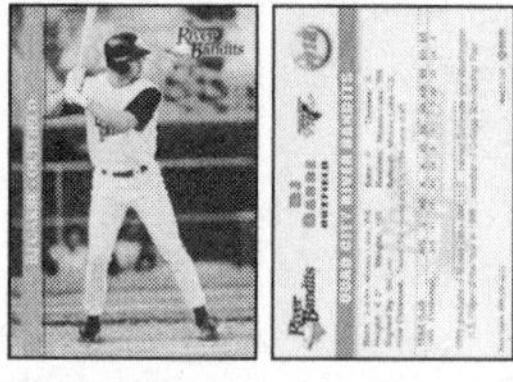

COMPLETE SET (30)............... 10.00 3.00

2000 Rancho Cucamonga Quakes Grandstand

An early card of Mike Bynum highlights this set.
COMPLETE SET (30)............... 10.00 3.00

2000 Reading Phillies Multi-Ad

COMPLETE SET (30)............... 15.00 4.50

2000 Richmond Braves Q-Cards/Blueline

John Rocker has a card in this set.
COMPLETE SET (36)............... 10.00 3.00

2000 Richmond Braves Richmond Camera

John Rocker's card highlights this set.
COMPLETE SET (25)............................ .00

2000 River City Rascals Team Issue

COMPLETE SET (30)............... 8.00 2.40

2000 Rochester Red Wings Grandstand

COMPLETE SET (25)............... 10.00 3.00

2000 Round Rock Express Multi-Ad

Cards of Morgan Ensberg, Roy Oswalt and team owner Nolan Ryan are among the keys in this set.
COMPLETE SET (30)............... 25.00 7.50

2000 Sacramento River Cats Grandstand

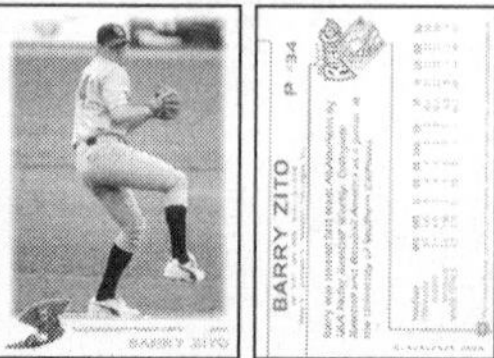

Barry Zito is the key card in this team set.
COMPLETE SET (30)............... 20.00 6.00

2000 Salem Avalanche Grandstand

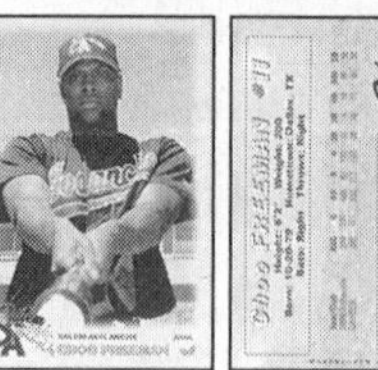

COMPLETE SET (31)............... 10.00 3.00

2000 Salem-Keizer Volcanoes Grandstand

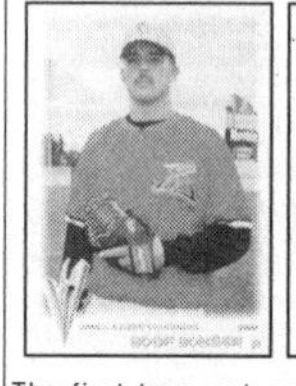

The first team set card of Lance Niekro highlights this set.
COMPLETE SET (36)............... 15.00 4.50

2000 Salt Lake Buzz Multi-Ad

COMPLETE SET (30)............... 8.00 2.40

2000 San Antonio Missions Grandstand

An early card of Chin-Feng Chen highlights this set.
COMPLETE SET (28)............... 15.00 4.50

2000 San Bernardino Stampede Grandstand

Some key people in this set include Jack Clark, Orle Hershiser and Hong-Chih Kuo.
COMPLETE SET (30)............... 12.00 3.60

2000 San Jose Giants Grandstand

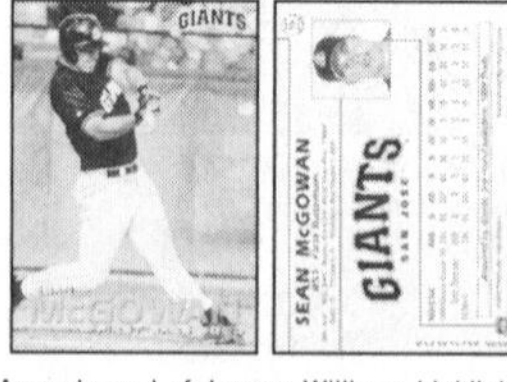

An early card of Jerome Williams highlights this set.
COMPLETE SET (30)............... 10.00 3.00

2000 Sarasota Red Sox Multi-Ad

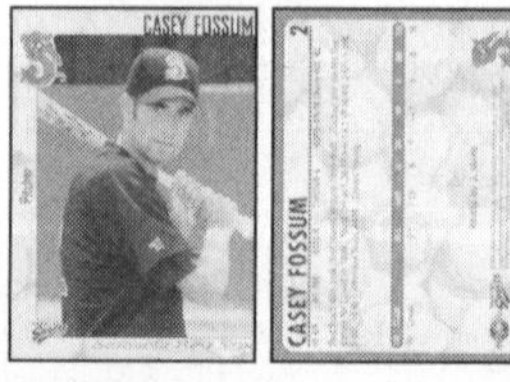

COMPLETE SET (30)............... 10.00 3.00

2000 Savannah Sand Gnats Multi-Ad

An early card of Hank Blalock highlights this set.
COMPLETE SET (29)............... 35.00 10.50

2000 Schaumburg Flyers Team Issue

COMPLETE SET (30)............... 5.00 1.50

2000 Scranton/Wilkes-Barre Red Barons Blueline

An early card of Pat Burrell highlights this set.
COMPLETE SET (30)............... 10.00 3.00

2000 Shreveport Captains Grandstand

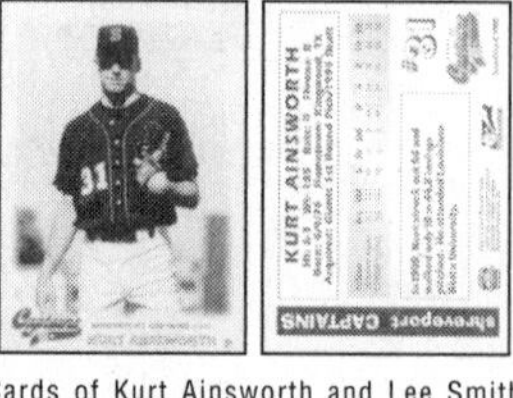

Cards of Kurt Ainsworth and Lee Smith highlight this set.
COMPLETE SET (30)............... 12.00 3.60

2000 Somerset Patriots Multi-Ad

Former Cy Young Award Winner Sparky Lyle is included in this set.
COMPLETE SET (27)............... 10.00 3.00

2000 South Atlantic League Top Prospect Multi-Ad

Among the prospects in this set are Bobby Bradley, Josh Hamilton, J.R. House and Chin-Hui Tsao.
COMPLETE SET (30)............... 15.00 4.50

2000 South Bend Silver Hawks Multi-Ad

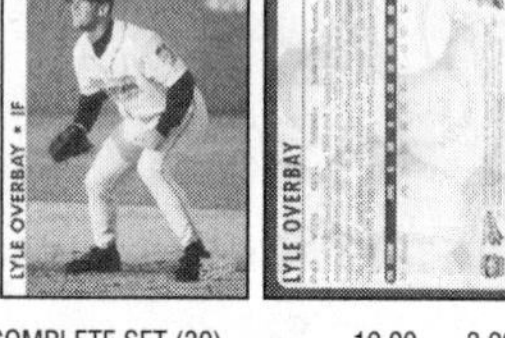

COMPLETE SET (30)............... 10.00 3.00

2000 Southern League Top Prospects Grandstand

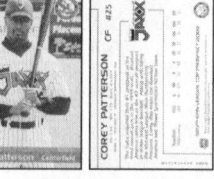

Among the prospects in this set are Sean Burroughs, Corey Patterson and Ben Sheets.
COMPLETE SET (31)............... 18.00 5.50

2000 SP Top Prospects Small Town Heroes

Randomly inserted in packs at one in 11, this 12-card insert set features the "small-town" feel of minor league baseball. Card backs carry a "S" prefix.
COMPLETE SET (12)............... 10.00 3.00

2000 Spokane Indians Grandstand

COMPLETE SET (37)............... 10.00 3.00

2000 St. Lucie Mets Grandstand

This 32-card set from Grandstand was released in August, 2000, and features players and coaches from the 2000 St. Lucie Mets team. Please note that these cards are not numbered and are listed below in alphabetical order. Also note that there were only 1000 of these sets produced, and a certificate came with the set stating which set out of 1000 you received.
COMPLETE SET (32)............... 10.00 3.00

2000 St. Paul Saints Team Issue

COMPLETE SET (31)............... 10.00 3.00

2000 St. Petersburg Devil Rays Multi-Ad

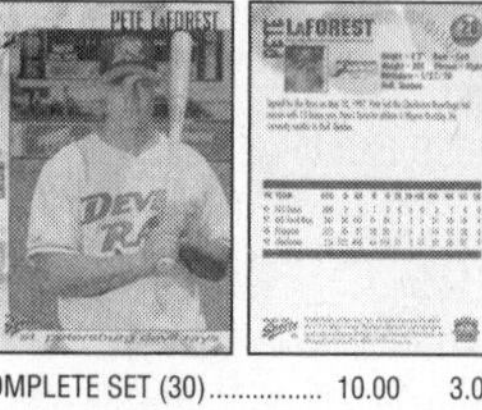

COMPLETE SET (30)............... 10.00 3.00

2000 Staten Island Yankees Multi-Ad

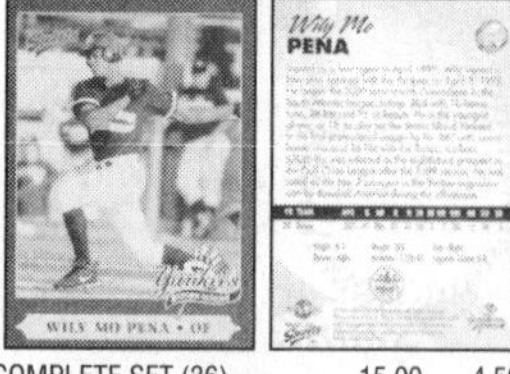

COMPLETE SET (36)............... 15.00 4.50

2000 Syracuse Skychiefs Grandstand

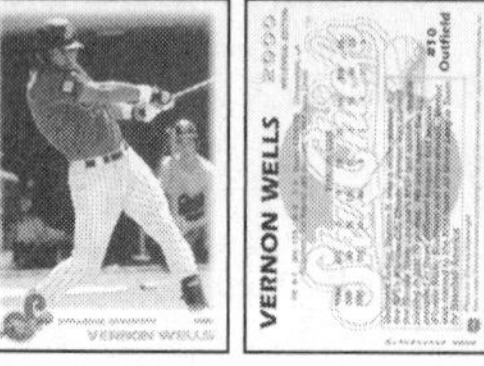

COMPLETE SET (47)............... 10.00 3.00

2000 Tacoma Rainiers Blueline

COMPLETE SET (30)............... 15.00 4.50

2000 Tampa Yankees Multi-Ad

A card of Derek Jeter highlights this set. In addition, key prospects include Andy Phillips and Juan Rivera.
COMPLETE SET (30)............... 20.00 6.00

2000 Tennessee Smokies Grandstand

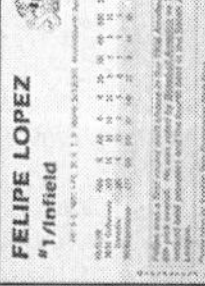

COMPLETE SET (28)............... 15.00 4.50

2000 Tennessee Volunteers Multi-Ad

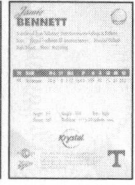

COMPLETE SET (32)............... 10.00 3.00

2000 Texas League Top Prospect Grandstand

Among the prospects in this set are Kurt Ainsworth, Chin-Feng Chen, Jason Hart and Bud Smith.
COMPLETE SET (24)............... 12.00 3.60

2000 Toledo Mudhens Grandstand

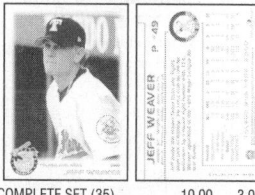

COMPLETE SET (35)............... 10.00 3.00

2000 Trenton Thunder Multi-Ad

COMPLETE SET (30)............... 10.00 3.00

2000 Tucson Sidewinders Grandstand

COMPLETE SET (30)............... 10.00 3.00

2000 Tulsa Drillers Oklahoma Highway

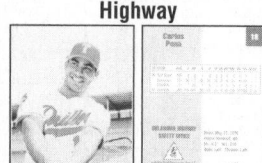

COMPLETE SET (28)............... 15.00 4.50

2000 Utica Blue Sox Multi-Ad

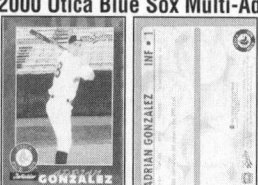

Adrian Gonzalez' first team set card and a card of Miguel Cabrera highlight this set.
COMPLETE SET (40)............... 40.00 4.50

2000 Vancouver Canadians Grandstand

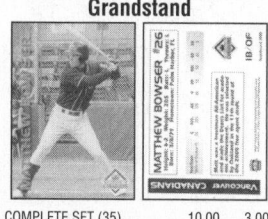

COMPLETE SET (35)............... 10.00 3.00

2000 Vermont Expos Grandstand

COMPLETE SET (34)............... 8.00 2.40

2000 Vero Beach Dodgers Multi-Ad

COMPLETE SET (30)............... 10.00 3.00

2000 Visalia Oaks Grandstand

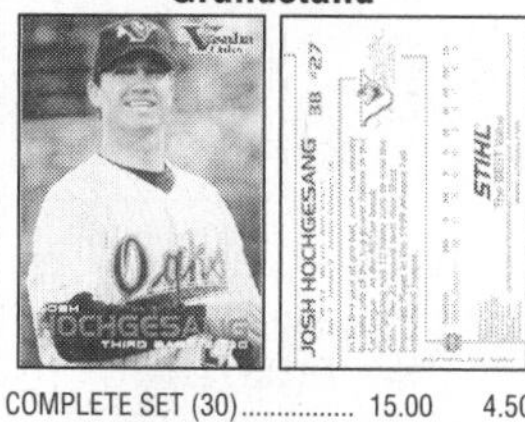

COMPLETE SET (30)............... 15.00 4.50

2000 West Michigan Whitecaps Multi-Ad

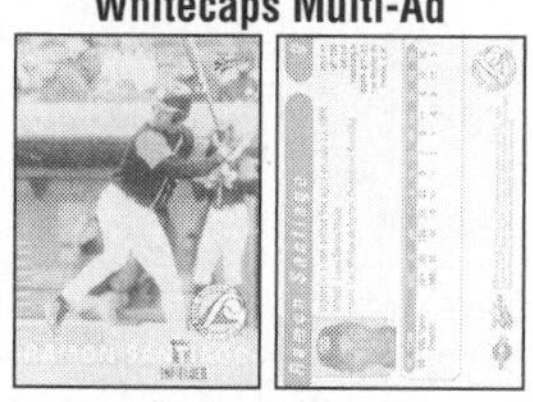

COMPLETE SET (31)............... 8.00 2.40

2000 West Tennessee Diamond Jaxx Champs Grandstand

750 sets produced.
COMPLETE SET (31)............... 20.00 6.00

2000 West Tennessee Diamond Jaxx Grandstand

Early cards of Eric Hinske, Corey Patterson and Carlos Zambrano highlight this set.
COMPLETE SET (30)............... 20.00 6.00

2000 Wichita Wranglers Choice

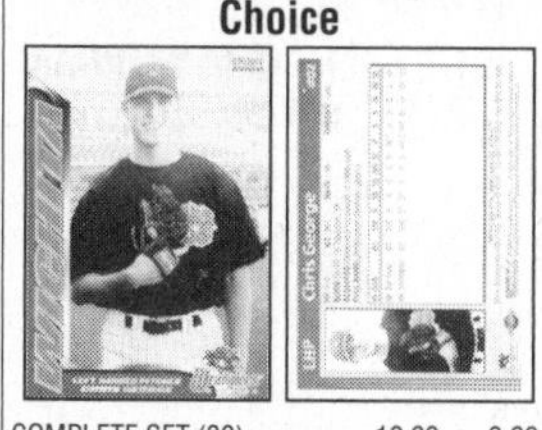

COMPLETE SET (30)............... 10.00 3.00

2000 Williamsport Crosscutters Multi-Ad

COMPLETE SET (30)............... 8.00 2.40

2000 Wilmington Blue Rocks Choice

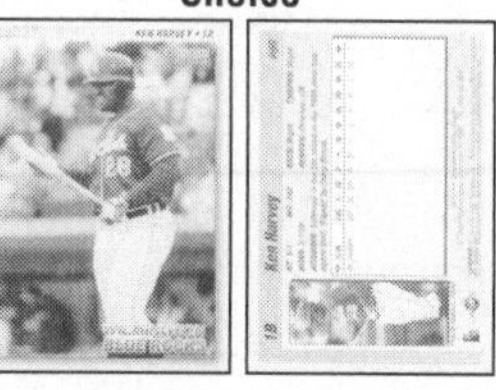

COMPLETE SET (30)............... 15.00 4.50

2000 Winnipeg Goldeyes Team Issue

COMPLETE SET (30)............... 10.00 3.00

2000 Winston-Salem Warthogs Choice

COMPLETE SET (30)............... 10.00 3.00

2000 Winston-Salem Warthogs Update Choice

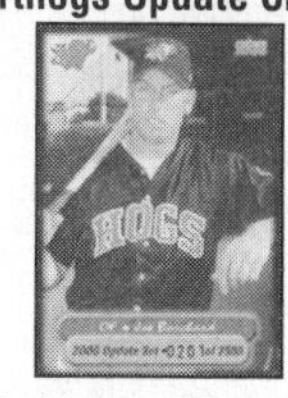

Cards of Joe Borchard and Tim Hummel are the keys to this set.
COMPLETE SET (30)............... 10.00 3.00

2000 Wisconsin Timber Rattlers Multi-Ad

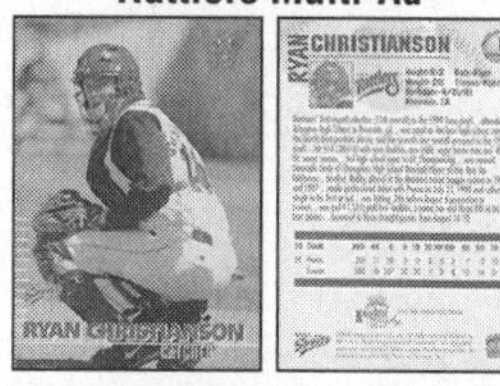

COMPLETE SET (30)............... 10.00 3.00

2000 Yakima Bears Grandstand

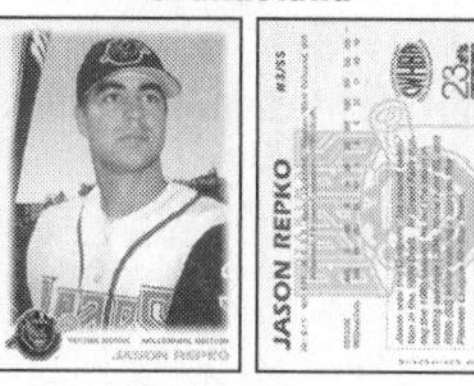

COMPLETE SET (31)............... 10.00 3.00

2001 Akron Aeros Anniversary Multi-Ad

COMPLETE SET (21)............... 15.00 4.50

2001 Akron Aeros Multi-Ad

COMPLETE SET (30)............... 10.00 3.00

2001 Altoona Curve Grandstand

COMPLETE SET (29)............... 10.00 3.00

2001 Appalachian League Top Prospect Grandstand

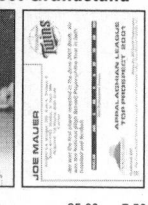

COMPLETE SET (30)............... 25.00 7.50

2001 Appalachian League Top Prospect Update Grandstand

Ten card update set distributed in November, 2001 in a loose, sealed, cello bag. The cards are unnumbered on back and checklisted in alphabetical order by player's last name. Joe Mauer, the first player chosen in the 2001 draft, highlights the set.
COMPLETE SET (10)............... 20.00 6.00

2001 Arkansas Travelers Multi-Ad

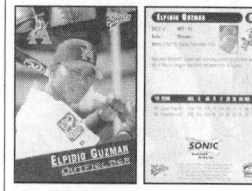

COMPLETE SET (30)............... 5.00 1.50

2001 Asheville Tourists Grandstand

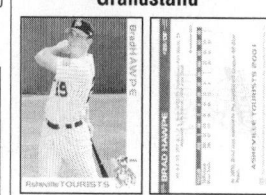

Cards of Brad Hawpe and Bryan Peck are the keys to this set.
COMPLETE SET (30)............... 20.00 6.00

2001 Auburn Doubledays Multi-Ad

COMPLETE SET (30)............... 8.00 2.40

2001 Augusta Greenjackets Multi-Ad

COMPLETE SET (30)............... 15.00 4.50

2001 Bakersfield Blaze Pepsi

COMPLETE SET (33)............... 10.00 3.00

2001 Batavia Muckdogs Agway

COMPLETE SET (15)............... 8.00 2.40

2001 Batavia Muckdogs Team Issue

COMPLETE SET (36)............... 15.00 4.50

2001 Beloit Snappers Multi-Ad

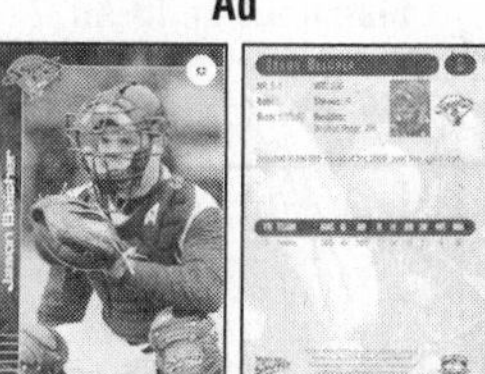

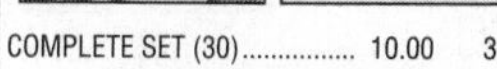

COMPLETE SET (30)............... 10.00 3.00

2001 Billings Mustangs Grandstand

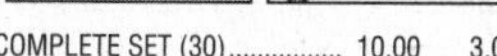

COMPLETE SET (30)............... 10.00 3.00

2001 Binghamton Mets Choice

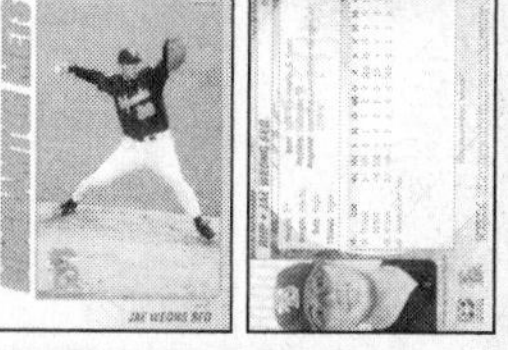

COMPLETE SET (30)............... 8.00 2.40

2001 Birmingham Barons Grandstand

COMPLETE SET (31)............... 40.00 12.00

2001 Bluefield Orioles Grandstand

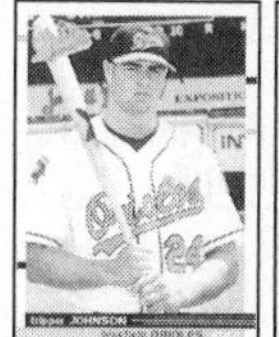

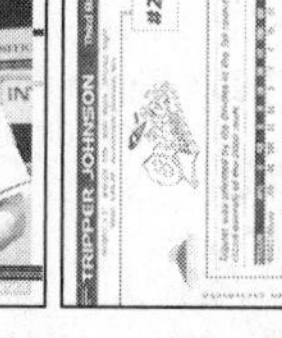

COMPLETE SET (37)............... 10.00 3.00

2001 Boise Hawks Grandstand

Cards of Angel Guzman, J.J. Johnson and Dontrelle Willis highlight this set.
COMPLETE SET (32)............... 30.00 5.50

2001 Bowie Baysox Grandstand

COMPLETE SET (31) 10.00 3.00

2001 Brevard County Manatees Multi-Ad

COMPLETE SET (30) 15.00 4.50

2001 Bristol White Sox Grandstand

COMPLETE SET (30) 10.00 3.00

2001 Brooklyn Cyclones Multi-Ad

An early card of Tsuyoshi Shinjo highlights this set.
COMPLETE SET (36) 25.00 7.50

2001 Buffalo Bisons Choice

COMPLETE SET (30) 10.00 3.00

2001 Burlington Bees Multi-Ad

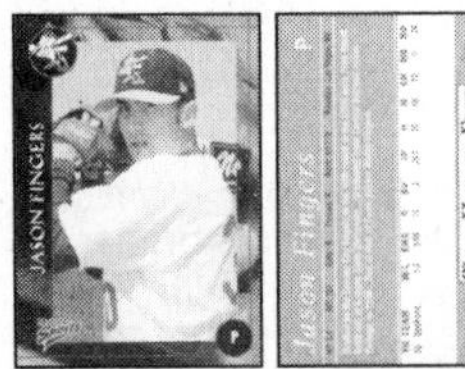

COMPLETE SET (31) 5.00 1.50

2001 Burlington Indians Grandstand

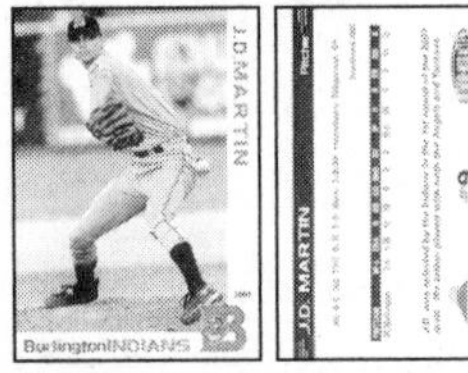

1000 sets were produced, each distributed in a cello team set bag with a small certificate from Minor Miracles hand-numbered to 1000. Cards are numbered on back by players jersey number.
COMPLETE SET (37) 15.00 4.50

2001 Cal State Fullerton Titans Team Issue

Kirk Saarloos highlights this set. These cards were given away at selected Cal State Fullerton Home games at a rate of one or two per game
COMPLETE SET (23) ....

2001 Calgary Cannons Bell Intrigna

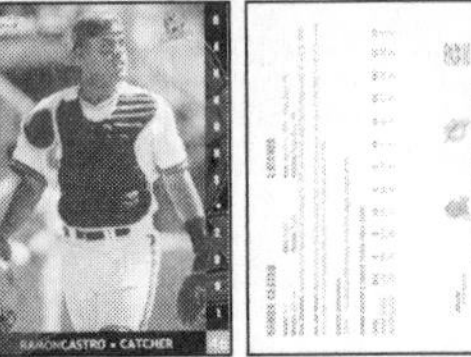

COMPLETE SET (31) 10.00 3.00

2001 California League Prospects Grandstand

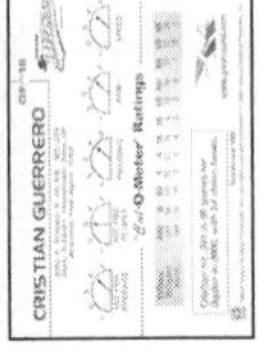

COMPLETE SET (31) 18.00 5.50

2001 California/Carolina League All-Stars Choice

COMPLETE SET (50) 18.00 5.50

2001 Canadian Junior National Team

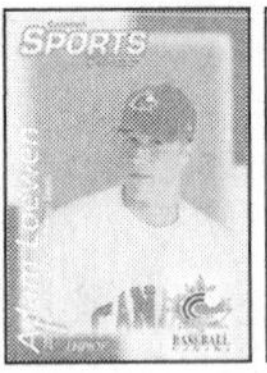

This 10 card standard-size set was included as a four card uncut sheet in each issue of the September 2001 Canadian Sportscard Collector. The unperforated sheets would measure the standard size if cut off the sheet.
COMPLETE SET (10) 5.00 1.50

2001 Capital City Bombers Minor Miracles

COMPLETE SET (1) 15.00 4.50

2001 Capital City Bombers Minor Miracles Autograph

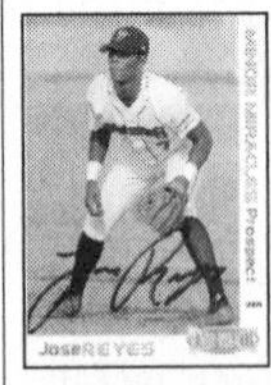
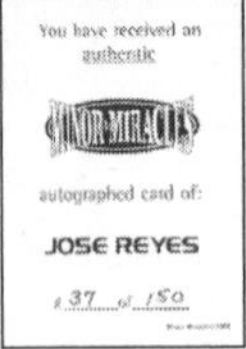

This card features Mets Phenom Jose Reyes who starred with Capital City in 2001. However, this card was not produced until early 2002 and thus has the copyright date of 2002. In addition, 25 of these cards were issued after being signed in a special gold pen.
COMPLETE SET (1) 40.00 12.00

2001 Capital City Bombers Multi-Ad

COMPLETE SET (30) 15.00 3.00

2001 Carolina League Top Prospects Choice

COMPLETE SET (30) 15.00 4.50

2001 Carolina Mudcats Walker-Ross

COMPLETE SET (30) 10.00 3.00

2001 Casper Rockies Grandstand

COMPLETE SET (31) 10.00 3.00

2001 Cedar Rapids Kernels Multi-Ad

COMPLETE SET (30) 10.00 3.00

2001 Charleston Alley Cats Multi-Ad

An early issue of Alexis Rios is featured in this set.
COMPLETE SET (30) 40.00 2.40

2001 Charleston River Dogs Multi-Ad

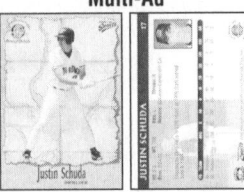

Cards of Rocco Baldelli, Mark Malaska and Seth McClung are the keys to this set.
COMPLETE SET (31) 20.00 6.00

2001 Charlotte Knights Choice

COMPLETE SET (30) 10.00 3.00

2001 Charlotte Rangers Multi-Ad

An early card of Hank Blalock highlights this set.
COMPLETE SET (31) 18.00 5.50

2001 Chattanooga Lookouts Grandstand

Early cards of Adam Dunn, David Gil, Austin Kearns and Corky Miller are featured in this set.
COMPLETE SET (31) 20.00 6.00

2001 Clearwater Phillies Multi-Ad

COMPLETE SET (30) 10.00 3.00

2001 Clinton Lumber Kings Grandstand

Grady Sizemore is featured in this set.
COMPLETE SET (31) 30.00 3.00

2001 Colorado Springs Sky Sox Team Issue

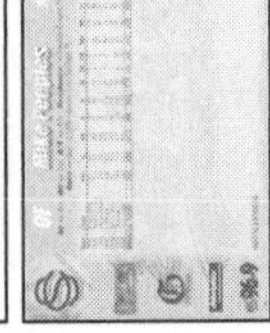

COMPLETE SET (32) 8.00 2.40

2001 Columbus Clippers Choice

COMPLETE SET (31) 10.00 3.00

2001 Columbus Redstixx Multi-Ad

COMPLETE SET (30) 12.00 3.60

2001 Danville Braves Grandstand

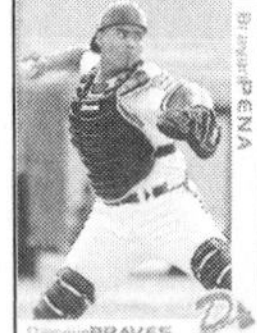

COMPLETE SET (35) 10.00 3.00

2001 Dayton Dragons Grandstand

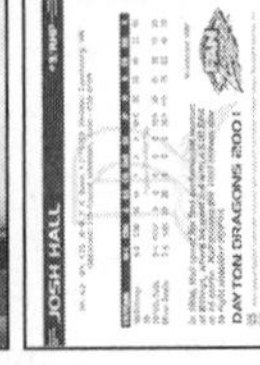

COMPLETE SET (30) 15.00 4.50

2001 Daytona Cubs Multi-Ad

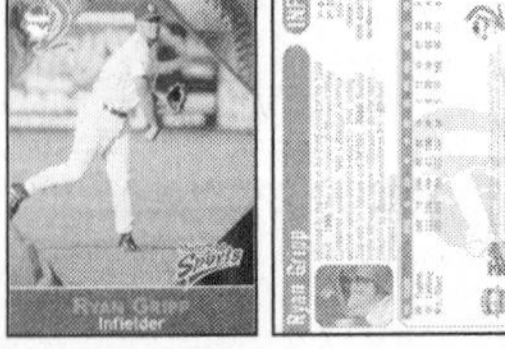

COMPLETE SET (30) 15.00 4.50

2001 Delmarva Shorebirds Multi-Ads

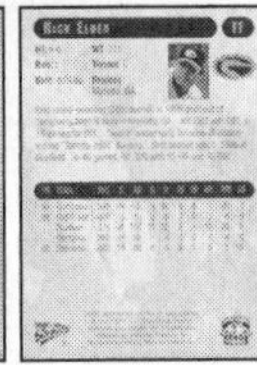

COMPLETE SET (30) 5.00 1.50

2001 Dunedin Blue Jays Grandstand

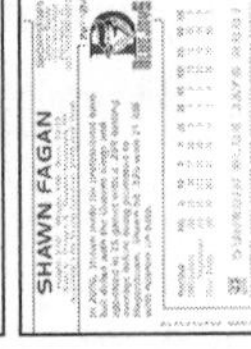

COMPLETE SET (30) 8.00 2.40

2001 Durham Bulls Choice

COMPLETE SET (30) 10.00 3.00

2001 Edmonton Trappers Team Issue

COMPLETE SET (30) 15.00 4.50

2001 El Paso Diablos Grandstand

COMPLETE SET (30) 10.00 3.00

2001 Elizabethton Twins Grandstand

Featured players in this set include Joseph Durbin, Joe Mauer and Sandy Tejada.
COMPLETE SET (30) 25.00 7.50

2001 Elizabethton Twins Update Grandstand

This 10 card set features 10 different cards of number one draft pick Joe Mauer.
COMPLETE SET (10) 25.00 7.50

2001 Erie Seawolves Multi-Ad

COMPLETE SET (30) 10.00 3.00

2001 Eugene Emeralds Grandstand

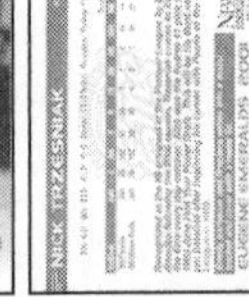

COMPLETE STET (35) 10.00 3.00

2001 Eugene Emeralds Greats Ortega

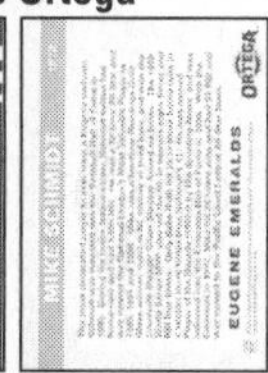

This 10-card set features a selection of major league stars that at one point in time played for the Eugene Emeralds. Each black-bordered card features crude painted images of the ballplayer. The set was produced the Ortega company and distributed within a loose, sealed cello bag in November, 2001.
COMPLETE SET 10.00 3.00

2001 Everett Aquasox Grandstand

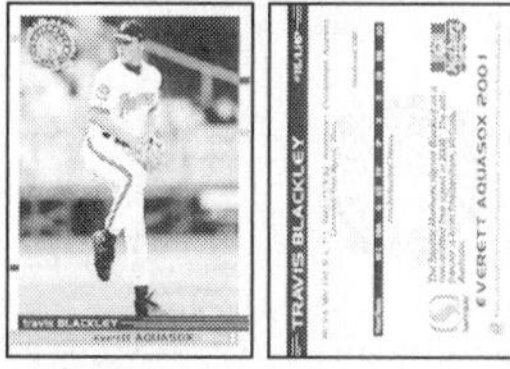

COMPLETE SET (32)................ 15.00 4.50

2001 Florida State League Gold Prospects Grandstand

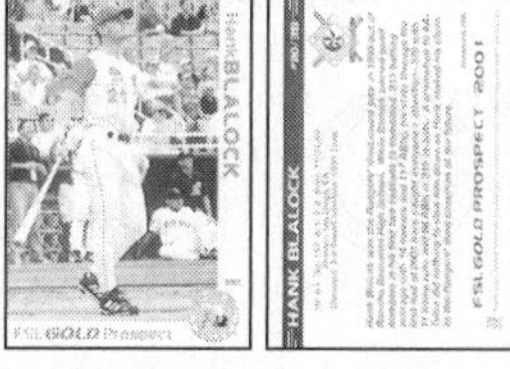

Only 500 sets were produced. Each set was distributed with a hand-numbered set identification card. Randomly seeded into sets were signed cards featuring super prospects Hank Blalock (of whom signed 75 copies) and Justin Morneau. Set price refers to sealed bags.
COMPLETE SET (9).................. 25.00 7.50

2001 Florida State League Prospects Grandstand

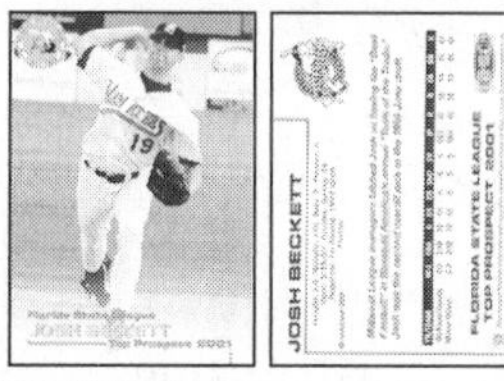

COMPLETE SET (31)................ 12.00 3.60

2001 Fort Myers Miracle Multi-Ad

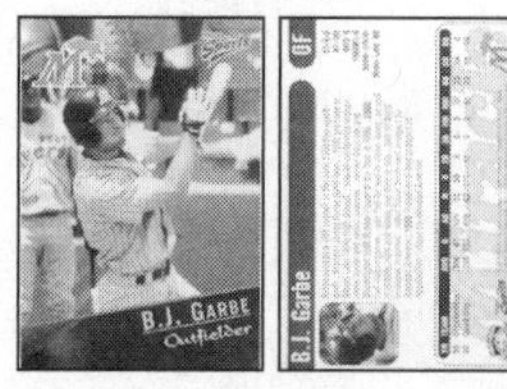

COMPLETE SET (30)................. 8.00 2.40

2001 Fort Wayne Wizards Grandstand

Key cards in this set include Jake Peavy, Oliver Perez and Dennis Tankersley.
COMPLETE SET (29)................ 18.00 5.50

2001 Frederick Keys Grandstand

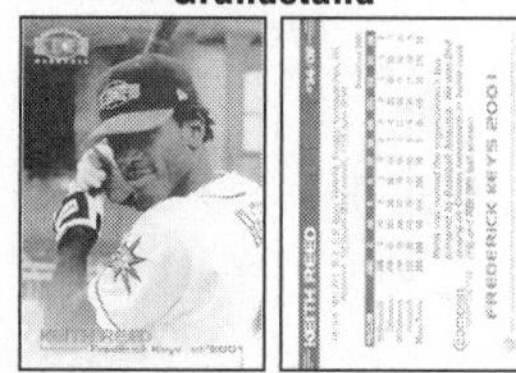

COMPLETE SET (31)................ 10.00 3.00

2001 Fresno Grizzlies Grandstand

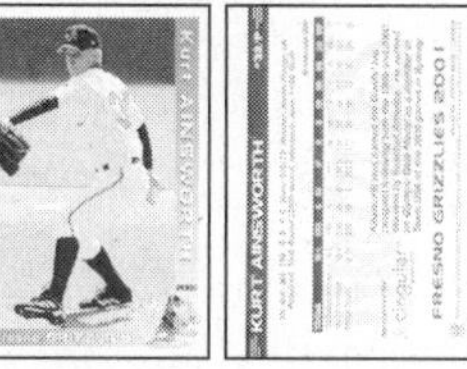

COMPLETE SET (30)................ 10.00 3.00

2001 Great Falls Dodgers Grandstand

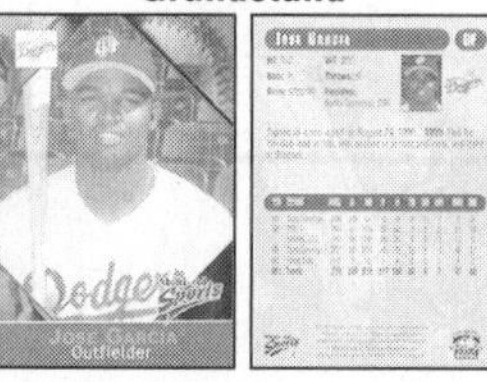

COMPLETE SET (30)................ 10.00 3.00

2001 Greensboro Bats Multi-Ad

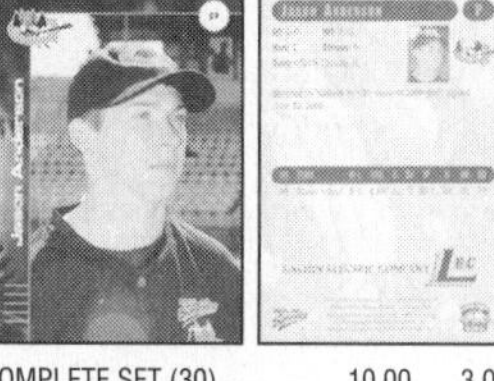

COMPLETE SET (30)................ 10.00 3.00

2001 Greenville Braves Grandstand

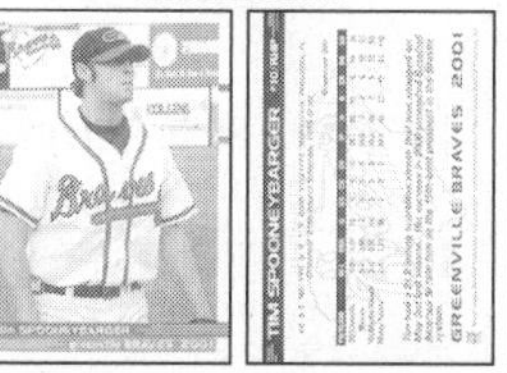

COMPLETE SET (38)................ 10.00 3.00

2001 Hagerstown Suns Multi-Ad

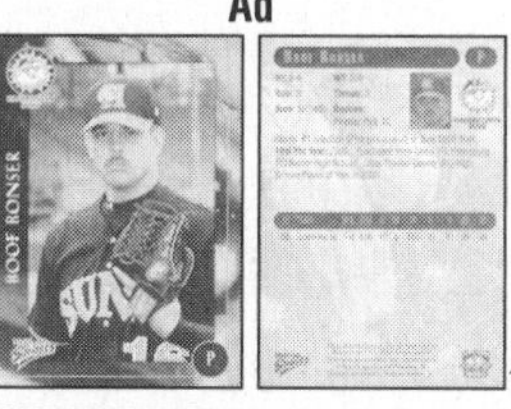

COMPLETE SET (30)................. 5.00 1.50

2001 Harrisburg Senators Multi-Ad

COMPLETE SET (30)................ 10.00 3.00

2001 Hickory Crawdads Black Multi-Ad

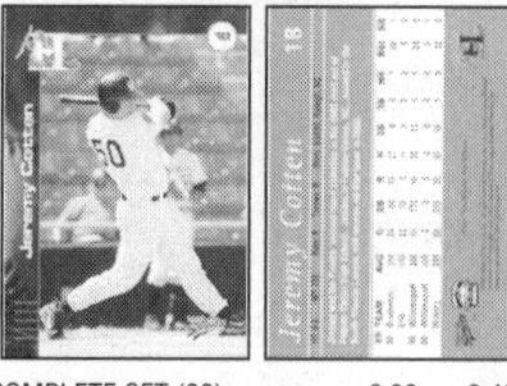

COMPLETE SET (30)................. 8.00 2.40

2001 Hickory Crawdads Multi-Ad

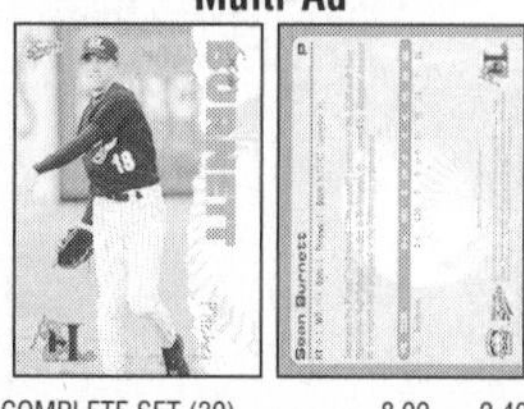

COMPLETE SET (30)................. 8.00 2.40

2001 High Desert Mavericks Grandstand

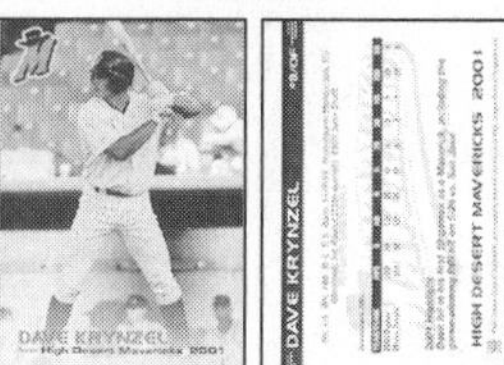

COMPLETE SET (31)................ 15.00 4.50

2001 Hudson Valley Renegades Multi-Ad

COMPLETE SET (33)................ 10.00 3.00

2001 Huntsville Stars Team Issue Burger King

COMPLETE SET (29)................ 10.00 3.00

2001 Indianapolis Indians Choice

COMPLETE SET (30)................. 8.00 2.40

2001 International League Top Prospects Choice

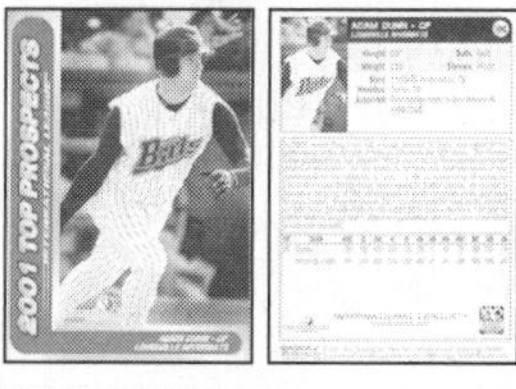

COMPLETE SET (30)................ 15.00 4.50

2001 Iowa Cubs Des Moines Register Oversize

COMPLETE SET (7)........................

2001 Iowa Cubs Multi-Ad

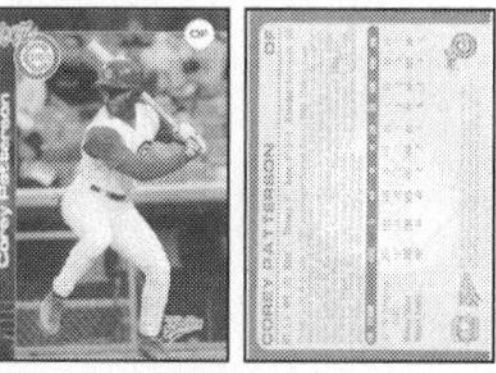

COMPLETE SET (30)................ 12.00 3.60

2001 Jacksonville Suns Grandstand

COMPLETE SET (31)................. 8.00 2.40

2001 Johnson City Cardinals Grandstand

COMPLETE SET (31)................ 10.00 3.00

2001 Jupiter Hammerheads Team Issue

Key cards in this set include Jason Bay, Cliff Lee and Brandon Phillips.
COMPLETE SET (36)................ 15.00 4.50

2001 Kane County Cougars Connie's Pizza

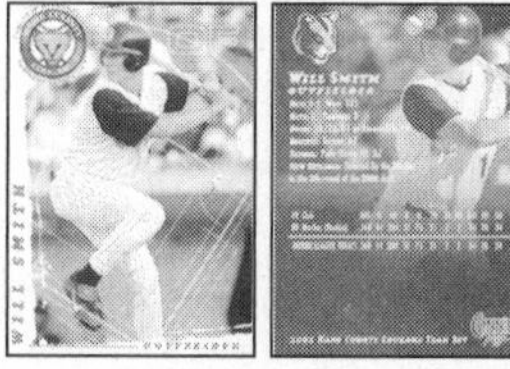

COMPLETE SET (33)................ 30.00 6.00

2001 Kane County Cougars Grandstand

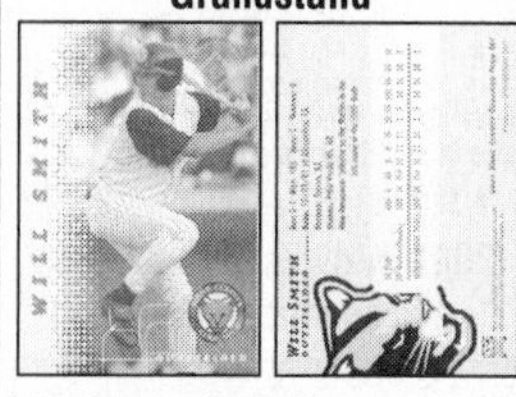

Adrian Gonzalez signed 100 cards which were randomly inserted in these sets.
COMPLETE SET (32)................ 25.00 4.50

2001 Kannapolis Intimidators Multi-Ad

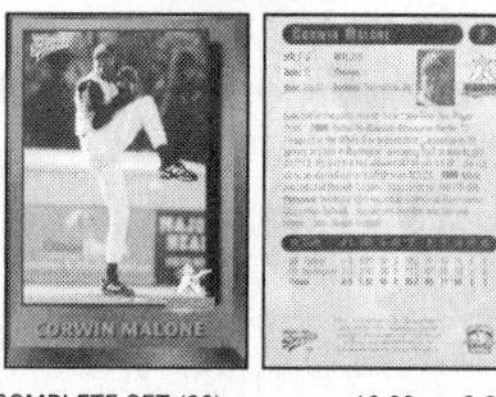

COMPLETE SET (30)................ 10.00 3.00

2001 Keene Swamp Bats

The set is unnumbered and checklisted in alphabetical order.
COMPLETE SET (26)................. 5.00 1.50

2001 Kinston Indians Choice

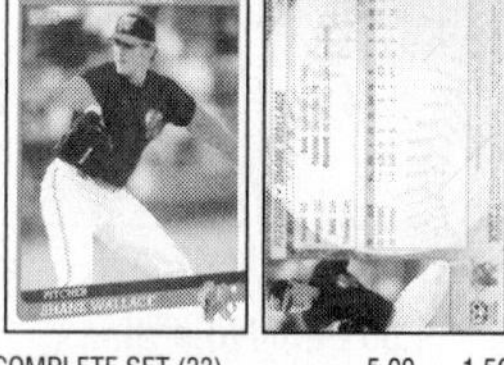

COMPLETE SET (33)................. 5.00 1.50

2001 Lake Elsinore Storm Grandstand

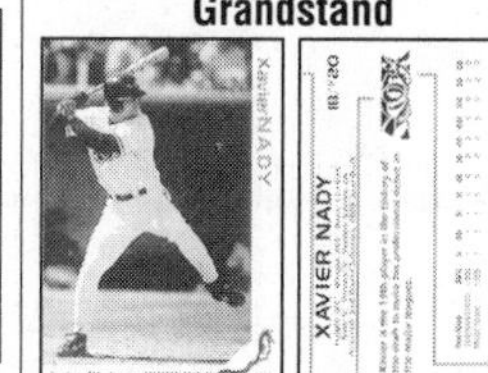

This set was loaded with prospects. Among the leading ones were Eric Cyr, Ben Howard, Xavier Nady, Jake Peavy and Dennis Tankersley.
COMPLETE SET (30)................ 20.00 6.00

2001 Lakeland Tigers Multi-Ad

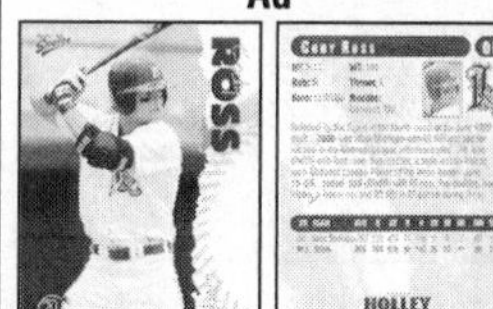

COMPLETE SET (30)................ 10.00 3.00

2001 Lakewood BlueClaws Multi-Ad

COMPLETE SET (32)................ 10.00 3.00

2001 Lancaster Jethawks Grandstand

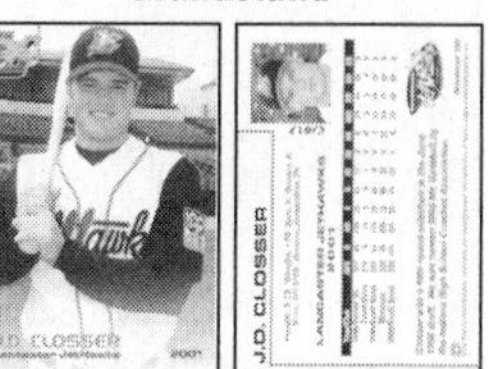

COMPLETE SET (30)................. 8.00 2.40

2001 Lansing Lugnuts Grandstand

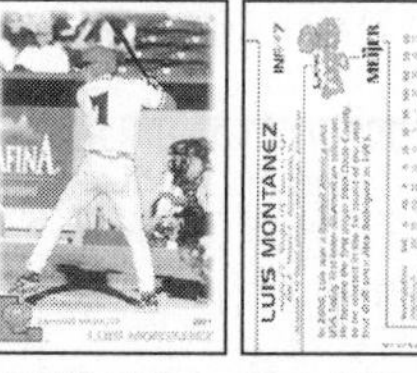

COMPLETE SET (30)................ 10.00 3.00

2001 Las Vegas 51's Multi-Ad

COMPLETE SET (30)................ 10.00 3.00

2001 Legends of Bowman

Given out one per selected games at Bowman Field. These cards honor players who were stars and passed through Bowman Field.
COMPLETE SET (4)................. 20.00 6.00

2001 Lexington Legends Multi-Ad

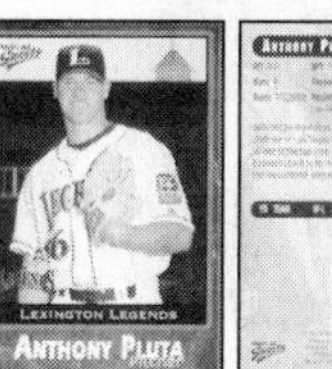

COMPLETE SET (30)................ 15.00 4.50

2001 Lincoln Saltdogs Grandstand

26-card set produced by Grandstand and distributed in a cello team set bag in November, 2001. The cards are numbered on back by uniform number, thus the set is checklisted in a skip-numbered fashion.
COMPLETE SET (26)................ 10.00 3.00

2001 Louisville Riverbats Choice

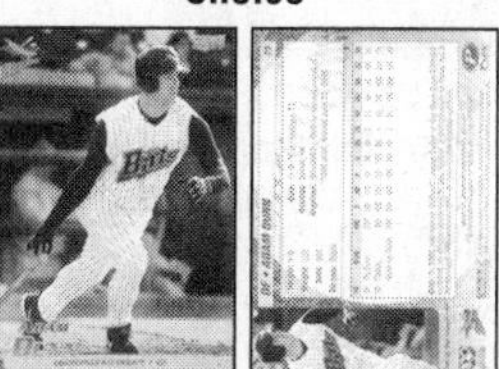

Cards number 29 and 30 do not exist. Key cards in this set include Adam Dunn, Brandon Larson and football star Deion Sanders.
COMPLETE SET (33)................ 15.00 4.50

2001 Lowell Spinners Multi-Ad

COMPLETE SET (30)................ 10.00 3.00

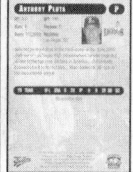

2001 LSU Tigers

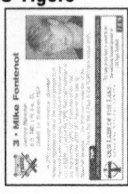

Todd Linden is the featured player in this set.
COMPLETE SET (16)................ 20.00 6.00

2001 Lynchburg Hillcats Choice

COMPLETE SET (30)................ 10.00 3.00

2001 Macon Braves Multi-Ad

COMPLETE SET (30)................ 15.00 4.50

2001 Mahoning Valley Scrappers Multi-Ad

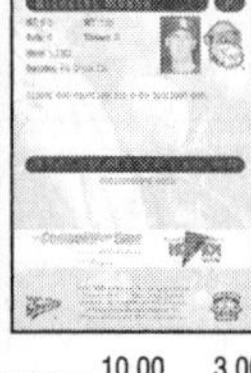

COMPLETE SET (30)................ 10.00 3.00

2001 Martinsville Astros Grandstand

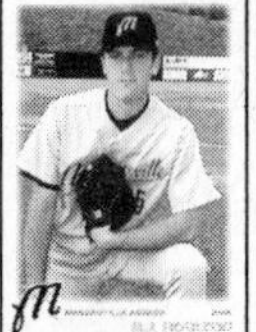
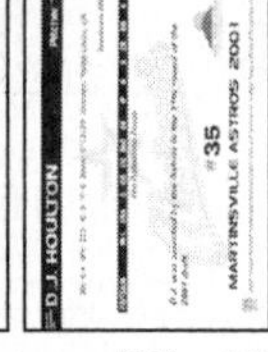

COMPLETE SET (30)................ 10.00 3.00

2001 Memphis Redbirds Post

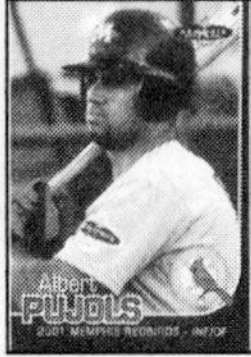
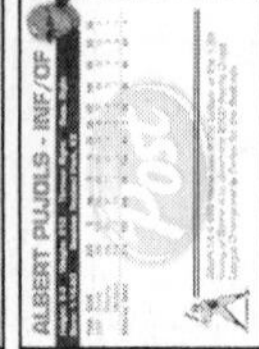

Key players in this set include Rick Ankiel, Albert Pujols and Bud Smith.
COMPLETE SET (30)................ 20.00 6.00

2001 Michigan Battlecats Team Issue

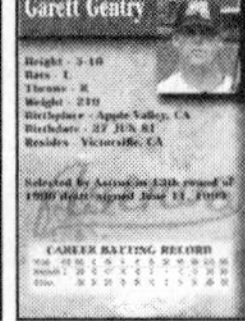

COMPLETE SET (30)................ 10.00 3.00

2001 Midland Rockhounds Grandstand

COMPLETE SET (27)................ 10.00 3.00

2001 Midland Rockhounds OHP

This 31-card set was issued by Walgreen's One Hour Photo. Each over-sized card measures 8" tall by 4" wide and features a full color player photo printed on glossy Kodak film stock. The backs are blank save for the Kodak logos. The cards are unnumbered and checklisted in alphabetical order by player's last name.
COMPLETE SET (31)................ 40.00 12.00

2001 Midwest League Top Prospect Multi-Ad

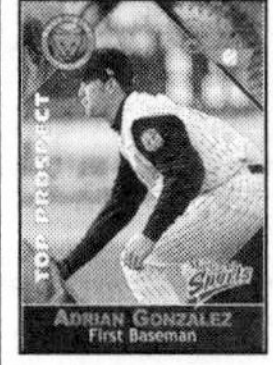

COMPLETE SET (29)................ 10.00 3.00

2001 Missoula Osprey Grandstand

Key players in this set include Jesus Cota, Lino Garcia and Scott Hairston.
COMPLETE SET (35)................ 20.00 6.00

2001 Modesto A's Grandstand

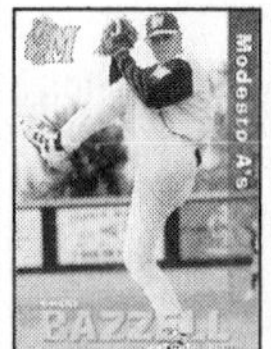

COMPLETE SET (30)................ 8.00 2.40

2001 Mudville Nine Grandstand

COMPLETE SET (30)................ 5.00 1.50

2001 Myrtle Beach Pelicans Multi-Ad

COMPLETE SET (30)................ 15.00 4.50

2001 Nashville Sounds Grandstand

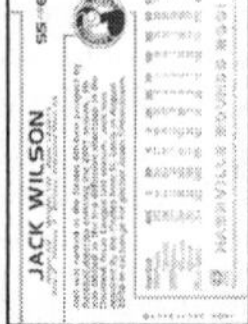

COMPLETE SET (30)................ 10.00 3.00

2001 New Britain Rock Cats Multi-Ad

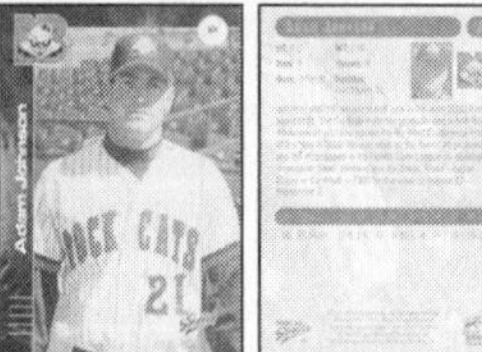

COMPLETE SET (30)................ 10.00 3.00

2001 New Haven Ravens Choice

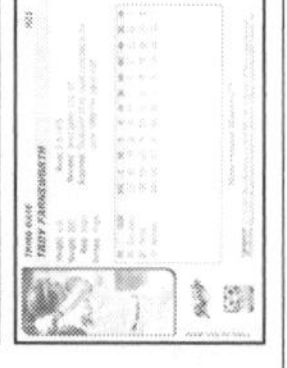

COMPLETE SET (29)................ 10.00 3.00

2001 New Jersey Cardinals Grandstand

COMPLETE SET (32)................ 8.00 2.40

2001 New Orleans Zephyrs Multi-Ad

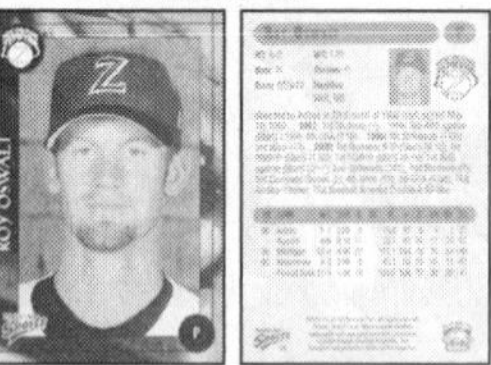

COMPLETE SET (30)................ 10.00 3.00

2001 Norfolk Tides Choice

COMPLETE SET (33)................ 8.00 2.40

2001 Norwich Navigators Grandstand

COMPLETE SET (26)................ 10.00 3.00

2001 Ogden Raptors N-Step

Key prospects in this set include J.J. Hardy, Corey Hart, Mike Jones and Matt Yeatman.
COMPLETE SET (43)................ 25.00 7.50

2001 Oklahoma Redhawks Multi-Ad

COMPLETE SET (29)................ 10.00 3.00

2001 Omaha Golden Spikes Choice

COMPLETE SET (26)................ 8.00 2.40

2001 Ottawa Lynx Choice

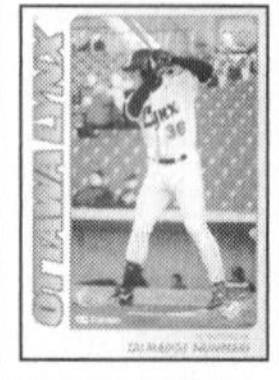

COMPLETE SET (31)................ 10.00 3.00

2001 Pawtucket Red Sox Choice

COMPLETE SET (30)................ 5.00 1.50

2001 Pawtucket Red Sox Dunkin' Donuts

This attractive set, sponsored by Dunkin' Donuts and The Providence Journal, consists of 30 standard-sized perforated cards and a jumbo photo montage cover sheet all distributed together as one giant fold-out sheet. The 30 cards feature members of the AAA Pawtucket Red Six and the jumbo montage features all-time Pawtucket greats like Nomar Garciaparra and Roger Clemens. The perforated cards are unnumbered and checklisted in alphabetical order by player's last name (save for the manager and coaches which begin the set).
COMPLETE SET (31)................ 15.00 4.50

2001 Penn State Nittany Lions Choice

COMPLETE SET (35)................ 10.00 3.00

2001 Peoria Chiefs Multi-Ad

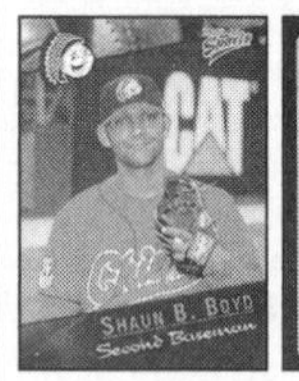

COMPLETE SET (30)................ 10.00 3.00

2001 Pittsfield Astros Multi-Ad

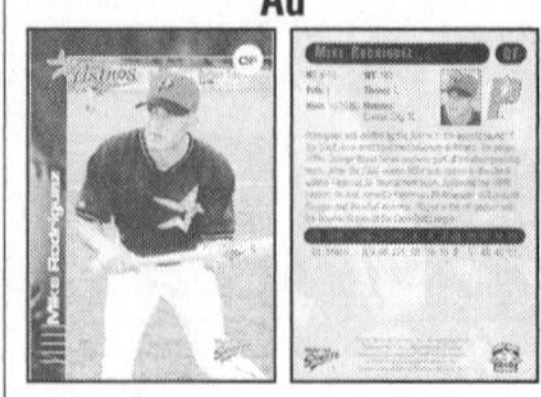

COMPLETE SET (31)................ 10.00 3.00

2001 Portland Sea Dogs Grandstand

COMPLETE SET (32)................ 15.00 4.50

2001 Potamac Cannons Choice

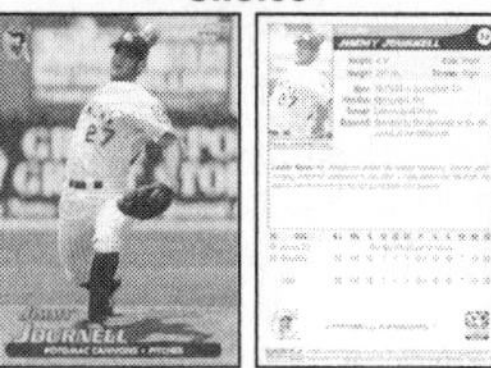

COMPLETE SET (30)................ 10.00 3.00

2001 Princeton Devil Rays Grandstand

Featured players in this set include Jonny Gomes and Greg "Toe" Nash.
COMPLETE SET (30)................ 20.00 6.00

2001 Provo Angels Grandstand

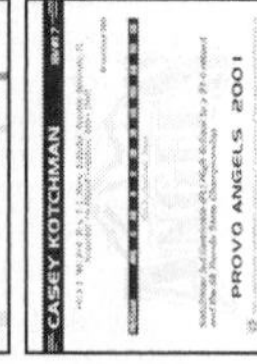

Casey Kotchman, Jeff Mathis and Dallas McPherson are the key prospects in this set.
COMPLETE SET (35)................ 30.00 9.00

2001 Pulaski Rangers Grandstand

COMPLETE SET (31)................ 10.00 3.00

2001 Quad City River Bandits Grandstand

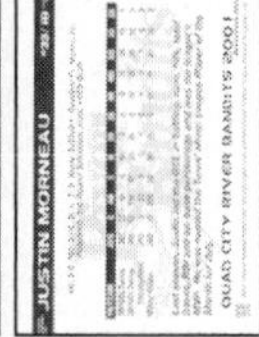

Key players in this set include Rob Bowen, Justin Morneau and Josh Rabe.
COMPLETE SET (30)................ 18.00 5.50

2001 Rancho Cucamonga Quakes

COMPLETE SET (30)................ 10.00 3.00

2001 Rancho Cucamonga Quakes Update Grandstand

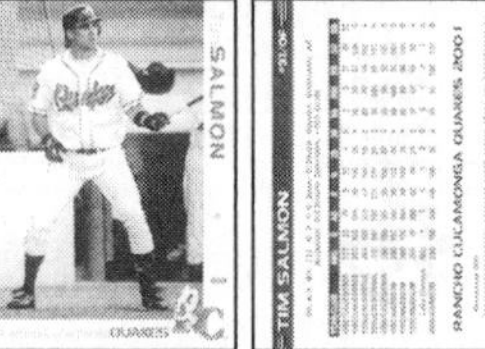

COMPLETE SET (17)................ 15.00 4.50

2001 Reading Phillies Multi-Ad

Marlon Byrd and Brett Myers are the key prospects in this set.
COMPLETE SET (30)................ 20.00 6.00

2001 Richmond Braves Choice

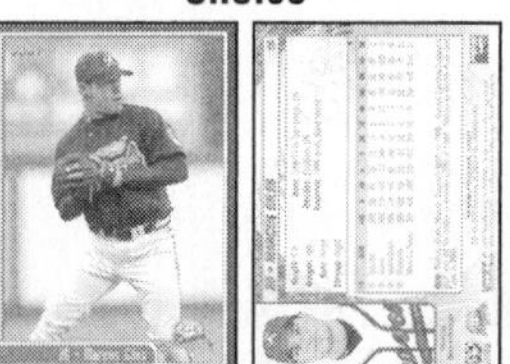

COMPLETE SET (32)................ 10.00 3.00

2001 Rochester Red Wings Choice

COMPLETE SET (30)................. 8.00 2.40

2001 Round Rock Express Multi-Ad

COMPLETE SET (30)............... 12.00 3.60

2001 Sacramento River Cats Grandstand

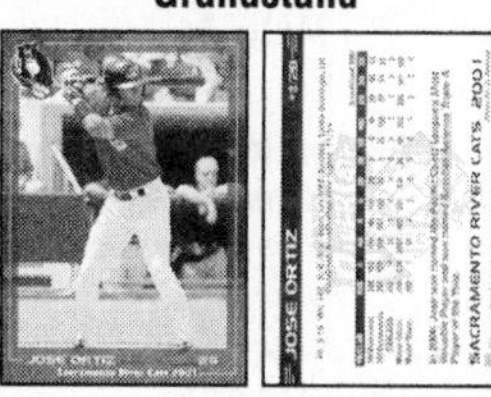

Eric Hinske is the featured prospect in this set.
COMPLETE SET (30)............... 20.00 6.00

2001 Salem Avalanche Grandstand

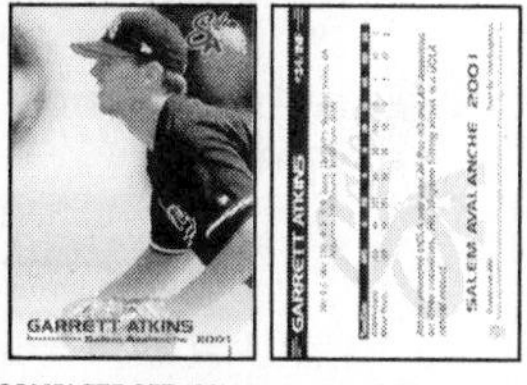

COMPLETE SET (30)................. 8.00 2.40

2001 Salem-Keizer Volcanoes Grandstand

Julian Benavidez is a late addition to this set. The key prospect in this set is Giant prospect Jesse Foppert.
COMPLETE SET (36)............... 12.00 3.60

2001 San Bernardino Stampede Grandstand

COMPLETE SET (29)............... 10.00 3.00

2001 San Jose Giants Grandstand

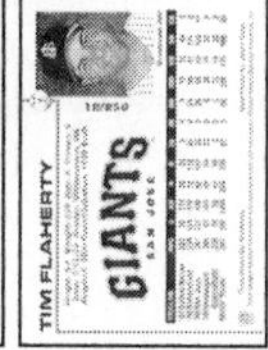

COMPLETE SET (30)................. 8.00 2.40

2001 Sarasota Red Sox Multi-Ad

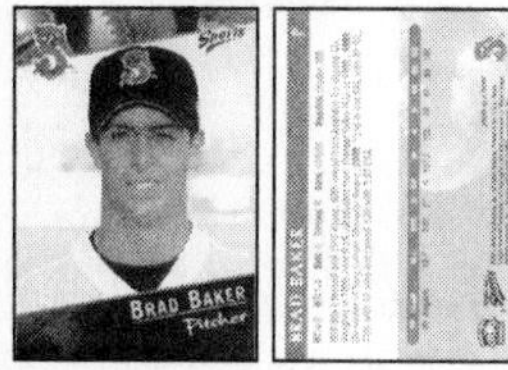

COMPLETE SET (30)................. 8.00 2.40

2001 Savannah Sand Gnats Multi-Ad

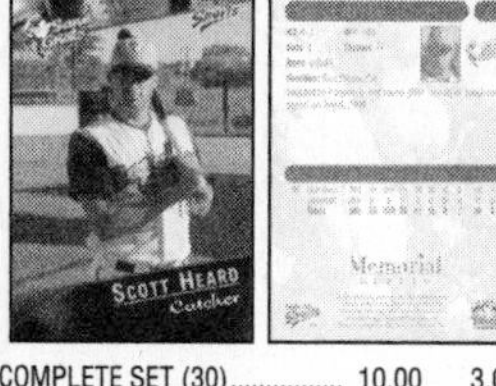

COMPLETE SET (30)............... 10.00 3.00

2001 Scranton/Wilkes-Barre Red Barons Choice

COMPLETE SET (30)............... 12.00 3.60

2001 Shreveport Swamp Dragons Team Issue

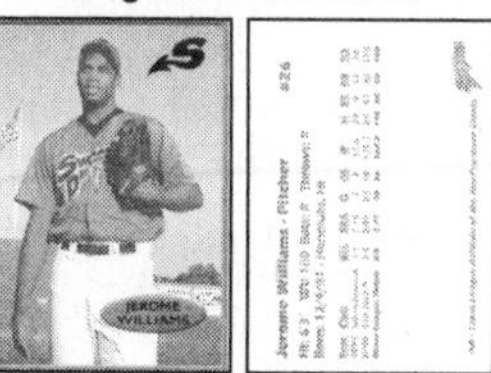

This 29-card set was produced by the team and distributed in a cello team set bag. The green bordered cards were cut from sheets in crude fashion, leaving most with uneven borders. The cards are numbered on back by uniform number, thus checklisting is skip-numbered. Jerome Williams is the key prospect in this set.
COMPLETE SET (29)............... 20.00 6.00

2001 South Atlantic League Top Prospect Multi-Ad

COMPLETE SET (32)............... 15.00 4.50

2001 Southern League Top Prospects Grandstand

COMPLETE SET (30)............... 15.00 4.50

2001 Spokane Indians Grandstand

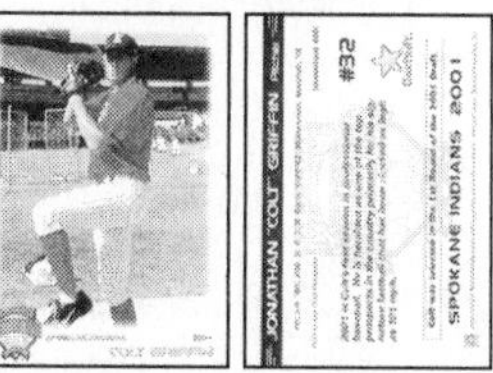

COMPLETE SET (35)............... 12.00 3.60

2001 St. Lucie Mets Grandstand

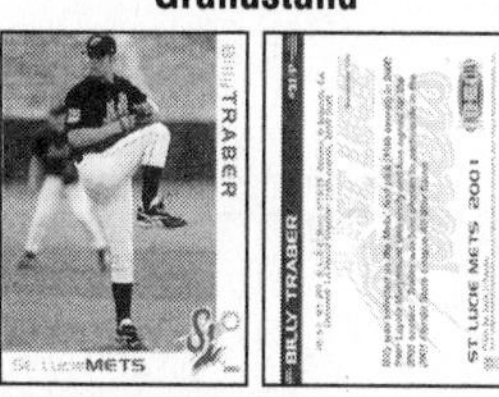

Billy Traber is the key to this set.
COMPLETE SET (32)............... 15.00 4.50

2001 St. Lucie Mets Update Grandstand

This one card set features Mets high draft pick Aaron Heilman.
COMPLETE SET (1)................. 5.00 1.50

2001 Staten Island Yankees Multi-Ad

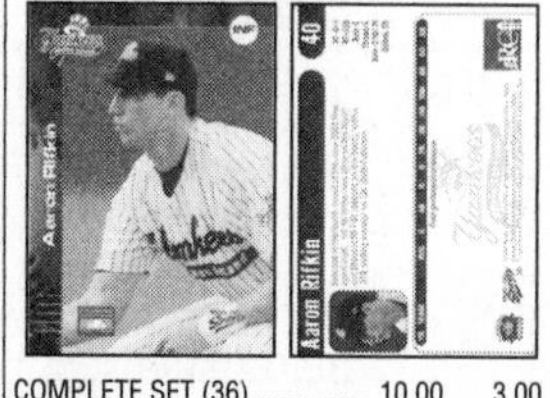

COMPLETE SET (36)............... 10.00 3.00

2001 Syracuse Skychiefs Choice

COMPLETE SET (30)............... 10.00 3.00

2001 Tacoma Rainiers Grandstand

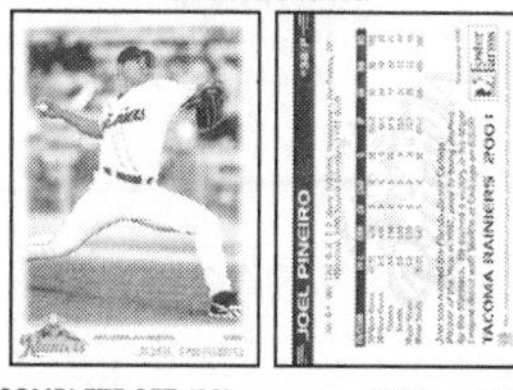

COMPLETE SET (30)............... 10.00 3.00

2001 Tampa Yankees Multi-Ad

COMPLETE SET (30)............... 15.00 4.50

2001 Tennessee Smokies Grandstand

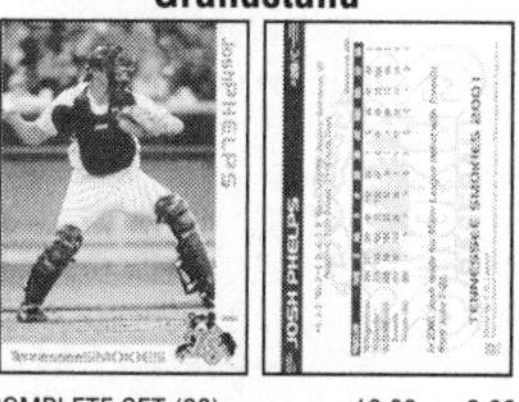

COMPLETE SET (28)............... 10.00 3.00

2001 Tennessee Volunteers Krystal

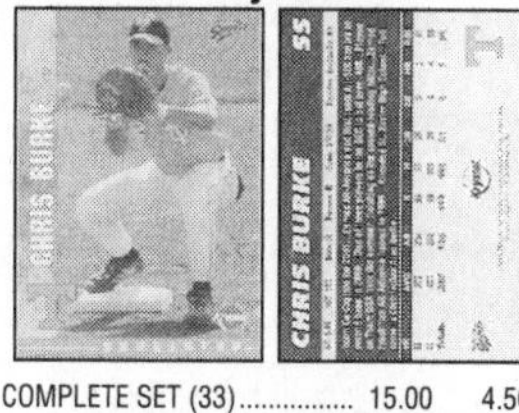

COMPLETE SET (33)............... 15.00 4.50

2001 Texas League Top Prospects Grandstand

COMPLETE SET (30)............... 15.00 4.50

2001 Toledo Mud Hens Choice

COMPLETE SET (30)............... 10.00 3.00

2001 Trenton Thunder Multi-Ad

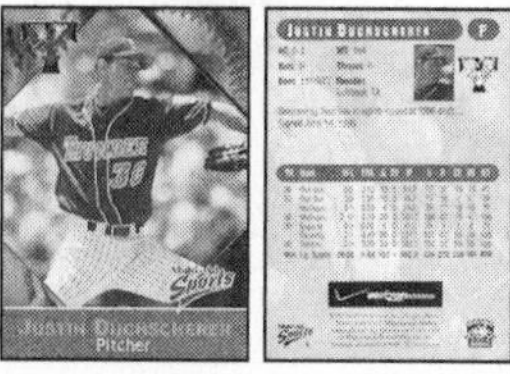

COMPLETE SET (30)............... 10.00 3.00

2001 Trenton Thunder Road to the Majors Multi-Ad

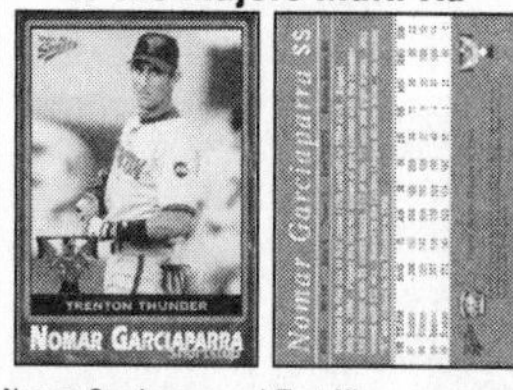

Nomar Garciaparra and Trot Nixon are among the players who have achieved sucsess in the major leagues.
COMPLETE SET (25)............... 20.00 6.00

2001 Tucson Sidewinders Grandstand

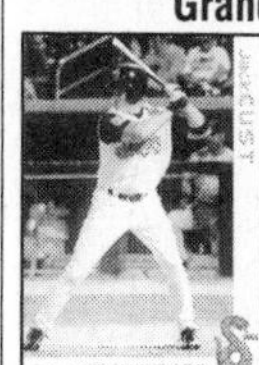
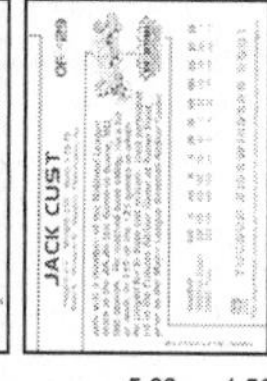

COMPLETE SET (30)................. 5.00 1.50

2001 Tulsa Drillers Hank Blalock Update Minor Miracles

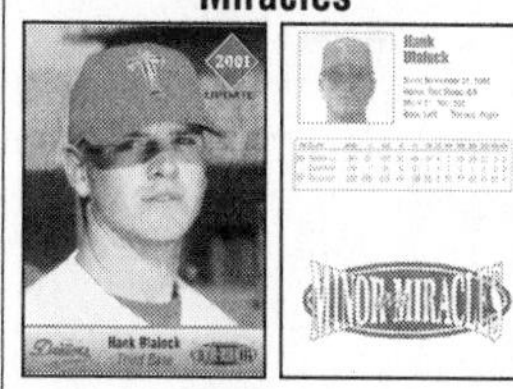

COMPLETE SET (1)................... 6.00 1.80

2001 Tulsa Drillers Oklahoma Highway

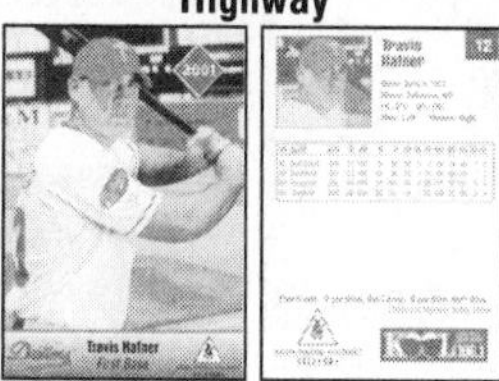

COMPLETE SET (31)............... 10.00 3.00

2001 Tulsa Drillers Update Oklahoma Highway

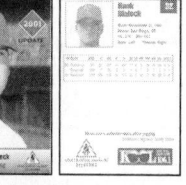

Hank Blalock signed 100 cards which were randomly inserted into sets.
COMPLETE SET (10)............... 12.00 3.60

2001 Vermont Expos Grandstand

COMPLETE SET (34)............... 10.00 3.00

2001 Vero Beach Dodgers Multi-Ad

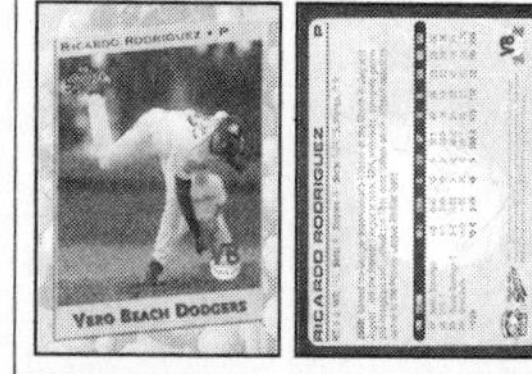

COMPLETE SET (35)............... 15.00 4.50

2001 Visalia Oaks Grandstand

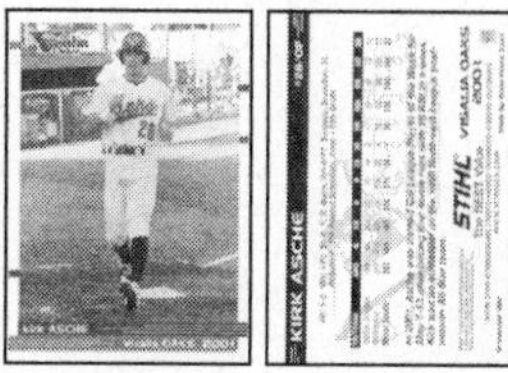

COMPLETE SET (30)............... 10.00 3.00

2001 West Michigan Whitecaps Multi-Ad

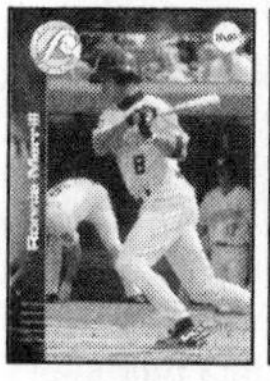
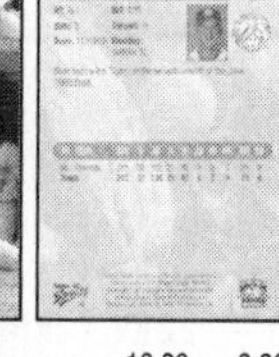

COMPLETE SET (30)............... 10.00 3.00

2001 West Tennessee Diamond Jaxx Grandstand

Juan Cruz and Bobby Hill are the keys to this set.
COMPLETE SET (30)............... 20.00 6.00

2001 Wichita Wranglers Grandstand

COMPLETE SET (31)................. 8.00 2.40

2001 Williamsport Crosscutters Multi-Ad

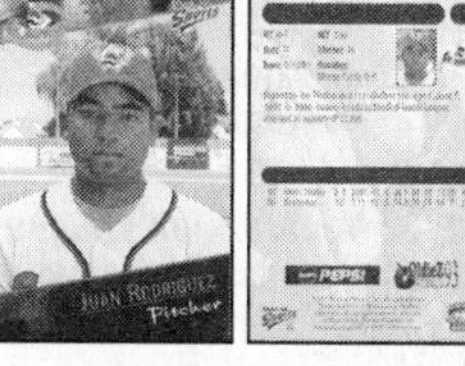

COMPLETE SET (30)............... 10.00 3.00

2001 Williamsport Pirates Multi-Ad

COMPLETE SET (30)............... 10.00 3.00

2001 Wilmington Blue Rocks Choice

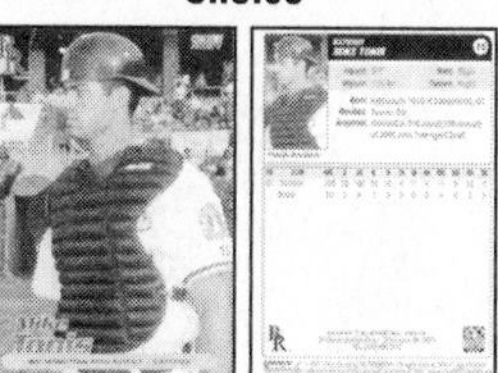

COMPLETE SET (30)................. 8.00 2.40

2001 Wilmington Waves Multi-Ad

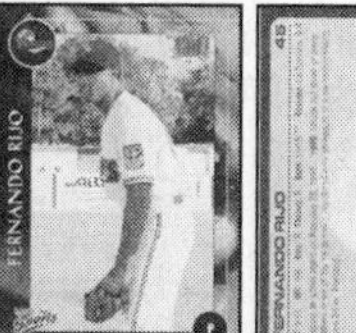

COMPLETE SET (30)............... 10.00 3.00

2001 Winston-Salem Warthogs Choice

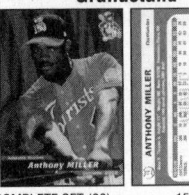

COMPLETE SET (1-31) 10.00 3.00

2001 Wisconsin Timber Rattlers Multi-Ad

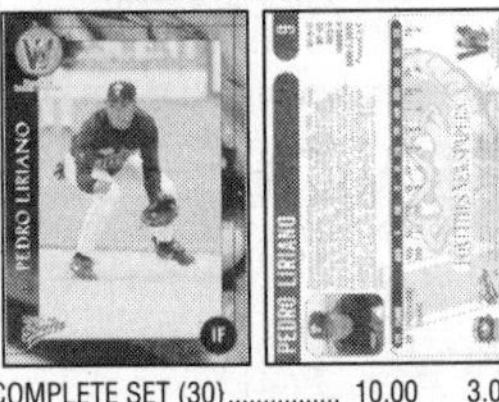

COMPLETE SET (30)............... 10.00 3.00

2001 Yakima Bears Grandstand

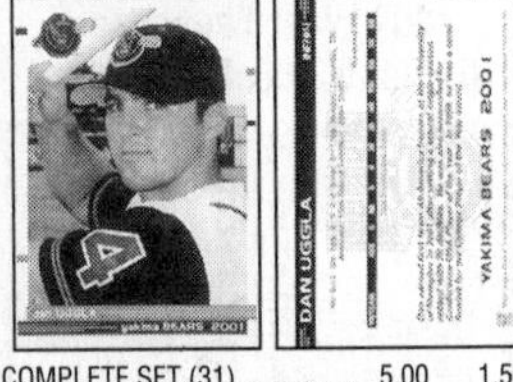

COMPLETE SET (31)................. 5.00 1.50

2002 Aberdeen Ironbirds Grandstand

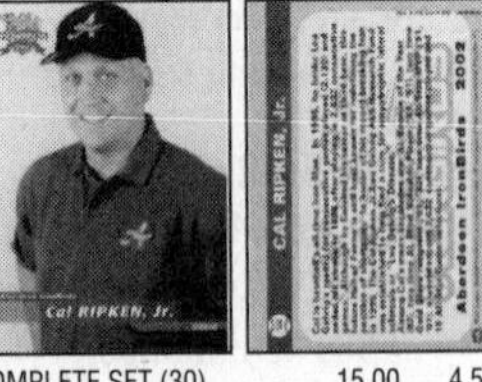

COMPLETE SET (30)............... 15.00 4.50

2002 Akron Aeros Multi-Ad

COMPLETE SET (30)............... 10.00 3.00

2002 Altoona Curve Grandstand

COMPLETE SET (30)............... 10.00 3.00

2002 Appalachian League Top Prospects Grandstand

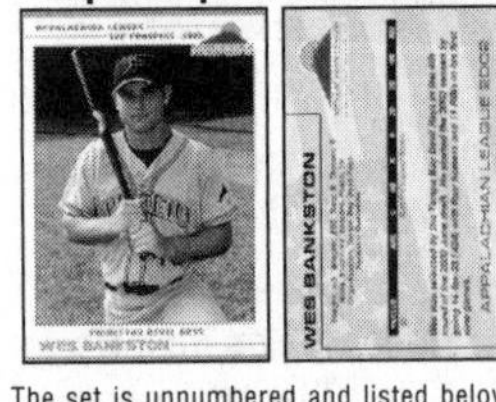

The set is unnumbered and listed below in alphabetical order.
COMPLETE SET (30)............... 15.00 4.50

2002 Arkansas Travelers Grandstand

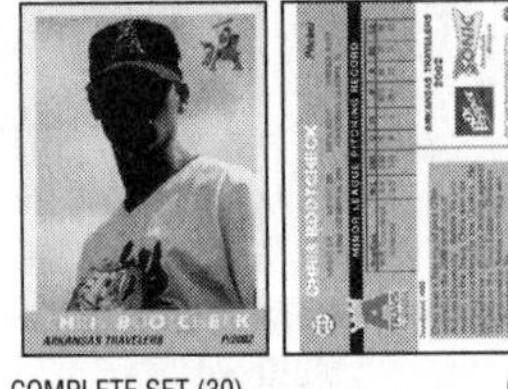

COMPLETE SET (30)................................. .00

2002 Asheboro Copperheads Grandstand

The set is unnumbered and checklisted below in alphabetical order.
COMPLETE SET (25)................. 8.00 2.40

2002 Asheville Tourists Grandstand

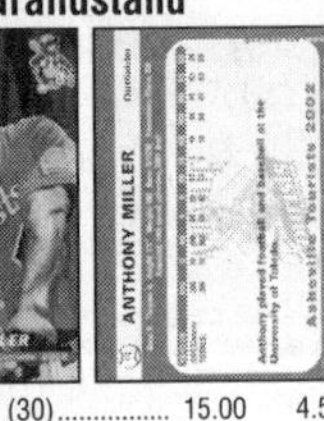

COMPLETE SET (30)............... 15.00 4.50

2002 Asheville Tourists Update Grandstand

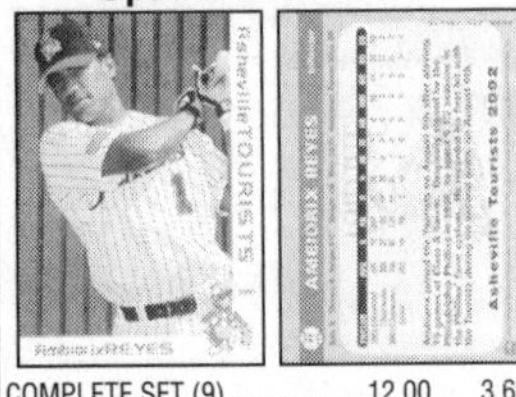

COMPLETE SET (9)................. 12.00 3.60

2002 Auburn Doubledays Team Issue

COMPLETE SET (33)............... 20.00 3.60

2002 Augusta Greenjackets Multi-Ad

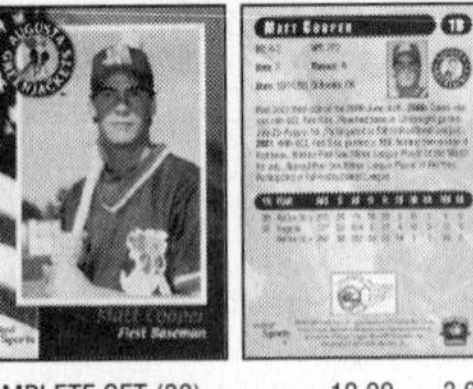

COMPLETE SET (30)............... 12.00 3.60

2002 Bakersfield Blaze Pepsi

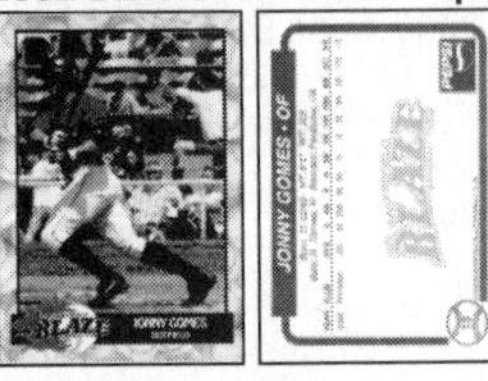

Early cards of Rocco Baldelli and Jonny Gomes highlight this set.
COMPLETE SET (32)............... 15.00 4.50

2002 Batavia Muckdogs Team Issue

COMPLETE SET (37)............... 12.00 3.60

2002 Beloit Snappers Multi-Ad

COMPLETE SET (31)............... 12.00 3.60

2002 Beloit Snappers Update Multi-Ad

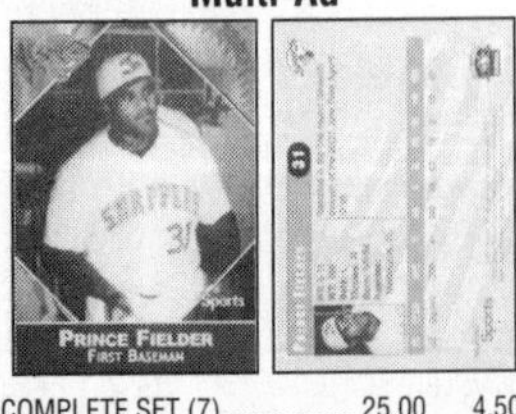

COMPLETE SET (7)................. 25.00 4.50

2002 Billings Mustangs Grandstand

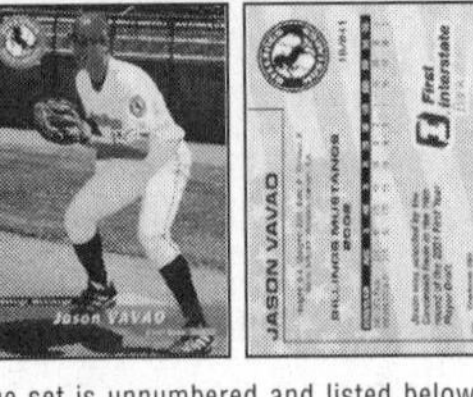

The set is unnumbered and listed below in alphabetical order.
COMPLETE SET (31)............... 12.00 3.60

2002 Binghamton Mets Choice

Team set was initially a 30-card set. Card No. 31 was issued as an update to the set.
COMPLETE SET (31)............... 12.00 3.60

2002 Birmingham Barons Grandstand

COMPLETE SET (30)............... 12.00 3.60

2002 Bluefield Orioles Grandstand

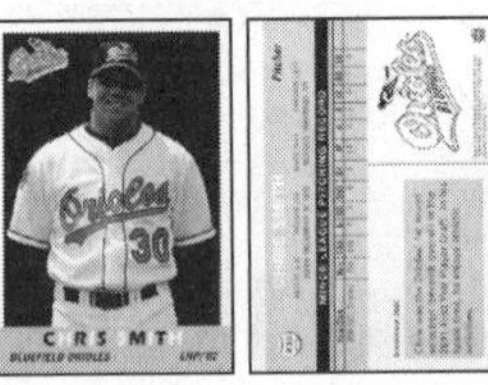

COMPLETE SET (36)............... 12.00 3.60

2002 Boise Hawks Grandstand

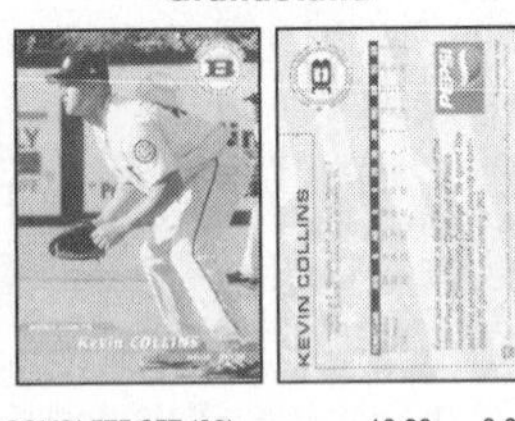

COMPLETE SET (30)............... 10.00 3.00

2002 Bowie Baysox Grandstand

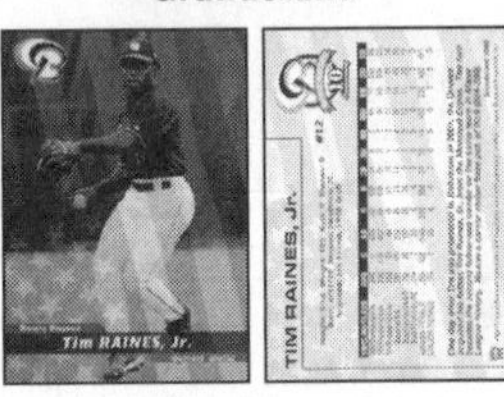

COMPLETE SET (29)............... 12.00 3.60

2002 Brevard County Manatees Multi-Ad

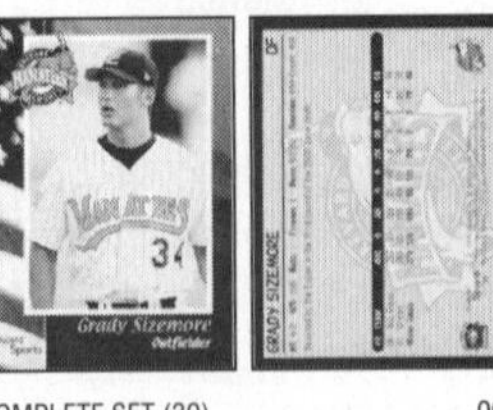

COMPLETE SET (30)............................ .00

2002 Bristol White Sox Grandstand

COMPLETE SET (30)............... 10.00 3.00

2002 Brooklyn Cyclones Multi-Ad

COMPLETE SET (34)............... 12.00 3.60

2002 Buffalo Bisons Choice

COMPLETE SET (30)................................. .00

2002 Burlington Bees Multi-Ad

COMPLETE SET (30)............... 12.00 3.60

2002 Calgary Cannons Multi-Ad

COMPLETE SET (27)............... 25.00 7.50

2002 California League Prospects Grandstand

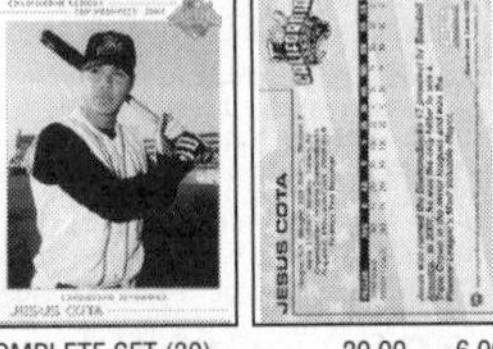

COMPLETE SET (30)............... 20.00 6.00

2002 California-Carolina League All Stars Choice

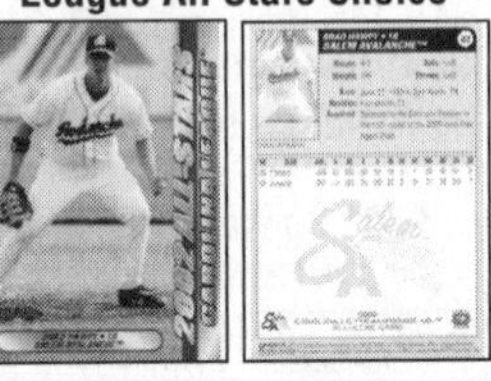

COMPLETE SET (50)............... 15.00 4.50

2002 Capital City Bombers Multi-Ad

COMPLETE SET (30)............... 15.00 4.50

2002 Carolina League Top Prospects Choice

COMPLETE SET (30)............... 12.00 3.60

2002 Carolina Mudcats Team Issue

COMPLETE SET (30)............... 12.00 3.60

2002 Casper Rockies Grandstand

COMPLETE SET (30)............... 12.00 3.60

2002 Cedar Rapids Kernels Perfect Game USA

COMPLETE SET (33)............... 12.00 3.60

2002 Charleston Alley Cats Multi-Ad

COMPLETE SET (30)............... 10.00 3.00

2002 Charleston River Dogs Multi-Ad

COMPLETE SET (30)............... 15.00 4.50

2002 Charlotte Knights Choice

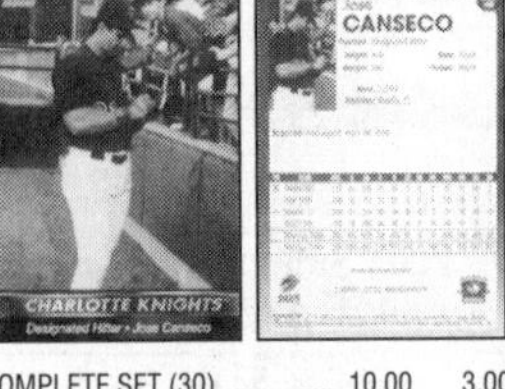

COMPLETE SET (30)............... 10.00 3.00

2002 Charlotte Rangers Grandstand

COMPLETE SET (30)............... 12.00 3.60

2002 Charlotte Rangers Minor Miracle Autograph

This one card set featured a signed card of Mark Teixeira. The front is the same as his Charlotte Rangers card, while the back states you have received an authentic "Minor Miracles" autograph card. Please note that this card does not have a certified stamp. This card was issued to a stated print run of 100 sets.
COMPLETE SET 30.00 9.00

2002 Chattanooga Lookouts Grandstand

The set is unnumbered and listed below in alphabetical order.
COMPLETE SET (30)............... 12.00 3.60

2002 Clearwater Phillies Grandstands

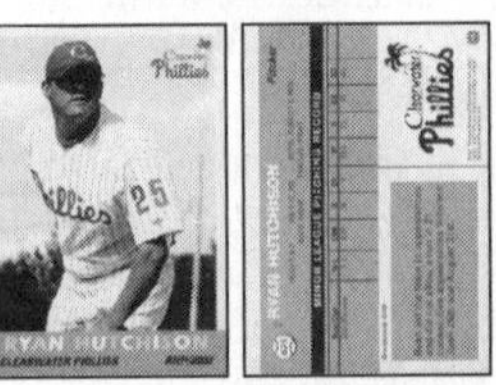

COMPLETE SET (30)............... 12.00 3.60

2002 Clinton Lumberkings Grandstand

COMPLETE SET (30)..................10.00 3.00

2002 College of St. Scholastica Saints

COMPLETE SET (10).................. 5.00 1.50

2002 Colorado Springs Sky Sox Multi-Ad

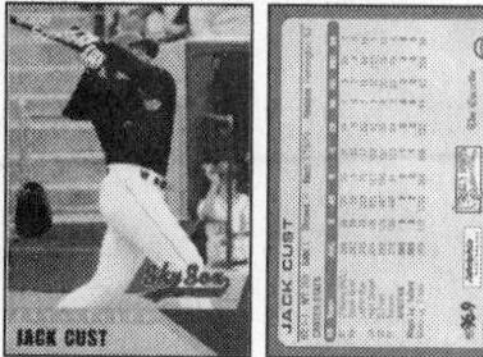

COMPLETE SET (30).................. 8.00 2.40

2002 Columbus Clippers Choice

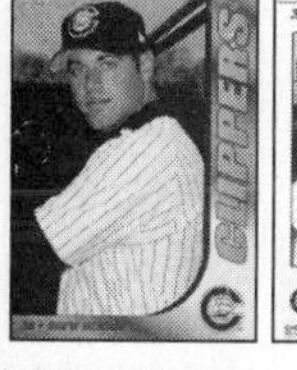

COMPLETE SET (30).................10.00 3.00

2002 Columbus RedStixx Multi-Ad

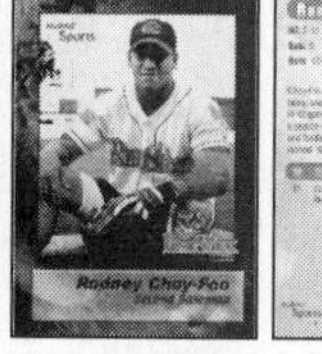

COMPLETE SET (30).................10.00 3.00

2002 Danville Braves Grandstand

The set is unnumbered and listed below in alphabetical order.
COMPLETE SET (33).................10.00 3.00

2002 Dayton Dragons Multi-Ad

COMPLETE SET (30)............... 15.00 4.50

2002 Daytona Cubs Choice

COMPLETE SET (30)............... 12.00 3.60

2002 Delmarva Shorebirds Multi-Ad

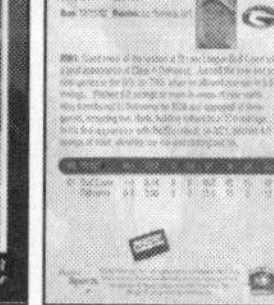

Key prospects in this set include Bryan Bass, David Crouthers and Tripper Johnson.
COMPLETE SET (30)............... 15.00 4.50

2002 Dunedin Blue Jays Grandstand

COMPLETE SET (30)............... 25.00 3.00

2002 Durham Bulls Choice

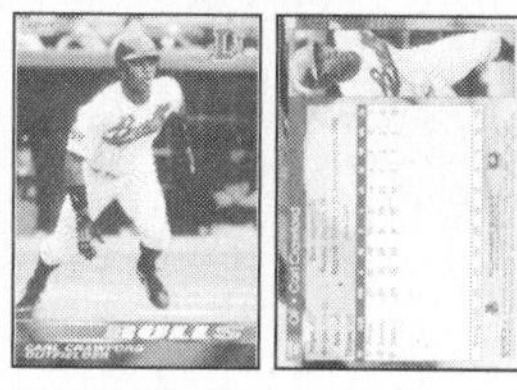

COMPLETE SET (30)............... 12.00 3.60

2002 Eastern League Prospects Grandstand

The checklist is unnumbered and listed below in alphabetical order.
COMPLETE SET (30)............... 10.00 3.00

2002 Edmonton Trappers Multi-Ad

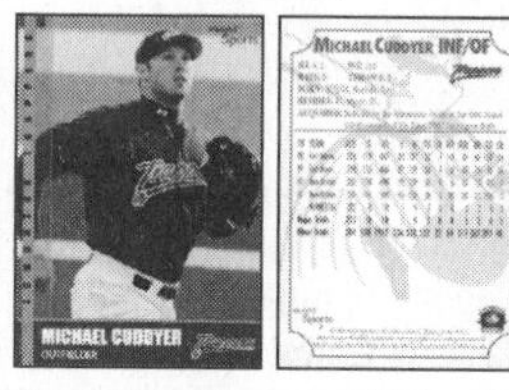

COMPLETE SET (30)............... 12.00 3.60

2002 El Paso Diablos Grandstand

The checklist is unnumbered and listed below in alphabetical order.
COMPLETE SET (30)............... 18.00 4.50

2002 Elizabethton Twins Grandstand

COMPLETE SET (27).................10.00 3.00

2002 Erie Seawolves Grandstand

COMPLETE SET (25)............... 10.00 3.00

2002 Eugene Emeralds Grandstand

COMPLETE SET (31)............... 15.00 4.50

2002 Everett AquaSox Grandstand

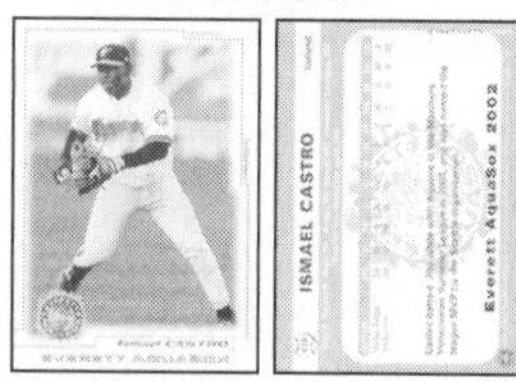

COMPLETE SET (30)............... 15.00 4.50

2002 Florida State League Prospects Grandstand

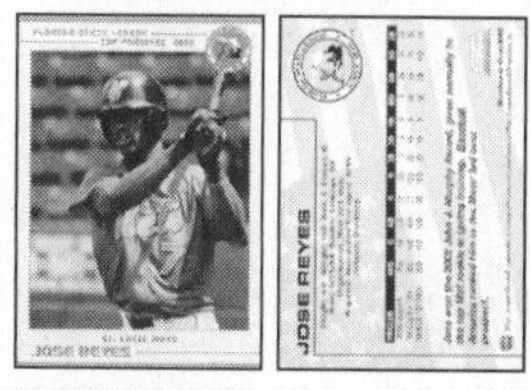

COMPLETE SET (24).............. 18.00 5.50

2002 Fort Wayne Wizards Grandstand

COMPLETE SET (31)............... 10.00 3.00

2002 Frederick Keys Grandstand

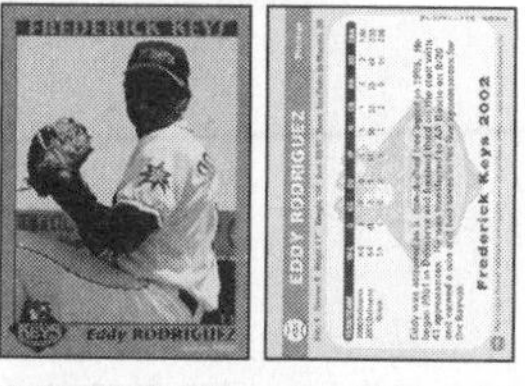

COMPLETE SET (30)............... 15.00 4.50

2002 Fresno Grizzlies Multi-Ad

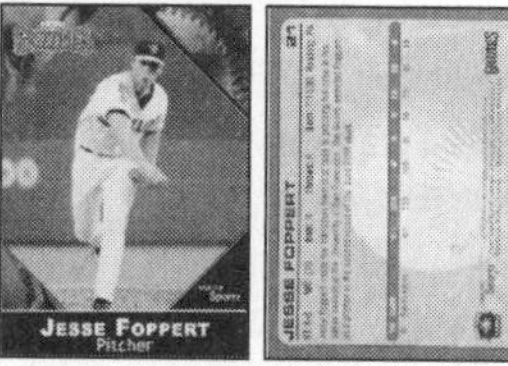

COMPLETE SET (29).................10.00 3.00

2002 Ft. Myers Miracle Multi-Ad

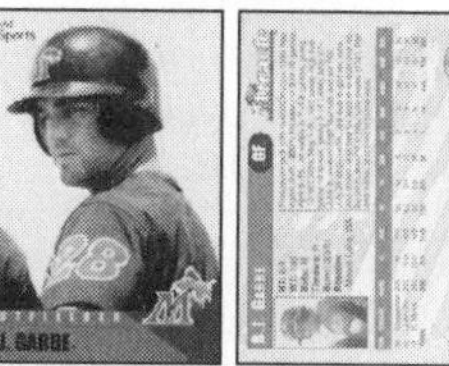

COMPLETE SET (30).................. 8.00 2.40

2002 FutureAngels.Com Grandstand

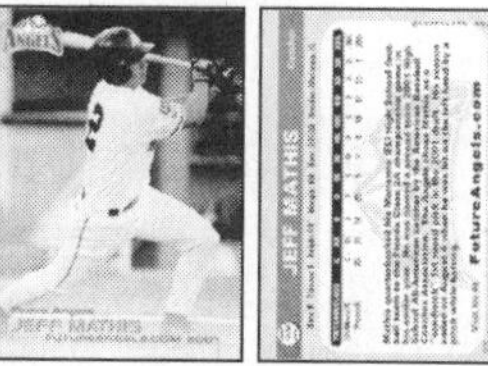

COMPLETE SET (30)............... 15.00 4.50

2002 Great Falls Dodgers Multi-Ad

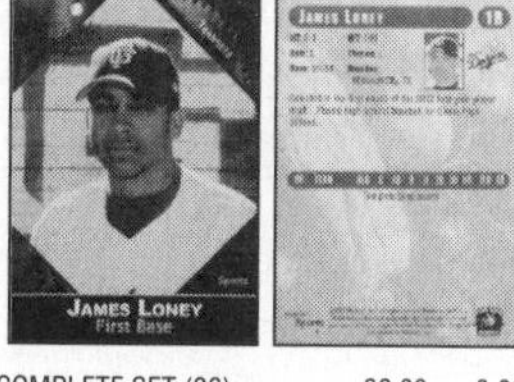

COMPLETE SET (36)............... 30.00 3.00

2002 Greensboro Bats Multi-Ad

COMPLETE SET (29)............... 12.00 3.60

2002 Greenville Braves Grandstand

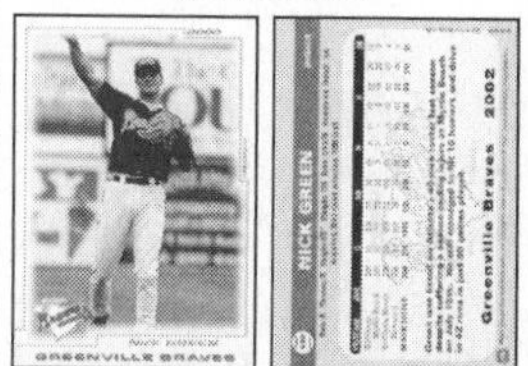

COMPLETE SET (30).......................... .00

2002 Hagerstown Suns Multi-Ad

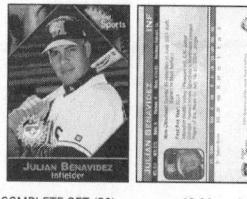

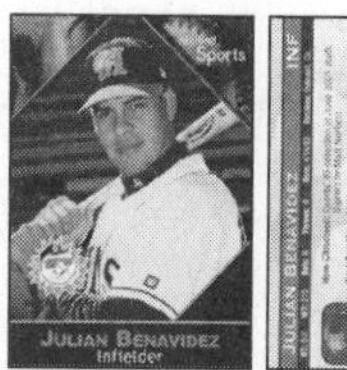

COMPLETE SET (29)............... 12.00 3.60

2002 Harrisburg Senators Grandstand

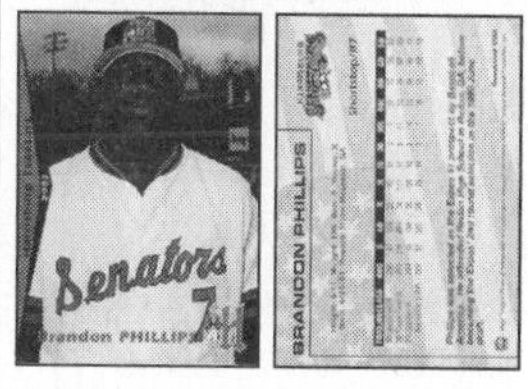

COMPLETE SET (28)............... 25.00 3.60

2002 Hickory Crawdads Multi-Ad

COMPLETE SET (30)............... 10.00 3.00

2002 Hickory Crawdads Update Multi-Ad

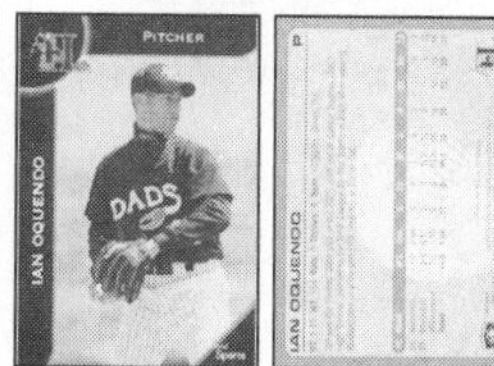

COMPLETE SET (30)............... 10.00 3.00

2002 High Desert Mavericks Grandstand

Key prospects in this set include Daryl Clark, Corey Hart and Dave Krynzel.
COMPLETE SET (32)............... 18.00 5.50

2002 High Desert Mavericks Update Autograph Minor Miracles

Under the auspices of Minor Miracles, Brad Nelson signed 100 cards honoring his stay as a member of the High Desert Maverick team.
COMPLETE SET 20.00 6.00

2002 High Desert Mavericks Update Grandstand

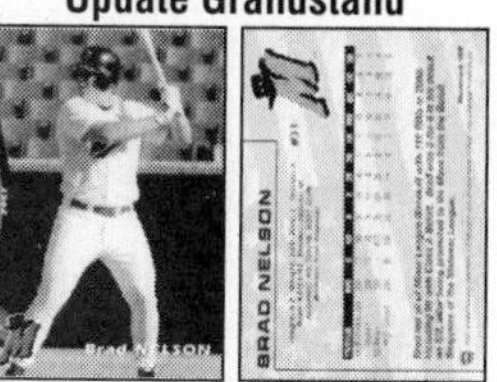

COMPLETE SET 5.00 1.50

2002 Hudson Valley Renegades Multi-Ad

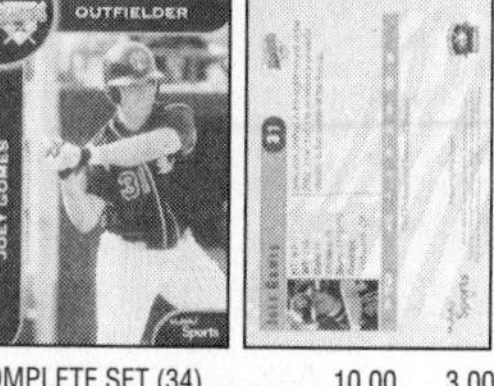

COMPLETE SET (34)............... 10.00 3.00

2002 Huntsville Stars Team Issue

COMPLETE SET (28).................10.00 3.00

2002 Indianapolis Indians Choice

COMPLETE SET (30)................. 8.00 2.40

2002 International League All-Stars Choice

COMPLETE SET (33)................. 15.00 4.50

2002 International League Top Prospects Choice

COMPLETE SET (30).................10.00 3.00

2002 Iowa Cubs Multi-Ad

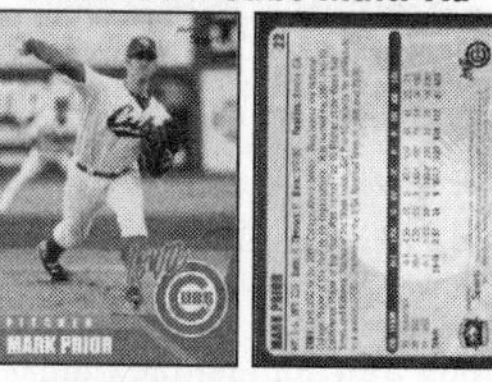

Hee Seop Choi and Mark Prior are the key players in this set.
COMPLETE SET (30).................25.00 7.50

2002 Jacksonville Suns Grandstand

COMPLETE SET (30)............... 10.00 3.00

2002 Johnson City Cardinals Grandstand

COMPLETE SET (35)............... 10.00 3.00

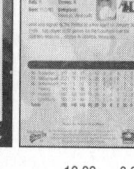

2002 Jupiter Hammerheads Team Issue

COMPLETE SET (36).......................... .00

2002 Kane County Cougars Authentic Signatures

This one card set features major league prospect Jason Stokes. Stokes signed 500 of these, inserted at a rate of 1 per every 4 Grandstand Team Sets. Althought they were inserted in Grandstand this independent card was inserted by the team with no Grandstand copyright. It is considered a Team Issue for this reason.

COMPLETE SET (1)................. 30.00 9.00

2002 Kane County Cougars Grandstand

Only 2,000 of these sets were produced. A Jason Stokes autograph was inserted at a rate of 1 per every 4 team sets.

COMPLETE SET (30).................15.00 4.50

2002 Kane County Cougars Home Run Inn

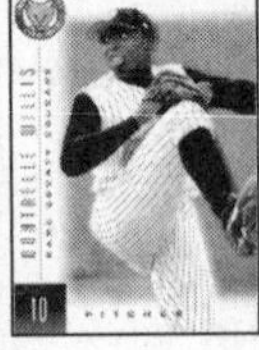

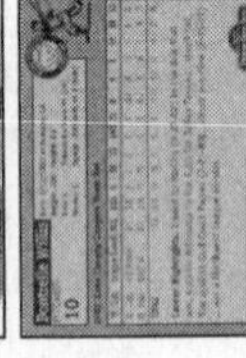

Unnumbered set.

COMPLETE SET (31)............... 20.00 6.00

2002 Kane County Cougars Old Navy

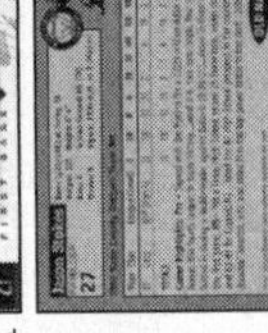

Cards are unnumbered.

COMPLETE SET (31)................. 30.00 9.00

2002 Kannapolis Intimidators Multi-Ad

COMPLETE SET (30)............... 12.00 3.60

2002 Kinston Indians Choice

COMPLETE SET (31)............... 15.00 4.50

2002 Lake Elsinore Storm Grandstand

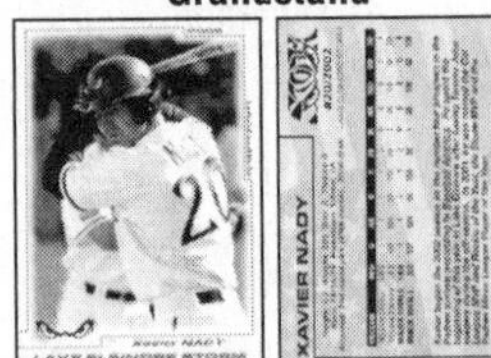

COMPLETE SET (31).................20.00 6.00

2002 Lakewood Blue Claws Multi-Ad

COMPLETE SET (30)............... 15.00 4.50

2002 Lancaster Jet Hawks Grandstand

COMPLETE SET (30)............... 12.00 3.60

2002 Lansing Lugnuts Grandstand

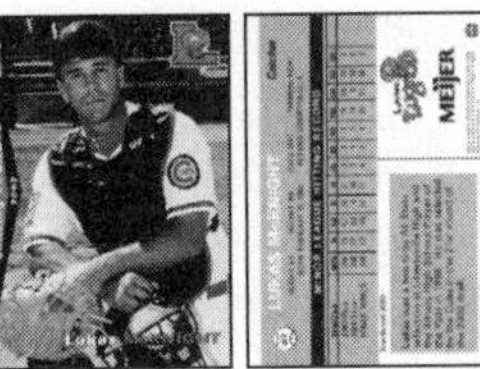

COMPLETE SET (30)............... 10.00 3.00

2002 Las Vegas 51s Multi-Ad

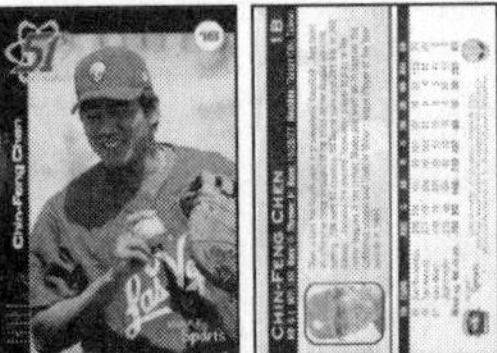

COMPLETE SET (30).................10.00 3.00

2002 Lexington Legends Multi-Ad

COMPLETE SET (30)............... 12.00 3.60

2002 Lowell Spinners Choice

COMPLETE SET (35).................15.00 4.50

2002 Lowell Spinners Legends Choice

COMPLETE SET (14)................. 5.00 1.50

2002 Lowell Spinners Update Choice

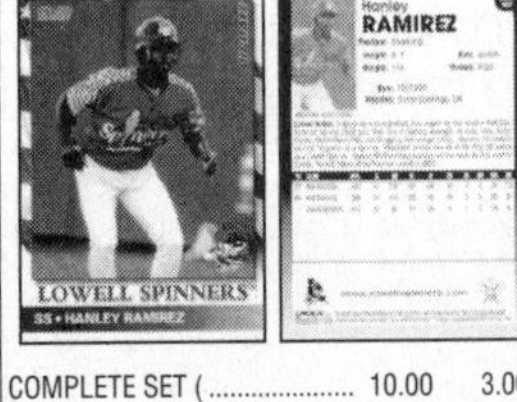

COMPLETE SET (................. 10.00 3.00

2002 Lowell Spinners Update Choice Autographs

COMPLETE SET 25.00 7.50

2002 Lynchburg Hillcats Choice

COMPLETE SET (30)............... 10.00 3.00

2002 Macon Braves Multi-Ad

COMPLETE SET (32).................10.00 3.00

2002 Mahoning Valley Scrappers Multi-Ad

COMPLETE SET (30).................10.00 3.00

2002 Martinsville Astros Grandstand

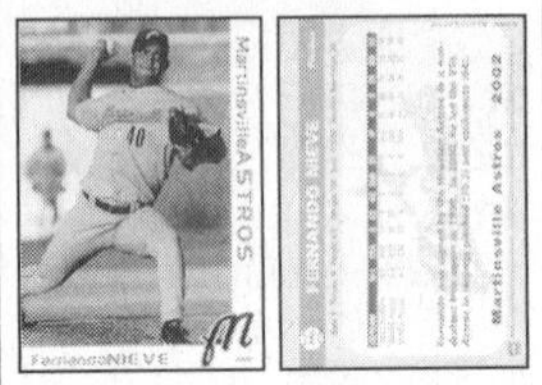

COMPLETE SET (32)............... 12.00 3.60

2002 Medicine Hat Blue Jays Burger King

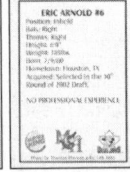

This set is skip-numbered. The numbering scheme is by jersey number. Cards have a tendency to be off-centered. Key prospects in this set include Eric Arnold, Brian Grant and Jason Perry.

COMPLETE SET (34)............... 20.00 6.00

2002 Memphis Redbirds Post

COMPLETE SET (30)............... 12.00 3.60

2002 Michigan Battlecats Multi-Ad

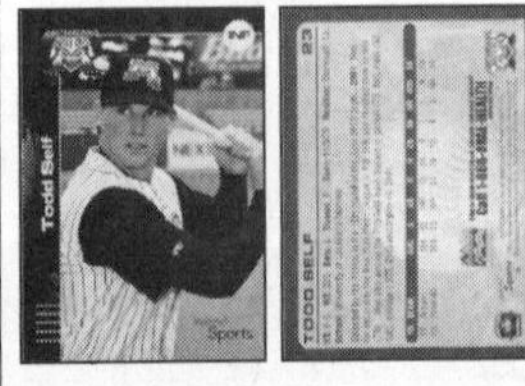

COMPLETE SET (30).................10.00 3.00

2002 Midland Rockhounds Grandstand

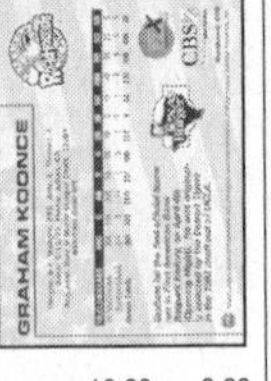

COMPLETE SET (29)............... 10.00 3.00

2002 Missoula Osprey Grandstand

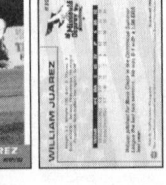

COMPLETE SET (33)................ 10.00 3.00

2002 Mobile BayBears Grandstand

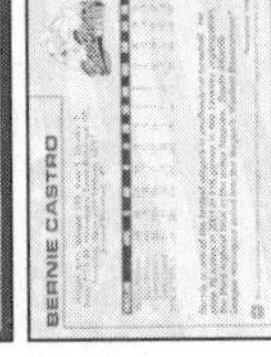

COMPLETE SET (30)............... 12.00 3.60

2002 Modesto A's Grandstand

Jeremy Bonderman has a card in this set.

COMPLETE SET (30).................18.00 5.50

2002 Myrtle Beach Pelicans Multi-Ad

COMPLETE SET (30)............... 12.00 3.60

2002 Nashville Sounds Multi-Ad

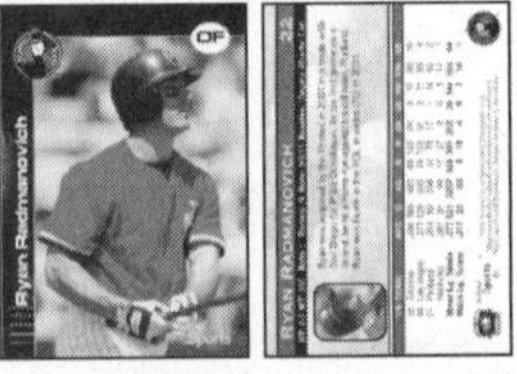

COMPLETE SET (30)............... 10.00 3.00

2002 New Britain Rock Cats Grandstand

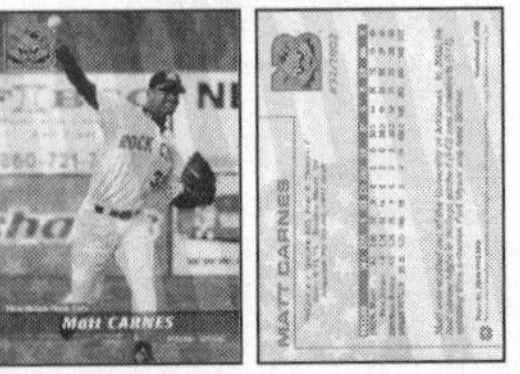

COMPLETE SET (30)............... 10.00 3.00

2002 New Britain Rock Cats Update Grandstand

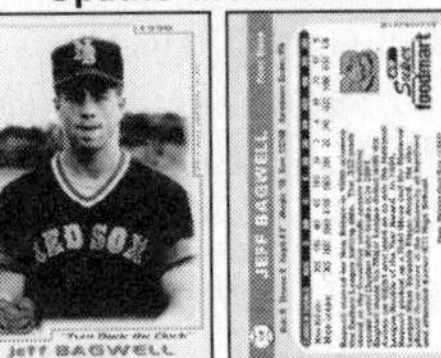

COMPLETE SET (9).................. 5.00 1.50

2002 New Haven Ravens Grandstand

COMPLETE SET (28)..................10.00 3.00

2002 New Jersey Cardinals Grandstand

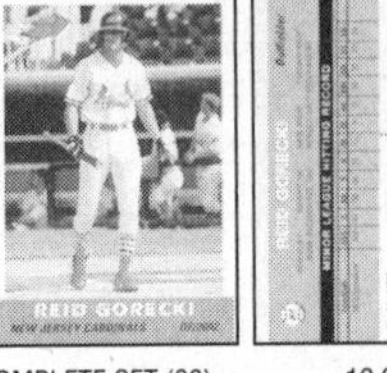

COMPLETE SET (30)............... 10.00 3.00

2002 New Orleans Zephyrs Multi-Ad

COMPLETE SET (30)............... 10.00 3.00

2002 Norfolk Tides Choice

COMPLETE SET (37)................ 10.00 3.00

2002 Norwich Navigators Grandstand

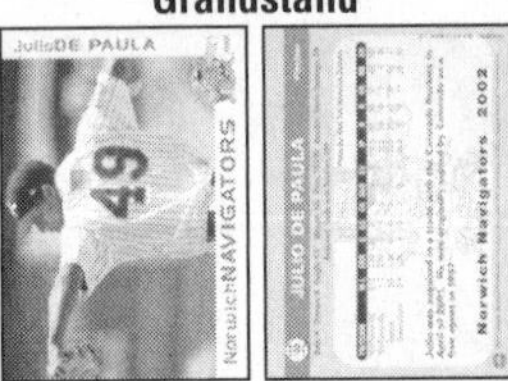

The set is unnumbered and listed below in alphabetical order.

COMPLETE SET (30)............... 10.00 3.00

2002 Ogden Raptors Multi-Ad

This set features prospects Callix Crabbe, John Vanden Berg and Prince Fielder. Prince is the son of Cecil Fielder, who hit 50 homers for the Detroit Tigers in 1990.

COMPLETE SET (36)............... 50.00 4.50

2002 Oklahoma Redhawks Multi-Ad

COMPLETE SET (36)................ 12.00 3.60

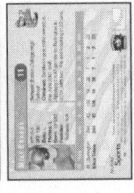

2002 Omaha Royals Multi-Ad
COMPLETE SET (30) 10.00 3.00

2002 Orlando Rays Multi-Ad
COMPLETE SET (29) 10.00 3.00

2002 Ottawa Lynx Choice
COMPLETE SET (29) 10.00 3.00

2002 Pacific Coast League All-Stars Multi-Ad
COMPLETE SET (30) 15.00 4.50

2002 Pacific Coast League Top Prospects
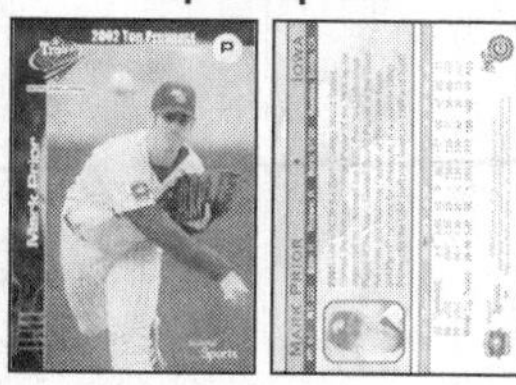
The set is unnumbered and listed below in alphabetical order.
COMPLETE SET (35) 12.00 3.60

2002 Pawtucket Red Sox Choice
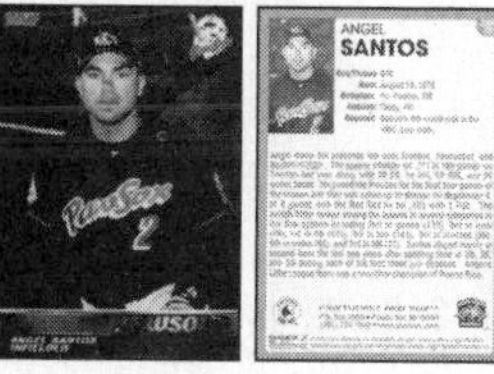
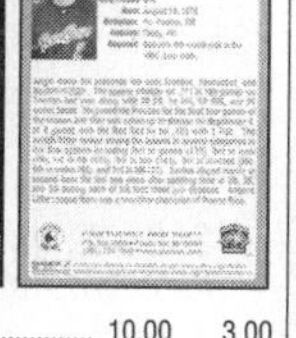
COMPLETE SET (30) 10.00 3.00

2002 Peoria Chiefs Multi-Ad
COMPLETE SET (30) 12.00 3.60

2002 Portland Beavers Multi-Ad

COMPLETE SET (29) 10.00 3.00

2002 Portland Sea Dogs Grandstand
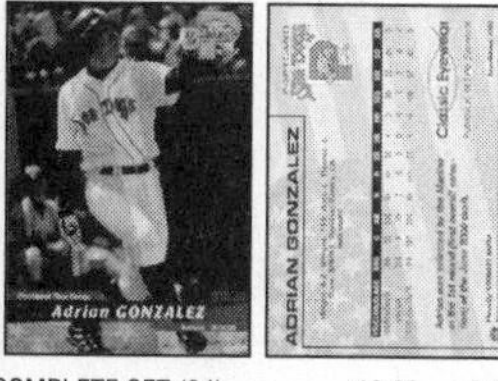
COMPLETE SET (34) 12.00 3.60

2002 Potomac Cannons Choice
COMPLETE SET (32) 10.00 3.00

2002 Princeton Devil Rays Grandstand
COMPLETE SET (30) 10.00 3.00

2002 Provo Angels Team Issue

COMPLETE SET (39) 10.00 3.00

2002 Pulaski Rangers Grandstand
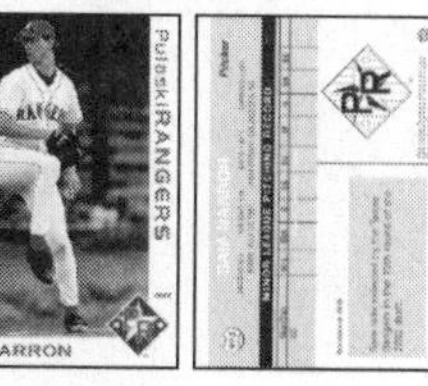
COMPLETE SET (32) 10.00 3.00

2002 Quad City River Bandits Grandstand
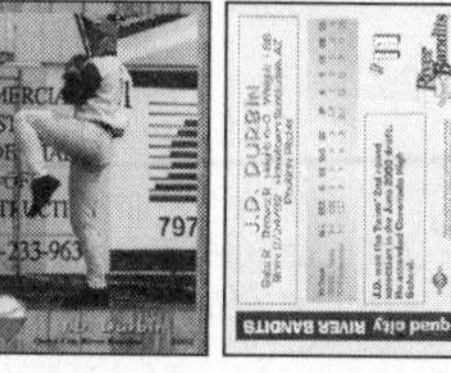
COMPLETE SET (30) 15.00 4.50

2002 Rancho Cucamonga Quakes Grandstand
The set is unnumbered and listed below in alphabetical order.
COMPLETE SET (30) 15.00 4.50

2002 Reading Phillies Legends Multi-Ad

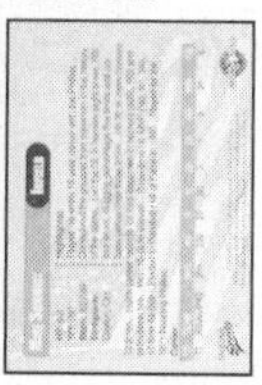
Rocky Colavito and Carl Furillo were hand pulled out of these sets after these cards were produced. However, a few of these cards did make it into the secondary market.
COMPLETE SET (18) 10.00 3.00

2002 Reading Phillies Multi-Ad

COMPLETE SET (30) 10.00 3.00

2002 Richmond Braves Choice
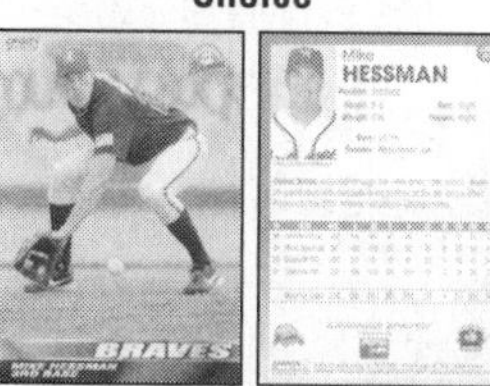
COMPLETE SET (30) 10.00 3.00

2002 Rochester Red Wings Choice
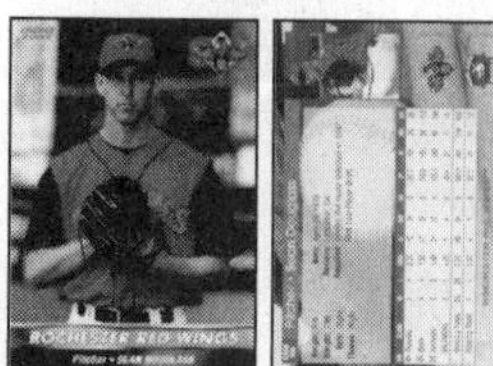
COMPLETE SET (29) 10.00 3.00

2002 Round Rock Express Team Issue
COMPLETE SET (30) 10.00 3.00

2002 Sacramento Rivercats Multi-Ad
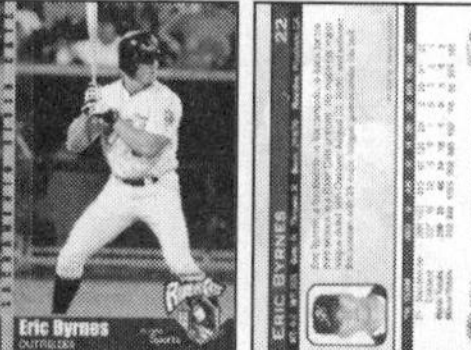

COMPLETE SET (31) 10.00 3.00

2002 Salem Avalanche Grandstand

COMPLETE SET (30) 10.00 3.00

2002 Salem-Keizer Volcanoes Grandstand
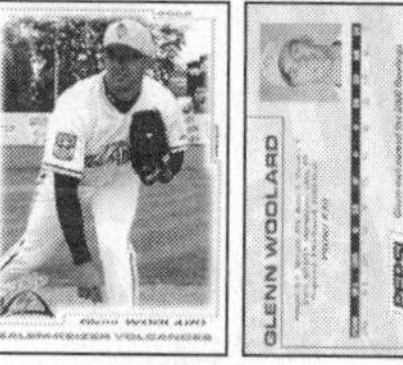
COMPLETE SET (35) 10.00 3.00

2002 Salt Lake Stingers Multi-Ad
COMPLETE SET (30) 12.00 3.60

2002 San Antonio Missions Grandstand
COMPLETE SET (30) 12.00 3.60

2002 San Bernardino Stampede Grandstand
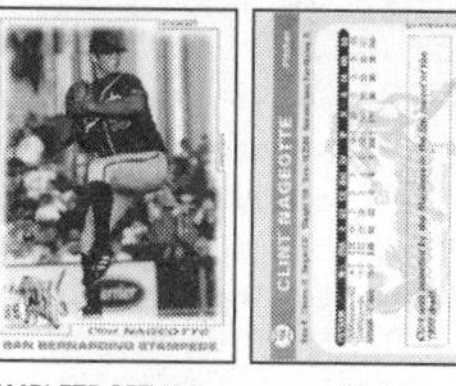
COMPLETE SET (30) 10.00 3.00

2002 San Jose Giants Grandstand
COMPLETE SET (30) 10.00 3.00

2002 Sarasota Red Sox Grandstand

COMPLETE SET (30) 10.00 3.00

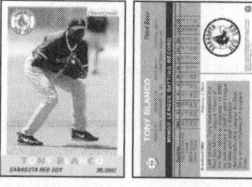

2002 Savannah Sand Gnats

COMPLETE SET (30) 15.00 4.50

2002 Scranton Wilkes-Barre Red Barons Choice
COMPLETE SET (30) 10.00 3.00

2002 Shreveport Swamp Dragons Grandstand
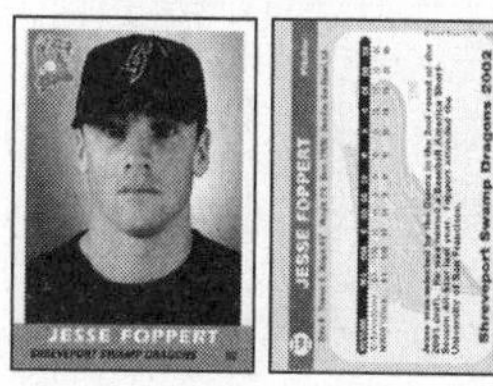
COMPLETE SET (26 .... 20.00 6.00

2002 Shreveport Swamp Dragons Minor Miracle Autograph
This signed card was issued by Minor Miracles. This card was issued to a stated print run of 112 copies.
COMPLETE SET 20.00 6.00

2002 South Atlantic League Prospects Multi Ad

COMPLETE SET (33) 15.00 4.50

2002 South Bend Silver Hawks Multi-Ad

COMPLETE SET (29) 10.00 3.00

2002 South Georgia Waves Multi-Ad
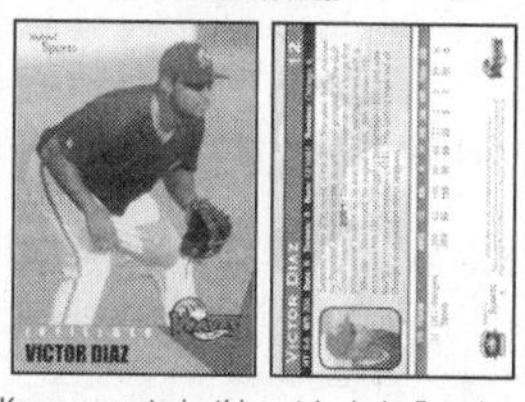
Key prospects in this set include Francisco Cruceta and Victor Diaz.
COMPLETE SET (30) 30.00 9.00

2002 Southern League Prospects Grandstand
The set is unnumbered and listed below in alphabetical order.
COMPLETE SET (30) 12.00 3.60

2002 Spokane Indians Grandstand
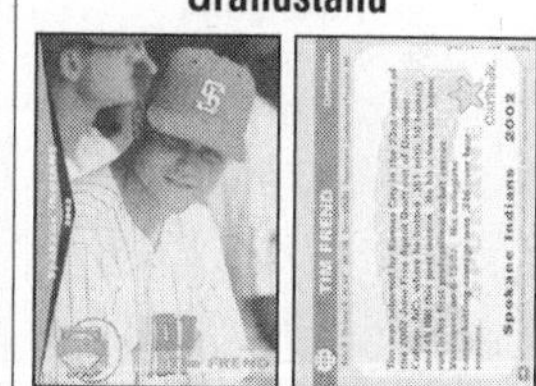
COMPLETE SET (32) 12.00 3.60

2002 St. Lucie Mets Grandstand
The set is unnumbered and listed below in alphabetical order. Justin Huber was issued via update making this a 34-card set. Craig Brazel and Jose Reyes are other important prospects in this set.
COMPLETE SET (34) 15.00 4.50

2002 St. Lucie Mets Minor Miracles Autograph
Issued by Minor Miracles, this card features New York Mets shortstop prospect Jose Reyes.

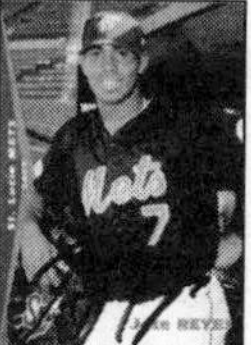

This card was issued to a stated print run of 150 signed sets.
COMPLETE SET (1) ....

2002 Staten Island Yankees Multi-Ad
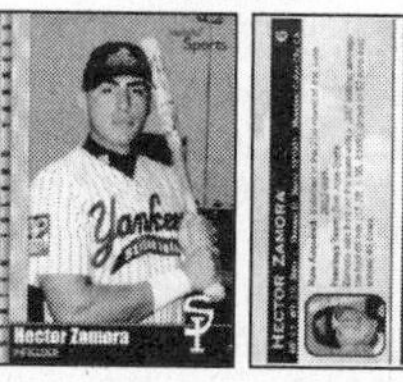
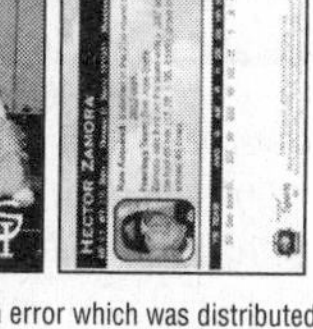
This set features an error which was distributed as a stadium give-away. Scott McClanahan is represented by Mike Meihls in the SGA set. This error was corrected with the correct photo of Scott McClanahan and was issued retail only. About 3,000 or each the SGA and the retail versions were produced.
COMPLETE SET (35) 10.00 3.00

2002 Stockton Ports Grandstand
The set is unnumbered and listed below in alphabetical order.
COMPLETE SET (30) 15.00 4.50

2002 Syracuse SkyChiefs Choice

COMPLETE SET (30) 10.00 3.00

2002 Syracuse SkyChiefs Update Grandstand
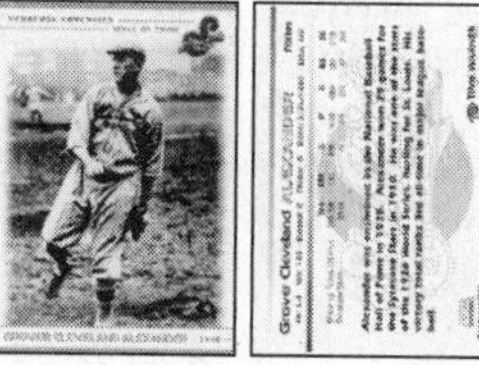
COMPLETE SET (30) 10.00 3.00

2002 Tacoma Rainiers Multi-Ad

COMPLETE SET (30) 10.00 3.00

2002 Tampa Yankees Multi-Ad

COMPLETE SET (30) 10.00 3.00

2002 Tennessee Smokies Grandstand

COMPLETE SET (30) 10.00 3.00

2002 Texas League Prospects Grandstand

The checklist is unnumbered and listed below in alphabetical order.
COMPLETE SET (24) 12.00 3.60

2002 Toledo Mud Hens Choice

COMPLETE SET (30) 10.00 3.00

2002 Trenton Thunder Multi-Ad

COMPLETE SET (29) 12.00 3.60

2002 Tri-City Dust Devils Team Issue

The set is unnumbered and listed below in alphabetical order. Beware of miscut singles.
COMPLETE SET (36) 10.00 3.00

2002 Tucson Sidewinders Multi-Ad

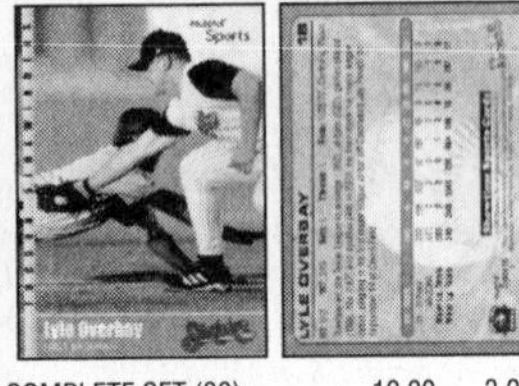

COMPLETE SET (30) 10.00 3.00

2002 Tulsa Drillers Associated Litho

COMPLETE SET (29) 10.00 3.00

2002 UCLA Bruins Team Issue

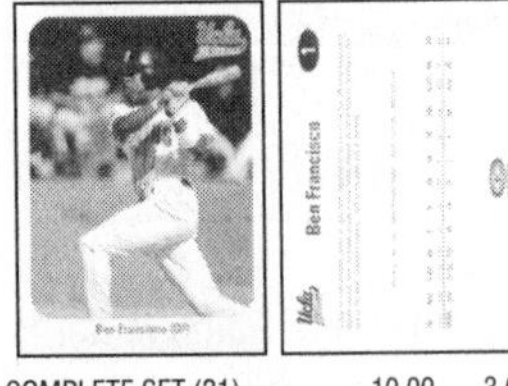

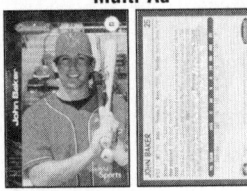

COMPLETE SET (21) 10.00 3.00

2002 Vancouver Canadians Multi-Ad

COMPLETE SET (42) 15.00 4.50

2002 Vermont Expos Grandstand

COMPLETE SET (36) 10.00 3.00

2002 Vero Beach Dodgers Grandstand

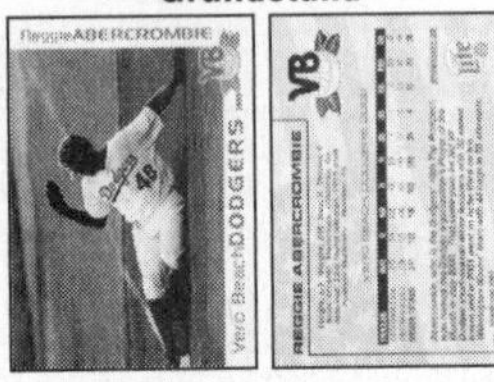

COMPLETE SET (31) 15.00 4.50

2002 Visalia Oaks Grandstand

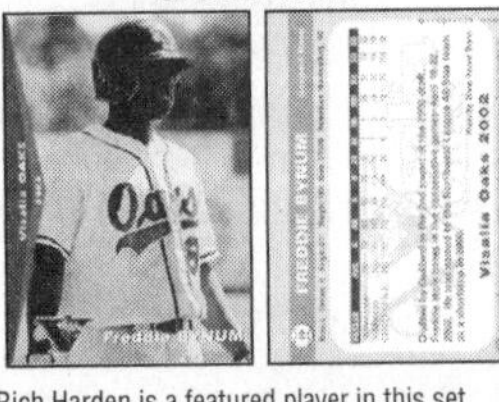

Rich Harden is a featured player in this set.
COMPLETE SET (30) 20.00 6.00

2002 West Michigan Whitecaps Multi-Ad

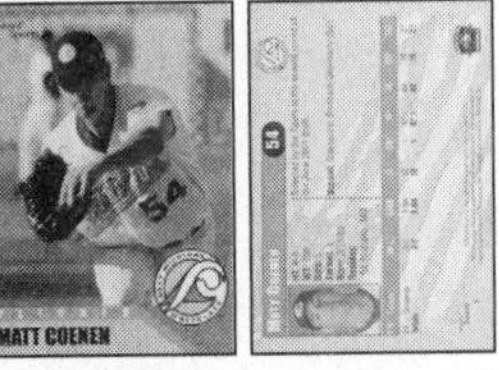

COMPLETE SET (30) 10.00 3.00

2002 West Tenn Diamond Jaxx Grandstand

This set features Nic Jackson, David Kelton and Mark Prior.
COMPLETE SET (30) 15.00 4.50

2002 West Tenn Diamond Jaxx Mark Prior Grandstand

These six cards feature Chicago Cub pitching prospect Mark Prior.
COMPLETE SET (6) 15.00 4.50

2002 Wichita Wranglers Grandstand

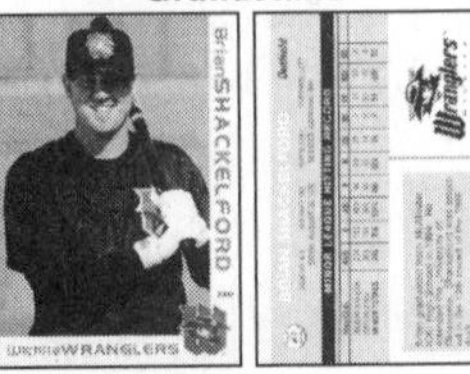

COMPLETE SET (24) .... 15.00 4.50.

2002 Williamsport Crosscutters Choice

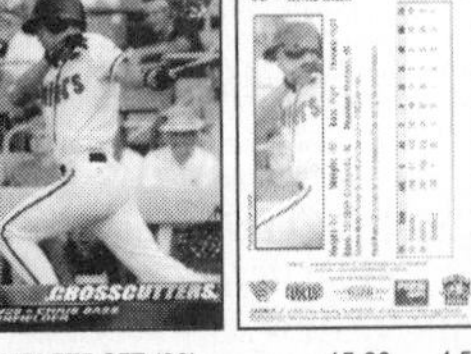

COMPLETE SET (33) 15.00 4.50

2002 Wilmington Blue Rocks Choice

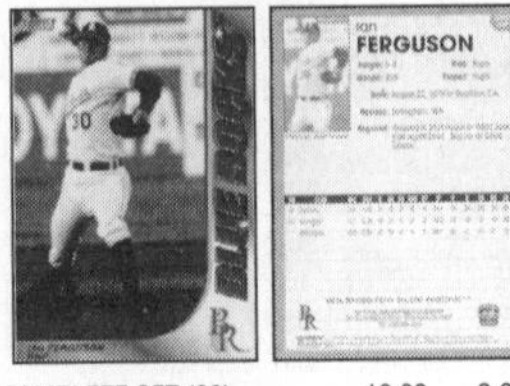

COMPLETE SET (30) 10.00 3.00

2002 Winston-Salem Warthogs Choice

COMPLETE SET (30) 12.00 3.60

2002 Winston-Salem Warthogs Update Choice

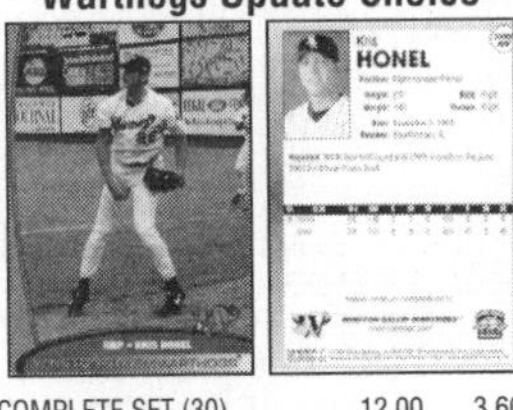

COMPLETE SET (30) 12.00 3.60

2002 Wisconsin Timber Rattlers Multi-Ad

COMPLETE SET (28) 10.00 3.00

2002 Yakima Bears Grandstand

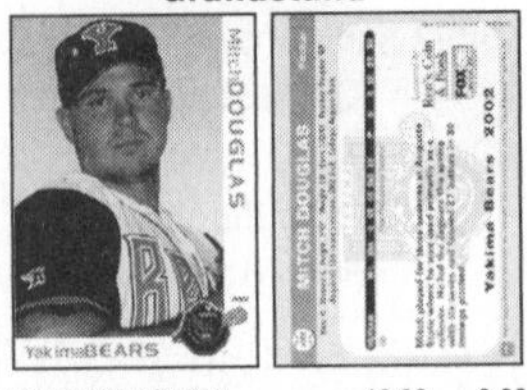

COMPLETE SET (34) 10.00 3.00

2003 Aberdeen Ironbirds Grandstand

COMPLETE SET (30) 15.00 4.50

2003 Aberdeen Ironbirds Update Grandstand

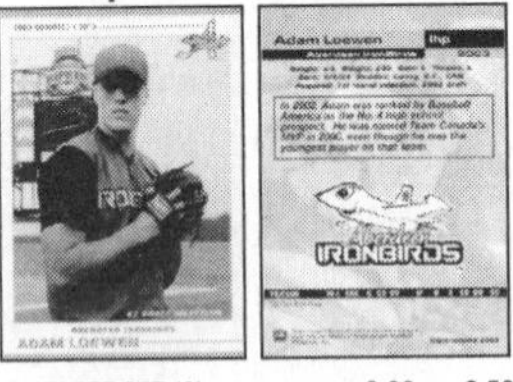

COMPLETE SET (3) 8.00 2.50

2003 Akron Aeros Multi-Ad

COMPLETE SET (29) 15.00 4.50

2003 Albuquerque Isotopes Multi-Ad

COMPLETE SET (31) 12.00 3.00

2003 Altoona Curve Grandstand

COMPLETE SET (30) 10.00 3.00

2003 Altoona Curve Update Grandstand

COMPLETE SET (6) 8.00 2.50

2003 Appalachian League Top Prospects Grandstand

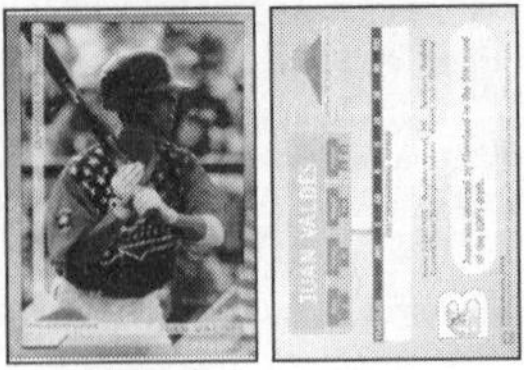

COMPLETE SET (30) 15.00 4.50

2003 Arkansas Travelers Grandstand

COMPLETE SET (34) 12.00 3.50

2003 Asheville Tourists Grandstand

COMPLETE SET (30) 15.00 4.50

2003 Asheville Tourists Update Grandstand

COMPLETE SET (12) 15.00 4.50

2003 Atlantic City Surf Operation Swatch

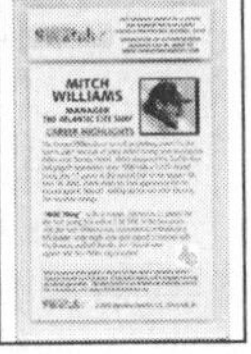

This one card set was given away for a donation to Scholarship America at an Atlantic City Surf game. This card featured a game-worn jersey swatch from Manager Mitch Williams and the back features information about Williams' time with the Surf. Please note that this card was issued in its own protective holder.
COMPLETE SET 15.00 4.50

2003 Auburn Doubledays Team Issue

COMPLETE SET (36) 10.00 3.00

2003 Augusta Greenjackets Multi-Ad

COMPLETE SET (33) 15.00 4.50

2003 Batavia Muckdogs Team Issue

COMPLETE SET (36) 12.00 3.50

2003 Battle Creek Yankees Choice

COMPLETE SET (30) 20.00 6.00

2003 Beloit Snappers Multi-Ad

COMPLETE SET (30) 20.00 6.00

2003 Beloit Snappers Prospects Multi-Ad

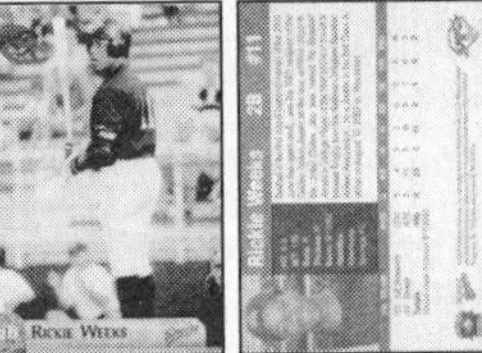

COMPLETE SET (6) 20.00 6.00

2003 Beloit Snappers Update Multi-Ad

COMPLETE SET (9) 20.00 6.00

2003 Billings Mustangs Grandstand

COMPLETE SET (30) 12.00 3.50

2003 Binghamton Mets Grandstand

COMPLETE SET (29) 12.00 3.50

2003 Birmingham Barons Grandstand

COMPLETE SET (29) 12.00 3.50

2003 Birmingham Barons Update Grandstand

COMPLETE SET (3) 12.00 3.50

2003 Bluefield Orioles Grandstand

COMPLETE SET (34) 12.00 3.50

2003 Boise Hawks Grandstand

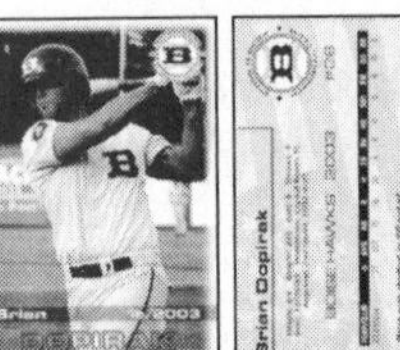

COMPLETE SET (30) 12.00 3.50

2003 Bowie Baysox Grandstand

COMPLETE SET (29) 12.00 3.50

2003 Brevard County Manatees Multi-Ad

COMPLETE SET (30) 12.00 3.50

2003 Bristol White Sox Grandstand

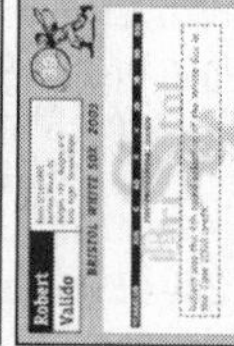

COMPLETE SET (31)............... 12.00 3.50

2003 Bristol White Sox Update Grandstand

Only 1,500 sets were produced.
COMPLETE SET (1)................ 12.00 3.50

2003 Brooklyn Cyclones Choice

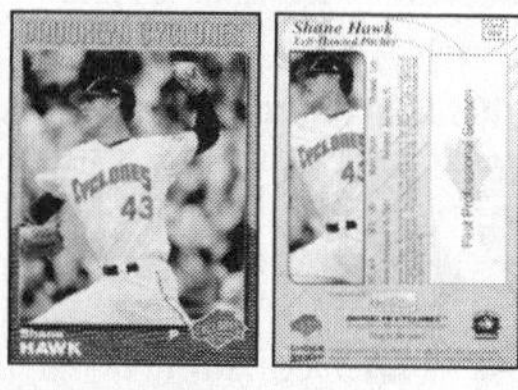
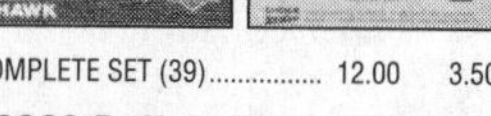

COMPLETE SET (39)............... 12.00 3.50

2003 Buffalo Bisons Choice

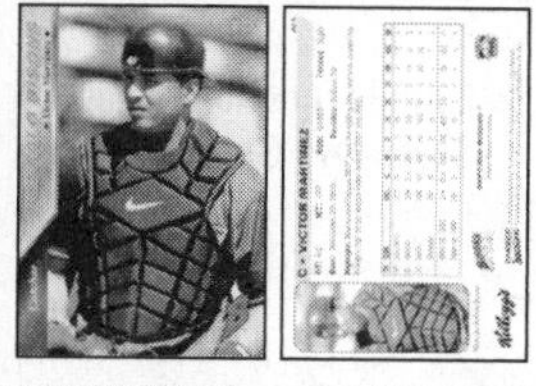

COMPLETE SET (30)................12.00 3.50

2003 Buffalo Bisons Classic Choice

COMPLETE SET (12)................12.00 3.50

2003 Burlington Bees Multi-Ad

COMPLETE SET (30)................12.00 3.50

2003 California-Carolina All-Star Grandstand

COMPLETE SET (50)................20.00 6.00

2003 Capital City Bombers Multi-Ad

COMPLETE SET (36)................10.00 3.00

2003 Carolina League Top Prospects Choice

COMPLETE SET (32)............... 12.00 3.50

2003 Carolina Mudcats Team Issue

COMPLETE SET (30)............... 15.00 4.50

2003 Casper Rockies Grandstand

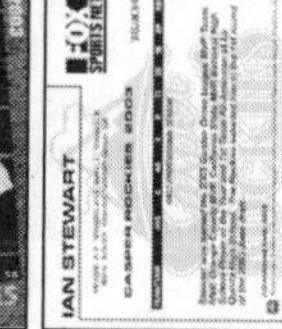

COMPLETE SET (32)............... 15.00 4.50

2003 Cedar Rapids Kernels Perfect Game USA

COMPLETE SET (31)................10.00 3.00

2003 Charleston Alley Cats Multi-Ad

COMPLETE SET (33)................10.00 3.00

2003 Charleston River Dogs Multi-Ad

COMPLETE SET (32)............... 20.00 6.00

2003 Charlotte Knights Choice

COMPLETE SET (29)................12.00 3.50

2003 Chattanooga Lookouts Grandstand

COMPLETE SET (29)................15.00 4.50

2003 Clearwater Phillies Grandstand

COMPLETE SET (30)................12.00 3.50

2003 Clinton Lumberkings Grandstand

COMPLETE SET (33)................10.00 3.00

2003 Colorado Springs Sky Sox Multi-Ad

COMPLETE SET (28)............... 10.00 3.00

2003 Columbus Clippers Choice

COMPLETE SET (30)............... 20.00 6.00

2003 Danville Braves Grandstand

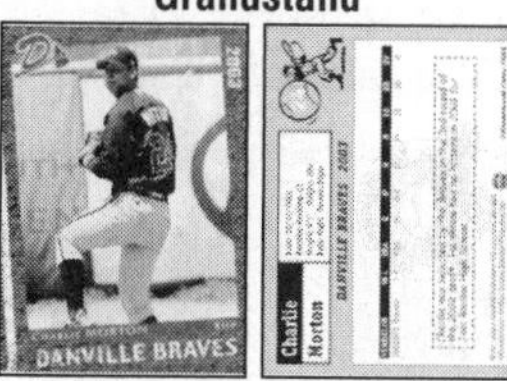

COMPLETE SET (32)............... 12.00 3.50

2003 Dayton Dragons Multi-Ad

COMPLETE SET (30)............... 15.00 4.50

2003 Daytona Cubs Choice

COMPLETE SET (30)................20.00 6.00

2003 Delmarva Shorebirds Multi-Ad

COMPLETE SET (30)............... 15.00 4.50

2003 Dunedin Blue Jays Grandstand

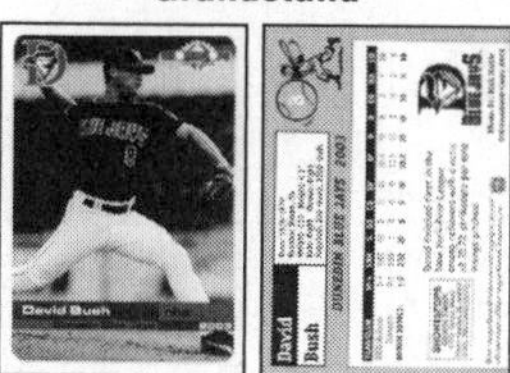

COMPLETE SET (30)............... 15.00 4.50

2003 Durham Bulls Choice

COMPLETE SET (29)............... 15.00 4.50

2003 Eastern League All-Time Greats Grandstand

This is a 20-card set. Cards 1-10 "A" were available at the New Britain Rock Cats Stadium Giveaway. Within that 10 card set, a redemption card was included that would give you the second portion of that set (11-20 "B"). The card could only have been redeemed at "Omni Comics and Cards" in Wethersfield, CT on May 17th, 2003 from 12 P.M. to 2 P.M..
COMPLETE SET (20)............... 40.00 12.00

2003 Eastern League Top Prospects Grandstand

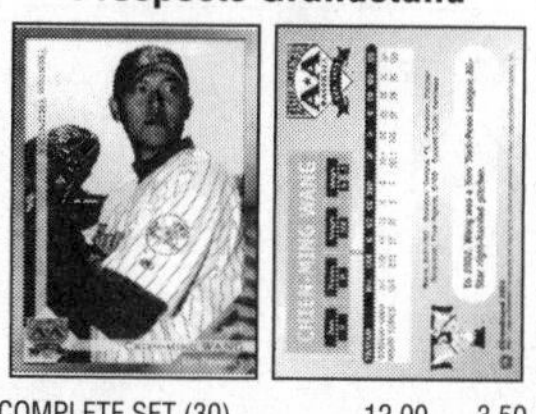

COMPLETE SET (30)............... 12.00 3.50

2003 Edmonton Trappers Multi-Ad

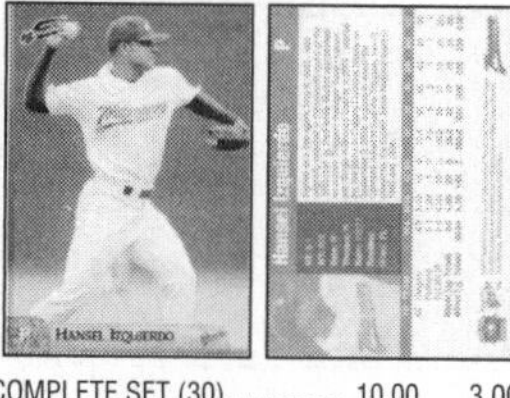

COMPLETE SET (30)............... 10.00 3.00

2003 El Paso Diablos Grandstand

COMPLETE SET (30)................10.00 3.00

2003 Elizabethton Twins Grandstand

COMPLETE SET (31)............... 12.00 3.50

2003 Erie Sea Wolves Grandstand

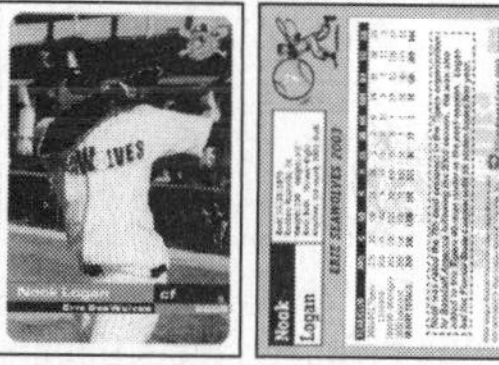

COMPLETE SET (28)............... 10.00 3.00

2003 Eugene Emeralds Grandstand

COMPLETE SET (32)............... 12.00 3.50

2003 Everett Aquasox Grandstand

COMPLETE SET (30)............... 18.00 5.50

2003 Florida State League Top Prospects Grandstand

COMPLETE SET (24)............... 12.00 3.50

2003 Fort Myers Miracle Grandstand

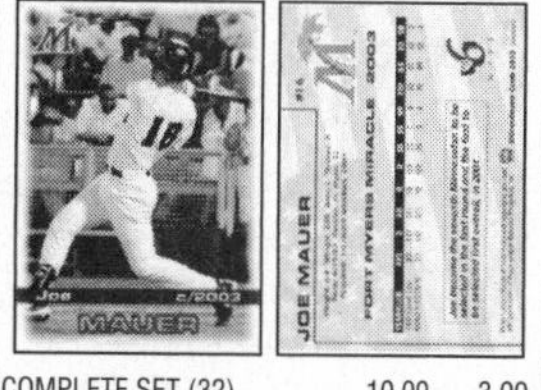

COMPLETE SET (32)............... 10.00 3.00

2003 Fort Wayne Wizards Grandstand

COMPLETE SET (29)............... 10.00 3.00

2003 Frederick Keys Grandstand

COMPLETE SET (30)............... 10.00 3.00

2003 Frederick Keys No Smoking Logo Grandstand

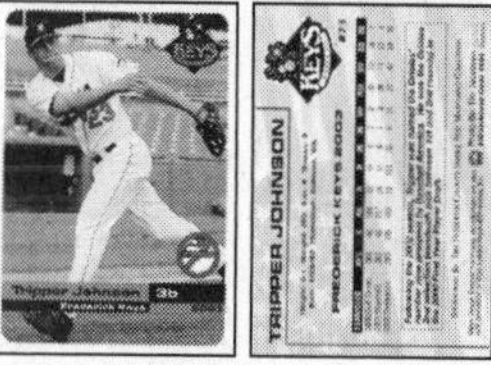

These sets feature the same design as the regular Grandstand issued set, with the exception of a No Smoking Logo on the bottom right hand corner of the card. These were given away to the first 1,000 kids under the age of 12 who attended the Frederick Keys on June 26, 2003 on behalf of The Frederick County-Smoke Free Maryland Coalition.
COMPLETE SET (30)............... 12.00 3.50

2003 Fresno Grizzlies Multi-Ad

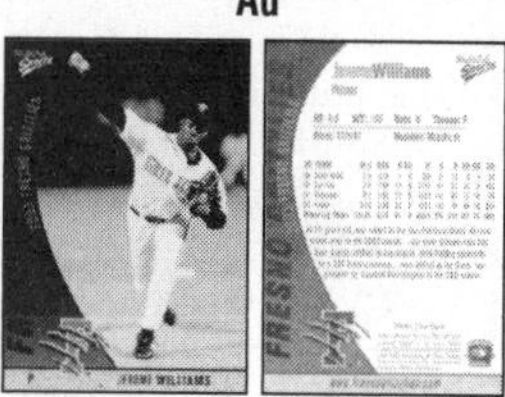

COMPLETE SET (31)............... 12.00 3.50

2003 Frisco Rough Riders Dallas Morning News

This set was available exclusively through the Sunday's edition of "The Dallas Morning News - Collin County Edition". This promotion went for six weeks, beginning on May 4, 2003; Prior to the first week just one card, Tim Ireland MGR, was distributed into the Collin County Edition branch of The Dallas Morning News to advertise this promotion. Each of the six weeks, a five-card perferated sheet was distributed. This was only available for home delivery papers.
COMPLETE SET (31)............... 25.00 8.00

2003 Frisco RoughRiders Grandstand

COMPLETE SET 20.00 6.00

2003 Great Falls White Sox Multi-Ad

COMPLETE SET (30)............... 12.00 3.50

2003 Greensboro Bats Multi-Ad

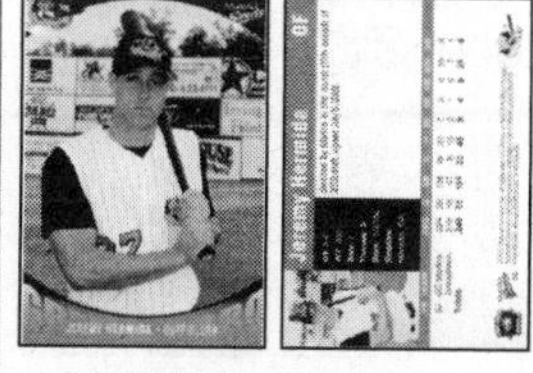

COMPLETE SET (30)............... 18.00 5.50

2003 Greenville Braves Grandstand

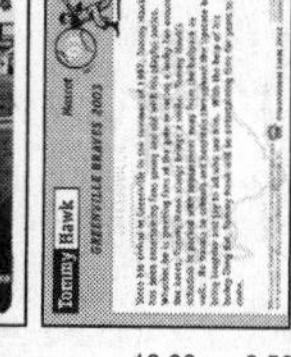

COMPLETE SET (30)............... 12.00 3.50

2003 Hagerstown Suns Multi-Ad

COMPLETE SET (36)............... 12.00 3.50

2003 Harrisburg Senators Grandstand

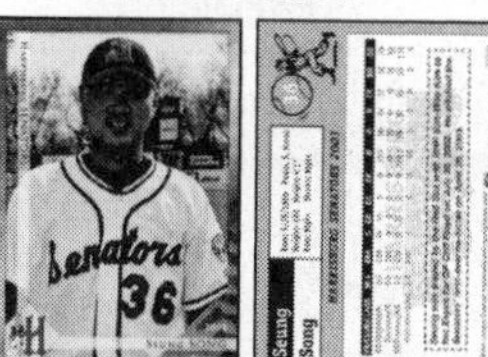

COMPLETE SET (30)............... 12.00 3.50

2003 Helena Brewers Grandstand

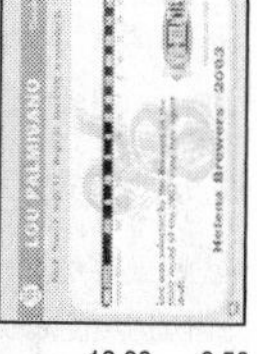

COMPLETE SET (4)................. 12.00 3.50

2003 Hickory Crawdads Multi-Ad

COMPLETE SET (32)............... 12.00 3.50

2003 Hickory Crawdads Update Multi-Ad

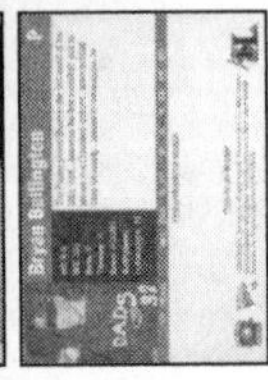

COMPLETE SET (33)............... 12.00 3.50

2003 High Desert Mavericks Grandstand

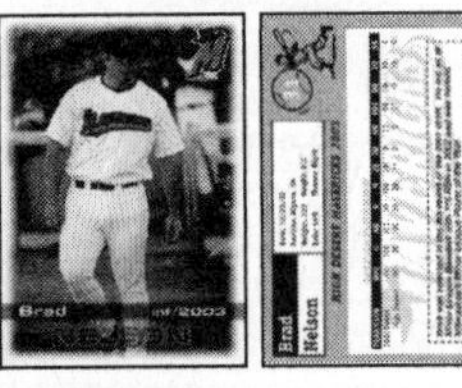

COMPLETE SET (34)............... 12.00 3.50

2003 Hudson Valley Renegades Grandstand

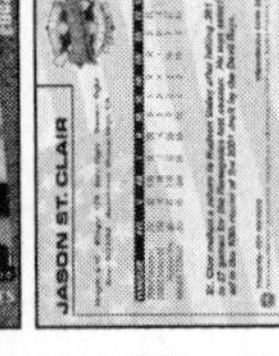

COMPLETE SET (35)............... 10.00 3.00

2003 Huntsville Stars Team Issue

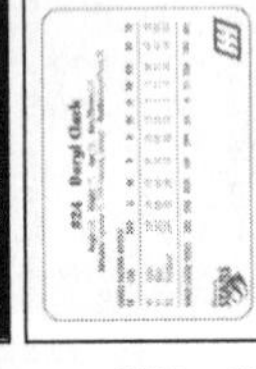

COMPLETE SET (29)............... 25.00 8.00

2003 Indianapolis Indians Choice

COMPLETE SET (30)............... 10.00 3.00

2003 Inland Empire 66ers Grandstand

COMPLETE SET (31)............... 12.00 3.50

2003 International League All-Stars Choice

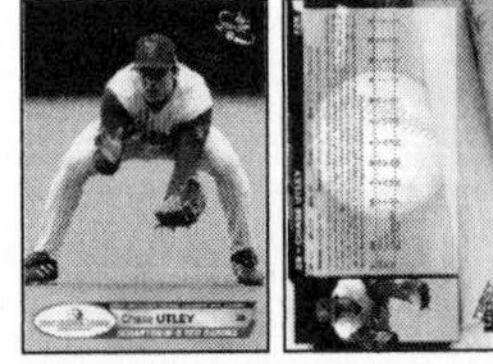

COMPLETE SET (31)............... 12.00 3.50

2003 International League Top Prospects Choice

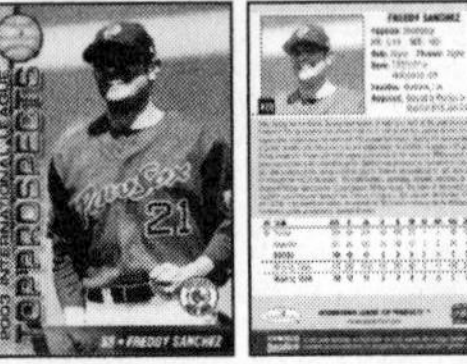

COMPLETE SET (30)............... 12.00 3.50

2003 Iowa Cubs Multi-Ad

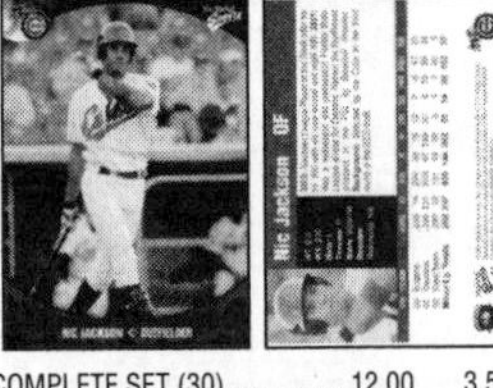

COMPLETE SET (30)............... 12.00 3.50

2003 Jacksonville Suns Grandstand

COMPLETE SET (30)............... 15.00 4.50

2003 Johnson City Cardinals Grandstand

COMPLETE SET (21)............... 12.00 3.50

2003 Jupiter Hammerheads Illustrated Properties

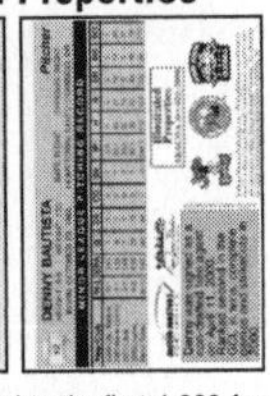

This set was distributed to the first 1,000 fans who attended Roger Dean Stadium on June 28, 2003. It was sponsored by Illustrated Properties of Abacoa which is signified by their logo on the bottom left hand corner of the cards. Card #1 (Team Checklist) has the serial number of each set numbered to 1000.

COMPLETE SET (37)............... 15.00 4.50

2003 Kane County Cougars Grandstand

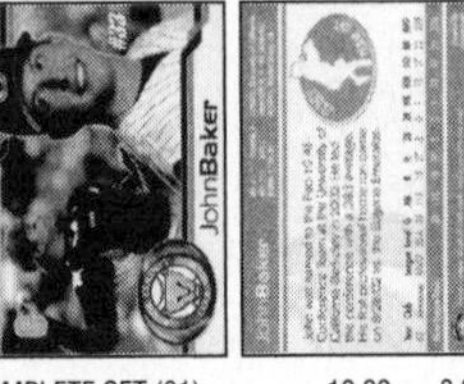

COMPLETE SET (31)............... 10.00 3.00

2003 Kane County Cougars Home Run Inn

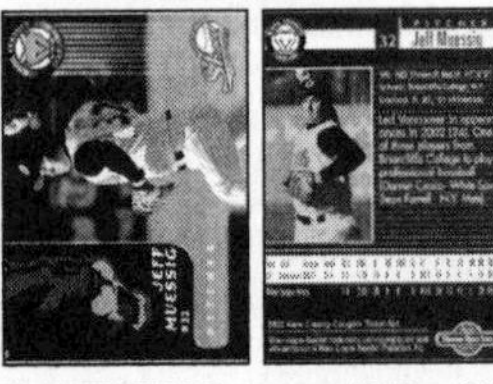

COMPLETE SET (30)............... 10.00 3.00

2003 Kane County Cougars Update Grandstand

COMPLETE SET (9)................. 25.00 8.00

2003 Kannapolis Intimidators Multi-Ad

COMPLETE SET (36)............... 12.00 3.50

2003 Kingsport Mets Choice

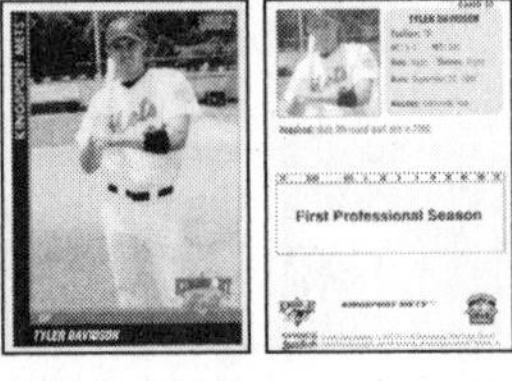

COMPLETE SET (40)............... 12.00 3.50

2003 Kingsport Mets Update Grandstand

COMPLETE SET (2)................. 12.00 3.50

2003 Kinston Indians Choice

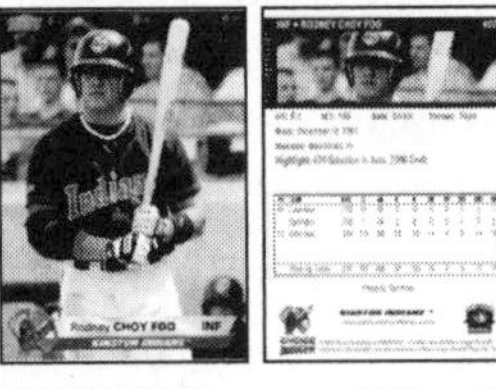

COMPLETE SET (30)............... 15.00 4.50

2003 Lake County Captains Choice

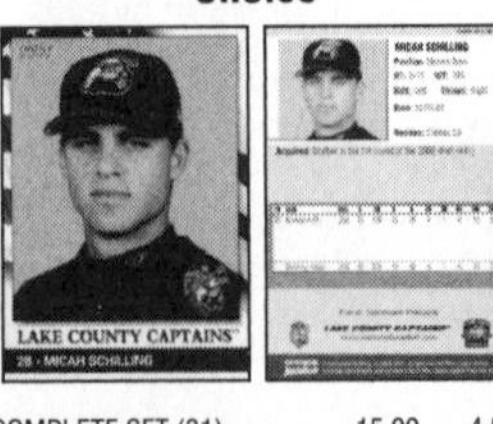

COMPLETE SET (31)............... 15.00 4.50

2003 Lake County Captains Choice Update

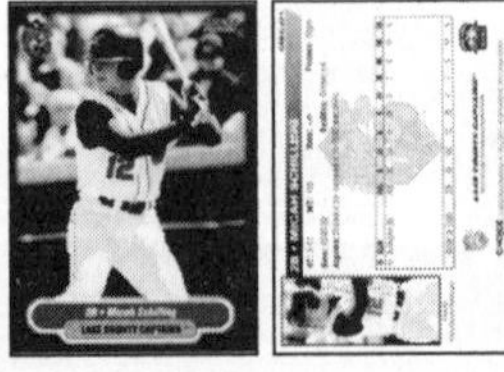

COMPLETE SET (30)............... 15.00 4.50

2003 Lake Elsinore Storm Grandstand

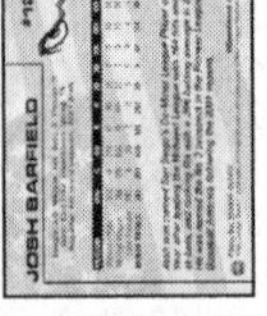

COMPLETE SET (30)............... 15.00 4.50

2003 Lakeland Tigers Grandstand

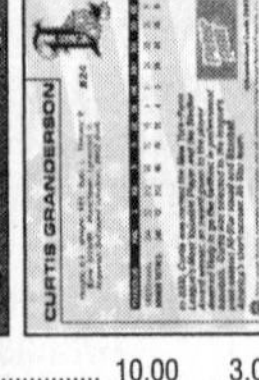

COMPLETE SET (29)............... 10.00 3.00

2003 Lakewood BlueClaws Multi-Ad

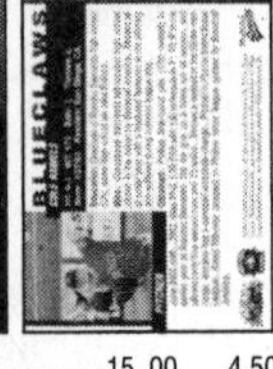

COMPLETE SET (35)...............15..00 4.50

2003 Lancaster JetHawks Grandstand

COMPLETE SET (30)............... 12.00 3.50

2003 Lansing Lugnuts Grandstand

COMPLETE SET (29)............... 10.00 3.00

2003 Las Vegas 51s Multi-Ad

COMPLETE SET (32)............... 10.00 3.00

2003 Lexington Legends Multi-Ad

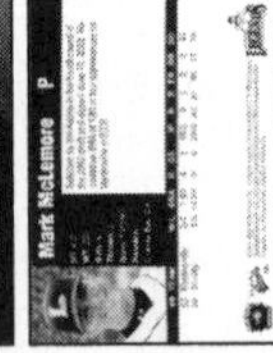

COMPLETE SET (31)............... 12.00 3.50

2003 Louisville Bats Choice

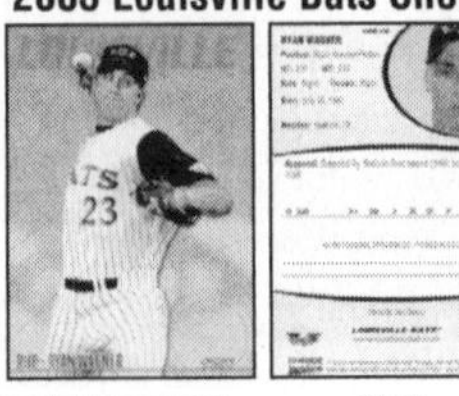

COMPLETE SET (36)............... 30.00 9.00

2003 Lowell Spinners Choice

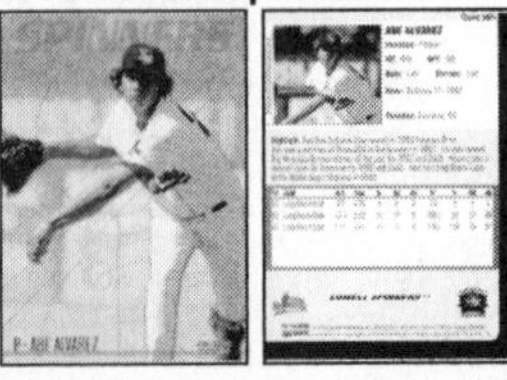

COMPLETE SET (38)............... 12.00 3.50

2003 Lowell Spinners Top Prospect Grandstand

COMPLETE SET (1)..................... 5.00 1.50

2003 Lowell Spinners Top Prospect Minor Miracles Autograph

COMPLETE SET (1)................. 25.00 8.00

2003 Lynchburg Hillcats Choice

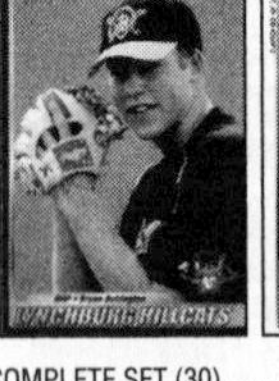
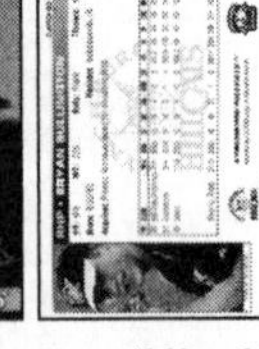

COMPLETE SET (30)............... 10.00 3.00

2003 Lynchburg Hillcats Litho

COMPLETE SET (30)............... 25.00 8.00

2003 Mahoning Valley Scrappers Grandstand

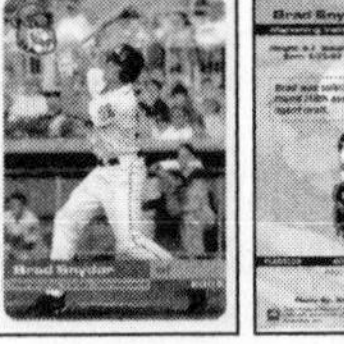

COMPLETE SET (26)............... 10.00 3.00

2003 Martinsville Astros Choice

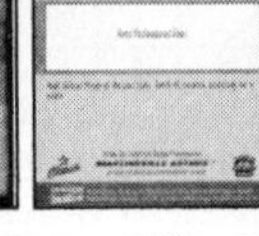

COMPLETE SET (35)............... 12.00 3.50

2003 Memphis Redbirds Multi-Ad

COMPLETE SET (30)............... 15.00 4.50

2003 Midland Rock Hounds Grandstand

COMPLETE SET (26)............... 10.00 3.00

2003 Midland Rockhounds One Hour Photo

COMPLETE SET (33)............... 60.00 18.00

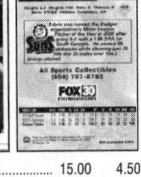

2003 Midwest League All-Star Choice

COMPLETE SET (68)............... 18.00 5.50

2003 Midwest League Top Prospects Grandstand

COMPLETE SET (28)............... 15.00 4.50

2003 Missoula Osprey Grandstand

COMPLETE SET (36)............... 10.00 3.00

2003 Mobile Baybears Grandstand

COMPLETE SET (29)............... 15.00 4.50

2003 Modesto A's Grandstand

COMPLETE SET (29)............... 10.00 3.00

2003 Myrtle Beach Pelicans Choice

COMPLETE SET (29)............... 12.00 3.50

2003 Nashville Sounds Multi-Ad

COMPLETE SET (30)............... 12.00 3.50

2003 New Britain Rock Cats Grandstand

COMPLETE SET (32)............... 12.00 3.50

2003 New Haven Ravens Grandstand

COMPLETE SET (29)............... 15.00 4.50

2003 New Jersey Cardinals Future Star Grandstand

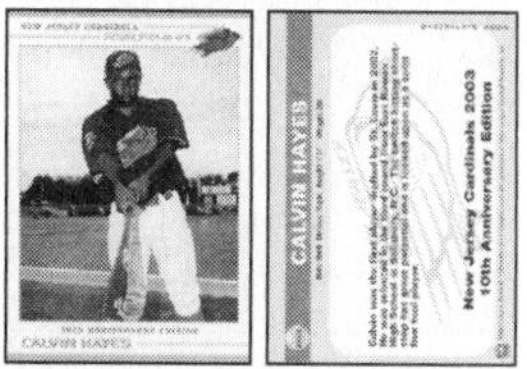

COMPLETE SET (5)................. 20.00 6.00

2003 New Jersey Cardinals Golden Great Grandstand

COMPLETE SET 10.00 3.00

2003 New Jersey Cardinals Grandstand

COMPLETE SET (29)............... 10.00 3.00

2003 New Orleans Zephyrs Multi-Ad

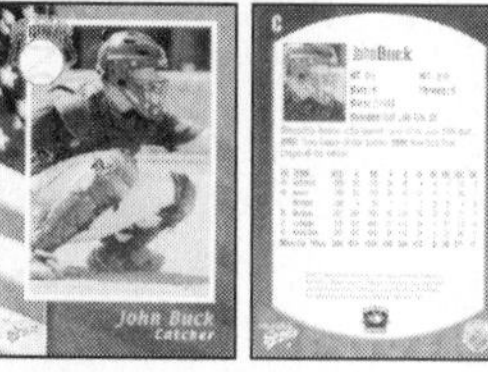

COMPLETE SET (31)............... 10.00 3.00

2003 Newark Bears Choice

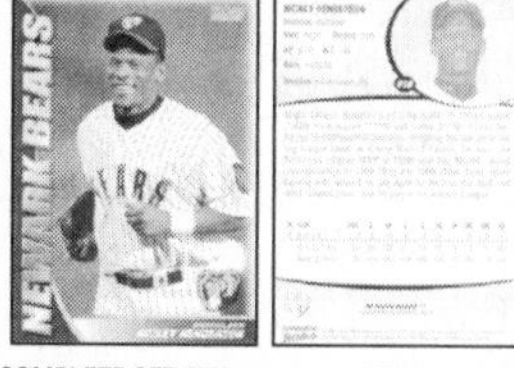

COMPLETE SET (30)............... 18.00 5.50

2003 Norfolk Tides Choice

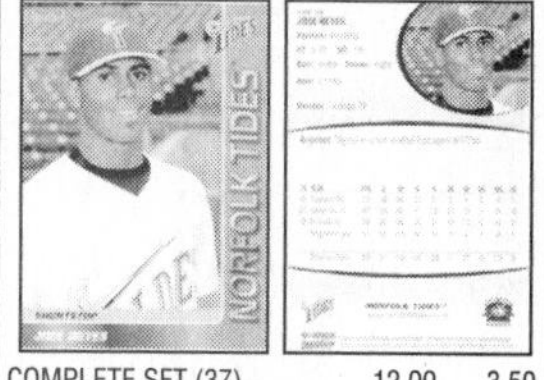

COMPLETE SET (37)............... 12.00 3.50

2003 Norwich Navigators Grandstand

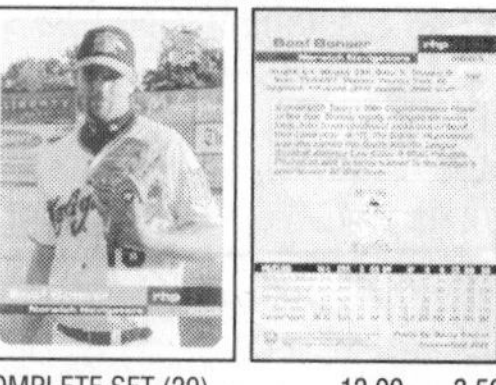

COMPLETE SET (29)............... 12.00 3.50

2003 Ogden Raptors Multi-Ad

COMPLETE SET (36)............... 15.00 4.50

2003 Oklahoma RedHawks Multi-Ad

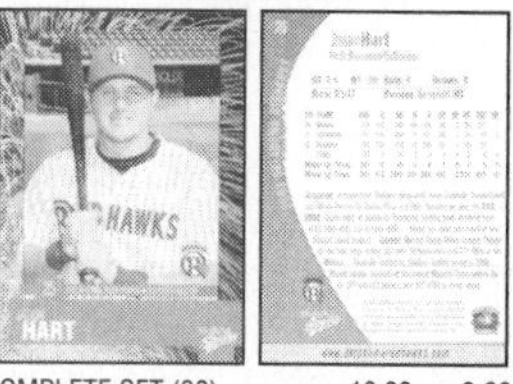

COMPLETE SET (30)............... 10.00 3.00

2003 Omaha Royals Multi-Ad

COMPLETE SET (26)............... 10.00 3.00

2003 Oneonta Tigers Prospects Grandstand

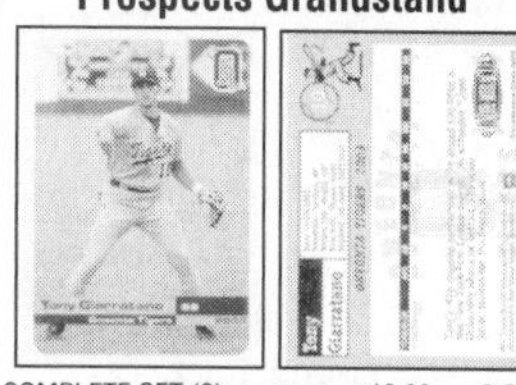

COMPLETE SET (3)................. 12.00 3.50

2003 Ottawa Lynx Choice

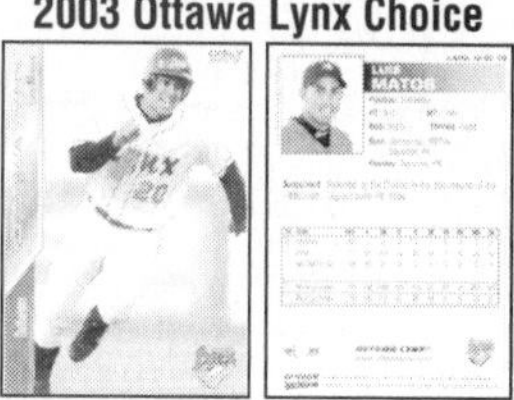

COMPLETE SET (29)............... 12.00 3.50

2003 Pacific Coast League All-Star Multi-Ad

COMPLETE SET (29)............... 15.00 4.50

2003 Pacific Coast League Top Prospects Multi-Ad

COMPLETE SET (35)............... 15.00 4.50

2003 Palm Beach Cardinals Team Issue

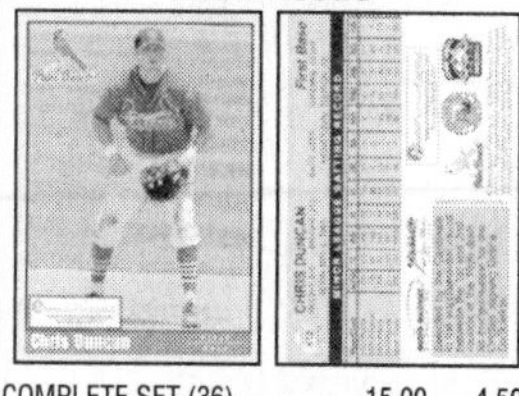

COMPLETE SET (36)............... 15.00 4.50

2003 Pawtucket Red Sox Choice

COMPLETE SET (30)............... 12.00 3.50

2003 Pawtucket Red Sox Dunkin Donuts

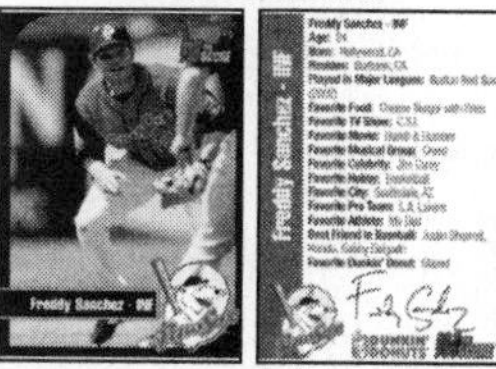

On June 6, 2003 all fans entering McCoy stadium received this Dunkin Donuts 30-card set featuring the 2003 PawSox Team. This is a 30-card perferated sheet, when detached, the card will feature blue borders with a Dunkin' Dounts logo in the upper-right hand corner with a 99.7/790 The Score logo just beneath it. The back of the card describes each players' favorite items as well as a facsimile autograph. This set is unnumbered.

COMPLETE SET (30)............... 15.00 4.50

2003 Peoria Chiefs Multi-Ad

COMPLETE SET (30)............... 15.00 4.50

2003 Portland Beavers Multi-Ad

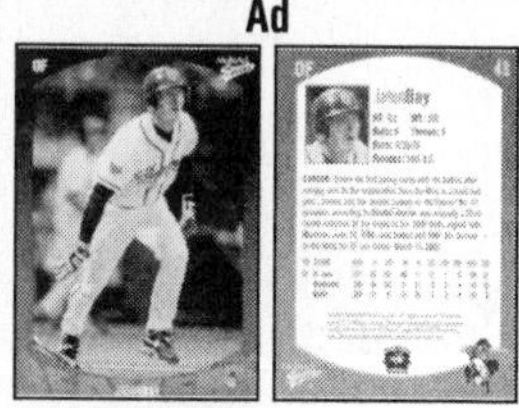

COMPLETE SET (28)............... 12.00 3.50

2003 Portland Sea Dogs Grandstand

COMPLETE SET (35)............... 10.00 3.00

2003 Potomac Cannons Choice

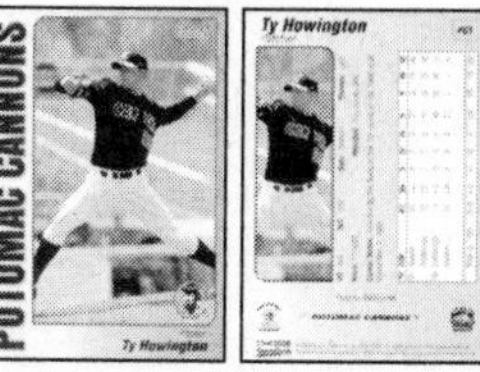

COMPLETE SET (30)............... 12.00 3.50

2003 Princeton Devil Rays Grandstand

COMPLETE SET (30)............... 12.00 3.50

2003 Princeton Devil Rays Police

This is an oversize set that features the listed players with a current student from the Mercer County Public Schools. The slogan "Character Counts" is in cursive from top to bottom on the card backs.

COMPLETE SET (4)................. 10.00 3.00

2003 Provo Angels Hobson

COMPLETE SET (30)............... 15.00 4.50

2003 Pulaski Blue Jays Choice

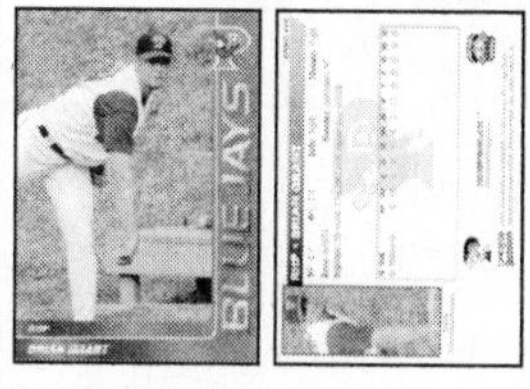

COMPLETE SET (36)............... 10.00 3.00

2003 Quad City River Bandits Grandstand

COMPLETE SET (30)............... 12.00 3.50

2003 Rancho Cucamonga Quakes Grandstand

COMPLETE SET (30)............... 12.00 3.50

2003 Reading Phillies Multi-Ad

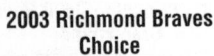

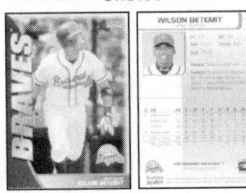

COMPLETE SET (30)................ 10.00 3.00

2003 Richmond Braves Choice

COMPLETE SET (30)................ 10.00 3.00

2003 Rochester Red Wings Choice

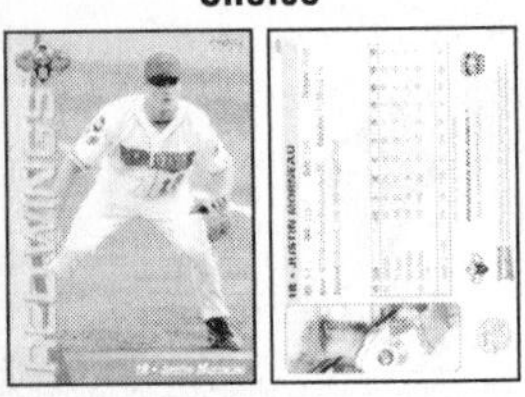

COMPLETE SET (31)................ 10.00 3.00

2003 Rome Braves Multi-Ad

COMPLETE SET (30)................ 15.00 4.50

2003 Round Rock Express Team Issue

COMPLETE SET (30)................ 15.00 4.50

2003 Sacramento River Cats Multi-Ad

COMPLETE SET (30)................ 15.00 4.50

2003 Salem Avalanche Grandstand

COMPLETE SET (30)................ 10.00 3.00

2003 Salem-Keizer Volcanoes Grandstand

COMPLETE SET (36)................ 12.00 3.50

2003 Salt Lake Stingers Multi-Ad

COMPLETE SET (34)................ 12.00 3.50

2003 San Antonio Missions Choice

COMPLETE SET (30)................ 12.00 3.50

2003 San Antonio Missions Update

COMPLETE SET (29)................ 12.00 3.50

2003 San Jose Giants Grandstand

COMPLETE SET (30)................ 10.00 3.00

2003 San Jose Giants Update Grandstand

COMPLETE SET (1)................ 10.00 3.00

2003 Sarasota Red Sox Grandstand

COMPLETE SET (30)................ 10.00 3.00

2003 Savannah Sand Gnats Golden Great Grandstand

COMPLETE SET 20.00 6.00

2003 Savannah Sand Gnats Multi-Ad

COMPLETE SET (30)................ 12.00 3.50

2003 Scranton Wilkes-Barre Red Barons Choice

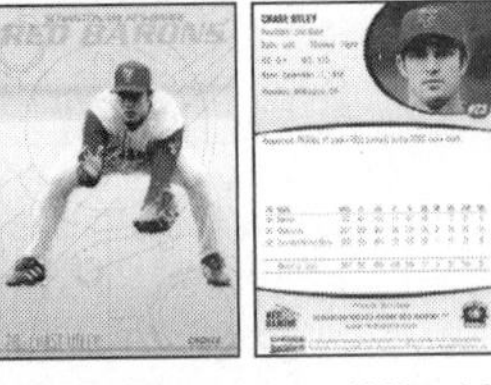

COMPLETE SET (30)................ 10.00 3.00

2003 South Atlantic League Prospects Multi Ad

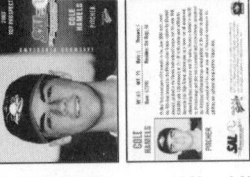

COMPLETE SET (36)................ 20.00 6.00

2003 South Bend Silver Hawks Grandstand

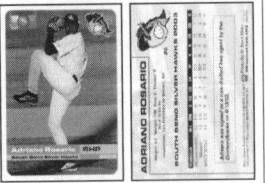

COMPLETE SET (35)................ 18.00 5.50

2003 Spokane Indians Grandstand

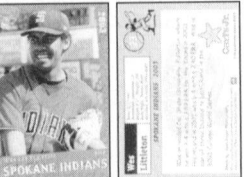

COMPLETE SET (32)................ 12.00 3.50

2003 St. Lucie Mets Grandstand

COMPLETE SET (35)................ 12.00 3.50

2003 St. Lucie Mets Update Grandstand

COMPLETE SET (8)................ 12.00 3.50

2003 Staten Island Yankees Multi-Ad

COMPLETE SET (35)................ 12.00 3.50

2003 Stockton Ports Multi-Ad

COMPLETE SET (30)................ 12.00 3.50

2003 Syracuse SkyChiefs Choice

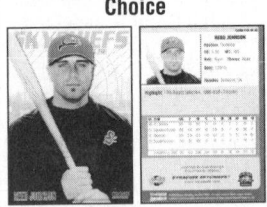

COMPLETE SET (30)................ 12.00 3.50

2003 Tacoma Rainiers Multi-Ad

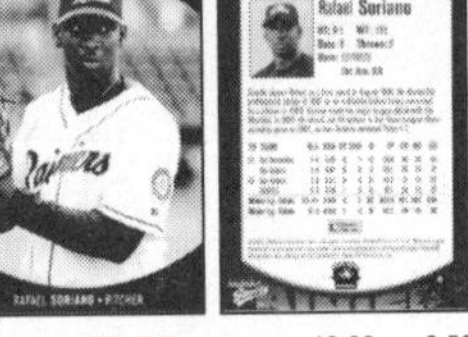

COMPLETE SET (31)................ 12.00 3.50

2003 Tampa Yankees Grandstand

COMPLETE SET (29)................ 10.00 3.00

2003 Tennessee Smokies Grandstand

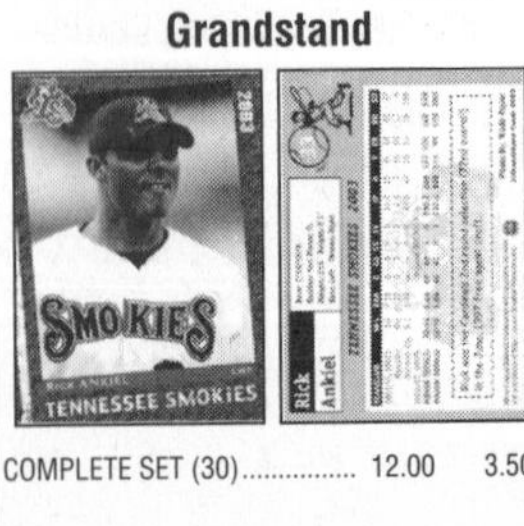

COMPLETE SET (30)................ 12.00 3.50

2003 Toledo Mud Hens Choice

COMPLETE SET (30)................ 12.00 3.50

2003 Trenton Thunder Multi-Ad

COMPLETE SET (31)................ 12.00 3.50

2003 Tri-City Dust Devils Grandstand

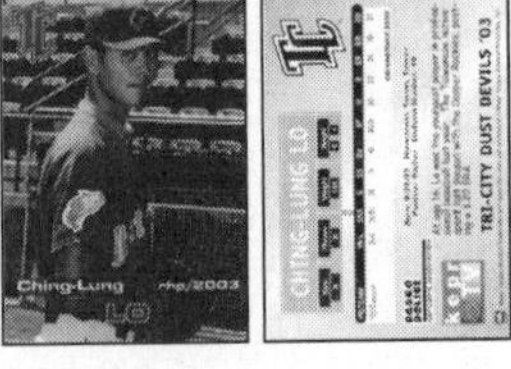

COMPLETE SET (32)................ 12.00 3.50

2003 Tri-City ValleyCats Choice

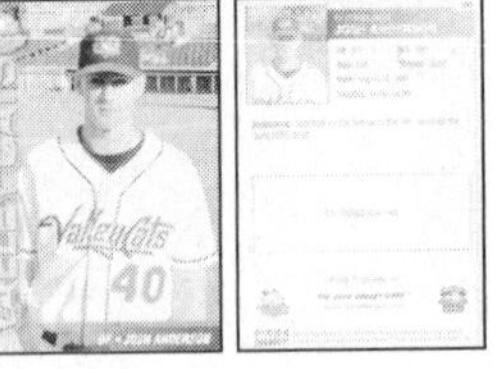

COMPLETE SET (38)................ 15.00 4.50

2003 Tucson Sidewinders Multi-Ad

COMPLETE SET 12.00 3.50

2003 Tulsa Drillers Team Issue

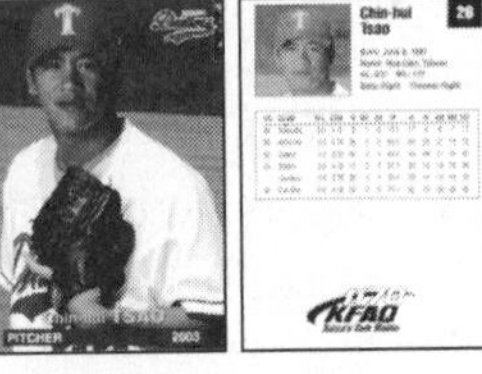

COMPLETE SET (29)................ 12.00 3.50

2003 Vancouver Canadians Infiniti Design

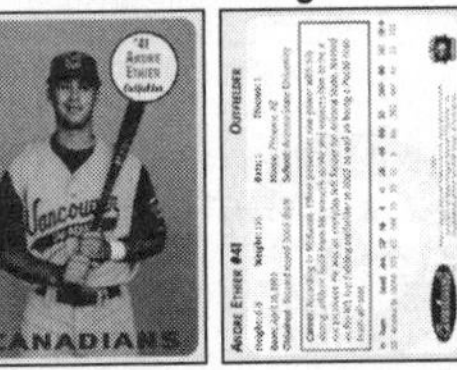

COMPLETE SET (38)................ 12.00 3.50

2003 Vermont Expos Grandstand

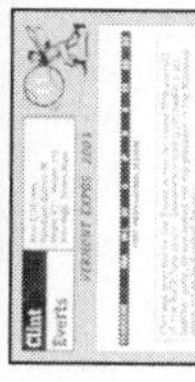

COMPLETE SET (34)............... 12.00 3.50

2003 Vero Beach Dodgers Grandstand

COMPLETE SET (29)............... 18.00 5.50

2003 Visalia Oaks Grandstand

COMPLETE SET (30)............... 10.00 3.00

2003 West Michigan WhiteCaps Choice

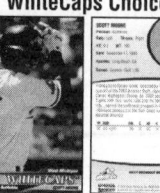

COMPLETE SET (30)............... 10.00 3.00

2003 West Tenn Diamond Jaxx Grandstand

COMPLETE SET (29)............... 15.00 4.50

2003 Wichita Wranglers Grandstand

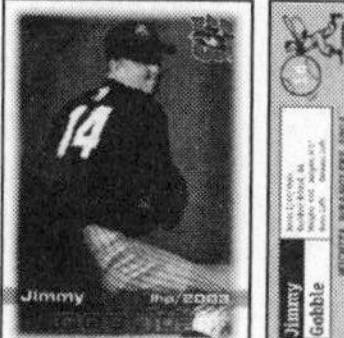

COMPLETE SET (29)............... 10.00 3.00

2003 Williamsport Crosscutters Choice

COMPLETE SET (35)............... 12.00 3.50

2003 Wilmington Blue Rocks Choice

COMPLETE SET (32)............... 15.00 4.50

2003 Wilmington Blue Rocks Rocks in the Show II

COMPLETE SET (24)............... 12.00 3.50

2003 Winston-Salem Warthogs Choice

COMPLETE SET (30)............... 15.00 4.00

2003 Wisconsin Timber Rattlers Choice

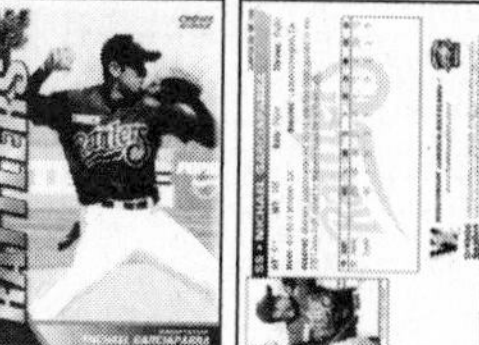

COMPLETE SET (30)............... 10.00 3.00

2003 Yakima Bears Grandstand

COMPLETE SET (34)............... 12.00 3.50

INTERNATIONAL

1909 Cuban Cabanas

These cards are arranged in alphabetical order by team.

Ex-Mt VG
COMPLETE SET............ 25000.00 12500.00
1 Rafael Almeida............ 500.00 250.00
2 Armando Cabanas............ 500.00 250.00
3 Alfredo Cabrera............ 400.00 200.00
4 Regino Garcia............ 800.00 400.00
5 Armando Marsans............ 600.00 300.00
6 Esteban Prats............ 400.00 200.00
7 Bebe Royer............ 500.00 250.00
8 Heliodoro Hidalgo............ 800.00 400.00
9 Luis Bustamante............ 1500.00 750.00
10 Chicho Gonzalez............ 400.00 200.00
11 Valentin Gonzalez............ 400.00 200.00
12 Ricardo Hernandez............ 400.00 200.00
13 Pete Hill............ 8000.00 4000.00
14 Angel Mesa............ 400.00 200.00
15 Carlos Moran............ 500.00 250.00
16 Luis Padron............ 2500.00 1250.00
17 Emilio Palomino............ 400.00 200.00
18 Pastro Pareda............ 300.00 150.00
19 Agustin Parpetti............ 1500.00 750.00
20 Bruce Petway............ 4000.00 2000.00
21 Inocencio Perez............ 400.00 200.00
22 Gonzalo Sanchez............ 400.00 200.00
23 Heinie Beckendorf............ 300.00 150.00
24 Donie Bush............ 500.00 250.00
25 Hopke............ 300.00 150.00
26 Davy Jones............ 400.00 200.00
27 Jack Lelivelt............ 300.00 150.00
28 Matty McIntyre............ 300.00 150.00
29 George Moriarty............ 400.00 200.00
30 George Mullin............ 600.00 300.00
31 Charley O'Leary............ 300.00 150.00
32 Boss Schmidt............ 300.00 150.00
33 Ed Willett............ 300.00 150.00
34 Silk O'Laughlin UMP............ 300.00 150.00
35 Tinti Molina............

1923-24 Cuban Billiken

These cards, which measure 1 15/16" by 2 5/8" feature members of the Cuban league. The fronts show the player in a posed shot to just below the waist. His name and team are on the bottom of the card. Unlike most Cuban sets, it is not known whether there is an album for these cards. Most cards say "Billiken" on the back but a few are known with "La Moda" on the back. We have sequenced this set in alphabetical order within team order.

Ex-Mt VG
COMPLETE SET (60)............ 35000.00 17500.00
1 Oscar Charleston............ 8000.00 4000.00
2 Rube Carrie............ 500.00 250.00
3 Pedro Dibut............ 250.00 125.00
4 Eddie Douglass............ 600.00 300.00
5 Frank Duncan............ 600.00 300.00
6 Oliver Marcelle............ 1500.00 750.00
7 Esteban Montalvo............ 250.00 125.00
8 Jose Mendez............ 2000.00 1000.00
9 Tinti Molina............ 250.00 125.00
10 Dobie Moore............ 600.00 300.00
11 Alejandro Oms............ 1000.00 500.00
12 Matias Rios............ 250.00 125.00
13 Julio Rojo............ 250.00 125.00
14 Red Ryan............ 250.00 125.00
15 Frank Warfield............ 300.00 150.00
16 Eufemio Abreu............ 250.00 125.00
17 John Bischoff............ 250.00 125.00
18 Danny Clark............ 250.00 125.00
19 Andy Cooper............ 250.00 125.00
20 Mack Eggleston............ 600.00 300.00
21 Hooks Jimenez............ 250.00 125.00
22 Marcelino Guerra............ 250.00 125.00
23 Oscar Levis............ 250.00 125.00
24 John Henry Lloyd............ 6000.00 3000.00
25 Juanelo Mirabal............ 250.00 125.00
26 Bartolo Portuando............ 250.00 125.00
27 Rafael Quintana............ 250.00 125.00
28 Buster Ross............ 250.00 125.00
29 Clint Thomas............ 500.00 250.00
30 Edgar Wesley............ 250.00 125.00
31 Bernardo Baro............ 250.00 125.00
32 Manuel Cueto............ 250.00 125.00
33 Valentin Dreke............ 600.00 300.00
34 Isidro Fabre............ 250.00 125.00
35 Jose Maria Fernandez............ 250.00 125.00
36 Oscar Fuhr............ 250.00 125.00
37 Hooks Jimenez............ 250.00 125.00
38 Snake Henry............ 250.00 125.00
39 Ramon Herrera............ 250.00 125.00
40 Jesse Hubbard............ 600.00 300.00
41 Armando Marsans............ 500.00 250.00
42 Jakie May............ 250.00 125.00
43 Eugenio Morin............ 250.00 125.00
44 Oscar Rodriguez............ 250.00 125.00
45 Nip Winters............ 250.00 125.00
46 Merito Acosta............ 250.00 125.00
47 Jose Acosta............ 250.00 125.00
48 James "Don" Brown............ 250.00 125.00
49 Eddie Brown............ 250.00 125.00
50 Rogelio Crespo............ 250.00 125.00
51 Hank DeBerry............ 300.00 150.00
52 Chuck Dressen............ 500.00 250.00
53 Freddie Fitzsimmons............ 500.00 250.00
54 Ivy Griffin............ 300.00 150.00
55 Ernie Krueger............ 250.00 125.00
56 Slim Love............ 250.00 125.00
57 Jose "Pepin" Perez............ 250.00 125.00
58 Rigal............ 250.00 125.00
59 Hank Schreiber............ 250.00 125.00
60 Cristobal Torriente............ 500.00 250.00

1923-24 Cuban Tomas Gutierrez

These cards, which measure 1 5/*" by 2 3/8" feature players who participated in the Cuban League in the 1923-24 season. These cards have the team name on top, the player photo in the middle and the player's name and position on the bottom. There was also an album issued to hold these cards. These cards have a sepia tone. We have sequenced them in alphabetical order by team.

Ex-Mt VG
COMPLETE SET............ 60000.00 30000.00
1 Dave Brown............ 1500.00 750.00
2 Oscar Charleston............ 10000.00 5000.00
3 Rube Currie............ 1200.00 600.00
4 Pedro Dibut............ 250.00 125.00
5 Bill Holland............ 1500.00 750.00
6 Oscar Johnson............ 1500.00 750.00
7 Frank Duncan............ 1200.00 600.00
8 Oliver Marcelle............ 1500.00 750.00
9 Jose Mendez............ 2500.00 1250.00
10 Pablo Mesa............ 250.00 125.00
11 Tinti Molina............ 250.00 125.00
12 Esteban Montalvo............ 600.00 300.00
13 Dobie Moore............ 1200.00 600.00
14 Alejandro Oms............ 1500.00 750.00
15 Eustaquio Pedroso............ 1500.00 750.00
16 Matias Rios............ 250.00 125.00
17 Julio Rojo............ 250.00 125.00
18 Frank Warfield............ 1200.00 600.00
19 Habana............ 250.00 125.00
Pennant
20 Eufemio Abreu............ 250.00 125.00
21 John Bischoff............ 250.00 125.00
22 Jacinto Calvo............ 400.00 200.00
23 Tatica Campos............ 250.00 125.00
24 Pelayo Chacon............ 250.00 125.00
25 Danny Clark............ 250.00 125.00
26 Mack Eggleston............ 250.00 125.00
27 Valentin Gonzalez UMP............ 250.00 125.00
28 Marcelino Guerra............ 600.00 300.00
29 Hooks Jimenez............ 250.00 125.00
30 Oscar Levis............ 250.00 125.00
31 Pop Lloyd............ 8000.00 4000.00
32 Dolph Luque............ 800.00 400.00
33 Juanelo Mirabal............ 250.00 125.00
34 Bartolo Portuando............ 250.00 125.00
35 Rafael Quintana............ 250.00 125.00
36 Buster Ross............ 250.00 125.00
37 Red Ryan............ 250.00 125.00
38 Clint Thomas............ 250.00 125.00
39 Cristobal Torriente............ 6000.00 3000.00
40 Edgar Wesley............ 250.00 125.00
41 Almendares............ 250.00 125.00
Pennant
42 Rafael Almeida............ 250.00 125.00
43 Bernardo Baro............ 250.00 125.00
44 Lucas Boada............ 250.00 125.00
45 Manuel Cueto............ 250.00 125.00
46 Valentin Dreke............ 250.00 125.00
47 Isidro Fabre............ 250.00 125.00
48 Jose Maria Fernandez............ 250.00 125.00
49 Willis Flournoy............ 250.00 125.00
50 Oscar Fuhr............ 250.00 125.00
51 Kakin Gonzalez............ 250.00 125.00
52 Papo Gonzalez............ 250.00 125.00
53 Snake Henry............ 250.00 125.00
54 Ramon Herrera............ 250.00 125.00
55 Jesse Hubbard............ 250.00 125.00
56 Armando Marsans............ 300.00 150.00
57 Jakie May............ 250.00 125.00
58 Eugenio Morin............ 250.00 125.00
59 Cheo Ramos............ 250.00 125.00
60 Jose Rodriguez............ 250.00 125.00
61 Oscar Rodriguez............ 250.00 125.00
62 Oscar Tuero............ 250.00 125.00
63 Marianao............ 250.00 125.00
Pennant
64 Merito Acosta............ 250.00 125.00
65 Jose Acosta............ 250.00 125.00
66 Otis Brannan............ 250.00 125.00
67 James D. Brown............ 250.00 125.00
68 Eddie Brown............ 250.00 125.00
69 Jimmy Cooney............ 300.00 150.00
70 Rogelio Crespo............ 250.00 125.00
71 Hank DeBerry............ 300.00 150.00
72 Chuck Dressen............ 500.00 250.00
73 Ernie Krueger............ 250.00 125.00
74 Slim Love............ 250.00 125.00
75 Hector Magrinat UMP............ 250.00 125.00
76 Harry McCurdy............ 250.00 125.00
77 Ed Morris............ 250.00 125.00
78 Emilio Palmero............ 250.00 125.00
79 Pepin Perez............ 250.00 125.00
80 Jess Petty............ 250.00 125.00
81 Art Phelan............ 250.00 125.00
82 Rosy Ryan............ 300.00 150.00
83 Hank Schreiber............ 250.00 125.00
84 Christobal Torriente............ 6000.00 3000.00

1924-25 Cuban Aguilitas Segundas

These cards which measure 1 7/32" by 2 3/8" feature players from the Cuban League. The player photo, name and the words "base ball" are featured on the front and set against a glossy photographic stock. Most cards are found with glue stains relating to being placed into album. These cards are part of a much larger series and are numbered from 841 through 900.

Ex-Mt VG
COMPLETE SET............ 20000.00 10000.00
841 Pablo Mesa............ 100.00 50.00
842 Armando Marsans............ 150.00 75.00
843 Cristobal Torriente............ 2000.00 1000.00
844 Merito Acosta............ 100.00 50.00
845 Cheo Ramos............ 100.00 50.00
846 Pop Lloyd............ 3000.00 1500.00
847 Matias Rios............ 100.00 50.00
848 Lucas Boada............ 100.00 50.00
849 Jose Mendez............ 100.00 50.00
850 Valentin Dreke............ 100.00 50.00
851 Eugenio Morin............ 100.00 50.00
852 Esteban Montalvo............ 100.00 50.00
853 Valentin Dreke............ 100.00 50.00
854 Julio Rojo............ 100.00 50.00
855 Rafael Almeida............ 150.00 75.00
856 Emilio Palmero............ 100.00 50.00
857 Dolf Luque............ 250.00 125.00
858 Isidro Fabre............ 100.00 50.00
859 Manuel Cueto............ 100.00 50.00
860 Pedro Dibut............ 100.00 50.00
861 Cheo Ramos............ 100.00 50.00
862 Jesse Hubbard............ 500.00 250.00
863 Kakin Gonzalez............ 100.00 50.00
864 Jose Maria Fernandez............ 100.00 50.00
865 Snake Henry............ 100.00 50.00
866 Ernie Krueger............ 100.00 50.00
Listed as Cruje on card
867 Manuel Parrado............ 100.00 50.00
Listed as Parrado on card
868 Chuck Dressen............ 250.00 125.00
869 Oscar Charleston............ 5000.00 2500.00
870 Pop Lloyd............ 3000.00 1500.00
871 Biz Mackey............ 2000.00 1000.00
872 Papo Gonzalez............ 100.00 50.00
873 Clint Thomas............ 500.00 250.00
874 Dobie Moore............ 500.00 250.00
875 Frank Duncan............ 500.00 250.00
876 Oscar Rodriguez............ 100.00 50.00
877 Lopito Lopez............ 100.00 50.00
878 Eustaquio Pedroso............ 600.00 300.00
879 Dick Lundy............ 2000.00 1000.00
880 Valentin Gonzalez............ 100.00 50.00
895 Oscar Tuero............ 100.00 50.00
897 Alejandro Oms............ 1000.00 500.00
898 Jess Petty............ 100.00 50.00
Listed as Peter on Card
899 Danny Clark............ 100.00 50.00

1924-25 Cuban Nacionales

These cards, which were issued as part of a much larger set of cards inserted into Nacionales cigarettes. These cards are all between number 21 and 60 in the set and all have a "C" prefix. A few cards; numbers 36 through 40 and numbers 56 through 60 were issued in an horizontal format.

Ex-Mt VG
COMPLETE SET............ 8000.00 4000.00
21 Rafael Almeida............ 150.00 75.00
22 Isidro Fabre............ 150.00 75.00
23 Eugenio Morin............ 100.00 50.00
24 Oscar Rodriguez............ 100.00 50.00
25 Joseito Rodriguez............ 100.00 50.00
26 Papo Gonzalez............ 100.00 50.00
27 J. Gutierrez............ 100.00 50.00
Photo is Cheo Ramos
28 Dreke............ 100.00 50.00
Photo is Lucas Boada
29 Jose Maria Fernandez............ 100.00 50.00
30 Cheo Ramos............ 100.00 50.00
31 Ramon Herrera............ 100.00 50.00
32 Bernardo Baro............ 150.00 75.00
33 Jose Cueto............ 100.00 50.00
34 Oscar Tuero............ 100.00 50.00
35 Kakin Gonzalez............ 100.00 50.00
36 Armando Marsans............ 150.00 75.00
37 Andy Cooper............ 400.00 200.00
38 Dolph Luque............ 300.00 150.00
39 Marcelino Guerra............ 100.00 50.00
40 Tatica Campos............ 100.00 50.00
41 Oscar Levis............ 100.00 50.00
42 Eufemio Abreu............ 100.00 50.00
43 Cristobal Torriente............ 2500.00 1250.00
44 Juanelo Mirabal............ 150.00 75.00
45 Merito Acosta............ 100.00 50.00
46 Jose Acosta............ 100.00 50.00
47 Rogelio Crespo............ 100.00 50.00
48 Jacinto Calvo............ 150.00 75.00
49 Emilio Palmero............ 100.00 50.00
50 Jose Mendez............ 2000.00 1000.00
51 Alejandro Oms............ 800.00 400.00
52 Pedro Dibut............ 100.00 50.00
53 Valentin Gonzalez UMP............ 100.00 50.00
54 Hector Magrinat UMP............ 100.00 50.00
55 Rafael Quintana............ 100.00 50.00
56 Hooks Jimenez............ 150.00 75.00
57 Bartolo Portuando............ 150.00 75.00
58 Pelayo Chacon............ 150.00 75.00
59 Red Ryan............ 150.00 75.00
60 Perico El Mano............ 100.00 50.00
Mascot

1926-27 Cuban Aguilitias

These cards, which measure 1 9/16" by 2 5/16" feature members of the Cuban League. These cards were issued in packs of Aguilitas brand cigarettes. These cards are part of a 900 card set which featured a mix of entertainers and athletes.

	Ex-Mt	VG
COMPLETE SET	4000.00	2000.00
751 Cheo Hernandez	60.00	30.00
752 Jose Maria Fernandez	60.00	30.00
756 Ricardo Torres	60.00	30.00
759 Jacinto Calvo	80.00	40.00
761 Emilio Palmero	60.00	30.00
763 Pablo Mesa	150.00	75.00
769 Carlos Zarza	60.00	30.00
771 Fernando Rios	60.00	30.00
772 Jose Rodriguez	60.00	30.00
774 Juanelo Mirabel	150.00	75.00
776 Lalo Rodriguez	60.00	30.00
777 Dolph Luque	250.00	125.00
778 Alejandro Oms	1200.00	600.00
779 Armando Marsans	150.00	75.00
782 Daniel Blanco	60.00	30.00
782 Alfredo Cabrera	60.00	30.00
787 Bartolo Portuando	60.00	30.00
791 Agustin Navarro	60.00	30.00
796 Rafael Quintana	60.00	30.00
797 Roberto Puig	60.00	30.00
817 Oscar Levis	60.00	30.00
819 Raul Atan	60.00	30.00
821 Pepin Perez	60.00	30.00
822 Isidro Fabre	60.00	30.00
823 Hooks Jimenez	150.00	75.00
824 Juanelo Mirabal	150.00	75.00
825 Tomas Calvo	60.00	30.00
826 Pelayo Chacon	150.00	75.00
829 Armando Marsans	150.00	75.00
832 Daniel Blanco	60.00	30.00
836 Valentin Dreke	60.00	30.00
838 Jose Echarri	60.00	30.00
839 Miguel Gonzalez	150.00	75.00
841 Oscar Estrada	60.00	30.00
846 Jose Acosta	60.00	30.00
847 Roberto Puig	60.00	30.00
849 Cesar Alvarez	60.00	30.00

1933 Sanella

This card of Babe Ruth, which measures approximately 2 3/4" by 4 1/8" features the famed Yankee slugger. The front is a colorized photo of the Babe swinging while the back has a significant amount of German type. These cards were originally designed to be put into an album.

	Ex-Mt	VG
COMPLETE SET	200.00	100.00
1 Babe Ruth	100.00	50.00
4 lines of type underneath Sanella		
2 Babe Ruth	100.00	50.00
Sanella in middle of card		

1970 Venezuelan Ovenca

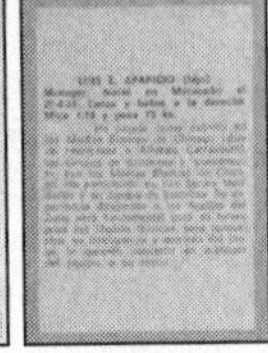

This standard-size set was printed in 1970 by Sport Grafico for Ovenca. The set includes many of the North Americans who played in the winter leagues. The fronts have the card number in the upper left hand corner. This checklist is incomplete so any additional information is greatly appreciated.

	NM	Ex
COMPLETE SET	1000.00	400.00
1 Cesar Gutierrez	6.00	2.40
3 Luis Rodriguez	5.00	2.00
4 Dave Concepcion	20.00	8.00
5 Roberto Munoz	5.00	2.00
6 Jesus Rizales	5.00	2.00
9 Cesar Garrido	5.00	2.00
10 Alejandro Tovar	5.00	2.00
11 William Salazar	5.00	2.00
13 Romulo Castillo	5.00	2.00
14 Victor Jimenez	5.00	2.00
15 Jose Saiz	5.00	2.00
17 Jesus Avila	5.00	2.00
18 Cruz Rodriguez	5.00	2.00
19 Julio Bracho	5.00	2.00
20 Cesar Gutierrez	10.00	4.00
Dave Concepcion		
23 Orlando Tavares	5.00	2.00
25 Jugada En 3a	5.00	2.00
Aragua		
26 Tigres al Acecho/c	5.00	2.00
Aragua		
27 Cesar Gutierrez Heri	6.00	2.40
28 Jugada en Home/Cesar	5.00	2.00
29 Joe Foy	6.00	2.40
Aragua		
30 Dennis Paepke	5.00	2.00
31 Fred Norman	6.00	2.40
Aragua		
32 John Purdin	5.00	2.00
Aragua		
33 Steve Huntz	5.00	2.00
34 Claide Mashore	5.00	2.00
Aragua		
35 Steve Mingori	5.00	2.00
Aragua		
36 Jim Breazale	5.00	2.00
Aragua		
37 Charles Day	5.00	2.00
Aragua		
38 Bob Stinson	5.00	2.00
Aragua		
39 Phil Hennigan	5.00	2.00
Aragua		
40 Checklist	5.00	2.00
Aragua		
42 Pablo Torrealba	5.00	2.00
Lara		
43 Erasmo Diaz	5.00	2.00
Lara		
44 Sebastian Martinez	5.00	2.00
Lara		
45 Nuedo Morales	5.00	2.00
Lara		
46 Iran Paz	5.00	2.00
Lara		
47 Franklyn Moreno	5.00	2.00
Lara		
48 Claudio Urdaneta	5.00	2.00
Lara		
49 Dario Chirinos	5.00	2.00
Lara		
50 Domingo Carrasquel	5.00	2.00
Lara		
51 Enrique Gonzalez	5.00	2.00
Lara		
52 Ednio Gonzalez	5.00	2.00
Lara		
53 Humberto Donquis	5.00	2.00
Lara		
54 Antonio Ruiz	5.00	2.00
Lara		
55 Efrain Urquiola	5.00	2.00
Lara		
57 Lucio Celis	5.00	2.00
Lara		
58 Domingo Barboza	5.00	2.00
Lara		
59 Zabala y Morales	5.00	2.00
Lara		
60 Jugada en la	5.00	2.00
Lara		
62 Lara Team Emblem	5.00	2.00
Lara		
63 Alexis Corro	5.00	2.00
Lara		
64 Novatos en Accion	5.00	2.00
Lara		
65 Jugada en Primera	5.00	2.00
Lara		
66 Jugada en Home	5.00	2.00
Lara		
67 Jugada en 3a	5.00	2.00
Lara		
68 Jim Shellenback	5.00	2.00
Lara		
69 Spizio Spinks	5.00	2.00
Lara		
70 Ken Forsch	8.00	3.20
Lara		
72 Ronald Cook	5.00	2.00
Lara		
73 Jackie Brown	5.00	2.00
Lara		
75 Bobby Watson	10.00	4.00
Lara		
77 Roger Metzger	5.00	2.00
Lara		
78 Tommy Reynolds	5.00	2.00
79 Cleo James	5.00	2.00
Lara		
80 Checklist	5.00	2.00
Lara		
81 Gus Gil	5.00	2.00
Magallanes		
82 Jesus Aristimuno	5.00	2.00
Magallanes		
83 Armando Ortiz	5.00	2.00
Magallanes		
87 Victor Colina	5.00	2.00
Magallanes		
89 Francisco Diaz	5.00	2.00
Magallanes		
90 Edito Arteaga	5.00	2.00
Magallanes		
91 Concepcion Escalona	5.00	2.00
Magallanes		
93 Luis A Serrano	5.00	2.00
Magallanes		
95 Raul Ortega	5.00	2.00
Magallanes		
97 Leopold Tovar	5.00	2.00
Magallanes		
99 Jugada en 3a	5.00	2.00
Magallanes		
101 Novatos del Magallan	5.00	2.00
Magallanes		
103 Marcano en la Lomita	5.00	2.00
Magallanes		
104 Fanaticos del Magall	5.00	2.00
Magallanes		
105 Jugada en 3a	5.00	2.00
Magallanes		
107 Hal King	6.00	2.40
Jim Holt		
Clarence Gaston		
Herman Hill		
108 Campeon del Caribe	5.00	2.00
Magallanes		
110 Herman Hill	5.00	2.00
111 Jim Holt	5.00	2.00
Magallanes		
113 Enzo Hernandez	5.00	2.00
Jugada en 1a		
114 Hal King	5.00	2.00
Magallanes		
117 Allan Closter	5.00	2.00
Magallanes		
118 Clarence Gaston	8.00	3.20
Magallanes		
119 John Morris	5.00	2.00
121 Victor Davalillo	5.00	2.00
Caracas leones		
122 Cesar Tovar	5.00	2.00
Caracas leones		
124 Luis Penalver	5.00	2.00
Caracas leones		
125 Alberto Cambero	5.00	2.00
Caracas leones		
126 Urbano Lugo	5.00	2.00
Caracas leones		
127 Juan Campos	5.00	2.00
Caracas leones		
128 William Castillo	5.00	2.00
Caracas leones		
129 Nelson Garcia	5.00	2.00
Caracas leones		
130 Ramon Guanchez	5.00	2.00
Caracas leones		
131 Manny Trillio	10.00	4.00
Jusus Marcano Trillo on the card		
132 Manuel Mendible	5.00	2.00
Caracas leones		
133 Teodoro Obregon	5.00	2.00
Caracas leones		
134 Jesus Padron	5.00	2.00
Caracas leones		
135 Ulises Urrieta	5.00	2.00
Caracas leones		
139 Alonso Olivares	5.00	2.00
Caracas leones		
140 Cesar Tovar in Action	6.00	2.40
Caracas leones		
141 Novatos en Accion	5.00	2.00
Caracas leones		
143 Andres Barrios	5.00	2.00
Caracas leones		
144 Heriberto Morillo	5.00	2.00
Caracas leones		
145 Angel Cordova	5.00	2.00
Caracas leones		
146 Freddy Rivero	5.00	2.00
Caracas leones		
147 Rafael Velasquez	5.00	2.00
Caracas leones		
152 Kurt Bevacqua	5.00	2.00
154 Larry Howard	5.00	2.00
Caracas leones		
155 Rick Scheinblum	5.00	2.00
Caracas leones		
157 Gregory Cooper	5.00	2.00
Caracas leones		
158 Richard Falker	5.00	2.00
Caracas leones		
159 Ed Sprague	5.00	2.00
Caracas leones		
160 Checklist Pompeyo Davil	5.00	2.00
Zulia		
161 Luis Aparicio	20.00	8.00
Zulia		
162 Teolindo Acosta	5.00	2.00
Zulia		
163 Gustavo Sposito	5.00	2.00
Zulia		
164 Juan Francia	5.00	2.00
Zulia		
165 Graciliano Parra	5.00	2.00
Zulia		
166 Simon Salaya	5.00	2.00
Zulia		
167 Nelson Castellanos	5.00	2.00
Zulia		
168 Edgar Urbina	5.00	2.00
Zulia		
169 Luis Gonzalez	5.00	2.00
Zulia		
170 Olinto Rojas	5.00	2.00
Zulia		
171 Everest Contramaestr	5.00	2.00
Zulia		
172 Juan Quiroz	5.00	2.00
Zulia		
173 Juan Quintana	5.00	2.00
Zulia		
174 Hugo Bello	5.00	2.00
Zulia		
175 Juses Ilamozas	5.00	2.00
Zulia		
176 Luis Aparicio	20.00	8.00
Zulia		
177 Luis Aparicio	20.00	8.00
Zulia		
179 Carlos Dickson Bell	5.00	2.00
Zulia		
181 Jugada en 3a	5.00	2.00
Zulia		
182 Las Aguilas Team Emblem	5.00	2.00
Zulia		
183 Nidio Sirit	5.00	2.00
Zulia		
184 Jugada en 1a	5.00	2.00
Zulia		
185 Las Aguilas Team	5.00	2.00
Zulia		
186 Bobby Cox in Action	10.00	4.00
Zulia		
187 Jugada en Home	5.00	2.00
Zulia		
188 Carrasquel Y Aparici	5.00	2.00
Zulia		
191 Bart Johnson	5.00	2.00
Zulia		
192 Jerry Crider	5.00	2.00
193 Getty Janesky	5.00	2.00
Zulia		
194 John Matias	5.00	2.00
Zulia		
195 Walter Williams	5.00	2.00
Zulia		
196 Steve Hovley	5.00	2.00
197 Frank Fernandez	5.00	2.00
Zulia		
198 John Donaldson	5.00	2.00
Zulia		
199 Donald Eddy	5.00	2.00
Zulia		
200 Checklist	5.00	2.00
Zulia		
207 Carlos Moreno	5.00	2.00
La Guaira		
208 Adolfo Philips	5.00	2.00
La Guaira		
209 Roberto Romero	5.00	2.00
La Guaira		
210 Euclides Camejo	5.00	2.00
La Guaira		
211 Oswaldo Troconis	5.00	2.00
La Guaira		
213 Victor Patino	5.00	2.00
La Guaira		
214 Hector Urbano	5.00	2.00
La Guaira		
216 Dave Garcia	5.00	2.00
La Guaira		
217 Graciano Ravelo	5.00	2.00
La Guaira		
219 Problema Entre Recepcion	5.00	2.00
La Guaira		
221 Tomas Liscano Arias	5.00	2.00
La Guaira		
223 Jesus Romero	5.00	2.00
La Guaira		
224 Julian Yanez	5.00	2.00
La Guaira		
225 Enrique Gutierrez	5.00	2.00
La Guaira		
226 Dionel Durand	5.00	2.00
La Guaira		
227 Jose Gregorio Salas	5.00	2.00
La Guaira		
228 Luis Camaleon Garcia	5.00	2.00
La Guaira		
229 Alfredo Ortiz	5.00	2.00
La Guaira		
230 Luis Contreras	5.00	2.00
La Guaira		
231 Ed Spiezio	5.00	2.00
La Guaira		
233 Mike Epstein	5.00	2.00
La Guaira		
234 Casey Cox	5.00	2.00
La Guaira		
236 Jerry Cram	5.00	2.00
La Guaira		
237 Danny Coombs	5.00	2.00
La Guaira		
238 Del Unser	5.00	2.00
239 Hector Brito	5.00	2.00
La Guaira		
240 Checklist	5.00	2.00
La Guaira		
241 Howard/Scheimblum in	5.00	2.00
242 Ed Spiezio in Action	5.00	2.00
La Guaira		
243 Clarence Gaston	8.00	3.20
CesarTovar in Action		
246 Pasion en el Juego	5.00	2.00
La Guaira		
247 Luis Aparicio in Action	20.00	8.00
La Guaira		
248 Angel Bravo in Action	5.00	2.00
La Guaira		
249 Bobby Watson in Action	10.00	4.00
La Guaira		
251 Enrique Fonseca	5.00	2.00
Veteranos		
252 Manuel Pollo Malpica	5.00	2.00
Immortales		
253 Emilio Cueche	5.00	2.00
Veteranos		
255 Felix Tirahuequito	5.00	2.00
Veteranos		
256 Heberto Leal	5.00	2.00
Veteranos		
258 Julian Ladera	5.00	2.00
Veteranos		
259 Carlos Ascanio	5.00	2.00
Veteranos		
260 Jose Perez Colmenare	5.00	2.00
Immortales		
262 Victor Garcia	5.00	2.00
Veteranos		
263 Valentin Arevalo	5.00	2.00
Immortales		
264 Adolfredo Gonzalez	5.00	2.00
Veteranos		
265 Hector Benitez Redon	5.00	2.00
Veteranos		
266 Ramon Fernandez	5.00	2.00
Veteranos		
267 Guillermo Vento	5.00	2.00
Veteranos		
268 Rafael Garcia Cedeno	5.00	2.00
Veteranos		
269 Luis Oliveros	5.00	2.00
Veteranos		
270 Luis Mono Zuloaga	5.00	2.00
Veteranos		
271 Carlos Santeliz	5.00	2.00
Immortales		
272 Aureliano Patino	5.00	2.00
Veteranos		
273 Rafael Olivares	5.00	2.00
Veteranos		
274 Tarzan Contreras	5.00	2.00
Veteranos		
276 Babbino Fuenmayor	5.00	2.00
Veteranos		
277 Rafael Galiz Tello	5.00	2.00
Veteranos		
278 Pantaleon Espinoza	5.00	2.00
Veteranos		
279 Miguel Sanabria	5.00	2.00
Veteranos		
281 Alfonso Carrasquel	5.00	2.00
Veteranos		
283 Balbino Inojosa	5.00	2.00
Veteranos		
284 Humberto Popita Leal	5.00	2.00
Veteranos		
285 Manuel Carrasquel	5.00	2.00
Veteranos		
286 Ignacio Florez	5.00	2.00
Veteranos		
287 Oscar Buzo Solorzino	5.00	2.00
Veteranos		
290 Micolas Berbesia	5.00	2.00
Veteranos		
291 Julio Bracho	5.00	2.00
Veteranos		
292 Dionisio Acosta	5.00	2.00
Veteranos		
293 Gualberto Acosta	5.00	2.00
Veteranos		
294 Winston Acosta	5.00	2.00
Veteranos		
295 Jose Manuel Tovar	5.00	2.00
Veteranos		
297 Luis Romero Petit	5.00	2.00
Veteranos		
298 Dalmiro Finol	5.00	2.00
Veteranos		

1976-77 Venezuelan League Stickers

This 330-sticker set measures approximately 2 3/8" by 3 1/8". The fronts feature color player portraits with rounded corners in a thin white frame surrounded by a different color border for each of the six featured teams. The team name is printed in the top border, with the card number and player's name below. The player's position is printed in a baseball in the lower right. The stickers are placed in a 9" by 12" album according to their number with the player's biography printed in his sticker space. The stickers are listed below according to teams as follows: Tigres de Aragua (1-36), Cardenales de Lara (37-72), Leones del Caracas (73-108), Tiburones de la Guaira (109-144), Navegantes del Magallanes (145-180), and Aguilas del Zulia (181-216). This is followed by a section with players from various teams (217-270). Stickers 271-324 in groups of nine form composite team photos. The album closes with team logo stickers (325-330).

	NM	Ex
COMPLETE SET (330)	3000.00	1200.00
1 Oswaldo Virgil MG	10.00	4.00
2 Patato Pascual CO	5.00	2.00
3 Jesus Avila CO	5.00	2.00
4 Raul Ortega CO	5.00	2.00
5 David Concepcion	50.00	20.00
6 Jesus Araujo	5.00	2.00
7 Preston Hanna	10.00	4.00
8 Victor Davalillo	10.00	4.00
9 Jesus Padron	5.00	2.00
10 Joseph Zdeb	10.00	4.00
11 Alfredo Ortiz	5.00	2.00
12 T. Acosta	5.00	2.00
13 Cesar Tovar	20.00	8.00
14 Craig Kusick	10.00	4.00
15 Angel Hernandez	5.00	2.00
16 Roberto Munoz	5.00	2.00
17 Fred Andrews	10.00	4.00
18 Rafael Alvarez	5.00	2.00
19 Jim Todd	10.00	4.00
20 Jeff Newman	10.00	4.00
21 Tommy Sandt	10.00	4.00
22 Simon Barreto	5.00	2.00
23 Willie Norwood	10.00	4.00
24 Juan Quiroz	5.00	2.00
25 Douglas Capilla	10.00	4.00
26 William Butler	10.00	4.00
27 William Castillo	5.00	2.00
28 Jugada for Robert Maneely	5.00	2.00
29 Peter Broberg	10.00	4.00
30 Jesse Jefferson	10.00	4.00
31 Carlos Avila	5.00	2.00
32 Jugada	5.00	2.00
33 Jugada	5.00	2.00
34 Terry Whitfield	10.00	4.00
35 Jugada	5.00	2.00
36 Gary Lance	10.00	4.00
37 Robert Cox MG	50.00	20.00
38 Leo Posada CO	10.00	4.00
39 Lucio Celis CO	5.00	2.00
40 Enrique Gonzalez CO	5.00	2.00
41 Jose (Musiu) Lopez	5.00	2.00
42 Jose Sandoval	5.00	2.00
43 Victor Correll	10.00	4.00
44 Pedro Lobaton	5.00	2.00
45 Jim Norris	10.00	4.00
46 Luis Aponte	10.00	4.00
47 Orlando Gonzalez	10.00	4.00
48 Eduardo Benitez	5.00	2.00
49 George Zeber	10.00	4.00
50 Carlos Rodriguez	5.00	2.00
51 Craig Robinson	10.00	4.00
52 Hernan Silva	5.00	2.00
53 Bob Oliver	10.00	4.00
54 Jose Herrera	10.00	4.00
55 Peter MacKanin	10.00	4.00
56 Roger Polanco	5.00	2.00
57 Stadium Lara	10.00	4.00
Por Gil Patterson		
58 A. Alvarado	5.00	2.00
59 Ron Selak	5.00	2.00
60 Nelson Canas	5.00	2.00
61 John Sutton	5.00	2.00
62 Nelson Garcia	5.00	2.00
63 Victor Patino	5.00	2.00
64 Francisco Navas	5.00	2.00
65 Robert Polinsky	10.00	4.00
66 Franklin Tua	5.00	2.00
67 Oscar Zamora	10.00	4.00
68 David Torres	5.00	2.00
69 Eddie Baez	10.00	4.00
70 Walter Williams	20.00	8.00
71 Cloyd Boyer CO	20.00	8.00
72 Carl Iorg	5.00	2.00
73 Pat Corrales MG	20.00	8.00
74 A. Carrasquel CO	10.00	4.00
75 Antonio Torres CO	5.00	2.00
76 Camilo Pascual CO	20.00	8.00
77 Tony Armas	50.00	20.00
78 Bo Diaz	20.00	8.00
79 Gary Beare	5.00	2.00
80 Steve Barr	10.00	4.00
81 Toribio Garboza	5.00	2.00
82 Mike Bacsik	10.00	4.00
83 Diego Segui	20.00	8.00
84 Jack Bastable	5.00	2.00
85 Ubaldo Heredia	5.00	2.00
86 Warren Cromartie	30.00	12.00
87 Elias Lugo	5.00	2.00
88 Mike Kelleher	10.00	4.00
89 Manny Trillo	20.00	8.00

90 Lenny Randle 20.00 8.00
91 Gonzalo Marquez 10.00 4.00
92 Jim Sadowski 5.00 2.00
93 Len Barker 20.00 8.00
94 Willi Quintana 5.00 2.00
95 Pablo Torrealba 10.00 4.00
96 Jim Hughes 10.00 4.00
97 Jose V. Caldera 5.00 2.00
98 Angel Vargas 5.00 2.00
99 Juan Gonzalez 5.00 2.00
100 Ulises Urrieta 5.00 2.00
101 Flores Bolivar 5.00 2.00
102 Robert Bowling 5.00 2.00
103 Rick Bladt 10.00 4.00
104 Luis Turner 5.00 2.00
105 Neldy Castillo 5.00 2.00
106 Adrian Garrett 10.00 4.00
107 Bob Davis 10.00 4.00
108 Jugada 5.00 2.00
109 P. Davalillo CO 10.00 4.00
110 Graciano Ravelo CO 5.00 2.00
111 Luis Lunar 5.00 2.00
112 Lester Morales 5.00 2.00
113 Enzo Hernandez 10.00 4.00
114 Aurelio Monteagudo 10.00 4.00
115 Angel Bravo 10.00 4.00
116 Carlos Moreno 5.00 2.00
117 Jose Cardenal 30.00 12.00
118 Rupert Jones 20.00 8.00
119 R. Blanco 5.00 2.00
120 Milton Ramirez 10.00 4.00
121 Antonio Correa 5.00 2.00
122 Clarence Gaston 20.00 8.00
123 Steve Luebber 10.00 4.00
124 Edwin Verheist 5.00 2.00
125 Robert Johnson 5.00 2.00
126 Earl Bass 5.00 2.00
127 Jose Salas 5.00 2.00
128 O. Blanco 5.00 2.00
129 Steve Staag 10.00 4.00
130 Steve Patchin 5.00 2.00
131 Michael Kekich 10.00 4.00
132 O. Troconis 5.00 2.00
133 Dave May 10.00 4.00
134 Luis Salazar 30.00 12.00
135 Larry Gura 20.00 8.00
136 Richard Dauer 20.00 8.00
137 Pastor Perez 5.00 2.00
138 Paul Siebert 10.00 4.00
139 Luis M. Sanchez 10.00 4.00
140 Victor Colina 5.00 2.00
141 Adrian Devine 10.00 4.00
142 Robert Marcano 5.00 2.00
143 Juan Berenger 10.00 4.00
144 Juan Monasterio 5.00 2.00
145 Donald Leppert MG 10.00 4.00
146 G. Machado CO 5.00 2.00
147 Mike Gonzalez CO 5.00 2.00
148 Wayne Granger 10.00 4.00
149 Remigio Hermoso 5.00 2.00
150 Rafael Cariel 5.00 2.00
151 Steve Dillard 10.00 4.00
152 Mitchell Page 10.00 4.00
153 Ramirez Y Rodriguez 10.00 4.00
154 Gary Wood 10.00 4.00
155 Ali Arape 5.00 2.00
156 Chris Batton 5.00 2.00
157 Gus Gil 10.00 4.00
158 Craig Reynolds 10.00 4.00
159 Jesus Aristimuno 5.00 2.00
160 Miguel Barreto 5.00 2.00
161 Alfonso Collazo 5.00 2.00
162 Steve Nicosia 10.00 4.00
163 O. Olivares 5.00 2.00
164 Robert Galasso 10.00 4.00
165 Alexis Ramirez 5.00 2.00
166 Craig Mitchell 10.00 4.00
167 Nelson Paiva 5.00 2.00
168 Ken Macha 10.00 4.00
169 Ruben Cabrera 5.00 2.00
170 Paul Reuschel 10.00 4.00
171 Edito Arteaga 5.00 2.00
172 Olinto Rojas 5.00 2.00
173 Jugada 5.00 2.00
174 Manny Sarmiento 10.00 4.00
175 Billy Moran 10.00 4.00
176 Eddie Watt CO 10.00 4.00
177 Michael Willis 10.00 4.00
178 Felix Rodriguez 5.00 2.00
179 James Easterly 10.00 4.00
180 Dave Parker 150.00 60.00
181 Luis Aparicio MG 150.00 60.00
182 Teodoro Obregon CO 5.00 2.00
183 D. Barboza CO 5.00 2.00
184 Orlando Pena CO UER 10.00 4.00
(Number printed on card is 190)
185 G. Marcano 5.00 2.00
186 Jose Alfaro 5.00 2.00
187 Jesus Reyes 5.00 2.00
188 Mike Scott 50.00 20.00
189 Dave Frost 5.00 2.00
190 Norm Shiera 10.00 4.00
Orlando Pena
191 Orlando Reyes 5.00 2.00
192 Milt Wilcox 20.00 8.00
193 Andrews Dyes 5.00 2.00
194 J. Hernandez 5.00 2.00
195 Dario Chirinos 5.00 2.00
196 Greg Shanahaln 10.00 4.00
197 Gustavo Sposito 5.00 2.00
198 S. Martinez 5.00 2.00
199 Leonel Carrion 5.00 2.00
200 Dennis Lewallyn 10.00 4.00
201 Charlie Moore 10.00 4.00
202 Steve Mallory 5.00 2.00
203 Gary Martz 5.00 2.00
204 Lamar Johnson 10.00 4.00
205 Tim Johnson 20.00 8.00
206 Levy Ochoa 5.00 2.00
207 Bill Dancy 5.00 2.00
208 Antonio Garcia 5.00 2.00
209 Nidio Dirit 5.00 2.00
210 Norman Shiera 5.00 2.00
211 Joe Chourio UER 5.00 2.00
(Card is numbered 221)
212 Jesus Alfaro 5.00 2.00
213 Bob Darwin 10.00 4.00
214 Jugada 5.00 2.00
215 Mike Seoane 5.00 2.00
216 Jim Gantner 30.00 12.00
217 Jugada 5.00 2.00
218 Jugada 5.00 2.00
219 Jugada 5.00 2.00
220 Jugada 5.00 2.00
221 Jugada 5.00 2.00
222 Jugada 5.00 2.00
223 Urrieta-Armas Y Trillo 30.00 12.00
224 Dogout 5.00 2.00
225 Hermoso y Gil 10.00 4.00
226 Jugada 5.00 2.00
227 Manny Trillo 50.00 20.00
Dave Concepcion
228 Jugada 5.00 2.00
229 Pizarra 5.00 2.00
230 Jugada 5.00 2.00
231 Jugada 5.00 2.00
232 Jugada 5.00 2.00
233 Jugada 5.00 2.00
234 Jugada 5.00 2.00
235 Publico 5.00 2.00
236 Jugada 5.00 2.00
237 Jugada 5.00 2.00
238 Jugada 5.00 2.00
239 Jugada 5.00 2.00
240 Jugada 5.00 2.00
241 Manny Trillo 50.00 20.00
Jose Cardenal
242 Davalillo Y Lacheman 10.00 4.00
243 Jugada 5.00 2.00
244 Jugada 5.00 2.00
245 Jugada 5.00 2.00
246 Jugada 5.00 2.00
247 Jugada 5.00 2.00
248 Jugada 5.00 2.00
249 Jugada 5.00 2.00
250 Jugada 5.00 2.00
251 Jugada 5.00 2.00
252 Jugada 5.00 2.00
253 Jugada 5.00 2.00
254 Jugada 5.00 2.00
255 Jugada 5.00 2.00
256 Jugada 5.00 2.00
257 Jugada 5.00 2.00
258 Jugada 5.00 2.00
259 Jugada 5.00 2.00
260 Jugada 5.00 2.00
261 Jugada 5.00 2.00
262 Club House 5.00 2.00
264 Club House 5.00 2.00
265 Club House 5.00 2.00
266 Jugada 5.00 2.00
267 Jugada 5.00 2.00
268 Jugada 5.00 2.00
269 Panoramica 5.00 2.00
270 Jugada 5.00 2.00
271 Tigres De Aragua 5.00 2.00
272 Tigres De Aragua 5.00 2.00
273 Tigres De Aragua 5.00 2.00
274 Tigres De Aragua 5.00 2.00
275 Tigres De Aragua 5.00 2.00
276 Tigres De Aragua 5.00 2.00
277 Tigres De Aragua 5.00 2.00
278 Tigres De Aragua 5.00 2.00
279 Tigres De Aragua 5.00 2.00
280 Cardenales De Lara 5.00 2.00
281 Cardenales De Lara 5.00 2.00
282 Cardenales De Lara 5.00 2.00
283 Cardenales De Lara 5.00 2.00
284 Cardenales De Lara 5.00 2.00
285 Cardenales De Lara 5.00 2.00
286 Cardenales De Lara 5.00 2.00
287 Cardenales De Lara 5.00 2.00
288 Cardenales De Lara 5.00 2.00
289 Leones Del Caracas 5.00 2.00
290 Leones Del Caracas 5.00 2.00
291 Leones Del Caracas 5.00 2.00
292 Leones Del Caracas 5.00 2.00
293 Leones Del Caracas 5.00 2.00
294 Leones Del Caracas 5.00 2.00
295 Leones Del Caracas 5.00 2.00
296 Leones Del Caracas 5.00 2.00
297 Leones Del Caracas 5.00 2.00
298 Tiburones De La Guaira 5.00 2.00
299 Tiburones De La Guaira 5.00 2.00
300 Tiburones De La Guaira 5.00 2.00
301 Tiburones De La Guaira 5.00 2.00
302 Tiburones De La Guaira 5.00 2.00
303 Tiburones De La Guaira 5.00 2.00
304 Tiburones De La Guaira 5.00 2.00
305 Tiburones De La Guaira 5.00 2.00
306 Tiburones De La Guaira 5.00 2.00
307 Navegantes Del Magallanes 5.00 2.00
308 Navegantes Del Magallanes 5.00 2.00
309 Navegantes Del Magallanes 5.00 2.00
310 Navegantes Del Magallanes 5.00 2.00
311 Navegantes Del Magallanes 5.00 2.00
312 Navegantes Del Magallanes 5.00 2.00
313 Navegantes Del Magallanes 5.00 2.00
314 Navegantes Del Magallanes 5.00 2.00
315 Navegantes Del Magallanes 5.00 2.00
316 Aguilas Del Zulia 5.00 2.00
317 Aguilas Del Zulia 5.00 2.00
318 Aguilas Del Zulia 5.00 2.00
319 Aguilas Del Zulia 5.00 2.00
320 Aguilas Del Zulia 5.00 2.00
321 Aguilas Del Zulia 5.00 2.00
322 Aguilas Del Zulia 5.00 2.00
323 Aguilas Del Zulia 5.00 2.00
324 Aguilas Del Zulia 5.00 2.00
325 Navegantes Emblema 5.00 2.00
326 Tigress Emblema 5.00 2.00
327 Leones Emblema 5.00 2.00
328 Aguilas Emblema 5.00 2.00
329 Cardenales Emblema 5.00 2.00
330 Tiburones Emblema 5.00 2.00
K263 Club House 5.00 2.00
XX Album 80.00 32.00

1980-81 Venezuelan League Stickers

This 288-sticker set measures approximately 2" by 2 3/4". The fronts feature color player portraits framed by white border. The player's name and sticker number are printed in a yellow bar below the picture. The stickers are placed according to number in an 8" by 10 1/2" album, with the player's biography printed in his sticker slot. The set is arranged according to teams as follows: Tigres de Aragua (1-45), Cardenales de Lara (46-90), Leones del Caracas (91-135), Navegantes del Magallanes (136-180), Tiburones del la Guaira (181-225), and Aguilas del Zulia (226-270). The set closes with action stickers (271-288). Andres Galarraga first ever card is in this set.

NRMT VG-E
COMPLETE SET (288) 1200.00 550.00
1 Carlos Pascual 3.00 1.35
2 Camilo Pascual 10.00 4.50
3 Jesus Avila 3.00 1.35
4 Raul Ortega 3.00 1.35
5 Francisco Herrera 3.00 1.35
6 Hector Rincones 3.00 1.35
7 Wilfredo Sarmiento 3.00 1.35
8 Richard Lysander 5.00 2.20
9 Roberto Espinoza 3.00 1.35
10 Dave Engle 5.00 2.20
11 Angel Hernandez 3.00 1.35
12 Wolfang Ramos 3.00 1.35
13 Jesus Alcala 3.00 1.35
14 Luis Bravo 3.00 1.35
15 Gary Ward 8.00 3.60
16 Diego Segui 8.00 3.60
17 Carlos Porter 3.00 1.35
18 Gregory Johnston 3.00 1.35
19 Robert Brenly 5.00 2.20
20 Graig Skok 3.00 1.35
21 Luis Martinez 3.00 1.35
22 Jack Perconte 5.00 2.20
23 Antonio Lopez 3.00 1.35
24 Alvaro Espinoza 5.00 2.20
25 David Moore 3.00 1.35
26 Jose Barrios 3.00 1.35
27 Marty Scott 3.00 1.35
28 Ted Power 5.00 2.20
29 Balor Moore 5.00 2.20
30 Bastidas Alcala y porte 3.00 1.35
31 Tim Corcoran 5.00 2.20
32 Richard Sofield 5.00 2.20
33 Victor Davalillo 5.00 2.20
34 Jefrey Johns 5.00 2.20
35 Salvatore Butera 5.00 2.20
36 Nelson Torres 3.00 1.35
37 Lester Straker 5.00 2.20
38 Wilfredo Flores 3.00 1.35
39 Accion 3.00 1.35
40 Accion 3.00 1.35
41 Accion 3.00 1.35
42 Accion 3.00 1.35
43 Accion 3.00 1.35
44 Panoramica 3.00 1.35
45 Stadium Perez Colmenares 3.00 1.35
46 Vernon Benson 5.00 2.20
47 Lucio Celis 3.00 1.35
48 Enrique Gonzalez 3.00 1.35
49 Leo Posada 5.00 2.20
50 Fred Manrique 5.00 2.20
51 Jose Escobar 3.00 1.35
52 R. Benson 3.00 1.35
53 Arturo Sanchez 3.00 1.35
54 Carlos Leal 3.00 1.35
55 Carlos Cabrera 3.00 1.35
56 Tobias Hernandez 3.00 1.35
57 Albert Castillo 3.00 1.35
58 Luis Aponte 5.00 2.20
59 Willie Upshaw 8.00 3.60
60 Ildemero Silva 3.00 1.35
61 William Ereu 3.00 1.35
62 Ernie Whitt 5.00 2.20
63 Richard Murray 3.00 1.35
64 Luis Leal 5.00 2.20
65 Franklin Tua 3.00 1.35
66 Arnaldo Alvarado 3.00 1.35
67 Onesimo Perez 3.00 1.35
68 Lloyd Moseby 8.00 3.60
69 Omar Malave 3.00 1.35
70 Chris Bourjos 5.00 2.20
71 Juan Aponte 5.00 2.20
72 Garth Iorg 5.00 2.20
73 Obdulio 3.00 1.35
74 Tom Brown 3.00 1.35
75 Phill Nastu 5.00 2.20
76 Mike Williams 3.00 1.35
77 George Scott 8.00 3.60
78 Dave Schrom 3.00 1.35
79 George Bjorkman 5.00 2.20
80 Acion 3.00 1.35
81 Acion 3.00 1.35
82 Nelson Garcia 3.00 1.35
83 Peter Ladd 5.00 2.20
84 Accion 3.00 1.35
85 Brown/Humprey y Aponte 5.00 2.20
86 Accion 3.00 1.35
87 Accion 3.00 1.35
88 Accion 3.00 1.35
89 Accion 3.00 1.35
90 Accion 3.00 1.35
91 William (Gates) Brown 5.00 2.20
92 Alfonso Carrasquel 3.00 1.35
93 Antonio (Loco) Torres 3.00 1.35
94 Manuel Gonzalez 3.00 1.35
95 Baudilio Diaz 5.00 2.20
96 Willibaldo Quintana 3.00 1.35
97 Luis Penalver 3.00 1.35
98 Gonzalo Marquez 5.00 2.20
99 Antonio Armas 8.00 3.60
100 Natalio Silva 3.00 1.35
101 Ubaldo Heredia 3.00 1.35
102 Luis Turnes 3.00 1.35
103 Leonardo Hernandez 5.00 2.20
104 Bruce Robbins 3.00 1.35
105 Levy Ochoa 3.00 1.35
106 Jhon Hobbs 3.00 1.35
107 Andres Galarraga 50.00 22.00
108 Anthony Brizzolara 5.00 2.20
109 Jesus Alfaro 3.00 1.35
110 Tom Dixon 5.00 2.20
111 Pablo Torrealba 5.00 2.20
112 Jeff Bertoni 3.00 1.35
113 Ruben Cabrera 3.00 1.35
114 Mark de John 3.00 1.35
115 Dan Rohn 5.00 2.20
116 Pedro J. Chavez 3.00 1.35
117 Emilio Carrasquel 3.00 1.35
118 Gene Roof 5.00 2.20
119 James Maler 5.00 2.20
120 Ed Miller 5.00 2.20
121 Dave Stewart 25.00 11.00
122 Dave Rucker 5.00 2.20
123 Jose Alfaro 3.00 1.35
124 Graig Ryan 3.00 1.35
125 Graig Eaton 3.00 1.35
126 Stu Cliburn 5.00 2.20
127 Mike Macha 3.00 1.35
128 Flores Bolivar 3.00 1.35
129 Dave Tobik 5.00 2.20
130 Armas/Baudilio 5.00 2.20
131 Leslie Filkins 3.00 1.35
132 Torres/Carrasquel 5.00 2.20
133 Gonzalez/Bolivar y Turnes 5.00 2.20
134 Hermanos Alfaro 3.00 1.35
135 Oyendo el Himno 5.00 2.20
136 Luis Aparicio 20.00 9.00
137 Remigio Hermoso 3.00 1.35
138 Gregorio Machado 3.00 1.35
139 Olinto Rojas 3.00 1.35
140 Alfredo Torres 3.00 1.35
141 Luis Jimenez 3.00 1.35
142 Alexis Ramirez 5.00 2.20
143 Carlos Hernandez 3.00 1.35
144 Felix Rodriguez 3.00 1.35
145 Fernando Guerra 3.00 1.35
146 Oswaldo Olivares 3.00 1.35
147 Miguel Barreto 3.00 1.35
148 Jesus Tiamo 3.00 1.35
149 Rene Nieto 3.00 1.35
150 Nelson Palva 3.00 1.35
151 Manuel Sarmiento 5.00 2.20
152 Carlos Gil 3.00 1.35
153 Jack Upton 5.00 2.20
154 Jhonny Gonzalez 3.00 1.35
155 Lawrence Rusch 3.00 1.35
156 Ernesto Gomez 3.00 1.35
157 Kim Allen 5.00 2.20
158 Scott Fletcher 5.00 2.20
159 Pat Dempsey 5.00 2.20
160 Mike Howard 3.00 1.35
161 Bryan Clark 5.00 2.20
162 Keith MacWhorter 5.00 2.20
163 Robert Myrick 5.00 2.20
164 Rick Jones 5.00 2.20
165 Billy Smithson 3.00 1.35
166 Randy Martz 5.00 2.20
167 Jim Neiper 5.00 2.20
168 Ralph Botting 5.00 2.20
169 Jim Dorsey 5.00 2.20
170 Accion 3.00 1.35
171 Mauro Pinto 3.00 1.35
172 Accion 3.00 1.35
173 Michael Grace 3.00 1.35
174 Luis Benitez 3.00 1.35
175 Accion 3.00 1.35
176 R. Walton 3.00 1.35
177 Donald Lyle 3.00 1.35
178 Jhon Hale 3.00 1.35
179 Accion 3.00 1.35
180 Stadium Jose B. Perez 3.00 1.35
181 Rene Lacheman 8.00 3.60
182 Pompeyo Davalillo 5.00 2.20
183 Graciano Ravelo 3.00 1.35
184 Carlos Mereno 3.00 1.35
185 Gustavo Polidor 5.00 2.20
186 Luis Alvarez 5.00 2.20
187 Paul Hartzell 5.00 2.20
188 Dan Graham 5.00 2.20
189 Rich Mahler 5.00 2.20
190 Antonio Cordova 3.00 1.35
191 Odell Jones 5.00 2.20
192 Oswaldo Blanco 3.00 1.35
193 Juan Eichelberger 5.00 2.20
194 O. Echenique 3.00 1.35
195 Francisco Leandro 3.00 1.35
196 Luis M. Sanchez 5.00 2.20
197 Raul Perez 3.00 1.35
198 Gavriel Ferrer 3.00 1.35
199 Albert Williams 5.00 2.20
200 Luis Salazar 5.00 2.20
201 Juan Monasterios 3.00 1.35
202 Victor Colina 3.00 1.35
203 Aurelio Monteagudo 5.00 2.20
204 Luis Lunar 3.00 1.35
205 Edwin Verheist 3.00 1.35
206 Juan Berenguer 5.00 2.20
207 Alfredo Pedrique 5.00 2.20
208 Mike Armstrong 5.00 2.20
209 Angel Salazar 5.00 2.20
210 Jesse Orozco 10.00 4.50
211 Roberto Marcano 3.00 1.35
212 James Anderson 5.00 2.20
213 Hector Rivas 3.00 1.35
214 Rick Lisi 5.00 2.20
215 Ted Cox 5.00 2.20
216 Tim Ireland 5.00 2.20
217 Bryan Harper 8.00 3.60
218 Antes Del Juego 3.00 1.35
219 Jugada 3.00 1.35
220 Safe! 3.00 1.35
221 Out en Segunda 3.00 1.35
222 Conferencia 3.00 1.35
223 Norman Shiera 3.00 1.35
224 Bryan Kingman 3.00 1.35
225 Daniel Garcia 5.00 2.20
226 Gus Gil 5.00 2.20
227 Marcos Sanchez 3.00 1.35
228 Domingo Barboza 3.00 1.35
229 Tom Brennan 5.00 2.20
230 Cesar Suarez 3.00 1.35
231 Gilberto Marcano 3.00 1.35
232 Dario Chirinos 3.00 1.35
233 Jose Alfaro 3.00 1.35
234 Antonio Garcia 3.00 1.35
235 Leonel Carrion 3.00 1.35
236 Gustavo Sposito 3.00 1.35
237 Rafael Cepeda 3.00 1.35
238 Marcos Campos 3.00 1.35
239 Jesus Alfaro 3.00 1.35
240 Justo Massaro 3.00 1.35
241 Omar Prieto 3.00 1.35
242 Alfredo Velazquez 3.00 1.35
243 Manuel Lunar 3.00 1.35
244 Toribio Garboza 3.00 1.35
245 Orlando Cepeda 15.00 6.75
246 Cesar Tovar 8.00 3.60
247 Jerry Reed 5.00 2.20
248 Gil Tovar 3.00 1.35
249 Accion 3.00 1.35
250 Bryn Smith 5.00 2.20
251 Porfirio Altamirano 5.00 2.20
252 Gustavo Quiroz 3.00 1.35
253 R. O'Keefe 3.00 1.35
254 Accion 3.00 1.35
255 Kevin Rhomberg 5.00 2.20
256 Robert Dernier 5.00 2.20
257 Tom Wieghaus 3.00 1.35
258 Todd Cruz 5.00 2.20
259 Mike Easler 8.00 3.60
260 Ron Clark 5.00 2.20
261 Accion 3.00 1.35
262 Jose V. Caldera 3.00 1.35
263 George Vukovich 5.00 2.20
264 Robert Sprowl 5.00 2.20
265 Accion 3.00 1.35
266 Accion 3.00 1.35
267 Accion 3.00 1.35
268 Accion 3.00 1.35
269 Accion 3.00 1.35
270 Accion 3.00 1.35
271 Accion 3.00 1.35
272 Accion 3.00 1.35
273 Accion 3.00 1.35
274 Accion 3.00 1.35
275 Accion 3.00 1.35
276 Accion 3.00 1.35
277 Accion 3.00 1.35
278 Accion 3.00 1.35
279 Accion 3.00 1.35
280 Accion 3.00 1.35
281 Accion 3.00 1.35
282 Accion 3.00 1.35
283 Accion 3.00 1.35
284 Accion 3.00 1.35
285 Accion 3.00 1.35
286 Accion 3.00 1.35
287 Accion 3.00 1.35
288 Accion 3.00 1.35
XX Album 20.00 9.00

1988-89 BYN Puerto Rico Winter League

Cards are numbered on the back as "X of 192", and each team set is also individually numbered as follows: Lobos De Arecibo, (A1-A32, 1-32) Criollos De Caguas, (C1-C32, 33-64) Indios De Mayaguez, (M1-M32, 65-96) Leones De Ponce, (P1-P32, 97-128) Metros De San Juan, (SJ1-SJ32, 129-160) and Cangrejeros De Santurce (S1-S32, 161-192).

Nm-Mt Ex-Mt
COMPLETE SET (192) 200.00 80.00
COMP.ARECIBO(1-32) 38.00 15.00
COMP.CAGUAS (33-64) 30.00 12.00
COMP.MAYAGUEZ (65-96) 38.00 15.00
COMP.PONCE (97-128) 38.00 15.00
COMP.SAN JUAN (129-160) 38.00 15.00
COMP.SANTURCE (161-192) 30.00 12.00
1 Marv Foley
2 Edwin Alicea
3 Saul Barreto
4 Jorge Candelaria
5 Luis Cruz
6 Fernando Figueroa
7 Willie Lozado
8 Juan Marina
9 Francico Melendez
10 Angel Miranda
11 Adalberto Pena
12 Benny Puig
13 German Rivera
14 Jesus Rivera
15 Jose Rivera
16 Angel Rodriguez
17 Edwin Rodreguez
18 Fernando Rodriguez
19 Aristalco Tirado
20 Miguel Torres
21 Hector Vargas
22 Jay Buhner
23 Mark Davis
24 Wayne Edwards
25 Bob Geren
26 Greg Hibbard
27 Donn Pall
28 Rick Raether
29 James Randall
30 Steve Rosenberg
31 Wolves Team Checklist
32 Wolves Logo
Substitutes
33 Santos Alomar
34 Roberto Alomar
35 Henry Cotto
36 Angelo Cuevas
37 Jose de Jesus
38 Edgar Diaz
39 Mario Diaz
40 Otto Gonzalez
41 Orestes Marrero
42 Vilato Marrero
43 Augustin Meizoso
44 Jose Melendez
45 Orlando Mercado
46 Jose Munoz
47 Omar Olivares
48 Francisco J. Olivera
49 Melvin Rosario
50 Ricky Torres
51 Hediberto Vargas
52 Chuck Cary
53 Danny Clay
54 Kevin Coffman
55 Rob Dibble
56 Cecil Espy
57 Ron Gant
58 Sam Horn
59 Bill Landrum

60 Mike Kinnunen
61 Van Snider
62 Ed Vosberg
63 Creoles Team Checklist
64 Croeles Logo
Substitutes
65 Tom Gamboa
66 Jose Birriel
67 Luis de Leon
68 Alex Diaz
69 Carlos Escalera
70 Roberto Hernandez
71 Luis Lopez
72 Luis Martinez
73 Charlie Montoyo
74 Lino Rivera
75 Javier Ocasio
76 Luis Raul Quinones
77 Luis Rivera
78 Julio Valera
79 Jeff Brantley
80 Ken Caminiti
81 Steve Davis
82 Jeff Facero
83 Steve Finley
84 Ken Gerhart
85 Don Heinkel
86 Chris Hoiles
87 Shawn Holman
88 Tom Howard
89 Ron Jones
90 Ricky Jordan
91 Alex Madrid
92 Kirt Manwaring
93 Tom McCarthy
94 Al Newman
95 Indians Team Checklist
96 Indians Logo
Substitutes
97 Jim Essian
98 Luis Aguayo
99 Ricky Bones
100 Francisco Burgos
101 Edgar Castro
102 Rafael Chavez
103 David Colon
104 Joey Cora
105 Juan Gonzalez
106 Ken Juarbe
107 Pedro Lopez
108 Johnny Monnell
109 Armando Moreno
110 Pedro Munoz
111 Adalberto Ortiz
112 Julian Perez
113 David Rivera
114 Gabriel Rodriguez
115 Victor Rodriguez
116 Hector Villanueva
117 Mike Felder
118 Marvin Freeman
119 Stan Jefferson
120 Ray Krawczyk
121 David Meads
122 Randy Milligan
123 John Pawlowski
124 Ernest Riles
125 Roger Samuels
126 Trevor Wilson
127 Lions Team Checklist
128 Lions Logo
Substitutes
129 Mako Oliveras
130 Miguel Alicea
131 Carlos Baerga
132 Hector Berrios
133 Mike Diaz
134 Ruben Escalera
135 Orlando Lind
136 Javy Lopez
137 Rafael Montalvo
138 Rafael Muratti
139 Carlos Rios
140 David Rosario
141 Elam Rossy
142 Hector Stewart
143 Jose Velez
144 Carlos Zayas
145 Tom Barrett
146 Joe Boever
147 Sherman Corbett
148 Doug Dascenzo
149 Joel Davis
150 Benny Distefano
151 Charlie Hayes
152 Rex Hudler
153 Morris Madden
154 Lonnie Smith
155 John Trautwein
156 Jeff Wetherby
157 Rick Wrona
158 Floyd Youmans
159 Metros Team Checklist
160 Metros Logo
Substitutes
161 Kevin Kennedy
162 Juan Jose Beniquez
163 John Burgos
164 Jose Calderon
165 Ivan De Jesus
166 Carlos LaBoy
167 Sixto Lezcano
168 Jose Lind
169 Luis Lopez
170 Angel Morris
171 Jaime Navarro
172 Jorge Ojeda
173 Mike Perez
174 Edgardo Romero
175 Geraldo Sanchez
176 Orlando Sanchez
177 Amilcar Valdez
178 John Valentin
179 Mike Basso
180 Dennis Burtt
181 Mike Devereaux
182 Mike Hartley
183 Dwayne Henry
184 Mike Jones
185 Jeff Manto
186 Mike Munoz
187 Javier Ortiz
188 Dwight Smith
189 John Wetteland
190 Rich Yett
191 Crabbers Checklist
192 Crabbers Logo
Substitutes

1988-89 BYN Puerto Rico Winter League Update

These cards are similar in design to the regular issue. The fronts are buys with a small player photo surrounded by a green border. The BYN logo is in the bottom left with the team identification on the upper left. The player's name is in the lower right. The back features biographical information as well as Puerto Rican league stats. An early Bernie Williams card is in this set.

	Nm-Mt	Ex-Mt
COMPLETE SET (64)	50.00	20.00

1 Darryl Boston
2 Mike Campbell
3 Reggie Dobie
4 Jeff Hull
5 Carlos Lezcano
6 Candido Maldonado
7 Roger Mason
8 Orlando Merced
9 Wally Ritchie
10 Tom Romano
11 Ricky Torres
12 Gene Walter
13 Bernie Williams
14 Shawn Abner
15 Wilfredo Cordero
16 Jack Daugherty
17 Mike Jeffcoat
18 Sixto Lezcano
19 Otis Nixon
20 Luis Ojeda
21 Rey Sanchez
22 Luis Aquino
23 Juan Belbru
24 John Cangelosi
25 Jeff Grey
26 Keith Hughes
27 Tom Pagnozzi
28 Rey Palacios
29 Keith Smith
30 Jay Aldrich
31 Duffy Dyer
32 Greg Harris
33 Ron Karkovice
34 Luis Martinez
35 Angel Ortiz
36 Rolando Roomes
37 Luis Alicea
38 Jose Anglero
39 Randy Kramer
40 Billy Moore
41 Ed Olwine
42 Stu Pederson
43 Mike Ramsey
44 Russ Swam
45 Dorn Taylor
46 Marcos Vazquez
47 Dave Clark
48 Tony Colon
49 Steve Davis
50 Jose Marzan
51 Dave Oliveras
52 Ruben Sierra
53 1988-89 Playoff Results
54 XIX Caribean
Championship Results
55 Batting Leaders
56 Home Run Leaders
57 Hits/Doubles Leaders
58 Triples Leaders
59 Win Leaders
60 CG/Shutout Leaders
61 Strikeout/Save Leaders
62 Starts Leaders
63 Checklist 1-32
64 Checklist 33-64

1989-90 BYN Puerto Rico Winter League

The cards are numbered on the back as "x of 201", and each team set is also individually numbered as follows: Metros De San Juan (SJ1-SJ34, 1-34), Criollos De Caguas (C1-C33, 35-67), Indios De Mayaguez (M1-M33, 68-100), Leones De Ponce (P1-P34, 101-134), Cangrejeros De Santurce (S1-S33, 135-167), and Lobos De Arecibo (A1-A34, 168-201). Early cards of Juan Gonzalez, Ivan Rodriguez and Bernie Williams are in this set.

	NRMT-MT	NM
COMPLETE SET (201)	200.00	90.00
COMP.SAN JUAN (1-34)	40.00	18.00
COMP.CAGUAS (35-67)	42.00	19.00
COMP.MAYAGUEZ (68-100)	22.00	10.00
COMP.PONCE (101-134)	30.00	13.50
COMP.SANTURCE (135-167)	35.00	16.00
COMP.ARECIBO (168-201)	38.00	17.00

1 Logo Card
2 Mako Oliveras
3 Miguel Alicea
4 Carlos Baerga
5 Hector Berrios
6 Ruben Escalera
7 Orlando Lind
8 Javy Lopez
9 Edgar Martinez
10 Rafael Montalvo
11 Adalberto Ortiz
12 Carlos Rios
13 Pablo Rivera
14 David Rosario
15 Elam Rossy
16 Rey Sanchez
17 Ricardo Ufret
18 Ramon Valdez
19 Marcos Vazquez
20 Hector Villanueva
21 Carlos Zayas
22 Dennis Burtt
23 Joaquin Contreras
24 Mike Hartley
25 Barry Jones
26 Paul McClellan
27 Mike Schwabe
28 Greg Tubbs
29 Don Vesling
30 Ramon L. Conde Jr. CO
31 Jesus Hernaiz CO
32 Luis Isaac CO
33 Jerry Morales CO
34 Checklist
35 Logo Card
36 Ramon Aviles
37 Henry Cotto
38 Angelo Cuevas
39 Jose De Jesus
40 Edgar Diaz
41 Mario Diaz
42 Juan Gonzalez
43 Gilberto Martinez
44 Agustin Meizoso
45 Jose Melendez
46 Orlando Mercado
47 Jose Munoz
48 Omar Olivares
49 Francisco J. Oliveras
50 Jorge Robles
51 Ivan Rodriguez
52 Victor Rodriguez
53 Melvin Rosario
54 Geraldo Sanchez
55 Hector Stewart
56 Beau Allred
57 Tom Barrett
58 Randy Bockus
59 George Canale
60 Pat Gomezz
61 Brad Moore
62 Andy Nezelek
63 Doug Strange
64 Luis Arroyo CO
65 Juan Lopez CO
66 Jaime Moreno CO
67 Checklist
68 Logo Card
69 Jim Riggleman
70 Juan Agosto
71 Luis Aquino
72 Jose Birriel
73 Luis De Leon
74 Alex Diaz
75 Luis Faccio
76 Leo Gomez
77 Roberto Hernandez
78 Juan Lopez
79 Luis Lopez Santos
80 Charlie Montoyo
81 Melvin Nieves
82 Javier Ocasio
83 Rey Palacios
84 Luis Raul Quinones
85 Lino Rivera
86 Luis Rivera
87 Roy Silver
88 Julio Valera
89 Billy Bates
90 Stan Clarke
91 Jeff Gray
92 Matt Kinzer
93 Ray Lankford
94 Jim Lindeman
95 Tim Meeks
96 Tom Pagnozzi
97 Dan Radison CO
98 Mark Riggins CO
99 Hector Valle CO
100 Checklist
101 Logo Card
102 Santos Alomar
103 Luis Aguayo
104 Roberto Alomar
105 Santos Alomar Jr.
106 Ricky Bones
107 Francisco Burgos
108 Ivan Calderon
109 Edgar Castro
110 Rafael Chavez
111 David Colon
112 Joey Cora
113 Felix Dedos
114 Luis Galindez
115 Otto Gonzalez
116 Jose Hernandez
117 Ken Juarbe
118 Pedro Lopez
119 Luis Martinez
120 Armando Moreno
121 Edwin Nunez
122 Julian Perez
123 Gabriel Rodriguez
124 Edwin Rosado
125 Terry Francona
126 Tom Howard
127 Ray Krawczyk
128 Dan Murphy
129 Greg Vaughn
130 Gary Lance CO
131 Efrain Maldonado CO
132 Abraham Martinez CO
133 Luis Melendez CO
134 Checklist
135 Logo Card
136 Ray Miller
137 Jose Anglero
138 Juan Belbru
139 Jose Calderon
140 Ivan De Jesus
141 Carlos Laboy
142 Jose Lebron
143 Jose Lind
144 Luis Lopez
145 Jose Marzan
146 Angel Morris
147 Jaime Navarro
148 Jorge Ojeda
149 Mike Perez
150 Rey Quinones
151 Jose Rivera
152 Tomas Rodriguez
153 Osvaldo Sanchez
154 Ulises Sierra
155 Jose Valentin
156 Albert Hall
157 Charlie Hayes
158 Randy Kramer
159 Terry McGriff
160 Rick Reed
161 Mike Roesler
162 Mark Ryal
163 Bob Sebra
164 Guillermo Montanez CO
165 Juan Pizarro CO
166 Eliseo Rodriguez
167 Checklist
168 Logo Card
169 Fernando Gonzalez
170 Edwin Alicea
171 Jorge Candelaria
172 Hernan Cortes
173 Luis Cruz
174 Fernando Figueroa
175 Victor Garcia
176 Javier Gonzalez
177 Wallace Gonzalez
178 Francisco Melendez
179 Orlando Merced
180 Angel Miranda
181 Roberto Munoz
182 Adalberto Pena
183 Benny Puig
184 David Rivera
185 Aristarco Tirado
186 Ricky Torres
187 Hector Vargas
188 Hediberto Vargas
189 Bernie Williams
190 Brian Giles
191 Erik Hanson
192 Gene Harris
193 Kelly Mann
194 Terry Taylor
195 Jim Wilson
196 Clint Zavaras
197 Carlos Arroyo CO
198 Jose Laboy CO
199 Carlos Lecano CO
200 Dan Warthen CO
201 Checklist

1989-90 BYN Puerto Rico Winter League Update

This standard-size set updates the regular 1989-90 Blanco Y Negro set issued before the 1989-90 Puerto Rican winter league season. An early card of Juan Gonzalez is in this set.

	NRMT-MT	NM
COMPLETE SET (75)	50.00	22.00

1 Tony Brown
2 Lenny Harris
3 Johny Maldonado
4 Reggie Ritter
5 Frenk Dimichele
6 Mike Kinnunen
7 Rafael Muratti
8 Rafael Novoa
9 Terry Shumpert
10 Nelson Simmons
11 Andy Stankiewicz
12 John Barfield
13 Danny Clay
14 Bill Fulton
15 Randy McCament
16 Armando Moreno
17 Carlos Rivera
18 Lou Thornton
19 Lee Tunnel
20 Gene Walter
21 Greg Harris
22 Allan Sadler
23 Roger Smithberg
24 Jeff Yurtin
25 Jose Birriel
26 Shawn Holman
27 Jim Hvizda
28 Luis Lopez Santos
29 Morris Madden
30 Bob Patterson
31 Scott Ruskin
32 Delvy Santiago
33 Osvaldo Virgil
34 Carlos Escalera
35 Jimmy Kremers
36 Chito Martinez
37 Ferdinand Rodriguez
38 Matt Sinatro
39 Mike Walker
40 Carlos Baerga MVP
Edgar Martinez MVP
41 Alex Diaz ROY
42 Ricky Bones
Pitcher of the Year
43 Ramon Aviles
Manager of the Year
44 Luis Aguayo
Comeback of the Year
45 Santos Alomar Jr. AS
46 Terry Francona AS
47 Carlos Baerga AS
48 Edgar Martinez AS
49 Joey Cora AS
50 Greg Vaughn AS
51 Henry Cotto AS
52 Juan Gonzalez AS
53 Roy Silver AS
54 Ricky Bones AS
55 David Rosario AS
56 Edgar Martinez LL
57 Luis Aguayo LL
Carlos Baerga LL
58 Greg Vaughn LL
59 Henry Cotto LL
60 Albert Hall LL
Carlos Baerga LL
61 Terry McGriff LL
62 Ray Lankford LL
63 Albert Hall LL
64 Ricky Bones LL
65 Randy Bockus LL
66 Rick Reed LL
67 Edwin Nunez LL
Brad Moore LL
Rick Reed LL
Aristarco Tirado LL
68 Rick Reed LL
69 Dan Murphy LL
70 Rick Reed LL
71 Julio Valera LL
Rick Reed LL
Ricky Bones LL
72 1989-90 Playoff Results
73 XX Caribean
Championship Results
74 Checklist 1-37
75 Checklist 38-75

1991 Adelaide Giants Futura

This 16-card set was produced by Futera for Pepsi. The standard-size cards have on the fronts glossy color player photos, with yellow borders that fade as one moves toward the card bottom. The "Pepsi/ABL" and team logos are superimposed at the top of the picture, with the Futera logo at the lower right corner. In a horizontal format, the backs have color head shots, biography, and 1989-90 ABL statistics.

	Nm-Mt	Ex-Mt
COMPLETE SET (16)	5.00	1.50

1 Glenn Jones
2 Gary Rice
3 Tony Harris
4 Tim Day
5 Nathan Davison
6 James Bushell
7 Dino Ebel
8 Bill Wengert
9 Brett Magnusson
10 John Knapp
11 Darren White
12 Phil Alexander CO
13 Phil White
14 Mark Van Pelt
15 Troy Scoble
16 Andrew Scott

1991 Brisbane Bandits Futura

This 19-card set was produced by Futera for Pepsi. The standard-size cards have on the fronts glossy color player photos, with yellow borders that fade as one moves toward the card bottom. The "Pepsi/ABL" and team logos are superimposed at the top of the picture, with the Futera logo at the lower right corner. In a horizontal format, the backs have color head shots, biography, and 1989-90 ABL statistics.

	Nm-Mt	Ex-Mt
COMPLETE SET (19)	5.00	1.50

1 John Bartorillo
2 Allan Albury CO
3 Gregory Suthers
4 Steven Devlin
5 Chris Welsh
6 Mathew Gates
7 David Kissick
8 Geoff Barden
9 Stuart Roebig
10 Ken MacDonald
11 Cameron Cairncross
12 John Boothby
13 Peter Vogler
14 Tim Worrell
15 Kim Jessop
16 David Hogan
17 Randy Johnson
18 Royal Thomas
19 Kevin Garner

1991 Daikyo Dolphins Futera

This 19-card standard-size set was produced by Futera for Pepsi. The fronts have glossy color player photos, with green borders that fade as one moves toward the card bottom. The "Pepsi/ABL" and team logos are superimposed at the top of the picture, with the Futera logo at the lower right corner. In a horizontal format, the backs have color head shots, biography, and 1989-90 ABL statistics.

	Nm-Mt	Ex-Mt
COMPLETE SET (19)	5.00	1.50

1 Bob Nilsson
Dave Nilsson
Gary Nilsson
2 Larry Montgomery
3 Mark Hess
4 David Foxover
5 Ron Johnson
6 Brett Cederblad
7 Gary Nilsson
8 Chris Maguire
9 Peter Yates
10 Bob Nilsson
11 Ian Burns
12 Charles Yang CO
13 Peter Hartas
14 Paul Gorman
15 Adrian Meagher
16 Travis Nicolau
17 Troy O'Leary
18 John Jaha
19 David Nilsson

1991 Melbourne Bushrangers Futura

This 19-card set was produced by Futera for Pepsi. The standard-size cards have on the fronts glossy color player photos, with orange borders that fade as one moves toward the card bottom. The "Pepsi/ABL" and team logos are superimposed at the top of the picture, with the Futera logo at the lower right corner. In a horizontal format, the backs have color head shots, biography, and 1989-90 ABL statistics.

	Nm-Mt	Ex-Mt
COMPLETE SET (19)	5.00	1.50

1 Greg Wharton
2 Neil Jones

3 Keith Gogas
4 Larry Gonzales
5 Jeff Oberdank
6 Marcus Moore
7 John Fritz
8 Leigh Walters
9 Mark Guy
10 George Bolin
11 Richard Vagg
12 Malcolm May
13 Mathew Wood
14 Bruce Morrison
15 Terry Reid
16 Howard Norsetter MGR
17 Wayne Pollock
18 Stephen Black
19 Glen Gambrell

1991 Parramatta Patriots Futera

This 20-card standard-size set was produced by Futera for Pepsi. The fronts have glossy color player photos, with purple borders that fade as one moves toward the card bottom. The "Pepsi/ABL" and team logos are superimposed at the top of the picture, with the Futera logo at the lower right corner. In a horizontal format, the backs have color head shots, biography, and 1989-90 ABL statistics.

	Nm-Mt	Ex-Mt
COMPLETE SET (20)	5.00	1.50

1 Ken Sharpe CO
2 Paul Elliot CO
3 Ben Shelton
4 Darian Lindsay
5 Darren Riley
6 Troy Halliday
7 Chris Hodkinson
8 Gary White
9 Grahame Cassel
10 John Gaynor
11 Gary Wales
12 Greg Johnston
13 Craig Summers
14 Steve Wilson
15 Stewart Bell
16 Scott Tunkin
17 Wayne Harvey
18 Chip Duncan
19 Tim McDowell
20 Austin Manahan

1991 Perth Heat Futera

This 19-card set was produced by Futera for Pepsi. The standard-size cards have on the fronts glossy color player photos, with orange borders that fade as one moves toward the card bottom. The "Pepsi/ABL" and team logos are superimposed at the top of the picture, with the Futera logo at the lower right corner. In a horizontal format, the backs have color head shots, biography, and 1989-90 ABL statistics.

	Nm-Mt	Ex-Mt
COMPLETE SET (19)	5.00	1.50

1 Simon Eissens
2 Mike Young MGR
3 Shaun Hrabar
4 Dave Rusin
5 John Moore
6 Todd Stephan
7 Pat Leinen
8 Tim Holland
9 Sean Jones
10 T.R. Lewis
11 Michael Moyle
12 Trevor Malcolm
13 Parris Mitchell
14 John Hearne
15 Peter Wood
16 Scott Metcalf
17 James Waddell
18 Tony Adamson
19 Scott Steed

1991 Sydney Wave Futera

This 20-card standard-size set was produced by Futera for Pepsi. The fronts have glossy color player photos, with purple borders that fade as one moves toward the card bottom. The "Pepsi/ABL" and team logos are superimposed at the top of the picture, with the Futera logo at the lower right corner. In a horizontal format, the backs have color head shots, biography, and 1989-90 ABL statistics.

	Nm-Mt	Ex-Mt
COMPLETE SET (20)	5.00	1.50

1 Mark Shipley
2 Brian Murphy
3 Matt Everingham
4 Troy Martin
5 Bevan James
6 Gregory Turner
7 Michael Dennis
8 Colin Barnes
9 Darren Fullerton
10 Billy White
11 Craig Johnston
12 Tad Powers
13 Brad DeJardin
14 Dodd Johnson
15 Peter Munro
16 Scott Barlow
17 Russell Haddan
18 Mike Gabbani
19 David Voit
20 James Donaldson
Owner

1991 Waverly Reds Futera

This 16-card standard-size set was produced by Futera for Pepsi. The fronts have glossy color player photos, with orange borders that fade as one moves toward the card bottom. The "Pepsi/ABL" and team logos are superimposed at the top of the picture, with the Futera logo at the lower right corner. In a horizontal format, the backs have color head shots, biography, and 1989-90 ABL statistics. The last two cards are unnumbered, and the player information is omitted altogether from one of the cards.

	Nm-Mt	Ex-Mt
COMPLETE SET (16)	5.00	1.50

1 Geoff Dunn
2 Dave McAuliffe
3 Pete Beeler
4 Mike Anderson
5 Ian Huble
6 Rob Hogan
7 Craig Kernick
8 David Buckthorpe
9 Mathew Sheldon-Collins
10 Richard King
11 Mark Respondek
12 Ron Carothers
13 Rohan Chapman
14 David Clarkson
xx x
Omitted player's name
xx Phil Dale

1993 Lime Rock Dominican Promos

This four-card promo set issued by Lime Rock introduces a premier 165-card set of Baseball Winter League cards that features players from the Professional Baseball League of the Dominican Republic, the largest source of foreign-born players to the major league teams in the United States. The cards are standard size and fronts feature a color player portrait bordered by speckled gray. The logo for the Professional Baseball League of the Dominican Republic appears in the upper right corner. The player's name is printed in white along the right border and the set title is printed below the photo. The black backs display a player head shot in the upper left corner with biography, statistics and team appearing in an orange, blue or purple box. The cards are numbered on the back with the prefix "P".

	Nm-Mt	Ex-Mt
COMPLETE SET (4)	4.00	1.20
P1 Jose Offerman	1.00	.30
P2 Denio Gonzalez	1.00	.30
P3 Omar Ramirez	2.00	.60
P4 Yorkis Perez	1.00	.30

1993 Lime Rock Dominican Winter Baseball

Issued by Lime Rock, this 166-card standard-size set of Baseball Winter League cards features players from the Professional Baseball League of the Dominican Republic, the largest source of foreign-born players for U.S. Major League teams. Each nine-card pack included a special offer card and a Diamond Star chase card. (The Diamond Star chase cards have a special gold foil emblem on their backs.). The cards are arranged according to teams as follows: Escogido Leones, (1-31) Estrellas de Oriente, (32-54) Licey Tigres, (55-86), Aguilas Cibaenas, (87-113) and Azucareros del Este (114-139). The set concludes with a Top Ten subset, (140-149) History cards, (150-151) and team checklist cards (152-161). Original Rookie cards are scattered throughout the set. Diamond Star cards are valued at 2X regular cards.

	Nm-Mt	Ex-Mt
COMPLETE SET (166)	20.00	6.00
1 Luis Encarnacion	.10	.03
2 Alberto Reyes	.10	.03
3 Victor Silverio	.10	.03
4 Wilfredo Tejada	.20	.06
5 Bienvenido Figueroa	.10	.03
6 Daniel Bautista	.30	.09
7 Fidel Compres	.10	.03
8 Miguel Batista	.10	.03
9 Mario Brito	.10	.03
10 Mariano de los Santos	.10	.03
11 Jose Nunez	.20	.06
12 Ramon Manon	.20	.06
13 Rafael Quirico	.10	.03
14 Mel Rojas	.30	.09
15 Sergio Valdez	.20	.06
16 Tony Eusebio	.30	.09
17 Carlos Mota	.10	.03
18 Fausto Cruz	.10	.03
19 Luis de los Santos	.20	.06
20 Mike Guerrero	.10	.03
21 Nelson Liriano	.20	.06
22 Junior Noboa	.20	.06
23 Ruben Santana	.10	.03
24 Domingo Martinez	.10	.03
25 Jose Oliva	.10	.03
26 Julio Peguero	.10	.03
27 Raul Mondesi	1.50	.45
28 Juan de la Rosa	.10	.03
29 Geronimo Berroa	.30	.09
30 Jesus Tavares	.10	.03
31 Samuel Sosa	5.00	1.50
32 Carlos de la Cruz	.10	.03
33 Julian Martinez	.10	.03
34 Norberto Martin	.20	.06
35 Luis Ortiz	.10	.03
36 Miguel Sabino	.10	.03
37 Mauricio Nunez	.10	.03
38 Roberto Rojas	.10	.03
39 Francisco de la Rosa	.10	.03
40 Armando Benitez	.30	.09
41 Julian Heredia	.10	.03
42 Josias Manzanillo	.20	.06
43 Jose Mercedes	.10	.03
44 Ben Rivera	.20	.06
45 Pedro Borbon	.20	.06
46 Francisco Cabrera	.10	.03
47 Ruben Rodriguez	.10	.03
48 Cesar Devares	.10	.03
49 Manny Alexander	.10	.03
50 Hector Roa	.10	.03
51 Cesar Bernhardt	.10	.03
52 Luis Mercedes	.20	.06
53 Sergio Cairo	.10	.03
54 Cesar Hernandez	.10	.03
55 Jose Luis Garcia	.10	.03
56 Jose Parra	.10	.03
57 Carlos Perez	.30	.09
58 Tito Bell	.10	.03
59 Miguel Santana	.10	.03
60 Pedro Astacio	.30	.09
61 Balbino Galvez	.20	.06
62 Jose Mesa	.30	.09
63 Gabriel Ozuna	.10	.03
64 Hipolito Pena	.20	.06
65 Vladimir Perez	.10	.03
66 Salomon Torres	.20	.06
67 Rafael Valdez	.10	.03
68 Yorkis Perez	.20	.06
69 Jose Segura	.20	.06
70 Efrain Valdez	.20	.06
71 Gilberto Reyes	.20	.06
72 Juan Guerrero	.20	.06
73 Jorge Alvarez	.10	.03
74 Gregorio Carmona	.10	.03
75 Freddy Gonzalez	.10	.03
76 Willie Otanez	.10	.03
77 Jose Offerman	.30	.09
78 Geronimo Pena	.30	.09
79 Bernie Brito	.20	.06
80 Braulio Castillo	.30	.09
81 Sil Campusano	.20	.06
82 Felix Jose	.20	.06
83 Jose Rafael Gonzalez	.10	.03
84 Henry Rodriguez	.50	.15
85 Mateo Ozuna	.10	.03
86 Miguel Jimenez	.10	.03
87 Jose Lima	.50	.15
88 Arturo Pena	.10	.03
89 Julian Tavarez	.30	.09
90 Elvin Paulino	.10	.03
91 Patricio Claudio	.10	.03
92 Miguel Garcia	.10	.03
93 Carmelo Castillo	.20	.06
94 Miguel Dilone	.20	.06
95 Jose Sued	.10	.03
96 Bernie Tatis	.10	.03
97 Miguel Fermin	.10	.03
98 Apolinar Garcia	.10	.03
99 Jose Bautista	.20	.06
100 Johnny Guzman	.20	.06
101 Manuel Fulcar	.10	.03
102 Victor Garcia	.20	.06
103 Fernando Hernandez	.10	.03
104 Jose Martinez	.10	.03
105 Tony Pena	.30	.09
106 Esteban Beltre	.20	.06
107 Felix Fermin	.20	.06
108 Carlos Fermin	.10	.03
109 William Suero	.10	.03
110 Quilvio Veras	.30	.09
111 Luis Polonia	.20	.06
112 Moises Alou	.50	.15
113 Omar Ramirez	.10	.03
114 Andy Araujo	.10	.03
115 Andres Lopez	.10	.03
116 Jose Cano	.10	.03
117 Cecilio Guante	.20	.06
118 Jesus Martinez	.10	.03
119 Sandy Guerrero	.10	.03
120 Domingo Michel	.10	.03
121 Manolo Mota	.10	.03
122 Ramon Sambo	.10	.03
123 Manny Jose	.10	.03
124 Wilson Heredia	.20	.06
125 Dario Perez	.10	.03
126 Pedro Martinez	5.00	1.50
127 Melido Perez	.20	.06
128 Hipolito Pichardo	.20	.06
129 Jose Ventura	.10	.03
130 Roberto Delgado	.10	.03
131 Henry Mercedes	.20	.06
132 Carlos Capellan	.20	.06
133 Domingo Cedeno	.20	.06
134 Julian Yan	.10	.03
135 Victor Rosario	.10	.03
136 Andujar Cedeno	.20	.06
137 Denio Gonzalez	.10	.03
138 Alberto de los Santos	.10	.03
139 Hensley Meulens	.20	.06
140 Miguel Batista	.50	.15
141 Fausto Cruz	.10	.03
142 Raul Mondesi	1.50	.45
143 Jose Lima	.50	.15
144 Luis Ortiz	.10	.03
145 Manny Alexander	.20	.06
146 Jose Oliva	.10	.03
147 Salomon Torres	.20	.06
148 Ruben Santana	.20	.06
149 Omar Ramirez	.10	.03
150 History Card	.10	.03
151 History Card	.10	.03
152 Checklist 1 Escogido Leones	.10	.03
153 Checklist 2 Escogido Leones	.10	.03
154 Checklist 3 Estrellas de Oriente	.10	.03
155 Checklist 4 Estrellas de Oriente	.10	.03
156 Checklist 5 Licey Tigres	.10	.03
157 Checklist 6 Licey Tigres	.10	.03
158 Checklist 7 Aguilas Cibaenas	.10	.03
159 Checklist 8 Aguilas Cibaenas	.10	.03
160 Checklist 9 Azucareros del Este	.10	.03
161 Checklist 10 Azucareros del Este	.10	.03
NNO Offer Card (Sports magazines)	.10	.03

1993-94 LineUp Venezuelan Baseball

This 350-card set was not available in the U.S. Cards have full-color fronts and backs with UV coating. Backs are in Spanish, with a player portrait, biography, statistics and large team logo at bottom. There are two subsets: Seven cards honoring former major leaguer and home run champ Tony Armas and 27 cards picturing the Caribbean Series. There are also autographed cards randomly inserted in the 14-card foil packs.

	Nm-Mt	Ex-Mt
COMPLETE SET (350)	45.00	13.50
1 Luis Salazar	.20	.06
2 Antonio Castillo	.10	.03
3 Pedro J. Chavez	.10	.03
4 Erick Ojeta Felix Leon	.10	.03
5 Ivan Arteaga	.10	.03
6 Wilson Alvarez	.40	.12
7 Ismael Rodriguez	.10	.03
8 Urbano Lugo	.20	.06
9 Todd Pratt	.40	.12
10 Jose Cardona	.10	.03
11 Luis Aparicio MG	1.00	.30
12 Frank Campos	.20	.06
13 Pedro P. Belmonte	.10	.03
14 Alejandro Alvarez	.10	.03
15 Juan F. Castillo	.10	.03
16 Jay Baller	.20	.06
17 Jose L. Zambrano	.10	.03
18 Argenis Conde	.10	.03
19 Yonni Naveda	.10	.03
20 Damaso Betancourt	.10	.03
21 Giovanni Carrara	.20	.06
22 Julio Franco	.40	.12
23 Omar Vizquel	1.00	.30
24 Jose Marchan	.10	.03
25 Edgar Naveda	.10	.03
26 Pedro Castellano	.10	.03
27 Jairo Ramos	.10	.03
28 Dave Burba	.40	.12
29 Pat Hentgen	.75	.23
30 Ramon Garcia	.10	.03
31 Robinson Garces	.10	.03
32 Remigio Hermoso	.10	.03
33 Malvin Matos	.10	.03
34 Miguel A. Garcia	.10	.03
35 Brad Holman	.20	.06
36 Johnny Malaver	.10	.03
37 Omar Daal	.40	.12
38 Edwin Hurtado	.10	.03
39 Ifrain Linares	.10	.03
40 Richard Delgado	.10	.03
41 Quinn Mack	.10	.03
42 Luis Lunar	.10	.03
43 Luis Gonzalez	.40	.12
44 Gilberto Clisanchez	.10	.03
45 Dave Masters	.10	.03
46 Jesus Hernandez	.10	.03
47 Johanne Manaure	.10	.03
48 Dean Hartgraves	.20	.06
49 Henrique A Gomez	.10	.03
50 Oscar Azocar	.20	.06
51 Edgar Herrera	.10	.03
52 Luis Dorante	.10	.03
53 Carlos Landines	.10	.03
54 Marcos Manrique	.10	.03
55 Dave Pavias	.20	.06
56 Jose Garcia	.10	.03
57 Mark Ohlms	.10	.03
58 Todd Jones	.40	.12
59 Julio Machado	.20	.06
60 Jose G. Urdaneta	.10	.03
61 Antonio Lopez	.10	.03
62 Alfredo Ortiz	.10	.03
63 Scott Cepicky	.20	.06
64 Gustavo Pinto	.10	.03
65 Tom McGraw	.20	.06
66 Oswald Peraza	.20	.06
67 Benito Malave	.10	.03
68 Esmily Guerra	.10	.03
69 Todd Trafton	.10	.03
70 Jesus Mendez	.10	.03
71 Amalio Carreno	.10	.03
72 Graciano Ravelo CO	.10	.03
73 Jose L. Ramos	.10	.03
74 Paul Marak	.20	.06
75 Oscar Sarmiento	.10	.03
76 Alfonzo Osuna	.20	.06
77 Felix Perez	.10	.03
78 Marlon Nava	.10	.03
79 Melvin Mora	.10	.03
80 Steve Wapnick	.20	.06
81 Ricky Rojas	.10	.03
82 Flores Bolivar	.10	.03
83 Donald Strange	.10	.03
84 Mike Soper	.10	.03
85 Juan C. Pulido	.10	.03
86 Daniel Rambo	.10	.03
87 Jorge Velandia	.10	.03
88 Silverio Navas	.10	.03
89 Trent Hubbard	.20	.06
90 Cliff Young	.20	.06
91 Julio C. Strauss	.10	.03
92 Cesar Tovar	.30	.09
93 Dilson Torres	.10	.03
94 Jose Villa	.10	.03
95 Jose Solarte	.10	.03
96 Francisco Munoz	.10	.03
97 Jesus Garces	.10	.03
98 Luis M. Sanchez	.20	.06
99 Jose Monzon	.10	.03
100 Luis Sojo	.40	.12
101 Ugueth Urbina	.40	.12
102 William Ereu	.10	.03
103 Mike Maksudian	.20	.06
104 Clemente Alvarez	.20	.06
105 Luis Portillo	.10	.03
106 Dan Urbina	.10	.03
107 Lester Straker	.20	.06
108 Jose Guarache	.10	.03
109 Miguel Soto	.10	.03
110 Henry Contreras	.10	.03
111 Jose Moreno	.10	.03
112 Luis Leal	.20	.06
113 Jesus Laya	.10	.03
114 Heberto Andrade	.10	.03
115 Angel Escobar	.10	.03
116 Jim Bruske	.20	.06
117 Edgar Marquez	.10	.03
118 Miguel Castellanos	.10	.03
119 Howard Battle	.20	.06
120 Amador Arias	.10	.03
121 Alexander Delgado	.10	.03
122 Omar Malave	.10	.03
123 Lipso Nava	.10	.03
124 Omar Bencomo	.10	.03
125 Oswaldo Olivares	.30	.09
126 Mahaly Carrera	.10	.03
127 Jesus Gonzalez	.10	.03
128 Doug Jennings	.20	.06
129 Edgardo Alfonzo	1.50	.45
130 Rob Natal	.20	.06
131 Joel Cartaya	.10	.03
132 Antonio Torres	.10	.03
133 Jose Betancourt	.10	.03
134 Carlos Lopez	.10	.03
135 Mario Gonzalez	.10	.03
136 Jose Stella	.10	.03
137 Oscar Escobar	.10	.03
138 Eddy Diaz	.10	.03
139 Mario Labastidas	.10	.03
140 Rafael Delima	.10	.03
141 Edgar Tovar	.10	.03
142 Gregorio Machado	.10	.03
143 Harry Guanchez	.10	.03
144 Jesus Alfaro	.10	.03
145 Asdrubal Estrada	.10	.03
146 Henry Centeno	.10	.03
147 Pedro Blanco	.10	.03
148 Kevin Noriega	.10	.03
149 Julio Armas	.10	.03
150 Cristobal Colon	.10	.03
151 Edgar Alfonzo	1.50	.45
152 Pablo Torrealba	.20	.06
153 Alexis Infante	.20	.06
154 Andres Espinoza	.20	.06
155 Jeff Grotewold	.20	.06
156 Robert Machado	.10	.03
157 Sherman Obando	.20	.06
158 Wilfredo Polidor	.20	.06
159 Henry Blanco	.10	.03
160 Jeff Kent	.75	.23
161 Alexander Sutherland	.20	.06
162 Noe Maduro	.10	.03
163 Jose G. Gil	.20	.06
164 Fernando Soto	.10	.03
165 Jose Leiva	.10	.03
166 Carlos Subero	.10	.03
167 Edgar Caceres	.10	.03
168 Rodolfo Hernandez	.10	.03
169 William Mota	.10	.03
170 Jesus Acevedo	.10	.03
171 Jose Leon	.10	.03
172 Cesar Gutierrez	.10	.03
173 Blas Cedeno	.10	.03
174 Fernando Ramsey	.10	.03
175 Marcos Armas	.10	.03
176 Roberto Castillo	.20	.06
177 Felipe Lira	.20	.06
178 Joe Hall	.20	.06
179 Freddy Torres	.10	.03
180 Juan Querecuto	.10	.03
181 Rouglas Odor	.10	.03
182 Ruben Amaro	.20	.06
183 Matt Maysey	.20	.06
184 Eduardo Perez	.20	.06
185 Freddy Gonzalez	.10	.03
186 Donald Harris	.20	.06
187 Ernesto Gomez	.10	.03
188 William Canate	.10	.03
189 Hector Rincones	.10	.03
190 Johnny Paredes	.20	.06
191 Roberto Espinoza	.10	.03
192 Jesus M. Trillo	.40	.12
193 Jaime Torres	.10	.03
194 Bob Abreu	1.00	.30
195 Jeff Frye	.30	.09
196 Shawn Jeter	.20	.06
197 Jesus Marquez	.10	.03
198 Scott Bryant	.20	.06
199 Robert Taylor	.10	.03
200 Carlos Garcia	.20	.06
201 Temis Liendo	.10	.03
202 Mauro Mendez	.10	.03
203 Jerry Kutzler	.20	.06
204 Troy O'Leary	.40	.12
205 Phil Regan MGR	.20	.06
206 Lino Connell	.10	.03
207 Luis R. Salazar	.20	.06
208 Len Picota	.10	.03
209 William Magallanes	.10	.03
210 Luis Gonzalez	.40	.12
211 Carlos Burguillos	.10	.03
212 Justo Massaro	.10	.03
213 Carlos T. Trillo	.10	.03
214 Richard Garces	.20	.06
215 Rick Sweet MG	.20	.06
216 Jim Newlin	.10	.03
217 Hector Ortega	.10	.03
218 Roger Cedeno	.40	.12
219 Eric Anthony	.20	.06
220 Jason Grimsley	.30	.09
221 Juan C. Abreu	.10	.03
222 Leonel Carrion	.10	.03
223 Alejandro Rodriguez	.10	.03
224 Jeff Pierce	.10	.03
225 Gustavo Polidor	.10	.03
226 Steve Pegues	.20	.06
227 William Pennyfeather	.10	.03
228 Eminson Soto	.10	.03
229 Karl Rhodes	.20	.06
230 Barry Manuel	.20	.06
231 Simon Pinango	.10	.03
232 Elias Lugo	.10	.03
233 Raul P. Tovar	.10	.03
234 Roberto Petaguine	.20	.06
235 Oswaldo Virgil MG	.20	.06
236 Gregory O'Halloran	.10	.03
237 Adrian Jordan	.10	.03
238 Orangel Lopez	.10	.03
239 Roberto Zambrano	.10	.03
240 Mauricio Ruiz	.10	.03
241 Igor Oviedo	.10	.03

242 Angel Leon .10 .03
243 Wilfredo Romero .10 .03
244 Richard Romero .10 .03
245 Pompeyo Davalillo MG .20 .06
246 Jack Voigt .20 .06
247 Danilo Leon .10 .03
248 Mike Draper .10 .03
249 Dan Urbina .10 .03
250 Carlos Hernandez .30 .09
251 Carlos Martinez .10 .03
252 Brian Keyser .10 .03
253 Jorge Uribe .10 .03
254 Jesus Delgado .10 .03
255 Garth Iorg .20 .06
256 Jose Centeno .10 .03
257 Douglas Moreno .10 .03
258 Jose F. Malave .10 .03
259 Oscar Henriquez .10 .03
260 Eduardo Zambrano .20 .06
261 Doug Linton .20 .06
262 Robert Perez .10 .03
263 Raul Chavez .10 .03
264 Darrin Chapin .20 .06
265 Mike Hart MG .10 .03
266 Ender Perozo .10 .03
267 Rick Polak .10 .03
268 Orlando Munoz .10 .03
269 Carlos Quintana .20 .06
270 Oswaldo Guillen .40 .12
271 Todd Stephan .10 .03
272 Manuel Gonzalez .10 .03
273 Terry Francona MG .20 .06
274 Jorge Mitchell .10 .03
275 Alfredo Pedrique .10 .03
276 Andres Galarraga .50 .15
Tovar
Olivares
Espinoza
277 Roger Cedeno .75 .23
Bob Abreu
Rob Natal
Jay Baller
Jennings
278 Roger Cedeno .75 .23
279 William Canate .10 .03
280 Andres Galarraga 1.50 .45
281 Antonio Armas .30 .09
282 Antonio Armas .30 .09
On Deck
283 Antonio Armas .30 .09
At Bat
284 Antonio Armas .30 .09
Awaiting Pitch
285 Antonio Armas .30 .09
Running to First
286 Antonio Armas .30 .09
Celebration
287 Antonio Armas .30 .09
El Slugger de Venezuela
288 Todd Pratt .30 .09
Rob Natal
O'Halloran
Perez
Hernandez
289 Aguilas del Zulia .10 .03
Team Card
290 Cangrejeros de Santurce .10 .03
Team Card
291 Venados de Mazatlan .10 .03
Team Card
292 Aguilas Cibaenas .10 .03
Team Card
293 Refuerzos Pitchers .10 .03
294 Refuerzos Jugadores .10 .03
295 Las Maximas Autoridades .10 .03
Umpires
296 Scott Bryant .20 .06
Jeff Grotewold
297 Hector Villanueva .20 .06
298 Tony Pena .30 .09
299 Jose Munoz .10 .03
300 Andujar Cedeno .20 .06
301 Cristobal Colon .20 .06
302 Edwin Alicea .10 .03
303 Moises Alou .75 .23
304 Matias Carrillo .10 .03
305 Dickie Thon .20 .06
306 Angel Moreno .10 .03
307 Mike Cook .10 .03
308 Luis Polonia .30 .09
309 Felix Fermin .20 .06
310 Adalberto Ortiz .10 .03
311 Alex Arias .20 .06
312 Fernando Valenzuela .50 .15
313 Johnny Paredes .30 .09
Moises Alou
314 Scott Bryant .20 .06
Hector Villanueva
315 Jim Wilson .20 .06
Nelson Simmons
316 Mako Olivares .20 .06
Pompeyo Davalillo
Ramon Montaya
Miguel Dilone
317 Hector Villanueva .20 .06
Alexander Delgado
Tony Pena
318 William Suero .20 .06
Edgar Naveda
Guillermo Velazquez
319 Cristobal Colon .20 .06
Luis Lopez Jr.
Andujar Ceceno
320 Luis Polonia .20 .06
Ruben Escalera
Robert Perez
321 Moises Alou .30 .09
William Canate
Erick Fox
322 Urbano Lugo .30 .09
Fernando Valenzuela
323 Liga Venezolana .10 .03
324 Asociasion de Peloteros .10 .03
325 Aguilas del Zulia .10 .03
326 Navegantes del Magallanes .10 .03
327 Leones del Caracas .10 .03
328 Cardenales de Lara .10 .03
329 Tiburones de la Guaira .10 .03
330 Tigres de Aragua .10 .03
331 Info: Caribes .10 .03
332 Petroleros de Cabimas .10 .03
333 Zulia TC .10 .03
334 Magallanes TC .10 .03
335 Caracas TC .10 .03
336 Lara TC .10 .03
337 La Guaira TC .10 .03
338 Aragua TC .10 .03
339 Caribes TC .10 .03
340 Cabimas TC .10 .03
341 Omar Vizquel .75 .23
342 William Canate .10 .03
343 Luis Salazar .20 .06
344 Andres Galarraga 1.00 .30
345 Musiu .10 .03
346 Wilson Alvarez .40 .12
347 Checklist .10 .03
348 Checklist 1-122 .10 .03
349 Checklist 247-350 .10 .03
350 Checklist 123-246 .10 .03

1994 Cuban League

Produced by Cubadeportes and printed in Canada, this 132-card set measures the standard size and features players from the 1994 Cuban baseball league. The cards are checklisted alphabetically according to team names as follows: Occidentales (1-33), Habana (34-66), Centrales (67-99), and Orientales (100-132). This set includes the first cards of Livan Hernandez, Orlando Hernandez and Omar Linares,

Nm-Mt Ex-Mt
COMPLETE SET (132) 20.00 6.00
1 Juan Manrique .10 .03
2 Lazaro Arturo Castro .10 .03
3 Pedro Luis Duenas .10 .03
4 Julio German Fernandez .10 .03
5 Alberto Peraza .10 .03
6 Yobal Duenas .10 .03
7 Alexander Ramos .10 .03
8 Omar Linares 5.00 1.50
9 Eduardo Cardenas .10 .03
10 Reniel Capote .10 .03
11 Alberto Diaz .10 .03
12 Lazaro Junco .10 .03
13 Jose Antonio Estrada .10 .03
14 Daniel Lazo .10 .03
15 Juan Carlos Linares .10 .03
16 Lazaro Madera .10 .03
17 Felix Isasi .10 .03
18 Eisler Livan Hernandez 8.00 2.40
19 Pedro Luis Lazo .10 .03
20 Faustino Corrales .10 .03
21 Omar Ajete .10 .03
22 Jorge Luis Valdez .10 .03
23 Carlos Yanes .10 .03
24 Lazaro Garro .10 .03
25 Jesus Bosmenier .10 .03
26 Carlos De La Torre .10 .03
27 Jorge Antonio Martinez .10 .03
28 Jorge Fuentes MG .10 .03
29 Pablo Pascual Abreu CO .10 .03
30 Nestor Perez CO .10 .03
31 Roman Suarez TR .10 .03
32 Armando Johnson .10 .03
33 Occidentales Team CL .10 .03
34 Pedro Luis Rodriguez .10 .03
35 Francisco Santiesteban .10 .03
36 Ricardo Miranda .10 .03
37 Roberto Colina .10 .03
38 Juan Carlos Millan .10 .03
39 Juan Padilla .10 .03
40 Oscar Macias .10 .03
41 Andy Morales .50 .15
42 Enrique Diaz .10 .03
43 German Mesa .10 .03
44 Juan Carlos Moreno .10 .03
45 Javier Mendez .10 .03
46 Gerardo Miranda .10 .03
47 Romelio Martinez .10 .03
48 Luis Enrique Piloto .10 .03
49 Carlos Tabares .10 .03
50 Orbe Luis Rodriguez .10 .03
51 Orlando Hernandez 10.00 3.00
52 Lazaro Valle .10 .03
53 Ariel Prieto 1.00 .30
54 Jorge Fumero .10 .03
55 Jose Ibar .10 .03
56 Vladimir Nunez 1.50 .45
57 Heriberto Collazo .10 .03
58 Jorge Garcia .10 .03
59 Euclides Rojas .10 .03
60 Osnel Blas Bocourt .10 .03
61 Jorge Trigoura MG .10 .03
62 Rene Bello CO .10 .03
63 Jorge Hernandez CO .10 .03
64 Antonio Jimenez TR .10 .03
65 Rene Rojas TR .10 .03
66 Habana Team CL .10 .03
67 Angel Lopez .10 .03
68 Jose Raul Delgado .10 .03
69 Ariel Pestano .10 .03
70 Lourdes Gurriel .10 .03
71 Jorge Luis Toca 1.00 .30
72 Jorge Diaz .10 .03
73 Lazaro Lopez .10 .03
74 Miguel Caldes .10 .03
75 Eduardo Paret .10 .03
76 Luis Ulacia .10 .03
77 Eusebio Miguel Rojas .10 .03
78 Victor Mesa .10 .03
79 Oscar Machado .10 .03
80 Eddy Rojas .10 .03
81 Pablo Primelles .10 .03
82 Rey Isaac .10 .03
83 Edel Pacheco .10 .03
84 Luis Rolando Arrojo .10 .03
85 Jose Ramon Riscart .10 .03
86 Teofilo Perez .10 .03
87 Adiel Palma .10 .03
88 Miguel Arnay Hernandez .10 .03
89 Omar Luis .10 .03
90 Felipe Fernandez .10 .03
91 Ramon Gardon .10 .03
92 Eliecer Montes de Oca .10 .03
93 Yovani Aragon .10 .03
94 Pedro Jova MG .10 .03
95 Luis Enrique Gonzalez CO .10 .03
96 Roberto Montero CO .10 .03
97 Pedro Perez TR .10 .03
98 Antonio Munoz TR .10 .03
99 Centrales Team CL .10 .03
100 Alberto Hernandez .10 .03
101 Luis Enrique Padro .10 .03
102 Carlos Barrabi .10 .03
103 Orestes Kindelan .10 .03
104 Pablo Bejerano .10 .03
105 Antonio Pacheco .10 .03
106 Gabriel Pierre .10 .03
107 Evenecer Godinez .10 .03
108 Manuel Benavides .10 .03
109 Marino Moreno .10 .03
110 Felix Benavides .10 .03
111 Ermidelio Urrutia .10 .03
112 Fausto Alvarez .10 .03
113 Luis Rodriguez .10 .03
114 Jorge Ochoa .10 .03
115 Juan Carlos Bruzon .10 .03
116 Leonel Bueno .10 .03
117 Osvaldo Fernandez .75 .23
118 Ernesto Leonel Guavara .10 .03
119 Jose Luis Aleman .10 .03
120 Osmani Tamayo .10 .03
121 Adolfo Canet .10 .03
122 Jose Miguel Baez .50 .15
123 Alfredo Fonseca .10 .03
124 Miguel Perez .10 .03
125 Ruben Rodriguez .10 .03
126 Misael Lopez .10 .03
127 Frangel Reynaldo .10 .03
128 Antonio Sanchez .10 .03
129 Miguel Giro .10 .03
130 Rafael Ramos TR .10 .03
131 Jesus Santiago Guerra .10 .03
132 Orientales Team CL .10 .03

1994-95 LineUp Venezuelan Baseball

This 300-card set features color photos of the players in the Venezuelan Baseball League and was not available in the United States. The backs carry player information and statistics. The cards are written in Spanish. Early cards of Edgardo Alfonso, Richard Hidalgo and Magglio Ordonez card are in this set.

Nm-Mt Ex-Mt
COMPLETE SET (300) 45.00 13.50
1 Carlos Garcia .20 .06
2 Ivan Artega .10 .03
3 Chris Hatcher .10 .03
4 Erick Ojeda .10 .03
5 Raul Chavez .10 .03
6 Cesar Morillo .10 .03
7 Brian L. Hunter .20 .06
8 Edgar Naveda .10 .03
9 Luis Raven .10 .03
10 R. "Tucupita" Marcano .10 .03
11 Jose Villa .10 .03
12 Oscar Azocar .20 .06
13 John Hudek .20 .06
14 Andres Espinoza .20 .06
15 Eddy Diaz .10 .03
16 Edgardo Alfonzo 5.00 1.50
17 Juan Fco. Castillo .10 .03
18 Melvin Mora .40 .12
19 Melcher Pacheco .10 .03
20 Richard Hidalgo 5.00 1.50
21 Clemente Alvarez .20 .06
22 Juan Carlos Pulido .10 .03
23 Al Osuna .20 .06
24 Ifrain Linares .10 .03
25 Jason Grimsley .20 .06
26 Alvaro Espinoza .20 .06
27 Tim Tolman .20 .06
28 Coaches Magallanes .10 .03
29 Henry Blanco .10 .03
30 Jose Centeno .10 .03
31 Francisco Munoz .10 .03
32 Ugueth Urbina 1.00 .30
33 Julio Strauss .10 .03
34 Terry Clark .20 .06
35 Omar Daal .40 .12
36 Kip Gross .20 .06
37 Bill Werts .10 .03
38 Jeff Shaw .40 .12
39 Brad Holman .10 .03
40 Urbano Lugo .20 .06
41 Andres Galarraga 2.00 .60
42 Omar Vizquel 2.00 .60
43 Tim Spehr .20 .06
44 E. "Charallave" Rios .10 .03
45 Rodolfo Hernandez .10 .03
46 Jose Stella .10 .03
47 Miguel Cairo .30 .09
48 Greg Briley .20 .06
49 Edgar Caceres .10 .03
50 Roberto Petagine .20 .06
51 Bob Abreu 3.00 .90
52 Edgar Alfonso .10 .03
53 Roger Cedeno .40 .12
54 Carlos Hernandez .30 .09
55 Jesus Alfaro .10 .03
56 Jorge Uribe .10 .03
57 Roger Cedeno 1.00 .30
Omar Vizquel
58 Phil Regan .30 .09
59 Coaches Caracas .10 .03
60 Luis Salazar .20 .06
61 Carlos "Cafe" Martinez .10 .03
62 Jose Monzon .10 .03
63 Miguel Soto .10 .03
64 Gustavo Polidor .20 .06
65 Alejandro Alvarez .10 .03
66 Juan Carlos Quero .10 .03
67 Andrew Lorraine .20 .06
68 Luis Gonzalez 1.00 .30
69 Gustavo Pinto .10 .03
70 Frank Campos .10 .03
71 Mark Zappelli .10 .03
72 Alejandro Prieto .10 .03
73 Igor Oropeza .10 .03
74 Steve Pegues .10 .03
75 Luis Dorante .10 .03
76 Johanne Manaure .10 .03
77 Jose Cardona .10 .03
78 Felipe Lira .20 .06
79 Dennis Moeller .20 .06
80 Raul Perez Tovar .10 .03
81 Freddy Torres .10 .03
82 Keith Lockhart .20 .06
83 Melvin Matos .75 .23
84 Hector Ortega .10 .03
85 Harry Guanchez .10 .03
86 Ronny Benavente .10 .03
87 Karl Rhodes .20 .06
88 Terry Shumpert .20 .06
89 Jairo Ramos .10 .03
90 Oswaldo Guillen 1.00 .30
91 Mario Gonzalez .10 .03
92 Carlos Subero .10 .03
93 Luis Vasquez .10 .03
94 Miguel Castellanos .10 .03
95 Jose Marchan .10 .03
96 Edwin Marquez .10 .03
97 Robert Guerra .10 .03
98 James Hurst .10 .03
99 Jeff Cox .20 .06
100 Coaches LaGuaira .10 .03
101 Derek Bell .40 .12
102 William Canate .10 .03
103 Jesus Marquez .10 .03
104 Alex Ramirez .30 .09
105 Howard Battle .20 .06
106 Asdrubal Estrada .10 .03
107 Jesus Azuaje .10 .03
108 Luis Sojo .30 .09
109 Alexis Infante .10 .03
110 Domingo Carrasquel .10 .03
111 Dilson Torres .10 .03
112 Oswald Peraza .20 .06
113 Juan Querfecuto .10 .03
114 Woody Williams .20 .06
115 Scott Brown .10 .03
116 Gilberto Clisanchez .10 .03
117 Jose Moreno .10 .03
118 Omar Sanchez .10 .03
119 Alex Gonzalez .30 .09
120 Mackey Sasser .20 .06
121 Edwin Hurtado .10 .03
122 Jose Montilla .10 .03
123 Marcos Armas .10 .03
124 Giovanni Carrara .20 .06
125 Robert Perez .20 .06
126 Doug Linton .20 .06
127 Antonio Castillo .10 .03
128 Huck Flener .20 .06
129 McLaren .10 .03
130 Coaches Cardenales .10 .03
131 Luis Gallardo .10 .03
132 Jesus Gonzalez .10 .03
133 Oscar Sarmiento .10 .03
134 Tow Maynard .10 .03
135 Todd Pratt .20 .06
136 Wilfredo Polidor .10 .03
137 Marcos Manrique .10 .03
138 L. Mercedes Sanchez .10 .03
139 Al Levine .20 .06
140 Agustin Gomez .10 .03
141 Familia Armas .10 .03
142 Rolando Caridad .10 .03
143 Simon Pinango .10 .03
144 Gilberto Roca .10 .03
145 Ronaldo Caridad .10 .03
146 Frank Merigiano .10 .03
147 Mike Robertson .10 .03
148 Nigel Alejo .10 .03
149 Magglio Ordonez 5.00 1.50
150 Johnny Paredes .20 .06
151 Carlos Lopez .10 .03
152 Brian Keyser .10 .03
153 John Barfield .20 .06
154 Argenis Conde .10 .03
155 Fred Manrique .20 .06
156 Jorge Mitchel .10 .03
157 Wilmer Montoya .10 .03
158 Julio Franco 1.00 .30
159 Felix Perez .10 .03
160 Pedro Jose Chavez .10 .03
161 Stuart Ruiz .40 .12
162 Victor Oramas .10 .03
163 Julio Armas .10 .03
164 Jeff Frye .30 .09
165 William Magallanes .10 .03
166 Fred Kendall .20 .06
167 Coaches Caribes .10 .03
168 Prospectos .10 .03
169 Alexis Infante .20 .06
170 Alfredo Pedrique .10 .03
171 Fernando Soto .10 .03
172 Matt Dunbar .10 .03
173 Marcos Bolanos .10 .03
174 Jesus "Chalao" Mendez .10 .03
175 Brad Woodall .20 .06
176 Jose Leon .10 .03
177 Jose Correa .10 .03
178 Jesus Garces .10 .03
179 Jalal Leach .10 .03
180 Edgar Tovar .10 .03
181 Kevin Jordan .20 .06
182 Leo Hernandez .20 .06
183 Luis Gallardo .10 .03
184 Ernesto Gomez .10 .03
185 Roberto Zambrano .10 .03
186 Miguel Angel Garcia .10 .03
187 Rafael De Lima .10 .03
188 German Gonzalez .20 .06
189 Lester Straker .20 .06
190 Roberto Castillo .10 .03
191 Temistockles Liendo .10 .03
192 Jaime Torres .10 .03
193 Silverio Navas .10 .03
194 Eduardo Perez .20 .06
195 Alexis Santaella .10 .03
196 Richard Garces .20 .06
197 Roberto Zambrano .10 .03
Armas
198 Rick Down .10 .03
199 Coaches Aragua .10 .03
200 Eduardo Zambrano .10 .03
201 Wilson Alvarez .40 .12
202 Jose Solarte .10 .03
203 Omar Bencomo .10 .03
204 Lipso Nava .10 .03
205 Henrique Gomez .10 .03
206 Jose Luis Zambrano .10 .03
207 Frank Gonzalez .10 .03
208 Robinson Garces .20 .06
209 Jimmy Williams .10 .03
210 Esmily Guerra .10 .03
211 Julio Machado .20 .06
212 Heath Haynes .10 .03
213 Jeremi Gonzalez .40 .12
214 Jose Gil .10 .03
215 Alexander Delgado .10 .03
216 Eminson Soto .10 .03
217 Ender Perezo .10 .03
218 Angel Escobar .10 .03
219 Jack Voigt .20 .06
220 Cesar Vargas .10 .03
221 Jeff Tackett .20 .06
222 Jesse Levis .20 .06
223 Dan Masteller .10 .03
224 Ken Ramos .10 .03
225 Pedro Castellanos .10 .03
226 Jorge Velandia .20 .06
227 Cristobal Colon .20 .06
228 William Mota .10 .03
229 Blas Cedeno .10 .03
230 Luis Portillo .10 .03
231 Omar Munoz .10 .03
232 Carlos Burguillos .10 .03
233 Carlos Quintana .20 .06
234 Jason Satre .10 .03
235 Richard Perez .10 .03
236 Pompeyo Davalillo .20 .06
237 Coaches Zulia .10 .03
238 Edgar Herrera .10 .03
239 Len Picota .10 .03
240 Nelson Portales .10 .03
241 Jose Amado .10 .03
242 Johan Strauss .10 .03
243 Oswaldo Villalobos .10 .03
244 David Mosquera .10 .03
245 Omer Munoz .10 .03
246 Jhonny Gonzalez .10 .03
247 Danilo Leon .10 .03
248 Ismael Zabala .10 .03
249 Joel Pozo .10 .03
250 Carlos Tovar Trillo .20 .06
251 Robert Machado .10 .03
252 Teo Majias .10 .03
253 Benito Malave .10 .03
254 Raul Herrera .10 .03
255 Luis Salazar .20 .06
256 Jose Graterol .10 .03
257 Joe Hall .20 .06
258 Mario Labastidas .10 .03
259 Rouglas Odor .10 .03
260 Jose Cheo Garcia .10 .03
261 Adrian Jordan .10 .03
262 Jose G. Gil .20 .06
263 Luis Gallardo .10 .03
264 Marlo Nava .10 .03
265 Steve Carter .20 .06
266 Jaime Dismuke .10 .03
267 Jeff Carter .20 .06
268 Jimmy Kremers .20 .06
269 Kelly Stinnett .20 .06
270 Coaches Petroleros .10 .03
271 Magallanes Checklist .10 .03
272 Caracas Checklist .10 .03
273 La Guaira Checklist .10 .03
274 Lara Checklist .10 .03
275 Caribes Checklist .10 .03
276 Tigres Checklist .10 .03
277 Zulia Checklist .10 .03
278 Petroleros Checklist .10 .03
279 Clasico LaChinita .10 .03
280 Garcia-Espinoza .20 .06
281 Calendario Magallanes .10 .03
282 Calendario Caracas .10 .03
283 Calendario LaGuaira .10 .03
284 Calendario Lara .10 .03
285 Calendario Caribes .10 .03
286 Calendario Aragua .10 .03
287 Calendario Zulia .10 .03
288 Calendario Cabimas .10 .03
289 Juego De Las Estrellas .10 .03
290 Juego De Las Estrellas .10 .03
291 Juego De Las Estrellas .10 .03
292 Juego De Las Estrellas .10 .03
293 Juego De Las Estrellas .10 .03
294 Juego De Las Estrellas .10 .03
295 Juego De Las Estrellas .10 .03
296 Juego De Las Estrellas .10 .03
297 Juego De Las Estrellas .10 .03
298 Checklist (1-100) .10 .03
299 Checklist (101-200) .10 .03
300 Checklist (201-300) .10 .03

1995-96 LineUp Venezuelan Baseball

This 325-card set features color photos of the players in the Venezuelan Baseball League and was not available in the United States. The backs carry player information and statistics. The cards are written in Spanish. A special memoriam card issued in the honor of Gus Polidor was later added to the set.

Nm-Mt Ex-Mt
COMPLETE SET (325) 45.00 13.50
1 Roger Cedeno .40 .12
2 Curtis Goodwin .20 .06
3 Reggie Williams .20 .06
4 David Davalillo .10 .03

5 Wiki Gonzalez .50 .15
6 Carlos Mendez .10 .03
7 Edgar Alfonzo .20 .06
8 Urbano Lugo .20 .06
9 Miguel Cairo .20 .06
10 Jorge Uribe .10 .03
11 Bob Abreu 2.00 .60
12 Tyrone Woods .10 .03
13 Omar Vizquel 2.00 .60
14 Andres Galarraga 2.00 .60
15 Wilfredo Romero .10 .03
16 Henry Blanco .20 .06
17 Giomar Guevara .20 .06
18 Jesus Alfaro .10 .03
19 Edgar Caceres .10 .03
20 Eduardo Rios .10 .03
21 Omar Daal .30 .09
22 Jose Centano .10 .03
23 John Desilva .10 .03
24 Pedro P. Belmonte .10 .03
25 Calvin Jones .10 .03
26 Carlos Hernandez .30 .09
27 Roberto Petaguine .20 .06
28 Jesus Hernandez .10 .03
29 Ugueth Urbina 1.00 .30
30 Dan Urbina .10 .03
31 Johan Lopez .10 .03
32 Terry Clark .20 .06
33 Marcos Ferreira .10 .03
34 Damaso Betancourt .10 .03
35 Flores Bolivar .10 .03
Henry Contreras
Dave Jauss CO
36 Pompeyo Davalillo MG .20 .06
37 Phil Regan MG .20 .06
38 Eminson Soto .10 .03
39 Lipso Nava .10 .03
40 Wilson Alvarez .40 .12
41 Johnny Carvajal .10 .03
42 Carlos Quintana .20 .06
43 Cristobal Colon .20 .06
44 J. Luis Zambrano .10 .03
45 David Montiel .10 .03
46 Orlando Munoz .10 .03
47 Alexander Delgado .10 .03
48 Pedro Castellano .10 .03
49 Jorge Velandia .20 .06
50 Lino Connell .10 .03
51 Carlos Burguillos .10 .03
52 A. Sutherland .10 .03
53 Jose Potro Gil .10 .03
54 Ender Perozo .10 .03
55 William Mota .10 .03
56 Richard Perez .10 .03
57 Jose Solarte .10 .03
58 Jeremi Gonzalez .20 .06
59 Heath Haynes .10 .03
60 Frank Gonzalez .10 .03
61 Hugo Pinero .10 .03
62 Blas Cedeno .10 .03
63 Omar Bencomo .10 .03
64 Danilo Leon .10 .03
65 Esmily Guerra .10 .03
66 Robinson Garces .10 .03
67 Ruben Amaro Jr. .20 .06
68 Luis H. Silva .10 .03
69 Clasico La Chinita .10 .03
70 Cesar Gutierrez CO .10 .03
Noel Maduro CO
71 Ruben Amaro MG .20 .06
72 Tucupita Marcano .10 .03
73 Oscar Azocar .20 .06
74 Edgar Naveda .10 .03
75 Melvin Mora .40 .12
76 Edgardo Alfonzo 2.00 .60
77 Orlando Miller .20 .06
78 Eddy Diaz .10 .03
79 Alvaro Espinoza .20 .06
80 Carlos Garcia .20 .06
81 Richard Hidalgo 2.00 .60
82 Luis Raven .20 .06
83 Andres Espinoza .20 .06
84 Jose F. Malave .10 .03
85 Amador Arias .10 .03
86 Clemente Alvarez .10 .03
87 Raul Chavez .10 .03
88 Cesar Morillo .10 .03
89 Cesar Diaz .10 .03
90 Luis Gonzalez 1.00 .30
91 Oscar Padron .10 .03
92 Ifrain Linares .10 .03
93 Juan Carlos Pulido .10 .03
94 Melchor Pacheco .10 .03
95 Ramon Garcia .10 .03
96 Ivan Artega .10 .03
97 Jose Villa .10 .03
98 Erick Ojeda .10 .03
99 Juan Francisco Castillo .10 .03
100 Antonio Torres CO .10 .03
Pablo Torrealba CO
Hector Rincones CO
101 Tim Tolman MG .20 .06
102 Los Hermanos Espinoza .10 .03
103 Chip Hale .20 .06
104 Silverio Navas .10 .03
105 Rafael D'Lima .10 .03
106 Jose Cheo Garcia .10 .03
107 J.T. Snow 1.00 .30
108 Jesus Chalao Mendez .10 .03
109 Mike Mordecai .20 .06
110 Jesus Garces .10 .03
111 Jaime Torres .10 .03
112 Edgar Tovar .10 .03
113 Rodolfo Hernandez .10 .03
114 Temis Liendo .10 .03
115 Kevin Noriega .10 .03
116 Eduardo Zambrano .20 .06
117 Roberto Zambrano .10 .03
118 Eduardo Perez .20 .06
119 Rene Pinto .10 .03
120 Richard Garces .20 .06
121 Miguel Angel Garcia .10 .03
122 Luis Colmenares .10 .03
123 Argenis Conde .10 .03
124 Julio Cesar Straus .10 .03
125 Fernando Mejias .10 .03
126 Lester Straker .20 .06
127 Alexis Santaella .10 .03
128 Darwin Cubillan .10 .03
129 Carlos Aguilar .10 .03
130 Angel Leon CO .10 .03
Alfredo Ortiz CO
Elias Lugo CO
Nelson Portales CO
131 Nigel Alejo .10 .03
132 Luis Merceds Sanchez .10 .03
133 Tony Armas Jr. 1.00 .30
134 Bryan Keyser .10 .03
135 Agustin Gomez .10 .03
136 Wilmer Montoya .10 .03
137 Francisco Munoz .10 .03
138 Alan Levine .20 .06
139 Roberto Castillo .10 .03
140 Richard Negrete .10 .03
141 Mauricio Ruiz .10 .03
142 Alexander Portillo .10 .03
143 Joe Hall .20 .06
144 Jesus Lugo .10 .03
145 Darren Bragg .40 .12
146 Carlos Lopez .10 .03
147 Wilfredo Polidor .20 .06
148 Luis Galindo .10 .03
149 William Magallanes .10 .03
150 Mike Robertson .10 .03
151 Magglio Ordonez 2.00 .60
152 Olmedo Saenz .20 .06
153 Henry Centeno .10 .03
154 Marcos Manrique .10 .03
155 Joe Oliver .20 .06
156 Alexander Ramirez .10 .03
157 Pedro Jose Chavez .10 .03
158 Rafael Betancourt .10 .03
159 Jesus Mendoza .10 .03
160 Carlos Alvarez .10 .03
161 Daniel Alzualde .10 .03
162 Angel Hernandez CO .20 .06
Tony Armas Sr. CO
Arquimedes Rojas CO
Jesus Tiamo CO
163 Luis Aponte MG .20 .06
164 Luis Sojo .50 .15
165 Alexis Infante .10 .03
166 Rob Butler .20 .06
167 Shawn Green 2.00 .60
168 Robert Perez .10 .03
169 Marcos Armas .10 .03
170 Howard Battle .20 .06
171 Jason Townley .10 .03
172 Domingo E. Carrasquel .10 .03
173 Juan Querecuo .10 .03
174 Omar Sanchez .10 .03
175 Jesus Marquez .10 .03
176 Jesus Gonzalez .10 .03
177 William Canate .10 .03
178 Richard Romero .10 .03
179 Jose Montilla .10 .03
180 Erick Perez .10 .03
181 Isbel Cardona .10 .03
182 Tim Crabtree .30 .09
183 Dilson Torres .10 .03
184 Edwin Hurtado .10 .03
185 Antonio Castillo .10 .03
186 Giovanni Carrara .20 .06
187 Doug Linton .20 .06
188 Jesus Delgado .10 .03
189 Kelvim Escobar .50 .15
190 William Ereu CO .10 .03
Juan Escobar CO
Luis Leal CO
191 Omar Malave MG .10 .03
192 Jesus Ugueto .10 .03
193 Miguel Soto .10 .03
194 Derek Wachter .10 .03
195 Jose Stella .10 .03
196 Asdrubal Estrada .10 .03
197 Robert Machado .20 .06
198 Jose Marchan .10 .03
199 Luis Ordaz .20 .06
200 Tomas Perez .20 .06
201 Jose Graterol .10 .03
202 Malvin Matos .10 .03
203 Rouglas Odor .10 .03
204 Jose Amado .10 .03
205 Marlon Nava .10 .03
206 Vicente Garcia .10 .03
207 Quinn Mack .10 .03
208 Adrian Jordan .10 .03
209 Luis Tinoco .10 .03
210 Luis Rafael Salazar .20 .06
211 Luis Lunar .10 .03
212 Nelson Canas .10 .03
213 Benito Malave .10 .03
214 Carlos Tovar Trillo .10 .03
215 Ismel Zabala .10 .03
216 Ivan Paz Montiel .10 .03
217 Johnny Gonzalez .10 .03
218 Jose Gonzalez .10 .03
219 Terry Burrows .20 .06
220 Mauro Mendez CO .10 .03
Amilcar Medina CO
Cesar Heredia CO
El Buchon (Mascot)
221 William Oropeza .10 .03
222 Carlos Cafe Martinez .10 .03
223 Jairo Ramos .10 .03
224 Carlos Subero .10 .03
225 Alex Cabrera .10 .03
226 Hector Ortega .10 .03
227 Johnny Paredes .20 .06
228 Homy Ovalles .10 .03
229 Luis Cartaya .10 .03
230 Mahali Carrera .10 .03
231 Miguel Castellanos .10 .03
232 Jose Monzon .10 .03
233 Harry Guanchez .10 .03
234 Frank Campos .20 .06
235 Edwin Marquez .10 .03
236 Heberto Andrade .10 .03
237 Robert Guerra .10 .03
238 Jorge Melendez .10 .03
239 Victor Lunar .10 .03
240 Alejandro Alvarez .10 .03
241 Gustavo Polidor .20 .06
242 Felipe Lira .20 .06
243 Jose Luis Ramos .10 .03
244 James Hurst .10 .03
245 Gustavo Pinto .10 .03
246 Johanne Manaure .10 .03
247 Mario Gonzalez .10 .03
248 Igor Oropeza .10 .03
249 Luis Vasquez .10 .03
250 Oswaldo Guillen .20 .06
251 Victor Colina CO .10 .03
Evilio Ovalles CO
Jeff Cox CO
252 Luis Salazar MG .20 .06
253 Luis Salazar .20 .06
254 Roberto Alomar 3.00 .90
255 Juego De Las Estrellas .10 .03
256 Juego De Las Estrellas .10 .03
257 Marcos Armas .20 .06
Tony Armas Sr.
Dave Concepcion
Luis Salazar
258 Robert Machado .10 .03
Carlos Hernandez
259 Henry Leon UMP .10 .03
Musulungo Herrera UMP
Emilo Velasquez UMP
Humberto Castillo UMP
260 Juego De Las Estrellas .10 .03
261 Cecil Fielder .50 .15
262 Los Compadres .10 .03
263 El Gran Dia .10 .03
264 El Alboroto .10 .03
265 Roberto Petaguine .10 .03
266 Carlos Garcia .20 .06
267 Omar Vizquel .75 .23
268 Carlos Martinez .20 .06
269 Eduardo Perez .20 .06
270 Darren Bragg .40 .12
271 J.D. Noland .10 .03
272 Robert Perez .10 .03
273 Antonio Castillo .10 .03
274 Andres Galarraga 1.00 .30
Vitico
275 Andres Galarraga 1.00 .30
Cesar Tovar
276 Los mas Valiosos .10 .03
277 Caimanera .10 .03
278 Caimanera .10 .03
279 Historia De La Caimanera .10 .03
280 Premio Victor Davalillo .20 .06
281 Eduardo Perez .20 .06
Vic Davalillo
282 Premio Carrao Bracho .10 .03
283 Richard Garces .20 .06
Vic Davalillo
284 Luis Sojo .20 .06
285 Fernando Mejias .10 .03
286 Eduardo Perez .20 .06
287 Richard Garces .20 .06
288 Carlos Martinez .20 .06
289 Carlos Martinez .20 .06
290 Checklist Caracas .10 .03
291 Checklist Zulia .10 .03
292 Checklist Magallanes .10 .03
293 Checklist Tigres .10 .03
294 Checklist Caribes .10 .03
295 Checklist Cardenales .10 .03
296 Checklist Pastora .10 .03
297 Checklist Tiburones .10 .03
298 Liga Venez. De Beisbol Prof. .10 .03
299 Urbano Lugo .20 .06
300 Senadores De San Juan B.B.C. .10 .03
301 Azucareros Del Este B.B.C. .10 .03
302 Naran. De Hermosillo B.B.C. .10 .03
303 Leones Del Caracas B.B.C. .10 .03
304 Art Howe .20 .06
Pompeyo Davalillo
Ralph Bryant
Luis Melendez
Luis Tiant
305 Felipe Lira .20 .06
Jeremi Gonzalez
Frank Gonzalez
Jimmy Haynes
Carlos Pulido
306 Luis Sojo .10 .03
Perez
Martinez
307 Roberto Petaguine 1.00 .30
Edgar Alfonzo
Omar Vizquel
Henry Blanco
308 Jose Rijo 1.00 .30
Urbano Lugo
Raul Mondesi
309 Domingo Cedeno .10 .03
Andujar Cedeno
310 Carlos Delgado 2.00 .60
Perez
Hernandez
311 Bob Abreu 2.00 .60
Juan Gonzalez
Martinez
Alfaro
312 Vinny Castilla .50 .15
Omar Vizquel
313 Ruben Sierra .50 .15
Carlos Delgado
314 Roberto Petaguine .20 .06
Henry Rodriguez
Henry Blanco
Hernandez
315 Roger Cedeno 1.00 .30
Raul Mondesi
316 Edgar Alfonzo 1.00 .30
Jose Offerman
Omar Vizquel
Henry Blanco
317 Carlos Baerga 1.00 .30
Omar Vizquel
318 Jose Rijo .10 .03
C. Martinez
319 Jose Rijo .10 .03
Urbano Lugo
320 Omar Vizquel 1.00 .30
Roberto Alomar
Luis Sojo
Sanchez
321 C. Martinez .20 .06
Ruben Sierra
322 Vinny Castilla 1.00 .30
323 Raul Mondesi 1.00 .30
Henry Blanco
324 Juan Gonzalez 3.00 .90
325 Roberto Alomar 1.00 .30
Carlos Baerga
330 Gustavo Polidor MEM 2.00 .60

1996-97 Lineup Venezuela

This 300 card set was issued in seven card wax packs. Included in the set is a special set honoring great shortstop Dave Concepcion who played for the Cincinnati Reds for nearly 20 years. The wrapper features Concepction on the cover.

	Nm-Mt	Ex-Mt
COMPLETE SET (300)	30.00	9.00

1 Checklist CL .10 .03
2 Alvaro Espinoza .25 .07
3 Eddy Diaz .10 .03
4 Carlos Hernandez .50 .15
5 Cesar Morillo .10 .03
6 Luis Raven .10 .03
7 Melvin Mora .50 .15
8 Carlos Guillen .75 .23
9 Jose Francisco Malave .10 .03
10 Alejandro Freire .10 .03
11 Edgardo Alfonzo 1.50 .45
12 Carlos Mendoza .10 .03
13 Carlos Garcia .25 .07
14 Raul Chavez .10 .03
15 Richard Hidalgo 1.50 .45
16 Cesar Diaz .10 .03
17 Clemente Alvarez .25 .07
18 Andres Espinoza .10 .03
19 Ifrain Linares .10 .03
20 Melchor Pacheco .10 .03
21 Oscar Henriquez .10 .03
22 Juan Carlos Pulido .10 .03
23 Erick Ojeda .10 .03
24 Juan Francisco Castillo .10 .03
25 Ramon Garcia .10 .03
26 Mauro Zerpa .10 .03
27 Ivan Arteaga .10 .03
28 Roberto Espinoza CO .10 .03
29 Hector Rincones .10 .03
30 Jesus Laya .10 .03
31 Gregorio Machado .10 .03
32 Luis Burelli .10 .03
33 Freddy Adrian Garcia .25 .07
34 Andy Vicentino .10 .03
35 Checklist CL .10 .03
36 Juan Munoz .10 .03
37 Miguel Cairo .25 .07
38 Luis Sojo .50 .15
39 Robert Perez .10 .03
40 Alexis Infante .10 .03
41 Juan Querecuto .10 .03
42 Jesus Gonzalez .10 .03
43 Raul Perez Tovar .10 .03
44 Jesus Marquez .10 .03
45 Omar Sanchez .10 .03
46 Domingo E. Carrasquel .10 .03
47 Jose Alguacil .10 .03
48 Jesus Azuaje .10 .03
49 Marcos Armas .10 .03
50 Antonio Castillo .10 .03
51 Giovanni Carrara .10 .03
52 Edwin Hurtado .10 .03
53 Erick Perez .10 .03
54 Jesus Delgado .10 .03
55 Kelvim Escobar .50 .15
56 Isbel Cardona .10 .03
57 Luis Leal CO .25 .07
58 Graterol .10 .03
Vargas
59 Omar Malave .10 .03
60 Checklist CL .10 .03
61 Oscar Azocar .10 .03
62 Roberto Zambrano .10 .03
63 Jose Cheo Garcia .10 .03
64 Temis Liendo .10 .03
65 Rene Pinto .10 .03
66 Silverio Navas .10 .03
67 Jesus Chalao Mendez .10 .03
68 Marlon Nava .10 .03
69 Jaime Torres .10 .03
70 Edgar Naveda .10 .03
71 Eduardo Perez .25 .07
72 Edgar Tovar .10 .03
73 Hector Ugueto .10 .03
74 Jesus Garces .10 .03
75 Eduardo Zambrano .10 .03
76 Amador Arias .10 .03
77 Carlos Aguilar .10 .03
78 Simon Pinango .10 .03
79 Alejandro Bracho .10 .03
80 Luis Colmenares .10 .03
81 Richard Garces .25 .07
82 Ronald Caridad .10 .03
83 Alexis Santaella .10 .03
84 Darwin Cubillan .10 .03
85 Fernando Mejias .10 .03
86 Julio Cesar Strauss .10 .03
87 Jose Correa .10 .03
88 Miguel Angel Garcia .10 .03
89 Lester Straker .25 .07
90 Argenis Conde .10 .03
91 Ismel Zabala .10 .03
92 Jesus Avila .10 .03
93 Elias Lugo CO .10 .03
94 Nelson Porte CO .10 .03
95 Angel Pocho Gomez CO .10 .03
96 Alfredo Ortiz MG .10 .03
97 Checklist CL .10 .03
98 Cristobal Colon .10 .03
99 Ruben Amaro Jr. .10 .03
100 Jose G. Urdaneta .10 .03
101 Carlos Burguillos .10 .03
102 Lino Connell .10 .03
103 Eminson Soto .10 .03
104 Carlos Quintana .10 .03
105 Lipso Nava .10 .03
106 Orlando Munoz .10 .03
107 Jose Luis Zambrano .10 .03
108 Alexander Delgado .10 .03
109 Pedro Castellano .10 .03
110 Jorge Velandia .10 .03
111 Johnny Carvajal .10 .03
112 David Montiel .10 .03
113 Johnny Paredes .10 .03
114 Hugo Pinero .10 .03
115 Omar Bencomo .10 .03
116 Wilson Alvarez .50 .15
117 Julio Machado .10 .03
118 Jose Solarte .10 .03
119 Danilo Leon .10 .03
120 Jeremy Gonzalez .25 .07
121 Blas Cedeno .10 .03
122 Esmili Guerra .10 .03
123 Noe Maduro CO .10 .03
124 Cesar Gutierrez CO .25 .07
125 Ruben Amaro Sr MG .25 .07
126 Clasico De La Chinita .10 .03
127 Boanerge Corzo .10 .03
128 Miguel Campos .10 .03
129 Didimo Bracho .10 .03
130 Checklist CL .10 .03
131 Roger Cedeno .10 .03
132 Bob Abreu 1.50 .45
133 Carlos Hernandez .50 .15
134 Roberto Petagine .25 .07
135 Eduardo Rios .10 .03
136 Edgar Alfonzo .10 .03
137 Wilfredo Romero .10 .03
138 Giomar Guevara .10 .03
139 Edgar Caceres .10 .03
140 Alex Gonzalez .25 .07
141 Luis Rodriguez .10 .03
142 Jorge Uribe .10 .03
143 Nestor Serrano .10 .03
144 Wiki Gonzalez .10 .03
145 Henry Blanco .10 .03
146 Carlos Mendez .10 .03
147 David Davalillo .10 .03
148 Omar Vizquel .75 .23
149 Andres Galarraga 1.50 .45
150 Urbano Lugo .10 .03
151 Jesus Hernandez .10 .03
152 Ronnie Sorzano .10 .03
153 Omar Daal .50 .15
154 Pedro Belmonte .10 .03
155 Jose Centeno .10 .03
156 Johan Lopez .10 .03
157 Ugueth Urbina .75 .01
158 Damaso Betancourt .10 .03
159 Gustavo Jose Gil .10 .03
160 Dilson Torres .25 .07
161 Dan Urbina .10 .03
162 David Jauss CO .10 .03
163 Jesus Alfaro CO .10 .03
164 Manuel Gonzalez CO .10 .03
165 Phil Regan MG .10 .03
166 Checklist CL .10 .03
167 Robert Machado .10 .03
168 Malvin Matos .10 .03
169 Tomas Perez .25 .07
170 Vicente Garcia .10 .03
171 Kevin Noriega .10 .03
172 Rafael DeLima .10 .03
173 Jose Amado .10 .03
174 Richard Romero .10 .03
175 Asdrubal Estrada .10 .03
176 Luis Ordaz .10 .03
177 Jesus Ugueto .10 .03
178 Ender Perozo .10 .03
179 Ramon Hernandez .10 .03
180 Luis Tinoco .10 .03
181 Adrian Jordan .10 .03
182 Darwin Bracho .10 .03
183 Raul Marval .10 .03
184 Jose Villa .10 .03
185 Luis Lunar .10 .03
186 Douglas Aguillar .10 .03
187 Benito Malave .10 .03
188 Luis Rafael Salazar .10 .03
189 Nelson Canas .10 .03
190 Guillermo Larreal .10 .03
191 Robinson Garces .10 .03
192 Jose Gonzalez .10 .03
193 Johnny Gonzalez .10 .03
194 Oswaldo Villalobos .10 .03
195 Justo Massaro CO .10 .03
Bob Humphryes CO
196 Domingo Carrasquel .10 .03
197 Checklist CL .10 .03
198 Raul Marcano .10 .03
199 Marcos Manrique .10 .03
200 Edwin Marquez .10 .03
201 Maggio Ordonez 1.50 .45
202 Victor Oramas .10 .03
203 Jesus Mendoza .10 .03
204 Alexander Ramirez .10 .03
205 Miguel Nieves .10 .03
206 Wuarnner Rincones .10 .03
207 Carlos Alvarez .10 .03
208 Marco Scutaro .10 .03
209 Jesus Lugo .10 .03
210 Fernando Lunar .10 .03
211 Henry Centeno .10 .03
212 Freddy Gonzalez .10 .03
213 Antonio Armas Jr. .10 .03
214 Jose Luis Ramos .10 .03
215 Nigel Alejo .10 .03
216 William Martinez .10 .03
217 Wilmer Montoya .10 .03
218 Richard Negrete .10 .03
219 Francisco Munoz .10 .03
220 Mauricio Ruiz .10 .03
221 Agustin Gomez .10 .03
222 Alexander Portillo .10 .03
223 Tomas Salazar .10 .03
224 Rigoberto Mendoza CO .10 .03
Jesus Tiamo CO
225 Arquimedes Rojas CO .10 .03
Gilberto Marcano CO
226 Pompeyo Davalillo MG .10 .03
227 Checklist CL .10 .03
228 William Oropeza .10 .03
229 Jairo Ramos .10 .03
230 Miguel Rendon .10 .03
231 Wilfredo Polidor .10 .03
232 Alex Cabrera .75 .23
233 Carlos Martinez .10 .03
234 Mario Gonzalez .10 .03

Card		
235 Jose Monzon	.10	.03
236 Carlos Subero	.10	.03
237 Rouglas Odor	.10	.03
238 William Canate	.10	.03
239 Hector Ortega	.10	.03
240 William Magallanes	.10	.03
241 Alejandro Prieto	.10	.03
242 Rafael Alvarez	.10	.03
243 Miguel Castellanos	.10	.03
244 Heberto Andrade	.10	.03
245 Oswaldo Guillen	.25	.07
246 Ivan Paz Montiel	.10	.03
247 Frank Campos	.25	.07
248 Carlos Tovar Trillo	.10	.03
249 Igor Oropeza	.10	.03
250 Alex Oviedo	.10	.03
251 Juan Carlos Moreno	.10	.03
252 Richard Fernandez	.10	.03
253 Felipe Lira	.25	.07
254 Alejandro Alvarez	.10	.03
255 Homer Baez	.10	.03
256 Remigio Hermoso CO	.10	.03
257 Luis Dorante CO	.10	.03
Carlos Moreno CO		
258 Los Hermanos Zambrano	.10	.03
A. Delgado		
Eduardo Perez		
259 Checklist CL	.10	.03
260 Premio Vitico Davalillo	.10	.03
261 Premio Carrao Bracho	.10	.03
262 Premio Pitcher Del Ano	.10	.03
263 Richard Garces	.25	.07
Premio Relevista Del Ano		
264 Ronnie Sorzano	.10	.03
Premio Novato Del Ano		
265 Carlos Martinez	.10	.03
Premio Prodcutor Del Ano		
266 Roberto Zambrano	.10	.03
Premio Regreso Del Ano		
267 J.E. Fielder	.10	.03
Leal		
268 J.E. Criollos	.10	.03
Importados		
269 J.E. Competencias	.10	.03
270 J.E. Jonrrones	.10	.03
Umpires		
271 J.E. Directiva	.10	.03
Delegados		
272 Luis Sojo	.25	.07
Vitico		
273 Los Grandes En La Serie	.10	.03
274 Huck Flener	.10	.03
Omar Daal		
Travis Baptist		
Edwin Hurtado		
Roger Cedeno		
Bob Abreu		
Miguel Cairo		
Los Grandes En La Serie		
275 Luis Raven	.10	.03
Guillermo Velasquez		
Roberto Alomar		
Alvaro Espinoza		
Los Grandes En La Serie		
276 Melvin Mora	.25	.07
Bernie Williams		
Omar Daal		
Roger Cedeno		
Los Grandes En La Serie		
277 Edwin Hurtado	.10	.03
Roberto Alomar		
Miguel Cairo		
Los Grandes En La Serie		
278 Roberto Alomar	.75	.23
Bob Abreu		
Roger Cedeno		
Raul Mondesi		
Omar Daal		
Los Grandes En La Serie		
279 Clemente Alvarez	.10	.03
Ivan Rodriguez		
Tony Pena		
Los Grandes En La Serie		
280 Omar Daal	.50	.15
281 Robert Machado	.10	.03
282 Carlos Quintana	.25	.07
283 Eddy Diaz	.10	.03
284 Miguel Cairo	.25	.07
285 Tomas Perez	.10	.03
286 Robert Perez	.10	.03
287 Roger Cedeno	.75	.23
288 Marvin Benard	.50	.15
289 David Concepcion 1/9	.25	.07
290 David Concepcion 2/9	.25	.07
291 David Concepcion 3/9	.25	.07
292 David Concepcion 4/9	.25	.07
293 David Concepcion 5/9	.25	.07
294 David Concepcion 6/9	.25	.07
295 David Concepcion 7/9	.25	.07
296 David Concepcion 8/9	.25	.07
297 David Concepcion 9/9	.25	.07
298 Checklist 1-100	.10	.03
299 Checklist 101-200	.10	.03
300 Checklist 201-300	.10	.03

1999-00 Gillette Venezuela

These cards, which were issued in five card cello packs, features 25 Venezulean players. The card has a color photo of the player in uniform while the back has a player portrait, and some biographical information. These cards were liscenced by Major League Baseball

	Nm-Mt	Ex-Mt
COMPLETE SET (25)	300.00	90.00
1 Andres Galarraga	20.00	6.00
2 Bob Abreu	20.00	6.00
3 Omar Daal	10.00	3.00
4 Melvin Mora	10.00	3.00
5 Henry Blanco	10.00	3.00
6 Omar Vizquel	15.00	4.50
7 Alex Gonzalez	10.00	3.00
8 Freddy Garcia	15.00	4.50
9 Wilson Alvarez	10.00	3.00
10 Felipe Lira	10.00	3.00
11 Luis Sojo	10.00	3.00
12 Eddie Perez	10.00	3.00
13 Miguel Cairo	10.00	3.00
14 Carlos Guillen	10.00	3.00
15 Richard Hidalgo	20.00	6.00
16 Eduardo Alfonzo	20.00	6.00
17 Ugueth Urbina	10.00	3.00
18 Carlos A. Hernandez	10.00	3.00
19 Roger Cedeno	12.00	3.60
20 Jorge Velandia	10.00	3.00
21 Ozzie Guillen	10.00	3.00
22 Kelvim Escobar	10.00	3.00
23 Magglio Ordonez	20.00	6.00
24 Jeremi Gonzalez	10.00	3.00
25 Carlos E. Hernandez	10.00	3.00

2000 Upper Deck Ovation Japan

The 2000 Upper Deck Ovation Japan product was released in late 2000, and offers a 90-card base set that is broken into tiers as follows: Rising Stars (1-30) individually serial numbered to 2000, and base veterans (31-90). Each pack contained five-cards and carried a suggested retail of $2.99.

	Nm-Mt	Ex-Mt
COMPLETE SET (90)	100.00	30.00
COMP.SET w/o SP's (60)	30.00	9.00
COMMON CARD (31-90)	.50	.15
COMMON RS (1-30)	3.00	.90
1 Daisuke Matsuzaka RS	3.00	.90
2 Koji Uehara RS	3.00	.90
3 Kosuke Fukudome RS	3.00	.90
4 Hidetaka Kawagoe RS	3.00	.90
5 Tomohiro Nioka RS	3.00	.90
6 Shinobu Fukuhara RS	3.00	.90
7 Yukio Tanaka RS	3.00	.90
8 Ryota Igarashi RS	3.00	.90
9 Akihiro Higashide RS	3.00	.90
10 Yoshinori Tateyama RS	3.00	.90
11 Naoyuki Shimizu RS	3.00	.90
12 Syogo Akada RS	3.00	.90
13 Soji Tanaka RS	3.00	.90
14 Naoki Matoba RS	3.00	.90
15 Hisashi Takayama RS	3.00	.90
16 Kazuo Yamaguchi RS	3.00	.90
17 Kaoru Takahashi RS	3.00	.90
18 Itsuki Shoda RS	3.00	.90
19 Kensuke Tanaka RS	3.00	.90
20 Daisuke Miyamoto RS	3.00	.90
21 Fumitoshi Takano RS	3.00	.90
22 Kenta Asakura RS	3.00	.90
23 Kenshin Kawakami RS	3.00	.90
24 Hisanori Takahashi RS	3.00	.90
25 Kazunori Tanaka RS	3.00	.90
26 Atsushi Kizuka RS	3.00	.90
27 Yoshiyuki Noguchi RS	3.00	.90
28 Takaya Kawauchi RS	3.00	.90
29 Tetsuto Tomabechi RS	3.00	.90
30 Kanichi Matoba RS	3.00	.90
31 Koji Akiyama	.50	.15
32 Kenji Jojima	.50	.15
33 Takayuki Shinohara	.50	.15
34 Rod Pedraza	.50	.15
35 Nobuhiko Matsunaka	.50	.15
36 Taisei Takagi	.50	.15
37 Daisuke Matsuzaka	.50	.15
38 Kazuo Matsui	.50	.15
39 Tony Fernandez	2.00	.60
40 Fumiya Nishiguchi	.50	.15
41 Ichiro Suzuki	10.00	3.00
42 Hidetaka Kawagoe	.50	.15
43 So Taguchi	.50	.15
44 Yoshitomo Tani	.50	.15
45 Masahiko Kaneda	.50	.15
46 Kiyoshi Hatsushiba	.50	.15
47 Tomohiro Kuroki	.50	.15
48 Hiroo Ishii	.50	.15
49 Makoto Kosaka	.50	.15
50 Brian Warren	.50	.15
51 Michihiro Ogasawara	.50	.15
52 Atsushi Kataoka	.50	.15
53 Tsutomu Iwamoto	.50	.15
54 Yukio Tanaka	.50	.15
55 Makoto Kaneko	.50	.15
56 Norihiro Nakamura	.50	.15
57 Phil Clark	.75	.23
58 Tuffy Rhodes	.75	.23
59 Akinori Ohtsuka	.50	.15
60 Akira Okamoto	.50	.15
61 Kosuke Fukudome	.50	.15
62 Leo Gomez	.75	.23
63 Koichi Sekikawa	.50	.15
64 Shigeki Noguchi	.50	.15
65 Hitoki Iwase	.50	.15
66 Hideki Matsui	4.00	1.20
67 Yoshinobu Takahashi	.50	.15
68 Koji Uehara	.50	.15
69 Akira Etoh	.50	.15
70 Kimiyasa Kudoh	.50	.15
71 Takeo Kawamura	.50	.15
72 Takashi Saito	.50	.15
73 Bobby Rose	.75	.23
74 Takanori Suzuki	.50	.15
75 Takuro Ishii	.50	.15
76 Kazuhisa Ishii	.50	.15
77 Shingo Takatsu	.50	.15
78 Roberto Petagine	.75	.23
79 Kenji Kawasaki	.50	.15
80 Atsuya Furuta	.75	.23
81 Tomonori Maeda	.50	.15
82 Koichi Ogata	.50	.15
83 Tomoaki Kanemoto	.50	.15
84 Shinji Sasaoka	.50	.15
85 Kenjiro Nomura	.50	.15
86 Makato Imaoka	.50	.15
87 Tsuyoshi Shinjo	4.00	1.20
88 Keiichi Yabu	.50	.15
89 Nobuyuki Hoshino	.50	.15
90 Tomochika Tsuboi	.75	.23

2000 Upper Deck Ovation Japan 40 Home Run Club

Inserted into packs at one in 12, this 18-card set features some of Japan's top power hitters. Card backs carry a "HR" prefix. Please note that Ken Griffey Jr. is also in the set.

	Nm-Mt	Ex-Mt
COMPLETE SET (18)	50.00	15.00
HR1 Roberto Petagine	5.00	1.50
HR2 Takeshi Yamasaki	2.00	.60
HR3 Hideki Matsui	8.00	2.40
HR4 Tomoaki Kanemoto	2.00	.60
HR5 Bobby Rose	3.00	.90
HR6 Tuffy Rhodes	3.00	.90
HR7 Sherman Obando	3.00	.90
HR8 Leo Gomez	3.00	.90
HR9 Domingo Martinez	2.00	.60
HR10 Koichi Ogata	2.00	.60
HR11 Hiroki Kokubo	2.00	.60
HR12 Nigel Wilson	5.00	1.50
HR13 Phil Clark	3.00	.90
HR14 Nobuhiko Matsunaka	2.00	.60
HR15 Akira Etoh	2.00	.60
HR16 Norihiro Nakamura	2.00	.60
HR17 Yoshinobu Takahashi	2.00	.60
HR18 Ken Griffey Jr.	20.00	6.00

2000 Upper Deck Ovation Japan Game Ball

Inserted into packs at one in 288, this 13-card insert features swatches of actual game-used baseballs. Included in the set are Ken Griffey Jr. and Japanese superstar Ichiro Suzuki. Card backs carry a "B" prefix followed by the player's initials.

	Nm-Mt	Ex-Mt
B-AF Atsuya Furuta	40.00	12.00
B-DM Daisuke Matsuzaka	40.00	12.00
B-HK Hiroki Kokubo	40.00	12.00
B-HM Hideki Matsui	60.00	18.00
B-HT Hiroshi Takamura	40.00	12.00
B-IS Ichiro Suzuki	150.00	45.00
B-KG Ken Griffey Jr.	150.00	45.00
B-KO Koichi Ogata	40.00	12.00
B-MO Michihiro Ogasawara	40.00	12.00
B-SN Shigeki Noguchi	40.00	12.00
B-TI Takuro Ishii	40.00	12.00
B-TK Tomohiro Kuroki	40.00	12.00
B-TT Tomochika Tsuboi	40.00	12.00

2000 Upper Deck Ovation Japan Game Ball/Shoe Combos

Randomly inserted into packs, this 13-card insert features swatches of actual game-used baseballs and shoes. Included in the set are Ken Griffey Jr. and Japanese superstar Ichiro Suzuki. Card backs carry a "C" prefix followed by the player's initials.

	Nm-Mt	Ex-Mt
C-DM Daisuke Matsuzaka	40.00	12.00
C-HK Hiroki Kokubo	40.00	12.00
C-HM Hideki Matsui	40.00	12.00
C-HT Hiroshi Takamura	40.00	12.00
C-IS Ichiro Suzuki	150.00	45.00
C-KG Ken Griffey Jr.	150.00	45.00
C-KI Kazuhisa Ishii	40.00	12.00
C-KO Koichi Ogata	40.00	12.00
C-MO Michihiro Ogasawara	40.00	12.00
C-SN Shigeki Noguchi	40.00	12.00
C-TI Takuro Ishii	40.00	12.00
C-TK Tomohiro Kuroki	40.00	12.00
C-TT Tomochika Tsuboi	40.00	12.00

2000 Upper Deck Ovation Japan Griffey Gallery

Inserted into packs at one in 10, this 6-card insert features American Superstar Ken Griffey Jr.. The set takes a look at some of Griffey's outstanding accomplishments. Card backs carry a "G" prefix.

	Nm-Mt	Ex-Mt
COMMON CARD (G1-G6)	5.00	1.50

2000 Upper Deck Ovation Japan Oendan Favorites

Inserted into packs at one in three, this 24-card insert takes a look at some of Japan's most popular players. Card backs carry an "OF" prefix.

	Nm-Mt	Ex-Mt
COMPLETE SET (24)	10.00	3.00
OF1 Ichiro Suzuki	4.00	1.20
OF2 Norihiro Nakamura	.50	.15
OF3 Toshio Haru	.50	.15
OF4 Daisuke Matsuzaka	.50	.15
OF5 Hideki Matsui	1.50	.45
OF6 Kenji Jojima	.50	.15
OF7 Tsutomu Iwamoto	.50	.15
OF8 Tuffy Rhodes	.75	.23
OF9 Koichi Ogata	.50	.15
OF10 Daisuke Motoki	.50	.15
OF11 Atsushi Kataoka	.50	.15
OF12 Kazuya Fukuura	.50	.15
OF13 Atsuya Furuta	.50	.15
OF14 So Taguchi	.50	.15
OF15 Kazuo Matsui	.50	.15
OF16 Hitoki Iwase	.50	.15
OF17 Kenji Morozumi	.50	.15
OF18 Shingo Takatsu	.50	.15
OF19 Kosuke Fukudome	.50	.15
OF20 Keiichi Yabu	.50	.15
OF21 Takahiro Saeki	.50	.15
OF22 Shinji Sasaoka	.50	.15
OF23 Tsuyoshi Shinjo	1.50	.45
OF24 Tadahito Iguchi	.50	.15

2000 Upper Deck Ovation Japan Shoe Card

Inserted into packs at one in 288, this 13-card insert features swatches of actual game-used shoes. Included in the set are Ken Griffey Jr. and Japanese superstar Ichiro Suzuki. Card backs carry a "S" prefix followed by the player's initials.

	Nm-Mt	Ex-Mt
S-DM Daisuke Matsuzaka	40.00	12.00
S-HK Hiroki Kokubo	40.00	12.00
S-HM Hideki Matsui	60.00	18.00
S-HT Hiroshi Takamura	40.00	12.00
S-IS Ichiro Suzuki	150.00	45.00
S-KG Ken Griffey Jr.	150.00	45.00
S-KI Kazuhisa Ishii	40.00	12.00
S-KO Koichi Ogata	40.00	12.00
S-MO Michihiro Ogasawara	40.00	12.00
S-SN Shigeki Noguchi	40.00	12.00
S-TI Takuro Ishii	40.00	12.00
S-TK Tomohiro Kuroki	40.00	12.00
S-TT Tomochika Tsuboi	40.00	12.00

2000 Upper Deck Ovation Japan Standing Ovation

Randomly inserted into packs, this 12-card insert features some of Japan's greatest players. Card backs carry a "SO" prefix. 2,500 serial-numbered sets were produced.

	Nm-Mt	Ex-Mt
COMPLETE SET (12)	120.00	36.00
SO1 Ichiro Suzuki	25.00	7.50
SO2 Bobby Rose	8.00	2.40
SO3 Shigeki Noguchi	5.00	1.50
SO4 Koji Uehara	5.00	1.50
SO5 Tsuyoshi Shinjo	10.00	3.00
SO6 Daisuke Matsuzaka	5.00	1.50
SO7 Tuffy Rhodes	8.00	2.40
SO8 Koichi Ogata	5.00	1.50
SO9 Kenji Jojima	5.00	1.50
SO10 Tomohiro Kuroki	5.00	1.50
SO11 Atsuya Furuta	5.00	1.50
SO12 Michihiro Ogasawara	5.00	1.50

2000 Upper Deck Victory Japan Superstar Showcase

Randomly inserted into packs, this nine-card insert set features some of Japan's finest athletes. Card backs carry a "SS" prefix.

	Nm-Mt	Ex-Mt
COMPLETE SET (9)	20.00	6.00
SS1 Ichiro Suzuki	8.00	2.40
SS2 Koji Uehara	2.00	.60
SS3 Koichi Ogata	2.00	.60
SS4 Daisuke Matsuzaka	2.00	.60
SS5 Tomohiro Kuroki	2.00	.60
SS6 Hideki Matsui	2.00	.60
SS7 Kenji Jojima	2.00	.60
SS8 Takanori Suzuki	2.00	.60
SS9 Atsuya Furuta	2.00	.60

2003 Topps Kanebo Japan

This 55-card standard-size set was issued in Japan. The cards were issued in three-card packs along with a stick of gum. These cards have a design similar to the 2002 Topps design but were issued with a 2003 copyright date. Please note that the fronts look like standard Topps cards but the backs are completely in Japanese. Silver parallel cards were issued at a stated rate of one in 10 and black

	Nm-Mt	Ex-Mt
COMPLETE SET (55)	30.00	9.00
1 Pedro Martinez	1.25	.35
2 Larry Walker	.50	.15
3 Jeff Bagwell	1.25	.35
4 Derek Jeter	5.00	1.50
5 Alfonso Soriano	1.25	.35
6 Vladimir Guerrero	1.25	.35
7 Doug Mientkiewicz	.50	.15
8 Manny Ramirez	1.25	.35
9 Magglio Ordonez	1.00	.30
10 Carlos Delgado	1.00	.30
11 Albert Pujols	2.50	.75
12 Jimmy Rollins	.50	.15
13 Ivan Rodriguez	1.25	.35
14 Shea Hillenbrand	.50	.15
15 Randy Johnson	1.50	.45
16 Ichiro Suzuki	2.50	.75
17 Masato Yoshii	.25	.07
18 Mike Lowell	.50	.15
19 Sammy Sosa	2.50	.75
20 Jorge Posada	.50	.15
21 Curt Schilling	1.00	.30
22 David Justice	.50	.15
23 Darin Erstad	1.00	.30
24 Nomar Garciaparra	2.00	.60
25 So Taguchi	.25	.07
26 Kazuhisa Ishii	.50	.15
27 Chris Singleton	.25	.07
28 Adam Dunn	.50	.15
29 Raul Ibanez	.25	.07
30 Lance Berkman	.50	.15
31 Shawn Green	1.00	.30
32 Hideki Irabu	.25	.07
33 Mike Piazza	2.50	.75
34 Derek Lowe	.50	.15
35 Tomo Ohka	.25	.07
36 Barry Bonds	3.00	.90
37 Roberto Alomar	1.00	.30
38 Tino Martinez	.50	.15
39 Freddy Garcia	.25	.07
40 Michael Tucker	.25	.07
41 Miguel Tejada	.75	.23
42 Kazuhiro Sasaki	.50	.15
43 Tim Salmon	.50	.15
44 Tsuyoshi Shinjo	.25	.07
45 Jason Giambi	1.00	.30
46 Jason Schmidt	.25	.07
47 Alex Rodriguez	2.50	.75
48 Raul Mondesi	.25	.07
49 Reggie Sanders	.25	.07
50 Shigetoshi Hasegawa	.25	.07
51 Brian Jordan	.25	.07
52 Hideo Nomo	2.00	.60
53 Cliff Floyd	.50	.15
54 Johnny Damon	.50	.15

2003 Topps Kanebo Japan Black

Randomly inserted in packs, these cards parallel the Topps Kanebo Japan set. Each of these cards can be differentiated from the regular cards by their black border.

	Nm-Mt	Ex-Mt
*STARS: 2X TO 5X BASIC CARDS		

2003 Topps Kanebo Japan Silver

These cards were inserted at a stated rate of one in 10. These cards parallel the regular Kanebo cards but have silver borders.

	Nm-Mt	Ex-Mt
*STARS: .75X TO 2X BASIC CARDS		

MULTI-SPORT

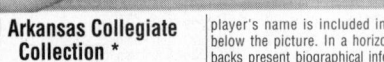

1991 Arkansas Collegiate Collection *

This 100-card multi-sport standard-size set was produced by Collegiate Collection. The fronts features a mixture of black and white or color player photos with black borders. The player's name is included in a black stripe below the picture. In a horizontal format the backs present biographical information, career summary, or statistics on a white background. Unless noted below, all players are from the sport of football.

	MINT	NRMT
COMPLETE SET (100)	15.00	6.75
1 Frank Broyles CO	.15	.07
2 Lance Alworth	.50	.23
3 Sidney Moncrief BK	.75	.35
4 Kevin McReynolds BB	.25	.11
5 John Barnhill CO	.10	.05
6 Dan Hampton	.50	.23
7 Mike Conley Track	.10	.05
8 John McDonnell CO Track	.10	.05
9 Miller Barber Golf	1.00	.45
10 Clyde Scott	.10	.05
11 Kendall Trainor	.10	.05
12 Les Lancaster BB	.10	.05
13 Tom Pagnozzi BB	.10	.05
14 Edrick Floreal Track	.10	.05
15 Tony Brown BK	.10	.05
16 Derek Russell	.10	.05
17 Niall O'Shaughnessy Track	.10	.05
18 Jimmy Walker	.10	.05
19 Ben Cowins	.10	.05
20 Keith Wilson BK	.10	.05

21 Tony Cherico .10 .05
22 Chip Hooper Tennis .10 .05
23 Tim Sherrill BB .10 .05
24 Paul Donovan Track .10 .05
25 Billy Ray Smith Jr. .15 .07
26 Steve Little .15 .07
27 Steve Atwater .10 .05
28 Roddie Haley Track .10 .05
29 Ron Faurot .10 .05
30 Peter Doohan Tennis .10 .05
31 Darrell Akerfelds BB .10 .05
32 Dickey Morton .10 .05
33 Lon Farrell CO .10 .05
34 Jerry Spencer Swimming .10 .05
35 Scott Hastings BK .10 .05
36 Dick Bumpas .10 .05
37 Johnny Ray BB .15 .07
38 Joe Kleine BK .10 .05
39 George Cole CO .10 .05
40 Bruce Lahay .10 .05
41 Jim Benton .10 .05
42 Stanley Redwine Track .10 .05
43 Jim Kremers BB .10 .05
44 Marvin Delph BK .10 .05
45 Joe Falcon Track .10 .05
46 Bill Montgomery .10 .05
47 Lou Holtz CO .25 .11
48 John Daly Golf 12.00 5.50
49 Bill McClard .10 .05
50 Gary Anderson RBK .15 .07
51 Alvin Robertson BK .15 .07
52 Glen Rose .10 .05
53 Ronnie Caveness .10 .05
54 Jeff King BB .10 .05
55 Bobby Joe Edmonds .10 .05
56 James Shibest .10 .05
57 Reuben Reina Track .10 .05
58 Martin Smith Swimming .10 .05
59 Wear Schoonover .10 .05
60 Bruce James .10 .05
61 Billy Moore .10 .05
62 Jim Mabry .10 .05
63 Ron Calcagni .10 .05
64 Wilson Matthews CO .10 .05
65 Martine Bercher .10 .05
66 Martin Terry BK .10 .05
67 Andrew Lang BK .10 .05
68 Mike Reppond .10 .05
69 Ron Brewer BK .10 .05
70 Ish Ordonez .10 .05
71 Steve Korte .10 .05
72 Jim Barnes .10 .05
73 Steve Cox .15 .07
74 Bud Brooks .10 .05
75 Roland Sales .10 .05
76 Chuck Dicus .10 .05
77 Rodney Brand .10 .05
78 Wayne Martin .10 .05
79 Greg Kolenda .10 .05
80 Ron Huery BK .10 .05
81 Brad Taylor .10 .05
82 Bill Burnett .10 .05
83 Glen Ray Hines .10 .05
84 Leotis Harris .10 .05
85 Darrell Walker BK .10 .05
86 Joe Ferguson .25 .11
87 Greg Horne .10 .05
88 Loyd Phillips .10 .05
89 James Rouse .10 .05
90 Ken Hatfield CO .15 .07
91 Bobby Crockett .10 .05
92 Quinn Grovey .10 .05
93 Wayne Harris .10 .05
94 Jim Mooty .10 .05
95 Barry Foster .25 .11
96 Mel McGaha BB .10 .05
97 Jim Lee Howell .10 .05
98 Jack Robbins .10 .05
99 Cliff Powell .10 .05
100 Checklist Card .10 .05

1990-91 Arizona Collegiate Collection *

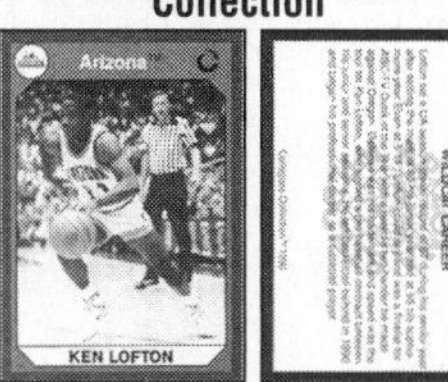

This 125-card standard-size set was produced by Collegiate Collection. We've included a sport initial (B-baseball, K-basketball, F-football) for players in the top collected sports.

	MINT	NRMT
COMPLETE SET (125)	12.00	5.50
1 Steve Kerr K	.50	.23
2 Sean Elliott K	1.00	.45
3 Vance Johnson F	.25	.11
4 Lute Olson CO K	.50	.23
5 Chris Singleton F	.25	.11
6 Robert Gamez	.10	.05
7 Ricky Hunley F	.10	.05
8 Terry Francona B	.10	.05
9 Chuck Cecil F	.25	.11
10 Craig Lefferts B	.15	.07
11 Warren Rustand K	.05	.02
12 Tommy Tunnicliffe F	.05	.02
13 Steve Strong B	.05	.02
14 Theo Bell F	.10	.05
15 Jerry Kindall CO B	.10	.05
16 Kevin Long B	.05	.02
17 Fred Snowden CO K	.05	.02
18 Anthony Smith F	.25	.11
19 Laurie Brunet	.05	.02
20 Wes Clements B	.05	.02
21 Larry Demic K	.10	.05
22 Peter Evans	.05	.02
23 Gilbert Heredia B	.25	.11
24 Chuck Cecil F	.25	.11
25 Todd Trafton B	.10	.05
26 Alan Durden F	.05	.02
27 Eric Meeks	.05	.02
28 Steve Kerr K	.50	.23
29 Rosie Wegrich	.05	.02
30 Danny Lockett F	.10	.05
31 Dana Wells F	.05	.02
32 Katrena Johnson	.05	.02
33 Anthony Cook K	.10	.05
34 Anita Moss	.05	.02
35 David Adams F	.05	.02
36 Eddie Leon B	.10	.05
37 Vance Johnson F	.25	.11
38 Sean Elliott K	1.00	.45
39 Alan Zinter K	.10	.05
40 Russell Brown K	.05	.02
41 Joe Magrane B	.25	.11
42 Derek Hill F	.25	.11
43 Hubie Oliver F	.10	.05
44 Scott Geyer F	.05	.02
45 Bill Wright	.05	.02
46 Max Zendejas F	.10	.05
47 Jim Young CO F	.10	.05
48 Mark Arneson F	.10	.05
49 Doug Pfaff F	.05	.02
50 George DiCarlo	.05	.02
51 Brad Henke F	.05	.02
52 Bruce Hill F	.25	.11
53 Ron Hassey B	.15	.07
54 Jim Gault	.05	.02
55 Bryon Evans F	.25	.11
56 Hoan Hansen	.05	.02
57 Pete Williams K	.05	.02
58 Frank Busch	.05	.02
59 David Wood F	.10	.05
60 Dave Murray	.05	.02
61 Carla Garrett	.05	.02
62 Ivan Lesnik F	.05	.02
63 J.T. Snow B	1.00	.45
64 Al Fleming K	.05	.02
65 Don Lee B	.05	.02
66 Dave Towne	.05	.02
67 Brad Anderson F	.05	.02
68 Chuck Cecil F	.25	.11
69 Mike Dawson F	.10	.05
70 Ed Vosberg B	.15	.07
71 Joe Tofflemire K	.10	.05
72 Rick LaRose	.05	.02
73 Larry Silveria	.05	.02
74 Lamonte Hunley F	.05	.02
75 June Olkowski	.05	.02
76 Dave Stegman B	.10	.05
77 Melissa McLinden	.05	.02
78 Chris Johnson	.05	.02
79 Kenny Lofton K	2.00	.90
80 Scott Erickson B	.50	.23
81 Martina Koch	.05	.02
82 Joel Estes	.05	.02
83 Diane Johnson	.05	.02
84 Jon Abbott F	.05	.02
85 Sean Elliott K	1.00	.45
86 Thom Hunt	.05	.02
87 Jeff Kiewel F	.05	.02
88 Morris Udall K	.30	.14
89 Becky Bell	.05	.02
90 Ruben Rodriguez F	.10	.05
91 Randy Robbins F	.10	.05
92 Eddie Smith K	.05	.02
93 Steve Kerr K	.50	.23
94 Dwight Taylor K	.05	.02
95 Mike Candrea	.05	.02
96 Vance Johnson RB F	.25	.11
97 Bob Elliott K	.05	.02
98 Glenn Parker DT F	.15	.07
99 Joe Nehls K	.05	.02
100 Checklist Card 1-99	.05	.02
101 Derek Huff	.05	.02
102 Dick Tomey CO F	.05	.02
103 Lute Olson CO K	.75	.35
104 Art Luppino F	.05	.02
105 Kevin Long B	.05	.02
106 Bob Elliott K	.05	.02
107 George Young	.05	.02
108 Don Pooley	.05	.02
109 Bryon Evans F	.25	.11
110 Sean Elliott K	1.00	.45
111 Kim Haddow	.05	.02
112 David Adams F	.05	.02
113 Bobby Thompson F	.10	.05
114 Brad Anderson F	.05	.02
115 Eddie Wilson F	.05	.02
116 Dan Pohl	.25	.11
117 Joe Hernandez F	.05	.02
118 J.F.(Pop) McKale CO B	.05	.02
119 Gayle Hopkins	.10	.05
120 Carl Cooper F	.05	.02
121 Ken Lofton K	2.00	.90
122 Robert Lee Thompson F	.10	.05
123 Robert Ruman F	.05	.02
124 Meg Ritchie	.05	.02
125 John Byrd Salmon F	.10	.05

1987-88 Arizona State *

Sponsored by the Valley of the Sun Kiwanis Club and "Our Quest: Their Best", this 22-card standard-size was produced by Sports Marketing Inc. The cards feature Arizona State athletes from various sports. The fronts have action color player photos against a white background. A maroon and wider yellow stripe appear below the picture, with the yellow stripe containing the player's name and sport. The words "Arizona State" are printed in maroon block letters above the photo and are underlined by a yellow stripe printed with the word "University". The Sun Devils mascot in the lower right corner rounds out the front. The backs are white with maroon print and include a player profile and a community service announcement from Sparky, the mascot. Sponsors' logos appear at the bottom. The sports represented are basketball (1, 4, 15, 18, 21), swimming (2), baseball (3, 8, 11), football (5, 10, 14, 16-17, 22), wrestling (6), softball (9), track and field (12), gymnastics (13), tennis (19), and volleyball (20). The cards are unnumbered and checklisted below in alphabetical order.

	MINT	NRMT
COMPLETE SET (22)	20.00	9.00
1 Mark Becker	1.00	.45
2 Peter Boden	1.00	.45
3 Jim Brock CO	2.50	1.10
4 Mark Carlino	1.00	.45
5 John Cooper CO	4.00	1.80
6 Aaron Cox	2.50	1.10
7 Mike Davies	1.00	.45
8 Bob Dombrowski	1.00	.45
9 Karen Fifield	1.00	.45
10 Darryl Harris	1.00	.45
11 Linty Ingram	1.00	.45
12 Gea Johnson	1.00	.45
13 Paul Linne	1.00	.45
14 Randall McDaniel	4.00	1.80
15 Shamona Mosley	1.00	.45
16 Anthony Parker	2.50	1.10
17 Shawn Patterson	1.00	.45
18 Steve Patterson CO	2.00	.90
19 Doug Sachs	1.00	.45
20 Regina Stahl	1.00	.45
21 Arthur Thomas	1.00	.45
22 Channing Williams	1.00	.45

1990-91 Arizona State Collegiate Collection Promos *

This ten-card standard size set was issued by Collegiate Collection to honor some of the leading athletes in all sports played at Arizona State. The front features a full-color photo while the back of the card has information or statistical information about the player featured. To help identify the player there is a two-letter abbreviation of the athlete's sport next to the player's name.

	MINT	NRMT
COMPLETE SET (10)	4.00	1.80
1 Reggie Jackson BB	2.00	.90
2 Lafayette Lever BK	.50	.23
3 Linty Ingram BB	.10	.05
4 Luis Zendejas FB	.25	.11
5 Byron Scott BK	.75	.35
6 Sam Williams BK	.10	.05
7 Lenny Randle BB	.25	.11
8 Brian Noble FB	.25	.11
9 Trace Armstrong FB	.50	.23
10 Sun Devil Stadium	.25	.11

1990-91 Arizona State Collegiate Collection *

This 200-card standard-size mulit-sport set was produced by Collegiate Collection. We've included a sport initial (B-baseball, K-basketball, F-football, WK-women's basketball) for players in the top collected sports. The key card is one of the few cards featuring all-time Baseball great Barry Bonds in a college uniform.

	MINT	NRMT
COMPLETE SET (200)	15.00	6.75
1 Reggie Jackson B	1.25	.55
2 Gerald Riggs F	.25	.11
3 John Jefferson F	.30	.14
4 Sam Williams K	.05	.02
5 Charley Taylor F	.40	.18
6 Mike Davies	.05	.02
7 Barry Bonds B	3.00	1.35
8 Byron Scott K	.50	.23
9 Fat Lever K	.20	.09
10 Oddibe McDowell B	.10	.05
11 Dan Saleaumua F	.15	.07
12 Lionel Hollins K	.15	.07
13 Donnie Hill B	.10	.05
14 Doug Allen F	.05	.02
15 Kurt Nimphius K	.10	.05
16 Mike Benjamin B	.10	.05
17 Mark Malone F	.25	.11
18 Scott Lloyd K	.10	.05
19 Fair Hooker F	.15	.07
20 Jim Brock CO B	.30	.14
21 Linty Ingram B	.05	.02
22 Larry Gordon F	.10	.05
23 Chris Beasley K	.05	.02
24 Bruce Hill F	.10	.05
25 Bump Wills B	.10	.05
26 Steve Beck K	.05	.02
27 Scott Stephen F	.05	.02
28 Mike Haynes F	.30	.14
29 Packard Stadium West	.05	.02
30 Vernon Maxwell F	.15	.07
31 Alton Lister K	.15	.07
32 Eric Allen F	.30	.14
33 Fat Lever K	.20	.09
34 Al Bannister B	.05	.02
35 Skip McClendon F	.05	.02
36 David Fulcher F	.15	.07
37 Todd Kalis F	.05	.02
38 Larry Gura B	.15	.07
39 Aaron Cox F	.10	.05
40 Bob Kohrs F	.10	.05
41 Mark Landsberger K	.10	.05
42 Mike Richardson F	.10	.05
43 Shawn Patterson F	.15	.07
44 Paul Williams K	.05	.02
45 Danny Villa F	.10	.05
46 Eddie Bane B	.10	.05
47 Mike Pagel F	.15	.07
48 Jim Jeffcoat F	.30	.14
49 John Harris F	.10	.05
50 Lenny Randle B	.10	.05
51 Jeff Van Raaphorst F	.10	.05
52 Alvin Davis B	.20	.09
53 Freddie Williams F	.05	.02
54 Kevin Higgins B	.05	.02
55 Brian Noble F	.25	.11
56 Junior Ah You F	.15	.07
57 Kendall Carter B	.05	.02
58 Tony Lorick F	.05	.02
59 Liz Aronshone	.05	.02
60 Buzz Hayes	.05	.02
61 Danny White F	.50	.23
62 John Mistler F	.05	.02
63 Heather Farr	.50	.23
64 Byron Scott K	.40	.18
65 Bill Mayfair	.30	.14
66 Tammy Webb	.10	.05
67 Curley Culp F	.30	.14
68 Mona Plummer Aquatic	.05	.02
69 Norris Stevenson F	.05	.02
70 Jay Barrs	.40	.18
71 Roger Schmuck B	.05	.02
72 Al Harris F	.15	.07
73 Pearl Sinn	.05	.02
74 John Finn B	.05	.02
75 Bruce Hardy F	.15	.07
76 Lisa Zeys	.05	.02
77 Andrew Parker	.05	.02
78 Ben Malone F	.10	.05
79 Brent McClanahan F	.15	.07
80 Sheri Rhodes	.05	.02
81 Mike Black F	.05	.02
82 Floyd Bannister B	.15	.07
83 Danielle Ammaccapone	.50	.23
84 Trace Armstrong F	.25	.11
85 Darryl Clack F	.10	.05
86 Steve Holden F	.10	.05
87 Pam Richmond	.05	.02
88 Whiteman Tennis	.05	.02
89 Art Malone F	.10	.05
90 Regina Stahl	.05	.02
91 Darryl Harris	.05	.02
92 Activity Center	.05	.02
93 Randall McDaniel F	.30	.14
94 Sun Devil Stadium	.10	.05
95 Luis Zendejas F	.15	.07
96 Sun Angel Track	.05	.02
97 J.D. Hill F	.15	.07
98 Rod Severn	.05	.02
99 Bobby Douglass CO	.15	.07
100 Checklist Card 1-99	.05	.02
101 1977 National Champs B	.10	.05
102 Bobby Winkles CO K	.25	.11
103 Zeke Jones	.05	.02
104 Christy Nore	.05	.02
105 Dan Devine CO F	.25	.11
106 Andy Astbury	.05	.02
107 Lisa Stuck	.05	.02
108 Dave Severn	.05	.02
109 JoAnne Carner	.50	.23
110 Doug Sachs	.05	.02
111 Bob Horner Hubie Brooks B	.15	.07
112 Herman Finzier	.05	.02
113 Football Team 1957 F	.10	.05
114 Lynda Tolbert	.05	.02
115 Baseball Team 1981 B	.10	.05
116 Bob Gilder	.05	.02
117 Ulis Williams	.05	.02
118 Tracy Cox	.05	.02
119 John Jefferson F	.25	.11
120 Mike Orn	.05	.02
121 Baseball Team 1965 B	.10	.05
122 Ron Brown F	.10	.05
123 Football Team 1986 F	.10	.05
124 Jim Gressley	.05	.02
125 Lucy Casazez	.05	.02
126 Dwayne Evans	.05	.02
127 Kathy Escarlega	.05	.02
128 Ned Wulk CO K	.10	.05
129 Jim Carter	.10	.05
130 Frank Covelli	.05	.02
131 Dan St. John	.05	.02
132 Jacinta Bartholomew	.05	.02
133 Baseball Team 1967 B	.10	.05
134 Jackie Brummer	.05	.02
135 Danny White F	.50	.23
136 Alan Waldan	.05	.02
137 Coleen Sommer	.05	.02
138 Football Team 1975 F	.10	.05
139 Eddie Urabano	.05	.02
140 Jane Bastanchury	.05	.02
141 Baseball Team 1969 B	.10	.05
142 Leon Burton F	.05	.02
143 Mona Plummer	.05	.02
144 Bob Mulgado F	.05	.02
145 Henry Carr F	.15	.07
146 Dan Severn	.05	.02
147 Milissa Belose	.05	.02
148 Ron Freeman	.05	.02
149 Kim Neal	.05	.02
150 Howard Twitty	.25	.11
151 Reggie Jackson B	1.25	.55
152 Lynn Nelson	.05	.02
153 Ken Landacox B	.05	.02
154 Joe Caldwell K	.10	.05
155 Bob Breunig F	.30	.14
156 Larry Lawson	.05	.02
157 Debbie Ochs	.05	.02
158 Mike Devereaux B	.30	.14
159 Mike Sodders B	.05	.02
160 Keith Russell	.05	.02
161 Art Becker K	.10	.05
162 Woody Green F	.10	.05
163 Ken Phelps B	.10	.05
164 Sherry Poole WK	.05	.02
165 Ricky Peters B	.10	.05
166 Sherri Norris	.05	.02
167 Paul Limne	.05	.02
168 Wilford Whizzer White F with Danny White	.40	.18
169 Maria Turjillo	.05	.02
170 Karli Urban	.05	.02
171 Chris Bando B	.25	.11
172 Bob Horner B	.25	.11
173 Hubie Brooks B	.25	.11
174 Mike Haynes F	.30	.14
175 Chris Jogis	.05	.02
176 Sal Bando B	.40	.18
177 Bernie Wrightson	.05	.02
178 Kevin Romine B	.10	.05
179 Cassandra Lander WK	.05	.02
180 1970 Football Team F	.10	.05
181 Sterling Slaughter B	.10	.05
182 Jerry Maddox B	.05	.02
183 Rick Monday B	.25	.11
184 Freddie Lewis K	.10	.05
185 Gary Gentry B	.10	.05
186 Tom Purtzer	.30	.14
187 Jodi Rathburn WK	.05	.02
188 Carl Donnelly	.05	.02
189 Frank Kush CO F	.10	.05
190 Glenn McMinn	.05	.02
191 Kym Hampton WK	.05	.02
192 Marty Barrett B	.15	.07
193 Rick McKinney	.05	.02
194 Michael Berlenheiter	.05	.02
195 Duffy Dyer B	.10	.05
196 Mary Littlewood	.05	.02
197 Ben Hawkins F	.10	.05
198 Dan Hayden	.05	.02
199 Cheryl Gibson	.05	.02
200 Checklist Card 101-200	.05	.02

1987-88 Auburn *

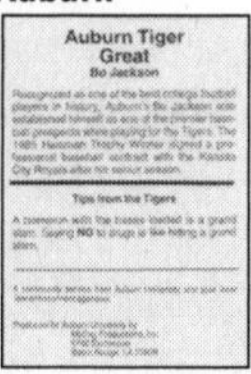

This 16-card standard-size set was issued by Auburn University and includes members from different sports programs. Reportedly only 5,000 sets were made by McDag Productions, and the cards were distributed by the Opelika, Alabama police department. The cards feature color player photos on white card stock. The backs present safety tips for children. The last three cards of the set feature "Tiger Greats," former Auburn athletes Bo Jackson, Rowdy Gaines, and Chuck Person. The key card in the set is Frank Thomas. The sports represented in this set are football (1, 3, 5, 11-13, 16), basketball (4, 6, 9-10, 14), baseball (2), and swimming (15). A card of Bo Jackson playing Football has been recently discovered. Since very few of these cards are known it is not considered part of the complete set

	MINT	NRMT
COMPLETE SET (16)	150.00	70.00
1 Pat Dye CO	2.50	1.10
2 Frank Thomas	80.00	36.00
3 Jeff Burger	1.50	.70
4 Sonny Smith CO	1.50	.70
5 Kurt Crain	1.00	.45
6 Joe Ciampi	1.50	.70
7 Aubie (Mascot)	1.00	.45
8 Tiger (Mascot)	1.00	.45
9 Jeff Moore	1.50	.70
10 Vickie Orr	1.50	.70
11 Tracy Rocker	1.50	.70
12 Brian Shulman	1.00	.45
13 Lawyer Tillman	2.50	1.10
14 Chuck Person	10.00	4.50
15 Rowdy Gaines	2.50	1.10
16A Bo Jackson Playing Baseball	20.00	9.00
16B Bo Jackson Playing Football	30.00	13.50

1987-88 Baylor *

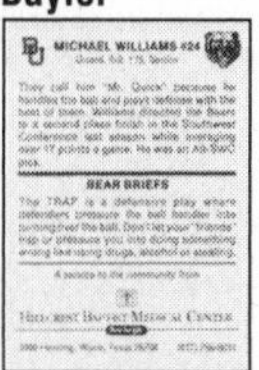

This 17-card standard-size set was sponsored by the Hillcrest Baptist Medical Center, the Waco Police Department, and the Baylor University Department of Public Safety. The cards represent several sports: baseball (1-3), basketball (4-6), track (7-10), and football (11-17). The front feature color action shots of the players on white card stock. At the top the words "Baylor Bears 1987-88" are printed between the Hillcrest and Baylor University logos. Player information is given below the picture. The back has more logos, brief career summaries, and "Bear Briefs," which consist of instructional sports information and an anti-drug or crime message.

	MINT	NRMT
COMPLETE SET (17)	30.00	13.50
1 Nate Jones	1.00	.45
2 Pat Combs	1.50	.70
3 Mickey Sullivan	1.00	.45
4 Micheal Williams	8.00	3.60
5 Darryl Middleton	2.00	.90
6 Gene Iba CO	2.00	.90
7 Victor Valen	1.00	.45
8 Raymond Pierre	1.00	.45
9 Darnell Chase	1.00	.45
10 Clyde Hart CO	1.00	.45
11 Ray Crockett	6.00	2.70
12 Joel Porter	1.00	.45
13 James Francis	8.00	3.60
14 Russell Sheffield	1.00	.45
15 Matt Clark	1.00	.45
16 Eugene Hall	1.00	.45
17 Grant Teaff CO	4.00	1.80

1990-91 Clemson Collegiate Collection Promos *

This ten-card standard-size set was issued by Collegiate Collection to honor some of the great athletes who played at Clemson. The front of the card features a full-color photo of the person featured while the back of the card has details about the person pictured. As this set is a multi-sport set we have used a two-letter identification of the sport next to the person's name.

	MINT	NRMT
COMPLETE SET (10)	4.00	1.80
C1 Tree Rollins BK	.75	.35
C2 CU-USC Series FB	.50	.23
C3 William Perry FB Bio	.75	.35
C4 Michael Dean Perry FB	.75	.35
C5 Orange Bowl FB	.25	.11
C6 Ken Hatfield CO FB	.50	.23
C7 Tim Teufel BB	.25	.11
C8 Dwight Clark FB	1.00	.45
C9 William Perry FB Stat	.75	.35
C10 Frank Howard CO FB	1.00	.45

1990-91 Clemson Collegiate Collection *

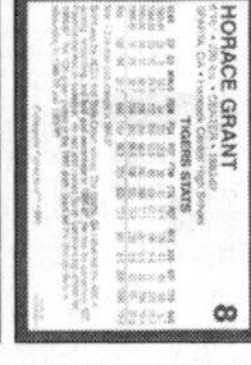

This 200-card standard-size set was produced by Collegiate Collection. We've included a sport initial (B-baseball, K-basketball, F-football, WK-women's basketball) for players in the top collected sports.

	MINT	NRMT
COMPLETE SET (200)	15.00	6.75
1 William Perry F	.40	.18
2 Kevin Mack F	.25	.11
3 Wayne(Tree) Rollins K	.25	.11
4 Donald Igwebuike F	.10	.05
5 Michael Dean Perry F	.40	.18
6 Larry Nance K	.50	.23
7 Steve Fuller F	.15	.07
8 Horace Grant K	1.00	.45
9 Frank Howard CO F	.40	.18
10 Orange Bowl Champs F	.15	.07
11 Brian Barnes B	.15	.07
12 Bobby Conrad K	.15	.07
13 John Phillips F	.05	.02
14 Kevin Johnson	.05	.02
15 Terry Allen F	.75	.35
16 Chris Morocco F	.05	.02
17 Elden Campbell K	.50	.23
18 Jimmy Key B	.75	.35
19 Tracy Johnson F	.10	.05
20 Bill Spiers B	.15	.07
21 Lawson Duncan	.05	.02
22 Eric Eichmann	.05	.02
23 Tim Teufel B	.15	.07
24 Vincent Hamilton K	.05	.02
25 Mike Eppley	.10	.05
26 Hans Koeleman	.05	.02
27 Tennis Facilities	.05	.02
28 Marvin Sim F	.05	.02
29 Tigers Win Classic K	.05	.02
30 Jim Riggs F	.10	.05
31 Adubarie Otorubio	.05	.02
32 Mike Milchin B	.10	.05
33 Bruce Murray	.25	.11
34 Banks McFadden F	.05	.02
35 Murray Jarman K	.05	.02
36 The Kick 1986 F	.10	.05
37 Gary Conner	.05	.02
38 Jason Griffith	.05	.02
39 Terrance Flagler F	.15	.07
40 Grayson Marshall K	.10	.05
41 David Treadwell F	.25	.11
42 Perry Tuttle F	.15	.07
43 Billy Williams K	.05	.02
44 Homer Jordan F	.10	.05
45 Dale Hatcher F	.15	.07
46 Steve Reese F	.05	.02
47 Ray Williams B	.10	.05
48 Obed Ariri F	.10	.05
49 Soccer Team Wins '87	.05	.02
50 Miguel Nido	.05	.02
51 Cliff Austin F	.10	.05
52 Chris Sherman	.05	.02
53 Jeff Nunamacher F	.05	.02
54 Steve Berlin F	.05	.02
55 Jess Neely CO F	.10	.05
56 Rick Rudeen	.05	.02
57 Jeff Bryant F	.15	.07
58 Jerry Butler F	.15	.07
59 Randy Mazey B	.05	.02
60 Bob Paulling F	.05	.02
61 Richard Matuszewski and Walters	.05	.02
62 James Farr F	.05	.02
63 Bob Boettner	.05	.02
64 Chuck McSwain F	.10	.05
65 Jim Stuckey B	.10	.05
66 Neil Simons B	.05	.02
67 Rodney Williams F	.10	.05
68 Butch Zatezalo K	.05	.02
69 Dr.I.M. Ibrahim	.05	.02
70 Richard Matuszewski	.05	.02
71 Dwight Clark F	.50	.23
72 Chuck Baldwin B	.05	.02
73 Kenny Flowers F	.10	.05
74 Michael Tait K	.10	.05
75 John Lee	.05	.02
76 Horace Wyatt K	.05	.02
77 Terrence Herrington	.05	.02
78 Gary Cooper F	.10	.05
79 Bert Hefferman B	.10	.05
80 Tigers with ACC Title K	.10	.05
81 Fred Cone F	.05	.02
82 Clarence Rose	.25	.11
83 Jean Desdunes	.05	.02
84 Donnell Woolford F	.25	.11
85 Ric Aronberg	.05	.02
86 Mike Brown B	.05	.02
87 Frank Howard CO F	.05	.02
88 Swimming Pool	.05	.02
89 Terry Kinard F	.15	.07
90 Chris Patton	.15	.07
91 Baseball Stadium B	.05	.02
92 Cliff Ellis CO K	.15	.07
93 1989 Senior Football F	.10	.05
94 The Clemson Tiger F	.10	.05
95 Howard's Rock F	.10	.05
96 Jeff Davis F	.10	.05
97 Derrick Forrest K	.10	.05
98 Mack Dickson	.05	.02
99 Clemson Wins Nebraska F	.10	.05
100 Checklist Card 1-99	.05	.02
101 Hill shot from field F	.05	.02
102 Ray Williams F	.10	.05
103 Jim McCollom B	.05	.02
104 Charlie Waters F	.50	.23
105 Soccer and Tennis Area	.05	.02
106 Bill Wilhelm B	.05	.02
107 Bubba Brown F	.05	.02
108 Ken Hatfield CO F	.15	.07
109 Lester Brown F	.05	.02
110 James Robinson F	.05	.02
111 Michael Dean Perry William Perry F	.30	.14
112 Nuamoi Nwokocha	.05	.02
113 Frank Howard CO F	.40	.18
114 Bill Foster CO K	.15	.07
115 Wesley McFadden F	.05	.02
116 Clemson 35 Penn State 10 F	.10	.05
117 Jay Berger	.25	.11
118 Andy Headen F	.15	.07
119 Fred Cone Frank Howard Banks McFadden Joe Blalock F	.10	.05
120 Hill Shot from Board F	.05	.02
121 Harry Olszewski F	.10	.05
122 CU clinches season F	.10	.05
123 Super Bowl Rings F	.10	.05
124 Otis Moore F	.05	.02
125 Kirk Howling K	.05	.02
126 Defensive Rankings F	.05	.02
127 Jeff Bostic Joe Bostic F	.25	.11
128 Bob Pollock	.05	.02
129 Randy Scott F	.05	.02
130 Noel Loban	.05	.02
131 Clemson VS. Stanford F	.05	.02
132 All-Americans	.10	.05
133 Danny Ford CO F	.10	.05
134 Larry Penley	.05	.02
135 Littlejohn Coliseum K	.05	.02
136 Clyde Browne	.05	.02
137 Clemson 13, Okla. 6 F	.10	.05
138 Clemson vs. W. Virginia F	.05	.02
139 Clemson and Notre Dame F	.10	.05
140 George Bush in jacket	1.00	.45
141 Steve Fuller and Jerry Butler F	.25	.11
142 Safety Celebration	.05	.02
143 Oswald Drawdy	.05	.02
144 John Phillips and Michael Dean Perry F	.15	.07
145 Chuck Kriese	.05	.02
146 Balloon Launch	.05	.02
147 William Perry F	.40	.18
148 Jim Davis WK	.10	.05
149 Jim Brennan K	.05	.02
150 Death Valley	.15	.07
151 Tina Krebs	.05	.02
152 Andy Johnston	.05	.02
153 Wayne Coffman	.05	.02
154 Andie Tribble WK	.05	.02
155 Mitzi Kremer	.05	.02
156 Rusty Adkins B	.05	.02
157 Choppy Patterson K	.05	.02
158 Jill Bakehorn	.05	.02
159 Baker vs. Tanner	.15	.07
160 Jerry Butler F	.25	.11
161 Championship Rings	.10	.05
162 Shawn Weatherly	.40	.18
163 Homecoming	.05	.02
164 Barbara Kennedy	.05	.02
165 Sports Facilities	.05	.02
166 Tommy Mahaffey K	.25	.11
167 Dillard Pruitt	.25	.11
168 Bill Yarborough K	.05	.02
169 Billy O'Dell B	.15	.07
170 Joe Blalock F	.05	.02
171 Ute Jamrozy	.05	.02
172 Jerry Pryor K	.05	.02
173 Susan Hill	.05	.02
174 Eddie Griffin	.05	.02
175 Jane Forman	.05	.02
176 Obed Ariri F	.10	.05
177 Richie Mahaffey K	.05	.02
178 Bobby Gage F	.05	.02
179 John Heisman CO F	.25	.11
180 Joe Landrum B	.05	.02
181 Soccer and Tennis	.05	.02
182 Clemson vs. USC F	.05	.02
183 Linda White	.05	.02
184 Denise Murphy	.05	.02
185 Mary Ann Cubelic WK	.05	.02
186 Pam Hayden	.05	.02
187 Coy Cobb	.05	.02
188 Randy Mahaffey K	.05	.02
189 Lou Cordileone F	.15	.07
190 1949 Gator Bowl F	.10	.05
191 Karen Ann Jenkins WK	.05	.02
192 Bobbie Mims WK	.05	.02
193 Janet Knight WK	.05	.02
194 Ray Matthews F	.05	.02
195 Gigi Fernandez	.50	.23
196 Joey McKenna	.05	.02
197 Denny Walling B	.10	.05
198 Janet Ellison	.05	.02
199 Donnie Mahaffey K	.05	.02
200 Director Card 101-200	.05	.02

1992-93 Clemson Schedules *

These ten cards measure approximately 2 1/4" by 3 1/2" and feature color action shots on their orange-bordered fronts. The white backs carry the various sport schedules in orange and black lettering. The name of the player depicted on the front appears at the bottom of the back. The cards are unnumbered and checklisted below in alphabetical order.

	MINT	NRMT
COMPLETE SET (11)	4.00	1.80
1 Kerry Boyatt-Hall Women's Basketball	.50	.23
2 Kim Graham Women's Track	.25	.11
3 Michael Green Men's Track	.25	.11
4 George Lampert Men's Tennis	.25	.11
5 Billy McMillon BB	1.00	.45
6 Mike Miller Wrestling	.25	.11
7 Andy Pujats Soccer	.25	.11
8 Jim Sheridan CO Men's and Women's Swimming	.25	.11
9 Chris Whitney BK	.75	.35
10 Amy Young Women's Tennis	.25	.11
11 Football Stadium	.50	.23

1990 Collegiate Collection Say No to Drugs *

This multi-sport set was released by Collegiate Collection for the "Say No To Drugs, Yes to Life" campaign. Each card is essentially a re-issue of a standard card from one of the college team sets along with a different card number and different copyright line.

	MINT	NRMT
COMPLETE SET (6)	12.00	5.50
AL1 Joe Namath	4.00	1.80
AL2 Bart Starr	2.00	.90
GA1 Herschel Walker	1.00	.45
NC1 Michael Jordan	8.00	3.60
LOU1 Johnny Unitas	2.00	.90
AU1 Bo Jackson	1.00	.45

1988-89 Florida *

This 14-card standard-size set was sponsored by University Athletic Association in conjunction with Burger King. The front features a color action shot of an athlete engaging in the particular sport highlighted on the card. The pictures are outlined by a thin black border on white card stock. The Burger King and the Gators' logo round out the card face. The back provides additional information on the sport as well as an anti-drug or crime message.

	MINT	NRMT
COMPLETE SET (14)	15.00	6.75
1 Men's Swimming	.75	.35
2 Baseball	1.00	.45
3 Men's Basketball	6.00	2.70
4 Women's Tennis	.75	.35
5 Women's Track and Field	.75	.35
6 Gymnastics	.75	.35
7 Cross Country	.75	.35
8 Women's Volleyball	.75	.35
9 Women's Swimming	.75	.35
10 Women's Basketball	4.00	1.80
11 Men's Track and Field	.75	.35
12 Men's Tennis	.75	.35
13 Women's Golf	1.00	.45
14 Men's Golf	2.00	.90

1990-91 Florida State Collegiate Collection *

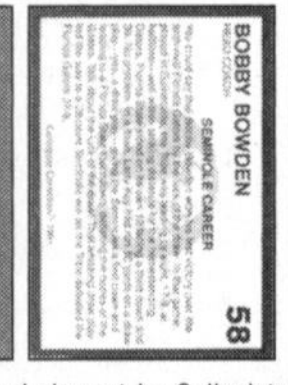

This 200-card standard-size set by Collegiate Collection features past and current athletes of Florida State University from a variety of sports.

	MINT	NRMT
COMPLETE SET (200)	15.00	6.75
1 Dick Howser BB	.25	.11
2 Edwin Alicea BB	.10	.05
3 Randy White	.05	.02
4 Steve Gabbard	.05	.02
5 Pat Tomberlin	.10	.05
6 Herb Gainer	.05	.02
7 Bobby Jackson	.10	.05
8 Redus Coggin	.05	.02
9 Pat Carter	.15	.07
10 Kevin Grant	.05	.02
11 Peter Tom Willis	.25	.11
12 Phil Carollo	.05	.02
13 Derek Schmidt	.05	.02
14 Rick Stockstill	.05	.02
15 Mike Martin BB	.05	.02
16 Terry Anthony	.05	.02
17 Darrin Holloman	.05	.02
18 John McLean	.05	.02
19 Rudy Maloy	.05	.02
20 Gary Huff	.15	.07
21 Jamey Shouppe BB	.05	.02
22 Isaac Williams	.05	.02
23 Weegie Thompson	.15	.07
24 Jose Marzan BB	.05	.02
25 Gerald Nichols	.05	.02
26 John Brown	.05	.02
27 Danny McManus	.15	.07
28 Parrish Barwick	.05	.02
29 Paul McGowan	.05	.02
30 Keith Jones	.05	.02
31 Alphonso Williams	.05	.02
32 Luis Alicea BB	.15	.07
33 Tony Yeomans	.05	.02
34 Michael Tanks	.05	.02
35 Stan Shiver	.05	.02
36 Willie Jones	.05	.02
37 Wally Woodham	.05	.02
38 Chip Ferguson	.05	.02
39 Sam Childers	.05	.02
40 Paul Piurowski	.05	.02
41 Joey Ionata	.05	.02
42 John Hadley	.05	.02
43 Tanner Holloman	.05	.02
44 Fred Jones	.05	.02
45 Terry Warren	.05	.02
46 John Merna	.05	.02
47 Jimmy Jordan	.05	.02
48 Dave Capellen	.05	.02
49 Martin Mayhew	.15	.07
50 Barry Barco	.05	.02
51 Ronald Lewis	.05	.02
52 Tom O'Malley	.10	.05
53 Rick Tuten	.10	.05
54 Ed Fulton BB	.05	.02
55 Marc Ronan BB	.05	.02
56 Bobby Bowden	.50	.23
57 Bobby Bowden	.50	.23
58 Bobby Bowden	.50	.23
59 Bobby Bowden	.50	.23
60 Bobby Bowden	.50	.23
61 John Grubb BB	.10	.05
62 Joe Wessel	.05	.02
63 Alphonso Carreker	.15	.07
64 Shelton Thompson	.05	.02
65 Tracy Sanders	.05	.02
66 Bobby Bowden	.50	.23
67 Bobby Bowden	.50	.23
68 Bobby Bowden	.50	.23
69 Bobby Bowden Jimmy Jordan Wally Woodham	.50	.23
70 Bobby Bowden	.50	.23
71 David Palmer	.10	.05
72 Jason Kuipers	.05	.02
73 Dayne Williams	.05	.02
74 Mark Salva	.05	.02
75 Bobby Butler	.10	.05
76 Bobby Bowden	.50	.23
77 Bobby Bowden	.50	.23
78 Bobby Bowden	.50	.23
79 Bobby Bowden	.50	.23
80 Bobby Bowden	.50	.23
81 Mike Loynd BB	.10	.05
82 Dexter Carter	.25	.11
83 Dedrick Dodge	.10	.05
84 Greg Allen	.05	.02
85 Barry Blackwell BB	.05	.02
86 Bobby Bowden	.50	.23
87 Bobby Bowden	.50	.23
88 Bobby Bowden	.50	.23
89 Bobby Bowden	.50	.23
90 Bobby Bowden	.50	.23
91 Bill Capece	.05	.02
92 Eric Hayes	.05	.02
93 Garth Jax	.15	.07
94 Odell Haggins	.05	.02
95 LeRoy Butler	.25	.11
96 Monk Bonasorte	.05	.02
97 Richie Lewis BB	.25	.11
98 Terry Kennedy BB	.25	.11
99 Hubert Green Golf	.25	.11
100 Checklist Card	.05	.02
101 Doc Hermann	.05	.02
102 Gary Futch	.05	.02
103 Tony Romeo	.05	.02
104 Lee Corso	.40	.18
105 Steve Bratton	.05	.02
106 Barry Rice	.05	.02
107 Jeff Hogan BK	.05	.02
108 John Wachtel	.05	.02
109 Dick Artmeier BK	.05	.02
110 Vic Szezepanik	.05	.02
111 Danny Litwhiler BB	.10	.05
112 Jack Fenwick	.05	.02
113 Nolan Henke Golf	.05	.02
114 Mark Meseroll	.05	.02
115 Jimmy Everett	.05	.02
116 Gary Schull BK	.05	.02
117 Les Murdock	.05	.02
118 Ron Schomburger	.05	.02
119 Scott Warren	.05	.02
120 Eric Williams	.05	.02
121 Buddy Strauss	.05	.02
122 Juan Bonilla BB	.10	.05
123 Rowland Garrett BK	.10	.05
124 Kenny Knox Golf	.10	.05
125 Bill Cappleman	.05	.02
126 Bill Kimber	.05	.02
127 Mike Fuentes BB	.10	.05
128 Bill Proctor	.05	.02
129 Kurt Unglaub	.05	.02
130 Woody Woodward BB	.25	.11
131 Dave Cowens BK	.50	.23
132 Lee Nelson	.05	.02
133 Robert Urich	.50	.23
134 Ron Fraser BB	.15	.07
135 Randy Coffield	.05	.02
136 Jimmy Lee Taylor	.05	.02
137 Max Wettstein	.05	.02
138 Brian Williams	.10	.05
139 T.K. Wetherell	.05	.02
140 Dale McCullers	.05	.02
141 Peter Tom Willis	.25	.11
142 Doug Little BB	.05	.02
143 J.T. Thomas	.15	.07
144 Hassan Jones	.15	.07
145 Deion Sanders	2.00	.90
146 Barry Smith	.05	.02
147 Hugh Durham BK	.15	.07
148 Bill Moremen	.05	.02
149 Gary Henry	.05	.02
150 John Madden	1.25	.55
151 J.T. Thomas	.15	.07
152 Tony Avitable BB	.05	.02
153 Keith Kinderman	.05	.02
154 Bill Dawson	.05	.02
155 Mike Good	.05	.02
156 Kim Hammond	.05	.02
157 Buddy Blankenship	.05	.02
158 Jimmy Black	.05	.02
159 Vic Prinzi	.05	.02
160 Bobby Renn	.05	.02
161 Mark Macek	.10	.05
162 Wayne McDuffie	.05	.02
163 Joe Avezzano	.25	.11
164 Hector Gray	.05	.02
165 Grant Guthrie	.05	.02
166 Tom Bailey	.05	.02
167 Ron Sellers	.10	.05
168 Dick Hermann	.05	.02
169 Bob Harbison	.05	.02
170 Winfred Bailey	.05	.02
171 James Harris	.05	.02
172 Jerry Jacobs	.05	.02
173 Mike Kincaid	.05	.02
174 Jimmy Heggins	.05	.02
175 Steve Kalenich	.05	.02
176 Del Williams	.10	.05
177 Fred Pickard	.05	.02
178 Walt Sumner	.10	.05
179 Bud Whitehead	.05	.02
180 Bobby Anderson	.05	.02
181 Paul Azinger Golf	.75	.35
182 Burt Reynolds	.75	.35
183 Ron King BK	.05	.02
184 H. Donald Loucks Tennis	.05	.02
185 Jim Lyttle BB	.10	.05
186 Richard Amman	.05	.02
187 Bobby Crenshaw	.05	.02
188 Bill Dawkins	.05	.02
189 Ken Burnett	.10	.05
190 Duane Carrell	.10	.05
191 Gene McDowell	.05	.02
192 Paul Wernke BK	.05	.02
193 Beryl Rice	.05	.02
194 Dave Fedor BK	.05	.02
195 Brian Schmidt	.05	.02
196 Rhett Dawson	.05	.02
197 Greg Futch	.05	.02
198 Joe Majors	.05	.02
199 Stan Dobosz	.05	.02
200 Checklist Card	.05	.02

1992-93 Florida State *

This 80-card multi-sport standard-size set features "Seminole Superstars" from various Florida State teams. The sports represented are golf (1-3), tennis (4-8), swimming and diving (9-14), track and field (15-21), softball (22-25), basketball (26-28, 39-42), volleyball (29-31), baseball (32-38), basketball (39-43), and football (44-75).

	MINT	NRMT
COMPLETE SET (80)	30.00	13.50
1 Ernest Lanford CO	.10	.05
2 Bobby Cochran	.10	.05
3 Debbie Dillman CO	.10	.05
4 Marie-Jose E. Rouleau	.10	.05
5 David Barron CO	.10	.05
6 Ken McKenzie	.10	.05
7 Alice Reen CO	.10	.05
8 Audra Brannon	.10	.05
9 Terry Maul CO	.10	.05
10 Gary Cole CO	.10	.05
11 Robert Caicedo	.10	.05
12 Missy Connolly	.10	.05
13 Brad Hoffman	.10	.05
14 Kiki Steinberg	.10	.05
15 Terry Long CO	.10	.05
16 Sue Addison CO	.10	.05
17 Jeff Bray	.10	.05
18 Sheryl Covington	.10	.05
19 Kevin Crist	.10	.05
20 Trinette Johnson	.10	.05
21 Patrice Verdun	.10	.05
22 Joanne Graf CO	.10	.05
23 Leslie Barton	.10	.05
24 Susan Buttery	.10	.05
25 Toni Gutierrez	.10	.05
26 Marynell Meadors CO	.10	.05
27 Allison Peercy	.20	.09
28 Ursula Woods	.20	.09
29 Cecile Reynaud CO	.20	.09
30 Adria Ciraco	.10	.05
31 Jennifer McCall	.10	.05
32 Mike Martin CO	.20	.09
33 Bryan Harris	.20	.09
34 Link Jarrett	.20	.09
35 Paul Wilson	3.00	1.35
36 Kevin McCray	.20	.09
37 Ty Mueller	.20	.09
38 Colby Weaver	.20	.09
39 Pat Kennedy CO	.50	.23
40 Sam Cassell	8.00	3.60
41 Rodney Dobard	.20	.09
42 Chuck Graham	.20	.09
43 Charlie Ward	8.00	3.60
44 Bobby Bowden CO	5.00	2.20
45 Clifton Abraham	.20	.09
46 Ken Alexander	.20	.09
47 Robbie Baker	.20	.09
48 Shannon Baker	.50	.23
49 Derrick Brooks	4.00	1.80

50 Lavon Brown .20 .09
51 Deondri Clark .20 .09
52 Richard Coes .20 .09
53 Chris Cowart .20 .09
54 John Davis .20 .09
55 Marvin Ferrell .20 .09
56 William Floyd 3.00 1.35
57 Dan Footman .50 .23
58 Leon Fowler .20 .09
59 Reggie Freeman .20 .09
60 Matt Frier .20 .09
61 Corey Fuller .20 .09
62 Felix Harris .20 .09
63 Tommy Henry .20 .09
64 Lonnie Johnson .50 .23
65 Marvin Jones 2.00 .90
66 Toddrick McIntosh .50 .23
67 Tiger McMillon .20 .09
68 Patrick McNeil .20 .09
69 Sterling Palmer .50 .23
70 Troy Sanders .20 .09
71 Corey Sawyer 1.00 .45
72 Carl Simpson .50 .23
73 Robert Stevenson .20 .09
74 Charlie Ward 8.00 3.60
75 Seminole Coaches .50 .23
76 Ad Card Motion Sports .10 .05
NNO Front Card .10 .05
NNO Back Card .10 .05
NNO Checklist 1-38 .10 .05
NNO Checklist 39-76 .10 .05

1991 Georgia Tech Collegiate Collection *

This 200-card set is standard sized. The fronts have a blue border with color action shots on each one. The school name and logo are found across the top border of the card. The featured player's name is found along the bottom border set against a yellow-gold background. The backs carry a small bio of the player and his/her statistics.

MINT NRMT
COMPLETE SET (200) 10.00 4.50
1 John Dewberry FB .05 .02
2 Ida Neal BK .05 .02
3 Lenny Horton BK .05 .02
4 Dennis Scott BK .25 .11
5 Steve Davenport FB .05 .02
7 Dante Jones FB .05 .02
8 Cory Collier FB .05 .02
9 LeeAnn Woodhull BK .05 .02
10 John Ivemeyer FB .05 .02
11 Ronny Cone FB .05 .02
12 George Malone FB .05 .02
13 Darrell Norton FB .05 .02
14 Roosevelt Isom FB .05 .02
15 Tom Hammonds BK .05 .02
16 Bobby Dodd FB CO .50 .23
17 Cindy Cochran BK .05 .02
18 Andre Thomas FB .05 .02
19 Chuck Easley FB .05 .02
20 Willie Burks FB .05 .02
21 Eric Thomas FB .05 .02
22 Jerry Mays FB .15 .07
23 Sammy Drummer FB .05 .02
24 Tory Ehle BK .05 .02
25 Rob Healy FB .05 .02
26 Brook Steppe BK .15 .07
27 Darrell Gast FB .05 .02
28 David Bell FB .05 .02
29 Keith Glanton FB .05 .02
30 Brian Oliver BK .10 .05
31 Sean Smith FB .05 .02
32 Cedric Stallworth FB .05 .02
33 Craig Neal BK .05 .02
34 Danny Harrison FB .05 .02
35 Duane Ferrell BK .05 .02
36 Eric Bearden FB .05 .02
37 Andy Hearn FB .05 .02
38 Jim Anderson FB .05 .02
39 Anthony Harrison FB .05 .02
40 Marielle Walker BK .05 .02
41 Dean Weaver FB .05 .02
42 Yvon Joseph BK .10 .05
43 Mike Kelley FB .05 .02
44 John Davis FB .05 .02
45 Mark Hogan FB .05 .02
46 Karl Brown BK .05 .02
47 Kyle Ambrose FB .05 .02
48 Steve Mullen FB .05 .02
49 Willis Crockett FB .05 .02
50 Jeff Mathis FB .05 .02
51 Ellis Gardner FB .05 .02
52 Larry Good FB .05 .02
53 Billy Lothridge FB .15 .07
54 Bill Kinard FB .05 .02
55 Brent Cunningham FB .05 .02
56 Ted Peeples FB .05 .02
57 Pat Swilling FB .40 .18
58 John Salley BK .50 .23
59 Lawrence Lowe FB .05 .02
60 Sheila Wagner BK .05 .02
61 Cam Bonifay FB .10 .05
62 George Brodnax FB .05 .02
63 Fred Braselton FB .05 .02
64 Joe Auer FB .15 .07
65 Franklin Brooks FB .05 .02
66 Rod Stephens FB .10 .05
67 Bill Curry FB CO .20 .09
68 Tim Manion FB .05 .02
69 Rick Strom FB .05 .02
70 Toby Pearson FB .05 .02
71 Jim Breland FB .05 .02
72 Don Bessillieu FB .05 .02
73 Craig Baynham FB .20 .09
74 Maxie Baughan FB .20 .09
75 Wade Mitchell FB .05 .02
76 Sammy Lilly FB .05 .02
77 Gary Lee FB .05 .02
78 Paul Jurgensen FB .05 .02
79 Robert Lavette FB .05 .02
80 Robert Jaracz FB .05 .02
81 Mike Oven FB .05 .02
82 Paul Menegazzi FB .05 .02
83 Billy Martin FB .10 .05
84 Bobby Moorhead FB .05 .02
85 Buck Martin FB .05 .02
86 Buzz FB MASCOT .05 .02
87 Malcolm King FB .05 .02
88 Bobby Ross FB CO .20 .09
89 Gary Lanier FB .05 .02
90 Bill Curry FB CO .20 .09
91 Bonnie Tate BK .05 .02
92 William Alexander FB CO .05 .02
93 Rick Lantz FB .05 .02
94 Eddie McAshan FB .05 .02
95 Kim King FB .05 .02
96 Cleve Pounds FB .05 .02
97 The Rambling Wreck FB .05 .02
98 Bud Carson FB CO .10 .05
99 Bobby Dodd Stadium FB .05 .02
100 Checklist .05 .02
101 Willie Burks FB .05 .02
102 Sheldon Fox FB .05 .02
103 Scott Erwin .05 .02
104 Danny Harrison FB .05 .02
105 Eric Thomas FB .05 .02
106 Kent Hill FB .05 .02
107 Ray Blemker BB .05 .02
108 Terry Randall .05 .02
109 Pete Silas BK .05 .02
110 Bob McDonnell .05 .02
Golf
111 Kevin Brown BB .75 .35
112 Ralph Malone FB .05 .02
113 Jerry Mays FB .15 .07
114 Mark Bradley FB .05 .02
115 Thomas Palmer FB .05 .02
116 Calvin Tiggle FB .05 .02
117 Roger Kinard BB .05 .02
118 Thomas Balkcom FB .05 .02
119 Steve Newbern BB .05 .02
120 Tripp Isenhour .05 .02
Golf
121 Rod Stephens FB .05 .02
122 Mark Price BK .50 .23
123 Keith Fleming BB .05 .02
124 Bobby Cremins BB CO .20 .09
125 Ivery Lee FB .05 .02
126 Darryl Jenkins FB .05 .02
127 Jerimiah McClary FB .05 .02
128 Dirk Morris .05 .02
Track & Field
129 Riccardo Ingram BB .05 .02
130 Lisa Neal .05 .02
Women's Softball
131 Robert Massey FB .05 .02
132 Cedric Stallworth FB .05 .02
133 Ty Griffin BB .10 .05
134 Bruce Dalrymple BK .05 .02
135 Johnny McNeil BK .05 .02
136 Stefen Scotton FB .05 .02
137 Jim Lavin FB .05 .02
138 Joe Siffri FB .05 .02
139 Gary Newsom BB .05 .02
140 Cristy Guardado .05 .02
Tennis
141 Scott Petway BK .05 .02
142 Jim Poole BB .10 .05
143 Kenneth Wilson FB .05 .02
144 Bridget Koster .05 .02
Track & Field
145 James Purvis .05 .02
Track & Field
146 Walt McConnell BB .05 .02
147 Jay Martin FB .05 .02
148 T.J. Edwards .05 .02
149 Chris Simmons FB .05 .02
150 Jennifer Beemsterboer .05 .02
Volleyball
151 Eric Smith .05 .02
Track & Field
152 George Paulson .05 .02
Tennis
153 Nacho Gervas .05 .02
Golf
154 Mark White .05 .02
Track & Field
155 Antonio McKay .05 .02
Track & Field
156 Taz Anderson FB .10 .05
157 Sam Bracken FB .05 .02
158 Kate Brandt BK .05 .02
159 Melvin Dold BK .05 .02
160 Tico Brown BK .05 .02
161 Lisa Kofskey .05 .02
Volleyball
162 Charlie Rymer .05 .02
Golf
163 Leigh Roberts .05 .02
Tennis
164 Scott Jordan BB .10 .05
165 Bill McDonald .05 .02
Golf
166 Harper Brown FB .05 .02
167 Jim Caldwell BK .05 .02
168 Buddy Blemker BK .05 .02
169 Bill Flowers FB .05 .02
170 Roger Kaiser BK .05 .02
171 Margaret Gales .05 .02
Volleyball
172 Kathy Harrison .05 .02
Track & Field
173 Kenny Thorne .05 .02
Tennis
174 Kim Lash .05 .02
Tennis
175 Jens Skjoedt .05 .02
Tennis
176 Bobby Kimmel BK .10 .05
177 Phil Wagner BK .05 .02
178 Jim Wood BK .05 .02
179 Rich Yunkus BK .15 .07
180 Tony Daykin FB .05 .02
181 Rick Lockwood BB .05 .02
182 Jay Nichols .05 .02
183 Paige Lord .05 .02
Women's Softball
184 Bryan Shelton .05 .02
Tennis
185 Carrie Ollar .05 .02
Tennis
186 Donnie Chisholm FB .05 .02
187 Floyd Faucette FB .05 .02
188 Jeff Ford .05 .02
189 Drew Hill FB .05 .02
190 Leon Hardeman FB .05 .02
191 Richy Gilbert .05 .02
Tennis
192 Roger Kinard BB .05 .02
193 K.G. White BB .05 .02
194 Andre Simm .05 .02
Tennis
195 Franz Sydow .05 .02
Tennis
196 Mackel Harris FB .05 .02
197 Eddie Lee Ivery FB .20 .09
198 Kris Kentera FB .05 .02
199 Lenny Snow FB .05 .02
200 Checklist .05 .02

1989-90 Kentucky Schedules *

This seven-card multi-sport set features schedule cards each measuring approximately 2 1/4" by 3 3/4". These schedule cards were passed out individually at games by booster clubs. The fronts feature full-bleed color action photos, some horizontally, some vertically oriented. The name "Kentucky" appears in either blue or white letters across the top of the card face on most cards. The backs carry the 1989-90 schedules for the respective sports. The cards are unnumbered and checklisted below with the named individuals listed first.

MINT NRMT
COMPLETE SET (7) 4.00 1.80
1 Melissa Nelson .25 .11
Women's Tennis schedule
2 Rick Pitino CO BK 3.00 1.35
3 Ian Skidmore .25 .11
Men's Tennis schedule
4 Mike Pfeifer FB 1.00 .45
5 Unidentified women's .25 .11
gymnast
Gymnastics schedule
6 Unidentified swimmer .25 .11
Swimming schedule
7 Painting of a baseball .50 .23
field
Baseball schedule

1992-93 Kentucky Schedules *

Sponsored by McDonald's, this ten-card multi-sport schedule features schedule cards each measuring 2 1/4" by 3 1/2". These schedule cards were passed out individually at games by booster clubs. The fronts feature a mix of color and black-and-white action player photos. Card numbers 1 and 2 are folded in the middle. The backs (or the insides) carry the 1992-93 schedules for the respective sports. The sponsor's logo appears either on the front or on the back. The cards are unnumbered and checklisted below in alphabetical order, with the schedule cards not featuring athletes listed at the end.

MINT NRMT
COMPLETE SET (10) 6.00 2.70
1 Jeff Abbott .50 .23
Jeff Michael
Brad Hindersman BB
2 Ann Hall .25 .11
Angela Salvatore
Womens's Volleyball
schedule
3 Pookie Jones FB .50 .23
4 Jamal Mashburn BK 3.00 1.35
5 Stacey Reed .25 .11
Women's Basketball
schedule
6 Maurice Stewart .25 .11
Swimming schedule
7 Chris Yario .25 .11
Women's Tennis Schedule
8 Basketball schedule .50 .23
9 Gymnastics schedule .25 .11
10 Men's Tennis schedule .25 .11

1985-86 LSU *

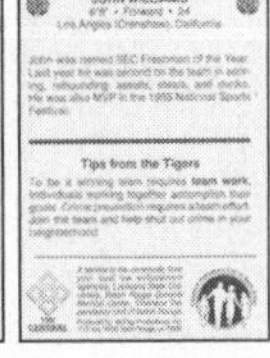

This 16-card standard-size set was sponsored by LSU, Baton Rouge General Medical Center, Chemical Dependency Unit of Baton Rouge, and various law enforcement agencies and was produced by McDag Productions. The General and the Chemical Dependency Unit logos adorn the top of the observe and the bottom of the reverse. The cards are unnumbered and we have checklisted them in alphabetical order. Since this set includes athletes from two different sports, we have indicated the sport after the player's name (B for baseball; BK for basketball). The set features Major League Baseball slugger Joey (Albert) Belle and other future Major Leaguers Mark Guthrie and Jeff Reboulet.

MINT NRMT
COMPLETE SET (16) 30.00 13.50
1 Joey (Albert) Belle B 20.00 9.00
2 Skip Bertman B CO 1.00 .45
3 Ricky Blanton BK 1.00 .45
4 Dale Brown BK CO 3.00 1.35
5 Ollie Brown BK .50 .23
6 Mark Guthrie B 1.00 .45
7 Rob Leary B .50 .23
8 Stan Loewer B .50 .23
9 Greg Patterson B .50 .23
10 Jeff Reboulet B 1.00 .45
11 Don Redden BK .50 .23
12 Derrick Taylor BK .50 .23
13 Jose Vargas BK .50 .23
14 John Williams BK 2.50 1.10
15 Nikita Wilson BK 1.00 .45
16 Anthony Wilson BK .50 .23

1987-88 LSU *

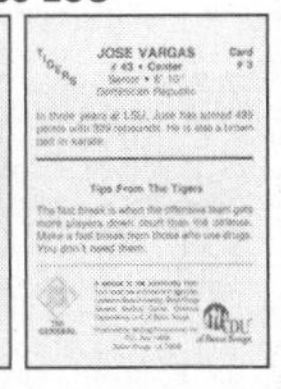

This 16-card standard-size set was sponsored by LSU, Baton Rouge General Medical Center, Chemical Dependency Unit of Baton Rouge, and various law enforcement agencies and was produced by McDag Productions. The General and the Chemical Dependency Unit logos adorn the bottom of both sides of the card. Six thousand sets were printed, and they were distributed by participating police agencies in the Baton Rouge area. The fronts feature borderless action or posed color photos of the players on white card stock. The upper left and right corners give the school name and player information. The backs have additional player information and "Tips from the Tigers", which consist of anti-drug or alcohol messages. This set includes athletes from basketball (1-7, 16) and baseball (8-15). Of special interest is card number 16, issued in memory of the late Pete Maravich, the all-time leading scorer in college basketball history. The set features the first card of Ben McDonald.

MINT NRMT
COMPLETE SET (16) 40.00 18.00
1 Dale Brown BK CO 3.00 1.35
2 Ricky Blanton BK 1.50 .70
3 Jose Vargas BK 1.00 .45
4 Fess Irvin BK 1.50 .70
5 Darryl Joe BK 1.00 .45
6 Bernard Woodside BK 1.00 .45
7 Neboisha Bukumirovich 1.00 .45
BK
8 Parker Griffin B 1.00 .45
9 Skip Bertman B CO 1.50 .70
10 Dan Kite B 1.00 .45
11 Russ Springer B 1.50 .70
12 Ben McDonald B 5.00 2.20
13 Richie Vasquez B 1.00 .45
14 Andy Galy B 1.00 .45
15 Pete Bush B 1.00 .45
16 Pete Maravich BK MEM 30.00 13.50

1988-89 LSU *

This 16-card standard-size set was sponsored by LSU, Baton Rouge General Medical Center, Chemical Dependency Unit of Baton Rouge, and various law enforcement agencies and was produced by McDag Productions. The General Medical Center and Chemical Dependency Unit logos adorn the bottom of both sides of the card. The cards were distributed in the Baton Rouge area by participating law enforcement agencies, the Medical Center, and the Chemical Dependency Unit. This set features athletes from basketball (1-8) and baseball (9-16). This set includes early cards of Chris Jackson, who played in the NBA, and of Ben McDonald, who pitched for the USA Olympic Baseball Team and the Baltimore Orioles.

MINT NRMT
COMPLETE SET (16) 12.00 5.50
1 Ricky Blanton 1.00 .45
2 Dale Brown CO 2.00 .90
3 Wayne Simms .50 .23
4 Chris Jackson 4.00 1.80
5 Kyle McKenzie .50 .23
6 Lyle Mouton 1.50 .70
7 Vernel Singleton 1.00 .45
8 Russell Grant .50 .23
9 Skip Bertman CO 1.00 .45
10 Ben McDonald 3.00 1.35
11 Pete Bush .50 .23
12 Mike Bianco .50 .23
13 Craig Cala .50 .23
14 Mat Gruver .50 .23
15 Keith Osik 1.00 .45
16 Russell Springer 1.50 .70

1988-89 LSU All-Americas *

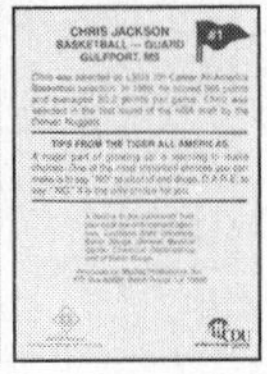

Produced by McDag Productions, this 16-card standard-size set was sponsored by LSU, Baton Rouge General Medical Center, Chemical Dependency Unit of Baton Rouge, and various law enforcement agencies. The General Medical Center and Chemical Dependency Unit logos adorn the bottom of both sides of the card. This set showcases athletes from basketball (1-2), baseball (3-5), track (6), volleyball (7), football (8-15) and golf (16). This set includes early cards of Chris Jackson, who was selected in the first round of the NBA draft by the Denver Nuggets, and of Ben McDonald, who was selected first by the Baltimore Orioles.

MINT NRMT
COMPLETE SET (16) 12.00 5.50
1 Chris Jackson 2.50 1.10
2 Durand(Rudy) Macklin 1.00 .45
3 Ben McDonald 3.00 1.35
4 Wes Grisham .50 .23
5 Barry Manuel 1.00 .45
6 Dawn Sowell .50 .23
7 Wendy Stammer .50 .23
8 Nacho Albergamo .50 .23
9 Wendell Davis 1.00 .45
10 Michael Brooks 1.50 .70
11 Lance Smith 1.00 .45
12 Eric Martin 1.50 .70
13 James Britt .50 .23
14 Albert Richardson .50 .23
15 Greg Jackson 1.00 .45
16 Rob McNamara .50 .23

1990 LSU Collegiate Collection *

This 200-card standard-size multi-sport set was produced by Collegiate Collection. Although a few color photos are included, the front features mostly black and white player photos, with borders in the team's colors of gold and purple. Unless noted below, all are football subjects.

MINT NRMT
COMPLETE SET (200) 15.00 6.75
1 Pete Maravich BK 1.50 .70
2 Chris Jackson BK .50 .23
3 Y.A. Tittle .75 .35
4 Ricky Blanton BK .25 .11
5 Charles Alexander .05 .02
6 Joe Dean BK .15 .07
7 Billy Cannon .25 .11
8 Dalton Hilliard .25 .11
9 Bert Jones .40 .18
10 Tommy Hodson .25 .11
11 Dale Brown CO BK .40 .18
12 Mike Archer CO F .15 .07
13 Jimmy Taylor .40 .18
14 John Williams BK .25 .11
15 Brian Kinchen .25 .11
16 Chris Carrier .05 .02
17 Jess Fatheree .05 .02
18 Chris Jackson BK .25 .11
19 Orlando McDaniel TRACK .05 .02
20 Billy Hendrix .05 .02
21 Eddie Ray .05 .02
22 Glenn Hansen BK .05 .02
23 Bo Strange .05 .02
24 Eric Hill .25 .11
25 Leonard Mitchell BK .05 .02
26 Larry Shipp TRACK .05 .02
27 Malcolm Scott .05 .02
28 A.J. Duhe .25 .11
29 George Brancato .05 .02
30 Jim Roshso .05 .02
31 Karl Wilson .25 .11
32 Ethan Martin BK .05 .02
33 Julie Gross WBK .05 .02
34 Lyman White .05 .02
35 Eddie Palubinskas BK .05 .02
36 Michael Brooks .25 .11
37 Frank Brian BK .05 .02
38 Gaynell Tinsley .10 .05
39 Mike Anderson .05 .02
40 Howard Carter BK .15 .07
41 Jerry Stovall .25 .11
42 Nikita Wilson BK .15 .07
43 Bill Fortier .05 .02
44 Mike V-Mascot .10 .05
45 Richard Granier .05 .02
46 DeWayne Scales BK .10 .05
47 Pinky Rohm .05 .02
48 Moore Stadium TRACK .05 .02
49 Toby Caston .25 .11
50 Durand Macklin BK .15 .07
51 John Ed Bradley .05 .02
52 Mark Lumpkin .05 .02
53 Joyce Walker WBK .05 .02
54 Bobby Lowther BK .05 .02
55 Al Sanders BK .05 .02
56 Curt Gore .05 .02
57 Eric Martin .25 .11
58 George Nattin BK .05 .02

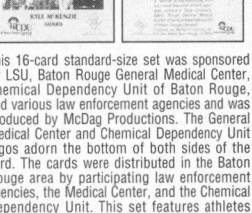

59 Roland Barray .05 .02
60 Craig Duhe .05 .02
61 Maree Jackson WBK .05 .02
62 Sparky Wade BK .05 .02
63 Karl Dunbar .10 .05
64 Mike Williams .05 .02
65 Al Green BK .05 .02
66 Lew Sibley .05 .02
67 John Sage .05 .02
68 Craig Burns .05 .02
69 Schwoonda Williams TRACK .05 .02
70 Wendell Davis .25 .11
71 Dick Maile BK .05 .02
72 Kenny Bordelon .05 .02
73 Rusty Jackson .05 .02
74 Pete Maravich BK 1.50 .70
75 Garry James .25 .11
76 Lance Smith .10 .05
77 Willie Teal .10 .05
78 John Wood .05 .02
79 Mike Robichaux .05 .02
80 Earl Leggett .10 .05
81 Alex Box Stadium .05 .02
82 Steve Cassidy .05 .02
83 Kenny Konz .10 .05
84 Wendell Harris .15 .07
85 Alan Risher .05 .02
86 Gerald Keigley .05 .02
87 Robert Dugas .05 .02
88 Chris Williams .05 .02
89 John DeMarie .05 .02
90 Eddie Fuller .05 .02
91 Chris Jackson BK .50 .23
92 Bo Harris .10 .05
93 Mel Lyle .05 .02
94 Greg Jackson .25 .11
95 Liffort Hobley .15 .07
96 Shawn Burks .05 .02
97 David Browndyke .10 .05
98 Jerry Reynolds BK .25 .11
99 Eric Andolsek .25 .11
100 Checklist Card 1-99 .05 .02
101 Jon Streete .05 .02
102 Barry Wilson .05 .02
103 Remi Prudhomme .10 .05
104 Abe Mickal .05 .02
105 Henry Thomas .40 .18
106 George Tarasovic .05 .02
107 Tiger Stadium .15 .07
108 Benjy Thibodeaux .05 .02
109 Jeffery Dale .05 .02
110 Sid Fournet .05 .02
111 John Adams .05 .02
112 Dennis Gaubatz .10 .05
113 Ben McDonald BB .40 .18
114 Joe Tuminello .05 .02
115 Billy Truax .15 .07
116 Warren Rabb .10 .05
117 Albert Richardson .05 .02
118 Jay Whitey .05 .02
119 Clinton Burrell RB .10 .05
120 Mike Miley BB .15 .07
121 Tommy Casanova .25 .11
122 George Bevan .05 .02
123 Binks Miciotto .05 .02
124 Joe Michaelson .05 .02
125 Mickey Mangham .05 .02
126 Ronnie Estay .05 .02
127 John Hazard .05 .02
128 Darrell Phillips .05 .02
129 Nacho Albergamo .05 .02
130 John Garlington .15 .07
131 Arthur Cantrelle .05 .02
132 Monk Guillot .05 .02
133 Gene Knight .05 .02
134 Gerry Kent .05 .02
135 Ron Sancho .05 .02
136 Kenny Higgs BK .10 .05
137 Billy Cannon .15 .07
138 Bob Pettit BK .75 .35
139 Mike Vincent .05 .02
140 Tyler LaFauci .05 .02
141 Richard Brooks .05 .02
142 Billy Booth .05 .02
143 Brad Davis .05 .02
144 Roy Winston .10 .05
145 Andy Hamilton .10 .05
146 Rene Bourgeois .05 .02
147 Terry Robiskie .15 .07
148 Godfrey Zaunbrecher .05 .02
149 George Atiyeh .05 .02
150 Billy Hardin TRACK .05 .02
151 Jeff Wickersham .15 .07
152 Charlie McClendon CO .10 .05
153 Hokie Gajan .25 .11
154 Pete Maravich Center BK .15 .07
155 Bill Arnsparger CO .15 .07
156 Max Fuglar .25 .11
157 Greg Lafleur .05 .02
158 George Rice .05 .02
159 Dave McCormick .05 .02
160 Fred Miller .05 .02
161 Steve Van Buren .50 .23
162 Sid Bowman TRACK .05 .02
163 Wes Grisham BB .05 .02
164 Jack Torrance TRACK .05 .02
165 Buddy Blair BK .05 .02
166 Doug Moreau .10 .05
167 Mike DeMarie .05 .02
168 James Britt .05 .02
169 Matt DeFrank .05 .02
170 Al Moreau TRACK .05 .02
171 Joe Bill Padcock BK .05 .02
172 Pat Screen .05 .02
173 Ralph Norwood .10 .05
174 Marcus Quinn .05 .02
175 Johnny Robinson .25 .11
176 Tony Moss .05 .02
177 Dan Alexander .05 .02
178 Norman Jefferson .05 .02
179 Bert Jones .40 .18
180 Joe LaBruzzo .05 .02
181 Jimmy Field .05 .02
182 David Woodley .15 .07
183 Paul Dietzel CO .15 .07
184 Abner Wimbley CO .05 .02
185 Steve Ensminger .05 .02
186 Carlos Carson .25 .11
187 Ken Kavnaugh Sr. CO .05 .02
188 Paul Ziegler .05 .02
189 Chris Jackson BK .50 .23
190 Chris Jackson BK .50 .23
191 W.T. Robinson Tennis .05 .02
192 Donnie Leaycraft TEN .05 .02
193 Fernando Perez TEN .05 .02
194 Steve Faulk TEN .05 .02
195 Warren Capone .05 .02
196 Howard Carter BK .15 .07
197 Glenn Hansen BK .05 .02
198 Durand Macklin BK .15 .07
199 Sam Grezaffi .10 .05
200 Checklist Card .05 .02

1986-87 Maine *

This 14-card set of Maine Black Bears is part of a "Kids and Kops" promotion, and one card was printed each Saturday in the Bangor Daily News. The cards measure approximately 2 1/2" by 4". The cards were to be collected from any participating plice officer. Once five cards had been collected (including card number 1), they could be turned in at a police station for a University of Maine ID card, which permitted free admission to selected university activities. When all 14 cards had been collected, they could be turned in at a police station to register for the Grand Prize drawing (bicycle) and to pick up a free "Kids and Kops" tee-shirt. The backs have tips in the form of an anti-drug or alcohol message and logos of Burger King, University of Maine and Pepsi across the bottom. With the exception of the rules card, the cards are numbered on the back.

MINT NRMT
COMPLETE SET (14) 15.00 6.75
1 Bananas Mascot 1.00 .45
2 Jack Capuano HK 1.00 .45
3 Amadou Coco Barry BK 1.00 .45
4 Doug Dorsey FB 1.00 .45
5 Dan Kane BB 1.00 .45
6 Michelle Duprey Softball 1.00 .45
7 Tina Ouellette Field Hockey 1.00 .45
8 Jeff Plympton BB 1.50 .70
9 Jim Boylen BK 1.00 .45
10 Bob Wilder FB 1.00 .45
11 Eric Weinrich HK 4.00 1.80
12 Lynn Hearty Softball 1.00 .45
13 Matt Rossignoi BK 1.00 .45
NNO Matt Rossignol BK 1.00 .45
Kids and Kops Rules

1987-88 Maine *

This 14-card set of Maine Black Bears is part of a "Kids and Kops" promotion, and one card was printed each Saturday in the Bangor Daily News. The cards measure approximately 2 1/2" by 4". The cards were to be collected from any participating police officer. Once five cards had been collected (including card number 1), they could be turned in at a police station for a University of Maine ID card, which permitted free admission to selected university activities. When all 14 cards had been collected, they could be turned in at a police station to register for the Grand Prize drawing (bicycle) and to pick up a free "Kids and Kops" tee-shirt. The backs have tips in the form of an anti-drug or alcohol message and logos of Burger King, University of Maine, and Pepsi across the bottom. With the exception of the rules card, the cards are numbered on the back. Sports represented in this set include hockey (2), basketball (3, 9, 13), tennis (4), baseball (5), swimming (6), soccer (7), track (8), football (10), field hockey (11), and softball (12).

MINT NRMT
COMPLETE SET (14) 15.00 6.75
1 Bananas (Mascot) and 5.00 2.20
K.C. Jones CO BK
2 Mike McHugh HK 2.00 .90
3 Matt Rossignoi BK 1.00 .45
4 Cindy Sprague Tennis 1.00 .45
5 Gary LaPierre BB 1.00 .45
6 Dana Billington Swimming 1.00 .45
7 Scott Atherley Soccer 1.00 .45
8 Elke Brutsaert Track 1.00 .45
9 Elizabeth(Liz) Coffin BK 1.00 .45
10 David Ingalls FB 1.00 .45
11 Wendy J. Nadeau Field Hockey 1.00 .45
12 Stacy Caron Softball 1.00 .45
13 Amadou Coco Barry BK 1.00 .45
NNO Matt Rossignoi BK 1.00 .45
Kids and Kops Rules

1989 McNeese State *

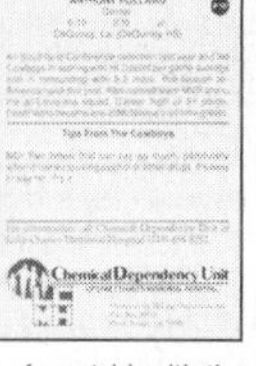

This 16-card standard-size set was sponsored by the Behavioral Health Unit of Lake Charles Memorial Hospital, and the sponsor's logo appears at the bottom of both sides of the card. This set was produced by McDag Productions. The front features a color posed player photo, with the McNeese logo and player information in the upper corners. The back presents biographical information and "Tips from The Cowboys," which consist of mental health tips. Sports represented in this set include basketball (1-6, 9-12), softball (7), golf (8), and baseball (13-15). Card number 13 Steve Boulet was missing from a number of sets and is believed to be somewhat tougher to find than other cards in the set.

MINT NRMT
COMPLETE SET (16) 10.00 4.50
1 Kevin Williams .75 .35
2 Terry Griggley .50 .23
3 Tab Harris .50 .23
4 Chandra Davis 1.00 .45
5 Tom McGrath .50 .23
6 Angie Perry 1.00 .45
7 Christine Lee .50 .23
8 Lawrence David 1.50 .70
9 Michael Cutright 1.00 .45
10 Anthony Pullard 1.50 .70
11 Mark Thompson .50 .23
12 Kim Turner .50 .23
13 Steve Boulet SP 1.50 .70
14 Charlie Phillips .50 .23
15 Mark Bowling .50 .23
16 David J. Drez .50 .23
Team Physician

1997 Miami (OH) Cradle of Coaches *

This set was produced by American Marketing Associates and features coaching greats from the University of Miami in Ohio. Football is the focus of the set although it also contains a few coaches from other sports as noted below. The cards are unnumbered and checklisted below in alphabetical order.

MINT NRMT
COMPLETE SET (19) 20.00 9.00
1 Walter Alston BB 2.00 .90
2 Bill Arnsparger 1.00 .45
3 Paul Brown 4.00 1.80
4 Carmen Cozza 1.00 .45
5 Dick Crum 1.00 .45
6 Paul Dietzel 2.00 .90
7 Wayne Embry BK 2.00 .90
8 Weeb Ewbank 3.00 1.35
9 Sid Gillman 3.00 1.35
10 Woody Hayes 4.00 1.80
11 Darrell Hedric BK 1.00 .45
12 Bill Mallory 1.00 .45
13 John McVay 1.00 .45
14 Ara Parseghian 3.00 1.35
15 John Pont 1.00 .45
16 Bo Schembechler 3.00 1.35
17 Richard Shrider BK 1.00 .45
18 Checklist 1.00 .45
19 Title Art Card 1.00 .45

1991 Michigan *

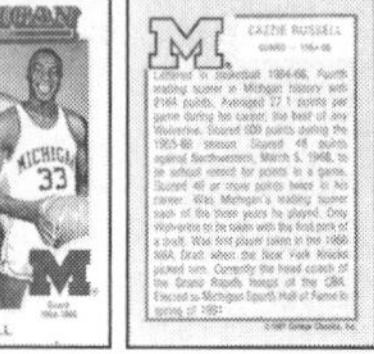

This 56-card multi-sport standard-size set was issued by College Classics. The fronts feature a mix of color or black and white player photos. This set features a card of Gerald Ford, center for the Wolverine football squad from 1932-34. Ford autographed 200 of his cards, one of which was to be included in each of the 200 cases of 50 sets. A letter of authenticity on Gerald Ford stationery accompanies each Ford autographed card. No price has been established for the Ford signed card. The cards are unnumbered and we have checklisted them below according to alphabetical order.

MINT NRMT
COMPLETE SET (56) 20.00 9.00
1 Jim Abbott B .75 .35
2 Moby Benedict B .10 .05
3 Red Berenson H .25 .11
4 John Blum H .10 .05
5 Marty Bodnar K .10 .05
6 Dave Brown F .10 .05
7 M.C. Burton K .10 .05
8 Andy Cannavino F .10 .05
9 Anthony Carter F .75 .35
10 Gil Chapman F .10 .05
11 Bob Chappuis F .10 .05
12 Casey Close B .10 .05
13 Evan Cooper F .10 .05
14 Tom Curtis F .10 .05
15 Diane Dietz WBK .10 .05
16 Dean Dingman F .25 .11
17 Mark Donahue F .10 .05
18 Donald Dufek CO F .25 .11
19 Bump Elliott F .25 .11
20 Greg Everson B .10 .05
21 Gerald Ford F 2.50 1.10
22 Wally Grant H .10 .05
23 Curtis Greer F .25 .11
24 Ali Haji-Sheikh F .25 .11
25 Elroy Hirsch F 1.00 .45
26 Stefan Humphries F .10 .05
27 Phil Hubbard K .75 .35
28 Ron Johnson F .75 .35
29 Brad Jones H .10 .05
30 Eric Kattus F .10 .05
31 Ron Kramer F .25 .11
32 Barry Larkin B 3.00 1.35
33 Michael Leach TEN .10 .05
34 Jim Mandich F .75 .35
35 Wilf Martin H .10 .05
36 Tim McCormick K .25 .11
37 Hal Morris B .75 .35
38 Jeff Norton H .10 .05
39 Frank Nunley F .25 .11
40 Calvin O'Neal F .10 .05
41 Steve Ontiveros B .25 .11
42 Bennie Oosterbaan F .50 .23
43 Richard Rellford K .10 .05
44 Steve Richmond H .10 .05
45 Cazzie Russell K .75 .35
46 Chris Sabo B .75 .35
47 Alicia Seegert SOFT .10 .05
48 Warren Sharples H .10 .05
49 Ted Sizemore B .25 .11
50 Lary Sorensen B .25 .11
51 Bob Timberlake F .25 .11
52 Rudy Tomjanovich K 1.50 .70
53 John Wangler F .10 .05
54 Gary Wayne B .25 .11
55 Tripp Welborne F .25 .11
56 Albert Wistert .10 .05
Alvin Wistert
Francis Wistert
AU21 Gerald Ford AU

1990-91 Michigan State Collegiate Collection 200 *

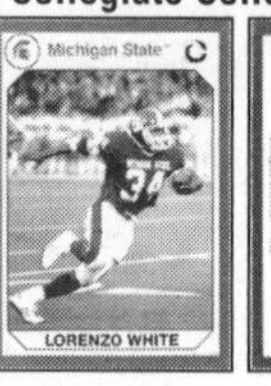

This 200-card standard-size set was produced by Collegiate Collection. The fronts feature black and white shots for earlier players or color shots for later players, with borders in the team's colors white and green. Since most cards are football, we've noted below which cards feature other sports. Although some players were famous in others sports, like Kirk Gibson and Steve Garvey, they do have football cards in this set.

MINT NRMT
COMPLETE SET (200) 15.00 6.75
1 Ray Stachowicz .05 .02
2 Larry Fowler .05 .02
3 Allen Brenner .05 .02
4 Greg Montgomery .15 .07
5 Ron Goovert .05 .02
6 Ed Bagdon .05 .02
7 Carl(Buck) Nystrom .05 .02
8 Earl Lattimer .05 .02
9 Bob Kula .05 .02
10 James Ellis .05 .02
11 Brad Van Pelt FB .25 .11
12 Andre Rison FB .40 .18
13 Sherman Lewis FB .10 .05
14 Eric Allen .05 .02
15 Robert Apisa .15 .07
16 Earl Morrall FB .25 .11
17 Danny Litwhiler CO BB .10 .05
18 Harold Lucas .05 .02
19 Lorenzo White FB .25 .11
20 Dorne Dibble .05 .02
21 Ronald Saul FB .10 .05
22 Ed Budde FB .10 .05
23 Gene Washington FB .25 .11
24 John S. Pingel .05 .02
25 Morten Andersen FB .40 .18
26 Lynn Chandnois FB .25 .11
27 Don Coleman .05 .02
28 Dave Behrman .05 .02
29 Bill Simpson .05 .02
30 LeRoy Bolden .05 .02
31 Lorenzo White FB .25 .11
32 Sidney P. Wagner .05 .02
33 Ellis Duckett .05 .02
34 Dick Tamburo .05 .02
35 Gerald Planutis .05 .02
36 Steve Juday .05 .02
37 Everett Grandelius .05 .02
38 Robert Apisa .25 .11
Clint Jones
Bubba Smith
Gene Washington
George Webster FB
39 George Perles CO FB .10 .05
40 Mark Brammer .05 .02
41 James Burroughs .05 .02
42 Harlon Barnett .15 .07
43 Charles(Bubba) Smith FB .40 .18
44 Percy Snow FB .10 .05
45 Norman Masters .05 .02
46 Jerry West .05 .02
47 Sam Williams .10 .05
Duffy Daugherty CO FB
48 Tom Yewcic FB .10 .05
49 Kirk Gibson FB .25 .11
50 Clinton Jones .25 .11
51 Frank E. Pellerin CO BB .05 .02
52 Don(Zippy) Thompson HK .05 .02
53 Kirk Gibson BB .25 .11
54 Edward Erickson BB .05 .02
55 Doug Roberts HK .05 .02
56 Percy Snow .10 .05
57 Dick Idzkowski .05 .02
58 Robert W.(Bob) Carey .05 .02
59 Clarence Biggie Munn CO .05 .02
60 Dan Currie .10 .05
61 Al Dorow .10 .05
62 Amo Bessone CO BK .05 .02
63 Joe DeLamielleure FB .25 .11
64 Tom Ross HK .05 .02
65 Steve Preston BB .05 .02
66 Kirk Gibson .25 .11
Steve Garvey BB
67 Eric Allen .05 .02
68 George Smith BB .05 .02
69 John Chandik HK .05 .02
70 Cordell Ross BB .05 .02
71 George Saimes FB .15 .07
72 Walt Kowalczyk .05 .02
73 Billy Joe Dupree FB .25 .11
74 Phil Fulton BB .05 .02
75 Weldon Olson HK .05 .02
76 Kirk Gibson FB .25 .11
77 Andre Rison FB .40 .18
78 Dean Look FB .10 .05
79 Hugh(Duffy) Daugherty CO FB .25 .11
80 Don McAuliffe .10 .05
81 Ronald Curl .05 .02
82 Percy Snow FB .10 .05
83 Carl Banks FB .25 .11
84 Joe Selinger HK .05 .02
85 Mel Behney BB .05 .02
86 Lorenzo White FB .25 .11
87 Ron Pruitt BB .10 .05
88 George Webster FB .25 .11
89 Tony Mandarich FB .10 .05
90 Ray Stachowicz .05 .02
91 Blake Miller .05 .02
92 Billy Joe DuPree .25 .11
Brad Van Pelt
Duffy Daugherty CO FB
93 Morten Andersen FB .40 .18
94 Kevin Dalson BB .05 .02
95 Norm Barnes HK .05 .02
96 Andre Rison FB .40 .18
97 Craig Simpson HK .15 .07
98 Kirk Gibson .25 .11
99 Ralf Mojsiejenko FB .10 .05
100 Checklist Card 1-99 .05 .02
101 Michael Robinson BK .05 .02
102 Jack Quiggle BK .05 .02
103 Robert Anderegg BK .05 .02
104 Rick Miller BB .05 .02
105 Steve Garvey FB .25 .11
106 John Herman Kobs CO BB .05 .02
107 Steve Garvey BB .25 .11
108 Vernon Carr .05 .02
109 Albert R. Ferrari .05 .02
110 Lance Olson .05 .02
111 Lee Lafayette .05 .02
112 Gregory Kelser BK .15 .07
113 Stan Washington .05 .02
114 Ron Perranoski BB .25 .11
115 Doug Volmar .05 .02
116 Robert Clancy .05 .02
117 Bob Boyd .10 .05
118 Lindsay Hairston .05 .02
119 Kevin Willis BK .25 .11
120 Bill Rapchak .05 .02
121 Marcus Sanders .05 .02
122 Mike Brkovich .05 .02
123 Jay Vincent BK .10 .05
124 Ron Scott .05 .02
125 Craig Simpson .10 .05
126 Mike Davidson .05 .02
127 Jim Watt .05 .02
128 Johnny Green BK .25 .11
129 Robert Chapman .05 .02
130 Pete Gent FB .25 .11
131 Magic Johnson BK 1.00 .45
132 Gregory Kelser BK .15 .07
133 Magic Johnson BK 1.00 .45
134 Bobby Reynolds .05 .02
135 Joe Murphy .25 .11
136 Mike Donnelly .05 .02
137 Bob Essensa HK .25 .11
138 Kevin Smith .05 .02
139 Kirk Manns .05 .02
140 Scott Skiles BK .25 .11
141 Matthew Aitch .05 .02
142 Rudy Benjamin .05 .02
143 Michael Robinson .05 .02
144 Kip Miller .15 .07
145 Kelly Miller .25 .11
146 Ron Mason CO .05 .02
147 Dan McFall .05 .02
148 Sam Vincent BK .10 .05
149 Carlton Valentine .05 .02
150 Ron Charles .05 .02
151 John Bennington .05 .02
152 Scott Skiles BK .25 .11
153 William Kilgore .05 .02
154 Dick Holmes .05 .02
155 Steven Colp .05 .02
156 Robert Ellis .05 .02
157 Brian Wolcott .05 .02
158 Ken Redfield .05 .02
159 Jud Heathcote CO BK .25 .11
160 Dave Fahs .05 .02
161 Pete Newell CO BK .25 .11
162 Larry Polec .05 .02
163 Kevin Willis BK .25 .11
164 Gaye Cooley .05 .02
165 Richard Vary .05 .02
166 Al Weston .05 .02
167 Scott Makarewicz .05 .02
168 Darryl Johnson .05 .02
169 Derek Perry .05 .02
170 Ralph Simpson BK .15 .07
171 Terry Furlow BK .10 .05
172 Forrest Anderson .05 .02
173 Ted Williams .05 .02
174 Dan Masteller .10 .05
175 Brad Lamont Jr. .05 .02
176 Steve Garvey BB .25 .11
177 Mike Eddington .05 .02
178 Jud Heathcote CO BK .25 .11
179 Kevin Willis BK .25 .11
180 Ben Van Alstyne .05 .02
181 Chet Aubuchon .05 .02
182 Magic Johnson BK 1.00 .45
183 Larry Hedden .05 .02
184 Larry Ike .05 .02
185 Frank Kush FB .10 .05
186 Magic Johnson BK 1.00 .45
187 Mitch Messier .05 .02
188 Julius McCoy .05 .02
189 Magic Johnson BK 1.00 .45
190 Forrest Anderson .05 .02
191 Gus Ganakas .05 .02
192 Jay Vincent BK .10 .05
193 Horace Walker .05 .02
194 Magic Johnson BK 1.00 .45
195 Tom Smith .05 .02

Card		
196 Don McSween	.05	.02
197 Rod Brind'Amour HK	.50	.23
198 Sam Vincent BK	.10	.05
199 Terry Donnelly BK	.10	.05
200 Checklist Card 101-199	.05	.02

1990-91 Michigan State Collegiate Collection Promos *

This ten-card standard size set features some of the great athletes from Michigan State History. Most of the cards in the set feature an action photograph on the front of the card along with either statistical or biographical information on the back of the card. Since this set involves more than one sport we have put a two-letter abbreviation to indicate the sport played.

	MINT	NRMT
COMPLETE SET (10)	4.00	1.80
1 Ron Scott HK	.10	.05
2 Steve Garvey BB	.75	.35
3 Percy Snow FB	.25	.11
4 Magic Johnson BK	2.50	1.10
5 Andre Rison FB	.75	.35
6 Lorenzo White FB	.10	.05
7 Kirk Gibson FB/BB	.75	.35
8 Tony Mandarich FB	.10	.05
9 Gregory Kelser BK	.50	.23
10 Kip Miller HK	.25	.11

1984-85 Nebraska *

This 31-card multi-sport set was distributed by the Lincoln Police Department. The cards measure approximately 2 1/4" by 3 5/8" and are printed on thin card stock. The sports represented are football (1-10), volleyball (11-12), gymnastics (13-15), basketball (16-19), baseball (20-24, 26, 28, 30), and track (25, 27, 29, 31).

	NRMT	VG-E
COMPLETE SET (31)	40.00	18.00
1 Mark Traynowicz	2.00	.90
2 Tom Osborne CO	15.00	6.75
3 Jeff Smith	3.00	1.35
4 Scott Strasburger	2.00	.90
5 Craig Sundberg	1.00	.45
6 Bill Weber	1.00	.45
7 Shane Swanson	1.00	.45
8 Neil Harris	1.00	.45
9 Mark Behning	2.00	.90
10 Dave Burke	1.00	.45
11 Mary Buysee	1.00	.45
12 Cathy Noth	1.00	.45
13 Terri Furman	1.00	.45
14 Char Hagamann	1.00	.45
15 Wes Suter	1.00	.45
16 Dave Hoppen	3.00	1.35
17 Debra Powell	1.00	.45
18 Ronnie Smith	2.00	.90
19 Angie Miller	1.00	.45
20 Bill McGuire	1.50	.70
21 Paul Meyers	1.00	.45
22 Jeff Carter	2.00	.90
23 Kurt Eubanks	1.00	.45
24 Mori Emmons	1.00	.45
25 Glen Cunningham	1.00	.45
26 Denise Eckert	1.00	.45
27 Angela Thacker	1.00	.45
28 Ann Schroeder	1.00	.45
29 Darren Burton	1.00	.45
30 Lori Sippel	1.00	.45
31 Rhonda Blanford	1.00	.45

1985-86 Nebraska *

This 37-card multi-sport set measuring 2 1/2" by 4" has on the fronts color action and posed player photos enclosed by a red border. The sports represented are football (2-11), volleyball (12, 14), gymnastics (13, 15-17), track (18, 20, 29-30), basketball (19, 21, 23, 26), baseball (20-24, 31-37), and swimming (22, 24, 27-28). The cards are numbered on the back. The key cards in the set are NBA draftee Rich King and NFL running back Tom Rathman.

	NRMT	VG-E
COMPLETE SET (37)	40.00	18.00
1 Title Card	1.50	.70
2 Doug DuBose	1.50	.70
3 Marc Munford	1.00	.45
4 Travis Turner	1.00	.45
5 Mike Knox	1.00	.45
6 Todd Frain	1.00	.45
7 Danny Noonan	2.50	1.10
8 Tom Rathman	8.00	3.60
9 Jim Skow	2.50	1.10
10 Stan Parker	1.00	.45
11 Bill Lewis	1.50	.70
12 Michelle Smith	1.00	.45
13 Wes Suter	1.00	.45
14 Karen Dahlgren	1.00	.45
15 Renee Gould	1.00	.45
16 Neil Palmer	1.00	.45
17 Racine Smith	1.00	.45
18 Gerard O'Callaghan	1.00	.45
19 Moe Iba CO	2.50	1.10
20 Angela Thacker	1.00	.45
21 Stacy Imming	1.00	.45
22 Ernie Duran	1.00	.45
23 Dave Hoppen	2.00	.90
24 Emily Ricketts	1.00	.45
25 Maurice Ivy	1.00	.45
26 Brian Carr	1.00	.45
27 Ed Jowdy	1.00	.45
28 Erin Hurley	1.00	.45
29 Von Sheppard	1.00	.45
30 Laura Wight	1.00	.45
31 Lori Sippel	1.00	.45
32 Paul Meyers	1.00	.45
33 Donna Deardorff	1.00	.45
34 Larry Mimms	1.00	.45
35 Lori Richins	1.00	.45
36 Rich King	2.50	1.10
37 Amy Love	1.00	.45

1986-87 Nebraska *

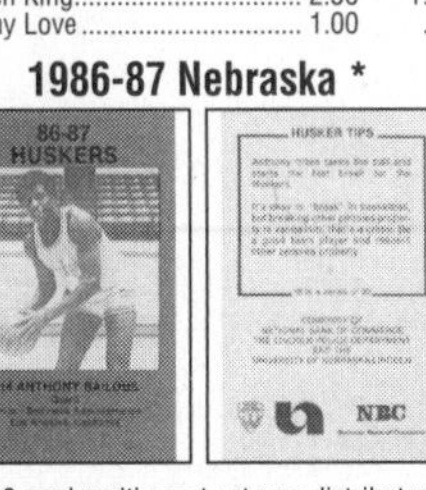

This 30-card multi-sport set was distributed by the Lincoln Police Department. The cards measure approximately 2 1/2" by 4" and are printed on thin card stock.

	MINT	NRMT
COMPLETE SET (30)	40.00	18.00
1 Bob Devaney McGruff the Crime Dog	4.00	1.80
2 Doug DuBose	2.50	1.10
3 Marc Munford	1.50	.70
4 Von Sheppard	1.50	.70
5 Dale Klein	1.50	.70
6 Robb Schnitzler	1.50	.70
7 Chris Spachman	1.50	.70
8 Brian Davis	1.50	.70
9 Ken Kaelin	1.50	.70
10 Karen Dahlgren	1.50	.70
11 Tisha Delaney	1.50	.70
12 Brian Carr	1.50	.70
13 Angie Miller	1.50	.70
14 Bill Jackman	1.50	.70
15 Maurtice Ivy	1.50	.70
16 Anthony Bailous	1.50	.70
17 Jeaneane Smith	1.50	.70
18 Neil Palmer	1.50	.70
19 Crystal Savage	1.50	.70
20 Tom Schlesinger	1.50	.70
21 John Hastings	1.50	.70
22 Jill Noel	1.50	.70
23 Regis Humphrey	1.50	.70
24 Tammy Thurman	1.50	.70
25 Lori Richins	1.50	.70
26 Todd Bunge	1.50	.70
27 Rhonda Gorraiz	1.50	.70
28 Jeff Taylor	1.50	.70
29 Marlys Handley	1.50	.70
30 Bruce Wobken	1.50	.70

1987-88 Nebraska *

This 26-card multi-sport set was distributed by the Lincoln Police Department. The cards measure approximately 2 1/2" by 4" and is printed on this cardboard stock.

	MINT	NRMT
COMPLETE SET (26)	40.00	18.00
1 Keith Jones	1.50	.70
2 Broderick Thomas	4.00	1.80
3 Dana Brinson	1.50	.70
4 John McCormick	1.50	.70
5 Steve Taylor	1.50	.70
6 Lee Jones	1.50	.70
7 Rod Smith	1.50	.70
8 Neil Smith	8.00	3.60
9 Kathi Deboer	1.50	.70
10 Virginia Stahr	1.50	.70
11 Henry T. Buchanan	1.50	.70
12 Maurtice Ivy	1.50	.70
13 Derrick Vick	1.50	.70
14 Stephanie Bolli	1.50	.70
15 Jeff Rekeweg	1.50	.70
16 Amy Stephens	1.50	.70
17 Beth Webster	1.50	.70
18 Regis Humphrey	1.50	.70
19 Linetta Wilson	1.50	.70
20 Terry Goods	1.50	.70
21 Ken Ramos	1.50	.70
22 Lori Sippel	1.50	.70
23 John Lepley	1.50	.70
24 Leeanna Miles	1.50	.70
25 Rocky Johnson	1.50	.70
26 Jane Kremer	1.50	.70

1988-89 Nebraska *

This 33-card multi-sport set measures approximately 2 1/2" by 4" and is printed on thin cardboard stock. The fronts feature black-and-white player action photos on a red card face. In black lettering the words "88- 89 Huskers" appear over the picture, while the player's name and other information are printed beneath the picture. The backs carry "Husker Tips," which consist of comments about the players combined with crime prevention tips. Sponsor names and logos at the bottom round out the back. The sports represented in this set are: football (1-9), volleyball (10- 11), gymnastics (12-15), basketball (16-21), track (22-25), baseball (26, 28, 30, 32), and softball (27, 29, 31, 33).

	MINT	NRMT
COMPLETE SET (33)	40.00	18.00
1 Steve Taylor	1.50	.70
2 Broderick Thomas	4.00	1.80
3 LaRoy Etienne	1.50	.70
4 Tyreese Knox	1.50	.70
5 Mark Blazek	1.50	.70
6 Charles Fryar	1.50	.70
7 Tim Jackson	1.50	.70
8 Andy Keeler	1.50	.70
9 John Kroeker	1.50	.70
10 Lori Endicott	4.00	1.80
11 Virginia Stahr	1.50	.70
12 Mike Epperson	1.50	.70
13 Crystal Savage	1.50	.70
14 Patrick Kirksey	1.50	.70
15 Jeaneane Smith	1.50	.70
16 Eric Johnson	1.50	.70
17 Amy Stephens	1.50	.70
18 Pete Manning	1.50	.70
19 Kim Harris	1.50	.70
20 Richard Van Poelgeest	1.50	.70
21 Amy Bullock	1.50	.70
22 James Morris	1.50	.70
23 Toyia Barnes	1.50	.70
24 Frank Graham	1.50	.70
25 Linetta Wilson	1.50	.70
26 Ken Sirak	1.50	.70
27 Jane Kremer	1.50	.70
28 Pat Leinen	1.50	.70
29 Ruth Chatwin	1.50	.70
30 Bruce Wobken	1.50	.70
31 Janelle Frese	1.50	.70
32 Bobby Benjamin	1.50	.70
33 Mary(Katy) Wolda	1.50	.70

1989-90 Nebraska *

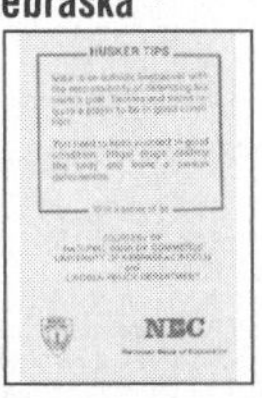

This 33-card multi-sport set measures approximately 2 1/2" by 4" and is printed on thin cardboard stock. The fronts feature color player action photos on a red card face. In black lettering the words "89-90 Huskers" appear over the picture, while the player's name and other information are printed beneath the picture. The backs carry "Husker Tips," which consist of comments about the players combined with crime prevention tips. Sponsor names and logos at the bottom round out the back. Two cards are not labeled (26 and 30) because we do not have the complete checklist. If any collector can help out, we would appreciate it.

	MINT	NRMT
COMPLETE SET (33)	40.00	18.00
1 Ken Clark	1.50	.70
2 Reggie Cooper	2.00	.90
3 Gerry Gdowski	1.50	.70
4 Monte Kratzenstein	1.50	.70
5 Gregg Barrios	1.50	.70
6 Morgan Gregory	1.50	.70
7 Jeff Mills	1.50	.70
8 Richard Bell	1.50	.70
9 Jake Young	1.50	.70
10 Mike Croel	4.00	1.80
11 Bryan Carpenter	1.50	.70
12 Kent Wells	1.50	.70
13 Sam Schmidt	1.50	.70
14 Virginia Stahr	1.50	.70
15 Carla Baker	1.50	.70
16 Patrick Kirksey	1.50	.70
17 Tami Bair	1.50	.70
18 Bob Stelter	1.50	.70
19 Michele Bryant	1.50	.70
20 Ray Richardson	1.50	.70
21 Ann Halsne	1.50	.70
22 Clifford Scales	2.50	1.10
23 Kelly Hubert	1.50	.70
24 Richard Van Poelgeest	1.50	.70
25 Kim Yancey	1.50	.70
27 Jill Rishel	1.50	.70
28 Dale Kistaitis	1.50	.70
29 Marie Bowie	1.50	.70
31 Lori Cook	1.50	.70
32 Mike Zajeski	1.50	.70
33 Joy Rishel	1.50	.70

1990-91 Nebraska *

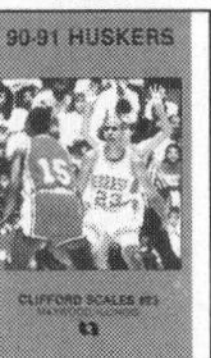

This 28-card set was sponsored by the National Bank of Commerce, the University of Nebraska-Lincoln, and the Lincoln Police Department. Sponsors' logos at the bottom round out the back. The sports represented in this set are football (2-13), volleyball (14-15), wrestling (16), gymnastics (17-20), basketball (21-24), softball (25, 27), and baseball (26, 28). The key cards in the set are these players with NFL experience: Mike Croel, Bruce Pickens, and Kenny Walker.

	MINT	NRMT
COMPLETE SET (28)	30.00	13.50
1 Bob Devaney AD	3.00	1.35
2 Reggie Cooper	1.50	.70
3 Terry Rodgers	1.50	.70
4 Kenny Walker	2.00	.90
5 Gregg Barrios	1.50	.70
6 Mike Croel	2.00	.90
7 Tom Punt	1.50	.70
8 Mike Grant	1.50	.70
9 Joe Sims	1.50	.70
10 Mickey Joseph	1.50	.70
11 Lance Lewis	1.50	.70
12 Bruce Pickens	2.00	.90
13 Nate Turner	1.50	.70
14 Linda Barsness	.75	.35
15 Becky Bolli	.75	.35
16 Jason Kelber	.75	.35
17 Brad Bryan	.75	.35
18 Ted Dimas	.75	.35
19 Nita Lichtenstein	.75	.35
20 Lisa McCrady	.75	.35
21 Clifford Scales	1.00	.45
22 Ann Halsne	.75	.35
23 Carl Hayes	1.00	.45
24 Kelly Hubert	.75	.35
25 Deanna Mays	.75	.35
26 Shawn Buchanan	.75	.35
27 Michelle Cuddeford	.75	.35
28 Eddie Anderson	2.00	.90

1991-92 Nebraska *

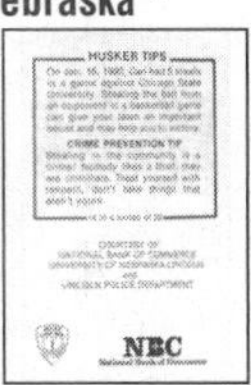

This 22-card multi-sport set was sponsored by the National Bank of Commerce, University of Nebraska, and the Lincoln Police Department. The sports represented are football (1-8), wrestling (9-10), volleyball (11-12), men's basketball (13-14, 16, 18), women's basketball (15, 17, 19), and baseball (20-22).

	MINT	NRMT
COMPLETE SET (22)	30.00	13.50
1 Mickey Joseph	2.00	.90
2 Pat Engelbert	1.50	.70
3 Jon Bostick	1.50	.70
4 Scott Baldwin	2.00	.90
5 Tim Johnk	1.50	.70
6 Tom Haase	1.50	.70
7 Erik Wiegert	1.50	.70
8 Chris Garrett	1.50	.70
9 John Buxton	1.00	.45
10 Chris Nelson	1.00	.45
11 Janet Kruse	1.00	.45
12 Cris Hall	1.00	.45
13 Danny Lee CO	1.50	.70
14 Carl Hayes	1.50	.70
15 Carol Russell	1.00	.45
16 Eric Piatkowski	6.00	2.70
17 Karen Jennings	1.00	.45
18 DaPreis Owens	1.00	.45
19 Sue Hesch	1.00	.45
20 Ann Halsne	1.00	.45
21 Misty Guenther	1.00	.45
22 Kris Vucurevic	1.00	.45

1992-93 Nebraska *

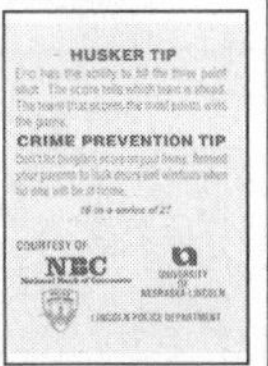

This 27-card multisport set was sponsored by the National Bank of Commerce, the University of Nebraska-Lincoln, and the Lincoln Police Department. The cards measure approximately 2 5/8" by 3 1/2" and are printed on thin card stock. Sponsor names and logos round out the back. The sports represented are football (1-9), women's volleyball (10, 11), basketball (12-17), gymnastics (18-20), track and field, (21-22) and baseball (23-27).

	MINT	NRMT
COMPLETE SET (27)	25.00	11.00
1 Will Shields	1.50	.70
2 Tyrone Hughes	2.50	1.10
3 Kenny Wilhite	1.00	.45
4 William Washington	1.00	.45
5 Mike Stigge	1.00	.45
6 Tyrone Byrd	.75	.35
7 Travis Hill	1.50	.70
8 John Parrella	1.50	.70
9 Jim Scott	1.00	.45
10 Eileen Shannon	.75	.35
11 Stephanie Thater	.75	.35
12 Derrick Chandler	1.00	.45
13 Karen Jennings	.75	.35
14 Jamar Johnson	.75	.35
15 Kristi Anderson	.75	.35
16 Eric Piatkowski	5.00	2.20
17 Rissa Taylor	.75	.35
18 Martha Jenkins	.75	.35
19 Dennis Harrison	.75	.35
20 Lori Phillips	.75	.35
21 Fran Ten Bensel	.75	.35
22 Kevin Coleman	.75	.35
23 Steve Boyd	.75	.35
24 Kris Vucurevic	.75	.35
25 Darin Petersen	.75	.35
26 Denise McMillan	.75	.35
27 Jed Dalton	.75	.35

1993-94 Nebraska *

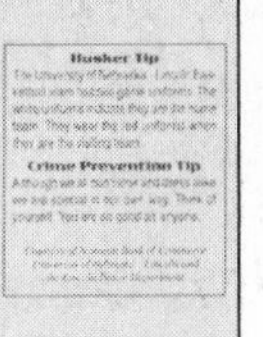

This 25-card multisport standard-size set was jointly sponsored by the National Bank of Commerce, the Lincoln Police Department, and the university. The cards are unnumbered and checklisted below alphabetically within sport as follows: football (1-9), basketball (men [10-11]; women [12-13]), gymnastics (14-17), baseball (18-19), women's softball (20-21), volleyball (22-23), and wrestling (24-25).

	MINT	NRMT
COMPLETE SET (25)	25.00	11.00
1 Trev Alberts	2.50	1.10
2 Mike Anderson	1.00	.45
3 Ernie Beler	1.00	.45
4 Byron Bennett	1.00	.45
5 Corey Dixon	1.00	.45
6 Troy Dumas	1.00	.45
7 Calvin Jones	2.00	.90
8 Bruce Moore	1.00	.45
9 David Noonan	1.50	.70
10 Jamar Johnson	.75	.35
11 Eric Piatkowski	4.00	1.80
12 NaFeesha Brown	.75	.35
13 Meggan Yedsena	.75	.35
14 Sumner Darling	.75	.35
15 Nicole Duval	.75	.35
16 Dennis Harrison	.75	.35
17 Lori Phillips	.75	.35
18 Troy Bromawn	.75	.35
19 Jed Dalton	.75	.35
20 Amy Erlenbusch	.75	.35
21 Denise McMillen	.75	.35
22 Laura Luther	.75	.35
23 Nikki Stricker	.75	.35
24 Mike Eierman	.75	.35
25 Frank Velazquez	.75	.35

1994-95 Nebraska *

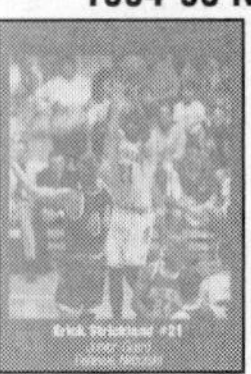
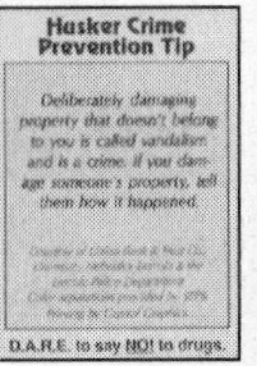

This 21-card multi-sport set was jointly sponsored by Union Bank, the Lincoln Police Department and the university. The unnumbered, attractive, full color cards are slightly wider than standard size and printed on very thin stock. Several sports are featured and are listed below alphabetically within sport as follows: baseball (1-2), men's basketball (3-4), women's basketball (5-6), football (7-14), men's gymnastics (15-16), women's gymnastics (17-18), softball (19) and women's volleyball (20-21). Future NBA player Erick Strickland has his first card in this set.

	MINT	NRMT
COMPLETE SET (21)	30.00	13.50
1 Jed Dalton	.75	.35
2 Darin Peterson	.75	.35
3 Jaron Boone	2.00	.90
4 Erick Strickland	4.00	1.80
5 Emily Thompson	.75	.35
6 Tanya Upthegrove	.75	.35
7 Terry Connealy	1.00	.45
8 Troy Dumas	1.00	.45
9 Donta Jones	2.50	1.10
10 Barron Miles	1.50	.70
11 Cory Schlesinger	4.00	1.80
12 Ed Stewart	1.00	.45
13 Zach Wiegart	2.00	.90
14 Rob Zatechka	1.50	.70
15 Richard Grace	.75	.35
16 Rick Kieffer	.75	.35
17 Nicole Duval	.75	.35
18 Joy Taylor	.75	.35
19 Cody Dusenberry	.75	.35
20 Kelly Aspegren	.75	.35
21 Billie Winsett	.75	.35

1997-98 Nebraska *

This 21-card standard-size set featured players who were seniors at Nebraska. The set features primarily football players, but a variety of other sports as well. We've included initials after each player's name that represent the sport in which they played.

	MINT	NRMT
COMPLETE SET (21)	20.00	9.00
1 Eric Anderson FB	1.50	.70
2 Scott Frost FB	2.50	1.10
3 Matt Hoskinson FB	1.00	.45
4 Vershan Jackson FB	1.00	.45
5 Jason Peter FB	1.50	.70
6 Fred Pollack FB	1.00	.45
7 Aaron Taylor FB	1.00	.45
8 Eric Warfield FB	1.50	.70
9 Grant Wistrom FB	2.50	1.10
10 Jon Zatechka FB	1.00	.45
11 Tyronn Lue BK	2.50	1.10
12 Venson Hamilton BK	1.00	.45
13 Ken Harvey BB	3.00	1.35
14 Mark Bennett	1.00	.45

Swimming
15 Chris Wright 1.00 .45
Track and Field
16 Anna DeForge BK 2.50 1.10
17 Ali Viola 1.00 .45
Women's Softball
18 Tressa Thompson 1.00 .45
Track and Field
19 Misty Oxford 1.00 .45
Gymnastics
20 Fiona Nepo 1.00 .45
Volleyball
21 Lisa Reitsma 1.00 .45
Volleyball

1998-99 Nebraska*

This 21-card set was sponsored by Union Bank and Trust Co, University of Nebraska-Lincoln and the Lincoln Police Department. Each includes a color photo of the player surrounded by a red and gray border with the the year "98 and '99" printed on the front. The unnumbered backs are a simple black print on white card stock. The set features primarily football players, but a variety of other sports as well. We've included initials after each player's name that represent the sport in which they played.

MINT NRMT
COMPLETE SET (21) 20.00 9.00
1 Kris Brown FB 1.25 .55
2 Monte Cristo FB 1.25 .55
3 Jose DeAnda Wrest. 1.00 .45
4 Keith Ebbert Swim 1.00 .45
5 Jay Foreman FB 1.25 .55
6 Venson Hamilton BK 1.00 .45
7 Josh Heskew FB 1.25 .55
8 Sheldon Jackson FB 1.25 .55
9 Brian Johnson BB 1.00 .45
10 Chad Kelsay FB 1.25 .55
11 Bill Lafleur FB 1.25 .55
12 Shane Lavy TR 1.00 .45
13 Joel Makovicka FB 3.00 1.35
14 Andy Markowski BK 1.00 .45
15 Cori McDill W-BK 1.00 .45
16 Laurie McLaghlin GYM 1.00 .45
17 Fiona Nepo VB 1.00 .45
18 Kelly Pinkepank SB 1.00 .45
19 Mike Rucker FB 3.00 1.35
20 Shevin Wiggins FB 1.00 .45
21 Monet Williams BK 1.00 .45

1999-00 Nebraska*

This 19-card set was sponsored by Union Bank and Trust Co, University of Nebraska-Lincoln and the Lincoln Police Department. The set features a variety of sports and we have the put an appropriate initial after each player's name.

MINT NRMT
COMPLETE SET (19) 20.00 9.00
1 Mike Brown FB 2.50 1.10
2 Ralph Brown FB 2.50 1.10
3 T.J. DeBates FB 1.50 .70
4 Lindsay Eddelman SO .75 .35
5 Paul Gomez Wrest. .75 .35
6 Dallhia Ingram TR .75 .35
7 Julius Jackson FB 2.00 .90
8 Nicole Kubik W-BK .75 .35
9 Jennifer Lizama SB .75 .35
10 Mandy Monson VB .75 .35
11 Sharolta Nonen SO .75 .35
12 Tony Ortiz FB 1.50 .70
13 David Riggert TR .75 .35
14 Charlie Rogers BK .75 .35
15 Brian Shaw FB 1.50 .70
16 James Sherman FB 1.50 .70
17 Jamal Strong BB 1.50 .70
18 Jenny Voss SB .75 .35
19 Steve Warren FB 1.50 .70

1991 Oklahoma State Collegiate Collection *

This 100-card multi-sport standard-size set was produced by Collegiate Collection. We've cataloged players from the top three sports using these initials: B-baseball, K-basketball, and F-football.

MINT NRMT
COMPLETE SET (100) 15.00 6.75
1 Henry Iba K .25 .11
2 Barry Sanders F 1.25 .55
3 Thurman Thomas F .75 .35
4 Robin Ventura B .50 .23
5 Bob Kurland F .40 .18
6 Athletic Tradition .05 .02
7 1959 NCAA Baseball .05 .02
Champions B
8 1945 NCAA Basketball .10 .05
Champions K
9 Bob Tway .50 .23
10 Allie Reynolds F .25 .11
11 Rodney Harling F .05 .02
12 Ed Gallagher .05 .02
13 Walt Garrison F .40 .18
14 Terry Miller F .15 .07
15 Bob Fenimore F .05 .02
16 Gerald Hudson F .05 .02
17 Hart Lee Dykes F .15 .07
18 1976 Big 8 Conference F .05 .02
19 Jimmy Johnson CO F .75 .35
20 Terry Brown F .05 .02
21 Derrel Gofourth F .05 .02
22 Paul Blair F .25 .11
23 John Little F .10 .05
24 1983 Bluebonnet Bowl F .05 .02
25 John Smith .05 .02
26 1976 Tangerine Bowl F .05 .02
27 Gary Cutsinger F .10 .05
28 Rusty Hilger F .10 .05
29 Ron Baker F .05 .02
30 Pat Jones F .15 .07
31 Phillip Dokes F .05 .02
32 Neil Armstrong F .05 .02
33 Joel Horlen B .15 .07
34 Jon Kolb F .10 .05
35 1958 NCAA Wrestling .05 .02
Champs
36 Doug Tewell .05 .02
37 Barry Hanna F .05 .02
38 Scott Verplank 2.00 .90
39 1946 Sugar Bowl F .05 .02
40 John Starks .50 .23
41 Liz Brown .05 .02
42 Thurman Thomas F .75 .35
43 Yojiro Uetake .05 .02
44 1988 Holiday Bowl F .05 .02
45 Ernest Anderson F .05 .02
46 Leslie O'Neal F .25 .11
47 Ken Monday .05 .02
48 Leonard Thompson F .10 .05
49 Jess(Cob) Rennick K .05 .02
50 Mike Gundy F .10 .05
51 Mark Moore F .05 .02
52 Clinette Jordan .05 .02
53 O.A.(Bum) Phillips F .50 .23
54 John Ward F .05 .02
55 Larry Roach F .05 .02
56 Jerry Sherk F .10 .05
57 Matt Monger F .05 .02
58 Dick Soergel F .05 .02
59 Ricky Young F .10 .05
60 Labron Harris and .05 .02
1963 NCAA
Championship Team
61 Barry Sanders F 1.25 .55
62 Gary Green B .10 .05
63 Henry Iba .25 .11
64 David Edwards .05 .02
65 Tom Chesbro .05 .02
66 Chris Rockins F .05 .02
67 Buddy Ryan F .25 .11
68 Thurman Thomas F .75 .35
69 Frank Lewis .05 .02
70 Doug Dascenzo B .10 .05
71 Pete Incaviglia B .25 .11
72 Willie Wood .25 .11
73 James Butler .05 .02
74 Lori McNeil .40 .18
75 Monty Farris B .10 .05
76 Barry Sanders F 1.25 .55
77 Mickey Tettleton B .25 .11
78 Barry Sanders 1.00 .45
Thurman Thomas F
80 Gale McArthur K .05 .02
81 Thurman Thomas F .75 .35
82 Danny Edwards .05 .02
83 Barry Sanders F 1.25 .55
84 Mike Sheets .05 .02
85 Jerry Adair B .15 .07
86 Thurman Thomas F .75 .35
87 Garth Brooks 4.00 1.80
88 John Farrell B .05 .02
89 Mike Holder and 1987 .05 .02
NCAA Championship Team
90 Jim Traber B .10 .05
91 Lindy Miller .05 .02
92 Mike Henneman B .25 .11
93 Thurman Thomas F .75 .35
94 John Washington F .05 .02
95 Michael Daniel B .05 .02
96 Ralph Higgins .05 .02
97 1987 Sun Bowl F .05 .02
98 War Pigs F .05 .02
Bryon Woodard
Chris Stanley
John Boisvert
Jason Kidder
Mike Wolfe
99 Eddie Sutton K .25 .11
100 Checklist Card .05 .02

1991 Southern Cal *

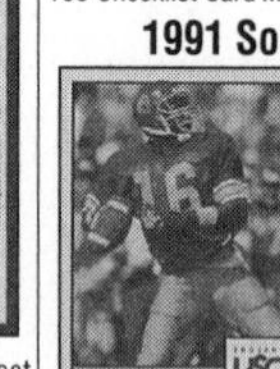

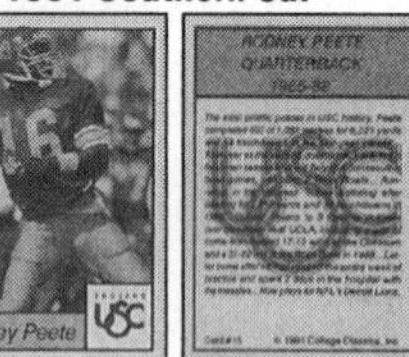

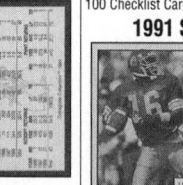

Produced by College Classics Inc., this 100-card standard-size set honors former Trojan Athletes of various sports. Most players are football, other sports are designated in the listings below. The complete set comes with a blank-backed white card that carries the set's production number out of a total of 20,000 produced. In addition, 1,400 cards autographed by John Naber, Ron Fairly, Tom Seaver, Charles White, Dave Stockton, Mike Garrett, Anthony Davis, and Fred Lynn were randomly inserted throughout 1,000 of these sets. Since these cards rarely appear in the secondary marketplace, they are not priced.

MINT NRMT
COMPLETE SET (100) 25.00 11.00
1 Charles White .50 .23
2 Anthony Davis .50 .23
3 Clay Matthews .30 .14
4 Hoby Brenner .20 .09
5 Mike Garrett .50 .23
6 Bill Sharman BK .75 .35
7 Bob Seagren .10 .05
(Track)
8 Mike McKeever .10 .05
9 Celso Kalache .10 .05
(Volleyball)
10 John Williams CO .10 .05
(Water polo)
11 John Naber .50 .23
(Swimming)
12 Brad Budde .20 .09
13 Tim Tyan .10 .05
14 Mark Tucker .10 .05
15 Rodney Peete .50 .23
16 Art Mazmanian BB .10 .05
17 Red Badgro BB .20 .09
18 Sue Habernigg .10 .05
(Women's Swimming)
19 Craig Fertig .10 .05
20 John Block BK .10 .05
21 Jen-Kai Liu .10 .05
(Volleyball)
22 Kim Ruddins .10 .05
(Women's volleyball)
23 Al Cowlings .50 .23
24 Ronnie Lott 1.50 .70
25 Adam Johnson .50 .23
(Volleyball)
26 Fred Lynn BB .30 .14
27 Rick Leach .30 .14
(Tennis)
28 Tim Rossovich .30 .14
29 Marvin Powell .30 .14
30 Ron Yary .30 .14
31 Ken Ruettgers .20 .09
32 Bob Yoder CO .10 .05
(Men's volleyball)
33 Megan McCallister .10 .05
(Women's volleyball)
34 Dave Cadigan .20 .09
35 Jeff Bregel .10 .05
36 Michael Wayman .10 .05
(Tennis)
37 Sippy Woodhead-Kantzer .10 .05
(Women's swimming)
38 Tim Hovland .30 .14
(Volleyball)
39 Steve Busby BB .20 .09
40 Tom Seaver BB 2.00 .90
41 Anthony Colorito .10 .05
42 Wayne Carlander BK .10 .05
43 Erik Affholter .20 .09
44 Jim Obradovich .10 .05
45 Duane Bickett .30 .14
46 Leslie Daland .10 .05
(Women's swimming)
47 Ole Oleson .10 .05
(Track)
48 Ed Putnam BB .10 .05
49 Stan Smith .75 .35
(Tennis)
50 Jeff Hart .10 .05
(Golf)
51 Jack Del Rio .30 .14
52 Bob Boyd CO BK .10 .05
53 Pat Haden 1.00 .45
54 John Lambert BK .10 .05
55 Pete Beathard .20 .09
56 Anna-Maria Fernandez .10 .05
(Women's tennis)
57 Marta Figueras-Dotti .10 .05
(Women's golf)
58 Don Mosebar .30 .14
59 Don Doll .10 .05
60 Dave Stockton .30 .14
(Golf)
61 Trisha Laux .10 .05
Women's tennis)
62 Roy Foster .20 .09
63 Bruce Matthews .30 .14
64 Steve Sogge .10 .05
65 Tracy Nakamura .10 .05
(Women's golf)
66 Marv Montgomery .10 .05
67 Jack Tingley .10 .05
(Swimming)
68 Larry Stevens .10 .05
69 Harry Smith .10 .05
70 Bill Bain .10 .05
71 Mark McGwire BB 10.00 4.50
72 Brad Brink BB .10 .05
73 Richard Wood .10 .05
74 Rod Dedeaux CO BB .20 .09
75 Paul Westphal BK 1.00 .45
76 Al Krueger .10 .05
77 James McConica .10 .05
(Swimming)
78 Rod Martin .30 .14
79 Bill Yardley .10 .05
(Volleyball)
80 Bill Stetson .10 .05
(Volleyball)
81 Ray Looze .10 .05
(Swimming)
82 Dan Jorgensen .10 .05
(Swimming)
83 Anna-Lucia Fernandez .10 .05
(Women's tennis)
84 Terri O'Loughlin .10 .05
(Women's Swimming)
85 John Grant .10 .05
86 Chris Lewis .10 .05
(Tennis)
87 Steve Timmons .75 .35
(Volleyball)
88 Dr. Dallas Long .10 .05
(Track)
89 John McKay CO .30 .14
90 Joe Bottom .10 .05
(Swimming)
91 John Jackson .10 .05
92 Paul McDonald .10 .05
93 Jimmy Gunn .10 .05
94 Rod Sherman .10 .05
95 Cecilia Fernandez .10 .05
(Women's tennis)
96 Doug Adler .10 .05
(Tennis)
97 Ron Orr .10 .05
(Swimming)
98 Debbie Landreth Brown .10 .05
(Women's volleyball)
99 Debbie Green .10 .05
(Women's volleyball)
100 Pat Harrison BB .10 .05

1991 South Carolina Collegiate Collection *

This 200-card set measures standard sized and features cards of all-time great South Carolina athletes. The fronts have a black border with color action shots on each one. The school name and logo are found across the top border of the card. The featured player's name is found along the bottom border set against a red background. The backs carry a small bio of the player and his/her statistics.

MINT NRMT
COMPLETE SET (200) 10.00 4.50
1 Frank McGuire BK CO .50 .23
2 Todd Ellis FB .05 .02
3 Alex English BK .50 .23
4 Cocky .05 .02
Mascot
5 Kevin Darmody BK .05 .02
6 Kent Hagood FB .05 .02
7 Duane Kendall .05 .02
8 Harold Green FB .10 .05
9 Linwood Moye BK .05 .02
10 George Rogers FB .50 .23
11 Hardin Brown BB .05 .02
12 Kent DeMars .05 .02
13 Bonnie Kenney .05 .02
Volleyball CO
14 Adrian Adkins BB .05 .02
15 George Felton BK CO .05 .02
16 Marty Baltzegar .05 .02
Soccer
17 Chris Wade .05 .02
18 Nancy Wilson BK .05 .02
19 James Seawright FB .05 .02
20 Lisa Diaz BK .05 .02
21 Kevin White FB .05 .02
22 June Raines BB CO .05 .02
23 Gretchen Koenig .05 .02
Women's Softball
24 Karlton Hilton BK .05 .02
25 Derrick Little FB .05 .02
26 Zam Fredrick BK .05 .02
27 Karen Sanchelli .05 .02
28 Ron Rabune FB .05 .02
29 Carolina Culik .05 .02
Tennis
30 Greg Kraft .05 .02
Track and Field CO
31 Warren Lipka .05 .02
Soccer
32 Martha Parker BK .05 .02
33 Vic McConnell FB .05 .02
34 Stephane Simian .05 .02
Tennis
35 Alex English BK .50 .23
36 Doug Allison .05 .02
Soccer
37 Brian Beatson .05 .02
38 Jimmy Hawthorne BK .05 .02
39 Fitzgerald Davis FB .05 .02
40 Linda Mescan .05 .02
Women's Golf CO
41 Rita Winebarger .05 .02
Tennis
42 Bill Hency .05 .02
Soccer
43 Mark Berson .05 .02
Men's Soccer CO
44 Todd Ellis FB .05 .02
45 Joyce Compton .05 .02
Women's Softball CO
46 Darlene Lowery .05 .02
Women's Softball
47 David Poinsett FB .05 .02
48 Schonna Banner .05 .02
Women's Basketball
49 Joe Cardwell BB .05 .02
50 Arlo Elkins .05 .02
Women's Tennis CO
51 Greg Morhardt BB .05 .02
52 Sparky Woods FB CO .05 .02
53 Charles Arndt .05 .02
Soccer
54 Joe Morrison FB CO .20 .09
55 Jeff Grantz FB .05 .02
56 Alfred H. Von Kolnitz FB .05 .02
57 Mike Caskey FB .05 .02
58 Tatum Gressette FB .05 .02
59 Alex Hawkins FB .15 .07
60 Phil Lavoie FB .05 .02
61 Lee Collins FB .05 .02
62 Jack Thompson BK .05 .02
63 Andrew Provence FB .05 .02
64 Kevin Joyce BK .20 .09
65 Brian Winstead .05 .02
Soccer
66 J. McIver Riley .05 .02
Track and Field
67 Bobby Heald .05 .02
Tennis
68 Cedrick Hordges BK .10 .05
69 Leon Cunningham FB .05 .02
70 Randy Martz BB .10 .05
71 Rex Enright FB CO AD .05 .02
72 Chris Boyle HK .05 .02
73 Grady Wallace BK .05 .02
74 Paul Hollins BB .05 .02
75 Norman Rucks .05 .02
Track and Field
76 Dan Reeves FB .75 .35
77 Tim Lewis FB .15 .07
78 Tom Riker BK .20 .09
79 King Dixon FB .05 .02
80 Bobby Cremins BK .20 .09
81 Billy Gambrell FB .10 .05
82 Rob Rinehart BB .05 .02
83 Max Runager FB .05 .02
84 Mike Cook BB .05 .02
85 Gary Gregor BK .10 .05
86 Bill Landrum BB .10 .05
87 Mark Van Bever BB .05 .02
88 Pat Dufficy .05 .02
89 Joe Datin BB .05 .02
90 Ronnie Collins BK .05 .02
91 Del Wilkes FB .05 .02
92 Earl Bass .05 .02
93 Johnny Gregory FB .05 .02
94 Lou Sossamon FB .05 .02
95 Lindi James .05 .02
Women's Softball
96 Sam Daniel .05 .02
Men's Tennis CO
97 Sharon Gilmore .05 .02
98 Steve Wadiak FB .05 .02
99 Joe Smith BK .05 .02
100 Checklist .05 .02
101 James Sumpter FB .05 .02
102 Mark Nelson BB .05 .02
103 Terry Dozier .05 .02
104 Scott Hagler FB .05 .02
105 Todd Berry FB .05 .02
106 Jack Gilloon BK .05 .02
107 Carl Hill FB .05 .02
108 Steve Liebler .05 .02
109 Earl Johnson FB .05 .02
110 Dominique Blasingame FB .05 .02
111 Jim Desmond FB .05 .02
112 Keith Bing FB .05 .02
113 Garrett Carter BB .05 .02
114 Ken Diller .05 .02
Tennis
115 Mike Durrah FB .05 .02
116 Jan Sandberg .05 .02
Tennis
117 Ron Bass FB .05 .02
118 Charlie Gowan FB .05 .02
119 Ray Carpenter FB .05 .02
120 Glen Thompson .05 .02
Soccer
121 Pat Mihm .05 .02
Soccer
122 Bryant Gilliard FB .05 .02
123 Darryl Martin .05 .02
124 Matt McKernan FB .05 .02
125 Mike Doyle BK .05 .02
126 Brad Jergenson BK .05 .02
127 Mark Fryer FB .05 .02
128 Michael Foster .05 .02
129 Anthony Smith FB .05 .02
130 Robert Robinson FB .05 .02
131 Mark Fleetwood FB .05 .02
132 Skeets Thomas BB .05 .02
133 Bobby Richardson BB CO .50 .23
134 Rodney Price FB .05 .02
135 Willie McIntee FB .05 .02
136 Kenny Haynes FB .05 .02
137 Ragnar Thorarinsson .05 .02
Soccer
138 Willie Scott FB .05 .02
139 Ricky Daniels FB .05 .02
140 Bill Barnhill FB .05 .02
141 Gordon Beckham FB .05 .02
142 Tim Dyches FB .05 .02
143 John Hudson BK .05 .02
144 Brian Williams BB .05 .02
145 Jim Walsh FB .05 .02
146 Keith Switzer .05 .02
Swimming CO
147 Thomas Dendy FB .05 .02
148 Gerald Peacock .05 .02
149 Bill Bradshaw FB .05 .02
150 Mike Brittain BK .05 .02
151 Tim Berra .15 .07
Soccer
152 Eric Poole FB .05 .02
153 Leonard Burton FB .05 .02
154 Danny Smith .05 .02
155 Scott Windsor FB .05 .02
156 Art Whisnant BK .05 .02
157 Jim Slaughter BK .05 .02
158 Skip Harlicka BK .10 .05
159 Bishop Strickland FB .05 .02
160 Marsi McAlister BK .05 .02
161 Larry Price BB .05 .02
162 Allen Mitchell FB .05 .02
163 Kenneth Robinson .05 .02
164 Paul Vogel FB .05 .02
165 Norman Floyd FB .05 .02
166 Carl Brazell FB .05 .02
167 Rod Carraway .05 .02
168 Fred Zeigler FB .05 .02
169 Frank Mincevich FB .05 .02
170 Bobby Bryant FB .15 .07
171 J.D. Fuller FB .05 .02
172 Harry South .05 .02
173 Tom O'Connor FB .05 .02
174 Kevin Hendrix FB .05 .02
175 Greg Philpot FB .05 .02
176 Warren Muir FB .05 .02
177 Chris Mayotte .05 .02
178 Ray Pericola BK .05 .02
179 Tommy Suggs FB .05 .02
180 Don Bailey FB .05 .02
181 Jones Andrews FB .05 .02
182 Chris Major FB .05 .02
183 Mike Hold .05 .02
184 Brendan McCormack FB .05 .02
185 David Taylor FB .05 .02
186 Hank Small BB .05 .02
187 Bryant Meeks FB .05 .02
188 Brantley Southers BK .05 .02
189 John Sullivan BB .05 .02
190 Evelyn Johnson BK .05 .02
191 Harry Skipper FB .05 .02
192 Derrick Frazier .05 .02
193 Raynard Brown FB .05 .02
194 Quinton Lewis FB .05 .02
195 Tony Guyton FB .10 .05
196 John Leheup FB .05 .02
197 Dick Harris FB .05 .02
198 Sheila Foster BK .05 .02
199 Johnny Gramling .05 .02
200 Checklist .05 .02

1986-87 Southwestern Louisiana *

This 16-card standard-size set was sponsored by the Chemical Dependency Unit of Acadiana in Lafayette, the University of Southwest Louisiana, and local law enforcement agencies and was produced by McDag Productions. Only 3,500 sets were produced. The cards were distributed by the CDU adolescent program and by law enforcement officers.The front features borderless color action player photos, on white card stock with black lettering. The CDU logo and the words "USL Ragin' Cajuns" appear on the top of the card, with player information below the picture. The back has biographical information and "Tips from the Ragin' Cajuns" which encourage children to avoid drug use. Sports represented in the set include basketball (1, 4, 9, 11, 15), baseball (2, 5, 8, 16), softball

7, 14), track (3), and tennis (6, 10, 12-13). The cards are unnumbered and we have checklisted them below in alphabetical order. The set includes a card of high jumper Hollis Conway, who competed for the 1992 United States Olympic team at Barcelona.

	MINT	NRMT
COMPLETE SET (16)	10.00	4.50
1 Stephen Beene	.75	.35
2 Eddie Citronnelli	.75	.35
3 Hollis Conway	1.50	.70
4 Teena Cooper	.75	.35
5 Herb Erhardt	.75	.35
6 Bret Garnett	.75	.35
7 Allison Gray	.75	.35
8 Bobby Hobbs	.75	.35
9 Brian Jolivette	.75	.35
10 Dianne Lowings	.75	.35
11 Rodney McNeil	.75	.35
12 Cathy O'Donovan	.75	.35
13 Ashley Rhoney	.75	.35
14 Alisa Smith	.75	.35
15 Randal Smith	.75	.35
16 Merv Waukau	.75	.35

1987-88 Southwestern Louisiana *

This 16-card standard-size set was sponsored by CDU of Acadiana in Lafayette, University of Southwestern Louisiana, and local law enforcement agencies. The fronts display color action player photos on a white card face. The CDU logo, school logo, and year appear above the picture, while player information is given below the picture. The backs carry player profile, advertisements, and "Tips From the Ragin' Cajuns," which consist of anti-drug and alcohol messages. Sports represented in this set include men's basketball (1-4), women's basketball (5-6), tennis (7-8), men's baseball (9-12), women's softball (14-16), and track (13). The set includes a card of high jumper Hollis Conway, who competed for the 1992 United States Olympic team at Barcelona. .

	MINT	NRMT
COMPLETE SET (16)	12.00	5.50
1 Randal Smith	.75	.35
2 Earl Watkins	.75	.35
3 Kevin Brooks	1.50	.70
4 Stephen Beene	.75	.35
5 Kim Perrot	6.00	2.70
6 Teena Cooper	.75	.35
7 Bret Garnett	.75	.35
8 Ashley Rhoney	.75	.35
9 Terry Fitzpatrick	.75	.35
10 Joe Turk	.75	.35
11 Brad Hebets	.75	.35
12 Ron Vincent	.75	.35
13 Hollis Conway	1.00	.45
14 Marria Blackwell	.75	.35
15 Stefni Whitton	.75	.35
16 Janine Johnson	.75	.35

1990 Texas *

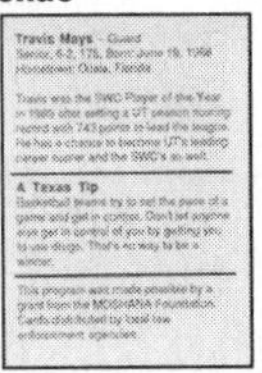

Financed by the MOSHANA Foundation and distributed by local law enforcement agencies, this 32-card multi-sport set measures 2 1/2" by 3 1/2" and is printed on thin card stock. The fronts display color action player photos inside a black frame on a white card face. The team name appears in a black bar above the picture, while the player's name and position are printed in the wider bottom border. The backs feature biographical information, player profile, and "A Texas Tip" in the form of anti-drug or alcohol messages. The sports represented are golf (1, 19), basketball (2-4, 8, 25-26, 29, 30), track and field (5-6, 15, 23), tennis (7, 28), baseball (9-10, 16, 32), swimming and diving (11, 13, 20-21), volleyball (12, 14, 18, 31), and football (17, 22, 24, 27). The cards are unnumbered and checklisted below in alphabetical order.

	MINT	NRMT
COMPLETE SET (32)	20.00	9.00
1 Brad Agee	1.50	.70
2 Susan Anderson	.75	.35
3 Ellen Bayer	.75	.35
4 Lance Blanks	1.50	.70
5 Patrik Boden	.75	.35
6 Angie Bradburn	.75	.35
7 Steve Bryan	.75	.35
8 Jody Conradt CO	2.00	.90
9 Brian Dare	.75	.35
10 Kirk Dressendorfer	1.00	.45
11 Leigh Ann Fetter	.75	.35
12 Annette Garza	.75	.35
13 Doug Gjertsen	.75	.35
14 Janine Gremmel	.75	.35
15 Carlette Guidry	1.00	.45
16 Cliff Gustafson CO	2.00	.90
17 Ken Hackenmack	.75	.35
18 Quandalyn Harrell	.75	.35
19 Michiko Hattori	1.00	.45
20 Andrea Hayes	.75	.35
21 Kelly Jenkins	.75	.35
22 Tony Jones	1.00	.45
23 Erin Keogh	.75	.35
24 Bobby Lilljedahl	.75	.35
25 Travis Mays	1.50	.70
26 Lyssa McBride	1.00	.45
27 David McWilliams CO	1.00	.45
28 Diane Merrett	.75	.35
29 George Muller	.75	.35
30 Tom Penders CO	2.00	.90
31 Dagmara Szyszczak	.75	.35
32 David Tollison	.75	.35

1991 Texas A and M Collegiate Collection *

This 100 card standard-size multi-sport set was produced by Collegiate Collection. Although a few color photos are included, the front features mainly black and white player photos with borders in the team's colors. All cards are of football players unless noted.

	MINT	NRMT
COMPLETE SET (100)	10.00	4.50
1 Rod Bernstine	.15	.07
2 Bear Bryant	1.50	.70
3 Shirley Furlong G	.10	.05
4 R.C. Slocum	.50	.23
5 Gary Kubiak	.20	.09
6 Larry Horton	.05	.02
7 Billy Cannon Jr.	.10	.05
8 John Beasley BK	.15	.07
9 Ray Childress	.10	.05
10 John David Crow	.75	.35
11 Bob Ellis G CO	.05	.02
12 Billy Hodge BB	.05	.02
13 Layne Talbot	.05	.02
14 Larry Stegent	.05	.02
15 Lisa Langston BK	.05	.02
16 Tom Chandler BB CO	.05	.02
17 Scott Livingstone BB	.15	.07
18 Jimmy Teal	.05	.02
19 Ted Nelson TR	.05	.02
20 Lance Pavlas	.05	.02
21 James "Hoot" Gibson BB	.05	.02
22 Mickey Washington	.15	.07
23 Rodney Hodde BB	.05	.02
24 Rob Swain BB	.05	.02
25 Thomas Sanders	.10	.05
26 Loyd Taylor	.05	.02
27 Danny Roberts TR	.05	.02
28 Bob Brock SOFT CO	.05	.02
29 Curtis Dickey	.20	.09
30 John Thornton BK	.05	.02
31 Matt McCall	.05	.02
32 David Kent TENNIS CO	.05	.02
33 Melinda Clark-Lechemiant TR	.05	.02
34 Brad Dusek	.10	.05
35 Mark Ross BB	.05	.02
36 Gary Oliver	.10	.05
37 Charles Milstead	.05	.02
38 Mark Johnson BB CO	.05	.02
39 Ever Magalles BB	.10	.05
40 Mark Thurmond BB	.15	.07
41 Keith Langston BB	.05	.02
42 Phillip Taylor BB	.05	.02
43 Jacob Green	.20	.09
44 Randy Matson TR	.20	.09
45 Sharon Andaya SOFT	.05	.02
46 Kevin Monk	.05	.02
47 Larry Kelm	.05	.02
48 Tory Parks SOFT	.05	.02
49 Barry Davis BK	.05	.02
50 Kitty Holley GOLF CO	.05	.02
51 Kent Adams	.05	.02
52 Randy Hall TRACK	.05	.02
53 Dave Goff BK	.05	.02
54 Rolf Krueger	.15	.07
55 Lynn Hickey BK CO	.05	.02
56 Sylvester Morgan	.05	.02
57 Bucky Sams	.05	.02
58 Jeff Nelson	.05	.02
59 Gary Jones	.05	.02
60 John Byington BB	.05	.02
61 Pat Thomas	.10	.05
62 Mark Dennard	.15	.07
63 James H. Heitmann BK	.05	.02
64 Kyle Field	.05	.02
Football Home of the Aggies		
65 Edd Hargett	.20	.09
66 Robert Slavens BB	.05	.02
67 Scott Slater	.05	.02
68 Louis Cheek	.05	.02
69 Ken Ford	.05	.02
70 Billy G. Hobbs	.05	.02
71 Bob Long	.05	.02
72 Jeff Payne	.05	.02
73 Garth Tenapel	.05	.02
74 David Bandy	.05	.02
75 Dennis Swilley	.05	.02
76 Mike Whitwell	.05	.02
77 Jim "Red" Cashion	.05	.02
78 Lisa "L.J." Jordon BK	.05	.02
79 Yvonne Van Brandt VB	.05	.02
80 Texas Aggie Band	.10	.05
81 Bobby Joe Conrad	.20	.09
82 Mike Mosley	.05	.02
83 Olsen Field	.05	.02
Baseball Field		
84 Jeff Schow BB	.05	.02
85 Al Givens VB CO	.05	.02
86 Steve Hughes BB	.05	.02
87 Lisa Herner BK	.05	.02
88 Traci Thomas BK	.05	.02
89 Karen Guerrero SOFT	.10	.05
90 Billy Pickard AAD	.05	.02
91 David Ogrin GOLF	.05	.02
92 Kim Bauer GOLF	.10	.05
93 Warren Trahan	.05	.02
94 Bobby Kleinecke TENN CO	.05	.02
95 Dave Elmendorf	.20	.09
96 Vicki A. Brown SWIM	.05	.02
97 Yvonne Hill BK	.05	.02
98 David Rollen BB	.10	.05
99 David Hardy	.05	.02
100 Checklist Card	.05	.02

1992-93 Virginia Tech *

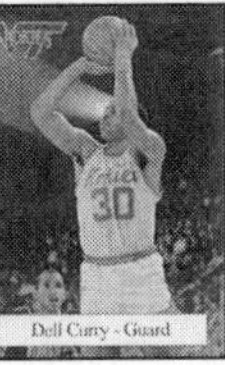

This 12-card multi-sport set measures the standard size and features full-bleed, color, action player photos. The sports represented in the set are football (1, 2, 5, 10-11), basketball (3, 7-8), baseball (4), soccer (6), and volleyball (9).

	MINT	NRMT
COMPLETE SET (12)	12.00	5.50
1 HokieBird (Mascot)	.50	.23
2 Will Furrer	1.50	.70
3 Phyllis Tonkin Dayna Sonovick Tisa Brown	.50	.23
4 David Dallas	.50	.23
5 Eugene Chung	1.00	.45
6 Eric McClellan	.50	.23
7 Thomas Elliott Jay Purcell	.50	.23
8 Dell Curry	6.00	2.70
9 Lisa Pikalek	.50	.23
10 Tony Kennedy	.50	.23
11 Vaughn Hebron	2.00	.90
12 Logo Card	.50	.23

1992 Washington Little Sun *

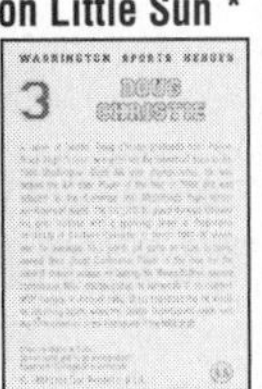

Produced by Little Sun and distributed by Snyder's Bakery of Spokane, Washington, this eight-card multi-sport standard-size set features former and current athletes from the state of Washington. The cards were available for eight weeks beginning Sept. 14. One card per week was inserted into loaves of Snyder's Premium White and Roman Meal bread. During the promotion, a total of 80,000 of each card were distributed. The bakery also made a donation to the Scholarship Fund of the Tacoma Athletic Commission in the names of the athletes included in the set. The sports represented in the set are baseball (1, 6), football (2, 8), basketball (3), bowling (4), skiing (5), and mountain climbing (7).

	MINT	NRMT
COMPLETE SET (8)	8.00	3.60
1 Ryne Sandberg	5.00	2.20
2 Mark Rypien	.75	.35
3 Doug Christie	2.00	.90
4 Leila Wagner	.50	.23
5 Phil Mahre and Steve Mahre	1.00	.45
6 John Olerud	1.50	.70
7 Lou Whitaker	.75	.35
8 Dana Hall	.50	.23

1994-95 Assets *

Produced by Classic, the 1994 Assets set features stars from basketball, hockey, football, baseball, and auto racing. The set was released in two series of 50 cards each. 1,994 cases were produced of each series. This standard-sized card set features a player photo with his name in silver letters on the lower left corner and the Assets logo on the upper right. The back has a color photo on the left side along with a biography on the right side of the card. A Sprint phone card is randomly inserted in each five-card pack.

	MINT	NRMT
COMPLETE SET (100)	15.00	6.75
1 Shaquille O'Neal	.50	.23
2 Hakeem Olajuwon	.25	.11
3 Troy Aikman	.50	.23
4 Nolan Ryan	.50	.23
5 Dale Earnhardt	2.00	.90
6 Glenn Robinson	.25	.11
7 Marshall Faulk	1.00	.45
8 Ed Jovanovski	.05	.02
9 Drew Bledsoe	.50	.23
10 Alonzo Mourning	.15	.07
11 Steve Young	.40	.18
12 Dan Wilkinson	.05	.02
13 Paul Wilson	.05	.02
14 Jason Kidd	1.00	.45
15 Charlie Garner	.25	.11
16 Derrick Alexander	.05	.02
17 Donyell Marshall	.05	.02
18 Ben Grieve	.75	.35
19 Eric Montross	.05	.02
20 Radek Bonk	.25	.11
21 Manon Rheaume	.50	.23
22 Jalen Rose	.40	.18
23 Antonio Langham	.05	.02
24 Greg Hill	.05	.02
25 Marshall Faulk CL	.50	.23
26 Shaquille O'Neal	.50	.23
27 Hakeem Olajuwon	.25	.11
28 Troy Aikman	.50	.23
29 Nolan Ryan	.50	.23
30 Dale Earnhardt	2.00	.90
31 Glenn Robinson	.30	.14
32 Marshall Faulk	1.00	.45
33 Ed Jovanovski	.05	.02
34 Drew Bledsoe	.50	.23
35 Alonzo Mourning	.15	.07
36 Steve Young	.40	.18
37 Dan Wilkinson	.05	.02
38 Paul Wilson	.05	.02
39 Jason Kidd	1.00	.45
40 Charlie Garner	.25	.11
41 Derrick Alexander	.05	.02
42 Donyell Marshall	.05	.02
43 Ben Grieve	.75	.35
44 Eric Montross	.05	.02
45 Radek Bonk	.25	.11
46 Manon Rheaume	.50	.23
47 Jalen Rose	.40	.18
48 Antonio Langham	.05	.02
49 Greg Hill	.05	.02
50 Glenn Robinson CL	.15	.07
51 Dikembe Mutombo	.05	.02
52 Rashaan Salaam	.05	.02
53 Anfernee Hardaway	.40	.18
54 Isaiah Rider	.05	.02
55 Emmitt Smith	.60	.25
56 Juwan Howard	.25	.11
57 Jeff O'Neill	.05	.02
58 Jamal Mashburn	.15	.07
59 Byron Bam Morris	.05	.02
60 Petr Sykora	.25	.11
61 Erict Rhett	.05	.02
62 Eric Fichaud	.15	.07
63 Heath Shuler	.05	.02
64 Doug Million	.05	.02
65 Barry Bonds	1.00	.45
66 William Floyd	.15	.07
67 Willie McGinest	.05	.02
68 Jeff Gordon	1.00	.45
69 Eddie Jones	.60	.25
70 Steve McNair	.75	.35
71 Ki-Jana Carter	.05	.02
72 Manon Rheaume	.50	.23
73 Shaquille O'Neal	.50	.23
74 Drew Bledsoe	.50	.23
75 Grant Hill CL	.25	.11
76 Dikembe Mutombo	.05	.02
77 Rashaan Salaam	.05	.02
78 Anfernee Hardaway	.50	.23
79 Isaiah Rider	.05	.02
80 Emmitt Smith	.60	.25
81 Juwan Howard	.15	.07
82 Jeff O'Neill	.05	.02
83 Jamal Mashburn	.15	.07
84 Byron Bam Morris	.05	.02
85 Petr Sykora	.25	.11
86 Errict Rhett	.05	.02
87 Eric Fichaud	.15	.07
88 Heath Shuler	.05	.02
89 Doug Million	.05	.02
90 Barry Bonds	1.00	.45
91 William Floyd	.15	.07
92 Willie McGinest	.05	.02
93 Jeff Gordon	1.00	.45
94 Eddie Jones	.50	.23
95 Steve McNair	.60	.25
96 Ki-Jana Carter	.05	.02
97 Manon Rheaume	.50	.23
98 Shaquille O'Neal	.50	.23
99 Drew Bledsoe	.50	.23
100 Steve Young CL	.15	.07

1994-95 Assets Silver Signature *

This 48-card standard-size set was randomly inserted at a rate of four per box. The cards are identical to the first twenty-four cards in the each series, except that these show a silver facsimile autograph on their fronts. The first 24 cards correspond to cards 1-24 in the first series while the second 24 cards correspond to cards 51-74 in the second series.

	MINT	NRMT
*SILVER SIGS: 1.2X TO 3X BASIC CARDS		

1994-95 Assets Die Cuts *

This 25-card standard-size set was randomly inserted into packs. DC1-10 were included in series one while DC11-25 were included in series two packs. These cards feature the player on the card and the ability to separate the player's photo. The back contains information about the player on the section of the card that is separable.

	MINT	NRMT
COMPLETE SET (25)	100.00	45.00
DC1 Shaquille O'Neal	10.00	4.50
DC2 Hakeem Olajuwon	2.00	.90
DC3 Troy Aikman	6.00	2.70
DC4 Nolan Ryan	10.00	4.50
DC5 Dale Earnhardt	15.00	6.75
DC6 Glenn Robinson	3.00	1.35
DC7 Marshall Faulk	10.00	4.50
DC8 Steve Young	3.00	1.35
DC9 Ed Jovanovski	1.00	.45
DC10 Manon Rheaume	5.00	2.20
DC11 Grant Hill	3.00	1.35
DC12 Jason Kidd	10.00	4.50
DC13 Eddie Jones	5.00	2.20
DC14 Heath Shuler	1.00	.45
DC15 Nomar Garciaparra	10.00	4.50
DC16 Byron Bam Morris	1.00	.45
DC17 Barry Bonds	10.00	4.50
DC18 Paul Wilson	1.00	.45
DC19 Jeff Gordon's Car	4.00	1.80
DC20 Isaiah Rider	1.00	.45
DC21 Steve McNair	6.00	2.70
DC22 Donyell Marshall	1.00	.45
DC23 Errict Rhett	1.00	.45
DC24 Eric Fichaud	1.00	.45
DC25 Emmitt Smith	8.00	3.60

1994-95 Assets Phone Cards One Minute/$2 *

Measuring 2" by 3 1/4", these cards have rounded corners and were inserted one per pack. Cards 1-24 were in first series packs while 25-48 were included with second series packs. The front features the player's photo and on the side is how long the card is good for. The Assets logo is in the bottom left corner. The back gives instructions on how to use the phone card. The first series cards expired on December 1, 1995 while the second series cards expired on March 31, 1996. The cards with a $2 logo are worth a mulitple of the regular cards. Please refer to the values below for these cards.

	MINT	NRMT
COMPLETE SET (48)	20.00	9.00
*PIN NUMB.REVEALED: .2X to .5X BASIC INS.		
*TWO DOLLAR: .5X TO 1.2X BASIC INSERTS		
1 Troy Aikman	1.25	.55
2 Derrick Alexander	.25	.11
3 Drew Bledsoe	.50	.23
4 Radek Bonk	.25	.11
5 Dale Earnhardt	3.00	1.35
6 Marshall Faulk	1.50	.70
7 Charlie Garner	.25	.11
8 Ben Grieve	1.00	.45
9 Greg Hill	.25	.11
10 Ed Jovanovski	.25	.11
11 Jason Kidd	1.25	.55
12 Antonio Langham	.25	.11
13 Donyell Marshall	.25	.11
14 Eric Montross	.25	.11
15 Alonzo Mourning	.50	.23
16 Hakeem Olajuwon	1.00	.45
17 Shaquille O'Neal	2.00	.90
18 Manon Rheaume	1.00	.45
19 Glenn Robinson	.50	.23
20 Jalen Rose	.50	.23
21 Nolan Ryan	2.00	.90
22 Dan Wilkinson	.25	.11
23 Paul Wilson	.25	.11
24 Steve Young	1.00	.45
25 Drew Bledsoe	1.00	.45
26 Barry Bonds	2.00	.90
27 Ki-Jana Carter	.25	.11
28 Eric Fichaud	.25	.11
29 William Floyd	.25	.11
30 Jeff Gordon	1.50	.70
31 Anfernee Hardaway	.75	.35
32 Juwan Howard	.75	.35
33 Eddie Jones	.75	.35
34 Jamal Mashburn	.75	.35
35 Willie McGinest	.25	.11
36 Steve McNair	1.00	.45
37 Doug Million	.25	.11
38 Byron Bam Morris	.25	.11
39 Dikembe Mutombo	.25	.11
40 Shaquille O'Neal	2.00	.90
41 Jeff O'Neill	.25	.11
42 Manon Rheaume	1.00	.45
43 Errict Rhett	.25	.11
44 Isaiah Rider	.25	.11
45 Rashaan Salaam	.25	.11
46 Heath Shuler	.25	.11
47 Emmitt Smith	1.50	.70
48 Petr Sykora	.50	.23

1994-95 Assets Phone Cards $5 *

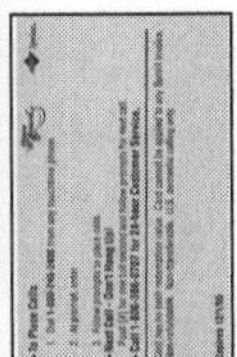

These cards measure 2" by 3 1/4", have rounded corners and were randomly inserted into packs. Cards 1-5 were inserted into first series packs while 6-15 were in second series packs. The front features the player's photo, with "Five Dollars" written in cursive script along the left edge. In the bottom left corner is the Assets logo. The back gives instructions on how to use the phone card. Series one cards expired on December 1, 1995 while second series cards expired on March 31, 1996.

	MINT	NRMT
COMPLETE SET (15)	25.00	11.00
*PIN NUMBER REVEALED: .2X TO .5X		
1 Troy Aikman	2.00	.90
2 Drew Bledsoe	1.25	.55
3 Jason Kidd	2.00	.90
4 Hakeem Olajuwon	1.25	.55
5 Nolan Ryan	3.00	1.35
6 Drew Bledsoe	1.25	.55
7 Barry Bonds	3.00	1.35
8 Ki-Jana Carter	.50	.23
9 Jeff Gordon	2.50	1.10
10 Jason Kidd	2.00	.90
11 Byron Bam Morris	.50	.23
12 Rashaan Salaam	.50	.23
13 Emmitt Smith	2.50	1.10
14 Manon Rheaume	1.50	.70
15 Glenn Robinson	.75	.35

1994-95 Assets Phone Cards $100 *

These 2" by 3 1/4" rounded corner cards were randomly inserted into packs. These cards were placed into series one packs. The front features the player's photo, with "One Hundred Dollars" written in cursive script along the left edge. The Assets logo is in the bottom left corner. The back gives instructions on how to use the phone card. These cards are listed in alphabetical order. These cards expired on December 1, 1995.

	MINT	NRMT
COMPLETE SET (5)	40.00	18.00
*PIN NUMBER REVEALED: .2X TO .5X		
1 Troy Aikman	12.00	5.50
2 Drew Bledsoe	10.00	4.50
3 Jason Kidd	10.00	4.50
4 Hakeem Olajuwon	8.00	3.60
5 Nolan Ryan	20.00	9.00

1994-95 Assets Phone Cards $200 *

These rounded corner cards were randomly inserted into second series packs and measure 2" by 3 1/4". The front features the player's photo, with "Two Hundred Dollars" written in cursive script along the left edge. In the bottom left corner is the Assets logo. The back gives instructions on how to use the phone card. These cards are arranged in alphabetical order. These cards expired on March 31, 1996.

	MINT	NRMT
COMPLETE SET (5)	50.00	22.00
*PIN NUMBER REVEALED: .2X TO .5X		
1 Drew Bledsoe	15.00	6.75
2 Barry Bonds	15.00	6.75
3 Ki-Jana Carter	10.00	4.50
4 Jason Kidd	15.00	6.75
5 Rashaan Salaam	10.00	4.50

1995 Assets Gold *

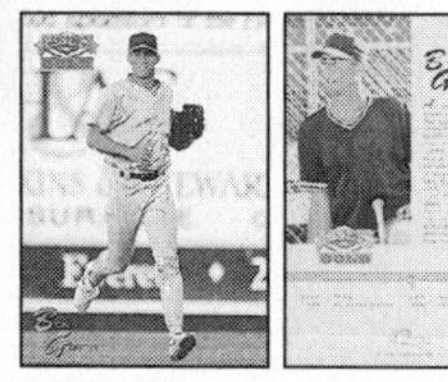

This 50-card set measures the standard size. The fronts feature borderless player action photos with the player's name printed in gold at the bottom. The backs carry a portrait of the player with his name, career highlights, and statistics. The Dale Earnhardt card was pulled from circulation early in the product's release. It is considered a Short Print (SP) but is not included in the complete set price.

	MINT	NRMT
COMPLETE SET (49)	15.00	6.75
1 Dale Earnhardt SP	15.00	6.75
2 Jeff O'Neill	.05	.02
3 Jeff Friesen	.15	.07
4 Aki-Petteri Berg	.05	.02
5 Todd Marchant	.15	.07
6 Blaine Lacher	.15	.07
7 Petr Sykora	.25	.11
8 David Oliver	.05	.02
9 Manon Rheaume	.50	.23
10 Ed Jovanovski	.15	.07
11 Nolan Ryan	1.50	.70
12 Barry Bonds	1.50	.70
13 Ben Grieve	.40	.18
14 Dustin Hermanson	.15	.07
15 Rashaan Salaam	.05	.02
16 Kyle Brady	.05	.02
17 J.J. Stokes	.30	.14
18 James O. Stewart	.50	.23
19 Michael Westbrook	.30	.14
20 Ki-Jana Carter	.15	.07
21 Steve McNair	1.00	.45
22 Kerry Collins	.40	.18
23 Byron Bam Morris	.05	.02
24 Errict Rhett	.25	.11
25 William Floyd	.15	.07
26 Drew Bledsoe	.25	.11
27 Marshall Faulk	1.00	.45
28 Troy Aikman	.60	.25
29 Steve Young	.40	.18
30 Trent Dilfer	.25	.11
31 Emmitt Smith	1.00	.45
32 Rasheed Wallace	.50	.23
33 Corliss Williamson	.15	.07
34 Tyus Edney	.05	.02
35 Ed O'Bannon	.05	.02
36 Damon Stoudamire	.50	.23
37 Eddie Jones	.25	.11
38 Khalid Reeves	.05	.02
39 Jason Kidd	.75	.35
40 Glenn Robinson	.15	.07
41 Juwan Howard	.15	.07
42 Jamal Mashburn	.15	.07
43 Shaquille O'Neal	1.00	.45
44 Alonzo Mourning	.25	.11
45 Donyell Marshall	.05	.02
46 Jalen Rose	.25	.11
47 Wesley Person	.05	.02
48 Grant Hill	.50	.23
49 Rasheed Wallace CL	.05	.02
50 Ki-Jana Carter CL	.05	.02
NNO Jason Kidd Grant Hill	10.00	4.50
NNO Jason Kidd Grant Hill DC	25.00	11.00

1995 Assets Gold Printer's Proofs *

These parallel cards were randomly seeded at the rate of 1:18 packs. They feature the words "Printer's Proof" on the cardfronts.

	MINT	NRMT
*PPs: 2X TO 5X BASIC CARDS		
1 Dale Earnhardt SP	25.00	11.00

1995 Assets Gold Silver Signatures *

These parallel cards were inserted one per pack. They feature a silver foil facsimile signature on the cardfronts.

	MINT	NRMT
*SILVER SIGS: .8X TO 2X BASIC CARDS		
1 Dale Earnhardt SP	12.00	5.50

1995 Assets Gold Die Cuts Silver *

This 20-card set was randomly inserted in packs at a rate of one in 18. The fronts feature a borderless player color action photo with a diamond-shaped top and the player's action taking place in front of the card name. The backs carry the card name, player's name and career highlights. The cards are numbered on the backs. Gold versions were inserted at a rate of one in 72 packs.

	MINT	NRMT
COMPLETE SET (20)	40.00	18.00
*GOLDS: 1.2X to 3X SILVERS		
SDC1 Ben Grieve	1.50	.70
SDC2 Shaquille O'Neal	4.00	1.80
SDC3 Kyle Brady	1.00	.45
SDC4 Glenn Robinson	1.00	.45
SDC5 Marshall Faulk	3.00	1.35
SDC6 Grant Hill	1.50	.70
SDC7 Rasheed Wallace	1.50	.70
SDC8 Ed O'Bannon	1.00	.45
SDC9 Barry Bonds	4.00	1.80
SDC10 Dale Earnhardt	5.00	2.20
SDC11 Ki-Jana Carter	1.50	.70
SDC12 Rashaan Salaam	1.00	.45
SDC13 Manon Rheaume	2.00	.90
SDC14 Jason Kidd	2.00	.90
SDC15 Emmitt Smith	4.00	1.80
SDC16 Drew Bledsoe	2.00	.90
SDC17 Kerry Collins	1.50	.70
SDC18 Nolan Ryan	6.00	2.70
SDC19 Michael Westbrook	1.00	.45
SDC20 Heath Shuler	1.00	.45

1995 Assets Gold Phone Cards $2 *

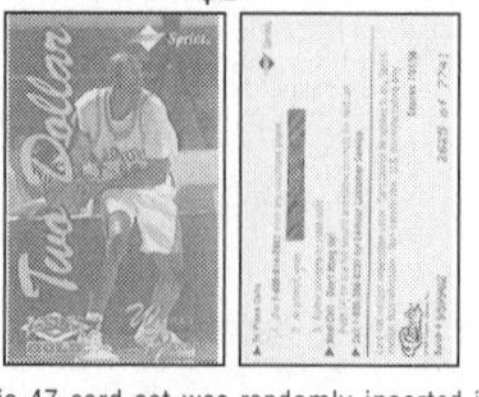

This 47-card set was randomly inserted in packs and measures 2 1/8" by 3 3/8". The fronts feature color action player photos with the player's name below. The $2 calling value is printed vertically down the left. The backs carry the instructions on how to use the cards which expired on 7/31/96. The cards are unnumbered.

	MINT	NRMT
COMPLETE SET (47)	50.00	22.00
*PIN NUMBER REVEALED: HALF VALUE		
1 Dale Earnhardt	5.00	2.20
2 Jeff O'Neill	.75	.35
3 Jeff Friesen	1.00	.45
4 Aki-Petteri Berg	.75	.35
5 Todd Marchant	.75	.35
6 Blaine Lacher	.75	.35
7 Petr Sykora	1.50	.70
8 David Oliver	.75	.35
9 Manon Rheaume	2.50	1.10
10 Ed Jovanovski	.75	.35
11 Nolan Ryan	5.00	2.20
12 Barry Bonds	4.00	1.80
13 Ben Grieve	1.50	.70
14 Dustin Hermanson	.75	.35
15 Rashaan Salaam	.75	.35
16 Kyle Brady	.75	.35
17 J.J. Stokes	1.50	.70
18 James O. Stewart	1.50	.70
19 Michael Westbrook	1.50	.70
20 Ki-Jana Carter	1.00	.45
21 Steve McNair	4.00	1.80
22 Kerry Collins	2.00	.90
23 Byron Bam Morris	.75	.35
24 Errict Rhett	.75	.35
25 William Floyd	.75	.35
26 Drew Bledsoe	1.50	.70
27 Marshall Faulk	1.50	.70
28 Troy Aikman	2.50	1.10
29 Steve Young	2.00	.90
30 Trent Dilfer	.75	.35
31 Emmitt Smith	3.00	1.35
32 Rasheed Wallace	1.50	.70
33 Corliss Williamson	.75	.35
34 Tyus Edney	.75	.35
35 Ed O'Bannon	.75	.35
36 Damon Stoudamire	1.50	.70
37 Eddie Jones	1.50	.70
38 Khalid Reeves	.75	.35
39 Jason Kidd	2.50	1.10
40 Glenn Robinson	1.00	.45
41 Juwan Howard	1.00	.45
42 Jamal Mashburn	.75	.35
43 Shaquille O'Neal	3.00	1.35
44 Alonzo Mourning	1.00	.45
45 Donyell Marshall	.75	.35
46 Jalen Rose	1.50	.70
47 Wesley Person	.75	.35

1995 Assets Gold Phone Cards $5 *

This 16-card set measures 2 1/8" by 3 3/8" and was randomly inserted in packs. The fronts feature color action player photos with the player's name below. The $5 calling value is printed vertically down the left. The backs carry the instructions on how to use the cards which expired on 7/31/96. The cards are unnumbered. The Microlined versions are inserted at a rate of one in 18 packs versus one in six packs for the basic $5 card.

	MINT	NRMT
COMPLETE SET (16)	60.00	27.00
*MICROLINED: .6X TO 1.5X BASIC INSERTS		
*PIN NUMBER REVEALED: HALF VALUE		
1 Drew Bledsoe	2.00	.90
2 Marshall Faulk	3.00	1.35
3 Manon Rheaume	2.00	.90
4 Nolan Ryan	6.00	2.70
5 Emmitt Smith	4.00	1.80
6 J.J. Stokes	1.00	.45
7 Damon Stoudamire	2.00	.90
8 Michael Westbrook	1.50	.70
9 Troy Aikman	3.00	1.35
10 Barry Bonds	5.00	2.20
11 Ki-Jana Carter	1.00	.45
12 Dale Earnhardt	6.00	2.70
13 Jason Kidd	2.50	1.10
14 Ed O'Bannon	1.00	.45
15 Shaquille O'Neal	5.00	2.20
16 Glenn Robinson	1.50	.70

1995 Assets Gold Phone Cards $25 *

This 5-card set measures 2 1/8" by 3 3/8" and was randomly inserted in packs. The fronts feature color action player photos of two different players with the player's name in gold below each photo. The $25 calling value is printed vertically in gold separating the two players. The backs carry the instructions on how to use the cards which expired on 7/31/96. The cards are unnumbered.

	MINT	NRMT
COMPLETE SET (5)	60.00	27.00
*PIN NUMBER REVEALED: HALF VALUE		
1 Marshall Faulk Ki-Jana Carter	12.00	5.50
2 Steve McNair Kerry Collins	12.00	5.50
3 Glenn Robinson Rasheed Wallace	10.00	4.50
4 Nolan Ryan Barry Bonds	20.00	9.00
5 Corliss Williamson Ed O'Bannon	8.00	3.60

1995 Assets Gold Phone Cards $1000 *

This five-card set measures 2 1/8" by 3 3/8". The fronts feature color action player photos with the player's name below. The $1000 calling value is printed on the left. The backs carry the instructions on how to use the cards which expired on 7/31/96. The cards are unnumbered and checklisted below in alphabetical order.

	MINT	NRMT
*PIN NUMBER REVEALED:HALF VALUE		
1 Drew Bledsoe	80.00	36.00
2 Dale Earnhardt	120.00	55.00
3 Marshall Faulk	80.00	36.00
4 Shaquille O'Neal	120.00	55.00
5 Nolan Ryan	200.00	90.00

1996 Assets *

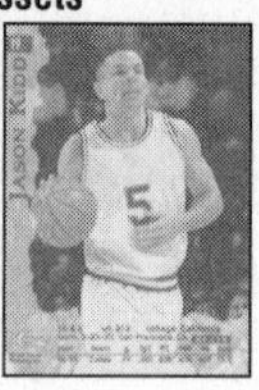

The 1996 Classic Assets was issued in one set totalling 50 cards. This 50-card premium set has a tremendous selection of the top athletes in the world headlines. Each card features action photos, up-to-date statistics and is printed on high-quality, foil-stamped stock. Hot Print cards are parallel cards randomly inserted in Hot Packs and are valued at a multiple of the regular cards below.

	MINT	NRMT
COMPLETE SET (50)	10.00	4.50
1 Troy Aikman	.50	.23
2 Drew Bledsoe	.40	.18
3 Todd Bodine	.15	.07
4 Barry Bonds	.75	.35
5 Isaac Bruce	.25	.11
6 Kerry Collins	.25	.11
7 Trent Dilfer	.15	.07
8 Radek Dvorak	.15	.07
9 Dale Earnhardt	2.50	1.10
10 Marshall Faulk	.75	.35
11 William Floyd	.15	.07
12 Joey Galloway	.15	.07
13 Kevin Garnett	2.00	.90
14 Brian Holzinger	.15	.07
15 Juwan Howard	.15	.07
16 Eddie Jones	.25	.11
17 Ed Jovanovski	.15	.07
18 Jason Kendall	.25	.11
19 Jason Kidd	.40	.18
20 Rebecca Lobo	.30	.14
21 Sterling Marlin	.25	.11
22 Mark Martin	.75	.35
23 Antonio McDyess	.75	.35
24 Steve McNair	.50	.23
25 Byron Bam Morris	.15	.07
26 Alonzo Mourning	.15	.07
27 Ted Musgrave	.15	.07
28 Dikembe Mutombo	.15	.07
29 Ed O'Bannon	.15	.07
30 Shaquille O'Neal	.75	.35
31 Hakeem Olajuwon	.25	.11
32 Cherokee Parks	.15	.07
33 Jay Payton	.15	.07
34 Scottie Pippen	.25	.11
35 Errict Rhett	.15	.07
36 Curtis Martin	.50	.23
37 Glenn Robinson	.15	.07
38 Jalen Rose	.25	.11
39 Nolan Ryan	1.00	.45
40 Darnay Scott	.15	.07
41 Emmitt Smith	.75	.35
42 Joe Smith	.25	.11
43 Jerry Stackhouse	.50	.23
44 Damon Stoudamire	.75	.35
45 Petr Sykora	.15	.07
46 Rasheed Wallace	.50	.23
47 Corliss Williamson	.15	.07
48 Paul Wilson	.15	.07
49 Steve Young	.40	.18
50 Eric Zeier	.15	.07

1996 Assets Hot Prints *

These parallel cards were randomly seeded in 1996 Assets Hot Packs. Each card is marked Hot Print on the cardfront.

	MINT	NRMT
*HOT PRINTS: .75X TO 2X BASIC CARDS		

1996 Assets A Cut Above *

The even cards were randomly inserted in retail packs at a rate of one in eight, and the odd cards were inserted in clear asset packs at a rate of one in 20, this 20-card die-cut set is composed of 10 phone cards and 10 trading cards. The cards have rounded corners except for one which is cut in a straight corner design. The fronts feature a color action player cut-out superimposed over a gray background with the words "cut above" printed throughout and resembled to be cut so it displays a basketball game behind it. The backs carry a color action player photo with the player's name and a short career summary.

	MINT	NRMT
COMPLETE SET (20)	50.00	22.00
CA1 Keyshawn Johnson	5.00	2.20
CA2 Troy Aikman	4.00	1.80
CA3 Shaquille O'Neal	8.00	3.60
CA4 Brian Holzinger	1.00	.45
CA5 Scottie Pippen	2.50	1.10
CA6 Mark Martin	3.00	1.35
CA7 Kevin Hardy	1.00	.45
CA8 Emmitt Smith	5.00	2.20
CA9 Jerry Stackhouse	1.50	.70
CA10 Barry Bonds	5.00	2.20
CA11 Marshall Faulk	4.00	1.80
CA12 Rasheed Wallace	2.50	1.10
CA13 Drew Bledsoe	2.50	1.10
CA14 Joe Smith	1.50	.70
CA15 Kevin Garnett	10.00	4.50
CA16 Jason Kidd	3.00	1.35
CA17 Sterling Marlin	2.50	1.10
CA18 Rebecca Lobo	3.00	1.35
CA19 Kerry Collins	1.50	.70
CA20 Glenn Robinson	1.50	.70

1996 Assets A Cut Above Phone Cards *

This 10-card set, which were inserted at a rate of one in eight, measures approximately 2 1/8" by 3 3/8" have rounded corners except for one corner which is cut out and made straight. The fronts feature a color action player cut-out superimposed over a gray background with the words "cut above" printed throughout and resembled to be cut so that it displays a game going on behind the background. The backs carry the instructions on how to use the card. The cards expired on 1/31/97.

	MINT	NRMT
COMPLETE SET (10)	60.00	27.00
*PIN NUMBER REVEALED: HALF VALUE		
1 Dale Earnhardt	15.00	6.75
2 Shaquille O'Neal	12.00	5.50
3 Scottie Pippen	5.00	2.20
4 Cal Ripken	15.00	6.75
5 Jerry Stackhouse	5.00	2.20
6 Marshall Faulk	6.00	2.70
7 Drew Bledsoe	6.00	2.70
8 Kevin Garnett	20.00	9.00
9 Ed O'Bannon	2.00	.90
10 Kerry Collins	3.00	1.35

1996 Assets Crystal Phone Cards *

Randomly inserted in retail packs at a rate of one in 250, this high-tech, 10-card insert set contains clear holographic phone cards worth five minutes of long distance calling time. The cards measure approximately 2 1/8" by 3 3/8" with rounded corners. The fronts display a color action double-image player cut-out on a clear crystal background with the player's name printed vertically on the side. The backs carry instructions on how to use the card. The cards expired January 31, 1997. Twenty dollar phone cards of these athletes were issued, they are valued as a multiple of the cards below.

	MINT	NRMT
COMPLETE SET (10)	50.00	22.00
*TWENTY DOLLAR CARDS: 1X TO 2.5X		
*PIN NUMBER REVEALED: HALF VALUE		
1 Troy Aikman	8.00	3.60
2 Drew Bledsoe	5.00	2.20
3 Dale Earnhardt	12.00	5.50
4 Marshall Faulk	6.00	2.70
5 Shaquille O'Neal	15.00	6.75
6 Scottie Pippen	5.00	2.20
7 Cal Ripken	15.00	6.75
8 Jason Kidd	6.00	2.70
9 Joe Smith	2.00	.90
10 Jerry Stackhouse	3.00	1.35

1996 Assets Phone Cards $2 *

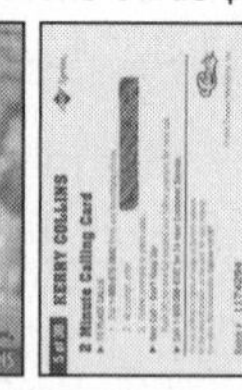

This 30-card set was inserted in retail packs at a rate of 1 per pack with a minimum value of $2 per phone card. The cards measure approximately 2 1/8" by 3 3/8" with rounded corners. The fronts display color aciton player photos with the player's name in a red bar below. The backs carry the instructions on how to use the cards and the expiration date of 1/31/97. Hot Print Cards parallel cards were randomly inserted in Hot Packs. These cards are valued as a mulitple of the cards below.

	MINT	NRMT
COMPLETE SET (30)	30.00	13.50
*$2 CARDS: .6X TO 1.5X $1 CARDS		
*PIN NUMBER REVEALED: HALF VALUE		

1996 Assets Phone Cards $5 *

This 20-card set was randomly inserted in retail packs at a rate of 1 in 5. The cards measure approximately 2 1/8" by 3 3/8" with rounded corners. The fronts display color action player photos with the player's name in a red bar below. The backs carry the instructions on how to use the cards and the expiration date of 1/31/97.

	MINT	NRMT
COMPLETE SET (20)	80.00	36.00
PIN NUMBER REVEALED: HALF VALUE		
Troy Aikman	4.00	1.80
Drew Bledsoe	2.50	1.10
Barry Bonds	2.50	1.10
Isaac Bruce	1.50	.70
Kerry Collins	1.50	.70
Dale Earnhardt	6.00	2.70
Marshall Faulk	3.00	1.35
Kevin Garnett	10.00	4.50
Jason Kidd	3.00	1.35
10 Mark Martin	3.00	1.35
11 Shaquille O'Neal	5.00	2.20
12 Hakeem Olajuwon	2.50	1.10
13 Scottie Pippen	2.50	1.10
14 Cal Ripken	3.00	1.35
15 Nolan Ryan	3.00	1.35
16 Emmitt Smith	5.00	2.20
17 Joe Smith	1.50	.70
18 Jerry Stackhouse	1.50	.70
19 Rasheed Wallace	1.00	.45
20 Steve Young	3.00	1.35

1996 Assets Phone Cards $10 *

This 10-card set was randomly inserted in packs at a rate of 1 in 20. The cards measure approximately 2 1/8" by 3 3/8" with rounded corners. The fronts display color action player photos with the player's name in a red bar below. The backs carry the instructions on how to use the cards and the expiration date of 1/31/97.

	MINT	NRMT
COMPLETE SET (10)	60.00	27.00
*PIN NUMBER REVEALED: HALF VALUE		
1 Troy Aikman	6.00	2.70
2 Drew Bledsoe	5.00	2.20
3 Dale Earnhardt	10.00	4.50
4 Marshall Faulk	5.00	2.20
5 Shaquille O'Neal	10.00	4.50
6 Scottie Pippen	5.00	2.20
7 Cal Ripken	8.00	3.60
8 Emmitt Smith	8.00	3.60
9 Joe Smith	4.00	1.80
10 Jerry Stackhouse	5.00	2.20
NNO Jackie Robinson	2.50	1.10

1996 Assets Phone Cards $20 *

This five card set measures approximately 2 1/8" by 3 3/8" with rounded corners and were randomly inserted in retail packs. The fronts display color action player photos with the player's name. The backs carry the instructions on how to use the cards and the expiration date of 1/31/97.

	MINT	NRMT
COMPLETE SET (5)	60.00	27.00
*PIN NUMBER REVEALED: HALF VALUE		
1 Dale Earnhardt	20.00	9.00
2 Scottie Pippen	8.00	3.60
3 Emmitt Smith	12.00	5.50
4 Cal Ripken	10.00	4.50
5 Shaquille O'Neal	15.00	6.75

1996 Assets Phone Cards $100 *

This five card set, randomly inserted in packs, measures approximately 2 1/8" by 3 3/8" with rounded corners. The fronts display color action player photos with the player's name. The backs carry the instructions on how to use the cards and the expiration date of 1/31/97.

	MINT	NRMT
COMPLETE SET (5)	80.00	36.00
*PIN NUMBER REVEALED: HALF VALUE		
9.00		
1 Dale Earnhardt	25.00	11.00
2 Marshall Faulk	15.00	6.75
3 Shaquille O'Neal	25.00	11.00
4 Scottie Pippen	15.00	6.75
5 Cal Ripken	40.00	18.00

1996 Assets Silksations *

Randomly inserted in retail packs at a rate of one in 100, this 10-card standard-size set features duplexed fabric-stock with top athletes. The fronts display a color action player cut-out with a two-tone background. The player's name is printed below. The backs carry a head photo of the player made to appear as if it is coming out of a square hole in gold cloth. The player's name and a short career summary are below. The cards are numbered with a "S" prefix and sequenced in alphabetical order.

	MINT	NRMT
COMPLETE SET (10)	80.00	36.00
1 Barry Bonds	25.00	11.00
2 Kerry Collins	8.00	3.60
3 Dale Earnhardt	25.00	11.00
4 Marshall Faulk	12.00	5.50
5 Jason Kidd	12.00	5.50
6 Shaquille O'Neal	25.00	11.00
7 Scottie Pippen	10.00	4.50
8 Emmitt Smith	20.00	9.00
9 Joe Smith	5.00	2.20
10 Jerry Stackhouse	8.00	3.60

1992-93 Classic C3 *

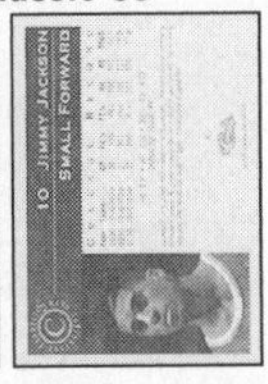

Limited to only 25,000 members, the Classic Collectors Club (also known as C3) featured two types of memberships: 1) the Presidential Charter membership (5,000), and 2) the Charter membership (20,000). As a bonus, the first 10,000 members received three packs of the bilingual edition of the 1991 Classic Draft Picks Collection. Exclusive to Presidential members were the following: a Brien Taylor autograph card (hand numbered "X/5,000"); an uncut sheet of either 1992 baseball, football, or hockey draft picks; and three special promo cards. In addition to other items (promo cards, T-shirt, newsletter, membership card, and posters), all members received a 30-card standard-size multi-sport set featuring tomorrow's future stars. Each set was accompanied by a certificate of limited edition, giving the set serial number and total production run (25,000). The sports represented are baseball (1-7, 25-27), basketball (8-13), football (14-20), hockey (21-24), track and field (28), and swimming (29).

	MINT	NRMT
COMP.FACT SET (30)	15.00	6.75
1 Phil Nevin	3.00	1.35
2 Jeffrey Hammonds	2.00	.90
3 Paul Shuey	1.00	.45
4 Derek Jeter	10.00	4.50
5 B.J. Wallace	1.00	.45
6 Ryan Luzinski	1.00	.45
7 Brien Taylor	1.00	.45
8 Alonzo Mourning	5.00	2.20
9 Christian Laettner	2.00	.90
10 Jimmy Jackson	2.00	.90
11 Harold Miner	2.00	.90
12 Billy Owens	2.00	.90
13 Dikembe Mutombo	2.00	.90
14 Desmond Howard	2.00	.90
15 David Klingler	1.00	.45
16 Quentin Coryatt	1.00	.45
17 Carl Pickens	2.00	.90
18 Tony Smith	1.00	.45
19 Rocket Ismail	2.00	.90
20 Terrell Buckley	1.00	.45
21 Roman Hamrlik	1.00	.45
22 Mike Rathje	1.00	.45
23 Manon Rheaume	2.00	.90
24 Viktor Kozlov	2.00	.90
25 David McCarty	1.00	.45
26 Mike Kelly	1.00	.45
27 Dmitri Young	3.00	1.35
28 Carl Lewis	2.00	.90
29 Pablo Morales	2.00	.90
30 Checklist	1.00	.45

1993-94 Classic C3 Gold Crown Cut Lasercut *

Along with the 20-card set checklisted below, the 10,000 members of the 1994 Classic Collectors Gold Crown Club received a 1994 C3 T-shirt, a TONX milk caps collectible sheet, a Classic Games magnet, and a 1994 C3 membership card. In later mailings they also received a 1993 Basketball Draft uncut sheet, a Chris Webber poster, and an autographed card of Jamal Mashburn, along with two promo cards. The sports represented are basketball (1-6), football (7-13), baseball (14-17), and hockey (18-20). The unnumbered checklist carries the set's production number out of the 10,000 produced.

	MINT	NRMT
COMPLETE SET (21)	25.00	11.00
1 Chris Webber	2.00	.90
2 Anfernee Hardaway	1.50	.70
3 Jamal Mashburn	1.00	.45
4 Isaiah Rider	1.00	.45
5 Rodney Rogers	1.00	.45
6 Toni Kukoc	1.00	.45
7 Drew Bledsoe	3.00	1.35
8 Rick Mirer	1.00	.45
9 Garrison Hearst	1.00	.45
10 Terry Kirby	1.00	.45
11 Glyn Milburn	1.00	.45
12 Reggie Brooks	1.00	.45
13 Jerome Bettis	2.00	.90
14 Jeff Granger	1.00	.45
15 Brooks Kieschnick	1.00	.45
16 Alex Rodriguez	15.00	6.75
17 Darren Dreifort	1.00	.45
18 Alexandre Daigle	1.00	.45
19 Chris Pronger	1.00	.45
20 Chris Gratton	1.00	.45
NNO Checklist	1.00	.45

1994 Classic C3 Gold Crown Club *

Part of a special issue to Classic Collector's Club members, these standard-size cards feature on their fronts color player action shots that are borderless, except at the bottom, where the player's name appears. His first name is shown at the bottom left within a gray rectangle, which is actually a vertically distorted and ghosted black-and-white player action shot. The last name is shown within a black rectangle edging the bottom right. Another vertically distorted black-and-white player action shot forms a stripe that roughly bisects the back. A color player action shot appears on the left side; the player's name and statistics are shown vertically within white and black panels on the right. As part of the 1994 Classic Collectors Gold Crown Club offer, members also received one of 10,000 individually numbered standard-size white bordered autographed card of Jamal Mashburn. His autograph in blue ink appears across the card face. The back carries the C3 logo and a congratulatory message.

	MINT	NRMT
COMPLETE SET (4)	15.00	6.75
CC1 Alonzo Mourning	5.00	2.20
Georgetown		
CC2 Brooks Kieschnick	2.00	.90
Texas		
CC3 Emmitt Smith	10.00	4.50
CC4 Donyell Marshall	3.00	1.35
NNO Jamal Mashburn	15.00	6.75
AUTO/10000		

1991 Classic Four-Sport *

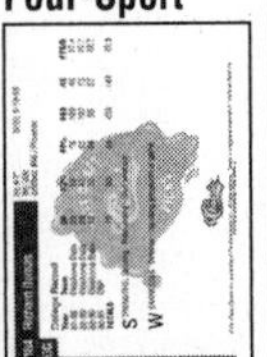

This 230-card multi-sport standard-size set includes all 200 draft picks players from the four Classic Draft Picks sets (football, baseball, basketball, and hockey), plus an additional 30 draft picks not previously found in these other sets. A subset within the 230 cards consists of five cards highlighting the publicized one-on-one game between Billy Owens and Larry Johnson. As an additional incentive to collectors, Classic randomly inserted over 60,000 autographed cards into the 15-card foil packs; it is claimed that each case should contain two or more autographed cards. The autographed cards feature 61 different players, approximately two-thirds of whom were hockey players. The production run for the English version was 25,000 cases, and a bilingual (French) version of the set was also produced at 20 percent of the English production. The major subdivisions of set are according to sport: hockey (2-50), baseball (51-101), football (102-148), and basketball (149-202).

	MINT	NRMT
COMPLETE SET (230)	10.00	4.50
*FRENCH VERSION: .4X TO 1X		
1 Larry Johnson	.40	.18
Brien Taylor		
Russell Maryland		
Eric Lindros		
2 Pat Falloon	.25	.11
3 Scott Niedermayer	.40	.18
4 Scott Lachance	.15	.07
5 Peter Forsberg	1.00	.45
6 Alex Stojanov	.15	.07
7 Richard Matvichuk	.25	.11
8 Patrick Poulin	.15	.07
9 Martin Lapointe	.25	.11
10 Tyler Wright	.15	.07
11 Philippe Boucher	.15	.07
12 Pat Peake	.15	.07
13 Markus Naslund	.25	.11
14 Brent Bilodeau	.15	.07
15 Glen Murray	.15	.07
16 Niklas Sundblad	.15	.07
17 Martin Rucinsky	.15	.07
18 Trevor Halverson	.15	.07
19 Dean McAmmond	.15	.07
20 Ray Whitney	.40	.18
21 Rene Corbet	.15	.07
22 Eric Lavigne	.15	.07
23 Zigmund Palffy	.50	.23
24 Steve Staios	.15	.07
25 Jim Campbell	.25	.11
26 Jassen Cullimore	.15	.07
27 Martin Hamrlik	.15	.07
28 Jamie Pushor	.25	.11
29 Donevan Hextall	.15	.07
30 Andrew Verner	.15	.07
31 Jason Dawe	.15	.07
32 Jeff Nelson	.15	.07
33 Darcy Werenka	.15	.07
34 Jozef Stumpel	.40	.18
35 Francois Groleau	.15	.07
36 Guy Leveque	.15	.07
37 Jamie Matthews	.15	.07
38 Dody Wood	.15	.07
39 Yanic Perreault	.25	.11
41 Yanick Dupre UER	.15	.07
(Yanic misspelled on both sides)		
42 Sandy McCarthy	.25	.11
43 Chris Osgood	.75	.35
44 Fredrik Lindquist	.15	.07
45 Jason Young	.15	.07
46 Steve Konowalchuk	.25	.11
47 Michael Nylander UER	.25	.11
48 Shane Peacock	.15	.07
49 Yves Sarault	.15	.07
50 Marcel Cousineau	.15	.07
51 Brien Taylor	.40	.18
52 Mike Kelly	.25	.11
53 David McCarty	.40	.18
54 Dmitri Young	.40	.18
55 Joe Vitiello	.15	.07
56 Mark Smith	.15	.07
57 Tyler Green	.25	.11
58 Shawn Estes UER	.40	.18
(Reversed negative)		
59 Doug Glanville	.40	.18
60 Manny Ramirez	1.50	.70
61 Cliff Floyd	1.00	.45
62 Tyrone Hill	.15	.07
63 Eduardo Perez	.25	.11
64 Al Shirley	.15	.07
65 Benji Gil	.25	.11
66 Calvin Reese	.25	.11
67 Allen Watson	.25	.11
68 Brian Barber	.15	.07
69 Aaron Sele	.40	.18
70 Jon Farrell UER	.15	.07
71 Scott Ruffcorn	.15	.07
72 Brent Gates	.15	.07
73 Scott Stahoviak	.15	.07
74 Tom McKinnon	.15	.07
75 Shawn Livsey	.15	.07
76 Jason Pruitt	.15	.07
77 Greg Anthony	.15	.07
Baseball		
78 Justin Thompson	.25	.11
79 Steve Whitaker	.15	.07
80 Jorge Fabregas	.25	.11
81 Jeff Ware	.15	.07
82 Bobby Jones	.25	.11
83 J.J. Johnson	.15	.07
84 Mike Rossiter	.15	.07
85 Dan Cholowsky	.15	.07
86 Jimmy Gonzalez	.15	.07
87 Trever Miller UER	.15	.07
88 Scott Hatteberg	.40	.18
89 Mike Groppuso	.15	.07
90 Ryan Long	.15	.07
91 Eddie Williams	.15	.07
92 Mike Durant	.15	.07
93 Buck McNabb	.15	.07
94 Jimmy Lewis	.15	.07
95 Eddie Ramos	.15	.07
96 Terry Horn	.15	.07
97 Jon Barnes	.15	.07
98 Shawn Curran	.15	.07
99 Tommy Adams	.15	.07
100 Trevor Mallory	.15	.07
101 Frank Rodriguez	.25	.11
102 Rocket Ismail	.40	.18
103 Russell Maryland	.25	.11
104 Eric Turner	.15	.07
105 Bruce Pickens	.15	.07
106 Mike Croel	.15	.07
107 Todd Lyght	.15	.07
108 Eric Swann	.15	.07
109 Antone Davis	.15	.07
110 Stanley Richard	.15	.07
111 Pat Harlow	.15	.07
112 Alvin Harper	.25	.11
113 Mike Pritchard	.25	.11
114 Leonard Russell	.15	.07
115 Dan McGwire	.15	.07
116 Bobby Wilson	.15	.07
117 Vinnie Clark	.15	.07
118 Kelvin Pritchett	.15	.07
119 Harvey Williams	.25	.11
120 Stan Thomas	.15	.07
121 Randal Hill	.25	.11
122 Todd Marinovich	.15	.07
123 Henry Jones	.25	.11
124 Mike Dumas	.15	.07
125 Ed King	.15	.07
126 Reggie Johnson	.15	.07
127 Roman Phifer	.25	.11
128 Mike Jones	.25	.11
129 Brett Favre	2.00	.90
130 Browning Nagle	.15	.07
131 Esera Tuaolo	.15	.07
132 George Thornton	.15	.07
133 Dixon Edwards	.25	.11
134 Terrell Brandon	.40	.18
135 Eric Bieniemy	.25	.11
136 Shane Curry	.15	.07
137 Jerome Henderson	.15	.07
138 Wesley Carroll	.15	.07
139 Nick Bell	.15	.07
140 John Flannery	.15	.07
141 Ricky Watters	.30	.14
142 Jeff Graham	.25	.11
143 Eric Moten	.15	.07
144 Jesse Campbell	.15	.07
145 Chris Zorich	.15	.07
146 Doug Thomas	.25	.11
147 Phil Hansen	.25	.11
148 Reggie Barrett	.25	.11
149 Larry Johnson	1.00	.45
150 Billy Owens	.40	.18
151 Dikembe Mutombo	1.00	.45
152 Mark Macon	.40	.18
153 Brian Williams	.25	.11
154 Terrell Brandon	.75	.35
155 Greg Anthony	.40	.18
Basketball		
156 Dale Davis	.75	.35
157 Anthony Avent	.25	.11
158 Chris Gatling	.40	.18
159 Victor Alexander	.25	.11
160 Kevin Brooks	.25	.11
161 Eric Murdock	.40	.18
162 LeRon Ellis	.25	.11
163 Stanley Roberts	.25	.11
164 Rick Fox	.75	.35
165 Pete Chilcutt	.40	.18
166 Kevin Lynch	.25	.11
167 George Ackles	.25	.11
168 Rodney Monroe	.25	.11
169 Randy Brown	.40	.18
170 Chad Gallagher	.15	.07
171 Donald Hodge	.15	.07
172 Myron Brown	.15	.07
173 Mike Iuzzolino	.25	.11
174 Chris Corchiani	.25	.11
175 Elliot Perry	.40	.18
176 Joe Wylie	.15	.07
177 Jimmy Oliver	.25	.11
178 Doug Overton	.15	.07
179 Sean Green	.15	.07
180 Steve Hood	.15	.07
181 Lamont Strothers	.15	.07
182 Alvaro Teheran	.15	.07
183 Bobby Phills	.40	.18
184 Richard Dumas	.25	.11
185 Keith Hughes	.15	.07
186 Isaac Austin	.40	.18
187 Greg Sutton	.15	.07
188 Joey Wright	.15	.07
189 Anthony Jones	.15	.07
190 Von McDade	.15	.07
191 Marcus Kennedy	.15	.07
192 Larry Johnson	.40	.18
(Number One Pick)		
193 Classic One on One II	.40	.18
194 Anderson Hunt	.15	.07
195 Darrin Chancellor	.15	.07
196 Damon Lopez	.15	.07
197 Thomas Jordan	.15	.07
198 Tony Farmer	.15	.07
199 Billy Owens	.40	.18
(Number Three Pick)		
200 Owens Takes 4-3 Lead	.40	.18
(Billy Owens)		
201 Johnson Slams for 6-6 Tie	.40	.18
(Larry Johnson)		
202 Score Tied with :49 Left	.40	.18
203 Gary Brown	.25	.11
204 Rob Carpenter	.15	.07
205 Ricky Ervins	.25	.11
206 Donald Hollas	.15	.07
207 Greg Lewis	.15	.07
208 Darren Lewis	.15	.07
209 Anthony Morgan	.15	.07
210 Chris Smith	.25	.11
211 Perry Carter	.25	.11
212 Melvin Cheatum	.25	.11
213 Jerome Harmon	.25	.11
214 Keith (Mr.) Jennings	.25	.11
215 Brian Shorter	.25	.11
216 Dexter Davis	.15	.07
217 Ed McCaffrey	.50	.23
218 Joey Hamilton	.25	.11
219 Marc Kroon	.15	.07
220 Moe Gardner	.15	.07
221 Jon Vaughn	.15	.07
222 Lawrence Dawsey	.15	.07
223 Michael Stonebreaker	.15	.07
224 Shawn Moore	.15	.07
225 Shawn Green	1.50	.70
226 Scott Pisciotta	.15	.07
227 Checklist 1	.15	.07
228 Checklist 2	.15	.07
229 Checklist 3	.15	.07
230 Checklist 4	.15	.07

1991 Classic Four-Sport Autographs *

The 1991 Classic Draft Collection Autograph set consists of 61 standard-size cards. They were randomly inserted throughout the foil packs. Listed after the player's name is how many cards were autographed by that player. An "A" suffix after card number is used here for convenience.

	MINT	NRMT
2A Pat Falloon/1100	6.00	2.70
3A Scott Niedermayer/1250	8.00	3.60
4A Scott Lachance/1100	2.00	.90
6A Alek Stojanov/950	2.00	.90
8A Patrick Poulin/1100	2.00	.90
10A Tyler Wright/950	2.00	.90
11A Philippe Boucher/1150	2.00	.90
12A Pat Peake/1100	5.00	2.20
14A Brent Bilodeau/1000	2.00	.90
15A Glen Murray/1100	5.00	2.20
16A Niklas Sundblad/900	2.00	.90
17A Martin Rucinsky/1100	2.00	.90
18A Trevor Halverson/1100	2.00	.90
19A Dean McAmmond/1100	2.00	.90
20A Ray Whitney/2600	6.00	2.70
21A Rene Corbet/950	2.00	.90
22A Eric Lavigne/1100	2.00	.90
24A Steve Staios/1100	2.00	.90
25A Jim Campbell/1100	6.00	2.70
26A Jassen Cullimore/1000	2.00	.90
28A Jamie Pushor/1050	2.00	.90
29A Donevan Hextall/1100	2.00	.90
30A Andrew Verner/1200	2.00	.90
31A Jason Dawe/950	2.00	.90
32A Jeff Nelson/1100	2.00	.90
33A Darcy Werenka/1150	2.00	.90

Card	MINT	NRMT
35A Francois Groleau/1150	2.00	.90
36A Guy Leveque/1150	2.00	.90
37A Jamie Matthews/1100	2.00	.90
38A Dody Wood/1050	2.00	.90
39A Yanic Perreault/1100	2.00	.90
40A Jamie Matthews/1100	2.00	.90
41A Yanick Dupre/1050	2.00	.90
42A Sandy McCarthy/1150	6.00	2.70
43A Chris Osgood/1100	15.00	6.75
44A Fredrick Lindquist/1100	2.00	.90
45A Jason Young/1200	2.00	.90
46A Steve Konowalchuk/1350	6.00	2.70
47A Michael Nylander/1100	2.00	.90
48A Shane Peacock/1150	2.00	.90
49A Yves Sarault/1150	2.00	.90
50A Marcel Cousineau/1100	2.00	.90
51A Brien Taylor/2600	5.00	2.20
52A Mike Kelly/2600	2.00	.90
53A David McCarty/2450	2.00	.90
54A Dmitri Young/2600	5.00	2.20
55A Joe Vitiello/1900	2.00	.90
56A Mark Smith/1700	2.00	.90
58A Shawn Estes/2000	5.00	2.20
59A Doug Glanville/2000	5.00	2.20
61A Cliff Floyd/2000	15.00	6.75
62A Tyrone Hill/1000	2.00	.90
63A Eduardo Perez/950	2.00	.90
101A Frank Rodriguez/1450	2.00	.90
102A Rocket Ismail/2000	10.00	4.50
103A Russell Maryland/1000	8.00	3.60
150A Billy Owens/2500	5.00	2.20
151A Dikembe Mutombo/1000	20.00	9.00
153A Brian Williams/1500	2.00	.90
163A Stanley Roberts/2000	2.00	.90
218A Joey Hamilton/2000	2.00	.90

1992 Classic Four-Sport Previews *

These five preview standard-size cards were randomly inserted in baseball and hockey draft picks foil packs. According to the backs, just 10,000 of each card were produced. The fronts display the full-bleed glossy color player photos. At the upper right corner, the word "Preview" surmounts the Classic logo. This logo overlays a black stripe that runs down the left side and features the player's name and position. The gray backs have the word "Preview" in red lettering at the top and are accented by short purple diagonal stripes on each side. Between the stripes are a congratulations and an advertisement. The cards are numbered on the back with a "CC" prefix.

	MINT	NRMT
COMPLETE SET (5)	20.00	9.00
CC1 Shaquille O'Neal	15.00	6.75
CC2 Desmond Howard	1.50	.70
CC3 Roman Hamrlik	1.00	.45
CC4 Phil Nevin	1.00	.45
CC5 Alonzo Mourning	3.00	1.35

1992 Classic Four-Sport *

The 1992 Classic Draft Picks Collection consists of 325 standard-size cards, featuring the top picks from football, basketball, baseball, and hockey drafts. According to Classic, 40,000 12-box foil cases were produced. Randomly inserted in the 12-card packs were over 100,000 autograph cards from over 50 of the top draft picks from basketball, football, baseball, and hockey, including cards autographed by Shaquille O'Neal, Desmond Howard, Roman Hamrlik, and Phil Nevin. Also inserted in the packs were "Instant Win Giveway Cards" that entitled the collector to the 500,000.00 sports memorabilia giveway that Classic offered in this contest. There was also a factory set produced with gold parallel cards.

	MINT	NRMT
COMPLETE SET (325)	15.00	6.75
COMP.FACT.GOLD SET (326)	100.00	45.00
FUT. SUPERSTARS AU/9500	50.00	22.00
*GOLDS: 1.5X TO 4X BASIC CARDS...		.07
1 Shaquille O'Neal	4.00	1.80
2 Walt Williams	.40	.18
3 Lee Mayberry	.25	.11
4 Tony Bennett	.25	.11
5 Litterial Green	.15	.07
6 Chris Smith	.15	.07
7 Henry Williams	.15	.07
8 Terrell Lowery	.25	.11
9 Curtis Blair	.15	.07
10 Randy Woods	.15	.07
11 Todd Day	.40	.18
12 Anthony Peeler	.40	.18
13 Darin Archibold	.15	.07
14 Benford Williams	.15	.07
15 Damon Patterson	.15	.07
16 Bryant Stith	.40	.18
17 Doug Christie	.40	.18
18 Latrell Sprewell	1.50	.70
19 Hubert Davis	.40	.18
20 David Booth	.25	.11
21 Dave Johnson	.25	.11
22 Jon Barry	.40	.18
23 Everick Sullivan	.15	.07
24 Brian Davis	.15	.07
25 Clarence Weatherspoon	.40	.18
26 Malik Sealy	.40	.18
27 Matt Geiger	.40	.18
28 Jimmy Jackson	.40	.18
29 Matt Steigenga	.25	.11
30 Robert Horry	.40	.18
31 Marlon Maxey	.15	.07
32 Chris King	.15	.07
33 Dexter Cambridge	.15	.07
34 Alonzo Jamison	.15	.07
35 Anthony Tucker	.15	.07
36 Tracy Murray	.40	.18
37 Vernel Singleton	.15	.07
38 Christian Laettner	.40	.18
39 Don MacLean	.40	.18
40 Adam Keefe	.25	.11
41 Tom Gugliotta	.40	.18
42 LaPhonso Ellis	.40	.18
43 Byron Houston	.25	.11
44 Oliver Miller	.25	.11
45 Popeye Jones	.25	.11
46 P.J. Brown	.40	.18
47 Eric Anderson	.15	.07
48 Darren Morningstar	.15	.07
49 Isaiah Morris	.15	.07
50 Stephen Howard	.15	.07
51 Elmore Spencer	.15	.07
52 Sean Rooks	.25	.11
53 Robert Werdann	.25	.11
54 Alonzo Mourning	1.00	.45
55 Steve Rogers	.15	.07
56 Tim Burroughs	.15	.07
57 Herb Jones	.15	.07
58 Sean Miller	.15	.07
59 Corey Williams	.15	.07
60 Duane Cooper	.15	.07
61 Brett Roberts	.15	.07
62 Elmer Bennett	.15	.07
63 Brent Price	.25	.11
64 Daimon Sweet	.15	.07
65 Darrick Martin	.15	.07
66 Gerald Madkins	.15	.07
67 Jo Jo English	.15	.07
68 Math Fish	.15	.07
69 Harold Miner	.40	.18
70 Greg Dennis	.15	.07
71 Jeff Roulston	.15	.07
72 Keir Rogers	.15	.07
73 Geoff Lear	.15	.07
74 Ron Ellis	.15	.07
75 Predrag Danilovic	.25	.11
76 Desmond Howard	.40	.18
77 David Klingler	.25	.11
78 Quentin Coryatt	.15	.07
79 Bill Johnson	.15	.07
80 Eugene Chung	.15	.07
81 Derek Brown	.15	.07
82 Carl Pickens	.40	.18
83 Chris Mims	.15	.07
84 Charles Davenport	.15	.07
85 Ray Roberts	.15	.07
86 Chuck Smith	.15	.07
87 Tony Smith RB	.15	.07
88 Ken Swilling	.15	.07
89 Greg Skrepenak	.15	.07
90 Phillippi Sparks	.15	.07
91 Alonzo Spellman	.15	.07
92 Bernard Dafney	.15	.07
93 Edgar Bennett	.40	.18
94 Shane Dronett	.15	.07
95 Jeremy Lincoln	.15	.07
96 Dion Lambert	.15	.07
97 Siran Stacy	.15	.07
98 Tony Sacca	.15	.07
99 Sean Lumpkin	.15	.07
100 Tommy Vardell	.15	.07
101 Keith Hamilton	.15	.07
102 Sean Gilbert	.25	.11
103 Casey Weldon	.15	.07
104 Marc Boutte	.15	.07
105 Arthur Marshall	.15	.07
106 Santana Dotson	.25	.11
107 Ronnie West	.15	.07
108 Mike Pawlawski	.15	.07
109 Dale Carter	.25	.11
110 Carlos Snow	.15	.07
111 Mark D'Onofrio	.15	.07
112 Matt Blundin	.15	.07
113 Patrick Rowe	.15	.07
114 Joel Steed	.15	.07
115 Erick Anderson	.15	.07
116 Rodney Culver	.15	.07
117 Chris Hakel	.15	.07
118 Kevin Smith	.15	.07
119 Robert Brooks	.40	.18
120 Bucky Richardson	.15	.07
121 Steve Israel	.15	.07
122 Marco Coleman	.15	.07
123 Johnny Mitchell	.15	.07
124 Scottie Graham	.25	.11
125 Keith Goganious	.15	.07
126 Tommy Maddox	.15	.07
127 Terrell Buckley	.15	.07
128 Dana Hall	.15	.07
129 Ty Detmer	.40	.18
130 Darryl Williams	.15	.07
131 Jason Hanson	.40	.18
132 Leon Searcy	.15	.07
133 Will Furrer	.15	.07
134 Darren Woodson	.40	.18
135 Corey Widmer	.15	.07
136 Larry Tharpe	.15	.07
137 Lance Olberding	.15	.07
138 Stacey Dillard	.15	.07
139 Anthony Hamlet	.15	.07
140 Mike Evans	.15	.07
141 Chester McGlockton	.25	.11
142 Marquez Pope	.15	.07
143 Tyrone Legette	.15	.07
144 Derrick Moore	.25	.11
145 Calvin Holmes	.15	.07
146 Eddie Robinson Jr.	.25	.11
147 Robert Jones	.15	.07
148 Ricardo McDonald	.15	.07
149 Howard Dinkins	.15	.07
150 Todd Collins	.15	.07
151 Roman Hamrlik	.15	.07
152 Alexei Yashin	.25	.11
153 Mike Rathje	.15	.07
154 Darius Kasparaitis	.15	.07
155 Cory Stillman	.15	.07
156 Robert Petrovicky	.15	.07
157 Andrei Nazarov	.15	.07
158 Jason Bowen	.15	.07
159 Jason Smith	.15	.07
160 David Wilkie	.15	.07
161 Curtis Bowen	.15	.07
162 Grant Marshall	.25	.11
163 Valeri Bure	.30	.14
164 Jeff Shantz	.15	.07
165 Justin Hocking	.15	.07
166 Mike Peca	.50	.23
167 Marc Hussey	.15	.07
168 Sandy Allan	.15	.07
169 Kirk Maltby	.25	.11
170 Cale Hulse	.15	.07
171 Sylvain Cloutier	.15	.07
172 Martin Gendron	.15	.07
173 Kevin Smyth	.15	.07
174 Jason McBain	.15	.07
175 Lee J. Leslie	.15	.07
176 Ralph Intranuovo	.15	.07
177 Martin Reichel	.15	.07
178 Stefan Ustorf	.15	.07
179 Jarkko Varvio	.15	.07
180 Martin Straka	.50	.23
181 Libor Polasek	.15	.07
182 Jozef Cierny	.15	.07
183 Sergei Krivokrasov	.40	.18
184 Sergei Gonchar	.40	.18
185 Boris Mironov	.25	.11
186 Denis Metyluk	.15	.07
187 Sergei Klimovich	.15	.07
188 Sergei Brylin	.15	.07
189 Andrei Nikolishin	.25	.11
190 Alexander Cherbayev	.15	.07
191 Vitali Tomilin	.15	.07
192 Sandy Moger	.25	.11
193 Darrin Madeley	.15	.07
194 Denny Felsner	.15	.07
195 Dwayne Norris	.15	.07
196 Joby Messier	.15	.07
197 Michael Stewart	.15	.07
198 Scott Thomas	.15	.07
199 Daniel Laperriere	.15	.07
200 Martin Lacroix	.25	.11
201 Scott LaGrand	.15	.07
202 Scott Pellerin	.15	.07
203 Jean-Yves Roy	.15	.07
204 Rob Gaudreau	.15	.07
205 Jeff McLean	.15	.07
206 Dallas Drake	.25	.11
207 Doug Zmolek	.15	.07
208 Duane Derksen	.15	.07
209 Jim Cummins	.15	.07
210 Lonnie Loach	.15	.07
211 Rob Zamuner	.25	.11
212 Brad Werenka	.25	.11
213 Brent Grieve	.15	.07
214 Sean Hill	.15	.07
215 Peter Ciavaglia	.15	.07
216 Jason Ruff	.15	.07
217 Shawn McCosh	.15	.07
218 Dave Tretowicz	.15	.07
219 Mike Vukonich	.15	.07
220 Kevin Wortman	.15	.07
221 Jason Muzzatti	.15	.07
222 Dmitri Kvartalnov	.15	.07
223 Ray Whitney	.40	.18
224 Manon Rheaume	1.00	.45
225 Viktor Kozlov	.30	.14
226 Phil Nevin	.40	.18
227 Paul Shuey	.25	.11
228 B.J. Wallace	.15	.07
229 Jeffrey Hammonds	.40	.18
230 Chad Mottola	.15	.07
231 Derek Jeter	5.00	2.20
232 Michael Tucker	.25	.11
233 Derek Wallace	.15	.07
234 Kenny Felder	.15	.07
235 Chad McConnell	.15	.07
236 Sean Lowe	.15	.07
237 Ricky Greene	.15	.07
238 Chris Roberts	.15	.07
239 Shannon Stewart	.40	.18
240 Benji Grigsby	.15	.07
241 Jamie Arnold	.15	.07
242 Rick Helling	.25	.11
243 Jason Kendall	.40	.18
244 Todd Steverson	.15	.07
245 Dan Serafini	.15	.07
246 Jeff Schmidt	.15	.07
247 Sherard Clinkscales	.15	.07
248 Ryan Luzinski	.15	.07
249 Shon Walker	.15	.07
250 Brandon Cromer	.15	.07
251 Dave Landaker	.15	.07
252 Michael Mathews	.15	.07
253 Brian Sackinsky	.15	.07
254 Jon Lieber	.25	.11
255 Jim Rosenbohm	.15	.07
256 DeShawn Warren	.15	.07
257 Mike Buddie	.15	.07
258 Chris Smith	.15	.07
259 Dwain Bostic	.15	.07
260 Bobby Hughes	.15	.07
261 Rick Magdellano	.15	.07
262 Bob Wolcott	.15	.07
263 Mike Gulan	.15	.07
264 Yuri Sanchez	.15	.07
265 Tony Sheffield	.15	.07
266 Dan Melandez	.15	.07
267 Jason Giambi	1.50	.70
268 Ritchie Moody	.15	.07
269 Trey Beamon	.15	.07
270 Tim Crabtree	.15	.07
271 Chad Roper	.15	.07
272 Mark Thompson	.15	.07
273 Marquis Riley	.15	.07
274 Tom Knauss	.15	.07
275 Chris Holt	.15	.07
276 Jon Nunnally	.15	.07
277 Everett Stull	.15	.07
278 Billy Owens	.15	.07
279 Todd Etler	.15	.07
280 Benji Simonton	.15	.07
281 Dwight Maness	.15	.07
282 Chris Eddy	.15	.07
283 Brant Brown	.15	.07
284 Kurt Ehmann	.15	.07
285 Chris Widger	.15	.07
286 Steve Montgomery	.15	.07
287 Chris Gomez	.25	.11
288 Jared Baker	.15	.07
289 Doug Hecker	.15	.07
290 David Spykstra	.15	.07
291 Scott Miller	.15	.07
292 Carey Paige	.15	.07
293 Dave Manning	.15	.07
294 James Keefe	.15	.07
295 Levon Largusa	.15	.07
296 Roger Bailey	.15	.07
297 Rich Ireland	.15	.07
298 Matt Williams	.15	.07
299 Scott Gentile	.15	.07
300 Hut Smith	.15	.07
301 Dave Brown	.15	.07
302 Bobby Bonds Jr.	.25	.11
303 Reggie Smith	.15	.07
304 Preston Wilson	.60	.25
305 John Burke	.15	.07
306 Rodney Henderson	.15	.07
307 Pete Janicki	.15	.07
308 Brien Taylor FLB	.15	.07
309 Mike Kelly FLB	.15	.07
310 Rocket Ismail FLB	.25	.11
311 Billy Owens FLB	.25	.11
312 Dikembe Mutombo FLB	.40	.18
313 Ty Detmer and Desmond Howard	.40	.18
314 Jim Pittsley	.15	.07
315 Christian Laettner JWA	.40	.18
316 Harold Miner JWA	.40	.18
317 Jimmy Jackson JWA	.40	.18
318 Shaquille O'Neal JWA	2.00	.90
319 Alonzo Mourning JWA	.40	.18
320 Checklist 1	.15	.07
321 Checklist 2	.15	.07
322 Checklist 3	.15	.07
323 Checklist 4	.15	.07
324 Checklist 5	.15	.07
325 Checklist 6	.15	.07

(Foil checklist includes LP's; jumbo checklist only list regular cards)

1992 Classic Four-Sport Autographs *

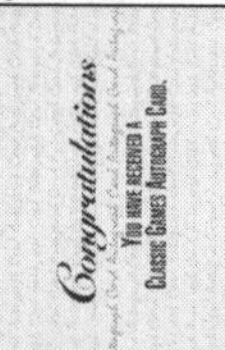

The 1992 Classic Draft Collection Autograph set consists of 56 standard-size cards. They were randomly inserted throughout the foil packs. Listed after the player's name is how many cards were autographed by that player. An "A" suffix after card number is used here for convenience. Jan Caloun and Jan Vopat were not included in the regular set and hence are unnumbered.

Card	MINT	NRMT
1A Shaquille O'Neal/150	600.00	275.00
2A Walt Williams/2550	10.00	4.50
3A Lee Mayberry/2575	5.00	2.20
11A Todd Day/1575	10.00	4.50
25A Clar.Weatherspoon/1575	10.00	4.50
26A Malik Sealy/1575	10.00	4.50
28A Jimmy Jackson/1575	15.00	6.75
36A Tracy Murray/1450	10.00	4.50
38A Christian Laettner/725	25.00	11.00
39A Don MacLean/2575	5.00	2.20
40A Adam Keefe/1575	5.00	2.20
54A Alonzo Mourning/975	40.00	18.00
69A Harold Miner/1475	10.00	4.50
76A Desmond Howard/975	5.00	2.20
77A David Klingler/1125	3.00	1.35
78A Quentin Coryatt/3500	5.00	2.20
82A Carl Pickens/1475	10.00	4.50
87A Tony Smith/3450	3.00	1.35
97A Siran Stacy/4325	3.00	1.35
98A Tony Sacca/1575	3.00	1.35
103A Casey Weldon/4350	3.00	1.35
108A Mike Pawlawski/1475	3.00	1.35
112A Matt Blundin/1575	3.00	1.35
126A Tommy Maddox/4575	20.00	9.00
127A Terrell Buckley/1475	3.00	1.35
129A Ty Detmer/1475	5.00	2.20
144A Derrick Moore/1575	3.00	1.35
151A Roman Hamrlik/1550	5.00	2.20
153A Mike Rathje/2075	3.00	1.35
155A Cory Stillman/2125	3.00	1.35
158A Jason Bowen/2075	3.00	1.35
159A Jason Smith/2075	3.00	1.35
165A Justin Hocking/2075	3.00	1.35
170A Cale Hulse/1850	3.00	1.35
181A Libor Polasek/1950	3.00	1.35
185A Boris Mironov/2075	3.00	1.35
192A Sandy Moger/1075	3.00	1.35
195A Dwayne Norris/1075	3.00	1.35
196A Joby Messier/1075	3.00	1.35
207A Doug Zmolek/1075	3.00	1.35
226A Phil Nevin/1475	10.00	4.50
227A Paul Shuey/4050	3.00	1.35
229A Jeffrey Hammonds/2950	5.00	2.20
231A Derek Jeter/1125	150.00	70.00
233A Derek Wallace/1475	3.00	1.35
241A Jamie Arnold/1575	3.00	1.35
242A Rick Helling/2875	5.00	2.20
245A Dan Serafini/1475	3.00	1.35
248A Ryan Luzinski/1575	3.00	1.35
253A Brian Sackinsky/1575	3.00	1.35
259A Dwain Bostic/2075	3.00	1.35
290A David Spykstra/1575	3.00	1.35
301A Dave Brown/1575	3.00	1.35
307A Pete Janicki/1875	3.00	1.35
NNO Jan Caloun/1975	3.00	1.35
NNO Jan Vopat/1775	3.00	1.35

1992 Classic Four-Sport BCs *

Inserted one per jumbo pack, these 20 bonus cards measure the standard size. The cards are numbered on the dark gray stripe and arranged according to sport as follows: basketball (1-6), hockey (7-12), football (13-17), and baseball (18-20). A randomly inserted Future Superstars card has a picture of all four players on its front, shot against a horizon with dark clouds and lightning; the back indicates that just 10,000 of these cards were produced.

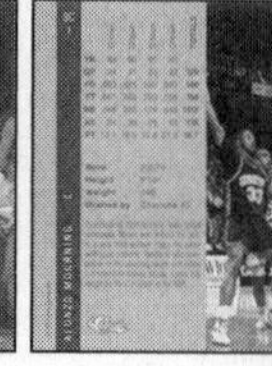

	MINT	NRMT
COMPLETE SET (20)	12.00	5.50
BC1 Alonzo Mourning	1.00	.45
BC2 Christian Laettner	.75	.35
BC3 Jimmy Jackson	.75	.35
BC4 Tom Gugliotta	.75	.35
BC5 Walt Williams	.75	.35
BC6 Harold Miner	.75	.35
BC7 Roman Hamrlik	.75	.35
BC8 Valeri Bure	.75	.35
BC9 Dallas Drake	.75	.35
BC10 Dmitri Kvartalnov	.75	.35
BC11 Manon Rheaume	1.00	.45
BC12 Viktor Kozlov	.75	.35
BC13 Desmond Howard	.75	.35
BC14 David Klingler	.75	.35
BC15 Terrell Buckley	.75	.35
BC16 Quentin Coryatt	.75	.35
BC17 Carl Pickens	.75	.35
BC18 Phil Nevin	.75	.35
BC19 Jeffrey Hammonds	.75	.35
BC20 Michael Tucker	.75	.35
FS1 Phil Nevin/10,000 Shaquille O'Neal Desmond Howard Roman Hamrlik	10.00	4.50

1992 Classic Four-Sport LPs *

Randomly inserted in foil packs, this 25-card standard-size insert set features full-bleed glossy color action player photos on the fronts. The sports represented are football (1-7, 16), basketball (8-14), baseball (17-21), and hockey (22-25). An 8 1/2" by 11" version of Shaquille O'Neal is known to exist.

	MINT	NRMT
LP1 Desmond Howard	.50	.23
LP2 David Klingler	.50	.23
LP3 Tommy Maddox	.50	.23
LP4 Casey Weldon	.50	.23
LP5 Tony Smith RB	.50	.23
LP6 Terrell Buckley	.50	.23
LP7 Carl Pickens	.50	.23
LP8 Shaquille O'Neal	10.00	4.50
LP9 Jimmy Jackson	.75	.35
LP10 Alonzo Mourning	2.00	.90
LP11 Christian Laettner	.50	.23
LP12 Harold Miner	.50	.23
LP13 Todd Day	.50	.23
LP14 Kareem Abdul-Jabbar Shaquille O'Neal	5.00	2.20
LP15 Phil Nevin Shaquille O'Neal Roman Hamrlik Desmond Howard	5.00	2.20
LP16 Matt Blundin David Klingler Tommy Maddox Mike Pawlawski Tony Sacca Casey Weldon	.50	.23
LP17 Phil Nevin	.50	.23
LP18 Jeffrey Hammonds	.50	.23
LP19 Paul Shuey	.50	.23
LP20 Ryan Luzinski UER	.50	.23
LP21 Brien Taylor	.50	.23
LP22 Roman Hamrlik	.50	.23
LP23 Mike Rathje	.50	.23
LP24 Valeri Bure	.50	.23
LP25 Alexei Yashin	.75	.35

1993 Classic Four-Sport Previews *

Issued as unnumbered inserts in '93 Classic hockey packs, these five cards measure the standard size. The fronts are similar in design to regular 1993 Classic Four-Sport cards. The backs carry a congratulatory message. The cards are unnumbered and checklisted below in alphabetical order.

	MINT	NRMT
COMPLETE SET (5)	15.00	6.75
CC1 Alexandre Daigle	.50	.23
CC2 Jeff Granger	.50	.23
CC3 Rick Mirer	.50	.23
CC4 Chris Webber	8.00	3.60
CC5 Toni Kukoc	3.00	1.35

1993 Classic Four-Sport *

The 1993 Classic Four-Sport Draft Pick Collection set consists of 325 standard-size cards of the top 1993 draft picks from football, basketball, baseball, and hockey. Just 49,500 sequentially numbered 12-box cases were produced. The set includes two topical subsets: John R. Wooden Award (310-314) and All-Rookie Basketball Team (315-319).

MINT NRMT
COMPLETE SET (325) 10.00 4.50
COMP.FACT.GOLD SET (329) 250.00 110.00
*GOLDS: 2.5X TO 6X BASIC CARDS...
1 Chris Webber 2.00 .90
2 Anfernee Hardaway 1.00 .45
3 Jamal Mashburn .75 .35
4 Isaiah Rider .40 .18
5 Vin Baker .40 .18
6 Rodney Rogers .40 .18
7 Lindsey Hunter .40 .18
8 Allan Houston .75 .35
9 George Lynch .40 .18
10 Toni Kukoc .75 .35
11 Ashraf Amaya .15 .07
12 Mark Bell .15 .07
13 Corie Blount .25 .11
14 Dexter Boney .15 .07
15 Tim Brooks .25 .11
16 James Bryson .15 .07
17 Evers Burns .15 .07
18 Scott Burrell .40 .18
19 Sam Cassell .40 .18
20 Sam Crawford .15 .07
21 Ron Curry .25 .11
22 William Davis .25 .11
23 Rodney Dobard .25 .11
24 Tony Dunkin .25 .11
25 Spencer Dunkley .25 .11
26 Bryan Edwards .25 .11
27 Doug Edwards .25 .11
28 Chuck Evans .25 .11
29 Terry Evans .25 .11
30 Will Flemons .25 .11
31 Alphonso Ford .25 .11
32 Josh Grant .25 .11
33 Eric Gray .25 .11
34 Geert Hammink .15 .07
35 Joe Harvell .15 .07
36 Scott Haskin .15 .07
37 Brian Hendrick .15 .07
38 Sascha Hupmann .15 .07
39 Stanley Jackson .25 .11
40 Ervin Johnson .40 .18
41 Adonis Jordan .25 .11
42 Malcolm Mackey .25 .11
43 Rich Manning .25 .11
44 Chris McNeal .15 .07
45 Conrad McRae .15 .07
46 Lance Miller .15 .07
47 Chris Mills .15 .07
48 Matt Nover .25 .11
49 Charles (Bo) Outlaw .40 .18
50 Eric Pauley .15 .07
51 Mike Peplowski .15 .07
52 Stacey Poole .15 .07
53 Anthony Reed .15 .07
54 Eric Riley .25 .11
55 Darrin Robinson .15 .07
56 James Robinson .25 .11
57 Bryon Russell .40 .18
58 Brent Scott .15 .07
59 Bennie Seitzer .15 .07
60 Ed Stokes .25 .11
61 Antoine Stoudamire .25 .11
62 Dirk Surles .15 .07
63 Justus Thigpen .15 .07
64 Kevin Thompson .15 .07
65 Ray Thompson .15 .07
66 Gary Trost .15 .07
67 Nick Van Exel .50 .23
68 Jerry Walker .15 .07
69 Rex Walters .25 .11
70 Chris Whitney .15 .07
71 Steve Worthy .15 .07
72 Luther Wright .15 .07
73 Mark Buford .15 .07
74 Mitchell Butler .15 .07
75 Brian Clifford .15 .07
76 Terry Dehere .25 .11
77 Acie Earl .25 .11
78 Greg Graham .25 .11
79 Angelo Hamilton .25 .11
80 Thomas Hill .25 .11
81 Khari Jaxon .15 .07
82 Darnell Mee .25 .11
83 Sherron Mills .15 .07
84 Gheorghe Muresan .40 .18
85 Eddie Rivera .15 .07
86 Richard Petruska .25 .11
87 Bryan Sallier .25 .11
88 Harper Williams .25 .11
89 Ike Williams .25 .11
90 Byron Wilson .25 .11
91 Drew Bledsoe .75 .35
92 Rick Mirer .25 .11
93 Garrison Hearst .50 .23
94 Marvin Jones .15 .07
95 John Copeland .15 .07
96 Eric Curry .15 .07
97 Curtis Conway .25 .11
98 Willie Roaf .15 .07
99 Lincoln Kennedy .15 .07
100 Jerome Bettis 1.00 .45
101 Mike Compton .15 .07
102 John Gerak .15 .07
103 Will Shields .15 .07
104 Ben Coleman .15 .07
105 Ernest Dye .15 .07
106 Lester Holmes .15 .07
107 Brad Hopkins .15 .07
108 Everett Lindsay .15 .07
109 Todd Rucci .15 .07
110 Lance Gunn .15 .07
111 Elvis Grbac .50 .23
112 Shane Matthews .15 .07
113 Rudy Harris .15 .07
114 Richie Anderson .15 .07
115 Derek Brown .25 .11
116 Roger Harper .15 .07
117 Terry Kirby .40 .18
118 Natrone Means .40 .18
119 Glyn Milburn .25 .11
120 Adrian Murrell .40 .18
121 Lorenzo Neal .25 .11
122 Roosevelt Potts .25 .11
123 Kevin Williams WR .25 .11
124 Fred Baxter .25 .11
125 Troy Drayton .25 .11
126 Chris Gedney .15 .07
127 Irv Smith .15 .07
128 Olanda Truitt .15 .07
129 Victor Bailey .25 .11
130 Horace Copeland .15 .07
131 Ron Dickerson Jr. .15 .07
132 Willie Harris .15 .07
133 Tyrone Hughes .15 .07
134 Qadry Ismail .25 .11
135 Reggie Brooks .25 .11
136 Sean LaChapelle .15 .07
137 O.J.McDuffie .40 .18
138 Kenny Shedd .15 .07
139 Brian Stablein .15 .07
140 Lamar Thomas .15 .07
141 Kevin Williams RB .15 .07
142 Othello Henderson .15 .07
143 Kevin Henry .15 .07
144 Todd Kelly .15 .07
145 Devon McDonald .15 .07
146 Michael Strahan .50 .23
147 Dan Williams .15 .07
148 Gilbert Brown .25 .11
149 Mark Caesar .15 .07
150 John Parrella .15 .07
151 Leonard Renfro .15 .07
152 Coleman Rudolph .15 .07
153 Ronnie Bradford .15 .07
154 Tom Carter .25 .11
155 Deon Figures .25 .11
156 Derrick Frazier .15 .07
157 Darrien Gordon .25 .11
158 Carlton Gray .25 .11
159 Adrian Hardy .15 .07
160 Mike Reid .15 .07
161 Thomas Smith .15 .07
162 Robert O'Neal .15 .07
163 Chad Brown .40 .18
164 Demetrius DuBose .15 .07
165 Reggie Givens .15 .07
166 Travis Hill .15 .07
167 Rich McKenzie .15 .07
168 Darrin Smith .25 .11
169 Steve Tovar .15 .07
170 Patrick Bates .15 .07
171 Dan Footman .15 .07
172 Ryan McNeil .15 .07
173 Danan Hughes .15 .07
174 Mark Brunell 1.00 .45
175 Ron Moore .25 .11
176 Antonio London .15 .07
177 Steve Everitt .15 .07
178 Wayne Simmons .15 .07
179 Robert Smith .50 .23
180 Dana Stubblefield .25 .11
181 George Teague .25 .11
182 Carl Simpson .25 .11
183 Billy Joe Hobert .25 .11
184 Gino Torretta .25 .11
185 Alexandre Daigle .15 .07
186 Chris Pronger .50 .23
187 Chris Gratton .15 .07
188 Paul Kariya 1.50 .70
189 Rob Niedermayer .40 .18
190 Viktor Kozlov .40 .18
191 Jason Arnott .50 .23
192 Niklas Sundstrom .25 .11
193 Todd Harvey .25 .11
194 Jocelyn Thibault .50 .23
195 Kenny Jonsson .25 .11
196 Denis Pederson .15 .07
197 Adam Deadmarsh .40 .18
198 Mats Lindgren .15 .07
199 Nick Stadjuhar .15 .07
200 Jason Allison .40 .18
201 Jesper Mattsson .15 .07
202 Saku Koivu .50 .23
203 Anders Eriksson .25 .11
204 Todd Bertuzzi .25 .11
205 Eric Lecompte .15 .07
206 Nikolai Tsulugin .15 .07
207 Janne Niinimaa .25 .11
208 Maxim Bets .15 .07
209 Rory Fitzpatrick .15 .07
210 Eric Manlow .15 .07
211 David Roche .15 .07
212 Vladimir Chebaturkin .15 .07
213 Bill McCauley .15 .07
214 Chad Lang .15 .07
215 Cosmo DuPaul .15 .07
216 Bob Wren .15 .07
217 Chris Simon .50 .23
218 Ryan Brown .15 .07
219 Mikhail Shtalenkov .15 .07
220 Vladimir Krechin .15 .07
221 Jason Saal .15 .07
222 Dion Darling .15 .07
223 Chris Helleher .15 .07
224 Antti Aalto .15 .07
225 Alain Nasreddine .15 .07
226 Paul Vincent .15 .07
227 Manny Legace .25 .11
228 Igor Chibirev .15 .07
229 Tom Noble .15 .07
230 Mike Bales .15 .07
231 Jozef Cierny .15 .07
232 Ivan Droppa .15 .07
233 Anatoli Fedotov .15 .07
234 Martin Gendron .15 .07
235 Daniel Guerard .15 .07
236 Corey Hirsch .40 .18
237 Steven King .15 .07
238 Sergei Krivokrasov .25 .11
239 Darrin Madeley .15 .07
240 Grant Marshall .25 .11
241 Sandy McCarthy .40 .18
242 Bill McDougall .15 .07
243 Dean Melanson .15 .07
244 Roman Oksiuta .15 .07
245 Robert Petrovicky .15 .07
246 Mike Rathje .15 .07
247 Eldon Reddick .25 .11
248 Andrei Trefilov .15 .07
249 Jiri Slegr .25 .11
250 Leonid Toropchenko .15 .07
251 Dody Wood .15 .07
252 Kevin Paden .15 .07
253 Manon Rheaume .75 .35
254 Cammi Granato .40 .18
255 Patrick Charboneau .15 .07
256 Curtis Bowen .25 .11
257 Kevin Brown .15 .07
258 Valeri Bure .40 .18
259 Janne Laukkanen .15 .07
260 Alex Rodriguez 5.00 2.20
261 Darren Dreifort .25 .11
262 Matt Brunson .15 .07
263 Matt Drews .15 .07
264 Wayne Gomes .15 .07
265 Jeff Granger .15 .07
266 Steve Soderstrom .15 .07
267 Brooks Kieschnick .25 .11
268 Daron Kirkreit .15 .07
269 Billy Wagner .40 .18
270 Alan Benes .15 .07
271 Scott Christman .15 .07
272 Willie Adams .15 .07
273 Jermaine Allensworth .15 .07
274 Jason Baker .15 .07
275 Brian Banks .15 .07
276 Marc Barcelo .15 .07
277 Jeff D'Amico IF .15 .07
(Redmond High;
see also card 306)
278 Todd Dunn .15 .07
279 Dan Ehler .15 .07
280 Tony Fuduric .15 .07
281 Ryan Hancock .15 .07
282 Vee Hightower .15 .07
283 Andre King .15 .07
(See also card 288A)
284 Brett King .15 .07
285 Derrek Lee .40 .18
286 Andrew Lorraine .15 .07
287 Eric Ludwick .15 .07
288A Ryan McGuire ERR .15 .07
(Card misnumbered 283;
should be 288)
288B Ryan McGuire COR .15 .07
(In jumbo packs)
289 Anthony Medrano .15 .07
290 Joel Moore .15 .07
291 Dan Perkins .15 .07
292 Kevin Pickford .15 .07
293 Jon Ratliff .15 .07
294 Bryan Rekar .15 .07
295 Andy Rice .15 .07
296 Carl Schulz .15 .07
297 Chris Singleton .40 .18
298 Cameron Smith .15 .07
299 Marc Valdes .15 .07
300 Joe Wagner .15 .07
301 John Wasdin .15 .07
302 Pat Watkins .15 .07
303 Dax Winslett .15 .07
304 Jamey Wright .25 .11
305 Kelly Wunsch .15 .07
306A Jeff D'Amico ERR .25 .11
(Northeast High;
card misnumbered 277,
should be 306)
306B Jeff D'Amico COR .25 .11
(In jumbo packs)
307 Brian Anderson .25 .11
308 Trot Nixon .40 .18
309 Kirk Presley .15 .07
310 John Wooden CO .75 .35
311 Chris Webber JWA .75 .35
312 Jamal Mashburn JWA .40 .18
313 Anfernee Hardaway JWA .40 .18
314 Terry Dehere JWA .25 .11
315 Shaquille O'Neal ART .40 .18
316 Alonzo Mourning ART .40 .18
317 Christian Laettner ART .25 .11
318 Jimmy Jackson ART .25 .11
319 Harold Miner ART .25 .11
320 Checklist 1 .15 .07
321 Checklist 2 .15 .07
322 Checklist 3 .15 .07
323 Checklist 4 .15 .07
324 Checklist 5 .15 .07
325 Checklist 6 .15 .07
NNO Jerome Bettis AU/3900 20.00 9.00
NNO Chris Gatton AU/3900 10.00 4.50
NNO Alonzo Mourning 20.00 9.00
AUTO/3900
NNO Alex Rodriguez 150.00 70.00
AUTO/3900
NNO Jamal Mashburn 2.00 .90
Draft Star Mail-In
PR1 Drew Bledsoe Promo 3.00 1.35
PR1 A.Hardaway Gold Promo 5.00 2.20

1993 Classic Four-Sport Acetates *

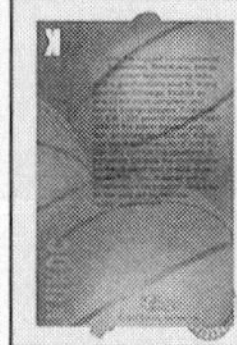

Randomly inserted throughout the 1993 Classic Four-Sport foil packs, this 12-card standard-size acetate set features on its fronts clear-bordered color player action cutouts set on basketball, football, baseball, or hockey stick backgrounds. The cards are unnumbered but carry letter designations. They are checklisted in the order that spells '93 Rookie Class.

MINT NRMT
COMPLETE SET (12) 20.00 9.00
1 Chris Webber 4.00 1.80
2 Anfernee Hardaway 2.50 1.10
3 Jamal Mashburn 1.00 .45
4 Isaiah Rider 1.00 .45
5 Toni Kukoc 2.00 .90
6 Drew Bledsoe 3.00 1.35
7 Rick Mirer 1.00 .45
8 Garrison Hearst 2.00 .90
9 Alex Rodriguez 8.00 3.60
10 Jeff Granger 1.00 .45
11 Alexandre Daigle 1.00 .45
12 Chris Pronger 2.00 .90

1993 Classic Four-Sport Autographs *

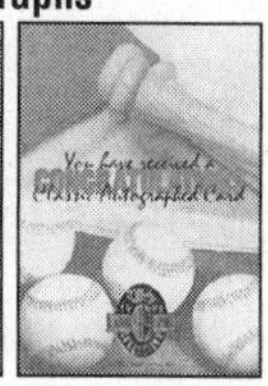

Randomly inserted in '93 Classic Four-Sport packs, these 26 standard-size cards feature on their fronts borderless color player action shots. The back carries a congratulatory message. The cards are listed below by their corresponding regular card numbers, except for Jennings and Klippenstein, which are shown as unnumbered cards (NNO) at the end of the checklist, since they are not in the regular set. The number of cards each player signed is shown. The Rider card may have been autopenned.

MINT NRMT
1A Chris Webber/550 80.00 36.00
3A Jamal Mashburn/800 30.00 13.50
4A Isaiah Rider/4100 10.00 4.50
6A Rodney Rogers/4000 10.00 4.50
77A Acie Earl/550 3.00 1.35
91A Drew Bledsoe/275 100.00 45.00
92A Rick Mirer/375 10.00 4.50
93A Garrison Hearst/650 20.00 9.00
94A Marvin Jones/3650 3.00 1.35
184A Gino Torretta/3200 3.00 1.35
189A Rob Niedermayer/4500 5.00 2.20
196A Denis Pederson/2050 3.00 1.35
197A Adam Deadmarsh/4250 5.00 2.20
218A Ryan Brown/900 3.00 1.35
222A Dion Darling/1500 3.00 1.35
253A Manon Rheaume/1250 25.00 11.00
260A Alex Rodriguez/4300 UER 150.00 70.00
Rodriguez is spelled Rodreguez
261A Darren Dreifort/3875 5.00 2.20
265A Jeff Granger/150 3.00 1.35
267A Brooks Kieschnick/450 3.00 1.35
268A Daron Kirkreit/275 3.00 1.35
310A John Wooden/150 100.00 45.00
315A Shaquille O'Neal/500 100.00 45.00
316A Alonzo Mourning/400 40.00 18.00
NNO Jason Jennings/1475 3.00 1.35
NNO Wade Klippenstein/800 3.00 1.35

1993 Classic Four-Sport Chromium Draft Stars *

Inserted one per jumbo pack, these 20 standard-size cards feature color player action cutouts on their borderless metallic fronts. The player's name, along with the production number (1 of 80,000), appear vertically in gold foil at the lower left. The cards are numbered on the back with a "DS" prefix.

MINT NRMT
COMPLETE SET (20) 20.00 9.00
DS41 Chris Webber 2.50 1.10
DS42 Anfernee Hardaway 1.25 .55
DS43 Jamal Mashburn 1.00 .45
DS44 Isaiah Rider 1.00 .45
DS45 Toni Kukoc 1.00 .45
DS46 Rodney Rogers 1.00 .45
DS47 Chris Mills 1.00 .45
DS48 Drew Bledsoe 2.00 .90
DS49 Rick Mirer 1.00 .45
DS50 Garrison Hearst 2.00 .90
DS51 Jerome Bettis 2.00 .90
DS52 Terry Kirby 1.00 .45
DS53 Glyn Milburn 1.00 .45
DS54 Reggie Brooks 1.00 .45
DS55 Alex Rodriguez 8.00 3.60
DS56 Brooks Kieschnick 1.00 .45
DS57 Jeff Granger 1.00 .45
DS58 Alexandre Daigle 1.00 .45
DS59 Chris Pronger 1.00 .45
DS60 Chris Gratton 1.00 .45

1993 Classic Four-Sport LP Jumbos *

Random inserts in hobby boxes, these five oversized cards measure approximately 3 1/2" by 5" and feature on their fronts borderless color player action shots. The player's name, statistics, biography, and career highlights, along with the card's production number out of 8,000 produced, appear on a gray lithic background to the left. The cards are numbered on the back as "X of 5."

MINT NRMT
COMPLETE SET (5) 50.00 22.00
1 Drew Bledsoe 8.00 3.60
2 Alexander Daigle 3.00 1.35
3 Alex Rodriguez 20.00 9.00
4 Chris Webber 8.00 3.60
5 Four in One 10.00 4.50

1993 Classic Four-Sport LPs *

Randomly inserted throughout the 1993 Classic Four-Sport foil packs, this 25-card standard-size set features the hottest draft pick players in 1993. The borderless fronts feature color player action shots. The player's name appears vertically in the lower left. The production number (1 of 63,400) appears in gold foil at the lower right. The cards are numbered on the back with an "LP" prefix.

MINT NRMT
COMPLETE SET (25) 40.00 18.00
LP1 Four-in-One Card 4.00 1.80
Chris Webber
Drew Bledsoe
Alex Rodriguez
Alexandre Daigle
LP2 Chris Webber 3.00 1.35
LP3 Anfernee Hardaway 2.50 1.10
LP4 Jamal Mashburn 2.00 .90
LP5 Isaiah Rider 1.00 .45
LP6 Shaquille O'Neal 5.00 2.20
LP7 Toni Kukoc 2.00 .90
LP8 Rodney Rogers 1.00 .45
LP9 Lindsey Hunter 1.00 .45
LP10 Drew Bledsoe 4.00 1.80
LP11 Rick Mirer 1.00 .45
LP12 Garrison Hearst 3.00 1.35
LP13 Jerome Bettis 3.00 1.35
LP14 Marvin Jones 1.00 .45
LP15 Terry Kirby 1.00 .45
LP16 Glyn Milburn 1.00 .45
LP17 Reggie Brooks 1.00 .45
LP18 Alex Rodriguez 8.00 3.60
LP19 Darren Dreifort 2.00 .90
LP20 Jeff Granger 1.00 .45
LP21 Brooks Kieschnick 1.00 .45
LP22 Alexandre Daigle 1.00 .45
LP23 Chris Pronger 2.00 .90
LP24 Chris Gratton 1.00 .45
LP25 Paul Kariya 5.00 2.20

1993 Classic Four-Sport Power Pick Bonus *

Issued one per jumbo sheet, these 20 standard-size cards feature on their borderless fronts color player action shots, the backgrounds for which are faded to black-and-white. The player's name and the sets production number (1 of 80,000) appear in green-foil cursive lettering near the bottom. The cards are numbered on the back with a "PP" prefix.

MINT NRMT
COMPLETE SET (20) 25.00 11.00
PP1 Chris Webber 2.00 .90
PP2 Anfernee Hardaway 1.50 .70
PP3 Jamal Mashburn 1.50 .70
PP4 Isaiah Rider 1.00 .45
PP5 Toni Kukoc 1.50 .70
PP6 Rodney Rogers 1.00 .45
PP7 Chris Mills 1.00 .45
PP8 Drew Bledsoe 2.00 .90
PP9 Rick Mirer 1.00 .45
PP10 Garrison Hearst 2.00 .90
PP11 Jerome Bettis 2.00 .90
PP12 Terry Kirby 1.00 .45
PP13 Glyn Milburn 1.00 .45
PP14 Reggie Brooks 1.00 .45
PP15 Alex Rodriguez 8.00 3.60
PP16 Brooks Kieschnick 1.00 .45
PP17 Jeff Granger 1.00 .45
PP18 Alexandre Daigle 1.00 .45
PP19 Chris Pronger 1.50 .70
PP20 Chris Gratton 1.00 .45
NNO Four in One Special 4.00 1.80

1993 Classic Four-Sport Tri-Cards *

Randomly inserted throughout the 1993 Classic Four-Sport foil packs, this set features five standard-size cards with three players on each card separated by perforations. The cards are numbered on the back with a "TC" prefix.

MINT NRMT
COMPLETE SET (5) 30.00 13.50
TC1 Anfernee Hardaway 8.00 3.60
TC6 Shaquille O'Neal

TC11 Chris Webber
TC2 Drew Bledsoe 6.00 2.70
TC7 Rick Mirer
TC12 Garrison Hearst
TC3 Jeff Granger 5.00 2.20
TC8 Brooks Kieschnick
TC13 Alex Rodriguez
TC4 Alexandre Daigle 4.00 1.80
TC9 Chris Pronger
TC14 Chris Gratton
TC5 Drew Bledsoe 8.00 3.60
TC10 Chris Webber
TC15 Alex Rodriguez

1993 Classic Four-Sport MBNA Promos *

This two-card set uses Classic's designs from its Four-Sport LPs "Four in One" insert number LP1. Card number 1 reproduces the Chris Webber/Alex Rodriguez side of LP1, card number 2 reproduces the Drew Bledsoe/Alexandre Daigle side. This set was issued exclusively to cardholders of the MBNA/ScoreBoard VISA. The backs contain congratulatory messages, information about the players depicted, and a notation than 10,000 sets were issued. Although the design and copyright reads 1993, these cards probably were first issued in 1994.

	MINT	NRMT
1 Chris Webber	10.00	4.50
Alex Rodriguez		
2 Drew Bledsoe	5.00	2.20
Alexander Daigle		

1993 Classic Four-Sport McDonald's *

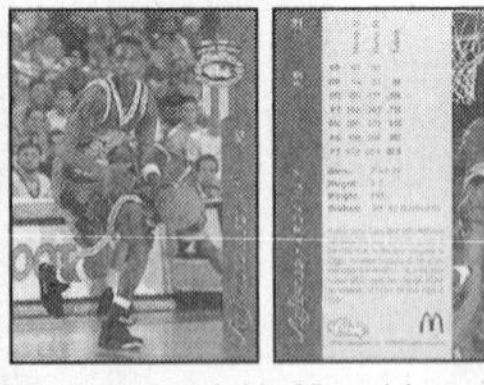

Classic produced this 35-card four-sport standard-size set for a promotion at McDonald's restaurants in central and southeastern Pennsylvania, southern New Jersey, Delaware, and central Florida. The cards were distributed in five-card packs. A five-card "limited production" subset was randomly inserted throughout these packs. The promotion also featured instant win cards awarding 2,000 pieces of autographed Score Board memorabilia. An autographed Chris Webber card was also randomly inserted in the packs on a limited basis. The set is arranged according to sports as follows: football (1-10), baseball (11, 26, 31-35), hockey (12-20), and basketball (21-25, 27-30). The cards are numbered on the back in the upper left, and the McDonald's trademark is gold foil stamped toward the bottom.

	MINT	NRMT
COMPLETE SET (35)	15.00	6.75
1 Troy Aikman	1.50	.70
2 Drew Bledsoe	1.00	.45
3 Eric Curry	.10	.05
4 Garrison Hearst	.50	.23
5 Lester Holmes	.10	.05
6 Marvin Jones	.10	.05
7 O.J. McDuffie	.20	.09
8 Rick Mirer	.20	.09
9 Leonard Renfro	.10	.05
10 Jerry Rice	1.50	.70
11 Darren Daulton	.10	.05
12 Vyacheslav Butsayev	.10	.05
13 Kevin Dineen	.10	.05
14 Andre Faust	.10	.05
15 Roman Hamrlik	.20	.09
16 Mark Recchi	.50	.23
17 Manon Rheaume	.75	.35
18 Dominic Roussel	.30	.14
19 Teemu Selanne	1.00	.45
20 Tommy Soderstrom	.30	.14
21 Anfernee Hardaway	1.25	.55
22 Jimmy Jackson	.20	.09
23 Christian Laettner	.20	.09
24 Jamal Mashburn	.50	.23
25 Harold Miner	.10	.05
26 Greg Luzinski	.10	.05
Ryan Luzinski		
27 Alonzo Mourning	.50	.23
28 Shaquille O'Neal	2.00	.90
29 Clarence Weatherspoon	.10	.05
30 Chris Webber	1.50	.70
31 Chad McConnell	.10	.05
32 Phil Nevin	.50	.23
33 Paul Shuey	.20	.09
34 Derek Wallace	.10	.05
35 Leonard Renfro	.10	.05
Lester Holmes		

1993 Classic Four-Sport McDonald's LPs *

Measuring the standard size, these five limited production cards were randomly inserted in 1993 Classic McDonald's five-card packs. Chris

Webber, the number one pick in the NBA draft, autographed 1,250 of his cards. Printed vertically, and parallel and next to the gold foil band, "1 of 16,750" appears in gold foil. The Classic Four Sport logo appears in the upper right. The cards are numbered on the back in gold foil with an "LP" prefix.

	MINT	NRMT
COMPLETE SET (5)	6.00	2.70
LP1 Darren Daulton	.75	.35
LP2 Trench Warfare	.25	.11
Leonard Renfro		
Lester Holmes		
LP3 Alonzo Mourning	.50	.23
LP4 Manon Rheaume	3.00	1.35
LP5 Steve Young	3.00	1.35
NNO Chris Webber AU/1250	60.00	27.00
(Certified autograph)		

1994 Classic Four-Sport Previews *

Randomly inserted in 1994-95 Classic hockey foil packs at a rate of three per case, these five standard-size preview cards show the design of the 1994-95 Classic Four-Sport series. The full-bleed color action photos are gold-foil stamped with the "4-Sport Preview" emblem and the player's name. The backs feature another full-bleed closeup photo, with biography and statistics displayed on a ghosted panel.

	MINT	NRMT
COMPLETE SET (5)	25.00	11.00
P1 Jeff O'Neill	1.00	.45
P2 Marshall Faulk	10.00	4.50
P3 Grant Hill	8.00	3.60
P4 Jason Kidd	5.00	2.20
P5 Ben Grieve	2.00	.90

1994 Classic Four-Sport *

Featuring top rookies from basketball, baseball, football and hockey, the 1994 Classic Four-Sport set consists of 200 standard-size cards. No more than 25,000 cases were produced. Over 100 players signed 100,000 cards that were randomly inserted four per case. Collectors who found one of 100 Glenn Robinson Instant Winner Cards received a complete Classic Four-Sport autographed card set. Also inserted on an average of one in every five cases were 4,695 hand-numbered 4-in-1 cards featuring all four number 1 picks. Classic's wrapper redemption program offered four levels of participation: 1) bronze-collect 20 wrappers and receive a 4-card Classic Player of the Year set, featuring Grant Hill, Shaquille O'Neal, Emmitt Smith, and Steve Young; 2) silver-collect 30 wrappers and receive the Classic Player of the Year set and a random autograph card; 3) gold-collect 144 wrappers and receive the Classic Player of the Year set and an autograph card by Muhammad Ali; and 4) platinum-collect 216 wrappers and receive the Classic Player of the Year set plus an autograph card by Shaquille O'Neal. The cards are numbered on the back and checklisted below by sport as follows: basketball (1-50), football (51-114), hockey (115-160), baseball (161-188), and Wooden Award Contenders (189-197).

	MINT	NRMT
COMPLETE SET (200)	15.00	6.75
COMPLETE GOLD SET (200)	30.00	13.50
*GOLDS: .75X TO 2X BASIC CARDS	.25	.11
COMP. PRINT PROOF (200)	100.00	45.00
*PRINT.PROOF: 2.5X TO 6X BASIC CARDS		
.90		
1 Glenn Robinson	1.00	.45
2 Jason Kidd	2.00	.90
3 Grant Hill	1.50	.70
4 Donyell Marshall	.40	.18
5 Juwan Howard	.40	.18
6 Sharone Wright	.15	.07
7 Billy McCaffrey	.15	.07
8 Brian Grant	.40	.18
9 Eric Montross	.15	.07
10 Eddie Jones	1.00	.45
11 Carlos Rogers	.15	.07
12 Khalid Reeves	.15	.07
13 Jalen Rose	1.00	.45
14 Yinka Dare	.15	.07
15 Eric Piatkowski	.40	.18
16 Clifford Rozier	.15	.07
17 Aaron McKie	.40	.18
18 Eric Mobley	.15	.07
19 Tony Dumas	.15	.07
20 B.J. Tyler	.15	.07
21 Dickey Simpkins	.15	.07
22 Bill Curley	.15	.07
23 Wesley Person	.40	.18
24 Monty Williams	.15	.07
25 Greg Minor	.15	.07
26 Charlie Ward	.40	.18
27 Brooks Thompson	.15	.07
28 Deon Thomas	.15	.07
29 Antonio Lang	.15	.07
30 Howard Eisley	.40	.18
31 Rodney Dent	.15	.07
32 Jim McIlvaine	.15	.07
33 Derrick Alston	.15	.07
34 Gaylon Nickerson	.15	.07
35 Michael Smith	.15	.07
36 Andrei Fetisov	.15	.07
37 Dontonio Wingfield	.15	.07
38 Darrin Hancock	.15	.07
39 Anthony Miller	.15	.07
40 Jeff Webster	.15	.07
41 Arturas Karnishovas	.15	.07
42 Gary Collier	.15	.07
43 Shawnelle Scott	.15	.07
44 Damon Bailey	.15	.07
45 Dwayne Morton	.15	.07
46 Jamie Watson	.15	.07
47 Jevon Crudup	.15	.07
48 Melvin Booker	.15	.07
49 Brian Reese	.15	.07
50 Lawrence Funderburke	.15	.07
51 Dan Wilkinson	.15	.07
52 Marshall Faulk	2.00	.90
53 Heath Shuler	.15	.07
54 Willie McGinest	.15	.07
55 Trev Alberts	.15	.07
56 Trent Dilfer	.40	.18
57 Bryant Young	.40	.18
58 Sam Adams	.15	.07
59 Antonio Langham	.15	.07
60 Jamir Miller	.15	.07
61 John Thierry	.15	.07
62 Aaron Glenn	.15	.07
63 Joe Johnson	.15	.07
64 Bernard Williams	.15	.07
65 Wayne Gandy	.15	.07
66 Aaron Taylor	.15	.07
67 Charles Johnson	.40	.18
68 Dewayne Washington	.15	.07
69 Todd Steussie	.15	.07
70 Tim Bowens	.15	.07
71 Johnnie Morton	.40	.18
72 Rob Fredrickson	.15	.07
73 Shante Carver	.15	.07
74 Thomas Lewis	.15	.07
75 Calvin Jones	.15	.07
76 Henry Ford	.15	.07
77 Jeff Burris	.15	.07
78 William Floyd	.40	.18
79 Derrick Alexander	.40	.18
80 Darnay Scott	.40	.18
81 Tre Johnson	.15	.07
82 Eric Mahlum	.15	.07
83 Errict Rhett	.40	.18
84 Kevin Lee	.15	.07
85 Andre Coleman	.15	.07
86 Corey Sawyer	.15	.07
87 Chuck Levy	.15	.07
88 Greg Hill	.15	.07
89 David Palmer	.15	.07
90 Ryan Yarborough	.15	.07
91 Charlie Garner	.75	.35
92 Mario Bates	.15	.07
93 Bert Emanuel	.40	.18
94 Thomas Randolph	.15	.07
95 Bucky Brooks	.15	.07
96 Rob Waldrop	.15	.07
97 Charlie Ward	.50	.23
98 Winfred Tubbs	.15	.07
99 James Folston	.15	.07
100 Kevin Mitchell	.15	.07
101 Aubrey Beavers	.15	.07
102 Fernando Smith	.15	.07
103 Jim Miller	.40	.18
104 Byron Bam Morris	.15	.07
105 Donnell Bennett	.15	.07
106 Jason Sehorn	.75	.35
107 Glenn Foley	.15	.07
108 Lonnie Johnson	.15	.07
109 Tyronee Drakeford	.15	.07
110 Vaughn Parker	.15	.07
111 Doug Nussmeier	.15	.07
112 Perry Klein	.15	.07
113 Jason Gildon	.50	.23
114 Lake Dawson	.15	.07
115A Ed Jovanovski ERR	.15	.07
115B Ed Jovanovski COR	.15	.07
116 Oleg Tverdovsky	.40	.18
117 Radek Bonk	.40	.18
118 Jason Bonsignore	.15	.07
119 Jeff O'Neill	.15	.07
120 Ryan Smyth	.15	.07
121 Jamie Storr	.40	.18
122 Jason Wiemer	.15	.07
123 Evgeni Ryabchikov	.15	.07
124 Nolan Baumgartner	.15	.07
125 Jeff Friesen	.40	.18
126 Wade Belak	.15	.07
127 Maxim Bets	.15	.07
128 Ethan Moreau	.15	.07
129 Alexander Kharlamov	.15	.07
130 Eric Fichaud	.15	.07
131 Wayne Primeau	.15	.07
132 Brad Brown	.15	.07
133 Chris Dingman	.15	.07
134 Craig Darby	.15	.07
135 Darby Hendrickson	.15	.07
136 Yan Golubovsky	.15	.07
137 Chris Wells	.15	.07
138 Vadim Sharifjanov	.15	.07
139 Dan Cloutier	.15	.07
140 Todd Marchant	.15	.07
141 David Roberts	.15	.07
142 Brian Rolston	.15	.07
143 Garth Snow	.40	.18
144 Cory Stillman	.15	.07
145 Chad Penny	.15	.07
146 Jeff Nelson	.15	.07
147 Michael Stewart	.15	.07
148 Mike Dunham	.15	.07
149 Joe Frederick	.15	.07
150 Mark DeSantis	.15	.07
151 David Cooper	.15	.07
152 Andrei Buschan	.15	.07
153 Mike Greenlay	.15	.07
154 Geoff Sarjeant	.15	.07
155 Pauli Jaks	.15	.07
156 Greg Andrusak	.15	.07
157 Denis Metlyuk	.15	.07
158 Mike Fountain	.15	.07
159 Brent Gretzky	.15	.07
160 Jason Allison	.50	.23
161 Paul Wilson	.15	.07
162 Ben Grieve	.75	.35
163 Doug Million	.15	.07
164 C.J. Nitkowski	.15	.07
165 Tommy Davis	.15	.07
166 Dustin Hermanson	.40	.18
167 Travis Miller	.15	.07
168 McKay Christiansen	.15	.07
169 Victor Rodriguez	.15	.07
170 Jacob Cruz	.15	.07
171 Rick Heiserman	.15	.07
172 Mark Farris	.15	.07
173 Nomar Garciaparra	4.00	1.80
174 Paul Konerko	2.00	.90
175 Trey Moore	.15	.07
176 Brian Stephenson	.15	.07
177 Matt Smith	.15	.07
178 Kevin Brown	.15	.07
179 Cade Gaspar	.15	.07
180 Bret Wagner	.15	.07
181 Mike Thurman	.15	.07
182 Doug Webb	.15	.07
183 Ryan Nye	.15	.07
184 Brian Buchanan	.15	.07
185 Scott Elarton	.15	.07
186 Mark Johnson	.15	.07
187 Jacob Shumate	.15	.07
188 Kevin Witt	.15	.07
189 Glenn Robinson JWA	.40	.18
190 Jason Kidd JWA	.75	.35
191 Grant Hill JWA	.60	.25
192 Donyell Marshall JWA	.15	.07
193 Eric Montross JWA	.15	.07
194 Khalid Reeves JWA	.15	.07
195 Jalen Rose JWA	.40	.18
196 Clifford Rozier JWA	.15	.07
197 Damon Bailey JWA	.15	.07
198 Checklist 1	.15	.07
199 Checklist 2	.15	.07
200 Checklist 3	.15	.07
FO1 4-in-1	5.00	2.20
Glenn Robinson		
Dan Wilkinson		
Paul Wilson		
Ed Jovanovski		
Number One Draft Picks		
PC1 Shaquille O'Neal	5.00	2.20
$25 Phone Card		

1994 Classic Four-Sport Autographs *

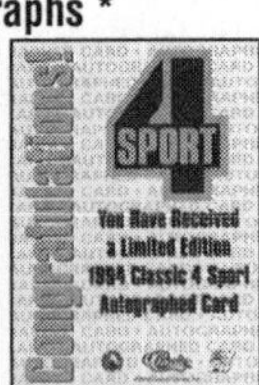

Randomly inserted in packs at a rate of one in 103, this standard-size set features players from the 1994 Classic Four-Sport set who autographed cards within the set. The fronts feature full-bleed color action player photos. The player's name is gold-foil stamped across the bottom of the picture. The backs have a congratulatory message about receiving an autographed card. Though the cards are unnumbered, we have assigned them the same number as their four-sport regular issue counterpart.

	MINT	NRMT
1A Glenn Robinson/1000	15.00	6.75
2A Jason Kidd/1300	25.00	11.00
5A Juwan Howard/940	12.00	5.50
9A Eric Montross/1000	5.00	2.20
11A Carlos Rogers/660	3.00	1.35
13A Jalen Rose/970	15.00	6.75
15A Eric Piatkowski/1090	5.00	2.20
16A Clifford Rozier/900	3.00	1.35
22A Bill Curley/1120	3.00	1.35
23A Wesley Person/1000	3.00	1.35
24A Monty Williams/1100	3.00	1.35
28A Deon Thomas/1090	3.00	1.35
30A Howard Eisley/970	5.00	2.20
32A Jim McIlvaine/965	3.00	1.35
33A Derrick Alston/1050	3.00	1.35
36A Andrei Fetisov/1080	3.00	1.35
39A Anthony Miller/1000	3.00	1.35
40A Jeff Webster/1070	3.00	1.35
41A Arturas Karnishovas/980	3.00	1.35
42A Gary Collier/1000	3.00	1.35
44A Damon Bailey/1050	3.00	1.35
45A Dwayne Morton/1000	3.00	1.35
46A Jamie Watson/1080	3.00	1.35
47A Jevon Crudup/1180	3.00	1.35
49A Brian Reese/960	3.00	1.35
53A Heath Shuler/1330	5.00	2.20
55A Trev Alberts/2520	3.00	1.35
56A Trent Dilfer/1495	25.00	11.00
81A Tre Johnson/1000	3.00	1.35
82A Eric Mahlum/1090	3.00	1.35
90A Ryan Yarborough/1020	3.00	1.35
93A Bert Emanuel/1100	5.00	2.20
96A Rob Waldrop/1095	3.00	1.35
97A Charlie Ward/1520	8.00	3.60
99A James Folston/1100	3.00	1.35
100A Kevin Mitchell/1090	3.00	1.35
103A Jim Miller/1030	10.00	4.50
108A Lonnie Johnson/1050	3.00	1.35
110A Vaughn Parker/750	3.00	1.35
115A Ed Jovanovski/1180	6.00	2.70
119A Jeff O'Neill/3000	5.00	2.20
124A Nolan Baumgartner/2900	3.00	1.35
134A Craig Darby/2990	3.00	1.35
139A Dan Cloutier/2980	6.00	2.70
140A Todd Marchant/3100	5.00	2.20
143A Garth Snow/3050	6.00	2.70
144A Cory Stillman/3000	3.00	1.35
148A Mike Dunham/2960	6.00	2.70
149A Joe Frederick/3000	3.00	1.35
150A Mark DeSantis/3000	3.00	1.35
154A Geoff Sarjeant/3000	3.00	1.35
156A Greg Andrusak/2970	3.00	1.35
157A Denis Metlyuk/2960	3.00	1.35
158A Mike Fountain/3000	3.00	1.35
161A Paul Wilson/2400	3.00	1.35
162A Ben Grieve/2500	6.00	2.70
163A Doug Million/1020	3.00	1.35
164A C.J. Nitkowski/970	3.00	1.35
165A Tommy Davis/960	3.00	1.35
166A Dustin Hermanson/1020	5.00	2.20
167A Travis Miller/760	3.00	1.35
169A Victor Rodriguez/1000	3.00	1.35
170A Jacob Cruz/990	3.00	1.35
171A Rick Heiserman/600	3.00	1.35
172A Mark Farris/1090	3.00	1.35
173A Nomar Garciaparra/1020	80.00	36.00
174A Paul Konerko/970	20.00	9.00
176A Brian Stephenson/1100	3.00	1.35
177A Matt Smith/1090	3.00	1.35
178A Kevin Brown/1090	3.00	1.35
179A Cade Gaspar/1090	3.00	1.35
180A Bret Wagner/970	3.00	1.35
181A Mike Thurman/990	3.00	1.35
183A Ryan Nye/1015	3.00	1.35
184A Brian Buchanan/950	3.00	1.35
186A Mark Johnson/1000	3.00	1.35
187A Jacob Shumate/980	3.00	1.35
188A Kevin Witt/970	3.00	1.35

1994 Classic Four-Sport BCs *

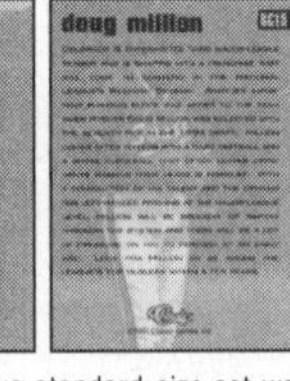

This 20-card bonus standard-size set was inserted one per '94 Classic Four-Sport jumbo packs. The fronts feature full color player photos. The backs carry biographical and statistical information about the player.

	MINT	NRMT
COMPLETE SET (20)	15.00	6.75
BC1 Marshall Faulk	2.50	1.10
BC2 Heath Shuler	.50	.23
BC3 Antonio Langham	.50	.23
BC4 Derrick Alexander	1.00	.45
BC5 Byron Bam Morris	.50	.23
BC6 Glenn Robinson	1.00	.45
BC7 Jason Kidd	2.00	.90
BC8 Grant Hill	1.25	.55
BC9 Jalen Rose	1.00	.45
BC10 Donyell Marshall	.50	.23
BC11 Juwan Howard	1.00	.45
BC12 Khalid Reeves	.50	.23
BC13 Paul Wilson	.50	.23
BC14 Ben Grieve	1.00	.45
BC15 Doug Million	.50	.23
BC16 Nomar Garciaparra	5.00	2.20
BC17 Ed Jovanovski	.50	.23
BC18 Radek Bonk	.50	.23
BC19 Jeff O'Neill	.50	.23
BC20 Ethan Moreau	.50	.23

1994 Classic Four-Sport Classic Picks *

This 10-card standard-size set was randomly inserted in packs at a rate of one in 72. The fronts feature full-color action player photos with the player's name and card title below. The backs carry a small player photo, the player's name, biographical information, and career highlights printed over a ghosted photo of the same player.

	MINT	NRMT
COMPLETE SET (10)	20.00	9.00
16 Paul Wilson	1.00	.45
17 Ben Grieve	2.00	.90
18 Trey Moore	1.00	.45
19 Nomar Garciaparra	10.00	4.50
20 Doug Million	1.00	.45
21 Dan Wilkinson	1.00	.45
22 Willie McGinest	1.00	.45
23 Khalid Reeves	1.00	.45
24 Grant Hill	4.00	1.80
25 Ethan Moreau	1.00	.45

1994 Classic Four-Sport High Voltage *

This 20-card sequentially-numbered standard-size set features the top draft picks. The cards are printed on holographic foil board with a striking design. 2,995 of each even-numbered card and 5,495 of each odd-numbered cards were produced. The cards were inserted on an average of 3 per case and had stated odds of one in 144 hobby packs. The fronts feature the players against a background of lightning while the backs feature a biography on the left side of the card. The right side shows more lightning and the player's photo.

	MINT	NRMT
COMPLETE SET (20)	150.00	70.00
COMMON CARD (HV1-HV20)	2.00	.90
COMMON SP (HV1-HV20)	5.00	2.20
HV1 Dan Wilkinson	2.00	.90
HV2 Glenn Robinson SP	12.00	5.50
HV3 Paul Wilson	2.00	.90
HV4 Ed Jovanovski SP	5.00	2.20
HV5 Marshall Faulk	15.00	6.75
HV6 Jason Kidd SP	25.00	11.00
HV7 Ben Grieve	3.00	1.35
HV8 Oleg Tverdovsky SP	5.00	2.20
HV9 Heath Shuler	3.00	1.35
HV10 Grant Hill SP	20.00	9.00
HV11 Dustin Hermanson	3.00	1.35
HV12 Radek Bonk SP	10.00	4.50
HV13 Trent Dilfer	4.00	1.80
HV14 Donyell Marshall SP	5.00	2.20
HV15 Doug Million	2.00	.90
HV16 Jason Bonsignore SP	5.00	2.20
HV17 Willie McGinest	2.00	.90
HV18 Juwan Howard SP	10.00	4.50
HV19 Jeff O'Neill	2.00	.90
HV20 Nomar Garciaparra SP	15.00	6.75

1994 Classic Four-Sport Phone Cards $1 *

This set of eight phone cards was randomly inserted in Four-Sport packs. Printed on hard plastic, each card measures 2 1/8" by 3 3/8" and has rounded corners. The fronts display full-bleed color action photos, with the phone time value ($1, $2, $3, $4 or $5) and the player's name printed vertically in red along the right edge. The horizontal backs carry instructions for use of the cards. The cards are unnumbered and checklisted below in alphabetical order. The $3 and $5 cards were inserted into retail packs. The phone cards could be used until November 30, 1995.

	MINT	NRMT
COMPLETE SET (8)	12.00	5.50
*TWO DOLLAR: .4X TO 1X BASIC INSERTS		
*THREE DOLLAR: .75X TO 2X BASIC INSERTS		
*FOUR DOLLAR: 1.2X TO 3X BASIC INSERTS		
*FIVE DOLLAR: 2X TO 5X BASIC INSERTS		
*PIN NUMBER REVEALED: HALF VALUE		
1 Trent Dilfer	1.00	.45
2 Marshall Faulk	4.00	1.80
3 Ben Grieve	1.00	.45
4 Ed Jovanovski	.50	.23
5 Jason Kidd	2.50	1.10
6 Jeff O'Neill	.50	.23
7 Glenn Robinson	2.00	.90
8 Paul Wilson	.50	.23

1994 Classic Four-Sport Tri-Cards *

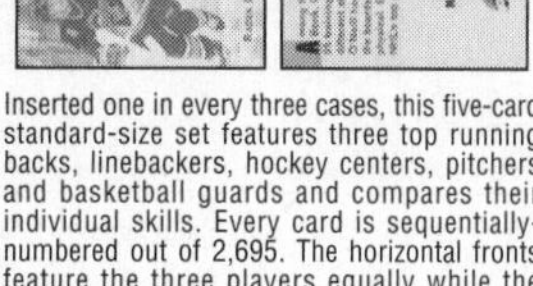

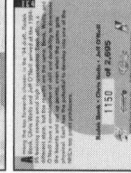

Inserted one in every three cases, this five-card standard-size set features three top running backs, linebackers, hockey centers, pitchers and basketball guards and compares their individual skills. Every card is sequentially-numbered out of 2,695. The horizontal fronts feature the three players equally while the backs gives a brief biography of why the three players are grouped together.

	MINT	NRMT
COMPLETE SET (5)	10.00	4.50
TC1 Marshall Faulk Calvin Jones Errict Rhett	5.00	2.20
TC2 Willie McGinest Trev Alberts Jamir Miller	1.00	.45
TC3 Jalen Rose Jason Kidd Khalid Reeves	3.00	1.35
TC4 Radek Bonk Chris Wells Jeff O'Neill	1.00	.45
TC5 Paul Wilson Doug Million Cade Gaspar	1.00	.45

1995 Classic Five-Sport Previews *

Randomly inserted in Classic hockey packs, this five-card standard-size set salutes the leaders and the up-and-coming rookies of the five sports. Borderless fronts have a full-color action shot with gold foil stamp of "preview" and the player's name, school and position printed vertically on the right side of the card. The player's sport's ball (or tire) is printed in a montage on the right. Backs have another full-color action shot and also a biography, statistics and profile. The cards are numbered with a "SP" prefix.

	MINT	NRMT
COMPLETE SET (5)	8.00	3.60
SP1 Dale Earnhardt	5.00	2.20
SP2 Joe Smith	1.00	.45
SP3 Michael Westbrook	1.00	.45
SP4 Bryan Berard	1.00	.45
SP5 Paul Wilson	1.00	.45

1995 Classic Five-Sport *

The 1995 Classic Five Sport set was issued in one series of 200 standard-size cards. Cards were issued in 10-card regular packs (SRP $1.99). Boxes contained 36 packs. One autographed card was guaranteed in each pack and one certified autographed card (with an embossed logo) appeared in each box. There were also memorabilia redemption cards included in some packs and were guaranteed in at least one pack per box. The cards are numbered and divided into the five sports as follows: Basketball (1-42), Football (43-92), Baseball (93-122), Hockey (123-160), Racing (161-180), Alma Maters (181-190), Picture Perfect (191-200).

	MINT	NRMT
COMPLETE SET (200)	15.00	6.75
COMP. SILVER DIE CUT(200)	30.00	13.50
*SILVER DCs: .75X TO 2X BASIC CARDS		
COMP. RED DIE CUT (200)	100.00	45.00
*RED DCs: 2X TO 5X BASIC CARDS		
*PROOFS: 4X TO 10X BASIC CARDS		
1 Joe Smith	.40	.18
2 Antonio McDyess	.50	.23
3 Jerry Stackhouse	.75	.35
4 Rasheed Wallace	.75	.35
5 Kevin Garnett	2.00	.90
6 Damon Stoudamire	.40	.18
7 Shawn Respert	.15	.07
8 Ed O'Bannon	.25	.11
9 Kurt Thomas	.40	.18
10 Gary Trent	.25	.11
11 Cherokee Parks	.15	.07
12 Corliss Williamson	.40	.18
13 Eric Williams	.15	.07
14 Brent Barry	.40	.18
15 Bob Sura	.40	.18
16 Theo Ratliff	.40	.18
17 Randolph Childress	.15	.07
18 Jason Caffey	.15	.07
19 Michael Finley	.50	.23
20 George Zidek	.15	.07
21 Travis Best	.25	.11
22 Loren Meyer	.15	.07
23 David Vaughn	.15	.07
24 Sherrell Ford	.15	.07
25 Mario Bennett	.15	.07
26 Greg Ostertag	.40	.18
27 Cory Alexander	.15	.07
28 Lou Roe	.15	.07
29 Dragan Tarlac	.15	.07
30 Terrence Rencher	.15	.07
31 Junior Burrough	.15	.07
32 Andrew DeClercq	.15	.07
33 Jimmy King	.15	.07
34 Lawrence Moten	.15	.07
35 Donny Marshall	.15	.07
36 Eric Snow	.40	.18
37 Anthony Pelle	.15	.07
38 Tyus Edney	.15	.07
39 Jerome Allen	.15	.07
40 Fred Hoiberg	.25	.11
41 Constantin Popa	.15	.07
42 Rebecca Lobo	.40	.18
43 Ki-Jana Carter	.25	.11
44 Tony Boselli	.25	.11
45 Steve McNair	1.00	.45
46 Michael Westbrook	.40	.18
47 Kerry Collins	.75	.35
48 Kevin Carter	.25	.11
49 Mike Mamula	.15	.07
50 Joey Galloway	.50	.23
51 Kyle Brady	.15	.07
52 J.J. Stokes	.40	.18
53 Derrick Alexander	.15	.07
54 Warren Sapp	.50	.23
55 Mark Fields	.15	.07
56 Ruben Brown	.15	.07
57 Ellis Johnson	.15	.07
58 Hugh Douglas	.40	.18
59 Tyrone Wheatley	.40	.18
60 Napoleon Kaufman	.40	.18
61 James O. Stewart	.40	.18
62 Luther Ellis	.15	.07
63 Rashaan Salaam	.15	.07
64 Tyrone Poole	.15	.07
65 Ty Law	.25	.11
66 Korey Stringer	.40	.18
67 Devin Bush	.15	.07
68 Mark Bruener	.25	.11
69 Derrick Brooks	1.00	.45
70 Craig Powell	.15	.07
71 Craig Newsome	.15	.07
72 Anthony Cook	.15	.07
73 Ray Zellars	.25	.11
74 Todd Collins	.15	.07
75 Sherman Williams	.15	.07
76 Frank Sanders	.40	.18
77 Corey Fuller	.15	.07
78 Kordell Stewart	1.00	.45
79 Curtis Martin	1.25	.55
80 Lorenzo Styles	.15	.07
81 Chris T. Jones	.15	.07
82 Zack Crockett	.25	.11
83 Stoney Case	.25	.11
84 Eric Zeier	.40	.18
85 Jimmy Hitchcock	.15	.07
86 Rodney Thomas	.25	.11
87 Rob Johnson	.75	.35
88 Tyrone Davis	.15	.07
89 Chad May	.15	.07
90 Ed Hervey	.15	.07
91 Terrell Davis	1.50	.70
92 John Walsh	.15	.07
93 Ben Grieve	.40	.18
94 Roger Cedeno	.25	.11
95 Michael Barrett	.50	.23
96 Ben Davis	.40	.18
97 Paul Wilson	.15	.07
98 Calvin Reese	.25	.11
99 Jermaine Dye	.40	.18
100 Alvie Shepherd	.15	.07
101 Ryan Jaroncyk	.15	.07
102 Mark Farris	.15	.07
103 Karim Garcia	.75	.35
104 Rey Ordonez	.40	.18
105 Jay Payton	.40	.18
106 Dustin Hermanson	.25	.11
107 Tommy Davis	.15	.07
108 C.J. Nitkowski	.15	.07
109 Todd Greene	.25	.11
110 Billy Wagner	.25	.11
111 Mark Redman	.15	.07
112 Brooks Kieschnick	.15	.07
113 Paul Konerko	.40	.18
114 Brad Fullmer	.25	.11
115 Vladimir Guerrero	3.00	1.35
116 Bartolo Colon	1.00	.45
117 Doug Million	.15	.07
118 Steve Gibralter	.15	.07
119 Tony McKnight	.15	.07
120 Derrek Lee	.25	.11
121 Nomar Garciaparra	2.00	.90
122 Chad Hermansen	.25	.11
123 Bryan Berard	.25	.11
124 Wade Redden	.25	.11
125 Aki-Petteri Berg	.15	.07
126 Nolan Baumgartner	.15	.07
127 Jason Bonsignore	.15	.07
128 Steve Kelly	.15	.07
129 George Breen	.15	.07
130 Terry Ryan	.15	.07
131 Greg Bullock	.15	.07
132 Jarome Iginla	.75	.35
133 Petr Buzek	.25	.11
134 Brad Church	.15	.07
135 Jay McKee	.15	.07
136 Jan Hlavac	.40	.18
137 Petr Sykora	.40	.18
138 Ed Jovanovski	.25	.11
139 Chris Kenady	.15	.07
140 Marc Moro	.15	.07
141 Kaj Linna	.15	.07
142 Aaron MacDonald	.15	.07
143 Chad Kilger	.15	.07
144 Tyler Moss	.15	.07
145 Christian Laflamme	.15	.07
146 Brian Mueller	.15	.07
147 Daymond Langkow	.40	.18
148 Brent Peterson	.15	.07
149 Chad Quenneville	.15	.07
150 Chris Van Dyk	.15	.07
151 Kent Fearns	.15	.07
152 Adam Wiesel	.15	.07
153 Marc Chouinard	.25	.11
154 Jason Doig	.15	.07
155 Denis Smith	.15	.07
156 Radek Dvorak	.25	.11
157 Donald MacLean	.15	.07
158 Shane Kenny	.15	.07
159 Brian Holzinger	.25	.11
160 Eric Flinton	.15	.07
161 Dale Earnhardt	2.00	.90
162 John Andretti	.15	.07
163 Derrike Cope	.15	.07
164 Richard Childress	.15	.07
165 Rusty Wallace	.60	.25
166 Bobby Labonte	.50	.23
167 Brett Bodine	.40	.18
168 Michael Waltrip	.15	.07
169 Sterling Marlin	.40	.18
170 Kyle Petty	.25	.11
171 Ricky Rudd	.40	.18
172 Jeff Burton	.40	.18
173 Dick Trickle	.15	.07
174 Ernie Irvan	.25	.11
175 Dale Jarrett	.60	.25
176 Darrell Waltrip	.25	.11
177 Geoff Bodine	.15	.07
178 Ted Musgrave	.15	.07
179 Morgan Shepherd	.15	.07
180 Todd Bodine	.15	.07
181 Jerry Stackhouse Jimmy Hitchcock	.40	.18
182 Antonio McDyess Sherman Williams	.40	.18
183 Nomar Garciaparra Travis Best	1.00	.45
184 Andrew DeClercq Ki-Jana Carter	.25	.11
185 Tyrone Wheatley Jimmy King	.40	.18
186 J.J. Stokes Ed O'Bannon	.40	.18
187 Warren Sapp Constantin Popa	.40	.18
188 Paul Wilson Derrick Brooks	1.00	.45
189 Eric Williams George Breen	.15	.07
190 Bob Sura Derrick Alexander	.15	.07
191 Steve Young	.60	.25
192 Hakeem Olajuwon	.40	.18
193 Barry Bonds	1.00	.45
194 Marshall Faulk	.75	.35
195 Troy Aikman	.60	.25
196 Drew Bledsoe	.50	.23
197 Emmitt Smith	.75	.35
198 Jason Kidd	.60	.25
199 Shaquille O'Neal	1.00	.45
200 Alonzo Mourning	.40	.18

1995 Classic Five-Sport Autographs *

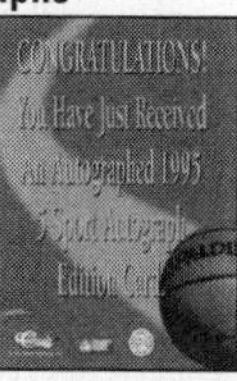

This set was randomly inserted into packs. Borderless fronts feature color player action photos. Balls of the sport run vertically down the right side with the player's name, position, and team name printed on them. The backs carry a "Congratulations" message stating that it is an autographed 1995 Five Sport Autograph Edition Card with the sport's ball pictured at the bottom. The cards are unnumbered. The set price is assumed to include the less valuable of cards with two versions.

	MINT	NRMT
*CLASSIC SIGNINGS: SAME VALUE		
1 Joe Smith	3.00	1.35
2 Antonio McDyess SP	25.00	11.00
4 Rasheed Wallace SP	30.00	13.50
6 Damon Stoudamire SP	20.00	9.00
8 Ed O'Bannon	2.00	.90
9 Kurt Thomas	3.00	1.35
11 Cherokee Parks	2.00	.90
14 Brent Barry SP	3.00	1.35
15 Bob Sura	3.00	1.35
16 Theo Ratliff	5.00	2.20
17 Randolph Childress SP	2.00	.90
19 Michael Finley	8.00	3.60
20 George Zidek	2.00	.90
24 Sherrell Ford	2.00	.90
27 Cory Alexander	2.00	.90
30 Terrence Rencher	2.00	.90
32 Andrew DeClercq SP	2.00	.90
35 Donny Marshall	2.00	.90
36 Eric Snow	3.00	1.35
37 Anthony Pelle	2.00	.90
38 Tyus Edney	2.00	.90
39 Jerome Allen	2.00	.90
40 Fred Hoiberg	2.00	.90
41 Constantin Popa	2.00	.90
45 Steve McNair	10.00	4.50
47 Kerry Collins	8.00	3.60
49 Mike Mamula	3.00	1.35
50 Joey Galloway	8.00	3.60
51 Kyle Brady	5.00	2.20
55 Mark Fields	2.00	.90
58 Hugh Douglas	2.00	.90
60 Napoleon Kaufman SP	8.00	3.60
64 Tyrone Poole	3.00	1.35
77 Corey Fuller	2.00	.90
84 Eric Zeier	5.00	2.20
87 Rob Johnson	6.00	2.70
89 Chad May	5.00	2.20
92 John Walsh	2.00	.90
93A Ben Grieve	3.00	1.35
93B Ben Grieve/295	8.00	3.60
94 Roger Cedeno SP	3.00	1.35
95 Michael Barrett	5.00	2.20
96A Ben Davis	3.00	1.35
97 Paul Wilson	2.00	.90
98 Calvin Reese	3.00	1.35
99 Jermaine Dye	5.00	2.20
100 Alvie Shepherd	2.00	.90
101 Ryan Jaroncyk	2.00	.90
102 Mark Farris	2.00	.90
103 Karim Garcia	5.00	2.20
104 Rey Ordonez	3.00	1.35
105 Jay Payton	3.00	1.35
106 Dustin Hermanson	3.00	1.35
109 Todd Greene	2.00	.90
110 Billy Wagner	3.00	1.35
111 Mark Redman	3.00	1.35
112 Brooks Kieschnick	2.00	.90
113 Paul Konerko	8.00	3.60
114 Brad Fullmer	3.00	1.35
115 Vladimir Guerrero	40.00	18.00
116 Bartolo Colon	8.00	3.60
117 Doug Million	2.00	.90
118 Steve Gibralter	2.00	.90
119 Tony McKnight	2.00	.90
120 Derrek Lee	3.00	1.35
121 Nomar Garciaparra	50.00	22.00
122 Chad Hermansen	2.00	.90
126 Nolan Baumgartner	2.00	.90
127 Jason Bonsignore	2.00	.90
128 Steve Kelly	2.00	.90
129 George Breen	2.00	.90
131 Greg Bullock	2.00	.90
132 Jarome Iginla	10.00	4.50
135 Jay McKee	2.00	.90
137 Petr Sykora SP	6.00	2.70
138 Ed Jovanovski	5.00	2.20
139 Chris Kenady	2.00	.90
140 Marc Moro	2.00	.90
142 Aaron MacDonald	2.00	.90
144 Tyler Moss	3.00	1.35
145 Christian Laflamme	2.00	.90
146 Brian Mueller	2.00	.90
148 Brent Peterson	2.00	.90
149 Chad Quenneville	2.00	.90
150 Chris Van Dyk SP	3.00	1.35
151 Kent Ferns	2.00	.90
153 Marc Chouinard SP	5.00	2.20
154 Jason Doig	3.00	1.35
155 Denis Smith	2.00	.90
156 Radek Dvorak	3.00	1.35
157 Don MacLean	2.00	.90
158 Shane Kenny	2.00	.90
161 Dale Earnhardt/635	350.00	160.00
192 Hakeem Olajuwon	25.00	11.00
193 Barry Bonds	100.00	45.00
195 Troy Aikman	2.00	.90
197 Emmitt Smith	2.00	.90
198 Jason Kidd SP	30.00	13.50
199 Shaquille O'Neal	100.00	45.00
200 Alonzo Mourning SP	25.00	11.00

1995 Classic Five-Sport Fast Track *

Randomly inserted in retail packs, this 20-card standard-size set spotlights the young stars of sports who are fast becoming major stars. Borderless fronts contain a player in full-color action while the rest of the shot is printed in colored foil. Backs have a color action shot in one box and two color separted boxes with the rest of the photo. A player profile appears underneath the photo. The cards are numbered with a "FT" prefix.

	MINT	NRMT
COMPLETE SET (20)	50.00	22.00
FT1 Joe Smith	3.00	1.35
FT2 Michael Westbrook	3.00	1.35
FT3 Jason Kidd	8.00	3.60
FT4 Kyle Brady	1.00	.45
FT5 Bryan Berard	1.00	.45
FT6 Jerry Stackhouse	5.00	2.20
FT7 Shawn Respert	1.00	.45
FT8 Napoleon Kaufman	4.00	1.80
FT9 Rasheed Wallace	3.00	1.35
FT10 Ed O'Bannon	1.00	.45
FT11 J.J. Stokes	3.00	1.35
FT12 Kevin Garnett	20.00	9.00
FT13 Ben Grieve	3.00	1.35
FT14 Petr Sykora	4.00	1.80
FT15 Tyrone Wheatley	3.00	1.35
FT16 Antonio McDyess	4.00	1.80
FT17 Rashaan Salaam	1.00	.45
FT18 Damon Stoudamire	4.00	1.80
FT19 Steve McNair	5.00	2.20
FT20 Corliss Williamson	4.00	1.80

1995 Classic Five-Sport Hot Box Autographs *

This set of six autographed standard-sized cards were randomly inserted in Hobby Hot boxes. The cards are identical to the regular Hot box inserts with the exception of a player's signature on the front.

	MINT	NRMT
COMPLETE SET (6)	500.00	220.00
1 Barry Bonds/630	100.00	45.00
2 Kerry Collins/625	25.00	11.00
3 Dale Earnhardt/635	400.00	180.00
4 Jason Kidd/650	25.00	11.00
5 Steve McNair/630	25.00	11.00
6 Shaquille O'Neal/655	80.00	36.00

1995 Classic Five-Sport Phone Cards $3 *

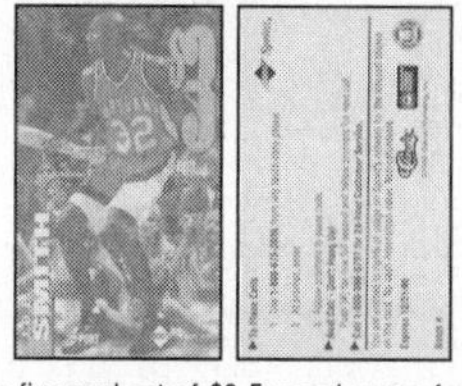

The five-card set of $3 Foncards were found one per 72 retail packs. The credit-card size plastic pieces have a borderless front with a full-color action player photo and the $3 emblem printed on the upper right in blue. The player's name is printed in white type vertically on the lower left. The Sprint logo appears on the bottom also. White backs carry information of how to place calls using the card.

	MINT	NRMT
COMPLETE SET (5)	8.00	3.60
1 Dale Earnhardt	5.00	2.20
2 C.J. Nitkowski	1.00	.45
3 Brian Holzinger	1.00	.45
4 Rashaan Salaam	1.00	.45
5 Joe Smith	1.50	.70

1995 Classic Five-Sport Phone Cards $4 *

These cards were inserted randomly into packs at a rate of one in 72 and featured the five top prospects or performers of the individual sports. The borderless fronts feature full-color action photos with the athlete's name printed in white across the bottom. The Sprint logo and $4 are printed along the top. White backs contain information about placing calls using the card.

	MINT	NRMT
COMPLETE SET (5)	15.00	6.75
1 Dale Earnhardt	6.00	2.70
2 Nomar Garciaparra	5.00	2.20

3 Wade Redden 1.00 .45
4 Jerry Stackhouse 2.50 1.10
5 Michael Westbrook 1.50 .70

1995 Classic Five-Sport Record Setters *

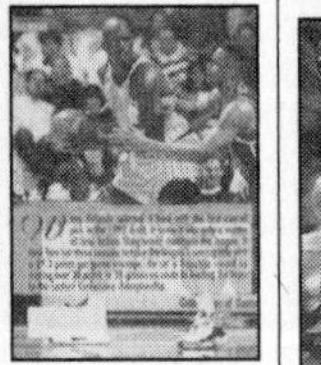

This 10-card standard-size set was inserted in retail packs and feature the stars and rookies of the five sports. The fronts display full-bleed color action photos; the set title "Record Setters" iin prismatic block lettering appears toward the bottom. On a sepia-tone photo, the backs carry a player profile. The cards are numbered on the back with an "RS" prefix and hand-numbered out of 1250.

MINT NRMT
COMPLETE SET (10) 40.00 18.00
RS1 Kerry Collins 2.50 1.10
RS2 Bryan Berard 2.00 .90
RS3 Ed O'Bannon 1.50 .70
RS4 Dale Earnhardt 10.00 4.50
RS5 Joe Smith 2.50 1.10
RS6 Jerry Stackhouse 4.00 1.80
RS7 Paul Wilson 1.50 .70
RS8 Rashaan Salaam 1.50 .70
RS9 Kevin Garnett 20.00 9.00
RS10 Jeff Gordon 8.00 3.60

1995 Classic Five-Sport Strive For Five *

This interactive game card set consists of 65 cards to be used like playing cards. Collector's gained a full suit of cards to redeem prizes. The odds of finding the card in packs were one in 10. Fronts are bordered in metallic silver foil and picture the player in full-color action. The cards are numbered on both top and bottom in silver foil and the player's name is printed vertically in silver foil. Backs have green backgrounds with the game rules printed in white type.

MINT NRMT
COMPLETE SET (65) 60.00 27.00
BA1 Paul Wilson .50 .23
BA2 Billy Wagner 1.00 .45
BA3 Ben Grieve 1.00 .45
BA4 Bartolo Colon 2.00 .90
BA5 Tommy Davis .50 .23
BA6 C.J. Nitkowski .50 .23
BA7 Mark Redman 1.00 .45
BA8 Todd Greene .50 .23
BA9 Jay Payton 1.00 .45
BA10 Nomar Garciaparra 5.00 2.20
BA11 Ben Davis 1.00 .45
BA12 Doug Million .50 .23
BA13 Dustin Hermanson .50 .23
BK1 Joe Smith 1.25 .55
BK2 Gary Trent 1.00 .45
BK3 Kurt Thomas .50 .23
BK4 Ed O'Bannon .50 .23
BK5 Shawn Respert .50 .23
BK6 Damon Stoudamire 2.00 .90
BK7 Kevin Garnett 5.00 2.20
BK8 Rasheed Wallace 1.50 .70
BK9 Antonio McDyess 1.50 .70
BK10 Hakeem Olajuwon 1.00 .45
BK11 Jason Kidd 1.50 .70
BK12 Rebecca Lobo 2.00 .90
BK13 Jerry Stackhouse 1.25 .55
FB1 Ki-Jana Carter .50 .23
FB2 Rashaan Salaam .50 .23
FB3 Napoleon Kaufman 1.00 .45
FB4 Tyrone Wheatley 1.00 .45
FB5 J.J. Stokes 1.00 .45
FB6 Joey Galloway 1.00 .45
FB7 Kerry Collins 1.00 .45
FB8 Michael Westbrook 1.00 .45
FB9 Steve McNair 2.00 .90
FB10 Drew Bledsoe 1.50 .70
FB11 Marshall Faulk 1.50 .70
FB12 Troy Aikman 2.00 .90
FB13 Steve Young 1.50 .70
HK1 Wade Redden .50 .23
HK2 Jan Hlavac 1.00 .45
HK3 Brad Church .50 .23
HK4 Steve Kelly .50 .23
HK5 Radek Dvorak 1.00 .45
HK6 Jason Bonsignore .50 .23
HK7 Petr Sykora 1.00 .45
HK8 Daymond Langkow 1.00 .45
HK9 Chad Kilger .50 .23
HK10 Nolan Baumgartner .50 .23
HK11 Brian Holzinger 1.00 .45
HK12 Aki-Petteri Berg .50 .23
HK13 Ed Jovanovski .50 .23
RC1 John Andretti .50 .23
RC2 Dick Trickle .50 .23
RC3 Kyle Petty 1.00 .45
RC4 Bobby Labonte 1.00 .45
RC5 Ricky Rudd 1.00 .45
RC6 Darrell Waltrip 1.00 .45
RC7 Dale Jarrett 1.00 .45
RC8 Brett Bodine 1.00 .45
RC9 Geoff Bodine .50 .23
RC10 Ernie Irvan .50 .23
RC11 Jeff Burton 1.00 .45
RC12 Sterling Marlin 1.00 .45
RC13 Rusty Wallace 1.00 .45

1993-94 Classic Images *

These 150 standard-size cards feature on their borderless fronts color player action shots with backgrounds that have been thrown out of focus. On the white background to the left, career highlights, biography and statistics are displayed. Just 6,500 of each card were produced. The set closes with Classic Headlines (128-147) and checklists (148-150). A redemption card inserted one per case entitled the collector to one set of basketball draft preview cards. This offered expired 9/30/94.

MINT NRMT
COMPLETE SET (150) 15.00 6.75
1 Drew Bledsoe .75 .35
2 Chris Webber 1.50 .70
3 Alex Rodriguez 5.00 2.20
4 Alexandre Daigle .15 .07
5 Rick Mirer .15 .07
6 Anfernee Hardaway .60 .25
7 Jeff D'Amico .15 .07
8 Chris Pronger .40 .18
9 Robert Smith .40 .18
10 Sherron Mills .15 .07
11 Alan Benes .15 .07
12 Warren Kidd .15 .07
13 Bryon Russell .40 .18
14 Mike Peplowski .15 .07
15 Jeff Granger .15 .07
16 Jim Montgomery .15 .07
17 Todd Marchant .15 .07
18 Doug Edwards .15 .07
19 Daron Kirkreit .15 .07
20 Mike Dunham .15 .07
21 Garth Snow .40 .18
22 Darnell Mee .15 .07
23 Billy Wagner .15 .07
24 Barry Richter .15 .07
25 Lincoln Kennedy .15 .07
26 Jerome Bettis .75 .35
27 Corie Blount .15 .07
28 Matt Martin .15 .07
29 Deon Figures .15 .07
30 Rob Niedermayer .15 .07
31 Brian Anderson .15 .07
32 Jesse Belanger .15 .07
33 George Teague .15 .07
34 Chris Schwab .15 .07
35 Peter Ferraro .15 .07
36 Shaquille O'Neal Rap 1.50 .70
37 Matt Brunson .15 .07
38 Ted Drury .15 .07
39 Glyn Milburn .15 .07
40 George Lynch .15 .07
41 Gheorghe Muresan .15 .07
42 Kirk Presley .15 .07
43 Derek Plante .15 .07
44 Gino Torretta .15 .07
45 Roger Harper .15 .07
46 Jim Campbell .15 .07
47 Chris Carpenter .15 .07
48 Victor Bailey .15 .07
49 Kelly Wunsch .15 .07
50 Isaiah Rider .15 .07
51 Jon Ratliff .15 .07
52 Wayne Gomes .15 .07
53 Thomas Smith .15 .07
54 Trot Nixon .75 .35
55 Andre King .15 .07
56 Chris Osgood 1.00 .45
57 Reggie Brooks .15 .07
58 Ron Moore .15 .07
59 Vin Baker .15 .07
60 Rodney Rogers .15 .07
61 Dan Footman .15 .07
62 Jason Arnott .40 .18
63 Darren Dreifort .15 .07
64 Tom Carter .15 .07
65 Qadry Ismail .40 .18
66 Josh Grant .15 .07
67 Luther Wright .15 .07
68 Allan Houston .60 .25
69 Brooks Kieschnick .15 .07
70 Marvin Jones .15 .07
71 Garrison Hearst .40 .18
72 John Copeland .15 .07
73 Darrien Gordon .15 .07
74 Jocelyn Thibault .40 .18
75 Lindsey Hunter .15 .07
76 Scott Burrell .15 .07
77 Torii Hunter 2.50 1.10
78 Chad Brown .15 .07
79 Sam Cassell .40 .18
80 Steve Soderstrom .15 .07
81 Jimmy Jackson .15 .07
82 Irv Smith .15 .07
83 Troy Drayton .15 .07
84 Chris Mills .15 .07
85 Derrek Lee .40 .18
86 Chris Gratton .15 .07
87 Carlton Gray .15 .07
88 Billy Joe Hobert .15 .07
89 Acie Earl .15 .07
90 Terry Dehere .15 .07
91 Carl Simpson .15 .07
92 Mike Rathje .15 .07
93 Jay Powell .15 .07
94 James Robinson .15 .07
95 Roosevelt Potts .15 .07
96 Jamal Mashburn .40 .18
97 Derek Brown RB .15 .07
98 Ed Stokes .15 .07
99 Ervin Johnson .15 .07
100 Nick Van Exel .40 .18
101 Martin Brodeur 1.00 .45
102 Curtis Conway .40 .18
103 Lamar Thomas .15 .07
104 Willie Roaf .15 .07
105 Matt Drews .15 .07
106 Paul Kariya 1.25 .55
107 Eric Curry .15 .07
108 Todd Kelly .15 .07
109 Rex Walters .15 .07
110 Chris Whitney .15 .07
111 Manon Rheaume .75 .35
112 Alonzo Mourning .40 .18
113 Lucious Harris .15 .07
114 Horace Copeland .15 .07
115 Scott Christman .15 .07
116 Terry Kirby .15 .07
117 Demetrius DuBose .15 .07
118 Will Shields .15 .07
119 Natrone Means .15 .07
120 O.J.McDuffie .40 .18
121 Felix Potvin .40 .18
122 Dino Radja .15 .07
123 Harold Miner .15 .07
124 Greg Graham .15 .07
125 Alexei Yashin .15 .07
126 Kevin Williams WR .15 .07
127 Lorenzo Neal .15 .07
128 Shaquille O'Neal B/W 1.25 .55
129 Drew Bledsoe B/W .75 .35
130 Alexei Yashin B/W .15 .07
131 Kirk Presley B/W .15 .07
132 Chris Webber B/W .75 .35
133 Rick Mirer B/W .15 .07
134 Anfernee Hardaway B/W .40 .18
135 Chris Pronger BW .15 .07
136 Alonzo Mourning B/W .40 .18
137 Jerome Bettis B/W .40 .18
138 Chris Gratton BW .15 .07
139 Trot Nixon B/W .40 .18
140 Terry Kirby BW .15 .07
141 Jamal Mashburn B/W .15 .07
142 Jason Arnott B/W .15 .07
143 Alex Rodriguez B/W 2.00 .90
144 Derek Brown RB BW .15 .07
145 Isaiah Rider B/W .15 .07
146 Harold Miner BW .15 .07
147 Manon Rheaume B/W .40 .18
148 Checklist 1 .15 .07
149 Checklist 2 .15 .07
150 Checklist 3 .15 .07
NNO BK Preview Redemption 1.00 .45

1993-94 Classic Images Chrome *

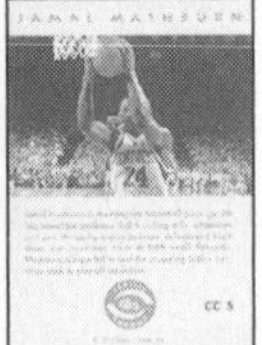

Randomly inserted one in every fourteen 1994 Classic Images packs, these 20 limited print (9,750 of each) cards measure the standard size and feature color player action shots on their borderless metallic fronts. The cards are numbered on the back with a "CC" prefix. This set was also available in uncut sheet form as a redeemed prize for the Marshall Faulk M5 card.

MINT NRMT
COMPLETE SET (20) 50.00 22.00
COMP. UNCUT SHEET 80.00 36.00
CC1 Chris Webber 8.00 3.60
CC2 Anfernee Hardaway 4.00 1.80
CC3 Jimmy Jackson 2.00 .90
CC4 Nick Van Exel 2.50 1.10
CC5 Jamal Mashburn 2.00 .90
CC6 Isaiah Rider 2.00 .90
CC7 Drew Bledsoe 6.00 2.70
CC8 Jerome Bettis 5.00 2.20
CC9 Terry Kirby 2.00 .90
CC10 Dana Stubblefield 2.00 .90
CC11 Rick Mirer 2.00 .90
CC12 Cammi Granato 5.00 2.20
CC13 Alexei Yashin 2.00 .90
CC14 Alexandre Daigle 2.00 .90
CC15 Manon Rheaume 3.00 1.35
CC16 Radek Bonk 2.00 .90
CC17 Alex Rodriguez 25.00 11.00
CC18 Kirk Presley 2.00 .90
CC19 Trot Nixon 3.00 1.35
CC20 Brooks Kieschnick 2.00 .90

1995 Classic Images *

Printed on 18-point micro-lined foil board, the 1995 Classic Images set consists of 120 standard-size cards, featuring the top draft picks from the four major sports. Classic produced 1,995 sequentially-numbered 16-box hobby cases. This series also features one "Hot Box" in every four cases; each pack in it included at least one card from five insert sets, plus the special Clear Excitement chase cards not found anywhere else, for a total of 24 inserts per Hot Box. The set subdivides according to sport as follows: basketball (1-37), football (38-75), baseball (76-93), and hockey (94-120). There was a promotional card issued, not inserted into '94-95 Assets packs, for Grant Hill numbered HP1. The front is the same as the card in the set, but the back has an orange background and describes the product's features.

MINT NRMT
COMPLETE SET (120) 15.00 6.75
1 Glenn Robinson .50 .23
2 Jason Kidd 1.50 .70
3 Grant Hill 1.00 .45
4 Donyell Marshall .25 .11
5 Juwan Howard .50 .23
6 Sharone Wright .25 .11
7 Brian Grant .50 .23
8 Eric Montross .25 .11
9 Eddie Jones .75 .35
10 Carlos Rogers .25 .11
11 Khalid Reeves .25 .11
12 Jalen Rose .75 .35
13 Yinka Dare .25 .11
14 Eric Piatkowski .25 .11
15 Clifford Rozier .25 .11
16 Aaron McKie .25 .11
17 Eric Mobley .25 .11
18 B.J. Tyler .25 .11
19 Dickey Simpkins .25 .11
20 Bill Curley .25 .11
21 Wesley Person .25 .11
22 Monty Williams .25 .11
23 Antonio Lang .25 .11
24 Darrin Hancock .25 .11
25 Michael Smith .25 .11
26 Rodney Dent .25 .11
27 Charlie Ward .75 .35
28 Jim McIlvaine .25 .11
29 Brooks Thompson .25 .11
30 Gaylon Nickerson .25 .11
31 Jamie Watson .25 .11
32 Damon Bailey .25 .11
33 Dontonio Wingfield .25 .11
34 Trevor Ruffin .25 .11
35 Greg Minor .25 .11
36 Dwayne Morton .25 .11
37 Shaquille O'Neal 1.00 .45
38 Dan Wilkinson .25 .11
39 Marshall Faulk .75 .35
40 Heath Shuler .25 .11
41 Willie McGinest .25 .11
42 Trev Alberts .25 .11
43 Trent Dilfer .40 .18
44 Bryant Young .25 .11
45 Sam Adams .25 .11
46 Antonio Langham .25 .11
47 Jamir Miller .25 .11
48 Aaron Glenn .25 .11
49 Bernard Williams .25 .11
50 Charles Johnson .25 .11
51 Dewayne Washington .25 .11
52 Tim Bowens .25 .11
53 Johnnie Morton .75 .35
54 Rob Fredrickson .25 .11
55 Shante Carver .25 .11
56 Henry Ford .25 .11
57 Jeff Burris .25 .11
58 William Floyd .25 .11
59 Derrick Alexander .25 .11
60 Darnay Scott .25 .11
61 Errict Rhett .25 .11
62 Greg Hill .25 .11
63 David Palmer .25 .11
64 Charlie Garner .40 .18
65 Mario Bates .25 .11
66 Bert Emanuel .75 .35
67 Thomas Randolph .25 .11
68 Aubrey Beavers .25 .11
69 Byron Bam Morris .25 .11
70 Lake Dawson .25 .11
71 Todd Steussie .25 .11
72 Aaron Taylor .25 .11
73 Corey Sawyer .25 .11
74 Kevin Mitchell .25 .11
75 Emmitt Smith 1.00 .45
76 Paul Wilson .25 .11
77 Ben Grieve .25 .11
78 Doug Million .25 .11
79 Bret Wagner .25 .11
80 Dustin Hermanson .25 .11
81 Doug Webb .25 .11
82 Brian Stephenson .25 .11
83 Jacob Cruz .25 .11
84 Cade Gaspar .25 .11
85 Nomar Garciaparra 5.00 2.20
86 Mike Thurman .25 .11
87 Brian Buchanan .25 .11
88 Mark Johnson .25 .11
89 Jacob Shumate .25 .11
90 Kevin Witt .25 .11
91 Victor Rodriguez .25 .11
92 Trey Moore .25 .11
93 Barry Bonds 2.50 1.10
94 Ed Jovanovski .25 .11
95 Oleg Tverdovsky .25 .11
96 Radek Bonk .75 .35
97 Jason Bonsignore .25 .11
98 Jeff O'Neill .25 .11
99 Ryan Smyth .75 .35
100 Jamie Storr .75 .35
101 Jason Wiemer .25 .11
102 Nolan Baumgarmer .25 .11
103 Jeff Friesen .75 .35
104 Wade Belak .25 .11
105 Ethan Moreau .25 .11
106 Alexander Kharlamov .25 .11
107 Eric Fichaud .75 .35
108 Wayne Primeau .25 .11
109 Brad Brown .25 .11
110 Chris Dingman .25 .11
111 Chris Wells .25 .11
112 Vadim Sharifjanov .25 .11
113 Dan Cloutier .25 .11
114 Jason Allison .75 .35
115 Todd Marchant .25 .11
116 Brent Gretzky .25 .11
117 Petr Sykora .75 .35
118 Manon Rheaume .50 .23
119 Grant Hill CL .75 .35
120 Marshall Faulk CL .75 .35
HP1 Grant Hill Promo 1.00 .45

1995 Classic Images Classic Performances *

Randomly inserted in hobby boxes at a rate of one in every 12 packs, this 20-card standard-size set relives great moments from the careers of 20 top athletes. Each card is numbered out of 4,495. The fronts feature the player against a gold background. The back contains on the left side a description of the great moment and on the right side a color player photo. The cards are numbered with a "CP" prefix.

MINT NRMT
COMPLETE SET (20) 50.00 22.00
CP1 Glenn Robinson 4.00 1.80
CP2 Grant Hill 6.00 2.70
CP3 Jason Kidd 8.00 3.60
CP4 Juwan Howard 2.00 .90
CP5 Shaquille O'Neal 10.00 4.50
CP6 Alonzo Mourning 4.00 1.80
CP7 Jamal Mashburn 1.00 .45
CP8 Steve Young 4.00 1.80
CP9 Marshall Faulk 8.00 3.60
CP10 Derrick Alexander 1.00 .45
CP11 William Floyd 1.00 .45
CP12 Errict Rhett 2.00 .90
CP13 Byron Bam Morris 1.00 .45
CP14 Heath Shuler 2.00 .90
CP15 Emmitt Smith 8.00 3.60
CP16 Paul Wilson 1.00 .45
CP17 Barry Bonds 6.00 2.70
CP18 Nolan Ryan 8.00 3.60
CP19 Ed Jovanovski 1.00 .45
CP20 Eric Fichaud 2.00 .90

1995 Classic Images Clear Excitement *

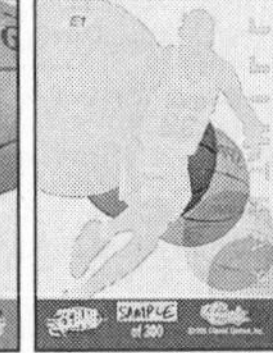

Randomly inserted at a rate of one in every 24 packs in hobby and retail hot boxes (1:1536 over the product run), these two five-card acetate sets each feature five notable athletes from different sports. Cards with the prefix "E" were inserted in hobby hot boxes, while cards with the prefix "C" were found in retail hot boxes. The cards are numbered out of 300.

MINT NRMT
COMPLETE SET (10) 200.00 90.00
C1 Shaquille O'Neal 40.00 18.00
C2 Emmitt Smith 30.00 13.50
C3 Troy Aikman 25.00 11.00
C4 Steve Young 20.00 9.00
C5 Nolan Ryan 50.00 22.00
E1 Grant Hill 25.00 11.00
E2 Marshall Faulk 30.00 13.50
E3 Drew Bledsoe 20.00 9.00
E4 Hakeem Olajuwon 20.00 9.00
E5 Manon Rheaume 20.00 9.00

1996 Classic Signings *

The 1996 Classic Signings set consists of 100 standard-size cards. This series is distinguished from the regular issue by a silver foil facsimile autograph and a silver-foil "Autograph Edition" toward the bottom. The die cut cards were inserted one in four packs. The blue and red signature cards were randomly inserted in regular five-sport Hot Boxes and are identical to the regular card with the exception of a red foil signature on the front.

MINT NRMT
COMPLETE SET (100) 15.00 6.75
*DIE CUTS: .75X TO 2X BASIC CARDS
*RED SIGS: 1.5X TO 4X BASIC CARDS
1995 FIVE-SPORT RED.SIG: SAME PRICE
*BLUE SIGS: 1.5X TO 4X BASIC CARDS
1 Joe Smith .50 .23
2 Antonio McDyess .50 .23
3 Jerry Stackhouse 1.00 .45
4 Rasheed Wallace .40 .18
5 Kevin Garnett 3.00 1.35
6 Damon Stoudamire .75 .35
7 Shawn Respert .15 .07
8 Ed O'Bannon .15 .07
9 Kurt Thomas .15 .07
10 Gary Trent .15 .07
11 Cherokee Parks .15 .07
12 Corliss Williamson .40 .18
13 Eric Williams .15 .07
14 Brent Barry .40 .18
15 Bob Sura .15 .07
16 Randolph Childress .15 .07

17 Michael Finley	.75	.35
18 George Zidek	.15	.07
19 Travis Best	.15	.07
20 David Vaughn	.15	.07
21 Mario Bennett	.15	.07
22 Greg Ostertag	.15	.07
23 Lou Roe	.15	.07
24 Junior Burrough	.15	.07
25 Andrew DeClercq	.15	.07
26 Lawrence Moten	.15	.07
27 Donny Marshall	.15	.07
28 Tyus Edney	.15	.07
29 Jimmy King	.15	.07
30 Rebecca Lobo	.40	.18
31 Ki-Jana Carter	.15	.07
32 Tony Boselli	.40	.18
33 Steve McNair	.60	.25
34 Michael Westbrook	.40	.18
35 Kerry Collins	.40	.18
36 Kevin Carter	.15	.07
37 Mike Mamula	.15	.07
38 Joey Galloway	.40	.18
39 Kyle Brady	.15	.07
40 J.J. Stokes	.40	.18
41 Derrick Alexander	.15	.07
42 Warren Sapp	.40	.18
43 Hugh Douglas	.15	.07
44 Tyrone Wheatley	.40	.18
45 Napoleon Kaufman	.40	.18
46 James O. Stewart	.40	.18
47 Rashaan Salaam	.15	.07
48 Ty Law	.15	.07
49 Mark Bruener	.15	.07
50 Derrick Brooks	.40	.18
51 Curtis Martin	1.00	.45
52 Todd Collins	.15	.07
53 Sherman Williams	.15	.07
54 Frank Sanders	.15	.07
55 Eric Zeier	.15	.07
56 Rob Johnson	.40	.18
57 Chad May	.15	.07
58 Terrell Davis	1.00	.45
59 Stoney Case	.15	.07
60 Ben Grieve	.40	.18
61 Paul Wilson	.15	.07
62 Calvin Reese	.15	.07
63 Karim Garcia	.50	.23
64 Mark Farris	.15	.07
65 Jay Payton	.15	.07
66 Dustin Hermanson	.15	.07
67 Michael Barrett	.50	.23
68 Ryan Jaroncyk	.15	.07
69 Ben Davis	.15	.07
70 Bryan Berard	.15	.07
71 Wade Redden	.15	.07
72 Aki-Petteri Berg	.15	.07
73 Nolan Baumgartner	.15	.07
74 Jason Bonsignore	.15	.07
75 Ed Jovanovski	.15	.07
76 Radek Dvorak	.40	.18
77 Brian Holzinger	.15	.07
78 Brad Church	.15	.07
79 Dale Earnhardt	1.50	.70
80 John Andretti	.15	.07
81 Rusty Wallace	.60	.25
82 Bobby Labonte	.50	.23
83 Michael Waltrip	.15	.07
84 Sterling Marlin	.40	.18
85 Brett Bodine	.15	.07
86 Kyle Petty	.15	.07
87 Ricky Rudd	.40	.18
88 Ernie Irvan	.40	.18
89 Darrell Waltrip	.15	.07
90 Geoff Bodine	.15	.07
91 Steve Young	.40	.18
92 Hakeem Olajuwon	.40	.18
93 Barry Bonds	1.25	.55
94 Marshall Faulk	.75	.35
95 Troy Aikman	.60	.25
96 Drew Bledsoe	.40	.18
97 Emmitt Smith	1.00	.45
98 Jason Kidd	.40	.18
99 Shaquille O'Neal	1.00	.45
100 Alonzo Mourning	.15	.07

1996 Classic Signings Etched in Stone *

This 10-card set, printed on 16-point foil board, was randomly inserted in Hot boxes only. Hot boxes were distributed at a rate of 1:5 cases.

	MINT	NRMT
COMPLETE SET (10)	150.00	70.00
1 Shaquille O'Neal	30.00	13.50
2 Jason Kidd	20.00	9.00
3 Scottie Pippen	12.00	5.50
4 Alonzo Mourning	8.00	3.60
5 Emmitt Smith	20.00	9.00
6 Troy Aikman	15.00	6.75
7 Steve Young	12.00	5.50
8 Barry Bonds	10.00	4.50
9 Mark Martin	6.00	2.70
10 Hakeem Olajuwon	12.00	5.50

1996 Classic Signings Freshly Inked *

This 30-card set was randomly inserted one in every ten 1996 Classic Signings packs. The fronts features borderless player color action photos with the player's name printed in gold foil across the bottom. The backs carry an artist's drawing of the player with the player's name at the top.

	MINT	NRMT
COMPLETE SET (30)	100.00	45.00
FS1 Joe Smith	5.00	2.20
FS2 Antonio McDyess	8.00	3.60
FS3 George Zidek	1.00	.45
FS4 Ed O'Bannon	1.00	.45
FS5 Damon Stoudamire	8.00	3.60
FS6 Jerry Stackhouse	8.00	3.60
FS7 Cherokee Parks	1.50	.70
FS8 Bob Sura	1.50	.70
FS9 Rasheed Wallace	6.00	2.70
FS10 Shawn Respert	1.00	.45
FS11 Hugh Douglas	1.00	.45
FS12 Curtis Martin	8.00	3.60
FS13 Michael Westbrook	2.50	1.10
FS14 Kerry Collins	5.00	2.20
FS15 Kevin Carter	1.50	.70
FS16 Joey Galloway	2.50	1.10
FS17 Eric Zeier	1.50	.70
FS18 Terrell Davis	8.00	3.60
FS19 Napoleon Kaufman	2.50	1.10
FS20 Rashaan Salaam	1.50	.70
FS21 Paul Wilson	2.50	1.10
FS22 Nomar Garciaparra	5.00	2.20
FS23 Brian Holzinger	1.50	.70
FS24 Radek Dvorak	1.50	.70
FS25 Petr Sykora	2.50	1.10
FS26 Daymond Langkow	6.00	2.70
FS27 John Andretti	2.50	1.10
FS28 Derrick Cope	1.00	.45
FS29 Todd Bodine	1.50	.70
FS30 Jeff Burton	8.00	3.60

1996 Clear Assets *

The 1996 Clear Assets set was issued in one series totaling 70 cards. The set features 75 upscale acetate cards of the most collectible athletes from baseball, basketball, football, hockey and auto racing. Also included is the debut appearance by many of the top players entering the 1996 football draft. Release date was April 1996.

	MINT	NRMT
COMPLETE SET (70)	15.00	6.75
1 Shaquille O'Neal	1.25	.55
2 Hakeem Olajuwon	.75	.35
3 Scottie Pippen	.75	.35
4 Alonzo Mourning	.25	.11
5 Damon Stoudamire	.60	.25
6 Jerry Stackhouse	1.00	.45
7 Joe Smith	.60	.25
8 Antonio McDyess	1.25	.55
9 Rasheed Wallace	.50	.23
10 Kevin Garnett	3.00	1.35
11 Shawn Respert	.25	.11
12 Ed O'Bannon	.25	.11
13 Kurt Thomas	.25	.11
14 Gary Trent	.25	.11
15 Cherokee Parks	.25	.11
16 Corliss Williamson	.25	.11
17 Eric Williams	.25	.11
18 Brent Barry	.25	.11
19 Bob Sura	.25	.11
20 Michael Finley	1.00	.45
21 Jimmy King	.25	.11
22 Jason Kidd	.75	.35
23 Dikembe Mutombo	.25	.11
24 Greg Ostertag	.25	.11
25 Cory Alexander	.25	.11
26 Glenn Robinson	.25	.11
27 Tyus Edney	.25	.11
28 Rebecca Lobo	.75	.35
29 Emmitt Smith	1.25	.55
30 Jeff Lewis	.25	.11
31 Joey Galloway	.75	.35
32 Steve McNair	.60	.25
33 Eric Moulds	.75	.35
34 Steve Young	.50	.23
35 Mike Alstott	.75	.35
36 Marshall Faulk	.50	.23
37 Kerry Collins	.75	.35
38 Kyle Brady	.25	.11
39 Drew Bledsoe	.40	.18
40 Troy Aikman	.75	.35
41 Duane Clemons	.25	.11
42 Napoleon Kaufman	.75	.35
43 Stanley Pritchett	.25	.11
44 Marcus Coleman	.25	.11
45 Amani Toomer	.60	.25
46 Richard Huntley	.25	.11
47 Tony Banks	.75	.35
48 Keyshawn Johnson	1.00	.45
49 Kevin Hardy	.25	.11
50 Karim Abdul-Jabbar	.25	.11
51 Manon Rheaume	.50	.23
52 Barry Bonds	2.50	1.10
53 Chad Hermansen	.25	.11
54 Ben Davis	.25	.11
55 Jay Payton	.25	.11
56 Bryan Berard	.25	.11
57 Petr Sykora	.25	.11
58 Ed Jovanovski	.25	.11
59 Radek Dvorak	.25	.11
60 Ricky Rudd	.25	.11
61 Bobby Hamilton	.25	.11
62 Dale Jarrett	.50	.23
63 Brett Bodine	.25	.11
64 Dale Earnhardt	1.50	.70
65 Sterling Marlin	.75	.35
66 Mark Martin	.60	.25
67 Ted Musgrave	.25	.11
68 Bobby Labonte	.50	.23
69 Ricky Craven	.25	.11
70 Kyle Petty	.25	.11

1996 Clear Assets 3X *

Randomly inserted in packs at a rate of one in 100, this 10-card set is another first from Classic. The cards resemble triplexed cards

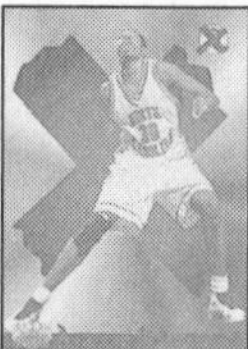

with acetate in the middle and an opaque covering.

	MINT	NRMT
COMPLETE SET (10)	120.00	55.00
X1 Mark Martin	12.00	5.50
X2 Rasheed Wallace	12.00	5.50
X3 Rebecca Lobo	12.00	5.50
X4 Barry Bonds	20.00	9.00
X5 Emmitt Smith	25.00	11.00
X6 Joe Smith	10.00	4.50
X7 Damon Stoudamire	25.00	11.00
X8 Keyshawn Johnson	20.00	9.00
X9 Jerry Stackhouse	15.00	6.75
X10 Troy Aikman	20.00	9.00

1996 Clear Assets Phone Cards $2 *

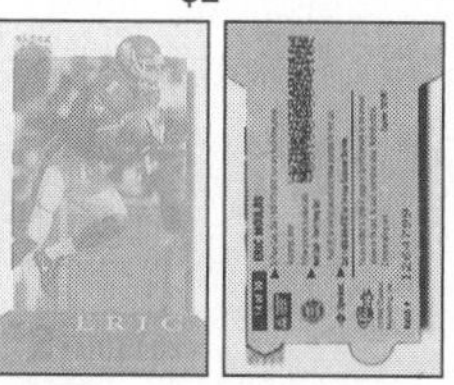

Inserted at a rate of one per pack, this 30-card set of acetate phone cards features many of the biggest names in sports. The Sprint phone cards carry expiration dates of 10/1/97.

	MINT	NRMT
COMPLETE SET (30)	20.00	9.00
*PIN NUMBER REVEALED: HALF VALUE		
ONE DOLLAR CARDS: HALF VALUE ...		
1 Shaquille O'Neal	3.00	1.35
2 Marshall Faulk	1.50	.70
3 Jerry Stackhouse	1.25	.55
4 Mark Martin	1.00	.45
5 Wade Redden	.50	.23
6 Barry Bonds	4.00	1.80
7 Troy Aikman	2.00	.90
8 Nolan Ryan	5.00	2.20
9 Jason Kidd	1.00	.45
10 Jeff Lewis	.50	.23
11 Manon Rheaume	1.50	.70
12 Drew Bledsoe	1.50	.70
13 Joe Smith	.75	.35
14 Eric Moulds	1.50	.70
15 Damon Stoudamire	1.00	.45
16 Cal Ripken	5.00	2.20
17 Hakeem Olajuwon	1.00	.45
18 Joey Galloway	1.50	.70
19 Dale Earnhardt	4.00	1.80
20 Dikembe Mutombo	.75	.35
21 Kerry Collins	.75	.35
22 Petr Sykora	1.00	.45
23 Mike Alstott	1.50	.70
24 Duane Clemons	.50	.23
25 Alonzo Mourning	1.00	.45
26 Stanley Pritchett	.50	.23
27 Steve Young	1.50	.70
28 Rasheed Wallace	1.00	.45
29 Ed O'Bannon	.50	.23
30 Michael Finley	2.00	.90

1996 Clear Assets Phone Cards $5 *

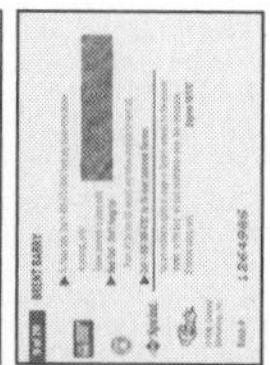

Inserted at a rate of 1:10 packs, this 20-card set of acetate phone cards features many of the biggest names in sports. The Sprint phone cards carry expiration dates of 10/1/97.

	MINT	NRMT
COMPLETE SET (20)	60.00	27.00
*PIN NUMBER REVEALED:HALF VALUE		
1 Shaquille O'Neal	5.00	2.20
2 Emmitt Smith	4.00	1.80
3 Jerry Stackhouse	2.00	.90
4 Dale Earnhardt	6.00	2.70
5 Barry Bonds	4.00	1.80
6 Troy Aikman	3.00	1.35
7 Keyshawn Johnson	2.50	1.10
8 Jason Kidd	2.50	1.10
9 Brent Barry	1.00	.45
10 Drew Bledsoe	2.00	.90
11 Joe Smith	1.25	.55
12 Cal Ripken	12.00	5.50
13 Hakeem Olajuwon	2.00	.90
14 Dikembe Mutombo	1.25	.55
15 Kerry Collins	2.00	.90
16 Petr Sykora	1.25	.55
17 Mike Alstott	2.50	1.10
18 Alonzo Mourning	1.25	.55
19 Steve Young	2.50	1.10
20 Marshall Faulk	2.50	1.10

1996 Clear Assets Phone Cards $10 *

Inserted at a rate of 1:30 packs, this 10-card set of acetate phone cards features many of the biggest names in sports. The Sprint phone cards carry expiration dates of 10/1/97.

	MINT	NRMT
COMPLETE SET (10)	60.00	27.00
*PIN NUMBER REVEALED:HALF VALUE		
1 Shaquille O'Neal	10.00	4.50
2 Troy Aikman	8.00	3.60
3 Dale Earnhardt	12.00	5.50
4 Keyshawn Johnson	5.00	2.20
5 Cal Ripken	12.00	5.50
6 Joe Smith	4.00	1.80
7 Napoleon Kaufman	3.00	1.35
8 Mark Martin	6.00	2.70
9 Scottie Pippen	5.00	2.20
10 Jason Kidd	6.00	2.70

1996 Clear Assets Phone Cards $1000 *

Inserted at a rate of 1:8,640 packs, this five-card set of acetate phone cards features many of the biggest names in sports. The Sprint phone cards carry expiration dates of 10/1/97.

	MINT	NRMT
1 Shaquille O'Neal	200.00	90.00
2 Troy Aikman	150.00	70.00
3 Kerry Collins	100.00	45.00
4 Keyshawn Johnson	100.00	45.00
5 Cal Ripken	50.00	22.00

1996-97 Score Board All Sport PPF *

The 1996-97 All Sport Past Present and Future set was issued in two series in six-card packs. The product contains original vintage and rookie cards of the top athletes from baseball, basketball, football and hockey as well as new cards of tomorrow's stars from each sport. Release date for series one was October 1996; series two was February 1997. There was also a gold parallel produced for this set. Series one gold cards were inserted 1:10 packs while series two had gold cards inserted at a 1:5 ratio.

	MINT	NRMT
COMPLETE SET (200)	15.00	6.75
*GOLDS: 1.2X TO 3X BASIC CARDS		
1 Shaquille O'Neal	1.00	.45
2 Scottie Pippen	.40	.18
3 Dikembe Mutombo	.40	.18
4 Damon Stoudamire	.40	.18
5 Brent Barry	.15	.07
6 Michael Finley	.40	.18
7 Allen Iverson	2.00	.90
8 Marcus Camby	.40	.18
9 Stephon Marbury	1.00	.45
10 Antonio McDyess	.40	.18
11 Kobe Bryant	3.00	1.35
12 Ray Allen	1.00	.45
13 Antoine Walker	1.00	.45
14 Erick Dampier	.15	.07
15 Vitaly Potapenko	.15	.07
16 Tony Delk	.40	.18
17 John Wallace	.40	.18
18 Roy Rogers	.15	.07
19 Jerome Williams	.40	.18
20 Travis Knight	.15	.07
21 Ryan Minor	.15	.07
22 Shawn Harvey	.15	.07
23 Jason Sasser	.15	.07
24 Doron Sheffer	.15	.07
25 Malik Rose	.15	.07
26 Jermaine O'Neal	.75	.35
27 Mark Hendrickson	.15	.07
28 Dontae Jones	.15	.07
29 Othella Harrington	.40	.18
30 Troy Aikman	.60	.25
31 Kerry Collins	.40	.18
32 Steve Young	.50	.23
33 Kordell Stewart	.40	.18
34 Kevin Hardy	.15	.07
35 Joey Galloway	.40	.18
36 Simeon Rice	.15	.07
37 Marcus Coleman	.15	.07
38 Eric Moulds	.50	.23
39 Ray Farmer	.15	.07
40 Chris Darkins	.15	.07
41 Amani Toomer	.40	.18
42 Daryl Gardener	.15	.07
43 Bobby Engram	.15	.07
44 Stepfret Williams	.15	.07
45 Eddie George	1.00	.45
46 Tony Brackens	.15	.07
47 Cedric Jones	.15	.07
48 Jason Dunn	.15	.07
49 Mike Alstott	.50	.23
50 Shaquille O'Neal CL (1-50)	.40	.18
51 Danny Kanell	.15	.07
52 Andre Johnson	.15	.07
53 Rickey Dudley	.15	.07
54 Jeff Hartings	.15	.07
55 Regan Upshaw	.15	.07
56 Alex Molden	.15	.07
57 Terry Glenn	.40	.18
58 Alex Van Dyke	.15	.07
59 Karim Abdul-Jabbar	.15	.07
60 Rey Ordonez	.15	.07
61 Todd Greene	.15	.07
62 Jermaine Dye	.40	.18
63 Karim Garcia	.15	.07
64 Todd Walker	.15	.07
65 Calvin Reese	.15	.07
66 Roger Cedeno	.15	.07
67 Ben Davis	.15	.07
68 Chad Hermansen	.15	.07
69 Vladimir Guerrero	.75	.35
70 Billy Wagner	.15	.07
71 Ed Jovanovski	.15	.07
72 Chris Phillips	.15	.07
73 Alexandre Volchkov	.15	.07
74 Adam Colagiacomo	.15	.07
75 Jonathan Aitken	.15	.07
76 Rico Fata	.15	.07
77 Andrei Zyuzin	.15	.07
78 Josh Holden	.15	.07
79 Boyd Devereaux	.15	.07
80 Allen Iverson	2.00	.90
81 Jason Kidd	.40	.18
82 Hakeem Olajuwon	.40	.18
83 Alonzo Mourning	.40	.18
84 Shareef Abdur-Rahim	.75	.35
85 Glenn Robinson	.15	.07
86 Rasheed Wallace	.15	.07
87 Emmitt Smith	.75	.35
88 Drew Bledsoe	.50	.23
89 Keyshawn Johnson	.50	.23
90 Marshall Faulk	.50	.23
91 Steve Young	.50	.23
92 Lawrence Phillips	.15	.07
93 Terry Glenn	.40	.18
94 Barry Bonds	1.00	.45
95 Vladimir Guerrero	.75	.35
96 Livan Hernandez	.50	.23
97 Bryan Berard	.15	.07
98 Dainius Zubrus	.15	.07
99 Radek Dvorak	.15	.07
100 Troy Aikman CL (51-100)	.40	.18
101 Hakeem Olajuwon	.40	.18
102 Alonzo Mourning	.40	.18
103 Rasheed Wallace	.40	.18
104 Glenn Robinson	.40	.18
105 Tyus Edney	.15	.07
106 Joe Smith	.40	.18
107 Jason Kidd	.40	.18
108 Shareef Abdur-Rahim	.40	.18
109 Kerry Kittles	.40	.18
110 Lorenzen Wright	.40	.18
111 Samaki Walker	.15	.07
112 Todd Fuller	.15	.07
113 Steve Nash	.40	.18
114 Jamie Feick	.15	.07
115 Walter McCarty	.15	.07
116 Jeff McInnis	.15	.07
117 Derek Fisher	.40	.18
118 Moochie Norris	.15	.07
119 Joseph Blair	.15	.07
120 Steve Hamer	.15	.07
121 Randy Livingston	.15	.07
122 Ron Riley	.15	.07
123 Mark Pope	.15	.07
124 Drew Barry	.15	.07
125 Brian Evans	.15	.07
126 Emmitt Smith	.75	.35
127 Drew Bledsoe	.50	.23
128 Steve McNair	.40	.18
129 Marshall Faulk	.50	.23
130 Keyshawn Johnson	.50	.23
131 Lawrence Phillips	.15	.07
132 Leeland McElroy	.15	.07
133 Tony Banks	.15	.07
134 Derrick Mayes	.15	.07
135 Jonathan Ogden	.15	.07
136 Zach Thomas	.50	.23
137 Tim Biakabutuka	.15	.07
138 Ray Mickens	.15	.07
139 Ray Lewis	1.00	.45
140 Marco Battaglia	.15	.07
141 John Mobley	.15	.07
142 Marvin Harrison	.75	.35
143 Duane Clemons	.15	.07
144 Lance Johnstone	.15	.07
145 Eddie Kennison	.15	.07
146 Bobby Hoying	.15	.07
147 Brett Favre	1.00	.45
148 Reggie Brown	.15	.07
149 Walt Harris	.15	.07
150 Kobe Bryant CL	1.50	.70
151 Marcus Jones	.15	.07
152 Je'Rod Cherry	.15	.07
153 Brian Dawkins	.15	.07
154 Johnny McWilliams	.15	.07
155 Brian Roche	.15	.07
156 Muhsin Muhammad	.40	.18
157 Lawyer Milloy	.15	.07
158 Jermane Mayberry	.15	.07
159 DeRon Jenkins	.15	.07
160 Barry Bonds	.75	.35
161 Jay Payton	.15	.07
162 Jose Cruz Jr.	1.00	.45
163 Richard Hidalgo	.40	.18
164 Bartolo Colon	.40	.18
165 Matt Drews	.15	.07
166 Kerry Wood	.50	.23
167 Ben Grieve	.40	.18
168 Wes Helms	.15	.07
169 Livan Hernandez	.15	.07
170 Dainius Zubrus	.15	.07
171 Joe Thornton	.40	.18
172 Daniel Briere	.15	.07
173 Radek Dvorak	.15	.07
174 Richard Jackman	.15	.07
175 Robert Dome	.15	.07
176 Sergei Samsonov	.40	.18
177 Jarome Iginla	.40	.18
178 Dan Cleary	.15	.07
179 Allen Iverson	1.00	.45
180 Antonio McDyess	.40	.18
181 Scottie Pippen	.40	.18
182 Dikembe Mutombo	.40	.18
183 Damon Stoudamire	.40	.18
184 Stephon Marbury	.40	.18
185 Kobe Bryant	1.50	.70
186 Marcus Camby	.40	.18
187 Steve Young	.50	.23
188 Kerry Collins	.40	.18
189 Kevin Hardy	.15	.07
190 Kordell Stewart	.40	.18
191 Joey Galloway	.40	.18
192 Simeon Rice	.15	.07
193 Eddie George	1.00	.45
194 Brett Favre	1.00	.45

	MINT	NRMT
195 Emmitt Smith	.75	.35
196 Todd Walker	.15	.07
197 Rey Ordonez	.15	.07
198 Todd Greene	.15	.07
199 Andrei Zyuzin	.15	.07
200 Eddie George CL	.40	.18

1996-97 Score Board All Sport PPF Retro *

Randomly inserted in series one packs at a rate of one in 35, this 10-card set was printed on old-style card stock.

	MINT	NRMT
COMPLETE SET (10)	30.00	13.50
R1 Allen Iverson	10.00	4.50
R2 Keyshawn Johnson	4.00	1.80
R3 Scottie Pippen	4.00	1.80
R4 Emmitt Smith	6.00	2.70
R5 Shaquille O'Neal	8.00	3.60
R6 Marcus Camby	4.00	1.80
R7 Troy Aikman	5.00	2.20
R8 Damon Stoudamire	2.00	.90
R9 Lawrence Phillips	1.00	.45
R10 Rey Ordonez	1.00	.45

1996-97 Score Board All Sport PPF Revivals *

Randomly inserted in series two packs at a rate of one in 35, this 10-card set was printed on old-style card stock.

	MINT	NRMT
COMPLETE SET (10)	50.00	22.00
REV1 Allen Iverson	10.00	4.50
REV2 Stephon Marbury	10.00	4.50
REV3 Alonzo Mourning	2.50	1.10
REV4 Shareef Abdur-Rahim	6.00	2.70
REV5 Kerry Kittles	2.00	.90
REV6 Emmitt Smith	6.00	2.70
REV7 Keyshawn Johnson	4.00	1.80
REV8 Eddie George	5.00	2.20
REV9 Brett Favre	8.00	3.60
REV10 Barry Bonds	4.00	1.80

1996-97 Score Board Autographed Collection *

Each box of Score Board Autographed Collection contains 16 packs containing six cards. The 50-card regular set includes top athletes from all four major team sports. According to Score Board, a total of 1,500 sequentially numbered cases were produced.

	MINT	NRMT
COMPLETE SET (50)	10.00	4.50
1 Damon Stoudamire	.15	.07
2 Scottie Pippen	.40	.18
3 Jason Kidd	.40	.18
4 Hakeem Olajuwon	.40	.18
5 Alonzo Mourning	.40	.18
6 Antonio McDyess	.15	.07
7 Allen Iverson	3.00	1.35
8 Rasheed Wallace	.40	.18
9 Glenn Robinson	.40	.18
10 Marcus Camby	.75	.35
11 Shareef Abdur-Rahim	1.00	.45
12 Stephon Marbury	1.00	.45
13 Kobe Bryant	5.00	2.20
14 Ray Allen	1.50	.70
15 Antoine Walker	1.00	.45
16 Kerry Kittles	.40	.18
17 John Wallace	.40	.18
18 Emmitt Smith	.75	.35
19 Kordell Stewart	.40	.18
20 Lawrence Phillips	.15	.07
21 Kerry Collins	.40	.18
22 Drew Bledsoe	.40	.18
23 Marshall Faulk	.60	.25
24 Steve Young	.50	.23
25 Joey Galloway	.40	.18
26 Keyshawn Johnson	.50	.23
27 Eddie George	1.00	.45
28 Karim Abdul-Jabbar	.15	.07
29 Terry Glenn	.40	.18
30 Marvin Harrison	.75	.35
31 Tim Biakabutuka	.15	.07
32 Leeland McElroy	.15	.07
33 Simeon Rice	.15	.07
34 Kevin Hardy	.15	.07
35 Rickey Dudley	.15	.07
36 Zach Thomas	.50	.23
37 Bobby Engram	.15	.07
38 Barry Bonds	1.00	.45
39 Vladimir Guerrero	.75	.35
40 Rey Ordonez	.15	.07
41 Jermaine Dye	.15	.07
42 Todd Walker	.15	.07
43 Billy Wagner	.15	.07
44 Karim Garcia	.15	.07
45 Joe Thornton	.40	.18
46 Dan Cleary	.15	.07
47 Robert Dome	.15	.07
48 Alexandre Volchkov	.15	.07
49 Adam Colagiacomo	.15	.07
50 Andrei Zyuzin	.15	.07

1996-97 Score Board Autographed Collection Autographs *

Each box of Autographed Collection contains an average of four autographed cards. There are two different varieties: regular foil stamped cards with no individual numbering inserted at a rate of 1:7 packs, and "SB Certified" autographs inserted at a rate of 1:16 packs.

	MINT	NRMT
1 Karim Abdul-Jabbar	5.00	2.20
2 Shareef Abdur-Rahim	25.00	11.00
3 Ray Allen	30.00	13.50
4 Drew Barry	5.00	2.20
5 Marco Battaglia	2.00	.90
6 Kobe Bryant	120.00	55.00
7 Marcus Camby	15.00	6.75
8 Michael Cheever	2.00	.90
9 Dan Cleary	2.00	.90
10 Adam Colagiacomo	2.00	.90
11 Chris Darkins	2.00	.90
12 Tony Delk	10.00	4.50
13 Robert Dome	2.00	.90
14 Donnie Edwards	2.00	.90
15 Ray Farmer	2.00	.90
16 Karim Garcia	5.00	2.20
17 Eddie George	50.00	22.00
18 Vladimir Guerrero	20.00	9.00
19 Kevin Hardy	2.00	.90
20 Othella Harrington	10.00	4.50
21 Jimmy Herndon	2.00	.90
22 Bobby Hoying	5.00	2.20
23 Allen Iverson	50.00	22.00
24 Dietrich Jells	5.00	2.20
25 DeRon Jenkins	2.00	.90
26 Andre Johnson	2.00	.90
27 Danny Kanell	5.00	2.20
28 Kerry Kittles	10.00	4.50
29 Travis Knight	5.00	2.20
30 Stephon Marbury	25.00	11.00
31 Derrick Mayes	5.00	2.20
32 Walter McCarty	5.00	2.20
33 Leeland McElroy	2.00	.90
34 Ray Mickens	2.00	.90
35 Roman Oben	2.00	.90
36 Jason Odom	2.00	.90
37 Rey Ordonez	2.00	.90
38 Vitaly Potapenko	5.00	2.20
39 Roy Rogers	5.00	2.20
40 Sergei Samsanov	12.00	5.50
41 Jamain Stephens	2.00	.90
42 Matt Stevens	2.00	.90
43 Kordell Stewart	20.00	9.00
44 Zach Thomas	25.00	11.00
45 Joe Thornton	15.00	6.75
46 Billy Wagner	5.00	2.20
47 Antoine Walker	25.00	11.00
48 Todd Walker	2.00	.90
49 John Wallace	10.00	4.50
50 Jerome Williams	10.00	4.50
51 Lorenzen Wright	10.00	4.50
52 Dainius Zubrus	5.00	2.20
53 Andrei Zyuzin	2.00	.90

1996-97 Score Board Autographed Collection Autographs Gold *

These parallel signed cards were seeded at the rate of 1:16 packs. They are Score Board Certified and individually numbered out of 280, 300 or 350.

	MINT	NRMT
COMMON GOLD/280-350	8.00	3.60
*UNLISTED GOLDS: .6X TO 1.5X BASIC AUTOS		
6 Kobe Bryant/300	200.00	90.00
18 Vladimir Guerrero	25.00	11.00
23 Allen Iverson/250	120.00	55.00
47 Antoine Walker/350	50.00	22.00

1996-97 Score Board Autographed Collection Game Breakers *

This 30-card insert set was printed on metallic stock and has two versions-- regular and gold. The insertion ratio is 1:10 packs for regular inserts and 1:50 for the gold foil version.

	MINT	NRMT
COMPLETE SET (30)	60.00	27.00
*GOLDS: .8X TO 2X BASIC CARDS		
GB1 Damon Stoudamire	1.00	.45
GB2 Scottie Pippen	2.00	.90
GB3 Jason Kidd	3.00	1.35
GB4 Ray Allen	8.00	3.60
GB5 Alonzo Mourning	1.00	.45
GB6 Joe Smith	1.00	.45
GB7 Allen Iverson	12.00	5.50
GB8 Rasheed Wallace	2.00	.90
GB9 Antoine Walker	5.00	2.20
GB10 Marcus Camby	5.00	2.20
GB11 Shareef Abdur-Rahim UER (Front Photo is Mystery Man)	5.00	2.20
GB12 Stephon Marbury	6.00	2.70
GB13 Kobe Bryant	15.00	6.75
GB14 Emmitt Smith	6.00	2.70
GB15 Kordell Stewart	3.00	1.35
GB16 Kevin Hardy	1.00	.45
GB17 Kerry Collins	2.00	.90
GB18 Drew Bledsoe	4.00	1.80
GB19 Marshall Faulk	4.00	1.80
GB20 Steve Young	3.00	1.35
GB21 Lawrence Phillips	1.00	.45
GB22 Keyshawn Johnson	5.00	2.20
GB23 Eddie George	6.00	2.70
GB24 Karim Abdul-Jabbar	1.00	.45
GB25 Terry Glenn	2.00	.90
GB26 Marvin Harrison	5.00	2.20
GB27 Tim Biakabutuka	1.00	.45
GB28 Rey Ordonez	1.00	.45
GB29 Joe Thornton	3.00	1.35
GB30 Alexandre Volchkov	1.00	.45

1997-98 Score Board Autographed Collection *

The 1998 Autographed Collection set was issued in one series totaling 50 cards with players from baseball, basketball, football and hockey. The product's major draw was an average of five autographed cards and one memorabilia redemption card per 18-pack box. The regular autographs were inserted 1:4.5 packs, the Blue Ribbon autographs were inserted 1:18 packs. The one-per box memorabilia redemption cards were not all redeemed due to the fact that Score Board, Inc. filed for bankruptcy a few months after the product's release. Score Board also released a "Strongbox Collection" that original retailed for around $125. Each Strongbox included a parallel of this 50 card set, one star player autographed baseball with holder, one star player autographed 8" x 10", one Athletic Excellence card and One Sports City USA card.

	MINT	NRMT
COMPLETE SET (50)	10.00	4.50
*STRONGBOX: .5X TO 1.2X BASIC CARDS		
1 Tim Duncan	1.25	.55
2 Brett Favre	1.00	.45
3 J.D.Drew	1.50	.70
4 Joe Thornton	.15	.07
5 Allen Iverson	1.00	.45
6 Emmitt Smith	.75	.35
7 Scottie Pippen	.40	.18
8 Steve Young	.40	.18
9 Stephon Marbury	.50	.23
10 Ike Hilliard	.40	.18
11 Matt White	.15	.07
12 Jay Payton	.15	.07
13 Darrell Russell	.15	.07
14 Keith Van Horn	.15	.07
15 Tiki Barber	.50	.23
16 Kobe Bryant	2.00	.90
17 Jake Plummer	.50	.23
18 Tim Thomas	.15	.07
19 Danny Wuerffel	.15	.07
20 Hakeem Olajuwon	.40	.18
21 Kordell Stewart	.40	.18
22 Clyde Drexler	.40	.18
23 Brandon Larson	.15	.07
24 Adonal Foyle	.15	.07
25 Alonzo Mourning	.40	.18
26 Warrick Dunn	.50	.23
27 Robert Dome	.15	.07
28 Jose Cruz Jr.	.40	.18
29 Rae Carruth	.15	.07
30 Joe Smith	.15	.07
31 Troy Aikman	.60	.25
32 Tony Battie	.15	.07
33 Peter Boulware	.15	.07
34 David LaFleur	.15	.07
35 Jim Druckenmiller	.15	.07
36 Sergei Samsonov	.40	.18
37 Chauncey Billups	.15	.07
38 Yatil Green	.15	.07
39 Tracy McGrady	1.25	.55
40 Orlando Pace	.15	.07
41 Antoine Walker	.75	.35
42 Byron Hanspard	.15	.07
43 Troy Davis	.15	.07
44 Reidel Anthony	.15	.07
45 Ron Mercer	.40	.18
46 Tony Banks	.40	.18
47 Antonio Daniels	.15	.07
48 Tony Gonzalez	.50	.23
49 Adrian Beltre	.40	.18
50 Kerry Kittles	.40	.18

1997-98 Score Board Autographed Collection Athletic Excellence *

These 3 1/2" x 5" cards, were inserted one per Score Board "Strongbox Collection" box that originally retailed for around $125. Each Strongbox also included a parallel of the 1998 Autograph Collection 50 card set, one star player autographed baseball with holder, one star player autographed 8" x 10" and one Sports City USA card. Each card is sequentially numbered out of 750.

	MINT	NRMT
COMPLETE SET (12)	25.00	11.00
AE1 Chauncey Billups	1.50	.70
AE2 Joe Thornton	1.50	.70
AE3 Warrick Dunn	3.00	1.35
AE4 Adrian Beltre	3.00	1.35
AE5 J.D.Drew	12.00	5.50
AE6 Tim Thomas	1.50	.70
AE7 Darrell Russell	1.50	.70
AE8 Jose Cruz Jr.	3.00	1.35
AE9 Tim Duncan	8.00	3.60
AE10 Nomar Garciaparra	10.00	4.50
AE11 Tracy McGrady	5.00	2.20
AE12 Keith Van Horn	3.00	1.35

1997-98 Score Board Autographed Collection Autographs *

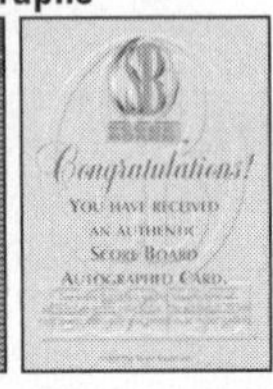

One autographed card was available in one in every 4.5 Score Board Autograph Collection packs. The cards have a circular player photograph in the middle with a white oval below that includes a player's autograph. The card backs read, "Congratulations! You have received an authentic Score Board autographed card." There was also a Kerry Wood card produced that made its way into the marketplace although it was not inserted into packs. It is priced at the end of set and is not included in the complete set price.The cards are unnumbered and listed below in alphabetical order.

	MINT	NRMT
COMPLETE SET (23)	150.00	70.00
1 John Allred	2.00	.90
2 Darnell Autry	2.00	.90
3 Pat Barnes	2.00	.90
4 Daniel Briere	2.00	.90
5 Dan Cleary	2.00	.90
6 Tony Delk	5.00	2.20
7 Robert Dome	2.00	.90
8 Jim Druckenmiller	2.00	.90
9 Ben Grieve	5.00	2.20
10 Wes Helms	2.00	.90
11 Richard Jackman	2.00	.90
12 Brevin Knight	5.00	2.20
13 Dexter McCleon	2.00	.90
14 Brad Otton	2.00	.90
15 Anthony Parker	2.00	.90
16 Jay Payton	2.00	.90
17 Jake Plummer	15.00	6.75
18 Scot Pollard	10.00	4.50
19 Antowain Smith	10.00	4.50
20 Charles Smith	2.00	.90
21 John Thomas	2.00	.90
22 Reinard Wilson	2.00	.90
23 Lorenzen Wright	2.00	.90
P1 Kerry Wood	15.00	6.75

1997-98 Score Board Autographed Collection Blue Ribbon Autographs *

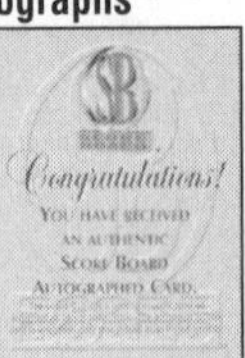

One Blue Ribbon autographed card was available in one in every 18 Score Board Autograph Collection packs. The cards have a circular player photograph with a blue ribbon border in the middle with a white oval below that includes a player's autograph. The cards are hand numbered out of the amounts listed below in the upper right hand corner. The card backs read, "Congratulations! You have received an authentic Score Board autographed card." The cards are unnumbered and listed below in alphabetical order. A Warrick Dunn card was later released through a home shopping network show. Some Kobe Bryant cards have surfaced in un-signed form and can often be found with forged autographs on the front. No unsigned Kobe signed and numbered cards are known although the Congratulations Score Board message is included on the cardbacks.

	MINT	NRMT
COMPLETE SET (16)	600.00	275.00
1 S.Abdur-Rahim/570	25.00	11.00
2 Tony Battie/650	5.00	2.20
3 Marcus Camby/675	10.00	4.50
4 Austin Croshere/1350	10.00	4.50
5 Jose Cruz Jr./1600	4.00	1.80
6 Tim Duncan/208	100.00	45.00
7 Danny Fortson/1350	5.00	2.20
8 Eddie George/240	60.00	27.00
9 Kerry Kittles/650	8.00	3.60
10 Stephon Marbury/1300	20.00	9.00
11 Tracy McGrady/670	60.00	27.00
12 Scottie Pippen/90	100.00	45.00
13 Emmitt Smith/120	150.00	70.00
14 Joe Thornton/1950	8.00	3.60
15 Steve Young/140	100.00	45.00
P1 Warrick Dunn/200	10.00	4.50
P2 Kobe Bryant Unsigned (no known signed cards exist)	2.00	.90

1997-98 Score Board Autographed Collection Sports City USA *

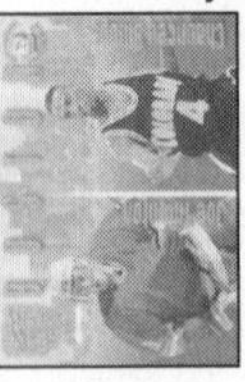

These multi-player, city-themed cards were inserted one in nine Autographed Collection packs. There is also a Strongbox parallel found one per Score Board "Strongbox Collection" box that originally retailed for around $125. Each Strongbox also included a parallel of the 1998 Autograph Collection 50 card set, one star player autographed baseball with holder, one star player autographed 8" x 10"and one Athletic Excellence jumbo card.. Each Strongbox parallel is embossed with "Strongbox" and is sequentially numbered out of 600. These cards are valued at 4 times the values listed below.

	MINT	NRMT
COMPLETE SET (15)	30.00	13.50
*STRONGBOX/600: .8X to 2X BASIC INSERTS		
SC1 Adonal Foyle Joe Smith Steve Young	1.00	.45
SC2 Matt White Warrick Dunn Reidel Anthony	1.00	.45
SC3 Hakeem Olajuwon Clyde Drexler Ricardo Hidalgo	1.00	.45
SC4 Kerry Wood Scottie Pippen Darnell Autry	1.00	.45
SC5 Ray Allen Brett Favre	5.00	2.20
SC6 Kobe Bryant Adrian Beltre	3.00	1.35
SC7 Tim Thomas Duce Staley J.D.Drew	2.50	1.10
SC8 Alonzo Mourning Yatil Green	1.00	.45
SC9 Joe Thornton Chauncey Billups	1.00	.45
SC10 Emmitt Smith Troy Aikman Richard Jackman	4.00	1.80
SC11 Kordell Stewart Robert Dome	1.00	.45
SC12 Wes Helms Bryan Hanspard Ed Gray	1.00	.45
SC13 Stephon Marbury Dwayne Rudd	1.00	.45
SC14 Jay Payton Tiki Barber Keith Van Horn	1.00	.45
SC15 Matt Drews Bryant Westbrook Scot Pollard	1.00	.45

1997 Score Board Players Club *

The 70 cards that make-up this set are grouping from baseball, basketball, football an hockey players. Card fronts are full colore action shots, with professional team names ai brushed out. The card backs contain 199 projected statistics and biographica information. Along with the number 1 Die-Cu and Play Back inserts, vintage cards were th major draw to this product. One in 32 pack contained a vintage card from 1909-1979 fro any of the four sports. An original Honu Wagner T206 card was offered as a redemptic in 1:153,600 packs. Also, one vintage wax pac was available via redemption card in one every 32 packs.

	MINT	NRMT
COMPLETE SET (70)	10.00	4.5
1 Brett Favre	1.00	.4
2 Duce Staley	.50	.2
3 Barry Bonds	1.50	.7
4 Shareef Abdur-Rahim	.40	.1
5 Karim Abdul-Jabbar	.15	.0
6 Robert Dome	.15	.0
7 Jose Cruz Jr.	.75	.3

8 Ray Allen .50 .23
9 Derek Anderson .15 .07
10 Kordell Stewart .30 .14
11 Mike Alstott .15 .07
12 Daniel Briere .15 .07
13 Peter Boulware .15 .07
R.Wilson
14 Troy Davis .15 .07
15 Tony Battie .15 .07
16 Kobe Bryant 1.50 .70
17 Matt Drews .15 .07
18 Marcus Camby .15 .07
19 Keith Van Horn .15 .07
20 Emmitt Smith .75 .35
21 Troy Aikman .50 .23
22 Joe Thornton .15 .07
23 Chauncey Billups .15 .07
24 Scottie Pippen .15 .07
25 Warrick Dunn .50 .23
26 Eddie George .50 .23
27 Wes Helms .15 .07
28 Joey Galloway .40 .18
29 Jacque Vaughn .15 .07
30 Tim Thomas .15 .07
31 Clyde Drexler .40 .18
32 Dainius Zubrus .15 .07
33 Darnell Autry .15 .07
34 Steve Young .40 .18
35 Joe Smith .15 .07
36 Antoine Walker .40 .18
37 Richard Hidalgo .40 .18
38 Tony Gonzalez .75 .35
39 Jim Druckenmiller .15 .07
40 Hakeem Olajuwon .40 .18
41 Alonzo Mourning .15 .07
42 Sergei Samsonov .40 .18
43 Stephon Marbury .40 .18
44 Corey Dillon .75 .35
45 Kerry Kittles .15 .07
46 Kerry Collins .40 .18
47 Byron Hanspard .15 .07
48 Jay Payton .15 .07
49 Allen Iverson 1.00 .45
50 Rae Carruth .15 .07
51 Jake Plummer .50 .23
52 Antonio Daniels .15 .07
53 Darrell Russell .15 .07
54 Shawn Springs .15 .07
55 Olivier Saint-Jean .15 .07
56 Bryant Westbrook .15 .07
57 Dan Cleary .15 .07
58 Tracy McGrady 2.00 .90
59 Orlando Pace .15 .07
60 Richard Jackman .15 .07
61 Ike Hilliard .40 .18
62 Johnny Taylor .15 .07
63 Reidel Anthony .15 .07
64 Austin Croshere .40 .18
65 Alexandre Volchkov .15 .07
66 Brevin Knight .15 .07
67 Zach Thomas .50 .23
68 Ron Mercer .40 .18
69 Kerry Wood 1.50 .70
70 Brett Favre CL .40 .18

1997 Score Board Players Club #1 Die-Cuts *

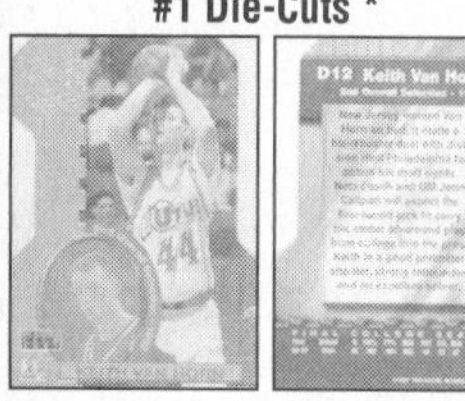

Each player in this 20 card set, inserted one in 32 packs, was at one time selected as a first round selection in the professional draft. The cards are die-cut in the shape of a "1" and have gold foil on the left border. The backs contain pre-professional biographical information and (if applicable) statistics from their last college or minor league season. The card numbers have a "D" prefix.

MINT NRMT
COMPLETE SET (20) 60.00 27.00
D1 Allen Iverson 10.00 4.50
D2 Troy Aikman 4.00 1.80
D3 Darrell Russell 1.00 .45
D4 Joe Thornton 2.00 .90
D5 Hakeem Olajuwon 2.00 .90
D6 Joe Smith 1.00 .45
D7 Orlando Pace 1.00 .45
D8 Shareef Abdur-Rahim 5.00 2.20
D9 Stephon Marbury 6.00 2.70
D10 Jose Cruz Jr. 2.00 .90
D11 Barry Bonds 4.00 1.80
D12 Keith Van Horn 2.00 .90
D13 Kobe Bryant 10.00 4.50
D14 Chauncey Billups 1.00 .45
D15 Jim Druckenmiller 1.00 .45
D16 Tim Thomas 2.00 .90
D17 Tony Battie 1.00 .45
D18 Warrick Dunn 3.00 1.35
D19 Emmitt Smith 6.00 2.70
D20 Antonio Daniels 1.00 .45

1995 Signature Rookies Club Promos *

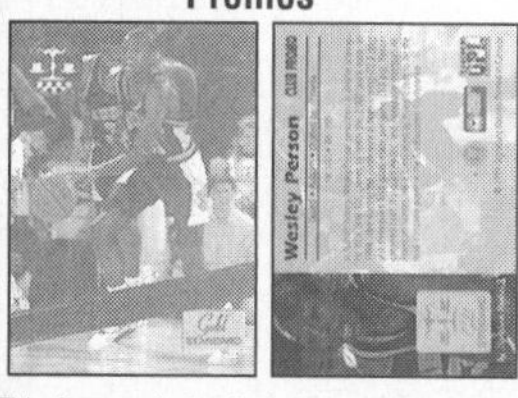

This five-card standard-size set was sent to members of the Signature Rookies collectors club to show what their 1995 products would be. This set has many different designs and several sports; the cards are listed below in alphabetical order.

MINT NRMT
COMPLETE SET (5) 5.00 2.20
S1 Josh Booty 1.00 .45
S2 Ki-Jana Carter 1.00 .45
S3 Karim Garcia 1.50 .70
S4 Wesley Person 2.00 .90
S5 Miracle on Ice 1.00 .45

1994 Signature Rookies Gold Standard *

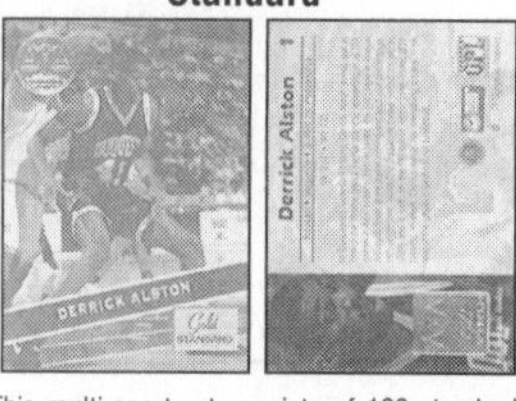

This multi-sport set consists of 100 standard-size cards. The fronts feature color action players photos with a circular gold foil seal at the upper left corner. The player's name appears on a diagonal black stripe edged by yellow. The horizontal backs carry a narrowly-cropped closeup photo and, on a ghosted panel, biography and player profile. The set is subdivided according to sport as follows: basketball (1-25), football (26-50), baseball (51-75), and hockey (76-100). Each sport is sequenced in alphabetical order.

MINT NRMT
COMPLETE SET (100) 12.00 5.50
1 Derrick Alston .05 .02
2 Damon Bailey .05 .02
3 Bill Curley .05 .02
4 Yinka Dare .05 .02
5 Rodney Dent .05 .02
6 Brian Grant .75 .35
7 Juwan Howard 1.00 .45
8 Askia Jones .05 .02
9 Eddie Jones 1.25 .55
10 Donyell Marshall .50 .23
11 Aaron McKie .50 .23
12 Greg Minor .05 .02
13 Eric Montross .05 .02
14 Wesley Person .25 .11
15 Eric Piatkowski .25 .11
16 Jalen Rose 1.00 .45
17 Clifford Rozier .05 .02
18 Dickey Simpkins .05 .02
19 Deon Thomas .05 .02
20 Brooks Thompson .05 .02
21 B.J. Tyler .05 .02
22 Charlie Ward .25 .11
23 Monty Williams .05 .02
24 Dontonio Wingfield .05 .02
25 Sharone Wright .05 .02
26 Sam Adams .05 .02
27 Trev Alberts .05 .02
28 Derrick Alexander .25 .11
29 Mitch Berger .05 .02
30 Tim Bowens .05 .02
31 Jeff Burris .05 .02
32 Shante Carver .05 .02
33 Lake Dawson .05 .02
34 Marshall Faulk 2.00 .90
35 Glenn Foley .05 .02
36 Rob Fredrickson .05 .02
37 Wayne Gandy .05 .02
38 Charles Johnson FB .25 .11
39 Tre Johnson .05 .02
40 Perry Klein .05 .02
41 Antonio Langham .25 .11
42 Eric Mahlum .05 .02
43 Willie McGinest .25 .11
44 Jamir Miller .05 .02
45 Byron Bam Morris .05 .02
46 Errict Rhett .25 .11
47 John Thierry .05 .02
48 Dewayne Washington .05 .02
49 Dan Wilkinson .05 .02
50 Bernard Williams .05 .02
51 Josh Booty .05 .02
52 Roger Cedeno .75 .35
53 Cliff Floyd .75 .35
54 Ben Grieve 1.00 .45
55 Joey Hamilton .05 .02
56 Todd Hollandsworth .05 .02
57 Brian L.Hunter .05 .02
58 Charles Johnson BB .50 .23
59 Brooks Kieschnick .05 .02
60 Mike Kelly .05 .02
61 Ray McDavid .05 .02
62 Kirk Miller .05 .02
63 James Mouton .05 .02
64 Phil Nevin .75 .35
65 Alex Ochoa .25 .11
66 Herbert Perry .05 .02
67 Kirk Presley .05 .02
68 Bill Pulsipher .05 .02
69 Scott Ruffcorn .05 .02
70 Paul Shuey .05 .02
71 Michael Tucker .25 .11
72 Terrell Wade .05 .02
73 Gabe White .05 .02
74 Paul Wilson .05 .02
75 Dmitri Young .50 .23
76 Nolan Baumgartner .05 .02
77 Wade Belak .05 .02
78 Radek Bonk .50 .23
79 Brad Brown .05 .02
80 Dan Cloutier .25 .11
81 Johan Davidsson .05 .02
82 Yannick Dube .05 .02
83 Eric Fichaud .25 .11
84 Johann Finnstrom .05 .02
85 Edvin Frylen .05 .02
86 Patrik Juhlin .05 .02
87 Valeri Karpov .05 .02
88 Nikolai Khabibulin .50 .23
89 Mattias Ohlund .25 .11
90 Jason Podollan .05 .02
91 Vadim Sharifjanov .05 .02
92 Ryan Smyth .25 .11
93 Dimitri Tabarin .05 .02
94 Nikolai Tsulygin .05 .02
95 Stefan Ustorf .05 .02
96 Paul Vincent .05 .02
97 Roman Vopat .05 .02
98 Rhett Warrener .05 .02
99 Vitali Yachmenev .05 .02
100 Vadim Yepenchinstev .05 .02

1994 Signature Rookies Gold Standard Autographs *

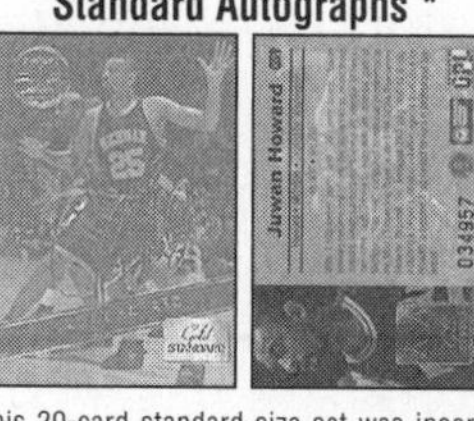

This 20-card standard-size set was inserted one per pack. The fronts display full-bleed color player photos. A facsimile autograph, the "Gold Standard" seal, and another emblem are gold-foil stamped on the fronts. Also a diagonal line carrying the player's name (also in gold foil) is edged by gold foil stripes. On the left side, the horizontal backs show a narrowly-cropped closeup of the front photo. The remainder of the backs carry biography, statistics, and player profile, all on a ghosted background. In addition to card number, each back carries a serial number.

MINT NRMT
COMPLETE SET (20) 10.00 4.50
GS1 Marshall Faulk 3.00 1.35
GS2 Josh Booty .50 .23
GS3 Radek Bonk .50 .23
GS4 Nolan Baumgartner .50 .23
GS5 Sam Adams .50 .23
GS6 Brooks Kieschnick .50 .23
GS7 Valeri Karpov .50 .23
GS8 Charles Johnson 1.00 .45
GS9 Juwan Howard 2.00 .90
GS10 Cliff Floyd 1.50 .70
GS11 James Mouton .50 .23
GS12 Eric Montross .50 .23
GS13 Willie McGinest 1.00 .45
GS14 Donyell Marshall 1.00 .45
GS15 Perry Klein .50 .23
GS16 Sharone Wright .50 .23
GS17 Dan Wilkinson .50 .23
GS18 Ryan Smyth 1.00 .45
GS19 Clifford Rozier .50 .23
GS20 Jalen Rose 2.00 .90

1994 Signature Rookies Gold Standard HOF *

MINT NRMT
HOF1 Nate Archibald 1.00 .45
HOF2 Rick Barry 1.00 .45
HOF3 Mike Bossy 2.00 .90
HOF4 Bob Cousy 2.00 .90
HOF5 Dave Cowens 1.25 .55
HOF6 Dave DeBusschere 1.25 .55
HOF7 Tony Esposito 1.50 .70
HOF8 Walt Frazier 1.00 .45
HOF9 Otto Graham 3.00 1.35
HOF10 Jack Ham 1.00 .45
HOF11 Connie Hawkins 1.00 .45
HOF12 Elvin Hayes 1.00 .45
HOF13 Paul Hornung 2.00 .90
HOF14 Sam Huff 1.00 .45
HOF15 Jim Hunter 1.25 .55
HOF16 Bob Lilly 1.50 .70
HOF17 Don Maynard 1.00 .45
HOF18 Ray Nitschke 1.25 .55
HOF19 Bob Pettit 1.00 .45
HOF20 Willie Stargell 1.25 .55
HOF21 Y.A.Tittle 1.50 .70
HOF22 Bill Walton 1.25 .55
HOF23 Paul Warfield 1.25 .55
HOF24 Randy White 1.50 .70

1994 Signature Rookies Gold Standard HOF Autographs *

Inserted at a rate of one per box, this 24-card standard-sized set is identical to the regular set except for the signatures inscribed across the front and the expression "Hall of Fame" gold-foil stamped at the upper left. Each card is numbered out of 2500. The collector could obtain unsigned versions by mailing in a redemption card that was randomly inserted in packs. These redemption cards are valued at 1/10 the value of the signed cards. The cards are numbered with an "HOF" prefix.

MINT NRMT
COMPLETE SET (24) 300.00 135.00
1 Nate Archibald 10.00 4.50
2 Rick Barry 10.00 4.50
3 Mike Bossy 25.00 11.00
4 Bob Cousy 15.00 6.75
5 Dave Cowens 10.00 4.50
6 Dave DeBusschere 10.00 4.50
7 Tony Esposito 20.00 9.00
8 Walt Frazier 10.00 4.50
9 Otto Graham 30.00 13.50
10 Jack Ham 10.00 4.50
11 Connie Hawkins 10.00 4.50
12 Elvin Hayes 10.00 4.50
13 Paul Hornung 25.00 11.00
14 Sam Huff 10.00 4.50
15 Jim Hunter 30.00 13.50
16 Bob Lilly 15.00 6.75
17 Don Maynard 10.00 4.50
18 Ray Nitschke 50.00 22.00
19 Bob Pettit 10.00 4.50
20 Willie Stargell 15.00 6.75
21 Y.A.Tittle 15.00 6.75
22 Bill Walton 10.00 4.50
23 Paul Warfield 15.00 6.75
24 Randy White 15.00 6.75

1994 Signature Rookies Gold Standard Legends *

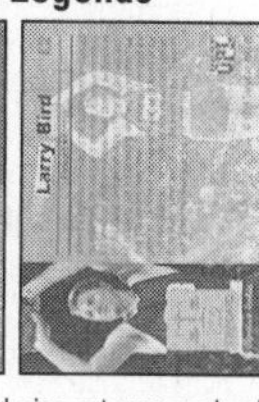

This five-card standard size set was randomly inserted into packs. This set has great athletes past and presents from all sports. The fronts have the word "Legends" on the top and the player's name on the bottom printed in silver ink against a black background. Meanwhile, the player's photo is shown against a gold background. The backs contains the player's photo on the left quarter with a biography about that player on the remainder of the card.

MINT NRMT
COMPLETE SET (5) 8.00 3.60
L1 Isiah Thomas 1.00 .45
L2 Larry Bird 3.00 1.35
L3 Nolan Ryan 4.00 1.80
L4 Pee Wee Reese 1.00 .45
L5 Brian Leetch 1.00 .45

1994 Signature Rookies Tetrad Previews *

Randomly inserted in Signature Rookies Football packs, these seven standard-size cards feature borderless color player action shots on their fronts. The player's name and position appear in gold-foil lettering near the bottom. The words "Promo, 1 of 10,000" appear in vertical gold-foil lettering within a simulated marble column near the left edge. On a ghosted background drawing of a Greek temple, the back carries the player's name, position, team, height and weight, and career highlights. The cards of this multisport set are numbered on the back with a "T" prefix.

MINT NRMT
COMPLETE SET (7) 5.00 2.20
T1 Eric Montross .25 .11
T2 Tim Taylor .25 .11
T3 Jeff Granger .25 .11
T4 Roger Cedeno .25 .11
T5 Charlie Ward .75 .35
T6 O.J. Simpson 3.00 1.35
NNO Header Card 1.00 .45

1994 Signature Rookies Tetrad *

These 120 standard-size cards feature borderless color player action shots on their fronts. The player's name appears in gold-foil lettering near the bottom. The words "1 of 45,000" appear in vertical gold-foil lettering within a simulated marble column near the left edge. The cards of this four-sport set are numbered on the back in Roman numerals and organized as follows: Football (1-40), Basketball (41-83), Baseball (84-103), and Hockey (104-118).

MINT NRMT
COMPLETE SET (120) 5.00 2.20
1 Jay Walker .15 .07
2 Ricky Brady .15 .07
3 Paul Duckworth .15 .07
4 Jim Flanigan .15 .07
5 Brice Adams .15 .07
6 William Floyd .40 .18
7 Charlie Garner .40 .18
8 Pete Bercich .15 .07
9 Frank Harvey .15 .07
10 Willie Clark .15 .07
11 Bernard Williams .15 .07
12 Kurt Haws .15 .07
13 Dennis Collier .15 .07
14 Filmel Johnson .15 .07
15 Zane Beehn .15 .07
16 Johnnie Morton .40 .18
17 Lonnie Johnson .15 .07
18 Jay Kearney .15 .07
19 Steve Shine .15 .07
20 Dexter Nottage .15 .07
21 Ervin Collier .15 .07
22 Dorsey Levens .40 .18
23 Kevin Knox .15 .07
24 Doug Nussmeier .15 .07
25 Bill Schroeder .40 .18
26 Winfred Tubbs .15 .07
27 Rodney Harrison .15 .07
28 Rob Waldrop .15 .07
29 Mike Davis .15 .07
30 John Burke .15 .07
31 Allen Aldridge .15 .07
32 Kevin Mitchell .15 .07
33 Greg Hill .40 .18
34 Ernest Jones .15 .07
35 Kevin Mawae .15 .07
36 John Covington .15 .07
37 Mike Wells .15 .07
38 Thomas Lewis .15 .07
39 Chad Bratzke .15 .07
40 Darren Studstill .15 .07
41 Derrick Alston .15 .07
42 Adrian Autry .15 .07
43 Damon Bailey .15 .07
44 Doremus Bennerman .15 .07
45 Melvin Booker .15 .07
46 Jevon Crudup .15 .07
47 Yinka Dare .15 .07
48 Rodney Dent .15 .07
49 Tony Dumas .15 .07
50 Dwayne Fontana .15 .07
51 Travis Ford .15 .07
52 Lawrence Funderburke .15 .07
53 Anthony Goldwire .15 .07
54 Brian Grant .40 .18
55 Kenny Harris .15 .07
56 Juwan Howard .40 .18
(Misspelled Juwon)
57 Askia Jones .15 .07
58 Eddie Jones .75 .35
59 Arturas Karnishovas .15 .07
60 Donyell Marshall .40 .18
61 Billy McCaffrey .40 .18
62 Jim McIlvaine .15 .07
63 Aaron McKie .15 .07
64 Greg Minor .15 .07
65 Eric Mobley .15 .07
66 Eric Montross .15 .07
67 Gaylon Nickerson .15 .07
68 Wesley Person .15 .07
69 Eric Piatkowski .40 .18
70 Kevin Rankin .15 .07
71 Shawnelle Scott .15 .07
72 Melvin Simon .15 .07
73 Dickey Simpkins .15 .07
74 Michael Smith .15 .07
75 Stevin Smith .15 .07
76 Deon Thomas .15 .07
77 Brooks Thompson .15 .07
78 B.J. Tyler .15 .07
79 Kendrick Warren .15 .07
80 Jeff Webster .15 .07
81 Monty Williams .15 .07
82 Dontonio Wingfield .15 .07
83 Sharone Wright .15 .07
84 Edgardo Alfonzo .75 .35
85 David Bell .40 .18
86 Chris Carpenter .15 .07
87 Roger Cedeno .40 .18
88 Phil Geisler .15 .07
89 Curtis Goodwin .15 .07
90 Jeff Granger .15 .07
91 Brian L.Hunter .40 .18
92 Adam Hyzdu .15 .07
93 Scott Klingenbeck .15 .07
94 Derrek Lee .40 .18
95 Calvin Murray .40 .18
96 Roberto Petagine .15 .07
97 Bill Pulsipher .15 .07
98 Marquis Riley .15 .07
99 Frank Rodriguez .15 .07
100 Scott Ruffcorn .15 .07
101 Roger Salkeld .15 .07
102 Marc Valdes .15 .07
103 Ernie Young .40 .18
104 Sven Butenschon .15 .07
105 Dan Cloutier .40 .18
106 Pat Jablonski .15 .07
107 Valeri Karpov .15 .07
108 Nikolai Khabibulin .40 .18
109 Sergei Klimentiev .15 .07
110 Krzysztof Oliwa .15 .07
111 Dmitri Riabykin .15 .07
112 Ryan Risidore .15 .07
113 Shawn Rivers .15 .07
114 Vadim Sharifjanov .40 .18
115 Mika Stromberg .15 .07
116 Tim Taylor .15 .07
117 Vitali Yachmenev .15 .07
118 Wendell Young .15 .07
NNO Checklist 1 .15 .07
NNO Checklist 2 .15 .07

1994 Signature Rookies Tetrad Autographs *

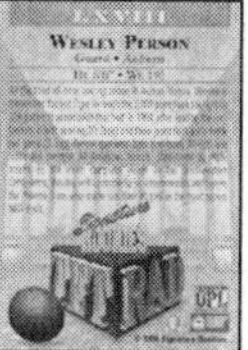

Inserted one card (or trade coupon) per pack, these 117 standard-size autographed cards comprise a parallel set to the regular '94 Tetrad set. Aside from the autographs and each card's numbering out of 7,750 produced, they are identical in design to their regular issue counterparts. The cards of this four-sport set are numbered on the back in Roman numerals and organized as follows: Football (1-40), Basketball (41-83), Baseball (84-103), and Hockey (104-118). Bernard Williams (card number 11) did not sign his cards.

MINT NRMT
COMPLETE SET (117) 250.00 110.00
1 Jay Walker 2.00 .90
2 Ricky Brady 2.00 .90
3 Paul Duckworth 2.00 .90
4 Jim Flanigan 2.00 .90
5 Brice Adams 2.00 .90
6 William Floyd 4.00 1.80
7 Charlie Garner 6.00 2.70
8 Pete Bercich 2.00 .90
9 Frank Harvey 2.00 .90
10 Willie Clark 2.00 .90
12 Kurt Haws 2.00 .90
13 Dennis Collier 2.00 .90
14 Filmel Johnson 2.00 .90
15 Zane Beehn 2.00 .90

16 Johnnie Morton 6.00 2.70
17 Lonnie Johnson 2.00 .90
18 Jay Kearney 2.00 .90
19 Steve Shine 2.00 .90
20 Dexter Nottage 2.00 .90
21 Ervin Collier 2.00 .90
22 Dorsey Levens 6.00 2.70
23 Kevin Knox 2.00 .90
24 Doug Nussmeier 2.00 .90
25 Bill Schroeder 10.00 4.50
26 Winfred Tubbs 2.00 .90
27 Rodney Harrison 2.00 .90
28 Rob Waldrop 2.00 .90
29 Mike Davis 2.00 .90
30 John Burke 2.00 .90
31 Allen Aldridge 2.00 .90
32 Kevin Mitchell 2.00 .90
33 Greg Hill 4.00 1.80
34 Ernest Jones 2.00 .90
35 Kevin Mawae 2.00 .90
36 John Covington 2.00 .90
37 Mike Wells 2.00 .90
38 Thomas Lewis 2.00 .90
39 Chad Bratzke 2.00 .90
40 Darren Studstill 2.00 .90
41 Derrick Alston 2.00 .90
42 Adrian Autry 2.00 .90
43 Damon Bailey 2.00 .90
44 Doremus Bennerman 2.00 .90
45 Melvin Booker 2.00 .90
46 Jevon Crudup 2.00 .90
47 Yinka Dare 2.00 .90
48 Rodney Dent 2.00 .90
49 Tony Dumas 2.00 .90
50 Dwayne Fontana 2.00 .90
51 Travis Ford 2.00 .90
52 Lawrence Funderburke 2.00 .90
53 Anthony Goldwire 2.00 .90
54 Brian Grant 8.00 3.60
55 Kenny Harris 2.00 .90
56 Juwan Howard 10.00 4.50
(Misspelled Juwon)
57 Askia Jones 2.00 .90
58 Eddie Jones 10.00 4.50
59 Arturas Karnishovas 2.00 .90
60 Donyell Marshall 6.00 2.70
61 Billy McCaffrey 4.00 1.80
62 Jim McIlvaine 2.00 .90
63 Aaron McKie 6.00 2.70
64 Greg Minor 2.00 .90
65 Eric Mobley 2.00 .90
66 Eric Montross 4.00 1.80
67 Gaylon Nickerson 2.00 .90
68 Wesley Person 4.00 1.80
69 Eric Piatkowski 4.00 1.80
70 Kevin Rankin 2.00 .90
71 Shawnelle Scott 2.00 .90
72 Melvin Simon 2.00 .90
73 Dickey Simpkins 2.00 .90
74 Michael Smith 2.00 .90
75 Stevin Smith 2.00 .90
76 Deon Thomas 2.00 .90
77 Brooks Thompson 2.00 .90
78 B.J. Tyler 2.00 .90
79 Kendrick Warren 2.00 .90
80 Jeff Webster 2.00 .90
81 Monty Williams 2.00 .90
82 Dontonio Wingfield 2.00 .90
83 Sharone Wright 2.00 .90
84 Edgardo Alfonzo 5.00 2.20
85 David Bell 4.00 1.80
86 Chris Carpenter 4.00 1.80
87 Roger Cedeno 4.00 1.80
88 Phil Geisler 2.00 .90
89 Curtis Goodwin 2.00 .90
90 Jeff Granger 2.00 .90
91 Brian L.Hunter 2.00 .90
92 Adam Hyzdu 2.00 .90
93 Scott Klingenbeck 2.00 .90
94 Derrek Lee 4.00 1.80
95 Calvin Murray 2.00 .90
96 Roberto Petagine 2.00 .90
97 Bill Pulsipher 2.00 .90
98 Marquis Riley 2.00 .90
99 Frank Rodriguez 2.00 .90
100 Scott Ruffcorn 2.00 .90
101 Roger Salkeld 2.00 .90
102 Marc Valdes 2.00 .90
103 Ernie Young 2.00 .90
104 Sven Butenschon 2.00 .90
105 Dan Cloutier 4.00 1.80
106 Pat Jablonski 2.00 .90
107 Valeri Karpov 2.00 .90
108 Nikolai Khabibulin 6.00 2.70
109 Sergei Klimentiev 2.00 .90
110 Krzysztof Oliwa 2.00 .90
111 Dmitri Riabykin 2.00 .90
112 Ryan Risidore 2.00 .90
113 Shawn Rivers 2.00 .90
114 Vadim Sharifjanov 4.00 1.80
115 Mika Stromberg 2.00 .90
116 Tim Taylor 2.00 .90
117 Vitali Yachmenev 2.00 .90
118 Wendell Young 2.00 .90

1994 Signature Rookies Tetrad Flip Cards *

Randomly inserted in packs, these five standard-size two-player cards feature a borderless color action shot of one player per side. The player's name appears in gold-foil lettering near the bottom. The words "1 of 7,500" appear in vertical gold-foil lettering within a simulated marble column near the left edge. The cards are numbered on both sides.

	MINT	NRMT
COMPLETE SET (5)	30.00	13.50
1 Charles Johnson BB Charles Johnson FB	3.00	1.35
2 Tony Dorsett Gale Sayers	8.00	3.60
3 Charlie Ward BK Charlie Ward FB	5.00	2.20
4 Juwan Howard UER (Misspelled Juwon) Jalen Rose	15.00	6.75
5 Glenn Williams UER (Misspelled Glen) Monty Williams	3.00	1.35

1994 Signature Rookies Tetrad Flip Cards Autographs *

Randomly inserted in packs, this three-card set features two-player cards with a borderless color action shot of one player per side. The player's name appears in gold-foil lettering near the bottom. Each card is autographed. The cards are numbered on both sides.

	MINT	NRMT
COMPLETE SET (3)	30.00	13.50
AU1 Charles Johnson BB/275	10.00	4.50
AU2 Glenn Williams Monty Williams 275	10.00	4.50
AU3 Charlie Ward FB/BK/275	15.00	6.75

1994 Signature Rookies Tetrad Top Prospects *

Randomly inserted in packs, these four standard-size cards feature borderless color player action shots on their fronts. The player's name appears in gold-foil lettering near the bottom. The words "1 of 20,000" appear in vertical gold-foil lettering within a simulated marble column near the left edge. On a ghosted background drawing of a Greek temple, the back carries the player's name, biography, statistics, and career highlights. The cards of this multisport set are numbered on the back in Roman numerals.

	MINT	NRMT
COMPLETE SET (4)	2.50	1.10
131 Charlie Ward	.75	.35
132 Willie McGinest	.75	.35
133 Shante Carver	.50	.23
134 Paul Wilson	.50	.23

1994 Signature Rookies Tetrad Top Prospects Autographs *

This four-card set was randomly inserted in packs. The fronts feature borderless color player action shots with the player's name in gold-foil lettering near the bottom. The cards are autographed on the fronts. The backs carry the player's name, biography, statistics, and career highlights on a ghosted background drawing of a Greek temple. The cards are numbered on the back in Roman numerals. Other than Shante Carver, the cards are numbered out of 2,000.

	MINT	NRMT
COMPLETE SET (4)	40.00	18.00
131A Charlie Ward	10.00	4.50
132A Willie McGinest	10.00	4.50
133A Shante Carver/2025	5.00	2.20
134A Paul Wilson	2.00	.90

1995 Signature Rookies Fame and Fortune *

The 1995 Fame and Fortune set was issued in one series totalling 100 cards and featured NBA and NFL draft picks. Cards were distributed in eight-card packs. Five insert card sets were produced with the set and include Collector's Pick, Top 5, Erstad, Star Squad and #1 Pick. The first 48 cards are basketball draft picks and the remaining 52 are football picks. Fronts have full-color action cutout photos with a black background with either a football or basketball. The player's first name is printed in gold foil horizontally while his last name is printed twice vertically in both gold foil and a larger green type on the left side. Backs have another action shot that is seprated with a color screen process. Backs include college statistics, a short biography and a player profile.

	MINT	NRMT
COMPLETE SET (100)	12.00	5.50
1 Cory Alexander	.15	.07
2 Jerome Allen	.15	.07
3 Brent Barry	.25	.11
4 Mario Bennett	.15	.07
5 Travis Best	.25	.11
6 Donie Boyce	.15	.07
7 Junior Burrough	.15	.07
8 Jason Caffey	.25	.11
9 Chris Carr	.15	.07
10 Randolph Childress	.15	.07
11 Mark Davis	.15	.07
12 Andrew DeClerco	.15	.07
13 Tyus Edney	.25	.11
14 Michael Finley	.50	.23
15 Sherell Ford	.15	.07
16 Kevin Garnett	1.25	.55
17 Alan Henderson	.25	.11
18 Fred Hoiberg	.15	.07
19 Jimmy King	.15	.07
20 Donny Marshall	.15	.07
21 Cuonzo Martin	.15	.07
22 Michael McDonald	.15	.07
23 Anthony McDyess	.15	.07
24 Loren Meyer	.15	.07
25 Lawrence Moten	.15	.07
26 Ed O'Bannon	.15	.07
27 Greg Ostertag	.25	.11
28 Cherokee Parks	.15	.07
29 Anthony Pelle	.15	.07
30 Constantin Popa	.15	.07
31 Theo Ratliff	.25	.11
32 Bryant Reeves	.25	.11
33 Don Reid	.15	.07
34 Terrance Rencher	.15	.07
35 Shawn Respert	.15	.07
36 Lou Roe	.15	.07
37 Joe Smith	.25	.11
38 Eric Snow	.15	.07
39 Jerry Stackhouse	1.00	.45
40 Damon Stoudamire	.25	.11
41 Bob Sura	.25	.11
42 Kurt Thomas	.25	.11
43 Gary Trent	.25	.11
44 David Vaughn	.15	.07
45 Rasheed Wallace	1.00	.45
46 Eric Williams	.15	.07
47 Corliss Williamson	.25	.11
48 George Zidek	.15	.07
49 Derrick Alexander DE	.15	.07
50 Joe Aska	.15	.07
51 Dave Barr	.15	.07
52 Tony Boselli	.25	.11
53 Kyle Brady	.15	.07
54 Derrick Brooks	.60	.25
55 Ruben Brown	.15	.07
56 Mark Bruener	.15	.07
57 Kevin Carter	.25	.11
58 Ki-Jana Carter	.25	.11
59 Stoney Case	.15	.07
60 Kerry Collins	1.25	.55
61 Terrell Davis	2.00	.90
62 Tyrone Davis	.15	.07
63 Hugh Douglas	.25	.11
64 David Dunn	.15	.07
65 Luther Elliss	.15	.07
66 Christian Fauria	.25	.11
67 Mark Fields	.15	.07
68 Joey Galloway	.40	.18
69 Eddie Goines	.15	.07
70 Jimmy Hitchcock	.15	.07
71 Stephen Ingram	.15	.07
72 Jack Jackson	.15	.07
73 Ellis Johnson	.15	.07
74 Chris T. Jones	.15	.07
75 Larry Jones	.15	.07
76 Mike Mamula	.15	.07
77 Curtis Martin	1.50	.70
78 Steve McNair	1.50	.70
79 Brent Moss	.15	.07
80 Craig Newsome	.15	.07
81 Tyrone Poole	.15	.07
82 Rashaan Salaam	.25	.11
83 Frank Sanders	.25	.11
84 Warren Sapp	.60	.25
85 J.J. Smith	.15	.07
86 Steve Stenstrom	.15	.07
87 James A. Stewart	.15	.07
88 James O. Stewart	1.00	.45
89 J.J. Stokes	.25	.11
90 Bobby Taylor	.25	.11
91 Rodney Thomas	.25	.11
92 John Walsh	.15	.07
93 Michael Westbrook	.40	.18
94 Zach Wiegert	.15	.07
95 Jerrott Willard	.15	.07
96 Billy Williams	.15	.07
97 Sherman Williams	.15	.07
98 Jamal Willis	.15	.07
99 Eric Zeier	.25	.11
100 Ray Zellars	.25	.11

1995 Signature Rookies Fame and Fortune #1 Pick *

Randomly inserted in packs at a rate of three in 16, this five-card set features the No. 1 pick in the NHL, the NFL, The NBA and Major leagues. The No. 5 card pictures all four of the picks. Fronts have a psychedelic background and feature the player in a full-color action cutout. "#1 Pick" appears in a sky blue and green type at the top and the bottom has a gold foil strip that contains the player's name, or names in the case of the #5 card, in raised white letters. Backs continue with the psychedelic background and picture the player or players in action. Player stats and biographies also appear on the back.

	MINT	NRMT
COMPLETE SET (5)	2.50	1.10
P1 Bryan Berard	.50	.23
P2 Ki-Jana Carter	.50	.23
P3 Darin Erstad	.75	.35
P4 Joe Smith	.50	.23
P5 Brian Berard K-Jana Carter Darin Erstad Joe Smith	.75	.35

1995 Signature Rookies Fame and Fortune Collectors Pick *

Randomly inserted in packs at a rate of one in 16, this 10-card set highlights the first five NBA picks and the first five NFL picks. Fronts are borderless with white backgrounds with "Collectors" on the top third and "Pick" in a vertically stretched type on the rest of the front. The player is pictured in a full-color action cutout in the foreground. His name is printed vertically in gold foil on the lower left. Backs have a small player head shot, and a faded screen action shot for a background. Player biography, statistics and profile appear on the back.

	MINT	NRMT
B1 Kerry Collins	1.50	.70
B2 Ed O'Bannon	.30	.14
B3 Cherokee Parks	.30	.14
B4 Bryant Reeves	.50	.23
B5 Rashaan Salaam	.50	.23
B6 Warren Sapp	.75	.35
B7 Joe Smith	.50	.23
B8 Jerry Stackhouse	1.50	.70
B9 J.J. Stokes	.50	.23
B10 Rasheed Wallace	1.50	.70

1995 Signature Rookies Fame and Fortune Darin Erstad *

Randomly inserted in packs at a rate of one in 4, this 5-card set highlights the college career of baseball's #1 draft pick. Borderless fronts have a full-color action shot of Erstad in his Nebraska uniform with "Erstad" printed in varying type sizes in the background. Erstad is also printed in gold foil vertically on the left side. The backs have a cropped action photo of Erstad at an angle with a white background for the rest of the back. Stats and biography appear on the back along with a short profile.

	MINT	NRMT
E1 Darin Erstad BB		
E2 Darin Erstad BB		
E3 Darin Erstad FB		
E4 Darin Erstad BB		
E5 Darin Erstad BB		

1995 Signature Rookies Tetrad Previews *

This five-card standard-size set was randomly inserted in SR BK autobilia packs. The fronts display borderless color action player photos. The named player stands out on a faded background with his name printed in gold below. The backs carry an elongated color action player photo on one side while a head photo, biographical information, position, college, and career statistics round out the backs.

	MINT	NRMT
COMPLETE SET (5)	2.00	.90
1 Ruben Rivera	.50	.23
2 Jim Carrey	.50	.23
3 Joe Smith	.75	.35
4 Jerry Stackhouse	1.50	.70
5 Ki-Jana Carter	.50	.23

1995 Signature Rookies Tetrad *

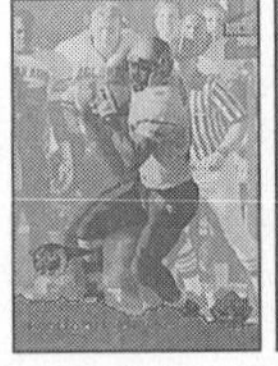

This 76-card standard-size set features borderless fronts with color action player photos. The named player stands out on a faded background with his name printed in gold below. The backs carry an elongated color action player photo on one side while a head photo, biographical information, position, college, and career statistics round out the backs.

	MINT	NRMT
COMPLETE SET (76)	15.00	6.75
1 Kevin Carter	.25	.11
2 Ruben Brown	.15	.07
3 Kyle Brady	.15	.07
4 Tony Boselli	.25	.11
5 Derrick Alexander	.15	.07
6 Mike Mamula	.15	.07
7 Ellis Johnson	.15	.07
8 Mark Fields	.15	.07
9 Luther Elliss	.15	.07
10 Hugh Douglas	.25	.11
11 Shawn Respert	.15	.07
12 Bryant Reeves	.15	.07
13 Cherokee Parks	.25	.11
14 Greg Ostertag	.25	.11
15 Ed O'Bannon	.15	.07
16 David Vaughn	.15	.07
17 Gary Trent	.25	.11
18 Kurt Thomas	.15	.07
19 Bob Sura	.25	.11
20 Damon Stoudamire	.50	.23
21 Brent Barry	.25	.11
22 Cory Alexander	.15	.07
23 Theo Ratliff	.25	.11
24 Loren Meyer	.15	.07
25 George Zidek	.15	.07
26 Alan Henderson	.15	.07
27 Michael Finley	1.00	.45
28 Randolph Childress	.15	.07
29 Jason Caffey	.15	.07
30 Mario Bennett	.15	.07
31 Andy Yount	.15	.07
32 Jose Cruz Jr.	.75	.35
33 Chad Hermansen	.25	.11
34 David Yocum	.15	.07
35 Dmitri Young	.40	.18
36 Kerry Wood UER Card front is Kevin	2.00	.90
37 Jonathan Johnson	.15	.07
38 Shea Morenz	.15	.07
39 Matt Morris	1.50	.70
40 Reggie Taylor	.25	.11
41 Antone Williamson	.15	.07
42 Derek Wallace	.15	.07
43 Ben Grieve	.25	.11
44 Benji Gil	.15	.07
45 Todd Walker	.40	.18
46 Jason Thompson	.15	.07
47 Scott Stahoviak	.15	.07
48 Chris Roberts	.15	.07
49 Dante Powell	.15	.07
50 Torii Hunter	1.50	.70
51 James O. Stewart	1.00	.45
52 Rashaan Salaam	.25	.11
53 Tyrone Poole	.15	.07
54 Craig Newsome	.15	.07
55 Devin Bush	.15	.07
56 Bryan Rekar	.15	.07
57 Jaime Jones	.15	.07
58 Todd Helton	2.00	.90
59 Joe Fontenot	.15	.07
60 Tony Clark	.25	.11
61 Alexei Morozov	.40	.18
62 Radek Dvorak	.25	.11
63 Corliss Williamson	.25	.11
64 Eric Williams	.15	.07
65 Sherell Ford	.15	.07
66 Terry Ryan	.15	.07
67 Shane Doan	.40	.18
68 Brad Church	.15	.07
69 Brian Boucher	1.50	.70
70 Dmitri Nabokov	.15	.07
71 Tony McKnight	.15	.07
72 Roy Halladay	1.00	.45
73 Mike Drumright	.15	.07
74 Ben Davis	.25	.11
75 Michael Barrett	.75	.35
NNO Checklist	.15	.07

1995 Signature Rookies Tetrad SR Force *

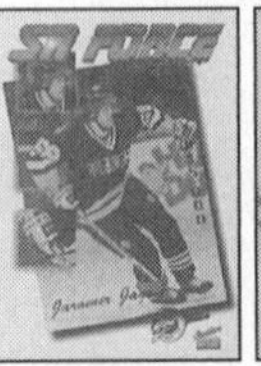
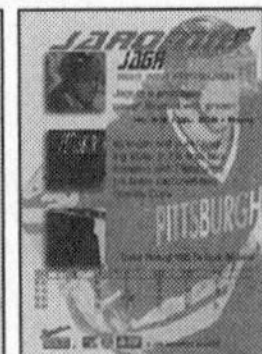

This 35-card standard-size set features color action player photos on the front on a white background. Pictures of one foot, the head, and one arm are set out as separate photos on the side of the main picture. The words, "SR Force," are printed in the white border at the top, while the player's name is in gold at the bottom of the picture. The backs carry the same photo as a faded background with photos of the head and parts of one leg. The player's name, position, team, biographical information, and statistics round out the back. The cards are numbered with an "F" prefix.

	MINT	NRMT
COMPLETE SET (35)	12.00	5.50
*AUTOGRAPHS: 8X TO 20X BASIC CARDS .45		
F1 Nolan Baumgartner	.25	.11
F2 Bryan Berard	.25	.11
F3 Aki-Petteri Berg	.25	.11
F4 Daymond Langkow	.50	.23
F5 Wade Redden	.25	.11
F6 Martin Brodeur	1.50	.70
F7 Jim Carey	.25	.11
F8 Jaromir Jagr	2.00	.90
F9 Maxim Kuznetsov	.25	.11
F10 Terry Ryan	.25	.11
F11 Manny Ramirez	.50	.23
F12 Jaret Wright	.25	.11
F13 Ruben Rivera	.25	.11
F14 Derek Jeter	3.00	1.35
F15 Monty Farris UER Back reads Farris	.25	.11
F16 Jason Isringhausen	.50	.23
F17 Marty Cordova	.25	.11
F18 Garret Anderson	.50	.23
F19 Alex Rodriguez	2.50	1.10
F20 Carlton Loewer	.25	.11
F21 Joe Smith	.50	.23
F22 Antonio McDyess	.50	.23
F23 Jerry Stackhouse	.60	.25
F24 Rasheed Wallace	.60	.25
F25 Kevin Garnett	1.00	.45
F26 Ki-Jana Carter	.25	.11
F27 Joey Galloway	.50	.23
F28 Michael Westbrook	.25	.11
F29 J.J. Stokes	.50	.23
F30 Eric Zeier	.25	.11
F31 Errict Rhett	.25	.11
F32 Steve McNair	2.00	.90
F33 Kerry Collins	.50	.23
F34 Stoney Case	.25	.11
F35 Mark Bruener	.25	.11

1995 Signature Rookies Tetrad Mail-In *

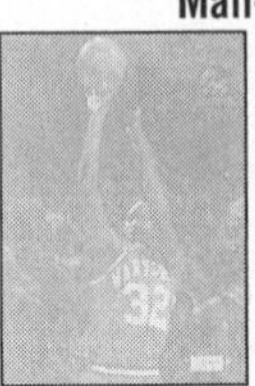
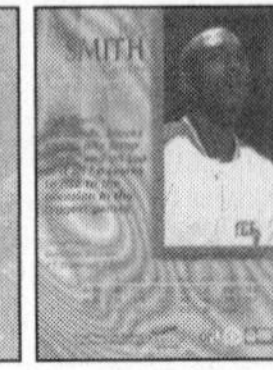

This five-card standard size set was available through the mail from Signature Rookies. The set highlights the 1995 first overall draft picks in basketball, football, baseball and hockey. The fronts picture color action photos blended with a fractal-swirling design. In a gold foil stamp, the players name is found vertically on the right, "Mail In" and "#1 Pick" adorn the top and bottom respectively on the left. The back has another color action photo in the upper-right corner. The rest is devoted to a player biography and statistics set on top of the same fractal-swirling design. The cards are numbered with a "P" prefix (P1-P5).

	MINT	NRMT
COMPLETE SET (5)	8.00	3.60
P1 Joe Smith	1.00	.45
P2 Ki-Jana Carter	1.00	.45
P3 Darin Erstad	2.00	.90
P4 Bryan Berard	1.00	.45

P5 Joe Smith 2.00 .90
Ki-Jana Carter
Darin Erstad
Bryan Berard

1995 Signature Rookies Tetrad Autobilia *

The 1995 Signature Rookies Tetrad Autobilia set was issued in one series with a total of 100 cards. The fronts feature a color action player cut-out on a background of a repeated action player photo with the player's name printed in a gold bar at the bottom. The words" Club Set" are printed in gold foil on the fronts as well. The backs carry two player photos with the player's name, position, biographical information, career statistics, and a player fact. Players signed the following items (sport specific where appropriate): 1,000 cards, 3,000 photos, 500 pennants, 500 hats, 3000 baseballs, 550 basketballs, 1000 footballs. Special items included 100 Darin Erstad signed bats, and an undisclosed amount of the following issues: Muhammad Ali signed boxing glove, Joe DiMaggio signed cards, Jaromir Jagr signed hockey stick, Jaromir Jagr signed practice jersey, and Jim Carey signed mask.

MINT NRMT
COMPLETE SET (100) 40.00 18.00
*SIGNED CARDS: 4X TO 10X BASIC CARDS
*SIGNED PHOTOS: 4X TO 10X BASIC CARDS
1 Travis Best .25 .11
2 Junior Burrough .25 .11
3 Randolph Childress .25 .11
4 Andrew DeClercq .25 .11
5 Michael Finley 1.00 .45
6 Alan Henderson .25 .11
7 Ed O'Bannon .25 .11
8 Cherokee Parks .25 .11
9 Bryant Reeves .25 .11
10 Shawn Respert .25 .11
11 Damon Stoudamire 2.00 .90
12 Bob Sura .50 .23
13 Scotty Thurman .25 .11
14 Gary Trent .50 .23
15 Corliss Williamson .50 .23
16 Donald Williams .25 .11
17 Eric Williams .25 .11
18 Juan Acevedo .50 .23
19 Trey Beamon .25 .11
20 Tim Belk .25 .11
21 Mike Bovee .25 .11
22 Brad Clontz .25 .11
23 Marty Cordova .50 .23
24 Johnny Damon .75 .35
25 Jeff Darwin .25 .11
26 Nick Delvecchio .25 .11
27 Ray Durham .75 .35
28 Jermaine Dye .75 .35
29 Jimmy Haynes .50 .23
30 Mark Hubbard .25 .11
31 Russ Johnson .25 .11
32 Andy Larkin .25 .11
33 Kris Ralston .25 .11
34 Luis Raven .25 .11
35 Desi Relaford .50 .23
36 Jeff Suppan .50 .23
37 Brad Woodall .25 .11
38 Nolan Baumgartner .25 .11
39 Bryan Berard .50 .23
40 Aki-Petteri Berg .25 .11
41 Dan Cleary .25 .11
42 Radek Dvorak .25 .11
43 Patrick Juhlin .25 .11
44 Jan Labraaten .25 .11
45 Daymond Langkow .75 .35
46 Sergei Luchinkin .25 .11
47 Cameron Mann .50 .23
48 Alexei Morozov .50 .23
49 Oleg Tverdovsky .75 .35
50 Johan Ramstedt .25 .11
51 Wade Redden .50 .23
52 Sami-Ville Salomaa .25 .11
53 Alexei Vasiljev .25 .11
54 Peter Wallin .25 .11
55 Dave Barr .25 .11
56 Brandon Bennett .25 .11
57 Kyle Brady .25 .11
58 Kevin Carter .25 .11
59 Terrell Davis 3.00 1.35
60 Luther Ellis .25 .11
61 Jack Jackson .25 .11
62 Frank Sanders .50 .23
63 Ki-Jana Carter .25 .11
64 Steve Stenstrom .25 .11
65 James A. Stewart .25 .11
66 James O. Stewart 1.00 .45
67 Bobby Taylor .25 .11
68 Michael Westbrook .75 .35
69 Rashaan Salaam .50 .23
70 Ray Zellars .25 .11
71 Antonio McDyess 2.00 .90
72 Ruben Rivera .25 .11
73 Joe Smith .75 .35
74 Jerry Stackhouse 1.50 .70
75 J.J. Stokes .50 .23
76 Sherman Williams .25 .11
77 Kevin Garnett 4.00 1.80
78 Juwan Howard .75 .35
79 Eddie Jones .75 .35
80 Kerry Collins 1.00 .45
81 Joey Galloway .75 .35
82 Steve McNair 1.50 .70
83 Errict Rhett .50 .23
84 Eric Zeier .50 .23
85 Jose Cruz Jr. 1.50 .70
86 Darin Erstad 3.00 1.35
87 Todd Helton 4.00 1.80
88 Chad Hermansen .50 .23
89 Jonathan Johnson .25 .11
90 Manny Ramirez .75 .35
91 Kerry Wood 3.00 1.35
92 Ben Davis .50 .23
93 Jaime Jones .50 .23
94 Brian Boucher 2.50 1.10
95 Martin Brodeur 1.00 .45
96 Brad Church .25 .11
97 Shane Doan .75 .35
98 Terry Ryan .25 .11
99 Ryan Smyth .50 .23
100 Checklist 1-100 .25 .11

1997 Scoreboard Talk N' Sports *

This product features phone cards with a couple twists, including trivia contests to win memorabilia and to check current sports scores. The 50-card regular set includes stars and prospects from all four major team sports. According to Score Board, a total of 1,500 sequentially numbered cases were produced.

MINT NRMT
COMPLETE SET (50) 10.00 4.50
1 Brett Favre 1.00 .45
2 Marshall Faulk .40 .18
3 Steve Young .40 .18
4 Troy Aikman .50 .23
5 Kordell Stewart .40 .18
6 Kerry Collins .15 .07
7 Keyshawn Johnson .40 .18
8 Eddie George .50 .23
9 Terry Glenn .15 .07
10 Kevin Hardy .15 .07
11 Emmitt Smith .75 .35
12 Karim Abdul-Jabbar .15 .07
13 Tony Banks .15 .07
14 Zach Thomas .40 .18
15 Mike Alstott .15 .07
16 Matt Stevens .15 .07
17 Troy Davis .15 .07
18 Warrick Dunn .50 .23
19 Yatil Green .15 .07
20 Rae Carruth .15 .07
21 Darrell Russell .15 .07
22 Peter Boulware .15 .07
23 Shawn Springs .15 .07
24 Clyde Drexler .40 .18
25 Scottie Pippen .40 .18
26 Hakeem Olajuwon .40 .18
27 Alonzo Mourning .15 .07
28 Joe Smith .15 .07
29 Antonio McDyess .15 .07
30 Allen Iverson 1.25 .55
31 Kerry Kittles .15 .07
32 Stephon Marbury .40 .18
33 Marcus Camby .15 .07
34 Ray Allen .50 .23
35 Shareef Abdur-Rahim .40 .18
36 Kobe Bryant 2.00 .90
37 Antoine Walker .40 .18
38 Glenn Robinson .15 .07
39 Dikembe Mutombo .15 .07
40 Barry Bonds 1.50 .70
41 Jay Payton .15 .07
42 Todd Walker .15 .07
43 Jose Cruz Jr. .75 .35
44 Kerry Wood 1.50 .70
45 Wes Helms .15 .07
46 Dainius Zubrus .15 .07
47 Sergei Samsonov .50 .23
48 Jay McKee .15 .07
49 Marcus Nilson .15 .07
50 Joe Thornton .50 .23

1997 Scoreboard Talk N' Sports Essentials *

These 10 plastic acetate cards were randomly inserted at a rate of 1:20 Talk N' Sports packs.

MINT NRMT
COMPLETE SET (10) 60.00 27.00
E1 Brett Favre 12.00 5.50
E2 Scottie Pippen 6.00 2.70
E3 Barry Bonds 4.00 1.80
E4 Emmitt Smith 10.00 4.50
E5 Clyde Drexler 6.00 2.70
E6 Kobe Bryant 30.00 13.50
E7 Eddie George 15.00 6.75
E8 Troy Davis 4.00 1.80
E9 Darrell Russell 4.00 1.80
E10 Dainius Zubrus 4.00 1.80

1997 Scoreboard Talk N' Sports Phone Cards $1 *

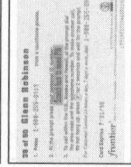

The $1 phone cards were inserted one per pack. The checklist of this 50-card set parallels the regular set. The phone time on these $1 phone cards can be combined. They expired 7/31/98.

MINT NRMT
COMPLETE SET (50) 25.00 11.00
*PHONE CARDS: .8X TO 2X BASIC CARDS
*PIN NUMBER REVEALED: HALF VALUE

1997 Scoreboard Talk N' Sports Phone Cards $10 *

These $10 phone cards allow users to choose trivia contests to win memorabilia in lieu of the phone time. Entrants who choose the trivia contest forfeit their phone time, but if they answer 9 of 10 questions, they win a baseball bat autographed by one of these six players: Willie Mays, Hank Aaron, Barry Bonds, Ken Griffey Jr., Pete Rose or Chipper Jones. The $10 cards were inserted at a rate of 1:12 packs and expire 5/20/98. Each card is sequentially numbered out of 3,960.

MINT NRMT
COMPLETE SET (10) 40.00 18.00
*PIN NUMBER REVEALED: HALF VALUE
1 Brett Favre 8.00 3.60
2 Hakeem Olajuwon 4.00 1.80
3 Keyshawn Johnson 4.00 1.80
4 Steve Young 4.00 1.80
5 Kordell Stewart 4.00 1.80
6 Cal Ripken 10.00 4.50
7 Eddie George 5.00 2.20
8 Troy Aikman 4.00 1.80
9 Clyde Drexler 4.00 1.80
10 Scottie Pippen 4.00 1.80

1997 Scoreboard Talk N' Sports Phone Cards $20 *

These $20 phone cards allow users to choose sports updates in lieu of the phone time. The time on the card can be used interchangably for either phone calls or sports updates. The $20 cards were inserted at a rate of 1:36 packs and expired 7/31/98. Each card is sequentially numbered out of 1,440.

MINT NRMT
COMPLETE SET (10) 60.00 27.00
*PIN NUMBER REVEALED: HALF VALUE
1 Brett Favre 15.00 6.75
2 Scottie Pippen 8.00 3.60
3 Barry Bonds 8.00 3.60
4 Cal Ripken 10.00 4.50
5 Clyde Drexler 8.00 3.60
6 Kobe Bryant 20.00 9.00
7 Eddie George 10.00 4.50
8 Troy Davis 5.00 2.20
9 Darrell Russell 5.00 2.20
10 Dainius Zubrus 5.00 2.20

1997 Scoreboard Talk N' Sports Phone Cards $1000 *

These rare cards are inserted at a rate of 1:11,000 packs. They are sequentially numbered out of 10. The phone time expired 7/31/98.

MINT NRMT
PIN NUMBER REVEALED: HALF VALUE
1 Cal Ripken 250.00 110.00
2 Scottie Pippen 120.00 55.00
3 Brett Favre 200.00 90.00
4 Allen Iverson 150.00 70.00
5 Eddie George 120.00 55.00

1997 Scoreboard Talk N' Sports Jackie Robinson $50 Phone Cards *

These phone cards pay tribute to the 50th anniversary of baseball legend Jackie Robinson breaking the sport's color barrier. Each of the five cards are sequentially numbered out of 499 and are randomly inserted at a rate of 1:200 packs. The phone card time expires 7/31/98.

MINT NRMT
COMPLETE SET (5) 150.00 70.00
COMMON ROBINSON (1-5) 30.00 13.50

2002-03 UD SuperStars *

This 300 card set was released in March, 2003. This set was issued in five card packs with an $3 SRP. The packs were issued in 24 pack boxes which came 12 boxes to a case. The final 50 cards of the set featured two rookies from different sports.

MINT NRMT
COMPLETE SET (300) 80.00 36.00
COMMON CARD (1-250) .40 .18
COMMON CARD (251-300) .50 .23
1 Tiger Woods 4.00 1.80
2 Troy Glaus .60 .25
3 Darin Erstad .60 .25
4 Garret Anderson .40 .18
5 Jarrod Washburn .40 .18
6 Paul Kariya 1.25 .55
7 Randy Johnson 1.00 .45
8 Curt Schilling .60 .25
9 Luis Gonzalez .40 .18
10 Jake Plummer .40 .18
11 Sean Burke .40 .18
12 Stephon Marbury .60 .25
13 Shawn Marion .60 .25
14 Tom Glavine 1.00 .45
15 Chipper Jones 1.00 .45
16 Greg Maddux 2.00 .90
17 Andruw Jones .60 .25
18 John Smoltz .40 .18
19 Gary Sheffield .40 .18
20 Shareef Abdur-Rahim .40 .18
21 Michael Vick 2.50 1.10
22 Ilya Kovalchuk .60 .25
23 Cal Ripken 3.00 1.35
24 Jay Gibbons .40 .18
25 Tony Batista .40 .18
26 Sergio Garcia 1.00 .45
27 Nomar Garciaparra 1.50 .70
28 Pedro Martinez 1.00 .45
29 Manny Ramirez .60 .25
30 Derek Lowe .40 .18
31 Cliff Floyd .40 .18
32 Shea Hillenbrand .40 .18
33 Johnny Damon .40 .18
34 Paul Pierce 1.00 .45
35 Antoine Walker .60 .25
36 Bobby Orr 2.50 1.10
37 Ray Bourque 1.00 .45
38 Tom Brady 1.50 .70
39 Antowain Smith .40 .18
40 Drew Bledsoe 1.00 .45
41 Jarome Iginla .40 .18
42 Sammy Sosa 1.50 .70
43 Mark Prior 2.00 .90
44 Kerry Wood .60 .25
45 Fred McGriff .60 .25
46 Corey Patterson .40 .18
47 Paul Konerko .40 .18
48 Frank Thomas .60 .25
49 Magglio Ordonez .60 .25
50 Carlos Lee .40 .18
51 Mark Buehrle .40 .18
52 Anthony Thomas .60 .25
53 Theoren Fleury .60 .25
54 Jack Nicklaus 1.50 .70
55 Ken Griffey Jr. 2.00 .90
56 Austin Kearns 1.00 .45
57 Adam Dunn 1.00 .45
58 Aaron Boone .40 .18
59 Sean Casey .60 .25
60 Corey Dillon .60 .25
61 C.C. Sabathia .40 .18
62 Omar Vizquel .40 .18
63 Tim Couch .40 .18
64 Todd Helton .60 .25
65 Larry Walker .60 .25
66 Juan Pierre .40 .18
67 Patrick Roy 2.00 .90
68 Joe Sakic 1.00 .45
69 Peter Forsberg 1.25 .55
70 Brian Griese .60 .25
71 Justin Leonard .60 .25
72 Dirk Nowitzki 1.25 .55
73 Emmitt Smith 2.00 .90
74 Quincy Carter .60 .25
75 Mike Modano 1.00 .45
76 Alex Rodriguez 2.00 .90
77 Ivan Rodriguez .60 .25
78 Juan Gonzalez 1.00 .45
79 Rafael Palmeiro .60 .25
80 Hank Blalock .60 .25
81 Gordie Howe 2.00 .90
82 Steve Yzerman 2.00 .90
83 Curtis Joseph .60 .25
84 Wayne Gretzky 3.00 1.35
85 Preston Wilson .40 .18
86 Josh Beckett .60 .25
87 Luis Castillo .40 .18
88 A.J. Burnett .40 .18
89 Mike Lowell .40 .18
90 Ricky Williams 1.00 .45
91 Johnny Miller .40 .18
92 Ahman Green .60 .25
93 Brett Favre 2.00 .90
94 Richie Sexson .40 .18
95 Geoff Jenkins .40 .18
96 Ben Sheets .40 .18
97 Ray Allen .60 .25
98 Roy Oswalt .60 .25
99 Richard Hidalgo .40 .18
100 Jeff Bagwell .60 .25
101 Lance Berkman .60 .25
102 Craig Biggio .60 .25
103 Steve Francis 1.25 .55
104 Reggie Miller 1.00 .45
105 Edgerrin James 1.00 .45
106 Peyton Manning 1.50 .70
107 Mark Brunell .60 .25
108 Jimmy Smith .40 .18
109 Mike Sweeney .40 .18
110 Carlos Beltran .40 .18
111 Priest Holmes 1.00 .45
112 Fred Couples 1.00 .45
113 Hideo Nomo 1.00 .45
114 Shawn Green .60 .25
115 Kevin Brown .40 .18
116 Brian Jordan .40 .18
117 Eric Gagne .40 .18
118 Adrian Beltre .40 .18
119 Kobe Bryant 3.00 1.35
120 Shaquille O'Neal 1.50 .70
121 Wilt Chamberlain 1.50 .70
122 Andre Miller .40 .18
123 Zigmund Palffy .40 .18
124 Pau Gasol .60 .25
125 Steve McNair .60 .25
126 Eddie George .60 .25
127 Torii Hunter .40 .18
128 Corey Koskie .40 .18
129 Doug Mientkiewicz .40 .18
130 Eric Milton .40 .18
131 Jacque Jones .40 .18
132 Kevin Garnett 1.50 .70
133 Daunte Culpepper .60 .25
134 Randy Moss 1.50 .70
135 Vladimir Guerrero 1.00 .45
136 Bartolo Colon .40 .18
137 Jose Vidro .40 .18
138 Jose Theodore .60 .25
139 Baron Davis .60 .25
140 Aaron Brooks .60 .25
141 Deuce McAllister 1.00 .45
142 Jesper Parnevik .40 .18
143 Jason Kidd 1.25 .55
144 Martin Brodeur 1.00 .45
145 Derek Jeter 3.00 1.35
146 Alfonso Soriano .60 .25
147 Mike Mussina 1.00 .45
148 Jason Giambi 1.00 .45
149 Robin Ventura .40 .18
150 Roger Clemens 2.00 .90
151 Bernie Williams .60 .25
152 Mickey Mantle 4.00 1.80
153 Joe DiMaggio 2.50 1.10
154 Raul Mondesi .40 .18
155 Mariano Rivera .60 .25
156 Hideki Matsui 15.00 6.75
157 Mike Piazza 1.50 .70
158 Roberto Alomar 1.00 .45
159 Edgardo Alfonzo .40 .18
160 Jeromy Burnitz .40 .18
161 Armando Benitez .40 .18
162 Mo Vaughn .40 .18
163 Curtis Martin .60 .25
164 Chad Pennington 1.00 .45
165 Pavel Bure .40 .18
166 Michael Peca .40 .18
167 Mark O'Meara .40 .18
168 Eric Chavez .40 .18
169 Miguel Tejada .60 .25
170 Tim Hudson .40 .18
171 Jermaine Dye .40 .18
172 David Justice .40 .18
173 Mark Mulder .40 .18
174 Ray Durham .40 .18
175 Barry Zito 1.00 .45
176 Jerry Rice 1.50 .70
177 Rich Gannon 1.00 .45
178 Jason Richardson 1.25 .55
179 Grant Hill .60 .25
180 Tracy McGrady 1.50 .70
181 Carl Crawford .40 .18
182 Bobby Abreu .40 .18
183 Pat Burrell 1.00 .45
184 Jimmy Rollins .40 .18
185 Marlon Byrd .40 .18
186 Mike Lieberthal .40 .18
187 Allen Iverson 1.50 .70
188 Julius Erving 1.50 .70
189 Donovan McNabb 1.00 .45
190 Jeremy Roenick .60 .25
191 Arnold Palmer 1.25 .55
192 Jason Kendall .40 .18
193 Brian Giles .40 .18
194 Aramis Ramirez .40 .18
195 Jerome Bettis .60 .25
196 Kordell Stewart .40 .18
197 Mario Lemieux 2.50 1.10
198 Rasheed Wallace .60 .25
199 Chris Webber 1.00 .45
200 Mike Bibby .60 .25
201 Tim Duncan 1.50 .70
202 Ryan Klesko .40 .18
203 Sean Burroughs .60 .25
204 Trevor Hoffman .40 .18
205 Phil Nevin .40 .18
206 LaDainian Tomlinson 1.00 .45
207 Nick Price .40 .18
208 Kenny Lofton .40 .18
209 J.T. Snow .40 .18
210 Barry Bonds 2.50 1.10
211 Rich Aurilia .40 .18
212 Reggie Sanders .40 .18
213 Robb Nen .40 .18
214 Jeff Garcia .60 .25
215 Terrell Owens 1.00 .45
216 Teemu Selanne 1.00 .45
217 Ichiro Suzuki 2.00 .90
218 Bret Boone .40 .18
219 John Olerud .40 .18
220 Freddy Garcia .40 .18
221 Edgar Martinez .60 .25
222 Rashard Lewis .40 .18
223 Gary Payton 1.00 .45
224 Shaun Alexander .40 .18
225 Byron Nelson 1.00 .45
226 Scott Rolen .60 .25
227 Tino Martinez .60 .25
228 Jim Edmonds .40 .18
229 Albert Pujols 1.50 .70
230 Mark McGwire 2.50 1.10
231 J.D. Drew .40 .18
232 Matt Morris .40 .18
233 Kurt Warner 1.25 .55
234 Marshall Faulk 1.00 .45
235 Keith Tkachuk .40 .18
236 Shannon Stewart .40 .18
237 Jose Cruz Jr. .40 .18
238 Carlos Delgado .40 .18
239 Vernon Wells .40 .18
240 Josh Phelps .60 .25
241 Roy Halladay .40 .18
242 Eric Hinske .40 .18
243 Vince Carter 1.25 .55
244 Mats Sundin .40 .18
245 Karl Malone 1.00 .45
246 Jerry Stackhouse .60 .25
247 Michael Jordan 5.00 2.20
248 Stephen Davis .40 .18
249 Jaromir Jagr 1.00 .45
250 Nick Faldo .40 .18
251 Josh McCown .75 .35
Jose Valverde
252 Doug Devore .50 .23
Wendell Bryant
253 T.J. Duckett 1.00 .45
Ilya Kovalchuk
254 Stanislav Chistov 1.00 .45
Melvin Ely
255 Dany Heatley 1.00 .45
John Ennis
256 Freddy Sanchez .75 .35
Rohan Davey
257 Julius Peppers 2.00 .90
Eric Cole
258 Jay Williams 2.00 .90
Francis Beltran
259 Kyle Kane .50 .23
Roger Mason Jr.
260 Edwin Almonte .75 .35
Adrian Peterson
261 Andre Davis 4.00 1.80
Rick Nash
262 Dajuan Wagner 2.00 .90
William Green
263 Cam Esslinger 4.00 1.80
Clinton Portis

264 Chad Hutchinson.................2.00 .90
Casey Jacobsen
265 Ashley Lelie.........................2.00 .90
Rene Reyes
266 Nene Hilario........................1.00 .45
Nick Rolovich
267 Joey Harrington...................4.00 1.80
Tayshaun Prince
268 Henrik Zetterberg.................4.00 1.80
Kalimba Edwards
269 Jay Bouwmeester.................2.50 1.10
Caron Butler
270 Mike Dunleavy.....................1.00 .45
Phillip Buchanon
271 Brandon Puffer......................50 .23
Jabar Gaffney
272 Bostjan Nachbar.....................50 .23
Jonathan Wells
273 David Carr.........................10.00 4.50
Yao Ming
274 Juan Brito............................50 .23
Ryan Sims
275 Kazuhisa Ishii......................1.50 .70
Kareem Rush
276 Drew Gooden.......................2.00 .90
Scottie Upshall
277 Luis Martinez..........................50 .23
Craig Nall
278 Marcus Haislip.....................1.50 .70
Javon Walker
279 Kevin Frederick......................50 .23
Shaun Hill
280 Donte' Stallworth..................2.00 .90
Curtis Borchardt
281 Tyler Yates.........................4.00 1.80
Jeremy Shockey
282 Jaime Cerda..........................75 .35
Tim Carter
283 Pierre-Marc Bouchard...........50 .23
Igor Rakocevic
284 Anderson Machado.................75 .35
John Salmons
285 Amare Stoudemire...............4.00 1.80
Jeremy Ward
286 Adrian Burnside....................2.00 .90
Antwaan Randle El
287 Ben Howard............................75 .35
Reche Caldwell
288 Oliver Perez.........................1.50 .70
Quentin Jammer
289 Luis Ugueto............................75 .35
Jerramy Stevens
290 Maurice Morris.......................75 .35
Matt Thornton
291 So Taguchi..........................1.00 .45
Lamar Gordon
292 Jason Simontacchi.................1.00 .45
Robert Thomas
293 Felix Escalona.........................75 .35
Marquise Walker
294 Brandon Backe.......................75 .35
Travis Stephens
295 Reed Johnson.........................50 .23
Chris Jefferies
296 Patrick Ramsey.....................2.00 .90
Juan Dixon
297 Jared Jeffries..........................50 .23
Steve Bechler
298 Charles Howell III..................2.00 .90
Jonathan Byrd
299 Luke Donald............................50 .23
Pat Perez
300 Scott McCarron.......................75 .35
Jerry Kelly

2002-03 UD SuperStars Gold *

Randomly inserted in packs, this is a parallel to the UD SuperStars set. These cards were issued to a stated print run of 250 serial numbered sets.

MINT NRMT
*GOLD 1-250: 2.5X TO 6X BASIC.......
*GOLD MATSUI: 6X TO 12X BASIC....
*GOLD 251-300: 2X TO 5X BASIC......

2002-03 UD SuperStars Benchmarks *

Inserted at a stated rate of one in 20, these 10 cards feature two athletes from different sports with something in common. It could be being a legendary figure in the sport or playing in the same city.

MINT NRMT
B1 Joe DiMaggio.........................8.00 3.60
Wayne Gretzky
B2 Barry Bonds..........................6.00 2.70
Jerry Rice
B3 Marshall Faulk.......................3.00 1.35
Tony Gwynn
B4 Bill Russell..........................10.00 4.50
Mickey Mantle
B5 Allen Iverson.........................2.50 1.10
Donovan McNabb
B6 Nomar Garciaparra.................4.00 1.80
Tom Brady
B7 Kevin Garnett........................4.00 1.80
Randy Moss
B8 Sammy Sosa..........................3.00 1.35
Anthony Thomas
B9 Mark McGwire........................6.00 2.70
Kurt Warner
B10 Kobe Bryant.........................8.00 3.60
Derek Jeter

2002-03 UD SuperStars City All-Stars Dual Jersey *

Inserted at a stated rate of one in 32, these 43 cards featured two jersey swatches from star athletes from the same city. Some cards were issued in smaller quantities and we have notated that information with an SP in our database.

MINT NRMT
ABBD Aaron Brooks..................15.00 6.75
Baron Davis
ABZP Adrian Beltre...................10.00 4.50
Zigmund Palffy
ADDM Andre Davis...................15.00 6.75
Darius Miles
ADPW Adam Dunn....................15.00 6.75
Peter Warrick
BGJS Brian Griese....................15.00 6.75
Joe Sakic
CDMS Carlos Delgado...............15.00 6.75
Mats Sundin
DBTH Drew Brees.....................15.00 6.75
Trevor Hoffman
DCTO Daunte Culpepper...........20.00 9.00
Torii Hunter
ECRG Eric Chavez.....................15.00 6.75
Rich Gannon
EJJO Edgerrin James...............15.00 6.75
Jermaine O'Neal
FPPL Felix Potvin......................15.00 6.75
Paul Lo Duca
GAPK Garret Anderson.............15.00 6.75
Paul Kariya
GSSA Gary Sheffield..................10.00 4.50
Shareef Abdur-Rahim
IRMF Ivan Rodriguez.................15.00 6.75
Michael Finley
JBJF Jay Fiedler........................15.00 6.75
Josh Beckett
JGCB Jabbar Gaffney................15.00 6.75
Craig Biggio
JGJS Jeff Garcia........................15.00 6.75
J.T. Snow
JLDS John LeClair.....................15.00 6.75
Duce Staley
JPLG Jake Plummer..................10.00 4.50
Luis Gonzalez
KPBA Keith Primeau..................10.00 4.50
Bob Abreu
LTRK LaDainian Tomlinson.......15.00 6.75
Ryan Klesko
MFJD Marshall Faulk.................20.00 9.00
J.D. Drew
MLBG Mario Lemieux................40.00 18.00
Brian Giles Pants
MMAR Mike Modano.................25.00 11.00
Alex Rodriguez
MPEL Mike Piazza.....................25.00 11.00
Eric Lindros
MRPP Manny Ramirez..............15.00 6.75
Paul Pierce
MVAJ Michael Vick....................40.00 18.00
Andruw Jones
PHMS Priest Holmes.................20.00 9.00
Mike Sweeney
PLAM Paul Lo Duca..................10.00 4.50
Andre Miller
RACP Roberto Alomar...............20.00 9.00
Chad Pennington
RCPB Roger Clemens................25.00 11.00
Pavel Bure
RDBW Ron Dayne......................15.00 6.75
Bernie Williams
RJSM Randy Johnson................15.00 6.75
Stephon Marbury
SAEM Shaun Alexander.............15.00 6.75
Edgar Martinez
SDJS Stephen Davis..................20.00 9.00
Jerry Stackhouse SP
SMPG Steve McNair..................15.00 6.75
Pau Gasol
SSAW Sergei Samsonov...........15.00 6.75
Antoine Walker
TCMO Tyson Chandler..............15.00 6.75
Magglio Ordonez
THJD Torry Holt........................15.00 6.75
J.D. Drew
THRB Todd Helton....................15.00 6.75
Rob Blake
TORA Terrell Owens..................15.00 6.75
Rich Aurilia
WGJG Wayne Gretzky..............60.00 27.00
Jason Giambi
WSMB Wally Szczerbiak...........15.00 6.75
Michael Bennett

2002-03 UD SuperStars City All-Stars Triple Jersey *

Randomly inserted in packs, these cards featured three game-used jersey swatches from all-stars from the same city. These cards were issued to a stated print run of 250 serial numbered sets.

MINT NRMT
CVT Chipper Jones...................50.00 22.00
Michael Vick
Jason Terry
DPE Darin Erstad......................25.00 11.00
Paul Kariya
Elton Brand
IGS Ichiro Suzuki.....................80.00 36.00
Gary Payton
Shaun Alexander
IMD Ivan Rodriguez..................40.00 18.00
Mike Modano
Dirk Nowitzki
JCK Ken Griffey Jr....................50.00 22.00
Corey Dillon
Kenyon Martin
JDW Jacque Jones....................25.00 11.00
Daunte Culpepper
Wally Szczerbiak
JDY Jeff Bagwell......................100.00 45.00
David Carr
Yao Ming
JKA Jason Kendall....................25.00 11.00
Kordell Stewart
Alexei Kovalev
JLP Jason Giambi.....................40.00 18.00
Latrell Sprewell
Pavel Bure
JMK J.D. Drew..........................25.00 11.00
Marshall Faulk
Keith Tkachuk
JSB Joey Harrington.................80.00 36.00
Steve Yzerman
Ben Wallace
MJA Mark Prior..........................50.00 22.00
Jay Williams
Anthony Thomas
MJC Mike Piazza.......................40.00 18.00
Jason Kidd
Curtis Martin
MJJ Miguel Tejada....................40.00 18.00
Jason Richardson
Jerry Rice
OTD Omar Vizquel.....................40.00 18.00
Tim Couch
Dajuan Wagner
PTP Pedro Martinez..................50.00 22.00
Tom Brady
Paul Pierce
REA Roger Clemens..................50.00 22.00
Eric Lindros
Allan Houston
RSS Randy Johnson.................30.00 13.50
Shawn Marion
Shane Doan
SWK Shawn Green..................120.00 55.00
Wayne Gretzky
Kobe Bryant

2002-03 UD SuperStars Dual Legendary Cuts *

Randomly inserted in packs, these two cards feature signatures from two legendary greats. Each of these cards were issued to a stated print run of one serial numbered set and no pricing is available due to market scarcity.

MINT NRMT
MMJU Mickey Mantle.........................
Johnny Unitas
WCWP Wilt Chamberlain....................
Walter Payton

2002-03 UD SuperStars Keys to the City *

Inserted at a stated rate of one in six. These 10 cards feature two star athletes from the same city.

MINT NRMT
COMPLETE SET (10)..................25.00 11.00
K1 Carlos Delgado.....................2.00 .90
Vince Carter
K2 Kobe Bryant..........................5.00 2.20
Kazuhisa Ishii
K3 Mark McGwire........................4.00 1.80
Kurt Warner
K4 Brian Urlacher.......................2.50 1.10
Sammy Sosa
K5 Pedro Martinez......................2.50 1.10
Tom Brady
K6 Patrick Roy...........................3.00 1.35
Todd Helton
K7 Mike Piazza...........................3.00 1.35
Curtis Martin
K8 Jeff Bagwell...........................4.00 1.80
David Carr
K9 Steve Yzerman........................4.00 1.80
Joey Harrington
K10 Alex Rodriguez....................3.00 1.35
Emmitt Smith

2002-03 UD SuperStars Legendary Leaders Dual Jersey *

Inserted at a stated rate of one in 96, these 20 cards feature game-worn jersey pieces from two star athletes from the same city.

MINT NRMT
AIDM Allen Iverson...................30.00 13.50
Donovan McNabb
DCJB David Carr........................25.00 11.00
Jeff Bagwell
EJJO Edgerrin James.................15.00 6.75
Jermaine O'Neal
ESAR Emmitt Smith...................40.00 18.00
Alex Rodriguez
ISDB Ichiro Suzuki....................120.00 55.00
David Beckham
JGKC Jason Giambi...................15.00 6.75
Kerry Collins
JKCP Jason Kidd........................20.00 9.00
Chad Pennington
JRCD Ken Griffey Jr...................30.00 13.50
Corey Dillon
JRJR Jerry Rice..........................25.00 11.00
Jason Richardson
JSTG Junior Seau.......................25.00 11.00
Tony Gwynn
JWAT Jay Williams......................15.00 6.75
Anthony Thomas
KGRM Kevin Garnett..................40.00 18.00
Randy Moss
KWMM Kurt Warner...................60.00 27.00
Mark McGwire
PMTB Pedro Martinez................25.00 11.00
Tom Brady
RMPM Reggie Miller...................25.00 11.00
Peyton Manning
SMRJ Shawn Marion..................25.00 11.00
Randy Johnson
SSBU Sammy Sosa.....................40.00 18.00
Brian Urlacher
SYJH Steve Yzerman...................40.00 18.00
Joey Harrington
TCOV Tim Couch.........................10.00 4.50
Omar Vizquel
ZPSG Zigmund Palffy..................15.00 6.75
Shawn Green

2002-03 UD SuperStars Legendary Leaders Dual Jersey Autograph *

Randomly inserted into packs, this card features not only event-used jersey swatches but also authentic signatures from the featured athletes. This card was issued to a stated print run of 25 serial numbered sets and no pricing is available due to market scarcity.

MINT NRMT
MJTW Michael Jordan.......................
Tiger Woods

2002-03 UD SuperStars Legendary Leaders Triple Jersey *

Randomly inserted in packs, these 18 cards feature game-used jersey swatches from three athletes. This set is significant by the usage of game-worn swatches of soccer great David Beckham.

MINT NRMT
ADJ Allen Iverson....................50.00 22.00
Donovan McNabb
Jeremy Roenick
AEM Alex Rodriguez.................60.00 27.00
Emmitt Smith
Mike Modano
CJS Cal Ripken..........................60.00 27.00
Jaromir Jagr
Stephen Davis
GMS Greg Maddux....................50.00 22.00
Michael Vick
Shareef Abdur-Rahim
IDK Ichiro Suzuki....................200.00 90.00
David Beckham
Kobe Bryant
IKD Ichiro Suzuki....................120.00 55.00
Kevin Garnett
David Beckham
JDM Jason Giambi.....................50.00 22.00
Drew Bledsoe
Mark Messier
JWL Joe DiMaggio...................350.00 160.00
Wayne Gretzky
Larry Bird
KJT Karl Malone.........................50.00 22.00
Jerry Rice
Tony Gwynn
LBP Larry Walker.......................40.00 18.00
Brian Griese
Patrick Roy
MCA Mike Piazza.......................50.00 22.00
Chad Pennington
Alexei Yashin
MPS Mark McGwire...................100.00 45.00
Peyton Manning
Steve Yzerman
PPT Pedro Martinez...................50.00 22.00
Paul Pierce
Tom Brady
RJM Roger Clemens...................80.00 36.00
Jerry Rice
Mario Lemieux
SEB Sammy Sosa.......................60.00 27.00
Eric Daze
Brian Urlacher
SKM Sammy Sosa.......................80.00 36.00
Kobe Bryant
Marshall Faulk
SWK Shawn Green...................120.00 55.00
Wayne Gretzky
Kobe Bryant
TEM Tony Gwynn.......................80.00 36.00
Emmitt Smith
Mario Lemieux

2002-03 UD SuperStars Magic Moments *

Inserted at a stated rate of one in five, this 20 card set featured a mix of active and retired players along with history about key moments in their career.

MINT NRMT
COMPLETE SET (20)..................25.00 11.00
MM1 Barry Bonds.......................4.00 1.80
MM2 Mark McGwire....................4.00 1.80
MM3 Roger Clemens...................3.00 1.35
MM4 Joe DiMaggio......................4.00 1.80
MM5 Cal Ripken..........................5.00 2.20
MM6 Ichiro Suzuki.......................3.00 1.35
MM7 Mickey Mantle.....................5.00 2.20
MM8 Sammy Sosa.......................2.50 1.10
MM9 Ken Griffey Jr......................2.50 1.10
MM10 Derek Jeter.......................5.00 2.20
MM11 Kurt Warner......................1.50 .70
MM12 Brett Favre........................3.00 1.35
MM13 Tom Brady.........................2.50 1.10
MM14 Michael Jordan..................6.00 2.70
MM15 Kobe Bryant......................4.00 1.80
MM16 Jay Williams......................2.00 .90
MM17 Bobby Orr.........................4.00 1.80
MM18 Wayne Gretzky..................5.00 2.20
MM19 Patrick Roy........................3.00 1.35
MM20 Tiger Woods......................5.00 2.20

2002-03 UD SuperStars Rookie Review *

Inserted at a stated rate of one in 20, these 10 cards feature two athletes who made their American professional debut in the same year.

MINT NRMT
R1 Mark Messier.........................5.00 2.20
Ozzie Smith
R2 Ichiro Suzuki.........................8.00 3.60
Michael Vick
R3 Josh Beckett..........................3.00 1.35
Steve Francis
R4 Vince Carter...........................3.00 1.35
Peyton Manning
R5 Emmitt Smith.........................5.00 2.20
Sammy Sosa
R6 Mark Prior..............................3.00 1.35
Drew Brees
R7 Jason Kidd..............................3.00 1.35
Alex Rodriguez
R8 Alfonso Soriano......................3.00 1.35
Shawn Marion
R9 Ken Griffey Jr.........................3.00 1.35
David Robinson
R10 Derek Jeter..........................5.00 2.20
Jerome Bettis

2002-03 UD SuperStars Spokesmen *

Issued as a three-card pack topper, these 30 cards feature a mix of players who were also serving as spokesmen for Upper Deck.

MINT NRMT
*BLACK: 1.25X TO 3X BASIC SPOKESMEN
BLACK: RANDOM IN SPOKESMEN PACKS
BLACK PRINT RUN 250 SERIAL #'d SETS
UD1 Ken Griffey Jr......................3.00 1.35
UD2 Ichiro Suzuki.......................4.00 1.80
UD3 Sammy Sosa........................3.00 1.35
UD4 Jason Giambi.......................3.00 1.35
UD5 Joe DiMaggio.......................5.00 2.20
UD6 Mark McGwire......................5.00 2.20
UD7 David Beckham.....................5.00 2.20
UD8 Michael Jordan...................10.00 4.50
UD9 Kobe Bryant.........................5.00 2.20
UD10 Jay Williams.......................3.00 1.35
UD11 Peyton Manning..................3.00 1.35
UD12 Bobby Orr...........................5.00 2.20
UD13 Gordie Howe.......................4.00 1.80
UD14 Wayne Gretzky....................6.00 2.70
UD15 Tiger Woods........................8.00 3.60
UD16 Ken Griffey Jr......................3.00 1.35
UD17 Ichiro Suzuki.......................4.00 1.80
UD18 Sammy Sosa........................3.00 1.35
UD19 Jason Giambi.......................3.00 1.35
UD20 Joe DiMaggio.......................5.00 2.20
UD21 Mark McGwire......................5.00 2.20
UD22 David Beckham.....................5.00 2.20
UD23 Michael Jordan...................10.00 4.50
UD24 Kobe Bryant.........................5.00 2.20
UD25 Jay Williams.........................3.00 1.35
UD26 Peyton Manning...................3.00 1.35
UD27 Bobby Orr.............................5.00 2.20
UD28 Gordie Howe.........................4.00 1.80
UD29 Wayne Gretzky.....................6.00 2.70
UD30 Tiger Woods.........................8.00 3.60

2002-03 UD SuperStars Spokesmen Gold *

Randomly inserted in Spokesman packs, this is a parallel to the Spokesman set. These cards were issued to a stated print run of 25 serial numbered sets and no pricing is available due to market scarcity. Peyton Manning and Mark McGwire signed all 25 cards for this set.

MINT NRMT
UD11 Peyton Manning AU..................
UD21 Mark McGwire AU....................

1996 Visions *

The 1996 Classic Visions set consists of 150 standard-size cards. The fronts feature full-bleed color action player photos. The player's position and name are presented in blue foil, while the Classic logo and set title "96 Visions" are stamped in gold foil. The back carries a second color photo, college statistics, biography, and a player fact.

MINT NRMT
COMPLETE SET (150)..................15.00 6.75
1 Shaquille O'Neal......................1.50 .70
2 Scottie Pippen...........................40 .18
3 Jason Kidd................................50 .23
4 Hakeem Olajuwon......................40 .18
5 Juwan Howard...........................40 .18
6 Alonzo Mourning........................40 .18
7 Glenn Robinson..........................40 .18
8 Rasheed Wallace........................60 .25
9 Ed O'Bannon..............................15 .07
10 Joe Smith.................................50 .23
11 Jerry Stackhouse....................1.00 .45
12 Damon Stoudamire...................50 .23
13 Cherokee Parks.........................15 .07
14 Gary Trent.................................15 .07
15 Shawn Respert..........................15 .07
16 Kevin Garnett..........................2.50 1.10
17 Kurt Thomas..............................15 .07
18 Jalen Rose.................................15 .07
19 Michael Finley...........................75 .35
20 Jason Caffey..............................15 .07
21 Randolph Childress...................15 .07
22 Tyus Edney................................15 .07
23 George Zidek.............................15 .07
24 Antonio McDyess...................1.25 .55
25 Corliss Williamson....................15 .07
26 Theo Ratliff...............................15 .07
27 Eric Williams.............................15 .07
28 Dikembe Mutombo....................40 .18
29 Lawrence Moten........................15 .07
30 Jimmy King................................15 .07
31 Donyell Marshall.......................15 .07
32 Brian Grant................................15 .07
33 Sharone Wright.........................15 .07
34 Eddie Jones................................40 .18
35 Greg Ostertag............................15 .07
36 Terrence Rencher.......................15 .07
37 David Vaughn.............................15 .07
38 Rebecca Lobo.............................40 .18
39 Troy Aikman...............................60 .25
40 Emmitt Smith..........................1.00 .45
41 Marshall Faulk............................40 .18
42 Kerry Collins...............................40 .18
43 Michael Westbrook.....................15 .07
44 Steve Young................................40 .18
45 Mike Mamula...............................15 .07
46 Joey Galloway.............................40 .18
47 Kyle Brady...................................15 .07
48 J.J. Stokes...................................15 .07
49 Steve McNair...............................60 .25
50 Kordell Stewart............................40 .18
51 Drew Bledsoe...............................40 .18
52 Hugh Douglas..............................15 .07
53 Curtis Martin................................50 .23
54 Ki-Jana Carter...............................15 .07
55 Tyrone Wheatley..........................40 .18
56 Napoleon Kaufman.......................40 .18
57 James Stewart...............................40 .18
58 Rashaan Salaam............................15 .07

59 Eric Zeier .15 .07
60 Bobby Taylor .15 .07
61 Ty Law .15 .07
62 Mark Bruener .15 .07
63 Devin Bush .15 .07
64 Frank Sanders .15 .07
65 Derrick Brooks .40 .18
66 Craig Powell .15 .07
67 Craig Newsome .15 .07
68 Trent Dilfer .40 .18
69 Sherman Williams .15 .07
70 Chris T. Jones .15 .07
71 Corey Fuller .15 .07
72 Luther Elliss .15 .07
73 Warren Sapp .40 .18
74 Isaac Bruce .40 .18
75 Tamarick Vanover .15 .07
76 Terrell Davis 1.00 .45
77 Byron Bam Morris .15 .07
78 Rodney Thomas .15 .07
79 Errict Rhett .15 .07
80 Kevin Carter .15 .07
81 Darnay Scott .15 .07
82 Bryan Berard .40 .18
83 Jeff Friesen .40 .18
84 Petr Buzek .40 .18
85 Nolan Baumgartner .15 .07
86 Jason Bonsignore .15 .07
87 Jan Hlavac .40 .18
88 Ethan Moreau .15 .07
89 Radek Dvorak .15 .07
90 Brian Holzinger .15 .07
91 Petr Sykora .50 .23
92 Ed Jovanovski .40 .18
93 Jeff O'Neill .15 .07
94 Manon Rheaume .50 .23
95 Barry Bonds 1.25 .55
96 Nolan Ryan 1.50 .70
97 Ben Grieve .15 .07
98 Ben Davis .15 .07
99 Paul Wilson .15 .07
100 C.J. Nitkowski .15 .07
101 Chad Hermansen .15 .07
102 Jason Kendall .15 .07
103 Todd Greene .15 .07
104 Dustin Hermanson .15 .07
105 Karim Garcia .40 .18
106 Doug Million .15 .07
107 Jay Payton .15 .07
108 Dale Earnhardt's Car .75 .35
109 Dale Jarrett .50 .23
110 Mark Martin .60 .25
111 Ernie Irvan .15 .07
112 Ricky Rudd .40 .18
113 Bobby Labonte .50 .23
114 Rusty Wallace's Car .40 .18
115 Michael Waltrip .15 .07
116 Sterling Marlin .40 .18
117 Dick Trickle .15 .07
118 John Andretti .15 .07
119 Darrell Waltrip .15 .07
120 Kyle Petty .15 .07
121 Shaquille O'Neal 1.50 .70
122 Troy Aikman .60 .25
123 Petr Sykora .50 .23
124 Dale Earnhardt 2.00 .90
125 Scottie Pippen .40 .18
126 Emmitt Smith 1.00 .45
127 Mark Martin .60 .25
128 Jason Kidd .40 .18
129 Marshall Faulk .50 .23
130 Nolan Ryan 1.50 .70
131 Joe Smith .50 .23
132 Rasheed Wallace .75 .35
133 Ed O'Bannon .15 .07
134 Michael Finley 1.00 .45
135 Jerry Stackhouse 1.00 .45
136 Tyus Edney .15 .07
137 Damon Stoudamire 1.25 .55
138 Antonio McDyess 1.25 .55
139 Kevin Garnett 2.50 1.10
140 Corliss Williamson .40 .18
141 Joey Galloway .40 .18
142 Kerry Collins .40 .18
143 Michael Westbrook .15 .07
144 Terrell Davis 1.00 .45
145 Kyle Brady .15 .07
146 Kordell Stewart .40 .18
147 Curtis Martin .50 .23
148 Tyrone Wheatley .40 .18
149 Napoleon Kaufman .40 .18
150 Rashaan Salaam .15 .07
V96 Damon Stoudamire 1.00 .45
Promo card

1996 Visions Signings *

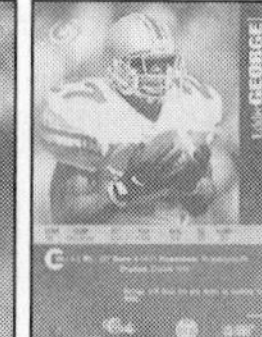

The 1996 Visions Signings set consists of 100 standard-size cards. The fronts feature full-bleed color action player photos. The player's position and name are stamped in prismatic foil along with the Classic logo and set title "96 Visions Signings." This set contains standouts from five sports grouped together in this order: basketball, football, hockey, baseball and racing. Cards were distributed in six-card packs. Release date was June 1996. The main allure to this product, in addition to the conventional inserts, were autographed memorabilia redemption cards inserted one per 10 packs.

MINT NRMT
COMPLETE SET (100) 15.00 6.75
1 Shaquille O'Neal 1.50 .70
2 Scottie Pippen .40 .18
3 Jason Kidd .50 .23
4 Hakeem Olajuwon .40 .18
5 Alonzo Mourning .15 .07
6 Glenn Robinson .15 .07
7 Rasheed Wallace .60 .25
8 Ed O'Bannon .15 .07
9 Joe Smith .40 .18
10 Damon Stoudamire .50 .23
11 Cherokee Parks .15 .07
12 Gary Trent .15 .07
13 Shawn Respert .15 .07
14 Kurt Thomas .15 .07
15 Michael Finley .75 .35
16 Jason Caffey .15 .07
17 Randolph Childress .15 .07
18 Tyus Edney .15 .07
19 George Zidek .15 .07
20 Antonio McDyess .75 .35
21 Corliss Williamson .40 .18
22 Theo Ratliff .15 .07
23 Eric Williams .15 .07
24 Brent Barry .15 .07
25 Lawrence Moten .15 .07
26 Bob Sura .15 .07
27 Travis Best .15 .07
28 Terrance Rencher .15 .07
29 Troy Aikman .75 .35
30 Emmitt Smith 1.00 .45
31 Marshall Faulk .50 .23
32 Kerry Collins .40 .18
33 Steve Young .40 .18
34 Drew Bledsoe .40 .18
35 Kyle Brady .15 .07
36 Steve McNair .40 .18
37 Napoleon Kaufman .40 .18
38 Karim Abdul-Jabbar .15 .07
39 Mike Alstott .40 .18
40 Tim Biakabutuka .15 .07
41 Duane Clemons .15 .07
42 Daryl Gardener .15 .07
43 Joey Galloway .40 .18
44 Eddie George 2.00 .90
45 Terry Glenn .15 .07
46 Kevin Hardy .15 .07
47 Bobby Hoying .15 .07
48 Keyshawn Johnson 1.25 .55
49 Derrick Mayes .15 .07
50 Eric Moulds 1.00 .45
51 Jonathan Ogden .15 .07
52 Simeon Rice .15 .07
53 Orpheus Roye .15 .07
54 Amani Toomer .40 .18
55 Chris Doering .15 .07
56 Jevon Langford .15 .07
57 Jeff Lewis .15 .07
58 Jamain Stephens .15 .07
59 Steve Taneyhill .15 .07
60 Alex Van Dyke .15 .07
61 Boyd Devereaux .15 .07
62 Alexandre Volchkov .15 .07
63 Trevor Wasyluk .15 .07
64 Luke Curtin .15 .07
65 Richard Jackman .15 .07
66 Jonathan Zukiwsky .15 .07
67 Geoff Peters .15 .07
68 Daniel Briere .40 .18
69 Chris Allen .15 .07
70 Jason Sweitezer .15 .07
71 Steve Nimigon .15 .07
72 Jay McKee .15 .07
73 Henry Kuster .15 .07
74 Jonathan Aitken .15 .07
75 Ed Jovanovski .40 .18
76 Petr Sykora .40 .18
77 Bryan Berard .15 .07
78 Manon Rheaume .50 .23
79 Radek Dvorak .15 .07
80 Barry Bonds 1.25 .55
81 Nolan Ryan 1.50 .70
82 Ben Davis .40 .18
83 Chad Hermansen .15 .07
84 Jason Kendall .15 .07
85 Todd Greene .15 .07
86 Karim Garcia .15 .07
87 Jay Payton .40 .18
88 Dale Jarrett .50 .23
89 Mark Martin .60 .25
90 Ernie Irvan .15 .07
91 Ricky Rudd .40 .18
92 Bobby Labonte .50 .23
93 Michael Waltrip .15 .07
94 Sterling Marlin .40 .18
95 Dick Trickle .15 .07
96 Darrell Waltrip .15 .07
97 Kyle Petty .15 .07
98 John Andretti .15 .07
99 Rusty Wallace's Car .40 .18
100 Dale Earnhardt's Car .75 .35

1996 Visions Signings Autographs Gold *

Certified autographed cards were inserted in Visions Signings packs at an overall rate of 1:12. Some players signed only the silver version while others signed both gold and silver cards. The Gold foil cards were not individually serial numbered. The quantity signed is unknown but assumed to be significantly higher than the corresponding number signed for the silver foil cards. We've listed the unnumbered cards alphabetically.

MINT NRMT
1 Karim Abdul-Jabbar 10.00 4.50
2 Jonathan Aitken 2.00 .90
3 Cory Alexander 2.00 .90
4 Chris Allen 2.00 .90
5 Mike Alstott 12.00 5.50
6 Brent Barry 5.00 2.20
7 Tim Biakabutuka 5.00 2.20
8 Daniel Briere 10.00 4.50
9 Junior Burrough 2.00 .90
10 Jerod Cherry 2.00 .90
11 Randolph Childress 2.00 .90
12 Sedric Clark 2.00 .90
13 Marcus Coleman 2.00 .90
14 Luke Curtin 2.00 .90
15 Chris Darkins 2.00 .90
16 Ben Davis 5.00 2.20
17 Boyd Devereaux 5.00 2.20
18 Chris Doering 2.00 .90
19 Tyus Edney 2.00 .90
20 Donnie Edwards 2.00 .90
21 Ray Farmer 2.00 .90
22 Michael Finley 10.00 4.50
23 Karim Garcia 2.00 .90
24 Randall Godfrey 2.00 .90
25 Scott Greene 2.00 .90
26 Todd Greene 5.00 2.20
27 Jeff Hartings 2.00 .90
28 Jimmy Herndon 2.00 .90
29 Fred Hoiberg 5.00 2.20
30 Richard Huntley 2.00 .90
31 Richard Jackman 5.00 2.20
32 Dietrich Jells 2.00 .90
33 Ed Jovanovski 10.00 4.50
34 Jason Kidd 20.00 9.00
35 Henry Kuster 2.00 .90
36 Jeff Lewis 2.00 .90
37 Jay McKee 2.00 .90
38 Ray Mickens 2.00 .90
39 Lawyer Milloy 5.00 2.20
40 Bryant Mix 2.00 .90
41 Alex Molden 2.00 .90
42 Lawrence Moten 2.00 .90
43 Alonzo Mourning 10.00 4.50
44 Steve Nimigon 2.00 .90
45 Jason Odom 2.00 .90
46 Hakeem Olajuwon 20.00 9.00
47 Shaquille O'Neal 80.00 36.00
48 Jay Payton 10.00 4.50
49 Geoff Peters 2.00 .90
50 Scottie Pippen 30.00 13.50
51 Constantin Popa 2.00 .90
52 Theo Ratliff 10.00 4.50
53 Jason Ritchey 2.00 .90
54 Brian Roche 2.00 .90
55 Orpheus Roye 2.00 .90
56 Jon Runyan 2.00 .90
57 Scott Slutzker 2.00 .90
58 Joe Smith 10.00 4.50
59 Jamain Stephens 2.00 .90
60 Matt Stevens 2.00 .90
61 Bob Sura 5.00 2.20
62 Jason Sweitezer 2.00 .90
63 Steve Taneyhill 2.00 .90
64 Zach Thomas 12.00 5.50
65 Alex Van Dyke 2.00 .90
66 Alexandre Volchkov 5.00 2.20
67 Kyle Wacholtz 2.00 .90
68 Trevor Wasyluk 2.00 .90
69 Stepfret Williams 2.00 .90
70 Jerome Woods 2.00 .90
71 Dusty Zeigler 2.00 .90
72 George Zidek 2.00 .90
73 Jonathan Zukiwsky 2.00 .90
82 Ben Davis 2.00 .90
85 Todd Greene 2.00 .90
86 Karim Garcia 5.00 2.20
87 Jay Payton 2.00 .90

1996 Visions Signings Autographs Silver *

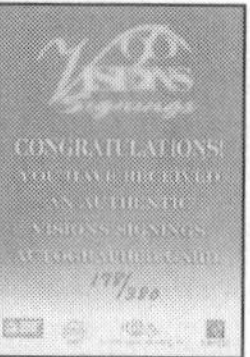

Certified autographed cards were inserted in Visions Signings packs at an overall rate of 1:12. Some players signed only silver cards while others signed gold and silver foil cards. The Silver cards were individually serial numbered as noted below. We've listed the unnumbered cards alphabetically.

MINT NRMT
1 Karim A.-Jabbar/365 10.00 4.50
2 Troy Aikman/190 50.00 22.00
3 Jonathan Aitken/360 2.00 .90
4 Cory Alexander/375 2.00 .90
5 Chris Allen/385 2.00 .90
6 Mike Alstott/345 20.00 9.00
7 Brent Barry/395 5.00 2.20
8 Tim Biakabutuka/390 10.00 4.50
9 Drew Bledsoe/110 50.00 22.00
10 Barry Bonds/240 100.00 45.00
11 Daniel Briere/390 5.00 2.20
12 Junior Burrough/395 2.00 .90
13 Jerod Cherry/355 2.00 .90
14 Randolph Childress/320 5.00 2.20
15 Sedric Clark/410 2.00 .90
16 Marcus Coleman/395 2.00 .90
17 Luke Curtin/370 2.00 .90
18 Chris Darkins/395 2.00 .90
19 Ben Davis/360 2.00 .90
20 Boyd Devereaux/350 5.00 2.20
21 Chris Doering/390 2.00 .90
22 Tyus Edney/375 5.00 2.20
23 Donnie Edwards/395 2.00 .90
24 Ray Farmer/395 2.00 .90
25 Marshall Faulk/185 30.00 13.50
26 Michael Finley/190 15.00 6.75
27 Karim Garcia/370 5.00 2.20
28 Randall Godfrey/380 2.00 .90
29 Scott Greene/395 2.00 .90
30 Todd Greene/385 2.00 .90
31 Jeff Hartings/380 2.00 .90
32 Jimmy Herndon/380 2.00 .90
33 Fred Hoiberg/395 5.00 2.20
34 Richard Huntley/380 2.00 .90
35 Ernie Irvan/265 5.00 2.20
36 Richard Jackman/400 5.00 2.20
37 Dietrich Jells/350 2.00 .90
38 Ed Jovanovski/405 10.00 4.50
39 Jason Kidd/145 40.00 18.00
40 Henry Kuster/415 2.00 .90
41 Jeff Lewis/385 2.00 .90
42 Mark Martin/315 30.00 13.50
43 Jay McKee/385 2.00 .90
44 Ray Mickens/390 2.00 .90
45 Lawyer Milloy/365 5.00 2.20
46 Bryant Mix/390 2.00 .90
47 Alex Molden/365 2.00 .90
48 Lawrence Moten/170 2.00 .90
49 Alonzo Mourning/405 10.00 4.50
50 Steve Nimigon/380 2.00 .90
51 Jason Odom/390 2.00 .90
52 Hakeem Olajuwon/270 40.00 18.00
53 Shaquille O'Neal/190 150.00 70.00
54 Jay Payton/365 2.00 .90
55 Geoff Peters/390 2.00 .90
56 Scottie Pippen/100 60.00 27.00
57 Constantin Popa/355 2.00 .90
58 Theo Ratliff/375 5.00 2.20
59 Jason Ritchey/360 2.00 .90
60 Brian Roche/395 2.00 .90
61 Orpheus Roye/350 2.00 .90
62 Ricky Rudd/285 10.00 4.50
63 Jon Runyan/430 2.00 .90
64 Scott Slutzker/385 2.00 .90
65 Emmitt Smith/90 100.00 45.00
66 Joe Smith/390 10.00 4.50
67 Jamain Stephens/380 2.00 .90
68 Matt Stevens/390 2.00 .90
69 Bob Sura/385 5.00 2.20
70 Jason Sweitezer/355 2.00 .90
71 Steve Taneyhill/420 2.00 .90
72 Zach Thomas/390 20.00 9.00
73 Dick Trickle/285 5.00 2.20
74 Alex Van Dyke/385 2.00 .90
75 Alexandre Volchkov/375 5.00 2.20
76 Kyle Wacholtz/385 2.00 .90
77 Michael Waltrip/285 5.00 2.20
78 Trevor Wasyluk/365 2.00 .90
79 Stepfret Williams/385 2.00 .90
80 Jerome Woods/430 2.00 .90
81 Steve Young/95 50.00 22.00
82 Dusty Zeigler/395 2.00 .90
83 George Zidek/365 2.00 .90
84 Jonathan Zukiwsky/375 2.00 .90

1997 Visions Signings *

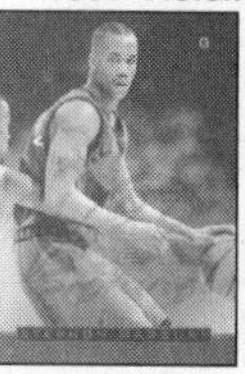

Score Board's follow-up to the 1996 Visions Signings debut product was released in June 1997. The second-year product had more of a memorabilia emphasis. According to Score Board, 1,700 sequentially numbered cases were produced with five cards per pack, 16 packs per box and 10 boxes per case. Each pack contains either an autographed card or an insert card. The 50-card regular set includes stars and prospects from all four major team sports. Also, one in every two packs contained a gold parallel card to the base set.

MINT NRMT
COMPLETE SET (50) 10.00 4.50
*GOLDS: .75X TO 2X BASIC CARDS
1 Barry Bonds 2.00 .90
2 Hakeem Olajuwon .40 .18
3 Glenn Robinson .15 .07
4 Steve Young .50 .23
5 Jose Cruz Jr. .75 .35
6 Ben Grieve .15 .07
7 Kerry Wood 2.00 .90
8 Erick Dampier .15 .07
9 Tony Delk .15 .07
10 Steve Nash .50 .23
11 Jerry Stackhouse .50 .23
12 Lorenzen Wright .15 .07
13 Vitaly Potapenko .15 .07
14 Allen Iverson 1.25 .55
15 Marcus Camby .15 .07
16 Shareef Abdur-Rahim .15 .07
17 Stephon Marbury .40 .18
18 Ray Allen .40 .18
19 Antoine Walker .50 .23
20 John Wallace .15 .07
21 Kobe Bryant 2.00 .90
22 Jermaine O'Neal .40 .18
23 Clyde Drexler .40 .18
24 Scottie Pippen .40 .18
25 Rasheed Wallace .40 .18
26 Joe Smith .40 .18
27 Antonio McDyess .15 .07
28 Alonzo Mourning .15 .07
29 Eddie George .50 .23
30 Warrick Dunn .75 .35
31 Darrell Russell .15 .07
32 Peter Boulware .15 .07
33 Shawn Springs .15 .07
34 Yatil Green .15 .07
35 David LaFleur .15 .07
36 Bryant Westbrook .15 .07
37 Rae Carruth .15 .07
38 Brett Favre 1.25 .55
39 Emmitt Smith .75 .35
40 Dainius Zubrus .15 .07
41 Joe Thornton .40 .18
42 Dan Cleary .15 .07
43 Sergei Samsonov .40 .18
44 Wes Helms .15 .07
45 Richard Hidalgo .15 .07
46 Jay Payton .15 .07
47 Leeland McElroy .15 .07
48 Troy Davis .15 .07
49 Tony Gonzalez .50 .23
50 Byron Hanspard .15 .07

1997 Visions Signings Autographs *

Each 1997 Visions Signings pack contains either an autographed card or an insert card. One in six packs contain a regular autograph card. Three cards, Troy Aikman, Allen Iverson, Emmitt Smith never made their way into packs as slated. Therefore the complete set only contains 63 cards.

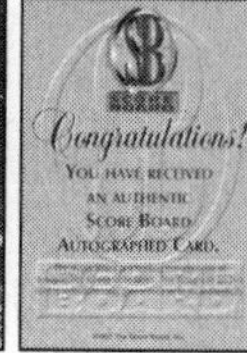

Congratulations!
You have received an authentic Score Board Autographed Card.

MINT NRMT
1 Shareef Abdur-Rahim 10.00 4.50
3 Ray Allen 15.00 6.75
4 Tony Banks 5.00 2.20
5 Michael Booker 2.00 .90
6 Peter Boulware 2.00 .90
7 Dante Calabria 2.00 .90
8 Rae Carruth 2.00 .90
9 Jose Cruz Jr. 8.00 3.60
10 Erick Dampier 2.00 .90
11 Tony Delk 2.00 .90
12 Koy Detmer 5.00 2.20
13 Corey Dillon 25.00 11.00
14 Warrick Dunn 15.00 6.75
15 Tyus Edney 5.00 2.20
16 Brian Evans 2.00 .90
18 Derek Fisher 10.00 4.50
19 Yatil Green 2.00 .90
20 Ben Grieve 5.00 2.20
21 Vladimir Guerrero 20.00 9.00
22 Steve Hamer 2.00 .90
23 Byron Hanspard 5.00 2.20
24 Kevin Hardy 5.00 2.20
25 Othella Harrington 2.00 .90
26 Wes Helms 2.00 .90
27 Richard Hidalgo 5.00 2.20
28 Josh Holden 2.00 .90
30 DeRon Jenkins 2.00 .90
31 Andre Johnson 2.00 .90
32 Greg Jones 2.00 .90
33 Danny Kanell 5.00 2.20
34 Jason Kendall 5.00 2.20
35 Pete Kendall 2.00 .90
36 Travis Knight 5.00 2.20
37 David LaFleur 2.00 .90
38 Jeff Lewis 2.00 .90
39 Stephon Marbury 10.00 4.50
40 Dave McCarty 2.00 .90
41 Walter McCarty 2.00 .90
42 Leeland McElroy 2.00 .90
43 Ray Mickens 2.00 .90
44 Jay Payton 2.00 .90
45 Vitaly Potapenko 2.00 .90
46 Trevor Pryce 2.00 .90
47 Efthimas Retzias 2.00 .90
48 Roy Rogers 2.00 .90
49 Malik Rose 2.00 .90
50 Darrell Russell 2.00 .90
51 Sergei Samsonov 10.00 4.50
52 Antowain Smith 10.00 4.50
54 Kurt Thomas 2.00 .90
55 Joe Thornton 10.00 4.50
56 Amani Toomer 5.00 2.20
57 Antoine Walker 10.00 4.50
58 John Wallace 5.00 2.20
59 Bryant Westbrook 2.00 .90
60 Jerome Williams 2.00 .90
61 Stepfret Williams 2.00 .90
62 Paul Wilson 2.00 .90
63 Kerry Wood 20.00 9.00
64 Lorenzen Wright 2.00 .90
65 Dainius Zubrus 5.00 2.20
66 Andrei Zyuzin 2.00 .90

1997 Visions Signings Artistry *

The cards in this 20-card set feature Score Board's "exclusive printing technology" and were inserted at a rate of 1:6 Vision Signings packs.

MINT NRMT
COMPLETE SET (20) 50.00 22.00
A1 Jose Cruz Jr. 1.50 .70
A2 Allen Iverson 8.00 3.60
A3 Marcus Camby 2.50 1.10
A4 Shareef Abdur-Rahim 2.50 1.10
A5 Stephon Marbury 2.50 1.10
A6 Ray Allen 5.00 2.20
A7 Antoine Walker 5.00 2.20
A8 Kobe Bryant 10.00 4.50
A9 Clyde Drexler 1.50 .70
A10 Scottie Pippen 1.50 .70
A11 Alonzo Mourning 1.50 .70
A12 Eddie George 4.00 1.80
A13 Warrick Dunn 2.50 1.10
A14 Darrell Russell 1.00 .45
A15 Peter Boulware 1.00 .45
A16 Shawn Springs 1.00 .45
A17 Yatil Green 1.00 .45
A18 Brett Favre 8.00 3.60
A19 Emmitt Smith 6.00 2.70
A20 Dainius Zubrus 1.00 .45

1997 Visions Signings Artistry Autographs *

These certified autographed cards feature Score Board's "exclusive printing technology" and were inserted at a rate of 1:18 packs. These 20 cards are autographed parallels of the Artistry insert set.

MINT NRMT
COMPLETE SET (20) 500.00 220.00
A1 Jose Cruz Jr. 8.00 3.60
A2 Allen Iverson 50.00 22.00
A3 Marcus Camby 15.00 6.75

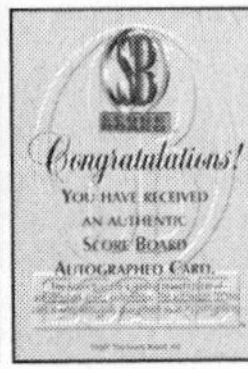

A4 Shareef Abdur-Rahim 15.00 6.75
A5 Stephon Marbury 20.00 9.00
A6 Ray Allen 25.00 11.00
A7 Antoine Walker 20.00 9.00
A8 Kobe Bryant 100.00 45.00
A9 Clyde Drexler 25.00 11.00
A10 Scottie Pippen 40.00 18.00
A11 Alonzo Mourning 20.00 9.00
A12 Eddie George 25.00 11.00
A13 Warrick Dunn 25.00 11.00
A14 Darrell Russell 8.00 3.60
A15 Peter Boulware 8.00 3.60
A16 Shawn Springs 8.00 3.60
A17 Yatil Green 8.00 3.60
A18 Brett Favre 120.00 55.00
A19 Emmitt Smith 100.00 45.00
A20 Dainius Zubrus 8.00 3.60

1956 Adventure R749 *

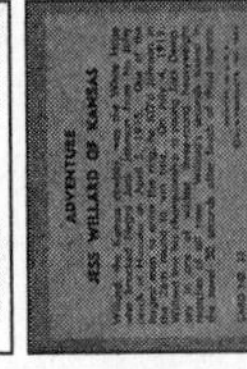

The Adventure series produced by Gum Products in 1956, contains a wide variety of subject matter. Cards in the set measure the standard size. The color drawings are printed on a heavy thickness of cardboard and have large white borders. The backs contain the card number, the caption, and a short text. The most expensive cards in the series of 100 are those associated with sports (Louis, Tunney, etc.). In addition, card number 86 (Schmelling) is notorious and sold at a premium price because of the Nazi symbol printed on the card. Although this set is considered by many to be a topical or non-sport set, several boxers are featured (cards 11, 22, 31-35, 41-44, 76-80, 86-90). One of the few cards of Boston-area legend Harry Agannis is in this set. The sports-related cards are in greater demand than the non-sport cards. These cards came in one-card penny packs where were packed 240 to a box.

NRMT VG-E
COMPLETE SET (100) 450.00 200.00
1 At The End Of 2.00 .90
Rainbow, Gold
2 The Porcupine 1.00 .45
Attack Proof
3 Indian Rope Trick 1.00 .45
Fake or Fact
4 Manolette 1.50 .70
Bullfighter Supreme
5 One Day Man 1.00 .45
Will Fly
6 The Space Man of 1.50 .70
the Future
7 The Greatest Show 1.00 .45
on Earth
8 Baskets and Rebounds 25.00 11.00
Makes Points
9 An Army of Ski 1.00 .45
Enthusiasts
10 Bobsledding 1.00 .45
Lake Placid Style
11 Willie Pep 8.00 3.60
12 Thousand-Thrill Sport 1.00 .45
13 Norkay 1.00 .45
Conqueror of Everest
14 Shy, Beautiful 1.00 .45
and Wild
15 Ivory Coast Snake 1.00 .45
Dance
16 Pan American 1.00 .45
Pacers Pant...
17 Devilfish and 1.00 .45
Child's Play
18 Over the Bounding 1.00 .45
Waves
19 A Tourist Paradise 1.00 .45
20 Not for Beginners 1.00 .45
21 Red-Stopper in Korea 1.00 .45
22 Sugar Ray Robinson 8.00 3.60
Bobo Olsen
23 Audie Murphy 5.00 2.20
Real Life Hero
24 Manning the Honest 1.00 .45
John ...
25 The Navy's Regulus 1.00 .45
26 Sunburns and Floor 1.00 .45
Burns
27 Bottlenosed Dolphin 1.00 .45
28 Mobile St. Bernards 1.00 .45
29 As American as the 1.00 .45
Hot Dog
30 Too Close for Comfort 1.00 .45
31 Tommy Burns 6.00 2.70
32 Jack Johnson 25.00 11.00
33 Jess Willard 12.00 5.50
34 Jack Dempsey 25.00 11.00
35 Gene Tunney 20.00 9.00
36 The Muskellunge 1.00 .45
Fighter
37 No Circus Stunt 1.00 .45
This ...
38 Dirt Track Hot-Rodders 3.00 1.35
39 One Down 1.00 .45
Zeros to Go
40 Mountain Climbing 1.00 .45
Monkey Style
41 Joe Louis 30.00 13.50
42 Ezzard Charles 8.00 3.60
43 Jersey Joe Walcott 12.00 5.50
44 Rocky Marciano 50.00 22.00
45 Rainmaking 1.00 .45
Scientific Magic
46 Aerial Torpedoes 1.00 .45
and Shellfire
47 The Stanley Steamer 1.00 .45
1906
48 Marquette and Priest 1.00 .45
Explorer
49 Skimming Over the Ice 2.00 .90
50 Happy Hunting 1.00 .45
Grounds ...
51 Boston's Skyline 2.00 .90
52 Racing 1.00 .45
With a Pinch of Salt
53 The Pilot Boat Pet 1.00 .45
54 Not All Pilots Fly 1.00 .45
55 Harry Agganis 20.00 9.00
56 Into the Air and Over 1.00 .45
57 Wedding of the 3.00 1.35
Year ... 1956
58 Leathernecks 1.00 .45
Courageous...
59 King of the Wild 1.50 .70
Frontier ...
60 The Navy's 1.00 .45
Flying Saucer
61 Flying at 3000 1.00 .45
Miles-an-Hour
62 Sitting on Top of 1.00 .45
the World
63 Hockey's Hardy 40.00 18.00
Perennials
Pictured are Chuck
Rayner and Gordie Howe
64 The Pintail Flyaway 1.00 .45
65 A Hunter's Dream 1.00 .45
Come True
66 British Navy 1.00 .45
African Style
67 Ride 'em Cowboy 1.00 .45
68 Breaking a Horse 1.00 .45
Cowboy Style
69 Shrine of Democracy 1.00 .45
70 Snowshoe Thompson 1.00 .45
Mailman
71 When a Feller 1.00 .45
Needs a Friend
72 A Fisherman's Life 1.50 .70
is Happy
73 The Groundhog's 1.00 .45
Northwest
74 In the Great 1.00 .45
Northwest
75 Famed for their 1.00 .45
Mimicry
76 John L.Sullivan 30.00 13.50
77 Jim Corbett 15.00 6.75
78 Bob Fitzsimmons 8.00 3.60
79 James J. Jeffries 8.00 3.60
80 Marvin Hart 6.00 2.70
81 Letting Loose on 1.50 .70
the Boards
82 A Boy's Best Friend 1.50 .70
83 The Ageless Sport 1.00 .45
84 Not Flying 1.00 .45
Just a-Jumpin'
85 Over Fence for New 1.00 .45
Record
86 Max Schmeling 200.00 90.00
Nazi Flag in Background
87 Jack Sharkey 6.00 2.70
88 Primo Carnera 6.00 2.70
89 Max Baer 8.00 3.60
90 James J. Braddock 6.00 2.70
91 Dead Heat-All 1.00 .45
the Way
92 Bob Mathias 6.00 2.70
Superman
93 First to Clear 2.00 .90
7-Foot Barrier
94 The Northern Light 1.00 .45
95 Alone with Gulls 1.00 .45
and Sea
96 Scramble, Men, 1.00 .45
Scramble
97 Cameramen 1.00 .45
Nervy Humans
98 Sea Firefighters- 1.00 .45
Lifesavers
99 Rusty Bacon at 1.00 .45
10 Dollars per Pound
100 Conestoga 1.50 .70
Pioneer Transport

1887 Allen and Ginter N28 *

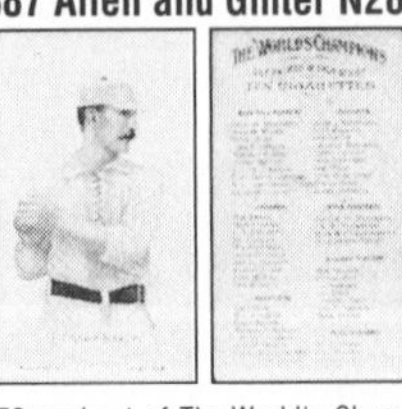

This 50-card set of The World's Champions was marketed by Allen and Ginter in 1887. The cards feature color lithographs of champion athletes from seven categories of sport, with baseball, rowing and boxing each having 10 individuals portrayed. Cards numbered 1 to 10 depict baseball players and cards numbered 11 to 20 depict popular boxers of the era. This set is called the first series although no such title appears on the cards. All 50 cards are checklisted on the reverse, and they are unnumbered. An album (catalog: A16) and an advertising banner (catalog: G20) were also issued in conjunction with this set.

EX-MT VG-E
COMPLETE SET (50) 10000.00 4500.00
1 Adrian C. Anson 2500.00 1100.00
2 Chas. W. Bennett 300.00 135.00
3 Robert L. Caruthers 400.00 180.00
4 John Clarkson 600.00 275.00
5 Charles Comiskey 1000.00 450.00
6 Capt.Jack Glasscock 400.00 180.00
7 Timothy Keefe 1000.00 450.00
8 Mike Kelly 1200.00 550.00
9 Joseph Mulvey 300.00 135.00
10 John M. Ward 1000.00 450.00
11 Jimmy Carney 125.00 55.00
12 Jimmy Carroll 125.00 55.00
13 Jack Dempsey 200.00 90.00
14 Jake Kilrain 150.00 70.00
15 Joe Lannon 125.00 55.00
16 Jack McAuliffe 125.00 55.00
17 Charlie Mitchell 150.00 70.00
18 Jem Smith 125.00 55.00
19 John L. Sullivan 400.00 180.00
20 Ike Weir 125.00 55.00
21 Wm. Beach 50.00 22.00
22 Geo. Bubear 50.00 22.00
23 Jacob Gaudaub 50.00 22.00
24 Albert Hamm 50.00 22.00
25 Ed. Hanlan 60.00 27.00
26 Geo. H. Hosmer 50.00 22.00
27 John McKay 50.00 22.00
28 Wallace Ross 50.00 22.00
29 John Teemer 50.00 22.00
30 E.A. Trickett 50.00 22.00
31 Joe Acton 80.00 36.00
32 Theo. Bauer 80.00 36.00
33 Young Bibby 100.00 45.00
(Geo. Mehling)
34 J.F. McLaughlin 80.00 36.00
35 John McMahon 80.00 36.00
36 Wm. Muldoon 100.00 45.00
37 Matsada Sorakichi 80.00 36.00
38 Capt. A.H. Bogardus 50.00 22.00
39 Dr. W.F. Carver 50.00 22.00
40 Hon. W.F. Cody 250.00 110.00
(Buffalo Bill)
41 Miss Annie Oakley 250.00 110.00
42 Yank Adams 75.00 34.00
43 Maurice Daly 75.00 34.00
44 Jos. Dion 75.00 34.00
45 J. Schaefer 75.00 34.00
46 Wm. Sexton 75.00 34.00
47 Geo. F. Slosson 75.00 34.00
48 M. Vignaux 75.00 34.00
49 Albert Frey 75.00 34.00
50 J.L. Malone 75.00 34.00

1888 Allen and Ginter N29 *

The second series of The World's Champions was probably issued in 1888. Like the first series, the cards are backlisted and unnumbered. However, there are 17 distinct categories of sports represented in this set, with only six baseball players portrayed (as opposed to 10 in the first series). Each card has a color lithograph of the individual set against a white background. An album (catalog: A17) and an advertising banner (catalog: G21) were issued in conjunction with the set. The numbering below is alphabetical within sport, e.g., baseball players (1-6), boxers (7-14), and other sports (15-50).

EX-MT VG-E
COMPLETE SET (50) 10000.00 4500.00
1 Wm.(Buck) Ewing 1200.00 550.00
2 Jas. H. Fogarty 700.00 325.00
3 Charles H. Getzien 700.00 325.00
4 Geo.F.(Doggie) Miller 700.00 325.00
5 John Morrell 700.00 325.00
6 James Ryan 800.00 350.00
7 Patsey Duffy 250.00 110.00
8 Billy Edwards 250.00 110.00
9 Jack Havlin 250.00 110.00
10 Patsey Kerrigan 250.00 110.00
11 George LaBlance 250.00 110.00
12 Jack McGee 250.00 110.00
13 Frank Murphy 250.00 110.00
14 Johnny Murphy 250.00 110.00
15 Capt. J.C. Daly 100.00 45.00
16 M.W. Ford 100.00 45.00
17 Duncan C. Ross 100.00 45.00
18 W.E. Crist 100.00 45.00
19 H.G. Crocker 100.00 45.00
20 Willie Harradon 100.00 45.00
21 F.F. Ives 100.00 45.00
22 Wm. A. Rowe 100.00 45.00
23 Percy Stone 100.00 45.00
24 Ralph Temple 100.00 45.00
25 Fred Wood 100.00 45.00
26 Dr. James Dwight 120.00 55.00
27 Thomas Pettit 120.00 55.00
28 R.D. Sears 120.00 55.00
29 H.W. Slocum Jr. 120.00 55.00
30 Theobaud Bauer 120.00 55.00
31 Edwin Bibby 120.00 55.00
32 Hugh McCormack 100.00 45.00
33 Axel Paulsen 100.00 45.00
34 T. Ray 100.00 45.00
35 C.W.V. Clarke 100.00 45.00
36 E.D. Lange 100.00 45.00
37 E.C. Carter 100.00 45.00
38 Wm. Cummings 100.00 45.00
39 W.G. George 100.00 45.00
40 L.E. Myers 100.00 45.00
41 James Albert 100.00 45.00
42 Patrick Fitzgerald 100.00 45.00
43 W.B. Page 100.00 45.00
44 C.A.J. Queckberner 100.00 45.00
45 W.J.M. Barry 100.00 45.00
46 Wm. G. East 100.00 45.00
47 Wm. O'Connor 100.00 45.00
48 Gus Hill 100.00 45.00
49 Capt. Paul Boyton 100.00 45.00
50 Capt. Matthew Webb

1888 Allen and Ginter N43 *

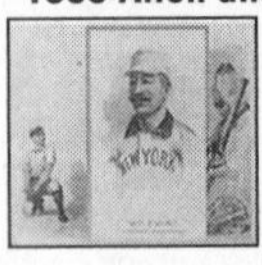

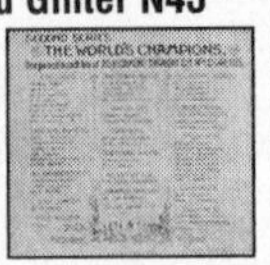

The primary designs of this 50-card set are identical to those of N29, but these are placed on a much larger card with extraneous background detail. The set was produced in 1888 by Allen and Ginter as inserts for a larger tobacco package than those in which sets N28 and N29 were marketed. Cards of this set, which is backlisted, are considered to be much scarcer than their counterparts in N29.

EX-MT VG-E
COMPLETE SET (50) 18000.00 8100.00
1 William(Buck) Ewing 2500.00 1100.00
2 Jas. J. Fogarty 1200.00 550.00
3 Charles H. Getzien 1200.00 550.00
4 Geo.F.(Doggie) Miller 1200.00 550.00
5 John Morrell 1200.00 550.00
6 James Ryan 1500.00 700.00
7 Patsey Duffy 500.00 220.00
8 Billy Edwards 500.00 220.00
9 Jack Havlin 500.00 220.00
10 Patsey Kerrigan 500.00 220.00
11 George LaBlanche 500.00 220.00
12 Jack McGee 500.00 220.00
13 Frank Murphy 500.00 220.00
14 Johnny Murphy 500.00 220.00
15 Capt. J.C. Daly 150.00 70.00
16 M.W. Ford 150.00 70.00
17 Duncan C. Ross 150.00 70.00
18 W.E. Crist 150.00 70.00
19 H.G. Crocker 150.00 70.00
20 Willie Harradon 150.00 70.00
21 F.F. Ives 150.00 70.00
22 Wm. A. Rowe 150.00 70.00
23 Percy Stone 150.00 70.00
24 Ralph Temple 150.00 70.00
25 Fred Wood 150.00 70.00
26 Dr. James Dwight 200.00 90.00
27 Thomas Pettitt 200.00 90.00
28 R.D. Sears 200.00 90.00
29 H.W. Slocum Jr. 200.00 90.00
30 Theobaud Bauer 200.00 90.00
31 Edwin Bibby 200.00 90.00
32 Hugh McCormack 150.00 70.00
33 Axel. Paulsen 150.00 70.00
34 T. Ray 150.00 70.00
35 C.W.V. Clarke 150.00 70.00
36 E.D. Lange 150.00 70.00
37 E.C. Carter 150.00 70.00
38 Wm. Cummings 150.00 70.00
39 W.G. George 150.00 70.00
40 L.E. Myers 150.00 70.00
41 James Albert 150.00 70.00
42 Patrick Fitzgerald 150.00 70.00
43 W.B. Page 150.00 70.00
44 C.A.J. Queckberner 150.00 70.00
45 W.J.M. Barry 150.00 70.00
46 Wm. G. East 150.00 70.00
47 Wm. O'Connor 150.00 70.00
48 Gus Hill 150.00 70.00
49 Capt. Paul Boyton 150.00 70.00
50 Capt. Matthew Webb

1968 American Oil Winners Circle*

This set of 12 perforated game cards measures approximately 2 5/8" by 2 1/8". There are "left side" and "right side" game cards which had to be matched to win a car or a cash prize. The "right side" game cards have a color drawing of a sports personality in a circle on the left, surrounded by laurel leaf twigs, and a short career summary on the right. There is a color bar on the bottom of the game piece carrying a dollar amount and the words "right side". The "left side" game cards carry a rectangular drawing of a sports personality or a photo of a Camaro or a Corvette. A different color bar with a dollar amount and the words "left side" are under the picture. On a dark blue background, the "right side" backs carry the rules of the game, and the "left side" cards show a "Winners Circle". The cards are unnumbered and checklisted below in alphabetical order.

NRMT VG-E
COMPLETE SET (12) 150.00 70.00
1 Julius Boros 5.00 2.20
right side
2 Gay Brewer 5.00 2.20
left side
3 Camaro 3.00 1.35
left side
4 Corvette 3.00 1.35
left side
5 Damascus 3.00 1.35
right side
6 Parnelli Jones 5.00 2.20
left side
7 Mickey Mantle 50.00 22.00
left side
8 Willie Mays 30.00 13.50
right side
9 Bob Richards 5.00 2.20
left side
10 Babe Ruth 50.00 22.00
right side
11 Gale Sayers 15.00 6.75
left side
12 Bart Starr 20.00 9.00
right side

1993 Anti-Gambling Postcards *

Measuring 5" by 7", these 13 postcards were produced and distributed to be sent to state and federal legislators to express the voters opinion on sports team based lotteries. The fronts feature color player photos, along with the league logo for the appropriate sport, the player's name and the words "Don't Gamble With Our Childrens' Heroes. Stop State-Sponsored Sports Betting". The backs have an area for comments and voter information, as well as an address area. The player's name, position, sport and team are printed across the comment section. The postcards are unnumbered and checklisted below in alphabetical order according to sports as follows: baseball (1-5), basketball (6-8), football (9-10), hockey (11-12), and tennis (13).

MINT NRMT
COMPLETE SET (13) 20.00 9.00
1 Will Clark 2.50 1.10
2 Glenn Davis 1.00 .45
3 Dennis Eckersley 2.00 .90
4 Dave Stewart 1.50 .70
5 Bob Welch 1.00 .45
6 Alex English 1.50 .70
7 Alvin Robertson 1.00 .45
8 Buck Williams 1.50 .70
9 Jim Kelly 2.50 1.10
10 Bernie Kosar 2.00 .90
11 Chris Chelios 2.50 1.10
12 Andy Moog 2.00 .90
13 Pam Shriver 2.00 .90

1991 Arena Holograms 12th National *

These standard-size cards have on their fronts a 3-D silver-colored emblem on a white background with orange borders. Though the back of each card salutes a different superstar, the players themselves are not pictured; instead, one finds pictures of a football; hockey stick and puck; basketball; and baseball in glove respectively. The cards are numbered on the front.

MINT NRMT
COMPLETE SET (4) 10.00 4.50
1 Joe Montana 3.00 1.35
2 Wayne Gretzky 3.00 1.35
3 Michael Jordan 5.00 2.20
4 Nolan Ryan 4.00 1.80

1991 Arena Holograms *

The 1991 Arena Hologram cards were distributed through hobby dealers and feature famous athletes. According to Arena, production quantities were limited to 250,000 of each card. The standard-size hologram cards have on the horozontially oriented backs a color photo of the player in a tuxedo. Ken Griffey Jr. Frank Thomas, David Robinson, Joe Montana and Barry Sanders all signed cards with each being serial numbered by hand. A card-sized certificate of authenticity was also issued with each signed card.

MINT NRMT
COMPLETE SET (5) 8.00 3.60
1 Joe Montana 2.00 .90
2 Ken Griffey Jr. 2.00 .90
3 Frank Thomas 1.50 .70
4 Barry Sanders 1.50 .70
5 David Robinson 1.00 .45
AU2 Ken Griffey Jr. AU/1000 75.00 34.00
AU3 Frank Thomas AU/1250 40.00 18.00
AU4 Barry Sanders AU/1000 75.00 34.00
AU5 David Robinson AU/250 75.00 34.00
AU6 Joe Montana AU/2500 75.00 34.00

1978 Atlanta Convention *

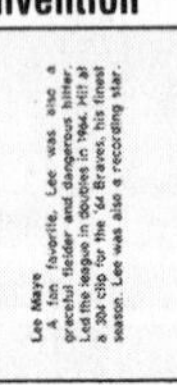

This 24-card standard-size set features circular black-and-white player photos framed in light green and bordered in white. The player's name is printed in black across the top with his position, team name, and logo at the bottom. The white backs carry the player's name and career information. The cards are unnumbered and checklisted below in alphabetical order. Almost all of the players in this set played for the Braves at one time.

NRMT VG-E
COMPLETE SET (24) 15.00 6.75
1 Hank Aaron 5.00 2.20

2 Joe Adcock .50 .23
3 Felipe Alou 1.00 .45
4 Frank Bolling .25 .11
5 Orlando Cepeda 1.50 .70
6 Ty Cline .25 .11
7 Tony Cloninger .25 .11
8 Del Crandall .25 .11
9 Fred Haney MG .25 .11
10 Pat Jarvis .25 .11
11 Ernie Johnson .50 .23
12 Ken Johnson .25 .11
13 Denver Lemaster .25 .11
14 Eddie Mathews 1.50 .70
15 Lee Maye .25 .11
16 Denis Menke .25 .11
17 Felix Millan .25 .11
18 Johnny Mize 1.50 .70
19 Tommy Nobis 1.50 .70
20 Gene Oliver .25 .11
21 Johnny Sain .50 .23
22 Warren Spahn 1.50 .70
23 Joe Torre 1.00 .45
24 Bob Turley .50 .23

1988 Athletes in Action *

The set features six Texas Rangers (1-6) and six Dallas Cowboys (7-12). The cards are standard size, 2 1/2" by 3 1/2". The fronts display color action player photos bordered in white. The words "Athletes in Action" are printed in black across the lower edge of the picture. The backs carry a player quote, a salvation message, and the player's favorite Scripture.

	MINT	NRMT
COMPLETE SET (12)	8.00	3.60
1 Pete O'Brien	.50	.23
2 Scott Fletcher	.50	.23
3 Oddibe McDowell	.50	.23
4 Steve Buechele	.50	.23
5 Jerry Browne	.50	.23
6 Larry Parrish	.50	.23
7 Tom Landry CO	2.50	1.10
8 Steve Pelluer	.50	.23
9 Gordon Banks	.50	.23
10 Bill Bates	1.00	.45
11 Doug Cosbie	.75	.35
12 Herschel Walker	1.50	.70

1994 Australian Futera NBL Promos *

This five-card cello-wrapped promo pack was given away at the 1994 National Sports Collectors Convention in Houston. Measuring the standard size, the fronts display full-bleed color action photos. Each card of the set is serially-numbered out of 5,000 sets produced. The cards are numbered on the back in gold foil in the upper right corner.

	MINT	NRMT
COMPLETE SET (5)	6.00	2.70
RC1 Allan Border (Cricket)	.75	.35
RC2 Conan Hayes (Surfing)	.75	.35
RC3 David Nilsson BB	2.50	1.10
RC4 Mark Bosnich (Soccer)	.75	.35
RC5 Andrew Gaze BK	2.50	1.10

1945 Autographs Playing Cards*

Cards from this set are part of a playing card game released in 1945 by Leister Game Co. of Toledo Ohio. The cards feature a photo of a famous person, such as an actor or writer, or athlete on the top half of the card with his signature across the middle. A photo appears in the upper left hand corner along with some biographical information about him printed in orange in the center. The bottom half of the cardfront features a drawing along with information about a second personality in the same field or vocation. Those two characters are featured on another card with the positions reversed top and bottom. Note that a card number was also used in the upper left corner with each pair being featured on two of the same card number. We've listed the player who's photo appears on the card first, followed by the personality featured at the bottom of the card.

	MINT	NRMT
COMPLETE SET (55)		
1 Lily Pons / Grace Moore	5.00	2.20
1 Grace Moore / Lily Pons	5.00	2.20
1A H.V. Kaltenborn / Lowell Thomas	5.00	2.20
1A Lowell Thomas / H.V. Kaltenborn	5.00	2.20
2 Jack Dempsey / Joe Louis	30.00	13.50
2 Joe Louis / Jack Dempsey	30.00	13.50
2A John Charles Thomas / Lauritz Melchoir	5.00	2.20
2A Lauritz Melchoir / John Charles Thomas	5.00	2.20
3 Kate Smith / Dinah Shore	10.00	4.50
3 Dinah Shore / Kate Smith	10.00	4.50
3A Clark Gable / Gary Cooper	25.00	11.00
3A Gary Cooper / Clark Gable	25.00	11.00
4 Bob Hope / Jack Benny	30.00	13.50
4 Jack Benny / Bob Hope	30.00	13.50
4A Bing Crosby / Frank Sinatra	30.00	13.50
4A Frank Sinatra / Bing Crosby	30.00	13.50
5 Dorothy Lamour / Claudette Colbert	15.00	6.75
5 Claudette Colbert / Dorothy Lamour	15.00	6.75
5A Irving Berlin / Jerome Kern	10.00	4.50
5A Jerome Kern / Irving Berlin	10.00	4.50
6 Walter Damrosch / Arturo Toscanini	5.00	2.20
6 Arturo Toscanini / Walter Damrosch	5.00	2.20
6A Kay Kyser / Paul Whiteman	5.00	2.20
6A Paul Whiteman / Kay Kyser	5.00	2.20
7 Byron Nelson / Walter Hagen	25.00	11.00
7 Walter Hagen / Byron Nelson	25.00	11.00
7A Bernie Bierman CO / Knute Rockne CO	20.00	9.00
7A Knute Rockne CO / Bernie Bierman	20.00	9.00
8 Robert Benchley / Irwin S. Cobb	5.00	2.20
8 Irwin S. Cobb / Robert Benchley	5.00	2.20
8A Franklin Roosevelt / Thomas E. Dewey	20.00	9.00
8A Thomas E. Dewey / Franklin Roosevelt	20.00	9.00
9 Dwight D. Eisenhower / Douglas MacArthur	25.00	11.00
9 Douglas MacArthur / Dwight D. Eisenhower	25.00	11.00
9A Joe DiMaggio / Babe Ruth	40.00	18.00
9A Babe Ruth / Joe DiMaggio	40.00	18.00
10 Red Grange / Tom Harmon	25.00	11.00
10 Tom Harmon / Red Grange	25.00	11.00
10A Don Budge / Bill Tilden	20.00	9.00
10A Bill Tilden / Don Budge	20.00	9.00
11 Joan Davis / Fanny Brice	5.00	2.20
11 Fanny Brice / Joan Davis	5.00	2.20
11A Katherine Cornell / Helen Hayes	15.00	6.75
11A Helen Hayes / Katherine Cornell	15.00	6.75
12 Ernie Pyle / Westbrook Pegler	5.00	2.20
12 Westbrook Pegler / Ernie Pyle	5.00	2.20
12A John Lewis / William Green	5.00	2.20
12A William Green / John Lewis	5.00	2.20
13 Bill Stern / Ted Husing	5.00	2.20
13 Ted Husing / Bill Stern	5.00	2.20
13A Roy Rogers / Gene Autry	20.00	9.00
13A Gene Autry / Roy Rogers	20.00	9.00
NNO Holding the Bag Cover Card	5.00	2.20
NNO Holding the Bag Rule Card	5.00	2.20
NNO Sgt. Edwin Rowlands / Autograph Collector	5.00	2.20

1932 C.A.Briggs Chocolate *

This set was issued by C.A. Brigss Chocolate company in 1932. The cards feature 31-different sports with each card including an artist's rendering of a sporting event. Although players are not named, it is thought that most were modeled after famous athletes of the time. The cardbacks include a written portion about the sport and an offer from Briggs for free baseball equipment for building a compete set of cards.

	EX-MT	VG-E
8 Basketball	250.00	110.00
11 Football (thought to be Red Grange)	1200.00	550.00
24 Baseball (thought to be Babe Ruth)	1500.00	700.00
25 Golf (thought to be Gene Sarazen)	250.00	110.00

1995 Classic National *

This 20-card multi-sport set was issued by Classic to commemorate the 16th National Sports Collectors Convention in St. Louis. The set included a certificate of limited edition, with the serial number out of 9,995 sets produced. One thousand Sprint 20-minute phone cards featuring Ki-Jana Carter were also distributed.

	MINT	NRMT
COMPLETE SET (20)	20.00	9.00
NC1 Shaquille O'Neal	5.00	2.20
NC2 Emmitt Smith	4.00	1.80
NC3 Troy Aikman	2.50	1.10
NC4 Dale Earnhardt	5.00	2.20
NC5 Nolan Ryan	4.00	1.80
NC6 Steve Young	2.00	.90
NC7 Glenn Robinson	.50	.23
NC8 Marshall Faulk	2.00	.90
NC9 Jason Kidd	2.50	1.10
NC10 Drew Bledsoe	2.00	.90
NC11 Ki-Jana Carter	.50	.23
NC12 Kerry Collins	1.00	.45
NC13 Barry Bonds	3.00	1.35
NC14 Alonzo Mourning	1.50	.70
NC15 Manon Rheaume	2.00	.90
NC16 Joe Smith	.50	.23
NC17 Rasheed Wallace	1.00	.45
NC18 Ed O'Bannon	.50	.23
NC19 Corliss Williamson	.50	.23
NC20 Checklist	.50	.23
NNO Ki-Jana Carter (Phone Card)	2.00	.90

1992 Classic Show Promos 20 *

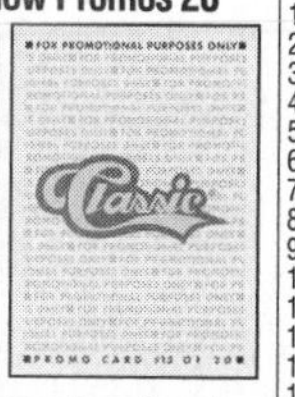

This 20-card standard-size set was issued one card at a time at the various shows throughout the year where Classic maintained a presence or booth. Typically the cards were given out free to attendees while supplies lasted. The cards all read "Promo Card x of 20" prominently on the card back. The cards are done in several different styles depending on the Classic issue that was being promoted by that particular card.

	MINT	NRMT
COMPLETE SET (20)	30.00	13.50
1 Billy Owens (1992 Sports Spectacular) Syracuse	.50	.23
2 Dikembe Mutombo (1992 SportsNet National) Georgetown	.75	.35
3 Brien Taylor (1992 SportsNet National) New York Yankees	.50	.23
4 David Klingler (1992 Sports Spectacular) Houston	.50	.23
5 Carl Lewis (July 1992 Arlington Marcus show)	1.50	.70
6 Quentin Coryatt (July 1992 Arlington Marcus show)	.50	.23
7 Brien Taylor (1992 Atlanta National Convention) New York Yankees	.50	.23
8 Frankie Rodriguez (1992 Atlanta National Convention) Boston Red Sox	.50	.23
9 Jimmy Jackson (July 9-12, 1992 at Atlanta National)	1.00	.45
10 Ken Griffey Jr. (July 9-12, 1992 at Atlanta National) Seattle Mariners	3.00	1.35
11 Shaquille O'Neal (July 9-12, 1992 at Atlanta National) LSU	5.00	2.20
12 Alonzo Mourning (July 9-12, 1992 at Atlanta National) Georgetown	2.00	.90
13 Christian Laettner (1992 East Coast National) Duke	.75	.35
14 Nolan Ryan (1992 East Coast National) Texas Rangers	5.00	2.20
15 Roman Hamrlik (1992 Tri-Star St. Louis)	.50	.23
16 Phil Nevin (1992 Tri-Star St. Louis) Cal State-Fullerton	2.00	.90
17 Shaquille O'Neal (1992 Tri-Star St. Louis)	5.00	2.20
18 David Klingler (1992 Tri-Star Houston) Houston	.50	.23
19 Phil Nevin (1992 Tri-Star Houston) Cal State-Fullerton	2.00	.90
20 Harold Miner (1992 Tri-Star Houston) USC	.50	.23

1993 Classic Superheroes *

This purple-bordered three-card standard-size subset features the art work of Neal Adams, who has produced sports and comics fantasy cards of various athletes. It is one of two insert sets included (randomly inserted) in Classic's Deathwatch 2,000 110-card set. The horizontal backs carry a color action player photo with a player profile on a purple background.

	MINT	NRMT
COMPLETE SET (3)	20.00	9.00
SS1 Shaquille O'Neal	8.00	3.60
SS2 Manon Rheaume	8.00	3.60
SS3 Ken Griffey Jr.	8.00	3.60

1935 Detroit Free Press *

This newsprint set of the 1935 Detroit Tigers and one boxer measures approximately 9" by 11" and was within the "The Detroit Free Press." The cards are unnumbered and checklisted below in alphabetical order. One boxer -- Joe Lewis is known to be issued as part of this set.

	EX-MT	VG-E
COMPLETE SET	325.00	145.00
1 Eldon Auker	10.00	4.50
2 Del Baker CO	10.00	4.50
3 Tommy Bridges	15.00	6.75
4 Flea Clifton	10.00	4.50
5 Mickey Cochrane	25.00	11.00
6 General Crowder	10.00	4.50
7 Frank Doljack	10.00	4.50
8 Carl Fischer	10.00	4.50
9 Pete Fox	10.00	4.50
10 Charlie Gehringer	20.00	9.00
11 Goose Goslin	20.00	9.00
12 Hank Greenberg	25.00	11.00
13 Luke Hamlin	10.00	4.50
14 Ray Hayworth	10.00	4.50
15 Chief Hogsett	10.00	4.50
16 Joe Lewis (Heavyweight Boxer)	50.00	22.00
17 Firpo Marberry	10.00	4.50
18 Marvin Owen	10.00	4.50
19 Cy Perkins	10.00	4.50
20 Bill Rogell	10.00	4.50
21 Schoolboy Rowe	15.00	6.75
22 Heinie Schuble	10.00	4.50
23 Victor Sorrell	10.00	4.50
24 Joe Sullivan	10.00	4.50
25 Gee Walker	10.00	4.50
26 Jo-Jo White	10.00	4.50

1972-83 Dimanche/Derniere Heure *

The blank-backed photo sheets in this multi-sport set measure approximately 8 1/2" by 11" and feature white-bordered color sports star photos from Dimanche Derniere Heure, a Montreal newspaper. The player's name, position and biographical information appear within the lower white margin. All text is in French. A white vinyl album was available for storing the photo sheets. Printed on the album's spine are the words, "Mes Vedettes du Sport" (My Stars of Sport).The photos are unnumbered and are checklisted below in alphabetical order according to sport or team as follows: Montreal Expos baseball players (1-117; National League baseball players (118-130); Montreal Canadiens hockey players (131-177); wrestlers (178-202); prize fighters (203-204); auto racing drivers (205-208); women's golf (209); Patof the circus clown (210); and CFL (211-278).

	NRMT	VG-E
COMPLETE SET (278)	800.00	350.00
1 Santo Alcala	2.00	.90
2 Bill Almon	2.00	.90
3 Bill Atkinson	2.00	.90
4 Stan Bahnsen	2.00	.90
5 Bob Bailey	2.00	.90
6 Greg Bargar	2.00	.90
7 Tony Bernazard	2.00	.90
8 Tim Blackwell	2.00	.90
9 Dennis Blair	2.00	.90
10 John Boccabella	2.50	1.10
11 Jim Brewer CO	2.00	.90
12 Hal Breeden	2.00	.90
13 Dave Bristol CO	2.00	.90
14 Jackie Brown	2.50	1.10
15 Ray Burris	2.00	.90
16 Don Carrithers	2.00	.90
17 Gary Carter	15.00	6.75
18 Dave Cash	2.00	.90
19 Jim Cox	2.00	.90
20 Warren Cromartie	2.00	.90
21 Terry Crowley	2.00	.90
22 Willie Davis	3.00	1.35
23 Andre Dawson	10.00	4.50
24 Boots Day UER (Reversed Negative)	2.00	.90
25 Don Demola	2.00	.90
26 Larry Doby CO	4.00	1.80
27 Hal Dues	2.00	.90
28 Duffy Dyer	2.00	.90
29 Jim Fairey	2.00	.90
30 Ron Fairly	3.00	1.35
31 Jim Fanning MG	2.00	.90
32 Doug Flynn	2.00	.90
33 Tim Foli	2.50	1.10
34 Barry Foote	2.00	.90
35 Barry Foote (Wearing chest protector and shin guards)	2.00	.90
36 Terry Francona	2.50	1.10
37 Pepe Frias	2.00	.90
38 Woodie Fryman	2.00	.90
39 Woodie Fryman / Jeff Reardon	2.50	1.10
40 Mike Garman	2.00	.90
41 Wayne Garrett	2.00	.90
42 Ross Grimsley	2.00	.90
43 Bill Gullickson	2.00	.90
44 Ed Herrmann	2.00	.90
45 Terry Humphrey	2.00	.90
46 Ron Hunt	2.50	1.10
47 Tommy Hutton	2.00	.90
48 Bob James	2.00	.90
49 Wallace Johnson	2.00	.90
50 Mike Jorgensen	2.00	.90
51 Joe Kerrigan	2.00	.90
52 Darold Knowles	2.00	.90
53 Coco Laboy	2.50	1.10
54 Charles Lea	2.00	.90
55 Bill Lee	2.50	1.10
56 Ron LeFlore	2.50	1.10
57 Larry Lintz	2.00	.90
58 Bryan Little	2.00	.90
59 Ken Macha	2.00	.90
60 Jerry Manuel	2.50	1.10
61 Mike Marshall	3.00	1.35
62 Clyde Mashore	2.00	.90
63 Jim Mason	2.00	.90
64 Gene Mauch MG	3.00	1.35
65 Rudy May	2.00	.90
66 Ernie McAnally	2.00	.90
67 Tim McCarver	4.00	1.80
68 Cal McLish CO	2.00	.90
69 Sam Mejias	2.00	.90
70 John Milner	2.00	.90
71 John Montague	2.00	.90
72 Willie Montanez	2.00	.90
73 Balor Moore	2.00	.90
74 Jose Morales	2.00	.90
75 Dan Norman	2.00	.90
76 Fred Norman	2.00	.90
77 Al Oliver	4.00	1.80
78 David Palmer	2.00	.90
79 Stan Papi	2.00	.90
80 Larry Parrish	2.50	1.10
81 Tony Perez	4.00	1.80
82 Tim Raines	4.00	1.80
83 Tim Raines / Andre Dawson / Warren Cromartie	4.00	1.80
84 Bobby Ramos	2.00	.90
85 Bob Reece	2.00	.90
86 Steve Renko	2.00	.90
87 Steve Rogers	3.00	1.35
88 Angel Salazar	2.00	.90
89 Scott Sanderson	2.00	.90
90 Dan Schatzeder	2.00	.90
91 Rodney Scott	2.00	.90
92 Norm Sherry CO	2.00	.90
93 Ken Singleton	2.50	1.10
94 Tony Solaita	2.00	.90
95 Elias Sosa	2.00	.90
96 Chris Speier	2.00	.90
97 Don Stanhouse	2.00	.90
98 Mike Stenhouse	2.00	.90
99 Bill Stoneman	2.50	1.10
100 John Strohmayer	2.00	.90
101 John Tamargo	2.00	.90
102 Frank Taveres	2.00	.90
103 Chuck Taylor	2.00	.90
104 Jeff Terpko	2.00	.90
105 Hector Torres	2.00	.90
106 Mike Torrez	2.50	1.10
107 Wayne Twitchell	2.00	.90
108 Del Unser	2.00	.90
109 Ellis Valentine	2.00	.90
110 Mickey Vernon CO	2.50	1.10
111 Bill Virdon MG	2.50	1.10
112 Tom Walker	2.00	.90
113 Tim Wallach	2.00	.90
114 Dan Warthen	2.00	.90
115 Jerry White	2.00	.90
116 Dick Williams MG	3.00	1.35
117 Bobby Wine	2.00	.90
118 Jim Wohlford	2.00	.90
119 Ron Woods	2.00	.90
120 Joel Youngblood	2.00	.90
121 Hank Aaron	10.00	4.50
122 Johnny Bench	6.00	2.70
123 Larry Bowa	2.50	1.10
124 Steve Carlton	4.00	1.80
125 Roberto Clemente	10.00	4.50
126 Willie Davis	2.00	.90
127 Bob Gibson	4.00	1.80
128 Ferguson Jenkins	4.00	1.80
129 Willie McCovey	4.00	1.80
130 Willie Montanez	2.00	.90
131 Pete Rose	8.00	3.60
132 Willie Stargell	4.00	1.80
133 Rusty Staub / Mike Jorgensen	3.00	1.35
134 Chuck Arnason	2.50	1.10
135 Jean Beliveau VP	4.00	1.80
136 Pierre Bouchard (Action)	2.50	1.10
137 Pierre Bouchard (Posed)	2.50	1.10
138 Scotty Bowman CO	4.00	1.80
139 Yvan Cournoyer (Action)	4.00	1.80
140 Yvan Cournoyer (Posed)	4.00	1.80
141 Ken Dryden	10.00	4.50
142 Bob Gainey	4.00	1.80
143 Dale Hoganson	2.50	1.10
144 Rejean Houle	3.00	1.35
145 Guy Lafleur (Action)	10.00	4.50
146 Guy Lafleur (Posed)	10.00	4.50
147 Yvon Lambert	3.00	1.35
148 Jacques Laperriere (Action)	4.00	1.80
149 Jacques Laperriere (Posed)	4.00	1.80
150 Guy Lapointe (Action)	4.00	1.80
151 Guy Lapointe (Posed)	4.00	1.80
152 Michel Larocque	4.00	1.80

153 Claude Larose 3.00 1.35
(Action)
154 Claude Larose 3.00 1.35
(Posed)
155 Chuck Lefley 2.50 1.10
(Action)
156 Chuck Lefley 2.50 1.10
(Posed)
157 Jacques Lemaire 4.00 1.80
(Action)
158 Jacques Lemaire 4.00 1.80
(Posed)
159 Frank Mahovlich 6.00 2.70
(Action)
160 Frank Mahovlich 6.00 2.70
(Posed)
161 Pete Mahovlich 3.00 1.35
(Action)
162 Pete Mahovlich 3.00 1.35
(Posed)
163 Bob J. Murdoch 2.50 1.10
164 Michel Plasse 4.00 1.80
(Action)
165 Michel Plasse 4.00 1.80
(Posed)
166 Henri Richard 6.00 2.70
(Action)
167 Henri Richard 6.00 2.70
(Posed)
168 Jim Roberts 3.00 1.35
(Action)
169 Jim Roberts 3.00 1.35
(Posed)
170 Larry Robinson 6.00 2.70
(Action)
171 Larry Robinson 6.00 2.70
(Posed)
172 Serge Savard 4.00 1.80
(Action)
173 Serge Savard 4.00 1.80
(Posed)
174 Steve Shutt 4.00 1.80
(Action)
175 Steve Shutt 4.00 1.80
(Posed)
176 Marc Tardif 3.00 1.35
177 Wayne Thomas 3.00 1.35
(Action)
178 Wayne Thomas 3.00 1.35
(Posed)
179 Murray Wilson 2.50 1.10
(Action)
180 Murray Wilson 2.50 1.10
(Posed)
181 The Assassins 2.00 .90
182 Dino Bravo 4.00 1.80
Gino Brito
183 Edouard Carpentier 4.00 1.80
184 Nick Carte 2.50 1.10
Sweet Williams
185 Serge Dumont 3.00 1.35
186 Johnny(War) Eagle 2.50 1.10
187 Edouard Ethifier 2.50 1.10
188 Jean Ferre 15.00 6.75
(Andre The Giant)
189 Bull Gregory 2.50 1.10
190 Don Leo Jonathan 4.00 1.80
191 Wladek(Killer) 4.00 1.80
Kowalski
192 Leronix et Patonix 2.50 1.10
193 Michel Pelletier 2.50 1.10
194 Gilles(The Fish) 2.50 1.10
Poisson
195 Yvon Robert 2.50 1.10
196 Yvon Robert 2.50 1.10
(Father and son)
197 Dale Roberts 2.50 1.10
Gerry Brown
198 Tokio Joe 2.50 1.10
199 Tarzan(La Bottine) 2.50 1.10
Tyler
200 U.F.O. 2.50 1.10
201 Maurice(Mad Dog) 4.00 1.80
Vachon
202 Paul(The Butcher) 4.00 1.80
Vachon
203 Viviane Vachon 4.00 1.80
204 Frank Valois 3.00 1.35
205 Yagi 2.50 1.10
206 Jean-Claude Leclair 2.50 1.10
207 Donato Paduano 2.50 1.10
208 Emerson Fittipaldi 6.00 2.70
209 Alan Jones 3.00 1.35
210 Jody Scheckter 4.00 1.80
211 Patrick Tambay 3.00 1.35
212 Jocelyne Bourassa 2.00 .90
(Canadian Women's Golf)
213 Jacques Desrosiers 2.00 .90
(Patof, circus clown)
214 Peter Dalla Riva 10/23/77 2.00 .90
215 Don Sweet 10/30/77 2.00 .90
216 Mark Jackson 11/6/77 2.00 .90
217 Tony Proudfoot 11/13/77 2.00 .90
218 Dan Yochum 11/20/77 2.00 .90
219 1977 Team Photo 11/27/77 2.00 .90
220 Wayne Conrad 12/77 2.00 .90
221 Vernon Perry 12/11/77 3.00 1.35
222 Carl Crennel 12/17/77 2.00 .90
223 Sonny Wade 10.00 4.50
Marv Levy 12/25/77
224 John O'Leary 8/6/78 2.00 .90
225 Dickie Harris 8/13/78 2.50 1.10
226 Glen Weir 8/20/78 2.00 .90
227 Gabriel Gregoire 8/27/78 2.00 .90
228 Larry Smith 9/3/78 2.00 .90
229 Gerry Dattilio 9/10/78 2.00 .90
230 Ken Starch 9/17/78 2.00 .90
231 Larry Uteck 9/24/78 2.00 .90
232 Jim Burrow 10/1/78 2.50 1.10
233 Randy Rhino 10/8/78 2.00 .90
234 Chuck McMann 10/15/78 2.00 .90
235 Gordon Judges 10/22/78 2.00 .90
236 Doug Payton 10/29/78 2.00 .90
237 Ty Morris 11/5/78 2.00 .90
238 Wally Buono 11/12/78 2.00 .90
239 1978 Team Photo 11/19/78 2.50 1.10
240 Ray Watrin 11/26/78 2.00 .90
241 Junior Ah You 12/3/78 4.00 1.80
242 David Green 10/7/79 2.50 1.10
243 Ron Calgagni 10/14/79 2.00 .90
244 Bobby Husea 10/21/79 2.00 .90
245 Nick Arakgi 10/28/79 2.00 .90
246 Joe Barnes 11/4/79 4.00 1.80
247 Keith Baker 11/11/79 2.00 .90
248 Tony Petruccio 11/18/79 2.00 .90
249 Tom Cousineau 11/25/79 4.00 1.80
250 Doug Scott 10/5/80 2.00 .90
251 Dickie Harris 10/12/80 2.50 1.10
252 Gabriel Gregoire 10/19/80 2.00 .90
253 Fred Biletnikoff 10/26/80 10.00 4.50
254 Tom Cousineau 11/2/80 4.00 1.80
255 Chuck McMann 11/9/80 2.00 .90
256 Junior Ah You 11/16/80 4.00 1.80
257 Gerry Dattilio 11/23/80 2.00 .90
258 Vince Ferragamo 7/19/81 4.00 1.80
259 Joe Scannella 7/26/81 2.00 .90
260 Billy Johnson 8/2/81 4.00 1.80
261 Joe Hawco 8/9/81 2.00 .90
262 Gerry McGrath 8/16/81 2.00 .90
263 Joe Taylor 8/23/81 2.00 .90
264 Doug Scott 8/30/81 2.00 .90
265 Tom Cousineau 9/6/81 4.00 1.80
266 Nick Arakgi 9/13/81 2.00 .90
267 Mike Hameluck 8/20/81 2.00 .90
268 Doug Payton 9/27/81 2.00 .90
269 James Scott 10/4/81 3.00 1.35
270 Keith Gary 10/11/81 2.00 .90
271 David Overstreet 10/18/81 4.00 1.80
272 Peter Dalla Riva 10/25/81 2.00 .90
273 Marc Lacelle 11/1/81 2.00 .90
274 Luc Tousignant 9/19/82 2.00 .90
275 Denny Ferdinand 9/26/82 2.00 .90
276 Joe Galat 10/3/82 2.00 .90
277 Lester Brown 10/10/82 2.00 .90
278 Dom Vetro 10/17/82 2.00 .90
279 Preston Young 10/24/82 2.00 .90
280 Eugene Beliveau 10/31/82 2.00 .90
281 Ken Miller 11/7/82 2.00 .90

1937 Dixie Lids *

This unnumbered set of lids is actually a combined sport and non-sport set with 24 different lids. The lids are found in more than one size, approximately 2 11/16" in diameter as well as 2 5/16" in diameter. The 1937 lids are distinguished from the 1938 Dixie Lids by the fact that the 1937 lids are printed in black or wine-colored ink where the 1938 lids are printed in blue ink. In the checklist below only the sports subjects are checklisted; non-sport subjects (celebrities) included in this 24-card set are Gene Autry, Freddie Bartholomew, Bill Boyd, Johnny Mack Brown, Madeleine Carroll, Nelson Eddy, Clark Gable, Jean Harlow, Carole Lombard, Myrna Loy, Fred MacMurray, Ken Maynard, Merle Oberon, Eleanor Powell, William Powell, Luisa Rainer, Charles Starrett and Robert Taylor. The catalog designation is F7-1.

	EX-MT	VG-E
COMPLETE SPORT (6)	350.00	160.00
1 Georgia Coleman	15.00	6.75
2 Charles Gehringer	100.00	45.00
3 Charles Hartnett	80.00	36.00
4 Carl Hubbell	120.00	55.00
5 Joe Medwick	80.00	36.00
6 Bill Tilden	25.00	11.00

1937 Dixie Premiums *

This is a parallel issue to the lids -- an attractive "premium" large picture of each of the subjects in the Dixie Lid set. The premiums are printed on thick stock and feature a large color drawing on the front; each unnumbered premium measures approximately 8" X 10". The 1937 premiums are distinguished from the 1938 Dixie Lid premiums by the fact that the 1937 premiums contain a dark green border whereas the 1938 premiums have a lighter green border completely around the photo. Also, on the reverse, the 1937 premiums have a large gray star and three light gray lines at the top. Only the sports personalities are checklisted below.

	EX-MT	VG-E
COMPLETE SPORT SET (6)	350.00	160.00
1 Georgia Coleman	15.00	6.75
2 Charles Gehringer	100.00	45.00
3 Charles Hartnett	80.00	36.00
4 Carl Hubbell	100.00	45.00
5 Joe Medwick	80.00	36.00
6 Bill Tilden	25.00	11.00

1938 Dixie Lids *

This unnumbered set of lids is actually a combined sport and non-sport set with 24 different lids. The lids are found in more than one size, approximately 2 11/16" in diameter as well as 2 5/16" in diameter. The catalog designation is F7-1. The 1938 lids are distinguished from the 1937 Dixie Lids by the fact that the 1938 lids are printed in blue ink whereas the 1938 lids are printed in black or wine-colored ink. In the checklist below only the sports subjects are checklisted; non-sport subjects (celebrities) included in this 24 card set are Don Ameche, Annabella, Gene Autry, Warner Baxter, William Boyd, Bobby Breen, Gary Cooper, Alice Fay, Sonja Henie, Tommy Kelly, June Lang, Colonel Tim McCoy, Tyrone Power, Tex Ritter, Simone Simon, Bob Steele, The Three Musquiteers and Jane Withers.

	EX-MT	VG-E
COMPLETE SPORT SET (6)	500.00	220.00
1 Sam Baugh	125.00	55.00
2 Bob Feller	80.00	36.00
3 Jimmie Foxx	80.00	36.00
4 Carl Hubbell mouth open	80.00	36.00
5 Wally Moses	40.00	18.00
6 Bronko Nagurski	150.00	70.00

1938 Dixie Premiums *

This is a parallel issue to the lids -- an attractive "premium" large picture of each of the subjects in the Dixie Lids set. The premiums are printed on thick stock and feature a large color drawing on the front; each unnumbered premium measures approximately 8" X 10". The 1938 premiums are distinguished from the 1937 Dixie Lid premiums by the fact that the 1938 premiums contain a light green border whereas the 1937 premiums have a darker green border completely around the photo. Also, on the reverse, the 1938 premiums have a single gray sline line at the top leading to the player's name in script. Again, we have only checklisted the sports personalities.

	EX-MT	VG-E
COMPLETE SET (6)	750.00	350.00
1 Sam Baugh	250.00	110.00
2 Bob Feller	80.00	36.00
3 Jimmie Foxx	80.00	36.00
4 Carl Hubbell	80.00	36.00
5 Wally Moses	40.00	18.00
6 Bronko Nagurski	250.00	110.00

1967-73 Equitable Sports Hall of Fame *

This set consists of copies of art work found over a number of years in many national magazines, especially "Sports Illustrated," honoring sports heroes that Equitable Life Assurance Society selected to be in its very own Sports Hall of Fame. The cards consists of charcoal-type drawings on white backgrounds by artists, George Loh and Robert Riger, and measure approximately 11" by 7 3/4". The unnumbered cards have been assigned numbers below using a sport prefix (BB-baseball, BK- basketball, FB- football, HK-hockey, OT-other).

	NRMT	VG-E
COMPLETE SET (95)	500.00	220.00
BB1 Ernie Banks	8.00	3.60
BB2 Roy Campanella	8.00	3.60
BB3 Johnny Evers	6.00	2.70
BB4 Bob Feller	6.00	2.70
BB5 Lou Gehrig	15.00	6.75
BB6 Lefty Grove	6.00	2.70
BB7 Tom Henrich	2.50	1.10
BB8 Carl Hubbell	6.00	2.70
BB9 Al Kaline	6.00	2.70
BB10 Jerry Koosman	4.00	1.80
BB11 Mickey Mantle	15.00	6.75
BB12 Ed Mathews	6.00	2.70
BB13 Willie Mays	12.00	5.50
BB14 Stan Musial	10.00	4.50
BB15 PeeWee Reese	8.00	3.60
BB16 Allie Reynolds	2.50	1.10
BB17 Robin Roberts	6.00	2.70
BB18 Brooks Robinson	8.00	3.60
BB19 Red Ruffing	4.00	1.80
BB20 Babe Ruth	15.00	6.75
BB21 Warren Spahn	6.00	2.70
BK1 Elgin Baylor	6.00	2.70
BK2 Wilt Chamberlain	10.00	4.50
BK3 Bob Cousy	6.00	2.70
BK4 Hal Grier	4.00	1.80
BK5 Jerry Lucas	4.00	1.80
BK6 George Mikan	6.00	2.70
BK7 Bob Pettit	6.00	2.70
BK8 Willis Reed	4.00	1.80
BK9 Bill Russell	10.00	4.50
BK10 Dolph Schayes	4.00	1.80
FB1 Jim Brown	8.00	3.60
FB2 Charley Conerly	4.00	1.80
FB3 Bill Dudley	2.50	1.10
FB4 Roman Gabriel	2.50	1.10
FB5 Red Grange	8.00	3.60
FB6 Elroy Hirsch	4.00	1.80
FB7 Jerry Kramer	4.00	1.80
FB8 Vince Lombardi	8.00	3.60
FB9 Earl Morrall	2.50	1.10
FB10 Bronko Nagurski	6.00	2.70
FB11 Gale Sayers	8.00	3.60
FB12 Jim Thorpe	8.00	3.60
FB13 Johnny Unitas	8.00	3.60
FB14 Alex Webster	4.00	1.80
HK1 Phil Esposito	6.00	2.70
HK2 Bernie Geoffrion	6.00	2.70
HK3 Gordie Howe	10.00	4.50
HK4 Ching Johnson	4.00	1.80
HK5 Stan Mikita	6.00	2.70
HK6 Maurice Richard	8.00	3.60
OT1 George Archer (Golf)	2.50	1.10
OT2 Frank Beard (Golf)	2.50	1.10
OT3 Patty Berg (Golf)	2.50	1.10
OT4 Julius Boros (Golf)	4.00	1.80
OT5 Don Budge (Tennis)	8.00	3.60
OT6 Dick Button (Skiing)	6.00	2.70
OT7 Don Carter (Bowling)	4.00	1.80
OT8 Billy Casper (Golf)	6.00	2.70
OT9 Florence Chadwick (Swimming)	4.00	1.80
OT10 Maureen Connolly (Tennis)	6.00	2.70
OT11 Glenn Cunningham (Track)	4.00	1.80
OT12 Ned Day (Bowling)	2.50	1.10
OT13 Jimmy Demaret (Golf)	4.00	1.80
OT14 Art Devlin (Skiing)	2.50	1.10
OT15 Harrison Dillard (Track)	2.50	1.10
OT16 Gertrude Ederle (Swimming)	4.00	1.80
OT17 Stein Eriksen (Skiing)	2.50	1.10
OT18 Buzz Fazio (Bowling)	2.50	1.10
OT19 Peggy Fleming (Skating)	8.00	3.60
OT20 Althea Gibson (Tennis)	4.00	1.80
OT21 Walter Hagen (Golf)	8.00	3.60
OT22 Carol Heiss (Skating)	8.00	3.60
OT23 Rafer Johnson (Track)	6.00	2.70
OT24 Billy Jean King (Tennis)	8.00	3.60
OT25 Jack Kramer (Tennis)	6.00	2.70
OT26 Bob Mathias (Track)	4.00	1.80
OT27 Cary Middlecoff (Golf)	2.50	1.10
OT28 Carlton Mitchell (Yachting)	2.50	1.10
OT29 Byron Nelson (Golf)	8.00	3.60
OT30 Jesse Owens (Track)	6.00	2.70
OT31 Penny Pitou (Skiing)	2.50	1.10
OT32 Wilma Rudolph (Track)	6.00	2.70
OT33 Gene Sarazen (Golf)	6.00	2.70
OT34 Don Schollander (Swimming)	4.00	1.80
OT35 Sam Snead (Golf)	8.00	3.60
OT36 Bill Talbert (Tennis)	4.00	1.80
OT37 Art Tokle (Skiing)	2.50	1.10
OT38 Tony Trabert (Tennis)	2.50	1.10
OT39 Andy Varipapa (Bowling)	4.00	1.80
OT40 Ken Venturi (Golf)	4.00	1.80
OT41 Cornelius Warmerdam Track	4.00	1.80
OT42 Dick Weber (Bowling)	6.00	2.70
OT43 Johnny Weissmuller (Swimming)	6.00	2.70
OT44 Frank Wycoff (Track)	2.50	1.10

1993 Fax Pax World of Sport *

The 1993 Fax Pax World of Sport set was issued in Great Britain and contains 40 standard size cards. This multisport set spotlights notable sports figures from around the world, who are the best in their respective sports. An Olympic subset of seven cards (28-34) is included. The full-bleed fronts feature color action and posed photos with a red-edged white stripe intersecting the photo across the bottom. Within the white stripe is displayed the athlete's name and his country's flag. The horizontal, white backs carry the athlete's name and sport at the top followed by biographical information. Career summary and statistics are printed within a gray box, edged in red.

	MINT	NRMT
COMPLETE SET (40)	15.00	6.75
1 Roger Clemens BB	1.50	.70
2 Ken Griffey Jr. BB	2.50	1.10
3 John Olerud BB	.50	.23
4 Nolan Ryan BB	3.00	1.35
5 Charles Barkley BK	1.00	.45
6 Patrick Ewing BK	.50	.23
7 Michael Jordan BK	4.00	1.80
8 Shaquille O'Neal BK	2.50	1.10
9 Riddick Bowe (Boxing)	.25	.11
10 Julio Cesar Chavez (Boxing)	.75	.35
11 Lennox Lewis (Boxing)	2.00	.90
12 Allan Border (Cricket)	.10	.05
13 Ian Botham (Cricket)	.50	.23
14 Vic Richards (Cricket)	.10	.05
15 Dan Marino FB	2.00	.90
16 Joe Montana FB	2.00	.90
17 Emmitt Smith FB	1.50	.70
18 Paul Gascoigne (Soccer)	.10	.05
19 John Harkes (Soccer)	.50	.23
20 Gary Lineker (Soccer)	.50	.23
21 Diego Maradona (Soccer)	.75	.35
22 Seve Ballesteros (Golf)	.50	.23
23 John Daly (Golf)	.75	.35
24 Jack Nicklaus (Golf)	3.00	1.35
25 Wayne Gretzky HK	3.00	1.35
26 Brett Hull HK	.25	.11
27 Eric Lindros HK	.75	.35
28 Linford Christie (Track and Field)	.25	.11
29 Oscar De La Hoya (Boxing)	1.50	.70
30 Sally Gunnell (Track and Field)	.10	.05
31 Jackie Joyner-Kersee (Track and Field)	.75	.35
32 Toni Kukoc BK	.25	.11
33 Carl Lewis (Track and Field)	.75	.35
34 Katarina Witt (Figure Skating)	1.00	.45
35 Nigel Mansell (Racing)	.75	.35
36 Richard Petty (Racing)	2.00	.90
37 Will Carling (Rugby)	.10	.05
38 Boris Becker (Tennis)	.75	.35
39 Steffi Graf (Tennis)	1.00	.45
40 John McEnroe (Tennis)	.75	.35

1993 FCA 50 *

This 50-card standard-size set was sponsored by Fellowship of Christian Athletes. The color player photos on the fronts are accented on three sides by a thin pink stripe; the card face itself shades from blue to white as one moves toward the bottom. The FCA logo, featuring a cross with two olive branches, is superimposed in the upper left corner, while the player's name is printed beneath the picture and his sport in the pink stripe on the left. On a blue background, the backs carry a close-up photo, biography, and the player's testimony.

	MINT	NRMT
COMPLETE SET (50)	10.00	4.50
1 Title Card	.15	.07
2 Zenon Andrusyshyn FB	.15	.07
3 Bobby Bowden CO FB	2.00	.90
4 Eric Boyles Volleyball	.15	.07
5 John Brandes FB	.15	.07
6 Dan Britton Lacrosse	.15	.07
7 Brian Cabral FB	.15	.07
8 Bobby Clampett Golf	.15	.07
9 Paul Coffman FB	.25	.11
10 Jeff Coston Golf	.15	.07
11 Tanya Crevier BK	.15	.07
12 Doug Dawson FB	.15	.07
13 Donnie Dee FB	.15	.07
14 Denise DeWalt Softball	.15	.07
15 Mitch Donahue FB	.15	.07
16 Curtis Duncan FB	.25	.11
17 Mike Gartner HK	.75	.35
18 Brian Harper BB	.25	.11
19 Janice Harrer Volleyball	.15	.07
20 Ed Hearn BB	.15	.07
21 Bobby Hebert FB	.25	.11
22 Julie Hermann CO Volleyball	.15	.07
23 David Dean FB	.15	.07
24 Steve Jones Golf	.25	.11
25 Brian Kinchen FB	.25	.11
26 Todd Kinchen FB	.25	.11
27 Jerry Kindall BB	.15	.07
28 Betsy King Golf	.40	.18
29 Tom Lehman Golf	1.25	.55
30 Neil Lomax FB	.40	.18
31 LaVonna Martin-Floreal Track	.15	.07
32 Dan Meers FB Mascot	.15	.07
33 Mike Merriweather FB	.25	.11
34 Ken Norton Jr. FB	.40	.18
35 Greg Olson C BB	.15	.07
36 Tim Peddie Cycling	.15	.07
37 Rob Pelinka BK	.15	.07
38 Steve Pelluer FB	.25	.11
39 Brent Price BK	.25	.11
40 Jan Ripple Cycling	.15	.07
41 Kyle Rote Jr. Soccer	.25	.11
42 Ted Schulz Golf	.15	.07
43 Scott Simpson Golf	.40	.18
44 R.C. Slocum CO FB	.25	.11
45 Grant Teaff CO FB	.25	.11
46 Pat Tilley FB	.25	.11
47 Bill Wegman BB	.25	.11
48 Wendy White Tennis	.15	.07
49 Charlton Young Kickboxing	.15	.07
50 Kay Yow CO BK	.15	.07

1988 Foot Locker Slam Fest *

This nine-card set was produced by Foot Locker to commemorate the "Foot Locker Slam Fest" slam dunk contest, televised on ESPN on May 17, 1988. The cards were given out in May at participating Foot Locker stores to

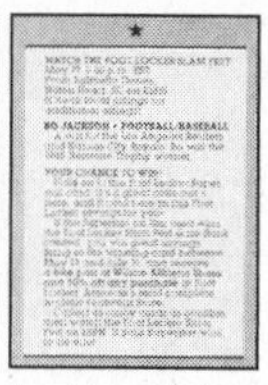

customers. Between May 18 and July 31, customers could turn in the winner's card (Mike Conley) and receive a free pair of Wilson athletic shoes and 50 percent off any purchase at Foot Locker. These standard size cards (2 1/2" by 3 1/2") feature color posed shots of the participants, who were professional athletes from sports other than basketball. The pictures have magenta and blue borders on a white card face. A colored banner with the words "Foot Locker" overlays the top of the picture. A line drawing of a referee overlays the lower left corner of the picture. The backs are printed in blue on white and promote the slam dunk contest and an in-store contest. The cards are unnumbered and checklisted below in alphabetical order.

	MINT	NRMT
COMPLETE SET (9)	30.00	13.50
1 Carl Banks FB	2.00	.90
2 Mike Conley SP	15.00	6.75
Track and Field		
3 Thomas Hearns	5.00	2.20
Boxing		
4 Bo Jackson BB/FB	6.00	2.70
5 Keith Jackson FB	2.00	.90
6 Karch Kiraly	5.00	2.20
Volleyball		
7 Ricky Sanders FB	2.00	.90
8 Dwight Stones	3.00	1.35
Track and Field		
9 Devon White BB	3.00	1.35

1989 Foot Locker Slam Fest *

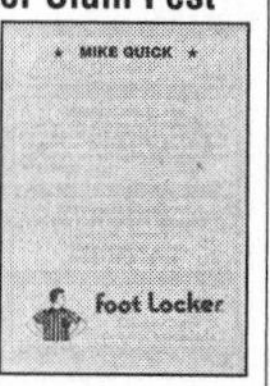

This ten-card standard-size set was produced by Foot Locker and Nike to commemorate the "Foot Locker Slam Fest" slam dunk contest, which was televised during halftimes of NBC college basketball games through March 12, 1989. The cards were wrapped in cellophane and issued with one stick of gum. They were given out at participating Foot Locker stores upon request with a purchase. The cards feature color posed shots of the participants, who were professional athletes from sports other than basketball. A banner with the words "Foot Locker" traverses the top of the card face. The cards are unnumbered and checklisted below in alphabetical order.

	MINT	NRMT
COMPLETE SET (10)	8.00	3.60
1 Mike Conley	.50	.23
Track and Field		
2 Keith Jackson FB	.50	.23
3 Vince Coleman BB	.50	.23
4 Eric Dickerson FB	1.50	.70
5 Steve Timmons	1.00	.45
Volleyball		
6 Matt Biondi	1.00	.45
Swimming		
7 Carl Lewis	1.50	.70
Track and Field		
8 Mike Quick	.50	.23
Football		
9 Mike Powell	1.00	.45
Track and Field		
10 Checklist Card	.50	.23

1991 Foot Locker Slam Fest *

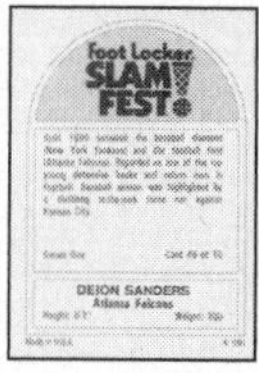

This 30-card standard-size set was issued by Foot Locker in three ten-card series to commemorate the "Foot Locker Slam Fest" dunk contest televised during halftimes of NBC college basketball games through March 10, 1991. Each set contained two Domino's Pizza coupons and a 5.00 discount coupon on any purchase of 50.00 or more at Foot Locker. The set was released in substantial quantity after the promotional coupons expired. The fronts feature both posed and action photos enclosed in an arch like double red borders. The card top carries a blue border with "Foot Locker" in blue print on a white background. Beneath the photo appears "Limited Edition" and the player's name. The backs present career highlights, card series, and numbers placed within an arch of double red borders. The player's name and team name appear in black lettering at the bottom. The cards are numbered on the back; the card numbering below adds the number 10 to each card number in the second series and 20 to each card number in the third series.

	MINT	NRMT
COMPLETE SET (30)	5.00	2.20
1 Ken Griffey Jr. BB	1.00	.45
2 Delino DeShields BB	.10	.05
3 Barry Bonds BB	1.50	.70
4 Jack Armstrong BB	.05	.02
5 Dave Justice BB	.40	.18
6 Deion Sanders BB/FB	.75	.35
7 Michael Dean Perry FB	.05	.02
8 Tim Brown FB	.50	.23
9 Mike Conley	.10	.05
Track and Field		
10 Mike Powell	.15	.07
Track and Field		
11 Wilt Chamberlain BK	3.00	1.35
12 Cal Ramsey BK	.05	.02
13 Bobby Jones BK	.05	.02
14 John Havlicek BK	1.00	.45
15 Calvin Murphy BK	.10	.05
16 Nate Thurmond BK	.25	.11
17 John Havlicek BK	1.00	.45
18 Series 1 Checklist	.05	.02
The Dunkers		
19 Series 2 Checklist	.05	.02
The Judges		
20 Series 3 Checklist	.05	.02
Fest Moments		
21 Jerry Lucas BK	.25	.11
22 Bo Jackson BB/FB	.25	.11
23 Elvin Hayes BK	.25	.11
24 Thomas Hearns	.25	.11
Boxing		
25 Matt Biondi	.05	.02
Swimming		
26 Earl Monroe BK	.25	.11
27 Eric Dickerson FB	.15	.07
28 Carl Lewis	.40	.18
Track and Field		
29 Wilt Chamberlain BK	1.00	.45
and Company		
30 TV Slam Fest Schedule	.05	.02

1963 Gad Fun Cards *

This set of 1963 Fun Cards were issued by a sports illustrator by the name of Gad from Minneapolis, Minnesota. The cards are printed on cardboard stock paper. The borderless fronts have black and white line drawings. A fun sport's fact or player career statistic is depicted in the drawing. The backs of the first six cards display numbers used to play the game explained on card number 6. The other backs carry a cartoon with a joke or riddle. Copyright information is listed on the lower portion of the card.

	NRMT	VG-E
COMPLETE SET (84)	75.00	34.00
1 Babe Ruth	8.00	3.60
2 Lost Baseballs Fact	.50	.23
3 Baseball Slang	.50	.23
Fireman		
4 Baseball Hurling Fact	.50	.23
5 Lou Gehrig	5.00	2.20
6 Number Game Directions	.50	.23
7 Baseball Fact	.50	.23
Consecutive Home Runs		
8 Old Hoss Radbourne	1.00	.45
9 Glen Gorbans	.50	.23
10 Joe Nuxhall	.75	.35
11 Ty Cobb	5.00	2.20
12 Baseball Slang	.50	.23
Jake		
13 Pop Schriver	.50	.23
14 Boston Red Sox	.50	.23
15 John Taylor	.50	.23
16 Cincinnati Red Stockings	.50	.23
17 Runs Scored in a Game	.50	.23
18 Baseball Slang	.50	.23
Duster		
19 1908 Baseball Fact	.50	.23
20 Evar Swanson	.50	.23
21 1929 World Series Pinch Hitters	.50	.23
22 Rogers Hornsby	1.50	.70
23 Highlanders	.50	.23
24 Baseball Slang	.50	.23
Strawberry		
25 Lew Flick	.50	.23
26 Cy Young	3.00	1.35
27 Jim Konstanty	.50	.23
28 Carl Weilman	.50	.23
29 Warren Rosar	.50	.23
30 Baseball Slang	.50	.23
Rabbit Ears		
31 Graham McNamee	.50	.23
32 Ty Cobb	5.00	2.20
Batting Record		
33 Joe DiMaggio	5.00	2.20
34 Babe Ruth	8.00	3.60
Earnings		
35 Baseball Slang	.50	.23
Chinese Homer		
36 Ed Delahanty	.75	.35
37 1912 Detroit Tiger Team Strike	.50	.23
38 Bobo Holloman	.50	.23
39 Walter Johnson	3.00	1.35
40 Sam Crawford	1.00	.45
41 Lifetime Record	.50	.23
Stolen Bases		
42 Baseball Slang	.50	.23
Showboat		
43 Lou Gehrig	5.00	2.20
23 Bases-loaded Homers		
44 Yankee Stadium	.50	.23
45 Nick Altrock	1.00	.45
46 Moses Walker	1.00	.45
Welday Waker		
47 Joseph Borden	.50	.23
48 Baseball Slang	.50	.23
Around the Horn"		
49 Hugh Duffy	1.00	.45
50 Longest Game	.50	.23
Baseball History		
51 Jim Scott	.50	.23
52 Longest Homer in 1919	.50	.23
53 Record	.50	.23
Runs Scored in One Inning		
54 Baseball Slang	.50	.23
Jockey		
55 Umpires in 1871	.50	.23
56 Bill Phillips	.50	.23
57 Eddie Collins	1.00	.45
58 Milwaukee Braves	.50	.23
59 Bill Wambsganss	.50	.23
60 Baseball Slang	.50	.23
Annie Oakley		
61 Bob Feller	1.00	.45
62 Wally Pipp	.50	.23
63 Shortest World Series Game	.50	.23
64 Chicago White Sox	.50	.23
65 Cleveland Indians	.50	.23
66 Baseball Slang	.50	.23
Baltimore Chop		
67 14 Pitchers Used in One Game	.50	.23
68 John Sigmund	.50	.23
69 Boomerang	.50	.23
70 Arthur Lehmann	.50	.23
71 Peter Tyler	.50	.23
Ellis Hodgkins		
72 Archer Davidson	.50	.23
73 Alex Wickham	.50	.23
74 Minnesota Football Team	.50	.23
1949		
75 George Washington	.50	.23
76 Buffalo Germans	.50	.23
Basketball Squad		
77 Gus Simmons	.50	.23
78 Tom Morris	.50	.23
79 Zoe Ann Olsen	.75	.35
80 Emperor of Rome Maxim	.50	.23
81 Highest Football Game Score	.50	.23
82 Harold Starkey	.50	.23
83 A Bowling Pin	.50	.23
84 Number of Bicycles in USA	.50	.23

1888 Goodwin N162 *

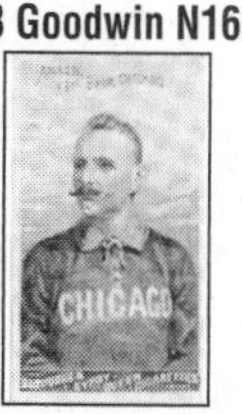

This 50-card set issued by Goodwin was one of the major competitors to the N28 and N29 sets marketed by Allen and Ginter. It contains individuals representing 18 sports, with eight baseball players pictured. Each color card is backlisted and bears advertising for "Old Judge" and "Gypsy Queen" cigarettes on the front. The set was released to the public in 1888 and an album (catalog: A36) is associated with it as a premium issue.

	EX-MT	VG-E
COMPLETE SET (50)	17500.00	7900.00
1 Ed Andrews: Phila.	700.00	325.00
2 Cap Anson: Chicago	4000.00	1800.00
3 Dan Brouthers:	1200.00	550.00
Detroit		
4 Bob Caruthers:	800.00	350.00
Brooklyn		
5 Fred Dunlap: Pittsburgh	700.00	325.00
6 Jack Glasscock:	800.00	350.00
Indianapolis		
7 Tim Keefe: New York	1200.00	550.00
8 King Kelly: Boston	2500.00	1100.00
9 Acton (Wrestler)	100.00	45.00
10 Albert (Pedestrian)	80.00	36.00
11 Beach (Oarsman)	80.00	36.00
12 Harry Beecher (Football)	2000.00	900.00
13 Beeckman (Lawn Tennis)	100.00	45.00
14 Bogardus (Marksman)	80.00	36.00
15 Buffalo Bill	400.00	180.00
Wild West Hunter		
16 Daly (Billiards)	100.00	45.00
17 Jack Dempsey	400.00	180.00
(Pugilist)		
18 D'oro (Pool)	100.00	45.00
19 James Dwight	100.00	45.00
(Lawn Tennis)		
20 Fitzgerald	80.00	36.00
(Pedestrian)		
21 Garrison (Jockey)	80.00	36.00
22 Gaudaur (Oarsman)	80.00	36.00
23 Hanlan (Oarsman)	100.00	45.00
24 Jake Kilrain	300.00	135.00
(Pugilist)		
25 MacKenzie (Chess)	100.00	45.00
26 McLaughlin (Jockey)	80.00	36.00
27 Charlie Mitchell	100.00	45.00
(Pugilist)		
28 Muldoon (Wrestler)	100.00	45.00
29 Isaac Murphy (Jockey)	100.00	45.00
30 Myers (Runner)	80.00	36.00
31 Page (High Jumper)	80.00	36.00
32 Prince (Bicyclist)	80.00	36.00
33 Ross (Broadswordsman)	80.00	36.00
34 Rowe (Bicyclist)	80.00	36.00
35 Rowell (Pedestrian)	80.00	36.00
36 Schaefer (Billiards)	100.00	45.00
37 R.D. Sears	100.00	45.00
(Lawn Tennis)		
38 Sexton (Billiards)	100.00	45.00
39 Slosson (Billiards)	100.00	45.00
40 Smith (Pugilist)	250.00	110.00
41 Steinitz (Chess)	120.00	55.00
42 Stevens (Bicyclist)	80.00	36.00
43 John L. Sullivan	500.00	220.00
(Pugilist)		
44 Taylor (Lawn Tennis)	100.00	45.00
45 Teemer (Oarsman)	80.00	36.00
46 Vignaux (Billiards)	100.00	45.00
47 Voss (Strongest Man	80.00	36.00
in the World)		
48 Wood (Bicyclist)	80.00	36.00
49 Charles Wood	80.00	36.00
Jockey		
50 Zukertort (Chess)	100.00	45.00

1962 H.F. Gardner Sports Stars PC768 *

This colorful 1960's set feature people of color stars only. The reverses can be identified by the line "Color by H.F. Gardner" at the lower left. A short biography of the subject player(s) is present on the reverse.

	NRMT	VG-E
COMPLETE SET (5)	100.00	45.00
1 Hank Aaron	50.00	22.00
Tommy Aaron		
2 Billy Bruton	5.00	2.20
3 Lee Maye	5.00	2.20
4 Billy Williams	20.00	9.00
5 Jesse Owens	25.00	11.00

1980 Italian American Sports Hall of Fame *

These exhibit-sized cards were issued to commemorate the first inductees into the Italian American Sports Hall of Fame. The fronts have sepia toned photos of the athlete as well as their name and identification in the lower left column. The bottom right of the card is dedicated to the "Unity" logo. The back is a standard postcard back. Since these cards are unnumbered we have sequenced them in alphabetical order.

	MINT	NRMT
COMPLETE SET	10.00	4.50
1 Eddie Arcaro	2.00	.90
2 Phil Cavaretta	1.00	.45
3 Joe DiMaggio	5.00	2.20
4 Ernie Lombardi	2.00	.90

1963 Jewish Sports Champions *

The 16 cards in this set, measuring roughly 2 2/3" x 3", are cut out of an "Activity Funbook" entitled Jewish Sports Champions. The set pays tribute to famous Jewish athletes from baseball, football, bull fighting to chess. The cards have a green border with a yellow background and a player close-up illustration. Cards that are still attached carry a premium over those that have been cut-out. The cards are unnumbered and listed below in alphabetical order with an assigned sport prefix (BB-baseball, BK- basketball, BX- boxing, FB- football, OT- other).

	NRMT	VG-E
COMPLETE SET (16)	150.00	70.00
BB1 Hank Greenberg BB	20.00	9.00
BB2 Johnny Kling BB	10.00	4.50
BB3 Sandy Koufax BB	40.00	18.00
BK1 Nat Holman BK	25.00	11.00
BK2 Dolph Schayes BK	20.00	9.00
BX1 Benny Leonard	12.00	5.50
Boxing		
BX2 Barney Ross	12.00	5.50
Boxing		
FB1 Benny Friedman FB	12.00	5.50
FB2 Sid Luckman FB	20.00	9.00
OT1 Herman Barron	6.00	2.70
Golf		
OT2 Lillian Copeland	6.00	2.70
Field Sports		
OT3 Bobby Fischer	12.00	5.50
Chess		
OT4 Sidney Franklin	6.00	2.70
Bull Fighting		
OT5 Irving Jaffee	8.00	3.60
Ice Racing		
OT6 Samuel Reshevsky	6.00	2.70
Chess		
OT7 Dick Savitt	8.00	3.60
Tennis		

1973 Jewish Sports Champions*

The 16 cards in this set, measuring roughly 2 2/3" x 3", are cut out of a sequel to the 1968 Activity Funbook. This time, the cards come from a funbook entitled "More Jewish Sports Champions". There are two variations to each card that are valued equally. One has a pink border with a yellow background and blue ink on the player close-up illustration. The other has a blue background and black ink on the player illustration. Cards that are still attached carry a premium over those that have been cut-out. The cards are unnumbered and listed below in alphabetical order.

	NRMT	VG-E
COMPLETE SET (16)	125.00	55.00
1 Arnold (Red) Auerbach BK	30.00	13.50
2 Isaac Berger	8.00	3.60
Weight Lifting		
3 James Bregman	5.00	2.20
Judo		
4 Dezso Gyarmati	5.00	2.20
Water Polo		
5 Vic Hershkowitz	5.00	2.20
Handball		
6 Israel Olympic Athletes	12.00	5.50
7 Agnes (Klein) Keletti	5.00	2.20
Gymnastics		
8 Emanuel Hasker	5.00	2.20
Chess		
9 Benny Leonard	12.00	5.50
Boxing		
10 Olympics in Munich	12.00	5.50
11 Angelica Roseanu	5.00	2.20
Table Tennis		
12 Al (Flip) Rosen BB	12.00	5.50
13 Fanny Rosenfeld	5.00	2.20
Track		
14 Ilona Schacherer-Elek	5.00	2.20
Fencing		
15 Mark Spitz	25.00	11.00
Swimming		
16 Henry Wittenberg	5.00	2.20
Wrestling		

1994-96 John Deere*

Over a three year period, the John Deere tractor company used professional athletes to promote their products and included cards of these athletes in their set. These five cards were issued in 1994 (Ryan and Novacek), 1995 (Jackson and Petty) and 1996 (Larry Bird). For our cataloguing purposes we are sequencing these cards in alphabetical order. Larry Bird signed some cards for this promotion but these cards are so thinly traded that no pricing is available

	MINT	NRMT
COMPLETE SET (5)	40.00	18.00
1 Larry Bird	10.00	4.50
2 Reggie Jackson	8.00	3.60
3 Jay Novacek	2.00	.90
4 Richard Petty	12.00	5.50
5 Nolan Ryan	15.00	6.75
AU1 Larry Bird AU		

1971 Keds KedKards *

This set is composed of crude artistic renditions of popular subjects from various sports from 1971 who were apparently celebrity endorsers of Keds shoes. The cards actually form a complete panel on the Keds tennis shoes box. The three different panels are actually different sizes; the Bing panel contains smaller cards. The smaller Bubba Smith shows him without beard and standing straight; the large Bubba shows him leaning over, with beard, and jersey number partially visible. The individual player card portions of the card panels measure approximately 2 15/16" by 2 3/4" and 2 5/16" by 2 3/16" respectively, although it should noted that there are slight size differences among the individual cards even on the same panel. The panel background is colored in black and yellow. On the Bench/Reed card (number 3 below) each player measures approximately 5 1/4" by 3 1/2". A facsimile autograph appears in the upper left corner of each player's drawing. The Bench/Reed was issued with the Keds Champion boys basketball shoe box, printed on the box top with a black broken line around the card to follow when cutting the card out.

	NRMT	VG-E
COMPLETE SET (3)	225.00	100.00
1 Dave Bing BK	75.00	34.00
Clark Graebner		
(Tennis)		
Bubba Smith FB		
Jim Maloney BB		
2 Willis Reed BK	75.00	34.00
Stan Smith		
(Tennis)		
Bubba Smith FB		
Johnny Bench BB		
3 Willis Reed BK	75.00	34.00
Johnny Bench BB		

1937 Kellogg's Pep Stamps *

Kellogg's distributed these multi-sport stamps inside specially marked Pep brand cereal boxes in 1937. They were originally issued in four-stamp blocks along with an instructional type tab at the top. The tab contained the sheet number. We've noted the sheet number after each athlete's name below. Note that six athletes appear on two sheets, thereby making those six double prints. There were 24-different sheets produced. We've catalogued the unnumbered stamps below in single loose form according to sport (AR- auto racing, AV- aviation, BB- baseball, BX- boxing, FB- football, GO- golf, HO- horses, SW- swimming, TN- tennis). Stamps can often be found intact in blocks of four along with the tab. Complete blocks of stamps are valued at roughly 50 percent more than the total value of the four individual stamps as priced below. An album was also produced to house the set.

	EX-MT	VG-E
COMPLETE SET (90)	2000.00	900.00
AR1 Billy Arnold 6	15.00	6.75
AR2 Bill Cummings 2	15.00	6.75
AR3 Ralph DePalma 14	20.00	9.00
AR4 Tommy Milton 8	15.00	6.75

AR5 Mauri Rose 10 25.00 11.00
AR6 Wilbur Shaw 24 25.00 11.00
AV1 Jimmy Doolittle 1 20.00 9.00
AV2 Dick Merrill 7 10.00 4.50
AV3 Clyde Pangborn 13 10.00 4.50
AV4 Eddie Rickenbacker 9/24 20.00 9.00
AV5 Al Williams 3 10.00 4.50
AV6 Roger Williams 18 10.00 4.50
BB1 Luke Appling 7 25.00 11.00
BB2 Mordecai Brown 22 25.00 11.00
BB3 Leo Durocher 3 25.00 11.00
BB4 Johnny Evers 17 25.00 11.00
BB5 Rick Ferrell 16 20.00 9.00
BB6 Lew Fonseca 15 10.00 4.50
BB7 Gabby Hartnett 5 25.00 11.00
BB8 Billy Herman 6 25.00 11.00
BB9 Walter Johnson 13 50.00 22.00
BB10 Ducky Medwick 1 25.00 11.00
BB11 Buddy Myer 19 10.00 4.50
BB12 George Selkirk 12 10.00 4.50
BB13 Tris Speaker 20/23 25.00 11.00
BB14 Bill Terry 11 25.00 11.00
BB15 Joe Tinker 21 25.00 11.00
BB16 Arky Vaughan 8 25.00 11.00
BB17 Paul Waner 9 25.00 11.00
BB18 Sam West 18 10.00 4.50
BX1 Jack Britton 11 10.00 4.50
BX2 Tony Canzoneri 6 20.00 9.00
BX3 James J. Corbett 19 25.00 11.00
BX4 Jack Delaney 22 10.00 4.50
BX5 Bob Fitzsimmons 23 20.00 9.00
BX6 Benny Leonard 1 25.00 11.00
BX7 Tommy Loughran 24 20.00 9.00
BX8 Barney Ross 16 20.00 9.00
BX9 Jack Sharkey 10 20.00 9.00
BX10 Gene Tunney 7 40.00 18.00
BX11 Mickey Walker 13 25.00 11.00
BX12 Jess Willard 15 25.00 11.00
FB1 Bill Alexander 2 20.00 9.00
FB2 Matty Bell 3 20.00 9.00
FB3 Fritz Crisler 14 40.00 18.00
FB4 Bill Cunningham 23 20.00 9.00
FB5 Red Grange 16/22 200.00 90.00
FB6 Howard Jones 18 25.00 11.00
FB7 Andy Kerr 4 25.00 11.00
FB8 Harry Kipke 19 20.00 9.00
FB9 Lou Little 8 40.00 18.00
FB10 Ed Madigan 12 20.00 9.00
FB11 Bronko Nagurski 15 200.00 90.00
FB12 Ernie Nevers 21 60.00 27.00
FB13 Jimmy Phelan 20 20.00 9.00
FB14 Bill Shakespeare 10 25.00 11.00
FB15 Frank Thomas 5 25.00 11.00
FB16 Tiny Thornhill 9 20.00 9.00
FB17 Jim Thorpe 17 200.00 90.00
FB18 Wallace Wade 11 20.00 9.00
GO1 Harry Cooper 15 15.00 6.75
GO2 Leo Diegel 16 15.00 6.75
GO3 Olin Dutra 4 15.00 6.75
GO4 Ralph Guldrahl 12 20.00 9.00
GO5 Walter Hagen 3 40.00 18.00
GO6 Henry Picard 1 15.00 6.75
GO7 Johnny Revolta 21 15.00 6.75
GO8 Paul Runyan 11 15.00 6.75
GO9 Gene Sarazen 2/23 50.00 22.00
GO10 Denny Shute 8 15.00 6.75
GO11 George Von Elm 14 15.00 6.75
GO12 Craig Wood 17 20.00 9.00
HO1 Equipoise 20 10.00 4.50
HO2 Exterminator 18 10.00 4.50
HO3 Gallant Fox 7 15.00 6.75
HO4 Pompoon 5 10.00 4.50
HO5 Sun Beau 22 10.00 4.50
HO6 Top Flight 19 10.00 4.50
SW1 Georgia Coleman 10/13 15.00 6.75
SW2 Buster Crabbe 14 20.00 9.00
SW3 Dick Degener 6 10.00 4.50
SW4 Helene Madison 4 10.00 4.50
SW5 Norman Ross 24 10.00 4.50
SW6 Lenore Wingard 2 10.00 4.50
TN1 Bruce Barnes 17 10.00 4.50
TN2 George Lott 5 10.00 4.50
TN3 Vincent Richards 20 20.00 9.00
TN4 Les Stoefen 21 10.00 4.50
TN5 Bill Tilden 4/12 50.00 22.00
TN6 Ellsworth Vines 9 20.00 9.00
NNO Stamp Album 25.00 11.00

1948 Kellogg's Pep *

MIKE TRESH
Catcher of Chicago White Sox. One of best throwers in major leagues and an artist on "squeeze play." A native of Detroit, Tresh is known as a "smart catcher" and currently works 100 or more games for White Sox.
Get Complete Series with Kellogg's PEP

These small cards measure approximately 1 7/16" by 1 5/8". The card front presents a black and white head-and-shoulders shot of the player, with a white border. The back has the player's name and a brief description of his accomplishments. The cards are unnumbered, but have been assigned numbers below using a sport (BB- baseball, FB- football, BK- basketball, OT- other) prefix. Other Movie Star Kellogg's Pep cards exist, but they are not listed below. The catalog designation for this set is F273-19. An album was also produced to house the set.

NRMT VG-E
COMPLETE SET (20) 1400.00 650.00
BB1 Phil Cavarretta BB 25.00 11.00
BB2 Orval Grove BB 20.00 9.00
BB3 Mike Tresh BB 20.00 9.00
BB4 Paul(Dizzy)Trout BB 30.00 13.50
BB5 Dick Wakefield BB 20.00 9.00
BK1 George Mikan BK 450.00 200.00
FB1 Lou Groza FB 120.00 55.00
FB2 George McAfee FB 40.00 18.00
FB3 Norm Standlee FB 30.00 13.50
FB4A Charley Trippi FB ERR 100.00 45.00
(Reversed negative)
FB4B Charley Trippi FB COR 60.00 27.00
FB5 Bob Waterfield FB 120.00 55.00
OT1 Donald Budge 20.00 9.00
(tennis)
OT2 James Ferrier 15.00 6.75
(golf)
OT3 Mary Hardwick 10.00 4.50
(tennis)
OT4 Adolph Kiefer 10.00 4.50
(swimming)
OT5 Lloyd Mangrum 40.00 18.00
(golf)
OT6 Sam Snead 250.00 110.00
(golf)
OT7A Tony Zale ERR 40.00 18.00
(Reversed negative)
(boxing)
OT7B Tony Zale COR 20.00 9.00
(boxing)

1987 Kentucky Bluegrass State Games*

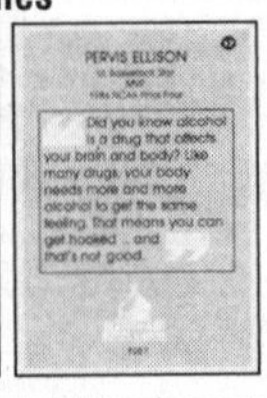

This 24-card set of standard size cards was co-sponsored by Coca-Cola and Valvoline, and their company logos appear on the bottom of the card face. The card sets were originally given out by the Kentucky county sheriff's departments and the Kentucky Highway Patrol. Reportedly about 350 sets were given to the approximately 120 counties in the state of Kentucky. One card per week was given out from May 25 to October 19, 1987. Once all 22 of the numbered cards were collected, they could be turned in to a local sheriff's department for prizes. The front features a color action player photo, on a blue card face with a white outer border. The player's name and the "Champions Against Drugs" insignia appear below the picture. The back has a anti-drug or alcohol tip on a gray background, with white border. The set commemorates Kentucky's hosting of the 1987 Bluegrass State Games and was endorsed by Governor Martha Layne Collins in Kentucky's Champions Against Drugs Crusade for Youth. The set features stars from a variety of sports as well as public figures. The two cards in the set numbered "SC" for special card were not distributed with the regular cards; they were produced in smaller quantities than the 22 numbered cards. The set features the first card of NBA superstar David Robinson. Reportedly the Robinson cards were distributed at the March 1987 Kentucky Boy's State High School Tournament in Rupp Arena, when David Robinson was in attendance.

MINT NRMT
COMPLETE SET (24) 60.00 27.00
1 Martha Layne Collins .50 .23
Governor of Kentucky
2 Kenny Walker K .75 .35
3 Dr. William DeVries .50 .23
4 Dan Issel K 4.00 1.80
5 Doug Flynn B .75 .35
6 Melinda Cumberledge .50 .23
7 Melvin Turpin 1.50 .70
Sam Bowie K
8 Darrell Griffith K 1.50 .70
9 Winston Bennett K .75 .35
10 Ricky Skaggs .75 .35
11 Wildcat Mascot .50 .23
12 Cardinal Mascot .50 .23
13 Pee Wee Reese B 4.00 1.80
14 Mary T. Meagher 1.50 .70
15 Jim Master K .75 .35
16 Kyle Macy K 1.00 .45
17 Pervis Ellison K 1.50 .70
18 Dale Baldwin K .50 .23
19 Frank Minniefield F .75 .35
20 Mark Higgs F .75 .35
21 Rex Chapman K 4.00 1.80
22 A.B.(Happy) Chandler B 1.00 .45
SC Billy Packer SP K 10.00 4.50
SC David Robinson SP K 40.00 18.00

1888 Kimball's N184 *

This set of 50 color pictures of contemporary athletes was Kimball's answer to the sets produced by Allen and Ginter (N28 and N29) and Goodwin (N162). Issued in 1888, the cards are backlisted but are not numbered. The cards are listed below in alphabetical order without regard to sport. There are four baseball players in the set. An album (catalog: A42) was offered as a premium in exchange for coupons found in the tobacco packages. The baseball players are noted in the checklist below by BB after their name; boxers are noted by BOX.

EX-MT VG-E
COMPLETE SET (50) 7000.00 3200.00
1 Wm. Beach 90.00 40.00
2 Marve Beardsley 90.00 40.00
3 Chas. P. Blatt 90.00 40.00
4 Blondin 100.00 45.00
5 Paul Boynton 90.00 40.00
6 E.A.(Ernie) Burch BB 700.00 325.00
7 Patsy Cardiff BOX 90.00 40.00
8 Phillip Casey 90.00 40.00
9 J.C. Cockburn 90.00 40.00
10 Dell Darling BB 700.00 325.00
11 Jack Dempsey BOX 300.00 135.00
12 Della Ferrell 90.00 40.00
13 Clarence Freeman 90.00 40.00
14 Louis George 90.00 40.00
15 W.G. George 90.00 40.00
16 George W. Hamilton 100.00 45.00
17 Edward Hanlan 100.00 45.00
18 C.H. Heins 90.00 40.00
19 Hardie Henderson BB 700.00 325.00
20 Thomas H. Hume 90.00 40.00
21 J.H. Jordon 90.00 40.00
22 Johnny Kane 90.00 40.00
23 James McLaughlin 90.00 40.00
24 John McPherson 90.00 40.00
25 Joseph Morsler 90.00 40.00
26 William Muldoon 100.00 45.00
27 S. Muller 90.00 40.00
28 Isaac Murphy 100.00 45.00
29 John Murphy 90.00 40.00
30 L.E. Myers 90.00 40.00
31 Annie Oakley 300.00 135.00
32 Daniel O'Leary 90.00 40.00
33 James O'Neil BB 800.00 350.00
Sic, O'Neill
34 Wm. Byrd Page 90.00 40.00
35 Axel Paulsen 90.00 40.00
36 Master Ray Perry 90.00 40.00
37 Duncan C. Ross 90.00 40.00
38 W.A. Rowe 90.00 40.00
39 Jacob Schaefer 90.00 40.00
40 M. Schloss 90.00 40.00
41 Jem Smith 90.00 40.00
42 Lillian Smith 90.00 40.00
43 Hattie Stewart 90.00 40.00
44 John L. Sullivan BOX 500.00 220.00
45 Arthur Wallace 90.00 40.00
46 Tommy Warren BOX 250.00 110.00
47 Ada Webb 90.00 40.00
48 John Wessels 90.00 40.00
49 Clarence Whistler 90.00 40.00
50 Charles Wood 90.00 40.00

1987 Marketcom/Sports Illustrated *

This 20-card white-bordered, multi-sport set measures approximately 3 1/16" by 4 14/16" and features color action photos of players in various sports produced by Marketcom. Cards #1-13 display Baseball players; cards #14-17, Basketball players; cards #18-10, Football players. The backs are blank. The set was issued to promote the Sports Illustrated sticker line. The cards are unnumbered and checklisted below alphabetically within each sport.

MINT NRMT
COMPLETE SET (20) 150.00 70.00
1 Wade Boggs 8.00 3.60
2 Gary Carter 4.00 1.80
3 Roger Clemens 20.00 9.00
4 Eric Davis 3.00 1.35
5 Andre Dawson 5.00 2.20
6 Dwight Gooden 3.00 1.35
7 Rickey Henderson 5.00 2.20
8 Don Mattingly 15.00 6.75
9 Dale Murphy 4.00 1.80
10 Kirby Puckett 15.00 6.75
11 Ryne Sandberg 15.00 6.75
12 Ozzie Smith 15.00 6.75
13 Darryl Strawberry 2.00 .90
14 Larry Bird 15.00 6.75
15 Magic Johnson 12.00 5.50
16 Michael Jordan 30.00 13.50
17 Dominique Wilkins 6.00 2.70
18 John Elway 25.00 11.00
19 Lawrence Taylor 3.00 1.35
20 Herschel Walker 3.00 1.35

1971 Mattel Mini-Records*

This 18-disc set was designed to be played on a special Mattel mini-record player, which is not included in the complete set price. Each black plastic disc, approximately 2 1/2" in diameter, features a recording on one side and a color drawing of the player on the other. The picture appears on a paper disk that is glued onto the smooth unrecorded side of the mini-record. On the recorded side, the player's name and the set's subtitle appear in arcs stamped in the central portion of the mini-record. The hand-engraved player's name appears again along with a production number, copyright symbol, and the Mattel name and year of production in the ring between the central portion of the record and the grooves. The ivory discs are the ones which are double sided and are considered to be much tougher than the black discs. They are currently valued at 2X the regular records. They were also known as "Mattel Show 'N Tell". The discs are unnumbered and checklisted below in alphabetical order.

NRMT VG-E
COMPLETE SET (18) 300.00 135.00
1 Hank Aaron 30.00 13.50
2 Hank Aaron 30.00 13.50
(Double-sided)
3 Ernie Banks 20.00 9.00
4 Ernie Banks 20.00 9.00
(Double-sided)
5 Al Kaline 20.00 9.00
6 Al Kaline 20.00 9.00
(Double-sided)
7 Willie Mays 30.00 13.50
8 Willie Mays 30.00 13.50
(Double-sided)
9 Willie McCovey 20.00 9.00
10 Willie McCovey 20.00 9.00
(Double-sided)
11 Tony Oliva 10.00 4.50
12 Tony Oliva 10.00 4.50
(Double-sided)
13 Frank Robinson 20.00 9.00
14 Frank Robinson 20.00 9.00
(Double-sided)
15 Tom Seaver 20.00 9.00
16 Tom Seaver 20.00 9.00
(Double-sided)
17 Willie Stargell 20.00 9.00
18 Willie Stargell 20.00 9.00
(Double-sided)

1982 Montreal News *

This 21-card set was cut out of the Montreal News and features various size color player photos of stars of different sports. The paper is printed in French. The cards are unnumbered and checklisted below in alphabetical order.

NRMT VG-E
COMPLETE SET (21) 40.00 18.00
1 Tracy Austin 2.00 .90
Tennis
2 Bjorn Borg 3.00 1.35
Tennis
3 Jimmy Connors 4.00 1.80
Tennis
4 Chris Chueden 1.00 .45
Soccer
5 Mario Cusson 1.00 .45
Boxing
6 Steve Garvey BB 3.00 1.35
7 Rejean Houle HK 2.00 .90
8 Mark Hunter HK 1.00 .45
9 Frantz Mathieu 1.00 .45
Soccer
10 Martina Navratilova 4.00 1.80
Tennis
11 Wilfrid Paiement HK 1.00 .45
12 Bob Rigby 1.00 .45
Soccer
13 Pete Rose BB 8.00 3.60
14 Mike Schmidt BB 8.00 3.60
15 Willie Stargell BB 3.00 1.35
16 Daniel Talbot 1.00 .45
Golf
17 Luc Tousignant FB 1.00 .45
18 Tony Towers 1.00 .45
Soccer
19 Thompson Usiyan 1.00 .45
Soccer
20 Fernando Valenzuela BB 2.00 .90
21 Dragan Vujovic 1.00 .45
Soccer

1976 Nabisco Sugar Daddy 1 *

This set of 25 tiny (approximately 1 1/16" by 2 3/4") cards features action scenes from a variety of popular sports from around the world. One card was included in specially marked Sugar Daddy and Sugar Mama candy bars. The set is referred to as "Sugar Daddy Sports World - Series 1" on the backs of the cards. The cards are in color with a relatively wide white border around the front of the cards.

NRMT VG-E
COMPLETE SET (25) 80.00 36.00
1 Hockey 10.00 4.50
2 High Jump 2.00 .90
3 Tennis 2.00 .90
4 Auto Racing 10.00 4.50
5 Hot Dog Ski 2.00 .90
6 Football 10.00 4.50
Sonny Jurgensen
7 Track and Field 2.00 .90
8 Pole Vault 2.00 .90
9 Swimming 2.00 .90
10 Gymnastics 2.00 .90
11 Basketball 10.00 4.50
12 Baseball 20.00 9.00
(Pete Rose batting)
13 Field Hockey 2.00 .90
14 Figure Skating 3.00 1.35
15 Tennis 2.00 .90
16 Track and Field 2.00 .90
17 Hurdles 2.00 .90
(Pamela Ryan)
18 Breast Stroke 2.00 .90
19 Broad Jump 2.00 .90
20 Slalom Ski 2.00 .90
21 Golf 10.00 4.50
22 Diving 2.00 .90
23 Volleyball 2.00 .90
24 Ski Jump 2.00 .90
25 Figure Skating 3.00 1.35

1976 Nabisco Sugar Daddy 2 *

This set of 25 tiny (approximately 1 1/16" by 2 3/4") cards features action scenes from a variety of popular sports from around the world. One card was included in specially marked Sugar Daddy and Sugar Mama candy bars. The set is referred to as "Sugar Daddy Sports World - Series 2" on the backs of the cards. The cards are in color with a relatively wide white border around the front of the cards.

NRMT VG-E
COMPLETE SET (25) 80.00 36.00
1 Cricket 2.00 .90
2 Yachting 2.00 .90
3 Diving 2.00 .90
4 Football 15.00 6.75
(Sonny Jurgensen)
5 Soccer 5.00 2.20
6 Lacrosse 2.00 .90
7 Track and Field 2.00 .90
8 Motorcycle 2.00 .90
9 Hang Gliding 2.00 .90
10 Tennis 2.00 .90
11 Hockey 10.00 4.50
12 Shot Put 2.00 .90
13 Basketball 10.00 4.50
14 Track and Field 2.00 .90
15 Gymnastics 2.00 .90
16 Power Boat Racing 2.00 .90
17 Bike Racing 2.00 .90
18 Golf 10.00 4.50
19 Hot Dog Ski 2.00 .90
20 Fishing 2.00 .90
21 Jai Alai 2.00 .90
22 Canoeing 2.00 .90
23 Gymnastics 5.00 2.20
(Cathy Rigby)
24 Steeple Chase 2.00 .90
25 Baseball 12.00 5.50
(Bobby Murcer)

2004 National Trading Card Day *

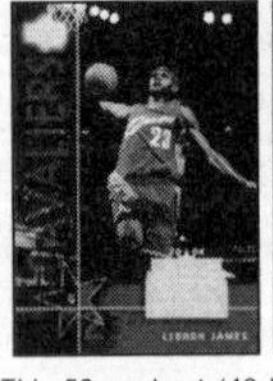

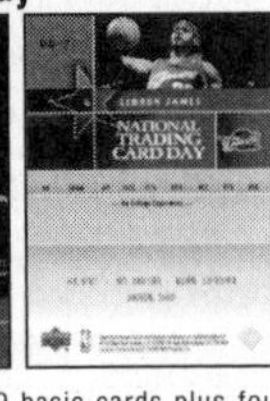

This 53-card set (49 basic cards plus four cover cards) was given out in five separate sealed packs (one from each of the following manufacturers: Donruss, Fleer, Press Pass, Topps and Upper Deck). One of the five packs was distributed at no cost to each patron that visited a participating sports card shop on April 3rd, 2004 as part of the National Trading Card Day promotion in an effort to increase awareness of collecting sports cards. The 50-card set is composed of 16 baseball, 9 basketball, 10 football, 4 golf, 5 hockey and 4 NASCAR cards. Of note, first year cards of NBA rookie stars LeBron James and Carmelo Anthony were included respectively within the UD and Fleer packs. An early Alex Rodriguez Yankees card was also highlighted within the Fleer pack.

MINT NRMT
COMPLETE SET (49) 15.00 6.75
F1-F9 ISSUED IN FLEER PACK
T1-T12 ISSUED IN TOPPS PACK
DP1-DP6 ISSUED IN DONRUSS PACK
PP1-PP7 ISSUED IN PRESS PASS PACK
UD1-UD15 ISSUED IN UPPER DECK PACK
FNNO Fleer Cover Card .10 .05
F1 Derek Jeter 1.50 .70
F2 Alex Rodriguez Yanks 3.00 1.35
F3 Nomar Garciaparra 1.00 .45
F4 Jose Reyes .50 .23
F5 Brett Favre 1.00 .45
F6 Marshall Faulk .50 .23
F7 Vince Carter .75 .35
F8 Carmelo Anthony 4.00 1.80
F9 Yao Ming .75 .35
TNNO Topps Cover Card .10 .05
T1 Rocco Baldelli .75 .35
T2 Mark Prior 1.00 .45
T3 Dontrelle Willis .40 .18
T4 Jason Giambi .75 .35
T5 Michael Vick 1.00 .45
T6 Charles Rogers .40 .18
T7 Rick Nash 1.00 .45
T8 Jean-Sebastian Giguere .40 .18
T9 Shaquille O'Neal 1.00 .45
T10 Kirk Hinrich 1.00 .45
T11 Tracy McGrady 1.00 .45
T12 Jaromir Jagr 1.00 .45
DPNNO DLP Cover Card .10 .05
DP1 Albert Pujols 1.00 .45
DP2 Roger Clemens 1.00 .45
DP3 Mike Piazza 1.00 .45
DP4 Alfonso Soriano .50 .23
DP5 Anquan Boldin .40 .18
DP6 Ricky Williams .75 .35
PP1 Press Pass Cover Card .10 .05
PP2 Jeff Gordon 1.00 .45
PP3 Jimmie Johnson .75 .35
PP4 Dale Earnhardt Jr. 1.25 .55
PP5 Tony Stewart .75 .35
PP6 Eli Manning 2.50 1.10
PP7 Roy Williams WR 1.50 .70
UDNNO UD Cover Card .10 .05
UD1 Annika Sorenstam 1.00 .45
UD2 Hideki Matsui 1.00 .45
UD3 Ichiro Suzuki 1.00 .45
UD4 Jack Nicklaus 1.00 .45
UD5 Ken Griffey Jr. 1.00 .45
UD6 Kevin Garnett 1.00 .45
UD7 LeBron James 8.00 3.60
UD8 Michael Jordan 1.50 .70
UD9 Michael Vick 1.00 .45
UD10 Patrick Roy 1.00 .45
UD11 Peyton Manning 1.00 .45
UD12 Sammy Sosa 1.00 .45
UD13 Sergio Garcia .75 .35
UD14 Tiger Woods 1.50 .70
UD15 Wayne Gretzky 1.50 .70

1974 New York News This Day in Sports *

These cards are newspaper clippings of drawings by Hollreiser and are accompanied by textual description highlighting a player's unique sports feat. Cards are approximately 2" X 4 1/4". These are multisport cards and aranged in chronological order.

NRMT VG-E
COMPLETE SET (40) 125.00 55.00
1 Johnny Bench 4.00 1.80
Yogi Berra
June 2, 1972; 1951
2 Byron Nelson 4.00 1.80
Ben Hogan
June 12, 1939
3 Ted Williams 4.00 1.80
June 13, 1957
4 Johnny Miller 2.00 .90
June 17, 1973
5 Ezzard Charles 4.00 1.80

Sandy Koufax
June 22, 1949; 1959
6 Bobby Murcer 2.00 .90
June 24, 1970
7 Gil Hodges 4.00 1.80
Ralph Kiner
June 25, 1949; 1950
8 Jim Ryun 2.00 .90
June 26, 1965
9 Dizzy Dean 2.50 1.10
July 1, 1934
10 Billie Jean King 2.50 1.10
Carl Hubbell
July 2, 1966; 1933
11 Yogi Berra 2.50 1.10
July 3, 1957
12 Arky Vaughan 4.00 1.80
Ted Williams
July 8, 1941
13 Tom Seaver 4.00 1.80
July 9, 1969; 1970
14 Willie Stargell 2.50 1.10
July 11, 1973
15 Nolan Ryan 10.00 4.50
July 15, 1973
16 Peter Revson 2.00 .90
July 25, 1971
17 Casey Stengel 4.00 1.80
July 26, 1916; 1955
18 Mickey Mantle 10.00 4.50
Whitey Ford
July 29, 1966; 1955
19 Robin Roberts 2.50 1.10
Aug. 19, 1955
20 Lou Gehrig 4.00 1.80
Aug. 21, 1935; 1937
21 Warren Spahn 2.50 1.10
Roy Face
Aug. 30. 1960; 1959
22 George Sisler 3.00 1.35
Pete Rose
Sept. 4, 1920; 1973
23 Sal Maglie 2.00 .90
Tommy Henrich
Sept. 9, 1950; 1941
24 Hank Aaron 4.00 1.80
Sept. 21, 1958
25 Doc Blanchard 3.00 1.35
Glenn Davis
Sept. 30, 1944
26 Dick Sisler 2.00 .90
Oct. 1, 1950
27 Archie Manning 3.00 1.35
Oct. 4, 1969
28 Pepper Martin 4.00 1.80
Yogi Berra
Oct. 7, 1931; 1961
29 Dizzy Dean 2.50 1.10
Daffy Dean
Oct. 9, 1934
30 Walter Johnson 2.50 1.10
Oct. 11, 1925
31 Harold Jackson 2.00 .90
Oct. 14, 1973
32 O.J. Simpson 3.00 1.35
Oct. 21, 1967
33 Doc Blanchard 2.00 .90
Nov. 11, 1944
34 Bobby Orr 4.00 1.80
Nov. 15, 1973
35 Bronko Nagurski 3.00 1.35
Nov. 23, 1929
36 Wilt Chamberlain 4.00 1.80
Dec. 6, 1963
37 New York Giants 2.00 .90
Dec. 9, 1934
38 John Brodie 2.00 .90
Dec. 20, 1970
39 Roger Staubach 4.00 1.80
Dec. 23, 1972
40 Paul Brown 3.00 1.35
Otto Graham
Dec. 26, 1954

1983-85 Nike Poster Cards *

The cards in this set measure approximately 5" by 7" and were produced for use by retailers of Nike full-size posters as a promotional counter display. The cards are plastic coated and feature color pictures of players posed in unique settings. The hole at the top was designed so that dealers could attach the cards to the display with a soft plastic fastener provided by Nike. The borders are black. Originally, 27-cards were issued together and others were added later as new posters were created. The backs are plain white and carry the poster name, item number, and the player names (except on group photos). The cards are numbered only by the item number on back and have been listed below according to the final two digits of that number.

NRMT VG-E
COMPLETE SET (43) 200.00 90.00
1 The Supreme Court 6.00 2.70
(Seventeen NBA players)
2 Iceman 10.00 4.50
George Gervin
4 No Finish Line 3.00 1.35
6 Dr. Dunkenstein 3.00 1.35
Darrell Griffith
12 Urban Runner 3.00 1.35
13 Runner in the Clouds 3.00 1.35
17 Truck 3.00 1.35
Leonard Robinson
18 MVP and CY 15.00 6.75
Mike Schmidt
Steve Carlton
19 Moses 6.00 2.70
Moses Malone
20 Jam Session 5.00 2.20
24 NBA players
some pictured with musical instruments)
21 The Williams 3.00 1.35
Ray Williams
Roseanne Williams
Gus Williams
22 McEnroe 10.00 4.50
John McEnroe
23 Fingers and Sutter 4.00 1.80
Rollie Fingers
Bruce Sutter
24 Penguin Power 3.00 1.35
Ron Cey
25 Silk 5.00 2.20
Jamaal Wilkes
26 Field Generals 12.00 5.50
(Eight NFL quarter-backs dressed in military garb)
27 Speedsters 12.00 5.50
(Thirteen NFL players)
28 Runner on the Beach 3.00 1.35
30 Board Room 5.00 2.20
(28 NBA players)
31 K-Lord 4.00 1.80
Gaylord Perry
33 Stormin' Norman 4.00 1.80
Norm Nixon
34 Secretary of Defense 5.00 2.20
Bobby Jones
35 Air Force I 10.00 4.50
Michael Cooper
Calvin Natt
Bobby Jones
Jamaal Wilkes
Moses Malone
37 Power Alley 4.00 1.80
Dale Murphy
38 Tigerrr Catcher 3.00 1.35
Lance Parrish
39 The Dodger Kid 3.00 1.35
Steve Sax
40 Steeler Pounder 20.00 9.00
Franco Harris
41 Atlanta Arsenal 6.00 2.70
Alfred Jackson
Steve Bartkowski
Alfred Jenkins
42 Texas Thunder 12.00 5.50
Ed(Too Tall) Jones
Harvey Martin
43 Sir Sid 5.00 2.20
Sidney Moncrief
44 Ruland 3.00 1.35
Jeff Ruland
46 No Passing 3.00 1.35
Mike Haynes
Vann McElroy
Mike Davis
Lester Hayes
47 Lofton 5.00 2.20
James Lofton
48 Battle of Atlanta 3.00 1.35
52 Dr. K 3.00 1.35
Dwight Gooden
54 Boss Boggs 8.00 3.60
Wade Boggs
55 Rick's World 3.00 1.35
Rick Sutcliffe
56 Stickball 5.00 2.20
Dwight Gooden
Dale Murphy
57 Air Force 20.00 9.00
Moses Malone
Charles Barkley
59 Football 3.00 1.35
Lester Hayes
Louis Lipps
61 The Judge 3.00 1.35
Lester Hayes
62 Manute Bol Growth Chart 3.00 1.35
5" by 13"
68 Shirts and Skins 3.00 1.35

1985 Nike *

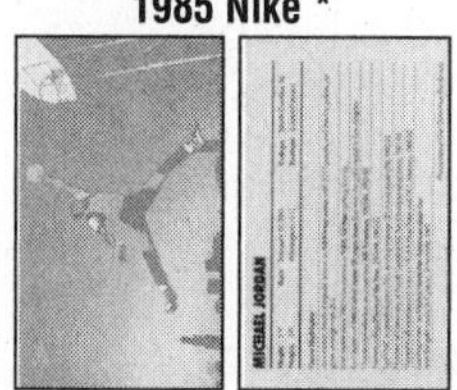

This oversized (slightly larger than 3x5 cards) multisport set was issued by Nike to promote athletic shoe sales. Although the set contains an attractive rookie-season card of Michael Jordan, the fairly plentiful supply has kept the market value quite affordable. Sets were distributed in shrinkwrapped form. The cards are unnumbered and are listed here in alphabetical order.

MINT NRMT
COMP.FACTORY SET (5) 100.00 45.00
COMPLETE SET (5) 50.00 22.00
1 Dwight Gooden 2.50 1.10
2 Michael Jordan 50.00 22.00
3 James Lofton 1.50 .70
4 John McEnroe 4.00 1.80
5 Lance Parrish 1.00 .45

1996 No Fear *

This eight-card jumbo-sized set was issued through No Fear. It is a multi-sport set that features a posed color player shot on the front and a white back featuring a slogan by No Fear. The mode of distribution is unclear. The cards are not numbered and checklisted below in alphabetical order.

MINT NRMT
COMPLETE SET (8) 12.00 5.50
1 Wade Boggs 2.00 .90
2 Theoren Fleury 1.00 .45
3 Grant Fuhr 3.00 1.35
4 Robby Gordon 1.00 .45
5 Tony Gwynn 4.00 1.80
6 Eric Karros 1.00 .45
7 Chris Mills 1.00 .45
8 Mo Vaughn 2.00 .90

1979 Open Pantry *

This set is an unnumbered, 12-card issue featuring players from Milwaukee area professional sports teams with five Brewers baseball (1-5), five Bucks basketball (6-10), and two Packers football (11-12). Cards are black and white with red trim and measure approximately 5" by 6". Cards were sponsored by Open Pantry, Lake to Lake, and MACC (Milwaukee Athletes against Childhood Cancer). The cards are unnumbered and hence are listed and numbered below alphabetically within sport.

NRMT VG-E
COMPLETE SET (12) 30.00 13.50
1 Jerry Augustine 2.00 .90
2 Sal Bando 3.00 1.35
3 Cecil Cooper 3.00 1.35
4 Larry Hisle 2.50 1.10
5 Lary Sorensen 2.00 .90
6 Kent Benson 4.00 1.80
7 Junior Bridgeman 4.00 1.80
8 Quinn Buckner 5.00 2.20
9 Marques Johnson 6.00 2.70
10 Jon McGlocklin 4.00 1.80
11 Rich McGeorge 2.00 .90
12 Steve Wagner 2.00 .90

1943-48 Parade Sportive *

These blank-backed photo sheets of sports figures from the Montreal area around 1945 measure approximately 5" by 8 1/4". They were issued to promote a couple of Montreal radio stations that used to broadcast interviews with some of the pictured athletes. The sheets feature white-bordered black-and-white player photos, some of them crudely retouched. The player's name appears in the bottom white margin and also as a facsimile autograph across the photo. The sheets are unnumbered and are checklisted below in alphabetical order within sport as follows: hockey (1-72), baseball (73-92) and various other sports (93-98). Additions to this checklist is appreciated. Many players are known to appear with two different poses. Since the values are the same for both poses, we have put a (2) next to the players name but have placed a value on only one of the photos.

EX-MT VG-E
COMPLETE SET 2500.00 1100.00
1 George Allen 25.00 11.00
2 Aldege(Bazz) Bastien 25.00 11.00
3 Bobby Bauer 50.00 22.00
Milt Schmidt
Woody Dumart
4 Joe Benoit 25.00 11.00
5 Paul Bibeault 25.00 11.00
6 Emile(Butch) Bouchard (2) 40.00 18.00
7 Butch Bouchard 40.00 18.00
Leo Lamoureux
Bill Durnan
8 Toe Blake 50.00 22.00
9 Lionel Bouvrette 25.00 11.00
10 Frank Brimsek 40.00 18.00
11 Turk Broda 50.00 22.00
12 Eddie Bruneteau 25.00 11.00
13 Modere Bruneteau 25.00 11.00
14 Jean Claude Campeau 25.00 11.00
15 J.P. Campeau 25.00 11.00
16 Bob Carse 25.00 11.00
17 Joe Carveth 40.00 18.00
18 Denys Casavant 25.00 11.00
19 Murph Chamberlain 25.00 11.00
20 Bill Cowley 25.00 11.00
21 Floyd Curry 25.00 11.00
22 Tony Demers 25.00 11.00
23 Connie Dion 25.00 11.00
24 Bill Durnan (2) 40.00 18.00
25 Normand Dussault 25.00 11.00
26 Frank Eddolls 25.00 11.00
27 Johnny Gagnon 25.00 11.00
28 Bob Fillion (2) 25.00 11.00
29 Johnny Gagnon 25.00 11.00
Aurel Joliat
Howie Morenz
30 Armand Gaudreault 25.00 11.00
31 Fernand Gauthier 25.00 11.00
32 Fernand Gauthier 25.00 11.00
Buddy O'Connor
Dutch Hiller
33 Jean-Paul Gladu 25.00 11.00
34 Leo Gravelle 25.00 11.00
35 Glen Harmon 25.00 11.00
36 Doug Harvey 40.00 18.00
37 Jerry Heffernan 25.00 11.00
Buddy O'Connor
Pete Morin
38 (Sugar) Jim Henry 30.00 13.50
39 Dutch Hiller 25.00 11.00
40 Rosario Joanette 25.00 11.00
41 Michael Karakas 25.00 11.00
42 Elmer Lach 50.00 22.00
43 Ernest Laforce 25.00 11.00
44 Leo Lamoureux 25.00 11.00
45 Edgar Laprade 25.00 11.00
46 Hal Laycoe 25.00 11.00
47 Roger Leger 25.00 11.00
48 Jacques Locas 25.00 11.00
49 Harry Lumley 40.00 18.00
50 Fernand Mageau 25.00 11.00
51 Georges Mantha (2) 25.00 11.00
52 Jean Marois 25.00 11.00
53 Mike McMahon 25.00 11.00
54 Gerry McNeil 25.00 11.00
55 Pierre(Pete) Morin 25.00 11.00
56 Ken Mosdell 25.00 11.00
57 Bill Mosienko 40.00 18.00
Max Bentley
Doug Bentley
58 Buddy O'Connor 25.00 11.00
59 Gerry Plamondon 25.00 11.00
60 Robert(Bob) Pepin 25.00 11.00
61 Jimmy Peters 25.00 11.00
62 Jerry Plamondon 25.00 11.00
63 Paul Raymond 25.00 11.00
64 Billy Reay 30.00 13.50
65 John Quilty 25.00 11.00
66 Kenny Reardon 30.00 13.50
67 Maurice Richard (2) 75.00 34.00
68 Maurice Richard 50.00 22.00
Elmer Lach
Toe Blake
69 Howie(Rip) Riopelle 25.00 11.00
70 Gaye Stewart 25.00 11.00
71 Phil Watson 30.00 13.50
72 Montreal Canadiens 25.00 11.00
Team Photo ($4)
73 Jack Banta 30.00 13.50
74 Stan Breard 25.00 11.00
75 Les Burge 25.00 11.00
76 Al Campanis 30.00 13.50
77 Red Durrett 25.00 11.00
78 Herman Franks 30.00 13.50
79 John Gabbard 25.00 11.00
80 Roland Gladu 25.00 11.00
81 Ray Hathaway 25.00 11.00
82 John Jorgenson 25.00 11.00
83 Paul Pepper Martin 25.00 11.00
84 Steve Nagy 25.00 11.00
86 Jackie Robinson 200.00 90.00
87 Marvin Rackley 25.00 11.00
88 Jean-Pierre Roy 25.00 11.00
89 Roland Gaddy 25.00 11.00
Jean-Pierre Roy
Stan Breard
90 Montreal Royals 1944 50.00 22.00
91 Montreal Royals 1945 25.00 11.00
92 Montreal Royals 1946 50.00 22.00
93 Gerard Cote 25.00 11.00
Racing
94 Harry Hurst 25.00 11.00
Boxing
95 Nik Kebedgy 25.00 11.00
Skiing
96 Jack Kramer 50.00 22.00
Tennis
97 Felix Miquet 25.00 11.00
Weight Lifting
98 Henri Rochon 25.00 11.00
Tennis
99 Barbara Ann Scott 40.00 18.00
Ice Skating

1968-70 Partridge Meats *

This black and white (with a little bit of red trim) photo-like card set features players from all three Cincinnati major league sports teams of that time, Cincinnati Reds baseball (BB1-BB18), Cincinnati Bengals football (FB1-FB4), and Cincinnati Royals basketball (BK1-BK2). The cards measure approximately 4" by 5", although there are other sizes sometimes found which are attributable to other years of issue. The cards are blank backed. In addition to the cards listed below, a "Mr. Whopper" card was also issued in honor of an extremely large spokesperson.

NRMT VG-E
COMPLETE SET (14) 800.00 350.00
BB1 Ted Abernathy 25.00 11.00
BB2 Johnny Bench 120.00 55.00
BB3 Jimmy Bragan CO 25.00 11.00
BB4 Dave Bristol MG 25.00 11.00
BB5 Don Gullett 30.00 13.50
BB6 Tommy Harper 30.00 13.50
BB7 Tommy Helms 25.00 11.00
BB8 Lee May 40.00 18.00
BB9 Denis Menke 25.00 11.00
BB10 Jim Merritt 25.00 11.00
BB11 Gary Nolan 25.00 11.00
BB12 Milt Pappas 30.00 13.50
BB13 Don Pavletich 25.00 11.00
BB14 Tony Perez 80.00 36.00
BB15 Mel Queen 25.00 11.00
BB16 Pete Rose 150.00 70.00
BB17 Jim Stewart 25.00 11.00
BB18 Bob Tolan 25.00 11.00
BK1 Adrian Smith 50.00 22.00
BK2 Tom Van Arsdale 60.00 27.00
FB1 Bob Johnson 20.00 9.00
FB2 Paul Robinson 40.00 18.00
FB3 John Stofa 40.00 18.00
FB4 Bob Trumpy 25.00 11.00

1992 Philadelphia Daily News *

This nine-card set, which is aptly subtitled "Great Moments in Philadelphia Sports," was sponsored by the Philadelphia Daily News. The fronts of the standard-size cards have red borders and feature miniature reproductions of newspaper front pages with famous headlines and memorable photos. Each card captures a great moment in the history of Philadelphia sports. Sports represented are baseball, (cards 1 and 7-8) hockey, (2) basketball, (3-4) football, (5-6) and boxing (9). The backs are printed in gray, black and white and provide text relating to the event commemorated on the card.

MINT NRMT
COMPLETE SET (9) 3.50 1.55
1 We Win .50 .23
Phillies win World Series
2 God Bless the Flyers .25 .11
Flyers win Stanley Cup
3 V .25 .11
Villanova wins
NCAA Championship
4 Hoopla .25 .11
Sixers win NBA Championship
5 Eagles Seek New CO and QB .25 .11
Eagles win
NFL Championship
6 Super .25 .11
Eagles win NFC Championship
7 Mike Schmidt 1.00 .45
announces retirement
8 City Wild .25 .11
Phillies win NL Championship
9 Joe Frazier 1.00 .45
defeats Muhammad Ali

1981-82 Philip Morris *

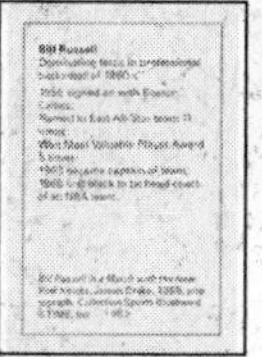

This 18-card standard-size set was included in the Champions of American Sport program and features major stars from a variety of sports. The program was issued in conjunction with a traveling exhibition organized by the National Portrait Gallery and the Smithsonian Institution and sponsored by Philip Morris and Miller Brewing Company. The cards are either reproductions of works of art (paintings) or famous photographs of the time. The cards are frequently found with a perforated edge on at least one side. The cards were actually obtained from two perforated pages in the program. There is no notation anywhere on the cards indicating the manufacturer or sponsor.

NRMT VG-E
COMPLETE SET (18) 80.00 36.00
1 Muhammad Ali 20.00 9.00
2 Arthur Ashe 8.00 3.60
3 Peggy Fleming 4.00 1.80
4 A.J. Foyt 8.00 3.60
5 Eric Heiden 1.00 .45
6 Bobby Hull 10.00 4.50
7 Sandy Koufax 10.00 4.50
8 Joe Louis 6.00 2.70
9 Bob Mathias 1.00 .45
10 Willie Mays 10.00 4.50
11 Joe Namath 15.00 6.75
12 Jack Nicklaus 15.00 6.75
13 Knute Rockne 8.00 3.60
14 Bill Russell 20.00 9.00
15 Jim Ryun 1.00 .45
16 Willie Shoemaker 2.50 1.10
17 Casey Stengel 2.50 1.10
18 Johnny Unitas 10.00 4.50

1998 Pinnacle Fanfest Elway*

This one card set, issued at the All-Star FanFest in Denver in 1998 honored long time Denver Bronco hero, John Elway. The front of the card features him in an Oneonta Yankee uniform while the back has a brief biography; a ghosted photo of Elway as a Bronco and his career minor league stats. The card was available for a small charity donation at the Pinnacle Booth.

MINT NRMT
NNO John Elway 20.00 9.00

1998 Pinnacle Team Pinnacle Collector's Club *

This four-card set originally to have been issued to members of the Pinnacle Collector's Club. Ultimately the cards were released after the company's bankruptcy. Each card reads "Team Pinnacle" at the bottom of the cardfront with the player's name above the image on the front.

	MINT	NRMT
COMPLETE SET (4)	30.00	13.50
1 John Elway	8.00	3.60
2 Ken Griffey Jr.	8.00	3.60
3 Derek Jeter	12.00	5.50
4 Eric Lindros	5.00	2.20

1950 Prest-o-Lite Postcards*

These two postcards were issued to promote the "Prest-O-Lite" batteries. The front contains an action photo of the star while the back has a promotion for those batteries. There might be more photos so any additions are appreciated.

	MINT	NRMT
1 Leon Hart	25.00	11.00
2 Ted Williams	60.00	27.00

1991 Pro Set Pro Files *

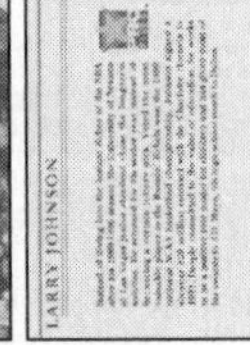

These cards measure the standard size. The fronts have full-bleed color photos, with facsimile autographs inscribed across the bottom of the pictures. Reportedly only 150 of each were produced and approximately 100 of each were handed out as part of a contest on the Pro Files TV show. Each week viewers were invited to send in their names and addresses to a Pro Set post office box. All subjects in the set made appearances on the TV show. The show was hosted by Craig James and Tim Brant and was aired on Saturday nights in Dallas and sponsored by Pro Set. The cards were subtitled "Signature Series". The cards are unnumbered and are listed in alphabetical order by subject in the checklist below. All of the cards were facsimile autographed except for Anne Smith who signed all of her cards personally.

	MINT	NRMT
COMPLETE SET (13)	300.00	135.00
1 Troy Aikman FB	150.00	70.00
2 Ben Crenshaw (Pro golfer)	25.00	11.00
3 James Donaldson BK holding saxophone)	10.00	4.50
4 Norm Hitzges ANN	10.00	4.50
5 Ferguson Jenkins BB	20.00	9.00
6 Larry Johnson BK	20.00	9.00
7 Rives McBee (Pro golfer)	10.00	4.50
8 Byron Nelson (Golf legend)	25.00	11.00
9 Anne Smith (Tennis player all personally signed)	20.00	9.00
10 Lanny Wadkins (Golfer)	20.00	9.00
11 Rusty Wallace (Auto racing)	25.00	11.00
12 Vernon Wells (Sports artist)	10.00	4.50
13 Herb Williams BK	10.00	4.50

1991 Pro Stars Posters *

These three posters were folded, cello wrapped, and inserted in Pro Stars cereal boxes. Through an offer on the side panel of the box, the collector could receive another poster by sending in three Pro Stars UPC symbols and 1.00 for postage and handling. In the cello packs, the posters measure approximately 4 1/2" by 4"; they unfold to a narrow poster that measures approximately 4 1/2" by 24". On a background of blue, purple, and bright yellow stars, a cartoon drawing portrays the athlete in an action pose. At the bottom of each poster appears a player profile in English and French. The backsides of all three posters combine to form a composite poster featuring all three players. The posters are unnumbered and listed below alphabetically.

	MINT	NRMT
COMPLETE SET (3)	10.00	4.50
1 Bo Jackson	1.50	.70
2 Michael Jordan	5.00	2.20
3 Wayne Gretzky	4.00	1.80

1954 Quaker Sports Oddities *

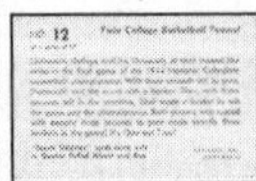

This 27-card set features strange moments in sports and was issued as an insert inside Quaker Puffed Rice cereal boxes. Fronts of the cards are drawings depicting the person or the event. In a stripe at the top of the card face appear the words "Sports Oddities." Two colorful drawings fill the remaining space: the left half is a portrait, while the right half is action-oriented. A variety of sports are included. The cards measure approximately 2 1/4" by 3 1/2" and have rounded corners. The last line on the back of each card declares, "It's Odd but True." A person could also buy the complete set for fifteen cents and two box tops from Quaker Puffed Wheat or Quaker Rice. If a collector did send in their material to Quaker Oats the set came back in a specially marked box with the cards in cellophane wrapping. Sets in original wrapping are valued at 1.25x to 1.5X the high column listings in our checklist.

	NRMT	VG-E
COMPLETE SET (27)	250.00	110.00
1 Johnny Miller (Incredible Punt)	6.00	2.70
2 Fred Snite Sr. (Two Holes-In-One)	12.00	5.50
3 George Quam (One Arm Handball)	5.00	2.20
4 John B. Maypole (Speedboating)	3.00	1.35
5 Harold(Bunny) Levitt (Free Throws)	20.00	9.00
6 Wake Forest College (Six Forward Passes)	6.00	2.70
7 Amos Alonzo Stagg (Three TD's No Score)	25.00	11.00
8 Catherine Fellmuth	3.00	1.35
9 Bill Wilson	12.00	5.50
10 Chicago Blackhawks	15.00	6.75
11 Betty Robinson	3.00	1.35
12 Dartmouth College/ University of Utah (1944 NCAA Basketball)	15.00	6.75
13 Ab Jenkins	6.00	2.70
14 Capt.Eddie Rickenbacker	6.00	2.70
15 Jackie LaVine	3.00	1.35
16 Jackie Riley	3.00	1.35
17 Carol Stokholm	3.00	1.35
18 Jimmy Smilgoff	3.00	1.35
19 George Halas	30.00	13.50
20 Joyce Rosenbom (A Girl Too Good For Men's Baseball)	3.00	1.35
21 Squatter's Rights	3.00	1.35
22 Richard Dwyer	3.00	1.35
23 Harlem Globetrotters	40.00	18.00
24 Everett Dean (Indiana basketball)	25.00	11.00
25 Texas University/ Northwestern University	6.00	2.70
26 Bronko Nagurski (All-American Team)	60.00	27.00
27 Yankee Stadium (No Homers Out)	15.00	6.75

1995 Real Action Pop-Ups *

This seven-card pop-up set was produced by Up Front Sports and Entertainment, Inc., a company started by baseball star Bert Blyleven. The fronts and backs measure 3" by 4" and are attached together at their tops by a hinge. The fronts display a color photo of a crowd at a sporting event. The backs show a full-bleed color photo of the athlete. When the cards are opened, the resulting 3" by 8" panel features biography, statistics, or highlights, along with a product advertisement and a 3" by 2 3/4" color pop-up picture. The cards are unnumbered and checklisted below in alphabetical order.

	MINT	NRMT
COMPLETE SET (7)	6.00	2.70
1 Bert Blyleven	.50	.23
2 John Elway	1.50	.70
3 Jackie Joyner-Kersee	1.00	.45
4 Pooh Richardson	.50	.23
5 Mike Schmidt	1.50	.70
6 Pernell Whitaker	1.00	.45
7 The Olympics	.50	.23

1993 Rice Council *

Sponsored by the USA Rice Council (Houston, Texas), this ten-card standard-size set of recipe trading cards was issued to promote the consumption of rice. These sets were originally available from the Rice Council for 2.00. The fronts feature color photos with either blue or red borders. The player's name appears in black lettering in an orange stripe beneath the picture. The backs present biographical information, career summary, a favorite rice recipe, an up-close trivia fact, and the athlete's favorite charity to which the profits generated from the sale of the cards will be donated. The sports represented in this set are baseball (1, 3, 7), football (2, 5), tennis (4), swimming (6), and bobsledding (8).

	MINT	NRMT
COMPLETE SET (10)	10.00	4.50
1 Steve Sax	.50	.23
2 Troy Aikman	4.00	1.80
3 Roger Clemens	3.00	1.35
4 Zina Garrison	.50	.23
5 Warren Moon	1.00	.45
6 Summer Sanders	.50	.23
7 Steve Sax	.50	.23
8 Brian Shimer	.25	.11
9 Food Guide Pyramid	.25	.11
10 Ten Tips to Healthy Eating for Kids	.25	.11

1930 Rogers Peet *

The Rogers Peet Department Store in New York released this set in early 1930. The cards were given out four at time to employees at the store for enrolling boys in Ropeco (the store's magazine club). Employees who completed the set, and pasted them in the album designed to house the cards, were eligible to win prizes. The blankbacked cards measure roughly 1 3/4" by 2 1/2" and feature a black and white photo of the famous athlete with his name and card number below the picture. Additions to this list are appreciated.

	EX-MT	VG-E
1 Walter Hagen Golf	400.00	180.00
2 Johnny Weissmuller Swimming	100.00	45.00
3 DeHart Hubbard Track	50.00	22.00
4 Unknown		
5 Dazzy Vance BB	100.00	45.00
6 Sabin Carr Track	50.00	22.00
7 John Van Ryn Tennis	50.00	22.00
8 Clarence Chamberlain Aviator	50.00	22.00
9 Lionel Conacher HK	125.00	55.00
10 Unknown		
11 Gene Tunney Boxing	100.00	45.00
12 Charles Lindbergh Aviator	100.00	45.00
13 Walter Johnson	400.00	180.00
14 H.O.D. Seagraves Aviator	50.00	22.00
15 Gar Wood Boating	50.00	22.00
16 Rogers Hornsby BB	200.00	90.00
17 Unknown		
18 Herb Pennock BB	100.00	45.00
19 Wilmer Allison Tennis	50.00	22.00
20 Francis Hunter Tennis	50.00	22.00
21 Unknown		
22 Frank Boucher HK	75.00	34.00
23 Richard Byrd Explorer	50.00	22.00
24 Bobby Jones Golf	800.00	350.00
25 Jack Sharkey Boxing	100.00	45.00
26 Frank Hawks Aviator	50.00	22.00
27 Thomas Hitchcock Jr. Polo	50.00	22.00
28 Lou Gehrig BB	750.00	350.00
29 Ching Johnson HK	125.00	55.00
30 Peter DePaolo Auto Racing	75.00	34.00
31 Red Grange FB	500.00	220.00
32 Walter Spence Swimming	50.00	22.00
33 Ken Strong NYU	200.00	90.00
34 Ty Cobb BB	500.00	220.00
35 Bill Tilden Tennis	250.00	110.00
36 Jack Dempsey Boxing	125.00	55.00
37 Ed Wittmer Football	125.00	55.00
38 Tris Speaker BB	125.00	55.00
39 George Kojac Swimming	50.00	22.00
40 Maurice McCarthy Golf	50.00	22.00
41 Chris Cagle FB	150.00	70.00
42 Bill Burch HK	50.00	22.00
43 Ray Ruddy Track	50.00	22.00
44 Edward Hamm Track	50.00	22.00
45 Paavo Nurmi Track	100.00	45.00
46 Bill Melhorn Golf	50.00	22.00
47 Max Schmeling Boxing	200.00	90.00
48 Babe Ruth BB	4000.00	1800.00

1994 Score Board National Promos *

Distributed during the 1994 National Sports Collectors Convention, this 20-card standard-size multi-sport set features four subsets: Salute to 1994 Draft Stars (1-5), Centers of Attention (6-9), Texas Heroes (10-13, 20), and Salute to Racing's Greatest (14-18). The borderless fronts feature color action cutouts on multi-colored metallic backgrounds. The players name, position, and team name appear randomly placed on arcs. The borderless backs feature a color head shot on a ghosted backgound. The players name and biography appear at the top with the player's stats and profile at the bottom. The cards are numbered on the back with an "NC" prefix. The sets were given away to attendees at Classic's National Convention Party. Each set included a certificate of authenticity, giving the set serial number out of a total of 9,900 sets produced. There were five different checklist cards created using the fronts of other cards in the set. The complete set price includes only one of the checklist cards.

	MINT	NRMT
COMPLETE SET (20)	40.00	18.00
1 Glenn Robinson	1.00	.45
2 Jason Kidd	3.00	1.35
3 Donyell Marshall	.50	.23
4 Juwan Howard	1.00	.45
5 Grant Hill	2.00	.90
6 Hakeem Olajuwon	1.50	.70
7 Patrick Ewing	1.50	.70
8 Dikembe Mutombo	.75	.35
9 Alonzo Mourning	1.50	.70
10 Troy Aikman	2.50	1.10
11 Nolan Ryan	4.00	1.80
12 Emmitt Smith	3.00	1.35
13 Hakeem Olajuwon Texas Heroes	1.50	.70
14 Dale Earnhardt 1979-1981	4.00	1.80
15 Dale Earnhardt 1982-1984	4.00	1.80
16 Dale Earnhardt 1985-1987	4.00	1.80
17 Dale Earnhardt 1988-1990	4.00	1.80
18 Dale Earnhardt 1991-1993	4.00	1.80
19 History of the National	.50	.23
20A Troy Aikman CL	2.50	1.10
20B Dale Earnhardt CL	3.00	1.35
20C Hakeem Olajuwon CL	1.50	.70
20D Nolan Ryan CL	3.00	1.35
20E Emmitt Smith CL	3.00	1.35

1981 7-Up Jumbos *

These thin-stock cards, measuring approximately 5 1/4" x 8 1/2", were given away at 7-Up point-of-purchase displays. With the slogan "Feelin' 7-Up", the cards were produced highlighting the cola's different sports spokesmen of that time. The fronts contain a full-bleed color posed player photograph and a facsimile autograph. The backs have a green border, and some highlights of the player inside a white box. The cards were first available during the 1980-81 basketball season, and therefore Magic Johnson's card is one of his earliest professional pieces. Ann Meyers, another basketball great in her own right, is also represented in the set. Any other additions to this checklist would be greatly appreciated. The cards are unnumbered and checklisted below in alphabetical order.

	MINT	NRMT
COMPLETE SET (7)	75.00	34.00
1 Tracy Austin Tennis	10.00	4.50
2 George Brett BB	20.00	9.00
3 Magic Johnson BK	25.00	11.00
4 Sugar Ray Leonard Boxing	20.00	9.00
5 Ann Meyers BK	15.00	6.75
6 Dave Parker BB	10.00	4.50
7 Mike Schmidt BB	20.00	9.00

1926 Sport Company of America *

This 151-card set encompasses athletes from a multitude of different sports. There are 49-cards representing baseball and 14-cards for football. Each includes a black-and-white player photo within a fancy frame border. The player's name and sport are printed at the bottom. The backs carry a short player biography and statistics. The cards originally came in a small glassine envelope along with a coupon that could be redeemed for sporting equipment and are often still found in this form. The cards are unnumbered and have been checklisted below in alphabetical order within sport. We've assigned prefixes to the card numbers which serves to group the cards by sport (BB-baseball, FB- football).

	EX-MT	VG-E
COMP.BASEBALL SET (49)	7000.00	3200.00
COMP.FOOTBALL SET (14)	3000.00	1350.00
COMMON OTHER SPORTS	200.00	90.00
BB1 Babe Adams	80.00	36.00
BB2 Grover Alexander	150.00	70.00
BB3 Nick Altrock	50.00	22.00
BB4 Dave Bancroft	150.00	70.00
BB5 Jesse Barnes	50.00	22.00
BB6 Ossie Bluege	50.00	22.00
BB7 Jim Bottomley	100.00	45.00
BB8 Max Carey	100.00	45.00
BB9 Ty Cobb	1000.00	450.00
BB10 Mickey Cochrane	150.00	70.00
BB11 Eddie Collins	150.00	70.00
BB12 Stan Coveleski	100.00	45.00
BB13 Kiki Cuyler	100.00	45.00
BB14 Hank DeBerry	50.00	22.00
BB15 Jack Fournier	50.00	22.00
BB16 Goose Goslin	100.00	45.00
BB17 Charley Grimm	80.00	36.00
BB18 Bucky Harris	100.00	45.00
BB19 Gabby Hartnett	100.00	45.00
BB20 Fred Hofmann	50.00	22.00
BB21 Rogers Hornsby	200.00	90.00
BB22 Waite Hoyt	100.00	45.00
BB23 Walter Johnson	400.00	180.00
BB24 Joe Judge	50.00	22.00
BB25 Willie Kamm	50.00	22.00
BB26 Tony Lazzeri	100.00	45.00
BB27 Rabbit Maranville	100.00	45.00
BB28 Firpo Marberry	50.00	22.00
BB29 Rube Marquard	100.00	45.00
BB30 Stuffy McInnis	50.00	22.00
BB31 Babe Pinelli	50.00	22.00
BB32 Wally Pipp	50.00	22.00
BB33 Sam Rice	100.00	45.00
BB34 Emory Rigney	50.00	22.00
BB35 Dutch Ruether	50.00	22.00
BB36 Babe Ruth	1500.00	700.00
BB37 Ray Schalk	100.00	45.00
BB38 Joe Sewell	100.00	45.00
BB39 Urban Shocker	80.00	36.00
BB40 Al Simmons	100.00	45.00
BB41 George Sisler	150.00	70.00
BB42 Tris Speaker	200.00	90.00
BB43 Pie Traynor	150.00	70.00
BB44 George Uhle	50.00	22.00
BB45 Paul Waner	150.00	70.00
BB46 Aaron Ward	50.00	22.00
BB47 Ken Williams	80.00	36.00
BB48 Glenn Wright	50.00	22.00
BB49 Emil Yde	50.00	22.00
BX1 Jim Corbett		
BX2 Jack Dempsey		
BX3 Gene Tunney		
FB1 Peggy Flournoy	200.00	90.00
FB2 Benny Friedman	300.00	135.00
FB3 Edgar "Ed" Garbisch	200.00	90.00
FB4 Homer Hazel	200.00	90.00
FB5 Walter Koppisch	250.00	110.00
FB6 Edward McGinley	200.00	90.00
FB7 Edward McMillan	250.00	110.00
FB8 Harry Stuhldreher	500.00	220.00
FB9 Harold "Brick" Muller	200.00	90.00
FB10 Ernie Nevers	600.00	275.00
FB11 Swede Oberlander	200.00	90.00
FB12 Edward Tryon	250.00	110.00
FB13 Ed Weir	200.00	90.00
FB14 George Wilson	250.00	110.00
OT1 Benny Hill Auto Racing	250.00	110.00
OT2 Paavo Nurmi Running	500.00	220.00
OT3 Charles Paddock Sprinter	250.00	110.00
OT4 Bill Tilden Tennis	800.00	350.00

1933 Sport Kings R338 *

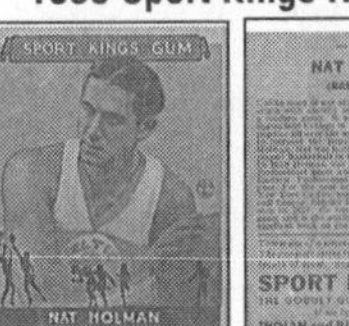

The cards in this 48-card set measure 2 3/8" by 2 7/8". The 1933 Sport Kings set, issued by the Goudey Gum Company, contains cards for the most famous athletic heroes of the times. No less than 18 different sports are represented in the set. The baseball cards of Cobb, Hubbell, and Ruth, and the football cards of Rockne and Thorpe command premium prices. The cards were issued in one-card penny packs along with a piece of gum. The catalog designation for this set is R338.

	EX-MT	VG-E
COMPLETE SET	15000.00	6800.00
1 Ty Cobb BB	2000.00	900.00
2 Babe Ruth BB	4000.00	1800.00
3 Nat Holman BK	400.00	180.00
4 Red Grange FB	800.00	350.00
5 Ed Wachter BK	120.00	55.00
6 Jim Thorpe (football)	800.00	350.00
7 Bobby Walthour Sr. (cycling)	60.00	27.00
8 Walter Hagen (golf)	300.00	135.00
9 Ed Blood (skiing)	60.00	27.00
10 Anton Lekang (skiing)	60.00	27.00
11 Charles Jewtraw (ice skating)	60.00	27.00
12 Bobby McLean (ice skating)	60.00	27.00
13 Laverne Fator (jockey)	60.00	27.00
14 Jim Londos (wrestling)	100.00	45.00
15 Reggie McNamara (bicycling)	60.00	27.00
16 Bill Tilden (tennis)	150.00	70.00
17 Jack Dempsey (boxing)	400.00	180.00
18 Gene Tunney (boxing)	300.00	135.00
19 Eddie Shore (hockey)	500.00	220.00
20 Duke Kahanamoku (swimming)	250.00	110.00
21 John Weissmuller (swimming)	400.00	180.00
22 Gene Sarazen (golf)	300.00	135.00
23 Vincent Richards (tennis)	60.00	27.00
24 Howie Morenz (hockey)	500.00	220.00
25 Ralph Snoddy (speedboat)	100.00	45.00
26 James R. Wedell (aviator)	100.00	45.00
27 Roscoe Turner (aviator)	100.00	45.00
28 Jimmy Doolittle (aviator)	150.00	70.00
29 Ace Bailey HK	400.00	180.00

30 Ching Johnson HK 400.00 180.00
31 Bobby Walthour Jr. 100.00 45.00
(cycling)
32 Joe Lapchick BK UER.......... 500.00 220.00
spelled Lopchick on front
33 Eddie Burke BK.................. 300.00 135.00
34 Irving Jaffee 100.00 45.00
(ice skating)
35 Knute Rockne FB............... 600.00 275.00
36 Willie Hoppe...................... 120.00 55.00
(billiards)
37 Helene Madison.................. 125.00 55.00
(swimming)
38 Bobby Jones 500.00 220.00
(golf)
39 Jack Westrope.................... 125.00 55.00
(jockey)
40 Don George........................ 125.00 55.00
(wrestling)
41 Jim Browning..................... 125.00 55.00
(wrestling)
42 Carl Hubbell BB................. 600.00 275.00
43 Primo Carnera.................... 200.00 90.00
(boxing)
44 Max Baer........................... 250.00 110.00
(boxing)
45 Babe Didrickson 800.00 350.00
(track)
46 Ellsworth Vines 150.00 70.00
(tennis)
47 J.H. Stevens...................... 125.00 55.00
(bob-sled)
48 Leonhard Seppala 150.00 70.00
(dog-sled)

1953 Sport Magazine Premiums *

This 10-card set features 5 1/2" by 7" color portraits and was issued as a subscription premium by Sport Magazine. These photos were taken by noted sports photographer Ozzie Sweet. Each features a top player from a number of different sports. The photo backs are blank and unnumbered. We've checklisted the set below in alphabetical order.

NRMT VG-E
COMPLETE SET (10)................ 60.00 27.00
1 Joe Black BB 10.00 4.50
2 Bob Cousy BK......................... 15.00 6.75
3 Elroy Hirsch FB...................... 15.00 6.75
4 Rocky Marciano 15.00 6.75
(boxing)
5 Bob Mathias........................... 12.00 5.50
(track)
6 Stan Musial BB...................... 15.00 6.75
7 John Olszewski FB 8.00 3.60
8 Allie Reynolds BB.................. 10.00 4.50
9 Robin Roberts BB.................. 15.00 6.75
10 Bobby Shantz BB.................. 8.00 3.60

1977-79 Sportscaster Series 1 *

NRMT VG-E
COMPLETE SET (24)................ 35.00 16.00
101 Roger De Coster..................... .50 .23
MotoCross
102 Bobby Orr.......................... 5.00 2.20
Ice Hockey
103 Muhammad Ali.................. 10.00 4.50
Boxing
104 Jesse Owens 2.50 1.10
1936 Olympics
Track and Field
105 Guy Drut............................ 1.00 .45
1976 Olympics
Track and Field
106 Faina Melnik........................ .50 .23
In the Discus
Track and Field
107 Mark Spitz .... 2.00 .90
Swimming
108 Michel Rousseau.................. .50 .23
Swimming
109 Fanny Blankers-Koen........... 1.00 .45
Track and Field
110 Bernard Thevenet .... 1.00 .45
Cycling
111 Michel Broillet .... .50 .23
Snatches 308 LBS
Weightlifting
112 Progress-For Better............... .50 .23
or Worse
A Ski Jumper
Nordic Skiing
113 Stream Fishing...................... .50 .23
Fisherman
Fishing
114 Frank Shorter .... 2.00 .90
1972 Olympics
Track and Field
115 Johnny Unitas FB 4.00 1.80
116 Anton Geesink....................... .50 .23
1965 World Champions
Judo
117 Pele.................................... 6.00 2.70
1970 World Cup
Soccer
118 Jimmy Connors................... 4.00 1.80
Tennis
119 The Weapons .... .50 .23
Four Weapons
Fencing
120 Jets vs. Colts...................... 1.50 .70
Football
121 Tom Seaver BB................... 4.00 1.80
122 Lasse Viren .... 1.00 .45
In the 5,000 M
Track and Field
123 Alberto Juantorena.............. 1.00 .45
1976 Montreal OG
Track and Field
124 Pete Maravich BK................ 5.00 2.20

1977-79 Sportscaster Series 2 *

NRMT VG-E
COMPLETE SET (24)................ 60.00 27.00
201 Une De Mai.......................... .50 .23
Horse Racing
202 Jack Nicklaus 6.00 2.70
Golf
203 Kareem Abdul-Jabbar BK 4.00 1.80
204 George Blanda FB................ 2.00 .90
205 Jacques Secretin .... .50 .23
Table Tennis
206 Gordie Howe 10.00 4.50
Ice Hockey
207 Off-side .... .50 .23
Line Judge
Soccer
208 Joe DiMaggio BB............... 10.00 4.50
209 USA-USSR .... 2.00 .90
USA vs. Russia
Basketball
Sergei Belov
210 Bernhard Russi .... .50 .23
Alpine Skiing
211 Vasaloppet .... .50 .23
Nordic Skiing
212 Sonja Henie......................... 2.00 .90
Figure Skating
213 The Stanley Cup .... 2.00 .90
Yvan Cournoyer
Serge Savard
Ice Hockey
214 Janet Lynn........................... 1.50 .70
Figure Skating
215 24 Hours at Le Mans........... 2.00 .90
1955 Crash
Auto Racing
216 1969 Mets......................... 10.00 4.50
Mets Win (Nolan Ryan)
Baseball
217 Johnny Cecotto .... .50 .23
Motorcycle Racing
218 Johnny Weissmuller............. 2.00 .90
Swimming
219 Eddy Merckx .... 1.00 .45
Milan-San Remo
Cycling
220 Bruce Lee.......................... 10.00 4.50
Lee Teaching
Karate
221 Kornelia Ender.................... 1.00 .45
Swimming
222 John Naber.......................... 1.00 .45
Swimming
223 Teofilo Stevenson................ 4.00 1.80
Boxing
224 Chris Evert.......................... 5.00 2.20
1974 Wimbledon
Tennis

1977-79 Sportscaster Series 3 *

NRMT VG-E
COMPLETE SET (24)................ 30.00 13.50
301 Toini Gustafsson .... .50 .23
1968 Olympics
Nordic Skiing
302 Adolfo Consolini.................... .50 .23
Track and Field
303 Group Gymnastics................. .50 .23
Gymnastics
304 Lightning Footwork .... .50 .23
Savate Action
Savate
305 Sheila Young .... 1.50 .70
Innsbruck/Istuno
Speed Skating
306 Chile-USSR .... .50 .23
Chile Stadium
Beyond Sports
307 O.J. Simpson FB................. 5.00 2.20
308 A Popular Sport..................... .50 .23
in Japan: Sumo Ceremony
Sumo
309 Variations on a .... .50 .23
Theme: Snow Racing
Motorcycle Racing
310 Daniel Morelon...................... .50 .23
Cycling
311 Dawn Fraser .... 1.50 .70
Aussie Swimmers
Swimming
312 Cornelius Warmerdam .... 1.00 .45
In Pole Vault
Track and Field
313 Avery Brundage.................. 1.00 .45
Beyond Sports
314 Rosi Mittermaier .... 1.00 .45
Alpine Skiing
315 Julius Erving BK.................. 6.00 2.70
316 Henry Aaron BB.................. 5.00 2.20
317 Soling.................................. .50 .23
The Long Ship
Yachting
318 Yukio Endo .... .50 .23
Parallel Bars
Gymnastics
319 Phil Esposito .... 2.00 .90
Tony Esposito HK
Two Bruins Stars
320 Joe Namath FB................... 5.00 2.20
321 Cathy Rigby........................ 2.00 .90
Gymnastics
322 Irena Szewinska .... .50 .23
Track and Field
323 Steve Williams....................... .50 .23
Track and Field
324 Dwight Stones.................... 1.00 .45
In High Jump
Track and Field

1977-79 Sportscaster Series 4 *

NRMT VG-E
COMPLETE SET (24)................ 30.00 13.50
401 Clay Regazzoni .... 1.00 .45
Auto Racing
402 Origin of the Game .... .50 .23
1890 Soccer Game
Soccer
403 Roger Menetrey................... 1.00 .45
Menetrey/Backus
Boxing
404 Jacques Anquetil .... .50 .23
Cycling
405 Track Racing .... 1.00 .45
Eddy Merckx
Sercu
Cycling
406 Anton Innauer .... .50 .23
Nordic Skiing
407 William Koch....................... 1.50 .70
1976 Olympics
Nordic Skiing
408 Eric Tabarly .... .50 .23
W/ Pen Duick VI
Yachting
409 Ireland's National .... .50 .23
Pastime
Dublin Stadium
Hurling
410 Earl Anthony....................... 2.00 .90
Bowling
411 Micki King .... 1.50 .70
Reverse Dive
Diving
412 Bill Russell BK.................... 6.00 2.70
413 A.Proell:Five .... 1.00 .45
World Cups
Annemarie Proell
Alpine Skiing
414 Dave Cowens BK................ 2.00 .90
415 Rick Barry BK..................... 2.00 .90
416 A Breakthrough For .... .50 .23
the E. Germans
Nehmer and Hausen
Bobsledding
417 Alberto Ascari......................... .50 .23
Auto Racing
418 Dr.Csaba Fenyvesi................. .50 .23
1972 Olympics
Fencing
419 An American........................... .50 .23
Invention
Blocking a Spike
Volleyball
420 Jonty Skinner .... 1.00 .45
Swimming
421 Hasely Crawford.................. 1.00 .45
1976 Olympics
Track and Field
422 Johnny Bench BB................ 4.00 1.80
423 Dorothy Hamill 4.00 1.80
Figure Skating
424 Bruce Jenner....................... 4.00 1.80
1976 Olympics
Track and Field

1977-79 Sportscaster Series 5 *

NRMT VG-E
COMPLETE SET (24)................ 25.00 11.00
501 Winter Triathlon .... .50 .23
On the Slalom
Triathlon
502 Mike Hailwood........................ .50 .23
Motorcycle Racing
503 Gymnaestrada .... .50 .23
Berlin in 1975
Gymnastics
504 Five Short Seconds .... 1.50 .70
Klaus Dibiasi
Diving
505 Skittles American .... .50 .23
Style
Bowler In Action
Bowling
506 A State of Mind .... .50 .23
Karate Action
Karate
507 Tourist Trophy......................... .50 .23
Isle of Man
Motorcycle Racing
508 Carlos Monzon .... 1.00 .45
Boxing
509 The USA vs........................ 1.50 .70
Czechoslovakia
Ice Hockey
510 Referee's Signals .... 1.50 .70
Olympic Action
Basketball
511 Babe Ruth BB..................... 8.00 3.60
512 It Requires More .... .50 .23
Than Speed
Trials Action
Trials
513 Karl Schranz........................ 1.00 .45
Alpine Skiing
514 Bobby Thomson BB .... 1.50 .70
515 World Cup Scorers................. .50 .23
Just Fontaine
Soccer
516 Timekeeping........................... .50 .23
Timing A Race
Beyond Sports
517 5 Rings and 1 Flame.............. .50 .23
Olympic Flame
Beyond Sports
518 Dick Fosbury .... 1.00 .45
Fosbury Flop
Track and Field
519 The 1969-70....................... 2.00 .90
Knickerbockers
Knicks vs. Lakers
Basketball
520 Bobby Hull HK 5.00 2.20
521 James Hunt......................... 1.50 .70
Auto Racing
522 The 1927 Yankees............... 2.00 .90
Baseball
523 Gale Sayers FB 4.00 1.80
524 World Championship............. .50 .23
for Sidecar
West Germany Win
Motorcycle Racing

1977-79 Sportscaster Series 6 *

NRMT VG-E
COMPLETE SET (24)................ 25.00 11.00
601 Abebe Bikila......................... 1.00 .45
Track and Field
602 Indianapolis.......................... 1.50 .70
Indy Raceway
Auto Racing
603 Jacky Ickx .... 1.50 .70
Auto Racing
604 Ron Clarke........................... 1.50 .70
1964 Olympics
Track and Field
605 A Mixed Team Sport.............. .50 .23
Game Action
Korfball
606 Record-Holder...................... 1.50 .70
in the Hour Race
Emil Zatopek
Track and Field
607 Gump Worsley HK............... 2.00 .90
608 The UCLA Dynasty 3.00 1.35
UCLA In Action
Basketball
609 Paula Sperber...................... 1.50 .70
Bowling
610 World Cup 6.00 2.70
Jack Nicklaus
Johnny Miller
Golf
611 Cresta Run .... .50 .23
Saint Moritz
Tobogganing
612 Joe Louis............................. 4.00 1.80
Boxing
613 Red Grange FB 4.00 1.80
614 Olympic Symbols.................... .50 .23
Olympic Flag
Beyond Sports
615 Aztec Stadium .... .50 .23
Beyond Sports
616 The Ten Members of .... 1.00 .45
10.0 Club
Armin Hary
Track and Field
617 The Javelin .... .50 .23
Nemeth
Track and Field
618 Jimmy Brown FB................. 5.00 2.20
619 Olympic Hierarchy.................. .50 .23
Olympic Committee
Beyond Sports
620 Alpine World Cup .... .50 .23
Thoeni Proell
Alpine Skiing
621 George McGinnis BK........... 1.50 .70
622 World Drivers....................... 2.00 .90
Champions 1976
Niki Lauda
Auto Racing
623 Lord Killanin........................ 1.00 .45
Beyond Sports
624 Johnny Vander Meer BB....... 1.50 .70

1977-79 Sportscaster Series 7 *

NRMT VG-E
COMPLETE SET (24)................ 30.00 13.50
701 Amateurism:........................... .50 .23
Article 26
Olympic Ceremony
Beyond Sports
702 Willie Shoemaker 4.00 1.80
Horse Racing
703 The 9.9 Club........................ 1.00 .45
Jim Hines
Track and Field
704 Don Schollander.................. 1.50 .70
Swimming
705 Eddy Merckx .... 1.00 .45
Sallanches Win
Cycling
706 Joel Robert............................. .50 .23
MotoCross
707 Marcel Cerdan..................... 1.50 .70
Cerdan and Tony Zale
Boxing
708 USSR .... 2.00 .90
1976 USSR Team
Ice Hockey
709 Refereeing............................. .50 .23
European Action
Australian Rules
710 Valeri Borzov....................... 1.50 .70
1972 Olympics
Track and Field
711 Olympic Programme .... .50 .23
The Tug-of-War
Sports of Past
712 A Laboratory Sport.............. 2.00 .90
USA vs. Russia
Basketball
713 Walt Frazier BK................... 3.00 1.35
714 The Morat to......................... .50 .23
Fribourg Race
Swiss Marathon
Track and Field
715 The 1967 Green Bay........... 1.50 .70
Packers
Football
716 Roger Maris 10.00 4.50
Mickey Mantle BB
717 Brad Park HK...................... 2.00 .90
718 Valeri Brumel....................... 1.50 .70
In the High Jump
Track and Field
719 Sugar Ray Robinson 4.00 1.80
Boxing
720 Wilt Chamberlain BK 10.00 4.50
721 The Rogallo Kite..................... .50 .23
Hang Glider
Hang Gliding
722 Jean-Claude Killy................. 2.00 .90
Alpine Skiing
723 Anders Garderud .... .50 .23
In Steeplechase
Track and Field
724 World Drivers .... .50 .23
Championship
Monza Race
Auto Racing

1977-79 Sportscaster Series 8 *

NRMT VG-E
COMPLETE SET (24)................ 25.00 11.00
801 Parry O'Brien....................... 1.00 .45
In the Shot Put
Track and Field
802 Juan Manuel Fangio .... 1.50 .70
Auto Racing
803 Rod Laver............................ 3.00 1.35
Tennis
804 Pete Rose BB 5.00 2.20
805 The 800-M............................. .50 .23
Sydney Wooderson
Track and Field
806 Fran Tarkenton FB 2.50 1.10
807 Triple Jump .... 1.00 .45
Victor Saneyev
Track and Field
808 Rocky Marciano 5.00 2.20
Boxing
809 Billie Jean King.................... 5.00 2.20
Tennis
810 Jerry West BK 5.00 2.20
811 Duke Kananamoku .... 1.50 .70
Swimming
812 A Game Played From............. .50 .23
One End
Curling Action
Curling
813 Boston Marathon.................. 1.00 .45
The 32nd Start
Track and Field
814 Glossary:A-G .... 1.00 .45
Bob Charles
Golf
815 A Game in a Walled .... .50 .23
Court
Jai Alai Player
Jai Alai (Pelota)
816 Equilibrium on a...................... .50 .23
Wave Crest
Surfing Action
Surfing
817 Murray Rose .... 1.00 .45
Swimming
818 No Push Shots .... .50 .23
Allowed
Billiards Player
Billiards
819 Navigation at 500 .... .50 .23
KM/H
Powerboat Race
Powerboat Racing
820 Target and .... .50 .23
Field Archery
An Archer
Archery
821 Secretariat........................... 4.00 1.80
Horse Racing
822 Ingemar Stenmark................ 1.50 .70
Alpine Skiing
823 Rafer Johnson...................... 2.00 .90
In the Shot Put
Track and Field
824 Niki Lauda 2.50 1.10
Auto Racing

1977-79 Sportscaster Series 9 *

NRMT VG-E
COMPLETE SET (24)................ 30.00 13.50
901 Tour De France........................ .50 .23
Aldo Parecchini
Cycling
902 The Classics .... .50 .23
Lahti and Finland
Nordic Skiing
903 Holmenkollen .... .50 .23
Nordic Skiing
904 Team Handball .... .50 .23
Team Action
Handball
905 Marking................................... .50 .23
Yukio Kasaya
Nordic Skiing
906 Football .... .50 .23
Australian Football
Australian Rules
907 Debbie Meyer .... 1.50 .70
Swimming
908 Francie Larrieu Lutz............. 1.50 .70
An Indoor Race
Track and Field
909 De Vlaeminck-......................... .50 .23
De Muynch
Vlaeminck/Muynck
Cycling
910 Joe Frazier........................... 4.00 1.80
Boxing
911 Johnny Miller .... 2.00 .90
Golf
912 Nate Archibald BK .... 2.00 .90
913 Vera Caslavska .... 1.00 .45
Balance Beam
Gymnastics
914 The Mile .... 2.00 .90
Roger Bannister
Track and Field
915 Stirling Moss........................ 2.00 .90
Auto Racing
916 A Game for Giants............... 2.50 1.10
USA vs. Russia
Basketball
917 An Eclectric .... .50 .23
Discipline

Cross-Country
Modern Pentathlon
918 Aquatic Handball .50 .23
Waterpolo Action
Waterpolo
919 Two Garmisch Races 1973 .50 .23
Roland Collombin
Alpine Skiing
920 Glossary:H-W .50 .23
Putting Action
Golf
921 Bjorn Borg 3.00 1.35
Tennis
922 The Rose Bowl 1.50 .70
Football
923 Jackie Robinson BB 15.00 6.75
924 Lise-Marie Morerod .50 .23
Alpine Skiing

1977-79 Sportscaster Series 10 *

NRMT VG-E
COMPLETE SET (24) 35.00 16.00
1001 European Circuits 1.50 .70
Monza Racing
Motorcycle Racing
1002 Rudolf Caracciola .50 .23
Auto Racing
1003 Nadia Comaneci 5.00 2.20
Montreal Olympics
Gymnastics
1004 Anything Goes .50 .23
Lacrosse Action
Lacrosse
1005 Nino Bibbia .50 .23
Tobogganing
1006 Sonia Lannaman .50 .23
Track and Field
1006 The Hall of Fame 1.50 .70
Cooperstown HOF
Beyond Sports
1007 Rod Carew BB 2.50 1.10
1008 William Tilden 2.50 1.10
Tennis
1009 Mario Andretti 10.00 4.50
Auto Racing
1010 Pierre Jonqueres .50 .23
D'Oriola
Competitions
1011 John Peterson 1.00 .45
Ben Peterson
1012 Pele 8.00 3.60
Pele/Bobby Moore
Soccer
1013 Jose Napoles 1.50 .70
Boxing
1014 Jean Beliveau HK 3.00 1.35
1015 Basic Regulations .50 .23
E. Gienger
Gymnastics
1016 Meta Antenen .50 .23
Track and Field
1017 Bob Beamon 2.00 .90
In Long Jump
Track and Field
1018 John Havlicek BK 3.00 1.35
1019 Kipchoge Keino 2.00 .90
1968 Olympics
Track and Field
1020 Ni Chih-Chin .50 .23
In the High Jump
Track and Field
1021 Times and Points 1.50 .70
Sheila Young
Speed Skating
1022 Thomas Magnusson .50 .23
Nordic Skiing
1023 Yves Saint-Martin .50 .23
W Allez France
Horse Racing
1024 Tony Dorsett FB 4.00 1.80

1977-79 Sportscaster Series 11 *

NRMT VG-E
COMPLETE SET (25) 40.00 18.00
1101 High Jump 1.50 .70
Ackermann/Jenner
Track and Field
1102 Joseph Siffert 1.00 .45
Auto Racing
1103 A Game for Gentle- .50 .23
men: Puc at Charlety
Rugby
1104 Karl Adam .50 .23
Sculling
1105 470 .50 .23
The 470
Yachting
1106 Willie Mays BB 5.00 2.20
1107 Aerial Sailing .50 .23
A Glider
Gliding
1108 Ard Schenk 1.00 .45
Speed Skating
1109 The Rules 3.00 1.35
Hank Aaron
Baseball
1110 Tour De France .50 .23
1975 Race
Cycling
1111 Olympic Trench and .50 .23
Skeet Shooting
Clay-Bird Shoot
Marksmanship
1112 Track Events .50 .23
Munich 6-Day
Cycling
1113 Larry Csonka 3.00 1.35
Jim Kiick FB
1114 1976 OG-4 x 10 KM .50 .23
Finnish Team
Nordic Skiing
1115 Richard Petty 20.00 9.00
Auto Racing
1116 Three-Day Events .50 .23
Endurance Action
Competitions
1117 The Boris 1.00 .45
Onischenko Affair
Boris Onischenko
Modern Pentathlon
1118 The Golden Ball .50 .23
A French Trophy
Soccer
1119 Hat Trick 1.00 .45
Bob Hodges
Ice Hockey
1120 Surfing on Wheels .50 .23
In Swimming Pool
Skateboarding
1121 Juha Mieto .50 .23
Nordic Skiing
1122 Ivo Van Damme 1.00 .45
1976 Olympics
Track and Field
1123 Steve Cauthen 2.00 .90
Horse Racing
1124A UCLA vs Houston ERR 20.00 9.00
Bill Walton
1124B UCLA vs. Houston COR 10.00 4.50
Lew Alcindor
Basketball

1977-79 Sportscaster Series 12 *

NRMT VG-E
COMPLETE SET (24) 25.00 11.00
1201 Graham Hill 5.00 2.20
Auto Racing
1202 Michel Rougerie .50 .23
Motorcycle Racing
1203 World Cyclocross .50 .23
Championship
Albert Sweifel
Cyclocross
1204 On the Fringe- .50 .23
Artist Gymnastics
Trampolining
1205 Angel Cordero 3.00 1.35
Horse Racing
1206 A Very Warlike Game 1.50 .70
Football Action
Football
1207 Ernie Banks BB 3.00 1.35
1208 World Professional .50 .23
Road Championships
1976 Ostuni
Cycling
1209 Joe Greene 4.00 1.80
Steelers/Vikings
Football
1210 Fear of Falling .50 .23
Rink at Sapporo
Speed Skating
1211 Ludmilla Bragina .50 .23
Leading the Pack
Track and Field
1212 Women's Horse Vault .50 .23
A Horse Vault
Gymnastics
1213 Wes Unseld BK 2.00 .90
1214 Walking .50 .23
1976 Olympics
Track and Field
1215 World Championship 1.50 .70
Czechs vs. USSR
Ice Hockey
1216 The Single-Paddle .50 .23
Canoe: Canoeing Action
Canoeing
1217 Smallbore .50 .23
Berno Klingner
Marksmanship
1218 John Curry 1.50 .70
Figure Skating
1219 Peter Mueller 1.00 .45
1976 Olympics
Speed Skating
1220 Jim Clark 4.00 1.80
Auto Racing
1221 Walter Steiner .50 .23
Nordic Skiing
1222 Stan Mikita HK 2.50 1.10
1223 Houston McTear 1.00 .45
Track and Field
1224 Two Opposite Styles .50 .23
Kung-Fu Action
Kung-Fu

1977-79 Sportscaster Series 13 *

NRMT VG-E
COMPLETE SET (24) 25.00 11.00
1301 All-American .50 .23
Futurity
1976 Race
Horse Racing
1302 Jack Dempsey 5.00 2.20
Boxing
1303 Ted Williams BB 8.00 3.60
1304 The European 1.00 .45
Championship Cup
Ignis Varese Tea
Basketball
1305 Glenn Davis 1.50 .70
Track and Field
1306 Archie Griffin FB 1.50 .70
1307 British Style .50 .23
Cricket Match
Cricket
1308 Women's Pentathlon .50 .23
Burglinde Pollack
Track and Field
1309 Boxing Before 1.00 .45
Boxing
John Gully& 1806
Sport of Past
1310 Lakers Win 33 In 4.00 1.80
A Row: Wilt Chamberlain
Jerry West
Basketball
1311 Bobby Morrow 1.00 .45
1956 Olympics
Track and Field
1312 India's Supremacy .50 .23
Challenged
1976 Olympics
Field Hockey
1313 Kathy Whitworth 2.00 .90
Golf
1314 It Deserves More .50 .23
Spectators
Game Action
Roller Hockey
1315 Ken Rosewall 1.50 .70
Tennis
1316 The European F2 .50 .23
Trophy
Silverstone Race
Auto Racing
1317 Ralph Boston 1.00 .45
In the Long Jump
Track and Field
1318 Olympic Games .50 .23
1906 Olympics
Beyond Sports
1319 A Mixture of Rugby .50 .23
and Soccer
Football Action
Gaelic Football
1320 Paavo Nurmi 1.00 .45
Track and Field
1321 Miami Dolphins vs. 2.00 .90
Kansas City
Garo Yepremian
Football
1322 Marie-Therese Nadig .50 .23
Alpine Skiing
1323 The Top Men Skating .50 .23
Jan Hoffman
Figure Skating
1324 Darrell Pace 1.00 .45
Archery

1977-79 Sportscaster Series 14 *

NRMT VG-E
COMPLETE SET (24) 35.00 16.00
1401 Yolanda Balas .50 .23
In the High Jump
Track and Field
1402 Nicknames 3.00 1.35
Jake La Motta
Boxing
1403 George Foreman 10.00 4.50
Boxing
1404 Dancing Football .50 .23
Volleying Action
Cycleball
1405 Wrestling .50 .23
Wrestling Action
Greco-Roman
1406 Seal Skins and .50 .23
Reindeer Bone
Canadian Pairs
Kayaking
1407 500 CC WCH .50 .23
500 CC Action
Motorcycle Racing
1408 Victor Saneev 1.00 .45
In Triple Jump
Track and Field
1409 The Oakland A's 2.50 1.10
1971-1975
Four A's Stars
Catfish Hunter
Rollie Fingers
Reggie Jackson
Sal Bando
Baseball
1410 Jim Hunter BB 2.50 1.10
1411 Maury Wills BB 1.50 .70
1412 Emil Zatopek 1.00 .45
Track and Field
1413 Nino Benvenuti 1.50 .70
Nino Benvenuti
Don Fullmer
Boxing
1414 The Forerunners of .50 .23
the Bicycle
1868 Race (FRA)
Cycling
1415 Ski Flying .50 .23
Tony Innauer
Nordic Skiing
1416 Eric Heiden 2.50 1.10
Speed Skating
1417 Henri Oreiller .50 .23
Alpine Skiing
1418 Oscar Robertson BK 4.00 1.80
1419 Miklos Nemeth .50 .23
Track and Field
1420 One of the Oldest .50 .23
Sports
Hans Rinn
Norbert Hahn
Luge
1421 Heini Hemmi .50 .23
Alpine Skiing
1422 The Oldest Sport .50 .23
of All
100 M Dash
Track and Field
1423 Ken Dryden HK 4.00 1.80
1424 Hans Hiltebrand .50 .23
Bobsledding

1977-79 Sportscaster Series 15 *

NRMT VG-E
COMPLETE SET (24) 25.00 11.00
1501 The European Cup .50 .23
Winners' Cup
Van Binst
Soccer
1502 GP Des Nations .50 .23
Ron Schuiten
Cycling
1503 Paavo Nurmi 1.00 .45
1924 Olympics
Track and Field
1504 The Derby .50 .23
Soap Box Derby
Soap Box
1505 Dick Weber 2.00 .90
Bowling
1506 Althea Gibson 2.00 .90
Tennis
1507 Willie Davenport 1.50 .70
In the Hurdles
Track and Field
1508 Alexander Medved 1.00 .45
Wrestling
1509 A Century and a 2.00 .90
Half of BB
Johnny Bench
Baseball
1510 Herbert McKenley 1.00 .45
Track and Field
1511 Tour of Switzerland .50 .23
Race Action
Cycling
1512 Single And Double .50 .23
Banked: 1976 Olympics
Sculling
1513 Yvan Cournoyer HK 2.50 1.10
1514 Henry Armstrong 2.00 .90
Boxing
1515 A Typically Belgian .50 .23
Game: Game Action
Balle Pelote
1516 Walking (Ron Laird .50 .23
Larry Young)
Track and Field
1517 Vaulting .50 .23
Gymnastics
1518 Tornado .50 .23
Olympic Boat
Yachting
1519 Maureen Connolly 2.50 1.10
Tennis
1520 Mac Wilkins 1.00 .45
In the Shot Put
Track and Field
1521 Billie Jean King 5.00 2.20
vs. Bobby Riggs
Tennis
1522 Heinz Gunthardt 1.00 .45
Tennis
1523 Levels of Horse .50 .23
Riding Competition
Horse Jumping
Competitions
1524 U.S. Women's 1.00 .45
Olympic Relay
Shirley Babashoff
Swimming

1977-79 Sportscaster Series 16 *

NRMT VG-E
COMPLETE SET (24) 30.00 13.50
1601 Roger De Vlaeminck .50 .23
Cycling
1602 Platform Tennis .50 .23
Game Action
Tennis
1603 Fair Play In The OG .50 .23
Lucien Gaudin
Beyond Sports
1604 Bobby Unser 8.00 3.60
Al Unser
Auto Racing
1605 Jim Ryun 1.50 .70
In the Mile Run
Track and Field
1606 Perhaps Art Rather .50 .23
than Sport
Individuals
Dressage
1607 Brooks Robinson BB 2.50 1.10
1608 The Other Rules of .50 .23
the Game
Mr. Risi/Dubach
Soccer
1609 The Breast and .50 .23
Butterfly Strokes
Swimming
1610 Some Dates in a 1.00 .45
Long History: Guy Drut
Track and Field
1611 Albert Zweifel .50 .23
Cyclocross
1612 Paul Hornung 3.00 1.35
Packers/Browns
Football
1613 The Asymmetric Bars 1.00 .45
Vera Caslavska
Gymnastics
1614 Elgin Baylor BK 2.50 1.10
1615 Evolution of Rules 1.00 .45
in Boxing: John Tate
Boxing
1616 Puig-Aubert .50 .23
Rugby
1617 Matter of Speed and .50 .23
Precision
Skiing in Air
Waterskiing
1618 Pancho Gonzales 2.00 .90
Tennis
1619 Christian D'Oriola .50 .23
Fencing
1620 Why Oval .50 .23
Shape of Ball
Rugby
1621 Raymond Ceulemans .50 .23
Billiards
1622 Patrick Pons .50 .23
Motorcycle Racing
1623 Fausto Radici .50 .23
Alpine Skiing
1624 Dick Button 2.00 .90
Figure Skating

1977-79 Sportscaster Series 17 *

NRMT VG-E
COMPLETE SET (24) 20.00 9.00
1701 Jimmy Taylor FB 2.50 1.10
1702 Speed Skating .50 .23
Speed Skaters
Roller Skating
1703 Chiquito De Cambo .50 .23
Jai Alai (Pelota)
1704 Randy Jones BB 1.00 .45
1705 A Fraternity in .50 .23
True Sense
L and G Camberabero
Rugby
1706 Forego 1.00 .45
Horse Racing
1707 Vitas Gerulaitis 3.00 1.35
Tennis
1708 50 and 125 CC WCH .50 .23
50/125 CC Races
Motorcycle Racing
1709 Denis Potvin HK 4.00 1.80
1710 Calculating The .50 .23
Gear-Ratio
Bicycle Gears
Cycling
1711 Hans Schmid .50 .23
Nordic Skiing
1712 UEFA Junior Cup .50 .23
USSR/Hungary
Soccer
1713 Regis Ovion .50 .23
Tour De L'Avenir
Cycling
1714 Jutta Heine .50 .23
Track and Field
1715 Ken Stabler FB 4.00 1.80
1716 1973 WCH 4.00 1.80
Jackie Stewart
Auto Racing
1717 Some Facts and .50 .23
Figures
Judging Performances
Figure Skating
1718 John B. Kelly 1.00 .45
Sculling
1719 World Team Tennis .50 .23
A Colored Court
Tennis
1720 World Cup .50 .23
Thomas Wassberg
Nordic Skiing
1721 Jean Prat .50 .23
Prat/Gachassin
Rugby
1722 The Forest Hills .50 .23
Tournament
Forest Hills& NY
Tennis
1723 Jean-Paul Coche .50 .23
Judo
1724 Star Class .50 .23
1980 Olympics
Yachting

1977-79 Sportscaster Series 18 *

NRMT VG-E
COMPLETE SET (24) 25.00 11.00
1801 Tour De Romandie .50 .23
Race Action
Cycling
1802 Wilma Rudolph 2.00 .90
In the Relays
Track and Field
1803 Janet Guthrie 3.00 1.35
Auto Racing
1804 Finn Class .50 .23
A Finn Boat
Yachting
1805 Joe Morgan BB 2.50 1.10
1806 An Efficacious .50 .23
Self Defense
Jui-Jitsu Match
Jiu-Jitsu
1807 Henri Desgrange .50 .23
Beyond Sports
1808 Toni Sailer 1.00 .45
Alpine Skiing
1809 The Brussels .50 .23
Disaster
USA Skating Team
Beyond Sports
1810 The Start of .50 .23
Competition Cycling
F. De Civry
Cycling
1811 Mark Fidrych BB 3.00 1.35
1812 Nadine and Martine 1.00 .45
Audin
Gymnastics
1813 Floyd Patterson 5.00 2.20
Muhammad Ali
Boxing
1814 Front Crawl and .50 .23
Backstroke
Swimming
1815 Cross-Country .50 .23
Artist Drawing
Track and Field
1816 Lingo II 1.50 .70
Earl Weaver
Baseball
1817 French GP .50 .23
Auto Racing
1818 Benoit Dauga .50 .23
Rugby
1819 Parnelli Jones 3.00 1.35
Auto Racing
1820 Jackie Chazalon BK 1.00 .45
1821 Michel Crauste .50 .23
Rugby
1822 Lee Trevino 8.00 3.60
Golf
1823 Garry Unger 1.00 .45
Ice Hockey
1824 French XV& 1977 .50 .23
French XV Team
Rugby

1977-79 Sportscaster Series 19 *

NRMT VG-E
COMPLETE SET (24) 50.00 22.00

1901 Feminine Artistic 1.50 .70
Nelly Kim
Gymnastics
1902 The Equipment .50 .23
Equipment Types
Table Tennis
1903 Arnold Palmer 12.00 5.50
Golf
1904 Arthur Ashe 10.00 4.50
In A Blue Shirt
Tennis
1905 First Strongman .50 .23
Joseph P. Bonnes
Weightlifting
1906 The Equipment .50 .23
Hockey Action
Field Hockey
1907 The History of .50 .23
Waterskiing
Using a %%Plank~
Waterskiing
1908 Steve Prefontaine 1.50 .70
1972 Olympics
Track and Field
1909 Sports Posters .50 .23
Before 1914
Beyond Sports
1910 1972 WCH 6.00 2.70
Emerson Fittipaldi
Auto Racing
1911 Penn Relays .50 .23
Steve Riddick/Williams
Track and Field
1912 Service, Rallies .50 .23
and Faults
Imano Yujiro
Table Tennis
1913 Basic Rules and .50 .23
Distances: The Start
Swimming
1914 Bob Pettit BK 2.00 .90
1915 World Championship 2.00 .90
1977 Canadians
Ice Hockey
1916 The Prix D'Amerique .50 .23
Vincennes
Horse Racing
1917 A.J. Foyt 10.00 4.50
Auto Racing
1918 The Origins .50 .23
Launching a Skif
Sculling
1919 Franz Klammer 2.00 .90
Alpine Skiing
1920 Gaylord Perry BB 1.50 .70
1921 Wyomia Tyus 1.00 .45
In the 100-M Dash
Track and Field
1922 The Hambleton .50 .23
Behind Pace Car
Horse Racing
1923 Rodeo .50 .23
Bullriding
Competitions
1924 The Dark Side of .50 .23
the Moon
S.F. Golden Gate
Bicycle Touring

1977-79 Sportscaster Series 20 *

NRMT VG-E
COMPLETE SET (24) 15.00 6.75
2001 Carol Heiss 2.00 .90
Figure Skating
2002 The Astrodome .50 .23
Beyond Sports
2003 The Monte-Carlo .50 .23
Rally Haren and Sure
Auto Racing
2004 Harness Racing and .50 .23
Saddle Trotting
Horse Racing
2005 Thurman Munson BB 3.00 1.35
2006 The World Champions .50 .23
Mechanics
Motorcycle Racing
2007 Earl Bell .50 .23
In Pole Vault
Track and Field
2008 Jan Kodes 1.00 .45
Tennis
2009 The History .50 .23
1910 Jumping
Jumping
2010 Sea Talk .50 .23
Sailing For Fun
Yachting
2011 The Expedite Rule .50 .23
and Doubles
Table Tennis
2012 The Classes .50 .23
Powerboat Racer
Powerboat Racing
2013 Judy Rankin 1.50 .70
Golf
2014 A TV Marathon At .50 .23
Moscow Olympics
Dynamo Stadium
Beyond Sports
2015 The Equipment .50 .23
Equipment Types
Waterskiing
2016 Stock vs. Charron .50 .23
Boxing
2017 The Foil .50 .23
F. Dal Zotto
Fencing
2018 5500 Practioners .50 .23
70 Areas
The Swiss
Hornuss
2019 Dunoyer De Segonzac .50 .23
Beyond Sports
2020 Ken Anderson FB 2.50 1.10
2021 24-Second Clock 1.50 .70
Sixers' Player
Basketball
2022 Match Specifics .50 .23
The Serve
Table Tennis
2023 World Records .50 .23
Backstroke Start
Swimming
2024 The Beam 1.00 .45
Vera Caslavska
Gymnastics

1977-79 Sportscaster Series 21 *

NRMT VG-E
COMPLETE SET (24) 30.00 13.50
2101 Olympic Downhill 1.50 .70
Franz Klammer
Alpine Skiing
2102 Karting In Europe .50 .23
A Karting Race
Auto Racing
2103 The Campbells 1.50 .70
Malcolm Campbell
Auto Racing
2104 Lingo I 1.00 .45
Dodger Pitcher
Baseball
2105 Joe Rudi BB 1.00 .45
2106 Bellino II .50 .23
Bellino Trotting
Horse Racing
2107 Archie Moore 2.00 .90
Moore and Joey Maxim
Boxing
2108 Gerhard Grimmer .50 .23
Nordic Skiing
2109 Vada Pinson BB 1.00 .45
2110 Tempest .50 .23
Yachting
2111 Ice Racing .50 .23
Swedish Racers
Motorcycle Racing
2112 The Equipment .50 .23
Fussen (WGE)
Ice Hockey
2113 Tour of Lombardy .50 .23
1976 Race
Cycling
2114 Clarence(Bevo) 1.00 .45
Francis
Basketball
2115 The All Blacks .50 .23
All Blacks Team
Rugby
2116 Stan Musial BB 4.00 1.80
2117 Dictionary .50 .23
A Smash
Volleyball
2118 College AS Game 2.00 .90
All-Stars vs. Steelers
Football
2119 World Heavyweight 10.00 4.50
Title
Joe Frazier
Muhammad Ali
Boxing
2120 Knock-On or Throw- .50 .23
Forward
Game Action
Rugby
2121 The Records 1.50 .70
Vassili Alexeiev
Weightlifting
2122 Monaco GP 1.50 .70
Jody Scheckter
Auto Racing
2123 Odd Martinsen .50 .23
Nordic Skiing
2124 The Horizontal Bar .50 .23
The High Bar
Gymnastics

1977-79 Sportscaster Series 22 *

NRMT VG-E
COMPLETE SET (24) 30.00 13.50
2201 Sam Snead 10.00 4.50
Golf
2202 Anne Henning 1.00 .45
Speed Skating
2203 Women Champions 4.00 1.80
Peggy Fleming
Figure Skating
2204 History of the Game .50 .23
Gillian Gilks
Badminton
2205 Major Tournaments .50 .23
Doubles Action
Badminton
2206 Raymond Poulidor .50 .23
Cycling
2207 WCH 1975 2.50 1.10
Niki Lauda
Auto Racing
2208 Milwaukee Bucks 3.00 1.35
1970-1971
Bucks vs. Knicks
Lew Alcindor
Basketball
2209 Ray Leonard 5.00 2.20
Boxing
2210 Roy Emerson 1.50 .70
Tennis
2211 The Garryowen or .50 .23
Up-and-Under
Attack Strategy
Rugby
2212 Sixteen Jernberg .50 .23
Nordic Skiing
2213 Oxford and .50 .23
Cambridge
Oxonians/Cantabs
Sculling
2214 The Fosbury Flop 1.00 .45
A Demonstration
Track and Field
2215 Vasaloppet .50 .23
Pierrat/Kaelin
Nordic Skiing
2217 Rules .50 .23
Game Action
Motorball
2218 Joan Joyce 1.00 .45
Softball
2219 Scoring Table for 2.00 .90
the Decathalon
Bruce Jenner
Track and Field
2220 Diana Nyad 2.00 .90
Swimming
2221 Points of Sail and .50 .23
Speed of Travel
A Stoarboard Tack
Yachting
2222 Water Just In Case 1.00 .45
Lasse Viren
Beyond Sports
2223 World Records .50 .23
Xavier Kurmann
Cycling
2224 Tracy Austin 3.00 1.35
1977 U.S. Open
Tennis

1977-79 Sportscaster Series 23 *

NRMT VG-E
COMPLETE SET (24) 40.00 18.00
2301 At-A-Glance .50 .23
Reference
Rugby Action
Ball Sports
2302 Peter Snell 1.50 .70
1964 Olympics
Track and Field
2303 Lingo 3.00 1.35
Pete Maravich
Basketball
2304 Nolan Ryan BB 30.00 13.50
2305 Glucose .50 .23
Hennie Kuiper
Beyond Sports
2306 Paris-Brussels .50 .23
W. Godefroot
Cycling
2307 2 CV-Cross .50 .23
Auto Racing
2308 Pierre De Coubertin 1.00 .45
Beyond Sports
2309 Dave Wottle 1.00 .45
Wearing His Hat
Track and Field
2310 The Marathon .50 .23
Track and Field
2311 Super Bowl 1.50 .70
Super Bowl Show
Football
2312 WCH 1969 4.00 1.80
Jackie Stewart
Auto Racing
2313 The Marquess of .50 .23
Exeter
Beyond Sports
2314 Jean-Pierre Wimille .50 .23
Auto Racing
2315 Lanny Bassham 1.00 .45
Rifle Shooting
2316 Pairs .50 .23
Soviet Pairs
Figure Skating
2317 The "Pen Duick" .50 .23
Series
Pen Duick IV
Yachting
2318 The Sport of Kings .50 .23
No Longer
Billiards Shot
Billiards
2319 Bruno Sammartino 3.00 1.35
Wrestling
2320 The Flying Dutchman .50 .23
1972 Olympics
Yachting
2321 The Equipment .50 .23
Squash Action
Squash
2322 The Evolution of .50 .23
the Rules
Australia/W. Germany
Soccer
2323 Warren Spahn BB 3.00 1.35
2324 Walter Bonatti .50 .23
Mountain Climbing

1977-79 Sportscaster Series 24 *

NRMT VG-E
COMPLETE SET (24) 20.00 9.00
2401 Steve Lobell 1.00 .45
Horse Racing
2402 Maurice Garin .50 .23
Cycling
2403 Little Brown Jug .50 .23
Wirtz/Chapman
Horse Racing
2404 Sport in Cuba 4.00 1.80
Fidel Castro
Beyond Sports
2405 Bert Jones 1.50 .70
Football
2406 The Tackle .50 .23
England vs Wales
Rugby
2407 Andre Carrus .50 .23
Beyond Sports
2408 The 1976 .50 .23
Continental Circus
Motorcycle Racing
2409 Arthur Augustus .50 .23
Zimmerman
Cycling
2410 Barrel Jumping .50 .23
At Grossinger's
Skating
2411 Single or .50 .23
Multihulls
Yachting
2412 Athens 1896 .50 .23
Masson (France)
Beyond Sports
2413 The Physically .50 .23
Handicapped and Sport
Wheelchair Archers
Beyond Sports
2414 The 3000-M .50 .23
Steeplechase
A Water-Hazard
Track and Field
2415 The "Pen Duick" .50 .23
Series
Pen Duick VI
Yachting
2416 Lou Brock BB 2.50 1.10
2417 America's Cup 1.00 .45
1977 Cup Race
Yachting
2418 Serving .50 .23
Serving Action
Volleyball
2419 Herve Filion 1.00 .45
Horse Racing
2420 Targa Florio .50 .23
Auto Racing
2421 Piero D'Inzeo .50 .23
With The Avenger
Jumping
2422 Some Herculean Goals .50 .23
P. Villepreux
Rugby
2423 Tim Shaw 1.00 .45
1975 Mundial
Swimming
2424 Alain Bombard .50 .23
Beyond Sports

1977-79 Sportscaster Series 25 *

NRMT VG-E
COMPLETE SET (24) 20.00 9.00
2501 Long-Distance .50 .23
Runners: Iditarod Race
Sled Dog Racing
2502 The 1st Channel Crossing .50 .23
Bleriot, 1909
Powered Flight
2503 Abdon Pamich .50 .23
Track and Field
2504 Alois Kaelin .50 .23
Nordic Skiing
2505 Uni-Bale .50 .23
Uni-Bale Team
Volleyball
2506 Chris McCarron 2.00 .90
Horse Racing
2507 The U.S. Open 2.00 .90
Jerry Pate
Golf
2508 Daniel Eckmann .50 .23
Handball
2509 WCH 1970 .50 .23
Jochen Rindt
Auto Racing
2510 Don Carter 4.00 1.80
Bowling
2511 Some of the Rules .50 .23
John Eaves
Freestyle Skiing
2512 Kingston, 1976 .50 .23
1976 Olympics
Yachting
2513 1977 Season At-A- .50 .23
Glance: England/Ireland
Rugby
2514 The NCAA .50 .23
Beyond Sports
2515 Jaroslav Drobny 1.00 .45
Tennis
2516 Hurdle Races 1.00 .45
Guy Drut
Track and Field
2517 Gunder Haegg 1.00 .45
Track and Field
2518 Frank Tanana BB 1.50 .70
2519 The Prix De L'Arc .50 .23
De Triomphe
Evanjica w/ Head
Horse Racing
2520 Willy Daume .50 .23
Killanin and Daume
Beyond Sports
2521 Dr. Paul Martin .50 .23
1924 Olympics
Track and Field
2522 David Hemery 1.00 .45
In 400 M Hurdles
Track and Field
2523 Charley Taylor FB 1.50 .70
2524 Blood Transfusion 1.00 .45
Lasse Viren
Beyond Sports

1977-79 Sportscaster Series 26 *

NRMT VG-E
COMPLETE SET (24) 30.00 13.50
2601 Suzanne Lenglen 2.00 .90
Tennis
2602 Walking on the .50 .23
Water
A Skiyaker
Skiyaking
2603 Six-Day Races .50 .23
Palais Des Sport
Cycling
2604 The Great Races .50 .23
Grand National
Horse Racing
2605 In the Bowels of .50 .23
the Earth: In A Cave
Spelunking
2606 Sir Gordon Richards .50 .23
1953 Derby
Horse Racing
2607 400 M Hurdles 2.00 .90
Edwin Moses
Track and Field
2608 Al Oerter 2.00 .90
Track and Field
2609 Manchester United 1.00 .45
1957 Manchester
Soccer
2610 Pan-American Games 1.00 .45
Cuba vs. Canada
Beyond Sports
2611 Presidents In 10.00 4.50
Sport
Gerald Ford
Beyond Sports
2612 David Broome .50 .23
With Heatwave
Jumping
2613 Jean-Pierre .50 .23
Beltoise
Auto Racing
2614 Walter Payton FB 8.00 3.60
2615 Jim Palmer BB 3.00 1.35
2616 WCH .50 .23
O. Mathisen
Speed Skating
2617 Rules .50 .23
Many Sailboats
Yachting
2618 Repelling the .50 .23
Invaders
Korean Action
Tae-Kwon-Do
2619 The Short Weapons .50 .23
5 Short Weapons
Martial Arts
2620 Dick Stockton 1.00 .45
Tennis
2621 Primo Carnera 2.00 .90
Carnera
Hans Schoenrath
Boxing
2622 Up From the Streets .50 .23
Game Equipment
Roller Hockey
2623 The Channel .50 .23
Crossing
David Morgan
Swimming
2624 Villeurbanne BK .50 .23

1977-79 Sportscaster Series 27 *

NRMT VG-E
COMPLETE SET (24) 25.00 11.00
2701 Petanque .50 .23
Petanque Action
Bowls
2702 Steve Carlton BB 3.00 1.35
2703 Aiming at Younger .50 .23
Generation
Master Aosaka
Shorinji-Kempo
2704 Wimbledon 1.00 .45
Tennis
2705 Ferdinand Kubler .50 .23
Cycling
2706 Packers vs. Bears 1.00 .45
(Wally Chambers)
Football
2707 Shane Gould 1.00 .45
Swimming
2708 As Old As The Hills .50 .23
Skiff-Fort Mahon
Sand Yachting
2709 Kyudo and Yabusame .50 .23
An Archer
Archery
2710 Gymnastics in .50 .23
Schools
Gymnastics w/ Children
Gymnastics
2711 French Enduro .50 .23
Riding in Water
Motorcycle Racing
2712 Brian Gottfried 1.00 .45
Serve and Volley
Tennis
2713 1974 WCH 6.00 2.70
Emerson Fittipaldi
Auto Racing
2714 The "Great Britain" .50 .23
Series
GB II
Yachting
2715 Robyn Smith 2.00 .90
Horse Racing
2716 The Nostalgia Craze .50 .23
Tiao-Tze-Ti Kick
Kung-Fu
2717 Pierre De Coubertin 1.00 .45
Beyond Sports
2718 AAU-NCAA .50 .23
High Jump Action
Beyond Sports
2719 Indoor Athletics .50 .23
1972 European
Championships
Track and Field
2720 Silvio Leonard 1.00 .45
Track and Field
2721 Dave Kingman BB 1.50 .70
2722 Nelly Kim 1.50 .70
The Vault
Gymnastics
2723 Jean-Louis Legrand .50 .23
Handball
2724 National Hockey 3.00 1.35
League: Black Hawks/Caps
(Dennis Hull)
Ice Hockey

1977-79 Sportscaster Series 28 *

NRMT VG-E
COMPLETE SET (24) 20.00 9.00
2801 Cale Yarborough 8.00 3.60
Auto Racing
2802 Three Types .50 .23
Boccie In Action
Boccie

2803 Gymnastics .50 .23
Acrobatics
Gymnastics
2804 Robert Vigier .50 .23
Rugby
2805 Sidecar-Cross .50 .23
Grogg (SWI)
Motorcycle Racing
2806 Parallel Bars .50 .23
Andrianov (USSR)
Gymnastics
2807 Jay Springsteen .50 .23
Motorcycle Racing
2808 Back To Fighting .50 .23
With Sticks
19th Century Art
The Cane
2809 The Rules .50 .23
Delvingt/Algisi
Judo
2810 Maurice Herzog .50 .23
Mountain Climbing
2811 Michel Jazy 1.00 .45
Jazy: Ron Clarke
Track and Field
2812 Janou Lefebvre .50 .23
Tissot
Tissot w/ Rocket
Jumping
2813 Kerry Cavazzi and .50 .23
Jane Puracchio
Dancing Pairs
Roller Skating
2814 Adriano Panatta 1.00 .45
Tennis
2815 Howard Davis 1.00 .45
Boxing
2816 Of Ringers and .50 .23
Leaners
Pitching Action
Horseshoe Pitching
2817 Alfred Bickel 1.00 .45
Soccer
2818 Nancy Greene 1.00 .45
Alpine Skiing
2819 The 400 M .50 .23
1968 Olympics
Track and Field
2820 The French Team of .50 .23
1968
Rugby
2821 Sylvain Saudan .50 .23
Alpine Skiing
2822 Harvey Smith .50 .23
Riding Askan
Jumping
2823 Rollerball 2.00 .90
Rollerball Action
Beyond Sports
2824 Bunkers .50 .23
A Bunker
Golf

1977-79 Sportscaster Series 29 *

NRMT VG-E
COMPLETE SET (24) 35.00 16.00
2901 Rucksacks .50 .23
A Climber
Mountain Climbing
2902 The Perfect Game 4.00 1.80
Sandy Koufax
Baseball
2903 Dieter Muller 1.00 .45
Muller/Beer
Soccer
2904 Lingo I 2.50 1.10
Secretariat
Horse Racing
2905 Catherine Lacoste 1.00 .45
Golf
2906 The 200-M 1.00 .45
Don Quarrie
Track and Field
2907 Defensive Formations 6.00 2.70
Harry Carson
Roger Staubach
Football
2908 The Power Play 2.00 .90
Phil Esposito
Ice Hockey
2909 The Rules .50 .23
Action
Singlestick
2910 From Cadine to 1.00 .45
Alexeiev
Vassili Alexeiev
Weightlifting
2911 Rosie Casals 1.50 .70
Tennis
2912 Sport and Diabetes .50 .23
Murray Halberg
Beyond Sports
2913 1967 WCH 1.50 .70
Denis Hulme
Auto Racing
2914 European Records .50 .23
David Wilkie
Swimming
2915 The UEFA Cup .50 .23
Iribar/Juventus
Soccer
2916 NFL History 1.50 .70
Packers/Browns
Football
2917 Speedway .50 .23
Challenge One
Motorcycle Racing
2918 Fleche Wallonne .50 .23
Joop Zoetemelk
Cycling
2919 Shooting I .50 .23
Hungary/France
Handball
2920 Shooting II .50 .23
Handball Shot
Handball
2921 Long Arms .50 .23
Warrior Regalia
Martial Arts
2922 At-A-Glance 2.00 .90
Reference
Tom Seaver
Ball Sports
2923 Jean-Marc Bourret .50 .23
Rugby League
2924 Lanny Wadkins 5.00 2.20
Golf

1977-79 Sportscaster Series 30 *

NRMT VG-E
COMPLETE SET (24) 25.00 11.00
3001 Roger Uttley .50 .23
Lions/Transvaal
Rugby
3002 Long Jump .50 .23
Hans Baumgartner
Track and Field
3003 Triple Crown 2.50 1.10
Carl Yastrzemski
Baseball
3004 Lingo II 2.00 .90
Steve Cauthen
Horse Racing
3005 Marathon 1.50 .70
Bill Rodgers
Track and Field
3006 The Discus 1.00 .45
Mac Wilkins
Track and Field
3007 Lionel Terray .50 .23
Mountain Climbing
3008 Women's WCH .50 .23
Liz A. Shetter
Waterskiing
3009 Robert Soro .50 .23
Rugby
3010 Fouls and Penalties 1.00 .45
Hawks vs. Bulls
Basketball
3011 Oxygen .50 .23
Eric Loder
Beyond Sports
3012 Podoloff Cup 3.00 1.35
Kareem Abdul-Jabbar
Basketball
3013 NBA All-Star Game 2.00 .90
Randy Smith
Basketball
3014 Kirkpinar .50 .23
Bout in Progress
Turkish Wrestling
3015 David Wilkie 1.00 .45
Swimming
3016 Ron Cey BB 1.50 .70
3017 Gheorghe Gruia .50 .23
Handball
3018 Soccer at the .50 .23
Olympics
E. Germany/Poland
3019 The Rules .50 .23
J. Barrington
Squash
3020 Henry Cooper 2.00 .90
Boxing
3021 The IFAB .50 .23
Dr. A. Franchi
Soccer
3022 Viet-Vo-Dao and .50 .23
Vo-Viet-Nam
Fighting Action
Martial Arts
3023 The Best School of .50 .23
Samba: Capoeira Action
Capoeira
3024 The Longest Match 2.00 .90
Pancho Gonzales
Charlie Pasarell
Tennis

1977-79 Sportscaster Series 31 *

NRMT VG-E
COMPLETE SET (24) 25.00 11.00
3101 Instruction 2.50 1.10
Rod Carew
Baseball
3102 Trick Plays 1.50 .70
Russ Francis
Football
3103 Penalty Killing 2.50 1.10
Bobby Clarke
Ice Hockey
3104 Liege-Bastogne- .50 .23
Liege
Bernard Hinault
Cycling
3105 Nicola Pietrangeli 1.00 .45
Tennis
3106 Linda Fratianne 3.00 1.35
Figure Skating
3107 The Sirens .50 .23
Clare Francis
Yachting
3108 The Rings .50 .23
Gymnastics
3109 Grasshopper Club .50 .23
The Zurich Club
Handball
3110 Honda and the GP .50 .23
Events
Mike Hailwood
Motorcycle Racing
3111 At-A-Glance .50 .23
Reference
Racing Action
Motorcycle Racing
3112 The Tour De France: .50 .23
The Mountain
F. Bahamontes
Cycling
3113 Dictionary .50 .23
Handball Action
Handball
3114 James Sullivan 2.00 .90
Memorial Trophy
John Naber
Beyond Sports
3115 Laura Baugh 4.00 1.80
Golf
3116 Sport for the .50 .23
Handicapped
Wheelchair Discussion
Beyond Sports
3117 Gianni Rivera .50 .23
Soccer
3118 World Records .50 .23
Kulikov/Muratov
Speed Skating
3119 From the Koka To .50 .23
the Ippon
Endo/Neureuther
Judo
3120 The Hammer .50 .23
A Spiridinov
Track and Field
3121 Jean Behra 1.00 .45
Auto Racing
3122 Lindbergh Crosses 6.00 2.70
the Atlantic
Charles Lindbergh
1927& Powered Flight
3123 Sport and Altitude 1.00 .45
Eddy Merckx
Beyond Sports
3124 Kate Schmidt 1.00 .45
In the Javelin
Track and Field

1977-79 Sportscaster Series 32 *

NRMT VG-E
COMPLETE SET (24) 35.00 16.00
3201 The 3000 Hit Club 20.00 9.00
Roberto Clemente
Baseball
3202 Facts about Jogging .50 .23
Run through Park
Track and Field
3203 Offensive 1.50 .70
Alignments
UCLA In Action
Football
3204 Tommy John BB 1.50 .70
3205 Micheline .50 .23
Ostermeyer
In the Discus
Track and Field
3206 Playground Sports .50 .23
Hitting A Ball
Softball
3207 Roger Bannister 2.00 .90
1954 Berne
Track and Field
3208 Growing in .50 .23
Popularity
Blow to the Knee
Kick-Boxing
3209 FC Nantes .50 .23
1977 FC Nantes
Soccer
3210 Daniel Bautista .50 .23
1976 Olympics
Track and Field
3211 Scottish RF Union .50 .23
Scottish Team
Rugby
3212 Winds and Currents .50 .23
In Atlantic
Fighting Winds
Yachting
3213 The "Course De .50 .23
L'Aurore"
Bernard Pallard
Yachting
3214 Equipment .50 .23
Mat and Scoreboard
Wrestling
3215 The 350 CC Category .50 .23
350 CC Rider
Motorcycle Racing
3216 A Change of .50 .23
Direction: Remfry/Zausz
Judo
3217 Cy Young Award 2.50 1.10
Tom Seaver
Baseball
3218 Pommel Horse .50 .23
S. Kato (Japan)
Gymnastics
3219 1971 WCH 4.00 1.80
Jackie Stewart
Auto Racing
3220 Ball Game on .50 .23
Horseback: Polo Action
Polo
3221 Tony Jacklin 2.00 .90
Golf
3222 Corinne Le Moal .50 .23
Sculling
3223 Roberto Bettega 1.00 .45
Soccer
3224 The 1977 Tour .50 .23
De France
Thurau/Pronk
Cycling

1977-79 Sportscaster Series 33 *

NRMT VG-E
COMPLETE SET (24) 20.00 9.00
3301 Holding 1.50 .70
Patriots/Raiders
Football
3302 J.P.R. Williams .50 .23
Rugby
3303 Lines in the Ice 1.50 .70
The Red Line
Ice Hockey
3304 Pivot Play 5.00 2.20
Bill Walton
Basketball
3305 Keeping Score .50 .23
Fan Scorekeeping
Baseball
3306 Manuel Orantes 1.00 .45
Tennis
3307 Stella-Sports .50 .23
Saint-Maur
Saint-Maur Team
Handball
3308 Robert Wurtz 1.00 .45
Soccer
3309 1968 WCH 4.00 1.80
Graham Hill
Auto Racing
3310 Specialist .50 .23
Equipment
Haessig (SWI)
Casting
3311 Roger Staub .50 .23
Alpine Skiing
3312 Men's World .50 .23
Championships
M. Hazelwood
Waterskiing
3313 The Irish RF Union .50 .23
Wales vs Ireland
Rugby
3314 Chuck Foreman FB 1.50 .70
3315 The Great Firms: .50 .23
MV Agusta
Giacomo Agostini
Motorcycle Racing
3316 Soaring .50 .23
A Glider
Gliding
3317 Technique .50 .23
1 of 8 Movements
Singlestick
3318 Claude Papi 1.00 .45
Soccer
3319 World Heavyweight 4.00 1.80
Championship
Joe Louis
3320 Angelo Parisi .50 .23
Judo
3321 The Black Power 2.00 .90
Salute
Tommie Smith
3322 Gene Upshaw 2.00 .90
Raiders vs Colts
Football
3323 The Sherpas .50 .23
Tenzing/Lambert
Mountain Climbing
3324 Gene Romero .50 .23
Daytona, 1975
Motorcycle Racing

1977-79 Sportscaster Series 34 *

NRMT VG-E
COMPLETE SET (24) 30.00 13.50
3401 Martini Challenge .50 .23
J. Hein
Fencing
3402 Four Home Runs In 8.00 3.60
A Game
Mike Schmidt
Baseball
3403 Roland-Garros .50 .23
Tennis
3404 Francis Chichester 1.00 .45
W/Gipsy Moth IV
Yachting
3405 How To Serve .50 .23
Overhead Serve
Volleyball
3406 Pone Kingpetch .50 .23
Pone Kingpetch
Boxing
3407 Dietmar Lorenz .50 .23
Montreal Olympics
Judo
3408 The 250 CC WCH .50 .23
Mario Lega (ITA)
Motorcycle Racing
3409 Roger Paschy .50 .23
Karate
3410 NCAA Championships 2.00 .90
Steve Prefontaine
Track and Field
3411 John Pullin .50 .23
Rugby
3412 Pierre-Albert .50 .23
Chapuisat
W. Germany/Switzerland
Soccer
3413 Floor Exercises .50 .23
S. Fujimoto
Gymnastics
3414 Defenses 1.00 .45
College Action
Basketball
3415 Dragsters .50 .23
A Dragster
Motorcycle Racing
3416 Jose Iribar 1.00 .45
1977 UEFA Cup
Soccer
3417 Joanne Carner 2.50 1.10
Golf
3418 Preston Pearson FB 1.50 .70
3419 All-Star Game 2.50 1.10
Joe Morgan
Steve Garvey
Baseball
3420 Ottavio Bottecchia .50 .23
Cycling
3421 Martina Navratilova 8.00 3.60
1975 French Open
Tennis
3422 George Best 2.00 .90
Soccer
3423 History .50 .23
Japan vs. USSR
Volleyball
3424 Greg Luzinski BB 1.00 .45

1977-79 Sportscaster Series 35 *

NRMT VG-E
COMPLETE SET (24) 30.00 13.50
3501 Sponsoring .50 .23
Gauloises II
Yachting
3502 Infield Fly Rule 1.50 .70
Bobby Grich
Baseball
3503 The Spengler Cup .50 .23
Davos, Switzerland
Ice Hockey
3504 John Candelaria BB 1.50 .70
3505 The Club of One .50 .23
Hundred
Brazil vs Italy
Soccer
3506 The Highest Scoring 6.00 2.70
Game
Julius Erving
Basketball
3507 Mike Boit 1.00 .45
1972 Olympics
Track and Field
3508 The Stramilano .50 .23
1977 Race
Track and Field
3509 Herbert Elliott 1.00 .45
1960 Olympics
Track and Field
3510 Ben Hogan 15.00 6.75
Golf
3511 Golden Gloves 1.00 .45
Boxing
3512 Peter Thomson 1.00 .45
Golf
3513 Birth of Alpine .50 .23
Skiing
Sir Arnold Lunn
Alpine Skiing
3514 Atmospheric .50 .23
Conditions
Col Du Geant
Mountain Climbing
3515 Interference 3.00 1.35
Johnny Bench
Baseball
3516 Volleyball at the .50 .23
Olympics
Poland vs. USSR
Volleyball
3517 World Cup 1.00 .45
Geoff Hurst
Soccer
3518 Jim Bakken FB 1.00 .45
3519 Ian O'Brien .50 .23
Swimming
3520 Olympic .50 .23
Commemorative Coins
Beyond Sports
3521 The Wightman Cup 1.50 .70
Joann Russell
Tennis
3522 Fred Perry 2.00 .90
Gottfried Von Cramm
Tennis
3523 The Components .50 .23
The Bows
Target Archery
3524 The First Kilometer .50 .23
Voisin Biplane
Powered Flight

1977-79 Sportscaster Series 36 *

NRMT VG-E
COMPLETE SET (26) 30.00 13.50
3601 Ron LeFlore BB 1.00 .45
3602 Driving on Wet .50 .23
Road Surfaces
R. Keegan
Auto Racing
3603 Jacques Laffite 1.50 .70
Auto Racing
3604 History .50 .23
With a Jump Rope
Trampolining
3605 Chamontix To Alpe .50 .23
D'Huez: Tour De France
Cycling
3606 Michel Pollentier .50 .23
Cycling
3607 Freddy Maertens 1.00 .45
Maertens/Merckx
Cycling
3608A Artis Gilmore ERR 3.00 1.35
Basketball
(Pictures Phil Ford
and the Four-corner
Offense; see 3612)
3608B Artis Gilmore COR 3.00 1.35
Basketball
3609 What is a Glider .50 .23
Glider Interior
Gliding
3610 The Italian Team .50 .23
'76 Italian Team
Waterpolo
3611 Great Contests .50 .23
Paris Six-Hour
Powerboat Racing
3612A The Four Corner ERR 3.00 1.35
Offense
Bulls vs. Bullets
Basketball
(Pictures Artis
Gilmore; see 3608)
3612B The Four Corner COR 3.00 1.35
Offense
Phil Ford
3613 Chris Chataway 1.00 .45
1955 White City
Track and Field
3614 Virginia Wade 2.00 .90
1977 Wimbledon
Tennis
3615 Raymond Domenech 1.00 .45

France/Denmark
Soccer
3616 The Jumps .50 .23
James Butts
Track and Field
3617 Goal Line Defense 1.50 .70
Bills vs Colts
Football
3618 Annapurna .50 .23
3 Climbers, 1974
Mountain Climbing
3619 Birger Ruud .50 .23
Nordic Skiing
3620 Two-Minute Offense 3.00 1.35
Ken Stabler
Football
3621 Larbi Ben Barek 1.00 .45
Portugal/France
Soccer
3622 The NCAA Tournament 5.00 2.20
Kentucky vs. Duke
Basketball
3623 The Paris "Relais" .50 .23
Race
Racing in Paris
Track and Field
3624 The Metric Mile 1.00 .45
Filbert Bayi, 1974
Track and Field

1977-79 Sportscaster Series 37 *

Please note that cards number 4 and 17 are not listed. Any information on the two missing cards is very appreciated.

NRMT VG-E
COMPLETE SET (24) 25.00 11.00
3701 Robert Schouckens .50 .23
Strasbourg-Paris
Track and Field
3702 The Shot Put .50 .23
A. Barichnikov
Track and Field
3703 John Akii-Bua 1.00 .45
In the Hurdles
Track and Field
3705 Hans Alser .50 .23
Table Tennis
3706 Hurdles .50 .23
In the Hurdles
Track and Field
3707 Philippe Thys .50 .23
Parc Des Princes
Cycling
3708 Lillian Board 1.00 .45
Track and Field
3709 Pickoff 1.50 .70
Luis Tiant
Baseball
3710 Nils Liedholm 1.00 .45
Liedholm/Buffon
Soccer
3711 Olympic Games 1.00 .45
Irina Press
Beyond Press
3712 Tai Babilonia and 4.00 1.80
Randy Gardner
Figure Skating
3713 Rocky 12.00 5.50
Rocky Stallone
(Sylvester Stallone
and Talia Shire)
Beyond Sports
3714 The Derby .50 .23
1971 Derby Day
Horse Racing
3715 Legal and Illegal .50 .23
Blocks: Blocking Action
Football
3716 Ivan Mauger .50 .23
His Trophies
Speedway
3718 Tom Watson 8.00 3.60
Golf
3719 Defense in Line .50 .23
France/Portugal
Soccer
3720 Defense in Line .50 .23
W. Germany/France
Soccer
3721 Vladimir Yaschenko .50 .23
In the High Jump
Track and Field
3722 NCAA Tournament 1.00 .45
Texas A and M/Texas
Baseball
3723 At-A-Glance .50 .23
Reference
The Rifle Range
Rifle Shooting
3724 Murren 1931 .50 .23
Walter Prager
Alpine Skiing

1977-79 Sportscaster Series 38 *

NRMT VG-E
COMPLETE SET (24) 40.00 18.00
3801 Robin Knox-Johnston .50 .23
W/ Suhaili
Yachting
3802 Eugene Criqui .50 .23
Criqui and Kilbane
Boxing
3803 The Weights .50 .23
The Shot Put
Track and Field
3804 Holding the Paddle .50 .23
Normal/Pen Holds
Table Tennis
3805 The British Open 6.00 2.70
Tom Watson
Golf
3806 Arnaud Massy .50 .23
Golf
3807 The Seven 3.00 1.35
Professional Trophies
Guy Lafleur
Ice Hockey
3808 Kriter-Craft .50 .23
Kriter II
Yachting
3809 George Brett BB 15.00 6.75
3810 Jim Rice BB 2.00 .90
3811 Paul Westphal 2.00 .90
Basketball
3812 Biddy-Basket 1.00 .45
Playground Game
Basketball
3813 Rules and Categories .50 .23
Starting A Race
Sand Yachting
3814 Wales .50 .23
Wales vs. France
Rugby
3815 Mary Rand 1.00 .45
Track and Field
3816 Murray Halberg .50 .23
In the Two-Mile
Track and Field
3817 Pope Paul VI 5.00 2.20
and Sport
Pope Paul
Eddy Merckx
Beyond Sports
3818 The Olympic Games .50 .23
At A Glance
Opening Ceremony
Beyond Sports
3819 Pierre Flamion 1.00 .45
Soccer
3820 Tony Roche 1.50 .70
1968 Wimbledon
Tennis
3821 Yamaha .50 .23
A Yamaha
Motorcycle Racing
3822 Jack Youngblood FB 2.00 .90
3823 Sweden .50 .23
Swedish Team
Handball
3824 The Federation Cup 2.50 1.10
Billie Jean King
Tennis

1977-79 Sportscaster Series 39 *

NRMT VG-E
COMPLETE SET (24) 15.00 6.75
3901 Roger Bambuck .50 .23
Track and Field
3902 Rundown 1.50 .70
Mets vs. Astros
Baseball
3903 The 5000-M .50 .23
Emil Puttemans
Track and Field
3904 Measurements .50 .23
Memorial Stadium
Baseball
3905 Golf and Television .50 .23
Televised Golf
Golf
3906 Links Between the .50 .23
USA and China
Peking Stadium
Table Tennis
3907 Willie Pep 2.00 .90
Boxing
3908 Johnny Giles .50 .23
Leeds vs Arsenal
Soccer
3909 Glossary From A-Z .50 .23
1972 World Champ
Karate
3910 Maccabi of Tel Aviv 1.00 .45
Maccabi Team
Basketball
3911 Roping Down .50 .23
'S' Double Rope
Mountain Climbing
3912 Edwin Moses 2.00 .90
In 400 M Hurdles
Track and Field
3913 Ann Davison and .50 .23
'Felicity Ann'
1952 In Plymouth
Yachting
3914 Passes and Passers .50 .23
Passing
Volleyball
3915 Doug Collins BK 3.00 1.35
3916 West Germany 1974 1.00 .45
1974 World Cup
Soccer
3917 Ball Control 1.50 .70
Packers vs Chiefs
Football
3918 Rugby Football .50 .23
Union
Twickenham Team
Rugby
3919 Bastia Sporting .50 .23
Club: SC Bastia
Soccer
3920 Played with the .50 .23
Fist: Playing Action
Faustball
3921 Grab Face Mask 1.50 .70
Colts vs Bills
Football
3922 Harvey Martin FB 2.00 .90
3923 Jousting on Water .50 .23
Jousting (FRA)
Sculling
3924 Cliff Diving .50 .23
A Cliff Diver
Diving

1977-79 Sportscaster Series 40 *

NRMT VG-E
COMPLETE SET (24) 20.00 9.00
4001 Garry Templeton BB 1.00 .45
4002 Jeff Burroughs BB 1.00 .45
4003 International .50 .23
Signals Code
Yachting
4004 Pass Interference 1.50 .70
Bob Chandler
Football
4005 The Smash .50 .23
Cuba vs. Poland
Volleyball
4006 Mt. Blanc .50 .23
Mountain Climbing
4007 Marques Johnson BK 4.00 1.80
4008 Equal Pacing .50 .23
G. Lohre
Track and Field
4009 Walter Davis BK 4.00 1.80
4010 Rick Upchurch FB 1.00 .45
4011 Roger Moens .50 .23
Moens: Michel Jazy
Track and Field
4012 Bill Shankly 1.00 .45
Charity Shield
Soccer
4013 Shirley Babashoff 1.00 .45
Swimming
4014 The Mainspring of .50 .23
Sport E. Germany
E. German Gymnastics
Beyond Sports
4015 Isotonic Training .50 .23
Isotonic
Beyond Sports
4016 Hill Climbs .50 .23
Rangiers
Auto Racing
4017 Kenny Dalglish 1.00 .45
Dalglish/Jardine
Soccer
4018 Karin Fischer- .50 .23
Muller
Swimming
4019 An Old-Established .50 .23
Sport: Jurg Boschung
Casting
4020 Nikolai Andrianov .50 .23
Parallel Bars
Gymnastics
4021 Roger Jouve 1.00 .45
Djebali/Jouve
Soccer
4022 Pedro Rodriguez 1.00 .45
Auto Racing
4023 Honda Endurance .50 .23
1976
Hubert Rigal
Motorcycle Racing
4024 The Stanley Cup 2.00 .90
Rangers/Blues
Ice Hockey

1977-79 Sportscaster Series 41 *

NRMT VG-E
COMPLETE SET (24) 40.00 18.00
4101 The Grand Slam 20.00 9.00
Bobby Jones
Golf
4102 Shep Messing 1.50 .70
Soccer
4103 Relief Pitching 1.00 .45
Mike Marshall
Baseball
4104 Pierre Barthes .50 .23
Tennis
4105 Putting 8.00 3.60
Arnie Palmer
Golf
4106 High Jump .50 .23
R. Skowronek
Track and Field
4107 Triple Play 1.00 .45
Bill Wambsganss
Baseball
4108 Don Quarrie 1.00 .45
Track and Field
4109 The Ryder Cup 2.50 1.10
Walter Hagen
Golf
4110 John Conteh 1.00 .45
Conteh and Bennett
Boxing
4111 Catamaran .50 .23
The Tornado
Yachting
4112 Robert Bobin .50 .23
Bobin/Bambuck
Track and Field
4113 Margaret Court 2.50 1.10
Tennis
4114 Dynamo Kiev 1.00 .45
Dynamo Kiev Team
Soccer
4115 Phil Read .50 .23
Motorcycle Racing
4116 Henri Courtine .50 .23
Judo
4117 South African Rugby .50 .23
Board
Springboks Team
Rugby
4118 Mao Tse-Tung and 5.00 2.20
Sport
Beyond Sports
4119 Laszlo Kubala 1.00 .45
Soccer
4120 Peter Radford .50 .23
1959-Hornchurch
Track and Field
4121 The Glider .50 .23
A Glider
Gliding
4122 Raymond Poulidor .50 .23
Tours-Versailles
Cycling
4123 Jean Boiteux .50 .23
Swimming
4124 Ernst Zullig .50 .23
Handball

1977-79 Sportscaster Series 42 *

NRMT VG-E
COMPLETE SET (24) 30.00 13.50
4201 The Masters 15.00 6.75
Jack Nicklaus
Golf
4202 Bernard King BK 2.00 .90
4203 Car Driving On Ice .50 .23
Race Tires
Auto Racing
4204 Rome Olympics .50 .23
100M Freestylers
Swimming
4205 The Diving Code .50 .23
Entering Water
Deep Sea Diving
4206 Four Important .50 .23
Changes
Refereeing
Rugby
4207 Tour De France - .50 .23
Green Jersey
J. Esclassan
Cycling
4208 Dave Parker 1.50 .70
Dave Kingman
Baseball
4209 Bert Blyleven BB 1.50 .70
4210 Rules .50 .23
Casting Action
Casting
4211 1934 WCH at St. .50 .23
Moritz
David Zogg
Alpine Skiing
4212 Novella Calligaris .50 .23
Swimming
4213 Curley Culp FB 1.00 .45
4214 Affirmed vs. Alydar 2.00 .90
The Belmont
Horse Racing
4215 Gordon Pirie .50 .23
Track and Field
4216 Chimney-Sweeping .50 .23
A Wide Chimney
Mountain Climbing
4217 Ghivi Onachvili .50 .23
Onachvili/Delaar
Judo
4218 Ezzard Charles 2.00 .90
Boxing
4219 Bob Beamon 1.50 .70
Track and Field
4220 The 3000-M .50 .23
Steeplechase
The Water-Jump
Track and Field
4221 The 110-M Hurdles 1.00 .45
Guy Drut
Track and Field
4222 The Galea Cup .50 .23
Argentine Team
Tennis
4223 The Par .50 .23
Tee Marker
Golf
4224 Cheerleading 1.50 .70
USC Cheerleaders
Football

1977-79 Sportscaster Series 43 *

NRMT VG-E
COMPLETE SET (24) 25.00 11.00
4301 The Washington 2.00 .90
Bullets
Bullets vs. Sonics
Basketball
4302 History of the .50 .23
World Cup
Yves Rimet
Soccer
4303 Pole Vault .50 .23
Dave Roberts
Track and Field
4304 Major and Minor 1.50 .70
Penalties
Maple Leafs/Caps
Ice Hockey
4305 Alexander Metreveli 1.00 .45
Tennis
4306 Rogie Vachon HK 2.00 .90
4307 Rick Reuschel BB 1.00 .45
4308 Techniques and .50 .23
Tactics
Helmet and Horn
Sand Yachting
4309 The Leader and .50 .23
Second Climber
Two Climbers
Mountain Climbing
4310 Long-Distance .50 .23
Yachting-France
The Mandrake
Yachting
4311 Nancy Lopez 8.00 3.60
Golf
4312 Holding the Ball 1.50 .70
For Placement
Roger Wehrli
Jim Bakken
Football
4313 Australian Rugby .50 .23
Football Union
Australian Team
Rugby
4314 A Little Like .50 .23
Volleyball
Equipment
Faustball
4315 The Glider .50 .23
A Glider
Gliding
4316 Tour De France: .50 .23
The Team Challenge
TI-Raleigh Team
Cycling
4317 Hendrikus Kuiper .50 .23
Tours-Versailles
Cycling
4318 Power Forward 2.50 1.10
Maurice Lucas
Basketball
4319 The United States .50 .23
Then Europe
The USA Team
Trampolining
4320 The First Races .50 .23
1984 Paris-Rouen
Auto Racing
4321 Decompression Table .50 .23
Equipment
Deep Sea Diving
4322 The French Team 1.00 .45
1958 World Cup
Soccer
4323 Yvon Duhamel .50 .23
650 CC Kawasaki
Motorcycle Racing
4324 The French Int'l. 2.50 1.10
at Roland-Garros
Guillermo Vilas
Tennis

1977-79 Sportscaster Series 44 *

NRMT VG-E
COMPLETE SET (24) 25.00 11.00
4401 Josef Walcher .50 .23
Alpine Skiing
4402 1976 WCH .50 .23
Three Skiers
Alpine Skiing
4403 Jaroslav Jirik 1.00 .45
Czechs vs. Swedes
Ice Hockey
4404 The Americans In .50 .23
The Lead
1977 WCH: Oliva
Bodybuilding
4405 The French Alpine .50 .23
Club: Couvercle Refuge
Mountain Climbing
4406 The European .50 .23
Championships
1977 Hungarians
Waterpolo
4407 Marcello Guarducci .50 .23
Swimming
4408 Rudolf Rominger .50 .23
Alpine Skiing
4409 Helen Wills 2.00 .90
Tennis
4410 The Winners of the 1.00 .45
Tour De France
Bernard Hinault
Cycling
4411 Phil Bennett .50 .23
Rugby
4412 The 1977 WCH 3.00 1.35
Niki Lauda
Auto Racing
4413 Filbert Bayi 1.00 .45
Track and Field
4414 Decathlon:The World 2.00 .90
Records
Bruce Jenner
Track and Field
4415 Jim Thorpe 5.00 2.20
In Shot Put
Track and Field
4416 Butch Lee BK 1.50 .70
4417 Hidden Ball Trick 1.50 .70
A's/Red Sox
Baseball
4418 Andres Gimeno .50 .23
1972 French Open
Tennis
4419 Johnny Rep .50 .23
Soccer
4420 Gerry Cheevers 2.00 .90
Ice Hockey
4421 3-Guard Offense 2.00 .90
Phil Chenier
Basketball
4422 Punting 2.50 1.10
Ray Guy
Football
4423 Just Fontaine 1.00 .45
Fontaine/Grosics
Soccer
4424 Special Team 1.00 .45
Defense
Kick Return
Football

1977-79 Sportscaster Series 45 *

Card number 11 is not in our checklist. Any information on this missing card is greatly appreciated.

NRMT VG-E
COMPLETE SET (24) 40.00 18.00
4501 The Ford-Cosworth 3.00 1.35
Engine: Formula 1 Engine
(A.J. Foyt's card)
Auto Racing
4502 Benny Briscoe 1.00 .45
Boxing
4503 Decathlon:The World .50 .23
Records
H.H. Sievert
Track and Field
4504 Throwing the Ball 3.00 1.35
Bob Griese
Football
4505 Gyula Grosics .50 .23
1954 World Cup
Soccer
4506 World Championships 5.00 2.20
Nancy Lopez
Golf
4507 Whirling Dervish .50 .23
Technique

A Squash Player
Squash
4508 Rodney Pattisson .50 .23
W/ Chris Davies
Yachting
4509 Punt Returns 2.00 .90
Lem Barney
Football
4510 Referee's Signals .50 .23
Refereeing
Karate
4512 Larry Holmes 5.00 2.20
Boxing
4513 Steve Shutt HK 2.00 .90
4514 Bob Hayes 3.00 1.35
1963 100 Yd Dash
Track and Field
4515 John H. Stracey 1.00 .45
Boxing
4516 Gary Player 8.00 3.60
Golf
4517 Hit and Run 1.50 .70
George Foster
Baseball
4518 David Jenkins .50 .23
Track and Field
4519 The Controlled Skid .50 .23
Skidding Racecar
Auto Racing
4520 Francesco Moser .50 .23
Moser/Dietrich
Cycling
4521 The Winger 1.00 .45
A. Simonsen
Soccer
4522 Hitting the Cutoff 1.50 .70
Man: Red Sox Player
Baseball
4523 Luis Pereira 1.00 .45
Soccer
4524 Walter Hagen 12.00 5.50
Golf

1977-79 Sportscaster Series 46 *

NRMT VG-E
COMPLETE SET (24) 25.00 11.00
4601 NFL Draft 2.50 1.10
Bubba Smith
Football
4602 Events Now Obsolete .50 .23
Swimming Action
Swimming
4603 Double Stringing .50 .23
A Tennis Racket
Tennis
4604 The Prague Scandal 4.00 1.80
Nadia Comaneci
Beyond Sports
4605 The 1950 World Cup 1.00 .45
Gaetjen/Williams
Soccer
4606 Ricky Bruch .50 .23
In the Discus
Track and Field
4607 Fighting Dress .50 .23
Kendo Action
Kendo
4608 Mike Hawthorn 1.00 .45
Auto Racing
4609 Ron Hill .50 .23
1972 Maxol
Track and Field
4610 Rosemarie Ackermann 1.00 .45
In the High Jump
Track and Field
4611 Yang Chuan-Kwang 1.00 .45
In the Shot Put
Track and Field
4612 Ole Olsen .50 .23
Motorcycle Racing
4613 Kickoff Returns 4.00 1.80
Gale Sayers
Football
4614 In the Corners 1.50 .70
Leafs/Capitals
Ice Hockey
4615 The "Cesta Punta" .50 .23
The Basque
Game Action
Jai Alai (Pelota)
4616 Geoff Hunt .50 .23
1975 British Open
Squash
4617 Ivar Formo .50 .23
Nordic Skiing
4618 The Three Ali- 10.00 4.50
Frazier Fights
Joe Frazier/Muhammad Ali
Boxing
4619 Sticks and Disks .50 .23
Game in Florida
Shuffleboard
4620 Fan And Fringe .50 .23
Cycling Action
Cycling
4621 Bryan Trottier HK 3.00 1.35
4622 Amateur Draft 1.00 .45
Rick Monday
Baseball
4623 Racetracks: .50 .23
Churchill Downs
The Twin Spires
Horse Racing
4624 Racetracks: Belmont .50 .23
Park: Belmont Oak Tree
Horse Racing

1977-79 Sportscaster Series 47 *

NRMT VG-E
COMPLETE SET (24) 35.00 16.00
4701 1972 WCH .50 .23
Three Skiers
Alpine Skiing
4702 Great Moments 2.00 .90
Ferguson Jenkins
Baseball
4703 Emerson Fittipaldi 8.00 3.60
Auto Racing
4704 Johan De Muynck .50 .23
1977 Giro
Cycling
4705 Great Moments 2.50 1.10
Bob Gibson
Baseball
4706 Racetracks: .50 .23
Hollywood Park
Horse Racing
4707 Noel Tijou .50 .23
Track and Field
4708 Marlies Olsner-Gohr .50 .23
Track and Field
4709 The Touquet Enduro .50 .23
Le Touquet Beach
Motorcycle Racing
4710 Helmut Fath and .50 .23
the Urs: Helmut Fath
Motorcycle Racing
4711 The Ball .50 .23
A Golf Ball
Golf
4712 Figure Competition .50 .23
Pairs Dancing
Cycling
4713 Racetracks: Santa .50 .23
Anita Park
Call To Track
Horse Racing
4714 Flemming Delfs .50 .23
Badminton
4715 Klaus Dibiasi 1.50 .70
Diving
4716 Trio Grande 8.00 3.60
(Bryan Trottier
Mike Bossy
Clark Gillies)
Ice Hockey
4717 Festivals of .50 .23
Sporting Films
Beyond Sports
4718 Darryl Sittler HK 3.00 1.35
4719 Rocky Graziano 2.00 .90
Graziano with Tony Zale
Boxing
4720 Rik Van Linden .50 .23
Tour De France
Cycling
4721 Tom Jackson 4.00 1.80
Jackson
O.J.Simpson
Football
4722 Peru in the World 1.00 .45
Cup: 1977 Peru Team
Soccer
4723 Austria in the 1.00 .45
World Cup
1977 Team
Soccer
4724 Christian Dalger 1.00 .45
Soccer

1977-79 Sportscaster Series 48 *

NRMT VG-E
COMPLETE SET (24) 20.00 9.00
4801 Bobby Charlton 4.00 1.80
1966 Manchester
Soccer
4802 Hans Gunter Winkler .50 .23
Show Jumping
4803 A Legacy of the Jeu .50 .23
De Paume
Mixed Doubles
Tennis
4804 The Tackle .50 .23
After the Tackle
Rugby League
4805 Walter Spanghero .50 .23
Rugby
4806 Alain Mimoun 1.00 .45
Track and Field
4807 The Snatch and The .50 .23
Clean and The Jerk
Two Movements
Weightlifting
4808 Lynn Davies 1.00 .45
In Long Jump
Track and Field
4809 Dominique Baratelli .50 .23
Baratelli/Tresor
Soccer
4810 The 4x400-M Relay 1.50 .70
1968 USA Team
Vince Matthews
Ron Freeman
Larry James
Lee Evans
Track and Field
4811 The Corrida of Sao .50 .23
Paulo
G. Roelants
Track and Field
4812 The Alpine Touring .50 .23
Certificate
Touring Action
Bicycle Touring
4813 Gustavo Thoeni .50 .23
Alpine Skiing
4814 Niels Fredborg .50 .23
Cycling
4815 John Newcombe 2.00 .90
Tennis
4816 The Competitions .50 .23
Posing Action
Bodybuilding
4817 European Origins .50 .23
English Play
Roller Hockey
4818 Vassili Alexeiev 1.50 .70
1976 Olympics
Weightlifting
4819 Denis Hulme 1.00 .45
Auto Racing
4820 The Fastnet .50 .23
American Eagle
Yachting
4821 Brendan Foster .50 .23
Track and Field
4822 The TT Races .50 .23
Mike Hailwood
Motorcycle Racing
4823 Frank Sedgman 1.00 .45
Tennis
4824 Bob Fitzsimmons 1.50 .70
Boxing

1977-79 Sportscaster Series 49 *

NRMT VG-E
COMPLETE SET (24) 40.00 18.00
4901 White City Stadium .50 .23
Beyond Sports
4902 The Olympic Games 2.00 .90
Jean Claude Killy
Huber/Matt
Beyond Sports
4903 Indianapolis 500 2.00 .90
Indy 500
Auto Racing
4904 Tatiana Kazankina .50 .23
1976 Olympics
Track and Field
4905 1972:The Rise of .50 .23
West Germany
West German Team
Soccer
4906 Gunnar Larsson .50 .23
Swimming
4907 The Mile 1.50 .70
John Walker
Track and Field
4908 Epsom .50 .23
Derby Day 1973
Horse Racing
4909 Alan Pascoe .50 .23
Track and Field
4910 Abas Arslanagic .50 .23
Handball
4911 Hans Schafer 1.00 .45
Schafer/Ramirez
Soccer
4912 Glossary .50 .23
Fencing Mask
Fencing
4913 Sue Barker 2.00 .90
1977 Wimbledon
Tennis
4914 Louis Martin .50 .23
Snatches 130 KG
Weightlifting
4915 World Champions .50 .23
Shozo Fujii
Judo
4916 Frew McMillan 1.00 .45
Bob Hewitt
1978 Wimbledon
Tennis
4917 Origins .50 .23
Atkins/Swallow
Rackets
4918 Manolete .50 .23
Bullfighting
4919 List of America's 5.00 2.20
Cup Winners: Ted Turner
Yachting
4920 Evonne Goolagong 4.00 1.80
Cawley
Tennis
4921 The 1934 World Cup 30.00 13.50
Peter Platzer
Soccer
4922 Nick Faldo 10.00 4.50
Golf
4923 The 1938 World Cup 1.00 .45
Amado/Raftl
Soccer
4924 Boy Charlton 1.00 .45
Andrew Charlton
Swimming

1977-79 Sportscaster Series 50 *

NRMT VG-E
COMPLETE SET (24) 30.00 13.50
5001 Equipment 1.50 .70
S.D. Chargers
Football
5002 John Pennel 1.00 .45
In Pole Vault
Track and Field
5003 Sticks 4.00 1.80
Bobby Hull
Harry Howell
Ice Hockey
5004 Facemasks 4.00 1.80
Two Facemasks
Ice Hockey
5005 Glossary .50 .23
Men's Helmet
Kendo
5006 Joe Louis 4.00 1.80
With Ezzard Charles
Boxing
5007 Dennis Eckersley BB 4.00 1.80
5008 Alexander .50 .23
Barishnikov
Track and Field
5009 Alan Minter 1.50 .70
Boxing
5010 Aladar Gerevich .50 .23
Fencing
5011 Referee's Signals .50 .23
Refereeing
Judo
5012 The Tires .50 .23
Motorcycle Tire
Motorcycle Racing
5013 Sandro Mazzola 1.00 .45
Soccer
5014 The Thirteen-A-Side .50 .23
Game: France/N.Zealand
Rugby League
5015 Rumania .50 .23
Rumanian Team
Handball
5016 Jean-Claude Killy 4.00 1.80
Alpine Skiing
5017 The American and 1.00 .45
European Circuits 1978
Graham Marsh
Golf
5018 Paul Elvstroem .50 .23
Yachting
5019 Dribbling 8.00 3.60
Pele/Mullery
Soccer
5020 Ernie Nevers FB 2.00 .90
5021 The Jockey's Room .50 .23
Jockeys Relaxing
Horse Racing
5022 The Blacksmith .50 .23
Blacksmith Tools
Horse Racing
5023 John Surtees 1.00 .45
Auto Racing
5024 The Penalty 1.00 .45
1974 World Cup
Soccer

1977-79 Sportscaster Series 51 *

NRMT VG-E
COMPLETE SET (24) 40.00 18.00
5101 Czechoslovakia 1977 1.50 .70
Czechs vs Soviet
Ice Hockey
5102 The Double Steal 1.50 .70
Davey Lopes
Baseball
5103 Cy Young BB 3.00 1.35
5104 28 Lost .50 .23
Pryce, Lafitte
Auto Racing
5105 Eddy Merckx 1.00 .45
Mont-Revard
Cycling
5106 Bobby Moore 1.50 .70
Moore/O'Hare
Soccer
5107 Ancient Game .50 .23
American Style
Newport, California
Lawn Bowls
5108 The 800 M Women's 1.50 .70
Freestyle
Petra Thumer
Swimming
5109 The 100 M Butterfly 2.50 1.10
Mark Spitz
Swimming
5110 Glossary .50 .23
The Courageous
Yachting
5111 Glossary .50 .23
Captain At Helm
Yachting
5112 Ray Moore .50 .23
Tennis
5113 Rosalyn Bryant .50 .23
Track and Field
5114 1,000,000 Folks in .50 .23
Waterways: Tubing Action
Tubing
5115 Seve Ballesteros 12.00 5.50
Golf
5116 Garrincha 1.00 .45
Soccer
5118 Guy Lafleur HK 3.00 1.35
5119 Jody Scheckter 3.00 1.35
Auto Racing
5120 The 10,000 Meters 1.00 .45
David Bedford
Track and Field
5121 Rule V:The Referee .50 .23
1974 World Cup
Soccer
5122 Lester Piggott 1.00 .45
Horse Racing
5123 The Outriders .50 .23
An Outrider
Horse Racing
5124 Graham Marsh 6.00 2.70
Golf

1977-79 Sportscaster Series 52 *

NRMT VG-E
COMPLETE SET (24) 20.00 9.00
5201 World Championship .50 .23
Inner Tube Race
Having Fun
Tubing
5202 Gene Tenace BB 1.00 .45
5203 The 4x100-M Relay .50 .23
1968 Olympics
Track and Field
5204 Vladimir Golubnichi .50 .23
In the 20-KM Walk
Track and Field
5205 North American 4.00 1.80
Soccer League
Kyle Rote Jr.
Soccer
5206 The 1950 World Cup 1.00 .45
Brazil/Uruguay
Soccer
5207 1974 WCH .50 .23
David Zwilling
Alpine Skiing
5208 The Origins .50 .23
1840 Laplander
Skiing
5209 Great Moments 1.50 .70
Mickey Lolich
Baseball
5210 The Corrida .50 .23
Pampelune Arena
Bullfighting
5211 Racetracks:Aqueduct .50 .23
The Big A
Horse Racing
5212 The Classes .50 .23
Karting Vehicle
Karting
5214 Dai Rees 8.00 3.60
Golf
5215 Sport In Nazi .50 .23
Germany
Tilly Fleischer
Beyond Sports
5216 Dave Bedford .50 .23
Track and Field
5217 Tom Pryce 1.00 .45
Auto Racing
5218 Clay Regazzoni 1.00 .45
Auto Racing
5219 The Beaufort Scale .50 .23
Francis Beaufort
Beyond Sports
5220 An Entertaining .50 .23
Sport Access
Centenary Final
Croquet
5221 Buster Mottram 1.00 .45
Tennis
5222 The Pioneers of .50 .23
Aviation
An Air Rescue
Powered Flight
5223 Anett Poetzsch 1.00 .45
Figure Skating
5224 Hank Luisetti BK 2.50 1.10

1977-79 Sportscaster Series 53 *

NRMT VG-E
COMPLETE SET (24) 30.00 13.50
5301 Alan Jones 1.50 .70
Auto Racing
5302 Lady Professionals 6.00 2.70
Judy Rankin
Golf
5303 1970 WCH 1.00 .45
Bernhard Russi
Alpine Skiing
5304 The New Rules For .50 .23
Judging
Yellow Cards
Handball
5305 Paddock Procedures 1.00 .45
Gustiness/Forego
Horse Racing
5306 Anatoly Bondartchuk .50 .23
Hammer Throw
Track and Field
5307 Andre Thornton BB 1.00 .45
5308 Origins .50 .23
Tommy O'Regan
Darts
5309 Sonny Liston 4.00 1.80
Liston/Floyd Patterson
Boxing
5310 The Sidelines 1.50 .70
S.D. Chargers
Football
5311 Marty Liquori 1.50 .70
Track and Field
5312 Richard Tison .50 .23
Trampolining
5313 Heikki Mikkola .50 .23
MotoCross
5314 Georges Carpentier 1.50 .70
Boxing
5315 Noble in Form and .50 .23
History
Wrestling Action
Breton Wresting
5316 Eddie Feigner 5.00 2.20
Softball
5317 Great Moments 3.00 1.35
Sonny Jurgensen
Football
5318 Kazimierz Deyna 1.00 .45
Poland/Italy
Soccer
5319 Equipment .50 .23
Equipment Type
Underwater Fishing
5320 Ann Jones 1.50 .70
At Wimbledon
Tennis
5321 The Women's 100-M .50 .23
1978 European
Championships
Track and Field
5322 Jack Sikma BK 2.50 1.10
5323 John Walker 1.50 .70
Track and Field
5324 BRM 1.00 .45
'75 Brands Hatch
Auto Racing

1977-79 Sportscaster Series 54 *

NRMT VG-E
COMPLETE SET (24) 30.00 13.50
5401 World Walking .50 .23
Records
Gerhard Weidner
Track and Field
5402 Dragsters 1.50 .70
A Dragster
Auto Racing
5403 Hot Walkers .50 .23
A Hot Walker
Horse Racing
5404 The ISDT .50 .23
300 Motorbikes
Motorcycle Racing
5405 The Classes .50 .23
Many Classes
Yachting
5406 Francis .50 .23
De Barbeyrac
Beyond Sports
5407 Eddie Hart 1.00 .45
In 100 M Dash
Track and Field
5408 Great Moments 2.50 1.10
Carl Yastrzemski

Baseball
5409 Freddie Patek BB 1.00 .45
5410 Boxe Francaise .50 .23
French Boxer
Boxing
5411 The Targe .50 .23
A Foil Hit
Fencing
5412 Eugenio Monti .50 .23
Bobsledding
5413 Ken Buchanan 1.00 .45
Boxing
5414 Joe Kapp 2.00 .90
Vikings/Colts
Football
5415 George Mikan BK 10.00 4.50
5416 Brooklands .50 .23
1930 Brooklands
Auto Racing
5417 David Lloyd 2.00 .90
John Lloyd
5418 Ulrike Meyfarth 1.00 .45
In the High Jump
Track and Field
5419 Michel Bernard .50 .23
Track and Field
5420 Jim Thorpe FB 8.00 3.60
5421 The Press Sisters 1.00 .45
Irina and Tamara
Track and Field
5422 Claudia Giordani .50 .23
Alpine Skiing
5423 Manuel Raga BK 1.50 .70
5424 The Way of the .50 .23
Sword: Ceremony
Kendo

1977-79 Sportscaster Series 55 *

NRMT VG-E
COMPLETE SET (24) 25.00 11.00
5501 Dave Casper FB 2.00 .90
5502 Synchronized .50 .23
Swimming
5503 Lyman Bostock BB 1.50 .70
5504 Russ Collins .50 .23
Motorcycle Racing
5505 Tony Trabert 2.50 1.10
Trabert/Nielson
Tennis
5506 Lead Ponies .50 .23
Two Lead Ponies
Horse Racing
5507 Rob Rensenbrink .50 .23
Soccer
5508 Georg Schwarzenbeck 1.00 .45
Soccer
5509 Sven-Ake Lundback .50 .23
S. Lundback
Nordic Skiing
5510 Klaus Wolfermann .50 .23
In the Javelin
Track and Field
5511 The Three Grips .50 .23
Interlock Grip
Golf
5512 North Face Extremes .50 .23
S. Cachat-Rosset
Alpine Skiing
5513 Barry Hoban .50 .23
Cycling
5514 Jiri Holik 2.00 .90
Jaroslav Holik
Two Czech Stars
Ice Hockey
5515 Bull Riding .50 .23
Rodeo
5516 Peter Oosterhuis 6.00 2.70
Golf
5517 Francoise Durr 1.00 .45
Tennis
5518 Leonard Robinson BK 1.50 .70
5519 The Sport in North .50 .23
America
Kayaking Action
Canoeing and Kayaking
5520 Cowes Week .50 .23
In The Solent
Yachting
5521 Arthur Wint 1.00 .45
Track and Field
5522 Hugo Corro 1.00 .45
Boxing
5523 World Hockey Assoc. 8.00 3.60
Bobby Hull
Ice Hockey
5524 Gillian Gilks .50 .23
Badminton

1977-79 Sportscaster Series 56 *

NRMT VG-E
COMPLETE SET (24) 75.00 34.00
5601 The Goalkeeper 2.00 .90
A Goalkeeper
Soccer
5602 The Monza Autodrome 2.00 .90
1976 Monza
Auto Racing
5603 Maracana 2.00 .90
Maracana Stadium
Soccer
5604 Cesta Punta 2.00 .90
A Pelota Player
Pelota
5605 Montreal Forum 5.00 2.20
Toronto/Montreal
Ice Hockey
5606 Piero Gros 3.00 1.35
Alpine Skiing
5607 Racetracks: Pimlico 2.00 .90
The Preakness
Horse Racing
5608 Olympic Medallists 2.00 .90
H. Uemura
Judo
5609 A Few Rules of the 2.00 .90
Game: Hockey Action
Field Hockey
5610 Felice Gimondi 2.00 .90
Cycling
5611 Marvin Webster BK 4.00 1.80
5612 Mark Cox 4.00 1.80
Tennis
5613 Carlton Fisk BB 10.00 4.50
5614 Donald Crowhurst 2.00 .90
Yachting
5615 Ray Guy FB 5.00 2.20
5616 Waldemar Cierpinski 4.00 1.80
In the Marathon
Track and Field
5617 St. Andrews 6.00 2.70
St. Andrews Club
Golf
5618 Great Moments 15.00 6.75
Joe Namath
Football
5619 Martin Lauer 2.00 .90
Lauer/May
Track and Field
5620 Derek Ibbotson 2.00 .90
With Bolotnikov
Track and Field
5621 Francois Cevert 2.00 .90
Auto Racing
5622 High Diving 2.00 .90
Acapulco
Diving
5623 Franz Beckenbauer 8.00 3.60
Germany/Holland
Soccer
5624 Mark McCormack 5.00 2.20
Beyond Sports

1977-79 Sportscaster Series 57 *

NRMT VG-E
COMPLETE SET (24) 80.00 36.00
5701 Willie Lanier FB 5.00 2.20
5702 Dave Winfield BB 12.00 5.50
5703 Ian Stewart 2.00 .90
1976 Olympics
Track and Field
5704 Davis Cup 2.00 .90
1955 Aussies
Tennis
5705 Zeno Cola 2.00 .90
Alpine Skiing
5706 Racetracks: Hialeah 2.00 .90
Park: Hialeah Flowers
Horse Racing
5707 Pele and 15.00 6.75
the Cosmos
Soccer
5708 The Courses 2.00 .90
St. Moritz
Bobsledding
5709 A Cousin of Tennis 2.00 .90
Badminton Action
Badminton
5710 Men's European Team 8.00 3.60
Championship
1977 Scottish Team
Golf
5711 Ruth Fuchs 3.00 1.35
In the Javelin
Track and Field
5712 The Sport in North 2.00 .90
America
A Parachute Jump
Parachute Jumping
5713 Vera Nikolic 2.00 .90
Track and Field
5714 Johann Cruyff 6.00 2.70
Soccer
5715 From Barrooms To 2.00 .90
Television: Refereeing
Wrist Wrestling
5716 The Formula 1 2.00 .90
Mechanics: Auto Mechanic
Auto Racing
5717 A New Sport 2.00 .90
Sailing on Sand
Wind Skating
5718 Max Faulrner 6.00 2.70
Golf
5719 Jack Brabham 4.00 1.80
Auto Racing
5720 The Sport of Kings 2.00 .90
Cutty Sark Open
Real Tennis
5721 Jai Alai in North 2.00 .90
America
American Jai Alai
Pelota
5722 Rules and History 2.00 .90
Nortlake Champions
Lawn Bowls
5723 The Equipment 6.00 2.70
Jay Schroeder
Golf
5724 Yvon Petra 2.00 .90
Tennis

1977-79 Sportscaster Series 58 *

NRMT VG-E
COMPLETE SET (24) 50.00 22.00
5801 Shea Stadium 2.00 .90
Baseball
5802 Busch Memorial 2.00 .90
Stadium
Baseball
5803 Max Decugis 2.00 .90
Tennis
5804 Four-Cyclinder 2.00 .90
Yamaha: Finnish GP
Motorcycle Racing
5805 Fenway Park 5.00 2.20
Baseball
5806 Fred Stolle 5.00 2.20
1963 Wimbledon
Tennis
5807 Jacques Rousseau 2.00 .90
In Long Jump
Track and Field
5808 Competition 2.00 .90
A Competitor
Skateboarding
5809 The Khans 2.00 .90
Mohibullah Khan
Squash
5810 Irina Rodnina 4.00 1.80
Aleksandr Zaitsev
Figure Skating
5811 Renate Stecher 4.00 1.80
1973 Dresden
Track and Field
5812 Baltimore Memorial 2.00 .90
Stadium
Baseball
5813 Gerd Muller 3.00 1.35
Soccer
5814 Yankee Stadium 5.00 2.20
Baseball
5815 Nenad Stekic 2.00 .90
In the Long Jump
Track and Field
5816 Kid Gavilan 4.00 1.80
Gavilan
Peter Waterman
Boxing
5817 Rugby in New 2.00 .90
Zealand
All Blacks/Lions
Rugby
5818 Candlestick Park 4.00 1.80
Baseball
5819 Lew Hoad 4.00 1.80
1968 Wimbledon
Tennis
5820 Betty Cuthbert 3.00 1.35
'62 Empire Games
Track and Field
5821 Veterans Stadium 2.00 .90
Baseball
5822 Amedeo Gordini 2.00 .90
Auto Racing
5823 Dodger Stadium 2.00 .90
Baseball
5824 Colette Besson 2.00 .90
1968 Olympics
Track and Field

1977-79 Sportscaster Series 59 *

NRMT VG-E
COMPLETE SET (24) 100.00 45.00
5901 Willy Frommelt 2.00 .90
Alpine Skiing
5902 Roger Staubach 12.00 5.50
Cowboys/Giants
Football
5903 Gottfried Von Cramm 4.00 1.80
Tennis
5904 Lee Evans 4.00 1.80
Track and Field
5905 David Thompson BK 8.00 3.60
5906 The International 2.00 .90
Championship
France vs. Wales
Rugby
5907 Jackie Stewart 10.00 4.50
Auto Racing
5908 Lingo 2.00 .90
A "Drop In"
Surfing
5909 Eclipse 4.00 1.80
Eclipse Painting
Horse Racing
5910 Dennis Ralston 5.00 2.20
1971 Wimbledon
Tennis
5911 Charles Rigoulot 2.00 .90
Lifting 156 KG
Weightlifting
5912 Alfons Brijdenbach 2.00 .90
Track and Field
5913 The Helicopter 2.00 .90
Route: Hans Gmoser
Skiing
5914 Henry Cotton 10.00 4.50
Golf
5915 Nadejda Chizova 2.00 .90
1972 Olympics
Track and Field
5916 Enzo Ferrari 5.00 2.20
Auto Racing
5917 Emile Griffith 5.00 2.20
Boxing
5918 The Two-Handed 8.00 3.60
Backhand
Jimmy Connors
Tennis
5919 Brad Lackey 2.00 .90
MotoCross
5920 Frank Robinson BB 8.00 3.60
5921 Mary Peters 4.00 1.80
In Pentathlon
Track and Field
5922 Ilona Gusenbauer 2.00 .90
In High Jump
Track and Field
5923 Kyle Rote Jr. 5.00 2.20
Soccer
5924 Roland Garros 2.00 .90
Powered Flight

1977-79 Sportscaster Series 60 *

NRMT VG-E
COMPLETE SET (24) 75.00 34.00
6001 Daniel Passarella 2.00 .90
Soccer
6002 Roscoe Tanner 5.00 2.20
1977 Wimbledon
Tennis
6003 Geoff Duke 2.00 .90
At Quarter Bridge
Motorcycle Racing
6004 Whizzer White 8.00 3.60
Beyond Sports
6005 Ben Jipcho 4.00 1.80
Track and Field
6006 The Skate 2.00 .90
Phenomenon
California Parks
Skateboarding
6007 Chay Blith 2.00 .90
W British Steel
Yachting
6008 Carol Blazejowski BK 6.00 2.70
6009 Nino Farina 2.00 .90
Auto Racing
6010 Marcello Fiasconaro 2.00 .90
Track and Field
6011 Jack Johnson 5.00 2.20
Johnson
Jack Jeffries
Boxing
6012 Bobby Clarke HK 8.00 3.60
6013 1962 WCH 2.00 .90
Marianne Jahn
Alpine Skiing
6014 The Fouls and 2.00 .90
Punishments
Austria vs. Dutch
Waterpolo
6015 Hale Irwin 12.00 5.50
Golf
6016 Bill Rodgers 4.00 1.80
Track and Field
6017 Andrea Lynch 2.00 .90
Track and Field
6018 Arkle 2.00 .90
Arkl/Mill House
Horse Racing
6019 Maria Filatova 2.00 .90
Balance Beam
Gymnastics
6020 Triple Crown 5.00 2.20
Seattle Slew
Horse Racing
6021 Peter Frenkel 2.00 .90
In the Walk
Track and Field
6022 Jean-Claude Nallet 2.00 .90
In the Hurdles
Track and Field
6023 Sandy Koufax BB 10.00 4.50
6024 British Lions 2.00 .90
Gareth Edwards
Rugby

1977-79 Sportscaster Series 61 *

NRMT VG-E
COMPLETE SET (24) 100.00 45.00
6101 The Smash 15.00 6.75
Arthur Ashe
Tennis
6102 Ron Guidry BB 4.00 1.80
6103 Lingo 5.00 2.20
Eddie Giacomin
Ice Hockey
6104 Angela Mortimer 2.00 .90
At Wimbledon
Tennis
6105 The 1938 World Cup 2.00 .90
Raftl (Germany)
Soccer
6106 National Sports 2.00 .90
Festival: Ceremonial Flame
Beyond Sports
6107 The Architecture of 8.00 3.60
Golf Course
Model of Course
Golf
6108 Brian Huggett 8.00 3.60
Golf
6109 Franklin Jacobs 3.00 1.35
In High Jump
Track and Field
6110 Bill Bradley 15.00 6.75
Beyond Sports
6111 Ann Packer 2.00 .90
Track and Field
6112 U.S. Open 2.00 .90
Flushing, NY
Tennis
6113 500-CC Champions 2.00 .90
Roger De Coster
MotoCross
6114 The History of Mont 2.00 .90
Blanc: 1838 Ascent
Mountain Climbing
6115 Maryvonne Dupureur 2.00 .90
Track and Field
6116 Roberto Clemente BB 25.00 11.00
6117 Steering 2.00 .90
Schaerer and Benz
Bobsledding
6118 Stein Eriksen 2.00 .90
Alpine Skiing
6119 Wembley 2.00 .90
Wembley Stadium
Soccer
6120 Heisman Trophy 10.00 4.50
Earl Campbell
Football
6121 Jocelyn Delecour 2.00 .90
At the Start
Track and Field
6122 Mario Kempes 2.00 .90
Soccer
6123 The French Open 2.00 .90
V. Tshabalala
Golf
6124 French Boxing 2.00 .90
French Boxer
Boxing

1977-79 Sportscaster Series 62 *

NRMT VG-E
COMPLETE SET (24) 80.00 36.00
6201 Ludvik Danek 2.00 .90
In the Discus
Track and Field
6202 Buzz Aldrin 12.00 5.50
Beyond Sports
6203 Berti Vogts 2.00 .90
Soccer
6204 Don Larsen's 5.00 2.20
Perfect Game
Baseball
6205 Glossary 2.00 .90
Skateboarding
6206 Alejandro Casanas 2.00 .90
1977 Universal Games
Track and Field
6207 Al Feuerbach 4.00 1.80
Track and Field
6208 Leon Spinks 10.00 4.50
Spinks
Muhammad Ali
Boxing
6209 Calvin Murphy BK 5.00 2.20
6210 African Games 2.00 .90
African Games Poster
Beyond Sports
6211 Real Tennis 2.00 .90
An Old Drawing
Sports of Past
6212 Guillermo Vilas 5.00 2.20
1977 French Open
Tennis
6213 Nicole Duclos 2.00 .90
Duclos/Meyer
Track and Field
6214 Eddie Lee Ivery FB 4.00 1.80
6215 Bill Ivy 2.00 .90
1967 Ulster GP
Motorcycle Racing
6216 The Principal 10.00 4.50
Punches: Muhammad Ali
Leon Spinks
Boxing
6217 Lester Patrick HK 5.00 2.20
6218 The Goalkeeper 2.00 .90
Goal-keeping
Handball
6219 Alexander Grigoriev 2.00 .90
In a High Jump
Track and Field
6220 John Watson 2.00 .90
Auto Racing
6221 Dragsters 2.00 .90
A Dragster
Auto Racing
6222 Scoring Methods 8.00 3.60
A Scoreboard
Golf
6223 Constance Appleby 2.00 .90
College Action
Field Hockey
6224 Peter Alliss 10.00 4.50
Golf

1977-79 Sportscaster Series 63 *

NRMT VG-E
COMPLETE SET (24) 60.00 27.00
6301 Udo Beyer 2.00 .90
In the Shot Put
Track and Field
6302 17-0 Dolphins 10.00 4.50
Bob Griese
Larry Csonka
Football
6303 Angel Nieto 2.00 .90
Motorcycle Racing
6304 1956 Winter 4.00 1.80
Olympics
Tony Sailer
Alpine Skiing
6305 First TV Game 2.00 .90
Burke Crotty
Basketball
6306 Tom Okker 4.00 1.80
Tennis
6307 Frank Baumgartl 2.00 .90
Track and Field
6308 The Corner Kick 2.00 .90
A Corner Kick
Soccer
6309 The Howe Family 12.00 5.50
Four Howes
Ice Hockey
6310 Glossary 2.00 .90
Skateboard Types
Skateboarding
6311 Origins 2.00 .90
18th Century Picture
Billiards
6312 Shirley Muldowney 8.00 3.60
Auto Racing
6313 Boris Zaichuk 2.00 .90
In Hammer Throw
Track and Field
6314 Roger Taylor 4.00 1.80
1973 Wimbledon
Tennis
6315 Moscow 1980 2.00 .90
Lenin Stadium
Beyond Sports
6316 Outland Award 2.00 .90
Brad Shearer
Football
6317 Flying Model Planes 2.00 .90
Safely
Model Airplanes
Model Airplanes
6318 Gil Hodges BB 8.00 3.60
6319 Fausto Coppi 2.00 .90
Cycling
6320 Austin Carr BK 4.00 1.80
6321 SPA-Francorchamps 2.00 .90
Auto Racing
6322 Rodrigo Valdes 4.00 1.80
Boxing
6323 The Clipper Race 2.00 .90
Great Britain II
Yachting
6324 Grazyna Rabsztyn 2.00 .90
In 80 M Hurdles
Track and Field

1977-79 Sportscaster Series 64 *

NRMT VG-E
COMPLETE SET (24) 50.00 22.00
6401 Pam Shriver 6.00 2.70
Tennis
6402 The 250-CC Prize .... 2.00 .90
List: Joel Robert
MotoCross
6403 The Commonwealth .... 2.00 .90
Games: '74 Commonwealth
Track and Field
6404 Chinese Tour .... 2.00 .90
Mu Tieh-Chu
Basketball
6405 Olympic Games 5.00 2.20
Honors Tables
USA vs. Russia
Basketball
6406 Single Sculls .... 2.00 .90
Karppinen/Kolbe
Sculling
6407 Pat Smythe .... 2.00 .90
Pat Smythe
Jumping
6408 Mate Parlov 4.00 1.80
Parlov and Fiol
Boxing
6409 Knut Knudsen .... 2.00 .90
Cycling
6410 The Flags in a Race .... 2.00 .90
Flag-Oil
Auto Racing
6411 Harvard Stadium 4.00 1.80
Football
6412 William Renshaw .... 2.00 .90
Ernest Renshaw
6413 Deena Brush .... 2.00 .90
In the Air
Waterskiing
6414 The Ratios .... 2.00 .90
B. Guyot
Cycling
6415 Origins .... 2.00 .90
Art by Bleuler
Mountain Climbing
6416 Sudden Death 5.00 2.20
Pete Stemkowski
Ice Hockey
6417 Henley Royal .... 2.00 .90
Regatta
Royal Regatta
Sculling
6418 Kornelia Ender 5.00 2.20
Swimming
6419 Floyd Little FB 5.00 2.20
6420 The History .... 2.00 .90
Start from Traps
Greyhound Racing
6421 Kjell Isaksson .... 2.00 .90
In Pole Vault
Track and Field
6422 The 1966 World Cup .... 2.00 .90
N. Korea/Italy
Soccer
6423 Olympic Games .... 2.00 .90
Prize List
Gu and Cowdell
Boxing
6424 Three Officials .... 2.00 .90
Three Referees
Basketball

1977-79 Sportscaster Series 65 *

NRMT VG-E
COMPLETE SET (24) 80.00 36.00
6501 Malcolm Forbes 8.00 3.60
Ballooning
6502 Wilt Chamberlain 12.00 5.50
In Volleyball
Volleyball
6503 The Eights .... 2.00 .90
1976 Olympics
Sculling
6504 Czechoslovakia .... 2.00 .90
1974 Czech Team
Soccer
6505 Winners at the .... 2.00 .90
Olympic Games
Spinks and Soria
Boxing
6506 1950 WCH .... 2.00 .90
G. Schneider
Alpine Skiing
6507 Marcia Frederick .... 2.00 .90
Uneven Bars
Gymnastics
6508 Wales in the 1970s .... 2.00 .90
Welsh Team
Rugby
6509 Bobby Wilson .... 2.00 .90
Tennis
6510 Nikolai Avilov 3.00 1.35
In the Long Jump
Track and Field
6511 By Split Seconds 4.00 1.80
Wilbur Shaw
Auto Racing
6512 The Continent vs. 10.00 4.50
Great Britain
1976 British Team
Golf
6513 The 1978 WCH 12.00 5.50
Mario Andretti
Auto Racing
6514 Robin Cousins 4.00 1.80
Figure Skating
6515 20,000 Point Club 5.00 2.20
Hal Greer
Basketball
6516 Ilie Nastase 8.00 3.60
Tennis
6517 Buyukdere Boronkay .... 2.00 .90
Instanbul
'78 Turkish Team
Volleyball
6518 Vida Blue BB 3.00 1.35
6519 Eraldo Pizzo .... 2.00 .90
Waterpolo
6520 Franco Causio .... 2.00 .90
Soccer
6521 Andreas Wenzel .... 2.00 .90
Alpine Skiing
6522 Jurgen Haase .... 2.00 .90
In the 10,000 M
Track and Field
6523 Maurice Hope 4.00 1.80
Boxing
6524 Franco Harris FB 10.00 4.50

1977-79 Sportscaster Series 66 *

NRMT VG-E
COMPLETE SET (24) 75.00 34.00
6601 Jimmy Carter 20.00 9.00
Beyond Sports
6602 Tracy Caulkins 5.00 2.20
Swimming
6603 Rod Milburn 4.00 1.80
In 110 M Hurdles
Track and Field
6604 The High Jump .... 2.00 .90
V. Yaschenko
Track and Field
6605 Heading the Ball .... 2.00 .90
Altobelli (Milan)
Soccer
6606 To Identify Boats .... 2.00 .90
When Racing
Many Sailboats
Yachting
6607 The Four Horsemen 15.00 6.75
Horsemen
Knute Rockne
Football
6608 Ludwig Jahn .... 2.00 .90
Beyond Sports
6609 The Backhand 5.00 2.20
Ken Rosewall
Tennis
6610 The Barbarians .... 2.00 .90
Barbarians/Lions
Rugby
6611 Hall of Fame 4.00 1.80
Basketball
6612 Christine .... 2.00 .90
Stuckelberger
Dressage
6613 Howard Clark 8.00 3.60
Golf
6614 Mike Wenden .... 2.00 .90
1970 In Edmonton
Swimming
6615 Designated Hitter 5.00 2.20
Rusty Staub
Baseball
6616 The 1966 World Cup 5.00 2.20
Bobby Moore/Stiles
Soccer
6617 The Olympic 4.00 1.80
Competition
Papp and Mate Parlov
Boxing
6618 Ian Thompson .... 2.00 .90
In the Marathon
Track and Field
6619 1968 Winter .... 2.00 .90
Olympics: Three Skiers
Alpine Skiing
6620 Ted Turner 20.00 9.00
Yachting
6621 Silverstone .... 2.00 .90
John Watson
Auto Racing
6622 Bebeto .... 2.00 .90
Volleyball
6623 The Rivers .... 2.00 .90
The Olry Brother
Canoeing
6624 Lucien Michard .... 2.00 .90
Cycling

1977-79 Sportscaster Series 67 *

NRMT VG-E
COMPLETE SET (24) 80.00 36.00
6701 Steve Garvey BB 5.00 2.20
6702 Nancy Lieberman BK 10.00 4.50
6703 Single-Hull .... 2.00 .90
Dinghies: The 505
Yachting
6704 25 November 1953 .... 2.00 .90
England/Hungary
Soccer
6705 The Bahr Family 5.00 2.20
Chris, Matt and Dad
Soccer-Football
6706 Jose Higueras 4.00 1.80
1978 Bournemouth
Tennis
6707 The 1976 .... 2.00 .90
Transatlantic Race
Club Mediterranean
Yachting
6708 Law 12: The Direct .... 2.00 .90
Free Kick: Michel Platini
Soccer
6709 Hole-In-One 25.00 11.00
Gene Sarazen
Golf
6710 Darrel McHargue .... 2.00 .90
Preakness Winner
Race Horsing
6711 Bob Morse BK 4.00 1.80
6712 Don Bragg 4.00 1.80
Track and Field
6713 Christine Caron .... 2.00 .90
Kiki Caron
Swimming
6714 Raelene Boyle .... 2.00 .90
Track and Field
6715 The Presidential 5.00 2.20
Ball: Pres.William Taft
Baseball
6716 Lotus 10.00 4.50
Mario Andretti
Auto Racing
6717 Carlos Reutemann .... 2.00 .90
Auto Racing
6718 The Deans Incident .... 2.00 .90
Bobby Deans
Rugby
6719 Christine Truman 4.00 1.80
Tennis
6720 Ricky McCormick .... 2.00 .90
The Slalom
Waterskiing
6721 Bill Chadwick 5.00 2.20
Ice Hockey
6722 The Club of Eleven 4.00 1.80
Nino Benvenuti
Luis Rodriguez
Boxing
6723 John McEnroe 15.00 6.75
Tennis
6724 Yordanka Blagoeva .... 2.00 .90
In the High Jump
Track and Field

1977-79 Sportscaster Series 68 *

NRMT VG-E
COMPLETE SET (24) 80.00 36.00
6801 Precision Landing .... 2.00 .90
Jump to 4~ Disc
Parachute Jumping
6802 Sandor Kocsis .... 2.00 .90
Soccer
6803 Sharif Khan 4.00 1.80
Squash
6804 Olga Morozova 4.00 1.80
1974 Wimbledon
Tennis
6805 Geoff Capes .... 2.00 .90
In Shot Put
Track and Field
6806 Incredible Playoff 4.00 1.80
Bill Osmanski
Football
6807 Walter McGowan 4.00 1.80
Boxing
6808 World Cup .... 2.00 .90
Championship
Soccer
6809 Louise Brough 4.00 1.80
1949 Wimbledon
Tennis
6810 7th Game of the 4.00 1.80
World Series
Bert Campaneris
Baseball
6811 Christy O'Connor 8.00 3.60
Golf
6812 Colin Chapman 5.00 2.20
Chapman and Andretti
Auto Racing
6813 PGA Championship 8.00 3.60
Dave Stockton
Golf
6814 Dorothy Hyman .... 2.00 .90
Track and Field
6815 Cliff Drysdale 5.00 2.20
Tennis
6816 Giorgio Chinaglia 6.00 2.70
Soccer
6817 Patrick Tambay .... 2.00 .90
Auto Racing
6818 Babe Ruth Baseball 4.00 1.80
Ed Figueroa
Baseball
6819 John Landy 4.00 1.80
1956 Olympics
Track and Field
6820 John Cappelletti 5.00 2.20
Rams/Falcons
Football
6821 Law 15:The Throw In .... 2.00 .90
Dave McCreery
Soccer
6822 Sara Simeoni .... 2.00 .90
In the High Jump
Track and Field
6823 Glossary 10.00 4.50
Muhammad Ali
Richard Dunn
Boxing
6824 1975-76 World Cup 5.00 2.20
Ingemar Stenmark
Alpine Skiing

1977-79 Sportscaster Series 69 *

NRMT VG-E
COMPLETE SET (24) 80.00 36.00
6901 Arnie Robinson 3.00 1.35
1976 Olympics
Track and Field
6902 Terry Bradshaw FB 10.00 4.50
6903 Bernard Pariset .... 2.00 .90
Judo
6904 The Service 8.00 3.60
Bjorn Borg
Tennis
6905 Stellan Bengtsson .... 2.00 .90
Table Tennis
6906 Roy Campanella BB 10.00 4.50
6907 Origins .... 2.00 .90
A Large Pitch
Shinty
6908 The 1978 WCH 5.00 2.20
Tracy Caulkins
Swimming
6909 Linda Fernandez .... 2.00 .90
Volleyball
6910 Ronnie Peterson .... 2.00 .90
Auto Racing
6911 Lucinda Prior- .... 2.00 .90
Palmer
Horse Racing
6912 First Televised .... 2.00 .90
Football Games
Skip Walz
Beyond Sports
6913 Glossary .... 2.00 .90
Amateur Fight
Boxing
6914 Kerry Reid 4.00 1.80
Tennis
6915 Indian HOF 8.00 3.60
Sonny Sixkiller
Beyond Sports
6916 The Emsley Carr .... 2.00 .90
Mile: John Robson
Track and Field
6917 Little League To 4.00 1.80
Big Leagues
Hector Torres
Baseball
6918 Hans Joachim Stuck .... 2.00 .90
Hans Stuck
Auto Racing
6919 The Format of 8.00 3.60
Competition Play
Paris Action
Golf
6920 Swiss Wrestling .... 2.00 .90
In Sawdust Ring
Wrestling
6921 Women's Marathon .... 2.00 .90
A New York Mini
Track and Field
6922 Panama Al Brown 4.00 1.80
Brown with Eugene Criqui
Boxing
6923 The Forehand 5.00 2.20
Ken Rosewall
Tennis
6924 The Vel'D'Hiv' .... 2.00 .90
Stadium
Beyond Sports

1977-79 Sportscaster Series 70 *

NRMT VG-E
COMPLETE SET (24) 60.00 27.00
7001 Dirceu .... 2.00 .90
Dirceu/Rossi
Soccer
7002 Racing Tires .... 2.00 .90
Rain Tires
Auto Racing
7003 Mark Roth 5.00 2.20
Bowling
7004 The Rules 8.00 3.60
A "Drop"
Golf
7005 Marita Koch .... 2.00 .90
Track and Field
7006 Hall of Fame 4.00 1.80
Toronto Hall of Fame
Ice Hockey
7007 The Bolt .... 2.00 .90
Karl Rappan
Soccer
7008 Bruce Woodcock .... 2.00 .90
Boxing
7009 Kjell Johansson .... 2.00 .90
Table Tennis
7010 Pro Bowl 5.00 2.20
Jan Stenerud
Football
7011 The 1977 WCH .... 2.00 .90
Gaston Rahier
MotoCross
7012 HRH Princess Anne 5.00 2.20
Equestrianism
7013 Daffy Dean 5.00 2.20
Dizzy Dean BB
7014 The Technique .... 2.00 .90
Roulette Bowl
Petanque
7015 Tessa Sanderson .... 2.00 .90
In the Javelin
Track and Field
7016 Henry Rono 4.00 1.80
In the Hurdles
Track and Field
7017 Glenn Cunningham 4.00 1.80
Track and Field
7018 Chris Brasher 4.00 1.80
1954 White City
Track and Field
7019 Billy Kidd 5.00 2.20
Alpine Skiing
7020 Left/Right Back .... 2.00 .90
Paul Breitner
Soccer
7021 Kurt Thomas 6.00 2.70
The Rings
Gymnastics
7022 Start and Finish .... 2.00 .90
A False Start
Swimming
7023 Jan Hoffman .... 2.00 .90
Figure Skating
7024 Lancia .... 2.00 .90
The Stratos
Auto Racing

1977-79 Sportscaster Series 71 *

NRMT VG-E
COMPLETE SET (24) 80.00 36.00
7101 Dave Jennings FB 4.00 1.80
7102 Yannick Noah 5.00 2.20
Tennis
7103 J.R. Richard BB 4.00 1.80
7104 Tommy Abrahamsson 4.00 1.80
Christian Abrhamsson
Two Whaler Stars
Ice Hockey
7105 Richard Bergmann .... 2.00 .90
Table Tennis
7106 Virginia Ruzici 4.00 1.80
Tennis
7107 The Bremen Disaster .... 2.00 .90
Italian Swimmer
Beyond Sports
7108 PGA School 30.00 13.50
Ben Crenshaw
Golf
7109 Sam Rabin .... 2.00 .90
Rabin Painting
Beyond Sports
7110 Henry Kissinger 12.00 5.50
Beyond Sports
7111 Manuel Santana 5.00 2.20
Tennis
7112 Anders Hedberg 5.00 2.20
Ulf Nilsson
Islanders/Rangers
Ice Hockey
7113 Vittorio Brambilla .... 2.00 .90
Auto Racing
7114 Public Golf 10.00 4.50
Courses: Saint-Aubin (FRA)
Golf
7115 Barbara Krause .... 2.00 .90
Swimming
7116 Karen Muir .... 2.00 .90
Swimming
7117 Hall of Fame 10.00 4.50
Johnny Weismuller
Swimming
7118 Ball Control .... 2.00 .90
Roberto Rivelino
Soccer
7119 The Double Mini- .... 2.00 .90
Tramp
Trampolining
7120 Stenmark 77-78 .... 5.00 2.20
Ingemar Stenmark
Alpine Skiing
7121 Olaf Beyer .... 2.00 .90
1978 European
Championship
Track and Field
7122 Liechtenstein .... 2.00 .90
Three Skiers
Alpine Skiing
7123 Chuck Noll 12.00 5.50
Terry Bradshaw FB
7124 1976-77 World Cup .... 2.00 .90
Lise Morerod
Alpine Skiing

1977-79 Sportscaster Series 72 *

NRMT VG-E
COMPLETE SET (24) 100.00 45.00
7201 Cynthia Woodhead 4.00 1.80
Swimming
7202 1978-79 World Cup .... 2.00 .90
Peter Luscher
Alpine Skiing
7203 Renaldo Nehemiah 5.00 2.20
In the Hurdles
Track and Field
7204 Gunnar Nilsson .... 2.00 .90
Nilsson& Peterson
Auto Racing
7205 Georges Carpentier 5.00 2.20
Jack Dempsey
1921 Fight
Boxing
7206 Carmen Salvino 5.00 2.20
Bowling
7207 Brian Phelps .... 2.00 .90
Diving
7208 Roberto 5.00 2.20
Soccer
7209 High School Record 4.00 1.80
Book: David Clyde
Beyond Sports
7210 Sten Stensen .... 2.00 .90
Speed Skating
7211 Harold Solomon 5.00 2.20
1978 French Open
Tennis
7212 Pietro Mennea .... 2.00 .90
1978 European
Championships
Track and Field
7213 Hitting Pitchers 8.00 3.60
Don Drysdale
Baseball
7214 The Origins .... 2.00 .90
Freestyle Skiing
7215 Lord's Cricket .... 2.00 .90
Ground: Marylebone Club
Crickett
7216 Game Fishing .... 2.00 .90
River Awe (Scot)
Fishing
7217 Joe Paterno FB 25.00 11.00
7218 Tommy Horton 10.00 4.50
Golf
7219 James Jim Corbett 6.00 2.70
Boxing
7220 Ulrika Knape .... 2.00 .90
Diving
7221 Greg Pruitt 5.00 2.20
Beyond Sports
7222 Joakim Bonnier .... 2.00 .90
Auto Racing
7223 Origins of .... 2.00 .90
Steeplechasing
Aintree& 1978
Horse Racing
7224 The 1958 World Cup 20.00 9.00
Brazilian Team
Soccer

1977-79 Sportscaster Series 73 *

NRMT VG-E
COMPLETE SET (24) 80.00 36.00
7301 USSR vs. NHL 8.00 3.60
Game Action
(Larry Robinson)
Ice Hockey
7302 The Towell Brothers .... 2.00 .90
Willie Towell
Boxing
7303 Rudy Tomjanovich BK 10.00 4.50
7304 World Championships .... 2.00 .90
1978: Elina Moukhina
Gymnastics
7305 Sport for the .... 2.00 .90

Disabled: Wheelchair Race
Beyond Sports
7306 Bear Bryant FB 20.00 9.00
7307 The Brooms 2.00 .90
1974 Swiss Team
Curling
7308 Gennadi Moisseev 2.00 .90
MotoCross
7309 Miki Gorman 4.00 1.80
In the Marathon
Track and Field
7310 The Three Patterson- 5.00 2.20
Johansson Fights
Ingemar Johansson
Floyd Patterson
Boxing
7311 Czechoslavakia 1976 5.00 2.20
1976 Championship Team
Ice Hockey
7312 Lingo 2.00 .90
A Bottom Turn
Surfing
7313 Diane Leather 2.00 .90
1958 White City
Track and Field
7314 Rob Shepherd 2.00 .90
Trials
7315 Emmett Ashford BB 4.00 1.80
7316 The Money Won By 10.00 4.50
Ladies' Champ
Chris Evert
Tennis
7317 Eero Mantyranta 2.00 .90
1976 Winter OG
Nordic Skiing
7318 Bobby Locke 12.00 5.50
Golf
7319 Stu Goldstein 2.00 .90
Squash
7320 Boats, Skis and Ropes 2.00 .90
The Slalom
Waterskiing
7321 Hjalmar Andersen 2.00 .90
Speed Skating
7322 Paolo Bertolucci 2.00 .90
Tennis
7323 Japanese GP 2.00 .90
Mount-Fuji Track
Auto Racing
7324 Guido Kratschmer 2.00 .90
1978 European
Championship
Track and Field

1977-79 Sportscaster Series 74 *

NRMT VG-E
COMPLETE SET (24) 400.00 180.00
7401 Forever Blowing 5.00 2.20
Bubbles
Davey Lopes
Baseball
7402 Jackie Paterson 2.00 .90
Paterson/Medina
Boxing
7403 Suzy Chaffee 40.00 18.00
Beyond Sports
7404 Wojtek Fibak 4.00 1.80
Tennis
7405 Walter Villa 2.00 .90
Motorcycle Racing
7406 Bernt Johansson 2.00 .90
Cycling
7407 A Pro Oddity 4.00 1.80
Eric Money
Basketball
7408 Bruno Giacomelli 2.00 .90
Auto Racing
7409 Sea Fishing 2.00 .90
South Africa
Fishing
7410 Phil Niekro BB 8.00 3.60
7411 Beppe Merlo 2.00 .90
Tennis
7412 Sandro Munari 2.00 .90
Auto Racing
7413 Max Schmeling 8.00 3.60
Boxing
7414 National Tennis 2.00 .90
Center: Helicopter View
Tennis
7415 Safety in a 8.00 3.60
Formula 1: Niki Lauda
Auto Racing
7416 Glossary 2.00 .90
Penholder Grip
Table Tennis
7417 The 1978 WCH 4.00 1.80
USSR 1978 Champs
Ice Hockey
7418 Larry Bird BK 300.00 135.00
7419 The Kick-off 2.00 .90
Soccer
7420 1948 Winter 2.00 .90
Olympics: Henri Oreiller
Alpine Skiing
7421 Pertti Karppinen 2.00 .90
Sculling
7422 ATP Classification 10.00 4.50
Jimmy Connors
Tennis
7423 Ken Forsch 4.00 1.80
Bob Forsch BB
7424 Vaclav Nedomansky 5.00 2.20
USSR vs. Czechs
Ice Hockey

1977-79 Sportscaster Series 75 *

NRMT VG-E
COMPLETE SET (24) 60.00 27.00
7501 Walter Schmidt 2.00 .90
In the Hammer
Track and Field
7502 Nick Buoniconti 5.00 2.20
Football
7503 The Canam 2.00 .90
Lola Racecar
Auto Racing
7504 Bernhard Kannenberg 2.00 .90
Track and Field
7505 Cindy Nelson 4.00 1.80
Alpine Skiing
7506 Cesar Luis Menotti 2.00 .90
Soccer
7507 Bjorn Borg 8.00 3.60
Vitas Gerulaitis
Tennis
7508 Long-Playing 8.00 3.60
Records
Arthur Ashe
Kuhnke
Tennis
7509 Tommy Lasorda BB 8.00 3.60
7510 United States GP 2.00 .90
Two Racetraks
Auto Racing
7511 Origins and History 2.00 .90
English/Aussies
Netball
7512 Serafino Antao 2.00 .90
1960 Olympics
Track and Field
7513 Fellowship of 4.00 1.80
Christian Athletes
Don Kessinger
Beyond Sports
7514 History and Rules 2.00 .90
of the Game
Game Action
Bandy
7515 Hack Wilson BB 5.00 2.20
7516 The WCH Amateur 8.00 3.60
Honors Tables
Teofilo Stevenson
Boxing
7517 Jim Montgomery 4.00 1.80
1976 Ceremony
Swimming
7518 Pekka Vasala 2.00 .90
1972 Olympics
Track and Field
7519 Corrado Barazzutti 3.00 1.35
Tennis
7520 Christian Leon 2.00 .90
J. Chemarin
Motorcycle Racing
7521 The 1954 World Cup 2.00 .90
Schmied (Austria)
Soccer
7522 Walter Kennedy 5.00 2.20
Award
Slick Watts
Beyond Sports
7523 Britain's Olympic 2.00 .90
Heroes
Parker/Mosolov
Modern Pentatholon
7524 The Firemen 8.00 3.60
Goose Gossage
Baseball

1977-79 Sportscaster Series 76 *

NRMT VG-E
COMPLETE SET (24) 60.00 27.00
7601 Kenny Roberts 2.00 .90
Motorcycle Racing
7602 Wilma Bardauskiene 2.00 .90
In the Long Jump
Track and Field
7603 NCAA Hockey 5.00 2.20
Champions
Minnesota/N. Dakota
(Bill Baker)
Ice Hockey
7604 The Origins of 2.00 .90
Tenpin Bowling
Bowling Action
Bowling
7605 NFL Hall of Fame 4.00 1.80
Canton, Ohio HOF
Football
7606 Phil Boggs 4.00 1.80
Diving
7607 Livio Berruti 2.00 .90
Track and Field
7608 The Longest Shot 2.00 .90
Rudy Williams
Basketball
7609 Vic Seixas 4.00 1.80
Tennis
7610 Bernard Gallacher 10.00 4.50
Golf
7611 Iron Mike 2.00 .90
Pitching Machine
Baseball
7612 Arthur Rowe 2.00 .90
Braemar Highland
Track and Field
7613 Yrjo Vesterinen 2.00 .90
On his Bike
Trials
7614 Inge Nissen BK 4.00 1.80
7615 Janis Lusis 2.00 .90
In the Javelin
Track and Field
7616 Serge Maury 2.00 .90
Yachting
7617 For The Revolution 2.00 .90
Sambo In Moscow
Sambo
7618 The 1954 World Cup 2.00 .90
Gyula Grosics
Soccer
7619 Training Camps 2.00 .90
Spring Training
Baseball
7620 The Swing 20.00 9.00
Tom Watson
Golf
7621 Richard Meade 2.00 .90
1976 Olympics
Equestrianism
7622 Santos FC 2.00 .90
Soccer
7623 Davis Cup 2.00 .90
Nicola Pietrangeli
Tennis
7624 Walter Camp All- 4.00 1.80
America Team
Walter Camp
Football

1977-79 Sportscaster Series 77 *

NRMT VG-E
COMPLETE SET (24) 300.00 135.00
7701 Didi 2.00 .90
Soccer
7702 1978 Commonwealth 8.00 3.60
Games
Daley Thompson
Beyond Sports
7703 Steve Baker 2.00 .90
1978 Mosport
Motorcycle Racing
7704 Outboard and 2.00 .90
Inboard
Two Boat Types
Powerboat Racing
7705 Kevin Porter BK 5.00 2.20
7706 The 1968 Norwegian 2.00 .90
Four Gold Medalists
Canoeing
7707 The World Cup 2.00 .90
Egil Johansen
Orienteering
7708 Monty Stratton BB 5.00 2.20
7709 Everest 2.00 .90
Dougal Haston
Mountain Climbing
7710 Wayne Gretzky HK 250.00 110.00
7711 Gigi Villoresi 2.00 .90
Auto Racing
7712 1977-78 World Cup 2.00 .90
Hanni Wenzel
Alpine Skiing
7713 Ron Taylor BB 4.00 1.80
7714 Plastics 2.00 .90
The 505
Yachting
7715 Brian Goodell 4.00 1.80
Swimming
7716 The Special 2.00 .90
Olympics
Beyond Sports
7717 Walt Chyzowych 2.00 .90
U.S. vs France
Soccer
7718 Rick Wohljuter 4.00 1.80
W/Alberto Juantorena
Track and Field
7719 Laila Schou Nilsen 2.00 .90
Alpine Skiing
7720 Carol Mann 10.00 4.50
Golf
7721 Nat Holman 8.00 3.60
Joe Lapchick BK
7722 Wimbledon 8.00 3.60
Bjorn Borg/Virginia Wade
Tennis
7723 Gilles Villeneuve 5.00 2.20
Auto Racing
7724 Expansion 4.00 1.80
Whalers/Oilers
Ice Hockey

1977-79 Sportscaster Series 78 *

NRMT VG-E
COMPLETE SET (24) 300.00 135.00
7801 Samson Kimobwa 2.00 .90
1977 Nice
Track and Field
7802 Earvin Johnson BK 200.00 90.00
7803 1957:Exit of the 2.00 .90
Italians
Colnago& 1957
Motorcycle Racing
7804 Real Cloutier 3.00 1.35
Ice Hockey
7805 Bruce Lietzke 10.00 4.50
Golf
7806 Christian Sarron 2.00 .90
Sarron/Pons
Motorcycle Racing
7807 Gene Tunney 10.00 4.50
Tunney
Jack Dempsey
Boxing
7808 The Top 12 2.00 .90
Jill Hammersley
Table Tennis
7809 Tom Landry FB 20.00 9.00
7810 Enrique Figuerola 2.00 .90
Track and Field
7811 Goliath or 2.00 .90
Regulation
View from Above
Trampolining
7812 Wladyslaw 2.00 .90
Kozakiewicz
In Pole Vault
Track and Field
7813 Timo Makinen 2.00 .90
Makinen and Liddon
Auto Racing
7814 Nancy Richey 4.00 1.80
Cliff Richey
1969 Wimbledon
Tennis
7815 Walking and the 2.00 .90
Olympic Games
V. Golubnichi
Track and Field
7816 Willie McCovey BB 8.00 3.60
7817 Steve Scott 2.00 .90
1977 NCAA Championship
Track and Field
7818 Brian Barnes 10.00 4.50
Golf
7819 The National Ski 2.00 .90
Patrol
Ski Patrol
Alpine Skiing
7820 Rating Passers 10.00 4.50
Dan Fouts
Football
7821 The Int'l Biennial 2.00 .90
of Sport Artists
Beyond Sports
7822 Marinho 2.00 .90
Soccer
7823 The 1973 WCH 2.00 .90
N. Calligaris
Swimming
7824 Dave Bing BK 8.00 3.60

1977-79 Sportscaster Series 79 *

NRMT VG-E
COMPLETE SET (24) 120.00 55.00
7901 Patrick Depailler 2.00 .90
Auto Racing
7902 Joan Benoit 8.00 3.60
In the Marathon
Track and Field
7903 Fuzzy Zoeller 15.00 6.75
Golf
7904 Bullfighting: 2.00 .90
Glossary
Bullfighting
Beyond Sports
7905 The Cochran Family 2.00 .90
B. and M. Cochran
Alpine Skiing
7906 Jochen Rindt 2.00 .90
Auto Racing
7907 Bruce Furniss 4.00 1.80
Swimming
7908 Naming A Horse 2.00 .90
Grey Legion Colt
Horse Racing
7909 Liesel Westermann 2.00 .90
In the Discus
Track and Field
7910 Ouliana Semenova BK 8.00 3.60
7911 Craig Swan BB 3.00 1.35
7912 Franco Nones 2.00 .90
Nordic Skiing
7913 Alwin Schockemoehle 2.00 .90
Show Jumping
7914 Martti Vainio 2.00 .90
1978 European
Championship
Track and Field
7915 Phil Ford BK 5.00 2.20
7916 Glossary 12.00 5.50
Chris Evert
Tennis
7917 Suzuki 2.00 .90
1977 Austrian GP
Motorcycle Racing
7918 Giacomo Agostini 2.00 .90
King Ago
Motorcycle Racing
7919 Women's Basketball 4.00 1.80
League
Randi Burdick
Basketball
7920 Isao Aoki 20.00 9.00
Golf
7921 Josy Barthel 2.00 .90
1952 Olympics
Track and Field
7922 College Football 25.00 11.00
Hall of Fame
Ronald Reagan
Football
7923 Greg Louganis 15.00 6.75
Diving
7924 3000 M Steeplechase 2.00 .90
1978 European
Championship
Track and Field

1977-79 Sportscaster Series 80 *

NRMT VG-E
COMPLETE SET (24) 125.00 55.00
8001 Disco 4.00 1.80
Disco Dancing
Roller Skating
8002 Track Events 4.00 1.80
Pietro Mennea
Track and Field
8003 Rick Mears 15.00 6.75
Auto Racing
8004 The 1958 World Cup 12.00 5.50
Brazilian Team
Soccer
8005 Leah Poulos Mueller 5.00 2.20
Speed Skating
8006 Scoring and Placing 6.00 2.70
Robin Cousins
Figure Skating
8007 Don Paige 4.00 1.80
Track and Field
8008 Dan Gable 12.00 5.50
Wrestling
8009 Bob Schul 5.00 2.20
Michel Jazy
Track and Field
8010 Lena Koppen 4.00 1.80
Badminton
8011 But Challenges The 4.00 1.80
Atlantic: Ondine/But
Yachting
8012 LPGA Caddies 12.00 5.50
Nancy Lopez/Jones
Golf
8013 The Straddle 4.00 1.80
V. Yaschenko
Track and Field
8014 The Field of Play 4.00 1.80
Olympic Stadium
Soccer
8015 Ragnhild Hveger 4.00 1.80
Swimming
8016 Grete Waitz- 6.00 2.70
Anderson
1977 World Cup
Track and Field
8017 Emile Puttemans 4.00 1.80
Track and Field
8018 John Davidson HK 6.00 2.70
8019 Jim Marshall 8.00 3.60
Larry Csonka FB
8020 Sebastian Coe 6.00 2.70
1978 European
Championship
Track and Field
8021 Umpires Strike 5.00 2.20
Ump Picket Line
(Ron Luciano and others)
Baseball
8022 The Women's Side 4.00 1.80
Penn St/Maryland
Lacrosse
8023 Al McGuire 12.00 5.50
Beyond Sports
8024 The Market Value 4.00 1.80
of a Win
World Cup Win
Beyond Sports

1977-79 Sportscaster Series 81 *

NRMT VG-E
COMPLETE SET (24) 125.00 55.00
8101 The 1976 4.00 1.80
Transatlantic Yacht
Race: Pen Duick
Yachting
8102 Lenny Wilkens BK 15.00 6.75
8103 Karl Hans Riehm 4.00 1.80
In the Hammer
Track and Field
8104 Alexander Pusch 4.00 1.80
Fencing
8105 Marv Albert 6.00 2.70
Beyond Sports
8106 George Woods 4.00 1.80
In Shot Put
Track and Field
8107 Tactical 4.00 1.80
Developments
1978 World Cup
Soccer
8108 Raul Ramirez 5.00 2.20
1978 French Open
Tennis
8109 Danny Seemiller 4.00 1.80
Table Tennis
8110 Mike Flanagan 4.00 1.80
Soccer
8111 Bob Lutz 5.00 2.20
Tennis
8112 The Lotus 79 10.00 4.50
Mario Andretti
Auto Racing
8113 Jesse Vassallo 5.00 2.20
Swimming
8114 The Women's 4.00 1.80
Pentathalon
N. Tkatchenko
Track and Field
8115 The World 4.00 1.80
Championships
USSR vs. Italy
Volleyball
8116 Women's Marathon 5.00 2.20
Kathy Switzer
Track and Field
8117 The World 4.00 1.80
Championships
Robert Muhlberger
Skibob
8118 Dan Pastorini FB 6.00 2.70
8119 Jacques Lemaire 10.00 4.50
Canadiens/Rangers
Ice Hockey
8120 The Women's Long 4.00 1.80
Jump: W. Bardauskiene
Track and Field
8121 Jim Hines 5.00 2.20
1968 Olympics
Track and Field
8122 Billy Sims FB 8.00 3.60
8123 Nick Rose 4.00 1.80
Track and Field
8124 Wrigley Marathlon 15.00 6.75
Mike Schmidt
Baseball

1977-79 Sportscaster Series 82 *

NRMT VG-E
COMPLETE SET (24) 100.00 45.00
8201 The 1978 Rum Route 4.00 1.80
Birch/Malinovsky
Yachting
8202 Moses Malone BK 15.00 6.75
8203 Jerome Holland 4.00 1.80
Brud Holland
Joe Holland
Beyond Sports
8204 Ilie Nastase 8.00 3.60
Stan Smith
Tennis
8205 Scotty Bowman 15.00 6.75
Ice Hockey
8206 Linda Jezek 4.00 1.80
Swimming
8207 Ivan Lendl 8.00 3.60
Tennis
8208 Candy Young 4.00 1.80
In the Hurdles
Track and Field
8209 The Women's Events 6.00 2.70
Nelly Kim
Gymnastics
8210 The Ligier Team 4.00 1.80
Ligier and Laffite
Auto Racing
8211 1971 European 5.00 2.20
Championships
Valeri Borzov
Track and Field
8212 Origins 4.00 1.80

Finnish "Jukola"
Orienteering
8213 Walter Cecchinel 4.00 1.80
Piolet-Traction
Mountain Climbing
8214 Luciano Susanj.................. 4.00 1.80
1974 European
Championships
Track and Field
8215 Academic Basketball 6.00 2.70
Team
Greg Kelser
Basketball
8216 Olympic Training............... 4.00 1.80
Centers
Olympic Equipment
Beyond Sports
8217 Pat Matzdorf...................... 5.00 2.20
In the High Jump
Track and Field
8218 British Grand Prix.............. 4.00 1.80
'78 British Grand Prix
Auto Racing
8219 Bobby Bonds BB 6.00 2.70
8220 Women's 100 M................ 4.00 1.80
Freestyle
Barbara Krause
Swimming
8221 Tom Cousineau FB 5.00 2.20
8222 Robbie Brightwell.............. 4.00 1.80
In One-Lap Race
Track and Field
8223 Dave Dryden HK................ 5.00 2.20
8224 IC4AS................................ 4.00 1.80
In the 800 M
Track and Field

1977-79 Sportscaster Series 83 *

	NRMT	VG-E
COMPLETE SET (24)..............	125.00	55.00

8301 Doris De Agostini 4.00 1.80
Alpine Skiing
8302 Grand National 4.00 1.80
B. Davis/W. Lucius
Horse Racing
8303 Paul Newman.................. 25.00 11.00
Auto Racing
8304 Connecticut Falcons 4.00 1.80
Playing in China
Softball
8305 Doris Hart.......................... 5.00 2.20
1951 Wimbledon
Tennis
8306 John Hencken 4.00 1.80
100M Breast Stroke
Swimming
8307 Three-Point Field............... 6.00 2.70
Goal: Louis Dampier
Basketball
8308 David Rigert 4.00 1.80
1976 Olympics
Weightlifting
8309 Billy Martin BB 8.00 3.60
8310 Ed Too Tall Jones.............. 8.00 3.60
At Football
Boxing
8311 Finland's Leading 4.00 1.80
Sport Person.
2 Winning Finns
Beyond Sports
8312 European........................... 4.00 1.80
Championships 1974
Brendan Foster
Track and Field
8313 Johns Hopkins 4.00 1.80
Hopkins/Cornell
Lacrosse
8314 World Championships........ 4.00 1.80
Eric Boggan
Table Tennis
8315 Patrick Vial 4.00 1.80
Vial vs. Landart
Judo
8316 Women's High Jump.......... 4.00 1.80
Sara Simeoni
Track and Field
8317 Dutch Dehnert BK.............. 6.00 2.70
8318 Origins of 4.00 1.80
Bullfighting
Arenas of Arles
Beyond Sports
8319 Eamonn Coghlan................ 6.00 2.70
Olympic Semis
Track and Field
8320 Olympic Hurdles................ 4.00 1.80
A Hurdles Race
Track and Field
8321 Joe Niekro 6.00 2.70
Baseball
8322 Lord Hesketh...................... 4.00 1.80
Hesketh, Galicia
Auto Racing
8323 Jack Kemp...................... 15.00 6.75
Beyond Sports
8324 European........................... 4.00 1.80
Championships 1962
Michel Jazy
Track and Field

1977-79 Sportscaster Series 84 *

	NRMT	VG-E
COMPLETE SET (24)..............	120.00	55.00

8401 Mike Bruner........................ 4.00 1.80
Swimming
8402 Jacek Wszola...................... 4.00 1.80
1976 Olympics
Track and Field
8403 The Take Off...................... 4.00 1.80
Gliding Take-Off
Hang Gliding
8404 Olympian Bouts................. 5.00 2.20
Leo Randolph
Boxing
8405 Alexander Grebeniuk.......... 4.00 1.80
Throwing Discuss
Track and Field
8406 Fines................................... 6.00 2.70
Doug Moe
Beyond Sports
8407 Karel Lismont..................... 4.00 1.80
1976 Olympics
Track and Field
8408 Triple Play 6.00 2.70
Rick Burleson
Baseball
8409 United Basketball............... 6.00 2.70
Association
Mike Riordan
Basketball
8410 The Records of.................. 4.00 1.80
Montreal
David Wilkie
Swimming
8411 Strength Coaches.............. 5.00 2.20
Carlos Alberto
Soccer
8412 1978-79 World Cup........... 4.00 1.80
D. DeAgostini
Alpine Skiing
8413 Mickey Wright.................. 12.00 5.50
Golf
8414 The Major........................... 4.00 1.80
Tournaments
Fencing Action
Fencing
8415 The Money Game 8.00 3.60
Dennis Eckersley
Baseball
8416 Olympic Decathlon 6.00 2.70
Bob Mathias
Track and Field
8417 Ron Delaney...................... 4.00 1.80
Delaney/Rawson
Track and Field
8418 Clemente Award 6.00 2.70
Andre Thornton
Beyond Sports
8419 Roscoe Case 4.00 1.80
Geoff Masters
Tennis
8420 The Women's Discus 4.00 1.80
Faina Melnik
Track and Field
8421 The 1975 WCH.................. 4.00 1.80
Ulrike Tauber
Swimming
8422 Elena Moukhina................. 4.00 1.80
Floor Exercises
Gymnastics
8423 World Golf Hall of............ 30.00 13.50
Fame: Walter Hagen
Golf
8424 Jacques-Yves.................... 8.00 3.60
Cousteau
Beyond Sports

1977-79 Sportscaster Series 85 *

	NRMT	VG-E
COMPLETE SET (24)..............	125.00	55.00

8501 Renee Richards................. 6.00 2.70
Tennis
8502 Barefoot Athletes............... 6.00 2.70
Tony Franklin
Football
8503 Bill Toomey 6.00 2.70
In Pole Vault
Track and Field
8504 Like Father......................... 5.00 2.20
Like Son
Roy Smalley
Baseball
8505 Brian Redman 4.00 1.80
Auto Racing
8506 Henri Cochet 6.00 2.70
Davis Cup Action
Tennis
8507 Harald Morpoth.................. 4.00 1.80
In the 5&000 M
Track and Field
8508 Records.............................. 4.00 1.80
Gerd Bonk
Weightlifting
8509 Marathon............................ 4.00 1.80
Central Park
Cycling
8510 Protecting the.................... 6.00 2.70
Quarterback
Craig Morton
Football
8511 The Colgate 12.00 5.50
European
LPGA Championship
Nancy Lopez
Golf
8512 Olympic Hammer and......... 4.00 1.80
Javelin
A Javelin Throw
Track and Field
8513 Walkie-Talkie.................... 12.00 5.50
Yogi Berra
Beyond Sports
8514 Sally Little 10.00 4.50
Golf
8515 Women's Draft.................. 4.00 1.80
Pat Colasurdo
Basketball
8516 Ralph Doubell.................... 4.00 1.80
'70 Commonwealth
Track and Field
8517 The Long Jump.................. 6.00 2.70
Bob Beamon
Track and Field
8518 Olympic Freestyle.............. 4.00 1.80
The Freestyle
Swimming
8519 1976 Winter Olympics....... 4.00 1.80
Helena Takalo
Nordic Skiing
8520 Lou Holtz FB.................... 20.00 9.00
8521 Jean Borotra...................... 6.00 2.70
W Basque Beret
Tennis
8522 F.P. Naismith Award.......... 6.00 2.70
Mike Scheib
Alton Byrd
Basketball
8523 Mamo Wolde...................... 5.00 2.20
1968 Olympics
Track and Field
8524 Riding 4.00 1.80
Scrambling
MotoCross

1977-79 Sportscaster Series 86 *

	NRMT	VG-E
COMPLETE SET (24)..............	100.00	45.00

8601 Grambling 6.00 2.70
Doug Williams
Football
8602 Jumbo Jim Elliott 5.00 2.20
W Korir and Paige
Track and Field
8603 Wimbledon Fashions......... 5.00 2.20
Tennis Attire
Tennis
8604 Frank Williams.................... 4.00 1.80
Auto Racing
8605 Olympic Shot Put 4.00 1.80
and Discus
John Powell
Track and Field
8606 Kiki Vandeweghe............... 6.00 2.70
Ernie Vandeweghe
Beyond Sports
8607 Dave Sime.......................... 5.00 2.20
Track and Field
8608 Danny Ainge BB/BK......... 50.00 22.00
8609 Olympic Sprints................. 4.00 1.80
Steve Williams
Track and Field
8610 Clowns 8.00 3.60
Al Schacht
Nick Altrock
Beyond Sports
8611 The Junior World 5.00 2.20
Records
Harvey Glance
Track and Field
8612 Rene Lacoste..................... 8.00 3.60
Tennis
8613 Japan 4.00 1.80
'76 Japanese Team
Volleyball
8614 The Brabham Stable........... 4.00 1.80
John Watson
Auto Racing
8615 Battling Siki....................... 5.00 2.20
Georges Carpentier
Boxing
8616 Benihana Grand Prix.......... 4.00 1.80
Aoki with Cougar
Powerboat Racing
8617 Jesse Owens.................... 10.00 4.50
1936 Olympics
Track and Field
8618 Speedball Golf................... 4.00 1.80
Speedball Action
Golf
8619 Levan Tediaschvili 4.00 1.80
Wrestling
8620 Trial Riding........................ 4.00 1.80
Going Uphill
Trials
8621 Daytona Speedway............ 6.00 2.70
Daytona Racing
Auto Racing
8622 Tie Break 4.00 1.80
1979 Wimbledon
Tennis
8623 Naftali Temu...................... 4.00 1.80
1968 Olympics
Track and Field
8624 Luther Lassiter 4.00 1.80
Billiards

1977-79 Sportscaster Series 87 *

This series contains two cards numbered 4.

	NRMT	VG-E
COMPLETE SET (24)..............	120.00	55.00

8701 Olympic 1500, 5000........... 4.00 1.80
and 10000 M
A Distance Run
Track and Field
8702 1976 Olympic Games......... 5.00 2.20
J. Chandler
Diving
8703 The Women's 200-M.......... 4.00 1.80
Marita Koch
Track and Field
8704 Georges Goven.................. 4.00 1.80
Tennis
8704 Olympic Long Jump........... 4.00 1.80
A Long Jump
Track and Field
8705 Mike Tully.......................... 5.00 2.20
In Pole Vault
Track and Field
8706 Olympic Backstroke........... 4.00 1.80
The Backstroke
Swimming
8707 Riding 4.00 1.80
Le Touquet
Enduro
8708 Sydney Wooderson 4.00 1.80
1946 1-Mile Race
Track and Field
8709 Madison Square 6.00 2.70
Garden: The 1st Garden
Beyond Sports
8710 Valdemar............................ 4.00 1.80
Bandolowski
Yachting
8711 Evgeny Arzanov................. 4.00 1.80
In the 800 M
Track and Field
8712 Lee Mazzilli BB 6.00 2.70
8713 The Organization 10.00 4.50
Golf Officials
Golf
8714 Open Pocket...................... 4.00 1.80
Championships
Jim Rempe
Billiards
8715 Betty Stove........................ 5.00 2.20
Tennis
8716 Lingo 1.............................. 4.00 1.80
Indy-Type Car
Auto Racing
8717 Charlie Greene.................. 5.00 2.20
In Dark Glasses
Track and Field
8718 Steve Dembowski BB 4.00 1.80
8719 The Dunlop Masters......... 10.00 4.50
Tommy Horton
Golf
8720 Hutch Award 15.00 6.75
Al Kaline
Beyond Sports
8721 Ingemar Johansson............ 6.00 2.70
Boxing
8722 The Matra Formula 1 .... 4.00 1.80
Engine
Matra Engine
Auto Racing
8723 1958 European.................. 4.00 1.80
Championships
Jocelyn Delecour
Track and Field
8724 Jerilyn Britz 10.00 4.50
Golf

1977-79 Sportscaster Series 88 *

	NRMT	VG-E
COMPLETE SET (24)..............	100.00	45.00

8801 Tom Stock.......................... 4.00 1.80
U.S. Champion
Weightlifting
8802 Mohamed Gammoudi......... 5.00 2.20
1972 Olympics
Track and Field
8803 Dave Winfield BB............. 15.00 6.75
8804 Ulrike Richter 4.00 1.80
Swimming
8805 Rod Dixon 5.00 2.20
Track and Field
8806 The 1962 World Cup 6.00 2.70
Brazilian Team
Soccer
8807 Donna Adamek................... 4.00 1.80
Bowling
8808 Dick Quax.......................... 4.00 1.80
In 5,000 M Race
Track and Field
8809 Pocono Raceway................ 4.00 1.80
A Pocono Race
Auto Racing
8810 Valentina Sidorova 4.00 1.80
Fencing
8811 Ernie Davis FB 15.00 6.75
8812 Sawao Kato 4.00 1.80
Parallel Bars
Gymnastics
8813 Physical Fitness................. 4.00 1.80
Running Children
Beyond Sports
8814 Markus Ryffel..................... 4.00 1.80
1978 European
Championships
Track and Field
8815 Ion Tiriac 6.00 2.70
Tennis
8816 Olympic Butterfly............... 4.00 1.80
The Butterfly
Swimming
8817 Randolph Turpin 5.00 2.20
Boxing
8818 Zoltan Magyar 4.00 1.80
Pommel Horse
Gymnastics
8819 Olympic Middle 4.00 1.80
Distances
The 800 M
Track and Field
8820 Bruce Devlin.................... 10.00 4.50
Golf
8821 The Tyrrell Stable 4.00 1.80
Ken Tyrrell
Auto Racing
8822 Lingo I................................ 4.00 1.80
Aquabats
Waterskiing
8823 Dougal Haston.................... 4.00 1.80
Mountain Climbing
8824 Cape Cod League 5.00 2.20
Jim Beattie
Baseball

1977-79 Sportscaster Series 101 *

	NRMT	VG-E
COMPLETE SET (24)..............	125.00	55.00

10101 The Women's 4x400-M.... 4.00 1.80
E. German Team
Track and Field
10102 John F. Kennedy............ 25.00 11.00
Beyond Sports
10103 Del Miller........................ 4.00 1.80
Horse Racing
10104 Talavera and.................... 4.00 1.80
Cassello
Jackie Cassello
Gymnastics
10105 Hank Pfister..................... 5.00 2.20
Tennis
10106 The Jyvaskyla................... 4.00 1.80
Two Winners
Auto Racing
10107 Carlos Alberto 6.00 2.70
Torres
New York Cosmos
Soccer
10108 Carlos Lopes 4.00 1.80
In the 10,000 M
Track and Field
10109 Jim Menges...................... 4.00 1.80
In the Sand
Volleyball
10110 Jimmy Jackson 4.00 1.80
Wrestling
10111 Irina Moisseieva 4.00 1.80
A. Minenkov
Ice Dancing
Figure Skating
10112 Oscar Fabbiani................. 5.00 2.20
Soccer
10113 Bob Braithwaite............... 4.00 1.80
Shooting
10114 Natalia 4.00 1.80
Chaposhnikova
Floor Exercises
Gymnastics
10115 Jean Balukas 5.00 2.20
Billiards
10116 Club Mediterranean.......... 4.00 1.80
78 Yards Long
Yachting
10117 Pat Haden......................... 6.00 2.70
Beyond Sports
10118 The Mille Miglia................ 4.00 1.80
Mercedes Racecar
Auto Racing
10119 Tarzan 15.00 6.75
John Weissmuller
Beyond Sports
10120 Alexander Romankov 4.00 1.80
1976 Olympics
Fencing
10121 Dorothy Round................ 4.00 1.80
Tennis
10122 400-Homer Club............... 8.00 3.60
Duke Snider
Baseball
10123 Vladimir Markelov 4.00 1.80
Pommel Horse
Gymnastics
10124 Youngest Champions..... 15.00 6.75
John McEnroe
Tracy Austin
Tennis

1977-79 Sportscaster Series 102 *

	NRMT	VG-E
COMPLETE SET (24)..............	150.00	70.00

10201 Mike Flanagan BB............ 6.00 2.70
10202 Ray Meyer BK................ 15.00 6.75
10203 The Women's 400-M....... 4.00 1.80
Marita Koch
Track and Field
10204 Eizo Kenmotsu 4.00 1.80
Gymnastics
10205 Mark Edmondson............. 4.00 1.80
Tennis
10206 Jan Egil Storholt.............. 4.00 1.80
Innsbruck OG
Speed Skating
10207 The Japanese 30.00 13.50
Circuit: Isao Aoki
Golf
10208 Johan Cruyff in.............. 10.00 4.50
America
Soccer
10209 Olga Korbut.................... 20.00 9.00
Balance Beam
Gymnastics
10210 Boston's Fenway 6.00 2.70
Fenway Park
Baseball
10211 Eddie Charlton................. 4.00 1.80
Snooker
10212 Flo Hyman 8.00 3.60
Volleyball
10213 The Women's 1500.......... 4.00 1.80
and Mile
Renate Stecher
Track and Field
10214 Charlamov, Petrov............ 8.00 3.60
Michailov
Russian Team
Ice Hockey
10215 Ballbirds........................... 4.00 1.80
Tennis
10216 1972 Olympic Games....... 4.00 1.80
Urika Knape
Diving
10217 Ricky Davis 6.00 2.70
Soccer
10218 Emilia Eberle 4.00 1.80
Floor Exercises
Gymnastics
10219 Japanese Track 4.00 1.80
Racing
1977 WCH Sprint
Cycling
10220 NCAA Records................. 6.00 2.70
Steve Owens
Football
10221 The Grand Prix and 20.00 9.00
Masters
John McEnroe
Tennis
10222 The McLaren Stable 5.00 2.20
Patrick Tambay
Auto Racing
10223 Don Cockell...................... 5.00 2.20
Boxing
10224 Jim Piersall BB................. 6.00 2.70

1977-79 Sportscaster Series 103 *

	NRMT	VG-E
COMPLETE SET (24)..............	175.00	80.00

10301 Jim Turner FB.................... 8.00 3.60
10302 Walter Cronkite 20.00 9.00
Yachting
10303 Bill Steinkraus 6.00 2.70
W Fleet Apple
Show Jumping
10304 Ann Meyers BK.............. 20.00 9.00
10305 Tim Wilkison 6.00 2.70
Tennis
10306 1979 Hall of Famers......... 6.00 2.70
Frank Sedgman
Tennis
10307 Mildred "Babe"............... 25.00 11.00

Zaharias
In the Hurdles
Track and Field
10308 Alexander Yakushev HK ... 8.00 3.60
10309 Airborne Model ... 5.00 2.20
Planes: Model Plane
Beyond Sports
10310 Bruce Tulloh ... 5.00 2.20
Running Barefoot
Track and Field
10311 Julia Bogdanova ... 5.00 2.20
Swimming
10312 In-Sook Bhushan ... 5.00 2.20
Table Tennis
10313 The Orange Bowl ... 12.00 5.50
Bjorn Borg
Tennis
10314 Wolfgang Schmidt ... 8.00 3.60
In the Discus
Track and Field
10315 Jean-Pierre Jarier ... 5.00 2.20
Auto Racing
10316 Longest Runs ... 8.00 3.60
Jack Tatum
Football
10317 The Pumas ... 5.00 2.20
Pumas vs France
Rugby
10318 Alan Willey ... 6.00 2.70
Soccer
10319 ESPN ... 15.00 6.75
TV College Action
Beyond Sports
10320 Gerd Wiltfang ... 5.00 2.20
W Romam
Show Jumping
10321 1979 NASL Champions ... 8.00 3.60
Trevor Whymark
Soccer
10322 World Championships ... 5.00 2.20
Crucible Theatre
Snooker
10323 John Marks ... 5.00 2.20
1978 Melbourne
Tennis
10324 Joe Bottom ... 5.00 2.20
100M Butterfly
Swimming

1987 Sports Cube Game *

3 1/2" by 5 3/8" cards with nine black and white portrait shots on front and questions on the back

MINT NRMT
COMPLETE SET (3) ... 20.00 9.00
1 James Naismith ... 15.00 6.75
Babe Ruth
America's Cup
Knute Rockne
Vince Lombardi
Herb Brooks
Jack Johnson
Bobby Jones
Jim Thorpe
2 Jack Dempsey ... 10.00 4.50
Ty Cobb
Gene Tunney
Willie Jones
Josh Gibson
Lou Gehrig
Harry Frazee
Eddie Gaedel
Red Rolfe
3 Joe Louis ... 8.00 3.60
Bill Klem
Ken Anderson
Thurman Munson
Earl Averill
Elston Howard
Arky Vaughan
Miller Huggins
Eddie Cicotte

1991 Stadium Club Charter Member *

This 50-card multi-sport standard-size set was sent to charter members in the Topps Stadium Club. The sports represented in the set are baseball (1-32), football (33-41), and hockey (42-50). The cards feature on the fronts full-bleed posed and action glossy color player photos. The player's name is shown in the light blue stripe that intersects the Stadium Club logo near the bottom of the picture. The words "Charter Member" are printed in gold foil lettering immediately below the stripe. The back design features a newspaper-like masthead (The Stadium Club Herald) complete with a headline announcing a major event in the player's season with copy below providing more information about the event. The cards are unnumbered and arranged below alphabetically within sports. Topps apparently made two printings of this set, which are most easily identifiable by the small asterisks on the bottom left of the card backs. The first printing cards have one asterisk, the second printing cards have two. The display box that contained the cards also included a Nolan Ryan bronze metallic card and a key chain. Very early members of the Stadium Club received a large size bronze metallic Nolan Ryan 1990 Topps card. It is valued below as well as the normal size Ryan metallic card. A third varation on the Ryan medallion has been found. This is another version of the 1991 Stadium Club charter member bronze medallion, except this one has a 24K logo on it. It is suspected that this might be a Home Shopping Newtork variety. No pricing is provided at this time for this piece due to lack of market information.

MINT NRMT
COMP.FACT SET (50) ... 20.00 9.00
1 Sandy Alomar ... .20 .09
2 George Brett ... 1.50 .70
3 Barry Bonds ... 1.50 .70
4 Ellis Burks ... .20 .09
5 Eric Davis ... .20 .09
6 Delino DeShields ... .10 .05
7 Doug Drabek ... .10 .05
8 Cecil Fielder ... .20 .09
9 Carlton Fisk ... .75 .35
10 Ken Griffey Jr. ... 3.00 1.35
Ken Griffey Sr.
11 Billy Hatcher ... .10 .05
12 Andy Hawkins ... .10 .05
13 Rickey Henderson ... .75 .35
A.L. Recognizes
Rickey As MVP
14 Rickey Henderson ... .75 .35
A.L.'s Leading Thief
15 Randy Johnson ... .75 .35
16 Dave Justice ... .50 .23
17 Mark Langston ... .10 .05
Mike Witt
18 Kevin Maas ... .10 .05
19 Ramon Martinez ... .20 .09
20 Willie McGee ... .20 .09
21 Terry Mulholland ... .10 .05
22 Jose Offerman ... .20 .09
23 Melido Perez ... .10 .05
24 Nolan Ryan ... 3.00 1.35
A No-Hitter For
The Ages
25 Nolan Ryan ... 3.00 1.35
Earns 300th Career Win
26 Ryne Sandberg ... 1.00 .45
27 Dave Stewart ... .10 .05
28 Dave Stieb ... .10 .05
29 Bobby Thigpen ... .10 .05
30 Fernando Valenzuela ... .20 .09
31 Frank Viola ... .10 .05
32 Bob Welch ... .10 .05
33 Ottis Anderson ... .10 .05
MVP of Super Bowl XXV
34 Ottis Anderson ... .10 .05
Reaches 10,000
35 Randall Cunningham ... .20 .09
36 Warren Moon ... .50 .23
37 Barry Sanders ... 2.50 1.10
38 Pete Stoyanovich ... .10 .05
39 Lawrence Taylor ... .50 .23
40 Derrick Thomas ... .50 .23
41 Richmond Webb ... .10 .05
42 Ed Belfour ... .50 .23
Cops The Vezina
43 Ed Belfour ... .50 .23
Is Top Goalie
44 Ray Bourque ... .50 .23
45 Paul Coffey ... .50 .23
46 Wayne Gretzky ... 3.00 1.35
Takes No. 2000
47 Wayne Gretzky ... 3.00 1.35
The 700 Club
48 Brett Hull ... .75 .35
Brett's All Hart
49 Brett Hull ... .75 .35
Joins 50-50 Club
50 Mario Lemieux ... 3.00 1.35
NNO Nolan Ryan Bronze ... 10.00 4.50
Medallion small
1991 Stadium Club
NNO Nolan Ryan Bronze ... 200.00 90.00
Medallion large
1990 Topps
NNO Nolan Ryan Bronze ... .10 .05
Medallion small
1991 Stadium Club
24K gold

1991 Stadium Club Members Only *

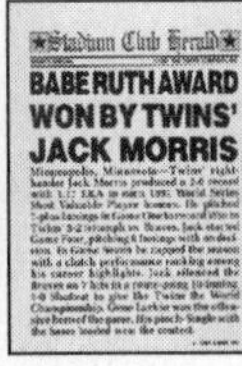

This 50-card multi-sport standard-size set was sent in three installments to members in the Topps Stadium Club. The first and second installments featured baseball players (card numbers 1-10 and 11-30), while the third spotlighted football (31-37) and hockey (38-50) players. The cards feature on the fronts full-bleed posed and action glossy color player photos. The player's name is shown in the light blue stripe that intersects the Stadium Club logo near the bottom of the picture. The words "Members Only" are printed in gold foil lettering immediately below the stripe. The back design features a newspaper-like masthead (The Stadium Club Herald) complete with a headline announcing a major event in the player's season with copy below providing more information about the event. The cards are unnumbered and arranged below alphabetically according to and within installments.

MINT NRMT
COMPLETE SET (50) ... 20.00 9.00
1 Wilson Alvarez ... .20 .09
2 Andy Ashby ... .10 .05
3 Tommy Greene ... .10 .05
4 Rickey Henderson ... 1.00 .45
Is Top Thief in History
5 Denny Martinez ... .20 .09
6 Paul Molitor ... .50 .23
7 Nolan Ryan ... 3.00 1.35
Extends Record
With 7th No-Hitter
8 Robby Thompson ... .10 .05
9 Dave Winfield ... .75 .35
10 Bob Milacki ... .10 .05
Mike Flanagan
Mark Williamson
Gregg Olson
Chris Hoiles
11 Jeff Bagwell ... 2.00 .90
12 Roger Clemens ... 1.50 .70
13 David Cone ... .30 .14
14 Carlton Fisk ... .75 .35
15 Julio Franco ... .20 .09
16 Tom Glavine ... .75 .35
17 Pete Harnisch ... .10 .05
18 Rickey Henderson ... 1.00 .45
Leads A.L. In
Thefts For 11th Time
19 Howard Johnson ... .10 .05
20 Chuck Knoblauch ... .40 .18
21 Ray Lankford ... .20 .09
22 Jack Morris ... .20 .09
23 Terry Pendleton ... .20 .09
NL's Leading Batsman
24 Terry Pendleton ... .20 .09
Close MVP Race
Favors Terry
25 Jeff Reardon ... .10 .05
26 Cal Ripken ... 3.00 1.35
27 Nolan Ryan ... 3.00 1.35
22nd Straight Year
With over 100 Strikeouts
28 Bret Saberhagen ... .10 .05
29 Cecil Fielder ... .40 .18
Jose Canseco
30 Kent Mercker ... .20 .09
Mark Wohlers
Alejandro Pena
31 Art Monk ... .20 .09
32 Warren Moon ... .40 .18
33 Leonard Russell ... .10 .05
34 Mark Rypien ... .10 .05
35 Barry Sanders ... 2.50 1.10
36 Emmitt Smith ... 2.50 1.10
37 Tony Zendejas ... .10 .05
38 Pavel Bure ... 1.50 .70
39 Guy Carbonneau ... .10 .05
40 Paul Coffey ... .40 .18
41 Mike Gartner ... .20 .09
Makes It Two
42 Mike Gartner ... .20 .09
Makes It 500
43 Michel Goulet ... .10 .05
44 Wayne Gretzky ... 3.00 1.35
45 Brett Hull ... 1.00 .45
46 Brian Leetch ... .30 .14
47 Mario Lemieux ... 3.00 1.35
Repeats As MVP
48 Mario Lemieux ... 3.00 1.35
Takes 3rd Ross Trophy
49 Mark Messier ... .40 .18
50 Patrick Roy ... 2.50 1.10

1992 Stadium Club Members Only *

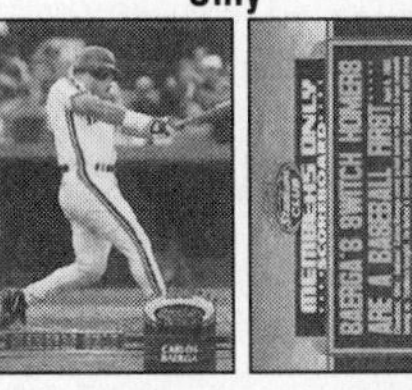

This 50-card standard-size set was sent to 1992 Stadium Club members in four installments. In addition to the Stadium Club cards, the first installment included one "Top Draft Picks of the '90s" card (as a bonus) and a randomly chosen "Master Photo" printed on 5" by 7" white card stock. The third and fourth installments included hockey and football players in addition to baseball players. The cards feature full-bleed glossy color player photos. The fronts of the regular cards have the words "Members Only" printed in gold foil at the bottom along with the player's name and the Stadium Club logo. The backs feature a stadium scene with the scoreboard displaying, in yellow neon, a career highlight. The cards are unnumbered and checklisted below alphabetically, with the two-player cards listed at the end.

MINT NRMT
COMPLETE SET (50) ... 30.00 13.50
1 Carlos Baerga ... .10 .05
2 Wade Boggs ... .75 .35
3 Barry Bonds ... 1.50 .70
4 Bret Boone ... .40 .18
5 Pat Borders ... .10 .05
6 George Brett ... 1.25 .55
7 George Brett ... 1.25 .55
8 Jim Bullinger ... .20 .09
9 Gary Carter ... .75 .35
10 Andujar Cedeno ... .10 .05
11 Roger Clemens ... .75 .35
Matt Young
12 Dennis Eckersley ... .20 .09
13 Dennis Eckersley ... .20 .09
14 Dave Eiland ... .10 .05
15 Ken Griffey Jr. ... 1.50 .70
16 Kevin Gross ... .10 .05
17 Bo Jackson ... .60 .25
18 Eric Karros ... .60 .25
19 Pat Listach ... .10 .05
20 Greg Maddux ... 1.50 .70
21 Mickey Morandini ... .10 .05
22 Jack Morris ... .20 .09
23 Eddie Murray ... .75 .35
24 Eddie Murray ... .75 .35
25 Bip Roberts ... .10 .05
26 Nolan Ryan ... 2.50 1.10
27 Seasons
27 Nolan Ryan ... 2.50 1.10
1993 Seasons His Finale
28 Gary Sheffield ... .40 .18
Dwight Gooden
29 Gary Sheffield ... .40 .18
Fred McGriff
30 Lee Smith ... .20 .09
31 Ozzie Smith ... 1.00 .45
(2,000th Hit)
32 Ozzie Smith ... 1.00 .45
(7,000th Career Assist)
33 Ozzie Smith ... 1.00 .45
34 Bobby Thigpen ... .10 .05
35 Dave Winfield ... .75 .35
36 Robin Yount ... .75 .35
37 Troy Aikman ... 1.25 .55
38 Dale Carter ... .10 .05
39 Art Monk ... .20 .09
40 Frank Reich ... .10 .05
41 Emmitt Smith ... 2.00 .90
42 Steve Young ... 1.00 .45
43 Neil Brady ... .10 .05
44 Mike Gartner ... .20 .09
45 Chris Kontos ... .10 .05
46 Jari Kurri ... .40 .18
47 Eric Lindros ... .75 .35
48 Reggie Savage ... .10 .05
49 Teemu Selanne ... .75 .35
Selanne Rewrites
Record Books
50 Teemu Selanne ... .75 .35
Teemu Bests Bossy

1993 Stadium Club Members Only *

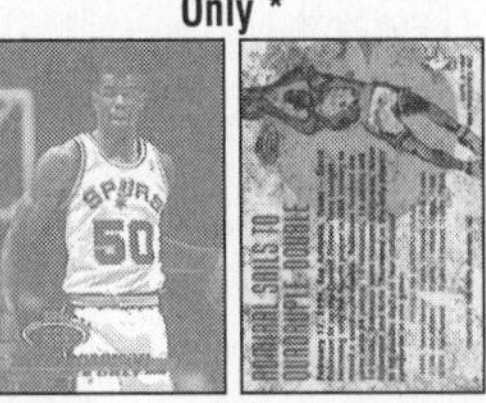

This 59-card standard-size set was mailed out to Stadium Club Members in four separate mailings. Each box contained several sports. The fronts have full-bleed color action player photos with the words "Members Only" printed in gold foil at the bottom along with the player's name and the Stadium Club logo. On a multi-colored background, the horizontal backs carry player information and a computer generated drawing of a baseball player. The cards are unnumbered and checklisted below alphabetically according to sport as follows: baseball (1-28), basketball (29-44), football (45-53), and hockey (54-59).

MINT NRMT
COMPLETE SET (59) ... 40.00 18.00
1 Jim Abbott ... .10 .05
2 Barry Bonds ... 1.50 .70
3 Chris Bosio ... .10 .05
4 George Brett ... 1.25 .55
5 Jay Buhner ... .40 .18
6 Joe Carter ... .20 .09
Belts 3 for Fifth
Time in Career
7 Joe Carter ... .20 .09
Dramatics Give Jays Series Crown
8 Carlton Fisk ... .75 .35
9 Travis Fryman ... .20 .09
10 Mark Grace ... .60 .25
11 Ken Griffey Jr. ... 1.50 .70
12 Darryl Kile ... .20 .09
13 Darren Lewis ... .10 .05
14 Greg Maddux ... 1.50 .70
15 Jack McDowell ... .10 .05
16 Paul Molitor ... .60 .25
17 Eddie Murray ... .75 .35
18 Mike Piazza ... 2.50 1.10
Home Run Record
for Rookie Catchers
19 Mike Piazza ... 2.50 1.10
NL Rookie Honors
20 Kirby Puckett ... .75 .35
21 Jeff Reardon ... .10 .05
22 Tim Salmon ... .40 .18
23 Curt Schilling ... .60 .25
24 Lee Smith ... .20 .09
25 Dave Stewart ... .20 .09
26 Frank Thomas ... .75 .35
27 Mark Whiten ... .10 .05
28 Dave Winfield ... .75 .35
29 Danny Ainge ... .20 .09
30 Mark Eaton ... .10 .05
31 Patrick Ewing ... .60 .25
32 Anfernee Hardaway ... .60 .25
33 Carl Herrera ... .20 .09
Rockets Tie Mark
for Best Start
34 Michael Jordan ... 3.00 1.35
35 Hakeem Olajuwon ... 1.00 .45
36 Shaquille O'Neal ... 2.00 .90
37 Cliff Robinson ... .20 .09
38 David Robinson ... 1.00 .45
39 Brian Shaw ... .10 .05
40 John Stockton ... .60 .25
41 Isiah Thomas ... .40 .18
42 Chris Webber ... 2.00 .90
43 Dominique Wilkins ... .40 .18
44 Micheal Williams ... .10 .05
45 Morten Andersen ... .10 .05
46 Jerome Bettis ... .75 .35
47 Steve Christie ... .10 .05
48 Jim Kelly ... .40 .18
49 Dan Marino ... 2.50 1.10
50 Sterling Sharpe ... .20 .09
51 Emmitt Smith ... 2.00 .90
52 Dana Stubblefield ... .20 .09
53 Steve Young ... 1.00 .45
54 Peter Bondra ... .40 .18
55 Mike Gartner ... .20 .09
56 Mario Lemieux ... 2.50 1.10
57 Mike Richter ... .40 .18
58 Patrick Roy ... 2.50 1.10
59 Teemu Selanne ... .60 .25

1980 Superstar Matchbook*

These collector issued matchbooks were issued in the New England area in 1980 and featured superstars from all sports but with an emphasis on players who made their fame in New England. Since these are unnumbered, we have sequenced them in alphabetical order.

MINT NRMT
COMPLETE SET ... 60.00 27.00
1 Hank Aaron ... 6.00 2.70
2 Larry Bird ... 10.00 4.50
3 Ray Bourque ... 8.00 3.60
4 Lou Brock ... 4.00 1.80
5 Gordie Howe ... 6.00 2.70
6 Al Kaline ... 4.00 1.80
7 Guy LaFleur ... 4.00 1.80
8 Willie Mays ... 8.00 3.60
9 Bobby Orr ... 10.00 4.50
10 Pete Rose ... 4.00 1.80
11 Duke Snider ... 6.00 2.70
12 Tom Yawkey ... 2.00 .90
13 Carl Yastrzemski ... 4.00 1.80

1948 Topps Magic Photos *

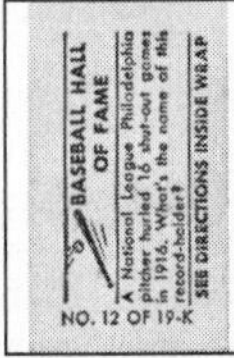

The 1948 Topps Magic Photos set contains 252 small (approximately 7/8" by 1 7/16") individual cards featuring sport and non-sport subjects. They were issued in 19 lettered series with cards numbered within each series. The fronts were developed, much like a photograph, from a "blank" appearance by using moisture and sunlight. Due to varying degrees of photographic sensitivity, the clarity of these cards ranges from fully developed to poorly developed. This set contains Topps' first baseball cards. A premium album holding 126-cards was also issued. The set is sometimes confused with Topps' 1956 Hocus-Focus set, although the cards in this set are slightly smaller than those in the Hocus-Focus set. The checklist below is presented by series. Poorly developed cards are considered in lesser condition and hence have lesser value. The catalog designation for this set is R714-27. Each type of card subject has a letter prefix as follows: Boxing Champions (A), All-American Basketball (B), All-American Football (C), Wrestling Champions (D), Track and Field Champions (E), Stars of Stage and Screen (F), American Dogs (G), General Sports (H), Movie Stars (J), Baseball Hall of Fame (K), Aviation Pioneers (L), Famous Landmarks (M), American Inventors (N), American Military Leaders (O), American Explorers (P), Basketball Thrills (Q), Football Thrills (R), Figures of the Wild West (S), and General Sports (T).

NRMT EXC
COMPLETE SET (252) ... 4000.00 1800.00
A1 Tommy Burns ... 15.00 6.75
A2 John L. Sullivan ... 40.00 18.00
A3 James J. Corbett ... 30.00 13.50
A4 Bob Fitzsimmons ... 20.00 9.00
A5 James J. Jeffries ... 30.00 13.50
A6 Jack Johnson ... 40.00 18.00
A7 Jess Willard ... 20.00 9.00
A8 Jack Dempsey ... 40.00 18.00
A9 Gene Tunney ... 30.00 13.50
A10 Max Schmeling ... 20.00 9.00
A11 Jack Sharkey ... 15.00 6.75
A12 Primo Carnera ... 15.00 6.75
A13 Max Baer ... 15.00 6.75
A14 James J. Braddock ... 15.00 6.75
A15 Joe Louis ... 50.00 22.00
A16 Gus Lesnevich ... 10.00 4.50
A17 Tony Zale ... 15.00 6.75
A18 Ike Williams ... 10.00 4.50
A19 Ray Robinson ... 40.00 18.00
A20 Willie Pep ... 15.00 6.75
A21 Rinty Monaghan ... 10.00 4.50
A22 Manuel Ortiz ... 10.00 4.50
A23 Marcel Cerdan ... 20.00 9.00
A24 Buddy Baer ... 10.00 4.50
B1 Ralph Beard ... 50.00 22.00
B2 Murray Weir ... 30.00 13.50
B3 Ed Macauley ... 80.00 36.00
B4 Kevin O'Shea ... 25.00 11.00
B5 Jim McIntyre ... 30.00 13.50
B6 Manhattan Beats ... 25.00 11.00
Dartmouth
C1 Barney Poole ... 25.00 11.00
C2 Pete Elliott ... 15.00 6.75
C3 Doak Walker ... 50.00 22.00
C4 Bill Swiacki ... 20.00 9.00
C5 Bill Fischer ... 15.00 6.75
C6 Johnny Lujack ... 50.00 22.00
C7 Chuck Bednarik ... 50.00 22.00
C8 Joe Steffy ... 15.00 6.75
C9 George Connor ... 30.00 13.50
C10 Steve Suhey ... 20.00 9.00
C11 Bob Chappuis ... 25.00 11.00
C12 Bill Swiacki ... 15.00 6.75
Columbia 23/Navy 14
C13 Army-Notre Dame ... 25.00 11.00
D1 Frank Gotch ... 15.00 6.75
D2 Hackenschmidt ... 10.00 4.50
D3 Stanuslaus Zbyszko ... 20.00 9.00
D4 Jim Browning ... 15.00 6.75
D5 Jim Londos ... 20.00 9.00
D6 Strangler Lewis ... 25.00 11.00
D7 George Becker ... 10.00 4.50
D8 Ernie Dusek ... 15.00 6.75
D9 Rudy Dusek ... 15.00 6.75

D10 Dean Detton 10.00 4.50
D11 Masked Marvel 20.00 9.00
D12 Maurice Tillet 10.00 4.50
D13 Olaf Swenson 10.00 4.50
D14 Tony Galento 20.00 9.00
D15 Frank Sexton 10.00 4.50
D16 George Calza 10.00 4.50
D17 Arm Lock 12.00 5.50
D18 Flying Dropkick 12.00 5.50
D19 Primo Carnera 20.00 9.00
D20 Gino Garabaldi 10.00 4.50
D21 Lord Jan Blears 25.00 11.00
D22 Joe Savoldi 12.00 5.50
D23 Dick Shikat 10.00 4.50
D24 Wadleslaw 10.00 4.50
D25 Steinke 12.00 5.50
E1 Jesse Owens 25.00 11.00
E2 Leo Steers 5.00 2.20
E3 Ben Eastman 5.00 2.20
E4 Harrison Dillard 10.00 4.50
E5 Greg Rice 5.00 2.20
E6 Kolehmainen 5.00 2.20
E7 Gunner Hagg 5.00 2.20
E8 Chas. Pores 5.00 2.20
E9 Grover Kelmmer 5.00 2.20
E10 Boyd Brown 5.00 2.20
E11 Pat Ryan 6.00 2.70
E12 Charlie Fonville 5.00 2.20
E13 Cornelius Warmerdam 5.00 2.20
E14 Army-Navy Tie 5.00 2.20
E15 Haaken Lidman 5.00 2.20
(Sweden)
E16 Morris-Army Wins 5.00 2.20
E17 M. Jarvinen and 5.00 2.20
Javelin
F1 Clark Gable 30.00 13.50
F2 Barbara Stanwyck 10.00 4.50
F3 Lana Turner 10.00 4.50
F4 Ingrid Bergman 15.00 6.75
F5 Betty Grable 10.00 4.50
F6 Tyrone Power 10.00 4.50
F7 Olivia DeHavilland 6.00 2.70
F8 Joan Fontaine 6.00 2.70
F9 June Allyson 8.00 3.60
F10 Dorothy Lamour 6.00 2.70
F11 William Powell 6.00 2.70
F12 Sylvia Sidney 5.00 2.20
F13 Van Johnson 6.00 2.70
F14 Virginia Mayo 6.00 2.70
F15 Claudette Colbert 10.00 4.50
F16 Eve Arden 5.00 2.20
F17 Lynn Bari 5.00 2.20
F18 Maureen O'Hara 6.00 2.70
F19 Jean Arthur 5.00 2.20
F20 Hazel Brooks 5.00 2.20
F21 Martha Vickers 6.00 2.70
F22 Noreen Nash 5.00 2.20
G1 Terrier 3.00 1.35
G2 Chow 3.00 1.35
G3 Cairn Terrier 3.00 1.35
G4 White Sealyham 3.00 1.35
G5 St. Bernard 3.00 1.35
G6 Boston Bull 3.00 1.35
G7 Greyhound 3.00 1.35
G8 Dalmation 3.00 1.35
G9 Pointer 3.00 1.35
G10 Cocker Spaniel 3.00 1.35
G11 English Bulldog 3.00 1.35
G12 Champion Pointer 3.00 1.35
G13 Setter 3.00 1.35
G14 Boxer 3.00 1.35
G15 Russian Wolfhound 3.00 1.35
G16 Doberman 3.00 1.35
G17 Collie 3.00 1.35
H1 George Remington 3.00 1.35
Mrs. George Remington
H2 Bernice Dossey 3.00 1.35
J1 Johnny Mack Brown 8.00 3.60
J2 Andy Clyde 6.00 2.70
J3 Roddy McDowall 10.00 4.50
J4 Keye Luke 8.00 3.60
J5 Jackie Coogan 8.00 3.60
J6 Joe Kirkwood Jr. 6.00 2.70
J7 Jackie Cooper 8.00 3.60
J8 Arthur Lake 6.00 2.70
J9 Sam Levine 6.00 2.70
J10 Binnie Barnes 6.00 2.70
J11 Gertrude Niesen 6.00 2.70
J12 Rory Calhoun 8.00 3.60
J13 June Lockhart 8.00 3.60
J14 Hedy Lamarr 8.00 3.60
J15 Robert Cummings 6.00 2.70
J16 Brian Aherne 6.00 2.70
J17 William Bendix 8.00 3.60
J18 Roland Winters 6.00 2.70
J19 Michael O'Shea 6.00 2.70
J20 Lois Butler 6.00 2.70
J21 Renie Riano 6.00 2.70
J22 Jimmy Wakely 6.00 2.70
J23 Audie Murphy 12.00 5.50
J24 Leo Gorcey 6.00 2.70
J25 Leon Errol 6.00 2.70
J26 Lon Chaney 12.00 5.50
J27 William Frawley 8.00 3.60
J28 Billy Benedict 6.00 2.70
J29 Rod Cameron 6.00 2.70
J30 James Gleason 6.00 2.70
J31 Gilbert Roland 6.00 2.70
J32 Raymond Hatton 6.00 2.70
J33 Joe Yule 6.00 2.70
J34 Eddie Albert 8.00 3.60
J35 Barry Sullivan 6.00 2.70
J36 Richard Basehart 6.00 2.70
J37 Claire Trevor 6.00 2.70
J38 Constance Bennett 6.00 2.70
J39 Gale Storm 6.00 2.70
J40 Elyse Knox 6.00 2.70
J41 Jane Wyatt 8.00 3.60
J42 Whip Wilson 6.00 2.70
J43 Charles Bickford 8.00 3.60
J44 Guy Madison 8.00 3.60
J45 Barton MacLane 6.00 2.70
K1 Lou Boudreau 60.00 27.00
K2 Cleveland Indians 40.00 18.00
K3 Bob Elliott 15.00 6.75
K4 Cleveland Indians 4-3 15.00 6.75
K5 Cleveland Indians 4-1 20.00 9.00
(Boudreau scoring)
K6 Babe Ruth 714 250.00 110.00
K7 Tris Speaker 793 60.00 27.00
K8 Rogers Hornsby 100.00 45.00
K9 Connie Mack 100.00 45.00
K10 Christy Mathewson 100.00 45.00
K11 Honus Wagner 100.00 45.00
K12 Grover Alexander 100.00 45.00
K13 Ty Cobb 150.00 70.00
K14 Lou Gehrig 150.00 70.00
K15 Walter Johnson 200.00 90.00
K16 Cy Young 150.00 70.00
K17 George Sisler 257 80.00 36.00
K18 Tinker and Evers 60.00 27.00
K19 Third Base 15.00 6.75
Cleveland Indians
L1 Colonial Airlines 8.00 3.60
L2 James Doolittle 12.00 5.50
L3 Wiley Post 12.00 5.50
L4 Eddie Rickenbacker 12.00 5.50
L5 Amelia Earhart 20.00 9.00
L6 Charles Lindbergh 25.00 11.00
L7 Doug Corrigan 10.00 4.50
L8 Chas. A. Levine 8.00 3.60
L9 Wright Brothers 12.00 5.50
M1 Niagara Falls 3.00 1.35
M2 Empire State Building 3.00 1.35
M3 Leaning Tower of Pisa 3.00 1.35
M4 Eiffel Tower 3.00 1.35
M5 Lincoln Memorial 3.00 1.35
M6 Statue of Liberty 5.00 2.20
M7 Geyser& Yellowstone 3.00 1.35
M8 Sphinx 3.00 1.35
M9 Washington Monument 3.00 1.35
N1 Eli Whitney 3.00 1.35
N2 Thomas A. Edison 5.00 2.20
N3 C.E. Duryea 3.00 1.35
N4 Benjamin Franklin 5.00 2.20
N5 V.K. Zworykin 3.00 1.35
N6 Robert Fulton 3.00 1.35
N7 Samuel Morse 3.00 1.35
N8 Alexander Graham Bell 5.00 2.20
O1 Joseph Stillwell 3.00 1.35
O2 Adm. Chester Nimitz 3.00 1.35
O3 George Patton 10.00 4.50
O4 General John Pershing 5.00 2.20
O5 Adm. David Farragut 3.00 1.35
O6 Jonathan Wainwright 3.00 1.35
O7 Douglas MacArthur 8.00 3.60
O8 General Omar Bradley 3.00 1.35
O9 George Dewey 3.00 1.35
O10 Gen.Dwight Eisenhower 8.00 3.60
P1 Adm. Robert Peary 3.00 1.35
P2 Richard E. Byrd 3.00 1.35
Q1 St. Louis Univ. 15.00 6.75
Q2 Long Island Univ. 15.00 6.75
Q3 Notre Dame 25.00 11.00
Q4 Kentucky 58-42 40.00 18.00
Q5 DePaul 75-64 50.00 22.00
(Mikan in picture)
R1 Wally Triplett 10.00 4.50
R2 Gil Stevenson 10.00 4.50
R3 Northwestern 10.00 4.50
R4 Yale vs. Columbia 10.00 4.50
R5 Cornell 10.00 4.50
S1 General Custer 20.00 9.00
S2 Buffalo Bill Cody 20.00 9.00
S3 Sitting Bull 20.00 9.00
S4 Annie Oakley 12.00 5.50
S5 Jessie James 15.00 6.75
S6 Geronimo 12.00 5.50
S7 Billy the Kid 20.00 9.00
T1 Soccer 20.00 9.00
T2 Motor Boat Racing 6.00 2.70
T3 Ice Hockey 30.00 13.50
T4 Water Skiing 5.00 2.20
T5 Gallorette 5.00 2.20
T6 Headlock 5.00 2.20
T7 Tennis 15.00 6.75

1981 Topps Thirst Break *

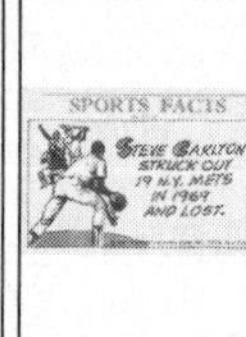

This 56-card set is actually a set of gum wrappers. These wrappers were issued in Thirst Break Orange Gum, which was reportedly only distributed in Pennsylvania and Ohio. Each of these small gum wrappers has a cartoon-type image of a particular great moment in sports. As the checklist below shows, many different sports are represented in this set. The wrappers each measure approximately 2 9/16" by 1 5/8". The wrappers are numbered in small print at the top. The backs of the wrappers are blank. The "1981 Topps" copyright is at the bottom of each card.

	NRMT	EXC
COMPLETE SET (56)	150.00	70.00

1 Shortest Baseball Game 1.00 .45
2 Lefty Gomez 1.50 .70
3 Bob Gibson 2.00 .90
4 Hoyt Wilhelm 1.50 .70
5 Babe Ruth 6.00 2.70
6 Toby Harrah 1.00 .45
7 Carl Hubbell 2.00 .90
8 Harvey Haddix 1.50 .70
9 Steve Carlton 2.00 .90
10 Nolan Ryan 12.00 5.50
Tom Seaver
Steve Carlton
11 Lou Brock 2.50 1.10
12 Mickey Mantle 8.00 3.60
13 Tom Seaver 4.00 1.80
14 Don Drysdale 2.00 .90
15 Billy Williams 1.50 .70
16 Wilt Chamberlain 5.00 2.20
100 Points One Game
17 Wilt Chamberlain 5.00 2.20
50.4 Avg/Game
18 Wilt Chamberlain 5.00 2.20
No Foulout Record
19 Kevin Porter 1.00 .45
20 Christy Mathewson 1.50 .70
21 Hank Aaron 4.00 1.80
22 Ron Blomberg 1.00 .45
23 Joe Nuxhall 1.00 .45
24 Reggie Jackson 4.00 1.80
25 John Havlicek 4.00 1.80
26 Oscar Robertson 4.00 1.80
27 Calvin Murphy 2.00 .90
28 Clarence(Bevo) Francis 1.00 .45
29 Garo Yepremian 1.00 .45
30 Bert Jones 2.00 .90
31 Norm Van Brocklin 2.50 1.10
32 Fran Tarkenton 5.00 2.20
33 Johnny Unitas 5.00 2.20
34 Bob Beamon 1.50 .70
35 Jesse Owens 2.50 1.10
36 Bart Starr 5.00 2.20
37 O.J. Simpson 2.00 .90
38 Jim Brown 5.00 2.20
Football Fact
39 Jim Marshall 2.50 1.10
40 George Blanda 2.50 1.10
41 Jack Tatum 2.50 1.10
42 Jim Brown UER 5.00 2.20
Touchdown Record
(Tim Brown on card)
43 Gerry Cheevers 2.00 .90
44 Dave Schultz 1.50 .70
45 Mark Spitz 1.00 .45
46 Byron Nelson 5.00 2.20
47 Soccer Attendance 3.00 1.35
48 Tom Dempsey 1.50 .70
49 Gale Sayers 4.00 1.80
50 Bobby Hull 4.00 1.80
51 Bobby Hull 4.00 1.80
52 Bobby Hull 4.00 1.80
Assist Record
53 Giorgio Chinaglia 1.00 .45
54 Muhammad Ali 8.00 3.60
55 Gene Tunney 4.00 1.80
Rocky Marciano
56 Roger Bannister 1.00 .45

1911 Turkey Red T3 *

The cards in this 126-card set measure approximately 5 3/4" by 8". The 1911 "Turkey Red" set of color cabinet style cards, designated T3 in the American Card Catalog, is named after the brand of cigarettes with which it was offered as a premium. Cards 1-50 and 77-126 depict baseball players while the middle series (51-76) portrays boxers. The cards themselves are not numbered but were assigned numbers for ordering purposes by the manufacturer. This list appears on the backs of cards in the 77-126 sub-series and has been used in the checklist below. The boxers (51-76) were formerly assigned a separate catalog number (T9) but have now been returned to the classification to which they properly belong and are indicated in the checklist below by BOX. This attractive set has been reprinted recently in 2 1/2" by 3 1/2" form. A small number of proofs were found in the early 1970's. Approximately 70 of the cards in the set have been discovered in proof form.

	EX-MT	VG-E
COMPLETE SET (126)	40000.00	18000.00
COMMON BASEBALL (1-50)	200.00	90.00
COMMON BOXING (51-76)	200.00	90.00
COMMON BASEBALL (77-126)	250.00	110.00

1 Mordecai Brown 500.00 220.00
2 Bill Bergen 200.00 90.00
3 Fred Leach 200.00 90.00
4 Roger Bresnahan 400.00 180.00
5 Sam Crawford 500.00 220.00
6 Hal Chase 250.00 110.00
7 Howie Camnitz 200.00 90.00
8 Fred Clarke 400.00 180.00
9 Ty Cobb 6000.00 2700.00
10 Art Devlin 200.00 90.00
11 Bill Dahlen 250.00 110.00
12 Bill Donovan 200.00 90.00
13 Larry Doyle 250.00 110.00
14 Red Dooin 200.00 90.00
15 Kid Elberfeld 200.00 90.00
16 Johnny Evers 500.00 220.00
17 Clark Griffith 400.00 180.00
18 Hughie Jennings 600.00 275.00
19 Addie Joss 600.00 275.00
20 Tim Jordan 200.00 90.00
21 Red Kleinow 200.00 90.00
22 Harry Krause 200.00 90.00
23 Napoleon Lajoie 1000.00 450.00
24 Mike Mitchell 200.00 90.00
25 Matty McIntyre 200.00 90.00
26 John McGraw 600.00 275.00
27 Christy Mathewson 1500.00 700.00
28 Harry McIntire 200.00 90.00
29 Amby McConnell 200.00 90.00
30 George Mullin 200.00 90.00
31 Sherry Magee 200.00 90.00
32 Orval Overall 200.00 90.00
33 Jack Pfeister 200.00 90.00
34 Nap Rucker 250.00 110.00
35 Joe Tinker 600.00 275.00
36 Tris Speaker 1000.00 450.00
37 Slim Sallee 200.00 90.00
38 Jake Stahl 250.00 110.00
39 Rube Waddell 500.00 220.00
40 Vic Willis 400.00 180.00
41 Hooks Wiltse 200.00 90.00
42 Cy Young 1200.00 550.00
43 Out At Third 200.00 90.00
44 Trying to Catch 200.00 90.00
Him Napping
45 Tim Jordan 200.00 90.00
Buck Herzog at First
46 Safe At Third 200.00 90.00
47 Frank Chance At Bat 500.00 220.00
48 Jack Murray At Bat 200.00 90.00
49 Close Play At Second 200.00 90.00
50 Chief Myers At Bat 200.00 90.00
(Sic, Meyers)
51 Jem Driscoll BOXING 250.00 110.00
52 Abe Attell BOX 400.00 180.00
53 Ad. Walgast BOX 200.00 90.00
54 Johnny Coulon BOX 200.00 90.00
55 James Jeffries BOX 600.00 275.00
56 Jack Sullivan BOX 300.00 135.00
Twin
57 Battling Nelson BOX 250.00 110.00
58 Packey McFarland BOX 200.00 90.00
59 Tommy Murphy BOX 200.00 90.00
60 Owen Moran BOX 250.00 110.00
61 Johnny Marto BOX 200.00 90.00
62 Jimmie Gardner BOX 200.00 90.00
63 Harry Lewis BOX 200.00 90.00
64 Billy Papke BOX 250.00 110.00
65 Sam Langford BOX 400.00 180.00
66 Knock-out Brown BOX 200.00 90.00
67 Stanley Ketchel BOX 600.00 275.00
68 Joe Jeannette BOX 300.00 135.00
69 Leach Cross BOX 250.00 110.00
70 Phil. McGovern BOX 200.00 90.00
71 Battling Hurley BOX 200.00 90.00
72 Honey Mellody BOX 200.00 90.00
73 Al Kaufman BOX 200.00 90.00
74 Willie Lewis BOX 200.00 90.00
75 Jack O'Brien BOX 300.00 135.00
Philadelphia
76 Jack Johnson BOX 1000.00 450.00
77 Red Ames: New York NL 250.00 110.00
78 Frank Baker: 400.00 180.00
Phila. AL
Picture probably
Jack Barry
79 George Bell 250.00 110.00
80 Chief Bender 500.00 220.00
81 Bob Bescher 250.00 110.00
82 Kitty Bransfield 250.00 110.00
83 Al Bridwell 250.00 110.00
84 George Browne 250.00 110.00
85 Bill Burns 300.00 135.00
86 Bill Carrigan 250.00 110.00
87 Eddie Collins 500.00 220.00
88 Harry Coveleski 250.00 110.00
89 Lou Criger 250.00 110.00
90 Mickey Doolan 250.00 110.00
91 Tom Downey 250.00 110.00
92 Jimmy Dygert 250.00 110.00
93 Art Fromme 250.00 110.00
94 George Gibson 250.00 110.00
95 Peaches Graham 250.00 110.00
96 Bob Groom 250.00 110.00
97 Bob Hoblitzel 250.00 110.00
98 Doc Hofman 250.00 110.00
99 Walter Johnson 1500.00 700.00
100 Davy Jones 250.00 110.00
101 Willie Keeler 800.00 350.00
102 Johnny Kling 250.00 110.00
103 Ed Konetchy 250.00 110.00
104 Ed Lennox 250.00 110.00
105 Hans Lobert 250.00 110.00
106 Bris Lord 250.00 110.00
107 Rube Manning 250.00 110.00
108 Fred Merkle 300.00 135.00
109 Pat Moran 250.00 110.00
110 George McBride 250.00 110.00
111 Harry Niles 250.00 110.00
112 Dode Paskert 250.00 110.00
113 Bugs Raymond 300.00 135.00
114 Bob Rhoads 300.00 135.00
115 Admiral Schlei 250.00 110.00
116 Boss Schmidt 250.00 110.00
117 Frank Schulte 250.00 110.00
118 Charlie Smith 250.00 110.00
119 George Stone 250.00 110.00
120 Gabby Street 250.00 110.00
121 Billy Sullivan 300.00 135.00
122 Fred Tenney 250.00 110.00
123 Ira Thomas 250.00 110.00
124 Bobby Wallace 500.00 220.00
125 Ed Walsh 500.00 220.00
126 Chief Wilson 250.00 110.00

1957-59 Union Oil Booklets *

These booklets were distributed by Union Oil. The front cover of each booklet features a drawing of the subject player. The booklets are numbered and were issued over several years beginning in 1957. These are 12-page pamphlets and are approximately 4" by 5 1/2". The set is subtitled "Family Sports Fun." This was apparently primarily a Southern California promotion.

	NRMT	VG-E
COMPLETE SET (44)	400.00	180.00

1 Elroy Hirsch FB 57 20.00 9.00
2 Les Richter FB 57 4.00 1.80
3 Frankie Albert FB 57 15.00 6.75
4 Y.A. Tittle FB 57 20.00 9.00
5 Bill Russell BK 57 40.00 18.00
6 Forrest Twogood BK57 12.00 5.50
7 Bob Richards 6.00 2.70
Body Conditioning 57
8 Phil Woolpert BK 58 12.00 5.50
9 Bill Sharman BK 58 20.00 9.00
10 Alf Engen 3.00 1.35
Skiing 58
11 Bob Mathias 5.00 2.20
Track 58
12 Duke Snider BB 58 20.00 9.00
13 Payton Jordan 3.00 1.35
Track 58
14 Bob Lemon BB 58 15.00 6.75
15 Red Schoendienst BB 58 20.00 9.00
16 Johnny Dieckman 3.00 1.35
Fishing 58
17 Pancho Gonzalez 6.00 2.70
Tennis 58
18 Mal Whitfield 3.00 1.35
Track 58
19 Mike Peppe 3.00 1.35
Swimming 58
20 Bill Rigney BB 58 6.00 2.70
21 Nancy Chaffee Kiner 3.00 1.35
Tennis 58
22 Lloyd Mangrum 15.00 6.75
Golf 58
23 Pat McCormick 3.00 1.35
Diving 58
24 Perry T. Jones 3.00 1.35
Tennis 58
25 Howard Hill 3.00 1.35
Archery 58
26 Herb Parsons 3.00 1.35
Hunting 58
27 Bob Waterfield FB 58 20.00 9.00
28 Pete Elliott FB 58 10.00 4.50
29 Elroy Hirsch FB 58 15.00 6.75
30 Frank Gifford FB 58 20.00 9.00
31 George Yardley BK 58 15.00 6.75
32 John Wooden BK 58 40.00 18.00
33 Ralph Borrelli 3.00 1.35
Tumbling 58
34 Bob Cousy BK 59 35.00 16.00
35 Yves Latreille 3.00 1.35
Skiing 59
36 Slats Gill BK 59 15.00 6.75
37 Jess Mortensen 3.00 1.35
Track 59
38 Jackie Jensen BB 59 12.00 5.50
39 Warren Spahn BB 59 20.00 9.00
40 Jack Kramer 4.00 1.80
Tennis 59
41 Ernie Banks BB 59 25.00 11.00
42 Cary Middlecoff 15.00 6.75
Golf 59
43 Greta Andersen 3.00 1.35
Swimming 59
44 Lon Garrison 3.00 1.35
Camping 59

1932 U.S. Caramel R328 *

The cards in this 32-card set measure 2 1/2" by 3". The U.S. Caramel set of "Famous Athletes" was issued in 1932. The cards contain black and white bust shots set against an attractive red background. Boxers and golfers are included in the set. The existence of card number 16, Fred Lindstrom has only recently been verified. The set price does not include the Lindstrom card.

	EX-MT	VG-E
COMPLETE SET (31)	80000.00	36000.00
COMMON BASEBALL	200.00	90.00
COMMON BOXING	150.00	70.00
COMMON GOLF	300.00	135.00

1 Eddie Collins 400.00 180.00
2 Paul Waner 400.00 180.00
3 Bobby Jones 500.00 220.00
4 Bill Terry 400.00 180.00
5 Earl Combs 400.00 180.00
6 Bill Dickey 400.00 180.00
7 Joe Cronin 400.00 180.00
8 Chick Hafey 300.00 135.00
9 Gene Sarazen 300.00 135.00
10 Rabbit Maranville 300.00 135.00
11 Rogers Hornsby 500.00 220.00
12 Mickey Cochrane 400.00 180.00
13 Lloyd Waner 300.00 135.00
14 Ty Cobb 1000.00 450.00
15 Gene Tunney 200.00 90.00
16 Fred Lindstrom 125000.00 56200.00
17 Al Simmons 400.00 180.00
18 Tony Lazzeri 300.00 135.00
19 Wally Berger 250.00 110.00
20 Red Ruffing 300.00 135.00
21 Chuck Klein 400.00 180.00
22 Jack Dempsey 300.00 135.00
23 Jimmie Foxx 500.00 220.00
24 Lefty O'Doul 200.00 90.00
25 Jack Sharkey 150.00 70.00
26 Lou Gehrig 1000.00 450.00
27 Lefty Grove 500.00 220.00
28 Edward Brandt 200.00 90.00
29 George Earnshaw 200.00 90.00
30 Frankie Frisch 400.00 180.00
31 Lefty Gomez 400.00 180.00
32 Babe Ruth 1200.00 550.00

1997 Upper Deck Shimano*

This six-card set features color photos of top fishermen on a background of fish images with side and bottom aqua borders. The backs carry a smaller head photo and information about the pictured fisherman.

	MINT	NRMT
COMPLETE SET (6)	4.00	1.80

1 Bob Izumi .10 .05
2 Jimmy Houston .50 .23
3 Jose Wejebe .10 .05
4 Larry Dahlberg .10 .05
5 Jay Buhner 1.00 .45
6 Tony Gwynn 3.00 1.35

1999 Upper Deck PowerDeck Athletes of the Century *

These CD-Rom cards featuring four of the most prominent athletes of the 20th century were issued by Upper Deck in one boxed set. The cards are inserted into a computer and display various highlights of the player's career and his stats and other information.

	MINT	NRMT
COMPLETE SET (4)	20.00	9.00

1 Babe Ruth 8.00 3.60
2 Michael Jordan 8.00 3.60
3 Joe Montana 6.00 2.70
4 Wayne Gretzky 4.00 1.80

2000 Upper Deck Hawaii *

These cards were issued by Upper Deck and given away at the Kit Young annual conference in Hawaii in 2000. These cards feature autographs of four athletes Upper Deck brought over to the conference. Each player signed a card serial numbered to 500. The card featuring all four players signed was not included in the factory set, but 100 cards featuring all four players were also signed and distributed. Two Kit Young cards were also included with the factory sets.

MINT NRMT
COMPLETE SET (6) 400.00 180.00
DR Julius Erving AU 150.00 70.00
GH Gordie Howe AU 100.00 45.00
JN Joe Namath AU 100.00 45.00
TS Tom Seaver AU 50.00 22.00
GAU Julius Erving AU 500.00 220.00
Gordie Howe AU
Joe Namath AU
Tom Seaver AU
Numbered to 100
KYA Kit Young AU 25.00 11.00
KYJH Kit Young GJ 10.00 4.50
Distibuted in Hawaii
KYJN Kit Young GJ 10.00 4.50
Distributed at the National Sports Card Convention

1928 W512 *

This set, referenced by the catalog designation W512, measures approximately 1 3/16" by 2 3/16". The cards are blank backed and the set includes most of the athletes that made the 1920s "The Golden Age of Sports," Babe Ruth, Bill Tilden, Johnny Weismuller, Walter Hagen, and Jack Dempsey. The cards are thought to have been issued about 1928. The set is sometimes titled as "Athletes, Aviators, Movie Stars and Boxers."

EX-MT VG-E
COMPLETE SET (50) 375.00 170.00
1 Dave Bancroft 15.00 6.75
2 Grover Alexander 30.00 13.50
3 Ty Cobb 60.00 27.00
4 Tris Speaker 30.00 13.50
5 Glenn Wright 8.00 3.60
6 Babe Ruth 120.00 55.00
7 Everett Scott 10.00 4.50
8 Frank Frisch 15.00 6.75
9 Rogers Hornsby 30.00 13.50
10 Dazzy Vance 15.00 6.75
31 Gladys Robinson 6.00 2.70
32 Lt. R.L. Maugham 6.00 2.70
33 Helen Wills 8.00 3.60
34 Jack Wardle 6.00 2.70
35 Clarence DeMar 6.00 2.70
36 Bill Tilden 10.00 4.50
37 Helen Wainright 6.00 2.70
38 Johnny Weismuller 12.00 5.50
39 Walter Hagen 8.00 3.60
40 Aileen Riggin 6.00 2.70
41 Jack Dempsey 12.00 5.50
42 Pancho Villa 12.00 5.50
43 Johnny Dundee 6.00 2.70
44 Gene Tunney 12.00 5.50
45 Mickey Walker 8.00 3.60
46 Luis Firpo 8.00 3.60
47 Geo. Carpentier 8.00 3.60
48 Benny Leonard 10.00 4.50
49 Abe Goldstein 8.00 3.60
50 Charley Ledoux 8.00 3.60

1928 W513 *

This set, referenced by the catalog designation W513, continues the numbering sequence started with W512. This set contains drawings and the cards which measure approximately 1 3/16" by 2 3/16" are blank backed. The most famous athletes outside the baseball players are Jack Sharkey, the heavyweight champion and Rene LaCoste, the famed tennis player and entrepeneur. The cards are thought to have been issued about 1928. The set is sometimes titled as "Athletes, Aviators, Movie Stars and Boxers."

EX-MT VG-E
COMPLETE SET (42) 4500.00 2000.00
61 Eddie Roush 20.00 9.00
62 Waite Hoyt 20.00 9.00
63 Gink Hundrick 10.00 4.50
64 Jumbo Elliott 10.00 4.50
65 John Miljus 10.00 4.50
66 Jumping Joe Dugan 10.00 4.50
67 Smiling Bill Terry 20.00 9.00
68 Herb Pennock 20.00 9.00
69 Rube Benton 10.00 4.50
70 Paul Waner 20.00 9.00
71 Adolfo Luque 10.00 4.50
72 Burleigh Grimes 20.00 9.00
73 Lloyd Waner 20.00 9.00
74 Hack Wilson 20.00 9.00
75 Hal Carlson 10.00 4.50
76 L. Grantham 10.00 4.50
77 Wilcey Moore 10.00 4.50
78 Jess Haines 20.00 9.00
79 Tony Lazzeri 20.00 9.00
80 Al De Vormer 10.00 4.50
81 Joe Harris 10.00 4.50
82 Pie Traynor 20.00 9.00
83 Mark Koenig 10.00 4.50
84 Babe Herman 12.00 5.50
85 George Harper 10.00 4.50
86 Earl Combs 20.00 9.00
87 Jack Sharkey 10.00 4.50
88 Paolino Uzcudun 8.00 3.60
89 Tom Heeney 8.00 3.60
90 Jack Delaney 8.00 3.60
91 Billy (Young) Stribling 8.00 3.60
92 Babe Herman 8.00 3.60
93 Phil Scott 8.00 3.60
94 Benny Touchstone 8.00 3.60
95 Sammy Mandell 8.00 3.60
96 Fedel La Barbra 8.00 3.60
97 Tony Canzoneri 10.00 4.50
98 Louis Kid Kaplan 8.00 3.60
99 Charlie Phil Rosenberg 8.00 3.60
100 Rene LaCoste 10.00 4.50

1928 W560 Playing Cards *

Cards in this set feature athletes from baseball and college football, along with a host of other sports and non-sports. The cards were issued in strips and follow a standard playing card design. Quite a few Joker cards were produced. We've numbered the cards below according to the suit and playing card number (face cards were assigned numbers as well). It is thought there were at least two different printings of 88-cards and that the baseball and football players were added in the second printing replacing other subjects. All are baseball players below unless otherwise noted. Many cards were printed in a single color red or single color black scheme (noted below as S) and a black/red dual color scheme (noted below as D), thereby creating two versions. The known variations are listed after the player's name. The set, with all variations, contains 128-different cards with 88-different photos/subjects. It is thought that the two-color cards are slightly tougher to find than the single color version.

EX-MT VG-E
COMPLETE SET (128) 2200.00 1000.00
C1 Kiki Cuyler D, S 40.00 18.00
C2A Fred McGuire S 8.00 3.60
C2B Walter Hagen D 25.00 11.00
(Golfer)
C3 Lou Gehrig D, S 250.00 110.00
C4 Max Bishop D, S 8.00 3.60
C5 Jim Bottomley D, S 25.00 11.00
C6A Buddy Myer S 8.00 3.60
C6B Monte Blue D 8.00 3.60
(Actor)
C7 Taylor Douthit D, S 8.00 3.60
C8A Bill Sherdel S 8.00 3.60
C8B Roger Williams D 8.00 3.60
(Aviator)
C9 Remy Kremer D, S 8.00 3.60
C10 Goose Goslin D, S 25.00 11.00
C11 Al Simmons D, S 50.00 22.00
C12A Vic Aldridge S 8.00 3.60
C12B Janet Gaynor D 8.00 3.60
(Actress)
C13 Lefty Grove D, S 60.00 27.00
D1A Dutch Loud S 8.00 3.60
(Yale football)
D1B Johnny Weismuller D 50.00 22.00
(Swimmer)
D2A Chris Cagle S 15.00 6.75
(Army football)
D2B Helen Willis D 25.00 11.00
(Tennis)
D3 Paul Waner D, S 40.00 18.00
D4A Benny Leonard S 40.00 18.00
(Boxer)
D4B Wilmer Allison D 8.00 3.60
(Tennis)
D5A George Uhle S 8.00 3.60
D5B Gene Tunney D 40.00 18.00
(Boxer)
D6 Tom Henney D, S 15.00 6.75
(Wrestler)
D7A Jack Delaney S 25.00 11.00
(Boxer)
D7B Bobby Jones D 60.00 27.00
(Golfer)
D8 Fred Lindstrom D, S 25.00 11.00
D9 Larry Benton D, S 8.00 3.60
D10A D.A. Lowry S 8.00 3.60
(misspelled Lowery)
(Princeton football)
D10B Tommy Hitchcock D 15.00 6.75
(Polo)
D11A Cy Williams S 8.00 3.60
D11B John Von Ryn D 15.00 6.75
(Tennis)
D12 Lloyd Waner D, S 25.00 11.00
D13 Fred Fitzsimmons D, S 15.00 6.75
H1 Watty Clark D, S 8.00 3.60
H2 Hugh Critz D, S 8.00 3.60
H3A Willie Kamm S 8.00 3.60
H3B Dolores Del Rio D 15.00 6.75
(Actress)
H4 Rogers Hornsby D, S 75.00 34.00
H5 Luke Sewell D, S 8.00 3.60
H6A B.T. Dumont S 8.00 3.60
(Colgate football)
H6B Tommy Loughran D 25.00 11.00
(Boxer)
H7 Babe Herman D, S 15.00 6.75
H8 Cl. Chamberlain D, S 8.00 3.60
(Aviator)
H9A Al Lassman S 8.00 3.60
(NYU football)
H9B Charles Ray D 8.00 3.60
(Actor)
H10 Sam Gray D, S 8.00 3.60
H11 Waite Hoyt D, S 25.00 11.00
H12A M.E. Sprague S 8.00 3.60
(Army football)
H12B Mary Brian D 8.00 3.60
(Actress)
H13 Andy Cohen D, S 8.00 3.60
S1A Glen Wright S 8.00 3.60
S1B Jean Assolant D 8.00 3.60
(Aviator)
S2 Walter Johnson D, S 100.00 45.00
S3A Flint Rhem S 8.00 3.60
S3B Jack Sharkey D 40.00 18.00
(Boxer)
S4A George Pipgras S 8.00 3.60
S4B Lewis Yancey D 8.00 3.60
(Aviator)
S5 Jim Wilson D, S 8.00 3.60
S6 Dazzy Vance D, S 40.00 18.00
S7A Max Schmeling D 60.00 27.00
(Boxer)
S7A Fred Marberry S 8.00 3.60
S8 Thomas Thevenow D, S 8.00 3.60
S9 Fresno Thompson D, S 8.00 3.60
S10 Jesse Haines D, S 25.00 11.00
S11 Guy Bush D, S 8.00 3.60
S12A Johnny Mostil S 8.00 3.60
S12B Dolores Costello D 15.00 6.75
(Actress)
S13 Del Bissonette D, S 8.00 3.60
JOK Lester Bell S 8.00 3.60
JOK Richard Byrd D, S 8.00 3.60
(Explorer)
JOK Mickey Cochrane D, S 40.00 18.00
JOK Jack Dempsey D, S 150.00 70.00
(Boxer)
JOK Dr. Eckener D 8.00 3.60
(Aviator)
JOK Charles Farrell D, S 8.00 3.60
(Actor)
JOK Jimmie Foxx D, S 125.00 55.00
JOK Hoot Gibson D 25.00 11.00
(Cowboy)
JOK Dale Jackson D 8.00 3.60
(Aviator)
JOK Henry Johnson S 8.00 3.60
JOK Charles Lindberg D, S 100.00 45.00
(Aviator)
JOK Forrest O'Brien D 8.00 3.60
(Aviator)
JOK Herb Pennock D, S 15.00 6.75
JOK Babe Ruth D, S 300.00 135.00
JOK Ken Strong D 40.00 18.00
(NYU Football)
JOK Rube Walberg S 8.00 3.60

1940 Wheaties M4 *

This set is referred to as the "Champs in the USA" The cards measure about 6" 8 1'4" and are numbered. The drawing portion (inside the dotted lines) measures approximately 6" X 6". There is a Baseball player on each card and they are joined by football players, football coaches, race car drivers, airline pilots, a circus clown, ice skater, hockey star and golfers. Each athlete appears in what looks like a stamp with a serrated edge. The stamps appear one above the other with a brief block of copy describing his or her achievements. There appears to have been three printings, resulting in some variation panels. The full panels tell the cereal buyer to look for either 27, 39, or 63 champ stamps. The first nine panels apparently were printed more than once, since all the unknown variations occur with those numbers.

EX-MT VG-E
COMPLETE SET (20) 800.00 350.00
1A Charles "Red" Ruffing 80.00 36.00
Lynn Patrick
Bob Feller
(27 stamp series)
1B Charles "Red" Ruffing 50.00 22.00
Lynn Patrick
Leo Durocher
(39 stamp series)
2A Joe DiMaggio 200.00 90.00
Hank Greenberg
Don Duge
(27 stamp series)
2B Joe DiMaggio 200.00 90.00
Mel Ott
Ellsworth Vines
(39 stamp series)
3 Jimmie Foxx 60.00 27.00
Bernie Bierman
Bill Dickey
4 Morris Arnovich 25.00 11.00
Earl "Dutch" Clark
Capt R.L. Baker
5 Joe Medwick 25.00 11.00
Matty Bell
Ab Jenkins
6A John Mize 25.00 11.00
Davey O'Brien
Ralph Guldahl
(27 stamp series)
6B John Mize 80.00 36.00
Bob Feller
Rudy York
(39 stamp series)
6C Gabby Hartnett 25.00 11.00
Davey O'Brien
Ralph Guldahl
(unknown series)
7A Joe Cronin 25.00 11.00
Cecil Isbell
Byron Nelson
(27 stamp series)
7B Joe Cronin 50.00 22.00
Hank Greenberg
Byron Nelson
(unknown series)
7C Paul Derringer 25.00 11.00
Cecil Isbell
Byron Nelson
(unknown series)
8A Jack Manders 25.00 11.00
Ernie Lombardi
George I. Myers
(27 stamp series)
8B Paul Derringer 25.00 11.00
Ernie Lombardi
George I. Myers
(39 stamp series)
9 Bob Bartlett 25.00 11.00
Terrell Jacobs
Captain R.C.Hanson
10 Adele Inge 25.00 11.00
Lowell "Red" Dawson
Billy Herman
11 Dolph Camilli 25.00 11.00
Antoinette Concello
Wallace Wade
12 Hugh McManus 25.00 11.00
Luke Appling
Stanley Hack
13 Felix Adler 25.00 11.00
Hal Trosky
Mabel Vinson

1941 Wheaties M5 *

This set is also referred to as "Champs of the U.S.A." These numbered cards made up the back of the Wheaties box; the whole panel measures 6" X 8 1/4" but the drawing portion (inside the dotted lines) is apparently 6" X 6". Each athlete appears in what looks like a stamp

with a serrated edge. The stamps appear one above the other with a brief block of copy describing his or her achievements. The format is the same as the previous M4 set -- even the numbering system continues where the M4 set stops.

EX-MT VG-E
COMPLETE SET (8) 350.00 160.00
14 Jimmie Foxx 50.00 22.00
Felix Adler
Capt. R.G. Hanson
15 Bernie Bierman 40.00 18.00
Bob Feller
Jessie McLeod
16 Hank Greenberg 40.00 18.00
Lowell "Red" Dawson
J.W. Stoker
17 Joe DiMaggio 200.00 90.00
Byron Nelson
Antoniette Concello
18 Pee Wee Reese 50.00 22.00
Capt. R.L. Baker
Frank "Buck" McCormick
19 W. Robbins 25.00 11.00
Gene Sarazen
20 Bucky Walters 25.00 11.00
Barney McCosky
21 Joe "Flash" Gordon 25.00 11.00
George I. Myers
Stan Hack

1951 Wheaties *

The cards in this six-card set measure approximately 2 1/2" by 3 1/4". Cards of the 1951 Wheaties set are actually the backs of small individual boxes of Wheaties. The cards are waxed and depict three baseball players, one football player, one basketball player, and one golfer. They are occasionally found as complete boxes, which are worth 50 percent more than the prices listed below. The catalog designation for this set is F272-3. The cards are blank-backed and unnumbered; they are numbered below in alphabetical order for convenience.

EX-MT VG-E
COMPLETE SET (6) 600.00 275.00
1 Bob Feller BB 80.00 36.00
2 Johnny Lujack FB 80.00 36.00
3 George Mikan BK 150.00 70.00
4 Stan Musial BB 120.00 55.00
5 Sam Snead 80.00 36.00
(golfer)
6 Ted Williams BB 120.00 55.00

1952 Wheaties *

The cards in this 60-card set measure 2" by 2 3/4". The 1952 Wheaties set of orange, blue and white, unnumbered cards was issued in panels of eight or ten cards on the backs of Wheaties cereal boxes. Each player appears in an action pose, designated in the checklist with an "A", and as a portrait, listed in the checklist with a "B". The catalog designation is F272-4. The cards are blank-backed and unnumbered, but have been assigned numbers below using a sport prefix (BB- baseball, BK- basketball, FB- football, OT- other).

EX-MT VG-E
COMPLETE SET (60) 1200.00 550.00
BB1A Larry (Yogi) Berra 30.00 13.50
BB1B Larry (Yogi) Berra 30.00 13.50
BB2A Roy Campanella 40.00 18.00
BB2B Roy Campanella 40.00 18.00
BB3A Bob Feller 30.00 13.50
BB3B Bob Feller 30.00 13.50
BB4A George Kell 20.00 9.00
BB4B George Kell 20.00 9.00
BB5A Ralph Kiner 20.00 9.00
BB5B Ralph Kiner 20.00 9.00
BB6A Bob Lemon 20.00 9.00
BB6B Bob Lemon 20.00 9.00
BB7A Stan Musial 60.00 27.00
BB7B Stan Musial 60.00 27.00
BB8A Phil Rizzuto 20.00 9.00
BB8B Phil Rizzuto 20.00 9.00
BB9A Elwin (Preacher) Roe 6.00 2.70
BB9B Elwin (Preacher) Roe 6.00 2.70
BB10A Ted Williams 80.00 36.00
BB10B Ted Williams 80.00 36.00
BK1A George Mikan 80.00 36.00
BK2B George Mikan 80.00 36.00
FB1A Glenn Davis 8.00 3.60
FB1B Glenn Davis 8.00 3.60
FB2A Tom Fears 8.00 3.60
FB2B Tom Fears 8.00 3.60
FB3A Otto Graham 20.00 9.00
FB3B Otto Graham 20.00 9.00
FB4A Johnny Lujack 8.00 3.60
FB4B Johnny Lujack 8.00 3.60
FB5A Doak Walker 15.00 6.75
FB5B Doak Walker 15.00 6.75
FB6A Bob Waterfield 20.00 9.00
FB6B Bob Waterfield 20.00 9.00
OT1A Alice Bauer 6.00 2.70
OT1B Alice Bauer 6.00 2.70
OT2A Marlene Bauer 6.00 2.70
OT2B Marlene Bauer 6.00 2.70
OT3A Patty Berg 6.00 2.70
OT3B Patty Berg 6.00 2.70
OT4A Bob Davies 20.00 9.00
OT4B Bob Davies 20.00 9.00
OT5A Ned Day 4.00 1.80
OT5B Ned Day 4.00 1.80
OT6A Charles Diehl 4.00 1.80
OT6B Charles Diehl 4.00 1.80
OT7A Gretchen Fraser 4.00 1.80
OT7B Gretchen Fraser 4.00 1.80
OT8A Ben Hogan 40.00 18.00
OT8B Ben Hogan 40.00 18.00
OT9A Jack Kramer 5.00 2.20
OT9B Jack Kramer 5.00 2.20
OT10A Lloyd Mangrum 15.00 6.75
OT10B Lloyd Mangrum 15.00 6.75
OT11A Jimmy Patterson 4.00 1.80
OT11B Jimmy Patterson 4.00 1.80
OT12A Jim Pollard 20.00 9.00
OT12B Jim Pollard 20.00 9.00
OT13A Sam Snead 40.00 18.00
OT13B Sam Snead 40.00 18.00

1951-53 Wisconsin Hall of Fame Postcards*

These 12 postcards were issued by the Wisconsin Hall of Fame and feature some of the leading athletes out of Milwaukee. The sepia illustrations have a relief of the player as well as some information about them. Since these cards are unnumbered, we have sequenced them in alphabetical order.

EX-MT VG-E
COMPLETE SET (12) 350.00 160.00
1 Addie Joss 60.00 27.00
2 Alvin Kraenzlein 15.00 6.75
3 Strangler Lewis 30.00 13.50
4 George McBride 15.00 6.75
5 Ralph Metcalfe 20.00 9.00
6 Ernie Nevers 80.00 36.00
7 Kid Nichols 50.00 22.00
8 Pat O'Dea 30.00 13.50
9 Dave Schreiner 15.00 6.75
10 Al Simmons 60.00 27.00
11 Billy Sullivan 20.00 9.00
12 Bob Zuppke CO 40.00 18.00

1993 World University Games*

This 10-card set features borderless photos of various sporting events at the World University Games in Buffalo in 1993. The backs display two different ways the collector could win prizes in two different scratch-off games. The cards are unnumbered and checklisted below alphabetically according to the sport pictured on the card front.

MINT NRMT
COMPLETE SET (10) 3.00 1.35
1 Baseball 1.00 .45
Charles Johnson batting
2 Basketball .25 .11
3 Gymnastics .25 .11
4 Pilot Field .25 .11
5 Rich Stadium .25 .11
6 Rowing .25 .11
7 Soccer .25 .11
8 Swimming .25 .11
9 Tennis .25 .11
10 Track and Field .25 .11

1992 Classic World Class Athletes *

Packaged in a high impact clam shell, this 60-card standard-size set features current and past world class athletes. The production run was 295,000 sets, and an enclosed certificate of limited edition carries the set serial number. A few athletes had autographs randomly inserted into the factory sets. We have noted those cards at the end of our checklist

MINT NRMT
COMP.FACT SET (60) 4.00 1.80
1 Carl Lewis .25 .11
Track and Field
2 Larry Bird BK .50 .23
3 Jennifer Capriati .50 .23
Tennis
4 Matt Biondi .15 .07
Swimming
5 Tom Jager .05 .02
Swimming
6 Janet Evans .20 .09
Swimming
7 Mark Spitz .25 .11
Swimming
8 Pablo Morales .05 .02
Swimming
9 Mike Barrowman .05 .02
Swimming
10 Anita Nall .05 .02
Swimming
11 Kent Ferguson .05 .02
Diving
12 Wendy Lucero-Schayes .20 .09
Diving
13 Wendy Lian Williams .20 .09
Diving
14 Leroy Burrell .05 .02
Track and Field
15 Michael Johnson .50 .23
Track and Field
16 Mike Powell .15 .07
Track and Field

Card		
17 Mark Lenzi	.05	.02
Diving		
18 Al Joyner	.15	.07
Track and Field		
19 Dave Johnson	.15	.07
Track and Field		
20 Jackie Joyner-Kersee	.30	.14
Track and Field		
21 Craig Wilson	.05	.02
Water Polo		
22 Florence Joyner	.30	.14
Track and Field		
23 Gwen Torrence	.20	.09
Track and Field		
24 Matt Scoggin	.05	.02
Diving		
25 Kim Zmeskal	.25	.11
Gymnastics		
26 Betty Okino	.05	.02
Gymnastics		
27 Nadia Comaneci	.25	.11
Gymnastics		
28 Bela Karolyi	.15	.07
Gymnastics		
29 Bart Conner	.15	.07
Gymnastics		
30 Chris Waller	.05	.02
Gymnastics		
31 Caren Kemner	.20	.09
Volleyball		
32 Steve Timmons	.25	.11
Volleyball		
33 Scott Fortune	.15	.07
Volleyball		
34 Muhammad Ali	2.00	.90
Boxing		
35 Bob Ctvrtlik	.05	.02
Volleyball		
36 Michael Chang	.25	.11
Tennis		
37 Pete Sampras	.50	.23
Tennis		
38 Mary Joe Fernandez	.25	.11
Tennis		
39 Norman Bellingham	.05	.02
Kayak		
40 Greg Barton	.05	.02
Kayak		
41 Oscar De La Hoya	1.00	.45
Boxing		
42 Tim Austin	.20	.09
Boxing		
43 Eric Griffin	.20	.09
Boxing		
44 Ivan Robinson	.20	.09
Boxing		
45 Jim Abbott BB	.15	.07
46 Jim Courier	.20	.09
Tennis		
47 Jennifer Azzi BK	.25	.11
48 Katrina McClain BK	.25	.11
49 Scottie Pippen BK	.50	.23
50 John Stockton BK	.25	.11
51 Patrick Ewing BK	.25	.11
52 Charles Barkley BK	.50	.23
53 Dan O'Brien	.20	.09
Track and Field		
54 Melvin Stewart	.05	.02
Swimming		
55 Desmond Howard FB	.15	.07
56 Raghib Ismail FB	.15	.07
57 Deion Sanders BB/FB	.25	.11
58 Carl Lewis	.15	.07
Life in the Fast Lane		
59 Pete Sampras	.25	.11
Pistol Pete		
60 Dave Johnson	.15	.07
Dan O'Brien		
To Be Settled		
AU3 Jennifer Capriati	30.00	13.50
Certified Autograph		
AU34 Muhammad Ali	100.00	45.00
Certified Autograph		
AU37 Pete Sampras	30.00	13.50
Certified Autograph		

1996 Upper Deck U.S. Olympic *

This multisport product was issued in June 1996, prior to the Centennial Olympic Games in Atlanta. Packs of 10 standard-size cards had a suggested retail price of $1.99. The set contains the following subsets: U.S. Olympic Moments (1-90), Future Champions (91-120) and Passing the Torch (121-135).

	MINT	NRMT
COMPLETE SET (135)	15.00	6.75
1 Matt Biondi	.15	.07
2 Janet Evans	.25	.11
3 Mark Spitz	.25	.11
4 Johnny Weismuller	.15	.07
5 Pablo Morales	.10	.05
6 Shirley Babashoff	.10	.05
7 Summer Sanders	.25	.11
8 Mary T. Meagher	.10	.05
9 Tracie Caulkins	.10	.05
10 John Naber	.10	.05
11 Michael Jordan	3.00	1.35
12 Larry Bird	1.00	.45
13 Teresa Edwards	.50	.23
14 Launi Meili	.05	.02
15 Ralph Boston	.10	.05
16 Floyd Patterson	.25	.11
17 Evander Holyfield	1.50	.70
18 Gwen Torrence	.25	.11
19 Alice Coachman	.05	.02
20 James Connolly	.05	.02
21 Mike Powell	.25	.11
22 Willie Banks	.05	.02
23 Valerie Brisco	.05	.02
24 Mike Conley	.10	.05
25 Jesse Owens	.25	.11
26 Bob Hayes	.15	.07
27 Wilma Rudolph	.25	.11
28 Bob Beamon	.15	.07
29 Babe Didrikson	.25	.11
30 Bobby Joe Morrow	.05	.02
31 Evelyn Ashford	.15	.07
32 Roger Kingdom	.15	.07
33 Betty Robinson	.05	.02
34 Al Oerter	.10	.05
35 Dick Fosbury	.10	.05
36 Denise Parker	.05	.02
37 Billy Mills	.10	.05
38 Joan Benoit-Samuelson	.10	.05
39 Frank Shorter	.10	.05
40 Bill Toomey	.10	.05
41 Bob Mathias	.15	.07
42 Rafer Johnson	.25	.11
43 Bruce Jenner	.25	.11
44 George Patton	.50	.23
45 Mary Lou Retton	.50	.23
46 Shannon Miller	.75	.35
47 Bart Conner	.25	.11
48 Mitch Gaylord	.15	.07
49 Kurt Thomas	.15	.07
50 Peter Vidmar	.10	.05
51 Will Clark	.50	.23
52 Jim Abbott	.15	.07
53 Karch Kiraly	.50	.23
54 Steve Timmons	.25	.11
55 Cobi Jones	.50	.23
56 Alexi Lalas	.50	.23
57 Greg Barton	.05	.02
58 John Michael Plumb	.05	.02
59 Terry Schroeder	.05	.02
60 Bruce Baumgartner	.10	.05
61 Dan Gable	.25	.11
62 Jeff Blatnik	.05	.02
63 Greg Louganis	.50	.23
64 Dr. Sammy Lee	.10	.05
65 Pat McCormick	.10	.05
66 Tracie Ruiz-Conforto	.15	.07
67 Peter Westbrook	.05	.02
68 Jim Craig	.25	.11
69 Mike Eruzione	.50	.23
70 Peggy Fleming	.50	.23
71 Kristi Yamaguchi	.75	.35
72 Nancy Kerrigan	.50	.23
73 Dick Button	.15	.07
74 Scott Hamilton	.25	.11
75 Rowdy Gaines	.10	.05
76 Eric Heiden	.15	.07
77 Eric Flaim	.05	.02
78 Dan Jansen	.25	.11
79 Bonnie Blair	.50	.23
80 Andrea Mead-Lawrence	.05	.02
81 Billy Kidd	.10	.05
82 Bill Johnson	.10	.05
83 Tommy Moe	.10	.05
84 Phil Mahre	.10	.05
85 Hilary Lindh	.05	.02
86 Mary Ellen Clark	.05	.02
87 Duncan Kennedy	.15	.07
88 Donna Weinbrecht	.10	.05
89 Bill Koch	.10	.05
90 Donna de Varona	.15	.07
91 Matt Ghaffari	.05	.02
92 Dominique Dawes	.75	.35
93 Anfernee Hardaway	.75	.35
94 Mark Crear	.10	.05
95 Jason Morris	.05	.02
96 Lisa Fernandez	.25	.11
97 Michael Gostigian	.05	.02
98 Wes Barnett	.05	.02
99 Chanda Rubin	.15	.07
100 Todd Martin	.10	.05
101 Jim Butler	.05	.02
102 Ned Overend	.05	.02
103 Fernando Vargas	1.00	.45
104 Mark Henry	.15	.07
105 Michael Johnson	1.00	.45
106 Sharon Monplaisir	.05	.02
107 Allen Johnson	.10	.05
108 Dan O'Brien	.25	.11
109 John Godina	.05	.02
110 Kim Batten	.05	.02
111 Derrick Adkins	.05	.02
112 Mia Hamm	1.50	.70
113 Marty Nothstein	.05	.02
114 Kevin Han	.05	.02
115 Eric Wunderlich	.05	.02
116 David Fox	.05	.02
117 Tripp Schwenk	.05	.02
118 Amy Van Dyken	.25	.11
119 Tracey Fuchs	.05	.02
120 Tami Jameson	.05	.02
121 Bob Beamon	.10	.05
Mike Powell		
122 Bill Johnson	.10	.05
Tommy Moe		
123 Jesse Owens	.50	.23
Michael Johnson		
124 Bruce Jenner	.15	.07
Dan O'Brien		
125 Peggy Fleming	.40	.18
Kristi Yamaguchi		
126 Eric Heiden	.15	.07
Bonnie Blair		
127 Dick Button	.15	.07
Scott Hamilton		
128 Al Oerter	.10	.05
Al Oerter		
129 Floyd Patterson	.75	.35
Evander Holyfield		
130 Mark Spitz	.10	.05
Matt Biondi		
131 Sammy Lee	.15	.07
Greg Louganis		
132 Wilma Rudolph	.15	.07
Gwen Torrence		
133 George Patton	.15	.07
Michael Gostigian		
134 Michael Jordan	1.50	.70
Anfernee Hardaway		
135 Mary Lou Retton	.40	.18
Shannon Miller		

MEMORABILIA

1967 Coke Caps All-Stars

These 1967 Coke caps were found on bottles of Coke, Tab, Sprite, and Fresca and were distributed in areas of the country without major league baseball teams. Collector sheets held 35 caps and could then redeemed at a Thom McAn Shoe Store for six autographed All-Star photos. Five collections could be redeemed for an Official Little League baseball. The caps measure about 1" in diameter and feature player head shots. The caps are numbered and checklisted below.

	NM	Ex
COMPLETE SET (35)	140.00	55.00
1 Richie Allen	4.00	1.60
2 Pete Rose	10.00	4.00
3 Brooks Robinson	8.00	3.20
4 Marcelino Lopez	2.00	.80
5 Rusty Staub	3.00	1.20
6 Ron Santo	5.00	2.00
7 Jim Nash	2.00	.80
8 Jim Fregosi	3.00	1.20
9 Paul Casanova	2.00	.80
10 Willie Mays	12.00	4.80
11 Willie Stargell	8.00	3.20
12 Tony Oliva	5.00	2.00
13 Joe Pepitone	3.00	1.20
14 Juan Marichal	8.00	3.20
15 Jim Bunning	8.00	3.20
16 Claude Osteen	2.00	.80
17 Carl Yastrzemski	8.00	3.20
18 Harmon Killebrew	8.00	3.20
19 Henry Aaron	12.00	4.80
20 Joe Torre	4.00	1.60
21 Ernie Banks	8.00	3.20
22 Al Kaline	8.00	3.20
23 Frank Robinson	8.00	3.20
24 Max Alvis	2.00	.80
25 Elston Howard	4.00	1.60
26 Gaylord Perry	6.00	2.40
27 Bill Mazeroski	6.00	2.40
28 Ron Swoboda	2.00	.80
29 Vada Pinson	3.00	1.20
30 Joe Morgan	8.00	3.20
31 Cleon Jones	2.00	.80
32 Willie Horton	2.00	.80
33 Leon Wagner	2.00	.80
34 George Scott	3.00	1.20
35 Ed Charles	2.00	.80

1967 Coke Caps All-Stars AL

These caps, measuring approximately 1" in diameter feature leading American League players. They were issued in cities which had American league teams. These caps were available on bottles of Coke, Fresca, Sprite and Tab. The caps have an "A" prefix.

	NM	Ex
COMPLETE SET (17)	50.00	20.00
19 Al Kaline	8.00	3.20
20 Frank Howard	3.00	1.20
21 Brooks Robinson	8.00	3.20
22 George Scott	2.00	.80
23 Willie Horton	2.00	.80
24 Jim Fregosi	3.00	1.20
25 Ed Charles	2.00	.80
26 Harmon Killebrew	8.00	3.20
27 Tony Oliva	5.00	2.00
28 Joe Pepitone	3.00	1.20
29 Elston Howard	4.00	1.60
30 Jim Nash	2.00	.80
31 Marcelino Lopez	2.00	.80
32 Frank Robinson	8.00	3.20
33 Leon Wagner	2.00	.80
34 Max Alvis	2.00	.80
35 Paul Casanova	2.00	.80

1967 Coke Caps All-Stars NL

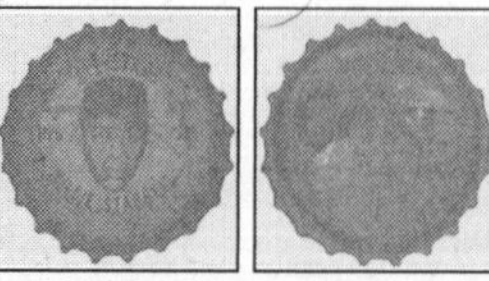

These caps feature leading National League players. They have an "N" prefix and were on Coke, Tab, Sprite and Fresca bottles. These caps were released in National League cities.

	NM	Ex
COMPLETE SET (17)	65.00	26.00
19 Hank Aaron	12.00	4.80
20 Jim Bunning	8.00	3.20
21 Joe Torre	5.00	2.00
22 Claude Osteen	2.00	.80
23 Ron Santo	5.00	2.00
24 Joe Morgan	8.00	3.20
25 Richie Allen	4.00	1.60
26 Ron Swoboda	2.00	.80
27 Ernie Banks	8.00	3.20
28 Bill Mazeroski	6.00	2.40
29 Willie Stargell	8.00	3.20
30 Pete Rose	10.00	4.00
31 Gaylord Perry	6.00	2.40
32 Rusty Staub	4.00	1.60
33 Vada Pinson	3.00	1.20
34 Juan Marichal	8.00	3.20
35 Cleon Jones	2.00	.80

1967 Coke Caps Astros

The caps, measuring approximately 1" in diameter, feature members of the Houston Astros. They were distributed in the Houston area. The caps have an "H" prefix.

	NM	Ex
COMPLETE SET (18)	40.00	16.00
1 Dave Giusti	2.00	.80
2 Bob Aspromonte	2.00	.80
3 Ron Davis	2.00	.80
4 Claude Raymond	2.00	.80
5 Barry Latman	2.00	.80
6 Chuck Harrison	2.00	.80
7 Bill Heath	2.00	.80
8 Sonny Jackson	2.00	.80
9 John Bateman	2.00	.80
10 Ron Brand	2.00	.80
11 Aaron Pointer	2.00	.80
12 Joe Morgan	8.00	3.20
13 Rusty Staub	5.00	2.00
14 Mike Cuellar	3.00	1.20
15 Larry Dierker	4.00	1.60
16 Dick Farrell	2.00	.80
17 Jim Landis	2.00	.80
18 Ed Mathews	6.00	2.40

1967 Coke Caps Athletics

These caps, measuring approximately 1" in diameter feature members of the Kansas City Athletics. They were distributed in the Kansas City area. The caps have a "K" prefix

	NM	Ex
COMPLETE SET (18)	35.00	14.00
1 Jim Nash	2.00	.80
2 Bert Campaneris	4.00	1.60
3 Ed Charles	2.00	.80
4 Wes Stock	2.00	.80
5 Johnny Odom	2.00	.80
6 Ozzie Chavarria	2.00	.80
7 Jack Aker	2.00	.80
8 Dick Green	2.00	.80
9 Phil Roof	2.00	.80
10 Rene Lachemann	2.00	.80
11 Mike Hershberger	2.00	.80
12 Joe Nossek	2.00	.80
13 Roger Repoz	2.00	.80
14 Chuck Dobson	2.00	.80
15 Jim Hunter	6.00	2.40
16 Lew Krausse	2.00	.80
17 Danny Cater	2.00	.80
18 Jim Gosger	2.00	.80

1967 Coke Caps Baseball Tips

These caps, show various plays made on a baseball diamond. These caps were issued in cities which didn't have a major league team.

	NM	Ex
COMPLETE SET (8)	15.00	6.00
COMMON PLAYER (19-26)	2.00	.80

1967 Coke Caps Braves

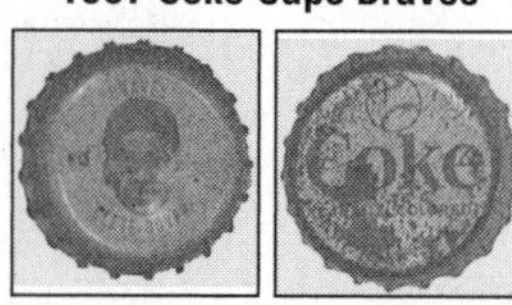

The caps, measuring approximately 1" in diameter, feature members of the Atlanta Braves. The caps were issued in the Atlanta are on bottles of Coke, Fresca, Sprite and Tab. The caps have a "B" prefix

	NM	Ex
COMPLETE SET (18)	40.00	16.00
1 Gary Geiger	2.00	.80
2 Ty Cline	2.00	.80
3 Hank Aaron	10.00	4.00
4 Gene Oliver	2.00	.80
5 Tony Cloninger	2.00	.80
6 Denis Menke	2.00	.80
7 Denny Lemaster	2.00	.80
8 Woody Woodward	2.00	.80
9 Joe Torre	5.00	2.00
10 Ken Johnson	2.00	.80
11 Bob Bruce	2.00	.80
12 Felipe Alou	4.00	1.60
13 Clete Boyer	3.00	1.20
14 Wade Blasingame	2.00	.80
15 Don Schwall	2.00	.80
16 Dick Kelley	2.00	.80
17 Rico Carty	3.00	1.20
18 Mack Jones	2.00	.80

1967 Coke Caps Cubs

These 1967 Coke caps were found on bottles of Coke, Tab, Sprite, and Fresca distributed in the Chicago area. The 35 caps could be affixed to a collector sheet and then redeemed at a Chicago area Thom McAn Shoe Store for six autographed Cubs photos. Five collections could be redeemed for an Official Little League baseball. The caps measure about 1" in diameter and feature player headshots. A baseball icon appears on each of the caps' crowns. Caps 1-18 below feature Cubs players and have "C" prefixes.

	NM	Ex
COMPLETE SET (18)	45.00	18.00
1 Fergie Jenkins	6.00	2.40
2 Ernie Banks	8.00	3.20
3 Glenn Beckert	3.00	1.20
4 Bob Hendley	2.00	.80
5 John Boccabella	2.00	.80
6 Ron Campbell	2.00	.80
7 Ray Culp	2.00	.80
8 Adolfo Phillips	2.00	.80
9 Don Bryant	2.00	.80
10 Randy Hundley	3.00	1.20
11 Ron Santo	5.00	2.00
12 Lee Thomas	2.00	.80
13 Billy Williams	6.00	2.40
14 Ken Holtzman	4.00	1.60
15 Cal Koonce	2.00	.80
16 Curt Simmons	2.00	.80
17 George Altman	3.00	1.20
18 Byron Browne	2.00	.80

1967 Coke Caps Dodgers

These 1967 caps feature members of the Los Angeles Dodgers. They measure 1" in diameter and have a "D" prefix.

	NM	Ex
COMPLETE SET (18)	35.00	14.00
1 Phil Regan	2.00	.80
2 Bob Bailey	2.00	.80
3 Ron Fairly	3.00	1.20
4 Joe Moeller	2.00	.80
5 Don Sutton	6.00	2.40
6 Ron Hunt	2.00	.80
7 Jim Brewer	2.00	.80
8 Lou Johnson	2.00	.80
9 John Roseboro	3.00	1.20
10 Jeff Torborg	3.00	1.20
11 John Kennedy	2.00	.80
12 Jim Lefebvre	2.00	.80
13 Wes Parker	3.00	1.20
14 Bob Miller	2.00	.80
15 Claude Osteen	2.00	.80
16 Ron Perranoski	2.00	.80
17 Willie Davis	3.00	1.20
18 Al Ferrara	2.00	.80

1967 Coke Caps Dodgers/Angels

These caps feature both members of the Los Angeles Dodgers and the California Angels. The caps, which measure approximately 1" in diameter, were issued in bottles of Coke, Fresca, Sprite and Tab. These caps have an "L" prefix.

	NM	Ex
COMPLETE SET (35)	65.00	26.00
1 Phil Regan	2.00	.80
2 Bob Bailey	2.00	.80
3 Ron Fairly	3.00	1.20
4 Joe Moeller	2.00	.80
5 Don Sutton	6.00	2.40
6 Ron Hunt	2.00	.80
7 Jim Brewer	2.00	.80
8 Lou Johnson	2.00	.80
9 John Roseboro	3.00	1.20
10 Jeff Torborg	2.00	.80
11 John Kennedy	2.00	.80
12 Jim Lefebvre	2.00	.80
13 Wes Parker	3.00	1.20
14 Bob Miller	2.00	.80
15 Claude Osteen	2.00	.80
16 Ron Perranoski	2.00	.80
17 Willie Davis	3.00	1.20
18 Al Ferrara	2.00	.04
19 Len Gabrielson	2.00	.80
20 Jackie Hernandez	2.00	.80
21 Paul Schaal	2.00	.80
22 Lou Burdette	3.00	1.20
23 Jimmie Hall	2.00	.80
24 Fred Newman	2.00	.80
25 Don Mincher	2.00	.80
26 Bob Rodgers	2.00	.80
27 Jack Sanford	2.00	.80
28 Bobby Knoop	2.00	.80
29 Jose Cardenal	2.00	.80
30 Jim Fregosi	3.00	1.20
31 George Brunet	2.00	.80
32 Marcelino Lopez	2.00	.80
33 Minnie Rojas	2.00	.80
34 Jay Johnstone	3.00	1.20
35 Ed Kirkpatrick	2.00	.80

1967 Coke Caps Giants

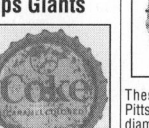

These caps featuring members of the San Francisco Giants were issued in the Bay area. The caps have a "G" prefix and measure approximately 1" in diameter.

	NM	Ex
COMPLETE SET (18)	50.00	20.00
1 Bob Bolin	2.00	.80
2 Ollie Brown	2.00	.80
3 Jim Davenport	2.00	.80
4 Tito Fuentes	2.00	.80
5 Norm Siebern	2.00	.80
6 Jim Hart	2.00	.80
7 Juan Marichal	6.00	2.40
8 Hal Lanier	2.00	.80
9 Tom Haller	2.00	.80
10 Bob Barton	2.00	.80
11 Willie McCovey	6.00	2.40
12 Mike McCormick	3.00	1.20
13 Frank Linzy	2.00	.80
14 Ray Sadecki	2.00	.80
15 Gaylord Perry	6.00	2.40
16 Lindy McDaniel	2.00	.80
17 Willie Mays	12.00	4.80
18 Jesus Alou	2.00	.80

1967 Coke Caps Indians

These caps feature members of the Cleveland Indians. They measure approximately 1" in diameter. The caps which were included on Coke, Tab, Sprite and Fresca boxes have an "I" prefix.

	NM	Ex
COMPLETE SET (18)	35.00	14.00
1 Luis Tiant	4.00	1.60
2 Max Alvis	2.00	.80
3 Larry Brown	2.00	.80
4 Rocky Colavito	5.00	2.00
5 John O'Donoghue	2.00	.80
6 Pedro Gonzalez	2.00	.80
7 Gary Bell	2.00	.80
8 Sonny Siebert	2.00	.80
9 Joe Azcue	2.00	.80
10 Lee Maye	2.00	.80
11 Chico Salmon	2.00	.80
12 Leon Wagner	2.00	.80
13 Fred Whitfield	2.00	.80
14 Jack Kralick	2.00	.80
15 Sam McDowell	3.00	1.20
16 Dick Radatz	2.00	.80
17 Vic Davalillo	2.00	.80
18 Chuck Hinton	2.00	.80

1967 Coke Caps Orioles

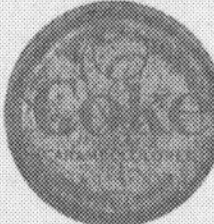

These caps feature members of the Baltimore Orioles. The caps, which measure approximatley 1" in diameter have an "O" prefix.

	NM	Ex
COMPLETE SET (18)	50.00	20.00
1 Dave McNally	3.00	1.20
2 Luis Aparicio	6.00	2.40
3 Paul Blair	2.00	.80
4 Frank Robinson	8.00	3.20
5 Jim Palmer	8.00	3.20
6 Russ Snyder	2.00	.80
7 Stu Miller	2.00	.80
8 Davey Johnson	4.00	1.60
9 Andy Etchebarren	2.00	.80
10 Brooks Robinson	8.00	3.20
11 Boog Powell	5.00	2.00
12 Sam Bowens	2.00	.80
13 Curt Blefary	2.00	.80
14 Eddie Fisher	2.00	.80
15 Wally Bunker	2.00	.80
16 Moe Drabowsky	2.00	.80
17 Larry Haney	2.00	.80
18 Tom Phoebus	2.00	.80

1967 Coke Caps Phillies

Included on bottles of Coke, Tab, Sprite and Fresca were these caps. They measured 1" in diameter, featured members of the Philadelphia Phillies and have a "P" prefix.

	NM	Ex
COMPLETE SET (18)	40.00	16.00
1 Richie Allen	5.00	2.00
2 Bob Wine	2.00	.80
3 John Briggs	2.00	.80
4 John Callison	4.00	1.60
5 Doug Clemens	2.00	.80
6 Dick Groat	3.00	1.20
7 Dick Ellsworth	2.00	.80
8 Phil Linz	2.00	.80
9 Clay Dalrymple	2.00	.80
10 Bob Uecker	5.00	2.00
11 Cookie Rojas	2.00	.80
12 Tony Taylor	3.00	1.20
13 Bill White	4.00	1.60
14 Larry Jackson	3.00	1.20
15 Chris Short	2.00	.80
16 Jim Bunning	6.00	2.40
17 Tony Gonzalez	2.00	.80
18 Don Lock	2.00	.80

1967 Coke Caps Pirates

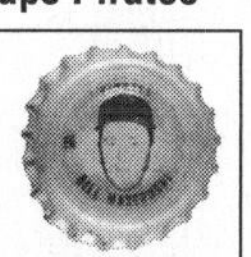

These caps portray members of the 1967 Pittsburgh Pirates. These caps measure 1" in diameter and were on Coke, Fresca, Tab and Sprite bottles. The caps have an "E" prefix.

	NM	Ex
COMPLETE SET (18)	50.00	20.00
1 Al McBean	2.00	.80
2 Gene Alley	2.00	.80
3 Donn Clendenon	2.00	.80
4 Bob Veale	2.00	.80
5 Pete Mikkelsen	2.00	.80
6 Bill Mazeroski	6.00	2.40
7 Steve Blass	2.00	.80
8 Manny Mota	3.00	1.20
9 Jim Pagliaroni	2.00	.80
10 Jesse Gonder	2.00	.80
11 Jose Pagan	2.00	.80
12 Willie Stargell	6.00	2.40
13 Maury Wills	4.00	1.60
14 Roy Face	3.00	1.20
15 Woodie Fryman	2.00	.80
16 Vernon Law	3.00	1.20
17 Matty Alou	3.00	1.20
18 Roberto Clemente	12.00	4.80

1967 Coke Caps Red Sox

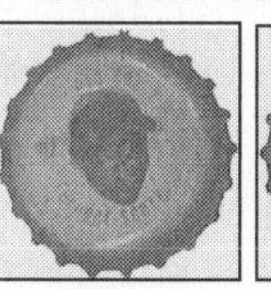

These caps, issued in various Coke products, featured members of the Boston Red Sox. The caps measure approximately 1" in diameter and have an "R" prefix.

	NM	Ex
COMPLETE SET (18)	35.00	14.00
1 Lee Stange	2.00	.80
2 Carl Yastrzemski	10.00	4.00
3 Don Demeter	2.00	.80
4 Jose Santiago	2.00	.80
5 Darrell Brandon	2.00	.80
6 Joe Foy	2.00	.80
7 Don McMahon	2.00	.80
8 Dalton Jones	2.00	.80
9 Mike Ryan	2.00	.80
10 Bob Tillman	2.00	.80
11 Rico Petrocelli	3.00	1.20
12 George Scott	3.00	1.20
13 George Smith	2.00	.80
14 Dennis Bennett	2.00	.80
15 Hank Fischer	2.00	.80
16 Jim Lonborg	3.00	1.20
17 Jose Tartabull	2.00	.80
18 George Thomas	2.00	.80

1967 Coke Caps Reds

These caps feature members of the Cincinnati Reds. They were issued in various Coke products, measure approximatley 1" in diameter and have "F" prefixes.

	NM	Ex
COMPLETE SET (18)	45.00	18.00
1 Milt Pappas	3.00	1.20
2 Leo Cardenas	3.00	1.20
3 Gordy Coleman	2.00	.80
4 Tommy Harper	2.00	.80
5 Tommy Helms	3.00	1.20
6 Deron Johnson	2.00	.80
7 Jim Maloney	3.00	1.20
8 Tony Perez	6.00	2.40
9 Don Pavletich	2.00	.80
10 John Edwards	2.00	.80
11 Vada Pinson	4.00	1.60
12 Chico Ruiz	2.00	.80
13 Pete Rose	10.00	4.00
14 Bill McCool	2.00	.80
15 Joe Nuxhall	4.00	1.60
16 Floyd Robinson	2.00	.80
17 Art Shamsky	2.00	.04
18 Dick Simpson	2.00	.80

1967 Coke Caps Senators

The 1967 Washington Senators are portrayed in this set. These caps, issued on bottles of Coke, Fresca, Tab and Sprite, measure approximately 1" in diameter. The caps have an "S" prefix.

	NM	Ex
COMPLETE SET (18)	35.00	14.00
1 Bob Humphreys	2.00	.80
2 Bernie Allen	2.00	.80
3 Ed Brinkman	2.00	.80
4 Pete Richert	2.00	.80
5 Camilo Pascual	3.00	1.20
6 Frank Howard	4.00	1.60
7 Casey Cox	2.00	.80
8 Jim King	2.00	.80
9 Paul Casanova	2.00	.80
10 Dick Lines	2.00	.80
11 Dick Nen	2.00	.80
12 Ken McMullen	2.00	.80
13 Bob Saverine	2.00	.80
14 Jim Hannan	2.00	.80
15 Darold Knowles	2.00	.80
16 Phil Ortega	2.00	.80
17 Ken Harrelson	3.00	1.20
18 Fred Valentine	2.00	.80

1967 Coke Caps Tigers

These caps measure approximately 1" in diameter. Members of the 1967 Detroit Tigers are remembered in this set. The caps have an "T" prefix.

	NM	Ex
COMPLETE SET (18)	40.00	16.00
1 Larry Sherry	2.00	.80
2 Norm Cash	4.00	1.60
3 Jerry Lumpe	2.00	.80
4 Dave Wickersham	2.00	.80
5 Joe Sparma	2.00	.80
6 Dick McAuliffe	3.00	1.20
7 Fred Gladding	2.00	.80
8 Jim Northrup	3.00	1.20
9 Bill Freehan	4.00	1.60
10 Earl Wilson	2.00	.80
11 Dick Tracewski	2.00	.80
12 Don Wert	2.00	.80
13 Jake Wood	2.00	.80
14 Mickey Lolich	4.00	1.60
15 Johnny Podres	3.00	1.20
16 Bill Monbouquette	2.00	.80
17 Al Kaline	8.00	3.20
18 Willie Horton	3.00	1.20

1967 Coke Caps Twins

These 1967 Coke Caps feature members of the Minnesota Twins. The caps, which measure approximately 1" in diameter, have an "M" prefix

	NM	Ex
COMPLETE SET (18)	40.00	16.00
1 Ron Kline	2.00	.80
2 Bob Allison	3.00	1.20
3 Earl Battey	2.00	.80
4 Jim Merritt	2.00	.80
5 Jim Perry	3.00	1.20
6 Harmon Killebrew	6.00	2.40
7 Dave Boswell	2.00	.80
8 Rich Rollins	2.00	.80
9 Jerry Zimmerman	2.00	.80
10 Al Worthington	2.00	.80
11 Cesar Tovar	2.00	.80
12 Sandy Valdespino	2.00	.80
13 Zoilo Versalles	2.00	.80
14 Dean Chance	3.00	1.20
15 Jim Grant	2.00	.80
16 Jim Kaat	4.00	1.60
17 Tony Oliva	5.00	2.00
18 Andy Kosco	2.00	.80

1967 Coke Caps White Sox

These 1967 Coke caps were found on bottles of Coke, Tab, Sprite, and Fresca distributed in the Chicago area. The 35 caps could be affixed to a collector sheet and then redeemed at a Chicago area Thom McAn Shoe Store for six autographed White Sox photos. Five collections could be redeemed for an Official Little League baseball. The caps measure about 1" in diameter and feature player headshots. A baseball icon appears on each of the caps' crowns. The caps are numbered with an "L" prefix.

	NM	Ex
COMPLETE SET (18)	35.00	14.00
1 Gary Peters	3.00	1.20
2 Jerry Adair	2.00	.80
3 Al Weis	2.00	.80
4 Pete Ward	2.00	.80
5 Hoyt Wilhelm	6.00	2.40
6 Don Buford	2.00	.80
7 John Buzhardt	2.00	.80
8 Wayne Causey	2.00	.80
9 Gerry McNertney	2.00	.80
10 Ron Hansen	2.00	.80
11 Tom McCraw	2.00	.80
12 Jim O'Toole	2.00	.80
13 Bill Skowron	3.00	1.20
14 Joel Horlen	2.00	.80
15 Tommy John	4.00	.16
16 Bob Locker	2.00	.80
17 Ken Berry	2.00	.80
18 Tommie Agee	2.00	.80

1967 Coke Caps Yankees and Mets

This 35-cap set was found on bottle tops of Coca-Cola and features both the New York Yankees and the Mets. The caps display a small head picture, with the player's name, team, and position surrounding it. The first 18 caps (V1-V18) picture the Yankees, while the last (V19-V35) picture the Mets.

	NM	Ex
COMPLETE SET (35)	100.00	40.00
V1 Mel Stottlemyre	4.00	1.60
V2 Ruben Amaro	2.00	.80
V3 Jake Gibbs	2.00	.80
V4 Dooley Womack	2.00	.80
V5 Fred Talbot	2.00	.80
V6 Horace Clarke	2.00	.80
V7 Jim Bouton	4.00	1.60
V8 Mickey Mantle	25.00	10.00
V9 Elston Howard	5.00	2.00
V10 Hal Reniff	2.00	.80
V11 Charley Smith	2.00	.80
V12 Bobby Murcer	5.00	2.00
V13 Joe Pepitone	4.00	1.60
V14 Al Downing	2.00	.80
V15 Steve Hamilton	2.00	.80
V16 Fritz Peterson	2.00	.80
V17 Tom Tresh	3.00	1.20
V18 Roy White	3.00	1.20
V19 Chuck Hiller	2.00	.80
V20 Johnny Lewis	2.00	.80
V21 Ed Kranepool	3.00	1.20
V22 Al Luplow	2.00	.80
V23 Don Cardwell	2.00	.80
V24 Cleon Jones	3.00	1.20
V25 Bob Shaw	2.00	.80
V26 John Stephenson	2.00	.80
V27 Ron Swoboda	3.00	1.20
V28 Ken Boyer	4.00	1.60
V29 Ed Bressoud	2.00	.80
V30 Tommy Davis	3.00	1.20
V31 Roy McMillan	2.00	.80
V32 Jack Fisher	2.00	.80
V33 Tug McGraw	4.00	1.60
V34 Jerry Grote	3.00	1.20
V35 Jack Hamilton	2.00	.80

1968 Coke Caps Astros

These caps remember members of the 1968 Houston Astros. Issued on bottles of Coke, Tab, Fresca and Sprite, these caps measure approximately 1" in diameter. They were issued with the prefix "H".

	NM	Ex
COMPLETE SET (18)	35.00	14.00
1 Dave Giusti	2.00	.80
2 Bob Aspromonte	2.00	.80
3 Ron Davis	2.00	.80
4 Julio Gotay	2.00	.80
5 Fred Gladding	2.00	.80
6 Lee Thomas	2.00	.80
7 Wade Blasingame	2.00	.80
8 Denis Menke	2.00	.80
9 John Bateman	2.00	.80
10 Ron Brand	2.00	.80
11 Doug Rader	3.00	1.20
12 Joe Morgan	5.00	2.00
13 Rusty Staub	4.00	1.60
14 Mike Cuellar	3.00	1.20
15 Larry Dierker	4.00	1.60
16 Denny Lemaster	2.00	.80
17 Jim Wynn	4.00	1.60
18 Don Wilson	3.00	1.20

1968 Coke Caps Braves

These caps remember members of the 1968 Atlanta Braves. Issued in bottles of Coke, Tab, Fresca and Sprite, these caps measure approximately 1" in diameter. They were issued with the prefix "B".

	NM	Ex
COMPLETE SET (18)	45.00	18.00
1 Cecil Upshaw	2.00	.80
2 Tito Francona	2.00	.80
3 Henry Aaron	12.00	4.80
4 Pat Jarvis	2.00	.80
5 Tony Cloninger	2.00	.80
6 Denis Menke	2.00	.80
7 Felix Millan	2.00	.80
8 Woody Woodward	2.00	.80
9 Joe Torre	5.00	2.00
10 Ken Johnson	2.00	.80
11 Marty Martinez	2.00	.80
12 Felipe Alou	4.00	1.60
13 Clete Boyer	2.00	.80
14 Sonny Jackson	2.00	.80
15 Deron Johnson	2.00	.80
16 Dick Kelley	2.00	.80
17 Rico Carty	3.00	1.20
18 Mack Jones	2.00	.80

1968 Coke Caps Orioles

These caps, which measure approximately 1" in diameter, portray members of the Baltimore Orioles. They were issued in various Coke products and have an "O" prefix.

	NM	Ex
COMPLETE SET (18)	50.00	20.00
1 Dave McNally	3.00	1.20
2 Luis Aparicio	6.00	2.40
3 Paul Blair	2.00	.80
4 Frank Robinson	8.00	3.20
5 Jim Palmer	8.00	3.20
6 John O'Donoghue	2.00	.80
7 Dave May	2.00	.80
8 Davey Johnson	3.00	1.20
9 Andy Etchebarren	2.00	.80
10 Brooks Robinson	8.00	3.20
11 Boog Powell	4.00	1.60
12 Pete Richert	2.00	.80
13 Curt Blefary	2.00	.80
14 Mark Belanger	3.00	1.20
15 Wally Bunker	2.00	.80
16 Moe Drabowsky	2.00	.80
17 Larry Haney	2.00	.80
18 Tom Phoebus	2.00	.80

1968 Coke Caps Red Sox

These caps were issued with coke products. They feature members of the Boston Red Sox and measure approximately 1" in diameter. These caps have an "R" prefix. Carl Yastrzemski is not in this set, probably because he is in the National set.

	NM	Ex
COMPLETE SET (18)	35.00	14.00
1 Lee Stange	2.00	.80
2 Gary Waslewski	2.00	.80
3 Gary Bell	2.00	.80
4 John Wyatt	2.00	.80
5 Darrell Brandon	2.00	.80
6 Joe Foy	2.00	.80
7 Ray Culp	2.00	.80
8 Dalton Jones	2.00	.80
9 Gene Oliver	2.00	.80
10 Jose Santiago	2.00	.80
11 Rico Petrocelli	4.00	1.60
12 George Scott	3.00	1.20
13 Mike Andrews	2.00	.80
14 Dick Ellsworth	2.00	.80
15 Norm Siebern	2.00	.80
16 Jim Lonborg	4.00	1.60
17 Jerry Adair	2.00	.80
18 Elston Howard	4.00	1.60

1968 Coke Caps Tigers

Included as a premium (Cap) with various Coke products (Coke, Tab, Fresca and Sprite), these caps measure approximately 1" in diameter. They have a "T" prefix.

	NM	Ex
COMPLETE SET (18)	50.00	20.00
1 Ray Oyler	2.00	.80
2 Norm Cash	4.00	1.60
3 Mike Marshall	3.00	1.20
4 Mickey Stanley	2.00	.80
5 Joe Sparma	2.00	.80
6 Dick McAuliffe	3.00	1.20
7 Gates Brown	2.00	.80
8 Jim Northrup	3.00	1.20
9 Bill Freehan	4.00	1.60
10 Earl Wilson	2.00	.80
11 Dick Tracewski	2.00	.80
12 Don Wert	2.00	.80
13 Dennis Ribant	2.00	.80
14 Mickey Lolich	4.00	1.60
15 Denny McLain	5.00	2.00
16 Ed Mathews	6.00	2.40
17 Al Kaline	8.00	3.20
18 Willie Horton	3.00	1.20

1962 Yankees Yoo-Hoo Bottle Caps

These six caps featured members of the 1962 Yankees and had the player's photo sandwiched between the words Me For on the top and Yoo-Hoo on the bottom. These caps can be dated to 1962 by the inclusion of both Tom Tresh and Bill Skowron as that is the only season the two of them played together. Since these caps are unnumbered, we have sequenced them in alphabetical order.

	NM	Ex
COMPLETE SET (6)	400.00	160.00
1 Yogi Berra	100.00	40.00
2 Whitey Ford	100.00	40.00
3 Mickey Mantle	200.00	80.00
4 Bobby Richardson	40.00	16.00
5 Bill Skowron	30.00	12.00
6 Tom Tresh	25.00	10.00

1959 Yankees Yoo Hoo Bottle Caps

Issued as Bottle Caps for Yoo Hoo products, these caps feature members of the New York Yankees. Since these caps are unnumbered, we have sequenced them in alphabetical order.

	NM	Ex
COMPLETE SET	400.00	200.00
1 Yogi Berra	80.00	40.00
2 Whitey Ford	80.00	40.00
3 Tony Kubek	40.00	20.00
4 Mickey Mantle	150.00	75.00
5 Gil McDougald	25.00	12.50
6 Bobby Richardson	40.00	20.00
7 Bill Skowron	30.00	15.00

2000 Alaska Goldpanners Coin

This coin was given out to fans that went to the World Famous Midnight Game played on June 21, 2000 in Fairbanks, Alaska. The coin is the same size as a quarter, and is gold.

	Nm-Mt	Ex-Mt
1 Midnight Game Coin	2.00	.60

1955 Armour Coins

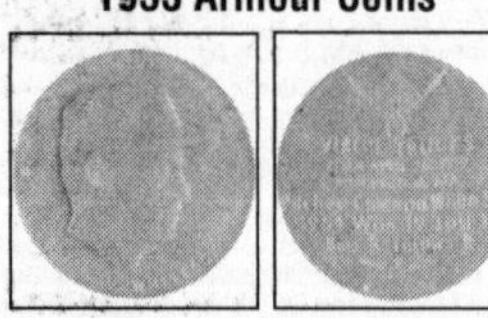

The front of each of the plastic baseball "coins" in this set contains a raised profile of a ballplayer. Each plastic coin measures approximately 1 1/2" in diameter. Although similar in design to the 1959 and 1960 issues by Armour, the 1955 set is distinguished by a number of details: the full team name under the profile, the listing of birthplace and date and batting and throwing preferences on the back and, of course, the 1954 batting or won-loss record located on the reverse. The coins are not numbered and come in colors of black, blue, blue-green, green, orange, red, yellow, tan and gold. Black, tan, and gold are the toughest color coins to find. Mantle and Kuenn exist in two variations each. These coins were inserted one per Armour Star Package of Hot Dogs. The set price below includes both variations.

	NM	Ex
COMPLETE SET (26)	600.00	300.00
1 Johnny Antonelli	10.00	5.00
2 Yogi Berra	40.00	20.00
3 Del Crandall	10.00	5.00
4 Larry Doby	20.00	10.00
5 Jim Finigan	10.00	5.00
6 Whitey Ford	30.00	15.00
7 Jim Gilliam	12.00	6.00
8 Harvey Haddix	10.00	5.00
9 Ransom Jackson	10.00	5.00
10 Jackie Jensen	12.00	6.00
11 Ted Kluszewski	15.00	7.50
12A Harvey Kuenn reg.	15.00	7.50
12B Harvey Kuenn cond.	50.00	25.00
13A Mickey Mantle ERR name spelled Mantel	125.00	60.00
13B Mickey Mantle COR	250.00	125.00
14 Don Mueller	10.00	5.00
15 Pee Wee Reese	30.00	15.00
16 Allie Reynolds	12.00	6.00
17 Al Rosen	15.00	7.50
18 Curt Simmons	10.00	5.00
19 Duke Snider	30.00	15.00
20 Warren Spahn	30.00	15.00
21 Frank Thomas	10.00	5.00
22 Virgil Trucks	10.00	5.00
23 Bob Turley	12.00	6.00
24 Mickey Vernon	10.00	5.00

1959 Armour Coins

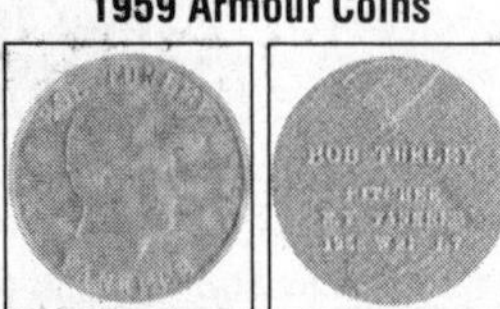

There are 20 coins in the 1959 Armour set, 10 from each league. Each coin measures 1 1/2" in diameter. In contrast to the 1955 set produced by this company, the raised profiles are not as finely detailed and the lettering is larger. In addition, the team nickname (for example, "Redlegs") is listed below the profile and the reverse does not record birth date and place or batting and throwing preferences. The coins are not numbered and are found in colors of dark and pale blue, dark and pale green, orange, red, pale yellow, pink and gray. These coins were inserted one per specially marked Armour Hot Dog packages. A collector could mail in two backboards for 10 assorted coins. It is believed that the same 10 coins were received each time. If true, this would verify the theory that some dealers believe about short printed coins. Those presumed to be shorter printed are: Antonelli, Ashburn, Banks, Crandall, Fox, Jensen, Kuenn, Podres, Thomas and Vernon.

	NM	Ex
COMPLETE SET (20)	300.00	150.00
1 Hank Aaron	60.00	30.00
2 Johnny Antonelli	10.00	5.00
3 Richie Ashburn	25.00	12.50
4 Ernie Banks	40.00	20.00
5 Don Blasingame	10.00	5.00
6 Bob Cerv	10.00	5.00
7 Del Crandall	10.00	5.00
8 Whitey Ford	40.00	20.00
9 Nellie Fox	25.00	12.50
10 Jackie Jensen	12.00	6.00
11 Harvey Kuenn	12.00	6.00
12 Frank Malzone	10.00	5.00
13 Johnny Podres	12.00	6.00
14 Frank Robinson	30.00	15.00
15 Roy Sievers	10.00	5.00
16 Bob Skinner	10.00	5.00
17 Frank Thomas	12.00	6.00
18 Gus Triandos	10.00	5.00
19 Bob Turley	12.00	6.00
20 Mickey Vernon	10.00	5.00

1960 Armour Coins

Although the 20 plastic baseball player coins produced by Armour in 1960 were identical in

style to those of the 1959 set, there was quite a turnover in personnel. Thirteen new subjects were depicted, with Aaron, Banks, Crandall, Ford, Fox, Malzone and Triandos the only returnees. The coins are the same size as the previous year, 1 1/2" in diameter. The reverse of these unnumbered coins lists the 1959 record for each individual. They are found in the following colors: two shades of blue, two shades of green, orange, red, salmon, tan and yellow. The complete set price below includes all variations. The Daley coin is regarded by serious Armour collectors as being quite scarce and has only been seen in two colors, yellow and orange. Again, as in 1959, a collector or a fan could send in two backboards and receive 10 assorted coins. Again, some Armour Coins may then be in short supply. Those coins include: Allison, Boyer, Colavito, Conley, Ford, Fox, Kaline, Mathews, Mays and Wynn.

	NM	Ex
COMPLETE SET (20)	900.00	350.00
COMMON COIN (1-20)	5.00	2.00
COMMON SP	600.00	240.00
1A Hank Aaron (Milwaukee)	80.00	32.00
1B Hank Aaron (Braves)	50.00	20.00
2 Bob Allison	5.00	2.00
3 Ernie Banks	25.00	10.00
4 Ken Boyer	12.00	4.80
5 Rocky Colavito	15.00	6.00
6 Gene Conley	5.00	2.00
7 Del Crandall	5.00	2.00
8 Bud Daley SP	600.00	240.00
9 Don Drysdale	20.00	8.00
10 Whitey Ford	25.00	10.00
11 Nellie Fox	20.00	8.00
12 Al Kaline	25.00	10.00
13A Frank Malzone (Boston)	40.00	16.00
13B Frank Malzone (Red Sox)	5.00	2.00
14 Mickey Mantle	100.00	40.00
15 Eddie Mathews	20.00	8.00
16 Willie Mays	50.00	20.00
17 Vada Pinson	8.00	3.20
18 Dick Stuart	5.00	2.00
19 Gus Triandos	5.00	2.00
20 Early Wynn	20.00	8.00

1966 Cardinals Coins

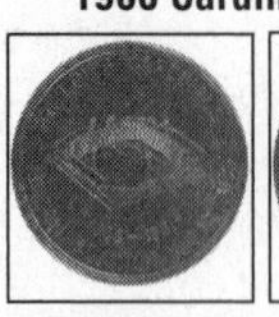

This 12-coin set measures approximately 1 1/2" in diameter and commemorates some of the all-time great St. Louis Cardinals. The gold coin fronts display a raised player image with the player's name, position, and why he was selected for this set. The backs carry an image of Busch Stadium with the team name and the words "Busch Stadium Immortals."

	NM	Ex
COMPLETE SET (12)	60.00	24.00
1 Dizzy Dean	8.00	3.20
2 Stan Musial	15.00	6.00
3 Johnny Mize	5.00	2.00
4 Dick Sisler	2.00	.80
5 Marty Marion	4.00	1.60
6 Chick Hafey	4.00	1.60
7 Frankie Frisch	5.00	2.00
8 Jesse Haines	4.00	1.60
9 Terry Moore	3.00	1.20
10 Joe Medwick	5.00	2.00
11 Enos Slaughter	5.00	2.00
12 Red Schoendienst	5.00	2.00

1969 Citgo Metal Coins

This set of metal coins was distributed at Citgo stations in 1969 to commemorate the 100th anniversary of professional baseball. Each metal coin measures 1" in diameter. Although the coins are not numbered, they are arranged in the checklist below according to numbers found on a display card (which could be obtained from the company via mail). Each coin depicts a ballplayer in a raised portrait; the brass-like metal plating is often found discolored due to oxidation. A saver sheet was issued for these coins and is valued at approximately $15.

	NM	Ex
COMPLETE SET (20)	45.00	18.00
1 Denny McLain	1.00	.40
2 Dave McNally	.50	.20
3 Jim Lonborg	1.00	.40
4 Harmon Killebrew	6.00	2.40
5 Mel Stottlemyre	1.00	.40
6 Willie Horton	1.00	.40
7 Jim Fregosi	1.00	.40
8 Rico Petrocelli	.50	.20
9 Stan Bahnsen	.50	.20
10 Frank Howard	1.00	.40
11 Joe Torre	2.00	.80
12 Jerry Koosman	1.00	.40
13 Ron Santo	2.00	.80
14 Pete Rose	15.00	6.00
15 Rusty Staub	1.50	.60
16 Henry Aaron	10.00	4.00
17 Richie Allen	2.00	.80
18 Ron Swoboda	.50	.20
19 Willie McCovey	5.00	2.00
20 Jim Bunning	4.00	1.60

1909-11 Colgan's Chips E254

This is list of the players issued by Colgan's chips. This is a combination of the E254. We have separated the Chips into the E254 and E270 listings.The "cards" measure 1 1/2" round and were inserted one per five cent package. The chips are unnumbered and we have sequenced them in alphabetical order.

	Ex-Mt	VG
COMPLETE SET	15000.00	7500.00
1 Ed Abbaticchio	40.00	20.00
2 Fred Abbott	40.00	20.00
3A Bill Abstein Pittsburg	40.00	20.00
3B Bill Abstein Jersey City	40.00	20.00
4 Babe Adams	50.00	25.00
5 Doc Adkins	40.00	20.00
6 Joe Agler	40.00	20.00
8A Dave Altizer Cincinnati	40.00	20.00
8B Dave Altizer Minneapolis	40.00	20.00
9 Nick Altrock	50.00	25.00
10B Red Ames New York Nat'l L	40.00	20.00
11 Jimmy Archer	50.00	25.00
14A Jimmy Austin New York Am.	50.00	25.00
14B Jimmy Austin St. Louis Am.	50.00	25.00
15A Charlie Babb Memphis	40.00	20.00
15B Charlie Babb Norfolk, Va.	40.00	20.00
16 Rudolph Baerwald	40.00	20.00
17 Bill Bailey	40.00	20.00
18 Frank Baker	80.00	40.00
19 Jack Barry	50.00	25.00
20 Bill Bartley	40.00	20.00
21A Johnny Bates Cincinnati	40.00	20.00
21B Johnny Bates Phila Nat'l L	40.00	20.00
22 Dick Bayless Atlanta	40.00	20.00
23A Ginger Beaumont Boston Nat'l L	40.00	20.00
23B Ginger Beaumont Chicago Nat'l	40.00	20.00
23C Ginger Beaumont St. Paul	40.00	20.00
24 Beals Becker	40.00	20.00
26 George Bell	40.00	20.00
27A Harry Bemis Cleveland	40.00	20.00
27B Harry Bemis Columbus	40.00	20.00
28A Heinie Berger Cleveland	40.00	20.00
28B Heinie Berger Columbus	40.00	20.00
29 Bob Bescher	50.00	25.00
30 Beumiller Louisville	40.00	20.00
31 Joe Birmingham	40.00	20.00
32 Kitty Bransfield	40.00	20.00
33A Roger Bresnahan St. Louis Nat'l	80.00	40.00
34 Al Bridwell	50.00	25.00
35 Lew Brockett New York Am L	40.00	20.00
37A Al Burch Brooklyn	40.00	20.00
38A William Burke Ft. Wayne	40.00	20.00
38B William Burke Indianapolis	40.00	20.00
40 Donie Bush	50.00	25.00
41 Bill Byers Baltimore	40.00	20.00
44 Howie Cammitz	40.00	20.00
46A Charlie Carr Indianapolis	40.00	20.00
46B Charlie Carr Utica	40.00	20.00
48A Frank Chance	120.00	60.00
49 Hal Chase	60.00	30.00
51 Clancy Baltimore	40.00	20.00
52 Nig Clarke	80.00	40.00
53 Fred Clarke Cincinnati	80.00	40.00
56 Clymer Minneapolis	40.00	20.00
57A Ty Cobb Detroit	800.00	400.00
57B Ty Cobb Detroit	800.00	400.00
58 Eddie Collins	120.00	60.00
59A Buck Congalton Columbus	40.00	20.00
60 Wid Conroy	40.00	20.00
64 Courtney Providence	40.00	20.00
65A Harry Coveleski	40.00	20.00
65B Stan Coveleski	80.00	40.00
66 Doc Crandall	40.00	20.00
67 Gavvy Cravath	50.00	25.00
69 Dode Criss	40.00	20.00
70 Bill Dahlen	40.00	20.00
72A Jake Daubert Memphis	50.00	25.00
72B Jake Daubert Brooklyn	50.00	25.00
73 Harry Davis	40.00	20.00
74 George Davis	80.00	40.00
75 Jim Delahanty	40.00	20.00
76A Ray Demmett New York Am. L.	40.00	20.00
76B Ray Demmett Montreal	40.00	20.00
76C Ray Demmett St. Louis Am. L	40.00	20.00
77 Art Devlin	40.00	20.00
80 Bill Donovan	50.00	25.00
82 Mickey Doolan	40.00	20.00
83 Patsy Dougherty	40.00	20.00
84 Tom Downey	40.00	20.00
85 Larry Doyle	50.00	25.00
87 Jack Dunn	50.00	25.00
88 Charles Eagan	40.00	20.00
89A Kid Elberfield Washington	40.00	20.00
89C Kid Elberfield New York Am. L	40.00	20.00
92 Rube Ellis	40.00	20.00
94A Clyde Engle New York Am. L	40.00	20.00
94B Clyde Engle Boston Am.	40.00	20.00
96 Steve Evans	40.00	20.00
97 Johnny Evers	125.00	60.00
98 George Ferguson	40.00	20.00
99 Hobe Ferris	40.00	20.00
100 Field Montreal	40.00	20.00
102 Matthew Fitzgerald	40.00	20.00
103A Patrick Flaherty Kansas City	40.00	20.00
103B Patrick Flaherty Atlanta	40.00	20.00
104 Flater Newark	40.00	20.00
105A Elmer Flick Cleveland	80.00	40.00
105B Elmer Flick Toledo	80.00	40.00
108A Freck Baltimore	40.00	20.00
108B Freck Toronto	40.00	20.00
109 Freeman Toledo	40.00	20.00
112 Art Froome Cincinnati	40.00	20.00
113A Larry Gardner Boston Am. L	40.00	20.00
113B Larry Gardner New York Am. L	40.00	20.00
114 Harry Gaspar	40.00	20.00
115A Gus Getz Boston Nat'l L.	40.00	20.00
115B Gus Getz Pittsburgh	40.00	20.00
116 George Gibson	40.00	20.00
120A Moose Grimshaw Toronto	40.00	20.00
120B Moose Grimshaw Louisville	40.00	20.00
122 Noodles Hahn	40.00	20.00
123 John Halla	40.00	20.00
124 Hally Rochester	40.00	20.00
125 Charles Hanford	40.00	20.00
126A Topsy Hartsel Phila. Am. L.	40.00	20.00
127A Roy Hartzell St. Louis Am. L.	40.00	20.00
127B Roy Hartzell New York Am.	40.00	20.00
128 Weldon Henley	40.00	20.00
129 Harry Hinchman	40.00	20.00
131 Solly Hofman	40.00	20.00
133A Harry Hooper Boston Am. L	80.00	40.00
133B Harry Hooper Boston Na'l	80.00	40.00
134 Del Howard	40.00	20.00
136B Hughes Louisville	40.00	20.00
136C Hughes Louisville as "c" but name and team in uniform	40.00	20.00
137 Hughes Rochester	40.00	20.00
138A Rudy Hulswitt St. Louis Nat'l L	40.00	20.00
138B Rudy Hulswitt Chattanooga	40.00	20.00
139 John Hummel	40.00	20.00
140 George Hunter	40.00	20.00
141 Joe Jackson	1000.00	500.00
142 Hugh Jennings	80.00	40.00
144 Davy Jones	50.00	25.00
145 Tom Jones	40.00	20.00
146B Jordon Atlanta	40.00	20.00
146C Jordon Atlanta.	40.00	20.00
146D Jordon Louisville	40.00	20.00
147 Joss Cleveland	80.00	40.00
148 Kaiser Louisville	40.00	20.00
150 Willie Keeler	80.00	40.00
151B Kelly Toronto	40.00	20.00
152A William Killefer St. Louis Am.	40.00	20.00
153A Ed Killian Detroit	40.00	20.00
153B Ed Killian Toronto	40.00	20.00
154 Johnny Kling	50.00	25.00
156 Otto Knabe	40.00	20.00
157A John Knight New York Am L	40.00	20.00
158 Ed Konetchy	40.00	20.00
160 Rube Kroh	40.00	20.00
161A Doc Lafitte Rochester	40.00	20.00
162 Nap Lajoie	200.00	100.00
163 Lakoff Louisville	40.00	20.00
164 Frank Lange	40.00	20.00
165A Frank LaPorte St. Louis Am	40.00	20.00
165B Frank LaPorte New York Am	40.00	20.00
166 Tommy Leach	50.00	25.00
168 William Lelivelt	40.00	20.00
169A Lewis Milwaukee	40.00	20.00
169B Lewis Indianapolis	40.00	20.00
170A Vivian Lindaman Boston Nat'l L	40.00	20.00
170B Vivian Lindaman Louisville	40.00	20.00
170C Vivian Lindaman Indianapolis	40.00	20.00
171 Bris Lord	40.00	20.00
172A Harry Lord Boston Am L	40.00	20.00
172B Harry Lord Chicago Am L	40.00	20.00
173A William Ludwig Milwaukee	40.00	20.00
173B William Ludwig St. Louis Nat'l L	40.00	20.00
175 Madden Montreal	40.00	20.00
176A Nicholas Maddox Pittsburg	40.00	20.00
177A Manser Jersey City	40.00	20.00
177B Manser Rochester	40.00	20.00
178 Rube Marquard	80.00	40.00
179 Al Mattern	40.00	20.00
180 Matthews Atlanta	40.00	20.00
182 George McBride	40.00	20.00
183 Alex McCathy	40.00	20.00
184 Ambrose McConnell Rochester	40.00	20.00
186 Moose McCormick	40.00	20.00
187 Dennis McGann	40.00	20.00
188 James McGinley	40.00	20.00
189 Joe McGinnity	80.00	40.00
190A Matty McIntyre Detroit	40.00	20.00
190B Matty McIntyre Chicago Am	40.00	20.00
191A Larry McLean Cincinnati	40.00	20.00
192 Fred Merkle	50.00	25.00
193A George Merritt Buffalo	40.00	20.00
193B George Merritt Jersey City	40.00	20.00
194 Lee Meyer	40.00	20.00
195 Chief Meyers	50.00	25.00
196 Clyde Milan	50.00	25.00
197 Dots Miller	40.00	20.00
199A Michael Mitchell Cincinnati	40.00	20.00
204 Pat Moran Atlanta	40.00	20.00
205 George Moriarty Detroit	50.00	25.00
206A George Moriarty Louisville	50.00	25.00
206B George Moriarty Omaha	50.00	25.00
207 Pat Mullen Detroit	40.00	20.00
208A Simmy Murch Chattanooga	40.00	20.00
208B Simmy Murch Indianapolis	40.00	20.00
209 Danny Murphy	40.00	20.00
210A Red Murray	40.00	20.00
210B Red Murray St. Paul	40.00	20.00
212 Bill Nattress Montreal	40.00	20.00
213A Red Nelson St. Louis Am L	40.00	20.00
213B Red Nelson Toledo	40.00	20.00
215 Rebel Oakes	40.00	20.00
216 Odwell Columbus	40.00	20.00
219B O'Rourke Columbus	40.00	20.00
220A Al Orth New York Am. L.	40.00	20.00
220B Al Orth Indianapolis	40.00	20.00
221 Wilfred Osborn	40.00	20.00
222 Orvie Overall	50.00	25.00
223 Frank Owens	40.00	20.00
225A Freddie Parent	40.00	20.00
226A Dode Paskert Cincinnati	40.00	20.00
226B Dode Paskert Phila. Nat'l L	40.00	20.00
227 Heinie Peitz	40.00	20.00
229 Robert A. Peterson	40.00	20.00
230 John Pfeister	40.00	20.00
231 Deacon Phillipe	40.00	20.00
232A Pickering Louisville	40.00	20.00
232B Pickering Minneapolis	40.00	20.00
232C Pickering Omaha	40.00	20.00
233A Billy Purtell Chicago Am L	40.00	20.00
233B Billy Purtell Boston	40.00	20.00
236 Bugs Raymond	40.00	20.00
237 Michael Regan	40.00	20.00
238 Thomas Reilly Chicago Am L	40.00	20.00
239 Thomas Reilly Louisville	40.00	20.00
240 Ed Reulbach	50.00	25.00
241 Claude Ritchey	40.00	20.00
242 Lou Ritter	40.00	20.00
243 Clyde Robinson	40.00	20.00
244 Royal Rock	40.00	20.00
245A Rowan Cincinnati	40.00	20.00
245B Jack Rowan	40.00	16.00

Phila Nat'l L
246 Nap Rucker 50.00 25.00
247A Dick Rudolph 40.00 20.00
New York Nat'l L
247B Dick Rudolph 40.00 20.00
Toronto
248 Buddy Ryan 40.00 20.00
St. Paul
250 Slim Sallee 40.00 20.00
252A Schardt 40.00 20.00
Birmingham
252B Schardt 40.00 20.00
Milwaukee
253 Jimmy Scheckard 40.00 20.00
254A George Schirm 40.00 20.00
Birmingham
254B George Schirm 40.00 20.00
Buffalo
255 Schlafly 40.00 20.00
Newark
256 Frank Schulte 50.00 25.00
257 Seabaugh 40.00 20.00
Nashville
258 Selby 40.00 20.00
Louisville
259A Cy Seymour 40.00 20.00
New York Nat'l L
259B Cy Seymour 40.00 20.00
Baltimore
262 Hosea Siner 40.00 20.00
263A Smith 40.00 20.00
Atlanta
263B Smith 40.00 20.00
Buffalo
265 George Smith 40.00 20.00
Montreal
266 Fred Snodgrass 50.00 25.00
267A Robert Spade 40.00 20.00
Cincinnati
267B Robert Spade 40.00 20.00
Newark N.J.
268A Tully Sparks 40.00 20.00
Phila. Nat'l L
268B Tully Sparks 40.00 20.00
Richmond, Va.
269A Tris Speaker 200.00 100.00
Boston Am.
269B Tris Speaker 200.00 100.00
Boston Nat'l
270 Spencer 40.00 20.00
St. Paul
271 Jake Stahl 40.00 20.00
272 Stansberry 40.00 20.00
Louisville
273 Harry Steinfeldt 50.00 25.00
274 George R. Stone 40.00 20.00
275 George Stovall 40.00 20.00
Cleveland
276 Gabby Street 50.00 25.00
Washington
278A Sullivan 40.00 20.00
Louisville
278B Sullivan 40.00 20.00
Omaha
281 Ed Summers 40.00 20.00
285 Lee Tannehill 40.00 20.00
286 Taylor 40.00 20.00
Kansas City
289A Joe Tinker 200.00 100.00
Chicago Nat'l L
290A John Titus 40.00 20.00
Phila. Nat'l
291 Terry Turner 40.00 20.00
292A Robert Unglaub 40.00 20.00
Washington Am L
292B Robert Unglaub 40.00 20.00
Lincoln Neb.
294A Rube Waddell 80.00 40.00
St. Louis Am L
294B Rube Waddell 80.00 40.00
Minneapolis
294C Rube Waddell 80.00 40.00
Newark, N.J.
295 Honus Wagner 500.00 250.00
296 Walker 40.00 20.00
Atlanta
298 Waller 40.00 20.00
Jersey City
301 Wauner 40.00 16.00
Memphis
302 Wiesman 40.00 20.00
Nashville
304 White 40.00 20.00
Buffalo
305 Kirby White 40.00 20.00
307 Ed Willett 40.00 20.00
308A Williams 40.00 20.00
Indianapolis
308B Williams 40.00 20.00
Minneapolis
309 Owen Wilson 50.00 25.00
310 Hooks Wiltse 40.00 20.00
312A Orville Woodruff 40.00 20.00
Indianapolis
312B Orville Woodruff 40.00 20.00
Louisville
313 Walter Woods 40.00 20.00
Buffalo
315 Cy Young 250.00 125.00
Cleveland
316 Heinie Zimmerman 60.00 30.00
Chicago Nat'l L
317A Heinie Zimmerman 60.00 30.00
Newark

1912 Colgan's Red Border

These chips look the same as the E254's, the only difference is that they have a red border. This set is skip numbered since the checklist is based on the E254 Colgan Chip checklist.

Ex-Mt VG
COMPLETE SET 20000.00 10000.00
1 Ed Abbaticchio 100.00 50.00
2 Fred Abbott 100.00 50.00
4 Babe Adams 125.00 60.00
10B Red Ames 100.00 50.00
New York Nat'l L
15B Charlie Babb 100.00 50.00
Norfolk, Va.
17 Bill Bailey 100.00 50.00
18 Frank Baker 200.00 100.00
19 Jack Barry 125.00 60.00
21A Johnny Bates 100.00 50.00
Cincinnati
22 Dick Bayless 100.00 50.00
24 Beals Becker 100.00 50.00
28B Heinie Berger 100.00 50.00
Columbus
30 Beumiller 100.00 50.00
Louisville
31 Joe Birmingham 100.00 50.00
Cleveland
32 Kitty Bransfield 100.00 50.00
Phila Nat'l
33A Roger Bresnahan 200.00 100.00
St. Louis Nat'l
35 Lew Brockett 100.00 50.00
37A Al Burch 100.00 50.00
Brooklyn
40 Donie Bush 125.00 60.00
42 Bobby Byrne 100.00 50.00
44 Howie Cammitz 100.00 50.00
46B Charlie Carr 100.00 50.00
Utica
48A Frank Chance 300.00 150.00
Chicago Nat'l L.
52 Fred Clarke 200.00 100.00
53 Tommy Clarke 200.00 100.00
56 Clymer 100.00 50.00
Minneapolis
57B Ty Cobb 2000.00 1000.00
Detroit
58 Eddie Collins 400.00 200.00
60 Wid Conroy 100.00 50.00
65B Stan Coveleski 100.00 50.00
67 Gavvy Cravath 125.00 60.00
69 Dode Criss 100.00 50.00
73 Harry Davis 100.00 50.00
Phila. Am. L.
74 George Davis 100.00 50.00
St. Paul
75 Jim Delahanty 100.00 50.00
Toronto
76B Ray Demmett 100.00 50.00
Montreal
78A Josh Devore 100.00 50.00
Cincinnati
80 Billi Donovan 125.00 60.00
82 Mickey Doolan 100.00 50.00
83 Patsy Dougherty 100.00 50.00
84 Tom Downey 100.00 50.00
85 Larry Doyle 125.00 60.00
87 Jack Dunn 125.00 60.00
88 Charles Eagen 100.00 50.00
Cincinnati
89A Kid Elberfield 100.00 50.00
Washington
92 Rube Ellis 100.00 50.00
St. Louis Nat'l
96 Steve Evans 100.00 50.00
97 Johnny Evers 300.00 150.00
98 George Ferguson 100.00 50.00
99 Hobe Ferris 100.00 50.00
101 Fisher 100.00 50.00
Louisville
102 Matthew Fitzgerald 100.00 50.00
106 Russ Ford 100.00 50.00
108A Freck 100.00 50.00
Baltimore
112 Art Froome 100.00 50.00
114 Harry Gaspar 100.00 50.00
116 George Gibson 100.00 50.00
120B Moose Grimshaw 100.00 50.00
Louisville
123 John Halla 100.00 50.00
Louisville
124 Hally 100.00 50.00
Rochester
125 Charles Hanford 100.00 50.00
Jersey City
126A Topsy Hartsel 100.00 50.00
Phila. Am. L.
128 Weldon Henley 100.00 50.00
Rochester
129 Harry Hinchman 100.00 50.00
Columbus
131 Solly Hofman 100.00 50.00
Chicago Nat'l
133A Harry Hooper 200.00 100.00
Boston Am. L
134 Del Howard 100.00 50.00
136C Hughes 100.00 50.00
Louisville
as "c" but name and
team in uniform
138C Rudy Hulswitt 100.00 50.00
Louisville
139 John Hummel 100.00 50.00
140 George Hunter 100.00 50.00
142 Hugh Jennings MG 200.00 100.00
145 Tom Jones 100.00 50.00
146B Jordon 100.00 50.00
Atlanta
152A William Killefer 100.00 50.00
St. Louis Am.
153B Ed Killian 100.00 50.00
Toronto
156 Otto Knabe 100.00 50.00
157A John Knight 100.00 50.00
New York Am L
158 Ed Konetchy 100.00 50.00
160 Rube Kroh 100.00 50.00
166 Tommy Leach 100.00 50.00
168 William Lelivelt 100.00 50.00
169A Lewis 100.00 50.00
Milwaukee
170B Vivian Lindaman 100.00 50.00
Louisville
171 Bris Lord 100.00 50.00
172B Harry Lord 100.00 50.00
173A William Ludwig 100.00 50.00
Milwaukee
176A Nicholas Maddox 100.00 50.00
Pittsburg
179 Al Mattern 100.00 50.00
182 George McBride 100.00 50.00
183 Alex McCathy 100.00 50.00
184 Ambrose McConnell 100.00 50.00
Rochester
186 Moose McCormick 100.00 50.00
188 James McGinley 100.00 50.00
189 Joe McGinnity 200.00 100.00
190B Matty McIntyre 100.00 50.00
Chicago Am
192 Fred Merkle 125.00 60.00
193A George Merritt 100.00 50.00
Buffalo
195 Chief Meyers 125.00 60.00
196 Clyde Milan 125.00 60.00
197 Dots Miller 100.00 50.00
Pittsburg
199A Michael Mitchell 100.00 50.00
Cincinnati
205 George Moriarty 100.00 50.00
Detroit
206B Moriarty 100.00 50.00
Omaha
207 Pat Mullen 125.00 60.00
Detroit
208A Murch 100.00 50.00
Chattanooga
209 Danny Murphy 100.00 50.00
210A Red Murray 100.00 50.00
New York Nat'l L
213A Red Nelson 100.00 50.00
St. Louis Am L
215 Rebel Oakes 100.00 50.00
222 Orvie Overall 125.00 60.00
223 Frank Owens 100.00 50.00
225A Freddie Parent 100.00 50.00
Chicago Am L
226B Dode Paskert 100.00 50.00
Phila. Nat'l L
227 Heinie Peitz 100.00 50.00
Louisville
229 Robert A. Peterson 100.00 50.00
232C Pickering 100.00 50.00
Omaha
236 Bugs Raymond 100.00 50.00
237 Michael Regan 100.00 50.00
243 Clyde Robinson 100.00 50.00
244 Royal Rock 100.00 50.00
245B Jack Rowan 100.00 50.00
Phila. Nat'l L
246 Nap Rucker 125.00 60.00
247A Dick Rudolph 100.00 50.00
New York Nat'l L
250 Slim Sallee 100.00 50.00
253 Jimmy Scheckard 100.00 50.00
254A George Schirm 100.00 50.00
Birmingham
256 Frank Schulte 125.00 60.00
257 Seabaugh 100.00 50.00
Nashville
258 Selby 100.00 50.00
Louisville
262 Hosea Siner 100.00 50.00
263A Smith 100.00 50.00
Atlanta
266 Fred Snodgrass 125.00 60.00
267B Robert Spade 100.00 50.00
Newark N.J.
268B Tully Sparks 100.00 50.00
Richmond, Va.
269A Tris Speaker 400.00 200.00
Boston Am.
274 George R. Stone 100.00 50.00
St. Louis Am. L.
275 George Stovall 100.00 50.00
Cleveland
276 Gabby Street 100.00 50.00
Washington
278B Sullivan 100.00 50.00
Omaha
280 J. Sullivan 100.00 50.00
Louisville
281 Ed Summers 100.00 50.00
Detroit
289A Joe Tinker 300.00 150.00
Chicago Nat'l L
290A John Titus 100.00 50.00
Phila. Nat'l
291 Terry Turner 100.00 50.00
Cleveland
294B Rube Waddell 300.00 150.00
Minneapolis
296 Walker 100.00 50.00
Atlanta
298 Waller 100.00 50.00
Jersey City
302 Wiesman 100.00 50.00
Nashville
304 White 100.00 50.00
Buffalo
308A Williams 100.00 50.00
Indianapolis
310 Hooks Wiltse 100.00 50.00
312A Woodruff 100.00 50.00
Indianapolis
314 Yeager 100.00 50.00
National
315 Cy Young 800.00 400.00
316 Heinie Zimmerman 100.00 50.00
Chicago Nat'l L

1913 Colgans Tin Tops

These chips are nicknames Tin Tops since the redemption offer on these chips asked for the Tin Tops to be included. That is how they are differentiated from the E-254's. This set is skip numbered since the checklist is based on the E-254 Colgan Chip checklist.

Ex-Mt VG
COMPLETE SET 22500.00 11200.00
5 Doc Adkins 100.00 50.00
7 Whitey Alperman 100.00 50.00
10A Red Ames 125.00 60.00
Cincinnati
10B Red Ames 125.00 60.00
New York Nat'l L
12A Atkins 100.00 50.00
Atlanta
12B Atkins 100.00 50.00
Fort Wayne
13 Atz 100.00 50.00
Providence
14B Jimmy Austin 125.00 60.00
St. Louis Am.
18 Frank Baker 200.00 100.00
21A Johnny Bates 100.00 50.00
Cincinnati
25 Fred Beebe 100.00 50.00
29 Bob Bescher 125.00 60.00
31 Joe Birmingham 100.00 50.00
33B Roger Bresnahan 200.00 100.00
Chicago Nat'l
35 Lew Brockett 100.00 50.00
37B Al Burch 100.00 50.00
Louisville
39 Burns 100.00 50.00
Toledo
40 Donie Bush 125.00 60.00
42 Bobby Byrne 100.00 50.00
43 Nixey Callahan 100.00 50.00
45 Vin Campbell 100.00 50.00
46C Charlie Carr 100.00 50.00
Kansas City
47 Cashion 100.00 50.00
Washington
48B Frank Chance 350.00 180.00
49 Hal Chase 150.00 75.00
50 Eddie Cicotte 300.00 150.00
52 Fred Clarke 200.00 100.00
Pittsburgh
53 Tommy Clarke 200.00 100.00
Cincinnati
54 Fred Clarke 200.00 100.00
Indianapolis
55 Clemons 100.00 50.00
Louisville
56 Clymer 100.00 50.00
Minneapolis
57A Ty Cobb 2000.00 1000.00
58 Eddie Collins 300.00 150.00
59B Buck Congalton 100.00 50.00
Omaha
59C Buck Congalton 100.00 50.00
Toledo
61 Cook 100.00 50.00
Columbus
62 Jack Coombs 125.00 60.00
63 Corcoran 100.00 50.00
Baltimore
68 Sam Crawford 200.00 100.00
70 Bill Dahlen 100.00 50.00
71 Bert Daniels 100.00 50.00
72B Jake Daubert 125.00 60.00
Brooklyn
78A Josh Devore 100.00 50.00
Cincinnati
78B Josh Devore 100.00 50.00
New York Nat'l
79 Mike Donlin 125.00 60.00
81 Red Dooin 100.00 50.00
82 Mickey Doolan 100.00 50.00
85 Larry Doyle 125.00 60.00
86 Drake 100.00 50.00
Kansas City
89B Kid Elberfield 100.00 50.00
Chattanooga
90 Ellam 100.00 50.00
Birmingahm
91 Elliott 100.00 50.00
Nashville
92 Rube Ellis 100.00 50.00
93 Elwert 100.00 50.00
Montgomery
94B Clyde Engle 100.00 50.00
Boston Am.
95 Esmond 100.00 50.00
Montreal
96 Steve Evans 100.00 50.00
97 Johnny Evers 300.00 150.00
Chicago Nat'l L
99 Ferris 100.00 50.00
Minneapolis
106 Russ Ford 100.00 50.00
107 Foster 100.00 50.00
Boston Am
110 Friel 100.00 50.00
St. Paul
111 Frill 100.00 50.00
Buffalo
112 Art Froome 100.00 50.00
115B Gus Getz 100.00 50.00
Pittsburgh
116 George Gibson 100.00 50.00
117 Graham 100.00 50.00
Toronto
118A Eddie Grant 100.00 50.00
Cincinnati
118B Eddie Grant 100.00 50.00
New York Nat'l
119 Grief 100.00 50.00
Columbus
121 Bob Groom 100.00 50.00
125 Charles Hanford 100.00 50.00
127A Topsy Hartzell 100.00 50.00
129 Harry Hinchman 100.00 50.00
130 Doc Hoblitzell 100.00 50.00
132 Hogan 100.00 50.00
St. Louis Am.
133A Harry Hooper 200.00 100.00
Boston Am. L
135 Miller Huggins 200.00 100.00
136A Hughes 100.00 50.00
Milwaukee
137 Hughes 100.00 50.00
Rochester
138C Hulswitt 100.00 50.00
Louisville
139 Hummel 100.00 50.00
Brooklyn
142 Hugh Jennings 200.00 100.00
143 Johns 100.00 50.00
Atlanta
144 Davy Jones 100.00 50.00
146A Jordon 100.00 50.00
Toronto
149 Keefe 100.00 50.00
Rochester
150 Willie Keeler 200.00 100.00
151A Kelly 100.00 50.00
Jersey City
152B William Killefer 100.00 50.00
Phila. Nat'l L
153B Ed Killian 100.00 50.00
Toronto
154A Johnny Kling 125.00 60.00
Boston Nat'l L
154B Johnny Kling 125.00 60.00
Cincinnati
155 Klipfer 100.00 50.00
Rochester
156 Otto Knabe 100.00 50.00
157B John Knight 100.00 50.00
Jersey City
158 Ed Konetchy 100.00 50.00
159 Paul Krichell 100.00 50.00
161B Doc Lafitte 100.00 50.00
Providence
162 Nap Lajoie 300.00 150.00
167 Lee 100.00 50.00
Newark
169A Lewis 100.00 50.00
Milwaukee
172B Harry Lord 100.00 50.00
Chicago Am L
174 John Lush 100.00 50.00
175 Thomas Madden 100.00 50.00
176B Nicholas Maddox 100.00 50.00
Louisville
177A Manser 100.00 50.00
Jersey City
181 McAllister 100.00 50.00
Atlanta
183 Alex McCathy 100.00 50.00
185 Ambrose McConnell 100.00 50.00
Toronto
191B Larry McLean 100.00 50.00
St. Louis Nat'l
192 Fred Merkle 125.00 60.00
195 Chief Meyers 125.00 60.00
197 Dots Miller 100.00 50.00
Pittsburg
198 Dots Miller 100.00 50.00
Columbus
199B Michael Mitchell 100.00 50.00
Chicago Nat'l
200 Mitchell 100.00 50.00
Providence
201 Mitchell 100.00 50.00
St. Louis Am.
202 Carlton Molesworth 100.00 50.00
203 Herbie Moran 100.00 50.00
205 George Moriarty 125.00 60.00
Detroit
209 Danny Murphy 100.00 50.00
211 Murray 100.00 50.00
Buffalo
214 Northrop 100.00 50.00
Louisville
217 Rube Oldring 100.00 50.00
218 Steve O'Neil 100.00 50.00
219A O'Rourke 100.00 50.00
St. Paul
225A Freddie Parent 100.00 50.00
Chicago Am L
226A Dode Paskert 100.00 50.00
Cincinnati
228 Perry 100.00 50.00
Providence
234 Bill Rariden 100.00 50.00
235 Morrie Rath 100.00 50.00
236 Bugs Raymond 100.00 50.00
249 Buddy Ryan 100.00 50.00
Cleveland
250 Slim Sallee 100.00 50.00
251 Ray Schalk 200.00 100.00
253 Jimmy Scheckard 100.00 50.00
260 Bob Shawkey 150.00 75.00
261 Shelton 100.00 50.00
Columbus
263A Smith 100.00 50.00
Atlanta
264 Smith 100.00 50.00
Newark
266 Fred Snodgrass 125.00 60.00
269A Tris Speaker 300.00 150.00
Boston Am.
271 Jake Stahl 100.00 50.00
272 Stansberry 100.00 50.00
Louisville
277 Amos Strunk 100.00 50.00
279 Sullivan 100.00 50.00
Indianapolis
282 Swacina 100.00 50.00
Newark
283 Sweeney 100.00 50.00
New York Am.
284 Sweeney 100.00 50.00
Boston Nat'l
287 Taylor 100.00 50.00
Montreal
288 Jim Thorpe 1500.00 750.00
289B Joe Tinker 300.00 150.00
290B John Titus 100.00 50.00
Boston Nat'l L
291 Terry Turner 125.00 60.00
292C Robert Unglaub 100.00 50.00
Minneapolis
293 Viebahn 100.00 50.00
Jersey City
294B Rube Waddell 200.00 100.00
Minneapolis
295 Honus Wagner 1000.00 500.00
297 Bobby Wallace 200.00 100.00
299 Ed Walsh 200.00 100.00
300 Jack Warhop 100.00 50.00
303 Zach Wheat 200.00 100.00
306 Kaiser Wilhelm 100.00 50.00
307 Ed Willett 100.00 50.00
309 Owen Wilson 100.00 50.00
310 Hooks Wiltse 100.00 50.00
311 Joe Wood 150.00 75.00
312A Woodruff 100.00 50.00
Indianapolis

314 Yeager	100.00	50.00
National		
317B Heinie Zimmerman	100.00	50.00
Newark		
318 Jameson	100.00	50.00
Buffalo		

1972 Esso Coins

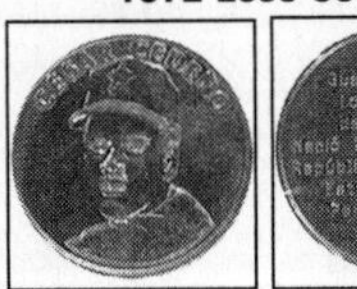
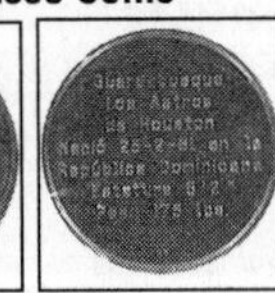

This 12-coin set measures approximately 1 1/4" in diameter and exclusively contains Latin players. The coins are silver in color with the fronts featuring an embossed head of the player below the player's name. The backs carry in Spanish biographical and personal information. The coins are unnumbered and checklisted below in alphabetical order.

	NM	Ex
COMPLETE SET (12)	30.00	12.00
1 Luis Aparicio	4.00	1.60
2 Rod Carew	10.00	4.00
3 Rico Carty	2.00	.80
4 Cesar Cedeno	2.00	.80
5 Orlando Cepeda	4.00	1.60
6 Mike Cuellar	2.00	.80
7 Juan Marichal	4.00	1.60
8 Felix Millan	1.00	.40
9 Willie Montanez	1.00	.40
10 Tony Oliva	3.00	1.20
11 Tony Perez	4.00	1.60
12 Manny Sanguillen	2.00	.80

1965 Old London Coins

The Old London set of metal baseball coins was distributed in that company's snack products in 1965. The coins were produced for Old London by Space Magic, Ltd. a Canadian firm which manufactured similar sets in 1964 and 1971. Each metal coin measures 1 1/2" in diameter. The silver-colored backs contain the company logo and a short biographical sketch of the player. Each team is represented by two ballplayers, except for the Mets (1) and the Cardinals (3) -- Tracy Stallard was traded from the former to the latter. The coins are unnumbered and hence they are listed below in alphabetical order within league, e.g., National Leaguers (1-20) and American Leaguers (21-40). Coins found still in their original cellophane wrappers are worth 25 percent more than the values listed below.

	NM	Ex
COMPLETE SET (40)	450.00	180.00
1 Hank Aaron	50.00	20.00
2 Richie Allen	8.00	3.20
3 Ernie Banks	30.00	12.00
4 Ken Boyer	6.00	2.40
5 Jim Bunning	15.00	6.00
6 Orlando Cepeda	10.00	4.00
7 Willie Davis	5.00	2.00
8 Ron Fairly	5.00	2.00
9 Dick Farrell	4.00	1.60
10 Bob Friend	4.00	1.60
11 Dick Groat	5.00	2.00
12 Ron Hunt	4.00	1.60
13 Ken Johnson	4.00	1.60
14 Willie Mays	50.00	20.00
15 Bill Mazeroski	10.00	4.00
16 Vada Pinson	5.00	2.00
17 Frank Robinson	30.00	12.00
18 Tracy Stallard	4.00	1.60
19 Joe Torre	8.00	3.20
20 Billy Williams	20.00	8.00
21 Bob Allison	4.00	1.60
22 Dean Chance	5.00	2.00
23 Rocky Colavito	10.00	4.00
24 Vic Davalillo	4.00	1.60
25 Jim Fregosi	5.00	2.00
26 Chuck Hinton	4.00	1.60
27 Al Kaline	40.00	16.00
28 Harmon Killebrew	40.00	16.00
29 Don Lock	4.00	1.60
30 Mickey Mantle	120.00	47.50
31 Roger Maris	40.00	16.00
32 Gary Peters	4.00	1.60
33 Boog Powell	8.00	3.20
34 Dick Radatz	5.00	2.00
35 Brooks Robinson	30.00	12.00
36 Leon Wagner	4.00	1.60
37 Pete Ward	4.00	1.60
38 Dave Wickersham	4.00	1.60
39 John Wyatt	4.00	1.60
40 Carl Yastrzemski	30.00	12.00

1962 Salada Plastic Coins

There are 221 different players in the 1962 plastic baseball coins marketed in Salada Tea and Junket Pudding mixes. Each plastic coin measures 1 3/8" in diameter. The initial production run consisted of 10 representatives from each of the 18 major league teams. A subsequent run added 20 players from the Mets and the Colt 45's and also dropped 21 of the original subjects, who were replaced by 21 new players assigned higher numbers. The "coin" itself is made of one-color plastic (light or dark) blue, black, orange, red or white) which has a color portrait printed on paper inserted into the obverse surface. A 10-coin, shield-like holder was available for each team. The complete set price below includes all variations. Many of the variations in the set are based on whether or not there are red buttons (RB) or white buttons (WB); these variation coin pairs are designated in the checklist below. Some of the tougher variations include Jackie Brandt listed as on the Orioles; Ed Bressoud with his name misspelled; Dick Williams with his name on the right; Gary Geiger with an "O" on the hat. A box was also issued by Salada to hold the first 180 coins issued.

	NM	Ex
COMPLETE SET (263)	5000.00	2000.00
COMMON COIN (1-180)	1.50	.60
COMMON COIN (181-221)	5.00	2.00
1 Jim Gentile	2.00	.80
2 Billy Pierce	150.00	60.00
3 Chico Fernandez	2.00	.80
4 Tom Brewer	30.00	12.00
5 Woody Held	1.50	.60
6 Ray Herbert	30.00	12.00
7A Ken Aspromonte	10.00	4.00
(Angels)		
7B Ken Aspromonte	2.00	.80
(Cleveland)		
8 Whitey Ford	25.00	10.00
9A Jim Lemon RB		
(does not exist)		
9B Jim Lemon WB	2.50	1.00
10 Billy Klaus	1.50	.60
11 Steve Barber	25.00	10.00
12 Nellie Fox	15.00	6.00
13 Jim Bunning	20.00	8.00
14 Frank Malzone	1.50	.60
15 Tito Francona	1.50	.60
16 Bobby Del Greco	1.50	.60
17A Steve Bilko RB	8.00	3.20
17B Steve Bilko WB	2.00	.80
18 Tony Kubek	60.00	24.00
19 Earl Battey	1.50	.60
20 Chuck Cottier	1.50	.60
21 Willie Tasby	1.50	.60
22 Bob Allison	2.00	.80
23 Roger Maris	40.00	16.00
24A Earl Averill RB	8.00	3.20
24B Earl Averill WB	2.50	1.00
25 Jerry Lumpe	1.50	.60
26 Jim Grant	30.00	12.00
27 Carl Yastrzemski	60.00	24.00
28 Rocky Colavito	8.00	3.20
29 Al Smith	1.50	.60
30 Jim Busby	30.00	12.00
31 Dick Howser	2.00	.80
32 Jim Perry	2.00	.80
33 Yogi Berra	30.00	12.00
34A Ken Hamlin RB	8.00	3.20
34B Ken Hamlin WB	2.00	.80
35 Dale Long	1.50	.60
36 Harmon Killebrew	30.00	12.00
37 Dick Brown	2.00	.80
38A Gary Geiger	500.00	200.00
(O on hat)		
38B Gary Geiger	2.00	.80
(no O on hat)		
39A Minnie Minoso	50.00	20.00
(White Sox)		
39B Minnie Minoso	25.00	10.00
(Cardinals)		
40 Brooks Robinson	40.00	16.00
41 Mickey Mantle	150.00	60.00
42 Bennie Daniels	1.50	.60
43 Billy Martin	8.00	3.20
44 Vic Power	1.50	.60
45 Joe Pignatano	1.50	.60
46A Ryne Duren RB	8.00	3.20
46B Ryne Duren WB	2.00	.80
47A Pete Runnels	8.00	3.20
(2nd base)		
47B Pete Runnels	3.00	1.20
(1st base)		
48A Dick Williams	1000.00	400.00
(name right)		
48B Dick Williams	5.00	2.00
(name left)		
49 Jim Landis	1.50	.60
50 Steve Boros	1.50	.60
51A Zoilo Versalles RB	8.00	3.20
51B Zoilo Versalles WB	2.00	.80
52A Johnny Temple	10.00	4.00
(Indians)		
52B Johnny Temple	5.00	2.00
(Orioles)		
53A Jackie Brandt	5.00	2.00
(Oriole)		
53B Jackie Brandt	1000.00	400.00
(Orioles)		
54 Joe McClain	1.50	.60
55 Sherman Lollar	1.50	.60
56 Gene Stephens	1.50	.60
57A Leon Wagner RB	8.00	3.20
57B Leon Wagner WB	2.00	.80
58 Frank Lary	1.50	.60
59 Bill Skowron	3.00	1.20
60 Vic Wertz	25.00	10.00
61 Willie Kirkland	1.50	.60
62 Leo Posada	1.50	.60
63A Albie Pearson RB	8.00	3.20
63B Albie Pearson WB	2.00	.80
64 Bobby Richardson	6.00	2.40
65A Marv Breeding	8.00	3.20
(Shortstop)		
65B Marv Breeding	3.00	1.20
(2nd Base)		
66 Roy Sievers	120.00	47.50
67 Al Kaline	40.00	16.00
68A Don Buddin	8.00	3.20
(Red Sox)		
68B Don Buddin	3.00	1.20
(Colt .45's)		
69A Lenny Green RB	8.00	3.20
69B Lenny Green WB	2.50	1.00
70 Gene Green	30.00	12.00
71 Luis Aparicio	15.00	6.00
72 Norm Cash	4.00	1.60
73 Jackie Jensen	50.00	20.00
74 Bubba Phillips	1.50	.60
75 James Archer	1.50	.60
76A Ken Hunt RB	8.00	3.20
76B Ken Hunt WB	2.00	.80
77 Ralph Terry	2.00	.80
78 Camilo Pascual	1.50	.60
79 Marty Keough	25.00	10.00
80 Clete Boyer	2.50	1.00
81 Jim Pagliaroni	1.50	.60
82A Gene Leek RB	8.00	3.20
82B Gene Leek WB	2.00	.80
83 Jake Wood	1.50	.60
84 Coot Veal	30.00	12.00
85 Norm Siebern	1.50	.60
86A Andy Carey	50.00	20.00
(White Sox)		
86B Andy Carey	3.00	1.20
(Phillies)		
87A Bill Tuttle RB	8.00	3.20
87B Bill Tuttle WB	2.00	.80
88A Jimmy Piersall	10.00	4.00
(Indians)		
88B Jimmy Piersall	6.00	2.40
(Senators)		
89 Ron Hansen	40.00	16.00
90A Chuck Stobbs RB	8.00	3.20
90B Chuck Stobbs WB	2.50	1.00
91A Ken McBride RB	8.00	3.20
91B Ken McBride WB	2.00	.80
92 Bill Bruton	2.00	.80
93 Gus Triandos	1.50	.60
94 John Romano	1.50	.60
95 Elston Howard	6.00	2.40
96 Gene Woodling	1.50	.60
97A Early Wynn	60.00	24.00
(pitching)		
97B Early Wynn	25.00	10.00
(portrait)		
98 Milt Pappas	1.50	.60
99 Bill Monbouquette	1.50	.60
100 Wayne Causey	1.50	.60
101 Don Elston	1.50	.60
102A Charlie Neal	8.00	3.20
(Dodgers)		
102B Charlie Neal	3.00	1.20
(Mets)		
103 Don Blasingame	1.50	.60
104 Frank Thomas	40.00	16.00
105 Wes Covington	1.50	.60
106 Chuck Hiller	1.50	.60
107 Don Hoak	1.50	.60
108A Bob Lillis	20.00	8.00
(Cardinals)		
108B Bob Lillis	5.00	2.00
(Colt .45's)		
109 Sandy Koufax	40.00	16.00
110 Gordy Coleman	1.50	.60
111 Eddie Matthews	25.00	10.00
(sic, Mathews)		
112 Art Mahaffey	1.50	.60
113A Ed Bailey (red)	10.00	4.00
113B Ed Bailey (white)	2.00	.80
114 Smoky Burgess	1.50	.60
115 Bill White	2.00	.80
116 Ed Bouchee	25.00	10.00
117 Bob Buhl	1.50	.60
118 Vada Pinson	2.00	.80
119 Carl Sawatski	1.50	.60
120 Dick Stuart	2.00	.80
121 Harvey Kuenn	35.00	14.00
122 Pancho Herrera	1.50	.60
123A Don Zimmer	8.00	3.20
(Cubs)		
123B Don Zimmer	3.00	1.20
(Mets)		
124 Wally Moon	1.50	.60
125 Joe Adcock	1.50	.60
126 Joey Jay	1.50	.60
127A Maury Wills	15.00	6.00
(blue number 3)		
127B Maury Wills	10.00	4.00
(red number 3)		
128 George Altman	1.50	.60
129A John Buzhardt	10.00	4.00
(Phillies)		
129B John Buzhardt	5.00	2.00
(White Sox)		
130 Felipe Alou	2.00	.80
131 Bill Mazeroski	2.00	.80
132 Ernie Broglio	1.50	.60
133 John Roseboro	1.50	.60
134 Mike McCormick	1.50	.60
135A Charlie Smith	8.00	3.20
(Philadelphia)		
135B Charlie Smith	3.00	1.20
(White Sox)		
136 Ron Santo	3.00	1.20
137 Gene Freese	1.50	.60
138 Dick Groat	2.00	.80
139 Curt Flood	2.00	.80
140 Frank Bolling	1.50	.60
141 Clay Dalrymple	1.50	.60
142 Willie McCovey	25.00	10.00
143 Bob Skinner	1.50	.60
144 Lindy McDaniel	1.50	.60
145 Glen Hobbie	1.50	.60
146A Gil Hodges	50.00	20.00
(Dodgers)		
146B Gil Hodges	25.00	10.00
(Mets)		
147 Eddie Kasko	1.50	.60
148 Gino Cimoli	40.00	16.00
149 Willie Mays	80.00	32.00
150 Roberto Clemente	100.00	40.00
151 Red Schoendienst	2.00	.80
152 Joe Torre	2.00	.80
153 Bob Purkey	1.50	.60
154A Tommy Davis	8.00	3.20
(Outfield)		
154B Tommy Davis	2.00	.80
(3rd Base)		
155A Andre Rogers ERR	8.00	3.20
(sic, Rodgers)		
155B Andre Rodgers COR	2.00	.80
156 Tony Taylor	1.50	.60
157 Bob Friend	1.50	.60
158A Gus Bell	8.00	3.20
(Reds)		
158B Gus Bell	3.00	1.20
(Mets)		
159 Roy McMillan	1.50	.60
160 Carl Warwick	1.50	.60
161 Willie Davis	2.00	.80
162 Sam Jones	40.00	16.00
163 Ruben Amaro	1.50	.60
164 Sammy Taylor	1.50	.60
165 Frank Robinson	30.00	12.00
166 Lew Burdette	2.00	.80
167 Ken Boyer	3.00	1.20
168 Bill Virdon	2.00	.80
169 Jim Davenport	1.50	.60
170 Don Demeter	1.50	.60
171 Richie Ashburn	40.00	16.00
172 Johnny Podres	2.00	.80
173A Joe Cunningham	50.00	20.00
(Cardinals)		
173B Joe Cunningham	20.00	8.00
(White Sox)		
174 Roy Face	2.00	.80
175 Orlando Cepeda	6.00	2.40
176A Bobby Gene Smith	8.00	3.20
(Philadelphia)		
176B Bobby Gene Smith	3.00	1.20
(Mets)		
177A Ernie Banks	50.00	20.00
(Outfield)		
177B Ernie Banks	25.00	10.00
(Shortstop)		
178A Daryl Spencer	8.00	3.20
(3rd Base)		
178B Daryl Spencer	3.00	1.20
(1st Base)		
179 Bob Schmidt	25.00	10.00
180 Hank Aaron	80.00	32.00
181 Hobie Landrith	5.00	2.00
182A Ed Broussard	400.00	160.00
(sic, Bressoud)		
182B Ed Bressoud	25.00	10.00
(correct)		
183 Felix Mantilla	5.00	2.00
184 Dick Farrell	5.00	2.00
185 Bob Miller	5.00	2.00
186 Don Taussig	5.00	2.00
187 Pumpsie Green	5.00	2.00
188 Bobby Shantz	6.00	2.40
189 Roger Craig	6.00	2.40
190 Hal Smith	5.00	2.00
191 Johnny Edwards	5.00	2.00
192 John DeMerit	5.00	2.00
193 Joe Amalfitano	5.00	2.00
194 Norm Larker	5.00	2.00
195 Al Heist	5.00	2.00
196 Al Spangler	5.00	2.00
197 Alex Grammas	5.00	2.00
198 Jerry Lynch	5.00	2.00
199 Jim McKnight	5.00	2.00
200 Jose Pagen	5.00	2.00
(sic, Pagan)		
201 Jim Gilliam	15.00	6.00
202 Art Ditmar	5.00	2.00
203 Bud Daley	5.00	2.00
204 Johnny Callison	6.00	2.40
205 Stu Miller	5.00	2.00
206 Russ Snyder	5.00	2.00
207 Billy Williams	25.00	10.00
208 Walt Bond	5.00	2.00
209 Joe Koppe	5.00	2.00
210 Don Schwall	10.00	4.00
211 Billy Gardner	6.00	2.40
212 Chuck Estrada	5.00	2.00
213 Gary Bell	5.00	2.00
214 Floyd Robinson	5.00	2.00
215 Duke Snider	50.00	20.00
216 Lee Maye	5.00	2.00
217 Howie Bedell	5.00	2.00
218 Bob Will	5.00	2.00
219 Dallas Green	8.00	3.20
220 Carroll Hardy	5.00	2.00
221 Danny O'Connell	5.00	2.00

1963 Salada Metal Coins

The 1963 baseball coin set distributed by Salada Tea and Junket Pudding marked a drastic change from the set of the previous year. The coins were made of metal, rather than plastic, with conspicuous red rims for National League players and blue rims for their American League counterparts. Each coin measures 1 1/2" in diameter. The subject's portrait was printed in color on the front, with his name, position, team and 1962 statistics listed on the back. Also on the reverse is located the coin number and the line "Save and Trade 63 All Star Baseball Coins."

	NM	Ex
COMPLETE SET (63)	600.00	240.00
1 Don Drysdale	15.00	6.00
2 Dick Farrell	4.00	1.60
3 Bob Gibson	15.00	6.00
4 Sandy Koufax	40.00	16.00
5 Juan Marichal	12.00	4.80
6 Bob Purkey	5.00	2.00
7 Bob Shaw	4.00	1.60
8 Warren Spahn	20.00	8.00
9 Johnny Podres	6.00	2.40
10 Art Mahaffey	4.00	1.60
11 Del Crandall	4.00	1.60
12 John Roseboro	6.00	2.40
13 Orlando Cepeda	10.00	4.00
14 Bill Mazeroski	10.00	4.00
15 Ken Boyer	8.00	3.20
16 Dick Groat	6.00	2.40
17 Ernie Banks	25.00	10.00
18 Frank Bolling	5.00	2.00
19 Jim Davenport	4.00	1.60
20 Maury Wills	8.00	3.20
21 Willie Davis	4.00	1.60
22 Willie Mays	60.00	24.00
23 Roberto Clemente	80.00	32.00
24 Hank Aaron	60.00	24.00
25 Matty Alou	6.00	2.40
26 Johnny Callison	6.00	2.40
27 Richie Ashburn	12.00	4.80
28 Eddie Mathews	20.00	8.00
29 Frank Robinson	20.00	8.00
30 Billy Williams	12.00	4.80
31 George Altman	5.00	2.00
32 Hank Aguirre	4.00	1.60
33 Jim Bunning	12.00	4.80
34 Dick Donovan	4.00	1.60
35 Bill Monbouquette	4.00	1.60
36 Camilo Pascual	6.00	2.40
37 Dave Stenhouse	4.00	1.60
38 Ralph Terry	5.00	2.00
39 Hoyt Wilhelm	12.00	4.80
40 Jim Kaat	8.00	3.20
41 Ken McBride	4.00	1.60
42 Ray Herbert	4.00	1.60
43 Milt Pappas	5.00	2.00
44 Earl Battey	4.00	1.60
45 Elston Howard	6.00	2.40
46 John Romano	4.00	1.60
47 Jim Gentile	5.00	2.00
48 Billy Moran	4.00	1.60
49 Rich Rollins	4.00	1.60
50 Luis Aparicio	12.00	4.80
51 Norm Siebern	5.00	2.00
52 Bobby Richardson	8.00	3.20
53 Brooks Robinson	20.00	8.00
54 Tom Tresh	5.00	2.00
55 Leon Wagner	4.00	1.60
56 Mickey Mantle	120.00	47.50
57 Roger Maris	30.00	12.00
58 Rocky Colavito	8.00	3.20
59 Frank Thomas	4.00	1.60
60 Jim Landis	4.00	1.60
61 Pete Runnels	4.00	1.60
62 Yogi Berra	25.00	10.00
63 Al Kaline	25.00	10.00

1983 Seven-Eleven Coins

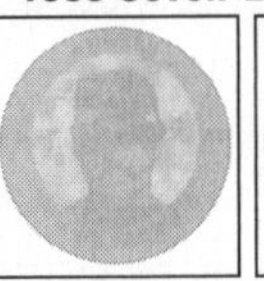
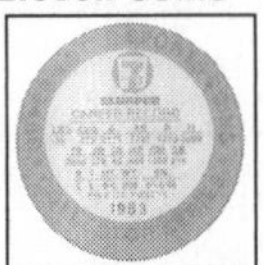

The coins in this 12-coin set measure approximately 1 3/4" diameter. This set of action coins was released by 7-Eleven stores in the Los Angeles area. Given out with large Slurpee drinks, the set features Los Angeles Dodgers (blue background) and California Angels (red background) on plastic discs. The fronts feature two pictures (portrait and action) of each player, each of which can be seen by moving the coin slightly to one side or another. Brief statistics fill the backs of these coins. The coins are numbered by uniform number on the front; in addition, an individual coin number can be found on the back.

	Nm-Mt	Ex-Mt
COMPLETE SET (12)	8.00	3.20
1 Rod Carew	2.00	.80
2 Steve Sax	.40	.16
3 Fred Lynn	.40	.16
4 Pedro Guerrero	.60	.24
5 Reggie Jackson	2.50	1.00
6 Dusty Baker	.40	.16
7 Doug DeCinces	.40	.16
8 Fernando Valenzuela	.75	.30
9 Tommy John	.60	.24
10 Rick Monday	.25	.10
11 Bobby Grich	.40	.16
12 Greg Brock	.25	.10

1984 Seven-Eleven Coins

The coins in this 72 coin set measure approximately 1 3/4" diameter. For the second year in a row, 7-Eleven issued sets of coins (officially called Slurpee Discs). The fronts feature two pictures (portrait and action) of each player, each of which can be seen by moving the coin slightly to one side or another. There were, in effect, three different sets of 24 coins corresponding to an East, Central and West region. The letter suffix after the number in the checklist below denotes the region of issue, East (E), Central (C), or West (W). Of the total 72 coins, only 60 different players appear. Six players appear in all three sets. The repeat players are Andre Dawson, Robin Yount, Dale Murphy, George Brett, Mike Schmidt and Eddie Murray. Each team is represented by at least one player and as one might expect, players within the three groups favor the teams of the geographical location in which that particular group was issued. Coins are numbered on the back, which is different from the uniform number which is on the front of the coin.

	Nm-Mt	Ex-Mt
COMPLETE SET (72)	80.00	32.00
C1 Andre Dawson	1.25	.50
C2 Robin Yount	2.50	1.00
C3 Dale Murphy	1.25	.50
C4 Mike Schmidt	3.00	1.20
C5 George Brett	4.00	1.60
C6 Eddie Murray	2.50	1.00
C7 Bruce Sutter	.75	.30
C8 Cecil Cooper	.75	.30
C9 Willie McGee	1.00	.40
C10 Mike Hargrove	.50	.20

C11 Kent Hrbek .75 .30
C12 Carlton Fisk 2.00 .80
C13 Mario Soto .50 .20
C14 Lonnie Smith .50 .20
C15 Gary Carter 2.50 1.00
C16 Lou Whitaker 1.00 .40
C17 Ron Kittle .50 .20
C18 Paul Molitor 2.50 1.00
C19 Ozzie Smith 4.00 1.60
C20 Fergie Jenkins 2.50 1.00
C21 Ted Simmons .75 .30
C22 Pete Rose 4.00 1.60
C23 LaMarr Hoyt .50 .20
C24 Dan Quisenberry .50 .20
E1 Andre Dawson 1.25 .50
E2 Robin Yount 2.50 1.00
E3 Dale Murphy 1.25 .50
E4 Mike Schmidt 3.00 1.20
E5 George Brett 4.00 1.60
E6 Eddie Murray 2.50 1.00
E7 Dave Winfield 2.50 1.00
E8 Tom Seaver 2.50 1.00
E9 Mike Boddicker .50 .20
E10 Wade Boggs 3.00 1.20
E11 Bill Madlock .75 .30
E12 Steve Carlton 2.50 1.00
E13 Dave Stieb .50 .20
E14 Cal Ripken 10.00 4.00
E15 Jim Rice .75 .30
E16 Ron Guidry .75 .30
E17 Darryl Strawberry 1.00 .40
E18 Tony Pena .75 .30
E19 John Denny .50 .20
E20 Tim Raines 1.00 .40
E21 Rick Dempsey .50 .20
E22 Rich Gossage 1.00 .40
E23 Gary Matthews .50 .20
E24 Keith Hernandez .75 .30
W1 Andre Dawson 1.25 .50
W2 Robin Yount 2.50 1.00
W3 Dale Murphy 1.25 .50
W4 Mike Schmidt 3.00 1.20
W5 George Brett 4.00 1.60
W6 Eddie Murray 2.50 1.00
W7 Steve Garvey 1.25 .50
W8 Rod Carew 2.00 .80
W9 Fernando Valenzuela .75 .30
W10 Bob Horner .50 .20
W11 Buddy Bell .75 .30
W12 Reggie Jackson 2.50 1.00
W13 Nolan Ryan 10.00 4.00
W14 Pedro Guerrero .75 .30
W15 Atlee Hammaker .50 .20
W16 Fred Lynn .75 .30
W17 Terry Kennedy .50 .20
W18 Dusty Baker .75 .30
W19 Jose Cruz .75 .30
W20 Steve Rogers .50 .20
W21 Rickey Henderson 3.00 1.20
W22 Steve Sax .75 .30
W23 Dickie Thon .50 .20
W24 Matt Young .50 .20

1985 Seven-Eleven Coins

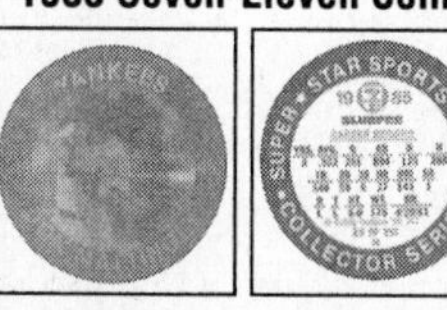

These "3-D" type coins are very similar to those of the preceding years except that in 1985 7-Eleven issued six subsets. The subsets are Central (C), Detroit (D), Eastern (E), Great Lakes (G), Southeast (S) and Western (W). The letter suffix after the number in the checklist below denotes the region of issue. Each of the six subsets is numbered and contains 16 coins except for the Tigers set which contains only 14 and was distributed in somewhat smaller supply. Each coin measures approximately 1 3/4" in diameter.

Nm-Mt Ex-Mt
COMPLETE SET (94) 100.00 40.00
C1 Nolan Ryan 10.00 4.00
C2 George Brett 4.00 1.60
C3 Dave Winfield 1.50 .60
C4 Mike Schmidt 3.00 1.20
C5 Bruce Sutter .40 .16
C6 Joaquin Andujar .20 .08
C7 Willie Hernandez .20 .08
C8 Wade Boggs 2.50 1.00
C9 Gary Carter .75 .30
C10 Jose Cruz .20 .08
C11 Kent Hrbek .60 .24
C12 Reggie Jackson 2.50 1.00
C13 Lance Parrish .40 .16
C14 Terry Puhl .20 .08
C15 Dan Quisenberry .20 .08
C16 Ozzie Smith 2.50 1.00
D1 Lou Whitaker .60 .24
D2 Sparky Anderson MG .40 .16
D3 Darrell Evans .40 .16
D4 Larry Herndon .20 .08
D5 Dave Rozema .20 .08
D6 Milt Wilcox .20 .08
D7 Dan Petry .20 .08
D8 Alan Trammell .75 .30
D9 Aurelio Lopez .20 .08
D10 Willie Hernandez .20 .08
D11 Chet Lemon .20 .08
D12 Jack Morris .40 .16
D13 Kirk Gibson .40 .16
D14 Lance Parrish .40 .16
E1 Eddie Murray 2.50 1.00
E2 George Brett 4.00 1.60
E3 Steve Carlton 2.50 1.00
E4 Jim Rice .40 .16
E5 Dave Winfield 2.50 1.00
E6 Mike Boddicker .20 .08
E7 Wade Boggs 2.50 1.00
E8 Dwight Evans .60 .24
E9 Dwight Gooden 2.50 1.00
E10 Keith Hernandez .40 .16
E11 Bill Madlock .40 .16
E12 Don Mattingly 6.00 2.40
E13 Dave Righetti .40 .16
E14 Cal Ripken 10.00 4.00
E15 Juan Samuel .20 .08
E16 Mike Schmidt 3.00 1.20
G1 Willie Hernandez .20 .08
G2 George Brett 4.00 1.60
G3 Dave Winfield 2.50 1.00
G4 Eddie Murray 2.50 1.00
G5 Bruce Sutter .60 .24
G6 Harold Baines .40 .16
G7 Bert Blyleven .60 .24
G8 Leon Durham .20 .08
G9 Chet Lemon .20 .08
G10 Pete Rose 4.00 1.60
G11 Ryne Sandberg 5.00 2.00
G12 Tom Seaver 2.50 1.00
G13 Mario Soto .20 .08
G14 Rick Sutcliffe .20 .08
G15 Alan Trammell .75 .30
G16 Robin Yount 2.50 1.00
S1 Dale Murphy .75 .30
S2 Steve Carlton 2.50 1.00
S3 Nolan Ryan 10.00 4.00
S4 Bruce Sutter .40 .16
S5 Dave Winfield 2.50 1.00
S6 Steve Bedrosian .20 .08
S7 Andre Dawson .75 .30
S8 Kirk Gibson .40 .16
S9 Fred Lynn .40 .16
S10 Gary Matthews .20 .08
S11 Phil Niekro 2.50 1.00
S12 Tim Raines .40 .16
S13 Darryl Strawberry .40 .16
S14 Dave Stieb .20 .08
S15 Willie Upshaw .20 .08
S16 Lou Whitaker .60 .24
W1 Mike Schmidt 3.00 1.20
W2 Jim Rice .40 .16
W3 Dale Murphy .75 .30
W4 Eddie Murray 2.50 1.00
W5 Dave Winfield 2.50 1.00
W6 Rod Carew 2.50 1.00
W7 Alvin Davis .20 .08
W8 Steve Garvey .60 .24
W9 Rich Gossage .60 .24
W10 Pedro Guerrero .40 .16
W11 Tony Gwynn 6.00 2.40
W12 Rickey Henderson 2.50 1.00
W13 Reggie Jackson 2.50 1.00
W14 Jeff Leonard .20 .08
W15 Alejandro Pena .20 .08
W16 Fernando Valenzuela .40 .16

1986 Seven-Eleven Coins

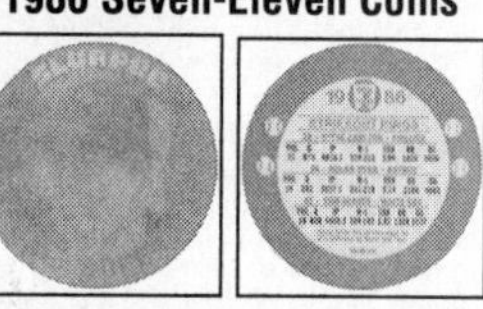

Four subsets of 16 coins each were distributed regionally by the 7-Eleven chain of convenience stores. The letter suffix after the number in the checklist below denotes the region of issue. The regions were Central (C), East (E), South (S) and West (W). The first eight coins in each region are the same; the last eight (9-16) in each region were apparently selected to showcase players from that area. Except for Dwight Gooden all other coins feature three players on each card depending on how you tilt the coin to see one of the three players. The three players are typically related by position. Each coin measures approximately 1 3/4" in diameter.

Nm-Mt Ex-Mt
COMPLETE SET (64) 60.00 24.00
C1 Dwight Gooden 1.50 .60
C2 Wade Boggs 3.00 1.20
George Brett
Pete Rose
C3 Keith Hernandez 5.00 2.00
Don Mattingly
Cal Ripken
C4 Harold Baines .40 .16
Pedro Guerrero
Dave Parker
C5 Dale Murphy .60 .24
Jim Rice
Mike Schmidt
C6 Ron Guidry .40 .16
Bret Saberhagen
Fernando Valenzuela
C7 Goose Gossage .40 .16
Dan Quisenberry
Bruce Sutter
C8 Steve Carlton 5.00 2.00
Nolan Ryan
Tom Seaver
C9 Willie Hernandez 1.50 .60
Ryne Sandberg
Robin Yount
C10 Bert Blyleven .40 .16
Jack Morris
Rick Sutcliffe
C11 Rollie Fingers .40 .16
Bob James
Lee Smith
C12 Carlton Fisk .40 .16
Lance Parrish
Tony Pena
C13 Shawon Dunston .40 .16
Ozzie Guillen
Earnie Riles
C14 Brett Butler .40 .16
Chet Lemon
Willie Wilson
C15 Tom Brunansky .25 .10
Cecil Cooper
Darrell Evans
C16 Kirk Gibson .40 .16
Paul Molitor
Greg Walker
E1 Dwight Gooden 1.50 .60
E2 Wade Boggs 3.00 1.20
George Brett
Pete Rose
E3 Keith Hernandez 5.00 2.00
Don Mattingly
Cal Ripken
E4 Harold Baines .40 .16
Pedro Guerrero
Dave Parker
E5 Dale Murphy .60 .24
Jim Rice
Mike Schmidt
E6 Ron Guidry .40 .16
Bret Saberhagen
Fernando Valenzuela
E7 Goose Gossage .40 .16
Dan Quisenberry
Bruce Sutter
E8 Steve Carlton 5.00 2.00
Nolan Ryan
Tom Seaver
E9 Steve Lyons .25 .10
Rick Schu
Larry Sheets
E10 Jeff Reardon .25 .10
Dave Righetti
Bob Stanley
E11 George Bell .75 .30
Darryl Strawberry
Dave Winfield
E12 Rickey Henderson .60 .24
Tim Raines
Juan Samuel
E13 Andre Dawson 1.50 .60
Dwight Evans
Eddie Murray
E14 Mike Boddicker .25 .10
Ron Darling
Dave Stieb
E15 Tim Burke .25 .10
Brian Fisher
Roger McDowell
E16 Jesse Barfield .40 .16
Gary Carter
Fred Lynn
S1 Dwight Gooden 1.50 .60
S2 Wade Boggs 3.00 1.20
George Brett
Pete Rose
S3 Keith Hernandez 5.00 2.00
Don Mattingly
Cal Ripken
S4 Harold Baines .40 .16
Pedro Guerrero
Dave Parker
S5 Dale Murphy 1.50 .60
Jim Rice
Mike Schmidt
S6 Ron Guidry .40 .16
Bret Saberhagen
Fernando Valenzuela
S7 Goose Gossage .40 .16
Dan Quisenberry
Bruce Sutter
S8 Steve Carlton 5.00 2.00
Nolan Ryan
Tom Seaver
S9 Vince Coleman .40 .16
Glenn Davis
Oddibe McDowell
S10 Buddy Bell 1.50 .60
Ozzie Smith
Lou Whitaker
S11 Mike Scott .25 .10
Mario Soto
John Tudor
S12 Jeff Lahti .25 .10
Ted Power
Dave Smith
S13 Jack Clark .40 .16
Jose Cruz
Bob Horner
S14 Bill Doran .25 .10
Tommy Herr
Ron Oester
S15 Tom Browning .25 .10
Joe Hesketh
Todd Worrell
S16 Willie McGee 1.50 .60
Jerry Mumphrey
Pete Rose
W1 Dwight Gooden 1.50 .60
W2 Wade Boggs 3.00 1.20
George Brett
Pete Rose
W3 Keith Hernandez 5.00 2.00
Don Mattingly
Cal Ripken
W4 Harold Baines .40 .16
Pedro Guerrero
Dave Parker
W5 Dale Murphy 1.50 .60
Jim Rice
Mike Schmidt
W6 Ron Guidry .40 .16
Bret Saberhagen
Fernando Valenzuela
W7 Goose Gossage .40 .16
Dan Quisenberry
Bruce Sutter
W8 Steve Carlton 5.00 2.00
Nolan Ryan
Tom Seaver
W9 Reggie Jackson .60 .24
Dave Kingman
Gorman Thomas
W10 Rod Carew 2.00 .80
Tony Gwynn
Carney Lansford
W11 Phil Bradley .25 .10
Mike Marshall
Graig Nettles
W12 Andy Hawkins .40 .16
Orel Hershiser
Mike Witt
W13 Chris Brown .25 .10
Ivan Calderon
Mariano Duncan
W14 Steve Garvey .40 .16
Bill Madlock
Jim Presley
W15 Jay Howell .25 .10
Donnie Moore
Edwin Nunez
W16 Karl Best .25 .10
Stu Cliburn
Steve Ontiveros

1987 Seven-Eleven Coins

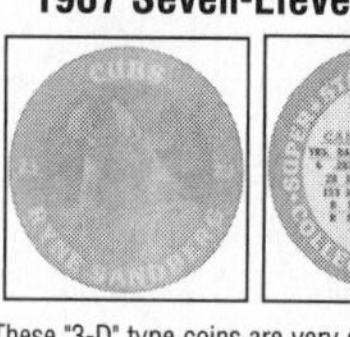

These "3-D" type coins are very similar to those of the preceding years except that in 1987 7-Eleven issued five subsets. The subsets are Detroit (D), East (E), Chicago (C), Mideast (M) and West (W). Each subset has a different color border on the back. The West subset is actually eight Dodgers and eight Angels. The Mideast subset is actually four each from the Mets, Cubs, Red Sox and Orioles. The East subset is actually five each from the Mets, Red Sox and Yankees. The letter prefix before the number in the checklist below denotes the region of issue. Each of the five subsets is numbered and contains between 12 and 16 coins. Each coin measures 1 3/4" in diameter.

Nm-Mt Ex-Mt
COMPLETE SET (75) 100.00 40.00
C1 Harold Baines 1.00 .40
C2 Jody Davis .50 .20
C3 John Cangelosi .50 .20
C4 Shawon Dunston .50 .20
C5 Dave Cochrane .50 .20
C6 Leon Durham .50 .20
C7 Carlton Fisk 3.00 1.20
C8 Dennis Eckersley 3.00 1.20
C9 Ozzie Guillen 1.00 .40
C10 Gary Matthews .50 .20
C11 Ron Karkovice .50 .20
C12 Keith Moreland .50 .20
C13 Bobby Thigpen .50 .20
C14 Ryne Sandberg 5.00 2.00
C15 Greg Walker .50 .20
C16 Lee Smith 1.25 .50
D1 Darnell Coles .50 .20
D2 Darrell Evans 1.00 .40
D3 Kirk Gibson 1.25 .50
D4 Willie Hernandez .50 .20
D5 Larry Herndon .50 .20
D6 Chet Lemon .50 .20
D7 Dwight Lowry .50 .20
D8 Jack Morris 1.00 .40
D9 Dan Petry .50 .20
D10 Frank Tanana .50 .20
D11 Alan Trammell 1.25 .50
D12 Lou Whitaker 1.00 .40
E1 Gary Carter 3.00 1.20
E2 Don Baylor 1.00 .40
E3 Rickey Henderson 3.00 1.20
E4 Lenny Dykstra 1.25 .50
E5 Wade Boggs 2.50 1.00
E6 Mike Pagliarulo .50 .20
E7 Dwight Gooden 1.50 .60
E8 Roger Clemens 8.00 3.20
E9 Dave Righetti .50 .20
E10 Keith Hernandez 1.00 .40
E11 Pat Dodson .50 .20
E12 Don Mattingly 6.00 2.40
E13 Darryl Strawberry 1.00 .40
E14 Jim Rice 1.00 .40
E15 Dave Winfield 3.00 1.20
M1 Gary Carter 3.00 1.20
M2 Marty Barrett .50 .20
M3 Jody Davis .50 .20
M4 Don Aase .50 .20
M5 Lenny Dykstra 1.25 .50
M6 Wade Boggs 3.00 1.20
M7 Keith Moreland .50 .20
M8 Mike Boddicker .50 .20
M9 Dwight Gooden 1.50 .60
M10 Roger Clemens 8.00 3.20
M11 Ryne Sandberg 5.00 2.00
M12 Eddie Murray 3.00 1.20
M13 Keith Hernandez 1.00 .40
M14 Jim Rice 1.00 .40
M15 Lee Smith 1.25 .50
M16 Cal Ripken 12.00 4.80
W1 Doug DeCinces .50 .20
W2 Mariano Duncan .50 .20
W3 Wally Joyner 1.50 .60
W4 Pedro Guerrero .50 .20
W5 Kirk McCaskill .50 .20
W6 Orel Hershiser 1.50 .60
W7 Gary Pettis .50 .20
W8 Mike Marshall .50 .20
W9 Dick Schofield .50 .20
W10 Steve Sax .50 .20
W11 Don Sutton 3.00 1.20
W12 Mike Scioscia 1.00 .40
W13 Devon White 1.25 .50
W14 Franklin Stubbs .50 .20
W15 Mike Witt .50 .20
W16 Fernando Valenzuela 1.25 .50

1991 Seven-Eleven 3-D Coins National

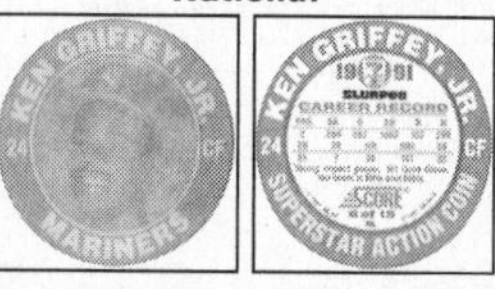

Measuring 1 3/4" in diameter, these 15 discs have 3-D color player photos on their fronts. Depending on how the disc is tilted, either a head shot or an action photo appears. The player's name, his number and position and the team name are printed in the red border around the photo. The backs carry the player's name, number, position, career record and the words "Superstar Action Coin" in yellow letters in the bottom part of the red border. The discs are numbered on the back as "X of 15."

Nm-Mt Ex-Mt
COMPLETE SET (15) 8.00 2.40
1 Wade Boggs 1.25 .35
2 Barry Bonds 3.00 .90
3 Roger Clemens 2.50 .75
4 Lenny Dykstra .50 .15
5 Dwight Gooden .50 .15
6 Ken Griffey Jr. 3.00 .90
7 Rickey Henderson 1.50 .45
8 Gregg Jefferies .25 .07
9 Roberto Kelly .25 .07
10 Kevin Maas .25 .07
11 Don Mattingly 2.50 .75
12 Mickey Morandini .25 .07
13 Dale Murphy 1.00 .30
14 Darryl Strawberry .50 .15
15 Frank Viola .25 .07

1991 Seven-Eleven Coins

This 120-coin set was produced by Score for 7-Eleven. The Superstar sport coins measure approximately 1 3/4" in diameter and they were attached to the bottom of specially-marked Slurpee cups. The coins were reportedly available through May, or while supplies lasted. These "magic motion" coins have color player pictures on the fronts and different colored borders. The backs have career statistics and brief player profiles. A total of 81 players are featured in the eight regional subsets issued. The subsets are Atlantic (A), Florida (F), Midwest (MW), Northern California (NC), Metro Northeast (NE), Northwest (NW), Southern California (SC) and Texas (T). Ken Griffey Jr. is the only player issued in all eight subsets. The letter suffix before the number in the checklist denotes the region of issue.

Nm-Mt Ex-Mt
COMPLETE SET (120) 100.00 30.00
A1 Glenn Davis .25 .07
A2 Dwight Evans .50 .15
A3 Leo Gomez .25 .07
A4 Ken Griffey Jr. 3.00 .90
A5 Rickey Henderson 1.25 .35
A6 Jose Canseco 1.00 .30
A7 Dave Justice .75 .23
A8 Ben McDonald .25 .07
A9 Randy Milligan .25 .07
A10 Gregg Olson .25 .07
A11 Kirby Puckett 1.25 .35
A12 Bill Ripken .25 .07
A13 Cal Ripken 5.00 1.50
A14 Nolan Ryan 5.00 1.50
A15 David Segui .25 .07
F1 Barry Bonds 3.00 .90
F2 George Brett 2.50 .75
F3 Roger Clemens 2.50 .75
F4 Glenn Davis .25 .07
F5 Alex Fernandez .25 .07
F6 Cecil Fielder .50 .15
F7 Ken Griffey Jr. 3.00 .90
F8 Dwight Gooden .50 .15
F9 Dave Justice .75 .23
F10 Barry Larkin 1.00 .30
F11 Ramon Martinez .25 .07
F12 Jose Offerman .25 .07
F13 Kirby Puckett 1.25 .35
F14 Nolan Ryan 5.00 1.50
F15 Terry Shumpert .25 .07
M1 George Brett 2.50 .75
M2 Andre Dawson .75 .23
M3 Cecil Fielder .50 .15
M4 Carlton Fisk 1.25 .35
M5 Travis Fryman .75 .23
M6 Mark Grace 1.00 .30
M7 Ken Griffey Jr. 3.00 .90
M8 Ozzie Guillen .50 .15
M9 Alex Fernandez .25 .07
M10 Ray Lankford .75 .23
M11 Ryne Sandberg 2.00 .60
M12 Ozzie Smith 1.25 .35
M13 Bobby Thigpen .25 .07
M14 Frank Thomas 2.00 .60
M15 Alan Trammell .75 .23
NE4 Lenny Dykstra .50 .15
NW4 Ken Griffey Jr. 1.25 .35
Ken Griffey Sr.
T1 Craig Biggio .75 .23
T2 Barry Bonds 3.00 .90
T3 Jose Canseco 1.00 .30
T4 Roger Clemens 2.50 .75
T5 Glenn Davis .25 .07
T6 Julio Franco .50 .15
T7 Juan Gonzalez 1.25 .35
T8 Ken Griffey Jr. 3.00 .90
T9 Mike Scott .25 .07
T10 Rafael Palmeiro 1.00 .30
T11 Nolan Ryan 5.00 1.50
T12 Ryne Sandberg 2.00 .60
T13 Ruben Sierra .50 .15
T14 Todd Van Poppel .25 .07
T15 Bobby Witt .25 .07
NC1 John Burkett .25 .07
NC2 Jose Canseco 1.00 .30
NC3 Will Clark 1.00 .30
NC4 Steve Decker .25 .07
NC5 Dennis Eckersley 1.25 .35
NC6 Ken Griffey Jr. 3.00 .90
NC7 Rickey Henderson 1.50 .45
NC8 Nolan Ryan 5.00 1.50
NC9 Mark McGwire 3.00 .90
NC10 Kevin Mitchell .25 .07
NC11 Terry Steinbach .25 .07
NC12 Dave Stewart .50 .15
NC13 Todd Van Poppel .25 .07
NC14 Bob Welch .25 .07

NC15 Matt Williams .75 .23
NE1 Wade Boggs 1.25 .35
NE2 Barry Bonds 3.00 .90
NE3 Roger Clemens 2.50 .75
NE5 Dwight Gooden .50 .15
NE6 Ken Griffey Jr. 3.00 .90
NE7 Rickey Henderson 1.50 .45
NE8 Gregg Jefferies .25 .07
NE9 Roberto Kelly .25 .07
NE10 Kevin Maas .25 .07
NE11 Don Mattingly 2.50 .75
NE12 Mickey Morandini .25 .07
NE13 Dale Murphy 1.00 .30
NE14 Darryl Strawberry .50 .15
NE15 Frank Viola .25 .07
NW1 George Brett 2.50 .75
NW2 Jose Canseco 1.00 .30
NW3 Alvin Davis .25 .07
NW5 Ken Griffey Jr. 3.00 .90
NW6 Erik Hanson .25 .07
NW7 Rickey Henderson 1.50 .45
NW8 Ryne Sandberg 2.00 .60
NW9 Randy Johnson 1.50 .45
NW10 Dave Justice .75 .23
NW11 Edgar Martinez .75 .23
NW12 Tino Martinez 1.00 .30
NW13 Harold Reynolds .50 .15
NW14 Nolan Ryan 5.00 1.50
NW15 Mike Schooler .25 .07
SC1 Jim Abbott .50 .15
SC2 Jose Canseco 1.00 .30
SC3 Ken Griffey Jr. 3.00 .90
SC4 Tony Gwynn 2.50 .75
SC5 Orel Hershiser .50 .15
SC6 Eric Davis .25 .07
SC7 Wally Joyner .50 .15
SC8 Ramon Martinez .25 .07
SC9 Fred McGriff .75 .23
SC10 Eddie Murray 1.25 .35
SC11 Jose Offerman .50 .15
SC12 Nolan Ryan 5.00 1.50
SC13 Benito Santiago .50 .15
SC14 Darryl Strawberry .50 .15
SC15 Fernando Valenzuela .50 .15

1992 Seven-Eleven Coins

These 26 discs, "Superstar Action Coins," measure approximately 1 3/4" in diameter and feature "Magic Motion" plastic-coated photos that alternate between a posed head shot and an action shot as the disc is moved. The photos are encircled by a yellow line and bordered in red. The player's name, team, position and uniform number appear in white lettering within the red border around the photo. The back carries the player's name in yellow lettering within the black border around the statistics table in the central yellow portion.

Nm-Mt Ex-Mt
COMPLETE SET (26) 12.00 3.60
1 Dwight Gooden .30 .09
2 Don Mattingly 1.50 .45
3 Roger Clemens 1.50 .45
4 Ivan Calderon .20 .06
5 Roberto Alomar .50 .15
6 Sandy Alomar Jr. .30 .09
7 Andy Van Slyke .20 .06
8 Lenny Dykstra .30 .09
9 Cal Ripken 3.00 .90
10 Dave Justice .50 .15
11 Nolan Ryan 3.00 .90
12 Craig Biggio .40 .12
13 Barry Larkin .50 .15
14 Ozzie Smith 1.00 .30
15 Ryne Sandberg .75 .23
16 Frank Thomas 1.00 .30
17 Robin Yount .75 .23
18 Kirby Puckett 1.00 .30
19 Cecil Fielder .30 .09
20 Will Clark .50 .15
21 Jose Canseco .75 .23
22 Jim Abbott .20 .06
23 Tony Gwynn 1.50 .45
24 Darryl Strawberry .20 .06
25 George Brett 1.50 .45
26 Ken Griffey Jr. 2.00 .60

2000 Seven-Eleven Coins

These 30 coins, issued by 7/11 featured one player from each major league team. They were available with the purchase of a "Slurpee" drink. The coins have a photo of the player on the front and some information about him on the back. The set is sequenced in alphabetical order by team.

Nm-Mt Ex-Mt
COMPLETE SET (30) 20.00 6.00
1 Tim Salmon .30 .09
2 Erubiel Durazo .30 .09
3 Chipper Jones 1.25 .35
4 Cal Ripken 3.00 .90
5 Nomar Garciaparra 1.50 .45
6 Mark Grace .60 .18
7 Frank Thomas .75 .23
8 Sean Casey .30 .09
9 Manny Ramirez .75 .23
10 Larry Walker .50 .15
11 Dean Palmer .30 .09
12 Alex Gonzalez .20 .06
13 Jeff Bagwell .75 .23
14 Carlos Beltran .50 .15
15 Gary Sheffield .75 .23
16 Jeromy Burnitz .30 .09
17 Corey Koskie .20 .06
18 Vladimir Guerrero 1.00 .30
19 Mike Piazza 1.50 .45
20 Roger Clemens 1.50 .45
21 Ben Grieve .20 .06
22 Scott Rolen .60 .18
23 Jason Kendall .30 .09
24 Mark McGwire 2.00 .60
25 Tony Gwynn 1.50 .45
26 Jeff Kent .50 .15
27 Jay Buhner .30 .09
28 Jose Canseco .60 .18
29 Ivan Rodriguez .75 .23
30 Carlos Delgado .75 .23

1962 Shirriff Plastic Coins

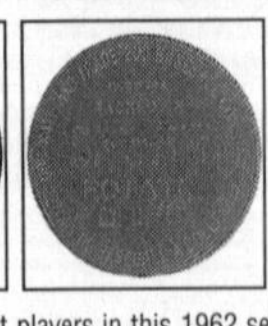

There are 221 different players in this 1962 set of plastic baseball coins marketed in Canada by Shirriff Potato Chips. The set is very similar to the American Salada coin set except for the printing on the reverse of the coin and the relative scarcitites of the coins in the set. Since the Shirriff coins were produced after the Salada coins, there are not the many gradations of scarcities and variations as in the Salada set. Each plastic coin measures approximately 1 3/8" in diameter. The "coin" itself is made of one-color plastic (light or dark) blue, black, orange, red or white) which has a color portrait printed on paper inserted into the obverse surface.

NM Ex
COMPLETE SET (221) 1600.00 650.00
1 Jim Gentile 5.00 2.00
2 Billy Pierce 5.00 2.00
3 Chico Fernandez 4.00 1.60
4 Tom Brewer 4.00 1.60
5 Woody Held 4.00 1.60
6 Ray Herbert 4.00 1.60
7 Ken Aspromonte 4.00 1.60
8 Whitey Ford 25.00 10.00
9 Jim Lemon 5.00 2.00
10 Billy Klaus 4.00 1.60
11 Steve Barber 5.00 2.00
12 Nellie Fox 15.00 6.00
13 Jim Bunning 15.00 6.00
14 Frank Malzone 5.00 2.00
15 Tito Francona 4.00 1.60
16 Bobby Del Greco 4.00 1.60
17 Steve Bilko 4.00 1.60
18 Tony Kubek 8.00 3.20
19 Earl Battey 4.00 1.60
20 Chuck Cottier 4.00 1.60
21 Willie Tasby 4.00 1.60
22 Bob Allison 5.00 2.00
23 Roger Maris 40.00 16.00
24 Earl Averill 4.00 1.60
25 Jerry Lumpe 4.00 1.60
26 Jim Grant 4.00 1.60
27 Carl Yastrzemski 25.00 10.00
28 Rocky Colavito 10.00 4.00
29 Al Smith 4.00 1.60
30 Jim Busby 5.00 2.00
31 Dick Howser 5.00 2.00
32 Jim Perry 5.00 2.00
33 Yogi Berra 30.00 12.00
34 Ken Hamlin 4.00 1.60
35 Dale Long 4.00 1.60
36 Harmon Killebrew 20.00 8.00
37 Dick Brown 4.00 1.60
38 Gary Geiger 5.00 2.00
39 Minnie Minoso 8.00 3.20
40 Brooks Robinson 25.00 10.00
41 Mickey Mantle 200.00 80.00
42 Bennie Daniels 4.00 1.60
43 Billy Martin 8.00 3.20
44 Vic Power 4.00 1.60
45 Joe Pignatano 4.00 1.60
46 Ryne Duren 5.00 2.00
47 Pete Runnels 5.00 2.00
48 Dick Williams 5.00 2.00
49 Jim Landis 4.00 1.60
50 Steve Boros 4.00 1.60
51 Zoilo Versalles 5.00 2.00
52 Johnny Temple 5.00 2.00
53 Jackie Brandt 5.00 2.00
54 Joe McClain 4.00 1.60
55 Sherman Lollar 4.00 1.60
56 Gene Stephens 4.00 1.60
57 Leon Wagner 4.00 1.60
58 Frank Lary 5.00 2.00
59 Bill Skowron 6.00 2.40
60 Vic Wertz 5.00 2.00
61 Willie Kirkland 4.00 1.60
62 Leo Posada 4.00 1.60
63 Albie Pearson 4.00 1.60
64 Bobby Richardson 8.00 3.20
65 Marv Breeding 4.00 1.60
66 Roy Sievers 5.00 2.00
67 Al Kaline 30.00 12.00
68 Don Buddin 4.00 1.60
69 Lenny Green 4.00 1.60
70 Gene Green 5.00 2.00
71 Luis Aparicio 15.00 6.00
72 Norm Cash 8.00 3.20
73 Jackie Jensen 6.00 2.40
74 Bubba Phillips 4.00 1.60
75 James Archer 4.00 1.60
76 Ken Hunt 4.00 1.60
77 Ralph Terry 5.00 2.00
78 Camilo Pascual 5.00 2.00
79 Marty Keough 5.00 2.00
80 Clete Boyer 5.00 2.00
81 Jim Pagliaroni 4.00 1.60
82 Gene Leek 4.00 1.60
83 Jake Wood 4.00 1.60
84 Coot Veal 4.00 1.60
85 Norm Siebern 4.00 1.60
86 Andy Carey 5.00 2.00
87 Bill Tuttle 5.00 2.00
88 Jimmy Piersall 6.00 2.40
89 Ron Hansen 5.00 2.00
90 Chuck Stobbs 4.00 1.60
91 Ken McBride 4.00 1.60
92 Bill Bruton 4.00 1.60
93 Gus Triandos 5.00 2.00
94 John Romano 4.00 1.60
95 Elston Howard 8.00 3.20
96 Gene Woodling 5.00 2.00
97 Early Wynn 15.00 6.00
98 Milt Pappas 5.00 2.00
99 Bill Monbouquette 4.00 1.60
100 Wayne Causey 4.00 1.60
101 Don Elston 4.00 1.60
102 Charlie Neal 4.00 1.60
103 Don Blasingame 4.00 1.60
104 Frank Thomas 5.00 2.00
105 Wes Covington 4.00 1.60
106 Chuck Hiller 4.00 1.60
107 Don Hoak 5.00 2.00
108 Bob Lillis 4.00 1.60
109 Sandy Koufax 40.00 16.00
110 Gordy Coleman 4.00 1.60
111 Eddie Mathews UER 25.00 10.00
(Misspelled Matthews)
112 Art Mahaffey 4.00 1.60
113 Ed Bailey 4.00 1.60
114 Smokey Burgess 5.00 2.00
115 Bill White 6.00 2.40
116 Ed Bouchee 5.00 2.00
117 Bob Buhl 4.00 1.60
118 Vada Pinson 6.00 2.40
119 Carl Sawatski 4.00 1.60
120 Dick Stuart 5.00 2.00
121 Harvey Kuenn 6.00 2.40
122 Pancho Herrera 4.00 1.60
123 Don Zimmer 5.00 2.00
124 Wally Moon 5.00 2.00
125 Joe Adcock 5.00 2.00
126 Joey Jay 4.00 1.60
127 Maury Wills 8.00 3.20
128 George Altman 4.00 1.60
129 John Buzhardt 5.00 2.00
130 Felipe Alou 6.00 2.40
131 Bill Mazeroski 10.00 4.00
132 Ernie Broglio 5.00 2.00
133 John Roseboro 5.00 2.00
134 Mike McCormick 4.00 1.60
135 Charlie Smith 4.00 1.60
136 Ron Santo 8.00 3.20
137 Gene Freese 4.00 1.60
138 Dick Groat 6.00 2.40
139 Curt Flood 6.00 2.40
140 Frank Bolling 4.00 1.60
141 Clay Dalrymple 4.00 1.60
142 Willie McCovey 20.00 8.00
143 Bob Skinner 4.00 1.60
144 Lindy McDaniel 4.00 1.60
145 Glen Hobbie 4.00 1.60
146 Gil Hodges 15.00 6.00
147 Eddie Kasko 4.00 1.60
148 Gino Cimoli 5.00 2.00
149 Willie Mays 50.00 20.00
150 Roberto Clemente 100.00 40.00
151 Red Schoendienst 15.00 6.00
152 Joe Torre 10.00 4.00
153 Bob Purkey 4.00 1.60
154 Tommy Davis 6.00 2.40
155 Andre Rodgers 4.00 1.60
156 Tony Taylor 5.00 2.00
157 Bob Friend 5.00 2.00
158 Gus Bell 5.00 2.00
159 Roy McMillan 4.00 1.60
160 Carl Warwick 4.00 1.60
161 Willie Davis 5.00 2.00
162 Sam Jones 5.00 2.00
163 Ruben Amaro 5.00 2.00
164 Sammy Taylor 4.00 1.60
165 Frank Robinson 25.00 10.00
166 Lew Burdette 5.00 2.00
167 Ken Boyer 8.00 3.20
168 Bill Virdon 5.00 2.00
169 Jim Davenport 4.00 1.60
170 Don Demeter 4.00 1.60
171 Richie Ashburn 15.00 6.00
172 Johnny Podres 5.00 2.00
173 Joe Cunningham 5.00 2.00
174 Roy Face 5.00 2.00
175 Orlando Cepeda 10.00 4.00
176 Bobby Gene Smith 4.00 1.60
177 Ernie Banks 30.00 12.00
178 Daryl Spencer 4.00 1.60
179 Bob Schmidt 5.00 2.00
180 Hank Aaron 50.00 20.00
181 Hobie Landrith 4.00 1.60
182 Ed Bressoud 5.00 2.00
183 Felix Mantilla 4.00 1.60
184 Dick Farrell 4.00 1.60
185 Bob Miller 4.00 1.60
186 Don Taussig 4.00 1.60
187 Pumpsie Green 4.00 1.60
188 Bobby Shantz 5.00 2.00
189 Roger Craig 8.00 3.20
190 Hal Smith 4.00 1.60
191 Johnny Edwards 4.00 1.60
192 John DeMerit 4.00 1.60
193 Joe Amalfitano 4.00 1.60
194 Norm Larker 4.00 1.60
195 Al Heist 4.00 1.60
196 Al Spangler 4.00 1.60
197 Alex Grammas 4.00 1.60
198 Jerry Lynch 4.00 1.60
199 Jim McKnight 4.00 1.60
200 Jose Pagan UER 4.00 1.60
(Misspelled Pagen)
201 Jim Gilliam 8.00 3.20
202 Art Ditmar 4.00 1.60
203 Bud Daley 4.00 1.60
204 Johnny Callison 5.00 2.00
205 Stu Miller 4.00 1.60
206 Russ Snyder 4.00 1.60
207 Billy Williams 20.00 8.00
208 Walt Bond 4.00 1.60
209 Joe Koppe 4.00 1.60
210 Don Schwall 4.00 1.60
211 Billy Gardner 4.00 1.60
212 Chuck Estrada 4.00 1.60
213 Gary Bell 4.00 1.60
214 Floyd Robinson 4.00 1.60
215 Duke Snider 40.00 16.00
216 Lee Maye 4.00 1.60
217 Howie Bedell 4.00 1.60
218 Bob Will 4.00 1.60
219 Dallas Green 4.00 1.60
220 Carroll Hardy 4.00 1.60
221 Danny O'Connell 4.00 1.60

1999 SkyBox Ozzie Smith Coin

This coin was distributed to attendees of the Hawaii XIV Trade Conference at a special dinner on February 23rd, 1999 featuring keynote speaker Ozzie Smith. The dinner was hosted at the famous Royal Hawaiian hotel in Honolulu and sponsored by Fleer/SkyBox. Each attendee received one of 500 serial numbered Ozzie coins next to their table settings. Similar in design to a casino chip, each coin front features a color headshot of Ozzie. The coins are serial numbered in gold foil on back. The coins came encased in a tight circular plastic holder.

Nm-Mt Ex-Mt
NNO Ozzie Smith 20.00 6.00

1994 Frank Thomas Coin

These coins contain one troy ounce of pure silver and are approximately 1 1/2" in diameter. Thomas' face appears on the front and his name, facsimile autograph, and uniform number are on the back. Backs also carry the logo for the MLBPA.

Nm-Mt Ex-Mt
NNO Frank Thomas 10.00 3.00

1987 Topps Coins

This full-color set of 48 coins contains a full-color photo of the player with a scroll at the bottom containing the player's name, position and team. The backs contain the coin number and brief biographical data. Some of the coins have gold rims and some have silver rims. Each coin measures approximately 1 1/2" in diameter. The 1987 set is very similar to the 1988 set of the following year; the 1988 coins have gold stars on the name scroll on the front of the coin.

Nm-Mt Ex-Mt
COMPLETE SET (48) 8.00 3.20
1 Harold Baines .15 .06
2 Jesse Barfield .05 .02
3 George Bell .05 .02
4 Wade Boggs .40 .16
5 George Brett 1.00 .40
6 Jose Canseco .75 .30
7 Joe Carter .25 .10
8 Roger Clemens 1.00 .40
9 Alvin Davis .05 .02
10 Rob Deer .05 .02
11 Kirk Gibson .10 .04
12 Rickey Henderson .40 .16
13 Kent Hrbek .10 .04
14 Pete Incaviglia .10 .04
15 Reggie Jackson .50 .20
16 Wally Joyner .40 .16
17 Don Mattingly 1.50 .60
18 Jack Morris .10 .04
19 Eddie Murray .50 .20
20 Kirby Puckett 1.25 .50
21 Jim Rice .10 .04
22 Dave Righetti .05 .02
23 Cal Ripken 2.50 1.00
24 Cory Snyder .05 .02
25 Danny Tartabull .05 .02
26 Dave Winfield .25 .10
27 Hubie Brooks .05 .02
28 Gary Carter .15 .06
29 Vince Coleman .05 .02
30 Eric Davis .15 .06
31 Glenn Davis .05 .02
32 Steve Garvey .15 .06
33 Dwight Gooden .15 .06
34 Tony Gwynn 1.50 .60
35 Von Hayes .05 .02
36 Keith Hernandez .10 .04
37 Dale Murphy .25 .10
38 Dave Parker .10 .04
39 Tony Pena .05 .02
40 Nolan Ryan 2.50 1.00
41 Ryne Sandberg 1.00 .40
42 Steve Sax .05 .02
43 Mike Schmidt .75 .30
44 Mike Scott .05 .02
45 Ozzie Smith .75 .30
46 Darryl Strawberry .15 .06
47 Fernando Valenzuela .10 .04
48 Todd Worrell .10 .04

1988 Topps Coins

This full-color set of 60 coins contains a full-color photo of the player with a gold-starred scroll at the bottom containing the player's name, position and team. The backs contain the coin number and brief biographical data. Some of the coins have gold rims and some have silver rims. Each coin measures approximately 1 1/2" in diameter. The 1988 set

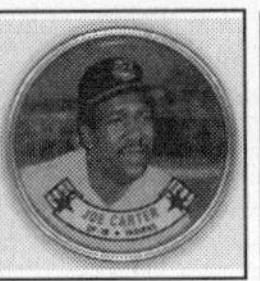

is very similar to the 1987 set of the previous year; the 1988 coins have gold stars on the name scroll on the front of the coin as well as a 1988 copyright at the bottom of the reverse.

Nm-Mt Ex-Mt
COMPLETE SET (60) 8.00 3.20
1 George Bell .05 .02
2 Roger Clemens 1.50 .60
3 Mark McGwire 2.00 .80
4 Wade Boggs .75 .30
5 Harold Baines .10 .04
6 Ivan Calderon .05 .02
7 Jose Canseco .75 .30
8 Joe Carter .25 .10
9 Jack Clark .10 .04
10 Alvin Davis .05 .02
11 Dwight Evans .10 .04
12 Tony Fernandez .10 .04
13 Gary Gaetti .10 .04
14 Mike Greenwell .05 .02
15 Charlie Hough .10 .04
16 Wally Joyner .10 .04
17 Jimmy Key .10 .04
18 Mark Langston .05 .02
19 Don Mattingly 1.50 .60
20 Paul Molitor .75 .30
21 Jack Morris .10 .04
22 Eddie Murray .50 .20
23 Kirby Puckett 1.00 .40
24 Cal Ripken 3.00 1.20
25 Bret Saberhagen .10 .04
26 Ruben Sierra .10 .04
27 Cory Snyder .05 .02
28 Terry Steinbach .05 .02
29 Danny Tartabull .05 .02
30 Alan Trammell .15 .06
31 Devon White .10 .04
32 Robin Yount .75 .30
33 Andre Dawson .25 .10
34 Steve Bedrosian .05 .02
35 Benny Santiago .10 .04
36 Tony Gwynn 1.50 .60
37 Bobby Bonilla .15 .06
38 Will Clark .50 .20
39 Eric Davis .10 .04
40 Mike Dunne .05 .02
41 John Franco .10 .04
42 Dwight Evans .10 .04
43 Pedro Guerrero .05 .02
44 Dion James .05 .02
45 John Kruk .10 .04
46 Jeffrey Leonard .05 .02
47 Carmelo Martinez .05 .02
48 Dale Murphy .25 .10
49 Tim Raines .10 .04
50 Nolan Ryan 3.00 1.20
51 Juan Samuel .05 .02
52 Ryne Sandberg 1.00 .40
53 Mike Schmidt .75 .30
54 Mike Scott .05 .02
55 Ozzie Smith .75 .30
56 Darryl Strawberry .10 .04
57 Rick Sutcliffe .10 .04
58 Fernando Valenzuela .10 .04
59 Tim Wallach .05 .02
60 Todd Worrell .10 .04

1989 Topps Coins

The 1989 Topps Coins set contains 60 coins, each measuring approximately 1 1/2" in diameter. The coins were issued in packs of three coins. The set is arranged by league order with the Most Valuable Player, Cy Young Award Winner, Rookie of the Year and Batting Leaders being first, then the rest of the league being arranged alphabetically within the league group. The National League players are 1-28 and the American League players are 29-60.

Nm-Mt Ex-Mt
COMPLETE SET (60) 8.00 3.20
1 Kirk Gibson .10 .04
2 Orel Hershiser .10 .04
3 Chris Sabo .05 .02
4 Tony Gwynn 1.50 .60
5 Bobby Bonilla .10 .04
6 Brett Butler .10 .04
7 Jack Clark .05 .02
8 Will Clark .50 .20
9 Eric Davis .10 .04
10 Glenn Davis .05 .02
11 Andre Dawson .25 .10
12 John Franco .10 .04
13 Andres Galarraga .25 .10
14 Dwight Gooden .10 .04
15 Mark Grace .40 .16
16 Pedro Guerrero .05 .02
17 Ricky Jordan .05 .02
18 Mike Marshall .05 .02
19 Dale Murphy .25 .10
20 Eddie Murray .50 .20
21 Gerald Perry .05 .02
22 Tim Raines .10 .04
23 Juan Samuel .05 .02
24 Benito Santiago .10 .04
25 Ozzie Smith .75 .30
26 Darryl Strawberry .10 .04
27 Andy Van Slyke .05 .02
28 Gerald Young .05 .02
29 Jose Canseco .50 .20
30 Frank Viola .05 .02

31 Walt Weiss .05 .02
32 Wade Boggs .75 .30
33 Harold Baines .10 .04
34 George Brett 1.50 .60
35 Jay Buhner .50 .20
36 Joe Carter .15 .06
37 Roger Clemens 1.50 .60
38 Alvin Davis .05 .02
39 Tony Fernandez .05 .02
40 Carlton Fisk .75 .30
41 Mike Greenwell .05 .02
42 Kent Hrbek .10 .04
43 Don Mattingly 1.50 .60
44 Fred McGriff .50 .20
45 Mark McGwire 2.00 .80
46 Paul Molitor .75 .30
47 Rafael Palmeiro .50 .20
48 Kirby Puckett 1.00 .40
49 Johnny Ray .05 .02
50 Cal Ripken 3.00 1.20
51 Ruben Sierra .10 .04
52 Pete Stanicek .05 .02
53 Dave Stewart .10 .04
54 Greg Swindell .05 .02
55 Danny Tartabull .05 .02
56 Alan Trammell .15 .06
57 Lou Whitaker .10 .04
58 Dave Winfield .75 .30
59 Mike Witt .05 .02
60 Robin Yount .75 .30

1990 Topps Coins

The 1989 Topps Coins set contains 60 coins, each measuring approximately 1 1/2" in diameter. The coins were issued in packs of three coins. The set is arranged by league order with the Most Valuable Player, Cy Young Award Winner, Rookie of the Year and Batting Leaders being first, then the rest of the league being arranged alphabetically within the league group. The American League players are 1-32 and the National League players are 33-60. This set was also issued in factory set form.

Nm-Mt Ex-Mt
COMPLETE SET (60) 8.00 2.40
COMP. FACT. SET (60) 8.00 2.40
1 Robin Yount .75 .23
2 Bret Saberhagen .10 .03
3 Gregg Olson .05 .02
4 Kirby Puckett .60 .18
5 George Bell .05 .02
6 Wade Boggs .75 .23
7 Jerry Browne .05 .02
8 Ellis Burks .15 .04
9 Ivan Calderon .05 .02
10 Tom Candiotti .05 .02
11 Alvin Davis .05 .02
12 Chili Davis .10 .03
13 Chuck Finley .10 .03
14 Gary Gaetti .10 .03
15 Tom Gordon .15 .04
16 Ken Griffey Jr. 2.00 .60
17 Rickey Henderson .75 .23
18 Kent Hrbek .10 .03
19 Bo Jackson .25 .07
20 Carlos Martinez .05 .02
21 Don Mattingly 1.50 .45
22 Fred McGriff .25 .07
23 Paul Molitor .75 .23
24 Cal Ripken 3.00 .90
25 Nolan Ryan 3.00 .90
26 Steve Sax .10 .03
27 Gary Sheffield .50 .15
28 Ruben Sierra .10 .03
29 Dave Stewart .10 .03
30 Mickey Tettleton .10 .03
31 Alan Trammell .15 .04
32 Lou Whitaker .10 .03
33 Kevin Mitchell .05 .02
34 Mark Davis .05 .02
35 Jerome Walton .05 .02
36 Tony Gwynn 1.50 .45
37 Roberto Alomar .25 .07
38 Tim Belcher .05 .02
39 Craig Biggio .30 .09
40 Barry Bonds 2.00 .60
41 Bobby Bonilla .10 .03
42 Joe Carter .10 .03
43 Will Clark .50 .15
44 Eric Davis .10 .03
45 Glenn Davis .05 .02
46 Sid Fernandez .05 .02
47 Pedro Guerrero .05 .02
48 Von Hayes .05 .02
49 Tom Herr .05 .02
50 Howard Johnson .05 .02
51 Barry Larkin .25 .07
52 Joe Magrane .05 .02
53 Dale Murphy .25 .07
54 Tim Raines .10 .03
55 Willie Randolph .10 .03
56 Ryne Sandberg 1.00 .30
57 Dwight Smith .05 .02
58 Lonnie Smith .05 .02
59 Robby Thompson .05 .02
60 Tim Wallach .05 .02

1989 A's Unocal 76 Pins

These pins were issued by Unocal in conjunction with the Oakland A's. These pins do not feature players, rather they feature symbols or evetnts significant to the A's.

Nm-Mt Ex-Mt
COMPLETE SET (5) 15.00 6.00
COMMON PIN (1-5) 3.00 1.20

1992 A's Unocal 76 Pins

These pins feature important events in the first quarter century of the Oakland A's. Many

prominent A's players are pictured on these pins.

Nm-Mt Ex-Mt
COMPLETE SET (5) 20.00 6.00
1 Jose Canseco 4.50 1.50
Mark McGwire
Walt Weiss
2 Vida Blue 5.00 1.50
Reggie Jackson
Jose Canseco
Rickey Henderson
3 Jim "Catfish" Hunter 4.00 1.20
Dave Stewart
4 Jim "Catfish" Hunter 4.00 1.20
Vida Blue
Mike Warren
Dave Stewart
5 Reggie Jackson 5.00 1.50
Harold Baines
Dave Henderson

1997 All-Star Game Pins

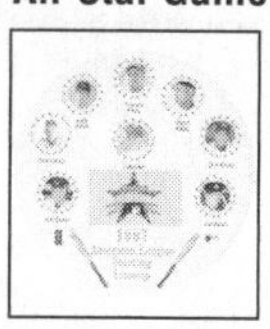

These two oversize pins were issued before the 1997 All-Star game and featured head shots of the players voted to the starting lineup in each league. The pins were produced before the starting pitchers were announced so neither pitcher is on the pin. The pins were approved by both Major League Baseball and the MLBPA and were produced by JKA Specialties in New Jersey.

Nm-Mt Ex-Mt
COMPLETE SET (2) 30.00 9.00
1 Ken Griffey Jr. 15.00 4.50
David Justice
Roberto Alomar
Tino Martinez
Ivan Rodriguez
Brady Anderson
Alex Rodriguez
Cal Ripken Jr.
2 Kenny Lofton 15.00 4.50
Tony Gwynn
Craig Biggio
Jeff Bagwell
Mike Piazza
Larry Walker
Barry Larkin
Ken Caminiti

1973-78 ASCCA Show Pins

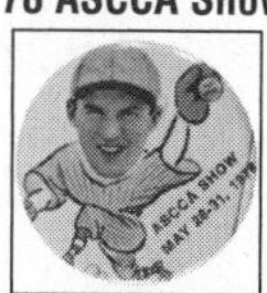

During the 1970's, these buttons were given away as an admission perk at the American Sports Cards Collector Association shows in New York City. These shows, which were run by the Gallagher brothers, were among the first and most sucsessful shows in the early days of the organized hobby. We have listed, when applicable, the player pictured as part of the button information.

NM Ex
COMPLETE SET 40.00 16.00
1 Jackie Robinson 5.00 2.00
Sept., 1973
2 Connie Mack 5.00 2.00
Sept., 1974
3 Babe Ruth 5.00 2.00
May, 1975
4 Joe Medwick 5.00 2.00
May, 1976
5 Sept 1976 5.00 2.00
6 Jackie Robinson 5.00 2.00
May, 1977
7 Yankee Pinstripes 5.00 2.00
Nov., 1977
8 Roy White 5.00 2.00
May, 1978
9 Yankee Pinstripes 5.00 2.00
Nov., 1978

1986 Baseball Star Buttons

This set features color player portraits of 124 Major League Baseball players printed on 1 7/16" diameter button pin-ons. The buttons were distributed two to a package. They are unnumbered and checklisted below in alphabetical order.

Nm-Mt Ex-Mt
COMPLETE SET (124) 35.00 14.00
1 Rick Aguilera .25 .10
2 Dave Anderson .10 .04
3 Alan Ashby .10 .04
4 Wally Backman .10 .04
5 Steve Balboni .10 .04
6 Don Baylor .25 .10
7 Buddy Bell .25 .10
8 George Bell .10 .04
9 Dave Bergman .10 .04
10 Buddy Biancalana .10 .04
11 Dann Bilardello .10 .04
12 Bud Black .10 .04
13 Wade Boggs 1.50 .60
14 Dennis Boyd .10 .04
15 George Brett 1.50 .60
16 Greg Brock .10 .04
17 Tom Browning .10 .04
18 Bill Buckner .25 .10
19 Sal Butera .10 .04
20 Gary Carter .75 .30
21 Jack Clark .25 .10
22 Vince Coleman .25 .10
23 Dave Concepcion .10 .04
24 Danny Cox .10 .04
25 Jose Cruz .25 .10
26 Ron Darling .25 .10
27 Chili Davis .25 .10
28 Glenn Davis .10 .04
29 Jody Davis .10 .04
30 John Denny .10 .04
31 Bob Dernier .10 .04
32 Bo Diaz .10 .04
33 Bill Doran .10 .04
34 Brian Downing .10 .04
35 Shawon Dunston .25 .10
36 Leon Durham .10 .04
37 Lenny Dykstra .60 .24
38 Dennis Eckersley .75 .30
39 Nick Esasky .10 .04
40 Sid Fernandez .10 .04
41 Carlton Fisk 1.00 .40
42 Scott Flecther .10 .04
43 Doug Frobel .10 .04
44 Phil Garner .10 .04
45 Steve Garvey .60 .24
46 Kirk Gibson .25 .10
47 Dan Gladden .10 .04
48 Rich Gossage .40 .16
49 Kevin Gross .10 .04
50 Pedro Guerrero .25 .10
51 Ron Guidry .25 .10
52 Tony Gwynn 2.00 .80
53 Atlee Hammaker .10 .04
54 Von Hayes .10 .04
55 Rickey Henderson 1.25 .50
56 Keith Hernandez .25 .10
57 Tom Herr .10 .04
58 Orel Hershiser .40 .16
59 Garth Iorg .10 .04
60 Bob James .10 .04
61 Tracy Jones .10 .04
62 Wally Joyner 1.00 .40
63 Charlie Kerfeld .10 .04
64 Dave Kingman .10 .04
65 Chet Lemon .10 .04
66 Jeff Leonard .10 .04
67 Charlie Liebrandt .10 .04
68 Fred Lynn .25 .10
69 Mike Marshall .10 .04
70 Gary Matthews .10 .04
71 Don Mattingly 2.00 .80
72 Roger McDowell .10 .04
73 Willie McGee .25 .10
74 Keith Moreland .10 .04
75 Jack Morris .25 .10
76 Dale Murphy .40 .16
77 Eddie Murray 1.25 .50
78 Pete O'Brien .10 .04
79 Ron Oester .10 .04
80 Bob Ojeda .10 .04
81 Jesse Orosco .25 .10
82 Tom Paciorek .10 .04
83 Dave Parker .25 .10
84 Darrell Porter .10 .04
85 Terry Puhl .10 .04
86 Dan Quisenberry .10 .04
87 Willie Randolph .25 .10
88 Shane Rawley .10 .04
89 Jerry Reuss .10 .04
90 Jim Rice .25 .10
91 Dave Righetti .10 .04
92 Cal Ripken Jr. 3.00 1.20
93 Pete Rose 1.00 .40
94 Nolan Ryan 3.00 1.20
95 Bret Saberhagen .25 .10
96 Ryne Sandberg 1.50 .60
97 Scott Sanderson .10 .04
98 Steve Sax .10 .04
99 Mike Schmidt 1.00 .40
100 Ted Simmons .25 .10
101 Don Slaught .10 .04
102 Lee Smith .40 .16
103 Lonnie Smith .10 .04
104 Ozzie Smith 1.50 .60
105 Mario Soto .10 .04
106 Darryl Strawberry .25 .10
107 Jim Sundberg .10 .04
108 Rick Sutcliffe .25 .10
109 Bruce Sutter .40 .16
110 Jay Tibbs .10 .04
111 Alan Trammell .60 .24
112 Manny Trillo .10 .04
113 John Tudor .10 .04
114 Tim Teufel .10 .04
115 Fernando Valenzuela .25 .10
116 Ozzie Virgil .10 .04
117 Tim Wallach .10 .04
118 Lou Whitaker .25 .10
119 Frank White .10 .04
120 Ernie Whitt .10 .04
121 Glenn Wilson .10 .04
122 Willie Wilson .10 .04
123 Dave Winfield 1.00 .40
124 Robin Yount .75 .30

1992 Blue Jays Pins

This 13-pin set features color player photos on tie tac type pins measuring approximately 1 1/16" by 1 3/8". The pins came one to a package with 2 1/2" by 4 3/4" cards with the checklist printed alphabetically on the card backs.

Nm-Mt Ex-Mt
COMPLETE SET (13) 50.00 15.00
1 Roberto Alomar 6.00 1.80
2 Pat Borders 3.00 .90
3 Joe Carter 6.00 1.80
4 Kelly Gruber 3.00 .90
5 Juan Guzman 4.00 1.20
6 Jimmy Key 6.00 1.80
7 Jack Morris 5.00 1.50
8 John Olerud 5.00 1.50
9 Dave Stieb 4.00 1.20
10 Todd Stottlemyre 3.00 .90
11 Duane Ward 3.00 .90
12 Devon White 4.00 1.20
13 Dave Winfield 6.00 1.80

2003 Bonds 600 Pin

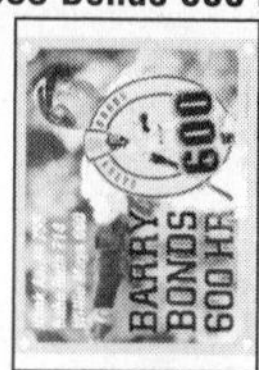

This one pin was issued to commemorate the 600th career homer of Barry Bonds. The pin is attached to a blank-backed 2 1/2" by 2" photo of Bonds along with the names of the players who are ahead of Bonds on the all-time homer list.

MINT NRMT
1 Barry Bonds 5.00 2.20

1992 Brewers U.S. Oil

Sponsored by U.S. Oil Co. Inc., this four-card set consists of 2 3/4" by 4 1/4" cards and commemorative pins. The pins are attached to an extension of the card that is perforated for removal. With this section attached, the cards measure 2 3/4" by 5 5/8" inches. The cards feature color action shots with bright yellow borders. The player's name appears in a bright blue stripe across the top. The event being commemorated is printed on a bright blue stripe across the bottom. The pins show a baseball player against a yellow home plate design. Blue banners across the top contain the event, and a blue bar at the bottom contains the player's name. The pin attached to the Milwaukee County Stadium card shows a bat, ball, and glove design, and has the words "American League Champions" at the top. The cards are unnumbered and checklisted below in alphabetical order.

Nm-Mt Ex-Mt
COMPLETE SET (4) 6.00 1.80
1 Milwaukee County 1.00 .30
Stadium - 1982
2 Paul Molitor 3.00 .90
3 Juan Nieves 1.50 .45
4 Robin Yount 3.00 .90

1898 Cameo Pepsin Gum Pins

The front of the pin is a player head shot with the player's name printed on the edge. The set is checklisted alphabetically below. Additions to this checklist are appreciated.

Ex-Mt VG
COMPLETE SET 30000.00 15000.00
1 Cap Anson 1200.00 600.00
2 Jimmy Bannon 300.00 150.00
3 Marty Bergen 300.00 150.00
4 Lou Bierbauer 300.00 150.00
5 Frank Bowerman 300.00 150.00
6 Ted Breitenstein 300.00 150.00
7 Buttons Briggs 300.00 150.00
8 Eddie Burke 300.00 150.00
9 Jesse Burkett 600.00 300.00
10 Cupid Childs 300.00 150.00
11 Willie Clark 300.00 150.00
12 Boileryard Clarke 300.00 150.00
13 Jack Clements 300.00 150.00
14 Cole 300.00 150.00
Cedar Rapids
14 Cozy Dolan 300.00 150.00
15 Tommy Corcoran 300.00 150.00
16 Lave Cross 300.00 150.00
17 Nig Cuppy 300.00 150.00
18 Bill Dammann 300.00 150.00
19 Tim Donahue 300.00 150.00
20 Donnelley 300.00 150.00
Cedar Rapids
21 Patsy Donovan 300.00 150.00
22 Frank Dwyer 300.00 150.00
23 Bones Ely 300.00 150.00
24 Buck Ewing 800.00 400.00
25 Fisher 300.00 150.00
Cedar Rapdis
26 Tim Flood 300.00 150.00
27 Fuller 300.00 150.00
Cedar Rapids
27 Bill Hoffer 300.00 150.00
28 Charlie Ganzel 300.00 150.00
29 Jot Goar 300.00 150.00
30 Mike Griffin 300.00 150.00
31 Billy Hamilton 800.00 400.00
32 Bill Hart 300.00 150.00
33 Pink Hawley 300.00 150.00
34 Belden Hill 300.00 150.00
35 Bug Holliday 300.00 150.00
36 Dummy Hoy 500.00 250.00
37 Jim Hughey 300.00 150.00
38 Hutchinson 300.00 150.00
Cedar Rapids
39 Charlie Irwin 300.00 150.00
40 Kennedy 300.00 150.00
Cedar Rapids
41 Frank Killen 300.00 150.00
42 Malachi Kittredge 300.00 150.00
43 Candy LaChance 300.00 150.00
44 Herman Long 400.00 200.00
45 Bobby Lowe 400.00 200.00
46 Denny Lyons 300.00 150.00
47 Mahaffey 300.00 150.00
Cedar Rapids
49 Jimmy McAleer 300.00 150.00
50 Willard Mains 300.00 150.00
51 McDougal 300.00 150.00
Cedar Rapids
52 Chippy McGarr 300.00 150.00
53 Ed McKean 300.00 150.00
54 Sadie McMahon 300.00 150.00
55 Bid McPhee 600.00 300.00
56 Dusty Miller 300.00 150.00
56 Bill Merritt 300.00 150.00
57 Frank Motz 300.00 150.00
58 Kid Nichols 600.00 300.00
59 Jack O'Connor 300.00 150.00
60 John Pappalau 300.00 150.00
61 Heinie Peitz 300.00 150.00
62 Jack Powell 300.00 150.00
63 Billy Rhines 300.00 150.00
64 Claude Ritchey 300.00 150.00
Sic, Richie
65 Jack Ryan 300.00 150.00
66 Pop Schriver 300.00 150.00
67 Tom Sharkey 300.00 150.00
Boxer
68 Billy Shindle 300.00 150.00
69 Aleck Smith 300.00 150.00
70 Elmer Smith 300.00 150.00
71 George Smith 300.00 150.00
72 Jake Stenzel 300.00 150.00
73 Jack Stivetts 300.00 150.00
75 Joe Sudgen 300.00 150.00
76 Jim Sullivan 300.00 150.00
77 Patsy Tebeau 400.00 200.00
78 Fred Tenney 400.00 200.00
79 Adonis Terry 300.00 150.00
80 Van Buren 300.00 150.00
Cedar Rapids
81 Farmer Vaughn 300.00 150.00
82 Bobby Wallace 600.00 300.00
83 Weaver 300.00 150.00
Milwaukee
84 Cy Young 1500.00 750.00
85 Brooklyn Baseball Club 400.00 200.00
1897
86 Buffalo Baseball Club 300.00 150.00
1897
87 New Castle Baseball Club 300.00 150.00
1897
88 Pittsburgh Baseball Club 400.00 200.00
1897
89 Toronto Baseball Club 300.00 150.00
1897

1994 Dean Chance Snapple

This pin and card honor the 1964 Cy Young Award-Winning pitching ace Dean Chance. The diamond-shaped pin measures about one inch from corner to corner and features a posed color photo of Chance. The card is 2 1/2" by 5 1/8" and features on its white-bordered front a photo of Chance in his windup. His lifetime pitching record appears below the photo in an area set off by a perforated line. The Snapple and California Angels logos rest at the bottom. The plain white back carries career highlights and the Snapple and Angels logos.

Nm-Mt Ex-Mt
1 Dean Chance 2.00 .60

1930 Chicago Evening American Pins

This set features 10 members of the Chicago Cubs and 10 members of the Chicago White Sox. These unnumbered pins are ordered below alphabetically by team, Chicago Cubs (1-10) and Chicago White Sox (11-20). The pins measure approximately 1 1/4" in diameter. The top of the pin gives the player's position, last name and team nickname. The photos are black and white on a white background. The player photos are head only with no neck shown. The set is thought to have been issued in 1930.

	Ex-Mt	VG
COMPLETE SET (20)	3000.00	1500.00
1 Les Bell	125.00	60.00
2 Kiki Cuyler	250.00	125.00
3 Woody English	125.00	60.00
4 Charlie Grimm	150.00	75.00
5 Gabby Hartnett	250.00	125.00
6 Rogers Hornsby	400.00	200.00
7 Joe McCarthy MG	250.00	125.00
8 Charlie Root	125.00	60.00
9 Riggs Stephenson	200.00	100.00
10 Hack Wilson	250.00	125.00
11 Moe Berg	500.00	250.00
12 Donie Bush MG	125.00	60.00
13 Bill Cissell	125.00	60.00
14 Red Faber	250.00	125.00
15 Bill Hunnefield	125.00	60.00
16 Smead Jolley	125.00	60.00
17 Willie Kamm	125.00	60.00
18 Jim Moore	125.00	60.00
19 Carl Reynolds	125.00	60.00
20 Art Shires	125.00	60.00

1929 Cubs Certified Ice Cream Pins

The pins in this unnumbered set are brown and white in color and measure 1" in diameter. The set features Chicago Cubs players only. The set was issued by Certified Ice Cream, the official Ice Cream of Wrigley Field. A 3" in dia. team photo pin was also issued during this 1929 season promotion. The set price below does not include the team photo pin.

	Ex-Mt	VG
COMPLETE SET (6)	3000.00	1500.00
1 Joe Bush	150.00	75.00
2 Kiki Cuyler	300.00	150.00
3 Rogers Hornsby	400.00	200.00
4 Riggs Stephenson	200.00	100.00
5 Hack Wilson	300.00	150.00
6 Team photo Pin (3")	1800.00	900.00

1933 Cracker Jack Pins

This 25-pin set is also known as the "PR4 Baseball Drawing Set" as the player portraits are actually line drawings. The pins measure approximately 13/16" in diameter. The pins are printed in gray and blue on a yellow background. The set was probably issued some time in the early thirties based on the selection of players in the set. Be careful not to get these pins wet as the inks are water soluble.

	Ex-Mt	VG
COMPLETE SET (25)	500.00	250.00
1 Charles Berry	15.00	7.50
2 Bill Cissell	15.00	7.50
3 Kiki Cuyler	25.00	12.50
4 Dizzy Dean	40.00	20.00
5 Wes Ferrell	15.00	7.50
6 Frankie Frisch	30.00	15.00
7 Lou Gehrig	100.00	50.00
8 Lefty Gomez	30.00	15.00
9 Goose Goslin	25.00	12.50
10 George Grantham	15.00	7.50
11 Charlie Grimm	20.00	10.00
12 Lefty Grove	30.00	15.00
13 Gabby Hartnett	30.00	15.00
14 Travis Jackson	25.00	12.50
15 Tony Lazzeri	25.00	12.50
16 Ted Lyons	25.00	12.50
17 Rabbit Maranville	25.00	12.50
18 Carl Reynolds	15.00	7.50
19 Red Ruffing	25.00	12.50
20 Al Simmons	30.00	15.00
21 Gus Suhr	15.00	7.50
22 Bill Terry	30.00	15.00
23 Dazzy Vance	25.00	12.50
24 Paul Waner	25.00	12.50
25 Lon Warneke	15.00	7.50

1911 Diamond Gum Pins

This set of 29 (the number of pins known at this time) pins is described on each pin as "Free with Diamond Gum." The border of each pin is

blue. Since the pins are unnumbered they are ordered below in alphabetical order. The player's name and team are given on the front of the pin on either side of the black and white player photo. Each pin measures approximately 7/8" in diameter.

	Ex-Mt	VG
COMPLETE SET	8000.00	4000.00
1 Babe Adams	150.00	75.00
2 Frank Baker	250.00	125.00
3 Chief Bender	250.00	125.00
4 Mordecai Brown	250.00	125.00
5 Donie Bush	150.00	75.00
6 Bill Carrigan	150.00	75.00
7 Frank Chance	300.00	150.00
8 Hal Chase	250.00	125.00
9 Ty Cobb	1500.00	750.00
10 Eddie Collins	300.00	150.00
11 Harry Davis	150.00	75.00
12 Red Dooin	150.00	75.00
13 Larry Doyle	175.00	90.00
14 Johnny Evers	250.00	125.00
15 Miller Huggins	250.00	125.00
16 Hugh Jennings	250.00	125.00
17 Napolean Lajoie	400.00	200.00
18 Harry Lord	150.00	75.00
19 Christy Mathewson	600.00	300.00
20 Dots Miller	150.00	75.00
21 George Mullen (Mullin)	150.00	75.00
22 Danny Murphy	150.00	75.00
23 Orval Overall	150.00	75.00
24 Eddie Plank	300.00	150.00
25 Hack Simmons Rochester	150.00	75.00
26 Ira Thomas	150.00	75.00
27 Joe Tinker	300.00	150.00
28 Honus Wagner	500.00	250.00
29 Cy Young	400.00	200.00

1987 Dodgers UNOCAL 76 Pins

This six-pin set features color lapel pins of important events in the history of the Los Angeles Dodgers team. The pins came attached to a 2" by 3" card explaining the significance of that particular pin.

	Nm-Mt	Ex-Mt
COMPLETE SET (6)	10.00	4.00
COMMON PIN (1-6)	2.00	.80

1989 Dodgers UNOCAL 76 Pins

This six-pin set features color lapel pins of important events in the history of the Los Angeles Dodgers team. The pins came attached to a 2" by 3" card explaining the significance of that particular pin.

	Nm-Mt	Ex-Mt
COMPLETE SET (6)	10.00	4.00
COMMON PIN (1-6)	2.00	.80

1990 Dodgers UNOCAL 76 Pins

This six-pin set features color lapel pins of important events in the history of the Los Angeles Dodgers team. The pins came attached to a 2" by 3" card explaining the significance of that particular pin.

	Nm-Mt	Ex-Mt
COMPLETE SET (6)	10.00	3.00
COMMON PIN (1-6)	2.00	.60

1991 Dodgers Unocal 76 Pins

Some leading events in Dodger history are featured in this set. Many leading Dodger players are featured in this set. This set was issued in conjunction with the Unocal 76 gas station chain.

	Nm-Mt	Ex-Mt
COMPLETE SET (6)	15.00	4.50
1 Ron Cey Steve Garvey Davey Lopes Bill Russell	3.00	.90
2 Manny Mota Lee Lacy	2.00	.60
3 Don Drysdale Orel Hershiser Fernando Valenzuela	3.00	.90
4 Sandy Koufax Bill Singer Jerry Reuss Fernando Valenzuela	5.00	1.50
5 Steve Garvey Reggie Smith Ron Cey Dusty Baker	3.00	.90
6 Sandy Koufax Ramon Martinez	5.00	1.50

1992 Dodgers Unocal 76 Pins

For the second straight year, Unocal 76 in conjunction with the Dodgers issued a set of pins featuring highlights of Dodger history. This set is less player specific than the previous season's set.

	Nm-Mt	Ex-Mt
COMPLETE SET (6)	12.00	3.60
COMMON PIN (1-6)	2.00	.60
5 Walter Alston Tommy Lasorda Dodger Managers	3.00	.90

1993 Dodgers UNOCAL 76 Pins

This six-pin set features color lapel pins of important events in the history of the Los Angeles Dodgers team. The pins came attached to a 2" by 3" card explaining the significance of that particular pin.

	Nm-Mt	Ex-Mt
C OMPLETE SET (6)	10.00	3.00
COMMON PIN (1-6)	2.00	.60

1932 Double Play Candy Pins PX3

These pins, which measure 1 3/4" in diameter, feature leading players of the early 1930's. Each pin has either a 1 or a 2 on the bottom. Since these pins are unnumbered, we have sequenced them in alphabetical order.

	Ex-Mt	VG
COMPLETE SET	1000.00	500.00
1 Sparky Adams	20.00	10.00
2 Dale Alexander	20.00	10.00
3 Earl Averill	40.00	20.00
4 Dick Bartell	25.00	12.50
5 Wally Berger	25.00	12.50
6 Jim Bottomley	40.00	20.00
7 Lefty Brandt	20.00	10.00
8 Owen Carroll	20.00	10.00
9 Lefty Clark	20.00	10.00
10 Mickey Cochrane	50.00	25.00
11 Joe Cronin	60.00	30.00
12 Jimmy Dykes	25.00	12.50
13 George Earnshaw	25.00	12.50
14 Wes Ferrell	30.00	15.00
15 Jimmie Foxx	100.00	50.00
16 Frankie Frisch	60.00	30.00
17 Charlie Gehringer	60.00	30.00
18 Goose Goslin	40.00	20.00
19 Johnny Hodapp	20.00	10.00
20 Frank Hogan	20.00	10.00
21 Si Johnson	20.00	10.00
22 Joe Judge	20.00	10.00
23 Chuck Klein	40.00	20.00
24 Al Lopez	40.00	20.00
25 Ray Lucas	20.00	10.00
26 Red Lucas	20.00	10.00
27 Ted Lyons	40.00	20.00
28 Fred Marberry	20.00	10.00
29 Oscar Melillo	20.00	10.00
30 Lefty O'Doul	30.00	15.00
31 George Pipgras	20.00	10.00
32 Flint Rhem	20.00	10.00
33 Sam Rice	40.00	20.00
34 Muddy Ruel	20.00	10.00
35 Harry Seibold	20.00	10.00
36 Al Simmons	60.00	30.00
37 Joe Vosmik	20.00	10.00
38 Gee Walker	20.00	10.00
39 Pinky Whitney	20.00	10.00
40 Hack Wilson	40.00	20.00

1969 Expos Pins

These nine round pins were manufactured by Best In Sports of Montreal, measure approximately 1 1/2" in diameter and feature players from the Montreal Expos debut season in 1969. The pins have white backgrounds and carry posed color player cutouts. The player's name appears in black lettering above the photo. The pins are unnumbered and checklisted below in alphabetical order.

	NM	Ex
COMPLETE SET (9)	30.00	12.00
1 John Bateman	2.50	1.00
2 Ron Brand	2.50	1.00
3 Ron Fairly	4.00	1.60
4 Coco Laboy	3.00	1.20
5 Gene Mauch MG	4.00	1.60
6 Steve Renko	2.50	1.00
7 Rusty Staub	8.00	3.20
8 Bill Stoneman	3.00	1.20
9 Bobby Wine	2.50	1.00

1970 Expos Pins

These 14 round pins measure approximately 1 1/2" in diameter and feature players from the 1970 Montreal Expos. The pins have red, white and blue backgrounds and carry circular posed color player headshots. The player's name appears in cursive black lettering below the photo. The pins are unnumbered and checklisted below in alphabetical order.

	NM	Ex
COMPLETE SET (14)	50.00	20.00
1 Expos Logo Pin	3.00	1.20
2 Bob Bailey	3.00	1.20
3 John Bateman	2.50	1.00
4 Ron Brand	2.50	1.00
5 Boots Day	2.50	1.00
6 Ron Fairly	4.00	1.60
7 Jim Gosger	2.50	1.00
8 Ron Hunt	3.00	1.20
9 Mack Jones	3.00	1.20
10 Coco Laboy	3.00	1.20
11 Gene Mauch MG	2.50	1.00
12 Dan McGinn	2.50	1.00
13 Carl Morton	3.00	1.20
14 Adolfo Phillips	2.50	1.00
15 Claude Raymond	3.00	1.20
16 Steve Renko	2.50	1.00
17 Marv Staehle	2.50	1.00
18 Rusty Staub	8.00	3.20
19 Bill Stoneman	3.00	1.20
20 Gary Sutherland	2.50	1.00
21 Bobby Wine	2.50	1.00

1998 FanFest Pins

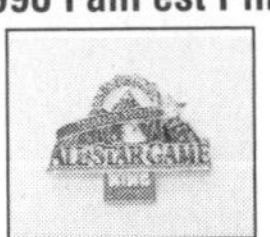

This four-pin set features lapel pins that could be obtained at the 1998 FanFest held in Denver, Colorado, and were sponsored by Aminco and King Soopers. Three of the pins were featured in a Limited Edition Collector Pin Set which could be bought for a suggested retail price of $7.99. A coupon came in the set that could be redeemed for the fourth pin at the Aminco or King Soopers booth at FanFest.

	Nm-Mt	Ex-Mt
COMPLETE SET (4)	8.00	2.40
COMMON PIN (1-4)	2.00	.60

1984 Fun Foods Pins

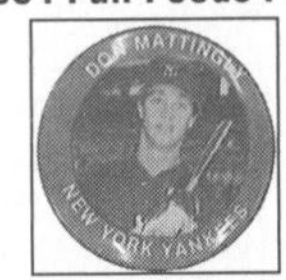

These pins were mass marketed in early 1985 (the copyright notice on the pin backs indicate 1984) and feature 133 pins of the current stars of baseball. Each pin measures approximately 1 1/8" in diameter. There are other related "proof" type items available for this issue. The color border around the photo is coded for the player's team. On the back each pins is numbered; the player's position and a statistic are given.

	Nm-Mt	Ex-Mt
COMPLETE SET (133)	15.00	6.00
1 Dave Winfield	.50	.20
2 Lance Parrish	.10	.04
3 Gary Carter	.75	.30
4 Pete Rose	.50	.20
5 Jim Rice	.10	.04
6 George Brett	1.50	.60
7 Fernando Valenzuela	.10	.04
8 Darryl Strawberry	.50	.20
9 Steve Garvey	.15	.06
10 Rollie Fingers	.25	.10
11 Mike Schmidt	1.00	.40
12 Kent Tekulve	.05	.02
13 Ryne Sandberg	1.25	.50
14 Bruce Sutter	.10	.04
15 Tom Seaver	.75	.30
16 Reggie Jackson	.50	.20
17 Rickey Henderson	1.00	.40
18 Mark Langston	.15	.06
19 Jack Clark	.10	.04
20 Willie Randolph	.10	.04
21 Kirk Gibson	.25	.10
22 Andre Dawson	.25	.10
23 Dave Concepcion	.10	.04
24 Tony Armas	.05	.02
25 Dan Quisenberry	.05	.02
26 Pedro Guerrero	.10	.04
27 Dwight Gooden	1.50	.60
28 Tony Gwynn	1.50	.60
29 Robin Yount	.75	.30
30 Steve Carlton	.75	.30
31 Bill Madlock	.10	.04
32 Rick Sutcliffe	.10	.04
33 Willie McGee	.15	.06
34 Greg Luzinski	.10	.04
35 Rod Carew	.40	.16
36 Dave Kingman	.10	.04
37 Alvin Davis	.10	.04
38 Chili Davis	.10	.04
39 Don Baylor	.10	.04
40 Alan Trammell	.25	.10
41 Tim Raines	.15	.06
42 Cesar Cedeno	.05	.02
43 Wade Boggs	.50	.20
44 Frank White	.10	.04
45 Steve Sax	.05	.02
46 George Foster	.05	.02
47 Terry Kennedy	.05	.02
48 Cecil Cooper	.10	.04
49 John Denny	.05	.02
50 John Candelaria	.05	.02
51 Jody Davis	.05	.02
52 George Hendrick	.05	.02
53 Ron Kittle	.05	.02
54 Fred Lynn	.10	.04
55 Carney Lansford	.05	.02
56 Gorman Thomas	.05	.02
57 Manny Trillo	.05	.02
58 Steve Kemp	.05	.02
59 Jack Morris	.10	.04
60 Dan Petry	.05	.02
61 Mario Soto	.05	.02
62 Dwight Evans	.10	.04
63 Hal McRae	.10	.04
64 Mike Marshall	.05	.02
65 Mookie Wilson	.10	.04
66 Graig Nettles	.10	.04
67 Ben Oglivie	.05	.02
68 Juan Samuel	.05	.02
69 Johnny Ray	.05	.02
70 Gary Matthews	.10	.04
71 Ozzie Smith	1.25	.50
72 Carlton Fisk	.75	.30
73 Doug DeCinces	.05	.02
74 Joe Morgan	.75	.30
75 Dave Stieb	.05	.02
76 Buddy Bell	.05	.02
77 Don Mattingly	1.50	.60
78 Lou Whitaker	.15	.06
79 Willie Hernandez	.05	.02
80 Dave Parker	.10	.04
81 Bob Stanley	.05	.02
82 Willie Wilson	.05	.02
83 Orel Hershiser	.50	.20
84 Rusty Staub	.10	.04
85 Goose Gossage	.15	.06
86 Don Sutton	.60	.24
87 Al Holland	.05	.02
88 Tony Pena	.10	.04
89 Ron Cey	.05	.02
90 Joaquin Andujar	.05	.02
91 LaMarr Hoyt	.05	.02
92 Tommy John	.10	.04
93 Dwayne Murphy	.05	.02
94 Willie Upshaw	.05	.02
95 Gary Ward	.05	.02
96 Ron Guidry	.10	.04
97 Chet Lemon	.05	.02
98 Aurelio Lopez	.05	.02
99 Tony Perez	.60	.24
100 Bill Buckner	.10	.04
101 Mike Hargrove	.05	.02
102 Scott McGregor	.05	.02
103 Dale Murphy	.25	.10
104 Keith Hernandez	.10	.04
105 Paul Molitor	1.00	.40
106 Bert Blyleven	.15	.06
107 Leon Durham	.05	.02
108 Lee Smith	.15	.06
109 Nolan Ryan	3.00	1.20
110 Harold Baines	.10	.04
111 Kent Hrbek	.10	.04
112 Ron Davis	.05	.02
113 George Bell	.10	.04
114 Charlie Hough	.05	.02
115 Phil Niekro	.60	.24
116 Dave Righetti	.05	.02
117 Darrell Evans	.10	.04
118 Cal Ripken	3.00	1.20
119 Eddie Murray	.75	.30
120 Storm Davis	.05	.02
121 Mike Boddicker	.05	.02
122 Bob Horner	.05	.02
123 Chris Chambliss	.10	.04
124 Ted Simmons	.10	.04
125 Andre Thornton	.05	.02
126 Larry Bowa	.05	.02
127 Bob Dernier	.05	.02
128 Joe Niekro	.05	.02
129 Jose Cruz	.10	.04
130 Tom Brunansky	.05	.02
131 Gary Gaetti	.15	.06
132 Lloyd Moseby	.05	.02
133 Frank Tanana	.10	.04

1992 Giants Chevron Hall of Famer Pins

This set features lapel pins of three San Francisco Giants players who are in the

Baseball Hall of Fame. Each pin is attached to the bottom margin of a 2 1/2" by 5" card with a color portrait of the player in a circle framed to look like a plaque. The backs display a small black-and-white head photo with information about the player and his career. The cards are unnumbered and checklisted below in alphabetical order.

	Nm-Mt	Ex-Mt
COMPLETE SET (3)	15.00	4.50
1 Willie Mays	10.00	3.00
2 Willie McCovey	5.00	1.50
3 Gaylord Perry	3.00	.90

1933 Gum Inc "Doubleheader" Discs

These metal discs were issued by Gum, Inc. circa 1933. The player's picture, name and team are on the front whereas the back is blank. Also on the front is a "1" or a "2". The wrapper says, "Put 1 and 2 together and make a Double Header." Each disc is approximately 1 1/4" in diameter.

	Ex-Mt	VG
COMPLETE SET	1100.00	550.00
1 Sparky Adams	15.00	7.50
2 Dale Alexander	15.00	7.50
3 Earl Averill	40.00	20.00
4 Dick Bartell	15.00	7.50
5 Wally Berger	25.00	12.50
6 Jim Bottomley	40.00	20.00
7 Lefty Brandt	15.00	7.50
8 Owen Carroll	15.00	7.50
9 Lefty Clark	15.00	7.50
10 Mickey Cochrane	80.00	40.00
11 Joe Cronin	50.00	25.00
12 Jimmy Dykes	25.00	12.50
13 George Earnshaw	25.00	12.50
14 Wes Ferrell	25.00	12.50
15 Neal Finn	15.00	7.50
16 Lew Fonseca	15.00	7.50
17 Jimmy Foxx	100.00	50.00
18 Frankie Frisch	60.00	30.00
19 Chick Fullis	15.00	7.50
20 Charley Gehringer	50.00	25.00
21 Goose Goslin	40.00	20.00
22 Johnny Hodapp	15.00	7.50
23 Frank Hogan	15.00	7.50
24 Si Johnson	15.00	7.50
25 Joe Judge	25.00	12.50
26 Chuck Klein	50.00	25.00
27 Al Lopez	40.00	20.00
28 Ray Lucas	15.00	7.50
29 Red Lucas	15.00	7.50
30 Ted Lyons	40.00	20.00
31 Firpo Marberry	15.00	7.50
32 Oscar Melillo	15.00	7.50
33 Lefty O'Doul	25.00	12.50
34 George Pipgras	15.00	7.50
35 Flint Rhem	15.00	7.50
36 Sam Rice	40.00	20.00
37 Muddy Ruel	15.00	7.50
38 Harry Seibold	15.00	7.50
39 Al Simmons	50.00	25.00
40 Joe Vosmik	15.00	7.50
41 Gerald Walker	15.00	7.50
42 Pinky Whitney	15.00	7.50
43 Hack Wilson	50.00	25.00

1962 Guy's Potato Chip Pins

This 20-pin set measures approximately 7/8" in diameter and features a team logo on the front and a Guy's Potato Chip sponsor ad on the back. The pins are unnumbered and checklisted below according to the team's city.

	NM	Ex
COMPLETE SET (20)	100.00	40.00
COMMON PIN (1-20)	5.00	2.00
1 Baltimore Orioles	6.00	2.40
2 Boston Red Sox	6.00	2.40
7 Detroit Tigers	6.00	2.40
8 Houston Colts	10.00	4.00
9 Kansas City A's	6.00	2.40
10 Los Angeles Angels	8.00	3.20
11 Los Angeles Dodgers	6.00	2.40
14 New York Mets	10.00	4.00
19 Washington Nationals	8.00	3.20
20 A Yankee Fan	8.00	3.20

1965 Guy's Potato Chip Pins

This 20-pin set measures approximately 7/8" in diameter and features a team logo on the front and a Guy's Potato Chip sponsor ad on the back. The pins are unnumbered and checklisted below according to the team's city.

	NM	Ex
COMPLETE SET (20)	100.00	40.00
COMMON PIN (1-20)	5.00	2.00
2 Boston Red Sox	6.00	2.40
3 Chicago Cubs	10.00	4.00
8 Houston Astros	6.00	2.40
9 Kansas City A's	6.00	2.40
10 Los Angeles Angels	6.00	2.40
14 New York Mets	10.00	4.00
18 St. Louis Cardinals	6.00	2.40
20 A Yankee Fan	10.00	4.00

1966 Guy's Potato Chip Pins

This 20-pin set measures approximately 7/8" in diameter and features a team logo on the front and a Guy's Potato Chip sponsor ad on the back. The pins are unnumbered and checklisted below according to the team's city. Each year there were subtle differences in the pin colors which helps collectors identify the year of issue.

	NM	Ex
COMPLETE SET (20)	100.00	40.00
COMMON PIN (1-20)	5.00	2.00
1 Baltimore Orioles	8.00	3.20
2 Boston Red Sox	6.00	2.40
4 Chicago Cubs	8.00	3.20
10 Kansas City A's	6.00	2.40
11 Los Angeles Dodgers	8.00	3.20
14 New York Mets	8.00	3.20
19 Washington Nationals	6.00	2.40
20 A Yankee Fan	10.00	4.00

1995 Gwynn Pin Ralph

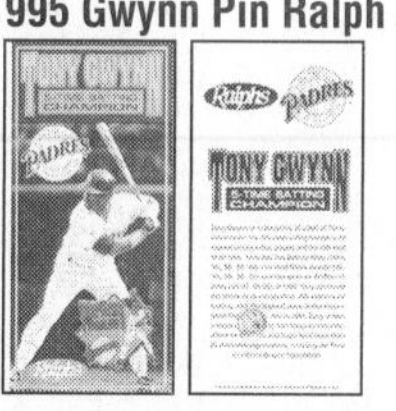

This combination pin/card was created by Imprinted Products and features a photo of Tony Gwynn as well as a pin commemorating his then five batting titles. The back has the "Ralph's" logo as well as the Padres logo and a description of Gwynn's career.

	Nm-Mt	Ex-Mt
1 Tony Gwynn	5.00	1.50

1994 Imprinted Products Pin-Cards

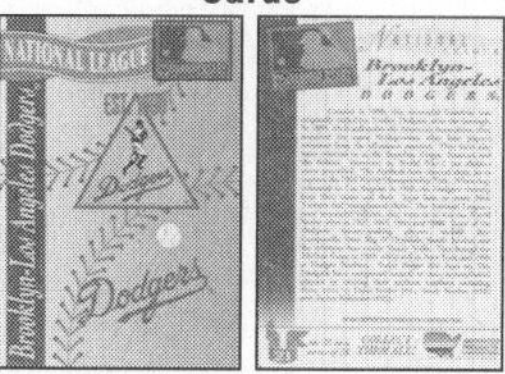

Made by Imprinted Products Corp., and distributed by Pinnacle Brands, these 28 pins and their accompanying cards feature American League (1-14) and National League (15-28) teams. Each pack contained one MLB team pin, one team card, and checklist. In all, 25,000 boxes were produced, with 36 single packs per box. 500 "Winner" pins were randomly inserted which could be redeemed for a free Diamond Series II set, valued at $250.00. The pins are made out of a soft bronzish metal. The pins, and their accompanying cards, are numbered on the back. The standard-size cards have on the front the team logos and the back summarize the beginnings and history of each franchise.

	Nm-Mt	Ex-Mt
COMPLETE SET	25.00	7.50
COMMON CARD (1-28)	1.00	.30

1969 Kelly's Potato Chips

This set of 20 red, white and blue pins has a very heavy emphasis on the National League and especially the midwestern city teams. The pins are unnumbered and hence are listed below in alphabetical order. The sponsor was Kelly's Potato Chips. Each pin measures approximately 1 3/16" in diameter. A black and white player photo is encircled by a blue (NL) or red (AL) band containing the player and team name as well as "Kelly's" and "ZIP".

	NM	Ex
COMPLETE SET	200.00	80.00
1 Luis Aparicio	12.00	4.80
2 Ernie Banks	15.00	6.00
3 Glenn Beckert	4.00	1.60
4 Lou Brock	15.00	6.00
5 Curt Flood	8.00	3.20
6 Bob Gibson	15.00	6.00
7 Joel Horlen	4.00	1.60
8 Al Kaline	20.00	8.00
9 Don Kessinger	4.00	1.60
10 Mickey Lolich	6.00	2.40
11 Juan Marichal	12.00	4.80
12 Willie Mays	40.00	16.00
13 Tim McCarver	6.00	2.40
14 Denny McLain	6.00	2.40
15 Pete Rose	50.00	20.00
16 Ron Santo	8.00	3.20
17 Joe Torre	8.00	3.20
18 Pete Ward	4.00	1.60
19 Billy Williams	12.00	4.80
20 Carl Yastrzemski	25.00	10.00

1922-23 Kolbs Mothers' Bread Pins PB4

These pins were issued over a two year period. The pins however are essentially indistinguishable as to which year they may have been produced. Pins measure approximately 7/8" in diameter. Players pictured in the set are from the Reading Baseball Club of the International League. The pins are styled in black and white with red trim.

	Ex-Mt	VG
COMPLETE SET (32)	1500.00	750.00
1 Spencer Abbott MG	60.00	30.00
2 Charles Babington	60.00	30.00
3 Bill Barrett	60.00	30.00
4 Raymond Bates	60.00	30.00
5 Chief Bender MG	250.00	125.00
6 Myrl Brown	60.00	30.00
7 Fred Carts	60.00	30.00
8 Justin Clarke	60.00	30.00
9 Thomas Connelly	60.00	30.00
10 Gus Getz	60.00	30.00
11 Frank Gilhooley	60.00	30.00
12 Ray Gordonier	60.00	30.00
13 Henry Haines	60.00	30.00
14 Francis Karpp	60.00	30.00
15 Joe Kelly	60.00	30.00
16 Andrew Kotch	60.00	30.00
17 William Lightner	60.00	30.00
18 Byrd Lynn	60.00	30.00
19 Al Mamaux	60.00	30.00
20 Pat Martin	60.00	30.00
21 Ralph Miller	60.00	30.00
22 Otto Pahlman	60.00	30.00
23 Sam Post	60.00	30.00
24 Al Schacht	100.00	50.00
25 John Scott	60.00	30.00
26 Walt Smallwood	60.00	30.00
27 Ross Swartz	60.00	30.00
28 Fred Thomas	60.00	30.00
29 Myles Thomas	60.00	30.00
30 Walt Tragesser	60.00	30.00
31 Roy Washburn	60.00	30.00
32 Walter Wolfe	60.00	30.00

1910 Luxello Cigar Pins

This set features members of both Philadelphia teams. They measure 7/8" around. We have sequenced this set in alphabetical order.

	Ex-Mt	VG
COMPLETE SET	4000.00	2000.00
1 Frank Baker	350.00	180.00
2 Jack Barry	200.00	100.00
3 John W. Bates	200.00	100.00
4 Eddie Collins	400.00	200.00
5 Jack Coombs	200.00	100.00
6 Harry Davis	200.00	100.00
7 Red Dooin	200.00	100.00
8 Mickey Doolan	200.00	100.00
9 James Dygert	200.00	100.00
10 Eddie Grant	250.00	125.00
11 William Heitmiller	200.00	100.00
12 Otto Knabe	200.00	100.00
13 Harry Krause	200.00	100.00
14 Paddy Livingston	200.00	100.00
15 George McQuillan	200.00	100.00
16 Earl Moore	200.00	100.00
17 Pat Moran	200.00	100.00
18 Danny Murphy	200.00	100.00
19 Eddie Plank	350.00	180.00
20 Tully Sparks	200.00	100.00
21 John Titus	200.00	100.00

1991 Major League Collector Pins

These gold-colored metal pins were issued by Ace Novelty and measure 1 1/8" by 1 7/8" and feature a color player photo on the fronts. The player's 1990 statistics are given on the reverse of the pin. Each pin was sold in a cardboard display package that included a '91 Score baseball card of the same player. The cards are listed below according to the checklist on the back of the cardboard display.

	Nm-Mt	Ex-Mt
COMPLETE SET (80)	60.00	18.00
1 Don Mattingly	2.50	.75
2 Kevin Maas	.25	.07
3 Hensley Meulens	.25	.07
4 Ken Griffey Jr.	3.00	.90
5 Ken Griffey Sr.	.50	.15
6 Randy Johnson	1.50	.45
7 Tino Martinez	1.00	.30
8 Roger Clemens	2.50	.75
9 Wade Boggs	1.25	.35
10 Mo Vaughn	.75	.23
11 Ellis Burks	.50	.15
12 Kirby Puckett	1.25	.35
13 Kevin Tapani	.25	.07
14 Carlton Fisk	1.25	.35
15 Bobby Thigpen	.25	.07
16 Sammy Sosa	3.00	.90
17 Frank Thomas	1.50	.45
18 Sandy Alomar Jr.	.50	.15
19 Mauro Gozzo	.25	.07
20 Bo Jackson	1.00	.30
21 George Brett	2.50	.75
22 Terry Shumpert	.25	.07
23 Jim Abbott	.25	.07
24 Lee Stevens	.25	.07
25 Mark Langston	.25	.07
26 Dave Stieb	.25	.07
27 John Olerud	.75	.23
28 Mark Whiten	.25	.07
29 Cal Ripken Jr.	5.00	1.50
30 David Segui	.50	.15
31 Ben McDonald	.25	.07
32 Cecil Fielder	.50	.15
33 Alan Trammell	.75	.23
34 Travis Fryman	.50	.15
35 Nolan Ryan	5.00	1.50
36 Juan Gonzalez	1.25	.35
37 Scott Chiamparino	.25	.07
38 Jose Canseco	1.00	.30
39 Mark McGwire	3.00	.90
40 Rickey Henderson	1.50	.45
41 Ozzie Canseco	.25	.07
42 Paul Molitor	1.25	.35
43 Robin Yount	1.25	.35
44 Eric Anthony	.25	.07
45 Andujar Cedeno	.25	.07
46 Dave Justice	1.00	.30
47 Ron Gant	.50	.15
48 Todd Zeile	.50	.15
49 Ozzie Smith	2.50	.75
50 Ray Lankford	.50	.15
51 Jose Offerman	.25	.07
52 Ramon Martinez	.25	.07
53 Eddie Murray	1.25	.35
54 Tony Gwynn	2.50	.75
55 Paul Faries	.25	.07
56 Bruce Hurst	.25	.07
57 Barry Bonds	3.00	.90
58 Orlando Merced	.25	.07
59 Doug Drabek	.25	.07
60 Len Dykstra	.50	.15
61 Mickey Morandini	.25	.07
62 Dale Murphy	1.00	.30
63 Will Clark	1.25	.35
64 Kevin Mitchell	.25	.07
65 Matt Williams	.75	.23
66 Mark Grace	1.00	.30
67 Andre Dawson	1.00	.30
68 Ryne Sandberg	1.25	.35
69 Derrick May	.25	.07
70 Eric Davis	.50	.15
71 Hal Morris	.25	.07
72 Glenn Sutko	.25	.07
73 Randy Myers	.25	.07
74 Dwight Gooden	.50	.15
75 Todd Hundley	.75	.23
76 Dave Magadan	.25	.07
77 Gregg Jefferies	.25	.07
78 Delino DeShields	.25	.07
79 Howard Farmer	.25	.07
80 Larry Walker	1.00	.30

1990 Mariners Red Apple Pins

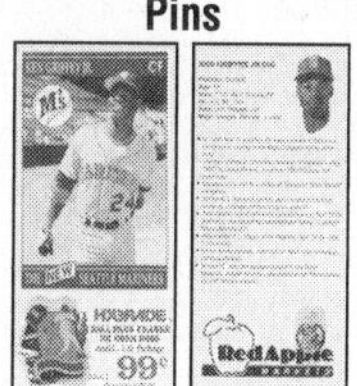

These pins features Seattle Mariner players. They were issued in conjunction with Red Apple. There might be more pins so any additions are appreciated.

	Nm-Mt	Ex-Mt
COMPLETE SET	12.00	3.60
1 Ken Griffey Jr.	10.00	3.00
2 David Valle	2.00	.60

1986 Mets World Series Pins

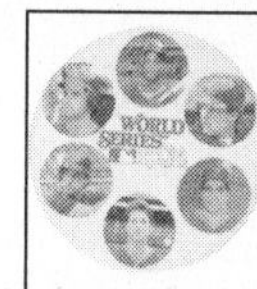

These three oversized pins feature six players each on the front. The photos are little head shots which surround the words "World Series 1986". We have sequenced the players by going clockwise from the top left corner. It is possible another pin or two exists in this set.

	Nm-Mt	Ex-Mt
COMPLETE SET (3)	50.00	20.00
1 Rick Aguilera Darryl Strawberry Lenny Dykstra Sid Fernandez Roger McDowell Danny Heep	20.00	8.00
2 Rafael Santana Tim Teufel Howard Johnson Ed Hearn Bob Ojeda Wally Backman	15.00	6.00
3 Mookie Wilson Ray Knight Lee Mazzilli Jesse Orosco Kevin Mitchell Doug Sisk	15.00	6.00

1996 MLB Pins

This set consists of 37 pins that measure approximately 2 15/16" each in diameter and features color photos of Major League Baseball players. The pins are unnumbered and checklisted below in alphabetical order. Pins were only made for teams which participated in the championship series: Atlanta Braves, Baltimore Orioles, St. Louis Cardinals and New York Yankees.

	Nm-Mt	Ex-Mt
COMPLETE SET (37)	100.00	30.00
1 Roberto Alomar	4.00	1.20
2 Brady Anderson	2.00	.60
3 Alan Benes	1.00	.30
4 Andy Benes	1.00	.30
5 Bobby Bonilla	2.00	.60
6 Pedro Borbon	1.00	.30
7 Mike Devereaux	1.00	.30
8 Jermaine Dye	4.00	1.20
9 Dennis Eckersley	5.00	1.50
10 Gary Gaetti	2.00	.60
11 Ron Gant	2.00	.60
12 Joe Girardi	1.00	.30
13 Tony Graffanino	1.00	.30
14 Marquis Grissom	1.00	.30
15 Chris Hoiles	1.00	.30
16 Derek Jeter	20.00	6.00
17 Brian Jordan	3.00	.90
18 Pat Kelly	1.00	.30
19 Ray Lankford	3.00	.90
20 Tino Martinez	4.00	1.20
21 Mike Mordecai	1.00	.30
22 Mike Mussina	5.00	1.50
23 Randy Myers	2.00	.60
24 Paul O'Neill	3.00	.90
25 Tom Pagnozzi	1.00	.30
26 Rafael Palmeiro	4.00	1.20
27 Eduardo Perez	1.00	.30
28 Tim Raines	2.00	.60
29 Cal Ripken	20.00	6.00
30 Ruben Rivera	1.00	.30
31 Dwight Smith	1.00	.30
32 Ozzie Smith	10.00	3.00
33 Todd Stottlemyre	1.00	.30
34 B.J. Surhoff	2.00	.60
35 John Wetteland	2.00	.60
36 Bernie Williams	4.00	1.20
37 Mark Wohlers	1.00	.30

1990 MLBPA Baseball Buttons (Pins)

These pins feature leading major league baseball players. They are sequenced by teams: Philadelphia Phillies (1-5), Los Angeles Dodgers (6-8), New York Mets (9-18), Cincinnati Reds (19-22), San Francisco Giants (23-29), Stl Louis Cardinals (30-35, 59), Pittsburgh Pirates (36-38), Houston Astros (39-45, 60), Chicago Cubs (46-54), San Diego Padres (55-58), New York Yankees (61-66, 92), Toronto Blue Jays (67), Boston Red Sox (68-73), Oakland A's (74-78, 115), Milwaukee Brewers (79-85), Detroit Tigers (86-91), California Angels (93-96), Minnesota Twins (97-100), Kansas City Royals (101-109), Baltimore Orioles (110-114, 119), Seattle Mariners (116-118, 120)

	Nm-Mt	Ex-Mt
COMPLETE SET (120)	15.00	4.50
1 Tom Herr	.10	.03
2 Von Hayes	.10	.03
3 Ricky Jordan	.10	.03
4 Dickie Thon	.10	.03
5 Lenny Dykstra	.20	.06
6 Kirk Gibson	.20	.06
7 Fernando Valenzuela	.20	.06
8 Orel Hershiser	.20	.06
9 Dwight Gooden	.20	.06
10 Keith Hernandez	.20	.06
11 David Cone	.50	.15
12 Kevin Elster	.10	.03
13 Darryl Strawberry	.20	.06
14 Ron Darling	.10	.03
15 Kevin McReynolds	.10	.03
16 Howard Johnson	.10	.03
17 Gary Carter	.75	.23
18 Gregg Jefferies	.10	.03
19 Chris Sabo	.10	.03
20 Tom Browning	.10	.03
21 Barry Larkin	.50	.15
22 Eric Davis	.20	.06
23 Rick Reuschel	.20	.06
24 Kevin Mitchell	.10	.03
25 Donell Nixon	.10	.03
26 Robby Thompson	.10	.03
27 Brett Butler	.20	.06
28 Will Clark	.75	.23
29 Todd Worrell	.20	.06
30 Ozzie Smith	1.25	.35
31 Tom Brunansky	.10	.03
32 Pedro Guerrero	.10	.03
33 Willie McGee	.20	.06
34 Tony Pena	.20	.06
35 Vince Coleman	.10	.03
36 Andy Van Slyke	.10	.03
37 Barry Bonds	2.00	.60
38 Bobby Bonilla	.20	.06
39 Alan Ashby	.10	.03
40 Gerald Young	.10	.03
41 Glenn Davis	.10	.03
42 Ken Caminiti	.50	.15
43 Mike Scott	.10	.03
44 Bill Doran	.10	.03
45 Kevin Bass	.10	.03
46 Shawon Dunston	.10	.03
47 Ryne Sandberg	1.00	.30
48 Mitch Williams	.10	.03
49 Greg Maddux	2.00	.60
50 Jerome Walton	.10	.03
51 Mark Grace	.50	.15
52 Damon Berryhill	.10	.03
53 Rick Sutcliffe	.10	.03
54 Andre Dawson	.50	.15
55 Tony Gwynn	1.50	.45
56 Jack Clark	.10	.03
57 Bruce Hurst	.10	.03
58 Benito Santiago	.20	.06
59 Jose Oquendo	.10	.03

60 Terry Puhl .10 .03
61 Jesse Barfield .10 .03
62 Steve Sax .10 .03
63 Don Mattingly 1.50 .45
64 Dave Winfield .75 .23
65 Don Slaught .10 .03
66 Steve Balboni .10 .03
67 George Bell .10 .03
68 Wade Boggs .75 .23
69 Roger Clemens 1.50 .45
70 Jim Rice .20 .06
71 Mike Greenwell .10 .03
72 Rich Gedman .10 .03
73 Carney Lansford .10 .03
74 Dave Stewart .20 .06
75 Dennis Eckersley .75 .23
76 Bob Welch .10 .03
77 Mark McGwire 2.00 .60
78 Jose Canseco .50 .15
79 Paul Molitor .75 .23
80 Rob Deer .10 .03
81 Jim Gantner .10 .03
82 Robin Yount .75 .23
83 Ted Higuera .10 .03
84 B.J. Surhoff .20 .06
85 Dan Plesac .10 .03
86 Matt Nokes .10 .03
87 Chet Lemon .10 .03
88 Alan Trammell .30 .09
89 Lou Whitaker .20 .06
90 Fred Lynn .10 .03
91 Mike Heath .10 .03
92 Mel Hall .10 .03
93 Wally Joyner .20 .06
94 Lance Parrish .20 .06
95 Jim Abbott .10 .03
96 Bert Blyleven .10 .03
97 Kent Hrbek .10 .03
98 Kirby Puckett .75 .23
99 Greg Gagne .10 .03
100 Gary Gaetti .20 .06
101 George Brett 1.50 .45
102 Kevin Seitzer .10 .03
103 Charlie Leibrandt .10 .03
104 Bo Jackson .50 .15
105 Mark Gubicza .10 .03
106 Kurt Stillwell .10 .03
107 Bob Boone .20 .06
108 Frank White .20 .06
109 Willie Wilson .10 .03
110 Jeff Ballard .10 .03
111 Mickey Tettleton .10 .03
112 Cal Ripken Jr. 3.00 .90
113 Billy Ripken .10 .03
114 Gregg Olson .10 .03
115 Terry Steinbach .10 .03
116 Alvin Davis .10 .03
117 Ken Griffey Jr. 2.00 .60
118 Harold Reynolds .20 .06
119 Brady Anderson .20 .06
120 Dave Valle .10 .03

1969 MLBPA Pins

This 1969 pin set of 60 was issued by the Major League Baseball Player's Association. Each pin is 7/8" in diameter. The pins are unnumbered and hence they are listed below in alphabetical order within each league, American Leaguers (1-30) and National Leaguers (31-60). This 60 pin set contains 30 pins each of National League players and American League players. The outer bands of the pins are red for American League players and blue for National League players. The pictures on the pins are black and white, head only photos. The line "c. 1969 MLBPA MFG. R.R. Winona, Minn." appears at the bottom of each pin. Many players were reprinted in 1983. The values of these players pins are therefore reduced.

NM Ex
COMPLETE SET (80) 375.00 150.00
1 Max Alvis 2.00 .80
2 Luis Aparicio 10.00 4.00
3 George Brunet 2.00 .80
4 Rod Carew 15.00 6.00
5 Dean Chance 2.50 1.00
6 Bill Freehan 3.00 1.20
7 Jim Fregosi 3.00 1.20
8 Ken Harrelson 3.00 1.20
9 Joel Horlen 2.00 .80
10 Tony Horton 2.00 .80
11 Willie Horton 3.00 1.20
12 Frank Howard 4.00 1.60
13 Al Kaline 12.00 4.80
14 Harmon Killebrew 12.00 4.80
15 Mickey Lolich 4.00 1.60
16 Jim Lonborg 2.50 1.00
17 Sam McDowell 2.50 1.00
18 Denny McLain 5.00 2.00
19 Rick Monday 2.50 1.00
20 Tony Oliva 4.00 1.60
21 Joe Pepitone 3.00 1.20
22 Boog Powell 5.00 2.00
23 Rick Reichardt 2.00 .80
24 Pete Richert 2.00 .80
25 Brooks Robinson 12.00 4.80
26 Frank Robinson 15.00 6.00
27 Mel Stottlemyre 3.00 1.20
28 Luis Tiant 4.00 1.60
29 Pete Ward 2.00 .80
30 Carl Yastrzemski 20.00 8.00
31 Hank Aaron 15.00 6.00
32 Felipe Alou 3.00 1.20
33 Richie Allen 4.00 1.60
34 Ernie Banks 15.00 6.00
35 Johnny Bench 25.00 10.00
36 Lou Brock 12.00 4.80
37 Johnny Callison 2.50 1.00
38 Orlando Cepeda 6.00 2.40
39 Roberto Clemente 30.00 12.00
40 Willie Davis 2.50 1.00
41 Don Drysdale 10.00 4.00
42 Ron Fairly 2.50 1.00
43 Curt Flood 5.00 2.00
44 Bob Gibson 12.00 4.80
45 Bud Harrelson 2.50 1.00
46 Jim Ray Hart 2.00 .80
47 Tommy Helms 2.00 .80
48 Don Kessinger 2.50 1.00
49 Jerry Koosman 5.00 2.00
50 Jim Maloney 2.50 1.00
51 Juan Marichal 8.00 3.20
52 Willie Mays 15.00 6.00
53 Tim McCarver 4.00 1.60
54 Willie McCovey 8.00 3.20
55 Pete Rose 30.00 12.00
56 Ron Santo 4.00 1.60
57 Ron Swoboda 2.00 .80
58 Joe Torre 4.00 1.60
59 Billy Williams 8.00 3.20
60 Jim Wynn 2.50 1.00

1983 MLBPA Pins

This pin set of 36 is apparently a reprinted set and is checklisted here in order to help collectors put a fair value on the pins that they are buying, selling and trading. These are frequently mistaken for the 1969 issue after which they are patterned. There is no indication that this set was authorized by the Major League Baseball Player's Association. Each pin is 7/8" in diameter. This 36 pin set contains 18 pins each of National League players and American League players. This unnumbered set is ordered below alphabetically within league, American Leaguers (1-18) and National Leaguers (19-36). The outer bands of the pins are red for American League players and blue for National League players. The pictures on the pins are black and white, head only photos. All of the players in the set had retired before 1984 and many had retired well before 1969. The line "c 1969 MLBPA MFG. in U.S.A." appears at the bottom of each pin, i.e., no reference to Winona as with the 1969 set.

Nm-Mt Ex-Mt
COMPLETE SET (36) 25.00 10.00
1 Bob Allison .25 .10
2 Yogi Berra 1.00 .40
3 Norm Cash .50 .20
4 Joe DiMaggio 4.00 1.60
5 Bobby Doerr .75 .30
6 Bob Feller 1.00 .40
7 Whitey Ford 1.00 .40
8 Nelson Fox .75 .30
9 Frank Howard .25 .10
10 Jim (Catfish) Hunter .75 .30
11 Al Kaline 1.00 .40
12 Mickey Mantle 4.00 1.60
13 Tony Oliva .50 .20
14 Satchel Paige 1.00 .40
15 Phil Rizzuto 1.00 .40
16 Brooks Robinson 1.00 .40
17 Bill Skowron .50 .20
18 Ted Williams 2.50 1.00
19 Hank Aaron 2.50 1.00
20 Roy Campanella 1.00 .40
21 Orlando Cepeda .50 .20
22 Roberto Clemente 3.00 1.20
23 Don Drysdale 1.00 .40
24 Sandy Koufax 2.00 .80
25 Juan Marichal 1.00 .40
26 Eddie Mathews 1.00 .40
27 Willie Mays 2.50 1.00
28 Willie McCovey .75 .30
29 Stan Musial 2.00 .80
30 Robin Roberts .75 .30
31 Jackie Robinson 2.50 1.00
32 Ron Santo .50 .20
33 Duke Snider 2.00 .80
34 Warren Spahn .75 .30
35 Billy Williams .75 .30
36 Maury Wills .50 .20

1920 Mrs. Sherlock's Pins PB5-1

This set of pins is subtitled "Mrs. Sherlocks Home Made Bread" at the top of each pin. Players pictured in the set are members of the Toledo Mud Hens. The pins measure approximately 7/8" in diameter and are done totally in black and white. Since the pins are unnumbered, they are listed below in alphabetical order.

Ex-Mt VG
COMPLETE SET (19) 1000.00 500.00
1 Brady 60.00 30.00
2 Roger Bresnahan MG 250.00 125.00
3 Dubuc 60.00 30.00
4 Dyer 60.00 30.00
5 Fox 60.00 30.00
6 Hyatt 60.00 30.00
7 J. Jones 60.00 30.00
8 J. H. Kelly 60.00 30.00
9 M. Kelly 60.00 30.00
10 Kores 60.00 30.00
11 McColl 60.00 30.00
12 McNeill 60.00 30.00
13 Middleton 60.00 30.00
14 Murphy 60.00 30.00
15 Nelson 60.00 30.00
16 Stryker 60.00 30.00
17 Thompson 60.00 30.00
18 Wickland 60.00 30.00
19 Wilhoit 60.00 30.00

1922 Mrs. Sherlock's Pins PB5-2

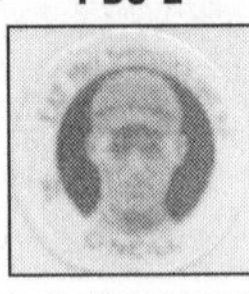

This set of pins is subtitled "Eat Mrs. Sherlocks Bread" at the top of each pin. Players pictured in the set are members of the Toledo Mud Hens. The pins measure approximately 5/8" in diameter and are done totally in brownish sepia (or green) and white. The catalog are numbered.

Ex-Mt VG
COMPLETE SET 1200.00 600.00
1 Roger Bresnahan MG 250.00 125.00
2 Kocher 60.00 30.00
3 Hill 60.00 30.00
4 C. Huber 60.00 30.00
5 Doc Ayers 60.00 30.00
6 Parks 60.00 30.00
7 J. Giard 60.00 30.00
8 Roy Grimes 60.00 30.00
9 P. McCullough 60.00 30.00
10 Shoup 60.00 30.00
11 A. Wickland 60.00 30.00
12 Baker 60.00 30.00
13 Schauffle 60.00 30.00
14 R. Wright 60.00 30.00
15 Lamar 60.00 30.00
16 Sallee 80.00 40.00
17 Luderus 60.00 30.00
18 Walgomat 60.00 30.00
19 E. Konetchy 60.00 30.00
20 B. O'Neill 60.00 30.00
21 Hugo Bedient 60.00 30.00

1924 Mrs. Sherlock's Bread Pins

This set of pins is subtitled "Mrs. Sherlocks Home Made Bread" at the top of each pin. Players pictured in the set are some of the legends of baseball. The pins measure approximately 7/8" in diameter and are done in black and white with a red border. Since these pins are unnumbered, they are listed below in alphabetical order.

Ex-Mt VG
COMPLETE SET 2500.00 1250.00
1 Grover C. Alexander 150.00 75.00
2 Ty Cobb 600.00 300.00
3 Rogers Hornsby 200.00 100.00
4 Walter Johnson 300.00 150.00
5 Rabbit Maranville 100.00 50.00
6 Paddy Moran 50.00 25.00
7 Babe Ruth 1000.00 500.00
8 George Sisler 125.00 60.00
9 Tris Speaker 200.00 100.00
10 Honus Wagner 300.00 150.00

1933 Mrs. Sherlock's Pins PB5-3

This set of pins is subtitled "Mrs. Sherlocks Home Made Bread" at the top of each pin. Players pictured in the set are members of the Toledo Mud Hens. The pins measure approximately 7/8" in diameter and are done in black and white with red subtitle at top. Since the pins are unnumbered, they are listed below in alphabetical order. In the set the position of each player is spelled out next to the player's last name at the bottom of the pin.

Ex-Mt VG
COMPLETE SET (18) 600.00 300.00
1 LeRoy Bachman 30.00 15.00
2 George Detore 30.00 15.00
3 Frank Doljack 30.00 15.00
4 Milt Galatzer 30.00 15.00
5 Walt Henline 30.00 15.00
6 Roxie Lawson 30.00 15.00
7 Thornton Lee 50.00 25.00
8 Montague 30.00 15.00
9 Steve O'Neill 40.00 20.00
10 Monte Pearson 40.00 20.00
11 Robert Reis 30.00 15.00
12 Hobart Scott 30.00 15.00
13 Bill Sweeney 30.00 15.00
14 Forrest Twogood 30.00 15.00
15 Hal Trosky 60.00 30.00
16 E. Turgeon 30.00 15.00
17 Max West 50.00 25.00
18 Ralph Winegarner 30.00 15.00

1990 M.V.P. Pins

These pins were issued along with a 1990 Score baseball card and were designed for

retail sale. The box calls this the "Major League Players Collector Pin series and a head shot of the player is on the pin against a diamond background. The back of the box gives the checklist for the set and says this is the "first edition" of this product. These pins were produced by the Ace Novelty Co.

Nm-Mt Ex-Mt
COMPLETE SET (108) 120.00 36.00
1 Tom Glavine 2.00 .60
2 Dale Murphy 1.50 .45
3 Lonnie Smith .50 .15
4 John Smoltz .75 .23
5 Gregg Olson .50 .15
6 Billy Ripken .50 .15
7 Cal Ripken 8.00 2.40
8 Mickey Tettleton .50 .15
9 Wade Boggs 2.00 .60
10 Roger Clemens 4.00 1.20
11 Mike Greenwell .50 .15
12 Lee Smith .75 .23
13 Jim Abbott .75 .23
14 Bert Blyleven .75 .23
15 Brian Downing .50 .15
16 Wally Joyner .75 .23
17 Andre Dawson 1.00 .30
18 Shawon Dunston .50 .15
19 Mark Grace 1.50 .45
20 Ryne Sandberg 4.00 1.20
21 Jerome Walton .50 .15
22 Mitch Williams .75 .23
23 Carlton Fisk 2.00 .60
24 Ozzie Guillen .75 .23
25 Bobby Thigpen .50 .15
26 Greg Walker .50 .15
27 Eric Davis .75 .23
28 Ken Griffey Sr. .75 .23
29 Danny Jackson .50 .15
30 Chris Sabo .50 .15
31 Brook Jacoby .50 .15
32 Doug Jones .50 .15
33 Cory Snyder .50 .15
34 Greg Swindell .50 .15
35 Chet Lemon .50 .15
36 Jack Morris .75 .23
37 Alan Trammell 1.00 .30
38 Lou Whitaker .75 .23
39 Craig Biggio 1.00 .30
40 Glenn Davis .50 .15
41 Bill Doran .50 .15
42 Mike Scott .50 .15
43 George Brett 4.00 1.20
44 Tom Gordon .75 .23
45 Bo Jackson 1.50 .45
46 Bret Saberhagen .75 .23
47 Kirk Gibson .75 .23
48 Orel Hershiser .75 .23
49 Mike Scioscia .75 .23
50 Fernando Valenzuela .75 .23
51 Teddy Higuera .50 .15
52 Paul Molitor 2.00 .60
53 B.J. Surhoff .75 .23
54 Robin Yount 2.00 .60
55 Gary Gaetti .75 .23
56 Dan Gladden .50 .15
57 Kent Hrbek .50 .15
58 Kirby Puckett 2.00 .60
59 Andres Galarraga 1.50 .45
60 Dennis Martinez .75 .23
61 Tim Raines .75 .23
62 Tim Wallach .50 .15
63 Sid Fernandez .50 .15
64 Doc Gooden .75 .23
65 Howard Johnson .50 .15
66 Darryl Strawberry .75 .23
67 Frank Viola .50 .15
68 Don Mattingly 4.00 1.20
69 Dave Righetti .50 .15
70 Steve Sax .50 .15
71 Dave Winfield 2.00 .60
72 Jose Canseco 1.50 .45
73 Dennis Eckersley 2.00 .60
74 Rickey Henderson 2.50 .75
75 Mark McGwire 5.00 1.50
76 Dave Stewart .75 .23
77 Lenny Dykstra .50 .15
78 Von Hayes .50 .15
79 Tom Herr .50 .15
80 Roger McDowell .50 .15
81 Barry Bonds 5.00 1.50
82 Bobby Bonilla .75 .23
83 Doug Drabek .50 .15
84 Andy Van Slyke .50 .15
85 Jack Clark .75 .23
86 Tony Gwynn 4.00 1.20
87 Dennis Rasmussen .50 .15
88 Benito Santiago .75 .23
89 Brett Butler .75 .23
90 Will Clark 1.50 .45
91 Kevin Mitchell .50 .15
92 Matt Williams 1.00 .30
93 Alvin Davis .50 .15
94 Ken Griffey Jr. 5.00 1.50
95 Jeffrey Leonard .50 .15
96 Harold Reynolds .75 .23
97 Tom Brunansky .50 .15
98 Pedro Guerrero .50 .15
99 Ozzie Smith 4.00 1.20
100 Todd Worrell .50 .15
101 Harold Baines 1.00 .30
102 Julio Franco .75 .23
103 Nolan Ryan 8.00 2.40
104 Ruben Sierra .75 .23
105 George Bell .50 .15
106 Tony Fernandez .75 .23
107 Fred McGriff 1.00 .30
108 Dave Stieb .50 .15

1991 M.V.P. Pins

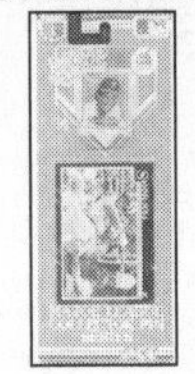

These pins were issued along with a 1991 Score baseball card and were designed for retail sale. The box calls this the "Major League Players Collector Pin series and a head shot of the player is on the pin against a diamond background. The back of the box gives the checklist for the set. These pins were produced by the Ace Novelty Co. We have followed the checklist on the back and listed the players in the team order but have made sure they are in alphabetical order within the team order.

Nm-Mt Ex-Mt
COMPLETE SET (80) 100.00 30.00
1 Kevin Maas .50 .15
2 Don Mattingly 4.00 1.20
3 Hensley Meulens .50 .15
4 Ken Griffey Jr. 5.00 1.50
5 Ken Griffey Sr. .75 .23
6 Randy Johnson 2.50 .75
7 Tino Martinez 1.00 .30
8 Wade Boggs 2.00 .60
9 Ellis Burks .75 .23
10 Roger Clemens 4.00 1.20
11 Mo Vaughn 1.50 .45
12 Kirby Puckett 1.50 .45
13 Kevin Tapani .50 .15
14 Carlton Fisk 2.00 .60
15 Sammy Sosa 5.00 1.50
16 Bobby Thigpen .50 .15
17 Frank Thomas 2.00 .60
18 Sandy Alomar Jr. .75 .23
19 Mauro Gozzo .50 .15
20 George Brett 4.00 1.20
21 Bo Jackson 1.50 .45
22 Terry Shumpert .50 .15
23 Jim Abbott .75 .23
24 Mark Langston .50 .15
25 Lee Stevens .50 .15
26 John Olerud 1.00 .30
27 Dave Stieb .50 .15
28 Mark Whiten .50 .15
29 Ben McDonald .50 .15
30 Cal Ripken Jr. 8.00 2.40
31 David Segui .75 .23
32 Cecil Fielder .50 .15
33 Travis Fryman .75 .23
34 Alan Trammell 1.00 .30
35 Scott Chiamparino .50 .15
36 Juan Gonzalez 1.50 .45
37 Nolan Ryan 8.00 2.40
38 Jose Canseco 1.50 .45
39 Ozzie Canseco .50 .15
40 Rickey Henderson 2.50 .75
41 Mark McGwire 5.00 1.50
42 Paul Molitor 2.00 .60
43 Robin Yount 2.00 .60
44 Eric Anthony .50 .15
45 Andujar Cedeno .50 .15
46 Ron Gant .50 .15
47 Dave Justice 1.50 .45
48 Ray Lankford .75 .23
49 Ozzie Smith 4.00 1.20
50 Todd Zeile .75 .23
51 Ramon Martinez .50 .15
52 Eddie Murray 2.00 .60
53 Jose Offerman .50 .15
54 Paul Faries .50 .15
55 Tony Gwynn 4.00 1.20
56 Bruce Hurst .50 .15
57 Barry Bonds 5.00 1.50
58 Doug Drabek .50 .15
59 Orlando Merced .50 .15
60 Lenny Dykstra .50 .15
61 Mickey Morandini .50 .15
62 Dale Murphy 1.00 .30
63 Will Clark 2.00 .60
64 Kevin Mitchell .50 .15
65 Matt Williams 1.00 .30
66 Andre Dawson 1.50 .45
67 Mark Grace 1.50 .45
68 Derrick May .50 .15
69 Ryne Sandberg 3.00 .90
70 Eric Davis .75 .23
71 Hal Morris .50 .15
72 Randy Myers .75 .23
73 Glenn Sutko .50 .15
74 Doc Gooden .75 .23
75 Todd Hundley .75 .23
76 Gregg Jefferies .50 .15
77 Dave Magadan .50 .15
78 Delino DeShields .75 .23
79 Howard Farmer .50 .15
80 Larry Walker 1.50 .45

1992 M.V.P. Pins

This set of 46 pins features color player photos in gold borders on a tie-tack pin design attached to a 3 1/2" by 5" card. The set was distributed one per card with a suggested retail price of $1.49 each and was produced by Ace Novelty Co. Inc. The pins are checklisted below according to the way they are sequenced on the package back.

Nm-Mt Ex-Mt

COMPLETE SET (46)	125.00	38.00
1 Don Mattingly	8.00	2.40
2 Kevin Maas	1.00	.30
3 Ken Griffey Jr.	10.00	3.00
4 Tino Martinez	3.00	.90
5 Roger Clemens	8.00	2.40
6 Phil Plantier	1.00	.30
7 Kirby Puckett	4.00	1.20
8 Scott Erickson	1.00	.30
9 Bo Jackson	3.00	.90
10 Alex Fernandez	1.00	.30
11 Frank Thomas	4.00	1.20
12 Sandy Alomar Jr.	1.50	.45
13 Brian McRae	1.00	.30
14 Mark Langston	1.00	.30
15 Jim Abbott	1.00	.30
16 Juan Guzman	1.00	.30
17 Kelly Gruber	1.00	.30
18 Cal Ripken	15.00	4.50
19 Ben McDonald	1.00	.30
20 Cecil Fielder	1.50	.45
21 Milt Cuyler	1.00	.30
22 Nolan Ryan	15.00	4.50
23 Juan Gonzalez	4.00	1.20
24 Rickey Henderson	5.00	1.50
25 Jose Canseco	4.00	1.20
26 Todd Van Poppel	1.00	.30
27 Robin Yount	4.00	1.20
28 Jeff Bagwell	5.00	1.50
29 Dave Justice	3.00	.90
30 Steve Avery	1.00	.30
31 Tom Glavine	4.00	1.20
32 Ray Lankford	1.50	.45
33 Todd Zeile	1.50	.45
34 Daryl Strawberry	1.50	.45
35 Ramon Martinez	1.00	.30
36 Tony Gwynn	8.00	2.40
37 Barry Bonds	10.00	3.00
38 Lenny Dykstra	1.00	.30
39 Will Clark	4.00	1.20
40 Matt Williams	2.00	.60
41 Andre Dawson	2.00	.60
42 Ryne Sandberg	5.00	1.50
43 Barry Larkin	3.00	.90
44 Chris Sabo	1.00	.30
45 Dwight Gooden	1.50	.45
46 Dennis Martinez	1.50	.45

1914 NY News Frank Chance Pin

This pin was issued around 1914 and features a photo of Frank Chance surrounded by the words "Members of the News -- Frank Chance Booster Club". The celluoid is 7/8" in diameter.

	Ex-Mt	VG
1 Frank Chance	200.00	100.00

1932-34 Orbit Gum Pins "Numbered"

These pins were thought to have been issued some time between 1932 and 1934. The catalog designation for these pins is PR2. These pins are skip-numbered which distinguishes them from the following set designated as PR3 which is unnumbered. Each pin is approximately 13/16" in diameter. On the front of the pin the team nickname is featured in all caps inside quotation marks. Player pictures are set against a green background with the player's name and team in a yellow strip.

	Ex-Mt	VG
COMPLETE SET	1200.00	600.00
COMMON PLAYER (1-72)	15.00	7.50
COMMON PLAYER (92-120)	20.00	10.00
1 Ivy Andrews	15.00	7.50
2 Carl Reynolds	15.00	7.50
3 Riggs Stephenson	20.00	10.00
4 Lon Warneke	15.00	7.50
5 Frank Grube	15.00	7.50
6 Kiki Cuyler	30.00	15.00
7 Marty McManus	15.00	7.50
8 Lefty Clark	15.00	7.50
9 George Blaeholder	15.00	7.50
10 Willie Kamm	15.00	7.50
11 Jimmy Dykes	20.00	10.00
12 Earl Averill	30.00	15.00
13 Pat Malone	15.00	7.50
14 Dizzy Dean	80.00	40.00
15 Dick Bartell	15.00	7.50
16 Guy Bush	15.00	7.50
17 Bud Tinning	15.00	7.50
18 Jimmy Foxx	50.00	25.00
19 Mule Haas	15.00	7.50
20 Lew Fonseca	15.00	7.50
21 Pepper Martin	25.00	12.50
22 Phil Collins	15.00	7.50
23 Bill Cissell	15.00	7.50
24 Bump Hadley	15.00	7.50
25 Smead Jolley	15.00	7.50
26 Burleigh Grimes	30.00	15.00
27 Dale Alexander	15.00	7.50
28 Mickey Cochrane	30.00	15.00
29 Mel Harder	20.00	10.00
30 Mark Koenig	15.00	7.50
31A Lefty O'Doul New York Giants	20.00	10.00
31B Lefty O'Doul Brooklyn Dodgers	100.00	50.00
32A Woody English	15.00	7.50
32B Woody English without bat	80.00	40.00
33A Billy Jurges	15.00	7.50
33B Billy Jurges without bat	80.00	40.00
34 Bruce Campbell	15.00	7.50
35 Joe Vosmik	15.00	7.50
36 Dick Porter	15.00	7.50
37 Charlie Grimm	25.00	12.50
38 George Earnshaw	15.00	7.50
39 Al Simmons	30.00	15.00
40 Red Lucas	15.00	7.50
51 Wally Berger	20.00	10.00
55 Jim Levey	15.00	7.50
58 Ernie Lombardi	30.00	15.00
64 Jack Burns	15.00	7.50
67 Billy Herman	30.00	15.00
72 Bill Hallahan	15.00	7.50
92 Don Brennan	20.00	10.00
96 Sam Byrd	20.00	10.00
99 Ben Chapman	20.00	10.00
103 Johnny Allen	20.00	10.00
107 Tony Lazzeri	40.00	20.00
111 Earle Combs	40.00	20.00
116 Joe Sewell	40.00	20.00
120 Lefty Gomez	50.00	25.00

1932-34 Orbit Gum Pins "Unnumbered"

These pins were thought to have been issued some time between 1932 and 1934. The catalog designation for these pins is PR3. These pins are unnumbered which distinguishes them from the set designated as PR2 which is skip-numbered. Each pin is approximately 13/16" in diameter. On the front of the pin the team nickname is featured in all caps inside quotation marks. Player pictures are set against a green background with the player's name and team in a yellow strip.

	Ex-Mt	VG
COMPLETE SET	2250.00	1100.00
1 Dale Alexander	30.00	15.00
2 Ivy Andrews	30.00	15.00
3 Earl Averill	60.00	30.00
4 (Dick) Bartell	30.00	15.00
5 Wally Berger	40.00	20.00
6 George Blaeholder	30.00	15.00
7 Jack Burns	30.00	15.00
8 Guy Bush	40.00	20.00
9 Bruce Campbell	30.00	15.00
10 Bill Cissell	30.00	15.00
11 Lefty Clark	30.00	15.00
12 Mickey Cochrane	80.00	40.00
13 Phil Collins	30.00	15.00
14 Kiki Cuyler	50.00	25.00
15 Dizzy Dean	100.00	50.00
16 Jimmy Dykes	40.00	20.00
17 George Earnshaw	40.00	20.00
18 Woody English	30.00	15.00
19 Lew Fonseca	30.00	15.00
20 Jimmy Foxx	100.00	50.00
21 Burleigh Grimes	50.00	25.00
22 Charlie Grimm	30.00	15.00
23 Lefty Grove	80.00	40.00
24 Frank Grube	30.00	15.00
25 Mule Haas	30.00	15.00
26 Bump Hadley	30.00	15.00
27 Chick Hafey	50.00	25.00
28 Jesse Haines	50.00	25.00
29 Bill Hallahan	30.00	15.00
30 Mel Harder	40.00	20.00
31 Gabby Hartnett	50.00	25.00
32 Babe Herman	40.00	20.00
33 Billy Herman	50.00	25.00
34 Rogers Hornsby	100.00	50.00
35 Roy Johnson	30.00	15.00
36 Smead Jolley	30.00	15.00
37 Billy Jurges	30.00	15.00
38 Willie Kamm	30.00	15.00
39 Mark Koenig	40.00	20.00
40 Jim Levey	30.00	15.00
41 Ernie Lombardi	50.00	25.00
42 Red Lucas	30.00	15.00
43 Ted Lyons	50.00	25.00
44 Connie Mack MG	60.00	30.00
45 Pat Malone	30.00	15.00
46 Pepper Martin	40.00	20.00
47 Marty McManus	30.00	15.00
48 Lefty O'Doul Brooklyn Dodgers	40.00	20.00
49 Dick Porter	30.00	15.00
50 Carl Reynolds	30.00	15.00
51 Charlie Root	40.00	20.00
52 Bob Seeds	30.00	15.00
53 Al Simmons	50.00	25.00
54 Riggs Stephenson	40.00	20.00
55 Bud Tinning	30.00	15.00
56 Joe Vosmik	30.00	15.00
57 Rube Walberg	30.00	15.00
58 Paul Waner	60.00	30.00
59 Lon Warneke	30.00	15.00
60 Pinky Whitney	30.00	15.00

1998 Orioles Pins Baltimore Sun

These three pins featuring all-time Oriole greats was issued by the Baltimore Sun. The pins feature black and white player photos and are set against an orange background. The pins are unnumbered so we are sequencing them alphabetically.

	Nm-Mt	Ex-Mt
COMPLETE SET (3)	15.00	4.50
1 Brooks Robinson	6.00	1.80
2 Frank Robinson	6.00	1.80
3 Earl Weaver MG	3.00	.90

1910-15 Ornate Oval Pins

These pins are very ornate. The issuer of these pins is unknown but it is thought that the pins were produced between 1910 and 1915 or shortly thereafter. The pins are oval shaped and are approximately 1 1/4" by 1 1/2" including the brass frame border. The photos in the middle are sepia tone. Since these pins are unnumbered, they are listed below in alphabetical order. In addition, since these pins were issued over a grouping of years, there are subtle differences in the known copies. However, there is no difference in pricing for any of these pins.

	Ex-Mt	VG
COMPLETE SET	10000.00	5000.00
1 Jimmy Archer	300.00	150.00
2 Frank Baker	600.00	300.00
3 Jack Barry	300.00	150.00
4 Chief Bender	600.00	300.00
5 Frank Chance	600.00	300.00
6 Ty Cobb	1500.00	750.00
7 Eddie Collins	800.00	400.00
8 Al Demaree	400.00	200.00
9 Johnny Evers	600.00	300.00
10 Dick Hoblitzel	300.00	150.00
11 Walter Johnson	800.00	400.00
12 Benny Kauff	300.00	150.00
13 Johnny Kling	300.00	150.00
14 Ed Konetchy	300.00	150.00
15 Nap Lajoie	600.00	300.00
16 Sherry Magee	400.00	200.00
17 Rube Marquard	500.00	250.00
18 Christy Mathewson	800.00	400.00
19 John McGraw	600.00	300.00
20 Tris Speaker	600.00	300.00
21 Jeff Tesreau	300.00	150.00
22 Joe Tinker	600.00	300.00

1912 PCL Pins

These Pacific Coast League (PCL) pins were produced around 1911. It is not known how these were produced or distributed. At present the checklist of known members of this set includes 22 members of Oakland but only one each from other PCL franchises of that time, e.g., Los Angeles, Portland, Sacramento and San Francisco. The pins are approximately 7/8" in diameter. The pins are black or blue and white. Since the pins are unnumbered, they are listed in alphabetical order below regardless of team affiliation.

	Ex-Mt	VG
COMPLETE SET (26)	3000.00	1500.00
1 Harry Ables	120.00	60.00
2 Claude Berry	120.00	60.00
3 Tyler Christian	120.00	60.00
4 Al Cook	120.00	60.00
5 Bert Coy	120.00	60.00
6 John Flater	120.00	60.00
7 Howard Gregory	120.00	60.00
8 Joseph Hamilton	120.00	60.00
9 August Hetling	120.00	60.00
10 Hille MG	120.00	60.00
11 Harry Hoffman	120.00	60.00
12 William Leard	120.00	60.00
13 William Malarkey	120.00	60.00
14 Elmer Martinoni	120.00	60.00
15 Walt McCredie MG	120.00	60.00
16 Carl Mitze	120.00	60.00
17 Roy Parkins	120.00	60.00
18 Ashley Pope	120.00	60.00
19 Bill Rapps	120.00	60.00
20 Tom Seaton	120.00	60.00
21 Bayard Sharpe MG	120.00	60.00
22 Tom Sheehan	120.00	60.00
23 Smith	120.00	60.00
24 John Tiedeman	120.00	60.00
25 Eddie Wilkinson	120.00	60.00
26 Elmer Zacher	120.00	60.00

1965 Phillies Pins

These 10 pins which measure 3 1/2" in diameter feature members of the 1965 Philadelphia Phillies. The buttons have a "Go! Phillies Go! Exclamation on the top and the player portrait directly underneath them. Since the buttons are unnumbered, we have sequenced them in alphabetical order.

	NM	Ex
COMPLETE SET (12)	80.00	32.00
1 Richie Allen	15.00	6.00
2 Ruben Amaro	5.00	2.00
3 Bo Belinsky	6.00	2.40
4 Jim Bunning	20.00	8.00
5 Johnny Callison	6.00	2.40
6 Wes Covington	5.00	2.00
7 Ray Culp	5.00	2.00
8 Cookie Rojas	5.00	2.00
9 Chris Short	6.00	2.40
10 Dick Stuart	5.00	2.00
11 Tony Taylor	5.00	2.00
12 Bobby Wine	5.00	2.00

1999 Pinheads

This set features life-like color head redentions of 30 top Baseball players illustrated by British sports artist Paul Trevillion and printed on lapel pins utilizing a patented "QuadraChrome Etching" printing process for a three-dimensional quality. The set is also available as key chains. The pins are unnumbered and checklisted below in alphabetical order.

	Nm-Mt	Ex-Mt
COMPLETE SET (30)	100.00	30.00
1 Moises Alou	1.50	.45
2 Jeff Bagwell	3.00	.90
3 Craig Biggio	2.00	.60
4 Barry Bonds	6.00	1.80
5 Kevin Brown	2.00	.60
6 David Cone	1.50	.45
7 Nomar Garciaparra	5.00	1.50
8 Juan Gonzalez	2.50	.75
9 Ben Grieve	1.00	.30
10 Ken Griffey Jr.	6.00	1.80
11 Tony Gwynn	5.00	1.50
12 Derek Jeter	10.00	3.00
13 Randy Johnson	3.00	.90
14 Chipper Jones	5.00	1.50
15 David Justice	2.50	.75
16 Barry Larkin	2.50	.75
17 Greg Maddux	6.00	1.80
18 Pedro Martinez	3.00	.90
19 Mark McGwire	8.00	2.40
20 Mike Piazza	6.00	1.80
21 Cal Ripken Jr.	10.00	3.00
22 Alex Rodriguez	5.00	1.50
23 Ivan Rodriguez	3.00	.90
24 Curt Schilling	2.50	.75
25 Sammy Sosa	5.00	1.50
26 Frank Thomas	2.50	.75
27 Larry Walker	2.00	.60
28 David Wells	1.50	.45
29 Bernie Williams	2.50	.75
30 Kerry Wood	1.00	.30

1999 Pinheads Update

This set, issued later in 1999, features life-like color head redentions of 10 top Baseball players illustrated by British sports artist Paul Trevillion and printed on lapel pins utilizing a patented "QuadraChrome Etching" printing process for a three-dimensional quality. The set is also available as key chains. The pins are unnumbered and checklisted below in alphabetical order.

	Nm-Mt	Ex-Mt
COMPLETE SET (10)	20.00	6.00
1 Roberto Alomar	2.50	.75
2 Dante Bichette	1.50	.45
3 Jose Canseco	2.50	.75
4 Roger Clemens	5.00	1.50
5 Todd Hundley	1.50	.45
6 Eric Karros	1.50	.45
7 Raul Mondesi	1.50	.45
8 Chan Ho Park	1.00	.30
9 Manny Ramirez	3.00	.90
10 Gary Sheffield	3.00	.90
11 Greg Vaughn	1.50	.45
12 Jaret Wright	1.00	.30
13 Eric Young	1.50	.45

2000 Pinheads

This set features life-like color head redentions of eight top Baseball players illustrated by British sports artist Paul Trevillion and printed on lapel pins utilizing a patented "QuadraChrome Etching" printing process for a three-dimensional quality. The set is also available as key chains. The pins are unnumbered and checklisted below in alphabetical order.

	Nm-Mt	Ex-Mt
COMPLETE SET (8)	40.00	12.00
1 Nomar Garciaparra	5.00	1.50
2 Shawn Green	2.50	.75
3 Ken Griffey Jr.	6.00	1.80
4 Derek Jeter	10.00	3.00
5 Chipper Jones	5.00	1.50
6 Mark McGwire	8.00	2.40
7 Mike Piazza	6.00	1.80
8 Sammy Sosa	5.00	1.50

1910 Pirates Hermes Ice Cream Pins

These 12 pins feature members of the defending World Champions Pittburgh Pirates. The pins measure 1 1/4" and feature black and white photos sets against blue and yellow borders. The players are not identified explicitly but all can be identified. The top of the pin identifies Hermes as the producer of these items. We have sequenced the pins in alphabetical order.

	Ex-Mt	VG
COMPLETE SET	2500.00	1250.00
1 Bill Abstein	200.00	100.00
2 Babe Adams	250.00	125.00
3 Bobby Byrne	200.00	100.00
4 Howie Camnitz	200.00	100.00
5 Fred Clarke	400.00	200.00
6 George Gibson	200.00	100.00
7 Tommy Leach	200.00	100.00
8 Sam Leever	200.00	100.00
9 Dots Miller	200.00	100.00
10 Mike Simon	200.00	100.00
11 Honus Wagner	600.00	300.00
12 J. Owen Wilson	200.00	100.00

1947-66 PM10 Stadium Pins 1 3/4"

These pins were sold at the stadiums by the souvenir vendors over a span of many years. The pins were produced in several sizes approximately 1 3/4" in diameter, 2" in diameter, or 2 1/4" in diameter. Most of these pins are in black and white; those showing color are so indicated in the checklist. Reproductions do exist but are fairly easy to spot. The reproductions usually look like they were manufactured yesterday with shiny metal rims and backs, and may have grainy photos. A raised union stamp on the reverse side is a sure sign of a pin's age and authenticity. We realize the foillowing checklist is incomplete. We urge anyone who might have pins that are not checklisted below to pass along the information to us so we can update our files. A simple photo will sufice. No complete set is printed since additions to this checklist are anticipated.

	EX-MT	VG-E
1 Hank Aaron	250.00	110.00
2 Sandy Amoros B on cap blue background	30.00	13.50
3 Harry Anderson P on cap	50.00	22.00
4 John Antonelli NY on cap	30.00	13.50
5 John Antonelli SF on cap	18.00	8.00
6 Richie Ashburn Phillies on shirt name across shoulders gray background	100.00	45.00
7 Ernie Banks Photographic Style	50.00	22.00
8 Dick Bartell white circle border	12.00	5.50
9 Gus Bell swinging bat)	60.00	27.00
10 Yogi Berra NY on cap light blue background	80.00	36.00
11 Yogi Berra NY on cap white background	60.00	27.00
12 Yogi Berra NY on cap gray background	80.00	36.00
13 Joe Black B on cap looking forward white background	30.00	13.50
14 Joe Black B on cap looking to side stands in background large print name	25.00	11.00
15 Joe Black B on cap looking to side no background smaller letters	60.00	27.00
16 Ewel Blackwell Name on chest	200.00	90.00
17 Don Bollweg A on cap	18.00	8.00
18 Lou Boudreau B on cap light gray background	15.00	6.75
19 Lou Boudreau name in red script cap in red and blue	125.00	55.00
20 Lou Bourdeau Circle border, name script	125.00	55.00
21 Bob Bowman	50.00	22.00
22 Eddie Bressoud B on cap gray background	18.00	8.00
23 Bill Bruton	18.00	8.00
24 Dolph Camilli Dodgers at top white circle border	18.00	8.00
25 Roy Campanella B on cap blue background	80.00	36.00
26 Roy Campanella B on cap white background	50.00	22.00
27 Roy Campanella B on cap teeth showing	50.00	22.00
28 Roy Campanella Circle border	200.00	90.00
29 Chico Carrasquel	80.00	36.00
30 Phil Cavaretta	80.00	36.00
31 Orlando Cepeda SF on cap large name teeth showing gray background	30.00	13.50
32 Orlando Cepeda SF on cap smaller name no teeth showing natural background	30.00	13.50
33 Roberto Clemente	40.00	18.00

We Remember
Clemente
Recordamos a Clemente
34 Gerry Coleman 12.00 5.50
NY on cap
light gray background
35 Tony Conigliaro 30.00 13.50
B on cap
no teeth showing
gray background
36 Tony Conigliaro 30.00 13.50
B on cap
teeth showing
gray background
37 Morton Cooper 12.00 5.50
STL on cap
white/black background
38 Billy Cox 30.00 13.50
Name on uniform
39 Billy Cox 12.00 5.50
B on cap
white background
white name background
40 Alvin Dark 12.00 5.50
41 Jim Davenport 80.00 36.00
SF on cap
42 Dizzy Dean 30.00 13.50
black background
43 Bill Dickey 120.00 55.00
44 Dom DiMaggio 30.00 13.50
black background
45 Dom DiMaggio 15.00 6.75
white background
46 Joe DiMaggio 200.00 90.00
green border
47 Joe DiMaggio 200.00 90.00
Yankees under name
facsimile autograph
48 Joe DiMaggio 70.00 32.00
NY on cap
light blue background
49 Joe DiMaggio 200.00 90.00
NY on cap
white background
50 Joe DiMaggio 200.00 90.00
NY on cap
black background
51 Joe DiMaggio 300.00 135.00
Yankees at top
white circle border
52 Larry Doby 50.00 22.00
C on cap
looking to side
black background
53 Larry Doby 80.00 36.00
Congratulations
54 Larry Doby 18.00 8.00
C on cap
looking forward
white background
55 Luke Easter 50.00 22.00
56 Del Ennis 80.00 36.00
P on cap
Phillies on shirt
gray background
57 Carl Erskine 30.00 13.50
B on cap
58 Ferris Fain 200.00 90.00
59 Bob Feller 15.00 6.75
white background
60 Bob Feller 150.00 70.00
gray background
61 Whitey Ford 80.00 36.00
NY on cap
white background
62 Nellie Fox 200.00 90.00
SOX on cap
foxes in border
63 Carl Furillo 80.00 36.00
stands in background
64 Carl Furillo 80.00 36.00
blue background
65 Carl Furillo 80.00 36.00
white background
66 Carl Furillo 80.00 36.00
natural background
67 Len Gabrielson 80.00 36.00
SF on cap
68 Ned Garver 120.00 55.00
StL on cap
Browns on shirt
white background
69 Ned Garver 120.00 55.00
StL on Cap
No team ID on shirt
70 Lou Gehrig 400.00 180.00
Yankees at top
white circle border
71 Lou Gehrig 300.00 135.00
Never Forgotten
72 Jim Gilliam 80.00 36.00
B on cap
white background
name in smaller print
73 Jim Gilliam 80.00 36.00
B on cap
natural background
name in larger print
74 Lefty Gomez 120.00 55.00
Yankees at top
75 Ruben Gomez 12.00 5.50
SF on cap
white circle border
76 Billy Goodman 50.00 22.00
B on cap
white background
77 Joe Gordon 200.00 90.00
Yankees
78 Granny Hamner 80.00 36.00
Phillies on shirt
name across shoulders
gray background
79 Ron Hansen 150.00 70.00
80 Jim Hart 80.00 36.00
SF on cap
black circle border
left ear missing
81 Gabby Hartnett 40.00 18.00
cap emblem not visible
black background
82 Grady Hatton 80.00 36.00
C on cap
Reds on shirt
83 Jim Hegan 120.00 55.00
name in red
team name in blue
84 Tom Henrich 30.00 13.50
NY on cap
name in border
85 Tom Henrich 18.00 8.00
NY on cap
name over shirt
86 Mike Higgins 12.00 5.50
B on cap
black background
87 Gil Hodges 80.00 36.00
B on cap
orange background
no teeth showing
88 Gil Hodges 50.00 22.00
B on cap
white background
no teeth showing
89 Gil Hodges 50.00 22.00
no teeth showing
90 Gil Hodges 80.00 36.00
B on cap
white background
teeth showing
91 Rogers Hornsby 200.00 90.00
92 Elston Howard 15.00 6.75
cap turned around
white background
chest protector on
TCMA
93 Carl Hubbell 80.00 36.00
sepia tone
94 Carl Hubbell 25.00 11.00
black and white
95 Monte Irvin 60.00 27.00
NY on cap
New York Giants(at top)
white circle border
96 Monte Irvin 30.00 13.50
NY on cap
black background
97 Monte Irvin 80.00 36.00
NY on cap
white background
name in white border
teeth plainly showing
98 Spook Jacobs 18.00 8.00
A on cap
black/white background
99 Jackie Jensen 80.00 36.00
no emblem on cap
name at top
white background
right ear missing
100 Jackie Jensen 25.00 11.00
black background
101 Jackie Jensen 30.00 13.50
B on cap
natural background
both ears showing
102 Jackie Jensen 120.00 55.00
Name at Top
103 Walter Johnson 200.00 90.00
104 Willie Jones 80.00 36.00
P on cap
Phillies on shirt
105 Harmon Killebrew 150.00 70.00
W on cap
batting stance
natural background
106 Ralph Kiner 120.00 55.00
107 Ted Kluszewski 50.00 22.00
C on cap
white background
108 Ted Kluszewski 200.00 90.00
Name on chest
109 Jim Konstanty 80.00 36.00
Phillies on shirt
name across shoulders
gray background
110 Ed Kranepool 18.00 8.00
TCMA
111 Hal Lanier 80.00 36.00
SF on cap
black circle border
112 Bill Lee 12.00 5.50
113 Bob Lemon 15.00 6.75
C on cap
114 Bob Lemon 80.00 36.00
pitching motion
115 Jim Lemon 80.00 36.00
W on cap
batting stance
116 Whitey Lockman 15.00 6.75
NY on cap
gray background
117 Stan Lopata 80.00 36.00
Phillies on shirt
name across shoulders
gray background
118 Sal Maglie 30.00 13.50
B on cap
natural background
119 Frank Malzone 50.00 22.00
B on cap
white background
both ears showing
120 Frank Malzone 15.00 6.75
B on cap
natural background
holding bat
right ear missing
121 Mickey Mantle 200.00 90.00
NY on cap
blue background
right ear missing
122 Mickey Mantle 120.00 55.00
NY on cap
stitched baseball
right ear missing
head and shoulders
123 Mickey Mantle 150.00 70.00
NY on cap
blue background
righty batting stance
left hand not visible
name starts at wrist
124 Mickey Mantle 100.00 45.00
NY on cap
white background
righty batting stance
left hand not visible
name starts at elbow
125 Mickey Mantle 50.00 22.00
NY on cap
white background
righty batting stance
both hands visible
126 Mickey Mantle 300.00 135.00
NY on cap
white background
name in white border
eyes almost closed
127 Mickey Mantle 60.00 27.00
I Love Mickey
no cap
with Teresa Brewer
each holding a bat
128 Juan Marichal 80.00 36.00
SF on cap
black border
129 Marty Marion 80.00 36.00
StL on cap
white circle border
130 Roger Maris 60.00 27.00
large NY on cap
salmon background
131 Roger Maris 40.00 18.00
normal NY on cap
yellow background
132 Roger Maris 120.00 55.00
no emblem on cap
white background
133 Willie Mays 30.00 13.50
NY on cap
white background
134 Willie Mays 150.00 70.00
NY on cap
New York Giants
white circle border
135 Willie Mays 150.00 70.00
NY on cap
natural background
136 Willie Mays 150.00 70.00
NY on cap
turquoise background
137 Willie Mays 100.00 45.00
SF on cap
gray background
white name background
left ear missing
eyes almost closed
138 Willie Mays 100.00 45.00
SF on cap
natural background
looking up
tongue showing
139 Willie Mays 250.00 110.00
SF on cap
stands in background
white name background
140 Willie McCovey 40.00 18.00
no emblem on cap
holding four bats
141 Gil McDougald 12.00 5.50
NY on cap
gray background
142 Cliff Melton 12.00 5.50
Giants at top
no emblem on cap
white circle border
143 Bill Meyer 80.00 36.00
144 Minnie Minoso 80.00 36.00
white circle border
name in script
145 Bill Monbouquette 12.00 5.50
146 Don Mueller 12.00 5.50
NY on cap
white background
no neck showing
147 Bobby Murcer 18.00 8.00
NY on cap
white background
head and shoulders
TCMA
148 Danny Murtaugh 80.00 36.00
white circle border
149 Stan Musial 160.00 70.00
StL on cap
white background
right ear noticeable
150 Stan Musial 50.00 22.00
StL on cap
yellow background
right ear missing
151 Stan Musial 250.00 110.00
Stan The Man
StL on cap
white background
152 Don Newcombe 50.00 22.00
B on cap
blue background
toothy smile
153 Don Newcombe 18.00 8.00
B on cap
white background
mouth slightly open
154 Don Newcombe 50.00 22.00
B on cap
white background
mouth closed
155 Don Newcombe 200.00 90.00
Circle boarder
156 Dan O'Connell 12.00 5.50
SF on cap
white circle border
157 Andy Pafko 100.00 45.00
158 Joe Page 30.00 13.50
NY on cap
white background
159 Satchel Paige 120.00 55.00
no emblem on cap
white background
160 Mel Parnell 12.00 5.50
B on cap
white background
161 Joe Pepitone 15.00 6.75
NY on helmet
white background
looking to side
head and shoulders
TCMA
162 Gaylord Perry 60.00 27.00
SF on cap
white background
163 Johnny Pesky 50.00 22.00
B on cap
white background
164 Rico Petrocelli 30.00 13.50
B on cap
light gray background
165 Billy Pierce White Sox 200.00 90.00
166 Jimmy Piersall 18.00 8.00
B on cap
white background
167 Johnny Podres 30.00 13.50
B on cap
gray/white background
168 John Pramesa 80.00 36.00
C on cap
Reds on shirt
gray background
169 Dick Radatz 25.00 11.00
B on cap
gray background
170 Vic Raschi 40.00 18.00
NY on cap
white background
171 Pee Wee Reese 80.00 36.00
B on cap
light gray background
172 Pee Wee Reese 100.00 45.00
B on cap
gray background
left ear missing
looking to side
173 Pee Wee Reese 80.00 36.00
B on cap
white background
174 Pee Wee Reese 80.00 36.00
B on cap
gray background
175 Pete Reiser 15.00 6.75
B on cap
Dodgers at top
white circle border
176 Bill Rigney 12.00 5.50
177 Phil Rizzuto 30.00 13.50
NY on cap
white background
178 Robin Roberts 18.00 8.00
P on cap
stands in background
179 Robin Roberts 80.00 36.00
P on cap
Phillies on shirt
name across shoulders
180 Brooks Robinson 250.00 110.00
181 Jackie Robinson 60.00 27.00
B on cap
yellow background
looking serious
182 Jackie Robinson 250.00 110.00
Dodgers at bottom
B on cap
red border
I'm Rooting For
Jackie Robinson
183 Jackie Robinson 150.00 70.00
B on cap
red border
Rookie of the Year 1947
184 Jackie Robinson 100.00 45.00
B on cap
blue background
looking to side
left ear missing
185 Jackie Robinson 200.00 90.00
B on cap
gray/white background
looking to side
left ear missing
186 Jackie Robinson 150.00 70.00
cap emblem not visible
white background
batting stance
Dodgers at bottom
187 Jackie Robinson 300.00 135.00
cap emblem not visible
right ear missing
white background
188 Jackie Robinson 100.00 45.00
B on cap
Dodgers on shirt
natural background
189 Preacher Roe 80.00 36.00
B on cap
Dodgers on shirt
pitching wind-up
white background
190 Saul Rogovin 12.00 5.50
SOX on cap
Chicago White Sox
white circle border
191 Stan Rojek 80.00 36.00
P on cap
Pittsburgh Pirates
white circle border
192 Al Rosen 15.00 6.75
193 Red Ruffing 18.00 8.00
middle name Herbert
194 Babe Ruth 400.00 180.00
195 Jack Sanford 50.00 22.00
196 Hank Sauer 200.00 90.00
197 Chuck Schilling 50.00 22.00
B on cap
white background
name at top
198 Chuck Schilling 50.00 22.00
name at bottom
199 George Scott 12.00 5.50
B on cap
left ear missing
white background
200 Andy Seminick 80.00 36.00
201 Bobby Shantz 80.00 36.00
gray background
202 Bobby Shantz 18.00 8.00
white background
203 Frank Shea 12.00 5.50
NY on cap
gray background
204 Curt Simmons 80.00 36.00
P on cap
Phillies on shirt
sepia tone
sepia background
205 Enos Slaughter 80.00 36.00
StL on cap
black background
206 Roy Smalley 80.00 36.00
C on cap
stars in border
white circle border
name in script
207 Duke Snider 120.00 55.00
blue background
208 Duke Snider 150.00 70.00
stands in background
209 Duke Snider 30.00 13.50
gray background
210 Dick Stuart 30.00 13.50
B on cap
light gray background
211 Hank Thompson 100.00 45.00
NY on cap
New York Giants
batting pose
white circle border
212 Bobby Thomson 30.00 13.50
NY on cap
white background
looking up
213 Gus Triandos 80.00 36.00
Oriole on cap
light gray background
214 Bob Trice 80.00 36.00
A on cap
natural background
left ear missing
215 Eddie Waitkus 80.00 36.00
Phillies on shirt
name across shoulders
gray background
216 Dixie Walker 30.00 13.50
cap emblem not visible
Dodgers (at top)
white circle border
217 Bill Werle 80.00 36.00
218 Sam White 12.00 5.50
partial B on cap
looking up
white background
219 Ted Williams 100.00 45.00
cap emblem not visible
name at top
Boston Red Sox
natural background
batting follow-through
220 Ted Williams 150.00 70.00
B on cap
white background
white name background
221 Ted Williams 150.00 70.00
B on cap
black background
name across shoulders
222 Ted Williams 150.00 70.00
B on cap
name at top
natural background
holding bat
white name background
223 Ted Williams 150.00 70.00
B on cap
white background
name across shoulders
224 Ted Williams 60.00 27.00
B on cap
name at bottom
natural background
holding bat
white name background
225 Gene Woodling 100.00 45.00
Oriole on cap
natural background
white name background
226 Whitlow Wyatt 12.00 5.50
B on cap
Dodgers (at top)
white circle border
227 Carl Yastrzemski 100.00 45.00
gray background
228 Carl Yastrzemski 100.00 45.00
white background
229 Gus Zernial 80.00 36.00
A on cap
Athletics on shirt
name across chest
gray background
230 Gus Zernial 120.00 55.00
Name on chest

1947-65 PM10 Stadium Pins 2 1/8'

This is more information on stadium pins. Celluoid foxing, cracks, dents, noticeable scratches or rusted metal rims can all reduce the worth of a button or pin. Rusting on the reverse side can sometimes be removed. A missing pin has no effefct on the price. Frequently, the pins were sold with red, white and blue ribbons and or/chains attached to a selection of miniature tin or plastic bats, balls and gloves. The miniature paraphanalia has very little effect on the values as these items are essentially interchangable. If the hanging ties features the same team or player name, this can affect the value of the pin. The pins checklisted below are those in the two larger sizes, close to 2 1/8" in diameter, most are slightly larger or smaller. The Phillies pins are approximately 2 1/4" in diameter, whereas the Yankees and other teams are about 2" in diameter. Again, additions to this checklist is appreciated. And as with the other PM 10 pins, no complete set price is listed.

EX-MT VG-E
1 Richie Allen 80.00 36.00
P on cap
light gray background
name across shoulders
2 Luis Arroyo 40.00 18.00
NY on cap
white background
name at top
3 Hank Bauer 60.00 27.00
NY on cap
white background
name at top
4 Yogi Berra 150.00 70.00
NY on cap
white background
name at top
5 Johnny Blanchard 50.00 22.00
NY on cap
white background
name at top
6 Clete Boyer 50.00 22.00
NY on cap
white background
name at top
7 Jim Bunning 100.00 45.00
P on cap
white background
white name background
8 Johnny Callison 40.00 18.00
P on cap
white background
white name background
9 Andy Carey 40.00 18.00
10 Gerry Coleman 40.00 18.00
NY on cap
white background
name at top
name in thin print
11 Joe Collins 40.00 18.00
NY on cap
white background
name at top
12 Del Crandall 40.00 18.00
M on cap
white background
name at top
13 Clay Dalrymple 40.00 18.00
P on cap
white background
white name background
14 Whitey Ford 125.00 55.00
NY on cap
light gray background
thin white border
15 Jim Gilliam 60.00 27.00
B on cap
white background
name at top
16 Ruben Gomez 40.00 18.00
NY on cap
white background
name at top
17 Elston Howard 80.00 36.00
NY on cap
white background
name at top
name in thin print
18 Billy Loes 40.00 18.00
B on cap
gray background
name at top
19 Ed Lopat 40.00 18.00
NY on cap
white background
name at top
20 Hector Lopez 40.00 18.00
NY on cap
white background
name at top
21 Mickey Mantle 250.00 110.00
NY on cap
light gray background
name at top
22 Roger Maris 150.00 70.00
NY on cap
white background
name at top
right ear missing
23 Roger Maris 120.00 55.00
NY on cap
white background
name at bottom
batting pose
24 Billy Martin 80.00 36.00
NY on cap
white background
name at top
right eye sleepy
25 Willie Mays 200.00 90.00
NY on cap
white background
name at top
26 Willie Mays 200.00 90.00
SF on cap
white background
name at top
27 Gil McDougald 40.00 18.00
NY on cap
white background
name at top
28 Bill Miller 40.00 18.00
29 Tom Morgan 40.00 18.00
NY on cap
light gray background
name at top
30 Don Newcombe 60.00 27.00
B on cap
white background
name at top
31 Irv Noren 40.00 18.00
NY on cap
white background
name at top
32 Johnny Podres 60.00 27.00
B on cap
white background
name at top
33 Allie Reynolds 60.00 27.00
33A Jackie Robinson 400.00 180.00
34 Phil Rizzuto 120.00 55.00
NY on cap
white background
name at top
35 Chris Short 40.00 18.00
P on cap
white background
white name background
36 Roy Sievers 40.00 18.00
P on cap
white background
white name background
37 Bill Skowron 40.00 18.00
38 Enos Slaughter 80.00 36.00
NY on cap
white background
name at top
39 Duke Snider 150.00 70.00
name at top)
40 Warren Spahn 100.00 45.00
M on cap
light gray background
name at top
41 Ted Williams 200.00 90.00
B on cap
light gray background
name print splotchy
42 Bobby Wine 40.00 18.00
P on cap
white background
white name background
43 Gene Woodling 60.00 27.00
NY on cap
black background
thin white border
lefty batting pose
44 Gene Woodling 40.00 18.00
NY on cap
white background
name at top

1935 Quaker Babe Ruth Pin

These pins were issued in 1935. The first version shows the Babe in a Yankee Hat. A second version has a photo of Babe Ruth in a Boston Braves cap. These pins were issued in black and white and comes with or without a scorer back.

Ex-Mt VG
1 Babe Ruth 250.00 125.00
Yankee Cap
2 Babe Ruth 250.00 125.00
Braves Cap

1994 Rangers All-Stars Pins

These pins along with the attached cards honor all Texas Rangers who were selected to the All-Star team during the Rangers stay in Arlington Stadium. The set is sequenced in year order. These pins were given out to all fans at the April 29th, 1994 Rangers game.

Nm-Mt Ex-Mt
COMPLETE SET (22) 20.00 6.00
1 Dave Nelson .... 1.00 .30
Jim Spencer
2 Jeff Burroughs .... 1.00 .30
Jim Sundberg
3 Mike Hargrove .... 1.50 .45
Toby Harrah
4 Toby Harrah .... 1.00 .30
5 Bert Campaneris .... 1.50 .45
6 Richie Zisk .... 1.00 .30
Jim Sundberg
7 Jim Kern .... 1.00 .30
8 Al Oliver .... 1.00 .30
Buddy Bell
9 Al Oliver .... 1.00 .30
Buddy Bell
10 Buddy Bell .... 1.00 .30
11 Rick Honeycutt .... 1.00 .30
12 Buddy Bell .... 1.00 .30
13 Gary Ward .... 1.00 .30
14 Charlie Hough .... 1.50 .45
15 Larry Parrish .... 1.00 .30
16 Jeff Russell .... 1.00 .30
17 Julio Franco 5.00 1.50
Ruben Sierra
Nolan Ryan
Jeff Russell
18 Julio Franco .... 1.50 .45
19 Rafael Palmeiro .... 2.00 .60
Ruben Sierra
Julio Franco
20 Ivan Rodriguez .... 2.50 .75
Ruben Sierra
Kevin Brown
21 Ivan Rodriguez .... 3.00 .90
Juan Gonzalez
22 Ivan Rodriguez .... 2.50 .75
Will Clark

1998 Rangers Pins MBNA

This four-pin set features action color photos of four of the 1998 Texas Rangers and printed on lapel pins measuring approximately 7/8" by 1 1/2". The pins are unnumbered and checklisted below in alphabetical order. They were given away on these dates: Rusty Greer June 14, Will Clark July 19, Juan Gonzalez August 26, Ivan Rodriguez September 5.

Nm-Mt Ex-Mt
COMPLETE SET (4) 10.00 3.00
1 Will Clark .... 3.00 .90
2 Juan Gonzalez 4.00 1.20
3 Rusty Greer .... 2.00 .60
4 Ivan Rodriguez 6.00 1.80

2003 Rangers Hall of Fame Pins

This set of four pins was given out at a 2003 Texas Ranger game to commemorate the induction of the first four members of the Texas Rangers Hall of Fame. Each pin has the player's uniform logo along with the Texas Rangers Hall of Fame logo. Since these pins are unnumbered, we have sequenced them in alphabetical order.

MINT NRMT
COMPLETE SET 8.00 3.60
1 Charlie Hough .... 1.00 .45
2 Johnny Oates MG .... 1.00 .45
3 Nolan Ryan 5.00 2.20
4 Jim Sundberg .... 1.00 .45

1904 Red Sox Union Pins

These pins measure 1 1/2" in diameter and feature members of the Boston team which won the first World Series in 1903. The pins have a black and white photo against a cream background. The pins also have a yellow border with a yellow ribbon under the photo and the label is in blue. The paper back mentions the manufacturer: A.R. Lopez of Boston.

Ex-Mt VG
COMPLETE SET 8000.00 4000.00
1 Jimmy Collins 800.00 400.00
2 Lou Criger 400.00 200.00
3 Bill Dineen 400.00 200.00
4 Patsy Dougherty 400.00 200.00
5 Duke Farrell 400.00 200.00
6 Hobe Ferris 400.00 200.00
7 Buck Freeman 400.00 200.00
8 Norwood Gibson 400.00 200.00
9 Candy LaChance 400.00 200.00
10 Bill O'Neill 400.00 200.00
11 Freddy Parent 400.00 200.00
12 Jake Stahl 400.00 200.00
13 Jesse Tannehill 400.00 200.00
14 George Winter 400.00 200.00
15 W.O Wolff 400.00 200.00
16 Cy Young 2000.00 1000.00

1992 Score Coke/Hardees Discs

This 24-disc set measures approximately 3" in diameter. The fronts feature color player action photos in different colored fading borders. The white backs carry player career totals. The cards are unnumbered and checklisted below in alphabetical order.

Nm-Mt Ex-Mt
COMPLETE SET (24) 20.00 6.00
1 Roberto Alomar .... 1.00 .30
2 Sandy Alomar Jr. .... .50 .15
3 Jeff Bagwell .... 3.00 .90
4 Brett Butler .... .50 .15
5 Roger Clemens 5.00 1.50
6 Chili Davis .... .50 .15
7 Andre Dawson .... 1.00 .30
8 Delino DeShields .... .25 .07
9 Ron Gant .... .50 .15
10 Tom Glavine .... 1.50 .45
11 Kelly Gruber .... .25 .07
12 Ozzie Guillen .... .50 .15
13 Dave Henderson .... .25 .07
14 Chuck Knoblauch .... 1.00 .30
15 Paul Molitor .... 1.25 .35
16 Hal Morris .... .25 .07
17 Rafael Palmeiro .... 1.00 .30
18 Terry Pendleton .... .25 .07
19 Benito Santiago .... .50 .15
20 Ozzie Smith 4.00 1.20
21 Andy Van Slyke .... .25 .07
22 Devon White .... .25 .07
23 Matt Williams .... .75 .23
24 Robin Yount .... 2.00 .60
25 Title Card CL .... .25 .07

1987 Sportflics Superstar Discs

These 18 discs, measuring approximately 4 5/8" in diameter, featured leading players. The player's photo was surrounded by a red border. Player information is located on the back

Nm-Mt Ex-Mt
COMPLETE SET (18) 40.00 16.00
1 Joe Carter 2.50 1.00
2 Mike Scott .... 1.00 .40
3 Ryne Sandberg 5.00 2.00
4 Mike Schmidt 2.50 1.00
5 Dale Murphy 2.50 1.00
6 Fernando Valenzuela .... 1.50 .60
7 Tony Gwynn 6.00 2.40
8 Cal Ripken Jr. 10.00 4.00
9 Gary Carter 3.00 1.20
10 Cory Snyder .... 1.00 .40
11 Kirby Puckett 4.00 1.60
12 George Brett 5.00 2.00
13 Keith Hernandez .... 1.50 .60
14 Rickey Henderson 3.00 1.20
15 Tim Raines .... 1.50 .60
16 Bo Jackson 2.50 1.00
17 Pete Rose 5.00 2.00
18 Eric Davis .... 2.00 .80

1991 Starshots Pinback Badges

These laminated badges were sold with 2" X 4 3/4" cardboard easels for displaying the badges. The easel is printed in red, white, and blue, and has biographical information and a five-year performance profile. The badges 2 3/16" in diameter, have a pin on the back, and feature color head and shoulders photos, encircled by a black border. The company initially issued 54 badges and planned to expand the collection to 200 or more players during the balance of the year. Both the cardboard easels and the badges are numbered on the front, but since the complete set of 200 was not issued, we have checklisted the first 54 badges below in alphabetical order.

Nm-Mt Ex-Mt
COMPLETE SET (54) 80.00 24.00
1 Jim Abbott .... .50 .15
2 Sandy Alomar Jr. .... .75 .23
3 Wade Boggs .... 2.50 .75
4 Barry Bonds 6.00 1.80
5 Bobby Bonilla .... .75 .23
6 George Brett 5.00 1.50
7 Jose Canseco .... 1.50 .45
8 Will Clark .... 1.50 .45
9 Roger Clemens 5.00 1.50
10 Eric Davis .... .75 .23
11 Glenn Davis .... .50 .15
12 Andre Dawson .... 1.50 .45
13 Delino DeShields .... .75 .23
14 Doug Drabek .... .50 .15
15 Shawon Dunston .... .50 .15
16 Len Dykstra .... .50 .15
17 Cecil Fielder .... .50 .15
18 Carlton Fisk .... 2.00 .60
19 Ron Gant .... .75 .23
20 Dwight Gooden .... .75 .23
21 Ken Griffey Jr. 6.00 1.80
22 Kelly Gruber .... .50 .15
23 Tony Gwynn 5.00 1.50
24 Rickey Henderson .... 3.00 .90
25 Orel Hershiser .... .75 .23
26 Wally Joyner .... .75 .23
27 Dave Justice .... 1.50 .45
28 Barry Larkin .... 1.50 .45
29 Don Mattingly 5.00 1.50
30 Mark McGwire 8.00 2.40
31 Kevin McReynolds .... .50 .15
32 Kevin Mitchell .... .50 .15
33 Paul Molitor .... 2.50 .75
34 Eddie Murray .... 2.00 .60
35 Dave Parker .... .75 .23
36 Kirby Puckett .... 2.00 .60
37 Billy Ripken .... .50 .15
38 Cal Ripken Jr. 10.00 3.00
39 Nolan Ryan 10.00 3.00
40 Bret Saberhagen .... .75 .23
41 Chris Sabo .... .50 .15
42 Ryne Sandberg 4.00 1.20
43 Benito Santiago .... .75 .23
44 Steve Sax .... .50 .15
45 Mike Scioscia .... .75 .23
46 Ruben Sierra .... .75 .23
47 Ozzie Smith 4.00 1.20
48 Dave Stieb .... .50 .15
49 Darryl Strawberry .... .75 .23
50 Alan Trammell .... 1.00 .30
51 Tim Wallach .... .50 .15
52 Bob Welch .... .50 .15
53 Matt Williams .... 1.00 .30
54 Dave Winfield .... 2.00 .60

1970 Sunoco Pins

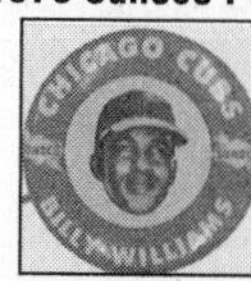

These pins feature members of the Chicago Cubs and Milwaukee Brewers. The pins are approximately 1 1/8" in diameter. The photo used is black and white but the border colors are either red and white (for Milwaukee Brewers players) or blue and white (for Chicago Cubs players. Since the pins are unnumbered they are ordered below in alphabetical order within team, Chicago Cubs (1-9) and Milwaukee Brewers (10-18).

NM Ex
COMPLETE SET (18) 100.00 40.00
1 Ernie Banks 20.00 8.00
2 Glenn Beckert 5.00 2.00
3 Jim Hickman 4.00 1.60
4 Randy Hundley 5.00 2.00
5 Ferguson Jenkins 10.00 4.00
6 Don Kessinger 5.00 2.00
7 Joe Pepitone 8.00 3.20
8 Ron Santo 8.00 3.20
9 Billy Williams 15.00 6.00
10 Tommy Harper 4.00 1.60
11 Mike Hegan 4.00 1.60
12 Lew Krausse 4.00 1.60
13 Ted Kubiak 4.00 1.60
14 Marty Pattin 4.00 1.60
15 Phil Roof 4.00 1.60
16 Ken Sanders 4.00 1.60
17 Ted Savage 4.00 1.60
18 Danny Walton 4.00 1.60

1910 Sweet Caporal "Domino" Discs

These discs were issued by Sweet Caporal Cigarettes and consist of a metal rim around cardboard. The discs come in a variety of colors: black, blue, brown, green and red. The player's picture, name, and team are on the front whereas the back shows a domino. Each disc is approximately 1 1/16" in diameter. The catalog designation for this set is PX7.

Ex-Mt VG
COMPLETE SET (136) 4000.00 2000.00
1 Red Ames 15.00 7.50
2 Jimmy Archer 15.00 7.50
3 Jimmy Austin 15.00 7.50
4 Frank Baker 40.00 20.00
5 Neal Ball 15.00 7.50
6 Cy Barger 15.00 7.50
7 Jack Barry 15.00 7.50
8 John Bates 15.00 7.50
9 Beals Becker 15.00 7.50
10 George Bell 15.00 7.50
11 Chief Bender 30.00 15.00
12 Bill Bergen 15.00 7.50
13 Bob Bescher 20.00 10.00
14 Dode Birmingham 15.00 7.50
15 Roger Bresnahan 30.00 15.00
16 Al Bridwell 15.00 7.50
17 Mordecai Brown 40.00 20.00
18 Robert Byrne 15.00 7.50
19 Nixey Callahan 15.00 7.50
20 Howie Camnitz 15.00 7.50
21 Bill Carrigan 15.00 7.50
22 Frank Chance 50.00 25.00
23 Hal Chase 30.00 15.00
24 Eddie Cicotte 40.00 20.00
25 Fred Clarke 40.00 20.00
26A Ty Cobb D on cap 500.00 250.00
26B Ty Cobb No D on cap 400.00 200.00
27 Eddie Collins 50.00 25.00
28 Doc Crandall 15.00 7.50
29 Birdie Cree 15.00 7.50
30 Bill Dahlen 20.00 10.00
31 Jim Delahanty 20.00 10.00
32 Art Devlin 15.00 7.50
33 Josh Devore 15.00 7.50
34 Red Dooin 15.00 7.50
35 Mickey Doolan 15.00 7.50
36 Patsy Dougherty 15.00 7.50
37 Tom Downey 15.00 7.50
38 Larry Doyle 20.00 10.00
39 Louis Drucke 15.00 7.50
40 Clyde Engle 15.00 7.50
41 Tex Erwin 15.00 7.50
42 Steve Evans 15.00 7.50
43 Johnny Evers 50.00 25.00
44 Cecil Ferguson 15.00 7.50
45 Russ Ford 15.00 7.50
46 Art Fromme 15.00 7.50
47 Harry Gaspar 15.00 7.50
48 George Gibson 15.00 7.50
49 Eddie Grant 15.00 7.50
50 Clark Griffith 40.00 20.00
51 Bob Groom 15.00 7.50
52 Bob Harmon 15.00 7.50
53 Topsy Hartsel 15.00 7.50
54 Arnold Hauser 15.00 7.50
55 Dick Hoblitzel 15.00 7.50
56 Danny Hoffman 15.00 7.50
57 Miller Huggins 40.00 20.00
58 John Hummell 15.00 7.50
59 Hugh Jennings 40.00 20.00
60 Walter Johnson 200.00 100.00
61 Ed Karger 15.00 7.50
62A John Knight Senators 40.00 20.00
62B John Knight Yankees 40.00 20.00
63 Ed Konetchy 15.00 7.50
64 Harry Krause 15.00 7.50
65 Nap Lajoie 120.00 60.00
66 Frank LaPorte 15.00 7.50
67 Tommy Leach 15.00 7.50
68 Sam Leever 15.00 7.50
69 Lefty Leifield 15.00 7.50
70 Paddy Livingston 15.00 7.50
71 Hans Lobert 15.00 7.50
72 Harry Lord 15.00 7.50
73 Nick Maddox 15.00 7.50
74 Sherry McGee 20.00 10.00
75 Rube Marquard 40.00 20.00
76 Christy Mathewson 200.00 100.00
77 Al Mattern 15.00 7.50
78 George McBride 15.00 7.50
79 John McGraw 50.00 25.00
80 Larry McLean 15.00 7.50
81 John McIntire 15.00 7.50
82 Matty McIntyre 15.00 7.50
83 Fred Merkle 20.00 10.00
84 Chief Meyers 20.00 10.00
85 Clyde Milan 20.00 10.00

86 Dots Miller	15.00	7.50
87 Mike Mitchell	15.00	7.50
88A Pat Moran Chicago Cubs	40.00	20.00
88B Pat Moran Philadelphia Phillies	40.00	20.00
89 George Mullen (Mullin)	15.00	7.50
90 Danny Murphy	15.00	7.50
91 Red Murray	15.00	7.50
92 Tom Needham	15.00	7.50
93 Rebel Oakes	15.00	7.50
94 Rube Oldring	15.00	7.50
95 Fred Parent	15.00	7.50
96 Dode Paskert	15.00	7.50
97 Barney Pelty	15.00	7.50
98 Eddie Phelps	15.00	7.50
99 Deacon Phillippe	20.00	10.00
100 Jack Quinn	20.00	10.00
101 Ed Reulbach	20.00	10.00
102 Lew Richie	15.00	7.50
103 Jack Rowan	15.00	7.50
104 Nap Rucker	20.00	10.00
105A Doc Scanlan Superbas	40.00	20.00
105B Doc Scanlan Phillies	40.00	20.00
106 Germany Schaefer	20.00	10.00
107 Boss Schmidt	15.00	7.50
108 Wildfire Schulte	20.00	10.00
109 Jimmy Sheckard	15.00	7.50
110 Hap Smith	15.00	7.50
111 Tris Speaker	120.00	60.00
112 George Stovall	15.00	7.50
113A Gabby Street Washington Senators	40.00	20.00
113B Gabby Street New York Yankees	40.00	20.00
114 George Suggs	15.00	7.50
115 Ira Thomas	15.00	7.50
116 Joe Tinker	50.00	25.00
117 John Titus	15.00	7.50
118 Terry Turner	15.00	7.50
119 Heine Wagner	15.00	7.50
120 Bobby Wallace	30.00	15.00
121 Ed Walsh	40.00	20.00
122 Jack Warhop	15.00	7.50
123 Zach Wheat	40.00	20.00
124 Doc White	15.00	7.50
125A Art Wilson Pirates	20.00	10.00
125B Art Wilson Giants	15.00	7.50
126A Owen Wilson Pirates	15.00	7.50
126B Owen Wilson Giants	15.00	7.50
127 Hooks Wiltse	15.00	7.50
128 Harry Wolter	15.00	7.50
129 Cy Young	120.00	60.00

1910 Sweet Caporal Tobacco Pins

This unnumbered set is numbered here for convenience in alphabetical order by team, e.g., Boston Red Sox (1-7), Chicago White Sox (8-15), Cleveland Naps (16-21), Detroit Tigers (22-31), New York Yankees (32-39), Philadelphia A's (40-50), St. Louis Browns (51-56), Washington Senators (57-64), Boston Rustlers NL (65-68), Brooklyn Superbas (69-78), Chicago Cubs (79-93), Cincinnati Reds (94-105), New York Giants (106-123), Philadelphia Phillies (124-132), Pittsburgh Pirates (133-144) and St. Louis Cardinals (145-152). Pins with larger letters are worth more. Large letter variations are indicated below by LL. These pins were produced and distributed roughly between 1910 and 1912. Each pin measures approximately 7/8" in diameter. The pins are essentially brown and white. The complete set price below reflects the inclusion of all variations.

	Ex-Mt	VG
COMPLETE SET	4200.00	2100.00
COMMON PINS	10.00	5.00
COMMON LARGE LETTERS	15.00	7.50
1A Bill Carrigan	10.00	5.00
1B Bill Carrigan LL	15.00	7.50
2 Ed Cicotte	40.00	20.00
3A Clyde Engle	10.00	5.00
3B Clyde Engle LL	15.00	7.50
4 Harry Hooper	30.00	15.00
5 Ed Karger	10.00	5.00
6A Tris Speaker	50.00	25.00
6B Tris Speaker LL	60.00	30.00
7 Heine Wagner	10.00	5.00
8 Nixey Callahan	10.00	5.00
9 Patsy Dougherty	10.00	5.00
10A Hugh Duffy	30.00	15.00
10B Hugh Duffy LL	50.00	25.00
11A Harry Lord	10.00	5.00
11B Harry Lord LL	15.00	7.50
12A Matty McIntyre	10.00	5.00
12B Matty McIntyre LL	15.00	7.50
13 Fred Parent	10.00	5.00
14 Ed Walsh	30.00	15.00
15 Doc White	10.00	5.00
16 Neal Ball	10.00	5.00
17 Joe Birmingham	10.00	5.00
18 Nap Lajoie	80.00	40.00
19A George Stovall	10.00	5.00
19B George Stovall LL	15.00	7.50
20 Terry Turner	10.00	5.00
21A Cy Young	50.00	25.00
21B Cy Young Old Cy Young	60.00	30.00
22A Ty Cobb	300.00	150.00
22B Ty Cobb LL	400.00	200.00
23 Jim Delahanty	20.00	10.00
24 Bill Donovan	60.00	30.00
25A Hugh Jennings	30.00	15.00
25B Hugh Jennings LL	40.00	20.00
26 Tom Jones	25.00	12.50
27 Ed Killian	25.00	12.50
28A George Mullen (Mullin)	10.00	5.00
28B George Mullen (Mullin) LL	15.00	7.50
29 Charley O'Leary	10.00	5.00
30A Boss Schmidt	10.00	5.00
30B Boss Schmidt LL	15.00	7.50
31 Oscar Stanage	10.00	5.00
32A Hal Chase	30.00	15.00
32B Hal Chase LL	40.00	20.00
33 Birdie Cree	10.00	5.00
34A Russ Ford	10.00	5.00
34B Russ Ford LL	15.00	7.50
35 Ira Hemphill	10.00	5.00
36A Jack Knight	10.00	5.00
36B Jack Knight LL	15.00	7.50
37 Jack Quinn	15.00	7.50
38 Jack Warhop	10.00	5.00
39 Harry Wolter	10.00	5.00
40 Frank Baker	30.00	15.00
41 Jack Barry	10.00	5.00
42A Chief Bender	30.00	15.00
42B Chief Bender LL	40.00	20.00
43A Eddie Collins	30.00	15.00
43B Eddie Collins LL	50.00	25.00
44 Jimmy Dygert	10.00	5.00
45 Topsy Hartsel	10.00	5.00
46 Harry Krause	10.00	5.00
47 Paddy Livingston	10.00	5.00
48 Danny Murphy	10.00	5.00
49 Rube Oldring	10.00	5.00
50A Ira Thomas	10.00	5.00
50B Ira Thomas LL	15.00	7.50
51A Jimmy Austin	10.00	5.00
51B Jimmy Austin LL	15.00	7.50
52 Danny Hoffman	10.00	5.00
53A Frank LaPorte	10.00	5.00
53B Frank LaPorte LL	15.00	7.50
54 Barney Pelty	10.00	5.00
55 George Stone	10.00	5.00
56A Bobby Wallace	30.00	15.00
56B Bobby Wallace LL	50.00	25.00
57A Kid Elberfeld	10.00	5.00
57B Kid Elberfeld LL	15.00	7.50
58 Dolly Gray	10.00	5.00
59 Bob Groom	10.00	5.00
60A Walter Johnson	100.00	50.00
60B Walter Johnson LL	120.00	60.00
61 George McBride	10.00	5.00
62 Clyde Milan	15.00	7.50
63 Herman Schaefer	15.00	7.50
64A Gabby Street	10.00	5.00
64B Gabby Street LL	15.00	7.50
65 Ed Abbaticchio	10.00	5.00
66 Cecil Ferguson	10.00	5.00
67 Buck Herzog	10.00	5.00
68A Al Mattern	10.00	5.00
68B Al Mattern LL	15.00	7.50
69 Cy Barger	10.00	5.00
70A George Bell	10.00	5.00
70B George Bell LL	15.00	7.50
71 Bill Bergen	10.00	5.00
72 Bill Dahlen LL	15.00	7.50
73 Tex Erwin	10.00	5.00
74 John Hummel	10.00	5.00
75A Nap Rucker	15.00	7.50
75B Nap Rucker LL	25.00	10.00
76 Doc Scanlon	20.00	10.00
77 Hap Smith	10.00	5.00
78A Zach Wheat	30.00	15.00
78B Zach Wheat LL	40.00	20.00
79A Jimmy Archer	10.00	5.00
79B Jimmy Archer LL	15.00	7.50
80A Mordecai Brown	30.00	15.00
80B Mordecai Brown LL	40.00	20.00
81A Frank Chance	40.00	20.00
81B Frank Chance LL	50.00	25.00
82 Johnny Evers	40.00	20.00
83 Rube Kroh	10.00	5.00
84 Harry McIntire	10.00	5.00
85 Tom Needham	10.00	5.00
86 Orval Overall	20.00	10.00
87 Jake Pfiester	10.00	5.00
88 Ed Reulbach	15.00	7.50
89 Lew Richie	10.00	5.00
90 Wildfire Schulte	15.00	7.50
91 Jimmy Sheckard	10.00	5.00
92 Harry Steinfeldt	15.00	7.50
93A Joe Tinker	40.00	20.00
93B Joe Tinker LL	50.00	25.00
94 Johnny Bates	10.00	5.00
95 Fred Beebe	10.00	5.00
96 Bob Bescher	15.00	7.50
97A Tom Downey	10.00	5.00
97B Tom Downey LL	15.00	7.50
98 Art Fromme	10.00	5.00
99 Harry Gaspar	10.00	5.00
100 Eddie Grant	10.00	5.00
101A Clark Griffith	30.00	15.00
101B Clark Griffith LL	40.00	20.00
102 Dick Hoblitzell	10.00	5.00
103A Larry McLean	10.00	5.00
103B Larry McLean LL	15.00	7.50
104 Mike Mitchell	10.00	5.00
105 George Suggs	10.00	5.00
106 Red Ames	10.00	5.00
107 Beals Becker	10.00	5.00
108 Al Bridwell	10.00	5.00
109 Doc Crandall	10.00	5.00
110 Art Devlin	10.00	5.00
111 Josh Devore	10.00	5.00
112A Larry Doyle	15.00	7.50
112B Larry Doyle LL	15.00	7.50
113 Louis Drucke	10.00	5.00
114 Buck Herzog	10.00	5.00
115 Arlie Latham	10.00	5.00
116 Rube Marquard	30.00	15.00
117A Christy Mathewson	100.00	50.00
117B Christy Mathewson LL	200.00	100.00
118A John McGraw	40.00	20.00
118B John McGraw LL	60.00	30.00
119 Fred Merkle	15.00	7.50
120 Chief Meyers	15.00	7.50
121 Red Murray	10.00	5.00
122A Art Wilson	10.00	5.00
122B Art Wilson LL	15.00	7.50
123 Hooks Wiltse	15.00	7.50
124 Kitty Bransfield	20.00	10.00
125A Red Dooin	10.00	5.00
125B Red Dooin LL	15.00	7.50
126A Mickey Doolan	10.00	5.00
126B Mickey Doolan LL	15.00	7.50
127 Hans Lobert	10.00	5.00
128 Sherry Magee	15.00	7.50
129 Pat Moran	10.00	5.00
130A Dode Paskert	10.00	5.00
130B Dode Paskert LL	15.00	7.50
131 Jack Rowan	10.00	5.00
132A John Titus	10.00	5.00
132B John Titus LL	15.00	7.50
133 Bobby Byrne	10.00	5.00
134A Howie Camnitz	10.00	5.00
134B Howie Camnitz LL	15.00	7.50
135A Fred Clarke	30.00	15.00
135B Fred Clarke LL	40.00	20.00
136 John Flynn	10.00	5.00
137 Geprge Gibson	10.00	5.00
138 Tommy Leach	10.00	5.00
138 Tommy Leach LL	15.00	7.50
139 Sam Leever	10.00	5.00
140 Lefty Leifield	10.00	5.00
141 Nick Maddox	10.00	5.00
142 Dots Miller	10.00	5.00
143 Deacon Phillippe	15.00	7.50
144 Owen Wilson	10.00	5.00
145A Roger Bresnahan	30.00	15.00
145B Roger Bresnahan LL different picture	80.00	40.00
146 Steve Evans	10.00	5.00
147 Bob Harmon	10.00	5.00
148 Arnold Hauser	10.00	5.00
149A Miller Huggins	30.00	15.00
149B Miller Huggins LL	40.00	20.00
150 Ed Konetchy	10.00	5.00
151A Rebel Oakes	10.00	5.00
151B Rebel Oakes LL	15.00	7.50
152 Eddie Phelps	10.00	5.00

1909 Tigers Morton's "Buster Brown" Bread Pins

These pins were produced by Morton's Bakery and have Morton's inside the pennant at the top of the pin. The pins are approximately 1 1/4" in diameter and show a black and white photo of the player surrounded by a yellow background. Also pictured on the pin is Buster Brown in a brightly colored outfit as well as Tige holding a baseball bat. The player on the pin is not explicitly identified on the pin. The pins are unnumbered so they are presented below in alphabetical order.

	Ex-Mt	VG
COMPLETE SET	4000.00	2000.00
1 Jimmy Archer	200.00	100.00
2 Heinie Beckendorf	200.00	100.00
3 Donie Bush	200.00	100.00
4 Ty Cobb	1200.00	600.00
5 Sam Crawford	400.00	200.00
6 Bill Donovan	200.00	100.00
7 Hugh Jennings MG	400.00	200.00
8 Tom Jones	200.00	100.00
9 Red Killefer	200.00	100.00
10 Matty McIntyre	200.00	100.00
11 George Moriarty	200.00	100.00
12 George Mullen (Mullin)	200.00	100.00
13 Claude Rossman	200.00	100.00
14 Herman Schaefer	250.00	125.00
15 Ed Summers	200.00	100.00
16 Ed Willett	200.00	100.00

1909 Tigers Morton's "Pennant Winner" Bread Pins

These are very attractive pins, approximately 1 1/4" in diameter. The rims are styled in black and white with blue and yellow trim. The catalog designation for this set is PB3. Since the player's name is not listed explicitly on the pin, there is still one player's pin who can not be identified positively; this pin is listed last in the checklist below in the otherwise alphabetized checklist.

	Ex-Mt	VG
COMPLETE SET	4000.00	2000.00
1 Donie Bush	200.00	100.00
2 Ty Cobb	1200.00	600.00
3 Sam Crawford	400.00	200.00
4 Bill Donovan	200.00	100.00
5 Hugh Jennings MG	400.00	200.00
6 Davy Jones	200.00	100.00
7 Matty McIntyre	200.00	100.00
8 George Moriarty	200.00	100.00
9 George Mullin	200.00	100.00
10 Claude Rossman	200.00	100.00
11 Herman Schaefer	250.00	125.00
12 Charles Schmidt	200.00	100.00
13 Oren Summers	200.00	100.00
14 Ed Willett	200.00	100.00
15 Unknown Player photo not recognizable	200.00	100.00

1934 Ward's Sporties Bread Pins

This eight pin set was put out by Ward Baking Co. around 1934. Each pin measures approximately 1 1/4" in diameter. The color scheme is red, white and blue. Since the pins are not numbered, they are ordered below alphabetically.

	Ex-Mt	VG
COMPLETE SET (8)	850.00	425.00
1 Dizzy Dean	250.00	125.00
2 Jimmie Dykes	50.00	25.00
3 Jimmy Foxx	250.00	125.00
4 Frankie Frisch	100.00	50.00
5 Charlie Gehringer	100.00	50.00
6 Charlie Grimm	50.00	25.00
7 Schoolboy Rowe	50.00	25.00
8 Jimmie Wilson	50.00	25.00

1952 White Sox Hawthorn-Mellody Dairy Pins

This set of 11 pins is described on each pin as "Club of Champs." The set was issued about 1952 by Hawthorn-Mellody Dairy in Chicago featuring members of the Chicago White Sox. The coloring of each pin is brownish sepia and white. Since the pins are unnumbered, they are ordered below in alphabetical order. The player's name only (no position) is given on the front of the pin. Each pin measures approximately 1 3/8" in diameter. The set also technically includes an eleventh pin, the "Club of Champs Member" pin. These pins were designed to be worn on a special "beanie" created to give a home for the pins. The set of 10 came in a small box with red lettering. The box featured a facsimile signature from football Hall of Famer Red Grange.

	NM	Ex
COMPLETE SET (11)	350.00	180.00
1 Ray Coleman	30.00	15.00
2 Sam Dente	30.00	15.00
3 Joe Dobson	30.00	15.00
4 Nellie Fox	60.00	30.00
5 Sherman Lollar	40.00	20.00
6 Billy Pierce	50.00	25.00
7 Eddie Robinson	30.00	15.00
8 Hector Rodriguez	30.00	15.00
9 Eddie Stewart	30.00	15.00
10 Al Zarilla	30.00	15.00
11 Club Membership Pin	25.00	12.50

1995 White Sox Pins

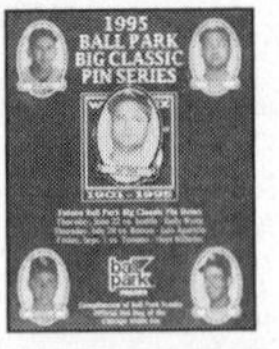

These four pins were given out at selected White Sox games during the 1995 season. The pin is attached to a black and white paper along with a photo of a great in each corner. This giveaway was sponsored by "Ball Park Franks". Since these pins are unnumbered, we have sequenced them in alphabetical order.

	Nm-Mt	Ex-Mt
COMPLETE SET	20.00	6.00
1 Luis Aparicio	6.00	1.80
2 Luke Appling	6.00	1.80
3 Hoyt Wilhelm	6.00	1.80
4 Early Wynn	6.00	1.80

1919 Winkleman's Quaker Bread Pin

This pin has a colorful yellow border surrounding the player's photo. There is also a turtle on the bottom of the pin. These pins are rarely seen in the hobby so any additional information is appreciated.

	Ex-Mt	VG
1 Bob Coulson	1200.00	600.00

1983 Yankees Roy Rogers Discs

This disc set features members of the 1983 New York Yankees team. The set was licensed by the Major League Baseball Players Association in conjunction with Mike Schechter Associates and was distributed at Roy Rogers Restaurants in the New York and New Jersey area. These round cards measure approximately 3 1/2" in diameter and were actually a round card with a red plastic rim. Cards were blank backed and the the player photo used is black and white. The discs are unnumbered and so they are ordered below in alphabetical order. These discs are also sometimes found with the printing of Roy Rogers missing at the top of the disc.

	Nm-Mt	Ex-Mt
COMPLETE SET (12)	30.00	12.00
1 Rick Cerone	2.00	.80
2 Rich Gossage	4.00	1.60
3 Ken Griffey	3.00	1.20
4 Ron Guidry	4.00	1.60
5 Steve Kemp	2.00	.80
6 Jerry Mumphrey	2.00	.80
7 Graig Nettles	4.00	1.60
8 Lou Piniella	4.00	1.60
9 Willie Randolph	4.00	1.60
10 Andre Robertson	2.00	.80
11 Roy Smalley	2.00	.80
12 Dave Winfield	6.00	2.40

1997 Yankees McDonald's Pins

These pins and card were issued in 1997 in New York area McDonalds. They are unnumbered and are sequenced in alphabetical order. The card has a player photo and talks about the McDonald charity. The pin lists the player and has Ronald McDonald Charity. There are nine pins in this set so this checklist is incomplete.

	Nm-Mt	Ex-Mt
COMPLETE SET (4)	5.00	1.50
1 Doc Gooden	1.00	.30
2 Tino Martinez	2.00	.60
3 Andy Pettitte	1.50	.45
4 Bernie Williams	2.00	.60

1998 Yankees Pins

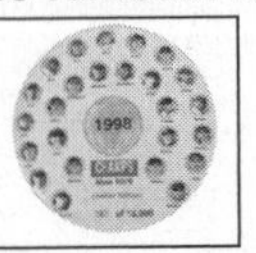

This two-card set features color head photos of the 1998 World Champs New York Yankees surrounded by red or blue stars placed in a circular fashion around a picture of the world and printed on two large pins. One pin measures approximately 4" in diameter and the other 6". Only 15,000 of the larger pin were produced and are serially numbered.

	Nm-Mt	Ex-Mt
COMPLETE SET (2)	15.00	4.50
1 1998 World Champions New York Yankees 4" pin	5.00	1.50
2 1998 World Champions New York Yankees 6" pin	10.00	3.00

1956 Yellow Basepath Pins

This relatively scarce set was probably issued around 1956 judging by the players included. If this set were produced in 1956, it would provide a possible explanation for the apparent scarcity of the Dale Long pin. Long was a relative unknown until going on his record-setting consecutive game homer-hitting spree in May 1956; perhaps he was a late addition to the set. These pins were supposedly issued as premiums or prizes in one-cent bubblegum machines. Each pin measures approximately 7/8" in diameter. The front of the pin also contains a green "infield" background with a black and white photo of the player in the center.

	NM	Ex
COMPLETE SET (32)	5500.00	2800.00
1 Hank Aaron	400.00	200.00
2 Joe Adcock	100.00	50.00
3 Luis Aparicio	150.00	75.00
4 Richie Ashburn	150.00	75.00
5 Gene Baker	80.00	40.00
6 Ernie Banks	250.00	125.00
7 Yogi Berra	300.00	150.00
8 Bill Bruton	80.00	40.00
9 Larry Doby	150.00	75.00
10 Bob Friend	80.00	40.00
11 Nellie Fox	150.00	75.00
12 Jim Greengrass	80.00	40.00
13 Steve Gromek	80.00	40.00
14 Johnny Groth	80.00	40.00
15 Gil Hodges	150.00	75.00
16 Al Kaline	250.00	125.00
17 Ted Kluzewski sic, Kluszewski	120.00	60.00
18 Johnny Logan	80.00	40.00
19 Dale Long	200.00	100.00
20 Mickey Mantle	1000.00	500.00
21 Eddie Matthews sic, Mathews	200.00	100.00
22 Minnie Minoso	120.00	60.00
23 Stan Musial	400.00	200.00
24 Don Newcombe	100.00	50.00
25 Bob Porterfield	80.00	40.00
26 Pee Wee Reese	250.00	125.00
27 Robin Roberts	150.00	75.00
28 Red Schoendienst	120.00	60.00
29 Duke Snider	300.00	150.00
30 Vern Stephens	80.00	40.00
31 Gene Woodling	100.00	50.00
32 Gus Zernial	80.00	40.00

1962 Auravision Records

These can be differentiated from the later (and more common) 1964 set by the stats only being listed through the 1961 season. Both this set and the 1964 set have a 1962 copyright date and the "Columbia" record trademark is NOT boxes in the 1962 set.

	NM	Ex
COMPLETE SET	1000.00	400.00
1 Ernie Banks	120.00	47.50
2 Whitey Ford	120.00	47.50
3 Jim Gentile	50.00	20.00
Orioles		
4 Mickey Mantle	250.00	100.00
5 Roger Maris	150.00	60.00
6 Willie Mays	200.00	80.00
7 Warren Spahn	120.00	47.50

1964 Auravision Records

These sixteen 33 1/3 RPM records feature a player photo on the front with biographical and statistical information on the back. When played on a record player, one could hear the player describe in his own voice, various parts of his career or giving advice. The records were distributed by Columbia Records. The Mays record seems to be in shorter supply and has been given an SP desgination. These unnumbered records have been sequenced in alphabetical order. These records were ordered through a premium with Milk Duds candy. The Mantle record has a different photo from the 1962 issue.

	NM	Ex
COMPLETE SET (16)	250.00	100.00
1 Bob Allison	5.00	2.00
2 Ernie Banks	15.00	6.00
3 Ken Boyer	8.00	3.20
4 Rocky Colavito	10.00	4.00
A's		
5 Don Drysdale	15.00	6.00
6 Whitey Ford	20.00	8.00
7 Jim Gentile	5.00	2.00
A's		
8 Al Kaline	15.00	6.00
9 Sandy Koufax	25.00	10.00
10 Mickey Mantle	80.00	32.00
11 Roger Maris	15.00	6.00
12 Willie Mays SP	120.00	47.50
13 Bill Mazeroski	8.00	3.20
14 Frank Robinson	15.00	6.00
15 Warren Spahn	15.00	6.00
16 Pete Ward	5.00	2.00

1996 Bally's HOF 1936 Chips

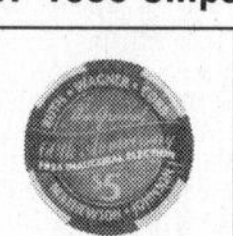

Distributed by Bally's in Atlantic City, New Jersey, this five-chip set commemorates the 60th anniversary of the 1936 HOF inaugural election and measures approximately 1 1/2" in diameter. One side of the chip features black-and-white player images on a red background with a red and yellow border printed on $5 gambling chips. The other side contains the last names of the players in a circle around the 60th anniversary banner. The chips are unnumbered and checklisted below in alphabetical order.

	Nm-Mt	Ex-Mt
COMPLETE SET (5)	50.00	15.00
1 Ty Cobb	15.00	4.50
2 Walter Johnson	10.00	3.00
3 Christy Mathewson	10.00	3.00
4 Babe Ruth	20.00	6.00
5 Honus Wagner	15.00	4.50

1979 Baseball Patches

This set features multi-color, three dimensional embroidered portraits of 100 of baseball's favorites displayed on patches. The patches could be ordered by mail for $2.50 each from Penn Emblem Co. of Philadelphia, Pennsylvania. The patches are unnumbered and checklisted below in alphabetical order.

	NM	Ex
COMPLETE SET (100)	400.00	160.00
1 Buddy Bell	3.00	1.20
2 Johnny Bench	8.00	3.20
3 Vida Blue	3.00	1.20
4 Bobby Bonds	3.00	1.20
5 Bob Boone	3.00	1.20
6 Larry Bowa	4.00	1.60
7 George Brett	15.00	6.00
8 Lou Brock	8.00	3.20
9 Rick Burleson	3.00	1.20
10 Jeff Burroughs	3.00	1.20
11 Bert Campaneris	3.00	1.20
12 John Candelaria	3.00	1.20
13 Rod Carew	8.00	3.20
14 Steve Carlton	8.00	3.20
15 Gary Carter	8.00	3.20
16 Dave Cash	3.00	1.20
17 Cesar Cedeno	3.00	1.20
18 Ron Cey	3.00	1.20
19 Chris Chambliss	4.00	1.60
20 Jack Clark	3.00	1.20
21 Dave Concepcion	3.00	1.20
22 Cecil Cooper	3.00	1.20
23 Jose Cruz	3.00	1.20
24 Andre Dawson	6.00	2.40
25 Dan Driessen	3.00	1.20
26 Rawly Eastwick	3.00	1.20
27 Dwight Evans	3.00	1.20
28 Mark Fidrych	5.00	2.00
29 Rollie Fingers	6.00	2.40
30 Carlton Fisk	8.00	3.20
31 George Foster	3.00	1.20
32 Steve Garvey	5.00	2.00
33 Rich Gossage	4.00	1.60
34 Bobby Grich	3.00	1.20
35 Ross Grimsley	3.00	1.20
36 Ron Guidry	4.00	1.60
37 Mike Hargrove	3.00	1.20
38 Keith Hernandez	4.00	1.60
39 Larry Hisle	3.00	1.20
40 Bob Horner	3.00	1.20
41 Roy Howell	3.00	1.20
42 Reggie Jackson	8.00	3.20
43 Tommy John	4.00	1.60
44 Jim Kern	3.00	1.20
45 Chet Lemon	3.00	1.20
46 Davey Lopes	4.00	1.60
47 Greg Luzinski	4.00	1.60
48 Fred Lynn	4.00	1.60
49 Garry Maddox	3.00	1.20
50 Bill Madlock	4.00	1.60
51 Jon Matlack	3.00	1.20
52 John Mayberry	3.00	1.20
53 Lee Mazzilli	4.00	1.60
54 Rick Monday	3.00	1.20
55 Don Money	3.00	1.20
56 Willie Montanez	3.00	1.20
57 John Montefusco	3.00	1.20
58 Joe Morgan	8.00	3.20
59 Thurman Munson	6.00	2.40
60 Bobby Murcer	3.00	1.20
61 Graig Nettles	4.00	1.60
62 Phil Niekro	8.00	3.20
63 Al Oliver	4.00	1.60
64 Amos Otis	3.00	1.20
65 Jim Palmer	8.00	3.20
66 Dave Parker	5.00	2.00
67 Fred Patek	3.00	1.20
68 Tony Perez	8.00	3.20
69 Lou Piniella	4.00	1.60
70 Biff Pocoroba	3.00	1.20
71 Darrell Porter	3.00	1.20
72 Jim Rice	4.00	1.60
73 Pete Rose	10.00	4.00
74 Joe Rudi	3.00	1.20
75 Rick Reuschel	3.00	1.20
76 Nolan Ryan	20.00	8.00
77 Manny Sanguillen	3.00	1.20
78 Mike Schmidt	8.00	3.20
79 George Scott	3.00	1.20
80 Tom Seaver	8.00	3.20
81 Ted Simmons	4.00	1.60
82 Reggie Smith	3.00	1.20
83 Willie Stargell	8.00	3.20
84 Rennie Stennett	3.00	1.20
85 Jim Sundberg	3.00	1.20
86 Bruce Sutter	5.00	2.00
87 Frank Tanana	3.00	1.20
88 Garry Templeton	3.00	1.20
89 Gene Tenace	3.00	1.20
90 Jason Thompson	3.00	1.20
91 Joe Torre	6.00	2.40
92 Ellis Valentine	3.00	1.20
93 Bob Watson	3.00	1.20
94 Frank White	3.00	1.20
95 Lou Whitaker	4.00	1.60
96 Bump Wills	3.00	1.20
97 Dave Winfield	8.00	3.20
98 Butch Wynegar	3.00	1.20
99 Carl Yastrzemski	8.00	3.20
100 Richie Zisk	3.00	1.20

1962 Baseball Pens

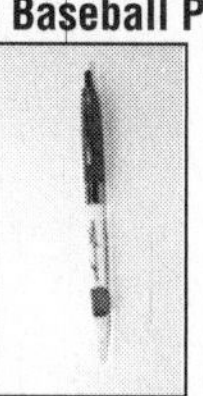

This four-pen set features player head photos with a facsimile autograph printed on a ball point pen with the team name and player's position. It is believed that this set might have been a Bazooka Gum premium offer made by Topps. The pens are unnumbered and checklisted below in alphabetical order.

	NM	Ex
COMPLETE SET (4)	400.00	160.00
1 Orlando Cepeda	50.00	20.00
2 Harmon Killebrew	50.00	20.00
3 Mickey Mantle	200.00	80.00
4 Roger Maris	100.00	40.00

1938 Baseball Tabs

The issuer of this set of baseball tabs is unknown. The tabs were produced about 1938 based on the players selected for the set. They measure approximately 3/4" in diameter and are shaped like a baseball with simulated stitching. The printing is in black and white with a solid background color, such as blue, green, orange, red, white or yellow. In the checklist below for these unnumbered tabs, the players are

checklisted first (1-27) in alphabetical order, followed by the teams (28-48) given in alphabetical order by team nickname, which is how the tabs are represented on the face of these tabs. The 48 tabs below may constitute the whole set; however any additions to the checklist would be welcome if other tabs from this set exist.

	Ex-Mt	VG
COMMON TEAM TAB (28-48)	5.00	2.50
1 Luke Appling	40.00	20.00
2 Earl Averill	40.00	20.00
3 Phil Cavarretta	25.00	12.50
4 Dizzy Dean	100.00	50.00
5 Paul Derringer	20.00	10.00
6 Bill Dickey	60.00	30.00
7 Joe DiMaggio	400.00	200.00
8 Bob Feller	100.00	50.00
9 Lou Fette	20.00	10.00
10 Jimmy Foxx	100.00	50.00
11 Lou Gehrig	400.00	200.00
12 Lefty Gomez	50.00	25.00
13 Hank Greenberg	60.00	30.00
14 Lefty Grove	80.00	40.00
15 Mule Haas	20.00	10.00
16 Gabby Hartnett	40.00	20.00
17 Rollie Hemsley	20.00	10.00
18 Chuck Klein	40.00	20.00
19 Red Kress	20.00	10.00
20 Tony Lazzeri	40.00	20.00
21 Ted Lyons	40.00	20.00
22 Joe Medwick	40.00	20.00
23 Van Lingle Mungo	25.00	12.50
24 Rip Radcliff	20.00	10.00
25 Schoolboy Rowe	20.00	10.00
26 Al Simmons	40.00	20.00
27 Lloyd Waner	40.00	20.00
32 St. Louis Browns	10.00	5.00
33 St. Louis Cardinals	10.00	5.00
35 Chicago Cubs	30.00	15.00
36 Brooklyn Dodgers	40.00	20.00
37 New York Giants	10.00	5.00
43 Boston Red Sox	10.00	5.00
46 Detroit Tigers	10.00	5.00
48 New York Yankees	20.00	10.00

1985 Blue Jays Coke Cups

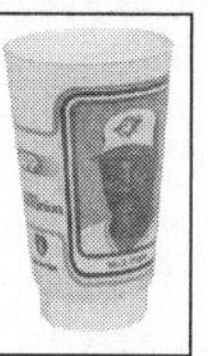

This nine-cup set features color portraits of the Toronto Blue Jays printed on plastic cups sponsored by Coke, A and P, the New Dominion, and the Variety Club of Ontario. The cups also carried player information and career averages. The cups are unnumbered and checklisted below in alphabetical order.

	Nm-Mt	Ex-Mt
COMPLETE SET (9)	18.00	7.25
1 Jesse Barfield	3.00	1.20
2 Bill Caudill	2.00	.80
3 Damaso Garcia	2.00	.80
4 Jimmy Key	5.00	2.00
5 Lloyd Moseby	2.00	.80
6 Rance Mulliniks	2.00	.80
7 Dave Stieb	3.00	1.20
8 Willie Upshaw	2.00	.80
9 Ernie Whitt	2.50	1.00

1979 Brewers Placemats Pizza Hut

These 17" by 11" placemats were issued to honor members of the 1979 Milwaukee Brewers. The players are drawn on the front and the back is a standard placemat design.

	NM	Ex
COMPLETE SET	30.00	12.00
1 Lary Sorenson	5.00	2.00
Billy Travers Larry Hisle Jim Gantner Bob McClure Sixto Lezcano		
2 Reggie Cleveland	10.00	4.00
Bob Galasso Ben Oglivie Don Money Robin Yount Moose Haas		
3 Gorman Thomas	10.00	4.00
Jim Slaton Dick Davis Buck Martinez Paul Molitor Jerry Augustine George Bamberger MG		
4 Jim Wohlford	5.00	2.00
Bill Castro Charlie Moore Cecil Cooper Sal Bando Mike Caldwell		

1983 Brewers Placemats McDonalds

These placemats were issued through McDonalds restaurants to honor members of the1982 American League champion Milwaukee Brewers. Two players are featured on each placemat along with their lifetime statistics. The back of the placemats have information on the Ronald McDonald houses for people in need.

	Nm-Mt	Ex-Mt
COMPLETE SET	35.00	14.00
1 Cecil Cooper	8.00	3.20
Pete Vuckovich		
2 Rollie Fingers	10.00	4.00
Paul Molitor		
3 Ben Oglivie	5.00	2.00
Charlie Moore		
4 Don Sutton	10.00	4.00
Ted Simmons		
5 Gorman Thomas	5.00	2.00
Mike Caldwell		

1983 Cardinals Pantera Placemats

This set of six placemats was liscensed by Major League Baseball, and issued by MSA for Pantera's Pizza in honor of the 1982 World Champion St. Louis Cardinals. Each placemat measures approximately 11" by 17", has a clear matte finish, and features head drawings of two players. The team logo, 1982 player statistics, and additional artwork along with a facsimile player autograph complete the placemat. The backs carry the Pantera's Pizza logo printed on a hot air balloon sailing under the St. Louis arch known as the Gateway to the West. The placemats are unnumbered and checklisted below in alphabetical order according to the name of the player appearing on the left of the placemat.

	Nm-Mt	Ex-Mt
COMPLETE SET (6)	15.00	6.00
1 Joaquin Andujar	5.00	2.00
Ozzie Smith		
2 George Hendrick	2.00	.80
Whitey Herzog MG		
3 Tom Herr	3.00	1.20
Keith Hernandez		
4 Willie McGee	4.00	1.60
Darrell Porter		
5 Ken Oberkfell	3.00	1.20
Bruce Sutter		
6 Lonnie Smith	2.00	.80
Bob Forsch		

1961 Chemstrand Patches

This nine-card set features color star player portraits on 2 1/2" diameter cloth patches which were included with the purchase of a boy's sport shirt for a short period in 1961. The patches were issued one to a cello package with instructions for ironing the patch onto the shirt. The package also offered the opportunity to trade the player patch for a different star. The patches are unnumbered and checklisted below in alphabetical order. Values for unopened cello packs are slightly higher.

	NM	Ex
COMPLETE SET (9)	350.00	140.00
1 Ernie Banks	40.00	16.00
2 Yogi Berra	40.00	16.00
3 Nellie Fox	40.00	16.00
4 Dick Groat	20.00	8.00
5 Al Kaline	40.00	16.00
6 Harmon Killebrew	40.00	16.00
7 Frank Malzone	20.00	8.00
8 Willie Mays	80.00	32.00
9 Warren Spahn	40.00	16.00

1970 Chemtoy Superball

These balls were originally issued late in 1969 at a cost of 29 cents per ball and were available at most five and dime stores. These "super" balls featured a photo of the player deep inside the ball along with some brief biographical information. We have sequenced this set in order by team. It is presumed a 12th person exists for the Twins, White Sox and A's, any further information on this set is appreciated. The National League Balls seem to be tougher than the American League balls and the Mets, Pilots, Pirates and Cardinal balls seem to be tougher as well.

	NM	Ex
COMPLETE SET	1600.00	650.00
1 Tom Griffin	4.00	1.60
2 Norm Miller	4.00	1.60
3 Larry Dierker	6.00	2.40
4 Joe Pepitone	6.00	2.40
5 Joe Morgan	15.00	6.00
6 Johnny Edwards	4.00	1.60
7 Jesus Alou	4.00	1.60
8 Hector Torres	4.00	1.60
9 Don Wilson	4.00	1.60
10 Doug Rader	4.00	1.60
11 Denis Menke	4.00	1.60
12 Denny Lemaster	4.00	1.60
13 Bill Stoneman	6.00	2.40
14 Ron Brand	4.00	1.60
15 Kevin Collins	4.00	1.60
16 Angel Hermoso	4.00	1.60
17 Gary Sutherland	4.00	1.60
18 Bobby Wine	4.00	1.60
19 Coco Laboy	4.00	1.60
20 John Boccabella	4.00	1.60
21 John Bateman	4.00	1.60
22 Bob Bailey	4.00	1.60
23 Ron Fairly	6.00	2.40
24 Rusty Staub	8.00	3.20
25 Billy Champion	4.00	1.60
26 Woody Fryman	4.00	1.60
27 Ron Stone	4.00	1.60
28 John Boozer	4.00	1.60
29 Billy Wilson	4.00	1.60
30 Larry Hisle	4.00	1.60
31 Johnny Briggs	4.00	1.60
32 Tommy Harmon	4.00	1.60
33 Rick Wise	4.00	1.60
34 Tony Taylor	4.00	1.60
35 Don Money	4.00	1.60
36 Lowell Palmer	4.00	1.60
37 Willie Mays	60.00	24.00
38 Gaylord Perry	15.00	6.00
39 Willie McCovey	25.00	10.00
40 Juan Marichal	25.00	10.00
41 Bobby Bonds	10.00	4.00
42 Tito Fuentes	4.00	1.60
43 Mike McCormick	4.00	1.60
44 Hal Lanier	4.00	1.60
45 Ron Hunt	4.00	1.60
46 Jim Ray Hart	4.00	1.60
47 Jim Davenport	4.00	1.60
48 Dick Dietz	4.00	1.60
49 Red Schoendienst MG	10.00	4.00
50 Steve Huntz	6.00	2.40
51 Julian Javier	6.00	2.40
52 Dal Maxvill	6.00	2.40
53 Carl Taylor	6.00	2.40
54 Cookie Rojas	6.00	2.40
55 Vada Pinson	8.00	3.20
56 Vic Davalillo	6.00	2.40
57 Nelson Briles	6.00	2.40
58 Jerry Johnson	6.00	2.40
59 Joe Torre	10.00	4.00
60 Lou Brock	30.00	12.00
61 Tom Seaver	50.00	20.00
62 Gil Hodges MG	20.00	8.00
63 Tommie Agee	8.00	3.20
64 Ron Swoboda	8.00	3.20
65 Ken Boswell	8.00	3.20
66 Jerry Koosman	8.00	3.20
67 Jerry Grote	8.00	3.20
68 Gary Gentry	8.00	3.20
69 Ed Kranepool	8.00	3.20
70 Cleon Jones	8.00	3.20
71 Bud Harrelson	8.00	3.20
72 Al Weis	8.00	3.20
73 Roberto Clemente	80.00	32.00
74 Rich Hebner	6.00	2.40
75 Manny Sanguillen	6.00	2.40
76 Jose Pagan	6.00	2.40
77 Gene Alley	6.00	2.40
78 Dock Ellis	6.00	2.40
79 Bob Veale	6.00	2.40
80 Bob Moose	6.00	2.40
81 Bill Mazeroski	10.00	4.00
82 Willie Stargell	40.00	16.00
83 Matty Alou	6.00	2.40
84 Al Oliver	10.00	4.00
85 Tony Perez	15.00	6.00
86 Bobby Tolan	6.00	2.40
87 Jack Fisher	6.00	2.40
88 Al Jackson	6.00	2.40
89 Tommy Helms	6.00	2.40
90 Lee May	6.00	2.40
91 Woody Woodward	6.00	2.40
92 Jim Merritt	6.00	2.40
93 Tony Cloninger	6.00	2.40
94 Jim Maloney	6.00	2.40
95 Clay Carroll	6.00	2.40
96 Pete Rose	60.00	24.00
97 Ron Santo	10.00	4.00
98 Leo Durocher MG	10.00	4.00
99 Willie Smith	4.00	1.60
100 Randy Hundley	4.00	1.60
101 Phil Regan	4.00	1.60
102 Ken Holtzman	6.00	2.40
103 Jim Hickman	4.00	1.60
104 Johnny Callison	4.00	1.60
105 Glenn Beckert	4.00	1.60
106 Ernie Banks	30.00	12.00
107 Don Kessinger	4.00	1.60
108 Billy Williams	15.00	6.00
109 Ivan Murrell	4.00	1.60
110 Clay Kirby	4.00	1.60
111 Gary Ross	4.00	1.60
112 Tommy Dean	4.00	1.60
113 Dick Kelley	4.00	1.60
114 Tommie Sisk	4.00	1.60
115 Jose Arcia	4.00	1.60
116 Jack Baldschun	4.00	1.60
117 Roberto Pena	4.00	1.60
118 Al Ferrara	4.00	1.60
119 Nate Colbert	4.00	1.60
120 Chris Cannizzaro	4.00	1.60
121 Len Gabrielson	4.00	1.60
122 Andy Kosko	4.00	1.60

123 Billy Grabarkewitz	4.00	1.60
124 Willie Crawford	4.00	1.60
125 Bill Sudakis	4.00	1.60
126 Willie Davis	4.00	1.60
127 Jim Brewer	4.00	1.60
128 Tom Haller	4.00	1.60
129 Claude Osteen	4.00	1.60
130 Jeff Torborg	4.00	1.60
131 Ted Sizemore	4.00	1.60
132 Pete Mikkelsen	4.00	1.60
133 Hank Aaron	50.00	20.00
134 Phil Niekro	15.00	6.00
135 Felix Millan	4.00	1.60
136 Bob Aspromonte	4.00	1.60
137 Clete Boyer	6.00	2.40
138 Pat Jarvis	4.00	1.60
139 Mike Lum	4.00	1.60
140 Ron Reed	4.00	1.60
141 Bob Tillman	4.00	1.60
142 Rico Carty	6.00	2.40
143 Milt Pappas	6.00	2.40
144 Orlando Cepeda	15.00	6.00
145 Frank Robinson	30.00	12.00
146 Brooks Robinson	30.00	12.00
147 Jim Palmer	30.00	12.00
148 Boog Powell	10.00	4.00
149 Tom Phoebus	4.00	1.60
150 Eddie Watt	4.00	1.60
151 Dave Johnson	4.00	1.60
152 Andy Etchebarren	4.00	1.60
153 Don Buford	4.00	1.60
154 Mike Cuellar	6.00	2.40
155 Mark Belanger	4.00	1.60
156 Paul Blair	4.00	1.60
157 Max Alvis	4.00	1.60
158 Dean Chance	4.00	1.60
159 Jose Cardenal	4.00	1.60
160 Ted Uhlaender	4.00	1.60
161 Zoilo Versalles	4.00	1.60
162 Duke Sims	4.00	1.60
163 Richie Scheinblum	4.00	1.60
164 Russ Snyder	4.00	1.60
165 Vern Fuller	4.00	1.60
166 Ray Fosse	4.00	1.60
167 Dick Ellsworth	4.00	1.60
168 Al Dark MG	4.00	1.60
169 Harmon Killebrew	30.00	12.00
170 Rod Carew	25.00	10.00
171 Jim Kaat	10.00	4.00
172 Tony Oliva	10.00	4.00
173 Leo Cardenas	4.00	1.60
174 Rich Reese	4.00	1.60
175 Cesar Tovar	4.00	1.60
176 Bob Allison	4.00	1.60
177 Jim Perry	6.00	2.40
178 George Mitterwald	4.00	1.60
179 Frank Quillici	4.00	1.60
180 Luis Aparicio	15.00	6.00
181 Tommy John	10.00	4.00
182 Ron Hansen	4.00	1.60
183 Ken Berry	4.00	1.60
184 Carlos May	4.00	1.60
185 Joel Horlen	4.00	1.60
186 Wilbur Wood	4.00	1.60
187 Bill Melton	4.00	1.60
188 Ed Herrmann	4.00	1.60
189 Billy Wynne	4.00	1.60
190 Walt Williams	4.00	1.60
191 Tony Conigliaro	10.00	4.00
192 Tom Satriano	4.00	1.60
193 Reggie Smith	8.00	3.20
194 Rico Petrocelli	6.00	2.40
195 Russ Gibson	4.00	1.60
196 Norm Siebern	4.00	1.60
197 Mike Andrews	4.00	1.60
198 Lee Stange	4.00	1.60
199 Jose Santiago	4.00	1.60
200 Jim Lonborg	6.00	2.40
201 George Scott	4.00	1.60
202 Dalton Jones	4.00	1.60
203 Ted Williams MG	40.00	16.00
204 Frank Howard	10.00	4.00
205 Ed Stroud	4.00	1.60
206 Chuck Hinton	4.00	1.60
207 Darold Knowles	4.00	1.60
208 Del Unser	4.00	1.60
209 Casey Cox	4.00	1.60
210 Ed Brinkman	4.00	1.60
211 Mike Epstein	4.00	1.60
212 Paul Casanova	4.00	1.60
213 Bernie Allen	4.00	1.60
214 Joe Coleman	4.00	1.60
215 Bobby Murcer	8.00	3.20
216 Mel Stottlemyre	8.00	3.20
217 Gene Michael	6.00	2.40
218 Roy White	6.00	2.40
219 Fritz Peterson	6.00	2.40
220 Tom Tresh	6.00	2.40
221 Steve Hamilton	6.00	2.40
222 Pete Ward	6.00	2.40
223 Jake Gibbs	6.00	2.40
224 Curt Blefary	6.00	2.40
225 Ralph Houk MG	6.00	2.40
226 Billy Cowan	6.00	2.40
227 Reggie Jackson	60.00	24.00
228 Rollie Fingers	25.00	10.00
229 Jim Hunter	30.00	12.00
230 Bert Campaneris	6.00	2.40
231 Sal Bando	6.00	2.40
232 Ramon Webster	4.00	1.60
233 Mike Hershberger	4.00	1.60
234 Don Mincher	4.00	1.60
235 Dick Green	4.00	1.60
236 Rick Monday	4.00	1.60
237 Joe Rudi	6.00	2.40
238 George Lauzerique	4.00	1.60
239 Mike Hegan	6.00	2.40
240 Jerry McNertney	6.00	2.40
241 Bob Locker	6.00	2.40
242 John Kennedy	6.00	2.40
243 Marty Pattin	6.00	2.40
244 Gene Brabender	6.00	2.40
245 Tommy Harper	6.00	2.40
246 Lew Krausse	6.00	2.40
247 Jim Pagliaroni	6.00	2.40
248 Rich Rollins	6.00	2.40
249 Wayne Comer	6.00	2.40
250 Lou Piniella	10.00	4.00
251 Pat Kelly	4.00	1.60
252 Moe Drabowsky	4.00	1.60
253 Jerry Adair	4.00	1.60
254 Tom Burgmeier	4.00	1.60
255 Mike Hedlund	4.00	1.60
256 Jim Campanis	4.00	1.60
257 Dave Morehead	4.00	1.60
258 Juan Rios	4.00	1.60
259 Bill Butler	4.00	1.60
260 Joe Keough	4.00	1.60
261 Mike Fiore	4.00	1.60
262 Al Kaline	25.00	10.00
263 Mickey Lolich	10.00	4.00
264 Denny McLain	8.00	3.20
265 Norm Cash	10.00	4.00
266 Dick McAuliffe	4.00	1.60
267 Bill Freehan	8.00	3.20
268 Joe Sparma	4.00	1.60
269 Willie Horton	6.00	2.40
270 Mickey Stanley	4.00	1.60
271 Mayo Smith MG	4.00	1.60
272 Jim Northrup	4.00	1.60
273 Earl Wilson	4.00	1.60
274 Rick Reichardt	4.00	1.60
275 Jim Fregosi	6.00	2.40
276 Jay Johnstone	4.00	1.60
277 Roger Repoz	4.00	1.60
278 Sandy Alomar	4.00	1.60
279 Bill Voss	4.00	1.60
280 Jose Azcue	4.00	1.60
281 Lefty Phillips MG	4.00	1.60
282 Joe Hicks	4.00	1.60
283 Eddie Fisher	4.00	1.60
284 Greg Washburn	4.00	1.60
285 Lloyd Allen	4.00	1.60

1966 Dodgers Records

This set of records, which are the size of the old 45 rpm singles but were played at 33 1/2 rpm feature interviews with various members of the Los Angeles Dodgers along with famed commentator Vin Scully. Each player is featured on one side of the record and it is believed that these records were used as premiums by Union 76. This set can be dated to 1966 as it was the only season that Maury Wills and Phil Regan were teammates.

	NM	Ex
COMPLETE SET	150.00	60.00
1 Buzzie Bavasi GM	10.00	4.00
Jim Gilliam		
2 Tommy Davis	10.00	4.00
Ron Perranoski		
3 Willie Davis|Al Ferrara	10.00	4.00
4 Don Drysdale	25.00	10.00
Jeff Torborg		
5 Ron Fairly	10.00	4.00
Howie Reed		
6 Sandy Koufax	30.00	12.00
John Kennedy		
7 Jim Lefebvre	10.00	4.00
Lou Johnson		
8 Bob Miller	10.00	4.00
John Roseboro		
9 Nate Oliver	10.00	4.00
Wes Parker		
10 Walter O'Malley OWN	15.00	6.00
Claude Osteen		
11 Phil Regan	15.00	6.00
Walt Alston MG		
12 Maury Wills	25.00	10.00
Don Sutton		

1966 Dodgers Volpe Tumblers

The 1966 Dodgers Volpe Tumblers were produced in conjuction with Union 76 gasoline stations. They feature the artwork of the noted artist Volpe, and show both a portrait and an action drawing, as well as a facsimile signature on each cup.

	NM	Ex
COMPLETE SET (12)	250.00	100.00
1 Tommy Davis	20.00	8.00
2 Willie Davis	20.00	8.00
3 Don Drysdale	30.00	12.00
4 Ron Fairly	20.00	8.00
5 John Kennedy	15.00	6.00
6 Sandy Koufax	50.00	20.00
7 Jim Lefebvre	15.00	6.00
8 Claude Osteen	15.00	6.00
9 Wes Parker	20.00	8.00
10 Ron Perranoski	15.00	6.00
11 John Roseboro	20.00	8.00
12 Maury Wills	30.00	12.00

1984 Expos Glasses

This set of the 1984 Montreal Expos features black-and-white player head photos printed on clear drinking glasses with red, white, and blue highlights. The glasses are unnumbered and checklisted below in alphabetical order. The two players listed may not be the only ones that were produced and any confirmed additions are appreciated.

	Nm-Mt	Ex-Mt
COMPLETE SET	15.00	6.00
1 Andre Dawson	5.00	2.00
2 Pete Rose	10.00	4.00

1985 Expos Cups

This set features color portraits of the Montreal Expos printed on plastic cups. The cups also carry player information. The cups are unnumbered and checklisted below in alphabetical order. The checklist may not be complete and any additions are appreciated.

	Nm-Mt	Ex-Mt
1 Tim Raines	5.00	2.00

1969 Fleer Team Plastics Trophy

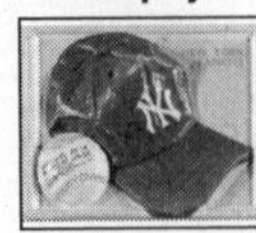

These standard-size flimsy plastic items were issued in one "card" packs. These plastics have the team name in the upper right corner, a fascimile cap and an "official" ball. Both the cap and the ball are set off in 3D fashion on the card. Since these are unnumbered, we have sequenced them in alphabetical order. This set can be dated to 1969 by the inclusion of the Seattle Pilots.

	NM	Ex
COMPLETE SET (24)	600.00	240.00
COMMON PLASTIC	20.00	8.00
2 Baltimore Orioles	25.00	10.00
3 Boston Red Sox	40.00	16.00
5 Chicago Cubs	30.00	12.00
11 Kansas City Royals	40.00	16.00
12 Los Angeles Dodgers	25.00	10.00
15 New York Mets	50.00	20.00
16 New York Yankees	40.00	16.00
20 San Diego Padres	40.00	16.00
23 Seattle Pilots	100.00	40.00
24 Washington Senators	50.00	20.00

1958 Giants Armour Tabs

This set of tabs features black-and-white player photos with a facsimile autograph lithographed on tin in a figural design in orange, black, and white. The checklist may be incomplete, however many additions have been added and more additions are welcome. The tabs are unnumbered and checklisted below in alphabetical order. On occasion, these tabs still exist in the original cellophane wrap which protected them from the hot dog and potential stains. There is no set size for these tabs which are all different sizes.

	NM	Ex
COMPLETE SET	350.00	180.00
1 Johnny Antonelli	40.00	20.00
2 Curt Barclay	25.00	12.50
3 Ray Crone	25.00	12.50
4 Whitey Lockman	30.00	15.00
5 Willie Mays	100.00	50.00
6 Don Mueller	30.00	15.00
7 Danny O'Connell	25.00	12.50
8 Hank Sauer	40.00	20.00
9 Darryl Spencer	25.00	12.50
10 Bobby Thomson	40.00	20.00

1952 H-O Instant Oatmeal Records

This very scarce set of four records measure 4 3/4" inches in diameter. The fronts feature a multi-color closeup with black and white portrait shots on the reverse. We have sequenced these in alphabetical order. Players from the NY area are featured in this set.

	NM	Ex
COMPLETE SET (4)	1000.00	500.00
1 Roy Campanella	250.00	125.00
2 Whitey Lockman	100.00	50.00
3 Allie Reynolds	200.00	100.00
4 Duke Snider	250.00	125.00

1973 Indians Arthur Treacher Cups

This six-cup set features color portraits of six members of the Cleveland Indians printed on trading cups. The set was issued by Arthur Treacher Restaurants in the Cleveland area. The cups are unnumbered and checklisted below in alphabetical order.

	NM	Ex
COMPLETE SET (6)	25.00	10.00
1 Buddy Bell	6.00	2.40
2 Jack Brohamer	4.00	1.60
3 Chris Chambliss	6.00	2.40
4 Dave Duncan	5.00	2.00
5 Gaylord Perry	10.00	4.00
6 Charlie Spikes	4.00	1.60

1966 Indians Volpe Tumblers

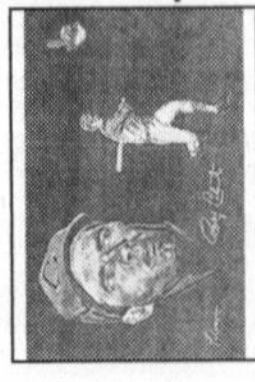

This 12-cup set features player portraits of the Cleveland Indians by artist Nicholas Volpe and printed on cups. The cups are unnumbered and checklisted below in alphabetical order.

	NM	Ex
COMPLETE SET (12)	200.00	80.00
1 Max Alvis	20.00	8.00
2 Joe Azcue	15.00	6.00
3 Larry Brown	15.00	6.00
4 Rocky Colavito	30.00	12.00
5 Vic Davalillo	15.00	6.00
6 Chuck Hinton	15.00	6.00
7 Dick Howser	20.00	8.00
8 Sam McDowell	25.00	10.00
9 Don McMahon	15.00	6.00
10 Sonny Siebert	15.00	6.00
11 Leon Wagner	20.00	8.00
12 Fred Whitfield	15.00	6.00

1960 Key Chain Inserts

These 1 1/8" by 1 1/2" "cards" are really key chain photos. These items are unnumbered, blank-backed and checklisted below in alphabetical order.

	NM	Ex
COMPLETE SET	500.00	200.00
1 Hank Aaron	25.00	10.00
2 Bob Allison	5.00	2.00
3 George Altman	3.00	1.20
4 Luis Aparicio	8.00	3.20
5 Richie Ashburn	8.00	3.20
6 Ernie Banks	15.00	6.00
7 Earl Battey	3.00	1.20
8 Hank Bauer	6.00	2.40
9 Gus Bell	5.00	2.00
10 Yogi Berra	15.00	6.00
11 Ken Boyer	8.00	3.20
12 Lew Burdette	5.00	2.00
13 Smoky Burgess	5.00	2.00
14 Orlando Cepeda	10.00	4.00
15 Gino Cimoli	3.00	1.20
16 Roberto Clemente	20.00	8.00
17 Del Crandall	5.00	2.00
18 Dizzy Dean	8.00	3.20
19 Don Drysdale	8.00	3.20
20 Sam Esposito	3.00	1.20
21 Roy Face	5.00	2.00
22 Nelson Fox	8.00	3.20
23 Bob Friend	5.00	2.00
24 Lou Gehrig	30.00	12.00
25 Joe Gibbon	3.00	1.20
26 Jim Gilliam	6.00	2.40
27 Fred Green	3.00	1.20
28 Pumpsie Green	3.00	1.20
29 Dick Groat	5.00	2.00
30 Harvey Haddix	5.00	2.00
31 Don Hoak	5.00	2.00
32 Glen Hobbie	3.00	1.20
33 Frank Howard	6.00	2.40
34 Jackie Jensen	6.00	2.40
35 Sam Jones	3.00	1.20
36 Al Kaline	8.00	3.20
37 Harmon Killebrew	8.00	3.20
38 Harvey Kuenn	3.00	1.20
39 Norm Larker	3.00	1.20
40 Vern Law	5.00	2.00
41 Mickey Mantle	40.00	16.00
42 Roger Maris	20.00	8.00
43 Eddie Mathews	8.00	3.20
44 Willie Mays	25.00	10.00
45 Bill Mazeroski	10.00	4.00
46 Willie McCovey	15.00	6.00
47 Lindy McDaniel	3.00	1.20
48 Roy McMillan	5.00	2.00
49 Minnie Minoso	6.00	2.40
50 Dan Murtaugh MG	3.00	1.20
51 Stan Musial	20.00	8.00
52 Rocky Nelson	3.00	1.20
53 Bob Oldis	3.00	1.20
54 Vada Pinson	5.00	2.00
55 Vic Power	3.00	1.20
56 Robin Roberts	8.00	3.20
57 Pete Runnels	3.00	1.20
58 Babe Ruth	40.00	16.00
59 Ron Santo	10.00	4.00
60 Dick Schofield	3.00	1.20
61 Bob Skinner	3.00	1.20
62 Hal Smith	3.00	1.20
63 Duke Snider	8.00	3.20
64 Warren Spahn	8.00	3.20
65 Dick Stuart	3.00	1.20
66 Willie Tasby	3.00	1.20
67 Tony Taylor	3.00	1.20
68 Bill Virdon	3.00	1.20
69 Ted Williams	30.00	12.00

1983 Major League Picture Balls

These baseballs, which are regulation size major league baseballs, have the pictures of four stars of each team on them. It is possible this list is incomplete so any additions to this checklist is appreciated.

	Nm-Mt	Ex-Mt
COMPLETE SET	50.00	20.00
1 Joe Morgan	30.00	12.00
Steve Carlton		
Pete Rose		
Mike Schmidt		
2 Rick Cerone	10.00	4.00
Dave Winfield		
Rich Gossage		
Ron Guidry		
3 Mookie Wilson	15.00	6.00
Tom Seaver		
Dave Kingman		
George Foster		

1966 Mets Volpe Tumblers

This 12-cup set features player portraits of the New York Mets by artist Nicholas Volpe and printed on cups. The cups are unnumbered and checklisted below in alphabetical order.

	NM	Ex
COMPLETE SET (12)	200.00	80.00
1 Larry Beranarth	15.00	6.00
2 Yogi Berra CO	25.00	10.00
3 Jack Fisher	15.00	6.00
4 Rob Gardner	15.00	6.00
5 Jim Hickman	15.00	6.00
6 Ron Hunt	15.00	6.00
7 Ed Kranepool	20.00	8.00
8 Johnny Lewis	15.00	6.00
9 Tug McGraw	20.00	8.00
10 Roy McMillan	15.00	6.00
11 Dick Stuart	15.00	6.00
12 Ron Swoboda	20.00	8.00

1977 Mets Nedicks Cups

Similar to the Yankees cups also issued in 1977, the Nedicks chain (home of world famous Hot Dogs), issued 10 cups featuring the leading players on the 1977 Mets. Since these are unnumbered, the ones we know are sequenced in alphabetical order. Also -- the information to complete this checklist would be appreciated.

	NM	Ex
COMPLETE SET	10.00	4.00
1 Lee Mazzilli	4.00	1.60
2 Tom Seaver	10.00	4.00

1991 MLBPA Key Chains

These key chains measure 2" by 3." A borderless color player photo appears inside a plastic case; the reverse of each picture has color logos of the team, MLB, and MLBPA. We have sequenced these unnumbered chains in alphabetical order.

	Nm-Mt	Ex-Mt
COMPLETE SET (4)	5.00	1.50
1 Bobby Bonilla	1.00	.30
2 Kevin Maas	.50	.15
3 Mark McGwire	4.00	1.20
4 Darryl Strawberry	1.00	.30

1984 MLBPA Pencils

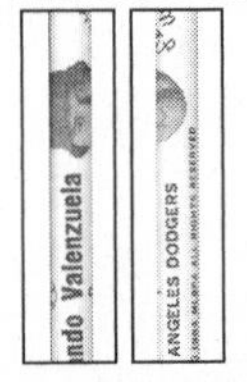

This 18-pencil set features head photos of major league players with facsimile autographs printed on different colored pencils.

	Nm-Mt	Ex-Mt
COMPLETE SET (18)	125.00	50.00
1 Cal Ripken	30.00	12.00
2 Dave Winfield	6.00	2.40
3 Reggie Jackson	10.00	4.00
4 Lou Whitaker	4.00	1.60
5 Ron Guidry	2.00	.80
6 Rusty Staub	1.00	.40
7 Rickey Henderson	15.00	6.00
8 Tom Seaver	6.00	2.40
9 George Brett	20.00	8.00
10 Carlton Fisk	6.00	2.40
11 Leon Durham	1.00	.40
12 Steve Carlton	6.00	2.40
13 Fernando Valenzuela	3.00	1.20
14 Ozzie Smith	15.00	6.00
15 Rich Gossage	2.00	.80
16 Mike Schmidt	6.00	2.40
17 Dale Murphy	4.00	1.60
18 Steve Garvey	3.00	1.20

2000 MLBPA Yoyo

These 10 Yoyo's were issued by Racing Champions and featured 10 of the leading players in Baseball.

	Nm-Mt	Ex-Mt
COMPLETE SET (10)	50.00	15.00
1 Kevin Brown	1.50	.45
2 Ken Griffey Jr.	6.00	1.80
3 Tony Gwynn	5.00	1.50
4 Derek Jeter	10.00	3.00
5 Greg Maddux	6.00	1.80
6 Mark McGwire	8.00	2.40
7 Mike Piazza	6.00	1.80
8 Cal Ripken	10.00	3.00
9 Ivan Rodriguez	3.00	.90
10 Sammy Sosa	5.00	1.50

1938 Our National Game Tabs

This set of 30 "tabs" (each measuring 7/8" in diameter) do not have a pin back but rather a tab or spike. They are frequently found with a paper back "holder". The catalog designation for these "tabs" is PM8. The set can be dated at approximately 1938 based on the selection of players in the set. The photo is in black and white but printed in blue tones. Since these tabs are unnumbered, they are listed below in alphabetical order.

	Ex-Mt	VG
COMPLETE SET (30)	800.00	400.00
1 Wally Berger	10.00	5.00
2 Lou Chiozza	8.00	4.00
3 Joe Cronin	15.00	7.50
4 Frank Crosetti	8.00	4.00
5 Dizzy Dean	50.00	25.00
6 Frank Demaree	8.00	4.00
7 Joe DiMaggio	200.00	100.00
8 Bob Feller	40.00	20.00
9 Jimmy Foxx	40.00	20.00
10 Charlie Gehringer	20.00	10.00
11 Lou Gehrig	200.00	100.00
12 Lefty Gomez	20.00	10.00
13 Hank Greenberg	20.00	10.00
14 Bump Hadley	8.00	4.00
15 Leo Hartnett	15.00	7.50

16 Carl Hubbell	20.00	10.00
17 Buddy Lewis	40.00	20.00
18 Gus Mancuso	8.00	4.00
19 Joe McCarthy MG	12.00	6.00
20 Joe Medwick	15.00	7.50
21 Joe Moore	8.00	4.00
22 Mel Ott	20.00	10.00
23 Jake Powell	8.00	4.00
24 Jimmy Ripple	8.00	4.00
25 Red Ruffing	15.00	7.50
26 Hal Schumacher	8.00	4.00
27 George Selkirk	8.00	4.00
28 Al Simmons	15.00	7.50
29 Bill Terry	20.00	10.00
30 Harold Trosky	8.00	4.00

2001 Pepsi All-Star Cans

These six cans, which feature players popular in Seattle and throughout the country, were issued to commemorate the 2001 All-Star game played in Seattle. Since these cans are unnumbered, we have sequenced them in alphabetical order.

	Nm-Mt	Ex-Mt
COMPLETE SET	15.00	4.50
1 Jason Giambi	2.50	.75
2 Ken Griffey Jr	5.00	1.50
3 Edgar Martinez	1.50	.45
4 Mike Piazza	4.00	1.20
5 Sammy Sosa	3.00	.90
6 Frank Thomas	2.00	.60

1976 Phillies Canada Dry Cans

These cands, featuring members of the 1976 Phillies were issued regionally in the Philadelphia area. Since these are unnumbered, we are sequencing them in alphabetical order. Dave Cash is not included in this set as he had signed with a rival soda maker. If a collector brought in 20 cans and a dollar, they could acquire a metal wall poster which included photos of all the cans in the set.

	NM	Ex
COMPLETE SET (26)	60.00	24.00
1 Dick Allen	4.00	1.60
2 Bob Boone	3.00	1.20
3 Larry Bowa	3.00	1.20
4 Ollie Brown	2.00	.80
5 Steve Carlton	6.00	2.40
6 Larry Christenson	2.00	.80
7 Gene Garber	2.00	.80
8 Terry Harmon	2.00	.80
9 Tom Hutton	2.00	.80
10 Jay Johnstone	2.00	.80
11 Jim Kaat	4.00	1.60
12 Jim Lonborg	2.50	1.00
13 Greg Luzinski	3.00	1.20
14 Garry Maddox	2.00	.80
15 Jerry Martin	2.00	.80
16 Tim McCarver	4.00	1.60
17 Tug McGraw	2.50	1.00
18 Johnny Oates	2.00	.80
19 Danny Ozark MG	2.00	.80
20 Ron Reed	2.00	.80
21 Mike Schmidt	8.00	3.20
22 Ron Schueler	2.00	.80
23 Tony Taylor	2.50	1.00
24 Bobby Tolan	2.00	.80
25 Wayne Twitchell	2.00	.80
26 Tom Underwood	2.00	.80

1976 Phillies Safelon Lunchbags

These four lunchbags feature a member of the 1976 Philadelpha Phillies. A player is featured on each side. Interestingly three of the four bags feature Dave Cash.

	NM	Ex
COMPLETE SET (4)	15.00	6.00
1 Greg Luzinski / Dave Cash	2.50	1.00
2 Tug McGraw / Dave Cash	3.00	1.20
3 Jim Lonborg / Dave Cash	2.00	.80
4 Mike Schmidt / Larry Bowa	8.00	3.20

1999 Pinheads Key Chains

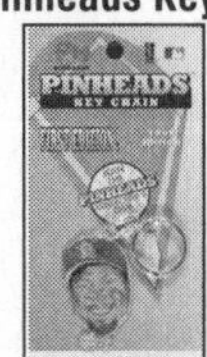

These key chains which use the same drawings as the 1999 Pinheads set, are another product of Pinheads Promotions.

	Nm-Mt	Ex-Mt
COMPLETE SET (30)	100.00	30.00
1 Moises Alou	1.00	.30
2 Jeff Bagwell	2.50	.75
3 Craig Biggio	2.00	.60
4 Barry Bonds	5.00	1.50
5 Kevin Brown	1.50	.45
6 David Cone	1.00	.30
7 Nomar Garciaparra	4.00	1.20
8 Juan Gonzalez	2.50	.75
9 Ben Grieve	1.00	.30
10 Ken Griffey Jr.	5.00	1.50
11 Tony Gwynn	4.00	1.20
12 Derek Jeter	8.00	2.40
13 Randy Johnson	3.00	.90
14 Chipper Jones	4.00	1.20
15 David Justice	1.00	.30
16 Barry Larkin	2.00	.60
17 Greg Maddux	5.00	1.50
18 Pedro Martinez	3.00	.90
19 Mark McGwire	6.00	1.80
20 Mike Piazza	5.00	1.50
21 Cal Ripken Jr.	8.00	2.40
22 Alex Rodriguez	5.00	1.50
23 Ivan Rodriguez	3.00	.90
24 Curt Schilling	2.00	.60
25 Sammy Sosa	4.00	1.20
26 Frank Thomas	2.50	.75
27 Larry Walker	1.50	.45
28 David Wells	1.00	.30
29 Bernie Williams	2.00	.60
30 Kerry Wood	2.00	.60
31 Roberto Alomar	2.00	.60
32 Dante Bichette	1.00	.30
33 Jose Canseco	2.00	.60
34 Roger Clemens	4.00	1.20
35 Todd Hundley	1.00	.30
36 Eric Karros	1.00	.30
37 Raul Mondesi	1.00	.30
38 Chan Ho Park	.50	.15
39 Manny Ramirez	3.00	.90
40 Gary Sheffield	2.50	.75
41 Greg Vaughn	1.00	.30
42 Jaret Wright	.50	.15
43 Eric Young	1.00	.30

2000 Pinheads Key Chains

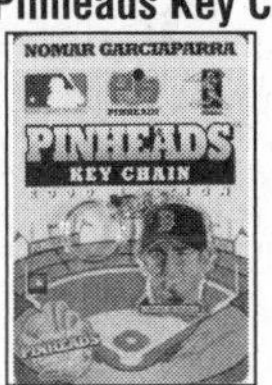

These key chains, which feature the same drawings as the regular Pinheads set were also produced by Pinhead Productions.

	Nm-Mt	Ex-Mt
COMPLETE SET (8)	30.00	9.00
1 Nomar Garciaparra	4.00	1.20
2 Shawn Green	3.00	.90
3 Ken Griffey Jr.	5.00	1.50
4 Derek Jeter	8.00	2.40
5 Chipper Jones	4.00	1.20
6 Mark McGwire	6.00	1.80
7 Mike Piazza	5.00	1.50
8 Sammy Sosa	4.00	1.20

1996 Rangers Cups

This four-cup set of the Texas Rangers features color portraits printed on plastic cups of Rangers pitchers who have pitched no hitters. The cups also carried player information. The cups are unnumbered and checklisted below in alphabetical order.

	Nm-Mt	Ex-Mt
COMPLETE SET (4)	8.00	2.40
1 Jim Bibby	1.00	.30
2 Bert Blyleven	2.00	.60
3 Kenny Rogers	1.50	.45
4 Nolan Ryan	5.00	1.50

1997 Rangers Cups

This four-cup set features black-and-white portraits of the Texas Rangers printed on plastic cups. The cups also carry player information and were distributed by Borden and Minyard Food Stores. The cups are unnumbered and checklisted below in alphabetical order.

	Nm-Mt	Ex-Mt
COMPLETE SET (4)	8.00	2.40
1 Will Clark	2.50	.75
2 Rusty Greer	1.50	.45
3 Mark McLemore	1.00	.30
4 Ivan Rodriguez	3.00	.90

1977 RC Cola Cans

This 70-can set features black-and white player head photos in white circles measuring 2 1/2" in diameter with no insignia on their caps indicating RC didn't pay the teams for the rights to reproduce their logos. The player's name was printed in red and player information was printed in black in a rectangle below the picture. The cans are unnumbered and checklisted below in alphabetical order. Cans opened from the bottom are worth twice the prices below.

	NM	Ex
COMPLETE SET (70)	200.00	80.00
1 Sal Bando	2.50	1.00
2 Mark Belanger	2.00	.80
3 Johnny Bench	6.00	2.40
4 Vida Blue	2.50	1.00
5 Bobby Bonds	3.00	1.20
6 Bob Boone	2.50	1.00
7 Larry Bowa	2.50	1.00
8 Steve Braun	2.00	.80
9 George Brett	15.00	6.00
10 Lou Brock	5.00	2.00
11 Bert Campaneris	2.50	1.00
12 Bill Campbell	2.00	.80
13 Jose Cardenal	2.00	.80
14 Rod Carew	5.00	2.00
15 Dave Cash	2.00	.80
16 Cesar Cedeno	2.50	1.00
17 Ron Cey	3.00	1.20
18 Chris Chambliss	2.50	1.00
19 Dave Concepcion	2.00	.80
20 Mark Fidrych	4.00	1.60
21 Rollie Fingers	5.00	2.00
22 George Foster	2.50	1.00
23 Wayne Garland	2.00	.80
24 Ralph Garr	2.00	.80
25 Steve Garvey	4.00	1.60
26 Bobby Grich	2.50	1.00
27 Ken Griffey	3.00	1.20
28 Don Gullett	2.00	.80
29 Mike Hargrove	2.50	1.00
30 Catfish Hunter	5.00	2.00
31 Randy Jones	2.00	.80
32 Dave Kingman	4.00	1.60
33 Dave LaRoche	2.00	.80
34 Ron LeFlore	2.00	.80
35 Greg Luzinski	2.50	1.00
36 Fred Lynn	2.50	1.00
37 Bill Madlock	2.50	1.00
38 Jon Matlack	2.00	.80
39 Gary Matthews	2.00	.80
40 Bake McBride	2.00	.80
41 Hal McRae	2.00	.80
42 Andy Messersmith	2.00	.80
43 Rick Monday	2.00	.80
44 John Montefusco	2.00	.80
45 Joe Morgan	5.00	2.00
46 Thurman Munson	4.00	1.60
47 Al Oliver	2.50	1.00
48 Amos Otis	2.00	.80
49 Jim Palmer	5.00	2.00
50 Dave Parker	3.00	1.20
51 Fred Patek	2.00	.80
52 Gaylord Perry	5.00	2.00
53 Marty Perez	2.00	.80
54 Tony Perez	5.00	2.00
55 J.R. Richard	2.50	1.00
56 Pete Rose	8.00	3.20
57 Joe Rudi	2.00	.80
58 Mike Schmidt	10.00	4.00
59 Tom Seaver	8.00	3.20
60 Bill Singer	2.00	.80
61 Rusty Staub	3.00	1.20
62 Don Sutton	5.00	2.00
63 Gene Tenace	2.00	.80
64 Luis Tiant	3.00	1.20
65 Ellis Valentine	2.00	.80
66 Claudell Washington	2.00	.80
67 Butch Wynegar	2.00	.80
68 Carl Yastrzemski	6.00	2.40
69 Robin Yount	8.00	3.20
70 Richie Zisk	2.00	.80

1978 RC Cola Cans

This 100-can set is indicated as Collector's Series Two on the cans and features black-and-white player head photos in a white circle with a red border. Player's biographical information is printed beneath in a white circle with red stitching to simulate a baseball. At the top of the ball is a facsimile autograph. The player's career highlights summary is written in paragraph form inside the ball. At the bottom of the ball is the can number, designated as, "No. x of 100." The cans are unnumbered and checklisted below in alphabetical order. Cans opened from the bottom are worth twice the prices below.

	NM	Ex
COMPLETE SET (100)	250.00	100.00
COMMON CARD (1-100)	2.00	.80
COMMON DP	4.00	1.60
1 Don Sutton	5.00	2.00
2 Bill Singer	2.00	.80
3 Pete Rose	8.00	3.20
4 Gene Tenace	2.00	.80
5 Dave Kingman	3.00	1.20
6 Dave Cash	2.00	.80
7 Joe Morgan DP	4.00	1.60
8 Mark Belanger	2.00	.80
9 Steve Braun	2.00	.80
10 Butch Wynegar	2.00	.80
11 Ken Griffey	3.00	1.20
12 Ron LeFlore	2.00	.80
13 George Foster	2.00	.80
14 Tony Perez	5.00	2.00
15 Thurman Munson	4.00	1.60
16 Bill Campbell	2.00	.80
17 Andy Messersmith	2.00	.80
18 Mike Schmidt	10.00	4.00
19 Ron Cey	2.50	1.00
20 Chris Chambliss	2.50	1.00
21 Ralph Garr	2.00	.80
22 Dave LaRoche	2.00	.80
23 George Brett	15.00	6.00
24 Bob Boone	2.50	1.00
25 Jeff Burroughs	2.00	.80
26 Bake McBride	2.00	.80
27 Gary Matthews	2.00	.80
28 Don Gullett	2.00	.80
29 Rick Monday	2.00	.80
30 Al Oliver	2.00	.80
31 Ellis Valentine	2.00	.80
32 Mike Hargrove	2.00	.80
33 Hal McRae	2.00	.80
34 Rollie Fingers	5.00	2.00
35 Dave Parker	4.00	1.60
36 Tom Seaver DP	4.00	1.60
37 Wayne Garland	2.00	.80
38 Jon Matlack	2.00	.80
39 Richie Zisk	2.00	.80
40 Joe Rudi	2.00	.80
41 Sal Bando	2.00	.80
42 Greg Luzinski	2.00	.80
43 Vida Blue	2.50	1.00
44 Bobby Bonds	2.50	1.00
45 Jim Palmer	5.00	2.00
46 Claudell Washington	2.00	.80
47 Dave Concepcion	2.00	.80
48 Rod Carew DP	4.00	1.60
49 J.R. Richard	2.00	.80
50 Goose Gossage	3.00	1.20
51 Cesar Cedeno	2.00	.80
52 Bert Campaneris	2.00	.80
53 Marty Perez	2.00	.80
54 Bill Madlock	2.00	.80
55 Amos Otis	2.00	.80
56 Robin Yount	5.00	2.00
57 Bobby Grich	2.00	.80
58 Catfish Hunter	5.00	2.00
59 Butch Hobson	2.00	.80
60 Larry Bowa	2.00	.80
61 Randy Jones	2.00	.80
62 Richie Hebner	2.00	.80
63 Fred Patek	2.00	.80
64 John Denny	2.00	.80
65 Johnny Bench DP	4.00	1.60
66 Doyle Alexander	2.00	.80
67 Dusty Baker	2.50	1.00
68 Bert Blyleven	3.00	1.20
69 Lyman Bostock	2.00	.80
70 Bill Buckner	2.00	.80
71 Steve Carlton	5.00	2.00
72 John Candelaria	2.00	.80
73 Andre Dawson	8.00	3.20
74 Al Cowens	2.00	.80
75 Eddie Murray	10.00	4.00
76 Dan Driessen	2.00	.80
77 Jim Rice	3.00	1.20
78 Garry Maddox	2.00	.80
79 Larry Hisle	2.00	.80
80 Al Hrabosky	2.00	.80
81 Reggie Jackson DP	6.00	2.40
82 Tommy John	3.00	1.20
83 Willie McCovey	5.00	2.00
84 Sparky Lyle	2.50	1.00
85 Tug McGraw	2.50	1.00
86 Paul Splittorff	2.00	.80
87 Bobby Murcer	2.00	.80
88 Graig Nettles	3.00	1.20
89 Phil Niekro	5.00	2.00
90 Lou Piniella	3.00	1.20
91 Rick Reuschel	2.00	.80
92 Frank Tanana	2.50	1.00
93 Nolan Ryan	15.00	6.00
94 Garry Templeton	2.00	.80
95 Reggie Smith	2.00	.80
96 Bruce Sutter	3.00	1.20
97 Jason Thompson	2.00	.80
98 Mike Torrez	2.00	.80
99 Rick Wise	2.00	.80
100 Bump Wills	2.00	.80

1966 Reds Volpe Tumblers

This 12-cup set features player portraits of the Cincinnati Reds by artist Nicholas Volpe and printed on cups. The cups are unnumbered and checklisted below in alphabetical order.

	NM	Ex
COMPLETE SET (12)	200.00	80.00
1 Leo Cardenas	15.00	6.00
2 Gordy Coleman	15.00	6.00
3 John Edwards	15.00	6.00
4 Sam Ellis	15.00	6.00
5 Tommy Harper	20.00	8.00
6 Deron Johnson	15.00	6.00
7 Jim Maloney	15.00	6.00
8 Bill McCool	15.00	6.00
9 Joe Nuxhall	15.00	6.00
10 Jim O'Toole	15.00	6.00
11 Vada Pinson	25.00	10.00
12 Pete Rose	50.00	20.00

1947 Red Sox Photo Records

These photo records were issued in the late 1940's and featured members of the Boston Red Sox. The picture sleeves feature a portrait of the player while the records are titled "How to play baseball". Since the records are unnumbered we have sequenced them in alphabetical order and it is possible there might be more records in this set so any further information is appreciated.

	Ex-Mt	VG
COMPLETE SET	600.00	300.00
1 Dom DiMaggio	200.00	100.00
2 Mel Parnell	120.00	60.00
3 Vern Stephens	100.00	50.00
4 Ted Williams	300.00	150.00

1978 Safelon Superstar Lunch Bags

There are six variations to the luch bags which were packed 40 per carton. These lunch bags were white plastic with black-and-white drawings on both sides. The player's name and team are printed in black beneath drawing. A facsimile autograph also appears on the bags. All players appear at least once with all the other players in the set.

	NM	Ex
COMPLETE SET (15)	75.00	30.00
1 Hank Aaron / Johnny Bench	8.00	3.20
2 Hank Aaron / Fred Lynn	3.00	1.20
3 Hank Aaron / Catfish Hunter	5.00	2.00
4 Hank Aaron / Pete Rose	12.00	4.80
5 Hank Aaron / Tom Seaver	8.00	3.20
6 Johnny Bench / Pete Rose	10.00	4.00
7 Johnny Bench / Jim(Catfish) Hunter	4.00	1.60
8 Johnny Bench / Fred Lynn	2.00	.80
9 Johnny Bench / Tom Seaver	10.00	4.00
10 Jim Hunter / Pete Rose	10.00	4.00
11 Jim Hunter / Fred Lynn	2.00	.80
12 Jim Hunter / Tom Seaver	8.00	3.20
13 Fred Lynn / Pete Rose	5.00	2.00
14A Fred Lynn / Tom Seaver / Lynn listed as MVP and ROY	3.00	1.20
14B Fred Lynn / Tom Seaver / Lynn listed as MVP	1.00	.40
15 Pete Rose / Tom Seaver	10.00	4.00

1972 Seven-Eleven Trading Cups

This 60-cup set features color player portraits of 60 top players printed on plastic cups which could be obtained from participating Seven-Eleven convenience stores by buying a specific size of one of their fountain drinks. The cups also carried player information. The cups are unnumbered and checklisted below in alphabetical order.

	NM	Ex
COMPLETE SET (60)	500.00	200.00
1 Henry Aaron	25.00	10.00
2 Tommie Agee	6.00	2.40
3 Rich Allen	8.00	3.20
4 Sal Bando	6.00	2.40
5 Johnny Bench	15.00	6.00
6 Steve Blass	6.00	2.40
7 Vida Blue	6.00	2.40
8 Lou Brock	15.00	6.00
9 Norm Cash	6.00	2.40
10 Cesar Cedeno	6.00	2.40
11 Orlando Cepeda	10.00	4.00
12 Roberto Clemente	30.00	12.00
13 Nate Colbert	6.00	2.40
14 Willie Davis	6.00	2.40
15 Ray Fosse	6.00	2.40
16 Ralph Garr	6.00	2.40
17 Bob Gibson	15.00	6.00
18 Bud Harrelson	6.00	2.40
19 Frank Howard	6.00	2.40
20 Ron Hunt	6.00	2.40
21 Reggie Jackson	25.00	10.00
22 Ferguson Jenkins	15.00	6.00
23 Alex Johnson	6.00	2.40
24 Deron Johnson	6.00	2.40
25 Al Kaline	15.00	6.00
26 Harmon Killebrew	15.00	6.00
27 Mickey Lolich	6.00	2.40
28 Jim Lonborg	6.00	2.40
29 Juan Marichal	15.00	6.00
30 Willie Mays	25.00	10.00
31 Willie McCovey	15.00	6.00
32 Denny McLain	6.00	2.40
33 Dave McNally	6.00	2.40
34 Bill Melton	6.00	2.40
35 Andy Messersmith	6.00	2.40
36 Bobby Murcer	6.00	2.40
37 Tony Oliva	8.00	3.20
38 Amos Otis	6.00	2.40
39 Jim Palmer	15.00	6.00
40 Joe Pepitone	6.00	2.40
41 Jim Perry	6.00	2.40
42 Lou Piniella	6.00	2.40
43 Vada Pinson	8.00	3.20
44 Dave Roberts	6.00	2.40
45 Brooks Robinson	15.00	6.00
46 Frank Robinson	15.00	6.00
47 Pete Rose	25.00	10.00
48 George Scott	6.00	2.40
49 Tom Seaver	15.00	6.00
50 Sonny Siebert	6.00	2.40
51 Reggie Smith	6.00	2.40
52 Willie Stargell	15.00	6.00
53 Bill Stoneman	6.00	2.40
54 Mel Stottlemyre	6.00	2.40
55 Joe Torre	8.00	3.20
56 Maury Wills	8.00	3.20
57 Don Wilson	6.00	2.40
58 Rick Wise	6.00	2.40
59 Wilbur Wood	6.00	2.40
60 Carl Yastrzemski	15.00	6.00

1973 Seven-Eleven Trading Cups

This 80-cup set features color player portraits of 60 Super Stars and 20 Hall of Fame stars printed on plastic cups which could be obtained from participating Seven-Eleven convenience stores by buying a specific size of one of their fountain drinks. The cups also carried player information. The cups are unnumbered and checklisted below in alphabetical order. The Slurpees at the time were costing 28 cents each.

	NM	Ex
COMPLETE SET (80)	750.00	300.00
1 Hank Aaron	20.00	8.00
2 Dick Allen	8.00	3.20
3 Dusty Baker	6.00	2.40
4 Johnny Bench	15.00	6.00
5 Yogi Berra	15.00	6.00
6 Larry Biittner	5.00	2.00
7 Steve Blass	5.00	2.00
8 Lou Boudreau	10.00	4.00
9 Lou Brock	15.00	6.00
10 Roy Campanella	15.00	6.00
11 Bert Campaneris	5.00	2.00
12 Rod Carew	15.00	6.00
13 Steve Carlton	15.00	6.00
14 Cesar Cedeno	5.00	2.00
15 Ty Cobb	20.00	8.00
16 Nate Colbert	5.00	2.00
17 Willie Davis	5.00	2.00
18 Bill Dickey	8.00	3.20
19 Bob Feller	10.00	4.00
20 Carlton Fisk	15.00	6.00
21 Bill Freehan	6.00	2.40
22 Ralph Garr	5.00	2.00
23 Lou Gehrig	20.00	8.00
24 Charlie Gehringer	8.00	3.20
25 Bob Gibson	15.00	6.00
26 Hank Greenberg	10.00	4.00
27 Bobby Grich	5.00	2.00
28 Lefty Grove	10.00	4.00
29 Toby Harrah	5.00	2.00
30 Rich Hebner	5.00	2.00
31 Ken Henderson	5.00	2.00
32 Carl Hubbell	10.00	4.00
33 Jim Hunter	15.00	6.00
34 Reggie Jackson	15.00	6.00
35 Walter Johnson	15.00	6.00
36 Don Kessinger	5.00	2.00
37 Leron Lee	5.00	2.00
38 Mickey Lolich	6.00	2.40
39 Greg Luzinski	8.00	3.20
40 Sparky Lyle	6.00	2.40
41 Mickey Mantle	25.00	10.00
42 Mike Marshall	5.00	2.00
43 Carlos May	5.00	2.00
44 Lee May	5.00	2.00
45 John Mayberry	5.00	2.00
46 Willie Mays	20.00	8.00
47 John McGraw	10.00	4.00
48 Joe Medwick	10.00	4.00
49 Joe Morgan	10.00	4.00
50 Thurman Munson	10.00	4.00
51 Bobby Murcer	6.00	2.40
52 Stan Musial	15.00	6.00
53 Gary Nolan	5.00	2.00
54 Tony Oliva	8.00	3.20
55 Al Oliver	6.00	2.40
56 Claude Osteen	5.00	2.00
57 Jim Palmer	15.00	6.00
58 Gaylord Perry	10.00	4.00
59 Lou Piniella	6.00	2.40
60 Vada Pinson	8.00	3.20
61 Brooks Robinson	15.00	6.00
62 Ellie Rodriguez	5.00	2.00
63 Joe Rudi	5.00	2.00
64 Red Ruffing	10.00	4.00
65 Babe Ruth	30.00	12.00
66 Nolan Ryan	30.00	12.00
67 Manny Sanguillen	5.00	2.00
68 Ron Santo	10.00	4.00
69 Richie Scheinblurn	5.00	2.00
70 Tom Seaver	15.00	6.00
71 Ted Simmons	8.00	3.20
72 Reggie Smith	5.00	2.00
73 Chris Speier	5.00	2.00
74 Don Sutton	15.00	6.00
75 Luis Tiant	8.00	3.20
76 Pie Traynor	10.00	4.00
77 Honus Wagner	15.00	6.00
78 Billy Williams	10.00	4.00
79 Wilbur Wood	5.00	2.00
80 Carl Yastrzemski	15.00	6.00

1982 Seven-Eleven Slurpee Cups

This 26-cup set features top player portraits printed on plastic cups that could be obtained with a Slurpee from Seven-Eleven stores. The player's name, team, and position are also printed on the cup. The cups are unnumbered and checklisted below in alphabetical order

	Nm-Mt	Ex-Mt
COMPLETE SET (26)	150.00	60.00
1 Doyle Alexander	2.00	.80
2 Alan Ashby	2.00	.80
3 Tony Armas	2.00	.80
4 Dusty Baker	2.50	1.00
5 Buddy Bell	2.50	1.00
6 Vida Blue	2.00	.80
7 Larry Bowa	2.00	.80
8 George Brett	10.00	4.00
9 Rod Carew	5.00	2.00
10 Gary Carter	5.00	2.00
11 Chris Chambliss	2.50	1.00
12 Jack Clark	2.50	1.00
13 Steve Comer	2.00	.80
14 Jose Cruz	2.50	1.00
15 Darrell Evans	2.50	1.00
16 Rollie Fingers	5.00	2.00
17 Carlton Fisk	5.00	2.00
18 Doug Flynn	2.00	.80
19 George Foster	2.50	1.00
20 Phil Garner	2.00	.80
21 Bobby Grich	2.00	.80
22 Rickey Henderson	12.00	4.80
23 Rick Honeycutt	2.00	.80
24 Burt Hooten	2.00	.80
25 Art Howe	2.50	1.00
26 Bob Knepper	2.00	.80
27 Ray Knight	2.00	.80
28 Carney Lansford	2.00	.80
29 Bill Madlock	2.50	1.00
30 Milt May	2.00	.80
31 John Mayberry	2.00	.80
32 Steve McCatty	2.00	.80
33 Doc Medich	2.00	.80
34 Mario Mendoza	2.00	.80
35 Joe Morgan	5.00	2.00
36 Eddie Murray	10.00	4.00
37 Joe Niekro	2.50	1.00
38 Al Oliver	2.50	1.00
39 Terry Puhl	2.00	.80
40 Jerry Reuss	2.00	.80
41 Craig Reynolds	2.00	.80
42 Pete Rose	10.00	4.00
43 Nolan Ryan	15.00	6.00
44 Mike Schmidt	10.00	4.00
45 Jim Sundberg	2.00	.80
46 Fernando Valenzuela	4.00	1.60
47 Dave Winfield	8.00	3.20

1979-80 Slush Puppies Cups

These cups, which were released between 1979 and 1980 feature leading baseball players. One side features the player in a drawing with a little "nickname" while the other side has the player's uniform number as well as the "Slush Puppie" logo. This list is incomplete, so any additions are appreciated.

	NM	Ex
COMPLETE SET (20)	50.00	20.00
2 Ron Cey	2.50	1.00
3 Tom Seaver	8.00	3.20
4 Steve Carlton	6.00	2.40
5 Jim Rice	4.00	1.60
7 Dave Kingman	2.50	1.00
8 J.R. Richard	2.50	1.00
9 Cecil Cooper	2.50	1.00
10 Jack Clark	2.50	1.00
11 Omar Moreno	2.00	.80
12 Richie Zisk	2.50	1.00
13 Ken Singleton	2.50	1.00
14 Ted Simmons	2.50	1.00
15 Don Baylor	3.00	1.20
16 Mike Schmidt	6.00	2.40
17 George Brett	10.00	4.00

1990 Superstar Action Marbles

These collectible action marbles measure approximately 1" across. Each marble contains a color action player photo inside, and on the backside one finds the team logo. The marbles were issued in four sets, and each set showcases players from one of the four major divisions: 1) AL West (1-5); 2) AL East (6-10); 3) NL West (11-15); and 4) NL East (16-20). The marbles are unnumbered.

	Nm-Mt	Ex-Mt
COMPLETE SET (20)	30.00	9.00
1 Jim Abbott	.50	.15
2 Jose Canseco	1.50	.45
3 Ken Griffey Jr.	6.00	1.80
4 Kirby Puckett	2.00	.60
5 Nolan Ryan	8.00	2.40
6 Robin Yount	2.00	.60
7 Cecil Fielder	.75	.23
8 Cory Snyder	.50	.15
9 Fred McGriff	1.00	.30
10 Cal Ripken Jr.	8.00	2.40
11 Ron Gant	.75	.23
12 Chris Sabo	.50	.15
13 Craig Biggio	1.50	.45
14 Fernando Valenzuela	.75	.23
15 Benito Santiago	.75	.23
16 Tim Raines	.75	.23
17 Darryl Strawberry	.75	.23
18 Len Dykstra	.50	.15
19 Barry Bonds	5.00	1.50
20 Ryne Sandberg	3.00	.90
XX Unopened Box	5.00	1.50

1988 Tara Plaques

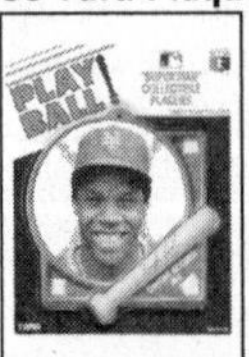

This 48-card set features color head photos of National and American League superstars printed on die-cut plaques with a baseball over a baseball diamond as background. The plaques were distributed one to a package with a display easel included in each. The set checklist was printed on the back of each package. The plaques are unnumbered and checklisted below in alphabetical order.

	Nm-Mt	Ex-Mt
COMPLETE SET (48)	80.00	32.00
1 Harold Baines	1.00	.40
2 Steve Bedrosian	.50	.20
3 George Bell	.50	.20
4 Wade Boggs	2.50	1.00
5 Bobby Bonilla	1.00	.40
6 George Brett	5.00	2.00
7 Jose Canseco	2.00	.80
8 Will Clark	2.00	.80
9 Roger Clemens	5.00	2.00
10 Vince Coleman	.50	.20
11 Eric Davis	1.00	.40
12 Andre Dawson	2.00	.80
13 Dennis Eckersley	2.50	1.00
14 Carlton Fisk	2.50	1.00
15 Kirk Gibson	1.00	.40
16 Dwight Gooden	.50	.20
17 Mike Greenwell	.50	.20
18 Tony Gwynn	5.00	2.00
19 Ricky Henderson	3.00	1.20
20 Keith Hernandez	1.00	.40
21 Orel Hershiser	1.00	.40
22 Pete Incaviglia	.50	.20
23 Wally Joyner	.50	.20
24 Mark Langston	.50	.20
25 Candy Maldonado	.50	.20
26 Don Mattingly	5.00	2.00
27 Mark McGwire	8.00	3.20
28 Paul Molitor	2.50	1.00
29 Jack Morris	1.00	.40
30 Dale Murphy	2.00	.80
31 Kirby Puckett	2.50	1.00
32 Tim Raines	1.00	.40
33 Cal Ripken Jr.	10.00	4.00
34 Nolan Ryan	10.00	4.00
35 Chris Sabo	.50	.20
36 Ryne Sandberg	4.00	1.60
37 Benny Santiago	1.00	.40
38 Mike Schmidt	2.50	1.00
39 Mike Scott	.50	.20
40 Kevin Seitzer	.50	.20
41 Ozzie Smith	5.00	2.00
42 Cory Snyder	.50	.20
43 Darryl Strawberry	1.00	.40
44 Alan Trammell	1.50	.60
45 Fernando Valenzuela	1.00	.40
46 Andy Van Slyke	.50	.20
47 Frank Viola	.50	.20
48 Dave Winfield	2.50	1.00

1989 Tara Plaques

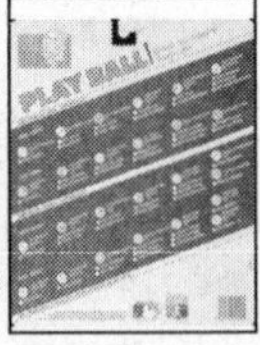

These plaques were issued in honor of the leading baseball players. The items feature a large player photos issued in a baseball against a green and red background. We have sequenced them the way in alphabetical order by team

	Nm-Mt	Ex-Mt
COMPLETE SET	80.00	32.00
1 Dale Murphy	2.00	.80
2 Eric Davis	1.00	.40
3 Chris Sabo	.50	.20
4 Nolan Ryan	10.00	4.00
5 Mike Scott	.50	.20
6 Tony Gwynn	5.00	2.00
7 Benito Santiago	1.00	.40
8 Will Clark	2.00	.80
9 Candy Maldonado	.50	.20
10 Kirk Gibson	1.00	.40
11 Orel Hershiser	1.00	.40
12 Fernando Valenzuela	.50	.20
13 Tim Raines	1.00	.40
14 Steve Bedrosian	.50	.20
15 Mike Schmidt	2.50	1.00
16 Bobby Bonilla	1.00	.40
17 Andy Van Slyke	.50	.20
18 Vince Coleman	.50	.20
19 Ozzie Smith	4.00	1.60
20 Dwight Gooden	1.00	.40
21 Keith Hernandez	1.00	.40
22 Darryl Strawberry	1.00	.40
23 Andre Dawson	2.00	.80
24 Ryne Sandberg	2.50	1.00
25 Wally Joyner	1.00	.40
26 Kirby Puckett	2.50	1.00
27 Frank Viola	.50	.20
28 Harold Baines	1.50	.60
29 Carlton Fisk	2.50	1.00
30 George Brett	5.00	2.00
31 Kevin Seitzer	.50	.20
32 Jose Canseco	2.00	.80
33 Dennis Eckersley	2.50	1.00
34 Mark McGwire	8.00	3.20
35 Mark Langston	.50	.20
36 Pete Incaviglia	.50	.20
37 Paul Molitor	2.50	1.00
38 Cory Snyder	.50	.20
39 Jack Morris	1.00	.40
40 Alan Trammell	1.50	.60
41 Wade Boggs	2.50	1.00
42 Roger Clemens	5.00	2.00
43 Mike Greenwell	.50	.20
44 Rickey Henderson	3.00	1.20
45 Don Mattingly	5.00	2.00
46 Dave Winfield	2.50	1.00
47 George Bell	.50	.20
48 Cal Ripken Jr	10.00	4.00

1966 Tigers Volpe Tumblers

This 12-cup set features player portraits of the Detroit Tigers by artist Nicholas Volpe and printed on cups. The cups are unnumbered and checklisted below in alphabetical order. These cups were available through Sunoco stations at a cost of 40 cents per with a purchase of gasoline.

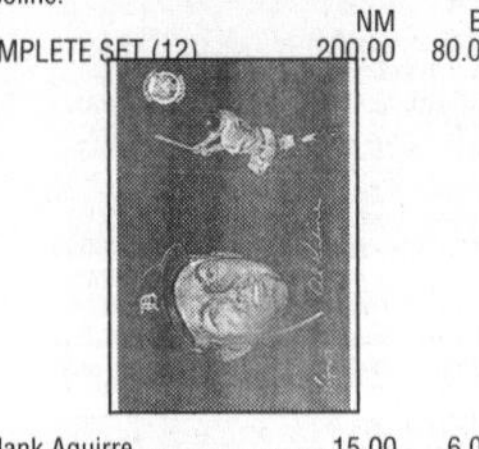

	NM	Ex
COMPLETE SET (12)	200.00	80.00
1 Hank Aguirre	15.00	6.00
2 Norm Cash	25.00	10.00
3 Don Demeter	15.00	6.00
4 Bill Freehan	25.00	10.00
5 Willie Horton	20.00	8.00
6 Al Kaline	30.00	12.00
7 Mickey Lolich	20.00	8.00
8 Dick McAuliffe	15.00	6.00
9 Denny McLain	25.00	10.00
10 Joe Sparma	15.00	6.00
11 Don Wert	15.00	6.00
12 Dave Wickersham	15.00	6.00

1985 Tigers Elias Brothers Placemats

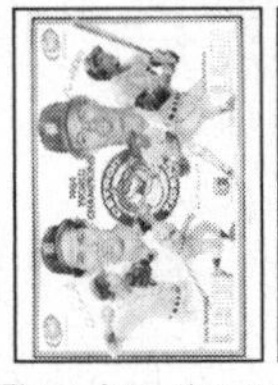

These four placemats, which measure approximately 18" by 11" feature eight of the stars of the 1984 World Champion Detroit Tigers. Each placemat features three drawings of two players (one portrait and two action) as well as the Tigers logo in the middle. The player's seasonal and career stats are also notated on each side of the placemat. Please note we have sequenced these placemats in alphabetical order of the player appearing on the left side of the placemat. The back of the placemat has pitching and hitting stats from members of both the 1968 and the 1984 Tigers World Championship teams.

	MINT	NRMT
COMPLETE SET	20.00	9.00
1 Chet Lemon Willie Hernandez	5.00	2.20
2 Jack Morris Lance Parrish	6.00	2.70
3 Dan Petry Kirk Gibson	6.00	2.70
4 Alan Trammell Lou Whitaker	10.00	4.50

1997 Topps Marbles

These marbles, which were issued in two marble packages, were issued by Topps as a test. These marbles have the player photo on the front and the players name, team identification and number on the back. The marbles are sequenced in alphabetical order.

	Nm-Mt	Ex-Mt
COMPLETE SET (60)	700.00	210.00
1 Roberto Alomar	8.00	2.40
2 Brady Anderson	5.00	1.50
3 Carlos Baerga	4.00	1.20
4 Jeff Bagwell	12.00	3.60
5 Albert Belle	5.00	1.50
6 Dante Bichette	5.00	1.50
7 Craig Biggio	5.00	1.50
8 Wade Boggs	12.00	3.60
9 Barry Bonds	30.00	9.00
10 Jay Buhner	5.00	1.50
11 Ken Caminiti	5.00	1.50
12 Jose Canseco	8.00	2.40
13 Roger Clemens	25.00	7.50
14 David Cone	5.00	1.50
15 Cecil Fielder	5.00	1.50
16 Travis Fryman	5.00	1.50
17 Andres Galarraga	8.00	2.40
18 Ron Gant	5.00	1.50
19 Bernard Gilkey	4.00	1.20
20 Tom Glavine	10.00	3.00
21 Juan Gonzalez	10.00	3.00
22 Mark Grace	8.00	2.40
23 Ken Griffey Jr	30.00	9.00
24 Tony Gwynn	25.00	7.50
25 Todd Hundley	5.00	1.50
26 John Jaha	4.00	1.20
27 Derek Jeter	50.00	15.00
28 Lance Johnson	4.00	1.20
29 Randy Johnson	12.00	3.60
30 Andruw Jones	15.00	4.50
31 Chipper Jones	25.00	7.50
32 Brian Jordan	5.00	1.50
33 Jason Kendall	8.00	2.40
34 Chuck Knoblauch	5.00	1.50
35 Ray Lankford	5.00	1.50
36 Barry Larkin	8.00	2.40
37 Kenny Lofton	5.00	1.50
38 Greg Maddux	30.00	9.00
39 Edgar Martinez	6.00	1.80
40 Fred McGriff	6.00	1.80
41 Mark McGwire	40.00	12.00
42 Paul Molitor	12.00	3.60
43 Raul Mondesi	5.00	1.50
44 Eddie Murray	12.00	3.60
45 Mike Mussina	15.00	4.50
46 Hideo Nomo	25.00	7.50
47 Rafael Palmeiro	8.00	2.40
48 Andy Pettitte	8.00	2.40
49 Mike Piazza	30.00	9.00
50 Cal Ripken Jr	50.00	15.00
51 Ivan Rodriguez	12.00	3.60
52 Tim Salmon	6.00	1.80
53 Ryne Sandberg	20.00	6.00
54 Gary Sheffield	12.00	3.60
55 John Smoltz	5.00	1.50
56 Sammy Sosa	25.00	7.50
57 Frank Thomas	12.00	3.60
58 Mo Vaughn	5.00	1.50
59 Bernie Williams	8.00	2.40
60 Matt Williams	6.00	1.80

1998 Topps SportzCubz

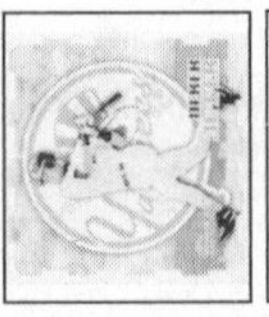
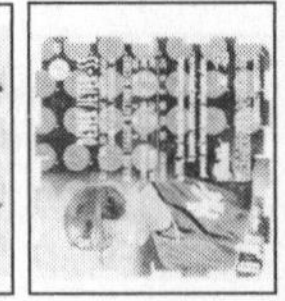

These plastic cards, which measure approximately 3" square were apparently issued by Topps to see if collectors would like this product. The fronts have a player photo set against their team's logo with the words "Topps SportzCubz" on the bottom left and the player's name located on the bottom right. The backs have biographical information as well as season and team stats. Any further information about these cards is appreciated. Since for now only one set is known, we are not providing any more information than a checklist.

	Nm-Mt	Ex-Mt
COMPLETE SET (25)		
1 Roberto Alomar		
2 Dante Bichette		
3 Barry Bonds		
4 Roger Clemens		
5 Juan Gonzalez		
6 Mark Grace		
7 Vladimir Guerrero		
8 Tony Gwynn		
9 Derek Jeter		
10 David Justice		
11 Chuck Knoblauch		
12 Barry Larkin		
13 Greg Maddux		
14 Paul O'Neill		
15 Mike Piazza		
16 Mo Vaughn		
17 Bernie Williams		
18 Albert Belle		
19 Ken Griffey Jr.		
20 Livan Hernandez		
21 Hideki Irabu		
22 Mark McGwire		
23 Raul Mondesi		
24 Andy Pettitte		
25 Tony Clark		

1999 Topps Action Flats

These 12 items were issued by Topps to take advantage of the burgeoning "statue" market. They were issued in a custom box featuring detailed miniature replicas of leading players. Also included in the box is a card showing the photography which was duplicated in the staute. Since the items are unnumbered we have sequenced them alphabetically. This is the first series with a second series expected to be out later in 1999. All of these flats were released with a $2.99 SRP. A few of the flats were printed in lesser quantity. The Sosa and Griffey classic away jerseys were inserted at a ratio of one in 24, while the McGwire away uniform was inserted at a rate of one in 36. These were packed 16 flats and six boxes to a case. Each box had the configuration of 3 McGwires, 2 Griffey and Sosa and one each of the other nine players in the set.

	Nm-Mt	Ex-Mt
COMPLETE SERIES 1 (12)	35.00	10.50
*AWAY UNIFORM: 5X BASIC FLATS ..		
*CLASSIC UNIFORMI 10X BASIC PLATS		
1 Barry Bonds	5.00	1.50
2 Nomar Garciaparra	4.00	1.20
3 Juan Gonzalez	2.00	.60
4 Ken Griffey Jr	5.00	1.50
5 Derek Jeter	8.00	2.40
6 Chipper Jones	4.00	1.20
7 Greg Maddux	5.00	1.50
8 Mark McGwire	6.00	1.80
9 Cal Ripken Jr	8.00	2.40
10 Alex Rodriguez	5.00	1.50
11 Sammy Sosa	4.00	1.20
12 Kerry Wood	1.50	.45

1999 Topps Jersey

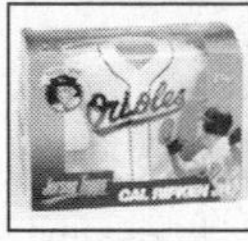

This six-item set features free-standing miniature replicas of top players' jerseys crafted from flexible vinyl. The McGwire, Ripken, Griffey and Sosa jerseys came three each to a case while the Chipper Jones and Derek Jeter came two to a case. Please note this fact while looking at our prices.

	Nm-Mt	Ex-Mt
COMPLETE SET (6)	60.00	18.00
1 Ken Griffey Jr. Home	10.00	3.00
2 Derek Jeter Away	15.00	4.50
3 Chipper Jones Home	8.00	2.40
4 Mark McGwire Home	12.00	3.60
5 Cal Ripken Home	15.00	4.50
6 Sammy Sosa Away	6.00	1.80

2001 Upper Deck Play Makers

These ten bobbing-head dolls were issued by Upper Deck in July, 2001 and featured a special card of the depicted player. Each doll stands about eight inches tall. Each doll carried a suggested retail price of $9.99.

	Nm-Mt	Ex-Mt
COMPLETE SET (10)	100.00	30.00
1 Alex Rodriguez	10.00	3.00
2 Cal Ripken	10.00	3.00
3 Derek Jeter	10.00	3.00
4 Ichiro Suzuki	10.00	3.00
5 Ken Griffey Jr.	10.00	3.00
6 Mark McGwire	10.00	3.00
7 Mike Piazza	10.00	3.00
8 Nomar Garciaparra	10.00	3.00
9 Pedro Martinez	10.00	3.00
10 Sammy Sosa	10.00	3.00

1971 White Sox Mugs

These four mugs, which were given away at various White Sox games during the 1971 season have two photos on them: an action shot as well as a portrait. Since these are unnumbered, we have sequenced them in alphabetical order.

	NM	Ex
COMPLETE SET	20.00	8.00
1 Mike Andrews	5.00	2.00
2 Tommy John	10.00	4.00
3 Carlos May	5.00	2.00
4 Bill Melton	5.00	2.00

1977 Yankees Nedicks Cups

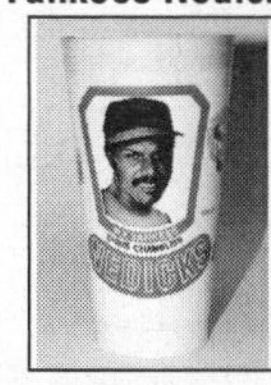

This set features black-and-white player head photos printed on plastic drinking cups. Player information was also printed on the cups. The cups are unnumbered, and the four currently known cups are checklisted below in alphabetical order. Ten cups are belived to be in this set so any help in completing this set is appreciated.

	NM	Ex
COMPLETE SET (4)	25.00	10.00
1 Chris Chambliss	4.00	1.60
2 Reggie Jackson	10.00	4.00
3 Thurman Munson	10.00	4.00
4 Willie Randolph	5.00	2.00

1933-99 All-Star Game Programs

Pre-War programs are difficult to obtain in top condition and are priced based on ex-mt condition.

	Ex-Mt	VG
1933 Chicago	4500.00	2200.00
1934 New York	6000.00	3000.00
1935 Cleveland	1500.00	750.00
1936 Boston	4000.00	2000.00
1937 Washington	2500.00	1250.00
1938 Cincinnati	2500.00	1250.00
1939 New York	3000.00	1500.00
1940 St. Louis	1500.00	750.00
1941 Detroit	1500.00	750.00
1942 New York	3500.00	1800.00
1943 Philadelphia	1000.00	500.00
1944 Pittsburgh	1500.00	750.00
1945 War Year - No Game		
1946 Boston	1500.00	750.00
1947 Chicago	600.00	300.00
1948 St. Louis	600.00	300.00
1949 Brooklyn	1000.00	500.00
1950 Chicago	400.00	200.00
1951 Detroit	300.00	150.00
1952 Philadelphia	250.00	125.00
Casey Stengel MG		
Leo Durocher MG		
1953 Cincinnati	300.00	150.00
1954 Cleveland	250.00	125.00
1955 Milwaukee	250.00	125.00
1956 Washington	250.00	125.00
Clark Griffith pictured		
1957 St. Louis	300.00	150.00
1958 Baltimore	250.00	125.00
1959 Pittsburgh	300.00	150.00
1959 Los Angeles	300.00	150.00
1960 Kansas City	200.00	100.00
1960 New York	150.00	75.00
1961 Boston	400.00	200.00
1961 San Francisco	425.00	210.00
1962 Washington	250.00	125.00
1962 Chicago	200.00	100.00
1963 Cleveland	200.00	100.00
1964 New York	200.00	100.00
1965 Minnesota	100.00	50.00
1966 St. Louis	175.00	90.00
1967 Anaheim	150.00	75.00
1968 Houston	125.00	60.00
1969 Washington	125.00	60.00
1970 Cincinnati	150.00	75.00
1971 Detroit	175.00	90.00
1972 Atlanta	75.00	38.00
1973 Kansas City	150.00	75.00
1974 Pittsburgh	50.00	25.00
1975 Milwaukee	50.00	25.00
1976 Philadelphia	35.00	17.50
1977 New York	20.00	10.00
1978 San Diego	50.00	25.00
1979 Seattle	25.00	12.50
1980 Los Angeles	35.00	17.50
1981 Cleveland	20.00	10.00
1982 Montreal	35.00	17.50
1983 Chicago	20.00	10.00
1984 San Francisco	10.00	5.00
1985 Minnesota	10.00	5.00
1986 Houston	10.00	5.00
1987 Oakland	15.00	7.50
1988 Cincinnati	15.00	7.50
1989 California	15.00	7.50
1990 Chicago	15.00	7.50
1991 Toronto	20.00	10.00
1992 San Diego	15.00	7.50
1993 Baltimore	15.00	7.50
1994 Pittsburgh	12.00	6.00
1995 Arlington	10.00	5.00
1996 Philadelphia	10.00	5.00
1997 Cleveland	10.00	5.00
1998 Colorado	10.00	5.00
1999 Boston	10.00	5.00
2000 Atlanta	10.00	5.00
2001 Seattle	10.00	5.00
2002 Milwaukee	10.00	5.00
2003 Chicago	10.00	5.00

1933-99 All-Star Game Ticket Stubs

Pre-War ticket stubs are difficult to obtain in top condition and are priced in ex-mt condition. Pre-1990 complete tickets are valued at 2 to 5 times that of a stub. In recent years, some tickets are no longer torn at the door. Rather they are scanned and the tickets are left complete. In these modern cases, the price of the stub actually refers to a full ticket.

	Ex-Mt	VG
1933 Chicago	700.00	350.00
1934 New York	800.00	400.00
1935 Cleveland	250.00	125.00
1936 Boston	500.00	250.00
1937 Washington	425.00	210.00
1938 Cincinnati	300.00	150.00
1939 New York	250.00	125.00
1940 St. Louis	350.00	180.00
1941 Detroit	250.00	125.00
1942 New York	300.00	150.00
1943 Philadelphia	250.00	125.00
1944 Pittsburgh	250.00	125.00
1945 War Year - No Game		
1946 Boston	200.00	100.00
1947 Chicago	125.00	60.00
1948 St. Louis	150.00	75.00
1949 Brooklyn	175.00	90.00
1950 Chicago	125.00	60.00
1951 Detroit	125.00	60.00
1952 Philadelphia	125.00	60.00
1953 Cincinnati	75.00	38.00
1954 Cleveland	75.00	38.00
1955 Milwaukee	100.00	50.00
1956 Washington	150.00	75.00
1957 St. Louis	100.00	50.00
1958 Baltimore	100.00	50.00
1959 Los Angeles	75.00	38.00
1959 Pittsburgh	125.00	60.00
1960 Kansas City	125.00	60.00
1960 New York	100.00	50.00
1961 San Francisco	100.00	50.00
1961 Boston	125.00	60.00
1962 Chicago	100.00	50.00
1962 Washington	75.00	38.00
1963 Cleveland	60.00	30.00
1964 New York	60.00	30.00
1965 Minnesota	50.00	25.00
1966 St. Louis	60.00	30.00
1967 Anaheim	50.00	25.00
1968 Houston	50.00	25.00
1969 Washington	50.00	25.00
1970 Cincinnati	50.00	25.00
1971 Detroit	60.00	30.00
1972 Atlanta	50.00	25.00
1973 Kansas City	60.00	30.00
1974 Pittsburgh	35.00	17.50
1975 Milwaukee	35.00	17.50
1976 Philadelphia	25.00	12.50
1977 New York	25.00	12.50
1978 San Diego	30.00	15.00
1979 Seattle	25.00	12.50
1980 Los Angeles	25.00	12.50
1981 Cleveland	30.00	15.00
1982 Montreal	25.00	12.50
1983 Chicago	20.00	10.00
1984 San Francisco	20.00	10.00
1985 Minnesota	20.00	10.00
1986 Houston	20.00	10.00
1987 Oakland	20.00	10.00
1988 Cincinnati	20.00	10.00
1989 California	20.00	10.00
1990 Chicago	20.00	10.00
1991 Toronto	20.00	10.00
1992 San Diego	20.00	10.00
1993 Baltimore	20.00	10.00
1994 Pittsburgh	20.00	10.00
1995 Arlington	20.00	10.00
1996 Philadelphia	20.00	10.00
1997 Cleveland	20.00	10.00
1998 Colorado	20.00	10.00
1999 Boston	20.00	10.00
2000 Atlanta	20.00	10.00
2001 Seattle	20.00	10.00
2002 Milwaukee	20.00	10.00
2003 Chicago	20.00	10.00

1937-99 All-Star Game Press Pins

	Ex-Mt	VG
1933 No Pin Issued		
1934 No Pin Issued		
1935 No Pin Issued		
1936 No Pin Issued		
1937 Washington		
1938 Cincinnati	4500.00	2200.00
1939 No Pin Issued		
1940 No Pin Issued		
1941 Detroit	1500.00	750.00
1942 No Pin Issued		
1943 Philadelphia	1500.00	750.00
1944 No Pin Issued		
1945 War Year - No Game		
1946 Boston	800.00	400.00
1947 Chicago	1800.00	900.00
1948 St. Louis	2500.00	1250.00
1949 Brooklyn	425.00	210.00
1950 Chicago	300.00	150.00
1951 Detroit	350.00	180.00
1952 Philadelphia	400.00	200.00
1953 Cincinnati	400.00	200.00
1954 Cleveland	300.00	150.00
1955 Milwaukee	350.00	180.00
1956 Washington	300.00	150.00
1957 St. Louis	300.00	150.00
1958 Baltimore	600.00	300.00
1959 Los Angeles	250.00	125.00
1959 Pittsburgh	250.00	125.00
1960 New York	350.00	180.00
1960 Kansas City	300.00	150.00
1961 San Francisco	500.00	250.00
1961 Boston	300.00	150.00
1962 Chicago	300.00	150.00
1962 Washington	250.00	125.00
1963 Cleveland	125.00	60.00
1964 New York	200.00	100.00
1965 Minnesota	125.00	60.00
1966 St. Louis	100.00	50.00
1967 Anaheim	75.00	38.00
1968 Houston	125.00	60.00
1969 Washington	100.00	50.00
1970 Cincinnati	100.00	50.00
1971 Detroit	100.00	50.00
1972 Atlanta	125.00	60.00
1973 Kansas City	75.00	38.00
1974 Pittsburgh	250.00	125.00
1975 Milwaukee	75.00	38.00
1976 Philadelphia	100.00	50.00
1977 New York	75.00	38.00
1978 San Diego	75.00	38.00
1979 Seattle	50.00	25.00
1980 Los Angeles	50.00	25.00
1981 Cleveland	50.00	25.00
1982 Montreal	75.00	38.00
1983 Chicago	35.00	17.50
1984 San Francisco	30.00	15.00
1985 Minnesota	50.00	25.00
1986 Houston	150.00	75.00
1987 Oakland	100.00	50.00
1988 Cincinnati	125.00	60.00
1989 California	50.00	25.00
1990 Chicago	125.00	60.00
1991 Toronto	100.00	50.00
1992 San Diego	75.00	38.00
1993 Baltimore	100.00	50.00
1994 Pittsburgh	125.00	60.00
1995 Arlington	125.00	60.00
1996 Philadelphia	125.00	60.00
1997 Cleveland	125.00	60.00
1998 Colorado	125.00	60.00
1999 Boston	125.00	60.00
2000 Atlanta	125.00	60.00
2001 Seattle	125.00	60.00
2002 Milwaukee	125.00	60.00
2003 Chicago	125.00	60.00

1969-99 American League Championship Series Programs

	NM	Ex
1969 Baltimore	75.00	30.00
1969 Minnesota	125.00	50.00
1970 Baltimore	35.00	14.00
1970 Minnesota	125.00	50.00
1971 Baltimore	35.00	14.00
1971 Oakland	30.00	12.00
1972 Oakland	35.00	14.00
1972 Detroit	100.00	40.00
1973 Oakland	25.00	10.00
1973 Baltimore	35.00	14.00
1974 Baltimore	35.00	14.00
1974 Oakland	425.00	170.00
1975 Boston	50.00	20.00
1975 Oakland	40.00	16.00
1976 Kansas City	20.00	8.00
1976 New York	15.00	6.00
1977 Kansas City	20.00	8.00
1977 New York	15.00	6.00
1978 New York	15.00	6.00
1978 Kansas City	20.00	8.00
1979 California	15.00	6.00
1979 Baltimore	50.00	20.00
1980 New York	15.00	6.00
1980 Kansas City	15.00	6.00
1981 New York	15.00	6.00
1981 Oakland	15.00	6.00
1982 Milwaukee	50.00	20.00
1982 California	15.00	6.00
1983 Baltimore	15.00	6.00
1983 Chicago	15.00	6.00
1984 Detroit	10.00	4.00
1984 Kansas City	15.00	6.00
1985 Toronto	25.00	10.00
1985 Kansas City	20.00	8.00
1986 California	10.00	4.00
1986 Boston	20.00	8.00
1987 Detroit	15.00	6.00
1987 Minnesota	10.00	4.00
1988 Oakland	30.00	12.00
1988 Boston	10.00	4.00
1989 Toronto	10.00	4.00
1989 Oakland	15.00	6.00
1990 Boston	10.00	4.00
1990 Oakland	10.00	4.00
1991 Toronto	15.00	6.00
1991 Minnesota	10.00	4.00
1992 Oakland	10.00	4.00
1992 Toronto	15.00	6.00
1993 Chicago	10.00	4.00
1993 Toronto	15.00	6.00
1994 No Series		
1994 No Series		
1995 Cleveland	10.00	4.00
1995 Seattle	10.00	4.00
1996 New York	10.00	4.00
1996 Baltimore	10.00	4.00
1997 Baltimore	10.00	4.00
1997 Cleveland	10.00	4.00
1998 Cleveland	10.00	4.00
1998 New York	10.00	4.00
1999 New York	10.00	4.00
1999 Boston	10.00	4.00
2000 Seattle	10.00	4.00
2000 New York	10.00	4.00
2001 Seattle	10.00	4.00
2001 New York	10.00	4.00
2002 Anaheim	10.00	4.00
2002 Minnesota	10.00	4.00
2003 Boston	10.00	4.00
2003 New York	10.00	4.00

1969-99 American League Championship Series Ticket Stubs

Ticket Stubs from historic ALCS Championship games such as 1976 game number 5 are valued higher. Pre-1990 Complete unused tickets are valued at twice that of a stub. Please note, that in recent years stadium scanners now let the ticket holders keep complete tickets. The values for these tickets are for the full tickets.

	NM	Ex
1969 Minnesota	25.00	10.00
1969 Baltimore	25.00	10.00
1970 Baltimore	25.00	10.00
1970 Minnesota	25.00	10.00
1971 Oakland	20.00	8.00
1971 Baltimore	25.00	10.00
1972 Oakland	20.00	8.00
1972 Detroit	25.00	10.00
1973 Baltimore	20.00	8.00
1973 Oakland	20.00	8.00
1974 Oakland	20.00	8.00
1974 Baltimore	20.00	8.00
1975 Oakland	20.00	8.00
1975 Boston	25.00	10.00
1976 New York	20.00	8.00
1976 Kansas City	15.00	6.00
1977 New York	15.00	6.00
1977 Kansas City	15.00	6.00
1978 New York	15.00	6.00
1978 Kansas City	15.00	6.00
1979 Baltimore	15.00	6.00
1979 California	15.00	6.00
1980 Kansas City	15.00	6.00
1980 Baltimore	15.00	6.00
1981 New York	18.00	7.25
1981 Oakland	15.00	6.00
1982 Milwaukee	15.00	6.00
1982 California	18.00	7.25
1983 Chicago	15.00	6.00
1983 Baltimore	15.00	6.00
1984 Kansas City	12.00	4.80
1984 Detroit	15.00	6.00
1985 Toronto	15.00	6.00
1985 Kansas City	12.00	4.80
1986 California	15.00	6.00
1986 Boston	15.00	6.00
1987 Minnesota	12.00	4.80
1987 Detroit	15.00	6.00
1988 Oakland	12.00	4.80
1988 Boston	15.00	6.00
1989 Oakland	15.00	6.00
1989 Toronto	10.00	4.00
1990 Boston	12.00	4.80
1990 Oakland	10.00	4.00
1991 Minnesota	10.00	4.00
1991 Toronto	12.00	4.80
1992 Oakland	10.00	4.00
1992 Toronto	12.00	4.80
1993 Chicago	12.00	4.80
1993 Toronto	10.00	4.00
1994 No Series		
1994 No Series		
1995 Cleveland	10.00	4.00
1995 Seattle	10.00	4.00
1996 New York	10.00	4.00
1996 Baltimore	10.00	4.00
1997 Cleveland	10.00	4.00
1997 Baltimore	10.00	4.00
1998 Cleveland	10.00	4.00
1998 New York	10.00	4.00
1999 New York	10.00	4.00
1999 Boston	10.00	4.00
2000 New York	10.00	4.00
2000 Seattle	10.00	4.00
2001 Seattle	10.00	4.00
2001 New York	10.00	4.00
2002 Minnesota	10.00	4.00
2002 Anaheim	10.00	4.00
2003 Boston	10.00	4.00
2003 New York	10.00	4.00

1969-99 National League Championship Series Programs

	NM	Ex
1969 New York	300.00	120.00
1969 Atlanta	30.00	12.00
1970 Pittsburgh	250.00	100.00
1970 Cincinnati	100.00	40.00
1971 San Francisco	500.00	200.00
1971 Pittsburgh	250.00	100.00
1972 Pittsburgh	40.00	16.00
1972 Cincinnati	35.00	14.00
1973 New York	100.00	40.00
1973 Cincinnati	175.00	70.00
1974 Los Angeles	250.00	100.00
1974 Pittsburgh	175.00	70.00
1975 Cincinnati	15.00	6.00
1975 Pittsburgh	20.00	8.00
1976 Cincinnati	60.00	24.00
1976 Philadelphia	15.00	6.00
1977 Philadelphia	15.00	6.00
1977 Los Angeles	50.00	20.00
1978 Los Angeles	15.00	6.00
1978 Philadelphia	15.00	6.00
1979 Cincinnati	10.00	4.00
1979 Pittsburgh	15.00	6.00
1980 Philadelphia	15.00	6.00
1980 Houston	40.00	16.00
1981 Los Angeles	15.00	6.00
1981 Montreal	25.00	10.00
1982 Atlanta	10.00	4.00
1982 St. Louis	10.00	4.00
1983 Los Angeles	50.00	20.00
1983 Philadelphia	10.00	4.00
1984 Chicago	15.00	6.00
1984 San Diego	25.00	10.00
1985 St. Louis	25.00	10.00
1985 Los Angeles	50.00	20.00
1986 Houston	15.00	6.00
1986 New York	25.00	10.00
1987 St. Louis	20.00	8.00
1987 San Francisco	10.00	4.00
1988 Los Angeles	10.00	4.00
1988 New York	10.00	4.00
1989 San Francisco	15.00	6.00
1989 Chicago	10.00	4.00
1990 Pittsburgh	10.00	4.00
1990 Cincinnati	10.00	4.00
1991 Atlanta	20.00	8.00
1991 Pittsburgh	10.00	4.00
1992 Pittsburgh	10.00	4.00
1992 Atlanta	20.00	8.00
1993 Philadelphia	10.00	4.00
1993 Atlanta	15.00	6.00
1994 No Series		
1994 No Series		
1995 Atlanta	10.00	4.00
1995 Cincinnati	10.00	4.00
1996 Atlanta	10.00	4.00
1996 St. Louis	10.00	4.00
1997 Florida	10.00	4.00
1997 Atlanta	10.00	4.00
1998 Atlanta	10.00	4.00
1998 San Diego	10.00	4.00
1999 Atlanta	10.00	4.00
1999 New York	10.00	4.00
2000 New York	10.00	4.00
2000 St Louis	10.00	4.00
2001 Atlanta	10.00	4.00
2001 Arizona	10.00	4.00
2002 San Francisco	10.00	4.00
2002 St. Louis	10.00	4.00
2003 Chicago	10.00	4.00
2003 Florida	10.00	4.00

1969-99 National League Championship Series Ticket Stubs

Tickets stubs from historic NLCS Championship games such as 1992 game seven are valued higher. Pre-1990 unused tickets are valued two times that of a stub. After 1990, many stadiums changed to a scanner system which entitled the ticket holder to keep the full ticket.

	NM	Ex
1969 New York	50.00	20.00
1969 Atlanta	25.00	10.00
1970 Cincinnati	25.00	10.00
1970 Pittsburgh	25.00	10.00
1971 San Francisco	25.00	10.00
1971 Pittsburgh	20.00	8.00
1972 Cincinnati	20.00	8.00
1972 Pittsburgh	20.00	8.00
1973 Cincinnati	20.00	8.00
1973 New York	25.00	10.00
1974 Pittsburgh	20.00	8.00
1974 Los Angeles	20.00	8.00
1975 Pittsburgh	20.00	8.00
1975 Cincinnati	25.00	10.00
1976 Cincinnati	15.00	6.00
1976 Philadelphia	15.00	6.00
1977 Philadelphia	15.00	6.00
1977 Los Angeles	15.00	6.00
1978 Los Angeles	15.00	6.00
1978 Philadelphia	15.00	6.00
1979 Cincinnati	15.00	6.00
1979 Pittsburgh	15.00	6.00
1980 Houston	15.00	6.00
1980 Philadelphia	15.00	6.00
1981 Monreal	15.00	6.00
1981 Los Angeles	15.00	6.00
1982 St. Louis	15.00	6.00
1982 Atlanta	15.00	6.00
1983 Los Angeles	15.00	6.00
1983 Philadelphia	15.00	6.00
1984 San Diego	12.00	4.80
1984 Chicago	18.00	7.25
1985 Los Angeles	12.00	4.80
1985 St. Louis	12.00	4.80
1986 New York	15.00	6.00
1986 Houston	12.00	4.80
1987 San Francisco	12.00	4.80
1987 St. Louis	12.00	4.80
1988 Los Angeles	10.00	4.00
1988 New York	12.00	4.80

1989 San Francisco	10.00	4.00
1989 Chicago	15.00	6.00
1990 Pittsburgh	10.00	4.00
1990 Cincinnati	10.00	4.00
1991 Pittsburgh	10.00	4.00
1991 Atlanta	10.00	4.00
1992 Pittsburgh	10.00	4.00
1992 Atlanta	10.00	4.00
1993 Atlanta	10.00	4.00
1993 Philadelphia	10.00	4.00
1994 No Series		
1994 No Series		
1995 Cincinnati	10.00	4.00
1995 Atlanta	10.00	4.00
1996 St. Louis	10.00	4.00
1996 Atlanta	10.00	4.00
1997 Atlanta	10.00	4.00
1997 Florida	10.00	4.00
1998 Atlanta	10.00	4.00
1998 San Diego	10.00	4.00
1999 Atlanta	10.00	4.00
1999 New York	10.00	4.00
2000 St Louis	10.00	4.00
2000 New York	10.00	4.00
2001 Atlanta	10.00	4.00
2001 Arizona	10.00	4.00
2002 San Francisco	10.00	4.00
2002 St Louis	10.00	4.00
2003 Chicago	10.00	4.00
2003 Florida	10.00	4.00

1921-78 Famous Slugger Yearbook

The Famous Slugger Yearbook was created as an advertising tool for Hillerich and Bradsby to sell its products. Each booklet contains information highlighted with player photos.

	Ex-Mt	VG
1921 Art Illustration	250.00	125.00
1927 Art Illustration	100.00	50.00
1928 Art Illustration	100.00	50.00
1929 Art Illustration	100.00	50.00
1930 Art Illustration	75.00	38.00
1931 Art Illustration	75.00	38.00
1932 Art Illustration	75.00	38.00
1933 Jimmy Foxx	60.00	30.00
Chuck Klein		
1934 Lou Gehrig	75.00	38.00
Paul Waner		
1935 Arky Vaughn	50.00	25.00
Buddy Myer		
1936 Lou Gehrig	75.00	38.00
Mel Ott		
1937 Charlie Gehringer	60.00	30.00
Joe Medwick		
1938 Art Illustration	60.00	30.00
1939 Jimmy Foxx	50.00	25.00
Ernie Lombardi		
1940 Joe DiMaggio	50.00	25.00
1941 Joe DiMaggio	50.00	25.00
1942 Joe DiMaggio	50.00	25.00
Ted Williams		
1943 Ted Williams	50.00	25.00
Ernie Lombardi		
1944 Stan Musial	50.00	25.00
1945 Dixie Walker	40.00	20.00
Lou Boudreau		
1946 Art Illustration	40.00	20.00
1947 Stan Musial	40.00	20.00
Mickey Vernon		
1948 Lefty O'Doul	30.00	15.00
1949 Ted Williams	35.00	17.50
Stan Musial		
1950 Jackie Robinson	35.00	17.50
Ted Williams		
1951 Ralph Kiner	30.00	15.00
1952 Art Illustration	25.00	12.50
1953 Art Illustration	25.00	12.50
1954 Art Illustration	20.00	10.00
1955 Ted Williams	25.00	12.50
1956 Al Kaline	25.00	12.50
Richie Ashburn		
1957 Mickey Mantle	30.00	15.00
Hank Aaron		
Ted Kluszewski		
1958 Ted Williams	25.00	12.50
1959 Stan Musial	25.00	12.50
1960 Rocky Colavito	20.00	10.00
1961 Ernie Banks	20.00	10.00
1962 Roger Maris	25.00	12.50
1963 Tommy Davis	18.00	9.00
Pete Runnels		
1964 Tommy Davis	20.00	10.00
Carl Yastremski		
1965 Roberto Clemente	25.00	12.50
Tony Oliva		
1966 Roberto Clemente	25.00	12.50
Tony Oliva		
1967 Frank Robinson	15.00	7.50
Matty Alou		
1968 Roberto Clemente	20.00	10.00
Carl Yastrzemski		
1969 Pete Rose	15.00	7.50
Carl Yastrzemski		
1970 Pete Rose	15.00	7.50
Rod Carew		
1971 Johnny Bench	15.00	7.50
Alex Johnson		
1972 Willie Stargell	10.00	5.00
1973 Dick Allen	10.00	5.00
1974 Hank Aaron	12.00	6.00
1975 Johnny Bench	10.00	5.00
1976 National League Salute	10.00	5.00
1977 Yankee Stadium	10.00	5.00
1978 Art Illustration	10.00	5.00

1883-41 Reach Baseball Guides

The Reach guide was the official guide of the American League. Spalding's parent, American Sports Publishing Company, retained the rights to the Reach guide after its 1934 edition, producing both from 1939 through 1939. Spalding combined both guides in 1940 and 1941. The Sporting News Baseball guide became the official baseball guide beginning in 1942. The majority of Reach covers feature a non-player design except for the years 1935 through 1938 when it was produced by Spalding. Reach guides from 1883 through 1929 are priced in Excellent condition, Guides from 1930 through 1941 are priced in Excellent-Mint condition.

	Ex-Mt	VG
1883 Non-Player	1500.00	750.00
1884 Non-Player	1200.00	600.00
1885 Non-Player	800.00	400.00
1886 Non-Player	600.00	300.00
1887 Non-Player	600.00	300.00
1888 Non-Player	600.00	300.00
1889 Non-Player	600.00	300.00
1890 Non-Player	600.00	300.00
1891 Non-Player	500.00	250.00
1892 Non-Player	500.00	250.00
1893 Non-Player	500.00	250.00
1894 Non-Player	500.00	250.00
1895 Non-Player	500.00	250.00
1896 Non-Player	500.00	250.00
1897 Non-Player	500.00	250.00
1898 Non-Player	500.00	250.00
1899 Non-Player	500.00	250.00
1900 Non-Player	400.00	200.00
1901 Non-Player	400.00	200.00
1902 Non-Player	400.00	200.00
1903 Non-Player	400.00	200.00
1904 Non-Player	500.00	250.00
1905 Non-Player	300.00	150.00
1906 Non-Player	400.00	200.00
1907 Non-Player	400.00	200.00
1908 Non-Player	300.00	150.00
1909 Non-Player	300.00	150.00
1910 Non-Player	300.00	150.00
1911 Non-Player	300.00	150.00
1912 Non-Player	300.00	150.00
1913 Non-Player	400.00	200.00
1914 Non-Player	400.00	200.00
1915 Non-Player	400.00	200.00
1916 Non-Player	400.00	200.00
1917 Non-Player	300.00	150.00
1918 Non-Player	300.00	150.00
1919 Non-Player	300.00	150.00
1920 Non-Player	300.00	150.00
1921 Non-Player	250.00	125.00
1922 Non-Player	250.00	125.00
1923 Non-Player	400.00	200.00
1924 Non-Player	400.00	200.00
1925 Non-Player	400.00	200.00
1926 Non-Player	300.00	150.00
1927 Non-Player	300.00	150.00
1928 Non-Player	250.00	125.00
1929 Non-Player	250.00	125.00
1930 Non-Player	200.00	100.00
1931 Non-Player	200.00	100.00
1932 Non-Player	200.00	100.00
1933 Non-Player	250.00	125.00
1934 Non-Player	200.00	100.00
1935 Lou Gehrig	250.00	125.00
1936 Mickey Cochrane	150.00	75.00
1937 Lou Gehrig	200.00	100.00
1938 Hank Greenberg	150.00	75.00
1939 Centennial Logo	150.00	75.00
1940 Spalding/Reach Combo	100.00	50.00
1941 Spalding/Reach Combo	100.00	50.00

1876-41 Spalding Baseball Guides

Spalding claimed to be the official guide of Major League Baseball. Except for a few issues in the 1930's, most of the Spalding guides featured a portaiture of an 18th century ballplayer, or in some cases, a generic baseball scene.

	Ex-Mt	VG
1876 Generic Ballplayer	2500.00	1250.00
1877 Generic Ballplayer	2000.00	1000.00
1878 Generic Ballplayer	1500.00	750.00
1879 Generic Ballplayer	1500.00	750.00
1880 Generic Ballplayer	1000.00	500.00
1881 Generic Ballplayer	1000.00	500.00
1882 Generic Ballplayer	750.00	375.00
1883 Generick Ballplayer	750.00	375.00
1884 Generic Ballplayer	750.00	375.00
1885 Generic Ballplayer	600.00	300.00
1886 Generic Ballplayer	600.00	300.00
1887 Generic Ballplayer	600.00	300.00
1888 Generic Ballplayer	600.00	300.00
1889 Generic Ballplayer	600.00	300.00
1890 Generic Ballplayer	600.00	300.00
1891 Generic Ballplayer	500.00	250.00
1892 Generic Ballplayer	500.00	250.00
1893 Generic Ballplayer	500.00	250.00
1894 Generic Ballplayer	500.00	250.00
1895 Generic Ballplayer	500.00	250.00
1896 Generic Ballplayer	400.00	200.00
1897 Generic Ballplayer	400.00	200.00
1898 Generic Ballplayer	400.00	200.00
1899 Generic Ballplayer	400.00	200.00
1900 Generic Ballplayer	350.00	180.00
1901 Generic Ballplayer	350.00	180.00
1902 Generic Ballplayer	350.00	180.00
1903 Generic Ballplayer	350.00	180.00
1904 Generic Ballplayer	400.00	200.00
1905 Generic Ballplayer	300.00	150.00
1906 Generic Ballplayer	300.00	150.00
1907 Generic Ballplayer	300.00	150.00
1908 Generic Ballplayer	300.00	150.00
1909 Generic Ballplayer	300.00	150.00
1910 Generic Ballplayer	250.00	125.00
1911 Generic Ballplayer	250.00	125.00
1912 Generic Ballplayer	250.00	125.00
1913 Generic Ballplayer	200.00	100.00
1914 Generic Ballplayer	200.00	100.00
1915 Generic Ballplayer	200.00	100.00
1916 Generic Ballplayer	200.00	100.00
1917 Generic Ballplayer	200.00	100.00
1918 Generic Ballplayer	200.00	100.00
1919 Generic Ballplayer	250.00	125.00
1920 Generic Ballplayer	300.00	150.00
1921 Generic Ballplayer	300.00	150.00
1922 Generic Ballplayer	250.00	125.00
1923 Generic Ballplayer	150.00	75.00
1924 Generic Ballplayer	150.00	75.00
1925 Generic Ballplayer	150.00	75.00
1926 Generic Ballplayer	150.00	75.00
1927 Generic Ballplayer	150.00	75.00
1928 Generic Ballplayer	150.00	75.00
1929 Generic Ballplayer	150.00	75.00
1930 Generic Ballplayer	150.00	75.00
1931 Generic Ballplayer	150.00	75.00
1932 Generic Ballplayer	150.00	75.00
1933 Generic Ballplayer	150.00	75.00
1934 Generic Ballplayer	150.00	75.00
1935 Dizzy Dean	175.00	90.00
1936 Generic Ballplayer	150.00	75.00
1937 Carl Hubbell	175.00	90.00
1938 Joe Medwick	150.00	75.00
1939 Centennial Logo	125.00	60.00
1940 Spalding/Reach Combo	100.00	50.00
1941 Spalding/Reach Combo	100.00	50.00

1942-99 The Sporting News Baseball Guide

This publication began as The Sporting News Record Book until 1948 when it changed its name to the The Sporting News Official Baseball Guide. A radio edition was published during the 1940's war years. The thinner radio editions are valued slightly less than the regular guides. Hardcover versions were produced for distribution to the baseball media. Hardover versions are valued slightly higher.

	Ex-Mt	VG
1942 Art Illustration	250.00	125.00
1943 Servicemen	125.00	60.00
1944 Bobo Newsom	100.00	50.00
Babe Dahlgren		
1945 Marty Marion	100.00	50.00
Hal Newhouser		
1946 Hal Newhouser	100.00	50.00
1947 Harry Brecheen	100.00	50.00
1948 Ewell Blackwell	100.00	50.00
1949 Lou Boudreau	75.00	38.00
1950 Phil Rizzuto	100.00	50.00
Pee Wee Reese		
1951 Red Schoendist	75.00	38.00
1952 Stan Musial	100.00	50.00
1953 Robin Roberts	75.00	38.00
1954 Casey Stengel	60.00	30.00
1955 Game Play	75.00	38.00
1956 Jerry Coleman	75.00	38.00
Billy Martin		
1957 Mickey Mantle	100.00	50.00
Yogi Berra		
1958 Ted Williams	100.00	50.00
1959 Spalding Advertisement	60.00	30.00
1960 Dodger Bum Mascot	60.00	30.00
1961 Relief Pitcher Award	50.00	25.00
1962 Babe Ruth	50.00	25.00
Roger Maris		
1963 Willard Mullin Artwork	50.00	25.00
1964 Stan Musial	50.00	25.00
1965 Brooks Robinson	40.00	20.00
Ken Boyer		
Dean Chance		
1966 Willie Mays	40.00	20.00
Sandy Koufax		
1967 Roberto Clemente	35.00	17.50
Sandy Koufax		
Frank Robinson		
1968 Orlando Cepeda	35.00	17.50
Jim Lonborg		
Carl Yastrzemski		
1969 Pete Rose	30.00	15.00
Denny McLain		
Bob Gibson		
1970 Willie McCovey	30.00	15.00
Harmon Killebrew		
1971 Johnny Bench	25.00	12.50
Bob Gibson		
Harmon Killebrew		
1972 Fergie Jenkins	25.00	12.50
Vida Blue		
Joe Torre		
1973 Steve Carlton	20.00	10.00
Johnny Bench		
Gaylord Perry		
1974 Jim Palmer	20.00	10.00
Barry Bonds		
Reggie Jackson		
1975 Lou Brock	20.00	10.00
Jim Hunter		
1976 Joe Morgan	15.00	7.50
Jim Palmer		
Tom Seaver		
1977 Thurman Munson	15.00	7.50
Jim Palmer		
1978 Rod Carew	15.00	7.50
Steve Carlton		
Nolan Ryan		
1979 Jim Rice	15.00	7.50
Ron Guidry		
Dave Parker		
1980 Keith Hernandez	10.00	5.00
Don Baylor		
1981 Steve Carlton	12.00	6.00
1982 Tom Seaver	12.00	6.00
1983 Robin Yount	12.00	6.00
1984 Ryne Sandberg	12.00	6.00
1985 Cal Ripken Jr.	15.00	7.50
1986 Willie McGee	10.00	5.00
1987 Roger Clemens	10.00	5.00
1988 Andre Dawson	10.00	5.00
1989 Jose Canseco	10.00	5.00
1990 Bret Saberhagen	10.00	5.00
1991 Bob Welch	10.00	5.00
1992 Will Clark	10.00	5.00
1993 Kirby Puckett	12.00	6.00
1994 Jack McDowell	10.00	5.00
1995 Ken Griffey Jr.	10.00	5.00
1996 Hideo Nomo	10.00	5.00
1997 John Smoltz	10.00	5.00
1998 Roger Clemens	10.00	5.00
1999 Derek Jeter	10.00	5.00
Tony Gwynn		
2000 Yankees Team	10.00	5.00
2001 Mike Piazza	10.00	5.00
2002 Ichiro Suzuki	10.00	5.00
2003 Angels Celebrate	10.00	5.00
Pedro Martinez		
Ichiro Suzuki		
Sammy Sosa		
2004 Ichiro Suzuki	10.00	5.00
Todd Helton		
Dontrelle Willis		
Esteban Loaiza		

1910-40 The Sporting News Baseball Record Book

In 1941, the pocket-sized Sporting News Record Book was replaced by the Sporting News Dope Book, later renamed One for the Book. The 1909 cover edition cover subject(s) are unknown to us.

	Ex-Mt	VG
1910 Ty Cobb	150.00	75.00
Honus Wagner		
1911 Philadelphia A's Player	125.00	60.00
1912 Eddie Collins	100.00	50.00
1913 Frank Chance	100.00	50.00
Frank Farrell OWN		
1914 Ban Johnson	100.00	50.00
1915 Charles Comiskey	75.00	38.00
1916 Joseph Lannin	75.00	38.00
1917 Joe Jackson	400.00	200.00
1918 St. Louis Brown	75.00	38.00
1919 Lt. Col. T.L. Huston	60.00	30.00
1920 Babe Ruth	150.00	75.00
1921 Babe Ruth	100.00	50.00
George Sisler		
1922 Rogers Hornsby	50.00	25.00
1923 George Sisler	40.00	20.00
1924 Everett Scott	35.00	17.50
1925 Walter Johnson	60.00	30.00
1926 Max Carey	30.00	15.00
1927 Bob O'Farrell	30.00	15.00
1928 Lou Gehrig	100.00	50.00
1929 Lou Gehrig	100.00	50.00
Babe Ruth		
1930 Mickey Cochrane	40.00	20.00
1931 Hack Wilson	40.00	20.00
1932 Lefty Grove	40.00	20.00
1933 Jimmy Foxx	40.00	20.00
1934 Carl Hubbell	35.00	17.50
1935 Dizzy Dean	35.00	17.50
1936 Hank Greenberg	30.00	15.00
1937 Joe McCarthy	25.00	12.50
1938 Joe Medwick	25.00	12.50
1939 Abner Doubleday	25.00	12.50
1940 Bucky Walters	25.00	12.50

1940-99 The Sporting News Baseball Register

The Sporting News Baseball Register became popular with autograph enthusiasts because it contained fascimile autographs for most current-day ball players. The Register ceased featuring sample signatures in the late 1960's. Hardcover versions were produced for distribution to the baseball media. Hardcover versions are valued at 1.5X the regular book value.

	Ex-Mt	VG
1940 Ty Cobb	200.00	100.00
1941 Paul Derringer	100.00	50.00
1942 Joe DiMaggio	150.00	75.00
1943 Uncle Sam	100.00	50.00
1944 Rube Waddell	120.00	60.00
1945 Billy Southworth	100.00	50.00
1946 Art Illustration	100.00	50.00
1947 Walter Johnson	100.00	50.00
1948 Art Illustration	80.00	40.00
1949 Art Illustration	80.00	40.00
1950 Joe DiMaggio	100.00	50.00
1951 Art Illustration	80.00	40.00
1952 Art Illustration	60.00	30.00
1953 Art Illustration	60.00	30.00
1954 Art Illustration	60.00	30.00
1955 Art Illustration	60.00	30.00
1956 Art Illustration	60.00	30.00
1957 Art Illustration	60.00	30.00
1958 Art Illustration	50.00	25.00
1959 Art Illustration	50.00	25.00
1960 Art Illustration	50.00	25.00
1961 Art Illustration	50.00	25.00
1962 Art Illustration	50.00	25.00
1963 Art Illustration	40.00	20.00
1964 Yankee Stadium	40.00	20.00
1965 Kenny Boyer	30.00	15.00
1966 Sandy Koufax	40.00	20.00
1967 Brooks Robinson	30.00	15.00
Frank Robinson		
1968 Jim Lonborg	25.00	12.50
1969 Willie Horton	25.00	12.50
1970 Tom Seaver	25.00	12.50
1971 Willie Mays	30.00	15.00
1972 Joe Torre	25.00	12.50
1973 Wilbur Wood	20.00	10.00
1974 Pete Rose	25.00	12.50
1975 Jim Hunter	20.00	10.00
1976 Jim Palmer	20.00	10.00
1977 Joe Morgan	20.00	10.00
1978 Rod Carew	20.00	10.00
1979 Ron Guidry	15.00	7.50
1980 Carl Yastrzemski	15.00	7.50
1981 George Brett	20.00	10.00
1982 Fernando Valenzuela	15.00	7.50
1982 Tom Seaver	15.00	7.50
1983 Robin Yount	15.00	7.50
1984 Cal Ripken Jr.	20.00	10.00
1984 John Denny	15.00	7.50
1985 Ryne Sandberg	12.00	6.00
1985 Willie Hernandez	12.00	6.00
1986 Willie McGee	10.00	5.00
1986 Don Mattingly	15.00	7.50
1987 Mike Schmidt	12.00	6.00
1987 Roger Clemens	10.00	5.00
1988 Andre Dawson	10.00	5.00
1988 George Bell	10.00	5.00
1989 Frank Viola	10.00	5.00
1989 Jose Canseco	10.00	5.00
1990 Kevin Mitchell	10.00	5.00
1991 Barry Bonds	10.00	5.00
1992 Frank Thomas	15.00	7.50
1993 Gary Sheffield	10.00	5.00
1994 Lenny Dykstra	10.00	5.00
1995 Bret Saberhagen	10.00	5.00
1996 Greg Maddux	10.00	5.00
1997 Frank Thomas	15.00	7.50
1998 Ken Griffey Jr.	15.00	7.50
1999 Sammy Sosa	10.00	5.00
2000 Pedro Martinez	10.00	5.00
2001 Jason Giambi	10.00	5.00
2002 Curt Schilling	10.00	5.00
2003 Barry Bonds	10.00	5.00
Albert Pujols		
Curt Schilling		
Rickey Henderson		
Miguel Tejada		
2004 Albert Pujols	10.00	5.00
Pedro Martinez		
Mark Prior		
Barry Bonds		
Garrett Anderson		

1941-99 Street and Smith Baseball Yearbook

Early Street and Smith Baseball Yearbooks are popular with uniform collectors and researchers because they were one of the few sources that provided player's uniform numbers. Street and Smith began publishing regional covers in 1963.

	Ex-Mt	VG
1941 Bob Feller	300.00	150.00
1942 Howard Pollett	200.00	100.00
1943 N.Y. Giants Game Play	200.00	100.00
1944 Joe McCarthy	150.00	75.00
1945 N.Y. Giants	175.00	90.00
Spring Training		
1946 Dick Fowler	150.00	75.00
1947 Leo Durocher	175.00	90.00
1948 Joe DiMaggio	200.00	100.00
1949 Lou Boudreau	125.00	60.00
1950 Ted Williams	200.00	100.00
Joe DiMaggio		
1951 Joe DiMaggio	175.00	90.00
Ralph Kiner		
1952 Stan Musial	150.00	75.00
1953 Mickey Mantle	200.00	100.00
1954 Eddie Mathews	125.00	60.00
1955 Yogi Berra	150.00	75.00
1956 Duke Snider	175.00	90.00
Mickey Mantle		
1957 Mickey Mantle	150.00	75.00
Don Larsen		
Yogi Berra		
1958 Bob Buhl	125.00	60.00
Lew Burdette		
1959 Lew Burdette	125.00	60.00
Mickey Mantle		
Warren Spahn		
1960 Nellie Fox	100.00	50.00
Luis Aparicio		
1961 Dick Groat	75.00	38.00
1962 Roger Maris	100.00	50.00
1963 Don Drysdale	75.00	38.00
1963 Tom Tresh	60.00	30.00
1963 Stan Musial	75.00	38.00
1964 Warren Spahn	60.00	30.00
1964 Mickey Mantle	75.00	38.00
1964 Sandy Koufax	60.00	30.00
1965 Dean Chance	50.00	25.00
1965 Ken Boyer	50.00	25.00
1965 Brooks Robinson	60.00	30.00
1966 Rocky Colavito	50.00	25.00
1966 Ron Swoboda	40.00	20.00
1966 Sandy Koufax	40.00	20.00
1967 Andy Etchebarren	40.00	20.00
1967 Juan Marichal	40.00	20.00
1967 Harmon Killebrew	40.00	20.00
1968 Jim Lonborg	40.00	20.00
1968 Orlando Cepeda	40.00	20.00
1968 Jim McGlothin	35.00	17.50
1969 Denny McLain	35.00	17.50
Bob Gibson		
1970 Harmon Killebrew	35.00	17.50
1970 Tom Seaver	40.00	20.00
1970 Bob Singer	35.00	17.50
1971 Boog Powell	30.00	15.00
1971 Johnny Bench	40.00	20.00
1971 Gaylord Perry	30.00	15.00
1972 Roberto Clemente	50.00	25.00
1972 Joe Torre	30.00	15.00
1972 Vida Blue	30.00	15.00
1973 Johnny Bench	30.00	15.00
1973 Steve Carlton	35.00	17.50
1973 Reggie Jackson	35.00	17.50
1974 Hank Aaron	35.00	17.50
1974 Nolan Ryan	50.00	25.00
1974 Pete Rose	35.00	17.50
1975 Lou Brock	25.00	12.50
1975 Catfish Hunter	30.00	15.00
1975 Mike Marshall	25.00	12.50
1976 Fred Lynn	25.00	12.50
1976 Joe Morgan	25.00	12.50
1976 Davey Lopes	20.00	10.00
1977 Mark Fidrych	25.00	12.50
1977 Thurman Munson	25.00	12.50
1977 Randy Jones	20.00	10.00
1978 Rod Carew	20.00	10.00
1978 Steve Garvey	20.00	10.00
1978 Reggie Jackson	20.00	10.00
1979 Ron Guidry	20.00	10.00
1979 J.R. Richard	20.00	10.00
1979 Burt Hooten	20.00	10.00
1980 Mike Flanagan	20.00	10.00
1980 Brian Downing	20.00	10.00
1980 Joe Niekro	12.00	6.00
1981 Mike Schmidt	20.00	10.00
1981 George Brett	20.00	10.00
1981 Rickey Henderson	20.00	10.00
1982 Pete Rose	20.00	10.00
Goose Gossage		
1982 Nolan Ryan	35.00	17.50
1982 Rollie Fingers	20.00	10.00
Tim Seaver		
1983 Steve Carlton	20.00	10.00
1983 Doug DeCinces	15.00	7.50
1983 Phil Niekro	15.00	7.50
1983 Robin Yount	20.00	10.00
1984 Dale Murphy	15.00	7.50
1984 Scott McGregor	15.00	7.50
Rick Dempsey		
1984 Carlton Fisk	15.00	7.50
1984 Pedro Guerrero	15.00	7.50
1985 Steve Garvey	15.00	7.50
1985 Tigers Celebrate	15.00	7.50
1985 Dwight Gooden	20.00	10.00
1986 Royals Celebrate	15.00	7.50
1986 Dwight Gooden	20.00	10.00
Don Mattingly		
1986 Jesse Barfield	15.00	7.50
Ernie Whitt		

1987 Wally Joyner	15.00	7.50
1987 Roger Clemens	20.00	10.00
1987 Joe Carter	15.00	7.50
1987 Gary Carter	15.00	7.50
Jesse Orosco		
1987 Mike Scott	15.00	7.50
1988 Dale Murphy	15.00	7.50
1988 Jeff Reardon	15.00	7.50
1988 Ozzie Smith	15.00	7.50
1988 Don Mattingly	20.00	10.00
1988 Benito Santiago	20.00	10.00
Mark McGwire		
1989 Kevin McReynolds	15.00	7.50
1989 Andres Galarraga	15.00	7.50
Fred McGriff		
1989 Mark Grace	15.00	7.50
Chris Sabo		
1989 Orel Hershiser	15.00	7.50
1990 50th Anniversary Issue	20.00	10.00
1991 Ryne Sandberg	15.00	7.50
1991 Lou Piniella	15.00	7.50
1992 Kirby Puckett	15.00	7.50
1992 Roger Clemens	15.00	7.50
1992 Bobby Bonilla	10.00	5.00
1993 Tom Glavine	10.00	5.00
1993 Roger Clemens	10.00	5.00
1994 David Justice	10.00	5.00
1994 Aaron Sele	10.00	5.00
1995 Bret Saberhagen	10.00	5.00
Jimmy Key		
1996 Greg Maddux	10.00	5.00
1996 Mo Vaughn	10.00	5.00
1997 Derek Jeter	10.00	5.00
1997 Gary Sheffield	10.00	5.00
1998 Livan Hernandez	10.00	5.00
1998 Tino Martinez	10.00	5.00
1999 David Wells	10.00	5.00
1999 Mark McGwire	10.00	5.00
Sammy Sosa		
2000 Brian Jordan	10.00	5.00
2000 Bob Abreu	10.00	5.00
2001 Jim Edmonds	10.00	5.00
2002 Randy Johnson	10.00	5.00
2003 Barry Bonds	10.00	5.00
2003 Austin Kearns	10.00	5.00
Adam Dunn		
2003 Ichiro Suzuki	10.00	5.00
2003 Garret Anderson	10.00	5.00
2003 Gary Sheffield	10.00	5.00
John Smoltz		
2003 Jim Thome	10.00	5.00
2003 Rodrigo Lopez	10.00	5.00
2003 Kerry Wood	10.00	5.00
Sammy Sosa		
2003 Alex Rodriguez	10.00	5.00
2003 Curt Schilling	10.00	5.00
Randy Johnson		
2003 Nomar Garciaparra	10.00	5.00
Manny Ramirez		
Pedro Martinea		
2003 Albert Pujols	10.00	5.00
2003 Josh Beckett	10.00	5.00
A.J.Burnett		
2003 Derek Jeter	10.00	5.00
2003 Torii Hunter	10.00	5.00

1933-52 Who's Who In Major League Baseball

The 1933 oversized hardback version (various colors) was edited by Speed Johnson. The publication was edited by John Carmichael from 1938 through 1952. Hardcover versions of the similar format also were available and are valued slightly higher.

	Ex-Mt	VG
1933 Speed Johnson Edition	500.00	250.00
1935 Mickey Cochrane	150.00	75.00
Charlie Grimm		
1936 Non-Player	125.00	60.00
1937 Carl Hubbell	100.00	50.00
Luke Appling		
1938 Joe DiMaggio	125.00	60.00
1939 Pitcher	100.00	50.00
1940 Joe DiMaggio	125.00	60.00
1941 Non-Player	75.00	38.00
1942 Non-Player	75.00	38.00
1943 Ted Williams	100.00	50.00
1944 Three Players	75.00	38.00
1945 Hal Newhouser	75.00	38.00
1946 Various Players	75.00	38.00
1947 Stan Musial	75.00	38.00
1948 Ted Williams	100.00	50.00
Joe DiMaggio		
1949 Non-Player	60.00	30.00
1950 Ralph Kiner	60.00	30.00
1951 Non-Player	60.00	30.00
1952 Joe DiMaggio	75.00	38.00
Ford Frick COMM		

1912-99 Who's Who In Baseball

Who's Who in Baseball contains lifetime records (including minor league) and personal photos for most current-day major leaguers. Editions from 1912 through 1929 are graded in Excellent Condition. 1929 through 1945 are graded in Excellent-Mint condition. 1946 through the present are graded in Near Mint condition.

	Ex-Mt	VG
1912 Ty Cobb	2000.00	1000.00
1916 Ty Cobb	1200.00	600.00
1916 Athletics Outfielder	800.00	400.00
1917 Tris Speaker	1200.00	600.00
1918 George Sisler	1000.00	500.00
1919 Grover C. Alexander	700.00	350.00
1920 Babe Ruth	800.00	400.00
1921 Babe Ruth	800.00	400.00
1922 Rogers Hornsby	400.00	200.00
1923 George Sisler	300.00	150.00
1924 Walter Johnson	300.00	150.00
1925 Dizzy Vance	250.00	125.00
1926 Max Carey	250.00	125.00
1927 Frankie Frisch	250.00	125.00
1928 Hack Wilson	200.00	100.00
1929 Bob O'Farrell	150.00	75.00
1930 Burleigh Grimes	150.00	75.00
1931 Lefty Grove	150.00	75.00
1932 Al Simmons	120.00	60.00
1933 Chuck Klein	120.00	60.00
1934 Bill Terry	100.00	50.00
1935 Dizzy Dean	100.00	50.00
1936 Hank Greenberg	100.00	50.00
1937 Lou Gehrig	150.00	75.00
1938 Joe Medwick	80.00	40.00
1939 Jimmie Foxx	100.00	50.00
1940 Bucky Walters	80.00	40.00
1941 Bob Feller	80.00	40.00
1942 Joe DiMaggio	100.00	50.00
1943 Ted Williams	80.00	40.00
1944 Stan Musial	80.00	40.00
1945 Hal Newhouser	50.00	25.00
Dizzy Trout		
1946 Hal Newhouser	50.00	25.00
1947 Eddie Dyer MG	40.00	20.00
1948 Johnny Mize	50.00	25.00
Ralph Kiner		
1949 Lou Boudreau	40.00	20.00
1950 Mel Parnell	35.00	17.50
1951 Jim Konstanty	35.00	17.50
1952 Stan Musial	40.00	20.00
1953 Hank Sauer	30.00	15.00
Bobby Shantz		
1954 Al Rosen	25.00	12.50
1955 Alvin Dark	25.00	12.50
1956 Duke Snider	35.00	17.50
1957 Mickey Mantle	75.00	38.00
1958 Warren Spahn	40.00	20.00
1959 Bob Turley	30.00	15.00
1960 Don Drysdale	30.00	15.00
1961 Roger Maris	35.00	17.50
1962 Whitey Ford	30.00	15.00
1963 Don Drysdale	25.00	12.50
1964 Sandy Koufax	30.00	15.00
1965 Ken Boyer	25.00	12.50
1966 Willie Mays	25.00	12.50
Sandy Koufax		
1967 Roberto Clemente	35.00	17.50
Sandy Koufax		
1968 Carl Yastrzemski	25.00	12.50
1969 Denny McLain	20.00	10.00
1970 Tom Seaver Blue Cover	20.00	10.00
1971 Johnny Bench Blue Cover	20.00	10.00
1971 Johnny Bench	20.00	10.00
1972 Joe Torre	15.00	7.50
1973 Steve Carlton	15.00	7.50
1973 Steve Carlton Blue Cover	15.00	7.50
1974 Nolan Ryan	25.00	12.50
Reggie Jackson		
Pete Rose		
1975 Lou Brock	15.00	7.50
1976 Fred Lynn	15.00	7.50
Joe Morgan		
1977 Thurman Munson	15.00	7.50
Joe Morgan		
1978 George Foster	15.00	7.50
Rod Carew		
1979 Ron Guidry	15.00	7.50
1980 Willie Stargell	10.00	5.00
Don Baylor		
Keith Hernandez		
1981 George Brett	15.00	7.50
1982 Fernando Valenzuela	10.00	5.00
Mike Schmidt		
1983 Robin Yount	10.00	5.00
1984 Cal Ripken	15.00	7.50
1985 Ryne Sandberg	10.00	5.00
1986 Dwight Gooden	10.00	5.00
Don Mattingly		
Willie McGee		
1987 Roger Clemens	10.00	5.00
Mike Schmidt		
1989 Jose Canseco	10.00	5.00
Kirk Gibson		
1990 Robin Yount	10.00	5.00
Kevin Mitchell		
1991 Nolan Ryan	10.00	5.00
Ryne Sandberg		
Cecil Fielder		
1992 Various Stars	8.00	4.00
1993 Dennis Eckersley	8.00	4.00
1994 Barry Bonds	8.00	4.00
1995 Frank Thomas	8.00	4.00
1996 Greg Maddux	8.00	4.00
1997 Alex Rodriguez	8.00	4.00
1998 Mark McGwire	8.00	4.00
1999 Mark McGwire	8.00	4.00
Sammy Sosa		
2000 Chipper Jones	8.00	4.00
2001 Pedro Martinez	8.00	4.00
2002 Barry Bonds	8.00	4.00
2003 Randy Johnson	8.00	4.00
2004 Barry Bonds	8.00	4.00

1903-99 World Series Programs

World Series program are the most popular item in the publication field. Programs prior to 1920 are difficult to find and command a premium in top condition. Programs prior to 1910 are quite scarce; only a few copies from 1903 are known to exist. Programs through 1935 are graded in Excellent/Excellent-Mint condition. Programs after 1935 are graded in Excellent-Mint/Near Mint condition.

	Ex-Mt	VG
1903 Pittsburgh Pirates	25000.00	12500.00
1903 Boston Red Sox	30000.00	15000.00
Then known as the Pilgrims		
1904 No Series		
1905 New York Giants	10000.00	5000.00
1905 Phil. Athletics	12000.00	6000.00
1906 Chicago White Sox	10000.00	5000.00
1906 Chicago Cubs	11000.00	5500.00
1907 Chicago Cubs	10000.00	5000.00
1907 Detroit Tigers	10000.00	5000.00
1908 Chicago Cubs	10000.00	5000.00
1908 Detroit Tigers	10000.00	5000.00
1909 Pittsburgh Pirates	10000.00	5000.00
1909 Detroit Tigers	10000.00	5000.00
1910 Phil. Athletics	9000.00	4500.00
1910 Chicago Cubs	8000.00	4000.00
1911 New York Giants	4500.00	2200.00
1911 Phil. Athletics	5000.00	2500.00
1912 New York Giants	4000.00	2000.00
1912 Boston Red Sox	3500.00	1800.00
1913 Philadelphia Athletics	4000.00	2000.00
1913 New York Giants	3500.00	1800.00
1914 Philadelphia Athletics	3500.00	1800.00
1914 Boston Braves	3000.00	1500.00
1915 Boston Red Sox	3500.00	1800.00
1915 Philadelphia Phillies	10000.00	5000.00
1916 Brooklyn Dodgers	6000.00	3000.00
1916 Boston Red Sox	4000.00	2000.00
1917 Chicago White Sox	8000.00	4000.00
1917 New York Giants	3500.00	1800.00
1918 Chicago Cubs	10000.00	5000.00
1918 Boston Red Sox	12000.00	6000.00
1919 Cincinnati Reds	4000.00	2000.00
1919 Chicago White Sox	12000.00	6000.00
1920 Cleveland Indians	6000.00	3000.00
1920 Brooklyn Dodgers	8000.00	4000.00
1921 New York Giants	2000.00	1000.00
1921 New York Yankees	2000.00	1000.00
1922 New York Yankees	2000.00	1000.00
1922 New York Giants	2000.00	1000.00
1923 New York Giants	2000.00	1000.00
1923 New York Yankees	2000.00	1000.00
1924 Washington Senators	1200.00	600.00
1924 New York Giants	1500.00	750.00
1925 Pittsburgh Pirates	5000.00	2500.00
1925 Washington Senators	1200.00	600.00
1926 St Louis Cardinals	1200.00	600.00
1926 New York Yankees	1500.00	750.00
1927 New York Yankees	3500.00	1800.00
1927 Pittsburgh Pirates	5000.00	2500.00
1928 New York Yankees	1500.00	750.00
1928 St Louis Cardinals	1200.00	600.00
1929 Philadelphia Athletics	1200.00	600.00
1929 Chicago Cubs	1000.00	500.00
1930 St Louis Cardinals	750.00	375.00
1930 Philadelphia Athletics	1000.00	500.00
1931 St Louis Cardinals	600.00	300.00
1931 Philadelphia Athletics	750.00	375.00
1932 New York Yankees	1000.00	500.00
1932 Chicago Cubs	600.00	300.00
1933 Washington Senators	600.00	300.00
1933 New York Giants	500.00	250.00
1934 Detroit Tigers	600.00	300.00
1934 St Louis Cardinals	500.00	250.00
1935 Chicago Cubs	500.00	250.00
1935 Detroit Tigers	700.00	350.00
1936 New York Yankees	500.00	250.00
1936 New York Giants	400.00	200.00
1937 New York Giants	400.00	200.00
1937 New York Yankees	500.00	250.00
1938 Chicago Cubs	350.00	180.00
1938 New York Yankees	400.00	200.00
1939 New York Yankees	400.00	200.00
1939 Cincinnati Reds	350.00	180.00
1940 Detroit Tigers	400.00	200.00
1940 Cincinnati Reds	350.00	180.00
1941 New York Yankees	350.00	180.00
1941 Brooklyn Dodgers	500.00	250.00
1942 New York Yankees	300.00	150.00
1942 St Louis Cardinals	250.00	125.00
1943 St Louis Cardinals	300.00	150.00
1943 New York Yankees	250.00	125.00
1944 St Louis Cardinals	250.00	125.00
1944 St Louis Browns	400.00	200.00
1945 Detroit Tigers	400.00	200.00
1945 Chicago Cubs	200.00	100.00
1946 St Louis Cardinals	200.00	100.00
1946 Boston Red Sox	200.00	100.00
1947 New York Yankees	300.00	150.00
1947 Brooklyn Dodgers	400.00	200.00
1948 Boston Braves	150.00	75.00
1948 Cleveland Indians	125.00	60.00
1949 New York Yankees	250.00	125.00
1949 Brooklyn Dodgers	300.00	150.00
1950 New York Yankees	150.00	75.00
1950 Philadelphia Phillies	125.00	60.00
1951 New York Yankee	150.00	75.00
1951 New York Giants	125.00	60.00
1952 New York Yankees	125.00	60.00
1952 Brooklyn Dodgers	300.00	150.00
1953 Brooklyn Dodgers	300.00	150.00
1953 New York Yankees	125.00	60.00
1954 New York Giants	250.00	125.00
1954 Cleveland Indians	200.00	100.00
1955 New York Yankees	150.00	75.00
1955 Brooklyn Dodgers	350.00	180.00
1956 Brooklyn Dodgers	250.00	125.00
1956 New York Yankees	175.00	90.00
1957 Milwaukee Braves	175.00	90.00
1957 New York Yankees	125.00	60.00
1958 Milwaukee Braves	175.00	90.00
1958 New York Yankees	125.00	60.00
1959 Chicago White Sox	225.00	110.00
1959 Los Angeles Dodgers	125.00	60.00
1960 New York Yankees	75.00	38.00
1960 Pittsburgh Pirates	100.00	50.00
1961 Cincinnati Reds	100.00	50.00
1961 New York Yankees	150.00	75.00
1962 San Francisco Giants	150.00	75.00
1962 New York Yankees	100.00	50.00
1963 New York Yankees	60.00	30.00
1963 Los Angeles Dodgers	60.00	30.00
1964 New York Yankees	75.00	38.00
1964 St Louis Cardinals	125.00	60.00
1965 Los Angeles Dodgers	40.00	20.00
1965 Minnesota Twins	100.00	50.00
1966 Baltimore Orioles	100.00	50.00
1966 Los Angeles Dodgers	40.00	20.00
1967 Boston Red Sox	125.00	60.00
1967 St Louis Cardinals	100.00	50.00
1968 St Louis Cardinals	100.00	50.00
1968 Detroit Tigers	225.00	110.00
1969 New York Mets	150.00	75.00
1969 Baltimore Orioles	40.00	20.00
1970 Cincinnati Reds	75.00	38.00
1970 Baltimore Orioles	40.00	20.00
1971 Pittsburgh Pirates	100.00	50.00
1971 Baltimore Orioles	40.00	20.00
1972 Cincinnati Reds	60.00	30.00
1972 Oakland A's	60.00	30.00
1973 New York Mets	35.00	17.50
1973 Oakland A's	60.00	30.00
1974 Los Angeles Dodgers	25.00	12.50
1974 Oakland A's	25.00	12.50
1975 Boston Red Sox	30.00	15.00
1975 Cincinnati Reds	25.00	12.50
1976 Cincinnati Reds	20.00	10.00
1976 New York Yankees	20.00	10.00
1977 New York Yankees	15.00	7.50
1977 Los Angeles Dodgers	15.00	7.50
1978 New York Yankees	15.00	7.50
1978 Los Angeles Dodgers	15.00	7.50
1979 Pittsburgh Pirates	15.00	7.50
1979 Baltimore Orioles	15.00	7.50
1980 Philadelphia Phillies	15.00	7.50
1980 Kansas City Royals	15.00	7.50
1981 Los Angeles Dodgers	15.00	7.50
1981 New York Yankees	15.00	7.50
1982 Milwaukee Brewers	20.00	10.00
1982 St Louis Cardinals	15.00	7.50
1983 Baltimore Orioles	15.00	7.50
1983 Philadelphia Phillies	20.00	10.00
1984 San Diego Padres	12.00	6.00
1984 Detroit Tigers	15.00	7.50
1985 St Louis Cardinals	12.00	6.00
1985 Kansas City Royals	12.00	6.00
1986 Boston Red Sox	15.00	7.50
1986 New York Mets	15.00	7.50
1987 Minnesota Twins	12.00	6.00
1987 St Louis Cardinals	12.00	6.00
1988 Los Angeles Dodgers	12.00	6.00
1988 Oakland A's	12.00	6.00
1989 San Francisco Giants	15.00	7.50
1989 Oakland A's	15.00	7.50
1990 Oakland A's	10.00	5.00
1990 Cincinnati Reds	10.00	5.00
1991 Minnesota Twins	10.00	5.00
1991 Atlanta Braves	10.00	5.00
1992 Toronto Blue Jays	10.00	5.00
1992 Atlanta Braves	10.00	5.00
1993 Toronto Blue Jays	10.00	5.00
1993 Philadelphia Phillies	10.00	5.00
1994 No Series		
1995 Cleveland Indians	10.00	5.00
1995 Atlanta Braves	10.00	5.00
1996 Atlanta Braves	10.00	5.00
1996 New York Yankees	10.00	5.00
1997 Florida Marlins	10.00	5.00
1997 Cleveland Indians	10.00	5.00
1998 New York Yankees	10.00	5.00
1998 San Diego Padres	10.00	5.00
1999 Atlanta Braves	10.00	5.00
1999 New York Yankees	10.00	5.00
2000 New York Mets	10.00	5.00
2000 New York Yankees	10.00	5.00
2001 Arizona Diamondbacks	10.00	5.00
2001 New York Yankees	10.00	5.00
2002 San Francisco Giants	10.00	5.00
2002 Anaheim Angels	10.00	5.00
2003 Florida Marlins	10.00	5.00
2003 New York Yankees	10.00	5.00

1903-99 World Series Ticket Stubs

The value for pre-1990 complete World Series tickets is generally double that of a stub. Complete World Series tickets prior to 1920 are valued even at a higher percentage. Ticket stubs for historic World Series contests, such as Don Larsen's 1956 perfect game, or Babe Ruth's famous called shot game, can command anywhere from 3 to 6 times that of a regular stub. Stubs prior to 1935 are graded in Excellent/Excellent-Mint Condition. Stubs after 1935 are graded in Excellent-Mint/Near-Mint condition.

	Ex-Mt	VG
1903 Pittsburgh Pirates	2500.00	1250.00
1903 Boston Red Sox	3500.00	1800.00
Then known as the Pilgrims		
1904 No Series		
1905 Philadelphia Athletics	1500.00	750.00
1905 New York Giants	1800.00	900.00
1906 Chicago Cubs	1200.00	600.00
1906 Chicago White Sox	1200.00	600.00
1907 Detroit Tigers	1000.00	500.00
1907 Chicago Cubs	1000.00	500.00
1908 Chicago Cubs	1000.00	500.00
1908 Detroit Tigers	1000.00	500.00
1909 Pittsburgh Pirates	800.00	400.00
1909 Detroit Tigers	1000.00	500.00
1910 Philadelphia Athletics	800.00	400.00
1910 Chicago Cubs	800.00	400.00
1911 Philadelphia Athtletics	800.00	400.00
1911 New York Giants	800.00	400.00
1912 New York Giants	800.00	400.00
1912 Boston Red Sox	1000.00	500.00
1913 Philadelphia Athletics	700.00	350.00
1913 New York Giants	800.00	400.00
1914 Boston Braves	800.00	400.00
1914 Philadelphia Athletics	700.00	350.00
1915 Boston Red Sox	800.00	400.00
1915 Philadelphia Phillies	700.00	350.00
1916 Boston Red Sox	800.00	400.00
1916 Brooklyn Dodgers	900.00	450.00
1917 New York Giants	700.00	350.00
1917 Chicago White Sox	700.00	350.00
1918 Chicago Cubs	700.00	350.00
1918 Boston Red Sox	800.00	400.00
1919 Cincinnati Reds	800.00	400.00
1919 Chicago White Sox	1500.00	750.00
1920 Cleveland Indians	600.00	300.00
1920 Brooklyn Dodgers	700.00	350.00
1921 New York Giants	500.00	250.00
1921 New York Yankees	600.00	300.00
1922 New York Giants	500.00	250.00
1922 New York Yankees	600.00	300.00
1923 New York Yankees	600.00	300.00
1923 New York Giants	500.00	250.00
1924 Washington Senators	400.00	200.00
1924 New York Giants	400.00	200.00
1925 Pittsburgh Pirates	400.00	200.00
1925 Washington Senators	400.00	200.00
1926 St Louis Cardinals	350.00	180.00
1926 New York Yankees	400.00	200.00
1927 New York Yankees	500.00	250.00
1927 Pittsburgh Pirates	300.00	150.00
1928 New York Yankees	350.00	180.00
1928 St Louis Cardinals	300.00	150.00
1929 Chicago Cubs	250.00	125.00
1929 Philadelphia Athletics	250.00	125.00
1930 St Louis Cardinals	250.00	125.00
1930 Philadelphia Athletics	250.00	125.00
1931 Philadelphia Athletics	250.00	125.00
1931 St Louis Cardinals	250.00	125.00
1932 Chicago Cubs	200.00	100.00
1932 New York Yankees	200.00	100.00
1933 Washington Senators	200.00	100.00
1933 New York Giants	150.00	75.00
1934 Detroit Tigers	175.00	90.00
1934 St Louis Cardinals	150.00	75.00
1935 Detroit Tigers	200.00	100.00
1935 Chicago Cubs	200.00	100.00
1936 New York Yankees	150.00	75.00
1936 New York Giants	150.00	75.00
1937 New York Giants	150.00	75.00
1937 New York Yankees	150.00	75.00
1938 New York Yankees	150.00	75.00
1938 Chicago Cubs	175.00	90.00
1939 Cincinnati Reds	150.00	75.00
1939 New York Yankees	125.00	60.00
1940 Cincinnati Reds	125.00	60.00
1940 Detroit Tigers	200.00	100.00
1941 Brooklyn Dodgers	200.00	100.00
1941 New York Yankees	125.00	60.00
1942 New York Yankees	150.00	75.00
1942 St Louis Cardinals	125.00	60.00
1943 New York Yankees	150.00	75.00
1943 St Louis Cardinals	125.00	60.00
1944 St Louis Browns	150.00	75.00
1944 St Louis Cardinals	150.00	75.00
1945 Detroit Tigers	200.00	100.00
1945 Chicago Cubs	150.00	75.00
1946 St Louis Cardinals	150.00	75.00
1946 Boston Red Sox	200.00	100.00
1947 Brooklyn Dodgers	200.00	100.00
1947 New York Yankees	150.00	75.00
1948 Boston Braves	125.00	60.00
1948 Cleveland Indians	125.00	60.00
1949 Brooklyn Dodgers	175.00	90.00
1949 New York Yankees	125.00	60.00
1950 New York Yankees	125.00	60.00
1950 Philadelphia Phillies	150.00	75.00
1951 New York Yankee	125.00	60.00
1951 New York Giants	90.00	45.00
1952 New York Yankees	125.00	60.00
1952 Brooklyn Dodgers	175.00	90.00
1953 New York Yankees	125.00	60.00
1953 Brooklyn Dodgers	175.00	90.00
1954 New York Giants	125.00	60.00
1954 Cleveland Indians	90.00	45.00
1955 New York Yankees	75.00	38.00
1955 Brooklyn Dodgers	250.00	125.00
1956 Brooklyn Dodgers	75.00	38.00
1956 New York Yankees	75.00	38.00
1957 Milwaukee Braves	75.00	38.00
1957 New York Yankees	75.00	38.00
1958 Milwaukee Braves	75.00	38.00
1958 New York Yankees	75.00	38.00
1959 Los Angeles Dodgers	75.00	38.00
1959 Chicago White Sox	75.00	38.00
1960 Pittsburgh Pirates	75.00	38.00
1960 New York Yankees	70.00	35.00
1961 New York Yankees	90.00	45.00
1961 Cincinnati Reds	70.00	35.00
1962 New York Yankees	75.00	38.00
1962 San Francisco Giants	75.00	38.00
1963 Los Angeles Dodgers	60.00	30.00
1963 New York Yankees	60.00	30.00
1964 New York Yankees	70.00	35.00
1964 St Louis Cardinals	60.00	30.00
1965 Los Angeles Dodgers	60.00	30.00
1965 Minnesota Twins	60.00	30.00
1966 Baltimore Orioles	60.00	30.00
1966 Los Angeles Dodgers	60.00	30.00
1967 St Louis Cardinals	60.00	30.00
1967 Boston Red Sox	75.00	38.00
1968 St Louis Cardinals	75.00	38.00
1968 Detroit Tigers	75.00	38.00
1969 New York Mets	75.00	38.00
1969 Baltimore Orioles	60.00	30.00
1970 Cincinnati Reds	60.00	30.00
1970 Baltimore Orioles	60.00	30.00
1971 Baltimore Orioles	60.00	30.00
1971 Pittsburgh Pirates	60.00	30.00
1972 Cincinnati Reds	60.00	30.00
1972 Oakland A's	60.00	30.00
1973 Oakland A's	60.00	30.00
1973 New York Mets	70.00	35.00
1974 Los Angeles Dodgers	50.00	25.00
1974 Oaklans A's	50.00	25.00
1975 Cincinnati Reds	45.00	22.00
1975 Boston Red Sox	55.00	28.00
1976 Cincinnati Reds	45.00	22.00
1976 New York Yankees	45.00	22.00
1977 Los Angeles Dodgers	45.00	22.00
1977 New York Yankees	45.00	22.00
1978 New York Yankees	45.00	22.00
1978 Los Angeles Dodgers	45.00	22.00
1979 Pittsburgh Pirates	40.00	20.00
1979 Baltimore Orioles	40.00	20.00
1980 Kansas City Royals	40.00	20.00
1980 Philadelphia Phillies	40.00	20.00
1981 New York Yankees	40.00	20.00
1981 Los Angeles Dodgers	40.00	20.00
1982 Milwaukee Brewers	40.00	20.00
1982 St Louis Cardinals	40.00	20.00
1983 Philadelphia Phillies	40.00	20.00
1983 Baltimore Orioles	40.00	20.00
1984 Detroit Tigers	45.00	22.00
1984 San Diego Padres	40.00	20.00
1985 St Louis Cardinals	40.00	20.00
1985 Kansas City Royals	40.00	20.00
1986 Boston Red Sox	45.00	22.00
1986 New York Mets	45.00	22.00
1987 St Louis Cardinals	40.00	20.00
1987 Minnesota Twins	40.00	20.00
1988 Los Angeles Dodgers	35.00	17.50
1988 Oakland A's	35.00	17.50
1989 Oakland A's	35.00	17.50
1989 San Francisco Giants	40.00	20.00
1990 Oakland A's	40.00	20.00
1990 Cincinnati Reds	35.00	17.50
1991 Minnesota Twins	35.00	17.50
1991 Atlanta Braves	35.00	17.50
1992 Atlanta Braves	35.00	17.50
1992 Toronto Blue Jays	35.00	17.50
1993 Toronto Blue Jays	35.00	17.50
1993 Philadelphia Phillies	35.00	17.50
1994 No Series		
1995 Atlanta Braves	35.00	17.50
1995 Cleveland Indians	35.00	17.50
1996 Atlanta Braves	35.00	17.50
1996 New York Yankees	35.00	17.50
1997 Florida Marlins	35.00	17.50
1997 Cleveland Indians	35.00	17.50
1998 San Diego Padres	35.00	17.50
1998 New York Yankees	35.00	17.50
1999 Atlanta Braves	35.00	17.50
1999 New York Yankees	35.00	17.50

2000 New York Yankees	35.00	17.50
2000 New York Mets	35.00	17.50
2001 Arizona Diamondbacks	35.00	17.50
2001 New York Yankees	35.00	17.50
2002 Anaheim Angels	35.00	17.50
2002 San Francisco Giants	35.00	17.50
2003 Florida Marlins	35.00	17.50
2003 New York Yankees	35.00	17.50

1938-99 World Series Phantom Press Pins

Major League Baseball allows teams it considers World Series contenders to produce post season materials prior to the end of the season. These materials include tickets, press pins, etc. Phantom World Series Press Pins were produced but never formerly released by non-title ballclubs

	Ex-Mt	VG
1938 Pittsburgh Pirates	900.00	450.00
1944 Detroit Tigers	400.00	200.00
1945 St Louis Cardinals	500.00	250.00
1946 Brooklyn Dodgers	200.00	100.00
1948 Boston Red Sox	1500.00	750.00
1948 New York Yankees	1500.00	750.00
1949 Boston Red Sox	700.00	350.00
1949 St Louis Cardinals	1500.00	750.00
1950 Boston Red Sox	1500.00	750.00
1950 Brooklyn Dodgers	2500.00	1250.00
1951 Cleveland Indians	1500.00	750.00
1951 Brooklyn Dodgers	500.00	250.00
1952 New York Giants	350.00	180.00
1955 Cleveland Indians	700.00	350.00
1956 Milwaukee Braves	125.00	60.00
1959 San Francisco Giants	400.00	200.00
1959 Milwaukee Braves	600.00	300.00
1960 Chicago White Sox	1200.00	600.00
1960 Baltimore Orioles	1000.00	500.00
1963 St Louis Cardinals	150.00	75.00
1964 Chicago White Sox	900.00	450.00
1964 Philadelphia Phillies	35.00	17.50
1964 Cincinnati Reds	200.00	100.00
1964 Baltimore Orioles	700.00	350.00
1965 San Francisco Giants	100.00	50.00
1966 San Francisco Giants	1000.00	500.00
1966 Pittsburgh Pirates	400.00	200.00
1967 Minnesota Twins	100.00	50.00
1967 Chicago White Sox	75.00	38.00
1969 Atlanta Braves	50.00	25.00
1969 San Francisco Giants	125.00	60.00
1969 Chicago Cubs	150.00	75.00
1969 Minnesota Twins	100.00	50.00
1970 California Angels	400.00	200.00
1970 Chicago Cubs	400.00	200.00
1971 San Francisco Giants	125.00	60.00
1972 Chicago White Sox	750.00	375.00
1974 Texas Rangers	450.00	220.00
1975 Oakland Athletics	400.00	200.00
1976 Philadelphia Phillies	50.00	25.00
1977 Boston Red Sox	75.00	38.00
1978 California Angels	200.00	100.00
1978 Cincinnati Reds	100.00	50.00
1978 San Francisco Giants	25.00	12.50
1979 California Angels	200.00	100.00
1979 Houston Astros	600.00	300.00
1979 Montreal Expos	50.00	25.00
1980 Houston Astros	150.00	75.00
1981 Oakland Athletics	100.00	50.00
1981 Philadelphia Phillies	50.00	25.00
1982 Los Angeles Dodgers	150.00	75.00
1983 Milwaukee Brewers	200.00	100.00
1983 Chicago White Sox	50.00	25.00
1983 Pittsburgh Pirates	200.00	100.00
1984 Chicago Cubs	150.00	75.00
1985 Toronto Blue Jays	200.00	100.00
1986 Houston Astros	200.00	100.00
1986 California Angels	200.00	100.00
1987 Detroit Tigers	150.00	75.00
1987 Boston Red Sox	100.00	50.00
1987 New York Yankees	200.00	100.00
1987 New York Mets	200.00	100.00
1988 Boston Red Sox	50.00	25.00
1990 Pittsburgh Pirates	225.00	110.00
1990 Boston Red Sox	50.00	25.00
1994 San Francisco Giants	100.00	50.00

1911-99 World Series Press Pins

World Series press pins were first introduced by the Philadelphia Athletics during the 1911 Fall Classic. The press pin was intended to keep non-press personnel out of the press box. Today, World Series press pins are given to members of the media more as a symbolic gesture.

	Ex-Mt	VG
1911 Phil. Athtletics	15000.00	7500.00
1912 Boston Red Sox	5000.00	2500.00
1912 New York Giants	9000.00	4500.00
1913 Philadelphia Athletics	6000.00	3000.00
1913 New York Giants	8000.00	4000.00
1914 Phil. Athletics	10000.00	5000.00
1914 Boston Braves	5000.00	2500.00
1915 Philadelphia Phillies	10000.00	5000.00
1915 Boston Red Sox	6000.00	3000.00
1916 Brooklyn Dodgers	4000.00	2000.00
1916 Boston Red Sox	4500.00	2200.00
1917 New York Giants	7500.00	3800.00
1917 Chicago White Sox	8000.00	4000.00
1918 Boston Red Sox	5000.00	2500.00
1919 Cincinnati Reds	4000.00	2000.00
1919 Chicago White Sox	10000.00	5000.00
1920 Cleveland Indians	3000.00	1500.00
1920 Brooklyn Dodgers	3200.00	1600.00
1921 New York Yankees	3000.00	1500.00
1921 New York Giants	3000.00	1500.00
1922 New York Yankees	3000.00	1500.00
1922 New York Giants	3000.00	1500.00
1923 New York Yankees	3200.00	1600.00
1924 Washington Senators	2000.00	1000.00
1924 New York Giants	1500.00	750.00
1925 Washington Senators	1250.00	600.00
1925 Pittsburgh Pirates	2500.00	1250.00
1926 New York Yankees	1250.00	600.00
1926 St Louis Cardinals	1500.00	750.00
1927 Pittsburgh Pirates	1200.00	600.00
1927 New York Yankees	2800.00	1400.00
1928 New York Yankees	1800.00	900.00
1928 St Louis Cardinals	800.00	400.00
1929 Chicago Cubs	2000.00	1000.00
1929 Philadelphia Athletics	900.00	450.00
1930 St Louis Cardinals	700.00	350.00
1930 Philadelphia Athletics	4000.00	2000.00
1931 Philadelphia Athletics	1000.00	500.00
1931 St Louis Cardinals	800.00	400.00
1932 New York Yankees	1000.00	500.00
1932 Chicago Cubs	2000.00	1000.00
1933 New York Giants	800.00	400.00
1933 Washington Senators	1000.00	500.00
1934 St Louis Cardinals	700.00	350.00
1934 Detroit Tigers	750.00	375.00
1935 Detroit Tigers	750.00	375.00
1935 Chicago Cubs	2500.00	1250.00
1936 New York Yankees	700.00	350.00
1936 New York Giants	350.00	180.00
1937 New York Yankees	800.00	400.00
1937 New York Giants	400.00	200.00
1938 New York Yankees	700.00	350.00
1938 Chicago Cubs	2000.00	1000.00
1939 New York Yankees	700.00	350.00
1939 Cincinnati Reds	400.00	200.00
1940 Cincinnati Reds	400.00	200.00
1940 Detroit Tigers	500.00	250.00
1941 Brooklyn Dodgers	800.00	400.00
1941 New York Yankees	700.00	350.00
1942 St Louis Cardinals	2500.00	1250.00
1942 New York Yankees	600.00	300.00
1943 St Louis Cardinals	2500.00	1250.00
1943 New York Yankees	600.00	300.00
1944 St Louis Browns	500.00	250.00
1944 St Louis Cardinals	600.00	300.00
1945 Chicago Cubs	600.00	300.00
1945 Detroit Tigers	600.00	300.00
1946 Boston Red Sox	600.00	300.00
1946 St Louis Cardinals	500.00	250.00
1947 New York Yankees	700.00	350.00
1947 Brooklyn Dodgers	900.00	450.00
1948 Cleveland Indians	500.00	250.00
1948 Boston Braves	600.00	300.00
1949 New York Yankees	600.00	300.00
1949 Brooklyn Dodgers	650.00	325.00
1950 New York Yankees	350.00	180.00
1950 Philadelphia Phillies	300.00	150.00
1951 New York Giants	200.00	100.00
1951 New York Yankee	300.00	150.00
1952 Brooklyn Dodgers	600.00	300.00
1952 New York Yankees	300.00	150.00
1953 Brooklyn Dodgers	400.00	200.00
1953 New York Yankees	300.00	150.00
1954 New York Giants	200.00	100.00
1954 Cleveland Indians	300.00	150.00
1955 Brooklyn Dodgers	600.00	300.00
1955 New York Yankees	300.00	150.00
1956 Brooklyn Dodgers	1500.00	750.00
1956 New York Yankees	300.00	150.00
1957 New York Yankees	200.00	100.00
1957 Milwaukee Braves	250.00	125.00
1958 New York Yankees	200.00	100.00
1958 Milwaukee Braves	250.00	125.00
1959 Chicago White Sox	250.00	125.00
1959 Los Angeles Dodgers	225.00	110.00
1960 Pittsburgh Pirates	325.00	160.00
1960 New York Yankees	175.00	90.00
1961 New York Yankees	175.00	90.00
1961 Cincinnati Reds	150.00	75.00
1962 San Francisco Giants	300.00	150.00
1962 New York Yankees	200.00	100.00
1962 San Francisco Giants	300.00	150.00
1963 New York Yankees	175.00	90.00
1963 Los Angeles Dodgers	200.00	100.00
1964 St Louis Cardinals	150.00	75.00
1964 New York Yankees	175.00	90.00
1965 Minnesota Twins	75.00	38.00
1965 Los Angeles Dodgers	100.00	50.00
1966 Baltimore Orioles	150.00	75.00
1966 Los Angeles Dodgers	75.00	38.00
1967 Boston Red Sox	150.00	75.00
1967 St Louis Cardinals	100.00	50.00
1968 St Louis Cardinals	75.00	38.00
1968 Detroit Tigers	150.00	75.00
1969 Baltimore Orioles	125.00	60.00
1969 New York Mets	350.00	180.00
1970 Cincinnati Reds	100.00	50.00
1970 Baltimore Orioles	100.00	50.00
1971 Baltimore Orioles	150.00	75.00
1971 Pittsburgh Pirates	125.00	60.00
1972 Oakland A's	250.00	125.00
1972 Cincinnati Reds	100.00	50.00
1973 New York Mets	150.00	75.00
1973 Oakland A's	250.00	125.00
1974 Los Angeles Dodgers	150.00	75.00
1974 Oakland A's	350.00	180.00
1975 Cincinnati Reds	150.00	75.00
1975 Boston Red Sox	250.00	125.00
1976 New York Yankees	150.00	75.00
1976 Cincinnati Reds	150.00	75.00
1977 Los Angeles Dodgers	100.00	50.00
1977 New York Yankees	150.00	75.00
1978 New York Yankees	100.00	50.00
1978 Los Angeles Dodgers	75.00	38.00
1979 Baltimore Orioles	100.00	50.00
1979 Pittsburgh Pirates	100.00	50.00
1980 Philadelphia Phillies	125.00	60.00
1980 Kansas City Royals	150.00	75.00
1981 Los Angeles Dodgers	75.00	38.00
1981 New York Yankees	100.00	50.00
1982 St Louis Cardinals	60.00	30.00
1982 Milwaukee Brewers	100.00	50.00
1983 Philadelphia Phillies	60.00	30.00
1983 Baltimore Orioles	60.00	30.00
1984 San Diego Padres	60.00	30.00
1984 Detroit Tigers	75.00	38.00
1985 St Louis Cardinals	75.00	38.00
1985 Kansas City Royals	100.00	50.00
1986 Boston Red Sox	75.00	38.00
1986 New York Mets	100.00	50.00
1987 Minnesota Twins	50.00	25.00
1987 St Louis Cardinals	50.00	25.00
1988 Los Angeles Dodgers	75.00	38.00
1988 Oakland A's	50.00	25.00
1989 Oakland A's	75.00	38.00
1989 San Francisco Giants	75.00	38.00
1990 Cincinnati Reds	125.00	60.00
1990 Oakland A's	125.00	60.00
1991 Atlanta Braves	100.00	50.00
1991 Minnesota Twins	100.00	50.00
1992 Atlanta Braves	100.00	50.00
1992 Toronto Blue Jays	125.00	60.00
1993 Philadelphia Phillies	125.00	60.00
1993 Toronto Blue Jays	125.00	60.00
1994 No Series		
1995 Cleveland Indians	150.00	75.00
1995 Atlanta Braves	150.00	75.00
1996 New York Yankees	150.00	75.00
1996 Atlanta Braves	150.00	75.00
1997 Florida Marlins	150.00	75.00
1997 Cleveland Indians	150.00	75.00
1998 San Diego Padres	150.00	75.00
1998 New York Yankees	150.00	75.00
1999 New York Yankees	150.00	75.00
1999 Atlanta Braves	150.00	75.00
2000 New York Mets	150.00	75.00
2000 New York Yankees	150.00	75.00
2001 Arizona Diamondbacks	150.00	75.00
2001 New York Yankees	150.00	75.00
2002 Anaheim Angels	150.00	75.00
2002 San Francisco Giants	150.00	75.00
2003 Florida Marlins	150.00	75.00
2003 New York Yankees	150.00	75.00

1934-99 World Series Black Bats

World Series Commemorative Black Bats are produced in limited numbers by Hillerich and Bradsby. The only bat not produced by H and B was the 1934 Tigers model. Black bats are given to various VIP's, league and team officials each December. Post 1937 Black Bats contain facsimile player signatures, usually in either green or gold ink. Pre-1938 bats are brown in color, rather than the traditional black. Beginning in 1991, the number of Black Bats issued fell sharply from previous years and command premium prices.

	Ex-Mt	VG
1934 St Louis Cardinals	3500.00	1800.00
1935 Chicago Cubs	3000.00	1500.00
1935 Detroit Tigers	3000.00	1500.00
1936 New York Giants	1500.00	750.00
1936 New York Yankees	2500.00	1250.00
1937 New York Giants	1200.00	600.00
1937 New York Yankees	2500.00	1250.00
1938 Chicago Cubs	1000.00	500.00
1938 New York Yankees	1200.00	600.00
1939 New York Yankees	1200.00	600.00
1939 Cincinnati Reds	1000.00	500.00
1940 Detroit Tigers	800.00	400.00
1940 Cincinnati Reds	1000.00	500.00
1941 Brooklyn Dodgers	1000.00	500.00
1941 New York Yankees	1500.00	750.00
1942 New York Yankees	600.00	300.00
1942 St Louis Cardinals	600.00	300.00
1943 New York Yankees	600.00	300.00
1943 St Louis Cardinals	800.00	400.00
1944 St Louis Cardinals	600.00	300.00
1944 St Louis Browns	600.00	300.00
1945 Detroit Tigers	800.00	400.00
1945 Chicago Cubs	500.00	250.00
1946 Boston Red Sox	700.00	350.00
1946 St Louis Cardinals	600.00	300.00
1947 New York Yankees	800.00	400.00
1947 Brooklyn Dodgers	1500.00	750.00
1948 Cleveland Indians	600.00	300.00
1948 Cleveland Indians	600.00	300.00
1949 New York Yankees	600.00	300.00
1949 Brooklyn Dodgers	600.00	300.00
1950 Philadelphia Phillies	500.00	250.00
1950 New York Yankees	500.00	250.00
1951 New York Giants	800.00	400.00
1951 New York Yankee	1500.00	750.00
1952 New York Yankees	600.00	300.00
1952 Brooklyn Dodgers	600.00	300.00
1953 Brooklyn Dodgers	600.00	300.00
1953 New York Yankees	500.00	250.00
1954 New York Giants	800.00	400.00
1954 Cleveland Indians	500.00	250.00
1955 New York Yankees	1000.00	500.00
1955 Brooklyn Dodgers	2000.00	1000.00
1956 Brooklyn Dodgers	800.00	400.00
1956 New York Yankees	600.00	300.00
1957 Milwaukee Braves	500.00	250.00
1957 New York Yankees	500.00	250.00
1958 New York Yankees	500.00	250.00
1958 Milwaukee Braves	500.00	250.00
1959 Chicago White Sox	800.00	400.00
1959 Los Angeles Dodgers	500.00	250.00
1960 Pittsburgh Pirates	500.00	250.00
1960 New York Yankees	500.00	250.00
1961 Cincinnati Reds	400.00	200.00
1961 New York Yankees	800.00	400.00
1962 New York Yankees	500.00	250.00
1962 San Francisco Giants	400.00	200.00
1963 Los Angeles Dodgers	500.00	250.00
1963 New York Yankees	400.00	200.00
1964 New York Yankees	400.00	200.00
1964 St Louis Cardinals	300.00	150.00
1965 Los Angeles Dodgers	400.00	200.00
1965 Minnesota Twins	300.00	150.00
1966 Los Angeles Dodgers	400.00	200.00
1966 Baltimore Orioles	400.00	200.00
1967 Boston Red Sox	500.00	250.00
1967 St Louis Cardinals	400.00	200.00
1968 St Louis Cardinals	500.00	250.00
1968 Detroit Tigers	800.00	400.00
1969 New York Mets	800.00	400.00
1969 Baltimore Orioles	400.00	200.00
1970 Cincinnati Reds	300.00	150.00
1970 Baltimore Orioles	300.00	150.00
1971 Pittsburgh Pirates	300.00	150.00
1971 Baltimore Orioles	250.00	125.00
1972 Oakland A's	300.00	150.00
1972 Cincinnati Reds	250.00	125.00
1973 New York Mets	400.00	200.00
1973 Oakland A's	300.00	150.00
1974 Los Angeles Dodgers	250.00	125.00
1974 Oakland A's	300.00	150.00
1975 Boston Red Sox	400.00	200.00
1975 Cincinnati Reds	250.00	125.00
1976 Cincinnati Reds	250.00	125.00
1976 New York Yankees	300.00	150.00
1977 Los Angeles Dodgers	300.00	150.00
1977 New York Yankees	400.00	200.00
1978 Los Angeles Dodgers	300.00	150.00
1978 New York Yankees	500.00	250.00
1979 Pittsburgh Pirates	300.00	150.00
1979 Baltimore Orioles	300.00	150.00
1980 Kansas City Royals	250.00	125.00
1980 Philadelphia Phillies	400.00	200.00
1981 Los Angeles Dodgers	300.00	150.00
1981 New York Yankees	300.00	150.00
1982 Milwaukee Brewers	250.00	125.00
1982 St Louis Cardinals	250.00	125.00
1983 Baltimore Orioles	250.00	125.00
1983 Philadelphia Phillies	300.00	150.00
1984 Detroit Tigers	500.00	250.00
1984 San Diego Padres	300.00	150.00
1985 Kansas City Royals	250.00	125.00
1985 St Louis Cardinals	250.00	125.00
1986 Boston Red Sox	300.00	150.00
1986 New York Mets	300.00	150.00
1987 Minnesota Twins	200.00	100.00
1987 St Louis Cardinals	200.00	100.00
1988 Los Angeles Dodgers	250.00	125.00
1988 Oakland A's	200.00	100.00
1989 Oakland A's	250.00	125.00
1989 San Francisco Giants	250.00	125.00
1990 Cincinnati Reds	200.00	100.00
1990 Oakland A's	200.00	100.00
1991 Atlanta Braves	800.00	400.00
1991 Minnesota Twins	1500.00	750.00
1992 Atlanta Braves	500.00	250.00
1992 Toronto Blue Jays	800.00	400.00
1993 Toronto Blue Jays	600.00	300.00
1993 Philadelphia Phillies	600.00	300.00
1994 No Series		
1995 Clevleland Indians	800.00	400.00
1995 Atlanta Braves	800.00	400.00
1996 New York Yankees	800.00	400.00
1996 Atlanta Braves	300.00	150.00
1997 Florida Marlins	500.00	250.00
1997 Cleveland Indians	500.00	250.00
1998 New York Yankees	500.00	250.00
1998 San Diego Padres	500.00	250.00
1999 Atlanta Braves	500.00	250.00
1999 New York Yankees	500.00	250.00
2000 New York Yankees	500.00	250.00
2000 New York Mets	500.00	250.00
2001 Arizona Diamondbacks	500.00	250.00
2001 New York Yankees	500.00	250.00
2002 Anaheim Angels	500.00	250.00
2002 San Francisco Giants	500.00	250.00
2003 Florida Marlins	500.00	250.00
2003 New York Yankees	500.00	250.00

1961-99 Anaheim Angels Yearbooks

The Angels did not issue Yearbooks between 1968 and 1982. Also, there was no Yearbook issued for the 1986 through 1991 season. The team was named the Los Angeles Angel from 1961 through 1965, the California Angels between 1966 and 1997, and the Anaheim Angels from 1998 to the present.

	NM	Ex
1961 First Season	125.00	50.00
1962 Yearbook	100.00	40.00
1963 Yearbook	50.00	20.00
1964 Yearbook	25.00	10.00
1965 Yearbook	25.00	10.00
1966 Yearbook	50.00	20.00
1967 Yearbook	15.00	6.00
1983 Yearbook	10.00	4.00
1984 Yearbook	10.00	4.00
1985 Yearbook	7.00	2.80
1992 To Present	10.00	4.00

1998-99 Arizona Diamondbacks Yearbooks

The Arizona Diamondbacks first season was 1998.

	Nm-Mt	Ex-Mt
1998 First Season	15.00	4.50
1999 To Present	10.00	3.00

1966-99 Atlanta Braves Yearbook

The Atlanta Braves did not issue a Yearbook for the 1989, 1991, or 1993 seasons.

	NM	Ex
1966 First Season	25.00	10.00
1967 Yearbook	15.00	6.00
1968 Yearbook	10.00	4.00
1969 Yearbook	15.00	6.00
1970 Yearbook	20.00	8.00
1971 Yearbook	10.00	4.00
1972 Yearbook	10.00	4.00
1973 Yearbook	15.00	6.00
1974 Yearbook	10.00	4.00
1975 Yearbook	12.00	4.80
1976 Yearbook	12.00	4.80
1977 Yearbook	12.00	4.80
1978 Yearbook	10.00	4.00
1979 Yearbook	12.00	4.80
1980 Yearbook	12.00	4.80
1981 Yearbook	12.00	4.80
1982 Yearbook	15.00	6.00
1983 Yearbook	10.00	4.00
1984 Yearbook	10.00	4.00
1985 Yearbook	10.00	4.00
1986 Yearbook	10.00	4.00
1987 Yearbook	10.00	4.00
1988 Yearbook	7.00	2.80
1990 Yearbook	7.00	2.80
1992 To Present	10.00	4.00

1954-99 Baltimore Orioles Yearbooks

The Orioles did not issue a yearbook between 1976 and 1979 or in 1985.

	NM	Ex
1954 First Season	250.00	125.00
1955 Yearbook	150.00	75.00
1956 Yearbook	150.00	75.00
1957 Yearbook	125.00	60.00
1958 Yearbook	150.00	75.00
1959 Yearbook	150.00	75.00
1960 Yearbook	125.00	60.00
1961 Yearbook	75.00	38.00
1962 Yearbook	100.00	50.00
1963 Oversize	75.00	38.00
1964 Oversize	75.00	38.00
1965 Oversize	75.00	38.00
1966 Yearbook	50.00	25.00
1966 Revised	50.00	25.00
1967 Yearbook	50.00	25.00
1968 Yearbook	35.00	17.50
1969 Yearbook	35.00	17.50
1970 Yearbook	25.00	12.50
1971 Yearbook	25.00	12.50
1972 Yearbook	20.00	10.00
1973 Yearbook	15.00	7.50
1974 Yearbook	15.00	7.50
1975 Yearbook	15.00	7.50
1980 Yearbook	10.00	5.00
1981 Yearbook	10.00	5.00
1982 Yearbook	12.00	6.00
1983 Yearbook	10.00	5.00
1984 Yearbook	10.00	5.00
1986 Yearbook	10.00	5.00
1987 To Present	10.00	5.00

1946-51 Boston Braves Yearbooks

This team did not issue Yearbooks during the 1948, 1949 or 1952 season. The Braves moved to Milwaukee after the 1952 season.

	Ex-Mt	VG
1946 First Year	325.00	160.00
1947 Yearbook	175.00	90.00
1950 Yearbook	150.00	75.00
1951 Yearbook	125.00	60.00

1912-99 Boston Red Sox Yearbooks

There were Yearbook-style publications issued for the Red Sox in 1912, 1936 and 1946. The team did not issue Yearbooks for the 1953 or 1954 seasons.

	Ex-Mt	VG
1912 Yearbook Style Publication		
1936 Yearbook Style Publication		
1946 Yearbook Style Publication		
1951 First Year	250.00	125.00
1952 Yearbook	125.00	60.00
1955 Yearbook	125.00	60.00
1956 Yearbook	100.00	50.00
1957 Yearbook	100.00	50.00
1958 Yearbook	75.00	38.00
1959 Yearbook	75.00	38.00
1960 Yearbook	75.00	38.00
1961 Yearbook	75.00	38.00
1962 Yearbook	50.00	25.00
1963 Yearbook	50.00	25.00
1964 Yearbook	50.00	25.00
1964 Yearbook Revised	60.00	30.00
1965 Yearbook	35.00	17.50
1966 Yearbook	50.00	25.00
1967 Yearbook	100.00	50.00
1968 Yearbook	35.00	17.50
1969 Yearbook	35.00	17.50
1970 Yearbook	35.00	17.50
1971 Yearbook	15.00	7.50
1972 Yearbook	15.00	7.50
1973 Yearbook	25.00	12.50
1974 Yearbook	10.00	5.00
1974 Yearbook Revised	10.00	5.00
1975 Yearbook	10.00	5.00
1976 Revised	10.00	5.00
1976 Yearbook	10.00	5.00
1977 Yearbook	10.00	5.00
1977 Revised	10.00	5.00
1978 Yearbook	10.00	5.00
1978 Revised	10.00	5.00
1979 Revised	12.00	6.00
1979 Yearbook	10.00	5.00
1980 Yearbook	10.00	5.00
1980 Yearbook Revised	10.00	5.00
1981 Yearbook	10.00	5.00
1982 Yearbook	10.00	5.00
1983 Yearbook	10.00	5.00
1984 Yearbook	7.00	3.50
1985 Yearbook	7.00	3.50
1986 Yearbook	7.00	3.50
1987 Yearbook	7.00	3.50
1988 Yearbook	7.00	3.50
1989 Yearbook	10.00	5.00
1990 Yearbook	10.00	5.00
1991 Yearbook	10.00	5.00
1992 To Present	10.00	5.00

1888-57 Brooklyn Dodgers Yearbooks

There was no Yearbook issued for the 1948 season. The Dodgers also had unofficial Yearbook-style publications published in 1888, 1940, 1941, 1942, and 1947. The Dodgers moved to Los Angeles after the 1957 season.

	Ex-Mt	VG
1888 Yearbook Style Publication		
1940 Yearbook Style Publication		
1941 Yearbook Style Publication		
1942 Yearbook Style Publication		
1947 First Year	125.00	60.00
1947 Yearbook Style Publication		
1949 Yearbook	250.00	125.00
1950 Yearbook	200.00	100.00
1951 Yearbook	150.00	75.00
1952 Yearbook	150.00	75.00
1953 Yearbook	150.00	75.00
1954 Yearbook	1500.00	750.00
1955 Revised	400.00	200.00
1955 Yearbook	400.00	200.00
1956 Yearbook	125.00	60.00
1957 Last Season	125.00	60.00

1919-99 Chicago Cubs Yearbooks

The Cubs did not issue Yearbooks between 1958 and 1984. There were unofficial Yearbook-style publications published in 1919, 1934, 1935, 1936, 1937, 1938, 1939, 1940, 1941, 1942 and 1946.

	Ex-Mt	VG
Yearbook		
Style Publication		
1919 Yearbook		
Style Publication		
1934 Yearbook		
Style Publication		
1935 Yearbook		
Style Publication		
1936 Yearbook		
Style Publication		
1937 Yearbook		
Style Publication		
1938 Yearbook		
Style Publication		
1939 Yearbook		
Style Publication		
1940 Yearbook		
Style Publication		
1941 Yearbook		
Style Publication		
1942 Yearbook		
Style Publication		
1948 First Year	125.00	60.00
1949 Yearbook	50.00	25.00
1950 Yearbook	50.00	25.00
1951 Yearbook	75.00	38.00
1952 Yearbook	50.00	25.00
1953 Yearbook	50.00	25.00
1954 Yearbook	50.00	25.00
1955 Yearbook	50.00	25.00
1956 Yearbook	75.00	38.00
1957 Yearbook	125.00	60.00
1985 Yearbook	10.00	5.00
1986 Yearbook	7.00	3.50
1987 Yearbook	7.00	3.50
1988 Yearbook	7.00	3.50
1989 Yearbook	7.00	3.50
1990 Yearbook	10.00	5.00
1991 Yearbook	10.00	5.00
1992 To Present	10.00	5.00

1915-99 Chicago White Sox Yearbooks

The White Sox did not issue Yearbooks from 1971 through 1981 and again in 1985, 1987 and 1989. There were unofficial Yearbook-style publications issued for the 1947, 1948, 1949 and 1950 seasons.

	Ex-Mt	VG
1915 Yearbook		
Style Publication		
1947 Yearbook		
Style Publication		
1948 Yearbook		
Style Publication		
1949 Yearbook		
Style Publication		
1950 Yearbook		
Style Publication		
1951 First Year	275.00	140.00
1952 Yearbook Revised	175.00	90.00
1952 Yearbook	150.00	75.00
1953 Yearbook	150.00	75.00
1953 Yearbook	125.00	60.00
1954 Yearbook Revised	150.00	75.00
1954 Yearbook	125.00	60.00
1955 Yearbook	100.00	50.00
1956 Yearbook	75.00	38.00
1957 Yearbook	100.00	50.00
1957 Yearbook Revised	75.00	38.00
1958 Yearbook	75.00	38.00
1959 Yearbook	125.00	60.00
1960 Yearbook	75.00	38.00
1961 Yearbook	50.00	25.00
1962 Yearbook	35.00	17.50
1963 Yearbook	20.00	10.00
1964 Pocket Book	30.00	15.00
1965 Yearbook	25.00	12.50
1966 Yearbook	35.00	17.50
1967 Yearbook	25.00	12.50
1968 Yearbook	25.00	12.50
1969 Yearbook	25.00	12.50
1970 Yearbook	35.00	17.50
1982 Yearbook	10.00	5.00
1983 Yearbook	10.00	5.00
1984 Yearbook	5.00	2.50
19865 Yearbook	10.00	5.00
1988 Yearbook	10.00	5.00
1990 Yearbook	10.00	5.00
1991 Yearbook	10.00	5.00
1992 To Present	10.00	5.00

1913-99 Cincinnati Reds Yearbooks

The Reds did not issue an Yearbook in 1950 and 1986. Unofficial Yearbook-style publications were issued in 1913, 1919 (2 different) and 1930. Very few copies of the 1913, 1919, 1930 and 1934 Yearbook style books are known so they are not priced.

	Ex-Mt	VG
1913 Yearbook		
Style Publication		
1919 Yearbook		
Style Publication		
1930 Yearbook		
Style Publicatoin		
1934 Yearbook		
Style Publication		
1947 First Year	250.00	125.00
1948 Yearbook	150.00	75.00
1949 Yearbook	225.00	110.00
1951 Yearbook	125.00	60.00
1952 Yearbook	125.00	60.00
1953 Yearbook	100.00	50.00
1954 Yearbook	100.00	50.00
1955 Red Cover	75.00	38.00
1955 Orange Cover	75.00	38.00
1956 Yearbook	75.00	38.00
1957 Yearbook Revised	75.00	38.00
1957 Yearbook	60.00	30.00
1958 Yearbook Revised	50.00	25.00
1958 Yearbook	50.00	25.00
1959 Yearbook	50.00	25.00
1959 Yearbook Spring	50.00	25.00
1960 Yearbook	35.00	17.50
1961 Yearbook	35.00	17.50
1962 Yearbook April/May	60.00	30.00
1962 Yearbook Spring	50.00	25.00
1962 Yearbook	35.00	17.50
1963 Yearbook	60.00	30.00
1963 Yearbook Revised	75.00	38.00
1964 Yearbook	35.00	17.50
1965 Yearbook	35.00	17.50
1966 Yearbook	35.00	17.50
1967 Yearbook	25.00	12.50
1968 Yearbook	25.00	12.50
1969 Yearbook	25.00	12.50
1970 Yearbook	25.00	12.50
1971 Yearbook	15.00	7.50
1972 Yearbook	10.00	5.00
1973 Yearbook	10.00	5.00
1974 Yearbook	15.00	7.50
1975 Yearbook	15.00	7.50
1976 Yearbook	15.00	7.50
1977 Yearbook	10.00	5.00
1977 Yearbook Revised	10.00	5.00
1978 Yearbook	10.00	5.00
1979 Yearbook	10.00	5.00
1980 Yearbook	10.00	5.00
1980 Yearbook Revised	10.00	5.00
1981 Yearbook	10.00	5.00
1982 Yearbook	10.00	5.00
1983 Yearbook	10.00	5.00
1984 Yearbook	10.00	5.00
1985 Yearbook	7.00	3.50
1987 Yearbook	7.00	3.50
1988 Yearbook	7.00	3.50
1989 Yearbook	7.00	3.50
1990 Yearbook	7.00	3.50
1991 Yearbook	7.00	3.50
1992 To Present	10.00	5.00

1918-99 Cleveland Indians Yearbooks

The Clevleland Indians did not issue a Yearbook between 1974 and 1983, and again between 1985 through 1988 and the strike season of 1994. The 1918 Yearbook is very rare so no pricing is provided.

	Ex-Mt	VG
1918 Yearbook		
Style Publication		
1928 Yearbook		
Style Publication		
1948 First Year	150.00	75.00
1949 Yearbook	60.00	30.00
1950 Yearbook	60.00	30.00
1951 Yearbook	75.00	38.00
1952 Yearbook	75.00	38.00
1953 Yearbook	100.00	50.00
1954 Yearbook	100.00	50.00
1955 Yearbook	75.00	38.00
1956 Yearbook	75.00	38.00
1957 Yearbook	100.00	50.00
1958 Yearbook	300.00	150.00
1959 Yearbook	200.00	100.00
1960 Yearbook	100.00	50.00
1961 Yearbook	100.00	50.00
1962 Oversize	75.00	38.00
1963 Oversize	100.00	50.00
1964 Yearbook	75.00	38.00
1965 Yearbook	75.00	38.00
1966 Yearbook	60.00	30.00
1967 Yearbook	60.00	30.00
1968 Oversize	40.00	20.00
1969 Yearbook	25.00	12.50
1970 Yearbook	15.00	7.50
1971 Yearbook	10.00	5.00
1972 Yearbook	10.00	5.00
1973 Yearbook	8.00	4.00
1984 Yearbook	10.00	5.00
1989 Yearbook	10.00	5.00
1990 Yearbook	10.00	5.00
1991 Yearbook	10.00	5.00
1992 To Present	10.00	5.00

1912-99 Detroit Tigers Yearbooks

The Tigers did not issue a Yearbook for the 1956 and 1993 seasons. There were Yearbook-style publications published for the Tigers in 1912, 1934, 1935 and 1939.

	Ex-Mt	VG
1912 Yearbook		
Style Publication		
1934 Yearbook		
Style Publication		
1934 Yearbook		
Style Publication		
1935 Yearbook		
Style Publication		
1939 Yearbook		
Style Publication		
1955 First Year	300.00	150.00
1957 Yearbook	150.00	75.00
1958 Yearbook	150.00	75.00
1959 Yearbook	150.00	75.00
1960 Yearboook	125.00	60.00
1961 Yearbook	100.00	50.00
1962 Yearbook	100.00	50.00
1963 Yearbook	100.00	50.00
1964 Yearbook	75.00	38.00
1965 Yearbook	75.00	38.00
1966 Yearbook	50.00	25.00
1967 Yearbook	50.00	25.00
1968 Yearbook	75.00	38.00
1969 Yearbook	50.00	25.00
1970 Yearbook	12.00	6.00
1971 Yearbook	20.00	10.00
1972 Yearbook	10.00	5.00
1973 Yearbook	10.00	5.00
1974 Yearbook	10.00	5.00
1975 Yearbook	12.00	6.00
1976 Yearbook	10.00	5.00
1977 Yearbook	12.00	6.00
1978 Yearbook	12.00	6.00
1979 Yearbook	10.00	5.00
1980 Yearbook	10.00	5.00
1981 Yearbook	10.00	5.00
1982 Yearbook	12.00	6.00
1983 Yearbook	7.00	3.50
1984 Yearbook	12.00	6.00
1985 Yearbook	10.00	5.00
1986 Yearbook	10.00	5.00
1987 Yearbook	10.00	5.00
1988 Yearbook	10.00	5.00
1989 Yearbook	10.00	5.00
1990 Yearbook	10.00	5.00
1991 Yearbook	10.00	5.00
1992 To Present	10.00	5.00

1962-99 Houston Astros Yearbooks

The Houston franchise was known as the Colt 45's between 1962 and 1964. The Astros did not issue a Yearbook for the 1967, 1980 or 1981 seasons. Also, no Yearbooks were issued between 1969-1971, 1973-1976 and 1983-1991.

	NM	Ex
1962 First Season	150.00	60.00
1963 Yearbook	150.00	60.00
1964 Yearbook	125.00	50.00
1965 Yearbook	100.00	40.00
1966 Yearbook	75.00	30.00
1968 Yearbook	50.00	20.00
1972 Yearbook	35.00	14.00
1977 Yearbook	15.00	6.00
1978 Yearbook	15.00	6.00
1979 Yearbook	15.00	6.00
1982 Yearbook	15.00	6.00
1992 To Present	10.00	4.00

1955-67 Kansas City Athletics Yearbooks

The Athletics played in Kansas City between 1955 and 1967. After the 1967 season, they moved to Oakland.

	NM	Ex
1955 First Season	150.00	75.00
Black Cover		
1955 First Season	125.00	60.00
Yellow Cover		
1956 Yearbook	125.00	60.00
1956 Yearbook Revised	150.00	75.00
1957 Yearbook Revised	150.00	75.00
1957 Yearbook	125.00	60.00
1958 Yearbook	150.00	75.00
1959 Yearbook	150.00	75.00
1960 Yearbook	125.00	60.00
1961 Yearbook	125.00	60.00
1962 Yearbook	100.00	50.00
1963 Yearbook	100.00	50.00
1964 Yearbook	100.00	50.00
1965 Yearbook	75.00	38.00
1966 Yearbook	75.00	38.00
1967 Final Season	50.00	25.00
1967R Final Season Revised	60.00	30.00

1969-99 Kansas City Royals Yearbooks

The Kansas City Royals begin playing in 1969. They did not issue Yearbooks between 1976 and 1982.

	NM	Ex
1969 First Season	25.00	10.00
1970 Yearbook	15.00	6.00
1971 Yearbook	15.00	6.00
1972 Yearbook	10.00	4.00
1973 Yearbook	10.00	4.00
1974 Yearbook	10.00	4.00
1975 Yearbook	15.00	6.00
1983 Yearbook	10.00	4.00
1984 Yearbook	10.00	4.00
1985 Yearbook	10.00	4.00
1986 Yearbook	10.00	4.00
1987 Yearbook	10.00	4.00
1988 Yearbook	10.00	4.00
1989 Yearbook	10.00	4.00
1990 Yearbook	10.00	4.00
1991 Yearbook	10.00	4.00
1992 To Present	10.00	4.00

1958-99 Los Angeles Dodgers Yearbooks

The Dodgers began playing in Los Angeles in 1958.

	NM	Ex
1958 First Season	175.00	90.00
1959 Yearbook	75.00	38.00
1960 Yearbook	50.00	25.00
1961 Yearbook	50.00	25.00
1962 Yearbook	25.00	12.50
1963 Yearbook	50.00	25.00
1964 Yearbook	10.00	5.00
1965 Yearbook	25.00	12.50
1966 Yearbook	20.00	10.00
1967 Yearbook	10.00	5.00
1968 Yearbook	10.00	5.00
1969 Yearbook	10.00	5.00
1970 Yearbook	10.00	5.00
1971 Yearbook	10.00	5.00
1972 Yearbook	15.00	7.50
1973 Yearbook	10.00	5.00
1974 Yearbook	10.00	5.00
1975 Yearbook	10.00	5.00
1976 Yearbook	10.00	5.00
1977 Yearbook	10.00	5.00
1978 Yearbook	10.00	5.00
1979 Yearbook	10.00	5.00
1980 Yearbook	10.00	5.00
1981 Yearbook	10.00	5.00
1982 Yearbook	10.00	5.00
1983 Yearbook	10.00	5.00
1984 Yearbook	10.00	5.00
1984 Yearbook Spanish	15.00	7.50
1985 Yearbook	10.00	5.00
1986 Yearbook	10.00	5.00
1987 Yearbook	10.00	5.00
1988 Yearbook	10.00	5.00
1989 Yearbook	10.00	5.00
1990 Yearbook	10.00	5.00
1991 Yearbook	10.00	5.00
1992 To Present	10.00	5.00

1953-65 Milwaukee Braves Yearbooks

The Braves played in Milwaukee between 1953 and 1965.

	NM	Ex
1953 First Season	150.00	75.00
1954 Yearbook	100.00	50.00
1954 Yearbook Revised	125.00	60.00
1955 Yearbook	75.00	38.00
1956 Yearbook	125.00	60.00
1957 Yearbook	125.00	60.00
1958 Yearbook	125.00	60.00
1959 Yearbook	75.00	38.00
1960 Yearbook	75.00	38.00
1961 Yearbook	60.00	30.00
1961 Yearbook Bob Allen	75.00	38.00
1962 Yearbook	50.00	25.00
1963 Yearbook	50.00	25.00
1964 Yearbook	50.00	25.00
1965 Yearbook	50.00	25.00

1970-99 Milwaukee Brewers Yearbooks

The Brewers moved to Milwaukee at the beginning of the 1970 season. The Brewers did not issue a Yearbook between 1971 and 1978 and in 1993.

	NM	Ex
1970 First Season	50.00	20.00
1979 Yearbook	10.00	4.00
1980 Yearbook	10.00	4.00
1981 Yearbook	10.00	4.00
1982 Yearbook	15.00	6.00
1983 Yearbook	10.00	4.00
1983 Yearbook Revised	10.00	4.00
1984 Yearbook	10.00	4.00
1985 Yearbook	10.00	4.00
1986 Yearbook	10.00	4.00
1987 Yearbook	10.00	4.00
1988 Yearbook	10.00	4.00
1989 Yearbook	10.00	4.00
1990 Yearbook	10.00	4.00
1991 Yearbook	10.00	4.00
1992 To Present	10.00	4.00

1961-99 Minnesota Twins Yearbooks

The Twins began playing in Minnesota in 1961. The Twins did not issued Yearbooks in 1983, 1984 and 1993.

	NM	Ex
1961 First Season	175.00	70.00
1962 Yearbook	125.00	50.00
1963 Yearbook	100.00	40.00
1964 Yearbook	50.00	20.00
1965 Yearbook	50.00	20.00
1966 Yearbook	50.00	20.00
1967 Yearbook	25.00	10.00
1968 Yearbook	20.00	8.00
1969 Yearbook	20.00	8.00
1970 Yearbook	15.00	6.00
1971 Yearbook	20.00	8.00
1972 Yearbook	15.00	6.00
1973 Yearbook	10.00	4.00
1974 Yearbook	20.00	8.00
1975 Yearbook	15.00	6.00
1976 Yearbook	25.00	10.00
1977 Yearbook	10.00	4.00
1978 Yearbook	10.00	4.00
1979 Yearbook	10.00	4.00
1980 Yearbook	10.00	4.00
1981 Yearbook	10.00	4.00
1982 Yearbook	10.00	4.00
1985 Yearbook	10.00	4.00
1986 Yearbook	10.00	4.00
1986 Yearbook	10.00	4.00
1987 Yearbook	10.00	4.00
1988 Yearbook	10.00	4.00
1989 Yearbook	10.00	4.00
1990 Yearbook	10.00	4.00
1991 Yearbook	10.00	4.00
1992 Yearbook	10.00	4.00
1994 To Present	10.00	4.00

1969-99 Montreal Expos Yearbooks

The Expos first season was 1969. The Expos revised its Yearbook three times each during the 1969 through 1972 seasons. All revisions have equal value. The team did not issue an Yearbook between 1973 and 1981 and again between 1987 and 1993.

	NM	Ex
1969 First Season	40.00	16.00
1970 Yearbook	50.00	20.00
1971 Yearbook	40.00	16.00
1972 Yearbook	40.00	16.00
1982 Yearbook	10.00	4.00
1983 Yearbook	10.00	4.00
1984 Yearbook	10.00	4.00
1985 Yearbook	10.00	4.00
1986 Yearbook	10.00	4.00
1994 To Present	10.00	4.00

1887-57 New York Giants Yearbooks

The Giants did not issue an Yearbook for the 1948 through the 1950 seasons. There were Yearbook-style publications issued for the Giants in 1887, 1888 and 1889. The Giants moved to San Francisco after the 1957 season.

	Ex-Mt	VG
1887 Yearbook Style Publication		
1888 Yearbook Style Publication		
1889 Yearbook Style Publication		
1947 First Year	150.00	75.00
1951 Yearbook	125.00	60.00
1952 Yearbook	100.00	50.00
1953 Yearbook	100.00	50.00
1954 Yearbook	100.00	50.00
1955 Yearbook	125.00	60.00
1956 Yearbook	100.00	50.00
1957 Final Season	100.00	50.00

1962-99 New York Mets Yearbooks

The New York Mets first season was 1962.

	NM	Ex
1962 First Season	350.00	140.00
1963 Yearbook	150.00	60.00
1963 Yearbook Edition 2	125.00	50.00
1963 Yearbook Edition 3	150.00	60.00
1964 Yearbook Edition 2	50.00	20.00
1964 Yearbook Edition 3	60.00	24.00
1964 Yearbook	50.00	20.00
1965 Yearbook Edition 2	60.00	24.00
1965 Yearbook	50.00	20.00
1965 Yearbook Edition 3	60.00	24.00
1966 Yearbook Edition 2	50.00	20.00
1966 Yearbook Edition 3	60.00	24.00
1966 Yearbook	50.00	20.00
1967 Yearbook Edition 2	50.00	20.00
1967 Yearbook	50.00	20.00
1967 Yearbook Edition 3	60.00	24.00
1968 Yearbook	50.00	20.00
1968 Yearbook Revised	50.00	20.00
1969 Yearbook	100.00	40.00
1970 Yearbook	35.00	14.00
1971 Yearbook	25.00	10.00
1971 Yearbook Revised	35.00	14.00
1972 Yearbook Revised	15.00	6.00
1972 Yearbook	15.00	6.00
1973 Yearbook Revised	15.00	6.00
1973 Yearbook	15.00	6.00
1974 Yearbook	15.00	6.00
1974 Yearbook Revised	15.00	6.00
1975 Yearbook	15.00	6.00
1975 Yearbook Revised	15.00	6.00
1976 Yearbook	15.00	6.00
1976 Yearbook Revised	15.00	6.00
1977 Yearbook Revised	10.00	4.00
1977 Yearbook	15.00	6.00
1978 Yearbook	10.00	4.00
1979 Yearbook	10.00	4.00
1980 Yearbook	20.00	8.00
1981 Yearbook	15.00	6.00
1982 Yearbook	15.00	6.00
1982 Yearbook Revised	10.00	4.00
1983 Yearbook	15.00	6.00
1983 Yearbook Revised	20.00	8.00
1984 Yearbook Revised	20.00	8.00
1984 Yearbook	20.00	8.00
1985 Yearbook	20.00	8.00
1985 Yearbook Revised	20.00	8.00
1986 Yearbook	20.00	8.00
1986 Yearbook Revised	20.00	8.00
1987 Yearbook Revised	15.00	6.00
1987 Yearbook	10.00	4.00
1988 Yearbook Revised	15.00	6.00
1988 Yearbook	10.00	4.00
1989 Yearbook	10.00	4.00
1989 Yearbook Revised	15.00	6.00
1990 Yearbook Revised	15.00	6.00
1990 Yearbook	10.00	4.00
1991 Yearbook Revised	15.00	6.00
1991 Yearbook	10.00	4.00
1992 To Present	10.00	4.00

1950-99 New York Yankees Yearbooks

Jay Publishing issued unofficial Yankee Yearbooks between 1952 and 1965. The Jay Yearbooks were available through various mail order sources and souvenir outlets outside Yankee Stadium.

	NM	Ex
1950 First Year	325.00	160.00
1951 Yearbook	200.00	100.00
1952 Yearbook	150.00	75.00
1952 Yearbook Jay	100.00	50.00
1953 Yearbook Jay	100.00	50.00
1953 Yearbook	150.00	75.00
1954 Yearbook Jay	100.00	50.00
1954 Yearbook	150.00	75.00
1955 Yearbook Jay	100.00	50.00
1955 Yearbook Revised	250.00	125.00
1955 Yearbook	275.00	140.00
1956 Yearbook Jay	75.00	38.00
1956 Yearbook	125.00	60.00
1956 Yearbook Revised	125.00	60.00
1957 Yearbook	225.00	110.00
1957 Yearbook Revised	225.00	110.00
1957 Yearbook Jay	75.00	38.00
1958 Yearbook Revised	150.00	75.00
1958 Yearbook	150.00	75.00
1958 Yearbook Jay	75.00	38.00
1959 Yearbook Revised	150.00	75.00
1959 Yearbook Jay	75.00	38.00
1959 Yearbook	150.00	75.00
1960 Yearbook	150.00	75.00
1960 Yearbook Jay	75.00	38.00
1960 Yearbook Revised	150.00	75.00
1961 Yearbook Revised	175.00	90.00
1961 Yearboook	150.00	75.00
1961 Yearbook Jay	75.00	38.00
1962 Yearbook Edition 2	100.00	50.00
1962 Yearbook Edition 3	100.00	50.00
1962 Yearbook	100.00	50.00
1962 Yearbook Edition 4	100.00	50.00
1962 Yearbook Jay	60.00	30.00
1963 Yearbook Jay	40.00	20.00
1963 Yearbook	75.00	38.00
1963 Yearbook Revised	75.00	38.00
1964 Yearbook Edition 2	75.00	38.00
1964 Yearbook Jay	35.00	17.50
1964 Yearbook Edition 4	75.00	38.00
1964 Yearbook Edition 3	75.00	38.00
1964 Yearbook	75.00	38.00
1965 Yearbook Jay	60.00	30.00
1965 Yearbook	35.00	17.50
1965 Yearbook Revised	60.00	30.00
1966 Yearbook Edition 2	50.00	25.00
1966 Yearbook	50.00	25.00
1966 Yearbook Edition 4	50.00	25.00
1966 Yearbook Edition 3	50.00	25.00
1967 Yearbook Revised	50.00	25.00
1967 Yearbook	50.00	25.00
1968 Yearbook	25.00	12.50
1969 Yearbook	40.00	20.00
1970 Yearbook	60.00	30.00
1971 Yearbook	7.00	3.50
1972 Yearbook	15.00	7.50
1973 Yearbook	15.00	7.50
1974 Yearbook	15.00	7.50
1975 Yearbook	15.00	7.50
1976 Yearbook	20.00	10.00
1977 Yearbook	10.00	5.00
1978 Yearbook	10.00	5.00
1979 Yearbook	10.00	5.00
1980 Yearbook	10.00	5.00
1981 Yearbook	15.00	7.50
1982 Yearbook	7.00	3.50
1983 Yearbook	7.00	3.50
1984 Yearbook	10.00	5.00
1985 Yearbook	7.00	3.50
1986 Yearbook	10.00	5.00
1987 Yearbook	7.00	3.50
1988 Yearbook	10.00	5.00
1989 Yearbook	10.00	5.00
1990 Yearbook	10.00	5.00
1991 Yearbook	10.00	5.00
1992 To Present	10.00	5.00

1968-99 Oakland Athletics Yearbooks

The Athletics began play in Oakland in 1968. The A's did not issue Yearbooks in 1978, 1980, 1981 or between the 1984 and the 1993 seasons.

	NM	Ex
1968 First Season	40.00	16.00
1969 Yearbook	20.00	8.00
1970 Yearbook	20.00	8.00
1971 Yearbook	20.00	8.00
1972 Yearbook	20.00	8.00
1973 Yearbook	20.00	8.00
1974 Yearbook	15.00	6.00
1975 Yearbook	15.00	6.00
1976 Yearbook	15.00	6.00
1977 Yearbook	10.00	4.00
1979 Yearbook	10.00	4.00
1982 Yearbook	10.00	4.00
1983 Yearbook	10.00	4.00
1984 To Present	10.00	4.00

1949-54 Philadelphia Athletics Yearbooks

The Athletics moved to Kansas City after the 1954 season.

	NM	Ex
1949 First Year	60.00	30.00
1950 Yearbook	50.00	25.00
1951 Yearbook	50.00	25.00
1952 Yearbook	50.00	25.00
1953 Yearbook	20.00	10.00
1954 Final Season	35.00	17.50

1949-99 Philadelphia Phillies Yearbooks

	NM	Ex
1949 First Year	250.00	125.00
1950 Yearbook	200.00	100.00
1951 Yearbook	425.00	210.00
1952 Yearbook	100.00	50.00
1953 Yearbook	30.00	15.00
1954 Yearbook	100.00	50.00
1955 Yearbook	125.00	60.00
1956 Yearbook	150.00	75.00
1957 Yearbook	100.00	50.00
1958 Yearbook	100.00	50.00
1959 Yearbook	75.00	38.00
1960 Yearbook	75.00	38.00
1961 Yearbook Revised	150.00	75.00
1961 Yearbook	125.00	60.00
1962 Yearbook	100.00	50.00
1963 Yearbook	100.00	50.00
1964 Yearbook Edition 2	100.00	50.00
1964 Yearbook	75.00	38.00
1964 Yearbook Edition 3	100.00	50.00
1965 Yearbook	60.00	30.00
1966 Yearbook	50.00	25.00
1967 Yearbook	50.00	25.00
1968 Yearbook	50.00	25.00
1969 Yearbook	50.00	25.00
1970 Yearbook	40.00	20.00
1971 Yearbook	40.00	20.00
1972 Yearbook	25.00	12.50
1973 Yearbook	35.00	17.50
1974 Yearbook	20.00	10.00
1975 Yearbook	25.00	12.50
1976 Yearbook	10.00	5.00
1977 Yearbook	10.00	5.00
1977 Yearbook Revised	12.00	6.00
1978 Yearbook	10.00	5.00
1979 Yearbook	10.00	5.00
1980 Yearbook	20.00	10.00
1981 Yearbook	20.00	10.00
1982 Yearbook	10.00	5.00
1983 Yearbook	10.00	5.00
1984 Yearbook	7.00	3.50
1985 Yearbook	7.00	3.50
1986 Yearbook	10.00	5.00
1987 Yearbook	7.00	3.50
1988 Yearbook	10.00	5.00
1989 Yearbook	10.00	5.00
1990 Yearbook	10.00	5.00
1991 Yearbook	10.00	5.00
1992 To Present	10.00	5.00

1951-99 Pittsburgh Pirates Yearbooks

	NM	Ex
1951 First Year	250.00	125.00
1952 Yearbook	150.00	75.00
1953 Yearbook	100.00	50.00
1954 Yearbook	100.00	50.00
1955 Yearbook	125.00	60.00
1956 Yearbook	100.00	50.00
1957 Yearbook	100.00	50.00
1958 Yearbook	75.00	38.00
1959 Yearbook	75.00	38.00
1960 Yearbook	75.00	38.00
1961 Yearbook	50.00	25.00
1962 Yearbook Revised	50.00	25.00
1962 Yearbook	35.00	17.50
1963 Yearbook	35.00	17.50
1964 Yearbook	20.00	10.00
1965 Yearbook	25.00	12.50
1966 Yearbook	25.00	12.50
1967 Yearbook	25.00	12.50
1968 Yearbook	20.00	10.00
1969 Yearbook	20.00	10.00
1970 Yearbook	60.00	30.00
1971 Yearbook	60.00	30.00
1972 Yearbook	15.00	7.50
1973 Yearbook	15.00	7.50
1974 Yearbook	15.00	7.50
1975 Yearbook	10.00	5.00
1976 Yearbook	7.00	3.50
1977 Yearbook	7.00	3.50
1978 Yearbook	7.00	3.50
1979 Yearbook	15.00	7.50
1980 Yearbook	7.00	3.50
1981 Yearbook	7.00	3.50
1982 Yearbook	7.00	3.50
1983 Yearbook	7.00	3.50
1984 Yearbook	7.00	3.50
1985 Yearbook	7.00	3.50
1986 Yearbook	10.00	5.00
1987 Yearbook	10.00	5.00
1988 Yearbook	10.00	5.00
1989 Yearbook	10.00	5.00
1990 Yearbook	10.00	5.00
1991 Yearbook	10.00	5.00
1992 To Present	10.00	5.00

1969-99 San Diego Padres Yearbooks

The Padres first season was 1969. The Padres did not issue Yearbooks from 1970 through 1978, 1981 or 1987 through 1991.

	NM	Ex
1969 First Season	75.00	30.00
1979 Yearbook	7.00	2.80
1980 Yearbook	7.00	2.80
1982 Yearbook	10.00	4.00
1983 Yearbook	10.00	4.00
1984 Yearbook	10.00	4.00
1985 Yearbook	10.00	4.00
1986 Yearbook	10.00	4.00
1992 To Present	10.00	4.00

1958-99 San Francisco Giants Yearbooks

The Giants first season in San Francisco was 1958. The Giants did not issue a Yearbook between 1977 and 1979, 1986, 1991 and 1993.

	NM	Ex
1958 First Season	275.00	140.00
1959 Yearbook Revised	125.00	60.00
1959 Yearbook	100.00	50.00
1960 Yearbook	60.00	30.00
1961 Yearbook	60.00	30.00
1962 Yearbook	50.00	25.00
1963 Yearbook	50.00	25.00
1964 Yearbook	35.00	17.50
1965 Yearbook	35.00	17.50
1966 Yearbook	40.00	20.00
1967 Yearbook	25.00	12.50
1968 Yearbook	25.00	12.50
1969 Yearbook	25.00	12.50
1970 Yearbook	25.00	12.50
1971 Yearbook	15.00	7.50
1972 Yearbook	10.00	5.00
1973 Yearbook	10.00	5.00
1974 Yearbook	10.00	5.00
1975 Yearbook	10.00	5.00
1976 Yearbook	15.00	7.50
1980 Yearbook	10.00	5.00
1981 Yearbook	15.00	7.50
1982 Yearbook	10.00	5.00
1983 Yearbook	10.00	5.00
1984 Yearbook	10.00	5.00
1985 Yearbook	10.00	5.00
1992 Yearbook	10.00	5.00
1994 To Present	10.00	5.00

1977-94 Seattle Mariners Yearbooks

The Mariners first season was 1977.

	NM	Ex
1977 First Season	50.00	20.00
1985 Yearbook	15.00	6.00
1994 To Present	10.00	4.00

1969 Seattle Pilots Yearbook

The Pilots only season in the American League was in 1969.

	NM	Ex
1969 First and Last Season	175.00	70.00

1937-53 St. Louis Browns Yearbooks

The Browns moved to Baltimore after the 1953 season. No pricing is provided for the 1937 style publication

	Ex-Mt	VG
1937 Yearbook Style Publication		
1944 First Year	300.00	150.00
1945 Yearbook	250.00	125.00
1946 Yearbook	250.00	125.00
1947 Yearbook	250.00	125.00
1948 Yearbook	200.00	100.00
1949 Yearbook	200.00	100.00
1950 Yearbook	275.00	140.00
1951 Yearbook	200.00	100.00
1952 Yearbook	250.00	125.00
1953 Final Season	250.00	125.00

1951-99 St. Louis Cardinals Yearbooks

The Cardinals did not issue a Yearbook in 1978 and from the 1981 through the 1988 seasons.

	NM	Ex
1951 First Year	250.00	125.00
1952 Yearbook	150.00	75.00
1953 Yearbook	150.00	75.00
1954 Yearbook	125.00	60.00
1955 Yearbook	100.00	50.00
1956 Yearbook	75.00	38.00
1957 Yearbook	75.00	38.00
1958 Yearbook	75.00	38.00
1959 Yearbook	60.00	30.00
1960 Yearbook	60.00	30.00
1961 Yearbook	50.00	25.00
1962 Yearbook	50.00	25.00
1963 Yearbook	50.00	25.00
1964 Yearbook	40.00	20.00
1965 Yearbook	40.00	20.00
1966 Yearbook	50.00	25.00
1967 Yearbook	60.00	30.00
1968 Yearbook	35.00	17.50
1969 Yearbook	25.00	12.50
1970 Yearbook	15.00	7.50
1971 Yearbook	15.00	7.50
1972 Yearbook	15.00	7.50
1973 Yearbook	20.00	10.00
1974 Yearbook	15.00	7.50
1975 Yearbook	20.00	10.00
1976 Yearbook	15.00	7.50
1977 Yearbook	15.00	7.50
1979 Yearbook	10.00	5.00
1980 Yearbook	10.00	5.00
1989 Yearbook	10.00	5.00
1990 Yearbook	10.00	5.00
1991 Yearbook	10.00	5.00
1992 To Present	10.00	5.00

1998-99 Tampa Bay Devil Rays Yearbooks

The Devil Ray first season was 1998.

	Nm-Mt	Ex-Mt
1998 First Season	15.00	4.50
1999 To Present	10.00	3.00

1976-99 Texas Rangers Yearbooks

The Rangers first season in Texas was 1972. The Rangers did not issue a Yearbook in the 1983 and 1986 through 1989 seasons.

	NM	Ex

1976 First Year	20.00	8.00
1977 Yearbook	15.00	6.00
1978 Yearbook	20.00	8.00
1979 Yearbook	10.00	4.00
1980 Yearbook	15.00	6.00
1981 Yearbook	10.00	4.00
1982 Yearbook	10.00	4.00
1984 Yearbook	10.00	4.00
1985 Yearbook	10.00	4.00
1990 Yearbook	10.00	4.00
1991 Yearbook	10.00	4.00
1992 To Present	10.00	4.00

1977-99 Toronto Blue Jays Yearbooks

The Blue Jays first season was 1977. The Blue Jays did not issue a Yearbook for the 1978 season.

	NM	Ex
1977 First Season	15.00	6.00
1979 Yearbook	10.00	4.00
1980 Yearbook	20.00	8.00
1981 Yearbook	15.00	6.00
1982 Yearbook	15.00	6.00
1983 Yearbook	15.00	6.00
1984 Yearbook	15.00	6.00
1985 Yearbook	15.00	6.00
1986 Yearbook	12.00	4.80
1987 Yearbook	10.00	4.00
1988 Yearbook	10.00	4.00
1989 Yearbook	10.00	4.00
1990 Yearbook	10.00	4.00
1991 Yearbook	12.00	4.80
1992 To Present	10.00	4.00

1947-69 Washington Senators Yearbooks

There were two different Senator franchises. The first one moved to Minnesota at the end of the 1960 season. The second one was created for the 1961 season and moved to Texas at the end of the 1971 season. The Washington team was also known as the Nationals in the 1940's and early 50's. The team did not issue a Yearbook in 1948, 1951, 1970 and 1971.

	NRMT	VG-E
1947 First Year	400.00	180.00
1949 Yearbook	300.00	135.00
1950 Yearbook	300.00	135.00
1952 Yearbook	120.00	55.00
1953 Yearbook	25.00	11.00
1954 Yearbook	80.00	36.00
1955 Yearbook	80.00	36.00
1956 Yearbook	100.00	45.00
1957 Yearbook	100.00	45.00
1958 Yearbook Revised	100.00	45.00
1958 Yearbook	80.00	36.00
1959 Yearbook	50.00	22.00
1960 Yearbook	50.00	22.00
1961 First Season	150.00	70.00
Second Franchise		
1962 Yearbook	60.00	27.00
1963 Yearbook	25.00	11.00
1963 Yearbook Revised	40.00	18.00
1964 Yearbook	25.00	11.00
1965 Yearbook	25.00	11.00
1966 Yearbook	20.00	9.00
1967 Yearbook	25.00	11.00
1968 Yearbook	20.00	9.00
1969 Yearbook	20.00	9.00

STATUES

2000 McFarlane Baseball

COMPLETE SET (6)	40.00	80.00
Barry Bonds	10.00	20.00
Chipper Jones	9.00	18.00
Mark McGwire	10.00	20.00
Manny Ramirez	9.00	18.00
Alex Rodriguez	9.00	18.00
Sammy Sosa	10.00	20.00

2000 McFarlane Baseball SportsPicks

BABBAGE'S EXCLUSIVE		
McGwire/Ramirez	18.00	30.00

2002 McFarlane Baseball

COMPLETE SERIES I (8)	50.00	90.00
COMPLETE SERIES II (9)	60.00	100.00
COMPLETE SERIES III (8)	40.00	70.00
PIECES IN ALPHA ORDER BY SERIES		
SERIES $ FOR COMMON VERSIONS ONLY		
Shawn Green White	6.00	10.00
Shawn Green Blue	15.00	25.00
Randy Johnson Black	7.00	12.00
R.Johnson Black w/Stripes		
Randy Johnson Purple	20.00	35.00
R.Johnson Purple w/Stripes		
Pedro Martinez White	7.00	12.00
Pedro Martinez Grey	15.00	25.00
Mike Piazza Black	7.00	12.00
Mike Piazza White	18.00	30.00
Albert Pujols Grey FP	10.00	18.00
Albert Pujols White	20.00	35.00
Ivan Rodriguez Grey	7.00	12.00
Ivan Rodriguez Blue	18.00	30.00
Sammy Sosa Blue	7.00	12.00
Sammy Sosa Grey	15.00	25.00
Ichiro Suzuki White FP	12.00	20.00
Ichiro Suzuki Grey	25.00	40.00
Barry Bonds Black	10.00	18.00
Barry Bonds Black Glossy	18.00	30.00
Barry Bonds White	20.00	40.00
Barry Bonds BLC	20.00	40.00
Roger Clemens Grey	7.00	12.00
Nomar Garciaparra White	7.00	12.00
Nomar Garciaparra Grey	12.00	20.00
Shawn Green BLC	15.00	25.00
Ken Griffey Jr. Grey	7.00	12.00
Derek Jeter White	7.00	12.00
Greg Maddux White	7.00	12.00
Greg Maddux Grey	15.00	25.00
Mike Piazza BLC	15.00	25.00
Manny Ramirez Grey	7.00	12.00
Manny Ramirez White	15.00	25.00
Alex Rodriguez White	7.00	12.00
Alex Rodriguez Blue	15.00	30.00
Kerry Wood Grey	6.00	10.00
Roberto Alomar Grey	6.00	10.00
Roberto Alomar White	10.00	18.00
Roger Clemens Red Sox	60.00	20.00
Adam Dunn Grey FP	6.00	10.00
Jason Giambi Grey	6.00	10.00
Juan Gonzalez Blue	6.00	10.00
Juan Gonzalez White	10.00	18.00
Ken Griffey Jr. Mariners	40.00	70.00
Vladimir Guerrero Grey	6.00	10.00
Vladimir Guerrero Blue	10.00	18.00
Chipper Jones Grey	6.00	10.00
Chipper Jones White	12.00	20.00
Chipper Jones BLC	10.00	18.00
R.Oswalt Red/White Astros FP	6.00	10.00
R.Oswalt Red/Grey Houston	12.00	20.00
Curt Schilling White	6.00	10.00
Curt Schilling Grey	10.00	18.00
Sammy Sosa BLC	12.00	20.00

2002 McFarlane Baseball Club Exclusives

COMP.SET (2)	20.00	40.00
Nomar Garciaparra BLC	12.00	20.00
Jason Giambi BLC	12.00	20.00

2003 McFarlane Baseball

COMPLETE SERIES IV (6)	30.00	50.00
COMPLETE SERIES V (8)	40.00	70.00
COMPLETE SERIES VI (7)	40.00	70.00
COMPLETE SERIES VII (6)	35.00	60.00
PIECES IN ALPHA ORDER BY SERIES		
SERIES $ INCLUDES COMMON VERSIONS		
Lance Berkman White FP	6.00	10.00
Lance Berkman Red	18.00	30.00
Eric Hinske Grey FP	7.00	12.00
Eric Hinske White	20.00	35.00
Trevor Hoffman Blue	6.00	10.00
Trevor Hoffman Grey	15.00	25.00
Matt Morris White FP	6.00	10.00
Matt Morris Grey	15.00	25.00
Ichiro Suzuki Blue	6.00	10.00
Ichiro Suzuki Grey	15.00	25.00
Larry Walker Purple	6.00	10.00
Barry Bonds White	7.00	12.00
Barry Bonds Grey	12.00	20.00
Barry Bonds Pirates	45.00	80.00
Pat Burrell Grey	6.00	10.00
Eric Gagne White FP	7.00	12.00
Eric Gagne Grey	15.00	25.00
Jason Giambi Pinstripes	7.00	12.00
Jason Giambi A's	20.00	35.00
J.Giambi w/o Patch		
T.Hoffman Camoflauge	15.00	25.00
T.Hunter Minnesota FP	6.00	10.00
Torii Hunter Twins	12.00	20.00
Derek Jeter Grey	7.00	12.00
D.Jeter w/o Patch		
Jason Kendall White	6.00	10.00
Jason Kendall Grey	15.00	25.00
Derek Lowe Grey FP	6.00	10.00
Derek Lowe Red	12.00	20.00
A.Soriano w/o Patch		
Greg Maddux Cubs	20.00	35.00
Curt Schilling Phillies	20.00	35.00
Alfonso Soriano Grey FP	7.00	12.00
Ichiro Suzuki White	15.00	25.00
Miguel Tejada Green FP	6.00	10.00
Miguel Tejada Grey	12.00	20.00
Roger Clemens Blue Jays	18.00	30.00
Jim Edmonds White	7.00	12.00
Jim Edmonds White	15.00	25.00
Luis Gonzalez White FP	6.00	10.00
Luis Gonzalez Black	15.00	25.00
Kazuhisu Ishii White FP	7.00	12.00
Kazuhisu Ishii Grey	15.00	25.00
Jorge Posada Grey	7.00	12.00
Alex Rodriguez Mariners	18.00	30.00
Sammy Sosa Grey	7.00	12.00
Sammy Sosa Pinstripes	18.00	30.00
Mike Sweeney Blue FP	6.00	10.00
Mike Sweeney White	15.00	25.00
Jim Thome Phillies	7.00	12.00
Jim Thome Indians	18.00	30.00
Troy Glaus White FP	6.00	10.00
T.Glaus White/Red Sleeves	40.00	90.00
Randy Johnson White	6.00	10.00
Randy Johnson Mariners	15.00	25.00
Mark Prior Grey FP	7.50	15.00
Scott Rolen Cards Grey	6.00	10.00
Scott Rolen Cards White	12.00	20.00
Scott Rolen Phillies	15.00	25.00
Bernie Williams Grey	6.00	10.00
Bernie Williams Pinstripes	10.00	18.00
Barry Zito White FP	6.00	10.00
Barry Zito Grey	12.00	20.00
Jim Edmonds Angels	10.00	18.00
Pedro Martinez Red	12.00	20.00
Ivan Rodriguez Marlins	20.00	40.00

2003 McFarlane Baseball Bonds World Series

STATED PRINT RUN 200 PIECES		
Barry Bonds World Series	400.00	600.00

2003 McFarlane Baseball FanFest Exclusives

COMPLETE SET (2)	30.00	50.00
Sammy Sosa	15.00	25.00
Frank Thomas	15.00	25.00

2004 McFarlane Baseball

SERIES $ FOR COMMON VERSIONS ONLY		
Jeff Bagwell	7.00	12.00
Jeff Bagwell White	17.50	35.00
K.Brown Dodgers	10.00	18.00
K.Brown Yankee	15.00	25.00
K.Brown Grey Dodgers	10.00	20.00
Hideki Matsui FP	10.00	18.00
H.Matsui Pinstripes	20.00	40.00
Mike Piazza Dodgers	15.00	30.00
Alex Rodriquez	10.00	20.00
Alex Rodriquez Grey	17.50	35.00
A-Rod HR Challenge	15.00	25.00
R.Sexson Brewers FP	10.00	18.00
R.Sexson Retro	15.00	25.00
John Smoltz	7.00	12.00
John Smoltz Grey	15.00	25.00
Alfonzo Soriano	10.00	18.00
A.Soriano Pinstripes	15.00	30.00
Sammy Sosa White Sox	25.00	50.00

2004 McFarlane Baseball 3-Inch Duals

COMPLETE SET (6)		
COMMON PIECE	4.00	10.00
E.Gagne/A.Rodriguez	4.00	10.00
Ichiro/J.Thome	5.00	12.00
D.Jeter/B.Zito	5.00	12.00
C.Jones/S.Sosa	4.00	10.00
M.Prior/I.Rodriguez	4.00	10.00
A.Soriano/R.Johnson	4.00	10.00

2004 MLB Sportsclix Promos

COMPLETE SET (6)	50.00	80.00
ISSUED TO DEALERS		
Ichiro Suzuki	2.00	5.00
Alfonso Soriano		
Alex Rodriguez	2.00	5.00
Randy Johnson		
Mark Prior	2.00	5.00
Barry Bonds	40.00	60.00

2004 MLB Sportsclix

COMMON DP	0.75	2.00
DP'S ISSUED IN ALL STARTER BOXES		
COMMON C	0.75	2.00
COMMON ODDS 1:108 FIGURES		
COMMON U	1.00	2.50
UNCOMMON ODDS 1:144 FIGURES		
COMMON R	1.25	3.00
RARE ODDS 1:216 FIGURES		
COMMON UNIQ	3.00	8.00
UNIQUE ODDS 1:432 FIGURES		
Roberto Alomar C	2.00	5.00
Hideki Matsui C	1.50	4.00
Juan Gonzalez R	1.50	4.00
Carlos Beltran C	1.25	3.00
Jorge Posada U	1.25	3.00
Rafael Palmeiro U	1.25	3.00
Jason Giambi U	1.50	4.00
Frank Thomas C	1.25	3.00
Troy Percival C	1.00	2.50
Mariano Rivera U	1.50	4.00
Derek Lowe C	1.25	3.00
Roger Clemens U	2.00	5.00
Tim Hudson U	1.50	4.00
Bret Boone U	1.25	3.00
Hank Blalock U	1.25	3.00
Garret Anderson C	1.00	2.50
Manny Ramirez UNIQ	5.00	12.00
Pedro Martinez UNIQ	5.00	12.00
Nomar Garciaparra UNIQ	5.00	12.00
Mike Mussina UNIQ	3.00	8.00
Derek Jeter UNIQ	8.00	20.00
Ichiro Suzuki UNIQ	5.00	12.00
Rocco Baldelli UNIQ	5.00	12.00
Alex Rodriguez UNIQ	6.00	15.00
Roy Halladay UNIQ	4.00	10.00
Ken Griffey U	1.50	4.00
Juan Pierre C	1.25	3.00
J.D. Drew C	1.25	3.00
Chipper Jones R	2.00	5.00
Jose Cruz Jr. R DP	1.25	3.00
Javy Lopez C	1.25	3.00
Dontrelle Willis C	1.25	3.00
Curt Schilling U	2.00	5.00
Eric Gagne U	1.50	4.00
John Smoltz C	1.50	4.00
Kerry Wood U DP	1.50	4.00
Jason Schmidt C	0.75	2.00
Barry Larkin U	1.25	3.00
Jose Reyes C	1.25	3.00
Edgar Renteria U	1.00	2.50
Marcus Giles U	1.00	2.50
Todd Helton C	1.50	4.00
Scott Rolen C	1.25	3.00
Gary Sheffield U	1.50	4.00
Randy Johnson UNIQ	4.00	10.00
Andruw Jones UNIQ	4.00	10.00
Greg Maddux UNIQ	5.00	12.00
Mark Prior UNIQ	2.00	12.00
Sammy Sosa UNIQ	6.00	15.00
Ivan Rodriguez UNIQ	3.00	8.00
Hideo Nomo UNIQ	3.00	8.00
Vladimir Guerrero UNIQ	4.00	10.00
Mike Piazza UNIQ	4.00	10.00
Jim Thome UNIQ	4.00	10.00
Albert Pujols UNIQ	6.00	15.00

2004 MLB Sportsclix Blue Base

BLUE BASE ODDS 1:1296 FIGURES		
Mike Sweeney	6.00	15.00
Bret Boone	6.00	15.00
Bret Boone Road	6.00	15.00
Hank Blalock	6.00	15.00
Jorge Posada	6.00	15.00
Garrett Anderson	6.00	15.00
Torii Hunter	6.00	15.00
Maggio Ordonez	6.00	15.00
Maggio Ordonez Road	6.00	15.00
Barry Zito	6.00	15.00
Nomar Garciaparra	8.00	20.00
Jim Thome	6.00	15.00
Jim Thome Road	6.00	15.00
Jim Thome BP Red		
Richie Sexson	6.00	15.00
Marcus Giles	6.00	15.00
Jose Vidro	6.00	15.00
Jose Vidro Road	6.00	15.00
Scott Rolen	6.00	15.00
Jose Reyes	6.00	15.00
Mike Piazza	8.00	20.00
Ivan Rodriguez	6.00	15.00
J.T. Snow	6.00	15.00
Lance Berkman	6.00	15.00
Albert Pujols	10.00	25.00
Sammy Sosa	10.00	25.00
Sammy Sosa Road	10.00	25.00
Luis Gonzalez	6.00	15.00
Luis Gonzalez Road	6.00	15.00
Andruw Jones	6.00	15.00
Kevin Millwood	6.00	15.00
Kevin Millwood Road	6.00	15.00
Eric Gagne	8.00	20.00
Edgar Renteria	6.00	15.00
Edgardo Alfonzo	6.00	15.00

2004 MLB Sportsclix Red Base

RED BASE ODDS 1:2160		
Alfonso Soriano	25.00	40.00
Ichiro Suzuki	30.00	50.00
Ichiro Suzuki Road	30.00	50.00
Alex Rodriguez	30.00	50.00
Randy Johnson	15.00	30.00
Randy Johnson Road	15.00	30.00
Mark Prior	25.00	40.00

AUTOGRAPHS

Current Active Signers

	Flat Item Show Fee	Authentic Jersey	Signed Bat	Signed Helmet	Single Signed Ball
ALOMAR, ROBERTO	$35	$150-$200	$100-$150	$65-$85	$40-$100
BAGWELL, JEFF		$225-$300	$100-$150	$75-$100	$60-$150
BALDELLI, ROCCO					$25-$60
BECKETT, JOSH	$70-$90	$200-$250	$100-$200		$40-$100
BIGGIO, CRAIG		$175-$225	$90-$125	$75-$100	$35-$50
BLALOCK, HANK	$20-$25				$20-$30
BONDS, BARRY		$400-$600	$300-$600	$200-$250	$150-$400
CABRERA, MIGUEL					$30-$60
CLEMENS, ROGER		$300-$600	$100-$150	$75-$100	$100-$250
DELGADO, CARLOS		$135-$175	$100-$125	$50-$75	$40-$60
DUNN, ADAM			$50-$80	$30-$40	$25-$60
GAGNE, ERIC					$30-$60
GARCIAPARRA, NOMAR		$200-$250	$90-$125	$80-$110	$75-$90
GIAMBI, JASON		$150-$250	$90-$150	$50-$80	$40-$60
GLAUS, TROY		$100-$150	$65-$80	$45-$60	$25-$35
GLAVINE, TOM	$35-$50	$150-$200	$60-$75	$50-$70	$40-$100
GONZALEZ, JUAN		$150-$200	$75-$125	$50-$75	$30-$60
GRIFFEY, KEN JR.		$200-$500	$150-$250	$125-$175	$60-$150
GUERRERO, VLADIMIR		$175-$225	$90-$125	$60-$80	$50-$100
HALLADAY, ROY					$20-$30
HARDEN, RICH	$20-$30		$75-$100		$20-$40
HELTON, TODD		$225-$300	$100-$150	$50-$70	$30-$80
HENDERSON, RICKEY		$225-$275	$125-$175	$60-$75	$75-$150
HUDSON, TIM	$30				$25-$50
JETER, DEREK		$300-$600	$200-$500	$150-$400	$150-$300
JOHNSON, RANDY		$225-$300	$90-$130	$75-$100	$100-$250
JONES, ANDRUW		$150-$200	$60-$150	$50-$70	$30-$80
JONES, CHIPPER		$125-$200	$75-$150	$60-$80	$30-$80
KEARNS, AUSTIN			$50-$100		$20-$50
LARKIN, BARRY		$125-$175	$35-$80	$40-$60	$20-$40
MADDUX, GREG		$275-$350	$100-$150	$70-$90	$100-$200
MARTINEZ, EDGAR		$125-$175	$75-$90	$45-$60	$40-$100
MARTINEZ, PEDRO		$200-$250	$100-$150	$75-$100	$100-$200
MATSUI, HIDEKI		$300-$500			$200-$400

	Flat Item Show Fee	Authentic Jersey	Signed Bat	Signed Helmet	Single Signed Ball
MAUER, JOE					$25-$50
MCGRIFF, FRED		$150-$200	$75-$100	$40-$60	$30-$40
MULDER, MARK	$30-$50				$25-$60
MUSSINA, MIKE		$150-$200	$75-$90	$50-$70	$30-$60
NOMO, HIDEO		$150-$200	$75-$100	$50-$70	$35-$45
PALMEIRO, RAFAEL	$160-$190	$150-$200	$125-$250	$50-$80	$100-$200
PETTITTE, ANDY		$150-$200	$75-$90	$50-$70	$45-$60
PIAZZA, MIKE		$225-$300	$100-$150	$80-$100	$100-$200
PRIOR, MARK		$300-$600	$60-$80	$50-$70	$75-$200
PUJOLS, ALBERT			$100-$200	$50-$70	$100-$200
RAMIREZ, MANNY		$150-$300	$90-$125	$70-$80	$40-$100
REYES, JOSE	$30		$75-$150		$30-$80
RIVERA, MARIANO		$200-$400	$60-$80	$65-$80	$50-$100
RODRIGUEZ, ALEX		$400-$600	$200-$400		$150-$300
RODRIGUEZ, IVAN	$80-$90	$200-$250	$75-$200	$50-$70	$30-$80
ROLEN, SCOTT		$150-$300	$75-$125	$40-$60	$30-$80
SALMON, TIM		$125-$175	$60-$80	$40-$60	$20-$30
SCHILLING, CURT		$200-$250	$75-$100	$70-$90	$100-$200
SHEFFIELD, GARY	$50-$100	$100-$200	$100-$200	$45-$60	$50-$100
SMOLTZ, JOHN		$125-$175	$40-$65	$45-$60	$40-$100
SORIANO, ALFONSO		$100-$200	$90-$125	$60-$80	$50-$100
SOSA, SAMMY		$250-$600	$200-$500	$175-$225	$125-$300
SUZUKI, ICHIRO		$300-$600	$200-$400		$200-$400
TEIXEIRA, MARK	$20				$20-$40
THOMAS, FRANK		$200-$250	$90-$125	$60-$80	$30-$80
THOME, JIM		$150-$200	$75-$90	$60-$75	$30-$40
WALKER, LARRY		$150-$200	$75-$100	$50-$75	$35-$50
WEEKS, RICKIE					$50-$100
WILLIAMS, BERNIE		$200-$250	$90-$125	$75-$90	$75-$150
WILLIS, DONTRELLE	$50-$80	$250-$500	$60-$150		$40-$100
WOOD, KERRY	$75	$150-$200	$65-$80	$45-$60	$40-$100
YOUNG, DELMON					$75-$150
ZITO, BARRY		$75-$100			$30-$50

Retired Active Signers

	Flat Item Show Fee	Authentic Jersey	Signed Bat	Signed Helmet	Single Signed Ball
AARON, HANK	$135	$300-$600	$200-$400		$75-$200
BANKS, ERNIE	$80-$90	$125-$250	$125-$200		$50-$100
BENCH, JOHNNY	$50-$60	$150-$300	$150-$200		$50-$100
BERRA, YOGI	$40-$55	$200-$300	$150-$250		$40-$100
BOGGS, WADE	$40-$60	$125-$300	$125-$175		$50-$100
BRETT, GEORGE	$95		$160-$200		$50-$100
BROCK, LOU	$40-$60	$125-$250	$150-$200		$30-$80
CANSECO, JOSE	$35-$50	$125-$300	$100-$150		$25-$60
CAREW, ROD	$50		$110-$150		$40-$100
CARLTON, STEVE	$35-$55		$75-$125		$30-$80
CARTER, GARY	$50-$70				$40-$100
CEPEDA, ORLANDO	$25-$40	$125-$300	$75-$125		$30-$80
COLAVITO, ROCKY					$30-$40
FELLER, BOB	$15-$40		$75-$125		$25-$60
FISK, CARLTON	$60	$125-$300	$100-$200		$60-$150
FORD, WHITEY	$50-$70	$125-$300	$90-$125		$40-$80
GIBSON, BOB	$50-$60	$125-$300	$75-$125		$40-$100
GRACE, MARK			$65-$80		$20-$30
GWYNN, TONY			$125-$200		$30-$80
JACKSON, BO	$60	$300-$500	$200-$300		$50-$100
JACKSON, REGGIE	$85-$100	$200-$500	$150-$300		$50-$100
KALINE, AL	$45		$75-$125		$30-$80
KILLEBREW, HARMON	$45-$60	$100-$250	$150-$200		$30-$80
KINER, RALPH	$20		$75-$100		$30-$60
KOUFAX, SANDY					$200-$400
KUBEK, TONY					$100-$150
MARICHAL, JUAN	$25-$50	$125-$300	$65-$80		$30-$50
MATTINGLY, DON	$60-$100	$200-$500			$40-$100
MAYS, WILLIE			$150-$300		$75-$150

	Flat Item Show Fee	Authentic Jersey	Signed Bat	Signed Helmet	Single Signed Ball
MAZEROSKI, BILL			$75-$100		$30-$60
MCCOVEY, WILLIE	$45-$80	$125-$300	$100-$150		$50-$100
MCGWIRE, MARK		$1000-$2000			$300-$600
MOLITOR, PAUL	$55-$75		$75-$125		$50-$100
MORGAN, JOE			$100-$150		$40-$60
MURPHY, DALE	$30		$75-$125		$30-$80
MURRAY, EDDIE	$100		$200-$500		$100-$200
MUSIAL, STAN	$60-$80	$150-$400	$200-$400		$50-$100
O'NEILL, PAUL	$85	$150-$300	$150-$300		$50-$100
PALMER, JIM	$30-$50	$125-$300	$75-$125		$25-$60
PUCKETT, KIRBY			$100-$150		$60-$100
RIPKEN, CAL JR.	$150	$250-$600	$250-$500	$150-$300	$100-$250
RIZZUTO, PHIL	$45	$200-$400	$100-$200		$35-$60
ROBINSON, BROOKS	$25-$60	$125-$300	$75-$150		$30-$60
ROBINSON, FRANK	$45-$55		$125-$250		$40-$80
ROSE, PETE	$50-$70	$200-$500	$100-$250	$50-$100	$40-$100
RYAN, NOLAN	$50-$100	$200-$500	$125-$200		$60-$150
SANDBERG, RYNE	$70		$125-$250		$50-$100
SCHMIDT, MIKE			$100-$200		$60-$150
SEAVER, TOM	$50-$75	$125-$300	$100-$200		$50-$100
SMITH, OZZIE	$75	$125-$300			$40-$100
SNIDER, DUKE	$50-$60	$125-$300	$100-$250		$30-$80
STRAWBERRY, DARRYL	$40				$20-$50
TORRE, JOE					$20-$40
TRAMMELL, ALAN					$20-$40
WINFIELD, DAVE		$150-$400	$100-$250		$40-$100
YASTRZEMSKI, CARL	$70	$150-$300	$150-$200		$60-$150
YOUNT, ROBIN			$100-$150		$50-$100

INDEX

Major League

Minor League Singles

Minor League Team Sets

ACKNOWLEDGEMENTS

Each year we refine the process of developing the most accurate and up-to-date information for this book. I believe this year's Price Guide is our best yet. Thanks again to all the contributors nationwide (listed below) as well as our staff here in Dallas.

Those who have worked closely with us on this and many other books have again proven themselves invaluable: Ed Allan, Frank and Vivian Barning, Levi Bleam and Jim Fleck (707 Sportscards), T. Scott Brandon, Peter Brennan, Ray Bright, Card Collectors Co., Dwight Chapin, Theo Chen, Barry Colla, Dick DeCourcy, Bill and Diane Dodge, Brett Domue, Dan Even, David Festberg, Fleer/SkyBox (Josh Pearlman), Steve Freedman, Gervise Ford, Larry and Jeff Fritsch, Tony Galovich, Dick Gilkeson, Steve Gold (AU Sports), Bill Goodwin, Mike and Howard Gordon, George Grauer, Steve Green (STB Sports), John Greenwald, Wayne Grove, Bill Henderson, Jerry and Etta Hersh, Mike Hersh, Neil Hoppenworth, Hunt Auction, Mike Jaspersen, Jay and Mary Kasper (Jay's Emporium), Jerry Katz, Pete Kennedy, David Kohler (SportsCards Plus), Terry Knouse (Tik and Tik), Tom Layberger, Tom Leon, Robert Lifsen, Lew Lipset (Four Base Hits), Mike Livingston, Mark Macrae, Bill Madden, Bill Mastro, Doug Allen and Ron Oser (MastroNet), Dr.William McAvoy, Michael McDonald, Mid-Atlantic Sports Cards (Bill Bossert), Gary Mills, Ernie Montella, Brian Morris, Mike Mosier (Columbia City Collectibles Co.), B.A. Murry, Ralph Nozaki, Mike O'Brien, Oldies and Goodies (Nigel Spill), Oregon Trail Auctions, Pacific Trading Cards (Mike Cramer and Mike Monson), Playoff Trading Cards (Ben Ecklar, Tracy Hackler, Steven Judd, David Porter, Scott Prusha and Rob Springs), Jack Pollard, Jeff Prillaman, Pat Quinn, Jerald Reichstein, Gavin Riley, Clifton Rouse, John Rumierz, Pat Blandford, Lonn Passon and Kevin Savage (Sports Gallery), Gary Sawatski and Jim Justus (The Wizards of Odd), Mike Schechter, Bill and Darlene Shafer, Barry Sloate, John E. Spalding, Phil Spector, Ted Taylor, Lee Temanson, Topps (Clay Luraschi), Ed Twombly, Upper Deck (Bill Bachman), Wayne Varner, Bill Vizas, Waukesha Sportscards, Brian and Mike Wentz (BMW Cards), Bill Wesslund (Portland Sports Card Co.), Kit Young, Rick Young, Ted Zanidakis, Robert Zanze (Z-Cards and Sports), Bill Zimpleman and Dean Zindler. Finally we give a special acknowledgment to the late Dennis W. Eckes, "Mr. Sport Americana." The success of the Beckett Price Guides has always been the result of a team effort.

It is very difficult to be "accurate" - one can only do one's best. But this job is especially difficult since we're shooting at a moving target: Prices are fluctuating all the time. Having several full-time pricing experts has definitely proven to be better than just one, and I thank all of them for working together to provide you, our readers, with the most accurate prices possible.

Many people have provided price input, illustrative material, checklist verifications, errata, and/or background information. We should like to individually thank AbD Cards (Dale Wesolewski), Action Card Sales, Jerry Adamic, Johnny and Sandy Adams, Mehdi Ahlei, Alex's MVP Cards & Comics, Will Allison, Dennis Anderson, Ed Anderson, Shane Anderson, Ellis Anmuth, Alan Applegate, Ric Apter, Clyde Archer, Randy Archer, Burl Armstrong, Neil Armstrong, Carlos Ayala, B and J Sportscards, Jeremy Bachman, Dave Bailey, Ball Four Cards (Frank and Steve Pemper), Bob Bartosz, Bubba Bennett, Carl Berg, Beulah Sports (Jeff Blatt), B..J. Sportscollectables, Al Blumkin, David Boedicker (The Wild Pitch Inc.), Louis Bollman, Tim Bond, Terry Boyd, Dan Brandenberry, Jeff Breitenfield, John Brigandi, Scott Brockleman, John Broggi, D.Bruce Brown, Virgil Burns, Greg Bussineau, David Byer, California Card Co., Capital Cards, Danny Cariseo, Carl Carlson (C.T.S.), Jim Carr, Ira Cetron, Sandy Chan, Ric Chandgie, Ray Cherry, Bigg Wayne Christian, Ryan Christoff (Thanks for the help with Cuban Cards), Josh Chidester, Michael and Abe Citron, Dr. Jeffrey Clair, Michael Cohen, Tom Cohoon (Cardboard Dreams), Gary Collett, Jay Conti, Rick Cosmen (RC Card Co.), Lou Costanzo (Champion Sports), Mike Coyne, Tony Craig (T.C. Card Co.), Solomon Cramer, Kevin Crane, Taylor Crane, Chad Cripe, Scott Crump, Allen Custer, Dave Dame, Scott Dantio, Dee's Baseball Cards (Dee Robinson), Joe Delgrippo, Mike DeLuca, Ken Dinerman (California Cruizers), Rob DiSalvatore, Cliff Dolgins, Discount Dorothy, Richard Dolloff, Joe Donato, Jerry Dong, Pat Dorsey, Double Play Baseball Cards, Joe Drelich, Richard Duglin (Baseball Cards-N-More), The Dugout, Ken Edick (Home Plate of Utah), Brad Englehardt, Terry Falkner, Mike and Chris Fanning, Linda Ferrigno and Mark Mezzardi, Jay Finglass, A.J. Firestone, Scott Flatto, Bob Flitter, Fremont Fong, Paul Franzetti, Ron Frasier, Tom Freeman, Bob Frye, Bill Fusaro, Chris Gala, David Garza, David Gaumer, Georgetown Card Exchange, David Giove, Dick Goddard, Jeff Goldstein, Ron Gomez, Rich Gove, Wayne Greene, Jay and Jan Grinsby, Bob Grissett, Gerry Guenther, Neil Gubitz, Hall's Nostalgia, Gregg Hara, Todd Harrell, Robert Harrison, Steve Hart, Floyd Haynes (H and H Baseball Cards), Kevin Heffner, Joel Hellman, Ron Hetrick, Hit and Run Cards (Jon, David, and Kirk Peterson), Vinny Ho, Johnny Hustle Card Co., John Inouye, Vern Isenberg, Dale Jackson, Marshall Jackson, Mike Jardina, Paul Jastrzembski, Jeff's Sports Cards, Donn Jennings Cards, George Johnson, Craig Jones, Chuck Juliana, Nick Kardoulias, Scott Kashner, Frank and Rose

Katen, Steven J Kerno, Kevin's Kards, Kingdom Collectibles, Inc., John Klassnik, Steve Kluback, Don Knutsen, Gregg Kohn, Mike Kohlhas, Bob & Bryan Kornfield, Carl and Maryanne Laron, Bill Larsen, Howard Lau, Richard S. Lawrence, William Lawrence, Brent Lee, Morley Leeking, Lelands (Simeon Lipman), Irv Lerner, Larry and Sally Levine, Larry Loeschen (A and J Sportscards), Neil Lopez, Kendall Loyd (Orlando Sportscards South), Steve Lowe, Leon Luckey, Ray Luurs, Jim Macie, Peter Maltin, Paul Marchant, Brian Marcy, Scott Martinez, James S. Maxwell Jr., McDag Productions Inc., Bob McDonald, Tony McLaughlin, Mendal Mearkle, Carlos Medina, Ken Melanson, William Mendel, Blake Meyer (Lone Star Sportscards), Tim Meyer, Joe Michalowicz, Lee Milazzo, Cary S. Miller, George Miller, Wayne Miller, Dick Millerd, Frank Mineo, Mitchell's Baseball Cards, John Morales, William Munn, Mark Murphy, Robert Nappe, National Sportscard Exchange, Roger Neufeldt, Steve Novella, Bud Obermeyer, John O'Hara, Glenn Olson, Scott Olson, Luther Owen, Earle Parrish, Clay Pasternack, Michael Perrotta, Bobby Plapinger, Tom Pfirrmann, Don Phlong, Loran Pulver, Bob Ragonese, Bryan Rappaport, Don and Tom Ras, Robert M. Ray, Phil Regli, Rob Resnick, Dave Reynolds, Carson Ritchey, Bill Rodman, Craig Roehrig, Mike Sablow, Terry Sack, Thomas Salem, Barry Sanders, Jon Sands, Tony Scarpa, John Schad, Dave Schau (Baseball Cards), Masa Shinohara, Eddie Silard, Mike Slepcevic, Sam Sliheet, Art Smith, Cary Smith, Jerry Smolin, Lynn and Todd Solt, Jerry Sorice, Don Spagnolo, Sports Card Fan-Attic, The Sport Hobbyist, Norm Stapleton, Bill Steinberg, Lisa Stellato (Never Enough Cards), Rob Stenzel, Jason Stern, Andy Stoltz, Rob Stenzel, Bill Stone, Ted Straka, Tim Strandberg (East Texas Sports Cards), Edward Strauss, Strike Three, Richard Strobino, Kevin Struss, Superior Sport Card, Dr. Richard Swales, George Tahinos, Brent Thorton, Ian Taylor, The The Thirdhand Shoppe, Dick Thompson, Brent Thornton, Paul Thornton, Jim and Sally Thurtell, Bud Tompkins (Minnesota Connection), Philip J. Tremont, Ralph Triplette, Umpire's Choice Inc., Eric Unglaub, Hoyt Vanderpool, Steven Wagman, T. Wall, Gary A. Walter, Dave Weber, Joe and John Weisenburger (The Wise Guys), Richard West, Mike Wheat, Louise and Richard Wiercinski, Don Williams (Robin's Nest of Dolls), Jeff Williams, John Williams, Kent Williams, Craig Williamson, Rich Wojtasick, John Wolf Jr., Jay Wolt (Cavalcade of Sports), Eric Wu, Joe Yanello, Peter Yee, Tom Zocco, Mark Zubrensky and Tim Zwick.

Every year we make active solicitations for expert input. We are particularly appreciative of help (however extensive or cursory) provided for this volume. We receive many inquiries, comments and questions regarding material within this book. In fact, each and every one is read and digested. Time constraints, however, prevent us from personally replying. But keep sharing your knowledge. Your letters and input are part of the "big picture" of hobby information we can pass along to readers in our books and magazines. Even though we cannot respond to each letter or email, you are making significant contributions to the hobby through your interest and comments.

The effort to continually refine and improve this book also involves a growing number of people and types of expertise on our home team. Our company boasts a substantial Sports Data Publishing team, which strengthens our ability to provide comprehensive analysis of the marketplace. SDP capably handled numerous technical details and provided able assistance in the preparation of this edition.

Our baseball analysts played a major part in compiling this year's book, traveling thousands of miles during the past year to attend sports card shows and visit card shops around the United States and Canada. The Beckett baseball specialists are, Brian Fleischer, Gabe Haro, Rich Klein, and Grant Sandground (Senior Price Guide Editor). Their pricing analysis and careful proofreading were key contributions to the accuracy of this annual.

Grant Sandground's coordination and reconciling of prices as Beckett Baseball Collector Price Guide Editor helped immeasurably. Rich Klein, as research analyst and primary accumulator of new information for this volume, contributed detailed pricing analysis and hours of proofing. They were ably assisted by Beverly Melian, who helped enter new sets and pricing information, and ably handled the ever-growing quantity of cards we need organized for efforts such as this.

The effort was led by the Manager of Sports Data Publishing Dan Hitt. They were ably assisted by the rest of the Price Guide analysts: Clint Hall and Keith Hower.

The price gathering and analytical talents of this fine group of hobbyists have helped make our Beckett team stronger, while making this guide and its companion monthly Price Guide more widely recognized as the hobby's most reliable and relied upon sources of pricing information.

The Beckett Interactive Division, led by Andrew Taylor's efforts, played a critical role in technology. He spent countless hours programming, testing, and implementing it to simplify the handling of millions of prices that must be checked and updated for each edition.

GeanPaul Figari was responsible for the typesetting and layout of the book. The reason this books looks as good as it does is due to the hard work and expertise he puts into making this volume each year.

In the years since this guide debuted, Beckett Publicatiins has grown beyond any rational expectation. A great many talented and hard working individuals have been instrumental in this growth and success. Our whole team is to be congratulated for what we together have accomplished.

The whole Beckett Publications team has my thanks for jobs well done. Thank you, everyone.